2013

National Trade and Professional Associations

of the United States

Managing Editor: Kathleen Anders
Senior Editor: Duncan Bell
Associate Editor: David Epstein
Project Manager: Matt Ouzounian

Columbia Books, Inc.
Bethesda, MD

ISBN-10: 0-974732-29-X
ISBN-13: 978-0-9747322-9-9
ISSN: 0734-0734

Columbia Books, Inc.
8120 Woodmont Ave., Suite 110
Bethesda, MD 20814
Toll-Free Customer Service: (888) 265-0600
Editorial Office: (202) 464-1662

2013 National
Trade and
Professional
Associations of
the United States

Table Of Contents

Associations in a Changing World

By John H. Graham IV, CAE
President and CEO, ASAE
Association TRENDS 2013 Association Executive of the Year

As the size of this directory suggests, associations represent virtually every industry, profession or cause in existence today. There is almost literally an association for everything.

Despite the breadth of the association community and the disparate interests they represent, associations share many common traits and face many of the same challenges. While the complexity of associations and their role has evolved, today's associations still share the purpose of coming together to produce positive results. People join and volunteer for associations because they want to learn from each other and work together to advance a common cause or interest.

But in today's rapidly changing world, associations need to be perpetually looking at their business model, their range of products and services and the way they communicate with their industry or profession, as well as the outside world. Because of the pace of change in the world today, associations need to be forecasters to some extent, to stop occasionally and ask "what's next?" – if only to avoid being overtaken by events.

Four years of prolonged economic uncertainty and slow recovery have changed the revenue model for many associations, perhaps permanently. At the same time, members' expectations of their associations have shifted as well. Even if membership dues are paid by a company and not directly by an individual, people and corporations are looking for more from their association to justify their continued investment. Many if not most associations provide educational programming, but are they giving their members exactly what they need to advance their professional development and in the format they want it? Increasing customization in the consumer marketplace extends to membership organizations. Members expect their associations to know who they are as individuals

and what they like. They expect their professional organizations to capture their attention if they want their involvement. Associations that truly know their members can focus their resources accordingly, and customize their products and services to serve every segment of their membership.

While associations know that their members are pressed for time and money, the successful organizations have been good at keeping their members engaged and invested in their profession. It's very easy nowadays to lose a member if they're not staying connected and plugged in to what's available and what's new in their association.

Changing demographics and a changing workforce are also impacting associations. While America is expected to add roughly 100 million people to its population by the middle of the 21st century, it won't have the same racial or gender profile as it does today. If recent trends continue, most of America's net population growth will come from its minorities. Hispanic and Asian populations are predicted to nearly triple over the next several decades. America's increasing diversity is already playing a major role in the workforce and associations need to understand how this impacts their membership recruitment, retention and engagement.

The New Year also brings a new Congress and new opportunities for associations that advocate on behalf of their industries and professions. Associations possess unique resources that can help solve many of the nation's most pressing issues. Among those resources, of course, are the millions of skilled professionals and experts in different fields who can share valuable perspectives, raise important questions and help formulate strategies to solve difficult problems. By leveraging these resources to address issues like disease prevention and research, consumer and product safety and disaster relief – just to name a few – associations directly benefit the public and improve the quality of life we all enjoy.

After an election, it's always essential for associations to introduce themselves to new policymakers and their staff to make sure they're aware of the knowledge and expertise that exists in the association community on a huge range of issues.

Despite changing market forces, associations remain as relevant and needed as ever. They have the collective power to enrich lives, keep America competitive, prepare for the future, and fuel the global economy. The associations found in this directory represent millions of people – those who are most knowledgeable and passionate about industries, professions and ideas. In virtually every business sector and industry, across the country, state to state, these associations turn change into progress one step at a time.

Organization and Use of This Directory

The main body of the book, called the Association Index, contains the full listing for each association in alphabetical order by organization name. Listings contain each association's:

- Year founded
- Historical Note & Membership Fees
- Headquarters
- Contact Information
- Staff & Membership Size
- Operating Budget Range
- Key Executives & Officers
- Upcoming Annual Meetings & Conventions
- Serial Publications
- Tax-Exempt Status
- Membership List Availability Indicator
- Continuing Education Enrolment
- Certification Designation
- Number of Non-convention events held per year (over 100 attendees)
- Name of Conference Chair
- Number of Exhibitors at Upcoming Conferences and Trade Shows

Following the Association Index are seven separate indices:

1. Subject Index
For users interested in particular industries or occupations, the Subject Index provides over 100 different categories. Associations may be listed under multiple categories. Organizations that make their membership lists available to non-members are denoted in this index with an asterisk (*).

2. Geographic Index
Associations are cross-referenced based on the city and state in which they are headquartered.

3. Budget Index
This index contains an alphabetical list of associations in each of the fourteen budget categories.

4. Executive Index
Each executive listed in NTPA is listed here alphabetically by last name with his or her association affiliation.

5. Association Acronym Index
Associations are often informally known by their acronyms. The Acronym Index lists all such acronyms, with the associations to which they refer.

6. Certification Acronym Index
Associations offering their own certification programs are indexed here under the acronym of the certification they confer.

7. Meeting Index
Organized by city within state, this index lists associations by the location of future annual meetings. Also included here are the facility, dates, and projected attendance and number of exhibitors for each meeting, when available.

8. Meeting Location Trends Index
Organized by city within state, this index lists associations by the location of the major meetings/conventions they have held within the past three years, providing the researcher with insight into these organizations' meeting location trends and preferences.

In addition to the indices, we've included breakdowns of associations based on state, budget, and subject in the front of the book, along with a handy calendar of events tailored to association executives, complete with dates, host organization, name of event, event location and host website.

NTPA is now available online at AssociationExecs.com. Frequently updated, AssociationExecs.com has customized search capabilities and allows for the exportation of data into desktop contact management programs. Please visit our websites at columbiabooks.com or associationexecs.com for more information and subscription options.

2013 National Trade and Professional Associations of the United States

Current Association Facts and Figures

Below is a breakdown of associations by state where they are headquartered, budget category and selected subjects.

ASSOCIATION HEADQUARTERS BY STATE

State	Number of Associations	State	Number of Associations
District of Columbia	1232	South Carolina	51
Virginia	980	Oklahoma	50
Illinois	657	Iowa	46
New York	586	Alabama	44
California	446	Utah	33
Maryland	427	New Mexico	31
Texas	338	Nebraska	29
Florida	257	Nevada	25
Pennsylvania	244	New Hampshire	24
Ohio	223	Mississippi	22
New Jersey	200	Arkansas	20
Colorado	195	Idaho	19
Wisconsin	165	Rhode Island	19
Georgia	159	Montana	17
North Carolina	153	Louisiana	17
Missouri	147	Delaware	14
Michigan	141	Vermont	14
Massachusetts	132	Maine	13
Minnesota	124	Hawaii	9
Indiana	112	South Dakota	8
Kentucky	107	Wyoming	8
Tennessee	96	North Dakota	7
Kansas	95	West Virginia	6
Arizona	74	Alaska	2
Washington	74	Virgin Islands	1
Connecticut	60	Palau	1
Oregon	54		

BUDGET CATEGORY

Budget Category	Number of Associations
Over $100,000,000	75
$50-100,000,000	85
$25-50,000,000	162
$10-25,000,000	380
$5-10,000,000	420
$2-5,000,000	870
$1-2,000,000	923
$500-1,000,000	988
$250-500,000	916
$100-250,000	998
$50-100,000	533
$25-50,000	353
$10-25,000	289
Under $10,000	342

DISTRIBUTION BY SELECTED SUBJECTS

Category	Number of Associations	Category	Number of Associations
Medicine/Health Care/Mental Health	2016	Animals	362
Education	1250	Agriculture/Agronomy	356
Science	757	Environment And Conservation	320
Manufacturers	661	Energy/Electricity	312
Communications	660	Law/Law Firms	310
Transportation	614	Computer/Technology	291
Government-Related	579	Law Enforcement/Security	291
Sports/Leisure/Entertainment	509	Natural Resources	289
Construction/ Construction Materials	451	Retail/Wholesale	281
Banking/Finance/Investments	436	Business	274
Arts, The	433	Industrial Relations	261
Engineering/Mathematics	397	Management	245
Food And Beverage Industry	388		

Association Executive Events Calendar 2013

Below is a calendar of key networking events scheduled in 2013 that are tailored to the association executive. Each listed item includes the dates, name, host, and city/state location of the event. The host's website, where you may find additional details about the event, is also provided wherever possible.

Date	Host	Event Name	Event Location	Host Website
Jan 13-16	Professional Conv. Mgmt Assn.	Annual Meeting	Orlando, FL	pcma.org
Jan 13-17	Public Affairs Council	Public Affairs Institute	Laguna Beach, CA	pac.org
Jan 16	FAR	Non Profit Financial	Washington, DC	far-roundtable.org
Jan 28	HSMAI	Adrian Awards	New York, NY	hsmai.org
Jan 29	Governing	Outlook in the States Conference	Washington, DC	governing.com
Jan 29	IL Soc of Assn. Execs	Annual Convention & Trade Show	Springfield, IL	isae.com
Jan 29-31	Legaltech	Trade Show	New York, NY	legaltechshow.com
Jan 31	CFO of the Year	Non Profit CFO of the year award lunch	Washington, DC	nonprofitcfoaward.com
Feb 1	Campaigns & Elections	Reed Awards	Washington, DC	politicsmagazine.com
Feb 5-8	Public Affairs Council	Grassroots Conference	Key West, FL	pac.org
Feb 6-8	AAP/PSP	Annual Conference	Washington, DC	pspcentral.org
Feb 7-8	Direct Mkg Assn.	Non Profit Conference	Washington, DC	the-dma.org
Feb 7-8	DMA Non Profit Federation	Issues conference	Washington, DC	nonprofitfederation.org
Feb 12-14	ASAE Online	Conference for Small-Staff Assn.	Virtual	asaecenter.org
Feb 13-15	AMC Institute Annual	Annual Conference	St. Pete Beach, FL	amci.conferencespot.org
Feb 15	Association TRENDS	Salute To Excellence Event	Washington, DC	associationtrends.com
Feb 20	FAR	Non Profit Financial	Washington, DC	far-roundtable.org
Feb 24-27	CESSE	Mid Winter CEO	Albuquerque, NM	cesse.org
Mar 10-12	ASAE	Great Ideas Conference	Washington, DC	asaecenter.org
Mar 13	DMAI	Foundation Dinner & Dream Auction	Washington, DC	destinationmarketing.org
Mar 14	Destinations Showcase	Conference & Expo	Washington, DC	destinationsshowcase.com
Mar 14-15	PA SAE	Education Summit & Expo	Harrisburg, PA	pasae.org
Mar 18-19	ASAE	American Associations Day	Washington, DC	asaecenter.org
Mar 20	FAR	Non Profit Financial	Washington, DC	far-roundtable.org
Mar 21-22	Legal & Tax	Washington Non Profit	Arlington, VA	legalandtaxconference.com
Apr 3-5	AAPC	Pollie Awards Conference	Washington, DC	theaapc.org
Apr 4-6	Digital Now	Annual Conference	Lake Buena Vista, FL	fusionproductions.com
Apr 5	ASAE	Annual Law Symposium	Chicago, IL	asaecenter.org
Apr 7-9	Assn. of Fundraising Pros	Conference	San Diego, CA	afpnet.org
Apr 8-10	Legal Mkg Association	Annual Conference	Las Vegas, NV	legalmarketing.org
Apr 9-11	Custom Content Council	Custom Content Conference	Chicago, IL	customcontentcouncil.com
Apr 10-14	ACRL	Conference	Indianapolis, IN	acrl.org
Apr 11-13	Non Profit Tech Network	Non Profit Technology Conference	Minneapolis, MN	nten.org
Apr 17-19	CA SAE	Annual	San Francisco, CA	calsae.org
Apr 23-24	HSMAI	MEET Mid-America	Chicago, IL	hsmai.org
Apr 24	FAR	Non Profit Financial	Washington, DC	far-roundtable.org

Date	Host	Event Name	Event Location	Host Website
Apr 24-26	Georgetown U	Representing & Managing Tax Exempts	Washington, DC	law.georgetown.edu
Apr 29-May 1	Chamber of Commerce	Small Business Summit & Fly-in	Washington, DC	uschambersummit.com
Apr 30-31	ASAE	Finance, HR, Business Operations Conf.	Washington, DC	asaecenter.org
Apr 30- May 2	STM	Spring Conference	Washington, DC	stm-assoc.org
May 3-6	CSE	Annual Meeting	Montreal, Canada	councilscienceeditors.org
Mar 4-7	National Public Affairs Council	Annual Conference	Miami Beach, FL	pac.org
May 8	Destinations Showcase	Chicago Expo	Chicago, IL	destinationsshowcase.com
May 9	Assn. Foundation Group	Nat'l Conference	Washington, DC	afgnet.org
May 14-16	FOSE	Annual Conference	Washington, DC	fose.com
May 14-16	ASAE International	Conference	Washington, DC	asaecenter.org
May 15	FAR	Non Profit Financial	Washington, DC	far-roundtable.org
May 16	ASAE	Springtime in Park	Washington, DC	asaecenter.org
May 16-18	Prometheus Retreat	Leadership Retreat	Monterey, CA	prometheusretreat.org
May 29	ECEF	Exhibit & Convention Forum	Washington, DC	eceforum.com
May 29-30	HSMAI	MEET West	Anaheim, CA	hsmai.org
June 4	ASAE	Mkg, Membership & Comm. Conference	Washington, DC	mmcconference.org
June 5-7	Soc of Scholarly Publishing	Annual Conference	San Francisco, CA	sspnet.org
June 5-7	SIPA	Annual Conference	Washington, DC	newsletters.org
June 11-13	AIBTM	Meetings Week	Chicago, IL	aibtm.com
June 13-14	New England Soc of Assn. Execs	Annual Management Conference	Lenox, MA	nesae.org
June 16-19	Soc of HR Mgmt.	Annual Conference	Chicago, IL	shrm.org
June 18	Assn. Forum	Annual Meeting	Chicago, IL	associationforum.org
June 19	FAR	Non Profit Financial	Washington, DC	far-roundtable.org
June 19-21	ASAE	Future Leaders	Lansdowne, VA	asaecenter.org
June 20-21	AICPA	National Not for Profit	Washington, DC	cpa2biz.com
June 24-27	HITEC	Annual Conference	Minneapolis, MN	hftp.org
July 8-10	MI ORGPRO	Annual Conference	Kalamazoo, MI	orgpro.info
July 10-12	FL Soc of Assn. Execs	Annual Conference	Tampa, FL	fsae.org
July 16-19	CESSE Annual	Annual	Providence RI	cesse.org
July 17-20	American Assn. Med Soc Execs	Conference	St. Louis, MO	aamse.org
July 20-23	MPI	Mtg. Planners World Edu. Congress	Las Vegas, NV	mpiweb.org
July 31	Direct Mkg Assn. of Washington	Bridge to Integrated Mkg/Fundraising Conf.	Washington, DC	bridgeconf.org
Aug 3-6	ASAE	Annual Meeting & Gold Awards	Atlanta GA	asaecenter.org
Aug 12-15	Nat'l Conference of State Legislatures	Legislative Summit	Atlanta, GA	ncsl.org
Aug 29-Sept 1	APSA	Annual Conference	Chicago, IL	apsanet.org
Sept 4-5	HSMAI	MEET National	Washington, DC	hsmai.org
Sept 22-24	TX Soc of Assn. Execs	New Ideas Annual Conference	Galveston, TX	tsae.org
Sept 23-25	Publishing Business	Conference & Expo	New York, NY	publishingbusiness.com
Oct 1	ASAE	Leaders	Chicago, IL	asaecenter.org
Oct 15-17	IMEX America	Annual Conference	Las Vegas, NV	meetingsnet.com
Nov 5-6	AICPA	Non Profit Forum	San Francisco, CA	aicpa.org
Dec 19	Assn. Forum	Holiday Showcase	Chicago, IL	associationforum.org

2013 National Trade and Professional Associations

Association Index

The following listings include over 7,900 active national trade associations, professional societies, technical organizations, and labor unions. For each organization, the latest pertinent information has been compiled. Included among the current listings are references to organizations previously listed in NTPA that have since ceased operations, and cross-references to track association name changes.

1394 Trade Association (*1994*)
315 Lincoln
Suite E
Mukilteo, WA 98275
Tel: (425) 870-6574 *Fax:* (425) 320-3897
E-Mail: tinal@1394ta.org
Website: 1394ta.org
Members: 130 Companies
Staff: 5

Personnel:
Contact, Public Relations, Marketing and Communications: Richard Davies
Administrator, Website Services: Jim Hicks
    E-Mail: jim@chromazone1.com
Manager, Operations and Member Support: Tina Lipscomb
    E-Mail: tinal@1394ta.org

Historical Note:
The 1394 Trade Association promotes the proliferation of the IEEE 1394 Serial Bus standard technology into the computer, consumer, peripheral, and industrial markets to enable a truly interoperable, standardized, universal I/O and back plane interconnect. Membership: $500-10,000/ year, based on the company's gross revenues.

Meetings/Conferences: Annual

Publications:
Membership Directory

AABB - American Association of Blood Banks (*1947*)
8101 Glenbrook Rd.
Bethesda, MD 20814-2749
Tel: (301) 907-6977 *Fax:* (301) 907-6895
E-Mail: aabb@aabb.org
Website: aabb.org
Members: 2000 institutions and 8000 individuals
Staff: 70
Annual Budget: $25-50,000,000
Tax: 501(c)(3)

Personnel:
Chief Executive Officer: Karen Shoos Lipton
    E-Mail: karen@aabb.org
Director, Membership and Sales: Angela Buscemi
    E-Mail: angela@aabb.org
Chief Financial Officer: Mark Conheady
    E-Mail: mconheady@aabb.org
Director, Public Relations and Communications: Jennifer Garfinkel
    E-Mail: jgarfinkel@aabb.org
Staff Counsel and Privacy and Security Officer: Diane Killion
    E-Mail: dkillion@aabb.org
Director, Education and Professional Development: Sharon Moffett
    E-Mail: smoffett@aabb.org
Editor: Laurie Munk
    E-Mail: laurie@aabb.org

Meetings Specialist: Lauren Pisner
    E-Mail: lpisner@aabb.org
Director, Management Information Systems: Dennis Sadler
    E-Mail: dennis@aabb.org
Division Director, Government Affairs, Operations and Business Development: Philip D. Schiff JD
    E-Mail: phil@aabb.org
Director, Marketing and Corporate Relations: Jackie Thomas
    E-Mail: jthomas@aabb.org
Director, Human Resources: Tamara Walker
    E-Mail: twalker@aabb.org
Manager, Corporate Relations: Tamara Zein
    E-Mail: tzein@aabb.org

Historical Note:
Formerly known as the American Association of Blood Banks. AABB's mission is to advance the practice and standards of transfusion medicine and cellular and related biological therapies. Membership: $218 (Physician); $108 (Health-care Professional/Physician in Residency); $1,150 (Institutional); $1,100 (Affiliate); 2,000 (Corporate Affiliate); $48 (E-member).

Meetings/Conferences: Annual
Conference Chair: Lauren Pisner
2013 - Denver, CO/Oct. 12 - 15
2014 - Philadelphia, PA/Oct. 25 - 28
2015 - Anaheim, CA/Oct. 24 - 27
2016 - Orlando, FL/Oct. 22 - 25
2017 - San Diego, CA/Oct. 7 - 10
2018 - Boston, MA/Oct. 13 - 16
Number of non-conference events/year: 6

Publications:
AABB CellSource; quarterly
AABB News; monthly
AABB SmartBrief; daily; adv.
AABB Weekly Report; weekly
AABB Weekly Report News Flash; weekly
Biovigilance Update; quarterly
TRANSFUSION Journal; monthly

AABC Commissioning Group
1518 K St. NW
Suite 503
Washington, DC 20005
Tel: (202) 737-7775 *Fax:* (202) 638-4833
E-Mail: info@commissioning.org
Website: commissioning.org
Staff: 1
Annual Budget: $500-1,000,000
Tax: 501(c)(6)

Personnel:
President: James Magee

Historical Note:
A subsidiary organization of the Associated Air Balance Council. ACG's mission is to promote ACG independent commissioning services to build owners and to design professionals. Membership and certification are open

to independent commissioning companies that meet the requirements for membership. Membership: $250 (Branch Office/Associate); $1,500 (Company Location).

Continuing Education:
Certification Designation/s: CxT, CxA, EMPs

Meetings/Conferences: Annual
2013 - Chicago, IL (InterContinental Hotels)/April 17 - 19
Number of non-conference events/year: 5

Publications:
Cx Journal Newsletter
Membership Directory; on-line

Membership List Available to Non-members

AACE International (*1956*)
1265 Suncrest Towne Centre Dr.
Morgantown, WV 26505-1876
Tel: (304) 296-8444 *Fax:* (304) 291-5728
E-Mail: info@aacei.org
Website: aacei.org
Members: 7500 individuals
Staff: 17
Annual Budget: $2-5,000,000
Tax: 501(c)(3)

Personnel:
Executive director: Dennis G. Stork
    E-Mail: dstork@aacei.org
Manager, Marketing and Meetings: Jennie Amos
    E-Mail: jamos@aacei.org
Managing Editor: Marvin Gelhausen
    E-Mail: mgelhausen@aacei.org
Coordinator, Member Services: Sharon Hardman
    E-Mail: shardman@aacei.org
Staff Director, Technical: Christian Heller
    E-Mail: cheller@aacei.org
Meetings Coordinator: Teri Jefferson
    E-Mail: tjefferson@aacei.org
Business Development Coordinator: Garth Leech
    E-Mail: gleech@aacei.org
Staff Director, Education and Administration: Charla Miller
    E-Mail: cmiller@aacei.org
Manager, Finance: Carol Sue Rogers
    E-Mail: crogers@aacei.org

Historical Note:
Founded as American Association of Cost Engineers; assumed its current name in 1991. A professional society of individuals interested in applying scientific principles to the solution of problems of cost management, engineering, estimating, cost control, planning and scheduling, project management and profitability. Membership: fees based on membership classification.

Continuing Education:
Certification Designation/s: CEP, CCC/CCE, CFCC, C3PM, EVP, CCT, PSP

Meetings/Conferences: Annual
Conference Chair: Jennie Amos

2013 - Washington, DC (Washington Marriott
    Wardman Park)/June 30 - July 3
2014 - New Orleans, LA (Sheraton New Orleans
    Hotel)/June 15 - 18
2015 - Las Vegas, NV (MGM Grand Hotel and Casino)/
    June 28 - July 1
2016 - Toronto, ON (Sheraton Centre Toronto Hotel)/
    June 26 - 29

Publications:
Cost Engineering journal; monthly; adv.

AAGL - Advancing Minimally Invasive Gynecology Worldwide *(1971)*
6757 Katella Ave.
Cypress, CA 90630-5105
Tel: (714) 503-6200 *Fax:* (714) 503-6201
TollFree: (800) 554-2245
E-Mail: generalmail@aagl.com
Website: aagl.com
Members: 5800 members
Staff: 13
Annual Budget: $500-1,000,000

Personnel:
Executive Vice President and Medical Director: Franklin D.
    Loffer MD
Executive Director: Linda Michels
Professional Education Manager: Art Arellano
Director, Information Systems and Project Development:
    Roman Bojorquez
    E-Mail: rbojorquez@aagl.org
Coordinator, Membership Services: Gerardo Galindo
    E-Mail: ggalindo@aagl.org
Director, Marketing and Strategic Initiatives: Barbara
    Hodgson
    E-Mail: bhodgson@aagl.org
Coordinator, Events: Jane Kalert
Graphic Designer, Communication Manager: Jennifer
    Sanchez
Administrator: Seth Spirrison

Historical Note:
*Founded as the American Association of Gynecologic
Laparoscopists, assumed its current name in 2005.
AAGL's mission is to advance diagnostic and therapeutic
techniques that provide less invasive treatments for
gynecologic conditions. It has affiliated societies worldwide.
Membership: $275 (Physician/Corporate); $115 (Resident/
Fellows/Retired Physician/Allied Healthcare Professionals).*

Meetings/Conferences:
Conference Chair: Jane Kalert
2013 - Cape Town, South Africa/April 9 - 13
2013 - Ft. Washington, MD (Gaylord National Resort
    and Convention Center-National Harbor)/Nov. 10 -
    14
Number of non-conference events/year: 9

Publications:
Membership Directory
NewsScope; quarterly
The Journal of Minimally Invasive Gynecology; bi-
    monthly; adv.

AASHTO: Transportation Center of Excellence
444 N. Capitol St. NW, Suite 249
Washington, DC 20001
Tel: (202) 624-5800 *Fax:* (202) 624-5806
E-Mail: info@aashto.org
Website: transportation.org
Members: 52 state governmental agencies
Staff: 131
Annual Budget: $50-100,000,000

Personnel:
Executive Director: John C. Horsley
    E-Mail: jhorsley@aashto.org
Director, Administration and Finance: Jenet Adem
    E-Mail: jadem@aashto.org
Manager, Marketing Campaign: Sherry Appel
    E-Mail: sappel@aashto.org
Director, Program Finance and Management: Jack Basso
    E-Mail: jbasso@aashto.org
Manager, Human Resource: Christine Beauvais
    E-Mail: cbeauvais@aashto.org
Director, Communications: Lloyd Brown
    E-Mail: lbrown@aashto.org
Information Systems Technical Specialist: Takaro J. Day
    E-Mail: tday@aashto.org
Director, Publications Production: Erin K. Grady
    E-Mail: egrady@aashto.org
Assistant Director, Publications Production: Linda Graves

    E-Mail: lindag@aashto.org
Meeting Planner: Sheri Johnson
    E-Mail: sherij@aashto.org
Director, Engineering and Technical Services: Anthony R.
    Kane PhD
    E-Mail: akane@aashto.org
Director, Policy and Government Relations: Janet Oakley
    E-Mail: joakley@aashto.org
Director, Meetings and Member Services: Monica Russell
    E-Mail: mrussell@aashto.org
Senior Editor: Lucas Wall
    E-Mail: lwall@aashto.org
Membership Coordinator and Meeting Planner: Brian
    Watson
    E-Mail: Bwatson@aashto.org

Historical Note:
*Formerly the American Association of State Highway
and Transportation Officials, the American Association
of State Highway and Transportation Officials advocates
transportation-related policies and provides technical
services to support states in their efforts to efficiently and
safely move people and goods. Membership: $2,000/year
(Associate).*

Meetings/Conferences: Annual
Conference Chair: Monica Russell
2013 - Denver, CO (Sheraton Denver West Hotel)/Oct.
    16 - 21
2014 - Charlotte, NC (Westin Charlotte)/Oct. 23 - 27

Publications:
AASHTO Email Newsletter; weekly
AASHTO Journal; weekly
Transportation Marketing E-News; monthly

AASP - The Palynological Society *(1967)*
Conoco Phillips
P.O. Box 2197
Houston, TX 77252-2197
Tel: (281) 293-3189 *Fax:* (281) 293-3833
Website: palynology.org
Members:
103 institutions
617 individuals
Staff: 8
Annual Budget: $25-50,000

Personnel:
President: Ian Harding
    E-Mail: ich@noc.soton.ac.uk
Secretary and Treasurer: Thomas D. Demchuk
    E-Mail: thomas.d.demchuk@conocophillips.com
Managing Editor: James B. Riding
    E-Mail: j.riding@bgs.ac.uk
Webmaster: Mohamed K. Zobaa
    E-Mail: mkzb79@mst.edu

Historical Note:
*In 2008, AASP changed its name from the American
Association of Stratigraphic Palynologists.to AASP - The
Palynological Society. AASP's mission is to promote the
study of palynology, or the study of pollen and spores,
especially as it relates to stratigraphic applications and
Biostratigraphy. Membership: $45 (Professional); $30
(Student); $15(Retired).*

Meetings/Conferences: Annual
2013 - San Francisco, CA/Oct. 20 - 24

Publications:
AASP Newsletter; quarterly
Membership Directory; annually

Abacus International *(2012)*
12050 SW 88 Ave.
Miami, FL 33176
Tel: (305) 389-9466
E-Mail: info@abacusworldwide.org
Website: abacusworldwide.org
Staff: 1

Personnel:
President and Chief Executive Officer: Julio Gabay

Historical Note:
*An international association of independent accounting,
consulting and legal firms focused on connecting like-
minded firms.*

ABC Children's Group *(1900)*
200 White Plains Rd.
Suite 600
Tarrytown, NY 10591
Tel: (800) 637-0037 *Fax:* (914) 591-2720
E-Mail: info@bookweb.org

Website: bookweb.org/membership/abc
Members: 600 individuals
Staff: 1
Annual Budget: $250-500,000
Tax: 501(c)(6)

Personnel:
Group Manager: Shannon O'Connor

Historical Note:
*Formerly known as the Association of Booksellers for
Children. It was absorbed by the American Booksellers
Assoication to form the ABC Children's Group. Members
have access to programs specifically aimed at growing
and expanding the reach of children's books to a wide
audience of both consumers and booksellers. Membership:
$200(Used/Auxiliary); $350(Associate/Provisional);*

Meetings/Conferences:
Number of non-conference events/year: 1

Publications:
Membership Directory; on-line

Membership List Available to Non-members

Abortion Care Network *(2008)*
1425 K St. NW
Suite 350
Washington, DC 20006
Tel: (202) 419-1444 *Fax:* (202) 587-5601
E-Mail: info@ncap.com
Website:
abortioncarenetwork.org
ncap.com
Members: 200 clinics
Staff: 3
Annual Budget: $100-250,000
Tax: 501(c)(4)

Personnel:
Director: Charlotte Taft
Treasurer: Dallas Schubert

Historical Note:
*ACN's founders were part of two organizations, the
Abortion Conversation Project and the National Coalition of
Abortion Providers (NCAP). NCAP is now dissolved. ACN
provides support for the credibility of the unique perspective
brought by abortion providers to the cultural conversation
surrounding abortion. Members are independently
owned clinics providing abortion services. Membership:
$500-4,000 (Provider); $150 (Allied).*

Meetings/Conferences: Annual

Publications:
ACN Newsletter; on-line
Membership Directory; on-line

Abrasive Engineering Society *(1957)*
144 Moore Rd.
Butler, PA 16001
Tel: (724) 282-6210 *Fax:* (724) 234-2376
E-Mail: aes@abrasiveengineering.com
Website: abrasiveengineering.com
Members: 300 individuals
Staff: 1
Annual Budget: Under $10,000
Tax: 501(c)(6)

Personnel:
Business Manager: Theodore L. Giese

Historical Note:
*AES distributes technical information about abrasives
minerals and their uses including abrasives grains and
products such as grinding wheels, coated abrasives and
thousands of other related tools and products that serve
manufacturers and the consumer. Membership: $55
(Individual); $350 (Organization).*

Publications:
International Journal of Abrasive Technology

ACA International, The Association of Credit and Collection Professionals *(1939)*
P.O. Box 390106
Minneapolis, MN 55439-0106
Tel: (952) 926-6547 *Fax:* (952) 926-1624
E-Mail: aca@acainternational.org
Website: acainternational.org
Members: 5000 third-party collection agencies,
asset buyers, attorneys, creditors and vendor
affiliates
Staff: 70
Annual Budget: $2-5,000,000
Tax: 501(c)(6)

Personnel:

Director, Federal Government Affairs: Adam J. Peterman
E-Mail: peterman@acainternational.org

Historical Note:
Formerly (2001) known as American Collectors Association, ACA promotes the general welfare of the credit and collection profession. Its activities include education, publishing, research, public affairs, group buying, public relations, conventions and trade shows and also sponsors and supports the American Collectors Political Action Committee (ACPAC). Membership: $750/year (Affiliate).

Continuing Education:
Certification Designation/s: PPMS, MCE, IFCCE

Meetings/Conferences:
2013 - Vail, CO (Vail Cascade Resort and Spa)/Jan. 5 - 8
2013 - Grand Cayman Island, United Kingdom (Westin Casuarina Resort and Spa)/Feb. 12 - 15
Number of non-conference events/year: 17

Publications:
ACA News Link; weekly
Collector; monthly; adv.
Consumer Trends Newsletter; monthly
MAPbulletin; monthly
Paper Newsletter
Pulse Newsletter; monthly

Academic Language Therapy Association (1986)
14070 Proton Rd.
Suite 100, LB Nine
Dallas, TX 75244
Tel: (972) 233-9107 Fax: (972) 490-4219
TollFree: (866) 283-7133
E-Mail: office@altaread.org
Website: altaread.org
Members: 800 individuals
Staff: 6
Annual Budget: $100-250,000
Tax: 501(c)(6)

Personnel:
President: Karen Avrit
Vice President, Website Services: Lexie Barefoot
Vice President, Programs: Christine Bedenbaugh
Treasurer: Kathleen Carlsen
Vice President, Public Relations: Lynne Fitzhugh
Vice President, Membership Services: Tim Odegard

Historical Note:
ALTA's purpose is to establish, maintain and promote standards of education, practice and professional conduct for Certified Academic Language Therapists. Academic Language Therapy is an educational, structured, comprehensive, phonetic, multisensory approach for the remediation of dyslexia and/or written-language disorders. Membership: $120 (Associate/Teacher Level); $150 (Therapist Level).

Continuing Education:
Certification Designation/s: CALT, CALP, ICALP, QI

Publications:
ALTA newsletter
Member Directory; on-line

Academic Pediatric Association (1962)
6728 Old McLean Village Dr.
McLean, VA 22101
Tel: (703) 556-9222 Fax: (703) 556-8729
E-Mail: info@academicpeds.org
Website: ambpeds.org
Members: 1800 individuals
Staff: 6
Annual Budget: $1-2,000,000
Tax: 501(c)(3)

Personnel:
Executive Director: Marge Degnon
E-Mail: marge@ambpeds.org
Research Associate: Nui Dhepyasuwan
E-Mail: nui@academicpeds.org
Administrative Assistant: Allison Hartle
E-Mail: allison@academicpeds.org
Manager, Accounts: Jennifer Padilla
E-Mail: jennifer@academicpeds.org
Director, Communications: Barry Solomon
E-Mail: bsolomo1@jhmi.edu

Historical Note:
APA is dedicated to improving the health of all children and adolescents through leadership in education of child health professionals, research and dissemination of knowledge, patient care, and advocacy, in partnership with children, families and communities. Membership: $250 (Physician); $125 (Non-Physician); $50 (In Training).

Meetings/Conferences: Annual
2013 - Washington, DC/May 4 - 7

Publications:
Academic Pediatrics; bi-monthly
APA Newsletter; bi-monthly

Academy for Eating Disorders (1993)
111 Deer Lake Rd.
Suite 100
Deerfield, IL 60015
Tel: (847) 498-4274 Fax: (847) 480-9282
E-Mail: info@aedweb.org
Website: aedweb.org
Members: 1300 individuals
Staff: 4
Annual Budget: $500-1,000,000
Tax: 501(c)(3)

Personnel:
Executive Director: Greg Schultz
Administrative Director: Annie Cox
E-Mail: acox@aedweb.org
Manager, Marketing and Communications: Jeff Keller
E-Mail: jkeller@aedweb.org
Director, Conferences: Jacky Schweinzger
E-Mail: jschweinzger@aedweb.org

Historical Note:
AED is an association committed to leadership in eating disorders research, education, treatment, and prevention. Membership: $189-245 (Regular/Affiliate Members); $245(Fellows); $58-123 (Student Members).

Meetings/Conferences: Annual
Conference Chair: Jacky Schweinzger
2013 - Montreal, QC (Hilton Montreal Bonaventure)/ May 2 - 4
2014 - New York City, NY (Sheraton New York Hotel and Towers)/March 27 - 29
2015 - Boston, MA (Boston Marriott Copley Place)/ April 23 - 25
2016 - San Francisco, CA (Hyatt Regency San Francisco)/May 5 - 7

Publications:
International Journal of Eating Disorders; adv.
Member Directory; on-line
The AED Forum; quarterly

Membership List Available to Non-members

Academy Health (2000)
1150 17th St. NW
Suite 600
Washington, DC 20036
Tel: (202) 292-6700 Fax: (202) 292-6800
E-Mail: info@academyhealth.org
Website: academyhealth.org
Members: 4000 individuals and organizations
Staff: 38
Annual Budget: $5-10,000,000
Tax: 501(c)(3)

Personnel:
President and Chief Executive Officer: Lisa Simpson FAAP, MPH
E-Mail: dawn.ferdinand@academyhealth.org
Director, Membership Services: Jane Brookstein
E-Mail: jane.brookstein@academyhealth.org
Senior Manager, Meeting Operations: Gennice T. Carter
E-Mail: gennice.carter@academyhealth.org
Chief Financial Officer: Deborah L. Edwards
E-Mail: deborah.edwards@academyhealth.org
Director, Information Technology: Stacy L. Halbert
E-Mail: stacy.halbert@academyhealth.org
Director, Human Resources: Teasha Powell
E-Mail: teasha.powell@academyhealth.org
Director, Communications: Kristin Rosengren
E-Mail: kristin.rosengren@academyhealth.org
Manager, Accounting: Wendy Smith
E-Mail: wendy.smith@academyhealth.org

Historical Note:
Founded as Association for Health Services Research; became Association for Health Services Research and Health Policy in 2000 and assumed its current name in 2002. Academy Health's mission is to improve health and health care by generating new knowledge and moving knowledge into action. Academy Health members are individuals and organizations concerned with health services research. Membership: $175 (Regular/International); $100 (Fellow); $40 (Student); $2,000-10,000 (Organization).

Meetings/Conferences: Annual

Conference Chair: Gennice T. Carter
2013 - Baltimore, MD/June 23 - 25/2400 attendees/26-50 exhibitors
2014 - San Diego, CA/June 8 - 10/2400 attendees/26-50 exhibitors
2015 - Minneapolis, MN/June 14 - 16/2400 attendees/51-100 exhibitors
2016 - Boston, MA/June 26 - 28

Publications:
Health Affairs; monthly
AcademyHealth Reports; quarterly
Health Services Research (HSR); on-line; adv.
Member Update; monthly
Partners; bi-monthly

Academy of Accounting Historians (1973)
Case Western Reserve University, Weatherhead School of Management
10900 Euclid Ave.
Cleveland, OH 44106-7235
Tel: (216) 368-2058 Fax: (216) 368-6244
E-Mail: acchistory@case.edu
Website: aahhq.org
Members: 850 individuals
Staff: 3
Annual Budget: $25-50,000

Personnel:
President: Joann Noe Cross
Vice President, Communications: Yvette Lazdowski
Treasurer: Jennifer Reynolds-Moehrle

Historical Note:
AAH's purpose is to encourage research, publication, teaching and personal interchanges in all phases of accounts and business. Members are individuals and institutional affiliates. Membership: $50 (Individual); $30 (Retired); $100 (Institution/Library); $10 (College/ Graduate/Doctoral Students).

Meetings/Conferences: Annual
2013 - Oshkosh, WI (University of Wisconsin Oshkosh)/Oct. 14 - 19
Number of non-conference events/year: 1

Publications:
Individual Directory; on-line
Membership Directory; on-line
The Accounting Historians Journal; semi-annually

Academy of Ambulatory Foot and Ankle Surgery (1972)
1601 Walnut St.
Suite 1005
Philadelphia, PA 19102
Tel: (215) 569-3303 Fax: (215) 569-3310
TollFree: (800) 433-4892
E-Mail: aafas@aol.com
Website: aafas.org
Members: 1500 individuals
Staff: 3
Annual Budget: $250-500,000

Personnel:
Program Coordinator: Harriet Waloff

Historical Note:
AAFAS is committed to offering patients a combination of high-tech, state- of-the-art medicine and surgery mixed with old fashioned caring and compassion and specialize in surgical procedures that do not require hospitalization. Members are doctors and podiatric surgeons. AAFAS' mission is to advocate ethical high quality treatment of patients by a group of morally motivated professionals. Membership: $345 (International); $495 (Fellow/ Associate); $50 (Resident/Student); $100 (Retired).

Meetings/Conferences: Annual

Publications:
Membership Directory; on-line

The Academy of American Poets (1934)
75 Maiden Ln.
Suite 901
New York, NY 10038
Tel: (212) 274-0343 Fax: (212) 274-9427
E-Mail: academy@poets.org
Website: poets.org
Staff: 16
Annual Budget: $1-2,000,000
Tax: 501(c)(3)

Personnel:
Executive Director: Jennifer Benka
Editor: Hanna Andrews

E-Mail: handrews@poets.org
Manager, Finance: Eric Engleson
  E-Mail: engleson@poets.org
Associate Director and Development Director: Beth Harrison
  E-Mail: bharrison@poets.org
Coordinator, Publicity and Outreach: Stacy Lasner
Web Developer: Billy Merrell CAE
  E-Mail: bmerrell@poets.org

Historical Note:
Mission is to support American poets at all stages of their careers and to foster the appreciation of contemporary poetry. Membership: $55 (Associate); $100 (Sustainer); $35 (Contributor); $250 (Patron); $500 (Sponsor); $1,000 (Benefactor); $2,500 minimum (Chairman's Circle).

Publications:
AAP Newsletter
American Poet; biennially; adv.
Poem-A-Day; daily
Poets.org Update; monthly

Academy of Aphasia (1962)
5130 W. Suffield Terrace
Skokie, IL 60077
Tel: (847) 467-7591 *Fax:* (847) 467-7377
E-Mail: contact@academyofaphasia.org
Website: academyofaphasia.org
Members: 200 individuals
Staff: 4
Annual Budget: $50-100,000
Tax: 501(c)(6)

Personnel:
Director, Administrative Services: Mejrima-Mary Cosic
  E-Mail: contact@academyofaphasia.org
Treasurer: Cindy Thompson

Historical Note:
AA's mission is to provide clinical services to help people improve their language skills following strokes or other illnesses. Membership: $100 (Regular); $50 (Associate).

Meetings/Conferences: Annual

Publications:
Aphasiology; monthly
Brain and Language; monthly
Cognitive Neuropsychology
Procedia

Academy of Applied Science (1963)
24 Warren St.
Concord, NH 03301
Tel: (603) 228-4530 *Fax:* (603) 228-4730
E-Mail: admin@aas-world.org
Website: aas-world.org
Members: 300 individuals
Staff: 6
Annual Budget: $2-5,000,000
Tax: 501(c)(3)

Personnel:
Program Director: Pamela Hampton
  E-Mail: phampton@aas-world.org
Administrative Assistant: Carol Hyslop
Business Administrator and Deputy Director: Kate Trojano
  E-Mail: ktrojano@aas-world.org

Historical Note:
AAS is an educational resource center offering enrichment programs for students, and professional development for teachers and educational administrators. Members are educators and professionals in applied science, engineering and similar disciplines. AAS sponsors programs that recognize and foster creativity and advancement in the applied sciences. Individuals become members of the Academy through nomination by current members.

Meetings/Conferences:
Conference Chair: Pamela Hampton

Academy of Behavioral Medicine Research (1978)
Department of Psychology, University of Miami
P.O. Box 248185, 5665 Ponce de Leon Blvd.
Coral Gables, FL 33124-0751
Tel: (305) 284-6698 *Fax:* (305) 284-2522
E-Mail: pmccabe@miami.edu
Website: academyofbmr.org
Members: 350 individuals
Staff: 3
Annual Budget: $25-50,000

Personnel:
President: Stephen Manuck
  E-Mail: manuck@pitt.edu

Treasurer: Ken Freedland
  E-Mail: freedlak@bmc.wustl.edu
Secretary: Maria Llabre
  E-Mail: mllabre@miami.edu

Historical Note:
ABMR's purpose is to provide service for established behavioral medicine researchers where ideas could be exchanged in an informal yet scientifically charges atmosphere. Membership: $125/year.

Meetings/Conferences: Annual

Publications:
Membership Directory; on-line

Academy of Breastfeeding Medicine (1993)
140 Huguenot St.
Third Floor
New Rochelle, NY 10801
Tel: (914) 740-2115 *Fax:* (914) 740-2101
E-Mail: abm@bfmed.org
Website: bfmed.org
Members: 500 individuals
Staff: 2
Annual Budget: $500-1,000,000
Tax: 501(c)(3)

Personnel:
Executive Director: Karla Shepard Rubinger
  E-Mail: krubinger@liebertpub.com
Treasurer: Timothy Tobolic

Historical Note:
Founded as Physicians Advocating Breastfeeding; became ABM in 1994. A worldwide organization of physicians dedicated to the promotion, protection and support of breastfeeding and human lactation. ABM's mission is to unite members of the various medical specialties with this common purpose. ABM provides education and technical information on breastfeeding and related medical issues for its members. Membership: $45-260 (General); $95 (Student); $600 (Gold); $5,000 (Lifetime).

Meetings/Conferences: Annual

Publications:
Breastfeeding Medicine

Academy of Certified Archivists (1989)
1450 Western Ave.
Suite 101
Albany, NY 12203
Tel: (518) 694-8471 *Fax:* (518) 463-8656
E-Mail: aca@caphill.org
Website: certifiedarchivists.org
Members: 725 individuals
Staff: 5
Annual Budget: $50-100,000
Tax: 501(c)(6)

Personnel:
Webmaster: Laura Botts
  E-Mail: webmaster@certifiedarchivists.org
Secretariat: Steve Grandin
Contact, Communications: Laura Lyons McLemore
  E-Mail: laura.mclemore@lsus.edu
Treasurer: Todd Welch

Historical Note:
ACA is an independent, nonprofit certifying organization of professional archivists. Individual members qualify for certification by meeting a series of defined professional standards.

Continuing Education:
Certification Designation/s: CA

Publications:
ACA News; quarterly
Membership Directory; on-line

Academy of Clinical Laboratory Physicians and Scientists (1966)
500 Chipeta Way
C/O ARUP Laboratories
Salt Lake City, UT 84108
Tel: (801) 583-2787 *Fax:* (801) 584-5207
E-Mail: karolynn.braden@aruplab.com
Website: aclps.org
Members: 300 individuals
Staff: 4
Annual Budget: $100-250,000

Personnel:
President: Eric D. Spitzer
Newsletter Editor: Geza S. Bodor
Administrative Assistant and Membership Contact: Karolynn Braden

  E-Mail: karolynn.braden@aruplab.com
Secretary and Treasurer: David Grenache

Historical Note:
ACLPS members are physicians, scientists and educators primarily engaged in teaching, research and service in academic laboratory medicine, also known as clinical pathology. Membership: $100/year.

Meetings/Conferences: Annual
2013 - Atlanta, GA (Emory University)/June 6 - 8

Publications:
ACLPS Newsletter
Membership Directory
The American Journal of Clinical Pathology; monthly

Academy of Clinical Research Professionals (1976)
500 Montgomery St.
Suite 800
Alexandria, VA 22314
Tel: (703) 254-8100 *Fax:* (703) 254-8101
E-Mail: office@acrpnet.org
Website: acrpnet.org
Members: 18000 individuals
Staff: 4
Annual Budget: $1-2,000,000
Tax: 501(c)(6)

Personnel:
President: Barbara J. Early RN
  E-Mail: earlybj@upmc.edu
Executive Director: James D. Thomasell
Treasurer: Susan Warne

Historical Note:
ACRP's mission is to provide global leadership to promote integrity and excellence for the clinical research profession. Membership: $100 (Resident); $60 (Student); $25(Chapter members).

Continuing Education:
Certification Designation/s: CRC, CRA, CPI, CTI

Meetings/Conferences: Annual
2013 - Orange, FL (Orange County Convention Center)/April 13 - 16/2000 attendees/over 100 exhibitors

Publications:
ACRP Newsletter; semi-annually; adv.
Member Directory; on-line

Academy of Country Music (1964)
5500 Balboa Blvd.
Encino, CA 91316
Tel: (818) 788-8000 *Fax:* (818) 788-0999
E-Mail: info@acmcountry.com
Website: acmcountry.com
Members: 4000 individuals
Staff: 15
Annual Budget: $5-10,000,000
Tax: 501(c)(6)

Personnel:
Chief Executive Officer: Bob Romeo
  E-Mail: bobromeo@acmcountry.com
Director, Finance: Alexa Fasheh
Senior Vice President, Membership Services and Industry Relations: Michelle Goble
Senior Vice President, Operations and Events: Erick Long
Senior Vice President, Publicity: Brooke Primero
  E-Mail: brooke@acmcountry.com

Historical Note:
Formerly, Country and Western Music Academy and then Academy of Country and Western Music. Assumed it's current name in 1970's. ACM's mission is to promote and support the industry and engage country music fans not just in the western states, but from coast to coast. Membership: $75/year (Individual).

Meetings/Conferences:
Conference Chair: Michelle Goble

Publications:
A-List newsletter; on-line

Academy of Criminal Justice Sciences (1963)
P.O. Box 960
Greenbelt, MD 20768-0960
Tel: (301) 446-6300 *Fax:* (301) 446-2819
TollFree: (800) 757-2257
E-Mail: info@acjs.org
Website: acjs.org
Members: 2700 individuals
Staff: 2

Annual Budget: $500-1,000,000
Tax: 501(c)(3)

Personnel:
Executive Director: Mittie D. Southerland
   E-Mail: execdir@acjs.org

Historical Note:
ACJS seeks to advance professional and scholarly activities in the field of criminal justice. It is composed of professors, practitioners, researchers and institutions who deal with criminology, criminal justice, corrections and law. Membership: $75 (Regular); $300 (Institution); $150 (Sustaining); $30 (Student); $1,125 (Lifetime).

Continuing Education:
Certification Designation/s: ACJS

Meetings/Conferences: Annual
2013 - Dallas, TX (Sheraton Dallas)/March 19 - 23
2014 - Philadelphia, PA (Philadelphia Marriott Downtown)/Feb. 18 - 22
2015 - Orlando, FL (Caribe Royale All-Suite Hotel and Convention Center)/March 3 - 7
2016 - Denver, CO (Sheraton Denver Downtown Hotel)/March 29 - April 2
2017 - Kansas City, MO (Kansas City Marriott Downtown)/March 28 - April 1

Publications:
ACJS Today; quarterly; adv.
Journal of Criminal Justice Education; quarterly; adv.
Justice Quarterly; bi-monthly; adv.
The ACJS Membership Directory; quarterly

Membership List Available to Non-members

Academy of Dental Materials (1941)
21 Grouse Ter.
Lake Oswego, OR 97035-1013
Tel: (503) 636-0861 *Fax:* (503) 675-2738
E-Mail: admtreas@comcast.net
Website: academydentalmaterials.org
Members: 350 individuals
Staff: 5
Annual Budget: $100-250,000
Tax: 501(c)(3)

Personnel:
President: Alvaro Della Bona
   E-Mail: dbona@upf.br
Interim Webmaster: Steve Bayne
Contact, Membership Services: Deanna Hilton
Treasurer: Thomas Hilton
   E-Mail: hiltont@ohsu.edu
Editor: David Watts

Historical Note:
Formerly (1983) American Academy for Plastics Research in Dentistry. ADM's aim is to provide a forum for the exchange of information on all aspects of dental materials. Membership: $40 (Student); $149-175 (Regular).

Meetings/Conferences: Annual

Publications:
Academy of Dental Materials Newsletter; annually
Dental Materials; monthly; adv.

Academy of Dentistry International (1974)
3813 Gordon Creek Dr.
Hicksville, OH 43526
Tel: (419) 542-0101 *Fax:* (419) 542-6883
E-Mail: rramus@bright.net
Website: adint.org
Members: 2935 individuals
Staff: 3
Annual Budget: $100-250,000
Tax: 501(c)(6)

Personnel:
Executive Director: Robert L. Ramus
Vice President, Finance &Administration: Ramon J. Baez
   E-Mail: rjbaez@gvtc.com
Vice President, Education: Ernesto Acuña E.
   E-Mail: dreacuna@prodiigy.net.mx

Historical Note:
ADI is dedicated to share knowledge in order to serve the dental and oral health needs and to improve the quality of life of the people throughout the world. Membership: $80/year.

Publications:
Australasian Section News
International Communicator
USA Section Newsletter; bi-annually

Academy of Doctors of Audiology (1977)
3493 Lansdowne Dr.
Suite two
Lexington, KY 40517
Fax: (859) 271-0607
TollFree: (866) 493-5544
E-Mail: info@audiologist.org
Website: audiologist.org
Members: 1000 individuals
Staff: 3
Annual Budget: $500-1,000,000
Tax: 501(c)(6)

Personnel:
Executive Director: Stephanie Czuhajewski CAE
   E-Mail: sczuhajewski@audiologist.org

Historical Note:
Formerly Academy of Dispensing Audiologists. ADA is dedicated to the advancement of practitioner excellence, high ethical standards, professional autonomy and sound business practices in the provision of quality audiologic care. Membership: $250 (Fellow); $210 (Associate); $25 (Student); $125-200 (Graduated); $125 (Lifetime-65 yrs and 15 or more yrs of membership).

Meetings/Conferences: Annual
2013 - Bonita Springs, FL (Hyatt Regency Coconut Point Resort and Spa)/Nov. 7 - 9
2014 - Las Vegas, NV (Red Rock Casino Resort and Spa)/Nov. 6 - 8

Publications:
AuDioGram; monthly
Audiologist Directory; on-line
Audiology Practices; quarterly; adv.

Membership List Available to Non-members

Academy of General Dentistry (1952)
211 E. Chicago Ave.
Suite 900
Chicago, IL 60611-1999
Tel: (312) 440-4300 *Fax:* (312) 440-0559
TollFree: (888) 243-3368
E-Mail: agdtech@agd.org
Website: agd.org
Members: 37000 individuals
Staff: 75
Annual Budget: $10-25,000,000
Tax: 501(c)(6)

Personnel:
President: Jeffrey M. Cole
Associate Executive Director, Public Affairs: Daniel Buksa CAE, JD
   E-Mail: daniel.buksa@agd.org
Director, Communications: Cathy McNamara
   E-Mail: cathy.mcnamara@agd.org
Director, Education: Rebecca M. Murray
   E-Mail: rebecca.murray@agd.org
Manager, Exhibits: Margery Palonis
   E-Mail: margery.palonis@agd.org
Managing Editor: Chris Zayner

Historical Note:
AGD's mission is to serve the needs and represent the interest of general dentists, and to promote the oral health of the public. Membership: $16-354/year.

Continuing Education:
Enrollment: 8456

Meetings/Conferences: Annual
Conference Chair: Margery Palonis
2013 - Nashville, TN/June 23 - 30
Number of non-conference events/year: 5

Publications:
AGD Impact; monthly; adv.
Dentalnotes; quarterly
General Dentistry; bi-monthly; adv.
Membership Directory; on-line
SmileLine; monthly

Academy of Homiletics (1965)
The Divinity School, Vanderbilt University
411 21st Ave. South
Nashville, TN 37240-1121
Tel: (615) 343-3989
E-Mail: homiletic@vanderbilt.edu
Website: homiletics.org
Members: 400 individuals
Staff: 5
Annual Budget: $25-50,000

Personnel:
President: Alyce McKenzie

   E-Mail: alycemck@smu.edu
Treasurer and Contact, Membership Services: Jennifer Lord
   E-Mail: jlord@austinseminary.edu
Editor: John S. McClure
   E-Mail: john.s.mcclure@vanderbilt.edu
Secretary and Contact News and Information: Luke Powery
   E-Mail: luke.powery@ptsem.edu
Editor and Contact Website: Andre Resner
   E-Mail: soht_e@yahoo.com

Historical Note:
AH's mission is to further homiletics as an academic discipline, and to promote scholarship and teaching excellence in the field. Members are faculty at graduate schools of theology, teaching courses in homiletics. Membership: $75 (Full Member); $35 (Associate - Graduate Students/Retired).

Meetings/Conferences: Annual

Publications:
Homiletic; bi-annually
Member Directory

Academy of Hospitality Industry Attorneys
14070 Proton Rd.
Suite 100, LB Nine
Dallas, TX 75244
Tel: (972) 233-9107 *Fax:* (972) 409-4219
E-Mail: becky@madcrouch.com
Website: ahiattorneys.org
Staff: 2
Annual Budget: $50-100,000
Tax: 501(c)(6)

Personnel:
Executive Director: Becky Tiemann
   E-Mail: becky@madcrouch.com
Treasurer: David Comeaux
   E-Mail: david.comeaux@ogletreedeakins.com

Historical Note:
AHIA strives to promote professionalism, education, and improved communication to create a network of competent, experienced attorneys to improve legal services to its clients in the industries. Membership is limited to those attorneys whom AHIA believes will represent the principles of leadership and excellence in providing quality legal services to its clients in the Industries. Membership: $300/year.

Meetings/Conferences:
Conference Chair: Becky Tiemann

Publications:
Membership Directory

Academy of International Business (1959)
C/O Michigan State University
Seven Eppley Center
East Lansing, MI 48824-1121
Tel: (517) 432-1452 *Fax:* (517) 432-1009
E-Mail: aib@aib.msu.edu
Website: aib.msu.edu
Members: 3170 individuals
Staff: 6
Annual Budget: $500-1,000,000
Tax: 501(c)(6)

Personnel:
Executive Director: G. Tomas M. Hult
Managing Editor: Anne Hoekman
Managing Director: Tunga Kiyak
Assistant, Office and Editorial: Meg Quine
   E-Mail: quinemar@msu.edu
Systems Analyst: Jamie Rytlewski

Historical Note:
Formerly (1959) Association for Education in International Business, AIB's mission is to facilitate the exchange of information and ideas among people in academic, business, and government professions who are concerned with education in international business. Members are teachers and executives in the field of international business. Membership: $100 (Individual); $50 (Student/Low Income); $25 (Electronic).

Meetings/Conferences: Annual
2013 - Istanbul, Turkey/July 3 - 6

Publications:
AIB Insights; quarterly
AIB Newsletter; quarterly; adv.
Conference Proceedings; annually
Journal of International Business Studies (JIBS)

Membership List Available to Non-members

Academy of Laser Dentistry (1993)
9900 W. Sample Rd.
Suite 400
Coral Springs, FL 33065
Tel: (954) 346-3776 *Fax:* (954) 757-2598
TollFree: (877) 527-3776
E-Mail: memberservices@laserdentistry.org
Website: laserdentistry.org
Members: 1100 individuals and 75 organizations
Staff: 2
Annual Budget: $500-1,000,000

Personnel:
Executive Director: Gail S. Siminovsky CAE
    E-Mail: laserexec@laserdentistry.org
Treasurer: John J. Graeber DMD
    E-Mail: hitekdr@mac.com

Historical Note:
ALD was formed by the merger of the American Academy of Laser Dentistry, the International Academy of Laser Dentistry and the North American Academy of Laser Dentistry in 1993. ALD promotes the advancement of research and education in laser applications in dentistry. Members are licensed dentists, auxiliaries, academic and research institutions, dental students, scientists and physicians. Membership: $950 (Corporate); $395 (Dentists/Institutional); $150 (Non-Practicing/Associate/ Affiliate); $50 (Student).

Continuing Education:
Certification Designation/s: SPC, APC, LCP

Meetings/Conferences: Annual
2013 - Rancho Mirage, CA (Rancho Las Palmas Resort and Spa)/Feb. 7 - 9

Publications:
Journal of Laser Dentistry; quarterly; adv.
Lightwaves Newsletter; quarterly; adv.
Membership Directory; on-line

Membership List Available to Non-members

Academy of Legal Studies in Business (1924)
Miami University, Department of Finance
3111-Farmer School of Business
Oxford, OH 45056
Fax: (513) 523-8180
TollFree: (800) 831-2903
Website: alsb.mobi
Members: 1000 individuals
Staff: 5
Annual Budget: $100-250,000

Personnel:
Executive Secretary: Daniel J. Herron
    E-Mail: herrondj@muohio.edu

Historical Note:
Formerly (1991) American Business Law Association. Members are teachers of business law, legal environment and other law-related courses in colleges and universities other than professional law schools. Membership: $30 (Emeritus); $60 (Regular).

Meetings/Conferences: Annual
2013 - Boston, MA (Fairmont Copley Plaza Hotel Boston)/Aug. 6 - 11

Publications:
ALSB Newsletter; quarterly
Journal of Legal Studies Education; bi-annually
The American Business Law Journal; quarterly
The Journal of Employment and Labor Law

Academy of Leisure Sciences (1980)
C/O Texas A&M University
College Station, TX 77840
Tel: (979) 845-3211
E-Mail: adsess@intrex.net
Website: academyofleisuresciences.org
Members: 100 individuals
Staff: 2

Personnel:
President: Rep. David A. Scott

Historical Note:
ALS's purpose is to recognize, support, and establish a network and forum for scholars committed to the intellectual advancement of the field. Members are academics specializing in the study of issues related to leisure, recreation, and management of businesses and agencies in the park, recreation, and tourism industries. Membership: $50 (New); $20 (Student).

Meetings/Conferences: Annual
2013 - Salamanca, Spain (Salamanca)/Oct. 4 - 10
Number of non-conference events/year: 4

Academy of Managed Care Pharmacy (1989)
100 N. Pitt St.
Suite 400
Alexandria, VA 22314
Tel: (800) 827-2627 *Fax:* (703) 683-8417
TollFree: (800) 827-2627
Website: amcp.org
Members: 6000 members
Staff: 30
Annual Budget: $10-25,000,000
Tax: 501(c)(6)

Personnel:
Chief Executive Officer: Edith Rosato IOM
    E-Mail: erosato@amcp.org
Director, Finance: Johann De Castro
Editor in Chief: Fred Curtiss CEBS, PhD, RPh
    E-Mail: fcurtiss@amcp.org
Vice President, External Relations: Robert Fulcher
Vice President of Government Affairs: Lauren Fuller
    E-Mail: lfuller@amcp.org
Director, Education and Meetings: Aimee Hickox
    E-Mail: ahickox@amcp.org
Director, Human Resources: Krista Kirk
Director, Communications: Neal Learner
    E-Mail: nlearner@amcp.org
Director, Membership Services and Marketing: Betty Whitaker

Historical Note:
AMCP's mission is to empower its members to serve society by using sound medication management principles and strategies to improve health care for all. Membership: $240 (Associate); $240 (Pharmacist/Health Care Practitioner); $35 (Student Pharmacist); $85 (Resident/Fellow/Graduate Student).

Meetings/Conferences: Semi-Annual
Conference Chair: Aimee Hickox
2013 - San Antonio, TX (Henry B. Gonzalez Convention Center and the Lila Cockrell Theatre)/ April 3 - 6
2013 - San Diego, CA (San Diego Convention Center)/ April 3 - 5
2014 - Tampa, FL (Tampa Convention Center)/April 2 - 4
2014 - Boston, MA (Hynes Convention Center)/Oct. 8 - 10
Number of non-conference events/year: 3

Publications:
AMCP Legislative/Regulatory Briefing; monthly
AMCP News; monthly; adv.
Daily Dose; daily; adv.
Journal of Managed Care Pharmacy; adv.
Journal of Manged Care Pharmacy; adv.
Membership Directory; annually; adv.
URAC & AMCP Quality Management News; quarterly

Membership List Available to Non-members

Academy of Managed Care Providers (1993)
1945 Palo Verde Ave.
Suite 202
Long Beach, CA 90815-3445
Tel: (562) 682-3559 *Fax:* (562) 799-3355
TollFree: (800) 297-2627
Website: academymcp.org
Members: 2500 individuals
Staff: 1

Personnel:
President: John K. Russell CEAP, PhD

Historical Note:
AMCP is a national association of clinicians, managed care organization staff and other healthcare industry professionals. AMCP goal is to help professionals maintain the ability to provide quality care within a cost- conscious environment. Its members are companies and individuals interested in the provision of quality managed care. It sponsors educational programs and other services. Membership: $125-175 (Individual/Affiliate); $35-45 (Student); $1,000 (Corporate/Institutional).

Publications:
Managed Care Times

Academy of Management (1936)
P.O. Box 3020
Briarcliff Manor, NY 10510-8020
Tel: (914) 923-2607 *Fax:* (914) 923-2615
E-Mail: membership@aom.pace.edu
Website: aomonline.org
Members: 19184 Individuals
Staff: 18
Annual Budget: $5-10,000,000
Tax: 501(c)(3)

Personnel:
Executive Director: Nancy Urbanowicz
    E-Mail: nurbanowicz@pace.edu
Coordinator, Communications and Publishing: Michael J. Davis
    E-Mail: mdavis@pace.edu
Specialist, Marketing and Social Media: Susan J. Fernandez
    E-Mail: sfernandez@pace.edu
Manager, Meetings: Taryn Fiore
    E-Mail: tfiore@pace.edu
Manager, Membership Services: Kerry Ignatz
    E-Mail: kignatz@pace.edu
Director, Finance: John P. Lozito
    E-Mail: jlozito@pace.edu
Managing Editor: Michael Malgrande
    E-Mail: mmalgrande@pace.edu
Database Developer and Programmer: Alina Matei
    E-Mail: amatei@aom.pace.edu
Associate Executive Director, Information Technology: Matthew Suppa
    E-Mail: msuppa@aom.pace.edu
Senior Managing Editor: Susan Zaid
    E-Mail: szaid@pace.edu

Historical Note:
AOM's mission is to build a vibrant and supportive community of scholars by markedly expanding opportunities to connect and explore ideas. Members are professors who research and teach management, as well as doctoral students in management and business professionals interested in principles of management. Membership: $182 (Academic/Executive/Practitioner); $91 (Student).

Meetings/Conferences: Annual
Conference Chair: Taryn Fiore
2013 - Orlando, FL/Aug. 9 - 13
2014 - Philadelphia, PA/Aug. 1 - 5
2015 - Vancouver, BC/Aug. 7 - 11
2016 - Anaheim, CA/Aug. 5 - 9
2017 - Atlanta, GA/Aug. 4 - 8
Number of non-conference events/year: 1

Publications:
Academy of Management Journal; on-line
Academy of Management News; quarterly
Membership Directory; on-line

Membership List Available to Non-members

Academy of Marketing Science (1971)
P.O. Box 3072
Ruston, LA 71272
Tel: (318) 257-2612 *Fax:* (318) 257-4253
E-Mail: ams@latech.edu
Website: ams-web.org
Members: 1500 individuals
Staff: 7
Annual Budget: $500-1,000,000

Personnel:
Executive Vice President and Director: Harold W. Berkman PhD
    E-Mail: ams@latech.edu
President-Elect: Linda Ferrell
    E-Mail: lferrell@mgt.unm.edu
Secretary and Treasurer: Lauren Skinner Beitelspacher
    E-Mail: beitel@pdx.edu
Vice President, Programs: Adilson Borges
    E-Mail: adilson.borges@reims-ms.fr
Director, Social Media: Colin Campbell
    E-Mail: mrcol@mac.com
Vice President, Publications: O. C. Ferrell
    E-Mail: OCferrell@mgt.unm.edu
Vice President, Membership Services: Constantine Katsikeas
    E-Mail: csk@lubs.leeds.ac.uk

Historical Note:
AMS's mission is to foster education in marketing, advancing the science of marketing and furthering professional standards in the discipline. It sponsors and supports the AMS Foundation which provides grants for both the advancement of the teaching of marketing and research in marketing. Membership: $90 (Regular); $60 (Student); $100 (Corporate).

Meetings/Conferences: Annual
Conference Chair: Adilson Borges
2013 - Monterey, CA/May 14 - 18
Number of non-conference events/year: 2

Publications:
AMS Quarterly; quarterly
AMS Review; quarterly
Journal of the Academy of Marketing Science;
    quarterly; adv.
Membership Directory; on-line

Membership List Available to Non-members

Academy of Medical-Surgical Nurses (1991)
E. Holly Ave.
P.O. Box 56
Pitman, NJ 08071-0056
Tel: (856) 256-2323 *Fax:* (856) 589-7463
TollFree: (866) 877-2676
E-Mail: amsn@ajj.com
Website: amsn.org
Members: 7600 individuals
Staff: 2
Annual Budget: $2-5,000,000
Tax: 501(c)(6)

Personnel:
Executive Director: Cynthia R. Nowicki Hnatiuk CAE,
    EdD, RN
    E-Mail: cyndee@ajj.com
Director, Association Services: Suzanne Stott
    E-Mail: sue.stott@ajj.com

Historical Note:
*AMSN's mission is to promote excellence in adult health.
Members are RNs, LPNs, LVNs, clinical nurse specialists,
nurse practitioners, educators, researchers, administrators,
and students. Membership: $84 (Full/Associate); $70 (New
Graduate); $45-50 (Student); $75 (Senior Associate).*

Continuing Education:
Certification Designation/s: CMSRN

Meetings/Conferences: Annual
2013 - Nashville, TN (Gaylord Opryland Resort
    and Convention Center)/Sept. 25 - 29/1000
    attendees/11-25 exhibitors
Number of non-conference events/year: 8

Publications:
Med-Surg Nursing Connection; monthly; adv.
MedSurg Matters!; bi-monthly; adv.
MEDSURG Nursing; monthly; adv.

Academy of Model Aeronautics
5161 E. Memorial Dr.
Muncie, IN 47302
Tel: (765) 287-1256
Website: modelaircraft.org
Staff: 58
Annual Budget: $5-10,000,000

Personnel:
Executive Director: Dave Mathewson
Director, Public Relations and Development: Chris Brooks
Contact, Human Resources: April Conner
Membership Director: Shawn Grubbs
Events Contact and Technical Director: Greg Hahn
Contact, Government and Regulatory Affairs: Rich Hanson
Director, Publications: Rob Kurek
Director, Marketing and Programs: Jeff Nance
Education Director: Bill Pritchett
Comptroller: Craig Schroeder

Historical Note:
*A self-supporting, non-profit organization whose purpose is
to promote development of model aviation as a recognized
sport and worthwhile recreation*

Meetings/Conferences: Annual
Conference Chair: Jeff Nance
2013 - Ontario, CA (Ontario Convention Center)/Jan.
    11 - 13

Publications:
AMA Flightline
AMA Today
Cloud 9
Model Aviation Magazine; monthly; adv.
Park Pilot Magazine; quarterly; adv.
Sport Aviator Magazine; on-line
The AMA Insider
The Nats News; daily

Academy of Molecular Imaging
5839 Green Valley Cir.
Suite 209
Los Angeles, CA 90230
Tel: (310) 215-9730 *Fax:* (310) 215-9731
Website: ami-imaging.org

Staff: 3
Annual Budget: $2-5,000,000
Tax: 501(c)(3)

Personnel:
Executive Director: Kim Pierce
    E-Mail: kpierce@ami-imaging.org
Administrative Director: Dova Levin
    E-Mail: dlevin@ami-imaging.org
Coordinator, Membership and Exhibitor Relations: B.
    Nichole Navar
    E-Mail: ami@ami-imaging.org

Historical Note:
*AMI aims to advance the field of molecular medicine.
Its goal is to establish a structure that best serves the
varied interests of the academy's changing membership,
and provide the means for IMIS, ICP, IMT and SNIDD
to evolve. Membership: $125-275 (Individual); $1,500
(Institutional); $10,000-200,000 (Corporate).*

Meetings/Conferences:
Conference Chair: B. Nichole Navar

Publications:
AMI Newsletter; quarterly
Molecular Imaging and Biology; bi-monthly

Membership List Available to Non-members

Academy of Motion Picture Arts and Sciences (1927)
8949 Wilshire Blvd.
Beverly Hills, CA 90211
Tel: (310) 247-3000 *Fax:* (310) 859-9619
E-Mail: ampas@oscars.org
Website: oscars.org
Members: 6500 artists and professionals
Staff: 136
Annual Budget: Over $100,000,000
Tax: 501(c)(6)

Personnel:
Chief Executive Officer: Dawn Hudson
Managing Director, Information Technology: Megan
    Clarke
*Managing Director, Educational Programs and Special
    Projects:* Randy Haberkamp
    E-Mail: rhaberkamp@oscars.org
Director, Exhibitions and Special Events: Ellen Harrington
Chief Finance Officer: Andrew Horn
Executive Administrator: Cheryl Marshall
Assistant General Counsel, Legal: Scott Miller
Director, Membership Services: Kimberly Roush

Historical Note:
*A professional honorary organization of motion picture
craftsmen and craftswomen founded to advance the arts
and sciences of motion pictures and to foster cooperation
among the creative leadership of the industry for cultural,
educational and technological progress.*

Meetings/Conferences:
Conference Chair: Ellen Harrington
Number of non-conference events/year: 8

Academy of Nutrition and Dietetics (1917)
120 S. Riverside Plaza
Suite 2000
Chicago, IL 60606-6995
Tel: (312) 899-0040 *Fax:* (312) 899-4845
TollFree: (800) 877-1600
E-Mail: knowledge@eatright.org
Website: eatright.org
Members: 74000 individuals
Staff: 155
Annual Budget: $2-5,000,000
Tax: 501(c)(6)

Personnel:
Chief Executive Officer: Patricia M. Babjak
    E-Mail: pbabjak@eatright.org
Director, Strategic Communications: Doris Acosta
    E-Mail: media@eatright.org
Editorial Director: Jennifer Herendeen
    E-Mail: jherendeen@eatright.org
Vice President and Chief Financial Officer: Paul Mifsud
    E-Mail: pmifsud@eatright.org
Director, Information Technology: Richard Newman
    E-Mail: rnewman@eatright.org
Director, Human Resources: Carrolyn Patterson
    E-Mail: HR@eatright.org
Coordinator, Professional Development: Caitlin Peters
    E-Mail: cpeters@eatright.org
Vice President, Member Services: Barbara Visocan LDN,
    MS, RD

    E-Mail: membrshp@eatright.org
Senior Manager, Meeting Services: Mary Wolski
    E-Mail: mwolski@eatright.org

Historical Note:
*Foremrly (2012) American Dietetic Association. ADA
works to empower members to be the nation's food and
nutrition leaders. Members are employed in health care
organizations, schools, colleges, and universities as well
as in business institutions and industry. Membership:
$50 (Student); $220 (Active); $110 (Retired); $170
(International).*

Continuing Education:
Certification Designation/s: RD, DTR

Meetings/Conferences: Annual
Conference Chair: Mary Wolski
Number of non-conference events/year: 2

Publications:
ADA News Bytes; on-line
ADA Student Scoop; on-line
CADE Newsletter; on-line

Academy of Organizational and Occupational Psychiatry (1990)
402 E. Yakima Ave.
Suite 330
Yakima, WA 98901
Tel: (509) 457-4611 *Fax:* (509) 454-3295
Website: aoop.org
Members: 150 individuals
Staff: 4
Annual Budget: $10-25,000

Personnel:
Administrator: Sandra Gabel-Onkels
Contact, Information Technology: C. Donald Williams
    E-Mail: cdonald@aol.com

Historical Note:
*AOOP's mission is to enhance psychiatry's contribution
to the well-being and productivity of workers, leaders
and work organizations. Members are psychiatrists
with an interest in the relationship of work to general
well-being and mental health. Membership: $690-790
(General/Associate); $345-395 (General Member-
Psychiatrists in first 5 years of post residency practice);
$150 (International).*

Meetings/Conferences: Annual
2013 - Chicago, IL (University Club)/April 20 - 21

Publications:
AOOP Online Membership Directory; on-line

Academy of Osseointegration (1982)
85 W. Algonquin Rd.
Suite 550
Arlington Heights, IL 60005
Tel: (847) 439-1919 *Fax:* (847) 439-1569
TollFree: (800) 656-7736
E-Mail: academy@osseo.org
Website: osseo.org
Members: 6,000 professionals
Staff: 12
Annual Budget: $5-10,000,000
Tax: 501(c)(6)

Personnel:
Executive Director: Kevin P. Smith
    E-Mail: kevinsmith@osseo.org
Assistant Director, Membership Services: Barbara
    Hartmann
    E-Mail: barbarahartmann@osseo.org
Director, Exhibits: Jean Lynch
    E-Mail: jeanlynch@osseo.org
Chief Financial Officer: John Nocera
    E-Mail: johnnocera@osseo.org
Manager, Education: Kimberly Scroggs
    E-Mail: kimberlyscroggs@osseo.org
Director, Meeting Services: Gina Seegers
    E-Mail: ginaseegers@osseo.org
Manager, Marketing Communications: Terri Vargulich
    E-Mail: terrivargulich@osseo.org

Historical Note:
*AO's mission is to advance, promote and improve the
art and science of rigid and living tissue interfaces
(osseointegration). Members are dental specialists and
general practitioners. Affiliate membership includes certified
dental technicians, nurses, auxiliary personnel and technical
representatives of manufacturing companies who have an
interest in implant dentistry. Membership: $355 (Active);
$200 (Affiliate); $75 (Student).*

Meetings/Conferences: Annual
Conference Chair: Gina Seegers

2013 - Tampa, FL/March 7 - 9
2014 - Seattle, WA/March 6 - 8
2015 - San Francisco, CA/March 12 - 14
2015 - San Francisco, CA/Sept. 12 - 14
2016 - San Diego, CA/Feb. 18 - 20

Publications:
Academy News; quarterly
AO e-News Weekly; weekly
Membership Directory; on-line
The International Journal of Oral & Maxillofacial
Implants; bi-monthly; adv.

Membership List Available to Non-members

Academy of Pharmaceutical Research and Science
(1852)
2215 Constitution Ave. NW
Washington, DC 20037
Tel: (202) 628-4410 *Fax:* (202) 783-2351
E-Mail: infocenter@aphanet.org
Website: pharmacist.com
Members: 3000 individuals
Staff: 9
Annual Budget: $100-250,000

Personnel:
Executive Vice President and Chief Executive Officer:
Thomas E. Menighan
E-Mail: tmenighan@aphanet.org
Senior Vice President, Professional Affairs: Anne Burns
E-Mail: aburns@aphanet.org
Contact, Marketing: Irica Cheeks
E-Mail: icheeks@aphanet.org
Senior Vice President, Government Affairs: Brian
Gallagher
E-Mail: bgallagher@aphanet.org
Contact, Membership Services: Tammy Hoff
E-Mail: thoff@aphanet.org
Chief Financial Officer: Joseph J. Janela
E-Mail: jjanela@aphanet.org
Contact, Meetings: Todd McDonald
E-Mail: tmcdonald@aphanet.org
Senior Vice President, Human Resources: Jule Miller
E-Mail: jmiller@aphanet.org
Senior Vice President, Communications: Karen K. Tracy
E-Mail: ktracy@aphanet.org

Historical Note:
*APhA-APRS advances the pharmaceutical sciences and
improves the quality of pharmacy practice by stimulating
research and promoting its dissemination to improve
patient care. It is a section of the American Pharmacists
Association (APhA).*

Meetings/Conferences: Annual
Conference Chair: Todd McDonald
2013 - Los Angeles, CA (Los Angeles Convention
Center)/March 1 - 4
2014 - Orlando, FL/March 28 - 31
2015 - San Diego, CA/March 27 - 30
2016 - Baltimore, MD/March 4 - 7

Publications:
APhA DrugInfoLine; weekly
Journal of Pharmaceutical Sciences; monthly; adv.
Journal of the American Pharmacists Association
Pharmacy Today
Student Pharmacist
Transitions; quarterly

Academy of Physicians in Clinical Research
(1993)
500 Montgomery St.
Suite 800
Alexandria, VA 22314
Tel: (703) 254-8100 *Fax:* (703) 254-8101
E-Mail: office@acrpnet.org
Website: apcrnet.org
Members: 20,000 physicians and clinical
researchers
Staff: 2

Personnel:
Executive Director: James D. Thomasell CPA
Manager, External Relations: Sara Kilkenny
E-Mail: sara@acrpnet.org

Historical Note:
*In 2005, The Association of Clinical Research Professionals
(ACRP) and the Academy of Pharmaceutical Physicians
and Investigators (APPI) - formerly known as the American
Academy of Pharmaceutical Physicians (AAPP) - merged to
become APCR, a global organization that unifies, certifies
and educates all members of the clinical research team.*

*APCR represents pharmaceutical physicians and physician
investigators.*

Continuing Education:
Certification Designation/s CPI, CTI

Meetings/Conferences: Annual
2013 - Orlando, FL (Orange County Convention
Center)/April 13 - 16

Publications:
AAPP Newsletter; monthly
Membership Directory; on-line

Membership List Available to Non-members

Academy of Political Science *(1880)*
475 Riverside Dr.
Suite 1274
New York, NY 10115-1274
Tel: (212) 870-2500 *Fax:* (212) 870-2202
E-Mail: apsa@apsanet.org
Website: apsanet.org
Members: 140 institutions
Staff: 6
Annual Budget: $500-1,000,000
Tax: 501(c)(3)

Personnel:
Executive Director: Michael A Brintnall
E-Mail: brintnall@apsanet.org
Director, Finance and Administration: Regina Chavis CPA
E-Mail: rchavis@apsanet.org
Manager, Membership Services: Linda Davis
Director, Communications and Publishing: Polly
Karpowicz
E-Mail: pkarpowicz@apsanet.org
Director, Educational, Professional and Diversity Initiatives:
Kimberly Mealy PhD
E-Mail: kmealy@apsanet.org
Director, Meetings and Conferences: Lauren West
E-Mail: lwest@apsanet.org

Historical Note:
*APS promotes objective, scholarly analyses of political,
social, and economic issues. Membership: $96-314
(Regular); $39-65 (Retired); $60 (Associate); $28 (Family);
$44 (High School Teacher/Student/Unemployed); $40
(Targeted International Member); $3,000 (Life).*

Meetings/Conferences:
Conference Chair: Lauren West
2013 - Long Beach, CA (Renaissance Long Beach
Hotel)/Feb. 8 - 10
2013 - Chicago, IL (Sheraton Chicago Hotel and
Towers)/Aug. 29 - Sept. 1
2014 - Washington, DC (Washington Marriott
Wardman Park)/Aug. 28 - 31
2015 - San Francisco, CA (Hilton San Francisco Union
Square)/Sept. 3 - 6
2016 - Philadelphia, PA (Philadelphia Marriott
Downtown)/Sept. 1 - 4

Publications:
Perspectives on Politics; quarterly; adv.
Political Science and Politics; quarterly; adv.
Political Science Quarterly; quarterly; adv.
The American Political Science Review; on-line; adv.

Academy of Prosthodontics *(1918)*
4425 Cass St.
Suite A
San Diego, CA 92109
Tel: (858) 272-1018 *Fax:* (858) 272-7687
E-Mail: ap@res-inc.com
Website: academyofprosthodontics.org
Members: 130 individuals
Staff: 2
Annual Budget: $100-250,000

Personnel:
President: Thomas D Taylor
Treasurer and Secretary: James C Taylor
E-Mail: jctaylor@istar.ca

Historical Note:
*Founded as National Society of Denture Prosthetists became
Academy of Denture Prosthetics in 1940 and assumed its
current name in 1991. AP's mission is to enhance the art
and science of prosthodontics to the profession and the
public to disseminate knowledge concerning prosthodontics
throughout the profession, to encourage study and
investigation of the various phases of prosthodontics and
related subjects.*

Meetings/Conferences: Annual
2013 - Maui, HI (Sheraton Maui Resort and Spa)/April
16 - 20

Publications:
Membership Directory; on-line
Newsletters; bi-annually

Academy of Psychosomatic Medicine *(1953)*
5272 River Rd.
Suite 630
Bethesda, MD 20816-1453
Tel: (301) 718-6520 *Fax:* (301) 656-0989
E-Mail: apm@apm.org
Website: apm.org
Members: 1000 individuals
Staff: 4
Annual Budget: $500-1,000,000

Personnel:
Executive Director: Norman E. Wallis PhD
E-Mail: nwallis@apm.org
Assistant, Membership Services: Rene Atkinson
E-Mail: membership@apm.org
Academy Coordinator: Kristen Flemming
E-Mail: kflemming@apm.org
Editor: Theodore A. Stern FAPM, MD

Historical Note:
*APM represents psychiatrists dedicated to the advancement
of medical science, education and healthcare for persons
with comorbid psychiatric. Membership: $225 (Full
Member); $175 (Associate); $55 (Postgraduate Fellow/
Resident/Intern/Student).*

Continuing Education:
Certification Designation/s: ACGME

Meetings/Conferences: Annual

Publications:
APM Directory; annually
APM Newsletter; biennially
Directory of US Consultation-Liaison Training
Programs; annually
Psychosomatics; bi-monthly; adv.

Academy of Radiology Research *(1995)*
1029 Vermont Ave. NW
Suite 505
Washington, DC 20005
Tel: (202) 347-5872 *Fax:* (202) 347-5876
E-Mail: acadrad@aol.com
Website: acadrad.org
Members: 27 organizational members
Staff: 4
Annual Budget: $1-2,000,000
Tax: 501(c)(6)

Personnel:
Executive Director: Renee Cruea MPA
E-Mail: rcruea@acadrad.org
Senior Director, Government Affairs: Michael J.
Kalutkiewicz
Administrative Assistant: Angela Quick
E-Mail: admin@acadrad.org
Policy and Programs Manager: Roxanne Yaghoubi

Historical Note:
*ARR seeks identification of sources of support for radiology
research and the use of that research to improve the
knowledge base, educational programs, and patient care
activities of radiology. Members are professional imaging
societies.*

Publications:
Membership Directory; on-line

Membership List Available to Non-members

Academy of Rail Labor Attorneys
4350 N. Fairfax Dr.
Suite 740
Arlington, VA 22203
Tel: (703) 465-2752
E-Mail: arla@gsbcom.com
Website: arla.org
Staff: 1
Annual Budget: $250-500,000
Tax: 501(c)(6)

Personnel:
President: Howard Spier

Historical Note:
*The organization is dedicated to getting the victims of rail
accidents the compensation they deserve.*

Meetings/Conferences: Annual

Academy of Rehabilitative Audiology *(1966)*
P.O. Box 2323

Albany, NY 12220-0323
Tel: (860) 486-3289 *Fax:* (866) 547-3073
E-Mail: ara@audrehab.org
Website: audrehab.org
Members: 385 individuals
Staff: 6
Annual Budget: $10-25,000
Tax: 501(c)(3)

Personnel:
President Elect: Kathleen M. Cienkowski PhD
    E-Mail: cienkowski@uconn.edu
President: Carol Cokely PhD
Secretary: Sarah Ferguson
Treasurer: Jan Moore PhD
Editor in Chief: Linda Thibodeau PhD
Contact, Parliamentarian: Laura Ann Wilber PhD

Historical Note:
ARA's mission is to promote excellence in hearing care through the provision of comprehensive rehabilitative and habilitative services. Members hold graduate degrees in audiology, speech pathology, language or related fields and have had a minimum of two years post-degree experience. Membership: $55 (Regular); $40 (Associate); $20 (Student); Free (Life).

Meetings/Conferences: Annual

Publications:
Journal of the Academy of Rehabilitative Audiology;
    annually
Membership Directory; on-line
Pinnacle Express
The News Flash E-Mail Update

Academy of Security Educators and Trainers
(1980)
16 Penn Plaza
Suite 1570
New York, NY 10001
Tel: (212) 268-4555 *Fax:* (212) 563-4783
TollFree: (800) 947-5827
Website: academyofsecurity.org
Members: 300 individuals
Staff: 2
Annual Budget: Under $10,000

Personnel:
Executive Director: Dr. Richard W. Kobetz CST
Vice President, Certification: Dr. H.H.A. Cooper CST

Historical Note:
ASET's mission is to advocate establishment of security degree program and training courses, aiding curriculum development, Sponsoring basic and applied research. Members are academics, trainers, students, law enforcement and government officials from national, state and local agencies, self-employed professionals and security officers, supervisors and directors from major international corporations, banks, transportation industry, security service organizations, communications, energy, retail, chemicals, insurance, petroleum and utility companies. Membership: $50 (Annual Member); $500 (Life).

Continuing Education:
Enrollment: 10
Certification Designation/s: CST

Publications:
Journal of Applied Security Research; quarterly; adv.

Academy of Surgical Research *(1982)*
7500 Flying Cloud Dr.
Suite 900
Eden Prairie, MN 55344
Tel: (952) 835-4180 *Fax:* (952) 835-4774
E-Mail: jrmanke@associationsolutionsinc.com
Website: surgicalresearch.org
Members: 400 individuals
Staff: 3
Annual Budget: $100-250,000

Personnel:
President: Teresa Gleason BS
Secretary and Treasurer: Tracie Rindfield
Editor: Luis Toledo-Pereyra

Historical Note:
ASR's mission is to encourage, foster, promote, and advance professional and academic standards, education, research, and development in the arts and sciences of experimental surgery. Membership: $245 (Individual); $100 (Associate).

Continuing Education:
Certification Designation/s: SRA, SRT, SRS

Meetings/Conferences: Annual
2013 - Clearwater, FL (Sandpearl Resort)/Sept. 26 - 28

Publications:
Journal of Investigative Surgery; bi-monthly

Academy of Veterinary Allergy and Clinical Immunology *(1960)*
330 Waukegan Rd.
Glenview, IL 60025
Tel: (847) 729-5200 *Fax:* (847) 729-5214
E-Mail: Richlge@aol.com
Members: 300 individuals
Staff: 3
Annual Budget: $25-50,000

Personnel:
President: Michael Groh
Chairman, Membership: Fredrick Feibel
Treasurer: Richard J. Rossman DVM

Historical Note:
Formerly (1993) Academy of Veterinary Allergy. AVACI members are veterinarians, physicians and other professionals with an interest in animal and comparative allergy research. Membership: $50/year (individual).

Academy of Veterinary Homeopathy *(1995)*
P.O. Box 232282
Leucadia, CA 92023-2282
Fax: (866) 652-1590
TollFree: (866) 652-1590
E-Mail: office@theavh.org
Website: theavh.org
Members: 206 veterinarians
Staff: 1
Tax: 501(c)(6)

Personnel:
Secretary: Kathy Combs

Historical Note:
AVH is comprised of veterinarians who share the common desire to restore true health to their patients through the use of homeopathic treatment. Members of the Academy are dedicated to understanding and preserving the principles of Classical Homeopathy. Membership: $125/year.

Continuing Education:
Certification Designation/s: CVH

Meetings/Conferences: Annual
2013 - Tampa, FL (Clearwater Beach Hotel)/April 26 - 28

Publications:
AVH Journal; quarterly
AVH Newsletter

Accordionists and Teachers Guild International
(1940)
4420 Morella Ave.
Studio City, CA 91607
Tel: (818) 766-3101
Website: accordions.com/atg
Members: 175 individuals
Staff: 2
Annual Budget: $10-25,000

Personnel:
First Vice President and Interim Chair: Liz Finch
    E-Mail: lizeef@aol.com
Secretary and Treasurer: Betty Jo Simon

Historical Note:
Formerly the Accordion Teachers' Guild International (1998). ATGI strives to improve teaching standards, music and all phases of music education. Members are accordion teachers, professional musicians, hobbyists and students. Membership: $45/year (Individual).

Meetings/Conferences: Annual
2013 - Chicago, IL (Hyatt Lisle)/July 17 - 21

Accreditation Association for Ambulatory Health Care *(1979)*
5250 Old Orchard Rd.
Suite 200
Skokie, IL 60077
Tel: (847) 853-6060 *Fax:* (847) 853-9028
E-Mail: info@aaahc.org
Website: aaahc.org
Members: 5250 Accredited organizations
Staff: 363
Annual Budget: $10-25,000,000
Tax: 501(c)(3)

Personnel:
Executive Vice President and Chief Executive Officer: John E. Burke PhD
Manager, Human Resources: Jacqueline Benitez

    E-Mail: jbenitez@aaahc.org
Director, Marketing and Communications: Geoffrey Charlton-Perrin
    E-Mail: gcp@aaahc.org
Vice President, Accreditation Services: Meg Gravesmill
    E-Mail: mgravesmill@aaahc.org
General Counsel and Vice President, Government and Public Affairs: Carolyn Kurtz JD
    E-Mail: ckurtz@aaahc.org
Meeting Planner: Pat Mead
Vice President and Chief Operating Officer: James "Jim" Pavletich CAE, MHA
Director, Information Technology: Janice Plack
    E-Mail: jplack@aaahc.org
Chief Financial Officer and Senior Director, Administration: Sergio Tumang
    E-Mail: stumang@aaahc.org

Historical Note:
AAAHC's mission is to advance and promote patient safety, quality, value and measurement of performance for ambulatory health care through peer-based accreditation processes, education and research.

Meetings/Conferences:
Conference Chair: Pat Mead
Number of non-conference events/year: 6

Publications:
Connection; bi-monthly
Update; quarterly

Accreditation Board for Engineering and Technology Inc. *(1932)*
111 Market Pl.
Suite 1050
Baltimore, MD 21202
Tel: (410) 347-7700 *Fax:* (410) 625-2238
E-Mail: info@abet.org
Website: abet.org
Members: 2031 volunteers and societies
Staff: 39
Annual Budget: $5-10,000,000

Personnel:
Executive Director: Michael K. J. Milligan MBA, PE, PhD
    E-Mail: executive-director@abet.org
Senior Specialist, Communications: Keryl M. Cryer MA
    E-Mail: kcryer@abet.org
Manager, Human Resources: Rachelle R. Daucher MS
    E-Mail: rdaucher@abet.org
Managing Director, Planning and Operations and Chief Financial Officer: Lance K. Hoboy CAE, MBA
    E-Mail: lhoboy@abet.org
Managing Director, Professional Services: Ashley Ater Kranov PhD
    E-Mail: akranov@abet.org
Meeting and Event Planner: Chantelle Murat
    E-Mail: cmurat@abet.org
Chief Information Officer: Joseph L. Sussman PhD
    E-Mail: jsussman@abet.org
Manager, Communications and Marketing: Erika A. Williams MA
    E-Mail: ewilliams@abet.org

Historical Note:
Formerly Engineers Council for Professional Development (ECPD). ABET's mission is to serve the public through the promotion and advancement of education in applied science, computing, engineering, and technology.

Meetings/Conferences:
Conference Chair: Chantelle Murat
Number of non-conference events/year: 4

Publications:
E-News; monthly

Accreditation Council for Accountancy and Taxation *(1973)*
1010 N. Fairfax St.
Alexandria, VA 22314-1574
Tel: (888) 289-7763 *Fax:* (703) 549-2512
E-Mail: info@acatcredentials.org
Website: acatcredentials.org
Staff: 3
Annual Budget: $250-500,000

Personnel:
President: Wanda Goodson ABA, ATA, CPA
Director, Education: Michael D. Kinkade
Secretary and Treasurer: Donald G. Yoder

Historical Note:

ACAT's mission is to accredit professionals who have demonstrated knowledge of the principles, practices, and ethical standards of accounting, taxation, information technology and related financial services in order to maintain the highest level of service to the public.

Continuing Education:
Certification Designation/s: IABA, ATA, ATP, ARA

Publications:
Action News; quarterly

Accreditation Council for Pharmacy Education
(1932)
135 S. LaSalle St.
Suite 4100
Chicago, IL 60603-4810
Tel: (312) 664-3575 *Fax:* (312) 664-4652
E-Mail: info@acpe-accredit.org
Website: acpe-accredit.org
Staff: 14
Annual Budget: $5-10,000,000
Tax: 501(c)(3)
Personnel:
Executive Director: Peter H. Vlasses BCPS, PharmD,
    FCCP, DSc
    E-Mail: pvlasses@acpe-accredit.org
Assistant Executive Director and Director, Operations and Human Resources: Sharon L. Hudson
    E-Mail: shudson@acpe-accredit.org
Assistant Executive Director, Professional Affairs, and Director, International Services: Michael J. Rouse MPS
    E-Mail: mrouse@acpe-accredit.org

Historical Note:
Established as the American Council on Pharmaceutical Education and chartered in Maryland in 1939, assumed its current name in 2003. ACPE's mission is to promote continuous quality improvement within its accredited groups and itself. Its sponsoring organizations are the American Association of Colleges of Pharmacy, the American Pharmaceutical Association, and the National Association of Boards of Pharmacy.
Meetings/Conferences:
Number of non-conference events/year: 2
Publications:
ACPE Update

Accredited Gemologists Association *(1974)*
C/O G-Force Services
3315 Juanita St.
San Diego, CA 92105
Tel: (619) 501-5444
E-Mail: 5444@accreditedgemologists.org
Website: accreditedgemologists.org
Members: 250 individuals
Staff: 3
Annual Budget: $50-100,000
Tax: 501(c)(3)
Personnel:
President: Donna Hawrelko
Treasurer: Monica Caldwell
Executive Administrator and Contact, Membership Services: Jan Giamanco
    E-Mail: AGAadmin@cox.net
Historical Note:
AGA is dedicated to gemological education and research, identification and evaluation of gem materials, development of professional standards of analysis, practice and ethics. Membership: $125 (Associate); $150 (Voting); $75 (Student); $200 (Supplier).
Meetings/Conferences: Annual
2013 - Tucson, AZ/Feb. 6
Publications:
Member Directory; on-line
Update; irregular

Accredited Medical Equipment Providers of America
20815 NE 16th Ave.
Suite B-32
Miami, FL 33179
Tel: (305) 654-5957 *Fax:* (866) 322-2060
Website: amepa.us
Staff: 1
Personnel:
President: Rob Brant
Historical Note:
Advocacy organization for medical equipment suppliers. Membership: $500/Year.

Publications:
Membership Directory; on-line

Accredited Pet Cemetery Society *(1993)*
P.O. Box 12073, 12200 N. Crooked Rd.
C/O Rolling Acres Memorial Gardens for Pets
Kansas City, MO 64152
Tel: (816) 891-8888 *Fax:* (816) 891-8781
TollFree: (888) 891-0988
E-Mail: nancypiper@visitrollingacres.com
Website: visitrollingacres.com/apcs.html
Members: 15 individuals
Staff: 3
Annual Budget: Under $10,000
Personnel:
Secretary: Nancy Piper
    E-Mail: nancypiper@visitrollingacres.com
Historical Note:
APCS's mission is to define standards to enhance public trust in the post-life care of animal companions.

Accredited Telematics Providers Association
1450 Pennsylvania Ave. NW
Washington, DC 20006
Tel: (703) 624-1206
E-Mail: info@atpausa.org
Website: atpausa.org
Staff: 2
Personnel:
Executive Director: William B. Smith
Manager, Programs: Scott Smith
Historical Note:
ATPA is an independent association established to promote the integrity of vehicle tracking system providers in support of end users.

Accrediting Bureau of Health Education Schools
7777 Leesburg Pike
Suite 314
Falls Church, VA 22043
Tel: (703) 917-9503 *Fax:* (703) 917-4109
E-Mail: info@abhes.org
Website: abhes.org
Members: 170 individuals
Staff: 15
Annual Budget: $2-5,000,000
Personnel:
Executive Director: Carol A. Moneymaker
    E-Mail: cmoneymaker@abhes.org
Director, Accreditation Development: Eileen M. Brennan
    E-Mail: ebrennan@abhes.org
Coordinator,Database: Jonathan Bridges
    E-Mail: jbridges@abhes.org
Office Manager: Judy Burke
    E-Mail: jburke@abhes.org
Distance Education and Communications Specialist: Christy Baily Byers
    E-Mail: cbyers@abhes.org
Associate Executive Director: Christopher J. Eaton
    E-Mail: ceaton@abhes.org
Executive Operations Coordinator: Holly Viar
    E-Mail: hviar@abhes.org
Historical Note:
ABHES strives to enhance the quality of education and training by promoting institutional and programmatic accountability through systematic and consistent program evaluation.
Meetings/Conferences: Annual
2013 - San Diego, CA (Manchester Grand Hyatt)/Feb. 13 - 15
Publications:
The Advantage-Newsletter

The Accrediting Commission of Career Schools and Colleges *(1993)*
2101 Wilson Blvd.
Suite 302
Arlington, VA 22201
Tel: (703) 247-4212 *Fax:* (703) 247-4533
E-Mail: info@accsct.org
Website: accsct.org
Members: 800 schools and institutions
Staff: 39
Annual Budget: $5-10,000,000
Personnel:
Executive Director: Michale S McComis EdD

    E-Mail: mccomis@accsct.org
Information Coordinator and Information Technology Assistant: Maurice Gatewood
    E-Mail: mgatewood@accsct.org
Accreditation and Volunteer Specialist: Mary Jolliffe-Henry
    E-Mail: mjolliffe@accsc.org
Coordinator, Executive Communication and Relations: Holly Miller
    E-Mail: hmiller@accsc.org
Coordinator, Conference and Events: Michelle Ragnetti
    E-Mail: mragnetti@accsc.org
Director, Accreditation: Corey Rosso
Director, Operations: Anne Santalla
    E-Mail: asantalla@accsc.org
Historical Note:
Founded as Accrediting Commission of the National Association of Trade and Technical Schools, became an independent organization in 1993. Formally called as Accrediting Commission of Career Schools & Colleges of Technology.ACCSC mission is to serve as a reliable authority on educational quality and to promote enhanced opportunities for students by establishing, sustaining, and enforcing valid standards and practices which contribute to the development of a highly trained and competitive workforce through quality career oriented education.
Meetings/Conferences:
Conference Chair: Michelle Ragnetti
Publications:
Directory

Accrediting Council for Continuing Education & Training *(1974)*
1722 N St. NW
Washington, DC 20036
Tel: (202) 955-1113 *Fax:* (202) 955-1118
E-Mail: info@accet.org
Website: accet.org
Members: 246 institutions
Staff: 12
Annual Budget: $2-5,000,000
Personnel:
Executive Director: Roger J. Williams
    E-Mail: rjwilliams@accet.org
Senior Accreditation Coordinator: Scott Faulstick
    E-Mail: sfaul@accet.org
Associate Executive Director: Charlie Matterson
    E-Mail: chmatterson@accet.org
Historical Note:
ACCET seeks to inspire and promote quality-oriented continuing education and training. Members are associations, private educational institutions, and companies who conduct continuing education and training programs, both to the general public and internal to their operations for employees.
Meetings/Conferences: Annual
Number of non-conference events/year: 5
Publications:
Membership Directory; on-line

Accrediting Council for Independent Colleges and Schools *(1912)*
750 First St. NE
Suite 980
Washington, DC 20002-4223
Tel: (202) 336-6780 *Fax:* (202) 842-2593
TollFree: (866) 510-0746
E-Mail: acics@acics.org
Website: acics.org
Members: 800 institutions, 800,000 students
Staff: 39
Annual Budget: $10-25,000,000
Tax: 501(c)(3)
Personnel:
Executive Director and Chief Executive Officer: Albert C. Gray PhD
    E-Mail: agray@acics.org
Director, Administration: Jeanine Ford
    E-Mail: jford@acics.org
Manager, Communications: Annette Headley
    E-Mail: aheadley@acics.org
Membership Data Specialist: Soo Ryun Kim
    E-Mail: skim@acics.org
Project Manager, Information Technology: Peter Kim
    E-Mail: pkim@acics.org
Director, Finance: Jeffrey S. Olszewski
    E-Mail: jolszewski@acics.org

Historical Note:
ACICS is a established national accreditor of academic institutions in the United States. It is recognized by the U.S. Department of Education and the Council for Higher Education Accreditation (CHEA). The mission of the ACICS is to advance educational excellence at independent, nonpublic career schools, colleges, and organizations in the United States and abroad. This is achieved through a deliberate and thorough accreditation process of quality assurance and enhancement as well as ethical business and educational practices.

Publications:
The Evaluator

Accrediting Council on Education in Journalism and Mass Communications *(1947)*
1435 Jayhawk Blvd.
Stauffer-Flint Hall
Lawrence, KS 66045-7575
Tel: (785) 864-3973 *Fax:* (785) 864-5225
Website: www2.ku.edu/~acejmc
Members: 133 Schools and associations
Staff: 4
Annual Budget: $100-250,000
Tax: 501(c)(3)

Personnel:
Executive Director: Susanne Shaw
   E-Mail: sshaw@ku.edu
President and Accrediting Council: Peter Bhatia
   E-Mail: pbhatia@oregonian.com
Office Staff: Cheryl Klug
   E-Mail: cklug@ku.edu
Assistant to the Executive Director: Cindy Reinardy
   E-Mail: creinardy@ku.edu

Historical Note:
ACEJMC's mission is to establish, preserve, and advance standards of quality in professional education in journalism and mass communications. Membership: $1,000 (Accredited School); $1,000-6,000 (Company).

Publications:
Accredited Journalism and Mass Communications Education; annually
ACEJMC Ascent Newsletter; on-line
Diversity: Best Practices; adv.

Membership List Available to Non-members

ACORD - Association for Cooperative Operations Research and Development
Two Blue Hill Plaza, Third Floor
P.O. Box 1529
Pearl River, NY 10965-8529
Tel: (845) 620-1700 *Fax:* (845) 620-3600
Website: acord.org
Members: 500 Insurance carriers, reinsurers, agents, brokers and financial services.
Staff: 60
Annual Budget: $10-25,000,000

Personnel:
President and Chief Executive Officer: Gregory A. Maciag
   E-Mail: gmaciag@acord.org
Vice President, General Counsel and Corporate Secretary: Gary Bel
   E-Mail: gbel@acord.org
Director, Member Operations: Dominic Caccioppoli
   E-Mail: dcaccioppoli@acord.org
Chief Learning Officer: Beth Grossman
   E-Mail: bgrossman@acord.org
Vice President and Chief Administrative Officer: Tanya J. Krochta
   E-Mail: tkrochta@acord.org
Chief Technology Officer: Peter Teresi
   E-Mail: pteresi@acord.org

Historical Note:
ACORD's mission is to facilitate the development of open consensus data standards and standard forms. ACORD members include hundreds of insurance and reinsurance companies, agents and brokers, software providers, and industry associations worldwide.

Meetings/Conferences: Annual
Number of non-conference events/year: 1

Publications:
ACORD Newsletter; weekly; adv.

The Acoustical Society of America *(1929)*
Two Huntington Quadrangle
Suite 1N01
Melville, NY 11747-4502
Tel: (516) 576-2360 *Fax:* (516) 576-2377

E-Mail: asa@aip.org
Website: acousticalsociety.org
Members: 7500 individuals
Staff: 12
Annual Budget: $5-10,000,000

Personnel:
Executive Director: Charles E. Schmid PhD
Treasurer: David Feit
Editor-In-Chief: Allan D. Pierce

Historical Note:
ASA, a member of the American Institute of Physics and primarily a voluntary organization, works to attract the interest, commitment, and service of a large number of professionals. Membership: $45 (Student/Corresponding Electronic Associate); $95 (Associate/Full).

Meetings/Conferences:
2013 - Montreal, QC (Palais Des Congres de Montreal)/June 2 - 7
2013 - Montreal, QC/July 2 - 7
2013 - San Francisco, CA/Dec. 2 - 6
2014 - Providence, RI/May 5 - 9
2014 - Indianapolis, IN/Oct. 27 - 31
2015 - Pittsburgh, PA/May 18 - 22
2015 - Jacksonville, FL/Nov. 2 - 6

Publications:
Acoustics Today; quarterly
ECHOES; quarterly
JASA Express Letters; monthly
Journal of the Acoustical Society of America; monthly; adv.
Proceedings of Meetings on Acoustics; on-line

ACPA College Student Educators International *(1924)*
One Dupont Cir. NW
Suite 300
Washington, DC 20036-1188
Tel: (202) 835-2272 *Fax:* (202) 296-3286
E-Mail: info@acpa.nche.edu
Website: www2.myacpa.org
Members: 7500 individuals
Staff: 14
Annual Budget: $2-5,000,000

Personnel:
Executive Director: Gregory Roberts
   E-Mail: gr@acpa.nche.edu
Assistant Director, Professional Development: Colleen Blevins
Director, Corporate Relations: Ron Campbell
Senior Director, Membership, Marketing and Media Relations: Stanton Cheah
Coordinator, Membership and Convention Services: Stephanie M. Gatson
Director, Fiscal Services and Human Resources: Tom Gentry
Director, Information Technology: Jon Gilmore
Senior Director, Professional Development, Research and Scholarship: Vernon A. Wall

Historical Note:
Formed in 1924 as the National Association of Appointment Secretaries (NAAS), later became the National Association of Personnel and Placement Officers (NAPPO), assumed its current name in 1931. ACPA is a comprehensive student affairs association that advances student affairs and engages students for a lifetime of learning and discovery. Membership: $29-55 (Student); $79-219 (Individual); $75 (Transitional); $225-1985 (College/University); $0 (Emeritus).

Meetings/Conferences: Annual
Conference Chair: Stephanie M. Gatson
2013 - Las Vegas, NV/March 4 - 8
2013 - Las Vegas, NV (Paris Hotel)/March 4 - 7
2014 - Indianapolis, IN/March 30 - April 2
Number of non-conference events/year: 1

Publications:
About Campus; bi-monthly; adv.
College/University and Organization Member Directory
Developments; quarterly
Journal of College Student Development; bi-monthly; adv.

Acrylonitrile Group, Inc. *(1981)*
1250 Connecticut Ave. NW
Suite 700
Washington, DC 20036
Tel: (202) 419-1500 *Fax:* (202) 659-8037

E-Mail: angroup@regnet.com
Website: angroup.org
Members: 7 companies
Staff: 1
Annual Budget: $2-5,000,000
Tax: 501(c)(6)

Personnel:
Executive Director: Robert J. Fensterheim CAE

Historical Note:
AN represents producers and users of the industrial chemical used to make plastics, fibers and synthetic rubber products.

Actors' Equity Association *(1913)*
165 W. 46th St.
New York, NY 10036
Tel: (212) 869-8530 *Fax:* (212) 719-9815
E-Mail: info@actorsequity.org
Website: actorsequity.org
Members: 48000 individuals
Staff: 120
Annual Budget: $50-100,000,000
Tax: 501(c)(5)

Personnel:
Executive Director: Mary McColl
Director, Information Technology: Doug Beebe
Assistant Executive Director, Finance and Administration: Steve DiPaola
National Director, Membership Services: John Fasulo
Director, Governance Policy and Support: Jack Goldstein
National Director, Communications: David Lotz

Historical Note:
AEA seeks to advance, promote and foster the art of live theater as an essential component of a society. Members include actors and stage managers in the United States. Membership: $118/year.

Publications:
Equity News

ACUTA - The Association for Information Communications Technology Professionals in Higher Education *(1971)*
152 W. Zandale
Suite 200
Lexington, KY 40503
Tel: (859) 278-3338 *Fax:* (859) 278-3268
Website: acuta.org/wcm/acuta
Members: 750 colleges and universities
Staff: 9
Annual Budget: $1-2,000,000

Personnel:
Executive Director: Corinne Hoch
   E-Mail: choch@acuta.org
Manager, Membership Marketing and Corporate Relations: Amy Burton
   E-Mail: aburton@acuta.org
Associate Executive Director: Tom Campbell
   E-Mail: tcampbell@acuta.org
Director, Information Technology: Aaron Fuehrer
   E-Mail: afuehrer@acuta.org
Director, Professional Development: Donna Hall
   E-Mail: dhall@acuta.org
Director, Communications: Pat Scott
   E-Mail: pscott@acuta.org
Director, Meetings and Events: Lisa Thornton CMP
   E-Mail: lthornton@acuta.org
Director, Membership Services: Michele West
   E-Mail: mwest@acuta.org

Historical Note:
ACUTA's mission is to support higher education information communications technology professionals in contributing to the achievement of the strategic mission of their institution. Members are institutions of higher education with members ranging from small schools and community colleges to institutions representing diverse Carnegie classifications in all 50 states, Canada, Australia, and New Zealand. Affiliate members represent all categories of communications technology vendors who serve the college/university market. Membership: $253-845 (College/University); $740-2,220 (Corporate Affiliate); $200 (Associate); $100 (Emeritus).

Meetings/Conferences: Annual
Conference Chair: Lisa Thornton CMP
2013 - San Diego, CA (Manchester Grand Hyatt San Diego)/April 14 - 17
2014 - Dallas, TX (Hyatt Regency Dallas at Reunion)/ March 30 - April 2

2015 - Atlanta, GA (Hyatt Regency Atlanta)/April 19 - 22

Number of non-conference events/year: 3

Publications:
ACUTA eNews; monthly; adv.
ACUTA Journal; quarterly; adv.
Legislative/Regulatory Update; monthly; adv.
Membership Directory; annually; adv.

Membership List Available to Non-members

Acute Long Term Hospital Association *(1996)*
1667 K St. NW
Suite 1050
Washington, DC 20006
Tel: (202) 266-9800 *Fax:* (703) 518-9980
E-Mail: info@altha.org
Website: altha.org
Members: 175 Hospitals
Staff: 11
Annual Budget: $2-5,000,000

Personnel:
Chief Executive Officer: William E. Walters
    E-Mail: william.walters@altha.org
Senior Director, Program Services: Kathy Anderson
Director, Membership Services: Jennifer Connors
    E-Mail: jennifer.connors@altha.org
Director, Government Relations: Michael O'Donnell

Historical Note:
ALTHA strives to promote the interests of long term acute care hospitals and their patients. ALTHA works to protect the rights of medically complex patients and the hospitals that treat them by educating federal and state regulators, members of Congress, and health care industry colleagues. Membership: $11,000 (Allied-Gold); $7,000 (Allied-Silver); $3,000 (Allied-Bronze).

Meetings/Conferences: Annual

Publications:
Continuum
Member Directory

Membership List Available to Non-members

ADARA *(1966)*
P.O. Box 480
Myersville, MD 21773
Tel: (301) 293-8969 *Fax:* (301) 293-9698
E-Mail: adaraorg@comcast.net
Website: adara.org
Members: 600 individuals
Staff: 3
Annual Budget: $50-100,000
Tax: 501(c)(3)

Personnel:
Office Manager: Sherri Fleishell
Web Administrator: Barry Blood
    E-Mail: webadmin@adara.org
Editor: David Feldman
    E-Mail: dfeldman@mail.barry.edu

Historical Note:
Formerly the American Deafness and Rehabilitation Association. ADARA works to promote the development and expansion of professional rehabilitation services to adult deaf individuals. Members are anyone interested in services to Deaf and Hard of Hearing people, and those who support the goals, mission, and intent of the organization. Membership: $30-175/year.

Meetings/Conferences: Biennial
2013 - Bloomington, MN (Embassy Suites Bloomington)/May 29 - June 1

Publications:
ADARA Update; quarterly; adv.
JADARA

ADED - The Association for Driver Rehabilitation Specialists *(1977)*
2425 N. Center
Suite 369
Hickory, NC 28601
Tel: (828) 855-1623 *Fax:* (828) 855-1672
TollFree: (866) 672-9466
E-Mail: info@driver-ed.org
Website: driver-ed.org
Members: 656 Individual members, Facility Members, Mobility Equipment Dealer members, and Corporate members.
Staff: 2
Annual Budget: $250-500,000

Tax: 501(c)(3)

Personnel:
Executive Director: Elizabeth Green CDRS, OTR/L
    E-Mail: elizabeth.green@driver-ed.org
Editor: Beth Anderson Gibson CDRS, OTR/L
    E-Mail: bgibson@freedomandmobility.com

Historical Note:
ADED's aim is to support professionals working in field of driver education/driver training and transportation equipment modifications for persons with disabilities through education and information dissemination. Membership: $95-960/year.

Continuing Education:
Certification Designation/s: CDRS

Meetings/Conferences: Annual
2013 - Detroit, MI/Sept. 16 - 18

Publications:
Member Directory; on-line
NewsBrake; quarterly; adv.

Adhesion Society *(1977)*
Two Davidson Hall - 0201
Blacksburg, VA 24061
Tel: (540) 231-7257 *Fax:* (540) 231-3971
E-Mail: adhesoc@vt.edu
Website: adhesionsociety.org
Members: 514 individuals
Staff: 6
Annual Budget: $100-250,000

Personnel:
Contact, Membership and Publicity: Alfred J. Crosby
    E-Mail: crosby@mail.pse.umass.edu

Historical Note:
AS's mission is to promote the advancement of the science and technology of adhesion and the dissemination of this knowledge. Members are chemists, engineers, biologists, mathematicians, physicists, physicians, dentists and other professionals involved in adhesion science. Membership: $75 (Individual); $30 (Student/Retiree).

Meetings/Conferences: Annual
Conference Chair: Greg Schueneman
2013 - Daytona Beach, FL (Hilton Daytona Beach Oceanfront Resort)/March 3 - 6

Publications:
Membership Directory; on-line
Newsletter

Adhesive and Sealant Council *(1958)*
7101 Wisconsin Ave.
Suite 990
Bethesda, MD 20814-2429
Tel: (301) 986-9700 *Fax:* (301) 986-9795
E-Mail: info@ascouncil.org
Website: ascouncil.org
Members: 130 companies
Staff: 7
Annual Budget: $2-5,000,000
Tax: 501(c)(6)

Personnel:
President: Matt Croson
    E-Mail: matt.croson@ascouncil.org
Senior Manager, Meetings and Tradeshows: Malinda Armstrong
    E-Mail: malinda.armstrong@ascouncil.org
Director, Government Relations: Mark Collatz
    E-Mail: mark.collatz@ascouncil.org
Senior Director, Membership Services: Steve Duren
    E-Mail: steve.duren@ascouncil.org
Contact, Marketing: Michael Socha
    E-Mail: msocha@kdgadvertising.com
Director, Finance and Administration: Kate Zando
    E-Mail: kate.zando@ascouncil.org

Historical Note:
ASC is bound by the collective efforts of its members, and strives to improve the industry operating environment and strengthen its member companies. Members are makers of adhesives and sealants. Membership: $1,900-30,000/year (Company) based on net sales.

Meetings/Conferences: Semi-Annual
Conference Chair: Malinda Armstrong
2013 - Atlanta, GA (Hyatt Regency Atlanta)/April 21 - 23
2013 - Napa, CA (Westin Verasa Napa)/June 25 - 26
2013 - Minneapolis, MN (Hilton Minneapolis)/Oct. 21 - 23

Number of non-conference events/year: 6

Publications:
Adhesives.org e-newsletter; on-line; adv.
e-Catalyst Newsletter; monthly; adv.
Member Directory; on-line
Washington Watch Newsletter; on-line

Membership List Available to Non-members

Adjutants General Association of the United States *(1912)*
P.O. Box 854
Norwell, MA 02061
Tel: (614) 336-7070 *Fax:* (614) 336-7074
Website: agaus.org
Members: 54 state and territorial commands
Staff: 2
Annual Budget: Under $10,000

Personnel:
President: Maj. Gen. William D. Wofford
    E-Mail: president@agaus.org
Treasurer: Maj. Gen. Dave Sprynczynatyk

Historical Note:
AGAUS's purpose is to promote and support adequate state and national security in facilitating and improving the administration of the foregoing National Guard and NGUS affairs through the agencies of the Department of Defense and the several States. Membership composed of the commander of the National Guard in each state, the District of Columbia, the Commonwealth of Puerto Rico, the Virgin Islands and Guam.

Meetings/Conferences:
Number of non-conference events/year: 2

ADSC: The International Association of Foundation Drilling *(1972)*
8445 Freeport Pkwy.
Suite 325
Irving, TX 75063
Tel: (469) 359-6000 *Fax:* (469) 359-6007
E-Mail: adsc@adsc-iafd.com
Website: adsc-iafd.com
Members: 1000 companies and individuals
Staff: 13
Annual Budget: $1-2,000,000
Tax: 501(c)(6)

Personnel:
Chief Executive Officer: Michael D. Moore
    E-Mail: mmoore@adsc-iafd.com
Director, Meetings: Jan Hall
    E-Mail: jhall@adsc-iafd.com
Coordinator, Education: Kathleen Jones
    E-Mail: kjones@adsc-iafd.com
Editor-in-Chief: S. Scot Litke
    E-Mail: slitke@adsc-iafd.com
Director, Operations: Antonio Marinucci MBA, P E, PhD
    E-Mail: tmarinucci@adsc-iafd.com
Controller: Cole Savage
    E-Mail: csavage@adsc-iafd.com
Administrator, Membership Services: B. D. Smith
    E-Mail: bdsmith@adsc-iafd.com

Historical Note:
Founded as the Association of Drilled Shaft Contractors, assumed its current name in 1995. ADSC's aim is to promote, foster, and advance the interests of persons, firms, or corporations engaged in the design, construction, equipment manufacture and distribution in and for the anchored earth retention, drilled shaft, micropiling, and corresponding industries. Membership: $95-4,640/year.

Meetings/Conferences: Annual
Conference Chair: Jan Hall

Publications:
Foundation Drilling Magazine
Membership Directory; annually

Membership List Available to Non-members

Advanced Biofuels Association
2099 Pennsylvania Ave. NW
Suite 100
Washington, DC 20006
Tel: (202) 469-5140
Website: advancedbiofuelsassociation.com
Members: 39 companies
Staff: 3
Annual Budget: $500-1,000,000
Tax: 501(c)(6)

Personnel:
President: Michael McAdams
Director, Communications: Tom Alexander

E-Mail: tom@alexanderstratcomm.com

Historical Note:
The Advanced Biofuels Association and its member companies represent a wide range of technologies, feedstocks, and molecules within the advanced biofuels. The Advanced Biofuels Association is focused on helping America transform to a low carbon economy.

Advanced Medical Technology Association (AdvaMed) *(1903)*
701 Pennsylvania Ave. NW
Suite 800
Washington, DC 20004
Tel: (202) 783-8700 *Fax:* (202) 783-8750
E-Mail: info@advamed.org
Website: advamed.org
Members: 1600 companies
Staff: 85
Annual Budget: $25-50,000,000

Personnel:
President and Chief Executive Officer: Stephen J. Ubl
Executive Vice President, Global Strategy and Analysis: Ralph Ives
    E-Mail: rives@advamed.org
Executive Vice President, Public Affairs: Gary Karr
Senior Executive Vice President and Chief Administrative Officer: Kenneth Mendez
Vice President, Policy Communications: Wanda Moebius
    E-Mail: wmoebius@advamed.org
Senior Executive Vice President: David H. Nexon
    E-Mail: dnexon@advamed.org
Executive Vice President, Technology and Regulatory Affairs: Janet Trunzo
Executive Vice President, General Counsel and Secretary: Christopher L. White
    E-Mail: cwhite@advamed.org
Senior Vice President, Membership and Marketing: Frank S. Wilton
    E-Mail: fwilton@advamed.org

Historical Note:
Formerly known as the Health Industry Manufacturers Association. Represents the medical device, diagnostics and healthcare information systems industry. Membership: $299-15,700/year.

Meetings/Conferences: Annual
Number of non-conference events/year: 5

Publications:
AdvaMed In Brief; monthly
AdvaMed SmartBrief; daily; adv.
Membership Directory; on-line

Advanced Transit Association *(1976)*
P.O. Box 293
Maple Valley, WA 98038
E-Mail: membership@advancedtransit.org
Website: advancedtransit.org
Members:
150 members
8 companies
Staff: 3
Annual Budget: $10-25,000
Tax: 501(c)(3)

Personnel:
President: Stan Young
Director, Membership: Lawrence J. Fabian
    E-Mail: lfabian21@gmail.com

Historical Note:
ATRA's mission is to help communities, agencies, and planners implement transit systems that serve the mobility needs of their citizens in a cost- effective, service-oriented fashion. ATRA's members are professionals from the research, planning, engineering, consulting, environmental, and government communities. Membership: $50 (Regular); $100 (Sustaining) ; $500 (Corporate); $35 (Student/Senior).

Publications:
Cities for Mobility
Journal of Advanced Transportation; quarterly
TransitPulse

Adventure Travel Trade Association *(1990)*
601 Union St.
Suite 4200
Seattle, WA 98101
Tel: (360) 805-3131 *Fax:* (360) 805-0649
E-Mail: info@adventuretravel.biz
Website: adventuretravel.biz

Members: 700 corporations
Staff: 4
Annual Budget: $250-500,000

Personnel:
Executive Director: Chris Doyle APR
    E-Mail: cdoyle@adventuretravel.biz
President: Shannon Stowell
Vice President, Business Development and Contact, Membership Services: Chris Chesak
    E-Mail: cchesak@adventuretravel.biz
Director, Event Operations: Amber Silvey

Historical Note:
Formerly (1997) Adventure Travel Society. Serves as a strategic membership organization for companies in the Adventure Travel arena. ATTA is dedicated to raising the profile of Adventure Travel in the world travel market and provides valuable services, knowledge and connections that will help members succeed in their businesses, thereby contributing to industry-wide growth. Membership: $100 (Individual); $500 (Operator/Agent/Accommodations); $750 (Industry Partner); $750-1,500 (Organization).

Meetings/Conferences: Annual
Conference Chair: Amber Silvey
2013 - Swakopmund and Windhoek, Namibia/Oct. 26 - 31

Publications:
AdventureTravelNews; monthly
Membership Directory; on-line

Advertising and Marketing International Network *(1932)*
3587 Northshore Dr.
Wayzata, MN 55391
Tel: (952) 457-1116 *Fax:* (952) 471-7752
E-Mail: vaughn.sink@shscom.com
Website: aminworldwide.com
Members: 65 agencies
Staff: 2
Annual Budget: $500-1,000,000

Personnel:
Manager, Membership Services: Janna Sperry Sundby
    E-Mail: jsundby@aminworldwide.com

Historical Note:
AMIN, the Advertising and Marketing International Network, is a global alliance of independently owned advertising agencies. Membership: $6,000 (Organization/Company, Initiation fee $2500 extra for first time).

Meetings/Conferences: Annual
Number of non-conference events/year: 4

Publications:
The AMIN Network

Advertising Council *(1942)*
815 Second Ave.
Ninth Floor
New York, NY 10017
Tel: (212) 922-1500 *Fax:* (212) 922-1676
TollFree: (800) 933-7727
E-Mail: info@adcouncil.org
Website: adcouncil.org
Members: 500 companies
Staff: 119
Annual Budget: $25-50,000,000

Personnel:
President and Chief Executive Officer: Peggy Conlon
Senior Vice President, National Accounts and Media Marketing: James Baumann
Senior Vice President and Director, Human Resources and Office Services: Regina Bradley
Executive Vice President and Chief Financial Officer: Jon Fish
Executive Vice President, Corporate Communications: Paula Veale
    E-Mail: pveale@adcouncil.org
Director, Special Events and Development: Jessica Wolin
    E-Mail: jwolin@adcouncil.org

Historical Note:
Founded as the War Advertising Council, reorganized after World War II and became the Advertising Council, Inc. Mission is to identify a select number of significant public issues and stimulate action on those issues through communications programs that make a measurable difference in society.

Meetings/Conferences:
Conference Chair: Jessica Wolin
Number of non-conference events/year: 6

Publications:

Ad Council Newsletter; on-line

Advertising Media Credit Executives Association *(1953)*
24600 Detroit Rd., Suite 100
P.O. Box 40036
Bay Village, OH 44140-0036
Tel: (972) 377-6335 *Fax:* (972) 755-6643
E-Mail: AMCEA@tx.rr.com
Website: amcea.org
Members:
300 companies
300 individuals
Staff: 3
Annual Budget: $10-25,000

Personnel:
Administrative Liaison: Nancy Reynolds

Historical Note:
AMCEA's purpose is to improve professionalism in the credit management field through the exchange of ideas, education and training in business techniques. Members are credit executives of newspapers, magazines, radio and television stations. Membership: $185-395/year.

Meetings/Conferences: Annual
Number of non-conference events/year: 1

Publications:
Member Roster; on-line
News and Views

The Advertising Research Foundation *(1936)*
432 Park Ave., South
Sixth Floor
New York, NY 10016-8013
Tel: (212) 751-5656 *Fax:* (212) 319-5265
E-Mail: info@thearf.org
Website: thearf.org
Members: 400 companies
Staff: 48
Annual Budget: $5-10,000,000

Personnel:
President and Chief Executive Officer: Robert L. Barocci
Manager, Membership Services: Rosie Aponte
Managing Editor: Catherine Gardner
    E-Mail: catherine@thearf.org
Director, Sales: Chris Kosar
    E-Mail: ckosar@thearf.org
Executive Vice President, Media: David Marans
Director, Events: Kelly McSorley
Senior Vice President: Dr. Raymond Pettit PhD
    E-Mail: rpettit@thearf.org
Director, Human Resources: Demi Williams
Chief Operating Officer: Felix Yang

Historical Note:
Founded in 1936 by the Association of National Advertisers and the American Association of Advertising Agencies, TARF's mission is to enhance profitable marketing through effective research. It improves the practice of advertising, marketing and media research in pursuit of more effective marketing and advertising communications. Membership is corporate and open to all employees. Membership: $5,000-37,000 (Advertiser/Company-Research/Media/Agency); $1,000 (Association); $300 (Academic); $3,000 (Individual Consultant).

Meetings/Conferences: Annual
Conference Chair: Chris Kosar
2013 - New York City, NY (New York Marriott Marquis)/March 17 - 20
2014 - New York City, NY (New York Marriott Marquis)/March 24 - 26
Number of non-conference events/year: 10

Publications:
Journal of Advertising Research; quarterly; adv.
Member Directory; on-line

Aerobics and Fitness Association of America *(1983)*
15250 Ventura Blvd.
Suite 200
Sherman Oaks, CA 91403-3297
Tel: (818) 905-0040 *Fax:* (818) 788-6301
TollFree: (877) 968-7263
E-Mail: contactafaa@afaa.com
Website: afaa.com
Members: 150000 individuals
Staff: 50

Personnel:
President: Linda D. Pfeffer

Director, Media Relations: Tom Ivicevic
 E-Mail: tomafaa@aol.com
Contact, Accreditation: Dorette Nysewander
 E-Mail: dorette@dgroupconsulting.com

Historical Note:
*AFAA is an international professional association for the
education, training and certification of fitness professionals.
AFAA provides comprehensive cognitive and practical
education for fitness professionals. Publishes standards
and guidelines in addition to provide educational materials,
continuing education programs and home study courses.
Membership: $68/year (Individual).*

Continuing Education:
Certification Designation/s: PGEC, KBC, PTC, SC

Publications:
American Fitness Magazine; adv.

Aeronautical Repair Station Association *(1984)*
121 N. Henry St.
Alexandria, VA 22314-2903
Tel: (703) 739-9543 *Fax:* (703) 739-9488
E-Mail: arsa@arsa.org
Website: arsa.org
Members:
700 companies
50 aviation maintenance facilities
Staff: 14
Annual Budget: $1-2,000,000

Personnel:
Executive Director: Sarah MacLeod
 E-Mail: sarah.macleod@arsa.org
*Vice President, Regulatory Affairs and Assistant General
 Counsel:* Craig Fabian
 E-Mail: craig.fabian@arsa.org
Managing Director and General Counsel: Marshall S.
 Filler
 E-Mail: Marshall.Filler@arsa.org
Director, Financial Services: Tambria Gariepy
 E-Mail: Tambria.Gariepy@arsa.org
Director, Communications : Jason Langford
 E-Mail: Jason.Langford@arsa.org
Vice President, Operations: Crystal Maguire
 E-Mail: Crystal.Maguire@arsa.org
Director, Publications and Web Content: Keith
 Mendenhall
 E-Mail: keith.mendenhall@arsa.org

Historical Note:
*Established and incorporated in Washington, DC.
in June 1984. ARSA represents entities certified by
national aviation authorities to perform maintenance and
alterations on civil aviation products. Absorbed Airline
Services Association in 1985. ARSA is the association
of the worldwide civil aviation community, it helps
develop guidance, policy and interpretations that are
clear, concise and consistent, and applied uniformly
to all similarly situated companies and individuals.
Membership: $600-3,600 (Regular, based on number of
employees); $1,200 (Associate); $18,000 (Corporate);
$300 (Individual).*

Meetings/Conferences:
Conference Chair: Keith Mendenhall
Number of non-conference events/year: 1

Publications:
Membership Directory; on-line
Staff Directory; on-line
The Hotline Newsletter; monthly; adv.

Membership List Available to Non-members

Aerospace & Flight Test Radio Coordinating Council *(1954)*
P.O. Box 1996
Independence, KS 67301
Tel: (620) 332-0432 *Fax:* (316) 206-8396
Website: aftrcc.org
Staff: 3
Annual Budget: $250-500,000

Personnel:
Chair: Danny Hankins
 E-Mail: chair@aftrcc.org

Historical Note:
*AFTRCC mission is to advance the arts and sciences of
radio communications, and the efficient allocation and
utilization of the electromagnetic spectrum, in connection
with the flight testing of aircraft, missiles and major
components thereof. Membership: $3000 (Member); $1000
(Associate).*

Aerospace Department Chairs Association *(1968)*

710 H.R. Bright Building
3141 TAMU
College Station, TX 77843-3141
Tel: (979) 845-1604 *Fax:* (979) 845-6051
Website: aerodeptchairs.org
Members: 80 individuals
Staff: 2
Annual Budget: Under $10,000

Personnel:
Secretary and Treasurer: Prof. Dimitris C. Lagoudas
 E-Mail: lagoudas@aero.tamu.edu

Historical Note:
*ADCA's mission is to advocate aerospace engineering
education and research to stimulate the growth of the
aerospace profession. Membership: $3/year.*

Meetings/Conferences: Annual

Aerospace Futures Alliance
14407 SE 266th St.
Kent, WA 98042
Tel: (253) 277-1844
Website: afa-wa.com
Staff: 2
Annual Budget: $100-250,000

Personnel:
President and Executive Director: Linda Lanham
 E-Mail: lindal@afa-wa.com

Historical Note:
*Aerospace Futures Alliance works to pursue measures
supporting a tax structure and tax policies that encourage
the growth and long-term health of the industry.*

Aerospace Industries Association of America *(1919)*
1000 Wilson Blvd.
Suite 1700
Arlington, VA 22209-3928
Tel: (703) 358-1000
E-Mail: aia@aia-aerospace.org
Website: aia-aerospace.org
Members:
102 regular members
174 associate members
Staff: 65
Annual Budget: $10-25,000,000

Personnel:
President and Chief Executive Officer: Marion C. Blakey
Director, Corporate Events: Garnett Black
 E-Mail: garnett.black@aia-aerospace.org
Secretary-Treasurer: Ginette C Colot
 E-Mail: ginette.colot@aia-aerospace.org
Director, Space Systems: Michael Conschafter
 E-Mail: mike.conschafter@aia-aerospace.org
Director, Human Resources and Administration: Brian
 Crowley
 E-Mail: brian.crowley@aia-aerospace.org
Administrative Assistant: Lourdes Fernandes
 E-Mail: lourdes.fernandes@aia-aerospace.org
Director, Space Systems: Dan Hendrickson
 E-Mail: daniel.hendrickson@aia-aerospace.org
Vice President, Membership and Business Development:
 David Mandell
 E-Mail: david.mandell@aia-aerospace.org
Assistant Vice President, Technical Operations: Rusty
 Rentsch
 E-Mail: rusty.rentsch@aia-aerospace.org
Vice President, Communications: Chip Sheller
 E-Mail: chip.sheller@aia-aerospace.org
Vice President, Legislative Affairs: Cord Sterling
 E-Mail: cord.sterling@aia-aerospace.org

Historical Note:
*Established as the Aeronautical Chamber of Commerce
of America, Inc. Name changed to Aircraft Industries
Association of America, Inc. in 1945 and to Aerospace
Industries Association of America in 1959. The National
Center for Advanced Technologies is its non-profit affiliate.
AIA's mission is to provide strong and steady advocacy
of the aerospace and defense industry with Congress,
the White House, the executive branch particularly
the departments of Defense, State, Transportation/
FAA, Commerce, Homeland Security. Membership:
$6,800-400,000 (Full); $3,000-5,000 (Associate).*

Meetings/Conferences: Annual
Conference Chair: Garnett Black
Number of non-conference events/year: 6

Publications:
Membership Directory; on-line

Aestheticians International Association *(1972)*
310 E. Interstate 30
Suite B107
Garland, TX 75043
Tel: (469) 429-9300 *Fax:* (469) 429-9301
TollFree: (877) 968-7539
Website: aiaprofessional.com
Members: 2000 individuals
Staff: 4
Annual Budget: $25-50,000

Personnel:
President: Patricia Strunk
Vice President and Director, Education: Michelle D'Allaird
Director, Operations: Melissa Gillette
Director, Membership and Human Resources: Melissa
 Lawrence

Historical Note:
*AIA's mission is to standardize education and licensing
through creating a national standard of licensing. Members
are individuals owning or working in a skin care salon,
together with manufacturers and distributors of skin care
products. Membership: $30 (Student); $125 (Professional).*

Continuing Education:
Certification Designation/s: NCP

AFCOM *(1980)*
742 E. Chapman Ave.
Orange, CA 92866
Tel: (714) 997-7966 *Fax:* (714) 997-9743
E-Mail: afcom@afcom.com
Website: afcom.com
Members: 4500 members
Staff: 10
Annual Budget: $2-5,000,000

Personnel:
President: Jill Yaoz
 E-Mail: jyaoz@afcom.com
Manager, Conference Services: Brittany Embler
 E-Mail: bembler@afcom.com
Membership Services and Event Manager: Robyn
 Goldstone
 E-Mail: rgoldstone@afcom.com
Manager, Events: Gina Jahn
 E-Mail: gjahn@afcom.com
Office Manager: Jennifer Moore
Manager, Sales: Patrick Peterman
 E-Mail: ppeterman@afcom.com
Managing Editor: Karen Riccio
 E-Mail: kriccio@afcom.com

Historical Note:
*Founded as Association for Computer Operations
Management, became Association for Data Center,
Network, and Enterprise Systems Management (1997);
assumed its current name in 2001. AFCOM members are
managers of corporate, institutional and internet computer
facilities. Membership: $300 (Individual); $690 (Site);
$1,020 (Corporate); $205 (Additional Site/Corporate).*

Meetings/Conferences:
Conference Chair: Gina Jahn

Publications:
Comminique Newsletter; on-line; adv.
Data Center Management Magazine; bi-monthly; adv.

AFL-CIO (American Federation of Labor and Congress of Industrial Organizations) *(1955)*
815 16th St. NW
Washington, DC 20006
Tel: (202) 637-5000 *Fax:* (202) 637-5058
E-Mail: info@workingamerica.org
Website: aflcio.org
Members:
13100000 individuals
53 Unions
Staff: 9
Annual Budget: $500-1,000,000

Personnel:
President: Richard L. Trumka
Associate General Counsel: James Bryan Coppess
 E-Mail: jcoppess@aflcio.org
Media Outreach Specialist: Josh Goldstein
 E-Mail: jgoldstein@aflcio.org
Chief of Staff and Executive Assistant to President:
 Jonathan P. Hiatt
Contact, Media Outreach and Organizing: Brenda Loya
Director, Government Affairs: William Samuel
Treasurer and Secretary: Elizabeth Shuler
Senior Legal and Policy Advisor: Heather Slavkin

E-Mail: Hslavkin@aflcio.org
Media Contact: Amaya Tune
    E-Mail: atune@aflcio.org

Historical Note:
A national trade union center. The American Federation of Labor and Congress of Industrial Organizations is an expression of the hopes and aspirations of the working people of America.

Publications:
Membership Directory; on-line

AFL-CIO - Building and Construction Trades Department
815 16th St. NW, Suite 600
Washington, DC 20006
Tel: (202) 347-1461
Website: bctd.org
Staff: 24
Annual Budget: $10-25,000,000

Personnel:
President: Edward C. Sullivan
Director, Government Affairs: Roderick Bennett

Historical Note:
Provides essential coordination and support to the work of its affiliated national.

AFL-CIO - Maritime Trades Department (1946)
815 16th St. NW, Sixth Floor
Washington, DC 20006
Tel: (202) 628-6300 Fax: (202) 637-3989
Website: maritimetrades.org
Staff: 2
Annual Budget: $250-500,000

Personnel:
President: Michael Sacco
Executive Secretary and Treasurer: Daniel Duncan

Historical Note:
A constitutionally mandated department of the AFL-CIO, the Maritime Trades Department, AFL-CIO has a special interest in preserving a strong U.S. maritime industry by promoting a comprehensive legislative agenda and in educating Congress, the administration, the international community and the American public about the benefits of this vitally important industry. AFLO-CIO is affiliated with Sailors' Union of the Pacific.

AFL-CIO Housing Investment Trust (1964)
2401 Pennsylvania Ave. NW
Suite 200
Washington, DC 20037
Tel: (202) 331-8055 Fax: (202) 331-8190
Website: aflcio-hit.com
Staff: 20

Personnel:
Chief Executive Officer: Stephen Coyle
Chief Operating Officer: Theodore S. Chandler
Director, Communications: Ann Kay
Chief Financial Officer: Erica Khatchadourian
General Counsel: Saul A. Schapiro
Director, Marketing: Lesyllee M. White

Historical Note:
AFL-CIO HIT's mission is to provide economic and social benefits coupled with primary mission of good returns for participants.

Publications:
Investor Newsletter

AFL-CIO Working for America Institute (1998)
815 16th St. NW
Washington, DC 20006
Tel: (202) 508-3717 Fax: (202) 508-3719
Website: workingforamerica.org
Staff: 7
Annual Budget: $1-2,000,000
Tax: 501(c)(3)

Personnel:
Executive Director: Robert Baugh
    E-Mail: bbaugh@aflcio.org
Office Manager: Shelia Marion
    E-Mail: smarion@workingforamerica.org

Historical Note:
AFL-CIO Working for America Institute is a union-sponsored, nonprofit organization dedicated to creating good jobs and building strong communities. It has made significant progress in articulating a vision of a high road economy, an economy that competes in today's global marketplace on the basis of innovation, quality and skill rather than on low wages and benefits.

Publications:
Connections; annually

Africa Travel Association (1975)
152 Madison Ave.
Suite 1702
New York, NY 10016
Tel: (212) 447-1357 Fax: (212) 213-4890
E-Mail: info@africatravelassociation.org
Website: africatravelassociation.org
Members: 760 individuals
Staff: 5
Annual Budget: $250-500,000
Tax: 501(c)(6)

Personnel:
Contact, Membership Services: Angela Gerrow

Historical Note:
ATA's mission is to promote the tourist attractions of the continent of Africa to the travel industry in North America and educate all interested travel agents, planners, and operators about the products and services offered by the travel and tourism industry in Africa. Works to strengthen intra-Africa partnerships. Membership: $50 (Student); $100 (Associate); $200 (Allied); $300 (Supplier); $1,000 (Corporate); $3,000-5,000 (Government).

Meetings/Conferences: Annual
Conference Chair: Sharon Roling
Number of non-conference events/year: 2

Publications:
Africa Travel Magazine; quarterly; adv.
Membership Directory; annually

African American Contractors Association
2910 S Wentworth Ave.
Chicago, IL 60616
Tel: (312) 915-5960
Members: 2500 individuals
Staff: 6

Personnel:
President: Omar S. Shareef

African Studies Association (1957)
C/O Rutgers University
54 Joyce Kilmer Ave.
Piscataway, NJ 08854-8045
Tel: (848) 445-8173 Fax: (732) 445-1366
E-Mail: members@rci.rutgers.edu
Website: africanstudies.org
Members: 1700 individuals
Staff: 6
Annual Budget: $500-1,000,000

Personnel:
Interim Executive Director: Suzanne Moyer Baazet
    E-Mail: ASAED@africanstudies.org
Program Manager, Annual Meetings: Kimme Carlos
    E-Mail: annualmeeting@africanstudies.org
Program Manager, Membership Services: Margaret McLaughlin
    E-Mail: members@africanstudies.org
Acting Program Manager, Publications and Information: Sharhonda Simpson
    E-Mail: publications@africanstudies.org
Contact, Financial Administration: Brandy Wakeman
    E-Mail: accounting@africanstudies.org

Historical Note:
ASA is a non profit organization open to all individuals and institutions interested in African affairs whose mission is to bring together people with a scholarly and professional interest in Africa. Membership: $115-180 (Individual); $2,400 (Lifetime); $70 (Student/Joint); 100 (Retiree).

Meetings/Conferences: Annual
Conference Chair: Kimme Carlos
2013 - Baltimore, MD (Baltimore Marriott Waterfront)/ Nov. 21 - 24
2014 - Indianapolis, IN (JW Marriott Indianapolis)/ Nov. 20 - 23
2015 - San Diego, CA (Sheraton San Diego Hotel and Marina)/Nov. 19 - 22
Number of non-conference events/year: 4

Publications:
ASA Online Membership Directory; on-line
History in Africa: A Journal of Method (HiA); annually
The African Studies Review

African-American Library and Information Science Association (1993)

UCLA Center for African-American Studies
Library
P.O. Box 951545
Los Angeles, CA 90095
Tel: (310) 825-6060 Fax: (310) 825-5019
E-Mail: information@irda.org
Members: 100 individuals
Annual Budget: Under $10,000

Personnel:
President: Itibari M. Zulu CAE, CPA
    E-Mail: imz@ucla.edu

Historical Note:
Formed to address issues of under-representation within the library sciences profession and access to information resources for the African-American community at large. Has no paid officers or full-time staff. Membership: $20/ year.

African-American Women's Clergy Association (1969)
1110 A. Sixth St. NE
Suite Four
Washington, DC 20002
Tel: (202) 518-8488 Fax: (202) 518-1273
E-Mail: imageneshelter@aol.com
Website: houseofimagene.org
Members: 175 individuals
Staff: 1

Personnel:
Executive Director: Imagene B. Stewart

Historical Note:
Formerly (1990) American Women's Clergy Association. AAWCA strives to provide shelter to battered women, the homeless, and the nation's veterans. Members are lay and ordained women clergy.

AFT - Public Employees (1916)
555 New Jersey Ave. NW
Washington, DC 20001
Tel: (202) 879-4400
E-Mail: pubemps@aft.org
Website: aft.org/pubemps
Members: 100000 individuals
Staff: 9

Personnel:
President: Randi Weingarten
Director, Communications: Kris Havens
Treasurer: Lorretta Johnson
Managing Editor: Kathy Nicholson

Historical Note:
Formerly (2002) Federation of Public Employees and a division of the American Federation of Teachers. AFT Public Employees works to improve the lives of its members and their families. It represents state and local government employees who are members of the AFT. AFT is affiliated with American Federation of Teachers (AFL-CIO). Membership: $40 (Associate); $60 (Working Teachers).

Publications:
Public Employee Advocate; adv.

AFT Healthcare (1978)
555 New Jersey Ave. N. W.
Washington, DC 20001
Tel: (202) 879-4400 Fax: (202) 879-4597
E-Mail: healthcare@aft.org
Website: aft.org
Members: 70000 health professionals
Staff: 9
Annual Budget: $100-250,000

Personnel:
Executive Vice President: Francine Lawrence
Managing Editor: Adrienne Coles
    E-Mail: acoles@aft.org
Director, Communications: Kris Havens
Director: Mary Lehman MacDonald
    E-Mail: mmacdona@aft.org

Historical Note:
Formerly (2002) Federation of Nurses and Health Professionals, AFT Healthcare is a union which organizes and represents a wide spectrum of health care professionals, including registered nurses, LPNs, medical technologists and technicians and school nurses.

Publications:
Healthwire; bi-monthly; adv.

AGN International North America, Inc (1978)
2851 S. Parker Rd.

Suite 850
Aurora, CO 80014-2729
Tel: (303) 743-7880 *Fax:* (303) 743-7660
TollFree: (800) 782-2272
Website: agn-na.org
Members: 54 firms
Staff: 6
Annual Budget: $1-2,000,000
Tax: 501(c)(6)

Personnel:
Executive Director: Rita J. Hood
  E-Mail: rhood@agn.org
Director, Member Information Services: Patsy L. Bowen
  E-Mail: pbowen@agn.org
Staff Training Coordinator: Irene Hayden
  E-Mail: ihayden@agn.org
Meeting Planner: Courtney Mino
  E-Mail: cmino@agn.org
Director, Internal Information Systems: Mark Pigg
  E-Mail: mpigg@agn.org

Historical Note:
Founded as Continental Association of CPA Firms, assumed its current name in 1997 and absorbed TAG International in 2002. AGN-NA is dedicated to enhancing the practice value of its members through the sharing of specialized knowledge and support. Member firms consist of any firm (including partnerships, professional corporations, limited liability companies or other formal forms of practice) engaged in the rendering of professional services, as defined from time to time by the Board of Directors. A firm who chooses to apply for membership shall submit an application to the Board of Directors in the form prescribed by the Board and the required entry fee as prescribed in the bylaws of the association and membership is open to non-competing CPA firms.

Meetings/Conferences: Semi-Annual
Conference Chair: Courtney Mino
Number of non-conference events/year: 4

Publications:
Membership Directory; on-line

Agribusiness Council (1967)
1312 18th St. NW
Suite 300
Washington, DC 20036
Tel: (202) 296-4563 *Fax:* (202) 887-9178
E-Mail: info@agribusinesscouncil.org
Website: agribusinesscouncil.org
Members: 400 companies and organizations
Staff: 3

Personnel:
President: Nicholas E. Hollis
Director, Enterprise Policy and Development: Frances Brigham Johnson
  E-Mail: agenergy@aol.com

Historical Note:
ABC is a consortium of companies, universities, foundations and individuals. Purpose is to stimulate and encourage agribusiness development both domestically and abroad. Identifies investment opportunities for agribusiness, supports research and serves as an information and networking resource for its members.

Agricultural & Applied Economics Association (1985)
555 E. Wells St.
Suite 1100
Milwaukee, WI 53202
Tel: (414) 918-3190 *Fax:* (414) 276-3349
E-Mail: info@aaea.org
Website: aaea.org
Members:
50 associations
2700 individuals
Staff: 5
Annual Budget: $1-2,000,000
Tax: 501(c)(3)

Personnel:
Executive Director: Kristin Agard
  E-Mail: kristin@aaea.org
Administrative Coordinator: Tess Heiderscheit
  E-Mail: Theiderscheit@aaea.org
Manager, Membership Services: Brian Mondragón Jones
  E-Mail: brian@aaea.org
Manager, Meetings: Kristen Wright
  E-Mail: Kwright@aaea.org

Historical Note:

AAEA is a not-for-profit association serving the professional interests of members working in agricultural and broadly related fields of applied economics. Members of the AAEA are employed by academic or government institutions, as well as in industry and not-for-profit organizations, and engage in a variety of teaching, research, and extension/outreach activities. Membership: $25-225/year.

Meetings/Conferences: Annual
Conference Chair: Kristen Wright
2013 - Washington, DC/Aug. 4 - 6
2014 - Minneapolis, MN/July 27 - 29
2015 - San Francisco, CA/July 26 - 28
Number of non-conference events/year: 3

Publications:
American Journal of Agricultural Economics (AJAE); semi-annually
Applied Economic Perspectives and Policy (AEPP)
Choices Magazine; quarterly
Journal of Natural Resources and Life Sciences Education (JNRLSE)
Policy Issues
The Exchange; bi-monthly

Agricultural and Food Transporters Conference (1995)
950 N. Glebe Rd.
Suite 210
Arlington, VA 22203
Tel: (703) 838-7955 *Fax:* (703) 838-1781
E-Mail: jsamson@trucking.org
Website: truckline.com/Federation/Conferences/AFTC
Members: 500 companies
Staff: 1
Annual Budget: $250-500,000

Personnel:
Executive Director: Jon Samson
  E-Mail: jsamson@trucking.org

Historical Note:
Formerly (2003) the Agricultural Transportation Conference. AFTC's mission is to increase the safety, security, profitability and efficiency of transporters of agricultural commodities, food, forest products and natural resources. It also represents motor carrier and allied members of the American Trucking Associations on critical issues affecting agricultural commodity and food transportation.

Agricultural History Society (1919)
C/O MSU History Department
P.O. Box H
Mississippi State, MS 39762
Tel: (662) 268-2247
Website: aghistorysociety.org
Members: 800 individuals and companies
Staff: 3
Annual Budget: $100-250,000
Tax: 501(c)(3)

Personnel:
Executive Secretary: James C. Giesen
  E-Mail: jgiesen@history.msstate.edu
Treasurer: Alan I. Marcus
  E-Mail: aimarcus@history.msstate.edu

Historical Note:
AHS's mission is to advocate the interest, study and research in the history of agriculture. Members are agricultural economists, anthropologists, economists, environmentalists, historians, historical geographers, rural sociologists, and a variety of independent scholars. Membership: $55-65 (Regular); $20-25 (Students); $25-30 (Retired); $1,000 (Life); $175 (Institutional); $20 (Overseas).

Meetings/Conferences: Annual
2013 - Banff, AB/June 12 - 15
Number of non-conference events/year: 1

Publications:
Agricultural History; quarterly

Agricultural Retailers Association (1955)
1156 15th St. NW
Suite 500
Washington, DC 20005
Tel: (202) 457-0825 *Fax:* (202) 457-0864
TollFree: (800) 535-6272
E-Mail: info@aradc.org
Website: aradc.org
Members: 2592 individuals

Staff: 8
Annual Budget: $2-5,000,000
Tax: 501(c)(6)

Personnel:
President and Chief Executive Officer: Daren Coppock
  E-Mail: dcoppock@aradc.org
Senior Vice President for Public Policy & Counsel: Richard Gupton
  E-Mail: richard@aradc.org
Director, Marketing and Communications: Michelle Hummel
  E-Mail: michelle@aradc.org
Associate Director, Membership Services and Office Administrator: Kelly Jones
  E-Mail: kelly@aradc.org
Director, Administration and Membership Relations: Tracey Kerns
  E-Mail: tracey@aradc.org

Historical Note:
ARA's mission is to advocate, influence, educate and provide services to support its members in their quest to maintain a profitable business environment, adapt to a changing world and preserve their freedom to operate. Membership: $800-60000 (Distributor); $1000-35000 (Industry).

Meetings/Conferences: Annual
Conference Chair: Kelly Jones
Number of non-conference events/year: 3

Publications:
Ag Professional Magazine; on-line
Membership Directory; on-line
Retailer Fact$

Agricultural Stewardship Association (1990)
14 Main St.
Suite 100
Greenwich, NY 12834
Tel: (518) 692-7285 *Fax:* (518) 692-7720
E-Mail: asa@agstewardship.org
Website: agstewardship.org
Staff: 3
Annual Budget: $500-1,000,000
Tax: 501(c)(3)

Personnel:
Executive Director: Teri Ptacek
  E-Mail: teri@agstewardship.org
Senior Manager, Communications and Programs: Meegan Finnegan
  E-Mail: meegan@agstewardship.org
Administrative Assistant: Sarah Kane
  E-Mail: sarah@agstewardship.org

Historical Note:
ASA works with landowners to protect the vital and irreplaceable farm and forest lands in Washington and Rensselaer counties for the benefit of the community and generations to come.

Meetings/Conferences: Annual
Conference Chair: Meegan Finnegan
Number of non-conference events/year: 2

Agriculture Council of America (1973)
11020 King St.
Suite 205
Overland Park, KS 66210
Tel: (913) 491-1895 *Fax:* (913) 491-6502
E-Mail: info@agday.org
Website: agday.org
Members: 2500 individuals and 300 individual and corporate members
Staff: 3
Annual Budget: $100-250,000
Tax: 501(c)(6)

Personnel:
President: Jenny Pickett
  E-Mail: jennyp@nama.org

Historical Note:
Works to promote and build public support on behalf of the industry. Serves as coordinator for National Agriculture Day. Absorbed Agricultural Relations Council in 1998. Members include producers, commodity groups/cooperatives, general farm organizations, railroads, port authorities, market development cooperators, private voluntary agencies, retailers and financial institutions, and food and agricultural companies. Membership fee varies according to type of membership.

Meetings/Conferences: Annual
Publications:

Membership Directory; on-line
Membership List Available to Non-members

AHS International - The Vertical Flight Society
(1943)
217 N. Washington St.
Alexandria, VA 22314-2538
Tel: (703) 684-6777 *Fax:* (703) 739-9279
TollFree: (855) 247-4685
E-Mail: staff@vtol.org
Website: vtol.org
Members: 6000 individuals and 100 companies
Staff: 8
Annual Budget: $1-2,000,000
Tax: 501(c)(6)

Personnel:
Executive Director: Mike Hirschberg
Office Manager, Membership Liaison and VFF Scholarship Coordinator: Holly Cafferelli
Director, Information Resources: Randy Johnson
 E-Mail: randy@vtol.org
Director, Membership Services: Liz Malleck
 E-Mail: liz@vtol.org
Director, Meetings and Advertising: David M. Renzi
 E-Mail: drenzi@vtol.org
Editor in Chief: L. Kim Smith

Historical Note:
AHS aims to promote traditional rotorcraft platform disciplines, and focuses on the multidisciplinary fields of vertical flight and related support industries. Membership: $65-85 (Regular); $40-60 (Regular, Age below 30); $35-55 (Retired/Active Military); $25-45 (Student); $500-12,500 (Corporate).

Meetings/Conferences: Semi-Annual
Conference Chair: David M. Renzi
2013 - Phoenix, AZ (Phoenix Convention Center)/May 21 - 23
Number of non-conference events/year: 8

Publications:
The Journal of the American Helicopter Society; quarterly
Vertiflite magazine; quarterly; adv.

AIB International *(1919)*
1213 Bakers Way
P.O. Box 3999
Manhattan, KS 66505-3999
Tel: (785) 537-4750 *Fax:* (785) 537-1493
TollFree: (800) 633-5137
E-Mail: aibmarketing@aibonline.org
Website: aibonline.org
Staff: 6
Tax: 501(c)(3)

Personnel:
President and Chief Executive Officer: James Munyon
 E-Mail: jmunyon@aibonline.org
Publication Coordinator: Kerry Beach
 E-Mail: kbeach@aibonline.org
Vice President, Education: Kirk O'Donnell
 E-Mail: kodonnell@aibonline.org
Senior Vice President, Audit and Technical Services: Maureen C. Olewnik PhD
Vice President, Administration: Gary Skrdlant
Vice President, Marketing and Sales: Brian Soddy
 E-Mail: bsoddy@aibonline.org

Historical Note:
Founded by the North American wholesale and retail baking industries as a technology transfer center for bakers and food processors. AIB's mission is to protect the safety of the food supply chain and delivering high value technical and educational programs. Membership: $500-10,000/year.

Continuing Education:
Certification Designation/s: CFDC, GFSI

Publications:
AIB Newsletter; monthly
Technical Bulletins; bi-monthly

AIM Global *(1972)*
One Landmark North, 20399 Route 19
Suite 203
Cranberry Township, PA 16066
Tel: (724) 934-4470 *Fax:* (724) 742-4476
E-Mail: info@aimglobal.org
Website: aimglobal.org
Members: 813 companies and chapters
Staff: 8

Personnel:
Chief Operating officer: Mary Lou Bosco
Manager, Finance and Administration: Diana Bowser
 E-Mail: diana@aimglobal.org
Director, Business Development: Linda Young
 E-Mail: l.young@aimglobal.org

Historical Note:
AIM global is involved with automatic identification, data collection and networking in a mobile environment. Manufacturers, major distributors and global resellers join AIM Global to pursue strategic efforts that will grow the market.

Meetings/Conferences: Semi-Annual

Publications:
AIM Connections; monthly; adv.
Career Center; on-line
RFID Connections; monthly; adv.
The Competitive Edge; monthly

Membership List Available to Non-members

AIM North America *(2003)*
One Landmark North
20399 Route 19, Suite 203
Cranberry Township, PA 16066
Tel: (724) 742-4473 *Fax:* (724) 742-4476
E-Mail: info@aim-na.org
Website: aim-na.org
Staff: 1

Personnel:
Chief Operating Officer: Mary Lou Bosco
 E-Mail: marylou@aim-na.org

Historical Note:
AIM North America's mission is to enhance its members' competitiveness, productivity, and profitability in the North American market while maintaining professionalism and inclusive industry partnerships. Membership: $1,200 (Council); $900 (Charter); $395 (Affiliate).

Continuing Education:
Certification Designation/s: RFID

Meetings/Conferences: Annual

Publications:
AIM Connections; monthly; adv.
Membership Directory; on-line
RFID Connections; monthly; adv.
The Competitive Edge; monthly; adv.

Air and Expedited Motor Carriers Association
9532 Liberia Ave.
Suite 705
Manassas, VA 20110
Tel: (703) 361-5208 *Fax:* (703) 361-5274
E-Mail: info@aemca.org
Website: aemca.org
Staff: 2
Annual Budget: $100-250,000
Tax: 501(c)(6)

Personnel:
Executive Director: Fiona J. Morgan
 E-Mail: fiona@aemca.org
Treasurer: Jeff Patterson
 E-Mail: jeffpat@aol.com

Historical Note:
AEMCA works to provide its members with timely, value added information, education, benefits and opportunities to promote business development through networking with members and industry groups. Members are firms using a variety of equipment including tractor-trailers and straight trucks, serving an entire region or group of state/provinces, firms using mainly straight trucks and vans, serving the metropolitan area around one major regional airport and firms working with airports nationwide, running line hauls day and night to provide connecting service on reliable schedules. Membership: $475-5,000 (Motor Carrier Member); $400 (Associate Member).

Meetings/Conferences: Annual
Conference Chair: Fiona J. Morgan
2013 - Las Vegas, NV (Red Rock Casino)/March 10 - 12/over 100 exhibitors

Publications:
e-Xpeditor Newsletter; monthly
Membership Directory; on-line

Air and Surface Transport Nurses Association
(1980)
7995 E. Prentice Ave.
Suite 100
Greenwood Village, CO 80111

Tel: (720) 488-0492 *Fax:* (303) 770-1614
TollFree: (800) 897-6362
E-Mail: astna@gwami.com
Website: astna.org
Members: 1850 individuals
Staff: 2
Annual Budget: $100-250,000

Personnel:
Executive Director: Karen M. Wojdyla
 E-Mail: kwojdyla@gwami.com
Administrator: Amanda Olaes
 E-Mail: aolaes@gwami.com

Historical Note:
Founded as National Flight Nurses Association; assumed its present name in 1999. ASTNA's mission is to advance the practice of transport nursing and enhance the quality of patient care. Members are hospital-based, public service, military and private providers of both emergency and non- emergency patient air and ground transport. Affiliate members include respiratory therapists, paramedics, pilots, and aircraft vendors/operators. Membership: $90 (Active); $85 (Affiliate); $75 (Student/Military); $115 (International); $95 (International Military); $1,000 (Lifetime).

Continuing Education:
Certification Designation/s: CFRN, CTRN

Meetings/Conferences: Annual
2013 - Virginia Beach, VA/Oct. 21 - 23
Number of non-conference events/year: 1

Publications:
Air Medical Journal; bi-monthly
Membership Directory; on-line
Wings, Wheels & Rotors; quarterly

Air and Waste Management Association *(1907)*
One Gateway Center
420 Ft. Duquesne Blvd., Third Floor
Pittsburgh, PA 15222-1435
Tel: (412) 232-3444 *Fax:* (412) 232-3450
E-Mail: info@awma.org
Website: awma.org
Members: 8000 organizations and individuals
Staff: 25
Annual Budget: $2-5,000,000
Tax: 501(c)(3)

Personnel:
Executive Director: Robert E. Hall
 E-Mail: bhall@awma.org
Director, Finance and Information Systems: Bill Braun
 E-Mail: bbraun@awma.org
Managing Editor: Lisa Bucher
 E-Mail: lbucher@awma.org
Conference and Events Manager: Dorothy Chmiel
 E-Mail: dchmiel@awma.org
Manager, Marketing: Emily Cope
 E-Mail: ecope@awma.org
Director, Membership Services and Human Resource: Stephanie Glyptis
 E-Mail: sglyptis@awna.org
Programs Planner: Carrie Hartz
 E-Mail: chartz@awma.org
Administrative Assistant: Mary Korzen
 E-Mail: mkorzen@awma.org
Senior Manager, Information Systems: Barry Rogers
 E-Mail: brogers@awma.org

Historical Note:
Formerly (1987) Air Pollution Control Association. A&WMA provides a neutral forum where environmental professionals share technical and managerial information about air pollution control and waste management. Members are drawn from a wide range of disciplines and represent all viewpoints on environmental issues. Membership: $180 (U.S. Individual); $93 (U.S. Young Professional); $35 (U.S. Student); $435 (Organizational); $65 (Individual Organizational).

Meetings/Conferences: Annual
Conference Chair: Carrie Hartz
2013 - Chicago, IL/June 25 - 28

Air Carrier Association of America *(1997)*
1776 K St. NW
Washington, DC 20006
Tel: (202) 719-7420 *Fax:* (202) 719-7049
E-Mail: info@acaa1.com
Website: acaa1.com
Members: 16 Airport Members, 1 Airline Members
Staff: 1

Annual Budget: $100-250,000
Tax: 501 (c)(6)

Personnel:
Executive Director: Edward P. Faberman
    E-Mail: epfaberman@acaa1.com

Historical Note:
ACAA's mission is to bring affordable airfare to the American traveler, promoting low-fare service.

AIR Commercial Real Estate Association (1960)
800 W. Sixth St.
Suite 800
Los Angeles, CA 90017
Tel: (213) 687-8777 Fax: (213) 687-8616
Website: airea.com
Members: 1700 real estate professionals 400 firms
Staff: 30
Annual Budget: $2-5,000,000

Personnel:
Executive Director: Tim Hayes
    E-Mail: thayes@airea.com
Staff Accountant: Ace Adriano
    E-Mail: aadriano@airea.com
Technical Support: David Gonzalez
    E-Mail: dgonzalez@airea.com
Marketing, Analyst: Matt Nelson
    E-Mail: mnelson@airea.com
Membership Support: Jobert Paz
    E-Mail: jobert@airea.com
Director, Training: Martin A. Vartanian
    E-Mail: mvartanian@airea.com
Executive Assistant: Maria Verdin
    E-Mail: mverdin@airea.com

Historical Note:
Formerly (2004) American Industrial Real Estate Association. AIR works for programs and services that are designed to advance the success of the members. Members are real estate brokers specializing in industrial/commercial properties. Membership: $270-600 (Affiliate Business Organization); $100 (Individual); $150 (Orientation Fee).

Publications:
AirWaves Newsletter; bi-monthly

Air Conditioning Contractors of America (1969)
2800 Shirlington Rd.
Suite 300
Arlington, VA 22206
Tel: (703) 575-4477
E-Mail: admin@acca.org
Website: acca.org
Members:
60000 professionals
4000 companies
Staff: 20
Annual Budget: $2-5,000,000
Tax: 501 (c)(6)

Personnel:
President and Chief Executive Officer: Paul T. Stalknecht
    E-Mail: paul.stalknecht@acca.org
General Counsel and Senior Vice President, Finance and Administration: Hilary Atkins
    E-Mail: atkins@acca.org
Director, Communications: Melissa Broadus
    E-Mail: Melissa.Broadus@acca.org
Director, Membership and Federation Relations: Kimya Bailey Cajchun
    E-Mail: kimya.cajchun@acca.org
Director, Information Systems: Craig Gotthardt
Vice President, Marketing and Business Development: Chris Hoelzel
Senior Vice President, Business Operations and Membership Services: Kevin W. Holland
    E-Mail: kevin.holland@acca.org
Senior Vice President, Technical, Accreditation and Educational Policy Development: Glenn Hourahan PE
    E-Mail: glenn.hourahan@acca.org
Director, Conferences and Training: Kimberly Hurley
    E-Mail: kimberly.hurley@acca.org
Director, Conferences and Events: Sandra Kyles CMP
    E-Mail: sandra.kyles@acca.org
Vice President, Government Relations: Charlie McCrudden
    E-Mail: charlie.mccrudden@acca.org

Historical Note:

ACCA is the trade association representing heating, ventilating, air conditioning and refrigeration contractors nationwide.

Continuing Education:
Certification Designation/s: NATE, EPA, EPIC

Meetings/Conferences: Semi-Annual
Conference Chair: Sandra Kyles CMP
2013 - Orlando, FL (Orlando World Center)/Feb. 27 - March 2
2013 - Mason, OH (Cincinnati)/March 6 - 8
Number of non-conference events/year: 16

Publications:
ACCA newsletter; on-line
Contractor Excellence; quarterly
Membership Directory; on-line

Air Conditioning, Heating and Refrigeration Institute (AHRI) (1997)
2111 Wilson Blvd.
Suite 500
Arlington, VA 22201
Tel: (703) 524-8800 Fax: (703) 562-1942
E-Mail: ahri@ahri.org
Website: ahrinet.org
Members: 300 companies
Staff: 11
Annual Budget: $25-50,000,000
Tax: 501 (c)(6)

Personnel:
President and Chief Executive Officer: Stephen R. Yurek
    E-Mail: ahri@ahrinet.org
IT Support Specialist: Clay Anderson
    E-Mail: CAnderson@ahrinet.org
Manager, Office Operations: Doug Burke
    E-Mail: dburke@ahrinet.org
Manager, Human Resources: Lisa Cardinal
    E-Mail: lcardinal@ahrinet.org
Director, Legislative and Regulatory Affairs: Don Davis
    E-Mail: ddavis@ari.org
Vice President, Public Affairs: Francis Dietz
    E-Mail: fdietz@ahrinet.org
Senior Vice President, Technical Services and Communications: Henry Hwong
    E-Mail: hhwong@ahrinet.org
Director, Meetings and Events: Carol Loughne
    E-Mail: cloughney@ahrinet.org
Director, Education: Warren Lupson
    E-Mail: wlupson@ahrinet.org
General Counsel and Secretary: Joseph Mattingly
    E-Mail: jmattingly@ahrinet.org
Chief Financial Officer: Stephanie Murphy
    E-Mail: smurphy@ahrinet.org
Membership Specialist: Freshta Rosario
    E-Mail: FRosario@ahrinet.org
Director, Information Technology: Bradley Slatten
    E-Mail: bslatten@ahrinet.org

Historical Note:
Trade Association for the air conditioning, heating and refrigeration industry

Continuing Education:
Certification Designation/s: HVACR

Meetings/Conferences: Annual

Publications:
AHRI Newsletter; on-line; adv.
AHRI Update; monthly
Membership Directory; on-line

Air Diffusion Council (1961)
1901 N. Roselle Rd.
Suite 800
Schaumburg, IL 60195
Tel: (847) 706-6750 Fax: (847) 706-6751
E-Mail: info@flexibleduct.org
Website: flexibleduct.org
Members: 50 companies
Staff: 2
Annual Budget: $50-100,000
Tax: 501 (c)(6)

Personnel:
Executive Director: Jack L. Lagershausen
    E-Mail: info@flexibleduct.org

Historical Note:
ADC's mission is to encourage, assist and support the development and maintenance of credible and efficient industry standards for the installation, use and performance of flexible duct products and to promote the use of those

standards by various code bodies, government agencies, architects, engineers, heating and cooling contractors, etc. Membership: $2,600/year (Active); $650 (Associate).

Continuing Education:
Certification Designation/s: TPCP

Publications:
Membership Directory; bi-annually

Air Distribution Institute (1947)
4415 W. Harrison St.
Suite 426
Hillside, IL 60162
Tel: (708) 449-2933 Fax: (708) 449-0837
E-Mail: info@steelduct.org
Website: steelduct.org
Members: 21 companies
Staff: 2
Annual Budget: $25-50,000

Personnel:
President: Rob Felton
    E-Mail: ADI-President@steelduct.org
General Manager: Patricia H. Keating
    E-Mail: adi-general-manager@steelduct.org

Historical Note:
ADI's mission is to advocate the use of fabricated steel duct pipe and fittings for air distribution products. Members are manufacturers of prefabricated ducts, pipes and fittings used in residential housing.

Meetings/Conferences: Annual

Air Force Association (1946)
1501 Lee Hwy.
Arlington, VA 22209-1198
Tel: (703) 247-5800 Fax: (703) 247-5853
TollFree: (800) 727-3337
E-Mail: grl@afa.org
Website: afa.org
Members: 130000 individuals
Staff: 65
Annual Budget: $10-25,000,000
Tax: 501 (c)(3)

Personnel:
President: Craig R. McKinley
Director, Government Relations: Douglas Birkey
    E-Mail: dbirkey@afa.org
Director, Policy and Communications: Chester Curtis
    E-Mail: ccurtis@afa.org
Director, Programs and Industry Relations: Mary Ellen Dobrowolski
    E-Mail: MDobrowolski@AFA.org
Chief, Media Services: Doreatha Major
    E-Mail: dmajor@afa.org
Manager, Meetings and Events: Meghan McClelland
    E-Mail: mmcclelland@afa.org
Contact, Information Technology: Ted Yorkshire
    E-Mail: tyorkshire@afa.org

Historical Note:
AFA's mission is to educate the public about the critical role of aerospace power in the defense of its nation and also seeks to advocate aerospace power and a strong national defense. Has military and civilian members. Membership: $45/year.

Meetings/Conferences:
Conference Chair: Mary Ellen Dobrowolski
2013 - Orlando, FL (Rosen Shingle Creek Hotel)/Feb. 21 - 22
2013 - Washington, DC (Gaylord National-Washington)/March 14 - 15
2013 - Washington, DC (Gaylord National-Washington)/Sept. 14 - 15
2013 - Washington, DC (Gaylord National-Washington)/Sept. 16 - 18
2014 - Washington, DC (Gaylord National-Washington)/March 27 - 29
2014 - Washington, DC (Gaylord National-Washington)/Sept. 13 - 14
2014 - Washington, DC (Gaylord National-Washington)/Sept. 15 - 17
2015 - Washington, DC (Gaylord National-Washington)/March 12 - 14
2015 - Washington, DC (Gaylord National-Washington)/Sept. 12
2015 - Washington, DC (Gaylord National-Washington)/Sept. 14 - 16
2016 - Washington, DC (Gaylord National-Washington)/Sept. 17 - 18

2016 - Washington, DC (Gaylord National-
Washington)/Sept. 19 - 21
2017 - Washington, DC (Gaylord National-
Washington)/Sept. 16 - 17
2017 - Washington, DC (Gaylord National-
Washington)/Sept. 18 - 20
2018 - Washington, DC (Gaylord National-
Washington)/Sept. 15 - 16
2018 - Washington, DC (Gaylord National-
Washington)/Sept. 17 - 19

Publications:
AE News; monthly
Air Force Magazine; monthly; adv.
Membership Directory; on-line

Air Force Sergeants Association (1961)
5211 Auth Rd.
Suitland, MD 20746
Tel: (301) 899-3500 *Fax:* (301) 899-8136
TollFree: (800) 638-0594
E-Mail: staff@hqafsa.org
Website: hqafsa.org
Members: 111000 individuals
Staff: 23
Annual Budget: $2-5,000,000
Tax: 501(c)(19)

Personnel:
Chief Executive Officer: John R. "Doc" McCaulsin Doc
    E-Mail: mccauslin@hqafsa.org
Director, Military and Government: Morgan Brown
    E-Mail: mbrown@hqafsa.org
Chief Financial Officer: Ernest Chriss
    E-Mail: echriss@hqafsa.org
Director, Marketing: Lisa Donor
    E-Mail: ldonor@hqafsa.org
Contact, Accounting Services: Judy McGraw
    E-Mail: jmcgraw@hqafsa.org
*Director, Communications and Technology and Contact,
    Publications:* David Mimms
    E-Mail: dmimms@hqafsa.org
Director, Government Affairs: Robert H. Price
    E-Mail: rprice@hqafsa.org
Director, Member and Field Relations and Planner, Events:
    Keith A. Reed MBA
    E-Mail: kreed@hqafsa.org
Executive Secretary: Teresa Young
    E-Mail: tyoung@hqafsa.org

Historical Note:
*AFSA works to represent members in more than 142
chapters worldwide before congressional and military
decisionmakers, voicing their concerns over pay, benefits,
advancement, retirement and living conditions. Members
are enlisted grades of Air Force Active Duty, Air National
Guard, and Air Force Reserve Command, retired, veteran
and family members. Membership: $24-25 (AFSA); $20
(Auxiliary/Auxiliary Affiliate); $25 (AFSA Associate).*

Meetings/Conferences: Annual
Conference Chair: Morgan Brown

Publications:
AFSA Enlisted Almanac; annually
Membership Directory; on-line
The Sergeants Magazine; bi-monthly; adv.
Weekly Newsletter; weekly; adv.

Air Line Pilots Association International (1931)
1625 Massachusetts Ave. NW
Washington, DC 20036
Tel: (703) 689-2270 *Fax:* (202) 797-4030
E-Mail: media@alpa.org
Website: alpa.org
Members: 53000 pilots
Staff: 947
Annual Budget: Over $100,000,000

Personnel:
Chief Counsel and Director, Legal Department: Jonathan
    Cohen CAE
Vice President, Finance and Treasurer: CAPT Randolph
    Helling
Michael Robbins
Contact, Communications: Linda Shotwell
    E-Mail: linda.shotwell@alpa.org

Historical Note:
*Organized in Chicago in 1931 by pilot representatives
of various air carriers under the leadership of David
Behncke and chartered by the American Federation of
Labor the same year. Once included the Air Line Employees
Association and the Association of Flight Attendants*

which became independent chartered affiliates in 1963
and 1973, respectively, absorbed Canadian Air Line
Pilots Association in 1997, and now represents pilots
at 49 airlines. ALPA's purpose is to promote the health
and welfare of the members of the association before all
governmental agencies and to be the guardian and defender
of the rights and privileges of the professional pilots who
are members of the association.

Meetings/Conferences:
Number of non-conference events/year: 4

Publications:
Air Line Pilot Magazine; on-line

Air Medical Operators Association (2009)
2200 Pennsylvania Ave. NW
Fourth Floor East
Washington, DC 20037
Tel: (703) 684-4447 *Fax:* (219) 743-3188
Website: airmedicaloperators.com
Staff: 1
Annual Budget: $250-500,000
Tax: 501(c)(6)

Personnel:
President: Christopher Eastlee
    E-Mail: ceastlee@airmedicaloperators.com

Historical Note:
*The Air Medical Operators Association (AMOA) is
committed to providing the highest level of safety in air
medical transport.*

Air Medical Physician Association (1992)
951 E. Montana Vista Ln.
Salt Lake City, UT 84124
Tel: (801) 263-2672 *Fax:* (801) 534-0434
E-Mail: patp@ampa.org
Website: ampa.org
Members: 400 individuals
Staff: 2
Annual Budget: $250-500,000

Personnel:
Executive Director: Patricia Petersen
    E-Mail: ppeter111@aol.com
Secretary And Treasurer: Christopher J. Fullagar FACEP,
    MD
    E-Mail: Fullagac@upstate.edu

Historical Note:
*AMPA is an association comprised of physicians and
professionals involved in medical transport who are
committed to promoting safe and efficacious patient
transportation through quality medical direction, research,
education, leadership, and collaboration. Membership:
$300 (Academic); $350 (Founding/Active Member); $125
(Affiliate); $75 (Medical Student/Resident).*

Publications:
Air Medical Journal; bi-monthly

Air Movement and Control Association International (1955)
30 W. University Dr.
Arlington Heights, IL 60004-1893
Tel: (847) 394-0150 *Fax:* (847) 253-0088
E-Mail: info@amca.org
Website: amca.org
Members: 300 members
Staff: 25
Annual Budget: $2-5,000,000
Tax: 501(c)(6)

Personnel:
Executive Director: Wade Smith
    E-Mail: wsmith@amca.org
Director, Certification Programs: Joseph Brooks
    E-Mail: jbrooks@amca.org
Director, Information Technology: Bruce Hackett
    E-Mail: bhackett@amca.org
Director, Finance: Robert Harris
    E-Mail: rharris@amca.org
Manager, Association Services: Rosann Jaffe
    E-Mail: rjaffe@amca.org
Director, Publications and Standards: Tim Orris
    E-Mail: torris@amca.org
Director, Membership, Marketing and Communications:
    Marian Vambreck
    E-Mail: mvambreck@amca.org

Historical Note:
*Formerly (1977) Air Moving and Conditioning Association.
AMCA's mission is to promote the health and growth
of the industries covered by its scope and the members
of the association consistent with the interests of the*

public. *Membership:* $4000 (AMCA North American/
International/Joint Member); $7,800 (CRP Affiliate);
$2,500 (Associate).

Continuing Education:
Certification Designation/s: CRP

Meetings/Conferences: Annual
Conference Chair: Rosann Jaffe
Number of non-conference events/year: 1

Publications:
AMCA Energy Focus; monthly
Greetings from the President-Newsletter; monthly
In Motion; biennially; adv.
Member Directory; on-line

Air Traffic Control Association (1956)
1101 King St.
Suite 300
Alexandria, VA 22314-2944
Tel: (703) 299-2430 *Fax:* (703) 299-2437
E-Mail: info@atca.org
Website: atca.org
Members: 2300 individuals
Staff: 10
Annual Budget: $2-5,000,000

Personnel:
President and Chief Executive Officer: Peter F. Dumont
    E-Mail: pete.dumont@atca.org
Administrator, Data Base: Keyvi Boyer
    E-Mail: keyvi.boyer@atca.org
Associate Director, Meetings and Expositions: Kenneth
    Carlisle
    E-Mail: ken.carlisle@atca.org
Director, Membership Services: Carrie Courter
    E-Mail: carrie.rowe@atca.org
Director, Communications: Marion Hixon
Chief Financial Officer: Christine Oster
    E-Mail: christine.oster@atca.org
Manager, Air Traffic Control Programs: Paul Planzer
    E-Mail: paul.planzer@atca.org
Vice President, Operations: Claire Rusk
    E-Mail: claire.rusk@atca.org
Director, Communications: Michele Townes
    E-Mail: michele.townes@atca.org

Historical Note:
*ATCA's serves as a forum for discussing issues and
exchanging ideas on all matters pertaining to global
airspace systems and flight safety. Membership: $130
(Professional Members); $26-130 (Armed Forces
Members); $52 (Student Members); $750- 2,000
(Organizational Members); $1,000-5,000 (Industry).*

Meetings/Conferences: Semi-Annual
Conference Chair: Paul Planzer
2013 - Madrid, Spain/Feb. 12 - 14
2013 - Ft. Washington, MD (Gaylord National Resort
    and Convention Center-National Harbor)/Oct. 20 -
    23/3000 attendees
2014 - Ft. Washington, MD (Gaylord National Resort
    and Convention Center-National Harbor)/Sept. 28 -
    Oct. 1
Number of non-conference events/year: 2

Publications:
ATCA Bulletin; monthly
Journal of Air Traffic Control; quarterly

Airborne Law Enforcement Association (1968)
50 Carroll Creek Way
Suite 260
Frederick, MD 21701
Tel: (301) 631-2406 *Fax:* (301) 631-2466
Website: alea.org
Members: 3500 individuals
Staff: 7
Annual Budget: $1-2,000,000
Tax: 501(c)(3)

Personnel:
Executive Director: Stephen J. Ingley
    E-Mail: singley@alea.org
Manager, Operations: Carrie Cosens
    E-Mail: ccosens@alea.org
Meeting Planner and Coordinator: Sherry W. Hadley CAE
    CMP
    E-Mail: shadley@alea.org
Legal Counsel: Paul J. Marino
    E-Mail: legalcounsel@alea.org
Manager, Training Program: Don Roby
    E-Mail: droby@alea.org
Chief Financial Officer: Daniel B. Schwarzbach

E-Mail: Schwarzbach@msn.com
Manager, Marketing: Jennifer Thornton
E-Mail: jthornton@alea.org

Historical Note:
ALEA's mission is to support, promote and advance the safe and effective utilization of aircraft by law enforcement agencies in support of law enforcement missions through training, networking, advocacy and educational programs. Membership: $45 (Individual-US); $65 (Individual-International); $375 (Corporate).

Meetings/Conferences: Annual
2013 - Orlando, FL/July 17 - 20
Number of non-conference events/year: 6

Publications:
Air Beat Magazine; bi-monthly; adv.
Air Beat Today; daily; adv.
ALEA E-Newsletter; monthly; adv.
Membership Directory; annually
Safety First; monthly; adv.

Aircraft Builders Council *(1955)*
4248 Park Glen Rd.
Minneapolis, MN 55416-4758
Tel: (952) 928-4662 *Fax:* (952) 767-0767
E-Mail: info@aircraftbuilders.com
Website: aircraftbuilders.com
Staff: 3
Annual Budget: $250-500,000

Personnel:
Contact, Conference: Sara Jensen
E-Mail: sjensen@harringtoncompany.com

Historical Note:
ABC's mission is to support and promote the continuity of an innovative, competitive aircraft products liability insurance facility and to communicate the existence of such insurance program to aerospace manufacturers and product suppliers and promote the use of the program's product safety and liability prevention seminars.

Meetings/Conferences: Annual
Conference Chair: Sara Jensen
2013 - San Diego, CA (Park Hyatt Aviara Resort)/Sept. 22 - 24
2014 - Manalapan, FL (The Ritz-Carlton Palm Beach)/Sept. 21 - 23

Publications:
ABC Newsletter; semi-annually

Aircraft Electronics Association *(1957)*
3570 NE Ralph Powell Rd.
Lee's Summit, MO 64064
Tel: (816) 347-8400 *Fax:* (816) 347-8405
E-Mail: info@aea.net
Website: aea.net
Members: 1300 companies
Staff: 14
Annual Budget: $2-5,000,000
Tax: 501(c)(6)

Personnel:
President: Paula Derks
E-Mail: paulad@aea.net
Director, Membership Services and Advertising for Specialized Publications: Linda Adams
E-Mail: lindaa@aea.net
Vice President, Membership Programs and Education: Mike Adamson
E-Mail: mikea@aea.net
General Counsel: Jason Dickstein
E-Mail: jason@washingtonaviation.com
Director, Communications: Geoff Hill
E-Mail: geoffh@aea.net
Executive Vice President: Debra A. McFarland
E-Mail: debbiem@aea.net
Manager, Marketing and Advertising: Lauren McFarland
E-Mail: laurenm@aea.net
Vice President, Government and Industry Affairs: Ric Peri
E-Mail: ricp@aea.net
Director, Information Services: Aaron Ward
E-Mail: aaronw@aea.net

Historical Note:
AEA's mission is to self-sustaining organization committed to enhancing the profitability of its members. Membership includes instruments facilities, manufacturers of avionics equipment, instrument manufacturers, airframe manufacturers, test equipment manufacturers, major distributors, and educational institutions. Membership: $345-905 (Repair station/Provisional, based on number of staff); $855-2895 (Associate, based on Avionics Sales);

$670-2,300 (Corporate/Commercial Operator, based on fleets); $325 (Academic); $475 (DER).

Meetings/Conferences: Annual
Conference Chair: Debra A. McFarland
2013 - Las Vegas, NV/March 25 - 28
2014 - Nashville, TN/March 12 - 15
2015 - Dallas, TX/April 8 - 11
2016 - Orlando, FL/April 27 - 30

Publications:
AEA Wired; semi-monthly
Avionics News magazine; monthly; adv.
Member Directory

Aircraft Locknut Manufacturers Association
994 Old Eagle School Rd.
Suite 1019
Wayne, PA 19087
Tel: (610) 971-4850 *Fax:* (610) 971-4859
E-Mail: info@almanet.org
Website: almanet.org
Members: 10 companies
Staff: 2
Annual Budget: $25-50,000
Tax: 501(c)(6)

Personnel:
Executive Director: Robert H. Ecker
E-Mail: rhecker@almanet.org

Historical Note:
ALMA's mission is to control the process of locknut manufacturing to ensure timely delivery of quality products. ALMA is comprised of North American manufacturers of self-locking nuts for the aerospace industry.

Meetings/Conferences:
Number of non-conference events/year: 1

Publications:
Member Directory; on-line

Membership List Available to Non-members

Aircraft Mechanics Fraternal Association *(1962)*
14001 E. Iliff Ave.
Suite 217
Aurora, CO 80014
Tel: (303) 752-2632 *Fax:* (303) 362-7736
TollFree: (800) 520-2632
Website: amfanatl.org
Staff: 2
Annual Budget: $2-5,000,000
Tax: 501(c)(5)

Personnel:
National Director and Media Contact: Sidney "Louie " L. Key
E-Mail: Louie.Key@amfanatl.org
National Secretary and Treasurer: Steven Nowak
E-Mail: steven.nowak@amfanatl.org

Historical Note:
The Aircraft Mechanics Fraternal Association (AMFA) is a independent union representing aircraft maintenance employees. Mission is to raise the standards of and increase recognition of the technician and related class or craft for the protection of the profession. Membership: $25 (Active Associate), $40 (Associate).

Publications:
The Grapevine Newsletter

Aircraft Owners and Pilots Association *(1939)*
421 Aviation Way
Frederick, MD 21701
Tel: (301) 695-2000 *Fax:* (301) 695-2375
TollFree: (800) 872-2672
E-Mail: aopahq@aopa.org
Website: aopa.org
Members: 400000 individuals
Staff: 130
Annual Budget: $25-50,000,000

Personnel:
President and Chief Executive Officer: Craig L. Fuller
Contact, Convention Sponsorship and Exhibit Sales: Liz Tarver
E-Mail: liz.tarver@aopa.org

Historical Note:
AOPA's mission is to preserve the freedom to fly by advocating on behalf of its members, educating pilots, nonpilots, and policy makers alike, supporting activities that ensure the long-term health of General Aviation. Membership: $39/year (Individual).

Meetings/Conferences: Annual
Conference Chair: Liz Tarver

Publications:
Airport Directory and Resources; on-line
AOPA Pilot Magazine; monthly; adv.
e-Pilot; weekly; adv.
Flight Training Magazine; monthly; adv.
Membership Directory; on-line

Airforwarders Association *(1990)*
750 National Press Bldg.
529 14th St. NW
Washington, DC 20045
Tel: (202) 393-2818 *Fax:* (202) 223-9741
Website: airforwarders.org
Members: 3000 offices and 275 companies
Staff: 5
Annual Budget: $500-1,000,000
Tax: 501(c)(6)

Personnel:
Executive Director: Brandon Fried
E-Mail: bfried@airforwarders.org
Contact, Publications: Tara McLaughlin
E-Mail: tmclaughlin@kellencompany.com

Historical Note:
Airforwarder Association members are air freight forwarding companies holding valid FAA Security Agreement Numbers. Associate members are airlines, truckers and other non-forwarders with an interest in the industry. The mission of AFA is to provide information and education to the air and expedited freight forwarding industry. Membership: $850-2,585 (Regular Member); $1,095-1,755 (Airline Member/Associate Member); $325-545 (Affiliate Member).

Meetings/Conferences: Annual
2013 - Las Vegas, NV/March 10 - 12
Number of non-conference events/year: 1

Publications:
FORWARD Magazine; quarterly
Press Releases; monthly

Airline Industrial Relations Conference *(1971)*
1300 19th St. NW
Suite 750
Washington, DC 20036-1561
Tel: (202) 861-7550 *Fax:* (202) 861-7557
E-Mail: staff@aircon.org
Website: aircon.org
Members: 18 companies
Staff: 5
Annual Budget: $1-2,000,000
Tax: 501(c)(6)

Personnel:
President: Michael H. Campbell
Chief Information Officer and Treasurer: Frederick W. Deck III
Vice President, General Counsel and Secretary: Robert J. DeLucia
E-Mail: rob@aircon.org

Historical Note:
AIRCON is a voluntary, non-profit association serving as the Washington-based labor policy organization of scheduled air carriers in the United States.

Publications:
AIR Conference Personnel Directory; on-line
Member Directory; on-line

Airlines Electronic Engineering Committee *(1949)*
2551 Riva Rd.
Annapolis, MD 21401-7435
Tel: (410) 266-4113 *Fax:* (410) 266-2047
Website: aviation-ia.com
Members: 30 companies
Staff: 14

Personnel:
Contact, Communication and Executive Secretary: Paul Prisaznuk
E-Mail: pjp@arinc.com

Historical Note:
The Airlines Electronic Engineering Committee (AEEC) creates value for airlines and the aviation industry by developing engineering standards and technical solutions for avionics, networks, and cabin systems that foster increased efficiency and reduced life cycle costs throughout the aviation community.

Meetings/Conferences: Annual
2013 - Orlando, FL (Hilton Orlando Lake Buena Vista)/April 22 - 24

Publications:

AeroLine; monthly
Newsletter

Airlines For America (1936)
1301 Pennsylvania Ave. NW
Suite 1100
Washington, DC 20004-1707
Tel: (202) 626-4000
E-Mail: a4a@airlines.org
Website: airlines.org
Members: 23 U.S. airlines and non-U.S. airlines
Staff: 11
Annual Budget: $10-25,000,000

Personnel:
President and Chief Executive Officer: Nicholas E. Calio
Senior Vice President, Chief Financial Officer and Treasurer:
Paul R. Archambeault
   E-Mail: parch@airlines.org
Senior Vice President and General Counsel: David A. Berg
   E-Mail: dberg@airlines.org
Vice President and Chief Economist: John P. Heimlich
Senior Vice President, Communications: Jean Medina
   E-Mail: jmedina@airlines.org
Kimberly Roberts

Historical Note:
*Formerly Air Transport Association of America. A4A's
mission is to vigorously advocate for America's airlines
as models of safety, customer service and environmental
responsibility.*

Publications:
ATA SmartBrief; daily
e-business; on-line

Airport Consultants Council (1978)
908 King St.
Suite 100
Alexandria, VA 22314
Tel: (703) 683-5900 *Fax:* (703) 683-2564
E-Mail: info@acconline.org
Website: acconline.org
Members: 240 companies
Staff: 6
Annual Budget: $500-1,000,000

Personnel:
President: Paula P. Hochstetler
   E-Mail: paulah@acconline.org
Executive Vice President: T. J. Schulz
   E-Mail: tjs@acconline.org
Manager, Marketing and Services: Colleen Flood
   E-Mail: colleenf@acconline.org
Assistant, Membership and Administration: Lara Lynch
   E-Mail: laral@acconline.org
Manager, Communications: John B. Reynolds
   E-Mail: johnr@acconline.org
Coordinator, Marketing and Membership: Emily
VanderBush
   E-Mail: emilyv@acconline.org

Historical Note:
*ACC's mission is to deliver excellence in airport
development. Represents firms that provide airport
architecture, design, engineering, security, marketing,
and environmental services, air service development.
Membership: $2,150 (Executive/Participating); $1,075
(Individual); $1,650 (Associate).*

Meetings/Conferences: Annual
2013 - New Orleans, LA/Feb. 6 - 8

Publications:
ACC Outlook; weekly; adv.
AirportConsulting; quarterly; adv.
Membership Directory; annually; adv.

Airport Ground Transportation Association
(1946)
154 University Center
One University Blvd.
St. Louis, MO 63121
Tel: (314) 516-7271 *Fax:* (314) 516-7272
E-Mail: admin@agtaweb.org
Website: agtaweb.org
Members: 350 individuals and 125 companies
Staff: 2
Annual Budget: $100-250,000

Personnel:
Executive Director: Ray Mundy
   E-Mail: rmundy@umsl.edu
Director, Administration: Sandra Mundy
   E-Mail: AGTA.smundy@gmail

Historical Note:
*AGTA's mission is to advance airport ground transportation
that is conducted cooperatively with airport authorities.
Members include airport authorities and operators and
industry suppliers of ground transportation at airports and
courtesy transportation providers. Membership: $400/year.*

Meetings/Conferences: Annual

Publications:
AGTA Newsletter; on-line
Membership Directory; on-line

Membership List Available to Non-members

Airport Minority Advisory Council (AMAC)
2345 Crystal Dr.
Suite 902
Arlington, VA 22202
Tel: (703) 414-2622 *Fax:* (703) 414-2686
E-Mail: amac.info@amac-org.com
Website: amac-org.com
Staff: 4
Annual Budget: $500-1,000,000
Tax: 501(c)(6)

Personnel:
Executive Director: Shelby Scales
   E-Mail: shelby.scales@amac-org.com
Manager, Membership Development: Alexandra Haynes
   E-Mail: alexandra.haynes@amac-org.com
Office Manager: Sonya Shakleford
   E-Mail: sonya.shakleford@amac-org.com

Historical Note:
*A non-profit trade association dedicated to promoting the
full participation of minority-owned, women-owned and
disadvantaged based enterprises in airport contracts and
employment opportunities. The Airport Minority Advisory
Council Educational and Scholarship program, Inc. is the
sister organization of AMAC. Membership: $25 (Student,
Non-Voting); $225 (Government, One-Vote); $500 (M/
W/DBE Business, Two votes); $1,500 (Airport, Two votes);
$2,000 (Corporate, NON-M/W/DBE).*

Meetings/Conferences: Annual
2013 - San Diego, CA/June 8 - 11
2014 - Denver, CO/June 7 - 10
2015 - Ft. Lauderdale, FL/June 6 - 9

Publications:
Newsletter

Airports Council International - North America
(1948)
1615 L St. NW
Suite 300
Washington, DC 20036
Tel: (202) 293-8500 *Fax:* (202) 331-1362
TollFree: (888) 424-7767
E-Mail: postmaster@aci-na.org
Website: aci-na.org
Members:
190 airport members
335 airports
Staff: 38
Annual Budget: $10-25,000,000

Personnel:
President: Gregory O. Principato
   E-Mail: gprincipato@aci-na.org
Vice President, Legal Affairs: James I. Briggs
   E-Mail: jbriggs@aci-na.org
Director, Marketing Communications: Stephenie Brooks
   E-Mail: sbrooks@aci-na.org
Vice President, Meetings, Conventions and Education:
Deirdre L. Clemmons
   E-Mail: dclemmons@aci-na.org
Senior Manager, Communications and Marketing: Morgan
Dye
   E-Mail: mdye@aci-na.org
General Counsel: Monica R. Hargrove
   E-Mail: mhargrove@aci-na.org
Senior Manager, Member Operations: Michelle Leslie
   E-Mail: mleslie@aci-na.org
Chief Financial Officer: Brett McAllister
   E-Mail: bmcallister@aci-na.org
Executive Vice President, Policy and External Affairs:
Deborah C. McElroy
   E-Mail: dmcelroy@aci-na.org
Senior Director, Digital Communications: Thomas J.
Smith
   E-Mail: tsmith@aci-na.org
Database Administrator and Chief Historian: Joseph
Weidlich

   E-Mail: jweidlich@aci-na.org
Senior Vice President - Human Resources and Operations:
Nancy Zimini
   E-Mail: nzimini@aci-na.org

Historical Note:
*ACI-NA works to advocate policies and provide services
that strengthen the ability of airports to serve their
passengers, customers and communities. Membership:
$800-128,192 (Airport Member); $3000-16500
(Associate); $1000 (Affiliate).*

Meetings/Conferences:
Conference Chair: Brett McAllister
2013 - Las Vegas, NV (Harrah's Las Vegas Casino
   Hotel)/Jan. 9 - 11
2013 - St. Petersburg, FL (Vinoy Renaissance St.
   Petersburg Resort and Golf Club)/March 5 - 7
2013 - Las Vegas, NV/March 10 - 11
2013 - Biloxi, MS (Beau Rivage Resort and Casino)/
   April 14 - 16
2013 - Portland, OR (Hilton Portland and Executive
   Tower)/April 22 - 24
2013 - Halifax, NS (The Lord Nelson Hotel and Suites)/
   May 12 - 15
2013 - Seattle, WA (Hyatt at Olive 8)/May 15 - 18
2013 - Atlanta, GA/June 4 - 5
2013 - San Jose, CA/Sept. 22 - 25
2013 - Budapest, Hungary/Oct. 1 - 3
2013 - Sacramento, CA (Hyatt Regency Sacramento)/
   Nov. 11 - 13
Number of non-conference events/year: 3

Publications:
Centerlines; quarterly
Centerlines Weekly Update; weekly
CEO Brief; monthly
Daily Clips; daily
Facts About Airports and Membership Directory;
   annually

Alarm Industry Communication Committee
8150 Leesburg Pike
Suite 700
Vienna, VA 22182
Tel: (703) 242-4670 *Fax:* (703) 242-4675
Website: csaaul.org/AICCCommittee.htm
Members: 19 Organizations
Staff: 6

Personnel:
Executive Vice President: Stephen P. Doyle
   E-Mail: director@csaaul.org
Vice President, Membership Services and Programs: Becky
Lane
   E-Mail: memberservices@csaaul.org
Vice President, Meetings and Conventions: John
McDonald
   E-Mail: meetings@csaaul.org
Senior Vice President, Finance and Administration:
Madeline Fullerton McMahon
   E-Mail: finance@csaaul.org
Director, Education and Training: Stephanie S. Morgan
PhD
   E-Mail: education@csaaintl.org
Director, Marketing and Communications: Monique C
Talbot IOM
   E-Mail: communications@csaaul.org

Historical Note:
*A committee composed of representatives of the Central
Station Alarm Association (CSAA), National Burglar &
Fire Alarm Association (NBFAA), the Security Industry
Association (SIA) and major alarm companies and
manufacturers.AICC's mission is to provide coordination
in a variety of areas between the alarm industry and the
FCC, other regulatory agencies, and members of Congress,
when needed. Membership: $1,500-11,500 (Regular)
$500-1,950 (Proprietary); $1,925-38,000 (Associate);
$825 (International); $500 (Consultant); $300 (Press).*

Publications:
CSAA Dispatch; quarterly; adv.
CSAA Signals; annually; adv.
Membership Directory; on-line; adv.

Alberta Beef Producers (1969)
320, 6715 - Eighth St. NE
Calgary, AB T2E 7H7
Tel: (403) 275-4400 *Fax:* (403) 274-0007
E-Mail: abpfeedback@albertabeef.org
Website: albertabeef.org
Members: 28,000 beef cattle producers
Staff: 5

Personel:
Executive Director: Rich Smith
  E-Mail: RichS@albertabeef.org
Policy Analyst: Fred Hays
  E-Mail: fredh@albertabeef.org
Controller: Laura Procunier
  E-Mail: LauraP@albertabeef.org
Office Assistant: Kaity Smith
Manager, Marketing and Education: Barb Sweetland
  E-Mail: BarbS@albertabeef.org

Historical Note:
ABP's mission is to strengthen the sustainability and competitiveness of the beef industry for the benefit of Alberta beef producers.

Meetings/Conferences: Annual

Publications:
ABP Newsletter; weekly

Algal Biomass Organization
125 Saint Paul St.
P.O. Box 369
Preston, MN 55965-0369
TollFree: (877) 531-5512
Website: algalbiomass.org
Members: 68 Companies
Staff: 4
Annual Budget: $500-1,000,000
Tax: 501(c)(6)

Personnel:
Executive Director: Mary Rosenthal
  E-Mail: mrosenthal@algalbiomass.org
General Counsel: Andrew Braff
Administrative Coordinator: Barb Scheevel
Media Contact: John Williams
  E-Mail: jwilliams@algalbiomass.org

Historical Note:
ABO promotes the development of viable commercial markets for renewable and sustainable commodities derived from algae. Membership: $100-12,000/year.

Meetings/Conferences: Annual

Publications:
ABO Newsletter
Membership Directory

Alkylphenols and Ethoxylates Research Council (1998)
1250 Connecticut Ave. NW
Suite 700
Washington, DC 20036
Tel: (202) 419-1500 *Fax:* (202) 659-8037
E-Mail: info@aperc.org
Website: aperc.org
Members: 4 companies
Staff: 2
Annual Budget: $250-500,000
Tax: 501(c)(6)

Personnel:
Executive Director: Robert J. Fensterheim CAE
Deputy Director: Barbara Losey
  E-Mail: blosey@regnet.com

Historical Note:
APERC's mission is to advocate the safe use of AP and AP derivatives through research, product stewardship and outreach efforts, within the framework of responsible chemical management. Members are manufacturers, processors, users and raw material suppliers of alkylphenols (AP) and alkylphenol derivatives. Membership: $10,000-20,000 (Producer/Distributor/Supplier).

All-America Rose Selections (1938)
P.O. Box 2612
Mill Valley, CA 94942
Tel: (415) 381-5055
E-Mail: rose@rose.org
Website: rose.org
Members: 15 commercial rose growers
Staff: 5
Annual Budget: $10-25,000

Personnel:
President: Henry Conklin
Contact, Communications: Karen Omholt
  E-Mail: karen@omholtassoc.com

Historical Note:
All-America Rose Selections is a nonprofit association dedicated to the introduction and promotion of exceptional roses. It also runs the horticultural testing program, and recognizes roses that will be easy to grow.

Publications:
Newsletter; on-line

Membership List Available to Non-members

Allergy and Asthma Network Mothers of Asthmatics (1985)
8201 Greensboro Dr.
Suite 300
McLean, VA 22102
Tel: (800) 878-4403 *Fax:* (703) 288-5271
Website: aanma.org
Staff: 13
Annual Budget: $1-2,000,000

Personnel:
President and Founder: Nancy Sander
Specialist, Membership and Resource: Lisa Cox-Black
  E-Mail: lcox-black@aanma.org
Manager, Business and Marketing Development: Larry H. Evans
  E-Mail: levans@aanma.org
Managing Editor: Gary Fitzgerald
  E-Mail: gfitzgerald@aanma.org
Director, Administration and Programs: Marcela Gieminiani
  E-Mail: mgieminiani@aanma.org

Historical Note:
AANMA's mission is to eliminate suffering and death due to asthma, allergies and related conditions. Membership: $35 (Individual/Family/Gift Member); $50 (Foreign Family); $100 (Medical Professional); $130 (Foreign Medical Professional).

Publications:
Allergy and Asthma Today; adv.
MA Report; monthly
Membership Directory

Alliance for Aging Research (1986)
750 17th St. NW
Suite 1100
Washington, DC 20006-1003
Tel: (202) 293-2856 *Fax:* (202) 255-8394
E-Mail: info@agingresearch.org
Website: agingresearch.org
Staff: 7
Annual Budget: $1-2,000,000
Tax: 501(c)(3)

Personnel:
President and Chief Executive Officer: Daniel P. Perry
Director, Communications: Catherine Behan
  E-Mail: cbehan@agingresearch.org
Director, Public Policy: Cynthia Bens
  E-Mail: cfarrell@agingresearch.org
Program Assistant, Publication Requests and Information: Kyle Jensen
Vice President, Finance and Administration: Ephraim Vega CPA
  E-Mail: evega@agingresearch.org
Executive Vice President: Debbie Zeldow
  E-Mail: dzeldow@agingresearch.org

Historical Note:
AAR advances scientific and medical discoveries to maximize healthy aging, independence and quality of life for older Americans. The Alliance serves as the voice for Baby Boomer health by developing, implementing and advocating programs in research, professional and consumer health education and public policy. ARR's mission is to Aging Research advances scientific and medical discoveries to maximize healthy aging, independence and quality of life for older Americans.

Meetings/Conferences:
2013 - Montreal, QC/Oct. 1 - 4
Number of non-conference events/year: 1

Publications:
At-A-Glance: Aging Research News; annually

Alliance for Children and Families (1998)
11700 W. Lake Park Dr.
Milwaukee, WI 53224-3099
Tel: (414) 359-1040 *Fax:* (414) 359-1074
TollFree: (800) 221-3726
E-Mail: policy@alliance1.org
Website: alliance1.org
Members: 350 agencies
Staff: 14
Annual Budget: $2-5,000,000
Tax: 501(c)(3)

Personnel:

President and Chief Executive Officer: Susan Dreyfus
  E-Mail: sndreyfus@alliance1.org
Director, Editorial Services, Families in Society and Intellectual Capital Division: Kirstin Anderson
  E-Mail: kanderson@alliance1.org
Manager, Product and Project: Mike Barylski
  E-Mail: mbarylski@alliance1.org
Chief Information Officer: Robert Cacace
  E-Mail: rcacace@alliance1.org
Manager, Membership Relations: Carey Drees
  E-Mail: cdrees@alliance1.org
Director, Conferences: Linda Freeman
  E-Mail: lfreeman@alliance1.org
Director of Communications and Special Projects: Malcolm McIntyre
  E-Mail: mmcintyre@alliance1.org
Manager, Marketing: Crystal Morgan
  E-Mail: cmorgan@alliance1.org
Director, Evaluation and Research Services: Laura Pinsoneault
  E-Mail: lpinsoneault@alliance1.org
Human Resources Specialist: Kim Schick
  E-Mail: kschick@alliance1.org
Chief Financial Officer: John Schmidt
  E-Mail: jschmidt@alliance1.org

Historical Note:
Alliance for Children and Families strives to fuse intellectual capital with better membership services in order to strengthen the capacities of North America's nonprofit child and family serving organizations to serve and to advocate for children, families and communities. Membership dues are tier-based according to the personnel budget of an organization.

Continuing Education:
Certification Designation/s: NAA

Meetings/Conferences: Annual
Conference Chair: Linda Freeman
2013 - Clearwater, FL (Clearwater Beach)/Feb. 16 - 19
Number of non-conference events/year: 2

Publications:
Alliance E-News; bi-weekly
Alliance Magazine; quarterly
Alliance Staff Directory; on-line
Families in Society E-Alerts; quarterly
Grant Directory; weekly
Magazine for Boards; quarterly
Member Directory; on-line
Social Work E-Alert; quarterly
Social Work Journal; quarterly
Social Work Practice; quarterly
The GrantStation Insider; weekly

Alliance for Continuing Medical Education (1975)
1025 Montgomery Hwy.
Southcrest Building, Suite 105
Birmingham, AL 35216
Tel: (205) 824-1355 *Fax:* (205) 824-1357
E-Mail: acehp@acehp.org
Website: acme-assn.org
Members: 2200 individuals
Staff: 12
Annual Budget: $2-5,000,000
Tax: 501(c)(3)

Personnel:
Executive Director: Robin R. King CAE
  E-Mail: rking@acehp.org
Manager, Meetings and Conferences: Jay Brown BA
  E-Mail: jbrown@acehp.org
Manager, Membership Services: Debrah Fisher BA
  E-Mail: dfisher@acehp.org
Manager, Membership Information Services: Marissa K. Green
  E-Mail: mgreen@acehp.org
Director, Professional Development and Meeting Management: Bernie Halbur PhD
  E-Mail: bhalbur@acehp.org
Interim Director, Strategic Communications: Mary Martin Lowe PhD
  E-Mail: mlowe@acehp.org
Manager, Database Administration and Web: Lauren Mallory BA
  E-Mail: lmallory@acehp.org
Director, Governance and Advocacy: Anne Marie Smith MBA
  E-Mail: amsmith@acehp.org
Interim Chief Operating Officer: Gregory Paulos MBA
  E-Mail: gpaulos@acehp.org

Manager, Program Development and Marketing: Jessica
  Romano Stout BS
  E-Mail: jromano@acehp.org

Historical Note:
*Formerly (2011) the Alliance for Continuing Medical
Education.The Alliance's mission is to provide professional
development opportunities for CME professionals, advocate
for CME profession and strive to improve health care
outcomes. Members include professionals working
in hospitals and health systems, academic medical
centers, medical specialty societies, medical education
communication companies, the government, and the
pharmaceutical/medical device/biotech industries and
anyone involved in the CE/CPD enterprize. Membership:
$365 (Active); Free (Emeritus).*

Continuing Education:
Certification Designation/s: MOC

Meetings/Conferences: Annual
Conference Chair: Jay Brown BA
2013 - San Francisco, CA (San Francisco Marriott
  Marquis)/Jan. 30 - Feb. 1

Publications:
Almanac; monthly; adv.
Journal of Continuing Education in the Health
  Professions (JCEHP); quarterly
Membership Directory; on-line

Alliance for Energy and Economic Growth *(2001)*
1615 H St. NW
Washington, DC 20062-2000
Tel: (202) 463-3130 *Fax:* (202) 463-5521
E-Mail: info@yourenergyfuture.org
Website: yourenergyfuture.org
Members: 1200 Individual
Staff: 3

Personnel:
Contact, Government Relations Membership: Robin
  Billings
  E-Mail: rbillings@uschamber.com
General membership: Charity Edgar
  E-Mail: cedgar@uschamber.com
Manager, Steering Committee: Jonathan Jackson
  E-Mail: jjackson@uschamber.com

Historical Note:
*Coalition whose members develop, deliver, or consume
energy from all sources. Seeks to build a national consensus
for a comprehensive U.S. energy strategy that balances
supply and demand without compromising environmental
safeguards. Membership is free.*

Alliance for Gray Market and Counterfeit Abatement *(2001)*
15466 Los Gatos Blvd.
Suite 109-167
Los Gatos, CA 95032
Tel: (252) 500-0123
Website: agmaglobal.org
Staff: 4
Annual Budget: $100-250,000

Personnel:
President and Director: Sally Nguyen
Operations Manager: Debbie Corr
  E-Mail: debbie@agmaglobal.org
Treasurer and Director: Franziska Hanreich
Media Contact: Dena Jacobson
  E-Mail: dena@lages.com

Historical Note:
*AGMA was formed in 2001 by founding members
Hewlett-Packard and Cisco Systems. AGMA's role is to
present members and the industry with strategic ideas
for addressing key IP protection issues, and to introduce
better controls or processes in mitigating threats to
IP. Membership: $15,000 (Manufacturer); $10,000
(Associate/Product/Service).*

Meetings/Conferences: Semi-Annual

Publications:
AGMA eMail Newsletter; on-line

The Alliance for Home Health Quality and Innovation
P.O. Box 7319
Washington, DC 20044
Tel: (202) 239-3983
Website: ahhqi.org
Staff: 1
Annual Budget: $1-2,000,000
Tax: 501(c)(6)

Personnel:

Executive Director: Teresa L. Lee J.D., MPH
  E-Mail: tlee@ahhqi.org

Historical Note:
*The Alliance for Home Health Quality and Innovation is a
national consortium of home health care organizations and
providers that raises awareness about home health care and
its proven ability to deliver quality, cost-effective, patient-
centered care for patients.*

Alliance for Massage Therapy Education *(2009)*
1760 Old Meadow Rd.
Suite 500
McLean, VA 22102
Tel: (855) 236-8331 *Fax:* (786) 522-2440
TollFree: (855) 236-8331
E-Mail: admin@afmte.org
Website: afmte.org
Staff: 4
Tax: 501(c)(3)

Personnel:
Executive Director: Kate Zulaski

Historical Note:
*The Alliance for Massage Therapy Education is an
independent non-profit organization established to serve as
the voice, advocate and resource for the education sector
from entry-level training programs through post-graduate
studies. Membership categories available for Massage
Schools, Teachers, Continuing Education Providers, and
Industry Partners.Membership: $50-100(Associate);
$100-500(Gold);$1,000(Allied);$50(Supporting).*

Meetings/Conferences: Annual
2013 - St. Charles, MO (St. Charles Convention
  Center)/July 18 - 20

Publications:
AMTE eNewsletter; on-line
CE Directory; on-line
Membership Directory; on-line

Alliance for Natural Health USA *(1992)*
6931 Arlington Rd.
Suite 304
Bethesda, MD 20814
Tel: (800) 230-2762 *Fax:* (202) 315-5837
E-Mail: office@anh-usa.org
Website: anh-usa.org
Members: 350 individuals
Staff: 9
Annual Budget: $250-500,000
Tax: 501(c)(4)

Personnel:
Executive Director and Legal Director: Gretchen DuBeau
  E-Mail: gretchen@anh-usa.org
Editor: Deborah A. Ray
Director, Campaigns and Communications: Darrell Rogers
Deputy Editor and Graphics Designer: Craig A. Smith
Director, Membership Services: Emily Stevenson

Historical Note:
*Formerly (2001) American Preventive Medical Association;
(2009) American Association for Health Freedom. ANH-
USA is dedicated to promoting sustainable health and
freedom of choice in healthcare through good science and
good law. Members are primarily health care practitioners
who use complementary therapies, nutritional supplements
or other alternatives to allopathic medicine, supplement
manufacturers and other individuals or businesses involved
in the preventive health care industry. Membership:
$15 (Friends of ANH-USA); $25 (Integrative Medical
Community).*

Publications:
Membership Directory; on-line
Newsletter

Membership List Available to Non-members

Alliance for Nonprofit Management *(1998)*
1899 L St. NW
Ninth Floor
Washington, DC 20036
Tel: (202) 955-8406 *Fax:* (202) 721-0086
E-Mail: info@allianceonline.org
Website: allianceonline.org
Members: 1100 individuals
Staff: 6
Annual Budget: $250-500,000
Tax: 501(c)(3)

Personnel:
Executive Director and Chief Executive Officer: Tangie
  Newborn
  E-Mail: tangie@allianceonline.org

Historical Note:
*Formerly (1998) Nonprofit Management Association.
The Alliance for Nonprofit Management is a professional
association of member organizations and individuals
devoted primarily to helping nonprofit organizations
increase their effectiveness and impact. Membership:
$200 (Individual); $50 (Full-Time Student); $250-1,000
(Organizational).*

Meetings/Conferences:
Number of non-conference events/year: 31

Membership List Available to Non-members

Alliance for Quality Care *(2005)*
467 Richmond Ave.
Maplewood, NJ 07040
Tel: (973) 761-4391 *Fax:* (800) 704-3714
E-Mail: info@afqcare.com
Website: afqcare.com
Staff: 2
Annual Budget: $50-100,000

Personnel:
Executive Director: Ann Laskowski
  E-Mail: annlaskowski@afqcare.com

Historical Note:
*AFQC is a coalition of healthcare providers, including
the ASC, orthopedic surgery, pain management, and
neurosurgery communities (the "Alliance"). Membership:
$750 (Individuals/Practices); $5,000 (Ambulatory Surgery
Centers).*

Alliance for Regenerative Medicine
525 Second St. NE
Washington, DC 20002
Tel: (202) 568-6240
E-Mail: info@alliancerm.org
Website: alliancerm.org
Staff: 4
Annual Budget: $500-1,000,000
Tax: 501(c)(4)

Personnel:
Executive Director: Michael Werner J D
  E-Mail: mwerner@alliancerm.org
Vice President, Operations: Bethany Kraynack
  E-Mail: bkraynack@alliancerm.org
Director, Development and Communications: Robert
  Margolin MBA
  E-Mail: rmargolin@alliancerm.org
Director, Membership Services: Luke Thorstenson
  E-Mail: lthorstenson@alliancerm.org

Historical Note:
*ARM promotes legislative, regulatory and reimbursement
initiatives necessary to facilitate access to life-giving
advances in regenerative medicine.*

Meetings/Conferences: Annual
2013 - San Francisco, CA/Jan. 7 - 9

Publications:
ARM Newsletter; on-line

Alliance for Responsible Atmospheric Policy *(1980)*
2111 Wilson Blvd.
Suite 850
Arlington, VA 22201-3058
Tel: (703) 243-0344 *Fax:* (703) 243-2874
E-Mail: info@arap.org
Website: arap.org
Members: 100 manufacturers and businesses
Staff: 3
Annual Budget: $500-1,000,000

Personnel:
Executive Director: David J. Stirpe
  E-Mail: stirpe@alcalde-fay.com
Special Counsel: Kevin J. Fay
Director, Membership Services: Tonya Hunt

Historical Note:
*Formerly (1995) Alliance for Responsible CFC Policy, the
association works to address the issue of stratospheric
ozone depletion and its mission is to coordinate industry
participation in the development of reasonable international
and U.S. government policies regarding ozone protection
and climate change.*

Publications:
Membership Directory; on-line

Membership List Available to Non-members

Alliance for Telecommunications Industry Solutions *(1983)*

1200 G St. NW
Suite 500
Washington, DC 20005
Tel: (202) 628-6380 *Fax:* (202) 393-5453
E-Mail: atispr@atis.org
Website: atis.org
Members: 900 companies and professionals
Staff: 37
Annual Budget: $5-10,000,000
Tax: 501(c)(6)

Personnel:
President and Chief Executive Officer: Susan M. Miller
   E-Mail: smiller@atis.org
Manager, Meetings and Events: Madelyn Foxworthy
   E-Mail: mfox@atis.org
General Counsel: Thomas Goode
   E-Mail: tgoode@atis.org
Manager, Membership Services: Jennifer Harrell
   E-Mail: jharrell@atis.org
Vice President, Finance and Operations: Bill Klein
   E-Mail: bklein@atis.org
Vice President, Marketing and Public Relations: Lauren
Layman
   E-Mail: llayman@atis.org
Associate, Finance and Human Resources: Alexandra
Mastrogiuseppe
   E-Mail: alexm@atis.org
Director, Technology Programs: Tom Payne
   E-Mail: tpayne@atis.org
Manager, Education and Conferences: Lois Rude
   E-Mail: lrude@atis.org
Chief Editor: Chad Underkoffler
   E-Mail: cunderkoffler@atis.org

Historical Note:
Formerly (1993) Exchange Carriers Standards Association. ATIS is committed to providing leadership for, and the rapid development and promotion of worldwide technical and operations standards for information, entertainment and communications technologies using a pragmatic, flexible and open approach. Represents an organization of telecommunications carriers, manufacturers, and service providers. Membership: $1,750 (Affiliate); $1,750-281,000 (Full).

Meetings/Conferences:
Conference Chair: Madelyn Foxworthy

Publications:
ATS Newsletter
Tech Beat; on-line

Alliance for Women in Media (1951)
1760 Old Meadow Rd.
Suite 500
McLean, VA 22102
Tel: (703) 506-3290 *Fax:* (703) 506-3266
E-Mail: info@allwomeninmedia.org
Website: allwomeninmedia.org
Members: 2800 individuals
Staff: 8
Annual Budget: $250-500,000

Personnel:
President: Erin M. Fuller CAE
   E-Mail: efuller@allwomeninmedia.org
Executive Vice President: Amy B. Lotz CAE
   E-Mail: alotz@allwomeninmedia.org
Executive Administrator: Michelle DelaRosa
   E-Mail: mdelarosa@allwomeninmedia.org
Specialist, Database: Hector Jimenez
   E-Mail: hjimenez@awrt.org
Manager, Communications and Awards: Kate Niswander
   E-Mail: kniswander@allwomeninmedia.org
Vice President, Events: Elisa Perodin CEM, CMP
   E-Mail: eperodian@awrt.org
Director, Media Relations: Andy Schwarz
   E-Mail: aschwarz@allwomeninmedia.org

Historical Note:
Formerly American Women in Radio and Television. AWM was formed when National Association of Broadcasters discontinued its women's division Association of Women Directors. AWM's mission is to harness the promise, passion and power of women in all forms of media to empower career development, engage in thought leadership, and drive positive change for the industry and societal progress. Membership: $110 (Professional); $85 (Entry Level); $50 (Retired); $30 (Student).

Meetings/Conferences:
Conference Chair: Elisa Perodin CEM, CMP
Number of non-conference events/year: 5

Publications:

News & Views; monthly

Alliance of Area Business Publications (1979)
1970 E. Grand Ave.
Suite 330
El Segundo, CA 90245
Tel: (310) 364-0193 *Fax:* (310) 364-0196
E-Mail: info@bizpubs.org
Website: bizpubs.org
Members:
15 alliance members
70 publications
Staff: 7
Annual Budget: $100-250,000

Personnel:
Executive Director: James C. Dowden
   E-Mail: administrator@bizpubs.org
Conference Coordinator: Chris Katterjohn
   E-Mail: ckatterjohn@comcast.net
Editor: Barton Ortberg
   E-Mail: bart.ortberg@dowdenmanagement.com

Historical Note:
AABP's mission is to advance the publishing niche of local and regional business publications and to help members achieve better profitability. Members are local and regional business newspapers and magazines. Membership: $1,500 (Associate); $695-5,560 (Regular, based on annual revenues).

Meetings/Conferences:
Conference Chair: Chris Katterjohn
2013 - Phoenix, AZ (Arizona Biltmore)/Jan. 25 - 27
2013 - Nashville, TN (Hilton Nashville Downtown)/
June 20 - 22

Publications:
AABP Newsletter; on-line
Associate Member Directory; on-line
Central Penn Business Journal; weekly; adv.
Corridor Business Journal; quarterly; adv.
Dbusiness Magazine; adv.
Ingram's Magazine; monthly; adv.
Membership Directory; on-line

Alliance of Artists Communities (1992)
255 S. Main St.
Providence, RI 02903
Tel: (401) 351-4320 *Fax:* (401) 351-4507
E-Mail: info@artistcommunities.org
Website: artistcommunities.org
Members: 250 organizations and individuals
Staff: 3
Annual Budget: $500-1,000,000
Tax: 501(c)(3)

Personnel:
Executive Director: Caitlin Strokosch
   E-Mail: cstrokosch@artistcommunities.org
Manager, Development and Programs: Adam Short
   E-Mail: ashort@artistcommunities.org
Director, Operations: Carla Wahnon

Historical Note:
AAC's mission is to advocate for and support artist's communities, in order to advance the endeavors of artists the Alliance gives a collective voice on behalf of its members, small and large, promotes successful practices in the field, and advocates for creative environments that support the work of today's artists. Membership comprises of a diverse field of artist's communities, residency programs, individuals, and institutions that support living artists in the creation of new work. Membership: $500-5,000 (Organization, based on budget); $250 (Emerging Program); $350-1,000 (Affiliate, based on annual budget); $100 (Individual).

Meetings/Conferences: Annual

Publications:
Alliance Newsletter
Artists' Communities, a Directory of Residencies;
  irregular
Member Directory; on-line

Membership List Available to Non-members

Alliance of Associations of Teachers of Japanese (1963)
1424 Broadway
Boulder, CO 80309-0366
Tel: (303) 492-5487 *Fax:* (303) 492-5856
E-Mail: ATJ@colorado.edu
Website: aatj.org
Members: 1000 individuals
Staff: 4

Annual Budget: $500-1,000,000
Tax: 501(c)(3)

Personnel:
Executive Director: Susan Schmidt
Director, Publications: Emi Ochiai Ahn
   E-Mail: emijk47751@mesacc.edu
Co-Director, Conference: Prof. Masahiko Minami
   E-Mail: mminami@sfsu.edu

Historical Note:
The Association of Teachers of Japanese merged with the National Council of Japanese Language Teachers to form the AATJ in 1999. Members have professional interests in the teaching of Japanese as a foreign language and in the allied fields of Japanese linguistics and literature. Membership: $40 (Regular); $20 (Student); $60 (Institution).

Meetings/Conferences: Annual
Conference Chair: Prof. Masahiko Minami
2013 - San Diego, CA/March 21

Publications:
ATJ Journal; adv.
ATJ Newsletter; quarterly; adv.

Membership List Available to Non-members

Alliance of Automobile Manufacturers (1999)
1401 Eye St. NW
Suite 900
Washington, DC 20005
Tel: (202) 326-5500 *Fax:* (202) 326-5598
Website: autoalliance.org
Members: 13 companies
Staff: 59
Annual Budget: $10-25,000,000

Personnel:
President and Chief Executive Officer: Mitch Bainwol
Vice President, Communications and Public Affairs: Gloria
Bergquist
   E-Mail: gbergquist@autoalliance.org
Vice President, Finance and Operations: Charles L.
Robinson
   E-Mail: execdirector@navyleague.org

Historical Note:
committed to developing and implementing constructive solutions to public policy challenges that promote sustainable mobility and benefit society in the areas of environment, energy and motor vehicle safety.

Alliance of Automotive Service Providers (1999)
1730 New Brighton Blvd.
Suite 170
Minneapolis, MN 55413
Tel: (612) 270-6696 *Fax:* (612) 623-1122
E-Mail: info@autoserviceproviders.com
Website: autoserviceproviders.com
Members: 8500 mechanical and collision repair
shops
Staff: 2
Annual Budget: $100-250,000
Tax: 501(c)(6)

Personnel:
Administrator: Judell Anderson CAE

Historical Note:
AASP's mission is to serve the automotive service industry and to strengthen its state and regional affiliates by promoting common business interests, forging strategic alliances and monitoring federal legislation and regulations. Membership: $250 (Associate); $100 (At-Large).

Publications:
Monthly Government Relations Update; monthly
Monthly Industry News; monthly

Membership List Available to Non-members

Alliance of Black Telecommunications Employees (1985)
P.O. Box 8136
Bridgewater, NJ 08807
E-Mail: able@ableinc.org
Website: ableinc.org
Staff: 4
Annual Budget: $50-100,000

Personnel:
Executive Director: Terrance Jamison
President and Chief Executive Officer: Reginald Lee
   E-Mail: able@ableinc.org
Contact, Communications and Public Relations: Dana
Fernandez

Contact, Membership and Information Technology:
Marcus Willams

Historical Note:
Formed from the merger of Association of Black Laboratory Employees, Committee of Black AT&T Employees, and Employee Focus Group, a second group of AT&T Employees. ABTE works to promote positive dialogue on career advancement possibilities for African-Americans in the telecommunications industry.ABTE's mission is to enhance the professional, educational, career, and cultural development of communities with people of African descent. Membership:$40(ABLE National dues).

Publications:
Member Directory; on-line

Alliance of Cardiovascular Professionals *(1957)*
P.O. Box 2007
Midlothian, VA 23112
Tel: (804) 632-0078 *Fax:* (804) 639-9212
Website: acp-online.org
Members: 3500 individuals
Staff: 5
Annual Budget: $100-250,000

Personnel:
President: Richard Beveridge
E-Mail: rbeveridge@rbaconsult.com
Executive Director: Peggy McElgunn
E-Mail: peggymcelgunn@comcast.net
Vice President, Advocacy: Susan Heilman
Vice President, Education: Linda Paxton

Historical Note:
ACVP is the product of a merger of the National Society of Cardiopulmonary Technologists, the American Cardiology Technology Association, and the National Alliance of Cardiovascular Technologists. Formerly National Society for Cardiovascular and Pulmonary Technology, became National Society for Cardiovascular Technology/National Society for Pulmonary Technology in 1988. Mission is to promote recognition of the cardiovascular profession. Membership: Based on Primary Specialty and Multiple Specialties, $85-105 (Active/Associate); $45 (Student).

Publications:
ACVP Newsletter; bi-monthly
Advance Magazine; bi-monthly
CP Digest; bi-monthly; adv.
CV Educator
Heart to Heart; quarterly
Strategies; quarterly
The Beat Goes On; quarterly

Alliance of Claims Assistance Professionals *(1998)*
9600 Escarpment
Suite 745-65
Austin, TX 78749
Tel: (512) 394-0008
E-Mail: capinfo@claims.org
Website: claims.org
Members: 40 individuals
Staff: 1
Annual Budget: Under $10,000
Tax: 501(c)(6)

Personnel:
Co-President: Rebecca Stephenson
E-Mail: capinfo@claims.org

Historical Note:
ACAP is a not-for-profit organization dedicated to the growth and development of the claims assistance industry. Membership: $245/year.

Continuing Education:
Certification Designation/s: CAP

Publications:
Membership Directory; on-line

Alliance of Hazardous Materials Professionals *(1995)*
9650 Rockville Pike
Bethesda, MD 20814-3999
Tel: (301) 634-7430 *Fax:* (301) 634-7431
TollFree: (800) 437-0137
E-Mail: academy@achmm.org
Website: achmm.org
Members: 4000 individuals
Staff: 4
Annual Budget: $500-1,000,000
Tax: 501(c)(3)

Personnel:
Executive Director: A. Cedric Calhoun

E-Mail: ccalhoun@achmm.org
Administrative Assistant: Nina Gilmore
E-Mail: ngilmore@ahmpnet.org
Database Manager: Vickie Haskins
E-Mail: vhaskins@ahmpnet.org
Director, Membership and Chapter Development: Alison Heron
E-Mail: aheron@ahmpnet.org

Historical Note:
Formerly the Academy of Certified Hazardous Materials Managers. AHMP's mission is to strengthen communications among members and stakeholders. Membership: $20-105/year.

Continuing Education:
Certification Designation/s: CHMM

Meetings/Conferences: Annual
Number of non-conference events/year: 1

Publications:
The Manager & Essential HazMat News

Alliance of Information and Referral Systems *(1973)*
11240 Waples Mill Rd.
Suite 200
Fairfax, VA 22030
Tel: (703) 218-2477 *Fax:* (703) 359-7562
E-Mail: info@airs.org
Website: airs.org
Members:
420 agencies
557 individuals
Staff: 6
Annual Budget: $500-1,000,000

Personnel:
Chief Operating Officer: Charlene Hipes CMP
E-Mail: charlenehipes@airs.org
Contact, Public Policy: Robert B. Blancato
E-Mail: rblancato@matzblancato.com
Director, Conferences: Sharon R. Galler CMP
E-Mail: sharong@airs.org
Coordinator, Communications and Editor: Charlene Kloos
E-Mail: charlenekloos@airs.org
Director, Certification: Maria Ledoux
E-Mail: marial@airs.org
Director, Membership Services: Moyad Zahralddin
E-Mail: moayad@airs.org

Historical Note:
AIRS is the international voice of Information and Referral (I&R) that works to provide leadership and support to its members and affiliates to advance the capacity of a standards-driven information and referral industry that brings people and services together. Members are organizations and individuals providing a contact point for those with various social problems so that they can be referred to others who can assist them. Membership: $575 (Premium); $250-375 (Standard); $25-75 (Basic).

Continuing Education:
Certification Designation/s: CIRS-A, CIRS, CRS

Meetings/Conferences: Annual
Conference Chair: Sharon R. Galler CMP
2013 - Portland, OR (Portland Hilton and Executive Tower)/June 2 - 5

Publications:
AIRS Newsletter; monthly
Member Directory; on-line

Alliance of Motion Picture & Television Producers *(1924)*
15301 Ventura Blvd., Building E
Sherman Oaks, CA 91403
Tel: (818) 995-3600 *Fax:* (818) 382-1793
Website: amptp.org
Members: 25 companies
Staff: 15
Annual Budget: $10-25,000,000
Tax: 501(c)(6)

Personnel:
President: Carol Lonbardini

Historical Note:
Merger of Association of Motion Picture Producers (1924) and Alliance of Television Film Producers (1951) and Society of Independent Producers. AMPTP is responsible for negotiating virtually all the industry-wide guild and union contracts.

Alliance of National Staffing and Employment Resources

4835 LBJ Fwy.
Suite 1000
Dallas, TX 75244
TollFree: (888) 932-6737
Website: anserteam.com
Members: 62 firms
Staff: 1

Personnel:
President: Natalie Davis-Runyan

Historical Note:
ANSERTEAM was formed to provide clients with national access to a team of independent staffing providers.

Alliance of Nonprofit Mailers *(1980)*
1211 Connecticut Ave. NW
Suite 610
Washington, DC 20036-2705
Tel: (202) 462-5132 *Fax:* (202) 462-0423
E-Mail: alliance@nonprofitmailers.org
Website: nonprofitmailers.org
Members:
200 nonprofit organizations
300 individuals
Staff: 3
Annual Budget: $250-500,000
Tax: 501(c)(4)

Personnel:
Executive Director: Anthony W. Conway
Legal Counsel: David M. Levy
E-Mail: dlevy@venable.com

Historical Note:
A national coalition of nonprofit organizations seeking to maintain reasonable and stable nonprofit mail rates and regulations.

Alliance of Professional Tattooists *(1992)*
215 W. 18th. St.
Suite 210
Kansas City, MO 64108
Tel: (816) 979-1300 *Fax:* (816) 979-1310
E-Mail: info@safe-tattoos.com
Website: safe-tattoos.com
Staff: 2
Annual Budget: $50-100,000

Personnel:
President: Mike Martin
Treasurer: Tim Corley

Historical Note:
APT's purpose is to address the health and safety issues facing the tattoo industry, promote safe practices in the profession and provide public education about tattooing. Membership: $75-150/year.

Meetings/Conferences:
Number of non-conference events/year: 1

Publications:
Membership Directory; annually
SkinScribe

Alliance of Work/Life Progress
14040 N. Northsight Blvd.
Scottsdale, AZ 85260
Tel: (480) 922-2007 *Fax:* (480) 603-0791
E-Mail: awlp@worldatwork.org
Website: awlp.org
Members: 550 individuals
Staff: 3
Annual Budget: Under $10,000

Personnel:
Contact, Communications: Marcia Rhodes APR
E-Mail: Marcia.Rhodes@worldatwork.org

Historical Note:
Formerly (2003) the Alliance of Work/Life Professionals. AWLP defines and acknowledges practices and innovation, facilitates dialogue, and elevates work-life thought leadership.

Meetings/Conferences: Semi-Annual

Allied Artists of America *(1914)*
15 Gramercy Park South
New York, NY 10003
Tel: (212) 582-6411
Website: alliedartistsofamerica.org
Members: 400 regular and 800 associates
Staff: 5
Annual Budget: $50-100,000

Personnel:

President: Thomas Valenti
E-Mail: thomasvalenti@alliedartistsofamerica.org
Vice President and Treasurer: Christina Debarry
Associates Chair, Membership: Lucille Berrill Paulsen
Editor: Roger Rossi
Exhibition Assistant: Claudia Seymour

Historical Note:
AAA's purpose is to advocate American art and furnish exhibition space for American artists. Membership consists of painters and sculptors. Membership: $40 (Individual/Associate).

Publications:
AAA Newsletter

Allied Finance Adjusters (1936)
P.O. Box 41368
Raleigh, NC 27629
Tel: (619) 981-6866 *Fax:* (888) 949-8520
Website: alliedfinanceadjusters.com
Members: 200 companies
Staff: 2
Annual Budget: $250-500,000

Personnel:
President: George Badeen
E-Mail: President@AlliedFinanceAdjusters.com
Executive Secretary: Stephanie Findley
E-Mail: Secretary@AlliedFinanceAdjusters.com

Historical Note:
AFAC is the trade association of recovery specialists in North America. Membership is composed of professional liquidators, repossessors, and skip tracers. Membership: $1600 (Individual); $100 (Associate); $375 (Vendor).

Continuing Education:
Certification Designation/s: RSIG

Meetings/Conferences: Semi-Annual

Publications:
AFA Newsletter; monthly

Allied Pilots Association (1963)
14600 Trinity Blvd.
Suite 500
Fort Worth, TX 76155-2512
Tel: (817) 302-2272
E-Mail: PUBLIC-COMMENT@alliedpilots.org
Website: alliedpilots.org
Members: 11500 members
Staff: 3
Annual Budget: $25-50,000,000
Tax: 501(c)(5)

Personnel:
President: CAPT Dave Bates
Chairman, Government affairs committee: Robert Coffman
E-Mail: bcoffman@alliedpilots.org
Director, Communications: Gregg Overman
E-Mail: goverman@alliedpilots.org

Historical Note:
Represents American airline pilots. APA provides all of the traditional union representation services for its members, including the lobbying of airline pilots views to Congress and government agencies.

Meetings/Conferences: Annual

Publications:
Flightline Magazine
Turning Final

Allied Trades of the Baking Industry (1920)
C/O Cereal Food Processors, Inc.
2001 Shawnee Mission Pkwy.
Mission Woods, KS 66205
E-Mail: info@cerealfood.com
Website: atbi.org
Members: 500 individuals
Staff: 3
Annual Budget: $25-50,000

Personnel:
President: Gary Edwards
First Vice President: Tim Miller
E-Mail: t.miller@cerealfood.com

Historical Note:
Allied Trades of the Baking Industry (ATBI) is a fraternal organization that serves all of the segments of the baking industry by providing financial support to a wide variety of local, regional, national and even international associations. Membership: $25 (Individual); $250 (Corporate).

Publications:
Membership Directory

The Allied Tradesman Newsletter

ALMA - The International Loudspeaker Association (1961)
55 Littleton Rd., 13B
Ayer, MA 01432
Tel: (978) 772-6977 *Fax:* (617) 848-9935
E-Mail: management@almainternational.org
Website: almainternational.org/
Members: 100 companies
Staff: 3
Annual Budget: $50-100,000

Personnel:
Executive Director: Carol Bousquet
E-Mail: cbousquet@almainternational.org
Counsel: J. Andrew McKinney
E-Mail: mail@jandrewmckinney.com

Historical Note:
Founded as American Loudspeaker Manufacturers Association, assumed its current name in 2001. ALMA's mission is to provide a worldwide loudspeaker industry forum for the exchange of technical and business information of practical value. Membership: $550 (Full); $225 (Educational); $100 (Individual); $35 (Student); $200 (Consultant I); $300 (Consultant II).

Meetings/Conferences:
2013 - Las Vegas, NV (Tuscany Suites and Casino)/Jan. 6 - 7
Number of non-conference events/year: 2

Publications:
ALMA News; adv.

Membership List Available to Non-members

Alpha Chi Sigma Fraternity, Inc. (1902)
2141 N. Franklin Rd.
Indianapolis, IN 46219-2435
Tel: (317) 357-5944
E-Mail: national@alphachisigma.org
Website: alphachisigma.org
Members: 64000 individuals
Staff: 4
Annual Budget: $250-500,000
Tax: 501(c)(3)

Personnel:
Secretary and Treasurer: Patrick J. Johanns
E-Mail: gr@alphachisigma.org
Administrative Assistant and Associate Editor: Teresa Clark
E-Mail: teresa@alphachisigma.org

Historical Note:
A professional fraternity of chemists and chemical engineers founded at the University of Wisconsin and incorporated in Wisconsin. Alpha Chi Sigma aims to bind its members with a tie of true and lasting friendship and strives for the advancement of chemistry both as a science and as a profession. Membership: $145/year (Lifetime).

Meetings/Conferences: Biennial

Publications:
The Chrome and Blue; monthly
The Hexagon; quarterly

Alpha Gamma Rho (1904)
10101 NW Ambassador Dr.
Kansas City, MO 64153-1395
Tel: (816) 891-9200 *Fax:* (816) 891-9401
E-Mail: agr@alphagammarho.org
Website: alphagammarho.org
Members: 55000 individuals
Staff: 6
Annual Budget: $100-250,000
Tax: 501(c)(3)

Personnel:
Executive Director: Philip Josephson
E-Mail: phil@alphagammarho.org
Coordinator, Communications: Stephanie Casey
E-Mail: scasey@alphagammarho.org
Executive Assistant, Conventions: Rachelle Delaurier
E-Mail: rachelle@alphagammarho.org
Development Specialist: Emily Harrison
E-Mail: emily@alphagammarho.org
Bookkeeper: Judy Schmuecker
E-Mail: judy@alphagammarho.org
Chief Recruitment Officer: Josh H. Wackler
E-Mail: wack@alphagammarho.org

Historical Note:

AGR's purpose is to enhance a wider acquaintance and a broader outlook on the part of agricultural men through fellowship in a national organization that works for their social, mental, and moral development.

Meetings/Conferences:
Conference Chair: Rachelle Delaurier
Number of non-conference events/year: 4

Publications:
AGR Action newsletter; monthly
SICKLE & SHEAF; quarterly

Alpha Kappa Psi (1904)
7801 E. 88th St.
Indianapolis, IN 46256-1233
Tel: (317) 872-1553 *Fax:* (317) 872-1567
E-Mail: mail@akpsi.org
Website: akpsi.org
Members: 228000 individuals
Staff: 14
Annual Budget: $50-100,000

Personnel:
Chief Executive Officer: Gary L. Epperson CAE
E-Mail: gary@akpsi.com
Contact, Member Services: Debby Orff
E-Mail: debby@akpsi.org
Managing Director, Operations: Brian D. Parker
E-Mail: brian@akpsi.org
Director, Education: Jason R. Pierce
E-Mail: jason@akpsi.org
Director, Communication and Information Services: Christopher W. Pye
E-Mail: chris@akpsi.org
Contact, Event Registration Services and Administrative Assistance: Melinda Rosenthall
E-Mail: melinda@akpsi.org
Managing Director, Student Services: Jessica R. Seitz
E-Mail: jessica@akpsi.com

Historical Note:
AKPsi is based on the principle of educating its members and the public to appreciate and demand higher ideals in business and to further the individual welfare of members during college and beyond. AKPSi provides leadership development, personal and professional training and the fundamental ingredient higher education misses experience. Membership: $400 (Life Loyal); $200 (Student).

Continuing Education:
Certification Designation/s: CPL, CFV

Meetings/Conferences: Annual
Conference Chair: Jessica R. Seitz
2013 - New Orleans, LA (Sheraton New Orleans Hotel)/Aug. 7 - 10
Number of non-conference events/year: 12

Publications:
e-Newsletter; monthly

Alpha Omega Alpha Honor Medical Society (1902)
525 Middlefield Rd.
Suite 130
Menlo Park, CA 94025
Tel: (650) 329-0291 *Fax:* (650) 329-1618
E-Mail: info@alphaomegaalpha.org
Website: alphaomegaalpha.org
Members: 150000 members
Staff: 1
Annual Budget: $2-5,000,000
Tax: 501(c)(3)

Personnel:
Executive Director: Dr. Richard L. Byyny

Historical Note:
A national medical honor society. AOA has 120 chapters in medical schools throughout the United States and has elected more than 150,000 members. Membership: $35 (1 Year, Student/Resident); $500 (Lifetime, Student/Resident); $50 (1 year, Faculty/Alumni); $750 (Lifetime, Faculty/Alumni).

Publications:
The Pharos; quarterly

Alpha Omega International Dental Fraternity (1907)
50 W. Edmonston Dr.
Suite 303
Rockville, MD 20850
Tel: (301) 738-6400 *Fax:* (301) 738-6403
TollFree: (877) 368-6326
E-Mail: headquarters@ao.org

Website: ao.org
Members: 9000 individuals
Staff: 3
Annual Budget: $500-1,000,000
Tax: 501(c)(3)

Personnel:
Association Director: Heidi Weber
    E-Mail: Hweber@ao.org

Historical Note:
Formed by the merger of the Ramach Fraternity and the
Alpha Omega Dental Fraternity. AO's mission is to promote
professional excellence, fraternalism and Judaic values.
Members are dentists and dental students. Membership:
$180/year (International).

Meetings/Conferences:
2013 - Zurich, Switzerland/June 19 - 23
Number of non-conference events/year: 4

Publications:
AO NOW
The Alpha Omegan; semi-annually
The Articulator; semi-annually

Alpha Tau Delta (1921)
1904 Poinsettia Ave.
Manhattan Beach, CA 90266
E-Mail: info@atdnursing.org
Website: atdnursing.org
Members: 11000 individuals
Staff: 4
Annual Budget: $10-25,000

Personnel:
Co-President and Treasurer: Joni Cohen PhD, RN
    E-Mail: bruinjoni@yahoo.com
National Secretary: Trisha Epperly BSN, RN
    E-Mail: trisha.epperly@gmail.com
Editor: Ashley Zamudio BSN, RN
    E-Mail: ashleyzamudio@gmail.com
Co-President and Vice President: Lynn Zeeman BSN, RN
    E-Mail: bilynzeman@yaho.com

Historical Note:
ATD is a professional nursing fraternity affiliated with the
Professional Fraternity Association whose mission is to
further better educational standars for those in the nursing
profession. It supports chapters which offer workshops,
seminars, scholarships, grants, and loans. Membership:
$35/year (individual).

Meetings/Conferences: Annual
2013 - Newport Beach, CA/Aug. 7 - 10

Alpha Zeta Omega (1919)
4422 Porpoise Dr.
Tampa, FL 33617
Tel: (813) 283-5040
E-Mail: drbruce@tampabay.rr.com
Website: azo.org
Members: 11000 individuals
Staff: 2
Annual Budget: $50-100,000

Personnel:
Director, Fraternal Affairs: Bruce Strell
    E-Mail: drbruce@tampabay.rr.com
Director, Financial Affairs: John Anciano

Historical Note:
AZO seeks to promote the profession of Pharmacy; to
develop high standards of Scholarship; to inculcate a spirit
of Fellowship amongst its members; to bring together a
body of men and women who, by the diligent maintenance
of ethical ideals and faithful service, have proven a credit
to their chosen profession. Members are Pharmacists and
Undergraduates in Pharmacy.

Alpines International Club (1958)
10447 Weld County Rd.
Suite 70
Windsor, CO 80550
Tel: (970) 686-6672
E-Mail: mammkey@sopris.net
Website: alpinesinternationalclub.com
Members: 100 individuals
Staff: 3

Personnel:
Membership Contact, Secretary and Treasurer: Hannah
    Larson
    E-Mail: vet2b@juno.com

Historical Note:

AIC works to preserve and promote the French and
American Alpine Dairy Goat. Membership: $15/year
(Individual).

Publications:
AIC Newsletter; quarterly; adv.

Alternative Fuel Vehicle Network (1986)
11621 San Antonio NE
Albuquerque, NM 87122-2437
Tel: (505) 856-8585 *Fax:* (505) 856-5904
Website: cgsm.org
Members: 77 individuals
Staff: 1

Personnel:
Executive Director: Frank Burcham
    E-Mail: frank.burcham@comcast.net

Historical Note:
AFVN is a non-profit trade association for alternative
fuels. Involved in compressed natural gas infrastructure
development; state alternative fuel energy policy and
analysis; electric vehicle promotion; ethanol and biodiesel
infrastructure development, promotion and community
education; and hydrogen industry development.

Publications:
Alternatives Fuel Newsletter; monthly

Aluminum Anodizers Council (1988)
1000 N. Rand Rd.
Suite 214
Wauconda, IL 60084
Tel: (847) 526-2010 *Fax:* (847) 526-3993
E-Mail: mail@anodizing.org
Website: anodizing.org
Members: 75 companies
Staff: 3
Annual Budget: $100-250,000
Tax: 501(c)(6)

Personnel:
Manager, Communications: Nancy Johnson

Historical Note:
Formerly (1992) Architectural Anodizers Council.
AAC promotes the common interest of its member
firms engaged in aluminum anodizing, suppliers of
products and services used in the anodizing of aluminum
products, or purchasers of anodized finishes. Members
are manufacturers of anodized aluminum products.
Membership: $550 (Associate); $750-2000 (Firm
Members); $120 (Professional); $1000-2100 (Supplier).

Meetings/Conferences: Annual

Publications:
Anodizing Newsline Newsletter; bi-monthly
Industry Guide Online; on-line
Member Directory; on-line
Regulatory Roundup; quarterly

The Aluminum Association, Inc. (1933)
1525 Wilson Blvd.
Suite 600
Arlington, VA 22209
Tel: (703) 358-2960 *Fax:* (703) 358-2961
Website: aluminum.org
Members: 90 companies
Staff: 15
Annual Budget: $5-10,000,000
Tax: 501(c)(6)

Personnel:
President: Heidi B. Brock
    E-Mail: hbrock@aluminum.org
Vice President, Statistics and Business Information and
    Membership Services: Nicholas Adams
    E-Mail: nadams@aluminum.org
Executive Assistant: Laura N. Benton
    E-Mail: lbenton@aluminum.org
Treasurer: Karen M. Bowden
    E-Mail: kbowden@aluminum.org
Director, Membership Services and Meetings and Corporate
    Secretary: Pamela Dorsey
    E-Mail: pdorsey@aluminum.org
Vice President, Communications: Stephen Gardner
    E-Mail: sgardner@aluminum.org
Director, Communications: John Simpson
    E-Mail: jsimpson@aluminum.org
Vice President, Technology: Michael Skillingberg
    E-Mail: mhskilli@aluminum.org
Vice President, Standards and Technology: John Weritz
    E-Mail: jweritz@aluminum.org
Manager, Publications and Production: Dennis Workman

    E-Mail: dworkman@aluminum.org

Historical Note:
Purpose is to provide value to its membership through its
leadership and services in promoting the growth of the
aluminum industry globally by continuously strengthening
aluminum's position versus competitive materials. Members
are manufacturers of aluminum mill products and producers
of aluminum. Associate members are suppliers to the
industry. Membership: $2,500-10,000/year (Producer/
Fabricator/Associate).

Meetings/Conferences: Annual
Conference Chair: Pamela Dorsey
Number of non-conference events/year: 1

Publications:
Aluminum Newsletter
Membership Directory; on-line
The Briefing; weekly

Membership List Available to Non-members

Aluminum Extruders Council (1950)
1000 N. Rand Rd.
Suite 214
Wancona, IL 60084
Tel: (847) 526-2010 *Fax:* (847) 526-3993
E-Mail: mail@aec.org
Website: aec.org
Members: 200 companies
Staff: 7
Annual Budget: $1-2,000,000
Tax: 501(c)(6)

Personnel:
President: Rand A. Baldwin CAE
Manager, Communications: Nancy Johnson
    E-Mail: nmolenda@tso.net
Director, Membership Services: Gregory T. Rajsky CAE

Historical Note:
AEC's mission is to provide opportunities to network with
peers and suppliers, address common internal and external
issues, share data, train, and sponsor research. Membership
dues are established by the Board of Directors.

Meetings/Conferences: Annual

Publications:
Essentials; on-line
Washington Report; monthly

Aluminum Foil Container Manufacturers Association (1955)
10 Vecilla Ln.
Hot Springs Village, AR 71909
Tel: (501) 922-7425 *Fax:* (501) 922-0383
E-Mail: info@afcma.org
Website: afcma.org
Members: 12 companies
Staff: 1
Annual Budget: $100-250,000

Personnel:
Executive Secretary and Treasurer: Coke Williams
    E-Mail: jcokewilliams@aol.com

Historical Note:
The Association works to promote aluminum foil as a
superior packaging material. AFCMA is engaged in the
manufacturing of aluminum foil containers in the U.S. and
Canada.

Membership List Available to Non-members

Amalgamated Printer's Association (1958)
135 E. Church St.
Clinton, MI 49236
Website: apa-letterpress.com
Members: 150 individuals
Staff: 3
Annual Budget: Under $10,000

Personnel:
President: Jim Daggs
Secretary and Treasurer: Phillip Driscoll
Archivist: David L. Kent

Historical Note:
The purpose of APA is to foster interest in the art of
letterpress printing, to encourage excellence in printing
and to provide a means for collective exchange of members
work. Membership is limited to 150. Officers change
biennially. Membership: $30/year (Individual).

Meetings/Conferences:
Number of non-conference events/year: 1

Publications:
APA Journal; monthly

Amalgamated Transit Union (1892)

5025 Wisconsin Ave. NW
Washington, DC 20016
Tel: (202) 537-1645 *Fax:* (202) 244-7824
TollFree: (888) 240-1196
E-Mail: dispatch@atu.org
Website: atu.org
Members: 190000 individuals
Staff: 25
Annual Budget: Over $100,000,000
Tax: 501(c)(5)

Personnel:
ATU International President: Lawrence J. Hanley
   E-Mail: lhanley@atu.org
International Executive Vice President: Robert H. (Bob) Baker
International Secretary and Treasurer: Oscar Owens
Director, Communications: Shawn Perry
   E-Mail: stp@atu.org
Director, Political and Regulatory Affairs: Jeffrey Rosenberg
   E-Mail: jrosenberg@atu.org
Assistant General Counsel: Dan Smith
Coordinator, Meetings and Events: Ynez Wells

Historical Note:
Formerly the Amalgamated Association of Street Railway Employees of America and affiliated with the American Federation of Labor in 1893, (1903) the Amalgamated Association of Street and Electric Railway Employees of America, the Amalgamated Association of Street, (1934) Electric Railway and Motor Coach Employees of America and assumed its present name in 1964. Holda national affiliation with AFL-CIO. Members are metropolitan, interstate, and school bus drivers; paratransit, light rail, subway, streetcar, and ferry boat operators; mechanics and other maintenance workers; clerks, baggage handlers, municipal employees, and others.

Meetings/Conferences:
Conference Chair: Ynez Wells
Number of non-conference events/year: 2

Publications:
ATU Mobile Updates
In Transit Magazine; bi-monthly

Ambulance Manufacturers Division (1976)

37400 Hills Tech Dr.
Farmington Hills, MI 48331-3414
Tel: (248) 489-7090 *Fax:* (248) 489-8590
TollFree: (800) 441-6832
E-Mail: info@ntea.com
Website: ntea.com/content.aspx?id = 3620
Members: 60 companies
Staff: 1

Personnel:
Executive Director: Steve Carey CAE
   E-Mail: steve@ntea.com

Historical Note:
AMD became an NTEA affiliate in 1986, works to expand and improve its market segment; acquire, preserve and disseminate information on the role of emergency vehicles; improve relationships with other industry segments; advocate new product innovations; and assist in the development of industry safety standards and programs.

Ambulatory Surgery Center Association (2008)

1012 Cameron St.
Alexandria, VA 22314
Tel: (703) 836-8808 *Fax:* (703) 549-0976
E-Mail: asc@ascassociation.org
Website: ascassociation.org
Members:
2200 members
230 companies
5708 individuals
Staff: 18
Annual Budget: $2-5,000,000
Tax: 501(c)(6)

Personnel:
Chief Executive Officer: William M. Prentice
Director, Administration: Dee Bellfield
Manager, Political Affairs: Brendan Davis
   E-Mail: bdavis@ascassociation.org
Director, Communications: Kay Tucker
   E-Mail: ktucker@ascassociation.org

Historical Note:
The Ambulatory Surgery Center Association (ASCA) is the national membership association that represents ambulatory surgery centers (ASCs) and provides advocacy and resources to assist ASCs in delivering quality, cost-effective ambulatory surgery to all the patients they serve. Membership: $500-3000 (Facility); $1,000 (Vendor).

Meetings/Conferences: Annual
2013 - Boston, MA (Hynes Convention Center)/April 17 - 20/2500 attendees
2014 - Nashville, TN (Gaylord Opryland Resort and Convention Center)/May 14 - 17/2500 attendees
2015 - Orlando, FL (Orlando World Center Marriott)/ May 13 - 16/2500 attendees
2016 - Washington, DC (Gaylord National Resort and Convention Center)/May 18 - 21/2500 attendees
2017 - Dallas, TX (Gaylord Texan Hotel and Convention Center-Dallas)/May 3 - 7/2500 attendees
Number of non-conference events/year: 1

Publications:
ASC Focus; bi-monthly

AMC Institute (1964)

100 N. 20th St.
Fourth Floor
Philadelphia, PA 19103-1443
Tel: (215) 320-3874 *Fax:* (215) 963-9785
E-Mail: info@amcinstitute.org
Website: amcinstitute.org
Members: 200 companies
Staff: 4
Annual Budget: $500-1,000,000
Tax: 501(c)(6)

Personnel:
Executive Director: Andrea Bower MBA
   E-Mail: abower@amcinstitute.org
Director, Administration: Mike Mirabella
   E-Mail: mmirabella@amcinstitute.org

Historical Note:
Founded as the Multiple Association Management Institute in 1964; changed its name to IAMC in 1977; became the International Association of Association Management Companies in August, 1996; assumed its present name in 2007. AMC Institute provides a means by which association management companies can coordinate their efforts to advance the status and scope of the industry. Membership consists of companies engaged in the management of two or more organizations on a professional client basis; member companies are located in the United States, Canada and Europe. Membership: $655-16,500/year (Ranges according to total AMC annual income).

Meetings/Conferences: Annual
2013 - St. Pete Beach, FL (Loews Don CeSar Hotel)/ Feb. 13 - 15
2014 - Tempe, AZ (The Buttes Resort)/Feb. 26 - 28
Number of non-conference events/year: 4

Publications:
Membership Directory; on-line

Membership List Available to Non-members

America Outdoors Association (1990)

P.O. Box 10847
Knoxville, TN 37939-0847
Tel: (865) 558-3595 *Fax:* (865) 558-3598
TollFree: (800) 524-4814
E-Mail: info@americaoutdoors.org
Website: americaoutdoors.org
Members: 550 professional companies
Staff: 3
Annual Budget: $500-1,000,000
Tax: 501(c)(6)

Personnel:
Executive Director: David L. Brown
   E-Mail: dbrown@telcocom.com
Director, Communications: Robin Beard Brown
   E-Mail: robin@americaoutdoors.org
Office Manager: Chrystal Graham

Historical Note:
Formed by the merger of the Western River Guides Association and the Eastern Professional River Outfitters Association, AOA's mission is to grow, protect and support America's outfitting businesses. Members are professional outdoor recreation outfitters. Membership: $245-995 (Domestic/Outfitter); $225-450 (International); $250 (Vendor).

Meetings/Conferences: Annual

Publications:
AOA Newsletter; quarterly; adv.

Membership List Available to Non-members

America's Blood Centers (1962)

725 15th St. NW
Suite 700
Washington, DC 20005
Tel: (202) 393-5725 *Fax:* (202) 393-1282
TollFree: (888) 872-5663
E-Mail: abc@americasblood.org
Website: americasblood.org
Members: 77 centers
Staff: 19
Annual Budget: $2-5,000,000
Tax: 501(c)(6)

Personnel:
Chief Executive Officer: Jim MacPherson
   E-Mail: jmacpherson@americasblood.org
Manager, Conferences and Executive Services: Lori Beaston
   E-Mail: lbeaston@americasblood.org
Manager, Communications: Mack C. Benton
   E-Mail: mbenton@americasblood.org
Director, Communications and Membership Services: Matt J. Granato LLM, MBA
   E-Mail: mgranato@americasblood.org
Director, Government Relations: Robert Kapler
   E-Mail: rkapler@americasblood.org

Historical Note:
Formerly (1971) Community Blood Bank Council and (1996) Council of Community Blood Centers. ABC provides blood products and services to hospitals and healthcare facilities. Members are non-profit regional and community centers that collect blood only from volunteer donors. Membership fee is based on annual blood collection. ABC's U.S. members are licensed and regulated by the U.S. Food and Drug Administration. Canadian members are regulated by Health Canada.

Meetings/Conferences:
Conference Chair: Lori Beaston

Publications:
Blood Bulletin; quarterly
Blood Counts; irregular
Membership Directory; on-line
The America's Blood Centers Newsletter; weekly

Membership List Available to Non-members

America's Health Insurance Plans (2003)

601 Pennsylvania Ave. NW.
South Building, Suite 500
Washington, DC 20004
Tel: (202) 778-3200 *Fax:* (202) 331-7487
TollFree: (877) 291-2247
E-Mail: ahip@ahip.org
Website: ahip.org
Members: 1300 companies
Staff: 206
Annual Budget: $50-100,000,000
Tax: 501(c)(3)

Personnel:
President and Chief Executive Officer: Karen M. Ignagni CAE
   E-Mail: kignagni@ahip.org
Vice President, Federal Affairs: Kate Callanan
Counsel: Diana Dennett
   E-Mail: ddennett@ahip.org
Special Counsel, Legal Affairs: Stephanie W. Kanwit
   E-Mail: skanwit@ahip.org
Senior Associate Counsel: Julie Simon Miller
   E-Mail: jumiller@ahip.org
Vice President, Communications: Susan Pisano
   E-Mail: spisano@ahip.org
Director, Digital Media: Brenda Weigel

Historical Note:
National trade association representing the health insurance industry

Continuing Education:
Certification Designation/s: CCMC

Meetings/Conferences:
2013 - Las Vegas, NV/June 12 - 14
2014 - Seatle, WA/Jan. 11 - 13
Number of non-conference events/year: 4

Publications:
AHIP HI-WIRE's e-newsletter; irregular
AHIP Solutions SmartBrief; daily; adv.
AHIP Wellness SmartBrief; on-line; adv.
AHIP's Washington Bulletin; on-line
e-Newsletter; on-line
Executive Updates; quarterly

Federal News; on-line
Vaccines and Immunization Newsletter; quarterly

America's Independent Truckers' Association, Inc. (1997)
P.O. Box 1250
Clinton, MS 39060
Tel: (601) 924-9606
Website: aitaonline.com
Staff: 12

Personnel:
President, Founder and Contact, Media Services: Larry Daniel
   E-Mail: larry@aitaonline.com
Contact, Sales: Wesley Daniel
   E-Mail: Sales@AITAonline.com
Contact, Membership Services: Reagan Law
   E-Mail: benefits@aitaonline.com
Contact, Financial Services: Christine McKenzie
   E-Mail: factoring@AITAonline.com
Coordinator, Information Services: Tommy Warner
   E-Mail: Corrections@AITAonline.com

Historical Note:
AITA's goal is to simplify every aspect of trucking, leaving the trucker free to do his job. Membership: $10/year (Individual).

America's Natural Gas Alliance
701 Eighth St. NW
Suite 800
Washington, DC 20001
Tel: (202) 789-2642 *Fax:* (202) 944-1920
E-Mail: info@anga.us
Website: anga.us
Members: 30 companies
Staff: 14
Annual Budget: $50-100,000,000

Personnel:
President and Chief Executive Officer: Regina Hopper
Vice President, State Affairs and Business Development: Michelle Bloodworth
Senior Vice President, Legislative and Regulatory Affairs: Peter D. Robertson
Director, Media Relations: Robert Sumner
Vice President, Strategic Communications: Dan Whitten
   E-Mail: dwhitten@anga.us

Historical Note:
ANGA seeks to inform and engage all stakeholders about the opportunities presented by greater use of this clean energy resource-improving air quality, adding jobs to our economy and enhancing our energy security.

Publications:
Membership Directory; on-line
Wall Street Journal (WSJ); quarterly; adv.

America's Small Business Development Center Network (1979)
8990 Burke Lake Rd.
Second Floor
Burke, VA 22015
Tel: (703) 764-9850 *Fax:* (703) 764-1234
E-Mail: info@asbdc-us.org
Website: asbdc-us.org
Members: 1000 service centers
Staff: 6
Annual Budget: $1-2,000,000
Tax: 501(c)(6)

Personnel:
President and Chief Executive Officer: Charles Edward Rowe III
   E-Mail: tee.rowe@asbdc-us.org
Vice President, Operations: Donna Ettenson
   E-Mail: donna@asbdc-us.org
Meeting Planner and Director, Membership Services: Betsy Kaufman
   E-Mail: betsy@asbdc-us.org
Director, Marketing and Communications: April Youngblut
   E-Mail: april@asbdc-us.org

Historical Note:
Formerly the Small Business Development Center Directors Association. Mission is to represent the collective interest of their members by promoting, informing, supporting and continuously improving the SBDC network, which delivers nationwide educational assistance to strengthen small/ medium business management, thereby contributing to the growth of local, state and national economies.

Meetings/Conferences: Annual
Conference Chair: Betsy Kaufman

American Abstract Artists (1936)
P.O.Box 1076
New York, NY 10013-0862
E-Mail: americanabart@aol.com
Website: americanabstractartists.org
Members: 95 individuals
Staff: 2
Annual Budget: Under $10,000

Personnel:
President: Don Voisine
Editor: Marthe Keller

Historical Note:
Mission of AAA's is to unite multi-generational American artists working abstractly. Members are abstract painters and sculptors. Membership: $35/year.

Publications:
American Abstract Artists Journal

American Academy for Cerebral Palsy and Developmental Medicine (1947)
555 E. Wells St.
Suite 1100
Milwaukee, WI 53202
Tel: (414) 918-3014 *Fax:* (414) 276-2146
E-Mail: info@aacpdm.org
Website: aacpdm.org
Members: 1200 individuals
Staff: 4
Annual Budget: $1-2,000,000
Tax: 501(c)(3)

Personnel:
Executive Director: Tracy Burr
   E-Mail: tburr@aacpdm.org
Coordinator, Project: Jesse Cunningham
   E-Mail: jcunningham@aacpdm.org
Manager, Meetings: Marie Grevsmuehl
Editor: Lynne Romeiser Logan PCS, PhD, PT
   E-Mail: loganl@upstate.edu

Historical Note:
AACPDM is a multidisciplinary scientific society devoted to the study of cerebral palsy and other childhood onset disabilities. Membership: $285 (Fellow); $45 (International Corresponding); $35 (Student/Resident/Trainee).

Meetings/Conferences: Annual
Conference Chair: Marie Grevsmuehl
2013 - Milwaukee, WI (Frontier Airlines Center)/Oct. 16 - 19

Publications:
AAPCOM Newsletter; quarterly
Developmental Medicine & Child Neurology (DMCN); adv.
Membership Directory; on-line

Membership List Available to Non-members

American Academy of Actuaries (1965)
1850 M St. NW
Suite 300
Washington, DC 20036-5805
Tel: (202) 223-8196 *Fax:* (202) 872-1948
E-Mail: info@actuary.org
Website: actuary.org
Members: 17000 individuals
Staff: 43
Annual Budget: $10-25,000,000
Tax: 501(c)(6)

Personnel:
Executive Director: Mary E. Downs
   E-Mail: downs@actuary.org
Director, Finance and Administration: Joanne B. Anderson
   E-Mail: anderson@actuary.org
Assistant Director, Marketing: Lou Baccam
   E-Mail: baccam@actuary.org
Assistant Director, Technology: Christopher Cassidy
   E-Mail: cassidy@actuary.org
Director, Communications: Mark Cohen
   E-Mail: cohen@actuary.org
Assistant Director, Communications and Public Affairs: Ellen C. Dadisman
   E-Mail: dadisman@actuary.org
Director, Public Policy: Craig Hanna
   E-Mail: hanna@actuary.org

General Counsel and Director, Professionalism: Keith Jones
   E-Mail: jones@actuary.org
Assistant General Counsel: Sheila J Kalkunte
   E-Mail: kalkunte@actuary.org
Manager, Programs: Erica Kennedy
   E-Mail: kennedy@actuary.org
Assistant Communications Director, Publications and Editor: Linda Mallon
   E-Mail: mallon@actuary.org
Assistant Director, Communications and Public Affairs: Andrew Simonelli
   E-Mail: simonelli@actuary.org
General Counsel, Director of Professionalism: Gino Vissicchio
Assistant, Membership Services: Denise Winston
   E-Mail: winston@actuary.org

Historical Note:
AAA's mission is to serve the public and the actuarial profession. Academy members include consultants, corporate executives and staff, regulators, government officials, academicians, and retired actuaries. Membership: $605 (Regular); $305 (Government); $115 (Partial Dues Waiver).

Meetings/Conferences: Annual
Conference Chair: Denise Winston
2013 - San Antonio, TX (JW Marriott San Antonio Hill Country Resort and Spa)/Oct. 20 - 23
2014 - Rancho Mirage, CA (The Westin Mission Hills)/ Oct. 19 - 22

Publications:
Academy Alerts; on-line
Actuarial Update; monthly
ASB Boxscore; quarterly
Contingencies; bi-monthly; adv.
Enrolled Actuaries Report; quarterly
HealthCheck; monthly
Inside the Academy; monthly
Life and Health Valuation Law Manual; annually
Media Update; on-line
Property/Casualty Loss Reserve Manual; annually
Record; annually
Retirement Account; quarterly
This Week; weekly
Yearbook; annually

American Academy of Addiction Psychiatry (1985)
400 Massasoit Ave.
Suite 307, Two Floor
Providence, RI 02914
Tel: (401) 524-3076 *Fax:* (401) 272-0922
E-Mail: information@aaap.org
Website: aaap.org
Members: 1000 individuals
Staff: 6
Annual Budget: $1-2,000,000
Tax: 501(c)(3)

Personnel:
Executive Director: Kathryn Cates-Wessel
   E-Mail: kcw@aaap.org
Coordinator, Membership Services and Outreach: Grace Archibald
   E-Mail: grace@aaap.org
Associate Managing Editor: Martha Bostick
   E-Mail: aja@aaap.org
Director, Professional Development: Miriam Giles
   E-Mail: Miriam@aaap.org
Director, Grants Administration and Compliance: Franc Lemire
   E-Mail: Franc@aaap.org
Director, Education and Program Development: Isabel Vieira
   E-Mail: Isabel@aaap.org

Historical Note:
Founded as American Academy of Psychiatrists in Alcoholism and Addictions, assumed its current name in 1996. AAAP's mission is to advocate high quality evidence-based screening, assessment and treatment for substance use and co-occurring mental disorders. Membership: $250 (Regular Members/Affiliate); $158 (Retired); $45 (Residents); $0 (Medical Students); $240 (International Members).

Meetings/Conferences: Annual

Publications:
AAAP Email Bulletin; monthly
AAAP News; adv.
The American Journal on Addictions; bi-monthly

Membership List Available to Non-members

American Academy of Adoption Attorneys
P.O. Box 33053
Washington, DC 20033
Tel: (202) 832-2222
E-Mail: info@adoptionattorneys.org
Website: adoptionattorneys.org
Members: 340 attorneys
Staff: 3
Annual Budget: $250-500,000

Personnel:
Treasurer: Steven M. Kirsh

Historical Note:
AAAA's purpose is to advocate reform of adoption laws and helps disseminate information on ethical adoption practices. Membership: $500/year.

Publications:
Agency Directory; on-line
Member Directory; on-line

American Academy of Advertising (1958)
24710 Shaker Blvd.
Beachwood, OH 44122
Fax: (866) 607-8512
E-Mail: director@aaasite.org
Website: aaasite.org
Members: 570 individuals
Staff: 2
Annual Budget: $100-250,000
Tax: 501(c)(3)

Personnel:
Executive Director: Patricia B. Rose
  E-Mail: rosep@fiu.edu
Treasurer: Nancy Mitchell
  E-Mail: treasurer@aaasite.org

Historical Note:
AAAT's mission is to provide an organization through which all persons interested in advertising education may coordinate their efforts to advance academic and professional advertising. Membership: $65 (Regular); $40 (Retiree); $35 (Student).

Meetings/Conferences:
Conference Chair: Patricia B. Rose
2013 - Albuquerue, NM (Hyatt Regency Albuquerque)/
  April 3 - 7/200 attendees/11-25 exhibitors
2013 - Honolulu, HI (University of Hawaii)/May 31 -
  June 2
2014 - Atlanta, GA/March 27 - 30

Publications:
Journal of Advertising; quarterly; adv.
Journal of Advertising Education
Members Directory; on-line
The Journal of Interactive Advertising; on-line
The AAA Newsletter; quarterly

Membership List Available to Non-members

American Academy of Allergy, Asthma, and Immunology (1943)
555 E. Wells St.
Suite 1100
Milwaukee, WI 53202-3823
Tel: (414) 272-6071 *Fax:* (414) 272-6070
E-Mail: info@aaaai.org
Website: aaaai.org
Members: 6600 individuals
Staff: 40
Annual Budget: $5-10,000,000
Tax: 501(c)(3)

Personnel:
Executive Director: Kay A. Whalen CAE, MBA
  E-Mail: kwhalen@aaaai.org
Manager, Membership Services: Shauna Barnes
  E-Mail: sbarnes@aaaai.org
Director, Communications and Membership: Marianne
  Canter CAE, MBA
  E-Mail: mcanter@aaaai.org
Director, Education: Steve Folstein
  E-Mail: sfolstein@aaaai.org

Historical Note:
Formed by a merger of the American Association for the Study of Allergy and the Association for the Study of Asthma and Related Conditions as the American Academy of Allergy; became the American Academy of Allergy and Immunology in 1982 and assumed its present name in 1982. AAAAI's mission is to advance the knowledge and practice of allergy, asthma and immunology for optimal patient care.

Continuing Education:
Certification Designation/s: ABAI

Meetings/Conferences: Annual
2013 - San Antonio, TX/Feb. 22 - 26/11-25 exhibitors
2014 - San Diego, CA/Feb. 28 - March 4
2015 - Houston, TX/Feb. 20 - 24
2016 - Los Angeles, CA/March 4 - 8

Publications:
AAAAI eNews; monthly
Journal of Allergy and Clinical Immunology; monthly
Membership Directory; on-line

Membership List Available to Non-members

American Academy of Ambulatory Care Nursing (1978)
East Holly Ave.
P.O. Box 56
Pitman, NJ 08071-0056
Tel: (856) 256-2350 *Fax:* (856) 589-7463
TollFree: (800) 262-6877
E-Mail: aaacn@ajj.com
Website: aaacn.org
Members: 2100 individuals
Staff: 6
Annual Budget: $500-1,000,000

Personnel:
Executive Director: Cynthia R. Nowicki Hnatiuk CAE,
  EdD, RN
  E-Mail: cyndee@ajj.com
*Coordinator, Membership Services and Manager,
  Registration:* Regina Donohue CMSRN, CPP, MN
  E-Mail: donohuer@ajj.com
Director, Marketing: Tom Greene
  E-Mail: greenet@ajj.com
Director, Education: Rosemarie Marmion
  E-Mail: rosemarie.marmion@ajj.com
Director, Association Services: Pat Reichart
  E-Mail: reichartp@ajj.com

Historical Note:
Formerly the American Academy of Ambulatory Nursing Administration, and in 1993, name changed to American Academy of Ambulatory Care Nursing. AAACN's mission is to advance the art and science of ambulatory care nursing. Membership: $70-1500/year.

Continuing Education:
Certification Designation/s: CCN, ANCE, CTN, TNC

Meetings/Conferences: Annual
Conference Chair: Pat Reichart
2013 - Las Vegas, NV (LVH-Las Vegas Hotel and
  Casino)/April 23 - 25
2014 - New Orleans, LA (Marriott New Orleans)/May
  20 - 22

Publications:
Email Newsletter; monthly
Membership Directory; on-line
ViewPoint Newsletter Continuing nursing education
  (CNE); on-line

American Academy of Anesthesiologist Assistants (1973)
2209 Dickens Rd.
Richmond, VA 23230-2005
Tel: (804) 565-6353 *Fax:* (804) 282-0090
TollFree: (888) 443-6353
E-Mail: aaaa@societyhq.com
Website: anesthetist.org
Members: 750 individuals
Staff: 8
Annual Budget: $250-500,000

Personnel:
Executive Director: Heather A. Spiess
  E-Mail: heather@societyhq.com
Administrative Assistant: Julie Hitt
  E-Mail: julie@societyhq.com
Treasurer: Barry Hunt, AAC
Director, Meetings and Conventions: Kevin Johns
  E-Mail: kevin@societyhq.com
Manager, Membership Services: Greg Leasure
  E-Mail: greg@societyhq.com
Contact, Website: Matt Martin
  E-Mail: matt@societyhq.com
Association Manager: Joye Stewart
Manager, Corporate and Educational Support: Matt Van
  Wie

E-Mail: mattv@societyhq.com

Historical Note:
AAAA's mission is to dedicate to the ethical advancement of the Anesthesiologist Assistant profession and to excellence in patient care through education, advocacy, and promotion of the Anesthesia Care Team. Membership: $400 (Fellow); $150 (Physician Affiliate); $100 (Student); $350 (Associate).

Continuing Education:
Certification Designation/s: AA

Meetings/Conferences: Annual
Conference Chair: Kevin Johns
2013 - Orlando, FL (Caribe Royale Orlando)/April 13 -
  16

Publications:
Membership Directory; on-line
Newsletter; quarterly

Membership List Available to Non-members

American Academy of Anti-Aging Medicine (1992)
1801 N. Military Trail
Suite 200
Boca Raton, FL 33431
Tel: (561) 997-0112 *Fax:* (773) 528-5390
TollFree: (800) 558-1267
Website: a4m.com
Members: 24000 individuals
Staff: 1
Annual Budget: $1-2,000,000
Tax: 501(c)(3)

Personnel:
President: Ronald Klatz DO, MD

Historical Note:
A4M is committed to the advancement of technology to detect, prevent, and treat aging related diseases. It advocates research into methods that retard and optimize the human aging process and educates physicians, scientists and members of the public on anti-aging issues. Membership: $249 (Scientific/Healthcare/Physician); $149 (Auxiliary Staff); $1,000 (Corporate).

Continuing Education:
Certification Designation/s: ABAAHP, ACASP, ABAARM
Meetings/Conferences:
Number of non-conference events/year: 9

Publications:
Longevity Magazine eJournal; weekly
Membership Directory; on-line

American Academy of Appellate Lawyers (1990)
9707 Key West Ave.
Suite 100
Rockville, MD 20850
Tel: (240) 404-6498 *Fax:* (301) 990-9771
E-Mail: info@appellateacademy.org
Website: appellateacademy.org
Members: 250 individuals
Staff: 4
Annual Budget: $100-250,000
Tax: 501(c)(3)

Personnel:
Executive Director: Beth W. Palys CAE
Senior Graphic Designer: Jon Benjamin
Vice President, Meetings: Grace L. Jan CAE, CMP
Senior Member Services Manager: Lynn Turner

Historical Note:
AAAL promotes the improvement of appellate advocacy through recognition of outstanding practitioners in the field. Membership, by invitation only, consists of lawyers who have focused substantially on appeals representation for at least 15 years.

Meetings/Conferences: Annual
Conference Chair: Grace L. Jan CAE, CMP
2013 - Ottawa, ON (Fairmont Chateau Laurier Hotel)/
  April 25 - 27

Publications:
Appellate Advocate

American Academy of Arts & Sciences (1780)
136 Irving St.
Cambridge, MA 02138-1205
Tel: (617) 576-5000 *Fax:* (617) 576-5050
E-Mail: aaas@amacad.org
Website: amacad.org
Members: 4600 fellows and foreign honorary
  members
Staff: 34
Annual Budget: $50-100,000,000

Tax: 501 (c)(3)

Personnel:
President: Leslie Cohen Berlowitz
   E-Mail: berlowitz@amacad.org
Publications Officer: Phyllis Bendell
   E-Mail: pbendell@amacad.org
Communications Officer: Paul Karoff
   E-Mail: pkaroff@amacad.org
Contact, Membership and Visiting Scholars Programs:
   Alexandra Oleson
   E-Mail: aoleson@amacad.org

Historical Note:
AAAS's mission is to promote service and study through analysis of critical, social and intellectual issues and the development of practical policy alternatives.

Meetings/Conferences: Annual
Number of non-conference events/year: 1

Publications:
Dædalus; quarterly

American Academy of Audiology *(1988)*
11730 Plaza America Dr.
Suite 300
Reston, VA 20190
Tel: (800) 111-2336 *Fax:* (703) 790-8631
TollFree: (800) 222-2336
E-Mail: infoaud@audiology.org
Website: audiology.org
Members: 11000 individuals and 20 organizations
Staff: 40
Annual Budget: $5-10,000,000

Personnel:
Executive Director: Cheryl Kreider Carey CAE
   E-Mail: ccarey@audiology.org
Senior Education Specialist, Business Practice: Debra Abel
   E-Mail: dabel@audiology.org
Senior Director, Finance and Administration: Amy
   Benham CPA
   E-Mail: abenham@audiology.org
Manager, Information Systems: Bill Kana
   E-Mail: bkana@audiology.org
Senior Director, Communications: Amy Miedema
   E-Mail: amiedema@audiology.org
Director, Education: Meggan Olek
   E-Mail: molek@audiology.org
Assistant Director, Membership Services: Sarah E.
   Sebastian
   E-Mail: ssebastian@audiology.org
Manager, Marketing: Angela Ugoji
   E-Mail: augoji@audiology.org
Senior Manager, Publications: Joyanna Wilson CAE
   E-Mail: jwilson@audiology.org
Senior Director, Meeting Services: Lisa Yonkers CMP
   E-Mail: lyonkers@audiology.org

Historical Note:
AAA promotes hearing and balance care by advancing the profession of audiology through leadership, advocacy, education, public awareness, and support of research. Membership is also available to international audiologists. Membership: $265 (Fellow/Affiliate); $55 (Fellow-Doctoral Candidate/Student); $165 (International Member and Fellow); $85 (International Associate); $159 (Life).

Continuing Education:
Certification Designation/s: ABA, CEU

Meetings/Conferences:
Conference Chair: Lisa Yonkers CMP
Number of non-conference events/year: 1

Publications:
Audiology Today; bi-monthly; adv.
Find an Audiologist Directory; on-line
Journal of the American Academy of Audiology
Membership Directory; on-line

Membership List Available to Non-members

American Academy of Child and Adolescent Psychiatry *(1953)*
3615 Wisconsin Ave. NW
Washington, DC 20016-3007
Tel: (202) 966-7300 *Fax:* (202) 966-2891
TollFree: (800) 333-7636
E-Mail: communications@aacap.org
Website: aacap.org
Members: 59000 individuals and 28 groups
Staff: 30
Annual Budget: $2-5,000,000
Tax: 501 (c)(3)

Personnel:
Executive Director: Virginia Q. Anthony
   E-Mail: vqanthony@aacap.org
Managing Editor: Mary Billingsley
   E-Mail: mbillingsley@jaacap.org
Director and Comptroller: Larry Burner
   E-Mail: lburner@aacap.org
Director, Research, Training and Education: Yoshie
   Davison
   E-Mail: ydavison@aacap.org
Director, Information Systems and Web Services: Colleen
   Dougherty
   E-Mail: cdougherty@aacap.org
Director, Human Resources and Operations: Maureen
   DuBois MBA, PHR
   E-Mail: mdubois@aacap.org
Senior Director, Meetings and Deputy Executive Director:
   Heidi Buttner Fiordi
   E-Mail: hfiordi@aacap.org
Director, Communications and Membership Services: Rob
   Grant
   E-Mail: rgrant@aacap.org
Supervisor, Membership Services: Jared Hoke
   E-Mail: jhoke@aacap.org
Director, Government Affairs: Kristin Kroeger Ptakowski
   E-Mail: kkrueger@aacap.org

Historical Note:
Established in February 1953 as American Academy of Child Psychiatry and incorporated in Delaware in 1959; assumed its present name in 1986. A professional medical organization comprised of child and adolescent psychiatrists trained to promote healthy development and to evaluate, diagnose, and treat children and adolescents and their families who are affected by disorders of feeling, thinking, learning, and behavior. Encourages medical contributions to the knowledge and treatment of psychiatric problems of children and their families.

Meetings/Conferences: Annual
Conference Chair: Heidi Buttner Fiordi
2013 - Orlando, FL (Walt Disney World Resort)/Oct. 22
   - 27
2014 - San Diego, CA (Manchester Grand Hyatt San
   Diego)/Oct. 21 - 26
2015 - San Antonio, TX (The Henry B. Gonzalez
   Convention Center)/Oct. 27 - Nov. 1
2016 - New York City, NY (Hilton New York and
   Towers)/Oct. 25 - 30
2017 - Washington, DC (Marriott Wardman Park/Omni
   Shoreham)/Oct. 24 - 29

American Academy of Clinical Neuropsychology *(1996)*
C/O Department of Psychiatry, University of
Michigan Health System
1500 E. Medical Center Dr. SPC 5295
Ann Arbor, MI 48109-5295
Tel: (734) 936-8269 *Fax:* (734) 936-9761
Website: theaacn.org
Members: 800 individuals
Staff: 4
Annual Budget: $250-500,000
Tax: 501 (c)(6)

Personnel:
Executive Director: Linas A. Bieliauskas PhD
   E-Mail: linas@umich.edu
Treasurer: Susan McPherson PhD

Historical Note:
AACN supports continued maintenance of standards in Clinical Neuropsychology through the established board certification process of ABCN. Members are psychologists who have achieved board certification in the specialty of Clinical Neuropsychology, under the auspices of the American Board of Clinical Neuropsychology (ABCN). Membership: $75/year (Affiliate).

Continuing Education:
Certification Designation/s: CE

Meetings/Conferences: Annual
2013 - Chicago, IL (Renaissance Chicago Downtown
   Hotel)/June 20 - 22
Number of non-conference events/year: 3

Publications:
Child Neuropsychology
Member Directory; on-line
The Clinical Neuropsychologist; bi-monthly

Membership List Available to Non-members

American Academy of Clinical Psychiatrists *(1975)*

144 Georgetown Dr.
Glastonbury, CT 06033
Tel: (860) 633-6023 *Fax:* (866) 668-9858
E-Mail: aacp@cox.net
Website: aacp.com
Members: 500 individuals
Staff: 4
Annual Budget: $25-50,000
Tax: 501 (c)(3)

Personnel:
Executive Director: Beverly Davidson

Historical Note:
AACP provides a forum to share information for psychiatrists engaged in direct patient care and to keep abreast of the latest scientific developments relevant to the practice of psychiatry. Members are mainly private clinicians and academicians. Disseminates scientific information relevant to clinical practice to its members. Emphasizes on practical knowledge that will inform clinical care. Membership: $225 (Active); $90 (Affiliate); $50 (Student/Resident/Early Career Member).

Meetings/Conferences: Annual
Conference Chair: Richard Balon MD

Publications:
AACP Newsletter
American Academy of Clinical Psychiatrists
Membership Directory; on-line

American Academy of Clinical Toxicology *(1968)*
6728 Old Mclean Village Dr.
McLean, VA 22101
Tel: (703) 556-9222 *Fax:* (703) 556-8729
E-Mail: admin@clintox.org
Website: clintox.org
Members: 630 individuals
Staff: 3
Annual Budget: $250-500,000
Tax: 501 (c)(3)

Personnel:
Executive Director: Sarah Shiffert
Editor-in-Chief: Dr. Barbara Kirrane
Association Manager: Christine Lusk

Historical Note:
AACT is a not-for-profit multi-disciplinary organization that unites scientists and clinicians in the advancement of research, education, prevention and treatment of diseases caused by chemicals, drugs and toxins. Members are physicians, research scientists, and analytical chemists, veterinarians and pharmacists active in clinical toxicology. Membership: $225 (Full); $125 (Student).

Continuing Education:
Enrollment: 90
Certification Designation/s: ABAT

Meetings/Conferences: Annual
2013 - Atlanta, GA (Hyatt Regency Atlanta)/Sept. 27 -
   Oct. 2

Publications:
AACTion Newsletter; monthly
Clinical Toxicology
Current Awareness in Clinical Toxicology; monthly
Membership Directory; on-line

American Academy of Cosmetic Dentistry *(1984)*
402 W. Wilson St.
Madison, WI 53703
Tel: (608) 222-8583 *Fax:* (608) 222-9540
TollFree: (800) 543-9220
E-Mail: info@aacd.com
Website: aacd.com
Members: 6,000 individuals
Staff: 29
Annual Budget: $5-10,000,000

Personnel:
Chief Executive Officer: Ed Simeone
   E-Mail: eds@aacd.org
Director, Membership and Marketing: Michael DiFrisco
   E-Mail: michaeld@aacd.com
Chief Operating Officer: S. John Hanson CPA
Director, Information Technology: Karin Langsdorf
Staff Accountant: Carolyn Madaus
Director, Professional Education: Kelly Radcliff CMP
   E-Mail: kellyr@aacd.com
Manager, Professional Education and Events: Carol
   Schwickrath CEM
Managing Editor: Tracy Skenandore
   E-Mail: tracys@aacd.com

Historical Note:

AACD's mission is to advance the art and science of cosmetic dentistry and encourage responsible patient care. Members are dental practitioners, educators and researchers with an interest in the field of cosmetic dentistry. Membership: $425 (Dentists/Laboratory Technicians or Owners/Supporting Members); $20 (Student); $95 (Resident/Hygienist/Recent Graduate Dentist/Dental Assistant); $115 (Full- Time Faculty/non practicing dentist); $2,500 (Corporate).

Meetings/Conferences: Annual
Conference Chair: Carol Schwickrath CEM
2013 - Seatle, WA/April 24 - 27
2014 - Orlando, FL/April 30 - May 3
2015 - San Francisco, CA/May 6 - 9
2016 - Toronto, ON/April 27 - 30

Publications:
AACD eUpdate; weekly
Journal of Cosmetic Dentistry (jCD); adv.
Membership Directory; on-line

American Academy of Cosmetic Surgery (1985)
737 N. Michigan Ave.
Suite 2100
Chicago, IL 60611-5641
Tel: (312) 981-6760 Fax: (312) 981-6787
E-Mail: info@cosmeticsurgery.org
Website: cosmeticsurgery.org
Members: 2000 individuals
Staff: 12
Annual Budget: $2-5,000,000

Personnel:
Executive Director: Gail Fairhall PhD
    E-Mail: gfairhall@cosmeticsurgery.org
Director, Education, Conferences and Membership Services: Shelia Buchanan
    E-Mail: sbuchanan@cosmeticsurgery.org
Manager, Marketing: Maggie Endres
    E-Mail: mendres@cosmeticsurgery.org
Operations Analyst: Luis Gomez
    E-Mail: lgomez@cosmeticsurgery.org
Communications Specialist: Larry Guthrie
    E-Mail: lguthrie@cosmeticsurgery.org
Manager, Membership Services: Brian Jones
    E-Mail: bjones@cosmeticsurgery.org
Coordinator, Education: LaTanya Stovall
    E-Mail: lstovall@cosmeticsurgery.org

Historical Note:
Formed by a merger of the American Association of Cosmetic Surgeons (1969) and the American Society of Cosmetic Surgeons (1982). The American Academy of Cosmetic Surgery is a professional medical society is dedicated to patient safety and physician education in cosmetic surgery. The mission of the American Academy of Cosmetic Surgery is to advance the specialty of cosmetic surgery and quality patient care. Membership: $620 (Fellow); $475 (Associate); $345 (Corresponding); $100 (Resident).

Meetings/Conferences: Annual
Conference Chair: Shelia Buchanan
2013 - Las Vegas, NV (Caesars Palace)/Jan. 16 - 19/700 attendees
Number of non-conference events/year: 3

Publications:
American Journal of Cosmetic Surgery (AJCS); quarterly
Surge; quarterly

American Academy of Craniofacial Pain (1985)
12100 Sunset Hills Rd.
Suite 130
Reston, VA 20190
Tel: (703) 234-4142 Fax: (703) 435-4390
TollFree: (800) 322-8651
E-Mail: central@aacfp.org
Website: aacfp.org
Members: 500 individuals
Staff: 5
Annual Budget: $1-2,000,000

Personnel:
President: Terry R. Bennett DMD
Contact, Communications: Bill Carney
    E-Mail: bcarney@drohanmgmt.com
Chairman, Programs: Stacy V. Cole DDS
Treasurer: Richard E. Klein DDS
Publications Editor: Gerald J. Murphy BS, DDS

Historical Note:
Formerly (2001) American Academy of Head, Neck and Facial Pain . AACP's mission is to commit for the relief of craniofacial pain and dysfunction, and the advancement of research and study in this field. Members are dentists and other professionals concerned with disorders of the temporo-mandibular region. Membership: $420 (U.S.); $445 (Canada); $465 (Other Countries).

Meetings/Conferences:
Conference Chair: Stacy V. Cole DDS
Number of non-conference events/year: 1

Publications:
Journal of Craniomandibular Practice; quarterly; adv.
Membership Directory; on-line
TMDiary; adv.

American Academy of Dental Group Practice (1973)
2525 E. Arizona Biltmore Cir.
Suite 127
Phoenix, AZ 85016-2129
Tel: (602) 381-1185 Fax: (602) 381-1093
E-Mail: info@aadgp.org
Website: aadgp.org
Members: 370 groups
Staff: 3
Annual Budget: $250-500,000
Tax: 501(c)(6)

Personnel:
Administrative Director: Neil Armitage

Historical Note:
AADGP, formed to address the unique needs of dental groups, acts as a national voice for the special interests of dental group practices. It also acts as a liaison to other national dental organizations. Membership: $100-500/year.

Continuing Education:
Certification Designation/s: PACE

Meetings/Conferences: Annual
2013 - New Orleans, LA (Hilton New Orleans Riverside)/Feb. 6 - 9

Publications:
CONTACT Newsletter; quarterly
Membership Directory; on-line

American Academy of Dental Practice Administration (1956)
1063 Whippoorwill Ln.
Palatine, IL 60067-7064
Tel: (847) 934-4404 Fax: (847) 934-4410
Website: aadpa.org
Members: 250 individuals
Staff: 2
Annual Budget: $250-500,000
Tax: 501(c)(6)

Personnel:
Executive Director: Kathleen S. Uebel
    E-Mail: executivedirector@aadpa.org
Webmaster: Rick Roesener
    E-Mail: webmaster@aadpa.org

Historical Note:
AADPA's mission is to enrich the lives of members and those they serve, by creating an environment, which uniquely facilitates fellowship, the exchange of knowledge, ideas, and professional growth. Membership: $825 (Active/Affiliate member).

Meetings/Conferences: Annual
Conference Chair: Kathleen S. Uebel
2013 - Las Vegas, NV (The Cosmopolitan Hotel)/March 6 - 10
2014 - Palm Spring, CA (Hyatt Grand Champions Resort and Spa)/March 5 - 8
Number of non-conference events/year: 1

Publications:
AADPA Membership Roster; on-line
Membership Directory; annually
The Communicator; quarterly; adv.

American Academy of Dental Sleep Medicine (1991)
2510 N. Frontage Rd.
Darien, IL 60561
Tel: (630) 737-9705 Fax: (630) 737-9790
E-Mail: info@aadsm.org
Website: aadsm.org
Members: 2,800 members
Staff: 2
Annual Budget: $1-2,000,000
Tax: 501(c)(3)

Personnel:

President: B. Gail Demko DMD
Secretary and Treasurer: Leslie C. Dort DDS

Historical Note:
Founded as Sleep Disorders Dental Society, assumed its current name in 2006. AADSM promotes research and the clinical use of oral appliances and upper airway surgery for the treatment of sleep-related breathing disorders (SBD) and provides training and resources for those who work directly with patients. Membership: $175 (Regular); Membership for students and Emeritus members is free.

Continuing Education:
Certification Designation/s: ADA

Meetings/Conferences: Annual
2013 - Baltimore, MD (Hilton Baltimore)/May 30 - June 1

Publications:
Dialogue; quarterly; adv.
E-news Update; monthly
Membership Directory; on-line
Sleep and Breathing; quarterly; adv.

American Academy of Dermatology (1938)
930 E. Woodfield Rd.
Schaumburg, IL 60173
Tel: (847) 240-1280 Fax: (847) 240-1859
TollFree: (866) 503-7546
E-Mail: mrc@aad.org
Website: aad.org
Members: 17000 individuals
Staff: 173
Annual Budget: $25-50,000,000

Personnel:
Director, Meetings and Conventions: Timothy Moses
    E-Mail: tmoses@aad.org
General Counsel: Robert M. Portman
Director, Communications: Allison Scherer

Historical Note:
AAD's mission is to work in the areas of patient care, medical and public education, research, professionalism and member service and support. The Academy promotes and advances the science and art of medicine and surgery related to the skin and promotes the possible standards in clinical practice, education and research in dermatology and related disciplines. Membership: $750 (Individual/Corporate, US & Canada); $450 (Researchers).

Meetings/Conferences: Annual
Conference Chair: Timothy Moses
2013 - Miami, FL (Miami Beach Convention Center)/March 1 - 5
2013 - New York City, NY/July 30 - Aug. 3
2014 - Denver, CO/March 21 - 25
2015 - San Francisco, CA/March 20 - 24
2016 - Washington, DC/March 4 - 8
Number of non-conference events/year: 1

Publications:
Academy E-newsletter; on-line; adv.
Derm Coding Consult Newsletter
Dermatology Advocate; bi-monthly
Dermatology Daily; daily
Dermatology World Magazine; monthly; adv.
Directions in Residency Newsletter; quarterly
Journal of the American Academy of Dermatology (JAAD); on-line; adv.
Membership Directory; on-line
Philanthrop-e Newsletter; bi-monthly
Skin E-News; monthly
Young Physician Focus; quarterly

Membership List Available to Non-members

American Academy of Diplomacy (1983)
1200 18th St. NW
Suite 902
Washington, DC 20036
Tel: (202) 331-3721 Fax: (202) 833-4555
E-Mail: academy@academyofdiplomacy.org
Website: academyofdiplomacy.org
Members: 170 individuals
Staff: 4
Annual Budget: $1-2,000,000
Tax: 501(c)(3)

Personnel:
President: Ronald E. Neumann
Director, Programs: Elizabeth Burrell
Assistant, Financial Services and Operations: Lenore Flower
General Counsel: Glenn Gerstell

Historical Note:

AAD's mission is to increase public understanding and appreciation of the contributions of diplomacy to the national interests of the United States. It also seeks to encourage the strengthening and improvement of American diplomatic representation abroad. Members are individuals who have served in high positions in the diplomatic corps or state department. Membership: $350/year.

Meetings/Conferences:
Conference Chair: Elizabeth Burrell
Number of non-conference events/year: 1

Publications:
AAD Newsletter; quarterly
The Diplomatic Pouch e-Newsletter; monthly

American Academy of Disability Evaluating Physicians (1987)
233 W. Jackson Blvd.
Suite 1104
Chicago, IL 60606-6900
Tel: (312) 663-1171 Fax: (312) 663-1175
TollFree: (800) 456-6095
E-Mail: aadep@aadep.org
Website: aadep.org
Members: 1400 individuals
Staff: 5
Annual Budget: $1-2,000,000
Tax: 501(c)(6)

Personnel:
Executive Director: Sandra L. Yost MBA
    E-Mail: sandyy@aadep.org
Manager, Accounting and Membership Services: Debra Frigo
    E-Mail: debraf@aadep.org

Historical Note:
Mission is to advance the science of the prevention and management of disability, as well as, disability and impairment evaluation and to serve its members. Members are medical doctors, doctors of osteopathy, doctors of chiropractic, nurses, attorneys, psychologists, case managers, and therapists. Membership: $295 (Associate); $4500 (Life).

Continuing Education:
Certification Designation/s: CEDIR

Meetings/Conferences: Annual
2013 - Hollywood, CA (Loews Hollywood Hotel)/Jan. 18 - 19/300 attendees
Number of non-conference events/year: 11

Publications:
AADEP Disability Newsletter; adv.
Membership Directory; on-line

American Academy of Emergency Medicine (1994)
555 E. Wells St.
Suite 1100
Milwaukee, WI 53202-3823
Tel: (414) 276-7390 Fax: (414) 276-3349
TollFree: (800) 884-2236
E-Mail: info@aaem.org
Website: aaem.org
Members: 5800 individuals
Staff: 8
Annual Budget: $2-5,000,000
Tax: 501(c)(6)

Personnel:
Executive Director: Kay A. Whalen CAE, MBA
    E-Mail: kwhalen@aaem.org
Manager, AAEM and RSA Program: Jody Bath
    E-Mail: jbath@aaem.org
Manager, Communications and Website: Marsha Berenson
Manager, Meetings and CME: Marcia Blackman
    E-Mail: mblackman@aaem.org
Manager, Membership Services: Ginger Czajkowski
    E-Mail: gczajkowski@aaem.org
Associate Executive Director: Janet Wilson
    E-Mail: jwilson@aaem.org

Historical Note:
AAEM strives to provide every individual an unencumbered access to emergency care provided by a specialist in emergency medicine. Membership: $365 (Fellow and Full Voting/Affiliate); $250 (Associate/Emeritus); $50 (Resident/Student); $150 (International).

Meetings/Conferences: Annual
Conference Chair: Marcia Blackman
2013 - Las Vegas, NV (Sugar Loaf Ct)/Feb. 11 - 13
Number of non-conference events/year: 10

Publications:
Common Sense; bi-monthly
Dollars & Common Sense; on-line
Journal of Emergency Medicine; monthly
Washington Sentinel; monthly

American Academy of Environmental Engineers (1955)
130 Holiday Ct.
Suite 100
Annapolis, MD 21401
Tel: (410) 266-3311 Fax: (410) 266-7653
E-Mail: info@aaee.net
Website: aaee.net
Members: 2600 individuals
Staff: 5
Annual Budget: $500-1,000,000
Tax: 501(c)(6)

Personnel:
Executive Director: Joseph S. Cavarretta CAE
    E-Mail: jcava@aaee.net
Production Manager, Publications: Yolanda Y. Moulden
    E-Mail: ymoulden@aaee.net
Manager, Special Projects: J. Sammi Olmo
    E-Mail: jsolmo@aaee.net
Accounting Manager: Lisa Pike
    E-Mail: lpike@aaee.net

Historical Note:
Originally (1955) the American Sanitary Engineering Intersociety Board, became the Environmental Engineering Intersociety Board in 1966 and assumed its present name in 1973. AAEE is committed to improving the practice, elevating the standards and advancing the cause of environmental engineering. Members are board-certified environmental engineers. Membership: $85 (Member); Free (Student).

Continuing Education:
Enrollment: 2600
Certification Designation/s: BCEE, BCEEM

Meetings/Conferences:
Conference Chair: J. Sammi Olmo

Publications:
Environmental Engineer; quarterly; adv.
Environmental Engineering Selection and Career Guide; annually; adv.
Who's Who in Environmental Engineering; annually

Membership List Available to Non-members

American Academy of Environmental Medicine (1965)
6505 E. Central Ave.
Suite 296
Wichita, KS 67206
Tel: (316) 684-5500 Fax: (316) 684-5709
E-Mail: administrator@aaemonline.org
Website: aaemonline.org
Members: 400 individuals
Staff: 3
Annual Budget: Under $10,000
Tax: 501(c)(3)

Personnel:
Executive Director: De Rodgers-Fox
    E-Mail: defox@aaemonline.org
Public Relations Chair: Amy Dean DO
    E-Mail: environmentalmed@yahoo.com
Editor: Lawrence Plumlee
    E-Mail: laplumlee@pol.net

Historical Note:
Originated as the Human Ecology Study Club and formerly (1984) Society for Clinical Ecology. AAEM is an international association of physicians and other professionals interested in the clinical aspects of humans and their environment. It provides research and education in the recognition, treatment and prevention of illnesses induced by exposures to biological and chemical agents encountered in air, food and water. Membership: $395 (Domestic Member); $285 (International Member/Doctoral Members/Allied Health Professional Members); $95 (Medical Student/Community); $1,000 (Corporate Member).

Continuing Education:
Certification Designation/s: ACCME

Meetings/Conferences: Annual

Publications:
Environmental Physician Newsletter; monthly; adv.
Membership Directory; annually; adv.

American Academy of Equine Art (1980)

117 N. Water St.
P.O. Box 1364
Georgetown, KY 40324
Tel: (859) 281-6031 Fax: (859) 281-6043
Website: aaea.net
Members: 90 individuals
Staff: 1
Annual Budget: $25-50,000
Tax: 501(c)(3)

Personnel:
Executive Director: Frances Clay Corner
    E-Mail: fcconner@aaea.net

Historical Note:
AAEA serves to educate and encourage a broad awareness and appreciation of equine art as a specific and distinctively worthy segment of contemporary fine art in America. Members are professional artists who are willing and qualified to exhibit works of equine art and to teach the subject. Membership: $175 (Associate-U.S.); $50 (Associate-Foreign); $350 (Full Member-U.S.); $100 (Full Member-Foreign/Donor); $25 (Friend of Academy); $50 (Supporting); $500 (Corporate).

Meetings/Conferences:
Number of non-conference events/year: 7

Publications:
Membership Directory; on-line
Newsletter

American Academy of Estate Planning Attorneys (1993)
9444 Balboa Ave.
Suite 300
San Diego, CA 92123
Tel: (858) 453-2128 Fax: (858) 874-5804
TollFree: (800) 846-1555
E-Mail: information@aaepa.com
Website: aaepa.com
Members: 120 law firms
Staff: 39

Personnel:
President: Robert G. Armstrong JD
    E-Mail: robert@aaepa.com
Chief Executive Officer and Co-Founder: Sanford M. Fisch JD, LLM
    E-Mail: sandyf@aaepa.com
Accounting Manager: Denise Ananian
    E-Mail: lorim@aaepa.com
Manager, Software Development and Training: Donna Hooper
    E-Mail: donna.hooper@aaepa.com
Coordinator, Events and Publicity: Erin Mathew
    E-Mail: erin@aaepa.com
Operations Manager: Traci Paul
    E-Mail: tracip@aaepa.com
Director, Membership Services, Recruiting and Marketing: Jennifer Price
    E-Mail: jenniferp@aaepa.com
Director, Education: Dennis Sandoval
    E-Mail: denniss@aaepa.com

Historical Note:
AAEPA's purpose is to promote estate planning by providing its exclusive membership of attorneys with up-to-date research, educational materials, and other vital practice management techniques. Members are lawyers and law firms specializing in estate planning practice. Membership: $9,500/year (Individual).

Meetings/Conferences:
Conference Chair: Erin Mathew

Publications:
AAEPA Newsletter; quarterly
Member Directory; on-line

American Academy of Esthetic Dentistry (1975)
303 W. Madison St .
Suite 2650
Chicago, IL 60606
Tel: (312) 981-6770 Fax: (312) 265-2908
E-Mail: info@estheticacademy.org
Website: estheticacademy.org
Members: 151 individuals
Staff: 6
Annual Budget: $500-1,000,000
Tax: 501(c)(6)

Personnel:
Executive Director: Joseph M. Jackson CAE
    E-Mail: jjackson@thesentergroup.com
Editor: Harald O. Heymann

Account Coordinator, Membership Services and Operations: Sara Porter
  E-Mail: sporter@thesentergroup.com
Director, Meetings and Education: Moira Twitty
  E-Mail: mtwitty@thesentergroup.com

Historical Note:
AAED's purpose is to advocate the integration of dental esthetics into the total spectrum of oral health care and provide a leadership role for the profession by defining the interdisciplinary clinical, scientific, artistic and ethical standards through research, publications and educational presentations. Membership: $1200/year.

Meetings/Conferences: Annual
Conference Chair: Moira Twitty
2013 - Washington, DC (The Ritz-Carlton)/Aug. 7 - 10

Publications:
Journal of Esthetic and Restorative Dentistry; bi-monthly; adv.
Journal of Prosthetic Dentistry; monthly; adv.
Member Directory; on-line

Membership List Available to Non-members

American Academy of Facial Plastic and Reconstructive Surgery *(1964)*
310 S. Henry St.
Alexandria, VA 22314-3524
Tel: (703) 299-9291 *Fax:* (703) 299-8898
E-Mail: mail@aafprs.org
Website: aafprs.org
Members: 2700 facial plastic and reconstructive surgeons
Staff: 14
Annual Budget: $1-2,000,000
Tax: 501(c)(6)

Personnel:
Executive Vice President: Stephen C. Duffy
  E-Mail: scduffy@aafprs.org
Assistant Manager, Meetings and Exhibits: Joanie Amorosi
  E-Mail: jamorosi@aafprs.org
Manager, Membership Services: Maria P. Atkins
  E-Mail: matkins@aafprs.org
Director, Development, Research and Humanitarian Programs: Ann K. Holton
  E-Mail: aholton@aafprs.org
General Vice President, Public and Regulatory Affairs: Corey S. Maas
Director, Publications and Marketing: Rita Chua Magness
  E-Mail: rcmagness@aafprs.org
Coordinator, Marketing and Information Services: Kim Middleton
  E-Mail: kmiddleton@aafprs.org
Director, Education (CME) and Training: Caryl Herrington Worthington
  E-Mail: cworthington@aafprs.org

Historical Note:
Formed by a merger (1964) of the American Society of Facial Plastic Surgery and the American Otorhinologic Society for Plastic Surgery. AAFPRS's mission is to promote the quality facial plastic surgery through education, dissemination of professional information, and the establishment of professional standards. Membership: $750 (Fellow); $700 (Physicians); $270 (International).

Meetings/Conferences: Semi-Annual
Conference Chair: Joanie Amorosi
Number of non-conference events/year: 1

Publications:
AAFPRS Buyers Guide; annually; adv.
Facial Plastic Surgery Today -Newsletter; quarterly
Membership Directory; annually

American Academy of Family Physicians *(1947)*
P.O. Box 11210
Shawnee, KS 66207-1210
Tel: (913) 906-6000 *Fax:* (913) 906-6075
TollFree: (800) 274-2237
E-Mail: capitol@aafp.org
Website: aafp.org
Members: 105,900 members
Staff: 8
Annual Budget: $50-100,000,000
Tax: 501(c)(6)

Personnel:
Executive Vice President and Chief Executive Officer: Douglas E. Henley FAAFP, MD
  E-Mail: dhenley@aafp.org

Vice President, Publications and Strategic Partnerships: Craig Doane
  E-Mail: cdoane@aafp.org
Vice President, Education: Perry A. Pugno MD, MPH
Vice President, Communications and Membership Services: Donna Valponi
Vice President, Financial and Administrative Services: Robert I. Watchinski CPA
  E-Mail: rwatchin@aafp.org

Historical Note:
Formerly (1971) the American Academy of General Practice. AAFP's purpose is to improve the health of patients, families and communities by serving the needs of members with professionalism and creativity. Membership: $30-395/year.

Continuing Education:
Certification Designation/s: CME

Meetings/Conferences:
Conference Chair: Donna Valponi

Publications:
FP Essentials; monthly
AAFP News Now (ANN)
American Family Physician (AFP); semi-monthly; adv.
Annals of Family Medicine; bi-monthly; adv.
CME Bulletin
Connect for Family Medicine
Environmental Scan; weekly
Family Practice Management (FPM); bi-monthly; adv.
Membership Directory; on-line
Washington Update; weekly

Membership List Available to Non-members

American Academy of Fertility Care Professionals *(1981)*
11700 Studt Ave.
Suite C
St. Louis, MO 63141
Tel: (402) 489-3733 *Fax:* (402) 488-6525
E-Mail: info@aafcp.org
Website: aafcp.org
Members: 413 individuals, organizations and associates
Staff: 5
Annual Budget: $50-100,000

Personnel:
President: Dorice Millar BSN, RN
  E-Mail: president@aafcp.org
Finance Officer: Candace Fier
  E-Mail: finances@aafcp.org
Vice President, Membership Services: Elizabeth Martinez BA, CFCP
  E-Mail: elizabethsmartinez@yahoo.com
Administrative Assistant: Minette Paltz BA, FCP
  E-Mail: adminassistant@aafcp.org
Vice President, Planning and Development: Maria Perkins CFCP
  E-Mail: planning@aafcp.org

Historical Note:
Founded as American Academy of Natural Family Planning, assumed its current name in 2001. AAFCP's mission is to support, advance, and advocate quality natural family planning through service, education, leadership, and research. Membership: $105 (Active/Organization); $26.25 (Student/Special); $47.25 (Associate).

Continuing Education:
Certification Designation/s: FCP

Meetings/Conferences: Annual
2013 - New Orleans, LA (Hotel Monteleone)/Aug. 7 - 10

Publications:
Academy Activity Newsletter; irregular
Membership. Directory; on-line

American Academy of Forensic Sciences *(1948)*
410 N. 21st St.
Colorado Springs, CO 80904
Tel: (719) 636-1100 *Fax:* (719) 636-1993
E-Mail: membship@aafs.org
Website: aafs.org
Members: 6260 individuals
Staff: 12
Annual Budget: $2-5,000,000
Tax: 501(c)(3)

Personnel:
Executive Director: Anne Warren
  E-Mail: awarren@aafs.org

Editor and Coordinator, Publications and Website: Sonya Bynoe
  E-Mail: sbynoe@aafs.org
Finance Manager: Debbie Crockett
  E-Mail: dcrockett@aafs.org
Manager, Meetings and Expositions: Sondra Doolittle
  E-Mail: sdoolittle@aafs.org
Coordinator, Membership Services: Cheryl Hunter
  E-Mail: chunter@aafs.org
Director, Development and Accreditation: Nancy Jackson
  E-Mail: njackson@aafs.org
Executive Assistant and Coordinator, Continuing Education: Kimberly Wrasse
  E-Mail: kwrasse@aafs.org

Historical Note:
AAFS's mission is to promote education, foster research, improve practice, and encourage collaboration in the forensic sciences. Also cooperates with regional, national, and international organizations dedicated to the use of science in the administration of justice. Membership: $145 (Individual); $55 (Student).

Meetings/Conferences: Annual
Conference Chair: Sondra Doolittle
2013 - Washington, DC (Washington Marriott Wardman Park)/Feb. 18 - 23/over 100 exhibitors
2014 - Seattle, WA (Washington State Convention Center)/Feb. 17 - 22/over 100 exhibitors
2015 - Orlando, FL (Hilton Orlando Lake Buena Vista)/ Feb. 16 - 21
2016 - Las Vegas, NV (Rio All-Suite Hotel and Casino)/ Feb. 15 - 20/over 100 exhibitors
2017 - New Orleans, LA (Hyatt Regency)/Feb. 13 - 18
2018 - Seattle, WA (Washington State Convention Center)/Feb. 19 - 24
Number of non-conference events/year: 12

Publications:
Journal of Forensic Sciences; bi-monthly; adv.
Member Directory; on-line

Membership List Available to Non-members

American Academy of Gnathologic Orthopedics *(1969)*
P.O. Box 646
Arnold, CA 95223
Fax: (209) 795-0125
TollFree: (800) 510-2246
E-Mail: aago@astound.net
Website: aago.com
Members: 160 individuals
Staff: 1
Annual Budget: $50-100,000

Personnel:
Executive Director: Jennifer Menefee

Historical Note:
Established in Portland, Oregon to promote the Crozat-Wiebrecht philosophy and incorporated in Wisconsin. AAGO is dedicated to advance Crozat method of orthodontics, which aims to bring about the potential of jaw growth and make room for all the teeth. Members are dentists specializing in non-extraction orthodontic treatment of malformations of the face and jaw. Membership: $350/year.

Meetings/Conferences: Annual

American Academy of Gold Foil Operators *(1952)*
One Woods End Rd.
Etna, NH 03750-4318
Tel: (603) 643-2899
Website: aagfo.org
Members: 300 individuals
Staff: 4
Annual Budget: $10-25,000

Personnel:
Secretary and Treasurer: Dr. Robert C. Keene
  E-Mail: dmdsmile@gmail.com

Historical Note:
AAGFO is an international dental organization dedicated to quality clinical dentistry through the development of technical skills via the study and manipulation of direct gold in the restoration of natural teeth. Membership: $50/year.

Meetings/Conferences: Annual

Publications:
Gold Leaf; irregular
Operative Dentistry; bi-monthly

American Academy of Health Care Providers-Addictive Disorders *(1988)*

314 W. Superior St.
Suite 508
Duluth, MN 55802
Tel: (218) 727-3940 *Fax:* (218) 722-0346
E-Mail: info@americanacademy.org
Website: americanacademy.org
Members: 2000 individuals
Staff: 6

Personnel:
Chief Executive Officer: Elizabeth M. George
Executive Director: Cheri L. Swensson
   E-Mail: cswensson@americanacademy.org
Program Director: Shannon Hursh

Historical Note:
AAHCPAD is committed to maintaining quality standards for the provision of treatment in the addictive disorders. AAHCPAD's mission is to establish and support the highest standards of professional ethics in the field of addictive disorders. Membership: 110/year.

Continuing Education:
Certification Designation/s: CAS, CGAS

Meetings/Conferences:
Conference Chair: Shannon Hursh

Publications:
Newsletter

American Academy of Health Physics *(1960)*
1313 Dolley Madison Blvd.
Suite 402
McLean, VA 22101
Tel: (703) 790-1745 *Fax:* (703) 790-2672
E-Mail: aahp@burkinc.com
Website: aahp-abhp.org
Members: 1600 individuals
Staff: 3
Annual Budget: $250-500,000
Tax: 501(c)(6)

Personnel:
Executive Secretary and Director, Program: Nancy Johnson
   E-Mail: njohnson@burkinc.com

Historical Note:
AAHP's purpose is to advance the profession of health physics and to encourage the standards of ethics and integrity in the practice of health physics.

Meetings/Conferences:
Conference Chair: Nancy Johnson
Number of non-conference events/year: 2

Publications:
CHP News and CHP Corner; monthly
Membership Directory; on-line

Membership List Available to Non-members

American Academy of Home Care Physicians
(1988)
P.O. Box 1037
Edgewood, MD 21040-0337
Tel: (410) 676-7966 *Fax:* (410) 676-7980
E-Mail: aahcp@comcast.net
Website: aahcp.org
Members: 1300 individuals and 10 companies
Staff: 5
Annual Budget: $250-500,000
Tax: 501(c)(3)

Personnel:
Executive Director: Constance F. Row FACHE
   E-Mail: Edrow@aahcp.org
Contact, Membership and Administrative Services: Audrey McDonough
   E-Mail: Audrey.McDonough@aahcp.org
Director, Financial Services: Bernie Sciuto
   E-Mail: AAHCP@comcast.net

Historical Note:
AAHCP serves the needs of physicians and related professionals and agencies interested in improving care of patients in home. Members are physicians and other home care professionals. AAHCP's mission is to advocate the art, science, and practice of medicine in the home. Membership: $195 (Physicians/Affiliate, USA/Medical Directors); $210 (Physicians, Outside USA); $115 (Associate, USA); $75 (Residents/Students); $2,000 (Corporate Sponsor).

Meetings/Conferences: Annual
2013 - Grapevine, TX (Gaylord Texan Resort)/May 2 - 3

Publications:
AAHCP e-Newsletter; weekly; adv.

Frontiers; bi-monthly; adv.
Membership Directory; on-line

American Academy of Hospice and Palliative Medicine *(1988)*
4700 W. Lake Ave.
Glenview, IL 60025-1485
Tel: (847) 375-4712 *Fax:* (847) 375-6475
E-Mail: info@aahpm.org
Website: aahpm.org
Members: 4600 physicians, nurses, and health care professionals
Staff: 21
Annual Budget: $5-10,000,000
Tax: 501(c)(3)

Personnel:
Chief Executive Officer and Executive Director: Steve R. Smith CAE
Administrator, Membership Services: Jennifer Bose
Director, Education and Training: Julie Bruno LCSW, MSW
Director, Marketing and Membership: Laura Davis CAE
Director of Health Policy and Government Relations: Jacqueline M. Kocinski MPP
   E-Mail: JKocinski@aahpm.org
Senior Managing Editor: Jerrod Liveoak
Accountant: Phyllis Milz
Senior Meetings Manager: Vanessa Mobley CMP

Historical Note:
Formerly the Academy of Hospice Physicians (1998), AAHPM members are physicians and other medical professionals dedicated to expanding access of patients and families to quality palliative care and advancing the discipline of Hospice and Palliative Medicine, through professional education and training, development of a specialist workforce, support for clinical practice standards, research and public policy. Membership: $415 (Physician); $205 (Affiliate); $130 (Fellow); $25 (Student). Free for International Corresponding category.

Continuing Education:
Certification Designation/s: AOA, ABMS

Meetings/Conferences: Annual
Conference Chair: Vanessa Mobley CMP
2013 - New Orleans, LA/March 13 - 16
2014 - San Diego, CA/March 12 - 15
2015 - Philadelphia, PA/Feb. 25 - 28

Publications:
AAHPM Bulletin; quarterly; adv.
AAHPM Quarterly; quarterly; adv.
Journal of Pain and Symptom Management; monthly; adv.
PC-FACS; monthly

American Academy of Implant Dentistry *(1951)*
211 E. Chicago Ave.
Suite 750
Chicago, IL 60611
Tel: (312) 335-1550 *Fax:* (312) 335-9090
TollFree: (877) 335-2243
E-Mail: info@aaid.com
Website: aaid-implant.org
Members: 3000 individuals
Staff: 7
Annual Budget: $2-5,000,000
Tax: 501(c)(6)

Personnel:
Executive Director: Sharon Bennett
   E-Mail: sbennett@aaid.com
Chief Financial Officer: Afshin Alavi
   E-Mail: afshin@aaid.com
Manager, Membership Services: Carolina Hernandez
   E-Mail: carolina@aaid.com
Director, Meetings: Jennifer Hopkins CMP
   E-Mail: jennifer@aaid.com
Director, Professional Development: Sara Cameron May
   E-Mail: sara@aaid.com
Director, Communications and Marketing: Max G. Moses
   E-Mail: max@aaid.com
Director, Credentialing: Joyce Sigmon CAE
   E-Mail: joyce@aaid.com

Historical Note:
Founded as the American Academy of Implant Dentures and incorporated in Minnesota in October 1952, name changed to American Academy of Implant Dentistry in 1966. AAID's mission is to advance the science and practice of implant dentistry through education, research support and to serve as the credentialing standard for implant dentistry for the

benefit of mankind. Membership: $295 (General); $25-50 (Student/Resident).

Meetings/Conferences: Annual
Conference Chair: Sara Cameron May
2013 - Phoenix, AZ (JW Marriott Phoenix Desert Ridge Resort and Spa)/Oct. 23 - 26/over 100 exhibitors
2014 - Orlando, FL (Peabody Orlando)/Nov. 5 - 8/over 100 exhibitors
2015 - Las Vegas, NV (Caesars Palace)/Oct. 21 - 24/over 100 exhibitors

Publications:
AAID Business Bite; monthly; adv.
AAID eGram; monthly
AAID Implant Insight; weekly; adv.
AAID News; quarterly; adv.
Journal of Oral Implantology; bi-monthly; adv.
Membership Directory; annually; adv.

American Academy of Matrimonial Lawyers
(1962)
150 N. Michigan Ave.
Suite 1420
Chicago, IL 60601
Tel: (312) 263-6477 *Fax:* (312) 263-7682
E-Mail: office@aaml.org
Website: aaml.org
Members: 1600 individuals
Staff: 3
Annual Budget: $1-2,000,000
Tax: 501(c)(6)

Personnel:
President: Kenneth Altshuler
Executive Director: Vicki L. West
Treasurer: Cary Mogerman

Historical Note:
AAML's purpose is to encourage the study, improve the practice, elevate the standards and advance the cause of matrimonial law, to the end that the welfare of the family and society be protected. Members are attorneys specializing in the field of marriage and family law. Membership: $325/year.

Meetings/Conferences: Semi-Annual
2013 - Fajardo, Puerto Rico (El Conquistador Hotel)/March 16 - 20
2013 - Chicago, IL (J.W. Marriott Hotel)/Nov. 6 - 9

Publications:
AAML Newsletters
Journal of the American Academy of Matrimonial Lawyers; semi-annually
Membership Brochure

American Academy of Maxillofacial Prosthetics
(1953)
981225 Nebraska Medical Center
Omaha, NE 68198-1225
Tel: (402) 559-8007
E-Mail: jcmarkt@cox.net
Website: maxillofacialprosth.org
Members: 260 individuals
Staff: 2
Annual Budget: $100-250,000
Tax: 501(c)(6)

Personnel:
Executive Secretary and Treasurer: Jeffery C. Markt, D.D.S.
   E-Mail: jcmarkt@cox.net

Historical Note:
AAMP's mission is to accumulate and disseminate knowledge and experience; to promote and maintain research programs involving methods, techniques and devices used in maxillofacial prosthetics. Membership: $260 (Individual); $250 (Organization/Company).

Meetings/Conferences: Annual
2013 - Santa Ana Pueblo, NM (Hyatt Regency Tamaya Resort & Spa)/Oct. 23 - 27
Number of non-conference events/year: 1

Publications:
AAMP Newsletter; annually
Journal of Prosthetic Dentistry; monthly; adv.

American Academy of Mechanics *(1969)*
Department of Mechanical Engineering
University of California
Santa Barbara, CA 93106
Tel: (805) 893-4459 *Fax:* (805) 893-4985
Website: aamech.org
Members: 1200 individuals

Staff: 4
Annual Budget: $1-2,000,000

Personnel:
Editor: Alberto M. Cuitino
Contact, Membership Services: Liz Montana
  E-Mail: liz@engineering.ucsb.edu

Historical Note:
AAM strives to advance in science and profession of mechanics. Members are individuals who have made significant contributions in the field of mechanics. Membership: $30-52 (Professional); $15-30 (Student); $100 (Organization); $15 (Retired).

Publications:
Mechanics; adv.

American Academy of Medical Acupuncture
(1987)
1970 E. Grand Ave.
Suite 330
El Segundo, CA 90245
Tel: (310) 364-0193 Fax: (310) 364-0196
E-Mail: administrator@medicalacupuncture.org
Website: medicalacupuncture.org
Members: 1900 individuals
Staff: 3
Annual Budget: $500-1,000,000
Tax: 501(c)(6)

Personnel:
Executive Administrator: James C. Dowden
  E-Mail: jdowden@prodigy.net
Coordinator, CME: Tracey Dowden
  E-Mail: tdowden44@hotmail.com
Editor: Barton Ortberg
  E-Mail: bart.ortberg@dowdenmanagement.com

Historical Note:
AAMA's purpose is to promote the integration of concepts from traditional and modern forms of acupuncture with Western medical training and thereby synthesize a more comprehensive approach to health care. Membership: $315 (Individual/Associate); $150 (Active Duty Military Personnel/Affiliate/International Affiliate/Application fee for Full/Associate); $85 (Student).

Continuing Education:
Certification Designation/s: CME, ABMA

Meetings/Conferences: Annual
Conference Chair: Tracey Dowden
2013 - Baltimore, MD (Renaissance Baltimore Harborplace)/May 3 - 5
Number of non-conference events/year: 2

Publications:
AAMA Newsletter
Medical Acupuncture; quarterly
Membership Directory; on-line

American Academy of Medical Administrators
(1957)
701 Lee St.
Suite 600
Des Plaines, IL 60016-4516
Tel: (847) 759-8601 Fax: (847) 759-8602
E-Mail: info@aameda.org
Website: aameda.org
Members: 3000 individuals
Staff: 9
Annual Budget: $500-1,000,000

Personnel:
President and Chief Executive Officer: Renee S. Schleicher CAE
  E-Mail: renee@aameda.org
Executive Online Editor: Laura Bowles
  E-Mail: executiveeditor@aameda.org
Director, Membership Services and Communications: Susan M. Eget
  E-Mail: sue@aameda.org
Chief Financial Officer: Rhonda Guptill
  E-Mail: rhonda@aameda.org
Meeting Planner: Merle Hedland
  E-Mail: merle@aameda.org
Director, Education: Guy Snyder MHA, RRT, CFAAMA
  E-Mail: guy@aameda.org
Administrator, Data and Information Technology: Leslie Talbert
  E-Mail: leslie@aameda.org

Historical Note:
Mission is to advance healthcare leadership through individual relationships, multi-disciplinary interaction, practical business tools and active engagement. AAMA

offers education, leadership training, credentialing, and networking opportunities to develop healthcare leaders. Members are healthcare administrators, including department heads, in both the federal and private sectors. Membership: $230 (Individual/Associate); $45 (Student).

Continuing Education:
Certification Designation/s: CAAMA

Meetings/Conferences: Annual
Conference Chair: Merle Hedland
2013 - Las Vegas, NV (Bally's Las Vegas Hotel and Casino)/April 10 - 12
Number of non-conference events/year: 1

Publications:
AAMA Executive Online; bi-monthly; adv.
AIM – Academy In Motion; bi-monthly; adv.
ExOn Express: Education and Inside Editions; semi-monthly; adv.
Membership Directory; annually

Membership List Available to Non-members

American Academy of Medical Hypnoanalysts
(1974)
P. O. Box 365
Winfield, IL 60190-0365
Tel: (720) 975-4485 Fax: (312) 604-5014
TollFree: (888) 454-9766
E-Mail: aamhinfo@aamh.com
Website: aamh.com
Members: 143 individuals
Staff: 1
Annual Budget: $10-25,000
Tax: 501(c)(6)

Personnel:
President: Jeanne Clark ACSW, LCSW, MSW

Historical Note:
Formerly the Society of Medical Hypnoanalysts. AAMH's mission is to develop and refine concepts and practices in the field of healthcare administration and to promote the advancement of its members in knowledge, professional development, credentialing, and personal achievements. Members include medical doctors, ministers, psychologists, social workers, marriage and family therapists, licensed counselors and nurses. Membership: $185 (Clinical); $135 (Associate).

Meetings/Conferences: Annual
2013 - Austin, TX (Hotel Allandale)/April 24 - 28

Publications:
E-Journal; annually; adv.
Membership Directory; on-line
News & Views

American Academy of Medical Management
(1987)
560 W. Crossville Rd.
Suite 104
Roswell, GA 30075
Tel: (770) 649-7150 Fax: (770) 649-7552
Website: epracticemanagement.org
Members: 4500 individuals
Staff: 28
Annual Budget: $5-10,000,000

Personnel:
President and Chief Executive Officer: Roger G. Bonds CMSR, FMSD, MBA
  E-Mail: rbonds@ePracticeManagement.org

Historical Note:
Formerly (2000) American College of Medical Staff Development; (2001) American College of Medical Practice Management. AAMM seeks to provide physicians with possible quality instruction and resources that is appropriate for both clinicians and administrators and in an environment which is conducive to the act of learning. Members are executives and managers in medical organizations. Membership: $378/year.

Continuing Education:
Certification Designation/s: EFPM, CMSR, CAPPM, PFPM, FMSD, RCMSR, MCPM, RCAPPM

Publications:
AAMM Newsletter

Membership List Available to Non-members

American Academy of Ministry (1992)
College of Christian Studies
Anderson University
Anderson, SC 29621
Tel: (864) 328-1809
Website: michaelduduit.com

Members: 1000 individuals
Staff: 2
Annual Budget: $25-50,000

Personnel:
Executive Director: Michael Duduit

Historical Note:
An interdenominational professional and scholarly organization, AAM is organized to help ministers enhance their ministry gifts. Membership: $39/year.

American Academy of Neurological and Orthopaedic Surgeons (1977)
1516 N. Lakeshore Dr.
Chicago, IL 60610
Tel: (800) 766-3427 Fax: (312) 787-9289
E-Mail: aanos@aanos.org
Website: aanos.org
Members: 269 individuals
Staff: 3
Annual Budget: $50-100,000

Personnel:
Executive Director: Nick Rebel
  E-Mail: nickrebel@ameritech.net

Historical Note:
AANOS is a scientific and educational association of neurosurgeons and orthopedists. Seeks to improve the quality of care for patients requiring expertise in these two major surgical specialties by setting standards for training, credentialing, peer review and ongoing surgical education. Membership: $300/year.

Meetings/Conferences: Annual
2013 - Jacksonville, FL/June 5 - 8

Publications:
The Journal of Neurological and Orthopaedic Medicine and Surgery; quarterly

Membership List Available to Non-members

American Academy of Neurology (1948)
201 Chicago Ave.
Minneapolis, MN 55415
Tel: (612) 928-6000 Fax: (612) 454-2746
TollFree: (800) 879-1960
E-Mail: memberservices@aan.com
Website: aan.com
Members: 24000 individuals
Staff: 18
Annual Budget: $2-5,000,000
Tax: 501(c)(6)

Personnel:
Executive Director and Chief Executive Officer: Catherine M. Rydell
  E-Mail: crydell@aan.com
Chief Financial Officer: Timothy Engel
  E-Mail: tengel@aan.com
Chief Membership and Strategy Officer: Christopher M Keran
  E-Mail: ckeran@aan.com
Chief Marketing and Technology Officer: Jason Kopinski
  E-Mail: jkopinski@aan.com
General Counsel: Bruce Levi JD
  E-Mail: blevi@aan.com
Deputy Executive Director, AAN Foundation: Christine E. Phelps
  E-Mail: cphelps@aan.com
Executive Editor: Andrea Weiss
  E-Mail: aweiss@aan.com

Historical Note:
Founded and incorporated in Minnesota in 1948, The American Academy of Neurology is a medical specialty society established to advance the art and science of neurology, and thereby promote the best possible care for patients with neurological disorders. Members are medical doctors who specialize in nerve and nervous system diseases. Membership: $130 (Junior); $205 (Research Scientists/Non-Neurologist/Business Administrators); $325 (US Associate/US Active/US Corresponding Active); $395 (International Associate/International Active/International Corresponding Active); $150 (Low/Low-Middle income countries, Associate/International/Active).

Meetings/Conferences: Annual
2013 - San Diego, CA (San Diego Convention Center)/March 16 - 23
2014 - Philadelphia, PA/April 26 - May 3
2015 - Washington, DC/April 18 - 25

Publications:
AANnews; monthly

Continuum: Lifelong Learning in Neurology; bi-
monthly
Neurology Journal; monthly
Neurology Today; bi-weekly

American Academy of Nurse Practitioners (1985)
P.O. Box 12846
Austin, TX 78711
Tel: (512) 442-4262 *Fax:* (512) 442-6469
E-Mail: dcoffice@aanp.org
Website: aanp.org
Members: 155000 nurse practitioners
Staff: 67
Annual Budget: $10-25,000,000
Tax: 501(c)(3)

Personnel:
Chief Operating Officer: Janice DeMartino
Director, Communications: Nancy McMurrey
    E-Mail: nmcmurrey@aanp.org

Historical Note:
*AANP works to promote excellence in NP practice,
education and research. Membership: $125 (Full/
Associate); $55 (Student/Retired); $95 (Recognized NP-
Student Member).*

Continuing Education:
Certification Designation/s: AANPCP

Meetings/Conferences: Annual
2013 - Las Vegas, NV (Venetian and Palazzo Resort,
    Hotel and Casinos)/June 19 - 23

Publications:
AANPSmartBrief; daily; adv.
Journal of the American Academy of Nurse
    Practitioners (JAANP); monthly

American Academy of Nursing (1973)
1000 Vermont Ave. NW
Suite 910
Washington, DC 20005
Tel: (202) 777-1170 *Fax:* (202) 777-0107
E-Mail: info@aanet.org
Website: aannet.org
Members: 1800 individuals
Staff: 17
Annual Budget: $2-5,000,000
Tax: 501(c)(3)

Personnel:
Chief Executive Officer: Cheryl G. Sullivan
Manager, Membership Services: Jocelyn Cunic
    E-Mail: Jocelyn_Cunic@AANnet.org
Manager, Policy: Kim Czubaruk
    E-Mail: Kim_Czubaruk@AANnet.org
Manager, Meetings and Events: Gale Guerrieri
    E-Mail: gguerrieri@aannet.org
Manager, Communications and Public Affairs: Kat
    Piscatelli
Administrative Assistant: Thomas Webb
    E-Mail: Thomas_Webb@AANnet.org

Historical Note:
*AAN's mission is to serve the public and the nursing
profession by advancing health policy and practice through
the generation, synthesis, and dissemination of nursing
knowledge. Members are invited on the basis of leadership
and accomplishments and designated as Fellows of the
American Academy of Nursing (FAAN). Membership:
$300/year (Individual).*

Meetings/Conferences: Annual
Conference Chair: Gale Guerrieri
2013 - Washington, DC (Hyatt Regency on Capitol
    Hill)/Oct. 17 - 19
Number of non-conference events/year: 2

Publications:
Membership Directory; on-line
Nursing Outlook; bi-monthly; adv.
Spotlight on the Academy E-Newsletter; quarterly; adv.

Membership List Available to Non-members

American Academy of Ophthalmic Executives (1979)
P.O. Box 7424
San Francisco, CA 94120-7424
Tel: (415) 561-8500 *Fax:* (415) 561-8533
E-Mail: aaoe@aao.org
Website: aao.org/aaoesite
Members: 29000 individuals
Staff: 7
Annual Budget: $500-1,000,000

Personnel:
Executive Director: Ernest Khirallah
    E-Mail: ekhirallah@aao.org
Manager, Administration: Peggy Coakley
    E-Mail: pcoakley@aao.org
Manager, Program and Content: Sangeeta Fernandes
    E-Mail: sfernandes@aao.org

Historical Note:
*AAOE's mission is to anticipate and meet the business
needs of ophthalmogy practices. Membership: $0-1,200/
year.*

Meetings/Conferences: Annual
Conference Chair: Sangeeta Fernandes
2013 - New Orleans, LA (Ernest N. Morial Convention
    Center)/Nov. 16 - 19
2014 - Chicago, IL (McCormick Place)/Oct. 18 - 21
2015 - Las Vegas, NV (Sands Expo and Venetian
    Hotel)/Nov. 14 - 17
2016 - Chicago, IL (McCormick Place)/Oct. 15 - 18
2017 - New Orleans, LA (Ernest N. Morial Convention
    Center)/Nov. 11 - 14
2018 - Chicago, IL (McCormick Place)/Oct. 27 - 30
2019 - San Francisco, CA (Moscone Center)/Oct. 12 -
    15

Publications:
AAO Newsbriefs; weekly
AAOE News; monthly
Coding Bulletin; monthly
EyeNet Magazine

American Academy of Ophthalmology (1979)
P.O. Box 7424
San Francisco, CA 94120-7424
Tel: (415) 561-8500 *Fax:* (415) 561-8533
E-Mail: comm@aao.org
Website: aao.org
Members: 29000 individuals
Staff: 180
Annual Budget: $25-50,000,000

Personnel:
Chief Executive Officer and Executive Vice President: David
    Parke II
Vice President, Communications: Siobhan Bunaes
    E-Mail: sbunaes@aao.org
Vice President, Governmental Affairs Division: Catherine
    Grealy Cohen
    E-Mail: ccohen@aaodc.org
Manager, Program and Contents: Sangeeta Fernandes
    E-Mail: sfernandes@aao.org
Director, Membership and Customer Service: Jill Hartle
    E-Mail: jhartle@aao.org
Vice President, Meetings and Exhibits: Debra
    Rosencrance CMP
    E-Mail: drosencrance@aao.org

Historical Note:
*American Academy of Ophthalmology evolved as part of
the AAOO, but incorporated as an independent organization
in 1979. AAO's mission is to advance the learning and
professional interests of ophthalmologists. Membership:
$400-875 (Active/Osteopathic); $160-495 (International);
$500 (Associate).*

Meetings/Conferences:
Conference Chair: Debra Rosencrance CMP
2013 - New Orleans, LA (Ernest N. Morial Convention
    Center)/Nov. 16 - 19
2014 - Chicago, IL (McCormick Place)/Oct. 18 - 21

Publications:
American Journal of Ophthalmology; monthly; adv.
British Journal of Ophthalmology; monthly; adv.
Journal of Academic Ophthalmology
Membership Directory; on-line
Ophthalmology Clinics
Survey of Ophthalmology
The Journal of Refractive Surgery; monthly

Membership List Available to Non-members

American Academy of Optometry (1922)
2909 Fairgreen St.
Orlando, FL 32803
Tel: (321) 710-3937 *Fax:* (407) 893-9890
E-Mail: aaoptom@aaoptom.org
Website: aaopt.org
Members: 5000 individuals
Staff: 11
Annual Budget: $2-5,000,000
Tax: 501(c)(3)

Personnel:

Executive Director: Lois Schoenbrun CAE, FAAO
    E-Mail: loiss@aaoptom.org
Database Administrator: Dana Edwards
    E-Mail: danae@aaoptom.org
Finance Director: Richard Jones CPA
    E-Mail: Richardj@aaoptom.org
Senior Director, Administration: Jana Kurtz
    E-Mail: janak@aaoptom.org
Contact, Membership Services: Stephen Morse
    E-Mail: StephenM@aaoptom.org
Manager, Exhibits: Betty Taylor
    E-Mail: bettyt@aaoptom.org
Senior Director, Programs: Helen Viksnins
    E-Mail: helenv@aaoptom.org
Managing Editor: Kurt Zadnik
    E-Mail: ovs@osu.edu

Historical Note:
*AAO is committed to promoting the art and science of vision
care through lifelong learning. Membership: $0-325/year.*

Meetings/Conferences: Annual
Conference Chair: Betty Taylor
2013 - Seatle, WA (Seattle Conference Center)/Oct. 23
    - 26
2014 - Denver, CO/Oct. 12 - 15
2014 - Denver, CO (Colorado Convention Center)/Nov.
    12 - 15
2015 - New Orleans, LA/Oct. 14 - 17
2016 - Anaheim, CA (Anaheim Convention Center)/
    Nov. 16 - 19
2017 - Boston, MA (Boston Convention and Exhibition
    Center)/Oct. 4 - 7
2018 - San Francisco, CA (Moscone West-Moscone
    Center)/Nov. 14 - 18

Publications:
AAO Newsletter
Eye-Mail® Monthly; monthly
Membership Directory; on-line
Optometry and Vision Science (OVS); monthly

American Academy of Oral and Maxillofacial Pathology (1950)
214 N. Hale St.
Wheaton, IL 60187
Tel: (630) 510-4552 *Fax:* (630) 510-4501
TollFree: (888) 552-2667
E-Mail: aaomp@b-online.com
Website: aaomp.org
Members: 700 individuals
Staff: 5
Annual Budget: $250-500,000

Personnel:
Executive Director: Janet Svazas
    E-Mail: jsvazas@integrated-solutions.com
Director, Administration: Karen Benton
    E-Mail: kbenton@integrated-solutions.com
Editor: Paul C. Edwards DDS, MSc
Director, Education: John W. Hellstein DDS, MS
Secretary and Treasurer: Steven D. Vincent

Historical Note:
*Formerly (1994) American Academy of Oral Pathology,
AAOMP endeavors to represent the interests of oral and
maxillofacial pathologists (OMPs) within the profession
itself, in the dental and medical community, and to the
public at large.*

Meetings/Conferences: Annual
2013 - Portland, OR (Hilton Portland and Executive
    Tower)/June 14 - 19

Publications:
AAOMP Newsletter; quarterly
Membership Directory; on-line

American Academy of Oral and Maxillofacial Radiology (1945)
3085 Stevenson Dr.
Suite 200
Springfield, IL 62703
Tel: (212) 342-5176 *Fax:* (212) 305-9313
Website: aaomr.org
Members: 400 individuals
Staff: 4
Annual Budget: $100-250,000

Personnel:
Executive Director: Dr. Christos Angelopoulos
    E-Mail: angelopoulosc@gmail.com
Exhibitor Coordinator: Christina Gordon
    E-Mail: Cgordon@associationcentral.org

Treasurer: Charles Hildebolt
   E-Mail: hildeboltc@mir.wustl.edu
Associate Executive Director: Gail Williamson
   E-Mail: gwilliam@iupui.edu

Historical Note:
Formerly (1949) American Academy of Dental Roentgenologists, (1951) American Academy of Oral Roentgenology, and then (1967) American Academy of Dental Radiology. Renamed in 1988 as the American Academy of Oral and Maxillofacial Radiology. AAOMR's mission is to promote and advance the art and science of radiology in dentistry, and to provide a forum for communication among and professional advancement of its members. Membership: $52-25,000/year.

Meetings/Conferences: Annual
Conference Chair: Christina Gordon
2013 - Los Angeles, CA (The Beverly Hilton, Beverly Hills)/Oct. 1 - 5

Publications:
AAOMR Newsletter; quarterly; adv.
Membership Roster; annually
Oral Surgery, Oral Medicine and Pathology, Oral Radiology and Endodontics; monthly; adv.

American Academy of Oral Medicine (1945)
23607 Hwy 99, Suite Two C
P.O. Box 2016
Edmonds, WA 98020-9516
Tel: (425) 778-6162 Fax: (425) 771-9588
E-Mail: info@aaom.com
Website: aaom.com
Members: 800 individuals
Staff: 2
Annual Budget: $250-500,000
Tax: 501(c)(6)

Personnel:
Executive Director: Eric Featherstone CAE
   E-Mail: eric@aaom.com

Historical Note:
Founded and incorporated in New York as the American Academy of Dental Medicine, assumed its present name in 1966. AAOM's purpose is to promote the study and dissemination of knowledge of the cause, prevention and control of diseases of the teeth and oral tissues and to foster increased scientific understanding and cooperation between the dental and medical professions. Membership: $295 (Regular); $145 (Affiliate/Student).

Meetings/Conferences: Annual
2013 - San Antonio, TX (Hyatt Regency San Antonio)/ April 23 - 27

American Academy of Orofacial Pain (1975)
174 S. New York Ave
P.O. Box 478
Oceanville, NJ 08231
Tel: (609) 504-1311 Fax: (609) 573-5064
E-Mail: aaopexec@aaop.org
Website: aaop.org
Members: 400 individuals
Staff: 2
Annual Budget: $250-500,000
Tax: 501(c)(3)

Personnel:
Executive Director: Kenneth Cleveland

Historical Note:
AAOP is an organization of health care professionals works towards alleviating pain and suffering through education, research and patient care in the field of orofacial pain and associated disorders. Membership: $217.50 (Active/ Physician Affiliate/Affiliate); $125.00 (Student/Initiatory Enrolled).

Meetings/Conferences: Annual
2013 - Lake Buena Vista, FL (Disney's Contemporary Resort)/April 23 - 28
Number of non-conference events/year: 6

Publications:
AAOP Newsletters
Journal of Orofacial Pain
Membership Directory; on-line

American Academy of Orthopaedic Surgeons (1933)
6300 N. River Rd.
Rosemont, IL 60018-4262
Tel: (847) 823-7186 Fax: (847) 823-8125
Website: aaos.org
Members: 36315 individuals
Staff: 282

Annual Budget: $25-50,000,000
Tax: 501(c)(3)

Personnel:
Chief Executive Officer: Karen L. Hackett CAE, FACHE
   E-Mail: hackett@aaos.org
Chief Education Officer: Constance Filling
   E-Mail: filling@aaos.org
Director, Publications: Marilyn L. Fox PhD
   E-Mail: fox@aaos.org
Director, Public Relations: Sandra R. Gordon
   E-Mail: gordon@aaos.org
Director, Marketing: Lewis Jenkins
   E-Mail: jenkins@aaos.org
Director, Conventions and Meeting Services: Susan McSorley
   E-Mail: mcsorley@aaos.org
Director, Information Services and Membership Services and Customer Relations: James A. Ogle
   E-Mail: ogle@aaos.org
General Counsel: Richard N. Peterson JD
   E-Mail: peterson@aaos.org
Director, Human Resources: Marita A. Powell SPHR
   E-Mail: powell@aaos.org
Chief Operating Officer and Chief Financial Officer: Richard J. Stewart
   E-Mail: stewart@aaos.org

Historical Note:
Founded in 1933 in Chicago. Incorporated in Illinois in 1948. AAOS's mission is to advance the highest quality musculoskeletal health through education of orthopedists and other health care providers; promotion of research; communication with other professionals and the public and leadership in the development of health care policy. Membership: $750 (Active Fellows); $300 (Candidate Members); $450 (International); $200 (International Resident Members).

Continuing Education:
Certification Designation/s: CME

Meetings/Conferences: Annual
Conference Chair: Susan McSorley
2013 - Chicago, IL (McCormick Place)/March 19 - 23
2013 - Austin, TX/Oct. 17 - 20
2014 - New Orleans, LA/March 11 - 15
2014 - IL/Oct. 30 - Nov. 2
2015 - Las Vegas, NV/March 24 - 28
2015 - IL/Oct. 29 - Nov. 1
Number of non-conference events/year: 2

Publications:
AAOS Now; monthly; adv.
Advocacy NOW
Advocacy NOW; on-line
Code X-tra Newsletter; on-line
he Journal of Bone & Joint Surgery (JBJS); semi-annually; adv.
Headline News Now
Headline News Now; on-line
Journal of the AAOS; monthly; adv.
Membership directory; annually
News in 10
Orthopaedic Knowledge Online; on-line
Resident's E-Letter; on-line
Residents' NewsLetters; monthly

American Academy of Orthotists and Prosthetists (1970)
1331 H St. NW
Suite 501
Washington, DC 20005
Tel: (202) 380-3663 Fax: (202) 380-3447
Website: oandp.org
Members: 3000 Individuals
Staff: 9
Annual Budget: $2-5,000,000

Personnel:
Executive Director: Peter D. Rosenstein
   E-Mail: prosenstein@oandp.org
Specialist, Communications and Program: Rachel Balick
   E-Mail: rbalick@oandp.org
Director, Publications and Marketing: Manisha S. Bhaskar
   E-Mail: mbhaskar@oandp.org
Deputy Executive Director: Chellie H. Blondes
   E-Mail: cblondes@oandp.org
Manager, Membership Services and Systems: Andrew B. Francis
   E-Mail: afrancis@oandp.org
Director, Meetings and Exhibits: Diane M. Ragusa

   E-Mail: dragusa@oandp.org

Historical Note:
AAOP's purpose is to promote professionalism and to advance the standards of patient care through education, literature, research, advocacy and collaboration. Members are individuals who have been certified for practice by the American Board for Certification in Orthotics and Prosthetics. Membership: $330 (Active/International Affiliate); $175 (Affiliate/Professional); $25 (Society); $36 (Candidate/Resident/Student); $300 (Associate).

Meetings/Conferences: Annual
Conference Chair: Diane M. Ragusa
2013 - Orlando, FL (Caribe Royal Resort)/Feb. 20 - 23
2014 - Chicago, IL (Hyatt Regency Chicago)/Feb. 26 - March 1
2015 - New Orleans, LA (Hyatt Regency New Orleans)/ Feb. 18 - 21
2016 - Orlando, FL (Caribe Royale Orlando)/March 9 - 12
2017 - Chicago, IL (Hyatt Regency Chicago)/March 1 - 4
2018 - New Orleans, LA (Hyatt Regency New Orleans)/ Feb. 14 - 17
2019 - Orlando, FL (Caribe Royale Orlando)/March 6 - 9

Publications:
Academy Today; quarterly
Journal of Prosthetics and Orthotics; quarterly
Membership Directory; on-line

American Academy of Osteopathy (1937)
3500 DePauw Blvd.
Suite 1080
Indianapolis, IN 46268
Tel: (317) 879-1881 Fax: (317) 879-0563
E-Mail: info@academyofosteopathy.org
Website: academyofosteopathy.org
Members: 2000 individuals
Staff: 7
Annual Budget: $1-2,000,000
Tax: 501(c)(3)

Personnel:
Interim Executive Director: Diana L. Finley CMP
   E-Mail: dfinley@academyofosteopathy.org
Director, Member Relations: Susan Lightle
   E-Mail: slightle@academyofosteopathy.org

Historical Note:
Founded in Chicago as The Section of Manipulative Therapeutics of the American Osteopathic Association. Name changed in 1938 to Osteopathic Manipulative Therapeutic and Clinical Research Association. Incorporated in 1944 as the Academy of Applied Osteopathy and became American Academy of Osteopathy in 1970. Affiliated with American Osteopathic Association. AAO's mission is to teach, advocate, and research the science, art and philosophy of osteopathic medicine, emphasizing the integration of osteopathic principles, practices and manipulative treatment in patient care. Membership: $248 (Active/Associate/Supporter); $88 (1st Year in Practice); $38 (Intern/Resident); $176 (2nd Year in Practice); $274 (Active/Associate/Supporter; International).

Continuing Education:
Certification Designation/s: FAAO, C-NMM/OMM

Meetings/Conferences: Annual
2013 - Orlando, FL (Rosen Shingle Creek Hotel)/March 20 - 24
2014 - Colorado Springs, CO (The Broadmoor)/March 19 - 23
2015 - Louisville, KY (Galt House Hotel and Suites)/ March 18 - 22
2016 - Orlando, FL (Rosen Shingle Creek Resort)/ March 16 - 20

Publications:
AAO Journal; quarterly
AAO Member Newsletter

American Academy of Otolaryngic Allergy (1941)
11130 Sunrise Valley Dr.
Suite 100
Reston, VA 20191
E-Mail: aaoa@aaoaf.org
Website: aaoaf.org
Members: 2700 individuals
Staff: 5
Annual Budget: $1-2,000,000

Personnel:
Director, Education, Meetings and Operations: Jeanne Procope

Historical Note:

AAOA's mission is to promote quality allergy care through member and public education. Membership: $375 (Fellow/Associate); $225 (Academic/Military); $175 (Allied Health).

Meetings/Conferences: Annual
Conference Chair: Matt Smith

Publications:
AAOA Today; quarterly
International Forum of Allergy & Rhinology; bi-monthly; adv.

American Academy of Otolaryngology-Head and Neck Surgery *(1896)*

1650 Diagonal Rd.
Alexandria, VA 22314-2857
Tel: (703) 836-4444 *Fax:* (703) 683-5100
Website: entnet.org
Members: 12000 individuals
Staff: 80
Annual Budget: $10-25,000,000
Tax: 501(c)(6)

Personnel:
Chief Executive Officer: David R. Nielsen MD
  E-Mail: dnielsen@entnet.org
Senior Director, Education and Meetings: Mary Pat Cornett
Chief Operating Officer and Chief Financial Officer: Brenda Hargett CAE, CPA
Director, Communications and Publications: Jeanne McIntyre
  E-Mail: jmcintyre@entnet.org
Senior Director, Development: Megan Schagrin
  E-Mail: mschagrin@entnet.org
Senior Manager, Media and Public Relations: Mary Stewart
  E-Mail: mstewart@entnet.org
Senior Director, Government Affairs: Joy Trimmer
  E-Mail: jtrimmer@entnet.org

Historical Note:

Affiliated with the International Federation of Oto-Rhino-Laryngological Societies and coordinates state and federal political action. AAO-HNS empowers otolaryngologist-head and neck surgeons to deliver quality patient care. Membership: $100-820 (Individual); $220 (Affiliate); $820 (Associate); $100-540 (International).

Continuing Education:
Enrollment: 30
Certification Designation/s: CPOP, MOC

Meetings/Conferences: Annual
Conference Chair: Mary Pat Cornett
2013 - Vancouver, BC (Vancouver Convention Centre)/Sept. 29 - Oct. 2
Number of non-conference events/year: 4

Publications:
Otolaryngology—Head and Neck Surgery; monthly; adv.
The Bulletin; monthly; adv.
The News; weekly; adv.

Membership List Available to Non-members

American Academy of Pain Management *(1988)*

975 Morning Star Dr.
Suite A
Sonora, CA 95370
Tel: (209) 533-9744 *Fax:* (209) 533-9750
E-Mail: aapm@aapainmanage.org
Website: aapainmanage.org
Members: 6000 individuals
Staff: 12
Annual Budget: $2-5,000,000
Tax: 501(c)(6)

Personnel:
Executive Director: Lennie Duensing MEd
  E-Mail: lduensing@aapainmanage.org
Controller: Jose Aguilera
Director, Publications: Carol Harper MA
  E-Mail: CHARPdesigns@comcast.net
Account Manager, Membership: Rosemary LeMay
  E-Mail: rosemary@aapainmanage.org
Director, Sales and Marketing: Jillian Manley
  E-Mail: jillian@yahoo.com
Director, Education: Debra Nelson-Hogan
  E-Mail: dhogan@seersha.com
Accounting Administrator: Mari Reddell
  E-Mail: mari@aapainmanage.org

Historical Note:

The mission of the American Academy of Pain Management is to advance the field of pain management using an integrative model of patient-centered care by providing evidence-based education for pain practitioners, as well as credentialing and advocacy for its members. Members are clinicians, students, hospitals, clinics, practices, other institutions and businesses that offer interdisciplinary pain management. Membership: $225 (General); $70 (Student); $1,500 (Health Care Provider); $7,500 (Corporate).

Continuing Education:
Certification Designation/s: CME, CE, CPE

Meetings/Conferences: Annual
Conference Chair: Jillian Manley
2013 - Orlando, FL (JW Marriott Orlando Grande Lakes)/Sept. 26 - 29

Publications:
Currents; monthly
The Pain Practitioner; quarterly; adv.

American Academy of Pain Medicine *(1983)*

4700 W. Lake Ave.
Glenview, IL 60025-1485
Tel: (847) 375-4731 *Fax:* (847) 375-6477
E-Mail: info@painmed.org
Website: painmed.org
Members: 2200 individuals
Staff: 12
Annual Budget: $2-5,000,000
Tax: 501(c)(6)

Personnel:
Executive Director: Phillip A. Saigh Jr.
Director, Communications: Susan M. Thompson
  E-Mail: sthompson@painmed.org

Historical Note:
Formerly the American Academy of Algology. AAPM's mission is to optimize the health of patients in pain and eliminate the major public health problem of pain by advancing the practice and the specialty of pain medicine. Members are physicians and surgeons who practice treating and studying pain disorders. Membership: $375 (Active); $190 (Affiliate); $250 (International); $0 (Student/Resident).

Continuing Education:
Certification Designation/s: ABPM, CME/CE

Meetings/Conferences: Annual
2013 - Ft. Lauderdale, FL (Greater Fort Lauderdale/Broward County Convention Center)/April 11 - 14/1-10 exhibitors

Publications:
AAPM eNews; bi-weekly
AAPMail; on-line
Membership Directory; annually
Pain Medicine Journal; semi-monthly; adv.

American Academy of Pediatric Dentistry *(1947)*

211 E. Chicago Ave.
Suite 1700
Chicago, IL 60611-2637
Tel: (312) 337-2169 *Fax:* (312) 337-6329
E-Mail: aapdinfo@aapd.org
Website: aapd.org
Members: 8401 members
Staff: 22
Annual Budget: $10-25,000,000
Tax: 501(c)(6)

Personnel:
Chief Executive Officer: John S. Rutkauskas CA, CAE, DDS
  E-Mail: jrutkauskar@aapd.org
Director, Meeting Services: Tonya Almond
Manager, Educational Affairs: Scott Dalhouse
  E-Mail: sdalhouse@aapd.org
Coordinator, Communications: Robert Gillmeiste
  E-Mail: rgillmeister@aapd.org
Manager, Publications: Cynthia Hansen
Chief Operating Officer and General Counsel: C. Scott Litch CAE, Esq.
  E-Mail: oed@aapd.org
Manager, Public Relations: Erika H. Skorupskas
  E-Mail: erika@aapd.org
Director, Membership Services and Marketing: Suzanne A. Wester
  E-Mail: swester@aapd.org
Director, Business Services: Margitta Winkler
  E-Mail: mw@aapd.org

Historical Note:
Formerly (1984) the American Academy of Pedodontics. Absorbed the Academy of Dentistry for Children in 2002.

AAPD's mission is to advocate policies, guidelines and programs that promote optimal oral health and oral health care for children. Also serves and represents its membership in the areas of professional development and governmental and legislative activities. Membership: $27-590/year.

Continuing Education:
Enrollment: 5

Meetings/Conferences: Annual
Conference Chair: Tonya Almond
2013 - Orlando, FL (Walt Disney World Resort)/May 23 - 26
2014 - Boston, MA (Sheraton Boston Hotel)/May 22 - 25

Publications:
Annual Session Program Book; annually; adv.
Journal of Dentistry for Children; adv.
Marketing Newsletter; on-line
Membership Directory; annually; adv.
Pediatric Dentistry; bi-monthly; adv.
Pediatric Dentistry Today; bi-monthly; adv.

American Academy of Pediatrics *(1930)*

141 N.W. Point Blvd.
Elk Grove Village, IL 60007-1098
Tel: (847) 434-4000 *Fax:* (847) 434-8000
TollFree: (800) 433-9016
E-Mail: kids1st@aap.org
Website: aap.org
Members: 60000 pediatricians
Staff: 441
Annual Budget: $50-100,000,000
Tax: 501(c)(3)

Personnel:
Executive Director: Errol R. Alden FAAP, MD
Washington Office Administrator: Katy Matthews
  E-Mail: kmatthews@aap.org
Director, Board Administration: Janice Page MPA
  E-Mail: jpage@aap.org
Manager, Medical Education: Theresa A. Woike
  E-Mail: twoike@aap.org

Historical Note:
AAP's mission is to attain optimal physical, mental, social health and well-being for all infants, children, adolescents, and young adults. Maintains a Washington office. Members include pediatricians, pediatric medical sub-specialists and pediatric surgical specialists. Membership: $579 (Fellow); $345 (Corresponding); $188 (Retired); $67 (Emeritus); $426 (Candidate); $314 (Associate); $177-345 (International); $90 (Resident/Post-Residency Training); $16 (Medical Student); $562 (Specialty Fellow).

Meetings/Conferences: Annual
2013 - Orlando, FL (Orange County Convention Center)/Oct. 26 - 29
2014 - San Diego, CA (San Diego Convention and Visitors Bureau)/Oct. 11 - 14
2015 - Chicago, IL/Oct. 17 - 20

Publications:
American Academy of Pediatrics Pediatric Coding Newsletter; monthly; adv.
Hospital Pediatrics; semi-annually; adv.
Membership Directory; on-line
PEDIATRICS; monthly; adv.
Red Book Online; on-line; adv.

American Academy of Periodontology *(1914)*

737 N. Michigan Ave.
Suite 800
Chicago, IL 60611-6660
Tel: (312) 787-5518 *Fax:* (312) 787-3670
Website: perio.org
Members: 8000 individuals
Staff: 43
Annual Budget: $10-25,000,000
Tax: 501(c)(6)

Personnel:
Executive Director: Alice DeForest
President: Pamela K. McClain
Senior Manager, Exhibits and Registration: Melodie Anderson
  E-Mail: melodie@perio.org

Historical Note:
Originated in Cleveland February 21, 1914 as the Academy of Oral Prophylaxis and Periodontology. Became the American Academy of Periodontology in 1919. AAP's mission is to provide members the expertise and resources to enhance the evaluation and diagnosis of oral conditions, assessment of risk for future disease, and delivery of specialty periodontal non-surgical, surgical and medical

care for patients. Membership: $890 (Active/Associate); $445 (International); $117 (Student).

Continuing Education:
Certification Designation/s: Diplomate

Meetings/Conferences:
Conference Chair: Melodie Anderson
2013 - Palm Spring, CA (JW Marriott Desert Springs Resort)/Feb. 8 - 10
2013 - Chicago, IL (Fairmont Hotel)/April 13 - 14
2013 - Boston, MA (Boston Marriott Copley Place)/ June 6 - 9
2013 - Philadelphia, PA/Sept. 28 - Oct. 1
2014 - San Francisco, CA/Sept. 19 - 22

Publications:
Clinical Advances in Periodontics; quarterly; adv.
E-news; monthly
Journal of Periodontology; monthly; adv.
Membership Directory; on-line

Membership List Available to Non-members

American Academy of Physical Medicine and Rehabilitation (1938)
9700 W. Bryn Mawr Ave.
Suite 200
Rosemont, IL 60018-5701
Tel: (847) 737-6000 Fax: (847) 737-6001
E-Mail: info@aapmr.org
Website: aapmr.org
Members: 8977 individuals
Staff: 32
Annual Budget: $10-25,000,000
Tax: 501(c)(3)

Personnel:
Executive Director: Thomas E. Stautzenbach CAE
Associate Director, Marketing and Communications: Joanne Constantine
    E-Mail: jconstantine@aapmr.org

Historical Note:
Founded as the American Society of Physical Therapy Physicians, became the American Society of Physical Medicine in 1944 and the present name was adopted in 1955. APM&R seeks to maximize the quality of life, while minimizing the incidence, severity, and prevalence of impairments, disabilities, and handicaps. Members are physiatrists practicing in the US and physicians who are Board-certified in physical medicine and rehabilitation. Membership: $0-645/year.

Meetings/Conferences: Annual
2013 - Washington, DC (Gaylord National-Washington)/Oct. 3 - 6
2014 - San Diego, CA (Marriott Convention Center)/ Nov. 13 - 16
2015 - Boston, MA (Marriott/Sheraton)/Oct. 1 - 4

Publications:
AAPM&R Connection E-Newsletter; semi-monthly
Membership Directory; on-line
PM&R Journal; monthly
PM&R Resident E-Newsletter; on-line
The Physiatrist Newsletter; adv.

Membership List Available to Non-members

American Academy of Physician Assistants (1968)
2318 Mill Rd.
Suite 1300
Alexandria, VA 22314
Tel: (703) 836-2272 Fax: (703) 684-1924
E-Mail: aapa@aapa.org
Website: aapa.org
Members: 39000 individuals
Staff: 87
Annual Budget: $10-25,000,000

Personnel:
Chief Executive Officer: Jennifer (Jenna) L. Dorn
    E-Mail: jdorn@aapa.org
Senior Vice President, Membership Services: Beth Bush
    E-Mail: bbush@aapa.org
Manager, Meetings and Events: Denise Cruse
    E-Mail: dcruse@aapa.org
Chief Financial Officer and Senior Vice President, Information Technology: Shyam Desigan
    E-Mail: sdesigan@aapa.org
Senior Vice President, Advocacy and Operations: James G. Potter
    E-Mail: jpotter@aapa.org
Senior Vice President and Chief Learning Officer: Mike Saxton, FACME, CCMEP MEd
    E-Mail: msaxton@aapa.org

Historical Note:
Formed by a group of physician assistants at Duke University in April 1968, sponsors the American Academy of Physician Assistants Political Action Committee and the Physician Assistant Foundation. AAPA's mission is to promote quality, cost-effective, accessible health care and to promote the professional and personal development of physician assistants. Membership: $75 (Student/ Sustaining/Affiliate/Physician); $275 (Fellow); $200 (Associate); $75 (Retired).

Continuing Education:
Certification Designation/s: CME

Meetings/Conferences: Annual
Conference Chair: Denise Cruse
2013 - Washington, DC/May 25 - 30
2014 - Boston, MA/May 24 - 29
2015 - San Francisco, CA/May 20 - 23
Number of non-conference events/year: 3

Publications:
AAPA Newsletter; on-line
Journal of the American Academy of Physician Assistants (JAAPA); monthly

American Academy of Physician Assistants in Occupational Medicine (1981)
174 Monticello Place
Elizabethtown, KY 42701
E-Mail: info@aapaoccmed.org
Website: aapaoccmed.org
Members: 250 individuals
Staff: 2
Annual Budget: $25-50,000

Personnel:
President: Thomas Powell PA-C
    E-Mail: oldnavypa@hotmail.com
Treasurer: Susan B. Golanski
    E-Mail: susangolanski@knology.net

Historical Note:
AAPA-OM is an educational organization representing physician assistants with an interest in the care of working people and the prevention of workplace illnesses and injuries. Administrative support provided by the American Academy of Physician Assistants. Membership: $75/year (Fellow/Physician); $10/year (Student); $50/year (Dual/ Associate).

Publications:
AAPA-OM Newsletter

American Academy of Podiatric Practice Management (1961)
1000 W. St Joseph Hwy.
Suite 200
Lansing, MI 48915
Tel: (517) 484-1930 Fax: (517) 485-9408
E-Mail: office@aappm.org
Website: aappm.com
Members: 800 individuals
Staff: 8
Annual Budget: $500-1,000,000
Tax: 501(c)(6)

Personnel:
Executive Director: Derek Dalling
    E-Mail: derek@aappm.org
Director, Meetings and Events: Kathe Biggs
    E-Mail: kathe@aappm.org
Administrative Assistant: Samantha Davis
Director, Membership Services: Michelle Dishaw
    E-Mail: michelle@aappm.org
Director, Finance: Denise Stone
    E-Mail: denise@aappm.org
Director, Graphic Design: Alicia Vazquez
    E-Mail: alicia@aappm.org

Historical Note:
Formerly (1993) American Academy of Podiatric Administration. Founded as American Academy of Practice Management in Podiatry and (1970) American Academy of Podiatric Management. AAPPM's mission is to positively change lives, practices and communities of podiatric physicians through leadership education, practice management education and sharing knowledge. AAPPM members are doctors of podiatric medicine interested in enhancing their professional efficiency and profits. Membership: $369 (Active); $169 (Associate 1 to 4-in practice 4 years or less/Senior Member); $139 (Executive Manager/Assistant Member); Free (Residents).

Continuing Education:
Certification Designation/s: CME

Meetings/Conferences: Annual
Conference Chair: Kathe Biggs

2013 - Coraopolis, PA (Pittsburgh Airport Marriott)/ Feb. 27 - March 3
Number of non-conference events/year: 2

Publications:
AAPPM Newsletter; quarterly
Membership Directory; on-line

American Academy of Podiatric Sports Medicine (1970)
3121 NE 26th St.
Ocala, FL 34470
Tel: (301) 845-9887
E-Mail: info@aapsm.org
Website: aapsm.org
Members: 700 individuals
Staff: 3
Annual Budget: $100-250,000
Tax: 501(c)(6)

Personnel:
Executive Director: Rita J. Yates
    E-Mail: ritayates2@aol.com

Historical Note:
Affiliated with the American Podiatric Medical Association, AAPSM serves to advance the understanding, prevention and management of lower extremity sports and fitness injuries. Membership: $200 (Individual); $25 (Student).

Meetings/Conferences: Annual
2013 - Las Vegas, NV/July 21 - 25
Number of non-conference events/year: 6

Publications:
Newsletter

American Academy of Political and Social Science (1889)
Annenberg Public Policy Center, 202 S. 36th St.
Philadelphia, PA 19104-3806
Tel: (215) 746-6500 Fax: (215) 573-2667
Website: aapss.org
Members: 2000 individuals
Staff: 2
Annual Budget: $500-1,000,000
Tax: 501(c)(3)

Personnel:
Executive Director: Tom Kecskemethy
    E-Mail: thomask@asc.upenn.edu
Managing Editor and Associate Director: Emily Wood
    E-Mail: ewood@asc.upenn.edu

Historical Note:
AAPSS seeks to advocate the progress of the social sciences and the use of social science knowledge in the enrichment of public understanding and in the development of public policy. Members are academics and others with an interest in the political and social sciences. Membership: $91- 659; $52-634 (Student).

Publications:
The Annals

American Academy of Professional Coders (1988)
2480 S. 3850 West
Suite B
Salt Lake City, UT 84120
Tel: (801) 236-2200 Fax: (801) 236-2258
TollFree: (800) 626-2633
E-Mail: aapc@aapc.com
Website: aapc.com
Members: 109000 members
Staff: 50

Personnel:
Chairman and Chief Executive Officer: Reed Pew
Vice President, Member Relations: Sherry Bernard
Director, Publishing and Warehouse: Brad Ericson
    E-Mail: brad.ericson@aapc.com
Officer, Member Relations: Melody S. Irvine CMRS, CPC
Director, Public Relations: Ben Jolley
    E-Mail: ben.jolley@aapc.com
Director, Conferences: Melanie Mestas
    E-Mail: melani.mestas@aapc.com
Director, Education: Nancy Reading RN
    E-Mail: nancy.reading@aapc.com

Historical Note:
Founded as American Academy of Procedural Coders, assumed its current name in 2001. AAPC was founded in an effort to elevate the standards of medical coding by providing certification, ongoing education, networking, and recognition. Members are medical coding professionals. Membership: $125 (Individual); $145 (International-

Individual); $70 (Student); $85 (International-Student); $750 (Corporate); $850 (International-Corporate).

Continuing Education:
Certification Designation/s: CPPM, CPC-H, CPC-P, CIRCC, CPMA, CPCO

Meetings/Conferences: Annual
Conference Chair: Melanie Mestas

Publications:
BillingInsider (e-Newsletter); monthly
Coding Edge; adv.
EdgeBlast (e-Newsletter); bi-monthly
ICD-10 Connect (e-Newsletter); monthly
Membership Directory; on-line

American Academy of Psychiatry and the Law
(1969)
One Regency Dr.
P.O. Box 30
Bloomfield, CT 06002
Tel: (860) 242-5450 *Fax:* (860) 286-0787
TollFree: (800) 331-1389
E-Mail: office@AAPL.org
Website: aapl.org
Members: 1500 individuals
Staff: 3
Annual Budget: $1-2,000,000
Tax: 501(c)(3)

Personnel:
Executive Director: Jacquelyn T. Coleman CAE
Editor: Ezra E.H. Griffith MD, CAE
Treasurer: Douglass Mossman MD

Historical Note:
AAPL seeks to promote scientific and educational activities in forensic psychiatry by facilitating the exchange of ideas and practical clinical experience through publications and regularly scheduled national and regional meetings. Members are forensic psychiatrists and general psychiatrists who have a professional interest in psychiatry and the law and are members of the American Psychiatric Association, the American Academy of Child and Adolescent Psychiatry or a national organization equivalent to the APA. Membership: $295 (General); $55 (Residents/Fellows); $95 (Correspondent).

Continuing Education:
Certification Designation/s: ABPN

Meetings/Conferences: Annual
2013 - Coronado, CA (Hotel del Coronado)/Oct. 24 - 27
2014 - Chicago, IL (Chicago Marriott Downtown Magnificent Mile)/Oct. 23 - 26
Number of non-conference events/year: 1

Publications:
AAPL Newsletter
Journal of the American Academy of Psychiatry and the Law

American Academy of Psychoanalysis and Dynamic Psychiatry *(1956)*
One Regency Dr.
P.O. Box 30
Bloomfield, CT 06002-0030
Fax: (860) 286-0787
TollFree: (888) 691-8281
E-Mail: info@aapdp.org
Website: aapdp.org
Members: 600 individuals
Staff: 4
Annual Budget: $100-250,000
Tax: 501(c)(3)

Personnel:
Executive Director: Jacquelyn T. Coleman CAE
Journal Editor: Douglas H. Ingram

Historical Note:
Formerly (1966) the Academy of Psychoanalysis and (2003) the American Academy of Psychoanalysis. AAPDP's mission to provide a forum for the expression of ideas, concepts, and research in psychodynamic psychiatry and psychoanalysis. Membership: $475/year.

Meetings/Conferences: Annual
2013 - San Francisco, CA/May 16 - 18
Number of non-conference events/year: 1

Publications:
Academy Forum
Academy News; bi-annually
Journal of the American Academy of Psychoanalysis and Dynamic Psychiatry; quarterly

Membership List Available to Non-members

American Academy of Psychotherapists *(1955)*
111 W. Main St.
Suite 100
Garner, NC 27529
Tel: (919) 779-5051 *Fax:* (919) 779-5642
E-Mail: aap@mgmt4u.com
Website: aapweb.com
Members: 600 individuals
Staff: 3
Annual Budget: $250-500,000
Tax: 501(c)(3)

Personnel:
Executive Director: Shaun Barbour CEO, PhD
    E-Mail: aap@mgmt4u.com
Editor: Wendy Graham

Historical Note:
AAP's mission is to advocate the development of experienced psychotherapists, to challenge the experienced practitioner to professional excellence and to explore the relationship of person and process to psychotherapy. Members are professional societies of practicing psychotherapists.

Meetings/Conferences: Annual
Conference Chair: Gordon Cohen PsyD
2013 - Boulder, CO (The Millennium Harvest House Hotel)/June 5 - 9

Publications:
AAP Newsletter; quarterly; adv.
Membership Directory; on-line

Membership List Available to Non-members

American Academy of Religion *(1909)*
825 Houston Mill Rd. NE
Suite 300
Atlanta, GA 30329-4205
Tel: (404) 727-3049 *Fax:* (404) 727-7959
E-Mail: aar@aarweb.org
Website: aarweb.org
Members: 10000 individuals
Staff: 19
Annual Budget: $2-5,000,000

Personnel:
Executive Director: John R. Fitzmier
    E-Mail: jfitzmier@aarweb.org
Coordinator, Membership Services: Paula Forte
    E-Mail: pforte@aarweb.org
Associate Director, Publications: Stephanie Gray
    E-Mail: sgray@aarweb.org
Chief Information Officer: Steve Herrick
    E-Mail: sherrick@aarweb.org
Director, Communications and Marketing: Aislinn Jones
    E-Mail: ajones@aarweb.org
Director, Finance and Administration: Deborah Minor
    E-Mail: dminor@aarweb.org
Director, Meetings: Robert Puckett
    E-Mail: rpuckett@aarweb.org
Coordinator, Conferences: Soraya Shahrak
    E-Mail: sshahrak@aarweb.org

Historical Note:
Formerly (1964) National Association of Biblical Instructors. A member of the American Council of Learned Socs. and the National Humanities Alliance. AAR's mission is to promote understanding of religious traditions, issues, questions, and values through excellence in scholarship and teaching in the field of religion. Members include students, persons who study religion outside the field and members of the profession in colleges, universities and seminaries. Membership: $50-200 (Professional/Retired); $50 (Student); $500 (Supporting Member); $1,000 (Sustaining Member); $15 (Special-International).

Meetings/Conferences: Annual
Conference Chair: Robert Puckett
2013 - Baltimore, MD/Nov. 23 - 26/10000 attendees/ over 100 exhibitors
2014 - San Diego, CA/Nov. 22 - 25/10000 attendees/ over 100 exhibitors
2015 - Atlanta, GA/Nov. 21 - 24/10000 attendees/over 100 exhibitors
2016 - San Antonio, TX/Nov. 19 - 22/10000 attendees/over 100 exhibitors
2017 - Boston, MA/Nov. 18 - 21/10000 attendees/over 100 exhibitors
2018 - Denver, CO/Nov. 17 - 20/10000 attendees/over 100 exhibitors
2019 - San Diego, CA/Nov. 23 - 26/10000 attendees/ over 100 exhibitors
2020 - Boston, MA/Nov. 21 - 24/10000 attendees/over 100 exhibitors
2021 - San Antonio, TX/Nov. 20 - 23/10000 attendees/over 100 exhibitors

Publications:
e-Bulletin; monthly; adv.
Journal of the American Academy of Religion:; quarterly; adv.
Membership Directory; on-line
Religious Studies News; quarterly; adv.
Religious Studies News (RSN); quarterly; adv.

Membership List Available to Non-members

American Academy of Research Historians of Medieval Spain *(1973)*
Department of History
Columbia University, 1180 Amsterdam Ave.
New York, NY 10027
E-Mail: mailbox@aarhms.org
Website: humweb.ucsc.edu/aarhms/index.php
Members: 200 individuals
Staff: 4
Annual Budget: Under $10,000
Tax: 501(c)(3)

Personnel:
President: Adam J. Kosto
    E-Mail: president@aarhms.org

Historical Note:
Founded as the Academy of American Research Historians on Medieval Spain, assumed its current name in 1980. AARHMS, an affiliated Society of the American Historical Association, serves to promote and facilitate the study of the history of the Iberian Peninsula during the Middle Ages. Membership is open to scholars of all relevant Humanities and Social Science disciplines, including but not limited to History, Literature, Art History, History of Science and Technology, Religious Studies, Jewish Studies, and Islamic Studies. Membership: $15/year (Individual).

Meetings/Conferences:
Conference Chair: James Todesca

Publications:
AARHMS Newsletter; bi-annually
Journal of Medieval Iberian Studies; semi-annually
Membership Directory

American Academy of Restorative Dentistry
(1921)
Dept. of Restorative Sciences
3302 Gaston Ave.
Dallas, TX 75246
Tel: (214) 828-8370 *Fax:* (214) 874-4544
Website: restorativeacademy.com
Members: 400 individuals
Staff: 1
Annual Budget: $250-500,000

Personnel:
President: Dr. Frank L. Higginbottom
    E-Mail: bottom@dallasesthetics.com

Historical Note:
Formerly known as the American Society of Dental Ceramics, the purpose of the Academy is to promote the improvement of the health of the public, and the quality of the art and science of restorative dentistry. Members are dentists in general practice with an interest in advanced restorative procedures and materials. Membership is by invitation only.

Meetings/Conferences: Annual
2013 - Chicago, IL (Ritz Carlton Hotel)/Feb. 23 - 24

Publications:
Journal of Prosthetic Dentistry; monthly; adv.

American Academy of Sanitarians *(1966)*
C/O Gary P. Noonan
1568 Le Grand Cir.
Lawrenceville, GA 30043-8191
Tel: (678) 407-1051 *Fax:* (678) 407-1051
E-Mail: sanitarians@sanitarians.org
Website: sanitarians.org
Members: 300 individuals
Staff: 1
Annual Budget: Under $10,000

Personnel:
Executive Secretary and Treasurer: Gary P. Noonan
    E-Mail: exec-sec@sanitarians.org

Historical Note:
AAS members are licensed sanitarians with at least an M.A. in environmental health sciences, environmental

management or public health. Membership: $50/year (Individual).

Continuing Education:
Certification Designation/s: DAAS

Meetings/Conferences: Annual
2013 - Washington, DC/July 9 - 11

Publications:
Membership Roster; on-line
Register of Diplomates; on-line

American Academy of Sleep Medicine *(1975)*
2510 N. Frontage Rd.
Darien, IL 60561
Tel: (630) 737-9700 Fax: (630) 737-9790
E-Mail: inquiries@aasmnet.org
Website: aasmnet.org
Members: 8742 individuals and 1173 centers
Staff: 50
Annual Budget: $10-25,000,000
Tax: 501(c)(6)

Personnel:
Executive Director: Jerome A. Barrett
    E-Mail: jbarrett@aasmnet.org
Director, Government Relations Activities: Bruce Blehart
    E-Mail: bblehart@aasmnet.org
Assistant Executive Director: Kathleen McCann RN, PhD
    E-Mail: kmccann@aasmnet.org
Director, Meeting Management: Becky Roberts
    E-Mail: broberts@aasmnet.org

Historical Note:
AASM was formerly (1975) American Association of Sleep Disorder Centers, (1987) Association of Sleep Disorders Centers, and (1999) American Sleep Disorders Association. AASM's mission is to serve its members and advance the field of sleep health care by setting the clinical standards for the field of sleep medicine. Membership: $125 (Individual-Regular/Affiliate); $20 (Student); $400 (Individual-Affiliate Industry); $20 (Emeritus); $125 (Fellow); $85 (Corresponding); $1,100 (Center).

Continuing Education:
Certification Designation/s: CBSM

Meetings/Conferences: Annual
Conference Chair: Becky Roberts

Publications:
SLEEP
Directory Listings; on-line
Journal of Clinical Sleep Medicine (JCSM); on-line; adv.
Membership Directory; on-line

Membership List Available to Non-members

American Academy of Somnology *(1986)*
P.O. Box 27077
Las Vegas, NV 89126-1077
Tel: (702) 371-0947
E-Mail: somnology@aol.com
Website: hopperinstitute.com/aas_intro.html
Members: 75 individuals
Staff: 6
Annual Budget: Under $10,000

Personnel:
President: David L. Hopper PhD
    E-Mail: drdavelv@aol.com

Historical Note:
AAS is an educational, scientific, and professional organization dedicated to advance the understanding of sleep and sleep related processes. AAS bestows the title "fellow" and other recognition on individuals who have made outstanding contributions to the field of somnology. Membership: $35-95/year.

American Academy of State Certified Appraisers
1438-F W. Main St.
Ephrata, PA 17522-1345
Tel: (717) 721-3500 Fax: (717) 721-3515
E-Mail: jjm@intercorpinc.net
Members: 4000 individuals
Staff: 2
Annual Budget: $100-250,000

Personnel:
Executive Director: John J. Matternas
    E-Mail: jjm@intercorpinc.net

Historical Note:
Works to advance the interests of state certified real estate appraisers.

American Academy of Teachers of Singing *(1922)*
777 W. End Ave.

Apartment 8A
New York, NY 10025-5551
Tel: (212) 666-1166
E-Mail:
info@americanacademyofteachersofsinging.org
Website:
    americanacademyofteachersofsinging.org
Members: 40 individuals
Staff: 3
Annual Budget: Under $10,000

Personnel:
Vice Chairman: Jan Eric Douglas
    E-Mail: jandouglas@aol.com
Publications Officer: Robert Gartside
    E-Mail: publications@
    americanacademyofteachersofsinging.org
Treasurer: Jeanne Goffi-Fynn
    E-Mail: jeanniegoffi@yahoo.com

Historical Note:
AATS acts as a consulting body to the profession on various topics of significance and interest. Members are faculty at prestigious universities, conservatories, or symposia and esteemed performers of classical and non-classical repertoire. Membership is exclusively by inner nomination and new members are nominated by current active members only when there is a vacancy. All nominees must have no more than two dissenting votes to become members, and when accepted, membership is for life.

American Academy of the History of Dentistry *(1951)*
284 Harvard St.
Brookline, MD 02446
Fax: (617) 731-8724
E-Mail: info@histden.org
Website: histden.org
Members: 400 individuals
Staff: 3
Annual Budget: $25-50,000
Tax: 501(c)(3)

Personnel:
Editor: David A. Chernin DMD, MLS
    E-Mail: editor@histden.org

Historical Note:
AAHD's mission is to support and encourage the study, teaching and appreciation of the history of dentistry. Membership: $95 (Regular); $105 (Foreign); $25 (Student); $125-150 (Institution); $1,500 (Lifetime).

Meetings/Conferences: Annual

Publications:
Journal of the History of Dentistry; annually; adv.

American Academy of Thermology *(1971)*
500 Duvall Dr.
Greenville, SC 29607
Tel: (864) 675-1031 Fax: (864) 675-1031
E-Mail:
info@americanacademyofthermology.org
Website: aathermology.org
Members: 250 individuals
Staff: 3
Annual Budget: Under $10,000

Personnel:
Executive Director: Jeff Lefko MHA
Vice President: Srini Govindan MD
President: Robert G. Schwartz MD

Historical Note:
Formed as the American Thermographic Society, assumed its present name in 1983. AAT'S purpose is to promote scientific development and clinical application of medical infrared imaging. Membership composed of physicians involved with the use of infrared and liquid cholesteric imaging in medical diagnosis. Membership: $150/year (Non-Physician); $250 (Physician); $100 (Student/Resident/Fellowship Training/New Member/Senior Member/Student/ Fellow) .

Continuing Education:
Certification Designation/s: AAT

Meetings/Conferences: Annual

Publications:
Thermology International

American Academy of Veterinary Acupuncture *(1998)*
P.O. Box 1058
Glastonbury, CT 06033
Tel: (860) 632-9911 Fax: (860) 659-8772
Staff: 2

Annual Budget: $100-250,000

Personnel:
Executive Director: Simon A. Flynn
Treasurer: Liane Sperlich CVA, DVM

Historical Note:
AAVA's mission is to improve animal health care by the advancement of veterinary acupuncture and Traditional Chinese Veterinary Medicine through education, research and leadership. Membership: $225/year.

Continuing Education:
Certification Designation/s: FAAVA

Meetings/Conferences: Annual
2013 - New Orleans, LA (Hotel Monteleone)/May 16 - 19

Publications:
American Journal of Traditional Chinese Veterinary Medicine (AJTCVM)
Member Directory; on-line
The Meridian; quarterly

American Academy of Veterinary and Comparative Toxicology *(1958)*
North Dakota State University, Veterinary Diagnostic Laboratory
P.O. Box 5406
Fargo, ND 58105-5406
Tel: (701) 231-7529 Fax: (701) 231-7514
E-Mail: acvs@acvs.org
Members: 220 individuals
Staff: 1
Annual Budget: $10-25,000

Personnel:
Secretary/Treasurer: Michelle S. Mostrom
    E-Mail: michelle.monstrom@ndsu.nodak.edu

Historical Note:
Organized in 1957, and incorporated Jan. 15, 1958 in Salt Lake City. Formerly (1984) the American College of Veterinary Toxicologists. Concerned with education, research and exchange of proven methods and procedures in the field of veterinary toxicology. Encourages the use of uniform toxicologic nomenclature. Membership: $60/year.

American Academy of Veterinary Pharmacology and Therapeutics *(1977)*
Dechra Development
7015 College Blvd., Suite 510
Overland Park, KS 66211
E-Mail: aavptst@hotmail.com
Website: aavpt.org
Members: 200 individuals
Staff: 4
Annual Budget: $25-50,000

Personnel:
Secretary: Susan L. Longhofer
    E-Mail: aavptsec@gmail.com
Editor: Jim E. Riviere

Historical Note:
Formerly (1981) American College of Veterinary Pharmacology and Therapeutics. AAVPT's purpose is to support and promote education and research in comparative pharmacology, clinical veterinary pharmacology and other aspects of pharmacology of interest to the veterinary profession. Members are veterinary pharmacologists and veterinarians. Membership: $45 (Fellow); $35 (Regular); $20 (Student).

Meetings/Conferences: Biennial
2013 - Potomac, MD (Bolger Center)/May 19 - 22

Publications:
AAPVT Newsletter; semi-annually
Journal of Veterinary Pharmacology and Therapeutics; bi-monthly; adv.
Membership Directory

American Academy of Wound Management *(1995)*
1155 15th St. NW
Suite 500
Washington, DC 20005
Tel: (202) 457-8408 Fax: (202) 530-0659
E-Mail: info@aawm.org
Website: aawm.org
Members: 1790 individuals
Staff: 5
Annual Budget: $500-1,000,000

Personnel:
Executive Director: Christopher M. Murphy
    E-Mail: cmurphy@aawm.org

Legal Counsel: Lynn D. Fleisher JD, PhD
   E-Mail: lfleisher@sidley.com
Director, Marketing: Carrie L. Hoffman
   E-Mail: choffman@abwmcertified.org
Manager, Certification and Administration: Luke Zorich
   E-Mail: lzorich@abwmcertified.org

Historical Note:
The purpose of the AAWM is to establish and administer a certification process to elevate the standard of care across the continuum of wound management. The Academy is dedicated to an interdisciplinary approach in promoting prevention, care and treatment of acute and chronic wounds. Membership: $400 (Certification); $150 (Certification Renewal).

Continuing Education:
Certification Designation/s: CWCA, CWS

Publications:
Newsletter

American Academy on Communication in Healthcare *(1993)*
201 E. Main St., Suite 1405
Lexington, KY 40507
Tel: (859) 514-9150 *Fax:* (859) 514-9207
E-Mail: info@aachonline.org
Website: aachonline.org
Members:
815 individuals
425 individuals
Staff: 12
Annual Budget: $500-1,000,000

Personnel:
Executive Director: Lisa Thompson
   E-Mail: lthompson@amrms.com
Finance Specialist: Robin Boucher
   E-Mail: boucher@aachonline.org
Vice President, Financial Services: Dianne Brncic
   E-Mail: brncic@aachonline.org
Coordinator, Education: Laura Cooley PhD
   E-Mail: cooley@aachonline.org
Director, Member Services: Sherry Erker
   E-Mail: erker@aachonline.org
Marketing and Communications Specialist: Laura Sienaski-Lancia
   E-Mail: laura@aachonline.org
Director, Meetings and Events: Miriam Yanders
   E-Mail: yanders@drakeco.com

Historical Note:
Formerly the American Academy on Physician and Patient. AACH is dedicated to research, education and professional standards in patient-clinician communication. Membership: $235 (Professional); $69 (Associate).

Meetings/Conferences: Semi-Annual
Conference Chair: Miriam Yanders
Number of non-conference events/year: 1

Publications:
Medical Encounter; quarterly; adv.
PEC Journal; monthly
The Scope; monthly; adv.

American Accordionists Association *(1938)*
152 Home Fair Dr.
Fairfield, CT 06825
Tel: (203) 335-2045 *Fax:* (203) 335-2048
E-Mail: aaa1938@aol.com
Website: ameraccord.com
Members: 17000 individuals
Staff: 3
Annual Budget: $50-100,000

Personnel:
President Emerita: Faithe Deffner
President: Linda Soley Reed
   E-Mail: lsoleyreed@aol.com
Secretary and Treasurer: Dr. Robert Young McMahan

Historical Note:
AAA's mission is to organize, sponsor and support workshops advancing educational and artistic levels of accordion enthusiasts. Members are teachers, manufacturers, importers, performers, amateurs and suppliers. Membership: $65 (Full); $35 (Associate).

Meetings/Conferences: Annual
Number of non-conference events/year: 4

Publications:
Membership Directory; on-line

American Accounting Association *(1916)*
5717 Bessie Dr.

Sarasota, FL 34233-2399
Tel: (941) 921-7747 *Fax:* (941) 923-4093
E-Mail: info@aaahq.org
Website: aaahq.org
Members: 8210 individuals
Staff: 24
Annual Budget: $5-10,000,000
Tax: 501(c)(3)

Personnel:
Executive Director: Tracey Sutherland
   E-Mail: tracey@aaahq.org
Manager, Web and Database Project: Kathy Casper
   E-Mail: Kathy@aaahq.org
Manager, Web and Social Media: Judy Cothern
   E-Mail: Judy@aaahq.org
Director, Meetings Planning: Debora Gardner
   E-Mail: debbie@aaahq.org
Director, Special Projects: Beverly Harrelson
   E-Mail: beverly@aaahq.org
Coordinator, Membership and Communications: Deirdre Harris
   E-Mail: deirdre@aaahq.org
Director, Publications: Diane Hazard CAE, PhD
   E-Mail: diane@aaahq.org
Director, Finance: Diane Leger
   E-Mail: Dianel@aaahq.org
Director, Meetings and Education Services: Gay F. Williams CAE
   E-Mail: GWilliams@aaahq.org

Historical Note:
Formerly (1935) the American Association of University Instructors in Accounting. AAA promotes accounting education, research and practice. Membership dues include online access to one, two, or three Association journals. Membership: $205 (Full); $30 (Emeritus); $20 (Life membership with electronic journal access); $35 (Student Member)

Meetings/Conferences:
Conference Chair: Debora Gardner
2013 - Ft. Lauderdale, FL (Bahia Mar – Fort Lauderdale Beach)/Jan. 10 - 12
2013 - New Orleans, LA (New Orleans Marriott)/Jan. 10 - 12
2013 - San Diego, CA (Westin San Diego)/Jan. 11 - 12
2013 - New Orleans, LA (New Orleans Marriott)/Jan. 17 - 19
2013 - San Diego, CA (DoubleTree San Diego Mission Valley)/Feb. 10 - 12
2013 - Savannah, GA (Hyatt Regency Savannah)/Feb. 21 - 23
2013 - St. Petersburg, FL (Hilton St. Petersburg Bayfront)/March 8 - 9
2013 - New Orleans, LA (Hyatt French Quarter)/March 22 - 23
Number of non-conference events/year: 1

Publications:
AAA Section Journal; adv.
AAA Section Newsletter; on-line; adv.
Accounting and the Public Interest; on-line; adv.
Accounting Education News; quarterly; adv.
Accounting Horizons; quarterly; adv.
Accounting Review; bi-monthly; adv.
Auditing: A Journal of Practice & Theory; quarterly; adv.
Behavioral Research in Accounting; semi-annually; adv.
Current Issues in Auditing; semi-annually; adv.
Issues in Accounting Education; quarterly; adv.
Journal of Emerging Technologies in Accounting; annually; adv.
Journal of Information Systems; semi-annually; adv.
Journal of International Accounting Research; semi-annually; adv.
Journal of Management Accounting Research; annually; adv.
Journal of the American Taxation Association; semi-annually

American Advertising Federation *(1968)*
1101 Vermont Ave. NW
Suite 500
Washington, DC 20005
Tel: (202) 898-0089 *Fax:* (202) 898-0159
TollFree: (800) 999-2231
E-Mail: aaf@aaf.org
Website: aaf.org

Members: 40000 professionals, 7500 undergraduate student, 225 affiliated chapters and 250 faculty advisers
Staff: 27
Annual Budget: $5-10,000,000

Personnel:
President and Chief Executive Officer: James Edmund Datri
   E-Mail: jdatri@aaf.org
Senior Vice President, Conference Services: Karen Cohn
   E-Mail: kcohn@aaf.org
Database Coordinator: Lucille Hill
   E-Mail: lhill@aaf.org
Executive Vice President, Government Affairs: Clark E. Rector
   E-Mail: crector@aaf.org
Executive Vice President, Club Services: Joanne Schecter
   E-Mail: jschecter@aaf.org

Historical Note:
Formed by a merger of the Advertising Federation of America and the Advertising Association of the West (formerly Pacific Advertising Association). AAF's mission is to protect and promote the well-being of advertising. Membership: $35/year (Student).

Meetings/Conferences: Annual
Conference Chair: Karen Cohn
2013 - Phoenix, AZ (Arizona Biltmore Resort and Spa)/June 5 - 8
Number of non-conference events/year: 2

Publications:
Internship Directory; on-line
Membership Directory; on-line

American Agents Alliance *(1962)*
1029 J. St.
Suite 120
Sacramento, CA 95814
Tel: (916) 283-9473 *Fax:* (916) 283-9479
TollFree: (866) 497-9222
E-Mail: info@agentsalliance.com
Website: agentsalliance.com
Members: 700 individuals
Staff: 5
Annual Budget: $500-1,000,000

Personnel:
President and Chief Executive Officer: Ken May
Contact, Membership Services: Martha Armas-Kelly
   E-Mail: martha@agentsalliance.com
Chief Operating Officer: Mike D'arelli

Historical Note:
The American Agents Alliance, a member-driven organization since 1962, empowers independent insurance agents and brokers to thrive through advocacy, education and networking.

Meetings/Conferences: Annual

American Aging Association *(1970)*
25373 Tyndall Falls Dr.
Olmsted Falls, OH 44138
Tel: (440) 793-6565 *Fax:* (440) 793-6598
E-Mail: americanaging@case.edu
Website: americanaging.org
Members: 200 individuals
Staff: 2
Annual Budget: $100-250,000
Tax: 501(c)(3)

Personnel:
President and Contact, Meeting: Michael J. Forster PhD
Secretary: Julie Mattison PhD

Historical Note:
AGE's mission is to promote biomedical aging studies directed towards increasing the functional life span of humans with one goal being to slow the aging process. Membership: $130 (Scientific); $60 (Trainee/Lay/Student).

Meetings/Conferences: Annual
Conference Chair: Michael J. Forster PhD

Publications:
American Aging Association Newsletter; monthly
Journal of the American Aging Association; quarterly

Membership List Available to Non-members

American Agricultural Editors Association *(1921)*
P.O. Box 156
New Prague, MN 56071
Tel: (952) 758-6502 *Fax:* (952) 758-5813

E-Mail:
aaea@gardnerandgardnercommunications.com
Website: ageditors.com
Members: 400 individuals
Staff: 4
Annual Budget: $100-250,000
Tax: 501(c)(6)

Personnel:
Executive Director: Den Gardner
 E-Mail:
 aaea@gardnerandgardnercommunications.com
Contact, Membership Renewal and Directory: Kathy Heyda
 E-Mail: kathyheyda@
 gardnerandgardnercommunications.com
Associate Director, Conferences and Co-Editor: Kenna Rathai
 E-Mail: kenna.rathai@kbrcommunications.com
Contact, Administration and Membership Services: Barbara Ulschmid
 E-Mail: barbaraulschmid@
 gardenandgardencommunications.com

Historical Note:
AAEA's mission is to provide opportunities for professional improvement and networking to agricultural editors, writers and photojournalists. Membership: $25 (Student); $87.50 (Retired); $100 (Active/Affiliate); $612.50 (Lifetime).

Meetings/Conferences: Annual
Conference Chair: Kenna Rathai
2013 - Buffalo, NY (Hyatt Regency Buffalo Hotel And Conference Center)/Aug. 3 - 7
2014 - Indianapolis, IN (Indianapolis Marriott Downtown)/July 26 - 30

Publications:
ByLine Newsletter
Membership Directory; annually

Membership List Available to Non-members

American Agricultural Law Association (1980)
127 Young Rd.
Kelso, WA 98626
Tel: (360) 200-5699 *Fax:* (360) 423-2287
Website: aglaw-assn.org
Members: 650 individuals
Staff: 1
Annual Budget: $100-250,000
Tax: 501(c)(6)

Personnel:
Executive Director: Robert P. Achenbach Jr.
 E-Mail: roberta@aglaw-assn.org

Historical Note:
AALA's mission is to focus on the legal needs of the agricultural community. Membership: $125 (Regular); $30 (Student); $75 (New Professional); $350 (Institutional); $200 (Sustaining).

Meetings/Conferences: Annual
Publications:
Membership Directory; on-line
Newsletter; monthly

Membership List Available to Non-members

American Agricultural Marketing Association (1960)
111 N. st.
Chicago, IL 57845
Staff: 1

Personnel:
Treasurer: Mark Jog

American Agriculture Movement, Inc. (1977)
3603 S. Hwy 78
Bonham, TX 75418
Tel: (903) 583-4388
E-Mail: adchaney@yahoo.com
Website: aaminc.org
Members: 42 state organizations
Staff: 6
Annual Budget: Under $10,000

Personnel:
Executive Vice President: Arthur Chaney
 E-Mail: adchaney@yahoo.com
President: Larry Matlack
 E-Mail: larry@stingerltd.com
Vice President, Political Action: Wayne Allen
Vice President, Marketing: Lynn Kirkpatrick

E-Mail: lynnkirk@nemr.net
Vice President, Communications: Christine Miller
 E-Mail: cemiller39@googlemail.com
Vice President, Membership: Marc Wetzel
 E-Mail: dcrain115@aol.com

Historical Note:
AAM is an umbrella organization composed of state organizations representing family farm producers for all sectors of agriculture. Membership: $21.25-100/year.

Meetings/Conferences: Annual

Publications:
The AAM Newsletter

American Alliance for Health, Physical Education, Recreation and Dance (1885)
1900 Association Dr.
Reston, VA 20191-1598
Tel: (703) 476-3400 *Fax:* (703) 476-9527
TollFree: (800) 213-7193
E-Mail: info@aahperd.org
Website: aahperd.org
Members: 4000 professionals
Staff: 98
Annual Budget: $10-25,000,000

Personnel:
Chief Executive Officer: LTGEN Paul Roetert
 E-Mail: proetert@aahperd.org
Director, Membership Services: Eric Berkowitz
 E-Mail: eberkowitz@aahperd.org
Senior Manager, Government Relations: Carly Braxton
 E-Mail: cbraxton@aahperd.org
Manager, Marketing: Vicki Santaniello
 E-Mail: vsantaniello@aahperd.org
Director, Events Management: Sandra Sumner
 E-Mail: ssumner@aahperd.org
Vice President, Programs: Judith Young
 E-Mail: jyoung@aahperd.org

Historical Note:
Formerly (1903) known as the American Association for Advancement of Physical Education; renamed to the American Alliance for Health, Physical Education and Recreation in 1974 and assumed its present name in 1979. AAHPERD's mission is to promote and support leadership, research, education, and best practices in the professions that support creative, healthy, and active lifestyles. It is composed of the American Association for Leisure and Recreation, American Association for Health Education, American Association for Active Lifestyles and Fitness, National Association for Girls and Women in Sports, National Association for Sport and Physical Education and the National Dance Association. Membership: $135 (Professional); $50 (Student).

Meetings/Conferences: Annual
Conference Chair: Sandra Sumner
2013 - Charlotte, NC (Charlotte Convention Center)/April 23 - 27/5000 attendees/1-10 exhibitors
2014 - St. Louis, MO (America's Center Convention Complex)/March 18 - 22/5000 attendees/1-10 exhibitors
2015 - Seatle, WA (Washington State Convention Center)/March 17 - 21/5000 attendees/1-10 exhibitors
2016 - Minneapolis, MN (Minneapolis Convention Center)/April 5 - 9/5000 attendees/1-10 exhibitors
Number of non-conference events/year: 5

Publications:
American Journal of Health Education; adv.
Et Cetera; weekly
Health Education Teaching Techniques Journal; on-line
International Journal of Health Education; on-line
Journal of Coaching Education; on-line
Journal of Physical Education, Recreation & Dance; adv.
Research Quarterly for Exercise and Sport; quarterly; adv.
Strategies; bi-monthly; adv.
UpdatePLUS; on-line; adv.
Women in Sport and Physical Activity Journal; on-line

Membership List Available to Non-members

American Alliance for Theatre and Education (1987)
4908 Auburn Ave.
Bethesda, MD 20814
Tel: (301) 200-1944 *Fax:* (301) 280-1682
E-Mail: info@aate.com
Website: aate.com
Members:

240 organizations
1000 individuals
Staff: 4
Annual Budget: $250-500,000
Tax: 501(c)(3)

Personnel:
Executive Director: Marcie Granahan
 E-Mail: marcie@aate.com
Managing Editor: Kate Marshall
 E-Mail: katherine.marshall@taylorandfrancis.com
Coordinator, Membership and Marketing: Kelly Prestel
 E-Mail: kelly@aate.com
Manager, Operations: Alexis Truitt
 E-Mail: alexis@aate.com

Historical Note:
Created by the merger of American Association of Theatre for Youth with American Association of Theatre in Secondary Education in 1987. Both organizations were originally divisions of the American Theatre Association (Children's Theatre Association and Secondary School Theatre Association) which were reorganized independently when ATA ceased operations in 1986. AATE connects and inspires a growing collective of theatre artists, educators, and scholars committed to transforming young people and communities through the theatre arts. Members are educators, artists, administrators and others serving young people in professional and community youth theatres and theatre educational programs. Membership: $115 (Individual); $220 (Organization); $60 (Students); $70 (Retired); $310 (University); $550 (Corporate).

Meetings/Conferences: Annual
Publications:
Incite/Insight; monthly; adv.
Youth Theatre Journal; semi-annually; adv.

Membership List Available to Non-members

American Alliance of Home Modification Professionals (AAHMP) (2009)
32-75 Steinway St.
Astoria, NY 11103
Tel: (718) 874-9475 *Fax:* (949) 267-1453
Website: aahmp.org
Staff: 1

Personnel:
Executive Director: Steven Gillan

Historical Note:
AAHMP is dedicated to the mission of aggregating the trained professional required to address the crisis.

Continuing Education:
Certification Designation/s: LMC

Publications:
Membership Directory; on-line
Newsletter; on-line

American Ambulance Association (1979)
8400 Westpark Dr.
Second Floor
McLean, VA 22102
Tel: (703) 610-9018 *Fax:* (703) 610-0210
TollFree: (800) 523-4447
Website: the-aaa.org
Members: 950 companies
Staff: 6
Annual Budget: $2-5,000,000
Tax: 501(c)(6)

Personnel:
Executive Vice President: Maria Bianchi CAE
 E-Mail: mbianchi@the-aaa.org
Director, Meetings: Kim Almstedt CMP
 E-Mail: kalmstedt@the-aaa.org
Director, Membership Services and Communications: Erin Fano
 E-Mail: efano@the-aaa.org
Senior Vice President, Government Affairs: Tristan M. North
 E-Mail: tnorth@the-aaa.org

Historical Note:
Product of a merger of the Ambulance Association of America formed in 1962 and the National Ambulance and Medical Services Association formed in 1963 and formerly (until 1979) known as the Ambulance and Medical Services Association of America. AAA strives to promote health care policies that ensure excellence in the ambulance services industry and provide research, education and communications programs to enable its members to address the needs of the communities they serve. Members are private ambulance services, but municipal and volunteer ambulance services can join as associate members.

Membership: $1216 (Affiliate); $287 (State Association Member); $8,774 (Active/Multi-State Provider); $218-807 (Associate).

Meetings/Conferences: Annual
Conference Chair: Kim Almstedt CMP
Number of non-conference events/year: 4

Publications:
AAA Weekly e-update; on-line
Ambulance Service Journal; on-line; adv.

American Amusement Machine Association
(1981)
450 E. Higgins Rd.
Suite 201
Elk Grove Village, IL 60007
Tel: (847) 290-9088 *Fax:* (847) 290-9121
TollFree: (866) 372-5190
E-Mail: information@coin-op.org
Website: coin-op.org
Members: 170 companies
Staff: 3
Annual Budget: $1-2,000,000
Tax: 501(c)(6)

Personnel:
President: John Schultz
  E-Mail: jschultz@coin-op.org
Administrative Assistant: Jennifer Anker
Manager, Business and Finance: Tina Schwartz
  E-Mail: tschwartz@coin-op.org

Historical Note:
Formerly known as the Amusement Device Manufacturers Association, assumed its present name in 1985. AAMA's mission is to preserve, protect and encourage the coin-operated entertainment industry. Members are manufacturers, distributors and parts suppliers of coin-operated games and machines. Membership: $1,800 (Manufacturer/Distributor); $745 (Associate).

Meetings/Conferences:
Conference Chair: Tina Schwartz
Number of non-conference events/year: 1

Publications:
Loose Change E-Newsletter; monthly
Membership Directory; on-line

American and Delaine-Merino Record Association
(1906)
7744 State Route 613
McComb, OH 45858
Tel: (740) 686-2172
Website: admra.org
Members: 200 flocks
Staff: 3
Annual Budget: Under $10,000

Personnel:
President: Bob Calvert
Secretary/Treasurer: Amy Schroeder

Historical Note:
ADMRA serves as a registry office for owners and breeders of Merino sheep. Membership: $15 (Lifetime); $20 (Individual).

Publications:
Membership Directory; on-line

American Angora Goat Breeder's Association
(1900)
P.O. Box 195
Rocksprings, TX 78880
Tel: (830) 683-4483 *Fax:* (830) 683-2559
E-Mail: aagba@swtexas.net
Website: aagba.org
Members: 700 individuals
Staff: 1
Annual Budget: $10-25,000
Tax: 501(c)(5)

Personnel:
President: Bonnie Naumann

Historical Note:
AAGBA is primarily concerned with maintaining registration records showing pedigrees of all registered Angoras and to keep records of all transfers showing ownership on all such goats. Members are Breeders and fanciers of Angora goats. Membership: $20/year.

Publications:
Membership Directory; annually

American Angus Association *(1883)*
3201 Frederick Ave.

St. Joseph, MO 64506
Tel: (816) 383-5100 *Fax:* (816) 233-9703
E-Mail: angus@angus.org
Website: angus.org
Members: 30000 individuals
Staff: 20
Annual Budget: $25-50,000,000
Tax: 501(c)(5)

Personnel:
Chief Executive Officer: Bryce Schumann
  E-Mail: bschumann@angus.org
Director, Information Systems: Lou Ann Adams
  E-Mail: ladams@angus.org
Director, Marketing and Public Relations: Katie Allen
  E-Mail: kallen@angusfoundation.org
Chief Operating Officer: Bill Bowman
  E-Mail: bbowman@angus.org
Director, Communications and Public Relations: Eric Grant
  E-Mail: egrant@angus.org
Director, Member Services: Don Laughlin
  E-Mail: dlaughlin@angus.org
Genetic Research Director, Performance Programs: Sally Northcutt
  E-Mail: snorthcutt@angus.org
Editor: Shauna Rose Hermel
  E-Mail: shermel@angusjournal.com
Director, Activities and Events: Shelia Stannard
  E-Mail: sstannard@angus.org
Chief Financial Officer: Richard Wilson
  E-Mail: rwilson@angus.org

Historical Note:
Formerly (1950) American Aberdeen-Angus Breeder's Association. Member of the National Pedigree Livestock Council, National Cattlemen's Beef Association. AAA's mission is to provide programs, services, technology and leadership to enhance the genetics of the Angus breed, broaden its influence within the beef industry, and expand the market for Angus beef worldwide. Membership: $20-1500/year.

Continuing Education:
Certification Designation/s: AIMS

Meetings/Conferences: Semi-Annual
Conference Chair: Shelia Stannard

Publications:
Angus Journal

American Animal Hospital Association *(1933)*
12575 W. Bayaud Ave.
Lakewood, CO 80228
Tel: (303) 986-2800 *Fax:* (303) 986-1700
TollFree: (800) 883-6301
E-Mail: info@aahanet.org
Website: aahanet.org
Members: 40000 individuals
Staff: 61
Annual Budget: $10-25,000,000
Tax: 501(c)(6)

Personnel:
Executive Director: Mike Cavanaugh DABVP, DVM
  E-Mail: mike.cavanaugh@aahanet.org
Director, Human Resources, Administration and Facilities: Rory Mohar Fisher
  E-Mail: rory.fisher@aahanet.org
Associate Public Relations Manager: Jason Merrihew
  E-Mail: jason.merrihew@aahanet.org
National Sales Manager: Stephanie Pates
  E-Mail: stephanie.pates@aahanet.org
Deputy Executive Director: Janice Trumpeter
  E-Mail: janice.trumpeter@aahanet.org,

Historical Note:
Incorporated (1935) in Illinois. AAHA's mission is to enhance the abilities of veterinarians to provide quality medical care to companion animals. Members are veterinarians, hospitals, support staff, accredited and non-accredited practice members. Membership: $475-800/year (Non accredited Practice Team Veterinarians).

Meetings/Conferences: Annual
Conference Chair: Janice Trumpeter
2013 - Phoenix, AZ (Phoenix Convention Center)/ March 14 - 17
2014 - Nashville, TN/March 20 - 23
2015 - Tampa, FL/March 12 - 15
2016 - Austin, TX/March 31 - April 3

Publications:
Membership Directory; on-line
Trends Magazine; adv.

Membership List Available to Non-members

American Anthropological Association *(1902)*
2200 Wilson Blvd.
Suite 600
Arlington, VA 22201
Tel: (703) 528-1902 *Fax:* (703) 528-3546
Website: aaanet.org
Members: 16000 individuals and institutional subscribers
Staff: 26
Annual Budget: $5-10,000,000
Tax: 501(c)(3)

Personnel:
Executive Director: Bill Davis
  E-Mail: bdavis@aaanet.org
Executive Office Assistant: Dexter K. Allen CAP
  E-Mail: dallen@aaanet.org
Director, Public Affairs: Damon A. Dozier
  E-Mail: ddozier@aaanet.org
Meetings Planner and Manager, Exhibits: Carla Fernandez
  E-Mail: cfernandez@aaanet.org
Deputy Executive Director and Chief Financial Officer: Elaine Lynch
  E-Mail: elynch@aaanet.org
Manager, Database and Web Services: Lisa Myers
  E-Mail: lmyers@aaanet.org
Manager, Marketing and Communications: Joslyn Osten
  E-Mail: josten@aaanet.org
Director, Publications: Oona Schmid
  E-Mail: oschmid@aaanet.org
Director, Academic Relations: Kathleen Terry-Sharp
  E-Mail: ksharp@aaanet.org
Manager, Membership Services: Richard Thomas
  E-Mail: rthomas@aaanet.org
Director, Meetings: Jason G. Watkins
  E-Mail: jwatkins@aaanet.org

Historical Note:
Established by members of the American Ethnological Society of New York, the Anthropological Society of Washington and Section H (Anthropology) of the American Association for the Advancement of Science. Membership: $135-306 (Professional); $70-306 (Student/Retired); $74-168 (Joint); $120 (Associate); $30-142 (International Professional), $35 (Undergraduate).

Meetings/Conferences:
Conference Chair: Carla Fernandez
2013 - Chicago, IL (Hilton Chicago)/Nov. 20 - 24
2014 - Washington, DC (Washington Marriott Wardman Park)/Dec. 3 - 7
2015 - Denver, CO (Colorado Convention Center)/Nov. 18 - 22

Publications:
American Anthropologist; adv.
Anthropology News; on-line; adv.
Membership Directory; on-line

Membership List Available to Non-members

American Antiquarian Society *(1812)*
185 Salisbury St.
Worcester, MA 01609-1634
Tel: (508) 755-5221 *Fax:* (508) 753-3311
E-Mail: library@americanantiquarian.org
Website: americanantiquarian.org
Members: 800 individuals
Staff: 56
Annual Budget: $10-25,000,000
Tax: 501(c)(3)

Personnel:
President: Ellen S. Dunlap
  E-Mail: edunlap@mwa.org
Recording Secretary: Richard D. Brown
Director, Information Technology: Nick Conti
  E-Mail: aconti@mwa.org
Director, Finance: Susan Forgit
  E-Mail: sforgit@mwa.org
Coordinator, Education: Kayla Haveles
  E-Mail: khaveles@mwa.org
Director, Human Resources: Carol-Ann P. Mackey
  E-Mail: cmackey@mwa.org
Outreach Director: James David Moran
  E-Mail: jmoran@mwa.org
Coordinator, Events: Ann-Cathrine Rapp
  E-Mail: arapp@mwa.org
Director, Book Publishing: Caroline F. Sloat
  E-Mail: csloat@mwa.org

Historical Note:

A learned society founded by Isaiah Thomas and others to collect and preserve materials related to American history before 1877. AAS's mission is to collect, preserve, and make available for study the printed record of what is now the United States of America from first European settlement. Members are scholars, educators, publishers, collectors, cultural administrators, civic leaders, journalists, writers, and filmmakers, as well as lay persons with an interest in the field of American history. Members are elected by their colleagues in recognition of scholarship, for support of cultural institutions, for manifest interest in bibliographical matters, or for distinction as community or national leaders in humanistic affairs.

Meetings/Conferences: Annual
Conference Chair: Ann-Cathrine Rapp

Publications:
Almanac; semi-annually
Common-place; quarterly
Members Directory; on-line

Membership List Available to Non-members

American Apitherapy Society (1989)
14942 S.Eagle Crest Dr.
Draper, UT 84020
Tel: (631) 470-9446 Fax: (631) 693-2528
E-Mail: info@apitherapy.org
Website: apitherapy.org
Members: 350 individuals
Staff: 3
Annual Budget: $25-50,000
Tax: 501(c)(3)

Personnel:
Executive Director: Marilyn Graham
Director, Public Relations: Priscilla Coe
Editor: Patsy McCook
 E-Mail: beeeditor@aol.com

Historical Note:
AAS's mission is to promote honey bee hive products for health as well as medicinal purposes and to educate the public and health care community, about both the traditional and scientifically valid uses of Apitherapy. Members are beekeepers, health professionals and others with an interest in therapeutic applications of honey bee products, particularly honey bee venom. Membership: $45 (Individual); $60 (Healthcare Professionals); $100 (Organization).

Publications:
AAS Newsletter; on-line
Journal of the American Apitherapy Society; quarterly

American Apparel & Footwear Association (1933)
1601 N. Kent St.
12th Floor
Arlington, VA 22209
Tel: (703) 797-9043 Fax: (703) 522-6741
TollFree: (800) 520-2262
E-Mail: lmasters@apparelandfootwear.org
Website: apparelandfootwear.org
Members: 450 companies
Staff: 16
Annual Budget: $5-10,000,000
Tax: 501(c)(6)

Personnel:
President and Chief Executive Officer: Kevin M. Burke
 E-Mail: kburke@apparelandfootwear.org
Director, Government Relations: Kurt Courtney
 E-Mail: kcourtney@apparelandfootwear.org
Director, Communications and Marketing: Scott Elmore
 E-Mail: selmore@apparelandfootwear.org
Vice President, International Trade: Nate Herman
 E-Mail: nherman@apparelandfootwear.org
Vice President, Industry Relations: Susan Lapetina
 E-Mail: Slapetina@apparelandfootwear.org
Vice President, Finance and Administration: Suzanne Shomers
 E-Mail: sshomers@wewear.org
Vice President, Membership Development: Maureen Storch
 E-Mail: mstorch@apparelandfootwear.org

Historical Note:
AAFA's mission is to promote and enhance its member's competitiveness, productivity and profitability in the global market by minimizing regulatory, legal, commercial, political and trade restraints. Members are apparel, footwear and other sewn products companies, and their suppliers.

Meetings/Conferences: Annual
Conference Chair: Susan Lapetina

Publications:

AAFA Newsbreaker; weekly
Membership Directory; on-line

American Apparel Producer's Network (1981)
P.O. Box 720693
Atlanta, GA 30358
Tel: (404) 843-3171 Fax: (404) 671-9456
E-Mail: source@aapnetwork.net
Website: aapnetwork.net
Members: 600 companies
Staff: 2
Annual Budget: $100-250,000

Personnel:
Executive Director: Sue C. Strickland
 E-Mail: sue@aapnetwork.net
Managing Director: Mike Todaro
 E-Mail: miketodaro@mindspring.com

Historical Note:
Formerly (1981) Southern Apparel Contractors and (1986) American Apparel Producers Association. AACA was established for the purpose of domestic apparel sourcing in direct competition with imports. Members are sewngoods and apparel sourcing managers, apparel/textile trim producers, suppliers, services and industry organizations. Membership: $1,600/year (Company).

Meetings/Conferences: Annual
2013 - Miami, FL (Eden Roc Renaissance Hotel)/May 5 - 7
Number of non-conference events/year: 2

Publications:
Membership Directory; on-line

American Arbitration Association (1926)
1633 Broadway
Tenth Floor
New York, NY 10019
Tel: (212) 716-5800 Fax: (212) 716-5905
TollFree: (800) 778-7879
Website: adr.org
Staff: 653
Annual Budget: $50-100,000,000

Personnel:
President and Chief Executive Officer: William K Slate II
 E-Mail: slatew@adr.org
Vice President, U.S. and International Mediation Services: Neil Carmichael
Administrator, Western Case Management Labor Center: Amie Chale
 E-Mail: chalea@adr.org
Vice President, AAA University: Harry Kaminsky
Vice President, Corporate Communications: Wayne Kessler
 E-Mail: kesslerw@adr.org
Vice President, Publications and ADR Resources: Ted E Pons

Historical Note:
Formed by a merger of the Arbitration Society of America and the Arbitration Foundation. AAA provides services to individuals and organizations who wish to resolve conflicts out of court. Members are individuals and organizations united to contribute the use of arbitration, mediation, conciliation, negotiation, democratic elections and other non- judicial processes for the settlement of all types of disputes.

American Architectural Foundation (1943)
1020 19th St. NW
Suite 525
Washington, DC 20006
Tel: (202) 787-1001 Fax: (202) 787-1002
E-Mail: info@archfoundation.org
Website: archfoundation.org
Staff: 13
Annual Budget: $2-5,000,000
Tax: 501(c)(3)

Personnel:
President and Chief Executive Officer: Ronald E Bogle Hon. AIA
 E-Mail: rbogle@archfoundation.org
Assistant, Digital Media Relations: Pamela Fernandez
 E-Mail: pfernandez@archfoundation.org
Director, Research: Mark de Groh
 E-Mail: mdegroh@archfoundation.org
Vice President, Finance and Administration: Bill Harris
 E-Mail: bharris@archfoundation.org
Manager, Events: Thom Minner
 E-Mail: tminner@archfoundation.org

Historical Note:
The mission of the AAF is to educate people about the power of architecture to improve lives and transform communities.

Meetings/Conferences: Annual
Conference Chair: Thom Minner
2013 - Washington, DC (Andrew W. Mellon Auditorium)/March 22
Number of non-conference events/year: 1

Publications:
AAF Newsletter

American Architectural Manufacturers Association (1936)
1827 Walden Office Sq.
Suite 550
Schaumburg, IL 60173-4268
Tel: (847) 303-5664 Fax: (847) 303-5774
E-Mail: customerservice@aamanet.org
Website: aamanet.org
Members: 300 companies
Staff: 17
Annual Budget: $2-5,000,000
Tax: 501(c)(6)

Personnel:
President and Chief Executive Officer: Richard G. Walker
Accounting Manager: Karen Allen
Manager, Technical Services: Ken Brenden
Chief Engineer, Certification Programs: Dean Lewis
 E-Mail: dlewis@aamanet.org
Coordinator, Membership Services: Jacqueline Luna
Manager, Meetings: Florence Nicolici
Supervisor, Technical Services: Andrea Rhodes
 E-Mail: arhodes@aamanet.org
Coordinator, Communications: Sam Sinkhorn
Director, Association Services: Janice Yglesias

Historical Note:
Formed by a merger (1962) of Sliding Glass Door and Window Institute (1954) and Aluminum Window Manufacturers Association (1936), name changed to the Architectural Aluminum Manufacturers Association and absorbed (1971) Aluminum Siding Association and assumed present name in 1984. Mission is to help its members serve better in the marketplace. Members are manufacturers of storm windows, residential/commercial windows and doors, as well as sliding glass doors, skylights, curtain walls and sun rooms. Dues are calculated based on a formula.

Continuing Education:
Certification Designation/s: FM, FA

Meetings/Conferences:
2013 - Tucson, AZ (Loews Ventana Canyon Resort)/ Feb. 24 - 27
2013 - Rosemont, IL (Hyatt Regency O'Hare)/June 9 - 12
2013 - Baltimore, MD (Baltimore Marriott Waterfront)/ Oct. 27 - 30

Publications:
AAMA E-news; monthly
Membership Directory; on-line

American Art Therapy Association, Inc. (1969)
4875 Eisenhower Ave.
Suite 240
Alexandria, VA 22304
Tel: (703) 548-5860 Fax: (703) 783-8468
TollFree: (888) 290-0878
E-Mail: info@arttherapy.org
Website: americanarttherapyassociation.org
Members:
5000 individuals
36 regional chapters
Staff: 7
Annual Budget: $1-2,000,000
Tax: 501(c)(3)

Personnel:
Executive Director: Susan Corrigan
 E-Mail: administration@arttherapy.org
Director, Membership Information and Programs: Michele Basham
 E-Mail: membership@arttherapy.org
Manager, Communications: Julia Connell
Director, Public Policy: Angela Foehl
 E-Mail: afoehl@arttherapy.org
Chief Financial Officer: Mary Ann Kibler

Historical Note:

AATA serves its members and the general public by providing standards of professional competence, and by disseminating knowledge relevant to the use of artistic processes and practices as tools for treatment, personal growth and the reconciliation of emotional conflict. Membership: $55 (Student); $72-164 (Professional); $210 (Contributing); $164 (Associate); $82 (Retired); $82 (International); $550 (Affiliate).

Meetings/Conferences: Annual
Conference Chair: Michele Basham
2013 - Seatle, WA/June 26 - 30
2014 - San Antonio, TX/July 9 - 13
2016 - Chicago, IL/July 6 - 10

Publications:
AATA Newsletter; quarterly; adv.
Art Therapy Journal; quarterly; adv.
Monthly Update; monthly; adv.

American Artists Professional League (1928)
47 Fifth Ave.
New York, NY 10003
Tel: (212) 645-1345 Fax: (212) 792-2275
E-Mail: aaplinc@gmail.com
Website: americanartistsprofessionalleague.org
Members: 750 individuals
Staff: 3
Annual Budget: $25-50,000
Tax: 501(c)(3)

Personnel:
President: Larry Mallory
Counsel: Michael J. Hughes Esq.
Treasurer: Gail Schulman

Historical Note:
AAPL's mission is to promote the standards of painting, sculpture and the graphic arts. Members are professional painters, sculptors and graphic artists working in style of traditional realism. Membership: $50 (Sponsor); $25 (Patron); $100 (Benefactor); $50 (Artist).

Meetings/Conferences: Annual

Publications:
AAPL Newsletter; semi-annually

American Assembly for Men in Nursing (1974)
P.O. Box 130220
Birmingham, AL 35213
Tel: (205) 956-0146 Fax: (205) 956-0149
E-Mail: aamn@aamn.org
Website: aamn.org
Members: 250 individuals
Staff: 5
Annual Budget: $100-250,000
Tax: 501(c)(6)

Personnel:
Executive Director: Byron W. McCain CAE
Secretary: Philip Julian
    E-Mail: julianp@ecu.edu
Treasurer: Danny Lee
    E-Mail: lee4185@bellsouth.net

Historical Note:
Founded as National Male Nurses Association and assumed its current name in 1982. The purpose of AAMN is to provide a framework for nurses as a group to meet, discuss, and influence factors which affect men as nurses. Membership: $100 (Full RN); $50 (1st Year Nurses, LPN/LVN, Retired/Disabled Nurse); $30 (Nursing Student); $350 (Corporate); $25 (NSNA Nursing Student Members); $15 (High School Students)

Meetings/Conferences: Annual
Number of non-conference events/year: 2

Publications:
AAMN Newsletter; on-line

American Association for Accreditation of Ambulatory Surgery Facilities (1980)
5101 Washington St., 2F Gurnee
P.O. Box 9500
Gurnee, IL 60031
Tel: (847) 775-1970 Fax: (847) 775-1985
TollFree: (888) 545-5222
E-Mail: info@aaaasf.org
Website: aaaasf.org
Members: 1000 individuals
Staff: 13
Annual Budget: $2-5,000,000

Personnel:
Executive Director: Jeff Pearcy CAE, MPA
    E-Mail: jeff@aaaasf.org

Director, Education: Theresa J. Griffin-Rossi CAE
    E-Mail: theresa@aaaasf.org
Accountant: Sam Kormoi
    E-Mail: sam@aaaasf.org
Contact, International Accreditation and Bookkeeper: Adriana Lomeli
    E-Mail: adriana@aaaasf.org
Director, Legislative and External Relations: Thomas "Tom" S. Terranova
    E-Mail: tom@aaaasf.org
Director, Marketing and Communications: Jaime Trevino
    E-Mail: jaime@aaaasf.org
Director, Information Technology and Staff: Jerome Unger
    E-Mail: jerome@aaaasf.org

Historical Note:
Formerly (1992) the American Association for Accreditation of Ambulatory Plastic Surgery Facilities, AAAASF's mission is to develop and implement standards to ensure patient care through an accreditation program. Members are ambulatory surgical facilities operated by American Board of Medical Specialties board certified surgeons. Membership: $750-6885 (Regular Accreditation); $1655-7410 (Medicare Accreditation).

Publications:
ASF SOURCE; quarterly; adv.

Membership List Available to Non-members

American Association for Adult and Continuing Education (1982)
10111 Martin Luther King Jr. Hwy.
Suite 200 C
Bowie, MD 20720
Tel: (301) 459-6261 Fax: (301) 459-6241
E-Mail: office@aaace.org
Website: aaace.org
Members: 1000 individuals
Staff: 1
Annual Budget: $250-500,000
Tax: 501(c)(3)

Personnel:
Association Manager: Cle Anderson
    E-Mail: office@aaace.org

Historical Note:
The product of a merger between the Adult Education Association (1951) and the National Association for Public and Continuing Adult Education (1952). Absorbed National Council of Administrators of Adult Education in 1992. AAACE's mission is to provide leadership for the field of adult and continuing education by expanding opportunities for adult growth and development, unifying adult educators, fostering the development and dissemination of theory, research, information, and best practices, promoting identity and standards for the profession, and advocating relevant public policy and social change initiatives. Membership: $85 (Individual); $30-60 (Student); $250 (Professional Association/Organization & Institution); $35 (Retiree).

Meetings/Conferences: Annual

Publications:
AAACE Newsletter
Adult Education Quarterly; quarterly
Adult Learning
Journal of Transformative Education (JTD)

American Association for Aerosol Research (1982)
15000 Commerce Pkwy.
Suite C
Mt. Laurel, NJ 08054
Tel: (877) 777-6753 Fax: (856) 439-0525
E-Mail: info@aaar.org
Website: aaar.org
Members: 1000 individuals
Staff: 5
Annual Budget: $1-2,000,000

Personnel:
Executive Director: Melissa Baldwin
    E-Mail: mbaldwin@ahint.com
Director, Administration and Membership Services: Deanna Bright
    E-Mail: dbright@ahint.com
Editor: B. Y. J. Liu
Meetings and Exhibits Manager: Ann Mitchell
    E-Mail: amitchell@ahint.com

Historical Note:
AAAR is a nonprofit professional organization for scientists and engineers who wish to promote and communicate technical advances in the field of aerosol research. Membership: $38-2,176/year.

Meetings/Conferences: Annual
Conference Chair: Ann Mitchell
2013 - Portland, OR (Oregon Convention Center)/Sept. 30 - Oct. 4

Publications:
Aerosol Science and Technology (AS&T); bi-annually
Particulars-Newsletter

American Association for Affirmative Action (1974)
888 16th St. NW
Suite 800
Washington, DC 20006
Tel: (202) 349-9855 Fax: (202) 355-1399
TollFree: (800) 252-8952
E-Mail: officeadministrator@affirmativeaction.org
Website: affirmativeaction.org
Members: 2000 members
Staff: 2
Annual Budget: $100-250,000
Tax: 501(c)(6)

Personnel:
Executive Director: Shirley J. Wilcher
    E-Mail: execdir@affirmativeaction.org
Office Administrator: Onenetta Williams
    E-Mail: officeadministrator@affirmativeaction.org

Historical Note:
AAAA is dedicated to promote the understanding and advocacy of affirmative action to enhance access and equality in employment, economic and educational opportunities. Represents managers of affirmative action programs. Membership: $250-475 (Organization); $125 (Individual); $50 (Retiree); $25 (Student).

Publications:
AAAA Newsletter; on-line

American Association for Agricultural Education (1960)
Clemson University
228 McAdams Hall
Clemson, SC 29634
Tel: (864) 656-5674 Fax: (864) 656-5675
Website: aaaeonline.org
Members: 300 individuals
Staff: 4
Annual Budget: $100-250,000

Personnel:
President: Greg W. Thompson
Vice-president, Communications: Emily B Rhoades
Editor: Grady Roberts
Treasurer: Roger Tormoehlen

Historical Note:
Formerly Teacher Trainers Section of the Agricultural Division of the American Vocational Association. AAAE is committed to studying, applying and advocating teaching and learning processes in agriculture. Membership: $115 (Regular); $20 (Student); $50 (Associate); $2300(Life Member).

Meetings/Conferences: Annual
2013 - Columbus, OH/May 21 - 24

Publications:
Journal of Natural Resources and Life Sciences Education; annually; adv.
AAAE Newsletter; biennially; adv.
The Journal of Agricultural Education; adv.
The Journal of Southern Agricultural Education Research (JSAER); adv.

Membership List Available to Non-members

American Association for Applied Linguistics (1977)
2900 Delk Rd.
Suite 700
Marietta, GA 30067-5350
Tel: (678) 229-2892 Fax: (678) 229-2777
TollFree: (866) 821-7700
E-Mail: info@aaal.org
Website: aaal.org
Members: 1300 individuals
Staff: 4
Annual Budget: $250-500,000
Tax: 501(c)(3)

Personnel:
President: Jane Zuengler
    E-Mail: zuengler@wisc.edu
Secretary and Treasurer: Linda Harklau

E-Mail: lharklau@uga.edu
Account Manager: Sarah Jackson
    E-Mail: sarah@aaal.org
Editor: Charlene Polio
    E-Mail: polio@msu.edu

Historical Note:
AAAL's mission is to facilitate the advancement and dissemination of knowledge and understanding regarding these language-related issues in order to improve the lives of individuals and conditions in society. Membership: $100 (Regular); $150 (Institution); $60 (Student Member within North America); $55 (Emeritus/Retired Member within North America); $155 (Joint Member within North America); $225 (Publisher); $115 (Regular Member outside North America); $165 (Institutional Member outside North America); $170 (Joint Member outside North America); $75 (Student Member outside North America); $70 (Emeritus/Retired Member outside North America).

Meetings/Conferences: Annual
2013 - Dallas, TX (Sheraton Dallas Hotel)/March 16 - 19
2014 - Portland, OR/March 22 - 25
2015 - Toronto, ON/March 21 - 24

Publications:
AAAL Newsletter
Annual Review of Applied Linguistics; annually
Applied Linguistics

American Association for Budget and Program Analysis (1976)
P.O. Box 1157
Falls Church, VA 22041
Tel: (703) 941-4300 Fax: (703) 941-1535
E-Mail: aabpa@aabpa.org
Website: aabpa.org
Members: 500 individuals
Staff: 6
Annual Budget: $100-250,000
Tax: 501(c)(3)

Personnel:
President:: Judy Thomas
    E-Mail: judy.thomas@aabpa.org
Director, Membership Services: Karen Kunz
    E-Mail: Karen.Kunz@mail.wvu.edu
Vice President, Symposia: Anthony Rainey
    E-Mail: anthony.rainey@opm.gov
General Counsel: Sheila Rajabiun
    E-Mail: srajabiun@bbg.gov
Treasurer and Secretary: Patrick Vallely
    E-Mail: vallelycp@gmail.com
Vice President, Communications and Newsletter: Juliet Vargas
    E-Mail: JulietVargas@aol.com

Historical Note:
The result of a merger between the Budget Officers Conference and the American Public Policy Association, AABPA was chartered as a non-profit educational corporation in Washington, DC. Members, largely in the DC area, have an interest in program management and budget analysis. Helps federal, state and local government managers and analysts, corporate executives and academic specialists members meet the unique challenges of their careers. Updates them on the latest developments in their fields and aids in establishing and maintaining contacts with colleagues. Membership: $45 (Individual); $150 (Corporate); $15 (Student).

Meetings/Conferences:
Conference Chair: Anthony Rainey
Number of non-conference events/year: 1

Publications:
Newsletter; quarterly
Public Budgeting and Finance
The Bottom Line

American Association for Cancer Education (1947)
C/O San Diego Hospice and Palliative Care
4311 Third Ave.
San Diego, CA 92103-1407
Tel: (619) 278-6164 Fax: (619) 278-6279
E-Mail: contactaace@aaceonline.com
Website: aaceonline.com
Members: 400 individuals
Staff: 2
Annual Budget: $50-100,000

Personnel:
Executive Secretary: Paula Frampton-Brown

Historical Note:

Formerly (1966) the Coordinators of Cancer Teaching. AACE's mission is to foster cancer education by individuals who either due to professional obligations or personal interest are involved in cancer education. Membership includes scientists, surgeons, internists, radiation oncologists, pediatricians, gynecologists, osteopathic physicians, dentists, oncology nursing educators and professional educators. Membership: $245 (Individual); $695 (Institutional); $65 (Senior-Over age 65); $40 (Student Associate with JCE); $20 (Student Associate without JCE).

Meetings/Conferences: Annual
Conference Chair: Jennifer Alluisi MA, Ed

Publications:
Journal of Cancer Education; quarterly

American Association for Cancer Research (1907)
615 Chestnut St.
17th Floor
Philadelphia, PA 19106-4404
Tel: (215) 440-9300 Fax: (215) 440-9313
TollFree: (866) 423-3965
E-Mail: aacr@aacr.org
Website: aacr.org
Members: 26000 individuals
Staff: 125
Annual Budget: $50-100,000,000
Tax: 501(c)(3)

Personnel:
Chief Executive Officer: Margaret Foti MD, PhD
    E-Mail: foti@aacr.org
Editorial Director: Helen Barsky Atkins
Director, Membership Services: Robin E. Felder
    E-Mail: felder@aacr.org
Director, Information Technology: Deighton E. Liverpool
Director, Human Resources: Vernetta J. Mitchell
Managing Director, Science Policy and Government Affairs: Jon G. Retzlaff
Director, Program Development: Jeffrey M. Ruben
Chief Financial Officer: Michael K. Stewart
Director, Meetings and Exhibits: Linda M. Still
Director, Government Relations: Mary Lee Watts MPH, RD
    E-Mail: marylee.watts@aacr.org
Senior Director, Communications: Christine Wilson
    E-Mail: christine.wilson@aacr.org

Historical Note:
Founded 1907 in Washington, DC and incorporated in New York in 1940. AACR's mission is to build bridges and unity among the leaders of the scientific and cancer survivor and patient advocacy communities worldwide. Membership: $280 (Active); $50 (Associate); $120 (Affiliate); $35 (Emeritus).

Meetings/Conferences:
Conference Chair: Linda M. Still
2013 - Maui, HI (Hyatt Regency Maui)/Feb. 21 - 25
2013 - San Diego, CA (Manchester Grand Hyatt San Diego)/Feb. 27 - March 2
2013 - Washington, DC (Walter E. Washington Convention Center)/April 6 - 10
2013 - Boston, MA/Oct. 19 - 23
2014 - San Diego, CA/April 5 - 9
2014 - Barcelona, Spain/Nov. 18 - 21
2015 - Philadelphia, PA/April 18 - 22
2016 - New Orleans, LA/April 16 - 20
Number of non-conference events/year: 26

Publications:
Cancer Discovery; on-line
CR magazine
Membership Directory; on-line

Membership List Available to Non-members

American Association for Career Education (1980)
2900 Amby Pl.
Hermosa Beach, CA 90254-2216
Tel: (310) 376-7378 Fax: (310) 376-2926
Members:
10 companies
500 individuals
Staff: 1
Annual Budget: Under $10,000
Tax: 501(c)(3)

Personnel:
President: Pat Nellor Wickwire PhD

Historical Note:
Incorporated in the District of Columbia in 1981. AACE connects education, work, and careers through Career

Education for all ages. AACE members are professional educators, community leaders, parents, business leaders, government leaders and other interested individuals. Membership: $15 (Regular); $100 (Sustaining); $25/2 years (Regular); $150/2 years (Sustaining). Has no full-time staff.

American Association for Chinese Studies (1959)
AACS R4/116, The City College, CUNY
Convent Ave., 138th St.
New York, NY 10031
Tel: (212) 650-8268 Fax: (212) 650-8287
E-Mail: aacs@mail.com
Website: 134.74.90.3/aacs/index.htm
Members: 350 individuals
Staff: 2
Annual Budget: Under $10,000

Personnel:
Executive Director: Peter C.Y. Chow
Editor: Thomas J. Bellows
    E-Mail: thomas.bellows@utsa.edu

Historical Note:
Formerly (1976) the American Association of Teachers of Chinese Language and Culture. The purpose of AACS is to encourage the study of subjects related to China, especially in American educational institutions. Membership: $60 (Individual/Institution); $80 (Joint); $500 (Life Member); $5 (Student); $40 (Retiree).

Meetings/Conferences: Annual

Publications:
American Journal of Chinese Studies (AJCS); bi-annually; adv.
Membership Directory; on-line
The American Association for Chinese Studies Newsletter

American Association for Clinical Chemistry, Inc. (1948)
1850 K St. NW
Suite 625
Washington, DC 20006
Tel: (800) 892-1400 Fax: (202) 887-5093
TollFree: (800) 892-1400
E-Mail: info@aacc.org
Website: aacc.org
Members: 8000 individuals
Staff: 60
Annual Budget: $10-25,000,000
Tax: 501(c)(3)

Personnel:
Chief Executive Officer and Executive Vice President: Lana Vukovljak
Director, Information Systems: Christina Elder
Director, Publications: Mac Fancher
Director, Membership Program: Michele Horwitz
    E-Mail: mhorwitz@aacc.org
Chief Financial Officer and Vice President, Finance and Administration: Nori Jones
    E-Mail: njones@aacc.org
Director, Professional Education: Penelope Jones
Director, Meetings: Gail E. Mutnik
    E-Mail: gmutnik@aacc.org
Director, Government Affairs: Vince Stine
    E-Mail: vstine@aacc.org
Director, Marketing: Dianne Vandivier

Historical Note:
Incorporated in New York in 1949. AACC's mission is to provide educational and professional development services to its members in order to improve the level at which chemistry is practiced in chemical laboratories. Members are chemists, physicians and other scientists specializing in clinical chemistry. Membership: $210 (Full); $120 (Affiliate); $35 (Student).

Meetings/Conferences: Annual
Conference Chair: Gail E. Mutnik
2013 - Baltimore, MD/April 18 - 19
2013 - La Jolla, CA/April 28 - May 2
2013 - Houston, TX/July 28 - Aug. 1
2014 - Chicago, IL/July 27 - 31/18000 attendees
2015 - Atlanta, GA/July 26 - 30/18000 attendees
2016 - Philadelphia, PA/July 24 - 28/18000 attendees/ over 100 exhibitors
2017 - San Diego, CA/July 30 - Aug. 3/18000 attendees
2018 - Houston, TX/July 23 - 27/18000 attendees
Number of non-conference events/year: 8

Publications:
AACC eNews; bi-monthly; adv.

Clinical and Forensic Toxicology News; quarterly
Clinical Chemistry Journal; monthly; adv.
Clinical Laboratory News; monthly; adv.
Clinical Laboratory Strategies; bi-monthly
Division Newsletters; annually
Government Affairs Update; bi-monthly

American Association for Crystal Growth (1969)
6986 S. Wadsworth Ct.
Littleton, CO 80128
Tel: (303) 539-6907 *Fax:* (303) 482-2775
Website: crystalgrowth.org
Members:
10 companies
600 members
Staff: 4
Annual Budget: Under $10,000

Personnel:
President: Peter Schunemann
Editor: Candace Lynch
 E-Mail: clynch@inradoptics.com
Executive Administrator: Shoshana Nash
 E-Mail: AACG@comcast.net
Treasurer: Dave Vanderwater

Historical Note:
Formerly (1970) American Committee for Crystal Growth. AACG's purpose is to organize and support activities which serve the technical and professional interests of its members and the crystal growth community. Membership: $50 (Individual); $20 (Student); $500 (Corporate Affiliation).

Meetings/Conferences: Annual
2013 - Keystone, CO (Keystone Resort and Conference Center)/July 21 - 26

Publications:
AACG Newsletter

American Association for Dental Research (1952)
1619 Duke St.
Alexandria, VA 22314-3406
Tel: (703) 548-0066 *Fax:* (703) 548-1883
E-Mail: research@aadronline.org
Website: aadronline.org
Members: 5000 individuals
Staff: 15
Annual Budget: $2-5,000,000
Tax: 501(c)(3)

Personnel:
Executive Director: Christopher H. Fox
Senior Manager, Membership Benefits: Marissa E. Naspinski
 E-Mail: mnaspinski@iadr.org
Senior Director, Marketing, Membership and Publications: Denise S. Streszoff
 E-Mail: dstreszoff@iadr.org
Manager, Marketing and Communications: Ingrid L. Thomas
 E-Mail: ithomas@iadr.org
Senior Director, Finance and Information Technology: R. Darin Walsh
 E-Mail: dwalsh@iadr.org
Director, Meetings: Leslie Zeck

Historical Note:
AADR is a division of International Association for Dental Research. AADR's mission is to advance research and increase knowledge for the improvement of oral health worldwide. Membership: $200 (Individual); $500-10,000 (Company), $550-2,500 (Educational, Government, and Non-profit Entities).

Meetings/Conferences: Annual
Conference Chair: Leslie Zeck
2013 - Seatle, WA/March 20 - 23
2014 - Charlotte, NC/March 19 - 22
2015 - Boston, MA/March 11 - 14

Publications:
Advances in Dental Research; on-line
Critical Reviews in Oral Biology and Medicine; bi-monthly
Global Research Update; monthly; adv.
IADR Reports; annually
Journal of Dental Research; on-line; adv.
Science Advocate; monthly; adv.

American Association for Employment in Education (1934)
947 E. Johnstown Rd.
Suite 170
Gahanna, OH 43230

Tel: (614) 485-1111 *Fax:* (360) 244-7802
E-Mail: info@aaee.org
Website: aaee.org
Members: 1000 institutions
Staff: 1
Annual Budget: $250-500,000
Tax: 501(c)(3)

Personnel:
Executive Director: Doug Peden
 E-Mail: execdir@aaee.org

Historical Note:
Formerly (1934) National Institutional Teacher Placement Association and (1962) Association for School, College and University Staffing. AAEE provides information and resources to assist schools, colleges and universities in the employment of educators for staffing excellence in education. AAEE's members are university career center directors and school system human resources administrators. Membership: $200 (College/School); $500 (For Profit Institutions); $50 (Institutional); $200 (Associate); $30 (Retired).

Meetings/Conferences: Annual

American Association for Geodetic Surveying (1981)
Six Montgomery Village Ave.
Suite 403
Gaithersburg, MD 20879
Tel: (240) 632-8943 *Fax:* (240) 632-1321
Website: aagsmo.org
Staff: 5
Tax: 501(c)(6)

Personnel:
Contact, Conferences: Kristi Audette
 E-Mail: kristi@allthedetailsinc.com
Managing Editor: Ilse Genovese
 E-Mail: ilse.genovese@acsm.net
Contact, Membership Services: Trisha Milburn
 E-Mail: trisha.milburn@acsm.net

Historical Note:
AAGS's mission is to promote a better understanding of geodesy as a science; create a better appreciation of the value of geodetic surveys and thus encourage greater use of such surveys. Membership: $175-220 (Regular); $124-140 (Associate); $28 (Student).

Meetings/Conferences: Annual
Conference Chair: Kristi Audette

Publications:
AAGS Newsletter
Membership Directory; on-line
Surveying and Land Information Science (SaLIS),; on-line

American Association for Geriatric Psychiatry (1978)
7910 Woodmont Ave.
Suite 1050
Bethesda, MD 20814-3004
Tel: (301) 654-7850 *Fax:* (301) 654-4137
E-Mail: main@aagponline.org
Website: aagponline.org
Members: 2000 geriatric psychiatrists, other health care professionals
Staff: 8
Annual Budget: $1-2,000,000

Personnel:
Chief Executive Officer: Christine DeVries
 E-Mail: cdevries@aagponline.org
Specialist, Membership Services: Janice Allen
 E-Mail: jallen@aagponline.org
Director, Finance and Administration: Bellinda D'Agostino
Editor-in-Chief: Dilip V. Jeste MD
Associate Director, Communications: Kate McDuffie
 E-Mail: kmcduffie@aagponline.org
Director, Governance: Carrie Stankiewicz
 E-Mail: cstankiewicz@aagponline.org

Historical Note:
The American Association for Geriatric Psychiatry is a national association representing and aid its members and the field of geriatric psychiatry. AAGP is an organization of psychiatrists interested in aging whose mission is to enhance the knowledge base and standard of practice in geriatric psychiatry through education and research and to advocate for meeting the mental health needs of older Americans. Membership: $300 (Psychiatrist Member); $150 (Retired); $75 (Member-in-Training); $10-45 (Student); $50-310 (International).

Meetings/Conferences:
2013 - Los Angeles, CA (Los Angeles Convention Center)/March 14 - 17
Number of non-conference events/year: 2

Publications:
American Journal of Geriatric Psychiatry; monthly; adv.
Geriatric Psychiatry News; bi-monthly

American Association for Hand Surgery (1970)
500 Cummings Center
Suite 4550
Beverly, MA 01915
Tel: (978) 927-8330 *Fax:* (978) 524-8890
TollFree: (800) 333-8835
E-Mail: contact@handsurgery.org
Website: handsurgery.org
Members: 1100 Individuals
Staff: 4
Annual Budget: $500-1,000,000
Tax: 501(c)(3)

Personnel:
Executive Director: Kris Haskin
 E-Mail: khaskin@handsurgery.org
Managing Editor: Anne Behrens
 E-Mail: visorient@comcast.net

Historical Note:
Mission of AAHS is to foster and promote the quality of hand care through the development and sponsorship of educational programs related to the hand and the upper extremity, through communications with health care professionals and the public, and through the endowment of research. Members are orthopedic surgeons, plastic surgeons, general surgeons, microsurgeons, hand therapists, nurses, and basic scientists. Membership: $440 (Active); $190 (Affiliate); $165 (International); $25 (Candidate).

Continuing Education:
Certification Designation/s: CME

Meetings/Conferences: Annual
2013 - Naples, FL (Naples Grande Resort and Club)/ Jan. 9 - 12/26-50 exhibitors
2014 - Kauai, HI (Grand Hyatt Kauai Resort and Spa)/ Jan. 8 - 11/26-50 exhibitors
2015 - Paradise Island, Bahamas (Atlantis Resort)/Jan. 21 - 24
2016 - Scottsdale, AZ (Westin Kierland Hotel)/Jan. 13 - 26
Number of non-conference events/year: 2

Publications:
HAND; quarterly; adv.
Hand Surgery Quarterly; quarterly; adv.
Member Directory; on-line

American Association for Health Education (1937)
1900 Association Dr.
Reston, VA 20191-1598
Tel: (703) 476-3400 *Fax:* (703) 476-9527
TollFree: (800) 213-7193
E-Mail: aahe@aahperd.org
Website: aahperd.org/aahe
Members: 7500 individuals
Staff: 4
Annual Budget: $2-5,000,000

Personnel:
Executive Director: Becky J. Smith CAE, CHES, PhD
 E-Mail: bsmith@aahperd.org
Advertising and Sponsorship Assistant: Vicki Santaniello
 E-Mail: vsantaniello@aahperd.org
President: Caile E. Spear
Vice President, Programs: Judy C. Young PhD
 E-Mail: jyoung@aahperd.org

Historical Note:
Formerly (1996) the Association for the Advancement of Health Education and until 1974 a division of the American Alliance for Health, Physical Education and Recreation. AAHE is now an independent member of the American Alliance for Health, Physical Education, Recreation and Dance whose mission is to advance the profession by serving health educators and other professionals who strive to promote the health of all people. A portion of the dues of AAHPERD goes to support the association.

Publications:
AAHE InfoSource; semi-monthly
American Journal of Health Education; bi-monthly; adv.
Health Education Teaching Techniques Journal; on-line

The Electronic Newsletter of the American Association
for Health Education; semi-monthly; adv.

American Association for Homecare (2000)
1707 L St. NW
Washington, DC 20036
Tel: (202) 372-0107 *Fax:* (202) 835-8306
E-Mail: info@aahomecare.org
Website: aahomecare.org
Members: 500 companies
Staff: 13
Annual Budget: $2-5,000,000
Tax: 501(c)(6)

Personnel:
Coordinator, Meetings and Education: Ashley Jackson
   E-Mail: ashleyj@aahomecare.org

Historical Note:
*A national association representing all elements of
homecare. Acquired the American Home Care Association
in 2002.*

Meetings/Conferences:
Conference Chair: Ashley Jackson

Publications:
Membership Directory; on-line
Weekly bulletins; weekly

American Association for Justice (1946)
777 Sixth St. NW
Suite 200
Washington, DC 20001
Tel: (202) 965-3500 *Fax:* (202) 625-7312
TollFree: (800) 424-2725
E-Mail: membership@justice.org
Website: justice.org
Members: 60000 individuals
Staff: 155
Annual Budget: $25-50,000,000
Tax: 501(c)(6)

Personnel:
Chief Executive Officer: Linda A. Lipsen
   E-Mail: linda.lipsen@justice.org
Chief Financial Officer: Kathi Berge
   E-Mail: kathi.berge@justice.org
General Counsel: Dan Cohen
   E-Mail: dan.cohen@justice.org
Chief Operating Officer: Charles Jeffress
   E-Mail: charles.jeffress@justice.org
Associate Director, National Affairs: Susan Steinman
   E-Mail: susan.steinman@atlahq.org

Historical Note:
*Founded as the NACCA Bar Association (National
Association of Claimant's Compensation Attorneys); became
the American Trial Lawyers Association in 1964 and the
Association of Trial Lawyers of America in 1972; assumed
its current name in 2007. Mission is to promote a fair and
effective justice system and to support the work of attorneys
in their efforts to ensure that their clinets recieve a fair trial.
Membership: $50-495 (Regular Members depending on
the number of years of practice); $125 (International);
$75 (Government/Paralegal Affiliate); $35 (Military/Law
Professor); $15 (Student).*

Continuing Education:
Certification Designation/s: CLE

Meetings/Conferences: Biennial
2013 - Miami, FL (Fountainebleau Hotel)/Feb. 9 - 13
2013 - San Francisco, CA (Hilton San Francisco)/July
   20 - 24
2014 - New Orleans, LA (Sheraton New Orleans
   Hotel)/Feb. 8 - 12
2014 - Baltimore, MD (Baltimore Convention Center)/
   July 26 - 30
2015 - Palm Spring, CA (JW Marriott Desert Springs
   Resort and Spa)/Feb. 14 - 18
2015 - Montreal, QC (Montreal Convention Centre)/
   July 11 - 15
Number of non-conference events/year: 1-10

Publications:
Class Action Law Reporter; monthly; adv.
Law Reporters; monthly; adv.
Membership Directory; on-line; adv.
Motor Vehicle Law Reporter; monthly; adv.
News Brief; daily; adv.
Products Liability Law Reporter; monthly; adv.
Professional Negligence Law Reporter,; monthly; adv.
Trial; monthly; adv.
Trial News; bi-monthly; adv.

Membership List Available to Non-members

American Association for Laboratory Accreditation (1978)
5301 Buckeystown Pike
Suite 350
Frederick, MD 21704
Tel: (301) 644-3248 *Fax:* (240) 454-9449
E-Mail: info@a2la.org
Website: a2la.org
Members: 1900 laboratories and individuals
Staff: 38
Annual Budget: $10-25,000,000
Tax: 501(c)(3)

Personnel:
President and Chief Executive Officer: Peter S. Unger
   E-Mail: punger@A2LA.org
Director, Quality: Teresa Barnett
   E-Mail: tbarnett@A2LA.org
Manager, Training and Membership Services: Julie Collins
   E-Mail: jcollins@A2LA.org
Director, Human Resources: Diana Elias
   E-Mail: delias@A2LA.org
Manager, Accreditation: Rob Miller
   E-Mail: rmiller@A2LA.org
Director, Finance: Tim Reachmack
   E-Mail: treachmack@A2LA.org
Vice President and Chief Operating Officer: Roxanne M.
   Robinson
   E-Mail: rrobinson@A2LA.org
Director, Medical and Marketing Affairs: Larnell Simpson
   E-Mail: lsimpson@A2LA.org
Director, Public Affairs: Philip Smith
   E-Mail: psmith@A2LA.org
Director, Information Technology: Daren Valentine
   E-Mail: dvalentine@A2LA.org

Historical Note:
*A2LA strives to achieve customer satisfaction through
meeting the needs of both laboratories and their users for
competent testing and calibration. Membership in A2LA is
open to any individual, institution or corporation interested
in supporting its mission. Membership: $100 (Individual);
$200 (Institutional); $400 (Organizational).*

Meetings/Conferences:
Conference Chair: Philip Smith

Publications:
A2LA Today; on-line

American Association for Laboratory Animal Science (1950)
9190 Crestwyn Hills Dr.
Memphis, TN 38125-8538
Tel: (901) 754-8620 *Fax:* (901) 753-0046
E-Mail: info@aalas.org
Website: aalas.org
Members:
600 institutions
11300 individuals
Staff: 39
Annual Budget: $5-10,000,000
Tax: 501(c)(3)

Personnel:
Executive Director: Ann T. Turner CAE, PhD
   E-Mail: ann.turner@aalas.org
Director, Meetings and Financial Services: Betty
   Cartwright
   E-Mail: betty.cartwright@aalas.org

Historical Note:
*Founded in 1950 and incorporated in Illinois in 1953
as the Animal Care Panel. Assumed its present name in
1966. Members are individuals professionally concerned
with the production, care and study of laboratory animals.
Membership: $0-600/year.*

Continuing Education:
Certification Designation/s: LATG, LAT, CMAR, ALAT

Meetings/Conferences: Annual
Conference Chair: Betty Cartwright
2013 - Baltimore, MD/Oct. 27 - 31
2014 - San Antonio, TX/Oct. 19 - 23
2015 - Phoenix, AZ/Nov. 1 - 5
2016 - Charlotte, NC/Oct. 30 - Nov. 3
2017 - Austin, TX/Oct. 15 - 19

Publications:
AALAS in Action; bi-monthly; adv.
Buyer's Guide; annually
Comparative Medicine; bi-monthly; adv.
Journal of the American Association for Laboratory
   Animal Science (JAALAS); bi-monthly; adv.

Tech Talk; bi-monthly; adv.

American Association for Marriage and Family Therapy (1942)
112 S. Alfred St.
Alexandria, VA 22314-3061
Tel: (703) 838-9808 *Fax:* (703) 838-9805
E-Mail: central@aamft.org
Website: inamft.org
Members: 24000 marriage and family therapists
Staff: 32
Annual Budget: $5-10,000,000

Personnel:
Manager, Government Affairs: Brian Rasmussen
   E-Mail: brasmussen@aamft.org
Director, Professional and Public Affairs Department: Tracy
   Todd
   E-Mail: ttodd@aamft.org

Historical Note:
*Founded as American Association of Marriage Counselors,
became American Association of Marriage and Family
Counselors in 1970 and assumed its present name in
1978. AAMFT represents the professional interests of
marriage and family therapists throughout the United
States, Canada and abroad. Members are clinical therapists
specially trained to conduct marriage and family therapy
with individuals, couples and families. Membership: $201
(Clinical Member, plus division dues); $146 (Associate,
plus division dues); $58 (Student, plus division dues); $161
(Affiliate, plus division dues).*

Meetings/Conferences: Semi-Annual
Number of non-conference events/year: 1

Publications:
AAMFT Electronic Newsletter; semi-monthly; adv.
AAMFT Member Directory; on-line
Family Therapy Magazine; bi-monthly; adv.
Journal of Marital and Family Therapy; quarterly; adv.

Membership List Available to Non-members

American Association for Paralegal Education (1981)
19 Mantua Rd.
Mt. Royal, NJ 08061
Tel: (856) 423-2829 *Fax:* (856) 423-3420
E-Mail: info@aafpe.org
Website: aafpe.org
Members: 450 universities, colleges, private
schools and institutions
Staff: 4
Annual Budget: $250-500,000
Tax: 501(c)(6)

Personnel:
Executive Director: Gene Terry
   E-Mail: gterry@talley.com
Director, Certificate Programs: Steve Dayton
   E-Mail: sdayton@fullcollege.edu
Contact, Conventions and Meetings: Kathryn Myers
   E-Mail: kmyers@smwc.edu

Historical Note:
*AAfPE promotes paralegal education, develops educational
standards and encourages professional growth, in order
to prepare graduates to perform a significant role in the
delivery of legal services. Members are institutions and
individuals who provide training or continuing education
to paralegals. Membership: $25 (Individual); $450
(Institution/Associate/Affiliate); $475 (Sustaining).*

Continuing Education:
Certification Designation/s: QPP

Meetings/Conferences: Annual
Conference Chair: Kathryn Myers
2013 - Phoenix, AZ/Nov. 6 - 9
2014 - Summerlin, NV/Oct. 15 - 18
2015 - Milwaukee, WI/Oct. 21 - 24

Publications:
AAfPE Bytes Newsletter; on-line
Member Directory; on-line
Sidebar
The Paralegal Educator magazine; semi-annually
The Sidebar

American Association for Pediatric Ophthalmology and Strabismus (1974)
P.O. Box 193832
San Francisco, CA 94119-3832
Tel: (415) 561-8505 *Fax:* (415) 561-8531
E-Mail: aapos@aao.org
Website: aapos.org

Members:
99 orthoptist members
37 associate members
842 active/honorary/charter members
268 international members
82 emeritus members
147 candidates-in-training
Staff: 3
Annual Budget: $1-2,000,000
Tax: 501(c)(3)

Personnel:
Client Program Manager: Jennifer Hull
    E-Mail: jhull@aao.org

Historical Note:
AAPOS's mission is to advance quality medical and surgical eye care worldwide for children and for adults with strabismus. Members are ophthalmologists certified in the United States or Canada who are in good standing with their respective national ophthalmology organization. Members should have completed one year of additional training in an AAPOS approved program in pediatric ophthalmology or strabismus.

Meetings/Conferences: Annual
Conference Chair: Maria A. Schweers, CO
2013 - Boston, MA (Westin Copley Place Boston)/April 3 - 7
2014 - Rancho Mirage, CA (Westin Mission Hills Resort and Spa)/April 2 - 6
2015 - New Orleans, LA (Hyatt Regency)/March 25 - 29

Publications:
e-mail Updates; on-line
Membership Directory; on-line

American Association for Physical Activity and Recreation

1900 Association Dr.
Reston, VA 20192-1598
Tel: (703) 476-3430 *Fax:* (703) 476-9527
E-Mail: aapar@aahperd.org
Website: aahperd.org/aapar
Staff: 2

Personnel:
Interim Executive Director: Christopher Neumann
President: Brad Strand

Historical Note:
Affiliated with the American Alliance for Health, Physical Education, Recreation and Dance. Promotes active living across the lifespan through professional members in school, community, corporate, and hospital settings.AAPAR's mission is to enhance quality of life by promoting creative and active lifestyles through meaningful physical activity, recreation, and fitness experiences across the lifespan, with particular focus on community based programs.

Meetings/Conferences:
2013 - Charlotte, NC (Westin Charlotte)/April 23 - 27

Publications:
Council on Safety and Risk Management; bi-annually
Measurement in Physical Education and Exercise Science
PAR for Life; quarterly
PARticipate; monthly

American Association for Public Opinion Research
(1947)
111 Deer Lake Rd.
Suite 100
Deerfield, IL 60015
Tel: (847) 205-2651 *Fax:* (847) 480-9282
E-Mail: info@aapor.org
Website: aapor.org
Members: 2400 Individuals
Staff: 6
Annual Budget: $1-2,000,000
Tax: 501(c)(6)

Personnel:
Executive Director: Susan L. Tibbitts
    E-Mail: stibbitts@aapor.org
Marketing and Communications Manager: Lindsay Arends
    E-Mail: larends@aapor.org
Membership Specialist: Tonya Cabrera
    E-Mail: tmcabrera@aapor.org
Manager, Conferences: Jacky Schweinzger
    E-Mail: jschweinzger@aapor.org
Director, Administration: Donna Tieberg
    E-Mail: dtieberg@aapor.org

Historical Note:
AAPOR is an organization of public opinion and survey research professionals in the U.S., with members from academia, media, government, the non-profit sector and private industry. Members are individuals engaged or interested in the methods and applications of public opinion and social research. Membership: $150 (Employer-paid); $55-130 (Individual-paid, based on annual income); $75 (Joint).

Meetings/Conferences:
Conference Chair: Jacky Schweinzger
2013 - Boston, MA (Seaport Boston Hotel)/May 16 - 19
2014 - Anaheim, CA (Anaheim Marriott)/May 15 - 18
2015 - Hollywood, FL (Westin Diplomat Resort and Spa)/May 14 - 17
2016 - Austin, TX (Hilton Austin)/May 12 - 15
2017 - New Orleans, LA (Sheraton New Orleans Hotel)/May 18 - 21

Publications:
Survey Practice; on-line

Membership List Available to Non-members

American Association for Respiratory Care
(1947)
9425 N. MacArthur Blvd.
Suite 100
Irving, TX 75063-4706
Tel: (972) 243-2272 *Fax:* (972) 484-2720
E-Mail: info@aarc.org
Website: aarc.org
Members: 49000 individuals
Staff: 40
Annual Budget: $10-25,000,000
Tax: 501(c)(6)

Personnel:
Chief Executive Officer and Executive Director: Thomas J. Kallstrom MBA, RRT
    E-Mail: kallstrom@aarc.org
Coordinator, Communications: Beth Binkley
    E-Mail: binkley@aarc.org
Manager, Conventions and Meetings: Kathy Blackmon
    E-Mail: blackmon@aarc.org
Editor: Marsha Cathcart
    E-Mail: cathcart@aarc.org
Coordinator, Marketing: Susan Gill
    E-Mail: gill@aarc.org
Associate Executive Director, Meetings and Conventions: Douglas Laher
    E-Mail: laher@aarc.org
Coordinator, Information Technology: Russell Leighton
    E-Mail: leighton@aarc.org
Associate Executive Director: Sherry Milligan
    E-Mail: milligan@aarc.org
Legislative Director: Miriam O'Day
    E-Mail: Oday@aarc.org
Associate Executive Director, Education: Shawna Strickland

Historical Note:
Formerly (1967) American Association for Inhalation Therapists, (1973) American Association for Inhalation Therapy, (1986) American Association for Respiratory Therapy. Sponsored by the American College of Chest Physicians, the American Society of Anaesthesiologists and the American Thoracic Society. AARC seeks to encourage and promote professional excellence, advance the science and practice of respiratory care, and serve as an advocate for patients, their families, the public, the profession and the respiratory therapist. Members are respiratory therapists in hospitals and with home care companies, managers of respiratory and cardiopulmonary services, and educators who provide respiratory care training. Membership: $90-125 (Active/Associate); $50 (Student); $93-165 (Associate - International); $90-125 (Special).

Meetings/Conferences: Annual
Conference Chair: Kathy Blackmon
2013 - Anaheim, CA/Nov. 16 - 19/5000 attendees/over 100 exhibitors
2014 - Las Vegas, NV/Dec. 9 - 12/5000 attendees/over 100 exhibitors
2015 - Tampa, FL/Nov. 7 - 10/5000 attendees/over 100 exhibitors

Publications:
AARC Online Buyer's Guide for Respiratory Car; on-line
AARC Times Magazine; monthly; adv.
News Now; on-line
Respiratory Care Journal; monthly; adv.

American Association for State and Local History
(1940)
1717 Church St.
Nashville, TN 37203-2991
Tel: (615) 320-3203 *Fax:* (615) 327-9013
E-Mail: membership@AASLH.org
Website: aaslh.org
Members: 6000 individuals and institutions
Staff: 10
Annual Budget: $1-2,000,000
Tax: 501(c)(3)

Personnel:
President and Chief Executive Officer: Terry Davis
    E-Mail: davis@aaslh.org
Vice President, Programs: Bob Beatty
    E-Mail: beatty@aaslh.org
Program Associate: Bethany Hawkins
    E-Mail: hawkins@aaslh.org
Finance and Business Manager: Sylvia McGhee
    E-Mail: mcghee@aaslh.org
Director, Advertising and Marketing: Rebecca Price
    E-Mail: price@aaslh.org
Data Entry and General Office Assistant: Mattie Rose
    E-Mail: rose@aaslh.org
Manager, Membership and Information Services: Gina Sawyer
    E-Mail: sawyer@aaslh.org

Historical Note:
Formerly the Council of Historical Societies. Absorbed the Association of Historic Sites Officials in 1963. AASLH provides leadership and support for its members who preserve and interpret state and local history in order to make the past more meaningful to all Americans. Membership: $25-250 (Individual Membership); $1,000 (Institutional Partner); $750 (Institutional Sustaining); $500 (Supporting Institutional); $250 (Contributing Institutional); $115 (Basic Institutional).

Meetings/Conferences: Annual
Conference Chair: Gina Sawyer
2013 - Birmingham, United Kingdom/Sept. 18 - 21

Publications:
Dispatch; monthly; adv.
History News; quarterly; adv.

Membership List Available to Non-members

American Association for the Advancement of Artificial Intelligence *(1979)*
2275 E. Bayshore Rd.
Suite 160
Palo Alto, CA 94303
Tel: (650) 328-3123 *Fax:* (650) 321-4457
E-Mail: info7contact@aaai.org
Website: aaai.org
Members: 6000 individuals
Staff: 5
Annual Budget: $1-2,000,000
Tax: 501(c)(3)

Personnel:
Executive Director: Carol M. Hamilton
Finance and Office Manager: Colleen Boyce
Senior Coordinator, Conferences: Karen Harvey
Editor: David B. Leake
Coordinator, Membership Services: Alanna Spencer

Historical Note:
Formerly American Association for Artificial Intelligence. AAAI strives to advance the scientific understanding of the mechanisms underlying thought and intelligent behavior and their embodiment in machines. Members are individuals interested in attempting to approximate the human thinking process with computers in such fields as visual data interpretation, expert systems, natural language processing, common sense reasoning, automated problem solving, and robotics. Membership: $140 (Individual); $1960 (Life Member); $70 (Student); $280 (Institution or Library).

Meetings/Conferences:
Conference Chair: Karen Harvey
2013 - Stanford, CA (Stanford University)/March 25 - 27
Number of non-conference events/year: 2

Publications:
AI Magazine; quarterly; adv.
Journal of Artificial Intelligence Research; semi-annually

American Association for the Advancement of Science *(1848)*
1200 New York Ave. NW

Washington, DC 20005
Tel: (202) 326-6400 *Fax:* (202) 371-9526
E-Mail: webmaster@aaas.org
Website: aaas.org
Members: 130000 individuals
Staff: 300
Annual Budget: $50-100,000,000
Tax: 501(c)(3)

Personnel:
Chief Executive Officer: Alan I. Leshner
Chief Financial Officer: Phillip 'Phil' Blair
Director, Center for Science, Technology and Congress:
   Joanne Padrón Carney
Meetings Assistant: Kim Klyberg
   E-Mail: kklyberg@aaas.org
Head, Directorate for Education and HR Programs: Shirley
   M. Malcom
   E-Mail: smalcom@aaas.org
Manager, Meetings: Nicole Maylett
   E-Mail: nmaylett@aaas.org
Senior Manager, Meetings, Marketing and Operations: Jill
   Perla
Director, Office of Public Programs: Ginger Pinholster
   E-Mail: gpinhols@aaas.org
Director, Meetings: Barbara Rice
   E-Mail: brice@aaas.org
Director, Science and Policy Programs: Albert H. Teich
   E-Mail: ateich@aaas.org

Historical Note:
*AAAS's mission is to advance science, engineering, and
innovation throughout the world for the benefit of all
people.. Membership: $149 (Professional); $75 (Student);
$99 (Postdoctoral/Resident/K-12 Teacher); $119 (NPA
Postdoctoral); $310 (Patron); $115 (Emeritus).*

Meetings/Conferences: Annual
Conference Chair: Nicole Maylett
2013 - Boston, MA/Feb. 14 - 18
2014 - Chicago, IL/Feb. 13 - 17
2015 - San Jose, CA/Feb. 12 - 16

Publications:
AAAS Advances; monthly
Annual Meeting Newsletter; annually
Bio-Med Roundup; monthly
Membership Directory; on-line
Science; weekly; adv.
Science Signaling
Science Translational Medicine Home

Membership List Available to Non-members

American Association for the Advancement of Slavic Studies *(1960)*
Univ.of Pittsburgh
203C Bellefield Hall
Pittsburgh, PA 15260-6424
Tel: (412) 648-9911 *Fax:* (412) 648-9815
Website: aseees.org
Members: 3,500 members
Staff: 6
Annual Budget: $500-1,000,000

Personnel:
Executive Director: Lynda Park
   E-Mail: lypark@pitt.edu
Communications Coordinator and Editor: Mary Arnstein
   E-Mail: newsnet@pitt.edu
Managing Editor: Jane T. Hedges
Finance Coordinator: Maureen Ryczaj
   E-Mail: aseeesfn@pitt.edu
Coordinator, Membership and Subscriptions Services:
   Jonathon Swiderski
   E-Mail: aseees@pitt.edu
Convention Coordinator: Wendy Walker
   E-Mail: wwalker@pitt.edu

Historical Note:
*Formerly, the American Association for the Advancement
of Slavic Studies and assumed its current name in 2010.
ASEEES is committed to the advancement of knowledge
about the former Soviet Union (including Eurasia)
and Eastern and Central Europe. Membership: $35
(Student); $45 (Affiliate); $85 (Affiliate/Joint Membership);
$150-600 (Institutional).*

Meetings/Conferences: Annual
Conference Chair: Wendy Walker
2013 - Boston, MA (Boston Marriot Copley Place)/Nov.
   21 - 24
2014 - San Antonio, TX (San Antonio Marriott
   Rivercenter)/Nov. 20 - 23

2015 - Philadelphia, PA (Philadelphia Marriott
   Downtown)/Nov. 19 - 22

Publications:
NewsNet Magazine; adv.
NewsNet Newsletter; bi-monthly
Slavic Review; quarterly; adv.

American Association for the History of Medicine *(1925)*
C/O Stony Brook University
Stony Brook, NY 11794
Tel: (631) 632-6000
E-Mail: aahm@kumc.edu
Website: histmed.org
Members: 1300 individuals
Staff: 3
Annual Budget: $100-250,000

Personnel:
President: Nancy Tomes
   E-Mail: nancy.tomes@stonybrook.edu

Historical Note:
*Incorporated in New York in 1958. AAHM is dedicated
to the study of the history of health, healing and disease.
Members include physicians and practitioners of other
health sciences, professional historians, laboratory
scientists, librarians and individuals from other disciplines.
Membership: $25-1,500/year.*

Meetings/Conferences: Annual
2013 - Atlanta, GA/May 16 - 19
2014 - Chicago, IL/May 8 - 11
2015 - New Haven, CT/April 29 - May 3

Publications:
AAHM Newsletter
Bulletin of the History of Medicine; quarterly; adv.

American Association for the History of Nursing *(1978)*
10200 W. 44th Ave.
Suite 304
Wheat Ridge, CO 80033
Tel: (303) 422-2685 *Fax:* (303) 422-8894
E-Mail: aahn@aahn.org
Website: aahn.org
Members: 500 individuals
Staff: 6
Annual Budget: $50-100,000
Tax: 501(c)(3)

Personnel:
Executive Director: David L. Stumph CAE, IOM
   E-Mail: dstumph@resourcenter.com
Editor: Patricia D'Antonio PhD, RN, CAE, IOM
   E-Mail: dantonio@nursing.upenn.edu
Director, Membership Services: Kristi Klinke
Director, Information Services: Ruth Gleason Roth

Historical Note:
*AAHN's purpose is to foster the importance of history as
relevant to understanding the past, defining the present and
influencing the future of nursing. Members are individuals
with an interest in the history of nursing. Membership:
$150 (Regular/Agency); $250 (Supporting); $75 (Student/
Retiree).*

Meetings/Conferences: Annual
2013 - Cleaveland, OH (Cleveland Clinic)/Sept. 26 - 29

Publications:
Bulletin- Newsletter; quarterly
Nursing History Review; annually

American Association for the Study of Hungarian History *(1970)*
St. Johns University, Department of
Administration and Economics
College of Professional Studies, 8000 Utopia
Pkwy.
Jamaica, NY 11439
Tel: (718) 990-6161 *Fax:* (718) 990-1882
E-Mail: glanzs@stjohns.edu
Website: h-net.org/~habsweb/aashh.htm
Members: 140 individuals
Staff: 2
Annual Budget: Under $10,000

Personnel:
Secretary and Treasurer: Susan Glanz
   E-Mail: glanzs@stjohns.edu

Historical Note:
*AASHH members are academics specializing in the history
of Hungary. Purpose is to further interest in Hungarian
history and to encourage research in this field. The*

*association also aims to cooperate with scholars and
institutions with similar interests in Hungary. Organizes
panels for participation at scholarly conferences with The
American Historical Association (Parent Organisation).
Membership: $10/year.*

Meetings/Conferences: Annual
Number of non-conference events/year: 2

Publications:
AASHH Newsletter; quarterly

American Association for the Study of Liver Diseases *(1949)*
1001 N. Fairfax St.
Suite 400
Alexandria, VA 22314
Tel: (703) 299-9766 *Fax:* (703) 299-9622
E-Mail: aasld@aasld.org
Website: aasld.org
Members: 3506 individuals
Staff: 35
Annual Budget: $10-25,000,000
Tax: 501(c)(3)

Personnel:
Executive Director: Sherrie Cathcart CAE
   E-Mail: scathcart@aasld.org
Director, Development: Heidi Bruce
   E-Mail: hbruce@aasld.org
Senior Manager, Publications: Ann Haran
   E-Mail: aharan@aasld.org
Director, Marketing: Yvonne Kassimatis
   E-Mail: ykassimatis@aasld.org
Director, Education: Janeil Klett
   E-Mail: jklett@aasld.org
Director, Membership Services: Joshua Lowe
   E-Mail: jlowe@aasld.org
*Senior Director, Information Technology and Business
   Analyst:* Paula McGraw
   E-Mail: pmcgraw@aasld.org
Director, Meetings and Conferences: Melissa Parrish
   E-Mail: mparrish@aasld.org
Chief Operations Officer: Nellie Sarkissian
   E-Mail: nsarkissian@aasld.org

Historical Note:
*AASLD's mission is to advance the science and practice of
hepatology, liver transplantation and hepatobiliary surgery,
thereby promoting liver health and optimal care of patients
with liver and biliary tract diseases. Membership: $375
(Regular/International); $135 (Associate); $700 (Corporate
Affiliate); $120 (Trainee).*

Meetings/Conferences: Annual
Conference Chair: Melissa Parrish
2013 - Washington, DC/Nov. 1 - 5
2014 - Boston, MA/Nov. 7 - 11

Publications:
AASLD Newsletter; bi-weekly
Hepatology; monthly; adv.
Liver Transplantation; monthly; adv.
Membership Directory; monthly

American Association for the Surgery of Trauma *(1938)*
633 N. Saint Clair St.
Suite 2600
Chicago, IL 60611
Tel: (312) 202-5252 *Fax:* (312) 202-5064
TollFree: (800) 789-4006
E-Mail: aast@aast.org
Website: aast.org
Members: 1200 individuals
Staff: 3
Annual Budget: $2-5,000,000
Tax: 501(c)(3)

Personnel:
Executive Director: Sharon Gautschy
   E-Mail: sgautschy@aast.org
Manager, Education: Sarah Cohen
Administrator, Programs: Tamara Jenkins
   E-Mail: tjenkins@aast.org

Historical Note:
*AAST's mission is to serve surgeons dedicated in the
field of trauma and the care of critically ill surgical
patients. AAST is dedicated in discovery, dissemination,
implementation, and evaluation of knowledge related
to acute care surgery (trauma, surgical critical care,
and emergency general surgery) by fostering research,
education, and professional development in an environment
of fellowship and collegiality.*

Meetings/Conferences: Annual

Conference Chair: Tamara Jenkins
2013 - San Francisco, CA (Hotel Adagio)/Sept. 18 -
   21/1000 attendees
2014 - Philadelphia, PA (Philadelphia Marriott
   Downtown)/Sept. 10 - 13/1000 attendees
2015 - San Diego, CA (Manchester Grand Hyatt San
   Diego)/Sept. 9 - 12/1000 attendees
2016 - Waikoloa, HI (Hilton Waikoloa Village)/Sept. 14
   - 17/1000 attendees

Publications:
Journal of Trauma; monthly
Membership Directory; on-line

American Association of Thoracic Surgery (1917)

500 Cummings Center
Suite 4550
Beverly, MA 01915
Tel: (978) 927-8330 Fax: (978) 524-8890
Website: aats.org
Members: 1200 individuals
Staff: 2
Annual Budget: $5-10,000,000

Personnel:
Executive Director: Elizabeth Dooley Crane CAE, CMP
Director, Meetings and Conventions: Jane Pimental
   E-Mail: jpimental@prri.com

Historical Note:
Organized in New York City. AATS's mission is to
promote and foster education and research in the field of
cardiothoracic surgery.

Meetings/Conferences: Annual
Conference Chair: Jane Pimental
2013 - Minneapolis, MN (Minneapolis Convention
   Center)/May 4 - 8
2014 - Toronto, ON (Metro Toronto Convention
   Centre)/April 26 - 30
2015 - Seatle, WA (Washington State Convention
   Center)/April 25 - 29
Number of non-conference events/year: 1

Publications:
Journal of Thoracic and Cardiovascular Surgery;
   monthly; adv.
Operative Techniques in Thoracic and Cardiovascular
   Surgery; quarterly; adv.
Pediatric Cardiac Surgery Annual; annually; adv.
Seminars in Thoracic and Cardiovascular Surgery;
   quarterly; adv.
Thoracic Surgery News; adv.
Thoracic Surgery News; monthly

American Association for Vocational Instructional Materials (1949)

220 Smithonia Rd.
Winterville, GA 30683-9527
Tel: (706) 742-5355 Fax: (706) 742-7005
TollFree: (800) 228-4689
Website: aavim.com
Members: 6 U.S. states
Staff: 4
Annual Budget: $100-250,000

Personnel:
President: Marion Fletcher
Business Manager: Kim Butler
Director: Gary Farmer
   E-Mail: gary@aavim.com

Historical Note:
AAVIM is a non-profit association whose mission is
to develop, produce and distribute quality instructional
materials for instructors, students and administrators.

American Association for Women in Community Colleges (1973)

765 Newman Springs Rd.
Lincroft, NJ 07738
E-Mail: info@aawccnatl.org
Website: aawccnatl.org
Members: 1000 individuals
Staff: 5
Annual Budget: $100-250,000

Personnel:
President: Maureen Murphy
   E-Mail: mmurphy@brookdalecc.edu

Historical Note:
Formerly (1993) American Association for Women in
Community and Junior Colleges. AAWCC's mission is to
champion women and maximizes their potential. Members
are women faculty, administrators, staff members, trustees,
students and others concerned with women's issues,
programs and professional development in the community,
junior or technical college setting. Membership: Dues based
on income (Individual); $450 (Institution).

Publications:
AAWCC Newsletter; on-line
Bulletien Board; on-line
Member Directory; on-line

American Association for Women Podiatrists (1965)

6042 Sierra Siena
Irvine, CA 92603
Tel: (949) 854-3636
Website: aawpinc.com
Members: 800 individuals
Staff: 2
Annual Budget: $25-50,000

Personnel:
President: Sheryl Strich DPM
   E-Mail: sstrich@americanwomenpodiatrists.com

Historical Note:
AAWP's mission is to advance the educational, political,
financial, social and emotional well-being of its members.
Membership: $100 (Active); $30 (Associate); $750 (Life);
$175 (Friends); $0 (Resident).

Meetings/Conferences:
2013 - Coral Gables, FL (Biltmore Resort)/April 26 - 28

Publications:
AAWP Newsletter; quarterly

American Association for Women Radiologists (1981)

4550 Post Oak Pl.
Suite 342
Houston, TX 77027
Tel: (713) 965-0566 Fax: (713) 960-0488
E-Mail: admin@aawr.org
Website: aawr.org
Members: 1100 individuals
Staff: 3
Annual Budget: $100-250,000
Tax: 501(c)(6)

Personnel:
President: Julia R. Fielding MD
Association Director: Angela Davis
   E-Mail: adavis@meetingmanagers.com
Treasurer: Margaret Szabunio MD

Historical Note:
Formerly (1991) American Association of Women
Radiologists, AAWR works to provide a forum for issues
to women in radiology, radiation oncology and related
professions. Membership: $125 (Active/Associate); $50
(First and Second Year in Practice in U.S. or Canada); $25
(Emeritus); $15 (International Member). Membership is free
for medical students and for members in training.

Publications:
AAWR Newsletter; quarterly

American Association for Wound Care Management (1998)

4109 Glenrose St.
Kensington, MD 20895
Website: aawcm.org
Staff: 2
Annual Budget: $100-250,000

Personnel:
Executive Director: Jule Crider
   E-Mail: jule.crider@gmail.com
Treasurer: Patricia Pasceri

Historical Note:
Association of wound care centers and clinics.

American Association of Acupuncture and Oriental Medicine (1981)

9650 Rockville Pike
Bethesda, MD 20814
Tel: (916) 443-4770 Fax: (301) 634-7099
TollFree: (866) 455-7999
E-Mail: info@aaaomonline.org
Website: aaaomonline.org
Members:
100 companies
1200 individuals
Staff: 5
Annual Budget: $250-500,000
Tax: 501(c)(6)

Personnel:
Contact, Member Services: Eleanor Peebles
   E-Mail: epeebles@aaaomonline.org
Administrative and Marketing Assistant: Tanisha Minor
Manager, Information Technology: Brian Smither BSEE

Historical Note:
Originally established in 1981. In 2007, the American
Association of Oriental Medicine (AAOM) and the AOM
Alliance reunited to form AAAOM. Mission is to promote
excellence and integrity in the professional practice of
acupuncture and Oriental medicine, in order to enhance
public health and well-being. AAAOM interacts with a
wide range of organizations, institutions and associations
that oversee, govern, advance or interact with the practice
of Acupuncture and Oriental Medicine within the United
States. Membership: $50-450/year.

Publications:
Membership Directory; on-line; adv.
The American Acupuncturist; quarterly

Membership List Available to Non-members

American Association of Advertising Agencies (1917)

1065 Avenue of the Americas
16th Floor
New York, NY 10018
Tel: (212) 682-2500 Fax: (212) 682-8391
TollFree: (800) 536-7346
Website: aaaa.org
Members: 1200 companies
Staff: 104
Annual Budget: $10-25,000,000

Personnel:
President and Chief Executive Officer: Nancy Hill
   E-Mail: nhill@aaaa.org
Senior Vice President, Communications: Portia E. Badham
   E-Mail: pbadham@aaaa.org
Chief Financial Officer and Chief Operating Officer: Laura
J. Bartlett
   E-Mail: lbartlett@aaaa.org
Senior Vice President and Chief Information Officer: Chick
Foxgrover
   E-Mail: cfoxgrover@aaaa.org
Senior Vice President, Digital Initiatives: Harold Geller
   E-Mail: hgeller@aaaa.org
Senior Vice President, Marketing: John Kaiser
   E-Mail: john@aaaa.org
Senior Vice President, Training Education and Development:
Bob Linden
   E-Mail: bobl@aaaa.org
Vice President, Conferences and Events: Gerald F. Longo
   E-Mail: glongo@aaaa.org
Vice President and Director, Production Services: Kathleen
Quinn
   E-Mail: kathleen@aaaa.org
Executive Vice President, Agency Relations and Membership
   Services: Jennifer Seidel
   E-Mail: jseidel@aaaa.org
Senior Vice President, Human Resources and
   Administration: Rhonda Steeg
   E-Mail: rhonda@aaaa.org
General Counsel: David Versfelt

Historical Note:
AAAA's mission is to work with Federal, state, and local
governments to help achieve desirable social and civic
goals, to influence public policy. Members are advertising
agencies or other organizations that create and/or places
advertising or marketing communications. Membership:
$3,000/year.

Continuing Education:
Certification Designation/s: IAAS

Meetings/Conferences:
Conference Chair: Gerald F. Longo
2013 - New Orleans, LA/March 11 - 13
Number of non-conference events/year: 1

Publications:
SmartBrief; daily

Membership List Available to Non-members

American Association of Airport Executives (1928)

601 Madison St.
Suite 400
Alexandria, VA 22314
Tel: (703) 824-0500 Fax: (703) 820-1395
Website: aaae.org
Members: 5,000 individual members

Staff: 72
Annual Budget: $10-25,000,000
Tax: 501(c)(6)

Personnel:
President: Charles Barclay AAE
 E-Mail: charles.barclay@aaae.org
Director, Electronic Publications: Holly Ackerman
 E-Mail: holly.ackerman@aaae.org
Director, Legislative and Regulatory Communication: Gwen Basaria
 E-Mail: gwen.basaria@aaae.org
Director, Human Resources: Calvin Crawford SPHR
 E-Mail: calvin.crawford@aaae.org
Director, Membership, Accreditation and Certification Programs: Cindy DeWitt
 E-Mail: Cindy.DeWitt@aaae.org
Senior Vice President, Finance and Administration: Tyra Harpster
 E-Mail: tyra.harpster@aaae.org
Senior Executive Vice President, Government Affairs and Senior Executive Producer, Aviation News Tod: Todd J Hauptli
 E-Mail: todd.hauptli@aaae.org
Senior Vice President, Communications: Joan Lowden
 E-Mail: joan.lowden@aaae.org
Senior Vice President, Information Systems: Patrick Osborne
 E-Mail: patrick.osborne@aaae.org
Director, Legislative and Regulatory Communications: Gwen Papineau-Basaria
 E-Mail: Gwen.Papineau@aaae.org
Vice President, Meetings: Jacky Sher Raker
 E-Mail: jacky.sher.raker@aaae.org
Director, Sales, Marketing and Meetings: Amy Trivette
 E-Mail: Amy.Trivette@aaae.org

Historical Note:
AAAE is dedicated to serve airports and the aviation industry, and provides critical support to the association through their participation in meetings and workshops. Membership: $40-850/year.

Continuing Education:
Certification Designation/s: ACE, AAEP, CM

Meetings/Conferences:
Conference Chair: Jacky Sher Raker
2013 - Reno, NV/May 5 - 7
2013 - Reno, NV (Reno-Sparks Convention Center)/ May 19 - 22
2014 - San Antonio, TX/May 18 - 21
Number of non-conference events/year: 79

Publications:
Airport Magazine; irregular
Airport Report Today; bi-weekly

Membership List Available to Non-members

American Association of Anatomists (1888)
9650 Rockville Pike
Bethesda, MD 20814-3998
Tel: (301) 634-7910 *Fax:* (301) 634-7965
E-Mail: exec@anatomy.org
Website: anatomy.org
Members: 1800 individuals
Staff: 7
Annual Budget: $1-2,000,000
Tax: 501(c)(3)

Personnel:
Executive Director: Andrea Pendleton
 E-Mail: apendleton@anatomy.org
Manager, Membership Services and Marketing: Melissa Kraft
 E-Mail: mkraft@anatomy.org
Program Manager, Membership Services and Accounting Coordinator: Liz Phares
 E-Mail: lphares@anatomy.org
Manager, Meetings: Colby Shultz
 E-Mail: cshultz@anatomy.org
Manager, Education and Professional Development: Wendy Zosh-McLean
 E-Mail: wzosh@anatomy.org

Historical Note:
Established as the Association of American Anatomists, Became the American Association of Anatomists in 1908. AAA serves as the professional home for an international community of biomedical researchers and educators focusing on anatomical form and function. Membership: $130 (Regular); $30 (Student/HAPS); $45 (Professional).

Meetings/Conferences: Annual
Conference Chair: Colby Shultz

2013 - Boston, MA/April 20 - 24
2014 - San Diego, CA/April 26 - 30
2015 - Boston, MA/March 28 - April 1
2016 - San Diego, CA/April 2 - 6
2017 - Washington, DC/April 22 - 26
2018 - San Diego, CA/April 21 - 25
Number of non-conference events/year: 32

Publications:
AAA Newsletter; quarterly; adv.
Anatomical Sciences Education(ASE); adv.
Developmental Dynamics (DD); adv.
E-Stratum; on-line
Membership Directory; on-line
The Anatomical Record (AR); adv.

Membership List Available to Non-members

American Association of Attorney-Certified Public Accountants (1964)
3921 Old Lee Hwy.
Suite 71-A
Fairfax, VA 22030
Tel: (703) 352-8064 *Fax:* (703) 352-8073
TollFree: (888) 288-9272
E-Mail: info@attorney-cpa.com
Website: attorney-cpa.com
Members: 1200 individuals
Staff: 4
Annual Budget: $250-500,000

Personnel:
Executive Director: Nicole E. Ratner CAE, CMP
 E-Mail: nratner@attorney-cpa.com
Administrator, Meetings: Melissa R. Benowitz CMP
 E-Mail: meetings@attorney-cpa.com
office Administrator: Katie Cammer
Coordinator, Chapter and Membership: Kimmy Livingston
 E-Mail: klivingston@attorney-cpa.com

Historical Note:
AAA-CPA's mission is to protect the rights of those dually qualified to practice as they see fit, be it law, accounting, or both. Membership: $240 (Regular/International); $40 (Associate/Student); $75 (Educator/Government); $2,750 (Life).

Continuing Education:
Certification Designation/s: CLE, MCLE, CPE

Meetings/Conferences:
Conference Chair: Melissa R. Benowitz CMP
2013 - Las Vegas, NV (Mandalay Bay Resort and Casino)/Nov. 6 - 10

Publications:
Attorney-CPA Update; weekly; adv.
Monthly Update; monthly
Networking & Referral Directory; annually; adv.
The Attorney-CPA Newsletter; quarterly; adv.

Membership List Available to Non-members

American Association of Automatic Door Manufacturers (1994)
1300 Sumner Ave.
Cleveland, OH 44115-2851
Tel: (216) 241-7333 *Fax:* (216) 241-0105
E-Mail: aaadm@aaadm.com
Website: aaadm.com
Members: 18 companies
Staff: 3
Annual Budget: $250-500,000
Tax: 501(c)(6)

Personnel:
Executive Director: Chris Johnson

Historical Note:
AAADM is a trade association of manufacturers of automatic pedestrian door systems. AAADM's mission is to increase education, training and professionalism among installers and service providers and to generally promote the safe use of automatic doors. Members are automatic door manufacturers who make their automatic doors and components in compliance with the ANSI/BHMA Standard for Power Operated Pedestrian Doors, ANSI A156.10-2005. Membership: $10,250/year (Company).

American Association of Avian Pathologists (1957)
12627 San Jose Blvd.
Suite 202
Jacksonville, FL 32223-8638
Tel: (904) 425-5735 *Fax:* (281) 664-4744
E-Mail: aaap@aaap.info
Website: aaap.info

Members: 1000 individuals
Staff: 2
Annual Budget: $500-1,000,000
Tax: 501(c)(6)

Personnel:
Executive Director: Bob Bevans-Kerr
Director, Membership Services: Janece Bevans-Kerr

Historical Note:
Affiliated with the American Veterinary Medical Association. Veterinarians specializing in poultry and their diseases. AAAP assures prevention and elimination of suffering and loss of poultry due to disease and the provision of a safe poultry-associated food supply through providing an open exchange of scientific and practical information. Membership: $110-130/year (Individual).

Meetings/Conferences: Annual
Number of non-conference events/year: 5

Publications:
Avian Diseases Journal; quarterly
Membership Directory; on-line

American Association of Bank Directors (1989)
1250 24th St. NW
Suite 700
Washington, DC 20037
Tel: (202) 463-4888 *Fax:* (202) 349-8080
E-Mail: info@aabd.org
Website: aabd.org
Staff: 3
Tax: 501(c)(6)

Personnel:
Executive Director: David H. Baris Esq.
 E-Mail: dbaris@aabd.org
Director, Marketing and Vice President: Andrew Baris
Director, Membership Services: Betty Pelton
 E-Mail: membership@aabd.org

Historical Note:
AABD's mission is to provide bank and savings institution directors the resources with which they can serve their institutions in a manner that will minimize risk of personal liability. Membership: $695 (Institution/Board Premium); $295 (Individual Premium); $750 (Individual Associate).

Continuing Education:
Certification Designation/s: BDEC, IBDE

Meetings/Conferences: Annual

Publications:
Bank Director Magazine
Bank Director News-Newsletter

American Association of Behavioral Therapists (1985)
P.O. Box 1737
Ormond Beach, FL 32175-1737
Tel: (386) 882-7999
Website: btherapy.net
Members: 1000 individuals
Staff: 1
Annual Budget: $25-50,000

Personnel:
President: Dan J. Allen PhD
 E-Mail: dallen50@aol.com

Historical Note:
AABT is dedicated to help mental health counselors and therapists achieve greater professional success and proficiency. Members are therapists and counselors who use behavioral science techniques, such as biofeedback, hypnosis, conditioned learning. Membership: $59/year.

Publications:
The Therapist Report; quarterly

American Association of Bioanalysts (1956)
906 Olive St.
Suite 1200
St. Louis, MO 63101
Tel: (314) 241-1445 *Fax:* (314) 241-1449
E-Mail: aab@aab.org
Website: aab.org
Members: 4000 individuals
Staff: 2
Annual Budget: $5-10,000,000
Tax: 501(c)(6)

Personnel:
Administrator: Mark S. Birenbaum PhD
Associate Administrator: Tammy Schalue PhD

Historical Note:

AAB is dedicated to serving the community clinical laboratory and the professionals involved in clinical laboratory operations. Its members are clinical laboratory directors, owners, managers, supervisors, technologists, technicians, and phlebotomists. Laboratories can also become members through AAB's National Independent Laboratory Association (NILA).

Continuing Education:
Certification Designation/s: BCLD, ELD, CC, GS, HCLD, TS, MLT, PBT, MT, POLT

Meetings/Conferences: Annual
2013 - Las Vegas, NV (Golden Nugget Hotel and Casino)/May 16 - 18

Publications:
The AAB Bulletin; quarterly; adv.

American Association of Birth Centers (1983)
3123 Gottschall Rd.
Perkiomenville, PA 18074
Tel: (215) 234-8068 Fax: (215) 234-8829
TollFree: (866) 542-4784
E-Mail: aabc@birthcenters.org
Website: birthcenters.org
Members:
180 birth centers
350 individuals
Staff: 3
Annual Budget: $250-500,000
Tax: 501(c)(6)

Personnel:
Executive Director: Kate E. Bauer MBA
    E-Mail: aabc@birthcenters.org
Administrative Assistant: Lisa Recke

Historical Note:
AABC's mission is dedicated to the promotion of the rights of healthy women and their families, in all communities, to birth their children in an environment which is safe, sensitive and economical with minimal intervention.Membership: $635-1560 (Birth Center Members); $47.50-2355 (Normal Birth Advocate Members).

Continuing Education:
Certification Designation/s: PSNA, CNM

Meetings/Conferences: Annual
Number of non-conference events/year: 1

Publications:
AABC News; quarterly; adv.
Legislative Alert; on-line
Membership Directory; annually; adv.

Membership List Available to Non-members

American Association of Blacks in Energy (1977)
1625 K St. NW
Suite 405
Washington, DC 20006
Tel: (202) 371-9530 Fax: (202) 371-9218
TollFree: (800) 466-0204
E-Mail: aabe@aabe.org
Website: aabe.org
Members: 1300 individuals
Staff: 3
Annual Budget: $1-2,000,000
Tax: 501(c)(3)

Personnel:
President and Chief Executive Officer: Arnetta McRae
    E-Mail: amcrae@aabe.org
Vice President, Operations: Paula Jackson
    E-Mail: pjackson@aabe.org
Director, Membership Services: Lakeesha Wilson
    E-Mail: lwilson@aabe.org

Historical Note:
AABE's mission is to ensure the input of African Americans and other minorities into the discussions and developments of energy policies regulations, R&D technologies, and environmental issues. Membership: $150 (Individual); $20 (Student); $200 (Sustaining); $250 (Board of Directors).

Meetings/Conferences:
Conference Chair: Lakeesha Wilson
Number of non-conference events/year: 1

Publications:
Newsletter; quarterly

American Association of Bovine Practitioners (1965)
P.O. Box 3610
Auburn, AL 36831-3610
Tel: (334) 821-0442 Fax: (334) 821-9532

TollFree: (800) 269-2227
E-Mail: aabphq@aabp.org
Website: aabp.org
Members: 6000 individuals
Staff: 4
Annual Budget: $1-2,000,000
Tax: 501(c)(3)

Personnel:
Executive Vice President: Dr. M. Gatz Riddell Jr.
    E-Mail: MGRiddell@AABP.ORG
Coordinator, Information Technology: Steve Johnson
    E-Mail: Steve@GPVEC.UNL.EDU
Administrative Assistant: Katie W. O'Neal
    E-Mail: aabphq@aabp.org

Historical Note:
AABP strives to enhance the professional lives of its members through relevant continuing education that will improve the well-being of cattle and the economic success of their owners, increase awareness and promote leadership for issues critical to cattle industries, and improve opportunities for careers in bovine medicine. Members are veterinarians. Membership: $125 (Active); $20 (Student); Free (Honor Roll/Honorary).

Meetings/Conferences: Annual
2013 - Milwaukee, WI/Sept. 19 - 21
2014 - Albuquerue, NM/Sept. 18 - 20
2015 - New Orleans, LA/Sept. 17 - 19
2016 - Charlotte, NC/Sept. 15 - 17
2017 - Omaha, NE/Sept. 14 - 16

Publications:
AABP Newsletter; monthly
Annual Membership Directory; annually
The Bovine Practitioner; semi-annually

American Association of Business Valuation Specialists (1995)
P.O. Box 13089
Tallahassee, FL 32317
Tel: (850) 878-3134 Fax: (850) 878-1291
E-Mail: ems-rac@nettally.com
Website: aabvs.com
Members: 180 individuals
Staff: 4
Annual Budget: $10-25,000

Personnel:
President and Chief Executive Officer: Robert S. Rhinehart

Historical Note:
Awards the designation BVS (Business Valuation Specialist). The purpose is to promote the interests and opportunities of individuals interested in the small business valuation field. Regardless of their prior business background, many individuals in the following fields (and others) are interested in engaging in the business valuation profession in the United States and internationally. Membership: $60/year.

American Association of Candy Technologists (1947)
711 W. Water St.
P.O. Box 266
Princeton, WI 54968
Tel: (920) 295-6969 Fax: (920) 295-6843
E-Mail: aactinfo@gomc.com
Website: aactcandy.org
Members: 650 individuals
Staff: 2
Annual Budget: $100-250,000

Personnel:
President: Randy Hofberger
    E-Mail: rdcandyc@wi.rr.com
Treasurer: Michael Allured
    E-Mail: mikea@gomc.com

Historical Note:
AACT's purpose is the advancement of the confectionery industry. AACT is a professional group of individual technologists, operations personnel, educators, students, business staff and others. Membership: $75 (U.S.); $80 (Canada); $135 (Other Countries).

Meetings/Conferences: Annual

Publications:
Newsletter

American Association of Cardiovascular and Pulmonary Rehabilitation (1985)
401 N. Michigan Ave.
Suite 2200
Chicago, IL 60611
Tel: (312) 321-5146 Fax: (312) 673-6924

E-Mail: aacvpr@aacvpr.org
Website: aacvpr.org
Members: 3000 individuals
Staff: 7
Annual Budget: $1-2,000,000

Personnel:
Executive Director: Joanne Ray
    E-Mail: jray@aacvpr.org
Manager, Development: Jessica Eustice
    E-Mail: jeustice@aacvpr.org
Senior Associate, Membership Services: Jonah Gorski
Senior Manager, Conventions: Eric Johnson
Administrative Associate: Erica Naranjo
Senior Director, Marketing and Communications: Linda Schwartz
Senior Manager, Information Technology: Rodney Stiegman

Historical Note:
AACVPR's mission is to reduce morbidity, mortality, and disability from cardiovascular and pulmonary diseases through education, prevention, rehabilitation, research, and aggressive disease management and thereby improve the quality of life for patients and their families. Members include cardiovascular and pulmonary physicians, nurses, exercise physiologists, physical therapists, behavioral scientists, respiratory therapists and nutritionists. Membership: $195 (Individual); $75 (Student).

Continuing Education:
Certification Designation/s: PPC, CRPC

Meetings/Conferences: Annual
Conference Chair: Eric Johnson
2013 - Nashville, TN/Oct. 3 - 5

Publications:
Journal of Cardiopulmonary Rehabilitation and Prevention(JCRP); bi-monthly; adv.
News & Views; bi-monthly

American Association of Cereal Chemists International (1915)
3340 Pilot Knob Rd.
St. Paul, MN 55121-2097
Tel: (651) 454-7250 Fax: (651) 454-0766
E-Mail: aacc@scisoc.org
Website: aaccnet.org
Members: 2500 individuals
Staff: 10
Annual Budget: $2-5,000,000
Tax: 501(c)(3)

Personnel:
Executive Vice President: Steve C. Nelson
    E-Mail: snelson@scisoc.org
Director, Membership and Communications: Michelle Bjerkness
    E-Mail: mbjerkness@scisoc.org
Marketing Manager, Meetings, Membership and Publications: Karen Deuschle
    E-Mail: kdeuschle@scisoc.org
Director, Meetings: Betty Ford
    E-Mail: bford@scisoc.org
Director, Publications: Greg Grahek
    E-Mail: ggrahek@scisoc.org
Contact, Continuing Education: Jody Grider
    E-Mail: jgrider@scisoc.org
Vice President, Operations: Amy Hope
    E-Mail: ahope@scisoc.org
Editor-in-Chief: R. Carl Hoseney
    E-Mail: choseney@scisoc.org
Vice President, Finance: Barbara Mock
    E-Mail: bmock@scisoc.org
Manager, Education: Tressa Patrias
    E-Mail: tpatrias@scisoc.org

Historical Note:
AACC International, formerly the American Association of Cereal Chemists, is a professional organization of members doing grain research and the use of grains in foods. Membership: $10-1,350/year.

Meetings/Conferences: Annual
Conference Chair: Betty Ford
2013 - Albuquerue, NM/Sept. 29 - Oct. 2/1000 attendees/11-25 exhibitors
2014 - Providence, RI/Oct. 5 - 8/1000 attendees/11-25 exhibitors
2015 - Minneapolis, MN/Oct. 18 - 21/1000 attendees/11-25 exhibitors
Number of non-conference events/year: 5

Publications:
Membership Directory

American Association of Certified Allergists
(1968)
85 W. Algonquin Rd.
Suite 550
Arlington Heights, IL 60005-4425
Tel: (847) 427-8111 *Fax:* (847) 427-9656
E-Mail: rslawney@surgonc.org
Members: 550 individuals
Staff: 2
Annual Budget: Under $10,000

Personnel:
Executive Director: Rick Slawny
Editor in Chief: Joseph A. Bellanti

Historical Note:
Membership: $75/year.

American Association of Certified Orthoptists
(1940)
3914 Nakoma Rd.
Madison, WI 53711
Tel: (608) 233-5383 *Fax:* (608) 263-4247
Website: orthoptics.org
Members: 300 individuals
Staff: 5
Annual Budget: $50-100,000

Personnel:
President: Bruce Furr
  E-Mail: bfurr@umich.edu
Contact, Website Services: Nikki Batra
  E-Mail: nnagarwa@yahoo.com
Contact, Membership Services: Neva Fukuda
  E-Mail: neva.fukuda@vanderbilt.edu
Secretary: Marlo Galli
  E-Mail: galli@vision.wustl.edu
Contact, Publications: Emily Miyazaki
  E-Mail: eamiyazaki@aol.com

Historical Note:
Founded in October 1940 in Cleveland as the American Association of Orthoptic Technicians; assumed its current name in 1966. AACO is the professional association for orthoptists in the United States. AACO is composed of a close network of orthoptists and orthoptic students across North America, dedicated to the support of the Profession and to the benefit of the individual orthoptist member. Membership: $150-200/year.

Continuing Education:
Certification Designation/s: C.O.

Meetings/Conferences: Annual
2013 - New Orleans, LA/Nov. 16 - 19
2014 - Chicago, IL/Oct. 18 - 21
Number of non-conference events/year: 1

Publications:
AOJ.org; on-line
DJO; on-line
Prism; on-line

Membership List Available to Non-members

American Association of Chairs of Departments of Psychiatry *(1967)*
c/o Lucille Meinsler, Suite 319
1594 Cumberland St.
Lebanon, PA 17042
Tel: (717) 270-1674 *Fax:* (717) 270-1673
E-Mail: aacdp@verizon.net
Website: aacdp.org
Members: 136 individuals
Staff: 3
Annual Budget: $50-100,000

Personnel:
President: Stuart Munro
Executive Secretary: Lucille F. Meinsler

Historical Note:
AACDP is a forum for professional exchange among teaching psychiatrists. AACDP's mission is to promote psychiatric education, research and clinical care.

Publications:
Academic Psychiatry
Member Directory; on-line

Membership List Available to Non-members

American Association of Children's Residential Centers *(1957)*
11700 W. Lake Park Dr.
Milwaukee, WI 53224
Tel: (877) 332-2272 *Fax:* (877) 362-2272
E-Mail: info@aacrc-dc.org

Website: aacrc-dc.org
Members:
106 agencies
160 individuals
Staff: 1
Annual Budget: $250-500,000

Personnel:
National Director: Kari Sisson
  E-Mail: kbehling@alliance1.org

Historical Note:
AACRC is engaged in maintaining and enhancing sound clinical practice in residential treatment for children with emotional problems. AACRC is Dedicated to Providing a Powerful National Voice for Residential Treatment through Leadership, Advocacy, and the Promotion of Best Practices. Membership includes psychologists, psychiatrists, social workers, educators and child care specialists, as well as residential treatment agencies. A member of the National Consortium for Child Mental Health Services. Membership: $110 (Individual); $1,200 (Agency).

Meetings/Conferences: Annual
Number of non-conference events/year: 1

Publications:
AACRC Journal
Membership Directory; on-line
Residential E-News; on-line

Membership List Available to Non-members

American Association of Christian Counselors
(2003)
P.O. Box 739
Forest, VA 24551
TollFree: (800) 526-8673
E-Mail: Advertising@AACC.net
Website: aacc.net
Members: 50,000 members
Staff: 8
Annual Budget: $500-1,000,000

Personnel:
President: Tim Clinton
Managing Editor and Director, Publications: Mark Camper
Assistant Vice President and Director, Operations: James D. Clinton
Director, Membership Services: Bob Cook
Executive Vice-President and Chief Administrative Officer: Jimmy Queen
Vice President, Professional Development: Eric Scalise LMFT, LPC
Chief Financial Officer: Alex Smith MA
Director, Technology: Johnny Smulik

Historical Note:
AACC is committed to assisting Christian counselors, the entire community of care, licensed professionals, pastors, and lay church members with little or no formal training. Their mission is to equip clinical, pastoral, and lay care-givers with biblical truth and psychosocial insights that minister to hurting persons and helps them move to personal wholeness, interpersonal competence, mental stability, and spiritual maturity. Membership: $69 (Regular); $39 (Student).

Publications:
AACC eNews; monthly
Christian Counseling Connection Newsletter; quarterly
Christian Counseling Today Magazine; quarterly

American Association of Christian Schools *(1972)*
602 Belvoir Ave.
E. Ridge, TN 37412
Tel: (423) 629-4280 *Fax:* (423) 622-7461
E-Mail: info@AACS.org
Website: aacs.org
Members: 171200 schools and students
Staff: 5
Annual Budget: $1-2,000,000
Tax: 501(c)(19)

Personnel:
Executive Director: Jeff Walton

Historical Note:
AACS works to aid in promoting, establishing, advancing, and developing Christian schools and Christian education in America. It also maintains school accreditation and teacher and administrator certification programs. Membership: $50 (Individual); $25 (Student/Faculty).

Publications:
AACS National Directory; on-line
Journal of Christian Educators
Washington Flyer; weekly

American Association of Classified School Employees *(1958)*
555 New Jersey Ave. NW
Washington, DC 20001
Tel: (202) 879-4400
Website: aacse.org
Members: 260000 school workers
Staff: 2
Annual Budget: $100-250,000

Personnel:
President: George Williams
Treasurer: Wayne Scott

Historical Note:
AACSE is an independent coalition of labor unions representing teaching and non-teaching employees of the nation's school systems and major emphasis is on national lobbying about educational issues.

Continuing Education:
Certification Designation/s: IDEA

Meetings/Conferences: Annual

American Association of Clinical Endocrinologists
(1991)
245 Riverside Ave.
Suite 200
Jacksonville, FL 32202
Tel: (904) 353-7878 *Fax:* (904) 353-8185
TollFree: (800) 393-2223
E-Mail: info@aace.com
Website: aace.com
Members: 6200 individuals
Staff: 48
Annual Budget: $10-25,000,000
Tax: 501(c)(6)

Personnel:
Chief Executive Officer: Donald C. Jones
Chief Financial Officer: Michael Avallone CPA
Director, AACE Education Services: Melinda Burdette
Director, Public and Media Relations: Bryan Campbell
  E-Mail: bcampbell@aace.com
Director, Communications and Publications: Lori Clawges
Director, Membership Services: Mandy Dean
Director, Information Technology and Network Administration: Ashley Horn
  E-Mail: wahorn@aace.com
Director, College Activities and Education: Lucille Killgore
Director, Business Development and Marketing: Kurt Laffy
Director, Meetings and Event Services: Matthew Marcial
Director, Administrative Services and Human Resources: Kim Neill
  E-Mail: kneill@aace.com
General Counsel: Christopher L. Nuland Esq.

Historical Note:
AACE's mission is to enhance the practice of clinical endocrinology. Members are physicians with special education, training and interest in the practice of clinical endocrinology. Membership: $179 (Active); $127 (First Year in Practice/Retired); Complimentary (Associate/ Affiliate).

Continuing Education:
Certification Designation/s: CME

Meetings/Conferences: Annual
Conference Chair: Matthew Marcial
Number of non-conference events/year: 12

Publications:
AACE on Line (internet); weekly
AACE's e-newsletter; on-line
Endocrine Practice Journal; bi-monthly; adv.
First Messenger Newsletter; bi-monthly; adv.
Membership Directory; annually; adv.

Membership List Available to Non-members

American Association of Clinical Urologists
(1968)
Two Woodfield Lake, 1100 E. Woodfield Rd.
Suite 520
Schaumburg, IL 60173
Tel: (847) 517-1050 *Fax:* (847) 517-7229
E-Mail: info@aacuweb.org
Website: aacuweb.org
Members: 4500 individuals
Staff: 6
Annual Budget: $500-1,000,000

Personnel:
Executive Director: Wendy J. Weiser
Secretary and Treasurer: Charles A. McWilliams MD

Historical Note:
AACU's mission is to promote the science of urology in the best interests of the public and the medical profession, by the study and evaluation of socioeconomic factors which affect the practice of urology, promoting and preserving the professional autonomy and financial viability of each of its members. Provides members with an opportunity to exert influence at a national level for the improvement of all aspects of the profession and to influence legislation and policies affecting the practice of medicine. Members are licensed physicians whose practices are devoted primarily to urology. Membership: $195/year (Active/Affiliate).

Meetings/Conferences: Annual

Publications:
AACU Sentinel; quarterly

The American Association of Code Enforcement
(1988)
114 Lakeshore Loop
Tow, TX 78672
Tel: (830) 613-4257
E-Mail: info@aace1.com
Website: aace1.org
Members: 1400 individuals
Staff: 1
Annual Budget: $100-250,000
Tax: 501(c)(6)

Personnel:
President: Donna Wisniewski
    E-Mail: dwisniewski@seminolesheriff.org

Historical Note:
AACE's mission is to educate, elevate and improve the profession of code enforcement. Membership: $75/year (Active/Associate).

Continuing Education:
Certification Designation/s: AACEPC

Meetings/Conferences: Annual

Publications:
Code Compliance Update; bi-monthly; adv.
Member Directory; on-line

American Association of Colleges for Teacher Education (1917)
1307 New York Ave. NW
Suite 300
Washington, DC 20005-4701
Tel: (202) 293-2450 Fax: (202) 457-8095
E-Mail: aacte@aacte.org
Website: aacte.org
Members: 780 institutions
Staff: 26
Annual Budget: $5-10,000,000
Tax: 501(c)(3)

Personnel:
President and Chief Executive Officer: Sharon P. Robinson
Vice President, Meetings and Events: Gail M Bozeman
    E-Mail: gbozeman@aacte.org
Manager, Communications: Lisa M. Johnson
Program Assistant, Membership: Gloriatine Jones
    E-Mail: gjones@aacte.org
Manager, State Programs and Policies: Kimberly T. Riley
    E-Mail: kriley@aacte.org
Director, Meetings, Events and Special Projects: Matthew J. Wales
    E-Mail: mwales@aacte.org
Senior Vice President of Policy, Programs and Professional Issues: Dr. Jane E. West PhD
    E-Mail: jwest@aacte.org
Chief Operating Officer and Chief Financial Officer: Jerry D. Wirth
    E-Mail: jwirth@aacte.org

Historical Note:
Formed by a merger of the American Association of Teachers Colleges, the National Association of Colleges and Departments of Education and the National Association of Teacher Education Institutions of Metropolitan Districts. AACTE's mission is to provide the learning of all PK-12 students through high-quality, evidence-based preparation and continuing education for all school personnel. Membership: $1,750-10,750/year.

Meetings/Conferences: Annual
Conference Chair: Matthew J. Wales
2013 - Orlando, FL (Rosen Shingle Creek)/Feb. 28 - March 2
2014 - Indianapolis, IN (JW Marriott Indianapolis)/ March 1 - 3
2015 - Atlanta, GA (Hilton Atlanta)/Feb. 27 - March 1
2016 - Las Vegas, NV (The Mirage)/Feb. 23 - 25

Publications:
AACTE Advisor; monthly; adv.
AACTE Directory of Members; annually
Journal of Teacher Education; quarterly; adv.

American Association of Colleges of Nursing
(1969)
One Dupont Cir. NW
Suite 530
Washington, DC 20036
Tel: (202) 463-6930 Fax: (202) 785-8320
E-Mail: info@aacn.nche.edu
Website: aacn.nche.edu
Members: 690 schools of nursing
Staff: 40
Annual Budget: $10-25,000,000
Tax: 501(c)(3)

Personnel:
Chief Executive Officer and Executive Director: Geraldine Bednash RN, PhD, FAAN
    E-Mail: pbednash@aacn.nche.edu
Chief Operating Officer: Jennifer Ahearn
    E-Mail: jahearn@aacn.nche.edu
Manager, Nursing CAS: Caroline Allen
    E-Mail: callen@aacn.nche.edu
Director, Membership Services: Beth Aronson
    E-Mail: baronson@aacn.nche.edu
Chief Operating Officer: Jennifer Butlin
    E-Mail: jbutlin@aacn.nche.edu
Director, Information Technology: Tony Dempsey
    E-Mail: tdempsey@aacn.nche.edu
Director, Government Affairs: Suzanne Miyamoto
    E-Mail: smiyamoto@aacn.nche.edu
Director, Publications: William O'Connor
    E-Mail: woconnor@aacn.nche.edu
Chief Communications Officer: Robert Rosseter
    E-Mail: rrosseter@aacn.nche.edu
Director, Finance and Administration: Heather Shelford
    E-Mail: hshelford@aacn.nche.edu
Senior Director, Education Policy: Joan Stanley
    E-Mail: jstanley@aacn.nche.edu
Coordinator, Conferences: Taren Wagner
    E-Mail: twagner@aacn.nche.edu

Historical Note:
Member of the Federation of Associations of Schools of the Health Professions. AACN serves the public interest by providing standards and resources, and by fostering innovation to advance professional nursing education, research, and practice. Members are schools of nursing at universities and four-year colleges. Membership: $2,136 (New); $4,273 (Regular).

Meetings/Conferences:
Conference Chair: Taren Wagner
2013 - New Orleans, LA (JW Marriott New Orleans)/ Jan. 17
2013 - New Orleans, LA (JW Marriott New Orleans)/ Jan. 17 - 19
2013 - San Diego, CA (Hotel del Coronado)/Jan. 23 - 26
2013 - San Diego, CA (Hotel del Coronado)/Jan. 24
2013 - Jacksonville, FL (Omni Jacksonville Hotel)/Feb. 7 - 9
2013 - Orlando, FL (Buena Vista Palace)/Feb. 20 - 23
2013 - Nashville, TN (Fairmont Washington)/March 15 - 16
2013 - Washington, DC (Fairmont Washington)/March 16 - 19
2013 - Washington, DC (Fairmont Washington)/March 17 - 19
2013 - Charlotte, NC/April 2 - 3
2013 - San Diego, CA (Omni San Diego Hotel)/April 5 - 6
2013 - St. Louis, MO (Sheraton Westport Chalet Hotel St. Louis)/April 11 - 13
2013 - Austin, TX (Omni Austin Hotel Downtown)/ April 17 - 19
2013 - Washington, DC (JW Marriott Washington, D.C.)/Oct. 26 - 29
2014 - Washington, DC (Fairmont Washington)/March 22 - 25
2014 - Washington, DC (JW Marriott Washington, D.C.)/Oct. 25 - 28
2015 - Washington, DC (Fairmont Washington)/March 21 - 24
2015 - Washington, DC (JW Marriott Washington, D.C.)/Oct. 24 - 27
2016 - Washington, DC (Fairmont Washington)/March 19 - 22

2016 - Washington, DC (JW Marriott Washington, D.C.)/Oct. 29 - Nov. 1
2017 - Washington, DC (Fairmont Washington)/March 18 - 21

Publications:
Journal of Professional Nursing; on-line
Membership Directory; on-line
News Watch newsletter; monthly; adv.
Syllabus Newsletter; on-line; adv.

Membership List Available to Non-members

American Association of Colleges of Osteopathic Medicine (1898)
5550 Friendship Blvd.
Suite 310
Chevy Chase, MD 20815-7231
Tel: (301) 968-4100 Fax: (301) 968-4101
Website: aacom.org
Members: 29 colleges
Staff: 8
Annual Budget: $10-25,000,000
Tax: 501(c)(3)

Personnel:
President and Chief Executive Officer: Stephen C. Shannon DO, MPH
    E-Mail: sshannon@aacom.org
Vice President, Finance and Administration and Chief Financial Officer: Nancy C. Cioffari
    E-Mail: ncioffari@aacom.org
Vice President, Communications and Marketing: Wendy Fernando
    E-Mail: wfernando@aacom.org
Vice President, Medical Education: Linda Heun PhD
    E-Mail: lheun@aacom.org
Editor and Associate, Communications: Lindsey Jurd
Database Administrator and Systems Analyst: Junhua (Lucy) Liu
Manager, Meetings and Events: Beth Martino
    E-Mail: bmartino@aacom.org
Vice President, Government Relations: Susan Eads Role JD, MSLS
    E-Mail: srole@aacom.org

Historical Note:
AACOM provides support and assistance to the nation's osteopathic medical schools, and serves osteopathic medical education. Membership represents the administration, faculty and students of all of the osteopathic medical colleges in the United States.

Meetings/Conferences: Annual
Conference Chair: Beth Martino
2013 - Baltimore, MD (Baltimore Marriott Waterfront)/ April 24 - 27
2014 - Washington, DC (Capital Hilton)/April 2 - 5

Publications:
Glossary of Osteopathic Terminology; semi-annually
Inside OME; monthly
MedEd Update; annually
Osteopathic Medical College Information Book; annually

American Association of Colleges of Pharmacy
(1900)
1727 King St.
Alexandria, VA 22314-2815
Tel: (703) 739-2330 Fax: (703) 836-8982
E-Mail: mail@aacp.org
Website: aacp.org
Members: 71500 students and faculty
Staff: 26
Annual Budget: $10-25,000,000
Tax: 501(c)(3)

Personnel:
Executive Vice President and Chief Executive Officer: Lucinda L. Maine
    E-Mail: lmaine@aacp.org
Editor: Joseph DiPiro PharmD
    E-Mail: jdipiro@cop.sc.edu
Associate, Member Services: Sandra Edwards
    E-Mail: aedwards@aacp.org
Vice President, Professional Affairs: Arlene A. Flynn PhD, RPh
    E-Mail: aflynn@aacp.org
Director, Meetings and Exhibits: Barbara A. Gustis CMP, MEd
    E-Mail: bgustis@aacp.org
Vice President, Policy Advocacy: William G. Lang MPH

E-Mail: wlang@aacp.org

Vice President, Research and Graduate Education and Chief Science Officer: Yuen-Sum (Vincent) Lau PhD
E-Mail: vlau@aacp.org

Director, Information Technology: Allan Lee
E-Mail: alee@aacp.org

Director, Financial Services: Sibu Ramamurthy
E-Mail: sramamurthy@aacp.org

Director, Communications and Marketing: Gerry Romano
E-Mail: gromano@aacp.org

Historical Note:
Founded as the American Conference of Pharmaceutical Faculties, became the American Association of Colleges of Pharmacy in August 1925. Mission is to guide and partner with members in advancing pharmacy education, research, scholarship, practice and service to improve societal health. Represents and advocates for the academic community in the profession of pharmacy. Members are accredited colleges and schools with pharmacy degree programs accredited by the Accreditation Council for Pharmacy Education. Membership: $100 (Individual); $15 (Student/Resident/Postdoctoral Fellow); $150 (Joint); $1600 (Lifetime).

Meetings/Conferences: Annual
Conference Chair: Barbara A. Gustis CMP, MEd
2013 - Chicago, IL (Hyatt Regency)/July 13 - 17
2014 - Grapevine, TX (Gaylord Texan Hotel and Convention Center, Dallas Texas)/July 26 - 30
2015 - Ft. Washington, MD (Gaylord National Hotel and Convention Center)/July 11 - 15
Number of non-conference events/year: 7

Publications:
AACP E-Lert Newsletters; bi-weekly
Academic Pharmacy Now; quarterly; adv.
American Journal of Pharmaceutical Education; quarterly
Member Directory; on-line

Membership List Available to Non-members

American Association of Colleges of Podiatric Medicine (1932)
15850 Crabbs Branch Way
Suite 320
Rockville, MD 20855
Tel: (301) 948-9760 *Fax:* (301) 948-1928
TollFree: (800) 922-9266
E-Mail: info@aacpm.org
Website: aacpm.org
Members:
200 hospitals and organizations
9 colleges
Staff: 7
Annual Budget: $1-2,000,000
Tax: 501(c)(3)

Personnel:
Chief Executive Officer: Thomas V. Melillo DPM
Secretary and Treasurer: Jeffrey Yung DPM

Historical Note:
Established as the American Association of Colleges of Chiropody, it then became the American Association of Colleges of Podiatry and assumed its present name in 1968. It is a member of the National Association of Advisors in the Health Professions, and the Federation of Associations of Schools of the Health Professions. AACPM's vision is to ensure, through collaboration and other appropriate means, that academic podiatric medicine is a vibrant community of schools and residency programs and other entities staffed with administrators, teachers and researchers capable of educating and training a podiatric workforce relevant to the needs of the public, generating new biomedical knowledge and providing academically based health services. Membership: $500/year (Organization).

American Association of Collegiate Registrars and Admissions Officers (1910)
One Dupont Cir. NW
Suite 520
Washington, DC 20036-1171
Tel: (202) 293-9161 *Fax:* (202) 872-8857
E-Mail: info@aacrao.org
Website: aacrao.org
Members:
2600 institutions
11,000 individuals
Staff: 16
Annual Budget: $10-25,000,000
Tax: 501(c)(3)

Personnel:
Executive Director: Michael Reilly

E-Mail: reillym@aacrao.org

Associate Director, Marketing: Saira Burki
E-Mail: burkis@aacrao.org

Associate Director, Meetings and Conferences: Melissa Ficek
E-Mail: ficekm@aacrao.org

Director, International Education Services: Dale Gough
E-Mail: goughd@aacrao.org

Specialist, Information Technology: Charles Han
E-Mail: hanc@aacrao.org

Director, Membership and Publications: Martha Henebry
E-Mail: henebrym@aacrao.org

Specialist, Public Relations and Marketing: Natalia Jimenez
E-Mail: jimenezn@aacrao.org

Associate Executive Director, External Relations: Barmak Nassirian
E-Mail: nassirianb@aacrao.org

Editor: Heather Zimar
E-Mail: zimarh@aacrao.org

Historical Note:
Founded as the American Association of Collegiate Registrars. AACRAO is a voluntary, nonprofit professional education association of degree-granting postsecondary institutions, government agencies and higher education coordinating boards, private educational organizations and education-oriented businesses. AACRAO's goal is to promote education and further the professional development of members working in admissions, enrollment management, financial aid, institutional research, records, and registration. Membership: $101.50-4000/year.

Meetings/Conferences:
Conference Chair: Melissa Ficek
2013 - San Francisco, CA (Moscone Center)/April 14 - 17
2013 - Tucson, AZ (JW Marriott Tucson Starr Pass Resort and Spa)/July 14 - 16
2013 - Chicago, IL (Hilton Chicago)/Nov. 10 - 13
2014 - Denver, CO (Colorado Convention Center)/ March 30 - April 2
2014 - Los Angeles, CA (JW Marriott Los Angeles L.A. LIVE)/Oct. 26 - 29
2015 - Baltimore, MD (Baltimore Convention Center)/ March 22 - 25
2015 - Hollywood, FL (Westin Diplomat Resort)/Nov. 1 - 4
2016 - Phoenix, AZ (Phoenix Convention Center)/ March 20 - 23
2016 - San Antonio, TX (JW Marriott San Antonio Hill Country Resort and Spa)/Nov. 6 - 9
2017 - Minneapolis, MN (Minneapolis Convention Center)/April 2 - 5
2017 - Phoenix, AZ (JW Marriott Phoenix Desert Ridge Resort and Spa)/Oct. 29 - Nov. 1
2018 - Orlando, FL (Orlando World Center Marriott)/ March 25 - 28
Number of non-conference events/year: 4

Publications:
College & University (C&U); quarterly; adv.

American Association of Community Colleges (1920)
One Dupont Cir. NW
Suite 410
Washington, DC 20036-1176
Tel: (202) 728-0200 *Fax:* (202) 833-2467
Website: aacc.nche.edu
Members: 1200 institutions
Staff: 61
Annual Budget: $10-25,000,000
Tax: 501(c)(3)

Personnel:
President and Chief Executive Officer: Dr. Walter G. Bumphus
E-Mail: wbumphus@aacc.nche.edu

Associate Vice President, Human Resources: Charisse Bazin Ash
E-Mail: cash@aacc.nche.edu

Senior Vice President for Government Relations and Policy Analysis: David S. Baime
E-Mail: dbaime@aacc.nche.edu

Senior Vice President, Chief Operations and Financial Officer: Donald O. Brown
E-Mail: dbrown@aacc.nche.edu

Director, Meetings and Council Relations: Tavia Cummings
E-Mail: tcummings@aacc.nche.edu

Editor, Community College Press: Deanna D'Errico

E-Mail: dderrico@aacc.nche.edu

Senior Accountant: Dei Dwamena
E-Mail: ddwamena@aacc.nche.edu

Associate, Membership Services: Wayne Horton
E-Mail: whorton@aacc.nche.edu

Associate Vice President, Finance: Ramsay Johnson
E-Mail: rjohnson@aacc.nche.edu

Senior Vice President, Communications and Advancement: Norma G. Kent
E-Mail: nkent@aacc.nche.edu

Manager, Marketing: Sarah Lawler CEM
E-Mail: slawler@aacc.nche.edu

Vice President, Workforce, Economic Development and International Programs: Dr. James F. McKenney
E-Mail: jmckenney@aacc.nche.edu

Chief Technology Officer: Johnathan "Mark" Nelson
E-Mail: jnelson@aacc.nche.edu

Director, Membership Services: Margaret Rivera
E-Mail: mrivera@aacc.nche.edu

Director, Service Learning: Gail Robinson
E-Mail: grobinson@aacc.nche.edu

Historical Note:
Formerly (1972) American Association of Community and Junior Colleges (AACJC) and assumed its current name in 1992. AACC's mission is to build a nation of learners by advancing America's Community Colleges. Membership: $715 (Educational Associate); $1,2490 (International Associate); $100 (Individual Associate); $1,650 (Lifetime Individual).

Meetings/Conferences: Annual
Conference Chair: Tavia Cummings
2013 - San Francisco, CA (Moscone Center)/April 20 - 23/2000 attendees
2014 - Washington, DC (Marriott Wardman Park/Omni Shoreham)/April 5 - 8
2015 - San Antonio, TX (The Henry B. Gonzalez Convention Center)/April 18 - 21

Publications:
Membership Directory; on-line
The Community College Journal; bi-monthly; adv.
The Community College Times; on-line; adv.

American Association of Community Psychiatrists (1984)
P.O. Box 570218
Dallas, TX 75357-0218
Tel: (972) 613-0985 *Fax:* (972) 613-5532
E-Mail: frda1@airmail.net
Website: communitypsychiatry.org
Members: 500 individuals
Staff: 5
Annual Budget: $100-250,000

Personnel:
President: Anita Everett
Administrative Director: Frances Roton Bell
Treasurer: Edward J. Maxwell MD
Contact, Conventions: Kenneth "Ken" Thompson MD
E-Mail: thompsonks@upmc.edu

Historical Note:
The Mission of AACP is to inspire, empower and equip community psychiatrists to promote and provide quality care and to integrate practice with policies that improve the well being of individuals and communities. Membership: $0-240/year.

Meetings/Conferences:
Conference Chair: Kenneth "Ken" Thompson MD

Publications:
AACP Community Psychiatrist; quarterly
Community Mental Health Journal; bi-monthly

Membership List Available to Non-members

American Association of Community Theatre (1986)
1300 Gendy St.
Fort Worth, TX 76107
Tel: (817) 732-3177 *Fax:* (817) 732-3178
TollFree: (866) 687-2228
E-Mail: info@aact.org
Website: aact.org
Members: 1000 organizations, 7000 theatres and 800 individuals
Staff: 4
Annual Budget: $250-500,000
Tax: 501(c)(3)

Personnel:
Executive Director: Julie Crawford
E-Mail: julie@aact.org

Assistant, Membership Services: Susan Austin
    E-Mail: info@aact.org
Webmaster: Stephen Peithman
    E-Mail: webmaster@aact.org
Director, Field Services: Ron Ziegler
    E-Mail: ron@aact.org

Historical Note:
AACT provides networking, resources and support to
suit the needs of all those involved in community theatre.
Members are community theatre organizations, theatre
professionals and volunteers interested in community
theatre. Membership: $30-55 (Individual); $55-450
(Organization); $500 (Commercial, Basic); $1,000
(Commercial, Elite).

Meetings/Conferences:
Conference Chair: Ron Ziegler

Publications:
Spotlight; bi-monthly; adv.
Membership Directory; on-line

American Association of Corporate and Public Practice Veterinarians (1954)
6060 Sunrise Vista Dr.
Suite 1300
Citrus Heights, CA 95610-7098
Tel: (916) 726-1560 Fax: (916) 722-8849
E-Mail: info@aacppv.org
Website: aacppv.org
Members: 500 individuals
Staff: 1
Annual Budget: $10-25,000
Tax: 501(c)(6)

Personnel:
Executive Director: MaryAnne P. Bobrow CAE, CMM, CMP
    E-Mail: maryanne@aacppv.org

Historical Note:
Formerly (1976) the American Association of Industrial
Veterinarians (AAIV). AACPPV is an AVMA allied
organization that works to advance the professional
standards of veterinarians engaged in any phase of
industrial employment. Members are veterinarians working
in corporate and public practice. Membership: $100/year.

Meetings/Conferences: Annual
2013 - Chicago, IL/July 22
Number of non-conference events/year: 6

Publications:
AmericanAssociation of Corporate and Public Practice
    Veterinarians Newsline
E-Newsline

American Association of Cosmetology Schools (1924)
9927 E. Bell Rd.
Suite 110
Scottsdale, AZ 85260
Tel: (480) 281-0431 Fax: (480) 905-0993
TollFree: (800) 831-1086
Website: beautyschools.org
Members: 1100 schools
Staff: 5
Annual Budget: $1-2,000,000
Tax: 501(c)(6)

Personnel:
Executive Director: Jim Cox
    E-Mail: jim@beautyschools.org
Manager, Membership Services: Chris Cox
    E-Mail: chris@beautyschools.org
Coordinator, Communications: Jenn Lyles
    E-Mail: jenn@beautyschools.org
Editor: Amber Mortensen
    E-Mail: editor@beautyschools.org
General Manager: Lisa Zarda
    E-Mail: lisa@beautyschools.org

Historical Note:
Formerly (1991) National Association of Cosmetology
Schools and (1993) Association of Accredited Cosmetology
Schools. AACS's mission is to develop and coordinate the
human and technological resources so that members can
exchange information about federal state and local issues.
Membership: $850 (Title IV Funded schools/Associate);
$550 (Privately Funded schools/Each Additional School).

Meetings/Conferences: Semi-Annual
Number of non-conference events/year: 2

Publications:
Beauty Link; quarterly; adv.

American Association of Credit Union Leagues
601 Pennsylvania Ave. NW, South Bldg.
Suite 600
Washington, DC 20004-5777
Tel: (202) 638-5777 Fax: (202) 638-7729
TollFree: (800) 356-9655
Website: aacul.org
Members: 200 individuals
Staff: 6
Annual Budget: $500-1,000,000
Tax: 501(c)(6)

Personnel:
Executive Director: Susan Newton
    E-Mail: snewton@cuna.coop
Manager, League Relations and Corporate Secretary: Alicia
    Valencia
      E-Mail: avalencia@cuna.coop

Historical Note:
Founded as Association of Credit Union League Executives,
assumed its current name in 1999 and administrative
support is provided by Credit Union National Association.
AACUL's mission is to create an environment that
perpetuates the success of leagues, both individually and
collectively and enhances their position as vital to the
future of the credit union system. Membership in AACUL is
comprised of state credit union leagues which are members
of the Credit Union National Association (CUNA).

Meetings/Conferences: Annual
Conference Chair: Alicia Valencia

American Association of Critical-Care Nurses (1969)
101 Columbia
Aliso Viejo, CA 92656-4109
Tel: (949) 362-2050 Fax: (949) 362-2020
TollFree: (800) 899-2226
E-Mail: info@aacn.org
Website: aacn.org
Members:
270 chapters
500000 individuals
Staff: 116
Annual Budget: $25-50,000,000
Tax: 501(c)(3)

Personnel:
Chief Executive Officer: Wanda L. Johanson MN, RN
Director, Corporate Relations and Exhibits: Randy Bauler
    E-Mail: randy.bauler@aacn.org
Director, Communications and Strategic Alliances: Ramon
    Lavandero
      E-Mail: ramon.lavandero@aacn.org
Chief Financial Officer: Michael Willett
    E-Mail: michael.willett@aacn.org
Director, Marketing and Strategy Integration: Dana
    Woods
      E-Mail: Dana.Woods@aacn.org

Historical Note:
Formerly (1972) the American Association of
Cardiovascular Nurses. AACN strives to provide its
members with the knowledge and resources necessary to
provide optimal care to critically ill patients. Members
are nurses in all areas of critical care, acute care, and
progressive care such as cardiac intensive care, medical/
surgical critical care, and trauma. Membership: $78
(Active/Affiliate); $52 (Student/Retired/Disabled); $59
(Emeritus); $78 (International Digital-Only).

Continuing Education:
Certification Designation/s: ACNPC, CNML, CCRN,
CCNS, PCCN, CMC, CSC, CCRN-E

Meetings/Conferences: Annual
Conference Chair: Randy Bauler
2013 - Boston, MA/May 18 - 23
2014 - Denver, CO/May 17 - 22
2015 - San Diego, CA/May 16 - 21
2016 - New Orleans, LA/May 14 - 19
Number of non-conference events/year: 15

Publications:
AACN Advanced Critical Care; quarterly
AACN Bold Voices; monthly; adv.
AACN News; monthly; adv.
American Journal of Critical Care; bi-monthly; adv.
Critical Care Newsline; weekly
Critical Care Nurse; bi-monthly; adv.
NTI Voices; on-line

American Association of Crop Insurers (1983)
One Massachusetts Ave. NW
Suite 800

Washington, DC 20001-1401
Tel: (202) 789-4100 Fax: (202) 408-7763
E-Mail: aaci@mwmlaw.com
Website: cropinsurers.com
Members: 9500 agents and 15 companies
Staff: 4
Annual Budget: $1-2,000,000
Tax: 501(c)(6)

Personnel:
Executive Director and General Counsel: Michael R.
    McLeod
Manager, Secretary and Senior Government Relations
    Representative: David R. Graves

Historical Note:
AACI's purpose is governmental relations with Congress,
the U.S. Department of Agriculture, and other executive
branch agencies whose decisions influence the program.
Governmental relations efforts include background
education, advocacy for program continuation, funding,
positive change, response to questions, media relations,
general information distribution, and influencing the
legislative and administrative rulemaking processes.
Membership: $2,500 (Associate Members/Agent Division-
Agent Advisory Committee); $5 (Affiliate); $100-1,000
(Agent Division-Standard).

Publications:
FarmPolicy

Membership List Available to Non-members

The American Association of Dental Boards (1883)
211 E. Chicago Ave.
Suite 760
Chicago, IL 60611
Tel: (312) 440-7464 Fax: (312) 440-3525
E-Mail: info@aadexam.org
Website: aadexam.org
Members: 725 individuals
Staff: 5
Annual Budget: $250-500,000
Tax: 501(c)(6)

Personnel:
Executive Director: Molly Nadler
    E-Mail: mnadler@dentalboards.org
Administrator: Bayley Milton
    E-Mail: bmilton@dentalboards.org

Historical Note:
Formerly (2009) the National Association of Dental
Examiners, AADB works to serve as a resource by
providing a national forum for exchange, development and
dissemination of information to assist dental regulatory
boards with their obligation to protect the public. Members
are present and former members of state dental examining
boards. Membership: $1,960 (Member Agency/Specialty
Board); $295 (Individual); $83 (Associate/Educator);
$1,500 (Lifetime); $304 (Active Member/Individual Active
Member).

Continuing Education:
Certification Designation/s: PGY-1

Meetings/Conferences: Semi-Annual
2013 - Chicago, IL (ADA Headquarters)/April 21 - 22
2013 - San Francisco, CA/Oct. 17 - 18
2013 - New Orleans, LA/Oct. 30 - 31
2014 - Chicago, IL (ADA Headquarters)/April 6 - 7
Number of non-conference events/year: 2

Publications:
The Bulletin; quarterly; adv.

American Association of Dental Consultants (1979)
10032 Wind Hill Dr.
Greenville, IN 47124
Tel: (812) 923-2600 Fax: (812) 923-2900
TollFree: (800) 896-0707
E-Mail: info@aadc.org
Website: aadc.org
Members: 450 individuals and 282 member
companies
Staff: 3
Annual Budget: $100-250,000

Personnel:
Executive Director: Judith "Judy" K. Salisbury
    E-Mail: jsalis913@aol.com
Secretary and Treasurer: Dr. Lawrence M. Hoffman
Editor: Dr. Harold J. Seiler

Historical Note:
AADC's mission is to promote competency and up-to-date
knowledge among dental benefits consultants. Members

are dentists, insurance consultants, benefits programs administrators, and other dental professionals. Membership: $225 (Active/Associate); $112.50 (Affiliate).

Continuing Education:
Enrollment: 6
Certification Designation/s: CDC

Meetings/Conferences: Annual
2013 - Lake Buena Vista, FL (Disney's BoardWalk Resort)/May 15 - 18
2014 - Santa Ana Pueblo, NM (Hyatt Regency Tamaya Resort and Spa)/May 7 - 10
2015 - Santa Ana Pueblo, NM (Hyatt Regency Tamaya Resort and Spa)/May 13 - 16

Publications:
Membership Directory; on-line

American Association of Dental Editors *(1931)*
750 N. Lincoln Memorial Dr.
Suite 422
Milwaukee, WI 53202
Tel: (414) 272-2759 *Fax:* (414) 272-2754
E-Mail: aade@dentaleditors.org
Website: dentaleditors.org
Members: 325 individuals
Staff: 2
Annual Budget: $25-50,000
Tax: 501(c)(6)

Personnel:
Executive Director: Detlef B. Moore

Historical Note:
AADE is dedicated to improve communication within the dental profession and to elevate the standards of dental journalism. Member publications represent state dental associations, component societies, dental specialty groups, dental schools, alumni, dental auxiliaries, students and commercial publications. Membership: $25-175/year.

Continuing Education:
Certification Designation/s: CDE

Meetings/Conferences: Annual
Number of non-conference events/year: 1

Publications:
AADE Newsletter; quarterly
Membership Directory; on-line

American Association of Diabetes Educators *(1973)*
200 W. Madison St.
Suite 800
Chicago, IL 60606
Tel: (312) 424-2426 *Fax:* (312) 424-2427
TollFree: (800) 338-3633
E-Mail: aade@aadenet.org
Website: diabeteseducator.org
Members: 12000 individuals
Staff: 54
Annual Budget: $10-25,000,000

Personnel:
Director, Human Resources: Christine Carter-Eggers SPHR
Editor: James Fain
Director, Meeting Services: Marian Long CMP
Vice President, Information Technology: Terry Merkley MBA
Director, Communications: Diana Pihos MA
  E-Mail: dpihos@aadenet.org
Co-Interim Chief Executive Officer and Chief Financial Officer: Ken Widelka CAE, CPA
  E-Mail: kwidelka@aadenet.org

Historical Note:
AADE's mission is to drive professional practice to promote healthy living through self-management of diabetes and related conditions. Members are nurses, dietitians, physicians, pharmacists and other allied health professionals involved in teaching self-management to people with diabetes. Membership: $125/year.

Continuing Education:
Certification Designation/s: BC-ADM, CDE

Meetings/Conferences: Annual
Conference Chair: Marian Long CMP

Publications:
AADE in Practice; quarterly
AADE's e-FYI Newsletter; monthly
The Diabetes Educator

American Association of Directors of Psychiatric Residency Training *(1971)*
1594 Cumberland St.

Suite 319
Lebanon, PA 17042
Tel: (717) 270-1673
E-Mail: aadprt@verizon.net
Website: aadprt.org
Members: 428 individuals
Staff: 3
Annual Budget: $250-500,000

Personnel:
Treasurer: Micheal Jibson MD, PhD
  E-Mail: mdjibson@med.umich.edu
Administrative Manager: Lucille F. Meinsler
  E-Mail: aadprt@verizon.net
President: Kathy Sanders MD
  E-Mail: ksanders@partners.org

Historical Note:
AADPRT's mission is to promote excellence in the education and training of future psychiatrists. Membership: $400 (Institutional); $300 (Affiliate).

Meetings/Conferences: Annual
2013 - Ft. Lauderdale, FL (Hilton Ft. Lauderdale Airport)/March 6 - 9
2014 - Tucson, AZ (Hilton El Conquistador)/March 12 - 15
2015 - Orlando, FL (Hilton Orlando Bonnet Creek)/March 4 - 7
2016 - Austin, TX (Hilton Austin)/March 2 - 5
2017 - San Juan, Puerto Rico (Hilton Caribe)/March 8 - 11
2018 - New Orleans, LA (Hilton New Orleans Riverside)/Feb. 28 - March 2
Number of non-conference events/year: 1

Publications:
Academic Psychiatry
Membership Directory; on-line

American Association of Early Childhood Educators *(1990)*
3612 Brent Branch Dr.
Falls Church, VA 22041-1006
Tel: (703) 941-4329 *Fax:* (703) 941-4329
Members: 5000 individuals
Staff: 3
Annual Budget: $10-25,000

Personnel:
Executive Director: Dr. William J. Tobin PhD
  E-Mail: tobwilliam@aol.com

Historical Note:
AAECE members are directors, teachers and teacher aides working in licensed childcare centers. Membership: $10 (Individual); $500 (Organization/Company).

American Association of Endodontists *(1943)*
211 E. Chicago Ave.
Suite 1100
Chicago, IL 60611-2691
Tel: (312) 266-7255 *Fax:* (866) 451-9020
TollFree: (800) 872-3636
E-Mail: info@aae.org
Website: aae.org
Members: 7500 endodontic professionals
Staff: 30
Annual Budget: $5-10,000,000

Personnel:
Executive Director: James M. Drinan JD
  E-Mail: jdrinan@aae.org
Coordinator, Education: Jill E. Forister
  E-Mail: jforister@aae.org

Historical Note:
AAE is dedicated to excellence and quality in the art and science of endodontics and to the good standard of patient care. Membership: $505-835 (Active); $215-380 (International); $278-443 (Educator); $215-380 (Associate); $50 (Resident/Predoctoral Student); $60 (Auxiliary/Auxiliary Group).

Continuing Education:
Certification Designation/s: ABE

Meetings/Conferences:
2013 - Honolulu, HI (Hawaii Convention Center)/April 17 - 20/4000 attendees/over 100 exhibitors
2014 - Washington, DC (Gaylord National Resort and Convention Center)/April 30 - May 3/400 attendees/over 100 exhibitors
2015 - Seattle, WA (Washington State Convention and Trade Center)/May 6 - 9/4000 attendees/over 100 exhibitors

2016 - San Francisco, CA (Moscone Center)/April 6 - 9
2017 - New Orleans, LA (Morial Convention Center)/ April 26 - 29
2018 - Denver, CO (Colorado Convention Center)/April 25 - 28

Publications:
AAE Communique
ENDODONTICS: Colleagues for Excellence Newsletter; bi-annually
Journal of Endodontics; monthly; adv.
PULP E-Newsletter; bi-monthly
The Diplomate; semi-annually

American Association of Engineering Societies *(1979)*
1801 Alexander Bell Dr.
Reston, VA 20191
Tel: (202) 296-2237 *Fax:* (202) 296-1151
E-Mail: info@aaes.org
Website: aaes.org
Members: 13 societies
Staff: 2
Annual Budget: $250-500,000
Tax: 501(c)(3)

Personnel:
Interim Executive Director: Carol W. Bowers CAE, P.G.
  E-Mail: cbowers@aaes.org

Historical Note:
Formerly the Engineers Joint Council. AAES is a multidisciplinary organization of engineering societies representing engineers in industry, government and education.

Meetings/Conferences:
Number of non-conference events/year: 2

Publications:
AAES eNewsletter; on-line
Engineering and Technology Degrees; annually
Engineering and Technology Enrollments; annually
Engineers' Salaries: Special Industry Report; annually
Salaries of Engineers in Education; biennially

American Association of Equine Practitioners *(1954)*
4075 Iron Works Pkwy.
Lexington, KY 40511
Tel: (859) 233-0147 *Fax:* (859) 233-1968
TollFree: (800) 443-0177
E-Mail: aaepoffice@aaep.org
Website: aaep.org
Members: 10000 veterinarians and veterinary students
Staff: 16
Annual Budget: $5-10,000,000
Tax: 501(c)(6)

Personnel:
Executive Director: David Foley
Director, Marketing and Public Relations: Sally J. Baker
  E-Mail: sbaker@aaep.org

Historical Note:
AAEP's mission is to improve health and welfare of the horse, to further the professional development of its members, and to provide resources and leadership for the benefit of the equine industry. Membership: $255 (Individual); $35 (Veterinary Students); $345 (Regular/ Veterinarian/International); $125 (Recent Graduates); $125 (Residents/Ph.D. Students).

Meetings/Conferences: Annual
2013 - Nashville, TN/Dec. 7 - 11
2014 - Salt Lake City, UT/Dec. 6 - 10
2015 - Las Vegas, NV/Dec. 5 - 9
Number of non-conference events/year: 3

Publications:
Equine Veterinary Education; monthly
Spur of the Moment; on-line
The AAEP Resource Guide and Membership Directory

American Association of Exporters & Importers *(1921)*
1050 17th St. NW
Suite 810
Washington, DC 20036
Tel: (202) 857-8009 *Fax:* (202) 857-7843
E-Mail: hq@aaei.org
Website: aaei.org
Members: 425 individuals
Staff: 4
Annual Budget: $1-2,000,000

Tax: 501(c)(6)

Personnel:
President and Chief Executive Officer: Marianne Rowden
    E-Mail: mrowden@aaei.org
Manager, Member and Media Affairs: Chris Enyart
    E-Mail: cenyart@aaei.org
Manager, Events: Michelle Measel
    E-Mail: mmeasel@aaei.org
Director, Government Affairs: Megan Montgomery
    E-Mail: mmontgomery@aaei.org

Historical Note:
Became the American Importers Association in 1967 and assumed its present name in 1981. AAEI seeks to achieve tangible benefits for members by promoting efficiency, economy and professionalism in global trade through advocacy, education and communication. Membership: $515 (Port Authority/Trade Association); $670-4,120 (Industry Service Provider); $618-6386 (Importers/Exporters); $567-4,120 (Law Firms).

Meetings/Conferences: Annual
Conference Chair: Michelle Measel
2013 - Washington, DC/June 16 - 18/11-25 exhibitors
Number of non-conference events/year: 2

Publications:
The ALERT; weekly

The American Association of Eye and Ear Centers of Excellence *(1983)*
1655 N. Fort Myer Dr.
Suite 700
Arlington, VA 22209
Tel: (703) 243-8848 *Fax:* (703) 351-5298
E-Mail: rbetz@aaeeh.org
Website: aaeece.org
Members: 2,550 physicians
Staff: 4

Personnel:
President: Robert Betz PhD
    E-Mail: rbetz@aaeeh.org
Vice President, Finance and Operations: Lorna Bradley
    E-Mail: lbradley@aaeeh.org

Historical Note:
Organized in 1983 as the American Association of Eye and Ear Hospitals (AAEEH), the forerunner of today's American Association of Eye and Ear Centers of Excellence (AAEECE). The Association delivers its membership a vast array of innovative programs and services to enhance their viability and to bolster quality patient care.

Meetings/Conferences: Annual
2013 - New Orleans, LA/Nov. 10 - 12
2014 - Chicago, IL/Nov. 16 - 18
2014 - Chicago, IL/Nov. 16 - 18

American Association of Family and Consumer Sciences *(1909)*
400 N. Columbus St.
Suite 202
Alexandria, VA 22314
Tel: (703) 706-4600 *Fax:* (703) 706-4663
TollFree: (800) 424-8080
E-Mail: info@aafcs.org
Website: aafcs.org
Members: 11000 individuals
Staff: 16
Annual Budget: $1-2,000,000
Tax: 501(c)(3)

Personnel:
Executive Director: Carolyn W. Jackson CFCS
    E-Mail: cjackson@aafcs.org
Director, Accreditation: Carol Anderson CFCS
    E-Mail: canderson@aafcs.org
Managing Editor: Debra Bass
    E-Mail: dbass@aafcs.org
Division Director, Operations and Membership Services: John Lord
    E-Mail: jlord@aafcs.org
Senior Manager, Communications: Gwynn Mason
    E-Mail: gmason@aafcs.org
Division Director, Credentialing, Professional Development and Public Policy: Gay Nell McGinnis CFCS
    E-Mail: gmcginnis@aafcs.org
Senior Manager, Member Relations and Contact, Conferences: Sophy Mott
    E-Mail: smott@aafcs.org
Database Manager: Sharon Wiltshire
    E-Mail: swiltshire@aafcs.org

Historical Note:

Formerly (1994) known as the American Home Economics Association, AAFCS's mission is to provide leadership and support to professionals whose work is to assist individuals, families and communities in making informed decisions about their well being, relationships, and resources to optimize their quality of life. Members are elementary, secondary and post-secondary educators and administrators, cooperative extension agents, other professionals in government, business and nonprofit sectors, and students preparing for the field. Membership: $60-250/year.

Continuing Education:
Certification Designation/s: CFCS-HDFS, CFCS-HNFS, CPFFE, CFCS

Meetings/Conferences:
Conference Chair: Sophy Mott
2013 - Houston, TX/June 26 - 29

Publications:
Family & Consumer Sciences Research Journal; quarterly; adv.
Journal of Family & Consumer Sciences; quarterly; adv.
Membership Directory; on-line

American Association of Feline Practitioners *(1974)*
390 Amwell Rd.
Suite 402
Hillsborough, NJ 08844
Tel: (908) 359-9351 *Fax:* (908) 292-1188
TollFree: (800) 874-0498
E-Mail: info@catvets.com
Website: catvets.com
Members: 2000 individuals
Staff: 3
Annual Budget: $500-1,000,000
Tax: 501(c)(6)

Personnel:
Executive Director: Rick Alampi
    E-Mail: rickaaamc@earthlink.net
Director, Communications and Public Relations: Paola Hernandez
    E-Mail: phernandez@association-partners.com
Assistant Executive Director: Heather O'Steen
    E-Mail: hosteen@association-partners.com

Historical Note:
AAFP's mission is to improve health and well-being of cats by supporting standards of practice, continuing education and scientific investigation. Members are veterinarians specializing in the treatment of cats. Membership: $205 (Individual Veterinarian); $125 (Recent Graduate); $115 (ISFM Member); $190 (Two Members in Practice); $180 (Three or More Members in Practice).

Meetings/Conferences:
Conference Chair: Heather O'Steen
2013 - Dallas, TX (The Sheraton Dallas)/Sept. 26 - 29

Publications:
AAFP Feline Weekly; weekly
Journal of Feline Medicine and Surgery (JFMS); on-line
Membership Directory; annually
The Scratching Post; bi-monthly; adv.

American Association of Food Hygiene Veterinarians *(1973)*
P.O. Box 550
Hoschton, GA 30548-0550
Tel: (770) 307-3862
Website: avma.org/About/AlliedOrganizations/Pages/AAFSV
Members: 600 veterinarians
Staff: 2
Annual Budget: $10-25,000

Personnel:
President: Dr. Bonnie J. Buntain
    E-Mail: aafsv.president@gmail.com
Executive President: Dr. Rex D. Holt
    E-Mail: aafsv.execvp@gmail.com

Historical Note:
AAFHV's purpose is to increase the knowledge of veterinarians in food animal practice, education and elevate the standards of food hygiene veterinarians and encourage them to communicate among the members of the association to share scientific and other relevant information. Membership : $45 (US, Canada & Mexico); $55 (Other International).

Publications:
News-O-Gram; bi-monthly

American Association of Franchisees and Dealers *(1992)*

P.O. Box 10158
Palm Desert, CA 92255-1058
Tel: (619) 209-3775 *Fax:* (866) 855-1988
TollFree: (886) 855-1988
E-Mail: benefits@aafd.org
Website: aafd.org
Members: 5000 individuals and companies
Staff: 2
Annual Budget: $250-500,000
Tax: 501(c)(6)

Personnel:
Chairman and Chief Executive Officer: Robert L. Purvin Jr.
Director, Member Support and Comptroller: Lorraine Nelson
    E-Mail: lorraine@aafd.org

Historical Note:
AAFD represents owners of franchised businesses whose mission is to promote fair and equitable franchising and dealer practices, to promote trade and exemplary trade practices, and to provide members with programs, services and products which enhance their ability to conduct their individual businesses and careers with competence and integrity. Membership: $290 (Franchisee); $119 (Associate); $500 (Supporting/Franchisor); $5,000 (Lifetime); $1000 (Associations); $25 (Affiliate).

American Association of Genitourinary Surgeons *(1886)*
Loyola University Medical Center, Department of Urology
Fahey Bldg. 54, Rm. 267, 2160 S. First Ave.
Maywood, IL 60153
Tel: (734) 232-4943 *Fax:* (734) 936-8037
E-Mail: sheskett@umich.edu
Website: aagus.org
Members: 200 individuals
Staff: 2
Annual Budget: $100-250,000

Personnel:
President: Carl A. Olsson
Secretary and Treasurer: Robert C. Flanigan MD

Historical Note:
AAGUS is an association of academic urologists from the United States, Canada and around the world, dedicated to the study of diseases of the genitourinary system. Membership: $260 (Active); $200 (Fellows/International); Free for Honorary .

Meetings/Conferences: Annual
2013 - New Orleans, LA (Ritz-Carlton)/April 3 - 6

Publications:
Newsletter

American Association of Grain Inspection and Weighing Agencies *(1944)*
P.O. Box 26426
Kansas City, MO 64196
Tel: (816) 569-4020 *Fax:* (816) 221-8189
E-Mail: info@aagiwa.org
Website: aagiwa.org
Members: 45 agencies and corporations
Staff: 2
Annual Budget: $50-100,000

Personnel:
Editor: Bob Petersen
    E-Mail: bob.petersen@aagiwa.org

Historical Note:
AAGIWA represents grain inspection and weighing agencies and provides a liaison between the Federal Grain Inspection Service and designated agencies. Members include federally-licensed private inspection agencies, official state agencies, and suppliers.

Meetings/Conferences: Annual
Number of non-conference events/year: 1

Publications:
Chaff Newsletter; monthly; adv.
Member Directory; on-line

American Association of Healthcare Administrative Management *(1968)*
11240 Waples Mill Rd.
Suite 200
Fairfax, VA 22030
Tel: (703) 281-4043 *Fax:* (703) 359-7562
E-Mail: info@aaham.org
Website: aaham.org
Members: 2500 individuals
Staff: 5

Annual Budget: $1-2,000,000
Tax: 501(c)(6)

Personnel:
Executive Director: Sharon R. Galler CMP
  E-Mail: sharon@aaham.org
Manager, Conventions: Danielle Burns
  E-Mail: danielle@aaham.org
Director, Certification: Maria Ledoux
  E-Mail: maria@aaham.org
Director, Membership Services: Moayad Zahralddin
  E-Mail: moayad@aaham.org

Historical Note:
AAHAM was founded in 1968 as the American Guild of Patient Account Management and later assumed its current name. AAHAM's mission is to provide education, certification, networking, and advocacy for healthcare revenue cycle professionals. It actively represents the interests of healthcare administrative management professionals through a comprehensive program of legislative and regulatory monitoring and its participation in industry groups such as ANSI, DISA and NUBC. Membership: $175 (Individual/National); $50 (Student/ Retired).

Continuing Education:
Enrollment: 2500
Certification Designation/s: CCAM, CPAT, CPAM, CCT, CCAT

Meetings/Conferences: Annual
Conference Chair: Danielle Burns
2013 - New Orleans, LA (Sheraton New Orleans Hotel)/Oct. 16 - 18

Publications:
Aksarben-Newsletter
Legislative Currents; bi-monthly
National News; monthly
The Journal of Healthcare Administrative Management; quarterly; adv.

Membership List Available to Non-members

American Association of Healthcare Consultants
(1949)
1205 Johnson Ferry Rd.
Suite 136-420
Marietta, GA 30068
Tel: (770) 635-8758 Fax: (770) 874-4401
E-Mail: info@aahcmail.org
Website: aahc.net
Members:
25 companies
100 individuals
Staff: 1
Annual Budget: $50-100,000

Personnel:
Executive Director: Linda Campbell CAE, CMP

Historical Note:
AAHC's mission is to serve as the preferred professional and practice development organization for consultants and advisors serving the healthcare industry; to advance the knowledge, practice standards, and quality pertaining to such consulting and advisory services. Membership: $695/year.

Meetings/Conferences:
Conference Chair: Linda Campbell CAE, CMP
Number of non-conference events/year: 1

Publications:
AAHC Newsletters
Member Directory

American Association of Heart Failure Nurses
15000 Commerce Pkwy.
Suite C
Mt. Laurel, NJ 08054
Tel: (856) 642-4408 Fax: (856) 439-0525
TollFree: (888) 452-2436
E-Mail: information@aahfn.org
Website: aahfn.org
Staff: 5
Annual Budget: $500-1,000,000
Tax: 501(c)(6)

Personnel:
Executive Director: Pete Pomilio
Manager, Membership and Certification: Pam Brown
Director, Sponsorship Sales: Sabina Gargiulo
Director, Membership and Client Services: Gail Haas
Director, Meetings and Exhibits: Clare MacNab CEM, CMP

Historical Note:

AAHFN seeks to create and maintain a professional association to unite individuals engaged in providing health care services relating to and in the support and advancement of heart failure care, education and research thus promoting optimal patient outcomes. Membership: $50-90/year.

Continuing Education:
Certification Designation/s: CHFN

Meetings/Conferences: Annual
Conference Chair: Clare MacNab CEM, CMP
2013 - Montreal, QC (Le Centre Sheraton Montreal Hotel)/June 27 - 29
2014 - Los Angeles, CA (Westin Bonaventure Hotel and Suites, Los Angeles)/June 26 - 28

Publications:
Membership Directory; on-line
The Connection

American Association of Hip and Knee Surgeons
(1991)
6300 N. River Rd.
Suite 615
Rosemont, IL 60018-4237
Tel: (847) 698-1200 Fax: (847) 698-0704
E-Mail: helpdesk@aahks.org
Website: aahks.org
Members: 1150 individuals
Staff: 6
Annual Budget: $2-5,000,000
Tax: 501(c)(6)

Personnel:
Executive Director: Robert A. Hall CAE, MEd
  E-Mail: bob@aahks.org
Director, Education and Meetings: Eileen Lusk
  E-Mail: eileen@aahks.org
Specialist, Membership and Coding: Krista Stewart
  E-Mail: krista@aahks.org

Historical Note:
AAHKS seeks to provide leadership in advocacy, education and research to achieve excellence in hip and knee patient care. Members are board-certified or board-eligible orthopaedic surgeons in the United States and Canada who devote at least 50% of their practice to hip and knee arthroplasty. Membership: $600(Fellow member); $200 (Active Military member); $500(Associate Member\Affiliate member); $300(candidate);

Meetings/Conferences: Annual
Conference Chair: Eileen Lusk
2013 - Dallas, TX (Sheraton Dallas)/Nov. 8 - 10
2014 - Dallas, TX/Nov. 7 - 9
2015 - Dallas, TX/Nov. 6 - 8
2016 - Dallas, TX/Nov. 4 - 6

Publications:
Membership Directory; on-line
The Journal of Arthroplasty; adv.

American Association of Home Inspectors *(1989)*
P.O. Box 53501
Lubbock, TX 79453-3501
Tel: (806) 794-1190 Fax: (806) 788-1525
E-Mail: aahi@aahionline.com
Website: aahionline.com
Staff: 1

Personnel:
President and Chief Executive Officer: Weldon Sikes

Historical Note:
AAHI's mission is to represent its membership in the Real Estate industry nationwide. Provide a Standards of Practice to enhance consumer protection. urnish Home Inspector Training that is within the reach, financially, of all who are interested in a career as a home inspector. *

Continuing Education:
Certification Designation/s: CHI

Publications:
AAHI Newsletter
Membership Directory; on-line

American Association of Homeopathic Pharmacists *(1923)*
4332 SE Logus Rd.
Milwaukie, OR 97222
Tel: (503) 654-1204 Fax: (503) 654-1204
E-Mail: homeopathicpharmacy@yahoo.com
Website: homeopathicpharmacy.org
Staff: 2
Annual Budget: $50-100,000

Personnel:

President: Mark Land
Treasurer: Mark Phillips

Historical Note:
The mission of the AAHP, an alliance of homeopathic manufacturers, pharmacists, and other qualified parties is to serve the homeopathic community by promoting excellence in the practice of homeopathic pharmacy, manufacturing and distribution, by supporting the requirements, criteria, and published guidelines in the HPRS, CPG, CFR, and other applicable regulations. Membership:$1,850 - 21,000 (Voting Member based on self-reported annual sales); $525 (Non-Voting Member); $100 (Individual).

Meetings/Conferences: Annual

Publications:
Homeopathy Today; quarterly; adv.
Journal of the American Institute of Homeopathy; adv.
Journal of the Homeopathic Academy of Naturopathic Physicians
Member Directory; on-line
The New England Journal of Homeopathy; semi-annually

American Association of Hospital and Healthcare Podiatrists *(1950)*
8508-18th Ave.
Brooklyn, NY 11214
Tel: (718) 259-1822 Fax: (718) 259-4002
E-Mail: info@hospitalpodiatrists.org
Website: hospitalpodiatrists.org
Members: 800 individuals
Staff: 1
Annual Budget: $25-50,000

Personnel:
Executive Director: Dr. Frank Rinaldi DPM, CAE

Historical Note:
Founded as American Association of Hospital Podiatrists. Purpose is to support, promote and provide educational programs in hospitals, health institutions and organizations as it pertains to foot health and podiatric medicine. Membership: $95 (Individual); $15 (Student).

Publications:
AAHHP Newsletter; on-line
The Hospital Podiatrist; on-line

American Association of Immunologists *(1913)*
9650 Rockville Pike
Bethesda, MD 20814-3994
Tel: (301) 634-7178 Fax: (301) 634-7887
E-Mail: infoaai@aai.org
Website: aai.org
Members: 7500 individuals
Staff: 9
Annual Budget: $10-25,000,000
Tax: 501(c)(3)

Personnel:
Executive Director and Executive Editor: M. Michele Hogan PhD
  E-Mail: infoaai@aai.org
Director, Communications and Development: Mary I. Bradshaw
  E-Mail: mbradshaw@aai.org
Director, Finance: Todd Breach CPA
  E-Mail: tbreach@aai.org
Administrative Assistant: James Finnerty
  E-Mail: jfinnerty@aai.org
Director, Public Policy and Government Affairs: Lauren G. Gross JD
  E-Mail: lgross@aai.org
Director, Publications: Kaylene J. Kenyon PhD
  E-Mail: kkenyon@aai.org
Senior Manager, Meetings: Diane E. Kovats CMP
  E-Mail: dkovats@aai.org
Director, Membership: Jan C. Massey CPA
  E-Mail: jmassey@aai.faseb.org
Manager, Content Licensing and Subscription Marketing and Sales: Clair O'Neil Sinks
  E-Mail: csinks@aai.org

Historical Note:
AAI was founded with 56 charter members, most of whom worked in the laboratories of Sir Almroth Wright, Mechnikov and Ehrlich and also a member of the Federation of American Societies for Experimental Biology since 1942. AAI's mission is to advance the knowledge of immunology and its related disciplines, support the interchange of ideas and information among investigators, and addressing the potential integration of immunologic principles into clinical practice. Membership: $260 (Active U.S. Residents); $266.25 (Active Non U.S. Residents); $125 (Emeritus U.S. Residents); $255 (Emeritus Non U.S.

Residents); $64 (Trainee U.S. Residents); $65.55 (Trainee Non U.S. Residents).

Continuing Education:
Certification Designation/s: AAI

Meetings/Conferences: Annual
Conference Chair: Diane E. Kovats CMP
2013 - Honolulu, HI (Hawaii Convention Center)/May 3 - 7/700 attendees/over 100 exhibitors
2014 - Pittsburgh, PA/May 2 - 6
2015 - New Orleans, LA/May 8 - 12

Publications:
AAI Newsletter
Journal of Immunology; semi-monthly; adv.
Membership Directory; on-line

Membership List Available to Non-members

American Association of Independent Claims Professionals (2002)
5746 Union Mill Rd.
P.O. Box 160
Clifton, VA 20124
E-Mail: info@aaicp.net
Website: aaicp.net
Members: 6 Organizations
Staff: 2
Annual Budget: $100-250,000

Personnel:
Association Director: Susan Murdock
    E-Mail: susan@murdockinc.com
Director, Finance: Robert Mason CPA
    E-Mail: rob@rfmasoncpa.com

Historical Note:
AAICP's mission is to advance a legal and regulatory environment that enables third-party administrators and independent adjustors to meet their responsibilities

Publications:
Newsletter

American Association of Independent Music
853 Brodway
Suite 1406
New York, NY 10003
Tel: (212) 999-6113 *Fax:* (928) 395-0871
E-Mail: newsletter@a2im.org
Website: a2im.org
Members: 350 Associate Members and Independent Music Label Members
Staff: 4
Annual Budget: $500-1,000,000

Personnel:
President: Rich Bengloff
    E-Mail: rich@a2im.org
Manager, Operations: Sheryl Cohen
    E-Mail: sheryl@a2im.org
Vice President: Jim Mahoney
    E-Mail: jim@a2im.org
Director, Membership Services: Jennifer Masset
    E-Mail: jen@a2im.org

Historical Note:
A2IM serves the Independent music community and represents a broad coalition of music labels from a sector that comprises over 30% of the music industry's market share in the U.S.

Meetings/Conferences: Annual

Publications:
Membership Directory; on-line

Membership List Available to Non-members

American Association of Individual Investors (1978)
625 N. Michigan Ave.
Chicago, IL 60611-3151
Tel: (312) 280-0170 *Fax:* (312) 280-9883
TollFree: (800) 428-2244
Website: aaii.com
Members: 150000 individuals
Staff: 25
Annual Budget: $5-10,000,000
Tax: 501(c)(3)

Personnel:
President: John Bajkowski
Managing Editor: Jean Henrich

Historical Note:
AAII's purpose is to assist individuals in becoming effective managers of their own assets through programs

of education, information and research. *Membership:* $29 (Basic); $49 (Enhanced); $290 (Lifetime).

Publications:
AAII Investor Update E-Newsletter; weekly
AAII Journal; monthly
AAII Tax Guide; annually
Computerized Investing; quarterly
Quarterly Mutual Fund Update; quarterly
Stock Investor Pro; on-line
Stock Superstars Report; weekly

American Association of Insurance Management Consultants (1979)
8980 Lakes At 610 Dr.
Suite 100
Houston, TX 77054
Tel: (713) 664-6424
Website: aaimco.com
Members: 35 companies
Staff: 2
Annual Budget: Under $10,000

Personnel:
President: Thomas M. Braniff
    E-Mail: thomas.braniff@aaimco.com
Director, Membership Services: Mary LaPorte
    E-Mail: malaporte@hughes.net

Historical Note:
AAIMCo's purpose is to promote the exchange of information, education, counsel and service between members serving as consultants to individuals and entities in order to help the insurance industry. Members are consultants to the insurance industry, including insurance companies, agents, brokers, and their consumers, as well as law firms that represent those constituencies. Membership: $240 (Regular); $90 (Retired Member); $180 (Associate).

Meetings/Conferences: Annual

American Association of Insurance Services (1975)
1745 S. Naperville Rd.
Wheaton, IL 60189-5898
Tel: (630) 681-8347 *Fax:* (630) 681-8356
TollFree: (800) 564-2247
E-Mail: info@AAISonline.com
Website: aaisonline.com
Members: 700 insurers
Staff: 7
Annual Budget: $5-10,000,000
Tax: 501(c)(6)

Personnel:
President and Chief Executive Officer: Edmund J. Kelly
Director, Member Relations: Kelly Grandy
    E-Mail: kellyg@AAISonline.com
Director, Corporate Communications: Joseph S. Harrington ARP, CPCU
    E-Mail: joeh@AAISonline.com
Vice President, Information Services: David Linton
Senior Director, Government Affairs: Kevin Ross Esq.
Manager, Human Resources: Karen Sheridan
    E-Mail: karens@AAISonline.com
Vice President, Marketing and Industry Relations: Joyce Tignino

Historical Note:
AAIS is a product development resource for insurance providers who need responsive, innovative information services. MEmbers are Insurance companies, reinsurers, software vendors, and other service providers who support AAIS member companies.

Meetings/Conferences: Annual
2013 - Ponte Vedra Beach, FL (Ponte Vedra Inn and Club)/April 7 - 9

Publications:
AAIS Advisory; bi-weekly
Viewpoint Magazine; quarterly; adv.

American Association of Integrated Healthcare Delivery Systems (1993)
4435 Waterfront Dr.
Suite 101
Glen Allen, VA 23060
Tel: (804) 747-5283 *Fax:* (804) 747-5316
E-Mail: info@aaihds.org
Website: aaihds.org
Members: 415 individuals
Staff: 16
Annual Budget: $100-250,000
Tax: 501(c)(6)

Personnel:
Managing Editor: Bill Edwards
    E-Mail: bill.edwards@douglasmurphy.com
Vice President, Sales and Marketing: Sloane Reed
Director, Communications: Jeremy Williams
    E-Mail: jwilliams@namcp.org

Historical Note:
Founded as American Association of Physician-Hospital Organizations, assumed its current name in 1997. An affiliate of National Association of Managed Care Physicians. AAIHDS is a non-profit organization dedicated to the educational advancement of provider-based managed care professionals involved in integrated healthcare delivery. Members are physicians, hospital administrators, health plan executives and other individuals with an interest in physician-hospital organizations. Membership: $275 (Individual); $750 (Group, includes 6 Membership); $500 (Partner); $1,000 (Benefactor); $5,000 (Corporate Patron); $2,500 (Patron); $10,000 (Grand Patron).

Continuing Education:
Certification Designation/s: CME

Publications:
Genomics Biotech E-News; on-line
Managed Care E-News; on-line

American Association of Intensive English Programs (1988)
P.O. Box 1158
Pacifica, CA 94044
Tel: (415) 926-1975 *Fax:* (415) 354-3322
E-Mail: info@aaiep.org
Website: aaiep.org
Members: 300 programs as members
Staff: 5
Annual Budget: $100-250,000
Tax: 501(c)(6)

Personnel:
Executive Director: Kathryn Kohut
Vice President, Outreach: Ann Aldrich
    E-Mail: outreach@aaiep.org
Secretary: Lisa Kraft
    E-Mail: secretary@aaiep.org
Vice President, Standards: Jane E. Robison
    E-Mail: standards@aaiep.org
Treasurer: Patricia Szasz
    E-Mail: treasurer@aaiep.org

Historical Note:
The purpose of AAIEP is to support ethical and professional standards for intensive English programs and to advocate for the value of English study in the United States. Membership in AAIEP is for programs, not individuals. At any time, only one person (normally the director) may be the designated representative for a program. Associate membership is open to any institution, organization, or business interested in supporting IEP issues and working with IEPs in the USA. Membership: $575 (New); $645 (Associate).

Meetings/Conferences: Annual
2013 - San Francisco, CA/Jan. 24 - 25
Number of non-conference events/year: 1

Publications:
AAIEP Newsletter; biennially
AAIEP Quarterly E-Newsletter; quarterly
Annual Memebership Directory; annually

American Association of International Healthcare Recruitment
2032 Exeter Rd.
Suite 2
Germantown, TN 38138
Tel: (855) 772-2447
E-Mail: info@aaihr.org
Website: aaihr.org
Staff: 3
Annual Budget: $100-250,000

Personnel:
President: Michael Le Monier
    E-Mail: mlemonier@medprostaffing.com
Treasurer: Tom Nichols
    E-Mail: TNichols@vintagehealth.net

Historical Note:
The mission of the American Association of International Healthcare Recruitment (AAIHR) includes the encouragement of high standards of ethical conduct in dealings with healthcare professionals, clients, and competitors. In furtherance of that mission, the AAIHR board of directors has adopted the following codes of ethics. Membership: $500 (Regular); $350 (Associate).

American Association of Jewish Lawyers and Jurists (1969)
2020 K St. NW
20006
Washington, DC 20036
Tel: (202) 775-0991 *Fax:* (202) 828-0909
E-Mail: iajlj@goldmail.net.il
Website: intjewishlawyers.org
Staff: 1

Personnel:
President: Alyza Lewin

Historical Note:
AAJLJ" was founded in 1983 and is affiliated with the International Association of Jewish Lawyers and Jurists (IAJLJ). The AAJLJ represents the American Jewish legal community, defending Jewish interests and human rights in the United States and abroad.

Meetings/Conferences: Annual

American Association of Kidney Patients (1969)
2701 N. Rocky Point Dr.
Suite 150
Tampa, FL 33607
Fax: (813) 636-8122
E-Mail: info@aakp.org
Website: aakp.org
Members: 20 members
Staff: 6
Annual Budget: $500-1,000,000
Tax: 501(c)(3)

Personnel:
Executive Director: Karen E. Ryals
    E-Mail: kryals@aakp.org
Communications Director: Jerome Bailey
Director, Office Operations: Valerie Gonzalez
    E-Mail: vgonzalez@aakp.org
Contact, Program Coordinator and Membership Services: Ecedra McGlone
    E-Mail: emcglone@aakp.org
Controller: Louis Scholl

Historical Note:
AAKP strive to educate and advance the health and well-being of chronic kidney disease (CKD) patients, those on hemodialysis, peritoneal dialysis and transplant recipients. The group originally called themselves NAPH (National Association of Patients on Hemodialysis, which later changed to AAKP) and set out to inform patients and the public about kidney disease. Membership: $25 (Patient/Family); $45 (Professional); $100 (Physician); $200 (Institutional); $1,000 (Life Member).

Meetings/Conferences: Annual

Publications:
AAKP Diet Tips & Bits; monthly; adv.
AAKP Public Policy Briefing; monthly; adv.
AAKP Renal Flash; monthly; adv.
aakpRENALIFE; on-line; adv.
At Home with AAKP; adv.
Kidney Beginnings: The Electronic Newsletter; monthly; adv.
Kidney Transplant Today; monthly; adv.
Taking Dialysis Home; quarterly; adv.

Membership List Available to Non-members

The American Association of Language Specialists (1957)
P.O. Box 27306
Washington, DC 20038-7306
Tel: (202) 580-5587
E-Mail: admin@taals.net
Website: taals.net
Members: 150 members
Staff: 1
Annual Budget: Under $10,000

Personnel:
President: Teresa G. Willett
    E-Mail: tereguz@aol.com

Historical Note:
Professional association representing interpreters and translators working at the international level, either for conferences on a free-lance basis or for international organizations as permanent staff. Has no paid officers or full-time staff. Membership: $100/year.

Publications:
Membership Directory; on-line

American Association of Law Libraries (1906)
105 W. Adams St.

Suite 3300
Chicago, IL 60603-6225
Tel: (312) 939-4764 *Fax:* (312) 431-1097
E-Mail: baish@law.georgetown.edu
Website: aallnet.org
Members: 5000 individuals
Staff: 12
Annual Budget: $5-10,000,000
Tax: 501(c)(3)

Personnel:
Executive Director: Kate Hagan
    E-Mail: khagan@aall.org
Director, Finance and Administration: Paula Davidson
    E-Mail: pdavidson@aall.org
Director, Membership Services, Marketing and Communications: Julia O'Donnell
    E-Mail: jodonnell@aall.org
Director, Meetings: Pamela Reisinger
    E-Mail: preisinger@aall.org
Director, Information Technology: Chris Siwa
    E-Mail: csiwa@aall.org
Director, Education: Celeste Smith
    E-Mail: csmith@aall.org

Historical Note:
AALL's mission is to promote and enhance the value of law libraries to the legal and public communities, to foster the profession of law librarianship, and to provide leadership in the field of legal information. Membership: $228 (Active/Associate); $58(Student/Retired/Unemployed).

Meetings/Conferences: Annual
Conference Chair: Pamela Reisinger
Number of non-conference events/year: 4

Publications:
AALL Biennial Salary Survey; biennially
AALL Directory and Handbook; annually
AALL E-newsletter; monthly; adv.
AALL Spectrum; monthly; adv.
Index to Foreign Legal Periodicals; quarterly
Law Library Journal; quarterly; adv.
Membership Directory; on-line

Membership List Available to Non-members

American Association of Legal Nurse Consultants (1989)
401 N. Michigan Ave.
Chicago, IL 60611-4267
Fax: (312) 673-6655
TollFree: (877) 402-2562
E-Mail: info@aalnc.org
Website: aalnc.org
Members:
20 companies
3500 individuals
Staff: 9
Annual Budget: $500-1,000,000
Tax: 501(c)(6)

Personnel:
Executive Director: Kevin Baliozian
    E-Mail: Kevin.Baliozian@aalnc.org
Director, Programs and Education: Pat Davis
    E-Mail: Patricia.Davis@aalnc.org
Manager, Operations: Kristin Dee
    E-Mail: Kristin.Dee@aalnc.org
Manager, Sales: Hallie Jaeger
    E-Mail: Hallie.Jaeger@aalnc.org
Associate, Membership Services: Jack Moulton
    E-Mail: Jack.Moulton@aalnc.org
Manager, Publications: Bonnie Rogers
Associate, Education and Communications: Kathryn Schafer
    E-Mail: Kathryn.Schafer@aalnc.org
Manager, Conventions: Mary Talbott-Field

Historical Note:
AALNC's mission is to encourage the professional advancement of Registered Nurses practicing in a consulting capacity in the legal profession and provides educational opportunities for legal nurse consultants. Membership: $160 (Active/Associate); $230 (Sustaining).

Continuing Education:
Certification Designation/s: LNCC

Meetings/Conferences: Annual
Conference Chair: Mary Talbott-Field
2013 - Chicago, IL (Palmer House a Hilton Hotel)/April 4 - 6

Publications:
Journal of Legal Nurse Consulting; quarterly; adv.

Membership Directory; on-line

American Association of Managed Care Nurses (1994)
4435 Waterfront Dr.
Suite 101
Glen Allen, VA 23060
Tel: (804) 747-9698 *Fax:* (804) 747-5316
Website: aamcn.org
Members: 2000 individuals
Staff: 10
Annual Budget: $250-500,000
Tax: 501(c)(6)

Personnel:
Executive Coordinator: Jennifer Turner
Vice President, Education: Katie Eads
Manager, Finance: Rene Enders
Director, Communications: Jeremy Williams

Historical Note:
AAMCN's mission is to establish standards for managed care nursing practice, to positively impact public policy regarding managed health care delivery and to assist in educating the public on managed care. AAMCN members are nurses and other professionals with an interest in managed healthcare. Membership: $70-85 (Individual); $100 (Other Professional); $300-5000 (Corporate); $15 (Student, Full Time).

Meetings/Conferences: Annual

Publications:
Journal of Managed Care Medicine; quarterly; adv.
Managed Care Weekly Update; on-line; adv.
Membership Directory; on-line
Nurses' Notes Newsletter; quarterly; adv.

American Association of Managing General Agents (1926)
610 Freedom Business Center
Suite 110
King of Prussia, PA 19406
Tel: (610) 992-0022 *Fax:* (610) 992-0021
Website: aamga.org
Members: 500 corporate members
Staff: 9
Annual Budget: $2-5,000,000
Tax: 501(c)(6)

Personnel:
Executive Director: Bernd G. Heinze Esq.
    E-Mail: bernie@aamga.org
Chief Financial Officer: Marty Bair
    E-Mail: marty@aamga.org
Director, Meetings: Martha A. Heinze CMP
    E-Mail: martha@aamga.org
Director, Education: Jeff Henry
    E-Mail: jeff@aamga.org
Director, Meetings and Projects: Caitlin Skelton
    E-Mail: caitlin@aamga.org

Historical Note:
AAMGA's mission is to advance managing general agencies as an economically efficient means of insurance distribution. Membership: 1,100 (Managing General Agents); $3,250 (Associate); $2,000 (Business Service).

Continuing Education:
Certification Designation/s: CMGA, CWIS, CIW

Meetings/Conferences: Annual
Conference Chair: Martha A. Heinze CMP
2013 - Scottsdale, AZ (Scottsdale Plaza Resort)/March 2 - 5
2013 - New Orleans, LA (New Orleans Downtown Marriott at the Convention Center)/May 19 - 22/720 attendees/51-100 exhibitors
2014 - Orlando, FL/March 1 - 4
2014 - Waikoloa, HI (Hilton Waikoloa Village)/May 18 - 21/720 attendees/51-100 exhibitors
2014 - Las Vegas, NV/Nov. 5 - 7
2015 - McHenry, MD (Wisp Resort)/May 17 - 20/720 attendees/51-100 exhibitors
2015 - Dallas, TX/Nov. 11 - 13
2016 - Scottsdale, AZ (J.W. Marriott Desert Ridge Resort)/May 22 - 25
Number of non-conference events/year: 14

Publications:
Communiqué; quarterly; adv.
Membership Directory; on-line

American Association of Meat Processors (1939)
One Meating Pl.
P.O. Box 269

Elizabethtown, PA 17022
Tel: (717) 367-1168 *Fax:* (717) 367-9096
E-Mail: aamp@aamp.com
Website: aamp.com
Members: 1325 firms
Staff: 8
Annual Budget: $500-1,000,000
Tax: 501(c)(6)

Personnel:
Executive Director: Jay Wenther PhD
    E-Mail: jay@aamp.com
Manager, Conventions: Jodi Bartlett
    E-Mail: jodi@aamp.com
Contact, Accounting and Finances: Jane Frey
Director, Regulatory and Legislative Affairs: Brynn Kepler
Coordinator, Membership Services: Katie Nolt
Contact, Membership Services: Nancy Stevens

Historical Note:
Small meat processor representation and consulting.
Membership: $99 (Operator); $325 (Supplier); $75
(Allied); $50 (Associate); $100 (Foreign).

Meetings/Conferences: Annual
Conference Chair: Jodi Bartlett
2013 - Charleston, SC (Embassy Suites Hotel and
    Convention Center)/July 18 - 20/800 attendees
2014 - Milwaukee, WI (Hilton Milwaukee City Center)/
    June 19 - 21
2015 - Springfield, IL (Priarie Capital Convention
    Center)/June 18 - 20
Number of non-conference events/year: 2

Publications:
Food Processing Magazine; monthly
Meat & Poultry Magazine; adv.
MeatingPlace Magazine
Prepared Foods Magazine; monthly
Render Magazine; bi-monthly
The Jerky Journal

American Association of Medical Assistants
(1955)
20 N. Wacker Dr.
Suite 1575
Chicago, IL 60606
Tel: (312) 899-1500 *Fax:* (312) 899-1259
E-Mail: info@aama-ntl.org
Website: aama-ntl.org
Members: 20000 individuals
Staff: 26
Annual Budget: $5-10,000,000

Personnel:
Executive Director: Donald A. Balasa CAE, JD
    E-Mail: dbalasa@aama-ntl.org
Executive Director, Accreditation: Anna Johnson CAE
    E-Mail: ajohnson@aama-ntl.org
Director, Continuing Education and Membership Services:
    David Knight
Meeting Planner: Kathy Langley
    E-Mail: klangley@aama-ntl.org
Director, Communications and Marketing: Jean Lynch

Historical Note:
AAMA's mission is to enable medical assisting professionals
to enhance and demonstrate the knowledge, skills and
professionalism required by employers and patients; protect
medical assistants right to practice and promote effective,
efficient health care delivery through optimal use of the
CMA (AAMA). Membership: $77-107 (Individual); $25-40
(Student).

Continuing Education:
Certification Designation/s: CMA (AAMA)

Meetings/Conferences: Annual
Conference Chair: Kathy Langley
2013 - Atlanta, GA (Sheraton Atlanta Hotel)/Sept. 27 -
    30

Publications:
CMA Today; bi-monthly

American Association of Medical Dosimetrists
2201 Cooperative Way
Suite 600
Herndon, VA 20171
Tel: (703) 677-8071 *Fax:* (703) 677-8071
E-Mail: aamd@medicaldosimetry.org
Website: medicaldosimetry.org
Staff: 4
Annual Budget: $500-1,000,000
Tax: 501(c)(6)

Personnel:
Executive Director: Gregg Robinson
    E-Mail: grobinson@drohanmgmt.com
Director, Operations: Spencer Boulter
    E-Mail: sboulter@medicaldosimetry.org
Director, Marketing: Stacey Wilson
    E-Mail: swilson@medicaldosimetry.org

Historical Note:
AAMD is an international society established to promote
and support the Medical Dosimetry profession. The
Society seeks to promote an ideal of professional conduct
to which its members should aspire and endorses the
highest standards of patient care. Membership: $200 (Full/
Professional); $150 (International); $120 (OJT); $60
(Student); $275 (Corporate); $150 (Retired).

Meetings/Conferences: Annual
2013 - San Antonio, TX/June 16 - 20
2014 - Seattle, WA/June 1 - 5
Number of non-conference events/year: 2

Publications:
emonitor — AAMD Newsletter
Medical Dosimetry Journal

American Association of Medical Milk Commissions *(1907)*
1824 N. Hillhurst Ave.
Los Angeles, CA 90027
Tel: (323) 664-1977 *Fax:* (323) 664-0870
E-Mail: fleiss@usc.edu
Members: 35 individuals
Staff: 2
Annual Budget: Under $10,000

Personnel:
President: Paul M. Fleiss MD
    E-Mail: fleiss@hsc.usc.edu

Historical Note:
Professional society of physicians on local Medical Milk
Commissions supervising production of certified milk
from dairies conforming to offical standards. Membership
includes physicians, pathologists, pediatricians and
veterinarians. Affiliated with the Certified Milk Producers
Association of America.

American Association of Medical Society Executives *(1946)*
555 E. Wells St.
Suite 1100
Milwaukee, WI 53202-3823
Tel: (414) 221-9275 *Fax:* (414) 276-3349
E-Mail: aamse@aamse.org
Website: aamse.org
Members: 390 member organizations
Staff: 4
Annual Budget: $500-1,000,000
Tax: 501(c)(6)

Personnel:
Executive Director: Rebecca Brandt, CAE
    E-Mail: rbrandt@aamse.org
Manager, Program: Kathryn E. Agard
    E-Mail: kagard@aamse.org
Manager, Meetings: Alisha T. Campbell MS
    E-Mail: acampbell@aamse.org
Director, Marketing: Jean M. Wenzel
    E-Mail: jwenzel@aamse.org

Historical Note:
Formerly Medical Society Executives Association. AAMSE's
mission is to advance profession and professionalism of
medicine by enhancing and recognizing the talent and work
of medical society executives. Membership: $195-1,500
(Based on tier level).

Meetings/Conferences: Annual
Conference Chair: Alisha T. Campbell MS
2013 - St. Louis, MO/July 17 - 20
2014 - Louisville, KY/July 30 - Aug. 2
2015 - Portland, OR/July 22 - 25
Number of non-conference events/year: 1

Publications:
Hotline; monthly; adv.
Membership Directory; on-line

American Association of Minority Businesses
(1992)
P.O. Box 35432
Charlotte, NC 28235
Members: 17000 businesses and corporations
Staff: 3
Annual Budget: $250-500,000

Personnel:
President and Chief Executive Officer: Charles L. Kelly

Historical Note:
AAMB is a network of minority business owners. AAMB
is supported by several minority organizations and
associations representing thousands of minority business
owners from across the nation. Membership: $60/year
(Business owner); $100/year (Associate); $1,000/year
(Corporate Member); $250/year (Alliance and Association
Members).

American Association of Motor Vehicle Administrators *(1933)*
4301 Wilson Blvd.
Suite 400
Arlington, VA 22203-1861
Tel: (703) 522-4200
E-Mail: inquiries@aamva.org
Website: aamva.org
Members: 150 agencies
Staff: 78
Annual Budget: $25-50,000,000
Tax: 501(c)(3)

Personnel:
President and Chief Executive Officer: Neil D. Schuster
    E-Mail: askneil@aamva.org
Senior Manager, Government Affairs: Cian Cashin
    E-Mail: ccashin@aamva.org
Senior Manager, Information and Knowledge Services:
    Janice Dluzynski
Coordinator, Marketing: Eric Dunn
Director, Contracts Administration: Hal Gollos
Director, Membership and Conference Services: Dianne
    Graham
Vice President, Membership Services and Public Affairs:
    Ian Grossman
Chief Information Officer and Vice President, Information
    Technology: Philippe Guiot
Electronic Communications Specialist: Amanda Mesones
Coordinator, Marketing: Claire O'Brien
Chief Financial Officer and Vice President , Finance: Mark
    Saitta
Manager, Membership Services and Public Affairs: Kim
    Sarkady
Vice President, Human Resources and Organizational
    Development: Anita Simmons
Coordinator, Membership Services and Public Affairs:
    Kathy Springer
Director, Law Enforcement: Brian Ursino
    E-Mail: bursino@aamva.org

Historical Note:
Mission is to improve motor vehicle administration, traffic
safety and law enforcement by providing a forum for
the exchange of idea. Members are state and provincial
agencies responsible for the administration and enforcement
of motor vehicle and traffic laws in the U.S. and Canada.
Membership: $750 (Local Governmental Units/Local
Government Law Enforcement); $1,100 (Category I-
Associations/not-for-profits/Educational Institutions/
Indian Nations/Governments other than United States,
Canada and Mexico); $2,400 (Category II-Business
Organizations).

Continuing Education:
Certification Designation/s: IDEC, CCE, CDE, CME, CTT

Meetings/Conferences: Annual
Conference Chair: Dianne Graham
2013 - Scottsdale, AZ (Westin Kierland Resort and
    Spa)/Aug. 26 - 28
2014 - Dover, DE (Dover Downs Hotel and Casino)/
    Aug. 25 - 27
Number of non-conference events/year: 10

Publications:
MOVE; quarterly; adv.
The Week in Review (TWIR); weekly; adv.

American Association of Museums *(1906)*
1575 Eye St. NW
Suite 400
Washington, DC 20005
Tel: (202) 289-1818 *Fax:* (202) 289-6578
E-Mail: infocenter@aam-us.org
Website: aam-us.org
Members: 250 corporate members, 18000
individuals and 3,000 institutions
Staff: 50
Annual Budget: $10-25,000,000
Tax: 501(c)(3)

Personnel:

President: Ford Bell
    E-Mail: fbell@aam-us.org
Director, Information Technology and Internet Services:
    Canan Abayhan
    E-Mail: cabayhan@aam-us.org
Assistant Director, Marketing and Communications: Susan
    Breitkopf
    E-Mail: sbreitkopf@aam-us.org
Coordinator, Communications: Ariana Carella
Director, External Relations: Eileen G. Goldspiel
    E-Mail: egoldspiel@aam-us.org
Vice President, Programs and Special Initiatives: Kim Igoe
    E-Mail: kigoe@aam-us.org
Chief Financial Officer and Director, Finance: Laura Lott
    E-Mail: llott@aam-us.org
Assistant Director, Human Resources: Katherine
    Mcnamee
    E-Mail: kmcnamee@aam-us.org
Director, Meetings and Professional Education: Dean
    Phelus
    E-Mail: dphelus@aam-us.org
Director, Government Relations: Gail Ravnitzky
    Silberglied
    E-Mail: gsilberglied@aam-us.org
Publisher, Print and Electronic Media: John Strand
    E-Mail: jstrand@aam-us.org
Senior Director, Membership Services: Janet Vaughan
    E-Mail: jvaughan@aam-us.org

Historical Note:
AAM's mission is to enhance value of museums to their
communities through leadership, advocacy, and service.
Membership: $50 (Student/Retired Professional); $90
(Professional); $100-15,000 (Institutional); $100 (Industry
Partner).

Meetings/Conferences: Annual
Conference Chair: Dean Phelus
2013 - Baltimore, MD/May 19 - 22/over 100 exhibitors
2014 - Seattle, WA/May 18 - 21/over 100 exhibitors
2015 - Atlanta, GA/April 26 - 29/over 100 exhibitors
Number of non-conference events/year: 3

Publications:
Aviso; monthly; adv.
Museum; bi-monthly; adv.

Membership List Available to Non-members

American Association of Naturopathic Physicians
(1985)
4435 Wisconsin Ave. NW
Suite 403
Washington, DC 20016
Tel: (202) 237-8150 Fax: (202) 237-8152
TollFree: (866) 538-2267
E-Mail: member.services@Naturopathic.org
Website: naturopathic.org
Members:
68 companies and official state affiliates
2000 students, physicians, supporting and
corporate members
Staff: 13
Annual Budget: $1-2,000,000

Personnel:
Chief Executive Officer: Jud Richland
Vice President, Marketing and Development: Terri Deerr
    E-Mail: terri.deerr@naturopathic.org
Associate, Marketing and Membership Services: Mandisa
    Jones
    E-Mail: mandisa.jones@naturopathic.org
Associate, Communications and Media Relations: Matthew
    Santoro
    E-Mail: matthew.santoro@naturopathic.org

Historical Note:
AANP's mission is to serve its members by advancing
the profession of naturopathic medicine and preserving
its integrity. Membership represents licensed/licensable
naturopathic physicians in the United States who are
graduates of four-year, residential graduates programs.
Membership: $60-654/year.

Meetings/Conferences: Annual
Number of non-conference events/year: 1

Publications:
AANP eNews; monthly
Membership Directory; on-line
Natural Medicine Journal; monthly; adv.
Referral Directory; annually; adv.

Membership List Available to Non-members

American Association of Neurological Surgeons
(1931)
725 15TH St. NW
Washington, DC 20005
Tel: (202) 628-2072 Fax: (202) 628-5264
TollFree: (888) 566-2267
E-Mail: info@aans.org
Website: aans.org
Members: 7200 individuals
Staff: 25
Annual Budget: $2-5,000,000
Tax: 501(c)(3)

Personnel:
Executive Director: Thomas A. Marshall
    E-Mail: tam@aans.org
Director, Meetings: Patricia Anderson CAE, IOM
    E-Mail: pla@aans.org
Director, Marketing: Martha Lara
    E-Mail: mal@aans.org
Director, Information Systems: Tony Macalindong
    E-Mail: ams@aans.org
Director, Washington Office: Katie O. Orrico JD
    E-Mail: korrico@aans.org
Director, Membership Services: Chris Ann Philips
    E-Mail: cap@aans.org
Associate Executive Director: Joni Shulman MPH
    E-Mail: jls@aans.org

Historical Note:
Founded as the Harvey Cushing Society. Incorporated in
Illinois in 1956 and assumed its current name in 1967.
AANS is dedicated to advance the specialty of neurological
surgery in order to promote the quality of patient care.
Membership: $495-875/year (Fellow/Provisional/Affiliate).

Meetings/Conferences: Annual
Conference Chair: Joni Shulman MPH
2013 - New Orleans, LA (Ernest N. Morial Convention
    Center)/April 27 - May 1
2014 - San Francisco, CA/April 5 - 9
2015 - Washington, DC/May 2 - 6

Publications:
AANS E-News; on-line
AANS Neurosurgeon
AANS Neurosurgeon; quarterly; adv.
Journal of Neurosurgery; monthly; adv.
Journal of Neurosurgery: Pediatrics; monthly; adv.
Journal of Neurosurgery: Spine; monthly; adv.
Neurosurgical Focus; on-line
The AANS Online Membership Directory; on-line

Membership List Available to Non-members

American Association of Neuromuscular and
Electrodiagnostic Medicine (1953)
2621 Superior Dr. NW
Rochester, MN 55901
Tel: (507) 288-0100 Fax: (507) 288-1225
E-Mail: aanem@aanem.org
Website: aanem.org
Members: 5200 individuals
Staff: 19
Annual Budget: $2-5,000,000
Tax: 501(c)(6)

Personnel:
Executive Director: Shirlyn A. Adkins JD
    E-Mail: sadkins@aanem.org
Director, Finance: Patrick Aldrich CPA
    E-Mail: paldrich@aanem.org
Manager, Communications and Foundation: Teresa
    Atkinson
    E-Mail: tatkinson@aanem.org
Director, Health Policy and Advocacy: Catherine French
    E-Mail: cfrench@aanem.org
Director, Education: Jackie Gunderson
    E-Mail: jgunderson@aanem.org
Administrative and Product Specialist: Ruth Michel
    E-Mail: rmichel@aanem.org
Director, Membership Services and Corporate Relations:
    Brenda L. Riggott
    E-Mail: briggott@aanem.org
Director, Meetings: Kathryn J. Smith CMP
    E-Mail: ksmith@aanem.org
Information Technology Analyst and Programmer: Jacob
    Sokol
    E-Mail: jsokol@aanem.org
Director, Product Development: Stacie C. Stucky

Historical Note:

Founded as the American Association of Electromyography
and Electrodiagnosis; became the American Association of
Electrodiagnostic Medicine in 1989; assumed its present
name in 2004. AANEM's goal is to increase the quality
of patient care, specifically of those patients with disorders
of skeletal muscle, neuromuscular function and the central
and peripheral nervous systems, by contributing to the
improvement in the methods of electrodiagnostic medicine
through programs in education, research and quality
assurance. Membership: $50-275/year.

Continuing Education:
Enrollment: 200
Certification Designation/s: ABEM, MOCP, CME, TPSAE

Meetings/Conferences: Annual
Conference Chair: Kathryn J. Smith CMP
2013 - San Antonio, TX (JW Marriott San Antonio Hill
    Country Resort and Spa)/Oct. 16 - 19
2014 - Savannah, GA (Savannah International Trade
    and Convention Center)/Oct. 29 - Nov. 1
2015 - Honolulu, HI (Hawaii Convention Center)/Oct.
    28 - 31
2016 - New Orleans, LA (Hilton New Orleans
    Riverside)/Sept. 14 - 17
Number of non-conference events/year: 2

Publications:
AANEM News; quarterly
Membership Directory; on-line
Muscle & Nerve; monthly; adv.

Membership List Available to Non-members

American Association of Neuropathologists
(1930)
Case Western Reserve University, Department of
Pathology
2103 Cornell Rd., WRB 5101
Cleveland, OH 44106
Tel: (216) 368-3671 Fax: (216) 368-8964
E-Mail: aanp@case.edu
Website: neuropath.org
Members: 800 members
Staff: 3
Annual Budget: $250-500,000

Personnel:
Business Manager: Peggy Harris
Secretary, Treasurer and Editor: C. Harker Rhodes BA,
    MS
    E-Mail: c.harker.rhodes@hitchcock.org

Historical Note:
Founded as the Club of Neuropatholgists, this professional
society of physicians assumed its present name in 1932.
AANP's purpose is to advance the science, teaching and
training of the diseases of the nervous system and the
practice of neuropathology. Membership: $140 (Affiliate);
$165 (Active).

Meetings/Conferences: Annual
2013 - Charleston, SC (Charleston Place Hotel)/June 20
    - 23

Publications:
Journal of Neuropathology and Experimental
    Neurology; monthly
Neuropathology Newsletter

American Association of Neuroscience Nurses
(1968)
4700 W. Lake Ave.
Glenview, IL 60025-1485
Tel: (847) 375-4733 Fax: (847) 375-6430
TollFree: (888) 557-2266
E-Mail: info@aann.org
Website: aann.org
Members: 4000 individuals
Staff: 13
Annual Budget: $1-2,000,000
Tax: 501(c)(6)

Personnel:
Executive Director: Joan Kram
    E-Mail: jkram@aann.org
Manager, Marketing and Membership Services: Angelisa
    Belden
    E-Mail: abelden@aann.org
Editor-in-Chief: V. Susan Carroll
    E-Mail: susan.carroll25@gmail.com
Administrator, Accounts: Patience Chiles
    E-Mail: pchiles@aann.org
Manager, Operations: Joe Lindahl
    E-Mail: jlindahl@aann.org
Senior Meetings Manager: Vanessa Mobley, CMP
    E-Mail: vmobley@aann.org

Senior Manager, Education: Jacki Van Oort
  E-Mail: jvanoort@aann.org

Historical Note:
AANN is committed to the advancement of neuroscience nursing by development and support of nurses to promote patient care. Membership is open to registered nurses who demonstrate an active or primary interest in neurosurgical or neurological nursing. Membership: $114 (Regular); $85 (Associate); $58 (Student).

Continuing Education:
Certification Designation/s: CNRN

Meetings/Conferences: Annual
Conference Chair: Vanessa Mobley, CMP
2013 - Charlotte, NC (Charlotte Convention Center)/
  March 9 - 12/800 attendees/1-10 exhibitors
Number of non-conference events/year: 4

Publications:
AANN Neuroscience News; weekly
Journal of Neuroscience Nursing; bi-monthly; adv.
Synapse E-News; on-line

Membership List Available to Non-members

American Association of Nurse Anesthetists
(1931)
222 S. Prospect Ave.
Park Ridge, IL 60068-4001
Tel: (847) 692-7050 *Fax:* (847) 692-6968
E-Mail: info@aanadc.com
Website: aana.com
Members: 40000 individuals
Staff: 16
Annual Budget: $25-50,000,000
Tax: 501(c)(6)

Personnel:
Executive Director: Wanda Wilson PhD, CRNA
  E-Mail: wwilson@aana.com
Senior Director, Communications: Christopher Bettin MA
  E-Mail: cbettin@aana.org
Contact, Membership Services: Mary Graf
  E-Mail: mgraf@aana.com
Senior Director, Finance and Administrative Services:
  Kenneth L. Hoffman CPA, CMA
  E-Mail: khoffman@aana.com
Director, Human Resources: Steven Penio
  E-Mail: spenio@aana.com
Senior Director, Education and Professional Development:
  John Preston CRNA, DNS.c
  E-Mail: jpreston@aana.com
Senior Director, Federal Government Affairs: Frank J.
  Purcell BS
  E-Mail: fpurcell@aanadc.com
Director, Information Systems: Timothy Rutter
  E-Mail: trutter@aana.com

Historical Note:
Formerly National Association of Nurse Anesthetists. AANA is dedicated to advancing patient safety and excellence in anesthesia.

Continuing Education:
Certification Designation/s: CRNA, NCE

Meetings/Conferences: Annual
2013 - Las Vegas, NV (The Mirage)/Aug. 10 - 13
2014 - Orlando, FL (Orlando World Center Marriott)/
  Sept. 13 - 16
Number of non-conference events/year: 4

Publications:
AANA Journal; bi-monthly; adv.
AANA NewsBulletin; monthly; adv.
Membership Directory; on-line

The American Association of Nurse Attorneys
(1977)
P.O. Box 14218
Lenexa, KS 66285-4218
Tel: (913) 895-4625 *Fax:* (913) 895-4652
TollFree: (877) 538-2262
E-Mail: taana_executive_office@goamp.com
Website: taana.org
Members: 575 individuals
Staff: 3
Annual Budget: $100-250,000

Personnel:
President: Nancy Hoffman J D, RN
Administrator: Liz Paulk
  E-Mail: lpaulk@goamp.com
Treasurer: Teressa M. Sanzio JD, MPA, RN

Historical Note:

TAANA's mission is to promote and enhance the profession of the nurse attorney and to provide educational programs, products and services to its members. Membership: $235 (Fellow); $190 (Affiliate); $25 (Student); $110 (First Year Post Graduate).

Meetings/Conferences: Annual
Conference Chair: Nancy Hoffman J D, RN

Publications:
Membership Directory; on-line
TAANA Newsletter; quarterly
The American Association of Nurse Attorneys; on-line

American Association of Nutritional Consultants
(1980)
220 Parker St.
Warsaw, IN 46580
Tel: (574) 269-6165 *Fax:* (574) 268-2120
Website: aanc.net
Members: 2000 individuals
Staff: 1

Personnel:
Registrar: Sherri Brock

Historical Note:
Professional association combating public ignorance and adverse legislation. Members are professional consultants in the field of nutrition. Also serves as administrative offices for the American Naturopathic Medical Association. Membership: $60/year (Association/ Professional/Diplomate Membership); $500/year (Corporate Membership).

Continuing Education:
Certification Designation/s: C.N.C.

Publications:
HealthKeepers Magazine; on-line; adv.

American Association of Occupational Health Nurses *(1942)*
7794 Grow Dr.
Pensacola, FL 32514
Tel: (850) 474-6963 *Fax:* (850) 484-8762
TollFree: (800) 241-8014
E-Mail: AAOHN@aaohn.org
Website: aaohn.org
Members: 6000 individuals and 137 chapters
Staff: 7
Annual Budget: $1-2,000,000
Tax: 501(c)(6)

Personnel:
Executive Director: Jon Dancy
  E-Mail: jon.dancy@dancyamc.com
Director, Convention Services: Donna Deans
Contact, Governance Services: Tracy Goodbred
  E-Mail: tracy.goodbred@dancyamc.com
President: Richard J. Kowalski

Historical Note:
Founded in Philadelphia and incorporated in New York in 1952, AAOHN is the professional association of occupational health nurses. Formerly (1977) the American Association of Industrial Nurses, Inc. AAOHN's mission is to advance and maximize the health, safety and productivity of domestic and global workforces by providing education, research, public policy and practice resources for occupational and environmental health nurses. Membership: $185 plus/year.

Continuing Education:
Certification Designation/s: PAC, CNE

Meetings/Conferences:
Conference Chair: Donna Deans
2013 - Las Vegas, NV (Cosmopolitan of Las Vegas)/
  April 15 - 18/1000 attendees

Publications:
AAOHN Journal; on-line
AAOHN News; quarterly; adv.

Membership List Available to Non-members

American Association of Oral and Maxillofacial Surgeons *(1918)*
9700 W. Bryn Mawr Ave.
Rosemont, IL 60018-5701
Tel: (847) 678-6200 *Fax:* (847) 678-6286
TollFree: (800) 822-6637
Website: aaoms.org
Members: 9000 individuals
Staff: 50
Annual Budget: $25-50,000,000
Tax: 501(c)(6)

Personnel:

Executive Director: Robert C. Rinaldi CAE, PhD
  E-Mail: brinaldi@aaoms.org
Associate Executive Director and General Counsel: Mark R
  Adams SPHR
*Associate Executive Director, Advanced Education and
  Professional Affairs:* Randi V. Andresen
  E-Mail: randesen@aaoms.org
*Associate Executive Director, Education, Meetings and
  Exhibits:* Barbara Choyke
  E-Mail: bchoyke@aaoms.org
Chief Financial Officer: Scott Farrell
  E-Mail: sfarrell@aaoms.org
*Associate Executive Director, Communications and
  Publications:* Janice Teplitz
  E-Mail: jteplitz@aaoms.org
*Associate Executive Director, Practice Management and
  Government Affairs:* Karin Wittich
  E-Mail: karinw@aaoms.org
Manager, Exhibitions: Valerie Wolf
  E-Mail: vwolf@aaoms.org

Historical Note:
Formerly (1978) the American Society of Oral Surgeons. AAOMS's mission is to promote, protect and advance oral and maxillofacial surgery to assure excellence for surgeons and their patients. Members are surgeons specializing in surgery of the mouth, face and jaws. Membership: $1,050 (Fellow/Individual/Faculty Fellow/Provisional Fellow); $450 (Affiliate); $55 (Allied Staff).

Meetings/Conferences:
Conference Chair: Barbara Choyke
2013 - Orlando, FL (Orange County Convention
  Center)/Oct. 7 - 12
2013 - Chicago, IL (Sheraton Chicago Hotel and
  Towers)/Dec. 5 - 8
2014 - Honolulu, HI (Hilton Hawaiian Village Waikiki
  Beach Resort)/Sept. 8 - 13
2014 - Chicago, IL (Sheraton Chicago Hotel and
  Towers)/Dec. 4 - 7
2015 - Washington, DC (Walter E. Washington
  Convention Center)/Sept. 28 - Oct. 3
2015 - Chicago, IL (Sheraton Chicago Hotel and
  Towers)/Dec. 3 - 6
Number of non-conference events/year: 1

Publications:
AAOMS Advocacy E-Newsletter; on-line
AAOMS Today; bi-monthly
Journal of Oral and Maxillofacial Surgery; monthly
Membership Directory; on-line

American Association of Orthodontists *(1900)*
401 N. Lindbergh Blvd.
St. Louis, MO 63141-7816
Tel: (314) 993-1700 *Fax:* (314) 997-1745
TollFree: (800) 424-2841
E-Mail: info@aaortho.org
Website: aaomembers.org
Members: 15000 individuals
Staff: 48
Annual Budget: $25-50,000,000
Tax: 501(c)(6)

Personnel:
Executive Director: Chris P. Vranas CAE
  E-Mail: cvranas@aaortho.org
Senior Manager, Marketing: Burton J. Bollinger III
  E-Mail: bbollinger@aaortho.org
Director, Education and Membership Services: Anita B.
  Craig
  E-Mail: acraig@aaortho.org
Assistant General Counsel: Kevin Dillard
  E-Mail: kdillard@aaortho.org
Assistant To The General Counsel: Kathy DiPrimo
  E-Mail: kdiprimo@aaortho.org
Editor: Gail Gardner
  E-Mail: ggardner@aaortho.org
Director, Communications and Marketing: Linda L.
  Gladden
  E-Mail: lgladden@aaortho.org
Senior Manager, Meetings and Exhibits: D.J. Haman
  E-Mail: dhaman@aaortho.org
Director, Finance And Administration: Nowak Jill
  E-Mail: jnowak@aaortho.org
Senior Manager, Information Systems: Eric P. Mutrux
  E-Mail: emutrux@aaortho.org
Coordinator, Membership Services: Sherry A. Nappier
  E-Mail: snappier@aaortho.org
Director, Leadership Entities and Chief Operating Officer:
  Julie Sutter

E-Mail: jsutter@aaortho.org

Historical Note:
Formed (1900) as The American Society of Orthodontists. Incorporated in Pennsylvania (1917) as The American Association of Orthodontists and later (1965) after the headquarters was established in St. Louis, incorporated in Missouri. AAO's mission is to advance the art and science of orthodontics and to make significant contributions to the health of the public. Membership: $20/year (Student and International Student).

Continuing Education:
Certification Designation/s: VC

Meetings/Conferences: Annual
Conference Chair: D.J. Haman
2013 - Palm Spring, CA (JW Marriott Desert Springs Resort and Spa)/Feb. 8 - 10
2013 - Philadelphia, PA (Philadelphia Convention Center)/May 3 - 7
2014 - New Orleans, LA/April 25 - 29
2015 - San Francisco, CA/May 15 - 20
2015 - San Francisco, CA/May 15 - 19
2016 - Orlando, FL/April 29 - May 2
2017 - San Diego, CA/April 21 - 25
Number of non-conference events/year: 2

Publications:
AAO eBulletin; on-line
American Journal of Orthodontics and Dentofacial Orthopedics; monthly; adv.

Membership List Available to Non-members

American Association of Orthopaedic Medicine
(1982)
600 Pembrook Dr.
Woodland Park, CO 80863
Tel: (800) 992-2063 *Fax:* (719) 687-5184
TollFree: (888) 687-1920
E-Mail: aaom@aaomed.org
Website: aaomed.org
Members: 600 individuals
Staff: 2
Annual Budget: $250-500,000
Tax: 501(c)(3)

Personnel:
Executive Director: Maelu Fleck
E-Mail: fleck@fleckcorporation.com
Secretary and Treasurer: Aris Barbadimos MD

Historical Note:
AAOM is dedicated to the education of physicians in the diagnosis and non-surgical treatment of musculoskeletal pain and functional limitations and promotes professional collaboration across multiple disciplines and creates public awareness of its integrative approach. Membership: $15-325/year.

Meetings/Conferences: Annual
2013 - Phoenix, AZ (Arizona Grand Resort)/April 24 - 27

Publications:
AAOM Newsletter; on-line

American Association of Osteopathic Women Physicians
1108 E. Patterson
Suite Three
Kirksville, MO 63501-2149
Tel: (660) 627-5175 *Fax:* (660) 626-5180
E-Mail: mtettambel@atsu.edu
Website: osteopathic.org/index.cfm?
  PageID = lcl_affil
Members: 64000 physicians
Staff: 1

Personnel:
President: Melicien A. Tettambel DO
E-Mail: mtettambel@atsu.edu

Historical Note:
An affiliate organization of AOA. AAOWP strives to advance osteopathic medicine at the state level, by medical specialty, through education at the colleges of osteopathic medicine and in many other ways.

American Association of Pastoral Counselors
(1963)
9504A Lee Hwy.
Fairfax, VA 22031-2303
Tel: (703) 385-6967 *Fax:* (703) 352-7725
E-Mail: info@aapc.org
Website: aapc.org
Members: 3000 individuals and 100 Centers

Staff: 8
Annual Budget: $500-1,000,000
Tax: 501(c)(3)

Personnel:
Executive Director: Douglas M. Ronsheim Dmin
E-Mail: doug@aapc.org
Director, Administrative Services: Ann L. Martin
E-Mail: Ann@aapc.org
Contact, Membership Services: Barbara Nyman
E-Mail: membership@aapc.org
Contact, Meetings and Publications: Sharon A. Sheflett
E-Mail: Sharon@appc.org

Historical Note:
AAPC's mission is to advocate the profession and the practice of Pastoral Counseling and to train future generations of the profession. Membership: $315 (Diplomate/Fellow); $254 (Certified Pastoral Counselor); $146 (Pastoral Counseling Educator/Pastoral Care Specialist/Member); $175 (Member); $24 (Member-International).

Continuing Education:
Certification Designation/s: CPC

Meetings/Conferences: Annual
Conference Chair: Sharon A. Sheflett

Publications:
Currents; quarterly
Journeys magazine
Sacred Spaces; on-line

American Association of Pathologists' Assistants
(1972)
2345 Rice St.
Suite 220
St. Paul, MN 55113-4036
Tel: (651) 697-9264 *Fax:* (651) 317-8048
TollFree: (800) 532-2272
E-Mail: info@pathologistsassistants.org
Website: pathologistsassistants.org
Members: 1200 fellow members
Staff: 2
Annual Budget: $500-1,000,000
Tax: 501(c)(6)

Personnel:
Executive Director: John E. Mitchell BA, MSBA
E-Mail:
  executivedirector@pathologistsassistants.org
Central Office Coordinator: Michelle Sok

Historical Note:
AAPA's mission is to provide members with high quality, targeted continuing medical education (CME) opportunities, as well as professional development and leadership activities to include networking and support. Membership: $140 (Fellow); $150 (Associate/Affiliate); $400 (Sustaining); $45 (Student); $300 (Institutional).

Continuing Education:
Certification Designation/s: PA(ASCP)

Meetings/Conferences: Annual
2013 - Portland, OR (Hilton Portland and Executive Tower)/Sept. 21 - 27
2014 - New York City, NY (Waldorf = Astoria)/Sept. 6 - 12

Publications:
AAPA Newsletter; quarterly
Member Directory; on-line

Membership List Available to Non-members

American Association of Petroleum Geologists
(1917)
P.O. Box 979
Tulsa, OK 74101-0979
Tel: (918) 584-2555 *Fax:* (918) 580-2665
TollFree: (800) 364-2274
E-Mail: join@aapg.org
Website: aapg.org
Members: 31000 individuals
Staff: 60
Annual Budget: $25-50,000,000
Tax: 501(c)(6)

Personnel:
Manager, Membership Department: Vicki Beighle
E-Mail: vbeighle@aapg.org
Executive Director: David R. Lange
E-Mail: dlange@aapg.org
Managing Editor, Technical Publications: Beverly Molyneux
Project Specialist, Communications: Susie Moore

Director, Education and Professional Development: Susan Nash
E-Mail: snash@aapg.org
Director, Communications: Larry M. Nation
E-Mail: lnation@aapg.org
Manager, Marketing: Julie Simmons
E-Mail: jsimmons@aapg.org
Director, Conventions: Alan Wegener
E-Mail: awegener@aapg.org

Historical Note:
Originally the Southwestern Association of Petroleum Geologists, assumed its current name in 1918. AAPG's purpose is to foster scientific research, to advance the science of geology, to promote technology, and to inspire high professional conduct, provides publications, conferences, and educational opportunities to geoscientists and disseminates the most current geological information available to the general public. Membership: $22.50-155 (Active/Associate); $10-25 (Student); $25-55 (Division).

Continuing Education:
Certification Designation/s: IACET, CEU

Meetings/Conferences:
Conference Chair: Alan Wegener
2013 - Pittsburgh, PA (David L. Lawrence Convention Center)/May 19 - 22
2013 - Cartagena, Colombia/Sept. 8 - 11
2014 - Houston, TX/April 6 - 9
2015 - Denver, CO/May 31 - June 3
2016 - Calgary, AB/June 19 - 22
2017 - Houston, TX/April 2 - 5
Number of non-conference events/year: 9

Publications:
Bulletin; monthly

Membership List Available to Non-members

American Association of Pharmaceutical Scientists *(1986)*
2107 Wilson Blvd.
Suite 700
Arlington, VA 22201-3042
Tel: (703) 243-2800 *Fax:* (703) 243-9650
E-Mail: aaps@aaps.org
Website: aaps.org
Members: 13000 individuals
Staff: 47
Annual Budget: $10-25,000,000
Tax: 501(c)(3)

Personnel:
Executive Director: John Lisack Jr., CAE
E-Mail: lisackj@aaps.org
Specialist, Communications: Joseph Catapano
E-Mail: catapanoj@aaps.org
Senior Manager, Distance Learning: Andy Cohn
E-Mail: cohna@aaps.org
Senior Manager, Marketing: Scott Didawick
E-Mail: didawicks@aaps.org
Associate Executive Director, Marketing and Member Services: Peter Inchauteguiz
E-Mail: inchauteguizp@aaps.org
Senior Manager, Membership Services: Connie Lee
Director, Information Technology: Sherry Martin
E-Mail: martins@aaps.org
Director, Public Outreach: Stacey May
E-Mail: mays@aaps.org
Director, Meetings: Sharon R. Pichon
E-Mail: pichons@aaps.org
Director, Publications: Todd Reitzel
Director, Finance and Administration: Alan Shutt
E-Mail: shutta@aaps.org

Historical Note:
AAPS provides a dynamic international forum for the exchange of knowledge among scientists to enhance their contributions to health, offers timely scientific programs, ongoing education, opportunities for networking, and professional development. Members are pharmaceutical scientists in academia, industry, government and other research institutions.Membership: $40 (Postdoctoral Fellow/Student); $60 (Retired); $165 (Regular Member).

Meetings/Conferences:
Conference Chair: Sharon R. Pichon
2013 - San Diego, CA (Sheraton San Diego Hotel and Marina)/May 20 - 22
2013 - San Antonio, TX (The Henry B. Gonzalez Convention Center)/Nov. 10 - 14
2014 - San Diego, CA (Sheraton San Diego Hotel and Marina)/May 19 - 21
2014 - San Diego, CA (San Diego Convention and Visitors Bureau)/Nov. 2 - 6

2015 - San Francisco, CA (Marriott Marquis San Francisco)/June 8 - 10
2015 - Orlando, FL (Orlando Convention Center)/Oct. 25 - 29
2016 - Denver, CO (Colorado Convention Center)/Nov. 12 - 17
2017 - San Diego, CA (San Diego Convention Center)/Nov. 12 - 16
2018 - Washington, DC (Washington Hilton)/Nov. 3 - 8
2019 - San Antonio, TX (The Henry B. Gonzalez Convention Center)/Nov. 3 - 7
2020 - New Orleans, LA (Ernest N. Morial Convention Center)/Oct. 25 - 29
2021 - Philadelphia, PA (Pennsylvania Convention Center)/Oct. 17 - 21
2022 - Boston, MA (Boston Convention and Exposition Center)/Oct. 16 - 20
2023 - Orlando, FL (Orlando Convention Center)/Oct. 22 - 26

Publications:
AAPS Newsmagazine
AAPS Newsmagazine; monthly; adv.
AAPS PharmSciTech
Membership Directory; on-line
Pharmaceutical Research

American Association of Philosophy Teachers
(1976)
California State University
6300 State University Dr., Suite 140
Long Beach, CA 90815
Tel: (562) 985-4346
E-Mail: aapt@philosphers.net
Website: philosophyteachers.org
Members: 400 individuals
Staff: 3
Annual Budget: $10-25,000
Tax: 501(c)(3)

Personnel:
Executive Director and Secretary: Emily Esch
    E-Mail: eesch@csbsju.edu
Chair, Communications committee: Kevin Hermberg
    E-Mail: kevin.hermberg@dc.edu
Treasurer: Rory Kraft
    E-Mail: rkraft1@ycp.edu

Historical Note:
AAPT is an international organization with members in the US, Canada, Japan, South Africa, and other countries whose purpose is to develop and improve philosophy teaching at all levels of schooling. It also sponsors a biennial international Workshop/Conference on Teaching Philosophy. Membership: $40 (Regular); $25 (Student/ Emeritus/Part- time/Adjunct); $500 (Life Time).

Meetings/Conferences: Annual
2013 - New Orleans, LA (Riverside Hilton)/Feb. 20 - 23

Publications:
AAPT Now; on-line
Teaching Philosophy; on-line

The American Association of Phonetic Sciences
(1973)
3185 Crystal Lake Dr.
St Louis, MO 63129
Tel: (314) 293-1940
E-Mail: aaps@phoneticsciences.com
Website: phoneticsciences.com
Members: 100 individuals
Staff: 2
Annual Budget: Under $10,000

Personnel:
Executive Secretary: Richard A. McGuire PhD
    E-Mail: mcguire@phoneticsciences.com

Historical Note:
AAPS's mission is to support and encourage teaching, learning, and research in phonetic sciences, to advocate cooperative research among scholars and scientists interested in this area, and to provide a forum for the exchange and development of information and ideas about phonetic sciences. Affiliated with International Society of Phonetic Sciences. Membership: $15 (Professional); $5 (Student).

Publications:
AAPS Newsletter; semi-annually

American Association of Physical Anthropologists
(1930)

Dept. of Anthropology
University of South Florida
Tampa, FL 33620-8100
Tel: (813) 974-0817 *Fax:* (813) 974-2668
E-Mail: aapamember@allenpress.com
Website: physanth.org
Members: 1700 individuals
Staff: 3
Annual Budget: $500-1,000,000

Personnel:
President: Lorena Madrigal
    E-Mail: madrigal@cas.usf.edu

Historical Note:
Founded in the District of Columbia in 1928. Affiliated with the International Association of Human Biologists, The American Association for The Advancement of Science (AAAS), and the Society for the Study of Human Biology. AAPA is the professional organization for physical anthropologists. Membership: $40 (Regular); $20 (Student).

Meetings/Conferences: Annual
2013 - Knoxville, TN/April 9 - 13
2014 - Calgary, AB/April 8 - 12
2016 - Atlanta, GA/April 12 - 16

Publications:
American Journal of Physical Anthropology; quarterly
Physical Anthropology; quarterly

American Association of Physician Specialists
(1952)
5550 W. Executive Dr.
Suite 400
Tampa, FL 33609
Tel: (813) 433-2277 *Fax:* (813) 830-6599
TollFree: (800) 447-9397
Website: aapsus.org
Members: 3123 individuals
Staff: 18
Annual Budget: $2-5,000,000
Tax: 501(c)(6)

Personnel:
Chief Executive Officer: William J. Carbone
    E-Mail: wcarbone@aapsus.org
Assistant Director, Certification: Andrea Balboa
    E-Mail: abalboa@aapsus.org
Director of CME, Meetings and Membership: Esther Berg
    E-Mail: eberg@aapsus.org
Director, Finance and Operations: Anthony Durante
    E-Mail: adurante@aapsus.org
Director, Public Relations and Marketing: James H. Marzano
    E-Mail: jmarzano@aapsus.org
Director, Communications and External Affairs: Jeff Morris
    E-Mail: jmorris@aapsus.org

Historical Note:
Formerly the American Academy of Osteopathic Surgeons, became American Association of Osteopathic Specialists in 1984, assumed its current name in 1994. AAPS was founded to fill a professional need among physicians practicing in medical specialties, providing a coordinated structure for affiliated academies of medicine. AAPS provides continuing medical education and board certification in numerous specialties. Membership: $450 (Regular); $795 (Diplomate); $350 (Military Regular/ Military Diplomate); $200 (Resident); $250 (Retired); $495 (Emeritus Diplomate).

Continuing Education:
Certification Designation/s: CME

Meetings/Conferences: Annual
Conference Chair: Esther Berg
2013 - San Juan, PR (Conrad San Juan Condado Plaza)/June 24 - 28

Publications:
American Journal of Clinical Medicine; quarterly; adv.

American Association of Physicians and Health Care Professionals
P.O. Box 13089
Tallahassee, FL 32317
Tel: (850) 878-3134 *Fax:* (850) 656-0510
Staff: 1
Annual Budget: $50-100,000

Personnel:
Executive Director: Robert S. Rhinehart

Historical Note:
Membership: $50/year.

American Association of Physicians of Indian Origin
600 Enterprise Dr.
Suite 108
Oakbrook Terrace, IL 60523
Tel: (630) 990-2277 *Fax:* (630) 990-2281
E-Mail: info@aapiusa.org
Website: aapiusa.org
Members: 3000 Individuals
Staff: 4
Annual Budget: $2-5,000,000

Personnel:
Executive Director: Mark Stone
    E-Mail: msstone@aapiusa.org
Director, Marketing and Communications: Sam Fulambarker
    E-Mail: sam@aapiusa.org
Associate Director, Accounts and Membership: Vijaya Kodali
    E-Mail: vkodali@aapiusa.org

Historical Note:
AAPI is a forum to facilitate and enable Indian American Physicians to excel in patient care, teaching and research and to pursue their aspirations in professional and community affairs

Meetings/Conferences: Annual
2013 - Chicago, IL (Sheraton Hotel)/May 23 - 27
2014 - San Antonio, TX/June 25 - 29
Number of non-conference events/year: 7

Publications:
AAPI E-Newsletter; monthly
AAPI Jounal; quarterly
Membership Directory; on-line

American Association of Physicists in Medicine
(1958)
One Physics Ellipse
College Park, MD 20740-3846
Tel: (301) 209-3350 *Fax:* (301) 209-0862
E-Mail: 2011.aapm@aapm.org
Website: aapm.org
Members: 5590 individuals and companies
Staff: 24
Annual Budget: $10-25,000,000
Tax: 501(c)(3)

Personnel:
Executive Director: Angela R. Keyser
    E-Mail: akeyser@aapm.org
Manager, Membership Services: Jennifer Hudson
Director, Finance and Administration: Cecilia A. Hunter
Manager, Meetings and Programs: Karen MacFarland
    E-Mail: karen@aapm.org
Manager, Education: Jacqueline Ogburn
Director, Meetings and Programs: Lisa Rose Sullivan
Manager, Programs: Nancy Vazquez
    E-Mail: nvazquez@aapm.org
Director, Information Services: Michael Woodward
    E-Mail: woodward@aapm.org

Historical Note:
Founded in Chicago and incorporated in Washington (1965). AAPM's mission is to advance the science, education and professional practice of medical physics. A member society of the American Institute of Physics and the American Institute for Medical and Biological Engineering. Membership: $285 (Full/Associate); $86 (Junior); $29 (Student); $86 (Junior/Resident); $114 (Corresponding/ International Affiliate).

Meetings/Conferences: Annual
Conference Chair: Lisa Rose Sullivan
2013 - Indianapolis, IN/Aug. 4 - 8
2014 - Austin, TX/July 20 - 24
2015 - Anaheim, CA/July 12 - 16
2016 - Washington, DC/July 31 - Aug. 4
Number of non-conference events/year: 1

Publications:
AAPM Newsletter; on-line; adv.
Medical Physics Journal; adv.
Membership Directory; on-line

Membership List Available to Non-members

American Association of Physics Teachers *(1930)*
One Physics Ellipse
College Park, MD 20740-3845
Tel: (301) 209-3311 *Fax:* (301) 209-0845
E-Mail: eo@aapt.org
Website: aapt.org

Members: 10000 individuals
Staff: 40
Annual Budget: $5-10,000,000

Personnel:
Executive Officer: Beth A. Cunningham
    E-Mail: bcunningham@aapt.org
Chief Finance Officer: Michael J. Brosnan
Director, Technology and Information Systems: Erwin
    Campbell
    E-Mail: ecampbell@aapt.org
Senior Production Editor: Jane Chambers
    E-Mail: jchamber@aapt.org
Associate Director, Membership: Rogers Fuller
    E-Mail: rfuller@aapt.org
Director, Communications and Membership: Marilyn
    Gardner
    E-Mail: mgardner@aapt.org
Director, Programs and Conferences: Tiffany Hayes
    E-Mail: thayes@aapt.org
Manager, Marketing: RaShonda Rosier

Historical Note:
*AAPT, a member of the American Institute of Physics,
is dedicated to advancing the teaching of physics and
furthering the role of physics in its culture. Members are
university, college, two-year college and high school physics
teachers, students and friends. Membership: $107-230
(Regular); $45 (Student); $800 (Sustaining).*

Meetings/Conferences:
Conference Chair: Tiffany Hayes
2013 - New Orleans, LA/Jan. 5 - 9
2013 - Portland, OR/July 13 - 17
2014 - Minneapolis, MN/July 26 - 30
Number of non-conference events/year: 4

Publications:
AAPT Membership Directory; on-line
American Journal of Physics; monthly; adv.
eNNOUNCER; monthly; adv.
Physical Review Special Topics - Physics Education
    Research; on-line
The Physics Teacher; adv.

American Association of Plastic Surgeons *(1921)*
500 Cummings Center
Suite 4550
Beverly, MA 01915
Tel: (978) 927-8330 *Fax:* (978) 524-8890
Website: aaps1921.org
Members: 780 individuals
Staff: 3
Annual Budget: $500-1,000,000
Tax: 501(c)(3)

Personnel:
Executive Director: Aurelie M. Alger JD
Associate Executive Director: Rebecca R. Bonsaint
    E-Mail: rbonsaint@prri.com
Director, Meetings: E. J. Weldon

Historical Note:
*Formerly (1942) American Association of Oral and Plastic
Surgeons. AAPS's purpose is to advance the science and
art of plastic surgery through surgical education, research,
scientific presentations, and professional interaction.*

Meetings/Conferences: Annual
Conference Chair: E. J. Weldon
2013 - New Orleans, LA (The Roosevelt Hotel)/April 20
    - 23

Publications:
AAPS Newsletter
Annals of Plastic Surgery; monthly; adv.
Membership Directory; on-line
Plastic and Reconstructive Surgery Journal; monthly;
    adv.
The Journal of Craniofacial Surgery; adv.

American Association of Poison Control Centers *(1958)*
515 King St.
Suite 510
Alexandria, VA 22314
Tel: (703) 894-1858 *Fax:* (703) 683-2812
E-Mail: info@aapcc.org
Website: aapcc.org
Members: 65 institutions and 20 individuals
Staff: 7
Annual Budget: $5-10,000,000
Tax: 501(c)(3)

Personnel:
Executive Director: Deborah A. Carr

    E-Mail: carr@aapcc.org
Administrative Assistant and Meetings Coordinator:
    Barbara Walker Bartlett
    E-Mail: walker@aapcc.org
Manager, Communications: Loreeta Canton
    E-Mail: canton@aapcc.org
Manager, Finance: Stephanie N. McIntyre
    E-Mail: mcintyre@aapcc.org
Executive Assistant and Office Manager: Julie Tufts
    E-Mail: tufts@aapcc.org
Manager, Public Education and National Outreach:
    Courtney Wilson MPH
    E-Mail: wilson@aapcc.org

Historical Note:
*AAPCC's mission is to advance poison centers in their
public health mission. Represents the poison control
centers of the United States and the interests of poison
prevention and treatment of poisoning. Certifies regional
poison centers and individual practitioners, and collects and
publishes data on poison exposure in the U.S. Maintains,
coordinates, and promotes a nationwide poison emergency
phone number. Membership: $2500 (Poison Center); $500
(Associate Institution); $1000 (Animal Poison Center);
$200 (Individual); $7500 (Sustaining).*

Meetings/Conferences: Annual
Conference Chair: Barbara Walker Bartlett
2013 - Washington, DC (Crystal City Marriott at
    Reagan National Airport)/Feb. 24 - 26

American Association of Police Officers
6605 Hollywood Blvd.
Suite 224
Los Angeles, CA 90028
Tel: (323) 465-5537 *Fax:* (800) 227-1042
Website: americanassociationofpoliceofficers.org
Staff: 32
Annual Budget: $250-500,000
Tax: 501(c)(3)

Personnel:
Chief Executive Officer: Phil LeConte
Administrative Officer: Paul Kutac

Historical Note:
*The American Association of Police Officers is a non-profit
educational organization dedicated to enhancing public
safety by bringing the wisdom of America's law enforcement
veterans to the next generation of Americans.*

American Association of Police Polygraphists *(1977)*
P.O. Box 657
Waynesville, OH 45068
Tel: (937) 728-7827 *Fax:* (937) 488-1046
TollFree: (888) 743-5479
Website: policepolygraph.org
Members: 700 individuals
Staff: 5
Annual Budget: $100-250,000
Tax: 501(c)(6)

Personnel:
Office Manager: Julie Gerspacher
    E-Mail: nom@policepolygraph.org

Historical Note:
*AAPP is dedicated to encourage and develop cooperation
among all American Law Enforcement Organizations
in the application and utilization of accepted polygraph
techniques. Members are polygraphists currently affiliated
with a law enforcement agency, investigative agency or
government service. Membership: $125-150/year.*

Continuing Education:
Certification Designation/s: CFLEPE
Meetings/Conferences:
Number of non-conference events/year: 1

Publications:
AAPP Journal; quarterly; adv.

American Association of Political Consultants *(1969)*
8400 Westpark Dr.
2nd Floor
McLean, VA 22102
Tel: (703) 245-8020 *Fax:* (703) 610-9005
E-Mail: info@theaapc.org
Website: theaapc.org
Members: 1200 individuals
Staff: 4
Annual Budget: $1-2,000,000

Personnel:
Executive Director: Alana Joyce CAE

    E-Mail: ajoyce@theaapc.org
Manager, Senior Meetings: Rebecca Fazzari
    E-Mail: rfazzari@theaapc.org
Manager, Program and Membership: Alecia Rives-DeWitt
    E-Mail: arives-dewitt@theaapc.org

Historical Note:
*AAPC's main purpose is to raise the standards of practice
in political consultation, thereby enhancing the political
process and improving public confidence in the American
political system. Membership: $60 (Student); $100
(Academic); $150 (Introductory); $250 (Individual); $500
(Gold); $1,000 (Platinum).*

Meetings/Conferences: Annual
Conference Chair: Rebecca Fazzari
2013 - Washington, DC (Hyatt Regency Washington on
    Capitol Hill)/April 3 - 5

Publications:
AAPC E-Newsletter; on-line
AAPC Update; irregular
Membership Directory; on-line

American Association of Port Authorities *(1912)*
1010 Duke St.
Alexandria, VA 22314-3589
Tel: (703) 684-5700 *Fax:* (703) 684-6321
E-Mail: info@aapa-ports.org
Website: aapa-ports.org
Members: 500 agencies and firms
Staff: 17
Annual Budget: $2-5,000,000

Personnel:
President and Chief Executive Officer: Kurt J. Nagle
    E-Mail: knagle@aapa-ports.org
Director, Communications: Aaron Ellis
    E-Mail: aellis@aapa-ports.org
Manager, Training and Programs: Jodi Gibson
    E-Mail: jgibson@aapa-ports.org
Executive Vice President and General Counsel: Jean C.
    Godwin
    E-Mail: jgodwin@aapa-ports.org
Vice President, Government Relations: Susan J.
    Monteverde
    E-Mail: smonteverde@aapa-ports.org
Coordinator, Finance and Human Resources: Teri Nagle
    E-Mail: tnagle@aapa-ports.org
Director, Membership Services: Edward L O'Connell
    E-Mail: eoconnell@aapa-ports.org
Director, Research and Information Services: Dr. Rex
    Sherman PhD
    E-Mail: rsherman@aapa-ports.org

Historical Note:
*AAPA's mission is to advocate governmental policies that
strengthen and expand opportunities for member ports,
advance professionalism in all facets of port management
and operations. Membership: $4,370 (Corporate); $1,495
(Sustaining); $100 (Associate).*

Continuing Education:
Certification Designation/s: AAPA/PPM

Meetings/Conferences:
2013 - Orlando, FL/Oct. 13 - 17/51-100 exhibitors
2014 - Houston, TX/Nov. 9 - 13/51-100 exhibitors

Publications:
AAPA Seaports Magazine; adv.
ADVISORY Newsletter; weekly
ALERT Newsletter; on-line
Port Industry Services Directory

American Association of Preferred Provider Organizations *(1983)*
222 S. First St.
Suite 303
Louisville, KY 40202
Tel: (502) 403-1122 *Fax:* (502) 403-1129
Website: aappo.org
Members: 500 individuals
Staff: 4
Annual Budget: $1-2,000,000
Tax: 501(c)(6)

Personnel:
President and Chief Executive Officer: Karen Greenrose
    E-Mail: kgreenrose@aappo.org
Manager, Membership Services: Pat Ciresi
    E-Mail: pciresi@aappo.org
Executive Vice President, Business Development: Julian
    Roberts
    E-Mail: jroberts@aappo.org

Project Specialist and Contact, Communications: Amy Seiler
E-Mail: aseiler@aappo.org

Historical Note:
AAPPO's mission is to advocate for the PPO Industry by educating and informing the federal and state legislative and regulatory bodies concerning the benefits and value the PPO delivery system provides in partnership with providers to consumers, employers and purchasers. Membership: $1,700 (Professional); $5,000-12,000 (Associate); $15,000-60,000 (Corporate).

Meetings/Conferences: Annual
2013 - Amelia Island, FL (The Ritz-Carlton)/Jan. 27 - 29
2014 - Laguna, CA (Ritz-Carlton)/Jan. 19 - 21

American Association of Presidents of Independent Colleges and Universities (1968)
Box 7070
Provo, UT 84602-7070
Tel: (801) 422-5624 Fax: (801) 422-0617
E-Mail: john_stohlton@byu.edu
Website: aapicu.org
Members: 300 individuals
Staff: 1
Annual Budget: $25-50,000

Personnel:
Executive Director: John B. Stohlton
E-Mail: john_stohlton@byu.edu

Historical Note:
Formerly known as the American Association of Independent College and University Presidents, assumed its current name in 1969. Mission is to provide the resources and opportunities presidents most need to be effective. AAPICU is committed to preserve the private sector of higher education. Membership: $200/year.

Meetings/Conferences: Annual
2013 - Scottsdale, AZ (Scottsdale Plaza Hotel)/Feb. 21 - 23

Publications:
Membership Directory; annually

American Association of Private Lenders (2009)
7509 NW Tiffany Springs Pkwy.
Kansas City, MO 64153
Tel: (913) 888-1250 Fax: (800) 695-8990
E-Mail: info@aaplonline.com
Website: aaplonline.com
Staff: 6

Personnel:
Executive Director: Wallace K. Groves
E-Mail: wgroves@AAPLonline.com
Director, Events: Timothy Bricker
E-Mail: tbricker@AAPLonline.com
General Counselor: Anthony Geraci
E-Mail: ageraci@AAPLonline.com
Contact, Membership and Conference Services: David Lang
E-Mail: dlang@aaplonline.com
Press Contact: Larry Muck
E-Mail: lmuck@aaplonline.com
Chief Financial Officer: Jack B. Rollins III, CPA
E-Mail: jrollins@AAPLonline.com

Historical Note:
A national organization representing the private real estate lending industry. Membership includes private money lenders, hard money lenders, mortgage fund managers, brokers, and service providers from around the United States. Membership: $400 (Individual); $80 (Premier Individual); $1,600 (Premier Corporate); $4000 (Premier Service Provider); $2,000 (Standard).

Meetings/Conferences: Annual
Conference Chair: Timothy Bricker

Publications:
The Journal of the American Association of Private Lending; bi-monthly; adv.

American Association of Private Railroad Car Owners (1977)
622 N. Reed St.
Joliet, IL 60435
Tel: (815) 722-8877
Website: aaprco.com
Members: 512 individuals
Staff: 1
Annual Budget: $250-500,000

Personnel:

Executive Director: Diane Elliott
E-Mail: execdirector@aaprco.com

Historical Note:
AAPRCO's mission is to promote the operation, ownership, and enjoyment of the private passenger railcar. Membership: $500 (Amtrak Certified Car Owner); $350 (Non-Amtrak Certified Car Owner); $90 (Associate/Non-owner); $150 (Trade/Non-owner).

Meetings/Conferences: Annual

Publications:
Private Varnish; quarterly
PV News Briefs- Newsletter; quarterly

American Association of Professional Farriers (2012)
PO Box 43802
Louisville, KY 40253-0802
Tel: (859) 533-1465 Fax: (859) 577-1403
E-Mail: AAPF@ProfessionalFarriers.com
Website: professionalfarriers.com
Staff: 1

Personnel:
Executive Director: Bryan Quinsey
E-Mail: AAPF@ProfessionalFarriers.com

Historical Note:
AAPF will promote the integrity of the farrier industry by strengthening the knowledge and skills of its members through continuing education and support at the state, national and international levels while improving overall equine health through collaboration with other industry professionals. Membership: $200 (Regular/Associate); $2000 (Regular Life/Associate Life); $100(Student).

Meetings/Conferences: Annual
2013 - Cincinnati, OH (Hyatt Regency Hotel)/Jan. 30

Publications:
AAEP News Bulletin; bi-weekly
AAPF Membership Directory
E-newsletter; monthly

American Association of Professional Hypnotherapists (1980)
16055 SW Walker Rd.
Suite 406
Beaverton, OR 97006
Tel: (503) 533-7106
Website: aaph.org
Members: 1500 individuals
Staff: 1
Annual Budget: Under $10,000

Personnel:
President: Katin B. Imes CCHt.

Historical Note:
AAPH's mission is to support hypnotherapists in establishing and successfully operating their own hypnotherapy businesses. Membership: $85 (Individual); $425 (Lifetime).

Publications:
Journal of the American Association of Professional Hypnotherapists; quarterly

American Association of Professional Landmen (1955)
4100 Fossil Creek Blvd.
Fort Worth, TX 76137
Tel: (817) 847-7700 Fax: (817) 847-7704
TollFree: (888) 566-2275
E-Mail: aapl@landman.org
Website: landman.org
Members: 12000 individuals
Staff: 19
Annual Budget: $5-10,000,000

Personnel:
Executive Vice President: Martin Schardt
E-Mail: mschardt@landman.org
Manager, Information Technology: Charles Armitage
E-Mail: carmitage@landman.org
Director, Education: Christopher Halaszynski
E-Mail: chalaszynski@landman.org
Controller: Alan Kottler
E-Mail: akottler@landman.org
Membership Administrator: Lahoma Long
E-Mail: llong@landman.org
Senior Director, Publications, Marketing and Media Relations: Le'ann Pembroke Callihan
E-Mail: leannc@landman.org
Event Meeting Manager and Information Technology Administrator: Kelly Robinson

E-Mail: krobinson@landman.org
Manager, Recruitment and Business Development: Brent Schreiber
E-Mail: bschreiber@landman.org

Historical Note:
Formerly (1992) the American Association of Petroleum Landmen. AAPL's mission is to advocate the highest standards of performance for all land professionals, to advance their stature and to encourage sound stewardship of energy and mineral resources. Membership: $100 (Active/Associate); $20 (Student); $2,500 (Life Membership).

Continuing Education:
Certification Designation/s: CPL, RL, RPL

Meetings/Conferences: Annual
Conference Chair: Kelly Robinson
2013 - Washington, DC (Grand Hyatt Washington)/ June 5 - 8

Publications:
Landman 2 Mini-Magazine; bi-monthly
Landman's Directory & Guidebook; annually; adv.
Membership Directory; on-line
The Landman Magazine; bi-monthly; adv.

American Association of Psychiatric Administrators (1961)
P.O. Box 570218
Dallas, TX 75357-0218
Tel: (972) 613-0985 Fax: (972) 613-5532
TollFree: (800) 650-5888
Website: psychiatricadministrators.org
Members: 413 individuals
Staff: 3
Annual Budget: $10-25,000

Personnel:
Executive Director: Frances Roton Bell
E-Mail: frda1@airmail.net
Treasurer: Wayne Creelman
Membership Committee Chair: Geetha Jayaram

Historical Note:
Affiliated with the American Psychiatric Association. Formerly (1975) Association of Medical Superintendents of Mental Hospitals. AAPA's mission is to promote medical standards in behavioral healthcare systems, including services for mental illness, substance use disorders and developmental disabilities. Membership: $75/year (National Dues)

Meetings/Conferences: Annual
Number of non-conference events/year: 1

Publications:
Psychiatrist Administrator; quarterly

American Association of Psychiatric Technicians (1991)
1220 S. St.
Suite 100
Sacramento, CA 95811-7138
Tel: (916) 443-1701 Fax: (916) 329-9145
TollFree: (800) 391-7589
E-Mail: aapt@psychtechs.net
Website: psychtechs.org
Members: 3500 individuals
Staff: 3

Personnel:
Executive Director: Debi Loger
President: Tony Myers
Secretary and Treasurer: Brad Leggs

Historical Note:
Administers an examination for mental health workers to receive the designation of Nationally Certified Psychiatric Technician.

Continuing Education:
Certification Designation/s: NCPT

American Association of Public Health Dentistry (1937)
3085 Stevenson Dr.
Suite 200
Springfield, IL 62703
Tel: (217) 529-6941 Fax: (217) 529-9120
E-Mail: natoff@aaphd.org
Website: aaphd.org
Members: 800 individuals and organizations
Staff: 3
Annual Budget: $250-500,000

Personnel:
Executive Director: Pamela J. Tolson CAE

E-Mail: pam@assn-srvs.com
Secretary and Treasurer: Christopher Okunseri BDS
Editor: Robert Weyant

Historical Note:
Formerly (1983) the American Association of Public Health Dentists. AAPHD's mission is to provide community awareness to future dental professionals and engage students in dialogue about current dental public health issues. Membership is open to all individuals concerned with improving the oral health of the public. Membership: $150/year.

Meetings/Conferences: Annual

Publications:
Communique; quarterly; adv.
Journal of Public Health Dentistry: Masthead; adv.
Membership Directory; on-line

American Association of Public Health Physicians
(1954)
1605 Pebble Beach Blvd.
Green Cove Springs, FL 32043-8077
Tel: (904) 860-9208 *Fax*: (904) 529-7761
E-Mail: aaphp@reachone.com
Website: aaphp.org
Members: 200 individuals
Staff: 3
Annual Budget: Under $10,000
Tax: 501(c)(6)

Personnel:
President: Virginia Dato
E-Mail: vmdato@aaphp.org
Treasurer: Dave Cundiff
Director, Membership: Sandra F. Magyar CHES, MEd
E-Mail: magyarsf@bellsouth.net

Historical Note:
AAPHP's mission is to foster public health, represent public health physicians and educate the nation on the role and importance of the public health physician's knowledge and skills in practicing population medicine. Membership: $15-95 (Physicians); $10-60 (Non-Physicians).

Meetings/Conferences: Annual

Publications:
AAPHP e-News; on-line
Membership Directory; on-line

American Association of Public Welfare Attorneys
(1967)
701 E. Jefferson St.
Phoenix, AZ 85034-2215
Tel: (602) 417-4008 *Fax*: (602) 253-9115
Website: aapwa.aphsa.org
Members: 200 individuals
Staff: 3
Annual Budget: Under $10,000

Personnel:
President: Matthew Devlin
E-Mail: matthew.devlin@azahcccs.gov
Conference Coordinator: Dee Gross
E-Mail: dee.gross@aphsa.org
Treasurer: Edward Watkins
E-Mail: ed.watkins@ocfs.state.ny.us

Historical Note:
An affiliate of the American Public Welfare Association. Mission of AAPWA is to provide a forum at national, state, and regional levels for the discussion of legal matters pertaining to public welfare and/or human services, and to provide for cordial exchange of experience and knowledge related to the development of public welfare and/or human services policy. Membership: $50/year.

Meetings/Conferences:
Conference Chair: Dee Gross

Publications:
Newsletter

The American Association of Radon Scientists and Technologists *(1986)*
P.O. Box 2109
Fletcher, NC 28732
Fax: (828) 890-8071
TollFree: (866) 772-2778
E-Mail: office@aarst.org
Website: aarst.org
Members: 1100 individuals
Staff: 6
Annual Budget: $250-500,000
Tax: 501(c)(6)

Personnel:

Treasurer: Calvin Murphy
E-Mail: Calvin@Alliedradon.com

Historical Note:
AARST's mission is to give standard of excellence and ethical performance of radon measurement, mitigation and transfer of information for the benefit of members, consumers and the public at large. Members are manufacturers, scientists and others concerned with radon gas testing and remediation. Membership: $150 (Individual); $260 (Company); $500 (Organization/Corporate); $1000 (Executive); $75 (Associate); $25 (Student).

Continuing Education:
Certification Designation/s: CE, NRPP

Meetings/Conferences: Annual
Number of non-conference events/year: 1

Publications:
AARST Member Directory; on-line; adv.
Briefly Speaking (e-newsletter); on-line; adv.
Radon Reporter; quarterly; adv.

Membership List Available to Non-members

American Association of Railroad Superintendents *(1881)*
P.O. Box 200
La Fox, IL 60147
Tel: (630) 762-0754 *Fax*: (630) 762-0755
E-Mail: aars@railroadsuperintendents.org
Website: railroadsuperintendents.org
Members: 500 individuals
Staff: 1
Annual Budget: $50-100,000
Tax: 501(c)(6)

Personnel:
Executive Director: Carrie Foor
E-Mail: aars@railroadsuperintendents.org

Historical Note:
AARS's mission is to gather, develop, evaluate and disseminate information for advocating railroad safety, reliability and efficiency by enhancing the knowledge, skills and professionalism of each member. Membership: $75 (Individual); $15 (Life Member).

Publications:
International Railway Journal; monthly; adv.
Railway Age Magazine; adv.
Trains Magazine; monthly; adv.

American Association of Residential Mortgage Regulators *(1989)*
1025 Thomas Jefferson St. NW
Suite 500 E
Washington, DC 20007
Tel: (202) 521-3999 *Fax*: (202) 833-3636
E-Mail: efreundel@aarmr.org
Website: aarmr.org
Members: 100 individuals
Staff: 2
Annual Budget: $250-500,000
Tax: 501(c)(3)

Personnel:
Executive Director: David A Saunders
E-Mail: dsaunders@aarmr.org
Manager, Membership Services: Erika Freundel
E-Mail: efreundel@aarmr.org

Historical Note:
AARMR's mission is to advocate the exchange of information between and among the executives and employees of the various states who are charged with the responsibility, pursuant to the laws of the individual states, for the administration and regulation of residential mortgage lending, servicing and brokering. Members are state employees responsible for administration of residential mortgage oversight. Membership: $750 (General); $1,000 (Affiliate).

Meetings/Conferences: Annual
2013 - Denver, CO (Sheraton Downtown Denver Hotel)/Aug. 6 - 9

Publications:
Newsletter; bi-annually

American Association of Retired Persons *(1958)*
601 E St. NW
Suite A1-200
Washington, DC 20049
Tel: (202) 434-7700 *Fax*: (202) 434-7710
TollFree: (888) 687-2277
E-Mail: member@aarp.org

Website: aarp.org
Staff: 10
Annual Budget: Over $100,000,000

Personnel:
Chief Executive Officer: A. Barry Rand
E-Mail: CEO@aarp.org
Senior Vice President and Editorial Director: Myrna Blyth
Vice President, Media Relations: Jeffrey Davis
Executive Vice President and Chief Communications Officer: Kevin J. Donnellan
E-Mail: kdonnellan@aarp.org
Executive Vice President and Chief Financial Office: Robert R. Hagans
Executive Vice President: Nancy LeaMond
E-Mail: nleamond@aarp.org
General Counsel: Cynthia M. Lewin
Executive Vice President and Chief Human Resources Officer.: Richard Randazzo
Executive Vice President, Policy: Debra Bailey Whitman

Historical Note:
AARP's mission is to promote independence, dignity and purpose for older persons and to enhance the quality of life for older persons. Membership: $16-63 (U.S.); $17-28 (International).

Meetings/Conferences: Semi-Annual
2013 - Las Vegas, NV (Las Vegas Convention Center)/ May 31 - June 1
2013 - Atlanta, GA (Georgia World Congress Center)/ Oct. 4 - 5

Publications:
AARP Magazine; bi-monthly; adv.
AARP Newsletter
AARP VIVA; quarterly

American Association of Retirement Communities
(1994)
P.O. Box 2931
Evans, GA 30809
Tel: (706) 496-7047 *Fax*: (912) 478-5581
TollFree: (866) 531-5567
Website: the-aarc.org
Staff: 1
Annual Budget: $25-50,000

Personnel:
Executive Director: Wade Adler

Historical Note:
AARC's mission is to advocate the economic enhancement of communities through the promotion of retiree attraction as an economic development strategy. Membership: $250.00 (Educational Institutions/Professional Associations); $250.00-350.00 (City Govt. Units/County Govt./Chambers, depending on the Population); $350.00 (Businesses/Developers, For ProfitOrganization); $500 (Media/Member Partner).

Meetings/Conferences: Annual

Publications:
Newsletter

American Association of School Librarians *(1951)*
50 E. Huron St.
Chicago, IL 60611-2795
Tel: (312) 280-4382 *Fax*: (312) 280-5276
TollFree: (800) 545-2433
E-Mail: aasl@ala.org
Website: aasl.org
Members: 9000 individuals
Staff: 325
Annual Budget: $25-50,000,000

Personnel:
Executive Director: Julie A. Walker
E-Mail: jwalker@ala.org
Manager, Communications: Stephanie Book
E-Mail: sbook@ala.org
Program Coordinator, Governance and Finance: Joshua Capp
E-Mail: jcapp@ala.org
Manager, Professional Development: Melissa Jacobsen
E-Mail: mjacobsen@ala.org
Manager, Meetings: Neela Johnston
E-Mail: njohnston@ala.org
Manager and Editor: Markisan Naso
E-Mail: mnaso@ala.org

Historical Note:
AASL's mission is to advocate, facilitate change, and develop leaders in the school library field. Membership is composed of school library media specialists. Membership:

$115 (Individual); $96 (Library Support Staff/Employed Full Time/Part-Time); $71 (Retired); $53 (Student).

Meetings/Conferences:
Conference Chair: Neela Johnston
2013 - Hartford, CT/Nov. 14 - 17
2015 - Columbus, OH/Oct. 15 - 18

Publications:
Hotlinks; monthly; adv.
Knowledge Quest; bi-monthly; adv.
School Library Media Research; on-line

Membership List Available to Non-members

American Association of School Personnel Administrators *(1940)*
11863 W. 112th St.
Suite 100
Overland Park, KS 66210
Tel: (913) 327-1222 *Fax:* (913) 327-1223
E-Mail: aaspa@aaspa.org
Website: aaspa.org
Members: 2000 individuals
Staff: 4
Annual Budget: $500-1,000,000
Tax: 501(c)(3)

Personnel:
Executive Director: Dr. Michael Redburn
    E-Mail: michael@aaspa.org
Specialist, Membership Services and Marketing: Emily Franzenburg
    E-Mail: emily@aaspa.org
Coordinator, Professional Development: Sandy Reigel
    E-Mail: sandy@aaspa.org

Historical Note:
Formerly the National Conference of Teacher Examiners, assumed its present name in 1959. AASPA's mission is to provide leadership in promoting effective human resources practices within education through professional development activities and a broad-based resource network. Membership: $55-375/year.

Continuing Education:
Certification Designation/s: NCP

Meetings/Conferences: Annual
2013 - San Antonio, TX/Oct. 1 - 4
2014 - Portland, OR/Oct. 13 - 17
Number of non-conference events/year: 8

Publications:
Best Practices; annually; adv.
Insider Legal Alert; monthly
Perspective; adv.

American Association of Sexuality Educators, Counselors and Therapists *(1967)*
1444 I St. NW
Suite 700
Washington, DC 20005
Tel: (202) 449-1099 *Fax:* (202) 216-9646
E-Mail: info@aasect.org
Website: aasect.org
Members: 2000 individuals
Staff: 4
Annual Budget: $100-250,000
Tax: 501(c)(3)

Personnel:
Executive Director: Dee Ann Walker
    E-Mail: dawalker@aasect.org
Director, Education and Certification: Alphonsus Baggett
    E-Mail: abaggett@bostrom.com
Chair, Membership Steering Committee: Stephanie Buehler
    E-Mail: drstephaniebuehler@gmail.com
Coordinator, Membership Services: Janet Huynh
    E-Mail: jhuynh@bostrom.com

Historical Note:
AASECT is a not-for-profit, interdisciplinary professional organization that is devoted to the promotion of sexual health by the development and advancement of the fields of sexual therapy, counseling, and education. Members include physicians, nurses, social workers, psychologists, allied health professionals, clergy members, lawyers, sociologists, marriage and family counselors and therapists, family planning specialists and researchers, as well as students in relevant professional disciplines. Membership: $100-525/year.

Continuing Education:
Certification Designation/s: AASECTCSE

Meetings/Conferences: Annual
Conference Chair: Dee Ann Walker

2013 - Miami, FL (Hilton)/June 5 - 9

Publications:
Contemporary Sexuality; monthly
Membership Directory; on-line

American Association of Sleep Technologists *(1978)*
2510 N. Frontage Rd.
Darien, IL 60561
Tel: (630) 737-9704 *Fax:* (630) 737-9788
E-Mail: aast@aastweb.org
Website: aastweb.org
Members: 4800 individuals
Staff: 4
Annual Budget: $1-2,000,000
Tax: 501(c)(6)

Personnel:
President: Melinda Trimble RPSGT
Secretary: David Gregory RPSGT

Historical Note:
Formerly (1978) the Association of Polysomnographic Technologists. AAST's mission is to advocate and advance the sleep technology profession through the continued development of educational, technical and clinical excellence in sleep disorders. Membership: $50 (Regular/Associate); $40 (Student).

Meetings/Conferences: Annual
Number of non-conference events/year: 1

Publications:
A2Zzz Magazine; quarterly; adv.
Membership Directory; on-line

Membership List Available to Non-members

American Association of Small Ruminant Practitioners *(1968)*
P.O. Box 3614
Montgomery, AL 36109
Tel: (334) 517-1233 *Fax:* (334) 270-3399
Website: aasrp.org
Members: 1000 individuals
Staff: 4
Annual Budget: $100-250,000
Tax: 501(c)(3)

Personnel:
Executive Director: Tom Johnson DVM
    E-Mail: tjohnson@aasrp.org
Coordinator, Membership Services: Linda Cargile
    E-Mail: Linda@Franzmgt.com
Director, Meetings and Membership Services: Roberta Norris
    E-Mail: Roberta@Franzmgt.com
Director, Public Relation and Communications: Melissa Williford
    E-Mail: Melissa@Franzmgt.com

Historical Note:
Formerly American Association of Sheep and Goat Practitioners. AASRP's mission is to improve the health and welfare of sheep, goats, cervids and camelids, to further the professional development of the members, provide resources to elevate the standards of small ruminant practice and to be the voice for small ruminant issues. Membership: $105-130 (Veterinarians/Non-Veterinary Associates); $15-20 (Veterinary Students).

Meetings/Conferences:
Number of non-conference events/year: 1

Publications:
Membership Directory; on-line
Wool & Wattles; quarterly

American Association of State Climatologists *(1976)*
Western Kentucky University, 1906 College Heights Blvd.
Suite 31066
Bowling Green, KY 42101-1066
Tel: (270) 745-5983
E-Mail: info@stateclimate.org
Website: stateclimate.org
Members: 150 individuals
Staff: 3
Annual Budget: $100-250,000
Tax: 501(c)(3)

Personnel:
President: Stuart A. Foster PhD
    E-Mail: stuart.foster@wku.edu

Historical Note:

AASC's mission is to promote cooperation between State Climatologists and those federal, state, and private agencies whose functions include the collection, analysis and dissemination of climate information. Members work closely with other climate services partners including NCDC, the NOAA Regional Climate Centers, and the National Weather Service. Membership: $100 (SC/RCC Director); $40 (Associate/New).

Meetings/Conferences: Annual

Publications:
Journal of Service Climatology; on-line
Membership Directory; on-line
The State Climatologist; annually

American Association of State Colleges and Universities *(1961)*
1307 New York Ave. NW
Fifth Floor
Washington, DC 20005-4701
Tel: (202) 293-7070 *Fax:* (202) 296-5819
E-Mail: info@aascu.org
Website: aascu.org
Members: 420 public colleges, universities and systems
Staff: 72
Annual Budget: $10-25,000,000
Tax: 501(c)(3)

Personnel:
President: Muriel A. Howard
    E-Mail: howardm@aascu.org
Director, Human Resources: Kathi Bailey
    E-Mail: baileyk@aascu.org
Vice President, Membership Services: Christina "Chris" Bitting
    E-Mail: bittingc@aascu.org
Vice President, Communications: Susan M. Chilcott
    E-Mail: chilcotts@aascu.org
Senior Vice President, Government Relations and Policy Analysis: Edward M. Elmendorf
    E-Mail: elmendorfe@aascu.org
Manager, Publications and Design: Trudy James
    E-Mail: jamest@aascu.org
Director, Meetings: Rosemary S. Lauth
    E-Mail: lauthr@aascu.org
Vice President, Academic Leadership and Change: George L. Mehaffy
    E-Mail: mehaffyg@aascu.org
Vice President, Administration and Finance: Celeste E. Regan
    E-Mail: reganc@aascu.org
Manager, Internet Communications: Ina Soepangkat
    E-Mail: soepangkati@aascu.org

Historical Note:
Formerly the Association of State Colleges and Universities, absorbed the Association of Upper Level Colleges and Universities and superseded the Association of Teachers of Education Institutions, founded in 1951. AASCU's mission is to promote understanding, appreciation and support for the public purpose of public higher education and the distinctive contributions of those institutions that comprise the AASCU membership. Membership fee based upon enrollment of institution.

Meetings/Conferences: Semi-Annual
Conference Chair: Rosemary S. Lauth
2013 - Point Clear, AL/Feb. 7 - 9
2013 - Baltimore, MD/July 25 - 27
Number of non-conference events/year: 4

Publications:
@aascu; bi-weekly
Membership Directory; on-line

American Association of State Troopers *(1989)*
1949 Raymond Diehl Rd.
Tallahassee, FL 32308
Tel: (850) 385-7904 *Fax:* (850) 385-8697
TollFree: (800) 765-5456
E-Mail: AASTPR@aol.com
Website: statetroopers.org
Members: 5500 individuals
Staff: 5
Annual Budget: $2-5,000,000

Personnel:
Executive Director: Ken Howes
    E-Mail: ken@statetroopers.org
Director, Membership Services: Christine Brasher
    E-Mail: christine@statetroopers.org
Director, Operations: Joan Breeding
    E-Mail: joan@statetroopers.org

Manager, Public Relations and Editor: Angie Ishee
  E-Mail: aastpr@aol.com

Historical Note:
AAST's purposes specifically include development of strong bonds of nationwide trooper camaraderie, providing benefits for all state troopers, highway patrol officers, and state police officers, as well as their families, promotion of professional law enforcement training and educational opportunities, securing financial support to subsidize scholarship stipends for members' dependents, and involvement in public safety and consumer information campaigns. Members are active and retired state troopers, highway patrol officers and state police officers. Membership: $35-75/year.

Publications:
Trooper Connection; quarterly

American Association of Suicidology *(1968)*
5221 Wisconsin Ave. NW
Washington, DC 20015
Tel: (202) 237-2280 *Fax*: (202) 237-2282
E-Mail: info@suicidology.org
Website: suicidology.org
Members:
250 organizations
1000 individuals
Staff: 8
Annual Budget: $1-2,000,000
Tax: 501(c)(3)

Personnel:
Executive Director: Alan L. Berman ABPP, PhD
  E-Mail: berman@suicidology.org
Communications Specialist: Justin Ferrese
  E-Mail: webmaster@suicidology.org
Office Manager: Holley Jackson
  E-Mail: hjackson@suicidology.org
Director, Training and Accreditation: Karen Kanefield
  E-Mail: kkanefield@suicidology.org
Deputy Director: Amy J. Kulp MS
  E-Mail: ajkulp@suicidology.org
Director, Project Development: Erin MacInnes
  E-Mail: emacinnes@suicidology.org

Historical Note:
The goal of AAS is to understand and prevent suicide. It also promotes research, public awareness programs, public education and training for professionals and volunteers. Members are multi-disciplinary organization of professionals and concerned lay people. Membership: $43-750/year.

Continuing Education:
Certification Designation/s: SSPA, CFS

Meetings/Conferences: Annual
Conference Chair: Erin MacInnes
2013 - Austin, TX (Hilton Austin)/April 24 - 27
2014 - Los Angeles, CA/April 9 - 12

Publications:
Newslink; quarterly
Suicide and Life-Threatening Behavior
Surviving Suicide; quarterly

American Association of Surgical Physician Assistants *(1973)*
P.O. Box 781688
Sebastian, FL 32978
Tel: (772) 388-0498 *Fax*: (772) 388-3457
E-Mail: aaspa@aaspa.com
Website: aaspa.com
Members: 540 individuals
Staff: 2
Annual Budget: $50-100,000

Personnel:
Executive Director: Linda Kotrba
  E-Mail: executivedirector@aaspa.com
Treasurer: J. Randy Thress MS, PA-C
  E-Mail: treasurer@aaspa.com

Historical Note:
AASPA provides a forum for the exchange of ideas for PAs in surgery. It also provides professional growth, networking opportunities and advocacy. Membership: $150 (Fellow); $80 (Resident); $75 (Student/Pre-PA).

Meetings/Conferences: Annual

Publications:
Sutureline; bi-monthly; adv.

American Association of Swine Veterinarians *(1969)*
830 26th St.
Perry, IA 50220-2328

Tel: (515) 465-5255 *Fax*: (515) 465-3832
E-Mail: aasv@aasv.org
Website: aasv.org
Members: 1300 individuals
Staff: 3
Annual Budget: $1-2,000,000
Tax: 501(c)(6)

Personnel:
Executive Director: Thomas J. Burkgren
  E-Mail: burkgren@aasv.org
Director, Communications: Harry Snelson
  E-Mail: snelson@aasv.org

Historical Note:
Formerly (2000) American Association of Swine Practitioners, AASV's mission is to increase the knowledge of swine veterinarians by promoting the development and availability of the resources which enhance the effectiveness of professional activities. Members are graduate veterinarians. Membership: $200 (Active/Associate); $15 (Student); $100 (Full-time Graduate Student).

Meetings/Conferences: Annual
2013 - San Diego, CA (Manchester Grand Hyatt San Diego)/March 2 - 5/900 attendees/51-100 exhibitors
2014 - Dallas, TX/March 1 - 4/900 attendees/51-100 exhibitors
2015 - Orlando, FL/Feb. 28 - March 3/900 attendees/51-100 exhibitors

Publications:
AASV e-Letter Newsletter; weekly
Journal of Swine Health and Production; bi-monthly; adv.
Membership Directory; annually; adv.

American Association of Teachers of Arabic *(1965)*
3416 Primm Ln.
Birmingham, AL 35216
Tel: (205) 822-6800 *Fax*: (205) 823-2760
E-Mail: info@aataweb.org
Website: aataweb.org
Members: 130 individuals
Staff: 5
Annual Budget: $10-25,000
Tax: 501(c)(3)

Personnel:
Executive Director: Elizabeth M. Bergman PhD
  E-Mail: admin@aataweb.org
Editor: Reem Bassiouney

Historical Note:
Affiliated in 1964 with the American Council on Teaching of Foreign Languages and in 1970 with the Middle East Studies Association. AATA's mission is to contribute to the enhancement of study, criticism and research in the field of Arabic language, literature and linguistics. Membership: $15-1,500/year.

Meetings/Conferences: Annual
Number of non-conference events/year: 1

Publications:
AATA Newsletter
Al-cArabiyya; annually
Member Directory; on-line

American Association of Teachers of French *(1927)*
Mailcode-4510
Southern Illinois University
Carbondale, IL 62901
Tel: (618) 453-5731 *Fax*: (618) 453-5733
E-Mail: aatf@frenchteachers.org
Website: frenchteachers.org
Members: 10000 individuals
Staff: 2
Annual Budget: $1-2,000,000
Tax: 501(c)(3)

Personnel:
Executive Director: Jayne Abrate
  E-Mail: abrate@siu.edu

Historical Note:
AATF's aim is to represent the French language in North America and to encourage the dissemination, both in the schools and in the general public, of knowledge concerning all aspects of the culture and civilization of France and the French-speaking world. Sponsors programs for students such as the French Honor Society at the high school level, a national French contest, summer scholarships, and a placement service. Membership: $55 (Regular); $65 (Foreign); $82 (Family); $27 (Student).

Meetings/Conferences: Annual
2013 - Providence, RI/July 11 - 14
2014 - New Orleans, LA/July 19 - 22

Publications:
French Review; adv.
membership Directory; on-line

Membership List Available to Non-members

American Association of Teachers of German *(1926)*
112 Haddontowne Ct.
Suite 104
Cherry Hill, NJ 08034-3668
Tel: (856) 795-5553 *Fax*: (856) 795-9398
E-Mail: headquarters@aatg.org
Website: aatg.org
Members: 5200 individuals
Staff: 7
Annual Budget: $1-2,000,000
Tax: 501(c)(3)

Personnel:
Executive Director: Keith Cothrun
  E-Mail: keith@aatg.org
Manager, Finance: Deborah DiAngelo
  E-Mail: deb@aatg.org
Coordinator, Communications: Mercedes Pokorny
  E-Mail: mercedes@aatg.org
Coordinator, Membership: Martha Williams
  E-Mail: martha@aatg.org

Historical Note:
AATG strives for the advancement and improvement of the language, literature, and culture of the German-speaking countries and sponsors a number of programs for students such as a national high school honor society, summer travel/study programs, and competitions. Members are teachers of German at all levels of instruction and those interested in the teaching of German. Membership: $10-1500/year.

Meetings/Conferences:
2013 - Orlando, FL (Orange County Convention Center-Rosen Centre Hotel)/Nov. 22 - 24
2014 - San Antonio, TX (The Henry B. Gonzalez Convention Center)/Nov. 21 - 23

Publications:
AATG Newsletter; quarterly
Die Unterrichtspraxis/Teaching German; semi-annually; adv.
German Quarterly; quarterly; adv.
Member Directory; on-line

Membership List Available to Non-members

American Association of Teachers of Italian *(1924)*
Department of Foreign languages and Literatures
Nazareth College 4245 E. Ave.
Rochester, NY 14618-3790
Tel: (585) 389-2688 *Fax*: (812) 855-8877
E-Mail: mrvittia@naz.edu
Website: aati-online.org
Members:
450 institutions
1500 individuals
Staff: 4
Annual Budget: $100-250,000
Tax: 501(c)(3)

Personnel:
Executive Director: Edoardo Lebano
  E-Mail: elebano@hotmail.com
Director, Communications, Secretary and Treasurer: Salvatore Bancheri
  E-Mail: salvatore.bancheri@utoronto.ca
Vice President: Maria Rosaria Vitti-Alexander
  E-Mail: mvittia6@naz.edu

Historical Note:
AATI's mission is to promote the study of Italian language, literature, and culture in schools, colleges and universities in North America. Membership: $25-165/year.

Meetings/Conferences:
Conference Chair: Salvatore Bancheri
2013 - Strasbourg, France (Palais universitaire)/May 30 - June 4

Publications:
Italica; quarterly
Member Directory
The AATI Newsletter; bi-annually

Membership List Available to Non-members

American Association of Teachers of Slavic and East European Languages (1941)

3501 Trousdale Pkwy.
THH 255L
Los Angeles, CA 90089-4353
Tel: (213) 740-2734 *Fax:* (213) 740-8550
E-Mail: aatseel@usc.edu
Website: aatseel.org
Members: 1000 individuals
Staff: 3
Annual Budget: $100-250,000
Tax: 501(c)(3)

Personnel:
Executive Director: Elizabeth Durst PhD
    E-Mail: aatseel@usc.edu

Historical Note:
AATSEEL's purpose is to advance study and promote the teaching of Slavic and East European languages, literatures, and cultures on all educational levels, elementary through graduate school. Members are teachers of Slavic and East European languages. Membership: $75 (Administrator/ Assistant/Non-Academic); $50 (Independent/Instructor & Lecturer/Retired and Emeritus/Secondary School Teacher); $100 (Associate); $125 (Full Professor); $25 (Joint); $20 (Student); $300 (Sustaining); $1,000 (Benefactor - Life Member).

Meetings/Conferences: Annual
Conference Chair: Dianna Murphy
2013 - Boston, MA (Hyatt Regency Boston)/Jan. 3 - 6
2014 - Chicago, IL/Jan. 9 - 12

Publications:
AATSEEL Newsletter; quarterly; adv.
membership directory
Slavic and East European Journal

American Association of Teachers of Spanish and Portuguese (1917)

900 Ladd Rd.
Walled Lake, MI 48390
Tel: (248) 960-2180 *Fax:* (248) 960-9570
E-Mail: corporate@aatsp.org
Website: aatsp.org
Members: 12500 individuals
Staff: 14
Annual Budget: $1-2,000,000

Personnel:
Executive Director: Emily Spinelli
    E-Mail: espinelli@aatsp.org
Director, Financial Services: Roberta Miller
    E-Mail: rmiller@aatsp.org
Coordinator, Membership Services: Debra Nigohosian
    E-Mail: dnigohosian@aatsp.org
Contact, Professional Development: Marcy Novak
    E-Mail: mnovak@aatsp.org
Editor: Mary-Anne Vetterling
    E-Mail: paintrock@aol.com

Historical Note:
AATSP's mission is to promote, develop, and advance the teaching of Hispanic, Luso-Brazilian and related languages, literatures, and cultures in the United States and in other countries from primary through graduate school. Membership: $65 (Regular); $25 (Student/Emeritus); $1950 (Life); $100 (Joint).

Meetings/Conferences: Annual
Conference Chair: Marcy Novak
2013 - San Antonio, TX (San Antonio Marriott Rivercenter)/July 8 - 11

Publications:
Enlace; annually
Hispania; quarterly; adv.
Portuguese Newsletter; semi-annually

American Association of Teachers of Turkic Languages (1985)

Near Eastern Studies, Princeton University
110 Jones Hall
Princeton, NJ 08544-1008
Tel: (609) 258-1435 *Fax:* (609) 258-1242
Website: princeton.edu/~turkish/aatt
Members: 185 individuals and organizations
Staff: 2
Annual Budget: Under $10,000
Tax: 501(c)(3)

Personnel:
Executive Secretary and Treasurer: Dr. Erika H. Gilson PhD
    E-Mail: ehgilson@princeton.edu

Historical Note:
Formerly the American Association of Teachers of Turkish, the objective of AATT is to advance and improve the teaching of the languages of the Turks. Members are individuals interested in the languages of the Turks. Membership: $25 (Individual); $50 (Regular); $10 (Student); $200 (Supporting); $500 (Sustaining); $15 (Faculty).

Meetings/Conferences: Annual

Publications:
Membership Directory; on-line
The AATT Newsletter & Bulletin; annually; adv.

American Association of Textile Chemists and Colorists (1921)

One Davis Dr.
P.O. Box 12215
Research Triangle Park, NC 27709-2215
Tel: (919) 549-8141 *Fax:* (919) 549-8933
Website: aatcc.org
Members: 250 organizations and 2000 individuals
Staff: 25
Annual Budget: $2-5,000,000
Tax: 501(c)(6)

Personnel:
Executive Vice President: John Y. Daniels
    E-Mail: danielsj@aatcc.org
Director, Business Development: Perry Grady
    E-Mail: gradyp@aatcc.org
Contact, Membership Services: Bonnie Green
    E-Mail: greenb@aatcc.org
Executive Assistant: Debra Hibbard
    E-Mail: hibbardd@aatcc.org
Technical Director: Chris Leonard
    E-Mail: leonardc@aatcc.org
Education Assistant: Kim Nicholson
    E-Mail: nicholk@aatcc.org
Director, Educational Programs: Peggy J. Pickett
    E-Mail: pickettp@aatcc.org
Director , Publications and Membership: Maria Thiry
    E-Mail: thirym@aatcc.org

Historical Note:
AATCC provides test method development and support application of colorants, chemicals, and polymers in the textile design, material, and processing industry. Membership: $110 (Senior/Associate); $330-5,280 (Corporate); $35 (Student).

Meetings/Conferences: Annual
2013 - Greenville, SC (Hyatt Regency Greenville)/April 9 - 11
Number of non-conference events/year: 7

Publications:
AATCC News; semi-monthly; adv.
AATCC Review Journal; bi-monthly; adv.
AATCC Technical Manual; annually

American Association of Tissue Banks (1976)

1320 Old Chain Bridge Rd.
Suite 450
McLean, VA 22101
Tel: (703) 827-9582 *Fax:* (703) 356-2198
E-Mail: aatb@aatb.org
Website: aatb.org
Members:
100 accredited tissue banks
1000 individual members
Staff: 15
Annual Budget: $2-5,000,000

Personnel:
Chief Executive Officer: P. Robert Rigney Jr.
    E-Mail: rigneyb@aatb.org
Chief Policy Officer: Scott Brubaker
    E-Mail: brubakers@aatb.org
Director, Financial Services: Kathy Crandall
    E-Mail: crandallk@aatb.org
Acting Chief Program Officer: Margaret A. Deuel RAC, RN
    E-Mail: deuelm@aatb.org
Manager , Meetings and Membership Services: Rebecca Hunter CMP
    E-Mail: hunterr@aatb.org
Manager, Accreditation: Debbie Butler Newman
    E-Mail: newmand@aatb.org
Director, Communications and Public Relations: Jim Warren
    E-Mail: warrenj@aatb.org

Historical Note:
AATB's mission is to enhance and save lives by promoting and facilitating the safety, quality and availability of donated human tissues. Members are individuals involved or interested in banking of tissues, cells or organs and institutions qualifying as accredited tissue banking facilities which participate in a tissue, cell or organ banking program including retrieval, processing, storage and distribution. Membership: $195/year (Individual).

Continuing Education:
Certification Designation/s: CTBS, CRCS

Meetings/Conferences:
Conference Chair: Rebecca Hunter CMP
2013 - Tucson, AZ (Westin La Paloma Resort and Spa)/ April 6 - 9
2013 - Ft. Washington, MD (Gaylord National Hotel and Convention Center)/Oct. 2 - 6
2014 - San Diego, CA (Hilton San Diego Bayfront)/ Sept. 16 - 20
2015 - Scottsdale, AZ (Westin Kierland Resort and Spa)/Sept. 15 - 19
Number of non-conference events/year: 2

Publications:
AATB E-Newsletter; on-line

American Association of University Administrators (1970)

214 Meadville St
Edinboro, PA 16412
Tel: (814) 460-6498 *Fax:* (814) 732-2623
Website: aaua.org
Members: 900 individuals
Staff: 1
Annual Budget: $50-100,000

Personnel:
Executive Director: Dan L. King EdD
    E-Mail: dking@mailâ "aaua.org

Historical Note:
AAUA mission is to develop and advance the standards for profession of higher education administration. Membership in AAUA is open to any individual interested in the field of higher education administration. Membership: $100 (Active); $250 (Sponsor); $150 (Sustaining); $35 (Student); $55 (Emeritus); $500-2,000 (Institution).

Meetings/Conferences:
Number of non-conference events/year: 1

Publications:
Journal Of Higher Education Management

American Association of University Professors (1915)

1133 19th St. NW
Suite 200
Washington, DC 20036
Tel: (202) 737-5900 *Fax:* (202) 737-5526
E-Mail: aaup@aaup.org
Website: aaup.org
Members: 45000 individuals
Staff: 35
Annual Budget: $5-10,000,000
Tax: 501(c)(3)

Personnel:
Senior Associate General Secretary: Martin D Snyder
    E-Mail: msnyder@aaup.org
Director, Communications: Gwendolyn Bradley
    E-Mail: gbradley@aaup.org
Director, Research and Public Policy: John Curtis AAP
    E-Mail: jcurtis@aaup.org
Chief Financial Officer: Tess Esposito
Director, Membership Services and Development: Katherine Isaac
    E-Mail: kisaac@aaup.org
Paralegal and Program Assistant: Elona M. Jouben
    E-Mail: ejouben@aaup.org
Executive Assistant: Susan Smee
    E-Mail: ssmee@aaup.org
Associate Counsel: Kathi Westcott

Historical Note:
AAUP provides economic and legislative information on higher education issues and advocates in the interest of faculty in all types of universities and colleges. Members are full and part-time teachers, scholars, graduate students, librarians and other academic professionals. Membership: $168 (Full-Time); $126 (Associate); $84 (Entrant/Joint/ Retired); $42 (Part-Time/Graduate).

Meetings/Conferences: Annual
Conference Chair: Susan Smee

2013 - Washington, DC (Mayflower Renaissance Hotel)/June 12 - 16
2014 - Washington, DC (Mayflower Renaissance Washington, D.C. Hotel)/June 11 - 15
Number of non-conference events/year: 3

Publications:
Academe Magazine; bi-monthly
Journal of Academic Freedom; on-line

Membership List Available to Non-members

American Association of University Women
(1881)
1111 16th St. NW
Washington, DC 20036-4873
Tel: (202) 785-7700 *Fax:* (202) 872-1425
TollFree: (800) 326-2289
E-Mail: helpline@aauw.org
Website: aauw.org
Members: 100000 members and 500 institutions
Staff: 112
Annual Budget: $10-25,000,000

Personnel:
President: Carolyn H. Garfein
Executive Director: Linda D. Hallman
Associate, Senior Media Relations and Marketing: Lisa Goodnight
    E-Mail: media@aauw.org
Director, Public Policy and Government Relations: Lisa M. Maatz
    E-Mail: maatzl@aauw.org
Director, Marketing and Communications: Cynthia Miller

Historical Note:
AAUW's mission is to advance equality for women and girls through advocacy, education, philanthropy, and research. Membership: $49 (Branch/National); $17 (Student).

Meetings/Conferences: Annual
2013 - New Orleans, LA (Sheratan New Orleans Hotel)/June 9 - 12

Publications:
AAUW Outlook; on-line; adv.
Good Housekeeping
Redbook

American Association of Variable Star Observers
(1911)
49 Bay State Rd.
Cambridge, MA 02138
Tel: (617) 354-0484 *Fax:* (617) 354-0665
E-Mail: aavso@aavso.org
Website: aavso.org
Members: 3000 individuals
Staff: 13
Annual Budget: $2-5,000,000
Tax: 501(c)(3)

Personnel:
Director: Arne Henden PhD
    E-Mail: aavso@aavso.org
Astronomical Technologist, Information Technology: Richard "Doc" Kinne
Membership Director and Development Officer: Mike Simonsen
Director, Science: Matthew Templeton
Director, Operations: Rebecca Turner
Senior Technical Assistant and Associate Editor: Elizabeth O. Waagen

Historical Note:
AAVSO's mission is to observe and analyze variable stars, to collect and archive observations for worldwide access, to forge strong collaborations between amateur and professional astronomers, and to promote scientific research and education using variable star data. Members are amateur and professional astronomers who gather and record data on stars which vary in brightness. Membership: $75 (Individual); $150 (Sustaining); $37.50 (Associate/Pension/Limited Income).

Meetings/Conferences: Annual
2013 - Boone, NC (Appalachian State University)/May 15 - 18

Publications:
AAVSO Newsletter
Membership Directory; on-line
The Journal of the American Association Of Variable Star Observers (JAAVSO); bi-annually; adv.

American Association of Veterinary Clinicians
(1958)

422 Peppers Ferry Rd.
Suite 309
Christiansburg, VA 24073
Tel: (614) 358-0417 *Fax:* (540) 242-3385
E-Mail: jaustin@aavcvet.org
Website: aavcvet.org
Members: 476 individuals
Staff: 3
Annual Budget: $250-500,000

Personnel:
Executive Director: Jonathan Austin
    E-Mail: jaustin@aavcvet.org

Historical Note:
AAVC's mission is to enhance the quality of and be an advocate for veterinary clinical teaching, service and research. Members are veterinary clinicians who are engaged in teaching and/or research at the professional, graduate or postgraduate level. Membership: $8/year (Individual).

Meetings/Conferences: Annual
2013 - Atlanta, GA (Westin Atlanta Airport)/March 21 - 22

Publications:
Membership Directory; on-line

American Association of Veterinary Immunologists
(1979)
University of Tennessee, Animal Science Department
114 McCord Hall, 2640 Morgan Cir.
Knoxville, TN 37996-4588
Tel: (865) 974-7225 *Fax:* (865) 974-9043
Website: theaavi.org
Members: 260 individuals
Staff: 3
Annual Budget: Under $10,000

Personnel:
President: Paul Coussens
    E-Mail: coussens@msu.edu
Editor: Kevin Lahmers
    E-Mail: klahmers@vetmed.wsu.edu
Secretary and Treasurer: Gina Pighetti
    E-Mail: pighetti@utk.edu

Historical Note:
AAVI is dedicated to the development, upliftment, and dissemination of knowledge in veterinary immunology. Its members are veterinarians and others with an interest in veterinary immunology. Membership: $50 (Individual); $20 (Student).

Meetings/Conferences: Annual
2013 - Honolulu, HI/May 3 - 7

Publications:
Membership Directory; on-line
Newsletter; bi-annually
Veterinary Immunology Immunopathology (VII)

Membership List Available to Non-members

American Association of Veterinary Laboratory Diagnosticians *(1958)*
P.O. Box 1770
Davis, CA 95617
Tel: (530) 754-9719 *Fax:* (530) 752-5680
Website: aavld.org
Members: 1200 individuals
Staff: 4
Annual Budget: $250-500,000

Personnel:
Secretary and Treasurer: John Adaska
    E-Mail: secretary-treasurer@aavld.org
Editor: Pat Blanchard
    E-Mail: pcblanchard@ucdavis.edu
Coordinator, Exhibitions: Jackie Cassarly
    E-Mail: jackie@planningconnection.com
Administrative Analyst: Reda Ozuna
    E-Mail: rozuna@cahfs.ucdavis.edu

Historical Note:
Formerly (1956) known as the Conference of Veterinary Laboratory Diagnosticians, AAVLD's purpose is dissemination of information relating to the diagnosis of animal disease, coordination of diagnostic activities of regulatory research in service laboratories, establishment of uniform diagnostic techniques and the improvement of existing ones, and the development of a body that could act in a consultant capacity to the United States Animal Health Association on uniform diagnostic criteria involved in regulatory animal disease programs. Membership: $150 (Full); $25 (Graduate Student/Resident/Retired/Vet Student/Undergraduate); $35 (Associate).

Meetings/Conferences: Annual
Conference Chair: Jackie Cassarly
2013 - San Diego, CA (Town and Country Resort Hotel)/Oct. 17 - 23

Publications:
Journal of Veterinary Diagnostic Investigation; bi-monthly
Membership directory; on-line

Membership List Available to Non-members

American Association of Veterinary Parasitologists *(1956)*
Pfizer Animal Health
7000 Portage Rd.
Kalamazoo, MI 49001
Tel: (269) 833-2674 *Fax:* (269) 833-3231
Website: aavp.org
Members: 450 individuals
Staff: 4
Annual Budget: $50-100,000

Personnel:
President: Alan Marchiondo
Secretary and Treasurer: Dr. Bob Arther
    E-Mail: Bob.Arther@bayer.com
Editor: Jenifer Edmonds
Contact, Membership Services: Bert Stromberg
    E-Mail: b-stro@umn.edu

Historical Note:
Affiliated with the American Veterinary Medical Association. AAVP's mission is to lead and partner with members in advancing veterinary parasitology education, research, practice and service to improve human and animal health. It serves as a professional society for the advancement of veterinary parasitology and the dissemination of current scientific information. Membership: $30 (Regular); $10 (Student).

Continuing Education:
Certification Designation/s: ACVM

Meetings/Conferences: Annual
2013 - Chicago, IL/July 20 - 23
2014 - Denver, CO/July 26 - 29

Publications:
American Association of Veterinary Parasitologists Newsletter
Membership Directory; on-line
Veterinary Parasitology; adv.

Membership List Available to Non-members

American Association of Veterinary State Boards *(1957)*
380 W. 22nd St.
Suite 101
Kansas City, MO 64108
Tel: (816) 931-1504 *Fax:* (816) 931-1604
TollFree: (877) 698-8482
E-Mail: aavsb@aavsb.org
Website: aavsb.org
Members: 57 jurisdictions
Staff: 9
Annual Budget: $2-5,000,000
Tax: 501(c)(3)

Personnel:
Executive Director: Robyn Kendrick
    E-Mail: rkendrick@aavsb.org
Manager, Membership Services: Jessica Haendler
    E-Mail: jhaendler@aavsb.org
Program Specialist: Jessica Klein
    E-Mail: jklein@aavsb.org
Office Administrator: Megan Pope
    E-Mail: mpope@aavsb.org
Manager, Marketing and Membership Services: Susan Rehm
    E-Mail: srehm@aavsb.org

Historical Note:
AAVSB's mission is to provide quality resources and accurate information for veterinary regulatory agencies and professionals and allied groups in the interest of public protection. Members are members of state boards of veterinary examiners.

Continuing Education:
Certification Designation/s: VTNE, VIVA, RACE, PAVE

Meetings/Conferences: Annual
Conference Chair: Jessica Haendler

Publications:
AAVSB Newsletter; on-line
Veterinary Regulation News

American Association of Wildlife Veterinarians (1979)

Idaho Dept. of Fish and Game
16569 S. Tenth Ave.
Caldwell, ID 83607
Website: aawv.net
Members: 250 individuals
Staff: 3
Annual Budget: $500-1,000,000
Tax: 501(c)(6)

Personnel:
President and Website Editor: Colin Gillin
    E-Mail: colin.m.gillin@state.or.us
Treasurer: Mark Drew
    E-Mail: mdrew@agri.idaho.gov
Editor: Jordan Mencher
    E-Mail: jmencher@myuw.net

Historical Note:
AAWV's mission is to encourage and enhance a philosophy of animal management and preventative medicine as it relates to free-ranging species. Members are veterinarians specializing in the health of wild animals in their natural habitat. Membership: $50 (Veterinarian Active/ Subscribing); $20 (Veterinary Student).

Meetings/Conferences: Annual

Publications:
AAWV Newsletter; on-line; adv.
Membership Directory; on-line

American Association of Women Dentists (1921)

216 W. Jackson Blvd.
Suite 625
Chicago, IL 60606
Tel: (800) 920-2293 *Fax:* (312) 750-1203
TollFree: (800) 920-2293
E-Mail: info@aawd.org
Website: aawd.org
Members: 1000 individuals
Staff: 3
Annual Budget: $100-250,000
Tax: 501(c)(6)

Personnel:
Executive Director: Debbie Gidley

Historical Note:
Founded (1921) as Federation of American Women Dentists. The mission of AAWD is to be the recognized resource for connecting and enriching the lives of women dentists. Membership: $215 (Active/Affiliate/International); $95 (Dental Office Team); $99 (Full Time Faculty/Federal Services); $45 (Students/Post Graduate/Resident).

Meetings/Conferences: Annual
2013 - Carlsbad, CA (LaCosta Resort and Spa)/July 18 - 21
Number of non-conference events/year: 3

Publications:
AAWD's Chronicle; quarterly
Membership Directory; annually; adv.

American Association of Woodturners (1986)

222 Landmark Center, 75 Fifth St., West
St. Paul, MN 55102
Tel: (651) 484-9094 *Fax:* (651) 484-1724
TollFree: (877) 595-9094
E-Mail: inquiries@woodturner.org
Website: woodturner.org
Members: 14,000 members
Staff: 9
Annual Budget: $1-2,000,000
Tax: 501(c)(3)

Personnel:
Executive Director: Phil McDonald
    E-Mail: phil@woodturner.org
Assistant, Administrative Services: Jane Charbonneau
    E-Mail: jane@woodturner.org

Historical Note:
AAW was first organized in 1986. The American Association of Woodturners is the organization dedicated to the advancement of woodturning. AAW's mission is to provide education, information, and organization to those interested in woodturning--a branch of woodworking centered around using the lathe to shape wood. Membership: $43 (Online); $24-58 (Individual); $79-1000 (Business/Professional); $58-73 (International).

Continuing Education:
Certification Designation/s: SCSC

Meetings/Conferences: Annual

2013 - Tampa, FL (Tampa Convention Center)/June 28 - 30

Publications:
American Woodturner Journal; bi-monthly
Resource Directory; biennially

American Association of Zoo Keepers (1967)

3601 SW 29th St.
Suite 133
Topeka, KS 66614-2054
Tel: (785) 273-9149 *Fax:* (785) 273-1980
Website: aazk.org
Members: 2800 individuals
Staff: 5
Annual Budget: $250-500,000
Tax: 501(c)(3)

Personnel:
Executive Director: Ed Hansen
    E-Mail: ed.hansen@aazk.org
Chair, Membership Resources: Jacque Blessington
    E-Mail: jacque.blessington@aazk.org
Managing Editor, AKF: Susan D. Chan
    E-Mail: susan.chan@aazk.org
Media Production Editor: Shane Good
    E-Mail: shane.good@aazk.org
Administrative Secretary: Barbara Manspeaker
    E-Mail: barbara.manspeaker@aazk.org

Historical Note:
AAZK is a nonprofit volunteer organization made up of professional zoo keepers and other interested persons dedicated to professional animal care and conservation. Members are professional zoo keepers and other interested persons for professional animal care and conservation. Membership: $30-150/year.

Meetings/Conferences: Annual
Conference Chair: Ed Hansen
2013 - Asheboro, NC/Sept. 22 - 26
2014 - Orlando, FL/Sept. 8 - 12
Number of non-conference events/year: 2

Publications:
Animal Keepers' Forum; monthly; adv.
Membership Directory; on-line

American Association of Zoo Veterinarians (1960)

581705 White Oak Rd.
Yulee, FL 32097
Tel: (904) 225-3275 *Fax:* (904) 225-3289
E-Mail: aazvorg@aol.com
Website: aazv.org
Members: 1200 individuals
Staff: 6
Annual Budget: $500-1,000,000
Tax: 501(c)(3)

Personnel:
Executive Director: Robert Hilsenroth
    E-Mail: RhilsenrothAAZV@aol.com
Administration Assistant: Pam Brownlee
    E-Mail: AAZVorg@aol.com
Webmaster: Dr. Tom Curro
    E-Mail: tgcurro@gmail.com
Treasurer: Chris Hanley
    E-Mail: chris.hanley@toledozoo.org
Executive Committee Representative: Thomas Meehan
    E-Mail: tomeehan@brookfieldzoo.org
Editor: Dr. Teresa Morishita
    E-Mail: JZWM_Editor@yahoo.com

Historical Note:
AAZV's mission is to enhance and uphold the professional ethics of veterinary medicine and to advocate the general welfare and conservation of captive and free-ranging wildlife. Members work in clinical zoo medical practice, diagnostic laboratories, reproductive and pathological laboratories, pharmaceutical companies, and governmental health and wildlife management agencies. Membership: $121 (Student); $158 (Active Family/Associate Family); $215 (Active/Associate); $15 (Foreign/Developing Nation Limited).

Meetings/Conferences: Annual
2013 - Salt Lake City, UT/Sept. 29 - Oct. 4
2014 - Orlando, FL (Walt Disney World Resort)/Oct. 18 - 24

Publications:
Journal of ZOO and WILDLIFE MEDICINE (JZWM); on-line; adv.
Membership Directory; on-line

American Astronautical Society (1954)

6352 Rolling Mill Pl.
Suite 102
Springfield, VA 22152-2370
Tel: (703) 866-0020 *Fax:* (703) 866-3526
E-Mail: aas@astronautical.org
Website: astronautical.org
Members: 1500 individuals and 40 corporations
Staff: 12
Annual Budget: $500-1,000,000

Personnel:
Executive Director: James R. Kirkpatrick
    E-Mail: jkirkpatrick@astronautical.org
Vice President, Publications: Richard Burns
Vice President, Membership Services: Randall Correll
Vice President, Strategic Communications and Outreach: Ken Davidian
Vice President, Education: Dustin Doud
Vice President, Programs: J. Walter Faulconer
Vice President, Finance: Carol S. Lane
Legal Counsel: Franceska O. Schroeder
President: Frank A. Slazer
Vice President, Public Policy: Marcia Smith
Vice President, Technical Services: David B. Spencer
Executive Vice President: Lyn D. Wigbels

Historical Note:
AAS is dedicated to the advancement of space science and exploration. Regular memberships are for professionals involved in the field of astronautics and general space enthusiasts. Membership: $100 (Regular/Affiliate); $115 (Senior/Fellow); $45 (K-12 Teacher/Student); $50 (Retired); $300-10,000 (Corporate); $300-1,000 (Institutional).

Meetings/Conferences:
Conference Chair: J. Walter Faulconer
2013 - Greenbelt, MD/March 19 - 21
Number of non-conference events/year: 4

Publications:
Journal of the Astronautical Sciences; quarterly
Membership Directory; on-line
Space Times; bi-monthly

American Astronomical Society (1899)

2000 Florida Ave. NW
Suite 400
Washington, DC 20009-1231
Tel: (202) 328-2010 *Fax:* (202) 234-2560
E-Mail: aas@aas.org
Website: aas.org
Members: 6700 individuals
Staff: 21
Annual Budget: $10-25,000,000
Tax: 501(c)(3)

Personnel:
Executive Officer: Kevin B Marvel PhD, CAE
    E-Mail: kevin.marvel@aas.org
Director, Publishing: Chris Biemesderfer
    E-Mail: biemesderfer@aas.org
Chief Financial Officer: Kelly E Clark
    E-Mail: kelly.clark@aas.org
Director, Meeting Services: Kim Earle
    E-Mail: earle@aas.org
Coordinator, Education, Outreach and Press Officer: Dr. Rick Fienberg
    E-Mail: fienberg@aas.org
Director, Information Technology: Scott Idem
    E-Mail: idem@aas.org
Contact, Public Policy: Bethany Johns
    E-Mail: bjohns@aas.org
Director, Communications: Judith M. Johnson
    E-Mail: johnson@aas.org
Director, Membership Services: Faye Peterson
    E-Mail: peterson@aas.org

Historical Note:
Organized September 6, 1899, at the Yerkes Observatory, Green Bay, Wisconsin, as the Astronomical and Astrophysical Society of America. Name changed to American Astronomical Society in 1914. Incorporated in Illinois in 1928 and incorporated in DC in 1986. A member of the American Institute of Physics. AAS's mission is to enhance and share humanity's scientific understanding of the Universe. Membership: $158 (Full/Associate); $58 (Junior); $80 (International Affiliate/Emeritus/Education Affiliate).

Meetings/Conferences:
Conference Chair: Kim Earle
2013 - Long Beach, CA (Long Beach Convention and Entertainment Center)/Jan. 6 - 10

2013 - Indianapolis, IN (Indiana Convention Center)/
June 2 - 6
2014 - Washington, DC/Jan. 5 - 9
2014 - Pasadena, CA/June 1 - 5
2015 - Seattle, WA/Jan. 4 - 8
2016 - Austin, TX/Jan. 10 - 14
2017 - Long Beach, CA/Jan. 8 - 12
2018 - Washington, DC/Jan. 7 - 11
2019 - Seattle, WA/Jan. 6 - 10
2020 - Austin, TX/Jan. 6 - 10
2022 - Washington, DC/Jan. 8 - 13
Number of non-conference events/year: 5

Publications:
AAS Membership Directory; annually; adv.
AJ/ApJ/ApJS; on-line
ApJ Supplement (ApJS); monthly
Astronomical Journal (AJ); monthly
Astrophysical Journal (ApJ); monthly
The AAS Newsletter; bi-monthly

Membership List Available to Non-members

American Auditory Society (1974)
19 Mantua Rd.
Mt. Royal, NJ 08061
Tel: (856) 423-3118 *Fax:* (856) 423-3420
E-Mail: aas@talley.com
Website: amauditorysoc.org
Members: 2000 individuals
Staff: 2
Annual Budget: $100-250,000
Tax: 501(c)(3)

Personnel:
Executive Director: Darla M. Eastlack
Treasurer: Linda Hood

Historical Note:
AAS seeks to increase knowledge and understanding of the
ear, hearing and balance, disorders of the ear, habilitation
and rehabilitation of individuals with hearing and balance
dysfunction. Membership: $55/year (Regular/Associate).

Meetings/Conferences: Annual
Conference Chair: Linda Hood
2013 - Scottsdale, AZ (Chaparral Suites Resort
Scottsdale)/March 7 - 9

Publications:
Membership Directory; on-line
The Bulletin of the American Auditory Society

Membership List Available to Non-members

American Auto Racing Writers and Broadcasters Association (1955)
922 N. Pass Ave.
Burbank, CA 91505-2703
Tel: (818) 842-7005 *Fax:* (818) 842-7020
Website: aarwba.org
Members: 525 individuals
Staff: 2
Annual Budget: Under $10,000

Personnel:
President and Executive Director: Norma "Dusty"
Brandel
E-Mail: dusty@aarwba.org
Secretary and Treasurer: Dr. George Peters
E-Mail: BarJean@prodigy.net

Historical Note:
AARWBA is dedicated to increase media coverage of motor
sports. Membership: $45 (Media); $65 (Affiliate); $300
(Associate/Corporate).

Publications:
AARWBA Newsletter

American Automatic Control Council (1957)
Department of Chemical and Biological
Engineering
129 Ricketts Building, 110 Eighth St.
Troy, NY 12180-3590
Tel: (518) 276-6683 *Fax:* (518) 276-4030
Website: a2c2.org
Members: 8 societies
Staff: 8
Annual Budget: $500-1,000,000
Tax: 501(c)(3)

Personnel:
President: R. Russell Rhinehart
Treasurer: Jordan Berg
E-Mail: jordan.berg@ttu.edu

Historical Note:
Founded as North American Control Council. AACC's
purpose is to enhance the role and contributions of
automation to the benefit of humankind. Membership:
$800/year (Organization).

Meetings/Conferences:
2013 - Washington, DC (Renaissance Washington)/
June 17 - 19/1100 attendees

Publications:
AACC Newsletter; semi-annually

American Automotive Leasing Association (1955)
675 N. Washington St
Suite 410
Alexandria, VA 22314
Tel: (703) 548-0777 *Fax:* (703) 548-1925
E-Mail: aalafleet@aol.com
Website: aalafleet.com
Members: 12 companies
Staff: 4
Annual Budget: $500-1,000,000
Tax: 501(c)(6)

Personnel:
Executive Director: Pamela Sederholm
E-Mail: sederholm@aalafleet.com
Legislative Associate: Courtney Groff
E-Mail: groff@aalafleet.com
Manager, Accounts: Traci Peters
E-Mail: peters@aalafleet.com
Director, Membership Services: Holly Walker
E-Mail: walker@aalafleet.com

Historical Note:
AALA's mission is to ensure that the business interests of
the fleet leasing industry are properly represented before
Congress, the Executive Branch and Regulatory Agencies.
Membership includes domestic and international companies
as well as family-owned businesses.

Meetings/Conferences: Annual
Publications:
Member Directory

American Automotive Policy Council
1401 H St. NW
Suite 780
Washington, DC 20005
Tel: (202) 789-0030 *Fax:* (202) 789-0054
E-Mail: info@americanautocouncil.org
Website: americanautocouncil.org
Staff: 5
Annual Budget: $1-2,000,000

Personnel:
President: Matt Blunt
E-Mail: mblunt@americanautocouncil.org
Assistant to the President, Legal Advisor to the Council:
Richard E. Coin
E-Mail: tcoin@americanautocouncil.org
Office Manager and Administrative Assistant: Peggy
Murphy
Vice President, International Policy: Charles D. Uthus
E-Mail: cuthus@autotradecouncil.org

Historical Note:
The American Automotive Policy Council, Inc. (AAPC) is a
Washington, D.C. association that represents the common
public policy interests of its member companies: Chrysler
Group LLC, Ford Motor Company and General Motors
Company. An expansion of The Automotive Trade Policy
Council.

American Backflow Prevention Association (1984)
P.O. Box 3051
Bryan, TX 77805-3051
Tel: (979) 846-7606 *Fax:* (979) 846-7607
TollFree: (877) 227-2127
Website: abpa.org
Staff: 5
Annual Budget: $250-500,000

Personnel:
President: Kenneth Kerr
E-Mail: ken@kerr-marketing.com
Director, Administrative Affairs: Shane Dillard
E-Mail: shane@abpa.org
Contact, Web and Forum Services: Gary Edwards
E-Mail: web@abpa.org
Certification Administrator: Ernest Havlina
E-Mail: certification@abpa.org

Historical Note:

ABPA's purpose is to involve all people in protecting public
health by protecting the drinking water through cross-
connection control and backflow prevention. Membership:
$60 (US); $74 (International); $300 (Affiliate).

Continuing Education:
Certification Designation/s: TCI, SCI

Meetings/Conferences: Annual
Conference Chair: Shane Dillard
2013 - Phoenix, AZ/May 6 - 8

American Bail Coalition (1992)
3857 Lewiston Pl.
Fairfax, VA 22030
Tel: (877) 385-9009 *Fax:* (703) 385-1809
TollFree: (877) 385-9009
E-Mail: dnabic@aol.com
Website: americanbailcoalition.com
Members: 12 companies
Staff: 2
Annual Budget: $100-250,000

Personnel:
President: William B. Carmichael
Executive Vice President: Dennis Bartlett
E-Mail: Dennis.Bartlett@americanbailcoalition.com

Historical Note:
Supersedes National Association of Bail Insurance
Companies (founded 1992). ABC's purpose is to protect
and expand the commercial surety bail market. Members
are companies who write contract and performance,
appearance, surety, and other related bond instruments.

Publications:
American Bail Coalition Newsletter

American Bakers Association (1897)
1300 I St. NW
Suite 700 W
Washington, DC 20005-3300
Tel: (202) 789-0300 *Fax:* (202) 898-1164
E-Mail: info@americanbakers.org
Website: americanbakers.org
Members: 300 companies
Staff: 9
Annual Budget: $5-10,000,000
Tax: 501(c)(6)

Personnel:
President and Chief Executive Officer: Robb S. MacKie II
E-Mail: rmackie@americanbakers.org
Manager, Finance: Teresa Grant
Director, Marketing and Membership Services: Kelly
Kotche
*Senior Vice President, Government Relations, Public Affairs
and Corporate Secretary:* Lee Sanders CAE
E-Mail: lsanders@americanbakers.org
Vice President, Membership Services: Karin M. Soyster
Fizgerald CAE, CMP
E-Mail: kfitzgerald@americanbakers.org

Historical Note:
ABA is a voluntary trade association designed to represent
the interests of the wholesale baking industry both on
national and state level. Membership: $1,500-400,000
(Baker Member, based on gross sales); $2000-4000 (Allied
Member, based on gross sales).

Meetings/Conferences: Annual
Conference Chair: Karin M. Soyster Fizgerald CAE, CMP
2013 - Aventura, FL (Fairmont Resort)/April 20 - 24
2013 - Las Vegas, NV (Las Vegas Convention Center)/
Oct. 6 - 9
2014 - Scottsdale, AZ (The Phoenician)/March 14 - 19

Publications:
ABA E-Newsletter; semi-annually
Membership Directory; on-line
What's New; weekly

American Bandmasters Association (1929)
The University of South Carolina
Columbia, SC 29208
Tel: (803) 787-6540 *Fax:* (803) 777-2151
Website: americanbandmasters.org
Members: 372 individuals
Staff: 2
Annual Budget: $50-100,000

Personnel:
President: Thomas G. Leslie
E-Mail: thomas.leslie@unlv.edu
Secretary and Treasurer: William J. Moody
E-Mail: wmoody4250@att.net

Historical Note:

Purpose of ABA is to recognize achievement in the field of concert band and its music and to promote standard of artistic excellence for the concert band, its performers, conductors and composers in USA and Canada. Membership: $300 (Member); $70 (Associate).

Meetings/Conferences: Annual
2013 - Tampa, FL (University of South Florida)/March 6 - 9
2014 - Montgomery, AL (The Renaissance Hotel)/ March 5 - 8

Publications:
Journal of Band Research; semi-annually

American Bankers Association (1875)
1120 Connecticut Ave. NW
Washington, DC 20036
Tel: (800) 226-5377
TollFree: (800) 226-5377
Website: aba.com
Members: 9000 individuals
Staff: 350
Annual Budget: Over $100,000,000
Tax: 501(c)(6)

Personnel:
President and Chief Executive Officer: Frank Keating
    E-Mail: fkeating@aba.com
Executive Director, Financial Institutions Policy and Regulatory Affairs: Wayne Abernathy
    E-Mail: wabernat@aba.com
Executive Vice President, Congressional Relations and Political Affairs: James Ballentine
    E-Mail: jballent@aba.com
Senior Vice President: John Blanchfield
    E-Mail: jblanchf@aba.com
General Counsel: Dawn Causey
    E-Mail: dcausey@aba.com
Executive Director, Communications: Virginia Dean
Senior Vice President, Tax, Accounting and Financial Management.: Donna J. Fisher
    E-Mail: dfisher@aba.com
Vice President, Business Development: Gail Kolakowski
    E-Mail: gkolakow@aba.com
Executive Vice President, Communications: Stephanie Matthews O'Keefe
Contact, Media: Marquita Powell
    E-Mail: mpowell@aba.com
Contact, Meetings: Eve Wallace
    E-Mail: ewallace@aba.com

Historical Note:
Trade Association representing nation's banking industry.

Continuing Education:
Certification Designation/s: CSOP, CTFA, CRSP, CFMP, CCSR, CLBB, CSOP, CBT, CISP, CPB, CFSSP, CRCM, CCTS

Meetings/Conferences:
Conference Chair: Eve Wallace
2013 - Orlando, FL (JW Marriott Orlando Grande Lakes)/Feb. 17 - 20
Number of non-conference events/year: 10

Publications:
ABA Bank Compliance; bi-monthly; adv.
ABA Bank Directors Briefing; monthly
ABA Bank Marketing; monthly; adv.
ABA Banking Journal; monthly; adv.
ABA Trust & Investments; bi-monthly; adv.
ABA Trust and Investments; bi-monthly; adv.
Community Banker; monthly
Membership Directory; on-line
Washington Perspective; weekly

American Bankers Association Securities Association (ABASA)
1120 Connecticut Ave. NW
Washington, DC 20036
Tel: (800) 226-5377
Website: aba.com/abasa/default.htm
Staff: 4

Personnel:
Executive Director and General Counsel: Cecelia Calaby
    E-Mail: ccalaby@aba.com
Associate General Counsel: Cristeena G. Naser
    E-Mail: cnaser@aba.com
Deputy General Counsel: Diana Preston
    E-Mail: dpreston@aba.com

Historical Note:

The ABA Securities Association (ABASA) is a separately chartered trade association and non-profit affiliate of the American Bankers Association whose mission is to develop policy and provide advocacy for banks underwriting and dealing in securities, proprietary mutual funds, and derivatives.

American Bankers Insurance Association (1875)
1120 Connecticut Ave. NW
Washington, DC 20036
Tel: (202) 663-5163   *Fax:* (202) 828-4546
TollFree: (800) 226-5377
E-Mail: bclimo@aba.com
Website: aba.com/abia
Staff: 7
Annual Budget: $1-2,000,000

Personnel:
President and Chief Executive Officer: Neal Aton
Executive Director: J. Kevin McKechnie
    E-Mail: kmckechni@aba.com
Treasurer: Peter Dunlap

Historical Note:
A full service trade association. An affiliate of the American Bankers Association (see separate listing) dedicated to improving financial services for consumers by supporting the sale of insurance by banking organizations.

Continuing Education:
Certification Designation/s: ICB

Meetings/Conferences: Annual

Publications:
ABIA Insurance News; bi-weekly
Membership Directory; on-line

American Bankruptcy Institute (1982)
44 Canal Center Plaza
Suite 400
Alexandria, VA 22314-1592
Tel: (703) 739-0800   *Fax:* (703) 739-1060
E-Mail: support@abiworld.org
Website: abiworld.org
Members: 13,000 individuals
Staff: 32
Annual Budget: $10-25,000,000
Tax: 501(c)(3)

Personnel:
Executive Director: Samuel J. Gerdano
    E-Mail: sgerdano@abiworld.org
Director, Marketing: Anne-Marie Corkran
    E-Mail: acorkran@abiworld.org
Conference Director, American Bankruptcy Institute: Jennifer Dugas
    E-Mail: jdugas@abiworld.org
Director, Interactive Media and Technology: Karim Guirguis
    E-Mail: kguirguis@abiworld.org
Senior Editor, American Bankruptcy Institute: Carolyn Kanon
    E-Mail: ckanon@abiworld.org
Chief Financial Officer: Kathy Sheehan
    E-Mail: ksheehan@abiworld.org
Director, Membership Services: Chris Thackston
    E-Mail: cthackston@abiworld.org

Historical Note:
ABI's mission is to provide Congress and the public with unbiased analysis of bankruptcy issues, dedicated to research and education on matters related to insolvency. Members are attorneys, auctioneers, bankers, judges, lenders, professors, turnaround specialists, accountants and other bankruptcy professionals. Membership: $275 (Individual); $95 (Government/Academic Individual/International/Auctioneer/Non-profit).

Meetings/Conferences: Semi-Annual
Conference Chair: Jennifer Dugas
Number of non-conference events/year: 30

Publications:
ABI Committee Newsletters; weekly
ABI Daily News; daily; adv.
ABI Journal; monthly; adv.
ABI Law Review; semi-annually
ABI Update; bi-weekly; adv.
Membership Directory; on-line

American Baptist Homes and Caring Ministries (1930)
Judson Park
23600 Marine View Dr. S
Des Moines, WA 98198
E-Mail: aundreia.alexander@abc-usa.org

Website: abhcm.org
Members: 130 Members
Staff: 2

Personnel:
President: Bill Painter
    E-Mail: Bpainter@abhow.com

Historical Note:
Formerly American Baptist Homes and Hospitals Association (ABHHA). Assumed its present name in 2006. ABHCM is an association of faith-based ministries founded to strengthen relationships and promote a standard of caring. Members are retirement/nursing homes, hospitals and children's homes.

American Bar Association (1878)
321 N. Clark St.
Chicago, IL 60654-7598
Tel: (312) 988-5522   *Fax:* (312) 988-6281
TollFree: (800) 285-2221
E-Mail: service@americanbar.org
Website: americanbar.org
Members: 400000 individuals
Staff: 900
Annual Budget: Over $100,000,000
Tax: 501(c)(6)

Personnel:
Executive Director and Chief Operating Officer: Jack L Rives
Director, Meeting Planning Services: Sarah Bolm
    E-Mail: Sarah.Bolm@americanbar.org
Division Director, Division for Public Education: Mabel McKinney Browning
    E-Mail:
    mabel.mckinneybrowning@americanbar.org
Director, Marketing and Program Planning: Angela Burke
    E-Mail: Angela.Burke@americanbar.org
Director, Membership Services and Marketing: Paula Cleave
    E-Mail: cleavep@staff.abanet.org
Program Manager and Editor: Catherine E. Hawke
    E-Mail: Catherine.Hawke@americanbar.org
Director, Publications and Marketing: Joanne O'Reilly
    E-Mail: oreillyj@staff.abanet.org
Information Research Specialist: Michael Ward
    E-Mail: michael.ward@americanbar.org
Director, Membership Development: Jill Werner
    E-Mail: Jill.Werner@americanbar.org

Historical Note:
ABA's mission is to serve members, profession and the public by defending liberty and delivering justice as the national representative of the legal profession. Represents more than 50% of practicing lawyers in the U. S. Federally approved accrediting agency for law schools. The American Law Student Association is a division of the ABA. Membership: Free (Judges/Lawyers/Practitioners); extra $35-100 to enrol in Sections/Divisions/Forums.

Meetings/Conferences:
Conference Chair: Sarah Bolm
2013 - Dallas, TX/Feb. 6 - 12
2013 - San Francisco, CA/Aug. 8 - 13
2014 - Chicago, IL/Feb. 5 - 11
2014 - Boston, MA/Aug. 7 - 14
2014 - Boston, MA/Aug. 7 - 12
2015 - Houston, TX/Feb. 4 - 10
2015 - Chicago, IL/July 30 - Aug. 4
2016 - San Diego, CA/Feb. 3 - 9
2016 - San Francisco, CA/Aug. 4 - 9
2017 - Miami, FL/Feb. 1 - 7
2017 - New York City, NY/Aug. 10 - 15
2018 - Vancouver, BC/Jan. 31 - Feb. 6
2018 - Chicago, IL/Aug. 2 - 7

Publications:
Litigation; quarterly
ABA Journal; monthly
Communications Lawyer; quarterly
Construct
Criminal Justice; quarterly
GPSolo
Human Rights; quarterly
Labor and Employment Law; quarterly
Probate & Property; bi-monthly
Student Lawyer; monthly
The Air and Space Lawyer; quarterly
The International Lawyer; quarterly
The Journal of Labor & Employment Law
The Urban Lawyer; quarterly
The Young Lawyer
TortSource; quarterly

The American Bar Association Rule of Law Initiative (2007)
740 15th St. NW
Washington, DC 20005
Tel: (202) 662-1950 Fax: (202) 662-1597
E-Mail: rol@americanbar.org
Website: abanet.org/rol/
Staff: 400

Personnel:
Director: Rob Boone
Director, Information Technology: Geoffrey Bentz
    E-Mail: geoffrey.bentz@americanbar.org
Director, Administration and Finance: Ingeborg Bock
    E-Mail: ingeborg.bock@americanbar.org
Director, Research and Assessments: Simon Conte
    E-Mail: simon.conte@americanbar.org
Director, Outreach and Communications: Anita Denning
    E-Mail: anita.denning@americanbar.org
Senior Criminal Law Advisor: Mary Greer
    E-Mail: mary.greer@americanbar.org

Historical Note:
The ABA established the program in 2007 to consolidate its five overseas rule of law programs, including the Central European and Eurasian Law Initiative (CEELI), which it created in 1990 after the fall of the Berlin Wall. The American Bar Association Rule of Law Initiative (ABA ROLI) is a mission-driven, non-profit program grounded in the belief that rule of law promotion is the most effective long-term antidote to the most pressing problems facing the world today, including poverty, conflict, endemic corruption and disregard for human rights.

Publications:
ABA Rule of Law Initiative Update; monthly

American Baseball Coaches Association (1945)
108 S. University Ave.
Suite Three
Mt. Pleasant, MI 48858-2327
Tel: (989) 775-3300 Fax: (989) 775-3600
E-Mail: abca@abca.org
Website: abca.org
Members: 6400 individuals
Staff: 5
Annual Budget: $1-2,000,000

Personnel:
Executive Director: Dave Keilitz
    E-Mail: dave@abca.org
Coordinator, Membership Services and Conventions: Nick Phillips
    E-Mail: phillips@abca.org

Historical Note:
Formerly (1985) the American Association of College Baseball Coaches. ABCA's mission is to promote the integrity of the profession and the development of the game of baseball. Includes members from every division of amateur baseball. Membership: $30 (USA); $35 (Canada); $40 (International).

Meetings/Conferences: Annual
Conference Chair: Nick Phillips
2013 - Chicago, IL (Hyatt Regency)/Jan. 3 - 6/6000 attendees/over 100 exhibitors
2014 - Dallas, TX (Hilton Anatole Dallas)/Jan. 2 - 5/6000 attendees/over 100 exhibitors
2015 - Orlando, FL (Marriott World Center)/Jan. 2 - 5/5500 attendees/over 100 exhibitors
2016 - Nashville, TN (Gaylord Opryland Hotel and Convention Center Nashville, Tennessee)/Jan. 7 - 10
2017 - Anaheim, CA (Anaheim Marriott)/Jan. 5 - 8

Publications:
Covering All Bases; adv.
Directory; annually; adv.

American Bashkir Curly Registry (1971)
2347 Hempfling Rd.
Morning View, KY 41063
Website: abcregistry.org
Members: 500 individuals
Staff: 3
Annual Budget: $10-25,000
Tax: 501(c)(5)

Personnel:
President and Registrar: Melinda Martino
    E-Mail: president@abcregistry.org

Historical Note:
Members are owners and breeders of rare horses with curly coats. Membership: $20 (Junior/Curly Cues Subscription); $35 (Adult) $90 (Family); $70 (Breeders License).

Meetings/Conferences: Annual
2013 - Kaufman, TX (Golden Curls)/Aug. 8 - 10

Publications:
Curly Cues (incorporated in the Equine Journal magazine); adv.

American Bearing Manufacturers Association (1933)
2025 M St. NW
Suite 800
Washington, DC 20036-3309
Tel: (202) 367-1155 Fax: (202) 367-2155
E-Mail: info@americanbearings.org
Website: abma-dc.org
Members: 40 Primary Manufacturer and Associate Member companies
Staff: 8
Annual Budget: $500-1,000,000
Tax: 501(c)(6)

Personnel:
President and Secretary: Scott Lynch
    E-Mail: slynch@americanbearings.org
Legal Counsel: Tod Ackerly
Technical Director: Jim Converse
    E-Mail: jconverse@americanbearings.org
Manager, Education: Delicia Hurdle
    E-Mail: dhurdle@americanbearings.org
Coordinator, Meetings and Events: Jessica Klapstein
    E-Mail: jklapstein@americanbearings.org
Associate, Membership Services: Kelly Sherrard
    E-Mail: ksherrard@americanbearings.org

Historical Note:
ABMA formerly known as the Anti-Friction Bearing Manufacturers Association till 1993. ABMA is a national trade association consisting of manufacturers of bearings, and components thereof who manufacture in the United States. ABMA's mission is to provide leadership, advocacy and education with a focus on membership value, industry outreach and issues impacting the global bearing industry. Membership: $1,410-46,000 (Company, based on net sales); $3,000 (Associate).

Meetings/Conferences:
Conference Chair: Jessica Klapstein
2013 - Carlsbad, CA (Park Hyatt Aviara)/April 25 - 27
Number of non-conference events/year: 3

Publications:
Newsletter

Membership List Available to Non-members

American Beefalo Association (2008)
P.O. Box 295
Benton City, WA 99320
E-Mail: OfficeManager@AmericanBeefalo.org
Website: americanbeefalo.org
Members: 50 individuals
Staff: 2
Annual Budget: Under $10,000

Personnel:
President: Andrew Hammer
Treasurer: Bret Green

Historical Note:
American Beefalo Association is a member driven organization. American Beefalo International and American Beefalo World Registry joined to form American Beefalo Association. Primary objective is the registration, improvement, and promotion of the Beefalo breed. Formed by the merger of American Beefalo International and American Beefalo World Registry. Membership: $25/year.

Meetings/Conferences: Annual

Publications:
The Beefalo Corral; monthly; adv.

American Beekeeping Federation (1943)
3525 Piedmont Rd.
Building Five, Suite 300
Atlanta, GA 30305
Tel: (404) 760-2875 Fax: (404) 240-0998
E-Mail: info@abfnet.org
Website: abfnet.org
Members: 1000 members
Staff: 4
Annual Budget: $500-1,000,000

Personnel:
Executive Director: Robin E. Dahlen CAE
    E-Mail: robindahlen@abfnet.org
Coordinator, Membership: Grayson Daniels
    E-Mail: graysondaniels@abfnet.org

Director, Government Relations: Troy Fore
    E-Mail: troyfore@abfnet.org
Senior Conference Planner: Tara Zeravsky CMP
    E-Mail: tarazeravsky@abfnet.org

Historical Note:
Formerly National Federation of Beekeepers Associations. Absorbed the Honey Industry Council of America in 1986. Members are honey producers, packers, shippers and suppliers. ABF acts on behalf of the beekeeping industry on issues affecting the interests and the economic viability of the various sectors of the industry. Membership: $250 (Commercial); $50 (Hobbyist); $100 (Sideliner); $500-1,500 (President's Club).

Meetings/Conferences: Annual
Conference Chair: Tara Zeravsky CMP
2013 - Hershey, PA (Hershey Lodge)/Jan. 8 - 12

Publications:
ABF E-Buzz; monthly
ABF Newsletter; bi-monthly
Membership Directory; on-line

American Benefits Council (2000)
1501 M St. NW
Suite 600
Washington, DC 20005
Tel: (202) 289-6700 Fax: (202) 289-4582
E-Mail: info@abcstaff.org
Website: appwp.org
Members: 347 companies
Staff: 12
Annual Budget: $2-5,000,000
Tax: 501(c)(6)

Personnel:
President: James A. Klein
    E-Mail: jklein@abcstaff.org
Senior Vice President, Policy: Lynn Dudley
    E-Mail: ldudley@abcstaff.org
Director, Communications: Jason Hammersla
    E-Mail: jhammersla@absstaff.org
Director, Membership Services: Deanna Johnson APR, CEBS
    E-Mail: djohnson@abcstaff.org
Senior Counsel, Health Policy: Kathryn Wilber
    E-Mail: kwilber@abcstaff.com

Historical Note:
Mission is to advocate for employer-sponsored benefit plans.

Publications:
Benefits Byte; annually

American Berkshire Association (1875)
2637 Yeager Rd.
West LaFayette, IN 47996-2436
Tel: (765) 497-3618 Fax: (765) 497-2959
E-Mail: berkshire@nationalswine.com
Website: americanberkshire.com
Members: 300 individuals
Staff: 3
Annual Budget: $500-1,000,000
Tax: 501(c)(5)

Personnel:
Secretary and Treasurer: Amy Smith

Historical Note:
Breeders and promoters of Berkshire swine. Member of the National Pedigree Livestock Council. Membership: $20/year.

Meetings/Conferences: Annual

Publications:
Breeders Directory; on-line
Breesders Digest; bi-monthly; adv.

American Beverage Association (1919)
1101 16th St. NW
Washington, DC 20036-4877
Tel: (202) 463-6732 Fax: (202) 659-5349
E-Mail: info@ameribev.org
Website: ameribev.org
Members: 300 firms
Staff: 40
Annual Budget: Over $100,000,000
Tax: 501(c)(6)

Personnel:
President and Chief Executive Officer: Susan K. Neely
    E-Mail: sneely@ameribev.org
Director, Communications: Maureen M. Beach

Vice President, Administration and Membership Services: Denise M. Burke

Vice President, Communications: Tracey A. Halliday

Senior Vice President and Chief Financial Officer: Mark Hammond

    E-Mail: mhammond@ameribev.org

Deputy General Counsel: Amy E. Hancock

Senior Vice President, Policy and Public Affairs: Kevin W. Keane

    E-Mail: kkeane@ameribev.org

Administrative Assistant: April Lee

Senior Vice President, Government Affairs: James A. McGreevy III

    E-Mail: jmcgreevy@ameribev.org

Federal Lobbyist: Antonio Moore

Office Assistant and Meetings Coordinator: Trudi Moore

Vice President, Scientific, Technical and Regulatory Affairs: Michael T. Redman

Director, Membership Services and Information Technology: Tara Spence

Senior Vice President, Science Policy: Maureen Storey PhD

Senior Vice President, Legal, Regulatory Affairs and General Counsel: Patricia Magee Vaughan

Historical Note:
Mission is to maximize consumer value by providing quality beverages in all classes of trade to meet the needs of its customers. Members are beverage producers, distributors, franchise companies. Membership: $300 (International Affiliate).

Meetings/Conferences: Annual
Conference Chair: Trudi Moore

Publications:
ABA SmartBrief; daily; adv.
Deposit News; quarterly
Membership Directory; on-line
Supplier Directory; on-line; adv.

American Beverage Institute (1991)
1090 Vermont Ave. NW
Suite 800
Washington, DC 20005
Tel: (202) 463-7110 *Fax:* (202) 463-7107
TollFree: (800) 843-8877
E-Mail: abi@abionline.org
Website: abionline.org
Members: 4500 individuals
Staff: 5
Annual Budget: $1-2,000,000
Tax: 501(c)(6)

Personnel:
Executive Director: Richard B. Berman
    E-Mail: Rick@bermanco.com
Managing Director: Sarah Longwell

Historical Note:
ABI strives to share accurate information with legislators, retailers, their employees, and the public regarding the responsible service and consumption of wine, beer, and distilled spirits.
Meetings/Conferences:
Number of non-conference events/year: 1

American Beverage Licensees (2002)
5101 River Rd.
Suite 108
Bethesda, MD 20816-1560
Tel: (301) 656-1494 *Fax:* (301) 656-7539
E-Mail: info@ablusa.org
Website: ablusa.org
Members: 20000 retailers
Staff: 3
Annual Budget: $500-1,000,000
Tax: 501(c)(6)

Personnel:
Executive Director: John D. Bodnovich
    E-Mail: bodnovich@ablusa.org
Director, Trade Relations and Operations: Susan Day Duffy
    E-Mail: day@ablusa.org
Manager, Communications and Public Relations: Rosanne Ferruggia

Historical Note:
Founded as National Retail Liquor Package Stores Association; became National Liquor Stores Association in 1964, and National Association of Beverage Retailers in 1992. ABL is an association representing off- premise licensees in the "open" or "license" states and on-premise proprietors in markets across the nation. It's mission is

---

to initiate and support laws, regulations and rules that preserve and protect the right of responsible on and off premise retailers of beverage alcohol to operate legitimate and lawful businesses without burdensome intrusion. Membership: $25,000 (Diamond); $15,000 (Platinum); $10,000 (Gold); $5,000 (Silver); $2,500 (Bronze); $15-25 (Affiliate).

Meetings/Conferences: Annual
Conference Chair: John D. Bodnovich
Number of non-conference events/year: 1

Publications:
ABL Insider; on-line

American Biological Safety Association (1984)
1200 Allanson Rd.
Mundelein, IL 60060-3808
Tel: (847) 949-1517 *Fax:* (847) 566-4580
TollFree: (866) 425-1385
E-Mail: info@absa.org
Website: absa.org
Members: 1000 individuals
Staff: 5
Annual Budget: $1-2,000,000
Tax: 501(c)(6)

Personnel:
Executive Director: Edward J. Stygar CAE, III, MBA
    E-Mail: ed@absaoffice.org
Educational Coordinator: KariAnn DeServi
    E-Mail: kariann@absaoffice.org
Membership, Exhibits Coordinator: Diane Johnson
    E-Mail: diane@absaoffice.org
Production Editor: Karen Savage
    E-Mail: karen@absaoffice.org
Vice President, Operations: Julie Savage
    E-Mail: julie@absaoffice.org

Historical Note:
ABSA provides members with information and research on practices in laboratory safety and related topics.The Association's goals are to provide a professional association that represents the interests and needs of practitioners of biological safety, and to provide a forum for the continued and timely exchange of biosafety information. Membership: $25 (Student), $210 (Individual); $735 (Corporate).

Continuing Education:
Certification Designation/s: CBSP

Meetings/Conferences: Annual
Conference Chair: Diane Johnson
2013 - Kansas City, MO (Hyatt Regency Crown Center)/Oct. 17 - 23
Number of non-conference events/year: 1

Publications:
Applied Biosafety: Journal of the American Biological Safety Association; quarterly; adv.
Member Directory; on-line

American Bladesmith Society (1976)
P.O. Box 160
Grand Rapids, OH 43522
Tel: (419) 832-0400
Website: americanbladesmith.com
Staff: 5
Annual Budget: $100-250,000

Personnel:
President and Contact, Events: Jim Batson
    E-Mail: jlbatson@mediastreamus.net
Webmaster: Dan Cassidy
    E-Mail: abswebmaster@americanbladesmith.com
Editor: Carolyn Hughes
    E-Mail: chughes@cableone.net
Office Manager: Cindy Sheely
    E-Mail: cindy@americanbladesmith.com

Historical Note:
Formed to operate for educational, scientific, and charitable purposes. The American Bladesmith Society was formed primarily to encourage and promote activities involving the art and science of forging metal, particularly tools, weapons, and art forms. Membership: $60 (Regular); $30 (Associate); $15 (Youth).

Meetings/Conferences: Annual
Conference Chair: Jim Batson
2013 - San Antonio, TX (Sheraton Gunter San Antonio)/Jan. 25 - 26

Publications:
American Bladesmith Journal
Newsletter

American Blonde D'Aquitaine Association (1973)
7407 VZ County Rd. 1507

Grand Saline, TX 75140
Tel: (903) 570-0568 *Fax:* (903) 569-1613
E-Mail: info@blondecattle.org
Website: blondecattle.org
Members: 70 individuals
Staff: 4
Annual Budget: $25-50,000

Personnel:
President: Doug Diebold
    E-Mail: doubledcattle@yahoo.com
Treasurer: Cliff R. Easley Jr.
    E-Mail: easley.cooper@ms.metrocast.net
Secretary: Janella H. Garrett
    E-Mail: janella@greenhillfarm.net

Historical Note:
Merged with the National Blonde D'Aquitaine Foundation in 1985. ABAA's mission is to develop and promote the Blonde d'Aquitaine breed of beef cattle in the United States. Members are breeders and fanciers of Blonde D'Aquitaine cattle. Membership: $50 (Associate/Active); $25 (Commercial); $5 (Junior); Free (Honorary).

Meetings/Conferences: Annual

Publications:
ABAA Newsletter
Membership Directory; on-line

American Bluefin Tuna Association
P.O. Box 854
Norwell, MA 02061
Tel: (802) 338-3124 *Fax:* (802) 338-3425
E-Mail: info@theabta.com
Website: theabta.com
Staff: 1

Personnel:
Executive Director: Rich Ruais

Historical Note:
Trade association of US bluefin tuna fishermen, pilots, processors and dealers.The American Bluefin Tuna Association (ABTA) was formed to protect the Atlantic Bluefin Tuna fishermen's traditional access and quota share. Membership: $50/Year.

American Board for Certification in Orthotics and Prosthetics, Inc. (ABC) (1948)
330 John Carlyle St., Suite 210
Alexandria, VA 22314
Tel: (703) 836-7114 *Fax:* (703) 836-0838
E-Mail: info@abcop.org
Website: abcop.org
Staff: 20
Annual Budget: $10-25,000,000
Tax: 501(c)(6)

Personnel:
Executive Director: Catherine Carter
    E-Mail: ccarter@abcop.org
Director, Public Relations and Marketing: Debbie Ayres
    E-Mail: dayres@abcop.org
Director, Information Services: Roxanne Bobb-Semple
    E-Mail: rbobbsemple@abcop.org
Specialist, Marketing and Communications Program: Megan Damewood
    E-Mail: mdamewood@abcop.org
Director, Continuing Education Programs: Heather Harris
    E-Mail: hharris@abcop.org
Manager, Credentialing Programs: Samlane Ketevong
    E-Mail: sketevong@abcop.org

Historical Note:
The mission of the American Board for Certification in Orthotics, Prosthetics and Pedorthics, Inc. (ABC) is to establish and promote better standards of organizational and clinical performance in the delivery of orthotic, prosthetic and pedorthic services. Members are certified orthotists, prosthetists, pedorthists and two public members who represent the interests of consumers, patients and other public groups.

Continuing Education:
Certification Designation/s: CT, CO, CP

Meetings/Conferences: Annual

Publications:
Facilitator
Mark of Merit Newsletter; quarterly

American Board of Anesthesiology (1941)
4208 Six Forks Rd.
Suite 900
Raleigh, NC 27609-5735
Fax: (866) 999-7503

TollFree: (866) 999-7501
Website: theaba.org
Staff: 5
Annual Budget: $10-25,000,000

Personnel:
Executive Director, Administrative Affairs: Mary Post
Corporate Meeting Planner: Amanda Barry
Senior Marketing and Communications Specialist: Cristalle Hinkle Dickerson
Chief Information Officer: Michael Eason
Chief Financial Officer: John Markey

Historical Note:
ABA's mission is to maintain the standards of practice by fostering educational facilities and training in anesthesiology.

Continuing Education:
Certification Designation/s: MOCA, CCMC, PMC, H&PMC, SMC, PAC

Meetings/Conferences:
Conference Chair: Amanda Barry

Publications:
ABA Newsletter; annually

The American Board of Facial Plastic and Reconstructive Surgery (1986)
115C S. St. Asaph St.
Alexandria, VA 22314
Tel: (703) 549-3223 Fax: (703) 549-3357
Website: abfprs.org
Staff: 3
Annual Budget: $500-1,000,000

Personnel:
Executive Director: Laurie Wirth
    E-Mail: lwirth@abfprs.org
Manager, Finance, Test and Administration: Missy Harp
    E-Mail: meharp@abfprs.org
Credentials Manager: Janice Knouse
    E-Mail: jknouse@abfprs.org

Historical Note:
ABFPRS's mission is to improve the quality of medical and surgical treatment available to the public by examining for professional expertise in facial plastic and reconstructive surgery.

Continuing Education:
Certification Designation/s: MOC

American Board of Family Medicine (1969)
1648 McGrathiana Pkwy.
Suite 550
Lexington, KY 40511-1247
Tel: (859) 269-5626 Fax: (859) 335-7501
TollFree: (888) 995-5700
E-Mail: help@theabfm.org
Website: theabfm.org
Staff: 67
Annual Budget: $10-25,000,000

Personnel:
President and Chief Executive Officer: James C. Puffer MD
    E-Mail: jpuffer@theabfm.org
Chief Operating and Financial Officer: Roger M. Bean
    E-Mail: rbean@theabfm.org
Manager, Communications: Robert Cattoi
    E-Mail: rcattoi@theabfm.org
Editor: Phil Lupo
    E-Mail: jabfm@med.wayne.edu
Coordinator, Certification: Debbie Medley
    E-Mail: dmedley@theabfm.org
Manager, Systems Programming and Development: Jin Xu
    E-Mail: jxu @theabfm.org

Historical Note:
Formerly American Board of Family Practice. ABFM's mission is to promote excellence in medical care through educational and scientific initiatives.The ABFM seeks to provide assurance to the public that certified family physicians possess the knowledge, skills and attitudes necessary to provide quality care to the individual, family and community through commitment to professional standing and competency in the field of family medicine.

Continuing Education:
Certification Designation/s: CAQ

Publications:
The Phoenix; bi-annually

American Board of Health Physics (1958)
1313 Dolley Madison Blvd.
Suite 402
McLean, VA 22101

Tel: (703) 790-1745 Fax: (703) 790-2672
E-Mail: abhpburkmgt@aol.com
Website: hps1.org
Staff: 1

Personnel:
Executive Secretary and Director, Programs: Nancy Johnson
    E-Mail: njohnson@burkinc.com

Historical Note:
The American Board of Health Physics is the certification body for the practice of professional health physics and is responsible for determining the qualifications of a Certified Health Physicist (CHP). Members are individuals who have been granted certification in Comprehensive Health Physics by the American Board of Health Physics (ABHP).

Continuing Education:
Certification Designation/s: CHP

American Board of Industrial Hygiene (1960)
6015 W. St. Joseph
Suite 102
Lansing, MI 48917-3980
Tel: (517) 321-2638 Fax: (517) 321-4624
E-Mail: abih@abih.org
Website: abih.org
Members: 11 board members
Staff: 6
Annual Budget: $1-2,000,000
Tax: 501(c)(6)

Personnel:
Executive Director: Lynn C. O'Donnell CIH
    E-Mail: LODonnell@ABIH.org
Contact, Examination: Ron Drafta CIH, CSP, SPHR
    E-Mail: rdrafta@abih.org
Contact, Marketing, Certification Maintenance and Accreditations: Tracy Parsons
    E-Mail: tparsons@abih.org
Contact Applications and Reapplications: Roger Smith CHMM, CIH
    E-Mail: rsmith@abih.org
Contact, Accounting and Office Administration: Charlotte Taylor
    E-Mail: ctaylor@abih.org
Contact, Fees, Office Administration, CM Worksheets and Audits: Pamela J. Trim
    E-Mail: ptrim@abih.org

Historical Note:
ABIH certifies professionals who evaluate health and safety in the workplace employed by industry, labor unions, state, provincial and local governments, federal agencies, uniformed services, as well as consulting organizations and academia in the U.S., Canada, Australia and other countries. Membership: $115/year (Individual).

Continuing Education:
Certification Designation/s: CIH, CAIH

Publications:
ABIH Newsletter
Member Directory; on-line
Newsletter

Membership List Available to Non-members

American Board of Internal Medicine (1936)
510 Walnut St.
Suite 1700
Philadelphia, PA 19106-3699
Tel: (215) 446-3500 Fax: (215) 446-3590
TollFree: (800) 441-2246
Website: abim.org
Members: 200000 certified physicians
Staff: 7
Annual Budget: $25-50,000,000
Tax: 501(c)(3)

Personnel:
President and Chief Executive Officer: Christine K. Cassel MD
Senior Vice President and Chief Information Officer: John K. Davis II
Senior Vice President and Chief Operating Officer: Lynn O. Langdon
Secretary-Treasurer: Stuart L. Linas MD
Vice President, Psychometrics and Research Analysis: Rebecca S. Lipner PhD
Senior Vice President , Finance and Chief Financial Officer: Vincent J. Mandes
Vice President, Communications: Lorie Slass

Historical Note:

Enhances the quality of health care by certifying internists and subspecialists who demonstrate the knowledge, skills, and attitudes essential for excellent patient care. Accountability is both to the profession of medicine and to the public.

Continuing Education:
Certification Designation/s: ABIM

Publications:
Membership Directory; on-line

American Board of Medical Specialties (1933)
222 N. LaSalle St.
Suite 1500
Chicago, IL 60601
Tel: (312) 436-2600 Fax: (312) 436-2700
TollFree: (866) 275-2267
Website: abms.org
Members: 24 organizations
Staff: 17
Annual Budget: $10-25,000,000
Tax: 501(c)(6)

Personnel:
Director, Communications and Meeting Services: Lori Boukas
    E-Mail: lboukas@abms.org
Director, Membership Services: JoAnn Ciatto
    E-Mail: jciatto@abms.org
Senior Vice President, Professional and Scientific Affairs: Richard E. Hawkins FACP, MD
Director, Information Services: James O. Jahrling
President and Chief Executive Officer: Lois Margaret Nora J D, MBA, MD
Director, Finance and Administration: Susan N. O'Connell

Historical Note:
ABMS's mission is to maintain and improve the quality of medical care by assisting the Member Boards in their efforts to develop and utilize professional and educational standards for the certification of physician specialists in the United States and internationally.

Continuing Education:
Certification Designation/s: MOC

Publications:
ABMS® Patient Safety Newsletter
e-newsletter; weekly

American Board of Multiple Specialties in Podiatry (1986)
1350 Broadway
Suite 1705
New York, NY 10018
Tel: (212) 356-0690 Fax: (212) 356-0678
TollFree: (888) 852-1442
E-Mail: abmsp@abmsp.org
Website: abmsp.org
Staff: 4

Personnel:
Executive Director: Joan Campbell CAE
    E-Mail: jcampbell@ptcny.com
Counsel: George Emershaw

Historical Note:
Incorporated in as the American Institute of Foot Medicine (AIFM), the name was changed to its current name in 1992 to better reflect its mission. ABMSP's purpose is to grant board certification to office-based or ambulatory surgeons.

Publications:
ABMSP Newsletter

American Board of Nursing Specialties (1991)
610 Thornhill Ln.
Aurora, OH 44202
Tel: (330) 995-9172 Fax: (330) 995-9743
E-Mail: abns@nursingcertification.org
Website: nursingcertification.org
Members: 23 organizations
Staff: 1
Annual Budget: $100-250,000
Tax: 501(c)(3)

Personnel:
Chief Executive Officer: Bonnie Niebuhr CAE, RN, MS
    E-Mail: abnsceo@aol.com

Historical Note:
ABNS's purpose is to promote the value of specialty nursing certification to all stakeholders . Members are Certified Registered Nurses. Membership: $2,000 (Regular); $1,500 (Associate); $2,500 (Affiliate).

Meetings/Conferences: Annual

Publications:
ABNS Newsletter
Membership Directory; on-line

The American Board of Opticianry and the National Contact Lens Examiners *(1979)*
6506 Loisdale Rd.
Suite 209
Springfield, VA 22150
Tel: (703) 719-5800 *Fax:* (703) 719-9144
TollFree: (800) 296-1379
E-Mail: mail@abo-ncle.org
Website: abo-ncle.org
Members: 38000 ophthalmic dispensers
Staff: 8
Annual Budget: $250-500,000

Personnel:
Executive Director: Michael H. Robey
    E-Mail: mrobey@abo-ncle.org

Historical Note:
The American Board of Opticianry (ABO) and the National Contact Lens Examiners (NCLE) are national organizations which administer voluntary certification examinations for dispensing opticians and contact lens technicians. Their purposes are to identify qualified eyewear providers by examination, urge growth of optical skills with continuing education, and approve continuing education programs.

Continuing Education:
Certification Designation/s: ABOC-AC, NCLE-AC, NOCE, CLRE, COT/COMT

Meetings/Conferences: Annual

American Board of Perianesthesia Nursing Certification Inc. *(1985)*
475 Riverside Dr.
Sixth Floor
New York, NY 10115-0089
Fax: (212) 367-4256
TollFree: (800) 622-7262
E-Mail: abpanc@proexam.org
Website: cpancapa.org
Staff: 5
Annual Budget: $1-2,000,000
Tax: 501(c)(6)

Personnel:
Chief Executive Officer: Bonnie Niebuhr CAE, RN, MS
    E-Mail: bniebuhr@proexam.org
Program Associate: Philip Godlewski
    E-Mail: pgodlewski@proexam.org

Historical Note:
Mission is to assure a certification process for perianesthesia nurses that validates knowledge gained through professional education and experience, ultimately promoting quality patient care.

Continuing Education:
Certification Designation/s: CPAN, CAPA

Publications:
CertificatioNEWS

American Board of Periodontology *(1939)*
877 Baltimore Annapolis Blvd.
Suite 111
Severna Park, MD 21146
Tel: (410) 647-1324 *Fax:* (410) 647-1260
E-Mail: staff@abperio.org
Website: abperio.org
Members: 8000 individuals
Staff: 4
Annual Budget: $500-1,000,000

Personnel:
Executive Director: Kent G. Palcanis
Associate Executive Director: Brenda J. Mayes
Coordinator, Examination: Barbara Robinette

Historical Note:
ABP was organized by the American Academy of Periodontology to elevate the standards and advance the science and art of periodontology by encouraging its study and advancing its practice. Membership: $125/year (Individual).

American Board of Physical Medicine and Rehabilitation *(1947)*
3015 Allegro Park Ln. SW
Rochester, MN 55902-4139
Tel: (507) 282-1776 *Fax:* (507) 282-9242
E-Mail: info@abpmr.org
Website: abpmr.org

Staff: 5
Annual Budget: $2-5,000,000

Personnel:
Executive Director: Anthony M. Tarvestad
    E-Mail: tarvestad@abpmr.org
Senior Computer Systems Programmer/Analyst: Diane C. Bur
    E-Mail: dbur@abpmr.org
Examinations Manager: Jill A. Hallman
    E-Mail: jhallman@abpmr.org
Communications and Editing Assistant: Kristina Kumar
    E-Mail: kkumar@abpmr.org
Administrator: Donna M. Morgan
    E-Mail: dmorgan@abpmr.org

Historical Note:
The ABPMR strives to improve training, and contributes to setting the standards for physical medicine and rehabilitation.

Continuing Education:
Certification Designation/s: MOC, CME

Publications:
ABPMR Newsletter; biennially

American Board of Podiatric Medicine *(1978)*
3812 Sepulveda Blvd.
Suite 530
Torrance, CA 90505
Tel: (310) 375-0700 *Fax:* (310) 375-1589
E-Mail: admin@abpoppm.org
Website: abpoppm.org
Members: 2850 individuals
Staff: 4
Annual Budget: $500-1,000,000

Personnel:
Executive Director: Marc A. Benard DPM
    E-Mail: mbenard@abpoppm.org
Treasurer: Michael P. DellaCorte DPM

Historical Note:
ABPM, Earlier (August 2012) known as American Board of Podiatric Orthopedics and Primary Podiatric Medicine-ABPOPPM, an affiliate of the American Podiatric Medical Association, works to delineate the skills, knowledge and attitudes necessary for the competent practice of podiatric medicine and orthopedics. All members, both qualified and certified, are required to pay yearly re-registration fees. Payment is due in January of each year and is subject to a late penalty if delinquent. Membership: $200 (Board-Qualified); $350 (Board-Certified).

Continuing Education:
Certification Designation/s: BQE, BCE

Publications:
Directory of Diplomates; annually; adv.
Membership Directory

American Board of Podiatric Surgery *(1975)*
445 Fillmore St.
San Francisco, CA 94117-3404
Tel: (415) 553-7800 *Fax:* (415) 553-7801
E-Mail: info@abps.org
Website: abps.org
Staff: 4
Annual Budget: $5-10,000,000

Personnel:
Executive Director: James A. Lamb
System Administrator: Tai Ngo
Associate Director, Administrative Services: Robert E. Perry
Associate Director, Credentials: John N. Venson

Historical Note:
Formerly National Board of Podiatric Surgery. ABPS's mission is to protect and improve the health and welfare of the public by the advancement of the art and science of podiatric surgery.

Continuing Education:
Certification Designation/s: FS, RRAS, F&AS

Publications:
Membership Directory; on-line

American Board of Preventive Medicine *(1948)*
111 W. Jackson Blvd.
Suite 1110
Chicago, IL 60604
Tel: (312) 939-2276 *Fax:* (312) 939-2218
E-Mail: abpm@theabpm.org
Website: theabpm.org
Members: 11 individuals
Staff: 3

Annual Budget: $2-5,000,000
Tax: 501(c)(6)

Personnel:
Executive Director: William W. Greaves
    E-Mail: execdir@theabpm.org
Administrator: Kristine Pasciak
    E-Mail: adminstrator@abpm.org
Assistant Office Manager: Pat Rimmer
    E-Mail: pat@theabpm.org

Historical Note:
ABPM's goal is to protect, promote and maintain health and well-being and to prevent disease, disability and death. Medicine specialists have core competencies in biostatistics, epidemiology, environmental and occupational medicine, planning and evaluation of health services management of health care organizations and research.

Continuing Education:
Certification Designation/s: EPIQ MOC

Publications:
Membership Directory; on-line

American Board of Professional Psychology *(1947)*
600 Market St.
Suite 300
Chapel Hill, NC 27516
Tel: (919) 537-8031 *Fax:* (919) 537-8034
E-Mail: office@abpp.org
Website: abpp.org
Members: 3500 individuals
Staff: 5
Annual Budget: $1-2,000,000

Personnel:
Executive Officer: David R. Cox ABPP, PhD
    E-Mail: drcox@abpp.org
Administrative Assistant: Diane Butcher
Manager, Information Systems and Accounts: Lanette Melville

Historical Note:
Formerly the American Board of Examiners in Professional Psychology, ABPP's mission is to increase consumer protection through the examination and certification of psychologists who demonstrate competence in approved specialty areas in professional psychology. Members must have a doctoral degree from a program in professional psychology which at the time the degree was granted was accredited by the APA, CPA, or was listed in the publication Doctoral Psychology Programs Meeting Designation Criteria.

Continuing Education:
Certification Designation/s: ABPP

Meetings/Conferences: Annual
2013 - Chicago, IL (Stouffer Renaissance Chicago Hotel)/June 20 - 22
2013 - Boston, MA/July 10 - 13

Publications:
ABPP Newsletter

American Board of Psychiatry & Neurology *(1934)*
2150 E. Lake Cook Rd.
Suite 900
Buffalo Grove, IL 60089
Tel: (847) 229-6500 *Fax:* (847) 229-6600
Website: abpn.com
Staff: 6
Annual Budget: $10-25,000,000

Personnel:
President and Chief Executive Officer: Larry R. Faulkner MD
Director, Administration and Chief Financial Officer: Robin Callen
    E-Mail: rcallen@abpn.com
Director, Credentials and Meetings: Pat Janda
    E-Mail: pjanda@abpn.com
Vice President, Research and Development: Dorthea Juul
    E-Mail: djuul@abpn.com
Manager, Human Resources: Valerie Pierce
    E-Mail: vpierce@abpn.com
Chief Information Officer: Paul Whittington
    E-Mail: pwhittinington@abpn.com

Historical Note:
ABPN is committed to serving the public interest and the professions of psychiatry and neurology by promoting excellence in practice through certification and maintenance of certification processes. The ABPN is a member of the American Board of Medical Specialties, an organization of 24 approved medical specialty boards.

Continuing Education:
Certification Designation/s: ABPN MOC

Meetings/Conferences:
Conference Chair: Pat Janda

American Board of Quality Assurance and Utilization Review Physicians, Inc. *(1977)*
6640 Congress St.
New Port Richey, FL 34653
Tel: (800) 998-6030 *Fax:* (727) 569-0195
TollFree: (800) 998-6030
E-Mail: info@abqaurp.org
Website: abqaurp.org
Members: 9000 certified members
Staff: 8
Annual Budget: $500-1,000,000
Tax: 501(c)(6)

Personnel:
Program Coordinator: Barbara Chalmers
　E-Mail: bchalmers@abqaurp.org
Advertising Director: Marvin Diamond
　E-Mail: marvin@lionhrtpub.com
Project Administrator, Exhibit/Sponsor Information: Kim Gorman
　E-Mail: kgorman@abqaurp.org
Coordinator, Education: Deborah Naser
　E-Mail: dnaser@abqaurp.org
Coordinator, Membership Services: Patti Rivers
　E-Mail: privers@abqaurp.org

Historical Note:
ABQAURP's purpose is to improve the overall quality of health care that is provided to the consuming public. Members include physicians and nurses of all specialties, medical directors, hospital administrators, care managers, pharmacists, risk managers and consultants. Membership: $150 (AIHQ Member); $2,500 (Corporate Partner-Silver); $5,000 (Corporate Partner-Gold); $10,000 (Corporate Partner-Platinum); $15,000 (Corporate Partner-Diamond); $150 (Affiliate).

Continuing Education:
Enrollment: 3000
Certification Designation/s: CHCQM

Meetings/Conferences: Annual
Conference Chair: Kim Gorman

Publications:
ABQAURP Diplomate Directory; on-line; adv.
Patient Safety and Quality Healthcare (PSQH); bi-
　monthly; adv.

Membership List Available to Non-members

American Board of Surgery *(1937)*
1617 John F. Kennedy Blvd.
Suite 860
Philadelphia, PA 19103
Tel: (215) 568-4000 *Fax:* (215) 563-5718
Website: absurgery.org
Staff: 20
Annual Budget: $5-10,000,000

Personnel:
Executive Director: Frank R. Lewis Jr. MD
General Counsel: Gabriel L. I. Bevilacqua Esq.
Manager, Information Technology: James F. Fiore
Manager, Operations: Jessica Schreader
Manager, Communications: Christine Shiffer

Historical Note:
ABS Purpose is to conduct examinations of acceptable candidates who seek certification or maintenance of certification by the board, and to issue certificates to all candidates meeting the board's requirements and satisfactorily completing its prescribed examinations and to improve and broaden the opportunities for the graduate education and training of surgeons.

Continuing Education:
Certification Designation/s: GS, VS

Publications:
ABS Newsletter; annually

American Board of Trial Advocates *(1957)*
2001 Bryan St.
Suite 3000
Dallas, TX 75201
Tel: (214) 871-7523 *Fax:* (214) 871-6025
TollFree: (800) 932-2682
E-Mail: national@abota.org
Website: abota.org
Members: 6300 members
Staff: 4

Annual Budget: $2-5,000,000
Tax: 501(c)(6)

Personnel:
Executive Director: Brian Tyson
　E-Mail: briant@abota.org
Coordinator, Professional Education: Jo Ann Murray
　E-Mail: joannm@abota.org
Coordinator, Meetings and Events: Sarah Wahlert
　E-Mail: sarahw@abota.org
Coordinator, Finance: Karan Wright
　E-Mail: karanw@abota.org

Historical Note:
ABOTA's mission is to advance improvement in the ethical and technical standards of practice in the field of advocacy to the end that individual litigants may receive representation and the general public will be benefited by administration of justice.

Meetings/Conferences: Semi-Annual
Conference Chair: Sarah Wahlert
Number of non-conference events/year: 1

Publications:
Membership Directory; on-line
Voir Dire; quarterly

American Board of Veterinary Practitioners *(1978)*
618 Church St.
Suite 220
Nashville, TN 37219-2321
Tel: (615) 250-7794 *Fax:* (615) 254-7047
TollFree: (800) 697-3583
E-Mail: abvp@xmi-amc.com
Website: abvp.com
Members: 850 individuals
Staff: 4
Annual Budget: $250-500,000

Personnel:
Executive Director: Marisa Hackemann
　E-Mail: mhackemann@xmi-amc.com

Historical Note:
ABVP advances the quality of veterinary medicine through certification of veterinarians who demonstrate excellence in species-oriented clinical practice.

Continuing Education:
Enrollment: 50

Meetings/Conferences:
2013 - Phoenix, AZ (Rennaissance Glendale Hotel &
　Spa)/Oct. 31 - Nov. 3

Publications:
ABVP Newsletter; quarterly

American Board of Vocational Experts *(1980)*
3540 Soquel Ave.
Suite A
Santa Cruz, CA 95062
Tel: (831) 464-4890 *Fax:* (831) 576-1417
E-Mail: abve@abve.net
Website: abve.net
Staff: 2
Annual Budget: $50-100,000
Tax: 501(c)(6)

Personnel:
Executive Director: Glenn Zimmermann BA, Esq.
　E-Mail: glenn@btfenterprises.com

Historical Note:
ABVE's mission is to promote forensic vocational credentialing, education, training and research through enhancing the competency of its members. Membership: $140 (Associate); $60 (Student); $220 (Certified).

Continuing Education:
Enrollment: 240
Certification Designation/s: ABVE/F, ABVE/D

Meetings/Conferences: Annual
2013 - Scottsdale, AZ (FireSky Resort and Spa)/April
　12 - 14
2014 - Nashville, TN (The Doubletree Hotel Nashville
　Downtown)/March 28 - 30

Publications:
ABVE Newsletter
Membership Directory; on-line
The Journal of Forensic Vocational Analysis; annually
The Vocational Expert; on-line

Membership List Available to Non-members

American Board of Vocational Experts *(1954)*

American Boat and Yacht Council *(1954)*

613 Third St.
Suite Ten
Annapolis, MD 21403
Tel: (410) 990-4460 *Fax:* (410) 990-4466
E-Mail: information@abycinc.org
Website: abycinc.org
Members: 4700 individuals and companies
Staff: 20
Annual Budget: $2-5,000,000
Tax: 501(c)(3)

Personnel:
President: John Adey
　E-Mail: jadey@abycinc.org
Manager, Educational Services: Crispina Gardner
　E-Mail: cgardner@abycinc.org
Director, Technical Department: Brian Goodwin
　E-Mail: bgoodwin@abycinc.org
Bookkeeper: Mary Lou Prokopchak
　E-Mail: mprokopchak@abycinc.org
Director, Membership Services: Judith Ramsey
　E-Mail: jramsey@abycinc.org
Contact, Marketing: Nina Ullrich
　E-Mail: nullrich@abycinc.org

Historical Note:
ABYC's mission is to develop quality technical practices and engineering standards for the design, construction, maintenance and repair of small craft with reference to their safety. Members are companies and individuals concerned with the design, construction, and maintenance of recreational boats and related equipment. Membership: $285 (Business Annual Member Service Fee and ABYC Foundation donation); $345 (Sustaining Annual Member Service Fee and ABYC Foundation donation); $425 (Manufacturer Annual Member Service Fee and ABYC Foundation donation); $500-5250 (Custom).

Continuing Education:
Certification Designation/s: DESSC, MCC, RAC, CBBC,
GESSC, MSC, EPA, MCC

Meetings/Conferences: Annual
Number of non-conference events/year: 5

Publications:
Membership Directory; on-line
Reference Point; quarterly; adv.

American Boat Builders and Repairers Association *(1943)*
3778 SW 30th Ave.
Ft. Lauderdale, FL 33312
Tel: (954) 654-7821 *Fax:* (954) 239-2600
E-Mail: info@abbra.org
Website: abbra.org
Members: 350 individuals and companies
Staff: 3
Annual Budget: $100-250,000

Personnel:
Executive Director: Gordon Connell
Program Coordinator: Nicole Hoekstra
　E-Mail: nicole@abbra.org
Treasurer: Peter Sabo

Historical Note:
Established as the Atlantic Coast Boat Builders and Repairers Association; assumed its present name in 1965. ABBRA's mission is to strengthen and encourage professionalism in the marine service industry. Membership: $290-525 (Active, based on number of employees); $230 (Professional); $530 (Associate); $345 (International); $75 (Student).

Continuing Education:
Certification Designation/s: MSM, CMF

Meetings/Conferences: Annual
2013 - Ft. Lauderdale, FL/Jan. 16 - 18

Publications:
ABBRACARD Cruising Directory; on-line
CAPSTAN Newsletter; adv.
Membership Directory; on-line

American Boiler Manufacturers Association *(1888)*
8221 Old Courthouse Rd.
Suite 202
Vienna, VA 22182
Tel: (703) 356-7172 *Fax:* (703) 356-4543
Website: abma.com
Members: 100 companies
Staff: 5
Annual Budget: $1-2,000,000
Tax: 501(c)(6)

Personnel:
President and Chief Executive Officer: W. Randall Rawson
    E-Mail: randy@abma.com
Director, Technical Affairs: Geoffrey Halley
    E-Mail: geoff@abma.com
Director, Meetings: Cheryl Jamall
    E-Mail: cheryl@abma.com
General Counsel: Hugh K. Webster
    E-Mail: hugh@abma.com

Historical Note:
Formerly (1960) American Boiler Manufacturers Association. Incorporated in New Jersey. ABMA is dedicated to the advancement and growth of the boiler and combustion equipment industry. It also provides a common ground for information sharing and to achieve better understanding and communication between manufacturers, their customers, government and the public. Members are manufacturers and suppliers of steam and hot water generating systems. Membership: $60-$14,935/year.

Meetings/Conferences: Semi-Annual
Conference Chair: Cheryl Jamall
2013 - Palm Beach Gardens, FL (PGA National Hotel, Resort and Spa)/Jan. 18 - 21
2013 - Colorado Springs, CO (Broadmoor)/June 21 - 24
Number of non-conference events/year: 2

Publications:
ABMA Directory of Members' Products & Services; annually; adv.
ABMA UPDATE e-mail Newsletter; on-line
Member Directory; on-line
Today's Boiler Magazine; semi-annually; adv.

American Bonanza Society *(1967)*
P.O. Box 12888
Wichita, KS 67277
Tel: (316) 945-1700
E-Mail: ABSMail@bonanza.org
Website: bonanza.org
Members: 10000 individuals
Staff: 2
Annual Budget: $100-250,000

Personnel:
Executive Director: J. Whitney Hickman
Advertising Contact: John Shoemaker
    E-Mail: johns@villagepress.com

Historical Note:
An association for Bonanza, Baron, Debonair, and Travel Air enthusiasts. Members own, fly, or have a sincere interest in these Hawker Beechcraft models. Membership: $25-1,200/year.

Meetings/Conferences: Annual

Publications:
ABS Magazine; monthly; adv.

American Book Producers Association *(1980)*
151 W. 19th St.
Third Floor
New York, NY 10011
Tel: (917) 741-1919 *Fax:* (212) 675-1364
E-Mail: office@abpaonline.org
Website: abpaonline.org
Members: 55 companies
Staff: 4
Annual Budget: $10-25,000
Tax: 501(c)(6)

Personnel:
President: Richard Rothschild
Administrator: Kirsten Hall
Treasurer: Valerie Tomaselli

Historical Note:
ABPA serves as a trade association for independent book producers called packagers in the United States and Canada. Members are companies or individuals that develop concepts for books based on a contractual agreement with a publisher, a business or other source. Membership: $595/year (Company).

Publications:
ABPA Bimonthly Newsletter; bi-monthly
ABPA Member Directory; on-line

Membership List Available to Non-members

American Booksellers Association *(1900)*
200 White Plains Rd.
Suite 600
Tarrytown, NY 10591
Tel: (914) 591-2665 *Fax:* (914) 591-2720
TollFree: (800) 637-0037

E-Mail: info@bookweb.org
Website: bookweb.org
Members: 2100 companies
Staff: 42
Annual Budget: $2-5,000,000
Tax: 501(c)(6)

Personnel:
Chief Executive Officer: Oren Teicher
    E-Mail: oren@bookweb.org
Chief Financial Officer: Eleanor Chang
    E-Mail: ellie@bookweb.org
Manager, Marketing and Designer: Greg Galloway
    E-Mail: greg@bookweb.org
Development Officer: Mark Nichols
    E-Mail: mark@bookweb.org
Meetings and Planning Officer: Jill Perlstein
    E-Mail: jill@bookweb.org
Membership and Marketing Officer: Meg Z. Smith
    E-Mail: meg@booksense.com
Director, Technology: Matt Supko
    E-Mail: matt@bookweb.org

Historical Note:
ABA's mission is to provide advocacy, education, opportunities for peer interaction, support services, and new business models to independent, professional booksellers. Membership: $299-10,000 (Regular); $350 (Foriegn/Provisional/Associate); $200 (Auxiliary/Bookstores); $199 (New Member/New Stores).

Meetings/Conferences: Annual
Conference Chair: Jill Perlstein
2013 - Kansas City, MO/Feb. 23 - 25
2013 - New York City, NY (Jacobs Javits Center)/May 30 - June 1/over 100 exhibitors
Number of non-conference events/year: 2

Publications:
Booksellers Resource Directory
Bookselling This Week; weekly; adv.
Membership Directory; on-line

Membership List Available to Non-members

American Border Leicester Association *(1973)*
692 Smithfield Rd.
Millerton, NY 12546
Tel: (518) 789-6113
E-Mail: info@ablasheep.org
Website: ablasheep.org
Members: 175 individuals
Staff: 10
Annual Budget: Under $10,000

Personnel:
Webmaster: JoAnne Tuncy
    E-Mail: webmaster@ablasheep.org

Historical Note:
ABLA's mission is to promote and register border leicester sheep in the United States and Canada. Membership: $20 (Individual); $15 (Junior).

Publications:
ABLA Newsletter
Membership Directory; on-line

American Botanical Council *(1988)*
P.O. Box 144345
Austin, TX 78714-4345
Tel: (512) 926-4900 *Fax:* (512) 926-2345
TollFree: (800) 373-7105
Website: abc.herbalgram.org
Staff: 16
Annual Budget: $1-2,000,000
Tax: 501(c)(3)

Personnel:
Founder and Executive Director: Mark Blumenthal
Education Coordinator: Becky Andrews LAc, ND
Coordinator, Membership Services: Janie Carter
Sales Representative: Lance Lawhon
Coordinator, Finance: Cecelia Thompson

Historical Note:
ABC is dedicated to providing accurate and reliable information for consumers, healthcare practitioners, researchers, educators, industry and the media. Membership: $50-70 (Individual); $100-120 (Academic); $150-170 (Professional).

Meetings/Conferences: Annual

Publications:
HerbalEGram; monthly; adv.
HerbalGram; quarterly; adv.
HerbClip; semi-monthly; adv.

American Brachytherapy Society *(1978)*
12100 Sunset Hills Rd.
Suite 130
Reston, VA 20190
Tel: (703) 234-4078 *Fax:* (703) 435-4390
E-Mail: abs@americanbrachytherapy.org
Website: americanbrachytherapy.org
Members: 1200 individuals
Staff: 3
Annual Budget: $500-1,000,000
Tax: 501(c)(6)

Personnel:
Executive Director: Rick A Guggolz
    E-Mail: rguggolz@drohanmgmt.com
Administrative Assistant: Colleen MacCutcheon
    E-Mail: cmaccutcheon@drohanmgmt.com
Program Manager: Melissa Pomerene

Historical Note:
ABS's mission is to benefit patients by providing information directly to the consumer, by promoting the highest possible standards of practice of brachytherapy, and to benefit health care professionals by encouraging improved and continuing education for radiation oncologists and other health care professionals involved in the treatment of cancer. Members are oncologists and physicists working in the field of brachytherapy. Membership: $180 (Regular); $100 (Associate); $90 (1st year Post Doctorate); $500 (Commercial); $0 (Resident).

Meetings/Conferences: Annual
2013 - New Orleans, LA (Hyatt Regency New Orleans)/April 18 - 20
2014 - San Diego, CA (Manchester Grand Hyatt San Diego)/April 3 - 5
Number of non-conference events/year: 2

Publications:
ABS Newsletter; semi-annually; adv.
Brachytherapy; bi-monthly; adv.

Membership List Available to Non-members

American Brahman Breeders Association *(1924)*
3003 S. Loop West
Suite 520
Houston, TX 77054
Tel: (713) 349-0854 *Fax:* (713) 349-9795
E-Mail: abba@brahman.org
Website: brahman.org
Members: 1200 individuals
Staff: 8
Annual Budget: $500-1,000,000
Tax: 501(c)(5)

Personnel:
Executive Vice President and Contact, Shows and Special Projects: Chris Shivers
    E-Mail: cshivers@brahman.org
Office Manager and Recording Secretary: Armelinda Ibarra
Director, Communications: Libby Williams
    E-Mail: lwilliams@brahman.org

Historical Note:
Represents breeders and fanciers of Brahman beef cattle. ABBA's mission is to maintain the purity of Brahman cattle and to use all possible and available means to promote interest in the breed. Membership: $100/year (Active).

Continuing Education:
Certification Designation/s: ABBA F-1

Meetings/Conferences: Annual
Conference Chair: Chris Shivers
Number of non-conference events/year: 2

Publications:
Brahman Journal; monthly; adv.
The American Brahman Review; quarterly; adv.

Membership List Available to Non-members

American Brahmousin Council
P.O. Box 88
Whitesboro, TX 76273
Tel: (903) 564-3995
E-Mail: info@brahmousin.org
Website: brahmousin.org
Members: 95 ranches
Staff: 1

Personnel:
Interim Director: Bob Cummins

Historical Note:

ABC's mission is to provide returns relative to feed efficiency and dressing percentage. Membership: $200 (Lifetime); $50 (Annual); $25 (Junior/Associate).

Publications:
Member Directory; on-line

American Bralers Association (1983)
P.O. Box 75
Burton, TX 77835
Tel: (409) 289-3021 *Fax:* (409) 289-0170
Members: 200 individuals
Staff: 1
Annual Budget: $25-50,000

Personnel:
President: Marcus Brosche

Historical Note:
Maintains a registry of Bralers (a crossbreed of Brahman and Salers cattle). Has no paid officers or full-time staff. Membership: $25/year.

American Bridge Teachers' Association (1957)
P. O. Box 232
Greenwood, MO 64034-0232
Tel: (816) 237-0519
E-Mail: info@abta.org
Website: atbahome.com
Members: 500 individuals
Staff: 3
Annual Budget: $25-50,000
Tax: 501(c)(6)

Personnel:
Webmaster: Luise Lee
     E-Mail: webmaster@abtahome.com
Business Secretary and Treasurer: Kathy Rolfe
     E-Mail: krolfe5@comcast.net
Editor: Charlie Williams
     E-Mail: slamhand@verizon.net

Historical Note:
ABTA's mission is to help those who teach bridge to do it better, more effectively, more knowledgeably, more professionally. Has members all over the world. Membership: $35 (Individual); $49 (Household).

Meetings/Conferences: Annual

Publications:
ABTA Quarterly Magazine; quarterly; adv.
Membership Directory; annually

American British White Park Association (1999)
2762 Hydro-Pondsville Rd
Smiths Grove, KY 42171
Tel: (270) 563-9733
E-Mail: office@whitecattle.org
Website: whitecattle.org
Members: 527 individuals
Staff: 2
Annual Budget: $10-25,000

Personnel:
President: Greg Powell
     E-Mail: gregpowell@sofwhitecattle.com

Historical Note:
Founded as White Park Cattle Association of America and assumed its current name in 1999. ABWPA is a Breeder and fancier of the Park cattle. Membership: $100 (Marketing Member/Adult Member/Associate); $10 (Junior); $20 (Transfer from British White Cattle Association); $50 (Gift Adult).

Meetings/Conferences: Annual

Publications:
MEmbeship Directory; on-line
White Cattle Journal; quarterly

American Broncho-Esophagological Association (1917)
730 Welch Rd.
Palo Alto, CA 94304
E-Mail: ABEA@facs.org
Website: abea.net
Members: 400 individuals
Staff: 5
Annual Budget: $50-100,000
Tax: 501(c)(3)

Personnel:
President: Dr. Peter J. Koltai MD
     E-Mail: pkoltai@ohns.stanford.edu

Historical Note:

Established as the American Bronchoscopic Society; assumed its present name in 1928. Affiliated with the American Academy of Otolaryngology - Head and Neck Surgery. ABEA's mission is to educate physicians regarding optimal evaluation and management of upper aerodigestive tract disorders. Membership: $185/year (Active members); $100/year (Associate members and Members who are on active duty in the US Military).

Meetings/Conferences: Annual
2013 - Orlando, FL (JW Marriott Orlando Grande Lakes)/April 10 - 14
2014 - Las Vegas, NV (Caesars Palace Las Vegas Hotel and Casino)/May 14 - 18
2015 - Boston, MA (Sheraton Boston Hotel)/April 22 - 26
Number of non-conference events/year: 2

Publications:
American Broncho-Esophagological Association Spring Newsletter
Membership Directory; on-line

American Brush Manufacturers Association (1917)
736 Main Ave.
Suite Seven
Aurora, CO 81301
Tel: (720) 392-2262 *Fax:* (866) 837-8450
E-Mail: info@abma.org
Website: abma.org
Members: 165 companies
Staff: 3
Annual Budget: $250-500,000
Tax: 501(c)(6)

Personnel:
Executive Director: David C. Parr

Historical Note:
Absorbed the National Broom and Mop Council in 1982. ABMA's mission is to help American brush manufacturers by enhancing industry knowledge, by providing networking opportunities for, and promoting profitability for, its members and to promote and strengthen value for its members to be the preferred and innovative source for broom, brush and mop products worldwide. Membership: $640-2,560 (International/Active, based on sales volume); $940-3,760 (Affiliate/Supplier, based on sales volume).

Meetings/Conferences: Annual
2013 - Miami, FL (Eden Roc Renaissance Miami Beach)/March 13 - 16
2014 - Rancho Mirage, CA (Westin Mission Hills Resort and Spa)/March 26 - 29
2015 - St. Petersburg, FL (Renaissance Vinoy Resort and Golf Club)/March 18 - 21
2016 - Bonita Springs, FL (Hyatt Coconut Point)/March 2 - 5
2017 - Orlando, FL (Hyatt Grand Cypress)/March 22 - 25
Number of non-conference events/year: 1

Publications:
Brush Up Monthly; monthly
Member Directory; on-line
The Freight Bulletin; monthly
Washington Update; monthly

American Bryological and Lichenological Society (1898)
Bureau of Land Management
1387 S. Vinnell Way
Boise, ID 83709
Tel: (208) 373-3824
Website: abls.org
Members: 625 individuals
Staff: 4
Annual Budget: $100-250,000
Tax: 501(c)(3)

Personnel:
President: Roger Rosentreter
     E-Mail: roger_rosentreter@blm.gov

Historical Note:
Originated in 1898 in Plymouth, New Hampshire, as the Sullivant Moss Chapter of the Agassiz Association, became independent in 1900 under the name of Sullivant Moss Society and name changed to American Bryological Society in 1949 and again changed to the American Bryological and Lichenological Society in 1969. ABLS, affiliated with American Institute of Biological Sciences, is devoted to the study of all aspects of bryophytes and lichen-forming fungi. Membership is open to all persons (professionals and amateurs) with an interest in these organisms. Membership:

$20 (Individual); $10 (Student); $25 (Family); $35 (Contributing Member).

Meetings/Conferences: Annual
Conference Chair: John J. Atwood
2013 - New Orleans, LA/July 26 - 31
Number of non-conference events/year: 3

Publications:
Evansia; quarterly
Membership Directory
The Bryologist; quarterly

American Buckskin Registry Association (1965)
1141 Hartnell Ave.
Redding, CA 96002-2113
Tel: (530) 223-1420 *Fax:* (530) 223-1420
Website: americanbuckskin.org
Members: 6000 individuals
Staff: 3
Annual Budget: $100-250,000

Personnel:
Executive Secretary and Treasurer: Georgi Jones
     E-Mail: georgijones@aol.com

Historical Note:
Established as the Buckskin Registry Association, assumed its present name in 1965. ABRA is a non-profit organization whose purpose is to collect, record and preserve the pedigrees of Buckskin, Dun, Red Dun and Grulla horses and ponies. Members are owners, breeders, and dealers of the Buckskin horse. Sponsors shows and other promotional events. Membership: $10-200/year.

Publications:
Membership Directory; on-line

American Bureau of Metal Statistics (1975)
P.O. Box 805
Chatham, NJ 07928
Tel: (973) 701-2299 *Fax:* (973) 701-2152
E-Mail: info@abms.com
Website: abms.com
Members: 5 companies
Staff: 3
Annual Budget: $100-250,000

Personnel:
Executive Director: Patricia T. Foley
Operations Manager: Christine Harashinski

Historical Note:
Created by a merger of the American Bureau of Metal Statistics (1920) with the Copper Institute (organized in 1927) and the United States Copper Association (established in 1934) ABMS collects and disseminates statistical industry data on copper, lead, zinc and other non-ferrous metals. It also collects and compiles statistical information for the Copper Development Association and other non-ferrous metal trade associations. Membership: dues assessed pro-rata.

Meetings/Conferences:
Number of non-conference events/year: 10

Publications:
Membership Directory

American Bureau of Shipping (1862)
16855 Northchase Dr.
Houston, TX 77060
Tel: (281) 877-5800 *Fax:* (281) 877-5803
E-Mail: abs-worldhq@eagle.org
Website: eagle.org
Members: 814 individuals
Staff: 1600
Annual Budget: Over $100,000,000
Tax: 501(c)(6)

Personnel:
President and Chief Executive Officer: Christopher J. Wiernicki
     E-Mail: cwiernicki@eagle.org
Vice President, Human Resources: T. Ray Bennett
     E-Mail: rbennett@eagle.org
Senior Vice President and Chief Information Officer: Gary A. Latin
     E-Mail: glatin@eagle.org
Publications Administrator: Carole McElroy
     E-Mail: abs_pubs@eagle.org
Senior Vice President, General Counsel and Corporate Secretary: Thomas A. Miller
     E-Mail: tmiller@eagle.org
Manager, Marketing and Communications: Rhonda Patterson
     E-Mail: rpatterson@eagle.org

Chairman: Robert D. Somerville
  E-Mail: rsomerville@eagle.org
Vice President, External Affairs: Stewart H. Wade
  E-Mail: abs-worldhq@eagle.org
Executive Vice President and Chief Financial Officer:
  Jeffrey J. Weiner
  E-Mail: jweiner@eagle.org

Historical Note:
ABS's mission is to serve the public interest as well as the needs of its clients by promoting the security of life, property and the natural environment.

Continuing Education:
Certification Designation/s: ISM, ISPS, MLC, HSQE, SOLAS

Meetings/Conferences:
Number of non-conference events/year: 15

Publications:
ABS International Directory; on-line
ABS Newsletter; quarterly
Surveyor; quarterly

American Burn Association *(1967)*
311 S. Wacker Dr.
Suite 4150
Chicago, IL 60606
Tel: (312) 642-9260 *Fax:* (312) 642-9130
TollFree: (800) 548-2876
E-Mail: info@ameriburn.org
Website: ameriburn.org
Members: 3500 individuals
Staff: 14
Annual Budget: $5-10,000,000

Personnel:
Chief Executive Officer and Executive Director: John A.
  Krichbaum JD
  E-Mail: krichbaum@ameriburn.org
Deputy Chief Executive Officer and Chief Operating Officer:
  Susan M. Browning MPH
  E-Mail: browning@ameriburn.org
Senior Director, Meeting Planning and Exhibitor Relations:
  M. Jane Burns
  E-Mail: burns@ameriburn.org
Coordinator, Membership Services: Rita Postilion
  E-Mail: rpostilion@ameriburn.org
Director, Accounting: Janet Turner
  E-Mail: turner@ameriburn.org

Historical Note:
ABA's mission is to advocate excellence in care by burn centers through a rigorous review process. ABA members include burn care physicians, nurses, physical and occupational therapists, social workers, psychologists, nutritionists, rehabilitation experts, and research personnel. Firefighters, attorneys, administrators, prevention educators, and burn patients also comprise the ABA membership. Membership: $340 (Physicians/Fellows); $140 (Non-Physicians/Nurses/Residents); $80 (Students).

Meetings/Conferences: Annual
Conference Chair: M. Jane Burns
2013 - Palm Spring, CA (Palm Springs Convention
  Center)/April 23 - 26
2014 - Boston, MA/March 25 - 28
2015 - Chicago, IL/April 21 - 24
2016 - Las Vegas, NV/May 3 - 6
2017 - Boston, MA/March 21 - 24
2018 - Chicago, IL/April 10 - 13
2019 - Las Vegas, NV/April 9 - 12
2021 - Chicago, IL/April 6 - 9

Publications:
ABA Newsletter; on-line
Journal of Burn Care and Research; bi-monthly
Membership Directory; on-line

American Bus Association *(1926)*
111 K St. NE
Ninth Floor
Washington, DC 20002
Tel: (202) 842-1645 *Fax:* (202) 842-0850
TollFree: (800) 283-2877
E-Mail: abainfo@buses.org
Website: buses.org
Members: 3800 companies and other
  organizations
Staff: 22
Annual Budget: $5-10,000,000
Tax: 501(c)(6)

Personnel:

President and Chief Executive Officer: Peter J. Pantuso
  CTIS
  E-Mail: ppantuso@buses.org
Chief Financial Officer: Eric Braendel
  E-Mail: ebraendel@buses.org
Membership Services Coordinator: Allison Brewer
  E-Mail: abrewer@buses.org
*Senior Vice President, Meetings, Education and Membership
  Services:* Lynn M. Brewer
  E-Mail: lbrewer@buses.org
Senior Director, Sponsorships and Meetings Planning: Jana
  Fields
  E-Mail: jfields@buses.org
Senior Vice President, Government Affairs and Policy:
  Clyde J. Hart Jr.
  E-Mail: chart@buses.org
Senior Director, Membership Services: Vicki Osman CTIS
  E-Mail: vosman@buses.org
Senior Director, Communications: Dan Ronan
  E-Mail: dronan@buses.org
*Senior Vice President, Communications, Marketing and
  Media Relations:* Eron Shosteck
  E-Mail: eshosteck@buses.org

Historical Note:
Formerly the Motor Bus Division and later the National Motor Bus Division of the American Automobile Association. Name changed to the National Association of Motor Bus Operators until 1960 when it became the National Association of Motor Bus Owners. Assumed its present name on Sept. 19, 1977. ABA's mission is to develop and promote methods, materials, and procedures to improve motorcoach safety. Members are privately owned bus companies, bus manufacturers, accessory manufacturers, travel-tourism businesses, and organizations and others concerned with bus service. Membership: $400-40,000 (Motorcoach Operator); $400 (Tour Operator); $350-1,000 (Travel Industry/Associate); $100 (Special Introductory Offer for New Bus Operator).

Continuing Education:
Enrollment: 75
Certification Designation/s: CTIS

Meetings/Conferences: Annual
Conference Chair: Jana Fields
2013 - Charlotte, NC (Charlotte Convention Center)/
  Jan. 5 - 9
2014 - Nashville, TN (Nashville Convention Center)/
  Jan. 11 - 15
2014 - Nashville, TN/Jan. 17 - 21

Publications:
ABA Insider; bi-weekly; adv.
Destinations; bi-monthly; adv.
Equip Magazine; on-line; adv.
Foundation Focus; bi-weekly
Market Place Today; daily
Member Alerts; on-line
The Motorcoach Marketer; annually; adv.
Top 100 Events In North America Magazine; annually;
  adv.

Membership List Available to Non-members

American Business Media *(1906)*
675 Third Ave.
Seventh Floor
New York, NY 10017-5704
Tel: (212) 661-6360 *Fax:* (212) 370-0736
E-Mail: info@abmmail.com
Website: americanbusinessmedia.com
Members: 200 companies
Staff: 21
Annual Budget: $2-5,000,000

Personnel:
President and Chief Executive Officer: Clark Pettit
Director, Research and Content: Michael Alterio
Vice President, Events: Michael Burns
Vice President, Recruitment and Retention: Claudia
  Flowers
Chief Financial Officer and General Manager: Todd Hittle
*Executive Manager, Membership Services and Business
  Development:* Debbie Humphreys
Vice President, Content and Programming: Matthew
  Kinsman
Manager, Marketing and Communications: Kate Patton

Historical Note:
Formed by a merger of Associated Business Publications (founded in 1906) and National Business Publications (founded in 1948). Absorbed Agricultural Publishers Association in 2002. ABM's mission is to enhance the knowledge and best practices of leading b-to-b media and

information companies and their employees. Members are specialized business magazines with audited circulation.

Meetings/Conferences:
Conference Chair: Michael Burns
2013 - Amelia Island, FL (Omni Amelia Island
  Plantation Resort)/April 28 - May 1
Number of non-conference events/year: 5

Publications:
Business-to-Business Magazine
Inside the Beltway; on-line; adv.
Member Directory

American Business Women's Association *(1949)*
11050 Roe Ave.
Suite 200
Overland Park, KS 66211
TollFree: (800) 228-0007
E-Mail: abwa@abwa.org
Website: abwa.org
Members: 545,000 individuals
Staff: 25
Annual Budget: $2-5,000,000
Tax: 501(c)(6)

Personnel:
Executive Director: Rene Street
Manager, Business Development: Cynthia Bell
  E-Mail: cbell@abwa.org

Historical Note:
ABWA strives to bring together businesswomen of diverse occupations and provides opportunities for them to help themselves and others grow personally and professionally through leadership, education, networking support and national recognition. Membership: $90 (Basic); $115 (Express Network).

Meetings/Conferences: Annual
Conference Chair: Cynthia Bell
Number of non-conference events/year: 6

Publications:
District Newsletters; semi-annually; adv.
Express Network Newsletter; bi-monthly; adv.

American Butter Institute *(1908)*
2101 Wilson Blvd.
Suite 400
Arlington, VA 22201
Tel: (703) 243-5630 *Fax:* (703) 841-9328
E-Mail: aminer@nmpf.org
Website: nmpf.org/ABI
Members: 31 companies
Staff: 2
Annual Budget: $100-250,000
Tax: 501(c)(6)

Personnel:
Executive Director: Jerry Kozak
  E-Mail: jkozak@nmpf.org
Senior Director, Executive Office and Membership Services:
  Anuja Miner
  E-Mail: aminer@nmpf.org

Historical Note:
Organized as the National Association of Creamery Butter Manufacturers. ABI's purpose is to promote and protect the interests and welfare of the industry.

Meetings/Conferences: Annual
2013 - Chicago, IL (Chicago Marriott Downtown
  Magnificent Mile)/April 28 - 30

American Cable Association *(1993)*
One Pkwy. Center
Suite 212
Pittsburgh, PA 15220
Tel: (412) 922-8300 *Fax:* (412) 922-2110
E-Mail: aca@americancable.org
Website: americancable.org
Members: 1100 companies
Staff: 9
Annual Budget: $2-5,000,000

Personnel:
President and Chief Executive Officer: Matthew M. Polka
  E-Mail: mpolka@americancable.org
Vice President, Communications: Ted Hearn
  E-Mail: thearn@americancable.org
Director, Meetings and Industry Affairs: Stacey DeLisio
  Leech
Vice President, Government Affairs: Ross Lieberman
  E-Mail: rlieberman@americancable.org

Vice President and Chief Operating Officer: Robert E. Shema
E-Mail: rshema@americancable.org
Director, Administration: Karen D. Yochum

Historical Note:
Through active participation in the legislative and regulatory process, ACA and its members advocate for the interests of their customers, their companies, and their communities. Membership is comprised of small, independent cable companies who provide broadband services for cable subscribers in rural and small suburban areas. Membership : $800/year (Associate).

Meetings/Conferences: Annual
Conference Chair: Stacey DeLisio Leech
2013 - Washington, DC (Grand Hyatt Washington)/ March 12 - 15
Number of non-conference events/year: 2

Publications:
ACAction Electronic Newsletter; on-line

Membership List Available to Non-members

American Camp Association (1910)
5000 State Rd. 67 North
Martinsville, IN 46151-7902
Tel: (765) 342-8456 Fax: (765) 342-2065
TollFree: (800) 428-2267
E-Mail: aca@acacamps.org
Website: acacamps.org
Members: 6000 individuals
Staff: 44
Annual Budget: $50-100,000
Tax: 501(c)(3)

Personnel:
Chief Executive Officer: Peg L. Smith
E-Mail: psmith@acacamps.org
Communications Editor: Julie Anderson
E-Mail: janderson@ACAcamps.org
Chief Financial Officer: Rhonda Begley
E-Mail: rbegley@acacamps.org
Director, Knowledge Systems: Kim Brosnan
E-Mail: kbrosnan@acacamps.org
Director, Program Development and Research Application: Barry Garst
E-Mail: bgarst@ACAcamps.org
Editor-in-Chief: Harriet Lowe
E-Mail: hlowe@ACAcamps.org
National Sales Associate: Paula McCarns
E-Mail: pmccarns@acacamps.org
Accountant: Denise McClure
E-Mail: dmcclure@acacamps.org
Director, Information Technology: Tom Schenk
E-Mail: tschenk@acacamps.org

Historical Note:
Formerly known as the Camp Directors' Association of America (1924) and the American Camping Association (1935). Assumed its current name in 2004. ACA's mission is to enrich the lives of children, youth and adults through the camp experience. It also sponsors accreditation programs for camps and educational programs for camp director/owners. Membership: $600 (Businesses); $200 (Individual); $95 (ACA Standards Visitor/Volunteer to My Organization/Educator/Expanded Learning Staff); $60 (Retiree); $35 (Student).

Meetings/Conferences: Annual
Conference Chair: Paula McCarns
2013 - Dallas, TX (Hyatt Regency Dallas at Reunion)/ Feb. 12 - 15/1-10 exhibitors
Number of non-conference events/year: 5

Publications:
Camping Magazine; bi-monthly; adv.
The CampLine

American Canoe Association (1880)
108 Hanover St.
Fredericksburg, VA 22401
Tel: (540) 907-4460 Fax: (888) 229-3792
E-Mail: aca@americancanoe.org
Website: americancanoe.org
Members: 50,000 members and over 300 Clubs and Affiliates
Staff: 17
Annual Budget: $500-1,000,000
Tax: 501(c)(3)

Personnel:
Executive Director: Wade Blackwood
E-Mail: wblackwood@americancanoe.org

Coordinator, Safety, Education, Instruction and Outreach: Kelsey Bracewell
E-Mail: kbracewell@americancanoe.org
Office Manager: Cireena Katto
E-Mail: ckatto@americancanoe.org
Chief Operating Officer: Christopher Stec
E-Mail: cstec@americancanoe.org
Coordinator, Membership Services: Rachel Vetterlein
E-Mail: rvetterlein@americancanoe.org

Historical Note:
ACA's mission is to serve the broader paddling public by providing education related to all aspects of paddling; stewardship support to help protect paddling environments; and sanctioning of programs and events to promote paddlesport competition and recreation.

Meetings/Conferences: Annual

Publications:
Adventure Kayak
Canoeroots
Kayak Angler
Rapid

American Case Management Association
11701 W. 36th St.
Little Rock, AR 72211
Tel: (501) 907-2262 Fax: (501) 227-4247
Website: acmaweb.org
Staff: 1
Annual Budget: $1-2,000,000
Tax: 501(c)(3)

Personnel:
Chief Executive Officer: Greg L. Cunningham MHA

Historical Note:
ACMA's mission is to offer solutions to support the evolving collaborative practice of Hospital/Health System Case Management and to provide innovative professional development services. Membership: $135/year.

Continuing Education:
Certification Designation/s: ACM, AMP, ACMA

Meetings/Conferences:
2013 - San Diego, CA (Manchester Hyatt San Diego)/ April 8 - 11

Publications:
ACMA e-Newsletter; monthly

American Cash Flow Association (1990)
255 S. Orange Ave.
Suite 600
Orlando, FL 32801
Tel: (407) 206-6523 Fax: (407) 206-6507
TollFree: (800) 253-1294
E-Mail: info@americancashflow.com
Website: association.americancashflow.com
Members:
1500 companies
25000 individuals
60 chapters
Staff: 4

Personnel:
President and Chief Executive Officer: Frederic Rewey

Historical Note:
Formerly (1997) the National Association of Entrepreneurs. ACFA manages the infrastructure of the cash flow industry. Members are professionals working in fields related to cash flow and debt instruments. Membership: $299/year.

Continuing Education:
Certification Designation/s: CFS, CCFC

American Catalog Mailers Association
P.O. Box 11173
Hauppauge, NY 11788-0941
Tel: (800) 509-9514
TollFree: (800) 509-9514
E-Mail: info@catalogmailers.org
Website: catalogmailers.org
Members: 129 Members
Staff: 7
Annual Budget: $500-1,000,000

Personnel:
President and Executive Director: Hamilton Davison
E-Mail: hdavison@catalogmailers.org
Vice President and Deputy Director: Paul Miller
E-Mail: pmiller@catalogmailers.org

Historical Note:
The American Catalog Mailers Association was formed by catalogers to advance catalog interests in commercial,

regulatory, and public relation venues. ACMA's mission is to provide their members with representation on issues that directly concern their immediate and long term commercial interests. Membership: $1,000-30,000 (Catalog); $2,500-30,000 (Supplier).

Publications:
E-Newsletter; on-line

American Catholic Correctional Chaplains Association (1952)
2522 Calle Delfino
Santa Fe, NM 87505
Tel: (505) 471-6089 Fax: (920) 324-6254
E-Mail: info@catholiccorrectionalchaplains.org
Website: catholiccorrectionalchaplains.org
Members: 150 individuals
Staff: 3
Annual Budget: Under $10,000

Personnel:
Treasurer: Teodoro Rael
E-Mail: teodororael@aol.com

Historical Note:
Formerly American Catholic Prison Chaplains Association. ACCCA is committed to promoting the principles of restorative justice for all involved with, or affected by, the criminal justice system. Membership: $40 (Individual); $25 (Retiree/Volunteer).

Continuing Education:
Certification Designation/s: ACCCA-CC

Publications:
Newsletter

American Catholic Historical Association (1919)
Dealy Hall, Room 637
441 E. Fordham Rd.
Bronx, NY 10458
Tel: (718) 817-3830 Fax: (718) 817-5690
E-Mail: acha@fordham.edu
Website: achahistory.org
Members: 2000 individuals
Staff: 3
Annual Budget: $50-100,000
Tax: 501(c)(3)

Personnel:
Executive Secretary and Treasurer: R. Bentley Anderson
Editor: Nelson H. Minnich

Historical Note:
A professional society of those interested in the history of the Catholic Church and the promotion of historical scholarship among Catholics. Sponsors the John Tarcy Ellis Dissertation Award, in support of graduate work on the history of the Catholic Church. Membership: $60 (Individual); $30 (Student); $40 (Retired/Emeritus).

Meetings/Conferences:
2013 - New Orleans, LA/Jan. 3 - 6
2013 - Easton, MA (Stonehill College)/April 5 - 6
2014 - Washington, DC/Jan. 2 - 5

Publications:
Catholic Historical Review; quarterly

American Catholic Philosophical Association (1926)
Center for Thomistic Studies, University of St. Thomas
3800 Montrose Blvd.
Houston, TX 77006
Tel: (713) 942-3483 Fax: (713) 525-6964
E-Mail: acpa@stthom.edu
Website: acpaweb.org
Members: 1600 members
Staff: 3
Annual Budget: $50-100,000

Personnel:
President: Richard C. Taylor
Secretary: Edward Houser
Treasurer: Steven Jensen

Historical Note:
ACPA's purpose is to promote the advancement of philosophy as an intellectual discipline consonant with Catholic tradition and strives to develop philosophical scholarship, to improve the teaching of philosophy and to communicate with other individuals and groups with similar aims. Members are scholars and individuals interested in Catholic philosophy. Membership: $53 (Professor/ Instructor/Lecturer); $1,000 (Life); $99 (Institution/ Library); $44 (Associate); $26 (Student).

Meetings/Conferences: Annual
2013 - Indianapolis, IN/Oct. 25 - 27

Publications:
American Catholic Philosophical Quarterly; quarterly; adv.

Membership List Available to Non-members

American Ceramics Society *(1898)*
600 N. Cleveland Ave.
Suite 210
Washington, OH 43082
Tel: (240) 646-7054 *Fax:* (240) 396-5637
TollFree: (866) 721-3322
E-Mail: customerservice@ceramics.org
Website: ceramics.org
Members: 9,500 scientists, engineers, researchers, manufacturers, plant personnel, educators, students, marketing and sales professionals
Staff: 38
Annual Budget: $5-10,000,000

Personnel:
Executive Director: Charles Spahr
  E-Mail: cspahr@ceramics.org
Director, Marketing and Membership Services: Megan Bricker
  E-Mail: mbricker@ceramics.org
Manager, Technical Content and Accreditation: Greg Geiger
  E-Mail: ggeiger@ceramics.org
Manager, Human Resources and Executive Assistant: Susan LaBute
  E-Mail: slabute@ceramics.org
Director, Technical Publications and Meetings: Mark Mecklenborg
  E-Mail: mmecklenborg@ceramics.org
Manager, Marketing: Andrea Silnes
  E-Mail: asilnes@ceramics.org
Director, Communications and Bulletin Editor: Peter Wray
  E-Mail: pwray@ceramics.org

Historical Note:
Incorporated in Ohio in 1905. ACerS's mission is to advance the study, understanding and use of ceramic and related materials, for the benefit of members and society. Members are scientists, engineers and industrialists who produce products related to ceramics and related materials. Membership: $120 (Individual/Associate); $325-1000 (Corporate).

Meetings/Conferences:
Conference Chair: Mark Mecklenborg
2013 - Daytona Beach, FL/Jan. 27 - Feb. 1
2013 - Portland, OR (Hilton Portland and Executive Tower)/Aug. 4 - 7
2013 - Montreal, QC (Palais Des Congres de Montreal)/Oct. 27 - 31
2014 - Daytona Beach, FL/Jan. 26 - 31
2014 - Pittsburgh, PA (David L. Lawrence Convention Center)/Oct. 12 - 16
2015 - Daytona Beach, FL/Jan. 25 - 30
2016 - Daytona Beach, FL/Jan. 24 - 29
2017 - Daytona Beach, FL/Jan. 22 - 27
Number of non-conference events/year: 13

Publications:
ACerS In Focus
Bulletin; on-line; adv.
Ceramic Arts Daily; daily
Ceramic Engineering & Science Proceedings
Ceramic Tech Today
e International Journal of Applied Ceramic Technology
Journal of the American Ceramic Society; monthly

American Chain of Warehouses *(1911)*
156 Flamingo Dr.
Beecher, IL 60401
Tel: (708) 946-9792 *Fax:* (708) 946-9793
E-Mail: info@acwi.org
Website: acwi.org
Members: 50 commercial warehouses
Staff: 2
Annual Budget: $100-250,000

Personnel:
Vice President, Sales and Marketing: William L. Jurus
  E-Mail: bjurus@acwi.org

Historical Note:
ACWI is an association of warehouses including privately owned and operated public and contract warehousing companies operating over 12 million square feet of warehouse space throughout North America. Warehouse members are providers of third party logistics services, providing personalized attention for a wide range of
supply chain, logistics, storage, and distribution solutions.
Membership: based on a formula.

Publications:
ACWI Newsletter; monthly
Membership Directory; on-line

American Chamber of Commerce Executives *(1914)*
4875 Eisenhower Ave.
Suite 250
Alexandria, VA 22304
Tel: (703) 998-0072 *Fax:* (703) 212-9512
TollFree: (800) 394-2223
E-Mail: info-central@acce.org
Website: acce.org
Members: 7000 individuals and 1400 chambers
Staff: 28
Annual Budget: $2-5,000,000
Tax: 501(c)(3)

Personnel:
President: Michael Fleming
  E-Mail: mfleming@acce.org
Chief Financial Officer: Jacqui Cook
  E-Mail: jcook@acce.org
Contact, Membership Services: Dana Ketterling
  E-Mail: dketterling@acce.org
Manager, Communications and Marketing: Tania Kohut
  E-Mail: tkohut@acce.org
Senior Vice President, Member and Sponsor Relations: Chris Mead
  E-Mail: cmead@acce.org
Vice President, Professional Development and Convention: Crystal Moore
  E-Mail: cmoore@acce.org
Director, Administration: Maryann Niner
  E-Mail: mniner@acce.org
Vice President, Communications and Networks: Ian Scott
  E-Mail: iscott@acce.org
Manager, Accounting: Debi Shifflet
  E-Mail: dshifflet@acce.org
Director, Research and Technology: Lisa Sohn

Historical Note:
Formerly National Association of Commercial Organization Secretaries. Absorbed the National Association for Membership Development in 2003. ACCE's mission is to support and develop chamber professionals to lead businesses and their communities. Membership: $275-4,650 (Dues are based on according to revenue from last completed fiscal year, including all income from non-dues revenue, sponsorships, special events etc).

Continuing Education:
Enrollment: 25
Certification Designation/s: CCE

Meetings/Conferences: Annual
Conference Chair: Crystal Moore
2013 - Oklahoma City, OK/July 24 - 27
Number of non-conference events/year: 1

Publications:
Chamber Executive; quarterly; adv.
Membership Directory; on-line

American Cheese Society *(1983)*
2696 S. Colorado Blvd.
Suite 570
Denver, CO 80222-5954
Tel: (720) 328-2788 *Fax:* (720) 328-2786
E-Mail: info@cheesesociety.org
Website: cheesesociety.org
Members: 1200 individuals
Staff: 6
Annual Budget: $1-2,000,000
Tax: 501(c)(6)

Personnel:
Executive Director: Nora Weiser
  E-Mail: nweiser@cheesesociety.org
Manager, Education and Outreach: Jane Bauer
  E-Mail: jbauer@cheesesociety.org
Assistant, Administration and Marketing: Steve Binns
  E-Mail: sbinns@cheesesociety.org
Specialist, Membership Services: Jana Hemphill
  E-Mail: jhemphill@cheesesociety.org
Director, Programs and Operations: Michelle Lee
  E-Mail: mlee@cheesesociety.org
Manager, Marketing and Communications: Rebecca Sherman CAE, MHA, RRT
  E-Mail: rsherman@cheesesociety.org

Historical Note:
ACS encourages the understanding, appreciation, and promotion of America's farmstead and specialty cheeses. Members include producers, distributors, retailers, and others with an interest in the cheese industry. Membership: $199 (Individual); $575 (Small Business); $995 (Corporate Sponsor); $150 (Enthusiast); $95 (Student).

Continuing Education:
Certification Designation/s: CCP

Meetings/Conferences: Annual

Publications:
CheeseBytes; monthly
Membership Directory; annually

American Chemical Society *(1876)*
1155 16th St. NW
Washington, DC 20036
Tel: (202) 872-4600
TollFree: (800) 227-5558
E-Mail: help@acs.org
Website: portal.acs.org
Members: 164000 individuals
Staff: 1981
Annual Budget: Over $100,000,000
Tax: 501(c)(3)

Personnel:
Executive Director and Chief Executive Officer: Madeleine Jacobs
Treasurer and Chief Financial Officer: Brian A. Bernstein
  E-Mail: b_bernstein@acs.org
President, ACS Publications Division: Brian Crawford
  E-Mail: b_crawford@acs.org
Director, Member and Scientific Advancement Division: Denise Creech
Exposition Associate: Amanda Frederick
  E-Mail: a_frederick@acs.org
Director, Education: Mary Kirchhoff
Secretary and General Counsel: Flint H. Lewis
  E-Mail: f_lewis@acs.org
Director, Human Resources: Scott Oliphant
Director, Office of Public Affairs: Glenn S. Ruskin
  E-Mail: g_ruskin@acs.org
Director, Communications: Jane Shure
  E-Mail: j_shure@acs.org
Senior Manager, Copyright, Permissions and Licensing: Eric C. Slater
  E-Mail: e_slater@acs.org
Chief Information Officer: John Sullivan

Historical Note:
Incorporated in 1877 and granted a national charter by the Congress in 1937. ACS's mission is to improve people's lives through the transforming power of chemistry. Membership: $148 (Regular or Re-instating Member/ Non-Scientist/Society Affiliate); $74 (Graduate Student); $25-47 (Undergraduate Student).

Continuing Education:
Certification Designation/s: CEC

Meetings/Conferences: Semi-Annual
Conference Chair: Amanda Frederick
2013 - New Orleans, LA/April 7 - 11
2013 - Indianapolis, IN/Sept. 8 - 12
2014 - Dallas, TX/March 16 - 20
2014 - San Francisco, CA/Aug. 10 - 14
2015 - Denver, CO/March 22 - 26
2015 - Boston, MA/Aug. 16 - 20
2016 - San Diego, CA/March 13 - 17
2016 - Philadelphia, PA/Aug. 21 - 25
2017 - San Francisco, CA/April 2 - 6
2017 - St. Louis, MO/Sept. 10 - 14
2018 - New Orleans, LA/March 18 - 22
2018 - Boston, MA/Aug. 19 - 23
2019 - Orlando, FL/March 31 - April 4
2019 - San Diego, CA/Aug. 25 - 29

Publications:
Accounts of Chemical Research; monthly; adv.
ACS Applied Materials & Interfaces; monthly; adv.
ACS Catalysis; monthly; adv.
ACS Chemical Biology; monthly; adv.
ACS Chemical Neuroscience; monthly; adv.
ACS Combinatorial Science; bi-monthly; adv.
ACS Medicinal Chemistry Letters; monthly; adv.
ACS Nano; monthly; adv.
Analytical Chemistry; semi-monthly; adv.
Biochemistry; quarterly; adv.
Bioconjugate Chemistry; monthly; adv.
Biomacromolecules; monthly; adv.
Biotechnology Progress; bi-monthly; adv.
C&EN Online; weekly; adv.

Chemical Research in Toxicology; monthly; adv.
Chemical Reviews; monthly; adv.
Chemistry of Materials; semi-monthly; adv.
Crystal Growth & Design; monthly; adv.
Energy & Fuels; monthly; adv.
Environmental Science & Technology; semi-monthly; adv.
Industrial & Engineering Chemistry; monthly; adv.
Industrial & Engineering Chemistry Research; semi-monthly; adv.
Inorganic Chemistry; semi-monthly; adv.
Journal of Agricultural and Food Chemistry; semi-monthly; adv.
Journal of Chemical & Engineering Data; monthly; adv.
Journal of Chemical Education; monthly; adv.
Journal of Chemical Information and Modeling; monthly; adv.
Journal of Chemical Theory and Computation; monthly; adv.
Journal of Medicinal Chemistry; semi-monthly; adv.
Journal of Natural Products; monthly; adv.
Journal of Proteome Research; monthly; adv.
Journal of the American Chemical Society; adv.
Langmuir; semi-monthly; adv.
Macromolecules; semi-monthly; adv.
Molecular Pharmaceutics; bi-monthly; adv.
Nano Letters; monthly; adv.
Organic Letters; bi-monthly; adv.
Organic Process Research & Development; bi-monthly; adv.
Organometallics; bi-monthly; adv.
The Journal of Organic Chemistry; semi-monthly; adv.
The Journal of Physical Chemistry A; adv.
The Journal of Physical Chemistry B; adv.
The Journal of Physical Chemistry C; adv.
The Journal of Physical Chemistry Letters; semi-monthly; adv.

American Chemical Society - Rubber Division (1909)

P.O. Box 499
Akron, OH 44309-0499
Tel: (330) 972-7814 Fax: (330) 972-5269
E-Mail: emiller@rubber.org
Website: rubber.org
Members: 3000 individuals
Staff: 10
Annual Budget: $1-2,000,000
Tax: 501(c)(3)

Personnel:
Executive Director: Edward L. Miller PE
    E-Mail: emiller@rubber.org
Meetings and Executive Assistant: Melanie Avdeyev
    E-Mail: melaniea@rubber.org
Manager, Accounting: Lakisha Barclay
    E-Mail: lb@rubber.org
Manager, Membership Services: Heather Maimone
    E-Mail: hmaimone@rubber.org
Manager, Technical and Student Programs: Linda McClure
    E-Mail: lmcclure@rubber.org
Manager, Education and Publications: Christie L. Robinson
    E-Mail: crobinson@rubber.org
Manager, Marketing: Gretchen Spear
    E-Mail: gspear@rubber.org

Historical Note:
Mission is to expand the elastomeric profession and individual development through educational, technical and interactive activities. Membership: $55-70 (Full/Affiliate); $14 (Student Affiliates).

Meetings/Conferences: Semi-Annual
Conference Chair: Melanie Avdeyev
2013 - Akron, OH (Hilton Akron/Fairlawn)/April 21 - 24
2013 - Cleaveland, OH (International Exposition Center)/Oct. 8 - 10/6000 attendees/over 100 exhibitors
Number of non-conference events/year: 2

Publications:
Innovations; on-line; adv.
Rubber Chemistry and Technology
Rubber Chemistry and Technology journal; quarterly

Membership List Available to Non-members

American Chemistry Council (1872)

700 Second St. NE
Washington, DC 20002

Tel: (202) 249-7000 Fax: (202) 249-6100
Website: americanchemistry.com
Members: 131 companies
Staff: 200
Annual Budget: Over $100,000,000
Tax: 501(c)(6)

Personnel:
President and Chief Executive Officer: Calvin M. Dooley
Deputy General Counsel: Donald D. Evans
Vice President, Communications: Anne Womack Kolton
    E-Mail: Anne_Kolton@AmericanChemistry.com
Director, Membership Services: Lora Ann Magruder
    E-Mail: lora_magruder@americanchemistry.com
Vice President, Federal Affairs: Walter K. Moore
Chief Financial Officer and Chief Administrative Officer: Raymond J. O'Bryan
Chief of Staff and General Counsel: Dell Perelman
Vice President, Regulatory and Technical Affairs: Michael P. Walls

Historical Note:
Merged with American Plastics Council in 2002. Represents chemical manufacturers with operations in the U.S. and Canada. ACC strives to brings together member company experts to help resolve public policy, technical and scientific problems. It communicates with government and the public and administers research studies and tests on chemical products and practices.

Meetings/Conferences: Annual
2013 - Colorado Springs, CO/June 3 - 5
Number of non-conference events/year: 2

Publications:
ACC SmartBrief; daily
ACC's Economics Report; weekly
Global Product Index Report; monthly
Membership Directory; on-line
Situation and Outlook Report; bi-annually

American Cheviot Sheep Society (1924)

10015 Flush Rd.
St. George, KS 66535
Tel: (785) 458-9174
E-Mail: cheviotorg@gmail.com
Website: cheviots.org
Members: 800 individuals
Staff: 1
Annual Budget: $10-25,000

Personnel:
Executive Secretary: Jeff Ebert
    E-Mail: ebertj@wamego.net

Historical Note:
ACSS's mission is to guard and maintain the purity and encourage the breeding of Cheviot Sheep, to keep and maintain a registry for the registration of purebred Cheviot Sheep and to issue certificates of registration and transfer of same. Member of the National Pedigree Livestock Council. Membership: $10/year (Lifetime).

Meetings/Conferences:
Number of non-conference events/year: 2

Publications:
Cheviot Journal; on-line

American Chianina Association (1972)

1708 N. Prairie View Rd.
P.O. Box 890
Platte City, MO 64079
Tel: (816) 431-2808 Fax: (816) 431-5381
E-Mail: amerchianina@earthlink.com
Website: chicattle.org
Members: 1044 individuals
Staff: 5
Annual Budget: $500-1,000,000
Tax: 501(c)(5)

Personnel:
Chief Executive Officer: Stan Comer
    E-Mail: amerchianina@earthlink.net
Publications Manager: Heather Counts
    E-Mail: acjeditor@earthlink.net
Director, Shows and Activities: Holly Hiebert
    E-Mail: acjeditor@earthlink.net
Director, Marketing and Performance Programs: Tyler Humphrey
    E-Mail: acamarketing@earthlink.net

Historical Note:
ACA's purpose is to register and transfer seedstock and maintain records of pedigrees in the breed's herdbook. Members are breeders and fanciers of Chianina beef cattle. Membership: $100 (Active Adult); $50 (Junior).

Meetings/Conferences: Annual
Conference Chair: Holly Hiebert
2013 - Grand Island, NE (Holiday Inn Midtown - Grand Island)/June 15 - 21

Publications:
ACJ; adv.
Membership Directory; on-line

American Chiropractic Association (1930)

1701 Clarendon Blvd.
Arlington, VA 22209
Tel: (703) 276-8800 Fax: (703) 243-2593
TollFree: (800) 986-4636
E-Mail: memberinfo@acatoday.org
Website: acatoday.com
Members: 18000 individuals
Staff: 43
Annual Budget: $5-10,000,000

Personnel:
Executive Vice President: William K. O'Connell
    E-Mail: boconnell@acatoday.org
Vice President, Communications and Marketing: Annette Pena Bernat
    E-Mail: apena@acatoday.org
Manager, Marketing: John Booze
    E-Mail: jbooze@acatoday.org
Director, Publications: Lori Burkhart
    E-Mail: lburkhart@acatoday.org
Vice President, Insurance Relations: Laurie Douglass
    E-Mail: ldouglass@acatoday.org
Senior Vice President, Government Relations: John Falardeau
    E-Mail: jfalardeau@acatoday.org
Director, Information Systems: Dean Millard
    E-Mail: dmillard@acatoday.org
Vice President, Finance: Steve Stoupa CPA
    E-Mail: sstoupa@acatoday.org

Historical Note:
Founded as the National Chiropractic Association and assumed its present name in 1963. ACA strives to promote the philosophy, science and art of chiropractic, and the professional welfare of its members. Membership: $639 (General); $1,200 (Governor's Advisory Cabinet); $319.50 (Family/Sustaining); $160 (International/Associate); $122-488 (New Practitioner, Licensed DC who is 2-5 years from graduation date); $60 (Student); $96 (Retired/Disabled).

Meetings/Conferences: Annual
Number of non-conference events/year: 1

Publications:
ACA News; monthly; adv.
ChiroHealth; monthly
In Touch; quarterly
Journal of the American Chiropractic Association (JACA) Online; on-line; adv.
The Journal of Manipulative and Physiological Therapeutics (JMPT)
Week in Review; weekly

Membership List Available to Non-members

American Chiropractic Registry of Radiologic Technologists (1982)

52 W. Colfax St.
Palatine, IL 60067
Tel: (847) 705-1178 Fax: (847) 705-1178
Website: acrrt.com
Members: 2000 individuals
Staff: 2
Annual Budget: $50-100,000

Personnel:
Executive Director: Dr. Lawrence Pyzik

Historical Note:
ACRRT's mission is to maintain standards of education, ethics and competency necessary and desirable to ensure appropriate knowledge and skill and to maintain a national registry for its members who have met the required standards of education and applied skills in the performance of applied technology in diagnostic radiology. Membership: $40.00 (Active); $25.00 (Inactive).

Continuing Education:
Certification Designation/s: R.T. (ACRRT)

Publications:
Wavelengths

American Choral Directors Association (1959)

545 Couch Dr.
Oklahoma City, OK 73102-2207

Tel: (405) 232-8161 *Fax:* (405) 232-8162
E-Mail: acda@acda.org
Website: acda.org
Members: 19000 individuals
Staff: 15
Annual Budget: $2-5,000,000
Tax: 501(c)(3)

Personnel:
Executive Director: Dr. Tim Sharp
    E-Mail: sharp@acda.org
Coordinator, Membership Services: Leane DeFrancis
    E-Mail: membership@acda.org
Director, Education and Communication: Dr. Scott W.
  Dorsey
Managing Editor: Ron Granger
    E-Mail: managingeditor@acda.org
National Accountant and Controller: Marvin Meyer
Manager, Information Systems: Jose Tellez
    E-Mail: webmaster@acda.org

Historical Note:
*ACDA strives to promote standards in choral music through
performance, composition, publication, research, and
teaching. Members are choral musicians from schools,
colleges and universities, community and industrial
organizations, churches and professional groups.
Membership: $95 (Active/Associate); $135 (International/
Industry); $45 (Retired); $35 (Student); $110 (Institution);
$2,000 (Life).*

Meetings/Conferences: Annual
2013 - Dallas, TX/March 13 - 16
Number of non-conference events/year: 7

Publications:
ChorTeach
Division Newsletters; on-line
National Accountant & Controller; monthly
State Chapter Newsletters; on-line

Membership List Available to Non-members

American Cinema Editors (1950)
100 Universal City Plaza, Verna Fields Building
2282
Room 190
Universal City, CA 91608
Tel: (818) 777-2900 *Fax:* (818) 733-5023
E-Mail: amercinema@earthlink.net
Website: ace-filmeditors.org
Members: 500 individuals
Staff: 3
Annual Budget: $250-500,000

Personnel:
President: Randy C. Roberts ACE
Treasurer: Ed Abroms

Historical Note:
*ACE's mission is to advance the art and science of the
editing profession and to increase the entertainment value
of motion pictures by attaining artistic pre-eminence
and scientific achievement in the creative art of editing.
Membership, though international, is concentrated in the
Los Angeles area. Membership: $250/year.*

Publications:
CinemaEditor Magazine; quarterly

American Classical League (1919)
Miami University
422 Wells Mill Dr.
Oxford, OH 45056
Tel: (513) 529-7741 *Fax:* (513) 529-7742
E-Mail: info@aclclassics.org
Website: aclclassics.org
Members: 4000 individuals
Staff: 5
Annual Budget: $1-2,000,000
Tax: 501(c)(3)

Personnel:
President: Peter Howard
    E-Mail: president@aclclassics.org
Administrative Secretary: Geri Dutra
Treasurer: Deb Heaton
    E-Mail: treasurer@aclclassics.org
Director, Placement Services: Sherwin Little
    E-Mail: president@aclclassics.org
Editor: Paul Properzio
    E-Mail: newsletter@aclclassics.org

Historical Note:
*ACL's purpose is to foster and study classical languages
in the United States and Canada. Members are teachers
of Latin, Greek and Classics on elementary, secondary and*

college levels. *Membership: $55 (Regular); $25 (Student);
$30 (Retired Teacher); $935 (Life) $82 (Joint); $1,400
(Joint Life).*

Continuing Education:
Certification Designation/s: NBCL

Meetings/Conferences: Annual
2013 - Memphis, TN (University of Memphis)/June 27
  - 29
Number of non-conference events/year: 1

Publications:
American Classical League Newsletter
Membership Directory; on-line
The Classical Outlook; quarterly; adv.

Membership List Available to Non-members

American Cleaning Institute (1926)
1331 L St. NW
Suite 650
Washington, DC 20005
Tel: (202) 347-2900 *Fax:* (202) 347-4110
E-Mail: info@cleaning101.com
Website: cleaning101.com
Members: 100 companies
Staff: 22
Annual Budget: $5-10,000,000
Tax: 501(c)(6)

Personnel:
President and Chief Executive Officer: Ernie Rosenberg
    E-Mail: erosenberg@cleaninginstitute.org
Chief Financial Officer: Helen Benz
    E-Mail: hbenz@cleaninginstitute.org
Senior Vice President, Meetings and Education: Nancy
  Bock MS
    E-Mail: nbock@cleaninginstitute.org
Staff Accountant and Coordinator, Human Resources:
  Edgar Chavez
    E-Mail: echavez@cleaninginstitute.org
Vice President, Communications and Membership Services:
  Brian T. Sansoni
    E-Mail: bsansoni@cleaninginstitute.org
*Executive Vice President, Technical and International
  Affairs:* Richard I. Sedlak
    E-Mail: rsedlak@cleaninginstitute.org
Manager, Meeting Services: Gail Tannenbaum CMP
    E-Mail: gtannenbaum@cleaninginstitute.org
*Vice President and General Counsel and Corporate
  Secretary:* Joanne Thelmo
    E-Mail: jthelmo@cleaninginstitute.org
Vice President and Counsel, Government Affairs: Douglas
  M. Troutman
    E-Mail: dtroutman@cleaninginstitute.org
Director, Information Technology: Ugur Usumi
    E-Mail: uusumi@cleaninginstitute.org

Historical Note:
*Formerly known as the Soap and Detergent Association -
SDA. ACI represents manufacturers of cleaning products
and product ingredients, providing research and publishing
technical information on behalf of the industry. Members
are manufacturers and marketers of household, industrial
and institutional cleaning products, their ingredients, and
finished packaging, oleochemical producers and chemical
distributors to the cleaning product industry who have any
measurable U.S. sales.*

Meetings/Conferences: Annual
Conference Chair: Nancy Bock MS
2013 - Orlando, FL (JW Marriott Orlando Grande
  Lakes)/Jan. 28 - Feb. 2/725 attendees
2014 - Orlando, FL (JW Marriott Orlando Grande
  Lakes)/Jan. 27 - Feb. 1/725 attendees
2015 - Orlando, FL (JW Marriott Orlando Grande
  Lakes)/Jan. 26 - 31/725 attendees
2016 - Orlando, FL (JW Marriott Orlando Grande
  Lakes)/Jan. 25 - 30/725 attendees
2017 - Orlando, FL (JW Marriott Orlando Grande
  Lakes)/Jan. 23 - 28/725 attendees
Number of non-conference events/year: 2

Publications:
ACI SmartBrief; weekly
Cleaning Matters; bi-monthly
Membership Directory; on-line

American Cleft Palate-Craniofacial Association (1943)
1504 E. Franklin St.
Suite 102
Chapel Hill, NC 27514-2820
Tel: (919) 933-9044 *Fax:* (919) 933-9604

E-Mail: info@aca-cpf.org
Website: acpa-cpf.org
Members: 2500 individuals
Staff: 6
Annual Budget: $500-1,000,000
Tax: 501(c)(3)

Personnel:
Executive Director: Nancy C. Smythe
    E-Mail: nsmythe@acpa-cpf.org
Deputy Director: Jeremy Baggish
    E-Mail: jbaggish@acpa-cpf.org
Administrative Assistant: Hillary Jones
    E-Mail: hjones@acpa-cpf.org
Coordinator, Meetings: Amatullah King
    E-Mail: meetings@acpa-cpf.org
Editor, Cleft Palate-Craniofacial Journal: Jack C. Yu Ed,
  MD, MS
    E-Mail: jyu@georgiahealth.edu

Historical Note:
*Formerly the American Academy of Cleft Prosthesis. Became
the American Association for Cleft Palate Rehabilitation
in 1949 and later assumed its present name. ACPA's
mission is to optimize interdisciplinary care of persons
affected by cleft lip, cleft palate and other craniofacial
anomalies. Members consist of doctors, dentists and others
concerned with facial birth defects. Membership: $200
(Active/Associate/Intl-Electronic); $235 (International);
$110 (International Student); $75 (Student/Intl Student-
Electronic).*

Continuing Education:
Certification Designation/s: ASHA, CEU, CME

Meetings/Conferences: Annual
Conference Chair: Amatullah King
2013 - Lake Buena Vista, FL (Hilton Orlando Lake
  Buena Vista)/May 5 - 10/1200 attendees
2014 - Indianapolis, IN (Indianapolis Marriott
  Downtown)/March 25 - 29
Number of non-conference events/year: 3

Publications:
ACPA/CPF Newsletter; quarterly; adv.
Cleft Palate-Craniofacial Journal; bi-monthly; adv.
Member Directory; biennially

Membership List Available to Non-members

American Clinical and Climatological Association (1884)
2320 Kleinert Ave.
Baton Rouge, LA 70806
Tel: (225) 215-1311 *Fax:* (225) 766-0218
Website: accasociety.org
Members: 175 individuals
Staff: 1
Annual Budget: $250-500,000
Tax: 501(c)(3)

Personnel:
Secretary, Treasurer: Frederic T. Billing III
    E-Mail: fredericb@marybird.com

Historical Note:
*The object of the Association is the clinical study of disease.
With the rapid advances in medicine, the Association
provides a place for the presentation and critical discussion
of progress in research, teaching and clinical aspects of
medicine.Association provides a place for the presentation
and critical discussion of progress in research, teaching and
clinical aspects of medicine. The members of the ACCA are
selected on the basis of leadership and excellence in their
chosen field.*

American Clinical Laboratory Association (1971)
1100 New York Ave. NW
Suite 725 W
Washington, DC 20005
Tel: (202) 637-9466 *Fax:* (202) 637-2050
E-Mail: info@clinical-labs.org
Website: acla.com
Members: 43 companies
Staff: 8
Annual Budget: $2-5,000,000
Tax: 501(c)(6)

Personnel:
President: Alan Mertz
    E-Mail: amertz@clinical-labs.org
Administrator: Cheryl Hawkins
    E-Mail: chawk@acla.com

Historical Note:
*ACLA's mission is to advocate laws and regulations that
recognize the essential role that laboratory services play in
delivering cost-effective health care.*

Meetings/Conferences: Annual
2013 - Washington, DC (Grand Hyatt Washington)/
April 3 - 4

American Clinical Neurophysiology Society
(1946)
One Regency Dr.
P.O. Box 30
Bloomfield, CT 06002-0030
Tel: (860) 243-3977 *Fax:* (860) 286-0787
E-Mail: info@acns.org
Website: acns.org
Members: 1450 individuals
Staff: 3
Annual Budget: $500-1,000,000

Personnel:
President: Susan T. Herman
Editor-in-chief: John S. Ebersole MD
Treasurer: Stephan Schuele

Historical Note:
Formerly American Electroencephalographic Society 1996. ACNS is a professional society of electroencephalographers and neurophysiologists. Association dedicated to fostering excellence in clinical neurophysiology and furthering the understanding of central and peripheral nervous system function in health and disease through education, research, and the provision of a forum for discussion and interaction. Membership: $150 (Physician-1st year of Practice); $275 (Physician-from 2nd year of Practice); $245 (Non-Physician); $95 (Junior); $165 (Corresponding).

Meetings/Conferences: Annual
2013 - Miami, FL (Miami Marriott Biscayne Bay)/Feb. 5 - 20

Publications:
Membership Directory; on-line

American Coal Ash Association *(1968)*
15200 E. Girard Ave.
Suite 3050
Aurora, CO 80014-3955
Tel: (720) 870-7897 *Fax:* (720) 870-7889
E-Mail: info@acaa-usa.org
Website: acaa-usa.org
Members: 123 companies
Staff: 4
Annual Budget: $500-1,000,000
Tax: 501(c)(6)

Personnel:
Executive Director: Thomas H. Adams
E-Mail: thadams@acaa-usa.org
Advisor and Member Recruitment: Harry Roof
E-Mail: harry.roof@acaa-usa.org
Coordinator, Communications: John Ward
E-Mail: communications@acaa-usa.org

Historical Note:
Incorporated as the National Ash Association in Washington, DC, ACAA moved to Alexandria, VA in 1994. ACAA has an international membership which includes both electric utility and non-utility producers of coal-combustion products (CCPs), marketers, consultants, and other organizations. ACAA's mission is to advance the management and use of coal combustion products in ways that are environmentally responsible, technically sound, commercially competitive and more supportive of a sustainable global community. Membership: $3,300 (Specialty CCP Marketer/Individual/Class Associate/Non-Electric Utility CCP Producer); $6,000-13,500 (General CCP Marketer); $1,650-15,000 (Electric Utility Producer).

Meetings/Conferences: Annual
Number of non-conference events/year: 1

Publications:
ASH at Work; semi-annually
Membership Directory; on-line

American Coal Council *(1982)*
1101 Pennsylvania Ave. NW
Suite 600
Washington, DC 20004
Tel: (202) 756-4540 *Fax:* (202) 756-7323
E-Mail: info@americancoalcouncil.org
Website: americancoalcouncil.org
Members: 170 member companies
Staff: 5
Annual Budget: $500-1,000,000
Tax: 501(c)(6)

Personnel:
Chief Executive Officer: Janet Gellici
E-Mail: jgellici@americancoalcouncil.org

Director, Education and Marketing: Ingrid Abrom CMP
E-Mail: tcoffer@americancoalcouncil.org
Director, Conferences and Meetings: Teresa Coffer
E-Mail: tcoffer@americancoalcouncil.org
Director, Communications: Jason Hayes
E-Mail: jhayes@americancoalcouncil.org
Administrative Assistant: Michele Rubin
E-Mail: mrubin@americancoalcouncil.org

Historical Note:
Founded in 1982 as the Western Coal Export Council (WCEC), the name was changed to the Western Coal Council (WCC) in 1986 and in the Spring of 2002 the WCC was changed from a regional to a national organization. ACC supports the business, marketing and management capabilities of American coal suppliers, coal consumers, coal transporters, coal traders and coal support service companies. Membership is open to all coal suppliers, coal consumers (utility & industrial), coal transporters, coal traders and coal support companies (rail, trucking, and ports/terminals), energy traders and suppliers/service providers with an interest in the American coal industry. Membership: $2,500 (Company Representatives); $750 (Subsidiary).

Meetings/Conferences: Annual
Conference Chair: Teresa Coffer
Number of non-conference events/year: 2

Publications:
2011 ACC Membership Directory; annually; adv.
ACC Members Update; on-line
American Coal Advisory eNewsLetter; quarterly; adv.
American Coal Magazine; quarterly; adv.

American Coatings Association *(1933)*
1500 Rhode Island Ave. NW
Washington, DC 20005
Tel: (202) 462-6272 *Fax:* (202) 462-8549
E-Mail: members@paint.org
Website: paint.org
Staff: 36
Annual Budget: $5-10,000,000

Personnel:
President and Chief Executive Officer: J. Andrew Doyle
E-Mail: adoyle@paint.org
Vice President, General Counsel and Corporate Secretary: Thomas J. Graves
E-Mail: tgraves@paint.org
Vice President, Government Affairs: Alison Keane
E-Mail: akeane@paint.org
Vice President, Events and Professional Development: Cheryl Matthews
E-Mail: cmatthews@paint.org
Senior Counsel: Heidi McAuliffe
E-Mail: hmcauliffe@paint.org
Vice President, Administration and Chief Financial Officer: Nathan Perrine
E-Mail: nperrine@paint.org
Vice President, Communications: Lisa Roman
E-Mail: lroman@paint.org
Senior Director, Information Technology: Kevin Sall
E-Mail: ksall@paint.org
Director,Technical Publications and Communications: Patricia Ziegler
E-Mail: pziegler@paint.org

Historical Note:
Formerly the NPCA/FSCT assumed its present name in 2010. ACA's mission is to advance the interests of the coatings industry and to serve as its chief advocate and spokesperson before the government and public. Membership in the association is open to both corporate companies and individuals in the paint and coatings industry. Membership: $150 (Professional); $45 (Educator).

Meetings/Conferences: Semi-Annual
Conference Chair: Cheryl Matthews
2013 - Rosemont, IL (Hyatt Regency O'Hare)/March 11 - 13
2013 - Nuremberg, Germany/March 19 - 21
2014 - Mumbai, India/March 6 - 8
2014 - Atlanta, GA (Georgia World Congress Center)/ April 7 - 10/7500 attendees/over 100 exhibitors

Publications:
Coatings Today; semi-monthly; adv.
CoatingsTech; monthly; adv.
Journal of Coatings Technology and Research (JCTR); bi-monthly

American Coke and Coal Chemicals Institute
(1944)
25 Massachusetts Ave. NW
Suite 800

Washington, DC 20001
Tel: (202) 452-7198 *Fax:* (202) 463-6573
E-Mail: information@accci.org
Website: accci.org
Members: 150 representatives and 45 companies
Staff: 3
Annual Budget: $500-1,000,000
Tax: 501(c)(6)

Personnel:
President: Bruce A. Steiner
E-Mail: bsteiner@accci.org
Director, Administration: Janis Deitch
E-Mail: jdeitch@accci.org
General Counsel: David E. Menotti Esq.

Historical Note:
ACCCI's purpose is to advance the interests of the metallurgical coke and coal chemicals industry by communicating industry positions to members of Congress and Federal regulatory officials. Membership: $80-40,000/ year.

Meetings/Conferences: Annual
2013 - Longboat Key, FL (Longboat Key Club and Resort)/May 3 - 4

Publications:
Membership Directory; on-line

American College Counseling Association *(1991)*
C/O Director of Counseling and Testing,
University of North Carolina at Pembroke
P.O. Box 1510
Pembroke, NC 28358
Tel: (910) 521-6202
E-Mail: accaorg@mindspring.com
Website: collegecounseling.org
Members: 2961 individuals
Staff: 4
Annual Budget: $10-25,000

Personnel:
President: Monica Z. Osburm LPC, NCC, PhD
E-Mail: Monica.osburn@uncp.edu

Historical Note:
ACCA is a division of the American Counseling Association which provides staff administrative support. ACCA's mission is to be the interdisciplinary and inclusive professional home that supports emerging and state of the art knowledge and resources for counseling professionals in higher education. Members are those in higher education who have a professional identity in counseling and whose primary purpose is fostering student development. Membership: $60 (Professional/Regular); $50 (New Professional/Student/Retired).

Meetings/Conferences: Annual
Conference Chair: Sylvia Shortt
2013 - New Orleans, LA/Sept. 25 - 28

Publications:
Member Directory; on-line
The Journal of College Counseling (JCC); bi-annually
Visions; quarterly

American College Dance Festival Association
(1960)
2275 Research Blvd.
Suite 500
Rockville, MD 20850
Tel: (301) 670-2820 *Fax:* (301) 330-0740
E-Mail: acdfa@verizon.net
Website: acdfa.org
Members: 100 Institutional organizations
Staff: 8
Annual Budget: $100-250,000

Personnel:
Executive Director: Diane DeFries
President: Holly Williams
E-Mail: hwdnce@mail.utexas.edu
Treasurer: Karen Dearborn
E-Mail: dearborn@muhlenberg.edu
Vice President, Policy and Procedures: Amy Ginsburg
E-Mail: ginsamy@gmail.com
Vice President, Membership: George Staib
E-Mail: gstaib@emory.edu

Historical Note:
ACDFA's mission is to support and affirm the role of dance in higher education primarily through the sponsorship of college/university regional conferences and national dance festivals. Membership: $250-300 (Institutional); $50 (Individual); $500 (Lifetime).

Meetings/Conferences: Biennial

Publications:
ACDFA Newsletter

American College for Advancement in Medicine
(1973)
8001 Irvine Center Dr.
Suite 825
Irvine, CA 92618
Tel: (949) 309-3520 *Fax:* (949) 309-3538
E-Mail: info@acam.org
Website: acamnet.org
Members: 1500 physicians
Staff: 6
Annual Budget: $1-2,000,000
Tax: 501(c)(6)

Personnel:
President and Chief Executive Officer: Mark O'Neal
Speight MD
Treasurer and Chief Financial Officer: Allen Green
Manager, Marketing and Events: Megan Marburger
E-Mail: megan.marburger@acam.org
Executive Vice President: Jeffrey Morrison MD
Senior Coordinator, Membership Services: Fatima
Quintero
E-Mail: fatima.quintero@acam.org
Executive Director: Rachel Weaver
E-Mail: rachel.weaver@acam.org

Historical Note:
*ACAM's mission is to educate physicians and other health
care professionals on the latest findings and emerging
procedures in complementary, alternative and integrative
(CAIM) medicine. Membership: $250-475/year.*

Continuing Education:
Enrollment: 200
Certification Designation/s: CCT, CME

Meetings/Conferences: Annual
Conference Chair: Megan Marburger

Publications:
The Voice - Newsletter; bi-monthly

Membership List Available to Non-members

American College Health Association *(1920)*
1362 Mellon Rd.
Suite 180
Hanover, MD 21076
Tel: (410) 859-1500 *Fax:* (410) 859-1510
E-Mail: contact@acha.org
Website: acha.org
Members: 2700 individuals and 800 institutions
Staff: 17
Annual Budget: $2-5,000,000
Tax: 501(c)(3)

Personnel:
Executive Director: Doyle E Randol USA (Ret.)
Director, Membership Programs and Services: Susan L
Ainsworth
E-Mail: sainsworth@acha.org
Director, Finance and Administration: Peggy Hayes
E-Mail: phayes@acha.org
Director, Research: Victor E Leino MA, PhD
E-Mail: vleino@acha.org
Coordinator, Communications: Rachel Mack
E-Mail: rmack@acha.org
Program Coordinator: Cynthia Perez
E-Mail: cperez@acha.org
Coordinator, Publications and Receptionist: Mandy
Valenzuela
E-Mail: mvalenzuela@acha.org

Historical Note:
*Formerly known as the American Student Health
Association. ACHA strives to advocate for college and
university health. Members are physicians, nurses, health
educators, administrative and support staff who manage
and staff college and university student health services.
Membership: $165- 190 (Regular); $195 (Associate);
$35-85 (Emeritus/Student); $375-2000 (Institution);
$425-1900 (Sustaining).*

Continuing Education:
Certification Designation/s: CE

Meetings/Conferences: Annual
Conference Chair: Cynthia Perez
2013 - Boston, MA (Boston Marriott Copley Place)/
May 28 - June 1
2014 - San Antonio, TX (San Antonio Marriott
Rivercenter)/May 27 - 31
2015 - Orlando, FL (Orlando World Center Marriott)/
May 26 - 30

2016 - San Francisco, CA (San Francisco Marriott
Marquis)/May 31 - June 4
Publications:
College Health in Action; quarterly
Membership Directory; on-line
The Journal of American College Health; bi-monthly;
adv.

Membership List Available to Non-members

American College of Allergy, Asthma and
Immunology *(1942)*
85 W. Algonquin Rd.
Suite 550
Arlington Heights, IL 60005-4460
Tel: (847) 427-1200 *Fax:* (847) 427-1294
E-Mail: mail@acaai.org
Website: acaai.org
Members: 5500 members
Staff: 20
Annual Budget: $5-10,000,000
Tax: 501(c)(3)

Personnel:
Executive Director: Rick Slawny
Director, Public Relations: Jo Ann Faber
E-Mail: joannfaber@acaai.org
Registration Director and Exhibits Manager: Dianne K.
Kubis
E-Mail: diannekubis@acaai.org

Historical Note:
*Formerly (1987) American College of Allergists and (1995)
American College of Allergy and Immunology. ACAAI's
mission is to promote excellence in the practice of the sub
specialty of allergy and immunology, and to improve the
quality of patient care in allergy and immunology through
research, advocacy and professional and public education.
Members are allergists/immunologists and allied health
professionals. Membership: $225-390 (Fellows); $100
(Allied/Associate). Free (International Affiliate/Fellows-in-
Training).*

Meetings/Conferences: Annual
Conference Chair: Dianne K. Kubis
2013 - Baltimore, MD/Nov. 7 - 12/51-100 exhibitors
2013 - Baltimore, MD/Nov. 7 - 12
2014 - Atlanta, GA/Nov. 6 - 11/51-100 exhibitors
2014 - Honolulu, HI/Nov. 6 - 11
2015 - San Antonio, TX/Nov. 5 - 10/51-100 exhibitors
2015 - San Antonio, TX/Nov. 5 - 10
2016 - San Francisco, CA/Nov. 10 - 15/51-100
exhibitors
2016 - San Francisco, CA/Nov. 10 - 15
Number of non-conference events/year: 5

Publications:
ACAAI eNews; monthly
ACAAI News
AllergyWatch; bi-monthly
Annals of Allergy
Asthma & Immunology
Membership Directory; on-line

American College of Apothecaries *(1940)*
Research and Education Resource Center
2830 Summer Oaks Dr.
Bartlett, TN 38134-3811
Tel: (901) 383-8119 *Fax:* (901) 383-8882
E-Mail: aca@acainfo.org
Website: americancollegeofapothecaries.com
Members: 1000 individuals
Staff: 5
Annual Budget: $250-500,000
Tax: 501(c)(6)

Personnel:
Executive Vice President: Edward J. Hesterlee PharmD
Director, Conferences: Susan M. Decker
Director, Business Development: Dana D. Easton CPA,
FACMPE, MD
Administrative Assistant: Terri E. Wade

Historical Note:
*ACA's purpose is the translation and dissemination
of knowledge, research data and recent developments
in professional pharmacy practice for the benefit of
pharmacists, pharmacy students and the public. Members
are pharmacists owning ethical prescription pharmacies.
Membership: $95 (Associate Fellowship); $250 (Full
Fellowship).*

Meetings/Conferences: Annual
Conference Chair: Susan M. Decker
2013 - Dana Point, CA (St. Regis Monarch Beach
Resort)/Feb. 6 - 9

Publications:
ACA Newsletter; monthly
Hospice Care & Pain Management News; quarterly
The Voice of the Pharmacist; quarterly
Women's Health News; quarterly

American College of Bankruptcy *(1989)*
11350 Random Hills Rd., Suite 800
P.O. Box 626A
Fairfax, VA 22030-6044
Tel: (703) 934-6154 *Fax:* (703) 802-0207
E-Mail: college@amercol.org
Website: amercol.org
Members: 650 individuals
Staff: 3
Annual Budget: $500-1,000,000
Tax: 501(c)(6)

Personnel:
Executive Director: Shari Bedker
E-Mail: sbedker@amercol.org
Contact, Counsel: William J. Perlstein

Historical Note:
*An honorary professional and educational association of
bankruptcy and insolvency professionals. ACB's fellows
include commercial and consumer bankruptcy attorneys,
insolvency accountants, corporate turnaround and renewal
specialists, law professors, judges, government officials,
and others involved in the bankruptcy and insolvency
community. Membership: $100-350/year.*

Publications:
ACB Directory; annually

American College of Cardiology *(1949)*
2400 N. St. NW
Washington, DC 20037
Tel: (202) 375-6000 *Fax:* (202) 375-7000
TollFree: (800) 253-4636
E-Mail: resource@acc.org
Website: cardiosource.org
Members: 39000 Members
Staff: 300
Annual Budget: $10-25,000,000
Tax: 501(c)(6)

Personnel:
Interim Chief Staff Officer: Thomas E. Arend Jr.
E-Mail: tarend@acc.org
Director, Legislative Policy: Patrick Hope
E-Mail: phope@acc.org
Ashvin Patel
Director, Member Leadership: Marthea Wilson
E-Mail: mwilson@acc.org

Historical Note:
*Society composed of cardiovascular physicians and
scientists around the world. ACC's mission is to advocate
for quality cardiovascular care through education, research
promotion, development and application of standards and
guidelines and to influence health care policy. Membership:
$670 (Physicians residing in Canada/United States/U.S.
Territories); $250 (Administrator); $125 (International
Associate/Cardiac care team member).*

Continuing Education:
Certification Designation/s: CE, MOC, CME

Meetings/Conferences:
2013 - Snowmass Village, CO (Westin Snowmass
Resort)/Jan. 14 - 18
2013 - Washington, DC (Heart House)/Feb. 8 - 9
Number of non-conference events/year: 9

Publications:
Cardiology Magazine
CV News Digest; daily
JACC Imaging; monthly
JACC Interventions; monthly
Journal of the American College of Cardiology; weekly;
adv.

Membership List Available to Non-members

American College of Cardiovascular
Administrators *(1957)*
701 Lee St.
Suite 600
Des Plaines, IL 60016-4516
Tel: (847) 759-8601 *Fax:* (847) 759-8602
E-Mail: info@aameda.org
Website: aameda.org
Members: 1000 individuals
Staff: 11

Personnel:

President and Chief Executive Officer: Renee S. Schleicher CAE
  E-Mail: renee@aameda.org
Editor: Laura Bowles
  E-Mail: executiveeditor@aameda.org
Director, Membership and Communications: Susan M. Eget
  E-Mail: sue@aameda.org
Chief Financial Officer: Rhonda Guptill
  E-Mail: rhonda@aameda.org
Meeting Planner: Merle Hedland
  E-Mail: merle@aameda.org
Director, Education: Guy Snyder MHA, RRT, CFAAMA
  E-Mail: guy@aameda.org
Data And IT Administrator: Leslie Talbert
  E-Mail: leslie@aameda.org

Historical Note:
ACCA is a specialty group of the American Academy of Medical Administrators. ACCA also serves as a forum for exchanging information, credentialing and networking among members. Members are administrators in cardiovascular care. AAMA's mission is to advance excellence in healthcare leadership through individual relationships, multi-disciplinary interaction, practical business tools and active engagement. Membership: $230 (Member); $230 (Associate Member); $45 (Student).

Continuing Education:
Certification Designation/s: CAAMA

Meetings/Conferences: Annual
Conference Chair: Merle Hedland
2013 - Las Vegas, NV (Bally's Las Vegas)/April 10 - 12

Publications:
AAMA Staff Directory; on-line
AIM (Academy in Motion) E-Newsletter; bi-monthly; adv.
Member Directory; on-line

Membership List Available to Non-members

American College of Certified Wound Specialists (2005)
P.O. Box 3421
Gettysburg, PA 17325
Fax: (717) 398-0357
TollFree: (877) 703-3274
E-Mail: info@theccws.org
Website: accws.org
Members: 2000 individuals
Staff: 1
Annual Budget: $50-100,000

Personnel:
Executive Director: Anthony J. McNevin

Historical Note:
ACCWS strives to promote the public and wound care community an enhanced awareness and understanding of the potential impact the Certified Wound Specialist (CWS) can have on the general health care environment. Membership: $25 (One Time Initiation Fee); $175 (Fellow/ Corresponding).

Continuing Education:
Certification Designation/s: CWS

Publications:
ACCWS Newsletter
The Journal Of The American College Of Certified Wound Specialists

Membership List Available to Non-members

American College of Chest Physicians (1935)
3300 Dundee Rd.
Northbrook, IL 60062-2348
Tel: (847) 498-1400 *Fax:* (847) 498-5460
TollFree: (800) 343-2227
E-Mail: accp@chestnet.org
Website: chestnet.org
Members: 16000 individuals
Staff: 60
Annual Budget: $25-50,000,000
Tax: 501(c)(3)

Personnel:
Executive Vice President and Chief Executive Officer: Paul A. Markowski CAE
  E-Mail: pmarkowski@chestnet.org
Director, Publications: Nicole Augustyn
Senior Vice President and Chief Financial Officer: P. Stratton Davies CPA
Senior Vice President, Educational Resources: Ed Dellert MBA, RN
  E-Mail: edellert@chestnet.org

Senior Vice President, Governance and Operations: Nancy MacRae
Director, Meetings: Heather Nash CMP
Director, Human Resources: Bill Rieser CCP, SPHR
Manager, Promotion and Membership: Linda Tomczynski
Vice President, Marketing: Richard Waters CAE
Senior Vice President, Communications: Stephen J. Welch
  E-Mail: swelch@chestnet.org

Historical Note:
ACCP's mission is to promote the prevention, diagnosis, and treatment of chest diseases through education, communication, and research. Membership: $372 (US/Canadian Member/US/Canadian Member); $198 (International Member/Fellow Member); $120 (US/ Canadian Allied Health Member); $60-144 (International Allied Health Member); $72-120 (International Member/ Fellow e-Member).

Continuing Education:
Certification Designation/s: CME

Meetings/Conferences: Annual
Conference Chair: Heather Nash CMP
2013 - Chicago, IL/Oct. 26 - 31
2014 - Austin, TX/Oct. 25 - 30
2015 - Montreal, QC/Oct. 24 - 29

Publications:
ACCP NewsBrief
CHEST Journal; monthly
CHEST Physician; monthly

Membership List Available to Non-members

American College of Chiropractic Orthopedists (1954)
1557 Weatherstone Ln.
Elgin, IL 60123
E-Mail: thomasmackdc@gmail.com
Website: accoweb.org
Members: 489 individuals
Staff: 2
Annual Budget: $25-50,000
Tax: 501(c)(3)

Personnel:
President: Joseph F. Ferstl DC
  E-Mail: ferstlchiro@msn.com

Historical Note:
ACCO's purpose is to assist in the advancement of chiropractic as a science and healing art. Members are chiropractic orthopedists and others with an interest in the field. Membership: $110 (Associate); $90 (Supporting); $25 (Student/Faculty); $200 (Business); $125 (Full Membership).

Meetings/Conferences: Annual
Conference Chair: Joseph F. Ferstl DC
2013 - Las Vegas, NV (Tropicana Casino)/April 25 - 27

Publications:
Journal of the ACCO; quarterly; adv.
Membership Directory; annually; adv.

American College of Clinical Pharmacology (1969)
P.O. Box 1637
Rockville, MD 20849
Tel: (240) 399-9070 *Fax:* (240) 399-9071
Website: accp1.org
Members: 1000 individuals
Staff: 4
Annual Budget: $1-2,000,000
Tax: 501(c)(3)

Personnel:
Chief Executive Officer: Stephen N. Keith MD, MSPH
Director, Marketing and Membership Services: Krista L. Levy
Editor: Daniel S. Sitar FCP, PhD
  E-Mail: m.spraycar@verizon.net
Manager, Meetings and Exhibits: Tami Stevens

Historical Note:
ACCP seeks to provide innovative, unbiased, quality educational programs and forums for the membership, fellow health professionals, students and the public. Members of the College are health care professionals and biomedical/pharmaceutical scientists employed in academia, the pharmaceutical industry, contract clinical research organizations, private practice or government. Membership: $300 (Fellowship); $175 (Individual); $150 (Associate); $50 (Student).

Meetings/Conferences: Annual
Conference Chair: Tami Stevens
2013 - Bethesda, MD (Bethesda North Marriott Hotel and Conference Center)/Sept. 22 - 24

2014 - Atlanta, GA (Westin Peachtree Plaza, Atlanta)/ Sept. 14 - 16

Publications:
ACCP Newsletter
Clinical Pharmacology in Drug Development
Journal of Clinical Pharmacology; monthly; adv.
Membership Directory; quarterly

Membership List Available to Non-members

American College of Clinical Pharmacy (1979)
13000 W. 87th St. Pkwy.
Lenexa, KS 66215-4530
Tel: (913) 492-3311 *Fax:* (913) 492-0088
E-Mail: accp@accp.com
Website: accp.com
Members: 10000 clinical pharmacists
Staff: 28
Annual Budget: $5-10,000,000
Tax: 501(c)(6)

Personnel:
Executive Director: Michael S. Maddux FCCP, PharmD
  E-Mail: mmaddux@accp.com
Business Manager, Pharmacotherapy: Ann Chella-Nigl
  E-Mail: achellanigl@accp.com
Manager, Operations: Richard Collins
  E-Mail: rcollins@accp.com
Director, Research Institute: Jaque Marinac PharmD, BCPS
  E-Mail: jmarinac@accp.com
Meetings Planner: Gretchen L. Miles CMP
  E-Mail: gmiles@accp.com
Project Manager, Education: Zangose Miti
  E-Mail: zmiti@accp.com
Project Manager, Publications: Janel Mosley
  E-Mail: jmosley@accp.com
Project Manager, Information Technology: Brent Paloutzian
  E-Mail: bpaloutzian@accp.com
Director, Professional Development: Nancy Perrin CAE, MA
  E-Mail: nperrin@accp.com
Project Manager, Membership: Jon Poynter PharmD
  E-Mail: jpoynter@accp.com

Historical Note:
ACCP promotes the rational use of medications in health care, the advancement of knowledge regarding drug therapy and the development of clinical pharmacy. Provides leadership, professional development, research opportunities, and advocacy to support important issues facing the profession. Membership: $220 (Full/Affiliate/ Associate + Out of Training); $75 (Associate Member - Fellow/Graduate Student/Resident); $35 (Associate Member - Student).

Continuing Education:
Certification Designation/s: LMCP

Meetings/Conferences: Semi-Annual
Conference Chair: Gretchen L. Miles CMP
2013 - Reno, NV (Peppermill Resort Spa Casino)/April 19 - 23
2013 - Albuquerue, NM (Albuquerque Convention Center)/Oct. 13 - 16
2014 - Rosemont, IL (Hyatt Regency O'Hare Hotel)/ April 11 - 15
2014 - Austin, TX (Austin Convention Center)/Oct. 12 - 15
2015 - Rosemont, IL (Hyatt Regency O'Hare Hotel)/ April 10 - 14
2015 - San Francisco, CA (Hilton San Francisco Union Square)/Oct. 18 - 21
Number of non-conference events/year: 3

Publications:
Membership Directory; on-line

American College of Construction Lawyers (1989)
P.O. Box 4646
Austin, TX 78765
Tel: (512) 343-1808 *Fax:* (512) 451-2911
E-Mail: contact@accl.org
Website: accl.org
Members: 160 individuals
Staff: 4
Annual Budget: $250-500,000
Tax: 501(c)(6)

Personnel:
Assistant Director: Bell Seward

Historical Note:

ACCL's mission is to improve and enhance the practice and understanding of construction law and to promote the positive role of lawyers as friends of the project. The group provides advanced professional workshops and educational programs. Membership: Based upon nomination and election.

Publications:
Journal of the American College of Construction
  Lawyers
Membership Directory; on-line

Membership List Available to Non-members

American College of Contingency Planners *(1998)*
1st Marine Logistics Group
Camp Pendleton, CA 92055
Website: aameda.org/Colleges/ACCP/
  contingency.html
Members: 400 individuals
Staff: 1

Personnel:
President: Thomas J. Sawyer
  E-Mail: thomas.sawyer@med.navy.mil

Historical Note:
ACCP is a national specialty group of the American Academy of Medical Administrators, focused on providing support and opportunity for those individuals who are in healthcare planning positions in contingency, emergency, and disaster response. Members are disaster, emergency, and contingency planners in healthcare organizations. ACCP also serves as a forum for exchanging information, credentialling and networking among members.

Continuing Education:
Enrollment: 42
Certification Designation/s: FACCP

Membership List Available to Non-members

American College of Counselors *(1976)*
Delano Village Apartments 8-N
630 Malcolm X Blvd.
New York, NY 10037-1253
Tel: (212) 281-6908
Website: acconline.us
Members: 150 individuals
Staff: 4
Annual Budget: $25-50,000
Tax: 501(c)(3)

Personnel:
President: Raymond Bazemore Croskey DPM
  E-Mail: csmith@mec.cuny.edu

Historical Note:
ACC strives to strengthen individuals, marriages, and family relationships through the counseling process while adhering to ethical standards. Members are professionals in counseling and related fields of human services. Membership: $25-120/year.

Continuing Education:
Certification Designation/s: CS, PG

Meetings/Conferences: Annual

Publications:
ACC Journal; annually
ACC Newsletter

American College of Dentists *(1920)*
839 Quince Orchard Blvd.
Suite J
Gaithersburg, MD 20878-1614
Tel: (301) 977-3223 *Fax:* (301) 977-3330
E-Mail: office@acd.org
Website: acd.org
Members: 7400 individuals
Staff: 6
Annual Budget: $1-2,000,000

Personnel:
Executive Director: Dr. Stephen A. Ralls DDS
  E-Mail: saralls@acd.org
Editor: David W. Chambers EdM, MBA, PhD
  E-Mail: dchamber@pacific.edu
*Subscriptions Coordinator and Meetings Registration
  Assistant:* Erica Royal
  E-Mail: erica@acd.org
Assistant, Financial Services : Sarah Shriver
  E-Mail: sarah@acd.org

Historical Note:
Founded in Cedar Rapids in 1920 and incorporated in Maryland in 1970, ACD seeks to advance excellence, ethics, professionalism, and leadership in dentistry. Membership in the American College of Dentists is by invitation only. Membership: $175/year.

Continuing Education:
Certification Designation/s: ADA CERP

Meetings/Conferences: Annual
Conference Chair: Erica Royal

Publications:
ACD News
Journal of the American College of Dentists; quarterly

American College of Emergency Physicians *(1968)*
1125 Executive Cir.
Irving, TX 75038-2522
Tel: (972) 550-0911 *Fax:* (972) 580-2816
TollFree: (800) 798-1822
E-Mail: membership@acep.org
Website: acep.org
Members: 25000 physicians, residents and
  medical students
Staff: 12
Annual Budget: $25-50,000,000
Tax: 501(c)(6)

Personnel:
Executive Director: Dean Wilkerson CAE, JD, MBA
  E-Mail: execdirector@acep.org
Senior Manager, Marketing: Buck Beighley
  E-Mail: bbeighley@acep.org
Senior Director, Membership Services and Development:
  Michele Byers CAE
  E-Mail: mbyers@acep.org
Director, Member Communications: Nancy Calaway
  E-Mail: ncalaway@acep.org
Director, Technology Services: Gabe Casey
  E-Mail: gcasey@acep.org
Manager, Human Resource: Mary Beth Collins
  E-Mail: mcollins@acep.org
Chief Financial Officer: Phyllis Edans CPA
  E-Mail: pedans@acep.org
Director, Governance Operations: Sonja Montgomery
  E-Mail: smontgomery@acep.org
Director, Conventions and Meetings: Debbie Smithey
  E-Mail: dsmithey@acep.org
Manager, Publications Sales and Marketing: Nicole
  Tidwell
  E-Mail: ntidwell@acep.org

Historical Note:
ACEP promotes emergency care for emergency physicians, patients, and the public. Members are emergency physicians. Membership: $105 (Resident/Fellowship); $55 (Medical Student); $141 (International); $283 (Military); $565 (Active).

Meetings/Conferences: Annual
Conference Chair: Debbie Smithey
2013 - Washington, DC (Omni Shoreham)/May 19 - 22
2013 - Seattle, WA/Oct. 14 - 17
2014 - Chicago, IL/Oct. 27 - 30
2015 - Boston, MA/Oct. 26 - 29

Publications:
ACEP News
Membership Directory; on-line

American College of Epidemiology *(1979)*
1500 Sunday Dr.
Suite 102
Raleigh, NC 27607
Tel: (919) 861-5573 *Fax:* (919) 787-4916
E-Mail: info@acepidemiology.org
Website: acepidemiology.org
Members: 850 individuals
Staff: 7
Annual Budget: $100-250,000

Personnel:
Executive Director: Peter Kralka
  E-Mail: pkralka@firstpointresources.com
Treasurer: Diana M. Bensyl MA, PhD
  E-Mail: zqg6@CDC.GOV
Director, Communications: Verena Rojas
  E-Mail: vrojas@firstpointresources.com

Historical Note:
ACE members are physicians and other health professionals with an interest in the study of human disease. The American College of Epidemiology was incorporated in 1979 to develop criteria for professional recognition of epidemiologists and to address their professional concerns. The College has benefited from the leadership of the leading epidemiologists in the world. Membership: $85 (Associate Member with Journal); $25 (Associate Member without Journal); $150 (Member with Journal); $195 (Fellow with Journal).

Meetings/Conferences: Annual
2013 - Louisville, KY (Galt House Hotel and Suites)/
  Sept. 21 - 24
Number of non-conference events/year: 2

Publications:
ACE Newsletter; quarterly
Annals of Epidemiology

American College of Eye Surgeons *(1987)*
334 E. Lake Rd.
Suite 135
Palm Harbor, FL 34685-2427
Tel: (727) 366-1487 *Fax:* (727) 836-9783
E-Mail: quality@aces-abes.org
Website: aces-abes.org
Members: 800 individuals,40 organizations
Staff: 1
Annual Budget: $100-250,000
Tax: 501(c)(6)

Personnel:
Assistant Executive Director: Laurel Fields
  E-Mail: quality@aces-abes.org

Historical Note:
ACES's mission is to promote, encourage, and enhance quality ophthalmic surgical care for the benefit of all patients. Membership: $750 (Physician); $100 (Academic); $300 (Corporate).

Meetings/Conferences: Annual
Conference Chair: Laurel Fields

Publications:
e-Newsletter; quarterly
Membership Directory; on-line

American College of Foot & Ankle Orthopedics & Medicine *(1940)*
5272 River Rd.
Suite 630
Bethesda, MD 20816
Tel: (301) 718-6505 *Fax:* (301) 656-0989
TollFree: (800) 265-8263
E-Mail: info@acfaom.org
Website: acfaom.org
Members: 1150 individuals
Staff: 6
Annual Budget: $250-500,000
Tax: 501(c)(6)

Personnel:
Executive Director: Norman E. Wallis PhD
  E-Mail: nwallis@acfaom.org
Membership Coordinator and Meetings Registrar: Robert
  Coneys
  E-Mail: rconeys@paimgmt.com
College Coordinator: Nick Hurwit
  E-Mail: nhurwit@paimgmt.com
Staff Accountant: Scott Recht MBA
  E-Mail: srecht@paimgmt.com

Historical Note:
Formerly (1951) American College of Foot Orthopedists. ACFAOM's purpose is to support scientific study and research to enhance the field of foot orthopedics and related matters in podiatric medicine. Membership: $350 (Fellow/ Associate); $250 (Member); Free (Student/Resident).

Meetings/Conferences: Annual
Conference Chair: Robert Coneys

Publications:
ACFAOM Newsletter; quarterly
Foot & Ankle; weekly
Member Directory; on-line
The Foot; quarterly; adv.

American College of Foot and Ankle Surgeons *(1942)*
8725 W. Higgins Rd.
Suite 555
Chicago, IL 60631-2724
Tel: (773) 693-9300 *Fax:* (773) 693-9304
TollFree: (800) 421-2237
E-Mail: info@acfas.org
Website: acfas.org
Members: 6500 Individuals
Staff: 16
Annual Budget: $5-10,000,000

Personnel:
Executive Director: J. C. (Chris) Mahaffey CAE, MS
  E-Mail: Mahaffey@acfas.org

Director, Finance and Administration: Nancy L. Anderson CAE, CPA, MBA
    E-Mail: nancy.anderson@acfas.org
Director, Membership Services: Michelle D. Brozell CAE, MS
    E-Mail: michelle.brozell@acfas.org
Journal Editor: D. Scot Malay DPM, FACFAS
    E-Mail: editorjfas@gmail.com
Director, Marketing and Communications: Melissa Matusek
    E-Mail: melissa.matusek@acfas.org
Director, Education Curriculum and Alliances: Mary V. Meyers
    E-Mail: meyers@acfas.org
Manager, Information Technology: Alfred D. Ticoalu
    E-Mail: alfred.ticoalu@acfas.org

Historical Note:
Formerly (1993) the American College of Foot Surgeons. ACFAS seeks to promote the art and science of foot, ankle, and related lower extremity surgery, address the concerns of foot and ankle surgeons, and advance and improve standards of surgical skill and patient care. Members are doctors of podiatric medicine who are board certified in foot and ankle surgery. Membership: $520 (Fellow/Associate); $112 (Resident); $175 (International Affiliate).

Meetings/Conferences: Annual
Conference Chair: Mary V. Meyers
2013 - Las Vegas, NV (Mandalay Bay Hotel)/Feb. 11 - 14
Number of non-conference events/year: 21

Publications:
Journal of Foot and Ankle Surgery; bi-monthly; adv.
Membership Directory; on-line
Scientific Literature Reviews; monthly
This Week @ACFAS; weekly
Update; adv.
Update Newsletter; monthly; adv.

American College of Forensic Examiners Institute
(1992)
2750 E. Sunshine St.
Springfield, MO 65804
Tel: (417) 881-3818   *Fax:* (417) 881-4702
TollFree: (800) 423-9737
E-Mail: cao@acfei.com
Website: acfei.com
Members: 11000 individuals
Staff: 25
Annual Budget: $1-2,000,000

Personnel:
Founder and Publisher: Robert L. O'Block PhD

Historical Note:
ACFEI members are forensic examiners, mostly from the United States, that engage in the scientific aspects of forensic examination. Membership: $165 (Individual); $65 (Student); $2500 (Life).

Continuing Education:
Certification Designation/s: ASC, CFP, CI, RI, AFC, CFSW, CSM, Cr.FA, CFN, CMI, CFC

Meetings/Conferences: Annual

Publications:
Membership Directory; on-line
The Forensic Examiner; quarterly; adv.

American College of Forensic Psychiatry *(1981)*
P.O. Box 130458
Carlsbad, CA 92013-0458
Tel: (760) 929-9777   *Fax:* (760) 929-9803
E-Mail: psychlaw@sover.net
Website: forensicpsychonline.com
Members: 350 individuals
Staff: 4

Personnel:
Executive Director and Editor-in-Chief: Debbie Miller

Historical Note:
ACFP is an association of psychiatrists and attorneys and other concerned scholars who have a common interest in the interface of psychiatry and law, with particular focus on forensic skills in their practice. Membership: $220/year.

Meetings/Conferences: Annual
Conference Chair: Debbie Miller

Publications:
American Journal of Forensic Psychiatry

American College of Gastroenterology *(1932)*
6400 Goldsboro Rd.
Suite 450

Bethesda, MD 20817
Tel: (301) 263-9000
E-Mail: info@acg.gi.org
Website: gi.org
Members: 12000 individuals
Staff: 27
Annual Budget: $10-25,000,000

Personnel:
Executive Director: Bradley C. Stillman
    E-Mail: bstillman@acg.gi.org
Director, Finance: Ernest Bomar
Federal Lobbyist: Thomas F. Fise JD
Director, Meetings and Exhibitions: Elaine McCubbin
    E-Mail: emccubbin@acg.gi.org
Vice President, Marketing: Martie Spath
    E-Mail: mspath@acg.gi.org
Vice President, Membership Services and Technology: Maria Susano
    E-Mail: msusano@acg.gi.org

Historical Note:
ACG's mission is to advance the medical treatment and scientific study of gastrointestinal disorders. Members are gastroenterologists, surgeons, radiologists, hepatologists, pediatricians, pathologists and others with a shared interest in the care of patients with digestive diseases. Membership: $25/year (Resident/Trainee Member).

Meetings/Conferences: Annual
Conference Chair: Elaine McCubbin
2013 - San Diego, CA/Oct. 11 - 16
Number of non-conference events/year: 5

Publications:
ACG Meeting News; adv.
ACG This Week, National Affairs News; weekly
ACG Update; bi-monthly
American College of Gastroenterology; monthly; adv.
Digestive Health SmartBrief; bi-weekly; adv.

American College of Health Care Administrators *(1962)*
1321 Duke St.
Suite 400
Alexandria, VA 22314
Tel: (202) 536-5120   *Fax:* (866) 874-1585
E-Mail: info@achca.org
Website: achca.org
Members: 2500 individuals
Staff: 6
Annual Budget: $100-250,000
Tax: 501(c)(3)

Personnel:
President and Chief Executive Officer: Marianna Kern Grachek CNHA, FACHCA, MSN
    E-Mail: mgrachek@achca.org
Manager, Media, Technology and Office Services: Michelle Berry
    E-Mail: mberry@achca.org
Coordinator, Financial Services: Katie Lynes
    E-Mail: klynes@achca.org
Coordinator, Membership Services: Whitney O'Donnell
    E-Mail: wodonnell@achca.org
Manager, Business Development: Becky Reisinger
    E-Mail: breisinger@achca.org
Director, Education and Professional Advancement: Janet Spence
    E-Mail: jspence@achca.org

Historical Note:
ACHCA's mission is to promote leadership among long-term care administrators. ACHCA provides educational programming, professional certification, and career development opportunities for its members. Membership: $295 (Full/Fellow); $195 (Associate); $145 (Bridge); $164 (Senior Retired); $45 (Student/Administrator-in-Training); $95 (Retired Member); $75 (Retired Fellow); $495 (Business Affiliate).

Continuing Education:
Certification Designation/s: CNHA, CALA

Meetings/Conferences:
Conference Chair: Janet Spence
2013 - Orlando, FL (Omni Orlando Resort at ChampionsGate)/April 12 - 16
Number of non-conference events/year: 1

Publications:
ACHCA eNews; semi-monthly
ACHCA Long Term Care Continuum; quarterly; adv.
Directory of Services; on-line
Membership Directory; on-line

Membership List Available to Non-members

American College of Health Plan Management
(1957)
701 Lee St.
Suite 600
Des Plaines, IL 60016
Tel: (847) 759-8601   *Fax:* (847) 759-8602
E-Mail: info@aameda.org
Website: my.aameda.org/AM/Template.cfm? Section = Home
Members: 400 individuals
Staff: 3

Personnel:
College President: Angela M Blackwell
    E-Mail: angela.blackwell@us.af.mil
College Membership Chair: Teresa Clark
    E-Mail: teresa.clark@lackland.af.mil
College Communications Chair: Wendy L. Mack
    E-Mail: bsg.wendy@gmail.com

Historical Note:
Formerly American College of Managed Care Administrators (ACMCA). ACHPM is a speciality group of the American Academy of Medical Administrators. ACHPM serves as a forum for exchanging information and networking among managed care professionals. Focuses on providing support and opportunity for healthcare leaders in the field of managed care in all types of healthcare institutions. Funding is provided by AAMA. Membership: $235 (Member/Associate); $45 (student).

Meetings/Conferences: Annual
2013 - Las Vegas, NV (Bally's Las Vegas)/April 10 - 12

Publications:
AIM (Academy in Motion); bi-monthly; adv.
Membership Directory; on-line
The AAMA Executive Online; bi-monthly; adv.

American College of Healthcare Architects
P.O. Box 14548
Lenexa, KS 66285-4548
Tel: (913) 895-4604   *Fax:* (913) 895-4652
E-Mail: acha-info@goamp.com
Website: healtharchitects.org
Staff: 2
Annual Budget: $250-500,000
Tax: 501(c)(3)

Personnel:
President: Wilbur "Tib" Tusler FACHA, FAIA
Secretary and Treasurer: Douglas Childs FAIA, FACHA

Historical Note:
ACHA's mission is to offer board certification within the specialized field of healthcare architecture.

Continuing Education:
Certification Designation/s: ACHA
Meetings/Conferences:
Number of non-conference events/year: 2

Publications:
ACHA Newsletter; quarterly
E-Voice; monthly

American College of Healthcare Executives
(1933)
One N. Franklin St.
Suite 1700
Chicago, IL 60606-3529
Tel: (312) 424-2800   *Fax:* (312) 424-0023
E-Mail: ache@ache.org
Website: ache.org
Members: 40000 individuals
Staff: 100
Annual Budget: $10-25,000,000
Tax: 501(c)(6)

Personnel:
President and Chief Executive Officer: Thomas C. Dolan CAE, FACHE, PhD
    E-Mail: tdolan@ache.org
Executive Vice President and Chief Operating Officer: Deborah J. Bowen CAE, FACHE
    E-Mail: dbowen@ache.org
Chief Financial Officer and Vice President: Joe Dietrich CAE, CPA
    E-Mail: jdietrich@ache.org
Vice President, Health Administration Press: Maureen C Glass CAE, FACHE
    E-Mail: mglass@ache.org
Vice President, Membership Services: Cynthia Hahn FACHE
    E-Mail: membership1@ache.org

Vice President, Education: Howard J. Horwitz
  E-Mail: hhorwitz@ache.org
Meeting Planner: Songi Kim

Historical Note:
ACHE's mission is to work toward its goal of improving the health status of society, by advancing healthcare management. Membership: $150 (Member); $115 (Faculty Associate); $150 (International Associate); $75 (Student/Retired).

Continuing Education:
Certification Designation/s: FACHE

Meetings/Conferences:
Conference Chair: Songi Kim
Number of non-conference events/year: 6

Publications:
Early Careerist Network; bi-monthly
Healthcare Executive Magazine
International Newsletter; quarterly
Journal of Healthcare Management; bi-monthly
Membership Directory; on-line

American College of Healthcare Information Administrators
C/O Lt Col Jerry A. Harvey, CAAMA
95th MDG
Edwards, CA 93524
E-Mail: info@aameda.org
Website: aameda.org/Boards/ACHIAboard.html
Members: 250 members
Staff: 2

Personnel:
College President: LTCOL Jerry A. Harvey
  E-Mail: jtjharvey@gmail.com

Historical Note:
ACHIA focuses on providing education, support and opportunity for information technology leaders in the healthcare industry. Members are IT professionals in healthcare organizations.

Meetings/Conferences: Annual

Publications:
AAMA Executive Online; bi-monthly; adv.
AIM (Academy in Motion); bi-monthly; adv.
Membership Directory; on-line

American College of International Physicians
(1975)
9323 Old Mt.Vernon Rd.
Alexandria, VA 22309
Tel: (703) 221-1500 *Fax:* (703) 221-1500
Website: acip.org
Members: 3000 individuals
Staff: 3
Annual Budget: $50-100,000
Tax: 501(c)(3)

Personnel:
President and Executive Director: Alex Yadao
  E-Mail: walkwithgod7@gmail.com

Historical Note:
ACIP's mission is to foster and advocate, equal opportunities, educational excellence, volunteerism and cooperation for all International Absorbed the National Association of Foreign Medical Graduates in 1976. Medical Graduates in the United States, and to participate in favorable non-discriminatory public policy development legislation and mainstream U.S. medical establishments. Members are physicians educated in foreign countries and the U.S. who are licensed and practicing in the U.S. Main interests of the College are medical education, research, ethics and international activities. Membership: $175 (Regular); $50 (Associate); $25 (Affiliate/Student).

Publications:
ACIP Newsletter
Membership Directory; on-line

American College of Laboratory Animal Medicine
(1957)
96 Chester St.
Chester, NH 03036
Tel: (603) 887-2467 *Fax:* (603) 887-0096
Website: aclam.org
Members: 700 individuals
Staff: 3
Annual Budget: $500-1,000,000
Tax: 501(c)(3)

Personnel:
Executive Director: Melvin W. Balk DACLAM, DVM, MS
  E-Mail: mwbaclam@gsi.net.net

Historical Note:
Founded as the American Board of Laboratory Animal Medicine, affiliated with the American Veterinary Medical Association and the American Association for Laboratory Animal Science. ACLAM seeks to encourage education, training, and research in laboratory animal medicine and to provide standards for veterinarians professionally concerned with the health of laboratory animals. Members are all veterinarians who are certified as ACLAM Diplomates. Membership: $300-400/year.

Continuing Education:
Certification Designation/s: ACLAMCE

Meetings/Conferences: Annual
2013 - Williamsburg, PA (Williamsburg Lodge)/April 14 - 17

Publications:
ACLAM Newsletter; quarterly
Membership Directory; on-line

Membership List Available to Non-members

American College of Legal Medicine *(1960)*
1100 E. Woodfield Rd.
Suite 520
Schaumburg, IL 60173
Tel: (847) 969-0283 *Fax:* (847) 517-7229
E-Mail: info@aclm.org
Website: aclm.org
Members: 1450 individuals
Staff: 3
Annual Budget: $250-500,000
Tax: 501(c)(3)

Personnel:
Executive Director: Wendy J. Weiser
Associate Director: Sue O'Sullivan
Editor: Ross D. Silverman JD, MPH

Historical Note:
ACLM's mission is to promote the continued professional advancement of its members, as well as non-member physicians, and other interested professionals, through education, research, publications, and interdisciplinary and collaborative exchanges of information. Members are doctors, lawyers, and other health care professionals interested in the interface between law and medicine. Fellows of the College must have both a medical and law degree or have performed significant service to the college over time. Membership: $295 (Fellow/International); $195 (Member/International); $35 (Student).

Meetings/Conferences: Annual
Conference Chair: Sue O'Sullivan
2013 - Las Vegas, NV (Planet Hollywood Resort and Casino)/Feb. 21 - 24

Publications:
Journal of Legal Medicine; quarterly
MEDICAL-LEGAL STUDIES eJOURNAL; on-line
Membership Directory; on-line

American College of Medical Genetics *(1991)*
7220 Wisconsin Ave.
Suite 300
Bethesda, MD 20814
Tel: (301) 718-9603 *Fax:* (301) 718-9604
E-Mail: acmg@acmg.net
Website: acmg.net
Members: 1400 individuals
Staff: 22
Annual Budget: $5-10,000,000
Tax: 501(c)(6)

Personnel:
Executive Director: Michael S. Watson PhD
  E-Mail: mwatson@acmg.net
Director, Public Relations: Kathy Beal MBA
  E-Mail: kbeal@acmg.net
Manager, Information Technology and Informatics: Bruce E. Bowdish
  E-Mail: bbowdish@acmg.net
Coordinator, Membership Services: Denise Calvert
  E-Mail: dcalvert@acmg.org
Director, Meetings and Exhibits: Jane Dahlroth CEM, CMP
  E-Mail: jdahlroth@acmg.net
Director, Administration: Melissa T. Forburger
  E-Mail: mforburger@acmg.net

Historical Note:
ACMG's purpose is to provide education, resources and a voice for the medical genetics profession. It also promote the development and implementation of methods to diagnose, treat and prevent genetic diseases. Members are physicians, laboratorians, and other health care professionals with an interest in genetics. Membership: $400-800 (Fellow); $275

(Affiliate Specialist/Candidate Fellow/Corresponding); $225 (Associate/Affiliate); $175 (Emeritus); $110 (Trainee); $30 (Student).

Meetings/Conferences: Annual
Conference Chair: Jane Dahlroth CEM, CMP
2013 - Phoenix, AZ/March 19 - 23/1-10 exhibitors
2014 - Nashville, TN/March 25 - 29

Publications:
ACMG Medical Geneticist; quarterly
Genetics in Medicine; monthly; adv.
Membership Directory; on-line
Standards and Guidelines For Clinical Genetics Laboratories; annually

Membership List Available to Non-members

American College of Medical Physics *(1982)*
One Physics Ellipse
College Park, MD 20740-3846
Tel: (301) 209-3360 *Fax:* (301) 209-3343
E-Mail: acmp@acmp.org
Website: acmp.org
Members: 475 individuals
Staff: 2
Annual Budget: $250-500,000

Personnel:
Editor: Eileen Cirino
  E-Mail: eileen.t.cirino@lahey.org
Executive Secretary: Corbi Foster
  E-Mail: corbi@aapm.org

Historical Note:
Founded with the support of the American Association of Physicists in Medicine (AAPM) in 1982. ACMP aims to enhance the quality of the practice of medical physics, engage in professional activities for the benefit of the medical physics community, and promote the continuing competence of practitioners of medical physics. Members are fully qualified or provisionally qualified clinical medical physicists. Membership: $275 (Full Members), $125 (Provisional Members), $25 (Trainee).

Meetings/Conferences: Annual

Publications:
ACMP Newsletter; on-line; adv.
Membership Directory; on-line

Membership List Available to Non-members

American College of Medical Quality *(1972)*
5272 River Rd.
Suite 630
Bethesda, MD 20816
Tel: (301) 718-6516 *Fax:* (301) 656-0989
E-Mail: acmq@acmq.org
Website: acmq.org
Members: 1000 individuals
Staff: 5
Annual Budget: $250-500,000
Tax: 501(c)(3)

Personnel:
Executive Director: Andrew Jerdonek
  E-Mail: ajerdonek@acmq.org
Membership Assistant: Rene Atkinson
  E-Mail: membership@acmq.org
Executive Vice President: Bridget Brodie
  E-Mail: bridget.brodie@acmq.org
Membership Coordinator and Meeting Registrar: Melynda Maurelus
  E-Mail: mmaurelus@acmq.org
Editor: David B. Nash MBA, MD
  E-Mail: David.nash@jefferson.edu

Historical Note:
Founded as the American College of Utilization Review Physicians. Became American College of Medical Quality (1991). ACMQ's mission is to provide leadership and education in healthcare quality management. Members are doctors, related health personnel, hospitals, and health plans. Membership: $145-295 (Physician); $1,500 (Organizational, for the first ten individuals); $80-125 (Affiliate); $25 (Student); $35 (Resident/Fellow).

Continuing Education:
Certification Designation/s: CQM, CMQ

Meetings/Conferences: Annual
Conference Chair: Melynda Maurelus
2013 - Phoenix, AZ/Feb. 20 - 23

Publications:
American Journal of Medical Quality; bi-monthly; adv.
Focus; bi-monthly
Membership Directory; on-line

Membership List Available to Non-members

American College of Medical Toxicology (1993)
10645 N. Tatum Blvd.
Suite 200-111
Phoenix, AZ 85028
Tel: (623) 533-6340 *Fax:* (623) 533-6520
E-Mail: info@acmt.net
Website: acmt.net
Members: 500 individuals
Staff: 3
Annual Budget: $500-1,000,000

Personnel:
Executive Director: Paul M. Wax FACMT, MD
  E-Mail: paul.wax@acmt.net
Educational Coordinator: Jim Wiggins
  E-Mail: jim.wiggins@acmt.net

Historical Note:
ACMT is a professional, non-profit organization of physicians, certified in medical toxicology, dedicated to advance the science and practice of medical toxicology. The mission of the American College of Medical Toxicology is to advance quality care of poisoned patients and public health through physicians who specialize in consultative, emergency, environmental, forensic, and occupational toxicology. Membership: $325 (Full); $100 (International); $75 (Associate).

Meetings/Conferences: Annual
2013 - San Juan, PR/March 17
Number of non-conference events/year: 3

Publications:
ACMT Newsletter; quarterly
The Journal of Medical Toxicology

American College of Mental Health Administration (1979)
7804 Loma del Norte Rd. NE
Albuquerque, NM 87109-5419
Tel: (505) 822-5038 *Fax:* (505) 822-5068
Website: acmha.org
Members: 235 individuals
Staff: 2
Annual Budget: $25-50,000
Tax: 501(c)(3)

Personnel:
Executive Director: Kris Ericson PhD
  E-Mail: executive.director@acmha.org

Historical Note:
ACMHA's mission is to further mental health administration as a practice and a profession, to foster research, and provide opportunities for professional education and communication. Members are clinician- administrators with knowledge and experience in both the administration of mental health programs and clinical care. Membership: $275/year.

Meetings/Conferences: Annual

Publications:
ACMHA eNewsletter; quarterly
Alcohol & Drug Abuse Weekly; weekly
Behavioral Healthcare; annually
Membership Directory; on-line
Mental Health Weekly; weekly

American College of Mohs Surgeons (1967)
555 E. Wells St.
Suite 1100
Milwaukee, WI 53202-3823
Tel: (414) 347-1103 *Fax:* (414) 276-2146
TollFree: (800) 500-7224
E-Mail: info@mohscollege.org
Website: mohscollege.org
Members: 810 individuals
Staff: 5
Annual Budget: $500-1,000,000

Personnel:
Executive Director: Kim Schardin CAE, MBA
  E-Mail: kschardin@mohscollege.org
Coordinator, Meetings and Membership Services: Josh de Beer
Manager, Communications and Projects: Erin O'Krongly
Manager, Meetings: Michelle Ridolfi
Education Manager: Susan Sadowski

Historical Note:
Formerly (1987) American College of Chemosurgery, (2007) American College of Mohs Micrographic Surgery and Cutaneous Oncology. Absorbed American College of Cryosurgery in 1997. Mission of ACMS is to promote and advance the standards of patient care with respect to Mohs surgery and cutaneous oncology through fellowship training, research, education and public advocacy. Membership open exclusively to physicians with fellowship training in Mohs surgery, utilizing Mohs micrographic for the microscopically controlled excision of skin cancers.

Meetings/Conferences: Annual
Conference Chair: Michelle Ridolfi
2013 - Washington, DC (Omni Shoreham)/May 2 - 5
2014 - Phoenix, AZ (JW Marriott Desert Ridge Resort)/May 1 - 4

Publications:
Membership Directory; on-line

American College of Mortgage Attorneys (1974)
9707 Key West Ave.
Suite 100
Rockville, MD 20850
Tel: (301) 990-9075 *Fax:* (301) 990-9771
E-Mail: acma@mgmtsol.com
Website: acmaatty.org
Members: 400 individuals
Staff: 4
Annual Budget: $250-500,000

Personnel:
Executive Director: Beverly I. Levy CAE
  E-Mail: blevy@mgmtsol.com
Manager, Communications: Jon Benjamin
Director, Meetings: Grace Jan CMP
  E-Mail: gjan@mgmtsol.com
Manager, Member Services: Lynn Turner

Historical Note:
Formed in 1974 by a group of lawyers. ACMA aims to improve and reform laws and procedures affecting real estate secured transactions and to raise the level of professional responsibility of lawyers practicing in this area. Members (Fellows) include in-house and government lawyers in addition to private practitioners.

Meetings/Conferences: Annual
Conference Chair: Grace Jan CMP
2013 - Teton Village, WY (Four Seasons Resort Jackson Hole)/Sept. 26 - 28
2014 - Bretton Woods, NH (Omni-Mount Washington Resort)/Sept. 18 - 20

Publications:
Membership Directory; on-line
The Abstract; bi-annually

American College of Musicians (1929)
P.O. Box 1807
Austin, TX 78767-1807
Tel: (512) 478-5775 *Fax:* (512) 478-5843
E-Mail: ngpt@aol.com
Website: pianoguild.com
Members: 118000 individuals
Staff: 12
Annual Budget: $2-5,000,000
Tax: 501(c)(3)

Personnel:
President: Richard Allison
Contact, Certification: Gloria Castro

Historical Note:
ACM's objective is to establish definite goals and awards in noncompetitive auditions for students of all levels. ACM grants degrees and diplomas to musicians, consists of two divisions: the National Guild of Piano Teachers and the National Fraternity of Student Musicians. Members are individuals whose qualifications make them eligible to judge. Membership: $75/year (Individual).

Continuing Education:
Certification Designation/s: ACM

Publications:
Piano Guild Notes; quarterly

American College of Neuropsychiatrists (1939)
28595 Orchard Lake Rd.
Suite 200
Farmington Hills, MI 48334-2979
Tel: (248) 553-0010 *Fax:* (248) 553-0818
E-Mail: acn-aconp@msn.com
Website: acn-aconp.webs.com/
Members: 800 Physicians
Staff: 2
Annual Budget: $250-500,000
Tax: 501(c)(3)

Personnel:
Executive Director: Sue Wesserling

Historical Note:
Affiliated with the American Osteopathic Association. Also known as American College of Osteopathic Neurologists and Psychiatrists. ACN's mission is to advocate the art and science of osteopathic medicine in the fields of neurology and psychiatry. Membership: $300 (Individual); $100 (Resident).

Meetings/Conferences: Annual

Publications:
ACN Newsletter; semi-annually
Journal of The American College Of Neuropsychiatrists; semi-annually; adv.

American College of Neuropsychopharmacology (1961)
5034-A Thoroughbred Ln.
Brentwood, TN 37027
Tel: (615) 324-2360 *Fax:* (615) 523-1715
E-Mail: acnp@acnp.org
Website: acnp.org
Members: 600 individuals
Staff: 15
Annual Budget: $2-5,000,000

Personnel:
Executive Director: Ronnie D Wilkins EdD
  E-Mail: rwilkins@acnp.org
Manager, Meetings: Eileen Cooke
Contact, Publications: Diane Drexler
  E-Mail: ddrexler@acnp.org
Project Manager: Laura Hill
  E-Mail: lhill@acnp.org
Coordinator, Finance and Meetings: Julie Magill
  E-Mail: jmagill@acnp.org

Historical Note:
ACNP's mission is to further research and education in neuropsychopharmacology and related fields. Promotes the interaction of a broad range of scientific disciplines of brain and behavior in order to advance the understanding of prevention and treatment of diseases of the nervous system.

Meetings/Conferences: Annual
Conference Chair: Julie Magill
2013 - Hollywood, FL (Westin Diplomat Resort and Spa)/Dec. 8 - 12
2014 - Phoenix, AZ (JW Marriott Phoenix Desert Ridge Resort and Spa)/Dec. 7 - 11
2015 - Hollywood, FL (Westin Diplomat Resort and Spa)/Dec. 6 - 10
2016 - Hollywood, FL (Westin Diplomat Resort and Spa)/Dec. 4 - 8
2017 - Palm Spring, CA (JW Marriott Desert Springs Resort)/Dec. 3 - 7
Number of non-conference events/year: 3

Publications:
Neuropsychopharmacology; monthly
Neuropsychopharmacology Reviews; annually

American College of Nuclear Medicine (2009)
1850 Samuel Morse Dr.
Reston, VA 20190-5316
Tel: (703) 326-1190 *Fax:* (703) 708-9015
Website: acnponline.org
Members: 500 individuals
Staff: 6
Annual Budget: $50-100,000

Personnel:
Chief Executive Officer: Virginia Pappas CAE
  E-Mail: vpappas@snm.org
Director, Health Policy and Regulatory Affairs: Sue Bunning
  E-Mail: sbunning@snm.org
Senior Manager, Membership Services: Christine Cachuela
  E-Mail: ccachuela@snmmi.org
Chief Financial Officer: Vince Pistilli
  E-Mail: vpistilli@snm.org

Historical Note:
The American College of Nuclear Physicians and the American College of Nuclear Medicine combined to form the American College of Nuclear Medicine. ACNM's mission is to foster better standards in Nuclear Medicine consultation and service to referring physicians, hospitals, and the public, advance the science of Nuclear Medicine through study, education, and improvement of the socioeconomic aspects of the practice of Nuclear Medicine and thereby to improve Nuclear Medicine consultation and service and to promote the continuing competence and socioeconomic awareness of practitioners of Nuclear Medicine through a program of continuing professional development emphasizing better standards of Nuclear Medicine practice. It is managed by the Society of Nuclear Medicine. Members

are physicians doing diagnostic work with radioactive pharmaceuticals. Members must pass a Specialty Board examination.Membership:$225 (Full Member); $100 (Corporate); $50 (Emeritus/Honorary/Affiliate); Free (Resident); $175 (Corresponding).

Meetings/Conferences: Annual
2013 - New Orleans, LA (Sheraton New Orleans Hotel)/Jan. 24 - 27

Publications:
Membership Directory; on-line
Online Clinical Nuclear Medicine Journal; monthly; adv.
Scanner
Scintillator
SNM-ACNM Health Policy & Regulatory Affairs Newsletter

American College of Nurse Practitioners *(1993)*
225 Reinekers Ln.
Suite 525
Alexandria, VA 22314
Tel: (703) 740-2529 *Fax:* (703) 740-2533
E-Mail: acnp@acnpweb.org
Website: acnpweb.org
Members:
3700 individuals
7 national affiliates
Staff: 7
Annual Budget: $1-2,000,000
Tax: 501(c)(6)

Personnel:
Chief Executive Officer: David E. Hebert
    E-Mail: David@acnpweb.org
Manager, Meetings: Tiffany Melton
    E-Mail: tiffany.melton@jspargo.com
Coordinator, Communications and Membership: Nick Rumberger
    E-Mail: nick@acnpweb.org
Director, Marketing and Meetings: Debra Swan
    E-Mail: Debra@acnpweb.org
Manager, Administrative Services: E. Timothy Wagner
    E-Mail: Tim@acnpweb.org

Historical Note:
Mission is to unite and represent nurse practitioners across the United States.

Continuing Education:
Certification Designation/s: NP

Meetings/Conferences: Annual
Conference Chair: Debra Swan
2013 - Las Vegas, NV/Oct. 2 - 6

Publications:
The Journal For Nurse Practitioners (JNP)
Washington Word; on-line

Membership List Available to Non-members

American College of Nurse-Midwives *(1955)*
8403 Colesville Rd.
Suite 1550
Silver Spring, MD 20910-6374
Tel: (240) 485-1800 *Fax:* (240) 485-1818
E-Mail: info@acnm.org
Website: midwife.org
Members: 7000 individuals
Staff: 30
Annual Budget: $5-10,000,000
Tax: 501(c)(6)

Personnel:
Executive Director: Lorrie Kline Kaplan
    E-Mail: lkaplan@acnm.org
Intern, Government Relations: Quinton Callahan
    E-Mail: qcallahan@acnm.org
Manager, Communications: Melissa Garvey
    E-Mail: mgarvey@acnm.org
Senior Policy Advisor, Education: Elaine Germano
    E-Mail: egermano@acnm.org
Director, Finance: Meredith Graham
    E-Mail: mgraham@acnm.org
Director, Membership Services: George Hamilton
    E-Mail: ghamilton@acnm.org
Director, Professional Practice and Health Policy: Christina Johnson CNM, MS
    E-Mail: profsvcs@midwife.org
Director, Government Relations: Joanna King
    E-Mail: jking@acnm.org
Editor-in-Chief: Frances Likis CNM, NP
    E-Mail: flikis@acnm.org

Manager, Information Technology: Fausto Miranda
    E-Mail: fmiranda@acnm.org

Historical Note:
Formerly (1969) American College of Nurse-Midwifery. Mission is to promote the health and well-being of women and infants within their families and communities through the development and support of the profession of midwifery as practiced by certified nurse-midwives and certified midwives. Membership: $5,025 (Life); $350 (Active); $135 (Associate/Student); $210 (Active-First Year); $187.50 (Active- Supporting).

Continuing Education:
Certification Designation/s: CNMs, CMs

Meetings/Conferences: Annual
2013 - Nashville, TN/May 30 - June 4
2014 - Denver, CO/May 12 - 17
2015 - Washington, DC/June 25 - 30
2017 - Chicago, IL/May 19 - 24
2019 - Washington, DC/May 31 - June 5
2022 - Chicago, IL/May 20 - 25
Number of non-conference events/year: 2

Publications:
Quick eNews; monthly
Quickening; quarterly
The Journal of Midwifery & Women's Health; bi-monthly

Membership List Available to Non-members

American College of Nutrition *(1959)*
300 S. Duncan Ave.
Suite 225
Clearwater, FL 33755
Tel: (727) 446-6086 *Fax:* (727) 446-6202
E-Mail: office@amcollnutr.org
Website: americancollegeofnutrition.org
Members: 1200 individuals
Staff: 4
Annual Budget: $250-500,000
Tax: 501(c)(3)

Personnel:
President: Harry G. Preuss CNS, MACN, MD
Office Manager: Santa Henriquez

Historical Note:
Merged with the American Nutritionists Association (1992). ACN's mission is to enhance nutrition and metabolism knowledge among physicians and professionals from all disciplines with a common interest in nutrition, and to promote the application of such knowledge to the maintenance of health and treatment of disease. Members are physicians, bachelor and advanced degree nutritionists, and registered dietitians. Membership: $150-190 (Fellows/Individual); $60 (Student/Trainee); $50 (Emeritus).

Continuing Education:
Certification Designation/s: CNS

Meetings/Conferences: Annual

Publications:
Membership Directory
Journal of the American College of Nutrition; bi-monthly

American College of Occupational and Environmental Medicine *(1916)*
25 Northwest Point Blvd.
Suite 700
Elk Grove Village, IL 60007-1030
Tel: (847) 818-1800 *Fax:* (847) 818-9266
E-Mail: acoeminfo@acoem.org
Website: acoem.org
Members: 4500 individuals
Staff: 8
Annual Budget: $5-10,000,000
Tax: 501(c)(3)

Personnel:
Executive Director: Barry S. Eisenberg CAE, MA
Director, Publications: Marianne Dreger
Manager, Membership Services: Miles Hoffman MA
Director, Finance: Julie Hofman
Director, Strategic Development: Doris L. Konicki MHS
    E-Mail: dkonicki@acoem.org
Director, Education: Joyce Paschall CAE, CMP
Director, Information Management and Technology: Bud J. Romano BS

Historical Note:
Established in Illinois in 1916 as the American Association of Industrial Physicians and Surgeons and chartered, became the Industrial Medical Association in 1951 and then the American Occupational Medical Association in

1974 and assumed its present name in 1988 on merging with the American Academy of Occupational Medicine, Organization for occupational and environmental medicine (OEM) physicians and other OEM health professionals in the world. ACOEM's purpose is to promote optimal health and safety of workers, workplaces, and environments by educating health professionals and the public, stimulating research, enhancing the quality of practice, guiding workplace and public policy and advancing the field of occupational and environmental medicine. Membership: $390 (Active); $225 (Associate/Affiliate); $45 (Resident).

Continuing Education:
Certification Designation/s: ABPM, AOBPM

Meetings/Conferences: Annual
2013 - Orlando, FL (Shingle Creek)/April 28 - May 1
2014 - San Antonio, TX (San Antonio Marriott Rivercenter)/April 27 - 30
2015 - Baltimore, MD (Hilton Baltimore)/May 3 - 6
2016 - Chicago, IL (Chicago Sheraton Hotel and Towers)/April 10 - 13
Number of non-conference events/year: 7

Publications:
CDME Review Newsletter; quarterly
Journal of Occupational and Environmental Medicine (JOEM); monthly
Membership Directory; on-line
MRO Update newsletter; quarterly

American College of Oral and Maxillofacial Surgeons *(1975)*
2025 M St. NW
Suite 800
Washington, DC 20036
Tel: (202) 367-1182 *Fax:* (202) 367-2182
TollFree: (800) 522-6676
E-Mail: admin@acoms.org
Website: acoms.org
Members: 2300 individuals
Staff: 6
Annual Budget: $500-1,000,000
Tax: 501(c)(3)

Personnel:
Executive Director: Steven C Kemp CAE
    E-Mail: Skemp@acoms.org
Manager, Education: Joyce Arawole
    E-Mail: jarawole@smithbucklin.com
Senior Director, Event Services: Tina Hochberg
    E-Mail: thochberg@smithbucklin.com
Senior Program Coordinator: Greg Maciog
    E-Mail: gmaciog@acoms.org
Manager, Conventions: Fred Moxley
Staff Accountant: Sunny Patel
    E-Mail: spatel@smithbucklin.com

Historical Note:
ACOMS's purpose is to enhance patient care through research and education in oral and maxillofacial surgery. Membership: $595/year (Fellows/Associate).

Meetings/Conferences: Annual
Conference Chair: Greg Maciog
2013 - Scottsdale, AZ (Phoenician Resort)/April 20 - 22
Number of non-conference events/year: 1

Publications:
OOOOE Journal; monthly

American College of Osteopathic Emergency Physicians *(1975)*
142 E. Ontario St.
Suite 1500
Chicago, IL 60611
Tel: (312) 587-3709 *Fax:* (312) 587-9951
TollFree: (800) 521-3709
Website: acoep.org
Members: 4500 individuals
Staff: 8
Annual Budget: $2-5,000,000
Tax: 501(c)(6)

Personnel:
Executive Director: Janice Wachtler
Editor: Drew A. Koch DO, FACOEP
Manager, Communications: Erin Sernoffsky
    E-Mail: esernoffsky@acoep.org
Manager, Membership Services: Sonya Stephens
    E-Mail: sstephens@acoep.org
Director, Information Technology: Brian Thommen
Director, Meetings: Kristin Wattonville
    E-Mail: kwattonville@acoep.org

Historical Note:
ACOEP's mission is to advance the philosophy and practice of osteopathic medicine through a system of quality and cost effective healthcare in a distinct, unified profession. *Membership:* $125-495 (Active, based on no. of years post residency); $250 (Associate).

Continuing Education:
Certification Designation/s: CCEM

Meetings/Conferences:
Conference Chair: Kristin Wattonville

Publications:
Member Directory; on-line
The Pulse; quarterly; adv.

Membership List Available to Non-members

American College of Osteopathic Family Physicians (1950)
330 E. Algonquin Rd.
Suite One
Arlington Heights, IL 60005
Tel: (847) 952-5108 *Fax:* (847) 228-9755
TollFree: (800) 323-0794
E-Mail: membership@acofp.org
Website: acofp.org
Members: 20000 individuals
Staff: 15
Annual Budget: $2-5,000,000

Personnel:
Executive Director: Peter L. Schmelzer CAE
   E-Mail: peters@acofp.org
Director, Membership Services and Administration: Tina Burk
   E-Mail: tinab@acofp.org
Manager, Marketing: Ashley Doyle
   E-Mail: ashleyd@acofp.org
Manager, Media and Design: Stacy Jacobs
   E-Mail: stacyj@acofp.org
Director, Education and Development: Kenneth Korber
   E-Mail: kenk@acofp.org
Controller: Richard Niebrzydowski
   E-Mail: richardn@acofp.org

Historical Note:
Formerly the American College of General Practitioners in Osteopathic Medicine and Surgery (1993). ACOFP works to promote excellence in osteopathic family medicine through responsible advocacy, quality education and visionary leadership. An affiliate of the American Osteopathic Association. *Members:* $325 (Physician); $150 (First-Year in Practice Physician/Associate); $60 (Military/Federal Health Member/Retired); Free (Students/Resident Physicians).

Continuing Education:
Certification Designation/s: CAQ, CME

Meetings/Conferences: Annual
2013 - Las Vegas, NV (The Cosmopolitan Hotel)/ March 21 - 24
2013 - Las Vegas, NV (Mandalay Bay Hotel)/Sept. 30 - Oct. 4
Number of non-conference events/year: 1

Publications:
Membership Directory; on-line
Osteopathic Family Physician; bi-monthly

American College of Osteopathic Internists (1941)
11400 Rockville Pike
Suite 801
Rockville, MD 20852
Tel: (301) 656-8877 *Fax:* (301) 231-6099
TollFree: (800) 327-5183
E-Mail: acoi@acoi.org
Website: acoi.org
Members: 3000 individuals
Staff: 8
Annual Budget: $2-5,000,000

Personnel:
Executive Director: Brian J. Donadio
   E-Mail: bjd@acoi.org
Assistant, Membership Services: Jennifer A. Bryant
   E-Mail: jenni@acoi.org
Coordinator, Membership Services and Certification Liaison: Keisha L. Oglesby
   E-Mail: keisha@acoi.org
Director, Administration and Finance: Susan B. Stacy
   E-Mail: susan@acoi.org

Historical Note:

ACOI's mission is to advance the practice of osteopathic internal medicine. *Membership:* $0-400/year.

Meetings/Conferences: Annual
Conference Chair: Susan B. Stacy
2013 - Indian Wells, CA (Renaissance Esmeralda Indian Wells Resort and Spa)/Oct. 9 - 13
2014 - Baltimore, MD (Baltimore Marriott Inner Harbor at Camden Yards)/Oct. 15 - 19

Publications:
ACOInformation; monthly
Resident Newsletter; quarterly

Membership List Available to Non-members

American College of Osteopathic Obstetricians and Gynecologists (1934)
8851 Camp Bowie West
Suite 275
Ft. Worth, TX 76116
Tel: (817) 377-0421 *Fax:* (817) 377-0439
TollFree: (800) 875-6360
E-Mail: info@acoog.org
Website: acoog.com
Members: 1000 individuals
Staff: 4
Annual Budget: $1-2,000,000
Tax: 501(c)(6)

Personnel:
Executive Director: Valerie Brennan CAE
   E-Mail: cme@acoog.org
Executive Vice President: Steve P. Buchanan DO
   E-Mail: stbuchan@hsc.unt.edu
Manager, Membership and Communications: Sherry Halm
   E-Mail: membership@acoog.org
Director, Administration: Helen Oberbeck
   E-Mail: postgraduate@acoog.org

Historical Note:
Formed in Wichita, Kansas during the annual meeting of the American Osteopathic Association by ten charter practicing obstetricians and gynecologists in the profession of osteopathic medicine. Originally the American College of Osteopathic Obstetricians, the present name was assumed in 1949. Chartered in the state of Missouri. Purpose is to improve the quality of life for women and promote educational programs that are innovative, visionary, inclusive and socially relevant. *Membership:* $200 (Regular); $50 (Associate); $25 (Affiliate).

Meetings/Conferences:
2013 - Clearwater, FL (Hilton Clearwater Beach)/April 7 - 12

Publications:
Newsletter; bi-annually

American College of Osteopathic Pediatricians (1940)
2209 Dickens Rd.
Richmond, VA 23230-2005
Tel: (804) 565-6333 *Fax:* (804) 282-0090
E-Mail: joye@acopeds.org
Website: acopeds.org
Members: 1000 individuals
Staff: 11
Annual Budget: $250-500,000
Tax: 501(c)(6)

Personnel:
Executive Director: Stewart A. Hinckley CMP
Contact, Membership Services: Kim Battle
   E-Mail: kim@acopeds.org
Editor in Chief: Michael Hunt DO, FACOP, CMP
Contact, Media Relations: Megan Renner

Historical Note:
ACOP's mission is to serve as the professional membership organization for all osteopathic pediatricians. *Membership:* $400 (Fellow/General/Associate); $20 (Intern); $30 (Resident/Fellow-in- Training/Student).

Meetings/Conferences: Annual
2013 - Columbus, OH (Renaissance Columbus Downtown Hotel)/April 25 - 28

Publications:
eJACOP; quarterly
Membership Directory; on-line
The Pulse Newsletter; quarterly; adv.

American College of Osteopathic Surgeons (1927)
123 N. Henry St.
Alexandria, VA 22314-2903
Tel: (703) 684-0416 *Fax:* (703) 684-3280

TollFree: (800) 888-1312
E-Mail: info@facos.org
Website: facos.org
Members: 2200 individuals
Staff: 8
Annual Budget: $1-2,000,000
Tax: 501(c)(6)

Personnel:
Executive Director: Guy D. Beaumont Jr.
   E-Mail: gbeaumont@facos.org
Director, Membership Recruitment and Retention: Sonjya Johnson
   E-Mail: sjohnson@facos.org
Director, Post-Doctoral Training Standards and Evaluation: Donald B. Kaveny
   E-Mail: dkaveny@facos.org
Director, Finance and Administration: Brandon Roberts
   E-Mail: broberts@facos.org
Director, Continuing Education and Meetings: Kendra E. Smith
   E-Mail: ksmith@facos.org

Historical Note:
Organized in June 1926 and incorporated in Missouri in 1927. ACOS is committed to assure excellence in osteopathic surgical care through education, advocacy, leadership development, and fostering of professional and personal relationships. *Membership:* $95-570 (Full); $150 (Resident); $20 (Student, one-time); $355 (U.S. Military/Public Health Service).

Continuing Education:
Certification Designation/s: AOBS, AOBOG, AOBOS, ABOO-HNS

Meetings/Conferences:
Conference Chair: Kendra E. Smith
2013 - Las Vegas, NV (Caesars Palace)/Nov. 14 - 17
2014 - Boston, MA (Westin Boston Waterfront)/Sept. 11 - 14
Number of non-conference events/year: 1

Publications:
ACOS News; monthly; adv.
Membership Directory; on-line

American College of Phlebology (1985)
101 Callan Ave.
Suite 210
San Leandro, CA 94577
Tel: (510) 346-6800 *Fax:* (510) 346-6808
E-Mail: info@acpmail.org
Website: phlebology.org
Members: 2000 phlebology professionals
Staff: 7
Annual Budget: $2-5,000,000
Tax: 501(c)(3)

Personnel:
Executive Director: Bruce A. Sanders CAE
   E-Mail: bsanders@acpmail.org
Director, Marketing And Communications: Michael "Mike" Armitage
   E-Mail: marmitage@acpmail.org
Director, Finance and Technology: Keith Darby MBA
   E-Mail: kdarby@acpmail.org
Director, Meeting Services: Dana Deponzi-Haas CMP
   E-Mail: ddeponzi@acpmail.org
Director, Continuing Medical Education: Heather Durband
   E-Mail: hdurband@acpmail.org
Administrative Assistant: Bernadette Hardy
   E-Mail: bhardy@acpmail.org
Director, Membership Services: Caryl G. Tynan CAE
   E-Mail: ctynan@acpmail.org

Historical Note:
ACP's mission is to strives to advance vein care. The College not only acts as a forum for physicians and other health professionals to exchange medical knowledge, it also offers education and training, and seeks to improve the standards of medical practitioners and the quality of patient care. *Membership:* $950 (Physician); $225 (Allied Healthcare); $50 (Physician Member in Training); $300 (International Physician/International Allied Healthcare).

Continuing Education:
Certification Designation/s: CME

Meetings/Conferences: Annual
Conference Chair: Dana Deponzi-Haas CMP
2013 - Boston, MA (John B. Hynes Veterans Memorial Convention Center)/Sept. 8 - 13
2014 - Phoenix, AZ (JW Marriott Desert Ridge Resort)/ Nov. 6 - 9

Publications:
IN THE VEIN e-newsletter; monthly
Membership Directory; on-line
Phlebology Journal; adv.
VeinLine E-Newsletter; quarterly; adv.
Venous Digest; monthly; adv.

American College of Physician Executives (1975)
400 N. Ashley Dr.
Suite 400
Tampa, FL 33602
Tel: (813) 287-2000 *Fax:* (813) 287-8993
TollFree: (800) 562-8088
E-Mail: acpe@acpe.org
Website: acpe.org
Members: 10000 individuals
Staff: 23
Annual Budget: $5-10,000,000

Personnel:
Chief Executive Officer: Peter Angood FACS, FCCM, FRCS, MD
  E-Mail: pangood@acpe.org
Faculty Coordinator and Contact, Onsite Education Development: Lisa Albrizzi
  E-Mail: lalbrizzi@acpe.org
Systems Administrator: Luke Barnes
  E-Mail: lbarnes@acpe.org
Professional Development and Career Counseling: Barbara Linney
  E-Mail: blinney@acpe.org
Contact, Production and Design Print: Debi Marsh
  E-Mail: dmarsh@acpe.org
Director, Membership Services: Judy Rochell
  E-Mail: jrochell@acpe.org
Contact, Marketing and Communications and Editor: Bill Steiger
  E-Mail: bsteiger@acpe.org
Director, Education Conference: Tonya Wade
  E-Mail: twade@acpe.org

Historical Note:
Formerly (1988) the American Academy of Medical Directors. ACPE strives to build physician leaders who can guide the direction of health care, through medical management education, professional growth and recognition programs. Members for physicians in management positions within all sectors of the health care field. Membership: $250 (Regular/International/Dental/Podiatry); $200 (Military/Public Health); $125 (Physician Assistant); $175 (Health Care Leader/Health Care Professional/Affiliate); $30 (Student); $45 (Resident); $50 (Masters Candidate/ Retired/Emeritus); $2,900 (Life); $225 (Group-10 physicians).

Continuing Education:
Certification Designation/s: CPE

Meetings/Conferences: Semi-Annual
Conference Chair: Tonya Wade
2013 - Orlando, FL (Loews Portofino Bay Hotel)/Jan. 25 - 27
2013 - New York City, NY (Hilton New York)/April 26 - 30
Number of non-conference events/year: 1

Publications:
ACPE Daily Digest; daily
Membership Directory; on-line
Physician Executive Journal; bi-monthly

Membership List Available to Non-members

American College of Physicians (1915)
190 N. Independence Mall West
Philadelphia, PA 19106-1572
Tel: (215) 351-2600 *Fax:* (215) 351-2829
TollFree: (800) 523-1546
Website: acponline.org
Members: 132000 internists, internal medicine sub-specialists, medical students, residents, and fellows.
Staff: 320
Annual Budget: $50-100,000,000

Personnel:
Executive Vice President and Chief Executive Officer: Steven E. Weinberger FACP, MD
  E-Mail: sweinberger@acponline.org
Chief Operating Officer: Wayne H. Bylsma PhD
  E-Mail: wbylsma@acponline.org
Director, Public Relations and Web Communications: Allison Ewing
  E-Mail: aewing@acponline.org

Chief Financial Officer: Ralph L. Hibbs CPA, Jr., MBA
  E-Mail: rhibbs@acponline.org
Vice President, Medical Education: D. Theresa Kanya
  E-Mail: tkanya@acponline.org
Director, Educational Meetings and Conferences: Barbara Licht
  E-Mail: Blicht@acponline.org
Senior Vice President, International Programs: James M. Ott
  E-Mail: jott@acponline.org
Senior Vice President, Publishing, Business Development and Marketing: David Sgrignoli
  E-Mail: dsgrignoli@acponline.org

Historical Note:
Merged with Congress of Internal Medicine in 1925 and American Society of Internal Medicine in 1999 and formerly American College of Physicians - American Society of Internal Medicine, assumed its current name in 2003, ACP's mission is to enhance the quality and effectiveness of health care by fostering professionalism in the practice of medicine. Members are practicing internists-physicians who specialize in the prevention, detection and treatment of illnesses in adults. "Fellows" are certified internists recognized by their colleagues for their scholarship and professional excellence. Membership: $109 (Associate); $99-255 (Individual); $265-445 (Fellow/Member/Master); $200 (Affiliate).

Continuing Education:
Certification Designation/s: ABIM, MOC

Meetings/Conferences: Annual
Conference Chair: Barbara Licht
2013 - San Francisco, CA (The Moscone Center)/April 11 - 13/1-10 exhibitors
2014 - Orlando, FL/April 10 - 12
2014 - Orlando, FL/April 10 - 14
2015 - Boston, MA/April 30 - May 2
2016 - Washington, DC/May 5 - 7
Number of non-conference events/year: 3

Publications:
ACP Hospitalist®; monthly
ACP Internist®; weekly; adv.
ACP Journal Club PLUS; on-line
Annals of Internal Medicine; semi-monthly
Hospitalist Weekly Online; on-line
Member Directory; on-line

American College of Physicians Services, Inc. (1915)
190 N Independence Mall West
Philadelphia, PA 19106-1572
Tel: (215) 351-2600
Website: acponline.org
Members: 133,000 individuals
Staff: 10
Annual Budget: $2-5,000,000
Tax: 501(c)(6)

Personnel:
Executive Vice President and Chief Executive Officer: Steven E. Weinberger FACP, MD
Senior Vice President, Medical Education: Patrick Alguire FACP, MD
  E-Mail: palguire@acponline.org
Chief Operating Officer: Wayne H. Bylsma PhD
  E-Mail: wbylsma@acponline.org
Director, Information Technology and Archives: Nancy Connors
  E-Mail: nconnors@acponline.org
Director, Public Relations and Web Communications: Allison Ewing
  E-Mail: aewing@acponline.org
Chief Financial Officer: Ralph L. Hibbs CPA, Jr., MBA
  E-Mail: aewing@acponline.org
Senior Vice President Editor-in-Chief: Christine Laine
  E-Mail: claine@acponline.org
Senior Vice President Publishing, Membership Development and Marketing: David L. Sgrignoli
  E-Mail: dsgrignoli@acponline.org
Director, Convention and Meeting Services: Bobbie Turner
  E-Mail: bturner@acponline.org

Historical Note:
ACP Services provides advocacy services to the American College of Physicians (ACP) in support of their public policy agenda.

Meetings/Conferences: Annual
Conference Chair: Bobbie Turner
2013 - San Francisco, CA/April 11 - 13/7000 attendees
2014 - Orlando, FL/April 10 - 12
2015 - Boston, MA/April 30 - May 2

Publications:

Member Directory
The Capitol Key; quarterly

American College of Podiatric Radiologists (1942)
423 E. 23rd St., Suite 112
New York, NY 10010
Tel: (212) 686-7500
Members: 65 individuals
Staff: 1
Annual Budget: Under $10,000

Personnel:
President: Michael P. DellaCorte DPM

Historical Note:
Established as the American College of Chiropodial Roentgenologists, it became the American College of Foot Roentgenologists in 1962 and assumed its present name in 1974. Affiliated with the American Podiatric Medical Association. Has no paid officers or full-time staff. Membership: $110/year (individual).

American College of Preventive Medicine (1954)
1307 New York Ave. NW
Suite 200
Washington, DC 20005
Tel: (202) 466-2044 *Fax:* (202) 466-2662
E-Mail: info@acpm.org
Website: acpm.org
Members: 2000 individuals
Staff: 9
Annual Budget: $2-5,000,000
Tax: 501(c)(3)

Personnel:
Executive Director: Michael A. Barry CAE
  E-Mail: mbarry@acpm.org
Director, Meetings and Education: Haydee Barno CMP, MBA
  E-Mail: hbarno@acpm.org
Manager, Information Technology: David Dauphinais
  E-Mail: ddauphinais@acpm.org
Director, Membership Services and Development: Jennifer Edwards
  E-Mail: jedwards@acpm.org
Controller, Finance and Human Resources: Amy Fleishman
  E-Mail: afleishman@acpm.org
Membership Manager: Camille Sanders
  E-Mail: csanders@acpm.org

Historical Note:
ACPM seeks to improve population health status through evidence-based disease prevention and health promotion research, policies, practices, and programs. Membership: $15-310/year.

Meetings/Conferences: Annual
Conference Chair: Haydee Barno CMP, MBA
2013 - Phoenix, AZ (Pointe Hilton Tapatio Cliffs Resort)/Feb. 20 - 23

Publications:
ACPM HEADLINES; on-line
American Journal of Preventive Medicine; monthly; adv.

Membership List Available to Non-members

American College of Prosthodontists (1970)
211 E. Chicago Ave.
Suite 1000
Chicago, IL 60611
Tel: (312) 573-1260 *Fax:* (312) 573-1257
E-Mail: acp@prosthodontics.org
Website: prosthodontics.org
Members: 3,300 members
Staff: 11
Annual Budget: $2-5,000,000
Tax: 501(c)(6)

Personnel:
Executive Director: Nancy Deal Chandler CAE, MA, RHIA
  E-Mail: dchandler@prosthodontics.org
Associate Executive Director, Membership Services and Outreach: Carla Baker CAE, MBA
  E-Mail: cbaker@prosthodontics.org
Associate Executive Director, Communications, Public Relations and Marketing: Lauren Dethloff
  E-Mail: ldethloff@prosthodontics.org
Managing Editor: Alethea Gerding
  E-Mail: alethea_gerding@dentistry.unc.edu
Director, Education and Meeting Services: Melissa Kabadian CMP, MA

E-Mail: mkabadian@prosthodontics.org
Manager, Finance and Administration: Jack Kanich
E-Mail: jkanich@prosthodontics.org

Historical Note:
*ACP is the professional association of dentists with
advanced specialty training in dental implants, dentures,
veneers, crowns and teeth whitening. Members are
prosthodontists and dentists specializing in implant,
esthetic, and reconstructive dentistry. Membership: $696
(Member/Fellow); $400 (Dental Technician Alliance); $495
(Global Alliance/Academic Alliance).*

Meetings/Conferences: Annual
Conference Chair: Melissa Kabadian CMP, MA
2013 - Las Vegas, NV (Caesars Palace Las Vegas Hotel
    and Casino)/Oct. 9 - 12
2014 - New Orleans, LA (Hyatt Regency New Orleans)/
    Nov. 5 - 8
Number of non-conference events/year: 2

Publications:
ACP Update
e-blasts; weekly
Journal of Prosthodontics
Messenger; quarterly

American College of Psychiatrists *(1963)*
122 S. Michigan Ave.
Suite 1360
Chicago, IL 60603
Tel: (312) 662-1020 *Fax:* (312) 662-1025
E-Mail: angel@acpsych.org
Website: acpsych.org
Members: 750 Psychiatrists
Staff: 4
Annual Budget: $1-2,000,000
Tax: 501(c)(3)

Personnel:
Executive Director: Maureen D. Shick
    E-Mail: maureen@acpsych.org
Manager, Programs: Kathy Ricker
    E-Mail: kathy@acpsych.org

Historical Note:
*ACP seeks to advocate and support psychiatry through
education, research, and clinical practice. Membership is
limited to practicing psychiatrists who have demonstrated
outstanding competence in the field of psychiatry, and who
have achieved national recognition in clinical practice,
research, academic leadership, and teaching. Membership:
$370/year (Individual).*

Continuing Education:
Certification Designation/s: PRITE, PIPE

Meetings/Conferences: Annual
2013 - Kohala Coast, HI (Hapuna Beach Prince Hotel)/
    Feb. 20 - 24
2014 - Antonio, TX (Grand Hyatt San Antonio)/Feb. 19
    - 23
2015 - Huntington Beach, CA (Hyatt Regency
    Huntington Beach Resort and Spa)/Feb. 18 - 22
2016 - Rio Grande, PR (Rio Mar Beach Resort and
    Spa)/Feb. 17 - 21

Publications:
Member Directory; on-line

American College of Psychoanalysts *(1969)*
C/O Frances Roton Bell
P.O. Box 570218
Dallas, TX 75357-0218
Tel: (972) 613-0985 *Fax:* (972) 613-5532
E-Mail: contact@acopsa.org
Website: acopsa.org
Members: 240 individuals
Staff: 2
Annual Budget: $25-50,000
Tax: 501(c)(6)

Personnel:
Executive Secretary: Frances Roton Bell
    E-Mail: frda1@airmail.net
Editor: David Dean Brockman MD
    E-Mail: deanbro@comcast.net

Historical Note:
*ACOPSA's mission is to honor outstanding physician-
psychoanalysts throughout the world. Members are medical
doctors practicing psychoanalysis.*

Publications:
ACP Newsletter; irregular
Membership Directory; on-line

American College of Radiation Oncology *(1989)*

5272 River Rd.
Suite 630
Bethesda, MD 20816
Tel: (301) 718-6515 *Fax:* (301) 656-0989
E-Mail: info@acro.org
Website: acro.org
Members: 1000 individuals
Staff: 6
Annual Budget: $1-2,000,000

Personnel:
Executive Director: Norman E. Wallis PhD
    E-Mail: nwallis@paimgmt.com
Assistant, Membership Services: Rene Atkinson
    E-Mail: membership@acro.org
Coordinator, Accreditation: Rachael Spencer
    E-Mail: rspencer@acro.org

Historical Note:
*ACRO strives to ensure quality care for radiation therapy
patients and promote success in the practice of radiation
oncology through education, responsible socioeconomic
advocacy, and integration of science and technology
into clinical practice. Members are radiation oncologists,
physicists and administrators. Membership: $375 (Active);
$255 (Associate); $100 (Corresponding Member); Free for
Resident.*

Meetings/Conferences: Annual

Publications:
Acro Alert; on-line; adv.
ACRO Bulletin; quarterly; adv.
American Journal of Clinical Oncology; bi-monthly
Legislative Update; monthly
RadOnc Weekly; weekly; adv.

Membership List Available to Non-members

American College of Radiology *(1924)*
1891 Preston White Dr.
Reston, VA 20191
Tel: (703) 648-8900
TollFree: (800) 227-5463
E-Mail: info@acr.org
Website: acr.org
Members: 34000 individuals
Staff: 200
Annual Budget: Over $100,000,000
Tax: 501(c)(3)

Personnel:
Chief Executive Officer: Harvey Neiman MD
    E-Mail: Hln@acr.org
*Senior Director, Marketing, Communications and Public
    Relations:* Diane Dunne
    E-Mail: ddunne@acr.org
Assistant Executive Director: Ronald Freedman
    E-Mail: rfreedman@acr.org
Senior Director, Publications: Becky Haines
    E-Mail: bhaines@acr.org
Senior Director, Finance: Elena Han
    E-Mail: ehan@acr-arrs.org
Associate General Counsel: Thomas Hoffman
    E-Mail: thoffman@acr-arrs.org
Chief Financial Officer: Kenneth Korotky
    E-Mail: kkorotky@acr.org
Senior Director, Association and Meeting Services: Pamela
    Mechler CAE, CMP
    E-Mail: pamechler@acr-arrs.org
Assistant Executive Director: James Morrison
    E-Mail: jmorrison@acr.org
Director, Membership Services: Heidi Salkeld
    E-Mail: hsalkeld@acr-arrs.org
Assistant Executive Director and General Counsel, Legal:
    William Shields
    E-Mail: bshields@acr.org
Senior Director, Human Resources: Hang Truong
    E-Mail: htruong@acr.org
Director, Information Technology: Ming-Jen Daniel Wu
    E-Mail: dwu@acr-arrs.org
Senior Director, Education: Elizabeth Yarboro

Historical Note:
*The principal organization of radiologists, radiation
oncologists, and clinical medical physicists in the United
States.*

Meetings/Conferences: Annual
Conference Chair: Pamela Mechler CAE, CMP
2013 - Washington, DC (Washington Hilton)/May 4 - 8
Number of non-conference events/year: 95

Publications:
ACR Bulletin
ACR News

Directory of Membership Anniversaries; on-line
Fellowship Directory; on-line
Journal of American College of Radiology (JACR); bi-
    weekly
Membership Directory; on-line
Staff Directory; on-line

American College of Real Estate Lawyers *(1978)*
11300 Rockville Pike
Suite 903
Rockville, MD 20852
Tel: (301) 816-9811 *Fax:* (301) 816-9786
Website: acrel.org
Members: 900 individuals
Staff: 2
Annual Budget: $500-1,000,000
Tax: 501(c)(6)

Personnel:
Executive Director and Editor: Jill H. Pace

Historical Note:
*ACREL's mission is to promote high standards of
professional and ethical responsibility in the practice of
real estate law, to seek to improve and reform real estate
law and practice. Members are attorneys with at least ten
years of specialization in real estate law. Membership is by
invitation.*

Meetings/Conferences: Semi-Annual
2013 - Naples, FL (Grande Resort)/March 14 - 17
2013 - Vancouver, BC (Four Seasons Hotel And
    Resorts)/Oct. 17 - 20
2014 - Kauai, HI (Grand Hyatt Kauai Resort and Spa)/
    March 27 - 30
2014 - Boston, MA (InterContinental Boston)/Oct. 16
    - 19

Publications:
ACREL Newsletter; quarterly
Membership Roster; on-line

American College of Rheumatology *(1934)*
2200 Lake Blvd. NE
Atlanta, GA 30319
Tel: (404) 633-3777 *Fax:* (404) 633-1870
E-Mail: acr@rheumatology.org
Website: rheumatology.org
Members: 6500 individuals
Staff: 40
Annual Budget: $50-100,000,000
Tax: 501(c)(6)

Personnel:
Executive Vice President: Mark Andrejeski
    E-Mail: mandrejeski@rheumatology.org
Vice President, Education: Donna Hoyne
    E-Mail: dhoyne@rheumatology.org
Coordinator, Membership Services: Janell Martin
    E-Mail: jmartin@rheumatology.org
Media Contact: Amy Molnar
    E-Mail: amolnar@wiley.com

Historical Note:
*Formerly (1989) American Rheumatism Association. ACR's
mission is to advance Rheumatology. Membership: $385
(Clinical/International/Fellow); $242 (Research); $100
(Fellow-In- Training/International Fellow-In-Training);
$25 (Resident/Medical Student); $50 (Special Members);
$30-60 (Emeritus).*

Continuing Education:
Certification Designation/s: CARE, CME, AIM

Meetings/Conferences: Annual
Number of non-conference events/year: 2

Publications:
Arthritis & Rheumatism; monthly
Arthritis Care & Research
Drug Safety; quarterly
Membership Directory; on-line
Rheumatology Morning Wire; daily; adv.
The Rheumatologist; adv.

Membership List Available to Non-members

American College of Sports Medicine *(1954)*
401 W. Michigan St.
Indianapolis, IN 46202-3233
Tel: (317) 637-9200 *Fax:* (317) 634-7817
E-Mail: publicinfo@acsm.org
Website: acsm.org
Members: 45000 Individuals
Staff: 40
Annual Budget: $10-25,000,000
Tax: 501(c)(3)

Personnel:
Manager, Meeting and Continuing Education: Dawn Hamilton
    E-Mail: dhamilton@acsm.org
Contact, Media Relations: Dan Henkel
    E-Mail: dhenkel@acsm.org
President: Janet Walberg Rankin
Director, Membership Services: Chris Sawyer
    E-Mail: csawyer@acsm.org
Executive Vice President: James R. Whitehead
    E-Mail: jwhitehead@acsm.org

Historical Note:
ACSM's mission is to promote and integrate scientific research, education, and practical applications of sports medicine and exercise science to maintain and improve physical performance, fitness and quality of life. Affiliated with the Federation Internationale de Medicine Sportive. Clinical Exercise Physiology Association (CEPA) and International Association for Worksite Health Promotion (IAWHP) originates as an affiliate society of the American College of Sports Medicine. Members are professionals and students wanting cutting-edge information in basic and applied exercise science and clinical sports medicine. Membership: $230 (Professional); $99 (Alliance of Health and Fitness Professional); $155 (Professional-in- Training); $10 (Student, must be enrolled in 6 + credit hours).

Continuing Education:
Certification Designation/s: CCET, RCEP, CPT, PAPHS, CHFS, CCES, CIFT

Meetings/Conferences: Annual
Conference Chair: Dawn Hamilton
2013 - Las Vegas, NV/March 12 - 15
2013 - Indianapolis, IN/May 29 - June 1
2014 - Atlanta, GA/April 2 - 5
2014 - Orlando, FL/May 28 - 31
2015 - San Diego, CA/May 27 - 30
2016 - Boston, MA/June 1 - 4
Number of non-conference events/year: 2

Publications:
Sports Medicine Bulletin; weekly
ACSM Fit Society® Page; quarterly
ACSM's Certified News; quarterly
ACSM's Health & Fitness Journal®; bi-monthly; adv.
Current Sports Medicine Reports
Exercise and Sport Sciences Reviews; quarterly; adv.
Medicine & Science in Sports & Exercise®; monthly; adv.
Member Directory; on-line

Membership List Available to Non-members

American College of Surgeons *(1913)*
633 N. Saint Clair St.
Chicago, IL 60611-3211
Tel: (312) 202-5000 *Fax:* (312) 202-5001
TollFree: (800) 621-4111
E-Mail: postmaster@facs.org
Website: facs.org
Members: 74000 individuals
Staff: 210
Annual Budget: Over $100,000,000
Tax: 501(c)(3)

Personnel:
Executive Director: Dr. David B. Hoyt MD
    E-Mail: dhoyt@facs.org
Director, Human Resources: Jean DeYoung
Editor-In-Chief: Timothy J. Eberlein
    E-Mail: jacsedit@facs.org
Director, Integrated Communications Division: Lynn Kahn
    E-Mail: lkahn@facs.org
Director, Conventions and Meetings: Felix Niespodziewanski
    E-Mail: fniespodziewanski@facs.org
Director, Education: Ajit K. Sachdeva MD, FACS
    E-Mail: asachdeva@facs.org
Director, Information Technology: Howard Tanzman
    E-Mail: htanzman@facs.org
Director, Membership Services: Patricia L. Turner
    E-Mail: pturner@facs.org
Director, Finance and Facilities: Gay L. Vincent
    E-Mail: gvincent@facs.org

Historical Note:
ACS's mission is to improve the care of the surgical patient and to safeguard standards of care in an optimal and ethical practice environment. Membership: $520 (Individual); $175 (Individual outside U.S); $200 (Associate); $20 (Resident).

Continuing Education:
Certification Designation/s: CME, RTTDC, SESAP

Meetings/Conferences:
Conference Chair: Felix Niespodziewanski

Publications:
ACS Cross Country; monthly
ACS NewsScope; weekly
ACS Surgery; monthly
Journal of the American College of Surgeons; monthly
Surgery News; weekly

Membership List Available to Non-members

American College of Surgeons Professional Association *(1913)*
633 N. Saint Clair St.,
Chicago, IL 60611-3211
Tel: (312) 202-5000 *Fax:* (312) 202-5001
TollFree: (800) 621-4111
Website: facs.org/acspa
Staff: 3
Annual Budget: $10-25,000,000
Tax: 501(c)(6)

Personnel:
Editor: Anne Magrath
Director, Division of Advocacy and Health Policy: Christian Shalgian
    E-Mail: cshalgian@facs.org

Historical Note:
Affiliated with the American College of Surgeons, the American College of Surgeons Professional Association is a trade association providing lobbying services on behalf of its members and the industry.ACS's mission is to improve the care of the surgical patient and to safeguarding standards of care in an optimal and ethical practice environment.

Meetings/Conferences: Annual

Publications:
Journal of the American College of Surgeons; monthly
Membership Directory; on-line

Membership List Available to Non-members

American College of Tax Counsel *(1980)*
529 14th St. NW
750 National Press Building
Washington, DC 20045
Tel: (202) 637-3243 *Fax:* (202) 331-2714
E-Mail: info@actconline.org
Website: actconline.org
Members: 700 individuals
Staff: 3
Annual Budget: $100-250,000
Tax: 501(c)(6)

Personnel:
Manager, Administration: Penny Alston
    E-Mail: palston@kellencompany.com
President: Victoria J. Perry

Historical Note:
ACTC strive to foster and recognize the excellence of its members and to elevate standards in the practice of the profession of tax law. It also provide additional mechanisms for input by tax professionals in the development of tax laws and facilitates scholarly discussion and examination of tax policy.

Meetings/Conferences: Annual
2013 - Orlando, FL/Jan. 24 - 26

Publications:
Members Directory; on-line

American College of Theriogenologists *(1971)*
P.O. Box 3065
Montgomery, AL 36109-3065
Tel: (334) 395-4666 *Fax:* (334) 270-3399
Website: theriogenology.org
Staff: 4
Annual Budget: $100-250,000
Tax: 501(c)(6)

Personnel:
Executive Director: Charles Franz DVM
    E-Mail: charles@franzmgt.com
Coordinator, Membership: Linda Cargile
    E-Mail: Linda@Franzmgt.com
Director, Meetings and Membership: Roberta Norris
    E-Mail: Roberta@Franzmgt.com
Director, Public Relations and Communications: Melissa Williford
    E-Mail: Melissa@Franzmgt.com

Historical Note:

Recognized by the American Veterinary Medical Association in 1971. ACT's purpose is to the advancement of knowledge, undergraduate, graduate and postgraduate education, research, and service in theriogenology.

Publications:
ACT Newsletter
Membership Directory; on-line

American College of Toxicology *(1977)*
9650 Rockville Pike
Bethesda, MD 20814
Tel: (301) 634-7840 *Fax:* (301) 634-7852
Website: actox.org
Members: 850 individuals
Staff: 3
Annual Budget: $1-2,000,000
Tax: 501(c)(3)

Personnel:
Executive Director: Carol L. Lemire
    E-Mail: clemire@actox.org
Editor-in-Chief: Mary Beth Genter PhD
    E-Mail: marybeth.genter@uc.edu
Director, Membership Services and Exhibits: Eve Gamzu Kagan
    E-Mail: ekagan@actox.org

Historical Note:
ACT's mission is to educate, lead and serve professionals in industry, government and related areas of toxicology by actively promoting the exchange of information and perspectives on the current status of safety assessment and the application of new developments in toxicology.

Meetings/Conferences: Annual
Conference Chair: Eve Gamzu Kagan
2013 - San Antonio, TX (JW Marriott San Antonio Hill Country Resort and Spa)/Nov. 3 - 6
2014 - Orlando, FL (Hyatt Regency Grand Cypress)/ Nov. 9 - 12

Publications:
International Journal of Toxicology; bi-monthly; adv.

American College of Trial Lawyers *(1950)*
19900 MacArthur Blvd.
Suite 530
Irvine, CA 92612
Tel: (949) 752-1801 *Fax:* (949) 752-1674
E-Mail: nationaloffice@actl.com
Website: actl.com
Members: 5700 fellows
Staff: 9
Annual Budget: $2-5,000,000
Tax: 501(c)(6)

Personnel:
Executive Director: Dennis J. Maggi CAE
    E-Mail: nationaloffice@actl.com
Manager, Membership: Brenda Bates
Manager, Information Technology and Web: Scott H.S. Bryan
Office Administrator: Cheryl E Castillo
Membership Manager: Geri Frankenstein
Manager, Meetings and Conference: Lindsey J.E. Mayfield
Controller: Mary Y Whitney

Historical Note:
An honorary society of lawyers, former lawyers and judges. ACTL is dedicated to maintain and improve the standards of trial practice, the administration of justice and the ethics of the profession.

Meetings/Conferences: Annual
Conference Chair: Lindsey J.E. Mayfield
2013 - Naples, FL (The Ritz - Carlton)/Feb. 28 - March 3
2013 - San Francisco, CA (San Francisco Marriott Marquis)/Oct. 24 - 27
2014 - La Quinta, CA (La Quinta Resort and Club)/ March 6 - 9
2015 - Chicago, IL (Fairmont Chicago Millenium Park)/ Oct. 1 - 4
2016 - Maui, HI (Grand Wailea)/March 3 - 6

Publications:
Attorney Directory; on-line

American College of Veterinary Anesthesiologists *(1975)*
22499 Polecat Hill Rd.
P.O. Box 1100
Middleburg, VA 20118
Tel: (540) 687-5270
Website: acva.org

Members: 220 members
Staff: 1
Annual Budget: $100-250,000
Tax: 501(c)(3)

Personnel:
Executive Secretary: Lydia L. Donaldson
   E-Mail: ldonldsn@earthlink.net

Historical Note:
ACVA aims to promote the advancement of veterinary anesthesiology and to assist the veterinary profession in providing exceptional service to all animals.

Continuing Education:
Certification Designation/s: ACVA-PC

Meetings/Conferences: Annual

Publications:
Member Directory; annually

American College of Veterinary Dermatology (1982)
5610 Kearny Mesa Rd.
Suite B
San Diego, CA 92111
Tel: (858) 560-9393 Fax: (858) 560-0926
E-Mail: itchypet@aol.com
Website: acvd.org
Members: 199 individuals
Staff: 1
Annual Budget: $100-250,000

Personnel:
Executive Secretary: Alexis Borich
   E-Mail: itchypet@aol.com

Historical Note:
Purpose of the ACVD is to advance and promote excellence in veterinary dermatology, oversee postgraduate training in veterinary dermatology, sponsor research, and organize scientific and educational programs for both veterinary dermatologists and general practitioners. ACVD members are veterinarians certified in veterinary dermatology.

Publications:
Veterinary Dermatology; adv.

American College of Veterinary Internal Medicine (1972)
1997 Wadsworth Blvd.
Suite A
Lakewood, CO 80214-5293
Tel: (303) 231-9933 Fax: (303) 231-0880
TollFree: (800) 245-9081
E-Mail: acvim@acvim.org
Website: acvim.org
Members: 1800 individuals
Staff: 10
Annual Budget: $2-5,000,000
Tax: 501(c)(6)

Personnel:
Executive Director: Roberta Herman
   E-Mail: Roberta@ACVIM.org
Manager, Membership Services: Terri Anglim
   E-Mail: terri@acvim.org
Director, Certification and Education: Nicole Faaborg MS
   E-Mail: nicole@acvim.org
Coordinator, Human Resources and Administrative Support:
   Desiree Fox
   E-Mail: Desiree@ACVIM.org
Director, Administration and Finance: Apollo Garcia
   E-Mail: Apollo@ACVIM.org
Education Specialist: Kathy Klaus
   E-Mail: kathy@acvim.org
Administrator, Publications: Ivy Leventhal
   E-Mail: Ivy@ACVIM.org
Director, Conference Management and Constituent Services:
   Mya Sadler
Director, Marketing and Publications: Christa Saracco
   E-Mail: Mya@ACVIM.org
Coordinator, Computer and Facility Support: Max Talley
   E-Mail: Max@ACVIM.org

Historical Note:
ACVIM's mission is to advance veterinary medical knowledge and improve the lives of animals by publication of authoritative scientific articles of animal diseases. Members are board-certified veterinary specialists. Membership: $350/year.

Meetings/Conferences: Annual
Conference Chair: Kathy Klaus
2013 - Seatle, WA/June 12 - 15
2014 - Nashville, TN/June 4 - 7
2015 - Indianapolis, IN/June 3 - 6

2016 - Denver, CO/June 8 - 11
2017 - Washington, DC/June 7 - 10

Publications:
Journal of Veterinary Internal Medicine; bi-monthly

American College of Veterinary Nutrition (1988)
16256 Ravenglen Rd.
Santa Clarita, CA 91387-4014
Website:
acvn.org
acvn.org
Members: 54 individuals
Staff: 3
Annual Budget: $10-25,000
Tax: 501(c)(6)

Personnel:
President: Sally Perea
Secretary: David Dzanis
Acting Treasurer: Lisa Weeth

Historical Note:
Formerly (1978) the American Association of Veterinary Nutritionists. ACVN's mission is to advance the area of veterinary nutrition and to increase the competence by enhancing the dissemination of new knowledge of veterinary nutrition through teaching and postgraduate programs. Membership: $25/year.

Meetings/Conferences: Annual
2013 - Seatle, WA/June 12 - 15

Publications:
Diplomate Directory; on-line

American College of Veterinary Ophthalmologists (1967)
P.O. Box 1311
Meridian, ID 83680
Tel: (208) 466-7624 Fax: (208) 466-7693
E-Mail: office12@acvo.org
Website: acvo.org
Members: 358 diplomates
Staff: 4
Annual Budget: $500-1,000,000

Personnel:
Executive Director: Stacee Daniel
Technical Administrator: Chris Daniel

Historical Note:
ACVO's mission is to advocate excellence in veterinary Ophthalmology through advanced training, certification, research and education. Membership: $600/year.

Continuing Education:
Certification Designation/s: DACVO

Meetings/Conferences: Annual
2013 - Rio Grande, PR (Rio Mar Beach Resort and
   Spa)/Nov. 4 - 9/51-100 exhibitors
2014 - Ft. Worth, TX (Omni Ft. Worth Hotel-Ft. Worth
   Convention Center)/Oct. 8 - 11

Publications:
ACVO View Newsletter; bi-annually; adv.
Directory; annually; adv.
Veterinary Ophthalmology; bi-monthly; adv.

Membership List Available to Non-members

American College of Veterinary Pathologists (1949)
2424 American Ln.
Madison, WI 53704
Tel: (608) 443-2466 Fax: (608) 443-2474
E-Mail: info@acvp.org
Website: acvp.org
Members: 1550 individuals
Staff: 4
Annual Budget: $500-1,000,000
Tax: 501(c)(3)

Personnel:
Executive Director: Wendy Coe
   E-Mail: wcoe@acvp.org
Editor: Tom Forest
   E-Mail: thomas_forest@merck.com
Contact, Meetings Department, Registrations and
   Exhibitions: Jane Shepard
   E-Mail: meetings@acvp.org
Contact, Membership: Molly Vanderlin
   E-Mail: membership@acvp.org

Historical Note:
ACVP is an organization of board-certified scientists. ACVP improves and protects human and animal health for the betterment of society. Membership: $170/year (Regular).

Continuing Education:
Enrollment: 80
Certification Designation/s: ACVP

Meetings/Conferences: Annual
Conference Chair: Jane Shepard
2013 - Montreal, QC (Montreal Convention Center and
   the LeWestin Montreal Hotel)/Nov. 16 - 20
2014 - Atlanta, GA (Atlanta Marriott Marquis)/Nov. 8
   - 12
2015 - Minneapolis, MN (Hyatt Regency Minneapolis)/
   Oct. 17 - 21

Publications:
ACVP Newsletter; quarterly
Membership Directory; on-line
Proceedings; annually
Veterinary Pathology Journal; bi-monthly; adv.

American College of Veterinary Radiology (1961)
777 E. Park Dr.
P.O. Box 8820
Harrisburg, PA 17105-8820
Tel: (717) 558-7865 Fax: (717) 558-7841
E-Mail: administration@acvr.info
Website: acvr.org
Members: 230 individuals
Staff: 5
Annual Budget: $500-1,000,000
Tax: 501(c)(6)

Personnel:
Executive Director: Dr. Robert D. Pechman Jr.
Administrative Secretary: J. Jacob Laughman
Treasurer: Dr. Rob McLear
Editor-in-Chief: Donald E. Thrall DVM, PhD
Manager, Meetings: Jessica Winger

Historical Note:
Originally established as a specialty board in veterinary radiology under the jurisdiction of the American Veterinary Medical Association, (1966) become the American Board of Veterinary Radiology and incorporated in Illinois. Assumed its present name in 1969. ACVR's mission is to promote veterinary radiology, radiation oncology and related sciences through education and research. Membership: $125/year.

Meetings/Conferences:
Conference Chair: Jessica Winger
2013 - Dallas, TX/April 13
2013 - Savannah, CA/Oct. 8
2013 - Savannah, GA (Savannah Marriott Riverfront)/
   Oct. 8 - 11
Number of non-conference events/year: 3

Publications:
ACVR Newsletter; monthly
Member Directory; on-line
Veterinary Radiology & Ultrasound Journal

American College of Veterinary Surgeons (1965)
19785 Crystal Rock Dr.
Suite 305
Germantown, MD 20874
Tel: (301) 916-0200 Fax: (301) 916-2287
TollFree: (877) 217-2287
E-Mail: acvs@acvs.org
Website: acvs.org
Members: 1471 individuals
Staff: 9
Annual Budget: $2-5,000,000
Tax: 501(c)(6)

Personnel:
Executive Director: Ann T. Loew CAE, EdM
   E-Mail: aloew@acvs.org
Executive Assistant: Lynne Marshall
   E-Mail: lmarshall@acvs.org
Manager, Marketing: Sue Nocitra
   E-Mail: snocitra@acvs.org
Manager, Accounting and Meeting Registrar: Christina
   Perkins
   E-Mail: cperkins@acvs.org
Manager, Conference: Teresa Perrell CMP
   E-Mail: tperrell@acvs.org
Director, Credentialing and Technology and Managing
   Editor: Kimberly E. Soehnlein
   E-Mail: ksoehnlein@acvs.org

Historical Note:
ACVS's mission is to advance the art and science of surgery and promote excellence in animal health care through research, education and service to the public.

Continuing Education:

Enrollment: 65
Certification Designation/s: DACVS

Meetings/Conferences: Annual
Conference Chair: Teresa Perrell CMP
2013 - San Antonio, TX (San Antonio Convention Center)/Oct. 23 - 26/over 100 exhibitors
2014 - San Diego, CA (San Diego Convention Center)/Oct. 16 - 18
2015 - Nashville, TN (Gaylord Opryland Resort and Convention Center)/Nov. 5 - 7
2016 - Seatle, WA (Washington State Convention Center)/Oct. 6 - 8
Number of non-conference events/year: 3

Publications:
Veterinary Surgery; adv.
ACVS Newsletter; semi-annually; adv.
Cut to the Point; monthly
Diplomate Directory; on-line
Membership List Available to Non-members

American College Personnel Association *(1924)*
One Dupont Cir. NW
Suite 300
Washington, DC 20036-1188
Tel: (202) 835-2272 *Fax:* (202) 296-3286
E-Mail: info@acpa.nche.edu
Website: www2.myacpa.org
Members: 7,500 members, 1,200 private and public institutions
Staff: 14
Annual Budget: $2-5,000,000
Tax: 501(c)(3)

Personnel:
Executive Director: Gregory Roberts
Senior Director, Membership Services, Marketing and Media Relations: Stanton Cheah
Executive Assistant and Office Manager: Marguerite Comfort
Coordinator, Membership and Convention Services: Stephanie M. Gatson
Director, Fiscal Services and Human Resources: Tom Gentry
Director, Information Technology: Jon Gilmore Jr.
Senior Director, Professional Development, Research and Scholarship: Vernon Wall

Historical Note:
ACPA's mission is to support college student learning through the generation and dissemination of knowledge, which informs policies, practices and programs for student affairs professionals and the higher education community. Membership: $29 (Full-time Undergraduate Student); $39-55 (Full-time Graduate Student); $75 (Transitional); $79 (Individual at Member College/University/Individual at Member Organization); $129 Individual at Non-Member College/University/Individual at Non-Member Organization).

Meetings/Conferences: Annual
Conference Chair: Stephanie M. Gatson
2013 - Las Vegas, NV (Planet Hollywood)/March 4 - 7
2014 - Indianapolis, IN/March 30 - April 2

Publications:
ACPA Newsletter; on-line
Membership Directory; on-line

American Collegiate Retailing Association *(1948)*
Sam Walton College of Business
University of Arkansas, WJWH 538
Fayetteville, AR 72701
Tel: (859) 257-7778 *Fax:* (859) 257-1275
Website: acraretail.org/
Members: 300 individuals
Staff: 5
Annual Budget: Under $10,000

Personnel:
President: Barry Berman
Contact, Conferences: Ann Fairhurst
    E-Mail: fairhurs@utk.edu
Treasurer: Susan S. Fiorito
Editor: Denise Ogden
    E-Mail: dto2@psu.edu

Historical Note:
ACRA seeks to foster quality retail education at four-year college and graduate schools. Members are faculty from business schools, liberal arts, economics, human ecology, textiles, design and apparel. Membership: $75 (Regular/Associate); $95 (International); Free (Honorary/Life members).

Meetings/Conferences: Annual
Conference Chair: Ann Fairhurst
2013 - Nashville, TN (The Gaylord Opryland)/March 20 - 23
Number of non-conference events/year: 2

Publications:
ACRA Newsletter; on-line

American Commodity Distribution Association
11358 Barley Field Way
Marriottsville, MD 21104
Tel: (410) 442-4612 *Fax:* (410) 442-4613
Website: commodityfoods.org
Staff: 2
Annual Budget: $100-250,000
Tax: 501(c)(6)

Personnel:
Executive Secretary: Ken Shifflett
    E-Mail: wkshifflett@verizon.net

Historical Note:
A non-profit professional trade association, ACDA's mission is to improve the U. S. Department of Agriculture (USDA) Commodity Food Distribution Program. Membership: $150 (Individual/Recipient Agency); $300 (State/Territory/Allied/Agricultural Organization); $400 (Industry/Associate)

Meetings/Conferences:
Number of non-conference events/year: 4

Publications:
Commodity Key
KEYNOTES
Membership Directory

American Comparative Literature Association *(1960)*
University of South Carolina, Dept of Languages, Literatures and Cultures
1620 College St. Rm 813A
Columbia, SC 29208
Tel: (803) 777-3021 *Fax:* (803) 777-3041
E-Mail: info@acla.org
Website: acla.org
Members: 1200 individuals
Staff: 2
Annual Budget: $250-500,000
Tax: 501(c)(3)

Personnel:
Administrative Assistant: Andy Anderson

Historical Note:
ACLA promotes the study of intercultural relations and interactions between literature and other forms of human activity. Membership: $25 (Regular/Faculty); $25-27 (Student); $30 (Emeritus); $35-37 (Institution);$35.00-77 (Individual, depending on the Income).

Meetings/Conferences: Annual
2013 - Toronto, ON (University of Toronto)/April 4 - 7
2013 - Paris, France (Université Paris-Sorbonne)/July 18 - 24

Publications:
Comparative Literature
Membership Directory; on-line
newsletter; annually

American Composers Alliance *(1937)*
802 W. 190th St.
First Floor
New York, NY 10040
Tel: (212) 925-0458 *Fax:* (212) 925-6798
E-Mail: info@composers.com
Website: composers.com
Members: 320 individuals
Staff: 4
Annual Budget: $100-250,000
Tax: 501(c)(3)

Personnel:
Executive Director and General Manager: Gina Genova

Historical Note:
ACA's mission is to publish and distribute the music of its composer members and to support and promote performances of their works. Membership in ACA is limited to BMI-affiliated composers writing music at a professional level of expertise, determined through an application process.

Meetings/Conferences:
Number of non-conference events/year: 2

Publications:
The ACA Bulletin

American Composers Forum *(1973)*
332 Minnesota St.
Suite E-145
St. Paul, MN 55101-1300
Tel: (651) 228-1407 *Fax:* (651) 291-7978
Website: composersforum.org
Members: 2000 members
Staff: 13
Annual Budget: $1-2,000,000
Tax: 501(c)(3)

Personnel:
President and Chief Executive Officer: John Nuechterlein
    E-Mail: jnuechterlein@composersforum.org
Manager, Education and Community Engagement: Suzanna Schlesinger Altman
    E-Mail: saltman@composersforum.org
Vice President, Finance and Administration: Paul Hanson
    E-Mail: phanson@composersforum.org
Director, Media Projects and Editor: John Michel
    E-Mail: jmichel@composersforum.org
Contact, Membership Services: Jay Walters
    E-Mail: jwalters@composersforum.org

Historical Note:
Formerly Minnesota Composers Forum. ACF's mission enriche lives by nurturing the creative spirit of composers and communities. They provide new opportunities for composers and their music to flourish, and engage communities in the creation, performance and enjoyment of new music. Membership: $65 (Regular); $45 (Student/Senior).

Publications:
Sounding Board; quarterly

American Composites Manufacturers Association *(1979)*
3033 Wilson Blvd.
Suite 420
Arlington, VA 22201
Tel: (703) 525-0511 *Fax:* (703) 525-0743
E-Mail: info@acmanet.org
Website: acmanet.org
Members: 3000 composites manufacturers and suppliers
Staff: 18
Annual Budget: $2-5,000,000
Tax: 501(c)(6)

Personnel:
Chief Staff Executive: Thomas Dobbins
    E-Mail: tdobbins@acmanet.org
Manager, Certification and Education: Anne Ashurst
    E-Mail: aashurst@acmanet.org
Senior Manager, Exhibit and Advertising Sales: Ryan Brown
    E-Mail: rbrown@acmanet.org
Senior Manager, Membership: Channing Daniel
    E-Mail: cdaniel@acmanet.org
Director, Marketing and Communications: Mary Johnson
    E-Mail: mjohnson@acmanet.org
Director, Finance and Administration: Judy Norton
    E-Mail: jnorton@acmanet.org
Director, Conventions and Education: Heather Rhoderick CMP
    E-Mail: hrhoderick@acmanet.org
Senior Director, Government Affairs: John Schweitzer
    E-Mail: jschweitzer@acmanet.org
Associate Director, Communications and Publications: Melinda Skea
    E-Mail: mskea@acmanet.org
Manager, Information Technology: Jesse Wrenn
    E-Mail: jwrenn@acmanet.org

Historical Note:
Formerly (1992) the Fiberglass Fabrication Association and then the Composites Fabricators Association, assumed its current name in 2003 and absorbed the Composites Institute in 2000. ACMA strives to provide a forum for the composites industry to develop and enhance shared opportunities and address common challenges. Membership is open to any person, firm or corporation performing the hand layup or sprayup method of fiberglass fabrication in open or closed molds or engaged in filament winding or resin transfer molding. Membership: $350-21,140 (Manufacturer); $0-1,000 (Supplier); $1,650-21,140 (Distributor); $0-500 (Affiliate).

Continuing Education:
Certification Designation/s: CCT-M, CCT-SS, CCT-I, CCT-C, CCT-CP, CCT-CM

Meetings/Conferences: Annual
Conference Chair: Heather Rhoderick CMP

2013 - Orlando, FL (Orange County Convention
    Center)/Jan. 29 - 31/3500 attendees/over 100
    exhibitors
2014 - San Antonio, TX/Feb. 18 - 20
2015 - Las Vegas, NV/Feb. 2 - 5
Number of non-conference events/year: 2

Publications:
ACMA Insider; bi-weekly
Composites; daily; adv.
Composites Manufacturing; bi-monthly; adv.
Composites Research Journal; quarterly
Insider; on-line; adv.

American Concrete Institute *(1904)*
P.O. Box 9094
Farmington Hills, MI 48333-9094
Tel: (248) 848-3700 *Fax:* (248) 848-3701
E-Mail: BKStore@concrete.org
Website: concrete.org
Members: 550 organizations and 16500
individuals
Staff: 110
Annual Budget: $10-25,000,000
Tax: 501(c)(3)

Personnel:
Executive Vice President: Ronald G. Burg
    E-Mail: ron.burg@concrete.org
Director, Sales and Membership Services: Diane L. Baloh
    E-Mail: Diane.Baloh@concrete.org
Director, Human Resources: Barbara Cheyne
    E-Mail: barb.cheyne@concrete.org
Editor-in-Chief: Rex C. Donahey PE
    E-Mail: rex.donahey@concrete.org
Managing Director, Finance and Administration: Donna
    G. Halstead
    E-Mail: Donna.Halstead@Concrete.org
Director, Publishing and Event Services: Renee J. Lewis
    CMP
    E-Mail: renee.lewis@concrete.org
Manager, Marketing and Director, Sustainability: Kevin P.
    Mlutkowski
    E-Mail: kevin.mlutkowski@concrete.org
Managing Director, Certification and Chapters: John W.
    Nehasil
    E-Mail: john.nehasil@concrete.org
Manager, Information Systems and Warehouse Operations:
    Jason J. Pennington
    E-Mail: Jason.Pennington@concrete.org
*Managing Director, Marketing, Sales and Industry
    Relations:* Douglas J. Sordyl
    E-Mail: douglas.sordyl@concrete.org
Coordinator, Information Systems: June F. Zimmerman
    E-Mail: june.zimmerman@concrete.org

Historical Note:
*Founded as the National Association of Cement Users,
became the American Concrete Institute in 1913 and
was incorporated in Michigan in 1964. ACI's mission is
to provide comradeship in finding ways to do concrete
work of all kinds and in spreading that knowledge.
Membership: $40-80 (Student); $990 (Organizational);
$222 (Individual); $124 (Young Professional) $0 (Student
E-Membership).*

Continuing Education:
Certification Designation/s: CCP, SN, TCP, FTCP, ICP,
ATCP, LTCP

Meetings/Conferences:
Conference Chair: Renee J. Lewis CMP
2013 - Minneapolis, MN (Hilton Minneapolis)/April 14
    - 17
2013 - Phoenix, AZ (Hyatt Regency Phoenix)/Oct. 20 -
    24
2014 - Reno, NV (Grand Sierra Resort and Casino)/
    March 23 - 27
2014 - Washington, DC (Heart House)/Oct. 26 - 30
2015 - Kansas City, MO (Kansas City Marriott
    Downtown)/April 12 - 15
2015 - Denver, CO (Scanticon Denver Inc)/Nov. 8 - 12
2016 - Milwaukee, WI (Hyatt Regency Milwaukee)/
    April 17 - 21
2016 - Philadelphia, PA (Philadelphia Marriott
    Downtown)/Oct. 23 - 27
2017 - Detroit, MI (Detroit Marriott at the Renaissance
    Center)/March 26 - 30
2018 - Louisville, KY (Hyatt and Kentucky International
    Convention Center)/March 25 - 29
Number of non-conference events/year: 5

Publications:

ACI Materials Journal; bi-monthly
ACI Structural Journal; bi-monthly
Certified Personnel Directory; on-line
Concrete International; monthly; adv.
Membership Directory; on-line

American Concrete Pavement Association *(1964)*
9450 Bryn Mawr
Suite 150
Rosemont, IL 60018
Tel: (847) 966-2272 *Fax:* (847) 966-9970
E-Mail: acpa@acpa.org
Website: pavement.com
Members: 500 companies
Staff: 14
Annual Budget: $2-5,000,000
Tax: 501(c)(6)

Personnel:
President and Chief Executive Officer: Gerald F. Voight
    E-Mail: jvoight@pavement.com
Vice President, Communications: Bill Davenport
    E-Mail: bdavenport@pavement.com
Membership Accountant: Marian Greco
    E-Mail: mgreco@acpa.org

Historical Note:
*Formerly the American Concrete Paving Association.
ACPA is dedicated to promoting concrete pavement for
use in interstate highways, state and county highways,
local roads and airports and advocates for the use of
concrete pavement in highways, airfields, and roadways
throughout the United States. Members are paving
contractors, cement companies, equipment manufacturers,
material and service suppliers, ready-mixed concrete
producers, allied associations/organizations, bonding and
insurance companies, consulting firms, and other allied
organizations and individuals. Membership dues depend
on the type of member company. Membership: $25-250
(Individual Affiliate); $400-1,825 (Association); $400-800
(Consultant/Service Business); $515 (Allied industry);
$2,000-18,000 (Equipment Manufacturer/Distributors/
Material Manufacturer/Supplier); $2,000 (International).*

Meetings/Conferences: Annual
2013 - Las Vegas, NV (Las Vegas Convention Center)/
    Feb. 5 - 8
2014 - Las Vegas, NV (Las Vegas Convention Center)/
    Jan. 21 - 24
Number of non-conference events/year: 30

Publications:
ACPA's flagship
Membership Directory; on-line

American Concrete Pipe Association *(1907)*
8445 Freeport Pkwy.
Suite 305
Irving, TX 75038
Tel: (972) 506-7216 *Fax:* (972) 506-7682
E-Mail: info@concrete-pipe.org
Website: concrete-pipe.org
Members: 125 companies and 40 countries
Staff: 13
Annual Budget: $2-5,000,000
Tax: 501(c)(6)

Personnel:
President: Matt Childs PE
    E-Mail: mchilds@concrete-pipe.org
Director, Technical Services: Josh Beakley PE
    E-Mail: jbeakley@concrete-pipe.org
Manager, Events: Wanda Cochran
    E-Mail: wcochran@concrete-pipe.org

Historical Note:
*Assumed its present name in 1914. ACPA's mission
is to contribute to the improvement of environment by
producing quality concrete pipe, engineered to provide a
lasting and economical solution to drainage and pollution
problems. There are currently over 400 plants operated
by ACPA members in the United States and Canada. Over
40 countries are represented in the membership of the
American Concrete Pipe Association. Membership: $1,650
(International); $150 (Professional).*

Continuing Education:
Certification Designation/s: QCAST

Meetings/Conferences:
Conference Chair: Wanda Cochran
2013 - Indianapolis, IN (Indianapolis Convention
    Center)/Jan. 11 - 13
2013 - Washington, DC (Washington Marriott
    Wardman Park)/Jan. 13 - 17
2013 - Palm Beach Gardens, FL (PGA National Resort
    and Spa)/March 10 - 12

2014 - Houston, TX (Hilton Americas-Houston)/March
    7 - 9
2015 - Orlando, FL (Rosen Shingle Creek Resort)/Feb.
    5 - 7
Number of non-conference events/year: 9

Publications:
Concrete Pipe News; quarterly
Membership Directory; on-line

American Concrete Pressure Pipe Association *(1949)*
3900 University Dr.
Suite 110
Fairfax, VA 22030-2513
Tel: (703) 273-7227 *Fax:* (703) 273-7230
E-Mail: info@acppa.org
Website: acppa.org
Members: 6 companies
Staff: 2
Annual Budget: $500-1,000,000
Tax: 501(c)(6)

Personnel:
President and Chief Executive Officer: Richard E. Lawhun
Treasurer: John Munro

Historical Note:
*Founded in 1949, the American Concrete Pressure Pipe
Association (ACPPA) is a nonprofit trade association
representing manufacturers of concrete pressure pipe on
the North American Continent. ACPPA sponsors research
projects and conducts educational programs to promote
and advance the use of concrete pressure pipe in water and
wastewater applications.*

Continuing Education:
Certification Designation/s: LRQA

American Concrete Pumping Association *(1974)*
606 Enterprise Dr.
Lewis Center, OH 43035
Tel: (614) 431-5618 *Fax:* (614) 431-6944
Website: concretepumpers.com
Members: 450 companies
Staff: 5
Annual Budget: $1-2,000,000
Tax: 501(c)(6)

Personnel:
Executive Director: Christie Collins
    E-Mail: christi@concretepumpers.com
Contact, Certification: Travis Collins
    E-Mail: travis@concretepumpers.com
Contact, Graphic Design and Marketing: Leah Duck
    E-Mail: leah@concretepumpers.com
Contact, Member Services: Janet Kasson
    E-Mail: janet@concretepumpers.com
Contact, Seminars and Certification: Sue Schumacher
    E-Mail: sue@concretepumpers.com

Historical Note:
*ACPA's mission is to expand and improve the concrete
pumping industry through leadership, education,
communication, and advocacy establishing concrete
pumping as the preferred method of placing concrete.
Membership: $125 (Individual); $500 (Affiliated
Professional); $665 (Distributor of Concrete Pumps);
$1,600-4,000 (Manufacturer); $300 (Trailer Pump
Operator, minimum); $335 (Boom Pump Operator,
minimum).*

Continuing Education:
Certification Designation/s: CCPO

Meetings/Conferences: Annual
Conference Chair: Sue Schumacher
2013 - Las Vegas, NV (World of Concrete)/Feb. 5

Publications:
Concrete Pumping Magazine; quarterly; adv.
Member Directory

Membership List Available to Non-members

American Conference for Irish Studies *(1960)*
GMU Department of History, Robinson Hall B,
Room 359
4400 University Dr. MSN 3G1
Fairfax, VA 22030
Website: acisweb.com/index.php
Members: 800 individuals
Staff: 5
Annual Budget: $10-25,000
Tax: 501(c)(3)

Personnel:
Web Master: Phillip Barron

E-Mail: pbarron@nicomediadesigns.com

Historical Note:
Formerly American Committe for Irish Studies (1988), affiliated with the American Historical Association and the Modern Language Association of America, ACIS works to encourage research and writing in Irish studies by establishing communication among scholars in Irish history, literature, folklore, language, social studies, and fine and applied arts. Members include scholars interested in Irish history, language and culture. Membership: $40 (Individual); $15 (Student); $45 (Institution/Library).

Publications:
ACIS Newsletter

American Conference of Academic Deans (1945)
1818 R St. NW
Washington, DC 20009
Tel: (202) 884-7419 Fax: (202) 265-9532
E-Mail: info@acad-edu.org
Website: acad-edu.org
Members: 600 individuals
Staff: 1
Annual Budget: $100-250,000
Tax: 501(c)(3)

Personnel:
Executive Director: Laura A. Rzepka
    E-Mail: rzepka@acad-edu.org

Historical Note:
ACAD's mission is to provide academic leaders who share a commitment to student learning and to the ideals of liberal education with networking and professional development opportunities and to support them in their work as educational leaders. Membership: $115 (Individual); $60 (International/Emeritus Membership); $100 (Group 2+).

Meetings/Conferences: Annual
2013 - Atlanta, GA/Jan. 23 - 26

Publications:
ACAD Newsletter; annually
Membership Directory; on-line

American Conference of Cantors (1953)
1305 Remington Rd.
Suite D
Schaumburg, IL 60173-4820
Tel: (847) 781-7800 Fax: (847) 781-7801
E-Mail: info@accantors.org
Website: accantors.org
Members: 465 individuals
Staff: 13
Annual Budget: $1-2,000,000
Tax: 501(c)(3)

Personnel:
Managing Director: Rachel B. Roth
    E-Mail: rroth@accantors.org
Director, Placement: Kay Greenwald
    E-Mail: kgreenwald@accantors.org
Director, Membership Support: Gail P. Hirschenfang
    E-Mail: ghirschenfang@accantors.org

Historical Note:
ACC supports its members in their sacred calling as emissaries for Judaism and for Jewish music. Members serve in Jewish congregations in the United States and Canada. Membership: 1.100-1.650% (Regular, based on salary); 0.825% of total salary and parsonage, or $350 (Associate, whichever is greater); $275 (ACC/CA Dual); $82.50 (Retired/Sustaining).

Meetings/Conferences: Annual
2013 - Minneapolis, MN (Marriott City Center Hotel)/ June 30 - July 4
Number of non-conference events/year: 2

Publications:
e-Koleinu; on-line
Membership Directory; annually

American Conference of Governmental Industrial Hygienists (1938)
1330 Kemper Meadow Dr.
Suite 600
Cincinnati, OH 45240-1634
Tel: (513) 742-2020 Fax: (513) 742-3355
E-Mail: mail@acgih.org
Website: acgih.org
Members: 3000 individuals
Staff: 14
Annual Budget: $2-5,000,000
Tax: 501(c)(6)

Personnel:

Executive Director: A. Anthony Rizzuto CAE
    E-Mail: trizzuto@acgih.org
Associate Executive Director: Amy B. Bloomhuff CAE, Esq.
    E-Mail: abloomhuff@acgih.org
Contact, Conferences and Events: Penny Martin

Historical Note:
Formerly (1945) the National Conference of Governmental Industrial Hygienists. ACGIH is a community of professionals that works to advance worker's health and safety through education and through development and dissemination of scientific and technical knowledge. Membership: $195 (Regular/Associate); $30 (Student/ Retired); $600 (Organization).

Continuing Education:
Certification Designation/s: CIH

Meetings/Conferences:
Conference Chair: Penny Martin
2013 - San Antonio, TX (Henry Gonzalez Convention Center)/March 11 - 13
2013 - Montreal, QC/May 20 - 22
2013 - Las Vegas, NV (Las Vegas Convention Center)/ June 24 - 26
Number of non-conference events/year: 9

Membership List Available to Non-members

American Congress of Community Supports and Employment Services (2007)
1501 M St. NW
Seventh Floor
Washington, DC 20005
Tel: (202) 349-4259 Fax: (202) 785-1756
Website: accses.org
Members: 80 partner organizations
Staff: 2

Personnel:
Director, Communications, Events and Membership Relations: Gary Goosman
    E-Mail: GGoosman@accses.org
Legislative Counsel: Peter W. Thomas
    E-Mail: peter.thomas@ppsv.com

Historical Note:
Mission of ACCSES is to promote and enhance community-based solutions that maximize employment and independent living opportunities for people with disabilities. Members are community organizations providing job training and related services.

Meetings/Conferences: Annual
Conference Chair: Gary Goosman

Publications:
ACCSES Member Directory; on-line
Newsletter; weekly

American Congress of Obstetricians and Gynecologists (1951)
409 12th St. SW
P.O. Box 70620
Washington, DC 20024-2188
Tel: (202) 638-5577 Fax: (202) 863-4980
E-Mail: communications@acog.org
Website: acog.org
Members: 55000 individuals
Staff: 218
Annual Budget: $10-25,000,000
Tax: 501(c)(6)

Personnel:
Executive Vice President: Hal C. Lawrence III
Senior Director of Government Affairs: Lucia DiVenere
    E-Mail: ldivenere@acog.org
Director, Communications: Penny Murphy MS
    E-Mail: pmurphy@acog.org
Director, Membership Services: Bernice Rose
    E-Mail: brose@acog.org

Historical Note:
Formerly (1956) the American Academy of Obstetrics and Gynecology. ACOG's mission is to be an advocate in the Commonwealth for lifelong health care for all women. Members are doctors who specialized in women's health care, including childbirth and female disorders. Membership: $3,000 (Corporate); $300 (Associate/ Associate International); $185 plus $10 as processing fee (Educational Affiliate); $150 (International Educational Affiliate).

Continuing Education:
Certification Designation/s: ACCME, AMA PRA

Meetings/Conferences: Annual
2013 - New Orleans, LA/May 4 - 8

Number of non-conference events/year: 1

Publications:
Gazette Newsletters
Membership Directory; on-line
The Coding and Practice Management Update; monthly
The Green Journal
Today Newsletter; on-line

American Congress of Rehabilitation Medicine (1923)
11654 Plaza America Dr.
Suite 535
Reston, VA 20190
Fax: (866) 692-1619
Website: acrm.org
Members: 815 companies and individuals
Staff: 6
Annual Budget: $1-2,000,000
Tax: 501(c)(3)

Personnel:
Chief Executive Officer: Jon W. Lindberg
    E-Mail: jlindberg@acrm.org
Chief Meetings Officer: Margo Holen
    E-Mail: mholen@acrm.org
Director, Membership Services: Jenny Richard
    E-Mail: jrichard@acrm.org
Coordinator, Marketing: Cindy Robinson
    E-Mail: crobinson@acrm.org
Director, Operations: Dinara Suleymanova
    E-Mail: dsuleymanova@acrm.org
Director, Publications: Fiona Williams
    E-Mail: fwilliams@acrm.org

Historical Note:
Formerly (1923) the American College of Radiology and Physiotherapy, (1926) the American College of Physical Therapy, (1930) the American Congress of Physical Therapy, (1945) the American Congress of Physical Medicine, (1953) the American Congress of Physical Medicine and Rehabilitation, assumed its current name in 1967. ACRM's mission is to enhance the lives of people living with disabilities through a multidisciplinary approach to rehabilitation. Membership: $295 (Regular/ International/Consumer); $150 (Early Career); $85 (Resident/Student/Fellow).

Meetings/Conferences: Annual
Conference Chair: Margo Holen
Number of non-conference events/year: 16

Publications:
ACRM eNews; bi-monthly
Archives of Physical Medicine and Rehabilitation; monthly
BI-ISIG Moving Ahead; semi-annually
Rehabilitation Outlook; bi-monthly

American Connemara Pony Society (1956)
Gately Farm
10501 Randall
Orange Park Acres, CA 92869-1644
Tel: (540) 886-2239 Fax: (540) 722-2277
E-Mail: connemaras@windstream.net
Website: acps.org
Members: 900 individuals
Staff: 3
Annual Budget: $25-50,000
Tax: 501(c)(3)

Personnel:
President: Kathy Lucas
    E-Mail: kathygatelyfarm@aol.com
Treasurer: Cathy Blackmon
    E-Mail: Pooka7@sbcglobal.net

Historical Note:
ACPS's mission is to assist and promote the breeding, registration, training, exhibition and general use of the Connemara. Members are breeders and trainers of the Connemara Pony. Sponsors shows and awards prizes for distinguished examples of the breed. Membership: $25 (Junior); $35 (Associate-Adult); $40 (Senior); $70 (Family); $600 (Life).

Meetings/Conferences: Annual
Conference Chair: Debbie Busta
Number of non-conference events/year: 1

Publications:
American Connemara Magazine; bi-monthly; adv.
Membership Directory; annually

American Construction Inspectors Association (1954)

530 S. Lake Ave.
Suite 431
Pasadena, CA 91101
Tel: (626) 797-2242 *Fax:* (626) 797-2214
E-Mail: office@acia.com
Website: acia.com
Members: 550 individuals
Staff: 1
Annual Budget: $100-250,000
Tax: 501(c)(3)

Personnel:
Executive Director: Dale Lacasella
    E-Mail: executivedirector@acia.com

Historical Note:
ACIA's mission is to promote educational opportunities, share information about construction and inspection, and to promote standards of knowledge and conduct for all construction inspectors regardless of their area of expertise or employment. Members are engineering, building, public works, and other specialized construction inspectors. Membership: $135 (General); $25 (Student/Retired); $100 (Associate); $1,500 (Life).

Continuing Education:
Enrollment: 685
Certification Designation/s: CCS, RCI

Meetings/Conferences: Annual
Conference Chair: Dale Lacasella
Number of non-conference events/year: 1

Publications:
Member Directory; on-line
The Inspector Magazine; semi-annually; adv.

The American Consultants League *(1983)*
C/O ETR
245 NE Fourth Ave., Suite 102
Delray Beach, FL 33483
Tel: (866) 344-7200
E-Mail: support@earlyrise.com
Members: 1025 individuals
Staff: 2
Annual Budget: $100-250,000

Personnel:
Copywriter and Consultant: Robert W. Bly

Historical Note:
An association of part-time and full-time consultants in every field of expertise from all over the United States, Canada, and all foreign countries. Assists consultants in the setting up and managing of the business end of their consultancies by providing educational materials and continuing education through the Consultants Institute, a home study course which is the education arm of the League. Membership: $139/year.

Continuing Education:
Certification Designation/s: CPC, APC

American Copper Council *(1975)*
Two S. End Ave.
Suite Four-C
New York, NY 10280
Tel: (212) 945-4990 *Fax:* (212) 945-4992
E-Mail: mary@americancopper.org
Website: americancopper.org
Members: 120 companies
Staff: 1
Annual Budget: $250-500,000

Personnel:
Executive Director: Mary C. Boland

Historical Note:
Organized in 1974 as the successor to the Committee for the Release of Stockpile Copper, the Council represents all segments of the copper industry. Member companies include producers, scrap dealers, brass and wire mills, fabricators, consumers, merchants and brokers. Membership: $1,000 (Producers/Scrap Dealers/Merchants/Brokers and Traders/Warehouses and Transportation Services); $500 (Copper Fabricators and Distributors of Copper/Refineries/ Foundries/Wire/Brass/ Tube and Cable Manufacturers/ Service Centers); $250 (Consumers/ Consultants/Services).

Publications:
Membership directory

Membership List Available to Non-members

American Corn Growers Association *(1987)*
P.O. Box 18157
Washington, DC 20036
Tel: (202) 835-0330 *Fax:* (202) 463-0862
Website: acga.org
Members: 14000 members

Staff: 3
Annual Budget: $50-100,000
Tax: 501(c)(6)

Personnel:
Executive Director: Pamela S. Horwitz

Historical Note:
ACGA is a progressive commodity association that strives to protect farm interests and rural communities. Membership: $50 (Corn Producer); $600 (Lifetime Corn Producer); $75 (Associate).

Publications:
Archive Smart-Newsletter; weekly

American Correctional Association *(1870)*
206 N. Washington St.
Suite 200
Alexandria, VA 22314
Tel: (703) 224-0000 *Fax:* (703) 224-0179
TollFree: (800) 222-5646
Website: aca.org
Members: 21000 individuals
Staff: 25
Annual Budget: $5-10,000,000
Tax: 501(c)(3)

Personnel:
Executive Director: James A Gondles Jr., CAE
    E-Mail: execoffice@aca.org
Director, Publications and Communications: Susan Clayton
    E-Mail: susanc@aca.org
Director, Standards and Accreditation: Kathy B. Dennis
    E-Mail: kathyd@aca.org
Manager, Sales and Customer Service: Roberta Gibson
    E-Mail: rgibson@aca.org
Manager, Information Technology: Ali Haidar
    E-Mail: ahaidar@aca.org
Director, Conventions and Meetings: Caitlin Mann
    E-Mail: CaitlinM@aca.org
Director, Professional Development: Kelli McAfee
    E-Mail: KelliM@aca.org
Director of Government and Public Affairs: Eric Schultz
    E-Mail: erics@aca.org
Deputy Executive Director: Jeff Washington
    E-Mail: jeffw@aca.org

Historical Note:
Formerly (1870), the National Prison Association, American Prison Association and assumed its present name in 1954. ACA's mission is to provide a professional organization for all individuals and groups, both public and private that share a common goal of improving the justice system. Membership: $35-115(Professional); $300 (Organizational/ Supporting); $15 (Associate); $100-150 (Gold).

Continuing Education:
Certification Designation/s: CCN, CCE, CCM, CCO, CCS

Meetings/Conferences: Annual
Conference Chair: Kelli McAfee
2013 - Houston, TX/Jan. 25 - 30
2015 - Austin, TX/Jan. 9 - 14
2016 - New Orleans, LA/Jan. 22 - 27
2017 - San Antonio, TX/Jan. 20 - 25
2018 - Orlando, FL (Orlando World Center Marriott)/ Jan. 5 - 10
2019 - New Orleans, LA/Jan. 11 - 16
2020 - San Diego, CA/Jan. 10 - 15

Publications:
Correctional Health Today
Corrections Compendium; quarterly; adv.
Corrections Today; adv.
Membership Directory; on-line
On the Line; monthly

Membership List Available to Non-members

American Correctional Chaplains Association *(1885)*
P.O. Box 85840
Seattle, WA 98145-1840
Tel: (206) 985-0577 *Fax:* (206) 526-7113
Website: correctionalchaplains.org
Members: 900 individuals and groups
Staff: 6
Annual Budget: Under $10,000
Tax: 501(c)(3)

Personnel:
Webmaster: Larry Bongiovi
Chairman, Communications: Gary Friedman
    E-Mail: GaryFriedman@msn.com

Vice President: Stephen Hall
    E-Mail: sthall@doc.in.gov
Secretary, Membership Services: Stephen G. Johnson
Treasurer: Steven E. Thomas

Historical Note:
An affiliate of American Correctional Association. ACCA serves as a professional organization for pastoral care personnel in the corrections field and provides a network for the sharing of information and resources amongst its members and with corrections administrators. Membership: $40 (Professional); $20 (Associate/Retired Professional); $25 (Auxiliary); $120 (Affiliate);$30 (Certified Professional); $500 (Lifetime).

Continuing Education:
Certification Designation/s: BCC, CCCC, CCC

Publications:
Newsletter

American Correctional Health Services Association *(1976)*
3990 Bullard Rd.
Monticello, GA 31064
Tel: (855) 825-5559 *Fax:* (866) 365-3838
Website: achsa.org
Members: 900 individuals
Staff: 1
Annual Budget: $50-100,000

Personnel:
Executive Director: Lori E. Roscoe

Historical Note:
Multidisciplinary society of health care professionals and representatives from diverse areas of the corrections field. An affiliate of the American Correctional Association. ACHSA's mission is to be the voice of the correctional healthcare profession, serving as an effective forum for communication addressing current issues and needs confronting correctional healthcare. Membership: $50/year.

Meetings/Conferences: Annual
2013 - Philadelphia, PA/March 14 - 17

Publications:
CorHealth Newsletter; quarterly; adv.

American Cotswold Record Association *(1878)*
18 Elm St.
P.O. Box 59
Plympton, MA 02367
Tel: (781) 585-2026 *Fax:* (781) 585-2026
E-Mail: acraregistry@cotswoldsheep.us.com
Website: cotswoldsheep.us.com
Members: 87 individuals
Staff: 2
Annual Budget: Under $10,000

Personnel:
Secretary and Treasurer: Vicki Rigel
    E-Mail: acraregistry@cotswoldsheep.us.com

Historical Note:
Formerly (1904) American Cotswold Sheep Association. Members are breeders of purebred Cotswold sheep. Maintains a breed registry. ACRA certifies the Cotswold breed of sheep, protecting consumers and producers of pure pedigreed Cotswolds.

American Cotton Shippers Association *(1924)*
88 Union Ave.
Suite 1204
Memphis, TN 38103
Tel: (901) 525-2272 *Fax:* (901) 527-8303
Website: acsa-cotton.org
Members: 300 individuals
Staff: 4
Annual Budget: $2-5,000,000
Tax: 501(c)(6)

Personnel:
President: William E. May
    E-Mail: bmay@acsa-cotton.org
Book Keeper: Laura Martin
    E-Mail: lmartin@acsa-cotton.org

Historical Note:
Provide a united voice for the cotton merchandising trade of the United States.

Meetings/Conferences: Annual
2013 - New Orleans, LA (Windsor Court Hotel)/May 8 - 10
Number of non-conference events/year: 4

Publications:
Membership Directory; on-line

American Council for Construction Education
(1974)
1717 N. Loop 1604 E.
Suite 320
San Antonio, TX 78232-1570
Tel: (210) 495-6161 *Fax:* (210) 495-6168
E-Mail: acce@acce-hq.org
Website: acce-hq.org
Members: 115 individuals and 68 4-year and 2-year schools
Staff: 2
Annual Budget: $250-500,000
Tax: 501(c)(3)

Personnel:
Executive Vice President: Michael M. Holland AIC, CPC
  E-Mail: mholland@acce-hq.org
Executive Assistant: Billye Hall
  E-Mail: bhall@acce-hq.org

Historical Note:
ACCE is the accrediting agency for post secondary construction education programs. ACCE's mission is to be a global advocate of quality construction education programs and to advocate, support, and accredit quality construction education programs. Recognized by the Council for Higher Education Accreditation. Membership: $150 (Individual); $1,500 (Organization); $4,400 (Association).

Meetings/Conferences: Semi-Annual
2013 - Baton Rouge, LA (Hilton Baton Rouge Capitol Center)/Feb. 20 - 23
2013 - Hartford, CT (Hartford Marriott Downtown)/ July 24 - 27

Publications:
ACCE Newletters

American Council for Southern Asian Art *(1966)*
211A Henry Hall , University of Illinois at Chicago
935 W. Harrison St.
Chicago, IL 60607-7039
Tel: (312) 996-3303 *Fax:* (312) 413-2460
Website: acsaa.us
Members: 280 individuals
Staff: 5

Personnel:
Secretary: Catherine Becker
  E-Mail: cathbeck@uic.edu

Historical Note:
American Council for Southern Asian Art (ACSAA) is an organization for advanced study and awareness of the art of South and Southeast Asia and the Himalayan regions. Membership: $15 (Student/Retired/Unemployed); $40 (Regular); $50 (Institutional); $60 (Contributing); $100 (Sustaining).

Meetings/Conferences: Biennial
Conference Chair: Cathleen Cummings

Publications:
ACSAA Newsletter; bi-annually

Membership List Available to Non-members

American Council of Christian Churches *(1941)*
P.O. Box 5455
Bethlehem, PA 18015
Tel: (610) 865-3009 *Fax:* (610) 865-3033
E-Mail: accc@juno.com
Website: amcouncilcc.org
Staff: 3
Annual Budget: $100-250,000
Tax: 501(c)(3)

Personnel:
President: Dr. John McKnight (EMC)
Executive Secretary: Dr. Ralph G. Colas (IBFNA)
Treasurer: Rev. Thomas Hamilton

Historical Note:
ACCC is a Fundamentalist multi-denominational organization whose purposes are to provide information, encouragement, and assistance to Bible-believing churches, fellowships and individuals; to preserve Christian heritage through exposure of, opposition to, and separation from doctrinal impurity and compromise in current religious trends and movements; to protect churches from religious and political restrictions, subtle or obvious, that would hinder their ministries for God; to promote obedience to the inerrant Word of God.

Meetings/Conferences: Annual
Conference Chair: Dr. Ralph G. Colas (IBFNA)
Number of non-conference events/year: 1

Publications:
Members Directory; on-line

American Council of Engineering Companies
(1909)
1015 15th St. NW
Eighth Floor
Washington, DC 20005-2605
Tel: (202) 347-7474 *Fax:* (202) 898-0068
E-Mail: acec@acec.org
Website: acec.org
Members: 5300 firms
Staff: 54
Annual Budget: $10-25,000,000

Personnel:
President and Chief Executive Officer: David A. Raymond
  E-Mail: draymond@acec.org
Vice President, Business Resources and Education: Jeffrey L. Beard
  E-Mail: jbeard@acec.org
Director, Public Relations and Communications: Alan Crockett
  E-Mail: acrockett@acec.org
Vice President, Operations and Membership Services: Mary Ann Emely CAE
  E-Mail: memely@acec.org
Director, Human Resources: Karen George
  E-Mail: kgeorge@acec.org
Director, Sales and MO Services: Nina Goldman
  E-Mail: ngoldman@acec.org
Director, Membership Recruitment: Leo H. Hoch
  E-Mail: lhoch@acec.org
Director, Policy and Strategic Planning and General Counsel: Charles Kim
  E-Mail: ckim@acec.org
Executive Director, Political Affairs: Greg Knopp
  E-Mail: gknopp@ACEC.org
Director, Administration: Steve Lim
  E-Mail: slim@acec.org
Chief Financial Officer: Kim Pham
  E-Mail: kpham@acec.org
Director, Meetings and Conventions: Michael E. Pramstaller CAE
  E-Mail: mpramstaller@acec.org
Manager, Publications: Jackie Pysarchuk
  E-Mail: jpysarchuk@acec.org
Corporate Secretary and Executive Assistant: Melissa J. Thompson
  E-Mail: mthompson@acec.org
Director, Information Technology: Yan Wiramidjaja
  E-Mail: ywiramidjaja@acec.org

Historical Note:
Formed by the merger of the American Institute of Consulting Engineers (1909) and the Consulting Engineers Council of the U.S.A. (1956), (2001) American Council of Engineering Companies. ACEC's mission is to contribute to prosperity and welfare by advancing the business interests of member firms. Members are independent private practice engineering companies.

Meetings/Conferences: Annual
Conference Chair: Michael E. Pramstaller CAE
2013 - Washington, DC (George Washington University)/April 21 - 24
2013 - Scottsdale, AZ (Fairmont Scottsdale Princess)/ Oct. 27 - 30
2014 - Washington, DC (George Washington University)/April 27 - 30
2014 - Waikoloa, HI (Hilton Waikoloa Village)/Oct. 22 - 25
2015 - Boston, MA (The Westin Copley Place)/Oct. 14 - 17
2016 - Colorado Springs, CO (The Broadmoor)/Oct. 19 - 22
2017 - Orlando, FL (Hilton Orlando Bonnet Creek)/Oct. 15 - 18
Number of non-conference events/year: 4

Publications:
Coalition Directory; on-line
Conference Compendium
Engineering, Inc.; bi-monthly; adv.
Last Word; weekly
Membership Directory; on-line
Suppliers Directory; on-line; adv.

Membership List Available to Non-members

American Council of Hypnotist Examiners *(1980)*
700 S. Central Ave.
Glendale, CA 91204
Tel: (818) 242-1159 *Fax:* (818) 247-9379
E-Mail: hypnotismla@earthlink.net

Website: hypnotistexaminers.org
Members: 9000 physicians, psychiatrists, psychologists
Staff: 5
Annual Budget: $100-250,000
Tax: 501(c)(6)

Personnel:
President: John Butler
Managing Editor, ACHE Newsletter: Cheryl Canfield
Administrative Director: Jon Young

Historical Note:
ACHE is an organization that certifies hypnotherapists worldwide, including numerous physicians, psychiatrists, psychologists and representatives of the healing arts, counseling and allied professions. Membership: $50-100/ year (Individual).

Continuing Education:
Certification Designation/s: CH, CCH

Publications:
Newsletter; monthly

American Council of Independent Laboratories
(1937)
1629 K St. NW
Suite 500
Washington, DC 20006
Tel: (202) 887-5872 *Fax:* (202) 887-0021
E-Mail: info@acil.org
Website: acil.org
Members: 250 Organizations
Staff: 4
Annual Budget: $500-1,000,000

Personnel:
Chief Executive Officer: Milton M. Bush JD, CAE
  E-Mail: mbush@acil.org
Chief Operating Officer: Richard Bright
  E-Mail: rbright@acil.org
Chief Communications Officer: Adrienne Bush
  E-Mail: abush@acil.org
Project Manager: Beth Horan CPA
  E-Mail: bhoran@acil.org

Historical Note:
Formerly (1937) American Council of Commercial Laboratories, American Council of Independent Laboratories (1994), ACIL: the Association of Independent Scientific, Engineering and Testing Firms (1995), and ACIL (1999) resumed using the name American Council of Independent Laboratories in 2000. ACIL's purpose is to promote code of ethics among members, working with standards and accrediting bodies on programs to improve laboratory performance. Members are third-party commercial engineering and scientific testing laboratories offering analytical, testing, R&D, and consulting services to industry, commerce, and government. Membership: $791-20,800 (Corporate); $500-1000 (Adjunct/Affiliate); $1,000-5,000 (Associate); $633-16,640 (Accreditation Body).

Meetings/Conferences: Annual
Conference Chair: Beth Horan CPA

Publications:
ACIL Newsletter; bi-monthly
Membership Directory; on-line

Membership List Available to Non-members

American Council of Learned Societies *(1919)*
633 Third Ave.
Eighth Floor
New York, NY 10017-6795
Tel: (212) 697-1505 *Fax:* (212) 949-8058
Website: acls.org
Members: 92 societies and affiliated associations
Staff: 24
Annual Budget: $50-100,000,000
Tax: 501(c)(3)

Personnel:
President: Pauline Yu
  E-Mail: paulineyu@acls.org
Program Assistant: Lauren Birnie
  E-Mail: lbirnie@acls.org
Director, Member Relations: Sandra Bradley
  E-Mail: sbradley@acls.org
Director, Web and Information Systems: Candace Frede
  E-Mail: cfrede@acls.org
Managing Editor: Nina Gielen
  E-Mail: ngielen@hebook.org
Director, Finance: Lawrence R. Wirth
  E-Mail: lwirth@acls.org

Historical Note:
ACLS works for advancement of humanistic studies in all fields of learning in the humanities and the social sciences and the maintenance and strengthening of relations among the national societies devoted to such studies. Membership: $990-9,900 (Constituent Learned Society); $1,765-7,030 (Associate); $1,200 (Affiliate).

Meetings/Conferences: Annual
2013 - Baltimore, MD (Renaissance Baltimore Harborplace Hotel)/May 9 - 11
2013 - Louisville, KY/Nov. 14 - 17
Number of non-conference events/year: 4

Publications:
ACLS News; on-line
Publications Directory; on-line

American Council of Life Insurers (ACLI) (1976)
101 Constitution Ave. NW
Suite 700
Washington, DC 20001-2133
Tel: (202) 624-2000
TollFree: (877) 674-4659
E-Mail: media@acli.com
Website: acli.com
Members: 400 Insurance Companies
Staff: 145
Annual Budget: $25-50,000,000

Personnel:
President and Chief Executive Officer: Dirk Kempthorne
    E-Mail: DIRKKempthorne@acli.com
Vice President, Media Relations: Jack F. Dolan
    E-Mail: jackdolan@acli.org
Senior Executive Vice President, Public Policy: Kimberly Olsen Dorgan
    E-Mail: kimdorgan@acli.com
Vice President, Communications: Jessica Hanson
Senior Vice President, Public Affairs and Publishing: Shawn Hausman
    E-Mail: shawnhausman@acli.com
Executive Vice President and General Counsel: Gary E. Hughes
    E-Mail: garyhughes@acli.com
Executive Vice President and Corporate Secretary: David C. Turner
    E-Mail: davidturner@acli.com
Senior Vice President, Administration and Chief Financial Officer: Donald Walker
    E-Mail: donwalker@acli.com

Historical Note:
A national trade association representing the interests of legal reserve life insurance companies in legislative, regulatory and judicial matters at the federal, state and municipal levels of government.

Meetings/Conferences:
2013 - Atlanta, GA (The Ritz-Carlton Buckhead)/Feb. 23 - 26
2013 - New Orleans, LA/April 15 - 17
2013 - St. Louis, MO/Oct. 27 - 29
2014 - Chicago, IL/April 7 - 9
Number of non-conference events/year: 12

Publications:
ACLI's Newsletters; weekly

Membership List Available to Non-members

American Council of Snowmobile Associations (1935)
271 Woodland Pass
Suite 216
East Lansing, MI 48823
Tel: (517) 351-4362 Fax: (517) 351-1363
E-Mail: info@snowmobilers.org
Website: snowmobilers.org
Staff: 2
Annual Budget: $100-250,000

Personnel:
Executive Director: Christine Jourdain
    E-Mail: cajourdain@aol.com

Historical Note:
ACSA is a national organization that was formed to unite the snowmobile community. Membership: $10 (individual); $15 (Family); $25 (Club); $100 (Business Contributor); $250 (Business Partner); $1000 (Associate).

Publications:
ACSA eNewsletter; on-line

American Council of State Savings Supervisors (1939)

1129 20th St. NW
Ninth Floor
Washington, DC 20036
Tel: (202) 728-5757
Website: acsss.org
Members: 130 individuals
Staff: 2
Annual Budget: Under $10,000
Tax: 501(c)(6)

Personnel:
Executive Director: Ed Smith

Historical Note:
Formerly (1987) National Association of State Savings and Loan Supervisors. ACSSS provides technical and supervisory training to state financial institution regulatory agencies and examiners nationwide.

American Council on Consumer Interests (1953)
P.O. Box 2528
Tarpon Springs, FL 34688-2528
Tel: (727) 493-2131
E-Mail: info@consumerinterests.org
Website: consumerinterests.org
Members:
420 institutions
350 individuals
Staff: 2
Annual Budget: $100-250,000
Tax: 501(c)(3)

Personnel:
Executive Director: Ginger Phillips
    E-Mail: gphillips@consumerinterests.org

Historical Note:
Formerly known as Council on Consumer Information; assumed its present name in 1969. Mission of ACCI is to enhance consumer and family economic well-being by promoting excellence in research and educational programs. Membership: $110 (Individual); $55 (Student/Retired).

Meetings/Conferences: Annual
2013 - Portland, OR (Benson Hotel)/April 10 - 12

Publications:
ACCI E-News; monthly
Consumer Interests Annual; annually
Journal of Consumer Affairs; on-line
Membership Directory; on-line

American Council on Education (1918)
One Dupont Cir. NW
Suite 800
Washington, DC 20036-1193
Tel: (202) 939-9300 Fax: (202) 833-4760
E-Mail: comments@ace.nche.edu
Website: acenet.edu
Members: 1825 Institutions, Associates and National and Regional Associations
Staff: 175
Annual Budget: $50-100,000,000
Tax: 501(c)(3)

Personnel:
President: Molly Corbett Broad
    E-Mail: president@ace.nche.edu
Director, Membership Services: Jennifer Adams
Director, Information Technology Services: Zenitta Anderson
    E-Mail: zanderson@acenet.edu
Account Manager: Michael Araujo
    E-Mail: maraujo@acenet.edu
Vice President, Advancement and Member Services: Ellen Babby
    E-Mail: ellen_babby@ace.nche.edu
Associate Director, Human Resources: Noreene Duggan
    E-Mail: nduggan@acenet.edu
Director, Publishing: Scott Harris
    E-Mail: sharris@acenet.edu
Senior Vice President, Government and Public Affairs: Terry W. Hartle
    E-Mail: t_w_hartle@ace.nche.edu
Program Manager: Debbie Knox
    E-Mail: dknox@acenet.edu
Director, Meeting Services: Stephanie Marshall
    E-Mail: smarshall@acenet.edu
Vice President, Public Affairs, Communications and Marketing: Timothy J. McDonough
    E-Mail: tmcdonough@acenet.edu
General Counsel: Ada Meloy
    E-Mail: ada_meloy@ace.nche.edu
President: David Ward

Historical Note:
ACE's mission is to provide leadership on key higher education issues and influences public policy through advocacy, research, and program initiatives and also fosters greater collaboration and new partnerships within and outside the higher education community to help colleges and universities.

Meetings/Conferences: Annual
Conference Chair: Stephanie Marshall
2013 - Washington, DC (Omni Shoreham Hotel)/March 2 - 5
2014 - San Diego, CA (Manchester Grand Hyatt San Diego)/March 8 - 11
2015 - Washington, DC (Washington Hilton)/March 14 - 17
Number of non-conference events/year: 5

Publications:
Higher Education and National Affairs (HENA)
Members and Associates Directory
President to President
The Presidency; adv.

Membership List Available to Non-members

American Council on Exercise (1985)
4851 Paramount Dr.
San Diego, CA 92123
Tel: (858) 576-6500 Fax: (858) 576-6564
TollFree: (888) 825-3636
E-Mail: support@acefitness.org
Website: acefitness.org
Members: 55000 individuals
Staff: 50
Annual Budget: $10-25,000,000
Tax: 501(c)(3)

Personnel:
President and Chief Executive Officer: Scott Goudeseune
Chief Science Officer: Cedric X. Bryant PhD
Chief Financial Officer: Alex Mirnezam MBA

Historical Note:
ACE is committed to enriching quality of life through safe and effective exercise and physical activity.

Continuing Education:
Certification Designation/s: ACE NCCA, AH + FSC, GFIC, PTC, L + WMCC, PFT
Meetings/Conferences:
Number of non-conference events/year: 5

Publications:
Health eTips; monthly; adv.

Membership List Available to Non-members

American Council on International Personnel (1972)
1101 15th St. NW
Suite 750
Washington, DC 20005
Tel: (202) 371-6789 Fax: (202) 371-5524
E-Mail: info@acip.com
Website: acip.com
Members:
500 employees
200 companies, universities and research institutions
Staff: 8
Annual Budget: $1-2,000,000

Personnel:
Executive Director: Lynn Frendt Shotwell
    E-Mail: lynn_shotwell@acip.com
Director and Counsel, Legislative Affairs: Rebecca Knowles Peters
    E-Mail: Rebecca_peters@acip.com
Legislative Assistant and Membership Coordinator: Kathryn Saville
    E-Mail: kathryn_saville@acip.com

Historical Note:
ACIP's mission is to provide the resources and support necessary to advance employment-based immigration of highly educated professionals worldwide. Membership is open to all companies and organizations that employ at least 500 persons worldwide, including overseas and U.S. affiliates and subsidiaries. Membership: $990/year.

Meetings/Conferences: Annual
Number of non-conference events/year: 1

Publications:
Immediate Alerts; weekly
Membership Directory; on-line

American Council on Science and Health (1978)

1995 Broadway
Suite 202
New York, NY 10023-5882
Tel: (212) 362-7044 *Fax:* (212) 362-4919
TollFree: (866) 905-2694
E-Mail: acsh@acsh.org
Website: acsh.org
Members: 2500 individuals
Staff: 11
Annual Budget: $1-2,000,000
Tax: 501(c)(3)

Personnel:
Medical and Executive Director: Gilbert Ross MD
Director, Development and Media: Jody Manley
Director, Publications: Alyssa Pelish
President: Elizabeth M. Whelan MPH, ScD

Historical Note:
ACSH is a consumer education organization providing the public with scientific evaluations of food, chemicals, environment and health. Membership: $50 (Member); $100 (Associate); $250 (Nader- Buster); $500 (Partner-In-Science); $1,000 (President's Club); $5,000 (Chairman's Circle); $10,000 (Leadership Council).

Publications:
Dispatch
Quarterly Updates; quarterly

American Council on the Teaching of Foreign Languages *(1967)*
1001 N. Fairfax St.
Suite 200
Alexandria, VA 22314
Tel: (703) 894-2900 *Fax:* (703) 894-2905
E-Mail: headquarters@actfl.org
Website: actfl.org
Members: 12000 foreign language teachers and administrators
Staff: 27
Annual Budget: $10-25,000,000

Personnel:
Executive Director: Marty Abbott
    E-Mail: mabbott@actfl.org
Director, Membership: Howie Berman
    E-Mail: hberman@actfl.org
Finance Manager: Zerihun Haile-Selassie
    E-Mail: zhaileselassie@actfl.org
Director, Conventions and Meetings: Julia Richardson
    E-Mail: jrichardson@actfl.org
Director, Professional Programs: Elvira Swender
    E-Mail: eswender@actfl.org

Historical Note:
Founded in 1967 as part of the Modern Language Association of America and incorporated in 1974, became a separate organization in 1977. ACTFL's mission is to provide vision, leadership and support for quality teaching and learning of languages. Membership: $75 (Regular); $50 (New Teacher/Adjunct/Part-Time Educators); $25 (Student/Retired); $20 (International/Joint); $5 (Special Interest Groups).

Meetings/Conferences: Annual
Conference Chair: Julia Richardson
2013 - Orlando, FL (Orange County Convention Center-Rosen Centre Hotel)/Nov. 22 - 24
2014 - San Antonio, TX (Hyatt Regency Hill Country Resort and Spa)/Nov. 21 - 23

Publications:
ACTFL Connection; on-line; adv.
Foreign Language Annals; quarterly
Membership Directory; on-line
SmartBrief; weekly
The Language Educator; adv.

Membership List Available to Non-members

American Councils for International Education *(1974)*
1828 L St. NW
Suite 1200
Washington, DC 20036
Tel: (202) 833-7522 *Fax:* (202) 833-7523
E-Mail: general@americancouncils.org
Website: americancouncils.org
Members: 1775 individuals and institutions
Staff: 232
Annual Budget: $50-100,000,000

Personnel:
President: Dr. Dan E. Davidson PhD
Vice President, Marketing: Kirsten Brecht

Vice President: Lisa Choate
Managing Director, Business and Program Development: Michael P. Curtis
Chief Financial Officer: John Henderson
Director, Human Resources and Office Manager: Suzanne LaFlair

Historical Note:
Formerly (2000) American Council of Teachers of Russian. ACTR strives to expand dialog among students, scholars, educators and professionals for the advancement of learning and mutual respect in the diverse communities and societies in which they work. Membership: $10-500/year.

Publications:
ACTR Newsletter
EURECA Chronicle; bi-weekly
Journal of Eurasian Research
Russian Language Journal

Membership List Available to Non-members

American Counseling Association *(1952)*
5999 Stevenson Ave.
Alexandria, VA 22304-3300
Tel: (800) 347-6647 *Fax:* (800) 473-2329
TollFree: (800) 347-6647
E-Mail: aca@counseling.org
Website: counseling.org
Members: 45000 individuals
Staff: 55
Annual Budget: $10-25,000,000
Tax: 501(c)(3)

Personnel:
Executive Director: Richard Yep
    E-Mail: ryep@counseling.org
Contact, Publications: Carolyn Baker
    E-Mail: cbaker@counseling.org
Chief Financial Officer: Deborah Barnes
    E-Mail: dbarnes@counseling.org
Director, Public Policy and Legislation: Scott Barstow
    E-Mail: sbarstow@counseling.org
Contact, Marketing: Debra Bass
    E-Mail: dbass@counseling.org
Contact, Professional Information Library: Vikki Cooper
    E-Mail: vcooper@counseling.org
Contact, Database Management: Mary Griffith
    E-Mail: mgriffith@counseling.org
Contact, Conference and Meetings: Robin Hayes
    E-Mail: rhayes@counseling.org
Contact, Membership Services: Jacki Walker
    E-Mail: jwalker@counseling.org
Contact, Human Resources and Office Services: Cindy Welch
    E-Mail: cwelch@counseling.org

Historical Note:
Formerly (1983) the American Personnel and Guidance Association and (1992) American Association for Counseling and Development. ACA's mission is to enhance the quality of life in society by encouraging the development of professional counselors, advancing the counseling profession and using the profession and practice of counseling to elevate respect for human dignity and diversity. Membership: $161 (Professional/Regular); $92 (New Professional/Student).

Meetings/Conferences: Annual
Conference Chair: Robin Hayes
2013 - Cincinnati, OH (Duke Energy Convention Center)/March 20 - 24/1-10 exhibitors
2014 - Honolulu, HI/March 26 - 30/1-10 exhibitors
2015 - Orlando, FL/March 11 - 15/1-10 exhibitors

Publications:
ACAeNews; bi-weekly
Counselling Today; daily; adv.
Journal of Counseling & Development; quarterly

American Court and Commercial Newspapers *(1997)*
P.O. Box 50301
Arlington, VA 22205
Tel: (703) 237-9801 *Fax:* (703) 237-9808
E-Mail: info@AmericanPressWorks.com
Website: americanpressworks.com
Members: 79 newspapers
Staff: 10
Annual Budget: $100-250,000

Personnel:
Executive Director: David Placher
President: Tonda F. Rush
Accountant: Russell Pierce

Communications Director: Stanley A. Schwartz
Manager, Membership Services: Gloria J. Watkins

Historical Note:
APW was founded in 1997 to provide management services and public affairs consulting for the communications industries and professions. Based in Arlington, Virginia, it works with organizations in the media world to shape opinion, build community and achieve group goals.

American Craft Council *(1943)*
1224 Marshall St. NE
Suite 200
Minneapolis, MN 55413-1036
Tel: (612) 206-3100 *Fax:* (612) 355-2330
TollFree: (800) 836-3470
E-Mail: council@craftcouncil.org
Website: craftcouncil.org
Members: 30000 individuals
Staff: 21
Annual Budget: $5-10,000,000
Tax: 501(c)(3)

Personnel:
Executive Director: Chris Amundsen
    E-Mail: camundsen@craftcouncil.org
Director, Finance and Administration: Greg Allen
    E-Mail: gallen@craftcouncil.org
Director, Marketing and Communications: Pamela Diamond
    E-Mail: pdiamond@craftcouncil.org
Director, Shows: Melanie Little
    E-Mail: mlittle@craftcouncil.org
Editor-in-Chief: Monica Moses
    E-Mail: mmoses@craftcouncil.org
Contact, Membership Inquiries: Alanna Nissen
    E-Mail: anissen@craftcouncil.org
Director, Education: Perry Price
    E-Mail: pprice@craftcouncil.org

Historical Note:
ACC works to promote understanding and appreciation of contemporary American craft. Membership: $40 (Individual, U.S.); $55 (Individual, Canada/International); $50 (Professional).

Meetings/Conferences:
Conference Chair: Melanie Little
2013 - Baltimore, MD (Baltimore Convention Center)/ Feb. 19 - 24
2013 - St. Paul, MN (St. Paul RiverCentre)/April 18 - 21
2013 - Atlanta, GA (Cobb Galleria Centre)/May 14 - 17
2013 - San Francisco, CA/Aug. 2 - 4
Number of non-conference events/year: 10

Publications:
American Craft Magazine; bi-monthly; adv.

American Cream Draft Horse Association *(1944)*
193 Crossover Rd.
Bennington, VT 05201
E-Mail: info@acdha.net
Website: acdha.org
Members: 125 individuals
Staff: 4
Annual Budget: Under $10,000

Personnel:
President: Frank Tremel
    E-Mail: rosehillcreams@aol.com
Secretary: Nancy H. Lively
    E-Mail: lively123@comcast.net
Editor: Nancy Phillps
    E-Mail: creamnewseditor@yahoo.com
Webmaster: Dean Tick

Historical Note:
ACDHA's mission is to preserve accurate records of the breeding and ancestry of American Cream Draft Horse. Members are owners and breeders of American Cream Draft Horses. Membership: $25-30/year (Individual).

Meetings/Conferences: Annual

Publications:
ACDHA Newsletter; on-line; adv.

American Credit and Collections Association *(1998)*
P.O. Box 40
Plymouth, NH 03264
Tel: (603) 744-9427
E-Mail: michelle@credit-and-collections.com
Website: credit-and-collections.com
Staff: 3

Personnel:

Founder: Michelle Dunn
   E-Mail: michelle@credit-and-collections.com

Historical Note:
American Credit and Collections Association's purpose is to provide resources and help to professionals in the credit & debt collection industry, including credit managers, people starting a collection agency, and business owners. Membership: $295/year (Professional Member).

American Criminal Justice Association Lambda Alpha Epsilon *(1937)*
P.O. Box 601047
Sacramento, CA 95860-1047
Tel: (916) 484-6553 *Fax:* (916) 488-2227
E-Mail: acjalae@aol.com
Website: acjalae.org
Members: 4500 individuals
Staff: 3
Annual Budget: $100-250,000
Tax: 501(c)(7)

Personnel:
Editor: Fred Campbell
   E-Mail: crimjust@jps.net
Executive Secretary: Karen K. Campbell

Historical Note:
Also known as Lambda Alpha Epsilon, ACJA/LAE's mission is to promote professional, academic and public awareness of criminal justice issues and to encourage the establishment and expansion of higher education and professional training in criminal justice. Membership is composed of individuals employed in the criminal justice system or taking a course of study in criminal justice at an accredited college or university at the time the application is submitted. Membership: $30/year (New Member).

Meetings/Conferences: Annual
2013 - Valley Forge, PA (Radisson Hotel Valley Forge)/
   April 21 - 26

Publications:
LAE Journal of the American Criminal Justice
   Association; annually
LAE Newsletter; annually

American Crossbred Pony Registry *(1957)*
152 Warbasse Junction Rd.
Lafayette, NJ 07848
Tel: (973) 383-0456
E-Mail: plumtreehill@nac.net
Website: njponybreeders.org/Crossbred/
   AmericanCrossbredPonyRegistry.htm
Members: 150 individuals
Staff: 2
Annual Budget: Under $10,000

Personnel:
President: Marian Smith
Registrar: Donna Raquet

Historical Note:
ACPR certifies and registers bloodlines of crossbred hunter and driving ponies. Mission is to serve and promote the pony industry in the state of New Jersey and the United States. Membership: $25 (Senior); $15 (Junior); $35 (Family); $100 (Life). All membership based on number of votes.

Publications:
Newsletter

American Crystallographic Association *(1949)*
Ellicott Stn.
P.O. Box 96
Buffalo, NY 14205-0096
Tel: (716) 898-8690 *Fax:* (716) 898-8695
E-Mail: aca@hwi.buffalo.edu
Website: amercrystalassn.org
Members: 2200 members
Staff: 5
Annual Budget: $500-1,000,000
Tax: 501(c)(3)

Personnel:
Chief Executive Officer: William L. Duax
   E-Mail: duax@hwi.buffalo.edu
Director, Administrative Services: Marcia Colquhoun
   E-Mail: marcia@hwi.buffalo.edu
Editor: Judy Flippen-Anderson
   E-Mail: acareflexions@gmail.com
Chief Financial Officer: S. N. Rao
   E-Mail: deanrao@gmail.com
Secretary, Membership Services: Crystal Towns
   E-Mail: ctowns@hwi.buffalo.edu

Historical Note:
Created in 1949 through a merger of the Crystallographic Society of America and the American Society of X-ray and Electron Diffraction, incorporated in New York in 1971. Member of the American Institute of Physics an affiliate member of the International Union of Crystallography. ACA's mission is to promote interaction among scientists who study the structure of matter at atomic (or near atomic) resolution. These interactions advance experimental and computational aspects of crystallography and diffraction. Membership: $100 (Regular); $25 (Student); $40 (Retired/Post Doc).

Meetings/Conferences: Annual
2013 - Honolulu, HI/July 20 - 24
2014 - Albuquerque, NM (Albuquerque Convention
   Center)/May 24 - 28

Publications:
ACA Reflexions; quarterly; adv.

Membership List Available to Non-members

American Culinary Federation *(1929)*
180 Center Pl. Way
St. Augustine, FL 32095
Tel: (904) 824-4468 *Fax:* (904) 825-4758
TollFree: (800) 624-9458
E-Mail: acf@acfchefs.net
Website: acfchefs.org
Members: 20000 individuals
Staff: 39
Annual Budget: $100-250,000
Tax: 501(c)(6)

Personnel:
Executive Director: Heidi Cramb
   E-Mail: hcramb@acfchefs.net
Director, Membership Development: Suzanne Bohle
   E-Mail: sbohle@acfchefs.net
Director, Communications: Patricia Carroll
   E-Mail: pcarroll@acfchefs.net
Director, Finance: Jim Denkler
   E-Mail: jdenkler@acfchefs.net
Director, Certification: Sandy Friend
   E-Mail: sfriend@acfchefs.net
Director, Business Development and Sales: Cheryl Hays
Manager, Membership Services: Linda Leo
   E-Mail: lleo@acfchefs.net
Director, Education and Professional Development: Kristy
   Nelson
   E-Mail: knelson@acfchefs.net
Editor: Kay Orde
   E-Mail: korde@acfchefs.net
Senior Events Manager: Tracy Smith
   E-Mail: tsmith@acfchefs.net
Manager, Information Technology: Michael Tadlock
   E-Mail: mtadlock@acfchefs.net

Historical Note:
ACF, a professional organization for culinarians in America, who work for culinarians internationally through education, apprenticeship and certification, while creating a fraternal bond of respect and integrity among culinarians everywhere. In addition, the ACF is the presidium for the World Association of Cooks Societies (WACS), the international network of chefs associations, with more that eight million members globally. Membership: $130 (Property Membership, 6- 10 members); $115 (Property Membership, 11-30 members); $95 (Property Membership,31 or more members); $75 (Military, E1-E5); $125 (Military, E6 and above/Culinary Enthusiast).

Continuing Education:
Certification Designation/s: CEC, CEPC, CCA, CCE, CMC

Meetings/Conferences: Annual
Conference Chair: Tracy Smith
Number of non-conference events/year: 4

Publications:
Center of the Plate; monthly; adv.
The Culinary Insider; bi-weekly

American Cultural Resources Association (ACRA) *(1995)*
5024-R Campbell Blvd.
Baltimore, MD 21236
Tel: (410) 931-8100 *Fax:* (410) 931-8111
Website: acra-crm.org
Members:
30 associate members
120 firms
Staff: 3
Annual Budget: $100-250,000

Personnel:

Executive Director: C.J. Summers
Association Manager and Webmaster: Ally Lancaster
Treasurer: Don Weir

Historical Note:
Supporting the business needs of the cultural resource management industry. ACRA's mission is to promote the professional, ethical, and business practices of the cultural resources consulting industry. Membership: $85 (Associates); $25 (Full/Part time student); $110-1975 (Corporate).

Meetings/Conferences: Annual
2013 - Washington, DC (Hyatt Regency Washington)/
   Oct. 10 - 13

Publications:
ACRA Edition; quarterly

American Custom Gunmakers Guild *(1983)*
Five Crescent Ct.
Midland, MI 48640
Tel: (989) 600-6135 *Fax:* (888) 959-0023
E-Mail: acgg@acgg.org
Website: acgg.org
Members: 350 individuals
Staff: 2
Annual Budget: $100-250,000
Tax: 501(c)(6)

Personnel:
Executive Director: Brett A. Schwenke
Treasurer: Roger Ferrell
   E-Mail: rogersgunworks@yahoo.com

Historical Note:
ACGG's mission is to educate the public and advance the trade as an acceptable art form. Membership: $45-2000/year.

Meetings/Conferences: Annual
Number of non-conference events/year: 1

Publications:
Directory of Custom Gunmaking Services; on-line
Gunmaker; quarterly; adv.
Membership Directory; on-line

American Dairy Goat Association *(1904)*
161 W. Main St.
P.O. Box 865
Spindale, NC 28160
Tel: (828) 286-3801 *Fax:* (828) 287-0476
E-Mail: info@adga.org
Website: adga.org
Members: 13000 individuals
Staff: 19
Annual Budget: $1-2,000,000
Tax: 501(c)(5)

Personnel:
Association Manager: Shirley C. McKenzie
   E-Mail: mckenzie@adga.org
Administrative Assistant: Paula Hughes
   E-Mail: hughes@adga.org
Manager, Information Systems: Kit Nevin
Coordinator, Performance Programs: Lisa Shepard
   E-Mail: shepard@thegrid.net

Historical Note:
Formerly American Milch Goat Record Association and American Milk Goat Record Association. ADGA aims to collect, record and preserve the pedigrees of dairy goats and to provide genetic, management and related services to dairy goat breeders. Member of the National Pedigree Livestock Council. Members are breeders and fanciers of dairy goats. Membership: $35 (Regular); $10 (Youth).

Meetings/Conferences: Annual
Conference Chair: Lisa Shepard
2013 - Asheville, NC/Oct. 12 - 19

Publications:
ADGA News and Events; quarterly
Membership Directory; annually; adv.

Membership List Available to Non-members

American Dairy Products Institute *(1986)*
116 N. York St.
Suite 200
Elmhurst, IL 60126
Tel: (630) 530-8700 *Fax:* (630) 530-8707
E-Mail: info@adpi.org
Website: adpi.org
Members: 225 companies
Staff: 5
Annual Budget: $1-2,000,000

Tax: 501(c)(6)
Personnel:
Chief Executive Officer: David Thomas
    E-Mail: dthomas@adpi.org
Director, Finance: Steve Griffin
    E-Mail: sgriffin@adpi.org
Director, Technical Services: Dan Meyer
    E-Mail: dmeyer@adpi.org
Director, Administration: Carl Roode
    E-Mail: carl@adpi.org
Director, Membership Communications: Beth Sutton
    E-Mail: bsutton@adpi.org

Historical Note:
Product of a merger between the American Dry Milk Institute and the Whey Products Institute in 1986; the Evaporated Milk Association merged into Institute in 1987; a cheese division was formed in 1997. ADPI's mission is to promote dairy products processing industry and it's products through relations with affiliated industry organizations and applicable government bodies. Membership: $2,750 (Associated Processor); $1,000 (International); $1,200 (Affiliate); $900 (Utilization).

Meetings/Conferences: Annual
Conference Chair: Carl Roode
2013 - Chicago, IL (Chicago Marriott Downtown Magnificent Mile)/April 28 - 30
2014 - Chicago, IL (Hyatt Regency Chicago)/April 27 - 30

Publications:
Member Directory; on-line

American Dairy Science Association *(1906)*
1800 S. Oak St.
Suite 100
Champaign, IL 61820-6974
Tel: (217) 356-5146 *Fax:* (217) 398-4119
E-Mail: adsa@assochq.org
Website: adsa.org
Members: 5200 individuals
Staff: 11
Annual Budget: $2-5,000,000
Tax: 501(c)(3)
Personnel:
Executive Director: Peter Studney CAE, MBA
    E-Mail: peters@assochq.org
Administrative Assistant: Vicki Paden
    E-Mail: vickip@assochq.org
Editor-in-Chief: Roger Shanks
Event Coordinator: Cara Tharp
    E-Mail: CaraT@assochq.org

Historical Note:
Formerly National Association of Dairy Instructors and Investigators, the name changed to Official Dairy Instructor's Association in 1908. Assumed its current name in 1916. ADSA's mission is to provide leadership in scientific and technical support to sustain and grow the global dairy industry through generation, dissemination, and exchange of information and services. Members are equipment manufacturers and suppliers, farmers, educators, researchers, and breeders interested in strengthening all aspects of the dairy industry. Membership: $110 (Professional); $890 (Corporate Sustaining); $5 (Undergraduate Student); $10 (Graduate Student); $55 (Post Doctorate).

Meetings/Conferences: Annual
Conference Chair: Cara Tharp
2013 - Indianapolis, IN/July 8 - 12
2014 - Kansas City, MO/July 20 - 24
Number of non-conference events/year: 3

Publications:
Animal & Dairy News; quarterly
Dair-e-news; weekly
Journal of Dairy Science; quarterly
Membership Directory; on-line

American Dance Guild *(1956)*
240 W. 14th St.
New York, NY 10011
Website: americandanceguild.org
Members: 400 individuals
Staff: 1
Annual Budget: $25-50,000
Personnel:
President: Gloria McLean
    E-Mail: gloria.mclean@earthlink.net

Historical Note:
Formerly known as (1956) Dance Teachers Guild, (1966) National Dance Teachers Guild, and (1968) National

Dance Guild before assuming its current name. ADG is dedicated to support artists and bringing the dance community together. Membership: $60 (Regular); $35 (Student/Retired); $100 (Supporting Member); $80-175 (Institute/Organization); $250 (Sponsoring Member); $600 (Life Member).

Publications:
ADG Newsletter

American Dance Therapy Association *(1966)*
10632 Little Patuxent Pkwy.
Suite 108
Columbia, MD 21044-3263
Tel: (410) 997-4040 *Fax:* (410) 997-4048
E-Mail: info@adta.org
Website: adta.org
Members: 1200 individuals
Staff: 5
Annual Budget: $100-250,000
Personnel:
President: Sharon Goodill BC-DMT, LPC, NCC, PhD
Co-Editor: Christina Devereaux BC-DMT, NCC, PhD
    E-Mail: christina@cd-photo.com
Director, Operations: Gloria J. Farrow
    E-Mail: gloria@adta.org
Policy Consultant: Myrna R. Mandlawitz J D, MEd
Administrative Assistant: Renee Wolfe BA

Historical Note:
ADTA's mission is to promote the use of dance and movement as powerful tools for mental and emotional health, maintaining high standards for education, training, and professional practice for dance/movement therapists. Membership: $50 (Associate/Associate International/ Professional/Professional International/Retired/Retired International/Student/Student High School/Student International); $255 (Institutional Member).

Continuing Education:
Certification Designation/s: R-DMT, BC-DMT
Meetings/Conferences: Annual
Conference Chair: Gloria J. Farrow
Publications:
American Journal of Dance Therapy; semi-annually
Membership Directory; on-line

Membership List Available to Non-members

American Dehydrated Onion and Garlic Association *(1956)*
1755 Creekside Oaks Dr.
Suite 250
San Francisco, CA 95833-3645
Tel: (916) 640-8150 *Fax:* (916) 640-8156
Members: 2 companies
Staff: 2
Annual Budget: $50-100,000
Tax: 501(c)(6)
Personnel:
Secretary-Treasurer: Bill Grigg
Office Manager: Allisa Rollm

Historical Note:
Members are U.S. companies that dehydrate onions and garlic serving industrial and food service customers.

American Dental Assistants Association *(1924)*
35 E. Wacker Dr.
Suite 1730
Chicago, IL 60601-2211
Tel: (312) 541-1550 *Fax:* (312) 541-1496
TollFree: (877) 874-3785
E-Mail: adaahelp@aol.com
Website: dentalassistant.org
Members: 30500 individuals
Staff: 10
Annual Budget: $1-2,000,000
Tax: 501(c)(6)
Personnel:
Executive Director: Lawrence H. Sepin
    E-Mail: lsepi@adaa1.com
Manager, Administration and Member Services: Erek Armentrout
    E-Mail: earmentrout@adaa1.com
Director, Education and Professional Relations: Jennifer K. Blake
    E-Mail: jenblakecda@indy.rr.com
Manager, Business Development: Shirley Idleman
    E-Mail: shirleyidleman@officemax.com
Consultant, Membership, Marketing and Editor: Douglas J. McDonough

    E-Mail: mcdono@adaa1.com
Director, Information Technology and Meeting Planner: Nancy Rodriguez
    E-Mail: nrod@adaa1.com
Managing Editor, The Dental Assistant: Michi Trota
    E-Mail: mtrota@adaa1.com

Historical Note:
ADAA's mission is to advance the careers of dental assistants and to promote the dental assisting profession in matters of education, legislation, credentialing and professional activities which enhance the delivery of quality dental health care to the public. Membership: $60 (Life Member); $35 (Students/Graduated); $125 (Active).

Meetings/Conferences: Annual
Conference Chair: Nancy Rodriguez
Number of non-conference events/year: 1

Publications:
ADAA's E-Newsletter; bi-monthly; adv.

American Dental Association *(1859)*
211 E. Chicago Ave.
Chicago, IL 60611-2678
Tel: (312) 440-2500
TollFree: (800) 621-8099
Website: ada.org
Members: 155000 Individuals
Staff: 400
Annual Budget: Over $100,000,000
Tax: 501(c)(6)
Personnel:
Executive Director: Kathleen T. O'Loughlin
    E-Mail: oloughlink@ada.org
Editor: Craig A. Palmer
    E-Mail: palmerc@ada.org
Manager, Communications: Robert Raible
    E-Mail: raibler@ada.org
Managing Vice President, Publishing Division: Michael Springer
    E-Mail: springerm@ada.org

Historical Note:
Founded August 3, 1859 in Niagara Falls. United with the Southern Dental Association in 1897 and changed its name to the National Dental Association; assumed its current name in 1922. ADA's mission is to foster the success of a diverse membership and advance the oral health of the public. Membership: $498 (Active); $75 (Affiliate); $125 (Associate); $30 (Graduate Student); $249 (Nonpracticing Member).

Meetings/Conferences:
2013 - Denver, CO (Four Seasons)/July 18 - 20
2013 - New Orleans, LA (Ernest N. Morial Convention Center)/Oct. 31 - Nov. 3
2014 - San Antonio, TX (The Henry B. Gonzalez Convention Center)/Oct. 9 - 14
2015 - Washington, DC (Walter E. Washington Convention Center)/Nov. 5 - 10
2017 - Atlanta, GA (Georgia World Congress Center)/ Oct. 19 - 24
2018 - San Francisco, CA (The Moscone Center)/Sept. 27 - Oct. 2
Number of non-conference events/year: 3

Publications:
ADA CERP Provider Newsletter; on-line
ADA e-pubs; on-line
JADA; monthly

Membership List Available to Non-members

American Dental Education Association *(1923)*
1400 K St. NW
Suite 1100
Washington, DC 20005
Tel: (202) 289-7201 *Fax:* (202) 289-7204
E-Mail: adea@adea.org
Website: adea.org
Members: 19000 students, faculty, staff, and administrators
Staff: 40
Annual Budget: $10-25,000,000
Tax: 501(c)(3)
Personnel:
Executive Director: Richard W. Valachovic DMD, MPH
    E-Mail: valachovicr@adea.org
Chief Policy Officer and Managing Vice President: Eugene L. Anderson
    E-Mail: andersone@adea.org
Director, Marketing and Communications: Kellie Bove
    E-Mail: BoveK@adea.org

Senior Vice President, Communications and Membership
  Services: Christopher Daniels
    E-Mail: DanielsC@adea.org
Senior Director, Meetings: Audra Franks
    E-Mail: FranksA@adea.org
Senior Vice President, Educational Research and Analysis:
  Gwen Garrison
    E-Mail: GarrisonG@adea.org
Deputy Director and Managing Vice President: Abigail W.
  Gorman
    E-Mail: gormana@adea.org
Recruitment Networking Associate: Joshua Hargrove
    E-Mail: HargroveJ@adea.org
Senior Vice President, Advocacy and Governmental
  Relations: Yvonne Knight
    E-Mail: KnightY@ADEA.org
Copyeditor and Publications Manager: Nancy Lang
    E-Mail: LangN@adea.org
Senior Director, Information Technology: Qi Li
    E-Mail: liq@adea.org
Director, Legislative Policy Development: Monette
  McKinnon
    E-Mail: mckinnonm@adea.org
Assistant Vice President, Division of Finance and
  Operations: Rowena Williams
    E-Mail: WilliamsR@adea.org

Historical Note:
Founded as American Association of Dental Schools
in Omaha, NE through a merger of the American
Institute of Dental Teachers, Canadian Dental Faculties'
Association, National Association of Dental Faculties and
the Dental Faculties' Association of American Universities,
incorporated in Illinois (1960) and assumed its current
name in 2000. ADEA fosters interconnected community
experiences that enable members to meet their individual
goals while leveraging their collective strength. Membership
includes all U.S. and Canadian dental schools and many
other dental and allied institutions in Canada and the U.S.,
provides an application service for people applying to dental
school. Membership: free to staff and students of member
institutions. Membership: $40-125 (Individua); $3,400
(Corporate); $945-25,522 (Institutional); $40 (Student).

Continuing Education:
Certification Designation/s: CERP

Meetings/Conferences:
Conference Chair: Audra Franks
2013 - Seatle, WA (Washington State Convention
  Center)/March 16 - 19
2013 - Portland, OR (Hilton Portland and Executive
  Tower)/June 8 - 11
2014 - San Antonio, TX (The Henry B. Gonzalez
  Convention Center)/March 15 - 18
2015 - Boston, MA (Hynes Convention Center)/March
  7 - 10
Number of non-conference events/year: 2

Publications:
Bulletin of Dental Education Online; monthly; adv.
Directory of Institutional Members; annually; adv.
Journal of Dental Education Online; monthly; adv.
Opportunities for Minority Students; biennially; adv.

American Dental Hygienists' Association (1923)
444 N. Michigan Ave.
Suite 3400
Chicago, IL 60611
Tel: (312) 440-8900 Fax: (312) 467-1806
E-Mail: mail@adha.net
Website: adha.org
Members: 35000 individuals
Staff: 40
Annual Budget: $5-10,000,000
Tax: 501(c)(6)

Personnel:
Executive Director: Ann Battrell MSDH(
Director, Finance: Isaac Carpenter
    E-Mail: finance@adha.net
Director, Administration and Human Resources
  Development: Karen Dunn Caspers CAE
    E-Mail: exec.office@adha.net
Director, Corporate Development and Conference Services:
  Maddie Hilpert "Oelkers"
    E-Mail: corp.dev@adha.net
Director, Communications: Jeff Mitchell
    E-Mail: jeffm@adha.net
Director, Membership Services: Katie Powell
    E-Mail: member.services@adha.net
Director, Education: Pamela Steinbach MS, RN
    E-Mail: education@adha.net

Historical Note:
ADHA's mission is to advance the art and science of
dental hygiene by ensuring access to quality oral health
care, to increase awareness of the cost-effective benefits
of prevention, to promote the standard of dental hygiene
education, licensure, practice and research and to represent
and promote the interests of dental hygienists. Membership:
$170/year.

Meetings/Conferences: Annual
Conference Chair: Maddie Hilpert "Oelkers"
2013 - Boston, MA (Sheraton Boston Hotel)/June 17 -
  27/over 100 exhibitors

Publications:
Access Magazine; monthly; adv.
ADHA Update Newsletter; bi-weekly; adv.
Liaison; monthly
Membership Directory; on-line
The Journal of Dental Hygiene; quarterly

Membership List Available to Non-members

American Dental Interfraternity Council (1923)
160 S. Bellwood Dr.
Suite Z
East Alton, IL 62024
Tel: (618) 307-5433 Fax: (618) 307-5430
E-Mail: odonto44@aol.com
Website: adifc.org
Members: 150 active alumni chapters and 4
dental fraternities
Staff: 1
Annual Budget: Under $10,000

Personnel:
Executive Secretary: Keith W. Dickey
    E-Mail: kdickey@siue.edu

Historical Note:
ADIFC is a federation of professional Greek letter societies
united to promote better public relations for the dental
profession. Goal is to encourage the ideals and standards of
its profession, to advance the professional knowledge and
welfare of its members.

American Dental Society of Anesthesiology
(1953)
211 E. Chicago Ave.
Suite 780
Chicago, IL 60611
Tel: (312) 664-8270 Fax: (312) 224-8624
E-Mail: adsahome@mac.com
Website: adsahome.org
Members: 3500 individuals
Staff: 3
Annual Budget: $2-5,000,000

Personnel:
Executive Director: Knight Charlton
    E-Mail: knightcharlton@mac.com
Director, Meetings: Barbra Josephson CMP
    E-Mail: barbra.josephson@mac.com
Director, Membership Services: Sandy Lieberman
    E-Mail: sandylieberman@mac.com

Historical Note:
ADSA is a group of dentists who are committed to the task
of making dental care more pleasant through a variety
of advanced pain and anxiety control techniques. It's
mission is to provide a forum for education, research and
recognition of achievement in order to advocate safe and
effective patient care for all dentists. Members are dentists
with a special interest in pain control. Membership: $175
(Active-Dentists); $26 (Students/Residents); $87.50 (Non-
Dentists).

Meetings/Conferences: Annual
Conference Chair: Barbra Josephson CMP
2013 - Manalapan, FL (Ritz Carlton Palm Beach)/April
  25 - 27
Number of non-conference events/year: 2

Publications:
Anesthesia Progress; quarterly

American Dermatological Association (1876)
P.O. Box 551301
Davie, FL 33355
Tel: (954) 452-1113 Fax: (305) 945-7063
E-Mail: ameriderm1930@aol.com
Website: amer-derm-assn.org
Staff: 1
Annual Budget: $250-500,000

Personnel:
Executive Manager: Julie Odessky

Historical Note:

ADA purpose was designated to promote the study
of dermatology, with the proviso that the science of
syphilology was not to be neglected. This was especially
important during the early days of arsenical and penicillin
therapy.

Meetings/Conferences: Annual
2013 - Scottsdale, AZ (Four Seasons Resort Scottsdale
  at Troon North)/Sept. 18 - 22
2014 - Williamsburg, VA (Colonial Williamsburg)/Oct.
  8 - 12

Publications:
ADA Newsletter
Membership Directory

American Design Drafting Association
International and American Digital Design
Association (1948)
105 E. Main St.
Newbern, TN 38059
Tel: (731) 627-0802 Fax: (731) 627-9321
E-Mail: corporate@adda.org
Website: adda.org
Members: 6000 individuals
Staff: 3
Annual Budget: $250-500,000
Tax: 501(c)(3)

Personnel:
Executive Director: Olen K. Parker
    E-Mail: okparker@adda.org

Historical Note:
Founded as the Bartlesville Draftsmen's Club and changed
to American Institute for Design and Drafting in 1960,
assumed its present name in 1989. ADDA's mission is to
strengthen the design graphics profession, through training
and educational opportunities. Membership includes
individuals, corporations and educational institutions and
students. It also administers a curriculum certification
program for schools with design/drafting programs.
Membership: $72-89 (Professional); $12-45 (Associate);
$225-675 (Institution); $600-1500 (Corporate Member);
$12-25 (Student/Former Student).

Continuing Education:
Enrollment: 750
Certification Designation/s: CD, DIT, ADDA, AD, CDD,
DD, CDT/CSD

Meetings/Conferences: Annual

Publications:
Design Drafting News
Membership Directory; on-line

American Devon Cattle Association (1918)
9272 Big Horn Rd.
Lakota Ranch
Remington, VA 22734
Tel: (641) 942-6430 Fax: (641) 942-6502
Website: americandevon.com
Members: 96 individuals
Staff: 2
Annual Budget: $100-250,000

Personnel:
President: Jeremy Anderson Engh
    E-Mail: Enghs@aol.com

Historical Note:
Formerly (1971) American Devon Cattle Club. ADCA's
mission is to maintain an accurate pure devon registry,
to preserve the purity of the breed, to disseminate general
information to the membership and to recruit new members
through general promotional activities. Membership: $100
(Individual); $5 (Junior); $40(Assosciation).

Meetings/Conferences: Annual

Publications:
ADCA Newsletter
Member Directory; on-line

American Dexter Cattle Association (1912)
17087 Dixie Farms Ln.
Iola, TX 77861
Tel: (936) 394-2606
E-Mail: adca@dextercattle.org
Website: dextercattle.org
Members: 450 individuals
Staff: 5
Annual Budget: $100-250,000

Personnel:
President: Pam Malcuit
    E-Mail: mornstarranch@cs.com

Historical Note:

Formerly (1957) American Kerry and Dexter Club. Indigenous to Ireland, the dexter is a breed used in both beef and dairy applications. ADCA seeks to encourage the breeding of high quality dexter cattle, to maintain a herd book and system of registry for registering such cattle and to assemble and disseminate information concerning the breed. Membership: $25 (Individual); $45 (Family/Partnership); $30 (Associate/Youth).

Meetings/Conferences: Annual
2013 - Springfield, MO (Ozark Empire Fairgrounds)/June 13 - 16

Publications:
ADCA Newsletter
Bulletin; quarterly; adv.
Farming Magazine; on-line
Membership Directory; on-line
Wall Street Journal

American Diabetes Association *(1940)*
1701 N. Beauregard St.
Alexandria, VA 22311
Tel: (703) 549-1500
TollFree: (800) 342-2383
E-Mail: customerservice@diabetes.org
Website: diabetes.org
Members: 390000 individuals
Staff: 1566
Annual Budget: Over $100,000,000

Personnel:
Chief Executive Officer: Laurence Hausner MBA
  E-Mail: lhausner@diabetes.org
Executive Vice President, Government Affairs and Advocacy: Shereen Arent
  E-Mail: sarent@diabetes.org
Chief Financial Officer: Debbie Johnson CPA
Senior Vice President, Human Resources: Don M. Laing
Senior Vice President and Chief Technology Officer: Rodney Sampson
Senior Vice President, Marketing and Communications: Lois A. Witkop MBA

Historical Note:
Formerly Professional Society of Medical Doctors; Became a voluntary health agency in 1965. ADA seeks to prevent and cure diabetes and to improve the lives of all people affected by diabetes by offering support, educate health professionals and the general public about the disease. Membership: $310-415 (Physicians); $140-205 (Category II).

Meetings/Conferences:
2013 - Denver, CO (Colorado Convention Center)/Feb. 9
2013 - Salt Lake City, UT (South Exhibition Center)/March 2
2013 - Chicago, IL (Hyatt Regency McCormick Place)/April 13
2013 - Seatle, WA (Seattle Conference Center)/April 13
2013 - Los Angeles, CA (Los Angeles Convention Center)/May 4
2013 - Portland, OR (Oregon Convention Center)/May 4
2013 - San Antonio, TX (The Henry B. Gonzalez Convention Center)/May 18
2013 - Minneapolis, MN (Minneapolis Convention Center)/Oct. 12
Number of non-conference events/year: 16

Publications:
ADA Membership Directory; on-line
Book News: Professional; monthly
Clinical Diabetes; monthly; adv.
Diabetes; monthly; adv.
Diabetes Advocate Action Alerts; weekly
Diabetes Care; monthly; adv.
Diabetes Spectrum; quarterly; adv.
DiabetesPro Smartbrief - for health care professionals; daily
Family Link eNews; quarterly
Professional Section Quarterly; quarterly
Stop Diabetes eNews; monthly

American Dialect Society *(1889)*
MacMurray College
Department of English
Jacksonville, IL 62650-2590
Tel: (217) 479-7014 *Fax:* (217) 245-0405
E-Mail: americandialect@mac.edu
Website: americandialect.org
Members: 400 individuals
Staff: 3
Annual Budget: $25-50,000

Tax: 501(c)(3)
Personnel:
Executive Secretary: Allan Metcalf
  E-Mail: aallan@aol.com
Vice President, Communications and Technology: Grant Barrett
  E-Mail: grantbarrett@gmail.com
Managing Editor: Charles E. Carson
  E-Mail: carson@duke.edu

Historical Note:
ADS is organized in the interest of the academic community and aims at the study of the English language in North America, together with other languages or dialects of other languages influencing it or influenced by it. Members are educators and others interested in the English language in North America. Sponsors the Dictionary of American Regional English. Membership: $50 (Individual); $25 (Student).

Meetings/Conferences: Annual
2013 - Boston, MA (Boston Marriott Copley Place)/Jan. 3 - 6
2014 - Minneapolis, MN (Hilton Minneapolis)/Jan. 2 - 5

Publications:
American Speech; quarterly; adv.
Newsletter of the American Dialect Society (NADS)
Publication of the American Dialect Society (PADS); annually

Membership List Available to Non-members

American Disc Jockey Association *(1992)*
20118 N. 67th Ave.
Suite 300-605
Glendale, AZ 85308
Tel: (805) 382-4676 *Fax:* (866) 310-4676
TollFree: (888) 723-5776
E-Mail: office@adja.org
Website: adja.org
Members: 900 individuals
Staff: 1

Personnel:
President: Dr. DJ Drax

Historical Note:
ADJA represents needs of professional mobile and night club DJ's and KJ's. It advocates common standards, procedures, and benefits for its members. Membership: $200 (Full National); $100 (Associate).

Meetings/Conferences: Annual

Publications:
Members Directory

American Donkey and Mule Society *(1967)*
P.O. Box 1210
Lewisville, TX 75067
Tel: (972) 219-0781 *Fax:* (972) 219-0781
E-Mail: lovelongears@hotmail.com
Website: lovelongears.com
Members: 5000 individuals
Staff: 8
Annual Budget: $100-250,000
Tax: 501(c)(3)

Personnel:
Contact, Membership Services: B. J. Ellison

Historical Note:
ADMS maintains five registries for donkeys, mules and zebra hybrids, stud books. It also prepares and disseminates educational books and literature. Members are breeders, owners, and organizations interested in donkeys and mules. Membership: $27 (Individual); $37 (Canada); $50 (International).

Publications:
The BRAYER - Magazine; bi-monthly; adv.

American Driver and Traffic Safety Education Association *(1963)*
1434 Trim Tree Rd.
Highway Safety Services, LLC
Indiana, PA 15701
Tel: (724) 801-8246 *Fax:* (724) 349-5042
TollFree: (877) 485-7172
E-Mail: office@adtsea.org
Website: adtsea.org/adtsea
Members:
100 companies
1000 individuals
Staff: 5
Annual Budget: $100-250,000

Tax: 501(c)(3)
Personnel:
Chief Executive Officer: Allen Robinson PhD
  E-Mail: arrobin@adtsea.org
Coordinator, On-Line Training: Christie Falgione
  E-Mail: christie@adtsea.org
Manager, Information Technology: Mark Ray
  E-Mail: mray@adtsea.org
Office Manager: Leslie Robinson
  E-Mail: office@adtsea.org

Historical Note:
Established as the American Driver and Safety Education Association, became the American Driver Education Association in 1957 and assumed its present name in 1963, ADTSEA advocates for quality traffic safety education, creates and publishes policies and guidelines for the discipline. Members include state supervisors of safety education, university professors, elementary and secondary school teachers, vocational rehabilitation specialists, commercial driving schoolteachers, police traffic safety personnel, and corporate representatives. Membership: $100 (Diamond); $50 (Professional); $75 (Presidential); $150 (Platinum); $1000 (Corporate).

Continuing Education:
Certification Designation/s: DTA, DDSC, DCK

Meetings/Conferences: Annual

Publications:
ADTSEA Newsletter; monthly
The Chronicle; on-line

American Economic Association *(1885)*
2014 Broadway
Suite 305
Nashville, TN 37203-2418
Tel: (615) 322-2595 *Fax:* (615) 343-7590
E-Mail: aeainfo@vanderbilt.edu
Website: aeaweb.org
Members: 4200 companies and 18000 Individuals
Staff: 93
Annual Budget: $5-10,000,000

Personnel:
President: Christopher A. Sims
Counsel: Terry Calvani
Manager, Conventions: Marlene Hight
Administrative Director: Regina Montgomery
  E-Mail: regina.montgomery@randerbilt.edu
Associate Secretary and Treasurer: Peter L. Rousseau
Director, Publication Services: Jane Emily Voros

Historical Note:
A Member of the American Council of Learned Societies and affiliated with the Social Science Research Council, the American Association for the Advancement of Science and the International Economic Association, AEA works for the encouragement of economic research, especially the historical and statistical study of the actual conditions of industrial life. Membership: $70-98 (Regular); $14 (Family); $35 (Student).

Meetings/Conferences: Annual
Conference Chair: Marlene Hight
2013 - San Diego, CA (Manchester Grand Hyatt San Diego)/Jan. 4 - 6/11-25 exhibitors
2014 - Philadelphia, PA/Jan. 3 - 5/over 100 exhibitors
2015 - Boston, MA/Jan. 3 - 5/over 100 exhibitors
2016 - San Francisco, CA (Hilton San Francisco Union Square)/Jan. 3 - 5
2017 - Chicago, IL (Hyatt Regency Chicago)/Jan. 6 - 8
2018 - Atlanta, GA (Atlanta Marriott Century Center)/Jan. 5 - 7

Publications:
American Economic Journal: Applied Economics; quarterly
American Economic Journal: Economic Policy; quarterly
American Economic Journal: Macroeconomics; quarterly
American Economic Journal: Microeconomics; quarterly
American Economic Review; adv.
Directory of Members; on-line
EconLit; on-line
Journal of Economic Literature; quarterly; adv.
Journal of Economic Perspectives; quarterly; adv.
The American Economic Review; adv.
Virtual Field Journals; on-line

Membership List Available to Non-members

American Edged Products Manufacturers Association *(1951)*

21165 Whitfield Pl.
Suite 105
Potomac Falls, VA 20165
Tel: (703) 433-9281 *Fax:* (703) 433-0369
E-Mail: info@aepma.org
Website: aepma.org
Members: 50 companies
Staff: 4
Annual Budget: $100-250,000
Tax: 501(c)(6)

Personnel:
Executive Director: David W. Barrack
Treasurer: Alan Peppel

Historical Note:
Formerly American Cutlery Manufacturers Association (2000). AEPMA's purpose is to serve the domestic edged products industry by providing educational services, promoting communication and cooperation between members and governmental agencies and by sponsoring meetings and trade shows. Membership: $1,685-4,460 (Manufacturer); $895-1,765 (Associate).

Meetings/Conferences: Semi-Annual
Number of non-conference events/year: 1

Publications:
AEPMA; adv.

American Education Finance Association *(1975)*
6703 Madison Creek
Columbia, MO 65203
Tel: (573) 814-9878
E-Mail: info@aefpweb.org
Website: aefpweb.org
Members: 650 individuals
Staff: 1
Annual Budget: $100-250,000
Tax: 501(c)(3)

Personnel:
Executive Director: Angela M. Hull
   E-Mail: Angela.M.Hull@mac.com

Historical Note:
AEFA's mission is to promote understanding of means by which resources are generated, distributed and used to enhance human learning. Membership: $125-150 (Regular); $125 (Retired); $55 (Student); $135 (International); $1,150 (Insititutional).

Meetings/Conferences: Annual
2013 - New Orleans, LA (InterContinental New
   Orleans)/March 14 - 16
2014 - San Antonio, TX (Marriott Rivercenter Hotel)/
   March 6 - 8
2015 - Washington, DC (Marriott Wardman Park
   Hotel)/Feb. 26 - 28

Publications:
AEFP Newsletter; quarterly
Education Finance and Policy; quarterly
Membership Directory; on-line

Membership List Available to Non-members

American Educational Research Association *(1916)*
1430 K St. NW
Suite 1200
Washington, DC 20005
Tel: (202) 238-3200 *Fax:* (202) 238-3250
Website: aera.net
Members: 26000 members
Staff: 28
Annual Budget: $10-25,000,000
Tax: 501(c)(3)

Personnel:
Executive Director: Dr. Felice J. Levine
   E-Mail: flevine@aera.net
Director, Meetings: Laurie Cipriano CMP
   E-Mail: lcipriano@aera.net
*Director, Membership, Constituent Relations and
   Governance:* Patricia A. Martin
   E-Mail: pmartin@aera.net
Director, Governmental Relations: Gerald E. Sroufe PhD
   E-Mail: jsroufe@aera.net
Director, Finance and Administration: Norman Tenorio
   E-Mail: ntenorio@aera.net
Director, Communications: Alicia Torres PhD
   E-Mail: atorres@aera.net
Director, Social Justice and Professional Development:
   George Wimberly PhD
   E-Mail: gwimberly@aera.net

Managing Editor: Martha Yager
   E-Mail: myager@aera.net
Director, Information Technology and Web Services: Tracy
   B. Young
   E-Mail: tyoung@aera.net

Historical Note:
Founded as the National Association of Directors of Educational Research and an affiliate of the National Education Association, assumed its current name in 1930. AERA a national research society, strives to advance knowledge about education, to encourage scholarly inquiry related to education, and to promote the use of research to improve education and serve the public good. Also sponsors and supports the National Council on Measurement in Education. Members are educators, administrators, directors of research, persons working with testing or evaluation in federal, state and local agencies, counselors, evaluators, graduate students and behavioral scientists. Membership: $150 (Regular/Affiliate); $40 (Graduate Student/Student Affiliate); $110 (International Affiliate).

Meetings/Conferences: Annual
Conference Chair: Laurie Cipriano CMP
2013 - Atlanta, GA/April 11 - 15
2013 - San Francisco, CA/April 27 - May 1
2014 - Philadelphia, PA/April 3 - 7
2015 - Chicago, IL/April 16 - 20

Publications:
American Educational Research Journal; bi-monthly;
   adv.
Educational Evaluation and Policy Analysis; quarterly;
   adv.
Educational Researcher; adv.
Journal of Educational and Behavioral Statistics; bi-
   monthly; adv.
Review of Educational Research; quarterly; adv.
Review of Research in Education; annually; adv.

American Educational Studies Association *(1968)*
University of Alabama, Department of Education
235 Morton Hall
Huntsville, AL 35899
Tel: (404) 651-1192
E-Mail: philip.kovacs@uah.edu
Website: educationalstudies.org
Members: 700 individuals
Staff: 10
Annual Budget: $100-250,000

Personnel:
Secretary: John Petrovic
Contact, Conference Exhibits: Julie Carter
   E-Mail: carterj@stjohns.edu
Editor: Rebecca Martusewicz
   E-Mail: rmartusew@emich.edu
Treasurer: Sandra Spickard Prettyman
   E-Mail: ssandra@uakron.edu
Director, Communications: Carolyn Vander Schee
   E-Mail: martusew@emich.edu

Historical Note:
AESA provides a cross-disciplinary forum wherein scholars gather to exchange and debate ideas in the field of education. AESA's purpose is to bring intellectual resources derived from these areas to bear in developing interpretive, normative, and critical perspectives on education, both inside of and outside of schools. Membership: $70 (Regular); $150 (Institution); $45 (Student); $55 (Emeritus); $125 (Joint/Regular); $75 (Joint/Student); $95 (Joint/Emeritus).

Meetings/Conferences: Annual
Conference Chair: Sandra Spickard Prettyman
2013 - Baltimore, MD (Engineers Club)/Oct. 31 - Nov.
   3
2014 - Toronto, ON/Oct. 28 - Nov. 2

Publications:
Educational Studies
Educational Theory

American Egg Board *(1973)*
1460 Renaissance Dr.
P.O. Box 738, Suite 301
Park Ridge, IL 60068
Tel: (847) 296-7043 *Fax:* (847) 296-7007
E-Mail: aeb@aeb.org
Website: aeb.org
Members: 1250 producers and companies
Staff: 20
Annual Budget: $10-25,000,000

Personnel:
President and Chief Executive Officer: Joanne C. Ivy
   E-Mail: jivy@aeb.org

Senior Vice President, Marketing: Kevin Burkum
   E-Mail: kburkum@acb.org
Director, Industry Communications: Ashley Richardson
   E-Mail: arichardson@aeb.org

Historical Note:
Formerly Poultry and Egg National Board, a federation of egg producers, assumed its current name in 1973. AEB's mission is to increase demand for egg and egg products on behalf of U.S. egg producers.

Meetings/Conferences:
Number of non-conference events/year: 1

Publications:
Eggs In The News
Eggstra! Newsletter; quarterly

American Electrology Association *(1958)*
Six Market Pl.
Suite One
Essex Junction, VT 05452
Tel: (802) 879-1898
E-Mail: infoaea@electrology.com
Website: electrology.com
Members: 1500 individuals
Staff: 3
Annual Budget: $250-500,000
Tax: 501(c)(6)

Personnel:
Contact, Membership Relations: Leslie Quinn Cody

Historical Note:
Founded in New Jersey in February 1958 as American Electrolysis Association, assumed its present name in 1986. AEA promotes standards in Electrology education, practice and ethics and champions state licensing and regulation of profession to protect public interest. Membership is composed of electrologists (permanent hair removers). Membership: $140/year (Individual).

Continuing Education:
Enrollment: 900
Certification Designation/s: CPE

Meetings/Conferences: Annual

Publications:
Electrology World; adv.
Journal of Electrology; semi-annually; adv.
Membership Directory; annually; adv.

The American Electrophoresis Society *(1980)*
1201 Ann St.
Madison, WI 53713
Tel: (608) 258-1565 *Fax:* (608) 258-1569
E-Mail: matt-aes@tds.net
Website: aesociety.org
Members: 100 individuals
Staff: 4
Annual Budget: $10-25,000
Tax: 501(c)(3)

Personnel:
Executive Director: Matt Hoelter
   E-Mail: matt-aes@tds.net
Associate Webmaster: Rafael Davalos
   E-Mail: davalos@vt.edu
Editor: Nancy C. Kendrick
   E-Mail: nancy@kendricklabs.com

Historical Note:
AES dedicated to the development, refinement of electrophoretic and detection technologies and Promoting scientific advancement in electrophoretic theory and applications. Membership: $75 (Full Member); $25 (Student); $500 (Corporate/Life); $35 (Postdoc/Emeritus); $2,500 (Platinum Sponsor); $1,000 (Gold Sponsor); $500 (Silver Sponsor); $300- 1,000 (Newsletter Sponsor).

Meetings/Conferences: Annual

Publications:
AES Newsletter; on-line
Membership Directory; on-line

American Embryo Transfer Association *(1981)*
1800 S. Oak St.
Suite 100
Champaign, IL 61820-6974
Tel: (217) 398-2217 *Fax:* (217) 398-4119
E-Mail: aeta@assochq.org
Website: aeta.org
Members: 363 companies and individuals
Staff: 3
Annual Budget: $250-500,000
Tax: 501(c)(5)

Personnel:

President: Glenn Engelland DVM
    E-Mail: glennengelland@gmail.com
Secretary and Treasurer: Chris Keim
    E-Mail: chris@sunshinegenetics.com
Certificate Administrator: Kathy Ruff
    E-Mail: kathyr@assochq.org

Historical Note:
AETA's purpose is to promote the use of embryo transfer as a means to improve livestock and encourages cooperative relationships among companies and individuals engaged in embryo transfer. Membership: $250 (Regular); $200 (Associate); $50 (Student).

Continuing Education:
Enrollment: 175
Certification Designation/s: ETB, AETAC, BEC

Meetings/Conferences: Annual
2013 - Reno, NV (Grand Sierra Resort and Casino)/
    Oct. 10 - 12

Publications:
Closer Look; quarterly; adv.
Membership Directory; on-line

American Emu Association *(1989)*
1201 W Main St.
Suite 2
Ottawa, IL 61350
Tel: (541) 332-0675
E-Mail: info@aea-emu.org
Website: aea-emu.org
Members: 680 individuals
Staff: 2
Annual Budget: Under $10,000
Tax: 501(c)(5)

Personnel:
Treasurer: Susan Wright
    E-Mail: susan.wright@aea-emu.org

Historical Note:
AEA is dedicated to develop structural support and visionary leadership for the emu industry. AEA promotes public awareness of emu products, fosters research. Affiliates are found for this Organization. Members are emu (a flightless bird) raisers. Membership: $100 (Individual/Renewal/Spouse); $350 (International); $10 (Junior); $75 (Contributing Member).

Meetings/Conferences: Annual

Publications:
Newsletter; bi-monthly

American Endodontic Society, Inc. *(1969)*
265 N. Main St.
Glen Ellyn, IL 60137
Tel: (773) 519-4879 *Fax:* (630) 858-0525
E-Mail: n2dontics@comcast.net
Website: aesoc.com
Members: 7000 individuals
Staff: 2
Annual Budget: $50-100,000

Personnel:
Executive Director: Earle F. Kuhn
    E-Mail: earle@earlekuhn.com
Treasurer: Alvin H. Arzt

Historical Note:
AES's mission is to provide educational and scientific information on simplified endodontic procedures. Members are dentists specializing in root canal work. Membership: $245 (Dentist/Active); $50 (Dentist/Retired/Student).

Meetings/Conferences: Annual

American Engineering Association *(1979)*
533 Waterside Blvd.
Monroe Township, NJ 08831
Tel: (972) 264-6428
E-Mail: aea@aea.org
Website: aea.org
Staff: 3
Tax: 501(c)(6)

Personnel:
President: Richard F. Tax
    E-Mail: rtax@aea.org
Treasurer and Contact, Membership Services: Harold
    Ruchelman
Contact, Communications: Alan Stolpen

Historical Note:
AEA is dedicated to the enhancement of the engineering profession and U.S. Engineering Capabilities. Membership: $30 (Individual/Associate); $20 (Academic/Retired/Unemployed); $15 (Student).

Publications:
AEA Newsletter

American Enterprise Institute for Public Policy Research *(1943)*
1150 17th St. NW
Washington, DC 20036
Tel: (202) 862-5800 *Fax:* (202) 862-7171
E-Mail: info@aei.org
Website: aei.org
Members: 354 institutions
Staff: 175
Annual Budget: $50-100,000,000
Tax: 501(c)(3)

Personnel:
President: Arthur C. Brooks
Executive Vice President: David Gerson
    E-Mail: david@aei.org
Vice President, Development: Jason Bertsch
    E-Mail: jbertsch@aei.org
Director, Conferences: Jessica Browning
    E-Mail: jbrowning@aei.org
Managing Editor: Bridget Johnson
    E-Mail: Bridget.Johnson@aei.org
Managing Editor: Sharon Kehnemui
    E-Mail: Sharon.Kehnemui@aei.org
Vice President and National Research Initiative Director:
    Henry Olsen
    E-Mail: holsen@aei.org
Vice President, Foreign and Defense Policy Studies:
    Danielle Pletka
    E-Mail: dpletka@aei.org
Director, Public Affairs: Veronique Rodman
    E-Mail: vrodman@aei.org

Historical Note:
The American Enterprise Institute (AEI) is dedicated to research and education on issues of government, politics, economics and social welfare.

Meetings/Conferences:
Conference Chair: Jessica Browning
Number of non-conference events/year: 5

Publications:
AEI Today; daily

American Entertainment Armories Association
9545 Wentworth St.
Sunland, CA 91040
Tel: (818) 951-5600 *Fax:* (818) 951-2850
Website: aeaa.us
Members: 100 individuals
Staff: 4
Annual Budget: $10-25,000
Tax: 501(c)(6)

Personnel:
President: Gregg Bilson Jr.
    E-Mail: issprops@aol.com
Secretary and Treasurer: Jennifer Scott
    E-Mail: jennifer@issprops.com

Historical Note:
A group currently comprised of seven companies and over 100 individual armorers working in the area of theatrical weapons. Membership: $5,000 (Gold Sponsorship); $2,500 (Silver Sponsorship); $1,000 (Corporate); $250 (Individual).

Publications:
AEAA's Newsletter; quarterly

American Entomological Society *(1859)*
Academy of Natural Sciences
1900 Benjamin Franklin Pkwy.
Philadelphia, PA 19103-1195
Tel: (215) 561-3978 *Fax:* (215) 299-1028
E-Mail: aes@ansp.org
Website: darwin.ansp.org/hosted/aes/
Members: 400 individuals
Staff: 3
Annual Budget: $50-100,000
Tax: 501(c)(3)

Personnel:
President: William J. Cromartie
Recording Secretary: Charles Bartlett
Editor: Daniel Otte
    E-Mail: otte@acnatsci.org

Historical Note:
Founded as the Entomological Society of Philadelphia, became American Entomological Society in 1967, the Society's library is housed and staffed by the Academy of

---

Natural Sciences of Philadelphia. AES promotes the study of insects and publishes the results of pure research in the systematics and morphology of insects. Membership: $20 (Regular); $12 (Student).

Meetings/Conferences:
Number of non-conference events/year: 2

Publications:
Entomological News; quarterly
Memoirs of the AES; irregular
Transactions of the AES; quarterly

American Epilepsy Society *(1946)*
342 N. Main St.
W. Hartford, CT 06117-2507
Tel: (860) 586-7505 *Fax:* (860) 586-7550
E-Mail: info@aesnet.org
Website: aesnet.org
Members: 2000 individuals
Staff: 10
Annual Budget: $5-10,000,000
Tax: 501(c)(3)

Personnel:
Executive Director: M. Suzanne C. Berry CAE, MBA
    E-Mail: sberry@aesnet.org
Association Administrator: Kate Flaherty
    E-Mail: kflaherty@aesnet.org
Director, Education: Jeffrey Melin CMP, MEd
    E-Mail: jmelin@aesnet.org
Director, Meetings and Events: Elizabeth Pillsworth CMP
    E-Mail: epillsworth@aesnet.org

Historical Note:
Formerly, American League Against Epilepsy; assumed its present name in 1959. AES's mission is to provide research and education for professionals dedicated to the prevention, cure and treatment of epilepsy. Members are physicians, nurses, and scientists engaged in research and practice in epilepsy or closely related fields. Membership: $250 (Active/Associate- Includes Epilepsia); $125 (Professionals in Epilepsy Care); $145 (Corresponding); $220 (Corresponding-Includes Epilepsia); $75 (Junior); $150 (Junior-Includes Epilepsia).

Meetings/Conferences: Annual
Conference Chair: Elizabeth Pillsworth CMP
2013 - Washington, DC (Walter E Washington
    Convention Center)/Dec. 6 - 9
2014 - Seatle, WA (Washington State Convention
    Center)/Dec. 5 - 9
2015 - Philadelphia, PA (Pennsylvania Convention
    Center)/Dec. 4 - 8
2016 - Houston, TX (George R. Brown Convention
    Center)/Dec. 2 - 6

Publications:
AES News; on-line
Epilepsia; monthly
Epilepsy Currents
Membership Directory; on-line

Membership List Available to Non-members

American Equilibration Society *(1955)*
207 E. Ohio St.
Suite 399
Chicago, IL 60611
Tel: (847) 965-2888 *Fax:* (609) 573-5064
Website: aes-tmj.org
Members: 1000 individuals
Staff: 6
Annual Budget: $250-500,000
Tax: 501(c)(6)

Personnel:
Executive Director: Kenneth S. Cleveland
    E-Mail: exec@aes-tmj.org
Web Master: James T Gavrilos
Editor: Tara M. Griffin
Exhibits Chair: Jason M Luchtefeld
Membership Chair: Curt W Ringhofer
Contact, Treasurer: Michael R Varley

Historical Note:
AES deals with the diagnosis and treatment of diseases of dental occlusion (bite problems) and disorders of the temporomandibular joint (TMJ) and associated muscles. Membership consists of dentists and physicians dealing with the diagnosis and treatment of diseases of dental occlusion (bite problems) and disorders of the temporomandibular region and related parts of the mouth. Membership: $625 (Active); $375 (Affiliate); $700 (New Member).

Meetings/Conferences:
Conference Chair: Jason M Luchtefeld

2013 - Chicago, IL (Chicago Downtown Marriott)/Feb.
20 - 21
2014 - Chicago, IL (Chicago Downtown Marriott)/Feb.
19 - 20

Publications:
AES Newsletter
Journal of Prosthetic Dentistry
Membership Directory; on-line

American Escrow Association (1980)
211 N. Union St.
Suite 100
Alexandria, VA 22314
Tel: (703) 519-1240
E-Mail: hq@a-e-a.org
Website: a-e-a.org
Staff: 3
Annual Budget: $100-250,000
Tax: 501(c)(6)

Personnel:
President: Jyl Meier
General Counsel and Executive Administrator: Arthur E.
Davis III
Treasurer: Sheryl Oldham

Historical Note:
*American Escrow Association (AEA) is the national
association of real estate settlement agents. AEA's mission
is to enhance the education of the escrow/settlement
professional and disseminate information as to the
differences in such services between states. Membership:
$150 (Associate); $500 (Affiliate); $1,000 (State Charter).*

Meetings/Conferences: Annual
2013 - Las Vegas, NV (Tuscany Suites Hotel and
Casino)/June 13 - 15

American Evaluation Association (1986)
16 Sconticut Neck Rd.
Suite 290
Fairhaven, MA 02719
Tel: (508) 748-3326 *Fax:* (508) 748-3158
TollFree: (888) 232-2275
E-Mail: info@eval.org
Website: eval.org
Members: 6500 individuals
Staff: 3
Annual Budget: $1-2,000,000
Tax: 501(c)(3)

Personnel:
Executive Director: Susan Kistler
E-Mail: susan@eval.org
Director, Communications: Gwen Fariss-Newman
E-Mail: gwen@eval.org
Director, Membership Services: Heidi Nye
E-Mail: heidi@eval.org

Historical Note:
*Formed in 1985 by the merger of the Evaluation Network
and the Evaluation Research Society. AEA's mission is
to improve evaluation practice and methods, increase
evaluation use and promote evaluation as a profession.
Members represent many different disciplines including
psychology, education, public administration and policy
analysis, economics, public relations and marketing,
auditing, health care, social work, sociology, and
measurement and statistics. Membership: $80 (Regular);
$60 (Joint CES); $30 (Student).*

Meetings/Conferences: Annual
Conference Chair: Heidi Nye
Number of non-conference events/year: 5

Publications:
AEA e-Newsletter; monthly
American Journal of Evaluation
Membership Directory; on-line

American Exploration & Production Council
(1975)
1350 Eye St. NW
Suite 510
Washington, DC 20005
Tel: (202) 652-2359
E-Mail: info@axpc.us
Website: axpc.us
Members: 32 companies
Staff: 1
Annual Budget: $500-1,000,000

Personnel:
President: V. Bruce Thompson

Historical Note:

*Formerly Domestic Petroleum Council. AXPC's mission
is to work for sound energy, environmental and related
public policies that encourage responsible exploration,
development and production of natural gas and crude oil to
meet consumer needs and fuel the economy. Members are
publicly-traded corporations.*

Meetings/Conferences: Annual
Number of non-conference events/year: 1

Publications:
Newsletter

American Factoring Association (2009)
2665 Shell Beach Rd.
Suite Three
Pismo Beach, CA 93449
Fax: (805) 773-0021
TollFree: (888) 425-2119
E-Mail: info@americanfactoring.org
Website: americanfactoring.org
Staff: 1
Annual Budget: $100-250,000
Tax: 501(c)(6)

Personnel:
Executive Director: Bert Goldberg

Historical Note:
*Trade association that educates the public and policymakers
on the availability of working capital for small businesses
through factoring. AFA's purpose is to educate the public
and policymakers on the availability of working capital for
financing America's small businesses and to conduct efforts
in support of increasing working capital financing.*

The American Fair Credit Council (2011)
100 W. Cypress Creek Rd.
Suite 700
Ft. Lauderdale, FL 33309
Tel: (888) 657-8272 *Fax:* (954) 343-6960
E-Mail: info@tascsite.org
Website: americanfaircreditcouncil.org
Staff: 3
Annual Budget: $1-2,000,000

Personnel:
President: Robby H. Birnbaum
*Vice President and Legal, transactional and regulatory
expert:* Bob Linderman

Historical Note:
*The AFCC was formed by a group of industry-leading
companies to advance the goal of an industry in full
compliance with the regulatory initiatives of the Federal
Trade Commission.Formally known as The Association of
Settlement Companies.*

Publications:
Membership Directory; on-line

American Family Therapy Academy (1977)
1608 20th St. NW
Fourth Floor
Washington, DC 20009
Tel: (202) 483-8001 *Fax:* (202) 483-8002
E-Mail: afta@afta.org
Website: afta.org
Members: 800 individuals
Staff: 2
Annual Budget: $250-500,000
Tax: 501(c)(3)

Personnel:
President: Hinda Winawer LCSW, MSW
Office Manager: Elishia Webster
E-Mail: afta@afta.org

Historical Note:
*Formerly American Family Therapy Association, AFTA's
purpose is to advance therapies and theories that regard
the family as a unit within a broader context. Members
are teachers, researchers, and clinical therapists specially
trained to work with couples and families. Membership:
$304 (Regular); $152 (Retired); $152 (Early Career/
International); $101 (Retired International/Student).*

Meetings/Conferences: Annual
2013 - Chicago, IL (Palmer House Hilton Hotel)/June 5
- 8

Publications:
AFTA Monograph Series
AFTA Newsletter
AFTA Update; semi-annually
Membership Directory; on-line

Membership List Available to Non-members

American Farm Bureau Federation (1919)
600 Maryland Ave. SW
Suite 1000 West
Washington, DC 20024
Tel: (202) 406-3600
Website: fb.org
Members: 5600000 million individuals worldwide
Staff: 100
Annual Budget: $25-50,000,000
Tax: 501(c)(5)

Personnel:
President: Robert Stallman
Director, Human Resources: Anne Bradley
Director, Human Resources: Anne Bradley
E-Mail: anneb@fb.org
Director, Information Technology and Communications:
Dave Francis
E-Mail: dave@fb.org
Human Resources Generalist: Stefanie Gambrell
E-Mail: stefphanieg@fb.org
Director, Conventions and Meetings: John Hawkins
E-Mail: jhawkins@fb.org
Executive Director, Accounting and Administrative Services:
Christy Lilja
E-Mail: christyl@fb.org
Executive Director, Public Relations: Don Lipton
E-Mail: donl@fb.org
Executive Director, Public Policy: Mark A. Maslyn
E-Mail: markm@fb.org
Director, Education: Curtis Miller
E-Mail: curtism@fb.org
Executive Vice President & Treasurer: Julie Anna Potts
Director, Membership and Leadership Development: Bob
Wilson
E-Mail: bobw@fb.org

Historical Note:
*AFBF works to enhance and strengthen the lives of rural
Americans engaged in agriculture.*

Meetings/Conferences: Annual
Conference Chair: John Hawkins
2013 - Nashville, TN (Opryland Hotel)/Jan. 13 - 16
2014 - San Antonio, TX/Jan. 12 - 15
2015 - San Diego, CA/Jan. 11 - 14

Publications:
Foodie News; monthly
Membership directory; on-line

American Farmland Trust (1980)
1200 18th St. NW
Suite 800
Washington, DC 20036
Tel: (202) 331-7300 *Fax:* (202) 659-8339
E-Mail: info@farmland.org
Website: farmland.org
Staff: 54
Annual Budget: $5-10,000,000
Tax: 501(c)(3)

Personnel:
President: Jon Scholl
E-Mail: jscholl@farmland.org
Chief Financial Officer: Vicki Edwards
E-Mail: vedwards@farmland.org
Manager of Member Engagement and Communications:
Gretchen Mais
E-Mail: gmais@farmland.org
General Counsel: Rick Monk
E-Mail: rmonk@farmland.org
Director, Federal Policy: Dennis R. Nuxoll
E-Mail: dnuxoll@farmland.org
Director, Research: Ann Sorensen
E-Mail: asorensen@niu.edu

Historical Note:
*Works to protect productive farm and ranchland through
public education, policy development and private land
conservancy transactions.*

Publications:
American Farmland
E-News; monthly
Farm Fresh News; bi-monthly

Membership List Available to Non-members

American Farrier's Association (1971)
4059 Iron Works Pkwy.
Suite One
Lexington, KY 40511
Tel: (859) 233-7411 *Fax:* (859) 231-7862

TollFree: (877) 268-4505
E-Mail: info@americanfarriers.org
Website: americanfarriers.org
Members: 3400 individuals
Staff: 3
Annual Budget: $500-1,000,000

Personnel:
President: Thomas N. Trosin
   E-Mail: trosinfarrier@gmail.com
Office Manager: Rachel Heighton

Historical Note:
An association of professional horseshoers, AFA promotes the profession and serves as a representative of farriery interests within the horse world. Membership: $150 (Regular/Associate).

Continuing Education:
Certification Designation/s: AFA CF, AFA CTF, AFA CJF

Meetings/Conferences: Annual
2013 - Baton Rouge, LA (The Belle of Baton Rouge Hotel)/Feb. 25 - March 2

Publications:
Membership Directory; annually
No Foot No Horse; bi-monthly

American Federation for Aging Research (1981)
55 W. 39th St.
16th Floor
New York, NY 10018
Tel: (212) 703-9977 *Fax:* (212) 997-0330
TollFree: (888) 582-2327
E-Mail: info@afar.org
Website: afar.org
Members: 2,600 scientists
Staff: 12
Annual Budget: $2-5,000,000

Personnel:
Executive Director: Stephanie Lederman EdM
Associate, Communications and Development Programs: Katherine Kelly Apple
Program Officer: Hattie Herman
Director, Development: Nancy O'Leary
Director, Finance: Jacalyn Schwartz

Historical Note:
AFAR's mission is to support and advance healthy aging through biomedical research. Members are physicians, scientists and others with an interest in research on aging.

Meetings/Conferences: Annual
Conference Chair: Hattie Herman

Publications:
AFAR Newsletter
Medical Student Training in Aging Research (MSTAR) Program Newsletter
The Week; weekly

American Federation for Medical Research (1940)
500 Cummings Center
Suite 4550
Beverly, MA 01915
Tel: (978) 927-8330 *Fax:* (978) 524-8890
Website: afmr.org
Members: 2500 individuals
Staff: 6
Annual Budget: $500-1,000,000
Tax: 501(c)(3)

Personnel:
Administrative Director: Elizabeth Chouinard
Editor-in-Chief: Michael J. McPhaul MD

Historical Note:
Formerly American Federation for Clinical Research (AFCR). The mission of AFMR is to promote understanding of recent advances in biomedical science for the prevention, diagnosis and treatment of disease; to facilitate the exchange of ideas and information among physicians and other investigators who are concerned with the treatment of disease; and to improve health by fostering research in all medical disciplines through public policy initiatives and educational programs. Member: $210-225 (Active); $90-110 (Associate); $75 (Medical Student); $0-105 (Emeritus).

Meetings/Conferences: Annual
2013 - Washington, DC (Omni Shoreham Hotel)/April 17 - 19
2014 - Boston, MA/April 20 - 24/14000 attendees
Number of non-conference events/year: 4

Publications:
AFMR Newsletters; on-line

Journal of Investigative Medicine; bi-monthly

American Federation of Astrologers, Inc. (1938)
6535 S. Rural Rd.
Tempe, AZ 85283-3746
Tel: (480) 838-1751 *Fax:* (480) 838-8293
TollFree: (888) 301-7630
E-Mail: info@astrologers.com
Website: astrologers.com
Members: 2554 individuals and foreign countries
Staff: 2
Annual Budget: $1-2,000,000
Tax: 501(c)(3)

Personnel:
Executive Director: Kris Brandt Riske
Manager, Operations: Jack Cipolla

Historical Note:
AFA's mission is to advance astrological education and research. Membership: $30-45 (Senior Associate U.S./Foreign); $45-60 (Associate U.S./International); $60-75 (Husband and Wife U.S./International); $50-60 (Group Affiliate U.S./International); $67-82 (Associate Research U.S./Foreign); $600-1,000 (Lifetime U.S./Foreign Associate Member); $1,000-1,400 (Lifetime Research U.S./Foreign).

Meetings/Conferences: Annual
2013 - Tempe, AZ (Embassy Suites)/May 2 - 4

Publications:
AFA Newsletter; monthly
Today's Astrologer; monthly

American Federation of Government Employees (1932)
80 F St. NW
Washington, DC 20001
Tel: (202) 737-8700
E-Mail: comments@afge.org
Website: afge.org
Members: 600,000 federal and D.C. government workers
Staff: 200
Annual Budget: $50-100,000,000
Tax: 501(c)(5)

Personnel:
Chief of Staff: Brian Dewyngaert
Director, Finance and Information Services: Faye Beardsley
Labor Relations Specialists: Charlie Bernhardt
   E-Mail: bernhc@afge.org
General Counsel: David Borer
   E-Mail: BORERD@afge.org
National Secretary and Treasurer: J. David Cox
Director, Communications: Enid Doggett
   E-Mail: doggee@afge.org
Director, Field Services and Education: Bill Fletcher
   E-Mail: fletcb@afge.org
National President: John Gage
Director, Information Services: Taylor Higley
Communications Specialist: Tim Kauffman
   E-Mail: kaufft@afge.org
Deputy Director, Membership Services: Cathie McQuiston
   E-Mail: mcquic@afge.org
Director, Legislative and Political Affairs: Beth Moten
   E-Mail: motenb@afge.org

Historical Note:
AFGE is the federal employee union representing federal and D.C. government workers nationwide and overseas.

Meetings/Conferences: Semi-Annual

Publications:
AFGE Action News
AFGE Week in Review
The Capitol Report
The Government Standard; bi-monthly
The Rep Wing; monthly

American Federation of Labor & Congress of Industrial Organizations (2009)
815 16th St. NW
Washington, DC 20006
Website: aflcio.org
Staff: 464
Annual Budget: Over $100,000,000

Personnel:
President: Richard L. Trumka
Secretary and Treasurer: Elizabeth Shuler

Historical Note:

AFL-CIO Mission is resolve to fulfill the yearning of the human spirit for liberty, justice and community; to advance individual and associational freedom; to vanquish - oppression, privation and cruelty in all their forms; and to join with all persons, of whatever nationality or faith, who cherish the cause of democracy and the call of solidarity, to grace the planet with these achievements.

Meetings/Conferences:
2013 - Philadelphia, PA (Sheraton Philadelphia Downtown Hotel)/Jan. 17 - 21

Publications:
Intern Journal Entries; weekly
Membership Directory
Newsletter; quarterly

American Federation of Musicians (1896)
1501 Broadway
Suite 600
New York, NY 10036
Tel: (212) 869-1330 *Fax:* (212) 764-6134
Website: afm.org
Members: 90000 members
Staff: 75
Annual Budget: $100-250,000

Personnel:
President: Ray Hair
   E-Mail: presoffice@afm.org
Director and Assistant to President: Janice Galassi
   E-Mail: jgalassi@afm.org
Manager, Information Systems: Gene Kosmark
   E-Mail: gkosmark@afm.org
Contact, Human Resources: Cindy Pellegrino
   E-Mail: cpellegrino@afm.org
Web Developer, Tech Support Specialist: Matt Plummer
   E-Mail: mplummer@afm.org
Director, Freelance Services and Membership Development: Paul Sharpe
   E-Mail: psharpe@afm.org
Director, Symphonic Services Division Canada: Mark Tetreault
   E-Mail: mtetreault@afm.org

Historical Note:
AFM's mission is to actively participate in the democratic institutions of its union and to work in dignity. AFM represents 130,000 professional recording, radio, television, motion picture, symphonic, country, pop, alternative, rock and jazz musicians.

Meetings/Conferences: Annual

Publications:
AFM Newsletter
Membership Directory; on-line
Music and Union News

American Federation of Musicians and Employers Pension Fund (1959)
One Penn Plaza
Suite 3115
New York, NY 10119
Tel: (212) 284-1314
TollFree: (800) 833-8065
Website: afm-epf.org
Staff: 2

Personnel:
Executive Director: Maureen B. Kilkelly
Director, Finance: Will Luebking

Historical Note:
The American Federation of Musicians and Employers' Pension Fund was established for the exclusive purpose of providing certain pension and related benefits to Covered Employees and their Beneficiaries under the Plan, and shall further provide the means for financing and maintaining the operation and administration of the Trust and the Plan in accordance with the Trust Agreement, the Plan, and applicable law.

Publications:
Pension Fund Notes
Officers' Edge

American Federation of Police and Concerned Citizens (1966)
6350 Horizon Dr.
Titusville, FL 32780
Tel: (321) 264-0911 *Fax:* (321) 264-0033
E-Mail: policeinfo@aphf.org
Website: afp-cc.org
Members: 130,000 donors and members
Staff: 6
Annual Budget: $2-5,000,000

Tax: 501(c)(3)

Personnel:
Chief Executive Officer: Donna M. Shepherd
    E-Mail: dshepherd@aphf.org
Executive Director: Barry Shepherd
    E-Mail: bshepherd@aphf.org
Chief Financial Officer: Debra Chitwood
    E-Mail: debbic@aphf.org
Executive Editor, Publications: Peter Connolly
    E-Mail: peterc@aphf.org
Director, Communications: Jamie Shepherd
    E-Mail: jshepherd@aphf.org
Director, Operations: Brent Shepherd
    E-Mail: brents@aphf.org

Historical Note:
Established as the United States Federation of Police, merged with the American Law Enforcement Officers Association in 1977, and added "and Concerned Citizens" to its name in 1996. AFP&CC is an educational organization, offering police survivor benefits, a placement service and various types of awards to its members. Membership: $36 (Active Individual, One Year); $90 (Active Individual, Three Year).

Publications:
Police Family Survivor Fund; quarterly
Police Times Magazine; quarterly

American Federation of School Administrators
(1971)
1101 17th St. NW
Suite 408
Washington, DC 20036
Tel: (202) 986-4209 *Fax:* (202) 986-4211
E-Mail: afsa@afsaadmin.org
Website: admin.org
Members: 20000 individuals
Staff: 4
Annual Budget: $1-2,000,000
Tax: 501(c)(5)

Personnel:
Executive Director: Paul Wolotsky
President: Diann Woodard
General Counsel: Bruce Bryant
Director, Operations and Government Affairs: Nick Spina

Historical Note:
Established as the School Administrators and Supervisors Organizing Committee. Assumed its present name on July 7, 1976. Affiliated with the AFL-CIO in 1976. AFSA's mission is to promote the professional, occupational, and economic interests of its members, and to fight for the highest quality public school education for all pupils. Membership: $72/ year.

Meetings/Conferences: Annual

Publications:
The Leader; quarterly

American Federation of State, County and Municipal Employees *(1936)*
1625 L St. NW
Seventh Floor
Washington, DC 20036-5687
Tel: (202) 429-1000 *Fax:* (202) 429-1293
Website: afscme.org
Members: 140000 individuals
Staff: 200
Annual Budget: Over $100,000,000
Tax: 501(c)(5)

Personnel:
Director, Financial Services: Charlie Jurgonis
Director, Federal Government Affairs: Charles M. Loveless
    E-Mail: cloveless@afscme.org
Director, Public Affairs: Chris Policano
    E-Mail: cpolicano@afscme.org
Secretary and Treasurer: Laura Reyes
President: Lee A. Saunders
    E-Mail: lsaunders@afscme.org
Assistant Legislative Advocacy and Specialist, Communications: Karl Stark
    E-Mail: kstark@afscme.org

Historical Note:
Chartered by the American Federation of Labor, Merged (1978) with the Civil Service Employees Association of New York. AFSCME's mission is to organize workers in general, public employees in particular, promoting the welfare of its members and providing a voice in determining the terms and conditions of employment by using the collective bargaining process, as well as legislative and political action, promoting civil service legislation and career service

in government, and assisting its members and affiliates through research and education.

Meetings/Conferences: Annual

Publications:
ACU Newsletter
AFSCME Governance
AFSCME Works; quarterly
PrimeTime; quarterly

American Federation of Teachers (AFL-CIO)
(1916)
555 New Jersey Ave. NW
Washington, DC 20001
Tel: (202) 879-4440 *Fax:* (202) 879-4576
E-Mail: online@aft.org
Website: aft.org
Members: 330,000 early childhood educators and retiree members
Staff: 250
Annual Budget: $50-100,000,000

Personnel:
President: Randi Weingarten
Director, Department of Legislation: Kristor W. Cowan
    E-Mail: tcowan@aft.org
Secretary and Treasurer: Lorretta Johnson
Director, Conventions, Meetings and Travel: Kitty Owens
    E-Mail: kowens@aft.org

Historical Note:
The Federation of Public Employees is a division of AFT. AFT's mission is to improve the lives of members and their families, to give voice to their legitimate professional, economic and social aspirations. Sponsors and supports the AFT Cope Political Action Committee. Membership: $30 (Basic); $60 (Advanced).

Meetings/Conferences: Annual
Conference Chair: Kitty Owens
2013 - Washington, DC (Washington Marriott)/July 22 - 24
2014 - Los Angeles, CA (Claremont Mckenna College)/ July 11 - 14
Number of non-conference events/year: 11

Publications:
AFT e-Activist Network; on-line
AFT Health and Safety; on-line
AFT Human Rights News; on-line
AFT On Campus; adv.
AFT Retiree e-News; on-line
AFT School Building Conditions; on-line
American Educator; quarterly
American Teacher; bi-monthly; adv.
Center for the Child Care Workforce; on-line
Early Childhood Educators; on-line
FACE Bulletin
Head Start Alert; on-line
Healthwire; adv.
Inside AFT Healthcare; on-line
Inside AFT PSRP; bi-weekly
International Rights Alert; on-line
PSRP Reporter; adv.
Tools For Teachers e-Newsletter; on-line

American Federation of Violin and Bow Makers
(1980)
1121 East Ave.
Red Wing, MN 55066
Tel: (507) 396-3411 *Fax:* (919) 233-4991
E-Mail: info@afvbm.org
Website: afvbm.org
Members: 170 instrument makers and restorers
Staff: 9
Annual Budget: $25-50,000

Personnel:
Secretary: Lisbeth Nelson Butler

Historical Note:
AFVBM seeks to enhance the public's understanding and appreciation of the violin and bow families, and of related areas of expertise, including the making of new instruments, as well as conservation and restoration of historical and modern instruments. Members are individuals who make and restore violins, violas, cellos and their bows. Membership: $300/year (Individual).

Meetings/Conferences: Biennial

Publications:
Membership Directory; annually

American Feed Industry Association *(1909)*
2101 Wilson Blvd.

Suite 916
Arlington, VA 22201
Tel: (703) 524-0810 *Fax:* (703) 524-1921
E-Mail: afia@afia.org
Website: afia.org
Members: 500 companies
Staff: 25
Annual Budget: $2-5,000,000
Tax: 501(c)(6)

Personnel:
President, Chief Executive Officer and Corporate Treasurer: Joel Newman
    E-Mail: jnewman@afia.org
Vice President, Manufacturing and Training: Keith Epperson
    E-Mail: kepperson@afia.org
Manager, Marketing And Websites: Lori Kaye
Director, Administration: Leanna Nail
    E-Mail: lnail@afia.org
Director, Membership Services and Public Relations: Sarah Novak
    E-Mail: snovak@afia.org
Director, Meetings And Events: Veronica Rovelli
Manager, Controller And Operations: Andrew M. Timmins
Director, Ingredients and State Legislative Affairs: Leah Wilkinson
    E-Mail: lwilkinson@afia.org

Historical Note:
Formerly (1985) American Feed Manufacturers Association. Absorbed Midwest Feed Manufacturers Association in 1975, National Feed Ingredients Association in 1992, and American Alfalfa Processors Association in 2001. AFIA is devoted exclusively to representing the business, legislative and regulatory interests of the U.S. animal feed industry and its suppliers. Members are firms which manufacture formula feed and pet food to sell; firms which manufacture formula feed only for their own poultry or livestock; and firms which provide ingredients, services, equipment, and supplies to feed manufacturers.

Meetings/Conferences: Annual
Conference Chair: Veronica Rovelli
2013 - Atlanta, GA (Georgia World Congress Center)/ Jan. 29 - 31
2013 - Ft. Worth, TX (Omni Ft. Worth Hotel)/March 13 - 15
2013 - St. Louis, MO (Hyatt Regency St. Louis at The Arch)/Sept. 10 - 12
2013 - Amelia Island, FL (Omni Amelia Island Plantation Resort)/Nov. 7 - 9
2014 - Las Vegas, NV (Caesars Palace Las Vegas Hotel and Casino)/March 12 - 14
Number of non-conference events/year: 1

Publications:
AFIA Journal
Membership Directory; on-line
Staff Directory; on-line

American Fence Association *(1962)*
800 Roosevelt Rd.
Building C, Suite 312
Glen Ellyn, IL 60137
Tel: (630) 942-6598 *Fax:* (630) 790-3095
TollFree: (800) 822-4342
Website: americanfenceassociation.com
Members: 1500 companies and 31 chapters
Staff: 7
Annual Budget: $2-5,000,000

Personnel:
Executive Vice President: Rick Church
    E-Mail: rickc@cmservices.com

Historical Note:
Formerly (1993) International Fence Industry Association. Organization representing the entire fence, deck, and railing industry in the U.S. and parts of Canada. AFA offers educational and certification options, along with providing networking opportunities to keep its members above and beyond their competition. Membership: $100-200/year.

Continuing Education:
Certification Designation/s: CFP, CAGOI.

Meetings/Conferences: Semi-Annual
Number of non-conference events/year: 2

Publications:
Across the Fence Newsletter
Deckworld Magazine
Fencepost Magazine; bi-monthly; adv.
FenceSense Newsletter; monthly

Membership Directory

American Fern Society (1893)
C/O Missouri Botanical Garden
P.O. Box 299
St. Louis, MO 63166-0299
Tel: (314) 577-9522 *Fax:* (314) 577-0830
Website: amerfernsoc.org
Members: 900 individuals
Staff: 11
Annual Budget: $25-50,000
Tax: 501(c)(3)

Personnel:
President: Michael D. Windham
   E-Mail: mdw26@duke.edu
Treasurer: James D. Caponetti
   E-Mail: jcaponet@utk.edu
Secretary, Membership Services: George Yatskievych

Historical Note:
Formerly (1905) Linnaean Fern Chapter of Aggasiz Association Affiliated with American Institute of Biological Sciences. AFS's mission is to advance ferns and fern allies. Members are pteridologists, botanists and others interested in growing or studying ferns. Membership: $12-19 (Regular); $20 (Organization); $25-32 (Journal Member); $300-430 (Life Member).

Meetings/Conferences:
Number of non-conference events/year: 1

Publications:
AFS Fern Journal; quarterly
Fiddlehead Forum Newsletter; bi-monthly
Pteridologia

Membership List Available to Non-members

American Fiber Manufacturers Association (1988)
1530 Wilson Blvd.
Suite 690
Arlington, VA 22209
Tel: (703) 875-0432 *Fax:* (703) 875-0907
E-Mail: afma@afma.org
Website: afma.org
Members: 27000 individuals
Staff: 7
Annual Budget: $500-1,000,000
Tax: 501(c)(5)

Personnel:
President and Counsel: Paul T. O'Day
   E-Mail: oday@afma.org
Manager, Information Technology and Trade Data: Kris Bayer
   E-Mail: kris@afma.org

Historical Note:
Established as the Rayon Institute with headquarters in New York. Formerly (1988) the Man-Made Fiber Producers Association, assumed its current name in 1988. Members are producers of chemically-based or cellulosic fibers such as polyester, nylon, rayon, etc. The membership is limited to U.S. producers that sell manufactured fiber in the open market.

Meetings/Conferences: Annual
Number of non-conference events/year: 2

Publications:
Fiber News; adv.
Fiber Organon; monthly
Fiber Society Newsletter; annually

American Filtration and Separations Society (1987)
7608 Emerson Ave., South
Richfield, MN 55423
Tel: (612) 861-1277 *Fax:* (612) 861-7959
E-Mail: afs@afssociety.org
Website: afssociety.org
Members: 300 members
Staff: 1
Annual Budget: $250-500,000

Personnel:
Executive Manager: Suzanne Sower
   E-Mail: afs@afssociety.org

Historical Note:
AFS's mission is to promote the recognition of fluid-particle processing as a branch of science and engineering. Members are engineers, scientists and others with an interest in fluid particle separation technology and is drawn from a wide variety of backgrounds, including end users, marketing and distribution engineers, product designers,

research scientists, raw material designers, company management, consultants, academicians, and officials of government. Membership: $125 (US Individual/Canada/Mexico/International); $2,500 (Corporate); $75 (Retiree); $50 (Student); $1,250 (Distributor/Manufacturer).

Meetings/Conferences:
2013 - Bloomington, MN/May 6 - 9

Publications:
AFS Newsletter; monthly
International Filtration News; bi-monthly; adv.
The Filtration Journal

Membership List Available to Non-members

The American Finance Association (1940)
Haas School of Business, University of California
Berkeley, CA 94729-1900
Tel: (781) 388-8401 *Fax:* (781) 388-8232
TollFree: (800) 835-6770
E-Mail: pyle@haas.berkeley.edu
Website: afajof.org
Members:
3500 corporations and libraries
5000 individuals
Staff: 4
Annual Budget: $2-5,000,000
Tax: 501(c)(3)

Personnel:
President: Sheridan Titman
Advertising Sales Representative: Kristin McCarthy
   E-Mail: kmccarthy@wiley.com
Executive Secretary and Treasurer: David H. Pyle
   E-Mail: pyle@haas.berkeley.edu
Editorial Assistant: Wendy Washburn
   E-Mail: editor@jfinance.org

Historical Note:
Incorporated in Illinois in 1952 and affiliated with Allied Social Sciences Association, AFA's purpose is to improve public understanding of financial problems and to provide a forum for the exchange of financial ideas through the distribution of periodical and other media. It also encourages the study of finance in colleges and universities. Membership consists of both individuals and institutions interested in finance. Membership: $11-351/year; $0 (3 Year Student Membership-Online Only).

Meetings/Conferences: Annual
Conference Chair: Sheridan Titman
2013 - San Diego, CA/Jan. 4 - 6
2013 - San Diego, CA (Marriot Marquis and Marina Hotel)/Jan. 4 - 6
2014 - Philadelphia, PA/Jan. 3 - 5
2015 - Boston, MA/Jan. 3 - 5
2016 - San Francisco, CA/Jan. 3 - 5
2017 - Chicago, IL/Jan. 6 - 8
2018 - Atlanta, GA/Jan. 5 - 7

Publications:
Membership Directory; on-line
The Journal of Finance; bi-monthly; adv.

American Financial Services Association (1916)
919 18th St. NW
Suite 300
Washington, DC 20006
Tel: (202) 296-5544 *Fax:* (202) 223-0321
E-Mail: afsa@afsamail.org
Website: afsaonline.org
Members: 530 companies
Staff: 23
Annual Budget: $5-10,000,000
Tax: 501(c)(6)

Personnel:
President and Chief Executive Officer: Christopher Stinebert
   E-Mail: cstinebert@afsamail.org
Senior Vice President, State Government Affairs: Danielle Fagre Arlowe
   E-Mail: dfagre@afsamail.org
Vice President, Membership Services: Sheilah J. Harrison CAE
   E-Mail: sharrison@afsamail.org
Director, Communications: Karen Klugh
   E-Mail: kklugh@afsamail.org
Vice President, Meetings and Conferences: Tom Morano
   E-Mail: tmorano@afsamail.org
Vice President and Chief Financial Officer: Tony Pelegrin
   E-Mail: tpelegrin@afsamail.org
Assistant, Communications and State Government Affairs: Susan J. Sullivan

   E-Mail: ssullivan@afsamail.org
Manager, Legal and Regulatory Affairs: Celia Winslow
   E-Mail: cwinslow@afsamail.org
Director, eBusiness Solutions: Mark Zalewksi

Historical Note:
AFSA's mission is to promote responsible, ethical lending to responsible, informed borrowers and to improve and protect consumers' access to credit. Membership: $39,500 (Commercial); $2,600 (Business Partner); $395 (Affiliate); $2000 (Foreign).

Meetings/Conferences: Annual
Conference Chair: Tom Morano
2013 - Orlando, FL (Convention Center/The Peabody Orlando)/Feb. 6 - 8

Publications:
AFSA Newsbriefs; weekly
Membership Directory; on-line

American Fire Safety Council (1973)
1909 K St. NW
Suite 1000-L
Washington, DC 20006
Tel: (202) 419-3269 *Fax:* (202) 955-6215
E-Mail: info@fire-safety.net
Website: fire-safety.net
Members: 40 companies
Staff: 3
Annual Budget: $250-500,000
Tax: 501(c)(3)

Personnel:
Program Manager: Mike Heimowitz
   E-Mail: michael.heimowitz@porternovelli.com

Historical Note:
Fire Retardant Chemicals Association, d/b/a American Fire Safety Council, promotes fire safety while creating and maintaining the best possible industry climate for member companies to individually market their products and services. Membership fee varies, based on sales volume.

American Fire Sprinkler Association (1981)
12750 Merit Dr.
Suite 350
Dallas, TX 75251
Tel: (214) 349-5965 *Fax:* (214) 343-8898
E-Mail: afsainfo@firesprinkler.org
Website: firesprinkler.org
Members: 750 companies
Staff: 17
Annual Budget: $100-250,000

Personnel:
President: Steve A. Muncy CAE
Director, Education Services and Meetings: Marlene Garrett CMP
Vice President, Engineering and Technical Services: Roland Huggins PE
Vice President, Marketing and Communications: Janet R. Knowles
   E-Mail: jknowles@firesprinkler.org
Director, Membership Services: Jeff Livaudais

Historical Note:
AFSA's mission is to aid the development of educational and training programs to maintain the quality and effectiveness of automatic fire sprinklers. Membership: $400-20,000 (Associate/Contractor, dues based on sales volume); $100 (Authority Having Jurisdiction); $200 (Designer).

Continuing Education:
Certification Designation/s: NICET

Meetings/Conferences: Annual
Conference Chair: Marlene Garrett CMP
2013 - Las Vegas, NV (Caesars Palace Las Vegas Hotel and Casino)/Sept. 18 - 22
2014 - Nashville, TN (Gaylord Hotels Resorts and Convention Centers-Nashville)/Sept. 17 - 21

Publications:
AFSA Technical Update Newsletter; monthly
SprinklerAge Weekly News Brief; weekly; adv.

American Fisheries Society (1870)
5410 Grosvenor Ln.
Suite 110
Bethesda, MD 20814-2199
Tel: (301) 897-8616 *Fax:* (301) 897-8096
E-Mail: main@fisheries.org
Website: fisheries.org
Members: 8500 individuals
Staff: 24

Annual Budget: $2-5,000,000
Tax: 501(c)(3)

Personnel:
Executive Director: Dr. Gus Rassam
  E-Mail: grassam@fisheries.org
Webmaster, Information Technology Coordinator, and Applications Architect: Farasha Euker
  E-Mail: farasha@farashaeuker.com
Administrative Coordinator: Shawn Johnston
  E-Mail: sjohnston@fisheries.org
Director, Publications: Aaron Lerner
  E-Mail: alerner@fisheries.org
Policy and Development Coordinator: Kevin Lynch
  E-Mail: klynch@fisheries.org
Accounting Assistant: Jackie Machado
  E-Mail: jmachado@fisheries.org
Coordinator, Membership Services: Eva Przygodzki
  E-Mail: eprzygod@fisheries.org
Coordinator, Continuing Education and Hutton Program: Kathryn Winkler
  E-Mail: kwinkler@fisheries.org

Historical Note:
Formerly (1878) known as American Culturists' Association, became (1884) American Fish Cultural Association. Incorporated in the District of Columbia in 1911. AFS's mission is to improve conservation, sustainability of fishery resources, aquatic ecosystems by advancing fisheries and aquatic science , promoting development of fisheries professionals. Membership: $10-1,737/year.

Continuing Education:
Enrollment: 150
Certification Designation/s: FPC

Meetings/Conferences: Annual
2013 - Little Rock, AR/Sept. 8 - 12
2014 - Québec, QC/Aug. 17 - 21

Publications:
Fisheries; monthly; adv.
Journal of Aquatic Animal Health; quarterly
Marine and Coastal Fisheries: Dynamics, Management, and Ecosystem Science; on-line
Member Directory; on-line
North American Journal of Aquaculture; quarterly
North American Journal of Fisheries Management; bi-monthly
Transactions of the American Fisheries Society; bi-monthly

Membership List Available to Non-members

American Flock Association (1984)
Six Beacon St.
Suite 1125
Boston, MA 02108
Tel: (617) 303-6288 *Fax:* (617) 542-2199
E-Mail: info@flocking.org
Website: flocking.org
Members: 150 companies
Staff: 2
Annual Budget: $100-250,000

Personnel:
Managing Director: Steve Rosenthal CAE, CMM, CMP
  E-Mail: srosenthal@flocking.org

Historical Note:
AFA provides positive leadership to foster a strong flock industry in North America. Represents the flock industry, including flock suppliers, manufacturers of roll-to-roll coated textiles, papers, and films as well as coaters of three dimensional objects and printers of apparel decoration and graphics art products. Membership: $925-2,750/year.

Membership List Available to Non-members

American Floorcovering Alliance (1979)
210 W. Cuyler St.
Dalton, GA 30720-8209
Tel: (706) 278-4101 *Fax:* (706) 278-5323
TollFree: (800) 288-4101
E-Mail: afa@americanfloor.org
Website: americanfloor.org
Members: 110 companies
Staff: 1
Annual Budget: $100-250,000

Personnel:
Executive Director: Wanda J. Ellis
  E-Mail: ellis@americanfloor.org

Historical Note:
Founded as Carpet Manufacturers Marketing Association; became Dalton Floor Covering Market Association in 1991

and assumed its current name in 2001. AFA's mission is to provide marketing services, employee benefits programs, and other services to members of the floor covering industry nationwide. Membership: $400 (Basic); $500 (Premium); $600 (Showcase).

Meetings/Conferences: Annual

Publications:
AFA Newsletter; on-line
Membership Directory; on-line

American Fly Fishing Trade Association
901 Front St.
Suite B-125
Louisville, CO 80027
Tel: (303) 604-6132 *Fax:* (302) 604-6162
Website: affta.com
Staff: 2
Annual Budget: $500-1,000,000
Tax: 501(c)(6)

Personnel:
Director, Show: Randi Swisher
General Manager: Ben Bulis

Historical Note:
The AFFTA is the sole trade organization for the fly-fishing industry representing more than 2000 manufacturers, retailers. AFFTA is a membership-based association for all sectors of the fly-fishing industry, from manufacturers to retailers. AFFTA's mission is to Promote the Sustained Growth of the Fly-Fishing Industry.

Meetings/Conferences:
Conference Chair: Randi Swisher

Publications:
AFFTA Connects; monthly
Member Directory

American Folklore Society (1888)
Ohio State University, Mershon Center
1501 Neil Ave.
Columbus, OH 43201-2602
Tel: (614) 292-4715 *Fax:* (614) 292-2407
Website: afsnet.org
Members: 2200 individuals
Staff: 4
Annual Budget: $500-1,000,000

Personnel:
Executive Director: Timothy Lloyd
  E-Mail: lloyd.100@osu.edu
Editor: Harris M. Berger
  E-Mail: jafolklore@tamu.edu
Contact, Meetings: Catherine McKemie
  E-Mail: catherine_mckemie@conferencedirect.com
Administrative Associate: Rob Vanscoyoc
  E-Mail: AmericanFolkloreSociety@gmail.com

Historical Note:
AFS was organized in Cambridge, MA to collect, publish and preserve original folklore material. Membership: $100 (Regular); $80 (Independent member of AFS/Retired); $35 (Student/Household/Partner); $65 (New Professional); $150 (Sustainer); $250 (Sponsor); $500 (Benefactor); $1,500 (Life).

Meetings/Conferences: Annual
Conference Chair: Catherine McKemie
2013 - Providence, RI (Westin Providence)/Oct. 16 - 19
2014 - Santa Fe, NM (Santa Fe Convention Center)/Nov. 5 - 8

Publications:
Journal of American Folklore; quarterly; adv.
Membership Directory; on-line

American Football Coaches Association (1921)
100 Legends Ln.
Waco, TX 76706
Tel: (254) 754-9900 *Fax:* (254) 754-7373
E-Mail: info@afca.com
Website: afca.com
Members: 11000 members
Staff: 16
Annual Budget: $2-5,000,000
Tax: 501(c)(6)

Personnel:
Executive Director: Grant Teaff
  E-Mail: grant@afca.com
Director, Education: Tai M. Brown
  E-Mail: tai@afca.com
Manager, Exhibits: Butch Gardner
  E-Mail: butch.afca@yahoo.com
Managing Director, Finance and Operations: Adam Guess

  E-Mail: adam@afca.com
Coordinator, Information Technologies: Kevin Morgan
  E-Mail: kevin@afca.com
Director, Marketing: Mel Pulliam
  E-Mail: mel@afca.com
Director, Special Events: Janet Robertson
  E-Mail: janet@afca.com
Director, Media Relations: Vince Thompson
  E-Mail: vince@afca.com
Contact, Membership Development, High Schools: Johnny Tusa
  E-Mail: jtusa@afca.com

Historical Note:
AFCA is a national organization solely dedicated to improving football coaches through ongoing education, interaction, and networking. Membership: $60-200/year.

Meetings/Conferences: Annual
Conference Chair: Janet Robertson
2013 - Nashville, TN (Gaylord Opryland Resort and Convention Center)/Jan. 6 - 9

Publications:
The AFCA Directory
This is AFCA

American Forage and Grassland Council (1944)
P.O. Box 867
Berea, KY 40403
Fax: (859) 623-8694
TollFree: (800) 944-2342
E-Mail: info@afgc.org
Website: afgc.org
Members: 2500 individuals
Staff: 2
Annual Budget: $100-250,000
Tax: 501(c)(3)

Personnel:
Executive Director: Tina Bowling
  E-Mail: tina.bowling@afgc.org

Historical Note:
AFGC was reorganized on December 19, 1957 as the American Grassland Council and changed its name to American Forage and Grassland Council on July 15, 1968. AFGC is dedicated to advancing the use of forage as a prime feed resource. Members represent the academic community, producers, private industry, institutes and foundations. Membership: $5-2,500/year.

Continuing Education:
Certification Designation/s: CGP

Meetings/Conferences: Annual
2013 - Covington, KY (Marriott RiverCenter)/Jan. 6 - 9

Publications:
Membership Directory; on-line
The Forage Leader; quarterly

American Foreign Law Association (1925)
C/O Soledad Matteozzi
150 E. 58th St., 20th Floor
New York, NY 10155
Website: afla-law.org
Members: 300 individuals
Staff: 2
Annual Budget: $10-25,000
Tax: 501(c)(3)

Personnel:
President: Elizabeth Van Schilfgaarde
  E-Mail: elizabeth.vanschilfgaarde@nautadutilh.com
Treasurer: Paul D. Downs
  E-Mail: aflatreasurer@gmail.com

Historical Note:
AFLA's purpose is to focus on relevant issues of foreign, international and comparative law of importance to the legal profession. Membership is open to all lawyers and jurists of all jurisdictions and to law students. Membership: $25-300/year.

Continuing Education:
Certification Designation/s: CLE

Publications:
Membership Directory; on-line; adv.

American Foreign Service Association (1924)
2101 E St. NW
Washington, DC 20037
Tel: (202) 338-4045 *Fax:* (202) 338-6820
TollFree: (800) 704-2372
E-Mail: member@afsa.org
Website: afsa.org
Members: 16000 individuals

Staff: 30
Annual Budget: $2-5,000,000
Tax: 501(c)(5)

Personnel:
Executive Director: Ian M. Houston
  E-Mail: houston@afsa.org
Editor: Donna Ayerst
  E-Mail: ayerst@afsa.org
Scholarship Assistant: Jonathan Crawford
  E-Mail: crawford@afsa.org
Director, Legislative Programs: Casey Frary
  E-Mail: frary@afsa.org
Director, Membership Services: Janet Hedrick
  E-Mail: hedrick@afsa.org
Editor: Steve Honley
  E-Mail: honley@afsa.org
President, Federal Lobbyist: Susan R. Johnson
  E-Mail: johnson@afsa.org
Director, Finance: Femi Oshobukola
  E-Mail: oshobukola@afsa.org
General Counsel: Sharon Papp
  E-Mail: PappS@state.gov
Director, Marketing and Outreach: Asgeir Sigfusson
  E-Mail: sigfusson@afsa.org
Director, Communications: Thomas Switzer
  E-Mail: switzer@afsa.org

Historical Note:
AFSA's missions are to enhance the effectiveness of the Foreign Service, to protect the professional interests of its members, to ensure the maintenance of high professional standards for both career diplomats and political appointees, and to promote understanding of the critical role of the Foreign Service. Represents 28,000 active duty and retired Foreign Service employees. Membership: $377.95 (Active); $64.15 (Retired); $104.80 (Associate).

Meetings/Conferences:
Number of non-conference events/year: 4

Publications:
AFSA Newsletter; bi-monthly; adv.
Foreign Service Journal; monthly; adv.
Membership Directory; on-line
Retiree Directory; adv.

American Foreign Service Protective Association (1929)
1716 N. St. NW
Washington, DC 20036-2902
Tel: (202) 833-4910 *Fax:* (202) 833-4918
E-Mail: afspa@afspa.org
Website: afspa.org
Members: 57000 individuals
Staff: 5
Annual Budget: $5-10,000,000
Tax: 501(c)(9)

Personnel:
Chief Executive Officer: Paula S. Jakub
Executive Vice President: John P. Shumate
Vice President, Operations: Gayle Bohorquez
Director, Accounting and Finance: Steve Stewart
Manager, Member Quality Services: Kathy R. Yeldell

Historical Note:
AFSPA is devoted to providing insurance and services specifically tailored to the unique needs of the Foreign Service and other Executive Branch personnel.

Publications:
AFSPA Newsletter
Special Health Newsletter

American Forensic Association (1949)
P.O. Box 256
River Falls, WI 54022-0256
Tel: (800) 228-5424 *Fax:* (888) 314-9533
E-Mail: amforensicassoc@aol.com
Website: americanforensics.org
Members: 1200 individuals
Staff: 3
Annual Budget: $100-250,000
Tax: 501(c)(3)

Personnel:
President: Rich Edwards
Webmaster: Allan D. Louden
  E-Mail: louden@wfu.edu
Executive Secretary: James W. Pratt
  E-Mail: amforensicassoc@aol.com

Historical Note:
AFA advocates effective and responsible oral communication. Membership composed primarily of college

and high school directors of debate and speech programs.
Membership: $75 (Individual/Institutional); $600 (Life Membership); $20 (Student); $50 (Non-Journal).

Meetings/Conferences:
Number of non-conference events/year: 1

Publications:
AFA members' directory; on-line
AFA Newsletter; quarterly
Argumentation and Advocacy; quarterly

American Forest & Paper Association (1993)
1111 19th St. NW
Suite 800
Washington, DC 20036
Tel: (202) 463-2700
TollFree: (800) 878-8878
E-Mail: info@afandpa.org
Website: afandpa.org
Members: 120 companies and trade associations
Staff: 99
Annual Budget: $10-25,000,000

Personnel:
President and Chief Executive Officer: Donna Akers Harman
  E-Mail: donna_harman@afandpa.org
Executive Director, Strategic Communications: Chuck Fuqua
  E-Mail: chuck_fuqua@afandpa.org
Vice President, Administration and Chief Financial Officer: Samuel Kerns
Director, Government Affairs: Suzanne Madden
  E-Mail: suzanne_madden@afandpa.org
Executive Director, Membership: Caroline Nealon
  E-Mail: membership@afandpa.org
Vice President, General Counsel & Corporate Secretary: Janet A. Poling

Historical Note:
AF&PA is committed to a sustainable, thriving forest and paper products industry that continues to improve tomorrow's environment today. Membership: $2000-4000 (General Association); $500 (State Level); $3000-25000 (Associate); $25000 (Partner Supplier).

Continuing Education:
Certification Designation/s: FC

American Forest Resource Council (2000)
5100 SW Macadam Ave.
Suite 350
Portland, OR 97239
Tel: (503) 222-9505 *Fax:* (503) 222-3255
E-Mail: info@amforest.org
Website: amforest.org
Members: 80 companies
Staff: 10
Annual Budget: $1-2,000,000
Tax: 501(c)(6)

Personnel:
President: Tom Partin
  E-Mail: tpartin@amforest.org

Historical Note:
AFRC seeks to advance its members' ability to practice socially and scientifically responsible forestry on both public and private forest lands.

Publications:
AFRC Newsletter

Membership List Available to Non-members

American Foundry Society (1896)
1695 N. Penny Ln.
Schaumburg, IL 60173-4555
Tel: (847) 824-0181 *Fax:* (847) 824-2174
TollFree: (800) 537-4237
Website: afsinc.org
Members: 7900 corporates and individuals
Staff: 25
Annual Budget: $5-10,000,000
Tax: 501(c)(6)

Personnel:
Executive Vice President: Jerry Call
  E-Mail: jcall@afsinc.org
Director, Membership Services: Leo J. Baran
  E-Mail: lbaran@afsinc.org
Director, Finance: Kris Drager
  E-Mail: kdrager@afsinc.org
Contact, Marketing and Assistant Editor: Jillian Knuerr
  E-Mail: jknuerr@afsinc.org

Director, Special Publications and Related Services: Laura Moreno
  E-Mail: lmoreno@afsinc.org
Vice President, Technical Services: Thomas Prucha
  E-Mail: tprucha@afsinc.org
Manager, Human Resources, Administration, Meetings and Exhibitions: Lynn Smith
  E-Mail: lsmith@afsinc.org
Director, Marketing, Public Relations and Communications: Alfred Spada
  E-Mail: aspada@afsinc.org

Historical Note:
Founded as the American Foundrymen's Association, became the American Foundrymen's Society (1948), assumed its present name in 2002. AFS is a U.S. based metalcasting society that assists member companies (metalcasting facilities, diecasters and industry suppliers) and individuals to manage all production operations, profitably market their products and services and to equitably manage their employees. Membership: $20-185/year.

Continuing Education:
Certification Designation/s: FMT, NFMT, MCT, GFT

Meetings/Conferences:
Conference Chair: Lynn Smith
2013 - St. Louis, MO (The Doubletree Hotel and Conference Center)/April 6 - 9/8000 attendees/over 100 exhibitors
2014 - Schaumburg, IL (Renaissance Schaumburg Convention Center Hotel)/April 8 - 11/1800 attendees/over 100 exhibitors
Number of non-conference events/year: 12

Publications:
AFS E-Connections; weekly
Casting Source Directory; on-line
Education Connections; bi-weekly
Forecast & Trends; annually
International Journal of Metalcasting; quarterly
Labor Agreement Settlement Data; quarterly
Member Connections; quarterly
Metal Casting Design and Purchasing; bi-monthly
Modern Casting Magazine; monthly
The Metalcaster Directory; on-line; adv.
Transactions; annually

American Fox Terrier Club (1885)
6838 Lake Shore Rd.
Derby, NY 14047
Website: aftc.org
Staff: 3
Annual Budget: $25-50,000

Personnel:
President: J. W. Smith
  E-Mail: President@AFTC.org
Treasurer: Susan Hogan
  E-Mail: Treasurer@AFTC.org
Contact, Membership Services: Anne E. Smith

Historical Note:
AFTC's mission is to promote the breeds of pure fox terriers, to define precisely the true type and to urge the adoption of such type by breeders, judges, dog show committees and others. Membership: $40-50 (United States); $45-55 (Canada/Mexico); $60-75 (Foreign Countries); $10-15 (Junior- United States/Canada/Mexico/Foreign Countries).

Publications:
AFTC Newsletter

American Franchisee Association (1975)
53 W. Jackson Blvd.
Suite 1256
Chicago, IL 60604
Tel: (312) 431-0545 *Fax:* (312) 431-1469
Website: franchisee.org
Staff: 1
Tax: 501(c)(6)

Personnel:
President: Susan Kezios
  E-Mail: spkezios@franchisee.org

Historical Note:
Formerly known as the National Franchise Association Coalition and merged with the National Alliance of Franchisees and Dealers to become American Franchisee Association.AFA's mission is to represent franchisees in all industries in the development of franchising; educate franchisees, potential franchisees, the government, the business community and the public as to the needs and requirements of franchisees. Membership: $2500 (Individuals); $2500-60000 (independent franchisee associations).

Publications:
AFA Enews; bi-monthly

American Fraternal Alliance *(1886)*
1301 W. 22nd St.
Suite 700
Oak Brook, IL 60523
Tel: (630) 522-6322 *Fax:* (630) 522-6326
E-Mail: info@FraternalAlliance.org
Website: fraternalalliance.org
Members: 70 societies
Staff: 9
Annual Budget: $2-5,000,000
Tax: 501(c)(6)

Personnel:
President and Chief Executive Officer: Joe Annotti
   E-Mail: jannotti@fraternalalliance.org
Executive Vice President: Allison Koppel
   E-Mail: AKoppel@fraternalalliance.org
Executive Administrator: Andrea Litewski
   E-Mail: alitewski@fraternalalliance.org
Director, Business Operations: Linda McLaughlin
   E-Mail: LMcLaughlin@fraternalalliance.org
Director, Public Affairs: Rose Riccetti-Andrikos
Director, Advocacy and Public Policy: Elizabeth Snyder
   E-Mail: ESnyder@fraternalalliance.org
Manager, Information Technology: Terry L. Whipple
   E-Mail: TWhipple@fraternalalliance.org

Historical Note:
Formerly known as National Fraternal Congress of America. AFA's mission is to provide advocacy, information, and operational products and services that help member societies make meaningful contributions to individual, communities, and society. Membership: $1,000/year (Associate).

Meetings/Conferences:
2013 - Hollywood, CA (Westin Diplomat Resort and Spa)/Sept. 5 - 7
2014 - Austin, TX (Hilton Austin)/Sept. 4 - 6
2015 - Indianapolis, IN (JW Marriott Indianapolis)/
   Sept. 10 - 12

Publications:
Member Directory; annually
Weekly Headlines; weekly
Yearbook; annually

American Friends of Turkey *(1974)*
1111 14th St. NW
Suite 1050
Washington, DC 20005
Tel: (202) 783-0483 *Fax:* (202) 783-0511
E-Mail: info@afot.us
Website: americanfriendsofturkey.org
Staff: 3
Annual Budget: $100-250,000

Personnel:
Executive Director: Dr. Elizabeth W. Shelton
General Counsel: Doreen Edelman Esq.
Treasurer: Louis Kahn

Historical Note:
The mission of the American Friends of Turkey, Inc. is to support and strengthen people-to-people relations between America and Turkey by deepening the understanding and appreciation of two centuries of friendship. AFOT's goal is to develop further a broad range of mutual interests including culture, education, the environment, literature and the arts.

American Frozen Food Institute *(1942)*
2000 Corporate Ridge Blvd.
Suite 1000
McLean, VA 22102-7805
Tel: (703) 821-0770 *Fax:* (703) 821-1350
E-Mail: info@affi.com
Website: affi.com
Members: 500 member companies
Staff: 18
Annual Budget: $2-5,000,000
Tax: 501(c)(6)

Personnel:
President and Chief Executive Officer: Kraig R. Naasz
   E-Mail: knaasz@affi.com
Director, Conferences: Mary Becton
   E-Mail: mbecton@affi.org
Vice President, Membership Services: Lucas R. Darnell
   E-Mail: ldarnell@affi.com
Vice President, Administration: Kathleen R. Greco

   E-Mail: kgreco@affi.com
Vice President, Communications: Corey Henry
   E-Mail: chenry@affi.com
Vice President, Finance: Tom Kearney
   E-Mail: tkearney@affi.com
Manager, Membership Services: Patrick Kendall
   E-Mail: pkendall@affi.com
Director, Industry and Public Affairs: Adrienne Richards
Vice President, Government Affairs: Kristin Pearson
   Wilcox
   E-Mail: kwilcox@affi.com

Historical Note:
Formerly (1970) National Association of Frozen Food Packers. Absorbed California Freezers Association in 1967. AFFI fosters industry development and growth, advocates on behalf of industry before legislative and regulatory entities, and provides additional value-added services for its members and for benefit of consumers. Membership: $2,400 (International Processor); $250 (Start-up Processor/Retail/Food service Operator); $1,000-1,900 (Associate).

Meetings/Conferences: Annual
Conference Chair: Mary Becton
2013 - Anaheim, CA (Hilton Anaheim)/Feb. 23 - 27

Publications:
Freeze Flash; weekly
Frozen Express; daily; adv.

American Fuel & Petrochemical Manufacturers *(1961)*
1667 K St. NW
Suite 700
Washington, DC 20006
Tel: (202) 457-0480 *Fax:* (202) 457-0486
E-Mail: info@npra.org
Website: npra.org
Members: 500 companies
Staff: 43
Annual Budget: $10-25,000,000

Personnel:
President: Charles T. Drevna
   E-Mail: cdrevna@npra.org
Coordinator, Membership Services: LaToya Blackburn
Director, Communications: David Egner
Director, Human Resources: Julia Gregg Kramer SPHR
Director, Convention Services: Helen M. Kutska
Manager, Information Technology: Carlos Lopez
General Counsel: Rich Moskowitz
Director, Industrial Relations and Programs: Dan Strachan
Chief Financial Officer: Gerry R. Van de Velde
Vice President, Advocacy: Brendan E. Williams
   E-Mail: bwilliams@npra.org
Vice President, Member Relations and Development: Susan Yashinskie

Historical Note:
Product of a merger of the National Petroleum Association (1902) and the Western Petroleum Refiners Association (1912), became the National Petroleum Refiners Association and assumed its present name in 2012. AFPM aims to provide a committee structure which provides counsel, expertise and support to the association and its activities.

Meetings/Conferences:
Conference Chair: Helen M. Kutska
2013 - San Antonio, TX (San Antonio Marriott Rivercenter)/March 17 - 19
2013 - San Antonio, TX (Grand Hyatt San Antonio)/
   March 24 - 26
2013 - The Woodlands, TX (Woodlands Waterway Marriott Hotel and Convention Center)/May 14 - 15
2013 - Orlando, FL (Orlando World Center Marriott)/
   May 21 - 24
2014 - San Antonio, TX (Grand Hyatt San Antonio)/
   March 30 - April 1
2014 - Antonio, TX (Grand Hyatt San Antonio)/May 14
   - 15
2014 - San Antonio, TX (San Antonio Convention Center)/May 20 - 23
2015 - San Antonio, TX (Grand Hyatt San Antonio)/
   March 29 - 31
Number of non-conference events/year: 7

Publications:
Fuel Line; on-line
Green Room Report; weekly
Membership Directory; on-line
Security Watch; on-line
Show Directory; adv.
Technical Update; monthly
The Daily Alert; daily

American Galvanizers Association *(1935)*
6881 S. Holly Cir.
Suite 108
Centennial, CO 80112
Tel: (720) 554-0900 *Fax:* (720) 554-0909
TollFree: (800) 468-7732
E-Mail: aga@galvanizeit.org
Website: galvanizeit.org
Members: 150 companies
Staff: 8
Annual Budget: $1-2,000,000

Personnel:
Technical Director: Thomas J. Langill PhD
   E-Mail: tlangill@galvanizeit.org
Manager, Marketing: Melissa Lindsley
   E-Mail: mlindsley@galvanizeit.org

Historical Note:
AGA was previously known as American Hot Dip Galvanizers Association till 1989. AGA's mission is to preserve, enhance, and protect the existence of the hot-dip galvanizing industry throughout North America, and to fulfill the needs of the industry for technical, marketing, and other services. Membership: $3,600 (Regular); $2,500-5,000(Associate); $1,680-14,000 (Sustaining); $100 (Professional/Retired).

Meetings/Conferences:
Number of non-conference events/year: 4

Publications:
Galvanizing Insights; quarterly

American Gaming Association *(1995)*
1299 Pennsylvania Ave. NW
Suite 1175
Washington, DC 20004
Tel: (202) 552-2675 *Fax:* (202) 552-2676
E-Mail: info@americangaming.org
Website: americangaming.org
Members: 50 companies
Staff: 7
Annual Budget: $5-10,000,000
Tax: 501(c)(6)

Personnel:
President and Chief Executive Officer: Frank J. Fahrenkopf Jr.
Senior Vice President and Executive Director: Judy L. Patterson
Contact, Membership Services: Ted Lynch
   E-Mail: tlynch@americangaming.org
Director, Research: Andrew Smith
   E-Mail: asmith@americangaming.org
Vice President , Communications: Holly Wetzel
   E-Mail: hwetzel@americangaming.org

Historical Note:
AGA's aim is to create a better understanding in the gaming entertainment industry by bringing facts about the industry to the general public, elected officials, other decision makers and the media through education and advocacy. A trade association representing the commercial casino industry.

Meetings/Conferences:
2013 - Las Vegas, NV (SandsExpo and Convention Center)/Sept. 24 - 26

Publications:
Gaming Legal Update
Inside the AGA
Responsible Gaming; quarterly

Membership List Available to Non-members

American Gas Association *(1918)*
400 N. Capitol St.
Suite 450
Washington, DC 20001
Tel: (202) 824-7000 *Fax:* (202) 824-9084
Website: aga.org
Members: 200 local energy companies
Staff: 85
Annual Budget: $50-100,000,000
Tax: 501(c)(6)

Personnel:
President and Chief Executive Officer: Hon. David K. McCurdy
General Counsel: Kevin B. Belford
   E-Mail: kbelford@aga.org
Editor: Tracy Burleson
Executive Vice President, Policy and Planning: Roger B. Cooper
   E-Mail: rcooper@aga.org

Senior Vice President, Policy and Planning: Paula Gant
  E-Mail: pgent@aga.org
Director, Information Technology, Conference and Industry Issues: Jim Linn
  E-Mail: jlinn@aga.org
Director, Rates and Regulatory Affairs: Cynthia Marple
  E-Mail: cmarple@aga.org
Contact, Human Resources and Industry Issues: Linda Nahin
Contact, Advertising and Communications: Jennifer O'Shea
Vice President, Communications and Marketing: George Sarkisian
  E-Mail: gsarkisian@aga.org
Director, Membership Services: Ysabel Suarez
  E-Mail: ysuarez@aga.org
Director, Meetings, Conferences and Expositions: Mary E. Weekley
  E-Mail: mweekley@aga.org

Historical Note:
Formed by a merger of the Gas Institute and the Commercial Gas Association. AGA represents companies delivering natural gas to customers to help meet their energy needs. Members are committed to delivering natural gas safely, reliably, cost-effectively and in an environmentally responsible way. Membership: $1250 (Associate); $25,000 (International); $6,250 (International Affiliate).

Meetings/Conferences:
Conference Chair: Mary E. Weekley
2013 - Orlando, FL (Gaylord Palms Resort and Convention Center-Orlando)/May 21 - 23
2013 - Washington, DC (Washington Court Hotel)/ Nov. 11
2014 - Pittsburgh, PA (Omni William Penn Hotel)/May 20 - 23
2014 - Las Vegas, NV (Red Rock)/Sept. 18 - 19
2015 - Grapevine, TX (Gaylord Hotels and Convention Centers)/May 19 - 21
2016 - Phoenix, AZ (Arizona Biltmore Resort and Spa)/ April 19 - 21
2016 - Nashville, TN (Omni Hotel)/Sept. 15 - 16
2017 - Grapevine, TX (Gaylord Hotels and Convention Centers)/April 25 - 28
2019 - Nashville, TN (The Gaylord Opryland)/April 30 - May 3
Number of non-conference events/year: 47

Publications:
AGA Legislative Directory
American Gas Magazine; adv.
Membership Directory; annually

American Gastroenterological Association *(1897)*
4720 Montgomery Ln.
Suite 430
Bethesda, MD 20814
Tel: (301) 654-2055 *Fax*: (301) 654-5920
E-Mail: member@gastro.org
Website: gastro.org
Members: 17000 individuals
Staff: 83
Annual Budget: $25-50,000,000
Tax: 501(c)(3)

Personnel:
Co-Executive Vice President: Thomas J. Serena CPA, MBA
  E-Mail: tserena@gastro.org
Senior Director, Finance: Arceli (Pinky) Bacsinila CPA
  E-Mail: pbacsinila@gastro.org
Senior Director, Scholarly Publishing: Erin Dubnansky
  E-Mail: edubnansky@gastro.org
Vice President, Communications: Jessica Duncan
  E-Mail: jduncan@gastro.org
Director, Human Resources: Lynn Grone
  E-Mail: lgrone@gastro.org
Vice president, Education and Training: Lori Marks PhD
  E-Mail: LMarks@gastro.org
Director, Membership Services: Theresa Remines
  E-Mail: tremines@gastro.org
Vice President, Public Policy: Michael Roberts
  E-Mail: mroberts@gastro.org
Co-Executive Vice President, Legal: Lynn P. Robinson JD
  E-Mail: lrobin@gastro.org
vice president, meetings and conventions: Ellen Silver
  E-Mail: esilver@gastro.org
Vice President, Marketing and Membership Services: Jeff Springer

  E-Mail: springer@gastro.org
Director, Information System: Leslie Waite
  E-Mail: lwaite@gastro.org

Historical Note:
AGA's mission is to promote the common business interests of its members by promoting the image of the industry as a whole and to serve as a central, unified voice for the specialty of gastroenterology. Membership: $395 (Physician/Scientist in U.S., Canada and Mexico); $450 (Physician/Scientist International); $95 (Trainees -First Year Free/International); $300 (Corporate); $175-215 (GI Nurse Practitioner/GI Nurse); $25 (Student/GI Practice Manager).

Meetings/Conferences:
Conference Chair: Ellen Silver
Number of non-conference events/year: 6

Publications:
AGA eDigest; weekly
AGA Perspectives; bi-monthly
AGA Quarterly: Practice; quarterly
AGA Quarterly: Quality; quarterly
Clinical Gastroenterology and Hepatology
Gastroenterology; monthly
GI & Hepatology; monthly
Membership Directory; on-line

American Gear Manufacturers Association *(1916)*
1001 N. Fairfax St.
Fifth Floor
Alexandria, VA 22314-1587
Tel: (703) 684-0211 *Fax*: (703) 684-0242
Website: agma.org
Members: 400 companies
Staff: 13
Annual Budget: $2-5,000,000
Tax: 501(c)(6)

Personnel:
Executive Director: Sandra Detwiler
  E-Mail: detwiler@agma.org
Manager, Education: Jan Alfieri
  E-Mail: alfieri@agma.org
Director, Marketing and Communications: Jenny Blackford
  E-Mail: blackford@agma.org
Vice President, Technical Division: Charles Fischer
  E-Mail: fischer@agma.org
Director, Membership Services: Jill Johnson
  E-Mail: jill.johnson@agma.org
Technical Editor: Amy Lane
  E-Mail: lane@agma.org
Manager, Meetings: Madelaine Morgan
  E-Mail: morgan@agma.org

Historical Note:
AGMA's mission is to help members compete more effectively in today's global marketplace. Members are gear manufacturers, makers of gear cutting and checking equipment, gearing teachers, suppliers to the industry and purchasers of gear products. Membership: $1,575-16,650 (Company); $1,575-14,000 (Associate, International Gear Manufacer) ; $2,625-9,725 (Associate, Suppliers to the Industry); $2,625 (End User, Associate Membership); $785 (Individual Technical Consultant); $55(Academic).

Meetings/Conferences:
Conference Chair: Madelaine Morgan
2013 - Carlsbad, CA (Park Hyatt Aviara)/April 25 - 27

Publications:
AGMA Business Journal
AGMA NewsBrief; weekly; adv.
Membership Directory

Membership List Available to Non-members

American Gelbvieh Association *(1971)*
10900 Dover St.
Westminster, CO 80021
Tel: (303) 465-2333 *Fax*: (303) 465-2339
E-Mail: info@gelbvieh.org
Website: gelbvieh.org
Members: 2000 individuals
Staff: 15
Annual Budget: $1-2,000,000
Tax: 501(c)(5)

Personnel:
Director, Administration: Dianne Coffman
  E-Mail: diannec@gelbvieh.org
Contact, Customer Services: Dolores Gravley
  E-Mail: doloresg@gelbvieh.org
Director, Communications: Jennifer Scharpe
  E-Mail: jennifers@gelbvieh.org

Director, Membership Services and Junior Programs: Dana Stewart
  E-Mail: danas@gelbvieh.org

Historical Note:
AGA is dedicated to enhancing member's prosperity through exceptional service and vision. Works towards recording, promoting and improving Gelbvieh cattle. Members are breeders and promoters of Gelbvieh cattle. Membership: $20-175/year.

Meetings/Conferences: Annual
2013 - Denver, CO (Red Lion Hotel on Quebec Street)/ Jan. 9 - 14
Number of non-conference events/year: 2

Publications:
AGA E-Newsletter; adv.
Gelbvieh World; monthly; adv.

The American Gem Society *(1934)*
8881 W. Sahara Ave.
Las Vegas, NV 89117-5865
Tel: (702) 255-6500 *Fax*: (702) 233-6122
TollFree: (866) 805-6500
Website: americangemsociety.org
Members:
3500 individuals and affiliates
1300 retails and 200 suppliers
Staff: 13
Annual Budget: $2-5,000,000
Tax: 501(c)(6)

Personnel:
Executive Director and Chief Executive Officer: Ruth Batson
  E-Mail: rbatson@ags.org
Director, Education: Diane Flora
  E-Mail: dflora@ags.org
Chief Financial Officer: Angela Fry CPA, CSA
  E-Mail: afry@ags.org
Coordinator, Marketing and Technology: Gregory Lyons
  E-Mail: glyons@ags.org
Director, Membership Services: Aashish Shah CG
  E-Mail: ashah@ags.org

Historical Note:
AGS is a professional association of US and Canadian Jewelers. Dedicated to maintain the possible standards of business ethics and professionalism in the jewelry industry.

Continuing Education:
Certification Designation/s: CGA, RJ, DQC, ICGA, CG, GSA

Meetings/Conferences: Annual
2013 - Phoenix, AZ (Arizona Biltmore Resort and Spa)/ April 24 - 27

Publications:
Spectra; quarterly

American Gem Trade Association *(1981)*
3030 LBJ Fwy.
Suite 840
Dallas, TX 75234
Tel: (214) 742-4367 *Fax*: (214) 742-7334
TollFree: (800) 972-1162
E-Mail: info@agta.org
Website: agta.org
Members: 1100 Members
Staff: 9
Annual Budget: $2-5,000,000

Personnel:
Chief Executive Officer: Douglas K. Hucker
  E-Mail: doug@agta.org
Chief Financial Officer: Joan Allen
  E-Mail: joan@agta.org
Manager, Membership Services: Joshua Garcia
  E-Mail: joshua@agta.org
Manager, Management Information Systems: Kelly George
  E-Mail: kelly@agta.org
Manager, Marketing: Adam Graham
  E-Mail: adam@agta.org
Manager, Trade Show: Mary Lou Keen
  E-Mail: marylou@agta.org
Manager, Operations: Kami S. Swinney
  E-Mail: kami@agta.org

Historical Note:
AGTA is a trade association for the colored gemstone industry in the United States and Canada, dedicated to promote the long term stability and integrity of the natural colored gemstone and Cultured Pearl industries through the combined use of educational programs, publicity, industry events, government and industry relations, and printed

materials for both the trade and consumer. *Membership:*
$1,000 (Firm); $350 (Retailer); $300 (Introductory
Member); $50 (Student).

Meetings/Conferences: Annual
Conference Chair: Mary Lou Keen
2013 - Tucson, AZ (Tucson Convention Center)/Feb. 5
 - 10/11-25 exhibitors

Publications:
Prism; weekly; adv.

American Genetic Association *(1903)*
2030 SE Marine Science Dr.
Newport, OR 97365
Tel: (541) 867-0334
E-Mail: agajoh@oregonstate.edu
Website: theaga.org
Members: 1500 institutions and 850 Individuals
Staff: 1
Annual Budget: $500-1,000,000
Tax: 501(c)(3)

Personnel:
Editor: C. Scott Baker
 E-Mail: scott.baker@oregonstate.edu

Historical Note:
Established as the American Breeders Association in
December 1903 in St. Louis by a committee from the
Association of Land Grant Colleges. Name changed in
1913 to the American Genetic Association when it was
incorporated in the District of Columbia. Affiliated with the
American Association for the Advancement of Science. AGA
strives to encourage the study of genetics and its application
to plant and animal improvement and human welfare.
Membership: $20(Student).

Meetings/Conferences: Annual

Publications:
Journal of Heredity

The American Geographical Society *(1851)*
32 Court St.
Suite 201
Brooklyn, NY 11201-4404
Tel: (718) 624-2212 *Fax:* (718) 624-2239
E-Mail: ags@amergeog.org
Website: amergeog.org
Members: 3000 fellows and subscribers
Staff: 4
Annual Budget: $500-1,000,000
Tax: 501(c)(3)

Personnel:
Executive Director: Timothy Heleniak
 E-Mail: timheleniak@amergeog.org
Editor and Manager, Subscription System: Peter Lewis
 E-Mail: pglewis@amergeog.org
Comptroller and Office Manager: Maria V. Rosa
 E-Mail: mvrosa@amergeog.org
Contact, Advertising: James Thomas
 E-Mail: JWThomas@amergeog.org

Historical Note:
Founded in 1851 and incorporated in 1854, in New York
as The American Geographical and Statistical Society,
assumed current name in 1871. AGS's mission is to link
business, professional and scholarly worlds in the creation
and application of geographical knowledge and techniques
to address economic, social and environmental problems.
Membership: $70 (Fellows); $85 (Institutions); $103
(Geographical Review Fellow); $65 (Focus on Geography
Fellow); $121 (Geographical Review Non-fellow); $74
(Focus on Geography Non-fellow).

Meetings/Conferences:
Conference Chair: James Thomas

Publications:
Annals of the Association of American Geographers
Focus on Geography; quarterly
Norwegian Journal of Geography
The Geographical Review; quarterly
The Professional Geographer
Ubique

American Geological Institute *(1948)*
4220 King St.
Alexandria, VA 22302-1502
Tel: (703) 379-2480 *Fax:* (703) 379-7563
E-Mail: agi@agiweb.org
Website: agiweb.org
Members: 46 Geoscientific and Professional
Associations,120000 Geologists and
Geophysicists
Staff: 55

Annual Budget: $5-10,000,000
Tax: 501(c)(3)

Personnel:
Executive Director: P. Patrick Leahy
 E-Mail: pleahy@agiweb.org
Director, Education, Outreach and Development: Ann E.
 Benbow
 E-Mail: aeb@agiweb.org
Director, Technology and Communications: Christopher
 M. Kane
 E-Mail: keane@agiweb.org
Senior Accountant: Katie Pfeifer
 E-Mail: kep@agiweb.org
Contact, Marketing and Advertising: John Rasanen
 E-Mail: jr@earthmagazine.org
Manager, Publications and Marketing: John P. Rasanen
 E-Mail: jr@agiweb.org
Director, Government Affairs: Linda Rowan
 E-Mail: rowan@agiweb.org
Managing Editor: Megan Sever
 E-Mail: msever@earthmagazine.org
Director, Information Systems: Sharon N. Tahirkheli
 E-Mail: snt@agiweb.org

Historical Note:
AGI's mission is to provide information services to
geoscientists, serve in its profession, strengthening
geoscience education, and to increase public awareness
about the geosciences society's use of resources, resilience
to natural hazards, and the health of the environment.
Membership: $10/year (Individual).

Publications:
Earth; monthly; adv.
The Geosciences Newsletter; quarterly

American Geophysical Union *(1919)*
2000 Florida Ave. NW
Washington, DC 20009-1277
Tel: (202) 462-6900 *Fax:* (202) 328-0566
TollFree: (800) 966-2481
E-Mail: service@agu.org
Website: agu.org
Members: 61000 individuals
Staff: 39
Annual Budget: $50-100,000,000
Tax: 501(c)(3)

Personnel:
Executive Director: Christine W. McEntee
 E-Mail: CMcEntee@agu.org
Assistant Director, Books and Publishing Services: Maxine
 Aldred
 E-Mail: MAldred@agu.org
Manager, Education and Public Outreach: Pranoti Asher
 E-Mail: pasher@agu.org
Director, Strategic Communications and Outreach: Ann
 Cairns
 E-Mail: acairns@agu.org
Director, Publications: William J. Cook
 E-Mail: wcook@agu.org
Manager, Advertising and Marketing: Christy Hanson
 E-Mail: CHanson@agu.org
Chief Financial Officer: Mark E. Hernick
 E-Mail: mhernick@agu.org
Director, Human Resources: Michael P. Hoagland CAE,
 SPHR
 E-Mail: mhoagland@agu.org
Manager, Administrative Services: Sue Kauffman
 E-Mail: SKauffman@agu.org
Chief Operating Officer: Frank Krause
 E-Mail: FKrause@agu.org
Public Affairs Manager: Elizabeth Landau
 E-Mail: elandau@agu.org
Controller, Accounting: Tonya McCray
 E-Mail: TMccray@agu.org
Chief Information Officer: Michael O'Brien
 E-Mail: mobrien@agu.org
Assistant Director, Membership Services: Jill Treby
 E-Mail: jtreby@agu.org
Director, Meetings: Brenda L. Weaver CMP
 E-Mail: bweaver@agu.org
Manager, Public Information: Peter Weiss
 E-Mail: pweiss@agu.org

Historical Note:
Incorporated in 1972. AGU's mission is to promote
discovery in earth and space science for the benefit of
humanity. Membership: $20 (Regular/Associate); $7
(Student); $300-600 (Life, one time payment based on
age); $120 (Supporting).

Meetings/Conferences: Annual
Conference Chair: Brenda L. Weaver CMP

Publications:
Geochemistry, Geophysics, Geosystems; daily

American Geriatrics Society *(1942)*
40 Fulton St.
18th Floor
New York, NY 10038
Tel: (212) 308-1414 *Fax:* (212) 832-8646
TollFree: (800) 247-4779
E-Mail: info.amger@americangeriatrics.org
Website: americangeriatrics.org
Members: 6000 individuals
Staff: 36
Annual Budget: $5-10,000,000

Personnel:
Chief Executive Officer: Jennie Chin Hansen
 E-Mail: jhansen@americangeriatrics.org
Assistant, Membership Services: Shirley Burnett
 E-Mail: sburnett@americangeriatrics.org
Manager, Website and Information Technology: Joseph
 Francese
 E-Mail: jfrancese@americangeriatrics.org
Assistant Director, Public Affairs and Advocacy: Alanna
 Goldstein
 E-Mail: agoldstein@americangeriatrics.org
Associate Vice President, Product Development and
 Marketing: Elvy Ickowicz
 E-Mail: eickowicz@americangeriatrics.org
Senior Coordinator, Products, Membership and
 Communications: Christine Polite
 E-Mail: ccampanelli@americangeriatrics.org
Senior Director, Professional Education and Special
 Projects: Linda Saunders
 E-Mail: lsaunders@americangeriatrics.org
Director, Finance and Administration: Phillip Washburne
 E-Mail: pwashburne@americangeriatrics.org

Historical Note:
Founded in Atlantic City, NJ, in 1942. Incorporated in
Rhode Island (1952) and later in New York (1963).
Mission is to improve the health, independence and quality
of life of all older people. Members are licensed physicians
and allied health care professionals whose practice
emphasis is in geriatric medicine and whose interests lie in
geriatric medicine and gerontology. Membership: $180-265
(Full Members); $60-95 (Trainee Members).

Meetings/Conferences: Annual
2013 - Grapevine, TX (Gaylord Texan Hotel and
 Convention Center-Grapevine)/May 3 - 5
2014 - Orlando, FL (Walt Disney World Swan And
 Dolphin)/May 14 - 17
Number of non-conference events/year: 19

Publications:
AGS Newsletter; quarterly
American Journal of Geriatric Pharmacotherapy
Annals of Long-Term Care: Clinical Care and Aging;
 monthly; adv.
Clinical Geriatrics; monthly; adv.
Journal of the American Geriatrics Society; monthly
Membership Directory; on-line

American Glovebox Society *(1986)*
526 SE St.
Santa Rosa, CA 95404-5138
Tel: (707) 527-0444 *Fax:* (707) 578-4406
TollFree: (800) 530-1022
E-Mail: ags@gloveboxsociety.org
Website: gloveboxsociety.org
Members: 300 individuals
Staff: 5
Annual Budget: $100-250,000
Tax: 501(c)(6)

Personnel:
President: Nate Levene
President Elect: Paul Contreras
 E-Mail: pcontreras@lanl.gov
Treasurer: Justin Dexter
Editor: Rodney B. Smith
 E-Mail: bsr@y12.doe.gov
Manager, Advertising: Crissy Willson

Historical Note:
AGS promotes safety and quality of glovebox systems.
Members are companies manufacturing equipment for
remote or safe handling of toxic, radioactive, or infectious
substances. Membership: $75 (Regular); $525 (Sustaining).

Meetings/Conferences: Annual

2013 - Lake Tahoe, NV (Harrah's Lake Tahoe)/July 29
- 31

Publications:
Enclosure; bi-monthly; adv.
Membership Directory; annually; adv.

American Goat Society (1936)
P.O. Box 63748
Pipe Creek, TX 78063-5658
Tel: (830) 535-4247 *Fax:* (830) 535-4561
E-Mail: agsoffice@earthlink.net
Website: americangoatsociety.com
Members: 1570 individuals
Staff: 1
Annual Budget: $50-100,000

Personnel:
Office Manager: Amy Y. Kowalik

Historical Note:
*Merged with the International Dairy Goat Record
Association (1925) in 1937. AGS's mission is to promote
the Dairy Goat Industry and support breeders interested
in maintaining the form and function of purebred dairy
goats. Maintains herdbooks on nine breeds: French Alpine,
Nubians, Saanens, Toggenburgs, Sabla, LaMancha,
Oberhasli, Pygmy and Nigerian Dwarf. Membership: $20
(Individual); $30 (Family); $15 (Senior); $10 (Junior);
$200 (Life).*

Meetings/Conferences: Annual
Number of non-conference events/year: 2

Publications:
Members Hand Book; annually
Roster of AGS Membership; annually
The Voice of AGS; quarterly

American Greyhound Track Operators Association (1987)
Palm Beach Kennel Club
1111 N. Congress Ave.
W. Palm Beach, FL 33409
Tel: (561) 688-5799 *Fax:* (801) 751-2404
Website: agtoa.com
Members: 40 tracks
Staff: 3
Annual Budget: $250-500,000
Tax: 501(c)(6)

Personnel:
President: Ed Braunger
Managing Coordinator: Dennis Bicsak
Counsel: Harold Purnell

Historical Note:
*AGTOA serves the interests of its members, and is the
American member organization of the World Greyhound
Racing Federation. Membership is open to all lawfully
licensed greyhound racetracks, whether they be individuals,
partnerships or corporations.*

Meetings/Conferences: Annual
2013 - Clearwater, FL (Sheraton Sand Key Resort)/Oct.
1 - 3

American Ground Water Trust (1986)
50 Pleasant St.
Concord, NH 03301
Tel: (603) 228-5444 *Fax:* (603) 228-6557
E-Mail: trustinfo@agwt.org
Website: agwt.org
Staff: 4
Annual Budget: $250-500,000
Tax: 501(c)(3)

Personnel:
Executive Director: Andrew Stone
E-Mail: astone@agwt.org

Historical Note:
*AGWT's mission is to protect ground water, promote public
awareness of the environmental and economic importance
of ground water, and provide accurate information to
assist public participation in water resources decisions and
management.*

Meetings/Conferences:
Number of non-conference events/year: 5

Publications:
Groundwater Information; on-line

American Group Psychotherapy Association (1942)
25 E. 21st St.
Sixth Floor
New York, NY 10010

Tel: (212) 477-2677 *Fax:* (212) 979-6627
TollFree: (877) 668-2472
E-Mail: info@agpa.org
Website: agpa.org
Members: 3000 individuals
Staff: 5
Annual Budget: $1-2,000,000
Tax: 501(c)(3)

Personnel:
Chief Executive Officer: Marsha S. Block CAE, CFRE
E-Mail: mblock@agpa.org
Associate, Membership Services and Credentials: Leah
Penney MBA
E-Mail: leahpenney@agpa.org
Director, Professional Development: Angela Moore
Stephens CAE
E-Mail: astephens@agpa.org

Historical Note:
*The American Group Psychotherapy Association is a
dynamic, thriving community of mental health professionals
of all disciplines dedicated to advancing knowledge,
and research, and providing quality training in group
psychotherapy and other group interventions, consultation
and direct services nationally and internationally.
Membership: $140 (Associate/Adjunct/Academic/
Research); $80 (New Professional); $65 (Student).*

Continuing Education:
Enrollment: 50
Certification Designation/s: CGP

Meetings/Conferences: Annual
2013 - New Orleans, LA (New Orleans Marriott Hotel)/
Feb. 25 - March 2

Publications:
Group Connections; monthly; adv.
International Journal of Group Psychotherapy;
quarterly; adv.
The Group Circle; quarterly; adv.
The Group Solution

Membership List Available to Non-members

American Guernsey Association (1877)
1224 Alton Darby Creek Rd.
Suite G
Columbus, OH 43228
Tel: (614) 864-2409 *Fax:* (614) 864-5614
E-Mail: info@usguernsey.com
Website: usguernsey.com
Members: 1427 individuals
Staff: 9
Annual Budget: $500-1,000,000
Tax: 501(c)(5)

Personnel:
Executive Secretary and Treasurer: Seth Johnson
E-Mail: sjohnson@usguernsey.com
*Records Director, Registrations, Transfers and Membership
Services:* Ida Albert
E-Mail: ialbert@usguernsey.com
Manager, Finance: Mary Ann D'Ippolito
E-Mail: mdippolito@usguernsey.com
Editor: Katie Hensen
E-Mail: khenson@usguernsey.com
Programs Coordinator: Brian Schewbly
E-Mail: bschewbly@usguernsey.com

Historical Note:
*Formerly (1877) American Guernsey Cattle Club. AGA's
mission is to provide and advocate programs and services
to enhance the value and profitability of the Guernsey breed
for the members, owners and dairy industry worldwide.
Members are breeders of Guernsey dairy cattle. Maintains
herd registry. Member of the National Pedigree Livestock
Council and the Purebred Dairy Cattle Association.
Membership: $10 (Junior); 150 (Lifetime).*

Publications:
The Guernsey Breeders' Journal; monthly; adv.

American Guild of Hypnotherapists (1975)
2200 Veterans Blvd.
Suite 108
Kenner, LA 70062-4005
Tel: (504) 468-2900 *Fax:* (504) 468-3213
Website: hypnotherapistcollege.com/guild.html
Members: 685 individuals
Staff: 2
Annual Budget: Under $10,000

Personnel:
President: Dr. Reg Sheldrick PhD
E-Mail: drreg@hypnotherapistcollege.com

Historical Note:
*AGH's purpose is to register, on a voluntary basis, persons
offering their services as Hypnotherapists or Professional
Hypnotists, and professionals whose governing bodies allow
the use of hypnosis in their practice. Membership: $50
(Registered Hypnotist); $60 (Registered Hypnotherapist).*

Publications:
Journal of Hypnotherapy
Newsletters

American Guild of Music (1901)
P.O. Box 599
Warren, MI 48090
Tel: (248) 686-1975
E-Mail: agm@americanguild.org
Website: americanguild.org
Members: 6000 individuals
Staff: 1
Annual Budget: $50-100,000

Personnel:
President: Richard Chizmadia
E-Mail: richard.chizmadia@americanguild.org

Historical Note:
*Formerly the American Guild of Banjoists, Mandolinists &
Guitarists. Present name adopted in 1954. AGM's mission
is to advance the study of music and to foster interest in,
promote and advance the artistic, educational, recreational
and commercial position of music of all kinds. Sponsors
regional and national competitions. AGM members are
music teachers, musicians, music retailers, music publishers,
store owners, manufacturers and others interested in
promoting music and music education. Membership: $55
(professional); $80 (Studio/Store); $30 (Professional
Associate); $75 (Music Publisher); $150 (Trade); $20
(College Student).*

Meetings/Conferences:
Number of non-conference events/year: 1-10

Publications:
Allegro Vivo e-newsletter; monthly
Member Directory; on-line
NEWS; quarterly; adv.

American Guild of Musical Artists (1936)
1430 Broadway
14th Floor
New York, NY 10018
Tel: (212) 265-3687 *Fax:* (212) 262-9088
E-Mail: agma@musicalartists.org
Website: musicalartists.org
Members: 6600 individuals
Staff: 20
Annual Budget: $2-5,000,000

Personnel:
National Executive Director: Alan S. Gordon
E-Mail: agmany@aol.com
Director, Operations: Gerry Angel
E-Mail: gerry@musicalartists.org
Supervisor, Membership Department: Candace Itow
E-Mail: candace@musicalartists.org

Historical Note:
*AGMA acts as a bargaining agent for concert musical
artists, opera singers, ballet dancers, modern dancers, and
stage personnel in those fields. Membership: A one-time
initiation fee of $500, plus annual due of $78 and working
dues equal to 2% of the first $100,000 of AGMA income in
any given year.*

Meetings/Conferences: Annual

Publications:
AGMAZINE

American Guild of Organists (1896)
475 Riverside Dr.
Suite 1260
New York, NY 10115
Tel: (212) 870-2310 *Fax:* (212) 870-2163
TollFree: (800) 246-5115
E-Mail: info@agohq.org
Website: agohq.org
Members: 20000 individuals
Staff: 10
Annual Budget: $25-50,000

Personnel:
Executive Director: James E. Thomashower
E-Mail: jet@agohq.org
Manager, Competitions and Educational Resources: Harold
Calhoun
E-Mail: hc@agohq.org
Financial Administrator: Karen Hamilton

E-Mail: hamilton@agohq.org
Editor: Todd R. Sisley
E-Mail: tsisley@agohq.org
Coordinator, Conventions and Meetings: Ronald Stolk
E-Mail: coordinator@ago2010.org
Coordinator, Membership Services: Justin Storms
E-Mail: jstorms@agohq.org
Director, Development and Communications: F. Anthony
Thurman
E-Mail: fathurman@agohq.org

Historical Note:
AGO's mission is to enrich lives through organ and choral music, and to provide a forum for mutual support, inspiration, education, and certification of Guild members. Membership: $92 (Regular/Regular Voting Member); $67 (Special/Partner Independent/Partner Voting Member/ Special Independent Member); $37 (Student/Student Independent Member); $36 (Dual Voting Member); $15 (Student Dual Member); $3000 (Lifetime).

Continuing Education:
Certification Designation/s: AGOC

Meetings/Conferences: Biennial
Conference Chair: Ronald Stolk
2014 - Boston, MA (Boston Marriott Copley Place)/
June 23 - 27
2014 - Boston, MA/June 24 - 27
2016 - Houston, TX (Hilton Americas-Houston)/June
23 - 26
2016 - Houston, TX/July 4 - 7
2018 - Kansas City, MO/July 1 - 5

Publications:
The American Organist Magazine; monthly; adv.

American Guild of Variety Artists (1939)
363 Seventh Ave.
17th Floor
New York, NY 10001-3904
Tel: (212) 675-1003 Fax: (212) 633-0097
E-Mail: agva@agvausa.com
Website: agvausa.com
Members: 5000 individuals
Staff: 19
Annual Budget: $500-1,000,000
Tax: 501(c)(5)

Personnel:
Executive President and Chief Executive Officer: Rod
McKuen
National Controller, Financial Department: Felix
Biberman
Executive Secretary and Treasurer: Susanne K. Doris
E-Mail: sdoris@agvausa.com
Director and Administrator, Membership Services: Lou Ann
Csaszar Salkin
E-Mail: lsalkin@agvausa.com

Historical Note:
AGVA is an autonomous component of Associated Actors and Artistes of America (AFL-CIO). It seeks to represent performing artists and stage managers for live performances in the variety field.

American Gynecological and Obstetrical Society
(2010)
230 W. Monroe
Suite 710
Chicago, IL 60606
Tel: (312) 676-3920 Fax: (312) 235-4059
Website: agosonline.org
Staff: 2
Annual Budget: $100-250,000

Personnel:
Executive Director: Jenna Cummins CMP
E-Mail: jennacummins@agosonline.org
Assistant, Education and Meetings: Mandy Marneris
E-Mail: mandymarneris@agosonline.org

Historical Note:
It was formed through the union of the American Gynecological Society and the American Association Obstetricians and Gynecologists.

Meetings/Conferences: Annual
2013 - Chicago, IL (InterContinental Hotel)/Sept. 18 -
21

American Hackney Horse Society (1891)
4059 Iron Works Pkwy.
Suite A-3
Lexington, KY 40511-8462
Tel: (859) 255-8694 Fax: (859) 255-0177

E-Mail: info@hackneysociety.com
Website: hackneysociety.com
Members: 900 individuals
Staff: 4
Annual Budget: $100-250,000

Personnel:
Secretary: Kathleen M. Barlow
E-Mail: RScrtRhythm@gmail.com
Legal Counsel: Harlan E Judd
Contact, Conventions: Anna Marie Knipp
E-Mail: Jdmamk@aol.com

Historical Note:
AHHS's mission is to advocate the breeding, registering and showing of registered Hackney horses and Hackney ponies. Membership: $50 (Individual); $25 (Junior); $75 (Family); $1,000 (Life).

Meetings/Conferences: Annual
Conference Chair: Anna Marie Knipp
Number of non-conference events/year: 2

Publications:
AHHS Newsletter; quarterly; adv.

Membership List Available to Non-members

The American Hair Loss Council
30 S. Main
Shenandoah, PA 17976
Tel: (570) 462-1101
E-Mail: info@ahlc.org
Website: ahlc.org
Members: 130 members of the hair restoration
industry
Staff: 2
Annual Budget: $25-50,000

Personnel:
Executive Director: Mike Mahoney
E-Mail: info@ahlc.org
Director, Membership Services: Betty Bugden
E-Mail: info@ahlc.org

Historical Note:
AHLC's mission is sorting through information, discovering what works and what doesn't, and presenting findings to the consumer. AHLC members specialize in surgical and non-surgical treatments for progressive or illness-related hair loss. Membership: $375 (Renewals); $425 (New).

Meetings/Conferences: Annual

Publications:
Hair Matters
Member Directory; on-line
The Link

American Hampshire Sheep Association (1889)
222 Main St.
P.O. Box 51
Milo, IA 50166
Tel: (641) 942-6402 Fax: (641) 942-6502
E-Mail: info@hampshires.com
Website: countrylovin.com/ahsa/index.html
Members: 900 individuals
Staff: 3
Annual Budget: $250-500,000
Tax: 501(c)(5)

Personnel:
Managing Editor: Carrie Taylor
E-Mail: heartbeat@hampshires.com

Historical Note:
AHSA is a national organization of registering hampshire sheep in US. Members are breeders and fanciers of Hampshire sheep. Membership: $26.25 (New Senior); $15.75 (New Junior).

Publications:
Hampshire Heartbeat - Newsletter; quarterly; adv.
Membership Directory; annually

American Handwriting Analysis Foundation
(1967)
P O Box 30
Santa Ynez, CA 93460
Tel: (805) 658-0109
E-Mail: ahaf@ahafhandwriting.org
Website: ahafhandwriting.org
Members: 250 individuals
Staff: 5
Annual Budget: $50-100,000
Tax: 501(c)(6)

Personnel:

President: Sheila Lowe CG
E-Mail: ahafpresident@gmail.com
Executive Treasurer: Gerry Shepherd

Historical Note:
AHAF's purpose is to provide information and services to its members with the goal of enriching their effectiveness as handwriting analysts and to educate the public about the handwriting sciences. Membership: $50 (Individual); $60 (Regular Mail Users).

Continuing Education:
Certification Designation/s: CG, CMG

Meetings/Conferences: Annual

Publications:
AHAF Journal; on-line
Directory of AHAF Professionals; on-line
In the Margin; monthly
Member Directory; on-line

American Hanoverian Society (1978)
4067 Iron Works Pkwy.
Suite One
Lexington, KY 40511-8462
Tel: (859) 255-4141 Fax: (859) 255-8467
E-Mail: ahsoffice@aol.com
Website: hanoverian.org
Members: 2000 individuals
Staff: 4
Annual Budget: $250-500,000

Personnel:
Executive Director: Hugh Bellis-Jones
E-Mail: hbj@hanoverian.org
Registrar: Sandy Clevenger
Publications Editor: Terri Ralenkotter
E-Mail: ahs_editor@hanoverian.org
Website Director: Sandra Werkheiser
E-Mail: admin@hanoverian.org

Historical Note:
AHS's goal is to promote and preserve the warmblooded Hanoverian horse in the North American continent. Members own and breed Hanoverian horses. Membership: $80 (Active); $55 (Associate); $25 (Junior); $800 (Life).

Meetings/Conferences: Annual
2013 - San Diego, CA (Hyatt Regency Mission Bay Spa
and Marina-San Diego)/Jan. 18 - 20

Publications:
AHS Services Directory; on-line
The American Hanoverian; quarterly; adv.
The American Hanoverian Breeders' Guide, Stallion
Directory and Mare Book; annually; adv.

American Hardware Manufacturers Association
(1901)
801 N. Plaza Dr.
Schaumburg, IL 60173
Tel: (847) 605-1025 Fax: (847) 605-1030
E-Mail: info@ahma.org
Website: ahma.org
Members: 800 individuals and organizations
Staff: 7
Annual Budget: $500-1,000,000
Tax: 501(c)(6)

Personnel:
President and Chief Executive Officer: Timothy S. Farrell
E-Mail: bfarrell@ahma.org
Vice President, Marketing and Communications: Connie
Dyer
E-Mail: cdyer@ahma.org
Manager, Communications and Editor and Publisher:
Terrence V. Gallagher
E-Mail: tgallagher@ahma.org
Manager, International and Industry Programs: John W.
Hasemann
E-Mail: jhasemann@ahma.org
Manager, Business Applications: Donna R. Liotta
E-Mail: dliotta@ahma.org
Vice President, Finance and Human Relations: Roger A.
Pettinger
E-Mail: rpettinger@ahma.org
Manager, Events: Cookie Walner
E-Mail: cwalner@ahma.org

Historical Note:
AHMA strives to serve the hardware/home improvement industry, seeking ways to bring supply channel partners together to increase industry efficiencies. Members include hardware producers, manufacturers' agents and industry trade publications. Membership: $500 (Regular); $450 (Associate).

Meetings/Conferences:
Conference Chair: Cookie Walner

Publications:
eAGLE; weekly
The Hard Fax International: Home Improvement
    Industry News; weekly
The Hard Fax: Home Improvement Industry News;
    weekly
Washington Report; on-line

American Hardwood Export Council *(1989)*
1825 Michael Faraday Dr.
Reston, VA 20190
Tel: (703) 435-2900 *Fax:* (703) 435-2537
Website: ahec.org
Members: 135 companies
Staff: 2
Annual Budget: $5-10,000,000
Tax: 501(c)(6)

Personnel:
Executive Director: Michael S. Snow
    E-Mail: msnow@ahec.org
Manager, International Programs: An Di H Nguyen
    E-Mail: dnguyen@ahec.org

Historical Note:
*Founded by the merger of Hardwood Export Trade
Council and National Lumber Exporters Association
(1989). AHEC's mission is to give its members a sharp
competitive edge in meeting the growing worldwide
demand for American hardwood products. Represents
companies and trade associations engaged in the export
of a full range of U.S. hardwood products, including -
lumber, veneer, plywood, flooring, molding and dimension
materials. Membership: $1500-7500 (Company Members);
$2600-9000 (Associate Members).*

Publications:
Membership Directory; on-line

American Harp Society *(1962)*
3416 Primm Ln.
Birmingham, AL 35216
Tel: (205) 795-7130 *Fax:* (205) 823-2760
Website: harpsociety.org
Members: 3300 individuals
Staff: 4
Annual Budget: $100-250,000
Tax: 501(c)(3)

Personnel:
Executive Secretary: Ashanti Pretlow
    E-Mail: execsecretary@harpsociety.org
Bookkeeper: Jan Bishop
    E-Mail: ahsbookkeeper@gmail.com
Web Editor: Cheryl Dungan Cunningham
    E-Mail: WebEditor@harpsociety.org

Historical Note:
*AHS strives to foster and cultivate the appreciation of the
harp as an instrument and to encourage the quality of
harp playing, harp composition and harp manufacturing.
Members are professionals, amateurs, folk harpers and all
those who have an interest in the harp. Affiliated with the
World Association of Harpists (Paris, France). Membership:
$50 (Regular); $65 (Regular-Foreign); $35 (Student); $80
(Contributing); $110 (Sustaining); $150 (Sponsor); $200
(Patron); $2,000 (Benefactor); $1,000 (Life).*

Meetings/Conferences: Biennial
2014 - New Orleans, LA (Astor Crowne Plaza New
    Orleans)/June 22 - 25
Number of non-conference events/year: 1

Publications:
American Harp Journal; semi-annually; adv.
Membership Directory; on-line
Regional Newsletters; annually; adv.
Unkle Knuckles Knews

American Head and Neck Society *(1959)*
11300 W. Olympic Blvd.
Suite 600
Los Angeles, CA 90064
Tel: (310) 437-0559 *Fax:* (310) 437-0585
E-Mail: admin@ahns.org
Website: headandneckcancer.org
Members: 1650 individuals
Staff: 2
Annual Budget: $500-1,000,000

Personnel:
President: Mark Wax MD
Treasurer: Ehab Hanna MD

Historical Note:
*The merger of two societies, the Society of Head and Neck
Surgeons (founded in 1954) and the American Society for
Head and Neck Surgery (founded in 1958), formed the
American Head and Neck Society. AHNS's purpose is to
promote and advance the knowledge, prevention, diagnosis,
treatment and rehabilitation of neoplasms and other
diseases of the head and neck. Membership: $300 (Active);
$100 (Associate/Corresponding); $25 (Candidate).*

Meetings/Conferences: Annual
2013 - Grande Lakes, FL (JW Marriott Orlando Grande
    Lakes)/April 10 - 11
2014 - New York City, NY (New York Marriott
    Marquis)/July 26 - 30
Number of non-conference events/year: 1

Publications:
AHNS e-newsletter; monthly
AHNS Newsletter; bi-annually
Otolaryngology - Head and Neck Surgery

Membership List Available to Non-members

American Headache Society *(1959)*
19 Mantua Rd.
Mt. Royal, NJ 08061
Tel: (856) 423-0043 *Fax:* (856) 423-0082
E-Mail: ahshq@talley.com
Website: americanheadachesociety.org
Members: 2400 individuals
Staff: 6
Annual Budget: $2-5,000,000
Tax: 501(c)(3)

Personnel:
Executive Director: Linda McGillicuddy
Editor: John Farr Rothrock MD
Legislative Liaison: Joel R. Saper

Historical Note:
*Formerly (2000) American Association for the Study of
Headache. AHS is a professional society of health care
providers dedicated to the study and treatment of headache
and face pain. Members are healthcare professionals
with an interest in the illness of headache. Membership:
$149-199 (Active); $75 (Associate); $65 (Trainee).*

Meetings/Conferences:
2013 - Scottsdale, AZ (Camelback Inn Resort and Spa)/
    Nov. 15 - 17
2014 - Los Angeles, CA (Hyatt Regency Century
    Plaza)/June 26 - 29
2014 - Scottsdale, AZ (Camelback Inn Resort and Spa)/
    Nov. 14 - 16
2015 - Scottsdale, AZ (Camelback Inn Resort and Spa)/
    Nov. 13 - 15
Number of non-conference events/year: 1

Publications:
AHS Membership Directory; on-line
Headache: The Journal of Head and Face Pain; adv.

American Health and Beauty Aids Institute *(1981)*
P.O. Box 19510
Chicago, IL 60619-0510
Tel: (708) 633-6328 *Fax:* (708) 633-6329
E-Mail: ahbai1@sbcglobal.net
Website: ahbai.org
Members: 11 companies
Staff: 3
Annual Budget: $250-500,000
Tax: 501(c)(6)

Personnel:
Executive Director: Geri Duncan-Jones

Historical Note:
*AHBAI's mission is to encourage and enhance the industry,
develop open lines of communication between members and
allied associations, cosmetologists, suppliers, retailers, the
media. Membership: $950/year (Associate).*

American Health Care Association *(1949)*
1201 L St. NW
Washington, DC 20005-4014
Tel: (202) 842-4444 *Fax:* (202) 842-3860
Website: ahcancal.org
Members: 10000 state licensed facilities
Staff: 93
Annual Budget: $25-50,000,000

Personnel:
President and Chief Executive Officer: Mark Parkinson
Senior Director, Public Relations: Tom Burke
    E-Mail: tburke@ahca.org

Vice President, Public Affairs: Greg Crist
*Director, Conference Programming and Educational
    Development:* Teresa Eyet
    E-Mail: teyet@ahca.org
Senior Vice President, Quality and Regulatory Affairs:
    David Gifford
Director, Convention and Meetings: Marilynn Maury
    E-Mail: mmaury@ahca.org
Director, Human Resources: Paul McGee
    E-Mail: pmcgee@ahca.org
Director, Membership Services: Christy Sharp
    E-Mail: csharp@ahca.org
Legal Counsel: Priscilla Shoemaker
    E-Mail: pshoemaker@ahca.org
Senior Editor: Suzanne Struglinski
    E-Mail: sstruglinski@ahca.org

Historical Note:
*A federation of state associations of health care facilities
formed by a merger of the American Association of Nursing
Homes and the National Association of Registered Nursing
Homes (1949). Formerly (1974) the American Nursing
Home Association. Absorbed (1984) National Council of
Health Centers. AHCA's mission is to provide a spectrum of
patient/resident-centered care and services which nurture
not only the individual's health, but their lives as well,
by preserving their connections with extended family and
friends. Membership: $2,200 (Associate Bronze); $5,500
(Associate Silver); $10,500 (Associate Gold).*

Continuing Education:
Certification Designation/s: QAPI

Meetings/Conferences: Annual
Conference Chair: Teresa Eyet
2013 - Phoenix, AZ/Oct. 6 - 9
2014 - Washington, DC/Oct. 5 - 8
2015 - San Antonio, TX/Oct. 4 - 7
2016 - Nashville, TN/Oct. 16 - 19

Publications:
AHCA Notes; monthly
Capitol Connection; weekly

American Health Information Management Association *(1928)*
233 N. Michigan Ave.
21st Floor
Chicago, IL 60601-5809
Tel: (312) 233-1100 *Fax:* (312) 233-1090
TollFree: (800) 335-5535
E-Mail: info@ahima.org
Website: ahima.org
Members: 61000 individuals
Staff: 130
Annual Budget: $25-50,000,000
Tax: 501(c)(6)

Personnel:
Chief Executive Officer: Lynne Thomas Gordon FACHE,
    MBA, RHIA
Senior Director, Human Resources: Dawn Dennie
Manager, Exhibits: Sarah Lawler CEM
    E-Mail: sarah.lawler@ahima.org
*Senior Vice President, Marketing and Strategic Business
    Development:* Robert Nelson CAE, FACE, MBA
Director, Education: Patt Peterson MA, RHIA
*Vice President, Education and Workforce Development and
    Editor:* William J. Rudman PhD, RHIA
    E-Mail: bill.rudman@ahimafoundation.org
Contact, Public Relations: Bridget Stratton
    E-Mail: bridget.stratton@ahima.org
Manager, Professional Practice Resources: Ann Zeisset
    CCS, CCSP, RHIT
    E-Mail: ann.zeisset@ahima.org

Historical Note:
*Founded as the Association of Record Librarians of North
America, became the American Association of Medical
Record Librarians (AAMRL) in 1938, the American
Medical Record Association in 1970 and assumed its
present name in 1991. AHIMA leads the health informatics
and information management community to advance
professional practice and standards. Membership:
$175-237.50 (Active); $35 (Student); $100 (New
Graduate); $60 (Emeritus).*

Continuing Education:
Enrollment: 6
Certification Designation/s: RHIA, RHIT, CCA, CCS, CCS-
P, CHDA, CHPS, CDI

Meetings/Conferences: Annual
Conference Chair: Sarah Lawler CEM
2013 - Atlanta, GA/Sept. 15 - 20
2013 - Atlanta, GA/Oct. 26 - 30
2014 - San Diego, CA/Sept. 27 - Oct. 2

Publications:
Academic Advisor; quarterly; adv.
AHIMA Advantage; bi-monthly; adv.
AHIMA Advantage E-alert; weekly; adv.
AHIMA Global News; on-line; adv.
AHIMA Resources; monthly; adv.
Certification Connection; quarterly; adv.
CodeWrite; monthly; adv.
ICD-Ten E-Newsletter; monthly; adv.
Journal of AHIMA; monthly; adv.
Long Term Care Insights; quarterly; adv.
Perspectives in Health Information Management; on-line
Student Connection; quarterly; adv.

American Health Lawyers Association (1971)
1620 Eye St. NW
Sixth Floor
Washington, DC 20006-4010
Tel: (202) 833-1100 Fax: (202) 833-1105
E-Mail: info@healthlawyers.org
Website: healthlawyers.org
Members: 10,000 members
Staff: 50
Annual Budget: $5-10,000,000
Tax: 501(c)(3)

Personnel:
Executive Vice President and Chief Executive Officer: Peter M. Leibold Esq.
E-Mail: pleibold@healthlawyers.org
Senior Manager, Communications and Membership Services: Allison E. Beard
E-Mail: abeard@healthlawyers.org
Senior Managing Editor: Bianca L. Bishop Esq.
E-Mail: bbishop@healthlawyers.org
Vice President, Professional Resources: Cynthia Conner
E-Mail: cconner@healthlawyers.org
Director, Information Technology: Maurice Harris
E-Mail: mharris@healthlawyers.org
Vice President, Membership Services and Public Interest: Kerry B. Hoggard CAE, PAHM
E-Mail: khoggard@healthlawyers.org
Vice President, Programs: Anne H. Hoover
E-Mail: ahoover@healthlawyers.org
Marketing and Editorial Administrator: Ana Mayer
E-Mail: amayer@healthlawyers.org
Deputy Executive Vice President and Chief Operating Officer: Wayne Miller
E-Mail: wmiller@healthlawyers.org
Executive and Human Resources Manager: Emily Morris
E-Mail: emorris@healthlawyers.org
Director, Finance: Michele Radell
E-Mail: mradell@healthlawyers.org

Historical Note:
Founded as National Health Lawyers Association, merged with American Academy of Healthcare Attorneys, and assumed its current name in 1998. AHLA's mission is to provide a collegial forum for interaction and information exchange to enable its members to serve their clients in a better manner. Members are private, corporate, government and institutional lawyers involved with or practicing law in the health care field. Membership is available to non-lawyers. Membership: $25-350/year.

Continuing Education:
Certification Designation/s: CLE

Meetings/Conferences: Annual
Conference Chair: Anne H. Hoover
2013 - San Diego, CA/June 30 - July 3

Publications:
AHLA Connections; monthly; adv.
Federal Healthcare Laws and Regulations; irregular
Health Law Digest; monthly
Health Lawyers; weekly
HIT Newsletter; irregular
Membership Directory; on-line
The Journal of Health and Life Sciences Law; quarterly

Membership List Available to Non-members

American Health Planning Association (1972)
Cameron Targeted Solutions
11451 Groves Rd.
New Kanet, VA 23124
E-Mail: info@ahpanet.org
Website: ahpanet.org
Members: 150 organizations
Staff: 2
Annual Budget: $10-25,000

Personnel:
Executive Director: Karen Cameron
E-Mail: kcameron@cvhpa.org

Historical Note:
AHPA strives to promote and improve the community-based health service planning and decision-making. Members are from state, regional and national health planning and other organizations. Membership: $75-500 (Individual); $500 (Organization); $250-500 (Affiliate); $25 (Student).

Publications:
Health Planning Today; quarterly
National Directory; on-line

American Health Quality Association (1973)
1776 I St. NW
Ninth Floor
Washington, DC 20006
Tel: (202) 331-5790 Fax: (202) 331-9334
E-Mail: info@ahqa.org
Website: ahqa.org
Members: 48 institutions and 1200 individuals
Staff: 7
Annual Budget: $1-2,000,000
Tax: 501(c)(6)

Personnel:
Executive Director: Todd D. Ketch
E-Mail: tketch@ahqa.org
Senior Director, Government Affairs and Executive Operations: Bruce Ehrle
E-Mail: behrle@ahqa.org
Director, Communications and Policy: Sofia Kosmetatos
E-Mail: skosmetatos@ahqa.org
Senior Director, Finance and Human Resources: Jacqueline Oglesby Cook
E-Mail: jcook@ahqa.org
Contact, Membership Services: Angela Theofilos
E-Mail: atheofilos@ahqa.org

Historical Note:
Promotes health care quality through community-based, independent quality evaluation and improvement programs.AHQA's mission is to advance quality of care and patient safety nationwide.

Meetings/Conferences: Annual
Number of non-conference events/year: 1

Publications:
Quality Update; bi-weekly

American Heart Association (1924)
7272 Greenville Ave.
Dallas, TX 75231
Tel: (214) 570-5935 Fax: (214) 706-5262
TollFree: (888) 242-2453
Website: heart.org
Members: 29506 Individuals
Staff: 4487
Annual Budget: Over $100,000,000

Personnel:
Chief Executive Officer: Nancy A. Brown
Director, Corporate and Media Communications: Carrie Thacker
E-Mail: carrie.thacker@heart.org

Historical Note:
AHA's mission is to build healthier lives, free of cardiovascular diseases and stroke.

Continuing Education:
Certification Designation/s: CPR, ECC

Meetings/Conferences: Annual
Number of non-conference events/year: 8

Publications:
Arteriosclerosis, Thrombosis, and Vascular Biology; on-line; adv.
Circulation; weekly; adv.
Circulation Research; bi-weekly; adv.
Circulation: Arrhythmia and Electrophysiology; bi-monthly; adv.
Circulation: Cardiovascular Genetics; bi-monthly; adv.
Circulation: Cardiovascular Imaging; bi-monthly; adv.
Circulation: Cardiovascular Interventions; bi-monthly; adv.
Circulation: Cardiovascular Quality and Outcomes; bi-monthly; adv.
Circulation: Heart Failure; bi-monthly; adv.
Hypertension; monthly; adv.
Journal of the American Heart Association; on-line; adv.
Membership Directory; on-line

Stroke; monthly; adv.

Membership List Available to Non-members

American Heartworm Society (1974)
5650 Wooldridge Rd.
Corpus Christi, TX 78414
E-Mail: info@heartwormsociety.org
Website: heartwormsociety.org
Members: 1200 individuals
Staff: 3
Annual Budget: $500-1,000,000

Personnel:
President: Dr. Wallace Graham
E-Mail: wallace.graham@heartwormsociety.org

Historical Note:
AHS's mission is the prevention, diagnosis and treatment of heartworm disease. Members are practitioners and research scientists dedicated to research and dissemination of knowledge about canine heartworm disease. Membership: $55/year.

Meetings/Conferences: Triennial
Number of non-conference events/year: 1

Publications:
AHS Bulletin; quarterly

American Hellenic Educational Progressive Association (AHEPA) (1922)
1909 Q St. NW
Suite 500
Washington, DC 20009-1007
Tel: (202) 232-6300 Fax: (202) 232-2140
E-Mail: ahepa@ahepa.org
Website: ahepa.org
Members: 500 active chapters
Staff: 7

Personnel:
Executive Director: Basil Mossaidis
E-Mail: bmossaidis@ahepa.org
Internet Strategist and Webmaster: Phil Attey
E-Mail: webmaster@ahepa.org
Executive Administrative Assistant: Stephanie Maniatis
E-Mail: stephanie@ahepa.org
Director, Membership Services: Rosalind Ofuokwu
E-Mail: rofuokwu@ahepa.org
Coordinator, Programs: Rory Puckerin
E-Mail: rpuckerin@ahepa.org

Historical Note:
AHEPA is a Greek American association and a major community service organization in North America. The mission of the AHEPA Family is to promote Hellenism, Education, Philanthropy, Civic Responsibility, and Family and Individual Excellence.

Publications:
AHEPA e-News Newsletter; weekly; adv.
The AHEPAN; quarterly; adv.

American Herb Association (1981)
P.O. Box 1673
Nevada City, CA 95959
Tel: (530) 265-9552
Website: jphein.com/ahaherb
Staff: 6

Personnel:
Director and Editor: Kathi Keville
Research Assistant: Beth Baugh

Historical Note:
AHA promotes the understanding and ecological use of medicinal herbs and aromatherapy. Membership: $22 (Regular); $35 (Supporting); $28 (Foreign); $24 (Canadian/Mexican); $4 (Sample Copy of Newsletter).

Publications:
American Herb Association Newsletter; quarterly

American Herbal Products Association (1982)
8630 Fenton St.
Suite 918
Silver Spring, MD 20910-5606
Tel: (301) 588-1171 Fax: (301) 588-1174
E-Mail: ahpa@ahpa.org
Website: ahpa.org
Members: 300 companies
Staff: 6
Annual Budget: $1-2,000,000
Tax: 501(c)(6)

Personnel:
President: Michael McGuffin

E-Mail: mmcguffin@ahpa.org
Chief Science Officer: Steven Dentali PhD
E-Mail: sdentali@ahpa.org
Director, Communications: Frank Lampe
E-Mail: flampe@ahpa.org
Chief Operations Officer: Devon Powell
E-Mail: dpowell@ahpa.org
General Counsel: Anthony Young
E-Mail: ayoung@kkblaw.com
Information Analyst: Merle Zimmermann PhD
E-Mail: mzimmermann@ahpa.org

Historical Note:
A trade association representing manufacturers, distributors, raw material suppliers and service associates of herbal products. AHPA's mission is to promote the responsible commerce of herbal products, maintain and improve market opportunities for companies that sell herbs, herbal products and other health-related products, and to ensure that consumers continue to enjoy informed access to a wide choice of goods. Membership: $1,000-50,000 (Organization); $1,000 (Associate).

Meetings/Conferences:
Number of non-conference events/year: 2

Publications:
Member Directory; on-line
The AHPA Report; monthly; adv.

American Herbalists Guild (1989)
P.O. Box 230741
Boston, MA 02123
Tel: (617) 520-4372
E-Mail: ahgoffice@earthlink.net
Website: americanherbalist.com
Members: 1100 individuals
Staff: 4
Annual Budget: $100-250,000
Tax: 501(c)(3)

Personnel:
President: Karta "K.P." Purkh Khalsa
E-Mail: president@americanherbalistsguild.com
Director, Education and Vice President: Bevin Clare
E-Mail: vice-president@americanherbalistsguild.com
Symposium Coordinator: Alexis Durham
E-Mail: symposium@americanherbalistsguild.com
Treasurer: David N. Harder
E-Mail: david.harder1@gmail.com

Historical Note:
AHG's mission is to encourage the development of high standards of education that promote well-trained professional practitioners who offer high quality herbal care and promote ecological health and increase awareness of issues surrounding plant sustainability. Membership: $120 (Professional); $60-80 (General) $50-70 (Student); $150 (School).

Meetings/Conferences: Semi-Annual
Conference Chair: Alexis Durham

Publications:
Journal of AHG
Newsletter

Membership List Available to Non-members

American Hereford Association (1881)
P.O. Box 014059
Kansas City, MO 64101
Tel: (816) 842-3757 *Fax:* (816) 842-6931
E-Mail: aha@hereford.org
Website: hereford.org
Members: 11000 individuals
Staff: 35
Annual Budget: $2-5,000,000
Tax: 501(c)(5)

Personnel:
Executive Vice President: Craig Huffhines
E-Mail: chuffhin@hereford.org
Editorial Designer and Assistant: Christy Benigno
E-Mail: cbenigno@hereford.org
Director, Communications: Angie Stump Denton
E-Mail: adenton@hereford.org
Chief Financial Officer: Leslie Mathews
E-Mail: lmathews@hereford.org
Chief Operating Officer and Director, Breed Improvement: Jack Ward
E-Mail: jward@hereford.org

Historical Note:
A member of the National Pedigreed Livestock Council and absorbed the American Polled Hereford Association in 1995. AHA's mission is to provide consumers with

consistently tender, juicy and flavorful beef products. Members are breeders of Hereford beef cattle. Membership: $1,000 (Lifetime); $30 (Recording Member); $15 (Adult/Junior).

Meetings/Conferences: Annual

Publications:
Advantage Newsletter; on-line
Cow-Calf; weekly
Hereford eNews; weekly; adv.
Hereford World Magazine; adv.
The Whiteface; on-line
Weekly Sales Digest; weekly; adv.

American Hernia Society (1997)
P.O. Box 4834
Englewood, CO 80155
Fax: (303) 771-2550
TollFree: (866) 798-5406
E-Mail: contact@americanherniasociety.org
Website: americanherniasociety.org
Members: 700 individuals
Staff: 5
Annual Budget: $500-1,000,000
Tax: 501(c)(6)

Personnel:
Executive Director: Carol A. Goddard

Historical Note:
AHS's mission is to provide a professional forum for the exchange of information and education regarding historic, current, and future methods of diagnosis and treatment of abdominal wall abnormalities. Membership: $160 (Active); $25 (Resident/Fellow).

Meetings/Conferences: Annual
2013 - Orlando, FL (JW Marriott Orlando Grande Lakes)/March 13 - 16

Publications:
Hernia Journal; quarterly; adv.

Membership List Available to Non-members

American Highland Cattle Association (1948)
Historic City Hall, 22 S. Fourth Ave.
Suite 201
Brighton, CO 80601-2030
Tel: (303) 659-2399 *Fax:* (303) 659-2241
E-Mail: info@highlandcattleusa.org
Website: highlandcattleusa.org
Members: 1500 individuals
Staff: 2
Annual Budget: $100-250,000

Personnel:
Contact, Membership Services: Nancy Coufal
Manager, Operations: Ginnah Moses

Historical Note:
Formerly (1994) American Scotch Highland Breeder's Association. AHCA's mission is to preserve integrity of the breed, maintain an American breed registry and assisting its members in creating value with their animals. Membership: $80 (US/Canada Individual); $100 (Overseas Individual).

Meetings/Conferences: Annual
2013 - Denver, CO/Jan. 22 - 27

Publications:
Membership Directory; on-line
The Bagpipe Highland Beef Cattle Quarterly; quarterly; adv.

American Highway Users Alliance (1970)
1101 14th St. NW
Suite 750
Washington, DC 20005
Tel: (202) 857-1200 *Fax:* (202) 857-1220
TollFree: (800) 483-4544
E-Mail: info@highways.org
Website: highways.org
Members: 300 companies and organizations
Staff: 2
Annual Budget: $500-1,000,000
Tax: 501(c)(6)

Personnel:
President and Chief Executive Officer: Gregory M. Cohen
E-Mail: gregcohen@highways.org
Project Manager: Daisy Singh
E-Mail: daisysingh@highways.org

Historical Note:
Formed as the Highway Users Federation for Safety and Mobility by the merger of three existing organizations: the National Highway Users Conference (1932), the

Automotive Safety Foundation (1937) and the Auto Industries Highway Safety Committee (1947), assumed its current name in 1995. The American Highway Users Alliance is a nonprofit advocacy organization serving as the united voice of the transportation community promoting safe, uncongested highways and enhanced freedom of mobility. Members are motorists, truckers and businesses who benefit from a safe and efficient national highway system. Membership: $500 (State & Local Advocate); $600 (Small Businesses/State/Regional Highway Users Coalition).

Meetings/Conferences: Annual

Publications:
Driving Ahead
Highway Users in Action

American Hiking Society (1976)
1422 Fenwick Ln.
Silver Spring, MD 20910
Tel: (301) 565-6704 *Fax:* (301) 565-6714
TollFree: (800) 972-8608
E-Mail: info@americanhiking.org
Website: americanhiking.org
Staff: 12
Annual Budget: $1-2,000,000
Tax: 501(c)(3)

Personnel:
President: Gregory A Miller PhD
E-Mail: gmiller@americanhiking.org
Director, Marketing and Development: Margie Cohen
E-Mail: mcohen@americanhiking.org
Director, Government Relations: Sheila Franklin
E-Mail: SFranklin@AmericanHiking.org
Vice President, Programs: Peter Olsen
E-Mail: polsen@americanhiking.org

Historical Note:
AHS's mission is to promote and protect America's hiking trails, the natural areas that surround them, and the hiking experience itself. Membership: $30 (Hiker); $50 (Pathfinder); $100 (Trail Leader); $250 (Explorer); $25 (Seniors/Alliance Clubs); $75-500 (Business); $1,000 (Life); $1,500 (Life-Couple).

Publications:
American Hiker
Newsletter

American Historical Association (1884)
400 A St. SE
Washington, DC 20003-3889
Tel: (202) 544-2422 *Fax:* (202) 544-8307
E-Mail: aha@historians.org
Website: historians.org
Members: 3500 Institutions and 14000 Individuals
Staff: 16
Annual Budget: $2-5,000,000
Tax: 501(c)(3)

Personnel:
Executive Director: Jim Grossman
Manager, Marketing: Kelly Elmore
Assistant Director, Women, Minorities and Teaching: Noralee Frankel
E-Mail: nfrankel@historians.org
Manager, Databases and Information Technology: Vernon Horn
Manager, Membership Services: Pamela Scott-Pinkney
Assistant Director, Research and Publications: Robert B. Townsend
E-Mail: rtownsend@historians.org
Director, Meetings and Administrative Operations: Sharon K. Tune

Historical Note:
AHA works for the promotion of historical studies, collection and preservation of historical documents and artifacts, and dissemination of historical research. Members include K-12 teachers, academics at two and four year colleges and universities, graduate students, historians in museums, historical organizations, libraries and archives, government and business, and independent historians. Membership: $40 (Student); $47-215 (Individual, based on income); $300 (Contributing); $89 (Associate); $50 (Joint Spouse/Partner); $72-103 (K-12 Teacher); $3,500 (Life Member).

Meetings/Conferences: Annual
Conference Chair: Sharon K. Tune
2013 - New Orleans, LA (New Orleans Marriott)/Jan. 3 - 6
2014 - Washington, DC (Washington Marriott Wardman Park)/Jan. 2 - 5

2015 - New York City, NY (Hilton and Sheraton)/Jan. 2 - 5

2016 - Atlanta, GA (Atlanta Marriott Marquis)/Jan. 7 - 10

2017 - Seatle, WA/Jan. 5 - 8

2018 - Washington, DC (Marriott Wardman Park/Omni Shoreham)/Jan. 4 - 7

2019 - New York City, NY (Hilton New York)/Jan. 3 - 6

2020 - New York City, NY (Hilton New York)/Jan. 3 - 6

Publications:

American Historical Review; on-line; adv.

Directory of Affiliated Societies; on-line

Directory of History Departments and Organizations; annually; adv.

Directory of History Journals; on-line

Grants and Fellowships of Interest to Historians; on-line

Perspectives on History; monthly; adv.

The Next Generation of History Teachers; on-line

Membership List Available to Non-members

The American Hockey Coaches Association (1947)

Seven Concord St.

Gloucester, MA 01930

Tel: (781) 245-4177 *Fax:* (781) 245-2492

E-Mail: ahcahockey@comcast.net

Website: ahcahockey.com

Members: 1300 individuals

Staff: 5

Annual Budget: $250-500,000

Personnel:

Executive Director: Joe Bertagna

Membership Administrator: Kathy Bertagna

    E-Mail: ahcahockey@comcast.net

Treasurer: Bruce Delventhal

    E-Mail: bflyfish@earthlink.net

Historical Note:

AHCA's mission is to maintain the standards in hockey, ice hockey, and the hockey profession and to maintain educational standards when coaching the game of ice hockey. Members include professional, junior, high school, and youth hockey coaches, as well as referees, administrators, sales representatives, journalists and fans. Membership: $85 (Allied Member); $25 (Youth- Amateur-High School); $210-340 (Active).

Meetings/Conferences: Annual

Conference Chair: Joe Bertagna

2013 - Naples, FL (The Naples Beach Hotel and Golf Club)/May 1 - 5

Number of non-conference events/year: 2

Publications:

Stops & Starts

American Hockey League (1936)

One Monarch Pl.

Suite 2400

Springfield, MA 01144

Tel: (413) 781-2030 *Fax:* (413) 733-4767

E-Mail: info@theahl.com

Website: theahl.com

Members: 27 clubs

Staff: 13

Annual Budget: $10-25,000,000

Tax: 501(c)(6)

Personnel:

President and Chief Executive Officer: David Andrews

Vice President, Communications: Jason Chaimovich

Director, Finance and Administration: Drew P. Griffin

Vice President, Licensing and Corporate Sales: Sean Lavoine

    E-Mail: slavoine@theahl.com

Executive Vice President, Marketing and Business Development: Chris Nikolis

    E-Mail: cnikolis@theahl.com

Historical Note:

The Canadian-American Hockey League and the International Hockey League merge in 1936, forming the International-American Hockey League. The present name was adopted in 1940. AHL is a professional ice hockey league functioning as a development league for the National Hockey League.

Meetings/Conferences:

2013 - Providence, RI (Dunkin Donuts Center Providence)/Jan. 27 - 28

Publications:

AHL's e-Newsletter

American Holistic Medical Association (1978)

27629 Chagrin Blvd

Suite 213

Woodmere, OH 44122

Tel: (216) 292-6644 *Fax:* (216) 292-6688

E-Mail: info@holisticmedicine.org

Website: holisticmedicine.org

Members: 800 individuals

Staff: 5

Annual Budget: $100-250,000

Tax: 501(c)(3)

Personnel:

Contact, Marketing Communications Intern: Trenton Chavez

    E-Mail: trent@holisticmedicine.org

Marketing Manager: Natalie Talis BA

    E-Mail: natalie@holisticmedicine.org

Administrative Assistant: Sarah Turell BM, MA

    E-Mail: admin@holisticmedicine.org

Historical Note:

Founded as an organization for physicians seeking to practice a broader form of medicine than what was (and is) currently taught in allopathic (MD and DO) medical schools. AHMA attempt toward creating fellowship and collaboration among practitioners and those they work with - bringing an understanding of how the mind, the body and the spirit all have a part to play in healing. Membership: $30 (Student Non-medical, full-time); $150-335 (Doctor); $150 (First-year after residency/Retired/Disabled); $20-50 (Intern/Resident, Medical student); $185 (Practitioner); $50 (Second Office Member); $100 (Friend/Supporter).

Meetings/Conferences: Annual

2013 - St. Louis, MO/April 18 - 21

Publications:

AHMA Newsletter; monthly; adv.

Member Directory; on-line

National Referral Directory; on-line

Membership List Available to Non-members

American Holistic Nurses Association (1981)

323 N. San Francisco St.

Suite 201

Flagstaff, AZ 86001

Tel: (928) 526-2196 *Fax:* (928) 526-2752

TollFree: (800) 278-2462

E-Mail: info@ahna.org

Website: ahna.org

Members: 5700 members

Staff: 14

Annual Budget: $1-2,000,000

Tax: 501(c)(3)

Personnel:

Interim Executive Director: Terri Roberts BSN, JD

    E-Mail: director@ahna.org

Director, Finance: Sandy Donlon

    E-Mail: accounting@ahna.org

Director, Education: Angela Krupica, BS

    E-Mail: education@ahna.org

Director, Communications and Marketing: Rebecca Lara BA

    E-Mail: communications@ahna.org

Editor: Lynne Nemeth

    E-Mail: editor@ahna.org

Director, Membership and Network Services: Shannon Sheffield-Saylor

    E-Mail: membership@ahna.org

Historical Note:

AHNA aims to foster a vital community that advances holistic health and nursing. Holistic nursing is recognized by the American Nurses Association as an official nursing specialty with defined scope and standards of practice. Members are nurses and other holistic healthcare professionals. Membership: $125 (Standard); $75 (Elder); $55-80 (Student); $135 (International); $85 (Recent Graduate).

Meetings/Conferences: Annual

2013 - Norfolk, VA/June 6 - 8

Publications:

Beginnings; bi-monthly; adv.

Connections in Holistic Nursing Research; quarterly

Journal of Holistic Nursing; quarterly; adv.

Member Directory; annually

News from AHNA-eNewsletter; semi-monthly; adv.

Membership List Available to Non-members

American Holistic Veterinary Medical Association (1982)

33 Kensington Pkwy.

P.O. Box 630

Abingdon, MD 21009-0630

Tel: (410) 569-0795 *Fax:* (410) 569-2346

E-Mail: office@ahvma.org

Website: ahvma.org

Members: 900 individuals

Staff: 5

Annual Budget: $500-1,000,000

Tax: 501(c)(3)

Personnel:

Executive Director: Nancy Scanlan DVM

Office Manager: Darlene Worley

Historical Note:

Formerly (1985) the American Veterinary Holistic Medical Association. AHVMA strives to explore and support alternative and complementary approaches to veterinary healthcare. Membership: $0-157/year.

Meetings/Conferences: Annual

Conference Chair: Darlene Worley

2013 - Kansas City, KS (Kansas City Marriott Downtown)/Aug. 24 - 27

2014 - Portland, OR (Red Lion Hotel on the River)/ Sept. 13 - 16

2015 - Augusta, GA (Augusta Marriott at the Convention Center)/Oct. 17 - 20

Publications:

AHVMA Journal; quarterly; adv.

American Holsteiner Horse Association (1978)

222 E. Main St.

Suite One

Georgetown, KY 40324-1712

Tel: (502) 863-4239 *Fax:* (502) 868-0722

Website: holsteiner.com

Staff: 2

Annual Budget: $100-250,000

Personnel:

President: Anke Magnussen

Vice President and Treasurer: Guy Mcelvain

Historical Note:

AHHA's mission is to assist breeders in producing quality horses with Holsteiner bloodlines. Membership: $85 (Full); $850 (Life); $50 (Associate); $35 (Junior).

Publications:

Holsteiner / Impulsion Magazine; quarterly; adv.

American Home Furnishings Alliance (1905)

317 W. High Ave.

Tenth Floor

High Point, NC 27260

Tel: (336) 884-5000 *Fax:* (336) 884-5303

Website: ahfa.us

Members: 400 companies

Staff: 14

Annual Budget: $1-2,000,000

Personnel:

Chief Executive Officer: Andy Counts

Vice President, Communications: Patricia Bowling

    E-Mail: pbowling@ahfa.us

Vice President, Public Relations and Marketing: Jaclyn C. Hirschhaut

    E-Mail: hirschhaut@aol.com

Vice President, Manufacturing, Information Technology, Human Resources, Transportation and Logistics: David Purvis

    E-Mail: dpurvis@ahfa.us

Coordinator, Conferences: Gail Stricklin

    E-Mail: gstricklin@ahfa.us

Historical Note:

AHFA is dedicated to foster the growth and global well being of its member companies. Members are manufacturers of household and international furniture. Membership: $750-3,000 (Supplier); $100-300 (Traditional Retailers); $2,500 (Other Retailers, catalog/internet); $100 (Single Designer/Sales Representative); $300 (Design Firm/Design Showroom); $1,200-44,675 + .04 per thousand in sales over $500,000,001 (Suppliers).

Meetings/Conferences: Semi-Annual

Conference Chair: Gail Stricklin

Number of non-conference events/year: 11

Publications:

Focus on Benefits; quarterly

Human Resources Close-Up; monthly

Suppliers on Demand; quarterly

The Furniture Executive; monthly

American Homebrewers Association *(1978)*
P.O. Box 1679
Boulder, CO 80306
Tel: (303) 447-0816 *Fax:* (303) 447-2825
TollFree: (888) 822-6273
E-Mail: info@brewersassociation.org
Website: homebrewersassociation.org
Members: 30000 individuals
Staff: 40
Tax: 501(c)(6)

Personnel:
Director, Finance: Tom Clark
Coordinator, Membership Services and Events: Kathryn
  Porter Drapeau
    E-Mail: kathryn@brewersassociation.org
Director, Sales and Marketing: Barbara Fusco
Director, Business Administration: Gary Glass
    E-Mail: gary@brewersassociation.org
Director, Events: Nancy Johnson
    E-Mail: nancy@brewersassociation.org
Editor: Jill Redding
    E-Mail: jill@brewersassociation.org
Director, Information Technology: Shane Wood

Historical Note:
*AHA's purpose is to advocate the community of home beer
brewers. Membership is open to everyone. Membership:
$38-97 (U.S. Member, for 1-3 years); $44 (Individual
International); $43-110 (Family, for 1-3 years); $600
(Life).*

Continuing Education:
Certification Designation/s: BJCP

Meetings/Conferences: Annual
Conference Chair: Nancy Johnson
2013 - Philadelphia, PA/June 27 - 29
Number of non-conference events/year: 3

Publications:
Membership Directory; on-line
Zymurgy Magazine; bi-monthly; adv.

Membership List Available to Non-members

American Honey Producers Association
P.O. Box 162
Power, MT 59468
Tel: (406) 463-2227 *Fax:* (406) 463-2583
Website: americanhoneyproducers.org
Staff: 3
Annual Budget: $250-500,000

Personnel:
President: Mark Jensen
    E-Mail: beeguy4jensen@yahoo.com

Historical Note:
*The American Honey Producers Association is an
organization dedicated to promoting the common interest
and general welfare of the American Honey Producer.
Membership: $500 (Commerical); $100 (Sideliner); $50
(Hobbyist); $150 (Associate, Firm / State); $40 (Associate,
Individual).*

Meetings/Conferences: Annual
2013 - San Diego, CA (Sheraton San Diego Hotel and
  Marina)/Jan. 8 - 13

Publications:
Honey Producer magazine; adv.

American Horse Council *(1969)*
1616 H St. NW
Seventh Floor
Washington, DC 20006
Tel: (202) 296-4031 *Fax:* (202) 296-1970
E-Mail: ahc@horsecouncil.org
Website: horsecouncil.org
Members: 1200 individuals and 160
organizations
Staff: 8
Annual Budget: $500-1,000,000

Personnel:
President: James J. Hickey Jr.
    E-Mail: ahc@horsecouncil.org
Director, Administration: Ashley Cole
Director, Communications: Bridget Harrison

Historical Note:
*AHP's mission is to promote and protect the equine industry
by representing its interests in Congress and in federal
regulatory agencies on national issues of importance.
Members are organizations and individuals who need to be
kept informed of tax and regulatory developments affecting
such matters as breeding, racing, showing, pleasure riding,*

*funding of livestock research, import-export restrictions
and similar matters affecting those who live by horses.
Membership: $25-5,000/year.*

Publications:
AHC Newsletter
Horse Industry Directory; on-line

American Horse Publications *(1970)*
49 Spinnaker Cir.
S. Daytona, FL 32119
Tel: (386) 760-7743 *Fax:* (386) 760-7728
E-Mail: ahorsepubs@aol.com
Website: americanhorsepubs.org
Members: 172 Corporate Members, 6 College/
University Members, 18 Student Members, 120
Publication Members, 6 Digital Publication
Members, 55 Equine-Related Website Members,
120 Individual Members
Staff: 3
Annual Budget: $100-250,000
Tax: 501(c)(6)

Personnel:
Executive Director and Contact, Membership Services:
  Christine W. Brune
    E-Mail: ahorsepubs@aol.com
Administrative Assistant and Contact, Publications: Judy
  Lincoln
    E-Mail: ahorsepubs2@aol.com
Webmaster: Christy West
    E-Mail: cmwest@thehorse.com

Historical Note:
*Association of horse-oriented publications in the U.S. and
Canada. AHP's mission is to improve communication and
cooperation through education and networking within
the equine publishing industry. Membership: $110-220
(Publication Member/Individual Member); $100 (Digital
Publication Member); $275 (Equine- Related/College and
University/Nonprofit Corporate); $110 (Associate Equine-
Related/Affiliate/Digital Publication); $385 (Corporate);
$25 (Student).*

Meetings/Conferences: Annual
Number of non-conference events/year: 1

Publications:
AHP For the Record; monthly
AHP Newsletter; adv.
Membership Directory; on-line

American Horticultural Society *(1922)*
7931 E. Boulevard Dr.
Alexandria, VA 22308
Tel: (703) 768-5700 *Fax:* (703) 768-8700
TollFree: (800) 777-7931
Website: ahs.org
Members: 36000 individuals
Staff: 25
Annual Budget: $2-5,000,000
Tax: 501(c)(3)

Personnel:
Executive Director: Tom Underwood
    E-Mail: tunderwood@ahs.org
Events and Facilities Manager: Janet Daniels
    E-Mail: jdaniels@ahs.org
Director, Communications and Editor: David J. Ellis
    E-Mail: dellis@ahs.org
Executive Assistant: Susan Galvin
    E-Mail: sgalvin@ahs.org
*Associate Director, Membership Services and Member
  Programs:* Nora K. MacDonald
    E-Mail: nmacdonald@ahs.org

Historical Note:
*AHS works to provide America's gardeners with better
quality gardening and horticultural education. Members
are individuals, scientific organizations, institutions and
commercial enterprises. Membership: $35 (National); $50
(Sustaining/Dual); $100 (Contributor).*

Meetings/Conferences:
Conference Chair: Janet Daniels

Publications:
Member Directory; on-line
The American Gardener; bi-monthly; adv.

American Horticultural Therapy Association
(1973)
610 Freedom Business Center
Suite 110
King of Prussia, PA 19406
Tel: (610) 992-0020 *Fax:* (610) 992-0021

Website: ahta.org
Members: 800 individuals
Staff: 2
Annual Budget: $100-250,000
Tax: 501(c)(3)

Personnel:
Executive Director: Martha A. Heinze CMP
    E-Mail: martha@ahta.org
Administrative Assistant: Donna Oxford
    E-Mail: donna@ahta.org

Historical Note:
*Formerly (1987) the National Council for Therapy and
Rehabilitation Through Horticulture. AHTA's mission is to
promote and advance the profession of horticultural
therapy. Members are professional therapists, rehabilitation
specialists and others using horticulture for rehabilitation.
Membership: $55-400/year.*

Continuing Education:
Certification Designation/s: HT

Meetings/Conferences: Annual

Publications:
Journal of Therapeutic Horticulture

American Hospital Association *(1898)*
155 N. Wacker Dr.
Chicago, IL 60606
Tel: (312) 422-3000 *Fax:* (312) 422-4796
Website: aha.org
Members: 40000 individuals and 5,000 hospitals,
health care systems, networks, other providers of
care.
Staff: 510
Annual Budget: Over $100,000,000
Tax: 501(c)(6)

Personnel:
President and Chief Executive Officer: Richard
  Umbdenstock
Senior Vice President and Chief Human Resources Officer:
  Lisa Allen
    E-Mail: lallen@aha.org
Senior Vice President and Chief Financial Officer: John
  Evans
    E-Mail: jevans@aha.org
Senior Vice President and General Counsel: Melinda Reid
  "Mindy" Hatton
    E-Mail: mhatton@aha.org
*Executive Vice President, Leadership and Business
  Development:* Neil J. Jesuele
    E-Mail: njesuele@aha.org
*Senior Vice President and President, Health Research and
  Educational Trust:* Maulik S. Joshi
    E-Mail: mjoshi@aha.org
Manager, Marketing and Communications: Mary LaRusso
    E-Mail: mlarusso@aha.org
Senior Vice President, Member Relations: Barbara Z.
  Lorsbach
    E-Mail: blorsbach@aha.org
Senior Vice President, Communications: Alicia Mitchell
    E-Mail: amitchell@aha.org
Executive Vice President, Advocacy and Public Policy:
  Richard J. Pollack
    E-Mail: rpollack@aha.org

Historical Note:
*Formerly(1899) Association of Hospital Superintendents
and changed to AHA in 1906. AHA's mission is to advance
the health of individuals and communities. It represents and
serves all types of hospitals, health care networks, and their
patients and communities. Membership: $500-10,000/year.*

Continuing Education:
Certification Designation/s: CAVS, CMRP, CPHRM, CHC,
CHFM, CHESP

Meetings/Conferences: Semi-Annual
2013 - Washington, DC (Heart House)/April 28 - May
  1
2013 - San Diego, CA (Manchester Grand Hyatt San
  Diego)/July 25 - 27
2014 - Washington, DC (Heart House)/May 4 - 7
2014 - San Diego, CA (Manchester Grand Hyatt San
  Diego)/July 20 - 22
2015 - San Francisco, CA (San Francisco Marriott
  Marquis)/July 23 - 25
2016 - San Diego, CA (Manchester Grand Hyatt San
  Diego)/July 17 - 19
2017 - San Diego, CA (Manchester Grand Hyatt San
  Diego)/July 27 - 29
Number of non-conference events/year: 2

Publications:

AHA Guide and Directory; annually
AHA News; bi-weekly; adv.
AHA News Now; daily; adv.
H&HN Newsletter; daily; adv.
Health Facilities Management; monthly; adv.
Hospitals & Health Networks; monthly; adv.
Trustee; monthly; adv.

American Hotel & Lodging Association (AH&LA)
(1910)
1201 New York Ave. NW
Suite 600
Washington, DC 20005-3931
Tel: (202) 289-3100 *Fax:* (202) 289-3199
E-Mail: eiinfo@ahla.com
Website: ahla.com
Members: 11,000 members
Staff: 60
Annual Budget: $5-10,000,000

Personnel:
President and Chief Executive Officer: Joseph A.
   McInerney CHA
   E-Mail: joe@ahla.com
Executive Vice President, Public Policy: Marlene M.
   Colucci
   E-Mail: mcolucci@ahla.com
Executive Vice President, Political Affairs & PAC Director:
   Lisa Costello
   E-Mail: lcostello@ahla.com
Director, Conventions and Events: Barbara DiRocco
   E-Mail: bdirocco@ahla.com
Director, Membership Services: Sandi Goad
   E-Mail: sgoad@ahla.com
Executive Vice President and Chief Financial Officer,
   President of AH&LEF: Joori Jeon CAE, CPA
   E-Mail: jjeon@ahla.com
Senior Director, Human Resources: Alice Laughlin
   E-Mail: alaughlin@ahla.com
Senior Vice President, Educational Foundation: Michelle
   Poinelli
   E-Mail: mpoinelli@ahla.com
Senior Vice President, Marketing and Communications:
   Kathryn Potter
   E-Mail: kpotter@ahla.com

Historical Note:
*Formerly American Hotel and Motel Association (1962)
and assumed its present name in 2000. AH&LA provides
members with national advocacy on Capitol Hill, public
relations and image management, education, research
and information. It represents sectors and stakeholders in
the lodging industry, individual hotel property members,
hotel companies, student, faculty members, and industry
suppliers. Membership: $1,500 (Allied); $45 (Student);
$250-450 (University/Faculty); $185-530 (International
Property, based on the number of rooms in the property).*

Continuing Education:
Certification Designation/s: CLSD, CHRE, CFBE, CHHE,
CEOE, CHSP, CHRM, CHT, CLSS, CHS, CLSO, HSC, CHA
Meetings/Conferences:
Number of non-conference events/year: 3

Publications:
Action Alerts
Advisories
AH&LA SmartBrief; adv.
Allied eNews; quarterly
Governmental Affairs Issue Briefs
Lodging
Lodging HR; bi-monthly
Media Advisories
Member eNews; monthly; adv.
The Gate; quarterly
WIL Connect; monthly; adv.

American Humor Studies Association *(1975)*
900 Havel Ct.
Charlotte, NC 28211
Website:
   americanhumorstudiesassociation.wordpress.c
Members: 400 individuals
Staff: 4
Annual Budget: Under $10,000
Tax: 501(c)(3)

Personnel:
Executive Director: Janice McIntire-Strasburg PhD
   E-Mail: mcintire@slu.edu
Secretary and Treasurer: Joe Alvarez
   E-Mail: ahsa@carolina.rr.com
Editor: Ed Piacento

E-Mail: epiacent@highpoint.edu
Webmaster: Tracy Wuster
   E-Mail: wustert@gmail.com

Historical Note:
*AHSA seeks to foster and promote study, criticism, and
research in American humor in all its varied aspects. An
allied organization of the Modern Language Association
of America and the American Literature Association.
Membership: $25 (Individual); $30 (Outside United States);
$10 (Graduate Students); $35 (Library/Institutional).*

Publications:
Studies in American Humor

American Hungarian Educators Association
(1974)
4515 Willard Ave.
Apartment 2210
Chevy Chase, MD 20815-3685
Tel: (301) 657-4759
Website: ahea.net
Members: 300 individuals
Staff: 2
Annual Budget: $10-25,000
Tax: 501(c)(3)

Personnel:
Executive Director and Treasurer: Eniko Molnar Basa
   E-Mail: eniko.basa@verizon.net
Editor: Louise Vasvari

Historical Note:
*AHEA is a professional organization devoted to the
teaching and dissemination of Hungarian culture. Provides
opportunities for those interested in Hungarian studies and
Hungarian heritage and works to further Hungarian studies
in American and Canadian universities. Members are
educators concerned with the teaching and dissemination
of Hungarian history, language, literature, art and music.
Membership: $25 (Regular); $40 (Couples/Joint); $10
(Students/Retired).*

Meetings/Conferences: Annual
2013 - New Brunswick, NJ (Rutgers)/May 2 - 5

Publications:
American Hungarian Educators Association
   Newsletters
E-Journal of the American Hungarian Educators
   Association; annually
Membership Directory; on-line

American Hydrogen Association *(1989)*
P.O. Box 4205
Mesa, AZ 85201
Tel: (602) 328-4238 *Fax:* (480) 967-6601
TollFree: (888) 493-7643
E-Mail: contact@clean-air.org
Website: clean-air.org
Members: 6200 individuals
Staff: 8
Annual Budget: Under $10,000
Tax: 501(c)(3)

Personnel:
President: Roy E. McAlister

Historical Note:
*AHA's mission is to test and report options for Civilization
to overcome dependence upon burning over one million
years' of fossil accumulations each year. Membership:
$29-400/year; $1000 (Life).*

Publications:
Hydrogen Today Newsletter; bi-monthly; adv.

American Hypnosis Association *(1972)*
18607 Ventura Blvd.
Suite 310
Tarzana, CA 91356-4158
Tel: (818) 758-2747 *Fax:* (818) 344-2262
TollFree: (800) 479-9464
E-Mail: aha@hypnosis.edu
Website: hypnosis.edu/aha
Members: 1500 individuals
Staff: 6
Annual Budget: $25-50,000

Personnel:
Director: George J. Kappas MA, MFT

Historical Note:
*The American Hypnosis Association (AHA) is a national
association of hypnotherapists. AHA's mission is to
provide continuing education in hypnotherapy and
introduce hypnotherapist to a wide variety of related
topics and specialties. Members are hypnotherapists, other*

*professionals and, private persons interested in hypnosis
and related fields. Membership: $149/year (Individual).*

Continuing Education:
Certification Designation/s: NLP, PLR, RLO, RLT, SS101C,
TIT, WL101
Meetings/Conferences:
Number of non-conference events/year: 25

Publications:
AHA Hypnotherapists Directory; on-line

American Immigration Lawyers Association
(1946)
1331 G St. NW
Suite 300
Washington, DC 20005-3142
Tel: (202) 507-7600 *Fax:* (202) 783-7853
Website: aila.org
Members: 11000 individuals
Staff: 50
Annual Budget: $10-25,000,000
Tax: 501(c)(6)

Personnel:
Executive Director: Crystal Williams Esq.
Director, Education: Grace Akers Esq.
Marketing Associate: Erin Carr
Director, Advocacy: Gregory Chen
   E-Mail: gchen@aila.org
Director, Liaison and Information: Robert P. Deasy Esq.
Director, Publications: Tatia L. Gordon-Troy Esq.
   E-Mail: pubs@aila.org
Legal Editor: Rizwan Hassan
   E-Mail: rhassan@aila.org
Director, Membership Services: Jennifer Lynch CAE
   E-Mail: membership@aila.org
Deputy Executive Director: Susan D. Quarles
   E-Mail: squarles@aila.org
Senior Director, Communications and Outreach: George P.
   Tzamaras
   E-Mail: gtzamaras@aila.org
Senior Director, Human Resources and Administration:
   Theresa A. Waters

Historical Note:
*Formerly (1981) the Association of Immigration and
Nationality Lawyers, AILA seeks to promote justice,
advocate for fair and reasonable immigration law and
policy, advance the quality of immigration and nationality
law and practice, and enhance the professional development
of its members. Members are attorneys practicing in the
field of immigration and nationality law. Membership:
$320-455 (Regular Active/Attorneys); $125 (Non Profit);
$227.50 (Senior/Non-Member International Associates);
$40 (Retired); $50 (Law Student).*

Meetings/Conferences: Annual
2013 - San Francisco, CA (Hilton San Francisco Union
   Square)/June 26 - 29
2014 - Boston, MA (Greater Boston Convention and
   Visitors Bureau)/June 18 - 21
2015 - Ft. Washington, MD (Gaylord National Hotel
   and Convention Center)/June 17 - 20
2016 - Las Vegas, NV/June 22 - 25
2017 - New Orleans, LA/June 21 - 24
Number of non-conference events/year: 2

Publications:
AILA Membership Directory and Resource Guide;
   annually; adv.
AILA's VOICE; on-line

Membership List Available to Non-members

American Import Shippers Association *(1987)*
662 Main St.
New Rochelle, NY 10801
Tel: (914) 633-3770 *Fax:* (914) 633-4041
E-Mail: info@aisaship.com
Website: aisaship.com
Members: 150 companies
Staff: 4
Annual Budget: $1-2,000,000
Tax: 501(c)(3)

Personnel:
Executive Director: Hubert Wiesenmaier
   E-Mail: h.wiesenmaier@aisaship.com
Accounting Manager: Edna Dela Pena
Vice President, Operations: Fred dela Pena
Assistant Vice President, Marketing and Operations: Kurt
   Wiesenmaier
   E-Mail: k.wiesenmaier@aisaship.com

Historical Note:

AISA's mission is to provide small and medium sized U.S. importers and overseas exporters with the leverage to secure discounted ocean freight rates and other freight incentives. Membership: $250/year plus service fee.

Meetings/Conferences: Annual

American Importers and Exporters/Meat Products Group (1955)

One Atlanta Plaza
Elizabeth, NJ 07206
Website: export-import-companies.com
Members: 30 companies
Staff: 3

Personnel:
President: James Chen

Historical Note:
Formerly (1983) Meat Products Group of the American Association of Exporters and Importers and (1992) American Importers Meat Products Group. Members are companies importing pork and pork products into the United States.

Publications:
Business Directory; on-line
Importers Directory; on-line
Membership Directory; on-line

American Independent Business Alliance (2001)

222 S. Black Ave.
Bozeman, MT 59715
Tel: (406) 582-1255
E-Mail: info@AMIBA.net
Website: amiba.net
Members: 30 Independent Business Alliances
Staff: 2
Annual Budget: $100-250,000
Tax: 501(c)(3)

Personnel:
Director: Jennifer Rockne
    E-Mail: jennifer@amiba.net
Operation Manager: Anna Hernandez

Historical Note:
Organized as an outgrowth of the Boulder Independent Business Alliance, AMIBA seeks to help communities establish Independent Business Alliances and to coordinate activities between IBAs nationwide. AMIBA provides resources to IBAs and works with them to help them succeed.

Publications:
Member Directory; on-line
Strength In Numbers; monthly

American Independent Writers (1975)

7817 Evening Ln.
Alexandria, VA 22306
Tel: (703) 660-9336 Fax: (703) 660-9321
Website: amerindywriters.org
Staff: 1

Personnel:
Executive Director: Donald O. Graul Jr.
    E-Mail: donald@aiwriters.org

Historical Note:
AIW's mission is to Create an open and inclusive community of authors, journalists, and other writers. Membership: $100/year (student/seniors); $125/year (Regular).

Publications:
Member Directory
Newsletter; monthly

American Indian Higher Education Consortium (1972)

121 Oronoco St.
Alexandria, VA 22314
Tel: (703) 838-0400 Fax: (703) 838-0388
E-Mail: info@aihec.org
Website: aihec.org
Members: 37 colleges
Staff: 14
Annual Budget: $2-5,000,000
Tax: 501(c)(3)

Personnel:
President and Chief Executive Officer: Carrie L. Billy J.D.
    E-Mail: cbilly@aihec.org
Director, Finance and Administration: Tina Cooper
    E-Mail: tcooper@aihec.org
Vice President, Advocacy: Meg Goetz
    E-Mail: mgoetz@aihec.org

Publisher: Rachael Marchbanks
    E-Mail: rachael@tribalcollegejournal.org

Historical Note:
AIHEC provides leadership and influences public policy on American Indian higher education issues through advocacy, research, and program initiatives; promotes and strengthens Indigenous languages, cultures, communities, and tribal nations.

Meetings/Conferences: Annual
Number of non-conference events/year: 1

Publications:
Tribal College Journal (TCJ)

American Indian Science and Engineering Society (1977)

P.O. Box 9828
Albuquerque, NM 87119-9828
Tel: (505) 765-1052 Fax: (505) 765-5608
E-Mail: info@aises.org
Website: aises.org
Members: 3000 individuals
Staff: 13
Annual Budget: $2-5,000,000
Tax: 501(c)(3)

Personnel:
Interim Chief Executive Officer: Marie Thames
    E-Mail: mthames@aises.org
Officer, Member Services and Communications: Benito Aragon
    E-Mail: baragon@aises.org
Coordinator, Information Services: April Armijo
    E-Mail: aarmijo@aises.org
Assistant Finance Officer: Debby Halterman
    E-Mail: deborah@aises.org
Marketing Officer: Krystal Harlow
    E-Mail: kharlow@aises.org
Director, Business Development: Rozella Kennedy
    E-Mail: rkennedy@aises.org
Administrator, Front Office: Elizabeth McPherson
    E-Mail: emcpherson@aises.org
Director, Member Services, Marketing and Events: Sheryl Wilkeson
    E-Mail: Sheryl@aises.org

Historical Note:
AISES's mission is to increase substantially the representation of American Indian and Alaskan Natives in engineering, science and other related technology disciplines. Membership: $25 (Student); $65 (Professional); (Retiree) $40.

Meetings/Conferences: Annual
Conference Chair: Sheryl Wilkeson

Publications:
Education Newsletter; bi-weekly; adv.
Winds of Change; quarterly

American Indonesian Chamber of Commerce (1949)

317 Madison Ave.
Suite 1619
New York, NY 10017
Tel: (212) 687-4505 Fax: (212) 687-5844
Website: aiccusa.org
Members:
175 companies
50 individuals
Staff: 2
Annual Budget: $100-250,000

Personnel:
President: Wayne Forrest
    E-Mail: wayne@aiccusa.org
Treasurer: Andrew Odell

Historical Note:
The Chamber works to increase business and understanding between the United States and Indonesia and serves organizations and individuals involved commercially with Indonesia. Membership: $7500 (Benefactor); $2500 (Sponsor); $1500 (Regular); $750 (Associate); $175 (Individual).

Meetings/Conferences:
Number of non-conference events/year: 3

American Industrial Hygiene Association (1939)

3141 Fairview Park Dr.
Suite 777
Falls Church, VA 22042
Tel: (703) 849-8888 Fax: (703) 207-3561
E-Mail: infonet@aiha.org

Website: aiha.org
Members:
200 companies and organizations
11600 individuals
Staff: 57
Annual Budget: $10-25,000,000
Tax: 501(c)(6)

Personnel:
Executive Director: Peter J. O'Neil CAE
    E-Mail: poneil@aiha.org
Director, Human Resources: Mary Ellen Brennan
    E-Mail: mbrennan@aiha.org
Chief Financial Officer: Russ Burnett
    E-Mail: rburnett@aiha.org
Manager, Meetings: Susan Dunbar
    E-Mail: sdunbar@aiha.org
Director, Continuing Education: Mary Ann Latko
    E-Mail: mlatko@aiha.org
Senior Manager and Webmaster: Jim Myers
    E-Mail: jmyers@aiha.org
Director, Marketing and Communications: Amita Patel
    E-Mail: apatel@aiha.org
Managing Editor: Ed Rutkowski
    E-Mail: erutkowski@aiha.org
Manager, Membership Services: Adam Seery
Director, Government Affairs: Aaron K. Trippler
    E-Mail: atrippler@aiha.org
Assistant Manager, Meetings: Stephanie Vichness
    E-Mail: svichness@aiha.org

Historical Note:
Formerly (1999) American Academy of Industrial Hygiene. AIHA's mission is to promote the study and control of environmental stresses arising in or from the work place or its products, in relation to the health or well-being of workers and the public. Membership: $10-990/year.

Continuing Education:
Certification Designation/s: CAIH, CSP, CIH

Meetings/Conferences: Semi-Annual
Conference Chair: Stephanie Vichness
Number of non-conference events/year: 4

Publications:
Journal of Occupational and Environmental Hygiene
Membership Directory; on-line

American Inns of Court (1985)

1229 King St.
Second Floor
Alexandria, VA 22314
Tel: (703) 684-3590 Fax: (703) 684-3607
TollFree: (800) 233-3590
E-Mail: info@innsofcourts.org
Website: home.innsofcourt.org
Members: 23,000 professionals
Staff: 13
Annual Budget: $2-5,000,000

Personnel:
Executive Director: BG Malinda E. Dunn USA (Ret.)
    E-Mail: mdunn@innsofcourt.org
Coordinator, Awards and Scholarships: Cindy Dennis
    E-Mail: cdennis@innsofcourt.org
Executive Assistant and Office Manager: Wanda Holmes
    E-Mail: wholmes@innsofcourt.org
Assistant, Membership Records: Howard L. Hurey III
    E-Mail: hhurey@innsofcourt.org
Director, Knowledge Resources: Andrew T. Young
    E-Mail: rzimmerman@innsofcourt.org
Coordinator, Communications: Rita Denniston Zimmerman
    E-Mail: rzimmerman@innsofcourt.org

Historical Note:
AIC's mission is to foster excellence in professionalism, ethics, civility and legal skills. Membership includes judges, lawyers, and in some cases, law professors and law students.

Meetings/Conferences: Annual
Conference Chair: Cindy Dennis
2013 - New Orleans, LA (Hilton New Orleans Riverside)/May 16 - 18

Publications:
Membership Directory; on-line

American Institute for Afghanistan Studies (2003)

Boston University, 232 Bay State Rd.
Room 426
Boston, MA 02215

Website: bu.edu/aias
Staff: 2
Annual Budget: $250-500,000

Personnel:
President: Thomas Barfield
Treasurer: Shah Mahmoud Hanifi

Historical Note:
AIAS's Mission is to improve the quality and quantity of research on Afghanistan by providing logistical and financial support for scholars in the United States, Afghanistan, and elsewhere. Membership: $500 (Institutional); $25 (Individual);

American Institute for Conservation of Historic and Artistic Works *(1973)*
1156 15th St.
Suite 320
Washington, DC 20005-1714
Tel: (202) 452-9545 *Fax:* (202) 452-9328
E-Mail: info@conservation-us.org
Website: conservation-us.org
Members: 3500 individuals
Staff: 13
Annual Budget: $1-2,000,000
Tax: 501(c)(6)

Personnel:
Executive Director: Eryl P. Wentworth
   E-Mail: ewentworth@conservation-us.org
Associate, Development and Education: Abigail
   Choudhury
   E-Mail: achoudhury@conservation-us.org
Communications Manager: Bonnie Naugle
   E-Mail: bnaugle@conservation-us.org
Finance Director: Sandy T. Nguyen
   E-Mail: snguyen@conservation-us.org
Director, Membership Services and Meetings: Ruth Seyler
   E-Mail: rseyler@conservation-us.org

Historical Note:
Formerly (until 1973) an affiliate of the International Institute for Conservation of Historic and Artistic Works, the AIC is a professional organization of conservators, curators, educators, librarians and scientists whose purpose is to disseminate information on conservation, establish and encourage standards of practice, and provide continuing education opportunities for conservators. Membership: $138 (Associate); $65 (Student/Retired); $208 (Institutional); $95 (Interim Year); $140 (JAIC Subscription Only); $15-30 (Specialty groups/Subgroups); $5-20 (Student); plus $30 for foreign postage.

Continuing Education:
Certification Designation/s: CM, CPM, CF

Meetings/Conferences: Annual
Conference Chair: Ruth Seyler
2013 - Indianapolis, IN (JW Marriott Indianapolis)/
   May 29 - June 1

Publications:
AIC Directory; annually
AIC News; bi-monthly
Journal of the American Institute for Conservation; bi-
   monthly

Membership List Available to Non-members

American Institute for CPCU - Insurance Institute of America *(1942)*
720 Providence Rd.
Suite 100
Malvern, PA 19355-3433
Tel: (800) 644-2101 *Fax:* (610) 640-9576
E-Mail: customerservice@TheInstitutes.org
Website: aicpcu.org
Members: 800 companies
Staff: 2
Annual Budget: $10-25,000,000

Personnel:
President and Chief Executive Officer: Peter L. Miller
Senior Vice President: Elizabeth A. Sprinkel

Historical Note:
Formerly (1992) the American Institute for Property and Liability Underwriters. The American Institute for CPCU (AICPCU) and the Insurance Institute of America (IIA) are independent organizations offering educational programs and professional certification to people in the property and liability insurance business. Chartered in 1942, AICPCU administers an education program that leads to the CPCU (Chartered Property Casualty Underwriter) designation. In 1953, the American Institute for CPCU and IIA (the Institutes) merged operations and now function as a single organization. IIA programs offer both general education in

insurance principles and specialist education in particular fields.

Continuing Education:
Certification Designation/s: AIS

Publications:
E-Updates; bi-monthly

American Institute for International Steel *(1950)*
701 W. Broad St.
Suite 301
Falls Church, VA 22046
Tel: (703) 245-8075 *Fax:* (703) 610-0215
E-Mail: phelps@aiis.org
Website: aiis.org
Members: 200 companies
Staff: 3
Annual Budget: $250-500,000

Personnel:
President: David H. Phelps
   E-Mail: phelps@aiis.org
Coordinator , Membership: Alexandra Jopp
   E-Mail: jopp@aiis.org

Historical Note:
AIIS is an information-gathering organization that keeps its members informed concerning trade and tariff legislation and importing concerns. Mission is to support free trade and economic growth in steel. Membership concentrated on the East, West and Gulf coasts. Membership: $8,000 (Regular/ Non-Sales Mills); $1,800 (Associate); $2,500 (Service Centers and Distributors).

Meetings/Conferences: Annual
2013 - New Orleans, LA (Hilton Riverside)/April 9 - 11

Publications:
Newsletter

American Institute for Maghrib Studies *(1984)*
C/O Center for Middle East Studies, 845 N. Park
Ave. Marshall Bldg., Rm. 470
P.O. Box 210158-B
Tucson, AZ 85721-0158
Tel: (520) 626-6498 *Fax:* (520) 621-9257
E-Mail: aimscmes@u.arizona.edu
Website: aimsnorthafrica.org
Members: 250 individuals and institutions
Staff: 1
Annual Budget: $1-2,000,000

Personnel:
Executive Director: Kerry Adams

Historical Note:
AIMS promotes the systematic study of North Africa among interested scholars, specialists, students, and others concerned with the region. Members are individuals and institutions with an interest in the study of the Maghrib region of North Africa. Membership: $40 (Student); $500 (Regular); $75 (Libraries).

Meetings/Conferences: Annual

Publications:
AIMS Newsletter; semi-annually
The Journal of North African Studies; quarterly

American Institute for Medical and Biological Engineering *(1991)*
1701 K St. NW
Suite 510
Washington, DC 20006
Tel: (202) 496-9660 *Fax:* (202) 466-8489
E-Mail: info@aimbe.org
Website: aimbe.org
Members: 50000 individuals
Staff: 4
Annual Budget: $500-1,000,000

Personnel:
Executive Director: Jennifer L. Ayers MPA
   E-Mail: jayers@aimbe.org
Policy Associate: Sean Gallagher
   E-Mail: sgallagher@aimbe.org
Coordinator, Program: Katie Goodman
   E-Mail: kgoodman@aimbe.org

Historical Note:
AIMBE works to ensure appropriate private and public investment to advance medical and biological engineering translational research and innovation.

Meetings/Conferences: Annual
Conference Chair: Katie Goodman
Number of non-conference events/year: 1

Publications:

Membership Directory; on-line

American Institute for Patristic and Byzantine Studies *(1967)*
12 Minuet Ln.
Kingston, NY 12401
Tel: (845) 336-8797 *Fax:* (845) 331-1002
Members: 319 individuals
Staff: 3
Annual Budget: Under $10,000

Personnel:
President: Constantine N. Tsirpanlis

Historical Note:
Promotes research in eastern Patristic literature, history, theology, and culture. Founded as the American Society for Neo-Hellenic Studies; assumed its present name in 1981. Membership: $65/year (individual); $90/year (organization).

American Institute for Shippers' Associations *(1960)*
P.O. Box 33457
Washington, DC 20033
Tel: (202) 628-0933 *Fax:* (202) 296-7374
E-Mail: info@shippers.org
Website: shippers.org
Members: 50 companies
Staff: 1
Annual Budget: $50-100,000

Personnel:
President: William Clark
   E-Mail: bclark@shippers.org

Historical Note:
AISA strives to market the benefits of shippers' associations to the international and domestic shipping community and to establish programs and services that will help shippers' associations have a better profit center.AISA's mission is to market the benefits of shippers' associations to the international and domestic shipping community and to establish programs and services that will help shippers' associations have a better and stronger profit center. Membership: $250-2,500/year (Based on gross revenues).

American Institute of Aeronautics and Astronautics *(1963)*
1801 Alexander Bell Dr.
Suite 500
Reston, VA 20191-4344
Tel: (703) 264-7500 *Fax:* (703) 264-7551
TollFree: (800) 639-2422
E-Mail: custserv@aiaa.org
Website: aiaa.org
Members: 35000 individuals
Staff: 100
Annual Budget: $25-50,000,000
Tax: 501(c)(3)

Personnel:
Executive Director: Sandra H. Magnus
Senior Editor: Heather Brennan
   E-Mail: heatherb@aiaa.org
Manager, Events: Cathy Chenevey
   E-Mail: cathyc@aiaa.org
Deputy Executive Director: Klaus Dannenberg
   E-Mail: klausd@aiaa.org
Director, Business Development: Craig Day
   E-Mail: craigd@aiaa.org
Manager, Exhibits: Chris Grady
   E-Mail: chrisg@aiaa.org
Manager, Public Policy: Steve Howell
   E-Mail: steveh@aiaa.org
Press Contact: Duane Hyland
   E-Mail: duaneh@aiaa.org
Chief Operations Officer and Treasurer: Angelo Iasiello
   E-Mail: angelo@aiaa.org
Marketing Strategist: Dominic Lapus
   E-Mail: dominicl@aiaa.org
Manager, Membership Services: Sonja Moore
   E-Mail: sonjam@aiaa.org

Historical Note:
Technical Professional Association-Aerospace Engineering

Meetings/Conferences:
Conference Chair: Cathy Chenevey
2013 - Daytona Beach, FL (Hilton Daytona Beach
   Resort/Ocean Walk Village)/March 25 - 28
2013 - Boston, MA (Boston Park Plaza Hotel and
   Towers)/April 8 - 11
2013 - San Diego, CA (Sheraton San Diego Hotel and
   Marina)/June 24 - 27

2013 - Vail, CO (Vail Marriott Mountain Resort)/July 14 - 18

2013 - San Jose, CA (San Jose Convention Center)/July 15 - 17

2013 - Los Angeles, CA (Hyatt Regency Century Plaza)/Aug. 12 - 14

2013 - Boston, MA (Boston Marriott Copley Place)/ Aug. 19 - 22

2013 - San Diego, CA (Hilton San Diego Bayfront)/ Sept. 10 - 12

2014 - Pasadena, CA (Pasadena Convention Center)/ May 5 - 9

Number of non-conference events/year: 10

Publications:
AIAA Journal; monthly
Journal of Aerospace Computing, Information, and Communication; monthly
Journal of Aircraft; bi-monthly
Journal of Guidance, Control, and Dynamics; bi-monthly
Journal of Propulsion and Power; bi-monthly
Journal of Spacecraft and Rockets; bi-monthly
Journal of Thermophysics and Heat Transfer; quarterly
Momentum; monthly
Wings of Liberty

Membership List Available to Non-members

The American Institute of Architects *(1857)*
1735 New York Ave. NW
Washington, DC 20006-5292
Tel: (202) 626-7300 *Fax:* (202) 626-7547
TollFree: (800) 242-3837
E-Mail: govaffs@aia.org
Website: aia.org
Members: 80000 individuals
Staff: 177
Annual Budget: $50-100,000,000

Personnel:
Executive Assistant, Government and Community Relations: Robin Stevenson
    E-Mail: rstevenson@aia.org
Vice President, Communications and Marketing: Kathy Compton
Executive Vice President and Chief Executive Officer: Robert Ivy
Manager, Federal Regulatory Relations: Biljana Kaumaya
    E-Mail: bkaumaya@aia.org
Manager, Federal Research and Policy Development: Cooper Martin
    E-Mail: coopermartin@aia.org
Vice President, Government and Community Relations: Paul Mendelsohn
    E-Mail: pmendelsohn@aia.org
Manager, Political Action Committee & Compliance: Wendy Perez Young
    E-Mail: wendyperezyoung@aia.org
Director, Federal Relations and Counsel: Jessica Salmoiraghi
    E-Mail: jessicasalmoiraghi@aia.org
Director, Corporate Sponsorship: Lori Sousa
    E-Mail: lsousa@aia.org
Editor: Stephanie Todd
    E-Mail: stephanietodd@aia.org

Historical Note:
Founded through education, government advocacy, community development, and public outreach activities. AIA serves as the architecture profession and the resource for its members in service to society.
Meetings/Conferences:
Number of non-conference events/year: 10

Publications:
AIArchitect; bi-weekly
Architect Finder; on-line

Membership List Available to Non-members

American Institute of Architecture Students *(1956)*
1735 New York Ave. NW
Washington, DC 20006-5209
Tel: (202) 626-7472 *Fax:* (202) 626-7414
E-Mail: mailbox@aias.org
Website: aias.org
Members: 6200 individuals
Staff: 9
Annual Budget: $1-2,000,000
Tax: 501(c)(3)

Personnel:
Chief Executive Officer: Joshua Caulfield
    E-Mail: executivedirector@aias.org
Contact, Programs and Membership Services: Yuriy Napelenok
    E-Mail: yuriynapelenok@aias.org
Associate, Communications: Amanda Santoro
    E-Mail: amandasantoro@aias.org

Historical Note:
Formerly (1985) Association of Student Chapters, American Institute of Architects and (1958) National Association of Students of Architecture. AIAS is an international organization for college-level students of architecture. The association helps to build interest and enrich the educational experience of students (of all ages) and others in architecture and design and it's mission is to advocate excellence in architecture education, training and practice. Membership: $45/year (Individual).

Meetings/Conferences:
Conference Chair: Yuriy Napelenok
Number of non-conference events/year: 5

Publications:
Crit; semi-annually; adv.

American Institute of Bangladesh Studies *(1989)*
203 Ingraham Hall, 1155 Observatory Dr.
Madison, WI 53706
Tel: (608) 261-1194
E-Mail: aibsinfo@aibs.net
Website: aibs.net
Members: 18 institutions
Staff: 2
Annual Budget: $250-500,000

Personnel:
Manager, Administrative Program: Laura Hammond

Historical Note:
A member of the Council of American Overseas Research Centers (CAORC), AIBS is a consortium of U.S. universities and colleges involved in research on Bangladesh whose mission is to improve the scholarly understanding of Bangladesh culture and society in U.S. and to promote educational exchange between the U.S. and Bangladesh. Membership: $250 (Institution); $25 (Individual Membership).

Publications:
Newsletter

American Institute of Biological Sciences *(1947)*
1900 Campus Commons Dr.
Suite 200
Reston, VA 20191
Tel: (703) 674-2500 *Fax:* (703) 674-2509
TollFree: (800) 992-2427
E-Mail: admin@aibs.org
Website: aibs.org
Members:
200 institutions
5000 individuals
Staff: 51
Annual Budget: $5-10,000,000
Tax: 501(c)(3)

Personnel:
Executive Director: Dr. Richard T. O'Grady PhD
    E-Mail: rogrady@aibs.org
Editor-in-Chief: Timothy M. Beardsley
    E-Mail: tbeardsley@aibs.org
Manager, Education Programs: Susan Musante
    E-Mail: smusante@aibs.org
Manager, Membership and Community Programs: Sheri Potter
    E-Mail: spotter@aibs.org

Historical Note:
Established within the National Academy of Sciences in 1946, incorporated as an independent, non-profit entity in the District of Columbia on January 12, 1955, absorbed the American Society of Professional Biologists in 1969. AIBS is dedicated to advance biological research and education for the welfare of society. Membership: $30-130 (Individual); $1,400-2,000 (Lifetime); $200-500 (Organization).

Meetings/Conferences: Annual
Conference Chair: Susan Musante
Number of non-conference events/year: 1

Publications:
AIBS News; on-line
BioScience; monthly; adv.
Public Policy Reports; bi-weekly

American Institute of Building Design *(1950)*
529 14th St. NW
Suite 750
Washington, DC 20045
Tel: (800) 366-2423 *Fax:* (866) 204-0293
TollFree: (800) 366-2423
E-Mail: info@aibd.org
Website: aibd.org
Members: 1400 individuals
Staff: 6
Annual Budget: $250-500,000

Personnel:
Executive Director: Steven Mickley CPBD
    E-Mail: steve.mickley@aibd.org
President: Dan Sater
    E-Mail: dan.sater@aibd.org
Chair, Membership Division: Paul Cole
    E-Mail: membership@aibd.org
Secretary and Treasurer: Kerry Dick
    E-Mail: kerry.dick@aibd.org
Internal Vice President: Alan Kent
    E-Mail: alan.kent@aibd.org
External Vice President: Viki Wooster
    E-Mail: viki.wooster@aibd.org

Historical Note:
Established in California as United Designers Association, assumed its present name in 1958. AIBD is dedicated to the enhancement, development and recognition of the residential and building design professions. Membership: $420-555 (New Professional); $305-480 (New General); $115-235 (New Educator); $25-50 (New Design Student); $95-545 (New Associate).

Continuing Education:
Certification Designation/s: CPBD, NCBDC

Meetings/Conferences:
Conference Chair: Dan Sater
Number of non-conference events/year: 1

Publications:
DESIGN LINES MAGAZINE; quarterly; adv.
Home Design Professional; monthly

American Institute of Certified Planners *(1978)*
1776 Massachusetts Ave. NW
Suite 400
Washington, DC 20036-1904
Tel: (202) 872-0611 *Fax:* (202) 872-0643
E-Mail: aicp@planning.org
Website: planning.org/aicp
Members: 10000 individuals
Staff: 7

Personnel:
Chief Executive Officer: Paul Farmer FAICP
    E-Mail: ExDir@planning.org
Director, Meetings and Conferences: Deene Alongi
Director, Information Technology: Mark Ferguson
Director, Certification and AICP Membership Programs: Monica Groh
Director, Publications: Sylvia Lewis
Chief Operating Officer and Chief Financial Officer: Ann Simms
Director, Finance: Arlis Withers

Historical Note:
AICP is the American Planning Association's professional institute, providing recognized leadership nationwide in the certification of professional planners, ethics, professional development, planning education, and the standards of planning practice. Membership: $35-110/year.

Continuing Education:
Certification Designation/s: CPC

Meetings/Conferences: Annual
Conference Chair: Deene Alongi
2013 - Chicago, IL (Hyatt Regency Chicago)/April 13 - 16
2014 - Atlanta, GA/April 26 - 29
Number of non-conference events/year: 1

Publications:
Planning; adv.

American Institute of Certified Public Accountants *(1887)*
1211 Avenue of the Americas
New York, NY 10036-8775
Tel: (212) 596-6200 *Fax:* (212) 596-6213
E-Mail: service@aicpa.org
Website: aicpa.org
Members: 350000 individuals

Staff: 791
Annual Budget: Over $100,000,000
Tax: 501(c)(6)

Personnel:
President and Chief Executive Officer: Barry C. Melancon
  E-Mail: bmelancon@aicpa.org
Senior Project Manager, Meetings and Conferences:
  Barbara L. Berman
  E-Mail: bberman@aicpa.org
Vice President, Information Technology: Diana Didia
  E-Mail: ddidia@aicpa.org
Vice President, Human Resources: Patricia Duane
  E-Mail: pduane@aicpa.org
Vice President, Communications and Media Channels:
  Janice Maiman
General Counsel and Secretary: Richard Miller
  E-Mail: rmiller@aicpa.org
Manager, Exhibit Sales: Alan R. Morris
  E-Mail: amorris@morrismarketinginc.com
Vice President, Students, Academics and Membership:
  Jeannie Patton
  E-Mail: jpatton@aicpa.org
Senior Vice President, Government Affairs: Mark G.
  Peterson
  E-Mail: mpeterson@aicpa.org
*Senior Vice President, Finance, Membership Services and
  Operations:* Anthony Pugliese
  E-Mail: athomas@aicpa.org

Historical Note:
*Founded as the American Association of Public
Accountants. Became the Institute of Accountants in the
U.S.A. in 1916 and the American Institute of Accountants
in 1917. Merged in 1937 with the American Society of
Certified Public Accountants. Became the American Institute
of Certified Public Accountants in 1957. AICPA's mission
is to provide members with the resources, information,
and leadership that enable them to provide services in
a professional manner to benefit the public as well as
employers and clients. Membership: $65-550/year.*

Continuing Education:
Certification Designation/s: CPA

Meetings/Conferences:
Conference Chair: Barbara L. Berman
Number of non-conference events/year: 5

Publications:
AICPA News Update; weekly
CPA Letter Daily; daily
Journal of Accountancy; on-line; adv.

American Institute of Chemical Engineers *(1908)*
Three Park Ave.
19th Floor
New York, NY 10016-5991
Tel: (203) 702-7660 *Fax:* (203) 775-5177
TollFree: (800) 242-4363
E-Mail: xpress@aiche.org
Website: aiche.org
Members: 40000 individuals
Staff: 25
Annual Budget: $50-100,000
Tax: 501(c)(3)

Personnel:
Executive Director: June Wispelwey
  E-Mail: junew@aiche.org
Director, Finance, Information Technology and Database:
  Rick Cain
  E-Mail: rickc@aiche.org
Director, Membership and Customer Service: Marty
  Clancy
  E-Mail: martc@aiche.org
Director, Human Resources and Foundation: Cathy Diana
  E-Mail: cathd@aiche.org
Editor-in-Chief: Cynthia Mascone
  E-Mail: cyntm@aiche.org
Director, Marketing: Tim McCreight
  E-Mail: timm@aiche.org
Executive Office Administrator: Susan Newton-Dunn
  E-Mail: susan@aiche.org
Contact, Continuing Education: Jackie Oppenheim
  E-Mail: oppenheimjs@asme.org
Director, Education: Anne Schaeffer
  E-Mail: annes@aiche.org
Director, Meetings: Jeffrey Wood
  E-Mail: jeffw@aiche.org
Director, Information Technology and Database: Steve
  Youn
  E-Mail: stevy@aiche.org

Historical Note:
*Organized on June 22, 1908 in Philadelphia and
incorporated in New York in 1910. AIChE's mission is to
promote excellence in chemical engineering education and
global practice. Membership: $199 (Professional); $100
(Young Professional); $50 (Graduate Student/Unemployed).*

Meetings/Conferences:
Conference Chair: Jeffrey Wood
2013 - Ft. Lauderdale, FL (Hyatt Pier)/Jan. 13 - 16
2013 - San Antonio, TX (The Grand Hyatt)/April 28 -
  May 2
2013 - Frankfurt, Germany (Marriott Frankfurt Hotel)/
  Aug. 26 - 29
2013 - San Francisco, CA (Hilton)/Nov. 3 - 8
Number of non-conference events/year: 5

Publications:
AIChE Activities Directory; on-line
AIChE eLibrary; on-line
AIChExtra; monthly
Membership Directory; on-line

Membership List Available to Non-members

American Institute of Chemists *(1923)*
315 Chestnut St.
Philadelphia, PA 19106-2702
Tel: (215) 873-8224 *Fax:* (215) 629-5224
E-Mail: info@theaic.org
Website: theaic.org
Members: 5000 individuals
Staff: 3
Annual Budget: $50-100,000

Personnel:
Treasurer: Dr. Saligrama Subbarao
  E-Mail: saligrama_subbarao@yahoo.com
Secretary: Rock J. Vitale
  E-Mail: rvitale@envstd.com

Historical Note:
*Incorporated in New York in 1926. AIC's mission is to
advance the chemical sciences and and to emphasize the
professional, ethical, economic, and social status of its
members for the benefit of society as a whole. Membership:
$2500 (Corporate); $3,500 (Charter Corporate Member);
$35 to $150 (Student/Fellow/Member); $70 (Retired).*

Continuing Education:
Certification Designation/s: NCCCCE, CPC, CChE

Meetings/Conferences: Annual

Publications:
The Chemist; quarterly

American Institute of Commemorative Art *(1951)*
Three N. Milpas St.
Santa Barbara, CA 93103
E-Mail: lelandb@monuments-aica.com
Website: monuments-aica.com
Members: 54 firms
Staff: 2
Annual Budget: $50-100,000

Personnel:
Executive Director: Jed A. Hendrickson
  E-Mail: jed@monuments-aica.com

Historical Note:
*AICA's mission is to promote excellence in commemorative
art and to enhance design and professional knowledge
through the exchange of ideas within an atmosphere of
trust. Membership: $400/year.*

Publications:
Member Directory; on-line

American Institute of Constructors *(1971)*
700 N. Fairfax St.
Suite 510
Alexandria, VA 22314
Tel: (703) 683-4999 *Fax:* (571) 527-3105
E-Mail: admin@aicnet.org
Website: professionalconstructor.org
Members: 1000 individuals
Staff: 4
Annual Budget: $500-1,000,000
Tax: 501(c)(6)

Personnel:
Contact, Membership: Kim Capra
Chief Operating Officer: Joseph Sapp
  E-Mail: Joe@professionalconstructor.org

Historical Note:
*AIC works to promote individual professionalism and
excellence throughout the related fields of construction.*

*Membership is free for students and honorary members.
Membership: $0-290/year.*

Continuing Education:
Certification Designation/s: CPC, AICC, AC

Meetings/Conferences:
Conference Chair: Joseph Sapp
2013 - Scottsdale, AZ/April 24 - 27

Publications:
Membership Directory; on-line

American Institute of Engineers, Inc. *(1990)*
4630 Appian Way
Suite 206
El Sobrante, CA 94803-1875
Tel: (510) 758-6240 *Fax:* (510) 758-6240
E-Mail: aie@aieonline.org
Website: aieonline.org
Members: 1250 individuals
Staff: 2

Personnel:
President and Co-Founder: Martin S. Gottlieb

Historical Note:
*AIE's mission is to improve and educate engineers,
scientists, researchers in all disciplines across professional
society. Membership: $100 (One Year); $300 (Supporting
Investment); $ 1,000 (Life Investment).*

Continuing Education:
Enrollment: 1250
Certification Designation/s: CE

Meetings/Conferences:
Number of non-conference events/year: 24

Publications:
AIE Alumni Directory, Statistical (US); biennially; adv.
AIE Geographic Distribution Directory, Statistical (US);
  biennially; adv.
AIE Perspectives; monthly; adv.
Directory of Professionals; annually; adv.
Membership Directory; annually; adv.

American Institute of Fishery Research Biologists *(1956)*
7909 Sleaford Pl.
Bethesda, MD 20814-4625
Tel: (301) 713-2363
Website: aifrb.org
Members: 1000 individuals
Staff: 5
Annual Budget: $10-25,000
Tax: 501(c)(3)

Personnel:
President: Steve Cadrin
  E-Mail: scadrin@umassd.edu
Editor: John Butler
  E-Mail: john.butler@noaa.gov
Webmaster: Tom Ihde
  E-Mail: tom.ihde@noaa.gov
Contact, Membership Services: Tom Keegan
  E-Mail: tkeegan@ecorpconsulting.com
Treasurer: Allen Shimada
  E-Mail: allen.shimada@noaa.gov

Historical Note:
*AIFRB's mission is to enhance conservation and proper
utilization of fishery resources through the use of fishery
and related sciences. Membership: $30 (New Student); $20
(Current Student); $50 (New); $40 (Current/Fellow).*

Publications:
Briefs; bi-monthly
E-Journal; on-line

American Institute of Floral Designers *(1965)*
720 Light St.
Baltimore, MD 21230
Tel: (410) 752-3318 *Fax:* (410) 752-8295
E-Mail: aifd@assnhqtrs.com
Website: aifd.org
Members: 550 individuals and 100 companies
Staff: 10
Annual Budget: $1-2,000,000

Personnel:
Executive Director: Thomas C. Shaner APR, CAE
  E-Mail: aifd@assnhqtrs.com
Director, Communications: Molly Baldwin
  E-Mail: mollybaldwin@assnhqtrs.com
Director, Membership Services: Kelly Mesaris
  E-Mail: kellymesaris@assnhqtrs.com
Bookkeeper: Susan Posluszny

E-Mail: susanposluszny@assnhqtrs.com
Director, Finance and Administration: Monica Shaner
E-Mail: monicashaner@assnhqtrs.com

Historical Note:
AIFD's mission is to advance the art of professional floral design through education, service and leadership, and to recognize the achievement of excellence in this art form. Membership: $275/year (Individual).

Meetings/Conferences: Annual
2013 - Las Vegas, NV (Paris Las Vegas Hotel and Casino)/June 28 - July 2
2014 - Chicago, IL (Hilton Chicago)/July 3 - 8
2015 - Denver, CO (Denver Downtown Sheraton)/June 30 - July 4
Number of non-conference events/year: 1

Publications:
AIFD Focal Points Newsletter; on-line
Membership Directory; on-line

American Institute of Graphic Arts (1914)
164 Fifth Ave.
New York, NY 10010-5900
Tel: (212) 807-1990 *Fax:* (212) 807-1799
E-Mail: robyn-jordan@aiga.org
Website: aiga.org
Members: 20000 individuals and firms
Staff: 19
Annual Budget: $2-5,000,000
Tax: 501(c)(3)

Personnel:
Executive Director: Richard Grefe
E-Mail: grefe@aiga.org
Director, Communications and Marketing: Jennifer Bender
Director, Events: Jonathan Feinberg
Director, Membership Services: George Fernandez
Managing Editor: Rebecca Sears
Director, Special Projects: Heather Strelecki
Chief Operating Officer: Denise Wood

Historical Note:
AIGA works to advance designing as a professional craft, strategic tool and vital cultural force. Members are communication design professions. Membership: $315 (Professional); $230 (Associate); $110 (Full-time faculty); $245 (Group/Person); $95 (Student).

Meetings/Conferences: Biennial
Conference Chair: Jonathan Feinberg
Number of non-conference events/year: 5

Publications:
AIGA Annual; annually
Member Directory; annually

American Institute of Homeopathy (1844)
401 Veterans Memorial Blvd.
Suite 203
Metairie, LA 70005
Tel: (504) 838-9804
E-Mail: admin@homeopathyusa.org
Website: homeopathyusa.org
Members: 150 individuals
Staff: 3
Annual Budget: $25-50,000

Personnel:
President: Irene Sebastian MD, PhD

Historical Note:
AIH is dedicated to the practice, promotion and improvement of homeopathic medicine. The organization places great emphasis on the dissemination of homeopathic medical knowledge through publishing, public speaking and education. Membership: $250 (Regular/Active); $150 (In-Training Active/Associate/Corresponding); $20 (Student).

Continuing Education:
Certification Designation/s: DSC

Meetings/Conferences: Annual
2013 - Chicago, IL (Hyatt Regency Chicago)/Feb. 8 - 10

Publications:
Membership Directory; on-line
The American Journal of Homeopathic Medicine (AJHM); adv.

American Institute of Hydrology (1981)
1230 Lincoln Dr.
Carbondale, IL 62901
Tel: (618) 453-7809 *Fax:* (618) 453-3044
E-Mail: aih@engr.siu.edu
Website: aihydrology.org
Members: 1000 organizations and individuals

Staff: 4
Annual Budget: $50-100,000
Tax: 501(c)(6)

Personnel:
Executive Director: Dr. Rolando Bravo
E-Mail: aih@engr.siu.edu
Vice President, Academic Affairs: John L. Nieber
E-Mail: nieber@umn.edu

Historical Note:
Incorporated in the state of Minnesota. AIH's mission is to enhance and strengthen the standing of hydrology as a science and a profession by establishing standards and procedures to certify individuals qualified in surface-water and groundwater etc. Membership: $150 (Hydrologist/ Hydrogeologist (certified)); $90 (Hydrologic Technician (certified)); $35 (Associate); $100 (Hydrologist-In-Training); $250 (Corporate/Institutional); $75 (Emeritus); Free (Students).

Continuing Education:
Certification Designation/s: HGW, HWQ, HTC, HSW

Publications:
AIH Bulletin; quarterly; adv.
Hydrological Science and Technology Journal

American Institute of Indian Studies (1961)
1130 E. 59th St.
Chicago, IL 60637
Tel: (773) 702-8638
E-Mail: aiis@uchicago.edu
Website: indiastudies.org
Members: 60 institutions
Staff: 2
Annual Budget: $2-5,000,000

Personnel:
U.S. Director: Dr. Elise Auerbach

Historical Note:
AIIS is dedicated to the advancement of knowledge of India and advocation of intellectual eengagement with India in American Colleges and Universities. Members include colleges and universities that support research in the art, archaeology and languages of India. Membership: $2,500 (Class A); $500 (Class B).

Publications:
Membership Directory; on-line

American Institute of Inspectors (1989)
P.O. Box 7243
S. Lake Tahoe, CA 96158
Tel: (800) 877-4770 *Fax:* (530) 577-1407
E-Mail: execdir@inspection.org
Website: inspection.org
Members: 280 individuals
Staff: 4
Annual Budget: $25-50,000

Personnel:
President: Perry Hawkins
Member Director: Larry Stamp
Treasurer: Michael Wicklund

Historical Note:
AII strives to promote professionalism in the inspection industry by certifying qualified individuals as inspectors and is accomplished through approved training and examination of those who apply for certification. Members are residential and commercial building inspectors. Membership: $300/ Year

Continuing Education:
Certification Designation/s: AII

Meetings/Conferences: Annual

Publications:
AAI Newsletter; monthly
Monday Morning Messenger; weekly
Roster; on-line

American Institute of Marine Underwriters (1898)
14 Wall St.
New York, NY 10005
Tel: (212) 233-0550 *Fax:* (212) 227-5102
E-Mail: aimu@aimu.org
Website: aimu.org
Members: 100 companies
Staff: 4
Annual Budget: $1-2,000,000
Tax: 501(c)(6)

Personnel:
President: James M. Craig
E-Mail: jcraig@aimu.org

Director, Financial Services: Frank Costa

Historical Note:
AIMU represents the marine insurance industry as an advocate, educator and information center. Its worldwide network of surveyors (Correspondents) aids its members in handling claims with speed and efficiency. Provides members with current information on maritime matters, media reports, legislation and court decisions. Testifies before congressional committees, works closely with organizations and participates in coalitions focused on improving safety and preventing cargo-related crime. Membership: $1,500 (Associate); $2,500 (Subscriber); $5,000 (Corporate).

Meetings/Conferences: Annual
Number of non-conference events/year: 15

The American Institute of Mining, Metallurgical, and Petroleum Engineers (1957)
12999 E. Adam Aircraft Cir.
Englewood, CO 80112
Tel: (303) 325-5185 *Fax:* (888) 702-0049
E-Mail: aime@aimehq.org
Website: aimehq.org
Members: 4 societies
Staff: 3
Annual Budget: $500-1,000,000
Tax: 501(c)(3)

Personnel:
Executive Director: L. Michele Lawrie-Munro
E-Mail: lawriemunro@aimehq.org
Manager, Information and Communications: Kathi Noland
E-Mail: noalnd@aimehq.org

Historical Note:
Founded in Wilkes-Barre, Pennsylvania as the American Institute of Mining Engineers to 'further the arts and sciences employed to recover the earth's minerals and convert them to useful products', incorporated in 1905, the name was changed in 1919 to the American Institute of Mining and Metallurgical Engineers after absorbing the American Institute of Metals. In 1957 the name American Institute of Mining, Metallurgical and Petroleum Engineers, Inc. was adopted and the Institute was reorganized into constituent societies: Minerals, Metals, & Materials Society; Society for Mining, Metallurgy, & Exploration; Society of Petroleum Engineers; and Iron and Steel Society. In 1985, these societies became separately incorporated, autonomous organizations. These are AIME's "members". AIME supports the advancement of member societies and represents them in the larger engineering and scientific communities. Publications of these societies should be obtained directly from the society in question. Individual or company and honorary membership is available.

Meetings/Conferences: Annual
Conference Chair: L. Michele Lawrie-Munro
2013 - Rio de Janeiro, Brazil/Oct. 8 - 10

Publications:
AIME eNews; quarterly

Membership List Available to Non-members

American Institute of Oral Biology (1943)
P.O. Box 1338
Loma Linda, CA 92354
Tel: (909) 558-4671 *Fax:* (909) 558-0285
Website: theaiob.org
Members: 4 individuals
Staff: 3
Annual Budget: $50-100,000
Tax: 501(c)(3)

Personnel:
President: Shahrokh Shabahang DDS, MS, PhD
Executive Secretary: June J. Barrientos
E-Mail: jbarrientos@llu.edu
Editor: Ted Splaver
E-Mail: theodoresplaver@comcast.net

Historical Note:
AIOB strives to provide a forum to emphasize the application of basic and clinical research to the prevention and treatment of oral disease.

Meetings/Conferences: Annual
Conference Chair: June J. Barrientos

Publications:
AIOB Newsletter; quarterly
Membership Directory; on-line

American Institute of Organbuilders (1974)
P.O. Box 35306
Canton, OH 44735
Tel: (303) 806-9011 *Fax:* (713) 529-2212
E-Mail: execsec@pipeorgan.org

Website: pipeorgan.org
Members: 380 individuals
Staff: 8
Annual Budget: $50-100,000

Personnel:
President: Fredrick W. Bahr
　　E-Mail: bahrman@aol.com
Coordinator, Conventions: David Beck
　　E-Mail: davebeck@sbcglobal.net
Contact, Membership Services: Matthew Bellocchio
　　E-Mail: mbellocchio@verizon.net
Treasurer: Charles Eames
　　E-Mail: crebuzco@aol.com
Contact, Outreach and Exhibits: John Nolte
　　E-Mail: john@nolteorgans.com
Executive Secretary: Robert Sullivan
　　E-Mail: robert_sullivan@ameritech.net
Contact, Education and Website Resources: Bryan Timm

Historical Note:
AIO's mission is to advance science and practice of pipe organbuilding by discussion, inquiry, research, experiment and other means, and to disseminate knowledge regarding pipe organbuilding through lectures, discussion and publication of technical information. Members are individuals professionally engaged in building, servicing and maintaining of pipe organs, including organ company executives, pipe and cabinet makers, and service and maintenance technicians. Membership: $95/year (Individual).

Continuing Education:
Certification Designation/s: AIO

Meetings/Conferences: Annual
Conference Chair: David Beck

Publications:
AIO Journal; quarterly; adv.
Membership Roster; on-line

American Institute of Parliamentarians (1958)
550M Ritchie Hwy.
Suite 271
Severna Park, MD 21146
Tel: (302) 762-1811 Fax: (410) 544-4640
TollFree: (888) 664-0428
E-Mail: aip@aipparl.org
Website: aipparl.org
Members: 1400 individuals
Staff: 4
Annual Budget: $100-250,000

Personnel:
President: Alison Wallis
　　E-Mail: President@aippparl.org
Treasurer: Mary Remson
　　E-Mail: Treasurer@aippparl.org
Editor: Ann Warner
　　E-Mail: Communicator@AIPparl.org
Director, Education: Jeanette Williams
　　E-Mail: education@aippparl.org

Historical Note:
AIP is a not-for-profit educational organization created for the advancement of parliamentary procedure. Members reside in the 50 states, the District of Columbia, Canada, Puerto Rico, and throughout the world. Membership: $20-105/year.

Continuing Education:
Certification Designation/s: CP-T, CPP-T, CP, CPP

Meetings/Conferences: Annual
2013 - Salt Lake City, UT/July 25 - 28

Publications:
Membership Directory; on-line
Parliamentary Journal; quarterly
The Communicator; quarterly

American Institute of Physics (1931)
One Physics Ellipse
College Park, MD 20740-3843
Tel: (301) 209-3100 Fax: (301) 209-0843
E-Mail: aipinfo@aip.org
Website: aip.org
Members:
10 societies
24 affiliates
135,000 scientists, engineers, and educators
Staff: 441
Annual Budget: $50-100,000,000
Tax: 501(c)(3)

Personnel:

Executive Director and Chief Executive Officer: H. Frederick Dylla
　　E-Mail: dylla@aip.org
Treasurer and Chief Financial Officer: Richard Baccante
　　E-Mail: rbaccant@aip.org
Contact, Media and Government Relations: Robert Boisseau
　　E-Mail: rboissea@aip.org
Vice President, Human Resources: Theresa C. Braun
　　E-Mail: tbraun@aip.org
Director, Corporate Communications: Liz Dart Caron
　　E-Mail: lcaron@aip.org
Associate Vice President, Physics Resources Center: Philip "Bo" Hammer
　　E-Mail: hammer@aip.org
Vice President, Publishing: John Haynes
　　E-Mail: jhaynes@aip.org
Director, Business Development: Terence Hulbert
　　E-Mail: thulbert@aip.org
Director, Web Strategy and Management: Jenny Krivanek
　　E-Mail: jkrivane@aip.org
Associate Director, Education: Gary White
　　E-Mail: gwhite@aip.org

Historical Note:
Organized in New York under the leadership of Karl Compton and George Pegram as a means of preserving communication within the community of physicists whose energies were being dispersed into an increasing number of special fields. A federation of ten societies in physics: Acoustical Society of America, American Association of Physicists in Medicine, American Association of Physics Teachers, American Astronomical Society, American Crystallographic Association, American Geophysical Union, American Physical Society, American Vacuum Society, Optical Society of America, and Society of Rheology. Incorporated in New York in 1932. AIP's purpose is to promote the advancement and diffusion of the knowledge of physics and its application to human welfare. Membership: $20 (Individual/Associate); $7 (Student).

Meetings/Conferences:
2013 - Chicago, IL/Jan. 14 - 18
2013 - Denver, CO/Nov. 4 - 8
2014 - Honolulu, HI/Nov. 3 - 7
Number of non-conference events/year: 1

Publications:
AIP Advances; on-line; adv.
AIP History of Physics Newsletter; semi-annually
APL: Organic Electronics and Photonics; monthly; adv.
Applied Physics Letters; daily
Applied Physics Reviews (APR)
Atomic Quantum Fluids; monthly
Biological Physics Research; semi-monthly
Biomicrofluidics; on-line; adv.
CHAOS: An Interdisciplinary Journal of Nonlinear Science; on-line
Computing in Science & Engineering; on-line; adv.
Journal of Applied Physics; daily; adv.
Journal of Chemical Physics
Nanoscale Science & Technology; weekly
Physics Today; on-line; adv.
Quantum Information; monthly
Review of Scientific Instruments; annually; adv.
Technical Physics Letters; on-line
Ultrafast Science; monthly
Virtual Journal of Applications of Superconductivity; bi-monthly; adv.

American Institute of Professional Bookkeepers (1987)
6001 Montrose Rd.
Suite 500
Rockville, MD 20852
Tel: (301) 770-7300 Fax: (800) 541-0066
TollFree: (800) 622-0121
E-Mail: info@aipb.org
Website: aipb.org
Members: 30000 individuals
Staff: 4

Personnel:
Co-President and Executive Director: Stanley I. Hartman
Manager, Educational Support Services: Barbara Regotti
Co-President and Director, Publishing: Stephen Sahlein
Director, Membership Services: Carol Watson

Historical Note:
AIPB's mission is to achieve recognition of bookkeepers as accounting professionals. Membership: $39/year.

Continuing Education:
Certification Designation/s: CB

Publications:
The General Ledger; monthly

Membership List Available to Non-members

American Institute of Professional Geologists (1963)
12000 Washington St.
Suite 285
Thornton, CO 80241-3134
Tel: (303) 412-6205 Fax: (303) 253-9220
E-Mail: aipg@aipg.org
Website: aipg.org
Members: 6000 individuals
Staff: 7
Annual Budget: $1-2,000,000
Tax: 501(c)(6)

Personnel:
Executive Director: William J. Siok
　　E-Mail: wsiok@aipg.org
Administrative Assistant: Dorothy K. Combs
　　E-Mail: dkc@aipg.org
Contact, Professional Services: Catherine L. Duran
　　E-Mail: cld@aipg.org
Contact, Membership Services: Vickie L. Hill
　　E-Mail: vlh@aipg.org

Historical Note:
AIPG, a member of the American Geological Institute, works to strengthen geological science as a profession and to provide continuing education and advocacy programs in support of the profession. Membership: $145 plus section dues (Certified Professional Geologist (CPG); $105 plus section dues (Member); $65 plus section dues (Associate); $500-6,000 (Corporate); $0 (Student); $50 (Young Professional).

Continuing Education:
Certification Designation/s: CPG

Meetings/Conferences: Annual
2013 - Broomfield, CO (Omni Interlocken Resort)/Oct. 23 - 26
Number of non-conference events/year: 3

Publications:
Membership Directory; annually; adv.
TPG Journal; bi-monthly; adv.

American Institute of Steel Construction (1921)
One E. Wacker Dr.
Suite 700
Chicago, IL 60601-1802
Tel: (312) 670-2400 Fax: (312) 670-5403
E-Mail: solutions@aisc.org
Website: aisc.org
Members:
4000 companies
10000 individuals
Staff: 60
Annual Budget: $10-25,000,000
Tax: 501(c)(6)

Personnel:
President: Roger E. Ferch
　　E-Mail: ferch@aisc.org
Vice President, Certifications: Jacques Cattan
Director, Education: Nancy Gavlin
　　E-Mail: gavlin@aisc.org
Director, Membership Services: Carly Hurd
　　E-Mail: hurd@aisc.org
Vice President, Communications: Scott Melnick
　　E-Mail: melnick@aisc.org
Director, Meetings and Conferences: Katey Preston CMP
　　E-Mail: preston@aisc.org
Director, Technical Marketing: Tabitha Stine LEED, PE, SE
　　E-Mail: stine@aisc.org

Historical Note:
AISC's mission is to make structural steel the material of choice for new structures. Membership: $137-550 (Full); $135-1,000 (Professional/Affiliate); $275-5,000 (Associate).

Meetings/Conferences: Annual
Conference Chair: Katey Preston CMP

Publications:
Engineering Journal; quarterly
Modern Steel Construction Magazine; monthly; adv.

American Institute of Stress (1978)
9112 Camp Bowie W. Blvd.
Suite 228
Fort Worth, TX 76116

Tel: (682) 239-6823 Fax: (817) 394-0593
E-Mail: stress125@optonline.net
Website: stress.org
Members: 5000 individuals
Staff: 4
Annual Budget: $25-50,000
Tax: 501(c)(3)

Personnel:
Executive Director: Kellie Marksberry
    E-Mail: kmarksberry@stress.org
Founder and Chairman: Paul J. Rosch FACP, MA, MD

Historical Note:
AIS is a multidisciplinary professional society composed of health professionals, academics and others with an interest in study of stress and its treatment. AIS's mission is to advance understanding of stress in health and illness. Membership: $100 (Fellow); $75 (Associate); $1000 (Sponsor); $100 (Sustaining).

Continuing Education:
Certification Designation/s: AIS

Meetings/Conferences: Annual

Publications:
Newsletter; monthly

American Institute of the History of Pharmacy
(1941)
777 Highland Ave.
Madison, WI 53705-2222
Tel: (608) 262-6234 Fax: (608) 262-3943
E-Mail: aihp@aihp.org
Website: pharmacy.wisc.edu/aihp
Members: 1000 individuals
Staff: 3
Annual Budget: $500-1,000,000
Tax: 501(c)(3)

Personnel:
Executive Director: Gregory J. Higby PhD

Historical Note:
AIHP fosters investigations, publications, teaching, and interest in the history of pharmacy; collects historical records and makes them available; and sponsors awards and educational grants. Membership: $50 (Regular); $20 (Student); $35 (Retired); $100 (Organization/Company); $350 (Patron); $1000 (Sponsor).

Continuing Education:
Certification Designation/s: SCP

Meetings/Conferences: Annual

Publications:
American Journal of Pharmaceutical Education
DISCOVERx Magazine
Email Listserv Directory; on-line
Faculty/Staff Internal User Directory; on-line
Membership Directory; on-line
New England Journal of Medicine
Newsletter; monthly

American Institute of Timber Construction
(1952)
7012 S. Revere Pkwy.
Suite 140
Centennial, CO 80112-3932
Tel: (303) 792-9559 Fax: (303) 792-0669
E-Mail: info@aitc-glulam.org
Website: aitc-glulam.org
Members: 510 companies and individuals
Staff: 7
Annual Budget: $500-1,000,000

Personnel:
Executive Vice President: Michael R. Caldwell PE
    E-Mail: rmc@aite-glulam.org
Director, Inspections Bureau: Ron Goff PE
    E-Mail: rgoff@aitc-glulam.org
Director, Technical Services: Jeffrey Linville PE
    E-Mail: linville@aitc-glulam.org
Manager, Accounts: Shirl V. Sieli
    E-Mail: svs@aitc-glulam.org

Historical Note:
AITC's mission is to educate and support small non-industrial forest landowners. Members are manufacturers and erectors of laminated structural timber and engineers, architects and other professionals involved in timber construction. Membership: $505 (Supplier); $155 (Associate); $55 (Professional); $30 (Student).

Continuing Education:
Certification Designation/s: IACET

American Institute of Ultrasound in Medicine
(1951)
14750 Sweitzer Ln.
Suite 100
Laurel, MD 20707-5906
Tel: (301) 498-4100 Fax: (301) 498-4450
TollFree: (800) 638-5352
E-Mail: info@aium.org
Website: aium.org
Members: 10000 individuals
Staff: 29
Annual Budget: $5-10,000,000
Tax: 501(c)(3)

Personnel:
Chief Executive Officer: Carmine. M Valente PhD, CAE
    E-Mail: cvalente@aium.org
Communications Specialist: Erin Chrapaty
    E-Mail: echrapaty@aium.org
Director, Professional Development: Jenny Clark
    E-Mail: jclark@aium.org
Director, Membership and Marketing: Jennifer Costello
    E-Mail: jcostello@aium.org
Manager, Publications: Lexie Cowger
    E-Mail: lcowger@aium.org
Chief Financial Officer: Diane Eberle
    E-Mail: deberle@aium.org
Secretary: Brian J. Fowlkes PhD
Director, Committees, Publications and Information
    Technology: Glynis Harvey
    E-Mail: gharvey@aium.org
Manager, Conventions: Brenda Kinney
    E-Mail: bkinney@aium.org
Director, Accreditation and Clinical Affairs: Paula Woletz
    E-Mail: pwoletz@aium.org

Historical Note:
AIUM's mission is to advance the safe and effective use of ultrasound in medicine through professional and public education, research, development of guidelines, and accreditation. Membership: $25-325/year.

Meetings/Conferences: Annual
Conference Chair: Brenda Kinney
2013 - New York City, NY (New York Marriott
    Downtown)/April 6 - 10/2000 attendees
2014 - Las Vegas, NV/March 29 - April 2
2015 - Orlando, FL/March 21 - 25
2016 - Las Vegas, NV/March 19 - 23
2016 - Las Vegas, NV/March 20 - 24
2017 - Orlando, FL/March 25 - 29
2018 - Las Vegas, NV/March 17 - 21
Number of non-conference events/year: 1

Publications:
Journal of Ultrasound in Medicine; monthly; adv.
Member Directory
New Member Newsletter; adv.
Sound Waves Newsletter; weekly

American Institutes for Research (1946)
1000 Thomas Jefferson St. NW
Washington, DC 20007-3835
Tel: (202) 403-5000 Fax: (202) 403-5454
TollFree: (877) 334-3499
Website: air.org
Staff: 23
Annual Budget: Over $100,000,000

Personnel:
President and Chief Executive Officer: David Myers
Senior Vice President and Chief Financial Officer: Marijo
    Ahlgrimm
Vice President, Communications and Public Affairs:
    Kathleen Courrier
Senior Vice President, Human Resources and
    Administration: Mark Fanning
Vice President, Education Research Program: Jane
    Hannaway
Vice President, Information Technology: Robert Holstein
Contact, General Counsel, Ethics Officer, and Board of
    Directors Secretary: Dona Kilpatrick
Director, Public Affairs: Larry McQuillan
Contact, Communications Strategist: Patrick R. Riccards

Historical Note:
AIR's mission is to conduct and apply the best behavioral and social science research and evaluation towards improving peoples' lives, with a special emphasis on the disadvantaged.

Publications:
CALDER; on-line

American Insurance Association (1964)
2101 L St. NW
Suite 400
Washington, DC 20037
Tel: (202) 828-7100 Fax: (202) 293-1219
E-Mail: info@aiadc.org
Website: aiadc.org
Members: 300 insurers
Staff: 120
Annual Budget: $10-25,000,000
Tax: 501(c)(6)

Personnel:
President and Chief Executive Officer: Leigh Ann Pusey
    E-Mail: Lpusey@aiadc.org
Manager, Membership Services: Joanne Brodt
    E-Mail: jbrodt@aiadc.org
Senior Vice President and General Counsel: J. Stephen
    Zielezienski

Historical Note:
Formed by a merger of the National Board of Fire Underwriters (1866), the Association of Casualty and Surety Companies (1927) and the old American Insurance Association (1953). AIA's mission is to advance the interests of its member companies in the public policy arena by providing communications and effective grassroots support to AIA and individual company programs. Membership fee based on market share.

Publications:
AIA E-Bulletin; on-line

American Insurance Marketing and Sales Society
(1968)
P.O. Box 35718
Richmond, VA 23235
Tel: (804) 674-6466 Fax: (703) 579-8896
TollFree: (877) 674-2742
E-Mail: info@aimssociety.org
Website: aimssociety.org
Members: 500 individuals
Staff: 2
Annual Budget: $100-250,000
Tax: 501(c)(6)

Personnel:
Executive Director: Kitty Ambers
    E-Mail: kitty@aimssociety.org

Historical Note:
Formerly Certified Professional Insurance Agents Society, assumed its current name in 2004. AIMS works to provide marketing and sales training and tools to property/casualty insurance agency owners, producers, support staff and insurance company personnel. Membership is open to anyone in the insurance industry. Membership: $95 (e-associate); $225 (Individual/Designee); $750-1,175 (Agency).

Continuing Education:
Certification Designation/s: CPIA

Meetings/Conferences: Annual
Number of non-conference events/year: 1

Publications:
Agency Ideas; annually
Extras; on-line
Membership Directory; on-line
Quik Sales Tip and Bright Ideas; on-line
Regular Sales, Marketing, Management and
    Motivational Tips; on-line

American Intellectual Property Law Association
(1897)
241 18th St. South
Suite 700
Arlington, VA 22202
Tel: (703) 415-0780 Fax: (703) 415-0786
E-Mail: aipla@aipla.org
Website: aipla.org
Members: 17000 individuals
Staff: 23
Annual Budget: $5-10,000,000

Personnel:
Executive Director: Q. Todd Dickinson
Deputy Executive Director: Vincent E. Garlock
    E-Mail: vgarlock@aipla.org
Director, Meetings and Events: Cathleen Clime
    E-Mail: cathleen@aipla.org
Director, Legal Affairs: James Crowne
    E-Mail: jcrowne@aipla.org
Manager, Membership Services: Bill Durante
    E-Mail: MemberServices@aipla.org

Coordinator, Online Continuing Legal Education and Communications: Wosene Gurmu
Director, Finance and Accounting: Pa Jallow
Director, Marketing and Communications: Lorri Ragan
    E-Mail: lragan@aipla.org
Manager, Information Technology: Randy Sagara

Historical Note:
Formerly (1914) known as the Patent Law Association of Washington and (1984) the American Patent Law Association. AIPLA serves the diverse IP community by enhancing knowledge and shaping the future of IP law. Membership is free for academic members. Membership: $345 (Regular/US Patent Agent Affiliate); $155 (Junior/US Patent Agent Affiliate Junior); $90 (Government Member); $370 (Foreign Lawyer Affiliate/Registered Foreign Patent/ Trademark Attorney/Agent Affiliate); $25 (Law Student/ Graduate Affiliate); $90 (US PTO Professional Affiliate).

Continuing Education:
Certification Designation/s: CLE

Meetings/Conferences: Annual
Conference Chair: Cathleen Clime
2013 - Tampa, FL (Tampa Marriott Waterside Hotel and Marina)/Jan. 30 - Feb. 2
2013 - Seatle, WA (Westin Seattle)/May 15 - 17
2013 - Washington, DC (Washington Marriott)/Oct. 24 - 26
2014 - Phoenix, AZ (Sheraton Wild Horse Pass Resort and Spa)/Jan. 29 - Feb. 1
2014 - Washington, DC (Washington Marriott)/Oct. 23 - 25
Number of non-conference events/year: 5

Publications:
The AIPLA Member Directory; on-line

American International Automobile Dealers Association (1970)
211 N. Union St.
Suite 300
Alexandria, VA 22314-1538
Tel: (800) 462-4232 Fax: (703) 519-7810
TollFree: (800) 462-4232
E-Mail: goaiada@aiada.org
Website: aiada.org
Members: 10,000 international nameplate automobile franchises
Staff: 12
Annual Budget: $2-5,000,000

Personnel:
Executive: Cody Lusk
    E-Mail: luskc@aiada.org
Director, Public Relations: Libby Krum
    E-Mail: kruml@aiada.org
Media Contact: Libby Newman
    E-Mail: NewmanL@aiada.org

Historical Note:
Initially the Volkswagen American Dealers Association. Assumed its present name in 1980. AIADA is dedicated to the economic and political interests of America's international nameplate automobile dealers and represents 500,000 employees who sell and service world- class automobiles.

Meetings/Conferences: Annual
Number of non-conference events/year: 2

Publications:
AutoDealer; quarterly; adv.
FirstUp Daily e-News; daily
Market Watch; monthly

American International Charolais Association (1957)
11700 NW Plaza Cir.
Kansas City, MO 64153
Tel: (816) 464-5977 Fax: (816) 464-5759
E-Mail: info@charolaisusa.com
Website: charolaisusa.com
Members: 2900 individuals
Staff: 12
Annual Budget: $1-2,000,000
Tax: 501(c)(5)

Personnel:
Executive Vice President: J. Neil Orth
    E-Mail: north@charolaisusa.com
Director, Activities: David Hobbs
    E-Mail: dhobbs@charolaisusa.com
Director, Communication: Molly Schoen
    E-Mail: mmader@charolaisusa.com

Director, Breed Improvement and Foreign Marketing: Robert Williams PhD
    E-Mail: rwilliams@charolaisusa.com

Historical Note:
Formed (1957) by merger of American Charolais Breeders Association and International Charolais Association. Absorbed (1967) American Charbray Breeders Association. AICA is the official registry of Charolais and Charbray cattle in the United States. Members are breeders and fanciers of Charolais beef cattle. Membership: $100 plus initial fee of $125 (Adult); $30 (Junior-First year).

Meetings/Conferences: Semi-Annual
Number of non-conference events/year: 2

Publications:
Charolais Journal; monthly; adv.
Membership Directory; on-line

Membership List Available to Non-members

American International Marchigiana Society (1973)
P.O. Box 198
Walton, KS 67151-0198
Tel: (620) 837-3303 Fax: (316) 283-8379
E-Mail: info@marky.willadsenfamily.org
Website: marchigiana.org
Members: 50 individuals
Staff: 1
Annual Budget: Under $10,000

Personnel:
Executive Secretary: Martie TenEyck

Historical Note:
Founded in 1973, AIMS is an association that fosters raising of the marchigiana breed of cattle in the United States. Also known as the Marky Cattle Association. AIMS is an organization dedicated to spreading the breed in the US. Membership: $100/year (initial fee per member); $25/year (per member, after first year); $10 (Junior Membership).

Meetings/Conferences:
Number of non-conference events/year: 1

American Iron and Steel Institute (1855)
25 Massachusetts Ave. NW
Suite 800
Washington, DC 20001
Tel: (202) 452-7100 Fax: (202) 463-6573
E-Mail: steelnews@steel.org
Website: steel.org
Members: 161 companies and associate members
Staff: 60
Annual Budget: $10-25,000,000
Tax: 501(c)(6)

Personnel:
President and Chief Executive Officer: Thomas J. J. Gibson
    E-Mail: tgibson@steel.org
Senior Vice President, Public Policy and General Counsel: Kevin M. Dempsey
    E-Mail: kdempsey@steel.org
Vice President, Communications: Nancy Gravatt
President, Steel Market Development Institute: Lawrence Kavanagh
    E-Mail: lkavanagh@steel.org

Historical Note:
Absorbed by the American Iron and Steel Association (1864). This, in turn, was absorbed (1912) by the American Iron and Steel Institute which had been incorporated in 1908 in New York. AISI's mission is to influence public policy, educate and shape public opinion in support of a strong, sustainable U.S. and North American steel industry committed to manufacturing products that meet society's needs. Membership: $1,000-5,000/year.

Meetings/Conferences: Annual
Number of non-conference events/year: 5

Publications:
AISI Newsletter; on-line

American Jail Association (1981)
1135 Professional Ct.
Hagerstown, MD 21740-5853
Tel: (301) 790-3930 Fax: (301) 790-2941
E-Mail: jails@aja.org
Website: aja.org
Members: 4200 individuals
Staff: 13
Annual Budget: $1-2,000,000
Tax: 501(c)(3)

Personnel:
Executive Director: Robert J. Kasabian
    E-Mail: robertk@aja.org
Director, Conferences and Corporate Relations: Chris Anderson
    E-Mail: chrisa@aja.org
Bookkeeper: Sandra Brown
    E-Mail: sandrab@aja.org
Coordinator, Marketing and Sales: Leslie Broznak
    E-Mail: leslieb@aja.org
Administrative Manager: Michele Florian
    E-Mail: michelef@aja.org
Manager, Membership Services: Steve Kendall
    E-Mail: stevek@aja.org
Director, Professional Development and Certification: Connie Lacy
    E-Mail: conniel@aja.org
Assistant Editor and Proofreader: Sandra Lunsford
    E-Mail: sandral@aja.org
Director, Administration and Communications: Rick Neimiller
    E-Mail: rickn@aja.org
Director, Marketing, Sales and Membership Services: Elizabeth Waybright
    E-Mail: elizabethw@aja.org

Historical Note:
AJA is dedicated exclusively to support those who work in and operate Nation's 3,200-plus jail facilities by offering good quality training, education, and networking. Membership: $48 (Individual); $54 (Canadian); $66 (Foreign); $300 (Agency); $350 (Corporate); $100 (Affiliate); $15 (Student); $36 (Retiree).

Continuing Education:
Certification Designation/s: CCT, CJO, CJM

Meetings/Conferences: Annual
Conference Chair: Michele Florian
2013 - Grand Rapids, MI (Amway Grand Plaza Hotel)/ May 5 - 9/1000 attendees
2014 - Dallas, TX (Hilton Anatole Dallas)/April 27 - 30/1000 attendees
2015 - Charlotte, NC (Sheraton Charlotte Airport Hotel)/April 19 - 22/1000 attendees
2016 - Austin, TX (Hilton Austin)/May 22 - 25
2017 - Louisville, KY/May 21 - 24
2018 - Dallas, TX/April 22 - 25

Publications:
American Jails Magazine; bi-monthly; adv.
Exploring Jail Operations
Product Service Resource Directory; annually
Who's Who in Jail Management (Jail Directory); adv.
Write It Right Bulletin; quarterly

Membership List Available to Non-members

American Jersey Cattle Association/National All-Jersey Inc. (1868)
6486 E. Main St.
Reynoldsburg, OH 43068-2362
Tel: (614) 861-3636 Fax: (614) 861-8040
E-Mail: info@usjersey.com
Website: usjersey.com
Members: 2381 individuals
Staff: 41
Annual Budget: $2-5,000,000

Personnel:
Executive Secretary and Chief Executive Officer: Neal Smith
    E-Mail: nsmith@usjersey.com
Director, Development: Cherie L. Bayer PhD
    E-Mail: cbayer@usjersey.com
Editor: Kimberly Billman
    E-Mail: kbillman@usjersey.com
Manager, Information Technology: Mark Chamberlain
    E-Mail: mchamberlain@usjersey.com
Manager, Marketing: Jason Robinson
    E-Mail: jrobinson@usjersey.com
Treasurer and Office Manager: Vickie White
    E-Mail: vwhite@usjersey.com
Director, Research and Genetic Program Development: Cari Wolfe
    E-Mail: cwolfe@usjersey.com

Historical Note:
A member of the National Pedigree Livestock Council, AJCA NAJ works to improve and promote the breed of Jersey cattle in the United States and to maintain such records and activities as the association deems necessary or conducive to the interests of the breeders of Jersey cattle. Members are persons who own a registered Jersey and who are interested

in improving and promoting the Jersey breed. Membership: $100/year (Lifetime Initiation Fee).

Meetings/Conferences: Annual
Conference Chair: Cherie L. Bayer PhD
2013 - Amarillo, TX (Ambassador Hotel)/June 24 - 29

Publications:
Jersey Directory Online (Membership Directory); on-line
Jersey Journal; monthly; adv.

American Jewish Correctional Chaplains Association *(1937)*
2445 Prior Ave.
Roseville, MN 55113
Tel: (651) 746-3414
Website: correctionalchaplains.org
Members: 50 individuals
Staff: 5
Annual Budget: Under $10,000

Personnel:
President: Dale L. Hale
    E-Mail: dale_hale@usc.salvationarmy.org
Webmaster: Larry Bongiovi
    E-Mail: webmaster@correctionalchaplains.org
Contact, Communications: Gary Friedman
    E-Mail: GaryFriedman@msn.com
Membership Secretary: Stephen G. Johnson
Treasurer: Steven E. Thomas

Historical Note:
Affiliated with the American Correctional Association and the American Correctional Chaplains Association. Formerly National Council of Jewish Correctional Chaplains and National Council of Jewish Prison Chaplains. Membership: $10/year.

Meetings/Conferences:
2013 - Houston, TX/Jan. 26 - 30

The American Jewish Historical Society *(1892)*
101 Newbury St.
Boston, MA 02116-3062
Tel: (617) 226-1245 *Fax:* (617) 226-1248
E-Mail: info@ajhs.cjh.org
Website: ajhs.org
Members: 4000 individuals
Staff: 21
Annual Budget: $1-2,000,000
Tax: 501(c)(3)

Personnel:
Executive Director: Jonathan Karp
    E-Mail: jkarp@ajhs.cjh.org
Controller: Jeffrey Kornstein
    E-Mail: jkornstein@ajhs.org
Director, Development: Rachel Lobovsky
    E-Mail: rlobovsky@ajhs.org
Director, Library and Archives: Susan Malbin
    E-Mail: smalbin@ajhs.org

Historical Note:
AJHS's mission is to foster awareness and appreciation of the American Jewish heritage. AJHS collects, preserves and disseminates materials relating to American Jewish history. Members are historians, scholars, and lay people. Membership: $60-500/year.

Publications:
American Jewish Historical; quarterly
Heritage Magazine; irregular
Heritage Newsletter; adv.
Living History Newsletter; on-line

American Jewish Press Association *(1944)*
107 S. Southgate Dr.
Chandler, AZ 85226-3222
Tel: (480) 403-4602
E-Mail: info@ajpa.org
Website: ajpa.org
Members: 50 individuals, 50 affiliates and 250 newspapers
Staff: 2
Annual Budget: $50-100,000
Tax: 501(c)(3)

Personnel:
President: Marshall Weiss
Treasurer: Richard Waloff

Historical Note:
AJPA's mission is to support the ethics, editorial quality and business standards to help its members navigate their challenges and responsibilities, especially those unique to the Jewish media. Membership: $525-730 (Full-based on

circulation); $315 (Associate/Website); $105 (Individual); $342 (Affiliate); $20 (Student); $50 (Student Paper).

Meetings/Conferences: Annual
Number of non-conference events/year: 1

Publications:
Freelancer Directory; on-line
Internet Resource Directory; on-line
Membership Bulletin Board; on-line
Membership Directory; on-line

Membership List Available to Non-members

American Journalism Historians Association *(1981)*
OBU Box 61201
500 W.Univ.
Shawnee, OK 74804-2590
Website:
ajhaonline.org
ajhaonline.org
Members: 160 institutional subscribers,360 individuals
Staff: 5
Annual Budget: $10-25,000

Personnel:
President: Therese Lueck
    E-Mail: tlueck@uakron.edu
Web Editor: David R. Davies
    E-Mail: dave.davies@usm.edu
Editor: Barbara Friedman
    E-Mail: bfriedman@unc.edu
Treasurer: Mavis Richardson
    E-Mail: mavis.richardson@mnsu.edu

Historical Note:
AJHA's purpose is to foster research and teaching of journalism history, to provide a forum and to be a resource. Members are academics and other individuals with an interest in the history of the media. Membership: $25 (Student/Retiree); $45 (Faculty/Professional); $55 (Institutional); $750 (Life).

Meetings/Conferences: Annual
Number of non-conference events/year: 1

Publications:
Intelligencer Newsletter; quarterly; adv.
American Journalism; quarterly; adv.
Membership Directory; on-line

Membership List Available to Non-members

American Judges Association *(1959)*
300 Newport Ave.
Williamsburg, VA 23185-4147
Tel: (757) 259-1841 *Fax:* (757) 259-1520
E-Mail: aja@ncsc.dni.us
Website: aja.ncsc.dni.us
Members: 3000 individuals
Staff: 1
Annual Budget: $250-500,000
Tax: 501(c)(6)

Personnel:
President: Kevin S. Burke

Historical Note:
Formerly (1965) the National Association of Municipal Judges and (1972) the North American Judges Association. AJA's mission is to advocate and improve the effective administration of justice, to maintain the status and independence of the judiciary, to provide a forum for the continuing education of its members and the general public, and for the interchange of ideas among all judges. Membership: $150 (Active); $50 (Retired).

Meetings/Conferences:
2013 - Kohala Coast, HI (The Fairmont Orchid)/Sept. 22 - 27

Publications:
AJA Benchmark; quarterly; adv.
Court Review; quarterly; adv.
Member Directory; on-line

American Judicature Society *(1913)*
The Opperman Center at Drake University
2700 University Ave.
Des Moines, IA 50311
Tel: (515) 271-2281 *Fax:* (515) 279-3090
TollFree: (800) 626-4089
Website: ajs.org
Members: 5000 individuals
Staff: 9
Annual Budget: $1-2,000,000

Tax: 501(c)(3)

Personnel:
Executive Director: Seth S. Andersen
    E-Mail: sandersen@ajs.org
Director, Center for Judicial Ethics: Cynthia Gray
    E-Mail: cgray@ajs.org
Coordinator, Membership Services and Manager, Human Resources: Laury Lieurance
    E-Mail: llieurance@ajs.org
Coordinator, Development and Events: Krista J. Maeder
    E-Mail: kmaeder@ajs.org
Interim Editor: Michael Ream
    E-Mail: manuscripts@ajs.org
Editor Emeritus: David Richert
    E-Mail: drichert@ajs.org
Director, Social Sciences, Center for Forensic Science and Public Policy: Gary Wells

Historical Note:
AJS works to maintain the independence and integrity of the courts and increase public understanding of the justice system. Members are judges, lawyers and other citizens interested in the administration of justice. Membership: $35-1,500 (Membership Levels) $5,000 (Life Time).

Meetings/Conferences: Annual
Conference Chair: Krista J. Maeder
Number of non-conference events/year: 4

Publications:
Judicatories; bi-monthly; adv.
Judicature; bi-monthly; adv.
Judicial Conduct Reporter; quarterly

American Karakul Sheep Registry *(1965)*
11500 Hwy. Five
Boonville, MO 65233
Tel: (660) 838-6340 *Fax:* (660) 838-6322
E-Mail: aksr@iland.net
Website: karakulsheep.com
Members: 24 individuals
Staff: 1
Annual Budget: Under $10,000

Personnel:
Registrar: Rey Perera
    E-Mail: drperera@iland.net

Historical Note:
Formerly Karakul Fur Sheep Registry, (1979) Empire Karakul Registry and (1985) American Karakul Fur Sheep Registry. AKSR encourages and perpetuates the Karakul purebred, originally imported from Russia. Membership: $15 (Individual); $5 (Junior).

Publications:
AKSR Newsletter; quarterly
Membership Directory; on-line

American Kennel Club *(1884)*
8051 Arco Corporate Dr.
Suite 100
Raleigh, NC 27617-3390
Tel: (212) 696-8200
E-Mail: info@akc.org
Website: akc.org
Members: 503 dog clubs
Staff: 449
Annual Budget: $50-100,000,000

Personnel:
President and Chief Executive Officer: Dennis B. Sprung
    E-Mail: dbs@akc.org
Vice President, Marketing: Michael J. Ganey
Vice President, Companion and Performance Events: Doug Ljungren
Vice President and Chief Information Officer: Connie Pearcy
Director, Communications: Lisa Peterson
    E-Mail: lxp@akc.org
General Counsel: Margaret H. Poindexter
Assistant Vice President, Human Resources: Vicki Lane Rees
    E-Mail: vlr@akc.org
Chief Financial Officer: James T. Stevens
    E-Mail: jts@akc.org
Assistant Vice President, Business Development,: Daphna Straus
    E-Mail: dxs@akc.org

Historical Note:
AKC's mission is to uphold the integrity of its Registry, to promote the sport of purebred dogs and breeding for type and function. Membership: $250/year.

Continuing Education:

Certification Designation/s: CGC, AFC, UDX, MXJ

Meetings/Conferences:
Conference Chair: Doug Ljungren

Publications:
Agility Judges Newsletter; quarterly
AKC Breeder Newsletter; quarterly
AKC Magazine
Membership Directory; on-line
Sirius Newsletter
Winners Galary; weekly

American Kinesiotherapy Association (1946)
118 College Dr.
Suite 5142
Hattiesburg, MS 39406
Tel: (800) 296-2582
TollFree: (800) 296-2582
E-Mail: info@aakta.org
Website: akta.org
Members: 500 individuals
Staff: 3
Annual Budget: $50-100,000

Personnel:
President: Lori Shuart
Director, Continuing Competency: Bridget Collins
    E-Mail: ccbkt@aol.com
Director, Registration: Doris Woods

Historical Note:
Formerly (1987) American Corrective Therapy Association
and (1967) Association for Physical and Mental
Rehabilitation. Professional society of kinesiotherapists
and exercise therapists. AKTA's mission is to promote
Kinesiotherapy and improve recognition of the profession
through the pursuit of legislation and public relations.
Kinesiotherapy is the application of scientifically based
exercise principles adapted to enhance the strength,
endurance and mobility of individuals with functional
limitations, and of individuals requiring extended physical
conditioning. Membership: $45 (Associate/Bridge); $15
(Student).

Meetings/Conferences: Annual
Conference Chair: Doris Woods

Publications:
Clinical Kinesiology
Mobility-Newsletter

American Knife & Tool Institute (1998)
22 Vista View Ln.
Cody, WY 82414-9606
Tel: (307) 587-8296 Fax: (307) 587-8296
E-Mail: akti@akti.org
Website: akti.org
Members: 300 individuals
Staff: 3
Annual Budget: $100-250,000
Tax: 501(c)(6)

Personnel:
Executive Director: Jan Billeb
Coordinator, Communications: David Kowalski
    E-Mail: communications@akti.org
President: Bill Raczkowski

Historical Note:
AKTI's mission is to ensure that Americans will always
be able to buy, sell, own, carry and use knives and edged
tools. Monitors legislative developments concerning the
use, manufacture, and distribution of knives and tools
in the U.S., and educates and informs the knife-using
community on important issues. Represents manufacturers,
distributors, retailers, custom knife artisans and journalists.
Membership: $5,000 (Advisory Board Member); $2,000
(Premier Member); $100- 1,000 (Associate Member); $35
(Ambassador); $750 (Individual Life Membership).

Publications:
Newsletter

American Ladder Institute (1947)
401 N. Michigan Ave.
Chicago, IL 60611-4267
Tel: (312) 644-6610 Fax: (312) 673-6929
Website: americanladderinstitute.org
Members: 34 companies
Staff: 1
Annual Budget: $250-500,000
Tax: 501(c)(6)

Personnel:
Executive Director: Janet Rapp
    E-Mail: jrapp@smithbucklin.com

Historical Note:

ALI's mission is to advocate the safe use of products
as well as advance the common business interests of
members through a commitment to develop and disseminate
appropriate standards, education of the public as to the
proper selection, care and safe users of ladders, and
representation of interests of its members. Members include
manufacturers of wood, metal and fiberglass ladders.
Membership: $1,008 (Associate); $2,600-29,000 (Regular,
based on sales).

Meetings/Conferences: Annual

Publications:
Member Directory; on-line

Membership List Available to Non-members

American Land Rights Association (1978)
30218 NE 82nd Ave.
P.O. Box 400
Battle Ground, WA 98604
Tel: (360) 687-3087 Fax: (360) 687-2973
Website: landrights.org
Members: 22000 individuals
Staff: 2
Annual Budget: $250-500,000

Personnel:
Founder and Executive Director: Charles S. Cushman
    E-Mail: ccushman@pacifier.com

Historical Note:
Founded as National Park Inholders Association, became
National Inholders Association in 1980. Adopted the
present name in 1995. ALRA's mission is to make wise-
use of resources, access to Federal lands and the protection
of private property rights. Membership: $35/year (Patron/
Sponsoring/Sustaining).

American Land Title Association (1907)
1828 L St. NW
Suite 705
Washington, DC 20036-5104
Tel: (202) 296-3671 Fax: (202) 223-5843
TollFree: (800) 787-2582
E-Mail: service@alta.org
Website: alta.org
Members: 4000 title agents, abstracters, and title
insurance companies
Staff: 17
Annual Budget: $5-10,000,000
Tax: 501(c)(6)

Personnel:
Chief Executive Officer: Michelle Larson Korsmo
    E-Mail: mkorsmo@alta.org
Vice President, Government and Regulatory Affairs: Justin
    B. Ailes
    E-Mail: jailes@alta.org
Legislative and Regulatory Counsel: Steve Gottheim
    E-Mail: sgottheim@alta.org
Meetings Coordinator: Erica Hampton
    E-Mail: ehampton@alta.org
Manager, Finance and Administration: Catherine Harold
    E-Mail: charold@alta.org
Vice President, Meetings and Conferences: Cornelia
    Horner
    E-Mail: chorner@alta.org
Manager, Membership Services: Taylor A. Morris
    E-Mail: tmorris@alta.org
Vice President, Education and Industry Technology: Kelly
    Lyn Romeo CAE
    E-Mail: kromeo@alta.org
Manager, Information Technology: Barry Sawyer
    E-Mail: bsawyer@alta.org
Director, Communications: Jeremy Yohe
    E-Mail: jyohe@alta.org

Historical Note:
ALTA members search, review and insure land titles to
protect home buyers and mortgage lenders who invest in
real estate. Membership: $460 (Associate); $460-1,391.50
(Abstracters/Abstract Companies and Agents of Title
Insurance/Title Guaranty Companies); $862.50-32,211.50
plus $63.25 per $100,000 over $25,000,000 (Title
Insurance Underwriter Companies).

Meetings/Conferences: Annual
Conference Chair: Cornelia Horner

Publications:
Title News; monthly; adv.

American Lands Access Association (1992)
P.O. Box 23
Tendoy, ID 83468-0023
Tel: (208) 756-2394

E-Mail: info@amlands.org
Website: amlands.org
Staff: 5
Tax: 501(c)(4)

Personnel:
President: Shirley Leeson
Treasurer: Ruth Bailley
Webmaster: John Martin
Editor: Jay Valle

Historical Note:
ALAA's mission is to promote and ensure the rights
for amateur fossil and mineral collecting, recreational
prospecting and mining, and the use of public and
private lands for educational and recreational purposes.
Membership: $50 (Clubs/Societies); $25 (Individual/
Family).

Publications:
ALAA Newsletter

American Laryngological Association (1878)
425 W 59th St.
Tenth Floor
New York, NY 10019
Tel: (212) 262-9500 Fax: (212) 523-6364
Website: alahns.org
Members: 250 individuals
Staff: 5
Annual Budget: $100-250,000

Personnel:
Secretary: Gaelyn C. Garrett MD
    E-Mail: gaelyn.garrett@vanderbilt.edu

Historical Note:
ALA's mission is to enhance the study of the science
of medicine and surgery. Members are individuals
concentrating on the advancement of medicine and surgery
of the upper aerodigestive tract. $150 (Active); $20
(Honorary); $10 (Corresponding); $30 (Associate).

Meetings/Conferences: Annual
2013 - Orlando, FL (JW Marriott Orlando Grande
    Lakes)/April 10 - 14

Publications:
American Laryngological Association Newsletter; bi-
annually
Membership Directory; on-line
The Laryngoscope

Membership List Available to Non-members

American Laryngological, Rhinological and Otological Society (1895)
13930 Gold Cir.
Suite 103
Omaha, NE 68144
Tel: (402) 346-5500 Fax: (402) 346-5300
E-Mail: info@triological.org
Website: triological.org
Members: 1100 individuals
Staff: 3
Annual Budget: $2-5,000,000

Personnel:
President: Jesus E. Medina FACS, MD
Publishing Liaison: Robert H. Miller
Treasurer: Myles L. Pensak MD, FACS

Historical Note:
Incorporated in December 5, 1917. The society provides
a forum for the international exchange of ideas and
knowledge in otolaryngology-head and neck surgery and
related fields of medicine and science. The Society promotes
research into the causes and treatments for otolaryngic
diseases by attracting promising physicians to scholarly
otolaryngology research and supporting their development,
providing financial support for the research efforts of young
scientists. Active Fellowship is achieved by presenting a
thesis in the field of otolaryngology. Membership: $85 (Post
Graduate); $55 (Resident).

Meetings/Conferences:
2013 - Scottsdale, AZ (Westin Kierland Resort and
    Spa)/Jan. 24 - 26
2013 - Orlando, FL (JW Marriott Orlando Grande
    Lakes)/April 10 - 14
Number of non-conference events/year: 4

Publications:
ENT Today; monthly; adv.
Senior Fellow Newsletters
The Laryngoscope; monthly; adv.

American Law Institute (1923)
4025 Chestnut St.

Philadelphia, PA 19104-3099
Tel: (215) 243-1600 *Fax:* (215) 243-1664
TollFree: (800) 253-6397
E-Mail: ali@ali.org
Website: ali-cle.org
Members: 4000 lawyers, judges, and law
professors
Staff: 18
Annual Budget: $50-100,000,000
Tax: 501(c)(3)

Personnel:
Director: Nancy Mulloy-Bonn
    E-Mail: nmulloy-bonn@ali-aba.org
Director, Office of Marketing and Design: Matthew Born
    E-Mail: mborn@ali-aba.org
Acting Chief, Operations: Mark T. Carroll
    E-Mail: mcarroll@ali-aba.org
Director, Office of Information and Web Technologies: John
Ceci
    E-Mail: jceci@ali-aba.org
Associate Deputy Director: Deanne Dissinger
Meetings Planner: Sandrine Forgeron
    E-Mail: sforgeron@ali.org
Director, Membership Services: Beth McGettigan
Goldstein
    E-Mail: bgoldstein@ali.org
Director, Human Resources: Diane Schnitzer
    E-Mail: dschnitzer@ali-aba.org
Chief Financial Officer: Julie Scribner
    E-Mail: jscribner@ali-aba.org
Director, Publications and Editor: Marianne M. Walker
    E-Mail: MWalker@ali.org

Historical Note:
*ALI's purpose is to promote the clarification and
simplification of the law and its better adaptation to social
needs, to secure the better administration of justice, and to
encourage and carry on scholarly and scientific legal work.
Membership : $250 (Attorneys); $125 (Employees).*

Meetings/Conferences: Annual
Conference Chair: Sandrine Forgeron

Publications:
Membership Directory; on-line

American League for Exports and Security Assistance (1976)
8150 Leesburg
Suite 840
Vienna, VA 22182
Website: alesa.org
Staff: 2
Annual Budget: $50-100,000

Personnel:
Senior Executive Vice President: Toby Roth Jr.
    E-Mail: Toby.roth@alesa.org

Historical Note:
*The mission of the American League for Exports and
Security Assistance is to support U.S. defense industry
trade priorities that are consistent with the national security
interests of the United States.*

American League of Anglers and Boaters
c/o Amer. Recreation Coalition
1225 New York Ave. NW, Suite 450
Washington, DC 20005
Tel: (202) 682-9530 *Fax:* (202) 682-9529
Website: funoutdoors.com/coalitions/alab
Staff: 1

Personnel:
Treasurer: Derrick A. Crandall
    E-Mail: dcrandall@funoutdoors.com

Historical Note:
*A federation of fishing and boating organizations. It returns
excise taxes to the fishing and boating communities in an
effort to enhance both groups.*

American League of Lobbyists (1979)
2121 Eisenhower Ave.
Suite 110
Alexandria, VA 22314
Tel: (703) 960-3011 *Fax:* (703) 960-4070
E-Mail: alldc.org@erols.com
Website: alldc.org
Members: 900 individuals
Staff: 4
Annual Budget: $250-500,000
Tax: 501(c)(6)

Personnel:

Executive Director: Danielle S. Abe
Federal lobbyist: Gina Bancroft
Legal Counsel: Penny Farthing
Treasurer: Katharine Calhoun Wood

Historical Note:
*ALL is dedicated to enhancing the profession of lobbying
throughout the United States. It also informs the
public about the substantive role of the lobbyist in the
American governmental process. Membership in the
League is open to anyone actively employed in the field
of government relations. Membership: $250 (Individual);
$750 (Organization); $85 (Government/Academic); $125
(Non-Resident); $99 (Young Leadership Network); $500
(Associate); $30 (Student/Emeritus).*

Continuing Education:
Enrollment: 300
Certification Designation/s: CLP, LCP

Meetings/Conferences: Annual

Publications:
Membership Directory; on-line

American Leather Chemists Association (1903)
1314 50th St.
Suite 103
Lubbock, TX 79412
Tel: (806) 744-1798 *Fax:* (806) 744-1785
E-Mail: alca@leatherchemists.org
Website: leatherchemists.org
Members: 500 individuals
Staff: 4
Annual Budget: $100-250,000
Tax: 501(c)(3)

Personnel:
President: Steven Gilberg
Executive Secretary: Carol Adcock
    E-Mail: carol.adcock@ttu.edu
Editor: Robert F. White
    E-Mail: jalcaeditor@prodigy.net

Historical Note:
*Founded in 1903 and incorporated in New Jersey in 1937,
ALCA is a member of the International Union of Leather
Chemists Societies. ALCA is to promote the advancement
of the knowledge of science and engineering especially in
regard to their application to problems facing the leather
and leather products industries, To encourage and promote
the full use of science and engineering in their applications
to the leather and leather product industries. Membership:
$130 (Active); $241 (Mutual); $65 (Student).*

Meetings/Conferences: Annual
2013 - Pinehurst, NC/June 20 - 23

Publications:
Journal of the American Leather Chemists Association;
    monthly; adv.
The ALCA Journal

Membership List Available to Non-members

American Legend Cooperative (1985)
P.O. Box 58308
Seattle, WA 98138
Tel: (425) 251-3200 *Fax:* (425) 251-3222
E-Mail: info@americanlegend.com
Website: americanlegend.com
Members: 800 individuals
Staff: 40
Annual Budget: $1-2,000,000

Personnel:
Chief Executive Officer: Joe Morelli

Historical Note:
*Formed by a merger of the Great Lakes Mink Association
and the Emba Mink Breeders Association (1942). ALC is
a producer-owned cooperative organization that promotes
ranch-raised mink and fox fur. Members are mink producers
from Canada and USA. Membership: 2% of gross sales per
year.*

American Library Association (1876)
50 E. Huron St.
Chicago, IL 60611
Tel: (312) 280-1392 *Fax:* (312) 440-9374
TollFree: (800) 545-2433
E-Mail: ala@ala.org
Website: ala.org
Members: 61198 individuals and libraries
Staff: 325
Annual Budget: $25-50,000,000
Tax: 501(c)(3)

Personnel:
Executive Director: Keith Michael Fiels

    E-Mail: kfiels@ala.org
*Associate Executive Director, Communications and
    Membership Relations:* Cathleen J. Bourdon
    E-Mail: cbourdon@ala.org
Director, Government Relations: Lynne E. Bradley
    E-Mail: lbradley@alawash.org
Manager , ALA Graphics Marketing: Diane Buck
    E-Mail: dbuck@ala.org
Director, Membership Development: John F. Chrastka
    E-Mail: jchrastka@ala.org
Director, Public Information Office: Mark R. Gould
    E-Mail: mgould@ala.org
Manager, Publications: Kathleen Marie Hughes
    E-Mail: khughes@ala.org
Manager, Computer Operations: Jim Kanis
    E-Mail: jkanis@ala.org
Director, Library Advocacy: Marci Merola
    E-Mail: mmerola@ala.org
Director, Human Resources: Cynthia Vivian
    E-Mail: cvivian@ala.org

Historical Note:
*ALA's mission is to provide leadership for the development,
promotion, and improvement of library and information
services and the profession of librarianship in order to
enhance learning and ensure access to information for all.
Membership: $33-78/year.*

Meetings/Conferences: Semi-Annual
Conference Chair: Alicia Babcock
2013 - Seattle, WA/Jan. 25 - 29
2013 - Chicago, IL/June 27 - July 2
2014 - Philadelphia, PA/Jan. 24 - 28
2014 - Las Vegas, NV/June 26 - July 1
2015 - Chicago, IL/Jan. 23 - 27
2015 - San Francisco, CA/June 25 - 30
2016 - Boston, MA/Jan. 22 - 26
2016 - Orlando, FL/June 23 - 28
2017 - Atlanta, GA/Jan. 20 - 24
2017 - Chicago, IL/June 22 - 27

Publications:
AL Direct (e-mail); weekly
American Libraries; monthly; adv.
Base Line; bi-monthly
Booklist magazine; adv.
Children's Programming Monthly; monthly

Membership List Available to Non-members

American Lighting Association (1945)
2050 Stemmons Fwy.
Unit 100
Dallas, TX 75207-3206
Tel: (214) 698-9898 *Fax:* (214) 698-9899
TollFree: (800) 605-4448
Website: americanlightingassoc.com
Members: 1200 Firms
Staff: 11
Annual Budget: $2-5,000,000

Personnel:
President and Chief Executive Officer: Richard D. Upton
CCE
    E-Mail: dupton@americanlightingassoc.com
Director, Conferences: Beth Bentley CMP
    E-Mail: bbentley@americanlightingassoc.com
Vice President, Membership Services: Eric Jacobson CAE
    E-Mail: ejacobson@americanlightingassoc.com
Director, Education: Nici Juneau
    E-Mail: njuneau@americanlightingassoc.com
Vice President, Communications: W. Larry "Lawrence"
Lauck
    E-Mail: llauck@americanlightingassoc.com
Director, Finance: Wendy E. Rollins IOM
    E-Mail: wrollins@americanlightingassoc.com

Historical Note:
*Formerly known as American Home Lighting Institute
1989. ALA is a trade association representing the lighting
industry. Members include lighting, dimming controls
and ceiling fan manufacturers, retail showrooms, sales
representatives and professional residential lighting
designers. Membership: $3,660-28,370 (Manufacturer);
$635 (Component Manufacturers); $420 (Associate/
Designer); $360-710 (Manufacturers' Representatives);
$470-4,320 (Showrooms).*

Continuing Education:
Certification Designation/s: LS, LA, CLC, CLMR, CS

Meetings/Conferences: Annual
Conference Chair: Beth Bentley CMP
2013 - Austin, TX (Hyatt Regency Lost Pines Resort
    and Spa)/Sept. 22 - 24

Publications:
Bright Ideas Newsletter; monthly; adv.
Lighting Magazine; annually; adv.
Lightrays Member Newsletter; bi-monthly; adv.
Membership Directory; annually; adv.
Proactive Showrooms; monthly
Rep Success; quarterly
Technology E-Newsletter; bi-monthly

Membership List Available to Non-members

American Literary Translators Association (1978)
800 W. Campbell Rd.
Mail Station JO51
Richardson, TX 75080-3021
Tel: (972) 883-2092 *Fax:* (972) 883-6303
Website: utdallas.edu/alta/
Members: 850 individuals
Staff: 3
Annual Budget: $100-250,000
Tax: 501(c)(3)

Personnel:
President: Gary Racz
    E-Mail: gregary.racz@liu.edu
Contact, Communications: Maria Suarez
    E-Mail: maria.suarez@utdallas.edu
Secretary and Treasurer: Russell Valentino
    E-Mail: russell-valentino@uiowa.edu

Historical Note:
ALTA is dedicated to the promotion of literary translation through services to literary translators, forums on the theory and practice of translation, collaboration with the international literary community, and advocacy on behalf of the literary translator. Members are translators into English of books in literature and the humanities. Membership: $80 (US and Canada); $100 (International/Joint Household/Library (US & Canada)); $20 (Student); $60 (Senior); $125 (Library, International); $150 (Institutional); $1500 (Lifetime).

Meetings/Conferences: Annual

Publications:
ALTA Newsletter; on-line

American Littoral Society (1961)
18 Hartshorne Dr.
Suite One
Highlands, NJ 07732
Tel: (732) 291-0055 *Fax:* (732) 291-3551
E-Mail: info@littoralsociety.org
Website: littoralsociety.org
Members: 6000 individuals
Staff: 10
Annual Budget: $1-2,000,000
Tax: 501(c)(3)

Personnel:
Executive Director: Tim Dillingham
Coordinator, Field Trip and Business Manager: Pat Coren
    E-Mail: pat@littoralsociety.org,
Director, Membership Services: Mary Ann Griesbach
    E-Mail: maryann@littoralsociety.org
Deputy Director: Eileen Kennedy
    E-Mail: eileen@littoralsociety.org
Coordinator, Communications and Technology: Dennis Reynolds
    E-Mail: reynolds@littoralsociety.org
Education and Outreach Coordinator: Stevie Thorsen
    E-Mail: stevie@littoralsociety.org

Historical Note:
Founded in 1961 at the Sandy Hook Marine Laboratory and incorporated in 1962 in New Jersey. ALS promotes the study and conservation of marine life and habitat, protects the coast from harm, and empowers others to do the same. Helps people to care for the coast through integrated programs focused on advocating, conserving, and learning. Membership: $25-500/year.

Meetings/Conferences: Annual

Publications:
Coastal Reporter; monthly
Littorally Speaking,

Membership List Available to Non-members

American Logistics Association (1972)
1133 15th St. NW
Suite 640
Washington, DC 20005
Tel: (202) 466-2520 *Fax:* (202) 296-4419
E-Mail: membership@ala-national.org
Website: ala-national.org

Members: 2500 individuals and 600 companies
Staff: 8
Annual Budget: $2-5,000,000
Tax: 501(c)(6)

Personnel:
President: Patrick B. Nixon
    E-Mail: pnixon@ala-national.org
Vice President, Operations: L. Maurice Branch
    E-Mail: maurice@ala-national.org
Director, Meetings and Expositions and Office Manager: Tracey Durand
    E-Mail: tracey@ala-national.org
Vice President, Exchange/MWR and Customer Relations: Bob Ellis
    E-Mail: bellis@ala-national.org
Manager, Accounting: Robin Sampson
    E-Mail: robin@ala-national.org
Vice President, Government Affairs: Len Williams
    E-Mail: en@ala-national.org

Historical Note:
ALA's mission is to promote, protect, and enhance the military resale and quality of life benefits on behalf of its members and the military community. Membership: $125-150 (Individual); $1,700-18,630 (Broker/ Manufacturer/Distributor/Manufacturer, Media/Service/ Affiliate).

Meetings/Conferences: Annual
Conference Chair: Tracey Durand
2013 - New Orleans, LA (Hyatt Regency New Orleans)/ Sept. 30 - Oct. 2
Number of non-conference events/year: 2

Publications:
Executive Briefing Newsletter; weekly
Worldwide Directory; annually

American Luggage Dealers Association (1970)
1817 Elmdale Ave.
Suite 310
Glenview, IL 60026
Tel: (847) 998-6869 *Fax:* (847) 998-6884
E-Mail: inquiry@nlda.com
Website: luggagedealers.com
Members: 130 luggage and travel stores
Staff: 4
Annual Budget: $2-5,000,000

Personnel:
Executive Director: Frank Fine
Coordinator, Membership Services: Bev Imbert
Chief Financial Officer: Andy Lubell
    E-Mail: andy@aceluggage.com

Historical Note:
ALDA seeks to develop a progressive merchandise program such as publication of catalogs and specific merchandise opportunities for independent luggage retailers. Members are cooperative of luggage, travel goods and leather goods retail stores. Membership: $250/year.

Publications:
Membership Directory; on-line

American Lung Association (1973)
1301 Pennsylvania Ave. NW
Suite 800
Washington, DC 20004
Tel: (202) 785-3355 *Fax:* (202) 452-1805
TollFree: (800) 586-4872
E-Mail: info@lungusa.org
Website: lung.org
Members:
57 constituents and 53 affiliate organization
10000 individuals
Staff: 130
Annual Budget: $25-50,000,000

Personnel:
Executive Director: Deborah Hoffman
    E-Mail: dhoffman@LungNewMexico.org
Vice President, National Policy And Advocacy: Paul Billings
    E-Mail: pbillings@lungusa.org
Director , Programs: JoAnna DeMaria
    E-Mail: jdemaria@lungnewmexico.org
Media Contact: Carrie Martin
    E-Mail: cmartin@lungusa.org

Historical Note:
Established as the National Association for the study and prevention of Tuberculosis, became the National Tuberculosis Association in 1918, the National Tuberculosis and Respiratory Disease Association in 1968 and assumed

its present name in 1973. ALA works to save lives by improving lung health and preventing lung disease.

Meetings/Conferences:
Conference Chair: JoAnna DeMaria

Publications:
FFS Online Weekly eNewsletter; weekly
ALA e-newsletter; irregular
Fighting for Air Online eNewsletter; monthly
Flu News eNewsletter; on-line
Promise of Research; quarterly
Tobacco Control Tribune; monthly

American Maine-Anjou Association (1969)
204 Marshall Rd.
P.O. Box 1100
Platte City, MO 64079-1100
Tel: (816) 431-9950 *Fax:* (816) 431-9951
E-Mail: maine@kc.rr.com
Website: maine-anjou.org
Members: 2500 individuals
Staff: 9
Annual Budget: $500-1,000,000
Tax: 501(c)(5)

Personnel:
Executive Vice President: John A. Boddicker
    E-Mail: amaajohn@kc.rr.com
Administrative Assistant: Rhonda Boddicker
    E-Mail: amaarhonda@kc.rr.com
Voice Editor and Director, Communications: Lindsey Broek
    E-Mail: voiceeditor@kc.rr.com
Director, Commercial Marketing: Dave Steen
    E-Mail: steen@metc.net

Historical Note:
Formerly (1971) the Maine-Anjou Society and (1975) the International Maine-Anjou Association and a member of the National Cattlemen's Association. Members are breeders and fanciers of Maine-Anjou Beef Cattle. Membership: $100 (Adult); $25 (Junior).

Publications:
The Voice Maine-Anjou; adv.

Membership List Available to Non-members

American Malting Barley Association (1945)
740 N. Plankinton Ave.
Suite 830
Milwaukee, WI 53203-2403
Tel: (414) 272-4640
E-Mail: info@ambainc.org
Website: ambainc.org
Members: 19 companies
Staff: 3
Annual Budget: $500-1,000,000
Tax: 501(c)(6)

Personnel:
President: Michael P Davis
Vice President and Technical Director: Scott E Heisel

Historical Note:
Founded as the Midwest Barley Improvement Association, became the Malting Barley Improvement Association in 1954 and assumed its present name in 1982. Absorbed Malt Research Institute. AMBA's purpose is to help ensure an adequate supply of malting barley for the malting and brewing industry. Membership: $4,800 (Regular/ Associate).

Meetings/Conferences: Annual

Publications:
Barley Genetics Newsletter
Barley Newsletter
Membership Directory; on-line

American Management Association (1923)
1601 Broadway
New York, NY 10019-7420
Tel: (212) 586-8100 *Fax:* (212) 903-8168
TollFree: (877) 566-9441
E-Mail: customerservice@amanet.org
Website: amanet.org
Members: 25000 individuals and 2500 corporate members
Staff: 406
Annual Budget: $50-100,000,000
Tax: 501(c)(3)

Personnel:
President and Chief Executive Officer: Edward T. Reilly
    E-Mail: ed.reilly@amanet.org

Senior Vice President, Global Human Resources: Manny Avramidis
Senior Vice President and Chief Information Officer: Richard J. Barton
Director, Instruction and Facilitation: Margaret Carney
  E-Mail: mcarney@amanet.org
Vice President, Event Management: Joan Castonguay
Executive Vice President, Chief Financial Officer and Treasurer: Vivianna Guzman
  E-Mail: vguzman@amanet.org
Manager, Public Relations: Roger Kelleher
  E-Mail: rkelleher@amanet.org
President and Publisher: Hank Kennedy
Senior Vice President, General Counsel and Corporate Secretary: Arthur J. Levy
Senior Vice President, Marketing and Membership Services: Robert G. Smith

Historical Note:
Resulted from the merger (1973) of the American Management Association (1923), the American Foundation for Management Research (1960), the International Management Association (1956), the Presidents Association (1961) and the Society for Advancement of Management (1912). Devoted to all types of management education. AMA fosters professional growth in any business climate and offers professional development and performance-based learning solutions. Members are both individuals as well as companies. Membership: $1,995 (Corporate/Small Business); $225 (Individual); $45 (E-Membership); $95 (Student).

Continuing Education:
Certification Designation/s: CEUs, PMI, NASBA, HRCI, CPE, CMA, IACET

Meetings/Conferences:
Conference Chair: Joan Castonguay
Number of non-conference events/year: 2

Publications:
Administrative Excellence; quarterly
Book Blast
Executive Matters; monthly
Leader's Edge; monthly
Management Update; monthly
Membership Directory; on-line
Moving Ahead; monthly
MWorld; quarterly
Performance & Profits; monthly
Thinking Management

Membership List Available to Non-members

American Manual Medicine Association
2040 Raybrook SE
Suite 103
Grand Rapids, MI 49546
Tel: (888) 375-7245 *Fax:* (616) 575-9066
TollFree: (888) 375-7245
E-Mail: info@americanmanualmedicine.com
Website: americanmanualmedicine.com
Staff: 1

Personnel:
Managing Director: Marie A. Ruberto

Historical Note:
AMMA seeks to advocate manual therapy as an allied health care profession. Membership: $100 (Association Affiliate); $100 (Fellowship Membership); $135 (Professional).

Continuing Education:
Certification Designation/s: Dipl.Ac., P.Ac.

Publications:
AMMA Journal

American Maritime Congress *(1977)*
444 N. Capitol St. NW
Suite 800
Washington, DC 20001
Tel: (202) 347-8020 *Fax:* (202) 347-1550
Website: americanmaritime.org
Members: 30 companies
Staff: 3
Annual Budget: $500-1,000,000
Tax: 501(c)(6)

Personnel:
Executive Director: James E. Caponiti
President: Lee Kincaid
  E-Mail: lkincaid@americanmaritime.org
Executive Assistant: Dianne Lauer

Historical Note:

Formerly (1977) Joint Maritime Congress. Assumed its current name in 1989. AMC strives to inform the public, media and its legislators in Washington on the issues and policy affecting the U.S Flag merchant marine and maritime industry. Members are U.S. ship operating companies having contracts with the Marine Engineers' Beneficial Association, a maritime union.

American Maritime Officers
601 S. Federal Hwy.
Dania Beach, FL 33004
TollFree: (800) 362-0513
E-Mail: webmaster@amo-union.org
Website: amo-union.org
Staff: 57
Annual Budget: $10-25,000,000

Personnel:
National Secretary and Treasurer: Jose E. Leonard
  E-Mail: jleonard@amo-union.org

Historical Note:
AMO protects its members' professional interests by helping to fend off persistent threats to laws and programs that sustain the fleet in foreign and domestic markets, and by promoting new opportunities for U.S.-flag vessel operators.

Publications:
AMO Currents
AMO Newspaper
Membership Directory; on-line

American Maritime Officers Plans
601 S. Federal Hwy.
Dania Beach, FL 33004
Website: amoplans.com
Staff: 1

Personnel:
National President: Thomas J. Bethel

Historical Note:
AMO's mission is to provide vacation, medical, pension, MPB, 401(k) and Safety and Education benefits to eligible employees of contributing employers.

American Maritime Officers Service
490 E. L'Enfant Plaza SW
Suite 7170
Washington, DC 20024
Tel: (202) 479-1133
E-Mail: amos@amoplans.com
Website: amos-maritime.com
Members: 30 Companies
Staff: 3
Annual Budget: $1-2,000,000

Personnel:
President and Chairman: F. Anthony Naccarato
Secretary and Treasurer: Edward Hanley
Legislative Consultant: Brenda Otterson

Historical Note:
AMOS's mission is to maintain a U.S. merchant fleet capable of meeting the economic, national security, diplomatic and humanitarian responsibilities assigned to it by U.S. history, geography and law, and to expand this fleet in domestic and international commerce.

Publications:
Membership Directory; on-line

American Marketing Association *(1937)*
311 S. Wacker Dr.
Suite 5800
Chicago, IL 60606
Tel: (312) 542-9000 *Fax:* (312) 542-9001
TollFree: (800) 262-1150
E-Mail: info@ama.org
Website: marketingpower.com
Members: 38000 individuals
Staff: 70
Annual Budget: $25-50,000

Personnel:
Chief Executive Officer: Dennis Dunlap

Historical Note:
Formerly (1915) National Association of Teachers of Advertising; (1926) National Association of Teachers of Marketing & Advertising; (1932) National Association of Teachers of Marketing; (1937) merged with American Marketing Society to form the American Marketing Association. The Academy of Health Service Marketing was absorbed by the AMA in 1994. AMA serves as a conduit to foster knowledge sharing, providing resources, education, career and professional development opportunities and promotes or supports marketing practice and thought leadership. Membership: $225 (First Year); $47 (College

Student), $210 (Doctoral Candidate/Academic/Research Professional/Marketing Professional), $90 (Young Professional).

Meetings/Conferences: Annual
2013 - New Orleans, LA (Sheraton New Orleans Hotel)/March 21 - 23/1-10 exhibitors
Number of non-conference events/year: 2

Publications:
AMA's Essential Marketing Directory; on-line
AMA's Flagship Newsletter; weekly
B2B Marketing; monthly
Career Update; monthly
Journal of International Marketing; quarterly
Journal of Marketing; bi-monthly
Journal of Marketing Research; bi-monthly
Journal of Public Policy & Marketing; semi-annually
Marketing Academics; semi-annually
Marketing Health Services; quarterly
Marketing Management; bi-monthly
Marketing News; monthly
Marketing News Exclusives; bi-weekly
Marketing Research; quarterly
Marketing Researchers; monthly
Marketing Thought Leaders; monthly
MarketingPower Today; bi-weekly
Membership Directory; on-line
Professional Development Digest; monthly

American Massage Therapy Association *(1943)*
500 Davis St.
Suite 900
Evanston, IL 60201-4695
Tel: (847) 864-0123 *Fax:* (847) 864-5196
TollFree: (877) 905-0577
E-Mail: info@amtamassage.org
Website: amtamassage.org
Members: 57000 individuals
Staff: 60
Annual Budget: $10-25,000,000
Tax: 501(c)(6)

Personnel:
Executive Director: Shelly Johnson
  E-Mail: sjohnson@amtamassage.org
Director, Marketing: David French
Associate Director, Information Technology: Dan Hickey
Program Manager, Convention and Meetings: Chris Kirbabas
  E-Mail: ckirbabas@amtamassage.org
Director, Membership Experience: Karen Kubek
Chief Financial Officer: Larry LaBoda
Program Manager, Human Resources: Diane Lazcano
Program Manager, Website and Database: Ian McNally
Manager, Communications: Ron Precht
  E-Mail: rprecht@amtamassage.org
Director, Knowledge Transfer: Jocelyn Pysarchuk
Director, Government and Industry Relations: Chris Studebaker

Historical Note:
AMTA's mission is to serve members while advancing the art, science and practice of massage therapy. Members are massage therapists and massage schools. Membership: $235 (Professional); $45 (Student); $89 (Graduate); $350 (School).

Meetings/Conferences: Annual
Conference Chair: Chris Kirbabas
2013 - Ft. Worth, TX (Fort Worth Convention Center)/ Sept. 25 - 28
2014 - Denver, CO (Colorado Convention Center)/Sept. 17 - 19
Number of non-conference events/year: 4

Publications:
AMTA School Advantage; quarterly
e-touch; quarterly; adv.
Hands On; monthly
Message Therapy Journal; quarterly; adv.
Student eSource; quarterly

Membership List Available to Non-members

American Mathematical Association of Two Year Colleges *(1974)*
Southwest Tennessee Community College
5983 Macon Cove
Memphis, TN 38134
Tel: (901) 333-6243 *Fax:* (901) 333-6251
E-Mail: amatyc@amatyc.org
Website: amatyc.org
Members:

150 institutions
3000 individuals
Staff: 5
Annual Budget: $500-1,000,000

Personnel:
Executive Director: Cheryl Cleaves
    E-Mail: ccleaves@amatyc.org
Coordinator, Conferences: Keven Dockter
    E-Mail: keven.dockter@anokaramsey.edu
Director, Accounting: Christy Hunsucker
    E-Mail: chunsucker@amatyc.org
Director, Publications: Christine Shott
    E-Mail: cshott@amatyc.org
Office Director: Beverly S. Vance
    E-Mail: bvance@amatyc.org

Historical Note:
AMATYC's mission is to promote and increase awareness of the role of two-year colleges in mathematics education and provide a forum that facilitates professional networking, communication, policy determination, and action among individuals, affiliates, and other professional organizations. Membership: $80 (Individual); $40 (Special); $1600 (Life).

Meetings/Conferences: Annual
Conference Chair: Keven Dockter
2013 - Anaheim, CA/Oct. 31 - Nov. 3
2014 - Nashville, TN/Nov. 13 - 16
2014 - Nashville, TN/Nov. 20 - 23
2015 - New Orleans, LA/Nov. 19 - 22
2016 - Denver, CO/Nov. 17 - 20
2017 - San Diego, CA/Nov. 9 - 12

Publications:
AMATYC News; quarterly
Mathamatyc Educator; irregular; adv.

American Mathematical Society (1888)
201 Charles St.
Providence, RI 02904-2294
Tel: (401) 455-4000 *Fax:* (401) 331-3842
TollFree: (800) 321-4267
E-Mail: ams@ams.org
Website: ams.org
Members: 30000 individuals and 553 institutions
Staff: 221
Annual Budget: $25-50,000,000
Tax: 501(c)(3)

Personnel:
Executive Director: Donald E. McClure
    E-Mail: dem@ams.org
Chief Information Officer: Thomas J. Blythe
Sales Administrator: Deborah Laroche
    E-Mail: dxl@ams.org
Director , Meetings and Conferences: Penny Pina CMP
    E-Mail: meet@ams.org
Chief Financial Officer: Emily D. Riley

Historical Note:
Formerly the New York Mathematical Society, (1894) the American Mathematical Society. Incorporated in the District of Columbia in 1923. AMS's mission is to promote mathematical research and its uses, strengthen mathematical education, and foster awareness and appreciation of mathematics and its connections to other disciplines and to everyday life. Membership: $84 (Foreign Reciprocity); $264 (Contributing); $16 (Affiliate); $44 (Student/Unemployed); $66-176 (Regular); $20-176 (Joint Family Member); $66 (Retired).

Meetings/Conferences: Annual
Conference Chair: Penny Pina CMP
2013 - San Diego, CA (San Diego Convention and Visitors Bureau)/Jan. 9 - 12
2014 - Baltimore, MD (Hilton Baltimore)/Jan. 15 - 18
2015 - San Antonio, TX (San Antonio Convention Center)/Jan. 10 - 13
2016 - Seatle, WA (Washington State Convention Center)/Jan. 6 - 9
2017 - Atlanta, GA (Hyatt Regency Atlanta)/Jan. 4 - 7
Number of non-conference events/year: 19

Publications:
AMS Journals Mailing Dates; weekly
Bulletin of the American Mathematical Society; quarterly; adv.
Electronic-Only Journals; adv.
Membership Directory; on-line
Notices; monthly; adv.
Primary Research Journals; adv.
Translation Journals

American Measuring Tool Manufacturers Association (1973)

8562 East Ave.
Mentor, OH 44060
Tel: (440) 974-6829 *Fax:* (440) 974-6828
E-Mail: amtma@amtma.com
Website: amtma.com
Members: 75 companies
Staff: 3
Annual Budget: $25-50,000
Tax: 501(c)(6)

Personnel:
Managing Director: James Popovic
    E-Mail: amtma@amtma.com

Historical Note:
AMTMA's mission is to encourage and further the interest of its members in manufacturing, engineering, research, safety, transportation and other problems of the industry. Members are companies that produce gauges and similar precision measuring tools for a wide variety of quality control applications. Membership: $613 (Associate); $613-1,712 (Individual Based on no. of Employees).

Publications:
AMTMA Newsletter; on-line
Membership Directory; on-line

Membership List Available to Non-members

American Meat Institute (1906)
1150 Connecticut Ave. NW
12th Floor
Washington, DC 20036
Tel: (202) 587-4200 *Fax:* (202) 587-4300
E-Mail: memberservices@meatami.com
Website: meatami.com
Members: 1100 companies
Staff: 33
Annual Budget: $5-10,000,000
Tax: 501(c)(6)

Personnel:
President and Chief Executive Officer: J. Patrick Boyle
    E-Mail: jpboyle@meatami.com
Manager, Public Affairs and Online Editor: Tonya Allen
    E-Mail: tallen@meatami.com
Senior Vice President, Regulatory Affairs and General Counsel: Mark Dopp
    E-Mail: mdopp@meatami.com
Vice President, Technical Services: Scott Goltry
Controller: Thao Grimes
Vice President, Convention and Exposition Services: Anne Halal
    E-Mail: ahalal@meatami.com
Director, Worker Safety and Human Resources: Dan McCausland
    E-Mail: dmccausland@meatami.com
Senior Vice President, Legislative Affairs: Dale Nellor
    E-Mail: dnellor@meatami.com
Chief Financial Officer: Ronald L. Nunnery
    E-Mail: rnunnery@meatami.com
Senior Vice President, Public Affairs and Member Services: Janet Riley
    E-Mail: jriley@meatami.com
Vice President, Public Affairs: Tom Super
    E-Mail: tsuper@meatami.com
Director, Professional Development: Marie D. Ternieden PhD
    E-Mail: mternieden@meatami.com

Historical Note:
AMI is the meat and poultry trade association. Dedicated to increase the efficiency, profitability and safety of meat and poultry trade worldwide. Membership: $40.15 (General/Per Employee); $1,125-15,000 (Supplier); $1,000 (Associate).

Meetings/Conferences: Annual
Conference Chair: Anne Halal
2013 - Atlanta, GA (Georgia World Congress Center)/Jan. 29 - 31/25000 attendees/over 100 exhibitors

Publications:
The Hazard Analysis and Critical Control Point System in the Meat and Poultry Industry

Membership List Available to Non-members

American Meat Science Association (1948)
201 W Springfield Ave.
Suite 1202
Champaign, IL 61820
Fax: (217) 356-5370
E-Mail: information@meatscience.org
Website: meatscience.org
Members: 1066 individuals
Staff: 3

Annual Budget: $500-1,000,000
Tax: 501(c)(3)

Personnel:
Executive Director: Thomas Powell CAE, PhD
    E-Mail: tpowell@meatscience.org
Director, Programs: Deidreax Mabry
    E-Mail: dmabry@meatscience.org

Historical Note:
Established as the Reciprocal Meat Conference and became the American Meat Science Association in 1964. Advocates education and research in meat and related subjects. AAMSA incorporates expertise from traditional animal science and food science disciplines. Members are individual meat scientists. Membership encompasses the entire meat industry including red meat and poultry. Membership: $170 (Professional); $80 (Graduate Student); $30 (Undergraduate).

Meetings/Conferences: Annual
Conference Chair: Deidreax Mabry
2013 - Auburn, AL (Auburn University)/June 16 - 19
2014 - Madison, WI (University of Wisconsin and Oscar Mayer/Kraft Foods)/June 15 - 18
2015 - Lincoln, NE (University of Nebraska, Lincoln)/ June 14

Publications:
AMSA Directory; on-line
AMSA eNews; on-line
Meat Science
Reciprocation

American Medallic Sculpture Association (1982)
P.O. Box 1201
Edmonds, WA 98020
Tel: (206) 542-0608
E-Mail: amsanews@verizon.net
Website: amsamedals.org
Members: 130 individuals
Staff: 3
Annual Budget: Under $10,000
Tax: 501(c)(3)

Personnel:
President: Eugene Daub
    E-Mail: eugenedaub@cox.net
Newsletter Editor and Contact, General Issues and Membership Services: Anne-Lise Deering
    E-Mail: supermedal@verizon.net
Treasurer: Sylvia Perle
    E-Mail: perlestudios@hotmail.com

Historical Note:
AMSA's purpose is to advocate improvement in the art of the medal. Sponsors exhibitions, symposia, and other events. Membership: $35 (Regular); $20 (Student); $45 (Foreign).

Publications:
Membership Directory; on-line

American Medical Association (1847)
515 N. State St.
Chicago, IL 60654
Tel: (312) 464-5000 *Fax:* (312) 464-4184
TollFree: (800) 621-8335
Website: ama-assn.org
Members: 270000 individuals
Staff: 1200
Annual Budget: Over $100,000,000
Tax: 501(c)(6)

Personnel:
Executive Vice President and Chief Executive Officer: Dr. James Madara
Editor-in-Chief: Howard Bauchner
Senior Vice President, Periodic Publications: Thomas Easley
Senior Vice President and General Counsel: Jon N. Ekdahl
Senior Vice President and Chief Financial Officer: Denise Hagerty
Senior Vice President, Publishing and Business: Robert A. Musacchio
    E-Mail: musacchio@ama-assn.org
Senior Vice President and Chief Marketing Officer: Marietta Parenti
Senior Division Counsel, Corporate Law Division: Joseph P. Thornton
    E-Mail: joseph.thornton@ama-assn.org
Senior Vice President, Professional Standards: Modena H. Wilson MD, MHP
    E-Mail: modena.wilson@ama-assn.org

Historical Note:

AMA's mission is to promote the art and science of medicine and the betterment of public health. Membership: $420 (Physicians); $45 (Residents/Fellows); $84 (Retired Physicians); $20 (Students).

Meetings/Conferences:
2013 - Washington, DC (Grand Hyatt Washington)/ Feb. 11 - 13
2013 - Chicago, IL (Hyatt Regency Chicago)/June 15 - 19
2013 - Ft. Washington, MD (Gaylord National Hotel and Convention Center)/Nov. 16 - 19
Number of non-conference events/year: 1

Publications:
AMA MedEd Update; monthly
AMA Morning Rounds; weekly
AMA Wire; weekly
American Medical News; bi-monthly
Archives of Dermatology; monthly
Archives of Facial Plastic Surgery; bi-monthly
Archives of General Psychiatry; monthly; adv.
Archives of Internal Medicine; adv.
Archives of Neurology; monthly
Archives of Ophthalmology; monthly
Archives of Otolaryngology—Head & Neck Surgery; monthly
Archives of Pediatrics & Adolescent Medicine; monthly
Archives of Surgery; monthly
Disaster Medicine and Public Health Preparedness; quarterly; adv.
eBookNews; bi-monthly
JAMA; weekly

American Medical Association Alliance, Inc. (1922)
515 N. State St.
Ninth Floor
Chicago, IL 60654
Tel: (312) 464-4470 *Fax:* (312) 464-5020
TollFree: (800) 549-4619
E-Mail: admin@amaalliance.org
Website: amaalliance.org
Members: 18000 individuals
Staff: 13
Annual Budget: $1-2,000,000
Tax: 501(c)(4)

Personnel:
Executive Director: Beth Kohr
   E-Mail: beth.kohr@ama-assn.org
Director, Communications: Rosetta Gervasi
   E-Mail: rosetta.gervasi@ama-assn.org
Director, Membership Services and Marketing: Julie Ziegler
   E-Mail: julie.ziegler@ama-assn.org

Historical Note:
AMAA's mission to support medical families through advocacy and education. Membership: $50/year.

Meetings/Conferences: Annual
Publications:
AMA Alliance E-Connection; monthly
Connections
Membership Directory; on-line

American Medical Directors Association (1976)
11000 Broken Land Pkwy.
Suite 400
Columbia, MD 21044
Tel: (410) 740-9743 *Fax:* (410) 740-4572
TollFree: (800) 876-2632
E-Mail: info@amda.com
Website: amda.com
Members: 7000 individuals
Staff: 30
Annual Budget: $2-5,000,000
Tax: 501(c)(6)

Personnel:
Interim Executive Director: Harvey Tillipman
Meeting Manager: Abby Giffin
   E-Mail: agiffin@amda.com
Director, Membership and Communications: Susan Hanf
   E-Mail: shanf@amda.com
Director, Professional Development and Meetings: Sheena Majette
   E-Mail: smajette@amda.com

Historical Note:
AMDA is dedicated to excellence in patient care and provides education, advocacy, information, and professional

development to promote the delivery of quality long term care medicine. Members are physicians and other practitioners who provide care to patients in long term care facilities. Membership: $131-337 (Physicians); $70-180 (Licensed Independent Practitioners); $57-148 (Interdisciplinary Team); $75 (Physicians in Training); $35 (Retired).

Continuing Education:
Certification Designation/s: CMD
Meetings/Conferences: Annual
Conference Chair: Abby Giffin
2013 - Ft. Washington, MD/March 21 - 24
2014 - Nashville, TN/Feb. 27 - March 2
Number of non-conference events/year: 27

Publications:
AMDA Reports; quarterly
Caring for the Ages; monthly; adv.
Health Policy Advisor
Journal of the American Medical Directors Association; adv.
Membership Directory; on-line
Weekly Round-Up; weekly

Membership List Available to Non-members

American Medical Group Association (1949)
One Prince St.
Alexandria, VA 22314-3318
Tel: (703) 838-0033 *Fax:* (703) 548-1890
Website: amga.org
Members: 370 medical groups
Staff: 32
Annual Budget: $100-250,000

Personnel:
President and Chief Executive Officer: Donald W. Fisher CAE, PhD
   E-Mail: dfisher@amga.org

Historical Note:
AMGA's mission is to improve health care for patients by supporting multispecialty medical groups and other organized systems of care.

Meetings/Conferences: Annual
2013 - Orlando, FL (Hilton Orlando Bonnet Creek)/ March 14 - 16
2014 - Grapevine, TX (Gaylord Texan Hotel and Convention Center, Dallas Texas)/April 9 - 12
2015 - Lake Tahoe, NV (Caesar's Palace Hotel and Casino)/March 23 - 26

Publications:
Advocacy Enews; on-line
Group Practice Journal; monthly; adv.
Inside AMGA; on-line
Medical Group Compensation and Financial Survey; annually
Membership Directory; annually

Membership List Available to Non-members

American Medical Informatics Association (1988)
4720 Montgomery Ln.
Suite 500
Bethesda, MD 20814
Tel: (301) 657-1291 *Fax:* (301) 657-1296
E-Mail: mail@amia.org
Website: amia.org
Members: 4000 individuals
Staff: 25
Annual Budget: $2-5,000,000

Personnel:
President and Chief Executive Officer: Kevin M. Fickenscher CPE, FAAFP, FACPE, MD
   E-Mail: drkevin@amia.org
Vice President, Public Policy and Government Relations: Meryl Bloomrosen
   E-Mail: meryl@amia.org
Director, Meetings: Dasha Cohen
   E-Mail: dasha@amia.org
Senior Advisor: Don E. Detmer MD
   E-Mail: detmer@mail.amia.org
Vice President, Corporate Relations and Development: Jonathan Grau
   E-Mail: jonathan@amia.org
Executive Vice President and Chief Operating Officer: Karen E. Greenwood
   E-Mail: karen@amia.org
Vice President, Marketing and Communications: Nancy Light
   E-Mail: nlight@amia.org

Director, Marketing and Communications: Krista Martin
   E-Mail: krista@amia.org
Director, Membership Services: Rob Rader
   E-Mail: rob@amia.org
Vice President, Education and Academic Affairs: Jeffrey Williamson
   E-Mail: jeff@amia.org

Historical Note:
AMIA aims at the development and application of biomedical and health informatics in United States. AMIA's mission is to lead the way in transforming health care through trusted science, education, and the practice of informatics. Members are individuals interested in the application of information science and computer technology to all aspects of biomedical and health care, teaching and research. Membership: $300 (Regular); $135 (Retired); $40 (Student); $75 (Affiliate).

Continuing Education:
Certification Designation/s: FACM
Meetings/Conferences: Annual
Conference Chair: Dasha Cohen
2013 - Washington, DC (Washington Hilton)/Nov. 16 - 20
2014 - Washington, DC (Washington Hilton)/Nov. 15 - 19
2015 - San Francisco, CA (Hilton San Francisco Union Square)/Nov. 14 - 18
2016 - Chicago, IL (Hilton Chicago)/Nov. 12 - 16
2017 - Washington, DC (Washington Hilton)/Nov. 4 - 8
2018 - San Francisco, CA (Hilton San Francisco Union Square)/Oct. 27 - 31
Number of non-conference events/year: 2

Publications:
AMIA e-News; weekly
JAMIA; bi-monthly
The Standards Standard; biennially

Membership List Available to Non-members

American Medical Rehabilitation Providers Association (1998)
1710 N St. NW
Washington, DC 20036
Tel: (202) 223-1920 *Fax:* (202) 223-1925
TollFree: (888) 346-4624
Website: amrpa.org
Members: 450 facilities
Staff: 6
Annual Budget: $2-5,000,000

Personnel:
Vice President: Magdalena Ramirez
   E-Mail: mramirez@amrpa.org
Accounts Manager: Amy Cheatham
   E-Mail: acheatham@firminc.com
Manager, Website: Susan Morris
   E-Mail: susan.morris@yahoo.com
Administrative Assistant: Lovelyn M. Robinson
   E-Mail: lrobinson@amrpa.org
Research Assistant: Rebecca Schnorf
   E-Mail: rschnorf@amrpa.org

Historical Note:
Formed by a merger of the Association of Rehabilitation Centers (founded in 1952 as the Conference of Rehabilitation Centers and Facilities) and the National Association of Sheltered Workshops and Homebound Programs (founded in 1954). AMRPA is devoted to the interests of inpatient rehabilitation hospitals and units and outpatient rehabilitation providers and establish a policy agenda for the field. Membership: $1,200-2,500 (Consultant, based on salary); $2587.32-20,279.94 (Institutional, based on salary).

Meetings/Conferences: Annual
Conference Chair: Amy Cheatham

Publications:
Action Advisory Alerts; on-line
AMRPA Magazine; monthly
Membership Directory; on-line
Off the Record; weekly

American Medical Society for Sports Medicine (1991)
4000 W. 114th St.
Suite 100
Leawood, KS 66211
Tel: (913) 327-1415 *Fax:* (913) 327-1491
E-Mail: office@amssm.org
Website: amssm.org
Members: 2100 individuals

Staff: 8
Annual Budget: $1-2,000,000

Personnel:
Executive Director: Jim Griffith
  E-Mail: jgriffith@amssm.org
Director and Editor: Chad Asplund
  E-Mail: newsletter@amssm.org
Contact, Membership: Joan Brown
  E-Mail: joanb@amssm.org
Director, Education: Sean Bryan MD
  E-Mail: education@amssm.org
Secretary and Treasurer: Katherine Dec MD
  E-Mail: secretarytreasurer@amssm.org
Director, Operations: Jody Gold
Website and Registration Inquiries: Michele Lane
  E-Mail: mlane@amssm.org
Director, Public Relations: Amy Powell MD
  E-Mail: publicrelations@amssm.org

Historical Note:
AMSSM seeks to foster a collegial relationship among dedicated, competent sports medicine specialists, to provide a quality educational resource for its members, other sports medicine professionals, and the general public. Membership is open to physician significantly involved in sports medicine, the "sports medicine physicians". Membership: $350 (Active/Associate); $225 (Fellowship/International); $150 (Resident); $30 (Student).

Meetings/Conferences: Annual
2013 - San Diego, CA (Manchester Grand)/April 17 - 21
2014 - New Orleans, LA (Hyatt Regency New Orleans)/April 5 - 9
2015 - Hollywood, FL (Westin Diplomat Resort and Spa)/April 15 - 19
2016 - Dallas, TX (Sheraton Dallas)/April 16 - 20
2018 - Orlando, FL (Walt Disney World Swan And Dolphin)/April 25 - 29
Number of non-conference events/year: 1

Publications:
AMSSM Newsletters

American Medical Student Association *(1950)*
45610 Woodland Rd.
Suite 300
Sterling, VA 20166
Tel: (703) 620-6600 *Fax:* (703) 620-6445
TollFree: (800) 767-2266
E-Mail: amsa@amsa.org
Website: amsa.org
Members: 68000 individuals
Staff: 35
Annual Budget: $5-10,000,000
Tax: 501(c)(6)

Personnel:
Executive Director: Carol Williams-Nickelson PsyD
  E-Mail: execdir@amsa.org
Director, Public Relations: Kim Cunningham
  E-Mail: pr@amsa.org
Senior Director, Communications and Marketing: Meeghan De Cagna
  E-Mail: mdecagna@amsa.org
Director, Education and Research: Jeff Koetje MD
Manager, Information Management: Jennifer Salehi
  E-Mail: jsalehi@amsa.org
Director, Events and Business Development: Jamie Thayer
  E-Mail: jthayer@amsa.org
Director, Publications: Pete Thomson
  E-Mail: pete_t@amsa.org
Associate Director, Membership Recruitment: Nicole White
  E-Mail: nwhite@amsa.org

Historical Note:
AMSA is committed to improving health care and healthcare delivery to all people, encouraging active improvement in medical education, involving its members in the social, moral and ethical obligations of the profession of medicine; assisting in the improvement and understanding of world health problems, contributing to the welfare of medical students, premedical students, interns, residents and post-MD/DO trainees, and advancing the profession of medicine. Members are medical students, premedical students, interns, residents and practicing physicians. Membership: (U.S. Medical Student/International Medical Student/Premedical Student); $50 (Supporting Affiliate); $10 (Graduate/Professional).

Meetings/Conferences: Annual
Conference Chair: Jamie Thayer
2013 - Washington, DC/March 14 - 17/1-10 exhibitors

Number of non-conference events/year: 10

Publications:
Global Pulse; adv.
Membership Directory; on-line
The New Physician Magazine; bi-monthly; adv.

American Medical Technologists *(1939)*
10700 W. Higgins Rd.
Suite 150
Rosemont, IL 60018
Tel: (847) 823-5169 *Fax:* (847) 823-0458
TollFree: (800) 275-1268
E-Mail: mail@amt1.com
Website: americanmedtech.org
Members: 46000 individuals
Staff: 21
Annual Budget: $2-5,000,000
Tax: 501(c)(6)

Personnel:
Executive Director: Christopher A. Damon JD
Director, Marketing: Kathy Cilia MBA
  E-Mail: kathy.cilia@amt1.com
Manager, Certifications: Geri Mulcahy
  E-Mail: geri.mulcahy@amt1.com
Director, Publications and Meetings: Diane Powell CMP
  E-Mail: diane.powell@amt1.com

Historical Note:
AMT's mission is to manage, promote, expand upon and continuously improve its certification programs for allied health professionals who work in a variety of disciplines and settings. Membership: $5-125/year.

Continuing Education:
Enrollment: 10000
Certification Designation/s: CMLA, RDA, RPT, RMA, CMAS, AHI, MLT, MT, CLC

Meetings/Conferences: Annual
Conference Chair: Diane Powell CMP

Publications:
AMT Events; quarterly; adv.
Journal of Continuing Education Topics & Issues; adv.

Membership List Available to Non-members

American Medical Women's Association *(1915)*
100 N. 20th St.
Suite 400
Philadelphia, PA 19103
Tel: (215) 320-3716 *Fax:* (215) 564-2175
TollFree: (866) 564-2483
E-Mail: info@amwa-doc.org
Website: amwa-doc.org
Members: 10000 individuals
Staff: 21
Annual Budget: $500-1,000,000
Tax: 501(c)(3)

Personnel:
President: Gayatri Devi MD

Historical Note:
Founded in November 1915 in Chicago and incorporated in Illinois in 1916 as the Medical Women's National Association. Reincorporated in New York in 1924 and name changed to American Medical Women's Association, Inc. in 1937. AMWA is an organization which functions at the local, national, and international level to advance women in medicine and improve women's health. Membership restricted to women physicians, interns, residents and medical and osteopathic students. Friends of AMWA Category is open to both females and males. U. S. affiliate of the Medical Women's International Association. Membership: $225 (Regular/Donor); $150 (Discounted and Non-Physician Member/Donor); $100 (Resident/Donor); $75 (Medical/Graduate Student Member/Donor); $25 (Undergraduate Student Member/Donor); $10,000 (Corporate).

Meetings/Conferences: Annual
2013 - New York City, NY (New York Palace)/March 15 - 17

Publications:
The Journal of Women's Health
Newsflash; monthly
The Connection; quarterly

American Medical Writers Association *(1940)*
30 W. Gude Dr.
Suite 525
Rockville, MD 20850-1161
Tel: (301) 294-5303 *Fax:* (301) 294-9006
E-Mail: amwa@amwa.org
Website: amwa.org

Members: 5600 individuals
Staff: 7
Annual Budget: $1-2,000,000
Tax: 501(c)(3)

Personnel:
Executive Director: Susan Krug CAE
  E-Mail: skrug@amwa.org
Staff Accountant and Benefits Administrator: Carol Griffin MS
  E-Mail: carol@amwa.org
Coordinator, Conference and Education: Becky Phillips
  E-Mail: becky@amwa.org
Deputy Director, Communications, Partnerships, Member and Chapter Relations: Shari Rager CAE
  E-Mail: srager@amwa.org
Coordinator, Membership Services and Database: Mark Rosol
  E-Mail: mark@amwa.org
Manager, Education: Dane Russo
  E-Mail: dane@amwa.org
Coordinator, Membership Services and Publications: Rachel Spassiani MA
  E-Mail: rachel@amwa.org

Historical Note:
Originated at Rock Island, IL as the Mississippi Valley Medical Editors' Association; assumed its current name in 1948. Incorporated in Illinois in 1951. AMWA's mission is to advocate excellence in medical communication and to provide educational resources in support of that goal. Membership: $160 (New Member); $55 (Student).

Continuing Education:
Certification Designation/s: PDC

Meetings/Conferences: Annual
Conference Chair: Becky Phillips
2013 - Columbus, OH/Nov. 6 - 9
Number of non-conference events/year: 9

Publications:
AMWA Journal; quarterly; adv.

American Membrane Technology Association *(1972)*
2409 SE Dixie Hwy.
Stuart, FL 34996
Tel: (772) 463-0820 *Fax:* (772) 463-0860
Website: amtaorg.com
Members: 750 individuals
Staff: 5
Annual Budget: $500-1,000,000
Tax: 501(c)(4)

Personnel:
Executive Director: Ian C. Watson PE
  E-Mail: iwatson@amtaorg.com
Administrative Director: Janet L. Jaworski CMP
  E-Mail: admin@amtaorg.com
Assistant, Events: Debi Levitt
  E-Mail: dlevitt@amtaorg.com
Coordinator, Events: Marilyn Medlock
  E-Mail: eventassist@amtaorg.com

Historical Note:
Formerly (1972) the National Water Supply Improvement Association, (1993) the Water Supply Improvement Association and (2000) the American Desalting Association. AMTA 's mission is to promote, advocate and advance the understanding and application of membrane technology to create safe, affordable and reliable water supplies, and to treat municipal, industrial, agricultural and waste waters for beneficial use. Membership: $50-2,500/year.

Meetings/Conferences: Annual
Conference Chair: Debi Levitt
2013 - San Antonio, TX (The Henry B. Gonzalez Convention Center)/Feb. 25 - 28
Number of non-conference events/year: 6

Publications:
Solutions; quarterly; adv.
Sourcebook and Membership Directory; annually

American Men's Studies Association *(1991)*
1507 Pebble Dr.
Greensboro, NC 27410
Tel: (336) 323-2672
E-Mail: mensstudies@umich.edu
Website: mensstudies.org
Members: 150 individuals
Staff: 5

Personnel:
President: Robert Heasley PhD

E-Mail: heasley@iup.edu
Treasurer: Jeff Cohen PhD
    E-Mail: jwcohen@me.com
Director, Outreach and Communications: Jan Deeds PhD
    E-Mail: jdeeds1@unl.edu
Webmaster: Robert N. Minor PhD
    E-Mail: rminor@ku.edu

Historical Note:
AMSA advances the critical study of men and masculinities by encouraging the development of teaching, research and clinical practice in the field of men's studies. Membership: $15 (Regular); $125 (Friend of AMSA).

Meetings/Conferences: Annual
2013 - Ann Arbor, MI (University of Michigan, Ann Arbor)/April 4 - 7

Publications:
AMSA E-Newsletter; on-line

American Mental Health Counselors Association
(1976)
801 N. Fairfax St.
Suite 304
Alexandria, VA 22314
Tel: (703) 548-6002 *Fax:* (703) 548-4775
TollFree: (800) 326-2642
Website: amhca.org
Members: 6300 individuals
Staff: 5
Annual Budget: $1-2,000,000
Tax: 501(c)(3)

Personnel:
Executive Director and Chief Executive Officer: W. Mark Hamilton PhD
    E-Mail: mhamilton@amhca.org
Director, Legislative Affairs: Julie A. Clements
    E-Mail: jclements@amhca.org
Office Administrator: Melissa Hobson
    E-Mail: mhobson@amhca.org
Manager, Membership Services and Member Relations: Linda Morano
    E-Mail: Lmorano@amhca.org

Historical Note:
AMHCA's mission is to enhance the profession of mental health counseling through licensing, advocacy, education and professional development. Membership: $169 (Clinical/Regular); $79 (Professional Associate/Student); $74 (Retired/Associate).

Meetings/Conferences: Annual
Number of non-conference events/year: 1

Publications:
Advocate; monthly; adv.
AMHCA Leadership Directory; on-line
Journal of Mental Health Counseling; quarterly
Membership Directory; on-line
Psychology Today's Therapy Directory

American Metal Detector Manufacturers Association *(1978)*
1881 W. State St.
Garland, TX 75042-6761
Tel: (972) 494-6151 *Fax:* (972) 494-1881
E-Mail: general@tsaweb.org
Members: 6 companies
Staff: 1
Annual Budget: Under $10,000

Personnel:
President: Charles Garrett
    E-Mail: sales@garrett.com

Historical Note:
Metal detector manufacturers. Objective is to assist members and the industry in dealing with common business problems. Presently inactive. Has no paid officers or full-time staff.

American Metalcasting Consortium
5300 International Blvd.
N. Charleston, SC 29418-6937
Tel: (843) 760-3591 *Fax:* (843) 760-3349
E-Mail: amc@aticorp.org
Website: amc.aticorp.org
Members: 230 companies
Staff: 12
Annual Budget: $25-50,000,000

Personnel:
Vice President, Metals Technology: Mike Gwyn
Manager, Programs: Thornton White
    E-Mail: thornton.white@scra.org

Historical Note:
AMC is a coalition of four metalcasting organizations which aims to reestablish manufacturing interests in specific areas. The Coalition includes the American Foundrymen's Society, the Non-Ferrous Founders Society, the North American Die Casting Association, and the Steel Founders Society of America. AMC's mission is to develop and apply new technologies that will rapidly deliver quality, cost-effective cast parts to support the warfighter.

Meetings/Conferences:
Conference Chair: Thornton White
Number of non-conference events/year: 4

American Meteorological Society *(1919)*
45 Beacon St.
Boston, MA 02108-3693
Tel: (617) 227-2425 *Fax:* (617) 742-8718
E-Mail: amsinfo@ametsoc.org
Website: ametsoc.org
Members: 14,000 professionals, students, and weather enthusiasts.
Staff: 50
Annual Budget: $10-25,000,000
Tax: 501(c)(3)

Personnel:
Executive Director: Keith L. Seitter
    E-Mail: kseitter@ametsoc.org
Director, Education: James Brey
    E-Mail: brey@ametsoc.org
Production Editor, AMS Books: Beth Dayton
    E-Mail: edayton@ametsoc.org
Director, Membership Services: Beth Farley
    E-Mail: bfarley@ametsoc.org
Director, Information Systems: Lee Gordon
    E-Mail: lgordon@ametsoc.org
Director, Meetings: Claudia Gorski
    E-Mail: cgorski@ametsoc.org
Director, Publications: Ken Heideman
    E-Mail: kheideman@ametsoc.org
Contact, Human Resources: Barry Mohan
    E-Mail: bmohan@ametsoc.org
Secretary and Treasurer: Richard D. Rosen
    E-Mail: amssectreas@ametsoc.org
Manager, Marketing and Special Programs: Kelly Savoie
    E-Mail: ksavoie@ametsoc.org

Historical Note:
Founded December 29, 1919 in St. Louis and incorporated in the District of Columbia in 1920. Permanent headquarters were established in Boston in 1946 and the Society was reincorporated in Massachusetts in 1958. AMS promotes the development, dissemination, information and education on the atmospheric and related oceanic and hydrologic sciences. Membership: $10-6,630/year.

Continuing Education:
Certification Designation/s: CCM, CBM

Meetings/Conferences: Annual
Conference Chair: Claudia Gorski
2013 - Austin, TX/Jan. 6 - 10
2014 - Atlanta, GA/Feb. 2 - 6
2015 - Phoenix, AZ/Jan. 4 - 8
2016 - New Orleans, LA/Jan. 10 - 14
2017 - Seatle, WA/Jan. 22 - 26
2018 - Austin, TX/Jan. 7 - 11
2019 - Phoenix, AZ/Jan. 6 - 10
2020 - Boston, MA/Jan. 12 - 16
2021 - New Orleans, LA/Jan. 10 - 14
2022 - Houston, TX/Jan. 23 - 27
2023 - Denver, CO/Jan. 8 - 12
2025 - New Orleans, LA/Jan. 12 - 16
2026 - Houston, TX/Jan. 25 - 29
2027 - Denver, CO/Jan. 10 - 14
2029 - New Orleans, LA/Jan. 7 - 11
2030 - Houston, TX/Jan. 27 - 31
2031 - Denver, CO/Jan. 12 - 16
Number of non-conference events/year: 17

Publications:
Earth Interactions; on-line
Journal of Applied Meteorology and Climatology; monthly
Journal of Atmospheric and Oceanic Technology; monthly
Journal of Climate; bi-monthly
Journal of Physical Oceanography; monthly
Journal of the Atmospheric Sciences; monthly
Monthly Weather Review; monthly
Weather and Forecasting; bi-monthly
Weather, Climate, and Society; quarterly

American Microchemical Society *(1935)*
Two June Way
Middlesex, NJ 08846
Website: microchem.org
Members: 125 individuals
Staff: 2
Annual Budget: Under $10,000

Personnel:
Treasurer: Herk Felder

Historical Note:
Formerly (1935) Metropolitan Microchemical Society. Absorbed its current name in 1963. AMS is a scientific, and educational organization with a focus upon encouraging the advancement of microchemistry. Members are analytic chemists with a special interest in the properties of chemicals when found in minute quantities. Membership: $10/year.

Publications:
Microchemical Journal

American Microscopical Society *(1878)*
1250 Bellflower Blvd.
C/O Department of Biol. Sciences, CSU, Long Beach
Long Beach, CA 90840
Tel: (562) 985-5378 *Fax:* (562) 985-8878
Website: amicros.org
Members: 510 individuals
Staff: 3
Annual Budget: $10-25,000

Personnel:
Editor-in-Chief: Dr. Bruno Pernet
    E-Mail: bpernet@csulb.edu

Historical Note:
AMS is an international society of biologists organized to encourage the use of microscopy. Its members are mostly scientists and educators who use various kinds of microscopes in their research and teaching light and electron microscopes, fluorescence and confocal microscopes, and other tools for visualizing the small. Membership: $25 (Student/Emeritus); $50 (Ordinary); $150 (Sustaining); $1,000 (Life).

Meetings/Conferences: Annual
2013 - San Francisco, CA (Hilton San Francisco Union Square)/Jan. 3 - 7
2014 - Austin, TX/Jan. 3 - 7

Publications:
AMS Newsletter; biennially
Invertebrate Biology; quarterly; adv.

American Mideast Business Associates *(1951)*
Four Kansas Rd.
Tuckerton, NJ 08087
Tel: (609) 296-4783
Members: 175 corporations
Staff: 2
Annual Budget: $500-1,000,000

Personnel:
President: I.F. Yusif CAE

Historical Note:
Established in New York, NY as the Egyptian American Society became (1960) American Arab Association for Commerce and Industry. Assumed its current name in 1987 to reflect growing membership interest in all Middle Eastern and North African countries. Members are both U.S and Arab transnationals. Provides consultation and translation services to non-members on a contract basis. Membership: $10,000/year (organization).

American Midwifery Certification Board
849 International Dr.
Suite 205
Linthicum, MD 21090
Tel: (410) 694-9424 *Fax:* (410) 694-9425
TollFree: (866) 366-9632
Website: amcbmidwife.org
Staff: 7
Annual Budget: $500-1,000,000

Personnel:
Executive Director: Carrie D. Bright CAE, IOM
    E-Mail: cbright@amcbmidwife.org
Director, Certification and Operations: Denise Smith
    E-Mail: dsmith@accmidwife.org

Historical Note:
Formerly the ACNM Certification Council, assumed its current name in 2005. AMCB's mission is to protect and serve the public by establishing and maintaining the

certification standards for individuals educated in the profession of midwifery.

Continuing Education:
Certification Designation/s: CM, CNM

American Military Retirees Association *(1973)*
5436 Peru St.
Suite One
Plattsburgh, NY 12901
Tel: (518) 563-9479 *Fax:* (518) 324-5204
TollFree: (800) 424-2969
E-Mail: info@amra1973.org
Website: amra1973.org
Members: 26,000 members
Staff: 6
Annual Budget: $250-500,000

Personnel:
Executive Director: Margaret "Peg" Bergeron
    E-Mail: info@amra1973.org
Staff writer, Coordinator Membership and Marketing:
    Kathy Baumgarten
    E-Mail: info@amra1973.org
Office Manager: Crystal Mang

Historical Note:
Founded in 1973. AMRA Mission is to works on behalf of military retirees and their families, to protect their rights and benefits under the law, and to lobby on their behalf in Washington, DC and elsewhere. Membership: $25 (Annual).

Meetings/Conferences: Annual
2013 - San Antonio, TX (El Tropicano Riverwalk
    Hotel)/June 7 - 8

Publications:
Newsletter; weekly; adv.

American Military Society *(1982)*
P.O. Box 90740
Washington, DC 20090-0740
Tel: (800) 379-6128 *Fax:* (301) 583-8717
TollFree: (800) 379-6128
Website: amsmilitary.org
Staff: 1
Annual Budget: $250-500,000

Personnel:
Executive Director: John P. May

Historical Note:
AMS's mission is to advocate improved quality-of-life and economic fairness that will support the well-being of the men and women of America's Uniformed Services and their families. Membership: $20-300 (Single); $30-400 (Joint).

Publications:
Advocate Newsletter; bi-monthly

American Milking Devon Cattle Association
(1978)
135 Old Bay Rd.
New Durham, NH 03855
Tel: (603) 859-6611 *Fax:* (860) 399-2485
E-Mail: mdevons@worldpath.net
Website: milkingdevons.org
Members: 85 individuals
Staff: 3
Annual Budget: Under $10,000

Personnel:
Registrar: Sue B. Randall

Historical Note:
AMDA works to promote American Milking Devon as the breed of cattle for sustainable healthy agriculture. Members are breeders and interested individuals. Membership: $20/ year (Voting/Associate).

Meetings/Conferences: Annual
2013 - Tunbridge, VT (Town Hall)/May 11

Publications:
Newsletter

American Milking Shorthorn Society *(1920)*
800 Pleasant St.
Beloit, WI 53511-5456
Tel: (608) 365-3332 *Fax:* (608) 365-6644
E-Mail: milkshorthorns@tds.net
Website: milkingshorthorn.com
Members: 350 individuals
Staff: 2
Annual Budget: $250-500,000
Tax: 501(c)(5)

Personnel:

Executive Secretary: David J. Kendall
    E-Mail: davetmb@tds.net

Historical Note:
Mission of AMSS is to recognize and welcome the diversity of the Milking Shorthorn as a unique feature of the breed, distinguishing it from all other breeds in the United States; to encourage each breeder to use all the Society programs which will benefit them individually and respect the rights of other breeders to have a different goal and to use different programs. Member of the National Pedigreed Livestock Council and the Purebred Dairy Cattle Association. Membership: $45 (Full); $30 (Associate); $25 (Junior).

Meetings/Conferences: Annual
2013 - McPherson, KS/May 29 - June 1

Publications:
AMSS Tails and Trails Newsletters
Breeders Directory; on-line
Member Directory; on-line
Milking Shorthorn Journal; adv.
State / Regional Newsletters

American Miniature Horse Association *(1978)*
5601 S. Interstate 35 West
Alvarado, TX 76009
Tel: (817) 783-5600 *Fax:* (817) 783-6403
E-Mail: information@amha.org
Website: amha.org
Members: 12000 members
Staff: 19
Annual Budget: $2-5,000,000
Tax: 501(c)(5)

Personnel:
President: Harry Elder
    E-Mail: president@amha.org
Contact, Information Technology: Quintin Boehmisch
    E-Mail: it@amha.org
Contact, Marketing and Public Relations: Stephanie
    Haselwander
    E-Mail: stephanie@amha.org
Controller: Randy Peacock
    E-Mail: randy@amha.org
Editor: Melissa Powell
    E-Mail: melissa@amha.org
Contact, Membership Services: Jamisen Robinson
    E-Mail: information@amha.org
Contact, Show Department: Christy Scott
    E-Mail: christy@amha.org

Historical Note:
Absorbed the International Miniature Horse Registry in 1985, AMHA's purpose is to encourage the breeding, exhibiting, use and perpetuation of the American Miniature Horse, separate and apart from ponies and other small equines. Membership: $65-100 (Regular-U.S./Canada/ Foreign); $65 (Associate); $10 (Youth).

Meetings/Conferences: Annual
Conference Chair: Christy Scott
2013 - Reno, NV (Peppermill Resort Spa Casino)/Feb.
    14 - 17
Number of non-conference events/year: 2

Publications:
AMHA Breeders Directory (Membership Directory)
Miniature Horse World; bi-monthly; adv.

American Mobile Telecommunications Association
200 N. Glebe Rd.
Suite 1000
Arlington, VA 22203
Tel: (202) 331-7773 *Fax:* (202) 331-9062
E-Mail: cschaar@atmausa.org
Website: amtaUSA.org
Staff: 1
Annual Budget: $250-500,000

Personnel:
President: Alan Shark

Historical Note:
Represents the interests of business wireless telecommunications systems.

American Mold Builders Association *(1973)*
3601 Algonquin
Suite 304
Rolling Meadows, IL 60008
Tel: (847) 222-9402 *Fax:* (847) 222-9437
Website: amba.org
Members: 300 organizations
Staff: 4
Annual Budget: $250-500,000

Tax: 501(c)(6)

Personnel:
Executive Director: Troy Nix
    E-Mail: tnix@amba.org
Contact, Emarketing, Web and Member Services: Sue
    Daniels
    E-Mail: sdaniels@amba.org
Coordinator, Business and Advertising: Shannon Merrill
    E-Mail: smerrill@amba.org

Historical Note:
AMBA's mission is to promote its member services and overall competitiveness in a world market, through membership participation. Membership: $400-1600/year (Organization).

Meetings/Conferences: Annual
2013 - Schaumburg, IL/April 24 - 26

Publications:
EBeat; bi-weekly; adv.
Membership Directory; annually; adv.
OEM eNewsletter; monthly; adv.
The American Mold Builder (TAMB); quarterly; adv.

American Montessori Society *(1960)*
116 E. 16th St.
New York, NY 10003
Tel: (212) 358-1250 *Fax:* (212) 358-1256
E-Mail: ams@amshq.org
Website: amshq.org
Members: 13,000 members
Staff: 23
Annual Budget: $2-5,000,000
Tax: 501(c)(3)

Personnel:
Executive Director: Richard A. Ungerer
    E-Mail: richard@amshq.org
Director, Membership Services: Carla Hofland MBA
    E-Mail: carla@amshq.org
Manager, Information Technology: Andrew Hofland
    E-Mail: andrew@amshq.org
Senior Director, Operations and Human Resources:
    Gregory A. Jones LMSW, SPHR
    E-Mail: gregory@amshq.org
Senior Director, Marketing and Communications: Marcy K.
    Krever
    E-Mail: marcy@amshq.org
Senior Director, Finance: Joan LaRacuente MBA
    E-Mail: joan@amshq.org
Senior Director, Teacher Education: Doris Sommer
    E-Mail: doris@amshq.org
Contact, Publications: Roger Williams
    E-Mail: orders@amshq.org
Conference Coordinator: Leah Zak
    E-Mail: leah@amshq.org

Historical Note:
AMS provides the leadership and inspiration to make Montessori a significant voice in education. A community of schools, teachers, families, and others determined to make Montessori a strong and positive force in education. Membership: $72-126 (Individual-U.S. Residents); $83-145 (Individual-International Residents); $16.75 -3900 (School-Regular); $10.85-710 (School-Family).

Meetings/Conferences: Annual
Conference Chair: Richard A. Ungerer
2013 - Orlando, FL (Hilton Orlando Destination
    Parkway)/March 14 - 17
2014 - Dallas, TX (Hilton Anatole Dallas)/March 27 -
    30
2015 - Philadelphia, PA (Philadelphia Marriott
    Downtown)/March 12 - 15

Publications:
Montessori Life; quarterly
Peace Seed Connection
The AMS Prism; quarterly

Membership List Available to Non-members

American Morgan Horse Association *(1909)*
4066 Shelburne Rd.
Suite Five
Shelburne, VT 05482
Tel: (802) 985-4944 *Fax:* (802) 985-8897
E-Mail: info@morganhorse.com
Website: morganhorse.com
Members: 10000 individuals
Staff: 13
Annual Budget: $1-2,000,000
Tax: 501(c)(5)

Personnel:
Executive Director: Julie Broadway
    E-Mail: execdir@morganhorse.com
Director, Publications: Julie Dicke
    E-Mail: julie@morganhorse.com
Senior Accountant: Sheila Knight
    E-Mail: sheila@Morganhorse.com
Communications Specialist: Christina Koliander
    E-Mail: chris@morganhorse.com
*Director, Membership Services, Information Technology and
    Registry:* Erica Richard
    E-Mail: erica@morganhorse.com

Historical Note:
*Established as the Morgan Horse Club, Inc., assumed
its present name in 1971. AMHA exists to preserve,
promote and perpetuate the Morgan breed. Members are
breeders, owners, trainers and friends of the Morgan horse.
Membership: $70 (General); $15 (Youth).*

Meetings/Conferences: Annual
2013 - Portland, OR (Benson Hotel)/Feb. 20 - 23
Number of non-conference events/year: 10

Publications:
Breed Magazine; monthly; adv.

American Mosquito Control Association (1935)
15000 Commerce Pkwy.
Suite C
Mt. Laurel, NJ 08054
Tel: (856) 439-9222 *Fax:* (856) 439-0525
E-Mail: amca@mosquito.org
Website: mosquito.org
Members: 2000 individuals
Staff: 2
Annual Budget: $500-1,000,000
Tax: 501(c)(3)

Personnel:
President: Tom Wilmot
    E-Mail: twilmot@co.midland.mi.us
Technical Advisor and Media Contact: Joe Conlon
    E-Mail: joec@mosquito.org

Historical Note:
*Established in 1935 as the Eastern Association of Mosquito
Control Workers and assumed its present name in 1944.
Incorporated in New Jersey (1948), California (1974)
and Louisiana (1986). Mission is to provide leadership,
information and education leading to the enhancement
of health and quality of life through the suppression
of mosquito and other vector-transmitted diseases.
Members are involved in the control of mosquitoes and
other vectors. Membership: $120 (Regular); $1,500
(Corporate Sustaining); $500 (Government Sustaining);
$50 (Associate); $30 (Student).*

Meetings/Conferences: Annual
2013 - Atlantic City, NJ (Trump Taj Mahal)/Feb. 24 - 28
2014 - Seatle, WA/Feb. 2 - 6
2015 - New Orleans, LA/March 29 - April 2
Number of non-conference events/year: 5

Publications:
AMCA Newsletter; quarterly
E-Newsletter; monthly
Journal of the American Mosquito Control Association;
    quarterly
Membership Directory; on-line
Wingbeats - Magazine for mosquito control; quarterly

American Motorcyclist Association (1924)
13515 Yarmouth Dr.
Pickerington, OH 43147
Tel: (614) 856-1900 *Fax:* (614) 856-1920
TollFree: (800) 262-5646
Website: americanmotorcyclist.com
Members: 290000 individuals
Staff: 311
Annual Budget: $10-25,000,000

Personnel:
President and Chief Executive Officer: Rob Dingman
Vice President, Administration: Robert Chaddock

Historical Note:
*AMA's mission is to promote the motorcycling lifestyle
and protect the future of motorcycling. Membership: $49
(Standard).*

Publications:
AMA Extra; on-line
American Motorcyclist Magazine

American Mountain Guides Association (1979)
P.O. Box 1739

Boulder, CO 80306
Tel: (303) 271-0984 *Fax:* (303) 271-1377
Website: amga.com
Staff: 31
Annual Budget: $500-1,000,000
Tax: 501(c)(3)

Personnel:
Executive Director: Betsy Winter
    E-Mail: betsy@amga.com
Director, Program: Henry Beyer
    E-Mail: henry@amga.com
Director, Climbing Instructor Program and Accreditation:
    Ed Crothers
    E-Mail: ed@amga.com
Director, Membership Services: Caroline McNally
    E-Mail: caroline@amga.com
Director, Technical Services: Dale Remsberg
    E-Mail: daleremsberg@mac.com

Historical Note:
*AMGA inspires client experience as source for training,
credentials, resource stewardship and services for
professional mountain guides and climbing instructors
in the United States. Membership: $110 (Individual);
$150-200 (IFMGA Guide); $45-65 (Associate); $125
(Certified Guide); $75 (Certified Single Pitch Instructor);
$250 (Accreditation).*

Continuing Education:
Certification Designation/s: CWI, SPI

Meetings/Conferences: Annual
Conference Chair: Henry Beyer

Publications:
E-news; monthly
E-newsletter; monthly
Mountain Bulletin - Newsletter; quarterly

American Moving and Storage Association (1920)
1611 Duke St.
Alexandria, VA 22314-3406
Tel: (703) 683-7410 *Fax:* (703) 683-7527
TollFree: (888) 849-2672
E-Mail: info@moving.org
Website: promover.org
Members: 3200 individual
Staff: 28
Annual Budget: $2-5,000,000
Tax: 501(c)(3)

Personnel:
President and Chief Executive Officer: Linda Bauer Darr
    E-Mail: ldarr@moving.org
Director, Conferences: Jaime Barnhart CMP
    E-Mail: jbarnhart@moving.org
*Chief Financial Officer and Senior Vice President,
    Membership Services, Finance and Administration:* John
    B. Brewer
    E-Mail: jbrewer@moving.org
Director, Advertising and Sales: Norma Gyovai
    E-Mail: ngyovai@moving.org
Manager, Computer and Building Services: Charles
    Holder
    E-Mail: cholder@moving.org
*Executive Vice President, Marketing, Communications,
    Training and Certification:* Sandy Lynch
    E-Mail: slynch@moving.org
Vice President, Military and Government Relations: Scott
    Michael
    E-Mail: smichael@moving.org
Senior Vice President, Government Affairs: Paul C. Oakley
    E-Mail: poakley@moving.org
Director, Training and Certification: Maryscott Tuck
    E-Mail: mtuck@moving.org
Manager, E-Media and Print Publications: Wayne
    Whitaker
    E-Mail: wwhitaker@moving.org

Historical Note:
*AMSA's mission is to represent the interest of the domestic
and international moving and storage industry and to help
the customers it serves.*

Continuing Education:
Certification Designation/s: COIC, CPM, RIM, CPL, CMC,
CCA, PMP

Meetings/Conferences:
Conference Chair: Jaime Barnhart CMP
2013 - Atlanta, GA (Atlanta Marriott Marquis)/March
    3 - 6
2014 - San Diego, CA (Manchester Grand)/Feb. 9 - 12

Publications:
AMSA Today; weekly; adv.

CPPC Newsletter; monthly; adv.
Direction; bi-monthly
Military Moving; on-line
Supply Line; quarterly

American Murray Grey Association (1971)
P.O. Box 43515
Louisville, KY 40253-0515
Tel: (502) 384-2335 *Fax:* (866) 571-2554
E-Mail: AMGAOffice@murraygreybeefcattle.com
Website: murraygreybeefcattle.com
Members:
200 individuals
108 Companies
Staff: 1
Annual Budget: $10-25,000

Personnel:
Executive Director: John Gerow
    E-Mail: johngerow@gmail.com

Historical Note:
*A member of the National Pedigree Livestock Council,
AMGA is the official registry for Murray Grey cattle in the
United States. Members are breeders and fanciers of Murray
Grey beef cattle. Membership: $50 (Active); $10 (Junior);
$25 (Associate).*

Publications:
Membership Directory; on-line
Murray Grey News; quarterly; adv.

American Mushroom Institute (1955)
One Massachusetts Ave. NW
Suite 800
Washington, DC 20001
Tel: (202) 842-4344 *Fax:* (202) 408-7763
E-Mail: ami@mwmlaw.com
Website: americanmushroom.org
Members: 325 companies
Staff: 3
Annual Budget: $1-2,000,000
Tax: 501(c)(5)

Personnel:
President: Laura Phelps
Secretary: Stephen Anania

Historical Note:
*AMI represents growers and marketers of cultivated
mushrooms in the United States. AMI's purposes are
research and information dissemination, the development
of better methods of growth and marketing of mushrooms,
representation of the industry to governmental bodies
and increasing the consumption of mushrooms. AMI is
a national voluntary trade association representing the
growers, processors, and marketers of cultivated mushrooms
in the United States and industry suppliers worldwide.
Membership is available to any person interested in
the mushroom industry. Categories of membership are
grower, associate, professional and retiree. Membership:
$350-16,000 (Growers); $350 (Non- Growers); $400
(Associate).*

Meetings/Conferences: Annual
Number of non-conference events/year: 1

Publications:
Membership Directory; on-line

American Music Center
90 John St.
Suite 312
New York, NY 10038
Tel: (212) 645-6949 *Fax:* (646) 490-0998
E-Mail: info@newmusicusa.org
Website: amc.net
Staff: 6
Annual Budget: $1-2,000,000

Personnel:
President and Chief Executive Officer: Ed Harsh
    E-Mail: eharsh@newmusicusa.org
Director, Finance and Administration: Chitra Arunasalam
    E-Mail: chitra@newmusicusa.org
Manager, Communications: Kevin Clark
    E-Mail: kevin@newmusicusa.org
Manager, IT Projects: Eddy Ficklin
    E-Mail: eficklin@newmusicusa.org
Composer Advocate, and Senior Editor: Frank J. Oteri
    E-Mail: fjo@newmusicusa.org
Director, Grant-Making Programs: Scott Winship
    E-Mail: swinship@newmusicusa.org

Historical Note:
*Formerly American Music Center and Meet The Composer,
November 8, 2011 both merged to form a new association*

New Music USA. New Music USA's mission is to increase opportunities for composers, performers and audiences by fostering the creation, dissemination, and enjoyment of new American music, both nationally and internationally. Membership: $65 (Individual); $25 (Student).

Meetings/Conferences:
Conference Chair: Scott Winship

Publications:
NewMusicBox; monthly; adv.

American Music Therapy Association (1950)
8455 Colesville Rd.
Suite 1000
Silver Spring, MD 20910
Tel: (301) 589-3300 Fax: (301) 589-5175
E-Mail: info@musictherapy.org
Website: musictherapy.org
Members: 5000 individuals
Staff: 10
Annual Budget: $1-2,000,000
Tax: 501(c)(3)

Personnel:
Executive Director: Andrea H. Farbman EdD
    E-Mail: farbman@musictherapy.org
Director, Communications and Conferences: Al Bumanis
    E-Mail: bumanis@musictherapy.org
Director, Professional Programs: Jane Creagan
    E-Mail: creagan@musictherapy.org
Director, Membership Services and Information Systems:
    Angie Elkins
    E-Mail: elkins@musictherapy.org
Director, Government Relations: Judy Simpson
    E-Mail: simpson@musictherapy.org
Coordinator, Administrative Services: Dianne Wawrzusin

Historical Note:
Founded as National Association for Music Therapy; merged with American Association for Music Therapy and assumed its current name in 1998. AMTA seeks to advance public awareness of the benefits of music therapy and increase access to quality music therapy services in a rapidly changing world. Membership: $235 (Professional/ Associate); $80 (Student); $125 (Retired); $650 (Patron); $350 (Affiliate).

Continuing Education:
Certification Designation/s: CMTE

Meetings/Conferences: Annual
Conference Chair: Al Bumanis

Publications:
Journal of Music Therapy; quarterly
Music Therapy Enews; monthly
Music Therapy Matters; quarterly
Music Therapy Perspectives; bi-annually

American Musicians Union (1948)
Eight Tobin Ct.
Dumont, NJ 07628
Tel: (201) 384-5378
Members: 200 individuals
Staff: 1
Annual Budget: Under $10,000

Personnel:
President and Treasurer: Ben Intorre

Historical Note:
Formed by a small group of musicians who chose to remain independent of the AFL-CIO merger of labor unions; joined the National Federation of Independent Unions in 1961. Membership is open to all musicians and vocalists; contract books are provided at a modest cost, but members are not required to use the official contract form nor a binding wage scale. Has no paid officers or full-time staff. Membership: $27/year, plus $10 initiation fee.

American Musicological Society (1934)
6010 College Stn.
Brunswick, ME 04011-8451
Tel: (207) 798-4243 Fax: (207) 798-4254
TollFree: (877) 679-7648
E-Mail: ams@ams-net.org
Website: ams-net.org
Members: 3600 individuals and 1100 institutions
Staff: 3
Annual Budget: $500-1,000,000
Tax: 501(c)(3)

Personnel:
Executive Director: Robert Judd
    E-Mail: rjudd@ams-net.org
Office Manager: Al Hipkins
    E-Mail: ahipkins@ams-net.org

Editor: Christopher Reynolds

Historical Note:
AMS's purpose is to advance research in the various fields of music as a branch of learning and scholarship. Membership: $110 (US/Canada; Regular); $200 (US/ Canada; Sustaining); $55 (US/Canada; Income less than 30K); $45 (US/Canada; Joint); $40 (US/Canada; Student); $50 (US/Canada; Emeritus); $130 (International; Regular); $220 (International; Sustaining); $75 (International; Income less than 30K); $65 (International; Joint); $60 (International; Student); $70 (International; Emeritus).

Meetings/Conferences: Annual
2013 - Pittsburgh, PA (Wyndham Grand Pittsburgh Downtown)/Nov. 7 - 10
2014 - Milwaukee, WI (Hilton Milwaukee City Center)/ Nov. 6 - 9
2015 - Louisville, KY (Galt House Hotel)/Nov. 12 - 15

Publications:
AMS Newsletter; semi-annually
Journal of the American Musicological Society; adv.

American Mustang Association (1962)
P.O. Box 338
Yucaipa, CA 92399
Tel: (661) 946-8308
E-Mail: mustang@netbox.com
Website: fp3.antelecom.net/fisherla
Members: 150 individuals
Staff: 1
Annual Budget: Under $10,000

Personnel:
Secretary: Mary Flory

Historical Note:
Members are owners and breeders of the Mustang horse of the Western plains. Membership: $10 (Individual Adult) $5 (Junior) $15 (Family) $100 (Individual Lifetime) $10 (Partnership/Corporation/Proprietorship).

American Name Society (1951)
Binghamton University, State University of New York
Office of the Provost (AD 711)
Binghamton, NY 13902-6000
Tel: (607) 777-2143 Fax: (607) 777-4830
Website: wtsn.binghamton.edu/ANS
Members: 750 individuals and institutions
Staff: 3
Annual Budget: $10-25,000
Tax: 501(c)(3)

Personnel:
President: Dr. Kemp Williams
    E-Mail: kempw@us.ibm.com
Treasurer: Michael F. McGoff
    E-Mail: mmcgoff@binghamton.edu
Editor: Dr. Frank Nuessel
    E-Mail: fhnues01@louisville.edu

Historical Note:
ANS is a professional society of onomastic scholars and others interested in the study of the origin and meaning of names, geographic, personal, scientific, etc. Membership: $40 (Domestic Active); $42 (Canadian and Mexican Active); $45 (Foreign); $35 (Foreign Student/Retired); $30 (Domestic Student/Retired).

Meetings/Conferences: Annual
Number of non-conference events/year: 1

Publications:
A Journal of Onomastics; quarterly

American Naprapathic Association (1907)
800 E S. St.
Woodstock, IL 60098
Tel: (312) 912-7984 Fax: (312) 380-4637
E-Mail: anarfordns@aol.com
Website: naprapathy.org
Members: 140 individuals
Staff: 4
Annual Budget: $10-25,000
Tax: 501(c)(6)

Personnel:
Editor: Dona A. Stretch CA, NA

Historical Note:
ANA strives to protect, preserve, enhance, expand and serve the naprapathic profession. Membership: $180 (Individual); $150 (Organization/Company); $175 (Licensed Doctors of Naprapathy); $45 (Student/Interns); $45 (Affiliated).

Publications:
Membership Directory; on-line

American National CattleWomen (1952)
P.O. Box 3881
Englewood, CO 80155
Tel: (303) 694-0313 Fax: (303) 694-2390
E-Mail: ancw@ancw.org
Website: ancw.org
Members: 2800 individuals
Staff: 4
Annual Budget: $500-1,000,000

Personnel:
President: Tammi Didlot
Contact, Advertising: Bonnie West
    E-Mail: bwest@beef.org

Historical Note:
ANCW seeks to support women in the beef industry and to mobilize a network of volunteers providing education and information to consumers about beef as a nutritious food. Members are women in the beef cattle industry. Membership: $50 (Basic); $75 (Sustaining); $20 (Collegiate/Junior); $100 (Associate); $200 (Affiliate).

Meetings/Conferences: Annual

Publications:
ANCW Newsletter; quarterly; adv.
Membership Directory; annually

American National Chamber of Commerce
1615 H St. NW
Washington, DC 20062-2000
Tel: (202) 659-6000
TollFree: (800) 638-6582
Website: uschamber.com
Staff: 9

Personnel:
President: Chester Chen
President and Chief Executive Officer: Thomas J. Donohue
Treasurer: John W. Bachmann
Senior Vice President, Chief Legal Officer, and General Counsel: Lily Fu Claffee
Senior Vice President, Communications and Strategy: Thomas Collamore
Senior Vice President, Administration: Shannon DiBari
Chief of Staff: Amanda Engstrom Eversole
Senior Vice President, Chief Financial Officer and Chief Information Officer: Stan Harrell
Executive Vice President, Government Affairs: R. Bruce Josten

Historical Note:
Assists enterprises to find U.S. products and services, travel to U.S. trade shows, and learn about new U.S. products. Membership in the U.S. Chamber is open to any company.

Publications:
Free Enterprise; weekly
Membership Directory; on-line

American National Standards Institute (1918)
1899 L St. NW
11th Floor
Washington, DC 20036
Tel: (202) 293-8020 Fax: (202) 293-9287
E-Mail: info@ansi.org
Website: ansi.org
Members:
3500000 professionals
125000 companies
Staff: 123
Annual Budget: $25-50,000,000
Tax: 501(c)(3)

Personnel:
President and Chief Executive Officer: S. Joe Bhatia
Vice President, Government Relations: Scott P. Cooper
    E-Mail: scooper@ansi.org
Senior Program Director, Personnel Certifier Accreditation Program: Dr. Roy Swift

Historical Note:
ANSI was originally established as the American Engineering Standards Committee (AESC), in 1928, it was reorganized and renamed as the American Standards Association (ASA) and in 1966 as the United States of America Standards Institute (USASI) the association adopted its present name in 1969. ANSI's mission is to enhance U.S. competitiveness and quality of life by promoting, facilitating, and safeguarding the integrity of the voluntary standardization system. Membership: $495-28,125/year.

Meetings/Conferences:
Conference Chair: Stephanie Carroll

Publications:
ANSI Congressional Standards Update; monthly
USNC News and Notes; quarterly
What's New?; weekly

American Nature Study Society (1908)
c/o Pocono Environmental Education Center
RR2 Box 1010
Dingmans Ferry, PA 18328-9614
Tel: (570) 828-2319 *Fax:* (570) 828-9695
E-Mail: peec@ptd.net
Website: peec.org
Members: 650 individuals
Staff: 4
Annual Budget: Under $10,000

Personnel:
Chief Executive Officer: Jeffrey Rosalsky
   E-Mail: jrosalsky@peec.org
Director, Marketing and Development: Flo Mauro
   E-Mail: fmauro@peec.org
Director, Education: Allison Owczarczak
   E-Mail: alozark@peec.org
Coordinator , Summer Camp, Special Events: Jessica Snyder
   E-Mail: jsnyder@peec.org

Historical Note:
Founded in 1908, ANSS quickly became the leading organization serving and strengthening the Nature Study movement. Its main concern is nature and conservation education. The Society works to forge a bond between each generation of students and their natural environment. Since 1997 ANS is managed at PEEC. ANSS is America's oldest environmental education organization. Members are science, nature study, and environmental education professionals. Membership: $30/year (individual); $50/year (organization); $30/year (Library).

Meetings/Conferences:
Conference Chair: Jessica Snyder

American Naturopathic Association
4435 Wisconsin Ave. NW, Suite 403
Washington, DC 20016
Staff: 1

Personnel:
Treasurer: Joha Mat

Historical Note:
Professional association representing the interests of naturopathic physicians (NDs).

American Navion Society (1960)
P.O. Box 335
16420 SE McGillivray, Suite 103
Vancouver, WA 98683-3461
Tel: (360) 833-9921 *Fax:* (360) 833-9921
E-Mail: flynavion@yahoo.com
Website: navionsociety.org
Members: 800 Members
Staff: 2
Annual Budget: $100-250,000

Personnel:
President: Gary Rankin
   E-Mail: N76V@aol.com
Secretary and Treasurer: Ken Whittall-Scherfee
   E-Mail: kwalaw@covad.net

Historical Note:
ANS was formed to bring the owners together in an organization where the members could participate in social events and share maintenance and technical information. Membership: $75 (United States); $85 (Canada); $90 (Other Country).

Meetings/Conferences: Annual
2013 - Paso Robles, CA/June 23 - 28

Publications:
Newsletter; bi-monthly; adv.

American Nephrology Nurses Association (1969)
E. Holly Ave.
P.O. Box 56
Pitman, NJ 08071-0056
Tel: (856) 256-2320 *Fax:* (856) 589-7463
TollFree: (888) 600-2662
E-Mail: anna@ajj.com
Website: annanurse.org
Members: 12165 individuals
Staff: 16
Annual Budget: $10-25,000,000
Tax: 501(c)(6)

Personnel:
Executive Director: Mike Cunningham
   E-Mail: cunninghamm@ajj.com
Director, Education Services: Hazel Dennison
   E-Mail: hazel.dennison@ajj.com
Director, Marketing: Tom Greene
   E-Mail: greenet@ajj.com
Manager, Conferences: Jeri Hendrie
   E-Mail: hendriej@ajj.com
Director, Membership Services: Lou Ann Leary
   E-Mail: learyl@ajj.com
Director, Fulfillment and Information Services: Rob McIlvaine
   E-Mail: rob.mcilvaine@ajj.com
Managing Editor: Kathleen E. Thomas
   E-Mail: kathy.thomas@ajj.com

Historical Note:
Formerly the American Association of Nephrology Nurses and Technicians, assumed its present name in 1984. ANNA's mission is to advance nephrology nursing practice and positively influence outcomes for individuals with kidney disease through advocacy, scholarship, and excellence. Members are nurses specializing in the structure, function and diseases of the kidneys, as well as dieticians, physicians, social workers and technicians. Membership: $75 (Full Member); $65 (Associate Member/Virtual International Member); $110 (International Member); $37.50 (Student Member).

Continuing Education:
Certification Designation/s: CNN, CNN-NP, CDN, CCHT, CEAB

Meetings/Conferences: Annual
Conference Chair: Jeri Hendrie
2013 - Las Vegas, NV (Rio All-Suite Hotel and Casino)/ April 21 - 24
Number of non-conference events/year: 4

Publications:
ANNA Update; bi-monthly; adv.
E-News/Association News; monthly
Membership Directory; on-line
Nephrology Nursing Journal; bi-monthly; adv.
RenalWEB Nephrology Nursing News; bi-weekly

American Network of Community Options and Resources (ANCOR) (1970)
1101 King St.
Suite 380
Alexandria, VA 22314
Tel: (703) 535-7850 *Fax:* (703) 535-7860
E-Mail: ancor@ancor.org
Website: ancor.org
Members: 775 agencies
Staff: 13
Annual Budget: $2-5,000,000
Tax: 501(c)(6)

Personnel:
Chief Executive Officer: Renee L. Pietrangelo
   E-Mail: rpietrangelo@ancor.org
Director, Communications and Marketing: Jocelyn Breeland
   E-Mail: jbreeland@ancor.org
Manager, Finance: Cynthia Allen de Ramos
   E-Mail: cramos@ancor.org
Director, Education and Foundation: Debra Langseth
   E-Mail: dlangseth@ancor.org
Director, Membership Relations and Board Development: Jerri McCandless
   E-Mail: jmccandless@ancor.org
Director, Government Relations: Jessica Sadowsky
   E-Mail: jsadowsky@ancor.org
Director, Web and Information Technology: Tony Yu
   E-Mail: tyu@ancor.org

Historical Note:
Formerly the American Network of Community Options and Resources, later became the National Association of Private Residential Resources and adopted its current name in 1993. ANCOR's mission is to inform, educate and network service providers to safeguard, develop, grow and extend their capacity to support the choices of people with disabilities. Membership: $50-3,675 (Associate, based on annual operating expenses); $1,260-7,430 (State Association); $470-11,775 (Full Member).

Meetings/Conferences:
2013 - Westminster, CO (Westin Westminster)/Nov. 3
Number of non-conference events/year: 2

Publications:
Links; monthly
Membership Directory; on-line

Washington Insiders Club (WICs); weekly
Membership List Available to Non-members

American Neurogastroenterology and Motility Society (1980)
45685 Harmony Ln.
Belleville, MI 48111
Tel: (734) 699-1130 *Fax:* (734) 699-1136
E-Mail: admin@motilitysociety.org
Website: motilitysociety.org
Members: 250 individuals
Staff: 1
Annual Budget: $500-1,000,000
Tax: 501(c)(3)

Personnel:
Executive Director: Lori Ennis

Historical Note:
Formerly American Motility Society, Mission of ANMS is to advance the study of neurogastroenterology and GI motility. Members are physicians with an interest in gastrointestinal motility. Membership: $150 (Regular-faculty/Industry/Other); $50 (Trainee/Associate/Fellow/Resident/Graduate Student/Postdoc).

Meetings/Conferences: Annual
2013 - Huntington Beach, CA/Sept. 20 - 22
Number of non-conference events/year: 1

Publications:
Neurogastroenterology and Motility
The Recorder-Newsletter

American Neurological Association (1875)
5841 Cedar Lake Rd.
Suite 204
Minneapolis, MN 55416
Tel: (952) 545-6284 *Fax:* (952) 545-6073
E-Mail: ana@llmsi.com
Website: aneuroa.org
Members: 1400 individuals
Staff: 7
Annual Budget: $5-10,000,000
Tax: 501(c)(3)

Personnel:
Executive Director: Linda Scher
   E-Mail: lindascher@llmsi.com
Accounting Assistant: Brenda Aschoff
   E-Mail: accounting@llmsi.com
Coordinator, Education: Laurie Dixon
   E-Mail: ana@iimsi.com
Director, Communications: Dave Spratt
   E-Mail: dspratt@umich.edu
Contact, Controller: Ron Steffens
   E-Mail: ronsteffens@llmsi.com
Meeting and Event Planner: Kayla Stidger
   E-Mail: kaylastidger@llmsi.com

Historical Note:
Founded in 1875 and incorporated in Minnesota. ANA is a professional society of academic neurologists and neuroscientists advancing the goals of academic neurology, training and educating neurologists and other physicians in the neurologic sciences and expanding the understanding of diseases of the nervous system and the ability to treat them. Membership: $390 (Active); $280 (Corresponding); $150 (Honorary/Senior).

Meetings/Conferences: Annual
Conference Chair: Kayla Stidger

Publications:
Annals of Neurology; monthly
Member Directory; on-line

American Neuropsychiatric Association (1988)
700 Ackerman Rd.
Suite 625
Columbus, OH 43202
Tel: (614) 447-2077 *Fax:* (614) 263-4366
E-Mail: anpa@osu.edu
Website: anpaonline.org
Members: 700 individuals
Staff: 2
Annual Budget: $250-500,000

Personnel:
Executive Director: Sandy Bornstein
   E-Mail: anpa@osu.edu
Treasurer: C. Edward Coffey

Historical Note:
ANPA is an organization of professionals in neuropsychiatry and clinical neurosciences. ANPA mission is to improve the lives of people with disorders at the interface

of psychiatry and neurology.Members are comprised of
professionals in neuropsychiatry, behavioral neurology,
neuropsychology, neuroradiology, neuropathology, and
neurosurgery as well as the basic neurosciences, who share
clinical and/or academic interests in neuropsychiatry.
Membership: $225 (Full); $65 (Junior).

Meetings/Conferences: Annual
2013 - Boston, MA (The Boston Park Plaza Hotel)/April
3 - 6

Publications:
Membership Directory; on-line
Newsletter

American Neurotology Society (1965)
1980 Warson Rd.
Springfield, IL 62704
Tel: (217) 638-0801 Fax: (217) 679-1677
E-Mail: neurotology65@yahoo.com
Website: americanneurotologysociety.com
Members: 500 individuals
Staff: 2
Annual Budget: $100-250,000
Tax: 501(c)(3)

Personnel:
Society Administrator: Kristen Bordignon
E-Mail: neurotology65@yahoo.com

Historical Note:
ANS is committed to improving public health care
through the provision of high-quality continuing medical
education (CME) to its members. Members are otologists/
neurotologists and allied health professionals as affiliate
members with an interest in hearing and balance disorders.

Meetings/Conferences: Annual
2013 - Washington, DC (Walter E. Washington
Convention Center)/April 12 - 14

Publications:
ANS Newsletter; on-line

American North Country Cheviot Sheep Association (1962)
1201 N 500 East
Rolling Prairie, IN 46371
Tel: (574) 323-3506
Website: northcountrycheviot.com
Members: 190 senior and junior members
Staff: 3
Annual Budget: Under $10,000

Personnel:
President: Brett Kessler

Historical Note:
Formerly North Country Sheep Breeders Association.
ANCCSA provides information on the North Country
Cheviot breed of sheep and works for registration,
exporting, promotion, and breed improvement. Members
are breeders of purebred North Country Cheviot Sheep.
Membership: $10/year.

American Nuclear Insurers (1957)
95 Glastonbury Blvd.
Suite 300
Glastonbury, CT 06033-4453
Tel: (860) 682-1301 Fax: (860) 659-0002
E-Mail: info@nuclearinsurance.com
Website: amnucins.com
Members: 100 companies
Staff: 79

Personnel:
President and Chief Executive Officer: George D. Turner
Vice President, Information Services: Daniel Antion

Historical Note:
ANI is the product of a merger (1974) of the Nuclear
Energy Property Insurance Association and the Nuclear
Energy Liability Insurance Association, both established
in 1957. From 1974 to 1978 known as the the Nuclear
Energy Liability Property Insurance Association assumed
its current name in 1978. ANI's purpose is to pool the
financial assets pledged by member companies to provide
the significant amount of property and liability insurance
required for nuclear power plants and related facilities
throughout the world.

Publications:
ANI Newsletter; monthly

American Nuclear Society (1954)
555 N. Kensington Ave.
La Grange Park, IL 60526
Tel: (708) 352-6611 Fax: (708) 352-0499
TollFree: (800) 323-3044

Website: ans.org
Members: 1600 corporations and 11000
individuals
Staff: 58
Annual Budget: $10-25,000,000

Personnel:
Executive Director: Robert C. Fine
Department Head, Public Information and Constituency:
Bonnifer Ballard
Department Head, Human Resources: Ann Marie
Gruszkowski
E-Mail: agruszkowski@ans.org
Department Head, Information Technology: Joseph
Koblich
E-Mail: jkoblich@ans.org
Director, Financial Operations: Staci B. Levy
Department Head, Meetings and Exhibits: Melissa
McKinzie
Department Head, Scientific Publications: Rick Michal
Department Head, Membership services and Marketing:
Gloria Naurocki
E-Mail: gnaurocki@ans.org
Administrator, Governance Services: Valerie Vasilievas

Historical Note:
Established as the National Academy of Sciences. Mission
is to promote the awareness and understanding of the
application of nuclear science and technology. Membership:
$28-262/year; $500-2800 (Lifetime).

Meetings/Conferences: Semi-Annual
Conference Chair: Melissa McKinzie
2013 - Atlanta, GA (Atlanta Marriott Marquis)/June 16
- 20
2013 - Washington, DC (Omni Shoreham Hotel,
Washington D.C.)/Nov. 10 - 14
2014 - Reno, NV (Grand Sierra Resort and Casino)/
June 15 - 19
2014 - Anaheim, CA (Disneyland Hotel)/Nov. 9 - 14
2015 - San Antonio, TX (Grand Hyatt San Antonio)/
June 7 - 11
2015 - Washington, DC (Omni Shoreham Hotel,
Washington D.C.)/Nov. 8 - 12
2016 - New Orleans, LA (Hyatt Regency New Orleans)/
June 12 - 16
2016 - San Diego, CA (Town and Country Resort
Hotel)/Nov. 13 - 17
2017 - San Francisco, CA (Hyatt Regency San
Francisco)/June 11 - 15
2017 - Washington, DC (Omni Shoreham Hotel,
Washington D.C.)/Nov. 12 - 16
Number of non-conference events/year: 25

Publications:
ANS News; on-line
Fusion Science and Technology
Membership directory; on-line
Nuclear News; monthly
Nuclear Science and Engineering
Nuclear Standards News; on-line
Nuclear Technology
Radwaste Solutions; bi-monthly

American Numismatic Society (1858)
75 Varick St.
11th floor
New York, NY 10013
Tel: (212) 571-4470 Fax: (212) 571-4479
E-Mail: info@numismatics.org
Website: numismatics.org
Members: 2112 individuals and institutions
Staff: 17
Annual Budget: $10-25,000,000
Tax: 501(c)(3)

Personnel:
Executive Director: Ute Wartenberg Kagan PhD
Director, Finance and Operations: Anna Chang
E-Mail: chang@numismatics.org
Manager, Membership and Events: Megan Fenselau
E-Mail: membership@numismatics.org

Historical Note:
ANS is dedicated to the study of coins, currency, medals,
tokens, and related objects from all cultures, past and
present. Members are academics, serious collectors and
professional numismatists. Membership: $50-755/year;
$2500-7,500 (Life).

Meetings/Conferences: Annual
Conference Chair: Megan Fenselau
Number of non-conference events/year: 2

Publications:

American Journal of Numismatics; annually
American Numismatic Society Magazine; adv.
Ancient Coins in North American Collections (ACNAC);
irregular
ANS E-News; monthly
ANS Magazine
Colonial Newsletter; quarterly
Numismatic Literature; semi-annually
Numismatic Notes & Monographs(ANSNNM); irregular
Numismatic Studies (ANSNS); irregular
Sylloge Nummorum Graecorum (SNGANS); irregular

American Nursery and Landscape Association (1876)
1200 G St. NW.
Suite 800
Washington, DC 20005
Tel: (202) 789-2900 Fax: (202) 789-1893
E-Mail: info@anla.org
Website: anla.org
Members: 1900 companies
Staff: 10
Annual Budget: $2-5,000,000
Tax: 501(c)(6)

Personnel:
Executive Vice President: Robert J. Dolibois CAE
Director, Marketing and Industry Relations: Jonathan
Bardzik
Director, Membership Services: Amanda Flynn
E-Mail: aflynn@anla.org
Manager, Meeting and Events: Ashley Giuda
E-Mail: agiuda@anla.org
Vice President, Government Relations and Research: Craig
J. Regelbrugge
E-Mail: cregelbrugge@anla.org
Director, Business Education: Stephanie Stockton CAE

Historical Note:
ANLA is a trade association for nursery and landscape
professionals. It provides education, research, public
relations, and representation services to members. ANLA
members are small, family-owned businesses that grow
nursery and greenhouse plants, sell lawn and garden
products, design/install/care for landscapes, and sell
supplies to the industry. Membership: $250 (New); $500
(Supplier Associate); $145 (Associate Professional); $275
(Canadian associate); $380 (International).

Meetings/Conferences:
Conference Chair: Ashley Giuda

Publications:
ANLA Member Directory; on-line
ANLA Newsletter; on-line

Membership List Available to Non-members

American Nurses Association (1896)
8515 Georgia Ave.
Suite 400
Silver Spring, MD 20910-3492
Tel: (301) 628-5000 Fax: (301) 628-5001
TollFree: (800) 274-4262
E-Mail: info@ana.org
Website: nursingworld.org
Members: 2900000 individuals and 54
associations
Staff: 239
Annual Budget: $25-50,000,000
Tax: 501(c)(3)

Personnel:
Chief Executive Officer: Marla J. Weston PhD, RN
E-Mail: marla.weston@ana.org
Director, Government Affairs: Rose Gonzalez MPS, RN
E-Mail: rose.gonzalez@ana.org
Senior Public Relations Specialist: Mary McNamara
E-Mail: mary.mcnamara@ana.org
Chief Financial Officer: Michael Pfeiffer
E-Mail: michael.pfeiffer@ana.org

Historical Note:
Incorporated in 1901 as the Nurses Associated Alumnae
of the United States and Canada. Became the American
Nurse's Association in 1911 and was incorporated in the
District of Columbia in 1917. ANA advances the nursing
profession by fostering better standards of nursing practice,
promoting the rights of nurses in the workplace, projecting
a positive and realistic view of nursing, and by lobbying
the Congress and regulatory agencies on health care issues
affecting nurses and the public.

Continuing Education:
Certification Designation/s: ANCC

Meetings/Conferences: Annual

2013 - Atlanta, GA/Feb. 6 - 8
Number of non-conference events/year: 1

Publications:
American Nurse Today; monthly; adv.
ANA eNewsletters
Capitol Update; semi-monthly
NursesBooks eNewsletter
NursingInsider e-Newsletter
The American Nurse; adv.
The Online Journal of Issues in Nursing

Membership List Available to Non-members

American Occupational Therapy Association, Inc. (1917)
4720 Montgomery Ln.
P.O. Box 31220
Bethesda, MD 20824-1220
Tel: (301) 652-2682 *Fax:* (301) 652-7711
TollFree: (800) 377-8555
E-Mail: fad@aota.org
Website: aota.org
Members: 42000 individuals
Staff: 14
Annual Budget: $10-25,000,000
Tax: 501(c)(6)

Personnel:
Executive Director: Frederick P. Somers
    E-Mail: fad@aota.org
Chief Public Affairs Officer: Christina A. Metzler
    E-Mail: cmetzler@aota.org
Director, Federal Affairs: Tim Nanof
    E-Mail: tnanof@aota.org

Historical Note:
AOTA advances the quality, availability, use, and support of occupational therapy through standard-setting, advocacy, education, and research on behalf of its members and the public. Members are occupational therapists, occupational therapy assistants, and OT students. Membership: $225 (Occupational Therapist/Individual Associate); $119-$175 (OT New Practitioner); $131 (Occupational Therapy Assistant); $95-$120 (OTA New Practitioner); $75 (Student); $387 (Organizational Associate Membership); $300-600 (Post-Professional Master's and Doctorate Degree).

Continuing Education:
Certification Designation/s: BC(OT), SC(OT&OTA), NBCOT

Meetings/Conferences: Annual
2013 - San Diego, CA (San Diego Convention Center)/ April 25 - 28/5000 attendees/over 100 exhibitors
2014 - Baltimore, MD (Baltimore Convention Center)/ April 3 - 6

Publications:
Administration & Management (AMSIS) Quarterlies; quarterly
American Journal of Occupational Therapy (AJOT)
Developmental Disabilities (DDSIS) Quarterlies; quarterly
E-Newsletters; on-line
Early Intervention & School (EISSIS) Quarterlies; quarterly
Education (EDSIS) Quarterlies; quarterly
Gerontology (GSIS) Quarterlies; quarterly
Home and Community Health (HCHSIS) Quarterlies; quarterly
Membership Directory; on-line
Mental Health (MHSIS) Quarterlies; quarterly
OT Practice Magazine; adv.
Physical Disabilities (PDSIS) Quarterlies; quarterly
Sensory Integration (SISIS) Quarterlies; quarterly
Special Interest Section Quarterly Newsletters; quarterly
Technology (TSIS) Quarterlies; quarterly
Work and Industry (WISIS) Quarterlies; quarterly

Membership List Available to Non-members

American Oil Chemists' Society (1909)
2710 S. Boulder
Urbana, IL 61802-6996
Tel: (217) 359-2344 *Fax:* (217) 351-8091
E-Mail: general@aocs.org
Website: aocs.org
Members: 4500 individuals
Staff: 41
Annual Budget: $5-10,000,000
Tax: 501(c)(3)

Personnel:

Chief Executive Officer: Patrick J. Donnelly
Registrar, Membership, Meetings and Subscriptions: Doreen Berning
    E-Mail: doreenb@aocs.org
Technical Director: Richard Mary Cantrill PhD
    E-Mail: rcantrill@aocs.org
Senior Director, Finance and Operations: Gloria Cook
    E-Mail: gloriac@aocs.org
Senior Director, Programs: Jeffrey L. Newman
    E-Mail: jnewman@aocs.org
Director, Publications: Jodey Schonfeld
    E-Mail: jodeys@aocs.org
Specialist, Public Relations and Marketing: Emily Wickstrom
    E-Mail: emilyw@aocs.org

Historical Note:
Founded in Memphis, TN as the Society of Cotton Products Analysts. Incorporated in Louisiana in 1922 as the American Oil Chemists' Society. AOCS's mission is to promote the successful exchange of ideas, information and experience while enhancing personal excellence and providing quality standards for those with a professional interest in the science and technology of fats, oils, surfactants and related materials. Membership: $775-10,000 (Corporate); $157 (Active); $145 (Individual); $92 (Retired); Free (Student/Emeritus).

Meetings/Conferences: Annual
Conference Chair: Doreen Berning
2013 - Montreal, QC (Palais Des Congres de Montreal)/April 28 - May 1
2014 - San Antonio, TX (The Henry B. Gonzalez Convention Center)/May 4 - 7
2015 - Orlando, FL (Rosen Shingle Creek Hotel)/May 3 - 6

Publications:
AOCS Agricultural Microscopy Division Newsletter
AOCS Analytical Division Newsletter; on-line
AOCS Biotechnology Division Newsletter
AOCS Edible Applications Technology Division Newsletter
AOCS Food Structure and Functionality Forum Newsletter; on-line
AOCS Industrial Oil Products Division Newsletter
AOCS LipidOxidation and Quality Division Newsletter; on-line
AOCS Phospholipid Division Newsletter; on-line
AOCS Processing Division Newsletter; on-line
AOCS Protein and Co-Products Division Newsletter; on-line
AOCS Resource Directory; on-line
AOCS Student Common Interest Group Newsletter; on-line
AOCS Surfactants and Detergents Division Newsletter; on-line
Inform Magazine; monthly; adv.
Journal of Surfactants and Detergents (JSD); quarterly
Journal of the American Oil Chemists' Society (JAOCS); monthly
Lipids; monthly

Membership List Available to Non-members

American Oilseed Coalition (1993)
1300 L St. NW
Suite 1020
Washington, DC 20005-4168
Tel: (202) 842-0463 *Fax:* (202) 842-9126
E-Mail: nopa@nopa.org
Website: nopa.org
Members: 6 associations
Staff: 4
Annual Budget: $100-250,000

Personnel:
President: Thomas A. Hammer
    E-Mail: thammer@nopa.org
Executive Vice President, Government Relations: David J. Hovermale
Office Administrator and Executive Assistant to the President: Kathleen A. Pennington CAE
    E-Mail: kpennington@nopa.org

Historical Note:
Successor to the Oilseed Council of America and a coalition of oilseed (canola, cottonseed, flaxseed, soybean, safflower and sunflower) growers, processors, handlers, exporters, and end users. The Council promotes long range government policies which ensure an adequate supply of oilseeds at economical prices. The AOC includes the American Soybean Association, the National Cottonseed Products Association, the National Oilseed Processors

Association, the National Sunflower Association, and the U.S. Canola Association.

Meetings/Conferences: Annual

American Ophthalmological Society (1864)
P.O. Box 193940
San Francisco, CA 94119
Tel: (415) 561-8578 *Fax:* (415) 561-8531
E-Mail: admin@aosonline.org
Website: aosonline.org
Members: 360 individuals
Staff: 2
Annual Budget: $250-500,000
Tax: 501(c)(3)

Personnel:
President: Richard K. Parrish
Editor: Emily Y. Chew

Historical Note:
AOS's mission is to promote patient care, education and research and to address essential issues in medicine. Membership: $400/year.

Meetings/Conferences: Annual
2013 - La Jolla, CA (Lodge at Torrey Pines)/May 16 - 19

Publications:
Electronic Newsletter; on-line
Membership Directory; on-line
Transactions of the AOS; annually

American Optometric Association (1898)
243 N. Lindbergh Blvd.
St. Louis, MO 63141-7851
Tel: (314) 991-4100 *Fax:* (314) 991-4101
TollFree: (800) 365-2219
Website: aoa.org
Members: 36000 individuals
Staff: 119
Annual Budget: $10-25,000,000
Tax: 501(c)(3)

Personnel:
Executive Director: Dr. Barry J. Barresi PhD
Contact, Finance: Debby Bartsch
Contact, Information Technology: Ken Burgdorf
Contact,Affiliate Relations and Membership Group: Sue Chiles
Contact, Administration and Human Resources: Wendy Harr
Manager, Meetings: Kellie Rodrigue
    E-Mail: kerodrigue@aoa.org
Associate Director, Public Relations: Susan Thomas
    E-Mail: SLThomas@aoa.org

Historical Note:
Founded as the American Optical Association and assumed its present name in 1919. AOA's mission is to improve the profession and to serve optometrists in meeting the eye care needs to the public. It also sets professional standards by conducting patient care efficiently and effectively, lobbies government and other organizations on behalf of the optometric profession. Membership: $368/year (Associate).

Continuing Education:
Certification Designation/s: CPOA, CPO, CPOT, CPC, CE

Meetings/Conferences: Annual
Conference Chair: Kellie Rodrigue
2013 - San Diego, CA/June 26 - 30
2014 - Philadelphia, PA/June 25

Publications:
AOA e-newsletter; on-line; adv.
AOA News; monthly; adv.
Membership Directory; on-line
Optometry: Journal of the AOA; irregular

American Optometric Student Association (1968)
243 N. Lindbergh Blvd.
St. Louis, MO 63141
Tel: (314) 983-4231 *Fax:* (314) 991-4101
Website: theaosa.org
Members: 6000 individuals
Staff: 2
Annual Budget: $500-1,000,000

Personnel:
Executive Director: Marlene Burle CMP
    E-Mail: mburle@theaosa.org

Historical Note:
AOSA's mission is to improve the visual welfare and health of the public, to promote the profession of optometry, and to enhance the education and welfare of optometry students. Membership: $40 (Individual); $130 (Group).

Meetings/Conferences: Annual
2013 - San Diego, CA/June 26 - 30
2014 - Philadelphia, PA/June 25

Publications:
AOSA newsletter; bi-annually
Optometry: Journal of the American Optometric
Association

American Orff-Schulwerk Association (1968)
P.O. Box 391089
Cleveland, OH 44139-8089
Tel: (440) 543-5366
E-Mail: info@aosa.org
Website: aosa.org
Members: 4500 art educators
Staff: 2
Annual Budget: $500-1,000,000
Tax: 501(c)(3)

Personnel:
Executive Director: Carrie Barnette
    E-Mail: execdir@aosa.org
Editor: Marjie Van Gunten
    E-Mail: communications@aosa.org

Historical Note:
*Formerly (1970) Orff Schulwerk Association. AOSA is
dedicated to the creative teaching approach developed by
Carl Orff and Gunild Keetman. Seeks to to demonstrate and
promote the value of Orff Schulwerk, support professional
development opportunities and align applications of the Orff
Schulwerk approach with the changing needs of American
society. Members are talented arts educators. Membership:
$0-120/year.*

Meetings/Conferences: Annual
2013 - Denver, CO/Nov. 13 - 16

Publications:
AOSA Approved Teacher Educators; on-line
The Orff Echo; on-line
The Orff Echo; quarterly

American Organization for Bodywork Therapies of Asia (1989)
45 Mill Race Place
Glen Mills, PA 19342
Tel: (610) 558-1591
E-Mail: office@aobta.org
Website: aobta.org
Members: 1400 individuals
Staff: 5
Annual Budget: $100-250,000
Tax: 501(c)(6)

Personnel:
President: Wayne Mylin
    E-Mail: president@aobta.org

Historical Note:
*Formerly (1990) known as American Shiatsu Association,
became American Oriental Bodywork Therapy Association
in 2001. AOBTA's mission is to serve its members with
educational and networking opportunities and to support
their personal and professional development and success.
Members are instructors, practitioners, schools and
programs, and students of Asian Bodywork Therapy (ABT).
Membership: $100 (Certified Practitioner Member); $25
(Student); $75 (Associate); $25-1,000 (Supporting); $500
(Professional Organization).*

Continuing Education:
Certification Designation/s: NCBTMB, NCCAOM

Meetings/Conferences: Annual
Conference Chair: Wayne Mylin
Number of non-conference events/year: 1

Publications:
AOBTA Pulse; quarterly; adv.
Membership Directory; on-line
Monthly Email updates; monthly

American Organization of Nurse Executives (1967)
155 N. Wacker Dr.
Suite 400
Chicago, IL 60606
Tel: (312) 422-2800 *Fax:* (312) 422-4503
E-Mail: aone@aha.org
Website: aone.org
Members: 8500 individual
Staff: 19
Annual Budget: $5-10,000,000

Personnel:
Chief Operating Officer: Susan Gergely MBA

E-Mail: sgergely@aha.org
Director, Educational Programs: Beverly Hancock DNP,
RN-BC
    E-Mail: bhancock@aha.org
Manager, Membership Services: Alyse Kittner
    E-Mail: akittner@aha.org
Senior Conference Management Specialist: Kourtney
Sproat
    E-Mail: ksproat@aha.org
Administrative Coordinator: Alexis Steele
    E-Mail: asteele@aha.org

Historical Note:
*Formerly (1978) American Society for Hospital Nursing
Service Administrators and (1985) American Society for
Nursing Service Administrators. AONE's mission is to
shape health care through innovative and expert nursing
leadership. Membership: $220 (Full/Affiliate Member); $95
(Student); $170 (Retired Member); $60-220 (International
Member); $180-210 (Group).*

Continuing Education:
Certification Designation/s: CENP, CNML

Meetings/Conferences: Annual
Conference Chair: Kourtney Sproat
2013 - Denver, CO/March 19 - 22
2013 - Denver, CO (Colorado Convention Center)/
    March 20 - 23
2014 - Orlando, FL/March 12 - 15
2015 - Phoenix, AZ/April 15 - 18

Publications:
AONE eNews; weekly
AONE Working for You; weekly
Journal of Nursing Administration
Nurse Leader; bi-monthly
Voice of Nursing Leadership; bi-monthly

Membership List Available to Non-members

American Oriental Society (1842)
University of Michigan
Hatcher Graduate Library
Ann Arbor, MI 48109-1190
Tel: (734) 647-4760 *Fax:* (734) 763-6743
Website: umich.edu/~aos
Members: 1350 individuals
Staff: 3
Annual Budget: $100-250,000

Personnel:
Editor-In-Chief: Stephanie Jamison
Secretary and Treasurer: Jonathan Rodgers
    E-Mail: jrodgers@umich.edu

Historical Note:
*Established to encourage research in the languages and
literatures of Asia and North Africa. Member of the
American Council of Learned Societies. Membership in the
Society is open to all persons interested in Oriental Studies.
Subscriptions to the JAOS is included in membership dues.
Membership: $80 (Regular); $2400 (Life); $40 (Student);
$20 (Associate/Joint).*

Meetings/Conferences: Annual
2013 - Portland, OR (Hilton Portland and Executive
    Tower)/March 15 - 18

Publications:
Journal of the American Oriental Society; quarterly
Membership Directory; on-line

Membership List Available to Non-members

American Ornithologists' Union (1883)
5405 Villa View Dr.
Farmington, NM 87402
Tel: (505) 326-1579
E-Mail: aou@aou.org
Website: aou.org
Members: 3000 individuals
Staff: 3
Annual Budget: $500-1,000,000

Personnel:
Executive Officer: Scott W. Gillihan
    E-Mail: executiveofficer@aou.org
Web Editor: Chris Merkord
    E-Mail: webeditor@aou.org
Editor: Cheryl L. Trine
    E-Mail: ctrine@andrews.edu

Historical Note:
*Affiliated with the American Association for the
Advancement of Science. AOU's mission is to advance the
scientific understanding of birds, to enrich ornithology as
a profession, and to promote a rigorous scientific basis for*

*the conservation of birds. Membership: $90 (Regular); $28
(Student/Family/Emeritus); $2,600 (Life).*

Meetings/Conferences: Annual
2013 - Chicago, IL/Aug. 14 - 19
2014 - Estes Park, CO/Sept. 24 - 27

Publications:
Checklist of North American Birds; irregular
Membership Directory; on-line
Ornithological Monographs; quarterly; adv.
The Auk; quarterly; adv.
The Ornithological Newsletter; bi-monthly

American Orthodontic Society
11884 Greenville Ave.
Suite 112
Dallas, TX 75243-3537
TollFree: (800) 448-1601
Website: orthodontics.com
Staff: 4
Annual Budget: $1-2,000,000

Personnel:
President and Board of Examiner: Mitchell S. Parker DDS
Secretary and Treasurer: W. Edward Gonzalez DMD, Jr.

Historical Note:
*AOS is committed to help its members stay up-to-date with
techniques, technology and products and also strives for
excellence in both the courses it sponsor and the services it
provides to its members. Membership: $245 (Active); $25
(Student-Associate); $1800 (lifetime).*

Meetings/Conferences: Annual

Publications:
The Journal of the American Orthodontic Society; on-
line

American Orthopaedic Association (1887)
6300 N. River Rd.
Suite 505
Rosemont, IL 60018
Tel: (847) 318-7330 *Fax:* (847) 318-7339
E-Mail: info@aoassn.org
Website: aoassn.org
Members: 1500 individuals
Staff: 14
Annual Budget: $2-5,000,000
Tax: 501(c)(3)

Personnel:
Executive Director: Kristin Olds Glavin JD
Program Manager, Own the Bone: Christina Boothby
    E-Mail: boothby@aoassn.org
Senior Director, Communications and Leadership Initiatives:
Jodene M. Brown
    E-Mail: brown@aoassn.org
Manager, Meetings and Fellowships: Marcia McIntyre
    E-Mail: mcintyre@aoassn.org
Manager, Marketing and Communications: Kari E.
McLean
    E-Mail: mclean@aoassn.org
Manager, Education and Membership Services: Jim Weiss
CAE
    E-Mail: weiss@aoassn.org

Historical Note:
*In 2003, the Academic Orthopaedic Society (AOS) was
incorporated into the AOA. Their mission is to identify,
develop, recognize and engage leadership in orthopaedics.
Candidates for active membership in the AOA must be
certified by the American Board of Orthopaedic Surgery
or a Fellow of the Royal College of Surgeons of Canada in
Orthopaedic Medicine. Membership: $950/year (Active/
Affiliate/Associate).*

Continuing Education:
Certification Designation/s: CME

Meetings/Conferences: Annual
Conference Chair: Marcia McIntyre
2013 - Denver, CO (Sheraton Denver Downtown
    Hotel)/June 12 - 15
2014 - Montreal, QC/June 18 - 21

Publications:
AOA News; quarterly
Community of Leaders; monthly
Membership Directory; annually

Membership List Available to Non-members

American Orthopaedic Foot and Ankle Society (1969)
6300 N. River Rd.
Suite 510
Rosemont, IL 60018-4264

Tel: (847) 698-4654 *Fax:* (847) 692-3315
TollFree: (800) 235-4855
E-Mail: aofasinfo@aofas.org
Website: aofas.org
Members: 1800 individuals
Staff: 8
Annual Budget: $2-5,000,000
Tax: 501(c)(3)

Personnel:
Executive Director: Lousanne (Zan) Lofgren CAE
    E-Mail: zlofgren@aofas.org
Director, Membership and Marketing: Lois Bierman
    E-Mail: LBierman@aofas.org
Finance and Administrative Support: Dianne Gilsenan
Director, Education: Judi Northrup
    E-Mail: jnorthrup@aofas.org
Manager, Information Technology: Rose Olea
    E-Mail: rolea@aofas.org

Historical Note:
Formerly (1983) American Orthopaedic Foot Society. AOFAS's mission is to promote quality, ethical and cost effective patient care through education, research and training of orthopaedic surgeons and other health care providers. Members are the members of American Academy of Orthopaedic Surgeons with an interest in the foot and ankle. Membership: $95-495/year.

Meetings/Conferences: Annual
2013 - Hollywood, FL (Westin Diplomat Resort)/July
    17 - 20
2014 - Chicago, IL (Hyatt Regency)/Sept. 21 - 23

Publications:
Foot & Ankle International; monthly
In-Stride Newsletter; quarterly

Membership List Available to Non-members

American Orthopaedic Society for Sports Medicine *(1972)*
6300 N. River Rd.
Suite 500
Rosemont, IL 60018-4229
Tel: (847) 292-4900 *Fax:* (847) 292-4905
TollFree: (877) 321-3500
E-Mail: aossm@aossm.org
Website: sportsmed.org
Members: 2500 individuals
Staff: 13
Annual Budget: $5-10,000,000
Tax: 501(c)(3)

Personnel:
Executive Director: Irvin E. Bomberger
    E-Mail: irv@aossm.org
Director, Finance: Richard Bennett
    E-Mail: richard@aossm.org
Manager, Membership Services and Programs: Debbie
    Czech
    E-Mail: debbie@aossm.org
Coordinator, Education and Meetings: Pat Kovach
    E-Mail: pat@aossm.org
Editor-in-Chief: Bruce Reider MD
    E-Mail: breider@ajsm.org
Coordinator, Exhibits and Administration: Michelle
    Schaffer
Director, Communications: Lisa Weisenberger
    E-Mail: lisa@aossm.org
Director, Education: Susan Brown Zahn PhD
    E-Mail: susan@aossm.org

Historical Note:
AOSSM enhances the prevention, recognition and orthopedic treatment of sports injuries and is formed primarily for education and research. Members are orthopaedic surgeons, physicians and allied health professionals. Membership: $150 (Active/Associate/MD Affiliate); $150 (Affiliate); $250 (Military).

Continuing Education:
Certification Designation/s: AOSSM-SC

Meetings/Conferences: Annual
Conference Chair: Pat Kovach
2013 - Chicago, IL (Sheraton Chicago Hotel and
    Towers)/July 11 - 14/51-100 exhibitors
2014 - Seatle, WA (Washington State Convention
    Center)/July 10 - 13/51-100 exhibitors
2015 - Orlando, FL (Hilton Orlando Bonnet Creek)/July
    9 - 12/51-100 exhibitors
Number of non-conference events/year: 4

Publications:
American Journal of Sports Medicine; monthly; adv.
AOSSM Membership Directory; quarterly

In Motion; quarterly
Online Self Assessment; on-line
Prevention of Non-Contact ACL Injuries
Sports Health; bi-monthly; adv.
Sports Medicine Update; bi-monthly; adv.

Membership List Available to Non-members

American Orthopsychiatric Association *(1924)*
C/O Clemson University, IFNL, 225 S.
Pleasantburg Dr.
Suite B-11
Greenville, SC 29607
Tel: (864) 250-4622 *Fax:* (864) 250-4668
E-Mail: orthocontact@aoatoday.com
Website: aoatoday.com
Members: 650 individuals
Staff: 5
Annual Budget: $250-500,000

Personnel:
Executive Officer: Robin Kimbrough-Melton JD
    E-Mail: rkimbro@clemson.edu
Director, Membership Services: Lori A. Bailey
    E-Mail: lbaile2@clemson.edu
Financial Director: Shelli Charles
Co-Editor: Gary B. Melton

Historical Note:
Incorporated in New York in 1937. Interdisciplinary association of mental health professionals concerned with the study of human behavior and development, and the promotion of mental health. Ortho's goal is based on the belief that fostering mental health in family, school and community contexts will reduce risk for mental disorder. Provides a common ground for collaborative study, research, and knowledge exchange among individuals engaged in preventive, treatment, and advocacy approaches to mental health. Membership: $150 (Individual, Regular); $115 (Fellow/Life Fellow); $60 (Retired); $45 (Student); $240 (AACP Dual).

Meetings/Conferences: Annual

Publications:
American Journal of Orthopsychiatry (AJO); quarterly
Membership Directory; on-line

American Orthotic and Prosthetic Association *(1917)*
330 John Carlyle St.
Suite 200
Alexandria, VA 22314
Tel: (571) 431-0876 *Fax:* (571) 431-0899
E-Mail: info@aopanet.org
Website: aopanet.org
Members: 2000 companies
Staff: 12
Annual Budget: $5-10,000,000
Tax: 501(c)(6)

Personnel:
Executive Director: Thomas F. Fise JD
    E-Mail: tfise@AOPAnet.org
Chief Operating Officer: Don J. DeBolt
    E-Mail: ddebolt@aopanet.org
Senior Director, Government Affairs: Kathleen A. Dodson
    E-Mail: kdodson@aopanet.org
Director, Advertising Sales, O&P Almanac: Dean Mather
    E-Mail: dmather@mrvica.com
*Director, Coding and Reimbursement Services, Education,
    and Programming:* Joseph "Joe" McTernan
    E-Mail: jmcternan@AOPAnet.org
*Senior Director, Membership Services, Operations and
    Meetings:* Tina M. Moran CMP
    E-Mail: tmoran@AOPAnet.org
Manager, Communications: Steven Rybicki
    E-Mail: srybicki@aopanet.org

Historical Note:
AOPA's mission is to work for favorable treatment of the O&P business in laws, regulation and services to help members improve their management and marketing skills and to raise awareness and understanding of the industry and the association. Membership: $1,745 (Patient Care Facility/Education and Research); $305 (Affiliate); $875 (International); $2,975-9,395 (Supplier).

Meetings/Conferences: Annual
Conference Chair: Tina M. Moran CMP

Publications:
AOPA in Advance Newsletter; bi-weekly
Insider Newsletter
Membership Directory; on-line
O&P Almanac Magazine; monthly

Membership List Available to Non-members

American Osteopathic Academy of Addiction Medicine
P.O. Box 280
La Grange, IL 60525-0280
Tel: (708) 572-8006 *Fax:* (708) 401-0360
E-Mail: info@aoaam.org
Website: aoaam.org
Staff: 2
Annual Budget: $100-250,000
Tax: 501(c)(3)

Personnel:
Executive Director: Nina Albano Vidmer
    E-Mail: nvidmer@aoaam.org
Secretary and Treasurer: Dr. Arlin Silberman DO

Historical Note:
AOAAM, an affiliate of American Osteopathic Healthcare Association that provides administrative support, works to give quality and competent multidisciplinary services to those afflicted with the disorders of substance abuse and addiction through the level of education for professionals and the community in the field of addiction medicine. AOAAM's mission is to improve the health of individuals and families burdened with the disease of addiction. Membership: $200 (Active); $75 (Associate); $50 (Resident/Fellow); $25 (Intern).

Meetings/Conferences: Annual
2013 - Seatle, WA (R and T Auditorium, Harborview
    Medical Center)/March 18

Publications:
Annual Membership Directory; annually
Journal of Addictive Diseases; quarterly

American Osteopathic Academy of Orthopedics *(1941)*
2209 Dickens Rd.
Richmond, VA 23230-2005
Tel: (804) 565-6370 *Fax:* (804) 282-0090
E-Mail: info@aoao.org
Website: aoao.org
Members: 1615 individuals
Staff: 6
Annual Budget: $1-2,000,000
Tax: 501(c)(6)

Personnel:
Manager, Information Technology: Daniel Gainyard
    E-Mail: daniel@aoao.org
Director, Operations: Stewart A. Hinckley CMP
    E-Mail: stewart@aoao.org
Director, Meetings and Conventions: Kevin Johns
    E-Mail: meetings@aoao.org
Manager, Membership: Greg Leasure
    E-Mail: membership@aoao.org
Financial Manager: Kimberly Robertson CPA
    E-Mail: kimberly@aoao.org

Historical Note:
Affiliated with the American Osteopathic Association. The American Osteopathic Academy of Orthopedics (AOAO) facilitates the training and continuous development of Osteopathic Orthopedic Surgeons (OOS) to positively improve the care, healing and quality of life of patients. Membership: 350 (Active); $200 (Associate/Military); $100 (Life/Disabled).

Meetings/Conferences: Annual
2013 - San Diego, CA (Sheraton San Diego Hotel and
    Marina)/Oct. 17 - 20
Number of non-conference events/year: 3

Publications:
Member Directory
The Journal of AOAC INTERNATIONAL
The Orthopod

American Osteopathic Academy of Sports Medicine *(1984)*
2424 American Ln.
Madison, WI 53704
Tel: (608) 443-2477 *Fax:* (608) 443-2474
E-Mail: info@aoasm.org
Website: aoasm.org
Members: 500 individuals
Staff: 2
Annual Budget: $100-250,000

Personnel:
Executive Director: Susan M. Rees
    E-Mail: srees@reesgroupinc.com

Historical Note:

AOASM's mission is to provide an educational forum for physicians and healthcare professionals to address the quality of health care for individuals in competitive, recreational, occupational, and industrial settings, leadership to establish, and promote fitness and exercise guidelines, and to guide health care policy relating to wellness, physical activities and sporting events and a collegial environment in which physicians and other healthcare professionals can expand their content knowledge and enhance their clinical skills in primary care sports medicine. Membership: $300-365 (Physician); $230 (Associate); $275-340 (Affiliate); $100-245 (Fellow/Resident/Intern); $145 (Student/Lifetime).

Meetings/Conferences:
2013 - Colorado Springs, CO (The Broadmoor)/March 6 - 9

Publications:
AOASM Newsletter
Member Directory; on-line

American Osteopathic Association (1897)
142 E. Ontario St.
Chicago, IL 60611-2864
Tel: (312) 202-8000 *Fax:* (312) 202-8200
TollFree: (800) 621-1773
E-Mail: govt-issues@osteopathic.org
Website: osteopathic.org
Members: 78,000 osteopathic physicians
Staff: 164
Annual Budget: $50-100,000,000
Tax: 501(c)(3)

Personnel:
Executive Director: John B. Crosby JD
Director, Education: Diane Burkhart PhD
  E-Mail: dburkhart@osteopathic.org
Director, Publications: Michael Fitzgerald
Director, Membership Services: Sherry McAuliffe
Director, Human Resources: Ollie McCarroll
Director, Quality and Research: Sharon McGill
General Counsel: Josh Prober
Director, Communications: Karyn Szurgot
Director, Information Technology: Mike Zarski

Historical Note:
Organized as the American Association for the Advancement of Osteopathic Medicine. Became the American Osteopathic Association in 1901 and was incorporated in Illinois in 1923. AOA's mission is to work towards and attain all things that will truly tend to the progression of Osteopathy. Membership: $683 (Regular); $513-171(Young Physician); $513 (Military Physicians); $104 (Retired Physicians); $99 (Associates); $69 (Interns and Residents).

Continuing Education:
Certification Designation/s: CME

Meetings/Conferences:
2013 - Las Vegas, NV/Sept. 30 - Oct. 4
2014 - Seatle, WA/Oct. 25 - 29
2015 - Orlando, FL/Oct. 17 - 21

Publications:
AOA Health Watch; monthly
JAOA—The Journal of the American Osteopathic Association; adv.
The DO; on-line; adv.
The Whole Patient

American Osteopathic Association of Prolotherapy Integrative Pain Management (1938)
303 S. Ingram Ct.
Middletown, DE 19709
Tel: (302) 530-2489 *Fax:* (302) 376-8081
TollFree: (800) 471-6114
E-Mail: admin@acopms.com
Website: acopms.com
Members: 190 individuals
Staff: 1
Annual Budget: $50-100,000

Personnel:
Executive Director: Linda J. Pavina
  E-Mail: lindapavina@verizon.net

Historical Note:
Formerly (1995) American Osteopathic Academy of Sclerotherapy. Founded in 1938 as the American Osteopathic Society of Herniologists and renamed as The American College of Osteopathic Academy of Sclerotherapy on June 26, 1953 due to the merger of the Central States Osteopathic Herniologists with the American Osteopatic Society of Herniologists. ACOSPM is dedicated towards improving the practice of, and disseminating knowledge

about Sclerotherapy. Members are physicians. Affiliated with American Osteopathic Association. Membership: $200/year (Individual).

Publications:
Membership Directory; on-line

American Osteopathic Board of Physical Medicine and Rehabilitation (1954)
142 E. Ontario St.
Fourth Floor
Chicago, IL 60611-2818
Tel: (312) 202-8103 *Fax:* (312) 202-8224
E-Mail: aobpmr@osteopathic.org
Website: aobpmr.org
Members: 323 individuals
Staff: 3
Annual Budget: $10-25,000
Tax: 501(c)(3)

Personnel:
Executive Director: Ellen Woods DO
  E-Mail: aobpmr@osteopathic.org
Contact, Education: Elaine Bell
  E-Mail: elaineb@osteopathic.org
Secretary and Treasurer: J. Michael Wieting DO

Historical Note:
Formerly (1995) the American Osteopathic Academy of Physical Medicine and Rehabilitation. The purpose of AOBPMR is to evaluate and recommend for Board certification in physical medicine and rehabilitation field. Affiliated with the American Osteopathic Association. Membership: $295/year.

Continuing Education:
Certification Designation/s: ACGME, AOA

Meetings/Conferences: Biennial

Publications:
AOCPMR News; quarterly

American Osteopathic College of Allergy and Immunology (1975)
16128 E. Kingstree Blvd.
Fountain Hills, AZ 85268-5618
Tel: (480) 585-1580 *Fax:* (480) 585-1581
Website: osteopathic.org/inside-aoa/about/affiliates/Pa
Members: 40 individuals
Staff: 2
Annual Budget: Under $10,000
Tax: 501(c)(6)

Personnel:
President: Barry A. Lampl DO
Secretary and Treasurer: William Higgins DO

Historical Note:
An affiliate of American Osteopathic Association, AOCAI provides opportunities for member osteopaths and students to continue studies as they relate to the field of allergy and immunology. Active members shall be graduates of a college of osteopathic medicine approved. Membership: $50/year.

Continuing Education:
Certification Designation/s: AOA-CME

American Osteopathic College of Anesthesiologists (1956)
2260 E. Saginaw St.
Suite B
East Lansing, MI 48823
Tel: (517) 339-0919 *Fax:* (517) 339-0910
E-Mail: osteoanest@aol.com
Website: aocaonline.org
Members: 575 individuals
Staff: 5
Annual Budget: $500-1,000,000
Tax: 501(c)(3)

Personnel:
Interim Executive Director: David C Lorms CAE
Secretary: Lesa Dugan
  E-Mail: lesa@aocaonline.org

Historical Note:
AOCA works to advance the standards of practice and service in the specialty of Anesthesiology, provides opportunities for study and training in this field, and establish standards for membership. Membership: $75 (Active); $20 (Resident); $10 (student)

Meetings/Conferences: Annual
2013 - Charleston, SC (Charleston Place Hotel)/Jan. 18 - 20
2013 - Chicago, IL (Wyndham Chicago)/March 15 - 17

2013 - Washington, DC (Omni Shoreham Hotel)/Sept. 22 - 25

Publications:
Member Directory; on-line

American Osteopathic College of Dermatology (1958)
1501 E. Illinois St.
P.O. Box 7525
Kirksville, MO 63501
Tel: (660) 665-2184 *Fax:* (660) 627-2623
TollFree: (800) 449-2623
E-Mail: info@aocd.org
Website: aocd.org
Members: 366 individuals
Staff: 3
Annual Budget: $500-1,000,000
Tax: 501(c)(3)

Personnel:
Executive Director: Marsha A. Wise BS
  E-Mail: execdirector@aocd.org

Historical Note:
AOCD's mission is to stimulate the study and extend knowledge in the field of dermatology and also promote the practice of osteopathic dermatology. AOCD is an affiliate of the American Osteopathic Association. Membership: $425 (Fellow/Associate/Affiliate); $75 (Resident); $25 (Student).

Continuing Education:
Enrollment: 290
Certification Designation/s: AOCD/AOA

Meetings/Conferences: Annual
2013 - Winter Park, CO (Winter Park Mountain Lodge)/Jan. 23 - 26

Publications:
AOCD Newsletter; quarterly; adv.
JAOCD; on-line
Membership Directory; annually; adv.

American Osteopathic College of Occupational and Preventive Medicine (1979)
P.O. Box 3043
Tulsa, OK 74101
Tel: (800) 558-8686 *Fax:* (918) 561-1431
TollFree: (800) 558-8686
Website: uale.org
Members: 350 individuals
Staff: 2
Annual Budget: $100-250,000

Personnel:
Executive Director: Jeffrey J. LeBoeuf CAE
  E-Mail: jeffrey@aocopm.org

Historical Note:
Originally chartered by the AOA in 1979 as the American Osteopathic Academy of Public Health and Preventive Medicine. Merged with the American Osteopathic Occupational Medicine Association in 1984, to form the American Osteopathic College of Preventive Medicine and assumed its current name in February, 1995. AOCOPM's purpose is to promote the public health and the practice of preventive medicine with the ultimate goal being to create better understanding of the relationship of health and prevention in regard to the wellness of the population.

Continuing Education:
Certification Designation/s: AOBPM, CAQ

Meetings/Conferences: Annual
Conference Chair: Joanna Drowos DO, MBA, MPH
2013 - Phoenix, AZ (Phoenix Sheraton Downtown)/Feb. 13 - 17

Publications:
Membership Directory; on-line
Newsletter

American Osteopathic College of Pathologists (1954)
142 E. Ontario St.
Chicago, IL 60611-8224
Tel: (312) 202-8197 *Fax:* (312) 202-8224
Website: doaocp.org
Members: 140 individuals
Staff: 2
Annual Budget: $10-25,000

Personnel:
President: Lillian Hynes Longendorfer D O
Secretary and Treasurer: Laura Michael

Historical Note:
AOCP's mission is to provide continuing education opportunities and support to member pathologists.

AOCP membership includes osteopathic pathologists and physicians, scientists, technologists, and lay persons who are interested in the practice of pathology. Membership is classified into seven different types. Membership: $300 (Active); $150 (1st year in practice); $100 (Retired/Associate); $10 (Candidate-Resident); Free (Students); $50 (Affiliate).

American Osteopathic College of Proctology

1090 Vermont Ave. NW
Suite 510
Washington, VA 20005
Tel: (202) 414-0140 *Fax:* (703) 684-3280
E-Mail: info@facos.org
Website: aocpr.org
Members: 41 individuals
Staff: 2
Annual Budget: Under $10,000

Personnel:
Executive Director, Secretary and Treasurer: Paul Broderick
    E-Mail: proctodoc55@hotmail.com
Contact: Sonjya Johnson

Historical Note:
AOCPr is dedicated to advancing and promoting the scientific, medical, and surgical practice of proctology. To become eligible for the certification from the AOA through the American Osteopathic Board of Proctology, certain criteria should be met by the applicants. Members are proctologists, colon and rectal surgeons, and other physicians related to the treatment of patients with diseases and conditions affecting the colon, rectum and anus. Members specialize in disorders of the lower gastrointestinal tract. Membership: $400/year.

American Osteopathic College of Radiology
(1941)
119 E. Second St.
Milan, MO 63556-1331
Tel: (660) 265-4011 *Fax:* (660) 265-3494
TollFree: (800) 258-2627
E-Mail: info@aocr.org
Website: aocr.org
Members: 900 individuals
Staff: 6
Annual Budget: $500-1,000,000

Personnel:
Executive Director: Pamela A. Smith
    E-Mail: pam@aocr.org
Director, Membership and Postdoctoral Training: Carol Houston
    E-Mail: carol@aocr.org
Executive Administrative Assistant: Erin Maulsby
    E-Mail: erin@aocr.org
Director, Communications: Jessica Roberts
    E-Mail: jessica@aocr.org

Historical Note:
AOCR is an affiliate organization of the American Osteopathic Association (AOA). AOCR's mission is to advance the practice of radiology by enhancing education, research and the delivery of quality, cost-effective healthcare while embracing the tenets of osteopathic medicine. Membership: $58-510/year.

Publications:
Membership Directory; on-line
Viewbox

American Osteopathic College of Rheumatology, Inc.

193 Monroe Ave.
Edison, NJ 08820-3755
Tel: (732) 494-6688 *Fax:* (732) 494-6689
E-Mail: bmaurer123@aol.com
Website: osteopathic.org
Members: 200 individuals
Staff: 3
Annual Budget: $25-50,000

Personnel:
President: Robert Speer DO
Executive Director: Robert S. Maurer
    E-Mail: bmaurer789@aol.com

Historical Note:
American Osteopathic College of Rheumatology, Inc strives to engage in and promote the study, research, and teaching of the diagnosis, prevention, and treatment of arthritis and allied diseases. Membership includes members of AOA and state societies who show definite interest in study of rheumatic diseases. Associate members are physicians whose interest in the purposes of the college are

outstanding, but who are unable to meet the qualifications for full membership.

American Osteopathic Colleges of Ophthalmology and Otolaryngology - Head and Neck Surgery
(1916)
4764 Fishburg Rd.
Suite F
Huber Heights, OH 45424
Tel: (937) 233-5653 *Fax:* (937) 233-5673
TollFree: (800) 455-9404
E-Mail: info@aocoohns.org
Website: aocoohns.org
Members: 565 individuals
Staff: 6
Annual Budget: $500-1,000,000

Personnel:
Administrative Director: Debra L. Bailey
    E-Mail: dbailey@aocoohns.org

Historical Note:
Formerly (1991) Osteopathic College of Ophthalmology and Otorhinolaryngology and (1993) Osteopathic Colleges of Ophthalmology and Otolaryngology and Head and Neck Surgery. AOCOO-HNS promotes the interests of Osteopathic Ophthalmologists and Osteopathic Otolaryngologists/Facial Plastic Surgeons, to continue to improve their quality of training, education and to advance the practice of osteopathic medicine through a system of quality and cost effective health care measures in the profession. Membership: $475/year.

Meetings/Conferences: Annual
2013 - Orlando, FL (Hyatt Regency Grand Cypress)/May 8 - 12
2014 - Scottsdale, AZ (JW Marriott Camelback Inn Scottsdale Resort and Spa)/May 7 - 11
2015 - Orlando, FL (Ritz Carlton)/May 6 - 10

Publications:
MembershipDirectory; on-line
Newsletter; quarterly; adv.

American Ostrich Association *(1987)*
P.O. Box 166
Ranger, TX 76470
Tel: (936) 333-6142 *Fax:* (936) 333-6142
E-Mail: aoa@ostriches.org
Website: ostriches.org
Members: 100 individuals
Staff: 3
Annual Budget: $500-1,000,000
Tax: 501(c)(5)

Personnel:
President: Glinda Cunningham
    E-Mail: glinda@wildcanyonostrich.com
Secretary and Treasurer: Sharon Birmingham
    E-Mail: srbirmingham@yahoo.com
Editor and Webmaster: Dianna Westmoreland
    E-Mail: ostrich@txcyber.com

Historical Note:
AOA's goal is to establish the standards for the quality American Ostrich products to ensure the long term viability of the industry. Supports the ostrich industry through government relations, promotions, referral services, and other programs. Membership: $150 (Domestic); $200 (International); $25 (Junior).

Meetings/Conferences:
Number of non-conference events/year: 1

Publications:
AOA Newsletter; quarterly
Membership Directory; annually

American Otological Society *(1868)*
1980 Warson Rd.
Springfield, IL 62704
Tel: (217) 638-0801 *Fax:* (217) 679-1677
E-Mail: segossard@aol.com
Website: americanotologicalsociety.org
Members: 301 individuals
Staff: 3
Annual Budget: $100-250,000
Tax: 501(c)(3)

Personnel:
President: Paul R. Lambert
Contact, Administrator: Kristen Bordignon
    E-Mail: otosociety@yahoo.com
Editor: Debara L. Tucci MD

Historical Note:
AOS's mission is to advance and advocate medical and surgical otology/neurotology and lateral skull base surgery

including the rehabilitation of individuals with hearing and balance disorders. Members are otologists and other health professionals with an interest in diseases of the ear. Membership : $425 (Active); $445 (Active International); $100 (Associate); $200 (Corresponding Member).

Meetings/Conferences: Annual
2013 - Orlando, FL (JW Marroitt Grande Lakes Resort)/April 12 - 14

Publications:
Newsletter; bi-annually
Otology & Neurotology; adv.
Transactions of the AOS; annually

Membership List Available to Non-members

American Pain Society *(1977)*
4700 W. Lake Ave.
Glenview, IL 60025-1485
Tel: (847) 375-4715 *Fax:* (847) 375-6479
E-Mail: info@ampainsoc.org
Website: ampainsoc.org
Members: 3400 individuals
Staff: 11
Annual Budget: $2-5,000,000
Tax: 501(c)(3)

Personnel:
Executive Director: Catherine Underwood CAE, MBA
    E-Mail: cunderwood@connect2amc.com
Senior Manager, Marketing: Erin Abbey
    E-Mail: eabbey@ampainsoc.org
Senior Manager, Education: Steve Biddle MEd
    E-Mail: sbiddle@ampainsoc.org
Manager, Meetings: Stephanie Dylkiewicz
    E-Mail: sdylkiewicz@connect2amc.com
Senior Manager, Membership Development: Carrie Gremer
    E-Mail: cgremer@ampainsoc.org
Managing Editor: June Pinyo
    E-Mail: jpinyo@ampainsoc.org

Historical Note:
A national chapter of the International Association for the Study of Pain and incorporated in the District of Columbia in 1978. APS's mission is to serve people in pain by advancing research, education, treatment and professional practice. Members are physicians, dentists, psychologists, nurses, physical and occupational therapists and scientists interested in pain research and treatment. Membership: $120-$325 (Regular); $50 (Student/Resident/Fellow Member); $150 (Individual Affiliate).

Meetings/Conferences: Annual
Conference Chair: Stephanie Dylkiewicz
2013 - New Orleans, LA/May 8 - 11
2014 - Tampa, FL (Tampa Convention Center)/April 30 - May 3

Publications:
APS E-News; monthly
Membership Directory; on-line
The Journal of Pain; monthly

American Paint Horse Association *(1962)*
P.O. Box 961023
Fort Worth, TX 76161-0023
Tel: (817) 834-2742 *Fax:* (817) 834-3152
E-Mail: askapha@apha.com
Website: apha.com
Members: 85000 individuals
Staff: 145
Annual Budget: $10-25,000,000
Tax: 501(c)(5)

Personnel:
Executive Director: Billy Smith
    E-Mail: billys@apha.com
Director, Administration: Theresa Brown
    E-Mail: tbrown@apha.com
Manager, Marketing and Public Relations: Cristin Conner
    E-Mail: cconner@apha.com
Managing Editor: Jessica Hein
    E-Mail: jhein@apha.com
Director, Human Resources: Judy Mitchell
    E-Mail: jmitchell@apha.com
Manager, Information Technology: Kelvin Oostra
    E-Mail: koostra@apha.com
Senior Director, Marketing and Communications: Karrie Patterson
    E-Mail: kpatterson@apha.com
Senior Managing Director: Lex Smurthwaite
    E-Mail: lex@apha.com
Director, Membership Services: Bob Steach

E-Mail: bsteach@apha.com

Historical Note:
Formed by a merger of American Paint Stock Horse, American Paint Quarter Horse Associations and a member of the National Pedigree Livestock Council and the American Horse Council. APHA's mission is to collect, record and preserve pedigrees of American Paint Horses. Membership: $500 (Lifetime); $20 (Junior); $100 (J-Term).

Meetings/Conferences:
Number of non-conference events/year: 4

Publications:
APHA Connection; quarterly
Breeders and Trainers Directory; annually
Paint Horse; monthly; adv.
Paint Horse Racing

American Pancreatic Association (1969)
Duke University Medical Center
DUMC 3919
Durham, NC 27710
Fax: (310) 824-5990
E-Mail: apa@umn.edu
Website: american-pancreatic-association.org
Members: 375 individuals
Staff: 3
Annual Budget: $250-500,000

Personnel:
President: Rodger Liddle MD
E-Mail: liddl001@mc.duke.edu

Historical Note:
Formerly (1975) American Pancreatic Study Group, APA is devoted to understanding the pancreas, its natural functions and disorders, benign or malignant. Members are medical professionals with an interest in diseases of the pancreas. Membership: $180 (Full); $120 (Training).

Meetings/Conferences: Annual

Publications:
Pancreas

American Pathology Foundation (1959)
1540 S. Coast Hwy.
Suite 203
Laguna Beach, CA 92651
Tel: (877) 993-9935 *Fax:* (949) 376-3456
E-Mail: info@apfconnect.org
Website: apfconnect.org
Members: 600 individuals
Staff: 3
Annual Budget: $250-500,000
Tax: 501(c)(6)

Personnel:
Executive Director: Bradley J. Lund
Associate Director: Melissa Lord-Toof
Director, Conferences: Gail Sunshine CMP

Historical Note:
Formerly Private Practitioners of Pathology Foundation. APF is dedicated to providing quality management and financial education, training and practice management resources for pathologists. Members are board certified pathologists concerned with private practice. Membership: $275-375 (Active Pathologist/Associate/Affiliate/Patron); $1,500 (Academic Institution); $1,000 (Industry Affiliate); $2,500 (Group).

Meetings/Conferences: Annual
Conference Chair: Gail Sunshine CMP

Publications:
American Pathology Review; quarterly; adv.
Membership Diretory; on-line

American Payroll Association (1982)
660 N. Main Ave.
Suite 100
San Antonio, TX 78205-1217
Tel: (210) 226-4600 *Fax:* (210) 226-4027
E-Mail: APA@americanpayroll.org
Website: americanpayroll.org
Members: 23000 individuals
Staff: 51
Annual Budget: $10-25,000,000

Personnel:
Executive Director: Daniel J. Maddux
Managing Editor, Membership Publications: Christine Avery
Specialist, Membership Services: Margie Garcia
Senior Director, Communications: Eileen Gaughran
Senior Manager, Meeting Planning: Beth Helberg CMP
Director, Marketing: Chrissy Meslener

Senior Director, Education Services: Jenny Provenzano CPP
Senior Manager, Human Resources: Sylvia Sanchez

Historical Note:
APA's mission is to increase the payroll professional's skill level through education and mutual support. Anyone engaged in payroll administration and/or related fields is eligible for APA membership. Membership: $254/year.

Continuing Education:
Certification Designation/s: FPC, CPP

Meetings/Conferences:
Conference Chair: Beth Helberg CMP
2013 - Grapevine, TX (Gaylord Texan Hotel and Convention Center, Dallas Texas)/May 7 - 11
Number of non-conference events/year: 2

Publications:
Payroll Compliance Newsletter; monthly
PAYTECH; monthly
PAYTECHonline; monthly
SSurvey of Salaries and the Payroll Profession; biennially

American Peanut Council (1997)
1500 King St.
Suite 301
Alexandria, VA 22314-2730
Tel: (703) 838-9500 *Fax:* (703) 838-9508
E-Mail: info@peanutsusa.com
Website: peanutsusa.com
Members: 225 producers and businesses
Staff: 6
Annual Budget: $2-5,000,000
Tax: 501(c)(6)

Personnel:
President: Patrick Archer
E-Mail: generalinfo@peanutsusa.com
Contact, Membership Services: Cindy Stickles
E-Mail: cstickles@peanutsusa.com

Historical Note:
Formerly National Peanut Council (1998). APC's mission is to serve as a forum for all segments of the peanut industry to discuss issues which impact the production, utilization and marketing of peanuts and peanut products worldwide. Membership: $495 (Small Manufacturer/Re-Packers of Peanuts); $1,650 (Allied/Broker/International); $55 (Individual/Research & Extension).

Meetings/Conferences: Semi-Annual
Conference Chair: Cindy Stickles

Publications:
American Peanut News; monthly

American Peanut Product Manufacturers, Inc. (1983)
One Massachusetts Ave. NW
Suite 800
Washington, DC 20001
Tel: (202) 842-2345 *Fax:* (202) 408-7763
Members: 6 companies
Staff: 2
Annual Budget: $100-250,000
Tax: 501(c)(6)

Personnel:
Director: Mike McLeod

Historical Note:
APPMI members are food processors of products using peanuts.

American Peanut Research and Education Society, Inc. (1968)
P.O. Box 15825
College Station, TX 77843-2132
Tel: (979) 845-8278 *Fax:* (979) 845-6483
E-Mail: contact@apresinc.com
Website: apresinc.com
Members: 550 individuals
Staff: 13
Annual Budget: $100-250,000
Tax: 501(c)(3)

Personnel:
Executive Officer: James L. Starr
E-Mail: jstarr@ag.tamu.edu

Historical Note:
Organized in Norfolk, Virginia as the American Peanut Research and Education Association as an outgrowth of the Peanut Improvement Working Group dating back to 1957. The present name was adopted in 1979. The purpose of this Society is to instruct and educate the public

on the properties, production, and use of the peanut ,and to provide consumers with wholesome peanuts and peanut products at reasonable prices. Membership: $25-1000/year.

Meetings/Conferences: Annual
Conference Chair: James L. Starr

Publications:
Newsletter; annually

American Peanut Shellers Association (1919)
2336 Lake Park Dr.
Albany, GA 31707
Tel: (229) 888-2508 *Fax:* (229) 888-5150
E-Mail: info@peanut-shellers.org
Website: peanut-shellers.org
Members: 200 companies
Staff: 4
Annual Budget: $2-5,000,000

Personnel:
Executive Director: John T. Powell
E-Mail: jtpowell@peanut-shellers.org
Director, Events and Publications: Miriam Crosby
E-Mail: mcrosby@peanut-shellers.org

Historical Note:
APSA's mission is to promote the common interests of those engaged in the peanut shelling industry and more particularly, those in the southeastern states. Members are commercial peanut shellers and crushers and other affiliated businesses. Membership: $400/year (Associate).

Meetings/Conferences: Semi-Annual
Conference Chair: Miriam Crosby

Publications:
APSA Newsletter; monthly
Membership Directory; on-line

American Pediatric Society (1888)
3400 Research Forest Dr.
Suite B-7
The Woodlands, TX 77381-4259
Tel: (281) 419-0052 *Fax:* (281) 419-0082
E-Mail: info@aps-spr.org
Website: aps-spr.org
Members: 3151 individuals
Staff: 13
Annual Budget: $1-2,000,000
Tax: 501(c)(3)

Personnel:
Executive Director: Debbie Anagnostelis
E-Mail: debbiea@aps-spr.org
Associate Executive Director: Kathy Cannon
E-Mail: kathyc@aps-spr.org
Accounting Manager: Kate Culliton
E-Mail: katec@aps-spr.org
Managing Editor: Stephanie Dean
E-Mail: stephanie.dean@pedres.org
Director, Information Technology: Antonio Moreno
E-Mail: antonio.moreno@aps-spr.org
Executive Secretary: Brenda Peat
E-Mail: brendap@aps-spr.org

Historical Note:
Organized and incorporated in New York in 1962. APS's purpose is to bring together men and women for the advancement of the study of children and their diseases and prevention of illness. Promotes pediatric education and research, coordinates meetings, research and further education of health professionals. Membership: $255/year.

Meetings/Conferences: Annual
Conference Chair: Kathy Cannon
2013 - Washington, DC/May 4 - 7
2015 - San Diego, CA/April 25 - 28
2016 - Baltimore, MD/April 30 - May 3
2017 - San Francisco, CA/May 6 - 9
2019 - Baltimore, MD/April 27 - 30
2020 - Philadelphia, PA/May 2 - 5

Publications:
American Pediatric Society & Society for Pediatric Research Newsletter
Membership Directory; on-line

American Pediatric Surgical Association (1970)
111 Deer Lake Rd.
Suite 100
Deerfield, IL 60015
Tel: (847) 480-9576 *Fax:* (847) 480-9282
E-Mail: eapsa@eapsa.org
Website: eapsa.org
Members: 800 individuals

Staff: 5
Annual Budget: $500-1,000,000
Tax: 501(c)(6)

Personnel:
Executive Director: Lee Ann Clark
    E-Mail: lclark@eapsa.org
Manager, Communications: Meagan Comerford
Director, Annual Meeting: Liz Freyn
Administrator: Maraina Petrulla

Historical Note:
APSA is a surgical specialty organization composed of surgeons specially trained in surgery for children and young adults, and dedicated to the care of the pediatric surgical patient. The organization represents specialists in pediatric surgery and the benefits derived from the services of qualified pediatric surgeons. Pediatric surgeons perform the surgical treatment of childhood cancer for all clinical trials of the Children's Oncology Group (COG), together with surgeons specifically trained in orthopedic surgery and neurological surgery. Membership: $75 (Candidate); $525 (Regular/ Associate/International).

Meetings/Conferences: Annual
Conference Chair: Liz Freyn
2013 - Marco Island, FL (Marco Island Marriott Beach Resort, Golf Club and Spa)/May 2 - 5
2014 - Phoenix, AZ (JW Marriott Phoenix Desert Ridge Resort and Spa)/May 29 - June 1
2015 - Ft. Lauderdale, FL (Harbor Beach Marriott Resort and Spa)/April 30 - May 3

Publications:
eNewsletter
Journal of Pediatric Surgery
Member Directory

American Peptide Society (1990)
P.O. Box 13796
Albuquerque, NM 87192
Tel: (505) 459-4808 Fax: (775) 667-5332
Website: ampepsoc.org
Members: 1000 individuals
Staff: 4
Annual Budget: $500-1,000,000

Personnel:
President: Ben M. Dunn
    E-Mail: apspresident@americanpeptidesociety.org
Editor: Ellen Terris Brenner
    E-Mail: apsnewsletter@americanpeptidesociety.org
Treasurer: Pravin T.P. Kaumaya
    E-Mail: apstreasurer@americanpeptidesociety.org
Association Manager: Becci Totzke
    E-Mail: APSmanager@americanpeptidesociety.org

Historical Note:
APS is a scientific and educational organization that provides a forum for advancing and promoting knowledge of the chemistry and biology of peptides. Members are involved in research in academia, industry and government covering all aspects of the chemistry and biology of peptides and small proteins. Membership for 2 years: $300 (Individual); $130 (Student); $190 (Postdoctoral/ Retired).

Meetings/Conferences: Annual
2013 - Waikoloa, HI (Hilton Waikoloa Village)/June 22 - 27

Publications:
American Peptide Society Newsletter; quarterly
Journal for Peptide Research and Therapeutics (IJPRT); adv.
Membership Directory; on-line

Membership List Available to Non-members

American Pet Products Association (1958)
255 Glenville Rd.
Greenwich, CT 06831-4148
Tel: (203) 532-0000 Fax: (203) 532-0551
TollFree: (800) 452-1225
Website: americanpetproducts.org
Members: 1013 Members
Staff: 17
Annual Budget: $5-10,000,000

Personnel:
President: Bob Vetere
    E-Mail: bob@americanpetproducts.org
Senior Vice President, Trade Shows: Andrew Darmohraj CAE
    E-Mail: andy@americanpetproducts.org
Senior Director, Regulatory Counsel and Legislative Director: Debora Eisen
    E-Mail: debora@americanpetproducts.org

Vice President, Member Relations and Business Development: Anne Ferrante
    E-Mail: aferrante@americanpetproducts.org
Chief Accountant: Miranda Jaffe
    E-Mail: miranda@americanpetproducts.org
Vice President, Government Affairs and General Counsel: Ed Rod
    E-Mail: ed@americanpetproducts.org
Manager, Communications Program: Jennifer Skelley
    E-Mail: jskelley@americanpetproducts.org
Associate Vice President, Sales, Marketing and Communications: Marian Thielsen
    E-Mail: mthielsen@americanpetproducts.org

Historical Note:
APPA's mission is to promote, develop and advance pet ownership and the pet products industry and to provide the services necessary to help its members prosper. Membership: $550-11,000 (Domestic Manufacturer/Domestic Livestock); $750-12,000 (International Manufacturer/International Livestock); $350 (Manufacturers Representatives).

Meetings/Conferences: Annual
Conference Chair: Andrew Darmohraj CAE
2013 - Orlando, FL (Orange County Convention Center)/Feb. 20 - 22/1-10 exhibitors

Publications:
APPA E-Update; weekly
APPA Smart Brief; weekly
Member Directory

American Petroleum Institute (1919)
1220 L St. NW
Washington, DC 20005-4070
Tel: (202) 682-8000
Website: api.org
Members: 500 companies
Staff: 200
Annual Budget: Over $100,000,000
Tax: 501(c)(6)

Personnel:
President and Chief Executive Officer: Jack N. Gerard
Executive Vice President, Government Affairs: Martin J. Durbin
Managing Counsel: Stacy Linden
Manager, Marketing: Prentiss Searles
    E-Mail: searlesp@api.org
Director, Media Relations: Eric Wohlschlegel

Historical Note:
API's mission is to influence public policy in support of a strong, viable US oil and natural gas industry essential to meet the energy needs of consumers in an efficient, environmentally responsible manner. API provides quality, environmental, and occupational health and safety management systems certification through APIQR. Membership dues based on market share volumes.

Continuing Education:
Certification Designation/s: ICP, EOLCS, APIQR, TPCP

Meetings/Conferences:
2013 - New Orleans, LA/Jan. 21 - 25
2013 - Las Vegas, NV/April 22 - 26
2013 - Houston, TX/July 16 - 17
2013 - New Orleans, LA/Nov. 11 - 15
Number of non-conference events/year: 5

Publications:
API SmartBrief; daily
API WorkSafe Directory; on-line

American Pharmacists Association (1852)
2215 Constitution Ave. NW
Washington, DC 20037
Tel: (202) 628-4410 Fax: (202) 783-2351
TollFree: (800) 237-2742
E-Mail: infocenter@aphanet.org
Website: pharmacist.com
Members: 62000 individuals
Staff: 100
Annual Budget: $25-50,000,000
Tax: 501(c)(6)

Personnel:
Chief Executive Officer: Thomas E. Menighan
    E-Mail: tmenighan@aphanet.org
Senior Director, Meetings and Expositions: Windy Christner
Senior Director, Education: Shelby Englert
    E-Mail: senglert@aphanet.org
Senior Director, Executive Office Operations and Corporate Secretary: Linda K. Gainey

Senior Vice President, Government Affairs: Brian Gallagher
    E-Mail: bgallagher@aphanet.org
Contact, Membership Services: Tammy Hoff
    E-Mail: thoff@aphanet.org
Chief Financial Officer: Joseph J. Janela
Chief Operating Officer: Elizabeth Keyes
    E-Mail: ekeyes@aphanet.org
Contact, Meetings: Todd McDonald
Senior Vice President, Human Resources: Jule Miller
    E-Mail: jmiller@aphanet.org
Senior Vice President, Communications and Marketing: Karen Tracy
    E-Mail: ktracy@aphanet.org

Historical Note:
Founded in Philadelphia, incorporated in the District of Columbia in 1888, APhA is a national professional society of pharmacists. Provides a forum for discussion, consensus building, and policy setting for the profession of pharmacy. Its constituent sections include: Academy of Pharmacy Practice and Management, Academy of Pharmaceutical Research and Science, and Academy of Student Pharmacists. Sponsors and supports the APhA Political Action Committee. APhA empowers its members to improve medication use and advance patient care. Membership: $235 (Pharmacist/Non- Pharmacist); $79-235 (New Practitioner); $117 (Federal/Canadian Pharmacist/Spouse Pharmacist); $62 (Technician); $114 (Retired); $79 (Post Graduate/Resident).

Meetings/Conferences: Annual
Conference Chair: Windy Christner
2013 - Los Angeles, CA (Los Angeles Convention Center)/March 1 - 4/over 100 exhibitors
2014 - Orlando, FL/March 28 - 31
2015 - San Diego, CA/March 27 - 30
2016 - Baltimore, MD/March 4 - 7

Publications:
APhA DrugInfoLine
Journal of Pharmaceutical Sciences
Journal of the American Pharmacists Association
Pharmacy Today
Student Pharmacist

Membership List Available to Non-members

American Philatelic Society (1886)
100 Match Factory Pl.
Bellefonte, PA 16823-1367
Tel: (814) 933-3803 Fax: (814) 933-6128
Website: stamps.org
Members: 34000 individuals
Staff: 8
Annual Budget: $5-10,000,000
Tax: 501(c)(3)

Personnel:
Executive Director: Ken Martin
Controller: Rick Banks
Editor: Barb Boal
Director, Shows and Exhibitions: Dana Guyer
Director, Sales Division: Thomas W. Horn
Manager, Membership Administration: Judy Johnson
Director, Education: Gretchen Moody
Director, Information Services: Tara Murray

Historical Note:
APS's purpose is to advocate stamp collecting for people of all ages and to offer services to its membership and to philately in general, including knowledge and education, which enhance the pleasure and friendliness of stamp collecting. Membership: $14.25-48 (U.S. Member); $16.75-58 (Canadian Member); $19.95-68 (Member, other countries); $8.75-25.50 (Associate); $750-1475 (Life- U.S.); $800-1550 (Life-Canada); $925-1700 (Life-Other Countries).

Meetings/Conferences:
Conference Chair: Dana Guyer
2013 - Louisville, KY (Kentucky International Convention Center)/Jan. 18 - 20
2013 - Louisville, KY/Jan. 24 - 26
2013 - Milwaukee, WI/Aug. 8 - 11
2014 - Riverside, CA/Jan. 24 - 26
2014 - Hartford, CT/Aug. 8 - 10
2014 - Hartford, CT/Aug. 21 - 24
2015 - Grand Rapids, MI/Aug. 20 - 23
Number of non-conference events/year: 5

Publications:
APS e-Newsletter; on-line
The American Philatelist; monthly

American Philological Association (1869)
University of Pennsylvania, 220 S. 40th St.

Suite 201E
Philadelphia, PA 19104-3512
Tel: (215) 898-4975 *Fax:* (215) 573-7874
E-Mail: apaclassics@sas.upenn.edu
Website: apaclassics.org
Members: 2900 individuals and 250 institutions
Staff: 5
Annual Budget: $1-2,000,000
Tax: 501(c)(3)

Personnel:
Executive Director: Adam D. Blistein PhD
   E-Mail: blistein@sas.upenn.edu
Director, Development: Julie A. Carew
   E-Mail: carewj@sas.upenn.edu
Director, Meetings: Heather Hartz Gasda
   E-Mail: heatherh@sas.upenn.edu
Information Architect: Samuel J. Huskey
   E-Mail: huskey@apaclassics.org
Placement Director: Renie Plonski
   E-Mail: plonskii@sas.upenn.edu

Historical Note:
Organized by "professors, friends, and patrons of linguistic science". APA seeks the study of ancient Greek and Roman languages, literatures, and civilizations. Majority of its members are university and college Classics teachers. Members also include scholars in other disciplines, primary and secondary school teachers, and interested lay people. Membership: $34-272 (Individual, based on salary); $33 (Student/Joint); $3000 (Life); $4000 (Joint Life).

Meetings/Conferences: Annual
Conference Chair: Heather Hartz Gasda
2013 - Seattle, WA (Sheraton Seattle Hotel)/Jan. 3 - 6/2800 attendees/51-100 exhibitors
2014 - Chicago, IL/Jan. 2 - 5
2015 - New Orleans, LA/Jan. 8 - 11
2016 - San Diego, CA/Jan. 7 - 11
2016 - San Francisco, CA/Jan. 7 - 10
2017 - Toronto, ON/Jan. 5 - 8
2019 - San Diego, CA/Jan. 3 - 6

Publications:
Amphora; semi-annually
APA Newsletter; quarterly; adv.
Membership Directory; irregular
Transactions of the American Philological Ass'n (TAPA); semi-annually; adv.

Membership List Available to Non-members

American Philosophical Association *(1900)*
University of Delaware
31 Amstel Ave.
Newark, DE 19716-4797
Tel: (302) 831-1112 *Fax:* (302) 831-8690
E-Mail: apaonline@udel.edu
Website: apaonline.org
Members: 10000 individuals
Staff: 9
Annual Budget: $1-2,000,000
Tax: 501(c)(3)

Personnel:
Executive Director: David E. Schrader
   E-Mail: dschrade@udel.edu
Coordinator, Information Technology: Vincent Monsen
   E-Mail: vfmonsen@udel.edu
Employment Services Coordinator: Mike Morris
   E-Mail: mpmorris@udel.edu
Coordinator, Membership Services: Janet Sample
   E-Mail: jsample@udel.edu
Coordinator, Publications: Erin Shepherd
   E-Mail: erinshep@udel.edu
Coordinator, Meetings: Linda Smallbrook
   E-Mail: lindas@udel.edu
Coordinator, Finance: Thomas Wiley
   E-Mail: twiley@udel.edu

Historical Note:
Merged in 1920 with the Western Philosophical Association and later with the Society of Philosophy, a Pacific Coast organization. Mission is to promote the exchange of ideas among philosophers, to encourage creative and scholarly activity in philosophy, to facilitate the professional work and teaching of philosophers, and to represent philosophy as a discipline. Members are professors of philosophy at the college level, graduate students and others with a special interest in the field. Membership: based on annual income $45-250 (Regular); $45 (Student- Overseas); $35 (International Associate/Student-U.S.); $2,500 (Life).

Meetings/Conferences:
Conference Chair: Linda Smallbrook

2013 - New Orleans, LA (Omni Royal Orleans Hotel)/ Feb. 20 - 23
2013 - San Francisco, CA/March 27 - 31
2013 - Baltimore, MD (Baltimore Marriott Waterfront)/ Dec. 27 - 30
2014 - Chicago, IL (Palmer House a Hilton Hotel)/Feb. 26 - March 1
2014 - San Diego, CA/April 14 - 19

Publications:
APA Newsletter; semi-annually
Jobs for Philosophers (JFP); adv.
Member Directory; on-line
Proceedings and Addresses

Membership List Available to Non-members

American Philosophical Society *(1743)*
104 S. Fifth St.
Philadelphia, PA 19106-3387
Tel: (215) 440-3400 *Fax:* (215) 440-3425
Website: amphilsoc.org
Members: 1004 members
Staff: 58
Annual Budget: $50-100,000,000
Tax: 501(c)(3)

Personnel:
Executive Officer: Keith Thomson
   E-Mail: kthomson@amphilsoc.org
Assistant Curator, Education and Museum: Jenni Drozdek
   E-Mail: jdrozdek@amphilsoc.org
Controller: Brunilda Matraku
   E-Mail: bmatraku@amphilsoc.org
Editor: Mary C. McDonald
   E-Mail: mmcdonald@amphilsoc.org
Director, Membership Services and Prizes: Nora Monroe
   E-Mail: nmonroe@amphilsoc.org
Public Information and Processing Archivist: Ann Reinhardt CAE, MEM
   E-Mail: areinhardt@amphilsoc.org
Director, Meetings and Annual Fund: Ann S. Westcott
   E-Mail: westcott@amphilsoc.org
Chief Financial Officer: John Wolfe
   E-Mail: jwolfe@amphilsoc.org
Assistant Technical Librarian and Technology Support Specialist: Scott Ziegler
   E-Mail: sziegler@amphilsoc.org

Historical Note:
Founded in Philadelphia by Benjamin Franklin, APS evolved in 1769 through a merger of the American Philosophical Society and the American Society for Promoting Useful Knowledge; chartered in 1780 in Pennsylvania. APS is held at Philadelphia for Promoting Useful Knowledge. Promotes and advances all useful branches of knowledge through scholarly and scientific meetings (semi-annual); financial assistance to scholars; scholarly books, monographs, articles and newsletter; a library specializing in the history of science in America and its European background; and community service. A member of the American Council of Learned Societies.

Meetings/Conferences: Annual
Conference Chair: Ann S. Westcott

Publications:
The Mendel Newsletter; annually

Membership List Available to Non-members

American Photographic Artists *(1985)*
P.O. Box 725146
Atlanta, GA 31139
Tel: (800) 272-6264 *Fax:* (888) 889-7190
TollFree: (800) 272-6264
E-Mail: office@apa-la.org
Website: apanational.com
Staff: 4
Annual Budget: $250-500,000

Personnel:
Chief Executive Officer: Stephen Best
   E-Mail: ceo@APAnational.com
Webmaster: Liz Roberts
Treasurer: George Simian
   E-Mail: Treasurer@APAnational.com

Historical Note:
Formerly Advertising Photographers of America . APA's goal is to establish, endorse, and promote professional practices, standards, and ethics in the photographic and advertising community.APA seeks to mentor, motivate, educate, and inspire in the pursuit of excellence. Members are established, independent advertising and commercial photographers. Membership: $350 (Professional Photographer); $225 (International Member/Emerging

Photographer); $125 (Assistant/Affiliate); $55 (Student); $75 (Educator); $500 (Educational Institution).

Publications:
InsideAPA; monthly; adv.
WRAPAROUND; quarterly; adv.

American Physical Society *(1899)*
One Physics Ellipse
College Park, MD 20740-3844
Tel: (301) 209-3200 *Fax:* (301) 209-0865
E-Mail: opa@aps.org
Website: aps.org
Members: 46000 Individuals
Staff: 170
Annual Budget: $50-100,000,000
Tax: 501(c)(3)

Personnel:
Program Administrator: Jacquelyn Beamon Kiene
   E-Mail: beamon@aps.org

Historical Note:
APS's mission is to provide effective programs in support of the physics community and the conduct of physics and to be an authoritative source of physics information for the advancement of physics and the benefit of humanity. Membership: $128 (Regular/Fellow); $1,920 (Life); $59 (Junior/Senior); $30 (Student).

Meetings/Conferences:
Conference Chair: Donna Baudrau
2013 - Baltimore, MD (Baltimore Convention Center)/ March 18 - 22
2013 - Denver, CO (Sheraton Denver Downtown Hotel)/April 13 - 16
2013 - Denver, CO/Nov. 11 - 15
2014 - Denver, CO/March 3 - 7
2014 - Savannah, GA/April 5 - 8
2014 - New Orleans, LA/Oct. 27 - 31
2015 - San Antonio, TX/March 2 - 6
2015 - Baltimore, MD/April 11 - 14
2015 - Baltimore, MD/May 2 - 5
2015 - Savannah, GA/Nov. 16 - 20
2016 - Baltimore, MD/March 14 - 18
2017 - New Orleans, LA/March 13 - 17
2018 - Los Angeles, CA/March 12 - 16
Number of non-conference events/year: 1

Publications:
APS Journal
Membership Directory; on-line
Physical Review

Membership List Available to Non-members

American Physical Therapy Association *(1921)*
1111 N. Fairfax St.
Alexandria, VA 22314-1488
Tel: (703) 683-6748 *Fax:* (703) 684-7343
TollFree: (800) 999-2782
Website: apta.org
Members: 80000 individuals
Staff: 160
Annual Budget: $25-50,000,000
Tax: 501(c)(6)

Personnel:
Chief Executive Officer: John D. Barnes
   E-Mail: johnbarnes@apta.org
Vice President, Finance and Business Development and Chief Financial Officer: Rob Batarla
Vice President, Communications and Marketing: Felicity Feather Clancy
Vice President of Public Policy, Practice and Professional Affairs: Justin Moore PT, DPT
   E-Mail: justinmoore@apta.org
Vice President, Membership Relations: Bonnie Polvinale CMP
Associate Director, Media Relations: Erin Wendel
   E-Mail: erinwendel@apta.org

Historical Note:
Formerly (1948) known as the American Women's Physical Therapeutic Association. APTA is a professional association of physical therapists, physical therapist assistants and physical therapy students. APTA's mission is to further the profession's role in the prevention, diagnosis, and treatment of movement dysfunctions and the enhancement of the physical health and functional abilities of members of the public. Membership: $60 (Life Member); $120 (Retired); $80 (Student); $150 (Post- professional Student); $190 (Physical Therapist Assistant); $295 (Physical Therapist).

Meetings/Conferences: Annual

Publications:

Membership Directory; on-line
On Target; monthly
Physical Therapy Reimbursement News; bi-monthly
PT in Motion; monthly
PT in Motion: News Now; weekly
PT-e Clips; on-line
Student E-News; monthly

American Physical Therapy Association - Private Practice Section (1955)
1055 N. Fairfax St.
Suite 204
Alexandria, VA 22314
Tel: (703) 299-2410 *Fax:* (703) 299-2411
TollFree: (800) 517-1167
E-Mail: privatepracticesection@apta.org
Website: ppsapta.org
Members: 4200 individuals
Staff: 249
Annual Budget: $25-50,000,000
Tax: 501(c)(6)

Personnel:
Executive Director: Laurie Kendall-Ellis PT
    E-Mail: lauriekendall-ellis@apta.org
Specialist, Education: Kathie St. Clair
    E-Mail: kathiestclair@apta.org
Managing Editor: Jeff Ostrowski PT

Historical Note:
PPS's mission is to foster the growth, economic viability, and business success, of physical therapist-owned physical therapy services provided for the benefit of the public, and to promote exclusive physical therapist ownership of physical therapy services. Membership in the APTA is a requirement for membership in the Private Practice Section. Membership: $175 (PT); $105 (PTA); $150 (PT Post Professional Student); $50 (Student); $60 (Life PT, Life PTA); $120 (Retired PT, Retired PTA).

Continuing Education:
Certification Designation/s: ACC

Meetings/Conferences: Annual
2013 - Memphis, TN/Feb. 21 - 23
2013 - New Orleans, LA (Hyatt Regency New Orleans)/ Nov. 6 - 9
2014 - Colorado Springs, CO (Antlers Hilton Colorado Springs)/Nov. 5 - 8

Publications:
Impact; adv.
Membership Directory; on-line
PPA E-news; on-line

American Physiological Society (1887)
9650 Rockville Pike
Bethesda, MD 20814-3991
Tel: (301) 634-7800 *Fax:* (301) 634-7241
E-Mail: info@the-aps.org
Website: the-aps.org
Members: 10500 individuals
Staff: 75
Annual Budget: $25-50,000,000
Tax: 501(c)(3)

Personnel:
Executive Director: Dr. Martin Frank PhD
    E-Mail: mfrank@the-aps.org
Manager, Membership Services: Linda Allen
    E-Mail: lallen@the-aps.org
Director, Information Technology: James Chapman
    E-Mail: jchapman@the-aps.org
Director, Communications: Donna Krupa
    E-Mail: dkrupa@the-aps.org
Director, Education Programs: Marsha Lakes Matyas PhD
    E-Mail: mmatyas@the-aps.org
Director, Finance: Robert Price
    E-Mail: rprice@the-aps.org
Director, Government Relations and Science Policy: Alice Hellerstein Ra'anan
    E-Mail: araanan@the-aps.org
Manager, Marketing: Sue Sabur
    E-Mail: ssabur@the-aps.org
Director, Publications and Executive Editor: Rita Scheman
    E-Mail: rscheman@schemanconsulting.com

Historical Note:
Founded in December 30, 1887 and incorporated in Missouri in 1923. APS's mission is to foster education, scientific research and dissemination of information in the physiological sciences. Members are individuals conducting original research in physiology. Membership: $140

(Regular); $95 (Affiliate); $10-20 (Students); $750-4,500 (Sustaining).

Meetings/Conferences: Annual
2013 - Boston, MA/April 20 - 24
2014 - San Diego, CA/April 26 - 30
2015 - Boston, MA/March 28 - April 1

Publications:
Advances in Physiology Education; annually; adv.
American Journal of Physiology (Consolidated); monthly; adv.
American Journal of Physiology: Endocrinology and Metabolism; monthly; adv.
American Journal of Physiology: Gastrointestinal and Liver Physiology; monthly; adv.
American Journal of Physiology: Heart and Circulatory Physiology; monthly; adv.
American Journal of Physiology: Lung Cellular and Molecular Physiology; monthly; adv.
American Journal of Physiology: Regulatory, Integrative and Comparative; monthly; adv.
American Journal of Physiology: Renal Physiology; monthly; adv.
American Physiological Society: Legacy Content; on-line
Journal of Applied Physiology; monthly; adv.
Journal of Neurophysiology; monthly; adv.
Membership Directory; on-line
News in Physiological Sciences; irregular; adv.
Physiological Genomics; quarterly; adv.
Physiological Reviews; quarterly; adv.
Physiology; bi-monthly
The American Journal of Physiology - Cell Physiology; monthly
The Physiologist; bi-monthly; adv.

Membership List Available to Non-members

American Phytopathological Society (1908)
3340 Pilot Knob Rd.
St. Paul, MN 55121-2097
Tel: (651) 454-7250 *Fax:* (651) 454-0766
E-Mail: aps@scisoc.org
Website: apsnet.org
Members: 60 companies and organizations and 5000 individuals
Staff: 23
Annual Budget: $2-5,000,000

Personnel:
Executive Vice President: Steve C. Nelson
    E-Mail: snelson@scisoc.org
Contact, Membership Services: Michelle Bjerkness
    E-Mail: mbjerkness@scisoc.org
Contact, Publications: Karen Cummings
    E-Mail: kcummings@scisoc.org
Contact, Meetings: Betty Ford
    E-Mail: bford@scisoc.org
Vice President, Operations: Amy Hope
    E-Mail: ahope@scisoc.org
Vice President, Finance: Barbara Mock
    E-Mail: bmock@scisoc.org
Contact, Marketing for Meetings, Membership Services and Publications: Sarah Wilson

Historical Note:
APS's mission is to encourage all aspects of knowledge of plant diseases, and promote their control. Membership: $78 (Professional/Regular/Group); $31 (Student); $54 (Post-Doc); $580-795 (Sustaining Associate).

Meetings/Conferences: Annual
Conference Chair: Betty Ford
2013 - Austin, TX/Aug. 10 - 14
2014 - Minneapolis, MN/Aug. 9 - 13

Publications:
Molecular Plant-Microbe Interactions; monthly; adv.
Phytopathology; monthly; adv.
Plant Disease; monthly; adv.

American Pianists Association (1979)
4603 Clarendon Rd.
Suite 030
Indianapolis, IN 46208
Tel: (317) 940-9945
E-Mail: APAinfo@americanpianists.org
Website: americanpianists.org
Staff: 5
Annual Budget: $500-1,000,000

Personnel:

Artistic Director and President and Chief Executive Officer: Joel Harrison
    E-Mail: joel@americanpianists.org
Director, Operations: Kim Lewis
    E-Mail: kim@americanpianists.org
Coordinator, Marketing and Administrative Assistant: Bridget Rawlins
    E-Mail: bridget@americanpianists.org

Historical Note:
Founded in 1979 as the Beethoven Foundation, the mission of the American Pianists Association is to discover, promote and advance the careers of young, American, world-class, jazz and classical pianists. Membership: $25-99 (Friend of the APA, One Person); $50-99 (Friend of the APA, Two People); $100-499 (Supporting Friend); $500- 999 (Sustaining Friend); $1000- Above (Grand Friend).

Meetings/Conferences:
Number of non-conference events/year: 13

American Pilots' Association (1884)
499 S. Capitol St. SW
Suite 409
Washington, DC 20003-4013
Tel: (202) 484-0700 *Fax:* (202) 484-9320
E-Mail: contact@americanpilots.org
Website: americanpilots.org
Members: 60 groups of state-licensed pilots
Staff: 4
Annual Budget: $2-5,000,000

Personnel:
Executive Director and General Counsel: Paul G. Kirchner
Executive Assistant: Lisa E. Powell
    E-Mail: lpowell@americanpilots.org
Secretary and Treasurer: Capt. Whit Smith
President: Capt. Michael R. Watson
    E-Mail: Captwatson@aol.com

Historical Note:
APA is a national trade association of professional maritime pilots. Members are groups or state licensed maritime pilots or federally licensed pilots in the Great Lakes region. Membership: $1,400/year (Individual).

Meetings/Conferences: Annual
Conference Chair: Lisa E. Powell

Publications:
ON STATION; quarterly

Membership List Available to Non-members

American Pinzgauer Association (1973)
1411 Hobo Ln.
Madisonville, TX 77864
Tel: (936) 443-9205
E-Mail: info@pinzgauers.org
Website: pinzgauers.org
Members: 500 individuals
Staff: 3
Annual Budget: $25-50,000
Tax: 501(c)(5)

Personnel:
President: Lisa Wamsley
    E-Mail: gertngauers@yahoo.com

Historical Note:
APA is the American Herdbook Affiliate for the Pinzgauer Cattle International. APA ensures that the Pinzgauer breed will make an important contribution to the improvement of the cattle industry in America. Membership is open to all cattle breeders who wish to import purebred Pinzgauer cattle and/or engage in a supervised pedigree program for the development of the Pinzgauer breed in the United States. Membership: $75 (Adult); $100 (Associate); $10 (Junior); $25 (Life Time).

Publications:
Breeder Directory; on-line

American Pipe Fittings Association (1938)
201 Park Washington Ct.
Falls Church, VA 22046-4527
Tel: (703) 538-1786 *Fax:* (703) 241-5603
E-Mail: info@apfa.org
Website: apfa.com
Members: 50 companies
Staff: 2
Annual Budget: $100-250,000

Personnel:
Executive Director: Clay D. Tyeryar CAE, MAM

Historical Note:
Formerly Pipe Fittings Manufacturers Association. Members are domestic producers of piping components and accessories and pipe hangers and supports. Seeks

to promote use of American pipe fittings, contribute to development of standards, collect statistics, and cooperate with government agencies on matters affecting the industry.

American Planning Association *(1909)*
97774 Eagle Way
Chicago, IL 60678-9770
Tel: (312) 786-6703 *Fax:* (312) 786-6700
E-Mail: apainfo@planning.org
Website: planning.org
Members: 40,000 national members
Staff: 119
Annual Budget: $10-25,000,000
Tax: 501(c)(3)

Personnel:
Chief Executive Officer: Paul Farmer FAICP
Director, Meetings and Conferences: Deene Alongi
    E-Mail: dalongi@planning.org
Director, Marketing and Promotions: Kenneth East
Director, Information Technology: Mark Ferguson
Director, Publications: Sylvia Lewis
    E-Mail: slewis@planning.org
Chief Operating Officer and Chief Financial Officer: Ann Simms
Director, Education and Citizen Engagement: Carolyn Torma
    E-Mail: ctorma@planning.org

Historical Note:
Founded as the National Conference on City Planning, assumed its present name in 1978. APA is an independent, not-for-profit educational organization that provides leadership in the development of vital communities by advocating excellence in community planning, promoting education and citizen empowerment, and providing the tools and support necessary to meet the challenges of growth and change. Membership: $45 (Planners/Student); $150-375 (Regular); $100 (Affiliate).

Meetings/Conferences: Annual
Conference Chair: Deene Alongi
2013 - Chicago, IL (Hyatt Regency Chicago)/April 13 - 17
2014 - Atlanta, GA/April 26 - 29
2014 - Atlanta, GA/April 26 - 30
2015 - Seattle, WA/April 18 - 22
Number of non-conference events/year: 10

Publications:
APA Interact; on-line
Journal of the American Planning Association; on-line
Planning & Environmental Law; monthly
Planning Magazine; adv.
Practicing Planner; quarterly
The Commissioner
The New Planner

Membership List Available to Non-members

American Podiatric Medical Association *(1912)*
9312 Old Georgetown Rd.
Bethesda, MD 20814-1621
Tel: (301) 581-9200 *Fax:* (301) 530-2752
TollFree: (800) 275-2762
E-Mail: askapma@apma.org
Website: apma.org
Members: 15000 individuals
Staff: 60
Annual Budget: $10-25,000,000
Tax: 501(c)(6)

Personnel:
Executive Director and Chief Executive Officer: Glenn B. Gastwirth DPM
    E-Mail: gbgastwirth@apma.org
Deputy Executive Director: Jay Levrio PhD
    E-Mail: jlevrio@ampa.org
Director, Finance: John A. Lieske CPA, MBA
    E-Mail: jalieske@apma.org
Administrator, Meetings: Anne R. Martinez CMP
    E-Mail: armartinez@apma.org
Director, Development and Corporate Relations: Heather Palmer MBA
    E-Mail: hepalmer@apma.org
Manager, Advertising: Rachel Richards
    E-Mail: rmrichards@apma.org
Director, Membership Services: Beth Shaub
    E-Mail: bshaub@apma.org
Director, Legislative Advocacy: Peter Stein
Director, Council on Podiatric Medical Education: Alan Tinkleman MPA
    E-Mail: artinkleman@apma.org

Director, Print and Online Communications: Peggy Tresky MA
    E-Mail: pstresky@apma.org

Historical Note:
Formerly the National Association of Chiropodists, (1958) the American Podiatry Association and assumed its current name in 1984. APMA's mission is to advance the growth and stability of podiatric medicine by increasing nationwide awareness of foot and ankle health through public education and legislative advocacy. Membership: $66 (Resident/Preceptor/Post-Graduate); $206 (Affiliate-Practitioners outside U.S.); $725 (Individual).

Meetings/Conferences: Annual
Conference Chair: Anne R. Martinez CMP
2013 - Las Vegas, NV (Venetian Resort Hotel Casino)/July 21 - 24
2014 - Honolulu, HI (Hilton Hawaiian Village Waikiki Beach Resort)/July 24 - 27
2015 - Orlando, FL (Orlando World Center Marriott)/July 23 - 26
2016 - Philadelphia, PA (Philadelphia Marriott Downtown)/July 14 - 17
Number of non-conference events/year: 1

Publications:
APMA News; adv.
Membership Directory; on-line
The APMA News Brief; weekly; adv.

American Podiatric Medical Students Association *(1954)*
9312 Old Georgetown Rd.
Bethesda, MD 20814
Tel: (301) 581-9200 *Fax:* (301) 530-2752
TollFree: (800) 275-2762
E-Mail: apmsajen@aol.com
Website: aacpm.org
Members: 2300 individuals
Staff: 3
Annual Budget: $250-500,000
Tax: 501(c)(6)

Personnel:
Executive Director: Dorothy Cahill McDonald
    E-Mail: apmsadcm@apma.org
Director, Development and Corporate Relations: Jessica Minder
    E-Mail: jessica.minder@my.rfums.org

Historical Note:
APMSA represents students enrolled in colleges of podiatric medicine in the U.S. APMSA provides issues and forum to discuss problems, to further the profession of podiatry on a national level.

Meetings/Conferences:
Number of non-conference events/year: 1

Publications:
First Step Winter 2011
Membership Directory; on-line

American Podiatric Medical Writers Association *(1985)*
P.O. Box 750129
Forest Hills, NY 11375
Tel: (718) 897-9700 *Fax:* (718) 896-5747
E-Mail: bblock@podiatrym.com
Members: 100 individuals
Staff: 3
Annual Budget: Under $10,000
Tax: 501(c)(6)

Personnel:
Executive Director: Barry Block
    E-Mail: bblock@prodigy.net

Historical Note:
APMWA's mission is to promote excellence in medical communication. Membership: $50 (Podiatrist); $25 (Non-Podiatrist).

American Polarity Therapy Association *(1984)*
122 N. Elm St.
Suite 504
Greensboro, NC 27401
Tel: (336) 574-1121 *Fax:* (336) 574-1151
E-Mail: aptaoffices@polaritytherapy.org
Website: polaritytherapy.org
Members: 900 individuals
Staff: 4
Annual Budget: $10-25,000
Tax: 501(c)(3)

Personnel:

Executive Director: MK Brennan
    E-Mail: mkbrennan@polaritytherapy.org
Marketing and Branding: Fran Kerg
    E-Mail: news@polaritytherapy.org
Director, Education: Nancy Lehto
    E-Mail: dofe@polaritytherapy.org
Director, Finance: Carrie Massey
    E-Mail: aptaoffices@polaritytherapy.org

Historical Note:
APTA is a national organization that supports the promotion and development of Polarity therapy as a field and as a profession. Membership: $70 (Student); $90 (General); $170 (Associate).

Continuing Education:
Enrollment: 900
Certification Designation/s: NCBTMB

Publications:
APTA Energy; quarterly

American Political Science Association *(1903)*
1527 New Hampshire Ave. NW
Washington, DC 20036-1206
Tel: (202) 483-2512 *Fax:* (202) 483-2657
E-Mail: apsa@apsanet.org
Website: apsanet.org
Members: 15000 individuals
Staff: 27
Annual Budget: $25-50,000,000
Tax: 501(c)(3)

Personnel:
Executive Director: Michael A Brintnall
    E-Mail: brintnall@apsanet.org
Director, Finance and Administration: Regina Chavis CPA
    E-Mail: rchavis@apsanet.org
Manager, Membership Services: Linda Davis
    E-Mail: ldavis@apsanet.org
Director, Communications and Publishing: Pauline Karpowicz CAE
    E-Mail: pkarpowicz@apsanet.org
Director, Educational, Professional and Minority Initiatives: Kimberly Mealy PhD
    E-Mail: kmealy@apsanet.org
Director, Membership Services and Development: Sean Twombly
    E-Mail: twombly@apsanet.org
Director, Meetings and Conferences: Lauren West
    E-Mail: lwest@apsanet.org

Historical Note:
APSA provides scholarly research and communication, domestically and internationally. Membership: $96-314 (Professional); $44 (Student/Unemployed/High School Teacher); $3,000 (Life Member); $39-65 (Retired); $60 (Associate); $40 (Targeted International Member); $28 (Family Member).

Meetings/Conferences: Annual
Conference Chair: Lauren West
2013 - Chicago, IL (Sheraton Chicago Hotel and Towers)/Aug. 29 - Sept. 1
2014 - Washington, DC (Washington Marriott Wardman Park)/Aug. 28 - 31
2015 - San Francisco, CA (Hilton San Francisco Union Square)/Sept. 3 - 6
2016 - Philadelphia, PA (Philadelphia Marriott Downtown)/Sept. 1 - 4
Number of non-conference events/year: 20

Publications:
Perspectives on Politics; quarterly; adv.
PS: Political Science and Politics; quarterly; adv.
The American Political Science Review; quarterly; adv.

Membership List Available to Non-members

American Polygraph Association *(1966)*
P.O. Box 8037
Chattanooga, TN 37414-0037
Tel: (423) 892-3992 *Fax:* (423) 894-5435
TollFree: (800) 272-8037
E-Mail: manager@polygraph.org
Website: polygraph.org
Members: 2500 individuals
Staff: 5
Annual Budget: $1-2,000,000
Tax: 501(c)(6)

Personnel:
President: Pam Shaw
    E-Mail: president@polygraph.org
Manager, National Office: Robbie S. Bennett
    E-Mail: manager@polygraph.org

Editor: Donald Krapohl
  E-Mail: editor@polygraph.org
Treasurer: Chad Russell
  E-Mail: treasurer@polygraph.org
General Counsel: Gordon L. Vaughan
  E-Mail: gvaughan@vaughandemuro.com

Historical Note:
APA is the product of a merger of Academy of Scientific Interrogation, American Academy of Polygraph Examiners, and National Board of Polygraph Examiners. A polygraph professional association, establishing standards of ethical practices, techniques, instrumentation, research, and advanced training and continuing educational programs. It's mission is to is to provide mankind with a valid and reliable means to verify the truth of the matter asserted by serving the cause of truth with integrity, objectivity and fairness to all persons. Members must acquire annual continuing education and training in order to maintain membership. Membership: $150/year.

Continuing Education:
Certification Designation/s: ASTC

Meetings/Conferences:
Conference Chair: Robbie S. Bennett
Number of non-conference events/year: 1

Publications:
APA Magazine
Member Directory; annually
Polygraph; quarterly
The Truth; bi-monthly

American Polypay Sheep Association *(1980)*
P.O. Box 51
222 Main St.
Milo, IA 50166
Tel: (641) 942-6402 *Fax:* (641) 942-6502
E-Mail: info@polppay.org
Website: countrylovin.com/polypay/
Members: 225 individuals
Staff: 4
Annual Budget: $25-50,000

Personnel:
Contact, Associated Sheep Registries: Karey Claghorn
Contact, Website Services: Carol Wise
  E-Mail: web@polypay.org

Historical Note:
APSA is engaged in the promotion, advancement and continued improvement of the polypay breed of sheep throughout the world. Members are breeders of polypay sheep, a breed developed to provide more productive sheep to make a profit. Membership: $50/year.

Publications:
APSA Newsletter; on-line
Breeders Directory; on-line

American Pomological Society *(1848)*
102 Tyson Building
University Park, PA 16802
Tel: (814) 863-6163 *Fax:* (814) 237-3407
E-Mail: aps@psu.edu
Website: americanpomological.org
Members: 950 individuals
Staff: 6
Annual Budget: $10-25,000
Tax: 501(c)(5)

Personnel:
President: Terence Robinson
Treasurer, Membership Contact and Business Manager: Dr. Robert Crassweller

Historical Note:
Formerly North American Pomological Convention and became American Pomological Congress in 1849 and then assumed its current name. APS's purpose is to promote the study and culture of fruit and nuts and to disseminate information pertaining to fruit and nut cultivars. Membership: $50-70 (Individual); $60-80 (Library and Institution Rate).

Publications:
Journal of the American Pomological Society

American Postal Workers Union *(1971)*
1300 L St. NW
Washington, DC 20005
Tel: (202) 842-4200 *Fax:* (202) 842-4297
Website: apwu.org
Members: 222000 private-sector mail workers and employees
Staff: 90
Annual Budget: $50-100,000,000

Tax: 501(c)(5)

Personnel:
President: Cliff Guffey
Executive Vice President: Greg Bell
Director, Human Relations: Sue Carney
Director, Communications: Sally Davidow
Secretary-Treasurer: Elizabeth Powell
Director, Legislative and Political Department: Myke Reid
  E-Mail: mreid@apwu.org
Director, Research and Education: Joyce B. Robinson
Director, Organization: Martha Shunn-King

Historical Note:
The American Postal Workers Union (APWU) is a labor union that negotiates a national Collective Bargaining Agreement and fights for its members' interests on Capitol Hill. Members are employees of the United States Postal Service who are clerks, maintenance employees, and motor vehicle service workers. Member dues vary from local to local. They include national dues established by the National Convention and local dues determined by the local union.

Meetings/Conferences: Annual
Conference Chair: Joyce B. Robinson

Publications:
APWU Web News; daily
Membership Directory; on-line
The American Postal Worker; bi-monthly

Membership List Available to Non-members

American Poultry Association *(1873)*
P.O. Box 306
Burgettstown, PA 15021-0306
Tel: (724) 729-3459
Website: amerpoultryassn.com
Members: 3000 individuals
Staff: 6
Annual Budget: $10-25,000

Personnel:
President: Sam Brush
  E-Mail: slbrush@verizon.net
Director-at-Large: CAPT Dave Anderson
  E-Mail: danderson@keygroupinc.com
Contact, Conventions and Meetings: Bill Brunschon
Secretary and Treasurer: Pat Horstman
  E-Mail: secretaryapa@yahoo.com
Coordinator, Youth Program: Doris Robinson
Contact, Website-Tech Support Issues: Patti Salmon
  E-Mail: psalmon@cafes.net

Historical Note:
The purpose of APA is to advocate and protect the standard-bred poultry industry in all its phases. Membership: $15 (Junior 18 and under); $20 (Individual); $25 (Associate/Outside US and Canada); $365 (Endowment Trust Life Member in US and Canada); $730 (International Endowment Trust Life Member).

Meetings/Conferences:
Conference Chair: Bill Brunschon

Publications:
Membership Directory; on-line
Newsletter; quarterly

American Poultry International Ltd. *(1970)*
5420 Interstate 55 N.
Suite A
Jackson, MS 39211
Tel: (601) 956-1715 *Fax:* (707) 988-1715
E-Mail: apiltd@apipoultry.com
Website: apipoultry.com
Staff: 2

Personnel:
President and Chief Executive Officer: Gerald W. Holaday
Secretary, Treasurer and Chief Financial Officer: Karla A. Ford

Historical Note:
API is an export trade association engaged in selling and shipping frozen poultry products from the USA to purchasers in foreign nations. In addition to frozen poultry and meat products for both export and domestic use, API offers a variety of services.

Publications:
Daily Industry News; daily

American Prepaid Legal Services Institute *(1976)*
321 N. Clark St.
19th Floor
Chicago, IL 60654
Tel: (312) 988-5751 *Fax:* (312) 988-5483

E-Mail: info@aplsi.org
Website: aplsi.org
Members: 500 individuals
Staff: 4
Annual Budget: $100-250,000
Tax: 501(c)(6)

Personnel:
Executive Director: Tori Jo Wible
Contact, Membership Services: Adrienne Tucker
Contact, Conference Services: Sara Walsh

Historical Note:
Founded by the American Bar Association to serve as a national umbrella organization. API is dedicated to the growth and development of prepaid legal services. Membership: $150 (Associate); $325 (Regular); $85 (Provider); $60 (Special ABA/GP).

Continuing Education:
Enrollment: 120
Certification Designation/s: NIA, CLEC

Meetings/Conferences: Annual
Conference Chair: Sara Walsh
2013 - Atlanta, GA (Hyatt Regency Atlanta)/May 2 - 4

Publications:
API Newsbriefs; monthly
Concise Guide to Prepaid Legal Services; on-line
Membership Directory
Regulation Reporter on Pre-Paid Legal Services; quarterly
Regulation State Pak; on-line
Who's Who in Prepaid Legal Services; annually

American Press Institute *(1946)*
11690 Sunrise Valley Dr.
Reston, VA 20191-1498
Tel: (703) 620-3611 *Fax:* (703) 620-5814
E-Mail: info@americanpressinstitute.org
Website: americanpressinstitute.org
Staff: 11
Annual Budget: $500-1,000,000
Tax: 501(c)(3)

Personnel:
Director, Finance: Evelyn Miyasato
  E-Mail: emiyasato@americanpressinstitute.org
Coordinator, Marketing and Seminars: Val Williamson
  E-Mail: vwilliamson@americanpressinstitute.org

Historical Note:
API works to develop educational programs for working media professionals.

Meetings/Conferences:
Conference Chair: Val Williamson

Membership List Available to Non-members

American Printing History Association *(1974)*
Grand Central Stn.
P.O. Box 4519
New York, NY 10163
Tel: (212) 930-9220 *Fax:* (212) 930-0079
E-Mail: secretary@printinghistory.org
Website: printinghistory.org
Members: 800 individuals
Staff: 4
Annual Budget: $50-100,000
Tax: 501(c)(3)

Personnel:
President: Robert McCamant
Executive Secretary: Lyndsi Barnes
Treasurer: David Goodrich
Editor: William T. La Moy
  E-Mail: newsletter@printinghistory.org

Historical Note:
APHA is an organization that encourages the study of the history of printing and related arts and crafts, including calligraphy, typefounding, typography, papermaking, bookbinding, illustration, and publishing. Works towards its goal through a variety of programs and services. Members are academics and others with an interest in the history of printing and its related skills and technologies. Membership: $50 (Individual); $75 (Institution); $100 (Contributing); $200 (Sustaining); $500 (Benefactor); $20 (Student).

Meetings/Conferences: Annual

Publications:
Printing History; semi-annually; adv.
The APHA Newsletter; quarterly; adv.

American Probation and Parole Association *(1975)*
P.O. Box 11910

Lexington, KY 40578-1910
Tel: (859) 244-8203 *Fax:* (859) 244-8001
E-Mail: appa@csg.org
Website: appa-net.org
Members: 3500 individuals
Staff: 18
Annual Budget: $1-2,000,000
Tax: 501(c)(3)

Personnel:
Executive Director: Carl Wicklund
    E-Mail: cwicklund@csg.org
Research Associate: Carrie Abner
    E-Mail: cabner@csg.org
Registrar: Krista Chappell
    E-Mail: kchappell@csg.org
Administrative Assistant: Lisa Ginter
    E-Mail: lginter@csg.org
Deputy Director and Information Specialist: Diane Kincaid
    E-Mail: dkincaid@csg.org
Manager, Corporate Relations, Exhibit, Sponsorship and Journal: Karen Mucci
    E-Mail: kmucci@csg.org

Historical Note:
APPA's mission is to support its member's interests in probation, parole and community corrections. Members are probation/parole professionals and others. Membership: $50-5,000/year; $300 (Lifetime).

Meetings/Conferences:
Conference Chair: Karen Mucci
Number of non-conference events/year: 2

Publications:
APPA Journal; quarterly
APPA Newsletter; semi-monthly

American Professional Society on the Abuse of Children *(1987)*
350 Poplar Ave.
Elmhurst, IL 60126
Tel: (630) 941-1235 *Fax:* (630) 359-4274
TollFree: (877) 402-7722
E-Mail: apsac@apsac.org
Website: apsac.org
Members: 2600 individuals
Staff: 6
Annual Budget: $500-1,000,000
Tax: 501(c)(3)

Personnel:
Executive Director: Michael L. Haney
    E-Mail: mhaney@apsac.org
Associate Director: Michael Bandy
    E-Mail: mbandy@apsac.org
Coordinator, Education: Jim Campbell
    E-Mail: apsaccolloquium@charter.net
Editor-in-Chief: Vincent J. Palusci

Historical Note:
APSAC's mission is to provide professional education that advocates effective, culturally sensitive and interdisciplinary approaches to the identification, intervetion, treatment and prevention of child abuse and neglect. Members include psychologists, social workers, physicians, attorneys, nurses, law enforcement officers, child protective service workers, administrators, researchers, and allied professionals who have dedicated a substantial portion of their professional lives to alleviating the problems caused by child maltreatment. Membership: $65 (Student); $75-125 (Individual).

Meetings/Conferences: Annual
Conference Chair: Jim Campbell
2013 - Las Vegas, NV (Caesar's Palace Hotel)/June 25 - 28
Number of non-conference events/year: 4

Publications:
Child Maltreatment Journal; quarterly
Member Directory; on-line
The APSAC Advisor; quarterly

American Property Tax Counsel
1970 E. Grand Ave.
Suite 330
El Segundo, CA 90245
Tel: (877) 829-2782 *Fax:* (877) 829-2782
E-Mail: bulletin@aptcnet.com
Website: aptcnet.com
Members:
100 attorneys
32 member firms
Staff: 1

Annual Budget: $250-500,000

Personnel:
Manager, Marketing and Communications: Anna Whitworth
    E-Mail: awhitworth@aptcnet.com

Historical Note:
APTC provides portfolio owners with property tax reporting and tax reduction needs.
Meetings/Conferences:
Number of non-conference events/year: 1

Publications:
APTC Newsletter

Membership List Available to Non-members

American Prosthodontic Society *(1928)*
303 W. Madison St.
Suite 2650
Chicago, IL 60606
Tel: (312) 981-6780 *Fax:* (312) 265-2908
E-Mail: aps@prostho.org
Website: prostho.org
Members: 450 individuals
Staff: 5
Annual Budget: $100-250,000
Tax: 501(c)(6)

Personnel:
Account Executive: Joseph M. Jackson CAE
    E-Mail: jjackson@thesentergroup.com
Account Coordinator, Membership and Operations: Sara Porter
    E-Mail: sporter@thesentergroup.com
Director, Meetings and Education: Moira Twitty
    E-Mail: mtwitty@thesentergroup.com
Senior Account Coordinator, Meetings and Education: Rachel Walsh
    E-Mail: rwalsh@thesentergroup.com

Historical Note:
APS's mission is is to promote the advancement of the discipline of prosthodontics. APS is an ADA CERP recognized provider of continuing education credits. Membership includes specialists, generalists, certified dental technologists and students. Membership: $435 (Active Practicing Dentist); $276 (Active Dental Technologist); $215 (Active Recent Graduate within 5 years); $25 (Graduate Student,Current).

Meetings/Conferences: Annual
Conference Chair: Moira Twitty
2013 - Chicago, IL (Swissotel Chicago)/Feb. 21 - 23

Publications:
Journal of Prosthetic Dentistry; monthly

Membership List Available to Non-members

American Psychiatric Association *(1844)*
1000 Wilson Blvd.
Suite 1825
Arlington, VA 22209-3901
Tel: (703) 907-7300
TollFree: (888) 357-7924
E-Mail: apa@psych.org
Website: psych.org
Members: 36000 physicians
Staff: 270
Annual Budget: $25-50,000,000
Tax: 501(c)(6)

Personnel:
Director, Communications and Public Affairs: Eve Herold
    E-Mail: press@psych.org
Director, Government Relations: Nicholas Meyers
    E-Mail: nmeyers@psych.org
Director, Psychiatric Research: Eve Moscicki
    E-Mail: emoscicki@psych.org
Chief Financial Officer: Terri Swetnam

Historical Note:
Founded in Philadelphia as the Association of Medical Superintendents of American Institutions for the Insane. In 1892 it became the American Medico-Psychological Association and in 1921 the American Psychiatric Association. Incorporated in the District of Columbia in 1927. APA's mission is to promote the highest quality care for individuals with mental disorders (including mental retardation and substance-related disorders) and their families; to promote psychiatric education and research and to advance and represent the profession of psychiatry. Membership: $105 (Member in Training, US); $65 (Member in Training, Canada); $125-565 (General Member); $345-565 (Fellow & Distinguished).$115-375 (Life-Status).

Continuing Education:
Certification Designation/s: AME
Meetings/Conferences: Annual
2013 - San Francisco, CA/May 18 - 22
2014 - New York City, NY/May 3 - 7
2015 - Toronto, ON/May 16 - 20
2016 - Atlanta, GA/May 14 - 18

Publications:
APA Newsletter
Membership Directory; on-line
Psychiatric News; bi-monthly
The American Journal of Psychiatry

American Psychiatric Nurses Association *(1987)*
1555 Wilson Blvd.
Suite 530
Arlington, VA 22209
Tel: (703) 243-2443 *Fax:* (703) 243-3390
TollFree: (866) 243-2443
E-Mail: inform@apna.org
Website: apna.org
Members: 8,000 individuals
Staff: 10
Annual Budget: $2-5,000,000
Tax: 501(c)(3)

Personnel:
Executive Director: Nicholas Croce Jr.
    E-Mail: ncroce@apna.org
Associate Executive Director: Patricia L Black
    E-Mail: pblack@apna.org
Coordinator, Membership Services: Patricia Federinko
    E-Mail: pfederinko@apna.org
Manager, Finance and Administration: Karla Lewis
    E-Mail: klewis@apna.org
Contact, Conferences: Keely McNerney
    E-Mail: keely@kmassociates.net
Specialist, Communications and Education: Meaghan Trimyer
    E-Mail: mtrimyer@apna.org

Historical Note:
APNA is committed to the specialty practice of psychiatric mental health nursing, health and wellness promotion through identification of mental health issues, prevention of mental health problems and the care and treatment of persons with psychiatric disorders. Members are registered nurses or students. Membership: $135 (Regular/Affiliate/International); $75 (Retired); $25 (Student).

Meetings/Conferences: Annual
Conference Chair: Keely McNerney
2013 - San Antonio, TX (The Henry B. Gonzalez Convention Center)/Oct. 9 - 12
Number of non-conference events/year: 1

Publications:
APNA News; monthly; adv.
Journal of the American Psychiatric Nurses Association; bi-monthly; adv.

Membership List Available to Non-members

American Psychoanalytic Association *(1911)*
309 E. 49th St.
New York, NY 10017-1601
Tel: (212) 752-0450 *Fax:* (212) 593-0571
E-Mail: info@apsa.org
Website: apsa.org
Members: 3500 individuals and 69 training institutes and societies
Staff: 13
Annual Budget: $2-5,000,000
Tax: 501(c)(3)

Personnel:
Executive Director: Dean K. Stein
    E-Mail: deankstein@apsa.org
Manager, Computer Information Systems: Brian Canty
    E-Mail: bcanty@apsa.org
Director, Scientific Program and Meetings: Carolyn Gatto
    E-Mail: cgatto@apsa.org
Director, Public Affairs: Geralyn Lederman
    E-Mail: glederman@apsa.org
Manager, Accounting Department: Nerissa Steele-Browne
    E-Mail: nsteele@apsa.org
Manager, Education and Membership Services: Debra Steinke Wardell
    E-Mail: dsteinke@apsa.org

Historical Note:
An Affiliate of the American Association for the Advancement of Science, APsaA focuses on education,

research and membership development. Membership is currently available to candidates and graduates of APsaA accredited training institutes and new training facilities and members of the International Psychoanalytical Association (IPA) or graduates of an institute of an IPA component society. Membership: $25 (Educator Associate/Student/Resident Associate); $75 (Psychotherapist Associate); $40 (Research Associate).

Meetings/Conferences:
Conference Chair: Carolyn Gatto
2013 - New York City, NY (Waldorf Towers)/Jan. 15 - 20

Publications:
The American Psychoanalyst; quarterly; adv.
The Journal of the American Psychoanalytic Association (JAPA); bi-monthly

Membership List Available to Non-members

American Psychological Association *(1892)*
750 First St. NE
Washington, DC 20002-4242
Tel: (202) 336-5500 *Fax:* (202) 336-6123
TollFree: (800) 374-2721
E-Mail: executiveoffice@apa.org
Website: apa.org
Members: 150000 individuals
Staff: 500
Annual Budget: Over $100,000,000
Tax: 501(c)(3)

Personnel:
Executive Vice President and Chief Executive Officer: Norman B. Anderson
    E-Mail: nanderson@apa.org
Education Directorate and Executive Director: Cynthia D. Belar PhD
    E-Mail: cbelar@apa.org
Executive Director, Public and Membership Communications: Rhea K. Farberman APR
    E-Mail: rfarberman@apa.org
General Counsel: Nathalie Gilfoyle JD
    E-Mail: ngilfoyle@apa.org
Deputy Chief Financial Officer: Susan B. Graves
    E-Mail: sgraves@apa.org
Chief Information Officer: Tony Habash CIO
    E-Mail: thabash@apa.org
Deputy Chief Executive Officer: Michael Honaker PhD
Director, Information Systems: Jerry McGlaughlin
    E-Mail: jmcglaughlin@apa.org
Executive Director, Governance Affairs: Nancy Gordon Moore PhD
    E-Mail: nmoore@apa.org
Chief Financial Officer: Archie L. Turner
    E-Mail: aturner@apa.org
Executive Director, Publications: Gary R. VandenBos PhD
    E-Mail: gary@apa.org

Historical Note:
Incorporated in the District of Columbia (1925). APA's mission is to advance the creation, communication and application of psychological knowledge to benefit society and improve people's lives. Membership: $80-287 (Member); $25-137 (Member Practice Assessment); $69-207 (Associate); $52 (Graduate Student); $27 (Undergraduate/High school Student/International); $40 (High School/Community College Teacher).

Meetings/Conferences: Annual
Number of non-conference events/year: 1

Publications:
APA Aging Issues Newsletter; monthly; adv.
APA Monitor; monthly; adv.
Behavioral Neuroscience; bi-monthly; adv.
Campus Representative Bulletin; on-line
Clinician's Research Digest Newsletter; monthly; adv.
CoA News and Actions; on-line
Communique; on-line
Consulting Psychology Journal: Practice and Research; quarterly; adv.
Contemporary Psychology; monthly; adv.
Cultural Diversity and Ethnic Minority Psychology; quarterly; adv.
CYF News; on-line
Developmental Psychology; bi-monthly; adv.
Dreaming; quarterly; adv.
Emotion; bi-monthly; adv.
European Psychologist; quarterly; adv.
Experimental and Clinical Psychopharmacology; bi-monthly; adv.
Families, Systems and Health; quarterly; adv.
GradPSYCH; quarterly; adv.

gradPSYCH: The Magazine of the American Psychological Association of Graduate Students; on-line
Group Dynamics: Theory, Practice & Research Journal; quarterly; adv.
Health Psychology Journal; bi-monthly; adv.
History of Psychology; quarterly; adv.
In the Public Interest
International Journal of Stress Management; quarterly; adv.
Journal of Abnormal Psychology; quarterly; adv.
Journal of Applied Psychology; bi-monthly; adv.
Journal of Comparative Psychology; quarterly; adv.
Journal of Consulting and Clinical Psychology; bi-monthly; adv.
Journal of Counseling Psychology; quarterly; adv.
Journal of Educational Psychology; quarterly; adv.
Journal of Experimental Psych: Human Perception & Performance; bi-monthly; adv.
Journal of Experimental Psychology: Animal Behavior Processes; quarterly; adv.
Journal of Experimental Psychology: Applied; quarterly; adv.
Journal of Experimental Psychology: General; quarterly; adv.
Journal of Experimental Psychology: Learning, Memory, & Cognition; bi-monthly
Journal of Family Psychology; bi-monthly; adv.
Journal of Occupational Health Psychology; quarterly; adv.
Journal of Personality and Social Psychology; monthly; adv.
Journal of Psychotherapy Integration; quarterly; adv.
Monitor on Psychology; monthly
Neuropsychology; bi-monthly; adv.
Prevention and Treatment; on-line
PsychMarketer
Psychoanalytic Abstracts Journal; quarterly; adv.
Psychological Abstracts; on-line
Psychological Assessment Journal; bi-monthly; adv.
Psychological Bulletin Journal; bi-monthly; adv.
Psychological Methods; quarterly; adv.
Psychological Review; quarterly; adv.
Psychological Science Agenda
Psychological Services; quarterly; adv.
Psychology and Aging; quarterly; adv.
Psychology and AIDS Exchange; quarterly; adv.
Psychology Giving, Newsletter of the American Psychological Foundation; on-line
Psychology International
Psychology of Addictive Behaviors Journal; quarterly; adv.
Psychology of Aesthetics, Creativity and the Arts; quarterly; adv.
Psychology of Men and Masculinity; quarterly; adv.
Psychology of Women Quarterly Journal; quarterly; adv.
Psychology Teacher Network
Psychology, Public Policy and Law; quarterly; adv.
Psychotherapy: Theory Research & Practice Journal; quarterly; adv.
PsycINFO News
PsycSCAN: Applied Psychology; on-line
PsycSCAN: Behavior Analysis and Therapy; semi-annually
PsycSCAN: Clinical Psychology; quarterly
PsycSCAN: Developmental Psychology; on-line
PsycSCAN: LD/MR; quarterly
Rehabilitation Psychology Journal; quarterly; adv.
Rehabilitation Psychology News Newsletter; quarterly
Review of General Psychology Journal; quarterly; adv.
School Psychology Quarterly; quarterly; adv.
Science Policy Insider News
Spotlight on Disability Newsletter
The Educator; on-line
The Pipeline Newsletter; on-line
The SES Indicator; on-line
Training and Education in Professional Psychology; quarterly; adv.
Variability Newsletter; on-line
Women's Psych-E Newsletter; on-line

Membership List Available to Non-members

American Psychological Association - Division of Psychoanalysis *(1979)*
2615 Amesbury Rd.
Winston-Salem, NC 27103

Tel: (336) 768-1113 *Fax:* (336) 768-4445
E-Mail: div39@namgmt.com
Website: division39.org
Members:
32 local chapters
4200 individuals
Staff: 702
Annual Budget: Over $100,000,000

Personnel:
Director, Administrator: Ruth Helein
    E-Mail: div39@namgmt.com
Co-chair, Conferences: Scott D. Pytluk
    E-Mail: spytluk@argosy.edu

Historical Note:
A semi-autonomous division of the American Psychological Association, division members participate professionally in psychoanalytic theory, research and practice. Sections include: Psychologist Psychoanalyst Practitioners, Childhood & Adolescence, Women, Gender, & Psychoanalysis, Local Chapters, Psychologist Psychoanalyst Clinicians, Psychoanalytic Research Society, Couple and Family Therapy and Psychoanalysis and Psychoanalysts for Social Responsibility. Membership: $65 (International Affiliates); $25 (Students); $95 (Regular/Associate/Allied Professional). Membership: $95 (Member/Affiliate/Other Mental Health Professional).

Meetings/Conferences: Semi-Annual
Conference Chair: Scott D. Pytluk
2013 - Boston, MA/April 24 - 28

Publications:
DIVISION/Review; quarterly
InSight eNews; monthly
Psychoanalytic Psychology; quarterly; adv.

American Psychological Association - Division of Psychotherapy *(1968)*
6557 E. Riverdale St.
Mesa, AZ 85215
Tel: (602) 363-9211 *Fax:* (480) 854-8966
E-Mail: assnmgmt1@cox.net
Website: divisionofpsychotherapy.org
Members: 4500 individuals
Staff: 702
Annual Budget: Over $100,000,000
Tax: 501(c)(3)

Personnel:
Administrator: Tracey A. Martin

Historical Note:
APA-DP is a semi-autonomous division of the American Psychological Association. This division is composed of individual members of the APA, who are interested in psychotherapy research, practice and training. Membership: $40 (Fellow/Associate/Psychologist); $20 (Student).

Continuing Education:
Certification Designation/s: CEC

Publications:
Psychotherapy; quarterly; adv.
Psychotherapy E-News; on-line

American Psychological Association - Society of Clinical Psychology *(1946)*
P.O. Box 1082
Niwot, CO 80544
Tel: (303) 652-3126 *Fax:* (303) 652-2723
E-Mail: div12apa@comcast.net
Website: div12.org
Members: 6600 individuals
Staff: 702
Annual Budget: Over $100,000,000

Personnel:
Administrative Officer: Lynell "Lynn" G. Peterson CAE
    E-Mail: div12apa@comcast.net

Historical Note:
A division 12 of APA, Society of Clinical Psychology works to encourage and support the integration of psychological science and practice in education, research, application, advocacy and public policy, attending to the importance of diversity. It has seven sections covering specific areas of interest. Members of Division 12 may also join one or more of the Sections. Some sections have categories for non-Division 12 members. APA members who are active in practice, research, teaching, administration, and/or study in the field of clinical psychology are invited to join the division. Membership: $61 (Affiliate); $25 (Student); $63 (Full); $40 (Early Career Psychologist).

Meetings/Conferences: Annual
Publications:

Clinical Psychology: Science and Practice; quarterly; adv.
The Clinical Psychologist; quarterly; adv.

American Psychological Association Practice Organization
750 First St. NE
Washington, DC 20002-4242
Tel: (800) 374-2723 *Fax:* (202) 336-5797
TollFree: (800) 374-2723
E-Mail: practice@apa.org
Website: apapracticecentral.org
Staff: 2
Annual Budget: $2-5,000,000
Tax: 501(c)(6)

Personnel:
Executive Director: Katherine C Nordal
Director, Field and state Operations: Jeff Cook
    E-Mail: jcook@apa.org

Historical Note:
Practice Central, a service of the APA Practice Organization (APAPO), provides information and resources for practicing psychologists in all settings.

Publications:
Good Company e-newsletter; on-line
Good Practice magazine; monthly
Practice Update E-newsletter; monthly

American Psychology-Law Society (1968)
P.O. Box 11488
Southport, NC 28461-3936
Tel: (910) 933-4018 *Fax:* (910) 933-4018
E-Mail: apls@ec.rr.com
Website: ap-ls.org
Members: 3000 individuals
Staff: 6
Annual Budget: Under $10,000
Tax: 501(c)(3)

Personnel:
President: William Foote
Treasurer: Eve Brank
    E-Mail: ebrank2@unl.edu
Newsletter Editor: Matthew Huss
    E-Mail: mhuss@creighton.edu
Conference Co-Chair: Stephanie Madon
Coordinator, Federal Advocacy: Beth Wiggins

Historical Note:
A division of the American Psychological Association in 1985. AP-LS is an inter-disciplinary organization devoted to scholarship, practice, and public service in psychology and law. Membership: $50 (Psychologists/Non-Psychologists); $15 (Student/Early Career Professionals).

Meetings/Conferences: Annual
Conference Chair: Stephanie Madon
2013 - Portland, OR (Hilton Portland & Executive Tower)/March 7 - 9

Publications:
AP-LS Newsletter; quarterly
Law and Human Behavior; annually

American Psychopathological Association (1910)
University Of Florida, 1225 Center Dr.
Room 3107, P.O. Box 100231
Gainesville, FL 32611
Fax: (352) 273-5365
Website: appassn.org
Members: 5000 individuals
Staff: 5
Annual Budget: $100-250,000

Personnel:
Treasurer: Linda B. Cottler PhD
    E-Mail: lbcottler@ufl.edu

Historical Note:
APPA's purpose is scientific investigation of disordered human behavior, and its biological and psychosocial substrates. Promotes research on problems of psychopathology. The APPA provides a forum for high level professional and social contact between established investigators, younger researchers, interested clinicians, and fellows. Special registration rates are available for students attending the meeting.Membership: $150(Fellows/Members/Corresponding); $50 (Life/Student).

Meetings/Conferences: Annual
2013 - New York City, NY (Grand Hyatt New York)/March 7 - 9

Publications:
Comprehensive Psychiatry; bi-monthly; adv.

American Psychosocial Oncology Society
154 Hansen Rd.
Suite 201
Charlottesville, VA 22911
Tel: (434) 293-5350 *Fax:* (434) 977-1856
E-Mail: info@apos-society.org
Website: apos-society.org
Members: 402 individuals
Staff: 6
Annual Budget: $250-500,000
Tax: 501(c)(3)

Personnel:
Executive Director: Allison Ball
    E-Mail: aball@apos-society.org
Director, Educational Programs: Jennifer Alluisi MA, Ed
    E-Mail: jalluisi@apos-society.org
Accountant: Patricia Cuthbert
    E-Mail: pcuthbert@apos-society.org
Manager, Membership Services: John Hamel
    E-Mail: jhamel@apos-society.org
Director, Publications and Web Services: Marilla Owens
Director, Conference Services: Lynne Valentic
    E-Mail: lvalentic@apos-society.org

Historical Note:
APOS's mission is to advance the science and practice of psychosocial care for people with cancer. Membership: $125 (Member-in-Training); $185 (Full Member/Associate Member).

Meetings/Conferences: Annual
Conference Chair: Lynne Valentic
2013 - Huntington Beach, CA/Feb. 14 - 16/400 attendees

Publications:
APOS Advocate; quarterly; adv.
Journal of Cancer Survivorship
Membership Directory
Psycho-Oncology; monthly; adv.

American Psychosomatic Society (1942)
6728 Old McLean Village Dr.
McLean, VA 22101-3906
Tel: (703) 556-9222 *Fax:* (703) 556-8729
E-Mail: info@psychosomatic.org
Website: psychosomatic.org
Members: 915 individuals
Staff: 5
Annual Budget: $500-1,000,000

Personnel:
Executive Director: George K. Degnon CAE
President: Michael R Irwin MD
Secretary and Treasurer: Mustafa al'Absi PhD
Editor-in-Chief: Willem J. Kop
Association Manager: Sarah Shiffert

Historical Note:
APS's mission is to enhance and advance the scientific understanding and multidisciplinary integration of biological, psychological, behavioral and social factors in human health and disease, and to foster the application of this understanding in education and improved health care. Membership: $190 (Regular); $50 (Corresponding Membership); $60 (Associate).

Meetings/Conferences: Annual
2013 - Miami, FL (InterContinental Miami)/March 13 - 16
2014 - San Francisco, CA (Hyatt Regency Embarcadero Hotel)/March 12 - 15

Publications:
APS journal, Psychosomatic Medicine; adv.
e-newsletter
Newsletter

American Psychotherapy Association (1997)
2750 E. Sunshine St.
Springfield, MO 65804
Tel: (417) 823-0173 *Fax:* (417) 823-9959
TollFree: (800) 205-9165
E-Mail: info@americanpsychotherapy.com
Website: americanpsychotherapy.com
Members: 5000 individuals
Staff: 7
Annual Budget: $100-250,000

Personnel:
Chair Person: Daniel J. Reidenberg
Editor: Laura Johnson
    E-Mail: editor@americanpsychotherapy.com

Historical Note:

The mission of the American Psychotherapy Association is to assume the leadership role in advancing the profession of psychotherapy. Its purpose is to establish a cohesive national organization that credentials ethical, highly-educated and well-trained psychotherapists. Membership: $65 (Student); $165 (Standard); $190 (International); $2500 (Life).

Continuing Education:
Certification Designation/s: CRS, MTAPA, DAPA, FAPA

Meetings/Conferences: Annual

Publications:
Annals; quarterly; adv.

American Public Communications Council (1988)
625 Slaters Ln.
Suite 104
Alexandria, VA 22314
Tel: (703) 739-1322 *Fax:* (703) 739-1324
E-Mail: apcc@apcc.net
Website: apcc.net
Members: 1300 member companies
Staff: 5
Annual Budget: $250-500,000

Personnel:
President: Willard "Randy" Nichols
    E-Mail: apcc@apcc.net
Corporate Counsel: Dan Collins
    E-Mail: dcollins@apcc.net
Office Manager and Database Administrator: Helly Shareefy
    E-Mail: hshareefy@apcc.net
Chief Financial Officer: Deborah Sterman
    E-Mail: dsterman@apcc.net

Historical Note:
APCC is dedicated to supporting a public communications environment that promotes the widest deployment of payphones for the use of the American public. Members are manufacturers, suppliers, distributors, owners and operators of public communications equipment.

Publications:
Perspectives Magazine; bi-monthly; adv.

American Public Gardens Association (1940)
351 Longwood Rd.
Kennett Square, PA 19348
Tel: (610) 708-3010 *Fax:* (610) 444-3594
E-Mail: info@publicgardens.org
Website: publicgardens.org
Members: 1850 individuals and institutions
Staff: 7
Annual Budget: $1-2,000,000
Tax: 501(c)(3)

Personnel:
Executive Director: Casey Sclar
    E-Mail: csclar@publicgardens.org
Coordinator, New Media and Communications: Aubree Davis
    E-Mail: adavis@publicgardens.org
Director, Development and Marketing: Madeline Dobbs
    E-Mail: mdobbs@publicgardens.org
Office Manager: Vivian Lovingood
    E-Mail: vlovingood@publicgardens.org
Manager, Membership Services: Sarah Maietta
    E-Mail: smaietta@publicgardens.org
Manager, Meetings: Sharon Malgire
    E-Mail: smalgire@publicgardens.org

Historical Note:
Formerly American Association of Botanical Gardens and Arboreta; assumed current name in 2005. APGA's mission is to Advance Public Gardens as a force for positive change in their communities through national leadership, advocacy and innovation. It serves and strengthens public gardens throughout North America by supporting and advocating their work in horticultural display, education, research and plant conservation. Membership: $80 (Individual); $65 (Affiliated/Retired/Volunteer); $35 (Student); $150-1,000 (Organization); $150-12000 (Institutional).

Meetings/Conferences: Annual
Conference Chair: Sharon Malgire
2013 - Phoenix, AZ/May 20 - 24
Number of non-conference events/year: 4

Publications:
Public Garden; quarterly
The APGA Newsletter; monthly

Membership List Available to Non-members

American Public Gas Association (1961)
201 Massachusetts Ave. NE

Suite C-4
Washington, DC 20002
Tel: (202) 464-2742 *Fax:* (202) 464-0246
TollFree: (800) 927-4202
Website: apga.org
Members: 700 members
Staff: 10
Annual Budget: $2-5,000,000
Tax: 501(c)(6)

Personnel:
President and Chief Executive Officer: Bert Kalisch
    E-Mail: bkalisch@apga.org
Director, Operations and Administration: Todd Brady
    E-Mail: tbrady@apga.org
Director, Membership Services and Finance: Sheila
    Deringis
    E-Mail: sderingis@apga.org
Director, Marketing and Communications: Kristin Gomez
    E-Mail: kgomez@apga.org
Director, Government Affairs: Nate Hill
    E-Mail: nhill@apga.org
General Counsel: William "Bud" Miller
Executive Vice President: David Schryver
    E-Mail: dschryver@apga.org

Historical Note:
APGA's mission is to be an advocate for publicly-
owned natural gas distribution systems, and educate and
communicate with members to promote safety, awareness,
performance and competitiveness. Membership: $575
(Associate); $330 (Small Member).

Meetings/Conferences:
2013 - Boston, MA (InterContinental Boston)/July 28 -
31
Number of non-conference events/year: 1

Publications:
The Source Magazine; quarterly

American Public Health Association *(1872)*
800 I St. NW
Washington, DC 20001-3710
Tel: (202) 777-2742 *Fax:* (202) 777-2534
E-Mail: comments@apha.org
Website: apha.org
Members: 50000 individuals and 53 state and
regional public health associations
Staff: 88
Annual Budget: $10-25,000,000

Personnel:
Executive Director: Georges C. Benjamin FACP, MD
    E-Mail: georges.benjamin@apha.org
Senior Administrative Assistant: Charlene Bright
    E-Mail: charlene.bright@apha.org
Director, Human Resource Services: Malinda Crowe MS
    E-Mail: malinda.crowe@apha.org
*Director, Center for Professional Development, Public Health
    Systems and Partnership:* Annette Ferebee MPH
    E-Mail: annette.ferebee@apha.org
Director, Communications: David Fouse
    E-Mail: david.fouse@apha.org
Manager, E-Marketing and Development: Glenn Griffin
    E-Mail: glenn.griffin@apha.org
Senior Manager, Marketing: David Hartogs
    E-Mail: david.hartogs@apha.org
Director, Information Technology: Violet Hohman MS
    E-Mail: violet.hohman@apha.org
Reporter: Teddi Johnson
    E-Mail: teddi.johnson@apha.org
Coordinator, Membership Services: Yvonne Kazim
    E-Mail: yvonne.kazim@apha.org
Executive Editor: Michele Late
    E-Mail: michele.late@apha.org
Director, Convention Services: T. J. McCabe CMP
    E-Mail: tj.mccabe@apha.org
Director, Membership Services: Sara Miller CAE, MBA
    E-Mail: sara.miller@apha.org
Chief Financial Officer: Kemi Oluwafemi CPA, MBA
    E-Mail: kemi.oluwafemi@apha.org
Communications Specialist: Audrey Pernik
    E-Mail: audrey.pernik@apha.org
Associate Executive Director, Public Affairs and Advocacy:
    Susan L. Polan PhD
    E-Mail: susan.polan@apha.org
Director, Publication Services: Nina Tristani
    E-Mail: nina.tristani@apha.org
Senior Editor, The Nation's Health: Charlotte Tucker MA
    E-Mail: charlotte.tucker@apha.org

Historical Note:
APHA's mission is to improve the health of the public
and achieve equity in health status. Members are health
professionals in disciplines in the development of health
standards and policies. Membership: $61-200/year.

Meetings/Conferences: Annual
Conference Chair: T. J. McCabe CMP
2013 - Boston, MA/Nov. 2 - 6/13000 attendees
2014 - New Orleans, LA/Nov. 15 - 19/13000 attendees
2015 - Chicago, IL/Nov. 7 - 11/13000 attendees
Number of non-conference events/year: 7

Publications:
American Journal of Public Health; monthly; adv.
Inside Public Health; monthly
Public Health Newswire
The Nation's Health; adv.

American Public Human Services Association
(1930)
1133 19th St. NW
Suite 400
Washington, DC 20036
Tel: (202) 682-0100 *Fax:* (202) 289-6555
Website: aphsa.org
Members: 4945 individuals and agencies
Staff: 60
Annual Budget: $5-10,000,000
Tax: 501(c)(3)

Personnel:
Executive Director: Tracy Wareing
    E-Mail: tracy.wareing@aphsa.org
ISM Associate: Mike Coulson
    E-Mail: michael.coulson@aphsa.org
Program Manager: Ursula Gilmore
    E-Mail: ursula.gilmore@aphsa.org
Director, Human Resources: Nicole Lobban
    E-Mail: nicole.lobban@aphsa.org
Director, Finance: Jay Phillips
    E-Mail: jay.phillips@aphsa.org
Manager, Publications: Amy Plotnick
    E-Mail: amy.plotnick@aphsa.org
Database Manager: Parthenia Purnell
    E-Mail: parthenia.purnell@aphsa.org
Director, Legislative Affairs: Ron Smith
    E-Mail: ron.smith@aphsa.org
Director, Membership and Communications: Jerome Uher
    E-Mail: jerome.uher@aphsa.org
Director , Finance and Administration: Raymond
    Washington III
    E-Mail: raymond.washington@aphsa.org
Manager, Membership and Marketing: Kristen
    Washington
    E-Mail: kwashington@aphsa.org
Manager, Conferences: Gloria Williams
    E-Mail: gloria.williams@aphsa.org

Historical Note:
Formerly American Public Welfare Association (1998).
APSHA's mission is to develop and promote policies and
practices that improve the health and well-being of families,
children, and adults. APSHA represents the 50 cabinet-
level, state human service departments, local public welfare
agencies, and individuals concerned with social welfare
policy and practice. Membership: $30-15,000/year.

Meetings/Conferences:
Conference Chair: Gloria Williams
Number of non-conference events/year: 6

Publications:
Policy and Practice; bi-monthly
Public Human Services Directory(on-line); annually
This Week in Washington; weekly

Membership List Available to Non-members

American Public Power Association *(1940)*
1875 Connecticut Ave. NW
Suite 1200
Washington, DC 20009
Tel: (202) 467-2900 *Fax:* (202) 467-2910
TollFree: (800) 515-2772
E-Mail: mrufe@appanet.org
Website: APPAnet.org
Members: 2000 utilities
Staff: 62
Annual Budget: $10-25,000,000
Tax: 501(c)(6)

Personnel:
President and Chief Executive Officer: Mark Crisson
    E-Mail: mcrisson@appanet.org

Vice President, Communications: Nicholas Braden
    E-Mail: nbraden@appanet.org
Director, Education: Kevin Cullather
    E-Mail: kcullather@APPAnet.org
Director, Membership Services and Information Technology:
    Jeff Haas
    E-Mail: jjhaas@publicpower.org
Senior Vice President, Engineering Services: Michael
    Hyland PE
    E-Mail: mhyland@APPAnet.org
General Counsel: Susan Kelly
    E-Mail: skelly@appanet.org
Senior Vice President, Publishing: Jeanne LaBella
    E-Mail: jlabella@appanet.org
Director, Database Systems and Analysis: Susan Lynch
    E-Mail: slynch@APPAnet.org
Director, Electric Reliability Standards and Compliance:
    Nathan Mitchell PE
    E-Mail: nmitchell@appanet.org
Senior Vice President, Government Relations: James
    Nipper
    E-Mail: jnipper@APPAnet.org
Director, Information Services: Mary Rufe
    E-Mail: mrufe@appanet.org
Director, Customer Programs: Ursula Schryver
    E-Mail: uschryver@appanet.org
Senior Vice President, Member Services: Jeffrey Tarbert
    E-Mail: jtarbert@appanet.org
Vice President, Human Resources and Administration:
    Deborah White
    E-Mail: dwhite@APPAnet.org
Director, Meetings Services: Jacqueline Williams
    E-Mail: jwilliams@appanet.org

Historical Note:
APPA's mission is to advance the public policy interests
of its members and their consumers. It also provides
member services to ensure adequate, reliable electricity
at a reasonable price with the proper protection of the
environment. Members are community-owned electric
utilities. Membership: $3,000 (Corporate Associate/
Federal Service Contracts Associate); $750 (Non-profit
Associate/Individual); $1,500 (International Associate);
$1,000 (Government Associate); $5,500 (Private Energy
Associate).

Continuing Education:
Certification Designation/s: PPMCP, KPPAE, EEMCP,
PPCSM, CSMCP

Meetings/Conferences:
Conference Chair: Jacqueline Williams
2013 - Nashville, TN (Gaylord Hotels Resorts and
    Convention Centers-Nashville)/June 15 - 19
2013 - Orlando, FL/Sept. 22 - 25
2014 - Denver, CO/Jan. 21 - 25
2014 - Portland, OR/Sept. 14 - 17
Number of non-conference events/year: 8

Publications:
APPA Customer Connector; on-line
Public Power Magazine; on-line; adv.
Public Power Weekly; weekly
Washington Report; on-line

American Public Transportation Association
1666 K St. NW
Suite 1100
Washington, DC 20006-1215
Tel: (202) 496-4800 *Fax:* (202) 496-4324
E-Mail: info@apta.com
Website: apta.com/Pages/default.aspx
Members: 1600 organizations and individuals
Staff: 17

Personnel:
President and Chief Executive Officer: Michael P.
    Melaniphy
    E-Mail: mmelaniphy@apta.com
President: William W. Millar
    E-Mail: wmillar@apta.com
*Vice President, Program Management and Educational
    Services:* Pamela L. Boswell
    E-Mail: pboswell@apta.com
Chief Financial Officer: Mary Childress
    E-Mail: mchildress@apta.com
Director, Marketing and Sales: Jack Gonzalez
    E-Mail: jgonzalez@apta.com
Director, Meetings and Conventions: Lenay Gore
    E-Mail: lgore@apta.com
Director, Human Resources: Karen W. Harvey
    E-Mail: kharvey@apta.com

Vice President, Government Affairs: Robert L. Healy Jr., Esq.
  E-Mail: rhealy@apta.com
Chief Counsel: James LaRusch
  E-Mail: jlarusch@apta.com
Chief of Staff: Petra Mollet
  E-Mail: pmollet@apta.com
Director, Educational Services: Joseph Niegoski
  E-Mail: jniegoski@apta.com
Manager, Editor: Susan Paisner
  E-Mail: spaisner@apta.com
Director, Information Technology: Jeff Popovich
  E-Mail: jpopovich@apta.com
Vice President, Communications and Marketing:
  Rosemary Sheridan
  E-Mail: rsheridan@apta.com
Vice President, Membership Services: Kathryn D. Waters
  E-Mail: kwaters@apta.com
Director, Advocacy Communications: Mantill Williams
  E-Mail: mwilliams@apta.com

Historical Note:
Works to improve and strengthen public transportation. APTA members are public organizations that are engaged in the areas of bus, paratransit, light rail, commuter rail, subways, waterborne passenger services, and high-speed rail.

Meetings/Conferences: Annual
Conference Chair: Lenay Gore
2013 - Chicago, IL/Sept. 29 - Oct. 2
2014 - Houston, TX/Oct. 12 - 15
2015 - San Francisco, CA/Oct. 4 - 7

Publications:
Membership Directory; on-line
Passenger Transport EXPRESS

American Public Works Association *(1894)*
2345 Grand Blvd.
Suite 700
Kansas City, MO 64108-2625
Tel: (816) 472-6100 *Fax*: (816) 472-1610
TollFree: (800) 848-2792
Website: www2.apwa.net
Members: 28500 workers
Staff: 59
Annual Budget: $10-25,000,000
Tax: 501(c)(3)

Personnel:
Executive Director: Peter B. King
  E-Mail: pking@apwa.net
Director, Human Resources and Office Manager: Julie
  Burrell
  E-Mail: jburrell@apwa.net
Editor: Kevin Clark
  E-Mail: kclark@apwa.net
Director, Marketing: David Dancy
  E-Mail: ddancy@apwa.net
Director, Credentialing: Ann Daniels
  E-Mail: adaniels@apwa.net
Manager, Publications: Connie Hartline
  E-Mail: chartline@apwa.net
Director, Finance and Controller: Teri Newhouse
  E-Mail: tnewhouse@apwa.net
Specialist, Membership Services: Kelly Price
  E-Mail: kprice@apwa.net
Director, Meetings: Dana Priddy
  E-Mail: dpriddy@apwa.net
Deputy Executive Director: Kaye Sullivan
  E-Mail: ksullivan@apwa.net
Director, Professional Development: Mabel Tinjacá
  E-Mail: mtinjaea@apwa.net
Information Technology Support Specialist: Keith Umsted
  E-Mail: kumsted@apwa.net

Historical Note:
Formed from the merger (1937) of American Society of Municipal Engineers and International Association of Public Works Officials. APWA works to promote professional excellence, understanding of, and competency and credibility in public works. Members are composed of government officials, engineers, administrators and others engaged in some aspect of public works. Membership: $145 (Individual); $232-5,800 (Public Group); $362-7176 (Corporate Group); $35 (Optional); $25 (Student); $100 (Student Group); $238-5950 (Public Agency); $278 (One-Call Center/System Membership).

Continuing Education:
Certification Designation/s: CSM, CPFP, CPII

Meetings/Conferences:
Conference Chair: Dana Priddy

2013 - Charlotte, NC (Charlotte Convention Center)/
  April 7 - 10
2013 - Chicago, IL (McCormick Place)/Aug. 25 - 28
2015 - Phoenix, AZ/Aug. 30 - Sept. 2
Number of non-conference events/year: 6

Publications:
American Historical Review
APWA Reporter; monthly; adv.
Board Directory; on-line
Journal of American History
Journal of Urban History; adv.
Membership Directory; on-line
Peer Resource Directory; on-line
Public Works History Newsletter
SHOT Newsletter; quarterly; adv.
Technology and Culture; quarterly; adv.
The Public Historian; adv.

American Purchasing Society *(1969)*
Eight E. Galena Blvd., Suite 203
P.O. Box 256
Aurora, IL 60506
Tel: (630) 859-0250 *Fax*: (630) 859-0270
E-Mail: propurch@propurch.com
Website: american-purchasing.com
Members: 4500 individuals
Staff: 7
Annual Budget: $500-1,000,000

Personnel:
President and Chief Executive Officer: Harry E. Hough
  E-Mail: hhough@propurch.com
Executive Vice President: Richard H. Hough
  E-Mail: rhough@propuch.com
Contact, Membership Services: Lynne M. Marlor
Contributing Editor: Robert Menard CPP

Historical Note:
APS's mission is to improve purchasing performance in business through the education of its membership and the development of ethical standards of conduct in the marketplace. Members include purchasing agents, buyers, procurement specialists, purchasing managers, purchasing executives and others who buy goods and services. Membership: $234 (Individual); $389 (Company).

Continuing Education:
Enrollment: 650
Certification Designation/s: CPPM, CPP, CPPC

Publications:
Member Directory; on-line
Professional Purchasing; monthly
Salary Report of Purchasing Professions; annually

American Pyrotechnics Association *(1948)*
P.O. Box 30438
Bethesda, MD 20824
Tel: (301) 907-8181 *Fax*: (301) 907-9148
Website: americanpyro.com
Members: 240 companies and 250 members
Staff: 3
Annual Budget: $500-1,000,000
Tax: 501(c)(6)

Personnel:
Executive Director: Julie L. Heckman
  E-Mail: jheckman@americanpyro.com
Manager, Administration and Membership Services:
  Annelise Gillespie
  E-Mail: agillespie@americanpyro.com
Manager, Safety Program: Gregg Smith
  E-Mail: gsmith@americanpyro.com

Historical Note:
Founded in 1948 and incorporated in Delaware. APA members are fireworks importers, distributors, suppliers and manufacturers. Absorbed the National Pyrotechnic Distributors Association in 1979. APA'S mission is to provide industry information and support to the members, encourage safety in the design and use of all types of fireworks, and promote responsible regulation of the fireworks industry. Membership: $1,300-8,300 (Full Member, based on annual sales); $1,300-5,700 (Foreign Manufacturer/Exporter); $1,000 (Supplier); $250-500 (Fire Service); $1,000-7,500 (Commercial User-Foreign).

Meetings/Conferences: Annual
Conference Chair: Annelise Gillespie
Number of non-conference events/year: 1

Publications:
Membership Directory; on-line

American Quarter Horse Association *(1940)*
P.O. Box 200

Amarillo, TX 79168
Tel: (806) 376-4811 *Fax*: (806) 349-6409
E-Mail: aqhamall@aqha.org
Website: aqha.com
Members: 342000 individuals
Staff: 330
Annual Budget: $50-100,000,000
Tax: 501(c)(5)

Personnel:
Executive Vice President: Don Treadway
Editor: Tonya Ratliff-Garrison

Historical Note:
AQHA's mission is to provide beneficial services for its members that enhance and encourage American Quarter Horse ownership and participation.

Meetings/Conferences: Annual
2013 - Houston, TX (Hyatt Regency Houston)/March 8
  - 11
2014 - New Orleans, LA (Hyatt Regency)/March 7 - 10
2015 - Ft. Worth, TX (Omni Hotels and Resorts)/
  March 6 - 9
2016 - Jacksonville, FL (Hyatt Regency Jacksonville
  Riverfront)/March 4 - 7
2017 - San Antonio, TX (The Grand Hyatt)/March 17
  - 20

Publications:
America's Horse Daily; daily; adv.
America's Horse Magazine; adv.
America's Horse Weekly e-newsletter; weekly; adv.
Journal Plus; monthly; adv.
The American Quarter Horse Journal; monthly; adv.

The American Quaternary Association *(1970)*
52801 E. 55 Rd.
Maramec, OK 74045
Tel: (405) 744-9585 *Fax*: (405) 744-5269
Website: amqua.org
Members: 1000 individuals
Staff: 4
Annual Budget: $10-25,000
Tax: 501(c)(3)

Personnel:
Treasurer: Brian Carter
  E-Mail: treasurer@amqua.org
Contact, Events: Steve Jackson
  E-Mail: jackson@uwyo.edu

Historical Note:
AQA's purpose is to encourage, initiate and sponsor the advancement of interdisciplinary research of the physical, biological and cultural environment and its history during the quaternary period through charitable, educational and scientific activities. Membership: $20 (Professional); $10 (Student/Retired).

Meetings/Conferences: Biennial
Conference Chair: Steve Jackson

Publications:
AMQUA newsletter; bi-annually

American Rabbit Breeders Association *(1910)*
P.O. Box 5667
Bloomington, IL 61702
Tel: (309) 664-7500 *Fax*: (309) 664-0941
E-Mail: info@arba.net
Website: arba.net
Members: 23,000 individuals
Staff: 6
Annual Budget: $500-1,000,000

Personnel:
Executive Director: Eric Stewart
  E-Mail: eric@arba.net

Historical Note:
Founded as American Pet Stock Association, became the National Breeders and Fanciers Association of America in 1923, the American Rabbit and Cavy Breeders Association in 1925 and assumed its present name in 1952. ARBA strives for the promotion, development and improvement of the domestic rabbit and cavy. Members are commercial or fancy breeders of rabbits and guinea pigs. Membership: $20 (Individual Adult); $30 (Husband and Wife Combination); $12 (Individual Youth); $20 (Single Adult Family); $30 (Husband and Wife Family).

Meetings/Conferences: Annual
2013 - Harrisburg, PA (Pennsylvania Historical and
  Museum Commission)/Oct. 19 - 23

Membership List Available to Non-members

American Radio Relay League *(1914)*

225 Main St.
Newington, CT 06111-1494
Tel: (860) 594-0200 *Fax:* (860) 594-0259
TollFree: (888) 277-5289
E-Mail: hq@arrl.org
Website: arrl.org
Members: 158000 members
Staff: 107
Annual Budget: $10-25,000,000
Tax: 501(c)(3)

Personnel:
Chief Executive Officer: David Sumner
  E-Mail: k1zz@arrl.org
Manager, Regulatory Information: Dan Henderson
  E-Mail: reginfo@arrl.org
Chief Development Officer: Mary Hobart
  E-Mail: k1mmh@arrl.org
Manager, Convention Programs: Gail Iannone
  E-Mail: hamfests@arrl.org
Manager, Marketing and Sales: Bob Inderbitzen
  E-Mail: rinderbitzen@arrl.org
Manager, Membership Services: Diane Petrilli
  E-Mail: membership@arrl.org
Chief Technology Officer: Brennan Price
  E-Mail: n4qx@arrl.org
Chief Financial Officer: Barry J. Shelley
  E-Mail: n1vxy@arrl.org
Specialist, Technical Relations: Jonathan Siverling

Historical Note:
ARRL's mission is to promote and advance the art, science and enjoyment of amateur radio. Membership: $8-1,550/ year.

Meetings/Conferences: Annual
Conference Chair: Gail Iannone

Publications:
Membership Directory; on-line
NCJ; bi-monthly; adv.
QEX; bi-monthly; adv.
QST; monthly; adv.
The ARRL Letter; weekly

American Radium Society (*1916*)
11300 W. Olympic Blvd.
Suite 600
Los Angeles, CA 90064
Tel: (310) 437-0581 *Fax:* (310) 437-0585
E-Mail: info@americanradiumsociety.org
Website: americanradiumsociety.org
Members: 500 individuals
Staff: 5
Annual Budget: $250-500,000
Tax: 501(c)(3)

Personnel:
Executive Director: Jaclyn Weinstein
Webmaster: Jason Levin
Membership Manager: Tressa MacKelvie
Coordinator, Fundraising and Exhibits: Jenay Root

Historical Note:
Founded in 1916 by physicians interested in radiation therapy. Promotes the study of cancer in all its aspects. Encourages liaison among the various medical specialists and allied scientists concerned with the treatment of cancer, and continues scientific study of the treatment of the cancer patient through its meeting and educational publications. Members include radiation oncologists, surgical oncologists, gynecologic oncologists and medical oncologists. Membership: $190 (Active-for the first year); $275 (Active-second year onwards); Free (Resident).

Continuing Education:
Certification Designation/s: SAM-MOC

Meetings/Conferences: Annual
Conference Chair: Jenay Root
2013 - Scottsdale, AZ (The Phoenician)/April 27 - May 1

Publications:
ARS Newsletter
Membership Directory; on-line

Membership List Available to Non-members

American Railway Development Association
(*1906*)
P.O. Box 255
Lecompton, KS 66050
Tel: (785) 393-8191
E-Mail: amraildev@gmail.com
Website: amraildev.com
Members: 200 individuals

Staff: 2
Annual Budget: $50-100,000

Personnel:
Executive Director: Ronald D. Skinner
Secretary and Treasurer: Luddy Arias

Historical Note:
ARDA works to foster the industrial, real estate, natural resources, market development activities and environmental concerns of the North American railroads. Members are marketing, real estate and industrial development officers of railroads. Membership also includes professionals from other associations, agencies, and railroad service partners that have a direct effect on rail business. Membership: $150/year (Active/Retired voting).

Meetings/Conferences: Annual
Conference Chair: Ronald D. Skinner
2013 - San Francisco, CA (Marines Memorial Club Hotel)/June 2 - 5
Number of non-conference events/year: 1

Publications:
ARDA Newsletter; semi-monthly
Member Directory; on-line

American Railway Engineering and Maintenance-of-Way Association (*1997*)
10003 Derekwood Ln.
Suite 210
Lanham, MD 20706
Tel: (301) 459-3200 *Fax:* (301) 459-8077
Website: arema.org
Members: 5000 individuals
Staff: 9
Annual Budget: $2-5,000,000
Tax: 501(c)(6)

Personnel:
Executive Director and Chief Executive Officer: Charles H. Emely CAE, CMP, PhD
Director, Administration: Beth Caruso CAE
Director, Membership and Information Systems: Janice Clements
Director, Finance: Vickie Fisher
Director, Marketing: Lisa Hall
  E-Mail: lhall@arema.org
Director, Conferences and Seminars: Desiree Knight CMP
  E-Mail: dknight@arema.org
Director, Committees and Technical Services: Stacy Spaulding CAE

Historical Note:
Formed by the merger of three engineering support associations, namely the American Railway Bridge and Building Association, the American Railway Engineering Association and the Roadmaster's and Maintenance of Way Association, along with functions of the Communications and Signals Division of the Association of American Railroads. AREMA's mission is the development and advancement of both technical and practical knowledge and recommended practices pertaining to the design, construction and maintenance of railway infrastructure. Membership: $158 (Full/Associate); $20 (Student).

Continuing Education:
Enrollment: 5500

Meetings/Conferences:
Conference Chair: Desiree Knight CMP
2013 - Indianapolis, IN (Indianapolis Convention Center)/Sept. 29 - Oct. 2
2014 - Chicago, IL (Hilton Chicago)/Sept. 28 - Oct. 1
2015 - Minneapolis, MN (Minneapolis Convention Center)/Oct. 4 - 7
2016 - Orlando, FL/Aug. 28 - 31
2017 - Indianapolis, IN (Indianapolis Convention Center)/Sept. 17 - 20
2018 - Chicago, IL/Sept. 16 - 19
2019 - Minneapolis, MN (Minneapolis Convention Center)/Sept. 22 - 25

Publications:
AREMA News; monthly
Membership Directory; on-line; adv.

The American Rambouillet Sheep Breeders Association (*1889*)
222 Main St.
P.O. Box 51
Milo, IA 50166
Tel: (641) 942-6402 *Fax:* (641) 942-6502
E-Mail: asregistry@yahoo.com
Website: countrylovin.com/ARSBA/index.htm
Members: 400 individuals
Staff: 3

Annual Budget: $50-100,000

Personnel:
President: Pete Willie
Contact, Website: Bernie Lattimore
  E-Mail: blewes@aol.com
Secretary: Burk Lattimore
  E-Mail: blewes@aol.com

Historical Note:
ARSBA's primary function is to register purebred Rambouillet sheep and secondarily to advertise and promote the breed. Members are breeders and fanciers of Rambouillet sheep. Membership: $30 (Adult); $20 (Junior).

Meetings/Conferences: Annual

Publications:
Membership Directory; annually

American Real Estate and Urban Economics Association (*1964*)
821 Academic Way, 248 RBB
PO Box 3061110
Tallahassee, FL 32306-1110
Tel: (850) 644-7898 *Fax:* (850) 644-4077
E-Mail: areuea@areuea.org
Website: areuea.org
Members: 1254 individuals
Staff: 3
Annual Budget: $100-250,000
Tax: 501(c)(3)

Personnel:
President: Timothy J. Riddiough
Treasurer: David H. Downs
Editor: Cinda Smith
  E-Mail: contactree@areuea.org

Historical Note:
Established and incorporated in 1965 as American Real Estate Association. Formerly American Real Estate and Urban Economics Association. AREUEA's purpose is to discuss and recognize a need for more information and analysis in the fields of real estate development, planning and economics. Members are individuals both academically and commercially involved in real estate and urban economics. Membership: $100 (Professional/Academic); $50 (Student/Retired); $750-999 (Contributing Member); $1,000-2,999 (Special Contributor); $3,000-9,999 (Contributing Sponsor); $10,000 (Partner).

Meetings/Conferences: Semi-Annual
Conference Chair: Cinda Smith
2013 - San Diego, CA (San Diego Marriott Marquis and Marina)/Jan. 4 - 6
2013 - Washington, DC (NAHB headquarters)/May 30 - 31

Publications:
AREUEA News Bytes
Real Estate Economics
Membership Directory; on-line

Membership List Available to Non-members

American Real Estate Society (*1985*)
2-210 Lee Hall
Clemson University
Clemson, SC 29634-1323
Tel: (864) 656-1373 *Fax:* (864) 656-7519
Website: aresnet.org
Members: 1150 companies and individuals
Staff: 5
Annual Budget: $500-1,000,000

Personnel:
Executive Director: Stephen A. Pyhrr
  E-Mail: spyhrr@kennedywilson.com
Director, Publications: William G. Hardin III
Director, Finance: Joseph B. Lipscomb
Coordinator, Membership Services: Diane Quarles
  E-Mail: equarle@clemson.edu
Meetings Planner: Arthur L. Schwartz Jr.
  E-Mail: baycityart@yahoo.com

Historical Note:
ARES's mission is to promote education in real estate, improve communication and exchange of information in real estate and allied matters among college/university faculty and practicing professionals, and facilitate the association of academic, practicing professional, and research persons in the area of real estate. Membership: $135-175 (Academic); $600-640 (Corporate); $1,500-6,000 (Major Real estate Companies and Organizations/Sponsor/ Regent/President's Council); $85-125 (Student/Retired); $300-340 (Professional).

Meetings/Conferences: Annual
Conference Chair: Arthur L. Schwartz Jr.

2013 - Kohala Coast, HI (Mauna Lani Bay Hotel and
  Bungalows Resort)/April 10 - 13
2014 - San Diego, CA (Marriott Coronado)/April 1 - 5
2015 - Ft. Myers, FL (Sanibel Harbour Marriott Resort
  and Spa)/April 14 - 18

Publications:
ARES Newsletter; semi-annually
Journal of Housing Research (JHR)
Journal of Real Estate Literature
Journal of Real Estate Portfolio Management
Journal of Real Estate Practice and Education
Journal of Real Estate Research
Journal of Sustainable Real Estate
Membership Directory; on-line

American Recovery Association (1965)
5525 N. MacArthur Blvd.
Suite 135
Irving, TX 75038
Tel: (972) 755-4755 *Fax:* (972) 870-5755
E-Mail: homeoffice@americanrecoveryassn.org
Website: repo.org
Members: 275 repossession agents
Staff: 3
Annual Budget: $1-2,000,000

Personnel:
Manager, Membership Services: Patricia Corkern
  E-Mail: tricia@americanrecoveryassn.org
Contact, Media Inquires: Dawn Wellington
  E-Mail: dawn@wellingtongrouppr.com

Historical Note:
*Formerly (1972) American Repossessors Association,
Inc. ARA seeks to provide the lender with not only
repossession and related services, but to provide these
services through members who are of the highest caliber in
professionalism, honesty, integrity, and expertise. Members
represent banks, credit unions, finance companies, leasing
companies, savings and loan associations and other
financial institutions involved in the recovery of collateral on
defaulted installment contracts. Membership: $600-1,300/
year (Dues are based on the Metropolitan Statistical Area
(MSA) of the city).*

Continuing Education:
Certification Designation/s: CRA, CCRS, CARS

Meetings/Conferences: Annual
Number of non-conference events/year: 1

Publications:
National Membership Directory; annually; adv.
News & Views; on-line

American Red Brangus Association (1956)
3995 E. Hwy. 290 ·
Dripping Springs, TX 78620-4205
Tel: (512) 858-7285 *Fax:* (512) 858-7084
E-Mail: info@americanredbrangus.com
Website: americanredbrangus.org
Members: 260 individuals
Staff: 1
Annual Budget: $100-250,000
Tax: 501(c)(5)

Personnel:
President: John Fischer
  E-Mail: jfischer@serv-alliance.com

Historical Note:
*Founded in Austin, Texas. Members are breeders and
fanciers of Red Brangus cattle, a crossbreed of Brahman
and Angus cattle. ARBA's aim is to identify Red Brangus
ancestry and record transfer of ownership, also encourage
Red Brangus cattle, provide communication among
the membership and compile performance information.
Membership: $75 (Active/Associate/Active Juniors); $30
(Junior).*

Meetings/Conferences: Annual
Number of non-conference events/year: 2

Publications:
ARBA Journal; adv.
Junior Newsletter
Mebership Directory; annually

Membership List Available to Non-members

American Red Poll Association (1883)
P.O. Box 847
Frankton, IN 46044
Tel: (765) 425-4515 *Fax:* (765) 754-8004
E-Mail: ARPA@americanredpolls.com
Website: redpollusa.org
Staff: 3

Annual Budget: $25-50,000

Personnel:
Executive Vice President: Ken Harwell
  E-Mail: kharwell@kc.rr.com

Historical Note:
*Formerly (1976) Red Poll Cattle Club of America. Member
of the National Pedigree Livestock Council. Absorbed The
Red Poll Beef Breeders International in 1979. ARPA's
mission is to reach out to breeders and consumers
to provide information about grass finish genetics,
management and marketing Members are breeders and
fanciers of Red Poll beef cattle. Membership: $35 (Non
Assessable); $25 (Junior).*

Meetings/Conferences: Annual
Number of non-conference events/year: 2

Publications:
Red Poll Beef Journal; adv.

American Registry for Diagnostic Medical Sonography (1975)
51 Monroe St.
Plaza East One
Rockville, MD 20850-2400
Tel: (301) 738-8401 *Fax:* (301) 738-0312
TollFree: (800) 541-9754
E-Mail: admin@ardms.org
Website: ardms.org
Members: 95000 individuals
Staff: 43
Annual Budget: $10-25,000,000

Personnel:
Deputy Chief Executive Officer: Jamie Blietz CAE
Chief Executive Officer and Executive Director: Dale R.
  Cyr CAE, MBA

Historical Note:
*ARDMS's mission is to promote quality care and patient
safety through the certification and continuing competency
of ultrasound professionals. It also offers voluntary
certification through examination to qualified sonographers
and vascular technologists.*

Continuing Education:
Certification Designation/s: RDCS, RDMS, RPVI, RVT

Publications:
News Wire; bi-weekly
Registry Reports; quarterly

Membership List Available to Non-members

American Registry for Internet Numbers (1997)
P. O. Box 79010
Baltimore, MD 21279-0010
Tel: (703) 227-9840 *Fax:* (703) 227-0671
E-Mail: info@arin.net
Website: arin.net
Members: 4254 members
Staff: 57
Annual Budget: $10-25,000,000

Personnel:
President and Chief Executive Officer: John Curran
  E-Mail: jcurran@arin.net
Executive Director, Government Affairs and Public Policy:
  Cathy Handley
Meeting Planner: De Harvey
  E-Mail: dharvey@arin.net
Public Relations Officer: Megan Kruse
Director, Human Resources and Administration: Mary K.
  Lee
Director, Financial Services: Bob Stratton

Historical Note:
*ARIN's mission is to provide services related to the
technical coordination and management of internet number
resources and participates in the international internet
community. Membership is open to any organization that
has a signed Registration Services Agreement or Legacy
Registration Services Agreement with ARIN and holds
Internet number resources from ARIN. Membership: $500/
year (General Members).*

Meetings/Conferences:
Conference Chair: De Harvey
2013 - Bridgetown, Barbados/April 21 - 24
2013 - Phoenix, AZ/Oct. 10 - 11

Publications:
Membership Directory; on-line

Membership List Available to Non-members

American Registry of Medical Assistants (1950)
61 Union St.
Suite 5

Westfield, MA 01085
Tel: (413) 562-7336 *Fax:* (413) 562-9021
TollFree: (800) 527-2762
E-Mail: arma@verizon.net
Website: arma-cert.org
Members: 11500 individuals
Staff: 8
Annual Budget: $250-500,000
Tax: 501(c)(6)

Personnel:
Executive Secretary: Michelle P. Lesieur
  E-Mail: mlesieur@arma-online.org

Historical Note:
*ARMA's purpose is to certify and advance the
professionalism of the qualified medical assistant, to
provide through publications, updated medical and social
information of interest to the assistant and to be of service
to its members whenever possible. Membership: $40
application fee; $30/year renewal and processing.*

Continuing Education:
Enrollment: 2400
Certification Designation/s: RMA

Publications:
Membership Directory; on-line
Newsletter; on-line

American Registry of Radiologic Technologists (1922)
1255 Northland Dr.
St. Paul, MN 55120
Tel: (651) 687-0048 *Fax:* (651) 994-8510
Website: arrt.org
Members: 290000 individuals
Staff: 60
Annual Budget: $10-25,000,000
Tax: 501(c)(6)

Personnel:
Executive Director: Jerry B. Reid PhD
Director, Education: Joey S. Battles

Historical Note:
*ARRT's mission is to promotes better standards of patient
care by recognizing qualified individuals in medical
imaging, interventional procedures and radiation therapy.
Establishes standards of professional behavior and
requirements for educational preparation and continuing
education of its members. Members are individuals
qualified in the use of both ionizing and nonionizing
radiation for the purposes of diagnostic medical imaging,
interventional procedures, and therapeutic treatment.
Membership: $20- 32/year*

Continuing Education:
Certification Designation/s: REREX, CT, NMT, MRI, BS,
MRI, RA, CI, RAD, QM, SON, BD, VS, VI, MAM, THR

Publications:
Educator Update; quarterly

Membership List Available to Non-members

American Rehabilitation Counseling Association (1957)
USF Counselor Education
4202 E. Fowler Ave., EDU 105
Tampa, FL 33620
Tel: (813) 974-0985
Website: arcaweb.org
Members: 1000 individuals
Staff: 3
Annual Budget: $50-100,000

Personnel:
President: Caroline Wilde
  E-Mail: cwilde4@gmail.com

Historical Note:
*ARCA, a division of the American Counseling Association
which provides administrative support, provides leadership
in advancing the profession and science of rehabilitation
counseling. Members are rehabilitation counselors working
with people with physical, mental or emotional disabilities.
Membership: $70/year (professional); $40/year (retired);
$20/year (student).*

Publications:
ARCA Newsletter; quarterly

American Rental Association (1955)
1900 19th St.
Moline, IL 61265-4179
Tel: (309) 764-2475 *Fax:* (309) 764-1533
TollFree: (800) 334-2177
Website: ararental.org
Members: 6100 companies

Staff: 36
Annual Budget: $10-25,000,000
Tax: 501(c)(6)

Personnel:
Chief Executive Officer: Christine Wehrman
  E-Mail: chris.wehrman@ararental.com
Senior Director, Education and Training: Carla Brozick
  CAE
  E-Mail: carla.brozick@ararental.org
Vice President, Marketing and Communications: Tom
  Hubbell
Publisher, Rental Management Group: Ken Hughes
Manager, Marketing: Connie Lannan
Director, Information Technology: John Sammon
Director, General Member Services: Debby Schaller
*Senior Vice President, Operations and Chief Financial
  Officer:* Kathy Schwartz
  E-Mail: kathy.schwartz@ararental.org

Historical Note:
*Founded as the National Rental Owners Mutual
Association, and formerly American Associated Rental
Operators (1961). In 1986, the National Rental Service
Association merged with ARA. ARA's mission is to promote
the success of its members and advance the growth of the
equipment rental industry. Represents owners of privately
owned or franchise rental businesses, and manufacturers
and suppliers of rental products. Covers most kinds of
tangible personal properties found in the market today
except apartments, cars, billboards or office space. Supports
ARAPAC, its political action committee. Membership:
$375-3,200 (General/CRA General); $375 (International);
$3,500 (Corporate); $500 (Associate); $300 (Independent
Manufacturer).*

Meetings/Conferences: Annual
2013 - Las Vegas, NV (Sands Expo and Convention
  Center)/Feb. 10 - 13/11-25 exhibitors

Publications:
ARA Advantage Newsletter; monthly
ARA Business Solutions Newsletter
ARA Event Pros Newsletters; quarterly
ARA Risk Management Newsletter
Rental Management; monthly; adv.

American Resort Development Association
(1969)
1201 15th St. NW
Suite 400
Washington, DC 20005-2842
Tel: (202) 371-6700 *Fax:* (202) 289-8544
Website: arda.org
Members: 1000 companies and corporations
Staff: 33
Annual Budget: $5-10,000,000

Personnel:
President and Chief Executive Officer: Howard C.
  Nusbaum
  E-Mail: hnusbaum@arda.org
Vice President, Marketing and Communications: Lou Ann
  Burney
  E-Mail: lburney@arda.org
Manager, Education: Anna Chongpinitchai
  E-Mail: achongpinitchai@arda.org
Vice President of Industry Relations: Bob Craycraft
  E-Mail: bcraycraft@arda.org
Vice President, Finance and Administration: Rob Dunn
  E-Mail: rdunn@arda.org
Communications Coordinator, State Affairs: Melissa
  Feeser
  E-Mail: mfeeser@arda.org
Vice President, State Government Affairs: Jason C. Gamel
  Esq.
  E-Mail: jgamel@arda.org
Associate Vice President, Membership Services: Randy
  Goodhope
  E-Mail: rgoodhope@arda.org
Vice President, Meetings and Conventions: Catherine
  Lacey ARP
  E-Mail: clacey@arda.org
Vice President, Management Information Systems: Keith
  Laurent
  E-Mail: klaurent@arda.org
Editor and Director, Publications: Kathryn Mullan
  E-Mail: kmullan@arda.org

Historical Note:
*ARDA represents the resort timeshare industry on issues
such as purchase or right of use of units and time at
resort condominiums/hotels. Membership: $1500 (Active/
Associate); $300-615 (Affiliate).*

Meetings/Conferences:
Conference Chair: Catherine Lacey ARP
2013 - Orlando, FL (Orlando World Center Marriott)/
  March 24 - 28
2013 - Hollywood, FL (Westin Diplomat Resort)/April
  7 - 11
2013 - Washington, DC (Fairmont Hotel)/Nov. 13 - 15
Number of non-conference events/year: 2

Publications:
ARDA Newsletter
Developments; adv.
Membership Directory; on-line

American Reusable Textile Association *(1982)*
P.O. Box 1142
Mission, KS 66222
Tel: (863) 660-5350
Website: arta1.com
Members: 70 companies and organizations
Staff: 1
Annual Budget: $50-100,000
Tax: 501(c)(6)

Personnel:
Executive Director, Secretary and Editor: Nancy Jenkins
  E-Mail: njenkins@arta1.com

Historical Note:
*ARTA aims to promote the value of and need for reusable
textiles with general and technical educational opportunities
for both consumers and producers of reusable textiles
through literature, seminars, and technical bulletins.
Members are producers and distributors of apparel, diapers,
and other reusable textiles, manufacturers of laundry
equipment, and suppliers to the industry. Membership:
$750/year.*

Meetings/Conferences: Annual
Conference Chair: Nancy Jenkins
2013 - New Orleans, LA (New Orleans Morial
  Convention Center)/June 20 - 22
Number of non-conference events/year: 1

Publications:
eNewsletter; bi-monthly
Reusable Textiles; quarterly

American Rhinologic Society *(1954)*
P.O. Box 495
Warwick, NY 10990-0495
Tel: (845) 988-1631 *Fax:* (845) 986-1527
E-Mail: arsinfo@american-rhinologic.org
Website: american-rhinologic.org
Members: 1100 individuals
Staff: 7
Annual Budget: $500-1,000,000

Personnel:
President: Michael Setzen
Assistants, Meetings and Development Liaison: Susan
  Arias
  E-Mail: arsoffice@optimum.net
Assistant, Treasurer's Office: Kathryn Bellucci
  E-Mail: ARSTreasurer@optonline.net
Assistant, Membership and Administration: Gloria
  Figueroa
  E-Mail: ars.administration@gmail.com
Contact , Membership Committee: Stephanie Joe
Editor-In-Chief: David W. Kennedy
Administrator: Wendi Perez
  E-Mail: wendi.perez@gmail.com

Historical Note:
*ARS's mission is to serve, represent and advance the
science and ethical practice of rhinology. Members are
physicians who are diplomates of the American Board of
Otolaryngology. Membership: $285 (Fellow/Active); $125
(Affiliate); $185 (International); Free (Resident).*

Meetings/Conferences: Annual
Conference Chair: Susan Arias
2013 - Orlando, FL (JW Marriott Orlando Grande
  Lakes)/April 10 - 14

Publications:
Nose News Newsletter
The IFAR journal

Membership List Available to Non-members

American Rights at Work *(2003)*
1616 P St. NW
Suite 150
Washington, DC 20036
Tel: (202) 822-2127 *Fax:* (202) 822-2168
E-Mail: info@americanrightsatwork.org

Website: americanrightsatwork.org
Staff: 8
Annual Budget: $500-1,000,000
Tax: 501(c)(4)

Personnel:
Executive Director: Sarita Gupta
Senior Adviser: Kimberly Freeman Brown
Director, Communications: Elizabeth Cattaneo
  E-Mail: lcattaneo@americanrightsatwork.org
Director, Communications: Liz Cattaneo
  E-Mail: lcattaneo@americanrightsatwork.org
Director, Development: Alicia Daly
  E-Mail: adaly@americanrightsatwork.org
Manager, Accounting and Human Resources: Nico
  Gittings
  E-Mail: ngittings@americanrightsatwork.org
Office Manager: Reese Jimenez
Director, Research: Erin Johansson

Historical Note:
*It is dedicated to improve the climate in which workers can
exercise their rights in the workplace.*

Membership List Available to Non-members

American Risk and Insurance Association *(1932)*
716 Providence Rd.
Malvern, PA 19355-3402
Tel: (610) 640-1997 *Fax:* (610) 725-1007
E-Mail: aria@cpcuiia.org
Website: aria.org
Members: 500 individuals
Staff: 2
Annual Budget: $250-500,000
Tax: 501(c)(3)

Personnel:
Executive Director: Tony Biacchi
  E-Mail: biacchi@cpcuiia.org

Historical Note:
*Formerly (1961) American Association of University
Teachers of Insurance. Association of insurance scholars
and other thoughtful risk management and insurance
professionals. ARIA is dedicated to advancing knowledge in
risk management and insurance and enhancing the career
development of its members. Membership is comprised of
academics, individual insurance industry representatives,
student and retirees. Membership: $135 (Professional
Member); $29- 56 (Student/Retired).*

Meetings/Conferences: Annual
2013 - Washington, DC (Washington Court Hotel on
  Capitol Hill)/Aug. 4 - 7

Publications:
ARIA Newsletter; semi-annually
Member Directory; on-line
Risk Management and Insurance Review; on-line; adv.
The Journal of Risk and Insurance; on-line

Membership List Available to Non-members

American Road and Transportation Builders Association *(1902)*
1219 28th St. NW
Washington, DC 20007-3389
Tel: (202) 289-4434 *Fax:* (202) 289-4435
E-Mail: hwebster@artba.org
Website: artba.org
Members: 5000 companies
Staff: 49
Annual Budget: $5-10,000,000
Tax: 501(c)(3)

Personnel:
President and Chief Executive Officer: Peter T. Ruane
  CAES
  E-Mail: pruane@artba.org
Senior Vice President of Government Affairs: David Bauer
  E-Mail: dbauer@artba.org
Assistant General Counsel and Director, Regulatory Affairs:
  Nick Goldstein
  E-Mail: ngoldstein@artba.org
Manager, Publications: Jaime Mahoney
  E-Mail: jmahoney@artba.org
Vice President, Safety and Education: Bradley Sant
  E-Mail: bsant@artba.org
Vice President, Meetings and Events: Edward Tarrant

Historical Note:
*American Road and Transportation Builders Association
(ARTBA).ARTBA's mision is to grow and protect
transportation infrastructure investment to meet the public
and business demand for safe and efficient travel.*

Continuing Education:
Certification Designation/s: YEDP

Meetings/Conferences:
Conference Chair: Edward Tarrant
Number of non-conference events/year: 9

Publications:
Member DIrectory; on-line
Trasportation Builder; quarterly

American Rock Mechanics Association *(1994)*
600 Woodland Terrace
Alexandria, VA 22302-3319
Tel: (703) 683-1808 *Fax:* (703) 683-1815
E-Mail: info@armarocks.org
Website: armarocks.org
Members:
5 companies
310 individuals
Staff: 1
Annual Budget: $250-500,000
Tax: 501(c)(6)

Personnel:
Executive Director: Peter H. Smeallie
    E-Mail: smeallie@armarocks.org

Historical Note:
ARMA serves as an advocate for firms and individuals who represent all aspects of rock mechanics and rock engineering. Membership: $85 (Individual); $2500 (Corporate); $15 (Student); $1,000 (Life).

Meetings/Conferences: Annual
2013 - San Francisco, CA (The Westin Milbrae)/June 23 - 26
Number of non-conference events/year: 1

Publications:
e-Newsletter

American Roentgen Ray Society *(1900)*
44211 Slatestone Ct.
Leesburg, VA 20176-5109
Tel: (703) 729-3353 *Fax:* (703) 729-4839
TollFree: (844) 940-2777
E-Mail: info@arrs.org
Website: arrs.org
Members: 20000 individuals
Staff: 34
Annual Budget: $5-10,000,000
Tax: 501(c)(3)

Personnel:
Executive Director: Susan Brown Cappitell CAE, MBA
Director, Information Technology: John Finney
    E-Mail: jfinney@arrs.org
Marketing Manager: Kelly Hansard
    E-Mail: Kelly.Hansard@gmail.com
Director, Communications and Development: Keri Sperry
    E-Mail: ksperry@arrs.org
Director, Membership and Meetings Services: Linda Thomas
    E-Mail: lthomas@arrs.org

Historical Note:
Formerly (1906) Roentgen Society of the United States. ARRS's mission is to improve health through a community committed to advancing knowledge and skills in radiology. Membership: $295 (Active/Associate); $375 (International). $85 (In-training); $155 (International In-training).

Continuing Education:
Certification Designation/s: MOC

Meetings/Conferences: Annual
Conference Chair: Linda Thomas
2013 - Washington, DC (Washington Marriott Wardman Park)/April 14 - 19
2014 - San Diego, CA (Manchester Grand Hyatt San Diego)/May 4 - 9
2015 - Toronto, ON (Metro Toronto Convention Centre)/April 19 - 24

Publications:
American Journal of Roentgenology; monthly; adv.
ARRS InPractice Insight; monthly; adv.
InPractice; quarterly; adv.

American Romagnola Association *(1974)*
704 S. Broadway, Suite Two
P.O. Box 8082
Portland, TN 37148
Tel: (615) 681-5225 *Fax:* (615) 325-3160
E-Mail: arabeef@aol.com

Website: americanromagnola.com
Members: 150 individuals
Staff: 1
Annual Budget: $50-100,000
Tax: 501(c)(5)

Personnel:
Chief Executive Officer: James Lyons DVM
    E-Mail: mwac@charter.net

Historical Note:
ARA is a association whose members are breeders of purebred Romagnola cattle. ARA's goal is to produce a breed that imparts a quiet nature to minimize the effects of shipping, feedlot conditions that could hinder weight gains. Membership: $100 (Active); $45 (Life).

American Romney Breeders Association *(1912)*
12775 NW Oak Ridge Rd.
Yamhill, OR 97148
Tel: (503) 662-4249
E-Mail: secretary@americanromney.org
Website: americanromney.org
Members: 500 individuals
Staff: 2
Annual Budget: $25-50,000
Tax: 501(c)(5)

Personnel:
Secretary and Treasurer: Christiane Payton
    E-Mail: secretary@americanromney.org

Historical Note:
ARBA is the promoter of Romney sheep in the United States and Canada. Members are breeders and fanciers of Romney sheep. Maintains a registry of pedigrees. ARBA registers both white and natural colored Romneys. Membership: $20 (Member); $10 (Junior).

Meetings/Conferences: Annual

Publications:
Membership Directory; on-line; adv.
Ramblings Online; on-line

American Running Association *(1968)*
4405 East- West Hwy.
Suite 405
Bethesda, MD 20814
Tel: (800) 776-2732 *Fax:* (301) 913-9520
TollFree: (800) 776-2732
E-Mail: arfarun@aol.com
Website: americanrunning.org
Staff: 5
Annual Budget: $250-500,000
Tax: 501(c)(3)

Personnel:
Executive Director: David Watt
    E-Mail: dave@americanrunning.org
Editor: Jeff Venables

Historical Note:
Originally founded as the National Jogging Association, became the American Running and Fitness Association in 1981 and changed to its current name in 1999. ARA's mission is to encourage all people, from youth to adults, to improve their health and fitness by walking and running, and maintaining an active and healthy lifestyle. Membership: $25 (Individual); $35 (Group); $55 (International).

Publications:
Running & FitNews; bi-monthly

American Running Association/American Medical Athletic Association *(1968)*
4405 East-West Hwy.
Suite 405
Bethesda, MD 20814-9139
Tel: (301) 913-9517 *Fax:* (301) 913-9520
TollFree: (800) 776-2732
E-Mail: run@americanrunning.org
Website: americanrunning.org
Staff: 2
Annual Budget: $250-500,000

Personnel:
Executive Director: David Watt
    E-Mail: dave@americanrunning.org
Editor: Jeff Venables

Historical Note:
Founded in 1968 as the National Jogging Association. Main goals include encouraging Americans to run and be fit; to keep health professionals up-to-date on the latest in sports medicine; and to mobilize parents and educators in fighting youth obesity with walk-run programs geared

toward improving fitness. Membership: $25 (Individual/ Family); $35 (Group); $55 (International).

Publications:
AMAA Journal; adv.
E-newsletters; on-line
Membership Directory; on-line
Running & FitNews; bi-monthly

American Saddlebred Horse Association *(1891)*
4083 Iron Works Pkwy.
Lexington, KY 40511
Tel: (859) 259-2742 *Fax:* (859) 259-1628
E-Mail: saddlebred@asha.net
Website: saddlebred.com
Members: 8000 individuals
Staff: 17
Annual Budget: $1-2,000,000
Tax: 501(c)(3)

Personnel:
Executive Director: Karen Winn
    E-Mail: k.winn@asha.net
Executive Secretary: Alan F. Balch
    E-Mail: a.balch@asha.net
Manager, Marketing and Communications: Brice Carr
    E-Mail: b.carr@asha.net
Senior Registry Associate and Program Manager: Patricia Edwards
    E-Mail: p.edwards@asha.net
Manager, Advertising: Dede Gatlin
    E-Mail: d.gatlin@asha.net
Technology Manager: William Wood Jr.
    E-Mail: w.wood@asha.net

Historical Note:
Formerly (1891) American Saddle-Horse Breeders' Association, assumed its current name in 1980. ASHA's mission is to safeguard the integrity of the American Saddlebred breed and to promote the use of Saddlebreds. Membership: $2,500 (Life Member); $100 (Contributing); $70 (Senior); $50 (Charter/Affiliate); $30 (Junior); $60 (Special Junior); $40 (Youth Club Affiliate).

Meetings/Conferences: Annual

Publications:
American Saddlebred; quarterly
Membership Directiory; on-line

The American Safe Deposit Association *(1924)*
P.O. Box 519
Franklin, IN 46131
Tel: (317) 738-4432 *Fax:* (317) 738-2571
E-Mail: tasda1@aol.com
Website: tasda.com
Members: 1800 banks
Staff: 5
Annual Budget: $100-250,000

Personnel:
Executive Director: Joyce A. McLin
    E-Mail: tasda1@aol.com
Treasurer: Linda Dunmire
    E-Mail: linda.dunmire@suncoastfcu.org
First Vice President: Winnifred Howard-Hammack
Secretary: Evelyn Ludgate
    E-Mail: Evbeanie2@aol.com
President: Wayne J. Merrill
    E-Mail: john_merrill@boonebank.com

Historical Note:
TASDA is a federation of regional and local associations of banks, trust companies and others engaged in the safe deposit business. Formerly (1947) National Safe Deposit Advisory Council. Membership: Associate Member : $110, Individual Member : $60, Corporate : $1,000 + $50 for each branch that will be members.

American Salers Association *(1974)*
19590 E. Main St.
Suite 104
Parker, CO 80138
Tel: (303) 770-9292 *Fax:* (303) 770-9302
E-Mail: salersinfo@salerusa.org
Website: salersusa.org
Members: 1000 individuals
Staff: 4
Annual Budget: $250-500,000
Tax: 501(c)(5)

Personnel:
Executive Vice President: Sherry Doubet
    E-Mail: sherry@salersusa.org
Director, Communications: Joe McDaniel

E-Mail: joe@salersusa.org
Director, Field Services: Dean Pike
   E-Mail: dcssalers@actcom.net

Historical Note:
ASA works for the development, registration and promotion of the Salers breed of cattle in the United States. Members are breeders and owners of Salers or Salers-influenced cattle. It also maintains registry of pedigreed Salers cattle. Membership: $100 (Individual); $25 (Associate/Junior).

Meetings/Conferences: Annual
2013 - Denver, CO (Holiday Inn Denver East-Stapleton)/Jan. 19 - 22
Number of non-conference events/year: 1

Publications:
American Salers Magazine; quarterly; adv.
Member Connection; weekly
Membership Ditrectory; on-line

American Salvage Pool Association *(1985)*
2100 Roswell Rd.
Suite 700 - PMB 321
Marietta, GA 30062
Tel: (678) 560-6678 *Fax:* (678) 229-2777
Website: aspa.com
Members: 180 companies
Staff: 2
Annual Budget: $250-500,000

Personnel:
Executive Director: Natalie Nardone CMP
   E-Mail: natalie@aspa.com
Contact, Conventions: Paula Kerr
   E-Mail: paula.kerr@salvagedirect.com

Historical Note:
Incorporated in Florida. Members are firms specializing in the brokering of totally wrecked, water and hail damaged, and other recovered vehicles in conjunction with insurance companies and recovery personnel. Membership: $500-5,600 (Regular); $300 (Associate).

Meetings/Conferences: Annual
Conference Chair: Paula Kerr

American Sand Association
P.O.Box 1872
Canyon Country, CA 91386
Tel: (805) 419-4544 *Fax:* (951) 242-1332
TollFree: (888) 540-7263
Website: americansandassociation.org
Members: 40000 Members
Staff: 2
Annual Budget: $250-500,000
Tax: 501(c)(4)

Personnel:
Executive Director: Nicole Gilles
Treasurer: Lloyd Misner

Historical Note:
ASA's mission is to Unite, Inform and Mobilize and support national cooperation of local and regional sand sport organizations.

Publications:
Newsletter; quarterly

American School Band Directors' Association *(1953)*
227 N. First St.
P.O. Box 696
Guttenberg, IA 52052-0696
Tel: (563) 252-2500
E-Mail: asbda@alpinecom.net
Website: asbda.com
Members: 1200 individuals
Staff: 3
Annual Budget: $25-50,000
Tax: 501(c)(6)

Personnel:
President: Kevin Beaber
   E-Mail: kevin.beaber@cck12.net
Office Manager: Dennis L. Hanna
Webmaster: Mekel Rogers
   E-Mail: m-rogers@earthlink.net

Historical Note:
Organized in 1953 Cedar Rapids, Iowa. ASBDA's mission is to promote, enhance and preserve quality school band programs through leadership and fellowship of exemplary band directors nationwide. Members are professionally trained instrumental music teachers. Membership: $75 (Individual); $65 (Institution); $70(Associate).

Meetings/Conferences: Annual

Publications:
ASBDA Newsletter; on-line
Bandworld Magazine
Member Directory; on-line

American School Bus Council *(2006)*
113 S. West St.
Fourth Floor
Alexandria, VA 22314
Tel: (866) 955-2722 *Fax:* (703) 684-3212
TollFree: (866) 955-2722
Website: americanschoolbuscouncil.org
Staff: 1

Personnel:
Contact, Communications: Clark Barrineau
   E-Mail: clark@americanschoolbuscouncil.com

Historical Note:
The American School Bus Council purpose is to educate parents, school officials and lawmakers about the essential role the yellow school bus plays in the safety, health, security and readiness of America?s schoolchildren.

Publications:
Newsletter

American School Counselor Association *(1952)*
1101 King St.
Suite 625
Alexandria, VA 22314
Tel: (703) 683-2722 *Fax:* (703) 683-1619
TollFree: (800) 306-4722
E-Mail: asca@schoolcounselor.org
Website: schoolcounselor.org
Members: 28000 individuals
Staff: 12
Annual Budget: $5-10,000,000
Tax: 501(c)(3)

Personnel:
Executive Director: Richard Wong CAE, EdD
   E-Mail: asca@schoolcounselor.org
Contact, Information Technology: Jeff Broderson
   E-Mail: jbroderson@schoolcounselor.org
Director, Public Policy: Amanda Fitzgerald
   E-Mail: afitzgerald@schoolcounselor.org
Administrator, Finance: Jane Fort
   E-Mail: jfort@schoolcounselor.org
Coordinator, Meetings: Kelly Frey
   E-Mail: kfrey@schoolcounselor.org
Director, Professional Development: Mark Kuranz
   E-Mail: mkuranz@schoolcounselor.org
Director, Communications: Kathleen M Rakestraw
   E-Mail: krakestraw@schoolcounselor.org
Contact, Membership Services: Stephanie J. Wicks
   E-Mail: swicks@schoolcounselor.org

Historical Note:
ASCA's mission is to represent professional school counselors and to promote professionalism and ethical practices and support relevant research and evaluation in school counseling. Membership: $115 (Professional/Affiliate); $60 (Student/Retired).

Meetings/Conferences: Annual
Conference Chair: Kelly Frey
2013 - Philadelphia, PA (Pennsylvania Convention Center)/June 30 - July 3
2014 - Orlando, FL (Walt Disney World Swan And Dolphin)/June 29 - July 2

Publications:
ASCA Aspects; monthly; adv.
ASCA School Counselor magazine; bi-monthly; adv.
Membership Directory; on-line
Professional School Counseling journal; bi-monthly

Membership List Available to Non-members

American School Health Association *(1927)*
4340 East West Hwy.
Suite 403
Bethesda, MD 20814
Tel: (330) 678-1601 *Fax:* (301) 652-8077
TollFree: (800) 445-2742
E-Mail: info@ashaweb.org
Website: ashaweb.org
Members: 2000 individuals
Staff: 5
Annual Budget: $500-1,000,000
Tax: 501(c)(3)

Personnel:
Executive Director: Stephen Conley PhD

   E-Mail: sconley@ashaweb.org
Coordinator, Communications: Heather W. Gibbons
   E-Mail: heatherwgibbons@mac.com
Director, Marketing and Conferences: Julie Greenfield CMP
   E-Mail: jgreenfield@ashaweb.org
Manager, Membership and Database: Lori Lawrence
   E-Mail: Llawrence@ashaweb.org

Historical Note:
Formerly (1927) the American Association of School Physicians, became the American School Health Association in 1936 and incorporated in Ohio in 1971. ASHA's mission is to build the capacity of its members to plan, develop, coordinate, implement, evaluate, and advocate for effective school health strategies that contribute to optimal health and academic outcomes for all children and youth. Members are those engaged in any aspect of the school health program. Membership: $60-500/year.

Continuing Education:
Enrollment: 750
Certification Designation/s: CME, CHES, CNE

Meetings/Conferences: Annual
Conference Chair: Julie Greenfield CMP
2013 - Myrtle Beach, SC (Hilton Myrtle Beach Resort)/Oct. 9 - 12

Publications:
Journal of School Health; monthly
Member Directory; on-line
The Pulse; bi-monthly

Membership List Available to Non-members

American Schools Association *(1914)*
P.O. Box 577820
Chicago, IL 60657-7820
Tel: (773) 732-0046 *Fax:* (773) 782-0113
TollFree: (800) 230-2263
E-Mail: asaceu@hotmail.com
Website: asaceu.com
Staff: 2
Annual Budget: $250-500,000
Tax: 501(c)(3)

Personnel:
President: Carl M. Dye
   E-Mail: asaceu@hotmail.com

Historical Note:
ASA works to develop and market continuing education on a home-study basis.

Continuing Education:
Certification Designation/s: LCSW-MFT, NBCC, CAADAC

American Schools of Oriental Research *(1900)*
Boston University, 656 Beacon St.
Fifth Floor
Boston, MA 02215-2010
Tel: (617) 353-6570 *Fax:* (617) 353-6575
E-Mail: asor@bu.edu
Website: asor.org
Members: 1515 individuals, institutions and affiliated overseas research institutes
Staff: 7
Annual Budget: $500-1,000,000
Tax: 501(c)(3)

Personnel:
Executive Director: Andrew G. Vaughn PhD
   E-Mail: asored@bu.edu
Director, Membership, Subscription, and Publication Services: Kevin Cooney
   E-Mail: asorsubs@bu.edu
Assistant, Publications: Jennifer Fitzgerald
   E-Mail: asormemb@bu.edu
Director, Meetings and Events: Kelley Herlihy CMP
   E-Mail: asorad@bu.edu
Financial Administrator: Selma Omerefendic
   E-Mail: asortoo@bu.edu
Specialist, Archivist and Information: Cynthia Rufo
   E-Mail: asorarch@bu.edu

Historical Note:
ASOR promotes the educational goals of Near Eastern studies disciplines and advocates academic standards in teaching and interdisciplinary research. Fosters original research, archaeological excavations and explorations. Members are universities and individuals involved in Middle Eastern research, especially Biblical archaeology, pre-history, ancient and medieval history. Membership: $90-130 (Individual); $50 (Associate); $255 (Sustaining); $125 (Contributing).

Meetings/Conferences: Annual
Conference Chair: Kelley Herlihy CMP

Publications:
ASOR Newsletter; quarterly
Journal of Cuneiform Studies (JCS); annually
Near Eastern Archaeology (NEA); adv.

American Scientific Glassblowers Society (1952)
P.O. Box 453
Machias, NY 14101
Tel: (716) 353-8062 *Fax:* (716) 353-4259
E-Mail: natl-office@asgs-glass.org
Website: asgs-glass.org
Members: 650 individuals
Staff: 2
Annual Budget: $100-250,000
Tax: 501(c)(6)

Personnel:
President: Curt Sexton
   E-Mail: william.sexton@srnl.doe.gov

Historical Note:
Incorporated in Delaware in 1954. ASGS's mission is to share the knowledge, techniques, and skills of scientific glassblowing to its worldwide membership. Activities include providing continuing education and maintaining the successful association between scientific glassblowers and all of the various enterprises which entail glass fabrication. Members are scientific glassblowers and associated members who are interested in the art of scientific glassblowing. Membership: $100 (Regular/ Associate/Artistic); $75 (Junior); $30 (Student); $125 (International); $50 (Retired).

Meetings/Conferences: Annual
Number of non-conference events/year: 1

Publications:
Fusion; quarterly; adv.
Proceedings; annually
Roster; annually

Membership List Available to Non-members

American Securitization Forum
One World Financial Center
30th Floor
New York, NY 10281
Tel: (212) 412-7100 *Fax:* (212) 313-1032
E-Mail: gmiller@americansecuritization.com
Website: americansecuritization.com
Members: 323 Organizations
Staff: 8

Personnel:
Executive Director: Tom Deutsch
   E-Mail: tdeutsch@americansecuritization.com
Vice President, Strategic Communications: Katrina Cavalli
   E-Mail: kcavalli@americansecuritization.com
Accounts Coordinator: Alyssa Chawdry
   E-Mail: achawdry@americansecuritization.com
Coordinator, Membership: Josh Gacek
   E-Mail: jgacek@americansecuritization.com
Managing Director, Public Policy: Jim Johnson
   E-Mail: jjohnson@americansecuritization.com
Director, Administration: Justin Ross
   E-Mail: jross@americansecuritization.com
Managing Director, Senior Counsel: Evan Siegert
   E-Mail: esiegert@americansecuritization.com
Coordinator, Events And Marketing: Wendy Zuluaga
   E-Mail: wzuluaga@americansecuritization.com

Historical Note:
ASF advocates the securitization industry's interests in various market practice, legal, accounting, tax, regulatory, legislative and policy issues. Builds consensus, coordinates advocacy efforts, and informs and educates the securitization community and related constituencies on issues of broad importance to the industry. Membership: $295-45,000/year.

Meetings/Conferences: Annual
Conference Chair: Wendy Zuluaga
2013 - Las Vegas, NV (ARIA Hotel and Convention Center)/Jan. 27 - 30

Publications:
The American Securitization; semi-annually; adv.

American Seed Trade Association (1883)
1701 Duke St.
Suite 275
Alexandria, VA 22314-3415
Tel: (703) 837-8140 *Fax:* (703) 837-9365
TollFree: (888) 890-7333
E-Mail: info@amseed.org
Website: amseed.com
Members: 700 companies

Staff: 11
Annual Budget: $2-5,000,000
Tax: 501(c)(6)

Personnel:
President and Chief Executive Officer: Andrew LaVigne
Vice President, Government Affairs: Leslie C. Cahill
   E-Mail: lcahill@amseed.org
Contact, Meetings: Jennifer Crouse
   E-Mail: jcrouse@amseed.org
Director, Membership Services: Jason Laney
   E-Mail: jlaney@amseed.org
Vice President, Scientific and International Affairs: Bernice Slutsky
   E-Mail: bslutsky@amseedl.org
Director, Administrative Services: Barbara Surian
   E-Mail: bsurian@amseed.org

Historical Note:
ASTA's mission is to provide service for development, marketing and free movement of seed, associated products and services throughout the world. Membership: $200-175,000/year.

Meetings/Conferences:
Conference Chair: Jennifer Crouse
2013 - Scottsdale, AZ (The Fairmont)/Jan. 26 - 29

Publications:
Membership Directory; on-line
Seed E-News; on-line

American Seminar Leaders Association (1988)
2405 E. Washington Blvd.
Pasadena, CA 91104-2040
Tel: (626) 791-1211 *Fax:* (626) 791-0701
TollFree: (800) 801-1886
E-Mail: info@asla.com
Website: asla.com
Members: 3500 individuals
Staff: 7
Annual Budget: $500-1,000,000

Personnel:
President: June Davidson
Senior Vice President, Communications, Marketing and Public Relations: Robbie Motter

Historical Note:
ASLA seeks to enhance the professional skills of its members and market their products and services effectively. Members are professional seminar and workshop leaders, coaches and trainers. ASLA's mission is to train excellence for certified seminar leaders and coaches. Membership: $447/year.

Continuing Education:
Certification Designation/s: CAC, CSL

Publications:
ASLA Newsletter; on-line
Membership Directory; on-line
Newsletter E-blasts; on-line

American Senior Benefits Association
P.O. Box 300777
Chicago, IL 60630-0777
Tel: (773) 714-7990
TollFree: (877) 906-2722
E-Mail: info@asbaonline.org
Website: asbaonline.org
Members: 700000 individuals
Staff: 4
Annual Budget: $1-2,000,000
Tax: 501(c)(3)

Personnel:
Executive Director: Eileen Philbin
   E-Mail: Eileen.Philbin@asbaonline.org

Historical Note:
Formerly American Small Businesses Association (ASBA). ASBA is focused on advocacy and education for men and women age 50 and above. Membership: Free.

Publications:
ASBA Newsletter; on-line
Member Directory; on-line

American Seniors Housing Association (1991)
5225 Wisconsin Ave. NW
Suite 502
Washington, DC 20015
Tel: (202) 237-0900 *Fax:* (202) 237-1616
Website: seniorshousing.org
Members: 250 firms
Staff: 5
Annual Budget: $2-5,000,000

Personnel:
President: David S. Schless
   E-Mail: dschless@seniorshousing.org
Vice President, Government Relations: Rachelle Bernstecker
   E-Mail: rbernstecker@seniorshousing.org
Chief Legislative Counsel: Randolf H. Hardock
   E-Mail: rhardock@seniorshousing.org
Vice President, Membership Services: Doris K. Maultsby
   E-Mail: dmaultsby@seniorshousing.org
Legal Counsel: Barbara A. Pate

Historical Note:
Formerly National Multi Housing Council. ASHA provides leadership for the seniors housing industry on legislative and regulatory matters, advances research, education and the exchange of strategic business information, and promotes the merits of seniors housing. Members are executives involved in the operation, development and finance of the entire spectrum of seniors housing â " independent living, assisted living, and continuing care retirement communities. Membership: $12,500 (Executive Board); $5,000 (Advisory Committee); $2,500 (Associate); $10,000 (State Association).

Meetings/Conferences: Annual
2013 - Phoenix, AZ (JW Marriott Desert Ridge Resort)/ Jan. 20 - 22
2013 - Washington, DC (Park Hyatt Washington)/April 25 - 26

Publications:
Brief
Capitol Connection Newsletter

American Sesame Growers Association (2006)
4308 Centergate St.
San Antonio, TX 78217-4804
Tel: (210) 590-3352
Website: sesamegrowers.org
Staff: 3
Tax: 501(c)(6)

Personnel:
Secretary and Treasurer: Ray Langham

Historical Note:
ASGA promotes and encourages the establishment and maintenance of conditions favorable to the production of non-dehiscent varieties of sesame in the U.S. and to the marketing, processing and use of U.S. grown sesame in both domestic and export markets. Provides growers and industry a voice in the development of sesame in the U.S. and in the development of U.S. farm policies affecting sesame. Membership: $10 (Producer/Associate Producer); $2,500 (Industry); $50 (Associate-Individual).

American Sexually Transmitted Diseases Association (1934)
P. O. Box 12665
Research Triangle Park, NC 27709
Tel: (919) 361-3125
Website: astda.org
Members: 450 individuals
Staff: 3
Annual Budget: $250-500,000

Personnel:
President: Bradley Stoner MD, PhD
   E-Mail: bstoner@wustl.edu
Secretary and Treasurer: Edward Hook III, MD
   E-Mail: ehook@uab.edu

Historical Note:
ASTDA strives to support the control and eradication of STDs. Membership: $100 (Physician/PhD); $50 (Clinician/ Laboratorian); $35 (Public Health Worker/Trainee).

Meetings/Conferences: Annual
Number of non-conference events/year: 1

Publications:
ASTDA Newsletters
Sexually Transmitted Diseases; monthly; adv.

American Sheep Industry Association (1865)
9785 Maroon Cir.
Suite 360
Englewood, CO 80112-2692
Tel: (303) 771-3500 *Fax:* (303) 771-8200
E-Mail: info@sheepusa.org
Website: sheepusa.org
Members: 82000 individuals and 45 sheep associations
Staff: 18
Annual Budget: $500-1,000,000
Tax: 501(c)(5)

Personnel:
Executive Director: Peter Orwick
  E-Mail: porwick@sheepusa.org
Assistant to Director: Mary Jensen
  E-Mail: mary@sheepusa.org
Project Manager, Human Resources and Finances: Zahrah Khan
  E-Mail: zahrah@sheepusa.org
Chief Financial Officer: Larry Kincaid
  E-Mail: larry@sheepusa.org
Director, Industry Information: Judy Malone
  E-Mail: judym@sheepusa.org
Deputy Director, Policy: Paul Rodgers
  E-Mail: prodgers2@earthlink.net
Director, International Wool and Pelt Marketing: Rita Kourlis Samuelson
  E-Mail: rita@sheepusa.org
Editor: Amy Trinidad
  E-Mail: amy@sheepusa.org

Historical Note:
Formerly (1989) the American Sheep Producers Council, ASI merged with the National Wool Growers Association in 1989. ASI's mission is to promote communication and cooperation between all segments of the industry, related business and government agencies. Members are sheep producers. Membership: $25 (Individual, minimum-based on no. of sheep); $2,500-10,000 (Industry Partner); $1,000 (Industry Supporter); $300 (Convention Sponsorship).

Meetings/Conferences: Annual
2013 - San Antonio, TX (Hyatt Regency San Antonio Riverwalk)/Jan. 23 - 26
2014 - Charleston, SC (Charleston Marriott)/Jan. 22 - 25
Number of non-conference events/year: 17

Publications:
ASI Newsletter; weekly
Sheep Industry News; monthly; adv.
State Association Newsletter; on-line
The Sheep & Goat Research Journal
Wool Journal; on-line

American Shetland Pony Club/American Miniature Horse Registry *(1888)*
81-B Queenwood Rd.
Morton, IL 61550-2923
Tel: (309) 263-4044 *Fax:* (309) 263-5113
E-Mail: info@shetlandminiature.com
Website: shetlandminiature.com
Members: 7500 individuals
Staff: 11
Annual Budget: $1-2,000,000

Personnel:
Director, Operations: Zona J. Schneider
  E-Mail: zona@shetlandminiature.com

Historical Note:
Founded by the American Shetland Pony Club and a member of the National Pedigree Livestock Council, ASPC/AMHR is a registry to keep the pedigrees for all the Shetlands that are being imported from Europe. Members are owners and breeders of of Shetland ponies. Membership: $65 (Individual); $20 (Secondary Members); $76 (International).
Meetings/Conferences:
Number of non-conference events/year: 47

Publications:
The Journal Magazine (Pony); bi-monthly
Your New Horse Magazine; annually; adv.

American Shire Horse Association *(1885)*
P.O. Box 408
Lake Delton, WI 53940
TollFree: (888) 302-6643
E-Mail: secretary@shirehorse.org
Website: shirehorse.org
Members: 650 individuals
Staff: 5
Annual Budget: $50-100,000

Personnel:
President: Daniel Todd Riedel
  E-Mail: traillightfarms@aol.com
Treasurer: Kimberly N. Parrington-Murchison
  E-Mail: thshire@sopris.net
Secretary: Myrna Rhinehart
  E-Mail: secretary@shirehorse.org

Historical Note:
ASHA records pedigrees of Shire draft horses and promotes their breeding. Members are owners and breeders of Shire horses. Membership: $50 (Individual-US); $60 (Individual-International); $600 (Lifetime-US); $700 (Lifetime-International); $275 (Corporate).

Publications:
Directory of Shire Owners and Breeders; annually
Newsletter; quarterly

American Short Line and Regional Railroad Association *(1913)*
50 F St. NW
Suite 7020
Washington, DC 20001-1536
Tel: (202) 628-4500 *Fax:* (202) 628-6430
E-Mail: aslrra@aslrra.org
Website: aslrra.org
Members: 450 short line and regional railroad members
Staff: 12
Annual Budget: $2-5,000,000
Tax: 501(c)(6)

Personnel:
Vice President and Executive Director: Stephen M. Sullivan
  E-Mail: sullivan@aslrra.org
Vice President and General Counsel: Keith T. Borman
  E-Mail: kborman@aslrra.org
Director, Marketing: Jenny M. Bourque
  E-Mail: jbourque@aslrra.org
Vice President, Meetings and Membership Services: Kathleen M. Cassidy
  E-Mail: kcassidy@aslrra.org
Chief Financial Officer: Eric J. O'Neill
  E-Mail: eoneill@aslrra.org
Executive Director, Federal and Industry Programs: Matthew B. Reilly Jr.
  E-Mail: mreilly@aslrra.org
President and Treasurer: Richard F. Timmons
  E-Mail: rftimmons@aslrra.org
Manager, Communications and Data Services: David C. Whorton
  E-Mail: dwhorton@aslrra.org

Historical Note:
Absorbed (1998) Regional Railroads of America, ASLRRA represents short line and regional railroads in legislative and regulatory matters and industry relations. Membership: $1,615-8,735 (Railroad Members); $1,145-1,750 (Associate Members).

Continuing Education:
Certification Designation/s: D and A, RWP, EC, CWR
Meetings/Conferences: Annual
Conference Chair: Kathleen M. Cassidy
2013 - Atlanta, GA (Atlanta Marriott Century Center)/ April 27 - 30/1500 attendees/51-100 exhibitors
2014 - San Diego, CA (Hilton San Diego Bayfront)/ April 22 - 25/1500 attendees/51-100 exhibitors
Number of non-conference events/year: 3

Publications:
Safety Bulletin; bi-monthly
Views & News; bi-weekly

American Shorthorn Association *(1846)*
8288 Hascall St.
Omaha, NE 68124
Tel: (402) 393-7200 *Fax:* (402) 393-7203
TollFree: (877) 272-0686
E-Mail: info@shorthorn.org
Website: shorthorn.org
Members: 3000 individuals
Staff: 10
Annual Budget: $500-1,000,000

Personnel:
Executive Secretary and Treasurer: Dr. Bert Moore
  E-Mail: bert@shorthorn.org
Director, Registrations: Gwen Crawford
  E-Mail: gwen@shorthorn.org
Director, Communication and Marketing: Amanda Reeson
  E-Mail: amandar@shorthorn.org

Historical Note:
Absorbed the American Polled Shorthorn Society in 1991. Members are breeders and promoters of Shorthorn Beef Cattle. A member of the National Pedigree Livestock Council, the US Beef Breeds Council and the National Cattlemen's Association. Membership: $35 (New Senior); $50 (New Junior).

American Shoulder and Elbow Surgeons *(1982)*
6300 N. River Rd.
Suite 727
Rosemont, IL 60018
Tel: (847) 698-1629 *Fax:* (847) 823-0536
E-Mail: ases@aaos.org
Website: ases-assn.org
Members: 206 individuals
Staff: 3
Annual Budget: $1-2,000,000
Tax: 501(c)(6)

Personnel:
President: Jon J.P. Warner MD
Secretary and Treasurer: George M. McCluskey III, MD
Society Manager: Susan Shannon
  E-Mail: shannon@aaos.org

Historical Note:
American Shoulder and Elbow Surgeons is nationally affiliated with American Academy of Orthopaedic Surgeons. ASES's mission is to foster and advance the science and practice of shoulder and elbow care. Members are orthopedic surgeons. Membership is by invitation only.

Meetings/Conferences:
2013 - Las Vegas, NV (Bellagio Hotel)/Oct. 12
2013 - Las Vegas, NV (Bellagio Hotel)/Oct. 13 - 15
2014 - Pinehurst, NC (Pinehurst Resort)/Oct. 9 - 12
Number of non-conference events/year: 2

Publications:
The Journal of Shoulder and Elbow Surgery; on-line

American Shrimp Processors Association *(1964)*
P.O. Box 4867
Biloxi, MS 39535
Tel: (228) 806-9600 *Fax:* (228) 385-2565
Website: americanshrimp.org
Members: 40 companies
Staff: 1
Annual Budget: $1-2,000,000
Tax: 501(c)(6)

Personnel:
Executive Director: C. David Veal
  E-Mail: director@americanshrimp.org

Historical Note:
Founded as the American Shrimp Canners Association. In 1979 the name was changed to the American Shrimp Processors Association. ASPA has been representing, protecting and promoting the interests of the U.S. domestic shrimp industry.

Publications:
Membership Directory; on-line
News & Notes

American Shropshire Registry Association *(1884)*
41 Bell Rd.
Leyden, MA 01337
Tel: (413) 624-9652 *Fax:* (413) 624-9652
E-Mail: shropsec@hotmail.com
Website: shropshires.org
Members: 1000 individuals
Staff: 3
Annual Budget: $25-50,000

Personnel:
Secretary: Becky Peterson
  E-Mail: shropsec@hotmail.com

Historical Note:
ASRA is composed of breeders and fanciers of Shropshire sheep, which were introduced into the U.S. in 1855 from England and are bred both for their meat and wool production. Registers and records the pedigrees of all purebred Shropshire sheep bred in America. Membership: $6-20/year.

Meetings/Conferences: Annual
Conference Chair: Mark McCabe
Number of non-conference events/year: 2

Publications:
Breeder's Index; on-line; adv.
Membership Directory; on-line
Shropshire Voice; adv.

Membership List Available to Non-members

American Simmental Association *(1969)*
One Simmental Way
Bozeman, MT 59715-9733
Tel: (406) 587-4531 *Fax:* (406) 587-9301
E-Mail: simmental@simmgene.com
Website: simmental.org
Members: 8702 individuals
Staff: 20

Annual Budget: $2-5,000,000
Tax: 501(c)(5)

Personnel:
Executive Vice President: Dr. Jerry Lipsey PhD
  E-Mail: jlipsey@simmgene.com
Contact, Membership and Mail Services: Nancy
  Chesterfield
  E-Mail: nchesterfield@simmgene.com
Executive Assistant, International Events, Information,
  Cost-Share and Check off: Paulette Cochenour
  E-Mail: pcochenour@simmgene.com
Chief Financial Officer and Contact, Human Resources:
  Linda Kesler
  E-Mail: lkesler@simmgene.com
Advertising Assistant and Webmaster: Jeneva Stene
  Lunceford
  E-Mail: jlunceford@simmgene.com
Director, Operations: Steve McGuire
  E-Mail: smcguire@simmgene.com
Software Developer: Sheldon Ross
  E-Mail: sross@simmgene.com
Chief Operations Officer and Director, Performance
  Programs: Dr. Wade Shafer PhD
  E-Mail: wshafer@simmgene.com

Historical Note:
ASA strives to effectively represent and serve the interests of its members, maintain credibility of information and integrity of the Simmental and Simbrah breeds. Also provides genetic evaluation, management information and marketing services of the possible quality to Simmental and Simbrah breeders, and develops a business climate designed to provide optimum economic opportunities. Members are breeders of Simmental and Simbrah cattle. Membership: $110 (Adult- plus one-time setup fee of $50 for all new adult members); $50 (Junior); $160 (Household).

Meetings/Conferences:
Conference Chair: Paulette Cochenour

Publications:
ASA weekly eNews newsletter; weekly
Membership Directory; annually
SimTalk; quarterly; adv.
Sire Source
State Association Newsletters
the Register; adv.

American Skin Association *(1987)*
Six E. 43rd St.
28th Floor
New York, NY 10017
Tel: (212) 889-4858 *Fax:* (212) 889-4959
TollFree: (800) 499-7546
E-Mail: info@americanskin.org
Website: americanskin.org
Members: 300 individuals
Staff: 4
Annual Budget: $1-2,000,000
Tax: 501(c)(3)

Personnel:
Managing Director, President and Founder: George W.
  Hambrick Jr.
Coordinator: Ashley R. Jutchenko
Executive Vice President: Kathleen Reichert

Historical Note:
ASA is a not-for-profit association that raises support money for research and educates the public, particularly children, on the prevention and treatment of skin disorders and it's mission is to drive public awareness about skin disease. Membership: $25/year.

Meetings/Conferences: Annual
Conference Chair: Ashley R. Jutchenko

Publications:
SKINFacts; semi-annually

Membership List Available to Non-members

American Sleep Apnea Association *(1990)*
6856 Eastern Ave. NW
Suite 203
Washington, DC 20012-2119
Tel: (202) 293-3650 *Fax:* (202) 293-3656
TollFree: (888) 293-3650
E-Mail: asaa@sleepapnea.org
Website: sleepapnea.org
Members: 3000 individuals and companies
Staff: 2
Annual Budget: $100-250,000
Tax: 501(c)(3)

Personnel:

Executive Director: Edward Grandi
  E-Mail: egrandi@sleepapnea.org
Treasurer: Burton Abrams

Historical Note:
ASAA is dedicated to reducing injury, disability, and death from sleep apnea and to enhancing well-being of those affected by this common disorder. It also encourages education and awareness, A.W.A.K.E. Network of voluntary mutual support groups, research, and continuous improvement in care. Membership: $25 (Member); $50 (Friend/Foreign Member); $100 (Contributor); $250 (Investor); $500 (Patron); $750 (Benefactor); $100 (Sponsor).

Meetings/Conferences: Annual

Publications:
ASAA Newsletter
Online Directory; on-line

American Small Manufacturers' Coalition
P.O. Box 15289
Washington, DC 20003
Tel: (202) 341-7066 *Fax:* (202) 315-3906
E-Mail: carrie.hines@smallmanufacturers.org
Website: smallmanufacturers.org
Members: 500 employees
Staff: 2
Annual Budget: $500-1,000,000
Tax: 501(c)(6)

Personnel:
Executive Director: Carrie Hines
  E-Mail: carrie.hines@smallmanufacturers.org
Director, Marketing and Communications: Kelly Pearl
  E-Mail: kelly.pearl@smallmanufacturers.org

Historical Note:
ASMC advocates for legislative and programmatic resources that allow small manufacturing clients to better compete in the global marketplace.

Meetings/Conferences: Annual

American Society for Adolescent Psychiatry *(1967)*
P.O. Box 570218
Dallas, TX 75357-0218
Tel: (972) 613-0985 *Fax:* (972) 613-5532
E-Mail: ADPSYCH@aol.com
Website: adolpsych.org
Members: 800 individuals
Staff: 3
Annual Budget: $50-100,000
Tax: 501(c)(6)

Personnel:
Executive Director: Frances Roton Bell
  E-Mail: frda1@airmail.net

Historical Note:
ASAP was before a group of New York psychiatrists that formed the Society for Adolescent Psychiatry (1958), thereafter same groups were set up in Philadelphia, Los Angeles and Chicago. ASAP works for the prevention and treatment of mental health disorders of adolescents and young adults and to the provision of optimal health care of patients. Membership: $275 (Regular); $150 (Associate Member); $45 (Members-in-Training).

Continuing Education:
Certification Designation/s: CME

Meetings/Conferences: Annual
2013 - Charleston, SC (Medical University Of South
  Carolina)/March 23 - 24

Publications:
Adolescent Psychiatry
Membership Directory; on-line
Newsletter; quarterly

American Society for Aesthetic Plastic Surgery *(1967)*
11262 Monarch St.
Garden Grove, CA 92841
Tel: (562) 799-2356 *Fax:* (562) 799-1098
TollFree: (800) 364-2147
E-Mail: asaps@surgery.org
Website: surgery.org
Members: 2500 individuals
Staff: 33
Annual Budget: $5-10,000,000
Tax: 501(c)(6)

Personnel:
Executive Director: Sue Dykema CAE
  E-Mail: sue@surgery.org

Director, Public Relations: Adeena Babbitt
  E-Mail: asaps@surgery.org
Director, Finance and Human Resources: Diana Guerrero
Director, Marketing and Public Education: John O'Leary
Webmaster: Lisa Orozco
Manager, Membership: Alicia Potochniak
Program Manager: Marissa Simpson
Director, Education: Debi Toombs

Historical Note:
ASAPS's mission is to advance the science, art, and safe practice of aesthetic plastic surgery among qualified plastic surgeons through support and direction of medical education and research, sponsor scientific meetings and dissemination of information on current aesthetic surgical techniques; to promote ethical conduct and responsible patient care among members; and to serve the public interest by providing accurate and timely information regarding aesthetic plastic surgery and promoting patient safety. Members are specialists in the area of aesthetic plastic surgery certified by the American Board of Plastic Surgery and to advance the medical profession and assure that aesthetic surgery maintains its proper place within the specialty of plastic surgery. Membership: $1089/year.

Continuing Education:
Certification Designation/s: CME

Meetings/Conferences: Annual
Conference Chair: Marissa Simpson
2013 - New York City, NY (Jacob K. Javits Convention
  Center)/April 11 - 16/2600 attendees/over 100
  exhibitors
2014 - San Francisco, CA (Moscone Center)/April 24 -
  29/2600 attendees
2015 - Montreal, QC (Palais Des Congres de
  Montreal)/May 14 - 19/2500 attendees
2016 - Las Vegas, NV (Mandalay Bay Resort &
  Casino)/April 2 - 7
2017 - San Diego, CA (San Diego Convention Center)/
  April 27 - May 1
Number of non-conference events/year: 5

Publications:
Beautiful Choice E-Newsletter; monthly
Aesthetic Surgery Journal; adv.

Membership List Available to Non-members

American Society for Aesthetics *(1942)*
C/O Dabney Townsend, Armstrong Atlantic State
University
P.O. Box 915
Pooler, GA 31322
Tel: (912) 921-2124 *Fax:* (912) 921-5740
E-Mail: asa@aesthetics-online.org
Website: aesthetics-online.org
Members:
1515 institutions, 809 consortia and 500
individuals
500 individuals
809 consortia
Staff: 2
Annual Budget: $500-1,000,000
Tax: 501(c)(3)

Personnel:
President: Paul Guyer
Secretary and Treasurer: Dabney Townsend
  E-Mail: secretary-treasurer@aesthetics-online.org

Historical Note:
Founded to advance the philosophical and scientific understanding of the arts and related fields, ASA promotes study, research, publication, and discussion of aesthetics. "Aesthetics" includes all studies of the arts and related types of experience from a philosophic, scientific, or other theoretical standpoint, including those of psychology, sociology, anthropology, cultural history, art criticism, and education. "The arts" include the visual arts, literature, music, and theater arts. Member of the Council of Learned Societies. Membership: $70 (Regular); $35-124/year.

Meetings/Conferences:
Number of non-conference events/year: 2

Publications:
ASA Newsletter
Journal of Aesthetics and Art Criticism; quarterly
Membership Directory; on-line

American Society for Apheresis *(1982)*
375 W. Fifth Ave.
Suite 201
Vancouver, BC V5Y 1J6
Tel: (604) 484-2851 *Fax:* (604) 874-4378
E-Mail: asfa@apheresis.org
Website: apheresis.org

Members: 1000 individuals
Staff: 6
Annual Budget: $500-1,000,000

Personnel:
Executive Director: Sarah McCarthy MBA, MSc
   E-Mail: sarah@apheresis.org
Meeting Manager: Paul Fogerty
Database Manager: Paul Kool BSc
   E-Mail: paul@apheresis.org
Treasurer: Bruce Sachais MD, PhD
President: Ravi Sarode MD
Editor: Robert Weinstein MD

Historical Note:
ASFA is an organization of physicians, scientists, and allied health professionals whose mission is to lead the field of apheresis through patient and donor care, research, education, and advocacy. Members are health professionals with an interest in the removal and separation of blood components. Membership: $135 (Physician/PhD/Corporate Supplier) ; $110 (Allied Health Professional/Physician).

Meetings/Conferences: Annual
Conference Chair: Paul Fogerty
2013 - Denver, CO (Sheraton Downtown Denver
   Hotel)/May 22 - 25

Publications:
Journal of Clinical Apheresis; bi-monthly
Membership Directory; on-line

American Society for Artificial Internal Organs
(1955)
7700 Congress Ave.
Suite 3107
Boca Raton, FL 33487-1356
Tel: (561) 999-8969 *Fax:* (561) 999-8972
E-Mail: info@asaio.com
Website: asaio.com
Members: 800 individuals
Staff: 2
Annual Budget: $500-1,000,000
Tax: 501(c)(3)

Personnel:
Executive Director: Karen Burke
Editor: Joseph B. Zwischenberger MD
   E-Mail: j.zwische@email.uky.edu

Historical Note:
A Society for physicians, scientists, engineers and entrepreneurs dedicated to the continually evolving field of artificial organs. ASAIO's mission is to increase the knowledge about artificial internal organs and their utilization. Membership: $345-365 (Senior Scientists and Faculty); $50 (Young Innovators, under 35); $100 (Young Innovators, under 40).

Meetings/Conferences: Annual
2013 - Chicago, IL/June 12 - 15

Publications:
ASAIO Journal; bi-monthly; adv.
Member Directory; on-line

American Society for Automation in Pharmacy
(1989)
492 Norristown Rd.
Suite 160
Blue Bell, PA 19422
Tel: (610) 825-7783 *Fax:* (610) 825-7641
E-Mail: will@computertalk.com
Website: asapnet.org
Members: 200 companies and 600 members
Staff: 4
Annual Budget: $250-500,000
Tax: 501(c)(6)

Personnel:
Executive Director: Bill A. Lockwood
   E-Mail: wal@computertalk.com

Historical Note:
ASAP provides a forum for sharing diverse knowledge and perspectives on the modern practice of pharmacy. Members are software solutions providers serving the pharmacy industry. Membership: $495 (Individual); $1,000 (Corporate).

Meetings/Conferences: Semi-Annual
2013 - Kiawah Island, SC (Sanctuary Hotel)/Jan. 24 -
   26
2013 - Louisville, KY (The Brown Hotel)/June 13 - 15
2014 - Amelia Island, FL (Ritz-Carlton, Amelia Island)/
   Jan. 16 - 18
2014 - Palm Beach, FL (Breakers Palm Beach)/June 26
   - 28

Publications:
Member Directory; on-line

American Society for Biochemistry and Molecular Biology *(1906)*
11200 Rockville Pk.
Suite 302
Rockville, MD 20852-3110
Tel: (240) 283-6600 *Fax:* (301) 881-2080
E-Mail: asbmb@asbmb.faseb.org
Website: asbmb.org
Members: 12000 members
Staff: 29
Annual Budget: $10-25,000,000

Personnel:
Executive Director: Barbara A. Gordon
   E-Mail: asbmb@asbmb.org
Director, Public Affairs: Benjamin Corb
   E-Mail: bcorb@asbmb.org
Manager, Meetings: Joan Geiling
   E-Mail: jgeiling@asbmb.org
Contact, Accounting, Membership and Subscription
   Support: Maria Hernandez
   E-Mail: mhernandez@asbmb.org
Director, Marketing: Jessica Homa
   E-Mail: jhoma@asbmb.org
Coordinator, Public Outreach: Geoff Hunt
   E-Mail: ghunt@asbmb.org
System Administrator: Ed Marklin
   E-Mail: emarklin@asbmb.org
Director, Finance: Steve Miller CPA
   E-Mail: smiller@asbmb.org
Director, Publications: Nancy Rodnan
   E-Mail: nrodnan@asbmb.org
Manager, Education and Professional Development: Weiyi
   Zhao MPH
   E-Mail: wzhao@asbmb.org

Historical Note:
Formerly (1987) American Society of Biological Chemists. ASBMB strives to advance the science of biochemistry and molecular biology through publication of scientific and educational journals. Members are scientists who hold doctoral degree or a post doctoral fellow or a student in the field of biochemistry and molecular biology. Membership: $140 (Regular); $70 (Associate); $20 (Undergraduate Student); $45 (Graduate).

Meetings/Conferences: Annual
Conference Chair: Joan Geiling
2013 - Boston, MA (Boston Convention and Exhibition
   Cente)/April 20 - 24/over 100 exhibitors
Number of non-conference events/year: 3

Publications:
ASBMB e-News; monthly
ASBMB Today; monthly
ASBMB Today; monthly; adv.
Membership Directory; on-line
Molecular and Cellular Proteomics(MCP); monthly
The Journal of Biological Chemistry (JBC); weekly; adv.
The Journal of Lipid Research (JLR); monthly; adv.

American Society for Bioethics and Humanities
(1998)
4700 W. Lake Ave.
Glenview, IL 60025-1485
Tel: (847) 375-4745 *Fax:* (847) 375-6482
E-Mail: info@asbh.org
Website: asbh.org
Members: 1515 individuals and organizations
Staff: 4
Annual Budget: $500-1,000,000
Tax: 501(c)(3)

Personnel:
President: Joseph J. Fins MD
Executive Director: Chris Welber MBA
   E-Mail: cwelber@asbh.org
Manager, Operations: Carolyn Burke
   E-Mail: cburke@asbh.org

Historical Note:
Founded through the consolidation of three existing associations in the field: the Society for Health and Human Values (SHHV), the Society for Bioethics Consultation (SBC), and the American Association of Bioethics (AAB). ASBH strives to promote the exchange of ideas and foster multidisciplinary, interdisciplinary, and interprofessional scholarship, research, teaching, policy development, professional development, and collegiality among people engaged in all of the endeavors related to clinical and academic bioethics and the health-related humanities.

Membership: $50-250 (Individual/AStudent); $30 (Full-
time graduate or undergraduate Student); $600 (Affiliate).

Meetings/Conferences: Annual

Publications:
ASBH Reader; biennially; adv.
Core Competencies; adv.
Membership Directory; on-line

American Society for Blood and Marrow Transplantation *(1993)*
85 W. Algonquin Rd.
Suite 550
Arlington Heights, IL 60005-4425
Tel: (847) 427-0224 *Fax:* (847) 427-9656
E-Mail: mail@asbmt.org
Website: asbmt.org
Members: 1600 individuals
Staff: 6
Annual Budget: $2-5,000,000
Tax: 501(c)(3)

Personnel:
Executive Director: Thomas L. Joseph CAE, MPS
   E-Mail: thomasjoseph@asbmt.org
Director, Finance: Sarah Adcock
   E-Mail: sarahadcock@asbmt.org
Director, Information Technology: Jeff Kiva
   E-Mail: jeffkiva@asbmt.org
Editor-in-Chief: Robert Korngold PhD
   E-Mail: rkorngold@humed.com
Director, Membership Services: Jean Lynch CAE, MPS
   E-Mail: jeanlynch@asbmt.org
Director, Membership: James Youkhanis
   E-Mail: jamesyoukhanis@asbmt.org

Historical Note:
ASBMT promotes dissemination of basic and clinical research related to hematopoietic stem cell transplantation and supports clinical guidelines and standards of care for marrow transplant patients. Membership represents cellular therapy and blood and marrow transplantation clinicians and investigators. Membership: $205 (Regular/Associate); $150 (Affiliate); $75 (In-Training); Free (Post-Doctoral Fellows).

Meetings/Conferences: Annual
2013 - Salt Lake City, UT (Salt Palace Convention
   Center)/Feb. 13 - 17/51-100 exhibitors
2014 - Orlando, FL/Feb. 19 - 23
2014 - Dallas, TX/Feb. 26 - March 2
2015 - San Diego, CA/Feb. 11 - 15
2016 - Honolulu, HI/Feb. 18 - 21

Publications:
ASBMT E-News; monthly
Biology of Blood and Marrow Transplantation;
   monthly; adv.
Blood and Marrow Transplantation Reviews; quarterly;
   adv.

Membership List Available to Non-members

American Society for Bone and Mineral Research
(1977)
2025 M St. NW
Suite 800
Washington, DC 20036-3309
Tel: (202) 367-1161 *Fax:* (202) 367-2161
E-Mail: asbmr@asbmr.org
Website: asbmr.org
Members: 4000 individuals
Staff: 20
Annual Budget: $10-25,000,000
Tax: 501(c)(3)

Personnel:
Executive Director: Ann L. Elderkin PA
   E-Mail: aelderkin@asbmr.org
Associate Executive Director: Douglas Fesler
   E-Mail: dfesler@asbmr.org
Director, Marketing and Communications: Amy Goetz
Senior Manager, Convention: Melissa Huston
Director, Development: Deborah Kroll
   E-Mail: dkroll@asbmr.org
Director, Finance: Brenda Malottke

Historical Note:
ASBMR is a society in the field of bone and mineral metabolism that promotes excellence in bone and mineral research, fosters integration of clinical and basic science, and facilitates the translation of that science to health care and clinical practice. Members are physicians and scientists who perform basic and clinical research in the

fields of metabolic bone diseases and mineral metabolism.
Membership: $245 (Full Member); $80 (In-Training).

Meetings/Conferences: Annual
Conference Chair: Melissa Huston
2013 - Baltimore, MD/Oct. 4 - 8
2013 - Baltimore, MD/Oct. 4 - 7/5000 attendees/over
  100 exhibitors
2014 - Houston, TX/Sept. 12 - 15/5000 attendees/over
  100 exhibitors

Publications:
ASBMR e-news; monthly
Journal of Bone and Mineral Research; monthly; adv.
Membership Directory; on-line

American Society for Cell Biology (1960)
8120 Woodmont Ave.
Suite 750
Bethesda, MD 20814-2762
Tel: (301) 347-9300 Fax: (301) 347-9310
E-Mail: ascbinfo@ascb.org
Website: ascb.org
Members: 10000 individuals
Staff: 22
Annual Budget: $10-25,000,000
Tax: 501(c)(3)

Personnel:
Executive Director: Stefano Bertuzzi
Director, Meetings: Trina Armstrong
  E-Mail: tarmstro@ascb.org
Director, Communications and Education: Thea Clarke
  E-Mail: tclarke@ascb.org
Senior Director, Finance and Administration: Cynthia
  Godes
  E-Mail: cgodes@ascb.org
Manager, Membership Services: Katherine Hempel
  E-Mail: khempel@ascb.org
Director, Publications: Mark Leader
  E-Mail: mleader@ascb.org
Executive Assistant: Cheryl Lehr
  E-Mail: clehr@ascb.org
Senior Manager, Minorities Affairs: Deborah McCall
  E-Mail: mac@ascb.org
Director, Information Technology: Michael McCormack
  E-Mail: mmccormack@ascb.org
Director, Exhibits and Sales: Edward Newman
  E-Mail: enewman@ascb.org
Director, Public Policy: Kevin M Wilson
  E-Mail: kwilson@ascb.org

Historical Note:
Incorporated in New York in 1961. ASCB is dedicated to
advance scientific discovery, advocating sound research
policies, improving education, promoting professional
development, and increasing diversity in the scientific
workforce. Membership in the ASCB is open to all
scientists who have education or research experience in cell
biology or an allied field. Membership: $145 (Regular);
$66 (Postdoctoral); $42 (Predoctoral Student); $22
(Undergraduate Student).

Meetings/Conferences: Annual
Conference Chair: Trina Armstrong
2013 - New Orleans, LA/Dec. 14 - 18
2014 - Philadelphia, PA/Dec. 6 - 10
2015 - San Diego, CA/Dec. 12 - 16
Number of non-conference events/year: 8

Publications:
ASCB Newsletter; monthly; adv.
CBE-Life Sciences Education Journal; quarterly; adv.
Membership Directory; on-line
Molecular Biology of the Cell; semi-monthly; adv.

Membership List Available to Non-members

American Society for Clinical Investigation (1908)
15 Research Dr.
Ann Arbor, MI 48103
Tel: (734) 222-6050 Fax: (734) 222-6058
E-Mail: staff@the-asci.org
Website: the-asci.org
Members: 2800 individuals
Staff: 21
Annual Budget: $2-5,000,000
Tax: 501(c)(3)

Personnel:
Executive Director: John Hawley
Editor: Howard A. Rockman
  E-Mail: h.rockman@duke.edu
Secretary and Treasurer: Theodora S. Ross
  E-Mail: theo.ross@utsouthwestern.edu

Historical Note:
Formerly (1908) as the American Society for the
Advancement of Clinical Investigation, assumed current
name in 1916. ASCI's objectives are to advance medical
science, cultivate clinical research through the methods of
natural science, correlate science with the art of medical
practice and encourage scientific spirit among its members.
Five classes of membership active, senior, foreign associate,
emeritus and honorary.

Meetings/Conferences: Annual
2013 - Chicago, IL (Fairmont Chicago Millenium Park)/
  April 26 - 28
2014 - Chicago, IL (Fairmont Chicago Millenium Park)/
  April 25 - 27

Publications:
Journal of Clinical Investigation; monthly

American Society for Clinical Laboratory Science (1933)
6701 Democracy Blvd.
Suite 300
Bethesda, MD 20817-1574
Tel: (301) 657-2768 Fax: (301) 657-2909
E-Mail: ascls@ascls.org
Website: ascls.org
Members: 11000 individuals
Staff: 5
Annual Budget: $1-2,000,000
Tax: 501(c)(6)

Personnel:
Executive Vice President: Elissa Passiment CLS
  E-Mail: elissap@ascls.org
Coordinator, Membership Services: Sherry Miner MLS
  E-Mail: sherrym@ascls.org

Historical Note:
Formerly (1933) the American Society of Clinical
Laboratory Technicians, the American Society of Medical
Technologists (1936), and the American Society for
Medical Technology (1973), assumed its present name
in 1993. ASCLS's mission is to promote all aspects
of clinical laboratory science practice, education and
management in the field of health care. Membership:
$78-99 (Professional); $45 (Collaborative/First Year
Professional); $25 (Student).

Meetings/Conferences: Annual
2013 - Houston, TX/July 28 - Aug. 1/19000 attendees/
  over 100 exhibitors
2013 - Houston, TX/July 30 - Aug. 3
2014 - Chicago, IL/July 27 - 31/19000 attendees/over
  100 exhibitors
2014 - Chicago, IL/July 29 - Aug. 2
2015 - Atlanta, GA/July 26 - 30/19000 attendees/over
  100 exhibitors
2015 - Atlanta, GA/July 28 - Aug. 1
2016 - Philadelphia, PA/July 24 - 28/19000 attendees/
  over 100 exhibitors
2016 - Philadelphia, PA/July 26 - 30
2017 - San Diego, CA/July 30 - Aug. 3/19000
  attendees/over 100 exhibitors
2017 - San Diego, CA/Aug. 1 - 4
2018 - Houston, TX/July 23 - 27/19000 attendees/
  over 100 exhibitors
2018 - Houston, TX/July 24 - 27
2019 - Philadelphia, PA/July 23 - 27
2020 - Chicago, IL/July 28 - Aug. 1
2022 - Anaheim, CA/July 26 - 30
2023 - Philadelphia, PA/July 25 - 29
2024 - Chicago, IL/July 23 - 27
Number of non-conference events/year: 3

Publications:
ASCLS Today; adv.
Clinical Laboratory Science; quarterly; adv.

Membership List Available to Non-members

American Society for Clinical Pathologists (2009)
33 W. Monroe St.
Suite 1600
Chicago, IL 60603
Tel: (312) 541-4999 Fax: (312) 541-4998
TollFree: (800) 267-2727
Website: ascp.org
Members: 130000 pathologists and laboratory
professionals.
Staff: 148
Annual Budget: $25-50,000,000

Personnel:
President: C. Bruce Alexander MD
Treasurer: Kenneth Emancipator MD

Historical Note:
ASCP's mission is to provide excellence in education,
certification and advocacy on behalf of patients,
pathologists and laboratory professionals across the globe.
Membership: $329 (ASCP Fellow); $176 (ASCP Medical
Affilliate).

Meetings/Conferences: Annual

Publications:
American Journal for Clinical Pathology
LabMedicine

American Society for Clinical Pathology (1922)
33 W. Monroe St.
Suite 1600
Chicago, IL 60603
Tel: (312) 541-4999 Fax: (312) 541-4998
TollFree: (800) 267-2727
E-Mail: info@ascp.org
Website: ascp.org
Members: 100,000 individuals
Staff: 137
Annual Budget: $25-50,000,000

Personnel:
Executive Vice President: Blair E. Holladay
Contact, Meetings: Terri Berkowitz
  E-Mail: tberkowitz@connect2amc.com
Manager, Media Relations: Gelasia Croom
  E-Mail: gelasia.croom@ascp.org
Vice President, Human Resources: Jean Marie Marden
  CFP, MA
Manager, Publishing Operations and API: Faye Ramsey
  E-Mail: faye.ramsey@ascp.org
Vice President: Joel M. Shilling MD
Vice President, Membership Services and Communications:
  Nanice Noie Thompson
  E-Mail: nanciet@ascp.org
Vice President, Continuing Professional Development:
  Suzanne Ziemnik MEd
  E-Mail: suzanne.ziemnik@ascp.org

Historical Note:
Formerly (1922) American Society of Clinical Pathologists;
assumed its current name in 2002. ASCP's mission
is to provide education, certification, and advocacy
on behalf of patients, pathologists, and laboratory
professionals. Members are pathologists, doctoral-
level laboratory scientists, and laboratory professionals,
including pathologists' assistants, medical technologists,
cytotechnologists, histotechnologists, histologic technicians,
phlebotomists, medical laboratory technicians, and
numerous laboratory specialists. Membership: $329
(Pathologist-Fellow); $89 (Laboratory Professionals/
Pathologist's Assistants/Clinical Scientists); $176 (Medical
Affiliate); $100 (International Physician and International
Medical Affiliate); $65 (International- Laboratory
Professional/Clinical Scientist); Free (Student/Resident).

Continuing Education:
Certification Designation/s: AT, BB, HT, BOC, CME, CMP,
MOC, PBT, DPT, HTL, MLT, MP, CT, ASCPi

Meetings/Conferences: Annual
Conference Chair: Suzanne Ziemnik MEd

Publications:
American Journal of Clinical Pathology (AJCP)
BOC Newsletter
Critical Values; quarterly
Daily Diagnosis; daily
eNewsBriefs; on-line
ePolicy News; on-line
Laboratory Medicine (LABMEDICINE)

American Society for Clinical Pharmacology and Therapeutics (1900)
528 N. Washington St.
Alexandria, VA 22314
Tel: (703) 836-6981 Fax: (703) 836-5223
E-Mail: info@ascpt.org
Website: ascpt.org
Members: 2300 individuals
Staff: 5
Annual Budget: $2-5,000,000
Tax: 501(c)(3)

Personnel:
Chief Executive Officer: Sharon J. Swan CAE
  E-Mail: sharon@ascpt.org
Director, Publications and Managing Editor: Elise
  Laffman-Johnson
  E-Mail: elise@ascpt.org
Senior Education Manager: Dianne Lee
  E-Mail: dianne@ascpt.org

Director, Membership Services: Ginny Stengel
E-Mail: ginny@ascpt.org

Historical Note:
Founded as the American Therapeutic Society, merged in 1969 with the American College of Clinical Pharmacology and Chemotherapy (1963) and was incorporated in the District of Columbia under its present name. ASCPT's mission is to provide forum for the exchange, development, and integration of translational science into the drug development continuum from discovery to safe and effective medication use. Members work in the field of clinical pharmacology. Membership: $405-440 (Full Members); $55-88(Trainee/Student Members); $560-595(Dual Members).

Meetings/Conferences: Annual
2013 - Indianapolis, IN (JW Marriott Indianapolis)/ March 6 - 9
2014 - Atlanta, GA (Atlanta Marriott Marquis)/March 19 - 22
2015 - New Orleans, LA (Hyatt Regency Austin)/March 4 - 7
2016 - San Diego, CA (The Bayfront Hilton)/March 9 - 12

Publications:
ASCPT Update; on-line
Clinical Pharmacology and Therapeutics (CPT); adv.
Member Directory; on-line

Membership List Available to Non-members

American Society for Colposcopy and Cervical Pathology *(1964)*
152 W. Washington St.
Hagerstown, MD 21740
Tel: (301) 733-3640 *Fax:* (301) 733-5775
TollFree: (800) 787-7227
Website: asccp.org
Members: 3800 individuals
Staff: 5
Annual Budget: $2-5,000,000
Tax: 501(c)(3)

Personnel:
Executive Director: Kerry Curtis
E-Mail: kcurtis@asccp.org
Director, Education: Cindy DeSirant
E-Mail: cdesirant@asccp.org
Coordinator, Membership Services: Amy Mason
E-Mail: amason@asccp.org
Coordinator, Technology and Training: Debbie McClain
E-Mail: dmcclain@asccp.org
Director, Administration: Ann Powell
E-Mail: apowell@asccp.org

Historical Note:
Founded as the American Society for Colposcopy and Colpomicroscopy. ASCCP's mission is to improve clinician competence and performance and patient outcomes through educational activities focused around the study, prevention, diagnosis, and management of lower genital tract disorders. Members are gynecologists, pathologists, family physicians and others interested in promoting the study of female lower genital tract disease. Membership: $200 (Active); $35 (Resident).

Meetings/Conferences: Biennial
Number of non-conference events/year: 8

Publications:
The Journal of Lower Genital Tract Disease; quarterly

American Society for Cytotechnology *(1979)*
1500 Sunday Dr.
Suite 102
Raleigh, NC 27607
Tel: (919) 861-5571 *Fax:* (919) 787-4916
TollFree: (800) 948-3947
E-Mail: info@asct.com
Website: asct.com
Members: 1800 individuals
Staff: 2
Annual Budget: $100-250,000

Personnel:
Executive Director: Beth Denny
E-Mail: bdenny@asct.com
Coordinator, Membership Services: Verena Rojas
E-Mail: vrojas@asct.com

Historical Note:
ASCT is committed to define and advocate cytotechnology by monitoring and evaluating legislative/regulatory issues and emerging technologies affecting the profession. Membership: $50 (General/Associate); $20 (Student); $30 (Retired).

Meetings/Conferences: Annual
Conference Chair: Beth Denny
2013 - Scottsdale, AZ (Hotel Valley Ho)/April 19 - 21
2014 - Charleston, SC (Charleston Marriott)/April 25 - 27

Publications:
E-Newsletter; on-line; adv.
Membership Directory; on-line

American Society for Dental Aesthetics *(1976)*
635 Madison Ave.
New York, NY 10022
Tel: (212) 751-3263 *Fax:* (212) 755-3263
TollFree: (800) 454-2732
E-Mail: info@asdatoday.com
Website: asdatoday.com
Members: 160 individuals
Staff: 4
Annual Budget: $100-250,000

Personnel:
Executive Vice President: Marvin A. Fier DDS
Chairman, Continuing Education: Paul Belvedere DDS
Director, Conferences: Howard S. Glazer DDS
Editor: Daniel H. Ward DDS

Historical Note:
ASDA is dedicated to improving the cosmetic dentistry field for patients and doctors and provides education seminars featuring aesthetic dentistry courses teaching the latest advancements in the industry. Members are dentists who have demonstrated excellence in an area of aesthetic dentistry. Membership: $200/year.

Continuing Education:
Certification Designation/s: PACE

Meetings/Conferences: Annual
Conference Chair: Howard S. Glazer DDS

Publications:
ASDA Today Journal; on-line

Membership List Available to Non-members

American Society for Dermatologic Surgery *(1970)*
5550 Meadowbrook Dr.
Suite 120
Rolling Meadows, IL 60008
Tel: (847) 956-0900 *Fax:* (847) 956-0999
Website: asds.net
Members: 5400 individuals
Staff: 17
Annual Budget: $5-10,000,000
Tax: 501(c)(3)

Personnel:
Executive Director: Katherine J. Duerdoth CAE
E-Mail: kduerdoth@asds.net
Director, Finance: William M. Brady CPA
E-Mail: bbrady@asds.net
Associate Executive Director: Debra Kennedy
E-Mail: dkennedy@asds.net
Director, Public Relations, Communications and Marketing: Jolene Kremer
E-Mail: jkremer@asds.net
Director, Education, Meetings and Research: Kim Santaniello
E-Mail: ksantaniello@asds.net

Historical Note:
Founded in 1970 as the American Society for Dermatologic Surgery (ASDS). ASDS was established to preserve and enhance the use of surgical modalities in the practice of dermatology. Mission is to foster, augment, develop and encourage investigative knowledge in Dermatologic Surgery, to maintain standards in clinical practice, continuing education and research in Dermatologic Surgery, to promote quality patient care and public interest relating to Dermatologic Surgery and to provide a forum for the exchange of ideas and methodology for Dermatologic Surgery and related basic sciences. Membership: $400 (Fellow/Corresponding Fellow/Associate/Osteopathic Affiliate); $35 (Fellows in Training Programs) with an application fee $95.

Continuing Education:
Certification Designation/s: CME

Meetings/Conferences: Annual
Conference Chair: Kim Santaniello
2013 - Chicago, IL (Hyatt Regency)/Oct. 3 - 6
2014 - San Diego, CA (Manchester Grand)/Nov. 6 - 9
2015 - Chicago, IL (Hyatt Regency Chicago)/Oct. 15 - 18
2016 - New Orleans, LA (Hyatt Regency New Orleans)/ Nov. 10 - 13

2017 - Chicago, IL (Hyatt Regency Chicago)/Oct. 5 - 7
Number of non-conference events/year: 1

Publications:
Currents-Newsletter
Dermatologic Surgery Journal

American Society for Eighteenth-Century Studies *(1969)*
C/O Wake Forest University
P.O. Box 7867
Winston-Salem, NC 27109
Tel: (336) 727-4694 *Fax:* (336) 727-4697
E-Mail: asecs@wfu.edu
Website: asecs.press.jhu.edu
Members: 3000 individuals
Staff: 2
Annual Budget: $250-500,000
Tax: 501(c)(3)

Personnel:
Executive Director: Byron R. Wells
E-Mail: asecs@wfu.edu

Historical Note:
ASECS's mission is to advance the study and research in the history from the later seventeenth through the early nineteenth century. Members are academics and others interested in the cultural history of the eighteenth century. Membership: $50-75 (Individual, based on income); $50 (Emeriti); $30 (Student); $85 (Joint); $100 (Sponsor); $125 (Joint Sponsor); $150 (Patron/Institutional); $175 (Joint Patron); $2500 (Lifetime Patron); $3000 (Joint Lifetime Patron).

Meetings/Conferences: Annual
2013 - Cleaveland, OH (Renaissance Cleveland Hotel)/ April 4 - 7
2014 - Williamsburg, VA (Colonial William Lodge)/ March 18 - 23
2015 - Los Angeles, CA (Webb Schools)/March 17 - 22
2016 - Pittsburgh, PA/March 29 - April 3

Publications:
ASECS News Circular; quarterly; adv.
Eighteenth-Century Studies; quarterly; adv.
Membership Directory; on-line
Studies in Eighteenth-Century Culture; annually

Membership List Available to Non-members

American Society for Engineering Education *(1893)*
1818 N St. NW
Suite 600
Washington, DC 20036-2479
Tel: (202) 331-3500 *Fax:* (202) 265-8504
E-Mail: aseexec@asee.org
Website: asee.org
Members: 13550 institutions and individuals
Staff: 50
Annual Budget: $50-100,000,000
Tax: 501(c)(3)

Personnel:
Executive Director: Dr. Norman Fortenberry ScD
E-Mail: n.fortenberry@asee.org
Deputy Executive Director: Robert H. Black
Director, Human Resources: Peggy Dolet
E-Mail: p.dolet@asee.org
Director, Conferences: Patricia Greenawalt
E-Mail: p.greenawalt@asee.org
Senior Program Manager: Artis Hicks
E-Mail: a.hicks@asee.org
Director, Communications: Nathan Kahl
Director, External Affairs: William Kelly
E-Mail: w.kelly@asee.org
Director, Editor: Mark Matthews
Director, Information Technology: Keith Mounts
E-Mail: k.mounts@asee.org
Chief Financial Officer: Sae Park
Director, Membership Services and Retention: Dwight Wardell
E-Mail: d.wardell@asee.org
Director, Corporate Marketing: Scott Williamson
E-Mail: s.williamson@asee.org
Director, Administration: Sandra Wingate-Bey

Historical Note:
Originated as the Society for the Promotion of Engineering Education. ASEE is committed to furthering education in engineering and engineering technology. Their mission is accomplished by promoting excellence in instruction, research, public service, and practice. Membership: $0-1200/year.

Continuing Education:
Certification Designation/s: HTCFP, NREIP, SMART, NRL PFP, NSF GRFP, NDSEG, SEAP, AF SFFP, ONR, S and EF, SLP, SFR

Meetings/Conferences: Annual
Conference Chair: Patricia Greenawalt
2013 - Atlanta, GA/June 23 - 26
2013 - Atlanta, GA (Georgia World Congress Center)/June 23 - 26/4000 attendees/over 100 exhibitors
2014 - Indianapolis, IN/June 15 - 18
2015 - Seattle, WA/June 14 - 17
2016 - New Orleans, LA/June 26 - 29
2017 - Columbus, OH/June 25 - 28
2018 - Salt Lake City, UT/June 24 - 25
2019 - Tampa, FL/June 16 - 19
2020 - Montreal, QC/June 21 - 24
Number of non-conference events/year: 9

Publications:
Advances of Engineering Education
ASEE Action; monthly
ASEE Connections Newsletter; monthly; adv.
Capitol Shorts; weekly
Chemical Engineering Education Journal; quarterly
Computers in Education Journal; quarterly
Connections; monthly; adv.
eGFI; on-line; adv.
Engineering Design Graphics Journal; on-line
First Bell; daily
Journal of Engineering Education; quarterly
Journal of Engineering Technology; bi-annually
PRISM Magazine; monthly; adv.
The Engineering Economist

American Society for Engineering Management
(1979)
1420 Austin Bluffs Pkwy.
Colorado Springs, CO 80918
Tel: (719) 255-8227
TollFree: (800) 990-8227
Website: asem.org
Members: 800 individuals
Staff: 2
Annual Budget: $100-250,000
Tax: 501(c)(6)

Personnel:
Executive Director: Dr. William Daughton
  E-Mail: daughton@mst.edu

Historical Note:
ASEM's mission is to provide engineering management solutions to leadership and management challenges to create and lead technical organizations and also promote the development and practice of the engineering management profession. Membership: $90 (Regular); $45 (Graduate Student); $20 (Undergraduate Students).

Continuing Education:
Certification Designation/s: EMPC, GPC, CKPP

Meetings/Conferences: Annual
Conference Chair: Dr. Rafael E. Landaeta
Number of non-conference events/year: 1

Publications:
Engineering Management Journal; adv.
Practice Periodical; adv.

American Society for Enology and Viticulture
(1950)
P.O. Box 1855
Davis, CA 95617-1855
Tel: (530) 753-3142 *Fax:* (530) 753-3318
E-Mail: society@asev.org
Website: asev.org
Members: 2500 members and Industrial Affiliates
Staff: 8
Annual Budget: $1-2,000,000
Tax: 501(c)(6)

Personnel:
Executive Director: Lyndie Boulton
Coordinator, Events and Tradeshows: Stephanie Bree
Administrative Assistant: Barbara Johns
Managing Editor: Judith McKibben

Historical Note:
Formerly (1984) the American Society of Enologists. ASEV's mission is to promote industry vitality through the exchange of information and the support of research and education. Membership: $170-305 (Full); $40-45 (Student); $600-730 (Industrial Affiliation).

Meetings/Conferences: Annual
Conference Chair: Stephanie Bree

2013 - Monterey, CA (Portola Hotel and Spa)/June 24 - 28
2014 - Austin, TX (Hyatt Regency Austin)/June 23 - 27

Publications:
American Journal of Enology and Viticulture; quarterly; adv.
ASEV Newsletter; adv.
Membership Directory; on-line
Technical Update

American Society for Environmental History
(1977)
C/O UW Interdisciplinary Arts and Sciences Program, University of Washington
P.O. Box 358436, 1900 Commerce St.
Tacoma, WA 98402-3100
E-Mail: director@aseh.net
Website: aseh.net
Members: 1200 individuals
Staff: 2
Annual Budget: $100-250,000

Personnel:
Executive Director: Lisa Mighetto
  E-Mail: director@aseh.net

Historical Note:
ASEH seeks to promote scholarship and teaching in environmental history, to support the professional needs of its members, and to connect its undertakings with larger communities. Works to foster dialogue between humanistic scholarship, environmental science, and other disciplines, and to support global environmental history efforts that benefit the public as well as the general scholarly community. Members are teachers and researchers with an interest in human ecology and environmental history. Membership: $65 (Basic Individual); $98 (Dual Household Member); $30 (Student); $100 (Supporting).

Meetings/Conferences: Annual
2013 - Toronto, ON (Fairmont Royal York Hotel)/April 3 - 6
2014 - San Francisco, CA/March 12 - 16
Number of non-conference events/year: 1

Publications:
ASEH News; quarterly
Environmental History; adv.

American Society for Ethnohistory *(1954)*
Duke University Press, Journals Fulfillment
P.O. Box 90660
Durham, NC 27708-0660
E-Mail: ase@indiana.edu
Website: ethnohistory.org
Members:
500 active members
700 institutions
Staff: 3
Annual Budget: $25-50,000

Personnel:
Secretary: Larry Nesper
  E-Mail: lnesper@wisc.edu

Historical Note:
Formerly American Indian Ethnohistoric Conference, ASE works to encourage the study of ethnohistory. Members are anthropologists, historians, art historians, geographers and other professionals interested in the research of the cultural history of non- industrial peoples. Has no paid officers or full-time staff. Membership: $50 (regular); $99 (Institution); $25 (Student/Retired); $700 (Life Time).

Continuing Education:
Certification Designation/s: EGCP

Meetings/Conferences: Annual
2013 - New Orleans, LA/Sept. 11 - 14

Publications:
Ethnohistory Quarterly; quarterly

Membership List Available to Non-members

American Society for Experimental NeuroTherapeutics *(1997)*
342 N. Main St.
W. Hartford, CT 06117
Tel: (860) 586-7570 *Fax:* (860) 586-7550
E-Mail: info@asent.org
Website: asent.org
Members: 275 individuals
Staff: 3
Annual Budget: $250-500,000

Personnel:
Executive Director: M. Suzanne C. Berry CAE, MBA

  E-Mail: sberry@asent.org
Treasurer: Robin A. Elliott MA
Secretary: Jacqueline A. French MD
  E-Mail: jacqueline.french@nyumc.org

Historical Note:
Organized by a consortium of leaders in academia, government, advocacy and the neurotherapeutic industry. ASENT's mission is to encourage and advance the development of improved therapies for diseases and disorders of the nervous system. Membership: $50-5,000/year.

Meetings/Conferences: Annual
Conference Chair: Jacqueline A. French MD
2013 - Bethesda, MD (Hyatt Regency Bethesda)/Feb. 28 - March 2

Publications:
Membership Directory; on-line
Neurotherapeutics Journal; quarterly

American Society for Gastrointestinal Endoscopy
(1941)
1520 Kensington Rd
Suite 202
Oak Brook, IL 60523
Tel: (630) 573-0600 *Fax:* (630) 573-0691
TollFree: (866) 353-2743
E-Mail: info@asge.org
Website: asge.org
Members: 12,000 members
Staff: 35
Annual Budget: $25-50,000,000
Tax: 501(c)(3)

Personnel:
Executive Director: Patricia Blake CAE
  E-Mail: pblake@asge.org
Manager, Education and Training: Marilyn Amador
  E-Mail: mamador@asge.org
Chief Operating Officer: Barbara Connell
  E-Mail: bconnell@asge.org
Director, Marketing: Therese Gray
  E-Mail: tgray@asge.org
Chief Financial Officer: Sam Haroz
  E-Mail: sharoz@asge.org
Manager, Accounting: Theresa Herrejon
  E-Mail: therrejon@asge.org
Director, Meeting Services: Vanessa Kizart
  E-Mail: vkizart@asge.org
Chief Communications Officer: Jennifer Michalek
  E-Mail: jmichalek@asge.org
Director, Membership Services: Jacqualine Price Osafo
  E-Mail: jpriceosafo@asge.org
Senior Director, Innovation and Human Capital: Larry Robertson
  E-Mail: lobertson@asge.org
Director, Marketing: Tamasha Williams
  E-Mail: twilliams@asge.org

Historical Note:
Formerly American Gastropic Club. ASGE's mission is to advance patient care and digestive health by promoting excellence and innovation in endoscopy. Membership: $290 (International/Group); $45 (Trainee); $25 (Associate/Special Interest Groups); $100-125 (Affiliate); 390 (Regular/Individual).

Meetings/Conferences:
Conference Chair: Vanessa Kizart

Publications:
ASGE Leading Edge; on-line
ASGE News; bi-monthly; adv.
Clinical Update; quarterly
GIE; monthly
Scope; monthly; adv.

American Society for Healthcare Engineering
(1962)
155 N. Wacker Dr.
Suite 400
Chicago, IL 60606
Tel: (312) 422-3800 *Fax:* (312) 422-4571
E-Mail: ashe@aha.org
Website: ashe.org
Members: 9000 individuals
Staff: 19
Annual Budget: $5-10,000,000

Personnel:
Executive Director: Dale Woodin CHFM, FASHE
  E-Mail: dwoodin@aha.org

Manager, Conferences and Seminars: Ilse Almanza CEM, CMP
  E-Mail: ialmanza@aha.org
Director, Business Development: Patrick J. Andrus MBA
  E-Mail: pandrus@aha.org
Director, Administration and Governance: Sharon Autrey CAP, CPS
  E-Mail: sautrey@aha.org
Senior Development Editor: Pamela James Blumgart
  E-Mail: pblumgart@aha.org
Financial Analyst: Chiquita Hodges
  E-Mail: chodges@aha.org
Senior Specialist, Membership Services: Charmaine Osborne
  E-Mail: cosborne@aha.org
Senior Specialist, Marketing and Communications: Susan Rubin MPH
  E-Mail: srubin@aha.org

Historical Note:
Formerly (1995) American Society for Hospital Engineering. For more than 50 years, the American Society for Healthcare Engineering (ASHE) of the American Hospital Association (AHA) has been the advocate and resource for continuous improvement in healthcare engineering and facilities management. ASHE is dedicated to optimize the healthcare physical environment. Membership: $175 (Associate); $25 (Educator/Student); $125 (Professional Active).

Continuing Education:
Certification Designation/s: CMRP, CPHRM, CHESP, CHFM, CHC

Meetings/Conferences: Annual
Conference Chair: Ilse Almanza CEM, CMP
2013 - Atlanta, GA/July 21 - 24/1-10 exhibitors
2014 - Chicago, IL/Aug. 3 - 6/1-10 exhibitors
2015 - Boston, MA/July 12 - 15/1-10 exhibitors
2016 - Denver, CO/July 10 - 13/1-10 exhibitors
Number of non-conference events/year: 1

Publications:
Advocacy Update and Special Alerts; monthly
ASHE e-News; weekly
ASHE Insider E-Newsletter; weekly
Building Health Newsletter; weekly
Career Flash; weekly
Health Facilities Management Magazine
Inside ASHE; bi-monthly
Membership Directory; on-line

American Society for Healthcare Environmental Services *(1986)*
155 N. Wacker
Suite 400
Chicago, IL 60606
Tel: (312) 422-3860 *Fax:* (312) 422-4578
E-Mail: ahe@aha.org
Website: ahe.org
Members: 2340 individuals
Staff: 5
Annual Budget: $500-1,000,000

Personnel:
Executive Director: Patti Costello
  E-Mail: pcostello@aha.org
Coordinator, Governance and Operations: Megan Burnette
Specialist, Membership and Chapter Relations: Marthe Lyngås Forster
Manager, Education: Sandra Rials MS
Coordinator, Marketing and Communications: Carrie Witt

Historical Note:
ASHES represents, defines, and advances the healthcare environmental services profession and mission is to be recognized globally on the healthcare environment. Membership: $115 (Professional Active/Transitional); $165 (Associate/Corporate Member).

Continuing Education:
Certification Designation/s: CHESP

Meetings/Conferences: Annual
Number of non-conference events/year: 1

Publications:
ASHES E-News; monthly; adv.
Membership Directory; on-line; adv.
The Phoenix Newsletter; quarterly; adv.

Membership List Available to Non-members

American Society for Healthcare Food Service Administrators
455 S. Four St.

Suite 650
Louisville, KY 40202
Website: ashfsa.org
Staff: 1
Annual Budget: $500-1,000,000

Personnel:
Director, Communication and Chapters: Maria Chapman
  E-Mail: mchapman@healthcarefoodservice.com

American Society for Healthcare Human Resources Administration *(1964)*
155 N. Wacker Dr.
Suite 400
Chicago, IL 60606
Tel: (312) 422-3720 *Fax:* (312) 422-4577
E-Mail: ashhra@aha.org
Website: ashhra.org
Members: 3350 individuals
Staff: 7
Annual Budget: $1-2,000,000

Personnel:
Executive Director: Stephanie H. Drake MBA
  E-Mail: sdrake@aha.org
Associate Executive Director: Sharon Allen MBA
  E-Mail: sallen@aha.org
Senior Governance Specialist: Shirley Armistead
  E-Mail: sarmistead@aha.org
Marketing Specialist: Ferdinand Libunao
  E-Mail: flibunao@aha.org
Senior Specialist, Education: Jamie Macander
  E-Mail: jmacander@aha.org
Specialist, Human Resources and Membership: Ursula Pawlowski
Manager, Communications: Marie-Clare Prisco
  E-Mail: mprisco@aha.org

Historical Note:
Formerly (1975) American Society for Hospital Personnel Directors. ASHHRA's mission is to serve its members to become effective, valued, and credible leaders in health care human resources administration. ASHHRA provides support through research, ongoing learning and development, products and resources, and opportunities for networking and collaboration. Membership: $160 (Practitioner); $210(Consultant); $50 (Student/Retired); $750-1,250 (Corporate).

Meetings/Conferences: Annual
Conference Chair: Ferdinand Libunao

Publications:
ASHHRA & IFD Hot Topics in Diversity eNews Brief; bi-weekly
ASHHRA eNews Brief; monthly; adv.
ASHHRA Weekly; weekly
HR Pulse; quarterly; adv.
Membership Directory; annually; adv.

American Society for Healthcare Risk Management *(1980)*
155 N. Wacker Dr.
Suite 400
Chicago, IL 60606
Tel: (312) 422-3980 *Fax:* (312) 422-4580
E-Mail: ashrm@aha.org
Website: ashrm.org
Members: 5400 individuals
Staff: 8
Annual Budget: $1-2,000,000

Personnel:
Executive Director: Kimberly Hoarle CAE, MBA
  E-Mail: khoarle@aha.org
Specialist, Membership Relations and Marketing: Rena Barron
  E-Mail: rbarron@aha.org
Manager, Education: Kelley Chrouser MA, PhD
  E-Mail: kchrouser@aha.org
Senior Planner, Meetings: Sara Giannoulias CMP
  E-Mail: sgiannoulias@aha.org
Manager, Marketing and Communications: Mary LaRusso
  E-Mail: mlarusso@aha.org
Writer and Editor: Kathleen Misovic
  E-Mail: kmisovic@aha.org

Historical Note:
Formerly (1987) American Society for Hospital Risk Management. ASHRM strives to advance safe and trusted patient-centered health care delivery. Members are hospital employees involved in risk management, insurance personnel, hospital administrators, attorneys, physicians and healthcare management consultants. Membership: $149 (Regular); $89 (Student/Retired).

Continuing Education:
Certification Designation/s: FASHRM, CPHRM, DFASHRM

Meetings/Conferences: Annual
Conference Chair: Sara Giannoulias CMP
Number of non-conference events/year: 8

Publications:
eNews; weekly
Forum Newsletter; on-line
Journal of Healthcare Risk Management; quarterly; adv.
Membership Directory; on-line

American Society for Histocompatibility and Immunogenetics *(1972)*
15000 Commerce Pkwy.
Suite C
Mt. Laurel, NJ 08054
Tel: (856) 638-0428 *Fax:* (856) 439-0525
E-Mail: info@ashi-hla.org
Website: ashi-hla.org
Members: 1150 individuals
Staff: 8
Annual Budget: $2-5,000,000

Personnel:
Executive Director: Kathy Miranda
  E-Mail: kmiranda@ahint.com
Coordinator, Membership Services: Cecilia Blair
  E-Mail: cblair@ahint.com
Director, Meetings and Exhibits: Clare MacNab
  E-Mail: cmacnab@ahint.com
Director, Finance: Maggie Ramirez
  E-Mail: mramirez@ahint.com
Managing Editor: Frank Scussa
  E-Mail: fscussa@ahint.com
Manager, Meetings: Nadege Toth
  E-Mail: ntoth@ahint.com
Manager, Accreditation: Melissa (McElroy) Weeks
  E-Mail: melissa@cmehelp.com

Historical Note:
Formerly until 1984 known as the American Association for Clinical Histocompatibility Testing. ASHI's mission is to advance the science, education and application of immunogenetics and transplant immunology. Members are clinical and research professionals including immunologists, geneticists, molecular biologists, transplant physicians and surgeons, pathologists and technologists. Membership: $40-126/year.

Continuing Education:
Certification Designation/s: ABHI

Meetings/Conferences: Annual
Conference Chair: Clare MacNab
2013 - Chicago, IL (Sheraton Chicago Hotel and Towers)/Nov. 18 - 22
2014 - Denver, CO (Sheraton Denver Downtown Hotel)/Oct. 20 - 24
Number of non-conference events/year: 2

Publications:
ASHI Quarterly; quarterly; adv.
Human Immunology; monthly
Membership Directory; semi-annually

American Society for Horticultural Science *(1903)*
1018 Duke St.
Alexandria, VA 22314
Tel: (703) 836-4606 *Fax:* (703) 836-2024
E-Mail: ashs@ashs.org
Website: ashs.org
Members: 4000 individuals
Staff: 11
Annual Budget: $2-5,000,000
Tax: 501(c)(3)

Personnel:
Executive Director: Michael W. Neff
  E-Mail: mwneff@ashs.org
Certified Professional Horticulturist (CPH) Program Coordinator and Production Assistant: Natasha Clark
  E-Mail: nclark@ashs.org
Managing Editor, Publications: Ruth Gaumond
  E-Mail: rgaumond@ashs.org
Director, Membership and Contact, Institutional Subscriptions: Fatema Gharzai
  E-Mail: fgharzai@ashs.org
Coordinator, Meetings and Conferences: Elizabeth Hernandez
  E-Mail: ehernandez@ashs.org
Administrative Assistant and Receptionist: Allison Uhlir
  E-Mail: auhlir@ashs.org

Historical Note:
ASHS strives to promote and encourage national and international interest in scientific research and education in all branches of horticulture production, marketing, processing, and utilization of fruits, nuts, vegetables, flowers, ornamental and landscape plants. Membership: $20-115/year.

Continuing Education:
Certification Designation/s: CPH

Meetings/Conferences: Annual
Conference Chair: Elizabeth Hernandez
2013 - Palm Desert, CA (JW Marriott Desert Springs Resort and Spa)/July 22 - 25
2014 - Orlando, FL (Rosen Plaza Hotel)/July 28 - 31
Number of non-conference events/year: 2

Publications:
ASHS Membership Directory; on-line
ASHS Newsletter; monthly; adv.
HortScience; monthly; adv.
HortTechnology; quarterly; adv.
Journal of the American Society for Horticultural Science; bi-monthly; adv.

American Society for Indexing (1968)
10200 W. 44th Ave.
Suite 304
Wheat Ridge, CO 80033
Tel: (303) 463-2887 Fax: (303) 422-8894
E-Mail: info@asindexing.org
Website: asindexing.org
Members: 900 individuals
Staff: 7
Annual Budget: $100-250,000
Tax: 501(c)(6)

Personnel:
Executive Director: David Stumph
    E-Mail: dstumph@asindexing.org
Account Manager: Thomas Farquhar
    E-Mail: tfarquhar@asindexing.org
Director, Membership Services: Kristi Klinke
    E-Mail: kklinke@asindexing.org
Key Words Editor: Judith Reveal
    E-Mail: keywords@asindexing.org
Manager, Information Technology: Ruth Gleason Roth
    E-Mail: rgleason@resourcecenter.com

Historical Note:
ASI works to advocate excellence in indexing and provides information, guidance and aid to indexers. Members include freelance and salaried indexers, abstracters, librarians, editors, publishers and organizations employing indexers. Membership: $150 (Individual); $130 (Retired); $500-1000 (Organization).

Meetings/Conferences: Annual
2013 - San Antonio, TX (Hotel Contessa)/April 17 - 19
2014 - North Charleston, SC (Charleston Convention Center)/April 30 - May 3

Publications:
Member Directory; on-line

Membership List Available to Non-members

American Society for Information Science and Technology (1937)
1320 Fenwick Ln.
Suite 510
Silver Spring, MD 20910
Tel: (301) 495-0900 Fax: (301) 495-0810
E-Mail: asis@asis.org
Website: asis.org
Members: 4000 individuals
Staff: 7
Annual Budget: $1-2,000,000
Tax: 501(c)(3)

Personnel:
Executive Director: Richard B Hill
    E-Mail: rhill@asis.org
Manager, Membership Services: Vanessa O Foss
    E-Mail: vfoss@asis.org
Treasurer: Vicki L Gregory
Director, Finance and Administration: Janice Hatzakos
    E-Mail: jan@asis.org
Accounting Assistant: Carline Haynes
    E-Mail: chaynes@asis.org
Office Assistant: Sandra Holder
    E-Mail: sholder@asis.org
Editor: Irene Travis
    E-Mail: bulletin@asis.org

Historical Note:

Founded in Washington, DC in 1937 as the American Documentation Institute and incorporated in Delaware the same year. Became the American Society for Information Science in 1968, and assumed its current name in 2000. ASIS&T promotes the creation and application of knowledge concerning information and its transfer. Mission is to advance the information sciences and related applications of information technology by providing focus, opportunity, and support to information professionals and organizations. Aims to increase public awareness of the information sciences and technologies and their benefits to society. Membership: $140 (Regular); $650 (Institutional Affiliate); $800 (Corporate Patron); $40 (Student); $70 (Retired).

Meetings/Conferences: Annual
Conference Chair: Vanessa O Foss
2013 - Montreal, QC (Le Centre Sheraton Montreal Hotel)/Nov. 1 - 6
Number of non-conference events/year: 1

Publications:
Bulletin of the American Society for Information Science and Technology; bi-monthly
Journal of the American Society for Information Science and Technology (JASIST)
Membership Directory; on-line

Membership List Available to Non-members

American Society for Investigative Pathology (1900)
9650 Rockville Pike
Suite E133
Bethesda, MD 20814-3993
Tel: (301) 634-7130 Fax: (301) 634-7990
E-Mail: asip@asip.org
Website: asip.org
Members: 2000 individuals
Staff: 28
Annual Budget: $5-10,000,000
Tax: 501(c)(3)

Personnel:
Executive Officer: Mark E. Sobel MD, PhD
    E-Mail: MESobel@asip.org
Manager, Membership: Ann Marie Bocus
    E-Mail: AMBocus@asip.org
Managing Editor: Audra E. Cox ELS, PhD
    E-Mail: ACox@asip.org
Chief Financial Officer: James S. Douglas CPA
    E-Mail: JDouglas@asip.org
Director, Scientific Affairs, Communications and Society Services: Priscilla S. Markwood CAE
    E-Mail: pmarkwood@asip.org
Educational Services Manager: Lisa McFadden
    E-Mail: lmcfadden@asip.org
Director, Marketing and Development: Laurie S. Menser
    E-Mail: lmenser@asip.org
Senior Director, Meetings and Society Services: Tara A. Snethen CAE, CMP
    E-Mail: tsnethen@asip.org
Administrative Assistant: Stacey Taylor
    E-Mail: STaylor@asip.org
Web Developer and Graphic Designer: Chris J. Wallington
    E-Mail: cwallington@asip.org
Accountant: Jody Zung
    E-Mail: jzung@asip.org

Historical Note:
Formed on July 1, 1976 by a merger of the American Society for Experimental Pathology (founded in 1913) and the American Association of Pathologists and Bacteriologists (founded in 1900) and formerly (1992) known as the American Association of Pathologists. ASIP promotes the discovery, advancement, and dissemination of knowledge in experimental pathology and related disciplines. Membership: $25-187/year.

Continuing Education:
Certification Designation/s: CME

Meetings/Conferences: Annual
Conference Chair: Tara A. Snethen CAE, CMP
2013 - Baltimore, MD/March 3
2013 - Boston, MA (Boston Convention and Exhibition Center)/April 20 - 24
2014 - San Diego, CA/April 26 - 30
2015 - Boston, MA/March 28 - April 1
2016 - San Diego, CA/April 2 - 6
2017 - Washington, DC/April 21 - 25
2018 - San Diego, CA/April 18 - 22

Publications:
American Journal of Pathology; monthly; adv.
ASIP Pathways; adv.
ASIP Pathways Newsletter

ASIP Trainee Newsletter; on-line
Journal of Molecular Diagnostics; bi-monthly; adv.

American Society for Laser Medicine and Surgery (1980)
2100 Stewart Ave.
Suite 240
Wausau, WI 54401
Tel: (715) 845-9283 Fax: (715) 848-2493
TollFree: (877) 258-6028
E-Mail: information@aslms.org
Website: aslms.org
Members: 4300 individuals
Staff: 8
Annual Budget: $2-5,000,000

Personnel:
Executive Director: Dianne Dalsky
    E-Mail: dianne@aslms.org
Coordinator, Program and Services: Barb Brown CPS
    E-Mail: barb@aslms.org
Assistant, Membership and Customer Service: Diane Dodds
    E-Mail: ddodds@aslms.org
Secretary: Richard O. Gregory MD
    E-Mail: zelicoo2@earthlink.net
Coordinator, Continuing Medical Education and Conferences: Michelle Theiler
    E-Mail: michelle@aslms.org

Historical Note:
Founded through an initial grant from the A. Ward Ford Memorial Institute in Wausau, and incorporated in the State of Wisconsin by 150 charter members. ASLMS's mission is to enhance excellence in patient care by advancing laser applications and related technologies. Membership: $220 (Fellow/Member-Physician/Industry); $120 (Fellow/Member-Scientist); $80 (Fellow/Member-Nursing/Allied Health); $70 (Student).

Meetings/Conferences: Annual
Conference Chair: Michelle Theiler
2013 - Boston, MA (Hynes Convention Center and Sheraton Boston Hotel)/April 3 - 7
2014 - Phoenix, AZ (Phoenix Convention Center)/April 2 - 6
2015 - Kissimmee, FL (Gaylord Palms Resort and Convention Center-Kissimmee)/April 22 - 26

Publications:
Lasers in Surgery and Medicine; on-line; adv.
Membership Directory; on-line; adv.

Membership List Available to Non-members

American Society for Legal History (1956)
C/O Western Michigan University
4301 Friedmann Hall
Kalamazoo, MI 49008-5334
Fax: (269) 387-4651
Website: legalhistorian.org
Members: 300 institutions and 930 individuals
Staff: 3
Annual Budget: $50-100,000
Tax: 501(c)(3)

Personnel:
Secretary: Sally Hadden
    E-Mail: shadden@mailer.fsu.edu
Treasurer: Craig Evan Klafter
    E-Mail: cklafter@ingenia.us

Historical Note:
ASLH, a member of the American Council of Learned Societies, works to foster the scholarship, teaching, and study concerning the law and institutions of all legal systems, both Anglo- American and those that do not operate in the Anglo-American tradition. Membership: $15-175/year.

Meetings/Conferences: Annual
2013 - Miami, FL (Hyatt Regency Miami)/Nov. 7 - 10

Publications:
ASLH Newsletter; biennially
H-Law; on-line
Law & History Review; quarterly; adv.

Membership List Available to Non-members

American Society for Mass Spectrometry (1969)
2019 Galisteo St.
Building I-1
Santa Fe, NM 87505
Tel: (505) 989-4517 Fax: (505) 989-1073
E-Mail: office@asms.org
Website: asms.org

Members: 7500 scientists
Staff: 6
Annual Budget: $2-5,000,000
Tax: 501(c)(3)

Personnel:
Executive Director: Judith A. Sjoberg
  E-Mail: judith@asms.org
Contact, Programs and Short Courses: Cindi Lilly
  E-Mail: cindi@asms.org
Contact, Exhibitors and Corporate Membership: Miquela Ortiz
  E-Mail: miquela@asms.org
Contact, Individual Membership and Conference Registration: Marin Walker
  E-Mail: marin@asms.org
Contact, Corporate Membership and Arrangements: Jennifer Watson
  E-Mail: jennifer@asms.org
Contact, Finance and Technical Services: Brent Watson
  E-Mail: brent@asms.org

Historical Note:
ASMS promotes and disseminates knowledge of mass spectrometry and allied topics. Members are academic and industrial chemists and scientists who use mass spectrometer as an analytical and physical tool. Membership: $65-75 (Regular); $40-50 (Student); $650 (Corporate).

Meetings/Conferences: Annual
Conference Chair: Jennifer Watson
2013 - Minneapolis, MN/June 9 - 13
2014 - Baltimore, MD/June 15 - 19
2015 - St. Louis, MO/May 31 - June 4
2016 - San Antonio, TX/June 5 - 9
2017 - Indianapolis, IN/June 4 - 8
Number of non-conference events/year: 1

Publications:
International Journal of Mass Spectrometry
Journal of the American Society for Mass Spectrometry; bi-monthly

---

American Society for Metabolic and Bariatric Surgery *(1983)*
100 S.W. 75th St.
Suite 201
Gainesville, FL 32607
Tel: (352) 331-4900 *Fax:* (352) 331-4975
E-Mail: info@asmbs.org
Website: asmbs.org
Members: 3350 individuals
Staff: 11
Annual Budget: $5-10,000,000
Tax: 501(c)(6)

Personnel:
Executive Director: Georgeann Mallory RD
Manager, Finance: Kim Carmichael
Coordinator, Graphic Art Design and Committee Liaison: Leslie Galloway
Director, Operations: Kristie Kaufman
Technology Specialist: James Osterhout
Director, Membership Services: Barbara Peck
Systems Administrator: Richard Russ
Associate, Communication and Grants: Natalie Squitiro
Director, Conventions: Pat Watson CMP

Historical Note:
ASMBS's mission is to improve the care and treatment of people with obesity and related diseases and to advance the science and understanding of metabolic surgery.

Continuing Education:
Certification Designation/s: CBN

Meetings/Conferences:
Conference Chair: Pat Watson CMP
2013 - Atlanta, GA (Georgia World Congress Center)/ Nov. 11 - 16
2014 - Boston, MA/Nov. 2 - 7
2015 - Los Angeles, CA/Nov. 1 - 7

Publications:
Membership Directory; on-line
Surgery for Obesity and Related Disorders; bi-monthly

Membership List Available to Non-members

American Society for Microbiology *(1899)*
1752 N St. NW
Washington, DC 20036
Tel: (202) 737-3600 *Fax:* (202) 942-9333
E-Mail: service@asmusa.org
Website: asm.org

Members: 43000 scientists
Staff: 19
Annual Budget: $50-100,000,000
Tax: 501(c)(3)

Personnel:
President: Bonnie L. Bassler
Executive Director: Michael I Goldberg
  E-Mail: mgoldberg@asmusa.org
Program Manager: Heather Garvey
Director, Communications: Barbara Hyde
  E-Mail: bhyde@asmusa.org
Deputy Executive Director: Nancy Sansalone
  E-Mail: NSansalone@asmusa.org
Director, Public Affairs: Janet Shoemaker
  E-Mail: jshoemaker@asmusa.org
Manager, Media Relations and Communications: James Sliwa
  E-Mail: jsliwa@asmusa.org

Historical Note:
ASM's mission is to advance the microbiological sciences for understanding life processes. Purpose is to enhance the contributions and promise of microbiological sciences and support programs of education, training and public information. Membership: $61 (Full); $41 (Transitional); $41 (Postdoctoral); $17 (Student).

Meetings/Conferences: Semi-Annual
2013 - Izmir, Turkey (Swissotel Grand Efes)/June 25 - 28
2013 - Boston, MA/Oct. 5 - 9

Publications:
Antimicrobial Agents and Chemotherapy; monthly
Applied and Environmental Microbiology; bi-monthly
Clinical and Vaccine Immunology; quarterly
Clinical Microbiology Reviews; quarterly
Eukaryotic Cell; monthly
Infection and Immunity; monthly
Journal of Bacteriology; bi-monthly
Journal of Clinical Microbiology; monthly
Journal of Microbiology and Biology Education; bi-annually
Journal of Virology; bi-monthly
Microbe Magazine; monthly
Microbiology and Molecular Biology Reviews; quarterly
Minority Microbiology Mentor Newsletter; monthly
Molecular and Cellular Biology; bi-monthly
Public Policy Reports; annually

Membership List Available to Non-members

American Society for Mohs Histotechnology *(1985)*
555 E. Wells St.
Suite 1100
Milwaukee, WI 53202
Tel: (414) 347-1103 *Fax:* (414) 276-3349
E-Mail: info@mohstech.org
Website: mohscollege.org/asmh
Staff: 1
Annual Budget: $100-250,000
Tax: 501(c)(3)

Personnel:
Executive Director: Kim Schardin CAE, MBA
  E-Mail: ASMH@mohscollege.org

Historical Note:
Founded in 1995 as an ancillary group to the American College of Mohs Surgery (ACMS). ASMH seeks to advance professional growth, standards, knowledge and performance in Mohs histotechnology through continuing and formal educational programs; to create mutual understanding and cooperation between the members; to safeguard the standards of histotechnology for processing micrographic surgery specimens and encourage research. Membership: $150/year.

Meetings/Conferences: Annual
2013 - Washington, DC (Omni Shoreham)/May 3 - 4

Publications:
ASMH Newsletter; quarterly; adv.
Membership Directory; on-line

American Society for Neurochemistry *(1969)*
9037 Ron Den Ln.
Windermere, FL 34786
Tel: (407) 909-9064 *Fax:* (407) 876-0750
E-Mail: amazing@iag.net
Website: asneurochem.org
Members: 1000 individuals
Staff: 4

Annual Budget: $250-500,000
Tax: 501(c)(3)

Personnel:
President: Steve Levison
  E-Mail: levison@asneurochem.org
Treasurer: Karen Chandross
  E-Mail: karen.chandross@sanofi-aventis.com
Secretary: Babette Fuss
  E-Mail: bfuss@vcu.edu
Professional Meeting Organizer: Sheilah Jewart

Historical Note:
Organized in 1968-1969 by US, Canadian and Mexican members of the International Society for Neurochemistry and incorporated in the District of Columbia, August 6, 1969. ASN's mission is to advance and promote cellular and molecular neuroscience knowledge. Members are zuroscientists. Membership: $125 (Ordinary); $30 (Student); $75 (Corresponding); $50 (Postdoctoral Member).

Meetings/Conferences: Annual
Conference Chair: Sheilah Jewart
2013 - Cancun, QR (Cancun Convention Center)/April 20 - 24
2014 - Long Beach, CA/March 8 - 14
2015 - Atlanta, GA/March 13 - 18
2016 - Denver, CO/March 19 - 23
Number of non-conference events/year: 2

Publications:
ASN NEURO
ASN Newsletter
Membership Directory; on-line
The Journal of Neurochemistry; monthly; adv.

American Society for Nondestructive Testing *(1941)*
1711 Arlingate Ln.
P.O. Box 28518
Columbus, OH 43228-0518
Tel: (614) 274-6003 *Fax:* (614) 274-6899
TollFree: (800) 222-2768
Website: asnt.org
Members:
500 companies
11000 individuals
Staff: 42
Annual Budget: $5-10,000,000

Personnel:
Executive Director: Wayne Holliday
Senior Manager, Marketing and Membership Services: Betsy Blazar
  E-Mail: bblazar@asnt.org
Specialist, Certifications: Tricia Davis
  E-Mail: tdavis@asnt.org
Senior Manager, Publications: Tim Jones
Senior Manager, Conferences: Michael O'Toole
Senior Manager, Accounting and Finance: Mary Potter
  E-Mail: mpotter@asnt.org
Manager, Information Systems: David Sentelle

Historical Note:
Founded in August 1941 with nine charter members as the American Industrial Radium and X-Ray Society; became Society for Nondestructive Testing in 1946 and assumed its current name in 1967. Incorporated in Ohio in 1988. ASNT's purpose is to create a safer world by promoting the profession and technologies of nondestructive testing. Members are engineers, metallurgists and managers in the field of nondestructive testing for a variety of industries: chemicals, aerospace, construction, electronics, nuclear, metals, petroleum, food processing, transportation and automotive. Membership: $75 (Individual); $15 (Student); $30 (Military); $410 (Corporate Partner).

Continuing Education:
Certification Designation/s: IRRSP, ACCP, ASNT

Meetings/Conferences: Annual
Conference Chair: Michael O'Toole
2013 - Memphis, TN (Peabody Memphis)/March 18 - 21
2013 - Las Vegas, NV (Rio All-Suite Hotel and Casino)/ Nov. 4 - 8/over 100 exhibitors
2014 - North Charleston, SC (Charleston Convention Center)/Oct. 27 - 30
Number of non-conference events/year: 4

Publications:
Materials Evaluation; monthly; adv.
Research in Nondestructive Evaluation; quarterly; adv.
TNT - The NDT Technican; quarterly; adv.

American Society for Nutrition *(2005)*

9650 Rockville Pike
Suite 4500
Bethesda, MD 20814
Tel: (301) 634-7050 *Fax:* (301) 634-7894
E-Mail: info@nutrition.org
Website: nutrition.org
Members: 3500 individuals
Staff: 29
Annual Budget: $5-10,000,000

Personnel:
Executive Officer: John E. Courtney PhD
  E-Mail: jcourtney@nutrition.org
Manager, Meetings and Individual Development: Katrina
Dunn
  E-Mail: KLD@nutrition.org
Vice President, Society Advancement: Paula
Eichenbrenner
  E-Mail: peichenbrenner@nutrition.org
Vice President, Publications: Karen King
  E-Mail: kking@nutrition.org
Administrator, Accounts: Tom Landicho
  E-Mail: tlandicho@nutrition.org
Director, Government Relations: Sarah D. Ohlhorst
  E-Mail: sohlhorst@nutrition.org
Manager, Communications: Suzanne Price
  E-Mail: sprice@nutrition.org
Managing Director, Professional Development: Gwen
Twillman
  E-Mail: gtwillman@nutrition.org
Manager, Membership and Marketing: Allanna Wallace
  E-Mail: awallace@nutrition.org

Historical Note:
*Founded as American Institute of Nutrition by members of
the American Society of Biological Chemists, reorganized
as a membership society in 1934, became American
Society for Nutritional Sciences in 1996, merged (2005)
with American Society for Clinical Nutrition and Society
for International Nutrition Research, and assumed its
current name the same year. ASN's mission is to develop
and extend knowledge of nutrition of all species through
fundamental, multidisciplinary, and clinical research.
Membership: $150 (Regular/Associate); $50 (Postdoctoral/
Young Professional/ Regular and Associate Members -
Residing in a Low, Lower-Middle, or Higher-Middle Income
Country); $30 (Students); $25 (Emeritus Members).*

Meetings/Conferences: Annual
Conference Chair: Katrina Dunn
2013 - Boston, MA (Boston Convention and Exhibition
Center)/April 20 - 24

Publications:
Advances in Nutrition; on-line; adv.
ASN Monthly eNewsletter; monthly; adv.
Membership Directory; on-line
Nutrition Notes; quarterly; adv.
Nutrition Today; bi-monthly; adv.
The American Journal of Clinical Nutrition; monthly;
  adv.
The Journal of Nutrition; adv.

American Society for Pain Management Nursing
(1990)
P.O. Box 15473
Lenexa, KS 66285-5473
Tel: (913) 895-4606 *Fax:* (913) 895-4652
TollFree: (888) 342-7766
E-Mail: aspmn@goamp.com
Website: aspmn.org
Members: 1700 individuals
Staff: 6
Annual Budget: $500-1,000,000
Tax: 501(c)(3)

Personnel:
Executive Director: Jerrie Lynn Kind
  E-Mail: jerrielynn@aspmn.org
Meeting Planner: Tonja Britt
  E-Mail: tonja.britt@goamp.com
Director, Government Affairs: Wade Delk
  E-Mail: wade@aspmn.org
Manager, Meetings: Joyce Miller CMP
  E-Mail: jmiller@goamp.com
Administrative Assistant: Tressie Nootz
  E-Mail: tnootz@goamp.com
Coordinator, Education Program: Christie Ross
  E-Mail: christie@aspmn.org

Historical Note:
*ASPMN's mission is to advance and promote optimal
nursing care for people affected by pain by promoting best*

nursing practices through education, standards, advocacy,
and research.

Continuing Education:
Certification Designation/s: PMNC

Meetings/Conferences: Annual
Conference Chair: Joyce Miller CMP
2013 - Indianapolis, IN/Oct. 9 - 12
2014 - San Diego, CA/Sept. 17 - 21

Publications:
Members Directory; on-line
Pain Management Nursing; quarterly; adv.

American Society for Parenteral and Enteral Nutrition *(1975)*
8630 Fenton St.
Suite 412
Silver Spring, MD 20910
Tel: (301) 587-6315 *Fax:* (301) 587-2365
TollFree: (800) 727-4567
E-Mail: aspen@nutr.org
Website: nutritioncare.org
Members: 5500 members
Staff: 18
Annual Budget: $2-5,000,000

Personnel:
Chief Executive Officer: Debra BenAvram CAE
  E-Mail: debrab@aspen.nutr.org
Director, Corporate Relations: Cheretta Clerkley
  E-Mail: cherettac@aspen.nutr.org
Manager, Education: Jennifer Green
  E-Mail: jenniferg@aspen.nutr.org
Senior Director, Finance: Joanne Kieffer
  E-Mail: joannek@aspen.nutr.org
Director, Education: Michelle Spangenburg MS, RD
  E-Mail: michelles@aspen.nutr.org
Program Director, Membership: Deborah Timmons
  E-Mail: deboraht@aspen.nutr.org

Historical Note:
*ASPEN's mission is to improve patient care by advancing
the science and practice of nutrition support therapy.
Members are physicians, dietitians, nurses, pharmacists,
nutritionists, researchers, hospital administrators and others
who work in specialized nutrition support. Membership:
$215-235 (Physician); $145-165 (Professional); $100
(Trainee/New Practitioner); $50-70 (Student).*

Continuing Education:
Certification Designation/s: NBNSC

Meetings/Conferences: Annual
2013 - Phoenix, AZ (Phoenix Convention Center)/Feb.
  9 - 13/2000 attendees/over 100 exhibitors
2014 - Savannah, GA (Savannah International Trade
  and Convention Center)/Jan. 18 - 21
Number of non-conference events/year: 7

Publications:
ASPEN Newsletter; on-line
Nutrition in Clinical Practice; bi-monthly; adv.
The Journal of Parenteral and Enteral Nutrition; bi-
  monthly; adv.

American Society for Pharmacology and Experimental Therapeutics *(1908)*
9650 Rockville Pike
Bethesda, MD 20814-3995
Tel: (301) 634-7060 *Fax:* (301) 634-7061
E-Mail: info@aspet.org
Website: aspet.org
Members: 4800 individuals
Staff: 20
Annual Budget: $5-10,000,000
Tax: 501(c)(3)

Personnel:
Executive Officer: Christine K. Carrico PhD
  E-Mail: ccarrico@aspet.org
Contact, Membership and Marketing: Gary Axelrod
  E-Mail: gaxelrod@aspet.org
Contact, Public Affairs: Jim Bernstein
  E-Mail: jbernstein@aspet.org
Director, Journals: Richard Dodenhoff
  E-Mail: rdodenhoff@aspet.org
Contact, Finance: Matthew Hilliker
  E-Mail: mhilliker@aspet.org
Contact, Membership and Marketing: Robert "Bobby"
Phipps
  E-Mail: rphipps@aspet.org
Contact, Meetings: Angelique Raptakis
  E-Mail: araptakis@aspet.org

Historical Note:
*ASPET members conduct basic and clinical pharmacological
research in academia, industry and the government to
develop new medicines and therapeutic agents to fight
existing and emerging diseases. Membership: $150
(Regular/Affiliate); $30 (Graduate Student/Semi- Retired);
$70 (Postdoctoral); Free (Undergraduates/Retired).*

Meetings/Conferences: Annual
Conference Chair: Angelique Raptakis
2013 - Boston, MA (Boston Convention and Exhibition
  Center)/April 20 - 24
2014 - San Diego, CA/April 26 - 30
2015 - Boston, MA/March 28 - April 1
2016 - San Diego, CA/April 2 - 6
2017 - Washington, DC/April 22 - 26
2018 - San Diego, CA/April 21 - 25
Number of non-conference events/year: 50

Publications:
Drug Metabolism and Disposition; monthly; adv.
Molecular Interventions; bi-monthly
Molecular Pharmacology; monthly; adv.
Pharmacological Reviews; quarterly; adv.
The Journal of Pharmacology and Experimental
  Therapeutics; adv.
The Pharmacologist; quarterly

American Society for Political and Legal Philosophy *(1955)*
1737 Cambridge St. CGIS
Knafel Building 437
Cambridge, MA 02138
Tel: (773) 702-8052 *Fax:* (773) 702-1689
Website: political-theory.org
Members: 500 individuals
Staff: 3

Personnel:
President: Nancy Rosenblum
  E-Mail: nrosenblum@gov.harvard.edu
Co-Editor: Jack Knight
  E-Mail: knight@law.duke.edu

Historical Note:
*ASPLP's mission is to share an interest in a range of
problems traditionally treated within the broad context of
interdisciplinary exploration and discussion of those issues
of political and legal philosophy. Members are academics
and others with an active professional interest in the field
of political/legal philosophy. Membership: $20 (Emeriti/
Retired/Graduate Students); $50 (Full-time).*

Meetings/Conferences: Annual
2013 - New Orleans, LA/Jan. 4 - 8

Publications:
Member Directory; on-line

American Society for Precision Engineering
(1986)
P.O. Box 10826
Raleigh, NC 27605-0826
Tel: (919) 839-8444 *Fax:* (919) 839-8039
Website: aspe.net
Members: 822 companies and individuals
Staff: 4
Annual Budget: $250-500,000
Tax: 501(c)(3)

Personnel:
Executive Director: Thomas A. Dow
  E-Mail: thomas_dow@ncsu.edu
Manager, Meetings: Erika Deutsch-Layne
  E-Mail: erika_layne@aspe.net
Contact, Publications and Office Manager: Ilka Lee
  E-Mail: ilka_lee@aspe.net
Manager, Meetings and Membership Services: Wendy
Shearon
  E-Mail: wendy_shearon@aspe.net

Historical Note:
*ASPE focuses on research, design, development,
manufacture and measurement of high accuracy
components and systems. Members represent a variety of
technical areas - from engineering (mechanical, electrical,
optical and industrial) to materials science, physics,
chemistry, mathematics and computer science - and
are employed in industry, academia and national labs.
Membership: $170 (Sustaining); $105 (Regular); $50
(Student); $1,500 (Corporate Sponsor); $2,000 (Sustaining
Corporate Sponsor).*

Meetings/Conferences: Annual
Conference Chair: Erika Deutsch-Layne
2013 - St. Paul, MN (Crowne Plaza St. Paul Riverfront)/
  Oct. 20 - 25

Number of non-conference events/year: 1

Publications:
ASPE Newsletter
Precision Engineering; quarterly

The American Society for Public Administration
(1939)
1301 Pennsylvania Ave. NW
Suite 700
Washington, DC 20004
Tel: (202) 393-7878 *Fax:* (202) 638-4952
E-Mail: info@aspanet.org
Website: aspanet.org
Members: 10000 individuals
Staff: 10
Annual Budget: $1-2,000,000
Tax: 501(c)(3)

Personnel:
Executive Director: Antoinette A. Samuel CAE, MPA
   E-Mail: tsamuel@aspanet.org
Director, Administrative Services: Duanne Crawley
   E-Mail: dcrawley@aspanet.org
Coordinator, Conferences: Amy Huber
   E-Mail: ahuber@aspanet.org
Editor: Christine Jewett McCrehin
   E-Mail: cjewett@aspanet.org
Senior Director, Professional Development: Judy Miller
   E-Mail: judymiller@aspanet.org
Director, Communications: Melissa Williams
   E-Mail: mwilliams@aspanet.org
Senior Director, Membership Services: Patricia Yearwood
   E-Mail: pyearwood@aspanet.org

Historical Note:
ASPA enhances the value of joining and elevating the public service profession, advances the art, science, teaching, and practice of public and non-profit administration and provides networking and professional development opportunities to those committed to public service values, and achieves solutions to the challenges of governance. Membership: $100 (Individual); $120 (Supporting Individual); $220 (Sustaining Individual); $75 (Full Student/New Professional); $55 (Senior); $35 (Family); $30-100 (International); $40 (Electronic Student).

Meetings/Conferences: Annual
Conference Chair: Amy Huber
2013 - New Orleans, LA (Hilton New Orleans Riverside)/March 15 - 19
2014 - Washington, DC (Mayflower Renaissance Hotel)/March 14 - 18
Number of non-conference events/year: 1

Publications:
Bridge e-newsletter; semi-monthly
PA TIMES Recruiter; monthly; adv.
Public Administration Review (PAR); bi-monthly
Public Integrity Journal
The Public Manager; quarterly

Membership List Available to Non-members

American Society for Quality *(1977)*
P.O. Box 3005
Milwaukee, WI 53201-3005
Tel: (414) 272-8575 *Fax:* (414) 272-1734
TollFree: (800) 248-1946
E-Mail: asq@asq.org
Website: asq.org
Members: 100000 individuals and organizations
Staff: 215
Annual Budget: $25-50,000,000
Tax: 501(c)(3)

Personnel:
Chief Executive Director: Paul E. Borawski CAE
   E-Mail: pborawski@asq.org
Administrator, Productions: Barb Mitrovic
   E-Mail: bmitrovic@asq.org
Executive Editor and Associate Publisher: Seiche Sanders
   E-Mail: ssanders@asq.org

Historical Note:
Formerly (1997) American Society for Quality Control. ASQ's mission is to facilitate continuous improvement and increase customer satisfaction by identifying, communicating and encouraging the use of quality principles, concepts and technologies. Membership: $138 (Full); $80 (Associate); $31 (Forum/Division); $27 (Student); $1,000 (Organization-Site); $350 (Organization-K-12- School); $750 (Organization-K-12-District).

Continuing Education:

Certification Designation/s: CQI, CBA, CCT, CHA, CMQ/OE, CQT, CQA, CQE, CQIA, CQPA, CRE, CSSBB, CSQE, CSSGB, CPGP, CMBB

Meetings/Conferences:
2013 - Phoenix, AZ (Pointe at Tapatio Cliffs)/March 4 - 5/500 attendees
2013 - Indianapolis, IN (Indiana Convention Center)/May 6 - 8
Number of non-conference events/year: 7

Publications:
ASQ Quality News Today; daily
ASQ Weekly e-newsletter; weekly; adv.
Journal for Quality and Participation; quarterly
Quality Progress Magazine; monthly

American Society for Reconstructive Microsurgery *(1983)*
20 N. Michigan Ave.
Suite 700
Chicago, IL 60602
Tel: (312) 456-9579 *Fax:* (312) 782-0553
E-Mail: contact@microsurg.org
Website: microsurg.org
Members: 500 individuals
Staff: 3
Annual Budget: $500-1,000,000
Tax: 501(c)(3)

Personnel:
Executive Director: Krista A. Greco
   E-Mail: greco@isms.org
Managing Editor, Newsletter: Anne Behrens
   E-Mail: visorient@comcast.net
Manager, Meetings: Susan Nicoletti
   E-Mail: susan@nhs-usa.org

Historical Note:
ASRM's mission is to encourage, foster and advance the art and science of microsurgical and other complex reconstructions, as well as, to establish a forum for teaching, research and free discussion of reconstructive microsurgical methods and principals among the members. Membership : $295 (Active); $245 (Associate); $0 (Candidate).

Continuing Education:
Certification Designation/s: CME

Meetings/Conferences: Annual
Conference Chair: Susan Nicoletti
2013 - Naples, FL (Napels Beach Hotel and Golf Club)/Jan. 12 - 15
2014 - Kauai, HI (Grand Hyatt Kauai)/Jan. 11 - 14
2015 - Paradise Island, Bahamas (Atlantis Paradise Island)/Jan. 24 - 27

Publications:
Reconstructive Microsurgery; semi-annually

Membership List Available to Non-members

American Society for Reproductive Medicine *(1944)*
1209 Montgomery Hwy.
Birmingham, AL 35216-2809
Tel: (205) 978-5000 *Fax:* (205) 978-5005
E-Mail: enicoll@asrm-dc.org
Website: asrm.org
Members: 8000 individuals
Staff: 23
Annual Budget: $10-25,000,000
Tax: 501(c)(3)

Personnel:
Executive Director: Robert W. Rebar MD
   E-Mail: rrebar@asrm.org
Manager, Membership Services: Julie Beckham
   E-Mail: jbeckham@asrm.org
Specialist, Education: Nancy Bowers MPH, RN
   E-Mail: nbowers@asrm.org
Chief Financial Officer: Daniel Carre
   E-Mail: dcarre@asrm.org
Editor: Alan H. DeCherney MD
   E-Mail: decherney@gmail.com
Director, Operations: Vickie Gamble
   E-Mail: vgamble@asrm.org
Director, Meetings and Exhibits: Deb Hanson
   E-Mail: dhanson@asrm.org
Coordinator, Human Resources and Assistant to the Director of Operations: Cherie Holverstott
   E-Mail: cholverstott@asrm.org
Director, Communications: Mitzi Mize MS
   E-Mail: mmize@asrm.org

Director, Public Affairs: Sean B. Tipton
   E-Mail: stipton@asrm-dc.org

Historical Note:
ASRM' mission is to advance the art, science, and practice of reproductive medicine. Membership: $275 (Doctoral); $125 (Associate/Allied Health Professional).

Meetings/Conferences: Annual
Conference Chair: Deb Hanson
2013 - Boston, MA (Boston Convention and Exhibition Cente)/Oct. 12 - 17
2014 - Honolulu, HI (Hawaii Convention Center)/Oct. 18 - 22
2015 - Baltimore, MD (Hilton Baltimore)/Oct. 17 - 21

Publications:
Fertility and Sterility; on-line
Journal of Assisted Reproduction and Genetics
Menopausal Medicine; irregular
Selected Articles from Fertility and Sterility
Sexuality, Reproduction and Menopause; quarterly

Membership List Available to Non-members

American Society for Stereotactic and Functional Neurosurgery *(1968)*
N1021 Doan Hall, 410 W. Ten Ave.
Columbus, OH 43210
Tel: (614) 366-2420 *Fax:* (614) 293-4281
Website: assfn.org
Members: 380 individuals
Staff: 6
Annual Budget: $25-50,000

Personnel:
President: Ali R. Rezai MD
   E-Mail: Ali.Rezai@osumc.edu
Coordinator, Membership and Newsletter Editor: Emad Eskandar MD
   E-Mail: eeskandar@partners.org
Website Coordinator: Kendall H. Lee MD, PhD
   E-Mail: Lee.Kendall@mayo.edu

Historical Note:
Formerly (1961) International Society for Research in Stereoencephalotomy, (1963) International Society for Research in Stereoencephalotomy, assumed current name in 1968. ASSFN's mission is to foster the use of stereotactic and functional neurological methods for the treatment of diseases of the nervous system. Members are surgeons using advanced localization of targets in the brain to diagnose and treat disease and injury. Membership: $325 (Active); $25 (Resident/fellow); Free (Senior); $50 (Associate).

Meetings/Conferences: Biennial

Publications:
ASSFN Newsletter; semi-annually
Brain; adv.
Lancet Neurology; adv.
Membership Directory; on-line
Stereotactic and Functional Neurosurgery; quarterly; adv.

American Society for Surgery of the Hand *(1946)*
822 W. Washington Blvd.
Chicago, IL 60607
Tel: (312) 880-1900 *Fax:* (847) 384-1435
E-Mail: info@assh.org
Website: assh.org
Members: 2700 individuals
Staff: 16
Annual Budget: $5-10,000,000
Tax: 501(c)(6)

Personnel:
Executive Vice President and Chief Executive Officer: Mark C. Anderson CAE, FASAE
   E-Mail: manderson@assh.org
Senior Coordinator, Membership Services: Jeanne Bloesch
   E-Mail: jbloesch@assh.org
Director, Communications: Tara Havenga
   E-Mail: thavenga@assh.org
Director, Finance and Administration: Dave Hood CPA
   E-Mail: dhood@assh.org
Director, Information Technology: Mike Lakas
Director, Meetings and Education: Angie Legaspi CMP
   E-Mail: alegaspi@assh.org
Coordinator, Publications and Communications: Alex Mitchell
Manager, Marketing and Publications: Nicole Renn

Historical Note:
Incorporated in Ohio in 1947. ASSH's mission is to advance the care of hand and upper extremity disorders

by supporting education and research through the efficient collection of donations and administration of grants.
Membership: $530 (Active/Supporting); $300 (Candidate); $250 (International); $220 (Affiliate).

Meetings/Conferences: Annual
Conference Chair: Angie Legaspi CMP
2013 - San Francisco, CA (Moscone West-Moscone Center)/Oct. 2
2013 - San Francisco, CA/Oct. 3 - 5
2014 - Boston, MA (John B. Hynes Veterans Memorial Convention Center)/Sept. 18 - 20
2015 - Seatle, WA/Sept. 10 - 12
2017 - San Francisco, CA/Sept. 7 - 9
2018 - Boston, MA/Sept. 13 - 15
Number of non-conference events/year: 3

Publications:
Business of Hand Surgery Newsletter
Journal of Hand Surgery
Membership Directory; on-line

Membership List Available to Non-members

American Society for the Advancement of Anesthesia and Sedation in Dentistry *(1929)*
Six E. Union Ave.
Bound Brook, NJ 08805
Tel: (732) 469-9050 *Fax:* (732) 271-1985
E-Mail: sedation4dentist@aol.com
Website: sedation4dentists.net
Members: 650 individuals
Staff: 1
Annual Budget: $25-50,000

Personnel:
Executive Secretary: David Crystal DDS
E-Mail: dacryst1@aol.com

Historical Note:
Formerly (1965) the American Society for the Advancement of General Anesthesia in Dentistry. ASAAD's purpose is to provide general dentists and dental specialists with a knowledge base and clinical experiences leading to competency in the provision of sedation for dental treatment. Membership: $85/year (Individual).

Continuing Education:
Enrollment: 10
Certification Designation/s: PCS

American Society for the Alexander Technique *(1987)*
P.O. Box 2307
Dayton, OH 45401-2307
Tel: (937) 586-3732 *Fax:* (937) 586-3699
TollFree: (800) 473-0620
E-Mail: info@amsatonline.org
Website: amsatonline.org
Members: 700 individuals
Staff: 3
Annual Budget: $100-250,000
Tax: 501(c)(3)

Personnel:
Treasurer: Ann Rodiger
Secretary: Jennifer Sielicki

Historical Note:
Founded as North American Society of Teachers of the Alexander Technique, assumed its current name in 2000. AmSAT's mission is to establish the Alexander Technique as a basic and recognized resource for health, productivity, and well being. Membership: $50 (Associates); $125 (International); $260 (Full Voting); $95-200 (Newly Certified Teachers).

Meetings/Conferences: Annual
2013 - Dublin, Ireland (Emmaus Retreat Centre)/March 22 - 29

Publications:
Membership Directory; on-line

American Society for Theatre Research *(1956)*
P.O. Box 1798
Boulder, CO 80306-1798
Tel: (303) 530-1838 *Fax:* (303) 530-1839
TollFree: (888) 530-1838
E-Mail: info@astr.org
Website: astr.org
Members: 750 individuals
Staff: 3
Annual Budget: $250-500,000
Tax: 501(c)(3)

Personnel:
President: Rhonda Blair

Administrator: Nancy Erickson
Editor: Matt Omasta

Historical Note:
ASTR advances scholarship on worldwide theatre and performance, both historical and contemporary. Membership: $200 (Individual); $75 (Retired/Student); $250 (Non-Member).

Meetings/Conferences: Annual

Publications:
ASTR Newsletter; on-line; adv.
Membership Directory; on-line
Theatre Journal; on-line; adv.

American Society for Therapeutic Radiology and Oncology *(1958)*
8280 Willow Oaks Corporate Dr.
Suite 500
Fairfax, VA 22031
Tel: (703) 502-1550 *Fax:* (703) 502-7852
TollFree: (800) 962-7876
E-Mail:
GovernmentRelationsDepartment@astro.org
Website: astro.org
Members: 10000 individuals
Staff: 73
Annual Budget: $10-25,000,000
Tax: 501(c)(3)

Personnel:
Chief Executive Officer: Laura Thevenot
Director, Government Relations: Dave Adler
Vice-President , Membership Services and Communications: Anna Arnone
E-Mail: annaa@astro.org
Managing Editor: Katherine Egan Bennett
Director, Communications: Beth Bukata
Director, Meetings: Michele Cordie
E-Mail: michelec@astro.org
Manager, Marketing: Kate Dodd
Director, Meetings: Michele Donohue
Senior Manager, Web Projects: Imola Ekart
General Counsel: Laura Gogal
Director, Information Technology: Jason Hoolsema
Vice-President, Finance and Administration: Terry Karras
Membership Coordinator: Todd Karstaedt
Marketing Manager: Barbara Moody
Director, Research: Barbara Muth
Director, Human Resources: Elizabeth Parks
Director, Development and Corporate Relations: Cheryl Reinhardt
Assistant Director, Information Technology: Mike Sullivan
E-Mail: mikes@astro.org
Senior Director, Education: Kathy Thomas

Historical Note:
ASTRO's mission is to advance the practice of radiation oncology by promoting excellence in patient care, providing opportunities for educational and professional development, promoting research and disseminating research results and representing radiation oncology in a rapidly evolving healthcare environment. Membership: $475 (Active/Allied/Affiliate); $300 (International); $60 (Associate/Nurse/Corresponding).

Meetings/Conferences:
Conference Chair: Michele Donohue
2013 - Atlanta, GA (Georgia World Congress Center)/Sept. 22 - 25
2013 - San Diego, CA (Hilton San Diego Bayfront)/Nov. 8 - 9
Number of non-conference events/year: 3

Publications:
ASTROgram; weekly
ASTROnews; quarterly
Membership Directory; on-line
Practical Radiation Oncology (PRO); quarterly
Red Journal; irregular

American Society for Training and Development *(1943)*
1640 King St.
P.O. Box 1443
Alexandria, VA 22313-1443
Tel: (703) 683-8100 *Fax:* (703) 683-8103
TollFree: (800) 628-2783
E-Mail: customercare@astd.org
Website: astd.org
Members: 70000 individuals
Staff: 125
Annual Budget: $25-50,000,000

Tax: 501(c)(3)

Personnel:
President and Chief Executive Officer: Tony Bingham
E-Mail: tony@astd.org
Vice President, External Relations: Jennifer Homer
E-Mail: jhomer@astd.org

Historical Note:
Formerly (1964) American Society of Training Directors. ASTD's mission is to empower professionals to develop knowledge and skills successfully. Membership: $90-489/year.

Continuing Education:
Certification Designation/s: CPLP

Meetings/Conferences: Semi-Annual
2013 - San Jose, CA/Jan. 30 - Feb. 1/1200 attendees
2013 - Dallas, TX/May 19 - 22/9000 attendees
2014 - Las Vegas, NV/Jan. 15 - 17
2014 - Washington, DC/May 4 - 7
2015 - Las Vegas, NV/Jan. 14 - 16
2015 - Orlando, FL/May 17 - 20

Publications:
Leader Connection Newsletter; monthly
Membership Directory; on-line

American Society for Virology *(1981)*
North Carolina State Univ.
1060 William Moore Dr.
Raleigh, NC 27607
E-Mail: asv@asv.org
Website: asv.org
Members: 3100 individuals
Staff: 3
Annual Budget: $250-500,000

Personnel:
President: Barbara Sherry
E-Mail: barbara_sherry@ncsu.edu

Historical Note:
ASV's mission is to advocate the exchange of information and stimulate discussion and collaboration among scientists active in all aspects of virology. ASV membership is open to any researcher interested or actively engaged in the study of viruses. Membership: $100 (Full); $30 (Associate); $15 (Associate Student); $1,000 (Lifetime/Full).

Meetings/Conferences: Annual
Conference Chair: Nancy Shiffler Eckard
2013 - University Park, PA (Pennsylvania State University)/July 20 - 24
2014 - Ft. Collins, CO (Colorado State University)/June 21 - 25
2015 - London, ON (The University of Western Ontario)/July 11 - 15
2016 - Blacksburg, VA (Virginia Polytechnic Institute and State University)/June 18 - 22
2017 - Madison, WI (Monona Terrace Convention Center)/June 24 - 28

Publications:
Membership Directory; on-line; adv.

American Society of Abdominal Surgeons *(1959)*
824 Main St., Second Floor
Suite One
Melrose, MA 02176
Tel: (781) 665-6102 *Fax:* (781) 665-4127
E-Mail: office@abdominalsurg.org
Website: abdominalsurg.org
Members: 2000 individuals
Staff: 3
Annual Budget: $50-100,000

Personnel:
Executive Editor: Louis F. Alfano Jr., MD
Editor-in-Chief: Demostene Romanucci MD

Historical Note:
Purpose of ASAS is to assist in improving the quality of graduate education in the field of abdominal surgery to establish minimum educational and training standards for the field of Abdominal Surgery. Membership: $175/year (Individual).

Continuing Education:
Certification Designation/s: CME

Meetings/Conferences: Annual

Publications:
Journal of Abdominal Surgery; annually
The Surgeon Newsletter; quarterly

American Society of Access Professionals *(1980)*
1444 I St. NW

Suite 700
Washington, DC 20005
Tel: (202) 712-9054 *Fax:* (202) 216-9646
E-Mail: asap@bostromdc.com
Website: accesspro.org
Members: 300 individuals
Staff: 2
Annual Budget: $500-1,000,000
Tax: 501(c)(3)

Personnel:
Executive Director: Claire Shanley
Director, Conference: Julie Elfand

Historical Note:
ASAP is a nongovernmental, independent, educational, not-for-profit association. A professional forum dedicated to bringing government FOIA and Privacy Act personnel in touch with the requester community and provides quality professional educational programs. Members are government employees, lawyers, journalists and others concerned with access to government data under current personal privacy and public information statutes. Membership: $35/year.

Meetings/Conferences: Annual
Conference Chair: Julie Elfand
Number of non-conference events/year: 1

Publications:
ASAP Newsletter

American Society of Addiction Medicine *(1954)*
4601 N. Park Ave.
Upper Arcade, Suite 101
Chevy Chase, MD 20815
Tel: (301) 656-3920 *Fax:* (301) 656-3815
E-Mail: email@asam.org
Website: asam.org
Members: 3000 Physicians
Staff: 19
Annual Budget: $2-5,000,000

Personnel:
Executive Vice President and Chief Executive Officer:
  Penny S. Mills MBA
  E-Mail: pmills@asam.org
Director, Finance: Frederica Browne
  E-Mail: fbrowne@asam.org
Administrator, Information Technology: Matthew Bryant
  E-Mail: mbryant@asam.org
Senior Director, Professional Development: Arlene C.
  Deverman CAE
  E-Mail: adeverman@asam.org
Director, Government Relations: Alexis Geier-Horan MPP
  E-Mail: ageier@asam.org
Director, Meetings and Conferences: John Hawkins
  E-Mail: jhawkins@asam.org
Chief Operating Officer: Carolyn C. Lanham
  E-Mail: clanham@asam.org
Staff Accountant: Noushin Shariati
  E-Mail: nshar@asam.org
Director, Marketing, Communications and Membership:
  Kate Volpe
  E-Mail: kvolpe@asam.org

Historical Note:
ASAM's mission is to improve the care and treatment of people with the disease of addiction and advance the practice of Addiction Medicine. Membership: $440 (Regular); $125 (Retired); $290 (International); $35 (Resident); $220 (Early Career Physicians).

Continuing Education:
Certification Designation/s: ASAM, ABAM, FASAM

Meetings/Conferences: Annual
Conference Chair: John Hawkins
2013 - Chicago, IL/April 25 - 28
2013 - Chicago, IL/April 25 - 28
2014 - Orlando, FL/April 10 - 13
2014 - Orlando, FL/April 10 - 13
Number of non-conference events/year: 3

Publications:
ASAM News; monthly; adv.
ASAM Weekly; weekly; adv.
Journal of Addiction Medicine; quarterly; adv.
Med-Sci Daily News; daily
Member Directory; adv.

American Society of Agricultural and Biological Engineers *(1907)*
2950 Niles Rd.
St. Joseph, MI 49085
Tel: (269) 429-0300 *Fax:* (269) 429-3852

TollFree: (800) 371-2723
E-Mail: hq@asabe.org
Website: asabe.org
Members: 9000 individuals
Staff: 29
Annual Budget: $2-5,000,000
Tax: 501(c)(3)

Personnel:
Executive Director: Darrin J. Drollinger
Director, Standards and Technical Activities: Scott
  Cedarquist
Director, Membership Services: Mark Crossley
Director, Publications: Donna M. Hull
Director, Public Affairs: Dolores Landeck
  E-Mail: landeck@asabe.org
*Contact, Continuing Education, Conference and Meeting
  Inquiries:* Sharon McKnight
  E-Mail: mcknight@asabe.org
Senior Director, Finance, Meetings and Human Resources:
  Mark D. Zielke

Historical Note:
Incorporated in Michigan in 1935 and assumed its current name in 2000. ASABE is a professional and technical society for engineering in agriculture, food and biological systems. ASABE's mission is to facilitate the exchange of technical information and to promote the science and art of engineering in agricultural, food and biological systems. Membership: $22 (Students/Preprofessionals); $35 (Graduate Student); $11-130 (Members Based On Age); $18-65 (Members, low income countries).

Continuing Education:
Certification Designation/s: PEI

Meetings/Conferences:
Conference Chair: Mark D. Zielke
2013 - Kansas City, MO (Kansas City Convention
  Center)/Jan. 28 - 30
2013 - Kansas City, MO/July 21 - 24
2014 - Montreal, QC/July 13 - 16
Number of non-conference events/year: 6

Publications:
Applied Engineering in Agriculture
ASABE Standards; annually
Biological Engineering; quarterly
Inside ASABE; monthly
Journal of Agricultural Safety & Health; quarterly
Resource Magazine; monthly; adv.
Transactions of the ASABE

Membership List Available to Non-members

American Society of Agricultural Appraisers *(1980)*
1126 Eastland Dr., North Suite 100
P.O. Box 186
Twin Falls, ID 83303-0186
Fax: (208) 733-2326
TollFree: (800) 488-7570
E-Mail: ag@amagappraisers.com
Website: amagappraisers.com
Members: 1200 individuals
Staff: 2
Annual Budget: $500-1,000,000

Personnel:
Executive Director: Jay Proost
Director, Education: Larry Lawson

Historical Note:
ASAA's mission is to provide educational and organizational support to members and to serve the public by producing qualified and ethical appraisers who are recognized authorities in the livestock and equipment appraisal fields. The Society consists of three divisions: International Society of Livestock Appraisers, American Society of Farm Equipment Appraisers, and American Society of Equine Appraisers. Membership: $395 (Individual/International); $495 (Dual).

Continuing Education:
Certification Designation/s: PPA

American Society of Agricultural Consultants *(1963)*
N78W14573 Appleton Ave.
Suite 287
Menomonee Falls, WI 53051
Tel: (262) 253-6902 *Fax:* (262) 253-6903
Website: agconsultants.org
Members: 125 individuals
Staff: 4
Annual Budget: $25-50,000
Tax: 501(c)(3)

Personnel:
President: Paige Gilligan
Executive Vice President: Carroll Merry
  E-Mail: cmerry@agconsultants.org
Vice President and Secretary: Russell Morgan
  E-Mail: russ.morgan@macsinc.biz
Chief Financial Officer: Erin Pirro

Historical Note:
ASAC's purpose is to foster the science of agricultural consulting, promote the profession and maintain high standards under which the members conduct their service to the public. It hold meetings for the exchange of ideas and the study of the profession of agricultural consulting. Membership: $210-350 (Certified); $195-325 (Individual); $500 (Sustaining); $50(Student); $75 (Retired).

Continuing Education:
Certification Designation/s: CAC, CACI

Meetings/Conferences:
Conference Chair: Carroll Merry

Publications:
ASAC News
Membership Directory; on-line

American Society of Agronomy (ASA, CSSA, SSSA) *(1907)*
5585 Guilford Rd.
Madison, WI 53711-5801
Tel: (608) 273-8080 *Fax:* (608) 273-2021
E-Mail: headquarters@agronomy.org
Website: agronomy.org
Members: 6408 individuals
Staff: 50
Annual Budget: $2-5,000,000
Tax: 501(c)(3)

Personnel:
Chief Executive Officer: Ellen G.M. Bergfeld
  E-Mail: ebergfeld@sciencesocieties.org
Manager, Science Communications: Teri Barr
  E-Mail: tbarr@sciencesocieties.org
Director, Membership Services: Susan Chapman
  E-Mail: schapman@sciencesocieties.org
Administrative Assistant: Rachael D. Jankowski
  E-Mail: rjankowski@sciencesocieties.org
Director, Publications: Mark Mandelbaum
  E-Mail: mmandelbaum@sciencesocieties.org
Chief Financial Officer: Wes Meixelsperger
  E-Mail: wm@sciencesocieties.org
Coordinator, Publications Marketing: Tricia Newell
  E-Mail: tnewell@sciencesocieties.org
Director, Information Technology and Operations: Ian
  Popkewitz
  E-Mail: ipopkewitz@sciencesocieties.org
Director, Meetings and Conventions: Keith Schlesinger
  E-Mail: kschlesinger@sciencesocieties.org
Director, Certification Programs: Luther Smith
  E-Mail: lsmith@sciencesocieties.org

Historical Note:
ASA is a scientific and educational organization, dedicated to fostering research, communications education, standards, and professionalism among people working in, or otherwise interested in agronomy and related activities. Members work for the conservation and wise use of natural resources to produce food, feed, and fiber crops while maintaining and improving the environment. Membership: $95-100 (Active); $35-40 (Graduate); $15 (Undergraduate); $47-62 (Emeritus).

Continuing Education:
Certification Designation/s: CPAg, CPSS/CPSC, CCA

Meetings/Conferences: Annual
2013 - Tampa, FL/Nov. 3 - 6
2014 - Long Beach, CA/Nov. 2 - 5
2015 - Minneapolis, MN/Nov. 15 - 18
2016 - Phoenix, AZ/Nov. 6 - 9
2017 - Tampa, FL/Oct. 22 - 25
2020 - Phoenix, AZ/Nov. 8 - 11
Number of non-conference events/year: 1

Publications:
Agronomy Journal; bi-monthly; adv.
Crop Science; bi-monthly; adv.
Crops and Soils; bi-monthly; adv.
CSA News Magazine; monthly; adv.
Journal of Environmental Quality; bi-monthly; adv.
Membership Directory; on-line
Methods of Introducing System Models into
  Agricultural Research
News Flash e-Newsletter; bi-weekly
Science Policy Newsletter; bi-weekly

Soil Science Society of America Journal; bi-monthly; adv.

Membership List Available to Non-members

American Society of Andrology *(1975)*
1100 E. Woodfield Rd.
Suite 520
Schaumburg, IL 60173
Tel: (847) 619-4909 *Fax:* (847) 517-7229
E-Mail: info@andrologysociety.com
Website: andrologysociety.com
Members: 775 members
Staff: 16
Annual Budget: $500-1,000,000
Tax: 501(c)(3)

Personnel:
Executive Director: Wendy J. Weiser
Manager, Information Technology and Web Development:
Marc Cakanic
Editor and Executive Editor: Ruth A. Gottmann MBA
Coordinator, Education: Lorene Harder
Meeting Planner: Maria Marchesi
Coordinator, Membership: Amy Meyer
Director, Operations: Debbie Roller
Accountant: Janet Ward

Historical Note:
ASA seeks to foster a multi-disciplinary approach to the study of male reproduction. Members are professionally qualified physicians, veterinarians, scientists, or laboratory technicians, graduate students, post-doctoral fellows, medical and veterinary students, medical residents, and fellows. Membership: $185-230 (Active); $40-55 (Trainee); $115-160 (Associate); $3,700 (Life Member).

Meetings/Conferences: Annual
Conference Chair: Maria Marchesi
2013 - San Antonio, TX (Hyatt Regency San Antonio)/
April 13 - 16
Number of non-conference events/year: 4

Publications:
Membership Directory
The Journal of Andrology; bi-monthly; adv.

American Society of Anesthesia Technologists and Technicians *(1989)*
7044 S. 13th St.
Oak Creek, WI 53154-1429
Tel: (414) 908-4942 *Fax:* (414) 768-8001
E-Mail: customercare@asatt.org
Website: asatt.org
Members: 1000 individuals
Staff: 1
Annual Budget: $250-500,000
Tax: 501(c)(6)

Personnel:
Executive Director: Mike Mcmanus
E-Mail: m.mcmanus@asatt.org

Historical Note:
ASATT was formed to address the needs of anesthesia support personnel and promote advances in anesthesia technology. ASATT's mission is to establish a professional entity for the field of Anesthesia Technology that will positively affect health care and quality standards, by raising the standards of patient care and by providing a safe anesthetic environment. Membership: $70 (Active), $80 (Associate/Individual/Physician/Nurse); $90 (International); $55 (Student); $135 (Corporate/ Institutional).

Continuing Education:
Enrollment: 100
Certification Designation/s: ASATT, CAT, CATT

Meetings/Conferences: Annual
Number of non-conference events/year: 7

Publications:
The Sensor; quarterly

Membership List Available to Non-members

American Society of Anesthesiologists *(1905)*
520 N. Northwest Hwy.
Park Ridge, IL 60068-2573
Tel: (847) 825-5586 *Fax:* (847) 825-1692
E-Mail: mail@asahq.org
Website: asahq.org
Members: 48000 individuals
Staff: 44
Annual Budget: $25-50,000,000
Tax: 501(c)(6)

Personnel:

Executive Vice President: John A. Thorner CAE, JD
E-Mail: j.thorner@asahq.org
Interim Director, Education and Professional Development Manager: Mary Carol Badat
E-Mail: m.badat@asahq.org
Chief Financial Officer: Thomas Conway CPA, MBA
E-Mail: t.conway@asahq.org
Manager, Human Resources: Sara Curtis MBA, SPHR
E-Mail: s.curtis@asahq.org
Director, Communications: Dawn M. Glossa
E-Mail: d.glossa@asahq.org
Manager, Sales and Marketing: Alexander Kahl MBA
E-Mail: a.kahl@asahq.org
Director, Member Services: Celeste Kirschner
E-Mail: c.kirschner@asahq.org
Director, Information Technology: Michael A. Parker
E-Mail: m.parker@asahq.org
Contact, Publications: Debbie Vena
E-Mail: d.vena@asahq.org
Director, Meetings and Exhibits: Christopher J. Wehking CMP
E-Mail: c.wehking@asahq.org

Historical Note:
Formerly (1905) the Long Island Society of Anesthetists, (1912) New York Society of Anesthetists, incorporated in 1936 as the American Society of Anesthetists, assumed its current name in 1945. ASA's mission is to elevate the standards of the specialty by fostering and encouraging education, research and scientific progress in anesthesiology.

Meetings/Conferences: Annual
Conference Chair: Christopher J. Wehking CMP
2013 - San Francisco, CA/Oct. 12 - 16
2014 - New Orleans, LA/Oct. 11 - 15
2015 - San Diego, CA/Oct. 24 - 28
2016 - Boston, MA/Oct. 15 - 19
2016 - Chicago, IL/Oct. 22 - 26
2017 - Orlando, FL/Oct. 14 - 18
2017 - Boston, MA/Oct. 21 - 25
2018 - San Francisco, CA/Oct. 13 - 17
2019 - Orlando, FL/Oct. 19 - 23
2019 - Chicago, IL/Oct. 26 - 30
2020 - San Antonio, TX/Oct. 17 - 21
Number of non-conference events/year: 2

Publications:
Anesthesiology
ASA Newsletter; monthly
Membership Directory; on-line
The Journal

American Society of Animal Science *(1908)*
P.O. 7410
Champaign, IL 61826-7410
Tel: (217) 356-9050 *Fax:* (217) 398-4119
E-Mail: asas@asas.org
Website: asas.org
Members: 5000 individuals
Staff: 10
Annual Budget: $2-5,000,000

Personnel:
Chief Executive Officer: Meghan C. Wulster-Radcliffe PhD
E-Mail: meghanwr@asas.org
Manager, Membership Services: Melissa Burnett
E-Mail: debis@assochq.org
Chief Operations Officer: Jacelyn Hemmelgarn
E-Mail: jacelynf@asas.org
Administrative Assistant: Judy McClughen
E-Mail: judym@assochq.org
Managing Editor: Susan Pollock
E-Mail: journals@assochq.org
Scientific Communications Associate: Madeline McCurry Schmidt
E-Mail: madelinems@asas.org
Executive Assistant and Event Coordinator: Debi Seymour
E-Mail: debis@assochq.org

Historical Note:
Formerly (1915)American Society of Animal Nutrition; (1961) American Society of Animal Production. ASAS seeks to discover, disseminate and apply knowledge for sustainable use of animals for food and other human needs. Membership: $375 (Individual Sustaining); $135 (Professional); $65 (Postdoctoral Fellow); $20 (Graduate Student Affiliate); Free (Undergraduate Student Affiliate).

Meetings/Conferences: Annual
Conference Chair: Debi Seymour
2013 - Indianapolis, IN (Indiana Convention Center)/
July 8 - 12/2700 attendees

2014 - Kansas City, MO/July 20 - 24

Publications:
Animal Frontiers; quarterly; adv.
Journal of Animal Science (JAS); monthly
Meeting Abstracts; on-line
Member Directory; on-line

American Society of Appraisers *(1952)*
11107 Sunset Hills Rd.
Suite 310
Reston, VA 20190
Tel: (703) 478-2228 *Fax:* (703) 742-8471
TollFree: (800) 272-8258
E-Mail: asainfo@appraisers.org
Website: appraisers.org
Members: 6000 individuals
Staff: 28
Annual Budget: $5-10,000,000
Tax: 501(c)(6)

Personnel:
Chief Executive Officer: James Hirt
E-Mail: jhirt@appraisers.org
Manager, Marketing: Andrea Burkhart
E-Mail: aburkhart@appraisers.org
Director, Membership Services and Reaccreditation: Susan Houchins
E-Mail: shouchins@appraisers.org
Associate Director, Accounting and Human Resources: Katrina Levesque
E-Mail: klevesque@appraisers.org
Director, Education and Accreditation: Sabri Math
E-Mail: smath@appraisers.org
Director, Marketing and Communications: Todd Paradis
E-Mail: tparadis@appraisers.org
Chief Operations Officer: Bonny F. Price
E-Mail: bprice@appraisers.org
Director, Government Relations: John G. Russell
E-Mail: jrussell@appraisers.org
Director, Information Technology: Sharlyne Tsai
E-Mail: stsai@appraisers.org
Chief Financial Officer: David Villani
E-Mail: dvillani@appraisers.org

Historical Note:
Formed by a merger of the Society of Technical Appraisers (founded in 1939) and the American Society of Technical Appraisers, ASA incorporated in 1952. Merged with the Association of Governmental Appraisers in 1985. Purpose is to appraise organization representing all the disciplines of appraisal specialists, ASA's office in Herndon, VA also serves as its international headquarters. Membership: $415/year (United States/Canada International).

Continuing Education:
Certification Designation/s: ASA, PEECP, CAVS

Publications:
ASA Fast-Read; bi-weekly
ASA Professional Magazine; quarterly; adv.

American Society of Architectural Illustrators *(1986)*
1022 Tait St.
Oceanside, CA 92054
Tel: (760) 453-2544 *Fax:* (760) 814-8448
E-Mail: hq@asai.org
Website: asai.org
Members: 350 individuals
Staff: 3
Annual Budget: $50-100,000

Personnel:
Executive Director: Tamara Horch-Prezioso
E-Mail: hq@asai.org
Website Manager: Jane Grealy
E-Mail: jane@janegrealy.com.au

Historical Note:
Formerly known as American Society of Architectural Perspectives. ASAI works to foster communication among architectural illustrators, to raise the standards of architectural illustration and to acquaint the public with the importance of such drawing as integral to the practice of architecture. Members are firms and individuals involved in architecture, and specifically in the art of architectural rendering as a design and presentation tool. Sponsors an annual juried competition, exhibitions and publications. Membership: $170 (Professional-North America/ International); $300 (Firm/Corporate); $35 (Student).

Publications:
Convergence; on-line

Membership List Available to Non-members

American Society of Artists (1972)

P.O. Box 1326
Palatine, IL 60078
Tel: (312) 751-2500
E-Mail: asoa@webtv.net
Website: americansocietyofartists.org
Members: 30000 individuals
Staff: 14
Annual Budget: $50-100,000

Personnel:
Membership Contact: Jury Material
   E-Mail: Asoaartists@aol.com

Historical Note:
ASA is an organization of professional artists, which sponsors art and crafts festivals and a lecture/ demonstration service and other services for members. Associate members are students, amateurs. Regular Membership based on the acceptance of jury only. Membership: $55/year.

Publications:
ASA Artisan; quarterly

American Society of Association Executives-The Center for Association Leadership (1920)

1575 I St. NW
12th Floor
Washington, DC 20005
Tel: (202) 371-0940 *Fax:* (202) 371-8315
TollFree: (888) 950-2723
E-Mail: asae@asaecenter.org
Website: asaecenter.org
Members:
10000 organizations
22,000 association executives
Staff: 161
Annual Budget: $25-50,000,000
Tax: 501(c)(6)

Personnel:
President and Chief Executive Officer: John Graham IV, CAE
   E-Mail: jgraham@asaenet.org
President ASAE Business Services, Inc.: Dixie Arthur
   E-Mail: darthur@asaecenter.org
Chief Learning Officer: Anne Blouin CAE
   E-Mail: ablouin@asaecenter.org
Manager, Meetings: Deborah Brawner CMP
   E-Mail: dbrawner@asaecenter.org
Marketing Manager: Taryn Burns
   E-Mail: tburns@asaecenter.org
Senior Vice President, Public Policy: James L. "Jim" Clarke CAE
   E-Mail: jclarke@asaenet.org
Director, Information Technology: Larry Covert
   E-Mail: lcovert@asaecenter.org
Representative, Member Services: Andrea Curry
   E-Mail: acurry@asaecenter.org
Senior Vice President and Publisher: Karl Ely CAE
   E-Mail: kely@asaecenter.org
Senior Director, Member Relations: Melody Jordan-Carr
   E-Mail: mcarr@asaecenter.org
Senior Manager, Public Relations: Sabrina Kidwai
   E-Mail: skidwai@asaecenter.org
Senior Vice President, Meetings and Expositions: Amy Ledoux CAE, CMP
   E-Mail: aledoux@asaecenter.org
Chief Marketing and Communications Officer: Robb Lee
   E-Mail: rlee@asaecenter.org
Vice President, Innovation and New Product Development: Mariah Burton Nelson CAE, MPH
   E-Mail: mnelson@asaecenter.org
Director, Marketing: Rosario Ortiz-Davis MBA CAE
   E-Mail: rortiz-davis@asaecenter.org
Chief Financial Officer: Heidi Robey
   E-Mail: hrobey@asaecenter.org
Manager, Information Technology: Carlos Shaw MCP
   E-Mail: cshaw@asaecenter.org
Senior Manager, Human Resources: Wiley Simons
   E-Mail: wsimons@asaecenter.org
Chief Administrative Officer: Robert Skelton CAE
   E-Mail: rskelton@asaecenter.org
Vice President, Publications: Keith Skillman CAE
   E-Mail: kskillman@asaecenter.org

Historical Note:
An organization of 25,000 professionals who manage 12,000 leading trade, individual, and voluntary organizations in the United States.

Continuing Education:
Certification Designation/s: CAE

Meetings/Conferences:
Conference Chair: Amy Ledoux CAE, CMP
2013 - Colorado Springs, CO (Broadmoor)/March 10 - 12/616 attendees
2013 - Washington, DC (Walter E. Washington Convention Center)/May 16
2013 - Washington, DC (Walter E. Washington Convention Center)/June 4 - 5
2013 - Atlanta, GA/Aug. 3 - 6
2014 - Nashville, TN/Aug. 9 - 12
2015 - Detroit, MI/Aug. 8 - 11
2016 - Salt Lake City, UT/Aug. 13 - 16
2017 - Toronto, ON/Aug. 12 - 15

Publications:
AMC Connection; quarterly
Association Law & Policy; monthly
Associations Now; monthly; adv.
Communication News; bi-monthly
Component Relations; bi-monthly
Consultants Connection; quarterly
Dollars & Cents; bi-monthly
Executive IdeaLink; bi-monthly
Global Link; bi-monthly
Government Relations; bi-monthly
Marketing Insights; bi-monthly
Meetings & Expositions; bi-monthly
Membership Developments; quarterly
Professional Development Forum Online; quarterly
TechnoScope; bi-monthly
Who's Who in Association Management; annually; adv.

American Society of Baking (1924)

P.O. Box 336
Swedesboro, NJ 08085
Tel: (800) 713-0462 *Fax:* (888) 315-2612
E-Mail: info@asbe.org
Website: asbe.org
Members: 2000 individuals
Staff: 4
Annual Budget: $500-1,000,000
Tax: 501(c)(6)

Personnel:
Executive Director: Kent Van Amburg
   E-Mail: kvanamburg@asbe.org
Director, Technology: Darla Eastlack
   E-Mail: deastlack@asbe.org
Manager, Membership: Amanda Gonzalez
   E-Mail: agonzalez@asbe.org
Director, Meetings and Operations: Tawnee Shuey CMP
   E-Mail: tshuey@asbe.org

Historical Note:
Formerly (1998) American Society of Bakery Engineers. ASB is a professional organization that brings together individuals in the grain-based food industry for personal development, recognition, networking, education and leadership. Membership: $185/year (Professional).

Meetings/Conferences: Annual
Conference Chair: Tawnee Shuey CMP
2013 - Chicago, IL (Chicago Marriott Downtown Magnificent Mile)/March 3 - 6

Publications:
E-newsletter; on-line
Member Directory; on-line

American Society of Bariatric Physicians (1950)

2821 S. Parker Rd.
Suite 625
Aurora, CO 80014
Tel: (303) 770-2526 *Fax:* (303) 779-4834
E-Mail: info@asbp.org
Website: asbp.org
Members: 1300 individuals
Staff: 6
Annual Budget: $1-2,000,000
Tax: 501(c)(6)

Personnel:
Executive Director: Laurie Traetow CPA, MAc
   E-Mail: laurie@asbp.org
Office Manager and Membership Coordinator: Karen Brenning
   E-Mail: karen@asbp.org
Director, Marketing and Communications: Heidi Gordon
   E-Mail: heidi@asbp.org
CME Director and Business Manager: Dana Mansell
   E-Mail: dana@asbp.org
Manager, Membership Services and Exhibit Sales: Anna Vanderkleed
   E-Mail: anna@asbp.org

Historical Note:
ASBP's mission is to advance and support the physician's role in treating overweight patients. Members are physicians specializing in the treatment of obesity. Membership: $475/ year (Physician); $325 (Associate); $150 (Affiliate); $125 (Student/Physician in training).

Continuing Education:
Enrollment: 1000
Certification Designation/s: CME

Meetings/Conferences: Annual
2013 - San Diego, CA/April 24 - 28

Publications:
American Journal of Bariatric Medicine - The Bariatrician; semi-annually; adv.
Newsletter; bi-monthly; adv.

Membership List Available to Non-members

American Society of Body Engineers (1945)

P.O. Box 80363
Rochester, MI 48308
Tel: (248) 219-4881
E-Mail: asbe@asbe.com
Members: 1600 individuals
Staff: 3
Annual Budget: $10-25,000

Personnel:
President: Richard George
   E-Mail: rgeorge@asbe.com
Secretary: Jeff Grundy
   E-Mail: jgrundy@asbe.com

Historical Note:
Founded as American Society of Body Engineers; became American Society of Body and Design Engineers in 1991, and reverted to its original name in 2000. Members are automotive engineers and auto body designers. Membership: $75/year (individual).

Continuing Education:
Certification Designation/s: CAT1AV5r12

American Society of Breast Disease (1976)

P.O. Box 1620
Frisco, TX 75034
Tel: (214) 368-6836 *Fax:* (214) 975-1832
Website: asbd.org
Members: 1200 individuals
Staff: 4
Annual Budget: $500-1,000,000
Tax: 501(c)(3)

Personnel:
President: Stephen A. Feig MD
Director, Operations: Chris Brockles
   E-Mail: cbrockles@asbd.org
Executive Administrator: Lynn Hamilton MD
Coordinator, Membership Services: Barb Hedinger
   E-Mail: barbh@asbd.org

Historical Note:
Formerly (1994) the Society for the Study of Breast Disease. ASBD's mission is to advocate a multidisciplinary team approach as the standard of excellence in managing benign and malignant breast conditions and provides professional education and advanced training in breast disease and cancer prevention, early detection, treatment, and survivorship. Membership: $0-10,000/year.

Meetings/Conferences: Annual
2013 - Amelia Island, FL (Ritz-Carlton, Amelia Island)/ Feb. 14 - 17

Publications:
ASBD Advisor; quarterly
Membership Directory; on-line

Membership List Available to Non-members

American Society of Brewing Chemists (1934)

3340 Pilot Knob Rd.
St. Paul, MN 55121
Tel: (651) 454-7250 *Fax:* (651) 454-0766
E-Mail: asbc@scisoc.org
Website: asbcnet.org
Members: 846 individuals
Staff: 22
Annual Budget: $500-1,000,000

Personnel:
Executive Officer: Steve C. Nelson

Director, Publications: Karen Cummings
  E-Mail: kcummings@scisoc.org
Manager, Education: Beth Elliott
  E-Mail: belliott@scisoc.org
Vice President, Finance: Barbara Mock
  E-Mail: bmock@scisoc.org

Historical Note:
ASBC was founded in 1934 to improve and bring uniformity to the brewing industry on a technical level. ASBC is represented by individual and corporate members worldwide representing large and small brewers, consultants, government agencies, academics, distillers, vintners and those working in allied industries (suppliers of malt, hops, enzymes, brewing syrups, chill proofing, filtration aids, C02 packaging materials, etc.). ASBC is dedicated to ensuring the quality, consistency and safety of malt-based beverages and their ingredients. Membership: $149 (Individual); $55 (Student); $325 (Corporate).

Meetings/Conferences:
Conference Chair: Beth Elliott
Number of non-conference events/year: 1

Publications:
ASBC Newsletter; adv.
Journal of the American Society of Brewing Chemists
Membership Directory; on-line

American Society of Business Publication Editors
(1964)
214 N. Hale St.
Wheaton, IL 60187
Tel: (630) 510-4588 *Fax:* (630) 510-4501
E-Mail: info@asbpe.org
Website: asbpe.org
Members: 800 individuals
Staff: 4
Annual Budget: $100-250,000

Personnel:
Executive Director: Janet Svazas
Secretary and Treasurer: Tina G. Barbaccia
Associate Director and Editor: Robin Sherman
  E-Mail: asbpe@bellsouth.net

Historical Note:
Formerly (1964) Society of Business Magazine Editors and (2000) American Society of Business Press Editors, ASBPE is the professional association for full-time and freelance editors and writers employed in the business, trade, and specialty press. Membership: $40-100/year.

Meetings/Conferences: Annual
Number of non-conference events/year: 1

Publications:
ASBPE News; on-line
ASBPE's online Membership Directory; on-line
Editor's Notes

American Society of Cataract and Refractive Surgery *(1974)*
4000 Legato Rd.
Suite 700
Fairfax, VA 22033-4003
Tel: (703) 591-2220 *Fax:* (703) 591-0614
E-Mail: ascrs@ascrs.org
Website: ascrs.org
Members: 9200 individuals
Staff: 13
Annual Budget: $10-25,000,000
Tax: 501(c)(6)

Personnel:
Executive Director: David A. Karcher
Director, Communications: John Ciccone
  E-Mail: JCiccone@ascrs.org
Director, Clinical Affairs: Paula Cooke
  E-Mail: pcooke@ascrs.org
Managing Editor: Christine Ford
  E-Mail: cford@ascrs.org
Director, Education: Laura R. Johnson
  E-Mail: ljohnson@ascrs.org
Contact, Membership Services: Michelle Martin
  E-Mail: mmartin@ascrs.org
Director, Government Relations: Nancey Kaplan McCann
  E-Mail: nmccann@ascrs.org
Director, Information System: Frank McDonough
  E-Mail: FMcDonough@ascrs.org
Director, Meetings and Conventions: Paula K. Schneider
  E-Mail: pschneider@ascrs.org
Director, Operations: Pattye Whitmer
  E-Mail: pwhitmer@ascrs.org

Historical Note:

Incorporated in California as the American Intraocular Implant Society, assumed its present name in 1986. ASCRS's mission is to advance the art and science of ophthalmic surgery and the knowledge and skills of ophthalmic surgeons. Membership is offered to physicians interested in anterior segment surgery working towards the advancement of ophthalmology. Membership: $485 (Domestic); $255 (International); $175 (Emeritus); $230((Military/Government).

Continuing Education:
Certification Designation/s: CME

Meetings/Conferences: Annual
Conference Chair: Paula K. Schneider
2013 - San Francisco, CA/April 19 - 23
2013 - San Francisco, CA/April 20 - 24
2014 - Boston, MA/April 25 - 29
2014 - Boston, MA/April 26 - 30
Number of non-conference events/year: 3

Publications:
ASCRS Washington Watch Weekly–Critical News from the Hill; weekly
EyeWorld Week; weekly
Journal of Cataract & Refractive Surgery; monthly
Membership Directory; on-line

American Society of Certified Engineering Technicians *(1964)*
P.O. Box 1536
Brandon, MS 39043-1356
Tel: (601) 824-8991 *Fax:* (913) 890-1021
Website: ascet.org
Members: 2000 individuals
Staff: 2
Annual Budget: $50-100,000
Tax: 501(c)(6)

Personnel:
President: Phil L. Gaughan CET
  E-Mail: Phil-Gaughan@ascet.org
Secretary, Treasurer and General Manager: Tim Latham
  E-Mail: tim-latham@ascet.org

Historical Note:
ASCET provides opportunities for technicians and technologists to magnify their status as vital members of the engineering team. Membership consists of certified and non-certified engineering technicians, technologists, registered professional engineers and land surveyors. Membership: $50/year (Certified/Registered/Regular).

Meetings/Conferences:
Number of non-conference events/year: 1

Publications:
ASCET Newsletter; quarterly; adv.
Member Directory; on-line

American Society of Cinematographers *(1919)*
P.O. Box 2230
Hollywood, CA 90078
Tel: (323) 969-4333 *Fax:* (323) 882-6391
TollFree: (800) 448-0145
E-Mail: office@theasc.com
Website: theasc.com
Members: 302 individuals
Staff: 20
Annual Budget: $2-5,000,000
Tax: 501(c)(3)

Personnel:
President: Stephen Lighthill

Historical Note:
ASC is dedicated to advance the art of film making. Membership is by invitation and is extended only to directors of photography with distinguished credits in the industry.

Meetings/Conferences:
Number of non-conference events/year: 1

Publications:
American Cinematographer Magazine; monthly; adv.

Membership List Available to Non-members

American Society of Civil Engineers *(1852)*
1801 Alexander Bell Dr.
Reston, VA 20191-4400
Tel: (703) 295-6300 *Fax:* (703) 295-6333
TollFree: (800) 548-2723
E-Mail: govwash@asce.org
Website: asce.org
Members: 147000 individuals
Staff: 295
Annual Budget: $25-50,000,000

Tax: 501(c)(3)

Personnel:
Executive Director: Patrick J Natale PE, CAE
  E-Mail: pnatale@asce.org
Chief Technology Officer: Joseph DeFiglia
Managing Director, Publications: Bruce Gossett
  E-Mail: bgossett@asce.org
Director, Communications: Jane Howell
  E-Mail: jhowell@asce.org
Managing Director, Government Relations and Infrastructure Initiatives: Brian T. Pallasch CAE
Managing Director, Human Resources: Kay Pulchiné
Deputy Executive Director: Lawrence H. Roth FAS, PE
  E-Mail: lroth@asce.org
Manager, Exhibits: Sean Scully
  E-Mail: sscully@asce.org
Chief Financial Officer: Pete Shavalay
Deputy Executive Director and General Counsel: Thomas Smith CAE

Historical Note:
Founded in New York City as the American Society of Civil Engineers and Architects. Dormant 1855-1867. Revived in 1868 as the American Society of Civil Engineers and incorporated in New York in 1877. ASCE's mission is to provide essential value to members, their careers, partners and the public by developing leadership, advancing technology, advocating lifelong learning and promoting the profession. Membership: $50-205/year.

Meetings/Conferences: Annual
Conference Chair: Sean Scully

Publications:
ASCE News; on-line
CE Magazine; monthly; adv.
Membership Directory; on-line

Membership List Available to Non-members

American Society of Clinical Hypnosis *(1957)*
140 N. Bloomingdale Rd.
Bloomingdale, IL 60108
Tel: (630) 980-4740 *Fax:* (630) 351-8490
E-Mail: info@asch.net
Website: asch.net
Members: 2500 individuals
Staff: 7
Annual Budget: $500-1,000,000
Tax: 501(c)(6)

Personnel:
Executive Vice President: John E. Kasper CAE, PhD
  E-Mail: asch-evp@www.asch.net
Manager, Membership and Certification: Elizabeth Kasper
  E-Mail: certification@asch.net
Director, Education: Emma Leighton
  E-Mail: eleighton@asch.net
Editor: Paul G. Taylor

Historical Note:
ASCH's mission is to provide and encourage education programs to further, in every ethical way, the knowledge, understanding, and application of hypnosis in health care and to encourage research and scientific publication in the field of hypnosis. Membership: $210 (Member/Associate/Researcher); $90 (Resident/Intern); $70 (Student); $185 (Canadian Membership); $77.50 (Resident/Intern-Canadian Members); $57.50 (Student-Canadian Members).

Continuing Education:
Certification Designation/s: CACP
Meetings/Conferences:
Number of non-conference events/year: 4

Publications:
American Journal of Clinical Hypnosis
ASCH Newsletter; quarterly

American Society of Clinical Oncology *(1964)*
2318 Mill Rd.
Suite 800
Alexandria, VA 22314
Tel: (571) 483-1300 *Fax:* (703) 299-1044
TollFree: (888) 282-2552
E-Mail: asco@asco.org
Website: asco.org
Members:
293 member groups
19 individuals
Staff: 13
Annual Budget: $50-100,000,000
Tax: 501(c)(3)

Personnel:
Chief Executive Officer: Allen Sollie Lichter MD

Senior Director, Finance and Administration update: Paul Aines CPA, MBA
Senior Director, Marketing: Suzanne Brach
Senior Director, Meeting and Membership Services: Jean Colvard
Director, Government Relations: Shelagh E. Foster
    E-Mail: foster@asco.org
Senior Counsel: Mary C. Hennessey
    E-Mail: mary.hennessey@asco.org
Senior Director, Communications and Patient Information: Kristin Ludwig
Vice President and General Counsel: Dina Michels Esq.
Senior Director, Education, Science and Professional Development: Cara Molinari
Senior Director, Human Resources: Kay Noll

Historical Note:
ASCO's mission is to advance the education of physicians and other professionals in the care of patients with cancer and supporting research and the development of clinical cancer researchers. Members are academicians in universities, medical centers, teaching and research facilities affiliated with cancer centers, major hospitals, as well as physicians in community practice. Membership: $520 (Active); $295 (Full); $140 (Allied); $115 (Affiliate); $50-210 (International Corresponding).

Continuing Education:
Certification Designation/s: MOC, CME

Meetings/Conferences: Annual
Conference Chair: Jean Colvard
2013 - Chicago, IL (McCormick Place)/May 31 - June 4
2014 - Chicago, IL/May 30 - June 3
2015 - Chicago, IL/May 29 - June 2
2016 - Chicago, IL/June 3 - 7
2017 - Chicago, IL/June 2 - 6
2018 - Chicago, IL/June 1 - 5
2019 - Chicago, IL/May 31 - June 4
2020 - Chicago, IL/May 29 - June 2
Number of non-conference events/year: 10

Publications:
ASCO Newsletter; monthly
ASCO Services; weekly
Journal of Clinical Oncology.
Membership Directory; on-line
The ASCO Daily News e-Digest; daily

Membership List Available to Non-members

American Society of Clinical Psychopharmacology (1992)
5034-A Thoroughbred Ln.
Brentwood, TN 37027
Tel: (615) 649-3085 *Fax*: (888) 417-3311
Website: ascpp.org
Members: 800 individuals
Staff: 2
Annual Budget: $500-1,000,000

Personnel:
President: John M. Kane MD
    E-Mail: psychiatry@lij.edu

Historical Note:
ASCP's mission is to advance the science and practice of clinical psychopharmacology. Membership: $100 (Physician/Doctoral level Scientist); Free (Residents).

Continuing Education:
Certification Designation/s: ASCP

Meetings/Conferences: Annual
2013 - Hollywood, FL (Westin Diplomat Resort and Spa)/May 28 - 31/1200 attendees
2014 - Hollywood, FL (Westin Diplomat Resort and Spa)/June 16 - 19
Number of non-conference events/year: 1

Publications:
Biological Therapies in Psychiatry; monthly
Journal of Clinical Psychiatry; monthly

Membership List Available to Non-members

American Society of Colon and Rectal Surgeons (1899)
85 W. Algonquin Rd.
Suite 550
Arlington Heights, IL 60005-4460
Tel: (847) 290-9184 *Fax*: (847) 290-9203
E-Mail: ascrs@fascrs.org
Website: fascrs.org
Members: 2700 members
Staff: 19
Annual Budget: $5-10,000,000

Tax: 501(c)(3)
Personnel:
Executive Director: Rick Slawny
    E-Mail: rickslawny@fascrs.org
Director, Finance: Sarah Adcock
    E-Mail: sarahadcock@fascrs.org
Editor: Dick Bragaw
    E-Mail: rbragaw@bragawpr.com
Director, Development: Linda Cullison
    E-Mail: lindacullison@fascrs.org
Contact, Information Technology: Jeff Kiva
    E-Mail: jeffkiva@fascrs.org
Director, Exhibits: Jean Lynch
    E-Mail: jeanlynch@fascrs.org
Chief Financial Officer: John Nocera
    E-Mail: johnnocera@fascrs.org
Director, Meetings and Conventions: Gina Seegers
    E-Mail: ginaseegers@fascrs.org

Historical Note:
Founded in Columbus, Ohio as the American Proctologic Society with 12 charter members. Incorporated in Delaware (1947). Became (1973) the American Society of Colon and Rectal Surgeons. Sponsored the formation of the American Board of Colon and Rectal Surgery and (1957) founded the American Society of Colon and Rectal Surgeons Research Foundation. ASCRS dedicated to assuring high quality patient care by advancing the science through research and education for prevention and management of disorders of the colon, rectum and anus. Members are surgeons and other professionals. Membership: $225/year (Individual).

Meetings/Conferences: Annual
Conference Chair: Gina Seegers
2013 - Phoenix, AZ (Phoenix Convention Center)/April 27 - May 1
2014 - Hollywood, FL (Westin Diplomat Resort and Spa)/May 17 - 21
2015 - Boston, MA (Hynes Convention Center and Sheraton Boston Hotel)/May 30 - June 3
2016 - Seatle, WA (Washington State Convention Center and Sheraton Seattle Hotel)/June 4 - 7

Publications:
ASCRS News; semi-annually
Diseases of the Colon & Rectum (DCR); monthly

American Society of Comparative Law (1951)
University of Connecticut School of Law
65 Elizabeth St.
Hartford, CT 06105
Tel: (860) 570-5172 *Fax*: (860) 570-5242
Website: comparativelaw.org
Members: 100 organizations
Staff: 3
Annual Budget: $50-100,000
Tax: 501(c)(3)

Personnel:
President: John C. Reitz
Treasurer: Richard S. Kay
Editor-in-Chief: Mathias W. Reimann
    E-Mail: purzel@umich.edu

Historical Note:
Formerly (1992) American Association for the Comparative Study of Law. ASCL's purpose is to promote the comparative study of law and the understanding of foreign legal systems and to establish, maintain and publish a comparative law journal and other publications related to the subject without a profit. Membership: $700 (Sponsor); $90 (Associate); $500 (Sustaining).

Meetings/Conferences: Annual
Number of non-conference events/year: 1

Publications:
American Journal of Comparative Law; quarterly
Membership Directory; on-line

American Society of Composers, Authors and Publishers (ASCAP) (1914)
One Lincoln Plaza
New York, NY 10023
Tel: (212) 621-6000 *Fax*: (212) 621-8453
TollFree: (800) 952-7227
E-Mail: info@ascap.com
Website: ascap.com
Members: 435000 individuals
Staff: 3
Annual Budget: $2-5,000,000

Personnel:
Chief Executive Officer: John LoFrumento
Treasurer: James M. Kendrick

Historical Note:
Membership association involved in musical performance rights.

Meetings/Conferences: Annual
2013 - Los Angeles, CA (Loews Hollywood Hotel)/April 18 - 20
Number of non-conference events/year: 2

Publications:
ASCAP Daily Brief; daily
Inside Music Newsletter

American Society of Concrete Contractors (1964)
2025 S. Brentwood Blvd.
Suite 105
St. Louis, MO 63144
Tel: (314) 962-0210 *Fax*: (314) 968-4367
TollFree: (866) 788-2722
E-Mail: ascc@ascconline.org
Website: ascconline.org
Members: 550 member companies
Staff: 7
Annual Budget: $1-2,000,000

Personnel:
Executive Director: Bev Garnant
    E-Mail: bgarnant@ascconline.org
Technical Director: Ward Malisch
    E-Mail: wmalisch@ascconline.org

Historical Note:
Formerly (1998) American Society for Concrete Construction. ASCC's mission is to enhance the capabilities of those who build with concrete. Members include contracting firms, manufacturers, suppliers, designers and other professionals. Membership: $450-995 (Contractor Companies); $250 (Professional); $850 (Associate); $2,000 (Sustaining).

Meetings/Conferences: Annual
2013 - West Palm Beach, FL (Breakers)/July 25 - 28
Number of non-conference events/year: 1

Publications:
ASCC Newsletter; monthly
Membership Directory; on-line
Troubleshooting Newsletter; weekly

Membership List Available to Non-members

American Society of Consultant Pharmacists (1965)
1321 Duke St.
Alexandria, VA 22314-3563
Tel: (703) 739-1300 *Fax*: (703) 739-1321
TollFree: (800) 355-2727
E-Mail: info@ascp.com
Website: ascp.com
Members: 11500 individuals
Staff: 34
Annual Budget: $5-10,000,000

Personnel:
Executive Director and Chief Executive Officer: Vera R. Jackson
    E-Mail: vjackson@ascp.com
Managing Editor: Marlene Bloom
    E-Mail: mbloom@ascp.com
Senior Director, Professional, Clinical and Government Affairs: Arnold Clayman
    E-Mail: aclayman@ascp.com
Director, Digital Communications: William Davis
    E-Mail: wdavis@ascp.com
Chief Financial Officer: Viresh Desai
    E-Mail: vdesai@ascp.com
Senior Director, Administration: Leslie Dykstra
    E-Mail: ldykstra@ascp.com
Senior Director, Membership and Chapter Relations: Debbie Furman
    E-Mail: dfurman@ascp.com
Senior Director, Educational Affairs: Joe Gerber
    E-Mail: jgerber@ascp.com
Manager, Data Systems: Dave Livingston
    E-Mail: dlivingston@ascp.com
Human Resources Representative: Susan Oswald
    E-Mail: soswald@ascp.com
Senior Director, Business Development and Events: Lee Anne Pirrello
    E-Mail: lpirrello@ascp.com

Historical Note:
ASCP empowers pharmacists to enhance quality of care for all older persons through the appropriate use of medication and the promotion of healthy aging. Membership: $122-12,500/year.

Continuing Education:
Certification Designation/s: CCP, CCGP, CGP

Meetings/Conferences: Annual
Conference Chair: Lee Anne Pirrello
2013 - Orlando, FL (Walt Disney World Resort)/May 15 - 17
2013 - Seatle, WA (Washington State Convention Center)/Nov. 19 - 22
2014 - Phoenix, AZ (JW Marriott Desert Ridge Resort)/ June 12 - 14
2014 - Orlando, FL (Gaylord Palms Resort and Convention Center-Orlando)/Nov. 4 - 7

Publications:
ASCP Clinical Connections; weekly
ASCP Insider
ASCP's Membership Enewsletter; monthly
The Consultant Pharmacist; monthly

Membership List Available to Non-members

American Society of Consulting Arborists *(1967)*
9707 Key West Ave.
Suite 100
Rockville, MD 20850
Tel: (301) 947-0483 *Fax:* (301) 990-9771
E-Mail: asca@mgmtsol.com
Website: asca-consultants.org
Members: 600 Consulting Arborists
Staff: 8
Annual Budget: $250-500,000
Tax: 501(c)(6)

Personnel:
Executive Director: Beth W. Palys CAE
Senior Graphic Designer: Jon Benjamin
  E-Mail: jbenjamin@mgmtsol.com
Registration Manager: Julie Burgess
Manager, Communications: Julie Hill
Vice President, Meetings: Grace L. Jan CAE, CMP
  E-Mail: gjan@mgmtsol.com
Contact, Accounts: Dawn Rosenfeld
Director, Education: Bill Scott
Manager, Membership Services: Shannon Sperati
  E-Mail: ssperati@mgmtsol.com

Historical Note:
ASCA is a society of individuals skilled in diagnosing problems and appraising the value of shade and ornamental trees. Members are professionals who bring comprehensive, objective viewpoints to the diagnosis, appraisal and evaluation of arboricultural issues. Membership: $440/year, includes a processing fee of $75.

Continuing Education:
Certification Designation/s: RCA

Meetings/Conferences: Annual
Conference Chair: Julie Burgess
2013 - Uncasville, CT (Mohegan Sun Conference Center)/Dec. 4 - 7
2014 - Palm Spring, CA (Westin Mission Hills Resort and Spa)/Dec. 2 - 5
Number of non-conference events/year: 1

Publications:
Membership Directory; on-line
The Arboricultural Consultant; quarterly

American Society of Crime Laboratory Directors *(1974)*
139-A Technology Dr.
Garner, NC 27529
Tel: (919) 773-2044 *Fax:* (919) 861-9930
Website: ascld.org
Members: 610 individuals
Staff: 3
Annual Budget: $250-500,000
Tax: 501(c)(3)

Personnel:
President: Jill Spriggs
Executive Director: John Collins
Treasurer: Jean Stover

Historical Note:
ASCLD's mission is to acquire, preserve and disseminate forensic based information and to promote, encourage and maintain the standards of practice in the field. Membership: $140 (Regular); $75 (Retired); $115 (Academic Affiliate).

Meetings/Conferences: Annual

Publications:
Crime Lab Minute; irregular
Membership Directory; on-line

American Society of Criminology *(1941)*
1314 Kinnear Rd.
Suite 212
Columbus, OH 43212-1156
Tel: (614) 292-9207 *Fax:* (614) 292-6767
E-Mail: asc@asc41.com
Website: asc41.com
Members: 3200 individuals
Staff: 2
Annual Budget: $1-2,000,000
Tax: 501(c)(3)

Personnel:
President: Robert Sampson
Contact, Membership Services: Susan Case
  E-Mail: asc@asc41.com

Historical Note:
Established in Berkeley, California as the Society for the Advancement of Criminology, it absorbed the Association of College Police Training Officials in 1947 and assumed its present name in 1956. Affiliated with the American Association for the Advancement of Science. ASC's mission is to stimulate the exchange, in a multidisciplinary setting, of those engaged in research, teaching, and practice so as to foster criminological scholarship, and to serve as a forum for the dissemination of criminological knowledge. Members are criminologists, psychologists, sociologists and students in institutions of higher learning. Membership: $50 (Student); $90 (Active); $55 (Retired/Student Partner); $95 (Joint- Partner/Spouse).

Meetings/Conferences: Annual
Conference Chair: Susan Case
2013 - Atlanta, GA (Atlanta Marriott Century Center)/ Nov. 20 - 23
2014 - San Francisco, CA (San Francisco Marriott Marquis)/Nov. 19 - 22
2015 - Washington, DC (Washington Hilton)/Nov. 18 - 21
2016 - New Orleans, LA (New Orleans Hilton)/Nov. 16 - 19
2017 - Philadelphia, PA (Philadelphia Marriott Downtown)/Nov. 15 - 18
2018 - Atlanta, GA (Atlanta Marriott Marquis)/Nov. 14 - 17
2019 - San Francisco, CA (San Francisco Marriott Marquis)/Nov. 20 - 23
2020 - Washington, DC (Washington Hilton)/Nov. 18 - 21
2021 - Chicago, IL (Palmer House Hilton Hotel)/Nov. 17 - 20
2022 - Atlanta, GA (Atlanta Marriott Marquis)/Nov. 16 - 19
2023 - Philadelphia, PA (Philadelphia Marriott Downtown)/Nov. 15 - 18
2024 - San Francisco, CA (San Francisco Marriott Marquis)/Nov. 13 - 16

Publications:
Criminology
Criminology and Public Policy
Member Directory; on-line
The Criminologist; irregular

Membership List Available to Non-members

American Society of Cytopathology *(1951)*
100 W. Tenth St.
Suite 605
Wilmington, DE 19801
Tel: (302) 543-6583 *Fax:* (302) 543-6597
E-Mail: asc@cytopathology.org
Website: cytopathology.org
Members: 3000 individuals
Staff: 6
Annual Budget: $2-5,000,000
Tax: 501(c)(3)

Personnel:
Executive Director: Elizabeth Jenkins
  E-Mail: bjenkins@cytopathology.org
Coordinator, Web Content and Administrative Assistant: Mark Bramble
  E-Mail: tclark@cytopathology.org
Contact, Membership Services and Financial Assistant: JoAnn Jenkins
  E-Mail: jjenkins@cytopathology.org
Coordinator, Cytotechnology Programs Review Committee and Editorial Assistant: Deborah MacIntyre
  E-Mail: dmacintyre@cytopathology.org
Coordinator, Educational Programs: Jodi Smith
  E-Mail: jsmith@cytopathology.org

Historical Note:
Formed as the Inter-Society Cytology Council. Incorporated in Delaware in 1966. Became American Society of Cytology in 1961; assumed current name in 1994. The American Society of Cytopathology is the premier organization for the promotion of cytopathology with its primary focus on: continuing medical education, public education, research, professional practice issues and standards, ethics, advocacy in Behalf of Members, Patients, Providers. Their members are physicians, cytotechnologists, and scientists employing the cytologic method of diagnostic pathology. Membership: $0-283/year

Meetings/Conferences: Annual
2013 - Orlando, FL (Hilton Orlando Bonnet Creek)/ Nov. 8 - 12
Number of non-conference events/year: 1

Publications:
eJournal; on-line
Vendor Directory; on-line

American Society of Dentist Anesthesiologists
2103 S. Tan Court, Unit C
Chicago, IL 60616
Tel: (312) 624-9591 *Fax:* (773) 304-9894
E-Mail: asda@asdahq.org
Website: asdahq.org
Members: 275 members
Staff: 2
Annual Budget: $250-500,000

Personnel:
Executive Director: Amy L. Brown MBA
  E-Mail: abrown@asdahq.org

Historical Note:
ASDA works to support and encourage the clinical practice of anesthesia by dentists and to promote the acquisition and dissemination of scientific knowledge associated therewith. Members are dentists who have completed a minimum of two years of full-time postdoctoral training in anesthesiology and who works to improve access to care. Membership: $495 (Active); $247.50 (Associate); $123.75 (Affiliate); $49.50 (Resident); $25 (Predocoral Dental Student).

Meetings/Conferences: Annual
2013 - San Diego, CA (Hard Rock Hotel San Diego)/ April 4 - 6

Publications:
Anesthesia Progress; quarterly
ASDA Newsletter; quarterly
Membership Directory; on-line

Membership List Available to Non-members

American Society of Dermatological Retailers *(1989)*
320 Superior Ave.
Suite 395
Newport Beach, CA 92663-3501
Tel: (949) 646-9098 *Fax:* (949) 646-7298
TollFree: (800) 469-3739
E-Mail: dermdoc58@aol.com
Members: 10 individuals
Staff: 2
Annual Budget: $25-50,000

Personnel:
Medical Director: Jeffrey Lauber MD
  E-Mail: dermdoc58@aol.com

Historical Note:
ASDR members are board-certified dermatologists concerned with marketing standards for skin care products.

American Society of Dermatology *(1992)*
First Financial Plaza, 1006
411 Hamilton Blvd.
Peoria, IL 61602
Tel: (309) 676-4074 *Fax:* (309) 676-3522
E-Mail: jeremy@aapsonline.org
Website: asd.org
Staff: 2
Annual Budget: $25-50,000

Personnel:
Executive Director: M. John Hanni CAE, Jr.

Historical Note:
ASD's mission is to facilitate optimal dermatologic care being available to all citizens of the country by preserving, promoting and enhancing the private practice of dermatology. Membership: $275 (Fellow/Affiliate/ Associate/Corporate); $12 (Student); $31 (Resident).

Publications:
Frontline Newsletter

American Society of Dermatopathology (1963)
111 Deer Lake Rd.
Suite 100
Deerfield, IL 60015
Tel: (847) 400-5820 *Fax:* (847) 480-9282
E-Mail: info@asdp.org
Website: asdp.org
Members: 1100 individuals
Staff: 5
Annual Budget: $1-2,000,000
Tax: 501(c)(6)

Personnel:
Executive Director: Leah McCrackin
 E-Mail: lmccrackin@asdp.org
Manager, Meetings and Exhibitions: Liz Freyn
 E-Mail: lfreyn@asdp.org
Specialist, Membership Services: Brenda Howe
 E-Mail: bhowe@asdp.org
Administrator: Maggie Substalae
 E-Mail: msubstalae@asdp.org
Manager, Marketing Communications: Patricia Sullivan
 E-Mail: psullivan@asdp.org

Historical Note:
ASDP seeks to improve the quality of dermatopathology as practiced by the dermatologists and pathologists. Members are pathologists or dermatologists who have extra training or expertise in the study of skin biopsies. Membership: $390 (Fellow/Associate); $100 (Non-Resident Associate).

Meetings/Conferences: Annual
Conference Chair: Liz Freyn
2013 - Washington, DC (Washington Marriott
 Wardman Park)/Oct. 3 - 6
2014 - Chicago, IL (Hilton Chicago)/Nov. 6 - 9
2015 - San Francisco, CA (Hilton San Francisco Union
 Square)/Oct. 8 - 11

Publications:
Journal of Cutaneous Pathology; monthly
Membership Directory; on-line

American Society of Dowsers (1961)
P.O. Box 24
184 Brainerd St.
Danville, VT 05828
Tel: (802) 684-3417 *Fax:* (802) 684-2565
E-Mail: asd@dowsers.org
Website: dowsers.org
Members: 3,000 members
Staff: 2
Annual Budget: $250-500,000

Personnel:
Bookkeeper and Membership Secretary: Lisa Lacoss
 E-Mail: bookkeeper@dowsers.org
Operations Manager: Nathan Platt
 E-Mail: asd@dowsers.org

Historical Note:
Purpose of ASD is to assemble all manner of dowsing theories, ideas, techniques, applications, instrumentation, experiences, etc. for study and evaluation. The American Society of Dowsers was founded to disseminate knowledge of dowsing (water witching, discovery of lost articles or persons, and related para-psychological phenomena), development of its skills, and recognition for its achievements. Memberships: $50 (Individual); $75 (Family Two); $60-80 (International); $250-1250 (Lifetime); $25-110 (Other).

Meetings/Conferences: Annual
2013 - Lyndonville, VT (Lyndon State College)/June 7
 - 9

Publications:
Newsletter; adv.
The American Dowser; quarterly; adv.

American Society of Echocardiography (1975)
2100 Gateway Centre Blvd.
Suite 310
Morrisville, NC 27560
Tel: (919) 861-5574 *Fax:* (919) 882-9900
E-Mail: asc@mercury.interpath.net
Website: asecho.org
Members: 9700 individuals
Staff: 25
Annual Budget: $5-10,000,000

Personnel:
Chief Executive Officer: Robin L. Wiegerink CAE
 E-Mail: rwiegerink@asecho.org
President: James D. Thomas MD
 E-Mail: president@asecho.org

Historical Note:
ASE's mission is to excel in cardiovascular ultrasound and its application to patient care through education, advocacy, research, innovation and service to its members and the public. Membership: $50 (Sonographer Student/ Medical Student); $75 (Retired/Early Career Cardiovascular Sonographer/Early Career Nurse/Fellow in Training); $95 (Cardiovascular Sonographer/Nurse); $125 (Early Career Physician/Early Career Scientist); $225 (Physician/Scientist/Lab Manager); $50-160 (International Membership).

Continuing Education:
Certification Designation/s: CME

Meetings/Conferences: Annual
2013 - Minneapolis, MN (Minneapolis Convention
 Center)/June 29 - July 2

Publications:
Journal of the American Society of Echocardiography;
 monthly; adv.
Membership Directory; on-line

Membership List Available to Non-members

American Society of Electroneurodiagnostic Technologists (1959)
402 E. Bannister Rd.
Suite A
Kansas City, MO 64131-3019
Tel: (816) 931-1120 *Fax:* (816) 931-1145
E-Mail: info@aset.org
Website: aset.org
Members: 3550 individuals and 149 institutions
Staff: 13
Annual Budget: $500-1,000,000
Tax: 501(c)(6)

Personnel:
Executive Director: Arlen Reimnitz
 E-Mail: arlen@aset.org
Manager, Marketing and Communications: Sarah Ecker
 E-Mail: sarah@aset.org
Manager, Governmental and Grassroots Advocacy:
 Bradley Hix
 E-Mail: bradley@aset.org
Director, Education: Faye McNall
 E-Mail: faye@aset.org
Director, Publications: Lucy Sullivan
 E-Mail: lucy@aset.org
Coordinator, Membership Services: Kathy Wolff
 E-Mail: taylor@aset.org

Historical Note:
ASET provides leadership, advocacy and resources that promote professional excellence and quality patient care in neurodiagnostics. Members include technologists, students, lab managers, physicians and institutions involved in EEG, evoked potentials, polysomnography, nerve conduction studies, intraoperative monitoring, and related neurodiagnostics. Membership: $50-100 (Active); $56-112 (Associate); $25-50 (Student); $218-435 (Institution).

Meetings/Conferences: Annual
2013 - Reno, NV (Peppermill Resort Spa Casino)/Aug.
 1 - 3
2014 - Asheville, NC (Grove Park Inn)/Aug. 20 - 23

Publications:
The American Journal of Electroneurodiagnostic
 Technology; quarterly; adv.

Membership List Available to Non-members

American Society of Emergency Radiology (1988)
4550 Post Oak Pl.
Suite 342
Houston, TX 77027
Tel: (713) 965-0566 *Fax:* (713) 960-0488
E-Mail: aser@meetingmanagers.com
Website: erad.org
Members: 430 individuals
Staff: 4
Annual Budget: $250-500,000
Tax: 501(c)(3)

Personnel:
Association Manager: Angela Davis
 E-Mail: ADavis@meetingmanagers.com
Meeting and Association Coordinator: Savanna Lott
 E-Mail: slot@meetingmanagers.com
Manager, Meetings: Jessica Whalen
 E-Mail: jwhalen@meetingmanagers.com
Editor-In-Chief: Ronald J. Zagoria MD

Historical Note:
The mission of the American Society of Emergency Radiology is to advance the quality of diagnosis and treatment of acutely ill or injured patients by means of medical imaging and to enhance teaching and research in Emergency Radiology.Members are practicing radiologists, scientists, imaging technologists, physician assistants in radiology, practice assistants in radiology, or non-radiological physicians, or physicians in training in the field of radiology with an interest in emergency radiology. Membership: $275 (Active/Associate); $55 (Member-in-Training).

Meetings/Conferences: Annual
Conference Chair: Jessica Whalen

Publications:
ASER Membership Directory; on-line
ASER Newsletter; annually
Emergency Radiology; bi-monthly

American Society of Equine Appraisers (1985)
1126 Eastland Dr. North, Suite 100
P.O. Box 186
Twin Falls, ID 83303-0186
Fax: (208) 733-2326
TollFree: (800) 704-7020
E-Mail: equine@equineappraiser.com
Website: equineappraiser.com
Staff: 2

Personnel:
Executive Director: Jay Proost
Director, Education: Larry Lawson

Historical Note:
A division of the American Society of Agricultural Appraisers. ASEA's mission is to provide educational and organizational support to ASEA members and to serve the public by producing qualified and ethical appraisers who are recognized authorities in the horse appraisal field. Membership: $395/year.

Publications:
Membership Directory; on-line

American Society of Extra-Corporeal Technology (1964)
2209 Dickens Rd.
Richmond, VA 23230-2005
Tel: (804) 565-6363 *Fax:* (804) 282-0090
Website: amsect.org
Members: 2000 individuals
Staff: 7
Annual Budget: $500-1,000,000
Tax: 501(c)(3)

Personnel:
Executive Director: Stewart A. Hinckley CMP
 E-Mail: stewart@amsect.org
Manager, Meetings and Conventions: Matt Carpenter
 E-Mail: mattc@societyhq.com
Contact, Membership Services: Greg Leasure
Association Manager: Donna Pendarvis
 E-Mail: donna@amsect.org
Managing Editor: Barbara Tolan
 E-Mail: jectedit@aol.com
Chairman, Government Relations: Michael Troike
 E-Mail: mtroike@bellsouth.net
Manager, Corporate and Educational Support: Matt Van
 Wie
 E-Mail: mattv@amsect.org

Historical Note:
Formerly (1968) the American Society of Extracorporeal Circulation Technicians. AmSECT strives to foster improved patient care by providing for the continuing education and professional needs of the extracorporeal circulation technology community. Membership: $15-225/year.

Continuing Education:
Certification Designation/s: CCP

Meetings/Conferences:
Conference Chair: Matt Carpenter
2013 - Las Vegas, NV (Red Rock Casino Resort and
 Spa)/March 6 - 9

Publications:
AmSECT Today; adv.
Journal of ExtraCorporeal Technology; adv.

Membership List Available to Non-members

American Society of Farm Managers and Rural Appraisers (1929)
950 S. Cherry St.
Suite 508
Denver, CO 80246-2664
Tel: (303) 758-3513 *Fax:* (303) 758-0190

E-Mail: Info@asfmra.org
Website: asfmra.org
Members: 2700 individuals
Staff: 10
Annual Budget: $1-2,000,000
Tax: 501(c)(6)

Personnel:
Executive Vice President: Brian Stockman
    E-Mail: bstockman@asfmra.org
Director, Finances and Administration: Meg Butcher
    E-Mail: mbutcher@asfmra.org
Manager, Information Technology and Communications:
    Cheryl L. Cooley
    E-Mail: ccooley@asfmra.org
Coordinator, Membership Services: Hope S. Evans
    E-Mail: hevans@asfmra.org
Director, Education: Mark Grace
    E-Mail: mgrace@asfmra.org

Historical Note:
ASFMRA members protect and serve their clients with
trustworthy valuation, management, consulting and
marketing services. ASFMRA members are agricultural
professionals with an interest in understanding the
interaction between the land and the forces that influence its
markets and products. Membership: $25-750/year.

Continuing Education:
Certification Designation/s: ARA, AAC, AFM, RPRA

Meetings/Conferences: Annual
Conference Chair: Cheryl L. Cooley
Number of non-conference events/year: 2

Publications:
Ag News; weekly
ASFMRA Updates; weekly
Journal of the ASFMRA; annually
LandOwner Newsletter; bi-monthly
Legislative Action News
Membership Directory; annually; adv.

The American Society of Forensic Odontology
(1970)
4414 82nd St., Suite 212
P. O. Box 121
Lubbock, TX 79424
Tel: (250) 426-2354
E-Mail: director@asfo.org
Website: asfo.org
Members: 1000 members
Staff: 4
Annual Budget: Under $10,000

Personnel:
Executive Director: Bruce A. Schrader
    E-Mail: director@asfo.org
Editor: Dr. Howard Cooper
    E-Mail: editor@asfo.org
Treasurer: Dr. Tom Gromling
    E-Mail: tgromling@asfo.org
Webmaster: Dane Johnson
    E-Mail: webmaster@asfo.org

Historical Note:
ASFO promotes the study of forensic dentistry. Members
are dentists and others interested in the study of teeth
for identification purposes, particularly in relation to
malpractice, child abuse and bite mark identification.
Membership: $75 (New Member); $15 (Student).

Meetings/Conferences: Annual
2013 - Washington, DC (Marriot Wardham Park)/Feb.
    19
Number of non-conference events/year: 1

Publications:
Newsletter

American Society of Furniture Designers (1981)
144 Woodland Dr.
New London, NC 28127
Tel: (910) 576-1273 Fax: (910) 576-1573
E-Mail: info@asfd.com
Website: asfd.com
Members: 200 individuals and corporations
Staff: 1
Annual Budget: $25-50,000
Tax: 501(c)(6)

Personnel:
Executive Director: Christine Evans

Historical Note:
The American Society of Furniture Designers is committed
to excellence, innovation, education and originality
in the practice of Furniture Design. Membership:

$225 (Professional/International Professional); $140
(Professional 'B'/Affiliate/Associate); $600 (Corporate/
International Corporate); $75 (Corporate Representative);
$35 (Student); $50 (Professional Retired).

Meetings/Conferences: Annual

Publications:
Membership Directory; annually
Newsletter

American Society of Gas Engineers (1954)
P.O. Box 66
Artesia, CA 90702
Tel: (949) 733-4304 Fax: (949) 733-4320
E-Mail: asgecge@aol.com
Website: asge-national.org
Members: 300 individuals
Staff: 2
Annual Budget: $25-50,000
Tax: 501(c)(6)

Personnel:
Executive Director and Certification Contact: Jerry Moore
Treasurer: Susan McCarthy

Historical Note:
Formerly (1958) Gas Appliance Engineers Society. ASGE's
objective is to promote the education and professionalism of
its members and to make available to the public technical
and scientific information and knowledge. Membership:
$50/year (Individual).

Continuing Education:
Enrollment: 142
Certification Designation/s: CGE

Publications:
ASGE Newsletter; quarterly
Member Roster; on-line

American Society of Gene & Cell Therapy (1996)
555 E. Wells St.
Suite 1100
Milwaukee, WI 53202
Tel: (414) 278-1341 Fax: (414) 276-3349
E-Mail: info@asgct.org
Website: asgct.org
Members: 1900 individuals
Staff: 6
Annual Budget: $1-2,000,000
Tax: 501(c)(3)

Personnel:
Executive Director: Mary Dean
    E-Mail: mdean@asgct.org
Coordinator, Membership Services and Administrative:
    David Finley
    E-Mail: dfinley@asgct.org
Manager, Education and Meetings: Ken Janowski
    E-Mail: kjanowski@asgct.org
Manager, Marketing: Shaun Kramer
    E-Mail: skramer@asgct.org
Coordinator, Membership Services and Website: Erin
    Larson
    E-Mail: elarson@asgct.org
Senior Program Manager: David Wood
    E-Mail: dwood@asgct.org

Historical Note:
ASGCT's mission is to advance knowledge, awareness, and
education leading to the discovery and clinical application
of genetic and cellular therapies to alleviate human
disease. ASGCT includes researchers, clinicians, and other
professionals dedicated to discover and develop new genetic
and cellular therapies. Membership: $220 (Active); $75
(Associate); $70-95 (Emeritus for Journal subscription).

Meetings/Conferences: Annual
Conference Chair: David Wood
2013 - Salt Lake City, UT (Salt Palace Convention
    Center)/May 15 - 19/2000 attendees
2014 - Washington, DC/May 21 - 24
2015 - New Orleans, LA/May 13 - 16
Number of non-conference events/year: 1

Publications:
ASGCT Newsletter; semi-annually
Member Directory; on-line
Molecular Therapy; monthly

Membership List Available to Non-members

American Society of General Surgeons (1993)
P.O. Box 4834
Englewood, CO 80155
Tel: (303) 771-5948 Fax: (303) 771-2550
TollFree: (800) 998-8322

E-Mail: asgs-info@theasgs.org
Website: theasgs.org
Members: 3600 individuals
Staff: 2
Annual Budget: $100-250,000
Tax: 501(c)(6)

Personnel:
Executive Director: Carol A. Goddard
    E-Mail: Carol@goddardassociates.com

Historical Note:
ASGS's mission is to achieve the political, economic,
and educational changes that benefit the welfare of the
general surgeons and their patients. Members are board
certified general surgeons and subspecialists who perform
general surgery. Membership: $125 (Active/Associate); $50
(Candidate); $25 (Resident); $100 (Senior).

Continuing Education:
Certification Designation/s: ASGS, CSEMIS

Meetings/Conferences: Annual
Number of non-conference events/year: 7

Publications:
ASGS Newsletter; monthly
Member Directory; on-line

Membership List Available to Non-members

American Society of Geolinguistics (1965)
Department of Modern Languages, Baruch
College (CUNY)
55 Lexington Ave., P.O. Box B6-280
New York, NY 10010-5585
Tel: (646) 312-4220 Fax: (646) 312-4211
Website: baruch.cuny.edu/wsas/academics/
    modern_l
Members: 30 organizations and 110 individuals
Staff: 1
Annual Budget: Under $10,000

Personnel:
Editor and Secretary: Wayne H. Finke PhD
    E-Mail: wayne.finke@baruch.cuny.edu

Historical Note:
ASG gathers and disseminates up-to-date knowledge
concerning the world's present-day languages, their
distribution and population use. Membership: $35
(Regular); $25 (Retired/Student); $40 (Organization/
Company).

Publications:
Geolinguistics; annually

American Society of Golf Course Architects
(1946)
125 N. Executive Dr.
Suite 302
Brookfield, WI 53005
Tel: (262) 786-5960 Fax: (262) 786-5919
E-Mail: info@asgca.org
Website: asgca.org
Members: 190 individuals
Staff: 5
Annual Budget: $250-500,000
Tax: 501(c)(6)

Personnel:
Executive Director: Chad Ritterbusch
    E-Mail: chad@asgca.org
Meeting Planner: Therese Johnston
    E-Mail: mike@asgca.org
Contact, Communications: Aileen Smith
    E-Mail: aileen@asgca.org

Historical Note:
ASGCA is an organization of golf course designers in
America whose mission is to foster the professionalism of its
members through education, promotion and fellowship.

Meetings/Conferences: Annual
Conference Chair: Therese Johnston
Number of non-conference events/year: 1

Publications:
By Design; quarterly
Membership Directory; on-line

American Society of Group Psychotherapy and
Psychodrama (1942)
301 N. Harrison St.
Suite 508
Princeton, NJ 08540
Tel: (609) 737-8500 Fax: (609) 737-8510
E-Mail: asgpp@asgpp.org
Website: asgpp.org

Members: 500 individuals
Staff: 1
Annual Budget: $100-250,000
Personnel:
Executive Director: Jennifer Reis
Historical Note:
ASGPP's purpose is to foster the national and international cooperation among all who are concerned with the theory and practice of psychodrama, sociometry, and group psychotherapy. Membership includes psychiatrists, psychologists, social workers, doctors, psychodramatists, sociologists and nurses. Membership: $120 (Regular); $60 (Student/Retiree).
Continuing Education:
Certification Designation/s: CEU
Meetings/Conferences: Annual
2013 - Arlington, VA (Crystal Gateway Marriott)/April 11 - 15
Publications:
Journal of Psychodrama, Sociometry and Group Psychotherapy
Membership Directory; on-line; adv.
Psychodrama Network News; quarterly; adv.

American Society of Hair Restoration Surgery
737 N. Michigan Ave.
Suite 2100
Chicago, IL 60611-5641
Tel: (312) 981-6773 *Fax:* (312) 981-6787
E-Mail: info@cosmeticsurgery.org
Website: cosmeticsurgery.org
Members: 300 individuals
Staff: 8
Personnel:
Organization Contact: Karena Rybarczyk
    E-Mail: krybarczyk@cosmeticsurgery.org
Historical Note:
ASHRS ia a part of the American Academy of Cosmetic Surgery. Membership: $399 (Physicians).
Publications:
American Journal of Cosmetic Surgery; quarterly

American Society of Hand Therapists *(1977)*
15000 Commerce Pkwy.
Suite C
Mt. Laurel, NJ 08054
Tel: (856) 380-6856 *Fax:* (856) 439-0525
E-Mail: asht@asht.org
Website: asht.org
Members: 3200 individuals
Staff: 7
Annual Budget: $1-2,000,000
Tax: 501(c)(3)
Personnel:
Executive Director: Karen Peterson CAE, SPHR
    E-Mail: kpeterson@asht.org
Manager, Membership Services: Michael Canino
    E-Mail: mcanino@asht.org
Manager, Publications: Erik Caplan
    E-Mail: ecaplan@asht.org
Director, Operations: Jess Ercolino
    E-Mail: jercolino@asht.org
Director, Sponsorship Sales: Sabina Gargiulo
    E-Mail: sgargiulo@asht.org
Director, Education and Research: Jessica Keenan Smith
    E-Mail: jsmith@asht.org
Director, Meetings and Exhibits: Meredith Weiner CMP
    E-Mail: mweiner@asht.org
Historical Note:
ASHT's mission is to advance the science and practice of hand therapy through education, advocacy, research and clinical standards. Members are registered or licensed occupational or physical therapists specializing in working with patients with hand problems. Membership: $45 (Student), $175(Affiliate/Step-up Member), $185 (New CHT), $225 (Active/Associate).
Continuing Education:
Certification Designation/s: CHT
Meetings/Conferences: Annual
Conference Chair: Meredith Weiner CMP
2013 - Chicago, IL/Oct. 24 - 27
2014 - Boston, MA/Sept. 18 - 20
Publications:
ASHT Times; quarterly
Journal of Hand Therapy; quarterly
Member Directory; on-line

Membership List Available to Non-members

American Society of Head and Neck Radiology *(1976)*
800 Enterprise Dr.,
Suite 205
Oak Brook, IL 60523-4216
Tel: (630) 574-0220 *Fax:* (630) 574-0661
Website: ashnr.org
Members: 520 individuals
Staff: 2
Annual Budget: $250-500,000
Tax: 501(c)(3)
Personnel:
Business Manager: Kenneth Cammarata
    E-Mail: kcammarata@asnr.org
Coordinator, Society and Membership Services: Bonnie Mack
    E-Mail: bmack@asnr.org
Historical Note:
ASHNR members are physicians who are board certified in general radiology with an interest in the field of head and neck radiology. Membership: $200 (Active/Associate/ Affiliate); Free (In-Training).
Meetings/Conferences: Annual
2013 - Milwaukee, WI (Pfister Hotel)/Sept. 25 - 29
2014 - Seatle, WA (Sheraton Seattle Hotel)/Sept. 10 - 14
Publications:
American Journal of Neuroradiology; monthly; adv.
ASHNR Newsletter; quarterly
Membership Directory; on-line

Membership List Available to Non-members

American Society of Health-System Pharmacists *(1942)*
7272 Wisconsin Ave.
Bethesda, MD 20814-1439
Tel: (301) 657-3000 *Fax:* (301) 664-8877
TollFree: (866) 279-0681
Website: ashp.org
Members: 35000 members
Staff: 200
Annual Budget: $25-50,000,000
Tax: 501(c)(6)
Personnel:
Chief Executive Officer: Paul W. Abramowitz PharmD
Executive Associate: Laura Gibbs
    E-Mail: lgibbs@ashp.org
Director, Government Affairs Division: Brian M. Meyer
    E-Mail: bmeyer@ashp.org
Director, ASHP Public Relations Division: Ellen Wilcox
    E-Mail: ewilcox@ashp.org
General Counsel and Vice President Human Resources: Fern Zappala
    E-Mail: fzappala@ashp.org
Historical Note:
Formerly (1994) American Society of Hospital Pharmacists. Founded as an outgrowth of the Sub-Section of Hospital Pharmacy of the American Pharmaceutical Association. Incorporated in the District of Columbia(1955), and reincorporated in Maryland(1984). ASHP's mission is to advance and support the professional practice of pharmacists in hospitals and health systems and serve on issues related to medication use and public health. Membership: $42-397/year.
Continuing Education:
Certification Designation/s: ACPE, ACCME
Meetings/Conferences:
2013 - Orlando, FL/Dec. 8 - 12
2014 - Anaheim, CA/Dec. 7 - 11
Number of non-conference events/year: 3
Publications:
AHFS Drug Information; annually
AJHP Online; on-line; adv.
American Journal of Health-System Pharmacy; irregular
ASHP Daily Briefing; on-line
ASHP e-newsletter; on-line
ASHP InterSections; quarterly
ASHP News and Views; daily

American Society of Heating, Refrigerating and Air Conditioning Engineers (ASHRAE) *(1894)*
1791 Tullie Cir. NE
Atlanta, GA 30329
Tel: (404) 636-8400 *Fax:* (404) 321-5478

TollFree: (800) 527-4723
E-Mail: ashrae@ashrae.org
Website: ashraeindia.org
Members: 53000 individuals
Staff: 103
Annual Budget: $50-100,000
Tax: 501(c)(3)
Personnel:
Manager, Education and Certifications: Joyce Abrams
Contact, Scholarship and Conferences: Lois Benedict
    E-Mail: lbenedict@ashrae.org
Director, Publications and Education: W. Stephen Comstock
Contact, Public Relations: Jodi Dunlop
    E-Mail: jdunlop@ashrae.org
Manager, Conference Programs: Anthony Giometti
Director, Membership Services: Carolyn Kettering
Manager, Human Resources: Sharon Priebe
Program Director, Government Affairs: Douglas E. Read
    E-Mail: dread@ashrae.org
Manager, Communications: Jodi Scott
Comptroller and Director, Administrative Services: Cindy Simmons
Manager, Information Technology: Dana Suffes
Historical Note:
ASHRAE fulfills its mission of advancing heating, ventilation, air conditioning and refrigeration to serve humanity and promote a sustainable world through research, standards writing, publishing and continuing education. Membership: $185 (Associate/Member); $20 (Student); $50 (Affiliate).
Continuing Education:
Enrollment: 300
Certification Designation/s: BEMP, HBDP, HFDP, BEAP, CPMP, OPMP
Meetings/Conferences: Semi-Annual
Conference Chair: Anthony Giometti
2013 - New York City, NY/Jan. 18 - 22
2013 - Dallas, TX (Headquarter Hotel)/Jan. 26 - 30
2013 - Denver, CO/June 22 - 26
2013 - Vancouver, BC (Renaissance Vancouver Hotel)/ Oct. 15 - 18
2014 - Seattle, WA/June 28 - July 2
Publications:
eSociety; on-line
ASHRAE Insights; monthly
ASHRAE Journal; monthly
Membership Directory; on-line
The HVAC&R Industry; weekly

Membership List Available to Non-members

American Society of Hematology *(1958)*
2021 L St. N. W.
Suite 900
Washington, DC 20036
Tel: (202) 776-0544 *Fax:* (202) 776-0545
E-Mail: ash@hematology.org
Website: hematology.org
Members: 15705 individuals
Staff: 69
Annual Budget: $25-50,000,000
Tax: 501(c)(3)
Personnel:
Executive Director: Martha L. Liggett Esq.
    E-Mail: mliggett@hematology.org
Director, Finance and Administration: Tiffany Ake CPA
    E-Mail: take@hematology.org
Manager, Membership Services: Ghennet Aklilu
    E-Mail: gaklilu@hematology.org
Senior Director, Government Relations, Practice, and Scientific Affairs: Mila Becker
    E-Mail: mbecker@hematology.org
Senior Director, Education and Training: Charles Clayton
Manager, Customer Relations: Kimberly Fayton
    E-Mail: kfayton@hematology.org
Senior Manager, Information Technology: Karina Fernandez MS
    E-Mail: kfernandez@hematology.org
Director, Communications: Jenifer Hamilton CAE
    E-Mail: jhamilton@hematology.org
Manager, Marketing: Keli Hammond
Senior Director, Publishing: Nina Hoffman
    E-Mail: nhoffman@hematology.org
Director, Meetings: Ayuko Kimura-Fay CMP
    E-Mail: akimura-fay@hematology.org
Director, Education: Mark A. Smith CAE, PhD
    E-Mail: msmith@hematology.org

Director, Publishing: Eleanore Tapscott
  E-Mail: etapscott@hematology.org

Historical Note:
ASH's mission is to further the understanding, diagnosis, treatment and prevention of disorders affecting the blood, bone marrow, and the immunologic, hemostatic and vascular systems, by promoting research, clinical care, education, training and advocacy in hematology. Membership: $325 (Active); $350 (International); $55 (Associate).

Meetings/Conferences: Annual
Conference Chair: Ayuko Kimura-Fay CMP
Number of non-conference events/year: 9

Publications:
ASH's Patient E-Newsletter; on-line
Membership Directory; on-line

Membership List Available to Non-members

American Society of Highway Engineers *(1958)*
65 Beacon Hill
Henderson, NC 27537
Tel: (252) 438-7723
E-Mail: euclid@embarqmail.com
Website: highwayengineers.org
Members: 6000 individuals
Staff: 4
Annual Budget: $100-250,000
Tax: 501(c)(6)

Personnel:
Secretary: Charles L. Flowe PE
  E-Mail: ashenational@embarqmail.com

Historical Note:
ASHE was incorporated in Pennsylvania in 1958 with the conception and inception of the first chartered section credited to a small group of dedicated engineers from the Pennsylvania Department of Highways, in association with a group of outstanding contractors, material suppliers and consulting engineers in the Harrisburg area. ASHE's mission is to provide a forum for members and partners of the highway industry to advocate a safe, efficient and sustainable highway system through education, innovation and fellowship. Membership: $6000/year.

Meetings/Conferences: Annual
2013 - Lake Placid, NY (Crowne Plaza Resort and Golf Club, Lake Placid)/June 5 - 8

Publications:
SCANNER Newsletter

American Society of Home Inspectors *(1976)*
932 Lee St.
Suite 101
Des Plaines, IL 60016
Tel: (847) 759-2820 *Fax:* (847) 759-1620
TollFree: (800) 743-2744
E-Mail: hq@ashi.org
Website: ashi.org
Members: 6000 individuals
Staff: 12
Annual Budget: $2-5,000,000
Tax: 501(c)(6)

Personnel:
Executive Director and Chief Executive Officer: Jeff Arnold
  E-Mail: jeffa@ashi.org
Director, Communications: Sandy Bourseau
  E-Mail: sandyb@ashi.org
Director, Membership Services and Chapter Relations: Russell Daniels
  E-Mail: russelld@ashi.org
Administrator, Membership and Marketing: Karen Davis
  E-Mail: karend@ashi.org
Manager, Education: Michele George
  E-Mail: micheleg@ashi.org
Director, Business Development: Bill Lewis
  E-Mail: bill@ashi.org
Manager, Information Technology: Mike Rostescu
  E-Mail: miker@ashi.org
Accounting Manager: Belienda Schultz
  E-Mail: beliendas@ashi.org
Manager, Membership Services: Sarah Walsh
  E-Mail: sarahw@ashi.org

Historical Note:
ASHI's mission is to build customer awareness of the importance of a quality home inspection and enhance the professionalism of home inspectors. Membership: $660 (Basic); $2,500 (Gold).

Continuing Education:
Certification Designation/s: NCCA

Meetings/Conferences: Annual
2013 - Las Vegas, NV (Bally's Las Vegas)/Jan. 13 - 16

Publications:
ASHI Reporter; monthly; adv.
Inspection Information For Inspectors From Inspectors; monthly

American Society of Human Genetics *(1948)*
9650 Rockville Pike
Bethesda, MD 20814-3998
Tel: (301) 634-7300 *Fax:* (301) 634-7079
TollFree: (866) 486-4363
E-Mail: society@ashg.org
Website: ashg.org
Members: 8000 members
Staff: 14
Annual Budget: $5-10,000,000
Tax: 501(c)(3)

Personnel:
Executive Vice President, Administration: Joann Boughman
  E-Mail: jboughman@ashg.org
Director, Information Technology: Yimang Chen
  E-Mail: ychen@ashg.org
Director, Education: Michael Dougherty
  E-Mail: mdougherty@ashg.org
Contact, Media Relations: Kristen Long
  E-Mail: klong@ashg.org
Director, Meetings and Exhibit Management: Pauline Minhinnett, CMP
  E-Mail: paulinem@ashg.org
Manager, Membership Services: Mary Shih
  E-Mail: mshih@ashg.org

Historical Note:
ASHG strives to provide leadership in research, education and service in human genetics. Members include researchers, academicians, clinicians, laboratory practice professionals, genetic counselors, nurses and others involved in or with special interest in human genetics. Membership: $190 (Regular); $230 (Spouse/Partner); $25-70 (Trainee).

Meetings/Conferences: Annual
Conference Chair: Pauline Minhinnett, CMP
2013 - Boston, MA/Oct. 22 - 26
2014 - San Diego, CA/Oct. 18 - 22
2015 - Baltimore, MD/Oct. 6 - 10
2016 - Vancouver, BC/Oct. 18 - 22
2017 - Orlando, FL/Oct. 17 - 21
2018 - San Diego, CA/Oct. 16 - 20
2019 - Toronto, ON/Oct. 22 - 26
2020 - San Diego, CA/Oct. 27 - 31
2021 - Montreal, QC/Oct. 19 - 23
2022 - Honolulu, HI/Oct. 18 - 22

Publications:
Membership Directory; on-line
The American Journal of Human Genetics (AJHG)

Membership List Available to Non-members

American Society of Hypertension, Inc. *(1985)*
148 Madison Ave.
Fifth Floor
New York, NY 10016
Tel: (212) 696-9099 *Fax:* (212) 696-0711
E-Mail: ash@ash-us.org
Website: ash-us.org
Members: 3000 individuals
Staff: 10
Annual Budget: $5-10,000,000
Tax: 501(c)(3)

Personnel:
Executive Director: Torry Mark Sansone
  E-Mail: tsansone@ash-us.org
Editor: Amy Bittle
  E-Mail: jash@ash-us.org
Director, Meetings and Exhibit Services: Gilda C. Caputo-Hansen
Manager, Communications and Related Marketing Service: Barbara E. Escobar
Manager, Financial Services: Kevin Lee
Associate Executive Director, Scientific Meetings and Professional Affairs: Melissa Levine
Manager, Membership and Marketing Services: Angel Loayza
Director, Education Services: Kathleen Sheridan

Historical Note:
ASH strives to translate and promote current research in hypertension and vascular disease into effective treatment strategies for patients with hypertension and associated disorders. ASH members are individuals who have undertaken and accomplished meritorious original scientific investigation in the field of hypertension and/or related cardiovascular disease, and/or those involved in the diagnosis and treatment of hypertension and related cardiovascular disease. Professionals, paraprofessionals and students with a demonstrated interest in the field are eligible for associate membership. Membership: $200(Individual); $75 (Member in Training).

Continuing Education:
Certification Designation/s: CME

Meetings/Conferences: Annual
Conference Chair: Gilda C. Caputo-Hansen
2013 - San Francisco, CA (San Francisco Marriott Hotel)/May 15 - 18
2014 - New York City, NY (Hilton New York)/May 17 - 20
2015 - New York City, NY (Hilton New York)/May 16 - 19
2016 - New York City, NY (Hilton New York)/May 14 - 17
Number of non-conference events/year: 2

Publications:
ASH Newsletter; on-line
Journal of Clinical Hypertension Online Access; monthly
Journal of the American Society of Hypertension Online Access; bi-monthly

American Society of Ichthyologists and Herpetologists *(1913)*
PO Box 1897
Lawrence, KS 66044-8897
Tel: (785) 843-1234 *Fax:* (785) 843-1274
TollFree: (800) 627-0326
E-Mail: asih@allenpress.com
Website: asih.org
Members: 1000 institutions and 2400 individuals
Staff: 4
Annual Budget: $250-500,000

Personnel:
President: Steven J. Beaupre
  E-Mail: sbeaupre@uark.edu
Editor: Christopher Beachy
  E-Mail: Christopher.Beachy@minotstateu.edu
Secretary: Maureen A. Donnelly PhD
  E-Mail: maureen.a.donnelly@gmail.com
Treasurer: Margaret A. Neighbors
  E-Mail: mneighbors@prodigy.net

Historical Note:
Incorporated in the District of Columbia. ASIH strives to increase knowledge about these organisms, to disseminate that knowledge through publications, conferences, symposia, and other means, and to encourage and support young scientists who will make future advances in these fields. The programs of the American Society of Ichthyologists and Herpetologists are part of a global effort to interpret, understand, and conserve the Earth's natural diversity and to contribute to the wise use of natural resources for the long-term benefit of humankind. Membership: $100 (Regular); $150 (Sustaining); $2,500 (Life Member); $85 (Student).

Meetings/Conferences: Annual
2013 - Albuquerue, NM/July 10 - 15
2014 - Chattanooga, TN/July 30 - Aug. 3

Publications:
Curation Newsletter
Membership Directory; on-line

American Society of Interior Designers *(1975)*
608 Massachusetts Ave. NE
Washington, DC 20002-6006
Tel: (202) 546-3480 *Fax:* (202) 546-3240
E-Mail: membership@asid.org
Website: asid.org
Members:
2,700 member firms
10,500 students
Staff: 13
Annual Budget: $100-250,000
Tax: 501(c)(3)

Personnel:
Executive Director: Michael C. Alin
  E-Mail: malin@asid.org
Executive Vice President and Chief Executive Officer: Randy W. Fisher

Vice President, Membership Services and Industry Development: Troy Adkins
Director, Information Technology: Wali Alawi
Chief Operating Officer: Thomas Banks
Director, Research and Knowledge Resources: Michael Berens
Vice President, Government and Public Affairs: Don Davis
Associate Executive Director, Customer Services: Kirstin Hellwig
    E-Mail: khellwig@asid.org
Senior Editor: Jennifer Lipner
    E-Mail: jlipner@asid.org
Vice President, Marketing and Communications: Kelly Nelson
Chief Financial Officer: Rick Peluso
    E-Mail: rpeluso@asid.org

Historical Note:
Formed as a product of a consolidation of the American Institute of Interior Designers (1931) and the National Society of Interior Designers (1957). ASID is a professional association representing the interests of interior designers. ASID's mission is to advise the interior design profession through knowledge generation and sharing advocacy of interior designers' right to practice professional and public education, and expansion of interior design markets. Membership: $430 (Allied/ Associate/ Professional/ International); $270 (Educator); $45 (Student); $75-445 (Student Advancement); $425-6,500 (Industry Partners).

Meetings/Conferences:
Number of non-conference events/year: 1

Publications:
Access; semi-annually
ASID Icon; quarterly
ASID News Flash; bi-weekly
Eye on Design; weekly

Membership List Available to Non-members

American Society of International Law (1906)
2223 Massachusetts Ave. NW
Washington, DC 20008-2864
Tel: (202) 939-6000
E-Mail: services@asil.org
Website: asil.org
Members: 4000 members
Staff: 17
Annual Budget: $2-5,000,000
Tax: 501(c)(3)

Personnel:
Executive Director and Executive Vice President: Elizabeth Andersen
    E-Mail: eandersen@asil.org
Director, Finance and Administration: Sara Dispenza CPA
    E-Mail: sdispenza@asil.org
Manager, Publications and Programs: Kate Doty
    E-Mail: kdoty@asil.org
Manager, Membership Services: Matthew Gomez
    E-Mail: mgomez@asil.org
Managing Editor: Djurdja Lazic
    E-Mail: dlazic@asil.org
Executive Office and Programs Manager: Veronica Onorevole
    E-Mail: vonorevole@asil.org
Contact, Web and Information Technology Support: Jimmy Steiner
    E-Mail: jsteiner@asil.org
Director, Communications and Member Relations: Sheila Ward
    E-Mail: sward@asil.org

Historical Note:
Incorporated in 1950 by a special act of Congress. ASIL's mission is to foster the study of international law and to promote the establishment and maintenance of international relations on the basis of law and justice. Membership: $55-210/year.

Meetings/Conferences: Annual
Conference Chair: Veronica Onorevole
2013 - Washington, DC (Marriott Renaissance Hotel)/ April 3 - 6/1200 attendees
2014 - Washington, DC/April 7 - 12
Number of non-conference events/year: 9

Publications:
American Journal of International Law; quarterly
ASIL Insight; on-line
ASIL Newsletter; quarterly
IL Post; bi-weekly
International Legal Materials; bi-monthly; adv.

American Society of Interventional Pain Physicians (1998)
81 Lakeview Dr.
Paducah, KY 42001
Tel: (270) 554-9412 *Fax:* (270) 554-5394
E-Mail: asipp@asipp.org
Website: asipp.org
Staff: 12
Annual Budget: $2-5,000,000
Tax: 501(c)(3)

Personnel:
Director, Operations: Melinda Martin
    E-Mail: mmartin@asipp.org
Director, Marketing and Public Relations: Ray Lane
    E-Mail: rlane@asipp.org
Coordinator, Editorial Services: Holly Long
    E-Mail: hlong@asipp.org
Administrative Assistant: Cindy Rogers
    E-Mail: crogers@asipp.org
Coordinator, Meetings: Paula Reynolds Spear
    E-Mail: paula@thepainmd.com

Historical Note:
ASIPP's mission is to promote the development and practice of safe, quality yet cost effective interventional pain management techniques for the diagnosis and treatment of pain and related disorders, and to ensure patient access to these interventions. Membership: $0-450/year; $6,000 (Life-Active); $3,000 (Life-Associate).

Continuing Education:
Enrollment: 200

Meetings/Conferences: Annual
Conference Chair: Paula Reynolds Spear
2013 - Arlington, VA (Crystal Gateway Marriott)/June 8 - 12
Number of non-conference events/year: 1

Publications:
ASIPP e-News; weekly; adv.
ASIPP News; quarterly; adv.
Pain Physician Journal; bi-monthly; adv.

American Society of Irrigation Consultants (1970)
503 Mall Ct.
Suite 293
Lansing, MI 48912-5200
Tel: (508) 763-8140 *Fax:* (866) 828-5174
Website: asic.org
Members: 300 individuals
Staff: 3
Annual Budget: $100-250,000
Tax: 501(c)(6)

Personnel:
Executive Director: Carol Colein
    E-Mail: carolc@asic.org
Director, Communications: Luke Frank
    E-Mail: lukefrank@comcast.net

Historical Note:
ASIC's mission is to enhance the role of the independent professional irrigation consultant. Their responsibility is to provide objective irrigation consulting services in the effective use and management of water and other natural resources. Membership: $55-2,750/year.

Meetings/Conferences: Annual
2013 - Scottsdale, AZ (Hilton Scottsdale Resort and Villas)/April 20 - 22

Publications:
Waterfront Newsletter; semi-annually

American Society of Journalists and Authors (1948)
1501 Broadway
Suite 403
New York, NY 10036
Tel: (212) 997-0947 *Fax:* (212) 937-2315
E-Mail: asjaoffice@asja.org
Website: asja.org
Members: 1400 individuals
Staff: 4
Annual Budget: $500-1,000,000
Tax: 501(c)(6)

Personnel:
Executive Director: Alexandra Owens
    E-Mail: director@asja.org
Editor: Barbara DeMarco-Barrett
Chair, Conferences: Linda Melone
Manager, Information Technology: Bruce W. Miller

Historical Note:
Established as the Society of Magazine Writers, became the American Society of Journalists and Authors in 1975. ASJA acts as an information center on freelance rights, and provides other services to members. Members are freelance nonfiction writers whose bylines appear on books and in leading periodicals. Membership: $70- 210/year.

Meetings/Conferences: Annual
Conference Chair: Linda Melone
2013 - New York City, NY/April 25 - 27/51-100 exhibitors

Publications:
Member Directory; on-line
The ASJA Monthly; monthly

Membership List Available to Non-members

American Society of Laboratory Animal Practitioners (1967)
9190 Crestwyn Hills Dr.
Memphis, TN 38125-8538
Tel: (901) 333-0498 *Fax:* (901) 753-0046
E-Mail: aslap-info@aslap.org
Website: aslap.org
Members: 778 individuals
Staff: 1
Annual Budget: $50-100,000

Personnel:
Coordinator: Darlene Brown
    E-Mail: darlene@aslap.org

Historical Note:
ASLAP seeks to provide a mechanism for the exchange of scientific and technical information among veterinarians engaged in laboratory animal practice. Membership in this organization is open to any veterinarian who is engaged in or interested in promoting and supporting laboratory animal practice or students, Residents or institutions that employ multiple veterinarians. Membership: $80 (Regular); $30 (Resident); $22.50 (Student); $70 (Programs with 3-6 veterinarians); $60 (Programs with more than 6 veterinarians).

Continuing Education:
Certification Designation/s: ACLAM

Publications:
Laboratory Animal Practitioner; quarterly
Membership Database; on-line

American Society of Landscape Architects (1899)
636 Eye St. NW
Washington, DC 20001-3736
Tel: (202) 898-2444 *Fax:* (202) 898-1185
TollFree: (888) 999-2752
E-Mail: info@asla.org
Website: asla.org
Members: 17000 individuals
Staff: 50
Annual Budget: $50-100,000
Tax: 501(c)(3)

Personnel:
Chief Executive Officer and Executive Vice President: Nancy C. Somerville
    E-Mail: nsomerville@asla.org
Manager, Marketing: Susan Apollonio
    E-Mail: sapollonio@asla.org
Managing Director, Information Technology and Professional Practice: Susan Aylward-Cahill
    E-Mail: scahill@asla.org
Director, Meetings and Special Programs: Joyce DePass
    E-Mail: jdepass@asla.org
Director, Membership and Chapter Services: Barbara Drobins
    E-Mail: bdrobins@asla.org
Manager, Education Programs: Clark Ebbert
    E-Mail: cebbert@asla.org
Director, Government Affairs: Julia Lent
    E-Mail: jlent@asla.org
Associate Director, Finance and Business Operations: Zandra Miller
    E-Mail: zmiller@asla.org
Legislative Analyst: Kevin O'Hara
    E-Mail: kohara@asla.org
Director, Public Relations and Communications: Terry Poltrack
    E-Mail: tpoltrack@asla.org
Managing Director, Publishing and Resource Development: Ann Looper Pryor
    E-Mail: alooper@asla.org

Historical Note:

Mission is to serve, educate, and to participate in the careful stewardship, wise planning, and artful design of the cultural and natural environments. Members include landscape architecture professionals, architects, planners, developers, engineers, product manufacturers and suppliers, and students from 48 professional chapters and 68 student chapters. Membership: $50-1,950/year.

Meetings/Conferences: Annual
Conference Chair: Joyce DePass
2013 - Boston, MA (Boston Convention and Exhibition Cente)/Nov. 15 - 18/over 100 exhibitors
2014 - Denver, CO (Colorado Convention Center)/Nov. 21 - 24/over 100 exhibitors
2015 - Chicago, IL (McCormick Place)/Nov. 6 - 9/over 100 exhibitors

Publications:
ASLA Newsletter
Business; quarterly
LAND Online; bi-weekly
Landscape Architecture Magazine; monthly; adv.
Membership Directory; on-line

American Society of Law, Medicine and Ethics (1911)
765 Commonwealth Ave.
Suite 1634
Boston, MA 02215
Tel: (617) 262-4990 Fax: (617) 437-7596
E-Mail: info@aslme.org
Website: aslme.org
Members: 4500 individuals
Staff: 5
Annual Budget: $500-1,000,000

Personnel:
Director, Publications and Executive Director: Ted Hutchinson
Director, Conferences: Katie Kenney Johnson
    E-Mail: kkenney@aslme.org
Director, Membership Services: Margo Smith
    E-Mail: margo@aslme.org

Historical Note:
An outgrowth of two founding organizations: the Massachusetts Society of Examining Physicians (1911) and the Massachusetts Society of Law and Medicine (1971). Formerly (1992) American Society of Law and Medicine. ASLME's mission is to provide high-quality scholarship, debate, and critical thought to the community of professionals at the intersection of law, medicine, and ethics. Membership: $230 (Doctoral); $150 (Non-Doctoral); $90 (Student).

Meetings/Conferences: Annual
Conference Chair: Katie Kenney Johnson

Publications:
American Journal of Law & Medicine (AJLM); adv.
Membership Directory; on-line
The Journal of Law, Medicine & Ethics (JLME); adv.

American Society of Limnology and Oceanography (1936)
5400 Bosque Blvd.
Suite 680
Waco, TX 76710-4446
Tel: (254) 399-9635 Fax: (254) 776-3767
TollFree: (800) 929-2756
E-Mail: business@aslo.org
Website: aslo.org
Members: 1500 Libraries and 3,800 members
Staff: 11
Annual Budget: $1-2,000,000

Personnel:
President: John Downing
    E-Mail: president@aslo.org
Manger, Journals: Lucille Doucette
    E-Mail: lo-manager@aslo.org
Editor-in-Chief: Everett Fee
Business Manager: Helen Schneider Lemay
Director, Public Policy: Adrienne Sponberg
    E-Mail: asponberg@aslo.org

Historical Note:
Founded January 1, 1936 in St. Louis as the Limnological Society of America. Assumed its present name in 1949 and was incorporated in Wisconsin in 1956. ASLO's purpose is to advance a diverse, international scientific community that creates, integrates and communicates knowledge across the full spectrum of aquatic sciences, advances public awareness and education about aquatic resources and research, and advocates scientific stewardship of aquatic resources for the public interest. Membership: $60-215 (Regular Member-Printed/Electronic); $15-170 (Early

Career Member- Printed/Electronic); $15-170 (Student Member- Printed/Electronic).

Meetings/Conferences: Annual
Conference Chair: Helen Schneider Lemay
2013 - New Orleans, LA (Ernest N. Morial Convention Center)/Feb. 17 - 22
2014 - Honolulu, HI/Feb. 23 - 28
2014 - Portland, OR/May 18 - 23
2015 - Granada, Spain/Feb. 22 - 27

Publications:
Limnology and Oceanography
Member Directory; annually

American Society of Lipo-Suction Surgery (1982)
737 N. Michigan Ave.
Suite 2100
Chicago, IL 60611-5405
Tel: (312) 981-6760 Fax: (312) 981-6787
E-Mail: info@cosmeticsurgery.org
Website: cosmeticsurgery.org
Members: 2000 Individuals
Staff: 8
Annual Budget: $2-5,000,000

Personnel:
Executive Vice President: Jeffrey P. Knezovich CAE
    E-Mail: jknezovich@cosmeticsurgery.org
Manager, Communications: Charlie Baase
    E-Mail: cbaase@cosmeticsurgery.org
Director, Meetings and Curriculum: Moira Twitty

Historical Note:
ASLSS's mission is to advance the specialty of cosmetic surgery and quality patient care. Members are dermatological surgeons, facial plastic surgeons, head and neck surgeons, oral and maxillofacial surgeons, general surgeons, plastic surgeons or ophthalmic plastic surgeons — all of whom specialize in cosmetic surgery.

Meetings/Conferences:
Conference Chair: Moira Twitty

Membership List Available to Non-members

American Society of Magazine Editors (1963)
810 Seventh Ave.
24th Floor
New York, NY 10019
Tel: (212) 872-3700 Fax: (212) 906-0128
E-Mail: asme@magazine.org
Website: magazine.org/asme
Members: 850 members
Staff: 4

Personnel:
Executive Director: Marlene Kahan
Treasurer: James Bennet
Program Coordinator: Nina Fortuna
    E-Mail: NFortuna@magazine.org
Chief Executive: Sid Holt
    E-Mail: sholt@magazine.org

Historical Note:
ASME is a non-profit professional organization for editors of print and online magazines which are edited, published and distributed in the U.S. ASME's mission is to preserve editorial independence and speaks out on public policy issues, particularly those pertaining to the First Amendment. Membership: $695 (Chief Editors) $395 (Regular); $95 (Junior Level Editors); $45 (Retired).

Publications:
Membership Directory; on-line
National Magazine

American Society of Mammalogists (1919)
810 E. Tenth St.
P.O. Box 1897
Lawrence, KS 66044-8897
Tel: (785) 843-1235 Fax: (785) 843-1274
E-Mail: asm@allenpress.com
Website: mammalsociety.org
Members: 4500 individuals
Staff: 3
Annual Budget: $500-1,000,000
Tax: 501(c)(3)

Personnel:
President: Edward J. Heske
    E-Mail: eheske@illinois.edu
Editor: Joseph F. Merritt
    E-Mail: jmerritt@illinois.edu
Secretary and Treasurer: Ronald A. Van Den Bussche
    E-Mail: ron.van_den_bussche@okstate.edu

Historical Note:

ASM's aim is to enhance the interests in study of mammals.
Membership: $20-5000/year.

Meetings/Conferences: Annual
2013 - Philadelphia, PA (Philadelphia Marriott Downtown)/June 14 - 18
2014 - Oklahoma City, OK (Renaissance Oklahoma City Convention Center Hotel)/June 6 - 10

Publications:
The Journal of Mammalogy

American Society of Marine Artists (1978)
P.O. Box 247
Smithfield, VA 23430
Tel: (757) 357-3785
E-Mail: asma1978@verizon.net
Website: americansocietyofmarineartists.com
Members: 625 individuals
Staff: 4
Annual Budget: $50-100,000
Tax: 501(c)(3)

Personnel:
President: Russ Kramer
    E-Mail: russ@russkramer.com
Treasurer: Peter Maytham
    E-Mail: asma1978@verizon.net
Editor: Robert C. Semler
    E-Mail: rcsart42@verizon.net
Vice President: Kim Shaklee
    E-Mail: russ@russkramer.com

Historical Note:
ASMA's mission is to advocate marine art and history, and to encourage cooperation among artists, historians, marine enthusiasts and others engaged in activities related to marine art and maritime history. Members are artists, collectors and historians. Galleries and museums can join as Regular Members. Membership: $50 (Regular); $150 (Supporting); $500 (Patron); $85 (Artist/Signature); $100 (Fellows); $15 (Student).

Publications:
ASMA News; quarterly

American Society of Master Dental Technologists (1973)
146-21 13th Ave.
Whitestone, NY 11357-2420
Tel: (718) 746-8355 Fax: (718) 746-8355
E-Mail: vinnie@asmdt.com
Website: asmdt.com
Members: 125 individuals
Staff: 4
Annual Budget: Under $10,000

Personnel:
Executive Director and Treasurer: Susan Heppenheimer
    E-Mail: sue@asmdt.com
Chairman, Education and Chief Executive Officer: Vincent V. Alleluia
Director, International Programs: Vladimir F. Kuznetsov
    E-Mail: vladimir@asmdt.com
Chief Information Officer and Marketing Director: Max Toth

Historical Note:
ASMDT is a professional society formed to raise the educational standards of dental technicians. ASMDT's mission is to provide educational resources, i.e., text materials, instructors and guidance, for technologists who are interested in becoming Master Dental Technologists. Membership: $125/year.

Continuing Education:
Certification Designation/s: MDT

Meetings/Conferences:
Conference Chair: Vladimir F. Kuznetsov

Publications:
ASMDT Newsletter

American Society of Maxillofacial Surgeons (1947)
500 Cummings Center
Suite 4550
Beverly, MA 01915
Tel: (978) 927-8330 Fax: (978) 524-8890
Website: maxface.org
Members: 350 individuals
Staff: 4
Annual Budget: $250-500,000
Tax: 501(c)(6)

Personnel:
President: Robert J. Havlik MD

Vice President, Administration: Arun K. Gosain
Vice President, Education: William Hoffman III
Vice President, Communications: Reza Jarrahy

Historical Note:
ASMS is devoted to stimulating interest, advancing knowledge, and providing leadership and direction within the areas of maxillofacial and craniofacial surgery. Members are surgeons actively engaged in the practice of maxillofacial and craniofacial surgery or individuals who have contributed to the understanding and treatment of disorders and/or trauma of the craniomaxillofacial region. Membership: $350 (Active); $200 (International/ Associate); $150 (Candidate For Membership).

Meetings/Conferences: Annual
Number of non-conference events/year: 3

Publications:
Membership Directory; on-line
Newsletter

American Society of Mechanical Engineers (ASME)
(1880)
Three Park Ave.
New York, NY 10016-5990
Tel: (212) 591-7000 *Fax:* (212) 591-7674
TollFree: (800) 843-2763
E-Mail: infocentral@asme.org
Website: asme.org
Members: 120,000 individuals
Staff: 405
Annual Budget: Over $100,000,000
Tax: 501(c)(3)

Personnel:
Executive Director: Thomas G. Loughin
    E-Mail: execdirector@asme.org
Director, Corporate Communications: Mel Torre
    E-Mail: torrem@asme.org
Editor: David Walsh
    E-Mail: WalshD@asme.org

Historical Note:
ASME's mission is to serve communities by advancing, disseminating and applying engineering knowledge for improving the quality of life and communicating the excitement of engineering. Membership: $140 (Individual/ Fellow/Affiliate); $70 (Retired); $56 (Automatic Student upgrade to member); $25 (Student); $0 (Life/Honorary).

Meetings/Conferences:
Conference Chair: Mel Torre
Number of non-conference events/year: 3

Publications:
Capitol Update; weekly
History & Heritage Newsletter; semi-annually
ME Today; daily
Membership Directory; on-line
Standards & Certification Update; quarterly

American Society of Media Photographers *(1944)*
150 N. Second St.
Philadelphia, PA 19106
Tel: (215) 451-2767 *Fax:* (215) 451-0880
E-Mail: info@asmp.org
Website: asmp.org
Members: 7000 individuals
Staff: 6
Annual Budget: $1-2,000,000
Tax: 501(c)(3)

Personnel:
Executive Director: Eugene Mopsik
    E-Mail: mopsik@asmp.org
Director, Education: Susan Carr
    E-Mail: carr@asmp.org
Bookkeeper: Christine Chandler
    E-Mail: chandler@asmp.org
Director, Communications: Peter Dyson
    E-Mail: dyson@asmp.org
General Manager: Elena Goertz
    E-Mail: goertz@asmp.org
Managing Director, Government Relations and General Counsel: Victor Perlman
    E-Mail: perlman@asmp.org

Historical Note:
Formerly (1979) ASMP - the Society of Photographers in Communications and after that name changed to simply the original ASMP and then became the American Society of Magazine Photographers and assumed its current name in 1992. ASMP seeks to support the education of its members and the creative community to which they belong, and encourages the professional and artistic growth of photographers. Membership: $45-335/year.

Continuing Education:
Enrollment: 10

Meetings/Conferences:
Conference Chair: Elena Goertz

Publications:
ASMP Bulletin; adv.
E-NewsLetter; monthly

American Society of Medical Association Counsel
6045 Shirley Dr
Oakland, CA 94611
Tel: (510) 482-2845 *Fax:* (510) 482-2845
Website: asmacnet.org
Staff: 3
Annual Budget: $50-100,000

Personnel:
President: Greg Abrams
    E-Mail: abrams@pacificwestlaw.com

Historical Note:
ASMAC is a unique legal organization consisting of lawyers whose central task is representing organized medicine. Members are employed by national, state and local medical societies throughout the United States. By networking, members can share ideas and documents in order to better represent organized medicine. Membership: $220 (Regular/ Special); $145 (Part-time).

Meetings/Conferences: Annual
Conference Chair: Leonard Nelson

Publications:
Member DIrectory; on-line

American Society of Military Comptrollers *(1948)*
415 N. Alfred St.
Alexandria, VA 22314-2269
Tel: (703) 549-0360 *Fax:* (703) 549-3181
TollFree: (800) 462-5637
Website: asmconline.org
Members: 20,000 members
Staff: 11
Annual Budget: $2-5,000,000
Tax: 501(c)(3)

Personnel:
Executive Director: Al Runnels
Associate Director, Certification: Claudia Carr CDFM
    E-Mail: carr@asmconline.org
General Counsel: Terry Elling
Manager, Information Systems: Michael Pickus
    E-Mail: pickus@asmconline.org
Contact, Special Projects: John Raines
    E-Mail: raines@asmconline.org
Associate Director, Finance, Administration and Human Resources: Riitta Silverman
    E-Mail: silverman@asmconline.org
Associate Director, Membership and Chapter Development: Jennifer Sizemore
    E-Mail: sizemore@asmconline.org
Communications Manager: Simone Toth
    E-Mail: toth@asmconline.org

Historical Note:
Formerly The Society of Military Accountants and Statisticians. ASMC is the non-profit educational and professional organization for persons, military and civilian, involved in the overall field of military comptrollership. ASMC promotes the education and training of its members, and supports the development and advancement of the profession of military comptrollership. Membership: $26 (Individual); $250-4,000 (Corporate).

Continuing Education:
Certification Designation/s: CDFM

Meetings/Conferences:
Conference Chair: John Raines

Publications:
Armed Forces Comptroller; quarterly; adv.
ASMC Connections; monthly
National Newsletter; monthly

American Society of Mining and Reclamation
(1973)
3134 Montavesta Rd.
Lexington, KY 40502
Tel: (859) 351-9032 *Fax:* (859) 335-6529
E-Mail: asmr@insightbb.com
Website: asmr.us
Members: 450 individuals
Staff: 2
Annual Budget: $100-250,000

Personnel:

President: Bruce Buchanan
Executive Secretary: Richard I. Barnhisel

Historical Note:
Formerly (1978) Council for Surface Mining and Reclamation Research in Appalachia and (1982) American Council for Reclamation Research; assumed its current name in 2001. ASMR's mission is to represent and serve a diverse national and international community of scientists, practitioners, private industry, technicians, educators, planners, and government regulators involved in mineral extraction and the reclamation of disturbed lands. Members are mining companies, federal and state agencies, academics and others with an interest in reclamation of mined land. Membership: $50 (Regular); $100 (Sustaining/ Corporate); $10 (Full-time Student); $25 (Part-time Student).

Meetings/Conferences: Annual
Conference Chair: Richard I. Barnhisel
2013 - Laramie, WY (Hilton Garden Inn)/June 1 - 6
Number of non-conference events/year: 1

Publications:
Membership Directory; on-line
Newsletters; irregular
Reclamation Matters; adv.

Membership List Available to Non-members

American Society of Missiology *(1973)*
Sioux Falls Seminary
2100 S. Summit Ave.
Sioux Falls, SD 57105
Tel: (605) 336-6588 *Fax:* (605) 335-9090
Website: asmweb.org
Members: 600 individuals
Staff: 4
Annual Budget: $100-250,000

Personnel:
Secretary and Treasurer: W. Jay Moon
    E-Mail: sec_treas@asmweb.org

Historical Note:
ASM strives to improve the scholarly study of theological, historical, social and practical questions relating to the missionary dimension of the Christian church; relate studies in Missiology to the other scholarly disciplines; enhance fellowship and cooperation among individuals and institutions engaged in activities and studies related to Missiology, facilitate mutual assistance and exchange of information among those thus engaged, encourage research and publication in the study of Christian missions, members are individuals interested in the scholarly study of theological, historical and social questions regarding the missionary dimension of the Christian church, member of the Council of Socs. for the Study of Religion, has no paid staff. Membership: $37 (Individual); $27 (Student); $19 (Retired).

Publications:
ASM Monographs
ASM newsletter
ASM Series
Missiology: An International Review; quarterly

American Society of Music Arrangers and Composers *(1938)*
5903 Noble Ave.
Van Nuys, CA 91411
Tel: (818) 994-4661 *Fax:* (818) 994-6181
E-Mail: asmac@properimageevents.com
Website: asmac.org
Members: 400 individuals
Staff: 3
Annual Budget: $10-25,000

Personnel:
President: Larry Blank
Director: Scherr Lillico

Historical Note:
Formerly American Society of Music Arrangers (ASMA). Assumed its current name in 1987. ASMAC is a professional society for musicians and composers specializing in arrangement and orchestration, working in film, television and other theater arts industries. Membership: $75 (Full); $50 (Associate); $25 (Student/ Initiation).

Publications:
Newsletter; monthly

The American Society of Naturalists *(1883)*
C/O Oregon State University
Corvallis, OR 97331
Tel: (541) 737-1000
E-Mail: asn@press.uchicago.edu

Website: asnamnat.org
Members: 1109 individuals
Staff: 3
Annual Budget: $50-100,000

Personnel:
President: Stevan J. Arnold
Editor in Chief: Mark A. McPeek

Historical Note:
ASN's purpose is to advance and diffuse knowledge of organic evolution and biological principles toward concept unification of the biological sciences. *Membership:* $75/year (US individuals); $95/year (foreign individuals); $100.25/year (Canadian individuals); $49/year (US students); $69/year (foreign students); $72.43/year (Canadian students).

Meetings/Conferences: Annual
2013 - Snowbird, UT/July 21 - 25
2014 - Pacific Grove, CA (Asilomar Conference Center)/Jan. 13 - 15

Publications:
Member Directory; on-line
The American Naturalist

American Society of Naval Engineers (1888)
1452 Duke St.
Alexandria, VA 22314-3458
Tel: (703) 836-6727 *Fax:* (703) 836-7491
E-Mail: asnehq@navalengineers.org
Website: navalengineers.org
Members: 5500 individuals
Staff: 10
Annual Budget: $2-5,000,000
Tax: 501(c)(3)

Personnel:
Executive Director: Capt. Dennis K. Kruse USN (Ret.)
    E-Mail: dkruse@navalengineers.org
Accounting Manager: Nancy Lackey
    E-Mail: nlackey@navalengineers.org
Manager, Membership Services: Danny C. Martin
    E-Mail: dmartin@navalengineers.org
Associate Director, Communications and Technical Media Relations: Maggie O'Brien
    E-Mail: mobrien@navalengineers.org
Communications Coordinator: Jared Pierce
    E-Mail: jpierce@navalengineers.org
Manager, Meetings: Joelle Ward
    E-Mail: jward@navalengineers.orgx

Historical Note:
ASNE's purpose is to advance the knowledge and practice of naval engineering in public and private applications and operations, to enhance the professionalism and well-being of members, and to promote naval engineering as a career field. *Membership:* $60-135 (Individual/Associate); $35 (Student); $25 (Spouse); $40 (Emeritus).

Meetings/Conferences: Annual
Conference Chair: Joelle Ward
2013 - Arlington, VA (Hyatt Regency Crystal City at Reagan National Airport)/Feb. 21 - 22
Number of non-conference events/year: 4

Publications:
Naval Engineers Journal; quarterly; adv.

American Society of Nephrology (1967)
1510 H St. NW
Suite 800
Washington, DC 20005
Tel: (202) 640-4660 *Fax:* (202) 637-9793
E-Mail: email@asn-online.org
Website: asn-online.org
Members: 13,000 members
Staff: 31
Annual Budget: $10-25,000,000
Tax: 501(c)(3)

Personnel:
Director, Operations: Danette Broughton
Marketing Associate: Amber Garner
Associate Director, Education: Jin Soo Kim
    E-Mail: jkim@asn-online.org

Historical Note:
ASN's mission is to fight against kidney disease by educating health professionals, sharing new knowledge, advancing research, and advocating the quality care for patients. Members are committed to preventing kidney diseases and making life better for patients. *Membership:* $296 (Corresponding/Affiliate/Active); $75 (Women in Nephrology); $0 (Medical Student/Resident/Fellow-in-Training/Retired Emeritus).

Continuing Education:
Certification Designation/s: CME

Meetings/Conferences: Annual
Conference Chair: Cele Fogarty
2013 - Atlanta, GA (Georgia World Congress Center)/Nov. 5 - 10
2014 - Philadelphia, PA (Pennsylvania Convention Center)/Nov. 11 - 16

Publications:
ASN Kidney News; monthly; adv.
CJASN; monthly; adv.
JASN; monthly; adv.
Kidney Daily; daily
Kidney Week; weekly

American Society of Neuroimaging (1977)
5841 Cedar Lake Rd.
Suite 204
Minneapolis, MN 55416
Tel: (952) 545-6291 *Fax:* (952) 545-6073
E-Mail: asn@llmsi.com
Website: asnweb.org
Members: 800 individuals
Staff: 2
Annual Budget: $250-500,000

Personnel:
Executive Director: Tisha Kehn
    E-Mail: asn@llmsi.com
Editor-in-Chief: Joseph Masdeu

Historical Note:
Established as the Society for Computerized Tomography and Neuroimaging; assumed its present name in 1980.The American Society of Neuroimaging (ASN) is an international, professional organization representing neurologists, neurosurgeons, neuroradiologists, and other neuroscientists who are dedicated to the advancement of any technique used to image the nervous system. The ASN supports the right of qualified physicians to utilize neuroimaging modalities for the evaluation and management of their patients, and the rights of patients with neurological disorders to have access to appropriate neuroimaging modalities and to physicians qualified in their use and interpretation. *Membership:* $100-525/year.

Continuing Education:
Certification Designation/s: NVTC, NC

Meetings/Conferences: Annual
2013 - Las Vegas, NV (Caesars Palace Las Vegas Hotel and Casino)/Jan. 17 - 20
Number of non-conference events/year: 1

Publications:
Journal Of Neuroimaging (JON); adv.
Membership Directory; on-line
Newsletter

American Society of Neuroradiology (1962)
2210 Midwest Rd.
Suite 207
Oak Brook, IL 60523-8205
Tel: (630) 574-0220 *Fax:* (630) 574-0661
E-Mail: bmack@asnr.org
Website: asnr.org
Members: 3200 individuals
Staff: 16
Annual Budget: $2-5,000,000
Tax: 501(c)(6)

Personnel:
Executive Director and Chief Executive Officer: James B. Gantenberg FACHE
    E-Mail: jgantenberg@asnr.org
Education Technologist: Arthur An
    E-Mail: aan@asnr.org
Director, Communications and Media Management: Angelo Artemakis MD, MPH
    E-Mail: aartemakis@asnr.org
Director, Specialty Societies and Membership Services: Kenneth Cammarata
    E-Mail: kcammarata@asnr.org
Director, Finance and Information Systems: Tina L. Cheng MD, MPH
    E-Mail: tcheng@asnr.org
Managing Editor: Karen Halm
    E-Mail: khalm@asnr.org
Office Manager and Executive Assistant: Karen Mansfield
    E-Mail: kmansfield@asnr.org
Director, Scientific Meetings: Lora Tannehill CMP
    E-Mail: ltannehill@asnr.org

Historical Note:

ASNR's purpose is to develop and support standards for training in the practice of neuroradiology. It also seeks to foster independent research, and to promote a closer fellowship and exchange of ideas among neuroradiologists. *Membership:* $425-750 (Senior); $215-330 (Senior Military); $313-600 (Member); $213-400 (1st year out of Neuroradiology fellowship); $140-255 (Member, Military Radiologists, and those outside North America).

Meetings/Conferences: Annual
Conference Chair: Lora Tannehill CMP
2013 - San Diego, CA (San Diego Convention and Visitors Bureau)/May 18 - 23
2014 - Montreal, QC (Palais Des Congres de Montreal)/May 17 - 22

Publications:
Membership Directory; on-line

Membership List Available to Non-members

American Society of Neurorehabilitation (1990)
5841 Cedar Lake Rd.
Suite 204
Minneapolis, MN 55416
Tel: (952) 545-6324 *Fax:* (952) 545-6073
E-Mail: asnr@llmsi.com
Website: asnr.com
Members: 500 individuals
Staff: 3
Annual Budget: $100-250,000
Tax: 501(c)(6)

Personnel:
President: Anna Barrett MD
Editor-in-Chief: Bruce Dobkin MD
    E-Mail: bdobkin@mednet.ucla.edu
Treasurer and Secretary: George Wittenberg MD, PhD

Historical Note:
ASNR's mission is to promote the medical and social wellbeing of persons with disabling neurological disorders and to advance training and research in the basic and clinical sciences that can lead to functional recovery of neurologically impaired persons and to disseminate the knowledge of this research among professionals and the general public. Members are physicians and other medical professionals with an interest in the rehabilitation of disorders of the nervous system. *Membership:* $260 (Active Physician); $185 (Active Non-Physician); $160 (Physician in Training); $60 (Student).

Continuing Education:
Certification Designation/s: ASNR

Meetings/Conferences: Annual

Publications:
Journal Watch
Neurorehabilitation and Neural Repair; adv.
Newsletter

Membership List Available to Non-members

American Society of News Editors (1922)
401 S. Ninth St.
Suite 209
Columbia, MO 65201
Tel: (573) 882-9854 *Fax:* (573) 884-3824
E-Mail: asne@asne.org
Website: asne.org
Members: 750 individuals
Staff: 9
Annual Budget: $500-1,000,000
Tax: 501(c)(3)

Personnel:
Accounting Manager: Jeanne Esmond
Director, Finance: Cindy L. Roe
    E-Mail: croe@asne.org

Historical Note:
ASNE is dedicated to the leadership of American journalism. It is committed to fostering the public discourse essential to democracy; helping editors maintain the highest standards of quality, improve their craft and better serve their communities; and preserving and promoting core journalistic values, while embracing and exploring change. *Membership:* $295 (First applicant); $125 (Retired); $1,000 (Retired Life Member).

Meetings/Conferences: Annual
2013 - Washington, DC (Jurys Washington Hotel)/April 14 - 17

Publications:
Membership Directory; on-line
The American Editor; quarterly; adv.

American Society of Notaries (1965)
P.O. Box 5707

Tallahassee, FL 32314-5707
Tel: (850) 671-5164 *Fax:* (850) 671-5165
E-Mail: info@asnnotary.org
Website: notaries.org
Members: 20000 individuals
Staff: 2
Annual Budget: $100-250,000
Tax: 501(c)(6)

Personnel:
Executive Director: Kathleen M. Butler
Director, Membership Services: Carly Heitz

Historical Note:
ASN's mission is to provide its members with education, professional service and technical support. Membership: $39-110 (Individual); $7 (ASN All-States Recordbook); $12 (Notarial Certificates on CD).

Publications:
American Notary newsletter
Hot Tips; semi-monthly

American Society of Nuclear Cardiology *(1993)*
4340 East-West Hwy.
Suite 1120
Bethesda, MD 20814-4578
Tel: (301) 215-7575 *Fax:* (301) 215-7113
E-Mail: info@asnc.org
Website: asnc.org
Members: 4700 individuals
Staff: 12
Annual Budget: $2-5,000,000
Tax: 501(c)(3)

Personnel:
Executive Director: Steve Carter
Director, Marketing and Membership Services: Karen DeSantis
Director, Communications: Beth Hodge
Senior Coordinator, Administration: Zachary Kesler
Managing Editor: Wendy Passerell
   E-Mail: J_Nucl_Cardiol@jnc.asnc.org
Director, Education and Meetings: Meridith Phillips
Director, Information Technology: Drita Tibbs
Director, Health Policy: Jenna Wilkes

Historical Note:
ASNC provides medical education programs related to nuclear cardiology and cardiovascular computed tomography (CT), promotes accreditation and certification in nuclear cardiology. Members comprised of physicians, scientists, technologists, and other personnel who work in the nuclear cardiology field. Membership: $230 (Domestic), $200 (International); $75 (Technologist); $95 (Associate).

Continuing Education:
Certification Designation/s: CME, CBCCT, CBNC, NMTCB

Meetings/Conferences: Annual
Conference Chair: Meridith Phillips
2013 - Chicago, IL/Sept. 27 - 30

Publications:
ASNC Newsletter; monthly
Journal of Nuclear Cardiology; bi-monthly
Membership Directory; on-line
SmartBrief; weekly

American Society of Ocularists *(1957)*
1001 Mohawk St.
Suite 16
Bakersfield, CA 93309
Tel: (661) 633-1746 *Fax:* (661) 458-1660
TollFree: (888) 973-4066
E-Mail: toniz@ocularist.org
Website: ocularist.org
Staff: 1
Annual Budget: $250-500,000

Personnel:
Executive Director: Cathi Guerrero
   E-Mail: info@ocularist.org

Historical Note:
ASO's mission is to foster, improve and promote research in and development of ophthalmic prosthetics. ASO members are technicians specializing in the fitting and fabrication of custom artificial eyes. Benefits of membership include research, education and standards. Membership: $250.

Meetings/Conferences:
2013 - Kohala Coast, HI (Mauna Lani Bay Hotel and Bungalows Resort)/May 9 - 17
2013 - New Orleans, LA/Nov. 15 - 19
2014 - Chicago, IL/Oct. 17 - 21
2015 - Phoenix, AZ (The Wigwam Hotel)/April 25 - May 1

Publications:
Journal of Ophthalmic Prosthetics

American Society of Ophthalmic Administrators *(1986)*
4000 Legato Rd.
Suite 700
Fairfax, VA 22033-4003
Tel: (703) 788-5777 *Fax:* (703) 547-8827
TollFree: (800) 451-1339
E-Mail: asoa@asoa.org
Website: asoa.org
Members: 2000 individuals
Staff: 7
Annual Budget: $1-2,000,000

Personnel:
Executive Director: Laureen Rowland
   E-Mail: laureen@asoa.org
Manager, Meetings and Program: Shannon Mueller
   E-Mail: shannon@asoa.org
Manager, Membership and Marketing: Lisa Marie Romano
   E-Mail: lisa@asoa.org
Administrative Assistant: Susan Younker
   E-Mail: susan@asoa.org

Historical Note:
A division of the American Society of Cataract and Refractive Surgery. ASOA's mission is to advance the skills and professionalism of ophthalmic practice management. Members are active administrators functioning in an ophthalmologists practice. Membership: $275/year (Individual).

Continuing Education:
Certification Designation/s: COE

Meetings/Conferences:
Conference Chair: Shannon Mueller
2013 - Aventura, FL (Turnberry Isle Miami)/Feb. 14 - 18
2013 - San Francisco, CA (Moscone Center/San Francisco Marriott Marquis)/April 19 - 23
2013 - San Francisco, CA/April 25 - 29
2014 - Boston, MA/April 9 - 13
2014 - Boston, MA/April 25 - 28
Number of non-conference events/year: 4

Publications:
Administrative Eyecare; quarterly; adv.
AE eZine; on-line; adv.
Coding Consult; monthly
COE Directory; on-line
EyeWorld; adv.
Health Insurance News; monthly
HR News; monthly
Insights; monthly
Membership Directory; on-line

American Society of Ophthalmic Plastic and Reconstructive Surgery *(1969)*
5841 Cedar Lake Rd.
Suite 204
Minneapolis, MN 55416
Tel: (952) 646-2038 *Fax:* (952) 545-6073
E-Mail: info@asoprs.org
Website: asoprs.org
Members: 500 individuals
Staff: 6
Annual Budget: $500-1,000,000
Tax: 501(c)(3)

Personnel:
President: Jill A. Foster FACS, MD
Editor-in-Chief: Jonathan J. Dutton MD, PhD
Treasurer: Jemshed A. Khan MD
Executive Secretary: Shannath L. Merbs
Secretary, Meetings: John D. Ng FACS, MD
Secretary, Education: Peter J. Sneed

Historical Note:
ASOPRS's mission is to advance training, research and patient care in the fields of aesthetic, plastic and reconstructive surgery specializing in the face, orbits, eyelids and lacrimal system. Members are surgeons specializing in plastic and reconstructive surgery of the eyelids, orbits and lacrimalsystem.

Meetings/Conferences: Annual
Conference Chair: John D. Ng FACS, MD
2013 - New Orleans, LA (Hyatt Regency)/Nov. 14 - 15
Number of non-conference events/year: 3

Publications:
Membership Directory; on-line

American Society of Ophthalmic Registered Nurses *(1976)*
P.O. Box 193030
San Francisco, CA 94119-3030
Tel: (415) 561-8513 *Fax:* (415) 561-8531
E-Mail: asorn@aao.org
Website: asorn.org
Members: 700 individuals
Staff: 4
Annual Budget: $250-500,000
Tax: 501(c)(3)

Personnel:
Executive Director: Lisa Brown
Manager, Programs: Sian Hillier
   E-Mail: shillier@aao.org
Director, Annual Meeting: Diane La Rosa
   E-Mail: Larosa.diane@yahoo.com
Secretary and Treasurer: Noreen Smith
   E-Mail: noreenelizabeth@comcast.net

Historical Note:
ASORN's mission is to foster excellence in ophthalmic patient care while supporting the ophthalmic team through individual development, education, and evidence based practice. Membership: $100 (Regular Member); $80 (Individual Affiliate); $65 (Retired); $1,000 (Corporates).

Continuing Education:
Enrollment: 400
Certification Designation/s: CRNO

Meetings/Conferences: Annual
Conference Chair: Diane La Rosa

Publications:
ASORN Connection; quarterly
Blink
Insight; monthly

Membership List Available to Non-members

American Society of Orthopedic Physician Assistants *(1976)*
8365 Keystone Crossing
Suite 107
Indianapolis, IN 46240
Tel: (800) 280-2390 *Fax:* (317) 205-9481
TollFree: (800) 280-2390
E-Mail: asopa@hp-assoc.com
Website: asopa.org
Staff: 3
Annual Budget: $100-250,000
Tax: 501(c)(6)

Personnel:
Executive Director: Lori Pearson
   E-Mail: lpearson@hp-assoc.com
Treasurer: Larry Eswein
   E-Mail: eswein@sbcglobal.net
Coordinator, Membership: Julie Schafer
   E-Mail: jschafer@hp-assoc.com

Historical Note:
ASOPAs mission is to enhance the quality of patient care by providing professional development to orthopaedic physician's assistants through continuing education, certification, networking, publications and meeting with peers and other allied health professionals. Membership: $200 (Fellow/Affiliate); $75 (Student).

Continuing Education:
Certification Designation/s: OPA-C

Meetings/Conferences: Annual
2013 - New Orleans, LA (Hyatt Regency)/July 31 - Aug. 3

Publications:
Membership Directory; on-line
Newsletter; quarterly

American Society of Papyrologists *(1961)*
Duke University, Department of Classical Studies
233 Allen Building, P O Box 90103
Durham, NC 27708-0103
E-Mail: asp@papyrology.org
Website: papyrology.org
Members: 175 individuals
Staff: 3
Annual Budget: $50-100,000
Tax: 501(c)(3)

Personnel:
President: Jennifer Sheridan Moss
   E-Mail: aa2191@wayne.edu
Secretary and Treasurer: William A. Johnson
   E-Mail: william.johnson@uc.edu

Editor in chief: Peter van Minnen
    E-Mail: peter.vanminnen@classics.uc.edu

Historical Note:
ASP is an association of scholars and students concerned
with classical and Egyptian antiquity, in particular with the
editing and study of texts preserved on papyrus. Affiliated
with the Association Internationale de Papyrologues,
Brussels, Belgium. Membership: $35 (Regular); $21
(Student); $10 (Spouse); $50 (Institutional); $100
(Sustaining); $1000 (Benefactor).

Publications:
Bulletin of the American Society of Papyrologists

American Society of Parasitologists (1924)
Department of Biological Sciences
Purdue University
West Lafayette, IN 47907-2054
Tel: (765) 494-8188 Fax: (765) 494-0876
Website: asp.unl.edu
Members: 1500 individuals
Staff: 3
Annual Budget: $100-250,000

Personnel:
President: Armand M. Kuris
Editor, Newsletter: Scott Lyell Gardner PhD
    E-Mail: nospam-slg@unl.edu
Secretary and Treasurer: Dennis J. Minchella
    E-Mail: dennism@purdue.edu

Historical Note:
Society started by Henry Baldwin Ward. Formed
in Washington under the leadership of a group of
parasitologists from the Baltimore-Washington area,
December 30, 1924 at a meeting of the American
Association for the Advancement of Science. Incorporated
in the District of Columbia in 1932. Purpose is to improve
teaching, promote investigation, and advance knowledge
of parasitology and related sciences. Membership: $20-50
(Student); $85 (Regular).

Meetings/Conferences: Annual
2013 - Québec, QC (Loews Hotel Le Concorde)/June 27
    - 30
2014 - New Orleans, LA (JW Marriott New Orleans)/
    July 24 - 27
2015 - Omaha, NE (Hilton Omaha)/June 25 - 28

Publications:
ASP Newsletter; quarterly; adv.
Journal of Parasitology; bi-monthly; adv.
Membership Directory; on-line

The American Society of Pediatric Hematology/Oncology (1981)
4700 W. Lake Ave.
Glenview, IL 60025-1485
Tel: (847) 375-4716 Fax: (847) 375-6483
E-Mail: info@aspho.org
Website: aspho.org
Members: 1650 individuals
Staff: 9
Annual Budget: $1-2,000,000
Tax: 501(c)(3)

Personnel:
Executive Director: Cynthia Porter
    E-Mail: cporter@aspho.org
Senior Manager, Marketing: Erin Abbey
    E-Mail: eabbey@aspho.org
Director, Education: Steve Biddle
    E-Mail: sbiddle@aspho.org
Senior Manager, Meetings: Stephanie Dylkiewicz
    E-Mail: sdylkiewicz@connect2amc.com
Senior Manager, Membership Development: Carrie
    Gremer
    E-Mail: cgremer@aspho.org
Manager, Operations: Amy Kephart
    E-Mail: akephart@aspho.org
Manager, Corporate Relations and National Sales: Mary
    Paulson
    E-Mail: mpaulson@connect2amc.com

Historical Note:
ASPHO's mission is to promote optimal care of children and
adolescents with blood disorders and cancer by advancing
research, education, treatment and professional practice.
Membership is open to qualified professionals from all
countries. Membership: $335 (Active); $115 (Trainees);
$150 (Allied).

Meetings/Conferences: Annual
Conference Chair: Stephanie Dylkiewicz
2013 - Miami, FL (Hyatt Regency)/April 24 - 27

2014 - Chicago, IL (Palmer House a Hilton Hotel)/May
    14 - 17

Publications:
ASPHO eNewsletter; bi-monthly
Pediatric Blood & Cancer; monthly

Membership List Available to Non-members

American Society of Pediatric Nephrology (1969)
3400 Research Forest Dr.
Suite B-7
The Woodlands, TX 77381
Tel: (281) 419-0052 Fax: (281) 419-0082
E-Mail: info@aspneph.com
Website: aspneph.com
Members: 600 Members
Staff: 1
Annual Budget: $250-500,000
Tax: 501(c)(6)

Personnel:
Executive Secretary: Lisa Thompson
    E-Mail: lthompson@aspneph.com

Historical Note:
ASPN seeks to advocate optimal care for children with
kidney disease through advocacy, education and research;
and to disseminate advances in clinical practice and
scientific investigation. Members are pediatric nephrologists
and affiliated health care professionals. Membership: $300
(Active); $150 (Associate); $35 (Affiliate).

Meetings/Conferences: Annual
2013 - Washington, DC/May 4 - 7
2014 - Vancouver, BC/May 3 - 6
2015 - San Diego, CA/April 25 - 28
2016 - Baltimore, MD/April 30 - May 3
2017 - San Francisco, CA/May 6 - 9
2018 - Toronto, ON/May 5 - 8
2019 - Baltimore, MD/April 27 - 30
2020 - Philadelphia, PA/May 2 - 5

Publications:
KIDney Notes; bi-monthly

The American Society of Pediatric Neurosurgeons (1978)
4800 Sand Point Way NE
Seattle, WA 98105
Tel: (206) 744-9321
Website: aspn.org
Members: 100 neurosurgeons
Staff: 5
Annual Budget: $100-250,000

Personnel:
President: Rick Abbott MD
President-Elect: Alan R. Cohen MD
Treasurer: James M. Drake

Historical Note:
ASPN's mission is to improve the neurosurgical care of the
children of the United States and Canada by encouraging
and advocating the specialty of Pediatric Neurosurgery.
Members are neurosurgeons who devote a substantial
majority of their practice to the care of pediatric patients.
Membership: $100/year.

Publications:
Membership Directory; on-line
The Journal of Neurosurgery - Pediatrics.

American Society of Pension Professionals & Actuaries (1966)
4245 N. Fairfax Dr.
Suite 750
Arlington, VA 22203
Tel: (703) 516-9300 Fax: (703) 516-9308
E-Mail: asppa@asppa.org
Website: asppa.org
Members: 10,000 career professionals
Staff: 46
Annual Budget: $10-25,000,000

Personnel:
Executive Director and Chief Executive Officer: Brian H.
    Graff Esq., APM
    E-Mail: bgraff@asppa.org
Director, Human Resources and Board of Directors Liaison:
    Troy L. Cornett
    E-Mail: tcornett@asppa.org
Assistant General Counsel and Director, Government
    Affairs: Debra Davis
    E-Mail: ddavis@asppa.org
Director, Political: James Dornan

    E-Mail: jdornan@asppa.org
General Counsel and Director, Regulatory Affairs: Craig P.
    Hoffman APM
    E-Mail: choffman@asppa.org
Senior Director, Business and Membership Development:
    Jeff Hoffman
    E-Mail: jhoffman@asppa.org
Chief Financial Officer: Tom Hopkins
    E-Mail: thopkins@asppa.org
Director, Information Technology Solutions: Vincent
    Huckle
    E-Mail: vhuckle@asppa.org
Chief of Marketing: John M. Phillips
    E-Mail: jphillips@asppa.org
Director, Media Relations: Melinda Semadeni
    E-Mail: msemadeni@asppa.org
Manager, Education and Publication Services: Beverly
    Shideler
    E-Mail: bshideler@asppa.org
Director, Conferences: Erin Stewart
    E-Mail: estewart@asppa.org
Director, Education Services: Catherine Williams
    E-Mail: cwilliams@asppa.org

Historical Note:
ASPPA is the national organization for career retirement
plan professionals. Members are part of the diversified,
technical, and regulated benefits industry. Membership:
$50-450 (Affiliate Member); $50-515 (Credentialed
Member).

Continuing Education:
Certification Designation/s: TGPC, APM, QPFC, QPA,
CPC, QKA

Meetings/Conferences:
Conference Chair: Erin Stewart
2013 - Los Angeles, CA (Sheraton Los Angeles
    Downtown)/Jan. 30 - Feb. 1
2013 - Las Vegas, NV (Caesars Palace Las Vegas Hotel
    and Casino)/March 3 - 5
2013 - Ft. Washington, MD (Gaylord National Resort
    and Convention Center-National Harbor)/Oct. 27 -
    30

Publications:
ENews; monthly
Membership Directory; on-line
The ASPPA Journal; on-line

American Society of Perfumers (1947)
P.O. Box 1551
W. Caldwell, NJ 07004
Tel: (201) 991-0040 Fax: (877) 732-0090
E-Mail: info@perfumers.org
Website: perfumers.org
Members: 300 individuals
Staff: 3
Annual Budget: $100-250,000

Personnel:
Chairman: Dennis Maroney
Administrator: Lisa Amatulli
Director, Financial Services: James Fassold

Historical Note:
ASP's mission is to foster and encourage art and science
of perfumery in United States while promoting professional
exchange and a high standard of professional conduct
within the fragrance industry. It is a sponsor of World
Perfumery Congress held every three years. Member are
qualified perfumers.

Meetings/Conferences: Annual
Number of non-conference events/year: 1

Publications:
Newsletter

Membership List Available to Non-members

American Society of PeriAnesthesia Nurses (1980)
90 Frontage Rd.
Cherry Hill, NJ 08034-1424
Tel: (856) 616-9600 Fax: (856) 616-9601
TollFree: (877) 737-9696
E-Mail: aspan@aspan.org
Website: aspan.org
Members: 55000 individuals
Staff: 10
Annual Budget: $2-5,000,000
Tax: 501(c)(3)

Personnel:
Chief Executive Officer: Kevin Dill
    E-Mail: kdill@aspan.org

Director, Programs and Project Development: Jane Certo
E-Mail: jcerto@aspan.org
Manager, Marketing and Communications: Douglas Hanisch
E-Mail: dhanisch@aspan.org
Manager, Accounting and Database: Jean Hess
E-Mail: jhess@aspan.org
Manager, Meetings: Courtney Papp
E-Mail: cpapp@aspan.org
Manager, Membership Services: Eileen Zeiger
E-Mail: ezeiger@aspan.org

Historical Note:
Formerly (1996) American Society of Post Anesthesia Nurses. ASPAN's purpose is to advance the unique specialty of perianesthesia nursing and also building integrity, modeling respect, honoring diversity, enhancing stewardship and mentorship, cultivating passion and supporting community. Members are post-anesthesia, pre-anesthesia and ambulatory surgery nurses. Membership: $80 (Active); $105 (Affiliate/International); $60 (Retired/Student).

Continuing Education:
Certification Designation/s: CAPA, CPAN

Meetings/Conferences: Annual
Conference Chair: Courtney Papp
2013 - Chicago, IL (Hilton Chicago)/April 14 - 18/2000 attendees/over 100 exhibitors
2014 - Las Vegas, NV/April 27 - May 1

Publications:
Breathline; bi-monthly; adv.
The Journal of PeriAnesthesia Nursing; bi-monthly; adv.

American Society of Pharmacognosy (1959)
3149 Dundee Rd.
Suite 260
Northbrook, IL 60062-2402
Tel: (773) 995-3748 Fax: (847) 656-2800
E-Mail: asphcog@aol.com
Website: pharmacognosy.us
Members: 1100 individuals
Staff: 2
Annual Budget: $500-1,000,000
Tax: 501(c)(6)

Personnel:
Ex--Officio: David J. Slatkin PhD
E-Mail: asphcog@aol.com
Editor: Edward J. Kennelly
E-Mail: kennelly@lehman.cuny.edu

Historical Note:
ASP strives to promote the study of the composition, production, use and history of drugs of natural origin. Membership: $75 (Full); $25 (Associate); $10 (Emeritus).

Meetings/Conferences: Annual
2013 - St. Louis, MO/July 12 - 18

Publications:
ASP Newsletter; quarterly
Journal of Natural Products; monthly; adv.
Membership Directory; on-line

Membership List Available to Non-members

American Society of Photographers (1937)
3120 N. Argonne Dr.
Milwaukee, WI 53222
Tel: (414) 871-6301 Fax: (414) 871-6600
E-Mail: jonallyn@aol.com
Website: asofp-online.com
Members: 800 individuals
Staff: 3
Annual Budget: $50-100,000
Tax: 501(c)(6)

Personnel:
Executive Director: Jon Allynn
President: James Churchill
E-Mail: jchurchill100@aol.com
Secretary and Treasurer: Kalen Henderson

Historical Note:
ASP's goal is to promote education, foster fellowship and perpetuate the ideals of photography as a science and an art. Members must be either a Master of Photography, a Photographic Craftsman, or a Photographic Specialist. Membership: $125/year (Individual).

Publications:
ASP Magazine
Membership Directory

American Society of Picture Professionals (1966)
217 Palos Verdes Blvd.

Suite 700
Redondo Beach, CA 90277
Tel: (424) 247-9944 Fax: (424) 247-9844
Website: aspp.com
Members: 750 individuals
Staff: 5
Annual Budget: $100-250,000

Personnel:
Executive Director: Jain Lemos
E-Mail: director@aspp.com
Contact, Membership Services: Doug Brooks
E-Mail: membership@aspp.com
Contact, Communications: Jennifer Davis Heffner
E-Mail: jennasppdc@gmail.com
Vice President: Sam Merrell
E-Mail: sam.merrell@gmail.com
Contact, Technology: Cecilia de Querol
E-Mail: galileopix@gmail.com

Historical Note:
ASPP provides networking and educational opportunities in the image transaction industry. Members are image producers (e.g. photographers), stock photo agencies, and image users (publishers and independent photo editors and researchers). Membership: $25 (Student); $125 (Regular); $95 (65 or Older); $135 (Foreign Regular); $105 (Foreign Senior).

Meetings/Conferences: Annual

Publications:
ASPP's eNewsletter; on-line
Membership Directory; on-line
The Picture Professional magazine; quarterly; adv.

Membership List Available to Non-members

American Society of Plant Biologists (1924)
15501 Monona Dr.
Rockville, MD 20855-2768
Tel: (301) 251-0560 Fax: (301) 279-2996
E-Mail: info@aspb.org
Website: my.aspb.org
Members: 5000 individuals
Staff: 22
Annual Budget: $5-10,000,000
Tax: 501(c)(3)

Personnel:
Executive Director: Crispin Taylor
E-Mail: ctaylor@aspb.org
Education Coordinator: Katie Engen
E-Mail: katie@aspb.org
Manager, Executive and Governance Affairs: Donna Gordon
E-Mail: dgordon@aspb.org
Director, Finance and Administration: Kim Kimnach
E-Mail: kkimnach@aspb.org
Director, Marketing, Meetings and Membership Services: Jean Rosenberg
E-Mail: jean@aspb.org
Director, Publications: Nancy Winchester
E-Mail: nancyw@aspb.org

Historical Note:
Formerly (1924) American Society of Plant Physiologists and incorporated in the District of Columbia the same year and assumed its current name in 2001. ASPB's mission is to promote the growth and development of plant biology, to encourage and publish research in plant biology, and to promote the interests and growth of plant scientists in general. Membership: $130 (Regular); $45 (Student); $65 (Postdoctoral Associate).

Meetings/Conferences: Annual
Conference Chair: Jean Rosenberg
2013 - Providence, RI/July 20 - 24
2014 - Portland, OR/July 12 - 16

Publications:
Membership Directory; on-line
The ASPB News; bi-monthly

American Society of Plant Taxonomists (1935)
University of Wyoming, Department of Botany
3165
1000 E. University Ave.
Laramie, WY 82071
Tel: (307) 766-2556 Fax: (307) 766-2851
E-Mail: aspt@uwyo.edu
Website: aspt.net
Members: 1400 individuals
Staff: 6
Annual Budget: $250-500,000
Tax: 501(c)(3)

Personnel:
Business Office Manager: Linda Brown
E-Mail: aspt@uwyo.edu
Treasurer: Steffi Ickert-Bond
E-Mail: smickertbond@alaska.edu
Contact, Membership: Kathy Kron
Contact, Public Relation: Austin R. Mast
Editor-in-Chief: Tom Ranker
President: Linda E. Watson
E-Mail: linda.watson10@okstate.edu

Historical Note:
ASPT promotes research and teaching of taxonomy, systematics, and phylogeny of vascular and nonvascular plants. ASPT members are professional plant systematists and others interested in plant taxonomy and evolution. Membership: $70 (Regular); $75 (Regular Family); $30 (Student/Postdoc); $35 (Student/Postdoc Family); $40 (Emeritus); $45 (Emeritus Family); $1,000 (Lifetime); $1250 (Family Life).

Meetings/Conferences: Annual
2013 - New Orleans, LA/July 21 - Aug. 1
2014 - Boise, ID/July 25 - 31
2015 - Edmonton, AB/July 24 - 30

Publications:
ASPT Membership Directory; biennially
ASPT Newsletter; semi-annually; adv.
Systematic Botany; quarterly; adv.

Membership List Available to Non-members

American Society of Plastic Surgeons (1931)
444 E. Algonquin Rd.
Arlington Heights, IL 60005-4654
Tel: (847) 228-9900 Fax: (847) 228-9131
E-Mail: registration@plasticsurgery.org
Website: plasticsurgery.org
Members: 6000 individuals
Staff: 96
Annual Budget: $10-25,000,000

Personnel:
President: Malcolm Z. Roth MD

Historical Note:
Founded as American Society of Plastic and Reconstructive Surgeons, assumed its current name in 1999. ASPS's mission is to advance quality care to plastic surgery patients by encouraging high standards of training, ethics, physician practice and research in plastic surgery.

Meetings/Conferences:
Number of non-conference events/year: 34

Publications:
Membership Directory; on-line
Plastic and Reconstructive Surgery
Plastic Surgery News
Plastic Surgery SmartBrief; weekly

American Society of Plumbing Engineers (1964)
2980 S. River Rd.
Des Plaines, IL 60018
Tel: (847) 296-0002 Fax: (847) 296-2963
E-Mail: info@aspe.org
Website: aspe.org
Members: 7000 individuals
Staff: 11
Annual Budget: $2-5,000,000
Tax: 501(c)(6)

Personnel:
Executive Director and Chief Executive Officer: Jim Kendzel CAE, MPH
E-Mail: jkendzel@aspe.org
Manager, Information Technology and Publications and Webmaster: Richard Albrecht
E-Mail: ralbrecht@aspe.org
Director, Membership Services: Stacey A. Kidd
E-Mail: skidd@aspe.org
Managing Director and Director, Education and Meetings: Cliff Reis
E-Mail: creis@aspe.org
Director, Finance and Administration: Donald Thurner
E-Mail: dthurner@aspe.org
Coordinator, Membership services and Meetings: Jinnie Yoo
E-Mail: jyoo@aspe.org

Historical Note:
ASPE is dedicated to the advancement of science of plumbing engineering to the professional growth and advancement of its members and the health, welfare and safety of the public. Membership: $165 (Associate); $185 (Full/Affiliate/Special/Governmental); $25 (Student).

Continuing Education:
Certification Designation/s: CPD

Meetings/Conferences: Annual
Conference Chair: Jinnie Yoo
2013 - Orlando, FL/Sept. 19 - 22
2014 - Chicago, IL/Sept. 19 - 24
2016 - Phoenix, AZ/Oct. 27 - Nov. 4

Publications:
ASPE Manufacturer Directory; on-line
Pipeline; bi-weekly; adv.
Plumbing Systems and Design; monthly; adv.

American Society of Podiatric Medical Assistants
(1964)
1616 N. 78th Ct.
Elmwood Park, IL 60707
Tel: (708) 456-4947 *Fax:* (630) 325-3594
E-Mail: aspmaex@aol.com
Website: aspma.org
Members: 1500 individuals
Staff: 4
Annual Budget: $25-50,000
Tax: 501(c)(3)

Personnel:
Executive Director: Karen Marie Keathley
    E-Mail: aspmaex@aol.com
Director, Communications and IT Technology: Jesus C.
    Vazquez
    E-Mail: jvazquezpmac@gmail.com

Historical Note:
*Formerly (1985) American Society of Podiatric Assistants.
An affiliate of the American Podiatric Medical Association.
ASPMA seeks to advocate, support, improve, sustain and
advance the profession of Podiatric Medical Assistants.
Members must be employed by podiatrists who are members
of APMA. Membership: $90/year.*

Continuing Education:
Certification Designation/s: DPM, PMAC

Publications:
ASPMA Journal; quarterly

American Society of Podiatric Medicine *(1944)*
1111 Lane Concourse Dr.
Suite 111
Bay Harbor, FL 33154
Tel: (305) 866-9608 *Fax:* (305) 866-1750
E-Mail: wsimmonds@msn.com
Website: aspmonline.net
Members: 110 individuals
Staff: 2
Annual Budget: Under $10,000

Personnel:
President: Elliot T. Udell DPM
Treasurer: Warren L. Simmonds

Historical Note:
*An affiliate of the American Podiatric Medical Association.
Formerly (1972) American College of Podiatric Medicine.
ASPM are Striving for technical and therapeutic
advancements within the scop of podiatric licensure for the
prevention and alleviation of pain and suffering.*

Meetings/Conferences:
2013 - Las Vegas, NV/July 21 - 25

American Society of Podiatry Executives
1296 W. 475 South
Farmington, UT 84025
Tel: (801) 599-8519 *Fax:* (801) 599-8519
Website: aspeonline.org/
Members: 35 individuals
Staff: 2
Annual Budget: Under $10,000

Personnel:
President: Candace Daly
    E-Mail: candacedaly.cjd@comcast.net
Secretary and Treasurer: Christian Kindsvatter

Historical Note:
*Founded as Conference of Podiatric Executives; assumed
its current name in 1996. ASPE is dedicated to working
on behalf of the medical and surgical specialists of the
foot and ankle through Education, Advocacy, Governance.
Members are directors of state podiatry associations. Has
no paid officers or full-time staff. Membership: $125/year
(individual).*

Meetings/Conferences: Semi-Annual
2013 - Washington, DC (JW Marriott Hotel -
    Washington)/March 15

American Society of Preventive Oncology *(1976)*
330 WARF Bldg
610 Walnut St.
Madison, WI 53726
Tel: (608) 263-9515 *Fax:* (608) 263-4497
Website: aspo.org
Members: 420 individuals
Staff: 2
Annual Budget: $250-500,000

Personnel:
Executive Director: Heidi A. Sahel
    E-Mail: hasahel@wisc.edu
Secretary and Treasurer: Amy Trentham-Dietz PhD
    E-Mail: trentham@wisc.edu

Historical Note:
*ASPO is a multi-disciplinary society committed to cancer
prevention and control through scientific conferences
and advocacy for cancer prevention and control research
funding. Promotes the exchange and dissemination of
information and ideas relating to cancer prevention and
control. Membership: $250 (Full Active-Individual); $35
(Student/Post-Doc Trainee); Free (Emeritus-Retired or > 70
yrs).*

Meetings/Conferences: Annual
2013 - Memphis, TN (Memphis Peabody Hotel)/March
    9 - 13

Publications:
Cancer Epidemiology, Biomarkers & Prevention (CEBP);
    monthly; adv.
Member Directory; on-line

American Society of Primatologists *(1976)*
Department of Psychology, Trinity University
One Trinity Pl.
San Antonio, TX 78212
Tel: (210) 999-7102 *Fax:* (210) 999-8386
Website: asp.org
Members: 750 individuals
Staff: 2
Annual Budget: $100-250,000
Tax: 501(c)(3)

Personnel:
Treasurer: Kimberley Phillips PhD
    E-Mail: kimberley.phillips@trinity.edu

Historical Note:
*ASP's mission is to promote and encourage the discovery
and exchange of information regarding primates. Members
are individuals specializing in the study of monkeys, apes,
and other primates. Membership: $90-115 (Full); $60-80
(Student); $25 (Retired).*

Meetings/Conferences: Annual
2013 - San Juan, PR/June 18 - 22

Publications:
Membership Directory; on-line
Newsletter

American Society of Professional Estimators *(1956)*
2525 Perimeter Place Dr.
Suite 103
Nashville, TN 37214
Tel: (615) 316-9200 *Fax:* (615) 316-9800
TollFree: (888) 378-6283
E-Mail: info@aspenational.org
Website: aspenational.org
Members: 3000 individuals
Staff: 6
Annual Budget: $500-1,000,000
Tax: 501(c)(3)

Personnel:
Executive Director: Patsy Smith
    E-Mail: psmith@aspenational.org
*Bookkeeper and Contact, Membership Database, Online
    Classes, Merchandise Orders:* Tina Cooke
    E-Mail: Tina@aspenational.org
Coordinator, Certification: Tanya Graham
    E-Mail: Tanya@aspenational.org
*Assistant Executive Director, Advertising, Marketing,
    Tradeshows and Education:* Christian Lutz
    E-Mail: christian@aspenational.org
*Coordinator, Publications, Graphics, Production and
    Website Management:* Corey M. Seaborn
    E-Mail: corey@aspenational.org

Historical Note:
*ASPE serves construction trade estimators by providing
education, fellowship and opportunity for professional
development. It is composed of construction trade
estimators. Membership: $220 (Estimator/Associate/
Affiliate/Constructor/Members-At-Large); $11 (Student).*

Continuing Education:
Enrollment: 100
Certification Designation/s: CPE

Meetings/Conferences: Annual
Conference Chair: Patsy Smith
2013 - Philadelphia, PA (Hyatt Regency)/July 17 - 20
Number of non-conference events/year: 3

Publications:
ASPE E-Newsletter; on-line
Estimating Today; monthly; adv.
Membership Directory; on-line
Standard Estimating Practice; annually

American Society of Psychoanalytic Physicians
(1985)
13528 Wisteria Dr.
Germantown, MD 20874
Tel: (301) 540-3197 *Fax:* (301) 540-3511
Website: aspp.net
Members: 280 individuals
Staff: 1
Annual Budget: Under $10,000
Tax: 501(c)(6)

Personnel:
Executive Director: Christine Cotter
    E-Mail: cfcotter@aspp.net

Historical Note:
*Formed by merging of American Society of Physician
Analysts and American Association of Psychoanalytic
Physicians. ASPP is an organization of physicians
established for non-profit education, scientific, and
professional purposes. Members are involved in private
practice of psychoanalysis and analytically-oriented
psychotherapy. Membership: $250/year (Individual).*

Publications:
The Bulletin

American Society of Questioned Document Examiners *(1942)*
P.O. Box 18298
Long Beach, CA 90807
Tel: (562) 901-3376 *Fax:* (562) 901-3378
Website: asqde.org
Members: 132 individuals
Staff: 5
Annual Budget: $50-100,000
Tax: 501(c)(3)

Personnel:
President: Linton A. Mohammed PhD
    E-Mail: lamqde@gmail.com
Editor: Kathleen Annunziata Nicolaides
    E-Mail: kan@afl-qd.com
Editor: Susan E. Morton
    E-Mail: semortonsf@aol.com
Administrator, Website: Farrell C. Shiver
    E-Mail: webeditor@asqde.org

Historical Note:
*ASQDE seeks to foster education, sponsor scientific
research and provide training in the field of questioned
document examination and promote justice in matters that
involve questions about documents. Membership: $200/
year (Individual).*

Meetings/Conferences: Annual
2013 - Indianapolis, IN (Embassy Suites Indianapolis-
    Downtown)/Aug. 24 - 29

Publications:
Journal of the American Society of Questioned
    Document Examiners; semi-annually
Membership Directory; on-line

American Society of Radiologic Technologists
(1920)
15000 Central Ave. SE
Suite A
Albuquerque, NM 87123-3909
Tel: (505) 298-4500 *Fax:* (505) 298-5063
TollFree: (800) 444-2778
E-Mail: customerinfo@asrt.org
Website: asrt.org
Members: 125000 individuals
Staff: 100
Annual Budget: $25-50,000,000
Tax: 501(c)(6)

Personnel:

Chief Executive Officer: Salvatore Martino
Contact, Human Resources: Dwanna Cooper
Director, Event Planning: Peggy Green
Director, Membership Services: Dina Hennessy
Chief Financial Officer: Mark Hoover
Chief Academic Officer: Myke Kudlas
Director, Professional development: Ellen Lipman
    E-Mail: elipman@asrt.org
Vice President, Government Relations And Public Policy:
    Christine Lung
    E-Mail: governmentrelations@asrt.org
Chief Communications and Membership Services Officer:
    Ceela McElveny
Director, Communications: Charles Poling
Director, Marketing and Business Development: Mark
    Ryerson
    E-Mail: mryerson@asrt.org
Director, Information Services: Sam Torrez

Historical Note:
*ASRT's mission is to advance the medical imaging and
radiation therapy profession and to enhance the quality
of patient care. Membership: $105 (Active/Associate/
Radiologist Assistant/International/Limited X-ray Machine
Operators); $30 (Student); $73.50 (Graduate Bridge);
$52.50 (Retired).*

Meetings/Conferences:
Conference Chair: Peggy Green
Number of non-conference events/year: 4

Publications:
ASRT Newsletters; monthly; adv.
ASRT Scanner; bi-monthly; adv.
Radiation Therapist; semi-annually; adv.
Radiologic Technology; bi-monthly; adv.

Membership List Available to Non-members

American Society of Regional Anesthesia and Pain Medicine *(1923)*
120 W. Center Ct.
Schaumburg, IL 60195
Tel: (847) 825-7246 *Fax:* (847) 825-5658
E-Mail: asra@asahq.org
Website: asra.com
Members: 5000 individuals
Staff: 5
Annual Budget: $2-5,000,000

Personnel:
Executive Director: Leonard Mafrica CAE
    E-Mail: lmafrica@kenes.com

Historical Note:
*In 1939, ASRA merged with the ASA. ASRA was reborn in
1975. ASRA's mission is to strive for patient care utilizing
regional anesthesia and pain medicine; and investigates the
scientific basis of the specialty. Membership: $195 (Active);
$95 (Associate); $30 (Resident/Fellow).*

Meetings/Conferences:
2013 - Phoenix, AZ/Nov. 21 - 24
Number of non-conference events/year: 1

Publications:
ASRA News - Newsletter; quarterly
E-News; bi-monthly
Regional Anesthesia and Pain Medicine; bi-monthly

American Society of Retina Specialists *(1982)*
20 N. Wacker Dr.
Suite 2030
Chicago, IL 60606
Tel: (312) 578-8760 *Fax:* (312) 578-8763
E-Mail: members@asrs.org
Website: asrs.org
Members: 2400 individuals
Staff: 7
Annual Budget: $50-100,000
Tax: 501(c)(6)

Personnel:
Executive Vice President: Jill F. Blim
    E-Mail: jill.blim@asrs.org
Manager, Finance and Administration: Mary Anne Difatta
    E-Mail: m.difatta@asrs.org
Director, Education: Stacy Kiff
    E-Mail: stacy.kiff@asrs.org
Director, Membership Relations: Robyn Lira
    E-Mail: Robyn.Lira@asrs.org
Website Manager: Chayal Patel
    E-Mail: chayal.patel@asrs.org
Director, Communications: Susan Raef
    E-Mail: susan.raef@asrs.org

Exhibit Manager: Deb Whalen
    E-Mail: deb.whalen@asrs.org

Historical Note:
*Founded as the Vitreous Society; assumed its current name
in 2002. ASRS's mission is to provide a collegial open
forum for education, to advance the understanding and
treatment of vitreoretinal diseases, and to enhance the
ability of its members to provide quality of patient care.*

Continuing Education:
Certification Designation/s: CME

Meetings/Conferences: Annual
Conference Chair: Deb Whalen

Publications:
Membership Directory; on-line
Retina Times; on-line

American Society of Safety Engineers *(1911)*
1800 E. Oakton St.
Des Plaines, IL 60018-2187
Tel: (847) 699-2929 *Fax:* (847) 768-3434
E-Mail: customerservice@asse.org
Website: asse.org
Members: 34000 individuals
Staff: 60
Annual Budget: $10-25,000,000
Tax: 501(c)(6)

Personnel:
Executive Director: Fred Fortman Jr.
Associate Editor: Tina Angley
    E-Mail: tangley@asse.org
Director, Membership Region and Affairs: Micah D'Orazio
    E-Mail: mdorazio@asse.org
Director, Marketing and Communications: Kelly Fanella
Manager, Education and Program Development: Trudy
    Goldman
Manager, Government Affairs and Policy: Dave Heidorn
    E-Mail: dheidorn@asse.org
Manager, Public Relations: Diane Hurns
Manager, Information Technology: Chris Kator
Manager, Human Resources and Benefits: Sally Madden
Manager, Conferences and Meetings: Stephanie Rennie-
    Sanchez
    E-Mail: sanchez@asse.org
Director, Finance and Controller: Bruce Sufranski

Historical Note:
*Founded in 1911 as the United Association of Casualty
Inspectors and merged with the National Safety Council
in 1924, becoming its Engineering Section and again
became independent in 1947 as the American Society of
Safety Engineers and incorporated in Illinois in 1962.
ASSE members manage, supervise and consult on safety,
health, and environmental issues in industry, insurance,
government and education. Membership is open to
individuals whose employment, education, and experience
are safety- related. Membership: $10-190/year.*

Continuing Education:
Certification Designation/s: CSM, EPSM, CSP, OHST

Meetings/Conferences:
Conference Chair: Stephanie Rennie-Sanchez
2013 - Las Vegas, NV/June 10 - 13
2013 - Las Vegas, NV (Las Vegas Convention Center)/
June 24 - 27
2014 - Orlando, FL/June 8 - 11
Number of non-conference events/year: 8

Publications:
Journal of Safety, Health and Environmental Research;
on-line; adv.
Membership Directory; on-line
Professional Safety; on-line; adv.
Society Update; monthly

American Society of Sanitary Engineering *(1906)*
901 Canterbury Rd.
Suite A
Westlake, OH 44145
Tel: (440) 835-3040 *Fax:* (440) 835-3488
E-Mail: info@asse-plumbing.org
Website: asse-plumbing.org
Members: 2750 individuals
Staff: 8
Annual Budget: $1-2,000,000

Personnel:
President: Donald R. Summers
Contact, Membership Services and Publication Sales:
    Elaine Mathieson
    E-Mail: membership@asse-plumbing.org
Communications Editor: Benjamin Ryan

    E-Mail: ben@asse-plumbing.org
Administrative Manager and Standards Coordinator: Ken
    Van Wagner
    E-Mail: ken@asse-plumbing.org

Historical Note:
*Originated in January 1906 in the District of Columbia
as the American Society of Inspectors of Plumbing and
Sanitary Engineers, became the American Society of
Sanitary Engineering in 1914 and incorporated in the
District of Columbia in 1937. ASSE's mission is to
continually improve the performance, reliability and safety
of plumbing systems. Membership: $85-120 (Individual);
$300 (Sustaining); $60-75 (Government); $25-50
(Student); $42.50 (New Member).*

Meetings/Conferences: Annual
2013 - Anaheim, CA/Nov. 5 - 9
Number of non-conference events/year: 1

Publications:
Plumbing Standards Magazine

American Society of Sephardic Studies *(1963)*
1225 Weaner St.
Wykagyl, NY 10804
Tel: (914) 633-3728 *Fax:* (914) 636-0608
Members: 120 individuals
Staff: 1
Annual Budget: Under $10,000

Personnel:
Director: M. Mitchell Serels PhD

Historical Note:
*ASOSS members are academics with an interest in
Sephardic Jewish history, culture or language.*

American Society of Sugar Beet Technologists *(1935)*
800 Grant St.
Suite 300
Denver, CO 80203
Tel: (303) 832-4460 *Fax:* (303) 832-4468
E-Mail: aa@bsdf-assbt.org
Website: bsdf-assbt.org
Members: 400 individuals
Staff: 4
Annual Budget: $100-250,000

Personnel:
Executive Vice President: Thomas K. Schwartz
    E-Mail: Tom@bsdf-assbt.org
Administrative Assistant: Linda Amerault
    E-Mail: Linda@bsdf-assbt.org
Manager, Business: Rebecca Lucy
    E-Mail: becky@bsdf-assbt.org

Historical Note:
*ASSBT strives to support all phases of sugar beet and
beet sugar research, advocates the dissemination of
resultant scientific knowledge. Membership: $200
(Individual-Biennially); $400 (Company- Biennially); $600
(Sustaining-Biennially); $12 (Retiree-Biennially).*

Meetings/Conferences: Biennial
2013 - Anaheim, CA (Disneyland Resort)/Feb. 27 -
    March 2
2015 - Clearwater, FL (Hilton Hotel)/Feb. 23 - 26

Publications:
Journal of Sugar Beet Research; biennially

American Society of Tax Professionals *(1985)*
P.O. Box 1213
Lynnwood, WA 98046-1213
Tel: (425) 774-1996 *Fax:* (425) 672-0461
TollFree: (877) 674-1996
Members: 150 individuals
Staff: 1
Annual Budget: $50-100,000
Tax: 501(c)(6)

Personnel:
Executive Director: Carol Kraemer
    E-Mail: carol-kraemer@comcast.net

Historical Note:
*Founded as National Association of Income Tax Preparers;
assumed its current name in 1987. ASTP provides
continuing education opportunities to its member tax
preparers. Supports the Accredited Tax Preparer (ATP)
program. Institute of Tax Consultants is the accrediting
board for ASTP.*

Publications:
Tax Professionals Update; irregular; adv.

American Society of Test Engineers *(1981)*

P.O. Box 389
Nutting Lake, MA 01865-0389
E-Mail: aste@earthlink.net
Website: astetest.org
Members: 500 individuals
Staff: 4

Personnel:
*Executive Director and Editor-in-Chief and Acting
    Treasurer:* Michael E. Keller
    E-Mail: mkeller@drc.com
Vice President, Information Systems: Michael Freeman
    E-Mail: mfreeman@broadcom.com
Vice President, Marketing: Bob Stasonis
    E-Mail: bob_stasonis@pickeringtest.com

Historical Note:
*ASTE's mission is to give professionals an opportunity
to meet and work with the leaders of the testing industry.
Members are engineers and companies involved in
test engineering and related fields. Membership: $40
(Individual); $400 (Corporate); $1000 (Individual,
Lifetime); $5000 (Corporate, Lifetime); $15 (Full Time
Student).*

Publications:
ASTE Newsletter; quarterly

American Society of Theatre Consultants (1983)
12226 Mentz Hill Rd.
St. Louis, MO 63128
Tel: (314) 843-9218 *Fax:* (314) 843-4955
Website: theatreconsultants.org
Members: 68 individuals
Staff: 2
Annual Budget: $10-25,000
Tax: 501(c)(6)

Personnel:
President: Michael McMackin
Secretary and Chief Financial Officer: Edgar L. Lustig
    E-Mail: elustig@swbell.net

Historical Note:
*ASTC's mission is to inform owners, users, and planners
about the services that theatre consultants offer and
about the value of those services to the achievement of
economically viable performance and assembly facilities.*

Publications:
Membership Roster; on-line
The ASTC Letter; annually

American Society of Transplant Surgeons (1974)
2461 S. Clark St.
Suite 640
Arlington, VA 22202
Tel: (703) 414-7870 *Fax:* (703) 414-7874
Website: asts.org
Members: 900 individuals
Staff: 7
Annual Budget: $2-5,000,000
Tax: 501(c)(3)

Personnel:
Executive Director: Kim Gifford MBA
    E-Mail: kim.gifford@asts.org
Director, Education: Mina Behari
    E-Mail: mina.behari@asts.org
Director, Communications: Chantay Parks Moye
    E-Mail: chantay.parks@asts.org
Meeting and Graphic Design Coordinator: Jamison
    Visone
    E-Mail: jamison.visone@asts.org
Manager, Finance and Membership Services: Joyce
    Williams
    E-Mail: joyce.williams@asts.org

Historical Note:
*ASTS's mission is to foster and advance the practice and
science of transplantation for the benefit of patients and
society. Members are surgeons, scientists and physicians
specializing in liver, heart, lung, pancreas, and kidney
transplants. Membership: $350/year (Individual); $125
(Surgical Associate).*

Continuing Education:
Certification Designation/s: CME

Meetings/Conferences: Annual
Conference Chair: Chantay Parks Moye
2013 - Miami, FL/Jan. 31 - Feb. 2
2013 - Seattle, WA (Washington State Convention and
    Trade Center)/May 18 - 21

Publications:
American Journal of Transplantation; monthly
ASTS Member Directory; on-line

The Chimera
Membership List Available to Non-members

American Society of Transplantation (1982)
15000 Commerce Pkwy.
Suite C
Mt. Laurel, NJ 08054
Tel: (856) 439-9986 *Fax:* (856) 439-9982
E-Mail: info@a-s-t.org
Website: a-s-t.org
Members: 3,126 members, 12 committees, 4
advisory councils and 10 community of practices
Staff: 14
Annual Budget: $5-10,000,000
Tax: 501(c)(3)

Personnel:
Executive Director: Libby McDannell
    E-Mail: emcdannell@ahint.com
Director, Government Relations: William Applegate
    E-Mail: bill@bryancavestrategies.com
Media and Public Relations: Sean Carney
    E-Mail: scarney@brownsteingroup.com
Administrative Director: Terri Hague
    E-Mail: thague@ahint.com
Accreditation and Grants Program Director: Elizabeth
    Maher
    E-Mail: emaher@ahint.com
Chief Learning Officer: Floyd Pennington PhD
    E-Mail: ctlassoc@mindspring.com
Director, Meetings: Tina Squillante
    E-Mail: tsquillante@ahint.com

Historical Note:
*AST is an international organization of professionals
dedicated to advancing the field of transplantation and
improving patient care by promoting research, education,
advocacy, and organ donation. Membership: $170-420
(Full, Doctoral); $90 (Full, Non-Doctoral/Trainee);
$120-300 (International).*

Meetings/Conferences:
Conference Chair: Tina Squillante
2013 - Seattle, WA/May 18 - 21
Number of non-conference events/year: 1

Publications:
American Journal of Transplantation; monthly; adv.
AST eNewsletter; bi-monthly; adv.
Membership List Available to Non-members

American Society of Transportation and Logistics (1946)
P.O. Box 3363
Warrenton, VA 20188
Tel: (202) 580-7270 *Fax:* (202) 962-3939
E-Mail: info@astl.org
Website: astl.org
Members: 1000 individuals
Staff: 2
Annual Budget: $250-500,000
Tax: 501(c)(6)

Personnel:
Executive Director: Laurie Denham CAE, PLS
    E-Mail: ldenham@astl.org
Editor: Evelyn Thomchick
    E-Mail: ethomchick@psu.edu

Historical Note:
*Organized in Chicago, and incorporated later in the
same year in the state of Indiana (1984) as the American
Society of Traffic and Transportation. A professional
society of individuals involved in or concerned with the
various management functions of transportation, physical
distribution and logistics. ASTL's membership of shippers,
carriers, educators, consultants and third-party logistics
individuals are dedicated to continuing education and
are committed to raising the professional standards in
the industry. Membership: $175 (Certified Member);
$145 (Associate); $100 (Affiliate); $75 (Educator); $30
(Student); $500 (Distinguished Logistics Professional);
$300 (HR/Recruiter Membership).*

Continuing Education:
Certification Designation/s: GLA, PLS, CTL, DLP

Meetings/Conferences: Annual

Publications:
Membership Directory; on-line
Transportation Journal; quarterly

American Society of Travel Agents (1931)
1101 King St.
Suite 200

Alexandria, VA 22314
Tel: (703) 739-2782
E-Mail: askasta@asta.org
Website: asta.org/Chapters/indvchapters.cfm?
    chapter = HAW
Members: 25500 individuals
Staff: 67
Annual Budget: $2-5,000,000

Personnel:
President and Chairman of the Board: Nina Meyer
    E-Mail: nrmmeyer@gmail.com
Senior Vice President, Market Development: Cheryl
    Ahearn CTIE
    E-Mail: cahearn@asta.org
Director, Market Development: Pamela Bonin
Senior Vice President, Legal and Industry Affairs: Paul M.
    Ruden
    E-Mail: pruden@asta.org
Vice President, Communications: Kristina Rundquist
    E-Mail: pr@asta.org

Historical Note:
Association of travel professionals.

Meetings/Conferences:
2013 - Dubai, United Arab Emirates/April 4 - 7
Number of non-conference events/year: 1

Publications:
ASTA Network Magazine; quarterly
Dateline Weekly; weekly; adv.
Member Directory; on-line
Smartbrief eNewsletter; weekly

American Society of Trial Consultants (1982)
1941 Greenspring Dr.
Timonium, MD 21093
Tel: (410) 560-7949 *Fax:* (410) 560-2563
E-Mail: astcoffice@astcweb.org
Website: astcweb.org
Members: 440 individuals
Staff: 2
Annual Budget: $100-250,000
Tax: 501(c)(6)

Personnel:
Executive Director: Ronald J. Matlon PhD
    E-Mail: matlon1005@earthlink.net
Editor, The Jury Expert: Rita R. Handrich PhD
    E-Mail: rhandrich@keenetrial.com

Historical Note:
*Formerly (1986) the Association of Trial Behavior
Consultants, ASTC assumed its present name in January,
1985. Members are trial consultants from a variety of
academic backgrounds who work within court systems
on jury selection, community surveys, continuing legal
education, courtroom visuals, witness preparation, language
and law, legal interviewing and negotiation, post trial juror
interviews, presentation strategy in the courtroom, trial
simulations, voir dire strategy, etc. Membership: $210
(Individual); $75 (Student).*

Meetings/Conferences: Annual
2013 - Las Vegas, NV (The M Resort Spa Casino)/May
    29 - June 1

Publications:
Court Call; quarterly
The Jury Expert; bi-monthly

American Society of Tropical Medicine and Hygiene (1903)
111 Deer Lake Rd.
Suite 100
Northbrook, IL 60015
Tel: (847) 480-9592 *Fax:* (847) 480-9282
E-Mail: info@astmh.org
Website: astmh.org
Members: 3000 individuals
Staff: 6
Annual Budget: $2-5,000,000
Tax: 501(c)(3)

Personnel:
Executive Director: Karen A. Goraleski
    E-Mail: kgoraleski@astmh.org
Senior Accountant: William Chandler
Administrator, Membership Services: Buffy Finn
    E-Mail: bfinn@astmh.org
Manager, Marketing and Communications: Jeff Keller
    E-Mail: jkeller@astmh.org
Director, Meetings: Lyn Maddox
    E-Mail: lmaddox@astmh.org

Managing Editor: Cathi Siegel

Historical Note:
Organized (1951) in Chicago as an amalgamation of the American Society of Tropical Medicine (1903) and the National Malaria Society (1916). Incorporated in Delaware in 1952. ASTMH's mission is to promote global health through the prevention and control of infectious and other diseases that disproportionately afflict the global poor. Membership: $195 (Regular); $25 (Post-Doctoral Student); $15 (Student); $3,900 (Life Member); $500-5000 (Affiliate Membership).

Continuing Education:
Certification Designation/s: CTropMed

Meetings/Conferences: Annual
Conference Chair: Lyn Maddox
2013 - Washington, DC (Washington Marriott Wardman Park)/Nov. 13 - 17
2014 - New Orleans, LA (Sheraton New Orleans Hotel)/Nov. 2 - 6
Number of non-conference events/year: 12

Publications:
ASTMH News
Membership Directory; on-line
The American Journal of Tropical Medicine and Hygiene

American Society of Wedding Professionals
(1992)
C/O Make an Impression
792 Kinderkamack Rd.
River Edge, NJ 07661
Tel: (973) 472-1800 *Fax:* (973) 574-7626
TollFree: (800) 274-3350
E-Mail: info@localtrafficbuilder.com
Website: sellthebride.com
Members: 100 individuals
Staff: 1
Annual Budget: $50-100,000

Personnel:
Executive Officer: Brian D. Lawrence

Historical Note:
SB members are wedding-related businesses. Membership: $149/year minimum (Individual).

American Society of Women Accountants (ACC)
(1938)
1760 Old Meadow Rd.
Suite 500
McLean, VA 22102
Tel: (703) 506-3265 *Fax:* (703) 506-3266
TollFree: (800) 326-2163
E-Mail: aswa@aswa.org
Website: aswa.org
Members: 4000 individuals
Staff: 9
Annual Budget: $500-1,000,000
Tax: 501(c)(6)

Personnel:
Executive Director: Lee K. Lowery
  E-Mail: llowery@aswa.org
Executive Administrator: Michelle DelaRosa
  E-Mail: mdelarosa@aswa.org
Database Specialist: Susan Martin
  E-Mail: smartin@aswa.org
Events Director: Elisa Perodin CEM, CMP
  E-Mail: eperodin@aswa.org

Historical Note:
ASWA seeks to enable women in all fields of accounting and related fields to achieve their full personal, professional, and economic potential as well as contributing to the future development of the profession. Members include partners in national, regional and local CPA firms, financial officers, controllers, academicians, financial analysts and data processing consultants, recent college graduates and women returning to the work force. Membership: $202 (Regular/ Affiliate); $57 (Student/Associate); $30-100 (Corporate).

Meetings/Conferences: Annual
Conference Chair: Elisa Perodin CEM, CMP

Publications:
Accountability; monthly; adv.
ASWA News Brief; weekly; adv.
Membership Directory; on-line

American Society on Aging *(1954)*
71 Stevenson St.
Suite 1450
San Francisco, CA 94105-2938
Tel: (415) 974-9600 *Fax:* (415) 974-0300

TollFree: (800) 537-9728
E-Mail: info@asaging.org
Website: asaging.org
Members: 5000 Individuals
Staff: 16
Annual Budget: $2-5,000,000
Tax: 501(c)(3)

Personnel:
President and Chief Executive Officer: Robert G. Stein CAE, MBA
  E-Mail: bstein@asaging.org
Vice President, Education: Carole Anderson
  E-Mail: canderson@asaging.org
Senior Director, Diversity and Member Inclusion: Anne Ornelas de Lemos
  E-Mail: adelemos@asaging.org
Director, Marketing and Educational Events: Linda Jones
  E-Mail: ljones@asaging.org
Manager, Conferences: Anna Kuvshinova
  E-Mail: annak@asaging.org
Senior Director, Operations and Information Technology: Robert R. Lowe
  E-Mail: rlowe@asaging.org
Senior Manager, Accounting: Vicky Nguyen
  E-Mail: vnguyen@asaging.org
Manager, Human Resources and Administration: Alesia Sheviakhova
  E-Mail: alesias@asaging.org

Historical Note:
Formerly (1954) Western Gerontological Society. ASA's mission is to support the commitment and enhance the knowledge and skills of those who seek to improve the quality of life of older adults and their families. Membership: $205 (Professional); $110 (Retired); $75 (Student); $525 (Organization); $175 (Organizational Affiliate).

Meetings/Conferences:
Conference Chair: Anna Kuvshinova
2013 - Chicago, IL (Hyatt Regency)/March 12 - 16
2014 - San Diego, CA (Manchester Grand Hyatt San Diego)/March 11 - 15
2015 - Chicago, IL (Hyatt Regency)/March 23 - 27
2016 - Washington, DC (Washington Marriott Wardman Park)/March 20 - 24
2017 - Chicago, IL (Hyatt Regency)/March 20 - 24

Publications:
Aging Today; bi-monthly; adv.
Aging Today Online; monthly
Generations; quarterly; adv.
Membership Directory; on-line

Membership List Available to Non-members

American Sociological Association *(1905)*
1430 K St. NW
Suite 600
Washington, DC 20005
Tel: (202) 383-9005 *Fax:* (202) 638-0882
Website: asanet.org
Members: 14000 individuals
Staff: 32
Annual Budget: $5-10,000,000
Tax: 501(c)(3)

Personnel:
Executive Officer: Sally T. Hillsman
  E-Mail: hillsman@asanet.org
Deputy Executive Officer, Administration and Technology: Janet L. Astner
  E-Mail: astner@asanet.org
Director, Finance: Les Briggs
  E-Mail: business@asanet.org
Director, Membership, Subscriptions, Publications and Customer Service: Karen Gray Edwards
  E-Mail: edwards@asanet.org
Director, Meetings Services Department: Kareem D. Jenkins
  E-Mail: meetings@asanet.org
Director, Public Affairs and Public Information Program: Bradley T. Smith
  E-Mail: public.affairs@asanet.org
Director, Research and Development Department: Roberta Spalter-Roth
  E-Mail: research@asanet.org

Historical Note:
ASA is dedicated to advance sociology as a scientific discipline and profession serving the public good. Membership: $20-196 (Regular); $47 (Associate/ International Associate/Emeritus); $20 (Student).

Meetings/Conferences: Annual
Conference Chair: Kareem D. Jenkins
2013 - New York City, NY (Hilton New York)/Aug. 10 - 13

Publications:
American Sociological Review; bi-monthly; adv.
ASA Footnotes; monthly; adv.
Contemporary Sociology; bi-monthly; adv.
Contexts; quarterly; adv.
Journal of Health and Social Behavior; quarterly; adv.
Social Psychology Quarterly; quarterly; adv.
Sociological Methodology; annually; adv.
Sociological Theory; quarterly; adv.
Sociology of Education; quarterly; adv.
Teaching Sociology; quarterly; adv.

Membership List Available to Non-members

American Solar Energy Society *(1954)*
4760 Walnut St.
Suite 106
Boulder, CO 80301
Tel: (303) 443-3130 *Fax:* (303) 443-3212
E-Mail: ases@ases.org
Website: ases.org
Members: 13,000 members
Staff: 18
Annual Budget: $2-5,000,000
Tax: 501(c)(3)

Personnel:
President: Susan Greene
Manager, Membership Services: Carolyn Beach
  E-Mail: cbeach@ases.org
Director, Sales: Annette Delagrange
Editor and Director, Communications: Seth Masia
  E-Mail: smasia@ases.org
Contact, Public Policy: Shaun McGrath
National Solar Conference Assistant: Joel Moore

Historical Note:
A U.S. Section of the International Solar Energy Society. ASES's mission is to inspire an era of energy innovation and speed the transition to a sustainable energy economy. Membership: $19-1200/year.

Meetings/Conferences: Annual
Conference Chair: Joel Moore
2013 - Baltimore, MD/April 15 - 20
2013 - Baltimore, MD/April 16 - 20

Publications:
Solar Today Magazine; adv.
Solar@Work; bi-weekly; adv.

American Southdown Breeders Association
(1882)
100 Cornerstone Rd.
Fredonia, TX 76842
Tel: (325) 429-6226 *Fax:* (325) 429-6225
E-Mail: southdown@ctesc.net
Website: southdownsheep.org
Members: 1000 individuals
Staff: 1
Annual Budget: $100-250,000
Tax: 501(c)(5)

Personnel:
President: L.C. Scramlin
  E-Mail: info@oakfair.org

Historical Note:
ASBA's purpose is to maintain registry and pedigree records. Members are breeders and fanciers of Southdown sheep. Membership: $20 (Adult/Family/Farm); $10 (Junior).

Meetings/Conferences: Annual
Number of non-conference events/year: 8

Publications:
Southdown Membership Directory; annually
The American Southdown Journal; quarterly; adv.

Membership List Available to Non-members

American Soybean Association *(1920)*
12125 Woodcrest Executive Dr.
Suite 100
St. Louis, MO 63141-5009
Tel: (314) 576-1770 *Fax:* (314) 576-2786
TollFree: (800) 688-7692
Website: soygrowers.com
Members: 27500 individuals
Staff: 26
Annual Budget: $10-25,000,000

Tax: 501(c)(5)

Personnel:
Executive Director, Membership Services and Industry Relations: Bill Schuermann
  E-Mail: bschuermann@soy.org
Chief Executive Officer: Steve Censky
  E-Mail: scensky@soy.org
Director, Communications: Patrick Delaney
  E-Mail: pdelaney@soy.org
Executive Assistant and Meeting Planner: Julie Hawkins
  E-Mail: julieh@soy.org
Director, Finance and Administration: Brian Vaught
  E-Mail: bvaught@soy.org
Director, Marketing and Planning: Jill Wagenblast
  E-Mail: jwagenblast@soy.org

Historical Note:
The American Soybean Association (ASA) is recognized for domestic and International policy advocate. ASA represents U.S. soybean farmers through policy advocacy and international market development. ASA's mission is to serve farmers by protecting and increasing the market value and opportunities for soybean farmers.

Meetings/Conferences: Annual
Conference Chair: Julie Hawkins
2013 - Orlando, FL/Feb. 28 - March 2
2014 - San Antonio, TX/Feb. 27 - March 1

Publications:
ASA Today Newsletter
ASA Weekly Leader Letter; weekly
The Progressive Farmer Magazine

American Specialty Toy Retailing Association
(1992)
432 N. Clark St.
Suite 401
Chicago, IL 60654
Tel: (312) 222-0984 *Fax:* (312) 222-0986
E-Mail: info@astratoy.org
Website: astratoy.org
Members: 1300 individuals and companies
Staff: 4
Annual Budget: $500-1,000,000

Personnel:
President: Kathleen McHugh CAE
Coordinator, Membership Services and Technology: Daniel Elacqua
Coordinator, Membership Services and Events: Caryn Giznik
Manager, Meetings and Exhibits: Amanda Zawad

Historical Note:
ASTRA's mission is to lead the way through play by providing quality products that help children have fun, achieve success and lead happy, healthy lives. Membership: $229-5,299 (Retailers, based on gross sales); $329-3,250 (Affiliate, based on gross sales); $329-7,999 (Manufacturer Member, based on gross sales); $75-350 (Manufacturers/Representative).

Meetings/Conferences: Annual
Conference Chair: Amanda Zawad
2013 - Nashville, TN/June 16 - 19

Publications:
ASTRA Newsletter; adv.
Membership Directory; on-line

Membership List Available to Non-members

American Speech-Language-Hearing Association
(1925)
2200 Research Blvd.
Rockville, MD 20850-3289
Tel: (301) 897-5700 *Fax:* (301) 296-8580
TollFree: (800) 498-2071
E-Mail: actioncenter@asha.org
Website: asha.org
Members: 150,000 members and affiliates
Staff: 250
Annual Budget: Over $100,000,000
Tax: 501(c)(6)

Personnel:
Executive Director: Arlene A. Pietranton PhD, CAE
  E-Mail: apietranton@asha.org
Contact, Corporate Partnership and Sponsorship: Barbara Lecker
  E-Mail: blecker@asha.org
Contact, Advertising: Pam Leppin
  E-Mail: pleppin@asha.org
Manager, Public Relations: Kimberly O'Sullivan
  E-Mail: kosullivan@asha.org

Chief Staff Officer, Communications: Martin J. Rome
  E-Mail: mrome@asha.org

Historical Note:
Formerly, American Academy of Speech Correction, American Academy of Speech Correction (1925), American Society for the Study of Disorders of Speech (1927), American Speech Correction Association (1934), American Speech and Hearing Association (1947) and assumed its current name in 1979. ASHA's mission is to empower and support speech-language pathologists, audiologists, speech, language, and hearing scientists by promoting effective human communication. Membership: $114 (Individual/ Research/Allied Professional); $170 (International Affiliate).

Continuing Education:
Certification Designation/s: CCC-A, CCC-SLP, CFCC

Meetings/Conferences: Annual
2013 - Chicago, IL/Nov. 14 - 16
2014 - Orlando, FL/Nov. 20 - 22

Publications:
Access Academics & Research; bi-monthly
Access Audiology; bi-monthly
Access Schools; bi-monthly
Access SLP Health Care; bi-monthly
ASHA Headlines; on-line
ASHA Leader; adv.
ASHA Leader Live; on-line
Membership Directory; on-line

Membership List Available to Non-members

American Spice Trade Association *(1907)*
1620 I St. NW
Suite 925
Washington, DC 20006
Tel: (202) 331-2461 *Fax:* (202) 463-8998
E-Mail: info@astaspice.org
Website: astaspice.org
Members: 175 members
Staff: 6
Annual Budget: $1-2,000,000

Personnel:
Executive Director: Cheryl A. Deem
Director, Government Relations: Julia Bellinger
  E-Mail: Jbellinger@astaspice.org
Association Associate: Meegan Kavanaugh
Meetings Coordinator: Whitney Thompson

Historical Note:
ASTA works to ensure clean, safe spice and address public policy on behalf of the global industry. Membership: $65 (Importers, Traders, Processors, Growers or Distributors); $4,000 (Brokers/Agents); $1,800 (Associate).

Meetings/Conferences: Annual
Conference Chair: Whitney Thompson
2013 - Manalapan, FL (Ritz-Carlton, Palm Beach Manalapan)/April 28 - May 1

Publications:
ASTA Advocate; monthly; adv.
FYI ASTA; monthly; adv.

American Spinal Injury Association *(1973)*
2020 Peachtree Rd. NW
Atlanta, GA 30309-1402
Tel: (404) 355-9772 *Fax:* (404) 355-1826
E-Mail: asia_office@shepherd.org
Website: asia-spinalinjury.org
Members: 500 physicians
Staff: 4
Annual Budget: $500-1,000,000
Tax: 501(c)(3)

Personnel:
Executive Director: Lesley M. Hudson
Coordinator, Administration: Patricia Duncan
  E-Mail: Pat_Duncan@shepherd.org
Manager, Projects: Marianne Kaplan

Historical Note:
ASIA strives to promote and establish standards for all aspects of health care of individuals with spinal cord injury from onset throughout life. Members are doctors of medicine and other allied health professionals. Membership: $200-375/year (Individual).

Continuing Education:
Enrollment: 500

Meetings/Conferences: Annual
2013 - Chicago, IL (Swissotel Chicago)/May 6 - 8

Publications:
E-Learning Center

Guidelines for Use of Durable Medical Equipment for Persons with Spinal Cord Injury and Dysfunction; annually
International Standards for Neurological Classification; annually

Membership List Available to Non-members

American Sportfishing Association *(1962)*
1001 N. Fairfax St.
Suite 501
Alexandria, VA 22314
Tel: (703) 519-9691 *Fax:* (703) 519-1872
E-Mail: info@asafishing.org
Website: asafishing.org
Members: 140 Sport Fishing Industry
Staff: 15
Annual Budget: $5-10,000,000
Tax: 501(c)(6)

Personnel:
President and Chief Executive Officer: J. Michael Nussman
  E-Mail: mnussman@asafishing.org
Director, Membership Services: Jill Calabria
  E-Mail: jcalabria@asafishing.org
Chief Financial Officer: Diane Carpenter
  E-Mail: dcarpenter@asafishing.org
Coordinator, Trade Show and Meetings: Teresa Denchfield
  E-Mail: tdenchfield@asafishing.org
Director, Communications: Mary Jane Williamson
  E-Mail: mwilliamson@asafishing.org

Historical Note:
The American Sportfishing Association is the sportfishing industry's trade association, uniting more than 650 members of the sportsfishing and boating industries with state fish and wildlife agencies, federal land and water management agencies, conservation organizations, angler advocacy group and outdoor journalists. ASA safeguards the enduring social, economic, and conservation values of sportfishing.

Meetings/Conferences: Annual
Conference Chair: Teresa Denchfield

Publications:
ASA Insider; monthly
ASA News; monthly

American Sports Builders Association *(1965)*
8480 Baltimore National Pike
Suite 307
Ellicott City, MD 21043
Tel: (410) 730-9595 *Fax:* (410) 730-8833
TollFree: (866) 501-2722
E-Mail: info@sportsbuilders.org
Website: sportsbuilders.org
Members: 360 companies
Staff: 4
Annual Budget: $500-1,000,000
Tax: 501(c)(6)

Personnel:
Executive Director: Fred Stringfellow CAE
  E-Mail: fred@stringfellowgroup.net
Financial Manager: Amy Chetelat, CAE
  E-Mail: amy@stringfellowgroup.net
Director, Meetings and Membership Services: Cynthia Jordan
  E-Mail: cjordan@sportsbuilders.org
Legal Counsel: David H. Pettit Esq.
  E-Mail: dhp@fpwlaw.com

Historical Note:
ASBA strives to represent builders, designers, and suppliers of materials for tennis courts, running tracks, synthetic and natural turf fields, and indoor and outdoor sport surfaces. Membership: $840 (Builder); $500 (Professional Member); $1,120 (Supplier); $450 (Provisional/Ancillary Member).

Continuing Education:
Certification Designation/s: CTB, CFB, CTCB

Meetings/Conferences: Semi-Annual
Conference Chair: Cynthia Jordan
2013 - Rio Grande, PR (Rio Mar Beach Resort and Spa)/Feb. 22 - 25
2013 - San Antonio, TX (Grand Hyatt San Antonio)/ Dec. 6 - 10
2014 - Ponte Vedra Beach, FL (Sawgrass Marriott Golf Resort and Spa)/Dec. 6 - 10
2015 - Scottsdale, AZ (Fairmont Scottsdale Princess)/ Dec. 4 - 8

Publications:

Newsline - Newsletter; quarterly
Organization Directory; on-line
Membership List Available to Non-members

American Sports Medicine Association (1978)
660 W. Duarte Rd.
Arcadia, CA 91007
Tel: (626) 445-1978
E-Mail: americansportsmedicine@hotmail.com
Members: 3550 individuals
Staff: 2
Annual Budget: Under $10,000

Personnel:
Chairman: Joe S. Borland
    E-Mail: americansportsmedicine@hotmail.com

Historical Note:
Members are sports medicine trainers, skilled in the prevention and care of injuries as well as physical therapy under a physician's direction. Members must maintain their professional license annually. Provides continuing education and awards the designation CSMT (Certified Sports Medicine Trainer). Membership: $40/year.

American Sportscasters Association (1979)
225 Broadway
Suite 2030
New York, NY 10007
Tel: (212) 227-8080 *Fax:* (212) 571-0556
E-Mail: info@americansportscastersonline.com
Website: americansportscastersonline.com
Members: 550 individuals
Staff: 3
Annual Budget: $50-100,000

Personnel:
President and Founder: Louis O. Schwartz
    E-Mail: LSchwa8918@aol.com
Associate Editor: Patrick Turturro

Historical Note:
ASA is a non-profit association to represent sportscasters by promoting, supporting and enhancing the needs and interests of the professional sports broadcaster. Members are radio and TV sportscasters. Membership: $50 (Individual); $35 (Student); $500 (Lifetime).

Publications:
ASA News; on-line
Insiders Sportsletter; quarterly
Newsletter

American Staffing Association (1966)
277 S. Washington St.
Suite 200
Alexandria, VA 22314
Tel: (703) 253-2020 *Fax:* (703) 253-2053
TollFree: (800) 315-3736
E-Mail: asa@americanstaffing.net
Website: americanstaffing.net
Members: 1600 companies
Staff: 29
Annual Budget: $5-10,000,000
Tax: 501(c)(6)

Personnel:
President and Chief Executive Officer: Richard A. Wahlquist
    E-Mail: rwahlquist@americanstaffing.net
Director, Membership Services: Simone Bielsker
    E-Mail: sbielsker@americanstaffing.net
General Counsel: Stephen C. Dwyer Esq.
    E-Mail: sdwyer@americanstaffing.net
Director, Publications: Marlene L. Hendrickson
    E-Mail: mhendrickson@americanstaffing.net
Coordinator, Marketing: Joshua Lamangan
    E-Mail: jlamangan@americanstaffing.net
Senior Manager, Education and Certification: Emily Lawson
    E-Mail: elawson@americanstaffing.net
Senior Vice President, Legal and Public Affairs: Edward A. Lenz Esq.
    E-Mail: elenz@americanstaffing.net
Director, Government Affairs: Elizabeth Meade
    E-Mail: emeade@staffingtoday.net
Assistant Vice President, Finance and Administration: Lyn Rawdon CPA
    E-Mail: lrawdon@americanstaffing.net
Director, Information Systems: Ray Richards
    E-Mail: rrichards@americanstaffing.net
Director, Meetings and Events: Lisa Simpson
    E-Mail: lsimpson@americanstaffing.net
Assistant Vice President, Membership Services and Sections: Kelly G. Verberg
    E-Mail: kverberg@americanstaffing.net

Historical Note:
ASA's mission is to advance the interests of staffing and recruiting firms of all sizes and across all sectors through legal and legislative advocacy, public relations, education and the promotion of high standards of legal, ethical, and professional practices. Membership: $520 (Active, based on annual gross revenues); $575 (Associate); $550 (International).

Continuing Education:
Certification Designation/s: WRC, TSC, CSP
Meetings/Conferences: Annual
Conference Chair: Lisa Simpson
2013 - Washington, DC/Oct. 8 - 11

Publications:
Sections Spotlight Newsletter; quarterly
Staffing Law Digest
Staffing Success Magazine; bi-monthly
Staffing Week Newsletter; weekly

Membership List Available to Non-members

American Stamp Dealers Association (1914)
217-14 Northern Blvd.
Suite 205
Bayside, NY 11361-3500
Tel: (718) 224-2500 *Fax:* (718) 224-2501
E-Mail: asda@asdaonline.com
Website: americanstampdealer.com
Members: 1000 individuals
Staff: 4
Annual Budget: $1-2,000,000

Personnel:
President: James Lee
Executive Vice President: Joseph B. Savarese
Secretary: Kim Kellermann
Editor: Randy L. Neil
    E-Mail: neilmedia1@sbcglobal.net

Historical Note:
ASDA is dedicated to promote integrity, honesty and reliability and are the hobby builders of philately. Membership: $300 (Regular); $240 (Provision).

Meetings/Conferences: Semi-Annual
2013 - Boynton Beach, FL (The Marriot Courtyard Hotel)/Feb. 8 - 10
2013 - New York City, NY (New Yorker Hotel)/April 11 - 14
2013 - New York City, NY (National Arts Club)/Oct. 10 - 13

Publications:
American Stamp Dealer & Collector Magazine; adv.
Membership Directory; annually

American Statistical Association (1839)
732 N. Washington St.
Alexandria, VA 22314-1943
Tel: (703) 684-1221 *Fax:* (703) 684-2037
TollFree: (888) 231-3473
E-Mail: asainfo@amstat.org
Website: amstat.org
Members: 18000 individuals
Staff: 36
Annual Budget: $5-10,000,000
Tax: 501(c)(3)

Personnel:
Executive Director: Ronald L. Wasserstein
    E-Mail: ron@amstat.org
Coordinator, Human Resources: Lynn Aikens
    E-Mail: lynn@amstat.org
Manager, Advertising: Claudine Donovan
    E-Mail: claudine@amstat.org
Director, Membership Development and Marketing: Amy Farris
    E-Mail: amy@amstat.org
Director, Information Technologies: Tim Gill
    E-Mail: tim@amstat.org
Manager, Communications: Megan Murphy
    E-Mail: megan@amstat.org
Director, Education: Rebecca Nichols
    E-Mail: rebecca@amstat.org
Associate Executive Director and Director, Operations: Stephen Porzio
    E-Mail: steve@amstat.org
Manager, Journals and Publications: Eric Sampson
    E-Mail: eric@amstat.org
Accounting Manager: Adriano Sarmiento
    E-Mail: adriano@amstat.org
Director, Meetings: Kathleen Wert
    E-Mail: kathleen@amstat.org

Historical Note:
ASA's mission is to promote excellence in the application of statistical science across the wealth of human endeavor. Members serve in industry, government, and academia, advancing research and promoting sound statistical practice to inform public policy and improve human welfare. Membership: $15-2200/year.

Meetings/Conferences: Annual
Conference Chair: Kathleen Wert
2013 - Montreal, QC (Palais Des Congres de Montreal)/Aug. 3 - 8/5000 attendees
2014 - Boston, MA (Boston Convention and Exhibition Center)/Aug. 2 - 7/5000 attendees
2015 - Seatle, WA (Washington State Convention Center)/Aug. 8 - 13
Number of non-conference events/year: 3

Publications:
American Statistician; quarterly; adv.
AMSTAT News; monthly; adv.
Chance Magazine; quarterly; adv.
Journal of Agricultural, Biological and Environmental Statistics; quarterly
Journal of Business and Economic Statistics; quarterly; adv.
Journal of Computational & Graphical Statistics; quarterly; adv.
Journal of Educational and Behavioral Statistics
Journal of Nonparametric Statistics
Journal of Quantitative Analysis in Sports; on-line
Journal of Statistical Software; on-line
Journal of Statistics Education; on-line
Journal of the American Statistical Association; quarterly; adv.
LINK Newsletter; quarterly
Membership Directory; on-line
Significance; quarterly; adv.
Statistical Analysis and Data Mining; on-line
Statistics in Biopharmaceutical Research; on-line
Statistics Surveys; on-line
Technometrics; quarterly

Membership List Available to Non-members

American String Teachers Association (1946)
4155 Chain Bridge Rd.
Fairfax, VA 22030-4102
Tel: (703) 279-2113 *Fax:* (703) 279-2114
E-Mail: asta@astaweb.com
Website: astaweb.com
Members: 11500 individuals, schools, universities and corporate members
Staff: 17
Annual Budget: $1-2,000,000
Tax: 501(c)(3)

Personnel:
Executive Director: Donna Sizemore Hale
    E-Mail: donna@astaweb.com
Coordinator, Membership Services: Amanda Bernhardt
    E-Mail: membership@astaweb.com
Deputy Director: Beth Danner-Knight
    E-Mail: beth@astaweb.com
Deputy Director, Communications: Mary Jane Dye
    E-Mail: maryjane@astaweb.com
Manager, Graphic Design: Sky Henderson
    E-Mail: sky@astaweb.com
Deputy Director, Finance and Administration: Jody McNamara
    E-Mail: jody@astaweb.com
Manager, Membership Services and Marketing and Chapter Liaison: Tami O'Brien
    E-Mail: tami@astaweb.com
Director, Conferences: Deanna Tompkins
    E-Mail: deanna@astaweb.com

Historical Note:
Incorporated in Iowa, absorbed National School Orchestra Association in 1998. ASTA's mission is to promote excellence in string and orchestra teaching and playing. Membership includes string and orchestra teachers and players. Membership is open to teachers and performers of all stringed instruments as well as students, universities, companies and suppliers of string industry products. Membership: $107 (Professional); $77 (Senior); $147 (Dual); $52 (Student).

Meetings/Conferences: Annual
Conference Chair: Deanna Tompkins

2013 - Providence, RI/Feb. 27 - March 2/11-25 exhibitors
2014 - Louisville, KY/March 5 - 8
Number of non-conference events/year: 8

Publications:
American String Teacher (AST); quarterly
String Research Journal (SRJ); biennially

Membership List Available to Non-members

American Student Dental Association *(1971)*
211 E. Chicago Ave.
Suite 700
Chicago, IL 60611-2687
Tel: (312) 440-2795 *Fax:* (312) 440-2820
TollFree: (800) 621-8099
E-Mail: asda@asdanet.org
Website: asdanet.org
Members: 18000 individuals
Staff: 11
Annual Budget: $2-5,000,000
Tax: 501(c)(6)

Personnel:
Executive Director: Nancy R. Honeycutt CAE
    E-Mail: Nancy@ASDAnet.org
Director, Membership Services: Danielle Bauer
    E-Mail: Danielle@ASDAnet.org
Manager, Meetings: Linda Cooper
    E-Mail: Linda@ASDAnet.org
Manager, Communications: Cheryl Graf
    E-Mail: Cheryl@ASDAnet.org
Administrator, Membership: Erin Kato
    E-Mail: Erin@ASDAnet.org
Manager, Accounting: Ruth Kerns
    E-Mail: Ruth@ASDAnet.org
Manager, Sales and Marketing: Barton Lewin
    E-Mail: Barton@ASDAnet.org
Office Manager: Angie Wines
    E-Mail: Angie@ASDAnet.org

Historical Note:
The American Student Dental Association seeks to involve its members in the inter professional activities of the dental profession, protects and advances the rights, interests, and welfare of students pursuing careers in dentistry. ASDA's mission is to protect and advance the rights, interests and welfare of dental students. Membership: $58 (Student-Predental/Associate); $75 (Predoctoral); $88 (International Dental Student).

Meetings/Conferences: Annual
Conference Chair: Linda Cooper
2013 - Atlanta, GA/March 6 - 10
2013 - Atlanta, GA (Westin Peachtree Plaza, Atlanta)/
    March 6 - 9/400 attendees/51-100 exhibitors
2013 - Chicago, IL (Holiday Inn Chicago Mart Plaza)/
    Nov. 15 - 17/51-100 exhibitors

Publications:
ASDA Leader; monthly
Mouth, Journal of the American Student Dental
    Association; quarterly
The Legislative Ledger; monthly
Word of Mouth; monthly

American Studies Association *(1951)*
1120 19th St. NW
Suite 301
Washington, DC 20036
Tel: (202) 467-4783 *Fax:* (202) 467-4786
E-Mail: asastaff@theasa.net
Website: theasa.net
Members: 5000 individuals and 2000 libraries
Staff: 5
Annual Budget: $1-2,000,000
Tax: 501(c)(3)

Personnel:
Executive Director: John F. Stephens PhD
    E-Mail: asastaff@theasa.net
Research Coordinator: Lawrence McMahon
    E-Mail: asastaff@theasa.net
Coordinator, Publications: Nathan Packard
Coordinator, Conventions: Gabriel Peoples
    E-Mail: annualmeeting@theasa.net

Historical Note:
Incorporated in 1951 to advance the study of American culture and civilization as an entity rather than from the viewpoint of a single discipline. ASA is devoted to the interdisciplinary study of American culture and history. Admitted to membership in the American Council of Learned Societies in 1958. Membership: $55-99 (Individual, vary

according to income); $20 (Student/Emeritus/Income under $12,000); $1,500 (Life Member).

Meetings/Conferences: Annual
Conference Chair: Gabriel Peoples
2013 - Washington, DC (Hilton Washington)/Nov. 21 -
    24
2014 - Los Angeles, CA (Westin Bonaventure Hotel and
    Suites, Los Angeles)/Nov. 6 - 9
2015 - Toronto, ON (Sheraton Centre Toronto Hotel)/
    Oct. 8 - 11

Publications:
American Quarterly
ASA Newsletter; adv.
Membership Directory

Membership List Available to Non-members

American Subcontractors Association *(1966)*
1004 Duke St.
Alexandria, VA 22314-3588
Tel: (703) 684-3450 *Fax:* (703) 836-3482
E-Mail: asaoffice@asa-hq.com
Website: asaonline.com
Members: 5500 companies
Staff: 9
Annual Budget: $100-250,000
Tax: 501(c)(6)

Personnel:
Executive Vice President: E. Colette Nelson
    E-Mail: cnelson@asa-hq.com
Manager, Education and Meetings: Veronica Allen
    E-Mail: vallen@asa-hq.com
Liaison, Sponsorship, Advertising and Sales: Richard
    Bright
    E-Mail: richard.bright@comcast.net
Director, Government Relations: Franklin Davis
    E-Mail: GovernmentRelations@asa-hq.com
Manager, Administration: April Hubbard
    E-Mail: ahubbard@asa-hq.com
Senior Director, Communications and Education: David
    Mendes
    E-Mail: dmendes@asa-hq.com

Historical Note:
ASA's mission is to improve the business environment for the construction industry and to serve as a steward for the community. Members: $425/year.

Meetings/Conferences:
Conference Chair: Veronica Allen
2013 - Las Vegas, NV (Planet Hollywood Resort and
    Casino)/March 21 - 23

Publications:
Membership Directory; on-line

American Suffolk Horse Association
4240 Goehring Rd.
Ledbetter, TX 78946-5004
Tel: (979) 249-5795
E-Mail: suffolks@cvtv.net
Website: suffolkpunch.com
Members: 200 individuals
Staff: 2
Annual Budget: Under $10,000
Tax: 501(c)(5)

Personnel:
Secretary: Mary Margaret Read
    E-Mail: suffolks@cvtv.net

Historical Note:
Members are owners and breeders of Suffolk horses. Membership: $45 (Individual, Initial); $40 (Individual, Renewal).

Meetings/Conferences: Annual

Publications:
ASHA Newsletter
Membership Directory; annually

American Sugar Alliance *(1983)*
2111 Wilson Blvd.
Suite 600
Arlington, VA 22201
Tel: (703) 351-5055 *Fax:* (703) 351-6698
E-Mail: info@sugaralliance.org
Website: sugaralliance.org
Members: 500 individuals
Staff: 5
Annual Budget: $1-2,000,000
Tax: 501(c)(6)

Personnel:

Executive Director: Vickie Rideout Myers
    E-Mail: vickie@sugaralliance.org
Director, Media Relations: Phillip W. Hayes
    E-Mail: phillip@sugaralliance.org
Staff Associate: Prescott Martin
    E-Mail: prescott@sugaralliance.org
Director, Economics and Policy Analysis: John C. "Jack"
    Roney
    E-Mail: jack@sugaralliance.org

Historical Note:
A national coalition supporting America's cane and beet farmers and dedicated to preserve a strong domestic sugar industry. Membership in the American Sugar Alliance ranges from the sweetener producers - including farmers all across the country, sugar processors and refiners to the implement dealers, local banks, community businesses of all types, fertilizer distributors, factory workers producing heavy equipment needed in sugar production, and others in services and supply. Works to assure that farmers and workers in the U.S. sugar industry survive in a world of heavily subsidized sugar. Membership: $2,500 (National Companies); $500 (Regional Companies); $150 (Local Companies/Sole Proprietors).

Meetings/Conferences: Annual
2013 - Napa, CA (Silverado Resort and Spa)/Aug. 2 -
    7
2014 - Stowe, VT (Stowe Mountain Lodge)/Aug. 1 - 6
2015 - Santa Ana Pueblo, NM (Hyatt Regency Tamaya
    Resort and Spa)/July 31 - Aug. 5

Publications:
Membership Directory; on-line

American Sugarbeet Growers Association *(1975)*
1156 15th St. NW
Suite 1101
Washington, DC 20005
Tel: (202) 833-2398 *Fax:* (240) 235-4291
E-Mail: info@americansugarbeet.org
Website: americansugarbeet.org
Members: 23 regional associations
Staff: 4
Annual Budget: $1-2,000,000
Tax: 501(c)(5)

Personnel:
Executive Vice President: Luther A Markwart
    E-Mail: lmarkwart@americansugarbeet.org
Director, Administration: Pamela Alther
    E-Mail: palther@americansugarbeet.org
Manager, Events and Communications: Brianne Blevins
    E-Mail: bblevins@americansugarbeet.org

Historical Note:
ASGA is a federation of state and regional associations of sugarbeet growers. Formerly (1975) National Sugarbeet Growers Association. ASGA's mission is to promote common interest of state and regional beet grower associations, which include legislative and international representation and public relations.

Meetings/Conferences: Annual
Conference Chair: Brianne Blevins
2013 - San Diego, CA (Hilton San Diego Bayfront)/Feb.
    3 - 5/350 attendees
2013 - Tampa, FL (Tampa Marriott Waterside Hotel
    and Marina)/Feb. 9 - 11
2015 - Long Beach, CA (Westin Long Beach)/Feb. 1 - 3

Publications:
Membership Directory; on-line

Membership List Available to Non-members

American Supply Association *(1894)*
1200 N. Arlington Heights Rd.
Suite 150
Itasca, IL 60143
Tel: (630) 467-0000 *Fax:* (630) 467-0001
E-Mail: info@asa.net
Website: asa.net
Members: 600 companies
Staff: 11
Annual Budget: $1-2,000,000
Tax: 501(c)(6)

Personnel:
Executive Director: Christopher Murin
    E-Mail: cmurin@asa.net
Executive Vice President: Michael Adelizzi
    E-Mail: madelizzi@asa.net
Director, Finance: Margaret Bean
    E-Mail: mbean@asa.net
Director, Meetings and Conventions: Ruth Mitchell
    E-Mail: ruth@asa.net

Director, Marketing and Communications: Benjamin Stephens
E-Mail: bstephens@asa.net

Historical Note:
Officially formed in December 1969 through the merger of two groups:The Central Supply Association (CSA) and the American Institute of Supply Associations (AI). ASA's mission is to drive the effective and consistent implementation of quality programs and services which improve the operational efficiency and marketing effectiveness of the wholesale distribution channel, resulting in market share growth and return-on-investment improvement for its members. Members are distributors, manufacturers, master distributors, independent manufacturers' representatives and service vendors who together create a powerful alliance of channel partners. Membership: $605-18,700/year.

Meetings/Conferences:
Conference Chair: Ruth Mitchell
2013 - Washington, DC (Renaissance Washington, D.C. Downtown Hotel)/Oct. 2 - 4
2014 - Las Vegas, NV (Bellagio Hotel and Casino)/ Sept. 9 - 12
2015 - Chicago, IL (Chicago Marriott Downtown Magnificent Mile)/Oct. 27 - 29

Publications:
ASA Insights Newsletter
Membership Directory; annually

Membership List Available to Non-members

American Surgical Association (1880)
500 Cummings Center
Suite 4550
Beverly, MA 01915
Tel: (978) 927-8330 Fax: (978) 524-8890
E-Mail: asa@prri.com
Website: americansurgical.info
Members: 1139 individuals
Staff: 1
Annual Budget: $1-2,000,000
Tax: 501(c)(6)

Personnel:
Executive Director: Jon Blackstone
E-Mail: jblackstone@prri.com

Historical Note:
ASA emerged as American Surgical Society, later gained current name. ASA's aim is to be the premier organization for surgical science and scholarship and to provide a national forum for presenting the developing state of the art and science of general and sub- specialty surgery and the elevation of the standards of the medical/surgical profession.

Meetings/Conferences: Annual
2013 - Indianapolis, IN (JW Marriott Indianapolis)/ April 4 - 6
2014 - Boston, MA (Boston Marriott Copley Place)/ April 10 - 12

Publications:
Annals of Surgery; monthly; adv.
ASA Newsletter; annually
Membership Directory; on-line

American Swimming Coaches Association (1958)
5101 NW 21st Ave.
Suite 200
Ft. Lauderdale, FL 33309
Tel: (954) 563-4930 Fax: (954) 563-9813
TollFree: (800) 356-2722
E-Mail: asca@swimmingcoach.org
Website: swimmingcoach.org
Members: 8001 individuals
Staff: 10
Annual Budget: $500-1,000,000
Tax: 501(c)(6)

Personnel:
Executive Director: John Leonard
E-Mail: JLeonard@swimmingcoach.org
Contact, Technical Programs: Guy Edson
E-Mail: gedson@swimmingcoach.org
General Counsel: Richard J. Foster
Director, Publications: Jen Johnson
E-Mail: publishing@swimmingcoach.org
Contact, Sales and Finance: Dianne Sgrignoli
E-Mail: dsgrignoli@swimmingcoach.org
Director, Membership Services: Melanie Wigren
E-Mail: membership@swimmingcoach.org
Director, Certification Services: Kim Witherington
E-Mail: certification@swimmingcoach.org

Historical Note:
ASCA is dedicated to create and enhance progressive and visible programs to strengthen and improve the coaching profession and build a stronger swimming community. It provides services like publications, educational programs, resources and general information about swimming related activities. Membership: $70-2000/year.

Continuing Education:
Certification Designation/s: ASCA, DSC

Meetings/Conferences: Semi-Annual
Conference Chair: Dianne Sgrignoli

Publications:
American Swimming Magazine; bi-monthly; adv.
ASCA Newsletter; monthly; adv.
The Club Newsletter; quarterly; adv.
The Journal of swimming Research; annually; adv.
Workout Wednesday; weekly

American Tarentaise Association (1973)
9150 N. 216th St.
Elkhorn, NE 68022
Tel: (402) 639-9808
E-Mail: info@americantarentaise.org
Website: americantarentaise.org
Members: 244 individuals
Staff: 4
Annual Budget: $10-25,000
Tax: 501(c)(5)

Personnel:
Office Manager: Sandy Brummund
E-Mail: info@americantarentaise.org

Historical Note:
Tarentaise cattle originated in Southeastern France, and were recognized as a breed in 1866. The association is the official breed registry for Tarentaise cattle. ATA's mission is to provide the beef cattle industry with the traits required to complement the British breeds and bring profitability and efficiency to commercial cattlemen. Membership: $50 (Active); $25 (Junior).

Meetings/Conferences: Annual

Publications:
Membership Directory; on-line
Tarentaise Talk - Newsletter; quarterly

American Technical Education Association (1928)
818 Dunwoody Blvd.
Minneapolis, MN 55403
Tel: (612) 381-3315
E-Mail: info@ateaonline.org
Website: ateaonline.org
Members: 2000 organizations and individuals
Staff: 2
Annual Budget: $100-250,000
Tax: 501(c)(3)

Personnel:
Executive Director: Sandra Krebsbach
E-Mail: skrebsbach@dunwoody.edu

Historical Note:
Established as American Association of Technical High Schools and Institutes; assumed its present name in 1950 and incorporated in New York (1960). Affiliated with the American Vocational Association from 1944 to 1969. ATEA's mission is to serve as the premier provider of professional development for postsecondary technical education. Membership: $75 (Regular); $30 (Retired); $15 (Student); $500 (Institutional/Corporate/Business Membership); $600 (Life); $1500 (Corporate/Business Sustaining); $1000 (Institutional Sustaining).

Meetings/Conferences: Annual
2013 - Chattanooga, TN (Chattanooga Convention Center)/March 20 - 21/51-100 exhibitors
Number of non-conference events/year: 8

Publications:
ATEA Journal; semi-annually
Member Directory; on-line

American Telemarketing Association (2010)
111 St.
New York, NY 56478
Website: ataconnect.org
Staff: 1
Annual Budget: $1-2,000,000

Personnel:
Treasurer: Hon Rack

American Telemedicine Association (1993)
1100 Connecticut Ave. NW
Suite 540

Washington, DC 20036
Tel: (202) 223-3333 Fax: (202) 223-2787
E-Mail: info@americantelemed.org
Website: americantelemed.org
Members: 2000 individuals and 60 companies
Staff: 11
Annual Budget: $2-5,000,000
Tax: 501(c)(3)

Personnel:
Chief Executive Officer: Jonathan D. Linkous
E-Mail: jlinkous@americantelemed.org
Senior Director, Programs: Jordana Bernard
E-Mail: jbernard@americantelemed.org
Associate Director, Sales and Marketing: Marcus Brady
E-Mail: mbrady@americantelemed.org
Senior Director, Communications: Benjamin R. Forstag
E-Mail: bforstag@americantelemed.org
Director, Meetings: Brian Lane
E-Mail: blane@americantelemed.org
Manager, Membership Services: Carmen Park
E-Mail: cpark@americantelemed.org
Manager, Finance and Administration: Mario R. Valdez Jr.
E-Mail: mvaldez@americantelemed.org
Chief Operating Officer: Alice J. Watland
E-Mail: awatland@americantelemed.org

Historical Note:
ATA's mission is to promote professional, ethical and equitable improvement in health care delivery through telecommunications and information technology. Members are individuals, companies and other organizations with an interest in promoting the deployment of telemedicine throughout the world. Membership: $220 (Individual); $1,400-2,050 (Institutional-for up to 7 individuals and to cover all employees in your institution); $500 (Sustaining); $2,050 (Regular Corporate); $10,000 (Sustaining President's Circle Sustaining); $6,750 (President's Circle).

Continuing Education:
Certification Designation/s: TPA

Meetings/Conferences: Annual
Conference Chair: Brian Lane
2013 - Austin, TX/May 5 - 7
2014 - Baltimore, MD/May 18 - 20
2015 - Los Angeles, CA/May 1 - 3
2015 - Los Angeles, CA/May 3 - 5
2016 - Minneapolis, MN/May 15 - 18
2016 - Minneapolis, MN/May 15 - 17
Number of non-conference events/year: 1

Publications:
Journal of Telemedicine and Telecare
Member Directory; on-line
Telemedicine and e-Health

Membership List Available to Non-members

American Teleservices Association (1983)
8500 Keystone Crossing
Suite 480
Indianapolis, IN 46240
Tel: (317) 816-9336
E-Mail: contact@ataconnect.org
Website: ataconnect.org
Members: 4,000 centers
Staff: 11
Annual Budget: $1-2,000,000

Personnel:
President and Chief Executive Officer: Phil Grudzinski
Vice President, Membership Development: Tom Chandler
E-Mail: tomchandler@ataconnect.org
Director, Digital Marketing: Tom Deeter
E-Mail: tom@ataconnect.org
Vice President, Conventions and Chapters: Lisa Nye Ford
E-Mail: lisa@ataconnect.org
Director, Finance: Bill Morris
Association Counsel: Mitchell Roth

Historical Note:
Founded as the American Telemarketing Association, assumed its current name in 1998. ATA is committed to serving the needs of its members by recommending the standards of quality for the channel and protecting the rights of consumers. Members are business executives who have significant management responsibilities for telephone-assisted marketing, sales and service activities, own or operate telemarketing service agencies, or are suppliers of goods and services to the telemarketing industry. Membership: $150-5,000/year.

Meetings/Conferences:
Conference Chair: Lisa Nye Ford

Publications:
eConnections; bi-weekly; adv.

Membership Directory; on-line

American Textile Machinery Association (1907)
201 Park Washington Ct.
Falls Church, VA 22046-4513
Tel: (703) 538-1789 *Fax:* (703) 241-5603
E-Mail: info@atmanet.org
Website: atmanet.org
Members: 100 companies
Staff: 4
Annual Budget: $500-1,000,000
Tax: 501(c)(6)
Personnel:
Executive Vice President and Secretary: Susan A. Denston
Management Counsel: Harry W. Buzzerd Jr., CAE, Jr. CAE
International Trade and Government Affairs Consultant: Carlos F. J. Moore
President and Assistant Treasurer: Clay D. Tyeryar CAE, MAM
 E-Mail: ctyeryar@atmanet.org
Historical Note:
Formerly (1933) National Association of Textile Machinery Manufacturers. Sponsors and supports the Textile Machinery Good Government Committee. ATMA is dedicated to the advancement of manufactures of textile machinery, parts and accessories in the textile industry. Membership: $595-1,675 (Single Entity); $510 (Affiliate).
Publications:
Newsletter

Membership List Available to Non-members

American Theatre and Drama Society
61 Carey Rd.
Needham, MA 02494
Tel: (850) 645-6858
Website: atds.org
Staff: 5
Personnel:
President: Mark Cosdon
 E-Mail: mcosdon@allegheny.edu
Editor: Sarah Bay-Cheng
 E-Mail: sbaycheng@mail.colgate.edu
Secretary: Cheryl Black
 E-Mail: blackc@missouri.edu
Conference Planner: James Cherry
 E-Mail: cherryj@wabash.edu
Secretary, Membership Services: Stuart J. Hecht
 E-Mail: hecht@bc.edu
Historical Note:
ATDS is an incorporated organization dedicated to the study of United States theater and drama, its varied histories, traditions, literatures, and performances within its cultural contexts. Membership: $30 (General); $20 (Student/Adjunct/Retired); $300 (Life Time for Faculty).
Meetings/Conferences:
Conference Chair: James Cherry
Publications:
The Journal of American Drama and Theatre (JADT)

American Theatre Critics Association (1974)
12809 Northern Sky NE
Albuquerque, NM 87111-8089
Tel: (505) 856-2101
E-Mail: atca_admin@msn.com
Website: americantheatrecritics.org
Members: 228 individuals
Staff: 2
Annual Budget: $10-25,000
Personnel:
Administrator: Barry Gaines
 E-Mail: bjgaines@unm.edu
Contact, Communications: Chris Rawson
 E-Mail: cchr@pitt.edu
Historical Note:
Organized at the O'Neill Theater Center in Waterford, CT in 1974. ATCA's purpose is to make possible greater communication among theater critics and to encourage freedom of expression in theater. Membership is open only to professional writers who have been actively employed reviewing theatre on a regular and continuing basis. Membership: $45/year.
Meetings/Conferences:
2013 - Indianapolis, IN/March 21 - 24

American Theological Library Association (1946)
300 S. Wacker Dr.

Suite 2100
Chicago, IL 60606-6701
Tel: (312) 454-5100 *Fax:* (312) 454-5505
TollFree: (888) 665-2852
E-Mail: atla@atla.com
Website: atla.com
Members: 1000 individual, institutional, and affiliate members.
Staff: 6
Annual Budget: $5-10,000,000
Tax: 501(c)(3)
Personnel:
Executive Director: Brenda Bailey-Hainer
 E-Mail: bbailey-hainer@atla.com
Director, Information Systems: Jim Butler
 E-Mail: jbutler@atla.com
Director, Member Programs: Miguel Figueroa
 E-Mail: mfigueroa@atla.com
Director, Financial Services: Marie Jacobsen
 E-Mail: mjacobsen@atla.com
Director, Business Development: Margot Lyon
 E-Mail: mlyon@atla.com
Specialist, Meetings: Denise McFarlin
 E-Mail: dmcfarlin@atla.com
Historical Note:
An outgrowth of a Round Table on Libraries of the American Association of Theological Schools held in 1947. ATLA's mission is to foster the study of theology and religion by enhancing the development of theological and religious studies libraries and librarianship. Membership: $15-150 (Individual/Student); $100 (Affiliates); $100-1000 (Institutional).
Meetings/Conferences: Annual
Conference Chair: Denise McFarlin
2013 - Charlotte, NC/June 19 - 22
2014 - New Orleans, LA/June 18 - 21
2015 - Denver, CO/June 17 - 20
Publications:
ATLA Newsletter; monthly

Membership List Available to Non-members

American Therapeutic Recreation Association (1984)
629 N. Main St.
Hattiesburg, MS 39401
Tel: (601) 450-2872 *Fax:* (601) 582-3354
E-Mail: national@atra-online.com
Website: atra-online.com
Members: 2100 individuals
Staff: 5
Annual Budget: $500-1,000,000
Tax: 501(c)(6)
Personnel:
President: Diane Skalko CTRS, MS
 E-Mail: dskalko@pittcoa.com
Association Manager: Lamar Evans
CEU Coordinator: Kelly Evans
 E-Mail: ceu@atra-online.com
Contact, Membership and Conference Registration: Tina Ignatiev
Contact, Conferences: Teddi Sisemore
Historical Note:
ATRA seeks to advance the field of therapeutic recreation as an effective and efficient component of health care. ATRA was incorporated in the District of Columbia in 1984 as a non-profit, grassroots organization in response to growing concern about the dramatic changes in the healthcare industry. Membership: $135 (Individual); $125 (Professional); $65 (Student); $1,000 (Lifetime).
Continuing Education:
Certification Designation/s: CEU
Meetings/Conferences: Semi-Annual
Conference Chair: Teddi Sisemore
2013 - Chattanooga, TN (Chattanooga Marriott at the Convention Center)/March 10 - 13
2013 - Pittsburgh, PA (Sheraton Station Square Hotel)/ Sept. 29 - Oct. 2
Number of non-conference events/year: 1
Publications:
ATRA Newsletter; semi-monthly; adv.
e-newslettter; bi-monthly

American Thoracic Society (1905)
61 Broadway
New York, NY 10006
Tel: (212) 315-8600 *Fax:* (212) 315-6498
E-Mail: atsinfo@thoracic.org

Website: thoracic.org
Members: 15000 individuals
Staff: 92
Annual Budget: $10-25,000,000
Personnel:
Executive Director: Stephen C. Crane MPH, PhD
 E-Mail: scrane@thoracic.org
Chief Financial Officer: Jo Anne Barry
Associate Director, Meeting Services: Emily Catanzaro
Senior Director, Scientific Meetings and Conferences: Francine Comi
Director, Editorial Production: Eric Gumpert
 E-Mail: egumpert@thoracic.org
Director, Human Resources: Rhina Guzman PHR
 E-Mail: rguzman@thoracic.org
Senior Manager, Education Programs: Barbara Horner
 E-Mail: bhorner@thoracic.org
Director, Membership Services and Chapter Relations: Jennifer A. Ian MBA
 E-Mail: jian@thoracic.org
Senior Director, Communications and Marketing: Brian Kell
 E-Mail: bkell@thoracic.org
Senior Director, Information Technology: Maribel Lim
Historical Note:
ATS emerged as American Sanatorium Association. In 1938 was renamed as American Trudeau Society. Gained its present name in 1960. ATS's mission is to improve health by advancing research, clinical care and public health in respiratory disease, critical illness and sleep disorders. Membership : $40-375/year.
Meetings/Conferences: Annual
Conference Chair: Emily Catanzaro
2013 - Philadelphia, PA/May 17 - 22
2014 - San Diego, CA/May 16 - 21
2015 - Denver, CO/May 15 - 20
2016 - San Francisco, CA/May 13 - 18
2017 - Washington, DC/May 17 - 24
2017 - Washington, DC/May 19 - 24
Publications:
American Journal of Respiratory and Critical Care Medicine; bi-weekly; adv.
American Journal of Respiratory Cell and Molecular Biology; monthly; adv.
ATS Coding & Billing Quarterly; quarterly
ATS News; monthly; adv.
Proceedings of the American Thoracic Society; quarterly; adv.

Membership List Available to Non-members

American Thyroid Association (1923)
6066 Leesburg Pike
Suite 550
Falls Church, VA 22041
Tel: (703) 998-8890 *Fax:* (703) 998-8893
TollFree: (800) 849-7643
E-Mail: thyroid@thyroid.org
Website: thyroid.org
Members: 1300 individuals
Staff: 7
Annual Budget: $1-2,000,000
Tax: 501(c)(3)
Personnel:
Executive Director: Barbara R. Smith CAE
 E-Mail: bsmith@thyroid.org
Senior Finance Officer: Shirlyn Barger
 E-Mail: sbarger@thyroid.org
Associate, Membership Services and Development: Sharleene E. Cano
Director, Meetings and Program Services: Adonia C. Coates CMP
 E-Mail: acoates@thyroid.org
Editor: Charles H. Emerson
Manager, Database Systems and Development: Kelly Hoff
 E-Mail: khoff@thyroid.org
Historical Note:
Formerly American Association for the Study of Goiter, it became the American Goiter Association in 1948 and assumed its present name in 1959. ATA is a professional organization of physicians and scientists dedicated to treatment, research and education regarding thyroid function and disease. Membership: $475 (Active); $100 (Corresponding); $90 (Senior); Free (Associate).
Continuing Education:
Enrollment: 1000
Meetings/Conferences: Annual
Conference Chair: Adonia C. Coates CMP

2013 - San Juan, PR (Sheraton Puerto Rico Hotel and
    Casino)/Oct. 16 - 20
2014 - Concord, CA (Sheraton Portland Airport Hotel)/
    Oct. 29 - Nov. 2/1000 attendees/11-25 exhibitors
2015 - Orlando, FL (Walt Disney World Swan And
    Dolphin)/Sept. 17 - 23
2016 - Denver, CO (Sheraton Denver Downtown
    Hotel)/Sept. 21 - 26/11-25 exhibitors
2017 - Victoria, BC (The Fairmont Empress and
    Victoria Conference Center)/Oct. 18 - 22
Number of non-conference events/year: 1

Publications:
ATA News Brief; quarterly; adv.
Clinical Thyroidology for Patients; monthly; adv.
Member Directory; on-line
Signal Newsletter; on-line
Thyroid, A Journal; monthly; adv.

American Tin Trade Association *(1928)*
P.O. Box 59
Richboro, PA 18954
Tel: (215) 504-9725 *Fax:* (555) 555-5555
E-Mail: americantintrade@gmail.com
Website: tintrade.org
Members: 60 companies
Staff: 1
Annual Budget: $10-25,000

Personnel:
Secretary: Karen Salberg
    E-Mail: Americantintrade@gmail.com

Historical Note:
*Purpose is to promote the best interests of those persons
engaged in the production, distribution, transportation,
consumption, purchase and sale of pig tin. Membership:
$350/year.*

American Tort Reform Association *(1986)*
1101 Connecticut Ave. NW
Suite 400
Washington, DC 20036
Tel: (202) 682-1163 *Fax:* (202) 682-1022
Website: atra.org
Members: 300 individuals
Staff: 6
Annual Budget: $5-10,000,000
Tax: 501(c)(6)

Personnel:
President: Sherman Joyce
    E-Mail: sjoyce@atra.org
Coordinator, Membership Services: Geneva Carney
    E-Mail: gcarney@atra.org
Director, Legislation: Matt Fullenbaum
    E-Mail: mfullenbaum@atra.org
Director, Communications: Darren McKinney
    E-Mail: dmckinney@atra.org

Historical Note:
*ATRA strives to repair America's civil justice system.
Members are individuals and organizations with a
professional interest in reforming the civil justice system.*
Meetings/Conferences:
Number of non-conference events/year: 2

Publications:
Member Directory; on-line
State Tort Reform Enactments; annually
Tort Reform Record; bi-annually

American Traffic Safety Service Association
(1969)
15 Riverside Pkwy.
Suite 100
Fredericksburg, VA 22406-1022
Tel: (540) 368-1701 *Fax:* (540) 368-1717
TollFree: (800) 272-8772
Website: atssa.com
Members: 1600 members
Staff: 28
Annual Budget: $5-10,000,000

Personnel:
President and Chief Executive Officer: Roger Wentz
Director, Communications and Public Relations: James
    Scott Baron
Director, Training and Products: Donna Clark
Director, Membership Services: Donald Ethier
Foundation Director: Melanie McKee
Director, Finance and Administration: Mitzi Osterhout

Historical Note:

*Formed as the the American Traffic Services Association,
assumed its current name in 1984. ATSSA's core purpose is
to advance roadway safety.*
Continuing Education:
Certification Designation/s: FIT, TCT, TCS
Meetings/Conferences: Semi-Annual
Conference Chair: Melanie McKee
2013 - San Diego, CA (San Diego Convention and
    Visitors Bureau)/Feb. 22 - 26
2013 - Nashville, TN (Loews Vanderbilt Hotel,
    Nashville)/Aug. 14 - 16
2014 - San Antonio, TX (Henry B. Gonzalez
    Convention Center and the Lila Cockrell Theatre)/
    Feb. 21 - 25
2014 - Kansas City, MO (Kansas City Hotel-
    InterContinental)/Aug. 20 - 22
2015 - Tampa, FL (Tampa Convention Center)/Feb. 6 -
    10
2016 - New Orleans, LA (Ernest N. Morial Convention
    Center)/Jan. 29 - Feb. 2
2017 - Phoenix, AZ (Phoenix Convention Center)/Feb.
    10 - 14

Publications:
ATSSA Flash; bi-weekly
ATSSA Membership Directory; annually
ATSSA Signal; quarterly

American Train Dispatchers Association *(1917)*
4239 W. 150th St.
Cleveland, OH 44135
Tel: (216) 251-7984 *Fax:* (216) 251-8190
Website: atdd.homestead.com/atddpg1.html
Members: 2600 individuals
Staff: 3
Annual Budget: $5-10,000,000
Tax: 501(c)(5)

Personnel:
President: F. L. McCann
Secretary and Treasurer: Gary L. Melton
Director, Research: R. M. Sermak

Historical Note:
*Formerly Western Train Dispatchers' Association and
assumed current name in 1918. Chartered by AFL-CIO in
1957. ATDA represents employees in the nation's railroad
industry who operate and dispatch trains, and supply the
electric power for those railroads which use electricity for
train propulsion and signalling. Membership: $729/year
(Individual).*
Publications:
ATDA Newsletter

American Trakehner Association *(1974)*
1536 W. Church St.
Newark, OH 43055
Tel: (740) 344-1111 *Fax:* (740) 344-3225
E-Mail: ata@americantrakehner.com
Website: americantrakehner.com
Members: 1400 individuals
Staff: 3
Annual Budget: $100-250,000

Personnel:
Executive Director: Kelly Gulick

Historical Note:
*Unified with North American Trakehner Association in
2001. ATA's mission is to establish, maintain, and operate
a non-profit association of breeders, owners and friends
for the promotion and preservation of the warmblood
horse of Trakehner origin in the Western Hemisphere.
In addition it maintains a public registry of the breed.
Members are owners and breeders of Trakehner horses, a
breed originating in Trakehnen, East Prussia. Membership:
$85 (Active); $850 (Lifetime); $35 (Youth).*
Meetings/Conferences: Annual
Publications:
Newsletter; adv.
The American Trakehner; adv.

American Translators Association *(1959)*
225 Reinekers Ln.
Suite 590
Alexandria, VA 22314
Tel: (703) 683-6100 *Fax:* (703) 683-6122
E-Mail: ata@atanet.org
Website: atanet.org
Members: 11000 members
Staff: 12
Annual Budget: $2-5,000,000
Tax: 501(c)(6)

Personnel:
Executive Director: Walter W. Bacak Jr., CAE
    E-Mail: walter@atanet.org
Member Benefits and Project Development Manager: Mary
    David CMT
    E-Mail: mary@atanet.org
*Deputy Executive Director and Manager, Certification
    Programs:* Terry Hanlen
    E-Mail: terry@atanet.org
Contact, Membership Relations and Office Manager:
    Kwana Ingram
    E-Mail: kwana@atanet.org
Manager, Meetings: Teresa C. Kelly
    E-Mail: teresak@atanet.org
Manager, Accounting: Kirk Lawson
    E-Mail: kirk@atanet.org
Manager, Public Relations and Marketing: Caron Mason
    CAE
    E-Mail: caron@atanet.org
Manager, Information Systems: Roshan Pokharel
    E-Mail: roshan@atanet.org
Manager, Publications: Jeff Sanfacon
    E-Mail: jeff@atanet.org

Historical Note:
*ATA's mission is to benefit translators and interpreters by
promoting recognition of their societal and commercial
value, facilitating communication among all its members,
establishing standards of competence and ethics, and
educating both its members and the public. Members are
translators and interpreters. Membership: $240 (Associate);
$300 (Institutional); $495 (Corporate); $120 (Student);
$440 (Joint Member).*

Continuing Education:
Certification Designation/s: CT

Meetings/Conferences: Annual
Conference Chair: Teresa C. Kelly
2013 - San Antonio, TX (San Antonio Marriott
    Rivercenter)/Nov. 6 - 9
2014 - Chicago, IL (Sheraton Chicago Hotel and
    Towers)/Nov. 5 - 8
2015 - Miami, FL (Hyatt Regency Coral Gables)/Nov. 4
    - 7
2016 - San Francisco, CA (Grand Hyatt San Francisco)/
    Nov. 2 - 5
Number of non-conference events/year: 17

Publications:
ATA Chronicle; monthly; adv.
ATA Newsbriefs; monthly; adv.
Directory of Language Services Providers; on-line; adv.
Directory of Translation and Interpreting Services; on-
    line
Member Directory; on-line

American Trauma Society *(1968)*
7611 S. Osborne Rd.
Suite 202
Upper Marlboro, MD 20772-2656
Tel: (301) 574-4300 *Fax:* (301) 574-4301
TollFree: (800) 556-7890
E-Mail: info@amtrauma.org
Website: amtrauma.org
Members: 3000 individuals
Staff: 4
Annual Budget: $1-2,000,000

Personnel:
Executive Director: Harry Teter
    E-Mail: hteter@amtrauma.org
Manager, Membership and Course: Theresa Smith
    E-Mail: tsmith@amtrauma.org

Historical Note:
*The mission of ATS is the elimination of needless death
and disability from injury. Membership includes both lay
and professional individuals, institutions, and corporations.
Membership: $30-160 (Individual); $100-2,900
(Institutional).*

Continuing Education:
Certification Designation/s: CSRT

Publications:
Membership Directory; on-line

Membership List Available to Non-members

American Truck Dealers *(1970)*
C/O National Automobile Dealers Association
8400 Westpark Dr.
McLean, VA 22102
Tel: (703) 821-7230 *Fax:* (703) 749-4700
TollFree: (800) 352-6232

E-Mail: atd@nada.org
Website: nada.org
Members: 2000 organizations
Staff: 35

Personnel:
Managing Director: Barbara Robinson
    E-Mail: brobinson@nada.org
Coordinator: Kim Carey
    E-Mail: kcarey@nada.org
Director, Public Relations: Charles Cyrill
    E-Mail: ccyrill@nada.org

Historical Note:
A division of National Automobile Dealers Association.
ATD represents medium and heavy truck dealers. ATD
members share in NADA's programs, services and benefits
and can take advantage of ATD 20 Groups, a performance-
based business forum for truck dealers. ATD membership is
open to any new-truck dealership holding a new truck sales
and service franchise. Membership: $245-620 (based on
the prior-calendar-year new vehicle sales of the dealership);
$100 (Affiliated).

Meetings/Conferences: Annual
2013 - Orlando, FL (Orange County Convention
    Center)/Feb. 8 - 11

Publications:
ATD Insider
ATD Newsletter; monthly

American Trucking Associations (1933)
950 N. Glebe Rd.
Suite 210
Arlington, VA 22203-4181
Tel: (703) 838-1700 Fax: (703) 838-1851
TollFree: (888) 333-1759
Website: truckline.com
Members: 37000 individuals
Staff: 205
Annual Budget: $25-50,000,000

Personnel:
President and Chief Executive Officer: Bill Graves
Controller: James 'Rusty" Duckworth
    E-Mail: rduckworth@trucking.org
Contact, Automobile Carriers Conference: Bob Farrell
    E-Mail: bfarrell@trucking.org
Executive Director: David Hershey
    E-Mail: dhershey@trucking.org
Chief Financial Officer: Karla Hulett
Contact, Membership Services: Greg Kohlrieser
    E-Mail: gkohlrieser@trucking.org
Vice President, Sales and Marketing: Don Lynn
Senior Vice President, Legislative Affairs: Mary Philips

Historical Note:
Formed as a merger of the American Highway Freight
Association and the Federated Truck Associations of
America. ATA's mission is to provide educational programs,
industry research and advance the trucking industry's
image, efficiency, competitiveness, and profitability. It
represents every type of motor carrier in the United States.
Sponsors and supports the political action committee
TRUCK-PAC. Membership: $500-9,756 (Hire Member);
$500-12,780 (Private Carrier Member); $2,856- 148,956
(Allied Member); $900-6,240 (Shipper).

Meetings/Conferences: Annual
2013 - Orlando, FL (Orlando World Center Marriott)/
    Oct. 19 - 22
2014 - San Diego, CA (San Diego Convention Center)/
    Oct. 17 - 20
Number of non-conference events/year: 1

Publications:
ATA Issues Update; quarterly
ATA State Laws Newsletter; weekly
Truckline; bi-weekly
Weekly Economic Recap; weekly

American Urogynecologic Society (1979)
2025 M St. NW
Suite 800
Washington, DC 20036
Tel: (202) 367-1167 Fax: (202) 367-2167
E-Mail: AUGS@sba.com
Website: augs.org
Members: 1400 Individuals
Staff: 5
Annual Budget: $250-500,000

Personnel:
Executive Director: Michelle Zinnert
Staff Accountant: Sarah Alcock

Senior Manager, Marketing and Communications: Kara
    Dress
Manager, Meetings: Tina Hochberg
Director, Education: Chris Peck

Historical Note:
AUGS dedicated to medical professional community for
individuals and companies in the field of urogynecology and
it's mission is to stimulate the highest quality patient care
through excellence in education, research and advocacy.
Members are practicing physicians, nurse practitioners,
physical therapists, nurses and health care professionals,
as well as researchers from many disciplines, all dedicated
to improving the urogynecologic health of women.
Membership: $365 (Physician); $170 (Student); $100
(Affiliate).

Continuing Education:
Certification Designation/s: FPMRS

Meetings/Conferences: Annual
Conference Chair: Tina Hochberg
2013 - Las Vegas, NV (Convention Center)/Oct. 16 -
    19/900 attendees/51-100 exhibitors
2014 - Chicago, IL (Hilton Chicago)/July 22 - 27
2015 - Chicago, IL (Hilton Chicago)/Oct. 6 - 9

Publications:
AUGS e-Xpress; monthly
Female Pelvic Medicine & Reconstructive Surgery
    (FPMRS); bi-monthly; adv.
Membership Directory; on-line

Membership List Available to Non-members

American Urological Association (1902)
1000 Corporate Blvd.
Linthicum, MD 21090
Tel: (410) 689-3700 Fax: (410) 689-3800
TollFree: (866) 746-4282
E-Mail: aua@auanet.org
Website: auanet.org
Members: 18000 individuals
Staff: 32
Annual Budget: $10-25,000,000

Personnel:
Executive Director: Michael Sheppard CAE, CPA
    E-Mail: sheppard@auanet.org
Manager, Advertising and Exhibits Sales: Jane Conway
    E-Mail: jconway@auanet.org
Generalist, Human Resources: Randi Cremmins
    E-Mail: rcremmins@auanet.org
Manager, Convention Operations: Andrew Niles
    E-Mail: aniles@auanet.org

Historical Note:
Founded in 1902 and incorporated in Maryland. AUA's
mission is to develop the standards of urological clinical
care through education, research and in the formulation of
health care policy. Membership: $425 (Active/Associate);
$115 (Candidate); $275 (International); $50-150
(International Residents-in-Training, based on country
classification); $150 (Allied/Affiliate)/ year.

Meetings/Conferences: Annual
Conference Chair: Andrew Niles
2013 - San Diego, CA (San Diego Convention Center)/
    May 4 - 8
2014 - Orlando, FL/May 17 - 21

Publications:
AUA Global Connections
AUANews; on-line
Health Policy Brief; monthly
Journal of Urology; monthly; adv.
Membership and Referral Directory; annually

Membership List Available to Non-members

American Veal Association (1984)
C/O Provitello Farms
5327 Watson Rd.
Elba, NY 14058
Tel: (585) 313-8466
E-Mail: info@americanveal.com
Website: americanveal.com
Staff: 2
Annual Budget: $50-100,000

Personnel:
President: Jurian Bartelse

Historical Note:
AVA members work together to promote the veal industry
through media, industry, consumer and policy outreach.

Continuing Education:
Certification Designation/s: VQA

American Venous Forum (1988)
555 E. Wells St.
Suite 1100
Milwaukee, WI 53202
Tel: (414) 918-9880 Fax: (414) 276-3349
E-Mail: info@veinforum.org
Website: veinforum.org
Members: 260 individuals
Staff: 4
Annual Budget: $500-1,000,000
Tax: 501(c)(6)

Personnel:
President: Rob McLafferty MD
Secretary: Lowell S. Kabnick MD

Historical Note:
AVF is dedicated to improving the care of patients with
venous and lymphatic disease. Membership: $150
(Associate/Candidate); $200 (Active).

Meetings/Conferences: Annual
2013 - Phoenix, AZ (Wigwam Resort)/Feb. 27 - March
    2

Publications:
Newsletter

American Veterinary Dental Society (1976)
P.O. Box 803
Fayetteville, TN 37334
Tel: (931) 438-0238 Fax: (931) 433-6289
TollFree: (800) 332-2837
E-Mail: avds@avds-online.org
Website: avds-online.org
Members: 25 companies and 1200 individuals
Staff: 2
Annual Budget: $250-500,000

Personnel:
President: Kevin Stepaniuk
    E-Mail: kstepani@umn.edu
Treasurer: Barden Greenfield
    E-Mail: memphispetdent@aol.com

Historical Note:
AVDS provides a forum for advancing the knowledge,
education, and awareness of veterinary dentistry among
veterinarians, students and the public. Members are
veterinarians, dentists, hygienists, technicians or individuals
interested in veterinary dentistry. Membership: $110
(Individual, U.S.); $120 (Individual, Outside U.S.).

Meetings/Conferences: Annual
2013 - New Orleans, LA (New Orleans Mariott)/Oct. 3
    - 6

Publications:
Journal of Veterinary Dentistry; quarterly; adv.
Membership Directory; on-line
The AVDS Newsletter; monthly

American Veterinary Distributors Association
(1976)
2105 Laurel Bush Rd.
Suite 200
Bel Air, MD 21015
Tel: (443) 640-1040 Fax: (443) 640-1086
Website: avda.net
Members: 75 companies
Staff: 4
Annual Budget: $250-500,000
Tax: 501(c)(6)

Personnel:
Executive Director: Jackie King
    E-Mail: jackie@@KINGmgmt.org
Director, Finance: Debbie Dacre
    E-Mail: Debbie @KINGmgmt.org
Legal Counsel: Neil Kuenn
    E-Mail: nkuenn@kkrlaw.com

Historical Note:
AVDA's mission is to serve businesses engaged in the
distribution of animal health products. Members are
distributors of animal healthcare products. Membership:
$1,500-5,000 (Active); $1,500 (Associate/Affiliate).

Meetings/Conferences: Annual
2013 - Bonita Springs, FL (Hyatt Coconut Point)/April
    28 - 30
2014 - Scottsdale, AZ (Fairmont Scottsdale Princess)/
    April 27 - 29

Publications:
Animal Health Distributor Online; quarterly
Membership Directory; on-line

American Veterinary Medical Association (1863)

1931 N. Meacham Rd.
Suite 100
Schaumburg, IL 60173-4360
Tel: (847) 925-8070 *Fax:* (847) 925-1329
TollFree: (800) 248-2862
Website: avma.org
Members: 82500 individuals
Staff: 117
Annual Budget: $25-50,000,000
Tax: 501(c)(6)

Personnel:
Executive Vice President: Dr. W. Ron DeHaven
Director, Marketing: Jim Flanigan
Assistant Director, Media Relations: Sharon Curtis
  Granskog
  E-Mail: sgranskog@avma.org
Director, Governmental Relations: Mark Lutschaunig
  E-Mail: mlutschaunig@avma.org

Historical Note:
Formerly, United States of Veterinary Medical Association and assumed current name in 1889. AVMA's mission is to improve animal and human health and advance the veterinary medical profession. Membership: $150 (Active/Associate/Family Obligation); $45,000 (Financial Hardship by reason of Extenuating Circumstances).

Meetings/Conferences: Annual
2013 - Chicago, IL/July 20 - 23
2014 - Denver, CO/July 26 - 29
2015 - Boston, MA/July 11 - 14
2016 - San Antonio, TX/Aug. 5 - 8

Publications:
Access PAC; quarterly
American Journal of Veterinary Research (AJVR); adv.
Animal Welfare Focus; quarterly
AVMA Advocate; monthly
AVMA@Work Newsletter; monthly
COE Standard; quarterly
ERC Newslink; monthly
Health News Bytes; monthly
JAVMA News; on-line; adv.
JAVMA News Bulletin; on-line
Journal of the AVMA (JAVMA); adv.
Membership Directory; on-line
State Legislative Update; monthly

American Veterinary Society of Animal Behavior (1976)

2715 N. Monticello Ave.
Chicago, IL 60647
Website: avsabonline.org
Members: 530 individuals
Staff: 3
Annual Budget: $10-25,000

Personnel:
Corresponding Secretary: Cheryl Kolus
  E-Mail: avsabe@gmail.com
Treasurer: Kari Krause
President: Valli Parthasarathy

Historical Note:
Formerly American Society of Veterinary Ethology. AVSAB is committed to improve the quality of life of all animals and strengthening the bond between animals and their owners. Members are veterinarians and research professionals who share an interest in understanding behavior in animals. Membership: $40 (Regular/Affiliate); $7.50 (Student).

Meetings/Conferences: Annual

Publications:
AVSAB Newsletter; quarterly

American Viola Society (1971)

14070 Proton Rd.
Suite 100, LB 9
Dallas, TX 75244-5737
Tel: (972) 233-9107
E-Mail: info@avsnationaloffice.org
Website: americanviolasociety.org
Members: 1000 individuals
Staff: 5
Annual Budget: $50-100,000

Personnel:
President: Nokuthula Ngwenyama
Editor: David M. Bynog
  E-Mail: dbynog@rice.edu
Webmaster and Media Coordinator: Adam Paul Cordle
  E-Mail: usviolasociety@gmail.com

General Manager: Madeleine Crouch
Treasurer: Michelle Sayles

Historical Note:
Formerly (1971) American Viola Research Society. AVS's mission is to promote interest in the viola by encouraging performance and recording at the artistic level and by providing a vehicle for the ongoing development of the fraternal bond among violists. Membership: $50 (Regular/Institutional); $23-32 (Student); $65 (Joint AVS/Canadian); $29 (Emeritus-Age 65 plus); $60 (International).

Meetings/Conferences:
Number of non-conference events/year: 1

Publications:
AVS E-Newsletter; on-line
Journal of the American Viola Society; on-line

Membership List Available to Non-members

American Voice Input/Output Society (1981)

P.O. Box 20817
San Jose, CA 95160
Tel: (408) 323-1783 *Fax:* (408) 323-1782
E-Mail: info@avios.org
Website: avios.com
Members: 470 individuals
Staff: 3
Annual Budget: $100-250,000

Personnel:
President: K. W. Scholz
  E-Mail: bill.scholz@comcast.net
Secretary: Sara Basson
  E-Mail: sbasson@us.ibm.com
Manager, Operations: Peggie Johnson
  E-Mail: Peggie@avios.com

Historical Note:
AVIOS is dedicated to the dissemination of knowledge and material essential to speech practitioners. Members are academics, engineers, hardware manufacturers and others. Membership: $125 (Individual); $800 (Corporate).

American Volleyball Coaches Association (1981)

2365 Harrodsburg Rd.
Suite A325
Lexington, KY 40504
Tel: (859) 226-4315 *Fax:* (859) 226-4338
TollFree: (866) 544-2822
E-Mail: members@avca.org
Website: avca.org
Members: 4400 individuals
Staff: 8
Annual Budget: $2-5,000,000
Tax: 501(c)(3)

Personnel:
Executive Director: Kathy DeBoer
  E-Mail: kathy.deboer@avca.org
Specialist, Events and Education: Kali Andress
  E-Mail: kali.andress@avca.org
*Director, Membership Services, Marketing and Board
  Relations:* Ashley Beil
  E-Mail: ashley.beil@avca.org
Senior Manager, Sales: Toby Bishop
  E-Mail: toby.bishop@avca.org
Senior Director, Internal Operations: Jason Jones
  E-Mail: ashley.beil@avca.org
Manager, Communications and Editor: Jackson Silvanik
  E-Mail: jackson.silvanik@avca.org

Historical Note:
AVCA's mission is to advance the sport of volleyball and its coaches. Members are coaches from all levels who are committed to the development and advancement of volleyball throughout America. Membership: $45-345/year.

Continuing Education:
Certification Designation/s: NFHS

Meetings/Conferences:
Conference Chair: Kali Andress
2013 - Los Angeles, CA (University of California, Los Angeles)/May 2 - 4
2013 - Seatle, WA/Dec. 18 - 22
2014 - Oklahoma City, OK/Dec. 17 - 21

Publications:
At the Net; bi-weekly
Coaching Volleyball; bi-monthly
Membership directory; on-line
Volleyball Ace Power Tips; bi-weekly
VolleyBiz; monthly

American Walnut Manufacturers Association (1912)

1007 N. 725 West
West LaFayette, IN 47906-9431
Tel: (614) 923-4421 *Fax:* (614) 923-4421
Website: walnutassociation.org
Members: 11 companies
Staff: 1
Annual Budget: Under $10,000

Personnel:
Executive Director: Liz Jackson
  E-Mail: jackson@purdue.edu

Historical Note:
AWMA's purpose is to help the industry build and maintain better markets for walnut and lead in efforts to ensure proper management, and sustainability of the timber supply, of all fine hardwoods, especially walnut. Represents manufacturers of walnut and other hardwood, lumber, dimension lumber, veneer, squares and gunstock blanks. Membership: $1800/year.

Publications:
Federal Regulatory Agency Updates

American Warmblood Registry (1981)

P.O. Box 89
Amenia, NY 12501-0089
Tel: (561) 693-5516 *Fax:* (775) 667-0516
E-Mail: info@americanwarmblood.com
Website: americanwarmblood.com
Members: 400 individuals
Staff: 2
Annual Budget: $250-500,000

Personnel:
Executive Director: Jody Jackson
President: Sonja Lowenfish
  E-Mail: namsportpony@aol.com

Historical Note:
AWR's mission is to record and preserve the pedigrees of the American Warmblood Registry Sporthorses while maintaining the integrity of the breed. Membership: $75 (Individual); $800 (Lifetime).

Continuing Education:
Enrollment: 12

Publications:
Breeder's Directory; on-line
Internet-with monthly upgrades of news; monthly; adv.
Stallions Roster; annually; adv.
Warmblood Newsletter; monthly

American Watch Association (1933)

1201 Pennsylvania Ave. NW
P.O. BOX 464
Washington, DC 20044-0464
Tel: (434) 963-7773 *Fax:* (434) 963-7776
Website: americanwatchassociation.com
Members: 45 companies
Staff: 2
Annual Budget: $250-500,000

Personnel:
Executive Director: Emilio G. Collado III
Contact, Communication: Deanna Tinsley

Historical Note:
A trade association of watch importers, assemblers and manufacturers.

American Watchmakers-Clockmakers Institute (1960)

701 Enterprise Dr.
Harrison, OH 45030-1696
Tel: (513) 367-9800 *Fax:* (513) 367-1414
TollFree: (866) 367-2924
Website: awci.com
Members: 3000 individuals and institutions
Staff: 8
Annual Budget: $500-1,000,000
Tax: 501(c)(3)

Personnel:
Executive Director: James E. Lubic
  E-Mail: jlubic@awci.com
Director, Marketing and Editor: Amy Dunn
  E-Mail: adunn@awci.com
Coordinator, Membership Services: Elizabeth Janszen
  E-Mail: ejanszen@awci.com
Coordinator, Education: Daniela Ott
  E-Mail: dott@awci.com

Director, Operations: Thomas Pack CPA
    E-Mail: tpack@awci.com

Historical Note:
*Formed by the merger of the Horological Institute of
America and United Horological Association of America,
assumed present name in 2003. AWCI seeks to preserve
and promote better standards of workmanship in the
horological crafts. It sets the standard of excellence
to be applied to the quality of instruction for both the
restoration and repair practices that are taught worldwide.
Membership: $149-4,470/year.*

Continuing Education:
Enrollment: 300
Certification Designation/s: WS, WT, CMC, CMI, CW,
CMW, CC

Publications:
AWCI Referral Directory; on-line
Horological Times; monthly; adv.

American Water Resources Association *(1964)*
P.O. Box 1626
Middleburg, VA 20118-1626
Tel: (540) 687-8390 *Fax:* (540) 687-8395
E-Mail: info@awra.org
Website: awra.org
Members: 2800 individuals
Staff: 9
Annual Budget: $1-2,000,000
Tax: 501(c)(3)

Personnel:
Executive Vice President: Kenneth D. Reid CAE
    E-Mail: ken@awra.org
Coordinator, Marketing: Mary S. Ashton
    E-Mail: mary@awra.org
Technical Director: Richard A. Engberg
    E-Mail: dick@awra.org
Director, Operations: Michael J. Kowalski CAE
    E-Mail: mike@awra.org
Manager, Membership Services: Christine McCrehin
    E-Mail: christine@awra.org
Director, Publications: Charlene E. Young
    E-Mail: charlene@awra.org

Historical Note:
*AWRA's mission is to advance research, planning,
management, development and education in water
resources. Membership includes engineers, hydrologists,
biologists, attorneys, chemists and social scientists.
Membership: $165 (Individual); $500-2000 (Associate);
$30 (Student); $100 (Transitional); $25 (International
Electronic); $82.50 (Retired).*

Continuing Education:
Certification Designation/s: CEU

Meetings/Conferences: Annual
2013 - Portland, OR (Red Lion Hotel on the River-
    Jantzen Beach)/Nov. 4 - 7

Publications:
AWRA Connections
Journal of the AWRA; bi-monthly; adv.
Membership Directory; on-line
Water Resources Impact; bi-monthly; adv.

Membership List Available to Non-members

American Water Works Association *(1881)*
6666 W. Quincy Ave.
Denver, CO 80235-3098
Tel: (303) 794-7711 *Fax:* (303) 347-0804
TollFree: (800) 926-7337
Website: awwa.org
Members:
4800 organizations
49500 individuals
Staff: 48
Annual Budget: $25-50,000,000
Tax: 501(c)(3)

Personnel:
Executive Director: David B. LaFrance
    E-Mail: dlafrance@awwa.org
Deputy Executive Director, Government Affairs: Tom
    Curtis
    E-Mail: tcurtis@awwa.org
Director, Conferences and Events: April DeBaker
    E-Mail: adebaker@awwa.org
Director, Publishing: Liz Haigh
    E-Mail: lhaigh@awwa.org
Technical and Educational Council: Rick Harmon
    E-Mail: rharmon@awwa.org
Chief Information Officer: Robert Huff

    E-Mail: bhuff@awwa.org
Director, Communications: Greg Kail
    E-Mail: gkail@awwa.org
Chief Financial Officer: Kevin Mann
    E-Mail: kmann@awwa.org
Senior Manager, Membership Services: Melanie Penoyar
    E-Mail: mpenoyar@awwa.org
Senior Publications Marketing Manager: Grant Price
    E-Mail: gprice@awwa.org

Historical Note:
*Organized at Washington University, St. Louis, MO
on March 29, 1881 and incorporated in Illinois in
1912. AWWA is an international nonprofit educational
association dedicated to safe water and serves as a forum
for water professionals to share information and learn
from each other for the common good. Membership: $170
(Individual); $99 (Young Professional); $70 (Operations/
Administrative); $28 (Student).*

Meetings/Conferences:
Conference Chair: April DeBaker
2013 - San Antonio, TX (The Henry B. Gonzalez
    Convention Center)/Feb. 25 - 28
2013 - Glendale, AZ (Renaissance Phoenix Glendale
    Hotel and Spa)/March 10 - 13
2013 - Denver, CO (Colorado Convention Center)/June
    9 - 13
Number of non-conference events/year: 3

Publications:
AWWA Streamlines; bi-weekly; adv.
e-Journal AWWA; monthly; adv.
IDA Journal; quarterly; adv.
Opflow; monthly; adv.

American Waterways Operators *(1944)*
801 N. Quincy St.
Suite 200
Arlington, VA 22203
Tel: (703) 841-9300 *Fax:* (703) 841-0389
Website: americanwaterways.com
Members: 375 companies
Staff: 38
Annual Budget: $5-10,000,000

Personnel:
President and Chief Executive Officer: Thomas A.
    Allegretti
    E-Mail: tallegretti@vesselalliance.com
Vice President, Public Affairs and Communications: Anne
    Davis Burns
    E-Mail: aburns@vesselalliance.com
Vice President, Finance and Administration: Lynn M.
    Craig
    E-Mail: lcraig@vesselalliance.com
Manager, Information Technology and Training: Jayson C.
    Larner
    E-Mail: jlarner@vesselalliance.com
Senior Vice President, Regional Advocacy: Lynn M.
    Muench
    E-Mail: lmuench@vesselalliance.com
Manager, Meetings and Membership Services: Ashley M.
    Smith
    E-Mail: asmith@vesselalliance.com
Vice President, Southern Region and Federal Lobbyist:
    Mark A. Wright
    E-Mail: mark@actweb.org

Historical Note:
*AWO's mission is to promote the long term economic
soundness of the industry, enhance the industry's ability
to provide safe, efficient, and environmentally responsible
transportation, through advocacy, public information, and
the establishment of safety standards. Represents the owners
and operators of tugboats, towboats, and barges serving the
waterborne commerce of the United States. It also supports
the American Waterways Operators PAC. Membership:
$4,000 (Corporate Businesses or Partnerships); $1,350
(Sole Proprietors); $540 (Affiliate Associate).*

Meetings/Conferences: Semi-Annual
Conference Chair: Ashley M. Smith
2013 - Washington, DC (Mandarin Oriental
    Washington D.C.)/April 16 - 19
2013 - Miami, FL (Fountainebleau Hotel)/Oct. 16 - 19
Number of non-conference events/year: 1

Publications:
AWO Newsletter; semi-monthly

Membership List Available to Non-members

American Weather and Climate Industry Association *(1990)*
1015 Waterwood Pkwy.

Suite J
Edmond, OK 73034
Tel: (405) 359-0773
E-Mail: CWSA@wpa.org
Website: awcia.org
Members: 21 companies
Staff: 1
Annual Budget: Under $10,000

Personnel:
President and Chief Executive Officer: Steven A. Root
    CCM
    E-Mail: sroot@weatherbank.com

Historical Note:
*Formerly (2009) Commercial Weather Services Association.
AWCIA's mission is to save lives and protect property,
and help people prosper while running a successful
business. Membership: $250-$3500 (Regular depending
on employees); $25-$500 (Associate); $75-$1150 (Related
depending on employees).*

Publications:
Membership Directory; on-line

American Welara Pony Registry *(1981)*
P.O. Box 3309
Landers, CA 92285-0309
Tel: (760) 364-2048 *Fax:* (760) 364-2048
E-Mail: info@WelaraRegistry.com
Website: WelaraRegistry.com
Members:
217 individuals
312 businesses
Staff: 13
Annual Budget: $10-25,000

Personnel:
Registrar: John H. Collins
    E-Mail: awps@copper.net
Main Secretary: Donna Valdez

Historical Note:
*AWPS collects, records and preserves the pedigrees of
Welara ponies (a cross of Arabian horse with Welsh pony),
to publish a stud book, and to stimulate all other matters
such as may pertain to the history, breeding, exhibiting,
publicity, sale and improvement of the breed throughout the
world. Membership: $28 (Individual); $40 (Associate); $16
(Senior); $14 (Junior).*

Publications:
Breeder Directory; on-line
Introduction to the Welara CD-Rom
Registry Stud Book; biennially; adv.
Welara Journal; semi-annually; adv.
Welara Journal CD-Rom; semi-annually; adv.

American Welding Society *(1919)*
550 NW LeJeune Rd.
Miami, FL 33126
Tel: (305) 443-9353 *Fax:* (305) 443-5647
TollFree: (800) 443-9353
E-Mail: info@aws.org
Website: aws.org
Members: 55000 individuals
Staff: 119
Annual Budget: $25-50,000,000

Personnel:
Executive Director: Ray Shook
    E-Mail: rshook@aws.org
Director, Information Technology Network: Armando
    Campana
    E-Mail: acampana@aws.org
Production Manager, Publications: Zaida Chavez
    E-Mail: zaida@aws.org
Director, Marketing and Communications: Ross Hancock
    E-Mail: rhancock@aws.org
Director, Membership Services: Rhenda Mayo Kenny
    E-Mail: rhenda@aws.org
Senior Coordinator, Certification: Vivian Pupo
    E-Mail: vpupo@aws.org
Director, Convention and Meeting Services: Matthew
    Rubin
    E-Mail: mrubin@aws.org
Director, Human Resources Department: Dora Shade
Chief Financial Officer: Gesana Villegas
    E-Mail: gvillegas@aws.org

Historical Note:
*Organized as an outgrowth of the Welding Committee of the
Emergency Fleet Corporation, U.S. Shipping Board. Mission
is to advance the science, technology and application of
welding and allied joining and cutting processes, including*

brazing, soldering and thermal spraying. *Membership:*
$15-800/year.

Continuing Education:
Certification Designation/s: RI, SCWI, CWI, CWE, CRAW,
CW, CAWI, CWF, CWS, CRI

Meetings/Conferences: Annual
Conference Chair: Matthew Rubin
2013 - Monterrey, NL (Cintermex)/May 7 - 9/9000
attendees/over 100 exhibitors
2013 - Chicago, IL/Nov. 18 - 21

Publications:
American Welder; bi-annually
Product Literature Review; bi-annually
Welding Journal; monthly
Welding Marketplace; bi-annually

American White American Creme Horse Registry
(1936)
202 Blaine St.
Apartment A
Wayne, NE 68787
Tel: (402) 740-2239
E-Mail: awachr@yahoo.com
Website: awachorseregistry.com
Members: 200 individuals
Staff: 2
Annual Budget: Under $10,000

Personnel:
Contact: Sandra Rivera

Historical Note:
*Founded as the American Albino Horse Club in 1936,
became American Albino Association in 1964, and
International American Albino Association in 1985. The
Association does business as the American White/American
Creme Horse Registry. Serves as a promotional agency for
the registered breeds American White and American Creme.
Membership: $15 (domestic individual); $25(domestic
family); $30 (overseas individual).*

American Wholesale Marketers Association
(1945)
2750 Prosperity Ave.
Suite 530
Fairfax, VA 22031
Tel: (703) 208-3358 *Fax:* (703) 573-5738
TollFree: (800) 482-2962
E-Mail: info@awmanet.org
Website: awmanet.org
Members: 1500 organizations
Staff: 9
Annual Budget: $2-5,000,000
Tax: 501(c)(6)

Personnel:
President and Chief Executive Officer: Scott Ramminger
  E-Mail: scottr@awmanet.org
Manager, Membership Services: Kimberly Bolin
  E-Mail: kimberlyb@awmanet.org
Associate Publisher, Business Manager and Editor: Joan
  Fay
  E-Mail: joanf@awmanet.org
Vice President, Communications: Bob Gatty
  E-Mail: bobg@awmanet.org
Vice President, Government Affairs: Anne Holloway
  E-Mail: anneh@awmanet.org
Director, Education and Research: Meredith Kimbrell
*Director, Administration, Information Technology and
  Internet Services:* Jennifer Moulton
  E-Mail: jenniferm@awmanet.org
*Vice president, Marketing, Membership and Industry
  Affairs:* Robert Pignato IOM
  E-Mail: robertp@awmanet.org

Historical Note:
*AWMA is an international trade organization working on
behalf of convenience distributors in the United States.
Associate members include manufacturers, brokers, retailers
and others allied to the convenience product industry.
Membership: $585-4,050 (Wholesale Distributors,
dues based on number of employees); $400-3,200
(Manufacturers/Suppliers/Importers, based on annual sales
volume); $210-635 (Brokers and Sales Representatives,
dues based on number of employees); $585 (Retailers/
Foreign Distributors/Other Allied).*

Meetings/Conferences: Annual
2013 - Orlando, FL (Peabody Orlando Hotel)/March 6
  - 8
2014 - Las Vegas, NV (Paris Las Vegas)/Feb. 25 - 27
2015 - Las Vegas, NV (Paris Las Vegas)/Feb. 24 - 26
2016 - Las Vegas, NV (Paris Las Vegas)/Feb. 16 - 18

Publications:
AWMA Executive Update; weekly
Convenience Distribution
Convenience Distribution; adv.
Tobacco Newsletter weekly e-mails; weekly

Membership List Available to Non-members

American Wind Energy Association (AWEA)
(1974)
1501 M St. NW
Suite 1000
Washington, DC 20005
Tel: (202) 383-2500 *Fax:* (202) 383-2505
E-Mail: windmail@awea.org
Website: awea.org
Members: 2400 members and advocates
Staff: 11
Annual Budget: $25-50,000,000
Tax: 501(c)(6)

Personnel:
Chief Executive Officer: Denise Bode
  E-Mail: dbode@americancleanskies.com
Manager, Social Media and Online Advocacy: Lauren
  Glickman
  E-Mail: lglickman@awea.org
Senior Vice President, Public Policy: Robert Gramlich
  E-Mail: rgramlich@awea.org
Deputy Executive Director and Director, Communications:
  Tom Gray
Senior Director, Human Resources: Diane Irving
Editor and Publications Manager: Carl Levesque
  E-Mail: clevesque@awea.org
Chief Information Officer: Thad Lurie
  E-Mail: tlurie@awea.org
*Senior Vice President, Conference, Membership and
  Business Development:* Stephen Miner
  E-Mail: sminer@awea.org
Chief Financial Officer: Pam Poisson
Director, Marketing and Sales: Lori Rugh
  E-Mail: lrugh@awea.org

Historical Note:
*Mission of AWEA is to promote wind power growth through
advocacy, communication, and education. Membership:
$250-150,000/year.*

Meetings/Conferences: Semi-Annual
Conference Chair: Stephen Miner
Number of non-conference events/year: 1

Publications:
Periodicals; weekly

Membership List Available to Non-members

American Wine Society *(1967)*
P.O. Box 279
Englewood, OH 45322
Tel: (888) 297-9070 *Fax:* (937) 529-7888
Website: americanwinesociety.org
Members: 4000 individuals
Staff: 2
Annual Budget: $250-500,000
Tax: 501(c)(3)

Personnel:
Executive Director: John Hames
  E-Mail: executivedirector@americanwinesociety.org
Member Service Manager: Diane Chappell
  E-Mail: diane@americanwinesociety.org

Historical Note:
*AWS is a non-profit, educational, consumer-oriented
organization for those interested in learning more about all
aspects of wine. Members include professional and amateur
wine growers, winemakers, distributors, retailers and others
with an interest in American or foreign wines. Membership:
$25-950/year.*

Meetings/Conferences: Annual
Conference Chair: John Hames

Publications:
AWS Journal; semi-annually; adv.
AWS News; bi-monthly; adv.

American Wire Cloth Institute *(1933)*
25 N. Broadway
Tarrytown, NY 10591
Tel: (914) 332-0040 *Fax:* (914) 332-1541
E-Mail: info@wireclothinstitute.org
Website: wireclothinstitute.org
Members: 16 companies
Staff: 2

Annual Budget: $25-50,000

Personnel:
Executive Director: Richard C. Byrne

Historical Note:
*Formerly (1978) the Industrial Wire Cloth Institute. It's aim
is to establish, sustain and advocate the standards for wire
cloth sold throughout North America.*

Publications:
Members Directory; on-line; adv.

American Wire Producers Association *(1981)*
801 N. Fairfax St.
Suite 211
Alexandria, VA 22314-1757
Tel: (703) 299-4434 *Fax:* (703) 299-9233
E-Mail: info@awpa.org
Website: awpa.org
Members: 94 companies
Staff: 5
Annual Budget: $1-2,000,000
Tax: 501(c)(6)

Personnel:
Director, Meetings and Membership Services: Emily M.
  Bardach

Historical Note:
*AWPA is a result of the merger between the Independent
Wire Producers Association and the Specialty Wire
Association. The mission of the American Wire Producers
Association is to assure free access to the global supply of
Carbon, Alloy and Stainless Steel Wire Rod. AWPA provides
an educational, interactive industry forum and lobby that
supports and enhances the global competitiveness, and acts
in the best interests, of the North American wire producers.
Membership: $1,200-7,200 (Wire Companies, based on
annual rod usage); $2,000-8,100 (Supplier Companies,
based on annual rod sales).*

Meetings/Conferences: Annual
Conference Chair: Emily M. Bardach
2013 - Orlando, FL (Hilton Orlando Bonnet Creek)/Feb.
  18 - 20

Publications:
The Wire-News & Events; bi-weekly

Membership List Available to Non-members

American Woman's Society of Certified Public
Accountants *(1933)*
136 S. Keowee St.
Dayton, OH 45402
Tel: (937) 222-1872 *Fax:* (937) 222-5794
TollFree: (800) 297-2721
E-Mail: info@awscpa.org
Website: awscpa.org
Members: 2000 Individuals
Staff: 6
Annual Budget: $100-250,000
Tax: 501(c)(6)

Personnel:
Executive Director: Kimberly Fantaci
  E-Mail: info@awscpa.org

Historical Note:
*AWSCPA is a national organization dedicated to serving
all women CPAs. The AWSCPA provides a supportive
environment and valuable resources for members to
achieve their personal and professional goals through
various opportunities including leadership, networking and
education. Membership: $125 (Individual/Professional);
$30 (Student); $25 (Affiliate).*

Meetings/Conferences:
Number of non-conference events/year: 1

Publications:
AWSCPA Newsletter; quarterly; adv.
Membership Directory; on-line

American Wood Council *(1968)*
222 Catoctin Cir. SE
Suite 201
Leesburg, VA 20175
Tel: (202) 463-2766 *Fax:* (202) 463-2791
E-Mail: info@awc.org
Website: awc.org
Staff: 27
Annual Budget: $2-5,000,000
Tax: 501(c)(6)

Personnel:
President: Robert W. Glowinski
  E-Mail: robert_glowinski@afandpa.org

Executive Director, Strategic Communications: Chuck Fuqua
  E-Mail: CFuqua@awc.org
Director, Government Affairs: Suzanne Madden
  E-Mail: SMadden@awc.org
Manager, Engineering Research: Loren Ross EIT
  E-Mail: LRoss@awc.org
Vice President, Technology Transfer: John "Buddy" Showalter PE
  E-Mail: buddy_showalter@afandpa.org

Historical Note:
AWC is part of the wood products group of the American Forest & Paper Association. AWC's mission is to increase the use of wood by assuring the broad regulatory acceptance of wood products, developing design tools and guidelines for wood construction, and influencing the development of public policies affecting the use of wood products. Membership: $100 (Design Professionals in US); $150 (Outside US & Canada); $50 (Student).

Meetings/Conferences:
Number of non-conference events/year: 2

Publications:
Membership Directory; on-line

American Wood-Protection Association *(1904)*
P.O. Box 361784
Birmingham, AL 35236-1784
Tel: (205) 733-4077 *Fax:* (205) 733-4075
E-Mail: email@awpa.com
Website: awpa.com
Members: 1000 individuals
Staff: 2
Annual Budget: $250-500,000
Tax: 501(c)(6)

Personnel:
Executive Vice President: Colin McCown

Historical Note:
AWPA is an international, nonprofit, technical society founded to provide a common forum for exchange of information for all segments of the industry. The association provides a link for technical interchange between industry, research and users of treated wood. Membership: $30-160/year.

Meetings/Conferences: Annual
2013 - Honolulu, HI (Sheraton Waikiki)/April 28 - May 1

Publications:
AWPA Proceedings; annually
Membership Directory; annually

American Wool Council *(1954)*
9785 Maroon Cir., Suite 360
C/O American Sheep Industry Association
Centennial, CO 80112
Website: sheepusa.org/main/pageID/191/do/get_page
Staff: 6

Personnel:
Executive Director: Peter Orwick
  E-Mail: porwick@sheepusa.org
International Marketing Coordinator: Carole Adams
  E-Mail: carole@sheepusa.org
Project Manager, Human Resources and Finances: Zahrah Khan
  E-Mail: zahrah@sheepusa.org
Chief Financial Officer: Larry Kincaid
  E-Mail: larry@sheepusa.org
Director, Industry Information: Judy Malone
  E-Mail: judym@sheepusa.org
Deputy Director, Policy: Paul Rodgers

Historical Note:
A division of ASI, the American Wool Council works to improve the American wool industry and to promote the usage of American wool both in domestic and international markets.

American Youth Hostels, Inc (Hostelling International USA) *(1934)*
8401 Colesville Rd.
Suite 600
Silver Spring, MD 20910
Tel: (301) 495-1240 *Fax:* (301) 495-6697
Website: hiusa.org
Members: 60 Hostels
Staff: 40
Annual Budget: $500-1,000,000
Tax: 501(c)(3)

Personnel:
Chief Executive Officer: Russ Hedge
Senior Vice President, Finance and Administration: Greg Coble

Historical Note:
HIUSA is a national organization of youth hostels. A Member of the International Youth Hostel Federation. Membership: $28 (Adult); $18 (Senior); $250 (Life).

American-European Soda Ash Shipping Association *(1991)*
C/O Baker and McKenzie LLP
1114 Ave. of the Americas
New York, NY 10036-7703
Tel: (212) 626-4496 *Fax:* (212) 626-4120
Members: 6 companies
Staff: 1

Personnel:
Acting Secretary: Charles H. Critchlow

Historical Note:
AESSA members are producers of soda ash in the United States. A Webb-Pomerene Act association, AESSA promotes the export of U.S. natural soda ash to countries in the European community through the provision of joint storage, transportation and other related logistical and technical support.

American-Israel Chamber of Commerce and Industry *(1953)*
PO Box 237205
New York, NY 10023
Tel: (212) 819-0430
Website: aicci.net
Members: 300 individuals
Staff: 3
Annual Budget: $50-100,000

Personnel:
Vice President and Treasurer: Alon Gev
Vice President and General Counsel: Ron B. Sitton

Historical Note:
AICCI's purpose is to support the growth and expansion of economic relations between the U.S. and Israel and to advocate U. S. investment in Israel, Israeli exports to the U.S. and U.S. exports to Israel. Membership: $375 (Individual); $750 (Small Business); $2000 (Corporate); $2500 (Sponsor).

American-Uzbekistan Chamber of Commerce *(1993)*
39 Old Ridgebury Rd.
Danbury, CT 06810
Tel: (203) 778-9420
E-Mail: info@aucconline.com
Website: aucconline.com
Members: 60 companies and individuals
Staff: 3
Annual Budget: $50-100,000
Tax: 501(c)(6)

Personnel:
President: Timothy Y. McGraw

Historical Note:
AUCC seeks to promote trade and investment ties, cultural exchanges and bonds of friendship between the United States of America and the Republic of Uzbekistan. Membership: $3,000/year (corporate); $1,250/year (small business); $500/year (nonprofit); $100/year (professional).

Meetings/Conferences: Annual

Publications:
AUCC Newsletter; on-line

Americas Association of Cooperative/Mutual Insurance Societies *(1979)*
8400 Westpark Dr.
Second Floor
McLean, VA 22102-5116
Tel: (703) 245-8077 *Fax:* (703) 610-0211
E-Mail: info@icmifamericas.org
Website: aacmis.org
Members: 56 companies
Staff: 1
Annual Budget: $500-1,000,000

Personnel:
Executive Director: Edward L. Potter CAE

Historical Note:
Formerly the North American Association of the International Cooperative Insurance Federation and Americas Association of Cooperative/Mutual Insurance Societies. ICMIF/Americas's mission is to support and develop effective and viable co-operative, popular-based insurance organizations throughout the Americas. Membership: $500-3,000 (Full, upto net income $250,000,000); $12 per million (Full, greater than net income $250,000,000); $500 (Associate); $1000 (Observer/Supporting).

Meetings/Conferences:
2013 - Capetown, South Africa/Nov. 6 - 8
Number of non-conference events/year: 3

Amerifax Cattle Association *(1977)*
P.O. Box 149
Hastings, NE 68902
Tel: (402) 463-5289 *Fax:* (402) 463-6652
E-Mail: spa@seaplanes.org
Members: 150 individuals
Staff: 1
Annual Budget: $25-50,000

Personnel:
Executive Secretary: John F. Quirk
  E-Mail: quirk@navix.net

Historical Note:
Promotes the Amerifax breed of cattle. Maintains a herd book. Membership: $20/year; $50 initiation fee.

AMT - The Association For Manufacturing Technology *(1902)*
7901 Westpark Dr.
McLean, VA 22102-4206
Tel: (703) 893-2900 *Fax:* (703) 893-1151
TollFree: (800) 524-0475
E-Mail: AMT@AMTonline.org
Website: amtonline.org
Members: 420 companies
Staff: 60
Annual Budget: $25-50,000,000
Tax: 501(c)(6)

Personnel:
President: Douglas K. Woods
  E-Mail: dwoods@amtonline.org
Vice President, Exhibitions and Communications: Peter R. Eelman
  E-Mail: peelman@amtonline.org
Vice President, Government Relations: Paul Freedenberg
  E-Mail: PFreedenberg@AMTonline.org
Manager, Strategic Information and Research: Kathryn "Kate" E. Fritz
  E-Mail: kfritz@amtonline.org
Director, Communications: Bonnie T. Gurney
  E-Mail: bgurney@AMTonline.org
Manager, Marketing and Communications: Monica J. Haley
  E-Mail: mhaley@amtonline.org
Coordinator, Communications: Pamela K. Kachel
  E-Mail: pkachel@amtonline.org
Director, Industry Engagement: Mark Kennedy
Director, Exhibitions: John J. Krisko
  E-Mail: jkrisko@AMTonline.org
Vice President, Industry Engagement: Steve Lesnewich
  E-Mail: SLesnewich@AMTonline.org
Vice President, Strategic Information and Research: Patrick W. McGibbon
  E-Mail: pmcgibbon@amtonline.org
Vice President, Finance and Human Resources: Linda G. Montfort
  E-Mail: lmontfort@AMTonline.org
Vice President, Meetings and Conferences: Christine T. Rasul
  E-Mail: crasul@AMTonline.org
Newsletter Editor: Ruth Sharpe
  E-Mail: rsharpe@amtonline.org
Vice President, Business Development: Jeffery H. Traver
  E-Mail: jtraver@amtonline.org
Vice President, Technology: Paul R. Warndorf
  E-Mail: pwarndorf@AMTonline.org

Historical Note:
Merged with The American Machine Tool Distributors' Association in 2012. Formerly (1992) the National Machine Tool Builders Association. AMT's mission is to promote technological advancements and improvements in the design, manufacture and sale of member's products in those markets and act as an industry advocate on trade matters to governments and trade organizations throughout the world. Membership: $400-9,500/year (based on Global Shipments).

Meetings/Conferences:
Conference Chair: Christine T. Rasul

2013 - Bangalore, India (Bangalore International
    Exhibition Centre)/Jan. 24 - 30
2013 - Waikaloa, HI (Hilton Waikaloa Village)/March
    5 - 8

Publications:
Directory of Member Products; biennially
Economic Handbook of Machine Tool Industry;
    annually
Membership Directory; on-line

Amusement & Music Operators Association
(1948)
600 Spring Hill Ring Rd.
Suite 111
Dundee, IL 60118
Tel: (847) 428-7699 *Fax:* (847) 428-7719
TollFree: (800) 937-2662
Website: amoa.com
Members: 1300 companies
Staff: 4
Annual Budget: $2-5,000,000
Tax: 501(c)(6)

Personnel:
Executive Vice President: Jack Kelleher
    E-Mail: jackamoa@aol.com
Manager, Programs: Maggie Kapinos
    E-Mail: mkapinos@amoa.com
Deputy Director: Lori Schneider
    E-Mail: lschneider@amoa.com

Historical Note:
*Formerly (1977) the Music Operators of America. AMOA
is a group of companies engaged in the coin-operated
amusement industry. Members are companies making,
servicing or selling coin operated amusement, music, and
vending equipment. Membership: $1580/year (Maximum
Dues).*

Meetings/Conferences: Annual
Conference Chair: Lori Schneider
2013 - Las Vegas, NV (Las Vegas Convention Center)/
    March 20 - 22
Number of non-conference events/year: 2

Publications:
Membership Directory; annually
Off-the-Top; weekly

Amusement Industry Manufacturers and Suppliers International *(1926)*
3026 S. Orange
Santa Ana, CA 92707
Tel: (714) 425-5747 *Fax:* (714) 276-9666
E-Mail: info@aimsintl.org
Website: aimsintl.org
Members: 61 companies
Staff: 2
Annual Budget: $50-100,000

Personnel:
President: Mike Gutknecht
    E-Mail: mike@rideentertainment.com
Contact, Membership Relations: Steve Laycock
    E-Mail: steve.laycock@rides.com

Historical Note:
*Formerly (1934) Manufacturers Division, National
Association of Amusement Parks and (1997) American
Recreational Equipment Association. AIMS's mission is
continuing safety in the Amusement Industry. Membership:
$360 (Active); $100 (Associate).*

Continuing Education:
Certification Designation/s: ARI, CRI, PRI, CMT, COT,
CAOT
Meetings/Conferences:
Number of non-conference events/year: 1

Analytical and Life Science Systems Association *(1988)*
500 Montgomery St.
Suite 400
Alexandria, VA 22314
Tel: (703) 647-6214 *Fax:* (703) 647-6368
Website: alssa.org
Members: 100 companies
Staff: 3
Annual Budget: $1-2,000,000
Tax: 501(c)(6)

Personnel:
President: Michael J. Duff

Historical Note:

*ALSSA is a trade association for suppliers of instruments,
consumables, reagents, software and technology used
in analysis and measurement in chemistry and the life
sciences. Mission is to be an advocate for industry and
a valuable aid to members' global business success by
providing industry-specific meetings and networking for
senior executives, global market and business intelligence,
and insight on optimization of business strategies for
worldwide competition. Membership: $2,625- 33,000
(Regular); $5,500 (Associate).*

Meetings/Conferences: Semi-Annual
2013 - Boston, MA/April 28 - 30
Number of non-conference events/year: 1

Publications:
Membership Directory; on-line
Newsletter; monthly

Analytical Laboratory Managers Association *(1980)*
2900 High Hill Rd.
Slatington, PA 18080
E-Mail: alma@labmanagers.org
Website: labmanagers.org
Members: 450 individuals
Staff: 5
Annual Budget: $100-250,000

Personnel:
Executive Director: John Sadowski
    E-Mail: jpsadowski@ptd.net

Historical Note:
*ALMA's mission is to provide a forum for improving
laboratory management skills worldwide through through
conferences, short courses, networks, discussion groups,
and other means of sharing ideas and knowledge.
Membership: $50 (Individual); $500 (Corporate
Organizational).*

Meetings/Conferences: Annual
Number of non-conference events/year: 5

Publications:
ALMA e-News; quarterly
Membership Directory; annually
Membership List Available to Non-members

Angel Capital Association *(2004)*
10977 Granada Ln.
Suite 103
Overland Park, KS 66211
Tel: (913) 894-4700
Website: angelcapitalassociation.org
Staff: 4
Annual Budget: $250-500,000

Personnel:
Executive Director: Marianne Hudson
    E-Mail: mhudson@angelcapitalassociation.org
Manager, Member Services: Sarah Dickey
    E-Mail: sdickey@angelcapitalassociation.org
Manager, Education: Chris Major
    E-Mail: cmajor@angelcapitalassociation.org

Historical Note:
*The Angel Capital Association was formed in January 2004
and incorporated as a professional association in August
2006. ACA's mission is to fuel the success of angel groups
and private investors that invest in high growth, early-stage
ventures. Membership: $750 (Individual Investor/Groups of
up to 70); $1100 (Groups of more than 70); $2000 (Family
Offices).*

Meetings/Conferences: Annual
2013 - San Francisco, CA/April 17 - 19
Number of non-conference events/year: 1

Animal Behavior Society *(1964)*
C/O Indiana University, 402 N. Park St.
Bloomington, IN 47408
Tel: (812) 856-5541 *Fax:* (812) 856-5542
E-Mail: aboffice@indiana.edu
Website: animalbehaviorsociety.org
Members: 2200 individuals
Staff: 4
Annual Budget: $250-500,000

Personnel:
Society Manager: Shan D. Duncan
    E-Mail: sdduncan@abs.animalbehavior.org
Office Manager and Contact, Membership Services: Lori
Pierce
    E-Mail: lopierce@indiana.edu

Historical Note:

*ABS's mission is to encourage and promote the study of
animal behavior. Members are professionals and students
involved in animal behavior research. Membership: $50-80
(Regular); $40-70 (Emeritus); $25-55 (Student); $30-60
(Post Doc); $1000-1600 (Lifetime Member); $20-50
(Developing Nation Member); $15-45 (Developing Nation
Student Member).*

Meetings/Conferences: Annual
Conference Chair: Dario Maestripieri
2013 - Boulder, CO/July 28 - Aug. 1
Number of non-conference events/year: 2

Publications:
ABS Newsletter
Animal Behaviour; monthly; adv.
Membership Directory; on-line

Animal Health Institute *(1941)*
1325 G St. NW
Suite 700
Washington, DC 20005-3104
Tel: (202) 637-2440 *Fax:* (202) 393-1667
Website: ahi.org
Members: 23 companies
Staff: 11
Annual Budget: $2-5,000,000
Tax: 501(c)(6)

Personnel:
President and Chief Executive Officer: Alexander S.
Mathews
    E-Mail: amathews@ahi.org
Vice President, Administration and Finance: Carolyn S.
Ayers
    E-Mail: cayers@ahi.org
General Counsel: Dr. Kent D. McClure DVM, JD
    E-Mail: Kmcclure@ahi.org
Vice President, Legislative and Public Affairs: Ronald B.
Phillips
    E-Mail: rphillips@ahi.org

Historical Note:
*AHI is the U.S. industry trade association representing
companies that promote and encourage continuing research
and development in the area of animal health.*
Meetings/Conferences:
Number of non-conference events/year: 2

Publications:
Membership Directory; on-line

Animal Transportation Association *(1976)*
12100 Sunset Hills Rd.
Suite 130
Reston, VA 20190
Tel: (703) 234-4106 *Fax:* (703) 435-4390
E-Mail:
info@animaltransportationassociation.org
Website: animaltransportationassociation.org
Members: 560 companies and 180 individuals
Staff: 2
Annual Budget: $50-100,000
Tax: 501(c)(6)

Personnel:
Executive Director: Robin Turner
    E-Mail: rturner@drohanmgmt.com

Historical Note:
*Formerly (1989) Animal Air Transportation Association,
ATA is an international association dedicated to the safe
and humane transport of animals. Members include
transport manufacturers, carriers, and shippers animal
welfare groups and breeders, zoos and animal forwarders.
Membership: $260(Individual); $775 (Gold Corporate);
$360 (Small Business Membership); $260 (Individual/
Library/Museum/Press/Trade Association); $525
(Corporate); $150 (Academic/Government).*

Meetings/Conferences: Annual
Number of non-conference events/year: 1

Publications:
Membership Directory; on-line
Newsletters - (weekly electronic e-blast); weekly

Membership List Available to Non-members

Ankole Watusi International Registry *(1983)*
22484 W. 239 St.
Spring Hill, KS 66083-9306
Tel: (913) 592-4050
E-Mail: watusi@aol.com
Website: awir.org
Members: 86 individuals
Staff: 3

Annual Budget: $10-25,000

Personnel:
Executive Secretary: Elizabeth Lundgren

Historical Note:
AWIR's mission is to recognize Ankole-Watusi cattle as a distinct breed in order to protect their ancient and unique heritage. It also works to preserve its purity through proper breed practices. Members are breeders and fanciers of African Ankole Watusi cattle and include individuals, firms, corporations, and other entities with a common interest in the promotion, advancement and preservation of the Ankole-Watusi breed of cattle. Membership: $250 (Lifetime, Voting); $25 (Annual, Voting); $20 (Associate, Non-Voting).

Publications:
WATUSI Magazine; quarterly; adv.

Antenna Measurement Techniques Association
(1979)
19730 Magellan Dr.
Torrance, CA 90502
Website: amta.org
Members: 400 individuals
Staff: 3
Annual Budget: $100-250,000

Personnel:
President: Kim Hassett
    E-Mail: president@amta.org
Editor: Lawrence L. Mandeville
    E-Mail: newsletter@amta.org
Coordinator, Meetings: Vince Rodgriguez
    E-Mail: meeting-coordinator@amta.org

Historical Note:
AMTA's mission is to provide a forum for the exchange of information on electromagnetic measurement techniques and problems. Members are institutions and individuals concerned with the design and measurement of antennas. Membership: $30/year (Individual).

Meetings/Conferences: Annual
Conference Chair: Vince Rodgriguez

Publications:
AMTA Newsletter; quarterly
Member Directory; on-line

Antiquarian Booksellers Association of America
(1949)
20 W. 44th St.
Suite 507
New York, NY 10036
Tel: (212) 944-8291 *Fax:* (212) 944-8293
E-Mail: hq@abaa.org
Website: abaa.org
Members: 450 companies
Staff: 3
Annual Budget: $250-500,000

Personnel:
Executive Director: Susan Benne
    E-Mail: sbenne@abaa.org

Historical Note:
ABAA's mission is to encourage ethical standards and professionalism in the antiquarian book trade, to encourage the collecting and preservation of rare and antiquarian books and related materials, to support educational programs and research into the study of rare books, and to facilitate collegial relations between booksellers, librarians, scholars, and collectors. Membership: $625/year (Individual).

Meetings/Conferences:
2013 - San Francisco, CA (Concourse Exhibition Center)/Feb. 15 - 17
2013 - New York City, NY (Park Avenue Armory)/April 11 - 14

Publications:
ABAA e-Newsletter; quarterly

Antique and Amusement Photographers International
(1993)
3395 S. Jones Blvd.
Suite Four
Las Vegas, NV 89146
Tel: (860) 578-2274 *Fax:* (877) 865-1052
E-Mail: info@oldtimephotos.org
Website: oldtimephotos.org
Members: 150 companies
Staff: 3
Annual Budget: $50-100,000
Tax: 501 (c)(6)

Personnel:
Executive Director: Susan K. Crutchfield
President: Mike Glasser
    E-Mail: buffalophoto@aol.com
Accounting Manager, Secretary and Treasurer: Scott Henry

Historical Note:
AAPI specializes in antique or "old time" photography, special event photography, re-enactments and costumed portraits. Members are photography studios and photographers, primarily in the U. S. and Canada, specializing in costume photography and suppliers to the industry. Membership: $199 (Studio); $250 (Vendor/Supplier).

Continuing Education:
Certification Designation/s: AFPh, DFPh, FPh

Meetings/Conferences: Annual
2013 - Las Vegas, NV (Gold Coast Hotel and Casino)/ Feb. 5 - 7

Publications:
AAPI Directory; quarterly; adv.
AAPI Newsletter

Anxiety Disorders Association of America *(1980)*
8701 Georgia Ave.
Suite 412
Silver Spring, MD 20910
Tel: (240) 485-1001 *Fax:* (240) 485-1035
E-Mail: information@adaa.org
Website: adaa.org
Members: 1500 individuals
Staff: 10
Annual Budget: $500-1,000,000
Tax: 501 (c)(3)

Personnel:
Executive Director: Alies Muskin
Business Manager: Sarah Gerfen
Coordinator, Marketing Communications: Kate Mewhiney
Coordinator, Membership Outreach: Lisa Patterson
Meetings Consultant: Jennifer Richards
Director, Communications and Media Relations: Jean Kaplan Teichroew

Historical Note:
Formerly (1990) Phobia Society of America. ADAA is dedicated to the prevention, treatment, and cure of anxiety disorders and to improving the lives of all people who suffer from them. ADAA members include people who suffer from anxiety disorders and professionals who study and treat them. Membership: $195 (Professional); $50 (Students); $100 (Trainee/Postdoctoral Fellow/Resident).

Meetings/Conferences: Annual
Conference Chair: Jennifer Richards
2013 - La Jolla, CA (Hyatt Regency La Jolla at Aventine)/April 4 - 7
2014 - Chicago, IL (Chicago Marriott Downtown Magnificent Mile)/March 27 - 30
2015 - Miami, FL (Hyatt Regency Miami)/April 9 - 12
2016 - Philadelphia, PA (Philadelphia Marriott Downtown)/March 31 - April 3

Publications:
Anxiety News & Updates; on-line
Depression and Anxiety; monthly; adv.
Find-a-Therapist; on-line

Membership List Available to Non-members

APA The Engineered Wood Association *(1933)*
7011 S. 19th St.
Tacoma, WA 98466-5333
Tel: (253) 565-6600 *Fax:* (253) 565-7265
Website: apawood.org
Members: 152 mills
Staff: 78
Annual Budget: $5-10,000,000
Tax: 501 (c)(6)

Personnel:
President: Dennis J. Hardman
    E-Mail: help@apawood.org
Director: Tom Kositzky
    E-Mail: tom.kositzky@apawood.org
Coordinator, Tradeshows: Tanya Rosendahl
    E-Mail: tanya.rosendahl@apawood.org
Secretary and Treasurer: Kim Sivertsen
    E-Mail: Kim.sivertsen@apawood.org
Contact, Media Relations: Marilyn Thompson
    E-Mail: marilyn.thompson@apawood.org
Coordinator, Programs, Website and Publications: LaDauna Wilson

E-Mail: ladauna.wilson@apawood.org

Historical Note:
Formerly (1964) Douglas Fir Plywood Association and (1994) American Plywood Association. Mission is to work in partnership with members to develop and maintain markets through excellence in APA trademarked product promotion, quality assurance, and technical and educational support. Members are producers of plywood, oriented strandboard, and other engineered wood products.

Meetings/Conferences: Annual
Conference Chair: Tanya Rosendahl
Number of non-conference events/year: 1

Publications:
APA News Alerts; on-line
APA Publication Update; monthly
Building Code Professionals (e-Newsletter); on-line
Engineered Wood; semi-annually; adv.
Industry Newsletter; monthly
Management Report; monthly
Membership Directory; on-line

APHSA - Information Systems Management
(1930)
1133 19th St. NW
Suite 400
Washington, DC 20036
Tel: (202) 682-0100 *Fax:* (202) 289-6555
E-Mail: ismsupport@radiowire.net
Website: aphsa-ism.org
Members: 800 individuals
Staff: 33
Annual Budget: $10-25,000

Personnel:
Executive Director: Tracy Wareing
    E-Mail: tracy.wareing@aphsa.org
Director, Membership and Communications: Jerome Uher
    E-Mail: jerome.uher@aphsa.org

Historical Note:
Formerly American Association of Public Welfare Information Systems Management and a constituent unit of the American Public Welfare Association that provides administrative support. APHSA pursues improvement in health and human services by supporting state and local agencies, informing policymakers, and working with its partners to drive innovative, integrated and efficient solutions in policy and practice. Members are agencies and individuals. It has 9 affiliate organizations. Membership: $361-8,990 (Local Agency); $7500-15,000 (Industry Partnership); $3,000 (University/Academic Partner); $35-290 (Individual).

Meetings/Conferences: Annual
Conference Chair: Gloria Williams

Publications:
APHSA Membership Directory
e-News Clipping Service; on-line
NAPCWA Weekly Update; weekly
Policy & Practice; bi-monthly
This Week in Washington (when Congress is in session); weekly

Apiary Inspectors of America *(1932)*
One Natural Resources Dr.
C/O Arkansas State Plant Board
Little Rock, AR 72205
Tel: (501) 225-1598 *Fax:* (501) 219-1697
Website: apiaryinspectors.org
Members: 60 individuals
Staff: 3
Annual Budget: Under $10,000

Personnel:
President: Don Hopkins
    E-Mail: don.hopkins@ncagr.gov
Secretary: Ed Levi
    E-Mail: ed.levi@aspb.ar.gov
Treasurer: Keith Tignor
    E-Mail: keith.tignor@vdacs.virginia.gov

Historical Note:
Formerly National Apiary Inspectors. The AIA's goal is to provide accurate and helpful information for the successful management of honey bees, while seeking new information and ideas in honey bee management and plant pollination. Membership: $35 (Individual); $100 (State).

Meetings/Conferences: Annual

Publications:
Apiarist directory

APICS The Association for Operations Management *(1957)*

8430 W. Bryn Mawr Ave.
Suite 1000
Chicago, IL 60631
Tel: (773) 867-1777 *Fax:* (773) 639-3000
TollFree: (800) 444-2742
E-Mail: service@apics.org
Website: apics.org
Members:
1800 companies
33000 professionals, academics and students
Staff: 100
Annual Budget: $25-50,000,000

Personnel:
Chief Executive Officer: Abe Eshkenazi CAE
    E-Mail: aeshkenazi@apics.org
Director, Professional Development: Bob Collins
    E-Mail: bcollins@apics.org
Senior Vice President and General Counsel: Dean
    Martinez
Contact, Media: Jane Pearson
    E-Mail: jpearson@apics.org
Executive Vice President: Sharon Rice

Historical Note:
*Formerly (1997) the American Production and Inventory
Control Society and then APICS - The Educational Society
for Resource Management; assumed current name on
January 1, 2005. APICS's mission is to build knowledge
and skills in operations management professionals to
enhance and validate abilities and accelerate careers.
Membership: $25-200/year.*

Continuing Education:
Certification Designation/s: CSCP, CIRM, CFPIM, CPIM,
APICS

Meetings/Conferences: Annual
Number of non-conference events/year: 2

Publications:
APICS e-News; semi-monthly
APICS magazine; bi-monthly; adv.
P&IM Journal

Membership List Available to Non-members

APMI International (1959)
105 College Rd., East
Princeton, NJ 08540-6992
Tel: (609) 452-7700 *Fax:* (609) 987-8523
E-Mail: apmi@mpif.org
Website: mpif.org/apmi/index_frame.html
Members: 2600 individuals
Staff: 4
Annual Budget: $250-500,000
Tax: 501(c)(3)

Personnel:
Executive Director and Chief Executive Officer: C. James
    Trombino CAE
Director and Technical Services: James P. Adams
    E-Mail: jadams@mpif.org
Editor: Dora L Schember
    E-Mail: dschember@mpif.org
Contact, Membership Services: Susan Wright CMP, CAE
    E-Mail: swright@mpif.org

Historical Note:
*Formerly (1994) American Powder Metallurgy Institute.
APMI is a nonprofit, professional society serving the
technical and informational needs of individuals interested
or involved in the science and art of powder metallurgy.
The association consists of professionals from all industries
who recognize the significance of powder metallurgy and
particulate materials as a modern metalworking process.
Membership: $105 (Member-U.S, Canada and Mexico);
$125 (Member- Overseas); $25 (Student-Full time); $40
(Student-Overseas).*

Continuing Education:
Certification Designation/s: PMT

Meetings/Conferences: Annual
Conference Chair: James P. Adams
Number of non-conference events/year: 30

Publications:
International Journal of Powder Metallurgy; bi-
    monthly; adv.

APPA - Leadership in Educational Facilities
(1914)
1643 Prince St.
Alexandria, VA 22314
Tel: (703) 684-1446 *Fax:* (703) 549-2772
Website: appa.org
Members: 5200 individuals

Staff: 12
Annual Budget: $2-5,000,000

Personnel:
Executive Vice President: E. Lander Medlin
    E-Mail: lander@appa.org
*Specialist, Information Technology, Web Services and
    Facilities:* Karen Aguilar
    E-Mail: karen@appa.org
Associate Vice President: John F. Bernhards
    E-Mail: john@appa.org
Chief Financial Officer: Chong-Hie Choi
    E-Mail: choi@appa.org
Manager, Accounting: William J. D'Costa
    E-Mail: william@appa.org
Manager, Publications: Anita Dosik
    E-Mail: anita@appa.org
Director, Knowledge Management: Steve Glazner
    E-Mail: steve@appa.org
Director, Professional Development: Suzanne M. Healy
    E-Mail: suzanne@appa.org
Manager, Membership and Outreach: Santianna Stewart
    E-Mail: santianna@appa.org

Historical Note:
*Organized originally as the Association of Superintendents
of Buildings and Grounds, the association later became the
Association of Physical Plant Administrators of Universities
and Colleges. In 1991, the name APPA: The Association of
Higher Education Facilities Officers was adopted to reflect
increased higher education-based campus responsibilities.
In 2005, the association focused on APPA, the letters
only, adding the tag line "serving educational facilities
professionals". In 2007, a new logo and tagline introduced
representing APPA's new brand personality. The name
remained as APPA, the letters only, and the new tagline
is "Leadership in Educational Facilities". APPA works to
support educational excellence with quality leadership and
professional management through education, research,
and recognition. Members are accredited non-profit
institutions of higher education with an independent
facilities department, and university or college systems
offices which supervise the physical plants of two or more
campuses. Membership: $190-2,260/year (based on
enrollment and gross institutional expenditures).*

Continuing Education:
Enrollment: 5000
Certification Designation/s: CEFP, EFP

Meetings/Conferences: Annual
Conference Chair: Suzanne M. Healy

Publications:
APPA E-Newsletter; bi-weekly
Membership Directory; on-line

Appaloosa Horse Club (1938)
2720 W. Pullman Rd.
Moscow, ID 83843
Tel: (208) 882-5578 *Fax:* (208) 882-8150
E-Mail: marketing@appaloosa.com
Website: appaloosa.com
Members: 17775 individuals
Staff: 12
Annual Budget: $2-5,000,000
Tax: 501(c)(5)

Personnel:
Chief Executive Officer: Steve Taylor
Show Secretary: Klancy Allen
Director, Appaloosa Journal Advertising: Hannah
    Hathaway
*Director, Marketing, Public Relations and Regional Club
    Coordinator:* Merida McClanahan
    E-Mail: mmcclanahan@appaloosa.com
Supervisor, Information Technology: Dave O'Keefe
*Treasurer and Supervisor, Data and Mail Processing and
    Supervisor, Membership Services:* Tina Rea
    E-Mail: membership@appaloosa.com

Historical Note:
*ApHC is the international breed registry serving ApHC
members and Appaloosa enthusiasts by recording and
preserving the horses' heritage and history, and by
providing services that promote, enhance and improve the
Appaloosa. Membership: $10-500/year.*

Meetings/Conferences: Annual
Conference Chair: Klancy Allen
Number of non-conference events/year: 1

Publications:
ApHC E-Newsletter; monthly
Appaloosa Journal; monthly
Appaloosa Journal Online Xpress (AJOX); on-line
Handbook of the Appaloosa Horse Club; annually
Racing Industry Directory; on-line

Membership List Available to Non-members

APPAM - The Association for Public Policy Analysis and Management (1979)
1029 Vermont Ave. NW
Suite 1150
Washington, DC 20005
Tel: (202) 496-0130 *Fax:* (202) 496-0134
E-Mail: appam@appam.org
Website:
appam.org
appam.org/
Members:
2000 individuals
104 institutions
Staff: 3
Annual Budget: $1-2,000,000
Tax: 501(c)(3)

Personnel:
Executive Director: Tara Sheehan
    E-Mail: tsheehan@appam.org
Coordinator, Membership and Business: Candace Escobar
    E-Mail: appam.office@appam.org
Program and Conference Coordinator: Jocelyn Mason
    E-Mail: jmason@appam.org

Historical Note:
*APPAM is dedicated to improving public policy and
management by fostering excellence in research, analysis,
and education. Membership in the association is open
to individuals and institutions. Membership: $70-125
(Individual); $35 (Student); $2,000 (Institution).*

Meetings/Conferences: Annual
Conference Chair: Jocelyn Mason
2013 - Washington, DC (Washington Marriott)/Nov. 7
    - 9
2014 - Albuquerue, NM (Albuquerque Convention
    Center)/Nov. 6 - 8

Publications:
Individual Directory Search (Membership Directory);
    on-line
Journal of Policy Analysis and Management; quarterly;
    adv.
Organization Directory Search (Membership
    Directory); on-line

Membership List Available to Non-members

Apparel Graphics Institute (1989)
58 Boston Dr.
Suite 1000
Ocean Pines, MD 21811
Tel: (410) 641-7300
E-Mail: mark@shopworx.com
Members: 600 individuals
Staff: 7

Personnel:
President: Mark L. Venit
    E-Mail: mark@shopworx.com

Historical Note:
*Formerly (1995) Apparel Decorators Association
International. AGI serves constituents in the apparel
graphics industry, including textile screen printers,
embroiderers and apparel retailers, as well as manufacturers
and distributors of garments, apparel decorating equipment
and supplies.*

Apple Processors Association (1987)
1666 K St. NW
Suite 260
Washington, DC 20006
Tel: (202) 785-6715 *Fax:* (202) 331-4212
E-Mail: info@agriwashington.org
Website: appleprocessors.org
Members:
25 companies
90 individuals
Staff: 3
Annual Budget: $100-250,000
Tax: 501(c)(6)

Personnel:
President: Paul S. Weller Jr.
Senior Director, Meetings and Administration: Andrea Ball
    Siok
    E-Mail: aball@agriwashington.org

Historical Note:
*APA is a national association of companies that
manufacture quality apple products from whole apples.
Members are apple grower/processor cooperatives and*

companies, and suppliers to the industry. Membership: $3,000-12,000 (Based on Sales); $3,500 (Suppliers of goods and/or services); $7,500 (Sustaining members); $15,000 (Brokers and Traders).

Meetings/Conferences: Annual
Conference Chair: Andrea Ball Siok
2013 - Palm Coast, FL (Hammock Beach Resort)/June 16 - 18
Number of non-conference events/year: 1

Publications:
APA Gram; bi-annually
APA News Notes; monthly

Apple Products Research and Education Council (1951)
1100 Johnson Ferry Rd.
Suite 300
Atlanta, GA 30342
Tel: (404) 252-3663 Fax: (404) 252-0774
E-Mail: info@appleproducts.org
Website: appleproducts.org
Members: 80 companies
Staff: 5
Annual Budget: $100-250,000

Personnel:
Contact, Communications: Allison Parker MS, RD

Historical Note:
Formerly the Processed Apples Institute, is a coalition of U.S.-based producers of processed apple products. APREC's mission is to join in appropriate collective efforts to profitably produce and market apples and apple products. Members are producers of processed apple products, suppliers of equipment, packaging or ingredients to the apple processing industry, brokers and concentrate manufacturers.

Appliance Parts Distributors Association (1937)
3621 N. Oakley Ave.
Chicago, IL 60618
Tel: (773) 230-9851 Fax: (888) 308-1423
Website: apda.com
Members: 66 companies
Staff: 2
Annual Budget: $100-250,000

Personnel:
Executive Vice President: Rosemary Jacobshagen CAE
E-Mail: RO@apda.com

Historical Note:
Formerly Appliance Parts Jobbers Association. APDA's mission is to create stronger relationships between industry stakeholders, to assume a key role in supporting service initiatives in order to enhance the consumer experience and to promote the development of processes and technology critical to the industry. Membership: $1,300/year.

Publications:
Membership Directory; on-line

Application Developers Alliance (2012)
1025 F St. NW
Suite 720
Washington, DC 20004
Website: appdevelopersalliance.org
Members: 4545 corporate members
Staff: 6

Personnel:
President: Jonathan Potter
Director, Membership Services: Laura Bolos
Director, Technology: Chris Green
Director, Marketing: Chelsea Larson
Senior Advisor, Law and Policy: Tim Sparapani
Senior Vice President, Communications: Jake Michael Ward

Historical Note:
A nonprofit services organization dedicated to supporting app developers of every type, across all languages and platforms. Anyone who creates software or is invested in bringing great ideas to market can be a member of the Apps Alliance. Membership: $50.

Applied Research Ethics National Association (1974)
126 Brookline Ave.
Suite 202
Boston, MA 02215-3920
Tel: (617) 423-4112 Fax: (617) 423-1185
E-Mail: info@primr.org
Website: primr.org
Members: 875 individuals

Staff: 15
Annual Budget: Under $10,000

Personnel:
Executive Director: Joan Rachlin JD, MPH
E-Mail: jrachlin@primr.org
Manager, Membership: Joanna Cardinal
E-Mail: jcardinal@primr.org
Manager, Accounts: David Carter
E-Mail: dcarter@primr.org
Senior Director, Program and publication: Amy L. Davis JD, MPH
E-Mail: adavis@primr.org
Assistant Director, Conferences: Mariellen Diemand
E-Mail: mdiemand@primr.org
Manager, Marketing and Communication Design: Catherine Rogers
E-Mail: crogers@primr.org

Historical Note:
PRIM&R has served the full array of individuals and organizations involved in biomedical, social science, behavioral, and educational research.Members include professionals from around the world responsible for overseeing the use of human and animal research subjects, including administrators, government officials, and academic department chairs. PRIM&R's mission is to advance the highest ethical standards in the conduct of biomedical, social science, behavioral, and educational research.Membership: $165 (Individual); $65 (Student/Retired/International).

Meetings/Conferences: Annual
Conference Chair: Mariellen Diemand
2013 - Baltimore, MD/March 18 - 19
2013 - Boston, MA/Nov. 7 - 9
2014 - Ft. Washington, MD/Dec. 5 - 7
2015 - Boston, MA/Nov. 13 - 15
2017 - Ft. Washington, MD/Dec. 1 - 3

Publications:
Journal of Empirical Research on Human Research Ethics (JERHRE).
Member Directory; on-line
PRIM&R Newsletter; monthly

Appraisal Foundation (1987)
1155 15th St. NW
Suite 1111
Washington, DC 20005
Tel: (202) 347-7722 Fax: (202) 347-7727
E-Mail: info@appraisalfoundation.org
Website: appraisalfoundation.org
Staff: 6
Annual Budget: $2-5,000,000

Personnel:
President: David S. Bunton
E-Mail: david@appraisalfoundation.org
Director, Finance and Administration: Cathy Johnson
E-Mail: cathy@appraisalfoundation.org
Manager, Publications and Programs: Mavis E. Kleso
E-Mail: mavis@appraisalfoundation.org
Staff Accountant: Edna Nkemgnu
E-Mail: edna@appraisalfoundation.org
Specialist, Information Technology: Abhilash Rajan
E-Mail: abhilash@appraisalfoundation.org
Executive Administrator: Paula Douglas Seidel
E-Mail: paula@appraisalfoundation.org

Historical Note:
The Appraisal Foundation is dedicated to promoting professionalism and ensuring public trust in the valuation profession. This is accomplished through the promulgation of standards, appraiser qualifications, and guidance regarding valuation methods and techniques.

Meetings/Conferences:
Conference Chair: Mavis E. Kleso

Publications:
Foundation eNews
Organization Directory; on-line
Q&A Newsletter

Appraisal Institute (1932)
200 W. Madison
Suite 1500
Chicago, IL 60606
Tel: (312) 335-4100 Fax: (312) 335-4400
TollFree: (888) 756-4624
E-Mail: aiservice@appraisalinstitute.org
Website: appraisalinstitute.org
Members: 24000 individuals
Staff: 100
Annual Budget: $10-25,000,000

Tax: 501(c)(6)

Personnel:
Chief Executive Officer: Frederick H. Grubbe
E-Mail: aiceo@appraisalinstitute.org
Director, Marketing and Member Resources: Hope Atuel
E-Mail: hatuel@appraisalinstitute.org
Director, Human Resources: Sheila Barnes
E-Mail: sbarnes@appraisalinstitute.org
Manager, Meeting Services: Paula Cappelletti CMP
E-Mail: pcappelletti@appraisalinstitute.org
Director, Communications: Ken Chitester
E-Mail: kchitester@appraisalinstitute.org
Senior Manager, Education Delivery: Jimmy Driskill
E-Mail: jdriskill@appraisalinstitute.org
Senior Programmer: Rick Hrubec
E-Mail: rhrubec@appraisalinstitute.org
General Counsel and Professional Resources: Jeff Liskar
E-Mail: jliskar@appraisalinstitute.org
Director, Information Technology: David May
E-Mail: dmay@appraisalinstitute.org
Senior Manager, Publications: Tep Shea-Joyce
E-Mail: tshea-joyce@appraisalinstitute.org
Director, Education Resources: Sue Siradas
E-Mail: ssiradas@appraisalinstitute.org
Supervisor, Accounting: Yolanda Smith
E-Mail: ysmith@appraisalinstitute.org
Senior Manager, Marketing: Kerry Spaedy
E-Mail: kspaedy@appraisalinstitute.org
Chief Financial Officer: Bill Zimmermann
E-Mail: bzimmermann@appraisalinstitute.org

Historical Note:
Mission is to advance professionalism and ethics, global standards, methodologies, and practices through the professional development of property economics worldwide. Membership: $40 (Student Affiliate); $20 (College student); $110 (Trainee Associate); $205 (Affiliate); $310 (Associate).

Continuing Education:
Certification Designation/s: SRA, MAI, SRPA

Meetings/Conferences:
Conference Chair: Paula Cappelletti CMP
Number of non-conference events/year: 10

Publications:
Appraiser Directory; on-line
Appraiser News Online (ANO); on-line
Residential Update; monthly
The Appraisal Journal; quarterly
Valuation; quarterly
Valuation Magazine; quarterly

Appraisers Association of America (1949)
386 Park Ave. South
Suite 2000
New York, NY 10016
Tel: (212) 889-5404 Fax: (212) 889-5503
E-Mail: aaa@appraisersassoc.org
Website: appraisersassoc.org
Members: 800 individuals
Staff: 6
Annual Budget: $250-500,000
Tax: 501(c)(6)

Personnel:
Executive Director: Aleya Lehmann-Bench
Design & Communications Coordinator: Vanessa Garver
Programs Manager: Lauren Gewolb
Programs, Services Coordinator: Elizabeth Huff
Assistant Director, Membership Services: Tiffany W. Niem
Manager, Membership Services: Rachel E. Talentino

Historical Note:
The mission and primary purpose of the Appraisers Association of America is to develop and promote standards of excellence in the profession of appraising through education and the application of the highest form of professional practice, which results in enhancing the visibility and standing of appraisers within the private and professional communities in which they serve. It is primarily composed of personal property appraisers. Membership: $525 (Individual/Certified Member); $100 (Friend); $75 (Student).

Meetings/Conferences: Annual
Conference Chair: Lauren Gewolb

Publications:
AAA NEWS
E-vents; weekly
Membership Directory; on-line

Membership List Available to Non-members

APSE: The Network on Employment (1988)

416 Hungerford Dr.
Suite 418
Rockville, MD 20850
Tel: (301) 279-0060 *Fax:* (301) 279-0075
Website: apse.org
Staff: 6
Annual Budget: $500-1,000,000

Personnel:
Executive Director: Laura A. Owens
    E-Mail: lowens@apse.org
Administrative Assistant: Marlyn Barrow
    E-Mail: marlyn@apse.org
Membership Associate: Cindi Clark
    E-Mail: cindi@apse.org
Communications/Membership Director: Jenny Levet
    E-Mail: jenny@apse.org

Historical Note:
A non-profit association promoting employment for individuals with disabilities. APSE's mission is to provide advocacy and education concerning the value of integrated employment, address issues to expand the growth and implementation of integrated employment services. $25-105 (based on annual income) $250 (Contributing Member); $500 (Sustaining Member); $700 (Basic Business Member); $900 (Contributing Business Member) $1500 (Gold Business Member).

Meetings/Conferences: Annual
2013 - Indianapolis, IN (JW Marriott)/June 25 - 27

Publications:
The Journal of Vocational Rehabilitation
theAdvance; annually

Aquacultural Engineering Society *(1993)*
C/O Terry Rakestraw, Virginia Tech -0418
Blacksburg, VA 24061
Tel: (540) 231-6805 *Fax:* (540) 231-9293
E-Mail: aquaengsociety@yahoo.com
Website: aesweb.org
Members: 250 individuals
Staff: 3
Annual Budget: $25-50,000
Tax: 501(c)(6)

Personnel:
Administrator: Terry T. Rakestraw
    E-Mail: rakestra@vt.edu

Historical Note:
AES serves as an authoritative source of information on aquacultural engineering and provides engineering support to initiatives from or for the aquaculture industry. AES members are aquacultural engineers and others with an interest in the field. Membership: $30-80/year (General).

Meetings/Conferences: Annual

Publications:
AES Newsletter; quarterly; adv.
Aquacultural Engineering; adv.
Membership Directory; annually

Aquarium and Zoo Facilities Association
3900 Wildlife Way
Cleveland, OH 44109
Website: azfa.org
Staff: 3

Personnel:
President: David Jarvis
    E-Mail: jarvis@stlzoo.org
Secretary: Katie Olsen
    E-Mail: olsen@stlzoo.org
Treasurer: Mike Patera
    E-Mail: map@clevelandmetroparks.com

Historical Note:
AZFA is dedicated to increasing the understanding and appreciation of the inherent worth of all life forms. Membership: $26 (Professional); $16 (Student); $103 (Commercial/Organizational); $21 (Associate).

Meetings/Conferences: Annual

Publications:
Membership Directory; on-line
The Outlet

Aquatic Plant Management Society, Inc. *(1961)*
P.O. Box 821265
Vicksburg, MS 39182-1265
Fax: (601) 634-2398
Website: apms.org
Members: 600 individuals
Staff: 3
Annual Budget: $250-500,000

Tax: 501(c)(5)

Personnel:
President: Terry Goldsby
    E-Mail: terryg@aquaservicesinc.com
Editor: Rob Richardson
    E-Mail: rob_richardson@ncsu.edu
Treasurer: Sherry Whitaker
    E-Mail: sherry.l.whitaker@usace.army.mil

Historical Note:
APMS's purpose is to promote environmental stewardship through operations, research, education and outreach related to integrated management of vegetation in aquatic systems. Membership reflects diversity of federal, state, and local agencies, universities and colleges around the world, corporations, and small businesses. Membership: $75 (Individual); $20 (Student); $500 (Sustaining).

Meetings/Conferences: Annual
Number of non-conference events/year: 5

Publications:
APMS Newsletter
Aquatic Plant News
Journal of Aquatic Plant Management; annually
Member Directory

Arabian Horse Association *(1950)*
10805 E. Bethany Dr.
Aurora, CO 80014
Tel: (303) 696-4500 *Fax:* (303) 696-4599
E-Mail: info@arabianhorses.org
Website: arabianhorses.org
Members: 40,000 members
Staff: 45
Annual Budget: $5-10,000,000
Tax: 501(c)(5)

Personnel:
President: Lance Walters
    E-Mail: lance.walters@arabianhorses.org
Secretary: Jan Decker
    E-Mail: jandecker1@sbcglobal.net
Senior Director, Marketing: Dan Lawrence

Historical Note:
Merged with the Arabian Horse Registry of America (founded 1908) and the International Arabian Horse Association (founded 1950) and incorporated in the year 2003. AHA's mission is to promote the growth in the interest in, and demand for the Arabian, Half-Arabian and Anglo-Arabian horse and preservation of the integrity of the breed. Membership: $25 (Adult); $20 (Youth); $55 (Business); $1,000 (Life).

Meetings/Conferences: Annual

Publications:
AHA e-News; on-line
Modern Arabian Horse Magazine

Membership List Available to Non-members

Archaeological Institute of America *(1879)*
656 Beacon St.
Sixth Floor
Boston, MA 02215-2006
Tel: (617) 353-9361 *Fax:* (617) 353-6550
E-Mail: aia@aia.bu.edu
Website: archaeological.org
Members: 250,000 individuals
Staff: 30
Annual Budget: $5-10,000,000
Tax: 501(c)(3)

Personnel:
Chief Executive Officer and Publisher: Peter R. Herdrich
    E-Mail: pherdrich@aia.bu.edu
Specialist, Communications: Lynette Aznavourian
    E-Mail: laznavourian@aia.bu.edu
Administrator, Membership Services and Societies: Deanna Baker
    E-Mail: dbaker@aia.bu.edu
Director, Conferences and Event Planning : Andri Cauldwell
    E-Mail: acauldwell@aia.bu.edu
Coordinator, Governance: Aimee Fairclough
    E-Mail: afairclough@aia.bu.edu
Director, Development: Jennifer Klahn
    E-Mail: jklahn@aia.bu.edu
Chief Operating Officer and Publisher: Kevin Quinlan
    E-Mail: kquinlan@aia.bu.edu

Historical Note:
AIA's mission is to promote archaeological inquiry and public understanding of the material record of the human past worldwide, and is committed to preserve the world's

archaeological resources and cultural heritage for the benefit of people. Membership: $30-135 (Students/ Educators/Active Military Personnel); $60-270 (Basic).

Meetings/Conferences: Annual
Conference Chair: Andri Cauldwell
2013 - Seattle, WA (Washington State Convention Center)/Jan. 3 - 6
Number of non-conference events/year: 9

Publications:
AIA Newsletter
ARCHAEOLOGY Magazine
Journal of Archaeology

Archery Range and Retailers Organization *(1981)*
156 N. Main St.
Suite D
Oregon, WI 53757
Tel: (608) 835-9060 *Fax:* (608) 835-9360
TollFree: (800) 234-7499
E-Mail: lynn@archeryretailers.com
Website: archeryretailers.com
Members: 130 companies
Staff: 4
Annual Budget: $50-100,000

Personnel:
Administrative Director and Executive Secretary: Lynn Stiklestad
    E-Mail: lynn@archeryretailers.com

Historical Note:
Formerly (1980) the Archery Lane Operators Association, ARRO is a cooperative buying association that is comprised of archery retail professionals. ARRO is a national organization of professional full time archery ranges and pro shops. Membership: $400/year (Company).

Meetings/Conferences: Annual
2013 - Louisville, KY/Jan. 5 - 6
Number of non-conference events/year: 1

Publications:
Directory

Archery Trade Association *(1946)*
101 N. German, Suite Three
P.O. Box 70
New Ulm, MN 56073
Tel: (507) 233-8130 *Fax:* (507) 233-8140
TollFree: (866) 266-2776
E-Mail: info@archerytrade.org
Website: archerytrade.org
Members: 700 companies
Staff: 12
Annual Budget: $2-5,000,000
Tax: 501(c)(6)

Personnel:
Contributing Editor: Patrick Durkin

Historical Note:
Founded as the Archery Manufacturers and Dealers Association, later named as Archery Manufacturers Organization in 1965 and assumed present name in 2002. ATA is the organization for manufacturers, retailers, distributors, sales representatives and others working in the archery and bowhunting industry. Dedicated to making the industry profitable by decreasing business overhead, reducing taxes and government regulation, and increasing participation in archery and bowhunting. Members are producers and sellers to the archery consumer including manufacturers, distributors, sales representatives, dealers and the archery media. Membership: $200-2,000 (Regular); $100 (Manufacturer's Supplier/International Distributor/Sales Representative/Basic Manufacturer); $200-600 (Regular Distributor); $50-600 (Retail); $200 (Supporting/Media).

Meetings/Conferences: Annual
Conference Chair: Maria Lewis
2013 - Louisville, KY (Kentucky Exposition Center)/Jan. 7 - 9
Number of non-conference events/year: 3

Publications:
e-Insight; monthly
Membership Directory; annually

Architectural Engineering Institute *(1998)*
1801 Alexander Bell Dr.
Reston, VA 20191-4400
Tel: (703) 295-6300 *Fax:* (703) 295-6222
TollFree: (800) 548-2723
E-Mail: aei@asce.org
Website: aeinstitute.org
Members: 8000 individuals

Staff: 2
Annual Budget: $100-250,000
Tax: 501(c)(3)

Personnel:
Manager: Jennifer Balsley PE
E-Mail: jbalsley@asce.org

Historical Note:
AEI's purpose is to serve the building community by promoting an integrated, multi-disciplinary approach to planning, design, construction and operation of buildings and by encouraging excellence in practice. Membership: $0-100 (Associate); $100 (Affiliate); $205 (ASCE/AEI); $750- 2,000 (Corporate); Free for Student.

Continuing Education:
Certification Designation/s: BSCP

Meetings/Conferences: Annual
2013 - State College, PA (Pennsylvania State University)/April 3 - 5
Number of non-conference events/year: 1

Publications:
Means, Methods & Trends Magazine; quarterly
The Team; bi-monthly

Architectural Precast Association (1966)
6710 Winkler Rd.
Suite Eight
Ft. Myers, FL 33919
Tel: (239) 454-6989 Fax: (239) 454-6787
E-Mail: info@archprecast.org
Website: archprecast.org
Members: 100 companies
Staff: 2
Annual Budget: $250-500,000
Tax: 501(c)(6)

Personnel:
Executive Director: Fred L. McGee
Project Manager and Event Planner: Cari Renfro

Historical Note:
APA's mission is to serve the international, technical and business needs of architectural precast concrete manufacturers and their suppliers and to provide standard workmanship throughout the industry . Membership: $5,600-7,100 (Producer-based on gross sales); $1,500 (Associate); $750 (Professional).

Continuing Education:
Certification Designation/s: APAPCP

Meetings/Conferences: Annual
Conference Chair: Cari Renfro
Number of non-conference events/year: 1

Publications:
Membership Directory; on-line
The Architectural Precaster; quarterly; adv.

Architectural Woodwork Institute (1953)
46179 Westlake Dr.
Suite 120
Potomac Falls, VA 20165-5874
Tel: (571) 323-3636 Fax: (571) 323-3630
E-Mail: info@awinet.org
Website: awinet.org
Members: 4000 individuals
Staff: 12
Annual Budget: $2-5,000,000
Tax: 501(c)(6)

Personnel:
Executive Vice President: Philip Duvic
E-Mail: pduvic@awinet.org
Project Manager: Katie Allen
E-Mail: kallen@awinet.org
Manager, Marketing and Membership Services: Cassey Gibson
E-Mail: cgibson@awinet.org
Chief Learning Officer: Greg Heuer
E-Mail: gheuer@awinet.org
Planner, Meetings and Events: Beth Holcomb
E-Mail: bholcomb@awinet.org
Contact, Sponsor and Advertisement Sales: Cheryl Stratos
E-Mail: adsales@awinet.org
Manager, Accounting: Barbara Wert
E-Mail: bwert@awinet.org

Historical Note:
Incorporated in Chicago, Illinois in 1954. AWI promotes the architectural woodwork industry and provides educational programs, publications and information, marketing opportunities, career skills, and technical advice to both members and the industry. Members consist of architectural woodworkers, suppliers, design professionals

and students from around the world. Membership: $600-2,400 (Manufacturer); $700-1,100 (Supplier); $75 (Affiliate); $20 (Student).

Continuing Education:
Certification Designation/s: QCP, QCC

Meetings/Conferences: Annual
Conference Chair: Cheryl Stratos
Number of non-conference events/year: 2

Publications:
AWI NewsBriefs; monthly
Design Solutions Magazine; quarterly; adv.
e-brief; semi-monthly
Membership Directory; on-line; adv.

Membership List Available to Non-members

Archivists and Librarians in the History of the Health Sciences (1975)
1216 Fifth Ave.
New York, NY 10029
Tel: (212) 822-7313
Website: alhhs.org
Members: 220 individuals
Staff: 3
Annual Budget: Under $10,000

Personnel:
President: Christopher Lyons
E-Mail: christopher.lyons@mcgill.ca
Editor: Stephen E. Novak
E-Mail: sen13@columbia.edu
Treasurer: Arlene Shaner
E-Mail: ashaner@nyam.org

Historical Note:
Formerly (1992) the Association of Librarians in the History of the Health Sciences. ALHHS's mission is to serve the professional interests of librarians, archivists, and other specialists actively engaged in the librarianship of the history of the health sciences by promoting the exchange of information and by improving standards of service. Members are librarians & archivists with responsibility for history of health science collections. Membership: $15 (Domestic); $21 (Overseas).

Meetings/Conferences: Annual
2013 - Atlanta, GA/May 15 - 16

Publications:
The Watermark; quarterly

Argentine-American Chamber of Commerce (1919)
630 Fifth Ave.
25th Floor, Rockefeller Center
New York, NY 10111
Tel: (212) 698-2238 Fax: (212) 698-2239
E-Mail:
argentinechamber@argentinechamber.org
Website: argentinechamber.org
Members: 450 companies
Staff: 3
Annual Budget: Under $10,000

Personnel:
Executive Director: Claudia Schaefer-Farre
Treasurer: Joseph Prikazky

Historical Note:
AACC provides its members with a unique source of contacts and updates information about Argentina; organizes quality events, and give its members the opportunity to meet not only with key business professionals of both countries but also with government officials and other individuals shaping bilateral relations. Members are American companies doing business with Argentina and Argentine companies with activities in the United States. Membership: $475 (Individual); $850 (Corporate); $1500 (Sponsor); $5000 (Patron).

Publications:
Membership Directory

ARMA International (2000)
11880 College Blvd.
Suite 450
Overland Park, KS 66210
Tel: (913) 341-3808 Fax: (913) 341-3742
TollFree: (800) 422-2762
E-Mail: hq@arma.org
Website: arma.org
Members: 11000 individuals
Staff: 33
Annual Budget: $5-10,000,000

Personnel:

Executive Director: Marilyn Bier CAE
Senior Manager, Education: Jacki Conn
Specialist, Communications: Mallorie Dautenhahn
Director, Administration: Connie Hardy
E-Mail: connieh@arma.org
Director, Information Technology: Dusty Kline
Managing Editor: Amy Lanter
Director, Member Services: Trevor Mitchell CAE
Senior Director, Marketing and Sales: Jeff Randolph
E-Mail: jrandolph@arma.org
Senior Application Developer: Scott Simon
Coordinator, Membership Services: Julie Tesch
Director, Government Relations and GARP Outreach: Bob Tillman
E-Mail: btillman@arma.org
Director, Publications: Vicki Wiler
Senior Manager, Conferences: Wanda Wilson

Historical Note:
Founded as American Records Management Association. Absorbed Association of Records Executives and Administrators and became Association of Records Managers and Administrators in 1985; assumed its current name in 2000. Mission is to educate, advocate, provide resources, and set standards that enable professionals to govern information as a critical element of organizational value. ARMA International develops and publishes standards and guidelines related to records management. Membership: $175 (Individual); $25 (Student).

Continuing Education:
Certification Designation/s: RIM, CRM

Meetings/Conferences: Annual
Conference Chair: Wanda Wilson
2013 - New York City, NY (Hilton New York)/Jan. 29 - 31

Publications:
Canadian Policy Brief; monthly
Global Policy Brief; monthly
Information Management Journal; bi-monthly; adv.
Marketing RIMinder
NewsWire; monthly
Washington Policy Brief; monthly

Armed Forces Broadcasters Association (1982)
P.O. Box 447
Sun City, CA 92586-0447
Tel: (951) 672-7299 Fax: (951) 679-5484
Members: 600 individuals
Staff: 1
Annual Budget: Under $10,000

Personnel:
President: Mary Carnes

Historical Note:
Enhances camaraderie among former, present, and future members of the military broadcasting community; provides employment search assistance. Membership: $20/year.

Armed Forces Communications and Electronics Association (1946)
4400 Fair Lakes Ct.
Fairfax, VA 22033-3899
Tel: (703) 631-6100 Fax: (703) 631-6169
TollFree: (800) 336-4583
E-Mail: service@afcea.org
Website: afcea.org
Members: 11000 corporate associates and 21, 400 corporate members and individuals
Staff: 6
Annual Budget: $10-25,000,000
Tax: 501(c)(6)

Personnel:
President and Chief Executive Officer: Kent Schneider
Vice President, Publications and Knowledge Sharing: Beverly Cooper
Vice President, Chief Information Officer and Chief Technology Officer: James L. Griggs Jr.
Executive Vice President, Chief Financial Officer: Pat Miorin CPA
Executive Vice President: Becky Nolan
Vice President, Human Resources: Nancy Temple

Historical Note:
Originated as the Army Signal Association. Name changed to Armed Forces Communications Association in 1948; assumed its current name in 1954. AFCEA's mission is to increase knowledge through the exploration of issues relevant to its members in information technology, communications, and electronics for the defense, homeland security and intelligence communities. Membership: $35

(Individual); $400-700 (Individual Life); $350-4,800 (Corporate).

Meetings/Conferences:
2013 - Washington, DC (Defense Intelligence Analysis Center)/April 17 - 18

Publications:
Cybersecurity Directory; on-line
Health IT Directory; on-line
Intelligence Directory; on-line
Membership Directory; on-line
SIGNAL Connections; bi-monthly; adv.
SIGNAL Magazine; monthly; adv.

Armed Forces Financial Network *(1985)*
11601 Roosevelt Blvd.
TA-94
St. Petersburg, FL 33716
Tel: (727) 227-2880 *Fax:* (727) 227-5773
E-Mail: info@affn.org
Website: affn.org
Staff: 7

Personnel:
President and Chief Executive Officer: David O. Weber
E-Mail: david.weber@affn.org
Treasurer: Roland A. Arteaga
E-Mail: aarteaga@cuna.com

Historical Note:
AFFN is a joint venture of Association of Military Banks and Defense Credit Union Council. AFFN's mission is to increase the versatility of participating financial institutions to better serve the U.S. Military. Members are financial institutions who wish to serve the military community.

Publications:
AFFN NEWS; on-line

Armed Forces Optometric Society *(1970)*
P.O. Box 261511
Plano, TX 75026-1511
Tel: (214) 533-0227
E-Mail: execdir@afos2020.org
Website: afos2020.org
Members: 800 individuals
Staff: 1
Annual Budget: $250-500,000
Tax: 501(c)(6)

Personnel:
Executive Director: Gina Borgognoni
E-Mail: flossdaily@juno.com

Historical Note:
AFOS's mission is to advance, enhance, and improve the eye care of designated federal services health care beneficiaries given by optometrists in federal service; to provide a forum for these optometrists; to improve the art and science of the practice of optometry and to elevate the standards of the practice. Membership: $45-100 (Active, based on years of services); $40 (Associate); $15 (Student); $250 (Retired Lifetime Member).

Publications:
AFOS News; quarterly
Member directory; on-line

Armed Forces Special Agents Association
P.O. Box 13001
Arlington, VA 22219
E-Mail: contact@afsaa.org
Website: afsaa.org
Staff: 1
Annual Budget: Under $10,000

Personnel:
President: David Glendinning

Historical Note:
Comprised of people who are either currently serving or previously served as special agents in the branches of the United States Armed Forces, including the Army Criminal Investigation Command (CID), Naval Criminal Investigative Service (NCIS), Air Force Office of Special Investigations (OSI) and the Coast Guard Investigative Service (CGIS). Membership: $15/year (associate), $30/year (regular).

Arms Control Association *(1971)*
1313 L St. NW
Suite 130
Washington, DC 20005
Tel: (202) 463-8270 *Fax:* (202) 463-8273
E-Mail: aca@amrscontrol.org
Website: armscontrol.org
Staff: 9
Annual Budget: $1-2,000,000

Tax: 501(c)(3)

Personnel:
Executive Director: Daryl G. Kimball
E-Mail: dkimball@armscontrol.org
Director, Research: Tom Collina
E-Mail: tcollina@armscontrol.org
Program Associate: Tim Farnsworth
Editor: Daniel Horner
Finance Officer: Merle Lee Newkirk

Historical Note:
A national membership organization advocating public education on arms control and disarmament. ACA provides policy-makers, the press and the interested public with authoritative information, analysis and commentary on arms control proposals, negotiations and agreements, and related national security issues. Membership: $70 (Regular/U.S only); $35 (Student); $100 (International/ Contributing); $250 (Supporting); $500 (Leadership).

Meetings/Conferences: Annual
Conference Chair: Tim Farnsworth

Publications:
Arms Control Today; monthly; adv.

Army Aviation Association of America *(1957)*
755 Main St.
Suite 4D
Monroe, CT 06468-2830
Tel: (203) 268-2450 *Fax:* (203) 268-5870
E-Mail: aaaa@quad-a.org
Website: quad-a.org
Members: 14500 individuals
Staff: 12
Annual Budget: $2-5,000,000

Personnel:
Executive Director: William R. Harris Jr.
Vice President, Membership Services: Mark W. Grapin

Historical Note:
AAAA's mission is to support the United States Army Aviation Soldier and Family. Quad-A represents active and retired U.S. Army aviators and defense contractors. Membership: $26 (Individual); $15 (Student); $475-975 (Industry); $150-480 (Life).

Meetings/Conferences:
Number of non-conference events/year: 12

Publications:
Army Aviation Magazine; monthly; adv.

Art and Antique Dealers League of America *(1926)*
P.O. Box 2066
Lenox Hill Station
New York, NY 10021
Tel: (212) 879-7558 *Fax:* (212) 772-7197
E-Mail: secretary@artantiquedealersleague.com
Website: artantiquedealersleague.org
Members: 110 dealers
Staff: 3
Annual Budget: $1-2,000,000

Personnel:
President: Clinton Howell
Executive Director and Secretary: David Mayer
Treasurer: Susan Kaplan Jacobson

Historical Note:
Member of the International Art Dealers Confederation (CINOA Confederation International des Negociantes en Oeuvres d'Art). AADLA's purpose is to bring the various members of the art and antiques trade closer together to promote understanding among themselves and with the public.

Publications:
Membership Directory; on-line

The Arts and Creative Materials Institute, Inc. *(1936)*
1280 Main St., Second Floor
P.O. Box 479
Hanson, MA 02341-0479
Tel: (781) 293-4100 *Fax:* (781) 294-0808
E-Mail: debbief@acminet.org
Website: acminet.org
Members: 210 companies
Staff: 5
Annual Budget: $500-1,000,000
Tax: 501(c)(6)

Personnel:
Executive Vice President: Deborah M. Fanning CAE
E-Mail: debbief@acminet.org

Director, Membership Services: Becky J. Beaudoin
Associate Director: Deborah S. Gustafson
E-Mail: debbieg@acminet.org
Director, Certification: Debbie J. Munroe
E-Mail: debbiem@acminet.org
Legal Counsel: Martin J. Neville Esq.
E-Mail: mjneville@verizon.net

Historical Note:
Formerly (1983) the Crayon, Water Color and Craft Institute and Art and Craft Materials Institute (1994). Members are makers of art and craft products. ACMI assist its members in providing the public with art and creative materials for children and artists that are non-toxic. It also seeks to provide leadership, guidance and education to individuals, organizations, and the society to achieve greater participation in art and creative. Membership: based on annual sales of products eligible for the certification program $775-44,325 (Active Member/Subscriber); $500 (Associate).

Publications:
Institute Items; monthly
List of Certified Products; quarterly
Member Directory; quarterly

Membership List Available to Non-members

Art Dealers Association of America *(1962)*
205 Lexington Ave.
Suite 901
New York, NY 10016
Tel: (212) 488-5550 *Fax:* (646) 688-6809
E-Mail: adaa@artdealers.org
Website: artdealers.org
Members: 175 galleries
Staff: 6
Annual Budget: $1-2,000,000

Personnel:
Executive Director: Linda Blumberg
Director, Administration: Patricia L. Brundage
Vice President, Administrative Services and Counsel: Gilbert S. Edelson
E-Mail: adaa@artdealers.org
Director, Communications: Lily A. Mitchem

Historical Note:
ADAA seeks to uphold the standards of connoisseurship, scholarship and ethical practice within the profession. Membership in ADAA is by invitation of the Board of Directors.

Meetings/Conferences: Annual
2013 - New York City, NY (Park Avenue Armory)/ March 6 - 10

Publications:
Membership Directory; on-line

Art Directors Club *(1920)*
106 W. 29th St.
New York, NY 10001
Tel: (212) 643-1440 *Fax:* (212) 643-4266
E-Mail: info@adcglobal.org
Website: adcglobal.org
Members: 500 Members
Staff: 15
Annual Budget: $2-5,000,000

Personnel:
Executive Director: Ignacio Oreamuno
Coordinator, Membership: Ariel Adkins
Director, Communication and Content: Brianna Graves
Director, Operations: Olga Grisaitis
Manager, Information: Kim Hanzich
Director, Awards Programs: Jen Larkin Kuzler
Contact, Media Relations: Jack Mello
E-Mail: jack.mello@gmail.com
Director, Education: Brendan Watson

Historical Note:
ADC produces a wide range of programs on advertising, design, and interactive media for professionals, students, and others with a serious interest in visual communications. It encourages students to explore the field of visual communications with year-round educational events. Membership: $225 (Professionals); $175 (Non Resident/ International); $100 (Young Professional); $75 (Platinum Student); $35 (Basic Student); $1,500 -10,000 (Corporate).

Continuing Education:
Certification Designation/s: ADCNS

Publications:
ADC Newsletter

Art Directors Guild/Scenic, Title and Graphic Artists (1960)
11969 Ventura Blvd.
Second Floor, Suite 200
Studio City, CA 91604
Tel: (818) 762-9995 *Fax:* (818) 762-9997
Website: artdirectors.org
Members: 1879 individuals
Staff: 35
Annual Budget: $2-5,000,000

Personnel:
Executive Director: Scott Roth
    E-Mail: scott@artdirectors.org
Director, Education and Training: Casey Bernay
    E-Mail: casey@artdirectors.org
Editor and Contact, Member Services and Website Services:
    Christian McGuire
    E-Mail: christian@artdirectors.org
Accountant: Nicole Oeuvray
    E-Mail: nicole@artdirectors.org
Manager, Activities, Events and Gallery 800: Debbie
    Patton
    E-Mail: debbie@artdirectors.org
Manager, Membership Department: Alexandra Schaaf
    E-Mail: alex@artdirectors.org
Director, Operations: Lydia Zimmer
    E-Mail: lydia@artdirectors.org

Historical Note:
Founded as the Society of Motion Picture Art Directors; became (1960) Society of Motion Picture and Television Art Directors and assumed its current name in 1999. ADG/STGA comprises the Art Directors Guild and the Scenic, Title and Graphic Artists. ADG/STA is part of the International Alliance of Theatrical Stage Employees and Moving Picture Machine Operators of the U.S. and Canada. Members are creatives in the motion picture industry, responsible for settings, props, backgrounds, and related areas.

Meetings/Conferences:
Conference Chair: Debbie Patton

Art Glass Association (1986)
P.O. Box 2537
Zanesville, OH 43702-2537
Tel: (740) 450-6547 *Fax:* (661) 264-5277
TollFree: (866) 301-2421
Website: artglassassociation.info
Members: 890 manufacturers and retailers
Staff: 6
Annual Budget: $10-25,000

Personnel:
Chairman: Bill Bird
    E-Mail: bbird@artglassassociation.com
Secretary: Craig Bradley
    E-Mail: craigb@artglassassociation.com
Director, Membership Services: Vickie Gillespie
    E-Mail: vicki@stainedglassnews.com

Historical Note:
Formerly (2003) Art Glass Suppliers Association International. AGA is the trade association of the art, decorative glass and ceramics industry and it seeks to create awareness, knowledge and involvement for the growth and prosperity of the art glass industry. Members are retailers, wholesalers, studios of art glass and suppliers. Membership: $35 (Associate); $125 (Professional); $300 (Patron); $500 (Benefactor).

Publications:
News Blasts; on-line
Newsletter; quarterly

Art Libraries Society of North America (1972)
7044 S. 13th St.
Oak Creek, WI 53154
Tel: (414) 768-8000 *Fax:* (414) 768-8001
TollFree: (800) 817-0621
E-Mail: info@arlisna.org
Website: arlisna.org
Members: 1000 individuals
Staff: 5
Annual Budget: $250-500,000
Tax: 501(c)(3)

Personnel:
Manager, Association and Conferences: Guadalupe
    Rodriguez
    E-Mail: g.rodriguez@arlisna.org
Editor, Web Site: Nedda H. Ahmed
    E-Mail: nedda@gsu.edu

Manager, Membership: Nicole Cheever
    E-Mail: n.cheever@arlisna.org
Association Specialist: Karen Olsen
    E-Mail: k.olsen@arlisna.org

Historical Note:
The mission of ARLIS/NA is to foster excellence in art and design librarianship and image management. Membership: $120 (Individual); $90 (Introductory); $50 (Student); $60 (Retired/Unemployed).

Meetings/Conferences: Annual
Conference Chair: Guadalupe Rodriguez
2013 - Pasadena, CA (Sheraton Pasadena Hotel)/April
    25 - 29

Publications:
Art Documentation; semi-annually
Membership Directory; on-line

Art Therapy Credentials Board (1993)
Three Terrace Way
Suite B
Greensboro, NC 27403-3660
Tel: (336) 482-2856 *Fax:* (336) 482-2852
TollFree: (877) 213-2822
E-Mail: atcb@nbcc.org
Website: atcb.org
Members: 4000 individuals
Staff: 1
Annual Budget: $250-500,000

Personnel:
Executive Director: Rita Maloy

Historical Note:
ATCB's mission is to protect the public by promoting the competent and ethical practice of art therapy. Membership: $100 (Annual); $65 (Maintenance).

Continuing Education:
Certification Designation/s: ATR, ATR-BC, ATCS

Publications:
ATCB Review

Arthroscopy Association of North America (1982)
6300 N. River Rd.
Suite 104
Rosemont, IL 60018-4228
Tel: (847) 292-2262 *Fax:* (847) 292-2268
E-Mail: info@aana.org
Website: aana.org
Members: 2500 individuals
Staff: 17
Annual Budget: $5-10,000,000
Tax: 501(c)(3)

Personnel:
Executive Director: Edward A. Goss
    E-Mail: ed@aana.org
Director, Meetings and Exhibits: Holly R. Albert
    E-Mail: holly@aana.org
Administrative Assistant: Marge Blahut
    E-Mail: marge@aana.org
Coordinator, Education and Meetings: Lauren Bouchard
    E-Mail: lauren@aana.org
Director, Education: Susan Carlson Ed, MS
    E-Mail: susan@aana.org
Director, Information Systems: Tiffiny J. Duensing
    E-Mail: tiffiny@aana.org
Director, Membership Services: Donna K. Nikkel
    E-Mail: donna@aana.org
Editor-in-Chief: Gary G. Poehling MD
    E-Mail: poehling@wfubmc.edu

Historical Note:
AANA's mission is to promote, encourage, support and foster through continuing medical education functions, the development and dissemination of knowledge in the discipline of arthroscopic surgery. Membership: $645 (Active); $50(Inactive); $85 (International); $100 (Student/Graduate Associate).

Meetings/Conferences: Annual
Conference Chair: Holly R. Albert
2013 - San Antonio, TX/April 25 - 27
2014 - Hollywood, FL/May 1 - 3
2015 - Los Angeles, CA/April 23 - 25
2016 - Boston, MA/April 14 - 16
Number of non-conference events/year: 2

Publications:
Arthroscopy, The Journal of Arthroscopic & Related
    Surgery
Inside AANA

Membership List Available to Non-members

Arthur W. Page Society (1983)
317 Madison Ave.
Suite 1607
New York, NY 10017
Tel: (212) 400-7959 *Fax:* (347) 474-7399
Website: awpagesociety.com
Members: 400 members
Staff: 6
Annual Budget: $1-2,000,000

Personnel:
President: Roger Bolton
    E-Mail: rbolton@awpagesociety.com
Vice President, Member Engagement: Mary Elliott
    E-Mail: melliott@awpagesociety.com
Director, Communications: Anuneha S. Mewawalla
    E-Mail: amewawalla@awpagesociety.com
Director, Professional Development and Communities:
    Daniel Strouhal
    E-Mail: dstrouhal@awpagesociety.com

Historical Note:
Arthur W. Page Society's mission is to strengthen the management policy role of the corporate public relations officer by providing a continuous learning forum and by emphasizing the highest professional standards. Membership: $1395 (Individual/Non Profit and Government); $595 (Educator).

Meetings/Conferences: Annual
Conference Chair: Daniel Strouhal

Publications:
Membership Directory; on-line

Artist Rights Society (1987)
536 Broadway
Fifth Floor
New York, NY 10012
Tel: (212) 420-9160 *Fax:* (212) 420-9286
E-Mail: info@arsny.com
Website: arsny.com
Staff: 11

Personnel:
President: Dr. Theodore H. Feder
    E-Mail: tfeder@arsny.com
Associate Counsel: Adrienne Fields
    E-Mail: afields@arsny.com
Director, Permissions and Contact, Membership: Janet
    Hicks
    E-Mail: jhicks@arsny.com
Accounts Manager: Katie Mishler

Historical Note:
Non-profit organization created to protect the rights of illustrators and fine artists. ARS is the preeminent copyright, licensing, and monitoring organization for visual artists in the United States. Artists Rights Society is a member of the International Confederation of Societies of Authors and Composers, also known by its French acronym, CISAC. Membership: Free.

Artist-Blacksmiths' Association of North America (1973)
259 Muddy Fork Rd.
Jonesborough, TN 37659
Tel: (423) 913-1022 *Fax:* (423) 913-1023
E-Mail: centraloffice@abana.org
Website: abana.org
Members: 5000 individuals
Staff: 3
Annual Budget: $250-500,000
Tax: 501(c)(3)

Personnel:
Central Office Administrator: JoAnn F. Bentley
    E-Mail: centraloffice@abana.org

Historical Note:
ABANA works to encourage and facilitate the training of blacksmiths. Members are professional blacksmiths, artists and others with an interest in blacksmithing techniques and the education of the craft. Membership: $55 (Regular); $50 (Senior, 65 + years); $45 (Student/Library); $150 (Contributory); $65 (Foreign); $250 (Educational Institution).

Meetings/Conferences: Annual
2013 - Lumpkin, GA (Columbus Ga Convention Center
    & Westville Village)/March 15 - 17

Publications:
Hammer's Blow; quarterly; adv.
The Anvil's Ring; quarterly; adv.

Membership List Available to Non-members

ArtTable (1980)
137 Varick St.
Suite 402
New York, NY 10013
Tel: (212) 343-1735 *Fax:* (866) 363-4188
E-Mail: membership@arttable.org
Website: arttable.org
Members: 1700 women
Staff: 7
Annual Budget: $250-500,000

Personnel:
Co-President: Jennifer Rissler
Vice President, Governance: Sally Block
Vice President, Membership: Stefanie Fedor
Manager, Programs: Karolyn Hatton
    E-Mail: khatton@arttable.org
Vice President, Communications: Kellie Honeycutt
Director, Development and Special Events: Laura Meli
    E-Mail: lmeli@arttable.org
Interim Treasurer: Lisa Podos

Historical Note:
ArtTable is dedicated to the visual arts and to advancing women's leadership in the field. Members are women in all stages of their careers who exemplify leadership in the administration, business, finance, management, promotion, scholarship and stewardship of the visual arts. Membership: $100-350 (Regular); $350 (Sponsor); $500 (Patron); $1,000 (Benefactor); $2,500 (Sustaining); $100 (Retired).

Meetings/Conferences:
Conference Chair: Laura Meli

Asbestos Cement Product Producers Association (1972)
P.O. Box 2227
Arlington, VA 22202-9227
Tel: (703) 560-2980 *Fax:* (703) 560-2981
E-Mail: ica@chrysotile.com
Members: 10 companies
Staff: 1
Annual Budget: Under $10,000
Tax: 501(c)(6)

Personnel:
Treasurer: Bob J. Pigg

Historical Note:
Formerly (1989) the Association of Asbestos Cement Pipe Producers, and (1996) the Asbestos Cement Pipe Producers Association. An international association incorporated in Pennsylvania in 1972. Represents international manufacturers of asbestos-cement products.

AscdiNatd (2012)
131 NW First Ave.
Delray Beach, FL 33444
Tel: (561) 266-9440 *Fax:* (561) 431-6302
Website: natd.com
Members: 175 companies
Staff: 4
Annual Budget: $250-500,000
Tax: 501(c)(6)

Personnel:
President: Joseph Marion
    E-Mail: jmarion@ascdi.com
Office Manager: Gail Goldstein
    E-Mail: ggoldstein@ascdi.com
Director, Meetings: Ruth Marion
    E-Mail: rmarion@natd.com

Historical Note:
Formerly (1994) the National Association of Telecommunications Dealers, merged with the Association of Service and Computer Dealers International in 2012 to form AscdiNatd. AscdiNatd represents its members through promotion and enforcement of professional business practices and by providing information, services and education to its members, the industry and the public. Membership: $900/year.

Meetings/Conferences: Quarterly
Conference Chair: Ruth Marion
2013 - Hong Kong, China/Jan. 23 - 25
2013 - Nashville, TN/March 6 - 8
2013 - Venice, Italy/June 19 - 21
Number of non-conference events/year: 2

Publications:
Membership Directory; annually; adv.
NATD Newsletter; monthly

Membership List Available to Non-members

Aseptic Packaging Council (1989)
2120 L St. NW
Suite 400
Washington, DC 20037
Tel: (202) 478-6158 *Fax:* (202) 478-0104
TollFree: (800) 277-8088
Website: aseptic.org
Members: 2 companies
Staff: 3
Annual Budget: $100-250,000
Tax: 501(c)(6)

Personnel:
Executive Vice President: Erich Parker

Historical Note:
Members are producers of drink-boxes and other aseptic (plastic-coated paper) products.

ASFE/The Geoprofessional Business Association (1969)
8811 Colesville Rd.
Suite G106
Silver Spring, MD 20910
Tel: (301) 565-2733 *Fax:* (301) 589-2017
E-Mail: info@asfe.org
Website: asfe.org
Members: 300 companies and 2000 branch offices
Staff: 6
Annual Budget: $1-2,000,000

Personnel:
Executive Vice President: John P. Bachner
    E-Mail: john@asfe.org
Director, Programs: Kristen Dineen
    E-Mail: kristen@asfe.org
Manager, Membership Services: Suzy Ford
    E-Mail: suzy@asfe.org
Director, Membership and Organizational Relations:
    Colleen Harper CAE
    E-Mail: colleen@asfe.org
Director, Operations: Sarah Lanning
    E-Mail: sarah@asfe.org

Historical Note:
Formerly (1975) the Associated Soil and Foundation Engineers, (1987) Association of Soil and Foundation Engineers, and assumed its current name in 1993. ASFE purpose is to help geoprofessionals maximize their importance and value to the marketplace, achieve business excellence, and manage risk. Membership: $550-11,900/ year based on their firm's applicable gross annual revenue.

Meetings/Conferences: Tri-annual
Conference Chair: Kristen Dineen
2013 - Englewood, CO (Inverness Hotel and
    Conference Center)/Jan. 25 - 26
2013 - Isle of Palms, SC (Wild Dunes Resort)/April 25
    - 27
2013 - Boston, MA (Boston Marriott Copley Place)/
    Oct. 10 - 12

Publications:
ASFE Resource Directory; on-line
NewsLog - Newsletter; bi-monthly

Membership List Available to Non-members

Asia America MultiTechnology Association (1979)
Three W. 37th Ave.
Suite 19
San Mateo, CA 94403-4470
Tel: (650) 350-1124 *Fax:* (650) 738-1486
E-Mail: aama@aamasv.com
Website: aamasv.com
Members:
10000 individuals
2000 companies
Staff: 3
Annual Budget: $100-250,000
Tax: 501(c)(6)

Personnel:
Executive Director: Tina Wang
Marketing Manager: Jaymee Liu
Board of Director: Michael C. Wu

Historical Note:
Formerly (2002) known as Asian American Manufacturers Association. AAMA is dedicated to the Asian American high-tech community. Having deep roots and a wide reach in the local silicon valley community and across pacific rim countries, as well as a proven track record of success as a silicon valley-based organization. Members manufacturer high technology computer-related products. Membership: $25 (Student); $100 (Individual); $1000 (Lifetime/Bronze Corporate); $2,000 (Silver Corporate);

$3,000 (Gold Corporate); $4,000 (Platinum Corporate); $5,000 (Diamond Corporate).

Meetings/Conferences:
Number of non-conference events/year: 1

Publications:
AAMA News; monthly

Membership List Available to Non-members

Asian American Convenience Stores Association (2005)
13014 N. Dale Mabry
Suite 109
Tampa, FL 33618
Tel: (813) 960-7429 *Fax:* (813) 908-1601
E-Mail: aacsai@aol.com
Website: aacsa.org
Staff: 2

Personnel:
Executive Director: Paul Rock
    E-Mail: aacsaprocessing@yahoo.com
President: Satya Shaw

Historical Note:
Represents the Asian American convenience retailing industry and assists retail members in increasing their current and future effectiveness and profitability. AACSA's mission is to provide knowledge, solutions and connections needed by the industry. International Retail Membership is open to all non-US convenience Stores and Petroleum marketing companies. Membership: $100/Store Owner/ year (Domestic Retail/International Retail).

Meetings/Conferences: Annual
Number of non-conference events/year: 5

Publications:
AACSA Magazine

Asian American Hotel Owners Association (1989)
7000 Peachtree Dunwoody Rd. NE
Building Seven
Atlanta, GA 30328
Tel: (404) 816-5759 *Fax:* (404) 816-6260
TollFree: (888) 692-2462
E-Mail: info@aahoa.com
Website: aahoa.com
Members: 9700 members
Staff: 15
Annual Budget: $5-10,000,000
Tax: 501(c)(6)

Personnel:
President: Fred Schwartz
    E-Mail: fred@aahoa.com
Director, Membership Services: Jonathan Albano
    E-Mail: jonathan@aahoa.com
Director, Meetings and Conventions: Jennifer Altman
    E-Mail: jennifer@aahoa.com
*Vice President, Fair Franchising, Government Affairs and
    General Counsel:* Laura Lee Blake
    E-Mail: lauralee@aahoa.com
Manager, Public Relations and Communications: Chris
    Carlson
    E-Mail: chris@aahoa.com
Office Manager: Fay Jacobson
    E-Mail: fay@aahoa.com
Director, Business Development: James Jenkins
    E-Mail: james@aahoa.com
Editor: Dan Marcec
    E-Mail: dmarcec@francepublications.com
Manager, Accounts: Laarni V. Mata
    E-Mail: laarni@aahoa.com

Historical Note:
Promote and protect the interests of members by inspiring excellence through programs and initiatives in advocacy, industry leadership, professional development, membership benefits, and community involvement. Membership:

Continuing Education:
Certification Designation/s: CHO

Meetings/Conferences:
Conference Chair: Jennifer Altman
2013 - Houston, TX (George R. Brown Convention
    Center)/March 26 - 29
Number of non-conference events/year: 1

Publications:
AAHOA Lodging Business Magazine

Asian American Journalists Association (1981)
Five Third St.
Suite 1108
San Francisco, CA 94103

Tel: (415) 346-2051 *Fax:* (415) 346-6343
E-Mail: national@aaja.org
Website: aaja.org
Members: 1400 individuals
Staff: 5
Annual Budget: $1-2,000,000
Tax: 501(c)(3)

Personnel:
Executive Director: Kathy Chow
   E-Mail: kathyc@aaja.org
Manager, Chapter Development and Membership Services:
   Antonio M. Salas MA
   E-Mail: antonios@aaja.org
Coordinator, Events and Fundraising: Annabelle A. Udo-O'Malley
   E-Mail: events@aaja.org
Coordinator, Student Programs: Nao Vang
   E-Mail: programs@aaja.org

Historical Note:
AAJA's mission is to provide encouragement, information, advice and scholarship assistance to Asian American and Pacific Islander students who aspire to professional journalism careers. Members are journalists who work as executives, reporters, editors, writers, photographers, producers, technicians and directors in news or news-oriented public affairs departments of print or broadcast companies. Members also include one time professional journalists and non- newsroom employers and students. Membership: $65 (Full/Associate); $25 (Retired/Student); $100 (Gold); $750 (Platinum Full/Platinum Associate); $1,500 (Corporate).

Meetings/Conferences: Annual
Conference Chair: Annabelle A. Udo-O'Malley

Publications:
AAJA Newsletter; quarterly; adv.
AAJA Online; weekly
Membership Roster; on-line

Asian American Psychological Association *(1972)*
Department of Psychology, N563 Elliot Hall
University of Minnesota, 75 E. River Rd.
Minneapolis, MN 55455
Tel: (612) 625-6357
E-Mail: aapainquiries@gmail.com
Website: aapaonline.org
Members: 400 individuals
Staff: 5
Annual Budget: Under $10,000
Tax: 501(c)(3)

Personnel:
President: Richard M. Lee PhD
   E-Mail: richlee@umn.edu

Historical Note:
AAPA's mission is to provide a network and forum for member psychologists and psychology professionals. Members are faculty, students, researchers, and practitioners interested in Asian American psychology. Membership: $6-70/year.

Meetings/Conferences: Annual

Publications:
Asian American Journal Of Psychology
Membership Directory; on-line
The Asian American Psychologist; adv.

Membership List Available to Non-members

Asian Pacific American Labor Alliance, AFL-CIO *(1992)*
815 16th St. NW
Washington, DC 20006
Tel: (202) 508-3733 *Fax:* (202) 508-3716
E-Mail: apala@apalanet.org
Website: apalanet.org
Staff: 5
Annual Budget: $250-500,000
Tax: 501(c)(5)

Personnel:
Executive Director: Gregory A. Cendana
   E-Mail: gcendana@apalanet.org
Coordinator, Membership and Chapter: Diana Bui
   E-Mail: dbui@apalanet.org
Director, Political: Gloria T. Caoile
   E-Mail: gtcaoile@cox.net

Historical Note:
APALA plays a unique role in addressing the workplace issues of union members and act as the bridge between the broader labor movement and the APA community.

Publications:

APALA e-Newsletter; on-line

Asian Women in Business *(1995)*
42 Broadway
Suite 1748
New York, NY 10004
Tel: (212) 868-1368 *Fax:* (877) 686-6870
E-Mail: info@awib.org
Website: awib.org
Members: 500 members
Staff: 6
Annual Budget: $250-500,000
Tax: 501(c)(3)

Personnel:
President: Bonnie Wong
Treasurer: Nancy Yieh

Historical Note:
AWIB assists women who are seeking information, education and networking opportunities to start or expand their businesses and provides technical assistance and support to entrepreneurs. Membership: $50 (Student); $175 (Individual); $275 (Sustaining); $500 (Small Business) $1,000 (Corporate); $5,000 (Patron); $15,000 (Benefactor).

Meetings/Conferences:
Number of non-conference events/year: 1

Publications:
AWIB E-Newsletter
AWIB Membership Directory; on-line

Asian/Pacific American Librarians Association *(1980)*
P.O. Box 1669
Goleta, CA 93116-1669
Tel: (805) 893-8067
Website: apalaweb.org
Members: 219 individuals
Staff: 2
Annual Budget: $10-25,000
Tax: 501(c)(3)

Personnel:
Executive Director: Buenaventura "Ven" Basco
   E-Mail: Buenaventura.Basco@ucf.edu
Treasurer: Shoko Tokoro
   E-Mail: stokoro@uncc.edu

Historical Note:
Formerly affiliated with American Library Association. APALA's mission is to provide vehicle whereby Asian/Pacific American librarians can cooperate with other associations and organizations having similar or allied interests. Members are librarians and other information specialists of Asian/Pacific heritage. Membership: $30 (Individual); $15 (Retiree/Library Support Staff); $10 (Student); $350 (Life); $60 (Institutional); $200 (Corporate).

Meetings/Conferences: Annual

Publications:
APALA Newsletter; adv.

Membership List Available to Non-members

ASIS International *(1955)*
1625 Prince St.
Alexandria, VA 22314-2818
Tel: (703) 519-6200 *Fax:* (703) 519-6299
E-Mail: asis@asisonline.org
Website: asisonline.org
Members: 37000 individuals
Staff: 103
Annual Budget: $25-50,000,000
Tax: 501(c)(6)

Personnel:
Chief Executive Officer: Michael J. Stack
Senior Editor: Teresa Anderson
   E-Mail: teresa.anderson@asisonline.org
Vice President of Government Affairs & Public Policy: Col. Jack D. P. Lichtenstein AUS (Ret.)
   E-Mail: jlichtenstein@asisonline.org
Media Contact: Leigh A. McGuire
   E-Mail: leigh.mcguire@asisonline.org
Vice President, Education: Susan A. Melnicove
   E-Mail: smelnicove@asisonline.org
Vice President, Marketing: Eileen Smith
   E-Mail: esmith@asisonline.org
Treasurer: Dave N. Tyson
Vice President, Publishing: Denny White
   E-Mail: dwhite@asisonline.org

Historical Note:

Formerly the American Society for Industrial Security. ASIS International is the preeminent organization for security professionals. ASIS is dedicated to increasing the effectiveness and productivity of security professionals by developing educational programs and materials that address broad security interests. Membership: $170 (Member/Associate); $25 (Student).

Continuing Education:
Certification Designation/s: CPP, PSP, PCI

Publications:
ASISPAC Newsletter
Dynamics; bi-monthly; adv.
Eurodynamics
Member Directory; on-line
Security Management Daily; daily; adv.
Security Management Magazine; monthly; adv.
Security Management Weekly; weekly; adv.

ASM International *(1913)*
9639 Kinsman Rd.
Materials Park, OH 44073-0002
Tel: (440) 338-5151 *Fax:* (440) 338-4634
TollFree: (800) 336-5152
E-Mail:
memberservicecenter@asminternational.org
Website: asminternational.org
Members: 36000 individuals
Staff: 65
Annual Budget: $10-25,000,000
Tax: 501(c)(3)

Personnel:
Managing Director: Shirley C. Theobald
   E-Mail: theobald@asminternational.org
Senior Manager, Marketing: Mark Barton
   E-Mail: mark.barton@asminternational.org
Senior Manager, Education: Norina Columbaro
   E-Mail: norina.columbaro@asminternational.org
Manager, Chapter Relations and Membership Services:
   Candace Cunningham
   E-Mail:
   candace.cunningham@asminternational.org
Senior Manager, Human Resources: Janice Farmwald
   E-Mail: janice.farmwald@asminternational.org
Senior Manager, Content Development: Scott Henry
   E-Mail: scott.henry@asminternational.org
Senior Manager, Events: Pamela Kleinman
   E-Mail: pamela.kleinman@asminternational.org
Director, Finance: Terry Mosier
   E-Mail: terry.mosier@asminternational.org
Director, Information Technology: Bill Raley
   E-Mail: bill.raley@asminternational.org
Director, Sales and Marketing: Erik Wolfe
   E-Mail: skip.wolfe@asminternational.org

Historical Note:
Originated in Detroit as the Steel Treaters Club; became the American Society for Steel Treating in 1920, the American Society for Metals in 1933 and assumed its present name in 1986. Incorporated in Ohio in 1920. ASM's mission is to gather, process and disseminate technical information on engineered materials through forums and meetings, education programs, publications and electronic media. Society of Carbide and Tool Engineers is a division of ASM. Membership: $113 (Professional); $25 (Student); $15 (ASM Student).

Meetings/Conferences: Annual
Conference Chair: Pamela Kleinman
2013 - Bellevue, WA (Meydenbauer CenterBellevue)/ April 2 - 5
2013 - San Antonio, TX (Sheraton Gunter)/April 3 - 5
2013 - Prague, Czech Republic (OREA Hotel Pyramida)/May 21 - 24
2013 - Indianapolis, IN (Indiana Convention Center)/ Sept. 16 - 18

Publications:
/MTRL; on-line
Advanced Materials & Processes® (AM&P); monthly; adv.
Alloy Digest; bi-monthly
AM&P eNews; on-line
e-Elastic; on-line
EDFA eNews - (Electronic Device Failure Analysis); on-line; adv.
HTPro; weekly; adv.
Journal of Failure Analysis and Prevention; bi-monthly; adv.
Journal of Materials Engineering and Performance
Journal of Phase Equilibria and Diffusion
Materials Solutions Update; on-line

MPMD (Materials and Processes for Medical Devices);
  bi-weekly; adv.
SMST e-Elastic; quarterly; adv.
TSS eNews; monthly; adv.

ASME International Gas Turbine Institute (1956)
6525 The Corners Pkwy.
Suite 115
Norcross, GA 30092
Tel: (404) 847-0072 *Fax:* (404) 847-0151
E-Mail: igti@asme.org
Website: igti.asme.org
Members: 125000 members
Staff: 454
Annual Budget: Over $100,000,000
Tax: 501(c)(3)

Personnel:
*Managing Director, Engineering Research and Technology
  Development:* Michael Ireland
    E-Mail: irelandm@asme.org
*Manager, Expositions and Communications and
  Membership Services:* Kristin Barranger
    E-Mail: barrangerk@asme.org
Manager, Professional and Member Development: Shirley
  Barton
    E-Mail: bartons@asme.org
Director, Operations: Charity Golden
    E-Mail: prenticec@asme.org
Coordinator, Office and Finance: Martha Quinlin
    E-Mail: quinlinm@asme.org
Administrator, Conferences and Expositions: Smita Solanki
    E-Mail: solankis@asme.org
Coordinator, Communications and Customer Relations:
  Rebecca Watrous
    E-Mail: watrousr@asme.org

Historical Note:
*ASMEIGTI is an educational and technical institute
of the American Society of Mechanical Engineers.
Dedicated to support the international exchange and
development of information to improve the design,
application, manufacture, operation and maintenance, and
environmental impact of all types of gas turbines, turbo
machinery and related equipment. Membership: $51-129/
year (Fees Varies Depending on the Year of Graduation).*

Continuing Education:
Certification Designation/s: BGTMRT, GTCCP

Meetings/Conferences: Annual

Publications:
Global Gas Turbine News Newsletter; quarterly
Journal of Engineering for Gas Turbines and Power;
  monthly
Journal of Turbomachinery; quarterly
Member Directory; on-line
Source GT; on-line; adv.

Asphalt Emulsion Manufacturers Association
(1973)
Three Church Circle
P.O. Box 250
Annapolis, MD 21401
Tel: (410) 267-0023 *Fax:* (410) 267-7546
E-Mail: krissoff@aema.org
Website: aema.org
Members: 163 companies and 6 Individuals
Staff: 4
Annual Budget: $500-1,000,000
Tax: 501(c)(6)

Personnel:
Executive Director: Mike Krissoff
    E-Mail: krissoff@aema.org
Director, Membership Services: Lisa Cerone
    E-Mail: cerone@aema.org
Co-Chair, Programs: Mark McCollough
    E-Mail: mark.mccollough@asphalt-materials.com

Historical Note:
*AEMA's mission is to expand the use and applications of
asphalt emulsions. Members are emulsion manufacturers,
materials and equipmemnt suppliers, contractors, consulting
engineers and government agencies. Membership: $3000
(North American Manufacturer); $300 (North American
Manufacturer Plants-each to a maximum annual payment
of $10,000); $3000 (International Manufacturer); $3,500
(Supplier); $500 (Associate); $100 (Individual).*

Meetings/Conferences:
Conference Chair: Mark McCollough
2013 - Indian Wells, CA (Renaissance Esmeralda
  Indian Wells Resort and Spa)/Feb. 19 - 22

2014 - Aventura, FL (Fairmont Turnberry Isle Resort
  and Club)/Feb. 24 - 27

Publications:
AEMA Newsletter; quarterly; adv.
Membership Database (Membership Directory); on-
line

Membership List Available to Non-members

Asphalt Institute (1919)
2696 Research Park Dr.
Lexington, KY 40511-8480
Tel: (859) 288-4960 *Fax:* (859) 288-4999
E-Mail: info@asphaltinstitute.org
Website: asphaltinstitute.org
Members: 97 companies
Staff: 32
Annual Budget: $5-10,000,000

Personnel:
President: Peter T. Grass CAE, P E
    E-Mail: pgrass@asphaltlnstltute.org
Meeting Planner and Event Manager: Katrina Tohle

Historical Note:
*Founded as the Asphalt Association, assumed its present
name in 1929. AI's mission is to enhance the use, benefits,
and quality performance of petroleum asphalt, through
environmental, marketing, research, engineering and
technical development, and through the resolution of issues
affecting the industry.*

Continuing Education:
Certification Designation/s: NBTC, MDTC

Meetings/Conferences: Annual
Conference Chair: Katrina Tohle

Publications:
Asphalt E-News; semi-monthly
Asphalt Magazine; adv.

Asphalt Recycling and Reclaiming Association
(1976)
Three Church Cir.
P.O. Box 250
Annapolis, MD 21401-1902
Tel: (410) 267-0023 *Fax:* (410) 267-7546
Website: arra.org
Members: 200 companies
Staff: 2
Annual Budget: $500-1,000,000
Tax: 501(c)(6)

Personnel:
Executive Director: Mike Krissoff
    E-Mail: krissoff@arra.org

Historical Note:
*ARRA promotes the collective interests of those individuals,
firms or corporations engaged in the asphalt recycling
industry as contractors, owners or manufacturers of
equipment, engineers, suppliers and public highway
officials. Membership: $3000 (Contractor/Supplier); $300
(Affiliate).*

Meetings/Conferences:
Conference Chair: Mike Krissoff
2013 - Indian Wells, CA (Renaissance Esmeralda
  Indian Wells Resort and Spa)/Feb. 19 - 22

Publications:
ARRA Newsletter; quarterly; adv.
Membership Directory; on-line

Membership List Available to Non-members

Asphalt Roofing Manufacturers Association
(1915)
750 National Press Building
529 14th St. NW
Washington, DC 20045
Tel: (202) 591-2450 *Fax:* (202) 591-2445
Website: asphaltroofing.org
Members: 42 companies
Staff: 4
Annual Budget: $1-2,000,000
Tax: 501(c)(6)

Personnel:
Executive Vice President: Reed B. Hitchcock
Coordinator, Membership Services: Kelly Franklin
    E-Mail: kfranklin@kellencompany.com

Historical Note:
*Formerly (1969) Asphalt Roofing Industry Bureau,
ARMA strives to promote and further the sale and use
of bituminous-based roofing products. Members are
manufacturers of roll roofing, built-up roofing, residential*

---

*roofing, asphalt shingles, and modified bitumen roofing.
Membership: $11,500-146,000 (Regular); $2,412-11,844
(Associate).*

Meetings/Conferences:
Number of non-conference events/year: 2

Publications:
Alert Bulletins; irregular
ARMA Newsletter; semi-annually
Membership Directory; on-line
Shipment Report; quarterly

ASPIRA Association, Inc.
1444 I St. NW
Suite 800
Washington, DC 20005
Tel: (202) 835-3600 *Fax:* (202) 835-3613
E-Mail: info@aspira.org
Website: aspira.org
Members: 5000 organizations
Staff: 6
Annual Budget: $2-5,000,000
Tax: 501(c)(3)

Personnel:
President and Chief Executive Officer: Ronald Blackburn-
  Moreno
    E-Mail: rblackburn@aspira.org
Executive Director: Carlos Valentin
Vice President, Public Policy and Federal Relations: Hilda
  Crespo
    E-Mail: hcrespo@aspira.org
Office Manager and Finance Director: Matthew
  Eisenstadt
    E-Mail: maeisenstadt@aspira.org
Director, Technology: Marco Antonio Villafañe
    E-Mail: mvillafane@aspira.org
Executive Vice President and Chief Information Officer:
  John Villamil-Casanova
    E-Mail: jvillamil@aspira.org

Historical Note:
*ASPIRA is dedicated to encouraging education and
leadership development among Hispanic youth.*

Publications:
ASPIRA Policy Brief
Membership Directory

Aspirin Foundation of America, Inc. (1981)
1299 Pennsylvania Ave. NW
Tenth Floor
Washington, DC 20004
Tel: (202) 508-9523 *Fax:* (202) 508-9700
Website: aspirin-foundation.com/about/
  worldwide.html
Members: 8 companies
Staff: 1
Annual Budget: $100-250,000
Tax: 501(c)(6)

Personnel:
Contact, Communications: Bruce Dickson

Historical Note:
*A nonprofit organization made up of companies engaged in
the manufacture, preparation, propagation, compounding
or processing of aspirin and aspirin products. It informs
members of scientific developments relating to aspirin and
encourages an understanding of the potential health benefits
of aspirin.*

ASPRS-The Imaging and Geospatial Information
Society (1934)
5410 Grosvenor Ln.
Suite 210
Bethesda, MD 20814-2160
Tel: (301) 493-0290 *Fax:* (301) 493-0208
E-Mail: asprs@asprs.org
Website: asprs.org
Members: 6500 individuals and 160 corporations
Staff: 17
Annual Budget: $2-5,000,000
Tax: 501(c)(3)

Personnel:
Executive Director and Secretary: James R. Plasker
    E-Mail: jplasker@asprs.org
Manager, Membership Services: Sokhan Hing
    E-Mail: sokhanh@asprs.org
Assistant Director, Publications: Rae Kelley
    E-Mail: rkelley@asprs.org
Manager, Finance: Kathy Konapelsky
    E-Mail: kkonapelsky@asprs.org

Manager, Meetings and Marketing: Heather Staverman
    E-Mail: hstaverman@asprs.org
Director, Communications and Associate Executive Director:
    Kimberly A. Tilley
    E-Mail: kimt@asprs.org
Manager, Programs: Jesse Winch
    E-Mail: jwinch@asprs.org

Historical Note:
*Originally the American Society of Photogrammetry,
later became the American Society for Photogrammetry
and Remote Sensing. ASPRS's mission is to promote the
ethical application of active and passive sensors, the
disciplines of photogrammetry, remote sensing, geographic
information systems, and other supporting geospatial
technologies. Membership: $135 (Active); $90 (Associate);
$45 (Student).*

Continuing Education:
Certification Designation/s: CPT, CRST, CP, CMS-GIS/LIS,
CGIS/LIST, CMS-RS

Meetings/Conferences: Annual
Conference Chair: Heather Staverman
2013 - Baltimore, MD (Baltimore Marriott Waterfront)/
    March 24 - 28
2013 - San Antonio, TX (Crowne Plaza San Antonio
    Riverwalk)/Oct. 29 - 31
2014 - Louisville, KY (Galt House Hotel and Suites)/
    March 23 - 27
2015 - Tampa, FL (Grand Hyatt Tampa Bay)/May 4 - 8
2016 - Reno, NV (Grand Sierra Resort and Casino)/
    April 18 - 22
Number of non-conference events/year: 1

Publications:
ASPRS Journal; monthly
ASPRS Newsletter; quarterly
Photogrammetric Engineering and Remote Sensing;
    monthly; adv.
The ASPRS Student Newsletter

ASPSN - American Society of Plastic Surgical Nurses *(1975)*
500 Cummings Center
Suite 4550
Beverly, MA 01915
Fax: (978) 524-8890
TollFree: (877) 337-9315
E-Mail: aspsn@dancyamc.com
Website: aspsn.org
Members: 900 individuals
Staff: 3
Annual Budget: $250-500,000
Tax: 501(c)(6)

Personnel:
Director, Convention Services: Donna Deans

Historical Note:
*Formerly the American Society of Plastic and Reconstructive
Surgical Nurses, ASPSN assumed its current name in 2001.
ASPSN's mission is to employ education and research to
promote practice excellence, nursing leadership, optimal
patient safety, and outcomes by using evidence-based
practice as a foundation of care. Membership: $125
(Regular); $80 (Associate); $75 (Retired); $50 (Student).*

Continuing Education:
Certification Designation/s: CPSN

Meetings/Conferences:
Conference Chair: Donna Deans
2013 - New York City, NY/April 13 - 14
2013 - San Diego, CA (San Diego Sheraton Hotel and
    Marina)/Oct. 11 - 14
2014 - Chicago, IL/Oct. 10 - 13
2015 - Boston, MA/Oct. 16 - 19
Number of non-conference events/year: 1

Publications:
ASPSN eNews; monthly; adv.
Membership Directory; on-line
PSN Journal; quarterly; adv.

Membership List Available to Non-members

Assembly of Episcopal Healthcare Chaplains *(1950)*
P.O. Box 51372
Knoxville, TN 37950-1372
Tel: (402) 223-7372
Website: episcopalchaplain.org
Members: 800 individuals
Staff: 6
Annual Budget: $10-25,000
Personnel:

Editor: James L. Risk
    E-Mail: james_l_risk@rush.edu
Communications Officer: Razz Waff
    E-Mail: razzw@aol.com

Historical Note:
*Founded as Assembly of Episcopal Hospitals and Chaplains,
assumed its current name in 1999. Mission is to foster
chaplaincy as an essential expression of the Church's
healing ministry in response to the gospel imperative.
Membership: $150 (Diocesan); $100 (Institutional); $50
(Professional); $25 (Associate).*

Meetings/Conferences: Annual

Publications:
Chaplair - AEHC newsletter

Membership List Available to Non-members

Assisted Living Federation of America *(1990)*
1650 King St.
Suite 602
Alexandria, VA 22314-2747
Tel: (703) 894-1805 *Fax*: (703) 894-1831
E-Mail: info@alfa.org
Website: alfa.org
Members: 500 companies providing assisted
living, 150 suppliers to assisted living companies
and 35 state affiliate members
Staff: 15
Annual Budget: $5-10,000,000
Tax: 501(c)(6)

Personnel:
President and Chief Executive Officer: Richard P. Grimes
    CAE
    E-Mail: rgrimes@alfa.org
Senior Vice President, Public Policy: Maribeth Bersani
    E-Mail: rgrimes@alfa.org
Senior Vice President, Professional Affairs: Jerry L.
    Cooper
    E-Mail: jcooper@alfa.org
Senior Vice President, Marketing and Communications:
    Jamison Gosselin
    E-Mail: jgosselin@alfa.org
Vice President, Finance: Gina Mamone
    E-Mail: gmamone@alfa.org
Director, Meetings: Amanda Shapiro
    E-Mail: Ashapiro@alfa.org

Historical Note:
*Formerly (1996) Assisted Living Facilities Association
of America, ALFA promotes business and operational
excellence through national conferences, research,
publications, and executive networks. It also works to
influence public policy by advocating for informed choice,
quality care, and accessibility for all Americans. Members
are companies which operate professionally managed
assisted living communities for seniors. Membership: $2000
(Associate); $8000 (President's Council).*

Meetings/Conferences: Annual
Conference Chair: Jerry L. Cooper
2013 - Charlotte, NC (Charlotte Convention Center)/
    May 7 - 9
2014 - Phoenix, AZ/May 20 - 22

Publications:
ALFA e-Newsletter; on-line

Assistive Technology Industry Association *(1998)*
401 N. Michigan Ave.
Chicago, IL 60611-4267
Tel: (312) 321-5172 *Fax*: (312) 673-6659
TollFree: (877) 687-2842
E-Mail: info@atia.org
Website: atia.org
Members: 100 organizations
Staff: 2
Annual Budget: $1-2,000,000
Tax: 501(c)(6)

Personnel:
Executive Director: David Dikter
    E-Mail: executive_director@atia.org
Chief Operating Officer: Caroline Van Howe
    E-Mail: coo@atia.org

Historical Note:
*ATIA provides a forum for education and communication
to professional practitioners serving those with disabilities
(teachers, occupational therapists, rehabilitation counselors,
physicians, psychologists, etc.), with the overarching goal
of providing enhanced benefits and opportunities to people
with disabilities. Membership: $650-4,600 (Regular); $650
(Associate Publisher); $200 (Associate Distributor).*

Meetings/Conferences: Annual

2013 - Orlando, FL (Caribe Royale Orlando All-
    Suite Hotel and Convention Center)/Jan. 30 - Feb.
    2/51-100 exhibitors
Number of non-conference events/year: 2

Publications:
ATIA e-newsletter; on-line
Member Directory; on-line

Associated Actors and Artistes of America *(1919)*
165 W. 46th St.
New York, NY 10036
Tel: (212) 869-0358 *Fax*: (212) 869-1746
E-Mail: actors1919@verizon.net
Members:
7 national unions
120000 individuals
Staff: 2
Annual Budget: $500-1,000,000
Tax: 501(c)(5)

Personnel:
President: Theodore Bikel

Historical Note:
*Affiliated with AFL-CIO. Chartered by the American
Federation of Labor on August 28, 1919, 4As is the
successor organization to the White Rats Actors Union of
America (established in 1910). An umbrella coordinating
organization comprising autonomous branches: Actors'
Equity Association, American Federation of Television and
Radio Artists, American Guild of Musical Artists, American
Guild of Variety Artists, Italian Actors Union and Screen
Actors Guild.*

Associated Air Balance Council *(1965)*
1518 K St. NW
Suite 503
Washington, DC 20005
Tel: (202) 737-0202 *Fax*: (202) 638-4833
E-Mail: info@aabc.com
Website: aabc.com
Members: 140 companies
Staff: 5
Annual Budget: $500-1,000,000
Tax: 501(c)(6)

Personnel:
Executive Director: Kenneth M. Sufka

Historical Note:
*AABC is a non-profit association of qualified, independent
test and balance agencies. AABC's foremost objective is to
safeguard the reputation and competence of the Council and
the TAB profession. Members are independent testers of air
handling systems. Membership: $500 (Individual).*

Continuing Education:
Certification Designation/s: CTE, CCA, TBE

Meetings/Conferences: Annual

Publications:
Membership Directory; on-line

Associated Bodywork and Massage Professionals *(1987)*
25188 Genesee Trail Rd.
Suite 200
Golden, CO 80401
Tel: (303) 674-8478 *Fax*: (800) 667-8260
TollFree: (800) 458-2267
E-Mail: expectmore@abmp.com
Website: abmp.com
Members: 77000 individuals
Staff: 42
Annual Budget: $10-25,000,000

Personnel:
President: Les Sweeney

Historical Note:
*ABMP serves the massage therapy community through
practice support, ethical standards, legislative advocacy,
and public education. Members are massage therapists
and bodyworkers practicing a wide variety of massage and
bodywork therapies. Membership: $229 (Certified); $199
(Professional/Practitioner); $75 (Supporting); $65 (Student,
with Liability Insurance); $45 (Student, without Liability
Insurance).*

Publications:
Body Sense Magazine
Different Strokes; bi-monthly
Knead to Know; quarterly
Massage and Bodywork Magazine; bi-monthly; adv.

Membership List Available to Non-members

Associated Builders and Contractors (1950)

4250 N. Fairfax Dr.
Suite 900, Ninth Floor
Arlington, VA 22203-1607
Tel: (703) 812-2000 Fax: (703) 812-8236
E-Mail: gotquestions@abc.org
Website: abc.org
Members: 23,000 merit shop construction and construction-related firms
Staff: 19
Annual Budget: $2-5,000,000
Tax: 501(c)(3)

Personnel:
President and Chief Executive Officer: Michael D. Bellaman
  E-Mail: bellaman@abc.org
Vice President, Federal Affairs: Geoffrey Burr
  E-Mail: burr@abc.org
Chief Financial Officer: Jason R. Daisey
  E-Mail: daisey@abc.org
Director, Communications: Gerry Fritz
  E-Mail: fritz@abc.org
Directory, Legal and Regulatory Affairs: Bob Hirsch
  E-Mail: hirsch@abc.org
Director, Membership Services: Jen Huber
  E-Mail: huber@abc.org
Director, Business Development: Mark Leibman
  E-Mail: leibman@abc.org
Director, Meetings: Tina Schneider
  E-Mail: schneider@abc.org

Historical Note:
ABC provides better training, government and legal representation, and programs to ensure members a competitive advantage, add value to the industry's clients, promote a safe work place and enhance the lives of the industry's employees. Membership fee varies by volume and is collected at chapter level.

Meetings/Conferences: Annual
Conference Chair: Tina Schneider
2013 - Ft. Lauderdale, FL (Marriott Harbor Beach Resort & Spa)/Feb. 19 - 20
2013 - Denver, CO (Westin Tabor Center)/July 31 - Aug. 2
2013 - Las Vegas, NV (Red Rock Casino Resort and Spa)/Nov. 5 - 7
2014 - Maui, HI (Grand Wailea)/Feb. 11 - 12
2014 - Nashville, TN (Loews Vanderbilt Hotel Nashville)/Aug. 6 - 8
2014 - Miami, FL (Eden Roc Renaissance Miami Beach)/Nov. 11 - 13
Number of non-conference events/year: 18

Publications:
Newsline

Associated Business Writers of America (1945)

10940 S. Parker Rd.
Suite 508
Parker, CO 80134
Tel: (303) 841-0246 Fax: (303) 841-2607
Members: 230 individuals
Staff: 1
Annual Budget: $10-25,000

Personnel:
Executive Director: Sandy Whelchel

Historical Note:
An affiliate of the National Writers Association. The Associated Business Writers of America was established in 1946. The ABWA is composed of freelance writers whose aim is to better the image of the profession, to improve relations and communication with editors and other clients, and to strive for higher pay scales and more considerate handling of manuscripts. Membership: $98 (Individual); $250 (Group).

Publications:
Authorship; quarterly; adv.
Flash Market News (online); monthly
NWA Newsletter; monthly

Associated Church Press (1916)

P.O. Box 621001
Oviedo, FL 32762-1001
Tel: (407) 341-6615 Fax: (407) 386-3236
E-Mail: associatedchurchpress@gmail.com
Website: theacp.org
Members:
200 periodicals
40 individuals

Staff: 3
Annual Budget: Under $10,000
Tax: 501(c)(3)

Personnel:
Executive Director: Joe Thoma
Manager, Membership Services: Catherine Kohn
Treasurer: Carlos Medley

Historical Note:
Formerly (1937) Editorial Council of the Religious Press. ACP strives to promote and to stimulate better standards of religious communication inorder to hold peace, justice and the common good in contemporary society. Members are former ACP editors, freelance writers, journalists, artists, designers and photographers. Membership: $30 (Former ACP Editors); $25 (Students); $40 (All Others); $125 (Affiliate Member).

Meetings/Conferences: Annual
Conference Chair: Joe Thoma
2013 - Indianapolis, IN (Sheraton Indianapolis City Centre Hotel)/April 3 - 5

Publications:
ACPwire
Member Directory

Membership List Available to Non-members

Associated Collegiate Press (1921)

2221 University Ave. SE
Suite 121
Minneapolis, MN 55414
Tel: (612) 625-8335 Fax: (612) 626-0720
E-Mail: info@studentpress.org
Website: studentpress.org/acp
Members: 20000 individuals
Staff: 6
Annual Budget: $250-500,000
Tax: 501(c)(3)

Personnel:
Executive Director: Logan Aimone
  E-Mail: logan@studentpress.org
Accountant: Kay Dawson
Administrative assistant: Jackie Flaum
Director, Membership Services: Emily Griesser
  E-Mail: emily@studentpress.org
Director, Communications and Technology: Marc Wood

Historical Note:
ACP's purpose is to promote the growth and quality of high school and college student publications. Became a separate division of NSPA in 1933. Offers resources to members to help improve their publications - newspapers, yearbooks, magazines, broadcast programs, and online publications. ACP operates as a division of the National Scholastic Press Association (NSPA). Membership is open to student newspapers, yearbooks, magazines, broadcast stations and online publications at any four-year or two-year college or university, technical, professional or graduate school, public or private. Membership: $109-139 (Publication, based on enrollment); $69 (Broadcast Station); $139 (ACP Critiques).

Meetings/Conferences: Quarterly
2013 - Minneapolis, MN (Radisson Plaza Hotel Minneapolis)/Feb. 8 - 10
2013 - San Francisco, CA (Westin San Francisco Airport)/Feb. 28 - March 3
2013 - New Orleans, LA (New Orleans Marriott Hotel)/Oct. 23 - 27
2014 - San Diego, CA/Feb. 27 - March 2
2014 - Philadelphia, PA (Marriott, Philadelphia)/Oct. 29 - Nov. 2
2015 - Austin, TX (Hilton, Hotel)/Oct. 28 - Nov. 1
Number of non-conference events/year: 1

Publications:
Best of the High School Press; annually
Member Directory; on-line
Trends in High School Media; quarterly

Associated Construction Distributors International (1968)

1605 SE Delaware Ave.
Suite B
Ankeny, IA 50021
Tel: (515) 964-1335 Fax: (515) 964-7668
E-Mail: acdi@acdi.net
Website: acdi.net
Members: 35 Individual
Staff: 5
Annual Budget: $50-100,000

Personnel:
Executive Vice President: Tom Goetz

  E-Mail: tgoetz@acdi.net
Planner, Meetings: Nancy Herselius CMP
  E-Mail: nherselius@acdi.net
Director, Sales and Marketing: Dave Hill
  E-Mail: dhill@acdi.net
Manager, Meeting: Linda Phipps
  E-Mail: lphipps@acdi.net
Controller: Jane Zieser
  E-Mail: jzieser@acdi.net

Historical Note:
ACD provides opportunities for its members to be more successful individually through networking and sharing information, professional training, and the cooperative purchase of construction materials and business services. Members are distributors of construction supplies and equipment.

Meetings/Conferences:
Conference Chair: Nancy Herselius CMP

Publications:
Member Directory; on-line
Vendor Directory; on-line

Associated Construction Publications (1938)

1200 Madison Ave., LL20
Indianapolis, IN 46225
Tel: (317) 423-7080 Fax: (317) 423-7094
E-Mail: acp@reedbusiness.com
Website: acppubs.com
Members: 14 regional publications
Staff: 48
Annual Budget: $2-5,000,000

Personnel:
National Editorial Contact: Greg Sitek
  E-Mail: gsitek@reedbusiness.com
National Advertising Contact: Kenny Veach

Historical Note:
ACP is a business unit of Reed Construction Data, provider of critical data to all members of the building team throughout the construction life cycle. It also delivers the construction industry audience maximum visibility to advertisers by providing the most current construction industry news and information.

Publications:
California Builder & Engineer magazine; adv.
Construction; adv.
Construction Digest; adv.
Construction News; adv.
Constructioneer
Dixie Contractor; adv.
Michigan Contractor & Builder; adv.
Midwest Contractor; adv.
New England Construction; adv.
Pacific Builder & Engineer; adv.
Rocky Mountain Construction; adv.
Texas Contractor; adv.
Western Builder

Associated Cooperage Industries of America (1934)

8923 Stone Green Way
Second Floor
Louisville, KY 40220-4073
Tel: (502) 499-9808 Fax: (502) 499-9788
E-Mail: acia@att.net
Website: acia.net
Members: 53 companies
Staff: 2
Annual Budget: $50-100,000

Personnel:
President: Brad Boswell
Secretary and Treasurer: Polly Wagner

Historical Note:
ACIA's purpose is to serve as a contact point for the membership, distribute available information about the wooden barrel and to promote the common interests of those in the industry. Members are Cooperage Firms, producers of Stave and Heading, several distillers and vintners and other firms whose business interests are allied to the wooden barrel.

Meetings/Conferences: Annual
Number of non-conference events/year: 1

Publications:
Membership Directory; on-line

Associated Equipment Distributors (1919)

600 22nd St.
Suite 220

Oak Brook, IL 60523
Tel: (630) 574-0650 *Fax:* (630) 574-0132
TollFree: (800) 388-0650
E-Mail: aeddc@aednet.org
Website: aednet.org
Members: 500 companies
Staff: 26
Annual Budget: $2-5,000,000

Personnel:
President and Chief Executive Officer: Toby Mack
   E-Mail: jtm@aednet.org
Staff Vice President, Finance and Administration: Garry
   Bartecki
Director, Communications: Jenny Choe
   E-Mail: jchoe@aednet.org
Director, Meetings and Conferences: Janet L. Dixon
   E-Mail: jdixon@aednet.org
Executive Vice President and Chief Operating Officer: Bob
   Henderson
Manager, Workforce and Education Program Logistics: Pat
   Novak
Programs Director and Executive Editor: Kim Phelan
   E-Mail: kphelan@aednet.org
Manager, Sales and Development: Rebecca Rakers
Director, Development: Carol Schrader
   E-Mail: cschrader@aednet.org
Senior Programmer Analyst: Chirag Shah
   E-Mail: cshah@aednet.org
Director, Finance: Patsy Stetter
   E-Mail: pstetter@aednet.org
Manager, Membership Services: Ben Yates
   E-Mail: byates@aednet.org

Historical Note:
*Formerly National Distributors Association of Construction
Equipment. Affiliated with the Canadian Association of
Equipment Distributors. Distributors and manufacturers
of construction, mining, logging, and road maintenance
equipment. AED's mission is to enhance the ongoing
success and profitability of its member companies and
related constituencies by creating and providing high quality
products, services and information. Membership: $650
(Distributors, based on gross annual revenues); $1,200
(Manufacturers, based on gross annual revenues starting);
$1,500 (Service Companies); $800 (Press).*

Meetings/Conferences: Annual
Conference Chair: Janet L. Dixon
2013 - Las Vegas, NV (LVH-Las Vegas Hotel and
   Casino)/Jan. 15 - 17/26-50 exhibitors
Number of non-conference events/year: 3

Publications:
AED Membership Directory; on-line

Associated Funeral Directors International
(1939)
P.O. Box 1347
Kingsport, TN 37662-1347
TollFree: (800) 346-7151
Members: 1700 funeral homes
Staff: 4
Annual Budget: $50-100,000

Personnel:
Executive Director: Richard A. Santore

Historical Note:
Formerly (1992) the Associated Funeral Directors Service.

Associated General Contractors of America (AGC)
(1918)
2300 Wilson Blvd.
Suite 400
Arlington, VA 22201
Tel: (703) 548-3118 *Fax:* (703) 548-3119
TollFree: (800) 242-1767
E-Mail: info@agc.org
Website: agc.org
Members: 30,000 firms
Staff: 75
Annual Budget: $25-50,000,000
Tax: 501(c)(6)

Personnel:
Chief Executive Officer: Stephen E. Sandherr
   E-Mail: sandhers@agc.org
*Senior Director, Product Sales & Development, Business
   Development, Programs & Industry Relations:* Jordan
   Ahmad
   E-Mail: ahmadj@agc.org

*Director, Municipal & Utilities Division, Business
   Development, Programs & Industry Relations:* Scott
   Berry
   E-Mail: berrys@agc.org
Executive Director, Chapter Support Services: Elisa
   Brewer-Pratt
   E-Mail: brewere@agc.org
Senior Director, Education and Certification: Allison
   Brotman CAE
   E-Mail: brotmana@agc.org
*Executive Director, Convention, Meeting Services and
   Production:* Richard Brown CAE
   E-Mail: brownr@agc.org
*Executive Director, Human Resources, Membership Services
   and Administration:* Carolyn Coker
   E-Mail: cokerc@agc.org
Chief Information Officer: Fara Francis
   E-Mail: francisf@agc.org
General Counsel: Michael E. Kennedy
   E-Mail: kennedym@agc.org
Chief Operating Officer: David R. Lukens
   E-Mail: lukensd@agc.org
Senior Executive Director, Government Affairs: Jeffrey D.
   Shoaf
   E-Mail: shoafj@agc.org

Historical Note:
*AGC serves construction professionals by promoting
the skill, integrity and responsibility of those who build
America. Membership: $25.76/year.*

Meetings/Conferences:
Conference Chair: Richard Brown CAE
2013 - Palm Spring, CA (JW Marriott Desert Springs
   Resort)/March 6 - 9
2013 - Colorado Springs, CO (Antlers Hilton Colorado
   Springs)/Oct. 16 - 19
Number of non-conference events/year: 1

Publications:
AGC Federal Report; bi-monthly
Building Material; bi-monthly
Constructor Magazine; bi-monthly; adv.
Data Digest; weekly
Environmental Observer; monthly
Human Resource & Labor News; bi-monthly
Membership Directory; adv.
News & Views; bi-monthly
Newsletter
SmartBrief (online); daily
Specialty News; bi-monthly
The Pipeline; bi-monthly

Associated Glass and Pottery Manufacturers
(1923)
520 Westchester Dr.
Greensburg, PA 15601-6002
Tel: (330) 965-8728
Members: 20 companies
Staff: 1
Annual Budget: Under $10,000
Tax: 501(c)(6)

Personnel:
President: Robert Gonze

Historical Note:
*Manufacturers of semi-vitrified and vitrified ceramic and
glass dinnerware and tableware. Membership: $75/year
(organization/company).*

Associated Locksmiths of America *(1956)*
3500 Easy St.
Dallas, TX 75247-6416
Tel: (214) 819-9733 *Fax:* (214) 819-9736
TollFree: (800) 532-2562
Website: aloa.org
Members: 10000 individuals
Staff: 16
Annual Budget: $2-5,000,000

Personnel:
Executive Director: David M. Lowell CML, CAE
   E-Mail: david@aloa.org
*Manager, Membership Services and Interim Executive
   Director:* Mary May
Manager, Conventions: Jo Anne Mims
   E-Mail: joanne@aloa.org

Historical Note:
*ALOA's mission is to protect the general public against
abuses by promoting ALOA's code of ethics and the
enforcement of legal business practices. Members are
engaged in consulting, sales, installation and maintenance*

*of locks, keys, safes, premises security, access controls,
alarms, and other security related endeavors. Membership:
$200 (US Active Member/Probationary Member); $215
(Non US Active/any Allied Member).*

Continuing Education:
Certification Designation/s: ACE, CML, CPS, CRL, CMST,
CPL, PRP, CAL, RL, CFDI

Meetings/Conferences: Annual
Conference Chair: Jo Anne Mims

Publications:
Keynotes; monthly
Weekly Update; weekly

Associated Luxury Hotels International *(1986)*
1275 K St. NW
Suite 810
Washington, DC 20005
Tel: (202) 887-7020 *Fax:* (202) 887-0085
E-Mail: midatlantic@alhi.com
Website: alhi.com
Members: 100 four and five star quality hotels
and resorts
Staff: 26

Personnel:
President and Chief Executive Officer: David Gabri
   E-Mail: dgabri@alhi.com
Executive Vice President and Chief Financial Officer: Mike
   Coutu
   E-Mail: mcoutu@alhi.com
Director, Sales: Pam Rodgers Dauth
   E-Mail: prodgers@alhi.com

Historical Note:
*ALHI serves meetings, conventions and incentive programs
for the members. Members are independent luxury hotels
and resorts.*

Meetings/Conferences:
Number of non-conference events/year: 1

Publications:
Membership Directory; on-line

Associated Owners and Developers *(1994)*
P.O. Box 4163
McLean, VA 22103-4163
Tel: (703) 734-2397 *Fax:* (703) 734-2908
TollFree: (888) 999-2536
E-Mail: aod@cbrmag.com
Website: constructionchannel.net/aod
Members: 1832 individuals and 200 companies
Staff: 4
Annual Budget: $100-250,000

Personnel:
Founder, Chairman and Chief Executive Officer: Harvey L.
   Kornbluh
General Counsel: Ira Genberg

Historical Note:
*AOD's mission is to support the facility and financial
interests of owners and developers by promoting education,
participation, and cooperation among the individuals
and organizations who support the design, development,
construction, and delivery of projects. Membership:
$250 (Individual/Group Government/University);
$500 (Company); $1,000 (Affiliates/per Region); $125
(Individual Government/University Member); Free
(Student).*

Publications:
AOD Newsletter; quarterly
Construction Business Review; bi-monthly

Associated Pipe Organ Builders of America
(1941)
P.O. Box 155
Chicago Ridge, IL 60415
Tel: (660) 747-3066
TollFree: (800) 473-5270
Website: apoba.com
Members: 32 companies
Staff: 1
Annual Budget: $50-100,000

Personnel:
President: Michael Quimby
   E-Mail: qpo1@earthlink.net

Historical Note:
*Formerly Associated Organ Builders of America. Formed
originally to set metal priorities during World War II. Has
no permanent address or staff; officers rotate triennially.
APOBA is a professional association of North American
firms engaged in building traditional pipe organs.*

Publications:
The American Organist Magazine; monthly; adv.

Associated Press Managing Editors (1933)
450 W. 33rd St.
New York, NY 10001
Tel: (212) 621-7007 *Fax:* (212) 506-6102
E-Mail: apme@ap.org
Website: apme.com
Members: 2000 individuals
Staff: 2
Annual Budget: $250-500,000
Tax: 501(c)(6)

Personnel:
President: Bob Heisse
Treasurer: Jan Touney
    E-Mail: jtouney@qctimes.com

Historical Note:
APME is a source of information and support for editors who produce vital, interesting newspapers day in and day out. Members are editors of Associated Press newspapers. Membership: $150/year.

Meetings/Conferences: Annual

Publications:
APME News
APME Newsletter

Associated Professional Sleep Societies (1986)
2510 N. Frontage Rd.
Darien, IL 60561
Tel: (630) 737-9700 *Fax:* (630) 737-9789
Website: sleepmeeting.org
Members: 2 societies
Staff: 50
Annual Budget: $2-5,000,000

Personnel:
Executive Director: Jerome A. Barrett
Editor in Chief: David F. Dinges
Director, Meetings, Membership and Marketing: Becky Roberts
    E-Mail: broberts@aasmnet.org
Director, Professional Education and Training: Richard Rosenberg PhD
    E-Mail: rrosenberg@aasmnet.org

Historical Note:
Formerly (1993) Association of Professional Sleep Societies and a partnership comprising two sleep societies, Sleep Research Society and the American Academy of Sleep Medicine. APSS provides a joint annual meeting and publications.

Meetings/Conferences: Annual
Conference Chair: Becky Roberts
2013 - Baltimore, MD (Hilton Baltimore)/June 1 - 5/5000 attendees/over 100 exhibitors

Publications:
Membership Directory; on-line
Sleep; monthly; adv.

Membership List Available to Non-members

Associated Risk Managers (1970)
Two Pierce Pl.
20th Floor
Itasca, IL 60143-3141
Tel: (630) 285-4324 *Fax:* (630) 285-3590
Website: armiweb.com
Members: 300 agency members
Staff: 3
Annual Budget: $500-1,000,000

Personnel:
Vice President: Scott Spangler
    E-Mail: Scott.Spangler@armiweb.com

Historical Note:
ARM's mission is to create marketing, educational and networking opportunities for the ARM affiliated agents. It also works to generate revenue opportunities from insurance programs, products and risk management services and to serve the insurance consumers in a professional manner.

Meetings/Conferences: Annual

Publications:
ARM News; on-line

Associated Schools of Construction (1965)
P.O. Box 1312
Ft. Collins, CO 80522
Tel: (970) 988-1130 *Fax:* (970) 282-0396
E-Mail: info@ascweb.org

Website: ascweb.org
Members: 150 schools
Staff: 4
Annual Budget: $250-500,000
Tax: 501(c)(3)

Personnel:
President: Jay P Christofferson
    E-Mail: jay_christofferson@byu.edu
Interim Operations Manager: Larry Grosse
    E-Mail: info@ascweb.org
Editor: David E. Gunderson
    E-Mail: dgunderson@acm.wsu.edu
Manager, Operations: Sue Wagner-Renner
    E-Mail: sue.asc@gmail.com

Historical Note:
ASC is a professional association for the development and advancement of construction education. ASC's mission is to have a professional association for the development and advancement of construction education, where the sharing of ideas and knowledge inspires, guides and promotes excellence in curricula, teaching, research and service. Membership: $250 (Individual/Associate); $550 (Institutional/Industry); $400 (Governmental)..

Meetings/Conferences: Annual
2013 - Shell Beach, CA (Cliffs Resort)/April 9 - 13

Publications:
International Journal of Construction Education and Research
Member Directory; on-line

Associated Specialty Contractors (1955)
Three Bethesda Metro Center
Suite 1100
Bethesda, MD 20814
Tel: (301) 657-3110 *Fax:* (301) 215-4500
Website: assoc-spec-con.org
Members: 9 organizations
Staff: 1
Annual Budget: Under $10,000

Personnel:
President: Daniel "Dan" G. Walter
    E-Mail: dgw@necanet.org

Historical Note:
Formerly (1973) Council of Mechanical Specialty Contracting Industries, Inc. ASC's mission is to promote efficient management and productivity and to improve contracting forms and practices. Membership: $2,750/year.

Associated Universities Inc. (1946)
1400 16th St. NW
Washington, DC 20036
Tel: (202) 462-1676
E-Mail: Info@aui.edu
Website: aui.edu
Staff: 4
Annual Budget: Over $100,000,000
Tax: 501(c)(3)

Personnel:
President: Ethan J. Schreier
    E-Mail: ejs@aui.edu
Treasurer, Vice President, Administration and Corporate Secretary: Patrick W. Donahoe
    E-Mail: pdonahoe@aui.edu
Vice President, Programs: John C. Mester
    E-Mail: jmester@aui.edu
Acting AUI Controller and Chief Financial Officer: Connie Williams
    E-Mail: ccwilliam@nrao.edu

Historical Note:
Manages astronomical observatories for universities and National Science Foundation, press releases and information.

Meetings/Conferences:
Conference Chair: John C. Mester

Associated Wire Rope Fabricators (1975)
P.O. Box 748
Walled Lake, MI 48390-0748
Tel: (248) 994-7753 *Fax:* (248) 994-7754
TollFree: (800) 444-2973
E-Mail: awrf@att.net
Website: awrf.org
Members: 300 companies
Staff: 3
Annual Budget: $1-2,000,000
Tax: 501(c)(6)

Personnel:

President: Tom Miller
Secretary: Scott St. Germain

Historical Note:
AWRF works to establish, acquire, preserve, and disseminate various technical information, and encourages the development of safety standards and programs, and product identification procedures. Membership : $550-1,980 (Regular, based on annual sales); $330 (Affiliate); 220 (Branch).

Meetings/Conferences: Semi-Annual
2013 - Ft. Worth, TX (Omni Ft. Worth Hotel)/April 28 - May 1
2013 - Los Angeles, CA (Century Plaza Hyatt Regency)/Oct. 20 - 23
2014 - Baltimore, MD (Marriott Waterfront)/April 27 - 30
2014 - St. Louis, MO (Hyatt Regency St. Louis at The Arch)/Oct. 26 - 29

Publications:
Slingmakers; quarterly; adv.

Association & Society Insurance Corporation (1974)
2301 Research Blvd.
Suite 300
Rockville, MD 20850
Tel: (301) 816-0045 *Fax:* (301) 816-1125
TollFree: (800) 638-2610
E-Mail: custsvc@asicorporation.com
Website: asicorporation.com
Staff: 4

Personnel:
President: Mort Perlroth
Chief Administrative Officer: Ingrid Aldred
Chief Financial Officer: Brian Saphier
Manager, Business Development and Marketing: Fayton Washington

Historical Note:
ASI's mission is dedicated to providing members with a quality TRICARE Supplemental Plan that will have a positive impact on the cost effectiveness and accessibility of their TRICARE benefits.

The Association for Academic Surgery (1967)
11300 W. Olympic Blvd.
Suite 600
Los Angeles, CA 90064
Tel: (310) 437-1606 *Fax:* (310) 437-0585
E-Mail: admin@aasurg.org
Website: aasurg.org
Members: 2500 member surgeons
Staff: 5
Annual Budget: $250-500,000
Tax: 501(c)(3)

Personnel:
Executive Director: Christina Kasendorf
    E-Mail: christina@aasurg.org
Meeting Planner: Matthew Clark
    E-Mail: matt@aasurg.org
Administrative Assistant: Erin Drummond
    E-Mail: erind@aasurg.org
Contact, Membership Services: Elaine Henninger
    E-Mail: membership@aasurg.org
Contact, Corporate Relations: Jill Smith
    E-Mail: jill@aasurg.org < jill@aasurg.org >

Historical Note:
AAS strives to serve the needs of academic surgeons, particularly those under 40 years of age. Membership: $50 (Medical Student/Candidate); $80 (Senior); $250 (Active International) $300 (Active).

Meetings/Conferences: Annual
Conference Chair: Matthew Clark

Publications:
Association for Academic Surgery Newsletters; quarterly
Journal of Surgical Research (JSR)
Membership Directory; on-line

Association for Accounting Administration (1984)
136 S. Keowee St.
Dayton, OH 45402
Tel: (937) 222-0030 *Fax:* (937) 222-5794
E-Mail: aaainfo@cpaadmin.org
Website: cpaadmin.org
Members: 900 individuals
Staff: 5
Annual Budget: $500-1,000,000

Personnel:
Executive Director: Kimberly Fantaci
  E-Mail: aaainfo@cpaadmin.org
Director, Information and Communications: Robert E.
  Biddle
  E-Mail: rbiddle@bowmanllp.com
Treasurer: Jim Fahey
  E-Mail: jfahey@applegrowth.com
Director, Membership Services and Growth: Ginny Fedrich
  E-Mail: ginny@hbla.com
Director , Education: Jane Johnson
  E-Mail: jjohnson@gccpas.net

Historical Note:
*Formerly Association of Accounting Administrators,
AAA seeks to enable accounting firm administrators
to communicate with one another. Members are
accounting administrators, high-level office managers
and administrative partners in accounting firms and
corporate accounting departments. Membership: $375
(Administrator/Consultant SIG/Vendor SIG); $150
(Accounting Technology Administrator's Special Interest
Group/Controller SIG); $275-325 (Subsequent Member).*

Meetings/Conferences: Annual
2013 - Detroit, MI/June 18 - 21

Publications:
AAA Report; bi-monthly
Membership Directory; annually

Association for Accounting Marketing *(1989)*
15000 Commerce Pkwy.
Suite C
Mt. Laurel, NJ 08054
Tel: (856) 380-6850 *Fax:* (856) 439-0525
E-Mail: info@accountingmarketing.org
Website: accountingmarketing.org
Members: 904 individuals
Staff: 5
Annual Budget: $500-1,000,000

Personnel:
Executive Director: Pete Pomilio
  E-Mail: ppomilio@ahint.com
Member Relationship Specialist: Allyson Clark
  E-Mail: aclark@ahint.com
Treasurer: Raissa Evans
  E-Mail: revans@pkftexas.com
Meeting Manager: Nadège Toth
  E-Mail: ntoth@ahint.com

Historical Note:
*Formerly (1993) Association of Accounting Marketing
Executives. AAM's mission is to act as a catalyst for
furthering the marketing and sales efforts of its participating
firms. Membership: $275 (Executive/Associate/Affiliate);
$150 (Educator/Student).*

Meetings/Conferences: Annual
Conference Chair: Nadège Toth
2013 - Las Vegas, NV (Bellagio Las Vegas)/June 9 - 12
Number of non-conference events/year: 2

Publications:
Growth Strategies: The Journal of Accounting
  Marketing and Sales; quarterly; adv.
MarkeTrends; bi-monthly; adv.
Membership Directory; on-line
The AAM Minute; monthly

Membership List Available to Non-members

Association for Adult Development and Aging
(1986)
5999 Stevenson Ave.
C/O American Counseling Association
Alexandria, VA 22304-3300
Tel: (703) 823-9800 *Fax:* (703) 461-9260
TollFree: (800) 347-6647
Website: aadaweb.org
Members: 1369 individuals
Staff: 5
Annual Budget: $25-50,000

Personnel:
President: Radha Horton-Parker
  E-Mail: rparker@odu.edu
Secretary: Robert Dobmeier
  E-Mail: rdobmeie@brockport.edu
Treasurer: Patricia Goodspeed Grant
  E-Mail: pgoodspe@brockport.edu
Webmaster: Jessica Kramer
  E-Mail: jkram009@odu.edu
Editor and Coordinator, Conference: Catherine B. Roland
  E-Mail: rolandc@mail.montclair.edu

Historical Note:
*AADA is a division of the American Counseling
Association. Purpose is to provide leadership, advice,
and counsel to counselors and service providers in the
helping professions, family members, legislators, and other
community agencies and persons on matters related to
the development of adults across the life span. AADA
serves as an advocate for quality professional services with
appropriate governmental agencies and in the legislative
process affecting these services. Members are individuals
who hold a masters degree in adult and/or gerontological
counseling or an equivalent. Membership: $40 (Regular/
Professional/Regular Associate); $24 (Student/New
Professional); $20 (Retired).*

Meetings/Conferences: Annual
Conference Chair: Catherine B. Roland

Publications:
ADULTSPAN Journal; semi-annually
The Adultspan Newsletter; quarterly; adv.

Membership List Available to Non-members

Association for Advanced Life Underwriting
(1957)
11921 Freedom Dr.
Suite 1100
Reston, VA 20190
Tel: (703) 641-9400 *Fax:* (703) 641-9885
E-Mail: info@aalu.org
Website: aalu.org
Members: 1900 individuals
Staff: 35
Annual Budget: $10-25,000,000

Personnel:
Senior Director, Meetings and Events: Grant Lebens
Vice President, Membership Services and Marketing:
  James Lee
  E-Mail: lee@aalu.org
*Chief Financial Officer and Vice President, Human
  Resources:* Tracy Mawyer
  E-Mail: mawyer@aalu.org

Historical Note:
*AALU has evolved over its fifty-year history, into an
organization that is protecting advanced life insurance
planning and the tax treatment of life insurance, as well
as unifying the industry's joint defense of life insurance.
AALU's mission is to preserve and protect advanced life
insurance planning for the benefit of its members, their
clients, the industry and the general public. Membership:
$1870/year.*

Meetings/Conferences:
Conference Chair: Grant Lebens
2013 - Washington, DC (Washington Marriott
  Wardman Park)/April 28 - May 1

Publications:
AALU Quarterly; quarterly; adv.

Association for Africanist Anthropology
2200 Wilson Blvd.
Suite 600
Arlington, VA 22201
Tel: (703) 528-1902 *Fax:* (703) 528-3546
Website: aaanet.org/sections/afaa
Staff: 4

Personnel:
President: Mwenda Ntarangwi
Editor: Jennifer Coffman
Webmaster: J.R. Osborn
Treasurer: Susan Pietrzyk

Historical Note:
*AfAA's mission is to promote the study of Africa, as well
as Africanist scholarship and the professional interests of
Africanist anthropologists in the U.S., and both in and
outside of the African Continent.*
Meetings/Conferences:
Number of non-conference events/year: 1

Publications:
AfAA Newsletter

Association for Ambulatory Behavioral Healthcare
(1965)
247 Douglas Ave.
Portsmouth, VA 23707
Tel: (757) 673-3741 *Fax:* (757) 966-7734
E-Mail: info@aabh.org
Website: aabh.org
Members: 300 members
Staff: 1
Annual Budget: $100-250,000

Personnel:
Executive Director: Mickey Wright
  E-Mail: mickey@aabh.org

Historical Note:
*Began in the 1960's as the Partial Hospitalization Study
Group and formerly known as the American Association
for Partial Hospitalization, adopted its present name in
1979. AAPH's mission is to promote partial hospitalization
and intensive outpatient programs as a vital component of
the behavioral healthcare continuum. Membership: $295
(Individual); $495 (Program); $695 (System).*

Meetings/Conferences: Annual
Number of non-conference events/year: 1

Publications:
Milieu; quarterly

Association for Applied and Clinical Sociology
(1978)
926 E. Forest Ave.
Ypsilanti, MI 48198
Tel: (734) 845-1206 *Fax:* (734) 487-7010
E-Mail: sac_aacs@emich.edu
Website: aacsnet.net
Members: 425 organizations
Staff: 2
Annual Budget: $25-50,000
Tax: 501(c)(3)

Personnel:
Executive Officer: Fonda Martin
Editor: Jay Weinstein
  E-Mail: jay.weinstein@emich.edu

Historical Note:
*Formerly (2005) Society for Applied Sociology. AACS's
mission is to provide a common meeting ground for
individuals interested in the application of sociological
knowledge and to enhance the understanding of the
interrelationship between sociological knowledge and
sociological practice. Membership: $100 (Regular); $45
(Student); $220 (Organizational); $100 (International
Regular); $60 (Retired/International Student).*

Meetings/Conferences: Annual
2013 - South Portland, ME (DoubleTree by Hilton Hotel
  Portland)/Oct. 3 - 5
2014 - Pittsburgh, PA (DoubleTree by Hilton Hotel and
  Suites Pittsburgh Downtown)/Oct. 9 - 11

Publications:
Journal of Applied Social Science (JASS)

Association for Applied and Therapeutic Humor
(1987)
65 Enterprise
Aliso Viejo, CA 92656
Tel: (949) 715-4681 *Fax:* (949) 715-6931
TollFree: (888) 747-2284
E-Mail: info@aath.org
Website: aath.org
Members: 500 individuals
Staff: 6
Annual Budget: $100-250,000
Tax: 501(c)(3)

Personnel:
Executive Director: Jerry Packer
  E-Mail: jerry.packer@aath.org
Treasurer: Adrienne Edmonson
  E-Mail: solutionshr@sbcgolbal.net
Contact, Website Services: Deb Gauldin
Contact, Press: Roberta Gold
  E-Mail: laf4u@sbcglobal.net
Membership Chair: David Jacobson
Conference Co-Chair: Jill Knox
  E-Mail: jillknox@hotmail.com

Historical Note:
*Formerly American Association for Therapeutic Humor.
AATH's mission is to educate health care, business, and
education professionals about the values and therapeutic
uses of humor and laughter. Membership: $130 (Regular);
$185 (Gold); $95 (Senior); $60 (Student).*

Meetings/Conferences: Annual
Conference Chair: Jill Knox
2013 - San Diego, CA (Westin San Diego)/April 4 - 7

Publications:
e-zine; monthly
Membership Directory; on-line
The Humor Connection; monthly; adv.

Association for Applied Psychophysiology and
Biofeedback *(1969)*

10200 W. 44th Ave.
Suite 304
Wheat Ridge, CO 80033-2840
Tel: (303) 422-8436 *Fax:* (303) 422-8894
TollFree: (800) 477-8892
E-Mail: info@aapb.org
Website: aapb.org
Members: 2000 members
Staff: 2
Annual Budget: $250-500,000
Tax: 501(c)(6)

Personnel:
Executive Director: David L. Stumph CAE, IOM
   E-Mail: dstumph@resourcenter.com

Historical Note:
Formerly the Biofeedback Society of America. AAPB's mission is to advance the development, dissemination and utilization of knowledge about applied psychophysiology and biofeedback to improve health and the quality of life through research, education and practice. Membership: $185 (Regular); $209 (Associate); $69 (Corresponding); $55 (Student); $655 (Corporate); $425 (Corporate Clinical).

Meetings/Conferences: Annual
2013 - Portland, OR (Hilton Portland Executive
   Towers)/March 14 - 16

Publications:
AAPB E-Newsletter; on-line
AAPB Provider Directory; on-line
Applied Psychophysiology and Biofeedback Journal;
   quarterly; adv.
Biofeedback & Neurofeedback Concepts in Sports
   Psychology
Biofeedback Magazine; quarterly
Biofeedback Mastery
Evidence-Based Practice in Biofeedback and
   Neurofeedback
Journal of Behavioral Medicine
Membership Directory; on-line
The Neurofeedback Book

Membership List Available to Non-members

Association for Applied Sport Psychology (1986)
8365 Keystone Crossing
Suite 107
Indianapolis, IN 46240
Tel: (317) 205-9225 *Fax:* (317) 205-9481
E-Mail: info@appliedsportpsych.org
Website: appliedsportpsych.org
Members: 1200 individuals
Staff: 4
Annual Budget: $250-500,000

Personnel:
Executive Director: Kent Lindeman CMP
   E-Mail: klindeman@hp-assoc.com
Manager, Accounting: Barbara Case
   E-Mail: bcase@hp-assoc.com
Manager, Meetings: Audra Stewart
   E-Mail: astewart@hp-assoc.com
Manager, Membership Services and Communications: Jill
   Thompson
   E-Mail: info@appliedsportpsych.org

Historical Note:
AASP promotes the development of psychological theory, research and intervention strategies in sport psychology and provides a forum for individuals who are interested in research and theory development. Membership: $150 (Professional); $90 (Student); $150 (Affiliate); $115 (Early Professional); $25 (Senior Member).

Meetings/Conferences: Annual
Conference Chair: Audra Stewart

Publications:
AAASP Newsletter; adv.
AASP Newsletter
Graduate Program Directory; on-line
Journal of Applied Sport Psychology; quarterly
Journal of Sport Psychology in Action; quarterly
Membership Directory; on-line
Position Papers; on-line

Association for Arid Lands Studies (1966)
ICASALS, Office of International Affairs
601 Indiana Ave., P.O. Box 45004
Lubbock, TX 79409-5004
Tel: (806) 742-3667 *Fax:* (806) 742-1286
Website: iaff.ttu.edu
Members: 250 individuals

Staff: 27
Personnel:
Executive Director: A.C. Correa
   E-Mail: ac.correa@ttu.edu

Historical Note:
AALS's mission is to encourage and increased general awareness of the problems and potentials of the arid and semiarid lands of the world and of human adjustment to and impact upon them. Members are scientists, social scientists and other academics with an interest in the study of arid and semi-arid lands. ICASALS' mission is to promote and facilitate multidisciplinary initiatives in research, education and regional development programs that address the understanding of processes caused by natural phenomena and by the human presence in arid and semiarid lands. Membership: $20/year.

Publications:
K-12 International Education Outreach Staff Directory;
   on-line
International Affairs Staff Directory; on-line
International Center for Arid & Semi Arid Land Studies
   Staff Directory; on-line
International Cultural Center of Operations Staff
   Directory; on-line
International Newsletter; annually
International Student & Scholar Service Staff Directory;
   on-line
Membership Directory; on-line
Study Abroad Staff Directory; on-line

Association for Asian American Studies (1979)
267 19th Ave. S
Minneapolis, MN 55455
Tel: (612) 625-4813
Website: aaastudies.org
Members: 810 individuals
Staff: 4
Annual Budget: $100-250,000

Personnel:
Secretary and Treasurer: Anna Gonzalez
   E-Mail: annakgonzalez@gmail.com
Secretariat: Saengmany Ratsabout
   E-Mail: secretariat@aaastudies.org
Editor: Min Song

Historical Note:
AAAS seeks to advance the professional standard of excellence in teaching and research in the field of Asian American Studies and promote better understanding and closer ties between and among various sub-components within Asian American Studies. Members are academics, students and others with an interest in the field. Membership: $40 (Undergraduate Student); $55 (Grad/Post Doc/Part-Time/Retired); $30 (Unemployed); $105 (Regular); $1,500 (Lifetime); $225 to $500 (Institutional).

Meetings/Conferences: Annual
2013 - Seatle, WA (The Afterlives of Empire)/April 17
   - 20

Publications:
AAAS Directory
AAAS Newsletter
Journal of Asian American Studies

Association for Asian Performance (1987)
Rhodes College, 2000 N. Pkwy.
Memphis, TN 38112
Tel: (901) 843-3000
Website: yavanika.org/aaponline
Staff: 7

Personnel:
President: Siyuan "Steven" Liu
   E-Mail: steven_liu@verizon.net
Coordinator , Membership and Outreach: Jennifer
   Goodlander
   E-Mail: jenngoodlander@yahoo.com
Conference Planner: Alexander Huang
*Coordinator, Information Technology and AAP Online
   Editor:* David Mason
   E-Mail: masond@rhodes.edu
Editor: Carol Fisher Sorgenfrei
   E-Mail: csorgenfrei2@aol.com
Vice President and Coordinator, Conferences: John Swain
   E-Mail: jds22925@csun.edu
Secretary and Treasurer: Kevin J. Wetmore
   E-Mail: kwetmore@lmu.edu

Historical Note:
AAP began as a California Public Benefit Corporation and is now an incorporated nonprofit organization. Membership: $40 (Regular); $25 (Student/Retiree).

Meetings/Conferences: Annual
Conference Chair: John Swain

Publications:
AAP Newsletter
Asian Theatre Journal
Membership Directory; annually

Association for Asian Studies (1941)
825 Victors Way
Suite 310
Ann Arbor, MI 48108
Tel: (734) 665-2490 *Fax:* (734) 665-3801
Website: asian-studies.org
Members: 8000 members
Staff: 14
Annual Budget: $2-5,000,000

Personnel:
Executive Director: Michael Paschal
   E-Mail: mpaschal@asian-studies.org
Assistant, Accounting: Lailai Chu
   E-Mail: lchu@asian-studies.org
Manager, Membership Services: Doreen Ilozor
   E-Mail: dilozor@asian-studies.org
Manager, Annual Conferences: Robyn Jones
   E-Mail: rjones@asian-studies.org
Contact, Advertising: Shilpa Kharecha
   E-Mail: skharecha@asian-studies.org
Chief Financial Officer: Alicia Williams
   E-Mail: awilliams@asian-studies.org
Manager, Publications and Website: Jonathan Wilson
   E-Mail: jwilson@asian-studies.org

Historical Note:
Organized as the Far Eastern Association. Assumed its present name in 1957 to reflect a growing interest in Asia east of the Middle East. A member of the American Council of Learned Socs. Membership: $35-125 (Regular); $25 (Associate); $2,000 (Patron).

Meetings/Conferences: Annual
Conference Chair: Robyn Jones
2013 - San Diego, CA (Manchester Grand Hyatt San
   Diego)/March 21 - 24/11-25 exhibitors
2014 - Philadelphia, PA/March 24 - 30

Publications:
Asian Studies Newsletter; quarterly; adv.
Education About Asia; adv.
Member Directory; on-line
The Journal of Asian Studies (JAS); quarterly; adv.

Membership List Available to Non-members

Association for Assessment and Accreditation of Laboratory Animal Care International (1965)
5283 Corporate Dr.
Suite 203
Frederick, MD 21703-2879
Tel: (301) 696-9626 *Fax:* (301) 696-9627
E-Mail: accredit@aaalac.org
Website: aaalac.org
Members: 868 companies and sponsoring
societies
Staff: 14
Annual Budget: $2-5,000,000
Tax: 501(c)(3)

Personnel:
Executive Director: Dr. Christian E. Newcomer
   E-Mail: cnewcomer@aaalac.org
Senior Program Analyst and Coordinator, Council: Sandy
   L. Dexter
   E-Mail: sdexter@aaalac.org
Program Assistant, Communications: Susan Lynch
   E-Mail: slynch@aaalac.org
Financial Manager: Jacob Meesarapu
   E-Mail: jmeesara@aaalac.org

Historical Note:
Formerly (1996) the American Association for Accreditation of Laboratory Animal Care. AAALAC's mission is to enhance the quality of research, teaching, and testing by promoting humane, responsible animal care and use. Member organizations are a select group of scientific, professional and educational groups with an interest in advancing biomedical research and animal well-being in science.

Meetings/Conferences: Annual
Conference Chair: Sandy L. Dexter
2013 - Barcelona, Spain (Barcelona International
   Convention Center)/June 10 - 13
Number of non-conference events/year: 2

Publications:

AAALAC Ag Update Newsletter
AAALAC Connection Newsletter; on-line
Membership Directory; on-line

Association for Assessment in Counseling and Education (1965)
P.O. Box 791006
Baltimore, MD 21279-1006
Fax: (800) 473-2329
TollFree: (800) 347-6647
Website: theaaceonline.com
Members: 1331 individuals
Staff: 2
Annual Budget: $25-50,000

Personnel:
President: Carl Sheperis
Treasurer: Stephanie Crockett

Historical Note:
A division of the American Counseling Association. Formerly (1984) the Association for Measurement and Evaluation in Guidance, and (1992) Association for Measurement and Evaluation in Counseling and Development. Membership: $40 (Professional/Regular); $30 (New Professional/Student/Retired).

Meetings/Conferences: Annual

Publications:
Counseling Outcome Research and Evaluation; bi-annually
Measurement and Evaluation in Counseling and Development; quarterly
NewsNotes-Newsletter; quarterly

Association for Behavior Analysis International (1974)
550 W. Centre Ave.
Suite One
Portage, MI 49024
Tel: (269) 492-9310 *Fax:* (269) 492-9316
E-Mail: mail@abainternational.org
Website: abainternational.org
Members: 5000 individuals
Staff: 23
Annual Budget: $2-5,000,000

Personnel:
Executive Director: Maria E. Malott PhD
  E-Mail: mmalott@abainternational.org

Historical Note:
Formerly (1979) Midwestern Association for Behavior Analysis. ABAI organizes events that promote dissemination of the science and provide continuing education opportunities for practitioners, and offers job placement services that facilitate employment for behavior analysts. Members are individuals interested in the applied experimental and theoretical analysis of behavior and the enhancement of behavior analysis as a profession. Full members of ABA have at least a Master's degree in psychology or a related discipline and have demonstrated competence in either applied or experimental behavior analysis. Membership: $45-308/year.

Meetings/Conferences:
2013 - Portland, OR (Portland Marriott Downtown Waterfront Hotel)/Jan. 25 - 27
2013 - Minneapolis, MN (Minneapolis Convention Center)/May 24 - 28
2013 - Mérida, YU (Hotel Fiesta Americana)/Oct. 6 - 8
Number of non-conference events/year: 2

Publications:
Behavior Analysis in Practice; adv.
Inside Behavior Analysis; quarterly; adv.
Membership Directory; on-line
The Analysis of Verbal Behavior; adv.
The Behavior Analyst; semi-annually; adv.

Association for Behavioral and Cognitive Therapies (1966)
305 Seventh Ave.
Suite 16th Fl.
New York, NY 10001-6008
Tel: (212) 647-1890 *Fax:* (212) 647-1865
E-Mail: membership@aabt.org
Website: abct.org
Members: 4500 individuals
Staff: 9
Annual Budget: $2-5,000,000

Personnel:
Executive Director: Mary Jane Eimer CAE
  E-Mail: mjeimer@aabt.org

Director, Administration and Conventions Manager: Mary Ellen Brown
  E-Mail: mebrown@aabt.org
Managing Editor and Advertising Manager: Stephanie Schwartz
  E-Mail: sschwartz@abct.org
Director, Publications: David Teisler CAE
  E-Mail: teisler@aabt.org
Bookkeeper: Damaris Williams
  E-Mail: dwilliams@abct.org
Manager, Membership Services: Lisa Yarde
  E-Mail: lyarde@abct.org

Historical Note:
Founded as the Association for Advancement of the Behavioral Therapies. Assumed its present name in 1968. AABT's mission is to advance scientific approach to the understanding and amelioration of problems of the human condition. Membership: $250 (Full); $170 (New Professional); $85 (Post-Baccalaureate); $59 (Student).

Meetings/Conferences: Annual
Conference Chair: Mary Ellen Brown
2013 - Nashville, TN/Nov. 21 - 24
2014 - Philadelphia, PA/Nov. 20 - 23
2016 - New York City, NY/Oct. 27 - 30

Publications:
Behavior Therapy; quarterly; adv.
Cognitive and Behavioral Practice; quarterly; adv.
Membership Directory; on-line
the Behavior Therapist; adv.

Membership List Available to Non-members

Association for Behavioral Health & Wellness (1994)
1325 G St. NW
Suite 500
Washington, DC 20005
Tel: (202) 449-7660 *Fax:* (202) 449-7659
E-Mail: info@abhw.org
Website: abhw.org
Members: 8 organizations
Staff: 1
Annual Budget: $250-500,000

Personnel:
President and Chief Executive Officer: Pamela Greenberg MPP
  E-Mail: greenberg@abhw.org

Historical Note:
ABHW formerly the American Managed Behavioral Healthcare Association (AMBHA). ABHW's mission is to strive to the national voice for behavioral health and wellness companies committed to improving health care access and outcomes. Membership: $5,000-70,000/year (Company).

Publications:
Member Directory; on-line

Association for Biblical Higher Education (2004)
5850 T.G. Lee Blvd.
Suite 130
Orlando, FL 32822
Tel: (407) 207-0808 *Fax:* (407) 207-0840
E-Mail: info@abhe.org
Website: abhe.org
Members: 35000 students and 200 colleges
Staff: 8
Annual Budget: $1-2,000,000
Tax: 501(c)(3)

Personnel:
President: Dr. Ralph E. Enlow Jr.
  E-Mail: renlow@abhe.org
Chief Information Officer, Systems Analyst: Lucian Chenard
  E-Mail: lchenard@abhe.org
Director, Operations and Communications: Carol Dibble
  E-Mail: carol@abhe.org
Executive Vice President, Resource Development and Student Programs: Dr. David Medders
  E-Mail: dmedders@abhe.org

Historical Note:
Formerly Accrediting Association of Bible Institutes and Bible Colleges; assumed its current name in 2004, to reflect its expansion of scope with graduate education accreditation and programmatic accreditation and in order to address its expansion of services to include affiliate institutions. ABHE's mission is to enhance the quality and credibility of higher educational institutions that engage students in biblical, transformational, experiential, and missional higher education.

Meetings/Conferences: Annual
Conference Chair: Carol Dibble
2013 - Orlando, FL (Hilton Orlando)/Feb. 13 - 16
2014 - Orlando, FL (Wyndham Orlando Resort)/Feb. 19 - 22
2015 - Orlando, FL (Wyndham Orlando Resort)/Feb. 19 - 22
Number of non-conference events/year: 2

Publications:
Membership Directory; on-line

Membership List Available to Non-members

Association for Birth Psychology (1978)
9115 Ridge Blvd.
Brooklyn, NY 11209
Tel: (347) 517-4607
E-Mail: birthpsychology@aol.com
Website: birthpsychology.org
Members: 360 individuals
Staff: 1
Annual Budget: Under $10,000

Personnel:
Executive Director: Leslie Feher PhD

Historical Note:
ABP's mission is to establish birth psychology as a viable specialty and to allow many diverse professionals to advance theoretical development, empirical research and clinical application, by obtaining a broad spectrum of inquiry into the psychological impact of birth experience and related stages on the individual throughout their life.

Publications:
BIRTH PSYCHOLOGY BULLETIN

Association for Bridge Construction and Design (1976)
Country Office Bldg.
Fifth Floor
Pittsburgh, PA 15219
Tel: (412) 350-4005
Website: abcdpittsburgh.org
Members: 30 companies and 250 individuals
Staff: 3
Annual Budget: $10-25,000

Personnel:
President: Stephen Shanley
  E-Mail: sshanley@abcdpittsburgh.org

Historical Note:
ABCD seeks to stimulate science of bridge design, construction, and reconstruction by providing a forum for members to exchange and develop new ideas and techniques. Has no paid staff. Members are engineering consultants, contractors, material suppliers, or governmental agencies or company or organization that is involved in the design or construction of bridges or students. Membership: $20 (Individual); $150 (Company).

Publications:
Newsletter

Association for Business Communication (1935)
P.O. Box 6143
Nacogdoches, TX 75962--6143
Tel: (936) 468-6280 *Fax:* (936) 468-6281
Website: businesscommunication.org
Members:
800 institutions
1800 individuals
Staff: 3
Annual Budget: $250-500,000

Personnel:
Executive Director: Jim Dubinsky
  E-Mail: exec_director@businesscommunication.org
Web Editor: Barbara D'Angelo
  E-Mail: abcweb@businesscommunication.org

Historical Note:
ABC is an international, interdisciplinary organization committed to advancing business communication research, education, and practice. Membership: $100 (Sustaining); $80 (Active); $60 (Limited Publications); $30 (Student/Retired).

Meetings/Conferences: Annual
2013 - Louisville, KY/March 6 - 9
Number of non-conference events/year: 1

Publications:
Business Communication Quarterly (BCQ); quarterly
The Journal of Business Communication (JBC)

Association for Business Simulation and Experiential Learning (1974)
C/O Wayne State University, Department of Marketing 5201 Cass
Suite 300
Detroit, MI 48202-3930
Fax: (313) 577-5486
Website: absel.org
Members: 225 individuals
Staff: 7
Annual Budget: $25-50,000

Personnel:
Dean, ABSEL Fellows: Hugh "Mac" Cannon CAE
  E-Mail: hugh.cannon@wayne.edu

Historical Note:
ABSEL is a professional association whose purpose is to develop and promote the use of experiential techniques and simulations in the field of business education and development. Membership: $60/year (Individual).

Meetings/Conferences: Annual
Conference Chair: Bill Wellington
2013 - Oklahoma City, OK (The Skirvin hotel)/March 6 - 8

Publications:
ABSEL Newsletter
The Journal of Simulation and Gaming; bi-monthly

Association for Canadian Studies in the United States (1971)
1740 Massachusetts Ave. NW
Nitze 516
Washington, DC 20036
Tel: (202) 775-9007 *Fax:* (202) 775-0061
E-Mail: info@acsus.org
Website: acsus.org
Members: 1000 individuals
Staff: 4
Annual Budget: $250-500,000
Tax: 501(c)(3)

Personnel:
Executive Director: David Archibald
Treasurer: Neal Carter
Communications Officer: Linda Docter
  E-Mail: lrdocter@aol.com
Managing Editor: Catherine O'Mara Wallace

Historical Note:
ACSUS's mission is to serves its members and the community by supporting teaching, research, and outreach on Canada and Canadian studies. Membership is comprised of university professors involved in teaching about Canada. Membership: $60 (Retiree); $30 (Student); $60-150 (Individual, based on Income); $140 (Institution); 1,500 (Life Time).

Meetings/Conferences: Biennial

Publications:
ACSUS e-dition; monthly
American Review of Canadian Studies; quarterly
American Review of Canadian Studiesq; quarterly
Think Canada; biennially

Association for Career and Technical Education Research (1966)
North Carolina State Univ., 13 Ricks Hall
P.O. Box 7607
Raleigh, NC 27695-7607
Tel: (919) 515-1759 *Fax:* (703) 683-7424
Website: agri.wsu.edu/acter
Members: 27,000 career and technical educators, administrators, researchers, guidance counselor
Staff: 1
Annual Budget: Under $10,000

Personnel:
President: Barry Croom
  E-Mail: barry_croom@ncsu.edu

Historical Note:
Formerly American Vocational Education Research Association, AVERA (2005). ACTER mission is to provide leadership in developing an educated, prepared, adaptable and competitive workforce. Membership: $80 (Professional); $60 (International); $31 (Retired).

Association for Chemoreception Sciences (1979)
5841 Cedar Lake Rd.
Suite 204
Minneapolis, MN 55416
Tel: (952) 646-2035 *Fax:* (952) 545-6073
E-Mail: info@achems.org

Website: achems.org
Members: 725 individuals
Staff: 2
Annual Budget: $250-500,000
Tax: 501(c)(3)

Personnel:
Executive Director: Tisha Kehn
  E-Mail: tishakehn@llmsi.com
Treasurer: Joe Travers

Historical Note:
AChemS seeks to advance the understanding of chemosensory mechanisms by bringing to one forum the variety of different scientific disciplines currently being used to approach the chemical senses. Members are scientists interested in the physiological reception of chemical stimuli. Has no paid officers or full-time staff. Membership: $143 (Regular); $40(Student); Free (Emeritus).

Meetings/Conferences: Annual
2013 - Huntington Beach, CA (Hyatt Regency)/April 17 - 21

Publications:
AChemS Newsletter
Chemical Senses; monthly
Member Directory; on-line

Association for Child Psychoanalysis (1965)
7820 Enchanted Hills Blvd.
Suite A-233
Rio Rancho, NM 87144
Tel: (505) 771-0372 *Fax:* (866) 534-7555
E-Mail: childanalysis@comcast.net
Website: childanalysis.org
Members: 600 individuals
Staff: 3
Annual Budget: $100-250,000
Tax: 501(c)(3)

Personnel:
President: Anita Schmukler
  E-Mail: anitagschmukler36@verizon.net
Administrator: Tricia Hall
Treasurer: Barbara Streeter
  E-Mail: BStreeter@hannaperkins.org

Historical Note:
Formerly (1971) American Association for Child Psychoanalysis. ACP advocates educational programs for its members as well as for other mental health professionals. It collaborates among members in different parts of the country and the world, for the development of strategies to inform the general public about the value of a psychoanalytic frame of reference to the understanding of childhood, adolescence, and parenting. Membership: $200 (Individual); $75 (Candidates).

Meetings/Conferences: Annual
2013 - San Diego, CA/May 3 - 5

Publications:
ACP Newsletter; bi-annually
Member Directory; on-line; adv.

Association for Childhood Education International (1931)
17904 Georgia Ave.
Suite 215
Olney, MD 20832-2277
Tel: (301) 570-2111 *Fax:* (301) 570-2212
TollFree: (800) 423-3563
E-Mail: aceihq@aol.com
Website: acei.org
Members: 7000 individuals and organisations
Staff: 15
Annual Budget: $2-5,000,000
Tax: 501(c)(3)

Personnel:
Executive Director: Diane Whitehead
Manager, Operations: Michelle Allen
Editor and Director, Publications: Anne Watson Bauer
  E-Mail: editorial@acei.org
Manager, Member Relations and Communications: Sheri Levin
  E-Mail: slevin@acei.org
Accounting Manager: Emebet G. Micheal
Director, Advocacy and Outreach: Yvette Murphy
Director, Conferences: Lisa Wenger

Historical Note:
Established in 1892 as the International Kindergarten Union, merged with the National Council of Primary Education in 1931 and assumed current name. ACEI's mission is to promote and support the optimal education and development of children, from birth through early

adolescence, and to influence the professional growth of educators and the efforts of others who are committed to the needs of children in a changing society. Members are educators and advocates. Membership: $30-179/year.

Meetings/Conferences: Annual
Conference Chair: Lisa Wenger

Publications:
ACEI Action; on-line
ACEI E-news; monthly
ACEI Exchange; on-line
Childhood Education; bi-monthly; adv.
International Research Bulletin; semi-annually
Journal of Research in Childhood Education (JRCE); quarterly; adv.

Association for Clinical Pastoral Education (1967)
1549 Clairmont Rd.
Suite 103
Decatur, GA 30033-4611
Tel: (404) 320-1472 *Fax:* (404) 320-0849
E-Mail: acpe@acpe.edu
Website: acpe.edu
Members: 3500 individuals
Staff: 10
Annual Budget: $2-5,000,000

Personnel:
Interim Executive Director: Deryck Durston
  E-Mail: deryck@acpe.edu
Senior Accounting Assistant: Tonya Beasley
  E-Mail: tonya@acpe.edu
Executive Administrative Assistant: Terry Izaguirre
  E-Mail: terry@acpe.edu
Special Projects Coordinator: John Michael Roch
  E-Mail: john@acpe.edu
Administrative Assistant, Accreditation: Beverly Shinholster
  E-Mail: beverly@acpe.edu
Coordinator, Membership Services: Tobey Willis
  E-Mail: tobey@acpe.edu

Historical Note:
Formed by a combination of four CPE organizations: the Lutheran Council of the U.S.A., the Association of Clinical Pastoral Educators, the Council for Clinical Training and the Institute of Pastoral Care. Assumed present name in 1968. ACPE is an association meant to advance experience-based theological education for seminarians, clergy and lay persons of diverse cultures, ethnic groups and faith traditions. Membership: $65(Student/ Affiliate), $110(Individual)

Meetings/Conferences:
2013 - Indianapolis, IN (Indianapolis Marriott Downtown)/May 11 - 15
2013 - Indianapolis, IN (Indianapolis Marriott Downtown)/May 15 - 18
Number of non-conference events/year: 1

Publications:
E-Newsletter; monthly

Membership List Available to Non-members

Association for Clinical Research Training (2002)
1500 Sunday Dr.
Suite 102
Raleigh, NC 27607
Tel: (919) 861-4538 *Fax:* (919) 787-4916
E-Mail: info@acrtraining.org
Website: acrtraining.org
Members: 50 institutions
Staff: 2
Tax: 501(c)(6)

Personnel:
Executive Director: Angela L. Kite
  E-Mail: admin@acrtraining.org
Meeting Registrar: Tracy Steadman

Historical Note:
ACRT's mission is to improve the health of the public by increasing the amount and quality of clinical research through expanding and continually improving clinical research training. Membership: $1,000/year (Institutional).

Meetings/Conferences: Annual
Conference Chair: Tracy Steadman
2013 - Washington, DC (Omni Shoreham Hotel)/April 17 - 19

Publications:
Clinical Research Perspective; adv.
Membership Directory; on-line

Association for Communication Administration

C/O University of Miami, Strategic
Communication
P.O. Box 249117
Coral Gables, FL 33124-9117
Tel: (305) 284-2211
Website: usca.edu/communications/Harpine/
  ACA/index.html
Staff: 3
Annual Budget: $10-25,000

Personnel:
President: William Harpine
Membership Contact: Dr. Jeanne Persuit
Editor: Don W. Stacks
  E-Mail: don.stacks@miami.edu

Historical Note:
Mission is to promote discussion, study, criticism, research, and application of effective principles of education administration for the communication disciplines.

Publications:
Journal of the Association for Communication
  Administration

Association for Communication Excellence (1913)
59 College Rd.
Durham, NH 03824
Tel: (603) 862-1564 *Fax:* (603) 862-1585
E-Mail: ace.info@unh.edu
Website: aceweb.org
Members: 600 individuals
Staff: 1
Annual Budget: $100-250,000
Tax: 501(c)(4)

Personnel:
Interim Executive Director: Holly Young
  E-Mail: ace.info@unh.edu

Historical Note:
Founded as American Association of Agricultural College Editors, became Agricultural Communicators in Education in 1978 and assumed its current name in 2003. Members are writers, editors, broadcasters, graphic designers, teachers and researchers who are involved in the dissemination of agricultural, food science and natural resource information. Membership: $50 (Active Members); $25 (Full-Time Students); $250 (Life/Retired Members).

Meetings/Conferences: Annual
Number of non-conference events/year: 1

Publications:
Journal of Applied Communications; quarterly
Newsletter

Membership List Available to Non-members

Association for Community Affiliated Plans (2001)
1015 15th St. NW
Suite 950
Washington, DC 20005
Tel: (202) 204-7508 *Fax:* (202) 204-7517
Website: communityplans.net
Members: 58 organizations
Staff: 9
Annual Budget: $2-5,000,000

Personnel:
Chief Executive Officer: Margaret A. Murray
  E-Mail: mmurray@communityplans.net
Director, Finance and Administration: Sharon Gibson
  E-Mail: sgibson@communityplans.net
*Vice President, Quality Management and Operational
  Support:* Deborah Kilstein
  E-Mail: dkilstein@communityplans.net
Director, Medicaid Policy: Andrea Maresca
  E-Mail: amaresca@communityplans.net
Program Associate: Tim Murphy
  E-Mail: tmurphy@communityplans.net
Senior Director, Communications: Jeff Van Ness
  E-Mail: jvanness@communityplans.net
Senior Program Associate: Joseph Person
  E-Mail: jperson@communityplans.net
Treasurer: Christina Severin

Historical Note:
ACAP's mission is to represent and strengthen not-for-profit, safety net health plans as they work with providers and caregivers in their communities to improve the health and well being of vulnerable populations in a cost effective manner.

Meetings/Conferences: Annual

Publications:
Newsletter

Association for Commuter Transportation (1976)
1341 G St. NW
Tenth Floor
Washington, DC 20005
Tel: (202) 719-5331
TollFree: (888) 719-5772
E-Mail: info@actweb.org
Website: netforum.avectra.com
Members: 800 individuals and organizations
Staff: 3
Annual Budget: $250-500,000
Tax: 501(c)(6)

Personnel:
Executive Director: Caryn R. Souza
  E-Mail: souza@actweb.org
Specialist, Marketing and Outreach: Kevin Oliff
  E-Mail: oliff@actweb.org
Administrative Assistant: Marlon Powell
  E-Mail: powell@actweb.org

Historical Note:
Formed in Savannah, Georgia in August 1976 by 31 charter van pool pioneers as the National Association of Van Pool Operators, assumed its present name in 1984 and absorbed the Association of Ridesharing Professionals in 1986. ACT supports individual mobility management professionals and organizational members in their efforts to reduce traffic congestion, conserve energy, and improve air quality. Members are corporations, employers, public agencies, transit authorities, van pool management companies, real estate developers and individuals involved in promoting alternatives to drive alone commuting. Membership: $375 (Individual); $575 (Organization/ Company); $40 (Student); $280 (New Individual); $430 (New Organizational); $30 (New Student).

Meetings/Conferences: Annual
2013 - San Antonio, TX (San Antonio Luxury Hotel)/
  July 27 - 31
2014 - San Francisco, CA (Grand Hyatt San Francisco)/
  Aug. 2 - 6
2015 - Baltimore, MD (AAA- Four Diamond Hotel)/July
  25 - 29

Publications:
ACT E-news; bi-weekly; adv.
TDM Review; quarterly; adv.

Association for Comparative Economic Studies (1972)
333 N. Pennington Dr. #57
Chandler, AZ 85224-8269
Website: acesecon.org
Members: 700 individuals
Staff: 4
Annual Budget: $100-250,000

Personnel:
President: Pekka Sutela

Historical Note:
Formed by a merger of the Association for the Study of Soviet-Type Economics (1959) and the Association for Comparative Economics (1963). ACES's mission is to provide scholarly exchange among persons interested in comparative studies of economic systems, institutions, economic performance and development and to further the growth of research and instruction on these topics. Membership includes academics, economists and political scientists employed by international agencies, government and private firms, banks and policy makers. Membership: $80 (Individual); $65 (Organization/Company).

Meetings/Conferences: Annual
2013 - San Diego, CA/Jan. 4 - 6
2014 - Philadelphia, PA/Jan. 3 - 5

Publications:
ACES Newsletter
Journal of Comparative Economics

Association for Competitive Technology (ACT)
1401 K St. NW
Suite 502
Washington, DC 20005
Tel: (202) 331-2130 *Fax:* (202) 331-2131
E-Mail: info@actonline.org
Website: actonline.org
Members: 5000 individuals
Staff: 5
Annual Budget: $2-5,000,000
Tax: 501(c)(6)

Personnel:
Executive Director: Morgan W. Reed III
  E-Mail: mreed@ACTonline.org

Vice President, Public Affairs: Mark Blafkin
  E-Mail: mblafkin@actonline.org
Director, Communications: Jonathan Godfrey
Director, Membership: Melissa Lee

Historical Note:
ACT advocates for an environment that inspires and rewards innovation while providing resources to help its members leverage their intellectual assets to raise capital, create jobs, and continue innovating. Members are small and mid-size app developers and information technology firms.

Meetings/Conferences: Annual

Publications:
Membership Directory; on-line

Association for Comprehensive Energy Psychology (1993)
233 E. Lancaster Ave.
Suite 104
Ardmore, PA 19003
Tel: (619) 861-2237 *Fax:* (484) 418-1019
E-Mail: admin@energypsych.org
Website: energypsych.org
Members: 600 individuals
Staff: 5
Annual Budget: $250-500,000
Tax: 501(c)(3)

Personnel:
Executive Director: Robert Schwarz PsyD, DCEP
  E-Mail: acep_ed@energypsych.org
Manager, Conferences: Lois Miller CAE
  E-Mail: ldmiller@optonline.net
Office Manager: Leslie Primavera
  E-Mail: acep@energypsych.org
Contact, Communications and Outreach: Emily Snider
  E-Mail: acepoffice@gmail.com
Coordinator, Certification: Debby Vajda LCSW, DCEP
  E-Mail: certification@energypsych.org

Historical Note:
ACEP's mission is to research, education, and promotion of energy psychology among health professionals and the public throughout the world. ACEP members are psychotherapists and other care professionals interested in the integration of traditional mind/body therapies with current practice. Membership: $95 (Regular/Associate); $45 (Student); $300 (Affiliate); $38-76 (International Member); $90 (Regular Canadian).

Continuing Education:
Certification Designation/s: EFT, CEHP, DCEP

Meetings/Conferences: Annual
Conference Chair: Lois Miller CAE

Publications:
E-Newsletter; quarterly
Membership Directory; on-line
The Energy Field; quarterly; adv.

Membership List Available to Non-members

Association for Computational Linguistics (1962)
209 N. Eighth St.
Stroudsburg, PA 18360
Tel: (570) 476-8006 *Fax:* (570) 476-0860
E-Mail: acl@aclweb.org
Website: aclweb.org
Members: 2100 individuals
Staff: 1
Annual Budget: $50-100,000

Personnel:
Business Manager: Priscilla Rasmussen

Historical Note:
Formerly (1968) Association for Machine Translation and Computational Linguistics. Association for Computational Linguistics is the international scientific and professional society for people working on problems involving natural language and computation. Affiliated with the International Committee on Computational Linguistics. Membership: $60 (Regular/Student-Employed); $30 (Retired/Student-Unemployed).

Meetings/Conferences: Annual

Publications:
Computational Linguistics; quarterly
Membership Directory; on-line

Association for Computers and the Humanities (1978)
C/O Boston University
One Silber Way
Boston, MA 02215

Tel: (617) 353-2000
Website: ach.org
Members: 380 individuals
Staff: 5
Annual Budget: Under $10,000
Tax: 501(c)(3)

Personnel:
President: Bethany Nowviskie
    E-Mail: bethany@virginia.edu
Webmaster: Jeremy Boggs
    E-Mail: jeremy@clioweb.org
Editor: Willard McCarty
    E-Mail: willard.mccarty@kcl.ac.uk
Treasurer: Jarom McDonald
    E-Mail: jarom_mcdonald@byu.edu
Executive Secretary: Vika Zafrin
    E-Mail: vzafrin@bu.edu

Historical Note:
Formed to foster computer-aided scholarship and teaching in the humanities and arts fields. Membership: $75/year.

Meetings/Conferences: Annual
2013 - Lincoln, NE (University of Nebraska, Lincoln)/
July 16 - 19

Publications:
ACH Newsletter
Digital Humanities; quarterly; adv.

Association for Computing Machinery (1947)
P.O. Box 30777
New York, NY 10087-0777
Tel: (212) 869-7440 *Fax:* (212) 944-1318
TollFree: (800) 342-6626
E-Mail: acmhelp@acm.org
Website: acm.org
Members: 75000 individuals
Staff: 94
Annual Budget: $50-100,000,000
Tax: 501(c)(3)

Personnel:
Executive Director and Chief Executive Officer: John R.
    White
    E-Mail: white@acm.org
*Associate Director, Policy and Administration and Manager,
    Human Resources:* Monique Chang
    E-Mail: chang@acm.org
Program Manager, Conference Operations: Ashley Cozzi
    E-Mail: acozzi@hq.acm.org
Coordinator, Public Relations: Virginia Gold
    E-Mail: gold@acm.org
Director, Information Systems: Wayne S. Graves
    E-Mail: graves@acm.org
Director, Financial Operations and Budgeting: Russell
    Harris
    E-Mail: rharris@acm.org
Director, Membership Services: Lillian Israel
    E-Mail: israel@acm.org
Senior Accountant: Craig Jacobson
    E-Mail: jacobson@acm.org
Director, Publications: Bernard Rouse
    E-Mail: rous@acm.org
Director, Public Policy: Cameron Wilson
    E-Mail: cameron.wilson@acm.org

Historical Note:
*Formerly the Eastern Association for Computing Machinery,
incorporated in Delaware(1954). ACM's mission is to
advance the skills of information technology professionals
and students. It operates several special interest groups that
offer conferences, publications, and activities for computing
professionals. Membership: $99 (Professional); $19-62
(Student); $74 (Retired).*

Continuing Education:
Certification Designation/s: ICCP

Publications:
ACM Inroads
Acmqueue
Communications of the ACM
Computers in Entertainment; quarterly
eLearn Magazine
Interactions
Ubiquity
XRDS

Membership List Available to Non-members

Association for Conflict Resolution (1972)
12100 Sunset Hills Rd.
Suite 130

Reston, VA 20190
Tel: (703) 234-4141 *Fax:* (703) 435-4390
E-Mail: membership@acrnet.org
Website: acrnet.org
Members: 5000 Individuals
Staff: 8
Annual Budget: $500-1,000,000
Tax: 501(c)(3)

Personnel:
Contact, Marketing: Valerie Bowman
    E-Mail: vbowman@acrnet.org
Contact, Conferences and Meetings: Suzanne Burnett
    E-Mail: sburnett@acrnet.org
Contact, Membership Services: Catalina Mercado
    E-Mail: cmercado@acrnet.org
Contact, Communications and Publications: Leah Retting
    E-Mail: lretting@acrnet.org

Historical Note:
*Founded as Society of Professionals in Dispute Resolution,
merged with Academy of Family Mediators and Conflict
Resolution Education Network to become ACR (2001). ACR
works to enhance the practice and public understanding
of conflict resolution. Members are specialists in labor,
environment, family, community and other types of
dispute resolution. Membership: $195 (Individual); $205
(Practitioner/Educator/Researcher); $230 (Advanced
Practitioner); $110 (Associate), $80 (Student); $325-1400
(Organizational Affiliate); $50 (Retiree); $35 (Youth), $63
(International Virtual).*

Continuing Education:
Enrollment: 500
Certification Designation/s: AP, CDP

Meetings/Conferences:
Conference Chair: Suzanne Burnett
2013 - Minneapolis, MN/Oct. 9 - 12
2014 - Cincinnati, OH/Oct. 8 - 11

Publications:
ACR Update; monthly; adv.
ACResolution; quarterly; adv.
Conflict Resolution Quarterly (CRQ); quarterly; adv.
Membership Directory; on-line

Membership List Available to Non-members

Association for Conservation Information (1938)
1720 Carey Ave.
Suite 520
Cheyenne, WY 82001
Tel: (304) 269-0524
Website: aci-net.org
Members: 65 individuals and 45 natural resource
    agencies
Staff: 3
Annual Budget: $10-25,000

Personnel:
President: Don King
    E-Mail: Don.King@state.tn.us
Treasurer: Chuck Schlueter
    E-Mail: chuck.schlueter@state.sd.us
Legal Counsel: Sean Scoggin

Historical Note:
*Formerly American Association for Conservation
Information. ACI serves to further natural resource
conservation and exchange. Membership consists of the
information, education, and public affairs staffs of state,
federal and Canadian wildlife conservation, parks and
natural resource agencies. Membership: $25 (Individual);
$200 (Organization) $50 (Associate/Non-Voting); $500
(Sponsors); $250 (Supporting); $100 (Sustaining).*

Meetings/Conferences: Annual

Publications:
Membership Directory; annually
The Balance Wheel; quarterly

The Association for Consortium Leadership (1968)
C/O Virginia Tidewater Consortium for Higher
Education
4900 Powhatan Ave.
Norfolk, VA 23529-0293
Tel: (757) 683-3183 *Fax:* (757) 683-4515
Website: national-acl.com
Members: 60 consortia of institutions
Staff: 2
Annual Budget: $25-50,000
Tax: 501(c)(3)

Personnel:
Executive Director: Dr. Lawrence G. Dotolo PhD

    E-Mail: lgdotolo@aol.com
Director, Programs and Administration: Nicola Vocola
    Beltz
    E-Mail: nicola@national-acl.com

Historical Note:
*Formerly known as the Cooperative Program of the
American Association for Higher Education, and the
Council for Interinstitutional Leadership (1994). ACL
encourages voluntary cooperation between colleges
and universities. ACL's purpose is to help colleges and
universities cooperate with one another to improve
education and strengthen management. Membership: $250
(Small Consortium); $500 (Regular Consortium); $1,000
(Sustaining); $5,000 (Corporate); $250 (Small).*

Meetings/Conferences: Annual
Conference Chair: Nicola Vocola Beltz

Publications:
ACL Consortium Directory; annually
Business Consortia eNewsletter; weekly
Higher Education Consortia Magazine
Membership Directory; on-line

Association for Consumer Research (1969)
C/O Labovitz School of Business and Economics,
University of Minnesota Duluth
11 E. Superior St., Suite 210
Duluth, MN 55802
Tel: (218) 726-7853 *Fax:* (218) 726-6338
E-Mail: acr@acrwebsite.org
Website: acrwebsite.org
Members: 1700 individuals
Staff: 4
Annual Budget: $500-1,000,000
Tax: 501(c)(3)

Personnel:
Executive Director: Rajiv Vaidyanathan
Executive Manager, Membership Services: Praveen
    Aggarwal
Contact, Communications: Eugen Cazacu
Coordinator, Communications: Ekant Veer

Historical Note:
*ACR's mission is to advance consumer research and
facilitate the exchange of scholarly information among
members of academia, industry, and government worldwide.
Members are business people, educators and government
officials interested in consumer research. Membership: $60
(Regular); $20 (Full-Time Student/Retired, over 65, not
employed).*

Continuing Education:
Enrollment: 1500

Meetings/Conferences: Annual
2013 - Chicago, IL/Oct. 3 - 6
2014 - Baltimore, MD/Oct. 23 - 26
2015 - New Orleans, LA/Oct. 1 - 4

Publications:
ACR Newsletter
Advances in Consumer Research; annually

Membership List Available to Non-members

Association for Continuing Higher Education (1939)
1700 Asp Ave.
OCCE Administration Building, Room 233
Norman, OK 73072-6400
Tel: (405) 329-0249 *Fax:* (405) 325-4888
TollFree: (800) 807-2243
E-Mail: admin@acheinc.org
Website: acheinc.org
Members: 1500 individuals and 400 institutions
Staff: 5
Annual Budget: $250-500,000
Tax: 501(c)(3)

Personnel:
Executive Vice President: James P. Pappas
    E-Mail: jpappas@ou.edu
Editor: James K. Broomall
*Coordinator, Membership Services and Administrative
    Assistant:* Rebekah Law
    E-Mail: rlaw@acheinc.org
Coordinator, Membership Services and Marketing: Tarra
    Walker
    E-Mail: twalker@acheinc.org
Manager, Operations: Ynez Walske
    E-Mail: ywalske@ou.edu

Historical Note:
*Formerly (1973) known as Association of University
Evening Colleges. ACHE is dedicated to promote*

lifelong learning and excellence in continuing higher education. Membership: $42.50 (Professional); $255-500 (Institution); $495 (Affiliate); $255 (Organizational); $12.50 (Student/Retired).

Meetings/Conferences: Annual

Publications:
Five Minutes with ACHE
Membership Directory; on-line
The Journal of Continuing Higher Education

Association for Continuing Legal Education
(1964)
P.O. Box 4646
Austin, TX 78765
Tel: (512) 453-4340 *Fax:* (512) 451-2911
E-Mail: aclea@aclea.org
Website: aclea.org
Members: 600 individuals
Staff: 4
Annual Budget: $500-1,000,000

Personnel:
Executive Director: Donna J. Passons
  E-Mail: donna@clesolutions.com

Historical Note:
Formerly (1964) National Association of Continuing Legal Education Administrators and then (1995) Association for Continuing Legal Education. ACLEA's mission is to serve the CLE profession worldwide through leadership, education, and development. Members are organizations and individuals involved in providing continuing legal education. Membership: $245 (Professional); $195 (Additional Members); $65 (Associate).

Meetings/Conferences: Semi-Annual
2013 - Clearwater, FL (Sheraton Sand Key Resort)/Feb. 2 - 5
2013 - Baltimore, MD (Baltimore Marriott Waterfront)/ Aug. 3 - 6
2014 - Boston, MA (Westin Copley Place Boston)/Aug. 2 - 5

Publications:
@CLEA News; on-line
In the Loop; quarterly
Membership Directory; on-line

Association for Convention Marketing Executives
(1990)
191 Clarksville Rd.
Princeton, NJ 08550
Tel: (609) 269-2461 *Fax:* (609) 799-7032
E-Mail: info@CSPIonline.org
Website: cspionline.org
Members: 175 individuals
Staff: 4
Annual Budget: $50-100,000
Tax: 501(c)(6)

Personnel:
Executive Director: Gabrielle Copperwheat
  E-Mail: gcopperwheat@cmasolutions.com
Contact, Membership Inquiries: Kristin Couch
  E-Mail: KCouch@cmasolutions.com
Contact, Media Inquiries: Kaitlin Friedmann
  E-Mail: kfriedmann@cmasolutions.com

Historical Note:
Formerly (2001) the Association for Convention Sales and Marketing Executives. ACME's mission is to enhance the collaboration and partnership between destination marketing organizations and convention center sales professionals by delivering education, developing best practices and tracking industry trends worldwide. Active members are convention marketing executives affiliated with convention bureaus and centers whose chief objective is to establish and foster an effective marketing partnership. Membership: $50-350 (Active); $500 (Affiliate); $100 (Faculty); $50 (Student).

Meetings/Conferences: Annual
2013 - Washington, DC (Carnegie Library)/March 12 - 13

Publications:
CSPI newsletter; quarterly

Association for Corporate Growth *(1954)*
125 S. Wacker Dr.
Suite 3100
Chicago, IL 60606
Tel: (877) 358-2220
TollFree: (877) 358-2220
Website: acg.org
Members: 14000 individuals

Staff: 11
Annual Budget: $10-25,000,000
Tax: 501(c)(6)

Personnel:
President and Chief Executive Officer: Gary A. LaBranche CAE
  E-Mail: glabranche@acg.org
Manager, Membership Services: Sarah Foresman
  E-Mail: sforesman@acg.org
Director, Leadership Services: Carol Jezierski
  E-Mail: cjezierski@acg.org
Director, Chapter and Membership Programs: Shannon Kimball
  E-Mail: skimball@acg.org
Vice President, Communications and Marketing: Christine Melendes
  E-Mail: cmelendes@acg.org
Chief Financial Officer: John O'Loughlin
  E-Mail: joloughlin@acg.org
Director, Conference and Program Services: Jessica Petri
  E-Mail: jpetri@acg.org
Director, Communications: Matt Switzer
  E-Mail: mswitzer@acg.org

Historical Note:
ACG is the global community for mid-market private equity and merger and acquisition professionals along with CEOs of growing companies and related service providers. Organized into 50 + chapters in North America, Europe and Asia, ACG provides access to capital, connections and deals.

Meetings/Conferences: Annual
Conference Chair: Jessica Petri
2013 - Orlando, FL (Rosen Shingle Creek)/April 22 - 25
2014 - Las Vegas, NV (ARIA Resort and Casino Hotel)/ April 28 - 30

Publications:
Achieving Corporate Growth E-Newsletter; monthly; adv.
Advisor Link; monthly
Corporate Call; monthly
Membership Directory; on-line; adv.
Mergers and Acquisitions Magazine; monthly; adv.
Private Capital Review; monthly

Membership List Available to Non-members

Association for Counselor Education and Supervision *(1940)*
5999 Stevenson Ave.
Alexandria, VA 22304
Tel: (703) 212-2237
TollFree: (866) 815-2237
Website: acesonline.net
Members: 2711 individuals
Staff: 2
Annual Budget: $100-250,000

Personnel:
President: Gerard Lawson LPC, PhD
  E-Mail: glawson@vt.edu
Treasurer: Brian Dew PhD
  E-Mail: bdew@gsu.edu

Historical Note:
ACES emphasizes the need for quality education and supervision of counselors for all work settings. A division of the American Counseling Association. Membership: $163 (Professional/Regular); $93 (Student/Retired/New Professional).

Meetings/Conferences: Semi-Annual
2013 - Denver, CO (Hyatt Regency Denver at Colorado Convention Center)/Oct. 17 - 20

Publications:
ACES' journal; adv.
Graduate Student Newsletter; adv.

Association for Death Education and Counseling
(1976)
111 Deer Lake Rd.
Suite 100
Deerfield, IL 60015
Tel: (847) 509-0403 *Fax:* (847) 480-9282
E-Mail: adec@adec.org
Website: adec.org
Members: 2000 individuals and institutions
Staff: 8
Annual Budget: $500-1,000,000

Personnel:
Chief Staff Officer: Rick Koepke

  E-Mail: rkoepke@adec.org
Administrative Director: Emily Burch
  E-Mail: eburch@adec.org
Manager, Marketing and Communications: Kasia Chalko
  E-Mail: Kchalko@adec.org
Conference Director: Liz Freyn
  E-Mail: LFreyn@adec.org
Specialist, Member Services: Brenda Howe
  E-Mail: bhowe@adec.org
Editor: Deanna Marchetti
Manager, Education: Kismet Saglam
  E-Mail: KSaglam@adec.org

Historical Note:
ADEC is a professional organization dedicated to promoting excellence and recognizing diversity in death education, care of the dying, grief counseling and research in thanatology. Based on quality research and theory, the association provides information, support and resources to its international, multicultural, multidisciplinary membership and through it, to the public. Members are individuals and institutions involved in counseling the dying and bereaved. Membership: $185 (Individual); $395 (Institutional); $85 (Student); $95 (Senior).

Continuing Education:
Certification Designation/s: CT, FT

Meetings/Conferences: Annual
Conference Chair: Liz Freyn
2013 - Hollywood, CA (Renaissance Hollywood Hotel and Spa)/April 24 - 27
2014 - Baltimore, MD (Renaissance Baltimore Harborplace Hotel)/April 23 - 26
2015 - San Antonio, TX (Grand Hyatt San Antonio)/ April 8 - 11
2016 - Minneapolis, MN (Hilton Minneapolis)/April 13 - 16

Publications:
ADEC Connects; bi-monthly
The Forum; quarterly; adv.

Membership List Available to Non-members

Association for Demand Response & Smart Grid
(2004)
1301 Connecticut Ave. NW
Suite 350
Washington, DC 20036
Tel: (202) 296-1641
Website: demandresponsesmartgrid.org
Staff: 4
Tax: 501(c)(3)

Personnel:
Executive Director: Dan Delurey
Treasurer: Susan Covino
Manager, Research: Paul Pietsch
Manager, Programs and Outreach: Jenny Cross Senff

Historical Note:
Formerly The Demand Response Coordinating Committee (DRCC). ADS's mission is to increase the knowledge base in the U.S. on demand response and to facilitate the exchange of information and expertise among demand response practitioners and policy makers. Membership: $350 (Individual); $5,000 (Small Group); $15,000 (Large Group).

Meetings/Conferences: Annual
2013 - Washington, DC (Ronald Reagan Building and International Trade Center)/July 9 - 11

Publications:
ADS newsletter; monthly
Membership Directory; on-line

Association for Direct Instruction *(1981)*
P.O. Box 10252
Eugene, OR 97440
Tel: (541) 485-1293 *Fax:* (541) 868-1397
TollFree: (800) 995-2464
E-Mail: info@adihome.org
Website: adihome.org
Members: 1200 individuals
Staff: 3
Annual Budget: $500-1,000,000
Tax: 501(c)(3)

Personnel:
Director, Training: Bryan Wickman
  E-Mail: brywick@adihome.org

Historical Note:
ADI is a non-profit organization dedicated to promote and support the use of direct Instruction programs. Membership: $60 (Regular); $40 (Student); $100 (Sustaining); $200 (Institutional).

Publications:
Direct Instruction News; semi-annually
The Journal of Direct Instruction; semi-annually; adv.

Association for Documentary Editing *(1978)*
P.O. Box 400117
Charlottesville, VA 22904-4117
Tel: (434) 924-3569
Website: documentaryediting.org
Members: 350 Individuals
Staff: 3
Annual Budget: $25-50,000

Personnel:
President: Carol DeBoer-Langworthy
    E-Mail: CDBL@brown.edu
Editor: Jennifer E. Steenshorne
    E-Mail: jes2137@columbia.edu
Webmaster: Jennifer Stertzer
    E-Mail: jes7z@virginia.edu

Historical Note:
ADE works to make the papers of important individuals and groups accessible to all audiences through print, microfilm and digital editions. Members are teachers, archivists, editors and full-time editors. Membership: $60 (Regular); $100 (Sponsor/Sustaining); $250 (Patron); $500 (Benefactor); $40 (Retired); $15 (Students).

Meetings/Conferences: Annual
2013 - Ann Arbor, MI (Sheraton Ann Arbor Hotel)/July 11 - 13

Publications:
ADE e-Newsletter; quarterly
Documentary Editing; annually

Association for Dressings and Sauces *(1926)*
1100 Johnson Ferry Rd.
Suite 300
Atlanta, GA 30342
Tel: (404) 252-3663 *Fax:* (404) 252-0774
E-Mail: ads@kellencompany.com
Website: dressings-sauces.org
Members: 153 companies
Staff: 7
Annual Budget: $1-2,000,000
Tax: 501(c)(6)

Personnel:
Executive Director: Pam Chumley
Contact, Meetings: Jacque Knight
    E-Mail: jknight@kellencompany.com

Historical Note:
Formerly (1973) Mayonnaise and Salad Dressings Institute. ADS's purpose is to serve the best interests of industry members, its customers, and consumers of its products. ADS Represents international manufacturers and suppliers of salad dressing, dips, marinades, mustard, mayonnaise, and salsa. Membership: $1,250-36,197 (Manufacturing Member, based on sales); $1,206-11,042 (Supplier, based on annual sales of industry products).

Meetings/Conferences: Annual
Conference Chair: Jacque Knight

Publications:
Membership Directory; on-line

Association for Education and Rehabilitation of the Blind & Visually Impaired *(1984)*
1703 N. Beauregard St.
Suite 440
Alexandria, VA 22311-1717
Tel: (703) 671-4500 *Fax:* (703) 671-6391
TollFree: (877) 492-2708
E-Mail: aer@aerbvi.org
Website: aerbvi.org
Members: 5000 individuals
Staff: 6
Annual Budget: $500-1,000,000
Tax: 501(c)(3)

Personnel:
Executive Director: Lou Tutt
    E-Mail: lou@aerbvi.org
Director, Membership Services and Marketing: Ginger Croce
    E-Mail: ginger@aerbvi.org
Manager, Membership Services: Barbara James
    E-Mail: barb@aerbvi.org

Historical Note:
Formed as the result of a consolidation of the American Association of Workers for the Blind (1895) and the Association for Education of the Visually Handicapped

(1905) in 1984. AER's mission is to support professionals who provide education and rehabilitation services to people with visual impairments, offering professional development opportunities, publications, and public advocacy. Membership: $162 (Regular/International); $136 (Same Residential Household); $87 (Support/Clerical/Student/Retired/Associate); $132 (Transition); $625 (Corporate).

Continuing Education:
Enrollment: 4750

Meetings/Conferences: Annual

Publications:
AER Report; quarterly
AER's Journal; quarterly
Job Exchange Online; on-line
Membership Directory; on-line

Association for Education in Journalism and Mass Communication *(1912)*
234 Outlet Pointe Blvd.
Suite A
Columbia, SC 29210-5667
Tel: (803) 798-0271 *Fax:* (803) 772-3509
E-Mail: aejmchq@aol.com
Website: aejmc.org
Members: 3700 individuals
Staff: 9
Annual Budget: $1-2,000,000
Tax: 501(c)(3)

Personnel:
Executive Director: Jennifer H. McGill
    E-Mail: aejmchq@aol.com
Association Business Manager: Richard Burke
    E-Mail: richaejmc@aol.com
Newsletter Editor and Project Manager: Lillian Coleman
    E-Mail: aejmcnews@aol.com
Coordinator, Membership Services: Pamela Price
    E-Mail: aejmcmemsub@aol.com
Manager, Meetings and Conferences: Fred Williams
    E-Mail: fredaejmc@aol.com

Historical Note:
Formerly (1951) American Association for Teachers of Journalism, later (1950) changed its name to the Association for Education in Journalism and added the words "and Mass Communication" in 1982. AEJMC's mission is to promote the possible standards for journalism and mass communication education. It also seeks to defend and maintain freedom of communication in an effort to achieve better professional practice and a better informed public. Membership: $0-120/year.

Meetings/Conferences: Annual
Conference Chair: Fred Williams
2013 - Washington, DC (Renaissance Washington)/Aug. 8 - 11
2014 - Montreal, QC/Aug. 6 - 9
2015 - San Francisco, CA (Marriott San Francisco Marquis)/Aug. 5 - 9

Publications:
AEJMC News; adv.
Journalism and Communication Monographs; quarterly
Journalism and Mass Communication Directory; annually; adv.
Journalism and Mass Communication Educator; quarterly; adv.
Journalism and Mass Communication Quarterly; quarterly; adv.

Membership List Available to Non-members

Association for Educational Communications and Technology *(1923)*
1800 N. Stonelake Dr.
P.O. Box 2447
Bloomington, IN 47402-2447
Tel: (812) 335-7675 *Fax:* (812) 335-7678
TollFree: (877) 677-2328
E-Mail: aect@aect.org
Website: aect.org
Members: 4500 individuals
Staff: 8
Annual Budget: $500-1,000,000
Tax: 501(c)(6)

Personnel:
Executive Director: Phillip Harris
    E-Mail: pharris@aect.org
Manager, Membership, Subscription Services and Administrative Assistant: Judy Tackitt
    E-Mail: aect@aect.org

Director, Electronic Services: Larry Vernon
    E-Mail: lvernon@aect.org

Historical Note:
Formerly (1974) Department of Visual Instruction of the National Education Association. AECT's mission is to provide international leadership by promoting scholarship and best practices in the creation, use, and management of technologies for effective teaching and learning in a wide range of settings. Membership: $125-170 (Regular); $75 (Student); $400 (Corporate); $60 (Retired).

Meetings/Conferences: Annual
Conference Chair: Phillip Harris
Number of non-conference events/year: 1

Publications:
ETR&D (Educational Technology Research and Development); bi-monthly
Instructional Science
International Journal of Designs For Learning; on-line
iTech Digest; quarterly
Membership Directory; on-line
TechTrends; bi-monthly; adv.
The Journal of Applied Instructional Design; on-line

Membership List Available to Non-members

Association for Electronic Healthcare Transaction *(2007)*
230 E. Ohio St.
Suite 500
Chicago, IL 60611-3269
Tel: (312) 664-4467 *Fax:* (312) 664-6143
E-Mail: afehct@aol.com
Website: afehct.org
Members: 70 individuals
Staff: 1

Personnel:
Chairperson: Sheila Schweitzer

Historical Note:
Founded by Healthcare Information and Management Systems Society (HIMSS) on July 1, 2007. Purpose is to focus on financial services, administrative transactions systems, related technologies, and emerging trends such as medical banking.

Association for Enterprise Information
2111 Wilson Blvd.
Suite 400
Arlington, VA 22201
Tel: (703) 247-9474 *Fax:* (703) 522-3192
Website: afei.org
Staff: 13
Annual Budget: $1-2,000,000

Personnel:
President: Dave Chesebrough
    E-Mail: DChesebrough@afei.org
Business Operations Manager: Tammy Kicker
    E-Mail: tkicker@afei.org
Director: Betsy Lauer
    E-Mail: BLauer@afei.org

Historical Note:
The Association for Enterprise Information (AFEI) is an affiliate to the National Defense Industrial Association (NDIA). AFEI's mission is to support the advancement of enterprise information environments for the CIO community through industry/government collaboration. Membership: $75 (Industry); $500 (Non-Profit); $250-10,000 (Corporate).

Meetings/Conferences:
Conference Chair: Betsy Lauer
Number of non-conference events/year: 1

Association for Enterprise Opportunity *(1991)*
1111 16th St. NW
Suite 410
Washington, DC 20036
Tel: (202) 650-5580
E-Mail: aeo@assoceo.org
Website: aeoworks.org
Members: 400 organizations
Staff: 8
Annual Budget: $1-2,000,000
Tax: 501(c)(3)

Personnel:
President and Chief Executive Officer: Connie Evans
    E-Mail: cevans@aeoworks.org
Manager, Marketing: Matthew Crandall
    E-Mail: mcrandall@aeoworks.org
Director, Communications and Marketing: Kathryn Gray

E-Mail: kgray@aeoworks.org
Senior Vice President, Membership and New Initiatives:
Tammy A. Halevy
E-Mail: thalevy@aeoworks.org

Historical Note:
AEO supports the development of strong and effective U.S. microbusiness initiatives to assist underserved entrepreneurs in starting, stabilizing, and expanding businesses. Membership: $200- 400 (Practitioner); $250-5000 (Associate); $100 (Individual); $250 (Non-profit organizations).

Membership List Available to Non-members

The Association for Environmental Health and Sciences (1989)

150 Fearing St.
Amherst, MA 01002
Tel: (413) 549-5170 *Fax:* (413) 549-0579
TollFree: (888) 540-2347
E-Mail: info@aehs.com
Website: aehs.com
Members: 600 individuals
Staff: 6
Annual Budget: $250-500,000

Personnel:
Executive Director: Dr. Paul T. Kostecki PhD
E-Mail: info@AEHS.com

Historical Note:
AEHS's mission is to facilitate communication and foster cooperation among environmental health and science professionals. Membership: $125 (Individual); $75 (Student).

Meetings/Conferences: Annual
Number of non-conference events/year: 2

Publications:
Human and Ecological Risk Assessment; bi-monthly
International Journal of Phytoremediation
Soil and Sediment Contamination

Association for Equine Sports Medicine (1982)

8386 FM 455 E.
Pilot Point, TX 76258
Tel: (940) 686-2118 *Fax:* (940) 686-9330
E-Mail: sjwickler@csupomona.edu
Website: equine-sportsmedicine.com
Members: 350 individuals
Staff: 2
Annual Budget: Under $10,000

Personnel:
Executive Director: Holly M. Greene
Contact, Communications: Gabbe Bimson

Historical Note:
AESM members are veterinarians, health professionals, horse owners, horse trainers and others interested in the medical treatment of horses involved in athletic competition. Membership: $60/year (United States).

Association for Evolutionary Economics (1965)

C/O Ketner Business School, Ketner 327
Catawba College, 2300 W. Innes St.
Salisbury, NC 28144-2488
Tel: (704) 637-4293 *Fax:* (704) 637-4491
E-Mail: erhake@catawba.edu
Website: afee.net
Members: 1300 libraries and organizations,550 individuals
Staff: 3
Annual Budget: $100-250,000
Tax: 501(c)(3)

Personnel:
President: James Galbraith
E-Mail: galbraith@mail.utexas.edu
Secretary: Eric R. Hake
E-Mail: erhake@catawba.edu
Treasurer: David Zalewski

Historical Note:
A member of the Allied Social Science Associations, AFEE helps to foster the development of economic study and of economics as a social science based on the complex interrelationships of man and society. Members include institutional economists from the United States, Canada, Latin America, Western Europe, and Asia. Membership: $45-55 (Individual); $15 (Student).

Meetings/Conferences: Annual
2013 - San Diego, CA (San Diego Marriott Marquis and Marina)/Jan. 4 - 6
Number of non-conference events/year: 1

Publications:
Journal of Economic Issues; quarterly
Member Directory; on-line

Association for Experiential Education (1972)

3775 Iris Ave.
Suite Four
Boulder, CO 80301-2043
Tel: (303) 440-8844 *Fax:* (303) 440-9581
TollFree: (866) 522-8337
E-Mail: admin@aee.org
Website: aee.org
Members: 2000 individuals and 600 organizations
Staff: 7
Annual Budget: $500-1,000,000
Tax: 501(c)(3)

Personnel:
Director, Operations: Shawn Tierney
E-Mail: shawn@aee.org
Coordinator, Conferences and Events: Caitlin Leahy
E-Mail: Caitlin@aee.org
Coordinator, Membership: Mallory Montazzoli
E-Mail: membership@aee.org
Office Manager: Leslie Stevens
E-Mail: leslie@aee.org

Historical Note:
Mission of AEE is to develop and promote experiential education and is committed to support professional development, theoretical advancement and the evaluation of experiential education worldwide. Membership: $15-600/ year.

Meetings/Conferences: Annual
Conference Chair: Caitlin Leahy

Publications:
Journal of Experiential Education
Member Directory

Membership List Available to Non-members

Association for Facilities Engineering (1954)

12801 Worldgate Dr.
Suite 500
Herndon, VA 20170
Tel: (571) 203-7171 *Fax:* (571) 766-2142
E-Mail: info@afe.org
Website: afe.org
Members: 5000 members
Staff: 10
Annual Budget: $500-1,000,000
Tax: 501(c)(6)

Personnel:
Executive Director: Wayne Carley PhD
E-Mail: WCarley@AFE.org
Director, Finance: Glenn Beales
Manager, Chapter and Council Relations: Jai Coleman
E-Mail: jcoleman@afe.org
Editor: Jane Jacobs
E-Mail: jjacobs@afe.org
Manager, Certification and Education: Carol Lawrence
E-Mail: clawrence@afe.org
Contact, Member Services and Certifications: Katrina McEwan
E-Mail: kmcewan@afe.org
Director, Professional Development: Jeanine Salifou
E-Mail: jsalifou@afe.org
Director, Marketing and Business Development: Richard Stukey
E-Mail: rstukey@afe.org
Specialist, Membership Services and Operations: Janet Tavara
E-Mail: janettavara@afe.org
Director, Membership and Operations: Talisa Thomas-Hall
E-Mail: tthomashall@afe.org

Historical Note:
Formerly (1996) American Institute of Plant Engineers. AFE's mission is to provide education, certification, technical information and other relevant resources to plant and facility engineering, operation and maintenance professionals worldwide. Members are facility managers incharge of engineering, operations, and maintenance of industrial plants, office buildings, campuses, and other workplaces. Membership: $235 (Individual); $100 (Young Professional); $15 (Student); $102.50-174 (Corporate, varies with members); $80-120 (Retired).

Continuing Education:
Certification Designation/s: CPS, CPMM, CPE

Meetings/Conferences:
Conference Chair: Jai Coleman
Number of non-conference events/year: 5

Publications:
AFE e-newsletter; weekly; adv.
Facilities Engineering Journal; bi-monthly; adv.
Membership Directory; on-line

Association for Federal Information Resources Management (1979)

400 N. Washington St.
Suite 300
Alexandria, VA 22314
Tel: (703) 778-4646 *Fax:* (703) 683-5480
E-Mail: info@affirm.org
Website: affirm.org
Members: 565 individuals
Staff: 2
Annual Budget: $250-500,000
Tax: 501(c)(3)

Personnel:
President: Kirit Amin
Treasurer,Industry: Sherry Weir

Historical Note:
AFFIRM's purpose is to improve the management of information and related systems and resources, within the Federal government, by providing educational forums for the government information technology community. Members include information resource management professionals from the Federal, academic, and industry sectors. Membership: $25 (Individual Government/ Academia); $170 (Individual Govt/Academia Training Program).

Publications:
AFFIRMation; monthly

Membership List Available to Non-members

Association for Feminist Anthropology (1988)

2200 Wilson Blvd.
Suite 600
Arlington, VA 22201
Tel: (703) 528-1902 *Fax:* (703) 528-3546
Website: aaanet.org/sections/afa/
Staff: 4

Personnel:
President: Jane Henrici
E-Mail: henrici@iwpr.org
Treasurer: Sandra Faiman-Silva
E-Mail: SFAIMANSILVA@bridgew.edu
Editor: Lauren Fordyce
E-Mail: fordycel@gmail.com
Contact, Website Coordinator: Jamie Sherman
E-Mail: misha-quill@uiowa.edu

Historical Note:
Association for Feminist Anthropology Executive Board consisting of elected and appointed members (the AFA Board) voices its concern for what appears to be a censure of breastfeeding and a lack of recognition of parental needs on academic campuses and in the wider society.

Publications:
VOICES; annually

Association for Financial Counseling and Planning Education (1983)

1940 Duke St.
Suite 200
Alexandria, VA 22314
Tel: (703) 684-4484 *Fax:* (703) 684-4485
Website: afcpe.org
Members: 810 individuals
Staff: 6
Annual Budget: $1-2,000,000

Personnel:
Interim Executive Director: Rebecca Wiggins
E-Mail: rwiggins@afcpe.org
Operations Officer: Katie Baylor
E-Mail: kbaylor@afcpe.org
Coordinator, Membership Services: Cara Defibaugh
E-Mail: cdefibaugh@afcpe.org
Manager, Certification Programs: Carol Hite
E-Mail: chite@afcpe.org
Editor: Jill Ladouceur
E-Mail: ladjill@hotmail.com
Coordinator, Certification Programs: Michelle Starkey
E-Mail: mstarkey@afcpe.org

Historical Note:

AFCPE provides professional development experiences for financial educators, practitioners and researchers to improve the economic wellbeing of individuals and families worldwide. Members are financial planners and counselors, educators, and other professionals involved in teaching budgetary and financial skills to consumers. Membership: $100 (2012 U.S. Membership); $35 (Student); $135 (Membership outside U.S.); $110 (2013 U.S. Membership).

Continuing Education:
Certification Designation/s: AFC, CHC

Meetings/Conferences: Annual
2013 - Greenville, SC/Nov. 20 - 22
2014 - Bellevue, WA/Nov. 19 - 21

Publications:
Journal of Financial Counseling and Planning; bi-annually
Membership Directory; on-line
The Standard; quarterly

Association for Financial Professionals, Inc. *(1979)*
4520 E.W. Hwy.
Suite 750
Bethesda, MD 20814
Tel: (301) 907-2862 *Fax:* (301) 907-2864
E-Mail: afp@afponline.org
Website: afponline.org
Members: 16000 individuals
Staff: 60
Annual Budget: $25-50,000,000
Tax: 501(c)(6)

Personnel:
President and Chief Executive Officer: James A. Kaitz
    E-Mail: jkaitz@afponline.org
Director, Government Relations and policy: Jeanine H. Arnett
    E-Mail: jarnett@afponline.org
Vice President and Chief Operating Officer: Thomas W. Derry
Chief Financial Officer: Joe DeSalvio
    E-Mail: jdesalvio@afponline.org

Historical Note:
Formerly the Cash Management Practitioners Association and National Corporate Cash Management Association, became the Treasury Management Association in 1991 and assumed its present name in 1999. AFP's mission is to ensure that the views of financial professionals are included in public debate on key policy issues facing the profession. Membership: $395/year (Individual)

Continuing Education:
Certification Designation/s: CTP, CTPA

Meetings/Conferences: Annual

Publications:
AFP Payments; on-line
EconWatch; weekly
Electronic Commerce Report; monthly
Exchange Magazine
FP&A Newsletter; on-line
Futures in Finance Newsletter; on-line
Governance, Accounting, & Compliance; on-line
Membership Directory; on-line
Online Headlines newsletter; weekly
Risk!; monthly

Association for Financial Technology *(1972)*
34 N. High St.
New Albany, OH 43054-8507
Tel: (614) 895-1208 *Fax:* (614) 895-3466
E-Mail: aft@aftweb.com
Website: aftweb.com
Members: 58 companies
Staff: 2
Annual Budget: $250-500,000
Tax: 501(c)(6)

Personnel:
Executive Director: James R. Bannister

Historical Note:
Formerly (1994) known as the Multi-Bank Data Processing Organization. AFT member companies provide systems applications and outsourcing services to banks, thrifts, credit unions and other financial institutions. Membership also includes suppliers of computer hardware and software, and other related products and services. Membership: $1,250/year.

Meetings/Conferences: Semi-Annual
2013 - Boca Raton, FL (Boca Raton Resort and Club)/
    March 17 - 19

2013 - Dana Point, CA (Ritz-Carlton, Laguna Niguel)/
    Sept. 22 - 24
2014 - San Antonio, TX (Hyatt Regency Hill Country Resort and Spa)/March 16 - 18
2014 - White Sulphur Springs, WV (The Greenbrier)/
    Sept. 12 - 14
2015 - Napa, CA (The Meritage Resort and Spa)/Sept. 20 - 22

Publications:
AFTech Letter; bi-annually
Member Directory; on-line

Association for Gay, Lesbian, Bisexual, and Transgender Issues in Counseling *(1975)*
5999 Stevenson Ave.
Alexandria, VA 22304-3300
Tel: (703) 823-9800 *Fax:* (703) 461-9260
Website: algbtic.org/
Members: 1103 individuals
Staff: 3
Annual Budget: $25-50,000

Personnel:
President: Pete Finnerty
    E-Mail: pfinnert@kent.edu

Historical Note:
Formerly the Caucus of Gay Counselors and the National Caucus of Gay and Lesbian Counselors, AGLBIC is an association of members of the American Counseling Association, which provides administrative support. AGLBIC educates counselors to the unique needs of client identity development. Membership: $47 (Professional/Regular); $15 (Student/Retired/New Professional).

Publications:
ALGBTIC Newsletter; adv.
Journal of LGBT Issues in Counseling; quarterly

Association for General and Liberal Studies *(1961)*
Ball State University, English Department
RB 2109
Muncie, IN 47306-0460
Tel: (765) 285-8406 *Fax:* (765) 285-2384
Website: web.oxford.emory.edu
Members: 300 individuals
Staff: 2
Annual Budget: $25-50,000
Tax: 501(c)(3)

Personnel:
Executive Director: Paul Ranieri
    E-Mail: pranieri@bsu.edu

Historical Note:
AGLS serves colleges and universities by helping students and faculty enjoy the benefits of a liberal education attained through quality general education. Members are individuals with an interest in higher education liberal arts and general education programs. Membership: $40 (Faculty/Administration); $10 (Student); $500 (Institution); $25 (Adjunct/Retirees).

Meetings/Conferences: Annual
Number of non-conference events/year: 1

Publications:
AGLS Newsletter, LISTSERV; bi-annually
Journal of General Education; quarterly

Membership List Available to Non-members

Association for Gnotobiotics *(1961)*
Dept. of Microbiology, Pathology & Parasitology, College of Veterinary Medicine, North Carolina State Univ.
4700 Hillsborough St.
Raleigh, NC 27606
Tel: (919) 513-6278 *Fax:* (919) 848-3166
Website: gnotobiotics.org
Members: 220 individuals
Staff: 2
Annual Budget: Under $10,000
Tax: 501(c)(3)

Personnel:
President: Leda Vieira
    E-Mail: lqvieira@icb.ufmg.br
Interim Executive Secretary and Treasurer: Dr. Philip B. Carter
    E-Mail: philipcarter@earthlink.net

Historical Note:
AG was founded by Philip C. Trexler (at that time with the Lobund Laboratory, University of Notre Dame) in response to the need for organization and standardization in the

rapidly expanding field of germfree research. AG's mission is to disseminate information relative to Gnotobiotics and to cooperate with local, national, and international organizations concerned with Gnotobiotics and other biological sciences. Members are scientists interested in germ-free research and applications. Membership: $30 (Professional); $15 (Student); $300 (Institutional); Free (Emeritus).

Publications:
AG Newsletter; annually
Annual Meeting Abstract; annually
Membership Directory; annually

Association for Governmental Leasing and Finance *(1981)*
19 Mantua Rd.
Mt. Royal, NJ 08061
Tel: (856) 423-3259 *Fax:* (856) 423-3420
E-Mail: aglfhq@talley.com
Website: aglf.org
Members:
175 companies
295 individuals
Staff: 5
Annual Budget: $250-500,000
Tax: 501(c)(3)

Personnel:
Executive Director: Haley J. Brust
    E-Mail: hbrust@talley.com
Manager, Meeting: Heather Glenn
Membership Liaison: Denise Smith
    E-Mail: dsmith@talley.com
Administrative Assistant: Linda Wright
    E-Mail: aglfhq@aglf.org

Historical Note:
AGLF strives to provide resources, educational forums and networking to expand business opportunities. The members are third party lessors, placement agents, investment bankers, government officials, vendors, manufacturers, captives, and commercial bankers. Membership: $350 (Individual/Governmental/Not-For-Profit Organization); $750 (Limited); $1,250 (Basic); $2,500 (Industry leader).

Meetings/Conferences: Annual
Conference Chair: Heather Glenn
2013 - Chicago, IL (DoubleTree Chicago Magnificent Mile)/May 7 - 11
Number of non-conference events/year: 1

Publications:
Membership Directory; on-line

Association for Graphic Arts Training *(1986)*
C/O Albert Le Blanc - McNaughton & Gunn, Inc.
960 Woodland Dr.
Saline, MI 48176
Tel: (734) 429-5411 *Fax:* (800) 677-2665
E-Mail: albertl@mcnaughton-gunn.com
Website: agatweb.org
Members: 100 individuals
Staff: 2

Personnel:
Contact, Membership and Communications: Gary Fisher
    E-Mail: gary.fisher@gossinternational.com
Director, Membership Services: Albert LeBlanc
    E-Mail: albertl@mcnaughton-gunn.com

Historical Note:
AGAT strives to increase the productivity of member companies through education, training, and support from suppliers, educational facilities, industry foundations and consulting resources. Members are graphic arts trainers employed by printing companies, teachers and other individuals and companies with an interest in graphic arts instruction. Membership: $75/year.

Association for Healthcare Documentation Integrity *(1978)*
4230 Kiernan Ave.
Suite 130
Modesto, CA 95356
Tel: (209) 527-9620 *Fax:* (209) 527-9633
TollFree: (800) 982-2182
E-Mail: ahdi@ahdionline.org
Website: ahdionline.org
Members: 7500 individuals
Staff: 13
Annual Budget: $2-5,000,000
Tax: 501(c)(6)

Personnel:
Chief executive Officer: Linda Brady

E-Mail: lbrady@ahdionline.org
Technical Services Coordinator: Jason Hatchell
   E-Mail: jhatchell@ahdionline.org
Coordinator, Credentialing and Education: Cathy Huber
   E-Mail: cuber@ahdionline.org
Professional Programs Manager: Kelly Kappmeier
Senior Programs Coordinator and Editor: Kristin Wall
   E-Mail: kwall@ahdionline.org
Business and Staff Manager: Terri White
   E-Mail: twhite@ahdionline.org
Senior Meetings and Marketing Coordinator: Andrew Wolf
   E-Mail: awolf@ahdionline.org

Historical Note:
Formerly American Association for Medical Transcription (AAMT). AHDI is a professional association for medical transcriptionists, supervisors, teachers, students, and other interested health personnel. AHDI's mission is to promote the integrity of healthcare documentation through development of an educated, prepared workforce in clinical documentation.Membership: $135 (Individual); $55 (Student); $85 (Postgraduate); $200 (Educational); $400 (Corporate) .

Continuing Education:
Certification Designation/s: CMT, CMT-R, RMT, AHDI-F

Meetings/Conferences: Annual
Conference Chair: Andrew Wolf
2013 - Columbia, MO (Boone Hospital Center)/April 12 - 13
Number of non-conference events/year: 2

Publications:
Matrix; quarterly
Plexus; bi-monthly

Association for Healthcare Foodservice *(2009)*
455 S. Fourth St.
Suite 650
Louisville, KY 40202
Fax: (502) 589-3602
TollFree: (888) 528-9552
E-Mail: info@healthcarefoodservice.org
Website: healthcarefoodservice.org
Members: 3300 individuals
Staff: 12
Annual Budget: $1-2,000,000

Personnel:
Executive Vice President: Billye Potts
   E-Mail: bpotts@healthcarefoodservice.org
Contact, Finance: John Bunker
   E-Mail: jbunker@hqtrs.com
Contact, Client Relations: Tony Butler
   E-Mail: tbutler@hqtrs.com
Director, Membership, Marketing and Communication: Maria Chapman
   E-Mail: mchapman@healthcarefoodservice.org
Contact, Public Relations and Social Media: Trish Dever
   E-Mail: tdever@hqtrs.com
Director, Sponsorship and Advertising Sales: Lorraine Houghton
   E-Mail: lhoughton@hqtrs.com
Director, Public Relations and Digital Media: Andrea Parr
   E-Mail: aparr@hqtrs.com
Contact, Event Services: Michelle Romero
   E-Mail: mromero@hqtrs.com
Director, Education and Chapters: Sarah Saar
   E-Mail: ssaar@healthcarefoodservice.org

Historical Note:
Formed by the merger of HFM and ASHFSA in 2009. AHF's mission is to advance healthcare foodservice professionals by assuring food and nutrition is a core competency. Members include healthcare foodservice operators and business partners in North America. Membership: $25-595/year; $250 (lifetime).

Meetings/Conferences: Annual
Conference Chair: Michelle Romero
2013 - New Orleans, LA/June 5 - 8

Publications:
AHF e-Newsletter; on-line; adv.
Membership Directory; on-line
S.O. Connected Magazine; quarterly; adv.

Association for Healthcare Philanthropy *(1967)*
313 Park Ave.
Suite 400
Falls Church, VA 22046
Tel: (703) 532-6243 *Fax*: (703) 532-7170
E-Mail: ahp@ahp.org
Website: ahp.org
Members: 5,000 members

Staff: 12
Annual Budget: $2-5,000,000
Tax: 501(c)(6)

Personnel:
President and Chief Executive Officer: William C McGinly PhD, CAE
   E-Mail: bill@ahp.org
Director, Meetings and Exhibits: Kate Farrington
   E-Mail: kate@ahp.org
Director, Membership Services and Business Development: Kelly Kim
   E-Mail: kelly_kim@ahp.org
Director, Finance and Human Resources: Lynn Murphy
   E-Mail: lynn@ahp.org
Chief Strategic Officer and Government Relations: Kathy Renzetti CAE
   E-Mail: kathy@ahp.org
Chief Operating Officer: Monika Schulz CAE
   E-Mail: monika@ahp.org
Director, Education: Katherine Shamapande
   E-Mail: kat@ahp.org

Historical Note:
Established as Developartners, became National Association for Hospital Development in 1968, and assumed its present name in 1991, AHPA is a professional association of hospital and health care executives involved in hospital development and fund-raising programs. Membership: $440 (Individual); $459-1841 (Affiliate, plus $128 for each additional staff person of more than 11); $992-3,337 (Institutional, plus $250 for each additional staff person of more than 11); $315 (Associate).

Continuing Education:
Certification Designation/s: FAHP, CFRE

Meetings/Conferences: Annual
Conference Chair: Kate Farrington
Number of non-conference events/year: 8

Publications:
AHP E-Connect; on-line; adv.
Healthcare Philanthropy Journal; semi-annually
Membership Directory; on-line

Association for Healthcare Resource and Materials Management *(1951)*
155 N. Wacker Dr.
Chicago, IL 60606
Tel: (312) 422-3840 *Fax*: (312) 422-4573
E-Mail: ahrmm@aha.org
Website: ahrmm.org
Members: 4000 individuals
Staff: 10
Annual Budget: $25-50,000

Personnel:
Executive Director: Deborah Sprindzunas
   E-Mail: dsprindzunas@aha.org
Senior Specialist, Membership Services and Chapter Relations: Catherine Carruth
   E-Mail: ccarruth@aha.org
Specialist, Education: Cathy Futrell Davis
   E-Mail: cfutrell@aha.org
Manager, Marketing and Membership: Brenda Jones
   E-Mail: bjones@aha.org
Specialist, Marketing and Communications: Agnes Lipowicz
   E-Mail: alipowicz@aha.org
Administrative Coordinator: Beth McCoy
   E-Mail: bmccoy@aha.org
Associate Executive Director: Sarah Oaks
   E-Mail: soaks@aha.org
Planner, Meetings: TaNisha Williams
   E-Mail: twilliams@aha.org

Historical Note:
Formerly (1975) American Society for Hospital Purchasing Agents, (1983) American Society for Hospital Purchasing and Materials Management, (1994) American Society for Hospital Materials Management, and (1998) American Society for Healthcare Materials Management. AHRMM's mission is to advance healthcare supply chain excellence through education, sharing and cultivation of knowledge, and advocacy for the profession. Affiliated with the American Hospital Association. Members are professionals in hospitals, health systems, and related organizations committed to health improvement. Membership: $125 (Supply Chain Provider/Active Duty Military); $90 (Student); $100 (Young Professional Associate/Retiree); $180 (Affiliate/Supplier); $170 (Supply Chain Executive).

Continuing Education:
Enrollment: 50
Certification Designation/s: CHC, CHESP, CHFM, CMRP, CPHRM, FAHRMM

Meetings/Conferences: Annual
Conference Chair: TaNisha Williams
2013 - San Diego, CA/July 28 - 31/1200 attendees

Publications:
AHRMM eNews; weekly; adv.
AHRMM Supply Chain Strategies & Solutions; bi-monthly; adv.
Materials Management in HealthCare Magazine; adv.
Member Directory

Membership List Available to Non-members

Association for Healthcare Volunteer Resource Professionals *(1968)*
155 N. Wacker Dr.
Suite 400
Chicago, IL 60606
Tel: (312) 422-3939 *Fax*: (312) 278-0884
E-Mail: ahvrp@aha.org
Website: ahvrp.org
Members: 1500 individuals
Staff: 5
Annual Budget: $250-500,000

Personnel:
Executive Director: Joan M. Miller MHA
   E-Mail: jmiller@aha.org
Manager, Education and Chapter Relations: Kiwani Cooper
   E-Mail: kcooper@aha.org
Program Specialist, e-Marketing: Noemi Escutia
   E-Mail: knescutia@aha.org
Coordinator, Education: Lisa Hinkle MS
   E-Mail: lhinkle@aha.org
Specialist, Membership and Marketing: Jada L. Peterson
   E-Mail: jpeterson@aha.org

Historical Note:
Formerly known as American Society of Directors of Volunteer Services. Sponsored by the American Hospital Association. AHVRP mission is to lead, represent and serve its members who empower volunteers to meet community healthcare needs. Membership: $150 (Regular); $400 (Vendor); $75 (Retired, Transitional and Full-Time Students).

Continuing Education:
Certification Designation/s: CAVS

Meetings/Conferences: Annual

Publications:
Member Directory; on-line
News You Can Use; monthly; adv.

Association for High Technology Distribution *(1985)*
N19 W24400 Riverwood Dr.
Waukesha, WI 53188
Tel: (262) 696-3645 *Fax*: (262) 696-3646
E-Mail: ahtd@ahtd.org
Website: ahtd.org
Members: 250 companies
Staff: 5
Annual Budget: $500-1,000,000
Tax: 501(c)(6)

Personnel:
Executive Director: Bryan Roessler
   E-Mail: bryan.roessler@mranet.org
Contact, Financial Services: Pam Estergard
   E-Mail: pame@mranet.org
Manager, Association Services: Leigha Schatzman
   E-Mail: leigha.schatzman@ahtd.org

Historical Note:
Formerly (1995) Association of High Technology Distributors. AHTD's mission is to maximize member profit and growth through education and networking and by fostering partnerships and alliances to help deliver solutions. AHTD members are distributors of industrial automation products, affiliate membership is available for manufacturers. Membership: $595/year (Company).

Continuing Education:
Certification Designation/s: IAP, ASP

Meetings/Conferences: Semi-Annual
2013 - La Quinta, CA (La Quinta Resort and Club)/ April 24 - 27

Publications:
AHTD eNewsletter; monthly
Membership Directory; quarterly

Association for Hose and Accessories Distribution *(1985)*
105 Eastern Ave.

Suite 104
Annapolis, MD 21403-3300
Tel: (410) 940-6350 *Fax:* (410) 263-1659
TollFree: (800) 624-2227
E-Mail: info@nahad.org
Website: nahad.org
Members: 510 distributors and manufacturers
Staff: 12
Annual Budget: $1-2,000,000
Tax: 501(c)(6)

Personnel:
Executive Vice President: Joseph M. Thompson Jr.
    E-Mail: jthompson@nahad.org
Marketing Specialist: Beth Hiltabidle
    E-Mail: bhiltabidle@nahad.org
Director, Membership Services: Amy Luckado
    E-Mail: aluckado@nahad.org
Office Manager: Janice Sunderland
    E-Mail: jsunderland@nahad.org
Director, Communications and Conferences: Kristin B.
    Thompson
    E-Mail: kthompson@nahad.org

Historical Note:
*NAHAD's mission is to promote a better standard
of professionalism and integrity within the hose
and accessories industry by providing a medium for
communications, education and training. Members are
distributors and manufacturers of industrial hose and
fittings. Membership: $599-799 (Distributor, dues based
on annual sales); $899 (Affiliate); $1399 (Associate/
Manufacturer).*

Continuing Education:
Enrollment: 1000

Meetings/Conferences: Annual
Conference Chair: Kristin B. Thompson
2013 - Washington, DC (Gaylord National Resort and
    Convention Center)/April 20 - 24
2014 - Phoenix, AZ (JW Marriott Desert Ridge Resort)/
    April 26 - 30

Publications:
HoseCONNECTIONS; bi-weekly; adv.
Membership Directory; on-line
NAHAD News; bi-monthly

Association for Hospital Medical Education
(1956)
109 Brush Creek Rd.
Irwin, PA 15642
Tel: (724) 864-7321 *Fax:* (724) 864-6153
E-Mail: info@ahme.org
Website: ahme.org
Members:
300 hospitals
700 individuals
Staff: 8
Annual Budget: $500-1,000,000
Tax: 501(c)(6)

Personnel:
Executive Director: Kimball Mohn MD
Director, Accounting: Roberta (BJ) Couch
Editor: Bruce Deighton
Director, Meeting Services: Sandi Parsons
    E-Mail: sandi@ahme.org
Coordinator, Membership Services: Karen S. Zagar
    E-Mail: karen@ahme.org

Historical Note:
*Formerly (1968) Association of Hospital Directors
of Medical Education. AHME seeks to promote the
improvement in medical education to meet health care,
develop professionals in the field of medical education.
Members are hospital staff and administrators concerned
with medical education, primarily at community hospitals.
Members are teaching hospitals, academic medical centers,
and consortia nationwide. Membership: $495 (Individual);
$2,000 (Institutional); $1,000 (Sustaining).*

Meetings/Conferences:
Conference Chair: Sandi Parsons

Publications:
AHME News; semi-annually

Membership List Available to Non-members

Association for Humanist Sociology *(1976)*
11 Gates Ave.
E. Brunswick, NJ 00816
Website: ccsu.edu/page.cfm?p = 6817
Members: 300 individuals
Staff: 6

Annual Budget: $10-25,000
Tax: 501(c)(6)

Personnel:
President: Deborah Burris-Kitchen
    E-Mail: dburriskitchen@tnstate.edu
Vice President, Publications: David Embrick
Program Chair: Kathleen Fitzgerald
    E-Mail: kfitzger@loyno.edu
Treasurer: Chuck Koeber
Vice President, Membership: Ottis Murray
Executive Editor: Janine Schipper
    E-Mail: humanityandsociety@nau.edu

Historical Note:
*AHS's purpose is to be an active support network for
sociologists and other scholars committed to humanist
values, to inspire, support, and learn from one another to
make the humanist practice more conscious and skillful.
Membership: $12-100 (Student Unemployed) ; $150
(Sponsor).*

Meetings/Conferences: Annual
Conference Chair: Kathleen Fitzgerald

Publications:
Humanity & Society
Newsletter: The Humanist Sociologist

Membership List Available to Non-members

Association for Humanistic Psychology *(1962)*
151 Petaluma Blvd. S.
Suite 227
Petaluma, CA 94952
Tel: (415) 435-1604 *Fax:* (707) 599-5030
E-Mail: ahpoffice@aol.com
Website: ahpweb.org
Members: 1240 individuals
Staff: 4
Annual Budget: $50-100,000
Tax: 501(c)(3)

Personnel:
Co-President: Carroy U. "Cuf" Ferguson
    E-Mail: cuferguson@aol.com
Treasurer: M.A. Bjarkman
    E-Mail: MABahp@aol.com
Contact, Membership Services and Editor: Kathleen
    Erickson
    E-Mail: ericksoneditorial@att.net

Historical Note:
*Formerly (1969) known as the American Association for
Humanistic Psychology. AHP's purpose is to enhance the
quality of human experience and to advance the evolution of
human consciousness. Membership: $69 (Individual); $149
(Organizational); $49 (Students & Limited Income).*

Continuing Education:
Certification Designation/s: CECS

Meetings/Conferences: Annual
Number of non-conference events/year: 3

Publications:
AHP Newsletter; monthly
AHP Perspective; bi-monthly; adv.
AHP Professional Directory; on-line
Journal of Humanistic Psychology; quarterly

Membership List Available to Non-members

Association for Informal Logic and Critical Thinking *(1983)*
Baker University
Center for Critical Thinking
Baldwin City, KS 66006-0065
Website: ailact.mcmaster.ca
Members: 150 individuals
Staff: 4
Annual Budget: Under $10,000
Tax: 501(c)(3)

Personnel:
President: Derek Allen
    E-Mail: derekallen@trinity.utoronto.ca
Editor: James Freeman
    E-Mail: jfreeman@hunter.cuny.edu
Webmaster: David Godden
    E-Mail: webmaster.ailact@gmail.com
Treasurer and Membership Contact: Donald L. Hatcher
    E-Mail: dhatcher@bakeru.edu

Historical Note:
*AILACT was established to promote the quality of research,
teaching, and testing of informal logic and critical thinking
at all levels and to facilitate discussion between its members.
AILACT sponsors sessions at each APA divisional meeting*

*and other meetings. AILACT members are academics and
teachers of courses in informal logic and critical thinking.
Membership: $10/year (Individual).*

Publications:
AILACT Newsletter; quarterly

Association for Information and Image Management International *(1943)*
1100 Wayne Ave., Suite 1100
Silver Spring, MD 20910
Tel: (301) 587-8202 *Fax:* (301) 587-2711
TollFree: (800) 477-2446
E-Mail: aiim@aiim.org
Website: aiim.org
Members: 65000 individuals
Staff: 25
Annual Budget: $5-10,000,000
Tax: 501(c)(6)

Personnel:
President and Chief Executive Officer: John F. Mancini
    E-Mail: jmancini@aiim.org
Chief Financial Officer: Felicia Dillard
Chief Information Officer: Laurence Hart
Production Manager, Infonomics Magazine: Maureen
    Hearn
    E-Mail: mhearn@aiim.org
Chief Operating Officer: Atle Skjekkeland
Vice President and Chief Marketing Officer: Peggy Winton

Historical Note:
*Formerly (1975) National Microfilm Association, (1995)
National Micrographics Association. Merged with the
International Information Management Congress in 1999.
AIIM strives to provide education, research, and better
practices to help organizations find, control, and optimize
their information. Members are users and manufacturers
of equipment, supplies and services for the document
management industry. Membership: $135 (Professional);
$1,000 (Trade).*

Continuing Education:
Certification Designation/s: IOA, E2.0, BPM, ECM, EMM,
ERM, CCP, CIP

Meetings/Conferences: Annual
Conference Chair: Atle Skjekkeland
2013 - New Orleans, LA (Hyatt Regency New Orleans)/
    March 20 - 22/1-10 exhibitors

Publications:
Connect at AIIM eNewsletter; bi-weekly
GetSmart at AIIM eNewsletter; bi-weekly
Infonomics; bi-monthly

Membership List Available to Non-members

Association for Information Media and Equipment *(1986)*
P.O. Box 9844
Cedar Rapids, IA 52409-9844
Tel: (319) 654-0608 *Fax:* (319) 654-0609
Website: aime.org
Members: 159 organizations
Staff: 1
Annual Budget: $25-50,000

Personnel:
Executive Director: Betty Gorsegner Ehlinger

Historical Note:
*AIME seeks to advocate appropriate use of the media
and equipment delivering information. Members are
producers and distributors of educational films and video,
schools, libraries, museums and companies who provide
related equipment and services, and others who work
with information video, interactive technologies, computer
software and equipment for educational and information
uses. Membership: $300-1,000 (Corporate); $200
(Institution).*

Publications:
AIME News; quarterly
Membership Directory; on-line

Association for Information Protection
1155 15th St. NW
Suite 500
Washington, DC 20005
Tel: (202) 580-6293 *Fax:* (202) 530-0659
E-Mail: info@aipinfo.org
Website: aipinfo.org
Staff: 1

Personnel:
Executive Director: Carrie Hoffman
    E-Mail: choffman@aipinfo.org

Historical Note:
AIP's mission is to act as an advocate for the information protection industry by shaping legislation and public policy through government relations. Membership categories available are Charter Members, Active Members, Associate Members and Affiliate Members.

Association for Information Systems (1994)
P.O. Box 2712
Atlanta, GA 30301-2712
Tel: (404) 413-7445 *Fax:* (404) 413-7443
E-Mail: onestop@aisnet.org
Website: home.aisnet.org
Members: 3000 Members
Staff: 9
Annual Budget: $1-2,000,000
Tax: 501(c)(3)

Personnel:
Executive Director: Pete Tinsley CAE
   E-Mail: pete@aisnet.org
Conference Registrar: Litika Coleman
   E-Mail: registrar@aisnet.org
Meeting Planner: Lise Fitzpatrick
   E-Mail: meetingplanner@aisnet.org
Director, Finance: Tenez Quarles
   E-Mail: finance@aisnet.org
Director, Technology: Jeff Rausch
   E-Mail: jeff@aisnet.org
Membership Coordinator: Mary Smith
   E-Mail: membership@aisnet.org
Director, Communications: Michelle Syen
   E-Mail: communications@aisnet.org

Historical Note:
AIS is a professional organization that works to serve as a global organization for academics specializing in information systems. Members are academics with an interest in information systems and related fields. Membership: $125 (Academic/Professional/Corporate); $62.50 (Retired); $85 (Student); $1,750-3,000 (Institutional).

Meetings/Conferences: Annual
Conference Chair: Lise Fitzpatrick
2013 - Chicago, IL/Aug. 15 - 18/3000 attendees
2014 - Savannah, GA/Aug. 7 - 10/3000 attendees

Publications:
MIS Quarterly; quarterly
AIS InSider; monthly
AIS Transactions on Human-Computer Interaction
Communications of the Association for Information Systems (CAIS)
Journal of Information Technology Theory and Application (JITTA)
Journal of the Association for Information Systems (JAIS); adv.
Membership Directory; on-line
MIS Quarterly Executive; quarterly
Revista Latinoamericana Y Del Caribe De La Association De Sistemas De Informacion (RELCASI)

Association for Institutional Research (1965)
1435 E. Piedmont Dr.
Suite 211
Tallahassee, FL 32308
Tel: (850) 385-4155 *Fax:* (850) 385-5180
E-Mail: air@airweb.org
Website: airweb.org
Members: 4000 members
Staff: 20
Annual Budget: $5-10,000,000
Tax: 501(c)(3)

Personnel:
Executive Director: Randy Swing PhD
   E-Mail: rswing@airweb.org
Project Coordinator: Meg Andraza
   E-Mail: mandraza@airweb.org
Coordinator, Membership Services: Donna Carlsen
   E-Mail: dcarlsen@airweb.org
Contact, Membership Services and Publications: Lisa Gwaltney
   E-Mail: lgwaltney@airweb.org
Chief Information Officer: Kashif Imran
   E-Mail: kashif@airweb.org
Director, Financial Operations: Jason Lewis
   E-Mail: jlewis@airweb.org
Director, Education: Anne Munson
   E-Mail: amunson@airweb.org
Senior Manager, Meetings: Brandice Pittard CMP
   E-Mail: bpittard@airweb.org

Manager, Finance: Cathy Sexton
   E-Mail: csexton@airweb.org
Executive Assistant: Missy Wiggins
   E-Mail: mwiggins@airweb.org

Historical Note:
Founded in 1965 and incorporated in Michigan in 1966. AIR's mission is to support quality data and decisions for higher education. Members are involved in research to improve institutions of postsecondary education. Membership: $125 (Individual/ Organization); $30 (Graduate Student).

Meetings/Conferences: Annual
Conference Chair: Brandice Pittard CMP
2013 - Long Beach, CA (Long Beach Convention and Entertainment Center)/May 18 - 22
Number of non-conference events/year: 2

Publications:
AIR Alerts; on-line
Assessment UPdate; bi-monthly
Electronic AIR; monthly
Innovative Higher Education
Journal of Higher Education; bi-monthly
Member Directory; on-line

Association for Integrative Studies (1979)
Miami University, Western College Program
501 E. High St.
Oxford, OH 45056-3653
Tel: (513) 529-2659 *Fax:* (513) 529-5849
E-Mail: aisorg@muohio.edu
Website: units.muohio.edu/aisorg
Members: 2500 individuals
Staff: 4
Annual Budget: $10-25,000
Tax: 501(c)(3)

Personnel:
Executive Director: William "Bill" H. Newell
   E-Mail: newellwh@muohio.edu

Historical Note:
AIS's mission is to promote the interchange of ideas among scholars, teachers, administrators, and the public regarding interdisciplinarity and integration. Members are primarily faculty and administrators engaged in interdisciplinary teaching and research or who are interested in exploring interdisciplinary topics and methodology. Membership: $100 (Library); $200 (Institution); $25 (Student); $50 (Regular/Individual).

Meetings/Conferences: Annual
2013 - Oxford, OH (Miami University)/Nov. 7 - 10

Publications:
Doctoral Program Directory; on-line
Integrative Pathways (Newsletter); quarterly; adv.
Issues in Integrative Studies; annually
Master's Program Directory; on-line
Membership Directory; on-line

Membership List Available to Non-members

Association for International Agricultural and Extension Education (1984)
Ohio State University, 113 Agricultural Administration Building
2120 Fyffe Rd.
Columbus, OH 43210
Website: aiaee.org
Members: 300 individuals
Staff: 3
Annual Budget: Under $10,000

Personnel:
Treasurer: J. Mark Erbaugh
   E-Mail: erbaugh.1@osu.edu
President: Theresa Murphrey
   E-Mail: t-murphrey@tamu.edu

Historical Note:
AIAEE's mission is to provide a professional association for agricultural and extension educators who share the common goal of strengthening agricultural and extension education programs and institutions worldwide. Membership: $70/ year.

Meetings/Conferences: Annual
2013 - Ft. Worth, TX (Stockyard Station)/May 19 - 22

Publications:
AIAEE Journal
The AIAEE Newsletter; quarterly
The Informer

The Association for International Agriculture and Rural Development (1964)

Horticulture CRSP, UC Davis
138 Oak Ave.
Woodland, CA 95695
Tel: (530) 752-7975 *Fax:* (530) 752-7182
E-Mail: acrump@ucdavis.edu
Website: aiard.org
Members: 220 individuals
Staff: 2
Annual Budget: $25-50,000
Tax: 501(c)(3)

Personnel:
President: Chuck Chopak
   E-Mail: chuck_chopak@dai.com
Secretary and Treasurer: Amanda Crump
   E-Mail: acrump@ucdavis.edu

Historical Note:
Formerly (1989) Association of United States Directors of International Agriculture Programs. AIARD's mission is to improve quality of life for all people by improving and developing global capacities to respond to new challenges and opportunities in helping to eliminate poverty, improve food security, and conserve and protect the environment, in order to stimulate broad-based economic growth and sustainable development. Membership: $20-1,000/year.

Meetings/Conferences:
Conference Chair: Chuck Chopak

Publications:
Membership Directory; on-line
Newsletters; annually

Association for Iron and Steel Technology (2004)
186 Thorn Hill Rd.
Warrendale, PA 15086-7528
Tel: (724) 814-3000 *Fax:* (724) 814-3001
E-Mail: info@aist.org
Website: aist.org
Members: 15000 individuals
Staff: 29
Annual Budget: $10-25,000,000
Tax: 501(c)(3)

Personnel:
Executive Director: Ronald E. Ashburn
Editor-in-chief: Joann Cantrell
   E-Mail: jcantrell@aist.org
Accounting Administrator: Gale Crawford
   E-Mail: gcrawford@aist.org
Manager, Administration: Mark Didiano
   E-Mail: mdidiano@aist.org
Managing Editor: Karen Hickey
   E-Mail: khickey@aist.org
Manager, Sales and Exposition: Gerry Kane
   E-Mail: gkane@aist.org
Manager, Meeting Services: Shannon Kiley
   E-Mail: skiley@aist.org
Manager, Information Technology: Bill Patterson
   E-Mail: bpatterson@aist.org
Manager, Membership Services: Stacy Varmecky
   E-Mail: svarmecky@aist.org

Historical Note:
Originated in 1907 as the Association of Iron and Steel Electrical Engineers, became the Association of Iron and Steel Engineers in 1936. Merged with Iron and Steel Society and assumed its current name in 2004. AIST works to advance the technical development, production, processing and application of iron and steel. Membership: $115 (Professional); $57.50 (Young Professional); $25 (Student).

Meetings/Conferences: Annual
Conference Chair: Gerry Kane
2013 - Detroit, MI (MGM Grand Detroit)/March 26 - 28
2013 - Pittsburgh, PA (David L. Lawrence Convention Center)/May 6 - 9/over 100 exhibitors
2013 - Pittsburgh, PA (Sheraton Station Square Hotel)/June 9 - 11
2014 - Indianapolis, IN (Indiana Convention Center)/May 5 - 8

Publications:
AIST Steel Library; semi-annually
AIST Update; monthly

Association for Jewish Studies (1969)
15 W. 16th St.
New York, NY 10011-6301
Tel: (917) 606-8249 *Fax:* (917) 606-8222
E-Mail: ajs@ajs.cjh.org
Website: ajsnet.org

Members: 1800 individuals and 32 institutional
members
Staff: 5
Annual Budget: $500-1,000,000
Tax: 501(c)(3)

Personnel:
Executive Director: Rona Sheramy PhD
    E-Mail: ajs@ajs.cjh.org
Associate, Conference and Program: Emma Barker
    E-Mail: ajs@ajs.cjh.org
President: Sara Horowitz
Coordinator, Program and Membership Services: Karen
    Terry
    E-Mail: ajs@ajs.cjh.org

Historical Note:
*AJS's mission is to encourage, maintain and improve
teaching, research and related endeavors in Jewish Studies
in colleges, universities and other institutions of higher
learning. Membership: $500-1,000 (Institutional); $45
(Joint Student); $50-160/Year (Based on Income Level);
$35 (Student).*

Meetings/Conferences: Annual
Conference Chair: Emma Barker

Publications:
AJS Perspectives; bi-annually; adv.
AJS Review; bi-annually; adv.
Member Directory

Membership List Available to Non-members

Association for Library and Information Science Education *(1915)*
65 E. Wacker Pl.
Suite 1900
Chicago, IL 60601-7246
Tel: (312) 795-0996 *Fax:* (312) 419-8950
E-Mail: contact@alise.org
Website: alise.org
Members:
60 Institutional members
500 individuals
Staff: 3
Annual Budget: $250-500,000
Tax: 501(c)(3)

Personnel:
Executive Director: Kathleen Combs
    E-Mail: kcombs@alise.org
Executive Assistant: Jessica Schleinzer

Historical Note:
*Founded (1915) as the Association of American Library
Schools, assumed its current name in 1983 and is
an affiliate of the American Library Association and
the International Federation of Library Associations,
the Medical Library Association, the Special Libraries
Association, and the American Association of Law Libraries.
ALISE's mission is to promote excellence in research,
teaching, and service and to provide an understanding of
the values and ethos of library and information science.
Members are all levels of faculty, administration, students,
librarians, researchers, educational institutions and
others interested in library and information science
education. Membership: $125 (Full-time faculty member/
Librarian/Researcher/Administrator); $75 (Retired/Part-
time/Student); $60 (Doctoral Students); $350-2,500
(Institutional Member); $350 (International Affiliate
Institutional Member/ Associate Institutional Member).*

Continuing Education:
Certification Designation/s: ALISE

Meetings/Conferences: Annual
2013 - Seatle, WA (Grand Hyatt Seattle)/Jan. 22 - 25
2014 - Philadelphia, PA/Jan. 21 - 24
2015 - Chicago, IL/Jan. 27 - 30
Number of non-conference events/year: 1

Publications:
ALISE Directory
ALISE News
ALISE Newsletter; quarterly
Journal of Education for Library and Information
    Science (JELIS)

Association for Library Collections and Technical Services *(1957)*
50 E. Huron St.
Chicago, IL 60611-2795
Tel: (800) 545-2433 *Fax:* (312) 280-5033
TollFree: (800) 545-2433
E-Mail: alcts@ala.org
Website: ala.org/ala/mgrps/divs/alcts
Members: 5000 individuals

Staff: 3
Annual Budget: $500-1,000,000

Personnel:
Executive Director: Charles Wilt
    E-Mail: cwilt@ala.org
Contact, Publications and Membership Services: Christine
    McConnell
    E-Mail: cmcconnell@ala.org
Contact, Continuing Education and Meetings: Julie Reese
    E-Mail: jreese@ala.org

Historical Note:
*A division of the American Library Association. Formerly
Resources and Technical Services Division. Adopted its
name in 1989. ALCTS mission is to shape and respond
nimbly to all matters related to the selection, identification,
acquisition, organization, management, retrieval, and
preservation of recorded knowledge through education,
publication, and collaboration. Membership: $50/year
(Individual).*

Meetings/Conferences: Annual
Conference Chair: Julie Reese

Publications:
ALCTS Newsletter; on-line; adv.

The Association for Library Service to Children *(1958)*
C/O American Library Association
50 E. Huron St.
Chicago, IL 60611-2795
Tel: (800) 545-2433 *Fax:* (312) 280-5271
TollFree: (800) 545-2433
E-Mail: alsc@ala.org
Website: ala.org/alsc
Members:
310 Organizations
4200 Organizations, Libraries, Children's etc
Staff: 6
Annual Budget: $500-1,000,000
Tax: 501(c)(3)

Personnel:
Executive Director: Aimee Strittmatter
    E-Mail: astrittmatter@ala.org
Program Coordinator: Marsha Burgess
    E-Mail: mburgess@ala.org
Program Officer, Projects and Partnerships: Linda Mays
    E-Mail: lmays@ala.org
Program Officer, Continuing Education: Jennifer Najduch
    E-Mail: jnajduch@ala.org
Marketing Specialist, Membership Services: Dan Rude
    E-Mail: drude@ala.org
Program Officer, Communications: Laura Schulte-Cooper
    E-Mail: lschulte@ala.org

Historical Note:
*Formerly(1958) Children's Services Division of the
American Library Association. ALSC is a division of
American Library Association providing specialized
resources for librarians incharge of libraries serving
children. Its network includes more than 4,200 children's
and youth librarians, children's literature experts,
publishers, education and library school faculty members,
and other adults dedicated to creating a better future for
children through libraries and lead the way in forging
excellent library service for all children. Membership: $45
(Personal/Organizational/Corporate); $18 (Student).*

Continuing Education:
Certification Designation/s: CPLA, LSSC

Meetings/Conferences: Annual
Conference Chair: Linda Mays
2013 - Chicago, IL/June 27 - July 2

Publications:
ALSConnect Newsletter; quarterly
Children and Libraries Journal; quarterly; adv.

Membership List Available to Non-members

Association for Linen Management *(1939)*
2161 Lexington Rd.
Suite Two
Richmond, KY 40475-7952
Tel: (859) 624-0177 *Fax:* (859) 624-3580
TollFree: (800) 669-0863
Website: almnet.org
Members: 1200 individuals
Staff: 4
Annual Budget: $500-1,000,000
Tax: 501(c)(6)

Personnel:
Executive Director, Academic Affairs: Linda Fairbanks

    E-Mail: lindaf@almnet.org
Specialist, Marketing and Communications: Eric Puckett
    E-Mail: epuckett@almnet.org
Manager, Membership Services: Kelly Werner
    E-Mail: kwerner@almnet.org

Historical Note:
*Formerly known as National Association of Institutional
Laundry Managers (NAILM). Also known as the National
Association of Institutional Laundry Managers till 1985.
ALM is an educational source for people and organizations
that purchase, process, distribute, and manage the use of
linens and other textile products. Mission is to provide a
network for the flow of information among its members
leading toward their professional development and the
advancement of the technologies they employ. Membership:
$150 (Individual); $220 (Facility); $20 (Retired); $500
(National).*

Continuing Education:
Certification Designation/s: RLLD, RESD, CLLM, CWT,
CLT, CESM

Meetings/Conferences: Annual
2013 - New Orleans, LA/June 20 - 22

Publications:
ALM Journal; bi-monthly
Membership Directory; annually

Association for Living History, Farm and Agricultural Museums *(1970)*
8774 Route 45 NW
N. Bloomfield, OH 44450-9701
Tel: (440) 685-4410 *Fax:* (440) 685-4410
E-Mail: info@alhfam.org
Website: alhfam.org
Members:
250 institutions
800 individuals
Staff: 2
Annual Budget: $50-100,000
Tax: 501(c)(3)

Personnel:
President: Pete Watson
Editor: Katie Boardman
    E-Mail: katie@cherryvalley.com

Historical Note:
*ALHFAM's mission is to share practical knowledge
and skills among those who make history relevant to
contemporary lives.Members include people working in
living history, farms, house museums, agricultural museums
and outdoor museums of history and folklife. Membership:
$30 (Basic); $50 (Supporting/Business Associate); $55
(Joint); $25 (Student/Retired); $60 (Small Institution/
Library); $120 (Large Institution); $100 (Patron).*

Meetings/Conferences: Annual
2013 - Bath, OH (Hale Farm Village)/June 14 - 18
Number of non-conference events/year: 5

Publications:
Membership Directory; on-line
Western Region Newsletter

Association for Management Information in Financial Services *(1980)*
14247 Saffron Cir.
Carmel, IN 46032
Tel: (317) 815-5857 *Fax:* (317) 815-5877
E-Mail: ami@amifs.org
Website: amifs.org
Members: 600 individuals
Staff: 5
Annual Budget: $100-250,000
Tax: 501(c)(6)

Personnel:
Executive Director: Kevin W. Link
    E-Mail: kevin.link@altiusllc.com
President: Andy Streiff
    E-Mail: andrew.streiff@bankofamerica.com
Treasurer: Lynn Courchaine
    E-Mail: Lynn.Courchaine@td.com
Assistant Executive Director: Krissa Hatfield
    E-Mail: plaidgolf@indy.rr.com
Chair, Conferences: Robert McDonald
    E-Mail: Robert.McDonald@wachovia.com

Historical Note:
*Formerly (1990) the National Association for Bank Cost
Analysis and (1997) National Association for Bank Cost
and Management Accounting. AMIfs's mission is to develop
and advance the profession of management information
for the financial services industry. Membership open
to individuals employed by any commercial bank, trust*

company, Federal Reserve bank, bank holding company, credit union or thrift institution. Membership: $350 (Individual); $1,200 (Corporate).

Continuing Education:
Certification Designation/s: CPE

Meetings/Conferences: Annual
Conference Chair: Andy Streiff
Number of non-conference events/year: 1

Publications:
Membership Directory; annually
The Bulletin; quarterly; adv.
The Journal of Performance Management; adv.

The Association for Manufacturing Excellence
(1985)
3701 Algonquin Rd.
Suite 225
Rolling Meadows, IL 60008-3127
Tel: (224) 232-5980 Fax: (224) 232-5981
E-Mail: info@ame.org
Website: ame.org
Members: 5000 individuals
Staff: 12
Annual Budget: $2-5,000,000
Tax: 501(c)(3)

Personnel:
President: Paul Kuchuris
    E-Mail: pkuchuris@ame.org
Coordinator, Membership Services: Sue Bouraoui
    E-Mail: sbouraoui@ame.org
Registrar and Coordinator, Conferences: Veronica Ceaser
    E-Mail: vceaser@ame.org
Administrative Assistant: Maureen Gilhooly
    E-Mail: mgilhooly@ame.org
Director, Finance, Human Resources and Information
    Technology: Rachel Miller
    E-Mail: rmiller@ame.org
Coordinator, Marketing and Communications: Sara
    O'Hara
    E-Mail: sohara@ame.org
Director, Marketing and Communications: Scott Schiave
    E-Mail: sschiave@ame.org
Production Manager and Editor: JoAnn Weitzenfeld
    E-Mail: jaweitz@ame.org

Historical Note:
AME's mission is to strive for enterprise excellence through shared learning and access to best practices. Members are executives, senior and middle managers who wish to improve both their organization's and their personal performance. Membership: $150 (Individual); $25 (Student); $190 (International); $259 (Combined AME and Society of Manufacturing Engineers Member); $600-25,000 (Corporate Member); $1500 (Life).

Continuing Education:
Certification Designation/s: LEAN

Meetings/Conferences: Annual
Conference Chair: Veronica Ceaser
2013 - Toronto, ON/Oct. 21 - 25
2014 - Jacksonville, FL/Nov. 10 - 14
2015 - Cincinnati, OH/Oct. 19 - 23
2016 - Dallas, TX/Oct. 24 - 28
Number of non-conference events/year: 29

Publications:
Sharing Excellence; bi-weekly
Target; quarterly; adv.

Association for Medical Imaging Management
(1973)
490B Boston Post Rd.
Suite 200
Sudbury, MA 01776
Tel: (978) 443-7591 Fax: (978) 443-8046
TollFree: (800) 334-2472
E-Mail: info@ahraonline.org
Website: ahraonline.org
Members: 4000 individuals
Staff: 10
Annual Budget: $2-5,000,000

Personnel:
Chief Executive Officer: Edward J. Cronin Jr.
Director, Publications: Debra Murphy
    E-Mail: dmurphy@ahraonline.org
Coordinator, Membership Services: Jillian Nanof
Senior Website Administrator: Ryan Ocampo
Coordinator, Accounting Services: Suzee Slatton
Director, Marketing: Mike Suddendorf

Historical Note:

AHRA was previously called as American Healthcare Radiology Administrators, earlier to that was known as American Hospital Radiology Administrators till 1986. AHRA's mission is to provide resource and catalyst for the development of professional leadership in medical imaging management and dedicated to developing products and services driven by member needs. The association will be a driving force toward improving the healthcare environment. Membership: $175 (Individual/International); $130-155 (Organizational, non-hospital); $325-1850 (Organizational hospital, one price); $175-875 (Organizational hospital, a la carte).

Continuing Education:
Enrollment: 600
Certification Designation/s: CRA

Meetings/Conferences:
2013 - Minneapolis, MN (Minneapolis Convention Center)/July 28 - 31
Number of non-conference events/year: 2

Publications:
Member Directory; on-line

Membership List Available to Non-members

Association for Middle Level Education (1973)
4151 Executive Pkwy.
Suite 300
Westerville, OH 43081
Tel: (614) 895-4730 Fax: (614) 895-4750
TollFree: (800) 528-6672
E-Mail: info@nmsa.org
Website: amle.org
Members: 30000 individuals
Staff: 20
Annual Budget: $5-10,000,000
Tax: 501(c)(3)

Personnel:
Executive Director: William D. Waidelich EdD
    E-Mail: wwaidelich@amle.org
Manager, Meetings and Events: Sally Ann DeBolt
    E-Mail: sdebolt@amle.org
Chief Financial Officer: Ann Eichel
    E-Mail: aeichel@nmsa.org
Senior Director, Advocacy and Affiliate Services: Doug
    Herlensky
    E-Mail: dherlensky@nmsa.org
Manager, Membership and Marketing: Derek Neal
    E-Mail: dneal@nmsa.org
Chief Communications Officer: April Tibbles
    E-Mail: atibbles@nmsa.org
Editor-in-Chief: Carla Weiland
    E-Mail: cweiland@amle.org

Historical Note:
Formerly (1973) Midwest Middle School Association then the National Middle School Association. AMLE's mission is to improve the educational experiences of young adolescents by providing vision, knowledge, and resources to all who serve them in order to develop healthy, productive, and ethical citizens. Membership: $60 (Individual e-Membership); $90 (Professional-Individual Membership); $110(Premier-Individual Membership); $220 (Institutional e-Membership); $280 (Professional-Institutional Membership); $600 (Premier-Institutional Membership); $40 (College Student/Parent/Retiree).

Meetings/Conferences: Annual
Conference Chair: Sally Ann DeBolt
2013 - Minneapolis, MN/Nov. 7 - 9
2014 - Nashville, TN/Nov. 6 - 8
2015 - St. Louis, MO/Nov. 5 - 7

Publications:
Middle E-Connections; monthly; adv.
Middle Ground; quarterly; adv.
Middle Level Education Research Annual; annually
Middle School Journal; quarterly; adv.
RMLE Online; monthly
The Family Connection; quarterly
What's New (e-Newsletter); monthly

Membership List Available to Non-members

Association for Molecular Pathology (1995)
9650 Rockville Pike
Suite E133
Bethesda, MD 20814-3993
Tel: (301) 634-7939 Fax: (301) 634-7990
E-Mail: amp@amp.org
Website: amp.org
Members: 1800 individuals
Staff: 16
Annual Budget: $2-5,000,000

Tax: 501(c)(3)

Personnel:
Executive Director: Mary Steele Williams MT (ASCP)
    E-Mail: mwilliams@amp.org
Manager, Membership Services: Ann Marie Bocus
    E-Mail: AMBocus@asip.org
Managing Editor: Audra E. Cox ELS, PhD
    E-Mail: ACox@asip.org
Manager, Marketing, Development and Exhibits:
    Catherine Davidge
    E-Mail: cdavidge@amp.org
Director, Finance: James S. Douglas
    E-Mail: JDouglas@asip.org
Manager, Meetings: Sara Hamilton
    E-Mail: shamilton@asip.org
Manager, Educational Services: Lisa McFadden
    E-Mail: lmcfadden@asip.org
Director, Meetings: Tara Snethen CAE, CMP
    E-Mail: tsnethen@asip.org

Historical Note:
AMP works for the advancement of clinical molecular diagnostic and prognostic medicine through education and training. Members are individuals interested in the educational, medical, scientific, economic, and regulatory aspects of molecular diagnostics, including but not limited to pathologists, clinical laboratory scientists, clinicians and other health care personnel, government employees, especially those involved in regulation of the field, and professionals in the in vitro diagnostics industry. Membership: $200 (Regular); $85 (Associate); $25 (Residents in HINARI-Eligible Countries/Emeritus Members).

Meetings/Conferences: Annual
Conference Chair: Tara Snethen CAE, CMP
2013 - Phoenix, AZ (Phoenix Convention Center)/Nov. 14 - 16/over 100 exhibitors
2014 - Ft. Washington, MD (Gaylord National Resort and Convention Center-National Harbor)/Nov. 13 - 15/over 100 exhibitors
Number of non-conference events/year: 4

Publications:
AMP Membership Directory; on-line
AMP Newsletter; on-line; adv.
The Journal of Molecular Diagnostics; bi-monthly; adv.

Membership List Available to Non-members

Association for Multicultural Counseling and Development (1971)
101 Auburn Ave.
Atlanta, GA 30303
Website: multiculturalcounseling.org/
Members: 3091 individuals
Staff: 4
Annual Budget: $25-50,000

Personnel:
Webmaster: Timothy D. Baker
    E-Mail: tdbaker@stcloudstate.edu
President: S. Kent Butler
    E-Mail: sylvester.butler@ucf.edu
JMCD Editor: Caroline S. Clauss-Ehlers
    E-Mail: editor@jmcdonline.org
Treasurer: Harrison Davis
    E-Mail: harrisond2@gmail.com

Historical Note:
Formerly (1985) Association for Non-White Concerns in Personnel and Guidance. AMCD strives to improve cultural, ethnic and racial empathy and understanding by designing programs to advance and sustain personal growth. AMCD is a division of the American Counseling Association, which provides administrative support. Membership: $33/year (professional); $20/year (student/retired).

Publications:
The AMCD newsletter; quarterly

The Association for Nursing Professional Development (1987)
401 N. Michigan Ave.
Chicago, IL 60611
Tel: (312) 673-5135 Fax: (312) 673-6835
TollFree: (800) 489-1995
E-Mail: info@nnsdo.org
Website: nnsdo.org
Members: 10000 individuals
Staff: 15
Annual Budget: $250-500,000
Tax: 501(c)(6)

Personnel:
Executive Director: Kaye Englebrecht CAE

E-Mail: KEnglebrecht@nnsdo.org
Senior Coordinator, Operations: Meredith Bono
    E-Mail: mbono@nnsdo.org
Contact, Event Services: Cynthia Cortis
    E-Mail: ccortis@nnsdo.org
Contact, Sales Services: Hallie Jaeger
    E-Mail: HJaeger@nnsdo.org
Contact, Financial Services: Alexia Malamis
    E-Mail: amalamis@nnsdo.org
Contact, Trade Show Services: Catherine Perkins
    E-Mail: cperkins@nnsdo.org
Contact, Publications: Kelly Rehan
    E-Mail: KRehan@nnsdo.org
Contact, Marketing and Communication Services: Jennifer Snider
    E-Mail: JSnider@smithbucklin.com
Contact, Education and Learning Services: Jaclyn Weinrauch
    E-Mail: JWeinrauch@nnsdo.org

Historical Note:
Formerly the National Nursing Staff Development Organization (NNSDO). ANPD advances the specialty practice of staff development for the enhancement of healthcare outcomes. Membership: $95 (Regular); $105 (Retired).

Meetings/Conferences: Annual
Conference Chair: Cynthia Cortis
2013 - Dallas, TX (Dallas Convention Center)/July 16 - 20
Number of non-conference events/year: 3

Publications:
Membership Directory; on-line
Nurses in Staff Development
NurseWeek Magazine
TrendLines Newsletter; bi-monthly; adv.

Association for Philosophy of the Unconscious
(1971)
Department of Philosophy, Georgetown University
Washington, DC 20057
Tel: (202) 687-7613 *Fax:* (202) 687-4493
Website: processpsychology.com/ Unconscious.html
Members: 150 individuals
Staff: 1
Annual Budget: Under $10,000

Personnel:
President: Wilfried Ver Eecke
    E-Mail: vereeckw@georgetown.edu

Historical Note:
APU members are academics and others with an interest in psychoanalysis and philosophy. Membership: $5 (Individual); $2 (Student).

Association for Play Therapy *(1982)*
3198 Willow Ave.
Suite 110
Clovis, CA 93612
Tel: (559) 294-2128 *Fax:* (559) 294-2129
E-Mail: info@a4pt.org
Website: a4pt.org
Members: 6000 individuals
Staff: 6
Annual Budget: $1-2,000,000
Tax: 501(c)(6)

Personnel:
President and Chief Executive Officer: William M. Burns CAE
    E-Mail: bburns@a4pt.org
Coordinator, Media and Branch Relations: Stephanie Carter
    E-Mail: scarter@a4pt.org
Coordinator, Credentialing and Products: Carol Guerrero
    E-Mail: cguerrero@a4pt.org
Coordinator, Advertising and Marketing: Amber Kreiter
    E-Mail: akreiter@a4pt.org
Vice President, Chief Operating Officer and Coordinator, Conferences: Kathryn Lebby CAE, CMP
    E-Mail: klebby@a4pt.org
Coordinator, Membership Services, Accounts Payable and Technology: Diane Leon
    E-Mail: dleon@a4pt.org

Historical Note:
APT's mission is to promote the value of play, play therapy, and credentialed play therapists by advancing the psychosocial development and mental health of all people.

Membership: $95 (Professional); $70 (International); $45-50 (Affiliate).
Continuing Education:
Enrollment: 1800
Certification Designation/s: RPT, RPT-S
Meetings/Conferences: Annual
Conference Chair: Kathryn Lebby CAE, CMP
2013 - Rancho Mirage, CA (Westin Mission Hills Resort and Spa)/Oct. 8 - 13
2014 - Houston, TX (Westin Galleria Houston)/Oct. 7 - 12
2015 - Atlanta, GA (Renaissance Waverly Atlanta Luxury Hotel)/Oct. 6 - 11
Publications:
APT Flash; weekly
Find Approved Providers Directory; on-line
Find Branches Directory; on-line
Find Play Therapists Directory; on-line
Find Play Therapy & Supervisor Training Directory; on-line
Find University Play Therapy Directory; on-line
International Journal of Play Therapy; quarterly; adv.
Plan Therapy Magazine; quarterly; adv.
Membership List Available to Non-members

Association for Politics and the Life Sciences
(1980)
School of Public Policy, University of Maryland
College Park, MD 20742
Tel: (301) 405-0184 *Fax:* (301) 775-0320
E-Mail: sprinkle@umd.edu
Website: apls.msj.edu
Members: 350 individuals
Staff: 3
Annual Budget: $25-50,000

Personnel:
Executive Director: David B. Goetze PhD
    E-Mail: david.goetze@usu.edu
Editor-in-Chief: Erik P. Bucy
    E-Mail: ebucy@indiana.edu
Webmaster: Ronald F. White
    E-Mail: APLSwebmaster@gmail.com

Historical Note:
APLS is an international and interdisciplinary association of scholars, scientists and policymakers concerned with problems or issues that involve politics or public policy and one or more of the life sciences. Membership: $75-215 (Full), $40 (Student), $25 (Online).

Meetings/Conferences: Annual
Publications:
APLS Directory; on-line
Politics and the Life Sciences (PLS); semi-annually

Association for Population/Family Planning Libraries and Information Centers, International
(1968)
426 Thompson St.
Ann Arbor, MI 48105
Tel: (734) 763-2152
E-Mail: info@aplici.org
Website: aplici.org
Members: 75 individuals
Staff: 2
Annual Budget: Under $10,000

Personnel:
President: Lori Rosman
    E-Mail: ctwose1@jhmi.edu
Chair, Membership: Yan Fu
    E-Mail: yanfu@umich.edu

Historical Note:
APLIC's is to provide opportunities for capacity and community building among population and reproductive health communication, information, and resource professionals. Individual members include communication and information specialists, librarians and documentalists from the population and reproductive health fields, as well as public health, medical and social sciences professionals. Membership: $50 (Individual, Developed Countries); $15 (Individual, Developing Countries/Student/Retired); $125 (Sustaining).

Meetings/Conferences: Annual
Publications:
APLIC Communicator; on-line
Membership List; on-line

Association for Postal Commerce *(1947)*
1421 Prince St.

Suite 410
Arlington, VA 22314-2806
Tel: (703) 524-0096 *Fax:* (703) 997-2414
E-Mail: info@postcom.org
Website: postcom.org
Members: 1180 individuals and companies
Staff: 4
Annual Budget: $1-2,000,000
Tax: 501(c)(6)

Personnel:
Executive Vice President: Jessica Lowrance
    E-Mail: jlowrance@postcom.org
President: Gene A. Del Polito PhD
    E-Mail: genedp@postcom.org
Director, Administrative Services: Caroline Miller
General Counsel: Ian D. Volner

Historical Note:
Formerly known as the Third Class Mail Association and then the Advertising Mail Marketing Association. POSTCOM represents those that support the use of mail as a medium for business communication and commerce.

Publications:
Membership Directory; on-line

Association for Practical and Professional Ethics
(1991)
618 E. Third St.
Indiana University
Bloomington, IN 47405-3602
Tel: (812) 855-6450 *Fax:* (812) 856-4969
E-Mail: appe@indiana.edu
Website: appeonline.com
Members: 650 individuals, 100 institutions
Staff: 3
Annual Budget: $100-250,000
Tax: 501(c)(3)

Personnel:
Executive Director: Dr. Stuart Yoak
    E-Mail: appe@indiana.edu
Administrative Assistant: Beth Works
    E-Mail: appe@indiana.edu

Historical Note:
APPE encourages interdisciplinary scholarship and teaching in practical and professional ethics by educators and practitioners who appreciate the theoretical and practical impacts of their subjects. APPE members are academic and other professionals with an interest in the field of practical and professional ethics. Membership: $40-265 (Individual); $200 (Institution); $550 (Sustaining Institutional); $500 (RCREC Organizational); $2,000 (RCREC Organizational Sponsor).

Meetings/Conferences: Annual
2013 - San Antonio, TX (St. Anthony Riverwalk Wyndham Hotel)/Feb. 28 - March 3

Publications:
Ethically Speaking Newsletter; semi-annually
International Journal of Applied Philosophy
Member Directory; annually

Membership List Available to Non-members

Association for Preservation Technology International *(1968)*
3085 Stevenson Dr.
Suite 200
Springfield, IL 62703
Tel: (217) 529-9039 *Fax:* (888) 723-4242
E-Mail: info@apti.org
Website: apti.org
Members: 1500 individuals
Staff: 7
Annual Budget: $500-1,000,000

Personnel:
President: Joan C. Berkowitz
Administrative Director: Nathela Chatara
Treasurer: Kyle Normandin
Conference Meeting Planner: Dana Saal
    E-Mail: dana@apti.org
Editor: Lynette Stuhlmacher AP, LEED

Historical Note:
Organized in Canada and relocated to the United States in 1988. APT's mission is to promote technology for conserving historic structures and their settings. Members are preservationists, architects, conservators, consultants, contractors, craftspersons, curators, developers, educators, engineers, historians, landscape architects, technicians and other persons directly involved in the application of methods and materials to maintain, conserve, and protect historic

structures and sites. *Membership:* $60-250/year; $4,500 (Life).

Meetings/Conferences: Annual
Conference Chair: Dana Saal
2013 - New York City, NY (New York Marriott Marquis)/Oct. 12 - 15

Publications:
APT Bulletin: The Journal of Preservation Technology; adv.
Communique; quarterly; adv.
Membership Directory; on-line

Association for Prevention Teaching and Research (APTR) *(1942)*
1001 Connecticut Ave. NW
Suite 610
Washington, DC 20036
Tel: (202) 463-0550 *Fax:* (202) 463-0555
TollFree: (866) 520-2787
E-Mail: info@atpm.org
Website:
aptr.org
aptrweb.org
Members:
500 individuals
150 institutions
Staff: 9
Annual Budget: $5-10,000,000
Tax: 501(c)(3)

Personnel:
Executive Director: Allison L. Lewis
    E-Mail: all@aptrweb.org
Associate Director, Training and Education: Vera Cardinale
    E-Mail: vsc@aptrweb.org
Director, Finance and Administration: Connie Eisaman
    E-Mail: cle@aptrweb.org
Coordinator, Membership and Communications: Lauren Lefebvre
    E-Mail: LCL@aptrweb.org
Coordinator, Finance: Robyn McDaniels
    E-Mail: rgm@aptrweb.org
Director, Program Management and Development: O. Kent Nordvig
    E-Mail: okn@aptrweb.org
Editor-in-Chief: Kevin Patrick MD, MS

Historical Note:
Formerly the Association of Teachers of Preventive Medicine. APTR develops curricular resources, professional development programs, and tools for its membership. Individual members include educators in preventive medicine and public health, physicians, nurses, health services researchers, and public health professionals. Organizational members include academic departments and programs, health agencies, and graduate programs of public health. Membership: $65-875/year.

Meetings/Conferences: Annual
Conference Chair: O. Kent Nordvig
Number of non-conference events/year: 3

Publications:
American Journal of Preventive Medicine; monthly; adv.
APTR Quarterly Newsletter; quarterly
News Now; weekly

Membership List Available to Non-members

Association for Professionals in Infection Control and Epidemiology *(1972)*
1275 K St. NW
Suite 1000
Washington, DC 20005-4006
Tel: (202) 789-1890 *Fax:* (202) 789-1899
E-Mail: info@apic.org
Website: apic.org
Members: 14000 individuals
Staff: 49
Annual Budget: $10-25,000,000

Personnel:
Chief Executive Officer: Katrina Crist MBA
Contact, Publications: Janiene Bohannon
    E-Mail: jbohannon@apic.org
Senior Director, Education: Shawn E. Boynes
    E-Mail: sboynes@apic.org
Senior Director, Communications: Elizabeth Garman
    E-Mail: egarman@apic.org
Senior Director, Marketing: Debbie Goldstein

Associate Director, Education and Contact, Annual Conferences: Sara Haywood
    E-Mail: shaywood@apic.org
Senior Director, Governance and Executive Affairs: Barbara Long
    E-Mail: blong@apic.org
Senior Manager, Information Technology: Charles Malry Jr.
    E-Mail: cmalry@apic.org
Chief Financial Officer: George Margula CPA, MBA
    E-Mail: gmargula@apic.org
Senior Director, Membership and Information Technology: Artesha Moore
    E-Mail: amoore@apic.org
Senior Director, Human Resources: Lynn Schneider
    E-Mail: lschneider@apic.org

Historical Note:
Formerly (1992) the Association for Practitioners in Infection Control. APIC's mission is to improve health and patient safety by reducing risks of infection and other adverse outcomes. Members are physicians, nurses, medical technologists, sanitarians and others professionally concerned with the practice and management of infection control and epidemiology in all health settings. Membership: $80-205/year.

Continuing Education:
Certification Designation/s: CIC

Meetings/Conferences: Annual
Conference Chair: Sara Haywood
2013 - Ft. Lauderdale, FL/June 7 - 10
2013 - Ft. Lauderdale, FL/June 8 - 10
2014 - Anaheim, CA/June 6 - 9
Number of non-conference events/year: 1

Publications:
American Journal of Infection Control
e-News; weekly
Infection Connection; quarterly
Membership Directory; on-line
Preventing Infection in Ambulatory Care; quarterly
Prevention Strategist; quarterly

Association for Psychoanalytic Medicine *(1942)*
41 Union Sq., West
Room 402
New York, NY 10003
Website: theapm.org
Members: 280 individuals
Staff: 3
Annual Budget: $50-100,000

Personnel:
President: Henry Schwartz MD
Treasurer: Lawrence Jacobsberg MD, PhD

Historical Note:
Formerly the Association for Psychoanalytic and Psychosomatic Medicine and affiliated with the American Psychoanalytic Association. APM's mission is to foster discussion, educate and to promote the acquisition of new knowledge among its members and those interested in the clinical practice of psychoanalysis, in psychoanalytic theories of mind, and in related interdisciplinary fields. Membership: $265/year.

Continuing Education:
Certification Designation/s: ACCME

Meetings/Conferences: Annual

Publications:
Membership Directory; on-line
Shrink Ink
The Bulletin; bi-annually

Association for Psychological Science *(1988)*
1133 15th St. NW
Suite 1000
Washington, DC 20005
Tel: (202) 293-9300 *Fax:* (202) 293-9350
E-Mail: APS@APS.Washington.dc.us
Website: psychologicalscience.org
Members: 23,000 members
Staff: 12
Annual Budget: $5-10,000,000
Tax: 501(c)(3)

Personnel:
Executive Director: Alan G. Kraut
    E-Mail: akraut@aps.washington.dc.us
Director, Publications: Aime Ballard-Wood
    E-Mail: aballardwood@psychologicalscience.org
Senior Manager, Membership Services: Brendan Breen
    E-Mail: bbreen@psychologicalscience.org

Deputy Director, Advertising News: Sarah Brookhart
    E-Mail: sarahb@aps.washington.dc.us
Director, Public Affairs: Tiffany Harrington
    E-Mail: tharrington@psychologicalscience.org
Director, Internal Affairs: Sara Hitzig
    E-Mail: hitzigs@psychologicalscience.org
Director, Meetings: Nathalie Rothert
    E-Mail: nrothert@psychologicalscience.org
Director, Finance and Administration: Jen Stauder
    E-Mail: jstauder@psychologicalscience.org
Director, Marketing and Advertising: Brian L. Weaver

Historical Note:
Formerly American Psychological Society. APS's mission is to promote, protect, and advance the interests of scientifically oriented psychology in research, application, teaching, and the improvement of human welfare. Membership: $37-5000/year.

Meetings/Conferences: Annual
Conference Chair: Alan G. Kraut
2013 - Washington, DC (Washington Marriott Wardman Park)/May 23 - 26/11-25 exhibitors
2014 - San Francisco, CA (Hilton San Francisco)/May 22 - 25

Publications:
Current Directions in Psychological Science; bi-monthly
Observer
Perspectives on Psychological Science; bi-monthly
Psychological Science; monthly; adv.
Psychological Science in the Public Interest

Membership List Available to Non-members

Association for Psychological Type International *(1979)*
2415 Westwood Ave.
Suite B
Richmond, VA 23230
Tel: (804) 288-2950 *Fax:* (804) 288-3551
E-Mail: info@aptinternational.org
Website: aptinternational.org
Members: 20 Chapters
Staff: 6
Annual Budget: $250-500,000
Tax: 501(c)(3)

Personnel:
Executive Director: Tony Doucet
    E-Mail: tdoucet@catapult-inc.com
Director, Finance: Sterling Bates
Director, Communications: Gene Bellotti
    E-Mail: bellotti@bellotti.com
Director, Marketing: M. Eileen Brown
Director, Membership: Casey Lovoy
Director, Training and Education: Mike Shur
    E-Mail: mikeshur@gmail.com

Historical Note:
APTi is the international membership organization for professional users of personality type and assessments. Membership: $110 (Regular); $75 (Retirees); $55 (Students).

Continuing Education:
Certification Designation/s: CAPT MBTI CP, CPP MBTI CP

Meetings/Conferences: Biennial
2013 - Miami, FL (Hyatt Regency)/July 10 - 14

Publications:
Journal of Psychological Type; monthly
The Bulletin; quarterly

Association for Quality Imaging (AQI) *(1997)*
1629 K St. NW
Suite 300
Washington, DC 20006
Tel: (202) 355-6406 *Fax:* (202) 355-6407
E-Mail: contact@aqimaging.net
Website: aqimaging.org
Staff: 2
Annual Budget: $500-1,000,000
Tax: 501(c)(6)

Personnel:
Executive Director: Margaret Sayre
    E-Mail: maggie@sayreconsulting.com

Historical Note:
Formerly the National Coalition for Quality Diagnostic Imaging Services (NCQDIS)), established in 1997, continues to provide an effective voice for the diagnostic imaging industry.

Publications:

Journal of Computer Assisted Tomography; bi-
monthly; adv.
American Journal of Neuroradiology; adv.
American Journal of Roentgenology; adv.
Journal of Vascular and Interventional Radiology
Journal of Women's Imaging; adv.
Radiology Today Magazine; adv.
RT Image Weekly Radiology Magazine; weekly

Association for Radiological and Imaging Nursing
(1981)
7794 Grow Dr.
Pensacola, FL 32514
Tel: (850) 474-7292 Fax: (850) 484-8762
TollFree: (866) 486-2762
E-Mail: arin@dancyamc.org
Website: arinursing.org
Members: 2100 individuals
Staff: 7
Annual Budget: $250-500,000
Tax: 501(c)(6)

Personnel:
Executive Director: Karen L. Green
Director, Convention Services: Donna Deans
    E-Mail: donna.deans@dancyamc.com
Administrative Executive: Harriet McClung CAE, CMA,
MBA
    E-Mail: harriet.mcclung@dancyamc.com
Supervisor, Membership Services: Alexander Muniz
Contact, Education Services: Haley Shelton
Specialist, Governance Support: Richelle Torres
Contact, Membership Services: Mirta Wallace

Historical Note:
ARIN's purpose is to support the growth of nurses who
advance the standard of care in the imaging environment.
ARIN members are professional nurses actively engaged
in radiological nursing or with a radiological nursing
background. Membership: $95/year (Individual/Associate);
$110 (International).

Continuing Education:
Certification Designation/s: RNCB

Meetings/Conferences: Annual
Conference Chair: Donna Deans
2013 - New Orleans, LA/April 14 - 17

Publications:
Journal of Radiology Nursing; quarterly
Vision; quarterly; adv.

Association for Recorded Sound Collections
(1966)
P.O. Box 543
Annapolis, MD 21404-0543
Tel: (410) 757-0488 Fax: (410) 349-0175
Website: arsc-audio.org
Members: 1100 individuals
Staff: 3
Annual Budget: $100-250,000

Personnel:
Executive Director: Peter Shambarger
    E-Mail: shambarger@sprynet.com
Editor: Barry R. Ashpole
Treasurer: Steven I Ramm

Historical Note:
ARSC fosters the development of discographic information
in all formats and periods of recording and encourages
the preservation of historical recordings. Membership:
$20 (Student); $45 (Individual); $75 (Institutional); $90
(Sustaining); $200 (Donor); $500 (Patron); $1,000
(Benefactor).

Meetings/Conferences: Annual
2013 - Kansas City, MO/May 15 - 18

Publications:
ARSC Journal; semi-annually
ARSC Newsletter; adv.

Membership List Available to Non-members

The Association for Research in Business Education - Delta Pi Epsilon (1936)
1914 Association Dr.
Reston, VA 20191-1596
Tel: (703) 860-8300 Fax: (703) 620-4483
E-Mail: dpe@ipa.net
Website: dpe.org
Members:
60 chapters
11000 individuals
Staff: 5

Annual Budget: $100-250,000

Personnel:
Executive Director: Robert B. Mitchell
    E-Mail: rbmitchell@ualr.edu
Office Manager: Donna Brunt
Editor: Dr. Margaret Erthal

Historical Note:
Founded at the New York University in 1936 and
incorporated in the State of New York, December 3,
1937 and reincorporated in Minnesota in 1983 and in
Arkansas in 1988, name changed to the Association for
Research in Business Education - Delta Pi Epsilon in
2011. DPE is a professional society in graduate business
education that promotes three ideals as symbolized by
its name Delta - Scholarship, Pi - Leadership, Epsilon -
Cooperation. Members are teachers of business subjects.
Membership: $80 (Professional); $110 (Professional /
International Society for Business Education (ISBE));
$140 (Professional / Delta Pi Epsilon (DPE)); $170
(Professional / ISBE / Delta Pi Epsilon (DPE)).

Meetings/Conferences: Annual

Publications:
Newsletters
Delta Pi Epsilon Journal
Journal of Applied Research for Business Instruction
(JARBI)

Membership List Available to Non-members

Association for Research in Nervous and Mental Disease (1920)
c/o Weill Medical College of Cornell Univ., Dept.
of Psychiatry
1300 York Ave., Room F-1231, Box 171
New York, NY 10021
Tel: (570) 839-0296 Fax: (570) 839-0297
E-Mail: arnmd@arnmd.org
Website: arnmd.org
Members: 500 individuals
Staff: 1
Annual Budget: $50-100,000

Personnel:
Executive Director: Annlouise Goodermuth

Historical Note:
Established as the Neuropsychiatric Research Society;
assumed its present name in 1922. Membership: $150/year
(individual).

Association for Research in Otolaryngology
(1973)
19 Mantua Rd.
Mt. Royal, NJ 08061
Tel: (856) 423-0041 Fax: (856) 423-3420
E-Mail: headquarters@aro.org
Website: aro.org
Members: 2100 individuals
Staff: 4
Annual Budget: $500-1,000,000

Personnel:
Executive Director: Darla Eastlack
Manager, Meetings: Lisa Astorga
    E-Mail: meetings@aro.org
Editor: Linda Hood PhD
Manager, Exhibits: Alex Springer
    E-Mail: aspringer@talley.com

Historical Note:
ARO is dedicated to scientific exploration among all of
the disciplines in the field of otolaryngology. Research
efforts involve the ear, nose, head, neck and related
functions including hearing, balance, speech, taste and
smell among others. A wide range of scientific approaches
is represented including biochemical, physiological,
behavioral, developmental and evolutionary. Membership:
$120 (Regular); $50 (Associate).

Meetings/Conferences: Annual
Conference Chair: Lisa Astorga
2013 - Baltimore, MD (Baltimore Marriott Waterfront)/
    Feb. 16 - 20
2014 - San Diego, CA (Manchester Grand Hyatt San
    Diego)/Feb. 22 - 26
2015 - Baltimore, MD (Baltimore Marriott Waterfront)/
    Feb. 21 - 25
2016 - San Diego, CA (Manchester Grand Hyatt San
    Diego)/Feb. 20 - 24

Publications:
ARO News
Journal of the Association for Research in
    Otolaryngology
Membership Directory; on-line

Association for Research in Vision and Ophthalmology (1928)
1801 Rockville Pike
Suite 400
Rockville, MD 20852-5622
Tel: (240) 221-2900 Fax: (240) 221-0370
E-Mail: arvo@arvo.org
Website: arvo.org
Members: 12750 individuals
Staff: 44
Annual Budget: $5-10,000,000

Personnel:
Interim Executive Director: Iris M. Rush CAE
    E-Mail: irush@arvo.org
Director, Publishing: Karen Colson
    E-Mail: kcolson@arvo.org
Director, Meeting Logistics: Lancey Cowan
    E-Mail: cowan@arvo.org
Director, Membership Services: Francis George
    E-Mail: fgeorge@arvo.org
Director, Communications, Marketing and Sales: Joanne
Olson
    E-Mail: jolson@arvo.org
Director, Finance: Venkatachlam Veerappan
    E-Mail: vveerappan@arvo.org
Director, Information Technology and Web Services: Chi
Wei
    E-Mail: cwei@arvo.org

Historical Note:
Founded as the Association for Research in Ophthalmology
and incorporated in New York in 1936; assumed its
present name in 1970. ARVO seeks to encourage and
assist research, training, publication, and dissemination of
knowledge in vision and ophthalmology. Works to enhance
research opportunities in the vision sciences. Members
are both clinical and basic researchers, Ophthalmologists,
optometrists, osteopaths, and veterinarians. Membership:
$220 (Regular); $275 (Associate/Sustaining); $100
(Student/Resident); $4,400 (Life Member).

Continuing Education:
Enrollment: 500
Certification Designation/s: CME

Meetings/Conferences: Annual
Conference Chair: Lancey Cowan
2013 - Seatle, WA (Washington State Convention
    Center)/May 5 - 9/12000 attendees
2014 - Orlando, FL/May 4 - 8
2015 - Denver, CO/May 3 - 7
2016 - Seatle, WA/May 1 - 5
2017 - Baltimore, MD/May 7 - 11
2018 - Honolulu, HI/April 29 - May 2
2019 - Vancouver, BC/April 28 - May 2
2020 - Baltimore, MD/May 3 - 7
2021 - San Francisco, CA/May 2 - 6
Number of non-conference events/year: 3

Publications:
Drug Discovery and Development; monthly
ESCRS-Euro Times
Eye World
Investigative Ophthalmology & Visual Science (IOVS);
    on-line; adv.
Journal of Vision (JOV); on-line; adv.
Membership Directory; on-line
Ophthalmology Times; on-line
Optometric Physician; weekly

Membership List Available to Non-members

Association for Research on Nonprofit Organizations and Voluntary Action (1971)
550 W. North St.
Suite 301
Indianapolis, IN 46202
Tel: (317) 684-2120 Fax: (317) 684-2128
Website: arnova.org
Staff: 6
Annual Budget: $500-1,000,000

Personnel:
Executive Director: Thomas Jeavons
    E-Mail: tjeavons@arnova.org
Coordinator, Membership Services: Rosalind Conners
    E-Mail: rconners@arnova.org
Specialist, Communications: Melissa Gibson
    E-Mail: mgibson@arnova.org
Editor: Femida Handy
    E-Mail: nvsq@sp2.upenn.edu
Manager, Meetings: Mary Kate Myers
    E-Mail: mkmyers@arnova.org

Accountant: Sandra Ray

Historical Note:
Formerly Association of Voluntary Action Scholars (AVAS) assumed its current name Association for Research on Nonprofit Organizations and Voluntary Action (ARNOVA) in 1990. ARNOVA's mission is to foster through research and education, application and dissemination of knowledge on nonprofit organizations, philanthropy, civil society and voluntary action. Membership: $55-500/year.

Meetings/Conferences: Annual
Conference Chair: Mary Kate Myers

Publications:
ARNOVA News; quarterly; adv.
Membership Directory; on-line
Nonprofit and Voluntary Sector Quarterly; quarterly
Nonprofit Quarterly; quarterly

Association for Retail Environments *(1956)*
4651 Sheridan St.
Suite 470
Hollywood, FL 33021
Tel: (954) 893-7300 *Fax:* (954) 893-7500
E-Mail: are@retailenvironments.org
Website: retailenvironments.org
Members: 600 store fixture suppliers and retail design firms
Staff: 10
Annual Budget: $2-5,000,000

Personnel:
Executive Director: Klein S. Merriman
    E-Mail: kleinmerriman@retailenvironments.org
Editor: Tracy Dillon
    E-Mail: tracydillon@retailenvironments.org
Director, Programming and Events: Karen Doodeman
    E-Mail: karendoodeman@retailenvironments.org
Director, Communications: Katherine Josephs
    E-Mail: katherinejosephs@retailenvironments.org
Manager, Membership Services: Marcia King-Gamble PHR
    E-Mail: marciaking-gamble@retailenvironments.org
Director, Finance and Administration: Leslie Melvin CAE, CMP
    E-Mail: lesliemelvin@retailenvironments.org
Director, Membership Services and Sales: Karen Schaffner
    E-Mail: karenschaffner@retailenvironments.org
Coordinator, Membership Services and Sales: Yajayra Wojtas
    E-Mail: yajayrasaunders@retailenvironments.org

Historical Note:
Formerly (2007) National Association of Store Fixture Manufacturers (NASFM). ARE's mission is to advance the retail environments industry and the success of its member companies. Member companies offer a full range of products and services for retail environments, and include store fixture suppliers, retail design firms, suppliers of visual merchandising products, and suppliers of materials and equipment for the retail environments industry. Member capabilities extend beyond fixture manufacturing to include importing, exporting, consolidating, installing, project management, engineering, design, and more. Membership: $1,300-2,400 (Regular); $1,575 (Associate); $325-1,100 (Designer); $750 (Visual Merchandising).

Meetings/Conferences: Annual
Conference Chair: Karen Doodeman

Publications:
Buyers' Guide and Membership Directory; annually; adv.
Industry Performance Report; annually
Retail Environments Magazine; bi-monthly; adv.

Association for Retail Technology Standards *(1993)*
325 Seventh St. NW
Suite 1100
Washington, DC 20004
Tel: (202) 783-7971 *Fax:* (202) 737-2849
TollFree: (800) 673-4692
E-Mail: info@nrf.com
Website: nrf-arts.org
Members: 230 individuals
Staff: 3

Personnel:
Executive Director: Richard E. Mader
    E-Mail: maderr@nrf.com
Senior Director, Membership Services: Jannise Corry
    E-Mail: CorryJ@nrf.com
Director, Media Relations: Kathy Grannis
    E-Mail: grannisk@nrf.com

Historical Note:
An affiliate of National Retail Federation, ARTS promotes the adoption of standards for technology solutions in the retail sector. Members are retailers and vendors of retail and business systems and software. Membership: $250 (New); 1,500-3,000 (Retail); 2,500-5,000 (Vendor).

Continuing Education:
Certification Designation/s: SAPSC

Meetings/Conferences: Quarterly

Publications:
ARTS e-Newsletter; on-line
Membership Directory; on-line
Stores; monthly

The Association for Science Teacher Education *(1953)*
9324 27th Ave.
Eau Claire, WI 54703
Tel: (715) 838-0893 *Fax:* (715) 838-0893
Website: theaste.org
Members: 800 members
Staff: 3
Annual Budget: $100-250,000

Personnel:
Executive Director: Bob Hollon
    E-Mail: ExecutiveDirector@TheASTE.org

Historical Note:
Founded as the Association for the Education of Teachers of Science and affiliated with the National Science Teachers Association, assumed its current name in 2004. ASTE promotes excellence in science teacher education world-wide through scholarship and innovation. Has no paid officers or full-time staff. Membership: $95 (Full); $55 (Student).

Meetings/Conferences: Annual
Conference Chair: William Veal
2013 - Charleston, NC (Francis Marion Hotel)/Jan. 9 - 12
2014 - San Antonio, TX/Jan. 15 - 18

Publications:
ASTE Newsletter; quarterly
Contemporary Issues in Technology and Teacher Education; on-line
Elementary Science Education; bi-annually
Journal of Science Teacher Education

Association for Skilled and Technical Sciences *(2006)*
1931 Mortimer Ct.
Boise, ID 83712
Tel: (703) 777-1740
E-Mail: asts@mindspring.com
Website: astsonline.org
Members: 196 individuals
Staff: 2
Annual Budget: Under $10,000

Personnel:
Executive Director: Don Esheley

Historical Note:
Formerly known as National Association for Trade and Industrial Education. NASSTIE and NATIE merged to form Association for Skilled and Technical Sciences (ASTS). Mission is skilled and technical sciences education through a structured program of training, networking, conferences, political action and recognition activities. Membership: $25 (Member); $20 (Members of Skills USA/ACTE/State Associations).

Continuing Education:
Certification Designation/s: CCTE

Meetings/Conferences: Annual

Publications:
Partner Activity Newsletter

Association for Slavic, East European, and Eurasian Studies *(1938)*
C/O University of Pittsburgh
315 S. Bellefield Ave., 203C Bellefield Hall
Pittsburgh, PA 15260-6424
Tel: (412) 648-9911 *Fax:* (412) 648-9815
E-Mail: aseees@pitt.edu
Website: aseees.org
Members: 3500 individuals
Staff: 6
Annual Budget: $500-1,000,000

Personnel:
Executive Director: Lynda Park
    E-Mail: lypark@pitt.edu
Editor and Communications Coordinator: Mary Arnstein

E-Mail: newsnet@pitt.edu
Finance Coordinator: Maureen Ryczaj
    E-Mail: aseeesfn@pitt.edu
Editor: Mark D. Steinberg
    E-Mail: steinb@illinois.edu
Coordinator, Membership and Subscriptions: Jonathon Swiderski
    E-Mail: aseees@pitt.edu
Coordinator, Conventions: Wendy Walker
    E-Mail: wwalker@pitt.edu

Historical Note:
Formerly the American Association for the Advancement of Slavic Studies, ASEEES seeks to advance scholarly study, publication, and teaching relating to the former Soviet Union and Eastern Europe. Membership is open to anyone interested in furthering the scholarly objectives of the AAASS and institutions with programs or interests in Slavic, Eurasian, and East European studies. Membership: $70-200 (Individual); $35 (Student); $45 (Affiliate); 600 (Institutional); $400 (For-Profit Institutions and Foundations); $300 (Non-Profit Organizations/Institutions granting the PhD and/or MA); $200 (Institutions granting the BA); $150 (Non-Profit Institutions in the Former Soviet Union and Eastern Europe).

Meetings/Conferences: Annual
Conference Chair: Wendy Walker
2013 - Boston, MA (Boston Marriott Long Wharf)/Nov. 21 - 24
2014 - San Antonio, TX (San Antonio Marriott Rivercenter)/Nov. 20 - 23
2015 - Philadelphia, PA (Philadelphia Marriott Downtown)/Nov. 19 - 22

Publications:
Membership Directory; on-line
NewsNet: News of the Association for Slavic, East European, and Eurasian Studies
Slavic Review: Interdisciplinary Quarterly of Russian, Eurasian, and East European Studies; quarterly

The Association for Social Anthropology in Oceania *(1967)*
2115 N. Rolfe St.
Arlington, VA 22209-1029
E-Mail: mmccutch@gmu.edu
Website: asao.org
Members:
30 institutions
375 individuals
Staff: 4
Annual Budget: $10-25,000
Tax: 501(c)(3)

Personnel:
Treasurer: Mary McCutcheon
    E-Mail: mmccutch@gmu.edu

Historical Note:
Formerly the Association for Social Anthropology in Eastern Oceania, ASAO is an international organization dedicated to comparative studies of topics and cultural anthropology in Oceania. Membership: $35 (Individual); $20 (Student/retried/unemployment).

Meetings/Conferences: Annual
Conference Chair: Michael A. Rynkiewich
2013 - San Antonio, TX (St. Anthony RiverWalk Hotel)/Feb. 5 - 9

Publications:
ASAO Membership Database (Membership Directory); on-line
ASAO Newsletter

Association for Spanish and Portuese Studies *(1969)*
310 First St.
Westfield, NJ 07090
Tel: (707) 664-2489 *Fax:* (707) 664-3920
Website: asphs.net
Members: 500 individuals
Staff: 3
Annual Budget: $10-25,000

Personnel:
General Secretary: Dan Crews
Editor: Jesus Cruz
    E-Mail: jesus@udel.edu
Secretary, Membership Services and Treasurer: Prof. David Ortiz Jr.
    E-Mail: davido@u.arizona.edu

Historical Note:
Formerly Society for Spanish and Portuguese Historical Studies. ASPHS's purpose is to promote research in

all aspects and epochs of Iberian history and related disciplines. Membership: $21 (Regular); $7 (Student); $23 (Overseas); $25 (Institutions).

Meetings/Conferences: Annual

Publications:
ASPS Newsletter; on-line
Bulletin; on-line

Association for Specialists in Group Work (1973)
Texas A&M University-Commerce
Binnion Hall 212A
Commerce, TX 75429
E-Mail: info@asgw.org
Website: asgw.org
Members: 3980 individuals
Staff: 4
Annual Budget: $50-100,000

Personnel:
Executive Director: Janice DeLucia-Waack
    E-Mail: jdelucia@buffalo.edu
Webmaster: Penny Proctor
    E-Mail: webmaster@asgw.org
Treasurer: Carmen Salazar
    E-Mail: carmen_salazar@tamu-commerce.edu

Historical Note:
ASGW provides professional leadership in the field of group work; establishes standards for professional and ethical practice; and supports research and dissemination of knowledge. A division of the American Counseling Association which provides administrative support. Membership: $25 (Professional); $12.50 (Student/Retired).

Meetings/Conferences: Biennial
2014 - Orlando, FL/Feb. 6 - 9

Publications:
Journal for Specialists in Group Work; quarterly
The Group Worker

Association for Spiritual, Ethical and Religious Values in Counseling (1955)
5999 Stevenson Ave.
Alexandria, VA 22304
Tel: (703) 823-9800 Fax: (703) 461-9260
E-Mail: info@aservic.org
Website: aservic.org
Members: 5100 individuals
Staff: 4
Annual Budget: $10-25,000

Personnel:
President: Shannon Ray
    E-Mail: Shanray@nova.edu
Treasurer: Jennifer Curry
    E-Mail: jcurry@lsu.edu
Secretary: Aisha Lusk MA
    E-Mail: aishalusk@yahoo.com

Historical Note:
A division of the American Counseling Association, which provides administrative support. Formerly (1958) Catholic Counselors in APGA; (1960) National Conference of Diocesan Guidance Councils; (1962) National Conference of Catholic Guidance Councils; (1978) National Catholic Guidance Conference; and (1993) Association for Religious and Value Issues in Counseling. ASERVIC is devoted to advocate professionals who believe that spiritual, ethical, religious and other human values are essential to the full development of the person, and to the discipline of counseling. Membership: $203 (Regular/Professional); $113 (Student/New Professional/Retired).

Meetings/Conferences: Annual

Publications:
C & V Journal
Newsletters

Association for Supervision and Curriculum Development (ASCD) (1943)
1703 N. Beauregard St.
Alexandria, VA 22311-1714
Tel: (703) 578-9600 Fax: (703) 575-5400
TollFree: (800) 933-2723
E-Mail: member@ascd.org
Website: ascd.org
Members: 150000 individual
Staff: 200
Annual Budget: $50-100,000,000
Tax: 501(c)(3)

Personnel:
Executive Director and Chief Executive Officer: Dr. Gene R. Carter EdD

E-Mail: gcarter@ascd.org
Chief Officer, Program Development: Mary Catherine Desrosiers

Historical Note:
ASCD's mission is to develop quality in education for all students. Members are curriculum coordinators and consultants, superintendents, professors of education, educational administrators, school board members, principals, teachers, students and parents. Membership: $219 (Premium/ Premium Online); $49 (Basic Online); $25 (Student); $2,413 (ASCD Institutional); $3,452 (ASCD Institutional Plus).

Meetings/Conferences: Semi-Annual
2013 - Chicago, IL (McCormick Place)/March 16 - 18
2013 - Washington, DC (National Harbor Marina)/June 28 - 30

Publications:
ASCD Express; bi-weekly
ASCD SmartBrief; daily
Education Update; monthly
Educational Leadership
International Journal of Education Policy and Leadership; on-line
Policy Priorities; quarterly

Association for Surgical Education (1980)
SIU School of Medicine, Department of Surgery
P.O. Box 19655
Springfield, IL 62794-9655
Tel: (217) 545-3835 Fax: (217) 545-2431
E-Mail: admin@surgicaleducation.com
Website: surgicaleducation.com
Members: 850 individuals
Staff: 2
Annual Budget: $250-500,000

Personnel:
Executive Director: Susan Kepner MEd
    E-Mail: skepner@siumed.edu
Treasurer: Mary Klingensmith MD

Historical Note:
ASE's mission is to promote, recognize, and reward excellence, innovation and scholarship in surgical education. Membership: $250 (Individual); $15 (Residents/ Student); $150 (Clerkship).

Continuing Education:
Certification Designation/s: SERF

Meetings/Conferences: Annual
2013 - Orlando, FL (Gaylord Palms Resort and Convention Center-Orlando)/April 23 - 27/700 attendees
2014 - Chicago, IL (Fairmont Chicago Millenium Park)/ April 8 - 12
2015 - Seatle, WA (Westin Seattle)/April 14 - 18

Publications:
FOCUS; annually
The American Journal of Surgery

Association for Symbolic Logic (1936)
Vassar College, 124 Raymond Ave.
P.O. Box 742
Poughkeepsie, NY 12604
Tel: (845) 437-7080 Fax: (845) 437-7830
Website: aslonline.org
Members: 1450 individuals
Staff: 4
Annual Budget: $250-500,000

Personnel:
President: Alex J. Wilkie
    E-Mail: awilkie@maths.man.ac.uk
Contact, Publisher: Richard A. Shore
    E-Mail: aslpub@math.cornell.edu
Secretary and Treasurer: Charles I. Steinhorn
    E-Mail: steinhorn@vassar.edu
Administrator: Fran Whitney
    E-Mail: asl@vassar.edu

Historical Note:
Founded and incorporated in Rhode Island. Affiliated with the American Mathematical Society, the Conference Board of the Mathematical Sciences and the International Union for the History and Philosophy of Science. ASL strives to promote research and studies in mathematical logic and related fields and to present current research in logic to all logicians in such a way as to preserve the essential integrity of the entire subject. Membership: $18-180 (Individual Outreach); $625-1,075 (Institution); $1100 (Corporate Associate); $3000 (Corporate); $44 (Student/Unemployed/ Emeritus); $130 (Institutional Outreach); $88 (Individual).

Meetings/Conferences: Semi-Annual

2013 - San Diego, CA/Jan. 11 - 12
2013 - New Orleans, LA/Feb. 20 - 23
2013 - Waterloo, ON/May 8 - 11
Number of non-conference events/year: 4

Publications:
ASL Newsletter; quarterly
The Bulletin of Symbolic Logic
The Journal of Symbolic Logic; quarterly
The Review of Symbolic Logic

Membership List Available to Non-members

Association for Technology in Music Instruction (1975)
C/O University of Tennessee, School of Music
2431 Dunford
Knoxville, TN 37996-4040
Website: atmionline.org
Members: 200 individuals
Staff: 5
Annual Budget: Under $10,000

Personnel:
Editor: Barbara Murphy
    E-Mail: bmurphy@utk.edu

Historical Note:
Formerly (1986) known as the National Consortium for Computer-Based Music Instruction. ATMI's mission is to improve music teaching and learning through the integration of current and emerging technologies into the music learning environment. Members are music teachers and others interested in the application of computers in music instruction. Membership: $40 (Individual).

Meetings/Conferences: Annual
2013 - Cambridge, MA/Oct. 31 - Nov. 3
2014 - St. Louis, MO/Oct. 29 - Nov. 2

Publications:
ATMI Newsletter; quarterly

Membership List Available to Non-members

Association for Textual Scholarship in Art History (1991)
C/O Dr. Liana De Girolami Cheney
112 Charles St., Beacon Hill
Boston, MA 02114
Tel: (617) 367-1670 Fax: (627) 557-2962
Website: atsah.wordpress.com
Members: 65 individuals
Staff: 2
Annual Budget: Under $10,000

Personnel:
President and Treasurer: Liana de Girolami Cheney
    E-Mail: lianachaney@earthlink.net
Editor and Secretary: Maureen Pelta
    E-Mail: mpelta@moore.edu

Historical Note:
ATSAH's mission is to promote study and publication of art- historical primary sources, and to facilitate communication among scholars working with art literature. ATSAH members are academics and others with an interest in the study and publication of primary sources for art history. Membership: $20/year.

Publications:
ATSAH Newsletter; on-line

Association for the Accreditation of Human Research Protection Programs (2001)
2301 M St. NW
Suite 500
Washington, DC 20037
Tel: (202) 783-1112 Fax: (202) 783-1113
E-Mail: accredit@aahrpp.org
Website: aahrpp.org
Staff: 7
Annual Budget: $2-5,000,000
Tax: 501(c)(3)

Personnel:
President and Chief Executive Officer: Marjorie A. Speers PhD
    E-Mail: mspeers@aahrpp.org
Chief Accreditation Operations Officer: Suzanne Y. Bushfield
    E-Mail: sbushfield@aahrpp.org
Chief Financial Officer: Sandra Jackson MBA
    E-Mail: accounting@aahrpp.org
Director, Business Development, Communications, and Public Relations: Sarah H. Kiskaddon
    E-Mail: skiskaddon@aahrpp.org

Manager, Programs: Nancy Matthes CAE, MS
    E-Mail: nmatthes@aahrpp.org

Historical Note:
*AAHRPP accredits human research protection programs
in order to promote ethically sound research. Through
partnerships with research organizations, researchers,
sponsors, and the public, AAHRPP encourages effective,
efficient, and innovative systems of protection for human
research participants. Membership: $250-1,000 (Tax-
exempt professional societies/Tax-exempt academic
associations, foundations, patient groups and health-
based organizations, or trade associations); $500-1,500
(Businesses and Non tax-exempt organizations).*

Meetings/Conferences: Annual
Conference Chair: Nancy Matthes CAE, MS
2013 - Miami, FL (Hyatt Regency Miami)/April 3 - 5

Publications:
ADVANCE Newsletter; quarterly

Association for the Advancement of Automotive Medicine (1957)

P.O. Box 4176
Barrington, IL 60011-4176
Tel: (847) 844-3880 *Fax:* (847) 844-3884
E-Mail: info@aaam.org
Website: aaam.org
Members: 600 individuals
Staff: 2
Annual Budget: $500-1,000,000
Tax: 501(c)(3)

Personnel:
President: Brian N. Fildes PhD
Secretary: Mary Pat-McKay MD, MPH

Historical Note:
*Formerly (1988) the American Association for Automotive
Medicine. AAAM's purpose is to encourage and promote
the growth and dissemination of new knowledge in the field
of traffic and highway safety. Members are physicians,
researchers, educators, engineers, administrators, and other
highway and traffic medicine professionals. Membership:
$260-295 (Regular/Associate-Individual); $2,500
(Sustaining); $35 (Student).*

Continuing Education:
Certification Designation/s: CAISS

Meetings/Conferences: Annual
Number of non-conference events/year: 2

Publications:
Membership Directory; on-line

Membership List Available to Non-members

Association for the Advancement of Baltic Studies (1968)

P.O. Box 353420
Seattle, WA 98195-3420
Tel: (301) 977-8491 *Fax:* (301) 977-8492
E-Mail: aabs@washington.edu
Website: depts.washington.edu/aabs
Members: 700 individuals
Staff: 6
Annual Budget: $500-1,000,000
Tax: 501(c)(3)

Personnel:
Administrative Executive Director: Irena Blekys
Treasurer: Marc Hyman
Vice President, Professional Development: Andres
    Kasekamp
Vice President, Publications: Daiva Markelis
Webmaster: Amanda Swain
    E-Mail: ajswain@u.washington.edu
Vice President, Conferences: Brad Woodworth

Historical Note:
*AABS formed to promote research and education in Baltic
studies (history, literature, linguistics, social sciences). Since
1991, it has been a constituent member of the American
Council of Learned Societies. Membership is open to anyone
wishing to support AABS endeavors. The association
works towards its goal by sponsoring meetings and
conferences, supporting publications, sustaining a program
of scholarships, grants, and prizes, and disseminating news
of current interest in Baltic Studies. Membership: $25-500/
year; $2,000 (Life Member).*

Meetings/Conferences: Annual
Conference Chair: Brad Woodworth
2014 - New Haven, CT (Yale University)/March 13 - 15
Number of non-conference events/year: 1

Publications:
Baltic Studies Newsletter; annually
Journal of Baltic Studies; quarterly; adv.

Membership Directory; on-line

Membership List Available to Non-members

Association for the Advancement of Computing in Education (1981)

P.O. Box 1545
Chesapeake, VA 23327-1545
Tel: (757) 366-5606 *Fax:* (703) 997-8760
E-Mail: info@aace.org
Website: aace.org
Staff: 17
Annual Budget: $2-5,000,000

Personnel:
Executive Director: Gary H. Marks

Historical Note:
*AACE is an international, educational and professional
organization dedicated to the advancement of the
knowledge, theory and quality of learning and teaching
at all levels with information technology. Members are
educators and academics interested in the application
of information technology. Membership: $115-175
(Professional); $45 (Student).*

Meetings/Conferences: Annual
2013 - Victoria, BC/June 24 - 28
2013 - Las Vegas, NV/Oct. 21 - 25
Number of non-conference events/year: 3

Publications:
AACE Journal; quarterly

Association for the Advancement of International Education (1966)

Nova Southeastern University
11501 N. Military Trail
Palm Beach Gardens, FL 33418
Tel: (561) 805-2193 *Fax:* (561) 805-2187
E-Mail: g.aaie@nova.edu
Website: aaie.org
Members:
400 schools & companies
550 individuals
Staff: 2
Annual Budget: $250-500,000
Tax: 501(c)(3)

Personnel:
Executive Director: Elsa Lamb
    E-Mail: g.elamb@nova.edu
Administrative Assistant: Elleana Austin

Historical Note:
*AAIE's mission is to provide a forum for the exchange
of ideas and research concerning development in the
field of international education, school leadership and to
advance international education through participation
with educational institutions and associations worldwide.
Members include head administrators, superintendents and
college/university deans, presidents and others who have
an interest in American international schools. Membership:
$390 (Institutional/Organizational); $115 (individual).*

Meetings/Conferences: Annual
Conference Chair: Elsa Lamb
2013 - San Francisco, CA (Hyatt Regency)/Feb. 14 - 17
Number of non-conference events/year: 2

Publications:
InterEd; bi-annually
Member Directory; on-line

Membership List Available to Non-members

Association for the Advancement of Medical Instrumentation (1967)

4301 N. Fairfax Dr.
Suite 301
Arlington, VA 22203-1633
Tel: (703) 525-4890 *Fax:* (703) 276-0793
Website: aami.org
Members: 7000 individuals
Staff: 43
Annual Budget: $10-25,000,000

Personnel:
President: Mary K. Logan
    E-Mail: mlogan@aami.org
*Senior Vice President, Communications, Marketing and
    Healthcare Technology Management:* Steve Campbell
    E-Mail: scampbell@aami.org
*Vice President, Information Technology and Membership
    Services:* Susan DeCourcey
    E-Mail: sdecourcey@aami.org
Vice President, Education: Chris Dinegar
    E-Mail: cdinegar@aami.org

Director, Meetings and Exhibits: Ed Leonardo
    E-Mail: eleonardo@aami.org
*Executive Vice President, Education and Membership
    Services:* Leah Lough
    E-Mail: customerservice@aami.org
Director, Publications: Sean Loughlin
    E-Mail: sloughlin@aami.org

Historical Note:
*Founded and incorporated in Massachusetts in 1967.
AAMI's mission is to provide multidisciplinary leadership
and programs that enhance the ability of the professions,
healthcare institutions and industry to understand, develop,
manage and use medical instrumentation and related
technologies safely and effectively. Membership: $220
(Individual); $280 (Individual out side US); $60 (New
Professional); $30 (Student); $500-1,000 (Corporate);
$620-1,600 (Institutional).*

Continuing Education:
Certification Designation/s: CLES, CRES, CBET

Meetings/Conferences: Annual
Conference Chair: Ed Leonardo
2013 - Long Beach, CA/June 1 - 3
2014 - Philadelphia, PA/May 31 - June 2

Publications:
AAMI News; monthly
AAMI News Weekly!; weekly
AAMI's Resource Catalog; annually
AAMI's Wall Calendar; annually
Biomedical Instrumentation & Technology; bi-monthly
Horizons; semi-annually
Standards Monitor Online

Association for the Advancement of Psychology (1974)

P.O. Box 38129
Colorado Springs, CO 80937-8129
Tel: (719) 520-0688 *Fax:* (719) 520-0375
TollFree: (800) 869-6595
Website: aapnet.org
Members: 6000 individuals
Staff: 3
Annual Budget: $100-250,000
Tax: 501(c)(6)

Personnel:
Executive Director: Stephen M. Pfeiffer PhD
    E-Mail: smpfeiffer@aapnet.org
Editor: Nanci Klein PhD
    E-Mail: nklein@sisna.com
Administrative Director: Karen Rivard
    E-Mail: krivard@aapnet.org

Historical Note:
*Merged with the Council for the Advancement of the
Psychological Professions and Sciences, AAP's mission
is to promote human welfare through the advancement
of the profession and science of psychology. Represents
psychologists before public and governmental bodies,
cooperates with other organizations and agencies in
furtherance of the profession, the science of psychology,
and the education and training of psychologists. Members
are psychologists and educators. Membership: $75
(Introductory/New Member); $180 (Sponsoring
Organization); $25 (Student); $124 (Individual).*

Publications:
AAP Advance; quarterly

Association for the Advancement of Psychotherapy (1939)

Belfer Educational Center
1300 Morris Park Ave., Room 405
Bronx, NY 10461
Tel: (718) 430-3503 *Fax:* (718) 430-8907
E-Mail: info@ajp.org
Website: ajp.org
Members: 350 individuals
Staff: 2
Annual Budget: $250-500,000
Tax: 501(c)(3)

Personnel:
President and Editor-in-Chief: T. Byram Karasu MD

Historical Note:
*AAP serves as a forum for clinical and theoretical findings
in the field of psychotherapy. Membership: $84 (Individual);
$119 (Organization).*

Publications:
American Journal of Psychotherapy; quarterly

Association for the Advancement of Wound Care (1995)

83 General Warren Blvd.
Suite 100
Malvern, PA 19355
Tel: (800) 237-7285 *Fax:* (610) 560-0502
E-Mail: info@aawconline.org
Website: aawconline.org
Members: 1800 individuals
Staff: 2
Annual Budget: $250-500,000
Tax: 501(c)(3)

Personnel:
Executive Director: Tina Thomas
    E-Mail: tthomas@aawconline.org
Contact, Membership Services: Sheila Donato
    E-Mail: sdonato@aawconline.org

Historical Note:
*AAWC's mission is to build a collaborative community to
facilitate optimal care for those who suffer with wounds.
Membership: $145 (Clinician/Individual); $60 (Student
Clinician/Retired Clinician); $360 (Clinic/Healthcare
Facility /Corporations/Manufacturers).*

Meetings/Conferences: Annual

Publications:
AAWC Membership Directory
Newsletter; quarterly
Ostomy Wound Management; adv.
WOUNDS: A Compendium of Clinical Research and
    Practice.; adv.

Association for the Behavioral Sciences and Medical Education *(1970)*
1460 N. Center Rd.
Burton, MI 48509
Tel: (810) 715-4365 *Fax:* (810) 715-4371
E-Mail: admin@absame.org
Website: absame.org
Members: 140 individuals
Staff: 3
Annual Budget: $25-50,000

Personnel:
Executive Director and Editor: Mark Vogel ABPP, PhD
    E-Mail: vogel@absame.org
Treasurer: Patrick C. Hardigan PhD
Contact, Membership Services: Barbara E. Moquin PhD

Historical Note:
*ABSAME's purpose is to improve the effectiveness,
efficiency, and quality of health care through the application
of social and behavioral science knowledge, skills and
perspectives. Membership: $125 (Regular); $50 (Student);
$550 (Institutional).*

Meetings/Conferences: Annual

Publications:
ABSAME Newsletter; bi-annually; adv.
Annals of Behavioral Science and Medical Education;
    bi-annually; adv.
Membership directory; annually

Association for the Bibliography of History *(1978)*
Lockwood Library, Room 321
SUNY at Buffalo
Buffalo, NY 14260
Tel: (716) 645-2817 *Fax:* (716) 645-3859
Website: h-net.org
Members: 400 individuals
Staff: 2
Annual Budget: Under $10,000
Tax: 501(c)(3)

Personnel:
Secretary, Treasurer: Charles A. D'Aniello
    E-Mail: lclcharl@acsu.buffalo.edu
President: Richard Ring
    E-Mail: richring@ukans.edu

Historical Note:
*Established in San Francisco at the 1978 annual meeting
of the American Historical Association. Members are
historians and librarians interested in developing better
bibliographic tools and skills for historical research. Its
purpose is to promote and facilitate the bibliography of
history and to provide a forum for collaboration at the
intersection of history, bibliography, and library and
information science. It is an affiliate of American Historical
Association.*

Association for the Calligraphic Arts *(1997)*
26 Main St.
E. Greenwich, RI 02818

Tel: (401) 884-4150
E-Mail: aca@calligraphicarts.org
Website: calligraphicarts.org
Members: 800 individuals
Staff: 2
Annual Budget: $25-50,000

Personnel:
Executive Administrator: Jane Parillo
    E-Mail: jane@janeparilloscribe.com
President: Deb Warnat

Historical Note:
*ACA's mission is to strengthen, support and unify the
calligraphic community worldwide through information,
inspiration, resources for education and opportunities
for development. Members are new learners, experienced
calligraphers and professional lettering artists from several
countries. Membership: $35-45 (Individual); $60 (Guild).*

Publications:
ACA Newsletter; quarterly

Association for the Sociology of Religion *(1938)*
618 SW Second Ave.
Galva, IL 61434-1912
Tel: (309) 932-2727 *Fax:* (309) 932-2282
Website: sociologyofreligion.com
Members: 800 individuals
Staff: 2
Annual Budget: $100-250,000

Personnel:
Executive Officer: William H. Swatos Jr., PhD
    E-Mail: bill4329@hotmail.com
Editor: Scott Schiemann

Historical Note:
*Formerly (1971) American Catholic Sociological Society.
ASR is an international scholarly association that seeks to
advance theory and research in the sociology of religion.
Membership: $30 (Individual); $85 (Institutional); $15
(Student); $35 (Constituent).*

Meetings/Conferences: Annual

Publications:
Membership Directory; on-line
Sociology of Religion; quarterly; adv.

Membership List Available to Non-members

Association for the Study of African American Life and History *(1915)*
2225 Georgia Ave. NW
Suite 331
Washington, DC 20059
Tel: (202) 238-5910 *Fax:* (202) 986-1506
E-Mail: info@asalh.net
Website: asalh.org
Members: 3300 individuals
Staff: 17
Annual Budget: $500-1,000,000
Tax: 501(c)(3)

Personnel:
Executive Director: Sylvia Y. Cyrus
    E-Mail: bydunn@asalh.net
Vice President, Programs and Publications: Dr. Daryl
    Michael Scott
Vice President, Membership Services: Dr. Janet Sims-
    Wood

Historical Note:
*Organized by Dr. Carter G. Woodson as the Association
for the Study of Negro Life and History. Assumed its
present name in 1973. ASALH strives to promote, research,
preserve, interpret and disseminate information about
Black life, history and culture to the global community.
Membership: $35-1500/year.*

Meetings/Conferences: Annual
2013 - Jacksonville, FL (Hyatt)/Oct. 2 - 6
2015 - Atlanta, GA (Sheraton Atlanta Hotel)/Sept. 21 -
    27
2016 - Richmond, VA (Marriott)/Oct. 4 - 9

Publications:
Black History Bulletin; semi-annually; adv.
Black History products; annually; adv.
Journal of African American History; quarterly; adv.
The Woodson Review: ASALH's Annual Theme
    Magazine; annually

Association for the Study of Classical African Civilizations *(1984)*
2274 W. 20th St.
Los Angeles, CA 90018
Tel: (718) 209-1036

Website: africa.upenn.edu/Org_Institutes/
    ASCAC.h
Members: 1000 individuals
Staff: 2
Annual Budget: $25-50,000

Personnel:
International President: Nzinga Ratibisha Heru
    E-Mail: queen@ascac.org

Historical Note:
*ASCAC's purpose is to promote the study of African
civilizations for the development of an African world view.
Membership: $50 (Individual); $25 (Student/Elders).*

Association for the Study of Food and Society *(1985)*
New York University. Dept. of Nutrition and Food
Studies
35 W. Fourth St., Tenth Floor
New York, NY 10012-1172
Tel: (212) 998-5580 *Fax:* (212) 995-4194
Website: food-culture.org
Members: 200 individuals
Staff: 3
Annual Budget: $10-25,000

Personnel:
Executive Director: Warren Belasco
President: Annie Hauck-Lawson
Treasurer and Membership Chair: Jennifer Berg

Historical Note:
*ASFS is an interdisciplinary international organization
dedicated to the complex relationship between food and
society. ASFS members are sociologists, anthropologists,
nutritionists, dieticians and others with an interest in
sociological aspects of food. Has no paid officers or full-
time staff. Membership: $55/year; $30/year (Student).*

Meetings/Conferences: Annual

Publications:
Food, Culture & Society; quarterly
Member Directory; on-line

Association for the Study of Higher Education *(1976)*
University of Nevada Las Vegas, 4505 S.
Maryland Pkwy.
P.O. Box 453068
Las Vegas, NV 89154-3068
Tel: (702) 895-2737 *Fax:* (702) 895-4269
E-Mail: ashe@unlv.edu
Website: ashe.ws
Members: 1800 individuals
Staff: 4
Annual Budget: $250-500,000
Tax: 501(c)(3)

Personnel:
Executive Director: Kim Nehls PhD
    E-Mail: kim.nehls@unlv.edu
Legal Counsel: Karen Miksch
    E-Mail: miksch001@umn.edu
Graduate Assistant: Holly Schneider
    E-Mail: holly.schneider@unlv.edu
Director, Finance and Administration: Brandy Smith
    E-Mail: brandy.smith@unlv.edu

Historical Note:
*ASHE's mission is to promote collaboration among its
members and others engaged in the study of higher
education through research, conferences, and publications.
Membership: $130 (Faculty/Administrator); $75 (Student/
Emeritus/Retired).*

Meetings/Conferences: Annual
2013 - St. Louis, MO (Hyatt at the Arch)/Nov. 13 - 16
2014 - Washington, DC (Washington Hilton)/Nov. 19
    - 22

Publications:
ASHE Listserv; weekly
ASHE Newsletter; irregular
The Review of Higher Education; quarterly

Membership List Available to Non-members

Association for the Study of Nationalities *(1971)*
Harriman Institute, Columbia University
420 W. 118th St., 12th Floor
New York, NY 10027
Tel: (212) 854-8487 *Fax:* (212) 666-3481
E-Mail: gnb12@columbia.edu
Website: nationalities.org
Members: 825 individuals

Staff: 5
Annual Budget: $250-500,000

Personnel:
President: Dominique Arel
  E-Mail: darel@uottawa.ca
Executive Director and Treasurer: Gordon N. Bardos
  E-Mail: gnbardos@gmail.com
Contact, Communications: Lydia Hamilton
  E-Mail: lch2111@columbia.edu
Secretary: Lisa Koriouchkina
  E-Mail: lisa_kor@brown.edu
Editor: Steve Sabol
  E-Mail: sosabol@uncc.edu

Historical Note:
ASN is the scholarly association for the study of ethnicity and nationalism from Europe to Eurasia. Members are academics and others with an interest in the study of nationalities issues and ethnic problems in eastern Europe and the former USSR. Membership: $70 (Individual); $40 (Student).

Meetings/Conferences: Annual

Publications:
ASNews; annually
Ethnopolitics; quarterly
Membership Directory; on-line
Nationalities Papers; bi-monthly

The Association for the Study of Play *(1973)*
Strong National Museum of Play
One Manhattan Sq.
Rochester, NY 14607
Tel: (585) 263-2700
E-Mail: taspmembership@museumofplay.org.
Website: tasplay.org
Members: 200 individuals and organizations
Staff: 4
Annual Budget: Under $10,000

Personnel:
Treasurer: Dorothy Sluss
  E-Mail: slussdj@jmu.edu
Contact, Membership Services and Senior Director, Public Relations and Advertising: Susan Trien

Historical Note:
Formerly (1987) Association for the Anthropological Study of Play, TASP's mission is to dedicate itself into interdisciplinary research and theory construction concerning play throughout the world. It has no paid officers or full-time staff. Membership: $75 (Professional, USA only); $80 (Professional, outside USA); $65 (Student/ Retiree, with TASP Annual); $85 (Institution, with TASP Annual); $25 (Student/Retiree/Institution without TASP Annual).

Meetings/Conferences: Annual
2013 - Newark, DE (University of Delaware & The Embassy Suite)/March 6 - 9

Publications:
Membership Directory; on-line
Play and Culture Studies; annually
TASP Newsletter; quarterly

Association for the Treatment of Sexual Abusers *(1984)*
4900 SW Griffith Dr.
Suite 274
Beaverton, OR 97005
Tel: (503) 643-1023 *Fax:* (503) 643-5084
E-Mail: atsa@atsa.com
Website: atsa.com
Members: 2700 individuals
Staff: 4
Annual Budget: $1-2,000,000

Personnel:
Executive Director: Maia Christopher
  E-Mail: maia@atsa.com
Consultant, Public Policy: Alisa Klein
  E-Mail: aklein@atsa.com
Administrator: Kelly McGrath
  E-Mail: kelly@atsa.com

Historical Note:
ATSA's purpose is to foster research, facilitate information exchange, further professional education and provide for the advancement of professional standards and practices in the field of sex offender evaluation and treatment. Members are professionals treating sexual offenders and/or their victims. Affiliations are found for this organization. Membership: $180 (Clinical/Research/Clinical Associate/Research Associate/Professional); $35 (Student/Affiliate).

Meetings/Conferences: Annual

2013 - Chicago, IL (Sheraton Chicago Hotel and Towers)/Oct. 30 - Nov. 2
2014 - San Diego, CA (Manchester Grand)/Oct. 28 - Nov. 1
2015 - Montreal, QC (Le Centre Sheraton Montreal Hotel)/Oct. 13 - 17

Publications:
Sexual Abuse: A Journal of Research and Treatment
The Forum- Newsletter

Association for Theatre in Higher Education *(1986)*
P.O. Box 1290
Boulder, CO 80306-1290
Tel: (303) 530-2167 *Fax:* (303) 530-2168
TollFree: (888) 284-3737
E-Mail: info@athe.org
Website: athe.org
Members: 1800 individuals
Staff: 6
Annual Budget: $500-1,000,000
Tax: 501(c)(3)

Personnel:
Executive Director: Nancy Erickson
  E-Mail: executivedirector@athe.org
Vice President, Conferences: Chase Bringardner
  E-Mail: conf2013@athe.org
Vice President, Professional Development: Kelly Carolyn Gordon
  E-Mail: profdev@athe.org
Vice President, Membership and Marketing: David Kaye
  E-Mail: mm@athe.org
Vice President, Research and Publications: Robert "Bob" Schanke
  E-Mail: rp@athe.org
Vice President, Advocacy: Gale Sheaffer
  E-Mail: advocacy@athe.org

Historical Note:
ATHE's mission is to support and advance the study and practice of theatre and performance in higher education. Members include college and university theatre departments and administrators, educators, graduate students, and theatre practitioners. Membership: $60-265/year.

Meetings/Conferences: Annual
Conference Chair: Chase Bringardner
2013 - Orlando, FL (Hyatt Regency Grand Cypress)/ Aug. 1 - 3/800 attendees/11-25 exhibitors

Publications:
ATHENEWS; on-line
Membership Directory; on-line; adv.
Theatre Journal; quarterly; adv.
Theatre Topics; semi-annually

Membership List Available to Non-members

Association for Transpersonal Psychology *(1971)*
P.O. Box 50187
Palo Alto, CA 94303
Tel: (650) 424-8764 *Fax:* (650) 618-1851
E-Mail: info@atpweb.org
Website: atpweb.org
Members: 1200 individuals
Staff: 4
Annual Budget: $100-250,000
Tax: 501(c)(3)

Personnel:
Executive Director: Daniel Gaylinn
  E-Mail: dan@atpweb.org
Co-President: David Lukoff
Editor: Marcie Boucouvalas
Treasurer: Haru Murakawa

Historical Note:
ATP members are professionals and others with an interest in transpersonal psychology. ATP's mission is to advocate eco-spiritual transformation through transpersonal inquiry and action. Membership: $55 (Student/Senior); $50 (International); $75 (General); $95 (Professional); $150 (Organizational); $175 (Supporting); $60 (Recent Graduate/Alumni); $500 (Library); $999 (Lifetime); $120 (International Professional Plus); $105 (International Professional); $35 (International Student Plus); $25 (International Student).

Continuing Education:
Certification Designation/s: CE

Meetings/Conferences: Annual
Number of non-conference events/year: 1

Publications:
Journal of Transpersonal Psychology; bi-annually; adv.

Reflections e-newsletter; on-line

Association for Tropical Biology and Conservation *(1963)*
National Museum of Natural History, Department of Botany, MRC-166
P.O. Box 37012
Washington, DC 20013-7012
Tel: (202) 633-0920 *Fax:* (202) 786-2563
Website: tropicalbio.org
Members: 1900 individuals and libraries
Staff: 3
Annual Budget: $50-100,000
Tax: 501(c)(3)

Personnel:
Executive Director: John W. Kress
  E-Mail: kressj@si.edu
Editor: Jennifer Lynch CAE
  E-Mail: cs-journals@wiley.com

Historical Note:
ATBC's mission is to promote research, education, conservation, communication and foster the exchange of ideas among biologists working in tropical environments. Membership: $65 (Individual); $120 (Institution); $50 (Student).

Meetings/Conferences: Annual
2013 - San Jose, Costa Rica (Ramada Plaza Herradura Hotel)/June 23 - 27

Publications:
Biotropica
Membership Directory; on-line

Membership List Available to Non-members

Association for University and College Counseling Center Directors *(1951)*
University Counseling Center, Colorado State University
4112 Attleboro Ct.
Ft. Collins, CO 80525
Tel: (970) 980-8779
Website: aucccd.org
Members: 600 individuals
Staff: 3
Annual Budget: $25-50,000

Personnel:
Treasurer: Charles Davidshofer PhD
  E-Mail: Charles.Davidshofer@colostate.edu

Historical Note:
AUCCCD's mission is to promote awareness of college student mental health through research, education, and training provided to members, professional organizations, and the public with special attention to issues of diversity and multiculturalism. Members are directors of counseling centers on college and university campuses. Membership: $130-260/year.

Meetings/Conferences: Annual
Conference Chair: Casey Earle

Publications:
AUCCCD Newsletter

Association for University Business and Economic Research *(1947)*
P.O. Box 3446
Missoula, MT 59806
Tel: (406) 243-2714
Website: auber.org
Members: 130 individuals
Staff: 3
Annual Budget: $50-100,000

Personnel:
President: Janet Harrah
  E-Mail: harrahj1@nku.edu
Secretary and Treasurer: Pat Barkey
  E-Mail: patrick.barkey@umontana.edu
Contact, Business Office and Webmaster: Debora Simmons
  E-Mail: debora.simmons@business.umt.edu

Historical Note:
AUBER is the professional association of business and economic research organizations in public and private universities. Membership: $225/year (Group).

Meetings/Conferences: Annual

Publications:
AUBER newletter; quarterly

Association for Unmanned Vehicle Systems International *(1972)*

2700 S. Quincy St.
Suite 400
Arlington, VA 22206
Tel: (703) 845-9671 *Fax:* (703) 845-9679
E-Mail: info@auvsi.org
Website: auvsi.org
Members: 7000 individuals and 2200 companies
Staff: 29
Annual Budget: $5-10,000,000
Tax: 501(c)(3)

Personnel:
President and Chief Executive Officer: Michael Toscano
     E-Mail: toscano@auvsi.org
Manager, Information Technology: Karen Blonder
Vice President, Conferences and Exposition Services: Staci
     Butler
     E-Mail: butler@auvsi.org
Vice President, Membership Services: Amy Crolius
     E-Mail: crolius@auvsi.org
Vice President, Communications and Publications: Brett
     Davis
Senior Manger, Advertising and Marketing: Lisa Fick
     E-Mail: fick@auvsi.org
Manager, Finance and Accounting: Belinda Miller
     E-Mail: bmiller@auvsi.org
Senior Research Analyst: Bill Rauch
     E-Mail: rauch@auvsi.org
Executive Vice President: Gretchen West
     E-Mail: west@auvsi.org

Historical Note:
Established in Dayton, Ohio as the National Association for Remotely Piloted Vehicles, assumed its present name in 1977. AUVSI's mission is to promote and support the unmanned systems community through communication, education and leadership. Membership: $85 (Individual); $30 (Senior); $15 (Student); $50 (Active/Retired Military or Government Employee); $250-10,000 (Corporate).

Meetings/Conferences: Annual
Conference Chair: Staci Butler
2013 - Washington, DC (Walter E. Washington
     Convention Center)/Aug. 13 - 16/8000 attendees/
     over 100 exhibitors
2014 - Orlando, FL (Orange County Convention
     Center)/May 13 - 16/8000 attendees/over 100
     exhibitors
2015 - Atlanta, GA (Georgia World Congress Center)/
     May 5 - 8/8000 attendees/over 100 exhibitors
2016 - New Orleans, LA (New Orleans Convention
     Center)/May 3 - 6/8000 attendees/over 100
     exhibitors

Publications:
Flight Unmanned Daily News; bi-weekly; adv.
Membership Directory; on-line
Mission Critical; quarterly; adv.
Unmanned Science newsletter; bi-weekly
Unmanned Systems; monthly; adv.
Unmanned Systems e Brief; weekly
Unmanned Systems Program Review; on-line; adv.

Association for Vascular Access *(1985)*

5526 W. 13400 South
Suite 229
Herriman, UT 84096
Tel: (801) 792-9079 *Fax:* (801) 601-8012
TollFree: (877) 924-2821
E-Mail: info@avainfo.org
Website: avainfo.org
Staff: 7
Annual Budget: $1-2,000,000
Tax: 501(c)(6)

Personnel:
Chief Executive Officer: Pamela J. Haylock Ph.D. R.N.
     E-Mail: pjhaylock@indian-creek.net
Director, Professional Development: Lois Davis MSN, RN
     E-Mail: ldavis@avainfo.org
Network Coordinator and Administrative Assistant: Cindy
     Egbert
     E-Mail: cegbert@avainfo.org
Manager, Exhibits and Sponsorship: Jennifer Kerhin
     E-Mail: jkerhin@conferencemanagers.com
Director, Marketing, Outreach and Membership Services:
     Jan Kinzler
     E-Mail: jkinzler@avainfo.org
Director, Operations: Tonya Miller
     E-Mail: tmiller@avainfo.org

Director, Finance: Lory Schantz
     E-Mail: lschantz@avainfo.org

Historical Note:
AVA is an association of healthcare professionals founded to promote the emerging vascular access specialty. Membership: $115 (Individual); $2,500-15,000 (Corporate).

Continuing Education:
Certification Designation/s: VACC

Meetings/Conferences: Annual
Conference Chair: Jennifer Kerhin
2013 - Nashville, TN (Gaylord OprylandResort and
     Convention Center)/Sept. 20
2014 - Washington, DC (Gaylord National-
     Washington)/Sept. 7 - 10
2015 - Dallas, TX (Gaylord Texan Hotel and
     Convention Center-Dallas)/Sept. 26 - 29

Publications:
E-VAN; bi-monthly; adv.
Journal of the Association for Vascular Access (JAVA);
     quarterly; adv.

Association for Wedding Professionals International *(1995)*

6700 Freeport Blvd.
Suite 202
Sacramento, CA 95822
Tel: (916) 392-5000 *Fax:* (916) 392-5222
TollFree: (800) 242-4461
Website: afwpi.com
Members:
1460 individuals
742 companies
Staff: 4
Annual Budget: $250-500,000

Personnel:
Association Director, Media Relations and Member Benefits:
     Richard Markel
     E-Mail: richard@afwpi.com
Vice President, Chief Financial Officer and Administrator:
     Julia Markel
     E-Mail: julia@afwpi.com

Historical Note:
AFWPI is dedicated to provide quality service and a central source of information and referrals for those planning weddings and those who service weddings. Provides referral and other promotional and professional services to wedding professionals. Membership: $240 (Regular); $360 (Associate); $65 (Student).

Meetings/Conferences: Annual

Publications:
AFWPI e-Newsletter; on-line
Membership Directory; on-line
Wedding Professionals Newsletter; on-line

Association for Women Geoscientists *(1977)*

12000 N. Washington St.
Suite 285
Thornton, CO 80741
Tel: (303) 412-6219 *Fax:* (303) 253-9220
E-Mail: office@awg.org
Website: awg.org
Members: 1200 individuals
Staff: 5
Annual Budget: $50-100,000
Tax: 501(c)(6)

Personnel:
Acting Webmaster: Laurie Scheuing
Coordinator, Advertisements: Cristie Valero

Historical Note:
Established as the Association of Women Geoscientists, assumed its present name in 1982 and was incorporated in California in 1983. AWG's mission is to promote the professional development of its members, and encourages women to become geoscientists. Membership includes men and women from petroleum and mineral industries, geotechnical and hydrogeologic consulting, academic faculty, regulatory agencies and research institutions. Membership: $20-200/year; $1,600 (Lifetime).

Meetings/Conferences: Annual
Number of non-conference events/year: 1

Publications:
AWG E-Mail News; bi-weekly; adv.
Gaea Newsletter; bi-monthly; adv.
Membership Directory; on-line

Association for Women in Communications *(1909)*

3337 Duke St.
Alexandria, VA 22314
Tel: (703) 370-7436 *Fax:* (703) 342-4311
E-Mail: info@womcom.org
Website: womcom.org
Members: 2500 Individuals
Staff: 3
Annual Budget: $250-500,000
Tax: 501(c)(6)

Personnel:
Executive Director: Pamela Valenzuela CAE
Membership Coordinator: Liz Booth
     E-Mail: members@womcom.org
Manager, Communications and Programs: Beth Veney

Historical Note:
Founded as Theta Sigma Phi; absorbed Women in Communications, Inc., and assumed its current name in 1996. AWC's mission is to serve for the advancement of women across all communications disciplines by recognizing excellence and promoting leadership and positioning its members at the forefront of the evolving communications era. Membership:$0-1895/year.

Meetings/Conferences:
Conference Chair: Beth Veney

Publications:
AWC Membership Directory; on-line
Communique; bi-monthly; adv.

Association for Women in Computing *(1978)*

P.O. Box 2768
Oakland, CA 94602
E-Mail: info@awc-hq.org
Website: awc-hq.org
Members:
14 chapters
800 individuals
Staff: 4
Annual Budget: $10-25,000

Personnel:
President: Jill Sweeney
Secretary: Crista Deniz
Vice President, Web Communications: Gabriela Levit
Treasurer: Bonnie Sherwood

Historical Note:
AWC is dedicated to the advancement of women in technological fields. Membership: $25 (Independent/Non-Chapter); $35-100 (Chapter).

Publications:
Membership Directories

Association for Women in Mathematics *(1971)*

11240 Waples Mill Rd.
Suite 200
Fairfax, VA 22030
Tel: (703) 934-0163 *Fax:* (703) 359-7562
E-Mail: awm@awm-math.org
Website: awm-math.org
Members: 3000 Members
Staff: 5
Annual Budget: $250-500,000
Tax: 501(c)(3)

Personnel:
Executive Director: Magnhild Lien
     E-Mail: mlien@awm-math.org
Coordinator, Meetings: Bettye Anne Case
     E-Mail: case@math.fsu.edu
Coordinator, Membership Services: Matthew Hundley
     E-Mail: matthew@awm-math.org
Treasurer: Ellen Kirkman
     E-Mail: kirkman@wfu.edu
Editor: Anne Leggett
     E-Mail: leggett@member.ams.org

Historical Note:
Formerly (1973) Association of Women Mathematicians. AWM's purpose is to encourage women and girls to study and to have active careers in the mathematical sciences, and to promote equal opportunity and the equal treatment of women and girls in the mathematical sciences. Membership: $65 (Individual); $30 (Retired/Part-time employed); $20 (Student/Unemployed) $175-325 (Organization).

Meetings/Conferences: Annual
Conference Chair: Bettye Anne Case
2013 - Santa Clara, CA (Santa Clara University)/March
     16 - 17

Association for Women in Psychology

Publications:
AWM Newsletter; adv.

Association for Women in Psychology (1969)

University of Delaware
209 Laurel Hall
Newark, DE 19716
Tel: (302) 832-8992
Website: awpsych.org
Members: 2000 individuals
Staff: 3
Annual Budget: $25-50,000

Personnel:
Coordinator, Membership Services: Dr. Nicole Boyd-
Douglas
E-Mail: ancboyd@UDel.edu

Historical Note:
*Formerly Association for Women Psychologists. AWP is
a scientific and educational organization, committed to
encourage feminist psychological research, theory and
activism. Membership: $95 (Individual); $30 (Institutional);
$15 (Student with Reduced Income).*

Meetings/Conferences: Annual
2013 - Salt Lake City, UT (Salt Lake City Marriott City
Center)/March 7 - 10

Publications:
Membership Directory; on-line; adv.
Winter Newsletter

Membership List Available to Non-members

Association for Women in Science (1971)

1321 Duke St.
Suite 210
Alexandria, VA 22314
Tel: (703) 894-4490 *Fax:* (703) 778-7807
TollFree: (800) 886-2947
E-Mail: awis@awis.org
Website: awis.org
Members: 6000 individuals
Staff: 7
Annual Budget: $1-2,000,000
Tax: 501(c)(3)

Personnel:
President: Susan Fitzpatrick
E-Mail: susan@jsmf.org
Executive Director and Chief Executive Officer: Janet
Bandows Koster
E-Mail: koster@awis.org
Director, Special Events: Keisha Byrd
E-Mail: byrd@awis.org
Public Policy Fellow: Erin Cadwalader
E-Mail: cadwalader@awis.org
Marketing and Communications Associate: Samantha
Lomax
E-Mail: lomax@awis.org
Director, Programs and External Relations: Cindy
Simpson
E-Mail: simpson@awis.org

Historical Note:
*AWIS is a national advocacy organization championing the
interests of women in science, technology, engineering, and
mathematics across all disciplines and employment sectors.
Membership: $25-1000/year.*

Meetings/Conferences:
Conference Chair: Keisha Byrd

Publications:
Advocacy & Public Policy Newsletter; monthly
AWIS Magazine; quarterly; adv.
Membership Directory; on-line

Association for Women in Sports Media (1987)

3899 N. Front St.
Harrisburg, PA 17110
Tel: (717) 703-3086
E-Mail: info@awsmonline.org
Website: awsmonline.org
Members: 400 individuals
Staff: 6
Annual Budget: $50-100,000
Tax: 501(c)(3)

Personnel:
Vice President, Outreach: Joanne C. Gerstner
E-Mail: development@awsmonline.org

Historical Note:
*AWSM's mission is to serve as a support network and
advocacy group for women who work in sports writing,*

editing, broadcast and production, public and media
relations. It also works to promote and increase diversity in
sports media through internship and scholarship programs.
Membership: $50 (Professionals); $25 (Student).

Meetings/Conferences:
Conference Chair: Nicole Vargas
2013 - Scottsdale, AZ (Montelucia Resort and Spa)/
June 20 - 23

Publications:
AWSM Newsletter; semi-annually
Membership Directory; on-line

Association for Women Veterinarians Foundation (1947)

Northern Illinois University
Lowden Hall 301
DeKalb, IL 60115
Tel: (815) 753-1883 *Fax:* (815) 753-1631
E-Mail: lfreeman1@niu.edu
Website: womenveterinarians.org
Members: 300 individuals
Staff: 1
Annual Budget: Under $10,000

Personnel:
Chair Person: Lisa C. Freeman
E-Mail: lfreeman1@niu.edu

Historical Note:
*Founded as the Women's Veterinary Association, it became
the Women's Veterinary Medical Association in 1950 and
Association for Women Veterinarians in 1980. Renamed
to Association for Women Veterinarians Foundation in
2005. Membership: $50 (Full); $5 (Student); $10 (New
Graduate); $10 (Associate); $5 (Retiree).*

Publications:
Membership Directory; on-line

Association Foundation Group (1988)

1760 Old Meadow Rd.
Suite 500
McLean, VA 22102
Tel: (703) 506-2890 *Fax:* (703) 506-3266
E-Mail:
info@www.associationfoundationgroup.org
Website: associationfoundationgroup.org
Staff: 1
Annual Budget: $50-100,000

Personnel:
Executive Director: Amy B. Lotz CAE
E-Mail: alotz@afgnet.org

Historical Note:
*AFG's mission is to serve association fundraising and
association foundation professionals by providing
education, research and information resources necessary
to meet the unique needs of this community. Membership:
$95/year.*

Meetings/Conferences: Annual
2013 - Washington, DC (FHI 360 Conference Center)/
May 9
Number of non-conference events/year: 1

Publications:
AFG newsletter; quarterly
Membership directory; on-line

Association Media and Publishing (1963)

1760 Old Meadow Rd.
Suite 500
McLean, VA 22102
Tel: (703) 506-3285 *Fax:* (703) 506-3266
E-Mail:
info@associationmediaandpublishing.org
Website: associationmediaandpublishing.org
Members: 1600 individuals
Staff: 11
Annual Budget: $500-1,000,000
Tax: 501(c)(6)

Personnel:
Executive Director: Amy E. Lestition CAE
E-Mail:
alestition@associationmediaandpublishing.org
Coordinator, Marketing and Communications: Hannah
Andrews
Editorial Director: Carla Kalogeridis
E-Mail: reachcarla@comcast.net
Association Media and Publishing: Nancy Lu
Vice President, Meetings: Elisa Perodin CEM, CMP

Historical Note:

Formerly known as Society of National Association
Publications (SNAP), assumed its new name in 2009.
Mission is to enhance the effectiveness of print and
electronic publications professionals to meet their
association's communication and business goals.
Membership: $495-1,295 (Individual, Non-Profit
Organization); $395-995 (Individual, Industry Service
Provider, based on annual gross revenues); $95 (Individual,
Industry Service Provider- Additional Member).

Meetings/Conferences:
Conference Chair: Elisa Perodin CEM, CMP

Publications:
Association Publishing; bi-monthly
Final Proof; bi-weekly
In Touch; bi-weekly
Membership Directory; on-line
Sidebar; weekly
Signature; bi-monthly; adv.
SNAPsight; weekly

Association Montessori International - United States of America (1929)

410 Alexander St.
Rochester, NY 14607-1028
Tel: (585) 461-5920 *Fax:* (585) 461-0075
TollFree: (800) 872-2643
E-Mail: montessori@amiusa.org
Website: amiusa.org
Members: 5000 Montessori schools
Staff: 6
Annual Budget: $500-1,000,000

Personnel:
Executive Director: Virginia McHugh Goodwin
Educational Program Coordinator: Carrie Baxter
E-Mail: carrie@amiusa.org
Treasurer: Harris Gordon
Manager, Database Program: Denise Wanits
E-Mail: denise@amiusa.org

Historical Note:
*AMI/USA's mission is to create services that support
their members and the general public to the same degree
that the Montessori method supports students in the
classroom. Membership: $75/year (U.S. resident); $95/
year (International).*

Publications:
AMI/USA Newsletter; adv.
Communications

Association of Academic Chairmen of Plastic Surgery

500 Cummings Center
Suite 4550
Beverly, MA 01915
Tel: (978) 927-8330 *Fax:* (978) 524-8890
Website: acaplasticsurgeons.org/
Members: 290 individuals
Staff: 4
Annual Budget: $100-250,000

Personnel:
President: Nicholas B. Vedder
Vice President, Education: C. Scott Hultman
Vice president, Finance and Communication: Jeffrey E.
Janis
Vice President, Academic Administration: W. John
Kitzmiller

Historical Note:
*The American Council of Academic Plastic Surgeons
(ACAPS) is composed of the program directors /
chairpersons and associates of American College of
Graduate Medical Education (ACGME) approved plastic
surgery residency programs in the United States. ACAPS's
mission is to provide leadership and support for educational
programs for plastic surgery residents.*

Meetings/Conferences:
Number of non-conference events/year: 1-10

Publications:
ACAPS newsletter; on-line
Member Directory; on-line

Association of Academic Health Centers (1980)

1400 16th St. NW
Suite 720
Washington, DC 20036
Tel: (202) 265-9600 *Fax:* (202) 265-7514
Website: aahcdc.org
Members: 102 institutions
Staff: 11
Annual Budget: $2-5,000,000

Personnel:
President and Chief Executive Officer: Steven Wartman MD, PhD
  E-Mail: swartman@acadhlthctrs.org
Director, Information Technology: Nathan Castellanos
Meetings Planner: Audra Franks MTA
Receptionist, Office Coordinator: Lisa Harrison
Senior Director, Policy and Strategy: Anthony J. Knettel JD
  E-Mail: aknettel@aahcdc.org
Director, Meetings and Membership Services: Alcenia McIntosh-Peters

Historical Note:
Founded in 1969 and incorporated in Indiana as the Organization of University Health Center Administrators. Formerly, Association for Academic Health Centers (1971) and assumed its current name in 1980. Mission of AAHC is to improve the nation's health care system by mobilizing and enhancing the strengths and resources of the academic health center enterprise in health professions, education, patient care, and research.

Meetings/Conferences: Annual
Conference Chair: Audra Franks MTA
2013 - Washington, DC (Fairmont Hotel)/April 22 - 23

Association of Academic Health Sciences Library
(1978)
2150 N. 107th St.
Suite 205
Seattle, WA 98133
Tel: (206) 367-8704 *Fax:* (206) 367-8777
E-Mail: office@aahsl.org
Website: aahsl.org
Members: 125 institutions
Staff: 3
Annual Budget: $100-250,000

Personnel:
Executive Director: Louise S. Miller
  E-Mail: aahsl@sbims.com
Treasurer: Jett McCann
  E-Mail: jm594@georgetown.edu
Webmaster: Paul Schoening
  E-Mail: paul.schoening@wustl.edu

Historical Note:
AAHSL seeks to improve the role of academic health sciences, librarians and information professionals by assessing, advancing, strengthening and reframing health sciences libraries in patient care, research and teaching. Membership: $2,400 (Full); $900 (Associate).

Meetings/Conferences: Annual
2013 - Philadelphia, PA/Nov. 1 - 6

Publications:
Newsletter

Association of Academic Museums & Galleries
(1980)
Association of Academic Museums and Galleries
511 Park Ave.
Galena, IL 61036
Tel: (612) 486-2264
E-Mail: art.washington.edu/jlg
Website: aamg-us.org
Members:
1000 institutions and individuals
100 individuals
Staff: 6
Annual Budget: $10-25,000

Personnel:
Executive Director: David Alan Robertson
  E-Mail: d-robertson@aamg-us.org

Historical Note:
Formerly known as Association of College and University Museums and Galleries. Promotes the welfare of college and university museums and galleries of all disciplines, as well as the welfare of the professional staffs of those museums and galleries. Membership: $40 (Individual); $100 (Institution); $125 (Corporate); $10 (Student).

Meetings/Conferences: Annual
2013 - Baltimore, MD (Gilman Hall)/May 18

Publications:
Membership Directory; on-line
News and Views

Membership List Available to Non-members

Association of Academic Physiatrists *(1967)*
7250 Pkwy. Dr.
Suite 130
Hanover, MD 21076
Tel: (410) 712-7120 *Fax:* (410) 712-7101
E-Mail: aap@physiatry.org
Website: physiatry.org
Members: 1200 individuals
Staff: 7
Annual Budget: $1-2,000,000
Tax: 501(c)(3)

Personnel:
Executive Director: Lawrence C. Pencak MA
  E-Mail: lpencak@physiatry.org
Manager, Membership Services and Meetings: Katie Adair
  E-Mail: kadair@physiatry.org
Deputy Director: Vincent A. Fields MBA, Sr.
  E-Mail: vfields@physiatry.org
Managing Editor: Brad Johns
  E-Mail: bjohns@physiatry.org
Manager, Communications and Marketing: Bernadette M. Rensing
  E-Mail: brensing@physiatry.org

Historical Note:
Affiliated with Association of American Medical Colleges. AAP's purpose is to promote the advancement of teaching and research in physical medicine and rehabilitation within an academic environment. Members are academic physicians specializing in physical medicine and rehabilitation. Membership: $395 (Diplomate); $325 (Affiliate); $300 (International); $155 (Emeritus); $97 (In-training); $240-395 (Associate).

Meetings/Conferences: Annual
2013 - New Orleans, LA (Hilton New Orleans Riverside Hotel)/March 6 - 10
2014 - Nashville, TN (Renaissance Nashville Hotel and Convention Center)/Feb. 25 - March 1
Number of non-conference events/year: 5

Publications:
Member Directory
Rehab in Review; monthly
The AAP E-Brief; monthly
The AAP Newsletter; quarterly; adv.
The American Journal of Physical Medicine & Rehabilitation

Association of Administrative Law Judges *(1970)*
601 Pinetree Dr.
Decatur, GA 30030-2327
Fax: (404) 584-6234
E-Mail: info@aalj.org
Website: aalj.org
Members: 830 individuals
Staff: 1
Annual Budget: $100-250,000

Personnel:
Secretary: Dale D. Glendening Jr.

Historical Note:
Incorporated in the State of Illinois in 1980, AALJ works to protect the decisional independence of Federal Administrative Law Judges, to provide ongoing judicial education, and defend the integrity of the hearing system. AALJ chose to affiliate with the International Federation of Professional and Technical Engineers, AFL-CIO, joining other federal judges and professional employees in order to advocate for agencies and members. Members are administrative law judges of the Social Security Agency of the U.S. Government. Membership: $18.95/year; $50 (Retiree).

Meetings/Conferences: Annual

Publications:
Membership Directory; on-line

Association of Administrators of the Interstate Compact on the Placement of Children *(1974)*
1133 19th St. NW
Suite 400
Washington, DC 20036
Tel: (202) 682-0100 *Fax:* (202) 289-6555
E-Mail: icpcinbox@aphsa.org
Website: icpc.aphsa.org
Members: 52 member jurisdictions
Staff: 4

Personnel:
Division Director and Web Manager: Carla Fults
  E-Mail: cfults@aphsa.org
Administrative Assistant: Robin Henderson
  E-Mail: rhenderson@aphsa.org
Conference Coordinator: Emily Jacobs
  E-Mail: ejacobs@aphsa.org
Director, Membership and Communications: Jerome Uher
  E-Mail: Jerome.Uher@aphsa.org

Historical Note:
An affiliate of the American Public Human Services Association, AAICPC members are state administrators of the uniform law for the placement of children across state lines.

Meetings/Conferences: Annual
Conference Chair: Emily Jacobs

Association of Advanced Rabbinical and Talmudic Schools *(1973)*
11 Broadway
Suite 405
New York, NY 10004-1392
Tel: (212) 363-1991 *Fax:* (212) 533-5335
Members: 64 institutions
Staff: 5
Annual Budget: $250-500,000

Personnel:
Executive Vice President: Bernard Fryshman PhD

Historical Note:
Formerly (1971) the Council of Roshei Yeshivas.

Association of AE Business Leaders *(1975)*
948 Capp St.
San Francisco, CA 94110-3911
Tel: (415) 713-5379
E-Mail: events@aebl.org
Website: aebl.org
Members: 350 individuals
Staff: 12
Annual Budget: $100-250,000

Personnel:
Executive Director: Kathryn Sprankle
  E-Mail: kathrynsprankle@aebl.org

Historical Note:
Members are business managers, owners and principals of professional service firms (i. e. engineering, architecture, landscape architecture, interior design, management consultants, etc.) seeking to promote the exchange of ideas and information and to establish guidelines in the field of professional service firm management. Membership: $750 (Basic Firm Membership); $2500 (Sustaining Membership).

Association of African American Museums *(1978)*
4130 Overland Ave.
Culver City, CA 90230
Tel: (202) 609-9755 *Fax:* (202) 640-2589
E-Mail: info@blackmuseums.org
Website: blackmuseums.org
Members: 100 institutions 200 individuals
Staff: 3
Annual Budget: $50-100,000

Personnel:
Administrative Coordinator: Gil Mars
  E-Mail: mars@blackmuseums.org

Historical Note:
Founded as African-American Museums Association; assumed its current name in 1998. AAAM is the national voice of black museums in the U.S. and helps its members in collecting, preserving, and interpreting the cultural objects and artifacts of black heritage worldwide. Membership is open to cultural organizations, historical societies and museums that collect, conserve, exhibit and interpret objects valuable to art, history, and science, as well as educational institutions and research centers. Membership: $25 (Student/Retiree); $55 (Individual); $75 (Trustee/Board); $65 (Scholar); $125-1,000 (Institutional); $500 (Lifetime); $125-500 (ANNUAL AFFILIATE); $1,000 (Corporate).

Meetings/Conferences: Annual
2013 - Charlotte, NC/Aug. 7 - 10

Publications:
E-mail Updates; monthly
Member Directory; on-line
Newsletter; quarterly; adv.

Association of African Studies Programs *(1972)*
Cornell University, Department of History
320 McGraw
Ithaca, NY 14850
Tel: (607) 254-5334 *Fax:* (607) 255-0469
Website: aasp.asrc.cornell.edu
Staff: 3
Annual Budget: Under $10,000

Personnel:
Chair: Amadou Fofona
  E-Mail: afofona@willamette.edu

Contact, Membership: Judith A. Byfield
Secretariat: Renee Milligan
E-Mail: ram25@cornell.edu

Historical Note:
AASP's purpose is to keep all members informed of
major national developments that impact African studies
programs and the organization is made up of Deans,
Directors, Chairpersons, Committee Heads, or individuals
who have the responsibility for organizing the African
Studies program at their college or university. Membership:
$50-300/year.

Meetings/Conferences: Semi-Annual

Association of Air Medical Services (1980)
909 N. Washington St.
Suite 410
Alexandria, VA 22314
Tel: (703) 836-8732 Fax: (703) 836-8920
E-Mail: information@aams.org
Website: aams.org
Members: 600 companies
Staff: 10
Annual Budget: $2-5,000,000
Tax: 501(c)(6)

Personnel:
Chief Executive Officer: Rick Sherlock
E-Mail: rsherlock@aams.org
Manager, Communications and Marketing: Blair Marie
Beggan
E-Mail: bbeggan@aams.org
Manager, Government Relations: Greg Lynskey
E-Mail: glynskey@aams.org
Manager, Education and Meetings: Natasha Ross CMP
E-Mail: nross@aams.org
Manager, Accounting and Finance: Yogendra Sheth
E-Mail: ysheth@aams.org
Manager, Membership Services: Elena Sierra
E-Mail: esierra@aams.org

Historical Note:
AAMS's mission is to advance safety and quality in
air medical and critical care transport. Membership:
$175-5,601 (Regular); $1,320 (Associate); $291-1,167
(Affiliate); $109(Personal).

Continuing Education:
Enrollment: 80
Certification Designation/s: CMTE

Meetings/Conferences: Annual
Number of non-conference events/year: 3

Publications:
AAMS News and Views; monthly; adv.
Air Medical Journal; bi-monthly; adv.
Capital Watch; monthly
On the Fly Newsletter; monthly

Association of Alternate Postal Systems (1973)
1725 Oaks Way
Oklahoma City, OK 73131
Tel: (405) 478-0006
E-Mail: aaps@cox.net
Website: aapsinc.org
Members: 110 companies
Staff: 1
Annual Budget: $50-100,000

Personnel:
Executive Director: John White

Historical Note:
Formerly (1990) the Association of Private Postal Systems.
AAPS is an association of advertising distribution service
companies. Members are companies delivering advertising
mail to consumers. Membership: $340/year.

Meetings/Conferences: Annual
2013 - Las Vegas, NV (Mandalay Bay Resort and
Casino)/April 27 - 30

Publications:
AAPS e-Newsletter; monthly
AAPS Update

Association of Alternative Newsweeklies (1978)
1156 15th St. NW
Suite 1005
Washington, DC 20005
Tel: (202) 289-8484 Fax: (202) 289-2004
Website: altweeklies.com
Members: 128 alternative news organizations
Staff: 4
Annual Budget: $500-1,000,000
Tax: 501(c)(6)

Personnel:
Executive Director: Tiffany Shackelford
Director, Meetings and Special Projects: Debra Silverstrin
E-Mail: debra@aan.org
Editor and Director, Advertising: Jason Zaragoza

Historical Note:
AAN works to promote editorial excellence among its
members. It represents alternative newspapers. Membership:
$500/year (Associate).

Meetings/Conferences: Annual
Conference Chair: Debra Silverstrin
Number of non-conference events/year: 2

Publications:
AAN Newsletter; on-line
Newsweekly Directory; on-line

Membership List Available to Non-members

Association of American Cancer Institutes (2010)
3708 Fifth Ave., Medical Arts Bldg.
Suite 503
Pittsburgh, PA 15213
Tel: (414) 647-6111 Fax: (412) 647-3659
E-Mail: mail@aaci-cancer.org
Website: aaci-cancer.org
Members: 95 cancer research centers
Staff: 6
Annual Budget: $1-2,000,000

Personnel:
Executive Director: Barbara Duffy Stewart
E-Mail: barbara@aaci-cancer.org
Associate Director, Finance and Administration: Sara B.
Arvay MBA
E-Mail: sara@aaci-cancer.org
Director, Development: Kate S. Burroughs CFRE
E-Mail: kate@aaci-cancer.org
Administrative Assistant: Andrea L. Dixon
E-Mail: andrea@aaci-cancer.org
Director, Programs: Janie K. Hofacker BSN, MS, RN
E-Mail: janie@aaci-cancer.org
Director, Communications and Public Affairs: Chris
Zurawsky
E-Mail: chris@aaci-cancer.org

Historical Note:
The Association is committed to advocating the nation's
leading research institutions' efforts to eradicate cancer
through a comprehensive and multidisciplinary program
of cancer research, treatment, patient care, prevention,
education and community outreach. Membership: $7,500/
year.

Meetings/Conferences: Annual
Conference Chair: Janie K. Hofacker BSN, MS, RN
2013 - Washington, DC/Sept. 29 - Oct. 1

Publications:
AACI Update Newsletter; monthly

Association of American Chambers of Commerce in Latin America (1967)
1615 H St. NW
Washington, DC 20062-2000
Tel: (202) 463-5485 Fax: (202) 463-3126
E-Mail: info@aaccla.org
Website: aaccla.org
Members: 20000 companies and individuals
Staff: 23
Annual Budget: $250-500,000
Tax: 501(c)(6)

Personnel:
Executive Vice President: Patrick Kilbride
Vice President, Membership Relations: Jaime Bazan
Vice President, Executive Management: Aldo Defilippi
Senior Manager, Programs: Maria Medrano
E-Mail: mmedrano@aaccla.org

Historical Note:
AACCLA's mission is to promote trade and investment
between the United States and the countries of the region
through free trade, free markets, and free enterprise.
Represents over 20,000 companies and individuals
managing the bulk of U. S. investments in the region.

Meetings/Conferences: Annual
Conference Chair: Maria Medrano

Association of American Colleges and Universities (1915)
1818 R St. NW
Washington, DC 20009
Tel: (202) 387-3760 Fax: (202) 265-9532
TollFree: (800) 297-3775

Website: aacu.org
Members: 1250 representatives
Staff: 45
Annual Budget: $5-10,000,000
Tax: 501(c)(3)

Personnel:
President: Carol Geary Schneider
E-Mail: cgs@aacu-edu.org
Director, Publications and Editorial Services: Shelley
Johnson Carey
E-Mail: carey@aacu.org
Senior Scholar: Alma R. Clayton-Pedersen
E-Mail: alma@nonprofitsuccess.net
Vice President, Finance and Administration: Michelle
Hannahs
E-Mail: hannahs@aacu.org
Vice President, Communications and Public Affairs: Dr.
Debra Humphreys
E-Mail: humphreys@aacu.org
Director, Annual Meeting and Marketing: Suzanne Hyers
E-Mail: hyers@aacu.org
Director, Human Resources and Administrative Services:
Janet McLaughlin
E-Mail: jdm@aacu.org
Director, Membership Services: Dennis W. Renner
E-Mail: memberservices@aacu.org
Director, Information Systems: Daniel Singh
E-Mail: singh@aacu.org

Historical Note:
Established as the Association of American Colleges (AAU),
assumed its current name in 1995. Mission is to make the
aims of liberal learning a constant influence on institutional
purpose and educational practice in higher education.
Membership dues varies with the category of institution.

Meetings/Conferences: Annual
Conference Chair: Suzanne Hyers
2013 - Atlanta, GA (Hyatt Regency Atlanta)/Jan. 23 -
26/1800 attendees/11-25 exhibitors
2014 - Washington, DC/Jan. 22 - 24
2014 - Washington, DC/Jan. 22 - 25/1800 attendees
2015 - Washington, DC/Jan. 21 - 24/1800 attendees
2016 - Washington, DC/Jan. 20 - 23/1800 attendees

Publications:
AAC&U News; on-line
Diversity & Innovations
Liberal Education; quarterly
On Campus With Women; quarterly
Peer Review; quarterly

Association of American Editorial Cartoonists (1957)
3899 N. Front St.
Harrisburg, PA 17110
Tel: (717) 703-3003 Fax: (717) 703-3008
E-Mail: info@acconline.org
Website: editorialcartoonists.com
Members: 350 individuals
Staff: 4
Annual Budget: $50-100,000
Tax: 501(c)(6)

Personnel:
Contact, Website: Anita Austin
President: John Cole
Secretary and Treasurer: R. C. Harvey

Historical Note:
AAEC is a professional association concerned with
promoting the interests of staff, freelance and student
editorial cartoonists in the United States. Membership:
$150 (Regular); $60 (Retired); $65 (Student); $150
(Associate).

Publications:
Membership Directory; on-line
Notebook; quarterly; adv.

Association of American Educators (1994)
27405 Puerta Real
Suite 230
Mission Viejo, CA 92691-6388
Tel: (949) 595-7979 Fax: (949) 595-7970
TollFree: (800) 704-7799
E-Mail: info@aaeteachers.org
Website: aaeteachers.org
Members: 10000 individuals
Staff: 19
Annual Budget: $500-1,000,000
Tax: 501(c)(6)

Personnel:

Executive Director: Gary Beckner
Director, Education Policy: Tracey Bailey
Associate Director: Heather Reams

Historical Note:
AAE advances the teaching profession through personal growth, professional development, teacher advocacy and protection. Membership: $180 (Professional, includes $2 Million insurance); $25 (Student includes $2 Million Insurance); $25 (Retired Educator/Associate/Support).

Publications:
Education Matters; monthly

Association of American Feed Control Officials
(1909)
1800 S. Oak St.
Suite 100
Champaign, IL 61820-6974
Tel: (217) 356-4221 *Fax:* (217) 398-4119
E-Mail: aafco@aafco.org
Website: aafco.org
Members: 325 individuals
Staff: 1
Annual Budget: $500-1,000,000

Personnel:
Contact, Membership and Publications: Jenna Stoia
E-Mail: jennas@assochq.org

Historical Note:
AAFCO's goal is to provide mechanism for developing and implementing uniform and equitable laws, regulations, standards and enforcement policies for regulating manufacture, distribution and sale of animal feeds.

Meetings/Conferences: Semi-Annual
2013 - Albuquerue, NM (Hyatt Regency Albuquerque)/ Jan. 22 - 24
2013 - St. Pete Beach, FL/Aug. 10 - 12

Publications:
Official Publication; annually

Membership List Available to Non-members

Association of American Geographers *(1904)*
1710 16th St. NW
Washington, DC 20009-3198
Tel: (202) 234-1450 *Fax:* (202) 234-2744
E-Mail: gaia@aag.org
Website: aag.org
Members: 10700 individuals
Staff: 24
Annual Budget: $10-25,000,000
Tax: 501(c)(3)

Personnel:
Executive Director: Douglas B. Richardson
E-Mail: drichard@aag.org
Director, Communications: David L. Coronado
E-Mail: dcoronado@aag.org
Coordinator, Special Projects and Editor: Jim Ketchum
E-Mail: jketchum@aag.org
Director, Conferences: Oscar Larson
E-Mail: olarson@aag.org
Senior Manager, Program Development: Candida Mannozzi
E-Mail: cmannozzi@aag.org
Director, Finance: Teri Martin
E-Mail: tmartin@aag.org
Technical Services Coordinator: Greg Osburn
E-Mail: gosburn@aag.org
Director, Educational Affairs: Michael Solem
E-Mail: msolem@aag.org
Director, Membership and Business Operations: Adam Thocher
E-Mail: athocher@aag.org

Historical Note:
Merged in 1948 with the American Society for Professional Geographers. AAG strives to conduct educational and research projects that advance geographic understanding, geographic literacy, and geographic learning. Members are scholars, researchers, and professionals in geography. Membership: $21-220/year.

Meetings/Conferences: Annual
Conference Chair: Oscar Larson
2013 - Los Angeles, CA (Los Angeles Marriott Downtown)/April 9 - 13
2014 - Tampa, FL/April 8 - 12
2015 - Chicago, IL/April 21 - 25

Publications:
AAG Newsletter; monthly; adv.
The Annals of the Association of American Geographers; quarterly; adv.

The Professional Geographer; quarterly; adv.

Membership List Available to Non-members

Association of American Indian Physicians *(1971)*
1225 Sovereign Row
Suite 103
Oklahoma City, OK 73108
Tel: (405) 946-7072 *Fax:* (405) 946-7651
Website: aaip.org
Staff: 3
Annual Budget: $2-5,000,000
Tax: 501(c)(3)

Personnel:
Executive Director: Margaret Knight
E-Mail: mknight@aaip.org
Contact, Conferences: Jame Eskew
E-Mail: jeskew@aaip.org
Contact, Accounts: Jacque Muncy
E-Mail: aaip_accountingtech@aaip.org

Historical Note:
AAIP's Mission is to pursue excellence in Native American healthcare by promoting education in the medical disciplines, honoring traditional healing principles and restoring the balance of mind, body, and spirit. Sponsors continuing education and other programs that reflect the cultural heritage of Native Americans. Membership: $50-150 (Full/Associate Physicians); $50 (Retired/Resident Physicians).

Meetings/Conferences: Annual
Conference Chair: Jame Eskew

Publications:
AAIP Newsletter

Association of American Law Schools *(1900)*
1201 Connecticut Ave. NW
Suite 800
Washington, DC 20036-2717
Tel: (202) 296-8851 *Fax:* (202) 296-8869
E-Mail: aals@aals.org
Website: aals.org
Members: 168 institutions
Staff: 33
Annual Budget: $2-5,000,000

Personnel:
Executive Director and Chief Executive Officer: Susan Westerberg Prager
E-Mail: sprager@aals.org
Manager, Registration: Kai Baker
E-Mail: kbaker@aals.org
Coordinator, Communications: Kelly S. Caulk
E-Mail: kcaulk@aals.org
Manager, Meetings: Mary E. Cullen
E-Mail: mcullen@aals.org
Manager, Technical Services: Brent Kimmel
E-Mail: bkimmel@aals.org
Business Manager and Administrative Coordinator, Membership Review: Barbara A. Studenmund
E-Mail: bstudenmund@aals.org

Historical Note:
AALS's purpose is the improvement of the legal profession through legal education. This goal is furthered in a number of ways, including professional development programs for law professors and administrators, a complement of over 90 sections organized by faculty and senior administrators, and a membership process that is designed to further the core values of the Association.

Meetings/Conferences: Annual
Conference Chair: Kai Baker
2013 - New Orleans, LA/Jan. 4 - 8
2013 - New Orleans, LA (Hilton New Orleans Riverside)/Jan. 4 - 7
2014 - New York City, NY/Jan. 3 - 6
2015 - Washington, DC/Jan. 2 - 6
Number of non-conference events/year: 6

Publications:
AALS Newsletter; quarterly
Clinical Law Review
Journal of Legal Education; quarterly

Association of American Medical Colleges *(1876)*
2450 N St. NW
Washington, DC 20037-1126
Tel: (202) 828-0400 *Fax:* (202) 828-1125
Website: aamc.org
Members: 75,000 medical students, 128,000 faculty members, 110,000 resident physicians
Staff: 350

Annual Budget: Over $100,000,000
Tax: 501(c)(3)

Personnel:
Director and Managing Editor: Anne Farmakidis
E-Mail: afarmakidis@aamc.org
Chief Financial and Administrative Officer: Bernard K. Jarvis
President: Darrell G. Kirch MD
E-Mail: dgkirch@aamc.org
Chief Information Officer: Jeanne L. Mella
E-Mail: jmella@aamc.org
Senior Director, Government Relations: David B. Moore
E-Mail: dbmoore@aamc.org
Director, Meetings: Kirsten Olean
E-Mail: kolean@aamc.org
Senior Vice President and Chief Communications Officer: Elisa K. Siegel
E-Mail: esiegel@aamc.org
Editor in Chief: David P. Sklar

Historical Note:
AAMC's mission is to serve the academic medicine community to improve the health of all. Represents all 136 accredited U.S. and 17 accredited Canadian medical schools. Membership: $130 (Individual).

Continuing Education:
Certification Designation/s: MERC

Meetings/Conferences:
Conference Chair: Kirsten Olean
2013 - Minneapolis, MN (Hennepin)/Aug. 9 - 11
2013 - Philadelphia, PA (Pennsylvania Convention Center)/Nov. 1 - 6
2014 - Chicago, IL (Hyatt Regency Chicago)/Nov. 7 - 12
Number of non-conference events/year: 38

Publications:
AAMC Reporter; monthly
AAMC STAT; weekly
Membership Directory; on-line

Membership List Available to Non-members

Association of American Pesticide Control Officials
(1947)
P.O. Box 466
Milford, DE 19963
Tel: (302) 422-8152 *Fax:* (302) 422-2435
E-Mail: info@aapco.org
Website: aapco.org
Members: 55 individuals
Staff: 3
Annual Budget: $250-500,000

Personnel:
Treasurer: Michael K. Fresvik
E-Mail: mkfresvik@comcast.net
Executive Secretary: H. Grier Stayton
E-Mail: aapco-sfireg@comcast.net

Historical Note:
AAPCO's mission is to represent state pesticide control officials in development, implementation and communication of sound public policies and programs related to the sale, application, transport and disposal of pesticides. Membership: $125/year.

Meetings/Conferences: Annual
2013 - Arlington, VA (Hyatt Regency, Crystal City)/ March 18 - 20

Publications:
Member Directory; on-line
Official Publication; annually

Association of American Physicians *(1885)*
45685 Harmony Ln.
Belleville, MI 48111
Tel: (734) 699-1217
E-Mail: admin@aap-online.org
Website: aap-online.org
Members: 550 emeritus and honorary members
Staff: 2
Annual Budget: $100-250,000
Tax: 501(c)(3)

Personnel:
Executive Director: Lori Ennis
Treasurer: Linda Fried

Historical Note:
Provides pursuit of medical knowledge and the advancement through experimentation and discovery of basic and clinical science and their application to clinical medicine. Members are medical school professors. Membership: $150/year.

Meetings/Conferences:
2013 - Chicago, IL (Fairmont Chicago Millenium Park)/
April 26 - 28
2014 - Chicago, IL (Fairmont Chicago Millenium Park)/
April 25 - 27

Publications:
Membership Directory
Proceedings of the Association of American Physicians;
bi-monthly

Association of American Physicians and Surgeons
(1943)
1601 N. Tucson Blvd.
Suite Nine
Tucson, AZ 85716-3450
Tel: (800) 635-1196 *Fax:* (520) 326-3529
TollFree: (800) 635-1196
E-Mail: aaps@aapsonline.org
Website: aapsonline.org
Members: 6000 individuals
Staff: 3
Annual Budget: $500-1,000,000

Personnel:
Executive Director: Jane M. Orient MD
E-Mail: janeorientmd@gmail.com

Historical Note:
AAPS is dedicated to preserving the sanctity of the patient-physician relationship and the practice of private medicine. Membership: $350 (Regular); $25-150 (Professional Associate); $390 (Builder); $550 (Sustainer); $2,000 (Life Time); $30 (House Officer).

Meetings/Conferences: Annual

Publications:
AAPS Newsletter; monthly
Journal of American Physicians and Surgeons;
quarterly

Association of American Plant Food Control Officials *(1946)*
C/O University of Kentucky
Division of Regulatory Services, 103 Regulatory
Services Building
Lexington, KY 40546-0275
Tel: (859) 257-2785 *Fax:* (859) 323-9931
Website: aapfco.org
Members: 185 individuals
Staff: 4
Annual Budget: $100-250,000

Personnel:
President: Stephen McMurry
E-Mail: smcmurry@uky.edu

Historical Note:
Formerly (1967) the Association of American Fertilizer Control Officials. Purpose of AAPFCO is to promote safe and effective use of fertilizers and protection of soil and water resources. Membership: $100/year.

Meetings/Conferences: Annual
2013 - St. Petersburg, FL/Aug. 1 - 4

Publications:
AAPFCO Official Publication

Association of American Publishers *(1970)*
71 Fifth Ave.
Second Floor
New York, NY 10003-3004
Tel: (212) 255-0200 *Fax:* (212) 255-7007
Website: publishers.org
Members: 300 companies
Staff: 27
Annual Budget: $10-25,000,000

Personnel:
President and Chief Executive Officer: Thomas H. Allen
E-Mail: tallen@publishers.org
Vice President: Tina Jordan
E-Mail: tjordan@publishers.org
Director, Membership Services and Marketing: Gail Kump
E-Mail: gkump@publishers.org
Director, Finance and Administration: Tony Laforgia
E-Mail: tlaforgia@publishers.org
Director, Professional and Scholarly Publishing: Sara Pinto
E-Mail: spinto@publishers.org
Counsel: R. Bruce Rich
Vice President, Communications: Andi Sporkin
E-Mail: asporkin@publishers.org
Vice President and Executive Director, Professional and Scholarly Publishing Division: John Tagler

E-Mail: jtagler@publishers.org

Historical Note:
Formed by a merger of the American Educational Publishers Institute (1942), formerly known as the American Textbook Publishers Institute and the American Book Publishers Council (1946) . AAP works to showcase the value of content and the critical role of the dynamic U.S. book publishing industry around the world. Represents the major commercial, educational and professional companies as well as independents, non-profits, university presses and scholarly societies.

Association of American Railroads *(1934)*
425 Third St. SW
Suite 1000
Washington, DC 20024
Tel: (202) 639-2100
Website: aar.org
Members: 65 railroads
Staff: 45
Annual Budget: $50-100,000,000
Tax: 501(c)(6)

Personnel:
President and Chief Executive Officer: Edward R.
Hamberger
E-Mail: ehamberger@aar.org
Assistant Vice President, Media and Public Affairs: Holly
Arthur
E-Mail: harthur@aar.org
Associate General Counsel and Corporate Secretary: Janet
L. Bartelmay
Contact, Human Resources: Carla Garcia
E-Mail: cgarcia@aar.org
Assistant Vice President, Technical Services: James P.
Grady
E-Mail: jgrady@aar.org
Director, Meeting Services: Stephanie A. Kilfeather
E-Mail: skilfeather@aar.org
Vice President, Finance and Administration: Jeff Marsh
Vice President, Communications: Patricia Reilly
E-Mail: preilly@aar.org
Associate General Counsel: Michael J. Rush
Assistant General Counsel: Daniel Saphire
Senior Vice President, Law and General Counsel: Louis P.
Warchot
E-Mail: lwarchot@aar.org

Historical Note:
AAR serves as the joint agency of its individual railroad members to assure an efficient nationwide rail system. AAR's subsidiaries, the Transportation Technology Center Inc. (TTCI) and the Railinc Corp. Membership: $15,000 (Associate Gold); $ 7,500 (Associate Silver); $ 5,000-100,000 (Affiliate Freight Carrier); $ 2,500-50,000 (Affiliate Passenger Carrier).

Meetings/Conferences: Semi-Annual
Conference Chair: Stephanie A. Kilfeather

Publications:
AAR Newsletter; quarterly
Membership Directory; on-line
Rail Traffic Report; weekly

Membership List Available to Non-members

The Association of American Seed Control Officials *(1949)*
Office of Indiana State Chemist Purdue University
175 S. University St.
West Lafayette, IN 47907-2063
Tel: (765) 494-1557 *Fax:* (765) 494-4331
E-Mail: neesl@purdue.edu
Website: seedcontrol.org
Members: 52 individuals
Staff: 4
Annual Budget: Under $10,000

Personnel:
President: John Heaton
Treasurer: Greg Helmbrecht
Secretary: Larry Nees
E-Mail: neesl@purdue.edu
Webmaster: Melinda Walsh
E-Mail: walshm@purdue.edu

Historical Note:
AASCO's mission is to sponsor, endorse, instigate, evaluate and suggest seed research designed to develop and standardize competent and expedient methods of seed testing. Members are U.S. and Canadian officials who administer state and provincial seed regulations. AASCO has one member from each state, one from Canada and

one from the U.S. Department of Agriculture. Membership:
$150/year (State Organization).

Meetings/Conferences: Annual

Publications:
AASCO Newsletter; bi-annually
Membership Directory; on-line

Membership List Available to Non-members

Association of American Shippers *(1951)*
200 W. Forsyth St.
Suite 1000
Jacksonville, FL 32202
Tel: (904) 355-2601 *Fax:* (904) 791-8836
TollFree: (800) 874-6422
Website: americanshipper.com
Staff: 2

Personnel:
Production Manager, Advertising: Melodie Crites
Manager, Sales: Lisa Martini

Historical Note:
Howard Publications was founded by David A. Howard in 1951 and has published magazines covering international logistics and transportation.

Publications:
American Shipper magazine; monthly; adv.
AS + and News Flash; daily

Association of American State Geologists *(1879)*
University of Minnesota
2642 University Ave. West
St. Paul, MN 55114-1057
Tel: (612) 627-4780
Website: stategeologists.org
Members: 51 individuals
Staff: 3
Annual Budget: $25-50,000
Tax: 501(c)(3)

Personnel:
President: Harvey Thorleifson

Historical Note:
Founded as the Association of State Geologists of the Mississippi Valley, assumed its present name May 12, 1908 in the District of Columbia. AASG is an organization of the chief executives of the state geological surveys that works to promote the state geological surveys as sources of important geoscience data to address local, state, and national issues. Members of the association are chief executives of State Geological Surveys in the 50 states and Puerto Rico.

Meetings/Conferences: Annual
2013 - Deadwood, SD/June 9 - 13
2014 - Lexington, KY/June 8 - 12
Number of non-conference events/year: 5

Publications:
Member Directory; on-line
The State Geologists Journal; annually

Membership List Available to Non-members

Association of American Universities *(1900)*
1200 New York Ave. NW
Suite 550
Washington, DC 20005
Tel: (202) 408-7500 *Fax:* (202) 408-8184
Website: aau.edu
Members: 61 public and private research
universities
Staff: 22
Annual Budget: $10-25,000,000
Tax: 501(c)(3)

Personnel:
President: Hunter R. Rawlings
Director, Information Technology: Tom Bozzo
Director, Human Resources and Administration: Roxanne
Murray
E-Mail: roxanne_murray@aau.edu
Vice President, Policy: Tobin Smith
E-Mail: toby_smith@aau.edu
Director, Finance and Benefits: Susan Staton
Vice President, Public Affairs and Media Relations: Barry
Toiv
E-Mail: barry_toiv@aau.edu
Executive Vice President: John C. Vaughn
E-Mail: john_vaughn@aau.edu
Manager, Meetings: Leslie Weekes
E-Mail: leslie_weekes@aau.edu

Historical Note:

AAU's mission is to focus on national and institutional issues that are important to research-intensive universities, including funding for research, research and education policy, and graduate and undergraduate education. Members are chief executives of major research universities. Affiliated with the Association of Graduate Schools.

Meetings/Conferences:
Conference Chair: Leslie Weekes

Publications:
AAU Community Services Directory; annually
AAU Reports
AAU Weekly Wrap-ups; weekly

Association of American University Presses
(1937)
28 W. 36th St.
Suite 602
New York, NY 10018
Tel: (212) 989-1010 Fax: (212) 989-0975
E-Mail: info@aaupnet.org
Website: aaupnet.org
Members: 133 presses
Staff: 10
Annual Budget: $1-2,000,000
Tax: 501(c)(3)

Personnel:
Executive Director: Peter J. Givler
    E-Mail: pgivler@aaupnet.org
Communications Coordinator: Regan Colestock
    E-Mail: rcolestock@aaupnet.org
Manager, Administration: Linda McCall
    E-Mail: lmccall@aaupnet.org
Director, Marketing and Communications: Brenna McLaughlin
    E-Mail: bmclaughlin@aaupnet.org
Coordinator, Membership and Marketing: Kim Miller
    E-Mail: kmiller@aaupnet.org
Manager, Membership Services: Susan Patton
    E-Mail: spatton@aaupnet.org

Historical Note:
AAUP's mission is to assist its members through professional education, cooperative services, and public advocacy. Membership: $2,579 (Full/Associate); $500 (Introductory).

Meetings/Conferences: Annual
2013 - Boston, MA (Seaport Boston Hotel)/June 20 - 23
2014 - New Orleans, LA (New Orleans Marriott)/June 22 - 24

Publications:
AAUP bulletin; monthly
AAUP Directory; annually
Coop Ad Newsletter; weekly
The Digital Digest; on-line
The Exchange Newsletter; quarterly

Membership List Available to Non-members

Association of American Veterinary Medical Colleges (1966)
1101 Vermont Ave. NW
Suite 301
Washington, DC 20005-3521
Tel: (202) 371-9195 Fax: (202) 842-0773
TollFree: (877) 862-2740
Website: aavmc.org
Members: 67 institutions
Staff: 18
Annual Budget: $2-5,000,000
Tax: 501(c)(3)

Personnel:
Executive Director: Dr. Andrew Maccabe
    E-Mail: amaccabe@aavmc.org
Editor-in-Chief: Dr. Henry Baker
    E-Mail: hbaker@aavmc.org
Project Manager: Matt Grogg
    E-Mail: mgrogg@aavmc.org
Director, Communications: Jeanne Johnson
    E-Mail: jjohnson@aavmc.org
Associate Executive Director, Academic and Research Affairs: Ted Mashima
    E-Mail: tmashima@aavmc.org
Director, Government Affairs: Brian T. Smith
    E-Mail: bsmith@aavmc.org

Historical Note:
Mission is to provide service in academic veterinary medicine to prepare the veterinary workforce with the scientific knowledge and skills required to meet societal

needs. AAVMC promotes veterinary medical education, animal health and welfare, biomedical research, and food safety.

Meetings/Conferences:
Conference Chair: Matt Grogg
2013 - Alexandria, VA (Westin Alexandria)/March 8 - 10

Publications:
ebulletin; quarterly
Journal of Veterinary Medical Education; quarterly; adv.

Association of Analytical Communities International (1884)
481 N. Frederick Ave.
Suite 500
Gaithersburg, MD 20877-2417
Tel: (301) 924-7077 Fax: (301) 924-7089
TollFree: (800) 379-2622
E-Mail: aoac@aoac.org
Website: aoac.org
Members: 3200 members
Staff: 31
Tax: 501(c)(3)

Personnel:
Executive Director: E. James Bradford PhD
    E-Mail: jbradford@aoac.org
Director, Meetings and Expositions: Lauren Chelf
    E-Mail: lchelf@aoac.org
Senior Director, Membership and Professional Development: Dawn Frazier
    E-Mail: dfrazier@aoac.org
Senior Director, Communications: Krystyna McIver
    E-Mail: kmciver@aoac.org
Executive, Scientific Business Development: Anita Mishra
    E-Mail: amishra@aoac.org
Senior Director, Publications: Robert Rathbone
    E-Mail: rrathbone@aoac.org
Senior Director, Human Resources and Administration: Garlon Riegler
    E-Mail: griegler@aoac.org
Chief Financial Officer: Joyce Schumacher
    E-Mail: jschumacher@aoac.org

Historical Note:
Founded in 1884 as the Association of Official Agricultural Chemists, became the Association of Official Analytical Chemists in 1965 and assumed its present name in 1991. AOAC International is an independent international association whose primary focus is coordination of the development and validation of chemical and microbiological analytical methods by expert scientists working in industry, academic, and government laboratories worldwide. These scientists work within three validation programs operated by AOAC International: the AOAC Official Methods Program, the AOAC Peer-Verified Methods Program, and the AOAC Performance-Tested Methods Program. Membership: $120 (Individual); $40 (Student); $750 to $5,000 (Sustaining/Partner Member Organizations); $10,000 (Organizational Affiliate).

Meetings/Conferences: Annual
Conference Chair: Lauren Chelf
2013 - Chicago, IL (Palmer House a Hilton Hotel)/Aug. 25 - 28
2014 - Boca Raton, FL (Boca Raton Resort and Club)/Sept. 7 - 10
2015 - Los Angeles, CA (Hyatt Regency Century Plaza)/Sept. 27 - 30
2016 - Dallas, TX (Sheraton Dallas Hotel)/Sept. 18 - 21
2017 - Atlanta, GA (Marriott Atlanta Marquis)/Sept. 24 - 27

Publications:
Member Directory; on-line
The Journal of AOAC International; bi-monthly

Association of Ancient Historians (1969)
Mercyhurst College, History Dept.
501 E. 38th St., P.O. Box 165
Erie, PA 16546-0001
Tel: (814) 824-2345 Fax: (814) 824-2182
Website: associationofancienthistorians.org
Members: 800 individuals
Staff: 3
Annual Budget: Under $10,000
Tax: 501(c)(3)

Personnel:
Webmaster: Patricia Dintrone
    E-Mail: pdintron@mail.sdsu.edu

Secretary, Treasurer and Editor: Cindy Nimchuk
    E-Mail: aah.nimchuk@gmail.com

Historical Note:
AAH is devoted to promoting teaching and scholarship in ancient history. Membership: $7.50-12.50 (Regular); $5-10 (Associate); $125 (Life Time/Retired).

Meetings/Conferences: Annual
2013 - Columbus, OH (Ohio State University)/May 16 - 19

Publications:
AAH Newsletter
Directory of Ancient Historians in the United States and Canada; on-line

Association of Applied IPM Ecologists (1967)
P.O. Box 1119
Coarsegold, CA 93614
Tel: (559) 761-1064
E-Mail: director@aaie.net
Website: aaie.net
Members: 200 individuals
Staff: 6
Annual Budget: $25-50,000

Personnel:
Executive Director: Bill Rothfuss
    E-Mail: director@aaie.net
President: Robert Walther
Treasurer / Secretary: Ken Schnider

Historical Note:
Founded as the Association of Applied Insect Ecologists, assumed its current name in 2002. AAIE's mission is to provide a forum for the exchange of information about effective and environmentally responsible pest management. Membership: $150 (Professional); $60 (Associate).

Meetings/Conferences: Annual
2013 - Napa, CA (Embassy Suites Napa Valley)/Feb. 3 - 5/1-10 exhibitors

Publications:
The AAIE E Blast

Association of Art Editors (1994)
3912 Natchez Ave., South
St. Louis Park, MN 55416
Tel: (952) 922-1374 Fax: (952) 922-1374
Website: artedit.org
Members: 90 individuals
Staff: 1
Annual Budget: $50-100,000

Personnel:
President: Phil Freshman
    E-Mail: pfreshman@mm.com

Historical Note:
An affiliate of College Art Association, the purpose of AAE is to advance and set standards for the profession of art editors and to provide service for the exchange of information among art editors and others involved in art-related publications. Members are art editors and others involved in art-related publications. Membership: $20/year.

Meetings/Conferences: Annual

Publications:
Membership Directory; on-line

Association of Art Museum Directors (1916)
120 E. 56th St.
Suite 520
New York, NY 10022
Tel: (212) 754-8084 Fax: (212) 754-8087
Website: aamd.org
Members:
199 individuals
40 emeritus
20 honorary
Staff: 4
Annual Budget: $1-2,000,000
Tax: 501(c)(6)

Personnel:
Executive Director: Christine Anagnos
Chief Administrator: Alison Wade

Historical Note:
The purpose of AAMD is to support its members in increasing the contribution of art museums to society. Membership consists of persons who serve as directors of art museums in the United States, Canada, and Mexico which, by purpose, size, and standards of operation meet the eligibility requirements established by the Trustees of the Association. Membership in the association is based on the qualifications of both the individual director and the specific

art museum and no museum may be represented by more than one individual.

Publications:
Membership Directory; on-line; adv.
Professional Practices in Art Museums; on-line

Association of Artisan Business (AAB) *(1996)*
3309 Robbins Rd.,188
Springfield, IL 62629
Tel: (217) 303-5393 *Fax:* (888) 839-7089
E-Mail: info@ArtisanBusinessGroup.com
Website: artisanbusinessgroup.com
Staff: 1

Personnel:
Chief Executive Officer and President: Brian Su

Historical Note:
Artisan Business Group, Inc., assists small and mid-sized business in capturing opportunities in China.

Association of Arts Administration Educators
(1975)
N4460 Allan Rd.
Portage, WI 53901
Tel: (608) 561-2040
E-Mail: info@artsadministration.org
Website: artsadministration.org
Members: 250 university departments, individuals and students
Staff: 1
Annual Budget: $50-100,000
Tax: 501(c)(3)

Personnel:
Administrative Director: Barbara Harkins
    E-Mail: bharkins@artsadministration.org

Historical Note:
AAAE's mission is to provide a forum for communication among its members and advocate formal training and high standards of education for arts administrators. Membership: $30 (Student); $75 (Individual/Affiliate); $250 (Associate); $350 (Full).

Meetings/Conferences: Annual
2013 - New Orleans, LA (Bourbon Orleans Hotel)/
    March 7 - 9
Number of non-conference events/year: 1

Publications:
Arts Management

The Association of Asian American Investment Managers *(2006)*
C/O LEIA, 50 California St.
Suite 2320
San Francisco, CA 94111
E-Mail: info@aaaim.org
Website: aaaim.org
Staff: 2
Annual Budget: $250-500,000
Tax: 501(c)(6)

Personnel:
President: Jan Le Chang
General Counsel: Wilson Chu

Historical Note:
AAAIM promotes excellence in Asian American investment professionals and fosters unity in the Asian American community.AAAIM's mission is to provide a forum for sharing expertise within the Asian American investment and business community. Membership: $500/year.

Publications:
Member Directory; on-line

Association of Asian-Pacific Community Health Organizations *(1987)*
300 Frank H. Ogawa Plaza
Suite 620
Oakland, CA 94612
Tel: (510) 272-9536 *Fax:* (510) 272-0817
Website: aapcho.org
Members: 14 organizations
Staff: 10
Annual Budget: $2-5,000,000
Tax: 501(c)(3)

Personnel:
Executive Director: Jeffrey B. Caballero MPH
    E-Mail: jeffc@aapcho.org
Director, Programs: Nina Agbayani Grewe
    E-Mail: nagrewe@aapcho.org
Director, Operations: Peter Ho

    E-Mail: peter@aapcho.org
Director, Communications: Stacy K. Lavilla
    E-Mail: slavilla@aapcho.org
Associate, Membership Relations: Grace-Sonia Melanio
    E-Mail: gsmelanio@aapcho.org

Historical Note:
AAPCHO's mission is to promote advocacy, collaboration and to improve the health status and access of Asian Americans, Native Hawaiians and Pacific Islanders within the United States. Members are community health organizations. Membership: $3,333 (Full); $667 (Associate).

Meetings/Conferences: Annual
Number of non-conference events/year: 1

Membership List Available to Non-members

Association of Asphalt Paving Technologists
(1924)
6776 Lake Dr.
Suite 215
Lino Lakes, MN 55014
Tel: (651) 293-9188 *Fax:* (651) 293-9193
E-Mail: aaptinfo@gmail.com
Website: asphalttechnology.org
Members: 800 individuals
Staff: 2
Annual Budget: $100-250,000

Personnel:
Executive Secretary and Office Manager: Eileen Soler
    E-Mail: aapt@aapt.comcastbiz.net
Secretary and Treasurer: Eugene L. Skok
    E-Mail: aapt@aapt.comcastbiz.net

Historical Note:
AAPT works for the advancement of asphalt paving technology. Membership: $150 (Individual/Associate); $50 (Student).

Meetings/Conferences: Annual
2013 - Denver, CO (Westin Denver Downtown)/April 7
    - 10
2014 - Atlanta, GA (Sheraton Atlanta Hotel)/March 16
    - 19
2015 - Portland, OR/March 15 - 18

Publications:
AAPT Journal; annually
Membership Directory; on-line

Association of Assistive Technology ACT Programs
(1997)
One W Old State Capitol Plaza
Suite 100
Springfield, IL 62701
Tel: (202) 643-2827 *Fax:* (202) 643-2827
Website: ataporg.org
Staff: 3
Annual Budget: $500-1,000,000
Tax: 501(c)(3)

Personnel:
Partner, Governmental Relations: Audrey Busch
Treasurer: Carolyn Phillips
    E-Mail: carolynphillips@mindspring.com

Historical Note:
ATAP sets the national direction and advocates for AT Act programs. It also works to promote and support quality performance of the State AT programs.

Association of Attorney-Mediators *(1989)*
P.O. Box 741955
Dallas, TX 75374-1955
Tel: (972) 669-8101 *Fax:* (972) 669-8180
TollFree: (800) 280-1368
E-Mail: aam@attorney-mediators.org
Website: attorney-mediators.org
Members: 300 individuals
Staff: 2
Annual Budget: $100-250,000
Tax: 501(c)(6)

Personnel:
Executive Director: Brenda Rachuig
    E-Mail: aam@attorney-mediators.org

Historical Note:
AAM's mission is to to support professional and qualified attorney-mediators who are committed to the proposition that the existing dispute resolution system can fulfill its intended purpose now through the use of voluntary and Court-annexed mediation Members are mediators who are also attorneys. Membership: $225/year.

Meetings/Conferences:

Number of non-conference events/year: 1

Publications:
AAM Newsletter; semi-annually
Membership Directory; on-line

Association of Authors' Representatives *(1991)*
676-A Ninth Ave.
Suite 312
New York, NY 10036
Tel: (212) 840-5777
E-Mail: aarinc@mindspring.org
Website: aaronline.org
Members: 350 individuals
Staff: 3
Annual Budget: $50-100,000

Personnel:
Administrative Secretary: Jody Klein

Historical Note:
Formerly the Society of Authors' Representatives. SAR merged with the Independent Literary Agents Association (est. 1977) to form the Association of Authors' Representatives. AAR's mission is to provide information and education about the conditions in publishing. AAR's membership is restricted to professional literary and dramatic agents. Membership: $150; (Full); $75 (Associate).

Publications:
The Pitch; on-line

The Association of Average Adjusters of the United States and Canada *(2011)*
126 Midwood Ave.
Farmingdale, NY 11735
Tel: (516) 753-0464 *Fax:* (516) 753-0546
E-Mail: averageadjusters@aol.com
Website: usaverageadjusters.org
Members: 800 individuals
Staff: 2
Annual Budget: $25-50,000

Personnel:
Secretary: Eileen M. Fellin
Chair, Membership Committee: Edward J. Flynn
    E-Mail: ed.flynn@american-club.com

Historical Note:
Formed (2011) through the merger of the Association of Average Adjusters of the United States and the Association of Average Adjusters of Canada. The Association of Average Adjusters of the United States and Canada's mission is to promote principles in the adjustment of marine hull claims and uniformity of practice among average adjusters. Membership is principally in New York area. Membership: $90-175/year.

Meetings/Conferences: Annual
Number of non-conference events/year: 6

Publications:
Membership Directory; on-line

Association of Avian Veterinarians *(1980)*
90 Madison St.
Suite 403
Denver, CO 80206
Tel: (303) 756-8380 *Fax:* (303) 759-8861
E-Mail: aavctrlofc@aol.com
Website: aav.org
Members: 3300 individuals
Staff: 3
Annual Budget: $500-1,000,000

Personnel:
Executive Director: Adina Rae Freedman CAE
*Contact, Publications, Conferences and Membership
    Services:* Caitlin Cowen
    E-Mail: office@aav.org
Executive: Debbie Cowen
    E-Mail: debbie@aav.org

Historical Note:
AAV's mission is to advance and promote avian medicine, surgery, stewardship, and conservation through education of its members, the veterinary community and those they serve. Membership: $140-175 (Active/Associate/Allied Professional); $85-120 (Graduate Students and Residents/ Veterinary Technicians); $25-60 (Student, enrolled in a professional veterinary curriculum).

Meetings/Conferences: Annual
Conference Chair: Caitlin Cowen
2013 - Jacksonville, FL/Aug. 3 - 7

Publications:
AAV Newsletter; monthly

AAV Newslink; on-line
Journal of Avian Medicine and Surgery; on-line
Membership Directory; on-line

Association of Aviation Psychologists (1964)
765 The City Dr.
Suite 110
Orange, CA 92868
Tel: (770) 471-6286
Website: avpsych.org
Members: 225 individuals
Staff: 1
Annual Budget: Under $10,000

Personnel:
President: Dennis Beringer

Historical Note:
AAP is an non-profit professional organization whose members are psychologists, behavioral scientists, and pilots concerned with aviation psychology including such topics as pilot/controller performance and flight safety and related fields. Has no paid officers or full-time staff. AAP's purpose is to promote aviation psychology and related aerospace disciplines. Membership: $40/year.

Publications:
AAP Newsletter

Association of Baccalaureate Social Work Program Directors
1725 Duke St.
Suite 500
Alexandria, VA 22314-3457
Tel: (703) 519-2045 *Fax:* (703) 683-8099
E-Mail: ascott@cswe.org
Website: bpdonline.org
Members: 1000 members
Staff: 3
Annual Budget: $250-500,000

Personnel:
President: Peggy Munke
Treasurer: Susan Grettenberger
Association Manager: Amanda Scott

Historical Note:
BPD is an association of BSW Program Administrators, Faculty, Field Directors, and others dedicated to the promotion of excellence in Baccalaureate social work education. Membership: $175 (Regular); $50 (emeriti).

Meetings/Conferences: Annual
2013 - Myrtle Beach, SC (Hilton and Embassy Suites Resort)/March 6 - 10

Publications:
BPD Update
Membership Directory; on-line
The Journal of Baccalaureate Social Work

Association of Battery Recyclers (1884)
P.O. Box 290286
Tampa, FL 33687
Tel: (813) 620-3260
E-Mail: info@batteryrecyclers.com
Website: americasbatteryrecyclers.org
Members: 25 companies
Staff: 2
Annual Budget: $500-1,000,000

Personnel:
Secretary and Treasurer: Joyce Morales-Caramella

Historical Note:
Formerly (1990) the Secondary Lead Smelters Association. Investigates means/methods to achieve compliance with OSHA and EPA regulations impacting the secondary lead smelting industry. Membership: $1,500/year (consultant); $4,500/year (associate); $2,500/month (secondary smelter).

Association of Biomedical Communications Directors (1974)
University of North Texas Health Science Center, 3500 Camp Bowie Blvd.
Fort Worth, TX 76107
Tel: (817) 735-2678 *Fax:* (817) 735-5086
Website: abcdirectors.org
Members: 95 individuals
Staff: 3
Annual Budget: $10-25,000
Tax: 501(c)(3)

Personnel:
Business Manager: Carol Gray
  E-Mail: carolgray@gmail.com

Treasurer: Joseph Smith
President: Robert Wright
  E-Mail: rwright@hsc.unt.edu

Historical Note:
ABCD seeks to boosts the establishment, growth and effective use of information, communications and educational technology to meet the growing needs of health education, patient care and biomedical research. Members are directors of bio-medical communications units in a school or in an academic health science center, that grants degrees in the field of health or life sciences. Membership: $110 (Active); $50 (Associate).

Meetings/Conferences: Annual

Publications:
Membership Directory
The Journal of Biocommunication (JBC); quarterly

Association of Biomolecular Resource Facilities (1988)
9650 Rockville Pike
Bethesda, MD 20814
Tel: (301) 634-7306 *Fax:* (301) 634-7455
E-Mail: abrf@abrf.org
Website: abrf.org
Members: 800 individuals
Staff: 3
Annual Budget: $500-1,000,000
Tax: 501(c)(3)

Personnel:
Contact, Business Office: Lisa Hetherington

Historical Note:
ABRF is an international society dedicated to advancing core and research biotechnology laboratories through research, communication, and education. Promotes the education and career advancement of scientists through conferences, a journal, publication of research group studies and conference travel awards. The society also sponsors multi-center research studies designed to help members incorporate new biotechnologies into their laboratories. Members are laboratories and other facilities with an interest in biomolecular research. Administrative support is provided by the Federation of American Socs. for Experimental Biology. Membership: $100 (Member); $35 (Student).

Meetings/Conferences: Annual
2013 - Palm Spring, CA (Renaissance Palm Springs Hotel)/March 2 - 5

Publications:
Communications; quarterly; adv.
Membership Directory; on-line
The Journal of Biomolecular Techniques; adv.

Association of Bituminous Contractors (1968)
1250 I St. NW
Suite 650
Washington, DC 20005
Tel: (202) 785-4440 *Fax:* (202) 331-8049
Members: 100 companies
Staff: 1
Annual Budget: $100-250,000

Personnel:
Secretary and General Counsel: William H. Howe

Historical Note:
Members are general and independent contractors constructing coal mines and coal mine facilities. Bargains with the United Mine Workers.

Association of Black Anthropologists (1970)
2200 Wilson Blvd.
Suite 600
Arlington, VA 22201-3357
Tel: (703) 528-1902 *Fax:* (703) 528-3546
Website: aaanet.org/sections/aba/contact
Staff: 5

Personnel:
President: Raymond Codrington
Webmaster: Orisanmi Burton
General Editor: Dawn Elissa Fischer
Contact, Membership Services: Oneka LaBennett
Secretary and Treasurer: Willie Lewis McKether

Historical Note:
ABA is nationally affiliated to American Anthropological Association. The purpose of ABA is to bring together Black Anthropologists and other scholars concerned with the goals of the ABA and support its activities. Membership: $40 (Professional); $10 (Student).

Meetings/Conferences: Annual

Publications:

Transforming Anthropology; semi-annually

Association of Black Cardiologists (1974)
2400 N St. NW
Suite 604
Washington, DC 20037
Tel: (202) 375-6618 *Fax:* (202) 375-6801
TollFree: (800) 753-9222
E-Mail: abcardio@abcardio.org
Website: abcardio.org
Members: 2500 health professionals and community health advocates
Staff: 10
Annual Budget: $2-5,000,000
Tax: 501(c)(3)

Personnel:
Executive Director: Andre D. Williams
  E-Mail: awilliams@abcardio.org
Chief Operating Officer: Cassandra McCullough
  E-Mail: cmccullough@abcardio.org
Specialist, Marketing and Membership Services: Jacquelyn Taylor
  E-Mail: jtaylor@abcardio.org

Historical Note:
ABC's mission is to champion the elimination of cardiovascular disparties through education, research and advocacy. Membership: $350 (Full); $175 (Associate Membership); $50 (Medical Student/Emeritus /Retired); $1,000 (Institutional); $88 (Cardiology Fellows); $125 (Clinical Care Associates).

Publications:
ABC Newsletter; monthly; adv.

Membership List Available to Non-members

Association of Black Foundation Executives (1971)
333 Seventh Ave.
14th Floor
New York, NY 10001
Tel: (646) 230-0306 *Fax:* (646) 230-0310
E-Mail: information@abfe.org
Website: abfe.org
Members: 200 individuals
Staff: 7
Annual Budget: $500-1,000,000
Tax: 501(c)(3)

Personnel:
President and Chief Executive Officer: Susan Taylor Batten
Coordinator, Professional Development: Lynne Algrant
Director, Membership Services and Development: Erika Davies
  E-Mail: edavies@abfe.org
Coordinator, Membership Services: Christine Nicholson
  E-Mail: cnicholson@abfe.org
Director, Administrative Services: Joshua Powers
Director, Programs: Marcus F. Walton
  E-Mail: mwalton@abfe.org

Historical Note:
ABFE's mission is to promote philanthropy in Black communities. Membership: $200 (Individual Voting); $100 (Associate).

Meetings/Conferences:
Conference Chair: Marcus F. Walton
Number of non-conference events/year: 3

Publications:
ABFE Newsletter; quarterly
Membership Directory; on-line

Association of Black Nursing Faculty (1987)
P.O. Box 580
Lisle, IL 60532
Tel: (630) 969-0221 *Fax:* (630) 969-3895
Website: abnf.net
Members: 175 individuals
Staff: 3
Annual Budget: $25-50,000

Personnel:
Founder: Dr. Sallie Tucker-Allen FAAN, RN
  E-Mail: drsallie@gmail.com
Treasurer: Dr. Bobbiejean Perdue

Historical Note:
Formerly known as Association of Black Nursing Faculty in Higher Education. ABNF seeks to form and maintain a group whereby black professional nurses with similar credentials, interests and concerns may work to promote certain health-related issues and educational interests

for the benefit of themselves and the black community. Members are Black registered nurses with an earned graduate degree in nursing. Membership: $100 (Individual); $25 (Student).

Meetings/Conferences: Annual

Publications:
ABNF Journal; quarterly; adv.
ABNF Newsletter; semi-annually

The Association of Black Psychologists (1968)
7119 Allentown Rd.
Suite 203
Ft. Washington, MD 20744
Tel: (202) 722-0808 Fax: (202) 722-5941
E-Mail: abpsi_office@abpsi.org
Website: abpsi.org
Members: 1500 individuals
Staff: 2
Annual Budget: $25-50,000
Tax: 501(c)(3)

Personnel:
Executive Director: Anisha N. Lewis
    E-Mail: alewis@abpsi.org
Office Manager: Alisa Jackson
    E-Mail: ajackson@abpsi.org

Historical Note:
Organized at San Francisco meeting of the American Psychological Association. ABPsi is an independent autonomous organization addressing the needs of black professionals and the mental health of the national black community by means of planning, programs, services, training and advocacy. Membership: $2500 (Life); $30-1500/year.

Continuing Education:
Certification Designation/s: CAC/BP

Meetings/Conferences: Annual
2013 - New Orleans, LA (Astor Crowne Plaza New Orleans)/July 23 - 27

Publications:
Current Directions in Psychological Science; bi-monthly
Membership Directory; on-line
Observer; monthly
Perspectives on Psychological Science; bi-monthly
Psych Discourse; monthly; adv.
Psychological Science
Psychological Science in the Public Interest
The Journal of Black Psychology (JBP); on-line; adv.
This Week in Psychological Science (TWiPS); weekly

Association of Black Sociologists (1970)
3473 S. Martin Luther King Dr.
Box #495
Chicago, IL 60616-4108
Tel: (312) 342-7618 Fax: (773) 955-8890
E-Mail: info@blacksociologists.org
Website: associationofblacksociologists.org
Members: 400 individuals
Staff: 2
Annual Budget: $100-250,000

Personnel:
Executive Officer: BarBara M. Scott
    E-Mail: bmscott@associationofblacksociologists.org
Treasurer: Wanda M. West
    E-Mail:
    wmwest@associationofblacksociologists.org

Historical Note:
Formerly (1977) Caucus of Black Sociologists. ABS's mission is to build a tradition of scholarship that will serve Black people in perpetuity. Membership: $75-115 (Full Member); $60-100 (Associate); $55 (Emeritus); $50 (Active Student); $1,000-2,500 (Life).

Membership List Available to Non-members

Association of Boarding Schools (1976)
One N. Pack Sq.
Suite 301
Asheville, NC 28801
Tel: (828) 258-5354 Fax: (828) 258-6428
E-Mail: tabs@tabs.org
Website: boardingschools.com
Members: 300 schools
Staff: 6
Annual Budget: $2-5,000,000
Tax: 501(c)(3)

Personnel:
Executive Director: Peter Upham

E-Mail: upham@schools.com
Director, Operations: Steve Banks
    E-Mail: banks@tabs.org
Executive Assistant and Manager, Member Relations: Jill Fletcher
    E-Mail: fletcher@tabs.org
Director, Marketing: Annie Lundahl
    E-Mail: lundahl@tabs.org
Director, Research and Strategic Resources: Richard Phelps
    E-Mail: phelps@TABS.org
Director, Professional Development: Liz Verhalen
    E-Mail: verhalen@tabs.org

Historical Note:
TABS is an independent, non-profit association that serves its member schools by improving public awareness of boarding schools, expanding the markets of students, and providing training for boarding school professionals. Membership: $1,494-3,768/year (based on the number of boarding students enrolled in the school on opening day of the school year during which the application is sent).

Meetings/Conferences: Annual
Number of non-conference events/year: 9

Publications:
E-Newsletter

Association of Boards of Certification (1972)
2805 SW Snyder Blvd.
Suite 535
Ankeny, IA 50023
Tel: (515) 232-3623 Fax: (515) 965-6827
E-Mail: abc@abccert.org
Website: abccert.org
Members: 94 agencies
Staff: 10
Annual Budget: $1-2,000,000
Tax: 501(c)(3)

Personnel:
Chief Executive Officer: Paul D. Bishop
    E-Mail: pbishop@abccert.org
Coordinator, Communications and Membership Services: Sheena Kennedy
    E-Mail: skennedy@abccert.org
Certification Program Administrator: Gavin Moore
    E-Mail: dloney@abccert.org
Director, Finance and Administration: William Morrison
    E-Mail: wmorrison@abccert.org

Historical Note:
Formerly (1982) Association of Boards of Certification for Operating Personnel in Water and Wastewater Utilities and (1986) Association of Boards of Certification for Operating Personnel. ABC's mission is to protect public health and the environment by advancing the quality and integrity of environmental certification programs. Members are government agencies certifying operating personnel and laboratory analysts concerned with water and pollution control. Membership: $250 (Associate); $300-1,800 (Regulatory/Voluntary).

Continuing Education:
Certification Designation/s: PMTC, LAC, OC, BLAC

Meetings/Conferences: Annual
2013 - San Diego, CA (San Diego Marriott Mission Valley)/Jan. 22 - 25

Publications:
The Certifier; on-line
The Directory; annually

Association of Bone and Joint Surgeons (1947)
6300 N. River Rd.
Suite 605
Rosemont, IL 60018-4237
Tel: (847) 720-4186 Fax: (847) 720-4013
E-Mail: abjs@abjs.org
Website: abjs.org
Members: 270 individuals
Staff: 8
Annual Budget: $2-5,000,000
Tax: 501(c)(3)

Personnel:
Executive Director: Colette Iocca Hohimer
    E-Mail: hohimer@abjs.org
Administrative Coordinator: Emily Clark
    E-Mail: clark@abjs.org

Historical Note:
ABJS's mission is to advance the science and practice of orthopedic surgery by creating, evaluating, and disseminating new knowledge and by facilitating interaction among all orthopaedic specialties.

Meetings/Conferences: Annual
2013 - Istanbul, Turkey/April 24 - 28

Publications:
Clinical Orthopaedics and Related Research; monthly

Association of Bridal Consultants (1955)
56 Danbury Rd.
Suite 11
New Milford, CT 06776
Tel: (860) 355-7000 Fax: (860) 354-1404
E-Mail: office@bridalassn.com
Website: bridalassn.com
Members: 4000 companies and individuals
Staff: 10
Annual Budget: $500-1,000,000

Personnel:
President: David M. Woods III
Director, Operations: Elayne Anderson
Director, Membership Records: Carol Carroll
    E-Mail: mob@bridalassn.com
Director, Marketing: Dena Davey
    E-Mail: corp@bridalassn.com
Director, Education: Elise Enloe
    E-Mail: eliseabcfl@aol.com

Historical Note:
ABC is a membership service organization, designed to increase awareness of the wedding business and improve the professionalism of members. Members are independent consultants as well as owners and employees of wedding related businesses. Membership: $185 (Novice); $265 (Consultant); $225 (Vendor); $170 (Auxiliary); $550 (Corporate).

Continuing Education:
Certification Designation/s: MBC, ABC, PBC

Meetings/Conferences: Annual
Conference Chair: Dena Davey
Number of non-conference events/year: 2

Publications:
ABC Dialogue; bi-monthly; adv.
Member Directory; on-line

Membership List Available to Non-members

Association of Business Owners of America
242 N. Yale Ave.
Arlington Heights, IL 60005
Tel: (224) 277-5961 Fax: (847) 398-4683
E-Mail: info@aoboa.net
Website: aoboa.net
Members: 7500 business owners
Staff: 5
Annual Budget: $250-500,000

Personnel:
President: Jim Wener
    E-Mail: j.wener@aoboa.net
Contact: Jeanne Barrett
    E-Mail: info@aoboa.net
Administrator: Dan Hostetler
Director, Membership: Susan Maxwell
    E-Mail: s.maxwell@aoboa.net
Manager, Research and Knowledge: Marc Spaulding PhD
    E-Mail: m.spaulding@aoboa.net

Historical Note:
AOBOA's goal is to discover and implement informative and protective initiatives that can be tangibly useful to its members, who are solely comprised of business owners. Membership: $50 (individual)

Continuing Education:
Enrollment: 800

Association of Cable Communicators (1985)
P.O. Box 75007
Washington, DC 20013-5007
Tel: (202) 222-2370 Fax: (202) 222-2371
TollFree: (800) 210-3396
E-Mail: services@cablecommunicators.org
Website: cablecommunicators.org
Members: 43 corporations
Staff: 3
Annual Budget: $250-500,000

Personnel:
Executive Director: Steven R. Jones
    E-Mail: sjones@cablecommunicators.org

Historical Note:
Formerly the Cable Television Public Affairs Association (CTPAA). Adopted its current name in 2007. ACC's mission is to develop and promote cable communications excellence through professional development to help

achieve industry and corporate goals. Members are communications and public affairs professionals within the cable industry. Membership: $200 (Individual); $5,000-15,000 (Corporate).

Publications:
CPR Facts; bi-weekly
Membershhip Directory; on-line
SmartBrief; daily

Association of Camp Nurses *(1980)*

8630 Thorsonveien NE
Bemidji, MN 56601
Tel: (218) 586-2633
E-Mail: acn@campnurse.org
Website: acn.org
Members: 1000 Members
Staff: 3
Annual Budget: $25-50,000
Tax: 501(c)(6)

Personnel:
Executive Director: Linda Ebner Erceg MS, PHN, RN
    E-Mail: erceg@campnurse.org

Historical Note:
ACN is a professional nursing organization established to work towards healthier camp communities through camp nursing practice. Membership: $55/year (Individual).

Meetings/Conferences: Annual
2013 - Dallas, TX (Hyatt Regency Dallas)/Feb. 11 - 13
Number of non-conference events/year: 1

Publications:
CompassPoint; quarterly; adv.

Association of Career and Technical Education *(1926)*

P.O. Box 758621
Baltimore, MD 21275-8621
Tel: (703) 683-3111 *Fax:* (703) 683-7424
TollFree: (800) 826-9972
E-Mail: acte@acteonline.org
Website: acteonline.org
Members: 28000 individuals
Staff: 30
Annual Budget: $25-50,000

Personnel:
Executive Director: Janet Bray
    E-Mail: jbray@acteonline.org
Associate, Membership Services: Stephani Anderson
    E-Mail: sanderson@acteonline.org
Manager, Database and Information Technology: Julia Bankerd
    E-Mail: jbankerd@acteonline.org
Education Research Analyst: Jason Kiker
    E-Mail: jkiker@acteonline.org
Manager, Meetings: Marguerite Leishman
    E-Mail: mleishman@acteonline.org
Senior Director, Strategic Partnerships: Peter Magnuson
    E-Mail: pmagnuson@acteonline.org
Manager, Media Relations: Ashley Parker
    E-Mail: aparker@acteonline.org
Manager, Sponsorship and Exhibit Sales: Jim Waterhouse
    E-Mail: jwaterhouse@acteonline.org
Chief Financial and Operations Officer: LeAnn Wilson
    E-Mail: lwilson@acteonline.org

Historical Note:
Mission is to provide leadership in developing a competitive workforce. Membership: $1200 (Associate); $500 (National Affiliate Organization); $60 (International); $80 (Professional); $31 (Retired); $0 (National ACTE Student).

Continuing Education:
Certification Designation/s: NTC

Meetings/Conferences: Annual
Conference Chair: Jim Waterhouse
2013 - Las Vegas, NV/Dec. 5 - 7
2014 - Nashville, TN/Nov. 20 - 22
Number of non-conference events/year: 2

Publications:
ACTE News; monthly
Career Tech Update; daily; adv.
Legislative Alerts; on-line
Legislative Updates; on-line
Techniques; adv.

The Association of Career Firms North America *(1982)*

8509 Crown Crescent Ct.
Suite ACF
Charlotte, NC 28227
Tel: (704) 849-2500 *Fax:* (704) 845-2420
Website: acf-northamerica.com
Members: 75 firms
Staff: 6
Annual Budget: $50-100,000

Personnel:
President: Bill Crigger
    E-Mail: Bcrigger@oipartners.net

Historical Note:
Formerly Association of Career Firms International. The Association of Career Firms North America (ACF-North America) was founded to bring together and represent the interests of the North American outplacement and career transition industry. Mission is to Monitor, gather and disseminate information relevant to the industry. Membership: $150 (For Headquarters); $75 (For Each Branch Office).

Publications:
ACF North America Newsletter

Association of Career Professionals International *(1989)*

204 East St. NE
Washington, DC 20002
Tel: (202) 547-6377 *Fax:* (202) 547-6348
E-Mail: info@acpinternational.org
Website: acpinternational.org
Members: 1250 individuals
Staff: 1
Annual Budget: $25-50,000

Personnel:
Executive Director: Annette Summers

Historical Note:
Formerly International Association of Outplacement Professionals (IAOP) and then became International Association of Career Management Professionals (IACMP) in 1994, before assuming the current name. ACPI is dedicated to advancing public awareness of the career management profession, as well as in promoting the international profile and credibility of its varied membership. Membership: $120 (International); $40 (Student); $230 (New England Professional); $170 (Dual Membership).

Association of Catholic Colleges and Universities *(1899)*

One Dupont Cir. NW
Suite 650
Washington, DC 20036
Tel: (202) 457-0650 *Fax:* (202) 728-0977
E-Mail: accu@accunet.org
Website: accunet.org
Members: 194 U.S. members and 19 international member institutions
Staff: 5
Annual Budget: $1-2,000,000
Tax: 501(c)(3)

Personnel:
President and Chief Executive Officer: Michael Galligan-Stierle PhD
    E-Mail: mgs@accunet.org
Coordinator, Membership and Conferences: Andy Costigan
    E-Mail: acostigan@accunet.org
Director, Operations: Kathleen Laddbush
    E-Mail: kladdbush@accunet.org
Director, Communications: Paula Moore
    E-Mail: pmoore@accunet.org

Historical Note:
ACCU works to promote and strengthen the mission and character of Catholic higher education in the United States. Encourages and facilitates sharing of ideas and cooperative efforts among its member institutions. Through research, publications, conferences, consultations, special programs, and standing relationships with other agencies. Membership dues are calculated on the basis of FTE (full-time equivalent) enrollment information.

Continuing Education:
Certification Designation/s: CEC

Meetings/Conferences: Annual
Conference Chair: Andy Costigan
2013 - Washington, DC (Ritz-Carlton Hotel Company, L.L.C.)/Feb. 2 - 4
Number of non-conference events/year: 1

Publications:
Journal of Catholic Higher Education; semi-annually
Update; quarterly

Membership List Available to Non-members

Association of Catholic Diocesan Archivists *(1979)*

114 Broad St., Rear Building
P.O. Box 818
Charleston, SC 29402
Tel: (843) 724-8372
Website: diocesanarchivists.org
Members: 300 individuals
Staff: 3
Annual Budget: $10-25,000

Personnel:
Treasurer: Brian Fahey
    E-Mail: bfahey@catholic-doc.org
Officer, Education: Ann Boltin
    E-Mail: aboltin@diobr.org
Editor: Peggy Lavelle
    E-Mail: mlavelle@archchicago.org

Historical Note:
ACDA strives to promote a regular system of education and training programs including both basic archival training for newly appointed archivists, and continuing education for those who are further advanced in the field. Members are individuals responsible for the preservation of diocesan records and historical materials. Membership: $25/year (Individual).

Meetings/Conferences: Biennial

Publications:
ACDA Newsletter
Membership Directory; annually

Association of Catholic Publishers *(1987)*

4725 Dorsey Hall Dr., Suite A
P.O.Box 709
Ellicott City, MD 21042
Tel: (410) 988-2926 *Fax:* (410) 571-4946
Website: cbpa.org
Members: 100 publishers and services and indivdual members
Staff: 2
Annual Budget: $100-250,000

Personnel:
Executive Director: Therese Brown
    E-Mail: tbrown@catholicpublishers.org
Event Manager: Andrea Massengile
    E-Mail: amassengile@catholicpublishers.org

Historical Note:
Formerly Catholic Book Publishers Association. ACP's mission is to support a viable, vibrant, and diverse Catholic publishing environment in and outside the US. Membership: $3000-5000(Voting Member); $1500-2500 (Full Member); $5000 (Associate); $100 (Individual).

Meetings/Conferences:
Conference Chair: Andrea Massengile

Publications:
Membership Directory; on-line
Newsletter; monthly

Association of Celebrity Personal Assistants *(1992)*

914 Westwood Blvd.
Suite 507
Los Angeles, CA 90024
Tel: (310) 281-7775
Website: acpa-la.com
Members: 150 individuals
Staff: 11
Annual Budget: $25-50,000

Personnel:
President: Drei Donnelly
    E-Mail: jobbank@celebrityassistants.org
Coordinator, Meeting: Fernando Cubillas
Contact, Membership Services: Trish Jurmain
Treasurer: Kelly Wade
Coordinator, Website: J. McGill winston "jw"

Historical Note:
A non-profit, membership-based organization representing personal assistants to celebrities and other notables. Membership: $150 (Resident); $75 (Non-Resident).

Meetings/Conferences:
Conference Chair: Fernando Cubillas

Publications:
E! News; on-line
Membership Directory; on-line
The Best of the Best; on-line

Association of Certified Fraud Examiners *(1988)*

The Gregor Building
716 West Ave.
Austin, TX 78701-2727
Tel: (512) 478-9000 *Fax:* (512) 478-9297
TollFree: (800) 245-3321
E-Mail: memberservices@ACFE.com
Website: acfe.com
Members: 65000 individuals
Staff: 50
Annual Budget: $50-100,000

Personnel:
President and Chief Executive Officer: James D. Ratley
CFE, CPA
Editor: Dick Carozza CFE
Controller: Marianne Fatter CFA, CPA
Vice President, Education: John D. Gill CFE, JD
Vice President, Administration: Jeanette LeVie
Manager, Conferences: Dianne Liston CMP, CFE
Research Director: Andi McNeal CFE, CPA
    E-Mail: amcneal@acfe.com
Director, Membership: Ross Pry CFE
Manager, Information Technology: Stephen Sebesta
Director, Events: Leslie Simpson CFE
    E-Mail: lsimpson@acfe.com
Director, Marketing and Business Development: Kevin
Taparauskas
    E-Mail: events@acfe.com
Vice President and General Counsel: John Warren CFE,
JD
Manager, Human Resources: LaDonna Wernli PHR, CFE,
SPHR
    E-Mail: hr@acfe.com

Historical Note:
*ACFE's mission is to reduce the incidence of fraud and
white-collar crime and to assist the membership in fraud
detection and deterrence. Membership: $25/year (Student
Associate).*

Continuing Education:
Certification Designation/s: CFE

Meetings/Conferences:
Conference Chair: Leslie Simpson CFE
2013 - Prague, Czech Republic (Prague Marriott)/
March 17 - 19
2013 - Las Vegas, NV (ARIA Resort and Casino Hotel)/
June 23 - 28
Number of non-conference events/year: 4

Publications:
ACFE Insights
Fraud Magazine; bi-monthly
FraudInfo; bi-weekly
Report to the Nations; bi-annually

Association of Chartered Accountants in the United States *(1980)*
3887 Punahele Rd.
Princeville, HI 96722
Tel: (508) 395-0224
E-Mail: admin@acaus.org
Website: acaus.org
Members: 6700 chartered accountants
Staff: 2
Annual Budget: $50-100,000

Personnel:
Executive Director: Michael J. Dexter-Smith
    E-Mail: executivedirector@acaus.org
Treasurer: Timothy Clackett ACA, CPA

Historical Note:
*ACAUS's mission is to facilitate the professional success
of its members and to promote the business community's
recognition of, and respect for the qualifications of the
"Chartered Accountant" ("CA") designation. Membership:
$95/year (Individual).*

Publications:
Membership Directory; on-line

Association of Children's Museums *(1962)*
2711 Jefferson Davis Hwy.
Suite 600
Arlington, VA 22202
Tel: (703) 224-3100 *Fax:* (703) 224-3099
E-Mail: acm@childrensmuseums.org
Website: childrensmuseums.org
Members: 500 museums and individuals
Staff: 11
Annual Budget: $500-1,000,000
Tax: 501(c)(3)

Personnel:
Executive Director: Janet Rice Elman
    E-Mail: janet.elman@childrensmuseums.org
Program Manager, Events: Sharon Chiat
    E-Mail: Sharon.Chiat@ChildrensMuseums.org
Program Officer, Membership Services: Victoria Garvin
    E-Mail: Victoria.Garvin@ChildrensMuseums.org
Director, Communication: Diane Kopasz
    E-Mail: diane.kopasz@childrensmuseums.org
Editor: Mary Maher
    E-Mail: mmaher2049@aol.com
Association Coordinator: Laura Thornton
Program Officer, Education: Korie Twiggs
    E-Mail: korie.twiggs@childrensmuseums.org
Director, Finance and Administration: Stephanie Yang
    E-Mail: Stephanie.Yang@ChildrensMuseums.org

Historical Note:
*Formerly (1967) Association of Youth Museum Directors,
(1988) American Association of Youth Museums; and
(2001) Association of Youth Museums. ACM strives to
enhance the capacity and further the vision of children's
museums in order to make them places for children and
families where play leads to lifelong learning. Membership
composed of museums with hands-on exhibits and
programs targeted toward the educational needs of children.
Membership: $330- 2,200 (Museum, based on annual
budget); $500-1,100 (Corporate); $45-500 (Individual);
$330 (Academic / Research Institution Benefits); $500
(Nonprofit Affiliate Members).*

Meetings/Conferences: Annual
Conference Chair: Sharon Chiat
2013 - Pittsburgh, PA/April 30 - May 2

Publications:
E-Forum; monthly; adv.
Membership Directory; on-line

Association of Children's Prosthetic-Orthotic Clinics *(1978)*
6300 N. River Rd.
Suite 727
Rosemont, IL 60018-4226
Tel: (847) 698-1637 *Fax:* (847) 823-0536
E-Mail: acpoc@aaos.org
Website: acpoc.org
Members: 475 members
Staff: 3
Annual Budget: $100-250,000
Tax: 501(c)(3)

Personnel:
Society Manager: Melody Raymond
    E-Mail: raymond@aaos.org

Historical Note:
*ACPOC works to raise the standard of prosthetic
care for children in the United States by evaluating
experimental components, disseminating information and
establishing criteria for clinics. Members are physicians.
Membership: $175 (Physician); $100 (Non-Physicians);
$60 (Corresponding).*

Meetings/Conferences: Annual
Conference Chair: Melody Raymond
2013 - Atlanta, GA (Grand Hyatt Atlanta In Buckhead)/
April 10 - 13

Publications:
ACPOC News; quarterly
Annual Meeting Abstracts; annually

Association of Chiropractic Colleges *(1977)*
4424 Montgomery Ave.
Suite 202
Bethesda, MD 20814
Tel: (800) 284-1062 *Fax:* (301) 913-9146
TollFree: (800) 284-1062
E-Mail: info@chirocolleges.org
Website: chirocolleges.org
Members: 20 institutions
Staff: 3
Annual Budget: $250-500,000

Personnel:
Executive Director: David S. O'Bryon CAE
    E-Mail: obyronco@aol.com
Editor: Bart Green
    E-Mail: JChiroEd@aol.com

Historical Note:
*Formerly (1985) Association of Chiropractic College
Presidents. Represents accredited chiropractic colleges in
North America and seeks to advance chiropractic education,
research and service. Members are presidents of chiropractic
colleges.*

Meetings/Conferences: Annual
2013 - Washington, DC/March 14 - 16
2014 - Washington, DC/March 14 - 16

Association of Christian Librarians *(1957)*
P.O. Box Four
Cedarville, OH 45314
Tel: (937) 766-2255 *Fax:* (937) 766-5499
E-Mail: info@acl.org
Website: acl.org
Members: 500 individuals
Staff: 4
Annual Budget: $100-250,000
Tax: 501(c)(3)

Personnel:
Executive Director: Janelle Mazelin
Office Manager: Racha Gruet
Manager, Conferences and Business Manager: April
VanPutten

Historical Note:
*Formerly (1981) Christian Librarians Fellowship. ACL's
mission is to strengthen libraries through professional
development of evangelical librarians, scholarship, and
spiritual encouragement for service in higher education.
Members are primarily evangelical Christian academic
librarians, as well as other interested librarians and
individuals who subscribe to the purposes and position of
the association. Membership: $25-90/year.*

Meetings/Conferences: Annual
Conference Chair: April VanPutten
2013 - San Diego, CA (Point Loma Nazarene
University)/June 10 - 13
Number of non-conference events/year: 1

Publications:
Christian Periodical Index; semi-annually; adv.
Membership Directory; on-line
The Christian Librarian

Association of Christian Schools International *(1978)*
P.O. Box 65130
Colorado Springs, CO 80962-5130
Tel: (719) 528-6906 *Fax:* (719) 531-0631
TollFree: (800) 367-5391
E-Mail: info@acsi.org
Website: acsi.org
Members: 24,000 schools
Staff: 150
Annual Budget: $25-50,000,000
Tax: 501(c)(3)

Personnel:
President: Brian S. Simmons
Vice President, Academic Affairs: Derek Keenan EdD
    E-Mail: derek_keenan@acsi.org
Vice President, Operations: Thomas A. Scott
    E-Mail: tom_scott@acsi.org

Historical Note:
*Formed by the merger of the Western Association of
Christian Schools, the Ohio Association of Christian
Schools and the National Christian School Education
Association. Mission is to enable Christian educators
and schools worldwide to effectively prepare students
for life. Members are privately funded schools with a
religious orientation that work to prepare students for life.
Membership: $440-1025 (Student); $75 (Administrators
and Board Members).*

Continuing Education:
Enrollment: 50000
Certification Designation/s: EEC, K-12C

Publications:
Christian Early Education; quarterly
Christian School Comment; monthly
Christian School Education; quarterly
Legal Legislative Update
Math by Design; quarterly
Membership Directory; on-line
National Notes
Prayer Guide; monthly
The Meantime; quarterly
World Report

Association of Christian Teachers and Schools *(1993)*
P.O. Box 8437
Rockford, IL 61126
Tel: (815) 239-6673 *Fax:* (815) 977-5806
E-Mail: actsschools@gmail.com
Website: actsschools.org

Staff: 1
Annual Budget: $100-250,000

Personnel:
Executive Director: Dr. R. Jay Nelson

Historical Note:
ACTS's mission is to assist the Christian schools to realize the highest level of educational credibility.

Publications:
Membership Directory; on-line

Association of Christian Therapists *(1975)*
6728 Old McLean Village Dr.
McLean, VA 22101
Tel: (703) 556-9222 *Fax:* (703) 556-8729
E-Mail: ACTheals@degnon.org
Website: actheals.org
Members: 1000 individuals
Staff: 1
Annual Budget: $100-250,000

Personnel:
President: Cheryl Marsh
    E-Mail: marshcdt68@comcast.net

Historical Note:
ACT mission is to support ACT members with resources to achieve this vision, including healing prayer, mentoring, education and training, fostering their spiritual and professional growth. Members are Physicians and Dentists (including chiropractors), Nurses, Allied Health (including physician's assistants, physical therapists, medical technicians, body work practitioners, nutritionists. Membership: $54-$104(Professional or Associate depending on the month of joining); $84-$164(Couple depending on the month of joining); $29-$54 (Student/ Non-salaried Clergy or Religious).

Meetings/Conferences: Annual

Publications:
InterACT; bi-monthly
Membership Directory; annually
The Journal of Christian Healing

Association of Cinema and Video Laboratories *(1953)*
1144 N. Las Palmas Ave.
Hollywood, CA 90038
Tel: (323) 308-3055 *Fax:* (323) 962-0321
Website: acvl.org
Members: 61 laboratories
Staff: 3
Annual Budget: $25-50,000

Personnel:
President: Kevin Dillon
    E-Mail: kevin@efilm.com

Historical Note:
Formerly Association of Cinema Laboratories. ACVL's mission is to provide an opportunity for the discussion and exchange of ideas in connection with the technical, administrative and managerial problems of the motion-picture and video laboratory. Members are motion picture film laboratories and associates with allied interests. Membership: $250/year.

Meetings/Conferences: Annual

Association of Civilian Technicians *(1960)*
12620 Lake Ridge Dr.
Lake Ridge, VA 22192
Tel: (703) 494-4845 *Fax:* (703) 494-0961
Website: actnat.com
Members: 23500 combinations
Staff: 13
Annual Budget: $1-2,000,000

Personnel:
President: Terry W. Garnett

Historical Note:
ACT's purpose is to provide training and understanding of labor practice charges and to promote legislation designed to meet the needs of its membership. Membership: 0.007% of base pay/bi- weekly; $150 (Lifetime); $30 (Retired).

Publications:
Membership Directory; on-line
The Technician; monthly

Membership List Available to Non-members

Association of Clean Water Administrators *(1961)*
1221 Connecticut Ave. NW
Second Floor
Washington, DC 20036

Tel: (202) 756-0600 *Fax:* (202) 756-0605
E-Mail: admin1@asiwpca.org
Website: acwa-us.org
Members: 56 state government and interstate organizations
Staff: 5
Annual Budget: $500-1,000,000

Personnel:
Executive Director and General Counsel: Alexandra Dunn Esq.
Director, Operations: Annette Ivey
    E-Mail: a.ivey@asiwpca.org
Deputy Director: Sean Rolland
    E-Mail: s.rolland@asiwpca.org

Historical Note:
Formerly Association of State and Interstate Water Pollution Control Administrators. ACWA strives to protect and restore watersheds to achieve clean water everywhere for everyone. It facilitates interaction of State and interstate water quality agencies with Federal agencies, Congress, and the Administration. Association members are the State, Interstate and Territorial officials who are responsible for the implementation of surface water protection programs throughout the nation. Membership: $2,000 (Legal Subscribers); $3,000 (Affiliates).

Meetings/Conferences: Annual
Conference Chair: Annette Ivey
2013 - Ft. Washington, MD (Westin Washington National Harbor)/March 3 - 5

Publications:
Membership Directory; on-line
The Weekly Wrap; weekly

Association of Clinical Research Organizations *(2002)*
915 15th St. NW
Second Floor
Washington, DC 20005
Tel: (202) 464-9340
E-Mail: info@acrohealth.org
Website: acrohealth.org
Staff: 5
Annual Budget: $1-2,000,000
Tax: 501(c)(6)

Personnel:
Executive Director: Douglas Peddicord
Vice President, Public Affairs: John J. Lewis
Government Relations Counsel: Kyle Peddicord

Historical Note:
ACRO is the professional association of companies that include clinical research as a major part of their business. ACRO members provide specialized services that are integral to the development of drugs, biologics and medical devices. ACRO advances clinical outsourcing to improve the quality, efficiency and safety of biomedical research. Membership: $1,20,000 (Regular); $30,000 (Associate); $10,000 (Affiliate).

Association of Clinical Research Professionals *(1976)*
500 Montgomery St.
Suite 800
Arlington, VA 22314
Tel: (703) 254-8100 *Fax:* (703) 254-8101
E-Mail: office@acrpnet.org
Website: acrpnet.org
Members: 18000 individuals
Staff: 37
Annual Budget: $5-10,000,000
Tax: 501(c)(3)

Personnel:
Executive Director: James D. Thomasell CPA
National Sales Manager: Kim Kelemen
    E-Mail: kkelemen@townsend-group.com

Historical Note:
Founded as Associates of Clinical Pharmacology, assumed its current name in 1997. ACRP's mission is to provide global leadership to advocate integrity and excellence for the clinical research profession. Membership: $150 (Individual); $60 (Student); $100 (Resident).

Continuing Education:
Certification Designation/s: CCRA, CPI, CRC, CRA, CTI

Meetings/Conferences: Annual
2013 - Orlando, FL/April 12 - 16
2013 - Orlando, FL (Orange County Convention Center)/April 13 - 16/2000 attendees

Publications:
ACRP Wire; bi-weekly

Membership Directory; on-line
The Monitor; bi-monthly; adv.

Membership List Available to Non-members

Association of Clinical Scientists *(1949)*
6431 Fannin, MSB2.292
Houston, TX 77030
Tel: (713) 234-6387 *Fax:* (713) 500-0732
E-Mail: clinsci@sover.net
Website: clinicalscience.org
Members: 380 individuals
Staff: 3
Annual Budget: $100-250,000
Tax: 501(c)(3)

Personnel:
President: Magali J. Fontaine MD, PhD
Treasurer: Roger L Bertholf PhD
Editor-in-chief: Nina MD, PhD Tatevian MD, PhD

Historical Note:
Assumed the name Association of Clinical Scientists in 1956. ACS provides a forum for physicians, researchers and clinical scientists to interact in a professional and collegial atmosphere dedicated to the advancement of research and learning in laboratory science. Membership: $180/year (Individual).

Meetings/Conferences: Annual
2013 - Boston, MA (Omni Parker House Hotel)/May 22 - 25
Number of non-conference events/year: 2

Publications:
Annals of Clinical and Laboratory Science; quarterly
Newsletter (Clinical Science Trumpet); quarterly

Association of College Administration Professionals *(1995)*
P.O. Box 1389
Staunton, VA 24402
Tel: (540) 885-1873 *Fax:* (540) 885-6133
E-Mail: acap@cfw.com
Website: acap.webstarts.com
Members: 3000 individuals and 300 institutions
Staff: 1
Annual Budget: $50-100,000
Tax: 501(c)(6)

Personnel:
President: Stan Clark
    E-Mail: acap@cfw.com

Historical Note:
ACAP members are administrators in the business, student and academic services areas of colleges and universities. Membership: $85 (Individual); $195 (Institution).

Publications:
ACAP Newsletter; monthly

Association of College and Research Libraries *(1938)*
50 E. Huron St.
Chicago, IL 60611-2795
Tel: (312) 280-2523 *Fax:* (312) 280-2520
TollFree: (800) 545-2433
E-Mail: acrl@ala.org
Website: ala.org/acrl
Members:
877 libraries
13000 individuals
Staff: 14
Annual Budget: $2-5,000,000

Personnel:
Executive Director: Mary Ellen K. Davis
    E-Mail: mdavis@ala.org
Manager, Professional Development: Margot Sutton Conahan
    E-Mail: mconahan@ala.org
Editor-in-Chief and specialist, Marketing and Communications: David Free
    E-Mail: dfree@ala.org
Senior Strategist, Special Initiatives: Kara Malenfant
    E-Mail: kmalenfant@ala.org
Senior Production Editor: Dawn Mueller
    E-Mail: dmueller@ala.org
Conference Supervisor: Tory Ondrla
    E-Mail: tondrla@ala.org
Associate Director: Mary Jane Petrowski
    E-Mail: mpetrowski@ala.org

Historical Note:

Formerly Association of College and Reference Libraries. A division of the American Library Association represents academic and research librarians and libraries. This includes all types of academic libraries, community, junior college, and university as well as comprehensive and specialized research libraries and their professional staffs. Individuals must belong to ALA in order to join ACRL. Membership: $36-186/year.

Meetings/Conferences: Biennial
Conference Chair: Margot Sutton Conahan
2013 - Indianapolis, IN (J.W.Marriott)/April 10 - 13/3000 attendees/11-25 exhibitors
2015 - Portland, OR/March 25 - 28
2017 - Nashville, TN/March 29 - April 1
Number of non-conference events/year: 4

Publications:
College & Research Libraries; bi-monthly
College & Research Libraries News; monthly

Association of College and University Auditors
(1958)
P.O. Box 14306
Lenexa, KS 66285-4306
Tel: (913) 895-4620 Fax: (913) 895-4652
E-Mail: ACUA-info@goAMP.com
Website: acua.org
Members: 500 institutions
Staff: 4
Annual Budget: $500-1,000,000

Personnel:
Executive Director: Karen R. Hinen CAE, IOM, CMP
President: Toni Messer Stephens
    E-Mail: tmesser@utdallas.edu
Secretary/Treasurer: Tom Dwyer
    E-Mail: gtdwyer@syr.edu
Coordinator, Events: Carol Ewing CMP
    E-Mail: cewing@acu.org

Historical Note:
ACUA's mission is to improve the internal operations and processes of the individual institutions. Members are educational institutions with their own auditing staffs. Individual membership is a restricted category. Membership: $375-$575 (Institution); $150 (Individual).

Meetings/Conferences: Annual
Conference Chair: Carol Ewing CMP
2013 - Norfolk, VA (Norfolk Waterside Marriott)/Sept. 22 - 26

Publications:
College and University Auditor
Membership Directory; on-line

Membership List Available to Non-members

Association of College and University Clubs
(1978)
1733 King St.
Alexandria, VA 22314
Tel: (703) 299-2630 Fax: (703) 739-0124
E-Mail: acuc@acuclubs.org
Website: acuclubs.org
Staff: 2
Annual Budget: $25-50,000

Personnel:
Managing Director: Erin Herzog Bisceglia
    E-Mail: acuc@acuclubs.org
Director, Membership Services: Marisu Jimenez CCM
    E-Mail: marisu.jimenez@caltech.edu

Historical Note:
Founded as Association of Faculty Clubs International; assumed its current name in 2002. Membership: $300 (Club); $400 (Company).

Publications:
The Globe Newsletter; on-line

Association of College and University Housing Officers-International (1951)
941 Chatham Ln.
Suite 318
Columbus, OH 43221-2416
Tel: (614) 292-0099 Fax: (614) 292-3205
E-Mail: office@acuho-i.org
Website: acuho-i.org
Members: 900 colleges and universities, 6400 individuals
Staff: 16
Annual Budget: $2-5,000,000

Personnel:
Executive Director: Sallie Traxler

Director, Communications and Marketing: James Baumann
Director, Development and Corporate Relations: Alison Jones
    E-Mail: alison@acuho-i.org
Manager, Meetings and Events: Lisa Martin
    E-Mail: lisa@acuho-i.org
Director, Finance and Administration: Sheila Meyer
    E-Mail: sheila@acuho-i.org
Public Relations and Marketing Manager: Olivea Oldham
    E-Mail: olivea@acuho-i.org
Managing Editor: Camille Perlman
Coordinator, Volunteer and Membership Services: Laura Pietrykowski
    E-Mail: laura@acuho-i.org
Manager, Education: Lori Sobota
    E-Mail: lori@acuho-i.org

Historical Note:
Organized at the University of California, Berkeley, as a direct outgrowth of the first National Campus Housing Conference held in 1949 at the University of Illinois, added International to its name in 1981. ACUHO-I members believe in developing exceptional residential experiences at colleges, universities, and other post-secondary institutions around the world. Membership: $677 (Corporate Member); $50 (Faculty Affiliate Member, U.S.); $40 (Faculty Affiliate Member, Non U.S.); $155 (Associate Affiliate Member, U.S.); $115 (Associate Affiliate Member, Non U.S.); $45(Emeritus/Student Affiliate Member, U.S.); $33 (Emeritus/Student Affiliate Member, Non U.S.);$248-1,526 (Institutional, U.S.); $198-1,221 (Institutional, Non U.S.).

Meetings/Conferences: Annual
Conference Chair: Lisa Martin
2013 - Minneapolis, MN/June 15 - 18
2014 - Washington, DC/June 28 - July 1
2015 - Orlando, FL/June 27 - 30
2016 - Seatle, WA/July 9 - 12

Publications:
Acuho-i Newsletter; quarterly
Membership Directory; on-line
The Journal of College and University Student Housing; on-line

Association of College and University Printers
(1964)
P.O. Box 285
Carrabelle, FL 32322
Tel: (850) 570-5241
E-Mail: iburxl@asu.edu
Website: acup-edu.org
Members: 140 individuals
Staff: 2
Annual Budget: $10-25,000

Personnel:
President: Lisa Hoover
    E-Mail: LHoover@bucknell.edu
Director, Administrative Services: Jennifer Bowers
    E-Mail: Jennifer.Bowers@acup-edu.org

Historical Note:
ACUP's mission is to promote communication, training and educational opportunities within the Higher Education in-plant printing and mailing industry. Membership: $250 (Individual); $600-800 (Institutional).

Meetings/Conferences: Annual
2013 - Minneapolis, MN (Radisson Plaza Hotel Minneapolis)/May 19 - 23/100 attendees

Publications:
Membership Directory; on-line

Association of College and University Religious Affairs (1959)
Center for Religious and Spiritual Life
1600 Grand Ave.
St. Paul, MN 55105
Tel: (651) 696-6293 Fax: (651) 696-6580
E-Mail: acuraonline@acuraonline.org
Website: site.acuraonline.net
Members: 95 individuals
Staff: 2
Annual Budget: Under $10,000

Personnel:
President: Lucy Forster-Smith
    E-Mail: forstersmith@macalester.edu

Historical Note:
Formerly (1991) Association for the Coordination of University Religious Affairs. An organization of personnel involved in religious affairs at institutions of higher

education. Members include college and university chaplains, deans of religious life, and directors and coordinators of religious affairs. Membership: $50 (Individual); $100 (Institution).

Meetings/Conferences: Annual

Publications:
Dialogue-Newsletter
Member Directory; on-line

Association of College Honor Societies (1925)
4990 Northwind Dr.
Suite 140
East Lansing, MI 48823-5031
Tel: (517) 351-8335 Fax: (517) 351-8336
Website: achsnatl.org
Members: 67 societies
Staff: 1
Annual Budget: $10-25,000
Tax: 501(c)(3)

Personnel:
Executive Director: Dorothy I. Mitstifer
    E-Mail: dmitstifer@achsnatl.org

Historical Note:
ACHS seeks to build a visibly cohesive community of national and international honor societies, individually and collaboratively exhibiting excellence in scholarship, service, programs, and governance. A certifying agency for college and university honor societies, it helps in chartering chapters in accredited colleges and universities.

Meetings/Conferences: Annual
2013 - Arlington, VA (Hyatt Regency Crystal City at Reagan National Airport)/Feb. 14 - 17

Publications:
Membership Directory; annually
Psi Beta

Association of College Unions International
(1914)
One City Center, 120 W. Seventh St.
Suite 200
Bloomington, IN 47404-3925
Tel: (815) 245-2284 Fax: (812) 245-6710
E-Mail: acui@acui.org
Website: acui.org
Members: 3613 individuals and 669 institutions
Staff: 25
Annual Budget: $2-5,000,000

Personnel:
Executive Director: Marsha Herman-Betzen
    E-Mail: mherman@acui.org
Programmer, Information Technology: Erick Adienge
    E-Mail: eadienge@acui.org
Director, Educational Programs and Resources: Elizabeth Beltramini
    E-Mail: ebeltram@acui.org
Director, Membership Services and Sales: Jason Cline
    E-Mail: jascline@acui.org
Manager, Financial Services: Karen Keith
    E-Mail: kjkeith@acui.org
Director, Meetings: Michelle Smith
    E-Mail: mjsmith1@acui.org
Associate Editor: Elizabeth Stringer
    E-Mail: elstring@acui.org

Historical Note:
Formerly Association of College Unions, assumed its present name in 1961. ACUI is a professional association dedicated to enhancing campus life through programs, services, and facilities with the goal of unifying the union and activities field. Members are college union and student activities professionals from hundreds of schools in seven countries. Membership: $55-299 (Individual); $55-110 (Retiree); $75 (Associate).

Meetings/Conferences: Annual
Conference Chair: Michelle Smith
2013 - St. Louis, MO (St. Louis Renaissance Grand Hotel & Convention Center)/March 10 - 14
2014 - Orlando, FL/April 5 - 10
2015 - San Antonio, TX/April 8 - 12
2016 - New Orleans, LA/March 20 - 24
2017 - Philadelphia, PA/March 19 - 23
2018 - Reno, NV/March 19 - 23
2019 - Indianapolis, IN/March 24 - 29
2020 - Atlanta, GA/March 15 - 19

Publications:
Associate Member Directory; on-line
Member Directory; on-line
The Bulletin; bi-monthly; adv.

Membership List Available to Non-members

Association of Collegiate Business Schools and Programs (1988)

11520 W. 119th St.
Overland Park, KS 66213-1524
Tel: (913) 339-9356 *Fax:* (913) 339-6226
E-Mail: info@acbsp.org
Website: acbsp.org
Members:
587 institutions
6300 individuals
Staff: 8
Annual Budget: $1-2,000,000

Personnel:
Executive Director: Doug Viehland
　　E-Mail: dviehland@acbsp.org
Manager, Communications: Melinda Dorning
　　E-Mail: mdorning@acbsp.org
Manager, Conferences and Meetings: Candace Jackson
　　E-Mail: cjackson@acbsp.org
Manager, Member Services: Eliza Guyol Meinrath
Director, Accreditation: Steve Parscale
　　E-Mail: sparscale@acbsp.org
Contact, Regional Meetings: Giles Rafol
　　E-Mail: grafol@acbsp.org

Historical Note:
Accrediting organization for business schools and programs in colleges and universities, ACBSP develops, promotes, and recognizes practices that contribute to continuous improvement of business education and accredits qualified business programs. Membership: $1250/year (Institution).

Meetings/Conferences:
Conference Chair: Candace Jackson
2013 - Salt Lake City, UT (Salt Lake Marriott Downtown at City Creek)/June 21 - 24
2013 - Brussels, Belgium (Marriott Brussels)/Nov. 29 - Dec. 1
2014 - Chicago, IL (Chicago Marriott Downtown Magnificent Mile)/June 27 - 30
2014 - Athens, Greece (Electra Palace Hotel Athens)/ Nov. 27 - 30
2015 - Philadelphia, PA (Philadelphia Marriott Downtown)/June 12 - 15
2015 - Barcelona, Spain/Nov. 25 - 29

Publications:
ACBSP Update; quarterly
Business Education Week; weekly

The Association of Collegiate Conference and Events Directors International (1980)

419 Canyon Ave.
Suite 311
Ft. Collins, CO 80521
Tel: (970) 449-4960 *Fax:* (970) 449-4965
TollFree: (877) 502-2233
E-Mail: info@acced-i.org
Website: acced-i.org
Members: 1500 individuals
Staff: 8
Annual Budget: $500-1,000,000
Tax: 501(c)(6)

Personnel:
Executive Director: Deborah Blom
　　E-Mail: deborah@acced-i.org
Manager, Electronic Communications: Lori Everhart
　　E-Mail: lori@acced-i.org
Accountant: Mindy Griggs
　　E-Mail: Mindy@acced-i.org
Treasurer: Perry Hacker CMP
　　E-Mail: phacker@guesthouse.utah.edu
Director, Membership Services: Diana Hakenholz CMP
　　E-Mail: diana@acced-i.org
Director, Marketing and Sales: Monica Nesbit Schultz
　　E-Mail: monica@acced-i.org
Project Consultant: Craig Sommer
　　E-Mail: acced-i.sommer@comcast.net
Manager, Database: Jordan Weber

Historical Note:
Formerly (1998) Association of Conference and Events Directors International. ACCED-I promotes and advances the collegiate conference and events profession and sets the industry standards of excellence. It has increased the visibility and enhanced the stature of the collegiate conference and events profession.Members are collegiate conference and events directors, professionals who design, coordinate and market conferences and special events at their institutions. Membership: $350 (Individual); $795

(Institution-for three Reps and one Student Rep); $495 (Associate); $85 (Student); $895 (Corporate); $175 (Alumni).

Continuing Education:
Certification Designation/s: CCEP

Meetings/Conferences: Annual
Conference Chair: Diana Hakenholz CMP
2013 - Toronto, ON (Fairmont Royal York)/March 16 - 20/600 attendees
2014 - New Orleans, LA (Sheraton Hotel New Orleans)/March 23 - 26
Number of non-conference events/year: 10

Publications:
ACCED-I Connections Newsletter; quarterly; adv.
ACCED-I Membership Directory; on-line

Association of Collegiate Schools of Architecture (1912)

1735 New York Ave. NW
Washington, DC 20006
Tel: (202) 785-2324 *Fax:* (202) 628-0448
E-Mail: info@acsa-arch.org
Website: acsa-arch.org
Members: 4250 individuals and schools
Staff: 7
Annual Budget: $1-2,000,000
Tax: 501(c)(3)

Personnel:
Executive Director: Michael J. Monti PhD
　　E-Mail: mmonti@acsa-arch.org
Manager, Development: Mary Lou Baily
　　E-Mail: mlbaily@acsa-arch.org
Director, Operations and Programs: Eric W. Ellis
　　E-Mail: eellis@acsa-arch.org
Manager, Conferences: Jonathan Halpin
　　E-Mail: jhalpin@acsa-arch.org
Coordinator, Publications and Advertising: Kevin Mitchell
　　E-Mail: kmitchell@acsa-arch.org
Director, Communications and Media Strategies: Pascale J. Vonier
　　E-Mail: pvonier@acsa-arch.org
Coordinator, Membership Services: Danielle V. Washington
　　E-Mail: dwashington@acsa-arch.org

Historical Note:
ACSA's mission is to advance architectural education through support of member schools, their faculty, and students. Members are U. S. and Canadian faculties of professional architectural degree programs. Membership includes over 200 colleges and universities worldwide. Membership: $4,883-11,440 (Schools); $321-396 (Affiliate); $325-5,000 (Corporate); $25-104 (Individual).

Meetings/Conferences:
Conference Chair: Mary Lou Baily
2013 - San Francisco, CA (California College of the Arts)/March 21 - 24

Publications:
Journal of Architectural Education; bi-annually
ACSA E-Newsletter; on-line
ACSA Update; weekly

Membership List Available to Non-members

Association of Collegiate Schools of Planning (1959)

6311 Mallard Trace Dr.
Tallahassee, FL 32312
Tel: (850) 385-2054 *Fax:* (850) 385-2084
E-Mail: ddodd@acsp.org
Website: acsp.org
Members: 125 schools
Staff: 1
Annual Budget: $500-1,000,000
Tax: 501(c)(3)

Personnel:
Association Manager and Conference Director: Donna Dodd
　　E-Mail: ddodd@acsp.org

Historical Note:
ACSP is a consortium of university-based programs offering degrees in urban and regional planning in the U.S. Supports research in planning curricula and instruction to promote the discipline. Membership: $350 (Full); $115 (Affiliate/ Corresponding); $85 (Individual); $50 (Faculty); $35 (Student).

Meetings/Conferences: Annual
Conference Chair: Donna Dodd

2014 - Philadelphia, PA (Loews Philadelphia Hotel)/ Oct. 30 - Nov. 2

Publications:
ACSP Newsletter
Journal of the American Planning Association
Journal of the United Nations Centre for Regional Development
Journal of Urban Design and Planning

Membership List Available to Non-members

Association of Commercial Finance Attorneys (1958)

One American Pl., 14th Floor
McGlinchey Stafford, PLLC
Baton Rouge, LA 70825
Tel: (225) 382-3651 *Fax:* (410) 581-7410
E-Mail: acfa@acfalaw.org
Website: acfalaw.org
Members: 350 individuals
Staff: 2
Annual Budget: $100-250,000

Personnel:
Treasurer: R. Marshall Grodner
　　E-Mail: mgrodner@mcglinchey.com

Historical Note:
ACFA furthers the practice of law applicable to commercial finance, including but not limited to asset-based lending, factoring, loan restructuring and insolvency. Members are attorneys specializing in commercial finance and bankruptcy law. Membership: $225 (Established Professional); $150 (If out of school less than five years); $0 (Judge or Emeritus).

Continuing Education:
Certification Designation/s: CLEW
Meetings/Conferences:
Number of non-conference events/year: 5

Publications:
Membership Directory; on-line

Association of Commercial Real Estate

P.O. Box 1437
Fair Oaks, CA 95628
Tel: (916) 446-0775 *Fax:* (916) 961-6884
E-Mail: info@acre.org
Website: acre.org
Staff: 4
Annual Budget: $100-250,000

Personnel:
Executive Director: Debbie Uhrenholt
　　E-Mail: debbieuhrenholt@comcast.net
Vice President, Membership: Bill Andrews
　　E-Mail: bandrews@theevergreencompany.com
Secretary and Treasurer: John Shelby
　　E-Mail: john.shelby@unionbank.com
Special Director, Newsletters: Julie Sherry
　　E-Mail: jasherry1@aol.com

Historical Note:
ACRE is a non-profit, professional association formed to promote working relationships and professionalism within the Sacramento commercial real estate community. It brings together commercial brokers and affiliated professionals for business networking, educational presentations and discussion of industry developments. Membership: $145 (Active/Affiliate/Associate); $75 (Active/Newly Licensed Broker).

Meetings/Conferences: Annual
Conference Chair: Debbie Uhrenholt

Publications:
ACRE Newsletter; on-line
Membership Directory; on-line

Association of Community Cancer Centers (1974)

11600 Nebel St.
Suite 201
Rockville, MD 20852-2557
Tel: (301) 984-9496 *Fax:* (301) 770-1949
Website: accc-cancer.org
Members: 17924 cancer care professionals
hospitals and state oncology societies
Staff: 12
Annual Budget: $5-10,000,000
Tax: 501(c)(3)

Personnel:
Executive Director: Gov. Christian G. Downs JD, MHA
　　E-Mail: cdowns@accc-cancer.org
Director, Corporate Relations: Mike Andrews
　　E-Mail: mandrews@accc-cancer.org
Senior Director, Programs and Meetings: Lu Anne Bankert

E-Mail: labankert@accc-cancer.org
Director, Provider Economics and Public Policy: Matthew
  Farber MA
  E-Mail: mfarber@accc-cancer.org
Senior Director, Membership Services and Marketing: Lori
  B. Gardner
  E-Mail: lgardner@accc-cancer.org
Director, Corporate Communications: Don Jewler MA
  E-Mail: djewler@accc-cancer.org
Director, Educational Services: Kim LeMaitre
  E-Mail: klemaitre@accc-cancer.org
Manager, Publications, Advertising and Corporate Relations:
  Malvin Milburn
  E-Mail: mmilburn@accc-cancer.org
Director, Finance: Lois Utterback CPA
  E-Mail: lutterback@c-managementinc.com

Historical Note:
*ACCC's mission is to focus on enhancing, promoting, and
protecting the entire continuum of quality cancer care for
its patients and its communities. Strives to be the education
and advocacy organization for the cancer team. Members
are state oncology organizations, cancer care providers,
and cancer programs that include hospital-based cancer
programs, physician group practices, and freestanding
clinics. Membership: $135 (Individual); $1,095 (Cancer
Program).*

Meetings/Conferences:
Conference Chair: Lu Anne Bankert
2013 - Washington, DC (Washington Marriott
  Wardman Park)/March 6 - 8
2013 - Boston, MA (Westin Boston Waterfront)/Oct. 2
  - 5
2014 - Arlington, VA (Hyatt Regency Crystal City at
  Reagan National Airport)/March 31 - April 2
2014 - San Diego, CA (Sheraton San Diego Hotel and
  Marina)/Oct. 8 - 11
2015 - Arlington, VA (Hyatt Regency Crystal City at
  Reagan National Airport)/March 15 - 18
2015 - San Diego, CA (Sheraton San Diego Hotel and
  Marina)/March 16 - 18
2015 - Portland, OR (Portland Marriott Downtown
  Waterfront)/Oct. 21 - 24

Publications:
ACConnect; weekly
Member Directory; on-line
Oncology Issues; bi-monthly; adv.

Membership List Available to Non-members

Association of Community College Trustees
(1972)
1233 20th St. NW
Suite 301
Washington, DC 20036
Tel: (202) 775-4667 *Fax:* (202) 223-1297
E-Mail: acctinfo@acct.org
Website: acct.org
Members:
6,500 individual trustees
1,200 community, technical and junior colleges
Staff: 22
Annual Budget: $5-10,000,000
Tax: 501(c)(3)

Personnel:
President and Chief Executive Officer: J. Noah Brown
  E-Mail: nbrown@acct.org
Specialist, Marketing and Communications: David
  Michael Conner
  E-Mail: dconner@acct.org
Operations Management Officer: Tonya Harley
  E-Mail: tharley@acct.org
Director, Public Policy: Jee Hang Lee
  E-Mail: jhlee@acct.org
*Vice President, Education, Research and Board Leadership
  Services:* Narcisa Polonio EdD
  E-Mail: npolonio@acct.org
Administrator, Systems and Finance: Angela Summers
  E-Mail: asummers@acct.org

Historical Note:
*ACCT's mission is to promote effective board governance
through advocacy, education and training programs.
Membership: $1,627-7,238 (Regular Members); $415
(Associate Members).*

Continuing Education:
Certification Designation/s: CCGRP
Meetings/Conferences:
Number of non-conference events/year: 5
Publications:

Membership Directory; on-line
Trustee Quarterly; quarterly

Association of Community Health Nursing Educators (1978)
10200 W. 44th Ave.
Suite 304
Wheat Ridge, CO 80033
Tel: (303) 422-0769 *Fax:* (303) 422-8894
E-Mail: ACHNE@resourcenter.com
Website: achne.org
Members: 400 individuals
Staff: 5
Annual Budget: $100-250,000

Personnel:
President: Angeline Bushy FAAN, PhD, RN
  E-Mail: abushy@mail.ucf.edu
Contact, Membership Services: Paula De Vinay
Vice President and Program Chair: Mary Hoke PhD
  E-Mail: mhoke@uiwtx.edu
Treasurer: Pamela Levin APRN, PhD, RN
  E-Mail: pamela_levin@rush.edu
Secretary: Mary Molle PhD
  E-Mail: mmolle@msmc.la.edu

Historical Note:
*ACHNE's mission is to promote quality community or
public health nursing education and research to improve the
health of communities and populations. Membership: $120
(Active); $500 (Corporate/Institutional); $80 (Retired/
Student/International).*

Continuing Education:
Certification Designation/s: C/PHN
Meetings/Conferences: Annual
Conference Chair: Mary Hoke PhD
2013 - Raleigh, NC/June 6 - 8

Publications:
ACHNE Newsletter; quarterly
Membership Directory; on-line

Membership List Available to Non-members

The Association of Community Pharmacists Congressional Network
122 C St. NW
Suite 500
Washington, DC 20001
Tel: (202) 628-0333
Website: acpcn.org
Staff: 3

Personnel:
President: Bill Rustin
Director, Government Affairs: Julie Philp

Historical Note:
ACP Pharmacy Committees are now operating in 44 states.

Publications:
Action Alert; on-line
Drug Topics
Email Alert; on-line
Fax Alerts; on-line
Pharmacy Times; monthly; adv.
Pink Sheet; daily; adv.

Association of Community Tribal Schools (1982)
P.O. Box 1518
220 Omaha St.
Mission, SD 57555
Tel: (605) 838-0424 *Fax:* (605) 838-0424
E-Mail: acts@acts-tribal.org
Website: acts-tribal.org
Members: 30 schools
Staff: 3
Annual Budget: $10-25,000

Personnel:
Executive Director: Dr. Roger C. Bordeaux
  E-Mail: drbordeaux@acts-tribal.org
Administrative Assistant: Rosa Bordeaux
  E-Mail: rosa@acts-tribal.org
Network Administrator: Ben R. Bordeaux
  E-Mail: webmaster@acts-tribal.org

Historical Note:
*Founded as Association of Contract Tribal Schools, ACTS's
mission is to assist Community Tribal Schools towards
their mission of ensuring that when students complete their
schools they are prepared for lifelong learning and that
these students will strengthen and perpetuate traditional
tribal societies. Membership: $250 (Affiliate); $500-1200
(Voting); $50 (Associate).*

The Association of Concert Bands (1977)
6613 Cheryl Ann Dr.
Independence, OH 44131-3718
Tel: (216) 524-1897
TollFree: (800) 726-8720
E-Mail: acbsec@sbcglobal.net
Website: acbands.org
Members: 800 bands, companies and individuals
Staff: 5
Annual Budget: $50-100,000

Personnel:
Coordinator, Publications: Nancy Michalek
Chief Information Officer: Michael Montgomery
Secretary: Nada Vencl Montgomery

Historical Note:
*Formerly (1983) Association of Concert Bands of America.
ACB is dedicated to the worldwide advancement of
adult concert and community bands. Membership: $30
(Individual); $150 (Corporate); $50 (Organization); $45
(Family); $1,000 (Life); $15 (Student);*

Meetings/Conferences: Annual
2013 - San Ramon, CA/April 3 - 7

Publications:
Membership Directory; annually
The ACB Journal; adv.

Association of Conservation Engineers (1961)
5400 Bishop Blvd.
C/O Wyoming Game and Fish Department
Cheyenne, WY 82006
Website: conservationengineers.org
Members: 300 individuals
Staff: 16
Annual Budget: $10-25,000

Personnel:
President: Dave Bumann
  E-Mail: david.bumann@wgf.state.wy.us
Secretary and Contact, Publications and Membership:
  Kathy Dillmon
  E-Mail: kathy.dillmon@wgf.state.wy.us
Treasurer: Champak Patel

Historical Note:
*ACE's mission is to promote the application of sound
engineering practices in the field of natural resource
protection and recreation development. Members are
engineers and allied personnel employed by state, federal
and provincial conservation and recreation departments,
who have a specialized interest in the areas of fish,
wildlife, parks, forests and related conservation-recreation
fields. Membership: $25/year (Honory/Life); $0 (Active/
Associate/Student).*

Meetings/Conferences: Annual
Conference Chair: Dave Bumann

Publications:
ACE Resources; quarterly

Association of Consulting Chemists and Chemical Engineers (1928)
P.O. Box 902
Murray Hill, NJ 07974-0902
Tel: (908) 464-3182 *Fax:* (908) 464-3182
E-Mail: accce@chemconsult.org
Website: chemconsult.org
Members: 150 individuals
Staff: 1
Annual Budget: $10-25,000

Personnel:
Executive Director: Dr. John Bonacci

Historical Note:
*Founded and chartered in 1928 in the state of New York.
ACC&CE's mission is to serve the scientific industries, using
expertise based on a wide variety of technical and business
knowledge. Members are engaged in consulting practice as
chemists or chemical engineers. Membership: $75/year.*

Publications:
Membership Directory; on-line
The Chemical Consultant; on-line

Association of Consulting Foresters of America (1948)
312 Montgomery St.
Suite 208
Alexandria, VA 22314
Tel: (703) 548-0990 *Fax:* (703) 548-6395
TollFree: (888) 540-8733
E-Mail: director@acf-foresters.com
Website: acf-foresters.org

Members: 679 individuals
Staff: 5
Annual Budget: $250-500,000
Personnel:
Executive Director: Lynn Wilson
    E-Mail: director@acf-foresters.org
Coordinator, Membership and Events: Mary W.
    Dannahey
    E-Mail: mary@acf-foresters.org
Contact, Member Services: Savannah Edwards
    E-Mail: membership@acf-foresters.org
Administrative Director: Colleen M. Hoffman
    E-Mail: colleen@acf-foresters.org
Director, Information Systems: Sarah O'Neil
    E-Mail: sarah@acf-foresters.org

Historical Note:
Mission of ACF is to promote ethical stewardship of forest
resources by advancing the profession of consulting forestry.
Members are technically trained foresters who own their
own businesses, demonstrate their professional competency
and whose services are available to the general public on a
fee or contract basis. Membership: $375/year.

Meetings/Conferences: Annual
Conference Chair: Mary W. Dannahey
Number of non-conference events/year: 1

Publications:
ACF Membership Specialization Directory; annually;
    adv.
ACF Newsletter; quarterly
The Consultant; annually; adv.

Association of Cooperative Educators (1965)
29630-109th Ave. North
Hanover, MN 55341
Tel: (763) 432-2032 Fax: (651) 355-5073
Website: ace.coop
Members: 200 individuals
Staff: 2
Annual Budget: $100-250,000
Personnel:
Executive Administrator: Sarah Pike
    E-Mail: pike@ace.coop
Director, Communications and Contact, Newsletter: Cathy
    L. Chamberlain
    E-Mail: chamberlain@ace.coop

Historical Note:
Founded as the Association for Cooperative Education,
the name was changed in 1970 and reorganized in
1997 as a non-profit organization. ACE seeks to bring
together educators, researchers, cooperative members,
and cooperative developers from across cooperative
sectors and national borders. Membership consists of
individuals and organizations professionally engaged in
educational, training or personnel programs of cooperative
organizations. Membership: $65 (Professional); $165
(Organization); $40 (Associate).

Meetings/Conferences: Annual

Publications:
ACE UpDate - Newsletter; quarterly

Association of Corporate Contributions Professionals
1150 Hungryneck Blvd.
Mt. Pleasant, SC 29464
Tel: (843) 216-3442 Fax: (843) 216-3396
E-Mail: mail@accprof.org
Website: accprof.org
Members: 77 Organizations
Staff: 8
Annual Budget: $500-1,000,000
Personnel:
President and Chief Executive Officer: Mark W. Shamley
    E-Mail: mshamley@accprof.org
Coordinator, Events and Marketing: Libby Anderson
    E-Mail: libby@accprof.org
Vice President, Member Services: Melinda Bostwick
    E-Mail: melinda@accprof.org
Manager, Communications, Marketing and Public Relations:
    Dawn Henry
    E-Mail: dawn@accprof.org
Director, Operations and Finance: Donna Kraemer
    E-Mail: donna@accprof.org

Historical Note:
ACCP's mission is to is dedicate to the development of
contributions professionals through education & training,
defining best practices for the field, building relationships
and benchmarking & measurement. Membership: $6,000/
year

Meetings/Conferences: Annual
Conference Chair: Libby Anderson
2013 - New Orleans, LA (The Hotel Monteleone)/
    March 10 - 13
Number of non-conference events/year: 2

Publications:
News & Analysis; bi-weekly

Association of Corporate Counsel (1982)
1025 Connecticut Ave. NW
Suite 200
Washington, DC 20036-5425
Tel: (202) 293-4103 Fax: (202) 293-4701
Website: acc.com
Members: 28000 individuals
Staff: 59
Annual Budget: $10-25,000,000
Tax: 501(c)(6)
Personnel:
President and Chief Executive Officer: Veta T Richardson
Assistant Editor: Maggy Baccinelli
    E-Mail: baccinelli@acc.com
Senior Vice President and Chief-of-Staff: Anne Bracken
    E-Mail: bracken@acc.com
Vice President and Chief Marketing Officer: Kevin Buck
    E-Mail: buck@acc.com
Chief Financial Officer: Russ Capps
    E-Mail: capps@acc.com
Manager, Marketing: Liang Ge
    E-Mail: ge@acc.com
Vice President, Membership Services, Chapters and
    Communications: Robin Grossfeld
    E-Mail: grossfeld@acc.com
Editor in Chief: Kimberly A. Howard
    E-Mail: howard@acc.com
Vice President and Chief Technology Officer: John
    McAndrew
    E-Mail: mcandrew@acc.com
Vice President and General Counsel: James 'Jim"
    Merklinger
    E-Mail: merklinger@acc.com
Director, Information Technology: Michaelle Shultz
    E-Mail: shultz@acc.com
Director, Education and Meetings: Liza Trey
    E-Mail: trey@acc.com
Director, Membership and Marketing: Jim Way
    E-Mail: way@acc.com

Historical Note:
Formerly known as the American Corporate Counsel
Association (ACCA). ACC seeks to promote the common
professional and business interests of in- house counsel
who work for corporations, associations and other private-
sector organizations through information, education,
networking opportunities, and advocacy initiatives.
Membership: $295 (Individual); $95 (Retired).

Continuing Education:
Certification Designation/s: CLE

Meetings/Conferences: Annual
Conference Chair: Liza Trey
Number of non-conference events/year: 3

Publications:
ACC Committee Newsletter; quarterly
ACC Executive Bulletin; on-line
ACC Member Update Newsletter; monthly
Membership Directory; on-line
The ACC Docket Magazine; monthly

Membership List Available to Non-members

Association of Corporate Credit Unions (1995)
601 Pennsylvania Ave. NW
S. Building, Suite 600
Washington, DC 20004
Tel: (202) 508-6731 Fax: (202) 638-7736
E-Mail: info@theaccu.org
Website: theaccu.org
Staff: 3
Annual Budget: Under $10,000
Tax: 501(c)(6)
Personnel:
Executive Director: Brad Miller
    E-Mail: bmiller@cuna.com
Coordinator, Programs: Margot Meyer
    E-Mail: mmeyer@cuna.com
Assistant Director and Compliance Counsel: Rhonda
    Whitley
    E-Mail: rwhitley@cuna.com

Historical Note:
ACCU is committed to creating and maintaining a climate
of safety, soundness, innovation and unity among corporate
credit unions in order to promote and enhance the initiatives
of the credit union movement.
Meetings/Conferences:
Conference Chair: Margot Meyer

Association of Corporate Travel Executives (ACTE) (1988)
510 King St.
Suite 220
Alexandria, VA 22314
Tel: (703) 683-5322 Fax: (703) 683-2720
E-Mail: info@acte.org
Website: acte.org
Members: 6000 individuals
Staff: 17
Annual Budget: $2-5,000,000
Tax: 501(c)(6)
Personnel:
Executive Director: Greeley S. Koch
Senior Director, Global Membership, Marketing and
    Business Development: Jennifer Bialek
    E-Mail: jbialek@acte.org
Managing Director: Megan Costello
    E-Mail: mcostello@acte.org
Director, Global Events: Melissa Edwards CMP
    E-Mail: medwards@acte.org
Senior Director, Global Education: Amber Kelleher
    E-Mail: akelleher@acte.org
Interim Finance Director: Russell Yates
    E-Mail: ryates@acte.org

Historical Note:
ACTE's mission is to provide global and regional leadership
for the advancement of the business travel industry
through the exchange of knowledge and opportunity and
the pursuit of excellence. Membership: $425 (Corporate
Buyers, Suppliers and Agencies/TMCs); Free (Press); $175
(Government/NGOs); $75 (Students).

Meetings/Conferences:
2013 - New York City, NY/April 21 - 23
Number of non-conference events/year: 27

Publications:
Travel Daily News; on-line; adv.
ACTE Global Business Journal; quarterly; adv.
Membership Directory; on-line

Association of Correctional Food Service Affiliates (1969)
210 N. Glenoaks Blvd.
Suite C
Burbank, CA 91502
Tel: (818) 843-6608 Fax: (818) 843-7423
Website: acfsa.org
Members: 1400 individuals
Staff: 5
Annual Budget: $50-100,000
Tax: 501(c)(6)
Personnel:
Executive Director: Jon Nichols
    E-Mail: jonnichols@acfsa.org
Contact, Membership Services: Amber Brown
    E-Mail: membership@acfsa.org
Contact, Certifications: Gillian Newell
    E-Mail: certification@acfsa.org

Historical Note:
ACFSA's mission is to develop and promote educational
programs and networking activities to improve
professionalism and provide an opportunity for broadening
knowledge. Membership: $79 (Professional Foodservice);
$144 (Institutional); $39 (Retired); $119 (Associate
Professional Partner); $384 (Professional Partner); $169
(Chapter Professional Partner).

Continuing Education:
Certification Designation/s: CCFP, CFSM

Meetings/Conferences: Annual

Publications:
INSIDER; quarterly; adv.
Membership Directory; annually

Association of Coupon Professionals (1988)
1051 Pontiac Rd.
P.O. Box 512
Drexel Hill, PA 19026
Tel: (610) 789-9993 Fax: (610) 789-5309
Website: couponpros.org

Members: 60 companies
Staff: 1
Annual Budget: $100-250,000

Personnel:
Executive Director: John Morgan
　　E-Mail: John.Morgan@acp-hq.org

Historical Note:
Founded as the Association of Coupon Processors, assumed its current name in 1996. ACP's mission is to provide an industry forum that fosters expertise, education, and leadership that enriches the development, distribution, and redemption of coupons, ensuring they remain a viable sales and marketing tool. Membership: $1,700-3,200/year.

Meetings/Conferences: Annual
Number of non-conference events/year: 3

Publications:
E-zine Newsletter; quarterly
Membership Directory; on-line

Association of Credit Union Internal Auditors
(1990)
P.O. Box 150908
Alexandria, VA 22315
Tel: (703) 688-2284 *Fax:* (703) 683-0295
TollFree: (866) 254-8128
E-Mail: acuia@acuia.org
Website: acuia.org
Members: 800 individuals
Staff: 1
Annual Budget: $250-500,000
Tax: 501(c)(6)

Personnel:
Treasurer: Barbara Franco CIA, CPA
　　E-Mail: barbara.franco@gecu-ep.org

Historical Note:
ACUIA's mission is to unify and encourage cooperative relationships among credit union internal auditors to facilitate the exchange of information and ideas. Membership: $100-200 (Regular, 1 to 4 Internal Auditors/ Credit Union); $125 (Supervisory/Audit Committee).

Meetings/Conferences: Annual
2013 - San Francisco, CA (Grand Hyatt San Francisco)/ June 25 - 28

Publications:
E-News; monthly; adv.
The Audit Report; quarterly; adv.
Vendor Directory; on-line; adv.

Association of Dark Leaf Tobacco Dealers and Exporters *(1947)*
C/O Hail & Cotton, Inc.
P.O. Box 638
Springfield, TN 37172-0638
Tel: (615) 384-9576 *Fax:* (615) 384-6461
Website: hailcotton.com
Members: 22 companies
Staff: 3
Annual Budget: Under $10,000

Personnel:
President: August Payne
Secretary and Treasurer: Belinda Heard
Contact: Tom Wilks

Historical Note:
An affiliate of Burley and Dark Leaf Tobacco Export Association, ADLTDE was organized to promote the use of dark-fired and dark air-cured tobaccos, both domestically and abroad.

Association of Defense Communities
1023 15th St. NW
Suite 200
Washington, DC 20005
Tel: (202) 822-5256 *Fax:* (202) 289-7499
E-Mail: info@defensecommunities.org
Website: defensecommunities.org
Members: 1200 members
Staff: 7
Annual Budget: $500-1,000,000
Tax: 501(c)(6)

Personnel:
Chief Executive Officer: Tim Ford
　　E-Mail: tford@defensecommunities.org
Managing Editor: Dan Cohen
　　E-Mail: dcohen@defensecommunities.org
Chief Operating Officer: Todd Herberghs
　　E-Mail: therberghs@defensecommunities.org
Contact, Membership Services: Brendan O'Hara

E-Mail: bohara@defensecommunities.org
Director, Conferences and Outreach: Blake Stave
　　E-Mail: bstave@defensecommunities.org

Historical Note:
Formerly National Association of Installation Developers. ADC works to bring together public and private-sector professionals involved with the redevelopment, and privitization of former military -bases. Members are communities with active military installations, communities with closed or closing installations who are working to redevelop the military property, private sector companies and organizations interested in playing an active role in base redevelopment, military real estate, privatization initiatives, and community-military collaboration and representatives of the Department of Defense, and federal and state agencies. Membership: $200-450 (Closed Base Communities, depends on budget); $200-575 (Active Base Communities, depends on population); $200-450 (Non-Profit Organizations); $200 (State Agencies); $600-1,500 (Private Companies); $200-325 (Special Categories).

Meetings/Conferences: Annual
Conference Chair: Blake Stave

Publications:
Defense Communities 360; on-line
Federal Directory; on-line
Membership Directory
Private Sector Services Directory; on-line

Association of Defense Trial Attorneys *(1941)*
4135 Topsail Trail
New Port Richey, FL 34652
Tel: (304) 344-1611 *Fax:* (727) 859-0350
E-Mail: pschultz@adtalaw.com
Website: adtalaw.com
Members: 700 individuals
Staff: 2
Annual Budget: $100-250,000

Personnel:
Executive Director: Peggy L. Schultz
　　E-Mail: pschultz@adtalaw.com
Treasurer: Matthew W. Bailey
　　E-Mail: mattbailey@walshbailey.com

Historical Note:
ADTA members are attorneys who regularly represent insurance companies and self-insurers and are expert in the fields of law pertaining to dispute resolution for the insurance industry. Membership is limited to one member selected from each city, town and municipality (with certain exceptions). Membership: $400 (Prime); $300 (Associate).

Meetings/Conferences: Annual
2013 - White Sulphur Springs, WV (Greenbrier)/April 17 - 21

Publications:
Newsletter

Association of Defensive Spray Manufacturers
(1992)
906 Olive St.
Suite 1200
St. Louis, MO 63101-1434
Tel: (314) 241-1445 *Fax:* (314) 241-1449
E-Mail: adsm@pepperspray.org
Website: pepperspray.org
Members: 3 Corporate members
Staff: 2
Annual Budget: Under $10,000

Personnel:
Executive Director: Mark S. Birenbaum PhD

Historical Note:
ADSM's purpose is to permit manufacturers of non-lethal chemical weapons to join together to promote the industry as well as to address safety, quality control, marketing and other issues relevant to the industry. Membership: $1,000/ year (Corporate).

Publications:
Member Listing; on-line

Association of Departments of English *(1962)*
26 Broadway
Third Floor
New York, NY 10004-1789
Tel: (646) 576-5130
Website: ade.org
Members: 840 departments
Staff: 3

Personnel:
Director: David E. Laurence
　　E-Mail: dlaurence@mla.org

Senior Administrative Assistant: Roy Chustek
　　E-Mail: rchustek@mla.org
Manager and Editor: Stephen Olsen
　　E-Mail: solsen@mla.org

Historical Note:
Formerly Association of Departments of English in American Colleges and Universities. ADE serves as a central source of information and support for chairs of college and university English departments throughout the United States and Canada. Members are administrators of college and university level departments of English. Membership: $225-2,475 (Units (or combinations of units) in four-year institutions)); $125 (No degree offered/Two-year colleges);

Meetings/Conferences: Annual
Number of non-conference events/year: 2

Publications:
ADE Bulletin; on-line
Membership Directory; on-line

Association of Departments of Foreign Languages
(1969)
26 Broadway
Third Floor
New York, NY 10004-1789
Tel: (646) 576-5140 *Fax:* (646) 458-0033
E-Mail: adfl@mla.org
Website: adfl.org
Members: 1050 academic departments
Staff: 4
Annual Budget: $50-100,000

Personnel:
Director: Nelly Furman
　　E-Mail: nfurman@mla.org
Senior Administrative Assistant: Roy Chustek
　　E-Mail: rchustek@mla.org
Manager and Editor: Stephen Olsen
　　E-Mail: solsen@mla.org

Historical Note:
ADFL is an association of departments of foreign languages and literatures and divisions of humanities. Members are administrators of foreign language departments at college and university level. Membership: $175-575 (Departments, varies with faculty members); $125 (Community College Department).

Meetings/Conferences: Semi-Annual

Publications:
ADFL Bulletin; on-line; adv.
Membership Directory; on-line

Membership List Available to Non-members

Association of Dermatology Administrators & Managers
1120 G St. NW
Suite 1000
Washington, DC 20005
Tel: (866) 480-3573 *Fax:* (800) 671-3763
E-Mail: adaminfo@shcare.net
Website: ada-m.org
Members: 650 managers, administrators, attorneys, accountants and physicians in private, group and academic practice
Staff: 2
Annual Budget: $250-500,000

Personnel:
Executive Director: Pam Kroussakis
　　E-Mail: pam.kroussakis@shcare.net
Association Manager: Kelsey Heinze
　　E-Mail: kelsey.heinze@shcare.net

Historical Note:
ADAM's mission is to serve the dermatology profession through education, resources and networking opportunities. Membership: $295 (Individual); $245 (Practice); $500 (Corporate).

Meetings/Conferences: Annual
2013 - Miami, FL/Feb. 27 - March 2
2013 - Miami, FL (Hyatt Regency)/Feb. 27 - March 1
2014 - Denver, CO/March 19 - 22
2015 - San Francisco, CA/March 17 - 22

Publications:
Executive Decisions in Dermatology- Newsletter; bi-monthly
Member Directory

Association of Destination Management Executives *(1995)*
P.O. Box 2307

Dayton, OH 45401-2307
Tel: (937) 586-3727 *Fax:* (937) 586-3699
E-Mail: info@adme.org
Website: adme.org
Members: 200 companies
Staff: 3
Annual Budget: $100-250,000

Personnel:
Executive Vice President: Francine "Fran" W.
  Rickenbach CAE, IOM
Manager, Meetings: Doug Conrad
Contact, Membership: Roxy West

Historical Note:
ADMEI's mission is to define the destination management industry, uphold professionalism, establish standard business and ethical practices, and promote the value of local destination management through member and industry education. Membership: $575 (DMC/Affiliate/Consortium/ Provisional); $750 (Supplier Partner); $150 (Faculty/ Student).

Meetings/Conferences: Annual
Conference Chair: Doug Conrad
2013 - Montreal, QC (Sheraton Center)/Feb. 7 - 9

Publications:
ADME Newsletter; on-line
Membership Directory; on-line

Association of Diesel Specialists (1956)
400 Admiral Blvd.
Kansas City, MO 64106
Tel: (816) 285-0810 *Fax:* (847) 770-4952
E-Mail: info@diesel.org
Website: diesel.org
Members: 750 companies
Staff: 6
Annual Budget: $1-2,000,000

Personnel:
Executive Director: David Fehling
  E-Mail: david@diesel.org
Director, Marketing: Greg Carlile
  E-Mail: gregc@diesel.org
Director, Meetings: Rosemary Hall
  E-Mail: rhall@diesel.org
Manager, Membership Services: Tiffany Mayo
Director, Operations and Forerunners Liaison: Ashley
  Mercurio
  E-Mail: ashley@diesel.org
Director, Training: Tony Salas
  E-Mail: tony.salas@diesel.org

Historical Note:
ADS's mission is to provide programs and services to its members that will assist them in achieving success in the operation of their businesses in the diesel industry throughout the world. Membership: $289-1360/year.

Meetings/Conferences: Annual
Conference Chair: Rosemary Hall
2013 - San Diego, CA (Manchester Hyatt San Diego)/
  July 30 - Aug. 2

Publications:
Membership Directory; annually; adv.
News @ ADS; weekly; adv.
Nozzle Chatter; bi-annually; adv.

Association of Direct Response Fundraising Counsel (1987)
1612 K St. NW
Suite 510
Washington, DC 20006-2802
Tel: (202) 293-9640 *Fax:* (202) 887-9699
E-Mail: adrfco@msn.com
Website: adrfco.org
Members: 40 companies
Staff: 2
Annual Budget: $100-250,000
Tax: 501(c)(6)

Personnel:
Contact, Member Services: Nicole Haggerty
  E-Mail: nicole_adrfco@msn.com
General Counsel: Robert Tigner

Historical Note:
ADRFCO is dedicated to educating the public about the positive impact direct response fundraising.

Publications:
In Brief Newsletter
Membership Directory; annually

Association of Directory Publishers (1898)
116 Cass St.
P.O. Box 1929
Traverse City, MI 49684
Fax: (231) 486-2182
TollFree: (800) 267-9002
E-Mail: hq@adp.org
Website: adp.org
Members: 277 companies
Staff: 5
Annual Budget: $500-1,000,000

Personnel:
President and Chief Executive Officer: R. Lawrence
  Angove
  E-Mail: larry.angove@adp.org
Contact, Conventions: Valerie Donn
Contact, Finance: Janice Norman
Contact, Membership Services: Kat Philips
Chief Operating Officer: Bonnie Pintozzi

Historical Note:
Formerly (1992) the Association of North American Directory Publishers. Represents the interests of telephone directory publishers. ADP's mission is to promote the common business interest, to improve the general business conditions and facilitate the exchange of information of importance to, businesses engaged in the publication of printed telephone and other directories. Membership: $500-25,000 (Publisher/Associate Publisher); $3,000 (International Publisher); $1,750 (Partner); $350 (CMR/ Agency).

Meetings/Conferences: Annual
Conference Chair: Valerie Donn

Publications:
TheEXTRA; on-line; adv.

Association of Diving Contractors International (1968)
5206 Cypress Creek Pkwy.
Suite 202
Houston, TX 77069
Tel: (281) 893-8388 *Fax:* (281) 893-5118
TollFree: (888) 232-4838
Website: adc-int.org
Members: 600 companies
Staff: 5
Annual Budget: $1-2,000,000
Tax: 501(c)(6)

Personnel:
Executive Director: Phil Newsum
  E-Mail: pnewsum@adc-int.org
Manager, Marketing and Communications: Rebecca
  Roberts
  E-Mail: rroberts@adc-int.org
Manager, Administrative Services: Barbara Treadway
  E-Mail: btreadway@adc-int.org

Historical Note:
ADCI is dedicated to the art and science of commercial diving and also seeks to establish and maintain industry-wide safe standards for commercial diving. Members are commercial diving and underwater contractors, manufacturers and suppliers of diving equipment, diving schools and ROV owners and operators. Membership: $25 (Individual); $500- 5,750 (General); $750 (Supporting); $500-1,000 (Associate).

Continuing Education:
Certification Designation/s: DSC

Meetings/Conferences:
Conference Chair: Rebecca Roberts

Publications:
eDive Newsletter; bi-weekly
Membership Directory; annually
Underwater Magazine; bi-monthly; adv.

Association of Donor Recruitment Professionals (2010)
P.O. Box 150790
Austin, TX 78715
Tel: (512) 658-9414 *Fax:* (866) 498-6527
Website: adrp.org
Members: 500 Individuals
Staff: 1
Annual Budget: $250-500,000

Personnel:
Executive Director: Deborah Swift
  E-Mail: dswift@adrp.org

Historical Note:

ADRP Mission is to commit being a leader in providing education, development and resources for the donor recruitment profession.

Meetings/Conferences: Annual
2013 - Scottsdale, AZ (Talking Stick Resort)/May 15 -
  17/11-25 exhibitors

Publications:
ADRP's Quarterly Newsletter; quarterly
Member Directory; on-line

Association of Earth Science Editors (1967)
554 Chess St.
Pittsburgh, PA 15205-3212
Tel: (412) 268-4708 *Fax:* (412) 268-5677
Website: aese.org
Members: 275 individuals
Staff: 7
Annual Budget: $10-25,000

Personnel:
President: Carole Ziegler
Treasurer: Phil Farquharson
Contact, Membership Services: Mary Ann Schmidt
  E-Mail: maryanns@andrew.cmu.edu

Historical Note:
AESE promotes the exchange of ideas on problems of selection, editing and publication of research manuscripts, journals, serials, periodicals and maps pertaining to earth sciences. Membership: $35/year (Individual).

Meetings/Conferences: Annual

Publications:
Membership Directory; on-line

Association of Ecosystem Research Centers (1987)
University of Alabama, Center for Freshwater
Studies
P.O. Box 870206
Tuscaloosa, AL 35487-0206
Tel: (205) 348-1796 *Fax:* (205) 348-1403
E-Mail: award@biology.as.ua.edu
Website: ecosystemresearch.org
Members: 43 centers
Staff: 3
Annual Budget: Under $10,000

Personnel:
Treasurer: Amelia K. Ward

Historical Note:
AERC's mission is to encourage and facilitate communication between scientists on ecosystem research methodology and theory and build-up data compatibility, storage, access, and sharing. Members are professional scientists. Membership: $250 (Center, first two years); $500 (Center, after two years).

Meetings/Conferences: Annual

Publications:
AERC Newsletter; annually

Association of Edison Illuminating Companies (1885)
600 N. 18th St.
P.O. Box 2641
Birmingham, AL 35291-0992
Tel: (205) 257-2530 *Fax:* (205) 257-2540
E-Mail: aeicdir@bellsouth.net
Website: aeic.org
Members: 156 member utilities
Staff: 4
Annual Budget: $500-1,000,000
Tax: 501(c)(6)

Personnel:
Executive Director, Secretary and Treasurer: Earl B.
  Parsons Jr.
  E-Mail: aeicdir@bellsouth.net
Administrative Assistant: Cindy McLeod
  E-Mail: secretaryaeic@bellsouth.net

Historical Note:
AEIC encourages research and the exchange of technical information through a committee structure, staffed with experts from management of member companies and also provides valued literature on load research and underground cable specifications. Membership: $13,775/ year (fee varies based on revenues).

Meetings/Conferences: Annual
Number of non-conference events/year: 7

Publications:
AEIC Newsletter; quarterly

Association of Educational Publishers (1895)
510 Heron Dr.
Suite 200
Logan Township, NJ 08085
Tel: (856) 241-7772 *Fax:* (302) 778-1110
E-Mail: mail@aepweb.org
Website: aepweb.org
Members: 1500 companies and individuals
Staff: 12
Annual Budget: $1-2,000,000

Personnel:
Chief Executive Officer: Charlene F. Gaynor
    E-Mail: cgaynor@aepweb.org
Director, Information Technology: Mike Dodson
    E-Mail: mdodson@aepweb.org
*Vice President, Sales, Marketing, and Business
    Development:* Jo-Ann McDevitt
    E-Mail: jmcdevitt@aepweb.org
Manager, Finance: Bhavika Patel
    E-Mail: finance@aepweb.org
Content Manager: Stacey Pusey
    E-Mail: spusey@aepweb.org
Director, Membership Services: Colleen Quigley
    E-Mail: cquigley@aepweb.org
Director, Operations: Brian Sime
    E-Mail: bsime@AEPweb.org

Historical Note:
*Formerly (1998) Educational Press Association of America.
AEP's mission is to promote the value of supplemental
materials in all media as essential learning resources.
Members are school and teacher publications, children's
magazines, software and supplemental publishers,
educational foundations and associations, schools and
school districts, and the education and trade press across
the media. Membership: $965 (Corporate Membership);
$635 (Non-profit/School Membership); $1,090-12,000
(Affiliate Membership); $335 (Freelance/Independent
Membership); $65 (Teacher/Student).*

Meetings/Conferences: Semi-Annual

Publications:
Membership Directory; on-line

Association of Educational Service Agencies (1976)
801 N. Quincy St.
Suite 750
Arlington, VA 22203
Tel: (703) 875-0739 *Fax:* (703) 807-1849
E-Mail: info@aesa.us
Website: aesa.us
Members:
553 agencies
607 individuals
Staff: 3
Annual Budget: $500-1,000,000

Personnel:
Executive Director: Lee Warne
Chief Financial Officer: Peter C. Young

Historical Note:
*Mission of AESA is to support and strengthen regional
educational service agencies by providing professional
growth opportunities, technical assistance, advocacy,
research and helping member agencies to promote,
distribute, and leverage knowledge, products and services.
Membership: $110 (Associate); $975 (Business); $340
(Institutional); $340-1,575 (Individual); $245-935
(Statewide).*

Meetings/Conferences: Annual
Number of non-conference events/year: 2

Publications:
AESA News; bi-monthly
AESA Online News; monthly
Exhibitor Directory; on-line
Membership Directory; on-line
NAMTC / AESA Big Deal Book of Technology
    Newsletter
Perspectives; annually

Association of Educational Therapists (1978)
7044 S. 13th St.
Oak Creek, WI 53154
Tel: (414) 908-4949 *Fax:* (414) 768-8001
E-Mail: aet@aetonline.org
Website: aetonline.org
Members: 900 individuals
Staff: 1
Annual Budget: $250-500,000

Tax: 501(c)(3)

Personnel:
President: Marcy Dann BCET, MA

Historical Note:
*AET is dedicated to defining the professional practice of
educational therapy, setting standards for ethical practice,
advancing the profession through ongoing professional
development and training programs and promoting public
awareness of and access to educational therapy services.
Membership: $125 (General); $45 (Student); $150 (Allied
Professional); $200 (Associate Educational Therapist).*

Meetings/Conferences: Annual

Publications:
Educational Therapist Journal

Membership List Available to Non-members

Association of Educators in Imaging and Radiologic Sciences, Inc (1967)
P.O. Box 90204
Albuquerque, NM 87199-0204
Tel: (505) 823-4740 *Fax:* (505) 823-4740
E-Mail: office@aeirs.org
Website: aeirs.org
Members: 500 individuals
Staff: 4
Annual Budget: $100-250,000
Tax: 501(c)(3)

Personnel:
Executive Secretary: Valerie Christensen
    E-Mail: office@aeirs.org
Managing Editor: Susan Carr
    E-Mail: susan_carr@mac.com
Webmaster: Griffin Granberg
Meeting Planner: Carole South-Winter
    E-Mail: csouthwinter@aeirs.org

Historical Note:
*AEIRS are employed in an educational position associated
with an accredited radiological sciences program.
Membership: $75/year (Active/Associate).*

Meetings/Conferences: Annual
Conference Chair: Carole South-Winter
2013 - Salt Lake City, UT (Radisson Hotel Salt Lake
    City Downtown)/July 11 - 12

Publications:
membership directory
Radiologic Science & Education; bi-annually; adv.
Spectrum; quarterly; adv.

Association of Eminent Domain Professionals
P.O. Box 332
Palm Beach, FL 33402
Tel: (561) 802-4310 *Fax:* (561) 659-1824
E-Mail: aedp@aedp.org
Website: aedp.org
Staff: 2
Annual Budget: $25-50,000

Personnel:
President: Michael Sexton P E
Treasurer: Maurice Gruber

Historical Note:
*AEDP's mission is to maintain a forum for the exchange of
ideas and information between professionals who provide
private and public clients with eminent domain services and
enhance the professionalism of the membership through
educational opportunities. The Association also promotes
the value of membership to the eminent domain community.
Membership: $200/year.*

Meetings/Conferences: Annual
Number of non-conference events/year: 2

Publications:
AEDP Newsletter
Membership Directory; on-line

Association of Energy Engineers (1977)
4025 Pleasantdale Rd.
Suite 420
Atlanta, GA 30340
Tel: (770) 447-5083 *Fax:* (770) 446-3969
E-Mail: info@aeecenter.org
Website: aeecenter.org
Members: 11000 individuals
Staff: 21
Annual Budget: $5-10,000,000
Tax: 501(c)(6)

Personnel:
Executive Director: Albert Thumann CEM, PE

E-Mail: al@aeecenter.org
Director, Membership Services: Patricia Ardavin
    E-Mail: patricia@aeecenter.org
Director, International Certification: Mary Elise Cox
    E-Mail: maryelise@aeecenter.org
Director, E-Commerce and Business Development: Brian
    Douglas
    E-Mail: brian@aeecenter.org
Manager, Exhibits: Ted Kurklis
    E-Mail: ted@aeecenter.org
Director, Events and Marketing: Lauren Lake
    E-Mail: lauren@aeecenter.org

Historical Note:
*AEE strives to promote the scientific and educational
interests of those engaged in the energy industry and to
foster action for sustainable development. Members are
licensed professional engineers, architects, utility managers
and consultants with experience in energy management and
environmental management, distributed generation, energy
services, facilities management and security management.
Membership: $185 (Individual/Senior/Affiliate); $15
(Student/Retired); $120 (Individual Corporate).*

Continuing Education:
Certification Designation/s: BESA, CCP, CDSM, REP,
CIAQP, EBCP, CTAB, CGDIT, CIAQT, CEA, CREA, CLEP,
DGCP, CGD, CMVP, CEP, BEP, CSDP, CEM, EMIT, CBCP,
GBE, CRM, CPQ, CIAQP

Meetings/Conferences:
Conference Chair: Ted Kurklis
Number of non-conference events/year: 2

Publications:
Alternative & Renewable Energy Development Institute
    News
Cogeneration & Distributed Generation Journal;
    quarterly; adv.
Council on Women in Energy and Environmental
    Leadership
Council on Women in Energy and Environmental
    Leadership Newsletter; adv.
Distributed Generation & Alternative Energy Journal;
    quarterly
Energy Engineering Journal; bi-monthly; adv.
Energy Services Marketing Institute News
Energy Services Marketing Institute News; adv.
Environmental Engineers and Managers Institute news;
    adv.
Facility Managers Institute News; adv.
International Journal of Green Energy
Strategic Planning for Energy and the Environment;
    adv.
Sustainable Facility Magazine
The Energy Insight; quarterly; adv.
The Energy, Facility, Power Newsletter; adv.
The Journal of Energy Efficiency and Reliability

Membership List Available to Non-members

Association of Energy Service Companies (1956)
14531 FM 529
Suite 250
Houston, TX 77095
Tel: (713) 781-0758 *Fax:* (713) 781-7542
TollFree: (800) 692-0771
Website: aesc.net
Members: 687 companies
Staff: 5
Annual Budget: $100-250,000

Personnel:
Executive Director: Kenneth Jordan
    E-Mail: kjordan@aesc.net
Publisher and Manager, Sales: Patty Jordan
    E-Mail: progers@aesc.net

Historical Note:
*Formerly Association of Oilwell Servicing Contractors
(1956). AESC's mission is to advocate the interests of
members in representing the energy service industry
to customers, employees, governmental agencies and
the general public. Membership: $35-650 (Sustaining,
based on trucks); $750 (Class I Associate); $650 (Class
II Associate); $800 (Class I Producer); $700 (Class II
Producer); $150 (Individual).*

Meetings/Conferences: Annual
2013 - Tucson, AZ (Loews Ventana Canyon Resort)/
    Feb. 20 - 22
Number of non-conference events/year: 2

Publications:
Membership Directory; on-line
Well Servicing Magazine; bi-monthly; adv.

Association of Energy Services Professionals, International (1989)

15215 S. 48th St.
Suite 170
Phoenix, AZ 85044
Tel: (480) 704-5900 *Fax:* (480) 704-5905
Website: aesp.org
Members: 1400 individuals
Staff: 7
Annual Budget: $500-1,000,000

Personnel:
President and Chief Executive Officer: Meg Matt
    E-Mail: meg@aesp.org
Manager, Member Services: Kim Burtraw
    E-Mail: kim@aesp.org
Vice President, Event Planning and Member Education:
    Kisha Gresham
    E-Mail: kisha@aesp.org
Vice President, Operations: Claudia Huss
    E-Mail: claudia@aesp.org
Vice President, Marketing: Suzanne M Jones
    E-Mail: suzanne@aesp.org
Administrative Assistant: Stephanie Kilgore
    E-Mail: stephanie@aesp.org
Manager, Marketing Communications: Adeline Lui

Historical Note:
Formerly (1994) Association of DSM Professionals, AESP is dedicated to improving the delivery and implementation of energy efficiency, energy management and distributed renewable resources. Members are professionals in the energy industry. Membership: $195 (Individual); $30 (Student); $2,000 (Bronze-Level); $5,000 (Silver-Level); $10,000 (Gold- Level); $20,000 (Platinum-Level).

Meetings/Conferences: Annual
Conference Chair: Kisha Gresham
2013 - Orlando, FL (Hyatt Regency Grand Cypress)/
    Jan. 28 - 31
2013 - Dallas, TX (Westin Galleria Dallas)/April 29 -
    May 1

Publications:
Member Directory
Strategies; monthly

Association of Environmental and Engineering Geologists (1957)

P.O. Box 460518
Denver, CO 80246
Tel: (303) 757-2926 *Fax:* (720) 230-4846
E-Mail: aeg@aegweb.org
Website: aegweb.org
Members: 3100 individuals
Staff: 4
Annual Budget: $500-1,000,000

Personnel:
Chief Operating Officer: Becky Roland
    E-Mail: broland@aegweb.org
Manager, Meetings: Heather Clark
    E-Mail: heather@aegweb.org

Historical Note:
Founded by 12 charter members in Sacramento, CA as the California Association of Environmental and Engineering Geologists; and later assumed its present name. AEG's mission is to contribute to its members' professional success and the public welfare by providing leadership, advocacy, and applied research in environmental and engineering geology. A member society of the American Geological Institute. Membership: $115 (New Member); $75 (Affiliate); $35-55 (International).

Continuing Education:
Certification Designation/s: CEUs, IACET

Meetings/Conferences: Annual
Conference Chair: Heather Clark
2013 - Denver, CO/May 16 - 17

Publications:
AEG News; bi-monthly
Environmental & Engineering Geoscience Journal;
    monthly
Membership Directory; on-line

Association of Environmental and Resource Economists (1979)

1616 P St. NW
Suite 600
Washington, DC 20036
Tel: (202) 328-5125 *Fax:* (202) 939-3460
E-Mail: info@aere.org
Website: aere.org

Members: 800 individuals
Staff: 3
Annual Budget: $100-250,000
Tax: 501(c)(3)

Personnel:
Executive Director: Marilyn M. Voigt
    E-Mail: voigt@rff.org
Treasurer: Dr. Juha Siikamäki
    E-Mail: siikamaki@rff.org

Historical Note:
AERE serves as an information resource for economists involved in natural resources policy planning and research. Membership: $72 (Individual); $17-27 (Student); $17.50 (Resident).

Meetings/Conferences: Annual
2013 - Banff, AB (Banff Centre)/June 6 - 9
Number of non-conference events/year: 7

Publications:
AERE Newsletter; semi-annually
Journal of Environmental Economics and Management;
    semi-annually
Membership Directory; on-line
Review of Environmental Economics and Policy; semi-
    annually

Association of Environmental Engineering and Science Professors (1963)

C/O Department of Civil and Environmental
Engineering, 301 Dupont Hall
Newark, DE 19716
Tel: (302) 831-8120 *Fax:* (302) 831-3640
E-Mail: info@aeesp2011.com
Website: aeesp.org
Members: 850 individuals
Staff: 5
Annual Budget: $10-25,000,000
Tax: 501(c)(6)

Personnel:
Secretary: Steve K. Dentel PhD
    E-Mail: dentel@udel.edu

Historical Note:
Formerly (1972) the American Association of Professors in Sanitary Engineering. AEESP's mission is to assist its members in the development and dissemination of knowledge in environmental engineering and science. Members are professors in academic programs throughout the world who provide education in the sciences and technologies of environmental protection. Membership: $15-500/year.

Meetings/Conferences: Annual

Publications:
AEESP Newsletter

Association of Episcopal Colleges (1962)

815 Second Ave.
New York, NY 10017-4594
Tel: (212) 716-6148 *Fax:* (212) 986-5039
E-Mail: cuacaec@aol.com
Website: cuac.anglicancommunion.org/aec.cfm
Members: 11 colleges
Staff: 3
Annual Budget: $100-250,000

Personnel:
General Secretary: Rev. James G. Callaway
    E-Mail: jcallaway@cuac.org

Historical Note:
Formerly (1965) Foundation for Episcopal Colleges, and (1966) Fund for Episcopal Colleges. The Association is a consortium of colleges with historic and current ties to the Episcopal Church. AEC's mission is to enhance international/intercultural understanding through education and to promote joint curricular development. Membership: $135-2,100 (Institution); $105 (Individual).

Publications:
AEC Newsletter

Association of Equipment Management Professionals (1982)

817 Colorado Ave., Suite 103
P.O. Box 1368
Glenwood Springs, CO 81602
Tel: (970) 384-0510 *Fax:* (970) 384-0512
E-Mail: info@aemp.org
Website: aemp.org
Members: 1200 individuals
Staff: 4
Annual Budget: $500-1,000,000

Personnel:
President and Chief Strategy Officer: Stan Orr CAE
    E-Mail: stan@aemp.org
Executive Vice President: Cindy Challis Orr CAE
    E-Mail: cindy@aemp.org
Vice President, Educational Services: Jim Phillips
    E-Mail: jim@aemp.org

Historical Note:
AEMP's mission is to continue education, serve end users as a clearinghouse for technical, industry, and regulatory information. Membership: $304 (Basic); $407 (Premier/ Product Support); $922 (Basic Group); $1,082 (Premier Group); $1025 (Dealer/Distributor/Service Provider); $2,163 (Manufacturer).

Continuing Education:
Certification Designation/s: CESP, CEM, EMS

Meetings/Conferences: Annual
Conference Chair: Cindy Challis Orr CAE
2013 - Jacksonville, FL/March 17 - 19
2014 - Las Vegas, NV/March 2 - 4
Number of non-conference events/year: 2

Publications:
AEMP e-Newsletter; on-line
Biweekly Enews; bi-weekly
Membership Directory; on-line
Oversees content of Equipment Manager; quarterly;
    adv.

Association of Equipment Manufacturers (1894)

6737 W. Washington St.
Suite 2400
Milwaukee, WI 53214-5647
Tel: (414) 272-0943 *Fax:* (414) 272-1170
TollFree: (866) 236-0442
E-Mail: aem@aem.org
Website: aem.org
Members: 850 companies
Staff: 75
Annual Budget: $25-50,000,000
Tax: 501(c)(6)

Personnel:
President: Dennis J. Slater
    E-Mail: aem@aem.org
Director, Meetings and Education Programs: Mary
    Bukovic
    E-Mail: mbukovic@aem.org
Senior Director, Human Resources and Administration:
    Judy Gaus
    E-Mail: jgaus@aem.org
Senior Director, Marketing: Nicole Hallada
    E-Mail: nhallada@aem.org
Senior Director, Public Relations: Rich Jefferson
    E-Mail: rjefferson@aem.org
Vice President, Government Affairs: Anne Forristall Luke
    E-Mail: afluke@aem.org
Director, Membership Services: Paul Malek
    E-Mail: pmalek@aem.org
Chief Financial Officer: John Nowak
    E-Mail: jnowak@aem.org
Director, Information Technology: Dean Perlberg
    E-Mail: dperlberg@aem.org
Vice President, Exhibitions and Events: Megan Tanel
    E-Mail: mtanel@aem.org

Historical Note:
Formerly Construction Industry Manufacturers Association. AEM's purpose is to elevate the level of awareness for careers in the industries such as construction, agriculture, forestry, mining and utilities. Membership: $1,200-96,100/ year.

Continuing Education:
Certification Designation/s: ACET

Meetings/Conferences:
Conference Chair: Megan Tanel
2013 - Orlando, FL (Hilton Bonnet Creek Resort)/Nov.
    3 - 5

Publications:
Advisor Brussels; on-line
Advisor China; on-line
Advisor D.C.; on-line
Advisor Latin America; on-line
Advisor Latin America - Agriculture; on-line
AEM Advisor
Ag Executive Advisor; on-line
Membership Directory; quarterly

Association of Executive and Administrative Professionals (1975)

900 S. Washington St., Suite G-13
Falls Church, VA 22046-4020
Tel: (703) 237-8616 *Fax:* (703) 533-1153
E-Mail: headquarters@theaeap.com
Website: theaeap.com
Members: 5000 individuals
Staff: 4
Annual Budget: $100-250,000

Personnel:
Executive Director: Ruth Ludeman
    E-Mail: ruth@theaeap.com

Historical Note:
Formerly (1997) National Association of Executive Secretaries and (2006) National Association of Executive Secretaries and Administrative Assistants. AEAP assists its members in achieving their career goals by keeping them informed of advances and changes in professional practice and technology. Membership: $43 (Basic); $39 (Basic-Online); $74 (Premium–US/Premium Online–US); $48 (Canada-Basic); $45 (Canada Online); $78 (Canada Premium); $75 (Canada Premium Online); $58 (Other Countries-Basic); $55 (Other Countries Online).

Meetings/Conferences: Annual

Publications:
Execulary Newsletter; adv.
Member Online Network Directory; on-line; adv.
The Exec-U-Tary; adv.

Association of Executive Search Consultants
(1959)
12 E. 41st St.
17th Floor
New York, NY 10017
Tel: (212) 398-9556 *Fax:* (212) 398-9560
E-Mail: aesc@aesc.org
Website: aesc.org
Members: 300 firms
Staff: 13
Annual Budget: $2-5,000,000

Personnel:
Associate, Data and Communications: TJ Andres
Director, Information Technology: Ethan Birchard
    E-Mail: ebirchard@aesc.org
Managing Director, Finance and Administration: Kathryn Braine
    E-Mail: kbraine@aesc.org
Director, Global Marketing: Eryn Feinsod
    E-Mail: efeinsod@aesc.org
Managing Director, Global Strategy and the Americas: Brian J. Glade
    E-Mail: bglade@aesc.org
Senior Manager, Training Programs: Maureen Manion-Leone

Historical Note:
Established as the Association of Executive Recruiting Consultants, assumed its present name in 1982. AESC's mission is to promote the professional standards in retained executive search consulting, broaden public understanding of the executive search process, and serve as an advocate for the interests of its member firms. Membership: Dues based on a graduating scale relating to the number of revenue producing consultants.

Continuing Education:
Certification Designation/s: AESC CRA

Meetings/Conferences: Annual

Publications:
AESC News: Search Wire; bi-weekly; adv.
AESC Researchers Forum Newsletter; monthly; adv.
BlueSteps Senior Executives Newsletter; monthly; adv.
Member Directory; on-line

Association of Family and Conciliation Courts
(1963)
6525 Grand Teton Plaza
Madison, WI 53719
Tel: (608) 664-3750 *Fax:* (608) 664-3751
E-Mail: afcc@afccnet.org
Website: afccnet.org
Members: 1800 individuals
Staff: 8
Annual Budget: $2-5,000,000
Tax: 501(c)(3)

Personnel:
Executive Director: Peter Salem MA
    E-Mail: psalem@afccnet.org
Office Manager and Conference Registrar: Dawn Holmes
    E-Mail: dholmes@afccnet.org

Operations Administrator: Dawn Holmes
    E-Mail: dholmes@afccnet.org
Business and Administrative Director: Chris Shanahan
    E-Mail: cshanahan@afccnet.org
Administrative Assistant: Carly Wieman BA
    E-Mail: cwieman@afccnet.org

Historical Note:
AFCC's mission is to improving the lives of children and families through the resolution of family conflict. Membership: $150 (Individual); $360 (Institution); $60 (Student).

Meetings/Conferences: Annual
Conference Chair: Dawn Holmes
2013 - Los Angeles, CA (JW Marriott Los Angeles L.A. LIVE)/May 29 - June 1
2014 - Toronto, ON (Westin Harbour Castle)/May 28 - 31
2015 - New Orleans, LA (Hilton New Orleans Riverside)/May 27

Publications:
AFCC Newsletter; quarterly; adv.
Membership Directory; on-line

Association of Family Medicine Administration
(1983)
11400 Tomahawk Creek Pkwy.
Leawood, KS 66211-2672
Tel: (800) 274-2237 *Fax:* (913) 906-6092
TollFree: (800) 274-2237
E-Mail: cestes@aafp.org
Website: afmaonline.org
Members: 352 individuals
Staff: 4
Annual Budget: $50-100,000
Tax: 501(c)(6)

Personnel:
Executive Secretary: Cristin Estes
    E-Mail: cestes@aafp.org

Historical Note:
Formerly (1983) Association of Family Practice Administrators. Assumed its current name in 2005. AFMA is dedicated to the professional growth and development of members with particular emphasis on administration and coordination of health care delivery, education and research within family medicine residency programs. Members are administrators of residency programs in family medicine. Membership: $75-150/year.

Publications:
AFMA Newsletter; on-line
Membership Directory; on-line

Association of Family Medicine Residency Directors *(1990)*
11400 Tomahawk Creek Pkwy.
Suite 670
Leawood, KS 66211
Tel: (913) 906-6000 *Fax:* (913) 906-6105
TollFree: (800) 274-2237
E-Mail: afmrd@aafp.org
Website: afmrd.org
Members: 420 individuals
Staff: 4
Annual Budget: $2-5,000,000
Tax: 501(c)(3)

Personnel:
Executive Vice President: Kevin Helm MBA
    E-Mail: khelm@aafp.org
Chief Administrative Officer: Vickie Greenwood
    E-Mail: vgreenwood@aafp.org
Manager, Education Services and Special Projects: Katy Jaksa
    E-Mail: kjaksa@aafp.org
Specialist, Graduate Medical Education Services: Sam Pener
    E-Mail: spener@aafp.org

Historical Note:
Formerly (2004) Association of Family Practice Residency Directors. AFMRD works to inspire and empower family medicine residency program directors to achieve excellence in family medicine residency training. Membership: $395 (Program Director); $195 (Associate Program Director/ Associate).

Meetings/Conferences: Annual
2013 - Scottsdale, AZ (Hotel Valley Ho)/Jan. 24 - 27
2013 - Kansas City, MO (Sheraton Kansas City Hotel at Crown Center)/April 5 - 9

Publications:

Membership Directory; on-line
Redi-Reference Clinical Update Newsletter; bi-weekly
Membership List Available to Non-members

Association of Farmworker Opportunity Programs *(1971)*
1726 M St. NW
Suite 602
Washington, DC 20036-4525
Tel: (202) 828-6006 *Fax:* (202) 828-6005
E-Mail: afop@afop.org
Website: afop.org
Members:
45052 farmworkers
51 member agencies
Staff: 14
Annual Budget: $1-2,000,000
Tax: 501(c)(3)

Personnel:
Executive Director: Daniel Sheehan
Director, Communications: Ayrianne Parks
    E-Mail: parks@afop.org
Director, Health and Safety Programs: Levy Schroeder
Program Associate: Meriel Shire
    E-Mail: shire@afop.org

Historical Note:
AFOP's mission is to advance the quality of life for migrant and seasonal farmworkers and their families by providing advocacy for the member organizations that serve them. Membership: $50/year(Individual, varies with organizational capacity).

Meetings/Conferences: Annual
Conference Chair: Meriel Shire

Publications:
Salud; quarterly
Washington Newsline; bi-monthly; adv.

Association of Federal Communications Consulting Engineers *(1948)*
20th St. Stn.
P.O. Box 19333
Washington, DC 20036-0333
Tel: (202) 898-0110 *Fax:* (202) 898-0895
Website: afcce.org
Members: 240 individuals
Staff: 3
Annual Budget: $50-100,000

Personnel:
President: Mark D. Neumann
Treasurer: Ronald Chase
Contact, Membership: John George

Historical Note:
AFCCE seeks to aid and promote the proper federal administration and regulation of those engineering and technical phases of communications which are regulated by the Federal Communications Commission, to uphold the honor and dignity of engineers before the FCC, and to provide for the mutual improvement and social intercourse of the members of the Association. Members composed of engineering executives of communications companies and radio equipment manufacturers. Membership: $180 (Full); $140 (Associate) $50 (Government Full/Associate); $20 (Life).

Meetings/Conferences: Annual
Number of non-conference events/year: 2

Publications:
Membership Directory; on-line

Association of Field Ornithologists *(1922)*
2081 E. Sierra Ave.
Fresno, CA 93710
Tel: (559) 868-6233
E-Mail: business@osnabirds.org
Website: afonet.org
Members: 1200 individuals
Staff: 4
Annual Budget: $100-250,000

Personnel:
President: Kathryn Purcell
    E-Mail: kpurcell@fs.fed.us

Historical Note:
AFO is dedicated to the study and conservation of birds and their natural habitats. Membership: $25 (Regular); $50 (Supporting); $15 (Student/Early Professional); $30 (Family); $650 (Life); $1000 (Patron).

Meetings/Conferences: Annual
2013 - Venus, FL/March 27 - 30

Publications:
AFO Afield
AFO Afield; semi-annually
Journal of Field Ornithology; quarterly
Ornithological Newsletter; bi-monthly

Association of Film Commissioners International
(1979)
8530 Wilshire Blvd.
Suite 210
Beverly Hills, CA 90211
Tel: (323) 461-2324 *Fax:* (413) 375-2903
E-Mail: info@afci.org
Website: afci.org
Members: 307 individuals
Staff: 5
Annual Budget: $1-2,000,000

Personnel:
Executive Director: Martin Cuff
    E-Mail: martin@afci.org
Director, Operations: Kevin Clark
    E-Mail: kevin@afci.org
Director, Business Relationships: Elyse Gammer
    E-Mail: elyse@afci.org
Communications Specialist: Jason LaBue
    E-Mail: jason@afci.org
Contact, Advertising: Nicki Webber
    E-Mail: nwebber@boutiqueeditions.com

Historical Note:
Formerly (1990) Association of Film Commissioners. AFCI is the official professional organization for film commissioners who assist film, television and video production throughout the world. Members serve as city, county, state, regional, provincial or national film commissioners for their respective governmental jurisdictions. Membership: $750/year.

Continuing Education:
Certification Designation/s: CFC
Meetings/Conferences:
Number of non-conference events/year: 1

Publications:
AFCI Newsletter; monthly; adv.
Locations Magazine; adv.
Membership Directory; on-line

Association of Finance and Insurance Professionals *(1989)*
4104 Felps Drive, Suite H-J
P.O. Box 1933
Colleyville, TX 76034-1933
Tel: (817) 428-2434 *Fax:* (817) 428-2534
E-Mail: info@afip.com
Website: afip.com
Members: 10000 individuals
Staff: 7
Annual Budget: $500-1,000,000
Tax: 501(c)(3)

Personnel:
Executive Director: David N. Robertson

Historical Note:
AFIP's mission is to give a voice to the F&I practitioner, to protect the interests of the F&I profession and to support the companies that serve the F&I function. Membership: $915 (Individual); $3,500 (Industry); $1,750 (General Agents).

Continuing Education:
Certification Designation/s: AFIP, IDC, CVC, NCC
Publications:
AFIP Newsletter; monthly

Association of Financial Guaranty Insurers *(1986)*
139 Lancaster St.
Albany, NY 12210-1903
Tel: (518) 449-4698 *Fax:* (518) 432-5651
E-Mail: tcasey@mackinco.com
Website: afgi.org
Members: 7 corporations
Staff: 1
Annual Budget: Under $10,000

Personnel:
Executive Director: Teresa M. Casey
    E-Mail: tcasey@mackinco.com

Historical Note:
AFGI provides service to the insurers and reinsurers of municipal bonds and asset-backed securities. Members are Monoline municipal bond insurers and reinsurers.

Association of Firearm and Toolmark Examiners *(1969)*
5230 Medical Center Dr.
Dallas, TX 75235
Tel: (214) 920-5978 *Fax:* (214) 920-5896
E-Mail: j5945k@lvmpd.com
Website: afte.org
Members: 850 individuals
Staff: 6
Annual Budget: $10-25,000
Tax: 501(c)(3)

Personnel:
President: Ray Cooper
    E-Mail: rballistic@sbcglobal.net

Historical Note:
AFTE is dedicated to the advancement of forensic science, firearm and tool Identification. Represents firearm and toolmark examiners engaged in firearm and toolmark idenitification for legal system.

Continuing Education:
Certification Designation/s: CPS, AFTE
Publications:
AFTE Journal
AFTE News
Membership Directory; on-line

Association of Fish and Wildlife Agencies *(1902)*
444 N. Capitol St. NW
Suite 725
Washington, DC 20001
Tel: (202) 624-7890 *Fax:* (202) 624-7891
E-Mail: info@fishwildlife.org
Website: fishwildlife.org
Members: 300 individuals
Staff: 28
Annual Budget: $2-5,000,000
Tax: 501(c)(6)

Personnel:
Executive Director: Ron Regan
    E-Mail: rregan@fishwildlife.org
General Counsel: Carol Bambery
    E-Mail: cbambery@fishwildlife.org
Manager, Accounting: John Bloom
    E-Mail: jbloom@fishwildlife.org
Contact, Science and Research Liaison: Dr. Arpita Choudhury
    E-Mail: achoudhury@fishwildlife.org
Director, Communications and Marketing: Laura MacLean
    E-Mail: lmaclean@fishwildlife.org
Director, Government Affairs: Jennifer Mock Schaeffer
    E-Mail: jenmock@fishwildlife.org

Historical Note:
Established as the National Association of Game Commissioners and Wardens, it became the International Association of Game, Fish and Conservation Commissioners in 1917 and assumed its previous name in 1976, and present name in 2006. IAFWA represents North America's fish and promotes sound management, conservation and speaks with a unified voice on important fish and wildlife issues. Membership: $25 (Individual); $250 (Organization).

Meetings/Conferences: Annual

Publications:
e-newsletter; weekly

Association of Flight Attendants - CWA *(1945)*
501 Third St. NW
Washington, DC 20001-2797
Tel: (202) 434-1300 *Fax:* (202) 434-1319
E-Mail: info@afacwa.org
Website: afanet.org
Members: 60,000 flight attendants
Staff: 65
Annual Budget: $10-25,000,000

Personnel:
International President: Veda Shook
    E-Mail: vshook@afanet.org
Media Contact: Corey Caldwell
    E-Mail: ccaldwell@afanet.org
International Secretary and Treasurer: Kevin P. Creighan
Vice President and Director, Government Affairs: George Donahue
    E-Mail: gdonahue@afanet.org
General Counsel: Ed Glmartin
    E-Mail: egilma1t@afanet.org

Historical Note:

Formerly (1973) the Steward and Stewardesses Division of the Air Line Pilots Association, International. AFA-CWA's mission is to maintain and improve wages, benefits and working conditions for flight attendants. Sponsors and supports the Flight PAC Political Action Committee.

Publications:
AFA-CWA Newsletter; on-line
Membership Directory; on-line

Association of Food and Drug Officials *(1896)*
2550 Kingston Rd.
Suite 311
York, PA 17402
Tel: (717) 757-2888 *Fax:* (717) 650-3650
E-Mail: afdo@afdo.org
Website: afdo.org
Members: 600 individuals
Staff: 3
Annual Budget: $500-1,000,000
Tax: 501(c)(3)

Personnel:
Executive Director: Joseph Corby
    E-Mail: jcorby@afdo.org
Assistant, Administration and Special Projects: Patty Myers
Administrator, Information Technology: Randy Young

Historical Note:
AFDO's mission is to encourage education, communication and cooperation among government, industry and consumers. Membership: $50-325/year.

Continuing Education:
Certification Designation/s: HACCP
Meetings/Conferences: Annual
2013 - Louisville, KY (Louisville Marriott Downtown)/
    June 8 - 12
Number of non-conference events/year: 2

Publications:
AFDO Journal; on-line

Association of Food Industries *(1906)*
3301 Route 66
Suite 205, Building C
Naponee, NJ 07753
Tel: (732) 922-3008 *Fax:* (732) 922-3590
E-Mail: info@afius.org
Website: afius.org
Members: 850 companies
Staff: 7
Annual Budget: $1-2,000,000

Personnel:
President: Bob Bauer
Secretary: Stephen O' Mara

Historical Note:
Formed by a merger of the Bean Association, the Dried Fruit Association of New York and the Food Brokers Association. Formerly (1982) Association of Food Distributors. The Association of Food Industries is a trade association serving the food import trade. AFI is committed to developing programs that facilitate the business of its member companies, encourage free and fair trade and foster compliance with United States laws and regulations for the food industry. Membership: $495 (Associate/Overseas); $1,040-1,940 (Import/Export Agents, based on sales); $1,040-2,685 (Importers and Exporters, based on annual sales).

Meetings/Conferences: Annual
2013 - Las Vegas, NV/April 18 - 21
Number of non-conference events/year: 2

Association of Food Journalists *(1974)*
Seven Avenida Vista Grande
Suite B7 Room 467
Santa Fe, NM 87508-9299
Tel: (505) 466-4742
E-Mail: caroldemasters@yahoo.com
Website: afjonline.com
Members: 300 individuals
Staff: 2
Annual Budget: $25-50,000

Personnel:
Executive Director: Carol DeMasters
    E-Mail: caroldemasters@yahoo.com
Treasurer: Patricia West-Barker
    E-Mail: pwestbarker@gmail.com

Historical Note:
Formerly (1994) the Newspaper Food Editors and Writers Association, AFJ's primary goal is to encourage

communication among food journalists. *Membership:* $75 (Active/Associate); $37.50 (Retired).

Meetings/Conferences: Annual
2013 - Park City, UT (Treasure Mountain Inn.)/Sept. 18 - 20

Publications:
AFJ's Membership Directory
AFJNewsletter; monthly

Association of Foreign Investors in U.S. Real Estate *(1988)*
Ronald Reagan Building
1300 Pennsylvania Ave. NW
Washington, DC 20004
Tel: (202) 312-1400 *Fax:* (202) 312-1401
E-Mail: afireinfo@afire.org
Website: afire.org
Members: 200 corporations
Staff: 5
Annual Budget: $1-2,000,000

Personnel:
Chief Executive Officer: James A. Fetgatter
    E-Mail: afireinfo@afire.org
Director, Meetings and Membership Services: Nancy Nicolaides Knight
Managing Director: Lexie Miller CAE

Historical Note:
Formerly (1998) the Association of Foreign Investors in United States Real Estate. AFIRE provides an exclusive environment where principals and senior executives can meet and exchange information through regularly scheduled meetings in the US, Europe and key cities around the world. Members are foreign investors in U. S. real estate, and domestic firms providing services in the field. Membership is on a corporate basis and by invitation only. Membership: $9,500 (Institutional/Associate/Supporting).

Meetings/Conferences:
Conference Chair: Nancy Nicolaides Knight
2013 - New York City, NY (Mandarin Oriental, New York)/Feb. 13 - 14
2013 - Cologne, Germany (Maritim Hotel)/June 19 - 20
2013 - San Francisco, CA (Ritz-Carlton)/Sept. 9 - 11
Number of non-conference events/year: 6

Publications:
AFIRE News; bi-monthly
Membership Directory; on-line

Association of Foreign Trade Representatives *(1984)*
P.O. Box 300, Planetarium Stn.
New York, NY 10024-0300
Tel: (212) 877-8900 *Fax:* (212) 877-1905
E-Mail: mccabe@whoswho.com
Members:
75 organizations
200 individuals
Staff: 2
Annual Budget: Under $10,000

Personnel:
Executive Director: John J. McCabe
    E-Mail: mccabe@whoswho.com

Historical Note:
Established in April, 1984 to provide a forum for the exchange of ideas and experiences relating to the advancement of trade. Members are consuls general, executive directors, trade commissioners, ministers and consuls, attaches, secretaries and officers from the commercial and information sections of state and provincial governments.

Association of Forensic Document Examiners *(1986)*
5432 E. Karen Dr.
Scottsdale, AZ 85254-8205
Website: afde.org
Members: 40 individuals
Staff: 3
Annual Budget: Under $10,000

Personnel:
President: Emily J. Will
Editor: M. Patricia Fisher
Director, Membership Services: John Gorajczyk

Historical Note:
Established and incorporated in Illinois. AFDE provides continuing education in the field of forensic document examination and a forum for the exchange of information among colleagues. Membership: $175 (Professional/ Certified); $75 (International/Affiliate); $50 (Associate).

Continuing Education:
Certification Designation/s: BFDE, FSAB, BCP

Meetings/Conferences: Annual

Publications:
Journal of Forensic Document Examination; annually

Association of Former Agents of the U.S. Secret Service *(1971)*
525 SW Fifth St.
Suite A
Des Moines, IA 50309-4501
Tel: (515) 282-8192 *Fax:* (515) 282-9117
E-Mail: afausss@assoc-mgmt.com
Website: oldstar.org
Members: 1400 individuals
Staff: 4
Annual Budget: $100-250,000

Personnel:
Executive Director: Kathy Rinkenberger

Historical Note:
AFAUSSS strives to bring together former and current employees of the Secret Service. Members are special agents, technical specialists and other support personnel who carry out the investigative and protective responsibilities of the United States Secret Service. Membership: $25 (Associate/Affiliate); $75 (Regular).

Association of Former Intelligence Officers *(1975)*
6723 Whittier Ave.
Suite 200
McLean, VA 22101
Tel: (703) 790-0320 *Fax:* (703) 991-1278
E-Mail: afio@afio.com
Website: afio.com
Members: 4500 individuals and 200 corporations
Staff: 5
Annual Budget: $250-500,000
Tax: 501(c)(3)

Personnel:
Executive Director, Secretary and Treasurer: Elizabeth A Bancroft
    E-Mail: bancroft@afio.com
Contact, Publications Research: Priscilla Adams
Director, Membership Services: Patricia S. Lebeau
Contact, Special Events: Arlene Wagner
Financial Counsel: Duvall Wheeler

Historical Note:
Chartered originally as the Association of Retired Intelligence Officers, present name was adopted in 1976. AFIO's mission is to build a public constituency for a sound, healthy and capable US intelligence system. Membership: $60 (Former US Intelligence/Former US Law Enforcement Professional/Business Intelligence/Intelligence Enthusiast/ Media Professionals/College Professors/Students/Other Academics); $95 (UK, Canada, Australia, or New Zealand Citizen); $1,000 (Donor); $2,000 (Corporate).

Meetings/Conferences:
Conference Chair: Arlene Wagner
Number of non-conference events/year: 1

Publications:
Intelligencer; bi-annually
Weekly Intelligence Notes (WINs); weekly

Association of Former OSI Special Agents *(1966)*
P.O. Box 523135
Springfield, VA 22152-5135
Tel: (703) 978-6198 *Fax:* (703) 978-6198
E-Mail: info@afosisa-ncc.org
Website: afosisa-ncc.org
Members: 2000 members
Staff: 4
Annual Budget: $50-100,000
Tax: 501(c)(3)

Personnel:
Executive Officer and Editor: Dick Law
Treasurer: Charles A. Costa

Historical Note:
AFOSISA's purpose is to maintain and further friendships emanating from service with or employment by the Air Force Office of Special Investigations (AFOSI). Members are former and current members of the Air Force Office of Special Investigations. Membership: $35 (Regular); $25 (Associate).

Publications:
The Informant

Association of Fraternity Advisors *(1976)*

P.O. Box 1369
Ft. Collins, CO 80522-1369
Tel: (970) 797-4361 *Fax:* (888) 855-8670
E-Mail: info@fraternityadvisors.org
Website: afa1976.org
Members: 1700 Individuals
Staff: 4
Annual Budget: $100-250,000
Tax: 501(c)(3)

Personnel:
Director, Events and Programs: Tricia Fechter
    E-Mail: tricia@afa1976.org
Director, Member Engagement: Kyle Jordan
    E-Mail: kyle@afa1976.org
Director, Education and Curriculum Design: Ryan O'Rourke
    E-Mail: ryan@afa1976.org

Historical Note:
AFA enhances its members ability to create fraternity and sorority experiences that positively affect students, host institutions, and communities. AFA's mission is to enhance its members abilities to support impactful fraternity/ sorority experiences and to secure, invest, and distribute the necessary resources to support the educational objectives of the Association of Fraternity/SororityAdvisors. Membership: $99 (Professional/Affiliate); $65 (Graduate Student/ Emeritus); $60 (Retired); $15 (Optional); $199 (Vendor Members).

Meetings/Conferences: Annual
Conference Chair: Tricia Fechter
2013 - Orlando, FL (Hilton Orlando Bonnet Creek)/ Dec. 4 - 8
2014 - Nashville, TN (Omni Nashville Hotel)/Dec. 3 - 7
2015 - Ft. Worth, TX (Omni Fort Worth Hotel)/Dec. 2 - 5

Publications:
Associate Quarterly; quarterly
Association Update; monthly
Essentials; monthly
Membership Directory; on-line
Oracle : The Research Journal of the Association of Fraternity Advisors; semi-annually
Perspectives; quarterly; adv.
The AFA Volunteer; monthly

Membership List Available to Non-members

Association of Free Community Papers *(1951)*
7445 Morgan Rd.
Suite 103
Liverpool, NY 13090
Fax: (781) 459-7770
E-Mail: afcp@afcp.org
Website: afcp.org
Members: 350 corporations
Staff: 3
Annual Budget: $500-1,000,000
Tax: 501(c)(6)

Personnel:
Executive Director: Loren Colburn
Administrative Assistant: Kristen Des Lauriers

Historical Note:
Formerly (1987) National Association of Advertising Publishers. AFCP's mission is to help its members enhance their profitability and lead in strengthening the free paper industry. Members are publishers of free- circulation community newspapers. It provides recognition, business solutions and educational programs to its members. Membership: $200/year (Associate).

Continuing Education:
Certification Designation/s: AAE, CAE, MAE

Meetings/Conferences: Annual
Conference Chair: Kristen Des Lauriers
2013 - Denver, CO (Denver Marriott City Center)/April 25 - 27
Number of non-conference events/year: 6

Publications:
Free Paper Ink; monthly; adv.
Membership Directory; on-line

Association of Free Standing Radiation Oncology Centers *(1987)*
12100 Sunset Hills Rd.
Suite 130
Reston, VA 20005
Tel: (703) 234-4050 *Fax:* (703) 435-4390
E-Mail: info@afroc.org
Website: afroc.org

Members: 350 individuals
Staff: 3
Annual Budget: $100-250,000
Tax: 501(c)(3)

Personnel:
Executive Director: Robin Turner
  E-Mail: rturner@drohanmgmt.com
Administrator: Alexandra D'Imperio
Legal Counsel: Diane Millman

Historical Note:
AFROC's focus is on regulatory, legislative and socio economic issues. It also promotes independent, non-hospital based cancer therapy centers, which are typically cost-effective for consumers and have better practice standards and is comprised of a network of physicians, physicists, administrators, and allied health care professionals involved with freestanding centers. Membership: $500 (Individual); $5,000-15,000 (Physicians).

Meetings/Conferences:
Conference Chair: Alexandra D'Imperio

Publications:
Membership Directory
The Source; bi-monthly

Association of Fund-Raising Distributors and Suppliers *(1992)*
1100 Johnson Ferry Rd. NE
Suite 300
Atlanta, GA 30342
Tel: (404) 252-3663 *Fax:* (404) 252-0774
E-Mail: afrds@kellencompany.com
Website: afrds.org
Members: 600 companies as manufacturers, suppliers or distributors
Staff: 5
Annual Budget: $500-1,000,000
Tax: 501(c)(6)

Personnel:
Executive Director: Jon Krueger
Executive Vice President and Senior Advisor: Russ Lemieux
Manager, Trade Shows and Operations: Jennifer Stone-Rogers
  E-Mail: jstone@kellencompany.com

Historical Note:
Formerly (2001) Association of Fund Raisers and Direct Sellers. Formed in 1992 by the merger of National Association of Product Fund Raisers and National Association of Direct Sellers. AFRDS's mission is to unify, promote and safeguard the fundraising industry. AFRDS members are distributors, manufacturers, suppliers, and brokers to the product fund raising industry. Membership: $295-1,530 (Distributor); $850-2,000 (Supplier); $850 (Affiliate).

Meetings/Conferences: Annual
Conference Chair: Jennifer Stone-Rogers

Publications:
AFRDS Advisor Newsletter; quarterly
Membership Directory; on-line
The Fundraising Edge; semi-annually

Association of Fundraising Professionals *(1960)*
4300 Wilson Blvd.
Suite 300
Arlington, VA 22203-4168
Tel: (703) 684-0410 *Fax:* (703) 684-0540
TollFree: (800) 666-3863
E-Mail: afp@afpnet.org
Website: afpnet.org
Members: 30000 individuals
Staff: 45
Annual Budget: $10-25,000,000
Tax: 501(c)(6)

Personnel:
President and Chief Executive Officer: Andrew Watt
  E-Mail: awatt@afpnet.org
Manager, Chapter Services: Margie Bennett
  E-Mail: mbennett@afpnet.org
Publisher and Editor in Chief: Jackie Boice
  E-Mail: jboice@afpnet.org
Chief Financial Officer: Mike Eason CPA
  E-Mail: meason@afpnet.org
Vice President, Membership and Chapter Services: Lori Gusdorf CAE
  E-Mail: lgusdorf@afpnet.org
Vice President, Communications, Public Relations and Media Relations: Michael Nilsen

E-Mail: mnilsen@afpnet.org
Chief Marketing Officer: Scott Pearl
  E-Mail: spearl@afpnet.org
General Counsel: Walter Sczudlo
  E-Mail: wsczudlo@afpnet.org
Chief Information Officer: Prabhash Shrestha CAE
  E-Mail: pshrestha@afpnet.org
Vice President, Meetings and International Conferences: Lynn Smith CMP
  E-Mail: lsmith@afpnet.org
Vice President, Education and Training: Rhonda Starr
  E-Mail: rstarr@afpnet.org

Historical Note:
Formerly Association of Fund-Raising Directors and then (1978) the National Society of Fund Raisers, assumed its current name in 2000. AFP fosters development and growth of fundraising professionals and promotes better ethical standards in the fundraising profession. Members are individual fund raisers with experience in directing, managing or counseling fund raising programs. Membership: $250 (Professional/Associate); $75 (Young Professional/Retired) ;$35 (Collegiate membership); $50(Global e-membership);$1,500-5,000 (AFP Business Membership); $2,000 (AFP's Nonprofit Organizational Membership).

Meetings/Conferences: Annual
Conference Chair: Lynn Smith CMP
2013 - San Diego, CA/April 7 - 10
2013 - San Diego, CA/April 7 - 9

Publications:
Advancing Philanthropy; adv.
AFP eWire; weekly; adv.
Kaleidoscope; quarterly
Membership Directory; on-line
Steward Newsletter; semi-annually
Te Informa; quarterly

Association of Gaming Equipment Manufacturers
P.O. Box 50049
Henderson, NV 89016-0049
Tel: (702) 812-6932
E-Mail: agem.org@cox.net
Website: agem.org
Members: 120 companies
Staff: 2
Annual Budget: $1-2,000,000
Tax: 501(c)(6)

Personnel:
Executive Director: Marcus Prater
General Counsel: Neil H. Friedman

Historical Note:
AGEM works to further the interests of gaming equipment manufacturers throughout the world.

Publications:
Membership Directory; on-line

Association of Gay and Lesbian Psychiatrists *(1985)*
4514 Chester Ave.
Philadelphia, PA 19143-3707
Tel: (215) 222-2800 *Fax:* (215) 222-3881
E-Mail: info@aglp.org
Website: aglp.org
Members: 650 individuals
Staff: 4
Annual Budget: $50-100,000
Tax: 501(c)(3)

Personnel:
Executive Director: Roy Harker
  E-Mail: rharker@aglp.org
Editor: George Harrison MD
  E-Mail: gharrison@aglp.org
Treasurer: Serena Volpp MD
  E-Mail: svolpp@aglp.org
Editor: Eric Yarbrough
  E-Mail: eyarbrough@aglp.org

Historical Note:
AGLP's mission is to educate and advocate on lesbian, gay, bisexual and transgender mental health issues and to provide valuable and accessible services to members. Membership: $225 (General/Associate); $15 (Medical Student); $45 (Resident); $100 (Ally/International/Early Career).

Meetings/Conferences: Annual
2013 - Orlando, FL (Walt Disney World Resort)/Oct. 22 - 27

Publications:
AGLP newsletter; quarterly

Membership Directory; on-line
The Journal of Gay and Lesbian Mental Health; quarterly; adv.

Association of Genetic Technologists *(1975)*
P.O. Box 19193
Lenexa, KS 66285
Tel: (913) 895-4605 *Fax:* (913) 895-4652
E-Mail: agt-info@goamp.com
Website: agt-info.org
Members: 1200 technologists, supervisors, and lab directors
Staff: 2
Annual Budget: $250-500,000
Tax: 501(c)(3)

Personnel:
Executive Director: Christie Ross CAE
  E-Mail: cross@goamp.com
Administrative Assistant: Diane Conner
  E-Mail: diane.conner@goamp.com

Historical Note:
AGT is established to advocate cooperation and exchange of information among those engaged in classical cytogenetics, molecular and biochemical genetics, and to stimulate interest in genetics as a career. Membership: $95 (Regular); $35 (Student); $40 (Emeritus/Collaborative).

Meetings/Conferences: Annual
2013 - Las Vegas, NV (The Cosmopolitan of Las Vegas)/June 6 - 8
Number of non-conference events/year: 2

Publications:
AGT e-Newsletter; quarterly; adv.
Journal of the Association of Genetic Technologists; quarterly; adv.

Membership List Available to Non-members

Association of Girl Scout Executive Staff *(1939)*
236 Carmichael Way
Suite 300-26
Chesapeake, VA 23322
E-Mail: admin@agses.org
Website: agses.org
Members: 500 individuals
Staff: 2
Annual Budget: $50-100,000

Personnel:
President: Tracy Keller
  E-Mail: tracyk@gsccc.org
Treasurer: Janet Kington
  E-Mail: janetkington@yahoo.com

Historical Note:
Formerly National Association of Girl Scout Executives and Association of Girl Scout Professional Workers. AGSES's purpose is to enhance professional excellence for all employed Girl Scout staff. Members are executive staff employed by the national headquarters and local Girl Scout Councils. Membership: $75 (Active/Associate); $750 (Lifetime).

Publications:
E-Newsletter; monthly
Membership Directory; on-line

Association of Global Automakers *(1964)*
1050 K St. NW
Suite 650
Washington, DC 20001
Tel: (202) 650-5555 *Fax:* (703) 525-3289
E-Mail: info@globalautomakers.org
Website: globalautomakers.org
Members: f 14 motor vehicle manufacturers
Staff: 17
Annual Budget: $5-10,000,000

Personnel:
President and Chief Executive Officer: Michael J. Stanton
Vice President and General Counsel: Ellen J. Gleberman
Senior Manager, Finance and Administrative Services: Kim J. Hutchinson
Director, Communications: Annemarie B. Pender
  E-Mail: apender@globalautomakers.org
Director, Government Affairs: Paul D. Ryan
  E-Mail: pryan@aiam.org

Historical Note:
Formerly the Association of International Automobile Manufacturers. AGA represents international motor vehicle manufacturers, original equipment suppliers and other automotive-related trade associations. AGA provides members with information, analysis and advocacy on a

wide variety of legislative and regulatory issues impacting the auto sector. Members are automobile manufacturers.

Membership List Available to Non-members

Association of Golf Merchandisers *(1989)*
P.O. Box 7247
Phoenix, AZ 85011-7247
Tel: (602) 604-8250 *Fax:* (602) 604-8251
E-Mail: info@agmgolf.org
Website: agmgolf.org
Members: 800 individuals and 140 companies
Staff: 2
Annual Budget: $250-500,000
Tax: 501(c)(3)

Personnel:
Executive Director: Desane Blaney
    E-Mail: desane@agmgolf.org
Administrative Assistant: Diane Blackmer
    E-Mail: diane@agmgolf.org

Historical Note:
AGM's mission is to educate golf retail buyers/ merchandisers and golf professionals, elevate the golf merchandising profession, and enhance communication between golf buyers and vendor partners. Active members are individuals representing private, public, resort and off-course golf specialty stores. Membership: $225 (Merchandiser); $100 (Associate Merchandiser/Student); $450 (Vendor Partners).

Meetings/Conferences:
Number of non-conference events/year: 8

Publications:
AGM e-Tailer; monthly
Membership Directory; on-line

Association of Governing Boards of Universities and Colleges *(1921)*
1133 20th St. NW
Suite 300
Washington, DC 20036
Tel: (202) 296-8400 *Fax:* (202) 223-7053
TollFree: (800) 356-6317
Website: agb.org
Members: 36000 individuals and 1250 institutions
Staff: 39
Annual Budget: $5-10,000,000
Tax: 501(c)(3)

Personnel:
President: Richard D. Legon
    E-Mail: rickl@agb.org
Editor-In-Chief and Director, Publications: Sarah
    Hardesty Bray
    E-Mail: sarahb@agb.org
Director, Web Communications: Ursula Gross
    E-Mail: ursulag@agb.org
Executive Vice President: Susan Whealler Johnston
    E-Mail: sjohnston@agb.org
Director, Membership Services: Cathy Josman
    E-Mail: cathy@agb.org
Vice President, Finance: Maria Nazareth
    E-Mail: marian@agb.org
Senior Vice President, Programs and Research: Richard
    Novak
    E-Mail: RichN@agb.org
Registrar, Events: Jessica Oplak
    E-Mail: jessicao@agb.org

Historical Note:
Founded originally as an informal organization of public university trustees, AGB established an office in Washington with its first full- time staff in 1964. AGB's purpose is to strengthen the performance of boards of higher education. AGB serves trustees and regents on some governing and coordinating boards of public and private colleges and universities. Annual dues for membership in AGB are based on total enrollment figures for the Fall term. Membership: $2,500-10,900 (Enrollment); $2,100-3,000 (Public Institution).

Meetings/Conferences: Annual
Conference Chair: Jessica Oplak
2013 - San Francisco, CA (Hyatt Regency San
    Francisco)/April 21 - 23
2014 - Orlando, FL (Convention Center/The Peabody
    Orlando)/April 13 - 15
2015 - Phoenix, AZ (Sugarloaf Animal Clinic)/April 10
    - 12
Number of non-conference events/year: 1

Publications:
Trusteeship Magazine; on-line

Association of Government Accountants *(1950)*
2208 Mount Vernon Ave.
Alexandria, VA 22301-1314
Tel: (703) 684-6931 *Fax:* (703) 548-9367
TollFree: (800) 242-7211
Website: agacgfm.org
Members: 16000 individuals
Staff: 23
Annual Budget: $5-10,000,000
Tax: 501(c)(3)

Personnel:
Executive Director: Relmond P. Van Daniker CPA, DBA
    E-Mail: rvandaniker@agacgfm.org
Director, Finance and Administration: Cristina Barbudo
    CPA, MS
    E-Mail: cbarbudo@agacgfm.org
Director, Meetings and Expositions: Jerome Bruce CAE,
    CEM, CMP
    E-Mail: jbruce@agacgfm.org
Manager, Publications: Christina M. Camara
    E-Mail: camara100@cox.net
Deputy Executive Director and Chief Operating Officer:
    Susan M. Fritzlen
    E-Mail: sfritzlen@agacgfm.org
Director, Education and Research: Kevin Johnson
    E-Mail: kjohnson@agacgfm.org
Director, Communications and Journal Editor: Maryann
    Malesardi
    E-Mail: mmalesardi@agacgfm.org
Manager, Membership Services: Jill Murphy
    E-Mail: jmurphy@agacgfm.org
Systems Administrator: David Payne
    E-Mail: dpayne@agacgfm.org
Director, Intergovernmental Relations: Helena Sims
    E-Mail: hsims@agacgfm.org

Historical Note:
AGA fosters learning, certification, leadership and collaboration for professionals and stakeholders committed to advancing government accountability. Members are government accountability professionals. Membership: $30-150/year.

Continuing Education:
Certification Designation/s: CGFM, CPE

Meetings/Conferences:
Conference Chair: Jerome Bruce CAE, CEM, CMP
2013 - Dallas, TX (Gaylord Texan Hotel and
    Convention Center-Dallas)/July 14 - 17
2014 - Orlando, FL (Orlando World Center Marriott)/
    July 13 - 16
Number of non-conference events/year: 4

Publications:
AGA Today; bi-weekly; adv.
Government Financial Management TOPICS; bi-
    weekly; adv.
Journal CPE Online; on-line; adv.
The Journal of Government Financial Management;
    quarterly; adv.

Association of Graduate Liberal Studies Programs *(1975)*
C/O Duke University
P.O. Box 90095
Durham, NC 27708-0095
Tel: (919) 684-1987 *Fax:* (919) 681-8905
E-Mail: info@aglsp.org
Website: aglsp.org
Members: 105 institutions
Staff: 4
Annual Budget: $50-100,000
Tax: 501(c)(3)

Personnel:
President: David L. Gitomer
    E-Mail: dgitomer@depaul.edu
Treasurer: Kathleen Forbes
    E-Mail: keforbes@uncg.edu
Administrative Manager: Ellen Levine
    E-Mail: info@aglsp.org
Editor: Ken Smith
    E-Mail: ksmith@iusb.edu

Historical Note:
AGLSP promotes the concept and goals of Graduate Liberal Studies, fosters standards in GLS programs, provides guidance for institutions considering initiating and improving such programs, and promotes public awareness of the program. Membership: $350 (Full); $300 (Associate); $40 (Individual); Free (Fellows).

Meetings/Conferences: Annual

Publications:
Confluence: The Journal of Graduate Liberal Studies;
    bi-annually

Association of Graduate Schools in Association of American Universities *(1948)*
1200 New York Ave. NW
Suite 550
Washington, DC 20005
Tel: (202) 408-7500 *Fax:* (202) 408-8184
Website: aau.edu/about
Members: 61 individuals
Staff: 2
Annual Budget: Under $10,000

Personnel:
Associate Vice President, Federal Relations: Carrie
    Wolinetz
Director, Information Technology: Tom Bozzo

Historical Note:
Members are deans of graduate studies of the sixty-one research universities belonging to the Association of American Universities. Purpose is to consider matters of common interest relating to graduate study and research.

Publications:
Weekly Wrap-ups; weekly

Association of Halfway House Alcoholism Programs of North America *(1966)*
401 E. Sangamon Ave.
Springfield, IL 62702
Tel: (217) 523-0527 *Fax:* (217) 698-8234
Website: ahhap.org
Members: 120000 individuals
Staff: 3
Annual Budget: $10-25,000

Personnel:
President: Susan O. Binns
Treasurer: Roger Glasgow
Secretary: Jessica Hayes
    E-Mail: jessica@iaodapca.org

Historical Note:
AHHAP's mission is to offer residential services and programs that promote recovery from alcoholism and drug addiction. Members are halfway house programs and individuals with an interest in the halfway house movement. Membership: $100 (Newcomer Agencies); $25 (Individual).

Continuing Education:
Certification Designation/s: NCRS

Publications:
Membership Dirtectory

Association of HazMat Shippers *(2002)*
1101 30th St. NW
Suite 500
Washington, DC 20007
Tel: (202) 625-8355 *Fax:* (240) 559-0920
Website: hazmatshippers.com
Staff: 3
Annual Budget: $50-100,000
Tax: 501(c)(6)

Personnel:
President: Michael Ryan
General Counsel: Larry "Lawrence" W. Bierlein Esq.
    E-Mail: larry@hazmat-lawyer.com
Treasurer: Rob Brogus

Historical Note:
AHS serves the interests of companies involved in the domestic and international shipment of non-bulk and limited quantity sizes of hazardous materials. Membership: $3000-5000 (Company), $8000 (Association) and $1500 (Associate).

Publications:
Membership Directory; annually

Association of Health Information Outsourcing Services *(1996)*
6875 Hwy. 65 NE
Fridley, MN 55432
Tel: (800) 688-9644 *Fax:* (763) 572-0902
E-Mail: info@ahios.org
Website: ahios.org
Staff: 3
Annual Budget: $50-100,000

Personnel:
Executive Director: Richard C. Logan MBA, RHIA

E-Mail: rlogan1042@aol.com
Chair, Public Relations: Bonnie J Coffey
    E-Mail: bcoffey@cminfospec.com
President: Mariela Twiggs MS, PhD CHP, RHIA
    E-Mail: mtt@velfile.com

Historical Note:
AHIOS's mission is to strengthen and enhance the health
information management outsourcing industry while
promoting excellence in the handling and dissemination of
confidential patient-identifiable information. Membership is
open to all companies providing outsourcing services to the
healthcare industry.

Continuing Education:
Certification Designation/s: CRIS

Association of Healthcare Internal Auditors
(1981)
10200 W. 44th Ave.
Suite 304
Wheat Ridge, CO 80033
Tel: (303) 327-7546 Fax: (303) 422-8894
TollFree: (888) 327-7546
E-Mail: ahia@ahia.org
Website: ahia.org
Members: 1000 individuals
Staff: 3
Annual Budget: $500-1,000,000

Personnel:
Executive Director: David L. Stumph CAE, IOM
    E-Mail: dstumph@resourcecenter.com
Executive, Accounting Services: Michelle Cunningham
    E-Mail: mcunningham@resourcecenter.com

Historical Note:
Formerly (1989) Healthcare Internal Audit Group. HIAG
was established to promote cost containment and increased
productivity in healthcare institutions through internal
auditing. AHIA promotes excellence in its members,
their institutions, and the healthcare internal audit
profession.Provides healthcare auditors with specialized
education, resources and networking opportunities.
Membership: $200 (Individual); $75 (Faculty); $40
(Student); $100-180 (Group);

Meetings/Conferences: Annual
2013 - Chicago, IL/Aug. 25 - 28
2014 - Austin, TX/Sept. 21 - 24

Publications:
E-News; on-line; adv.
Membership Directory; on-line

Membership List Available to Non-members

Association of Hispanic Advertising Agencies
(1996)
8400 Westpark Dr.
Second Floor
McLean, VA 22102
Tel: (703) 610-9014 Fax: (703) 610-0227
E-Mail: info@ahaa.org
Website: ahaa.org
Members: 275 companies
Staff: 3
Annual Budget: $500-1,000,000
Tax: 501(c)(6)

Personnel:
Executive Director: Horacio Gavilan
    E-Mail: hgavilan@ahaa.org
Contact, Marketing, Media and Press Enquiries: Liz
Jayankura-Jones
    E-Mail: ljones@ahaa.org
Contact, Membership Directory: Fulvia Lee
    E-Mail: flee@ahaa.org

Historical Note:
AHAA's mission is to grow, strengthen and protect the
hispanic marketing and advertising industry by providing
leadership in raising awareness of the value of the hispanic
market opportunities and enhancing the professionalism of
the industry. Membership: $2,250-11,000 (General, based
on annual billings); $2,500-25,000 (Associates); $100
(Faculty); $25 (Student); $500 (Individuals).

Meetings/Conferences: Annual
Conference Chair: Fulvia Lee

Publications:
ConexiónAHAA; monthly

Association of Hispanic Healthcare Executives
(1988)
P.O Box 230832, Ansonia Stn.
New York, NY 10023
Tel: (212) 877-1615 Fax: (212) 877-2406

Website: ahhe.org
Members: 415 individuals and 17 organizations
Staff: 1
Annual Budget: $2-5,000,000

Personnel:
President and Chief Executive Officer: George
Zeppenfeldt Cestero
    E-Mail: gzeppenfeldt@ahhe.org

Historical Note:
AHHE's mission is to advance programs and policies to
increase the presence of Hispanics in health administration
professions. Membership $100 (one year); $25 (Students/
seniors/disabled); $3,000 (corporate charter) $750-2,500
(Affiliate); $5,000-10,000(Healthcare round table).

Publications:
Latino Health and Business E-News; on-line

Association of Home Appliance Manufacturers
(1967)
1111 19th St. NW
Suite 402
Washington, DC 20036
Tel: (202) 872-5955 Fax: (202) 872-9354
E-Mail: info@aham.org
Website: aham.org
Members: 173 companies
Staff: 15
Annual Budget: $2-5,000,000
Tax: 501(c)(6)

Personnel:
President: Joseph M. McGuire
    E-Mail: jmcguire@aham.org
Manager, Communications and Membership: Nick Baker
    E-Mail: nbaker@aham.org
Vice President, Finance and Administration: Peter Frank
    E-Mail: pfrank@aham.org
Vice President, Policy and Government Relations: Kevin
Messner
    E-Mail: kmessner@aham.org
Vice President, Technical Operations and Standards:
Wayne Morris
    E-Mail: wmorris@aham.org
Vice President, Communications and Marketing: Jill A.
Notini
    E-Mail: jnotini@aham.org

Historical Note:
Formed by a merger of the Consumer Products Division
of the National Electrical Manufacturers Association and
the American Home Laundry Manufacturers' Association.
AHAM's mission is to serve the home appliance industry
while delivering value to consumers through leadership,
education and advocacy. Members are manufacturers
of major, portable and floor care home appliances, and
suppliers to the industry.

Meetings/Conferences:
Number of non-conference events/year: 1

Publications:
PLUG; bi-weekly

Association of Home Office Underwriters (1930)
2300 Windy Ridge Pkwy.
Suite 600
Atlanta, GA 30339-8443
Tel: (770) 984-3715 Fax: (770) 984-6419
E-Mail: ahou@loma.org
Website: ahou.org
Members: 1200 individuals
Staff: 6
Annual Budget: $1-2,000,000
Tax: 501(c)(6)

Personnel:
President: Deb Schmidt
    E-Mail: president@ahou.org
Vice President, Publications and Secretary: Cheryl Johns
    E-Mail: secretary@ahou.org
Vice President, Membership Services: Norm Leblond
    E-Mail: membershipvp@ahou.org
Vice President, Marketing: Peter Speers
    E-Mail: peter.speers@rbc.com
Vice President, Technology Development: Bill Swarner
    E-Mail: bill.swarner@lfg.com
Vice President, Treasurer: Steve Tizzano
    E-Mail: treasurer@ahou.org

Historical Note:
AHOU exists to advocate a thorough knowledge of
mortality and morbidity as it relates to risk selection.
Members are insurance professionals who are responsible

for risk assessment in the life, health and disability
insurance industries. Membership: $50-75 (Basic);
$100-125 (Full).

Continuing Education:
Certification Designation/s: FALU

Meetings/Conferences: Annual
Conference Chair: Peter Speers
2013 - Phoenix, AZ (The Arizona Baltimore)/April 7 -
10

Publications:
Membership Directory; on-line

Association of Image Consultants International
(1990)
1255 SW Prairie Trail Pkwy.
Suite 330
Ankeny, IA 50023-7068
Tel: (515) 282-5500 Fax: (515) 334-1164
E-Mail: info@aici.org
Website: aici.org
Members: 1300 individuals
Staff: 7
Annual Budget: $500-1,000,000
Tax: 501(c)(6)

Personnel:
President: Kimberly Law AICI, CIP
    E-Mail: kim@personalimpact.ca
Vice President, Marketing: Yasmin Anderson-Smith AICI
    E-Mail: yasmin@kymsimage.com
Vice President, Conferences: Helena Chenn AICI, CIP
    E-Mail: hc@helenachenn.com
Vice President, Member Communications: Magoe Johnson
AICI, CIP
    E-Mail: info@imagesbymagoe.com
Vice President, Education: Hitomi Ohmori AICI, CIP
    E-Mail: hohmori@ohmori-method.co.jp
Treasurer: Joanne Rae AICI, CIP
    E-Mail: Joanne@younique-image.com
Vice President, Membership Services: Cecelia Stoeckiht
AICI, CIP
    E-Mail: imageatelier@comcast.net

Historical Note:
Formed by the merger of the Association of Image
Consultants (1982) and the Association of Fashion and
Image Consultants (1983). AICI's mission is to set the
professional standards for the industry and members.
Membership: $285 (Associate/Affiliate); $165 (Student).

Continuing Education:
Certification Designation/s: AICI FLC, CIM, CIP

Meetings/Conferences: Annual
Conference Chair: Helena Chenn AICI, CIP
2013 - Glendale, AZ (Renaissance Glendale Hotel and
Spa)/May 16 - 19

Publications:
AICI Connections; quarterly; adv.
Image Update Magazine; bi-annually; adv.
Member Minutes; weekly
Membership Directory; on-line

Association of Independent Colleges of Art and Design (1991)
3957 22nd St.
San Francisco, CA 94114-3205
Tel: (415) 642-8595 Fax: (415) 642-8590
Website: aicad.org
Members: 35 institutions
Staff: 2
Annual Budget: $500-1,000,000

Personnel:
Executive Director: Deborah Obalil
Assistant Director: Rebecca Deans

Historical Note:
AICAD is a consortium of 41 leading art schools in the
United States and Canada. AICAD's mission is to help
strengthen the member colleges individually and collectively,
and to inform the public about these colleges and the value
of studying art and design.

Association of Independent Commercial Producers (1972)
Three W. 18th St.
Fifth Floor
New York, NY 10011
Tel: (212) 929-3000
E-Mail: info@aicp.com
Website: aicp.com
Members: 575 companies

Staff: 13
Annual Budget: $25-50,000

Personnel:
President and Chief Executive Officer: Matt Miller
    E-Mail: mattm@aicp.com
Vice President, Business Affairs and Non-Trade Media Issues: Denise Gilmartin
    E-Mail: deniseg@aicp.com
Director, Events: Ileana Montalvo
    E-Mail: ileanam@aicp.com
Office Manager: Laurie R. Nichtern
    E-Mail: laurier@aicp.com
Vice President, Labor Relations: Jane Nunez
    E-Mail: janen@aicp.com
Manager, Membership Information and Systems: David Stewart
    E-Mail: davids@aicp.com
Chief of Staff: Kristin Wilcha
    E-Mail: kristinw@aicp.com

Historical Note:
AICP is an independent producer of television commercials. Membership: $2,000 (General); $500-1,000 (Associate).

Meetings/Conferences: Annual
Conference Chair: Ileana Montalvo
Number of non-conference events/year: 1

Publications:
Membership Directory; on-line

Association of Independent Corrugated Converters (1974)
P.O. Box 25708
Alexandria, VA 22313
Tel: (703) 836-2422 *Fax:* (703) 836-2795
TollFree: (877) 836-2422
E-Mail: info@aiccbox.org
Website: aiccbox.org
Members: 1100 companies
Staff: 7
Annual Budget: $2-5,000,000
Tax: 501(c)(6)

Personnel:
President: A. Steve Young
    E-Mail: syoung@aiccbox.org
Vice President, Operations: John Bacot
    E-Mail: jbacot@aiccbox.org
Director, Meetings: Cindy Guarino
    E-Mail: cguarino@aiccbox.org
Director, Membership Services: Taryn Pyle
    E-Mail: tpyle@aiccbox.org
Contact, Technical Services: Ralph Young
    E-Mail: askralph@aiccbox.org

Historical Note:
Represents a majority of the independent corrugated packaging manufacturers and their suppliers. AICC's purpose is to provide a forum for the independent corrugated converter on legitimate matters of mutual interest, to enhance the level of professionalism in the operation of his or her business. Membership: $1077-4146 (General-Companies); $1,360-4146 (Associate); $475 (Overseas Regular Member).

Meetings/Conferences: Semi-Annual
Conference Chair: Cindy Guarino
2013 - Orlando, FL (Hilton Bonnet Creek Resort)/April 24 - 26
2013 - Las Vegas, NV (Encore)/Sept. 23 - 25

Publications:
BoxScore Newsletter; adv.
Journal on Corrugated Graphic Design; adv.
Membership Directory; annually; adv.

Association of Independent Information Professionals (1987)
8550 United Plaza Blvd.
Suite 1001
Baton Rouge, LA 70809
Tel: (225) 408-4400 *Fax:* (225) 408-4422
E-Mail: office@aiip.org
Website: aiip.org
Members: 700 individuals
Staff: 18
Annual Budget: $100-250,000

Personnel:
President: Scott Brown
    E-Mail: President@aiip.org
Treasurer: Marilyn Harmacek
Director, Membership Development: Arthur Weiss

    E-Mail: Membership@aiip.org
Secretary: Joann M. Wleklinski
Director, Marketing and Web: Debbie Wynot
    E-Mail: Marketing@aiip.org

Historical Note:
AIIP strives to advance the knowledge and understanding of the information profession and also seeks to promote and maintain professional and ethical standards among its members. Members are owners of firms providing information-related services including online and manual research, document delivery, database design, library support, consulting, writing and publishing. Membership: $50-500/year.

Meetings/Conferences: Annual
2013 - Denver, CO (Westin Denver Downtown)/April 3 - 7

Publications:
AIIP Connections; quarterly; adv.
Membership Directory; annually

Association of Independent Manufacturers'/Representatives, Inc. (1972)
2262 N. Penn Rd.
P.O. Box 68
Hatfield, PA 19440
Tel: (267) 308-0500 *Fax:* (267) 308-0505
E-Mail: info@aimr.net
Website: aimr.net
Members: 350 firms
Staff: 15
Annual Budget: $100-250,000
Tax: 501(c)(6)

Personnel:
President: Mark Creyer
    E-Mail: mcreyer@landrassocinc.com

Historical Note:
Formerly (1987) the Association of Independent Manufacturers Representatives. AIM/R benefits independent sales representatives in the plumbing, HVAC/R, kitchen/bath, waterworks, irrigation and related industries by promoting the proper utilization of the rep function. Provides its members with a competitive advantage through education, information exchange, networking and a wide array of quality member services. Membership: $495 (Agent); $395 (Associate).

Meetings/Conferences: Annual
Conference Chair: Alan Guidish

Publications:
News & Views; quarterly; adv.
REP Locator; annually

Association of Independent Research Institutes (1961)
C/O DAI Management, Inc.
P.O. Box 844
Westminster, MD 21158
Tel: (410) 751-8900 *Fax:* (410) 751-2662
Website: airi.org
Members: 89 research institutions
Staff: 2
Annual Budget: $500-1,000,000

Personnel:
Executive Director: David A. Issing
    E-Mail: davidissing@airi.org

Historical Note:
AIRI is a biomedical and behavioral research institute whose mission is to enhance the ability of its members to improve human health and advance knowledge. Membership: $500-4,800/year.

Meetings/Conferences: Annual
Conference Chair: David A. Issing
2013 - Washington, DC/Sept. 8 - 11

Association of Independent Trust Companies (1989)
2313 N. Bwy.
Ada, OK 74820
Tel: (405) 680-7869 *Fax:* (580) 332-4714
E-Mail: aitco@gss.net
Website: aitco.net
Members: 150 companies
Staff: 4
Annual Budget: $100-250,000

Personnel:
President: Marcia Williams
General Counsel: Thomas Blank
Treasurer: Tony Guthrie

Historical Note:
Formerly, Association of Independent Trust Companies. ATO's mission is to provide a forum for leaders, owners and operators of trust organizations to network and grow as an industry. ATO attracts professionals from across the country, providing opportunities for networking, business development, continuing education and information on key industry issues. Membership: $2,500 (Platinum Council); $1000 (Trust Leader); $500 (Investor).

Publications:
AITCO Advisor Newsletter; quarterly
Member Directory; on-line

Association of Independents in Radio (1988)
P.O. Box 220400
Boston, MA 02122
Tel: (617) 825-4400 *Fax:* (617) 825-4422
E-Mail: inquiry@airmedia.org
Website: airmedia.org
Members: 800 producers
Staff: 5
Annual Budget: $250-500,000

Personnel:
Executive Director: Sue Schardt
    E-Mail: sue@airmedia.org
Operations Associate: Lo Audley
    E-Mail: lo@AIRmedia.org
Media Strategist: Jessica Clark
    E-Mail: jessica@airmedia.org
Director, Membership: Erin Mishkin
    E-Mail: erin@AIRmedia.org
Manager, Publications: Samantha Schongalla
    E-Mail: airblast@airmedia.org

Historical Note:
AIR is advocate for producers in public and commercial media and through its training programs, it helps to hone the technical, editorial, and strategic skills of hundreds of media professionals. Members are producers, independent and those employed by media organizations belonging to disciplines, from NPR news journalists and reporters, to sound artists, station station-based producers, podcasters, gearheads, media activists, and more. Membership: $125 (Producer); $500 (Company/Station); $2000 (Network); $45 (Student).

Publications:
AIR's Talent Directory; on-line
AIRblast; monthly

Association of Industrial Metallizers, Coaters and Laminators (1970)
201 Springs St.
Ft. Mill, SC 29715
Tel: (803) 948-9470 *Fax:* (803) 948-9471
E-Mail: aimcal@aimcal.org
Website: aimcal.org
Members: 230 companies
Staff: 6
Annual Budget: $1-2,000,000
Tax: 501(c)(6)

Personnel:
Executive Director: Craig Sheppard
    E-Mail: aimcal@aimcal.org
Manager, Communications: Steve Bright
Event Planner: Erin Davis
Senior Administrator: Tracey Ingram
Editor-in-Chief: Mark Spaulding

Historical Note:
Formerly (1973) Vacuum Metallizers Association, AIMCAL's mission is to serve as global forum for the flexible metalizing, coating and laminating industry by providing resources, services and information. Membership is on a Company basis and includes all employees of the Company. Membership: $1,995 (Basic); $935 (Trade Press); Free (College/University); $2,495 (Premium).

Meetings/Conferences: Annual
Conference Chair: Erin Davis
2013 - Rancho Mirage, CA (Rancho Las Palmas Resort and Spa)/March 9 - 13
2013 - Munich, Germany (Munich Trade Fair Center)/March 19 - 21
2013 - Orlando, FL (Orange County Convention Center)/April 9 - 11
Number of non-conference events/year: 4

Publications:
AIMCAL newsletter; on-line

Membership List Available to Non-members

Association of Information Technology Professionals *(1951)*
401 N. Michigan Ave.
Suite 2400
Chicago, IL 60611-4267
Tel: (312) 245-1070 *Fax:* (312) 673-6659
TollFree: (800) 224-9371
E-Mail: aitp_hq@aitp.org
Website: aitp.org
Members: 12000 individuals and students
Staff: 3
Annual Budget: $500-1,000,000
Tax: 501(c)(6)

Personnel:
Manager, Operations: Melissa Kiser
    E-Mail: mreznik@aitp.org
Association Assistant: Melissa McArdle
    E-Mail: mmcardle@aitp.org

Historical Note:
Formerly (1951) the National Machine Accountants Association, (1962) the Data Processing Management Association, and (1996) the DPMA: the Association of Information Systems Professionals. AITP strives to promote the management of information technology to the benefit of its members, their employers and society. Members serve in technical positions in business, industry and governmental organizations throughout the world. Membership dues depend on area wise chapters. Membership: $40 (Student); $80-215 (Enterprise Member); $35-70 (Student to Professional Member).

Meetings/Conferences: Annual
Conference Chair: Melissa McArdle
2013 - St. Louis, MO (The Millennium Hotel)/April 4 - 7
Number of non-conference events/year: 6

Publications:
Bulletin; monthly

Association of Insolvency and Restructuring Advisors *(1983)*
221 Stewart Ave.
Suite 207
Medford, OR 97501
Tel: (541) 858-1665 *Fax:* (541) 858-9187
E-Mail: aira@aira.org
Website: aira.org
Members: 2100 individuals
Staff: 9
Annual Budget: $1-2,000,000
Tax: 501(c)(6)

Personnel:
Executive Director: Grant W. Newton PhD
    E-Mail: gnewton@aira.org
Director, Information Technology: Lorren Biffin
    E-Mail: lbiffin@aira.org
Coordinator, Conferences and Marketing: Lauren Cypher
Director, CIRA and CDBV Programs: Terry Jones
    E-Mail: tjones@aira.org
Administrative Assistant: Michele Michael
    E-Mail: mmichael@aira.org

Historical Note:
Formerly National Association of Accountants in Insolvency. Mission is to unite and support professionals providing business turnaround, restructuring and bankruptcy services. Members are certified and licensed public accountants, lawyers, examiners, financial advisors, turnaround consultants, trustees and receivers concerned with the application and procedures to insolvency proceedings. Membership: $225 (Regular); $300 (CIRA Designee); $150 (Associate); $75 (Government/Education Member).

Continuing Education:
Certification Designation/s: CDBV, CIRA

Meetings/Conferences: Annual
2013 - New York City, NY (Arno Ristorante)/Jan. 31
2013 - Chicago, IL (Westin Chicago Northwest)/June 5 - 8
2014 - Denver, CO/June 4 - 7

Publications:
AIRA Journal; bi-monthly
AIRA Weekly Advisor; weekly
CIRA & CDBV Directory; annually
Membership Directory; on-line

Membership List Available to Non-members

Association of Institutional Investors
One Financial Center
Boston, MA 02111

Tel: (617) 748-1748
Website: association.institutionalinvestors.org
Staff: 2
Annual Budget: $25-50,000

Personnel:
Chairman: John Gidman

Historical Note:
Association of Institutional Investors is comprised of some of the oldest, largest, and most trusted investment advisers in the United States. Members manage pension, 401K, mutual fund, and personal investments on behalf of more than 100 million American workers and retirees.

Membership List Available to Non-members

Association of Insurance Compliance Professionals *(1985)*
12100 Sunset Hills Rd.
Suite 130
Reston, VA 20190
Tel: (703) 437-4377 *Fax:* (703) 435-4390
E-Mail: aicp@aicp.net
Website: aicp.net
Members: 1300 individuals
Staff: 3
Annual Budget: $500-1,000,000
Tax: 501(c)(6)

Personnel:
Executive Director: Rick A Guggolz
    E-Mail: rguggolz@drohanmgmt.com

Historical Note:
Formerly Society of State Filers (1998). AICP is dedicated to promoting regulatory competence and awareness for the improvement of regulatory compliance within the insurance industry. Serves members by promoting relationships, exchanging information, and providing learning opportunities within a dynamic regulatory environment. Members are property, casualty, life and health insurers, regulatory agencies, consultants. Associate members are consultants, attorneys, association managers, education/service organizations and other interested individuals. Membership: $190 (Industry/Associate); $50 (Regulator).

Continuing Education:
Certification Designation/s: ACP, CCP, CE

Meetings/Conferences: Annual
2013 - Toronto, ON (Westin Harbour Castle)/Oct. 6 - 9
2014 - Phoenix, AZ (JW Marriott Desert Ridge Resort)/ Sept. 14 - 17
2015 - New Orleans, LA (Hilton New Orleans Riverside)/Oct. 10 - 14
2016 - Orlando, FL (Convention Center/The Peabody Orlando)/Oct. 2 - 5

Publications:
Membership Directory; on-line
The Journal for Insurance Compliance Professionals; quarterly; adv.

Association of Internal Management Consultants *(1971)*
824 Caribbean Ct.
Marco Island, FL 34145
Tel: (239) 642-0580 *Fax:* (239) 642-1119
E-Mail: info@aimc.org
Website: aimc.org
Members: 500 individuals
Staff: 4
Annual Budget: $50-100,000

Personnel:
President: Neil Wilson
Treasurer and Secretary: Perry Hitt

Historical Note:
Established in Baltimore on February 19, 1971 by forty-two charter members under the leadership of Walter J. Sistek of the Maryland National Bank. Incorporated in the state of New York in 1975. AIMC provides valuable insights regarding how to effectively utilize external consulting capabilities and optimize the organization's overall consulting spend. Members are individuals engaged in the practice of internal management consulting, with five or more years experience and operating at a senior or project leader level. Membership: $250 (Individual); $750 (Corporate); $50 (Academic/Research Membership).

Meetings/Conferences: Annual
2013 - Marco Island, FL (Marco Island Hilton Beach Resort and Spa)/April 21 - 24

Publications:
Membership Directory; on-line
Newsletter; bi-annually; adv.

Association of International Education Administrators *(1982)*
Duke University
Campus Box 90404, 107 Franklin Center, 2204 Erwin Rd.
Durham, NC 27708-0404
Tel: (919) 668-1928 *Fax:* (919) 684-8749
E-Mail: aiea@duke.edu
Website: aieaworld.org
Members: 400 individuals
Staff: 6
Annual Budget: $500-1,000,000
Tax: 501(c)(6)

Personnel:
Executive Director: Dr. Darla K. Deardorff
Accountant: Robert Buser
Editor: Dr. Harvey Charles
Program Associate: Rosemary Holland
Treasure: Dr. Gilbert W. Merkx
Web Developer: Chris Telling

Historical Note:
AIEA purpose is to provide an effective voice on significant issues within international education at all levels, improve and promote international education programming and administration within institutions of higher education and establish and maintain a professional network among international education institutional leaders. Membership: $400 (Academic Institutional/Other Organizations Supporting International Education/Non-affiliated Individual); $100 (Individual).

Meetings/Conferences: Annual
2013 - New Orleans, LA (The New Orleans Marriott)/ Feb. 17 - 20
2014 - Washington, DC (JW Marriott Washington, D.C.)/Feb. 16 - 19
2015 - Washington, DC (JW Marriott Washington, D.C.)/Feb. 15 - 18

Publications:
Membership Directory; on-line
Newsletter

The Association of International Photography Art Dealers *(1979)*
2025 M St. NW
Suite 800
Washington, DC 20036
Tel: (202) 367-1158 *Fax:* (202) 367-2158
E-Mail: info@aipad.com
Website: aipad.com
Members: 200 Organizations and 125 individuals
Staff: 5
Annual Budget: $1-2,000,000

Personnel:
Executive Director: Meredith Young
Web Editor: Jennifer DeCarlo
    E-Mail: editor@aipad.com
Marketing and Advertising Manager: Kevin Hurley
Press Contact: Nicole Straus
    E-Mail: pr@aipad.com
Show Director: Dave Weil

Historical Note:
AIPAD's mission is to create and maintain standards in the business of exhibiting, buying and selling photographs as art. Members are galleries and private dealers in fine art photography who have been in business for at least three years. Membership: Dues prorated based on the date of acceptance of application.

Meetings/Conferences: Annual
Conference Chair: Dave Weil
2013 - New York City, NY (Park Avenue Armory)/April 4 - 7
Number of non-conference events/year: 1

Publications:
Membership Directory; annually

Membership List Available to Non-members

Association of Investment Management Sales Executives *(1977)*
12100 Sunset Hills Rd.
Suite 130
Reston, VA 20190
Tel: (703) 234-4098 *Fax:* (703) 435-4390
Website: aimse.com
Members: 1400 individuals
Staff: 6
Annual Budget: $1-2,000,000

Personnel:
Executive Director: Kathy Hoskins
  E-Mail: khoskins@drohanmgmt.com
Director, Finance: Glenn Beales
  E-Mail: gbeales@drohanmgmt.com
Administrative Assistant: Challee Blackwelder
Director, Communications: Micki Francis
  E-Mail: mfrancis@drohanmgmt.com
Director, Meetings: Lauren Papageorge
  E-Mail: lpapageorge@drohanmgmt.com

Historical Note:
Incorporated in 1981. AIMSE is dedicated to serve the needs of investment management sales and marketing professionals. Members are people involved in marketing or selling of investment management products/services. Membership: $350 (Active); $450 (Associate).

Meetings/Conferences:
Conference Chair: Lauren Papageorge
2013 - Toronto, ON (Sheraton Centre Toronto Hotel)/ Jan. 29 - 30
2013 - Scottsdale, AZ (Fairmont Scottsdale Princess)/ April 28 - 30
2014 - Boca Raton, FL (Boca Raton Resort and Club)/ April 27 - 29
Number of non-conference events/year: 3

Publications:
AIMSE Newsletter; on-line

Association of Jesuit Colleges and Universities
(1970)
One Dupont Cir. NW
Suite 405
Washington, DC 20036-1140
Tel: (202) 862-9893 *Fax:* (202) 862-8523
E-Mail: blkrobe@aol.com
Website: ajcunet.edu
Members: 28 institutions
Staff: 9
Annual Budget: $2-5,000,000
Tax: 501(c)(3)

Personnel:
President: Gregory Lucey SJ
  E-Mail: glucey@ajcunet.edu
Vice President, Communications: Melissa C. DiLeonardo
  E-Mail: mdileonardo@ajcunet.edu
Vice President, Federal Relations: Cynthia A. Littlefield
  E-Mail: clittlefield@ajcunet.edu
Executive Director, Jesuit Distance Education Network (JesuitNET): Dr. Richard Vigilante
  E-Mail: vigilante@ajcunet.edu

Historical Note:
Formed when the Jesuit Educational Association split to form the Association of Jesuit Colleges and Universities and the Jesuit Secondary Education Association. AJCU's mission is to support and promote U.S. Jesuit higher education by facilitating cooperative efforts among and providing services to its 28 member institutions, to provide a forum for the exchange of experience and information and represent the work of U.S. Jesuit higher education at the national and international levels. A national voluntary service organization whose institutional members are the Jesuit colleges and universities in the United States.

Publications:
AJCU Higher Ed News; weekly
Membership Directory; on-line

Association of Jewish Aging Services *(1960)*
2519 Connecticut Ave. NW
Washington, DC 20008
Tel: (202) 543-7500
E-Mail: info@ajas.org
Website: ajas.org
Members: 125 facilities
Staff: 2
Annual Budget: $500-1,000,000
Tax: 501(c)(3)

Personnel:
Director, Program: Monica Wolfe

Historical Note:
Formerly the North American Association of Jewish Homes and Housing for the Aging (NHAJHA), assumed its current name in 1997. AJAS's mission is to advocate and support elder services in the context of Jewish values through education, professional development, advocacy and community relationships. Members are non-profit organizations providing long term care and housing services for the aged.

Continuing Education:

Enrollment: 100

Meetings/Conferences: Annual
2013 - Beverly Hills, CA/March 3 - 6

Publications:
Directory; biennially; adv.
E-update; monthly
Ground Breaking; annually; adv.
Journal on Jewish Aging; semi-annually; adv.
The Scribe; quarterly
Washington/CEO Update; quarterly

Association of Jewish Family & Children's Agencies *(1973)*
5750 Park Heights Ave.
Baltimore, MD 21215
Tel: (732) 432-7120 *Fax:* (410) 664-0551
TollFree: (800) 634-7346
E-Mail: ajfca@ajfca.org
Website: ajfca.org
Members: 125 Jewish Family and Children's Agencies
Staff: 8
Annual Budget: $1-2,000,000
Tax: 501(c)(3)

Personnel:
President and Chief Executive Officer: Lee Sherman
  E-Mail: lsherman@ajfca.org
Manager, Membership Services and Communications: Megan Manelli
  E-Mail: mmyers@ajfca.org
Director, Meetings and Conferences: Ann Zeller
  E-Mail: azeller@ajfca.org

Historical Note:
Incorporated in 1972, the Association of Jewish Family and Children's Agencies. AJFCA's mission is to provide a wide range of needed social services to strengthen individuals and families; JF and CS agencies spend over $570,000,000 to assist a broad range of children, adults and elderly. Members provide social services to children, adults and the elderly in the Jewish and general community. Membership dues are calculated based on the size of the agency's revenue.

Meetings/Conferences: Annual
Conference Chair: Ann Zeller
2013 - Phoenix, AZ (Biltmore Hotel)/May 19 - 21
Number of non-conference events/year: 1

Publications:
AJFCA E-Newsletter; monthly; adv.
Membership Directory; on-line

Association of Jewish Libraries *(1966)*
P.O. Box 1118
Teaneck, NJ 07666
Tel: (201) 371-3255 *Fax:* (917) 591-8252
E-Mail: ajlibs@osu.edu
Website: jewishlibraries.org
Members: 1095 individuals
Staff: 2
Annual Budget: $100-250,000
Tax: 501(c)(3)

Personnel:
Vice President, Membership Services: Laurie Haas
  E-Mail: lhaas@torahacademy.org
Vice President, Publications: Debbie Stern
  E-Mail: dstern@rrc.edu

Historical Note:
Formed by the merger of the Jewish Library Association (founded in 1946) and the Jewish Librarians Association (founded in 1962). AJL's mission is to promote Jewish literacy through enhancement of libraries and library resources and through leadership for the profession and practitioners of Judaica librarianship. Membership: $75-100 (Institutional); $70 (Personal/Corporate);$35 (Retiree/Student); $10 (Trial).

Meetings/Conferences: Annual
2013 - Houston, TX/June 16 - 19

Publications:
AJL Newsletter; quarterly; adv.
Judaica Librarianship

Association of Junior Leagues International *(1921)*
80 Maiden Ln.
Suite 305
New York, NY 10038-4609
Tel: (212) 951-8300 *Fax:* (212) 481-7196
E-Mail: info@ajli.org

Website: ajli.org
Members: 160292 women and leagues
Staff: 26
Annual Budget: $5-10,000,000
Tax: 501(c)(3)

Personnel:
Executive Director: Susan E. Danish
  E-Mail: sdanish@ajli.org
Director, Meeting Management: Dee Brinkley
  E-Mail: dbrinkley@ajli.org
Director, Marketing and Development: Laurie Dodge
  E-Mail: ldodge@ajli.org
Chief Operating Officer: Maureen Mackey
  E-Mail: mmackey@ajli.org
Director, Education and Programs: Janine Le Sueur
  E-Mail: jlesuer@ajli.org
Director, Administrative Services: Pamela Antoine Weekes
  E-Mail: pweekes@ajli.org

Historical Note:
AJLI's mission is to develop the potential of women and improve communities through the effective action and leadership of trained volunteers.

Meetings/Conferences: Annual
Conference Chair: Dee Brinkley
Number of non-conference events/year: 5

Publications:
Membership Directory; on-line

Association of Kentucky Fried Chicken Franchisees, Inc. *(1974)*
9520 Poplar Hill Dr.
Crestwood, KY 40014
Tel: (502) 241-7871 *Fax:* (866) 329-0412
TollFree: (888) 868-4750
Website: akfcf.com
Members: 2,500 Individuals
Staff: 4

Personnel:
Treasurer, AKFCF Political Action Committee: Peg Duenow
Administrative Director: Debbi Newton
  E-Mail: debbienewton@bellsouth.net

Historical Note:
The AKFCF is focused on protecting and promoting its members' investments in a healthy KFC organization.

Meetings/Conferences: Annual
2013 - New Orleans, LA (Hyatt Regency)/Feb. 13 - 16

Publications:
AKFCF Quarterly; quarterly; adv.

Association of Labor Relations Agencies *(1951)*
495 W. State St.
C/O New Jersey Public Employment Relations
Trenton, NJ 08618-5663
Tel: (609) 292-9830
Website: alra.org
Members: 75 agencies
Staff: 3
Annual Budget: $10-25,000

Personnel:
President: Robert A Hackel
  E-Mail: rhackel@perc.state.nj.us
Vice President, Finance: Scot Beckenbaugh
  E-Mail: sbeckenbaugh@fmcs.gov
Vice President, Professional Development: Ginette Brazeau
  E-Mail: ginette.brazeau@cirb-ccri.gc.ca

Historical Note:
Formerly (1963) the Association of State Mediation Agencies, and (1978) the Association of Labor Mediation Agencies. Member agencies include those at the federal, state and local levels in the U.S. and federal and provincial levels in Canada. Has no paid officers or full-time staff. Membership: $250/year (Organization/Company).

Publications:
ALRA Advisor; bi-annually
Membership Directory; on-line

The Association of Language Companies *(2002)*
9707 Key West Ave.
Suite 100
Rockville, MD 20850
Tel: (240) 404-6511 *Fax:* (301) 990-9771
TollFree: (800) 338-4155
E-Mail: info@alcus.org

Website: alcus.org
Staff: 1
Annual Budget: $100-250,000
Tax: 501(c)(6)

Personnel:
Executive Director: Beth W. Palys CAE
    E-Mail: bpalys@mgmtsol.com

Historical Note:
ALC's mission is to promote professional stature and economic position of its US-based member language companies through industry advocacy and professional development of language company owners and senior management. Membership: $575 (Active/Affiliate); $790 (Industry Partner).

Meetings/Conferences: Annual
2013 - Boston, MA (Boston Park Plaza Hotel and
    Towers)/May 15 - 18
Number of non-conference events/year: 1

Publications:
ALC Update; monthly; adv.
Membership Directory; on-line

Association of Large Distribution Cooperatives
C.O. Walton EMC
P.O. Box 260
Monroe, GA 30655
Tel: (770) 267-2505
Staff: 1
Annual Budget: $25-50,000
Tax: 501(c)(6)

Personnel:
D. Ronnie Lee

Historical Note:
An association of electric distribution cooperatives.

Association of Latina and Latino Anthropologists (1990)
2200 Wilson Blvd.
Suite 600
Arlington, VA 22201
Tel: (703) 528-1902 *Fax:* (703) 528-3546
Website: aaanet.org/sections/alla
Staff: 1

Personnel:
Executive Director: Bill Davis
    E-Mail: bdavis@aaanet.org

Historical Note:
Association of Latino and Latina Anthropologists, a section of the American Anthropological Association. ALLA's mission includes working with professional and community based organizations, anthropologists outside of academe, and community leaders to promote excellence in scholarship and advocacy about and for Latino/Latina peoples, and for indigenous, queer, and Black allies.

Association of Latino Professionals in Finance and Accounting (1972)
801 S. Grand Ave.
Suite 650
Los Angeles, CA 90017
Tel: (213) 243-0004 *Fax:* (213) 243-0006
E-Mail: info@nationalalpfa.org
Website: alpfa.org
Members: 15000 individuals
Staff: 19
Annual Budget: $5-10,000,000
Tax: 501(c)(6)

Personnel:
Chief Executive Officer: Manny Espinoza
    E-Mail: ceo@national.alpfa.org
Chief Operating Officer: Pamela Ravare Browne
    E-Mail: pamela.ravarebrowne@national.alpfa.org
Chief Financial Officer: Steve Calderon
    E-Mail: steve.calderon@national.alpfa.org
Director, Student Affairs: Geraldine Contreras
    E-Mail: geraldine.contreras@national.alpfa.org
Director, Corporate Development: Amber Martinez
    E-Mail: amber.martinez@national.alpfa.org
Vice President, Marketing and Branding: Zenaida Avelar
    Mendoza
    E-Mail: zenaida.mendoza@national.alpfa.org
Vice President, Corporate Development: Anita Nunez
    E-Mail: anita.nunez@national.alpfa.org

Historical Note:
Formerly (2001) American Association of Hispanic Certified Public Accountants. ALPFA's mission is to create opportunities, add value, build relationships for its members, the community and its business partners while expanding Latino leadership in the global workforce. Membership: $120 (General/Associate) ; $20-30 (Student)

Meetings/Conferences: Annual
2013 - Washington, DC/Aug. 3 - 7

Publications:
ALPFA IMPACT E-Newsletter; weekly; adv.

Association of Leadership Educators (1990)
University of Florida
P.O. Box 110540
Gainesville, FL 32611-0540
Tel: (352) 294-1999
Website: leadershipeducators.org
Members: 180 individuals
Staff: 5
Annual Budget: $50-100,000
Tax: 501(c)(3)

Personnel:
President: Tony Andenoro
    E-Mail: andenoro@gonzaga.edu

Historical Note:
ALE's mission is to strengthen and sustain the expertise of professional leadership educators. Membership: $100 (Regular); $50 (Student).

Meetings/Conferences: Annual
2013 - New Orleans, LA (Astor Crowne Plaza)/July 7 -
    10

Publications:
Journal of Leadership Education; on-line
Member Directory; on-line
The Forum; quarterly

Association of Legal Administrators (1971)
75 Tri-State International
Suite 222
Lincolnshire, IL 60069-4435
Tel: (847) 267-1252 *Fax:* (847) 267-1329
E-Mail: ala@alanet.org
Website: alanet.org
Members: 9500 individuals
Staff: 35
Annual Budget: $10-25,000,000
Tax: 501(c)(6)

Personnel:
Executive Director: Oliver P. Yandle CAE
    E-Mail: oyandle@alanet.org
Director, Marketing and Communications: Gwen Biasi
Director, Membership Services: Debbie Curtis
    E-Mail: dcurtis@alanet.org
Manager, Information Technology: Murray Freeman
    E-Mail: mfreeman@alanet.org
Legal Management Information Specialist: Nancy
    Gronlund
    E-Mail: ngronlund@alanet.org
Director, Conferences and Meetings: Lisa J. Mikita
    E-Mail: lmikita@alanet.org
Manager, Exhibits and Sponsorships: Jacqueline Stasch
    E-Mail: jstasch@alanet.org
Director, Professional Development: Pam Stong
    E-Mail: pstong@alanet.org
Director, Accounting and Finance: Debbie Thormas
    E-Mail: dthormas@alanet.org

Historical Note:
ALA's mission is to promote and enhance the competence and professionalism of all members of the legal management team. Members are managers and administrators of private law firms, corporate legal departments and government agencies. Membership: $105-385 (Regular, depending on month of joining); $105-315 (Associate, depending on month of joining).

Continuing Education:
Certification Designation/s: CLM

Meetings/Conferences: Annual
Conference Chair: Lisa J. Mikita
2013 - Ft. Washington, MD (Gaylord National Resort
    and Convention Center-National Harbor)/April 15 -
    18
2014 - Toronto, ON (Metro Toronto Convention
    Centre)/May 19 - 22
2015 - Nashville, TN (Music City Center)/May 17 - 20
2016 - Los Angeles, CA (Los Angeles Convention
    Center)/May 22 - 25
Number of non-conference events/year: 5

Publications:
ALA Currents; semi-monthly

ALA Membership Resource Directory; annually
ALA News; bi-monthly; adv.
ALA News International; quarterly
Just the Facts
Legal Management; bi-monthly

Association of Library Trustees, Advocates, Friends and Foundations (1979)
109 S. 13th St.
Suite 3-N
Philadelphia, PA 19107
Tel: (312) 280-2161 *Fax:* (215) 545-3821
TollFree: (800) 545-2433
E-Mail: altaff@ala.org
Website: ala.org
Staff: 3

Personnel:
Executive Director: Sally Gardner Reed
Director, Marketing and Communications: Beth
    Nawalinski
    E-Mail: bnawalinski@ala.org

Historical Note:
Formerly Friends of Libraries U.S.A., ALTAFF's mission is to provide leadership for the development, promotion, and improvement of library and information services and the profession of librarianship in order to enhance learning and ensure access to information for all. Membership: $50-125 (Board of Trustees Group/Friends of the Library Group/ Library Foundation Group); $59 (Personal).

Publications:
The Voice; bi-monthly

Association of Life Insurance Counsel (1913)
14350 Mundy Dr.
Suite 800
Noblesville, IN 46060
Tel: (317) 774-7500
Website: alic.cc
Members: 850 individuals
Staff: 1
Annual Budget: $100-250,000
Tax: 501(c)(6)

Personnel:
Administrator: Paula Carey CAE
    E-Mail: pcarey@alic.cc

Historical Note:
ALIC is the association for life insurance counsel. ALIC's mission is to advocate the effectiveness of legal service to life insurance companies and to further the education and professional abilities of life insurance lawyers. Members are legal counsels of life insurance companies. Membership: $195/year (Individual).

Meetings/Conferences: Annual
2013 - Amelia Island, FL (The Ritz-Carlton, Amelia
    Island)/May 5 - 7

Publications:
Member Directory; on-line

The Association of Literary Scholars, Critics, and Writers (1994)
650 Beacon St.
Suite 510
Boston, MA 02215
Tel: (617) 358-1990 *Fax:* (617) 358-1995
E-Mail: office@alscw.org
Website: bu.edu/literary
Members: 1100 individuals
Staff: 3
Annual Budget: $100-250,000
Tax: 501(c)(3)

Personnel:
President: John Burt
Secretary: Lee Oser
Treasurer: Timothy Peltason

Historical Note:
A professional society for the study of literature. ALSCW serves as a forum for anyone with serious critical or scholarly interests in literature. ALSCW 's seeks to advocate excellence in literary criticism and scholarship, and ensures that literature thrives in both scholarly and creative environments. Membership: $74 (Standard); $58 (Reduced); $37 (Senior/ New Member); $32 (Student); $100 (Individual, Contributing); $200 (Individual, Patron); $600 (Individual-Lifetime); $80 (Standard, Joint-Domestic); $750 (Lifetime, Joint-Domestic).

Meetings/Conferences: Annual
2013 - Athens, GA (University Of Georgia)/April 5 - 7

Publications:

Literary Matters; quarterly
Membership Directory; on-line

Association of Litigation Support Professionals
401 N. Michigan Ave.
Suite 2400
Chicago, IL 60611-4267
Tel: (713) 375-2728 *Fax:* (312) 673-6949
E-Mail: info@alsponline.org
Website: alsponline.org
Staff: 11
Tax: 501(c)(3)

Personnel:
Executive Director: Chris Hansen
    E-Mail: chansen@alsponline.org
President: Robin Thompson
    E-Mail: rthompson@alsponline.org
Vice President, Membership: Lisa Clements
    E-Mail: lclements@alsponline.org
Vice President, Education: Michael Dalewitz
    E-Mail: mdalewitz@alsponline.org
Vice President, Communications and Website Services:
    Victoria Edelman
    E-Mail: vedelman@alsponline.org
Secretary and Treasurer: Stephen Goldstein
    E-Mail: sgoldstein@alsponline.org
Vice President, Conferences: Michael Landau
    E-Mail: mlandau@techlawsolutions.com
Manager, Membership and Administration: Barbara
    O'Connor
    E-Mail: boconnor@alsponline.org
Manager, Events: Peggy Sloyan
    E-Mail: psloyan@alsponline.org

Historical Note:
ALSP is dedicated to establish global professional standards for the litigation support profession through collaboration, education and certification. Membership: $25 (Student); $125 (Individual).

Meetings/Conferences:
Conference Chair: Peggy Sloyan

Publications:
ALSP Newsletter

Association of Lutheran Development Executives
(2010)
1737 Beach Rd.
Verona, WI 53593-9120
TollFree: (888) 630-2533
E-Mail: staff@alde.org
Website: alde.org
Staff: 3
Annual Budget: $250-500,000

Personnel:
Executive Director: Phyllis Castens Wiederhoeft
    E-Mail: phyllisw@alde.org
Associate Director, Membership Services: Pat Agoudemos
    E-Mail: pata@alde.org
Associate Director, Communications: Jon Nelson
    E-Mail: jonn@alde.org

Historical Note:
ALDE is an international community of fundraising and communications professionals that is rooted in the Lutheran tradition of the Christian faith and dedicated to serving God's people in the church and the world as it inspires, connects and equips Christians for excellence in philanthropy. Membership: $175 (Full Members); $100 (Volunteer Leader); $50 (Student).

Meetings/Conferences: Annual
2013 - Indianapolis, IN (Indianapolis Marriott
    Downtown)/Feb. 8 - 11

Publications:
ALDE News; quarterly
ALDE Newsletter

Association of Lutheran Secondary Schools
(1944)
12800 N. Lake Shore Dr.
Mequon, WI 53097-2402
Tel: (262) 243-4519 *Fax:* (262) 243-2942
Website: alss.org
Members: 90 schools
Staff: 2
Tax: 501(c)(3)

Personnel:
Executive Director: Ross E. Stueber
    E-Mail: rstueber@cuw.edu
Administrative Assistant: Shannon Carr
    E-Mail: shannon.carr@cuw.edu

Historical Note:
ALSS is committed to serving the needs of Lutheran high schools and their leaders by enabling them to improve and expand the ministry of Christian Education. Membership $450/year per school.

Meetings/Conferences: Annual
2013 - San Antonio, TX (Sheraton Gunter Hotel San
    Antonio)/March 7 - 10
Number of non-conference events/year: 1

Publications:
E-Compass; bi-monthly
Membership Directory; on-line

Association of Machinery and Equipment Appraisers (1983)
315 S. Patrick St.
Alexandria, VA 22314
Tel: (703) 836-7900 *Fax:* (703) 836-9303
TollFree: (800) 537-8629
E-Mail: amea@amea.org
Website: amea.org
Members: 300 individuals
Staff: 3
Annual Budget: $100-250,000

Personnel:
Director, Membership Services: Pamela J. Reid
    E-Mail: pamela.reid@amea.org

Historical Note:
AMEA's mission is to certify and accredit qualified capital equipment appraisers in the appraisal industry through promotion of standards of professional practice, ethical conduct and market-based experience. Members are appraisers of all different types of machinery and capital equipment. It also conducts accreditation and certification programs for members and offers accredited and certified membership. Membership: $395 (Regular); $600 (Associate).

Continuing Education:
Certification Designation/s: CEA, AEA
Meetings/Conferences:
Number of non-conference events/year: 1

Publications:
AMEA Appraiser; quarterly
Membership Directory; annually

Association of Mailing, Shipping, and Office Automation Specialists
11310 Wornall Rd
Kansas City, MO 64114
Tel: (888) 750-6245 *Fax:* (888) 836-9561
Website: aimedweb.org
Members: 300 dealerships
Staff: 1

Personnel:
Executive Director: Rick Chambers
    E-Mail: rick@aimedweb.org

Historical Note:
AIMED's mission is to provide opportunities for members in the areas of industry specific benchmarking, education and information. Membership: $275-350 (Dealer); $350-1500 (Associate).

Meetings/Conferences: Annual

Publications:
Member Directory; on-line
The network; quarterly

Association of Major City and County Building Officials (1972)
505 Huntmar Park Dr.
Suite 210
Herndon, VA 20170
Tel: (703) 481-2038 *Fax:* (703) 481-3596
Website: ncsbcs.org/newsite/AMCBO/
    amcbo_main_page.htm
Members: 36 Cities and Counties
Staff: 2
Annual Budget: Under $10,000
Tax: 501(c)(3)

Personnel:
Secretary: Robert Wible
    E-Mail: rwible@ncsbcs.org
Chairman and Building Commissioner: Claude Cooper
    E-Mail: coopercg@ci.richmond.va.us

Historical Note:
AMCBO's mission is to provide a forum for the building officials of major cities and counties in the U.S. to discuss mutual interests and seek solutions to common problems in building code and public safety issues. Membership: $300/year.

Publications:
AMCBO Newsletter; irregular

Association of Managed Care Dentists (1992)
2355 Westwood Blvd.
Suite 260
Los Angeles, CA 90064
Tel: (310) 709-2677
E-Mail: info@amcd.org
Website: amcd.org
Staff: 2

Personnel:
Executive Director: Maxine Shapiro
Treasurer: John J. Maguire DDS

Historical Note:
Formerly (1997) Association of Managed Care Providers. AMCD provides education, representation and a forum for dentists, AMCD is interested in influencing plan design, quality assurance procedures, and quality patient care. Membership: $150 (AMCD Dentist/Administrator); $95 (Recent Graduate).

Association of Management Consulting Firms (1929)
370 Lexington Ave.
Suite 2209
New York, NY 10017
Tel: (212) 262-3055 *Fax:* (212) 262-3054
E-Mail: info@amcf.org
Website: amcf.org
Members: 50 firms
Staff: 6
Annual Budget: $500-1,000,000
Tax: 501(c)(6)

Personnel:
President and Chief Executive Officer: John Furth
    E-Mail: jfurth@amcf.org
Director, Operations and Programming: Sally Caputo
    E-Mail: scaputo@amcf.org
Director, Public Relations and Marketing: Patricia
    O'Connell
    E-Mail: poconnell@amcf.org
Contact, Membership Services and Administrative Support:
    Jack Underwood
    E-Mail: junderwood@amcf.org

Historical Note:
Previously ACMF Association of Management Consulting Firms, merged with Institute of Management Consultants to form Council of Consulting Organizations(1989); split in 1999. AMCF's mission is to promote an environment which fosters the success of management consulting firms and the value they deliver to their clients. Membership: $1,000-45,000 (Firm); $2,500-12,500 (Associate).

Meetings/Conferences:
Conference Chair: Sally Caputo
Number of non-conference events/year: 1

Publications:
AMCF eNewsletter; on-line

Association of Management/International Association of Management (1975)
P.O. Box 64841
Virginia Beach, VA 23467-4841
Tel: (757) 482-2273 *Fax:* (757) 482-0325
E-Mail: aomgt@inter-source.org
Website: aom-iaom.org
Members: 3800 individuals
Staff: 12
Annual Budget: $1-2,000,000

Personnel:
Co-Founder, President and CEO: Willem Arthur Hamel
    PhD
    E-Mail: aomgt@inter-source.org
Counsel: Jane Quincy Bryant
*Editor-in-Chief and Co-Founder Journal, Management
    Systems:* Karin Klenke
Comptroller, Conference Director: D.T.J Mills
    E-Mail: aomgt@inter-source.org
Administrator, Secretary: Catherine S. Rogers
    E-Mail: aomgt@inter-source.org

Historical Note:
Formerly the Association of Management (AoM). Assumed its present name in 1996. AoM/IAoM serves academics, researchers, professionals, corporate and practitioners

of management, education (higher), leadership and technology. Membership: $150/year.

Meetings/Conferences:
Conference Chair: D.T.J Mills
Number of non-conference events/year: 1

Publications:
Journal of information technology Management; quarterly
Journal of management Systems; quarterly

Association of Marina Industries *(1986)*
50 Water St.
Warren, RI 02885
Tel: (202) 737-9775 *Fax:* (401) 247-0074
TollFree: (866) 367-6622
E-Mail: info@marinaassociation.org
Website: marinaassociation.org
Members: 800 companies
Staff: 5
Annual Budget: $500-1,000,000
Tax: 501(c)(6)

Personnel:
President: Jim Frye CMM
Coordinator, Membership Services: Merritt Alves
  E-Mail: malves@marinaassociation.org
Coordinator, Training: Kayce Cashill-Florio
  E-Mail: kflorio@marinaassociation.org
Treasurer: Brad Gross CMM
Co-Coordinator, Conferences: Rachel LaMarre
  E-Mail: imbc@marinaassociation.org

Historical Note:
The Association of Marina Industries (AMI) was created by the merger of Marina Operators Association of America (MOAA) and International Marina Institute (IMI). AMI members provide millions of recreational boaters each year the wide variety of goods and services, ranging from fuel and oil sales to boat repairs and food and lodging, that allow recreational boating to continue to grow in popularity with sportsmen and women. AMI strives to offer timely industry publications, and legislative support and updates to members. Membership: $300-525 (U.S. Marina Facility); $150 (International Marina Facility); $550 (Suppliers of Products and Services); $385 (Marina Related Individuals); $275 (Associate); $75 (Student).

Continuing Education:
Certification Designation/s: CMM, MSMC, CMO

Meetings/Conferences: Annual
Conference Chair: Rachel LaMarre
2013 - Ft. Lauderdale, FL (Greater Fort Lauderdale/ Broward County Convention Center)/Jan. 30 - Feb. 1/over 100 exhibitors
2014 - Ft. Lauderdale, FL (Greater Fort Lauderdale/ Broward County Convention Center)/Jan. 29 - 31
Number of non-conference events/year: 5

Publications:
E-News-Letter; monthly
Membership Directory; on-line
NewsFax; bi-weekly
NewsWatch emails; weekly

Association of Marketing Service Providers *(1920)*
1421 Prince St.
Suite 410
Alexandria, VA 22314-2806
Tel: (703) 836-9200 *Fax:* (703) 548-8204
TollFree: (800) 333-6272
E-Mail: mfsa@mfsanet.org
Website: mfsanet.org
Members: 500 companies
Staff: 10
Annual Budget: $1-2,000,000
Tax: 501(c)(6)

Personnel:
President and Chief Executive Officer: Ken Garner
  E-Mail: kgarner@mfsanet.org
Director, Membership Development: Tyler T. Keeney
  E-Mail: tkeeney@mfsanet.org
Manager, Communications: Kimberly Kight
  E-Mail: kkight@mfsanet.org
Vice President, Postal and Membership Relations: Leo Raymond
  E-Mail: lraymond@mfsanet.org
Director, Conferences and Education: Jennifer Root
  E-Mail: jroot@mfsanet.org
Director, Communications and Marketing: Bill Stevenson
  E-Mail: bstevenson@mfsanet.org

Historical Note:
Formerly (2001) Mail Advertising Service Association International. MFSA's mission is to improve the business environment for mailing and fulfillment companies and to provide opportunities for the learning and professional development of the managers of these companies. Membership: $1,575-7,400/year.

Meetings/Conferences:
Conference Chair: Jennifer Root

Publications:
Postal Points
PostalPoints; adv.
Postscripts Newsletter; monthly; adv.

Membership List Available to Non-members

Association of Maternal and Child Health Programs (AMCHP) *(1944)*
2030 M St. NW
Suite 350
Washington, DC 20036
Tel: (202) 775-0436 *Fax:* (202) 775-0061
E-Mail: info@amchp.org
Website: amchp.org
Members: 600 individuals
Staff: 23
Annual Budget: $2-5,000,000
Tax: 501(c)(3)

Personnel:
Chief Executive Officer: Michael Fraser CAE, PhD
  E-Mail: mfraser@amchp.org
Program Manger, Online Media and Information Technology: Julio Arguello Jr.
  E-Mail: jarguello@amchp.org
Director, Public Policy and Government Affairs Team: Brent Ewig MHA
  E-Mail: bewig@amchp.org
Associate Director, Organizational Performance and Membership Services: Adriana Houk
  E-Mail: ahouk@amchp.org
Senior Program Manager, Children and Youth with Special Health Care Needs: Grace Williams
  E-Mail: gwilliams@amchp.org

Historical Note:
AMCHP supports state maternal and child health programs and provides national leadership on issues affecting women and children. Membership: $120 (Individual/Associate/ Regular); $850 (Organizational).

Meetings/Conferences: Annual
2013 - Washington, DC (Omni Shoreham Hotel)/Feb. 9 - 12

Publications:
AMCHP Member Briefs; semi-monthly
AMCHP Pulse eNewsletter; monthly
Membership Directory; on-line

Membership List Available to Non-members

Association of Medical Device Reprocessors
600 New Hampshire Ave. NW
Suite 500
Washington, DC 20037
Tel: (202) 518-6796 *Fax:* (202) 234-0399
E-Mail: info@amdr.org
Website: amdr.org
Staff: 3
Annual Budget: $500-1,000,000

Personnel:
President Chief Executive Officer: Daniel J. Vukelich Esq.
  E-Mail: dvukelich@amdr.org
Counsel: Kathryn E. Balmford Esq.
Manager, Government Relations: Brandon Matson
  E-Mail: bcmatson@amdr.org

Historical Note:
AMDR's mission to promote the proper reprocessing of medical devices labeled for single-use an ensure the standards of regulatory and professional conduct by its members and to reduce the cost of health care while maintaining patient safety and care.

Association of Medical Diagnostic Manufacturers *(1973)*
555 13th St. NW
Suite Seven W
Washington, DC 20004
Tel: (202) 617-0164 *Fax:* (317) 974-1832
E-Mail: amdminfo@email.amdm.org
Website: amdm.org
Members: 83 companies

Staff: 2
Annual Budget: $100-250,000

Personnel:
Executive Secretary: Blake Jeffery CAE

Historical Note:
Formerly (1995) Association of Microbiological Diagnostic Manufacturers. AMDM's purpose is to raise the standards of excellence by free exchange of technical information among members of the industry. Members are companies who manufacture and distribute in vitro diagnostic products, consultants and other suppliers providing essential materials and services to the industry. Membership: $300-2,200/ year.

Meetings/Conferences: Annual

Association of Medical Education and Research in Substance Abuse *(1976)*
P.O. Box 20160
Cranston, RI 02920
Tel: (401) 243-8460 *Fax:* (877) 418-8769
E-Mail: admin@amersa.org
Website: amersa.org
Members: 300 individuals
Staff: 3
Annual Budget: $100-250,000
Tax: 501(c)(3)

Personnel:
Director, National Office: Doreen MacLane-Baeder
  E-Mail: doreen@amersa.org
Editor-in-Chief: Marc Galanter MD
  E-Mail: marcgalanter@nyu.edu
Treasurer: Kate Driscoll Malliarakis CNP, MAc, MSM, RN
  E-Mail: Kate.malliarakis@gmail.com

Historical Note:
AMERSA is a multidisciplinary organization of health care professionals whose mission is to provide leadership and improve training for all health care professionals in the management of problems related to alcohol, tobacco and other drugs. Membership: $195 (Full Member); $125 (Associate); $50 (Emeritus); $1,000 (Corporate).

Meetings/Conferences: Annual

Publications:
Membership Directory; on-line
Substance Abuse; quarterly; adv.

Membership List Available to Non-members

The Association of Medical Illustrators *(1945)*
201 E. Main St.
Site 1405
Lexington, KY 40507
Fax: (859) 514-9166
TollFree: (866) 393-4264
E-Mail: hq@ami.org
Website: ami.org
Members: 800 individuals
Staff: 2
Annual Budget: $500-1,000,000
Tax: 501(c)(6)

Personnel:
Executive Director: Tracy Tucker
  E-Mail: ttucker@amrms.com
Executive, Accounts: Melanie Bowzer

Historical Note:
AMI furthers the use of visual media to advance life sciences, medicine, and healthcare through a network of specialized interdisciplinary professionals. Membership: $275 (Professional/Emeritus/Associate); $100 (Student/ Associate - Trial Basis).

Continuing Education:
Certification Designation/s: CMI

Meetings/Conferences: Annual
2013 - Salt Lake City, UT (Sheraton Salt Lake City Hotel)/July 17 - 20

Publications:
AMI News; quarterly; adv.
The Journal of Biocommunication (JBC); adv.

Association of Medical School Pediatric Department Chairs *(1961)*
6728 Old McLean Village Dr.
McLean, VA 22101
Tel: (703) 556-9222 *Fax:* (703) 556-8729
E-Mail: info@amspdc.org
Website: amspdc.org
Members: 146 Member Schools
Staff: 2

Annual Budget: $250-500,000

Personnel:

Executive Director: Laura Degnon

   E-Mail: laura@amspdc.org

Historical Note:

AMSPDC's mission is to pursue optimal health of children through the development of successful academic pediatric departments across North America. Members are chairs of pediatrics of U.S. and Canadian accredited medical schools. Membership: $510/year (Institution).

Meetings/Conferences: Annual

2013 - Atlanta, GA (Hyatt Regency Atlanta)/Feb. 28 - March 3

Publications:

The Journal of Pediatrics

Association of Meeting Professionals *(1982)*

2025 M St. NW

Suite 800

Washington, DC 20036

Tel: (202) 973-8686 *Fax:* (202) 973-8722

E-Mail: amps@courtesyassoc.com

Website: ampsweb.org

Members: 400 planner and service providers

Staff: 5

Annual Budget: $100-250,000

Tax: 501(c)(3)

Personnel:

Executive Director: Meredith Young CMP

Coordinator, Membership and Golf Tournament: Sarah Bookwalter

Coordinator, Monthly Meeting and Special Event: Elizabeth Haxton

Coordinator, Meetings: Emily O'Connor

Associate, Membership and Administrative Services: Audrey Sedlacek

Historical Note:

AMP's mission is to provide local affordable opportunities for its members to gather and share information, and to promote excellence in and strengthen the value and credibility of the meeting profession. Membership: $150 (Planner); $25 (Student); $295 (Allied/Associate).

Meetings/Conferences: Annual

Conference Chair: Emily O'Connor

Number of non-conference events/year: 5

Publications:

AMPs Newsletter; monthly; adv.

Membership Directory; annually

Membership List Available to Non-members

Association of Mental Health Librarians *(1964)*

Alliant International University Library, One Beach St.

Suite 100

San Francisco, CA 94133

Tel: (415) 955-2157 *Fax:* (415) 955-2180

Website: mhlib.org

Members: 68 individuals

Staff: 2

Annual Budget: Under $10,000

Personnel:

President: Joseph Tally

   E-Mail: jtally@alliant.edu

Treasurer: Brian Seguin

   E-Mail: bseguin@alliant.edu

Historical Note:

Formed as the Society of Mental Health Librarians; assumed its present name in 1980. AMHL is a organization of individuals working in the field of mental health information delivery. AMHL's mission is providing an opportunity for the exchange of information and the continuing education of its members. Members are Librarians, library assistants, library associates or any other individual interested in the field of mental health librarianship. Membership: $15/year.

Meetings/Conferences: Annual

Publications:

Membership Directory; on-line

Membership List Available to Non-members

Association of Metropolitan Planning Organizations

444 N. Capitol St. NW

Suite 345

Washington, DC 20001

Tel: (202) 624-3680 *Fax:* (202) 624-3685

Website: ampo.org

Staff: 2

Annual Budget: $500-1,000,000

Tax: 501(c)(4)

Personnel:

Executive Director: DeLania Hardy

Director, Technical Programs: Rich Denbow

Historical Note:

AMPO advocates for metropolitan regions and is committed to enhance MPOs' abilities to improve metropolitan transportation systems. Membership: $22,000 (Individual); $2,500 (Associate); $150 (Individual Associate); $50 (Student/Intern).

Meetings/Conferences: Annual

2013 - Portland, OR (Embassy Suites Portland)/Oct. 22 - 25

Publications:

aMPO eMAIL; bi-weekly

Association of Metropolitan Water Agencies *(1981)*

1620 I St. NW

Suite 500

Washington, DC 20006

Tel: (202) 331-2820 *Fax:* (202) 785-1845

Website: amwa.net

Members: 200 agencies

Staff: 8

Annual Budget: $1-2,000,000

Tax: 501(c)(6)

Personnel:

Deputy Executive Director: Michael N. Arceneaux

   E-Mail: arceneaux@amwa.net

Executive Director: Diane VanDe Hei

   E-Mail: vandehei@amwa.net

Manager, Regulatory Affairs and Scientific Program Development: Scott Biernat

Manager, Office Administration and Conferences: Eugenia Cadena

   E-Mail: cadena@amwa.net

Director, Legislative Affairs: Daniel Hartnett

   E-Mail: hartnett@amwa.net

Director, Communications and Public Affairs: Carolyn Peterson

   E-Mail: peterson@amwa.net

Historical Note:

AMWA's mission is to serve the nation's publicly owned drinking water systems on regulatory, legislative and security issues. Members are publicly-owned metropolitan, county and city water supply agencies serving populations of more than 100,000. Membership is based on population served.

Meetings/Conferences: Semi-Annual

Conference Chair: Eugenia Cadena

2013 - Washington, DC (Washington Court Hotel)/ March 17 - 20

2013 - St. Petersburg, FL (Vinoy Renaissance St. Petersburg Resort and Golf Club)/Oct. 27 - 30

Publications:

Congressional Report; on-line

Member Directory; on-line

Monday Morning Briefings; weekly

Regulatory Report; on-line

Water Security Scan; bi-monthly

Water Utility Executive; bi-monthly

Association of Military Banks of America *(1959)*

P.O. Box 3335

Warrenton, VA 20188

Tel: (540) 347-3305 *Fax:* (540) 347-5995

E-Mail: info@ambahq.org

Website: ambahq.org

Members: 120 banks

Staff: 2

Annual Budget: $2-5,000,000

Tax: 501(c)(6)

Personnel:

President and Chief Executive Officer: Andrew M. Egeland Jr.

   E-Mail: andrew.egeland@ambahq.org

Historical Note:

AMBA operates on military installations, banks not located on military installations but serving military customers, and military banking facilities designated by U. S. Treasury. Members are banks specializing in providing services to military personnel and banks operating on military bases. Membership: $175-325 (Regular Corporate, based on total Parent Bank Assets); $200 (Associate Corporate);

$50 (Associate Individual); $400 (Associate Corporate/ Industrial).

Publications:

AMBA Newsletter

Association of Military Colleges and Schools of the United States *(1914)*

3604 Glenbrook Rd.

Fairfax, VA 22031

Tel: (703) 272-8406

E-Mail: amcsus@cox.net

Website: amcsus.org

Members: 45 institutions

Staff: 1

Annual Budget: $100-250,000

Tax: 501(c)(3)

Personnel:

Executive Director: Dr. Rudy Ehrenberg Jr.

   E-Mail: amcsus@cox.net

Historical Note:

AMCSUS serves as an advocate for military colleges and schools and acts as a liaison with the Departments of Defense and Education. Members are group of schools, college preparatory schools; two-year colleges; and colleges and universities which provide education in a military environment.

Meetings/Conferences: Annual

2013 - Alexandria, VA (Westin Hotel)/Feb. 24 - 26

Publications:

Directory of Military Schools & Military Colleges; on-line

Association of Military Surgeons of the United States *(1891)*

9320 Old Georgetown Rd.

Bethesda, MD 20814-1653

Tel: (301) 897-8800 *Fax:* (301) 530-5446

TollFree: (800) 761-9320

E-Mail: amsus@amsus.org

Website: amsus.org

Members: 9000 individuals

Staff: 9

Annual Budget: $2-5,000,000

Personnel:

Executive Director: George K. Anderson USAF (Ret.)

   E-Mail: george.anderson@amsus.org

Coordinator, Membership Services: Susan Bachenheimer

   E-Mail: membership@amsus.org

Coordinator, Meetings: Lindsey Bloom

   E-Mail: lindsey.bloom@amsus.org

Financial Manager: Diana Hedrick

   E-Mail: amsus@amsus.org

Journal Administrator: Tonya Lira

   E-Mail: milmed@amsus.org

Coordinator , Meeting: Jeanette Naiman

   E-Mail: meetings@amsus.org

Historical Note:

Incorporated by an act of Congress in 1903. AMSUS's mission is to advance the knowledge of federal healthcare and increases the effectiveness and efficiency of its membership by mutual association and by the consideration of matters pertaining to constituent services both in peace and war. Sustaining Members are companies and their representatives. Membership consists of health care professionals or civilians employed by the armed services, the Public Health Service or Dept. of Veterans Affairs, or medical consultants. Membership: $60 (Active); $27 (Student); $1200 (Life); $650-2,200 (Sustaining).

Meetings/Conferences: Annual

Conference Chair: Lindsey Bloom

2013 - Seattle, WA/Oct. 31 - Nov. 8

2014 - Boston, MA/Oct. 26 - 31

2015 - Minneapolis, MN/Nov. 1 - 5

Publications:

AMSUS; on-line

AMSUS Newsletter; quarterly; adv.

Military Medicine; monthly; adv.

Association of Millwork Distributors *(1935)*

10047 Robert Trent Jones Pkwy.

New Port Richey, FL 34655-4649

Tel: (727) 372-3665 *Fax:* (727) 372-2879

Website: amdweb.com

Members: 1100 companies

Staff: 7

Annual Budget: $2-5,000,000

Tax: 501(c)(6)

Personnel:
Chief Executive Officer and Secretary: Rosalie Leone
    E-Mail: rleone@amdweb.com

Historical Note:
Formally known as National Sash & Door Jobbers Association. AMD provides leadership, education, promotion, networking and advocacy to, and for, the millwork distribution industry. Membership: $1,000 (Associate Member Manufacturer); $500 (Associate Member Manufacturer's Representative).

Continuing Education:
Certification Designation/s: AMDC

Meetings/Conferences: Annual

Publications:
AMD Connected; weekly
AMD Millwork Magazine; monthly
Membership Directory and Products Guide; annually;
    adv.

Association of Minority Health Professions Schools *(1976)*
P.O. Box 13778
Atlanta, GA 30324
Tel: (678) 904-4217 *Fax:* (678) 904-4518
TollFree: (877) 895-0902
E-Mail: info@minorityhealth.org
Website: minorityhealth.org
Members: 12 historically black medical, dental, pharmacy and veterinary schools
Staff: 4
Annual Budget: $500-1,000,000
Tax: 501(c)(3)

Personnel:
Director, Finance and Administration: Breggie Jame
    E-Mail: bjames@minorityhealth.org
Director, Program and Operations: Thomas Adams
    E-Mail: tadams@minorityhealth.org

Historical Note:
AMHPS is comprised of nine minority health professions schools in the U.S. whose mission is to help career development of health care professionals who come from disadvantaged backgrounds.

Publications:
Newsletter

The Association of Mortgage Investors
900 19th St. NW
Suite 800
Washington, DC 20006
Tel: (202) 327-8100 *Fax:* (202) 327-8101
E-Mail: info@the-ami.org
Website: the-ami.org
Staff: 1
Annual Budget: $500-1,000,000
Tax: 501(c)(6)

Personnel:
Executive Director: Christopher J. Katopis
    E-Mail: katopis@the-ami.org

Historical Note:
The Association of Mortgage Investors (AMI) was formed to serve as the industry voice for institutional investors and investment professionals with interests in mortgage securities.

Publications:
Membership Directory; on-line

Association of Moving Image Archivists *(1990)*
1313 N. Vine St.
Hollywood, CA 90028
Tel: (323) 463-1500 *Fax:* (323) 463-1506
E-Mail: amia@amianet.org
Website: amianet.org
Members: 750 individuals and institutions
Staff: 3
Annual Budget: $500-1,000,000
Tax: 501(c)(3)

Personnel:
Managing Director: Laura Rooney
    E-Mail: lrooney@amianet.org
Manager, Membership Services: Beverly Graham
    E-Mail: bgraham@amianet.org
Manager, Events and Operations: Kristina Kersels
    E-Mail: kkersels@amianet.org

Historical Note:
Founded as Film and Television Archives Advisory Committee, assumed its current name in 1991. AMIA's mission is to advance the field of moving image archiving

by cultivating cooperation among individuals and organizations concerned with the acquisition, description, preservation, exhibition and use of moving image materials. Membership: $95 (Individual); $55 (Student); $300 (Non-Profit Institutional); $600 (Profit Institutional).

Meetings/Conferences:
Conference Chair: Kristina Kersels

Publications:
AMIA Membership Directory; annually; adv.
AMIA Newsletter; quarterly; adv.
AMIA Tech Review
The Moving Image; semi-annually; adv.

Association of Muslim Social Scientists of North America *(1972)*
P.O. Box 5502
Herndon, VA 20172
Tel: (703) 471-1133 *Fax:* (703) 471-3922
Website: amss.net
Members: 300 individuals
Staff: 2
Annual Budget: Under $10,000
Tax: 501(c)(3)

Personnel:
President: Safi Kaskas
    E-Mail: president@amss.org
Treasurer: Ahsun Dasti
    E-Mail: treasurer@amss.org

Historical Note:
AMSS's mission is to provide a forum through which Islamic positions on various academic disciplines can be promoted, with an emphasis on the social sciences and humanities. Membership: $60 (Full Membership); $40 (Associate); $100 (Associate Institutional).

Association of National Advertisers *(1910)*
708 Third Ave.
33rd Floor
New York, NY 10017
Tel: (212) 697-5950 *Fax:* (212) 687-7310
E-Mail: info@ana.net
Website: ana.net
Members: 400 companies
Staff: 61
Annual Budget: $10-25,000,000

Personnel:
President and Chief Executive Officer: Bob Liodice
    E-Mail: bliodice@ana.net
Director, Marketing Knowledge Center: Susan Burke
    E-Mail: sburke@ana.net
Senior Vice President, Marketing and Communications:
    Duke Fanelli
    E-Mail: dfanelli@ana.net
Vice President, Information Services: Kathleen Hunter
Chief Operating Officer: Christine Manna
    E-Mail: cmanna@ana.net
Senior Director, Conferences and Forums: Kristen
    McDonough
    E-Mail: kmcdonough@ana.net
Senior Manager, Human Resources: Alba Rivera
    E-Mail: arivera@ana.net
Senior Vice President and Chief Information Officer: Robert
    Rothe
General Counsel: Douglas Wood
Executive Vice President, Member Relations: William
    Zengel

Historical Note:
ANA strives to communicate marketing practices, lead industry initiatives, influence industry practices, manage industry affairs and advance, promote and protect all advertisers and marketers. Maintains a Washington office to lobby against restrictions of advertisers' rights.

Meetings/Conferences: Annual
Conference Chair: Kristen McDonough
Number of non-conference events/year: 7

Publications:
ANA Magazine; bi-monthly; adv.

Association of Natural Bio-Control Producers *(1990)*
P.O. Box 1609
Clovis, CA 93613-1609
Tel: (559) 360-7111 *Fax:* (800) 553-4817
Website: anbp.org
Staff: 3
Tax: 501(c)(6)

Personnel:

Executive Director: Lynn LeBeck
    E-Mail: exdir@anbp.org
Technical Advisor and Production Manager: Kim
    Gallagher Horton
General Manager, Sales and Administration: Rene Ruiter

Historical Note:
ANBP's mission is to address key issues of the augmentative biological control industry through advocacy, education, and quality assurance. Membership includes producers, distributors, suppliers, practitioners, general members, industry supporters, researchers, and government representatives. Membership: $35 (Associate); $250 (Distributor); $550 (Producer); $125 (Practitioner); $500 (Life time Associate).

Meetings/Conferences: Annual

Publications:
ANBP Newsletter; semi-annually
Member Directory; on-line

Membership List Available to Non-members

Association of Natural Resource Enforcement Trainers *(1986)*
402 W. Washington St.
Indianapolis, IN 46204
Tel: (317) 232-4010
Website: anret.org
Members: 50 Agencies
Staff: 3

Personnel:
Interim President: Cpt. Dave Windsor
    E-Mail: DWindsor@dnr.IN.gov
Executive Secretary: Scotty Roxburgh
    E-Mail: roxburgh_scotty@shaw.ca
Webmaster: Derick W. Stoddard
    E-Mail: stoddadw@gov.ns.ca

Historical Note:
ANRET's mission is to provide a medium for the collection and dissemination of training information. Membership: $50/year (Regular/Associate/Agency).

Publications:
ANRET Newsletter; semi-annually

Association of Naval Aviation *(1975)*
2550 Huntington Ave.
Suite 202
Alexandria, VA 22303-1499
Tel: (703) 960-6806 *Fax:* (703) 960-6807
E-Mail: anahqtr@aol.com
Website: anahq.org
Members: 7000 individuals
Staff: 3
Annual Budget: $100-250,000
Tax: 501(c)(3)

Personnel:
President: VADM Walter B. Massenburg USN (Ret.)

Historical Note:
ANA's purpose is to educate the general public about the overall military status of the United States and to encourage widespread interest as to the importance of Naval Aviation in the defense of the United States and its allies. Membership: $40 (Retired Military/Former Military/Civilian); $25 (Military Officer-Active or Reserve duty); $15 (Military Enlisted- Active or Reserve duty); $10 (Student/Officer Candidate); $14 (Overseas Members).

Meetings/Conferences:
Number of non-conference events/year: 6

Publications:
Wings of Gold; quarterly; adv.

Membership List Available to Non-members

Association of Neurosurgical Physician Assistants *(1991)*
P.O. Box 17781
Tampa, FL 33682
Tel: (813) 988-7795 *Fax:* (813) 988-7796
E-Mail: ANSPA@Focus-ED.net
Website: anspa.org
Members: 200 physician assistants
Staff: 2
Annual Budget: Under $10,000
Tax: 501(c)(3)

Personnel:
Treasurer: Damon Jordan PA-C
    E-Mail: Dmjhockey13@aol.com

Historical Note:
ANSPA is Nationally affiliated with the American Academy of Physician Assistants. ANSPA's mission is the

enhancement of the education of both professional and lay people with respect to neurological surgery and Physician Assistants. Membership: $100 (Fellow/Associate); $20 (Student).

Continuing Education:
Certification Designation/s: CME

Meetings/Conferences: Annual

Publications:
Brainwaves; quarterly; adv.
eBlasts; on-line
Membership Directory; on-line

Association of Nurses in AIDS Care (1987)
3538 Ridgewood Rd.
Akron, OH 44333-3122
Tel: (330) 670-0101 *Fax:* (330) 670-0109
TollFree: (800) 260-6780
E-Mail: anac@anacnet.org
Website: nursesinaidscare.org
Members: 2500 individuals
Staff: 5
Annual Budget: $1-2,000,000
Tax: 501(c)(3)

Personnel:
Executive Director: Adele A. Webb PhD, RN
    E-Mail: adele@anacnet.org
Director, Policy and Interim Chief Operating Officer:
    Kimberly Carbaugh
    E-Mail: kimberly@anacnet.org
Director, Meetings: Kathy Reihl
    E-Mail: kathy@anacnet.org

Historical Note:
ANAC's mission is to promote the individual and collective professional development of nurses involved in the delivery of health care to persons infected or affected by the Human Immunodeficiency Virus (HIV) and to promote the health and welfare of infected persons. Members are nurses and other health professionals with an interest in the care of individuals with HIV. Membership: $90 (Active/Affiliate); $70 (Associate/Disabled Nurses); $80 (International); $25 (Electronic).

Continuing Education:
Certification Designation/s: AACRN, ACRN

Meetings/Conferences: Annual
Conference Chair: Kathy Reihl

Publications:
HIV + Nurse Newsletter
Journal of the Association of Nurses in AIDS Care
    (JANAC); bi-monthly; adv.
Membership Directory; on-line

Membership List Available to Non-members

Association of Nutrition & Foodservice Professionals (1960)
406 Surrey Woods Dr.
St. Charles, IL 60174-2386
Tel: (630) 587-6336 *Fax:* (630) 587-6308
TollFree: (800) 323-1908
E-Mail: info@dmaonline.org
Website: anfponline.org
Members: 14000 individuals
Staff: 23
Annual Budget: $2-5,000,000
Tax: 501(c)(6)

Personnel:
President and Chief Executive Officer: William St. John
    CAE
Director, Information Systems: LeAnn Barlow
Coordinator, Events and Special Projects: Karen Cassidy
Editor: Diane Everett
Manager, Marketing: Kim Harden
Director, Professional Development Services: Pam Himrod
    CAE, CDM, CFPP, RD
Executive Vice President and Chief Operating Officer:
    Marla Isaacs CAE
Director, Finance: Jennifer Karson CAE
Manager, Professional Development Services: Keri Lilly
Executive Administrative Assistant: Allison Pate
Coordinator, Marketing: Magen Wielgus

Historical Note:
Formerly (1984) the Hospital, Institution and Educational Food Service Society, and then Dietary Managers Association. Assumed its present name in 2012. ANFP's mission is to promote career development, setting standards for food service practices, and enhancing and strengthening the overall profession of food service management. Membership: $105 (Professional/Allied Professional); $60 (Pre-Professional).

Continuing Education:
Certification Designation/s: CDM, CFPP

Meetings/Conferences: Annual
Conference Chair: Karen Cassidy
2013 - Savannah, GA (Westin Savannah Harbor Golf
    Resort and Spa)/July 28 - 31

Publications:
ANFP eNews; on-line
Dietary Manager; adv.

Association of Occupational and Environmental Clinics (1987)
1010 Vermont Ave. NW
Suite 513
Washington, DC 20005
Tel: (202) 347-4976 *Fax:* (202) 347-4950
TollFree: (888) 347-2632
E-Mail: aoec@aoec.org
Website: aoec.org
Members:
60 clinics
250 individuals
Staff: 19
Annual Budget: $2-5,000,000
Tax: 501(c)(3)

Personnel:
Executive Director: Katherine Kirkland Dr. P.H.
    E-Mail: kkirkland@aoec.org
Coordinator, Programs: Ingrid Denis MA
Health Educator: Paula Wilborne-Davis CHES, MPH
    E-Mail: pdavis@aoec.org

Historical Note:
AOEC is established to enhance the practice of occupational/environmental medicine through information sharing and research. Membership criteria include commitment to teaching, research and public health response to occupational and environmental conditions. Individual membership is open to those who share the goals of AOEC. Membership: $40 (Individual); $500 (Clinic); $300 (Associate).

Publications:
AOEC Clinic Directory; on-line
AOEC Newsletter; quarterly

Membership List Available to Non-members

Association of Occupational Health Professionals in Healthcare (1981)
109 VIP Dr.
Suite 220
Wexford, PA 15090
Tel: (724) 935-6612 *Fax:* (724) 935-1560
TollFree: (800) 362-4347
E-Mail: info@aohp.org
Website: aohp.org
Members: 1135 individuals
Staff: 1
Annual Budget: $250-500,000
Tax: 501(c)(6)

Personnel:
Executive Director and Director, Accounts: Judy Lyle

Historical Note:
Formerly (1994) known as Association of Hospital Employee Health Professionals. AOHP's mission is to is dedicated to promoting the health and safety of workers in healthcare. Membership: $125 (Active); $50 (Student); $25 (Retired).

Continuing Education:
Enrollment: 1000
Certification Designation/s: ANCC

Meetings/Conferences: Annual
2013 - Orlando, FL (Walt Disney World Resorts)/Sept.
    11 - 14

Publications:
AOHP e-Bytes; monthly
Journal of the AOHP; quarterly; adv.
Make a Difference e-Newsletter; quarterly
Membership Directory; on-line

Membership List Available to Non-members

Association of Official Racing Chemists (1947)
1021 Storrs Rd.
Storrs, CT 06268
Tel: (860) 487-3755 *Fax:* (860) 487-3756
Website: aorc-online.org
Members: 200 individuals
Staff: 1
Annual Budget: $25-50,000

Personnel:
Executive Director: Dennis Hill

Historical Note:
Founded in Chicago by a group of chemists from the United States and several other countries, AORC's mission is to encourage the advancement of drugs detection in biological materials. Membership of the AORC consists of individuals, not laboratories, and is limited to those concerned with the detection of drugs in racing animals.

Publications:
RCI Newsletter

Association of Official Seed Analysts, Inc. (1908)
101 E. State St.
Suite 214
Ithaca, NY 14850
Tel: (607) 256-3313 *Fax:* (607) 273-1638
E-Mail: aosa.office@twcny.rr.com
Website: aosaseed.com
Members: 59 individuals
Staff: 4
Annual Budget: $50-100,000

Personnel:
Editor: Cindy Finneseth
    E-Mail: Cindy.Finneseth@uky.edu
Executive Director: Anita Hall
Secretary and Treasurer: Janine Maruschak
    E-Mail: jmaruschak@inspection.gc.ca

Historical Note:
AOSA's mission is to serve the seed industry by maintaining and encouraging the professional standards and proficiency among its members and promoting uniform seed testing methods through accreditation, research and method development, and maintaining and updating the Rules for Testing Seeds. Members include official state, federal, and university seed laboratories across the United States and Canada. Membership: $150 (Individual); $500 (Organization).

Meetings/Conferences: Annual

Publications:
Member Directory; on-line
Seed Technology; annually

Association of Official Seed Certifying Agencies (1919)
1601 52nd Ave.
Suite One
Moline, IL 61265
Tel: (309) 736-0120 *Fax:* (309) 736-0115
Website: aosca.org
Members: 495 individuals and agencies
Staff: 2
Annual Budget: $1-2,000,000
Tax: 501(c)(5)

Personnel:
Chief Executive Officer: Chet Boruff
    E-Mail: cboruff@aosca.org
Administrative Assistant: Peggy Gromoll
    E-Mail: pgromoll@aosca.org

Historical Note:
Formerly (1968) The International Crop Improvement Association. AOSCA's mission is to promote and facilitate the movement of seed or plant products in local, national, and international markets through the coordinated efforts of official seed certification agencies acting to evaluate, document, and verify that a seed or plant product meets certain accepted standards. Membership: $50/year (Affiliate/Associate).

Meetings/Conferences: Annual
2013 - Dearborn, MI/June 23 - 26

Publications:
AOSCA Newsletter

Association of Oil Pipe Lines (1947)
1808 Eye St. NW
Suite 300
Washington, DC 20006
Tel: (202) 408-7970 *Fax:* (202) 280-1949
E-Mail: aopl@aopl.org
Website: aopl.org
Members: 48 companies
Staff: 6
Annual Budget: $2-5,000,000
Tax: 501(c)(6)

Personnel:
President and Chief Executive Officer: Andrew M. Black
Director, Programs and Administration: Heather Keith
    E-Mail: hkeith@aopl.org

General Counsel: Steven M. Kramer
E-Mail: skramer@aopl.org
Director, Government Relations: John Stoody
E-Mail: jstoody@aopl.org

Historical Note:
Formerly Committee for Pipe Line Companies; assumed its current name in 1960. AOPL represents common carrier crude and petroleum product pipelines, as well as carbon dioxide pipelines, before Congress, regulatory agencies, and the courts.

Meetings/Conferences: Annual
Conference Chair: Heather Keith

Association of Old Crows (1964)
1000 N. Payne St.
Suite 200
Alexandria, VA 22314-1652
Tel: (703) 549-1600 *Fax:* (703) 549-2589
Website: crows.org
Members: 13500 Individuals and 180 Organizations
Staff: 18
Annual Budget: $2-5,000,000
Tax: 501(c)(6)

Personnel:
Executive Director: Donald N. Richetti
E-Mail: richetti@crows.org
Director, Operations: Norm Balchunas
E-Mail: balchunas@crows.org
Director, Education: Mike Dolim
E-Mail: dolim@crows.org
Director, Convention and Meeting Services: Shelley Frost
E-Mail: frost@crows.org
Manager, Information Technology: Keith Jordan
E-Mail: jordan@crows.org
Director, Government and Industry Affairs: Kenneth Miller
E-Mail: kmiller@crows.org
Director, Membership Operations: Glorianne O'Neilin
E-Mail: oneilin@crows.org
Director, Marketing: Brock Sheets
E-Mail: sheets@crows.org
Manager, Marketing and Exhibits: J. Stewart Taylor
E-Mail: taylor@crows.org
Assistant, Marketing and Communications: Bridget Whyde
E-Mail: whyde@crows.org

Historical Note:
AOC will advocate the need for a strong defense capability emphasizing electronic warfare and information operations to government, industry, academia, and the public. $500 (Life); $15 (Student/Retired).

Continuing Education:
Certification Designation/s: AOC

Meetings/Conferences: Annual
Conference Chair: Shelley Frost
2013 - Washington, DC (Marriott Wardman Park Hotel)/Oct. 27 - 30
2014 - Indianapolis, IN (Indianapolis Convention Center)/Oct. 12 - 16
Number of non-conference events/year: 4

Publications:
E-Crow; weekly
IO Journal; quarterly; adv.
Journal of Electronic Defense; monthly; adv.

Association of Oncology Social Work (1984)
100 N. 20th St.
Suite 400
Philadelphia, PA 19103
Tel: (215) 599-6093 *Fax:* (215) 564-2175
E-Mail: info@aosw.org
Website: aosw.org
Members: 1000 members
Staff: 3
Annual Budget: $250-500,000
Tax: 501(c)(3)

Personnel:
Managing Director: Jessica Widing
E-Mail: jwiding@fernley.com
Planner, Meetings: Tina Phelan
E-Mail: tphelan@fernley.com

Historical Note:
Formerly the National Association of Oncology Social Workers. AOSW's mission is to advance excellence in the psychosocial care of persons with cancer, their families, and caregivers through networking, education, advocacy, research and resource development. Membership: $145

(Full); $115 (Full-time Student/Retired/Post Graduate); $85 (Associate/Friend).

Meetings/Conferences: Annual
Conference Chair: Tina Phelan
2013 - San Diego, CA (Loews Coronado Bay Resort)/ June 5 - 7

Publications:
Journal of Psychosocial Oncology; quarterly
Membership Directory; on-line

Association of Opinion Journalists (1947)
3899 N. Front St.
Harrisburg, PA 17110
Tel: (717) 703-3015 *Fax:* (717) 703-3014
E-Mail: aoj@pa-news.org
Website: opinionjournalists.org
Members: 545 individuals
Staff: 8
Annual Budget: $100-250,000

Personnel:
Web Manager: Thea Joselow
E-Mail: tjoselow@nutgraf.net
Editor: Lois Kazakoff
E-Mail: lkazakoff@sfchronicle.com
Manager: Lisa Strohl

Historical Note:
Formally (2012) National Conference of Editorial Writers. AOJ is dedicated to advancing the craft of opinion journalism through education, professional development, exploration of issues of public importance and vigorous advocacy within journalism organizations. Members are opinion writers and editors. Membership: $25 (Students); $75 (Academics/Associate/Broadcast/Columnist/Online/ Print); $45 (Retired).

Meetings/Conferences: Annual
Number of non-conference events/year: 1

Publications:
Membership Directory; on-line
The Masthead; quarterly

Association of Organ Procurement Organizations (1984)
8500 Leesburg Pike
Suite 300
Vienna, VA 22182
Tel: (703) 556-4242 *Fax:* (703) 556-4852
E-Mail: aopo@aopo.org
Website: aopo.org
Members: 58 organizations
Staff: 6
Annual Budget: $1-2,000,000
Tax: 501(c)(3)

Personnel:
Executive Director: Elling Eidbo
E-Mail: eeidbo@aopo.org
Manager, Accreditation and Programs: Carol O'Neill
E-Mail: coneill@aopo.org
Information Technology Officer: Mark Paster
E-Mail: mpaster@aopo.org

Historical Note:
Formerly (1988) Association of Independent Organ Procurement Agencies. AOPO represents and serves OPOs through advocacy, support, and development of activities that will maximize the availability of organs and tissues and enhance the quality, effectiveness, and integrity of the donation process. Members are certified OPO or private, non-profit health, medical, or scientific organizations engaged in organ donation or transplantation.

Meetings/Conferences: Annual
2013 - Indianapolis, IN (JW Marriott Indianapolis)/ June 18 - 21
2014 - Baltimore, MD (Baltimore Marriott Inner Harbor at Camden Yards)/June 17 - 20
Number of non-conference events/year: 4

Publications:
Member News; on-line

Association of Osteopathic State Executive Directors (1918)
2007 Apalachee Pkwy.
Tallahassee, FL 32302
Tel: (850) 878-7364 *Fax:* (850) 942-7538
E-Mail: admin@foma.org
Website: osteopathic.org/inside-aoa/about/ affiliates/Pa
Members: 75 individuals
Staff: 1

Annual Budget: $10-25,000

Personnel:
Coordinator: Michelle Winn CMP, CAE

Historical Note:
AOSED works for the purpose of strengthening AOA-affiliated state divisional societies, promoting coordination of divisional society programs, providing assistance for the development of divisional society leadership, and aiding with efforts of the AOA in the advancement of the osteopathic profession in the United States. Regular members are Osteopathic State executive directors, affiliate members include related medical associations. Has no paid officers or full-time staff. Membership: $400/year (allied); $400/year (international); $90/year (associate/ retired); $60/year (postdoctoral); $590/year (regular); complimentary for students.

Meetings/Conferences:
Conference Chair: Michelle Winn CMP, CAE

Association of Otolaryngology Administrators (1982)
2400 Ardmore Blvd.
Suite 302
Pittsburgh, PA 15221
Tel: (412) 243-5156 *Fax:* (412) 243-5160
E-Mail: info@AOAnow.org
Website: aoanow.org
Members: 1000 individuals
Staff: 5
Annual Budget: $500-1,000,000
Tax: 501(c)(6)

Personnel:
Executive Director: Robin L. Wagner CMPE, COPM
E-Mail: rwagner@cmemanage.com
Contact, Accounting: Elaine Ehalt
E-Mail: EEhalt@cmemanage.com
Contact, Meetings and Events: Susan "Suzy" Murton
E-Mail: smurton@cmemanage.com
Coordinator, Communications: Caitlin Price
E-Mail: cprice@cmemanage.com
Contact, Membership Services: Marcia Seiffert
E-Mail: marcia@cmemanage.com

Historical Note:
AOA's purpose is to support professional development, networking and education in otolaryngology practice management. Members are individuals responsible for the business aspects of an otolaryngology practice. Membership: $345 (Professional/Corporate); $295 (Active-Secondary); $175 (Associate); $100 (Coder or Auxiliary); $640 (Leadership Team); $650 (Multi-Year Professional).

Continuing Education:
Certification Designation/s: COPM

Meetings/Conferences: Annual
Conference Chair: Susan "Suzy" Murton
2013 - Vancouver, BC/Sept. 25 - 28

Publications:
AOA e-newletter; on-line
AOA Today; on-line
Fast Practice; monthly
Membership Directory; on-line
Oto's Scope Magazine; quarterly

Association of Paroling Authorities International (1970)
C/O Sam Houston State University
George J. Beto Criminal Justice Center
Huntsville, TX 77341-2296
Tel: (936) 294-1706 *Fax:* (936) 294-1671
TollFree: (877) 318-2724
E-Mail: info@apaintl.org
Website: apaintl.org
Members: 464 individuals
Staff: 2
Annual Budget: $100-250,000
Tax: 501(c)(3)

Personnel:
Chief Administrative Officer: Keith Hardison
E-Mail: keith@apaintl.org
Secretariat: Natalie Payne
E-Mail: npayne@shsu.edu

Historical Note:
APAI seeks to demonstrate through embracing APAI's values that the parole process of the criminal justice system is an essential element for making the society a safer and better place to live. Membership: $40 (Associate); $60 (Individual); $350-550 (Organization); $15 (Student); $1,000 (Corporate).

Meetings/Conferences: Annual

Conference Chair: Natalie Payne
2013 - Providence, RI (Renaissance Providence
  Downtown Hotel)/May 19 - 22
Number of non-conference events/year: 1

Publications:
E-forum Newsletter; quarterly; adv.

Association of Partners for Public Lands (1977)
2401 Blueridge Ave.
Suite 303
Wheaton, MD 20902
Tel: (301) 946-9475 *Fax:* (301) 946-9478
E-Mail: appl@appl.org
Website: appl.org
Members: 87 organizations
Staff: 5
Annual Budget: $500-1,000,000
Tax: 501(c)(3)

Personnel:
Executive Director: Donna L. Asbury
  E-Mail: dasbury@appl.org
Coordinator, Education: Chuck Benjamin
  E-Mail: cbenjamin@appl.org
Coordinator, Membership Services: Nancy Kotz
  E-Mail: nkotz@appl.org
Coordinator, Marketing and Outreach: Amy Matthews
  E-Mail: amatthews@appl.org
Coordinator, Trade Shows: Amy Norris
  E-Mail: norris@acmeetingevents.com

Historical Note:
*APPL seeks to support its members in their service and
stewardship of America's public lands through education,
information, and representation. APPL fosters stewardship
and appreciation of public lands and historic sites through
effective partnerships. Membership: $350-8,500 (Nonprofit
Member); $250-1500 (Associate Member).*

Meetings/Conferences: Annual
Conference Chair: Amy Norris
2013 - Portland, OR/March 10 - 14

Publications:
Membership Directory; on-line
Newswire; monthly

Association of Pathology Chairs (1967)
9650 Rockville Pike
Bethesda, MD 20814-3993
Tel: (301) 634-7880 *Fax:* (301) 634-7990
E-Mail: apc@asip.org
Website: apcprods.org
Members: 180 Academic Departments of
Pathology
Staff: 3
Annual Budget: $250-500,000
Tax: 501(c)(3)

Personnel:
Executive Director: Priscilla S. Markwood CAE
  E-Mail: pmarkwood@asip.org
Coordinator, Membership Services and Meetings: Ashlie
  Doran
  E-Mail: adoran@asip.org
Manager, Meetings: Sara Hamilton
  E-Mail: shamilton@asip.org

Historical Note:
*Formerly American Association of Chairmen of Medical
School Departments of Pathology (1976). APC provides
education, training, information resources and networking
opportunities for pathology chairs, residency program
directors, undergraduate medical educators, and department
administrators. Membership: $1,100 (Regular Member);
$600 (Affiliate Member).*

Meetings/Conferences: Annual
Conference Chair: Sara Hamilton
2013 - Boston, MA (Seaport Boston Hotel)/July 10 -
  12/11-25 exhibitors
2014 - Boston, MA (Seaport Boston Hotel)/July 9 - 11
2015 - San Diego, CA (Rancho Bernardo Inn)/July 15 -
  17
2016 - San Diego, CA (Rancho Bernardo Inn)/July 13 -
  15
Number of non-conference events/year: 1

Publications:
APC Newsletter; semi-annually
Membership Directory; on-line

Association of Pedestrian and Bicycle Professionals (1995)
P.O. Box 93

Cedarburg, WI 53012-0093
Tel: (262) 228-7025 *Fax:* (866) 720-3611
E-Mail: info@apbp.org
Website: apbp.org
Members: 800 individuals
Staff: 5
Annual Budget: $250-500,000
Tax: 501(c)(6)

Personnel:
Executive Director: Kit Keller
  E-Mail: kit@apbp.org
Contact, Membership Services: Debra Goeks
  E-Mail: deb@apbp.org
Manager, Complete Streets Program: Linda Tracy
  E-Mail: linda@apbp.org

Historical Note:
*APBP's purpose is to promote excellence in the emerging
professional discipline of pedestrian and bicycle
transportation. Membership: $100 (Professional); $80
(Advocate); $30 (Student/Retired).*

Meetings/Conferences: Annual

Publications:
Consultant and Supplier Directory; on-line
Member Directory; on-line
The Bike/Ped Professional Newsletter; on-line

Membership List Available to Non-members

Association of Pediatric Hematology/Oncology Nurses (1976)
4700 W. Lake Ave.
Glenview, IL 60025-1485
Tel: (847) 375-4724 *Fax:* (847) 375-6478
E-Mail: info@aphon.org
Website: aphon.org
Members: 3200 individuals
Staff: 9
Annual Budget: $1-2,000,000
Tax: 501(c)(3)

Personnel:
Executive Director: David J. Bergeson CAE, PhD
  E-Mail: dbergeson@connect2amc.com
Senior Manager: Nicole Wallace
  E-Mail: nwallace@connect2amc.com

Historical Note:
*APHON is dedicated to promoting optimal nursing care for
children, adolescents, and young adults with cancer and
blood disorders, and their families. Members are nurses
specializing in care for children and adolescents with
cancer and blood disorders and their families. Membership:
$25-130/year.*

Continuing Education:
Certification Designation/s: CPHON

Meetings/Conferences: Annual
2013 - Louisville, KY (Kentucky International
  Convention Center)/Sept. 19 - 21

Publications:
APHON Counts; quarterly; adv.
Journal of Pediatric Oncology Nursing; bi-monthly

Membership List Available to Non-members

Association of Pediatric Oncology Social Workers (1977)
Nemours Children's Clinic
807 Children's Way
Jacksonville, FL 32207
Tel: (904) 697-3786 *Fax:* (904) 697-3790
E-Mail: info@aposw.org
Website: aposw.org
Members: 380 individuals
Staff: 3
Annual Budget: $100-250,000
Tax: 501(c)(6)

Personnel:
Treasurer: Helena Gutierrez-Richards ACSW, LCSW
  E-Mail: hrichards@nemours.org

Historical Note:
*APOSW's mission is to advance pediatric psychosocial
oncology care through clinical social work practice,
research, advocacy, education, and program development.
Members are professional social workers employed in the
field of pediatric oncology. Membership: $95 (Full); $75
(Associate); $50 (Student/Non-North American Associate/
Retired Member).*

Meetings/Conferences: Annual
Conference Chair: Carolyn McCarley

2013 - Minneapolis, MN (Hilton Minneapolis)/May 15
  - 17

Publications:
APOSW newsletter; on-line
Member Directory; on-line

Association of Pediatric Program Directors (1980)
6728 Old McLean Village Dr.
McLean, VA 22101
Tel: (703) 556-9222 *Fax:* (703) 556-8729
E-Mail: info@appd.org
Website: appd.org
Members: 1100 Individuals
Staff: 3
Annual Budget: $500-1,000,000

Personnel:
Executive Director: Laura E. Degnon CAE
Director, Communications and Newsletter Editor: Jerry
  Rushton MD, MPH
  E-Mail: jrushton@iupui.edu

Historical Note:
*APPD is committed to pediatric graduate medical
education to ensure the health and well-being of children.
Membership: $1600/year.*

Meetings/Conferences:
2013 - Nashville, TN (Renaissance Nashville Hotel and
  Nashville Convention Center)/April 9 - 13
2013 - Arlington, VA/Oct. 2 - 4

Publications:
Academic Pediatrics; bi-monthly
APPD Newsletter
Membership Directory; on-line

Association of Performing Arts Presenters (1957)
1211 Connecticut Ave. NW
Suite 200
Washington, DC 20036
Tel: (202) 833-2787 *Fax:* (202) 833-1543
TollFree: (888) 820-2787
E-Mail: info@artspresenters.org
Website: apap365.org
Members: 2000 members
Staff: 23
Annual Budget: $250-500,000
Tax: 501(c)(3)

Personnel:
President and Chief Executive Officer: Maria Garcia
  Durham
  E-Mail: mdurham@artspresenters.org
Editor: Alicia Anstead
  E-Mail: aanstead@artspresenters.org
Programs Manager: Laura Benson
  E-Mail: lbenson@artspresenters.org
Director, Conference and Meetings: Gil Gonzalez
  E-Mail: ggonzalez@artspresenters.org
Director, Marketing and Communications: Lynne Kingsley
  E-Mail: lkingsley@artspresenters.org
Director, Finance and Administration: Malinda Lambert
  E-Mail: mlambert@artspresenters.org
Director, Membership Services: Susan Noseworthy
  E-Mail: snoseworthy@artspresenters.org
Project Manager, Information Technology: Phil Seeman
  E-Mail: pseeman@artspresenters.org
Communications and Government Affairs Associate: Emily
  Travis
  E-Mail: etravis@artspresenters.org

Historical Note:
*Formerly (1974) Association of College and University
Concert Managers and (1989) Association of College,
University and Community Arts Administrators. APAP is
dedicated to developing and supporting a robust performing
arts presenting field and the professionals who work within
it. Members are arts organizations, touring performing arts
and managers of artists involved in the performing arts.
Membership: $300-2,475/year.*

Meetings/Conferences: Annual
Conference Chair: Gil Gonzalez
2013 - New York City, NY (Hilton New York)/Jan. 11 -
  15

Publications:
Inside Arts; quarterly; adv.
Membership Directory; on-line
Presenting Matters; monthly

Membership List Available to Non-members

Association of periOperative Registered Nurses
(1954)
2170 S. Parker Rd.
Suite 400
Denver, CO 80231-5711
Tel: (303) 755-6304 *Fax:* (303) 750-3212
TollFree: (800) 755-2676
E-Mail: custsvc@aorn.org
Website: aorn.org
Members: 41000 individuals
Staff: 95
Annual Budget: $10-25,000,000
Tax: 501(c)(6)

Personnel:
Executive Director and Chief Executive Officer: Linda K.
  Groah CNAA, MSN, RN, FAAN
  E-Mail: executives@aorn.org
Manager, Meetings: Sandy Abbott CMP
  E-Mail: sabbott@aorn.org
Chief Financial Officer and Chief Operating Officer: James
  L. Cousin CPA, MBA
  E-Mail: accounting@aorn.org
Manager, Corporate Communications: Gayle Davis
  E-Mail: gdavis@aorn.org
Senior Manager, Marketing: Paula Felten
Chief Information Technology Officer: Karen Kemerling
Director, Membership Development: Brain Tepp
  E-Mail: btepp@aorn.org

Historical Note:
*AORN is a professional association that empowers the
OR nurse with education, standards of practice, and peer
networking. Members are perioperative nurses. Membership:
$125-1,000 (Standard-RN); $125 (Associate-Non-RN);
$20 (Student); $40 (Retired).*

Meetings/Conferences: Annual
Conference Chair: Sandy Abbott CMP
2013 - San Diego, CA/March 2 - 7/5500 attendees/
  over 100 exhibitors
2014 - Chicago, IL/March 29 - April 3
2015 - Denver, CO/March 7 - 12
2016 - Anaheim, CA/April 2 - 7
2017 - Boston, MA/April 1 - 6
2018 - New Orleans, LA/March 24 - 29

Publications:
AORN Connections; monthly; adv.
AORN Journal; monthly; adv.
Management Connections; monthly
Membership Directory; on-line
Periop Insider eNewsletter; weekly

Association of Personal Computer User Groups
(1987)
13940 Cedar Rd.
Suite 447
Cleveland, OH 44118-3204
Tel: (803) 272-8411 *Fax:* (952) 479-3627
Website: apcug.net
Members:
100000 users
280 User groups
Staff: 2
Annual Budget: $10-25,000

Personnel:
President: David Steward
Treasurer: Sandy Hart

Historical Note:
*APCUG's mission is to provide assistance and resources
to member organizations. Membership: $50/year (Full/
Associate).*

Publications:
APCUG Newsletter

Association of Personal Historians (1995)
3208 E. 25th St.
Minneapolis, MN 55406
E-Mail:
operationsmanager@personalhistorians.biz
Website: personalhistorians.org/
Staff: 8
Annual Budget: $100-250,000

Personnel:
Executive Director: Linda Coffin
  E-Mail: linda.coffin@personalhistorians.biz
Director, Marketing: Marcy Davis
  E-Mail: marcy.davis@personalhistorians.biz
Director, Communications: cj Madigan

  E-Mail: cj.madigan@personalhistorians.biz
Director, Education: Pat McNees
  E-Mail: pat.mcnees@personalhistorians.biz
Editor: Fran Morley
  E-Mail: fran.morley@personalhistorians.biz
Director, Membership Services: Annie Payne
  E-Mail: annie.payne@personalhistorians.biz
Director, Conference: Marianne Waller
  E-Mail: marianne.waller@personalhistorians.biz
Treasurer: Marty Walton
  E-Mail: marty.walton@personalhistorians.biz

Historical Note:
*Founded in 1995, Members of APH help other people
create personal histories, including memoirs, video
tributes, autobiographies, biographies, family histories,
heritage cookbooks, community histories, corporate
and organizational histories, legacy letters and ethical
wills. Members have backgrounds in fields as varied
as journalism, publishing, broadcasting, social work,
education, law, medicine and graphic design. Membership:
$200 (Full); $150 (Associate); $125 (Introductory); &120
(Partner).*

Meetings/Conferences: Annual
Conference Chair: Marianne Waller

Publications:
Members' Directory; on-line

Membership List Available to Non-members

Association of Pet Dog Trainers (1993)
104 S. Calhoun St.
Suite 610
Greenville, SC 29601
Tel: (866) 245-2742 *Fax:* (864) 331-0767
TollFree: (800) 738-3647
E-Mail: information@apdt.com
Website: apdt.com
Members: 6000 individuals
Staff: 9
Annual Budget: $1-2,000,000

Personnel:
President and Chief Executive Officer: Mychelle Blake
  MSW, CDBC
  E-Mail: mblake@apdt.com
Coordinator, Advertising Sales: Pamela Christy
  E-Mail: pamela@apdt.com
Coordinator, Membership Services: M. J. Glasby
  E-Mail: mj@apdt.com
Managing Editor: Adrienne Hovey
  E-Mail: adrienne@apdt.com
Coordinator, Education Programs: Katenna Jones
  E-Mail: katenna@apdt.com
Director, Operations: Alicia Reynolds
  E-Mail: alicia@apdt.com

Historical Note:
*APDT promotes relationships between dogs and people
by educating trainers in canine behavior and emphasizing
professionalism and reward- based training. Membership:
$150 (Professional); $100 (Full/Associate).*

Continuing Education:
Certification Designation/s: DTC

Meetings/Conferences: Annual
Conference Chair: Mychelle Blake MSW, CDBC
Number of non-conference events/year: 3

Publications:
Chronicle of the Dog; bi-monthly; adv.
Membership Directory; annually

Association of Physician Assistants in
Cardiovascular Surgery (1981)
P.O. Box 674867
Marietta, GA 30006
Tel: (877) 221-5651 *Fax:* (770) 509-0027
E-Mail: kim@oneillcommunications.com
Website: apacvs.org
Members: 700 individuals
Staff: 5
Annual Budget: $250-500,000

Personnel:
Manager, Marketing: Carmel Hearn
Finance Officer: Nancy O'Neill
Association Manager: Kim Shapland

Historical Note:
*APACVS strives to represent the interests of Cardiovascular
and Thoracic Surgical Physician Assistants. Members are
surgical physician assistants specializing in cardiovascular
surgery. Membership: $165 (Active); $25 (Student); $75
(Resident).*

Meetings/Conferences: Annual
2013 - Los Angeles, CA/Jan. 23 - 27
2013 - Los Angeles, CA (Sheraton Los Angeles
  Downtown Hotel)/Jan. 24 - 27
2014 - Orlando, FL/Jan. 22 - 26
Number of non-conference events/year: 2

Publications:
CardioVision; quarterly; adv.
Membership Directory; on-line

Membership List Available to Non-members

Association of Physician Assistants in Obstetrics
and Gynecology (1991)
563 Carter Ct.
Suite B
Kimberly, WI 54136
Tel: (920) 560-5620 *Fax:* (920) 882-3655
TollFree: (800) 545-0636
E-Mail: apaog@paobgyn.org
Website: paobgyn.org
Members: 200 individuals
Staff: 2
Annual Budget: $50-100,000
Tax: 501(c)(3)

Personnel:
Executive Director: Eric Ostermann
  E-Mail: eric@badgerbaymanagement.com
Director, Association Services: Shawn Sornson
  E-Mail: shawn@badgerbay.co

Historical Note:
*APAOG is a organization for physician assistants in OB-
GYN affiliated with the American Academy of Physician
Assistants. APAOG's mission is to improve the health
care of women by supporting physician/PA teams who
provide cost effective, quality care to female patients
and by promoting a network of communication and
education between providers dedicated to women's health.
Membership: $75 (Fellow/Associate/Affiliate); $25
(Student).*

Continuing Education:
Certification Designation/s: CME

Publications:
Membership Directory; on-line
The Monitor; quarterly; adv.

Association of Plastic Surgery Assistants (1974)
227 Oleander Ct.
Panama City, FL 32413
Tel: (850) 234-9044 *Fax:* (850) 234-9044
E-Mail: apsa@plasticassistants.info
Website: plasticassistants.info
Members: 650 individuals
Staff: 3
Annual Budget: $100-250,000

Personnel:
President: P.J. Watner
  E-Mail: pjsvettelady@yahoo.com

Historical Note:
*APSA's objective is to benefit the specialty of plastic and
reconstructive surgery by educating individuals working
for or with board certified/eligible plastic surgeons and to
encourage public interest and confidence in plastic surgery
assistants. Membership: $150/year.*

Meetings/Conferences:
Number of non-conference events/year: 1

Publications:
APSA Newsletter - the Network; adv.
Network; annually; adv.

Association of Pool and Spa Professionals (1956)
2111 Eisenhower Ave.
Suite 500
Alexandria, VA 22314-4695
Tel: (703) 838-0083 *Fax:* (703) 549-0493
E-Mail: memberservices@apsp.org
Website: apsp.org
Members: 4000 companies
Staff: 21
Annual Budget: $5-10,000,000
Tax: 501(c)(6)

Personnel:
President and Chief Executive Officer: Bill Weber
  E-Mail: bweber@apsp.org
Director, Membership Services and Operations: Terry
  Brown
  E-Mail: tbrown@apsp.org

Senior Director, Technical Services and Standards: Carvin DiGiovanni
   E-Mail: cdigiovanni@apsp.org
Director, Marketing and Communications: Lisa S. Grepps
   E-Mail: lgrepps@apsp.org
Director, Government Affairs: Jennifer Hatfield
   E-Mail: jhatfield@apsp.org
Director, Professional Development: Michael Reed
   E-Mail: mreed@apsp.org
Coordinator, Educational Publications: Nina Schwartz
   E-Mail: nschwartz@apsp.org
Director, Industry Relations: Lauren Stack
   E-Mail: lstack@apsp.org
Director, Finance: Leona Taylor
   E-Mail: ltaylor@apsp.org

Historical Note:
Formerly (1956) National Swimming Pool Institute. Absorbed the International Spa and Tub Institute in 1983. APSP's mission is to enhance the business success of its members. APSP provides professional practices through education, certification, standards, research, and safety. Membership: $1-565/Year.

Continuing Education:
Certification Designation/s: CST, CRSA, CBP, CSP
Meetings/Conferences:
Number of non-conference events/year: 2

Publications:
AQ Magazine; quarterly; adv.
MyAPSP News; weekly

Association of Postgraduate Physician Assistant Programs (1988)
300 N. Washington St.
Suite 710
Alexandria, VA 22314
Tel: (703) 778-5570 Fax: (703) 548-5539
E-Mail: appap@appap.org
Website: appap.org
Staff: 3

Personnel:
President: Jennie McKown
   E-Mail: jmckown1@jhmi.edu
Staff Liaison: Lynn Heitzman
Secretary and Treasurer: Mary Pugh
   E-Mail: Mary.Pugh2@imail.org

Historical Note:
Affiliated with the American Academy of Physician Assistants and the Association of Physician Assistant Programs. APPAP member programs are postgraduate programs that offer structured curricula, including didactic and clinical components, to educate physician assistants for a defined period of time in a medical specialty. Membership: $400 (Active Program/Provisional Program); $200 (Inactive Program); $50 (Affiliate Member/Individual Member).

Meetings/Conferences: Annual
Conference Chair: Lynn Heitzman
Number of non-conference events/year: 1

Publications:
APPAP News; adv.

Association of Presbyterian Colleges and Universities (1983)
100 Witherspoon St.
Louisville, KY 40202-1396
Tel: (502) 569-5364 Fax: (502) 569-8766
TollFree: (888) 728-7228
E-Mail: apcu@pcusa.org
Website: presbyteriancolleges.org
Members: 61 institutions
Staff: 2
Annual Budget: $100-250,000
Tax: 501(c)(3)

Personnel:
Executive Director: Gary W. Luhr
   E-Mail: gluhr@ctr.pcusa.org

Historical Note:
Product of a merger of the Association of Presbyterian Colleges and the Presbyterian College Union. APCU is an independent, not-for-profit organization that exists to strengthen the mission of colleges and universities related to the Presbyterian Church (U.S.A.).

Publications:
APCU Newsletter; on-line

Association of Private Club Directors (1997)
PO Box 9445
Laguna Beach, CA 92652

Tel: (949) 376-8889 Fax: (949) 376-6687
Website: apcd.com
Staff: 6

Personnel:
President and Chief Executive Officer: John Fornaro
   E-Mail: johnf@apcd.com
Vice President. Business Development: Kelly Herrera
   E-Mail: kelly@apcd.com
Controller and Accounting: Rameka Symons CAE
Executive Vice President: Bill Thomas
Editor, The BoardRoom: Dave White
   E-Mail: dave@boardroommagazine.com

Historical Note:
Mission is to assist private clubs in their day-to-day operations, strategic planning and continuing education for board members, especially newly elected board members. Founded in 1997, the APCD supplies education and resources to America's 7,000 private golf, country, yacht and city clubs.

Publications:
The BoardRoom magazine

Association of Private Enterprise Education (1974)
313 Fletcher Hall, Department 6106
615 McCallie Ave.
Chattanooga, TN 37403-2598
Tel: (423) 425-4118 Fax: (423) 425-5218
E-Mail: J-Clark@utc.edu
Website: apee.org
Members: 362 scholars and entrepreneurs
Staff: 4
Annual Budget: $100-250,000

Personnel:
Secretary and Treasurer: J.R. Clark
   E-Mail: j-clark@utc.edu

Historical Note:
APEE is an association of teachers and scholars from colleges and universities, public policy institutes, and industry with a common interest in studying and supporting the system of private enterprise. Mission is to put into action accurate and objective understandings of private enterprise. Membership: $75 (Individual); $255 (Institutional); $755 (Supporter); $1,005 (Sponsor).

Meetings/Conferences: Annual
Conference Chair: J.R. Clark
2013 - Maui, HI/April 14 - 16

Publications:
Journal of Private Enterprise; semi-annually
Membership Directory; annually

Association of Private Sector Colleges and Universities (Career College Association) (1991)
1101 Connecticut Ave. NW
Suite 900
Washington, DC 20036
Tel: (202) 336-6700 Fax: (202) 336-6828
TollFree: (866) 711-8574
E-Mail: cca@career.org
Website: career.org
Members: 1400 members
Staff: 49
Annual Budget: $10-25,000,000

Personnel:
President and Chief Executive Officer: Hon. Steve Gunderson
Vice President, Conferences and Professional Development: Katie A. Calabrese CMP
   E-Mail: katiec@career.org
Senior Vice President, Communications: Bob Cohen
   E-Mail: bobc@career.org
Vice President, Membership Services: Lauren Corbin CAE
   E-Mail: lauren.corbin@apscu.org
Database Manager: Stephen Holman
Executive Vice President, Government Relations and General Counsel: Brian Moran
   E-Mail: brian.moran@apscu.org
Vice President, Membership Services and Communications: Mark E. Robbins
   E-Mail: markr@career.org
Chief Financial Officer: Pamela Smith
   E-Mail: pam.smith@apscu.org

Historical Note:
Formerly Career College Association. APSCU provides crucial information and public policy recommendations that promote access to career education and the importance of workforce development. A trade association representing

private, postsecondary schools, institutes, colleges and universities that provide career-specific education programs. Membership: $500 (International); $15,000 (Allied Plus); $1,500-3,300 (Allied); $1,350 (Financial Advisory Council).

Meetings/Conferences: Annual
Conference Chair: Katie A. Calabrese CMP
2013 - Orlando, FL (Rosen Shingle Creek)/June 5 - 7/11-25 exhibitors

Publications:
APSCU Update Newsletter; irregular
Fact Book; bi-annually
The Link; quarterly; adv.

Association of Procurement Technical Assistance Centers (1986)
360 Sunset Island Tr.
Gallatin, TN 37066
Tel: (615) 268-6644
Website: aptac-us.org
Members: 500 individuals
Staff: 2
Annual Budget: $500-1,000,000

Personnel:
President: Gunnar Schalin
   E-Mail: president@aptac-us.org
Treasurer: Jason Porch
   E-Mail: treasurer@aptac-us.org

Historical Note:
Provides information and support for persons and organizations active in government procurement.

Meetings/Conferences: Semi-Annual
2013 - Atlanta, GA (Sheraton Atlanta Hotel)/April 21 - 25
2013 - Washington, DC (Hyatt Regency Washington)/ Nov. 11 - 13
2014 - San Francisco, CA (Westin San Francisco Market Street)/March 24 - 27
2014 - Washington, DC (Hyatt Regency Washington)/ Nov. 10 - 12
2015 - Denver, CO (Denver Marriott City Center)/ March 16 - 19
Number of non-conference events/year: 1

Publications:
Membership Directory; on-line

Association of Productivity Specialists (1976)
521 Fifth Ave.
Suite 1700
New York, NY 10175
Tel: (212) 286-0943
Website: a-p-s.org
Members: 1230 individuals and companies
Staff: 2
Annual Budget: $10-25,000
Tax: 501(c)(6)

Personnel:
Treasurer: James Quinn
Secretary: Edward Whistler Goh

Historical Note:
APS strives to stimulate and advocate public knowledge and understanding of the field of productivity improvement and to provide a vehicle for open communications between the Association members' clients and the general public. Membership: $1,500-4,000/year (Organization/ Company).

Continuing Education:
Certification Designation/s: MPS, CPS, APS

Publications:
The APS Review

Association of Professional Art Advisors (1980)
433 Third St.
Suite Three
Brooklyn, NY 11215
Tel: (718) 788-1425 Fax: (718) 788-1425
E-Mail: info@artadvisors.org
Website: artadvisors.org
Staff: 1
Annual Budget: $25-50,000

Personnel:
Executive Director: Kimberly Maier

Historical Note:
National Association for Corporate Art Management merged with APPA in 2005. APAA seeks to establish and disseminate principles and guidelines for acquiring, maintaining and presenting art, in relationships with

corporations, public art projects, and private collections. Anyone with five years of experience working as an art advisor, with a demonstrated knowledge of professional art practices, can become member. Affiliates are individuals and companies that support art advisors and corporate art curators in their work.

Publications:
Member Directory; on-line

Association of Professional Ball Players of America (1924)
101 S. Kraemer Ave.
Suite 112
Placentia, CA 92870
Tel: (714) 528-2012 *Fax:* (714) 528-2037
E-Mail: ballplayersassn@aol.com
Website: apbpa.org
Members: 11000 individuals
Staff: 2
Annual Budget: $250-500,000
Tax: 501(c)(3)

Personnel:
President: Roland Hemond
Secretary and Treasurer: Dick Beverage
   E-Mail: ballplayersassn@aol.com

Historical Note:
APBPA provides financial assistance for professional baseball players, coaches, umpires, scouts and clubhouse men who are in need. Members are professional baseball players, managers, coaches, scouts, and umpires. Membership: $125 (Members-Major League); $20 (Members-Minor League/Members inactive in the game/ Scouts/Administrative personnel).

Association of Professional Chaplains (1947)
1701 E. Woodfield Rd.
Suite 400
Schaumburg, IL 60173
Tel: (847) 240-1014 *Fax:* (847) 240-1015
E-Mail: info@professionalchaplains.org
Website: professionalchaplains.org
Members: 4000 members
Staff: 9
Annual Budget: $1-2,000,000
Tax: 501(c)(3)

Personnel:
Executive Director and Chief Executive Officer: Patricia F. Appelhans JD
   E-Mail: pat@professionalchaplains.org
Coordinator, Certification: Ewa Aksamit
   E-Mail: ewa@professionalchaplains.org
Coordinator, Membership: Diane Gerard
   E-Mail: diane@professionalchaplains.org
Manager, Marketing and Education: Rita Schauer Kaufman CAE
   E-Mail: rita@professionalchaplains.org
Manager, Conference and Meetings: Donna M. Kraar CMP
   E-Mail: donna@professionalchaplains.org
Manager, Operations: Carol A. Pape
   E-Mail: carol@professionalchaplains.org

Historical Note:
APC advocates professional chaplaincy care through advocacy, education, standards of practice and service to its members. Membership: $105 (APC Member/Retired Life Member/Institutional Life Member) /year.

Continuing Education:
Enrollment: 250
Certification Designation/s: BCC, PCC

Meetings/Conferences: Annual
Conference Chair: Donna M. Kraar CMP
2013 - Orlando, FL (Walt Disney World Resort)/June 27 - 30

Publications:
APC e-News; on-line; adv.
Chaplaincy Today; semi-annually; adv.
Leaders Link; quarterly

Membership List Available to Non-members

Association of Professional Communication Consultants (1983)
9840 Westpoint Dr.
Suite 200
Indianapolis, IN 46256
Tel: (317) 616-1810
Website: consultingsuccess.org/wp
Members: 140 individuals
Staff: 1

Annual Budget: Under $10,000

Personnel:
Association Manager: Reva Daniel
   E-Mail: Reva@DBWriting.com

Historical Note:
Formerly (1995) Association of Professional Writing Consultants. APCC's mission is to create a professional community to help communication consultants. Members are full-time independent writing and communications consultants, part-time consultants who primarily teach in colleges and universities, in-company consultants, training professionals, and freelance writers and editors. Membership: $50 (individual); $15 (student).

Publications:
Membership Directory; on-line

Association of Professional Design Firms (1985)
1448 E. 52nd St.
Suite 201
Chicago, IL 60615
Tel: (773) 643-7052 *Fax:* (773) 643-7054
E-Mail: cbrownlee@apdf.org
Website: apdf.org
Members: 100 companies
Staff: 1
Annual Budget: $100-250,000
Tax: 501(c)(6)

Personnel:
Executive Director: Cathy Brownlee
   E-Mail: cbrownlee@apdf.com

Historical Note:
APDF's mission is to elevate the standards of professional business practices for design consulting firms through education and the exchange of knowledge. Membership is open to firms engaged in graphic, industrial, and commercial interior design. Membership: $1,750/year (Independent Design Firm).

Meetings/Conferences:
Number of non-conference events/year: 4

Publications:
Membership Directory; on-line
Temperature Check; quarterly

Association of Professional Flight Attendants (1977)
1004 W. Euless Blvd.
Euless, TX 76040
Tel: (817) 540-0108 *Fax:* (817) 540-2077
Website: apfa.org
Members: 18000 Professional Flight Attendants
Staff: 3
Annual Budget: $5-10,000,000
Tax: 501(c)(5)

Personnel:
President: Laura Glading
Representative, Government Affairs: Julie Frederick
   E-Mail: legislation@apfa.org
Editor: Jeff Pharr

Historical Note:
APFA is an independent flight attendants union.

Publications:
APFA HotLine; on-line
Skyword Magazine

Association of Professional Genealogists (1979)
P.O. Box 350998
Westminster, CO 80035-0998
Tel: (303) 465-6980 *Fax:* (303) 456-8825
E-Mail: admin@apgen.org
Website: apgen.org
Members: 2200 individuals
Staff: 1
Annual Budget: $100-250,000
Tax: 501(c)(6)

Personnel:
Executive Director: Kathleen W. Hinckley CG

Historical Note:
APG purpose is to support professional genealogists in all phases of their work. Members include family historians, professional researchers, librarians, archivists, writers, editors, consultants, indexers, instructors, lecturers, columnists, booksellers, publishers, computer specialists and geneticists. Membership: $35-65 (US); $38-70 (Canada/ Mexico); $47-85 (International).

Meetings/Conferences: Annual

Publications:
APG Mail List; on-line

APG Membership Directory; on-line
APG Quarterly; quarterly; adv.

Association of Professional Investment Consultants (1991)
8826 Santa Fe Dr.
Suite 208
Overland Park, KS 66212
Tel: (913) 381-4458 *Fax:* (913) 381-9308
E-Mail: apic@sbcglobal.net
Website: apicsb.com
Members: 500 individuals
Staff: 2
Annual Budget: $500-1,000,000

Personnel:
Executive Director: Sandra Sabanske
   E-Mail: sabanske@apicsb.com

Historical Note:
APIC provides a forum for members to exchange ideas, knowledge, information and to enhance their professional skills. Members actively create and introduce technique and methods to provide cutting-edge services. Membership: $425 (Individual); $675 (Team); $300 (Firm Associate/ Additional Team Members).

Meetings/Conferences: Annual
2013 - La Jolla, CA (Hilton La Jolla Torrey Pines)/June 4 - 7

Publications:
Newsletter-Oracle; quarterly

Association of Professional Landscape Designers (1989)
4305 N. Sixth St.
Suite A
Harrisburg, PA 17110
Tel: (717) 238-9780 *Fax:* (717) 238-9985
E-Mail: info@apld.org
Website: apld.org
Members: 1400 individuals
Staff: 6
Annual Budget: $250-500,000
Tax: 501(c)(6)

Personnel:
Executive Director: Denise Calabrese
Director, Membership Services: Angela Burkett
   E-Mail: membership@apld.org
Director, Conferences and Events: Jen Cramer
   E-Mail: events@apld.org
Associate Executive Director: Lisa Frye
   E-Mail: assoced@apld.org
Coordinator, Exhibitor, Advertising and Sponsorships: Julie Sullivan
   E-Mail: ads@apld.org
Director, Communications: Stacy Zimmerman
   E-Mail: communications@apld.org

Historical Note:
APLD's mission is to advance the profession of landscape design and to promote the recognition of landscape designers as qualified and dedicated professionals. Members are professional landscape designers, allied vendors and students of landscape design. Membership: $25-400/year.

Continuing Education:
Certification Designation/s: APLDC

Meetings/Conferences: Annual
Conference Chair: Jen Cramer
Number of non-conference events/year: 1

Publications:
APLD Designer Newsletter; quarterly; adv.
APLD e-Newsletter; on-line
Member Directory; on-line

Membership List Available to Non-members

Association of Professional Material Handling Consultants (1959)
8720 Red Oak Blvd.
Suite 201
Charlotte, NC 28217-3992
Tel: (704) 676-1190 *Fax:* (704) 676-1199
E-Mail: theisey@mhia.org
Website: mhia.org/about/societies/apmhc
Members: 40 individuals
Staff: 1
Annual Budget: Under $10,000
Tax: 501(c)(6)

Personnel:
Membership Contact: Jeff Woroniecki

E-Mail: jworoniecki@mhia.org

Historical Note:
APMH promotes and coordinates the exchange of ideas and information among members; encourages the improvement of analysis, synthesis, installation, and training; advances the profession through the development of standards of performance; and assists other groups in promoting material handling generally, and the consulting profession specifically. Members are classified as either general members or associate members. Membership: $2000/year.

Publications:
Industry Newsletter; bi-monthly
Membership Directory; on-line

Association of Professional Model Makers *(1993)*
P.O. Box 165
Hamilton, NY 13346
Tel: (877) 663-2766 *Fax:* (877) 765-6950
E-Mail: info@modelmakers.org
Website: modelmakers.org
Members: 800 members
Staff: 6
Annual Budget: $50-100,000
Tax: 501(c)(6)

Personnel:
Executive Director: Samanthi Martinez
    E-Mail: samanthi@modelmakers.org
Vice President, Communications: Dennis Heinzeroth
    E-Mail: communications@modelmakers.org
Treasurer: Chris Lewis
    E-Mail: treasurer@modelmakers.org
Vice president , Education: Peter Mack
    E-Mail: education@modelmakers.org
Vice President , Technology: Michael Nixon
    E-Mail: technology@modelmakers.org
Vice President , Conferences: Bruce Willey
    E-Mail: conference@modelmakers.org

Historical Note:
APMM's mission is to offer members, and the model making community at large, professional communication, education, leading edge technology, and resource connection while honoring the traditional skills vital to model making and the realization of new ideas. Membership: $125 (Professional); $100 (Professional Group); $600 (Model Shop/Studio); $500 (Educational); $25 (Student).

Meetings/Conferences: Annual
Conference Chair: Bruce Willey

Publications:
APMM e-Newsletter; quarterly; adv.
Member Directory; on-line
Vendor Directory; on-line; adv.

Association of Professional Office Managers *(2002)*
P.O. Box 1926
Rockville, MD 20849
Tel: (240) 654-9108 *Fax:* (240) 331-0439
Website: apomonline.org
Members: 8000 members
Staff: 1
Tax: 501(c)(3)

Personnel:
Executive Director: Jim Lynch
    E-Mail: jim@apomhq.org

Historical Note:
APOM's mission is to advocate excellence in office management and is committed to being the leading information resource for office managers and recognized authority in office management ideas and best practice. Membership: Free (Regular/Promotional/APOM Affiliate/ Charitable/Vendor business).

Continuing Education:
Certification Designation/s: OMC, POM

Publications:
OfficeOurs; adv.

Association of Professional Researchers for Advancement *(1987)*
401 N. Michigan Ave.
Suite 2200
Chicago, IL 60611
Tel: (312) 321-5196 *Fax:* (312) 673-6966
E-Mail: info@aprahome.org
Website: aprahome.org
Members: 2500 Individuals
Staff: 17
Annual Budget: $500-1,000,000
Tax: 501(c)(6)

Personnel:
Interim Executive Director: Janet Rapp
    E-Mail: jrapp@aprahome.org
Coordinator, Conferences: Dana Almdale
    E-Mail: dalmdale@aprahome.org
Senior Accountant: Jennifer Buzalski
    E-Mail: jbuzalski@smithbucklin.com
Editorial Manager: Dennis Coyle
    E-Mail: dcoyle@aprahome.org
Manger, Education Program: Ariane Daniels
    E-Mail: adaniels@aprahome.org
Senior Manager, Marketing and Communications: Kara Dress
    E-Mail: kdress@aprahome.org
Manager, Information Technology: Denis Janis
Coordinator, Education: Carrie Johnson
    E-Mail: cjohnson@aprahome.org
Coordinator, Operations: Sarah Murphy
    E-Mail: smurphy@aprahome.org
Senior Coordinator, Marketing and Communications: Jennifer Snider
    E-Mail: jsnider@aprahome.org
Associate, Membership Services: Maggie Zimmerman
    E-Mail: mzimmerman@aprahome.org

Historical Note:
An outgrowth of the Minneapolis Prospect Research Association(1987) and formerly (1995) American Prospect Research Association. APRA's mission is to promote the value and impact of its members. Members are professionals (including prospect researchers, directors of development, executive directors and consultants) who work in donor research at non- profit institutions throughout the world. Membership: $195/year (Individual/Institutional).

Meetings/Conferences: Annual
Conference Chair: Dana Almdale
2013 - Baltimore, MD (Baltimore Marriott Waterfront)/ Aug. 7 - 10/11-25 exhibitors
Number of non-conference events/year: 1

Publications:
Connections; quarterly; adv.
Membership Directory; annually

Association of Professional Schools of International Affairs *(1989)*
3141 Van Munching Hall
College Park, MD 20742
Tel: (301) 405-5238 *Fax:* (301) 403-4675
E-Mail: apsia@apsia.org
Website: apsia.org
Members: 60 affiliate members and institutions (full members)
Staff: 2
Annual Budget: $250-500,000

Personnel:
Executive Director: Leigh Morris Sloane
    E-Mail: sloane@apsia.org
Program Associate: Margaret B. Brown
    E-Mail: mbrown@apsia.org

Historical Note:
APSIA's mission is to improve professional education in international affairs and the advancement thereby of international understanding, prosperity, peace, and security. Members are professional graduate schools of international affairs in the U.S., Europe and Asia. Membership: $1,000-5,000/year (Institution).

Meetings/Conferences:
Conference Chair: Margaret B. Brown

Association of Professors of Gynecology and Obstetrics *(1962)*
2130 Priest Bridge Dr.
Suite Seven
Crofton, MD 21114
Tel: (410) 451-9560 *Fax:* (410) 451-9568
E-Mail: apgoadmin@apgo.org
Website: apgo.org
Members: 1500 individuals
Staff: 6
Annual Budget: $1-2,000,000
Tax: 501(c)(3)

Personnel:
Executive Director: Donna Wachter
    E-Mail: apgoadmin@apgo.org
Director, Member Services: Bonnie Fetsko
    E-Mail: apgoadmin@apgo.org
Administrative Assistant: Adryon Montgomery
    E-Mail: amontgomery@apgo.org
Specialist, Communications: Anne Murphy
    E-Mail: amurphy@apgo.org
Specialist, Program and Grants: Marianne Poe
    E-Mail: mkpoe@apgo.org
Specialist, Meetings: Kelly Toepper
    E-Mail: ktoepper@apgo.org

Historical Note:
APGO mission is to promote excellence in women's health care by providing optimal resources and support to educators who inspire, instruct, develop and empower women's health care providers of tomorrow. Members are drawn from faculties of medical school departments of obstetrics and gynecology. Membership: $2,000 (Member/ Institutional Departments); $225-270 (Individual); $50 (Subscriber); Free (Student).

Meetings/Conferences: Annual
Conference Chair: Kelly Toepper
2013 - Phoenix, AZ (JW Marriott Desert Ridge Resort)/ Feb. 27 - March 2
2014 - Atlanta, GA (Hyatt Regency Atlanta)/Feb. 26 - March 1
Number of non-conference events/year: 1

Publications:
APGO Reporter; quarterly

Association of Professors of Medicine *(1954)*
330 John Carlyle St.
Suite 610
Alexandria, VA 22314
E-Mail: APM@im.org
Website: im.org/apm
Members: 200 Members
Staff: 10
Annual Budget: $1-2,000,000
Tax: 501(c)(3)

Personnel:
Executive Vice President: Bergitta E. Smith

Historical Note:
APM's mission is to provide the primary leadership and direction to academic internal medicine, including education, research, and patient care and to promote cooperation among the members of the internal medicine community. Membership: $4,250-6,250 (US Institutional, based on the size of the department of medicine); $3,300 (Canadian Institutional); $2,125 (US Affiliate); $1,650 (Canadian Affiliate).

Meetings/Conferences: Annual
2013 - Charleston, SC (Charleston Place Hotel)/Feb. 27 - March 2
Number of non-conference events/year: 1

Publications:
The American Journal of Medicine

Association of Professors of Mission *(1952)*
109 Brookwood Ln.
Wilmore, KY 40390
Website: asmweb.org
Members: 190 individuals
Staff: 3
Annual Budget: Under $10,000

Personnel:
President: Craig van Gelder
Treasurer: Duane Brown
    E-Mail: duane@drduanebrown.com

Historical Note:
APM's mission is to advocate among its members Christian fellowship, spiritual life and professional usefulness. APM members are professors and educators, including retirees and graduate students, teaching in the field of Christian mission in universities, seminaries, and other educational settings. It is a member of the Council on the Study of Religion and the International Association of Mission Studies. Membership: $10/year (Active).

Meetings/Conferences:
Number of non-conference events/year: 1

Publications:
Missiology: An International Review; quarterly

Association of Program Directors in Internal Medicine *(1977)*
330 John Carlyle St.
Suite 610
Alexandria, VA 22314
Tel: (703) 341-4540 *Fax:* (703) 519-1893
E-Mail: apdim@im.org
Website: im.org/APDIM
Members: 1870 individuals and institutions
Staff: 4
Annual Budget: $2-5,000,000

Personnel:
President: Paul B. Aronowitz, MD
Treasurer: Diana B. McNeill, MD

Historical Note:
APDIM's mission is to educate, support, empower and represent internal medicine program directors and to support program directors in their career development. Membership: $1,500 (per year).

Meetings/Conferences: Annual
2013 - Lake Buena Vista, FL (Disney's Coronado Springs Resort)/April 21 - 24

Publications:
Membership Directory; on-line

Association of Program Directors in Radiology
(1993)
820 Jorie Blvd.
Oak Brook, IL 60523-2251
Tel: (630) 368-3737 *Fax:* (630) 571-7837
E-Mail: apdr@rsna.org
Website: apdr.org
Members: 417 individuals
Staff: 6
Annual Budget: $50-100,000
Tax: 501(c)(3)

Personnel:
President: Jocelyn D. Chertoff MD, MS
President-Elect: J. Mark McKinney MD
    E-Mail: jmmckinney@utmck.edu
Secretary and Treasurer: Janet E. Bailey MD
Account Manager: Kristin Jacob
Editor: Brandi T. Nicholson MD
    E-Mail: bte6v@virginia.edu
Account Executive: Stephanie Taylor

Historical Note:
APDR's mission is to support the administrative, educational, recruitment and supervisory roles of radiology residency and fellowship program directors through the sponsorship of meetings, development of educational materials and policy statements. Membership: $190 (Active); $75 (Coordinating).

Publications:
Membership Directory

Association of Program Directors in Surgery
(1977)
6400 Goldsboro Rd.
Suite 450
Bethesda, MD 20817-5846
Tel: (301) 320-1200 *Fax:* (301) 263-9025
E-Mail: apds@mindspring.com
Website: apds.org/
Members: 500 individuals
Staff: 2
Annual Budget: $500-1,000,000
Tax: 501(c)(3)

Personnel:
President: Paula Termuhlen MD
    E-Mail: ptermuhlen@mcw.edu
Treasurer: Richard Damewood MD
    E-Mail: rdamewood@wellspan.org

Historical Note:
The purpose APDS is to provide a forum for the exchange of information and for discussion on a wide range of subjects related to post-graduate surgical education. Membership: $400 (Program Directors); $225 (Associate Program Directors/Residency Coordinators); $50 (Residents).

Meetings/Conferences: Annual
2013 - Orlando, FL (Gaylord Palms Resort and Convention Center-Orlando)/April 23 - 27
2014 - Chicago, IL (Fairmont Chicago Millenium Park)/April 8 - 12
2015 - Seatle, WA (Westin Seattle)/April 14 - 18

Publications:
Membership Directory; on-line

Membership List Available to Non-members

Association of Programs for Female Offenders
(1960)
P.O. Box 5293
Columbia, SC 29250-5293
E-Mail: info@apfonews.org
Website: apfonews.org
Members: 150 individuals
Staff: 2
Annual Budget: Under $10,000
Tax: 501(c)(3)

Personnel:
President: Gregory V. Smith
Treasurer: Judy Anderson

Historical Note:
Formerly, Women's Correctional Association (1960), then Association on Programs for Female Offenders. Assumed its current name in 2010. APFO's mission is to provide advocacy and professional support to improve programming for women and girls under criminal justice supervision. Members are correction professionals and others with an interest in programs for female offenders. Membership: $25 (Individual); $50 (Supporting).

Publications:
APFO Newsletter

Association of Progressive Rental Organizations
(1980)
1504 Robin Hood Trail
Austin, TX 78703
Tel: (512) 794-0095 *Fax:* (512) 794-0097
TollFree: (800) 204-2776
Website: rtohq.org
Members: 4500 companies
Staff: 10
Annual Budget: $10-25,000
Tax: 501(c)(6)

Personnel:
Executive Director: Bill Keese
    E-Mail: bkeese@rtohq.org
Director, Marketing: Cindy Ferguson
    E-Mail: cferguson@rtohq.org
Publications Editor and Art Director: Neil Ferguson
    E-Mail: nferguson@rtohq.org
Director, Information Technology and Web Director: Laurie Hill
    E-Mail: lhill@rtohq.org
Director, Administrative Services: Jeannie Hutchison
Director, Membership Services: Shelley Martinek CMP
    E-Mail: smartinek@aprovision.org
Director, Public Affairs: Richard May
    E-Mail: rmay@rtohq.org
General Counsel: Ed Winn III
    E-Mail: edwinn@mwvmlaw.com

Historical Note:
APRO offers services and resources for both RTO dealers and vendors, including education programs, annual meetings, seminars and a buying show. Members are television, appliance and furniture dealers who rent merchandise with an option to purchase. Membership: $225-375 (Rent-to-Own Dealers, based on number of stores); $600 (Vendors).

Meetings/Conferences: Annual
Conference Chair: Shelley Martinek CMP
2013 - New Orleans, LA (Astor Crowne Plaza and Morial Convention Center)/July 15 - 18
Number of non-conference events/year: 25

Publications:
Membership Directory; annually; adv.
RTO Today; weekly; adv.
RTOHQ: The Magazine; bi-monthly; adv.

Association of Proposal Management Professionals
P.O. Box 77272
Washington, DC 20013-7272
Tel: (202) 450-2549
E-Mail: apmpinfo@apmp.org
Website: apmp.org
Members: 3500 individuals
Staff: 4
Annual Budget: $1-2,000,000
Tax: 501(c)(6)

Personnel:
Executive Director: Rick Harris
    E-Mail: rick.harris@apmp.org
Editor: Ali Paskun
    E-Mail: apmpjournal@apmp.org
Director, Marketing and Communications: Patrice D. Scheyer
    E-Mail: patrice.scheyer@apmp.org
Coordinator, Membership and Chapter Services: Lauren Williams

Historical Note:
APMP's mission is to advance the arts, sciences, and technology of new business acquisition and to advocate the professionalism of those engaged in those pursuits. Members are executives and professionals who author

or evaluate funding proposals. Membership: $100-125 (Individual); $75 (Retiree/ Fulltime Student)

Meetings/Conferences: Annual
2013 - Atlanta, GA (The Westin Peachtree Plaza)/May 28 - 31
2014 - Chicago, IL/May 26 - 29
2015 - Seattle, WA/May 26 - 29
2016 - Boston, MA/May 25 - 28

Publications:
Journal of the Association of Proposal Management Professionals; semi-annually
Perspective Newsletter; quarterly

Membership List Available to Non-members

Association of Psychology Postdoctoral and Internship Centers
(1968)
17225 El Camino Real
Suite 170
Houston, TX 77058-2784
Tel: (832) 284-4080 *Fax:* (832) 284-4079
E-Mail: appic@appic.org
Website: appic.org
Staff: 3
Annual Budget: $500-1,000,000

Personnel:
Secretary: Lisa K. Kearney
    E-Mail: Lisa.Kearney3@va.gov
Contact, Membership Conferences: Arnold Abels PhD
    E-Mail: abelsa@umkc.edu
Editor: Emil Rodolfa PhD
    E-Mail: errodolfa@ucdavis.edu

Historical Note:
Formerly (1990) the Association of Psychology Internship Centers, APPIC's mission is to enhance internship and postdoctoral training in professional psychology. Membership consists of independent agencies conducting or sponsoring internship or postdoctoral training programs. Membership: $400 (Single-Doctoral/Postdoctoral); $600 (Combined- Doctoral and Postdoctoral); $275 (Annual).

Meetings/Conferences: Annual
Conference Chair: Arnold Abels PhD
Number of non-conference events/year: 1

Publications:
APPIC Directory; on-line
APPIC Newsletter; on-line
Training and Education in Professional Psychology

Membership List Available to Non-members

Association of Public and Land-Grant Universities (APLU)
(1887)
1307 New York Ave. NW
Suite 400
Washington, DC 20005-4722
Tel: (202) 478-6040 *Fax:* (202) 478-6046
Website: aplu.org
Members: 218 member institutions
Staff: 12
Annual Budget: $10-25,000,000
Tax: 501(c)(3)

Personnel:
President: M. Peter McPherson BA, JD, MBA
    E-Mail: pmcpherson@aplu.org
Director, Electronic Media and Associate Director, Public Affairs: David Edelson
    E-Mail: dedelson@aplu.org
Chief-of-Staff and Coordinator, National Meetings: Jean R. Middleton
    E-Mail: jmiddleton@aplu.org
Vice President, Congressional and Governmental Affairs: Jennifer Poulakidas
    E-Mail: jpoulakidas@aplu.org
Representative, Public Affairs: Troy Donté Prestwood
    E-Mail: tprestwood@aplu.org
Director, Extension and Outreach: Jane Schuchardt PhD
    E-Mail: jschuchardt@aplu.org
Director, Information Technology: Henry M. Wong
    E-Mail: hwong@aplu.org
Director, Finance and Benefits Administration: Tamera A. Wyatt
    E-Mail: twyatt@aplu.org

Historical Note:
Formerly National Association of State Universities and Land-grant Colleges (NASULGC). Mission of A.P.L.U is advancing learning, discovery, engagement and to provide forum for the discussion and development of policies and programs affecting higher education and the public interest.

Meetings/Conferences: Annual
Conference Chair: Jean R. Middleton
2013 - Washington, DC (Washington Marriott
   Wardman Park)/Nov. 10 - 12
2014 - Orlando, FL (Hilton Orlando Bonnet Creek)/
   Nov. 2 - 4
Publications:
A Public Voice; on-line

Association of Public Data Users
P.O. Box 100155
Arlington, VA 22210
Tel: (703) 522-4980 *Fax:* (703) 522-4985
E-Mail: info@apdu.org
Website: apdu.org
Members: 550 individuals and organizations
Staff: 1
Annual Budget: $50-100,000
Tax: 501(c)(3)
Personnel:
Administrator: Sean McNamara
Historical Note:
*APDU is a national network that links users, producers,
and disseminators of government statistical data.
APDU's purpose is to serve the users, producers and
disseminators of government statistical data by: assisting
users in identifying and applying public data; establishing
communication linkages between data producers and users;
and bringing the perspectives and concerns of public data
users to bear on issues of government information and
statistical policy. Members share a vital concern about the
collection, dissemination, preservation, and interpretation
of public data. Membership: $375(Organizational); $200
(Additional Representative/Individual).*
Meetings/Conferences: Annual
Publications:
APDU Newsletter; bi-monthly
APDU Weekly Update; weekly
Membership Directory; on-line

Association of Public Health Laboratories (1951)
8515 Georgia Ave.
Suite 700
Silver Spring, MD 20910
Tel: (240) 485-2745 *Fax:* (240) 485-2700
E-Mail: info@aphl.org
Website: aphl.org
Members: 750 delegates and other individuals,
Institutional members (states/counties/other
governmental labs impacting the public's health)
and corporate members
Staff: 108
Annual Budget: $25-50,000,000
Tax: 501(c)(3)
Personnel:
Executive Director: Scott J. Becker MS
   E-Mail: scott.becker@aphl.org
Director, Human Resources: Lisa Chilcote MBA, PHR
   E-Mail: lisa.chilcote@aphl.org
Senior Specialist, Media Relations: Michelle Forman
   E-Mail: michelle.forman@aphl.org
Director, Membership and Marketing: Linette Granen MT
   (ASCP)
   E-Mail: linette.granen@aphl.org
Manager, Health Information Technology: Wes
   Kennemore MS
   E-Mail: wes.kennemore@aphl.org
Senior Director, Public Policy: Peter Kyriacopoulos
   E-Mail: peter.kyriacopoulos@aphl.com
Senior Director, Professional Development: Eva Perlman
   MPH
   E-Mail: eva.perlman@aphl.org
Senior Specialist, Meetings: Terry Reamer
   E-Mail: terry.reamer@aphl.org
Senior Specialist, Communications: Kim Ross
   E-Mail: kim.ross@aphl.org
Historical Note:
*Formerly (1998) known as Association of State and
Territorial Public Health Laboratory Directors. APHL's
purpose is to safeguard the public's health via leadership-
through-science. Membership: $35-9,500/year (Based on
population served by the laboratory).*
Continuing Education:
Certification Designation/s: ASCLS
Meetings/Conferences: Annual
Conference Chair: Terry Reamer
Number of non-conference events/year: 4

Publications:
Bridges, APHL Environmental Health Newsletter
E-Update, APHL E-Newsletter; on-line
Lab Matters; quarterly; adv.

Association of Public Health Nurses (1935)
P.O. Box 7440
Oklahoma City, OK 73153
E-Mail: askastdn@astdn.org
Website: astdn.org
Members:
145 members
90 voting members and associates and alumni
Staff: 4
Annual Budget: $25-50,000
Tax: 501(c)(6)
Personnel:
Executive Director: Karen O'Brien DNP, RN
   E-Mail: ExDirector@PHNurse.org
Administrative Assistant: Janet DeVeny-Edwards CPM
   E-Mail: AdminAsst@phnurse.org
Coordinator, Communications: Glenda Kelly, MSN, RN
   E-Mail: glenda.kelly@astdn.org
Historical Note:
*Established as a council of the American Public Health
Association, it later became the Association of State and
Territorial Directors of Public Health Nursing and in 1966
the name was changed to ASTDN whose mission is to
protect and promote the health and safety of the public
through public policy efforts, leadership development and
advocacy for the preparation, practice and role of public
health nursing. Membership: $25-400/year.*
Meetings/Conferences: Annual
2013 - Cary, NC (Embassy Suites Raleigh-Durham/
   Research Triangle)/June 6 - 8
Number of non-conference events/year: 1
Publications:
Membership Directory; on-line

Association of Public Television Stations (1979)
2100 Crystal Dr.
Suite 700
Arlington, VA 22202
Tel: (202) 654-4200 *Fax:* (202) 654-4236
Website: apts.org
Members: 146 stations
Staff: 14
Annual Budget: $2-5,000,000
Tax: 501(c)(3)
Personnel:
President and Chief Executive Officer: Patrick Butler
   E-Mail: pbutler@apts.org
Manager, Networks and Technology: Kenneth Blunt
   E-Mail: kwblunt@apts.org
*Manager, Member Services and Executive Assistant to the
   President:* Tela Hansom-Pitt
   E-Mail: tpitt@apts.org
Legal Assistant and Human Resources Generalist: Tammye
   F. Heatley
   E-Mail: theatley@apts.org
Director, Communications: Stacey Karp
   E-Mail: skarp@apts.org
Director, Government Relations: Jennifer Kieley
   E-Mail: jkieley@apts.org
Vice President, Finance and Administration: Emil Mara
   E-Mail: emara@apts.org
Manager, Facilities and Events: Joyce Burgess Schwarz
   E-Mail: jschwarz@apts.org
*Executive Vice President, Chief Operating Officer and
   General Counsel:* Lonna Thompson
   E-Mail: lthompson@apts.org
Historical Note:
*Formerly the Association for Public Broadcasting, (1980)
National Association of Public Television Stations, assumed
its present name in 1991. APTS's mission is to support
the continued growth and development of a strong and
financially sound noncommercial television service for the
American public. It provides advocacy for public television
interests at the national level, as well as consistent
leadership and information in marshaling grassroots and
congressional support for its members.*
Meetings/Conferences: Annual
Conference Chair: Joyce Burgess Schwarz
2013 - Arlington, VA (The Hyatt Regency Crystal City
   Hotel)/Feb. 24 - 26
Publications:
APTS News; on-line

Association of Public Treasurers of the United States and Canada (1965)
962 Wayne Ave.
Suite 910
Silver Spring, MD 20910
Tel: (301) 495-5560 *Fax:* (301) 495-5561
E-Mail: info@aptusc.org
Website: aptusc.org
Members: 1920 individuals
Staff: 3
Annual Budget: $250-500,000
Tax: 501(c)(3)
Personnel:
Executive Director: Lindsay J. Dively
   E-Mail: ldively@aptusc.org
Office Administrator: Felicia Smith
   E-Mail: accounting@aptusc.org
Historical Note:
*Founded as Municipal Treasurers Association of the United
States and Canada, assumed its current name in 2001.
APT US&C's mission is to provide quality education
and training, professional certification, and networking
opportunities for public treasury and financial officials.
Membership: $140-375 (Towns/Villages/Cities/Counties/
States/Provinces); $140-374 (Special District/Retirement
System); $100 (Active); $409 (Primary Associate);
$600 (Corporate); (Additional Associate Member); $100
(Corporate); $57 (Sustaining).*
Continuing Education:
Certification Designation/s: CPFIM, CPFA, ACPFA
Meetings/Conferences: Annual
Conference Chair: Lindsay J. Dively
Number of non-conference events/year: 2
Publications:
Membership Directory; on-line
Spotlights; bi-monthly
Technical Topics; quarterly; adv.
Treasury Notes; bi-monthly; adv.

APCO (Association of Public-Safety Communications Officials) International (1935)
351 N. Williamson Blvd.
Daytona Beach, FL 32114-1112
Tel: (386) 322-2500 *Fax:* (386) 322-2501
TollFree: (888) 272-6911
E-Mail: apco@apcointl.org
Website: apcointl.org
Members: 15000 individuals
Staff: 60
Annual Budget: $2-5,000,000
Personnel:
Contact, Accounting: Doreen Geary
   E-Mail: gearyd@apcointl.org
Contact, Events: Patricia Giannini
   E-Mail: gianninip@apcointl.org
Contact, Technology and Support Operations: Ricky
   Marshall
   E-Mail: marshallr@apcointl.org
Contact, Media Relations and Publications: Meghan
   McCluskey
   E-Mail: mccluskeym@apcointl.org
Contact, Membership Services: Annie Russo
   E-Mail: russoa@apcointl.org
Director: Candice Solie
Contact, Communications: Stephen Wisely
   E-Mail: wiselys@apcointl.org
Historical Note:
*APCO committed to providing complete public safety
communications expertise, professional development,
technical assistance, advocacy and outreach to benefit
members and the public. Membership: $154 (Commercial);
$69-120 (Individual); $331-2920 (Group).*
Continuing Education:
Certification Designation/s: APCO
Meetings/Conferences:
Conference Chair: Patricia Giannini
2013 - Anaheim, CA/Aug. 18 - 21
2014 - New Orleans, LA (Ernest N. Morial Convention
   Center)/Aug. 3 - 7
Publications:
Membership Directory; on-line
Newsletter

Association of Racing Commissioners International (1934)
1510 Newtown Pike
Suite 210

Lexington, KY 40511-1222
Tel: (859) 224-7070 *Fax:* (859) 224-7071
E-Mail: info@arci.com
Website: arci.com
Members: 53 jurisdictions and neighboring
territories or countries
Staff: 6
Annual Budget: $500-1,000,000

Personnel:
President: Edward J. Martin
Vice President, Technology: Kevin Crum

Historical Note:
*Formerly National Association of State Racing
Commissioners, assumed its current name in 1988. RCI'
mission is to protect the integrity of the pari-mutuel
sports of horse racing, dog racing and jai-alai through an
informed membership, by encouraging forceful and uniform
regulation, by promoting the health and welfare of the
industry through various programs and projects.*

Publications:
Membership Directory; on-line
RCI bulletin; on-line

Association of Railway Museums (1961)
P.O. Box 1189
Covington, GA 30015
Tel: (770) 278-0088 *Fax:* (770) 388-7772
Website: railwaymuseums.org
Members: 202 museums
Staff: 2
Annual Budget: $25-50,000

Personnel:
Executive Director: Suzanne Grace
    E-Mail: scg@lagniappeassociates.com

Historical Note:
*ARM's purpose is to commit in the advancement of railway
heritage through education and advocacy, guided by the
principles set forth in "Recommended Practices for Railway
Museums," and incorporating other practices generally
accepted in the wider museum community.*

Meetings/Conferences: Annual
Publications:
Membership Directory; on-line
Railway Museum Quarterly; quarterly; adv.

Association of Real Estate License Law Officials
(1930)
150 N. Wacker Dr.
Suite 920
Chicago, IL 60606
Tel: (312) 300-4800 *Fax:* (312) 300-4807
E-Mail: support@arello.org
Website: arello.org
Members: 73 jurisdictions
Staff: 7
Annual Budget: $1-2,000,000
Tax: 501(c)(6)

Personnel:
Chief Executive Officer: William Wald CAE, MBA, MS
    E-Mail: Bill@arello.org
Chief Financial Operations Officer: Dean Comber
    E-Mail: dean@arello.org
Director, Professional and Membership Development:
    Karen Gamperl
    E-Mail: karen@arello.org
Manager, Education and Certification: Meloney Gwin
    E-Mail: meloney@arello.org
Director, Administration and Meetings: Jessica Sivels
    E-Mail: jessica@arello.org
Senior Director, Information Technology: Rich Sloan
    E-Mail: rich@arellohq.org

Historical Note:
*Formerly (1930) National Association of License Law
Officials (NALLO), and later (1965) the National
Association of Real Estate License Law Officials
(NARELO). 1993, it become the Association of Real
Estate License Law Officials (ARELLO). An association of
all the Real Estate Commissions in the United States and
territories. ARELLO's mission is to support jurisdictions in
the administration and enforcement of real estate license
laws to promote and protect the public interest. Strives to
upgrade the states' regulation of the real estate industry.
The organization also has international members in
Australia, Africa, Asia, the Caribbean and Central America
as well as the United States. Membership: $195-2,880
(Full); $75 (Associate); $150 (Affiliate-Individual); $750
(Affiliate-Institutional); $80-620 (Full Member-Other
countries).*

Continuing Education:
Certification Designation/s: AECCP, ECC, CREI
Meetings/Conferences: Semi-Annual
Conference Chair: Jessica Sivels
2013 - Scottsdale, AZ (DoubleTree Resort by Hilton
    Hotel Paradise Valley-Scottsdale)/April 10 - 13
2013 - Seatle, WA (Westin Seattle)/Sept. 18 - 22

Publications:
Boundaries; monthly
Digest of Real Estate License Laws and Issues;
    annually
International Directory of Real Estate Regulators and
    Organizations; annually
Membership Directory; on-line

Association of Real Estate Women (1978)
1201 Wakarusa Dr.
Suite C3
Lawrence, KS 66049
Tel: (212) 599-6181 *Fax:* (785) 832-1551
TollFree: (888) 329-2739
E-Mail: info@arew.org
Website: arew.org
Members: 210 individuals
Staff: 3
Annual Budget: $250-500,000

Personnel:
President: Jennifer Carey
    E-Mail: jcarey@jlcenvironmental.com
Treasurer: Rochelle Crespi
Secretary: Julia Glazer
    E-Mail: jglazer@tekus.com

Historical Note:
*AREW's mission is to provide outstanding educational
programs and networking opportunities that contribute to
the career growth of both men and women in all segments
and levels of the real estate industry. Membership: $625
(Full Member);$425(Associate);$180 (Student).*

Continuing Education:
Certification Designation/s: PRDP
Meetings/Conferences:
Number of non-conference events/year: 1

Publications:
AREW NEWSLETTER; quarterly
CREWbiz Membership Directory; on-line

Association of Regulatory Boards of Optometry
(1919)
200 S. College St.
Suite 2030
Charlotte, NC 28202
Tel: (704) 970-2710 *Fax:* (704) 970-2720
E-Mail: arbo@arbo.org
Website: arbo.org
Members: 56 boards
Staff: 7
Annual Budget: $500-1,000,000
Tax: 501(c)(3)

Personnel:
Executive Director: Lisa Fennell
    E-Mail: lfennell@arbo.org
Finance Chair: Ron Cassel
Web Developer and Database Administrator: Tony
    Mancuso
Manager, Programs: Anita Matthews
    E-Mail: amatthews@arbo.org

Historical Note:
*Formerly (1999) International Association of Boards of
Examiners in Optometry. ARBO's mission is to represent
and assist member licensing agencies in regulating the
practice of optometry for the public welfare.*

Meetings/Conferences: Annual
Conference Chair: Anita Matthews
2013 - San Diego, CA (San Diego Mariott Marquis and
    Marina)/June 23 - 25
2014 - Philadelphia, PA/June 22 - 24
2015 - Seatle, WA/June 21 - 23

Publications:
Directory of Optometry Boards; on-line
The Greensheet

Membership List Available to Non-members

Association of Rehabilitation Nurses (1974)
4700 W. Lake Ave.
Glenview, IL 60025-1485
Tel: (847) 375-4710 *Fax:* (847) 375-6481

TollFree: (800) 229-7530
E-Mail: info@rehabnurse.org
Website: rehabnurse.org
Members: 5700 individuals
Staff: 10
Annual Budget: $2-5,000,000
Tax: 501(c)(6)

Personnel:
President: Susan Wirt CCM, CRP, RN
National Sales Manager: Terri Berkowitz
    E-Mail: tberkowitz@connect2amc.com

Historical Note:
*ARN's mission is to promote and advance professional
rehabilitation nursing practice through education, advocacy,
collaboration, and research to enhance the quality of life
for those affected by disability and chronic illness. Members
are registered nurses concerned with or involved in the
practice of rehabilitation nursing; non-voting membership
is available for others interested in the field. Membership:
$115 (Nonvoting/Voting); $2,500 (Corporate/Facility
Member).*

Continuing Education:
Certification Designation/s: CRRN
Meetings/Conferences: Annual
Publications:
ARN Network; bi-monthly; adv.
Membership Directory; on-line
Rehabilitation Nursing; bi-monthly; adv.

Association of Rehabilitation Programs in
Computer Technology (1978)
Educational Leadership, Research and
Technology Department, Sangren Hall
Western Michigan University
Kalamazoo, MI 49008
Tel: (269) 387-2053 *Fax:* (269) 387-3696
Website: arpct.org
Members: 80 organizations
Staff: 2
Annual Budget: $10-25,000
Tax: 501(c)(3)

Personnel:
President: Dot Kret
    E-Mail: dkret@dkajobs.com
Contact, Membership Services: Robert Leneway
    E-Mail: bob.leneway@wmich.edu

Historical Note:
*Formerly (1994) Association of Rehabilitation Programs
in Data Processing. ARPCT's mission is to promote
communication and support among programs designed
to train and place people with disabilities in areas related
to computer technology and information processing.
Membership includes rehabilitation programs. Membership:
$50 (Associate); $395 (Member Program).*

Publications:
ARPCT Newsletter; quarterly
Membership Directory

Association of Reporters of Judicial Decisions
(1982)
5711 Nevada St.
College Park, MD 20740
Tel: (360) 357-2090 *Fax:* (360) 357-2099
Website: arjd.washlaw.edu
Members: 60 individuals
Staff: 2
Annual Budget: $10-25,000

Personnel:
President: Leah A. Walker
Treasurer: Truman S. Fuller

Historical Note:
*ARJD's mission is to improve the accuracy and efficiency of
the reporting of judicial decisions. The Association serves as
a forum for communication and cooperation among official
reporters and others in the legal publishing profession.
ARJD is composed of attorneys and their staff who edit
and publish judicial opinions. Membership: $50 (Active
Reporter); $30 (Associate Staff); Free (Retired).*

Publications:
Catchline; quarterly
Directory; annually

Association of Reproductive Health Professionals
(1963)
1901 L St. NW
Suite 300
Washington, DC 20036
Tel: (202) 466-3825 *Fax:* (202) 466-3826

E-Mail: ARHP@arhp.org
Website: arhp.org
Members: 11000 individuals
Staff: 15
Annual Budget: $2-5,000,000
Tax: 501(c)(3)

Personnel:
President and Chief Executive Officer: Wayne C. Shields
   E-Mail: wshields@arhp.org
Assistant, Membership: Ann E. Checkley
   E-Mail: membership@arhp.org
Director, Education: Ellen L. Cohen
   E-Mail: ecohen@arhp.org
Manager, Information technology: Jeff Glispie
   E-Mail: jglispie@arhp.org
Director, Communications: Beth Robbins MBA
   E-Mail: brobbins@ARHP.org
Vice President, Operations: Amy M. Swann MA
   E-Mail: aswann@arhp.org

Historical Note:
Formerly the Association of Planned Parenthood
Physicians. ARHP is a multidisciplinary association of
professionals who provide reproductive health services
or education, conduct reproductive health research, or
influence reproductive health policy. Educates healthcare
professionals, policy makers and the public. Membership:
$200 (Physicians); $125 (Advanced Practice Clinicians/
Researcher/Educator); $50 (Retired/Student/Resident).

Continuing Education:
Certification Designation/s: CME

Meetings/Conferences: Annual
Conference Chair: Ellen L. Cohen
Number of non-conference events/year: 19

Publications:
Contraception: An International Reproductive Health
Journal; monthly

Association of Research Directors (1972)
C/O University of Maryland Eastern Shore
Princess Anne, MD 21853
Tel: (410) 200-4566 Fax: (410) 621-3550
Website: umes.edu/ard
Members: 18 universities
Staff: 1

Personnel:
Executive Director: Carolyn B. Brooks
   E-Mail: cbbrooks@umes.edu

Historical Note:
Formerly Association of 1890 Research Directors, ARD
is a federation of eighteen (18) autonomous land-grant
universities, that provides coordination of research
initiatives among member 1890 Institutions in cooperation
with federal, state and private partners. ARD is integrally
involved in creating a society where all people have
opportunities for wholesome living and learning through
responsible pursuits of their goals.

Meetings/Conferences:
2013 - Jacksonville, FL (Hyatt Regency Jacksonville
   Riverfront)/April 6 - 10

Association of Research Directors of 1890s Colleges and Universities
University of Maryland Eastern Shore
Princess Anne, MD 21853
Tel: (410) 651-6072 Fax: (410) 621-3550
Website: umes.edu/ard/Default.aspx?id = 11342
Staff: 2

Personnel:
Executive Director: Carolyn B. Brooks
   E-Mail: cbbrooks@umes.edu

Historical Note:
The ARD is integrally involved in creating a society where
all people have opportunities for wholesome living and
learning through responsible pursuits of their goals and
aspirations.

Meetings/Conferences: Annual
2013 - Jacksonville, FL (Hyatt Regency Jacksonville
   Riverfront)/April 6 - 10

Association of Research Libraries (1932)
21 Dupont Cir. NW
Suite 800
Washington, DC 20036
Tel: (202) 296-2296 Fax: (202) 872-0884
E-Mail: arlhq@arl.org
Website: arl.org
Members: 120 libraries

Staff: 40
Annual Budget: $5-10,000,000
Tax: 501(c)(3)

Personnel:
Executive Director: Charles B. Lowry
   E-Mail: clowry@arl.org
Associate Executive Director, Federal Relations and
   Information Policy: Prudence S. Adler
   E-Mail: prue@arl.org
Deputy Executive Director: Sue Baughman
   E-Mail: sue@arl.org
Assistant Executive Director, Scholarly Communication:
   Julia Blixrud
   E-Mail: jblix@arl.org
Assistant Executive Director, Finance and Administration:
   Mary Jane Brooks
   E-Mail: maryjane@arl.org
Program Officer, Publications: Lee Anne George
   E-Mail: leeanne@arl.org
Assistant Executive Director, Research, Teaching and
   Learning: Karla Hahn
   E-Mail: karla@arl.org
Director, Diversity and Leadership Programs: Mark A.
   Puente
   E-Mail: mpuente@arl.org
Director, Information Technology: Gary Roebuck
   E-Mail: gary@arl.org
Program Officer, Information Technology: Beth Secrist
   E-Mail: beth@arl.org

Historical Note:
ARL's primary function is to identify and solve problems
fundamental to large research libraries. Membership:
$18,550/year.

Meetings/Conferences:
2013 - Chapel Hill, NC (Chapel Hill Hotel)/April 30 -
   May 3
2013 - Washington, DC/Oct. 8 - 11
2014 - Columbus, OH/April 29 - May 2
Number of non-conference events/year: 7

Membership List Available to Non-members

Association of Residents in Radiation Oncology (1983)
8280 Willow Oaks Corporate Dr.
Suite 500
Fairfax, VA 22031
Tel: (703) 502-1550 Fax: (703) 502-7852
TollFree: (800) 962-7876
E-Mail: arro@arro.org
Website: astro.org/ARRO/Index.aspx
Members: 10000 Members
Staff: 3
Annual Budget: $50-100,000
Tax: 501(c)(3)

Personnel:
Senior Advisor: Luqman K. Dad MD
   E-Mail: luqman.dad@roswellpark.org
Education Officer and ARROgram and Survey Coordinator:
   Vinai Gondi
   E-Mail: gondi@humonc.wisc.edu
Director, Membership Services: Steven M. Smith MBA

Historical Note:
The objectives of ARRO are to formalize resident input
into professional organizations affecting radiation
oncology residents, to disseminate information and
to foster communication among residents. An affiliate
of American Society for Therapeutic Radiology and
Oncology. Membership: $525(Active/Allied/Affiliate); $330
(International); $65 (Associate/Nurse/Corresponding);

Meetings/Conferences:
Conference Chair: Luqman K. Dad MD

Membership List Available to Non-members

Association of Retail Travel Agents (1963)
4320 N. Miller Rd.
Scottsdale, AZ 85251-3606
Fax: (615) 985-0600
TollFree: (866) 369-8969
Website: arta.travel
Members: 1200 companies and 2200 individuals
Staff: 4
Annual Budget: $10-25,000

Personnel:
Vice Chairman and Treasurer: John Faulds
Editor: Pat Funk
   E-Mail: pat@artaonline.com

Historical Note:
ARTA strives to provide educational and training
opportunities to agents and represents their point of view
before industry, governmental and consumer organizations.
Members are small and independent professional travel
agents. Membership: $99 (Individual); $250 (Agency);
$1000 (Lifetime).

Publications:
ARTA's Daily Newsletter; daily

Membership List Available to Non-members

Association of Rheumatology Health Professionals (1965)
2200 Lake Blvd. NE
Atlanta, GA 30319
Tel: (404) 633-3777 Fax: (404) 633-1870
E-Mail: arhp@rheumatology.org
Website: rheumatology.org
Members: 750 individuals
Staff: 7
Annual Budget: $500-1,000,000

Personnel:
Executive Director: Steve Echard CAE, IOM, REF
   E-Mail: sechard@rheumatology.org
Executive Director: David Haag CAE, MSM
   E-Mail: dhaag@rheumatology.org
Specialist, Program Services: Ramona Hilliard
   E-Mail: rhilliard@rheumatology.org
Director and Managing Editor: Nancy Parker
   E-Mail: nparker@rheumatology.org

Historical Note:
Formerly (1994) Arthritis Health Professions Association, a
professional membership society composed of non-physician
health care professionals specializing in rheumatology,
such as advanced practice nurses, nurses, occupational
therapists, physical therapists, psychologists, social
workers, epidemiologists, physician assistants, educators,
clinicians, and researchers. ARHP's mission is to advance
rheumatology. ARHP is a division of the American College
of Rheumatology (ACR). Membership: $130 (Individual/
International); $80 (Associate); $30 (Emeritus); $25
(Student).

Continuing Education:
Certification Designation/s: RMCC

Meetings/Conferences: Annual

Publications:
Arthritis & Rheumatism; monthly; adv.
Arthritis Care & Research; monthly; adv.
Drug Safety Quarterly; quarterly
The Rheumatologist; on-line; adv.

Membership List Available to Non-members

Association of Rotational Molders International (1976)
800 Roosevelt Rd.
Suite C-312
Glen Ellyn, IL 60137
Tel: (630) 942-6589 Fax: (630) 790-3095
E-Mail: info@rotomolding.org
Website: rotomolding.org
Members: 425 companies
Staff: 5
Annual Budget: $500-1,000,000

Personnel:
Executive Director: Rick Church
Legal Counsel: William C. Ives

Historical Note:
ARM serves its members by focusing on the needs of
designers, customers, educators, suppliers, member
company employees and regulators. Members include
manufacturers of rotationally molded plastic products,
suppliers to the industry, designers, and professionals.
Membership: $670-4,060/year.

Meetings/Conferences: Annual
2013 - Orlando, FL (Hyatt Regency Grand Cypress)/
   March 17 - 19
2013 - Cleaveland, OH (Renaissance Hotel)/Sept. 28 -
   Oct. 1
2014 - Rosemont, IL (Donald E. Stephens Convention
   Center)/Oct. 7 - 9

Publications:
Membership Directory; on-line

Membership List Available to Non-members

Association of School Business Officials International (1910)
11401 N. Shore Dr.

Reston, VA 20190-4200
Tel: (866) 682-2729 *Fax:* (703) 708-7060
TollFree: (866) 682-2729
E-Mail: asboreq@asbointl.org
Website: asbointl.org
Members: 5000 individuals
Staff: 18
Annual Budget: $5-10,000,000
Tax: 501(c)(3)

Personnel:
Executive Director: John D. Musso CAE, RSBA
   E-Mail: jmusso@asbointl.org
Coordinator, Publications: Lauren A. Konopka
   E-Mail: lkonopka@asbointl.org
Director, Membership, Marketing and Communications:
   Siobhan McMahon
   E-Mail: smcmahon@asbointl.org
Director, Professional Development: Arlene H. Olkin PhD
   E-Mail: aolkin@asbointl.org
Assistant Executive Director, Government and Public
   Affairs: Ronald A. Skinner
   E-Mail: rskinner@asbointl.org
Director, Events: Maureen C. Thompson
   E-Mail: mthompson@asbointl.org
Director, Certification: Pam Weber, FInstAM CAE
   E-Mail: pweber@asbointl.org
Manager, Accounting: Melissa Williams
   E-Mail: mwilliams@asbointl.org

Historical Note:
ASBO's mission is to provide programs and services to promote the standards of school business management practices, professional growth, and the effective use of educational resources. Members are school district-level business executives, professors of business and education, students, and businessmen of school-related firms. Membership: $211 (Active); $370-1,150 (Corporate); $225 (Associate); $140 (Publications); $99 (Student); $2,700 (Life); $60 (Emeritus).

Continuing Education:
Certification Designation/s: COE, SBMP, SFO

Meetings/Conferences: Annual
Conference Chair: Maureen C. Thompson
2013 - New Orleans, LA (The Ritz-Carlton, New
   Orleans)/Feb. 14 - 16
2013 - Boston, MA (Hynes Convention Center)/Oct. 25
   - 28
2014 - Kissimmee, FL (Gaylord Palms Resort and
   Convention Center-Kissimmee)/Sept. 19 - 22
Number of non-conference events/year: 1

Publications:
Accents Online; bi-weekly; adv.
Membership Directory; on-line
School Business Affairs; monthly; adv.
School Business Daily; daily

Association of Schools and Colleges of Optometry (1941)
6110 Executive Blvd.
Suite 420
Rockville, MD 20852
Tel: (301) 231-5944 *Fax:* (301) 770-1828
Website: opted.org
Members: 19 schools and colleges
Staff: 7
Annual Budget: $1-2,000,000

Personnel:
Executive Director: Martin A. Wall CAE
   E-Mail: mwall@opted.org
Manager, Administrative Services and Executive Assistant:
   Christina Doyle
   E-Mail: cdoyle@opted.org
Managing Editor: Desiree Ifft
   E-Mail: difft@opted.org
Manager, Programs: Lashawn Sidbury
   E-Mail: lsidbury@opted.org
Manager, Data and Surveys: Joanne Zuckerman
   E-Mail: jzuckerman@opted.org

Historical Note:
ASCO's mission is to serve the public through the continued advancement and promotion of all aspects of academic optometry.

Meetings/Conferences:
Conference Chair: Lashawn Sidbury
Number of non-conference events/year: 1

Publications:
Eye on Education; on-line
Optometric Education; quarterly

Association of Schools of Allied Health Professions (1967)
4400 Jenifer St. NW
Suite 333
Washington, DC 20015
Tel: (202) 237-6481 *Fax:* (202) 237-6485
TollFree: (800) 497-8080
Website: asahp.org
Members: 112 academic institutions, 200
individual members and 2 professional
associations
Staff: 3
Annual Budget: $1-2,000,000
Tax: 501(c)(3)

Personnel:
Executive Director: Thomas W. Elwood Dr. P.H.
   E-Mail: thomas@asahp.org
Managing Editor: Jessica Marino Kaplowitz MS
   E-Mail: jessicakaplowitz@asahp.org
Director, Programs: Kyle Williams
   E-Mail: kyle@asahp.org

Historical Note:
Formerly (1974) Association of Schools of Allied Health Professions and (1992) American Society of Allied Health Professions. ASAHP strives to influence governmental health and education policy. It also strives to promote quality education, encourage collaboration and partnerships, strengthen research and scholarship, develop academic leaders, and enhance global outreach. Membership includes allied health schools and programs, associations, and individual educators. Membership: $5,250 (Institutional); $138 (Individual); $77 (Senior/Student); $1,325 (Agency Affiliate); $171 (Individual Affiliate).

Meetings/Conferences:
Conference Chair: Kyle Williams
2013 - San Diego, CA (Catamaran Resort Hotel and
   Spa)/March 19 - 20
2013 - San Diego, CA (Catamaran Resort Hotel and
   Spa)/March 21 - 22
2013 - Nashville, TN (Hilton Nashville Downtown)/
   Oct. 21 - 22
2013 - Nashville, TN (Hilton Nashville Downtown)/
   Oct. 23 - 24
2013 - Nashville, TN (Hilton Nashville Downtown)/
   Oct. 23 - 25
Number of non-conference events/year: 1

Publications:
ASAHP Update; bi-weekly
Journal of Allied Health; quarterly; adv.
Membership Directory; on-line
Trends; monthly; adv.

Membership List Available to Non-members

Association of Schools of Journalism and Mass Communication (1917)
234 Outlet Pointe Blvd.
Columbia, SC 29210-5667
Tel: (803) 798-0271 *Fax:* (803) 772-3509
E-Mail: aejmchq@aol.com
Website: asjmc.org
Members: 202 institutions
Staff: 8
Annual Budget: $100-250,000

Personnel:
Executive Director: Jennifer H. McGill
   E-Mail: aejmchq@aol.com

Historical Note:
Founded as the Association of Accredited Schools and Departments of Journalism became the American Association of Schools and Departments of Journalism in 1954 and assumed its present name in 1983. Absorbed the American Society of Journalism School Administrators in 1984. Shares administrative offices with Association for Education in Journalism and Mass Communication. Membership: $50 (Individual); $350-700 (School Membership Based on Program Size); $100 (International Program).

Meetings/Conferences: Annual
2013 - Washington, DC (Renaissance Washington)/
   Aug. 8 - 11
2014 - Montreal, QC/Aug. 6 - 9
2015 - San Francisco, CA (Marriott San Francisco
   Marquis)/Aug. 5 - 9

Publications:
ASJMC Administrator
ASJMC Insights
Membership Directory; on-line

Association of Schools of Public Health (1953)
1900 M St. NW
Suite 710
Washington, DC 20036
Tel: (202) 296-1099 *Fax:* (202) 296-1252
E-Mail: info@asph.org
Website: asph.org
Members: 49 schools
Staff: 46
Annual Budget: $10-25,000,000

Personnel:
President and Chief Executive Officer: Dr. Harrison C.
   Spencer CPH, MD, MPH
   E-Mail: rkelliher@asph.org
Manager, Accounting Services: Bill Benz CPA
   E-Mail: wbenz@asph.org
Deputy Executive Director: Allison J. Foster CAE, MBA
   E-Mail: afoster@asph.org
Senior Director, Government and External Programs: Rita
   M. Kelliher
   E-Mail: rkelliher@asph.org
Manager, Communications and Project: Heather Kileff
   E-Mail: hkileff@asph.org
Manager, Program: Jessica H. Petrush
   E-Mail: jpetrush@asph.org
Director, Information Technology: Eduardo A. Ruiz
   E-Mail: eruiz@asph.org
Director, Special Projects: Elizabeth M. Weist CPH, MA,
   MPH
   E-Mail: eweist@asph.org

Historical Note:
ASPH promotes the efforts of schools of public health to improve the health of every person through education, research and policy. Members are administration, faculty, and students of the country's accredited schools of public health. Membership: $14,000/year (Organization).

Continuing Education:
Certification Designation/s: CPH

Meetings/Conferences: Annual
Conference Chair: Jessica H. Petrush
Number of non-conference events/year: 2

Publications:
Public Health Reports; bi-monthly
Student Services Council Newsletter; bi-annually
The Friday Letter; weekly

Association of Science Museum Directors (1960)
Illinois State Museum
502 S. Spring
Springfield, IL 62706-5000
Tel: (217) 782-5969 *Fax:* (217) 557-9226
Website: asmd.org
Members: 80 institutions
Staff: 2
Annual Budget: Under $10,000
Tax: 501(c)(3)

Personnel:
President and Director, Membership Services: Bonnie W.
   Styles
   E-Mail: director@museum.state.il.us

Historical Note:
An affiliate member of the American Association Of Museums. ASMD's mission is to represent and promote the interests of natural history museums and science centers. Members are science museums, science centers, science and technology centers, zoological parks, aquariums, botanical gardens, and other organizations that have significant collections, exhibitions, or educational programs relating to the physical or natural sciences, technology, or anthropology. Membership: $100-200/year (depending on museum operating budget).

Meetings/Conferences: Annual
2013 - Ft. Worth, TX (Botanical Research Institute of
   Texas)/Feb. 21 - 23

Membership List Available to Non-members

Association of Science-Technology Centers (1973)
1025 Vermont Ave. NW
Suite 500
Washington, DC 20005-6310
Tel: (202) 783-7200 *Fax:* (202) 783-7207
E-Mail: info@astc.org
Website: astc.org
Members: 600 members
Staff: 23
Annual Budget: $2-5,000,000
Tax: 501(c)(3)

Personnel:
Chief Executive Officer: Anthony (Bud) Rock
  E-Mail: brock@astc.org
Manager, Conference and Exhibit Hall: David Corson
  E-Mail: conference@astc.org
Accountant: Binaya Dhakal
Director, Membership Services: Diane Frendak
  E-Mail: dfrendak@astc.org
Manager, Professional Development Services: Wendy Hancock
Communications Strategist: Larry Hoffer
Editor: Emily Schuster
Director, Government and Public Relations: Sean Smith
  E-Mail: ssmith@astc.org

Historical Note:
ASTC works to improve the operation and delivery of services of member institutions, with a special interest in informal education and programs targeted to traditionally underserved communities and constituencies. Members are science museums and related institutions united to increase public understanding of science and technology. Members also include nature centers, aquariums, planetariums, zoos, botanical gardens, space theaters, and natural history and children's museums. Membership: $520- 4,380 (Science Center/Museum, based on annual operating income); $800 (Sustaining); $350 (Independent Contractor/Consultant).

Meetings/Conferences: Annual
Conference Chair: David Corson
2013 - Albuquerue, NM (Embassy Suites Albuquerque- Hotel and Spa)/Oct. 19 - 22
2014 - Raleigh, NC (North Carolina State University)/ Oct. 18 - 21
2015 - Montreal, QC (Montréal Science Centre)/Oct. 17 - 20

Publications:
Dimensions magazine; bi-monthly

Association of Senior Anthropologists
12 Willow Glen NE
Atlanta, GA 30342-1341
Tel: (404) 252-6956
Website: aaanet.org/sections/Association-of-Senior-Anthropologists.cfm
Staff: 3

Personnel:
President: J. Anthony Paredes
  E-Mail: janthonyparedes@bellsouth.net

Historical Note:
ASA is a section of the American Anthropological Association. Offers senior and retired anthropologists, curators, researchers, linguists, archaeologists, and museum technicians a continuing presence and voice in the discipline, allowing them to put their accumulated knowledge and insights to significant use. Membership: $30-306/year.

Association of Service and Computer Dealers International *(1981)*
131 NW First Ave.
Delray Beach, FL 33444
Tel: (561) 266-9016 *Fax:* (561) 431-6302
Website: ascdi.com
Members: 400 companies
Staff: 4
Annual Budget: $500-1,000,000
Tax: 501(c)(6)

Personnel:
President: Joseph Marion
  E-Mail: jmarion@ascdi.com
Director, Meetings: Ruth Marion
  E-Mail: rmarion@ascdi.com

Historical Note:
The ASCDI merged with the Computer Dealers and Lessors Association (CDLA) and the Eurpean Computer and Lessors Association (ECLAT) in 2000. The Association of Service and Computer Dealers International and the North American Association of Telecommunications Dealers merged in 2012 forming the AscdiNatd. ASCDINATD's mission is to promote a viable independent Information Technology industry, enforce high ethical standards of business conduct within the industry. Members are IT companies that provide hardware, software, maintenance services, leasing services, business solutions, technical support and value added services. Membership: $900/year.

Meetings/Conferences:
Conference Chair: Ruth Marion
2013 - Hong Kong, China (Kowloon Shangri-La)/Jan. 23 - 25
2013 - Nashville, TN (Renaissance Nashville Hotel)/ March 6 - 8

2013 - Venice, Italy/June 19 - 21
Number of non-conference events/year: 3

Publications:
Membership Directory; annually; adv.

Association of Seventh-Day Adventist Librarians *(1981)*
Walla Walla University Libraries
104 S. College Ave
Walla Walla, WA 99324
Website: asdal.org
Members: 150 individuals
Staff: 6
Annual Budget: Under $10,000

Personnel:
President: Lauren Matacio
  E-Mail: matacio@andrews.edu
Editor: Sallie Alger
  E-Mail: salger@andrews.edu
Coordinator, Web Site: Kieren Bailey
  E-Mail: kbailey@cauc.ca
Coordinator, Distance Education: Katie McGrat
  E-Mail: kmcgrath@southern.edu
Treasurer: Annette Melgosa
  E-Mail: Annette.Melgosa@wallawalla.edu
Contact, Communications: Lee Wisel
  E-Mail: lwisel@wau.edu

Historical Note:
Encourages librarianship and library services to Seventh-Day Adventist institutions. Sponsors the D. Glenn Hilts Scholarship Program. Has no paid officers or full-time staff. Membership: $20 (Regular); $10 (Student/Retiree).

Meetings/Conferences: Annual

Publications:
ASDAL Action Newsletter; quarterly; adv.
Membership Directory; on-line
Seventh-Day Adventist Periodical Index; annually

Association of Sewing and Design Professionals *(1989)*
2885 Sanford Ave. SW
Suite 19588
Grandville, MI 49418
E-Mail: admin@sewingprofessionals.org
Website: paccprofessionals.org
Members: 500 members
Staff: 8
Annual Budget: $100-250,000

Personnel:
Vice President, Conferences: Helen Haughey
  E-Mail: conference@sewingprofessionals.org
Webmaster: CJ Kipper
  E-Mail: webmaster@sewingprofessionals.org
Vice President, Communications: Rachel Kurland
  E-Mail: communications@sewingprofessionals.org
Treasurer: Kathy Levy
  E-Mail: treasurer@sewingprofessionals.org

Historical Note:
Formerly Professional Association of Custom Clothiers, ASDP is a non- profit organization that works to provide networking and referral opportunities for professionals engaged in sewing and design related businesses. Members are custom clothiers, designers, sewing educators, authors, costumers, wearable artists, image consultants, pattern makers, production sewing and other sewing professionals. Membership: $150 (Formal Education Institution); $100 (Intern); $60 (Retired); $30 (Student); $70 (Friend of ASDP Membership Application).

Continuing Education:
Certification Designation/s: MC

Meetings/Conferences: Annual
Conference Chair: Helen Haughey

Publications:
Membership Directory; on-line
Perspectives; monthly; adv.

Association of Shareware Professionals *(1987)*
P.O. Box 1522
Martinsville, IN 46151
Tel: (765) 349-4740 *Fax:* (815) 301-3756
Website: asp-shareware.org
Members: 1400 individuals
Staff: 4
Annual Budget: $50-100,000
Tax: 501(c)(6)

Personnel:
Executive Director: Richard Holler

Treasurer: Terry Jepson
Editor: Jerry Stern
Webmaster: Don Waterfield

Historical Note:
ASP's mission is to inform users about shareware programs and about shareware as a method of distributing and marketing software. Members are developers and distributors of shareware software for computers. Membership: $100 (Standard Member); $250 (Supporting Member).

Meetings/Conferences: Annual
2013 - Reno, NV (Atlantis Casino Resort Spa)/Sept. 27 - 29

Publications:
ASPects; monthly; adv.

Association of Ship Brokers and Agents (U.S.A.) *(1934)*
510 Sylvan Ave.
Suite 201
Englewood Cliffs, NJ 07632
Tel: (201) 569-2882 *Fax:* (201) 569-9082
E-Mail: asba@asba.org
Website: asba.org
Members: 152 companies
Staff: 4
Annual Budget: $500-1,000,000

Personnel:
President: Bill Stewart
Treasurer: Mike Black
Secretary: Jeanne L. Cardona
Legal Counsel: Pat Martin

Historical Note:
Formerly (1970) Association of Ship Brokers and Agents. ASBA's mission is to advance and foster the ideals and standards of professional conduct and practices. It also serves as a medium through which members with common interests can communicate. Membership: $450-800/year (Company/Affiliate).

Continuing Education:
Certification Designation/s: ASBASAM

Meetings/Conferences: Annual
2013 - Miami Beach, FL (Eden Roc Renaissance Hotel)/ Oct. 2 - 4

Publications:
American Tanker Rate Schedule; biennially
ASBA Desk Book
ASBA News and Newsletter; quarterly
Member Directory; on-line

Membership List Available to Non-members

Association of SIDS and Infant Mortality Programs *(1987)*
612 W. Lake Lansing Rd.
Suite 800
Lansing, MI 48823
Tel: (800) 930-7437 *Fax:* (517) 485-0163
E-Mail: asip@asip1.org
Website: asip1.org
Members: 75 individuals
Staff: 2
Annual Budget: $250-500,000

Personnel:
President: Anne Harvieux MSW
Treasurer: Christy Schunn MSW

Historical Note:
ASIMP provides national leadership to establish and promote policy and practice for professionals who respond to infant and child death and is committed to bereavement support, risk reduction and prevention services. Membership: $65 (Individual); $130 (Gold Institution); $260 (Platinum Institution).

Meetings/Conferences: Annual
2013 - Minneapolis, MN (Depot Renaissance Minneapolis Hotel)/April 18 - 21

Publications:
Newsletter; semi-annually

Association of Small Business Development Centers
8990 Burke Lake Rd.
Second Floor
Burke, VA 22015
Tel: (703) 764-9850 *Fax:* (703) 764-1234
E-Mail: info@asbdc-us.org
Website: asbdc-us.org
Staff: 6

Annual Budget: $2-5,000,000
Tax: 501(c)(6)

Personnel:
President/Chief Executive Officer: Charles "Tee" Rowe
    E-Mail: tee.rowe@asbdc-us.org
Meeting Planner and Director, Membership Services: Betsy Kaufman
    E-Mail: betsy@asbdc-us.org
Director, Government Relations: Laurie D. Rains
    E-Mail: laurie@asbdc-us.org
Director, Marketing and Communications: April Youngblut
    E-Mail: april@asbdc-us.org

Historical Note:
The Association of Small Business Development Centers (ASBDC) represents America's Small Business Development Center Network -- the most comprehensive small business assistance network in the United States and its territories.

Meetings/Conferences: Annual
Conference Chair: Betsy Kaufman
2013 - Orlando, FL (Hilton Orlando Lake Buena Vista)/ Sept. 9 - 12

Association of Small Foundations (1995)
1720 North St. NW
Washington, DC 20036
Tel: (202) 580-6560 *Fax:* (202) 580-6579
TollFree: (888) 212-9922
E-Mail: asf@smallfoundations.org
Website: smallfoundations.org
Members: 3000 individuals
Staff: 19
Annual Budget: $5-10,000,000
Tax: 501(c)(3)

Personnel:
Chief Executive Officer: Henry L. Berman
    E-Mail: henry@smallfoundations.org
Director, Marketing and Communications: Ted Adams
    E-Mail: ted@smallfoundations.org
Senior Manager, Marketing and Communications: Kim Adkinson
    E-Mail: kim@smallfoundations.org
Senior Program Manager: Sara Beggs
    E-Mail: sara@smallfoundations.org
Director, Member Services: Hanh Le
    E-Mail: hanh@smallfoundations.org
Managing Director: Kathryn Petrillo-Smith
    E-Mail: kathryn@smallfoundations.org
Manager, Operations: Peter Tajat
    E-Mail: peter@smallfoundations.org

Historical Note:
ASF's mission is to enhance the power of philanthropy by providing donors, trustees, and professionals with peer learning opportunities, resources, and a collective voice in and beyond the philanthropic community. Members are donors, trustees, employees and consultants of foundations. Membership: $695/year.

Meetings/Conferences: Annual
Conference Chair: Sara Beggs
Number of non-conference events/year: 6

Publications:
ASF Newsletter; quarterly
Membership Directory; on-line

Association of Social Work Boards (1979)
400 S. Ridge Pkwy.
Suite B
Culpeper, VA 22701
Tel: (540) 829-6880 *Fax:* (540) 829-0142
TollFree: (800) 225-6880
E-Mail: info@aswb.org
Website: aswb.org
Members: 61 states, Canadian provinces and territories
Staff: 21
Annual Budget: $5-10,000,000
Tax: 501(c)(3)

Personnel:
Executive Director: Donna DeAngelis ACSW, LICSW
Director, Office Operations: Christine Breeden
Coordinator, Publications and Web Applications: Bobbie Hartman
    E-Mail: bhartman@aswb.org
Meetings Planner: Jennifer Hoffman
Director, Board Services: Dwight Hymans LCSW
Director, Candidate Services: Pat Olinger
Manager, Information Technology: Dan Sheehan

    E-Mail: dsheehan@aswb.org
ACE Coordinator: Jennifer Ward
    E-Mail: jward@aswb.org
Manager , Communications: Jayne Wood

Historical Note:
Formerly American Association of State Social Work Boards in 1979, assumed its current name in 2000. ASWB develops and administers the social work licensing examinations, and supports social work licensing boards in the protection of the public through legal regulation.

Meetings/Conferences: Annual
Conference Chair: Jennifer Hoffman
Number of non-conference events/year: 8

Publications:
Association News; on-line

Association of Specialized and Cooperative Library Agencies (1944)
50 E. Huron St.
Chicago, IL 60611
Tel: (312) 280-4395 *Fax:* (312) 280-5273
TollFree: (800) 545-2433
E-Mail: ascla@ala.org
Website: ala.org/ascla
Members: 800 Members
Staff: 3
Annual Budget: $50-100,000

Personnel:
Executive Director: Susan Hornung
    E-Mail: shornung@ala.org
Manager, Web Services: Andrea Hill
Manager, Marketing and Programs: Liz Markel
    E-Mail: lmarkel@ala.org

Historical Note:
A division of the American Library Association. Formerly known as the Association of State Library Agencies, Association of Hospital and Institution Libraries, and then (1974) Health and Rehabilitative Library Services before assuming its current name in 1978. An ALA member can only join in ASCLA as a member. ASCLA enhances the effectiveness of library service by providing networking, enrichment and educational opportunities for its diverse members, who represent state library agencies, libraries serving special populations, multitype library organizations and independent librarians. Membership: $51 (Individual) plus the cost of ALA membership; $20 (Student); $60 (Organization); $500 (State Library Agency) plus the cost of ALA membership.

Meetings/Conferences: Annual
Conference Chair: Liz Markel
2013 - Seatle, WA/Jan. 25 - 29

Publications:
Interface; quarterly; adv.
Magazine; quarterly
Membership Directory; on-line
Newsletter; quarterly

Association of Specialized and Professional Accreditors (1993)
3304 N. Broadway St.
Suite 214
Chicago, IL 60657
Tel: (773) 857-7900 *Fax:* (773) 857-7901
E-Mail: aspa@aspa-usa.org
Website: aspa-usa.org
Members: 60 organizations
Staff: 1
Annual Budget: $250-500,000
Tax: 501(c)(3)

Personnel:
Executive Director: Joseph Vibert

Historical Note:
ASPA fosters good practice in accreditation of educational programs. ASPA also represents the interests of, and provides information about, specialized and professional accreditation organizations to higher education and to government. Mission is to promote quality and integrity in non-governmental specialized and professional accreditation of post- secondary programs and institutions, provide a forum for discussion and analysis and a mechanism for common action for members, address accreditation issues in educational, governmental, and public policy contexts, and facilitate collaboration among members. Members must meet definitions posted on web site. Membership: $4,265 (Member, based on no. of institutions that sponsor programs or units accredited by the agency).

Meetings/Conferences: Annual
2013 - Chicago, IL (Millennium Knickerbocker Hotel Chicago)/April 7 - 9

2014 - Washington, DC/March 30 - April 1
2015 - Chicago, IL/March 29 - 31
2015 - Washington, DC/March 29 - 30
2016 - Washington, DC/April 3 - 5
2017 - Chicago, IL/April 2 - 4
2018 - Washington, DC/April 8 - 10

Publications:
Newsletter; bi-annually

Membership List Available to Non-members

Association of Specialty Cut Flower Growers (1988)
17.5 W. College St.
MPO Box 268
Oberlin, OH 44074
Tel: (440) 774-2887 *Fax:* (440) 774-2435
E-Mail: ascfg@oberlin.net
Website: ascfg.org
Members: 600 individuals
Staff: 2
Annual Budget: $100-250,000

Personnel:
Executive Director: Judy M. Laushman
    E-Mail: ascfg@oberlin.net
Treasurer: Andrea Gagnon
    E-Mail: andrea@lynnvale.com

Historical Note:
ASCFG's mission is to unite and inform growers in the production and marketing of field and greenhouse specialty floral crops. Membership: $175 (Primary); $110 (Educator); $45 (Student); $2,000 (Lifetime Member).

Meetings/Conferences: Annual

Publications:
Short Cuts Newsletter; on-line
The Cut Flower; quarterly; adv.

Association of Specialty Professors
330 John Carlyle St.
Suite 610
Alexandria, VA 22314
Tel: (703) 341-4540 *Fax:* (703) 519-1893
E-Mail: asp@im.org
Website: im.org/asp
Members: 1259 members,10 societal members.
Staff: 10
Annual Budget: $1-2,000,000
Tax: 501(c)(3)

Personnel:
President: Scott D. Gitlin MD
Treasurer: David Daikh MD, PhD

Historical Note:
ASP is a division of Alliance for Academic Internal Medicine (AAIM). Mission is to support new initiatives in education, medical research, and patient care, to form public policy and influence legislation related to subspecialty internal medicine, to develop common resources and a uniform voice among subspecialty internal medicine professors and divisions. Members are division chiefs and program directors of ACGME-accredited internal medicine subspecialty training programs in the U.S. and Canada. Membership: $3,200/year (Societal).

Publications:
AAIM Connection; weekly
Insight; quarterly; adv.
Membership Directory; on-line

Association of State and Provincial Psychology Boards (1961)
P. O. Box 3079
Peachtree City, GA 30269
Tel: (678) 216-1175 *Fax:* (678) 216-1176
TollFree: (800) 448-4069
E-Mail: asppb@asppb.org
Website: asppb.net
Members:
62 agencies
64 jurisdictions
Staff: 9
Annual Budget: $2-5,000,000
Tax: 501(c)(6)

Personnel:
Executive Officer and General Counsel: Stephen T. Demers EdD
    E-Mail: sdemers@asppb.org
Associate Executive Officer: Amy C. Hilson CAE
    E-Mail: ahilson@asppb.org
Director, Member Services: Janet Pippin Orwig MBA

E-Mail: jpippin@asppb.org
Financial Officer: Mark Russell CPA
E-Mail: russell@asppb.org
Director, Meeting Management: Anita L. Scott CMP
E-Mail: ascott@asppb.org
Director, Professional Affairs: Alex M. Siegel J D, PhD
E-Mail: asiegel@asppb.org
Director, Regulatory Affairs: Matt Turner PhD
E-Mail: mturner@asppb.org

Historical Note:
Formerly (1992) the American Association of State Psychology Boards. ASPPB's mission is to enhance services and support its member jurisdictions in fulfilling their goal of advancing public protection. Membership: $350-2,750 (Agency); $35 (Individual).

Continuing Education:
Certification Designation/s: ASPPB/NR, IPC, CPQ, EPPP

Meetings/Conferences: Annual
Conference Chair: Anita L. Scott CMP
2013 - Stockholm, Sweden/July 7 - 9
2013 - Las Vegas, NV (Paris Las Vegas Hotel and Casino)/Oct. 16 - 20
2014 - Washington, DC/Aug. 7 - 10
Number of non-conference events/year: 9

Association of State and Territorial Dental Directors *(1948)*
1838 Fieldcrest Dr.
Sparks, NV 89434
Tel: (775) 626-5008 *Fax:* (775) 626-9268
E-Mail: info@astdd.org
Website: astdd.org
Members: 59 individuals
Staff: 4
Annual Budget: $500-1,000,000
Tax: 501(c)(6)

Personnel:
Executive Director: Christine Wood BS, RDH
E-Mail: cwood@astdd.org
Manager, Business: Cheryl Thomas
E-Mail: astddct@aol.com

Historical Note:
An affiliate of Association of State and Territorial Health Officials. ASTDD provides leadership to advocate for a governmental oral health presence in each state and territory, to formulate and promote sound oral health policies, to increase awareness of oral health issues, and to assist in the development of initiatives for prevention and control of oral diseases. Members are a small group of dedicated public health professionals, the majority of whom are either dentists or dental hygienists. Membership: $100 (Full Member); $50 (Associate); $300 (Organization).

Meetings/Conferences: Annual

Publications:
Membership Roster; on-line
Oral Health Matters; quarterly

Association of State and Territorial Health Officials *(1942)*
2231 Crystal Dr.
Suite 450
Arlington, VA 22202
Tel: (202) 371-9090 *Fax:* (571) 527-3189
E-Mail: psteib@astho.org
Website: astho.org
Members: 100000 public health professionals
Staff: 23
Annual Budget: $10-25,000,000
Tax: 501(c)(3)

Personnel:
Executive Director: Paul E. Jarris MBA, MD
E-Mail: pjarris@astho.org
Senior Director, Communications and Marketing: Scott Briscoe
E-Mail: sbriscoe@astho.org
Senior Analyst, Performance Improvement: Joya Coffman
E-Mail: jcoffman@astho.org
Senior Director, Human Resources: Diane Coontz
E-Mail: dcoontz@astho.org
Chief Program Officer, Member Services: Lacy M. Fehrenbach MPH
E-Mail: lfehrenbach@astho.org
Meetings Planner and Member Services Contact: Linda Holmsten
E-Mail: lthomas@astho.org
Director, Information Technology: Corey Hughley
E-Mail: chughley@astho.org

Chief Financial Officer: Rose-Ella Slavin
E-Mail: rslavin@astho.org

Historical Note:
Mission is to transform public health within states and territories to help members dramatically improve health and wellness. Represents the interests of senior health officials in the states and territories of the U.S.

Meetings/Conferences: Annual
Conference Chair: Linda Holmsten
Number of non-conference events/year: 1

Association of State and Territorial Public Health Nutrition Directors *(1952)*
P.O. Box 1001
Johnstown, PA 15907-1001
Tel: (814) 255-2829 *Fax:* (814) 255-6514
Website: astphnd.org
Members: 200 individuals
Staff: 3
Annual Budget: $250-500,000
Tax: 501(c)(3)

Personnel:
Executive Director: Karen L. Probert MS, RD
E-Mail: karen@astphnd.org
Director, Special Projects: Joan M. Atkinson MS, RD
E-Mail: joan@astphnd.org
Director, Operations: Cynthia Atterbury MPA, RD, LDN
E-Mail: cyndi@astphnd.org

Historical Note:
ASTPHND develops leaders in public health nutrition who strengthen policy, programs and environments making it possible for everyone to make healthy food choices and achieve healthy, active lifestyles. Members are directors of nutrition programs in the state and territorial public health agencies, coordinators and other public health nutrition professionals. Membership: $50/year (Associate).

Continuing Education:
Certification Designation/s: MCH

Meetings/Conferences: Annual
Conference Chair: Cynthia Atterbury MPA, RD, LDN

Publications:
e-newsletter; quarterly
Membership Directory; on-line

Association of State and Territorial Solid Waste Management Officials *(1974)*
444 N. Capitol St. NW
Suite 315
Washington, DC 20001
Tel: (202) 624-5828 *Fax:* (202) 624-7875
E-Mail: swmbarb@sso.org
Website: astswmo.org
Members: 56 states and territories
Staff: 7
Annual Budget: $2-5,000,000
Tax: 501(c)(6)

Personnel:
Executive Director: Mary Zdanowicz
E-Mail: maryz@astswmo.org
Information Staff Associate: Allison Goldberg
E-Mail: allisong@astswmo.org
Federal Facilities and Tanks Senior Staff Associate: Charles Reyes
E-Mail: charlesr@astswmo.org
Deputy Executive Director and Contact, Meeting Planning: Dania Rodriguez
E-Mail: daniar@astswmo.org

Historical Note:
ASTSWMO's mission is to enhance and promote effective state and territorial waste management programs and affect national waste management policies.

Meetings/Conferences: Annual
Conference Chair: Dania Rodriguez

Publications:
The ASTSWMO Newsletter; quarterly

Association of State Chamber Professionals *(1960)*
P.O. Box 149
Jefferson City, MO 65101
Tel: (573) 634-3511 *Fax:* (573) 634-8855
E-Mail: joycel@mainechamber.org
Website: statechamberpros.org
Members: 85 individuals
Staff: 5
Annual Budget: $25-50,000

Personnel:

President: Joyce LaRoche
E-Mail: joycel@mainechamber.org
Second Vice President, Membership: Barbara Beckham
E-Mail: barbara.beckham@scchamber.net
Contact, Website and Communications: Tim Brewer
E-Mail: tbrewer@indianachamber.com
Contact, Sponsorships: Leisa Fox
E-Mail: lfox@iowaabi.org
Secretary and Treasurer: Sean Heiner
E-Mail: seanh@awb.org

Historical Note:
Formerly known as Association of Membership and Marketing Executives (AMME). ASCP is dedicated to the growth and professional development of its members; membership, marketing, communications, and non-dues professionals from state chambers of commerce and business associations across the country. Membership: $275/Year.

Meetings/Conferences: Annual
Conference Chair: Joyce LaRoche

Publications:
ASCP e-newsletter; monthly
Membership Directory; on-line

Association of State Correctional Administrators *(1970)*
1110 Opal Ct.
Suite 5
Hagerstown, MD 21740
Tel: (301) 791-2722 *Fax:* (301) 393-9494
E-Mail: exec@asca.net
Website: asca.net
Members: 60 individuals
Staff: 5
Annual Budget: $1-2,000,000

Personnel:
Administrative Assistant: Lorna Bock
Project Manager: Jill Brooks
Accounts Manager: Tammy Kissinger

Historical Note:
Formerly (1967) Correctional Administrators Association of America. ASCA's mission is to provide leadership and direction on national correctional policy and practice, promotes and facilitates the exchange of ideas and philosophies at the top administrative level of correctional planning and policy-making, works for the advancement of correctional techniques, particularly in the areas of development, design of correctional facilities, staff training, and correctional management facilities. Members consists of the directors of all fifty state correctional agencies, the Federal Bureau of Prisons, and several large urban prison systems. Membership: $750/year.

Meetings/Conferences: Annual

Publications:
Corrections Directions; irregular; adv.

Association of State Dam Safety Officials *(1983)*
450 Old Vine St.
Lexington, KY 40507
Tel: (859) 257-5140 *Fax:* (859) 323-1958
E-Mail: info@damsafety.org
Website: damsafety.org
Members: 3279 individuals and 1041 associate affiliates
Staff: 6
Annual Budget: $2-5,000,000

Personnel:
Executive Director: Lori Cannon Spragens
E-Mail: lspragens@damsafety.org
Office Administrator: Jennifer Burns
E-Mail: jburns@damsafety.org
Information Specialist: Sarah McCubbin Cain
E-Mail: smc@damsafety.org
Contact, Marketing and Conference Management: Maureen Chinn Hogle
E-Mail: mhogle@damsafety.org
Director, Meetings and Membership Services: Susan Amato Sorrell
E-Mail: sasorrell@damsafety.org

Historical Note:
ASDSO's mission is to advance and improve the safety of dams by supporting the dam safety community and state dam safety programs, raising awareness of dam safety issues, facilitating cooperation, providing a forum for the exchange of information and representing dam safety interests before governments. Membership: $468 (State/ Voting); $49 (Associate/Affiliate Company Employee); $360 (Affiliate Company); $92 (Affiliate Individual); $38 (Retired/Senior); $22 (Student); $2,730 (Sustaining).

Continuing Education:
Certification Designation/s: TADS

Meetings/Conferences: Annual
Conference Chair: Susan Amato Sorrell
2013 - Providence, RI (Rhode Island Convention
  Center)/Sept. 8 - 12
2014 - San Diego, CA (San Diego Convention Center)/
  Sept. 20 - 25
2015 - New Orleans, LA (Hyatt Regency)/Sept. 13 - 17
Number of non-conference events/year: 2

Publications:
ASDSO eNews; monthly
Journal of Dam Safety; quarterly; adv.
Member Directory; on-line

Association of State Drinking Water Administrators *(1984)*
1401 Wilson Blvd.
Suite 1225
Arlington, VA 22209
Tel: (703) 812-9505 *Fax:* (703) 812-9506
E-Mail: info@asdwa.org
Website: asdwa.org
Members: 50 states and territories
Staff: 6
Annual Budget: $1-2,000,000
Tax: 501(c)(3)

Personnel:
Executive Director: James Taft
Specialist, Information Management: Anthony DeRosa
Manager, Projects: Deirdre Mason
Office Manager: Tom Maves

Historical Note:
*ASDWA's purpose is to support states in their efforts to
protect public health through the assurance of high quality
drinking water. Membership: $100/year (Associate).*

Meetings/Conferences: Semi-Annual
2013 - Alexandria, VA (Hilton Alexandria Old Town)/
  March 10 - 13
2013 - Long Beach, CA (Hilton Long Beach and
  Executive Meeting Center)/Oct. 27 - 31
2014 - Albuquerue, NM (Hyatt Regency Albuquerque)/
  Oct. 19 - 23

Publications:
ASDWA Weekly Update; weekly

Association of State Energy Research and Technology Transfer Institution
455 Science Dr.
Suite 200
Madison, WI 53711
Tel: (608) 238-8276 *Fax:* (608) 238-8733
Website: asertti.org
Staff: 3
Annual Budget: $250-500,000

Personnel:
Executive Director: David Terry
Director, Program: Sarah Ruen Blanchard
  E-Mail: sarah@asertti.org
Senior Project Manager, Technical Services: Abby Vogen
  E-Mail: avogen@ecw.org

Historical Note:
*ASERTTI's mission is to increase the effectiveness of
energy research efforts in contribution to economic growth,
environmental quality, and energy security.*

Meetings/Conferences:
2013 - Washington, DC (Fairmont Hotel)/Feb. 5 - 8

Publications:
Newsletter; on-line

Association of State Floodplain Managers *(1977)*
2809 Fish Hatchery Rd.
Suite 204
Madison, WI 53713-5020
Tel: (608) 274-0123 *Fax:* (608) 274-0696
E-Mail: asfpm@floods.org
Website: floods.org
Members:
2500 chapter affiliates
6500 individuals
Staff: 16
Annual Budget: $2-5,000,000

Personnel:
Executive Director: Chad Berginnis CFM
Manager, Outreach and Events: Diane Alicia Brown
Coordinator, Membership Services: Kevin Currie

E-Mail: memberhelp@floods.org
Manager, Financial Services: Bob Geenen
Coordinator, Certification: Anita Larson
  E-Mail: cfm@floods.org
Planner, Conferences and Special Events: Chad M. Ross
  E-Mail: ross@floods.org
Manager, Information Technology: Jason Scheeberger
  E-Mail: jason@floods.org
Technical Editor: Katrien Werner

Historical Note:
*The mission of ASFPM is to promote education, policies,
and activities that mitigate current and future losses, costs,
and human suffering caused by flooding, and to protect the
natural and beneficial functions of floodplains - all without
causing adverse impacts. Membership: $100 (Individual);
$250 (Agency); $175-700 (Corporate); $25 (Student).*

Continuing Education:
Certification Designation/s: CFM

Meetings/Conferences: Annual
Conference Chair: Chad M. Ross
2013 - Hartford, CT (Connecticut Convention Center)/
  June 9 - 14
2014 - Seatle, WA (Washington State Convention
  Center)/June 1 - 6
2015 - Atlanta, GA (Hyatt Regency Atlanta)/May 31 -
  June 1

Publications:
Membership Directory; annually
News & Views; bi-monthly

Association of State Supervisors of Mathematics *(1960)*
Wisconsin Department of Public Instruction
P.O. Box 7841
Madison, WI 53707-7841
Website: assm.us
Members: 173 Individuals
Staff: 5
Annual Budget: $100-250,000

Personnel:
President: Diana Kasbaum
  E-Mail: diana.kasbaum@dpi.wi.gov

Historical Note:
*ASSM promotes interest in the study and teaching of
mathematics. Membership: $50/year (Regular and
Associate).*

Meetings/Conferences:
Conference Chair: Diana Suddreth

Publications:
ASSM newsletter

Association of State Wetland Managers *(1983)*
32 Tandberg Trail
Suite 2A
Windham, ME 04062
Tel: (207) 892-3399 *Fax:* (207) 892-3089
E-Mail: aswm@aswm.org
Website: aswm.org
Members: 950 individuals
Staff: 6
Annual Budget: $250-500,000
Tax: 501(c)(3)

Personnel:
Executive Director: Jeanne Christie
  E-Mail: jeanne.christie@aswm.org
Senior Staff Policy Analyst: Peg Bostwick
  E-Mail: peg.bostwick@aswm.org
Program Assistant: Laura Burchill
  E-Mail: laura@aswm.org
Associate Director: Jon Kusler
  E-Mail: jon.kusler@aswm.org
Writer and Editor: Leah Stetson
  E-Mail: leah@aswm.org
Webmaster: Sharon Weaver
  E-Mail: sharon@aswm.org

Historical Note:
*ASWM's mission is to promote and enhance protection
and management of wetland resources and to promote the
application of sound science to wetland management efforts
and to provide training and education for members and
the public. Members are professionals involved in wetlands
protection and management programs including members
of the federal, state, local, private, not-for- profit and
academic communities addressing wetland protection issues.
Membership: $60 (Individual); $25 (Student); $150-500
(Corporate/Agency).*

Meetings/Conferences: Annual

Conference Chair: Laura Burchill
Number of non-conference events/year: 24

Publications:
Wetland News; bi-monthly
Insider's Edition; weekly
Legal Issues; on-line
Wetland Breaking News; monthly

Association of Statisticians of American Religious Bodies *(1935)*
C/O Research Center, Church of the Nazarene
17001 Prairie Star Pkwy.
Lenexa, MO 66220
Tel: (913) 577-0651 *Fax:* (913) 577-0651
E-Mail: sagesweb@sages.org
Website: asarb.org
Members: 30 individuals and 25 religious
organizations
Staff: 2
Annual Budget: Under $10,000

Personnel:
President: Richie Stanley
Secretary and Treasurer: Dale Jones
  E-Mail: djones@nazarene.org

Historical Note:
*ASARB works to bring together professionals in
denominations and other religious bodies who gather and
publish statistics on their groups. Members are persons at
the denominational or national level with responsibility for
gathering, compiling and publishing statistics of and for
their religious bodies. Membership: $15/year.*

Meetings/Conferences: Annual

Publications:
Membership Directoy; on-line

Association of Steel Distributors *(1943)*
401 N. Michigan Ave.
Suite 2200
Chicago, IL 60611
Tel: (312) 673-5793 *Fax:* (312) 527-6705
E-Mail: headquarters@steeldistributors.org
Website: steeldistributors.org
Members: 180 Companies
Staff: 4
Annual Budget: $250-500,000
Tax: 501(c)(3)

Personnel:
Executive Director: Ron Pietrzak
  E-Mail: rpietrzak@steeldistributors.org
Coordinator, Membership Services: Alyssa Anfuso
  E-Mail: aanfuso@steeldistributors.org
Editor: Frances Moffett
  E-Mail: fmoffett@steeldistributors.org
Coordinator, Conference: Courtney Toms
  E-Mail: ctoms@steeldistributors.org

Historical Note:
*ASD is designed to promote the important role of
distribution in the steel market by providing valuable
industry information and strives to educate and facilitate
interaction that benefit members in order to strengthen and
grow their business. Members are involved in distribution
of steel products. Membership: $2,100 (Regular); $1,900
(Associate/Mill Associate/Allied).*

Meetings/Conferences:
Conference Chair: Courtney Toms
Number of non-conference events/year: 7

Publications:
Membership Directory; on-line
Steel Distributor Update; on-line; adv.

Association of Strategic Alliance Professionals, Inc. *(1998)*
960 Turnpike St.
Canton, MA 02021-2818
Tel: (781) 562-1630 *Fax:* (781) 562-0354
E-Mail: info@strategic-alliances.org
Website: strategic-alliances.org
Members: 2000 individuals
Staff: 8
Annual Budget: $500-1,000,000
Tax: 501(c)(6)

Personnel:
President and Executive Director: Art Canter
  E-Mail: acanter@strategic-alliances.org
Director, Media Relations: John W. DeWitt
  E-Mail: jdewitt@asapmedia.org
Senior Manager, Membership Services: Lori Gold

E-Mail: lgold@strategic-alliances.org
Vice President, Operations: Pam Goodell
   E-Mail: pgoodell@strategic-alliances.org
Editorial Director: Jon Lavietes
   E-Mail: jlavietes@asapmedia.org
Senior Meeting and Event Manager: Michele Shannon CMP
   E-Mail: mshannon@strategic-alliances.org
Coordinator, Certification: Jennifer Silver
   E-Mail: jsilver@strategic-alliances.org
Coordinator, Administrative and Information Technology: Brendan Ward
   E-Mail: bward@strategic-alliances.org

Historical Note:
ASAP is dedicated to alliance formation and practice. Membership: $385/year.

Continuing Education:
Enrollment: 1000
Certification Designation/s: CA-AM, CSAP

Meetings/Conferences: Annual
Conference Chair: Michele Shannon CMP
Number of non-conference events/year: 1

Publications:
ASAP Alliances Best Practices Guidebook
ASAP Alliances Best Process Workbook
ASAP in Action (e-newsletter); monthly; adv.
Best Practice Bulletin; monthly
Membership Directory; on-line
Strategic Alliances Magazine; quarterly

Association of Supervisory and Administrative School Personnel *(1989)*
1300 Caraway Ct.
Suite 204
Largo, MD 20774
Tel: (301) 925-7047 *Fax:* (301) 925-2774
E-Mail: asasp@asasp.org
Website: asasp.org
Members: 625 individuals
Staff: 4
Annual Budget: $500-1,000,000

Personnel:
Executive Director: Doris A. Reed
Office Manager: Barbara Jolly

Historical Note:
Formerly (1994) Association of School Based Administrators and Supervisors. ASASP's purpose is to improve the educational process for students by helping members become more effective in their various roles as educational leaders.

Publications:
Membership Directory; on-line

The Association of Suppliers to the Paper Industry *(1933)*
15 Technology Pkwy., South
Norcross, GA 30092
Fax: (770) 209-7581
Website: aspinet.org
Members: 32 companies
Staff: 5
Annual Budget: $100-250,000
Tax: 501(c)(3)

Personnel:
Executive Director: Eric Fletty
   E-Mail: efletty@aspinet.org
Director, Membership Relations and Editor: Colleen Walker
   E-Mail: cwalker@aspinet.org

Historical Note:
Formerly (1971) Pulp and Paper Machinery Association, (1989) Pulp and Paper Machinery Manufacturers Association, and (2004) American Paper Machinery Association. ASPI is focused on providing membership benefits to companies supplying the global pulp and paper industry. Members are companies offering goods and services to commercial paper producers. Membership: $2,500-3,500 (Company, based on annual sales); $450 (Principal/Emeritus).

Meetings/Conferences: Annual
2013 - St. Pete Beach, FL (Don CeSar Beach Hotel)/ Feb. 28 - March 1

Publications:
ASPI Newsletter; on-line

Association of Surfing Professionals - North America *(1983)*

300 Pacific Coast Highway, Suite 114
P.O. Box 309
Huntington Beach, CA 92648
Tel: (714) 536-3500 *Fax:* (714) 536-4482
Website: aspnorthamerica.org
Members: 1200 individuals
Staff: 5
Annual Budget: $250-500,000

Personnel:
Executive Manager: Meg Bernardo
   E-Mail: meg@aspworldtour.com
Head Judge: Jeff Klugel
   E-Mail: jeff@aspworldtour.com
Manager, Media: Bobby Shadley
   E-Mail: bobby@aspworldtour.com

Historical Note:
ASPNA seeks to promote the sport of professional surfing for the benefit of its members, the sanctioned World Tour events, professional surfers and the public. North American arm of an international organization headquartered in Queensland, Australia. Membership is open to professional and amateur surfers. Membership: $75-1,400/year.

Publications:
ASP Newsletter

Association of Surgical Assistants
Six W. Dry Creek Cir.
Littleton, CO 80120
Tel: (303) 694-9130 *Fax:* (303) 694-9169
TollFree: (800) 637-7433
Website: surgicalassistant.org
Staff: 2

Personnel:
President: Dennis Stover
Treasurer: Greg Salmon

Historical Note:
ASA represents a broad coalition of surgical assistant practitioners, who share several common goals, including optimizing surgical patient care, promoting the recognition of all surgical assistants, advancing legislative strategies and providing relevant continuing education experiences.

Continuing Education:
Certification Designation/s: CSA

Publications:
ASA Newsletter; quarterly
ASA e-News; on-line

Association of Surgical Technologists *(1969)*
Six W. Dry Creek Cir.
suite 200
Littleton, CO 80120-8031
Tel: (303) 694-9130 *Fax:* (303) 694-9169
TollFree: (800) 637-7433
E-Mail: ast@ast.org
Website: ast.org
Members: 55000 individuals
Staff: 22
Annual Budget: $2-5,000,000

Personnel:
Chief Executive Officer: William J. Teutsch BA, CAE
   E-Mail: bteutsch@ast.org
Coordinator, Member Services, Meetings and PAE: Michele Frey
   E-Mail: mfrey@ast.org
Director, Continuing Education: Kevin Frey CST, MS
Accounting Manager: Kelley Hay
Database Specialist: Sean Irish
Network Administrator: Hyung Lim
Director, Publishing: Karen Ludwig BA
   E-Mail: kludwig@ast.org
Director, Government Affairs: Catherine Sparkman JD
   E-Mail: catherine.sparkman@ast.org

Historical Note:
AST's primary concerns center on ensuring that surgical technologists are educationally qualified to administer surgical patient care through the support of accreditation, certification and continuing education. Membership: $80 (Active/Associate/Affiliate); $45 (Student); $45 (Retired / Disabled).

Continuing Education:
Certification Designation/s: CST, CSFA

Meetings/Conferences: Annual
Conference Chair: Michele Frey
2013 - New Orleans, LA (Hilton New Orleans Riverside)/May 21 - 25
2014 - Denver, CO (Hyatt Regency Denver at Colorado Convention Center)/May 26 - 30

Publications:
ASA News; quarterly
ASTSA News; quarterly
Instructors Newsletter; bi-monthly
The Surgical Technologist; monthly

Association of Talent Agents *(1937)*
9255 Sunset Blvd.
Suite 930
Los Angeles, CA 90069
Tel: (310) 274-0628 *Fax:* (310) 274-5063
Website: agentassociation.com
Members: 120 companies
Staff: 9
Annual Budget: $500-1,000,000
Tax: 501(c)(6)

Personnel:
Executive Director: Karen Stuart
   E-Mail: atastuart@aol.com
Director, Administration: Shellie Jetton
   E-Mail: shellie@agentassociation.com
General Counsel: George A. Stohner Esq.

Historical Note:
Formerly (1937) Artists Managers Guild, assumed its present name in 1979. ATA's mission is to represent the talent agencies in the industry. It provides interpretation, construction and advice dispute resolution to member agencies. Membership: $1000 (Application Fee).

Meetings/Conferences:
Number of non-conference events/year: 2

Publications:
Membership Directory; on-line

Membership List Available to Non-members

Association of Teacher Educators *(1920)*
P.O. Box 793
Manassas, VA 20113
Tel: (703) 331-0911 *Fax:* (703) 331-3666
E-Mail: info@ate1.org
Website: ate1.org
Members: 3000 individuals
Staff: 2
Annual Budget: $500-1,000,000
Tax: 501(c)(3)

Personnel:
Executive Director: David A. Ritchey PhD, CAE
   E-Mail: dritchey@ate1.org

Historical Note:
ATE's mission is to improve effectiveness of teacher education through leadership in development of quality programs, by analyzing issues and by providing opportunities for personal and professional growth of association members. Membership: $100 (Regular); $260 (Library); $1,900 (Life); $35 (Retired/Student).

Meetings/Conferences:
2013 - Atlanta, GA (Hyatt Regency Atlanta)/Feb. 15 - 19
2013 - Washington, DC (Hyatt Regency Capitol Hill)/ Aug. 2 - 6
2014 - St. Louis, MO (Hyatt Regency)/Feb. 14 - 18
2015 - Phoenix, AZ (Hyatt Regency and Phoenix Convention Center)/Feb. 13 - 17
2016 - Chicago, IL (Hilton Chicago)/Feb. 11 - 17
2017 - Orlando, FL (Caribe Royale Orlando)/Feb. 10 - 14

Publications:
Action in Teacher Education; quarterly; adv.
ATE Newsletter; quarterly; adv.
The New Educator; quarterly; adv.

Membership List Available to Non-members

Association of Teachers of Maternal and Child Health *(1968)*
1900 M St. NW
Suite 710
Washington, DC 20036
Tel: (202) 296-1099 *Fax:* (202) 296-1252
Website: atmch.org
Members: 200 individuals
Staff: 3
Annual Budget: $25-50,000
Tax: 501(c)(3)

Personnel:
President: Douglas Taren PhD
   E-Mail: taren@email.arizona.edu
Contact, Media and Membership: Jessica Petrush

E-Mail: jpetrush@asph.org
Treasurer: Martha Wingate
E-Mail: mwingate@ms.soph.uab.edu

Historical Note:
ATMCH aims to provide education, research, and service in field of maternal and child health. Members are academics in the field of maternal and child health. Membership: $75 (Faculty/Community); $10 (Student).

Publications:
ATMCH Newsletter
Membership Directory; on-line

Association of Teachers of Technical Writing
(1973)
4125 W. Loch Alpine Dr.
Ann Arbor, MI 48103
Tel: (940) 565-2115
Website: attw.org
Members: 1000 Individuals
Staff: 7
Annual Budget: $10-25,000
Tax: 501(c)(3)

Personnel:
President: Bill Hart-Davidson
Treasurer: Ann Blakeslee
Coordinator, Conferences: Michelle Eble
Officer, Information Services: TyAnna Herrington
Editor: Amy Koerber
Membership Chair: Susan Popham
Secretary: Brenda Sims
E-Mail: sims@unt.edu

Historical Note:
ATTW's mission is to provide communication among teachers of technical writing and develop technical communications as an academic discipline. Membership includes teachers and students from all levels and all types of educational institutions, and technical writers from government and industry. Has no paid staff. Membership: $50 (USA); $55 (Foreign); $75 (Library); $20 (Student).

Meetings/Conferences: Annual
Conference Chair: Michelle Eble
2013 - Las Vegas, NV/March 13

Publications:
ATTW Membership Directory; on-line
ATTW Bulletin; semi-annually
Technical Communication Quarterly; quarterly; adv.

Association of Technical and Supervisory Professionals *(1974)*
153 Nettie Ln.
McDonough, GA 30252
Tel: (815) 439-0072
E-Mail: ATSPmail@aol.com
Website: atsp74.net
Members: 420 individuals
Staff: 2
Annual Budget: $25-50,000
Tax: 501(c)(6)

Personnel:
President: Luis Zamora
National Treasurer: Larry Hortert
E-Mail: larry@atsp74.net

Historical Note:
ATSP's mission is to promote the welfare of its members having as a primary purpose the improvement of working conditions among technical and supervisory professionals employed by the Agency. Members are individuals involved in the Department of Agriculture's meat and poultry inspection programs. Membership: $62.50/year (Individual).

Publications:
ATSP Newsletter; on-line

Association of Technical Personnel in Ophthalmology *(1969)*
2025 Woodlane Dr.
St. Paul, MN 55125-2998
Fax: (651) 731-0410
TollFree: (800) 482-4858
E-Mail: atpomembership@jcahpo.org
Website: atpo.org
Members: 1300 individuals
Staff: 2
Annual Budget: $250-500,000

Personnel:
President: Martha Finch Moos BS

Historical Note:

ATPO is dedicated to the success of ophthalmic medical technicians. Represents a diverse group of OMT, including (but not limited to) ophthalmic assistants, technicians, technologists, surgical and keratorefractive techs, photographers, nurses, and orthoptists. Membership: $75 (Regular/Non-Certified Associate); $55 (Group); $20 (Student).

Publications:
Viewpoints Magazine; semi-annually
Viewpoints Newsletter

Association of Technology Act Projects *(1997)*
1 W Old State Capitol Plaza
Suite 100
Springfield, IL 62701
Fax: (410) 554-9237
Website: ataporg.org/
Staff: 2

Personnel:
Executive Director: Anne Blackfield
E-Mail: ablackfield@mdtap.org
Treasurer: Carolyn Phillips

Historical Note:
ATAP will advocate and support quality performance of the State AT programs.

Publications:
Electronic Newsletter; monthly
Newsletter; quarterly

Association of Telehealth Service Providers *(1996)*
4702 SW Scholls Ferry Rd.
Suite 400
Portland, OR 97225-2008
Tel: (503) 922-0988 *Fax:* (315) 222-2402
Website: atsp.org
Members:
200 organizations
1000 individuals
Staff: 3

Personnel:
Executive Director: William Engle

Historical Note:
Founded as Association of Telemedicine Service Providers and assumed its current name in 2000. ATSP promotes and supports the use of telecommunications services and technology to expand health care options for patients and providers. Strives to advance the field of telehealth through advocacy, removal of barriers, health care delivery, health education and telemedicine business development. Membership: $1,250 (Organization); $195 (Individual).

Publications:
ATSP On-line Newsletter; quarterly

Association of TeleServices International, Inc. *(1942)*
12100 Sunset Hills Rd.
Suite 130
Reston, VA 20190
Tel: (703) 234-4111 *Fax:* (703) 435-4390
E-Mail: admin@atsi.org
Website: atsi.org
Members: 400 companies
Staff: 3
Annual Budget: $500-1,000,000
Tax: 501(c)(6)

Personnel:
Executive Vice President: Bill Carney
E-Mail: bcarney@drohanmgmt.com
Co-Chair, Annual Conventions: Marcy Hewlett

Historical Note:
Formerly (1986) Associated Telephone Answering Exchanges, then (1998) the Association of Telemessaging Services International. ATSI's mission is to enhance the value of association member's businesses by promoting fair competition through the pursuit of appropriate regulation and legislation. Members provide a variety of services to businesses, governmental agencies, local emergency respondents and the general public. Membership: $150-600/year.

Continuing Education:
Certification Designation/s: CSR

Meetings/Conferences: Annual
Conference Chair: Marcy Hewlett

Publications:
Connections; bi-monthly; adv.
Membership Directory; annually

Association of Test Publishers *(1992)*
601 Pennsylvania Ave. NW
S. Building, Suite 900
Washington, DC 20004
Tel: (866) 240-7909 *Fax:* (717) 755-8962
TollFree: (866) 240-7909
Website: testpublishers.org
Members: 120 companies
Staff: 5
Annual Budget: $1-2,000,000
Tax: 501(c)(6)

Personnel:
Chief Executive Officer: Dr. William G. Harris PhD
E-Mail: wgharris@testpublishers.org
General Counsel: David W. Arnold JD, PhD
Editor: Chad W. Buckendahl
E-Mail: chad.buckendahl@alpinetesting.com
Treasurer: Marten Roorda
Media Contact: Lauren Scheib
E-Mail: lscheibatatp@aol.com

Historical Note:
Formerly (1993) Association of Personal Test Publishers. ATP's mission is to promote and develop testing and assessment best practices and to facilitate an environment that would benefit test-takers, businesses, educational organizations, and society in general. Members are publishers of standardized tests for use in educational, industrial, and clinical situations, as well as providers of assessment services and products. Membership: $750-20,000 (Regular); $1,100-5,500 (Associate); $75 (Subscriber).

Meetings/Conferences:
2013 - Ft. Lauderdale, FL (The Westin Diplomat Resort and Spa)/Feb. 3 - 6

Publications:
Journal of Applied Testing Technology (JATT)
Membership Directory; on-line
Test Publisher industry newsletter; quarterly

Association of the United States Army *(1950)*
2425 Wilson Blvd.
Arlington, VA 22201-3385
Tel: (703) 841-4300 *Fax:* (703) 841-1050
TollFree: (800) 336-4570
E-Mail: ausa-info@ausa.org
Website: ausa.org
Members: 102000 individuals
Staff: 110
Annual Budget: $25-50,000,000

Personnel:
President and Chief Operating Officer: Gen. Gordon R. Sullivan USA(Ret)
E-Mail: gsullivan@ausa.org
Manager, System Support: Michael Coleman
E-Mail: mcoleman@ausa.org
Director, Marketing: Millie Hurlbut
E-Mail: mhurlbut@ausa.org
Director, Public Affairs and Communications: David Liddle
E-Mail: DLiddle@ausa.org
Manager, Human Resources: Merna Lipson
E-Mail: mlipson@ausa.org
Director, Government Affairs: William Loper
E-Mail: wloper@ausa.org
Editor: Peter Murphy
E-Mail: pmurphy@ausa.org
USA (Ret.), Vice President Finance and Administration: Lt. Gen Thomas G. Rhame
E-Mail: trhame@ausa.org
Contact, Legislative Affairs: Julie Rudowski
E-Mail: jrudowski@ausa.org
Administrator, Membership Services: Teshaka Stanley
E-Mail: tstanley@ausa.org
Vice President, Education: Lt. Gen Theodore G. Stroup Jr., USA (Ret.)
E-Mail: tstroup@ausa.org
Vice President, Membership Services and Meetings: Lt. Gen Roger G. Thompson USA (Ret.)
E-Mail: rthompson@ausa.org

Historical Note:
Formed by a merger of the U.S. Infantry Association and the U.S. Field Artillery Association in 1950, (1955) the U.S. Antiaircraft Association. AUSA's mission is to represent every American Soldier by being the voice for all components of America's Army. Members are active, retired and reserve military personnel. Membership: $14-39 (Individual); $150-1500 (Corporate); $6,000 (Sustaining); $250-525 (Life).

Meetings/Conferences:
Conference Chair: Lt. Gen Roger G. Thompson USA (Ret.)
2013 - Ft. Washington, MD (Gaylord National Resort and Convention Center-National Harbor)/Jan. 9 - 11
2013 - Ft. Lauderdale, FL (Greater Fort Lauderdale/ Broward County Convention Center)/Feb. 20 - 22
2013 - Honolulu, HI (Hilton Hawaiian Village Waikiki Beach Resort)/April 7 - 9
2013 - Richmond, VA (Greater Richmond Convention Center)/May 7 - 9
2013 - Washington, DC (Walter E. Washington Convention Center)/Oct. 21 - 23
2014 - Washington, DC (Walter E. Washington Convention Center)/Oct. 13 - 15
2015 - Washington, DC (Walter E. Washington Convention Center)/Oct. 12 - 14
2016 - Washington, DC (Walter E. Washington Convention Center)/Oct. 10 - 12
2017 - Washington, DC (Walter E. Washington Convention Center)/Oct. 9 - 11
2018 - Washington, DC (Walter E. Washington Convention Center)/Oct. 8 - 10
2019 - Washington, DC (Walter E. Washington Convention Center)/Oct. 14 - 16
2020 - Washington, DC (Walter E. Washington Convention Center)/Oct. 12 - 14
Number of non-conference events/year: 5

Publications:
ARMY Magazine; monthly; adv.
AUSA Industry Affairs Directory; on-line
Directory of Resources; on-line
Directory of Retiree and Veteran Resources; on-line
Directory of Veteran Benefits Info Web-Sites; on-line
Membership Directory; on-line
NSW
State Veteran's Benefits Directory; on-line
Sustaining Member Directory; on-line

Association of the United States Navy, Inc. (1954)
1619 King St.
Alexandria, VA 22314
Tel: (703) 548-5800 Fax: (866) 683-3647
TollFree: (877) 628-9411
Website: ausn.org
Members: 25000 individuals
Staff: 10
Annual Budget: $2-5,000,000
Tax: 501(c)(19)

Personnel:
Executive Director: Casey Coane RADM
    E-Mail: casey.coane@ausn.org
Contact, Navy Magazine: Linda Bautista
    E-Mail: navy@ausn.org
Director, Marketing and Communications: Jean Byrd
    E-Mail: jean.byrd@ausn.org
Director, Membership Services: Jerry Featherstone
    E-Mail: jerry.featherstone@ausn.org
Director, Business Development: Kenya Houston
    E-Mail: kenya.houston@ausn.org
Chief Financial Officer: Robert H. Lyman
    E-Mail: bob.lyman@ausn.org
Director, Legislation: Anthony A. Wallis
    E-Mail: anthony.wallis@ausn.org

Historical Note:
Formerly the Naval Reserve Association, assumed its current name in 2009 to the Association of the United States Navy (AUSN). AUSN's mission is to advance the interests of all members of the Navy community and supports the needs of the Navy. Membership: $40-105 (Regular); $35-90 (Associate); $12-28 (Spouse Associate).

Meetings/Conferences: Annual

Publications:
Association of the United States Navy Magazine; monthly; adv.
Membership Directory; on-line

Association of the Wall and Ceiling Industry (1918)
513 W. Broad St.
Suite 210
Falls Church, VA 22046-3108
Tel: (703) 538-1600 Fax: (703) 534-8307
E-Mail: info@awci.org
Website: awci.org
Members: 2200 companies, 17 chapters
Staff: 17

Annual Budget: $2-5,000,000

Personnel:
Executive Vice President and Chief Executive Officer: Steven A. Etkin CAE
Advertising Business Manager: Maggie Baker
Director, Conventions and Conferences: Karen Bilak
Director, Accounting Services: Bahman Kheradmand
Director, Communications and Editor: Laura M. Porinchak
Director, Technical Services: Don Smith
Associate Publisher: Brenton C. Stone

Historical Note:
AWCI's mission is to provide services and undertake activities that enhance the member's ability to operate a successful business. AWCI represents acoustics systems, ceiling systems, drywall systems, exterior insulation/ finishing systems, fireproofing, flooring systems, insulation and stucco contractors, suppliers and manufacturers, and those in allied trades. Membership: $585 (Contractor Headquarters Office, U.S.); $295 (Contractor Headquarters Office, Canada & International); $585 (Supplier or Distributor/Manufacturer Headquarters Office); $295 (General Interest).

Continuing Education:
Certification Designation/s: CEM, CEP, CEI, EIFS-IP, EIFS-M, EIFS-I

Meetings/Conferences:
Conference Chair: Karen Bilak
2013 - San Antonio, TX/March 18 - 22/over 100 exhibitors
2014 - Las Vegas, NV/March 23 - 27/over 100 exhibitors
Number of non-conference events/year: 6

Publications:
AWCI Members Only; monthly
AWCI's Construction Dimensions; monthly
AWCI's Tech Update; bi-monthly
Membership Directory; on-line

Membership List Available to Non-members

The Association of Theatre Movement Educators (1972)
Finger Lakes Community College, Department of Visual and Performing Arts
3325 Lakeshore Dr.
Canandaigua, NY 14424
Tel: (585) 785-1242
Website: atmeweb.org
Members: 170 individuals
Staff: 9

Personnel:
President: Deborah Robertson
    E-Mail: drobertson@niu.edu'
Vice President: Annette Thornton
    E-Mail: annette.thornton@cmich.edu
Editor: Sarah Barker
    E-Mail: sabarker@gwm.sc.edu
Website Coordinator: Judith Chaffee
    E-Mail: judith@commedia-dell-arte.com
Secretary: Beth Johnson
    E-Mail: atmesecretary@gmail.com
Treasurer: Marianne Kubik
    E-Mail: mmk4g@virginia.edu
Contact, Communications: Ted Morin
    E-Mail: ttmnyc@aol.com

Historical Note:
Formerly the Society of Theatre Movement Specialists, a focus group of the Association for Theatre in Higher Education and incorporated as an independent organization in 1993. ATME's mission is to promote the highest possible standards for theatre movement training and the application of those standards to educational and professional theatre. Membership: $25-45/year (Student).

Publications:
ATME Newsletter; bi-annually
Membership Directory; on-line
Performance; on-line
Rehearsal; on-line
Using a Period Movement Score in Actor Training; on-line

Association of Theatrical Press Agents and Managers (1928)
62 W. 45th St.
Suite 901
New York, NY 10036
Tel: (212) 719-3666 Fax: (212) 302-1585
E-Mail: info@atpam.com

Website: atpam.com
Members: 850 individuals
Staff: 5
Annual Budget: $1-2,000,000

Personnel:
President: David R. Calhoun
    E-Mail: dcalhoun@atpam.com
Consultant, Computer Services and Website Support: Roger Anderson
    E-Mail: randerson@atpam.com
Contact, Member Services: Fran Brando
    E-Mail: fbrando@atpam.com
Secretary and Treasurer: Nick Kaledin
    E-Mail: nkaledin@atpam.com

Historical Note:
Labor Union affiliated with the IATSE AFL-CIO. ATPAM members are press agents, publicity and marketing specialists company managers and house and facilities managers who are devoted to the health, vitality and success of staged entertainment of all types. Membership: $200/year (Individual).

Meetings/Conferences:
2013 - New York City, NY (Sardi's Restaurant)/Jan. 25
Number of non-conference events/year: 8

Association of Third World Studies (1983)
C/O Louisiana State University Shreveport
Shreveport, LA 71115-2301
Tel: (318) 797-5349 Fax: (318) 795-4203
Website: itc.gsw.edu/atws
Members: 600 individuals
Staff: 1
Annual Budget: $25-50,000

Personnel:
Executive Director: Dr. William D. Pederson
    E-Mail: william.pederson@lsus.edu

Historical Note:
ATWS works to provide an international structure for the humane and scientific study of third world peoples, problems and issues, with the ultimate goal of improving the quality of life. Members are academics, development specialists and others with an interest in third world countries. Membership: $30 (Student/Third World Resident); $60 (Regular); $90 (Husband and Wife); $75 (Sustainer); $100 (Patron); $150 (Third World Resident Life); $400 (Individual Life); $600 (Husband and Wife Life); $1,000 (Institutional).

Meetings/Conferences: Annual
Number of non-conference events/year: 1

Publications:
Membership Directory
Newsletter; annually

Association of Threat Assessment Professionals (1992)
1215 K St.
Suite 2290
Sacramento, CA 95814
Tel: (916) 231-2146 Fax: (916) 231-2141
E-Mail: ecardwell@atapworldwide.org
Website: atapworldwide.org
Members: 780 individuals
Staff: 8
Annual Budget: $250-500,000

Personnel:
President: Rachel Solov
    E-Mail: president@atapworldwide.org
Treasurer: Paul Bristow

Historical Note:
ATAP's mission is to share and facilitate the experiences and techniques of professionals in the field of threat assessment and/or threat management. Members are law enforcement officers, prosecutors, mental health professionals, and corporate security experts. Membership: $100/year.

Meetings/Conferences: Annual

Publications:
ATAP Newsletter; on-line
Membership Directory; on-line

Membership List Available to Non-members

Association of Transportation Professionals (1929)
P.O. Box 5407
Annapolis, MD 21403
Tel: (410) 268-1311 Fax: (410) 268-1322
E-Mail: info@atlp.org
Website: atlp.org

Members: 700 individuals
Staff: 1
Annual Budget: $100-250,000

Personnel:
Executive Director: Lauren Michalski
 E-Mail: info@atlp.org

Historical Note:
Formerly (1994) Association for Transportation Law, Logistics and Policy. ALTP's mission to equip its members with the necessary tools to be vital resources for their companies, firms, customers and clients who compete in a constantly changing and increasingly global transportation and logistics marketplace. Membership: $260 (Attorney/ Non-attorney); $115 (Government Employees/University/ College Faculty); $50 (Student).

Meetings/Conferences: Annual

Publications:
Association Highlights; bi-monthly; adv.
Journal of Transportation Law, Logistics & Policy; adv.
Membership Roster; on-line

Association of Traumatic Stress Specialists
(1987)
C/O MHANJ
88 Pompton Ave.
Verona, NJ 07044
Tel: (973) 559-9200
E-Mail: admin@atss.info
Website: atss.info
Members:
30 teams
800 individuals
Staff: 2
Annual Budget: $50-100,000
Tax: 501(c)(3)

Personnel:
President: Kent G. Laidlaw
 E-Mail: kent@canuckcare.com
Office Administrator: Annie N. James

Historical Note:
Founded as International Association of Trauma Counseling; assumed its current name in 1997. ATSS's mission is to help the traumatized through international service, education and professional development. ATSS members are actively engaged in the field of trauma counseling treatment. Membership: $85 (Individual); $325 (Agency); $50 (Senior); $45 (Student).

Continuing Education:
Certification Designation/s: CTSS, CTR, CTS

Meetings/Conferences: Annual

Publications:
E-Newsletter
International Journal of Mental Health
Membership Directory; on-line
Newsletter

Association of Travel Marketing Executives
(1980)
P.O. Box 3176
W. Tisbury, MA 02575
Tel: (508) 693-0550 *Fax:* (508) 693-0115
E-Mail: admin@atme.org
Website: atme.org
Members: 400 individuals
Staff: 2
Annual Budget: $100-250,000

Personnel:
Executive Director: Kristin Zern
Treasurer: Jacqueline Johnson

Historical Note:
ATME's mission is to provide members with an ongoing forum for the exchange of creative ideas and effective marketing solutions within the travel industry. Membership: $200 (Special ATME Conference); $295 (Active Travel Marketers/Marketing Solution Providers); $395 (Media); $195 (Educators).

Meetings/Conferences:
Number of non-conference events/year: 4

Publications:
Membership Directory; on-line
Travel Marketing Decisions; quarterly; adv.

Association of United States Night Vision Manufacturers *(1980)*
7040 Highfields Farm Dr.
Roanoke, VA 24018
Tel: (540) 774-8933 *Fax:* (540) 774-1802

Website: nightvisionassociation.org
Members: 19 companies
Staff: 1
Annual Budget: $50-100,000

Personnel:
President: Robert G. Williams
 E-Mail: bobjoe9134@aol.com

Historical Note:
ANVM's mission is to support an open dialog between the night vision industry and the government regarding military posture, budget actions, requirements, acquisition planning and export policy. It also serves as a common resource for persons involved in the development, manufacture or use of night vision systems as well as those involved in the manufacture of critical components for these systems. Members manufacture night vision devices, systems, or components.

Meetings/Conferences: Annual

Publications:
Membership Directory; on-line

Membership List Available to Non-members

Association of Universities for Research in Astronomy, Inc. *(1957)*
1212 New York Ave. NW
Suite 450
Washington, DC 20005
Tel: (202) 483-2101 *Fax:* (202) 483-2106
Website: aura-astronomy.org
Members: 39 institutions and 7 international affiliates
Staff: 1112
Annual Budget: Over $100,000,000

Personnel:
President and Chief Executive Officer: William S. Smith Jr.
 E-Mail: wsmith@aura-astronomy.org
Vice President, Administration: Deborah Narcisso
 E-Mail: dnarcisso@aura-astronomy.org
Senior Systems Administrator: Ryan L. Richmond
 E-Mail: rrichmond@aura-astronomy.org

Historical Note:
AURA is a consortium of universities, and educational and other non-profit institutions, that operates astronomical observatories. AURA's mission is to promote excellence in astronomical research by providing access to state-of-the-art facilities. Membership: $10000-initial (University).

Meetings/Conferences: Annual
2013 - Tucson, AZ/April 17 - 20
Number of non-conference events/year: 8

Publications:
AURA Monthly Activity Reports; monthly

Membership List Available to Non-members

Association of University Anesthesiologists
(1953)
520 N. Northwest Hwy.
Park Ridge, IL 60068-2573
Tel: (847) 825-5586 *Fax:* (215) 615-3898
E-Mail: aua@asahq.org
Website: auahq.org
Members: 700 individuals
Staff: 5
Annual Budget: $100-250,000

Personnel:
Executive Director: Chris Dionne
 E-Mail: c.dionne@asahq.org
Ex-Officio and Newsletter Editor: William A. Kofke MD
 E-Mail: kofkea@uphs.upenn.edu

Historical Note:
Formerly (1990) Association of University Anesthetists. AUA's mission is to advance the Art & Science of Anesthesiology by encouragement of its members to pursue original investigations in the clinic and in the laboratory, by the development of the method of teaching (Anesthesia). Membership: $200/year (Individuals).

Meetings/Conferences: Annual
2013 - Miami, FL (JW Marriott Marquis)/April 4 - 6
2014 - Stanford, CA/April 24 - 26

Publications:
AUA Newsletter; quarterly
Membership Directory; on-line

Association of University Centers on Disabilities (AUCD) *(1968)*
1100 Wayne Ave.
Suite 1000

Silver Spring, MD 20910
Tel: (301) 588-8252 *Fax:* (301) 588-2842
E-Mail: aucdinfo@aucd.org
Website: aucd.org
Members: 100 universities
Staff: 9
Annual Budget: $5-10,000,000
Tax: 501(c)(3)

Personnel:
Executive Director: George S. Jesien PhD
 E-Mail: gjesien@aucd.org
Director, Web Services: Oksana Klimova MSc
 E-Mail: oklimova@aucd.org
Director, Operations: Laura Martin
 E-Mail: lmartin@aucd.org
Director, Legislative Affairs: Kim E. Musheno
 E-Mail: kmusheno@aucd.org
Director, Materials Development and Special Projects:
 Crystal K. Pariseau MSSW
 E-Mail: cpariseau@aucd.org
Meetings Intern: Maria Velasco
 E-Mail: mvelasco@aucd.org

Historical Note:
Formerly the American Association of University Affiliated Programs for Persons with Developmental Disabilities. A member organization of the Coalition for Health Funding in Washington. AUCD's mission is to advance policy and practice for and with people with developmental and other disabilities, their families, and their communities by supporting members in research, education, and service activities that achieve vision.

Meetings/Conferences: Annual
Conference Chair: Crystal K. Pariseau MSSW
2013 - Washington, DC (Washington, DC, Renaissance Hotel)/Nov. 16 - 20
2014 - Washington, DC (Washington, DC, Renaissance Hotel)/Nov. 9 - 12
Number of non-conference events/year: 5

Publications:
AUCDigest; monthly
Developments; quarterly
Health & Disability Digest; monthly
Legislative News In Brief; weekly
Membership Directory; on-line
State Disability & Health Grantees Directory; on-line

Association of University Interior Designers
(1979)
C/O The Ohio State University, Office of Student Life, Facility Management and Logistics
1800 Cannon Drive, Suite 710
Columbus, OH 43210-1230
Tel: (812) 855-1764 *Fax:* (859) 323-1017
Website: auid.org
Members: 87 individuals
Staff: 2
Annual Budget: $10-25,000
Tax: 501(c)(6)

Personnel:
President: Julie Lenczycki
Treasurer: Carlos Lugo

Historical Note:
AUID provides a network and resource for the sharing of information, discussion of issues, resolution of problems related to interior design work at Universities, and the management of interior design work at institutions of higher education. Members are designers, architects, facility managers. Membership: $40/year (Individual).

Publications:
Membership Directory; on-line
The Clearstory

Association of University Professors of Ophthalmology *(1966)*
Department of Ophthalmology, University of Nebraska Medical Center
985540 Nebraska Medical Center
Omaha, NE 68198-5540
Tel: (415) 561-8548 *Fax:* (415) 561-8531
E-Mail: aupo@aao.org
Website: aupo.org
Members: 303 individuals
Staff: 4
Annual Budget: $2-5,000,000

Personnel:
Treasurer and Membership services: Kathy Austin
 E-Mail: keaustin@unmc.edu

Historical Note:
AUPO's mission is to serve, strengthen, and represent academic departments of ophthalmology; to provide support, information and leadership opportunities to departmental chairs, program directors, and other faculty members; to promote excellence in ophthalmic education; to foster vision research and to promote ethical practice and excellence in eye care in order to ensure the best possible vision for the public. Membership: $300/year (Research Director/Medical Student Education Director).

Meetings/Conferences: Annual
Conference Chair: Rebekah Stout
2013 - San Diego, CA (Loews Coronado Bay Resort)/ Jan. 31 - Feb. 2

Publications:
Membership Directory; annually
News & Views; quarterly

Membership List Available to Non-members

Association of University Programs in Health Administration *(1948)*
2000 14th St. North
Suite 780
Arlington, VA 22201
Tel: (703) 894-0940 *Fax:* (703) 894-0941
E-Mail: aupha@aupha.org
Website: aupha.org
Members: 400 colleges and universities
Staff: 8
Annual Budget: $1-2,000,000
Tax: 501(c)(3)

Personnel:
President and Chief Executive Officer: Lydia Middleton Reed CAE, MBA
    E-Mail: lmiddleton@aupha.org
Senior Director, Professional Affairs: Kristi Donovan CAE
    E-Mail: kdonovan@aupha.org
Director, Meetings and Events: Lucinda Flowers
    E-Mail: lflowers@aupha.org
Manager, Membership Services: Lacey Meckley
    E-Mail: lmeckley@aupha.org
Chief Operating Officer: Liane Pinero-Kluge CAE
    E-Mail: lianep.kluge@aupha.org
Director, Finance and Administration: Kimberly Starks
    E-Mail: kstarks@aupha.org
Administrative Assistant, Marketing, Membership and Meetings: Stephanie Williams
    E-Mail: swilliams@aupha.org

Historical Note:
AUPHA fosters innovation in healthcare management education, research and practice by providing opportunities for member programs to learn from each other, by influencing practice and by promoting the value of healthcare management education. Membership: $110-11,000/year.

Continuing Education:
Certification Designation/s: UC

Meetings/Conferences: Semi-Annual
Conference Chair: Lucinda Flowers
2013 - Chicago, IL (Palmer House a Hilton Hotel)/ March 12
2013 - Monterey, CA (Portola Hotel and Spa)/June 20 - 23
Number of non-conference events/year: 1

Publications:
AUPHA Exchange Quarterly Newsletter; quarterly; adv.
Directory of Healthcare Management Education; bi-annually
Directory of Healthcare Management Programs; on-line
The Journal of Health Administration Education (JHAE); quarterly; adv.

Membership List Available to Non-members

Association of University Programs in Occupational Health and Safety *(1981)*
1665 University Blvd.
Birmingham, AL 35205
Members: 14 universities
Staff: 1
Annual Budget: $25-50,000

Personnel:
President: Dr. Jacqueline Agnew

Historical Note:
Members are fourteen universities who have graduate, NIOSH-funded programs in such areas as occupational medicine, nursing, industrial hygiene and safety engineering.

Association of University Radiologists *(1953)*
820 Jorie Blvd.
Oak Brook, IL 60523
Tel: (630) 368-3730 *Fax:* (630) 571-7837
E-Mail: aur@rsna.org
Website: aur.org
Members: 4257 individuals
Staff: 3
Annual Budget: $1-2,000,000
Tax: 501(c)(6)

Personnel:
Accounts Executive: Stephanie Taylor

Historical Note:
AUR is committed to advance the interests of academic radiology, enhancing careers in academic radiology and advancing radiological science, research and education. Membership: $260 (Full Membership); $75 (Associate Membership); $60 (Junior); $0 (Student).

Meetings/Conferences: Annual
2013 - Los Angeles, CA (JW Marriott Los Angeles L.A. LIVE)/April 9 - 12

Publications:
Academic Radiology; on-line; adv.
AUR Newsletter
Membership Directory; on-line

Association of University Research Parks *(1986)*
6262 N. Swan Rd.
Suite 100
Tucson, AZ 85718
Tel: (520) 529-2521 *Fax:* (520) 529-2499
E-Mail: info@aurp.net
Website:
aurrp.org
aurp.net
Members: 320 companies and institutions
Staff: 5
Annual Budget: $500-1,000,000
Tax: 501(c)(6)

Personnel:
President: Harold Strong Jr.
Chief Executive Officer: Eileen Walker
    E-Mail: eileenwalker@aurp.net
Treasurer: Curt Hess
Manager, Events: Victoria Palmer
Manager, Marketing and Membership: Chelsea Simpson
    E-Mail: chelseasimpson@aurp.net

Historical Note:
Formerly (2001)Association of University Research Parks. AURP's mission is to fostering innovation, commercialization and economic growth in a global economy through university, industry and government partnerships. Membership: $2,000 (Sustaining Research/ Associate); $895 (Research/Associate).

Meetings/Conferences: Annual
Conference Chair: Victoria Palmer
2013 - Philadelphia, PA/Sept. 24 - 27
Number of non-conference events/year: 2

Publications:
AURP Newsletter; on-line; adv.
Membership Directory; on-line
Park Post; monthly
Research Park Forum; monthly

Association of University Technology Managers *(1974)*
111 Deer Lake Rd.
Suite 100
Deerfield, IL 60015
Tel: (847) 559-0846 *Fax:* (847) 480-9282
E-Mail: info@autm.net
Website: autm.net
Members: 3500 individuals
Staff: 12
Annual Budget: $2-5,000,000
Tax: 501(c)(6)

Personnel:
Executive Director: Vicki Loise CAE, CMP
    E-Mail: vloise@autm.net
Director, Administration: Aaron Adair
    E-Mail: aadair@autm.net
Accountant: William Chandler
    E-Mail: wchandler@autm.net
Manager, Professional Development: Barbara Gunderson

    E-Mail: bgunderson@autm.net
Editor: Lisa Richter
    E-Mail: lrichter@autm.net
Director, Annual Meetings: Jacky Schweinzger CMP
    E-Mail: jschweinzger@autm.net
Director, Communications: Jodi Talley
    E-Mail: jtalley@autm.net

Historical Note:
Incorporated as a non-profit group in the state of Connecticut and formerly (1989) known as the Society of University Patent Administrators, AUTM's mission is to promote, support and improve academic technology transfer worldwide and demonstrate its benefits globally through education, advocacy, networking and communication. Membership: $285 (Regular Member); $50 (Student Member); $130 (Electronic Member).

Continuing Education:
Certification Designation/s: CLP

Meetings/Conferences: Annual
Conference Chair: Aaron Adair
2013 - San Antonio, TX (The Henry B. Gonzalez Convention Center)/Feb. 27 - March 2
2014 - San Francisco, CA (Moscone West-Moscone Center)/Feb. 19 - 22
2015 - New Orleans, LA (Hyatt Regency New Orleans)/ Feb. 22 - 25
2016 - San Diego, CA (Manchester Grand Hyatt San Diego)/Feb. 14 - 17
2017 - Hollywood, FL (Westin Diplomat Resort and Spa)/March 12 - 15
Number of non-conference events/year: 10

Publications:
Membership Directory; on-line

Association of Vacuum Equipment Manufacturers *(1969)*
201 Park Washington Ct.
Falls Church, VA 22046-4527
Tel: (703) 538-3543 *Fax:* (703) 241-5603
E-Mail: aveminfo@avem.org
Website: avem.org
Members: 86 companies
Staff: 7
Annual Budget: $50-100,000
Tax: 501(c)(6)

Personnel:
Executive Director: Dawn M. Shiley CAE, MAM
Management Counsel: Harry W. Buzzerd Jr., CAE, Jr. CAE
    E-Mail: hbuzzerd@avem.org
Assistant Treasurer: Clay D. Tyeryar CAE, MAM
    E-Mail: ctyeryar@avem.org
Membership Assistant and Database Coordinator: Debbie Vincent
    E-Mail: avemmemsvcs@avem.org

Historical Note:
AVEM's mission is to promote member interests and provides services to enhance membership value and understanding of the global market. Members must be vacuum equipment manufacturers or persons, firms or corporations that engage in business in the vacuum equipment industry. Membership: $450 (Associate); $900-3,000 (Regular).

Publications:
AVEM newsletter; quarterly
Membership Directory; on-line

Association of Vascular and Interventional Radiographers *(1988)*
12100 Sunset Hills Rd.
Suite 130
Reston, VA 20190-3221
Tel: (703) 234-4055 *Fax:* (703) 435-4390
E-Mail: info@avir.org
Website: avir.org
Members: 110 individuals
Staff: 3
Annual Budget: $100-250,000
Tax: 501(c)(6)

Personnel:
President: Tony Walton RT
Executive Director: Carol Wynne
Secretary and Treasurer: Robert M. Sheridan

Historical Note:
AVIR is made up of interventional technologists, radiology nurses, cardiovascular technologists, radiology physician assistants, vendor representatives and other associated

professionals. Membership: $75 (Active); $65 (Clinical and Corporate Associate); $45 (Student); $85 (International).

Meetings/Conferences: Annual
2013 - New Orleans, LA/April 13 - 18

Publications:
Memberhsip Directory; on-line
Newsletter; quarterly

Association of Veterinary Biologics Companies

6849 Old Dominion Dr.
Suite 225
McLean, VA 22101
Tel: (703) 506-1260
Website: avbc.net
Members: 37 companies.
Staff: 2
Annual Budget: $100-250,000

Personnel:
Counsel: John Thomas
    E-Mail: jthomas@lltmlaw.com

Historical Note:
The Association of Veterinary Biologics Companies (AVBC) is an industry association which was organized in 1995 to support U.S. standards for licensing of veterinary biological products in domestic and international forums. Any person holding or applying for a USDA license or import permit for a veterinary biological product is eligible for voting membership in the association. Companies, consultants, and persons in related industries are eligible to become associate members. Membership: $100-6,300/year.

Meetings/Conferences: Annual

Publications:
AVBCurrent

Association of Vision Science Librarians *(1968)*

M.B. Ketchum Memorial Library
2575 Yorba Linda Blvd.
Fullerton, CA 92831
Website: avsl.org
Members: 150 individuals and 100 institutions
Staff: 3
Annual Budget: Under $10,000

Personnel:
Chair: D.J. Matthews
    E-Mail: djmatthews@scco.edu

Historical Note:
Members are librarians whose collections or services collections provide information services in the field of vision science. Has no paid officers or staff.

Meetings/Conferences: Annual

Publications:
Membership Directory; on-line

Membership List Available to Non-members

Association of Volleyball Professionals *(1983)*

6100 Center Dr.
Ninth Floor
Los Angeles, CA 90045
Tel: (310) 426-8000 *Fax:* (310) 426-8010
E-Mail: contact@avp.com
Website: avp.com
Members: 150 individuals
Staff: 15
Annual Budget: $5-10,000,000

Personnel:
Chief Executive Officer: Jason Hodell
Director, Tours: Matt Gage
Executive Vice President: Justin Kamm
Chief Marketing Officer: Paul Tedeschi

Historical Note:
Co-sponsors the AVP Tour, negotiates broadcast coverage of Tour events, and represents the Tour's players and sponsors. Membership: $10 (Individual); $200 (Gold).

Meetings/Conferences:
Conference Chair: Matt Gage

Association of Waldorf Schools of North America *(1968)*

2344 Nicollet Ave S.
Minneapolis, MN 55404
E-Mail: awsna@awsna.org
Website: whywaldorfworks.org
Members: 265 schools and teacher education institutes
Staff: 23
Annual Budget: $1-2,000,000

Personnel:
Leader, Association Administration: Frances Kane
    E-Mail: fkane@awsna.org
Contact,Renewal Subscriptions and Advertising: Anamyn Turowski
    E-Mail: subs_adsrenewal@awsna.org

Historical Note:
AWSNA provides leadership to schools by facilitating resources, networks and research as they strive towards excellence and build healthy school communities.

Meetings/Conferences: Annual
2013 - Austin, TX/June 24 - 27

Publications:
Renewal Magazine; semi-annually
Science Newsletters
Waldorf Journal Projects

Association of Water Technologies *(1985)*

9707 Key West Ave.
Suite 100
Rockville, MD 20850
Tel: (301) 740-1421 *Fax:* (301) 990-9771
TollFree: (800) 858-6683
E-Mail: awt@awt.org
Website: awt.org
Members: 500 water treatment companies and 2000 professionals
Staff: 9
Annual Budget: $1-2,000,000
Tax: 501(c)(6)

Personnel:
Executive Director: Heidi J. Zimmerman CAE
    E-Mail: hzimmerman@awt.org
Senior Graphic Designer: Jon Benjamin
    E-Mail: jbenjamin@mgmtsol.com
Manager, Marketing: Julie Hill
    E-Mail: jhill@mgmtsol.com
Vice President, Meetings: Grace L Jan CAE, CMP
    E-Mail: gjan@mgmtsol.com
Senior Manager, Membership Services: Angela Pike
    E-Mail: apike@awt.org
Accountant: Dawn Rosenfeld
    E-Mail: drosenfeld@mgmtsol.com
Vice President, Operations and Communications: Penny Willocks
    E-Mail: pwillocks@mgmtsol.com

Historical Note:
AWT seeks to provide small to medium-sized independent commercial water treatment companies with technical education, industry communication, access to information, group purchasing discounts, legislative affairs, and sound management techniques. Membership: $775 (Associate); $510 (Consultants/Manufacturers Representatives/Full Member); $675 (Combined Full).

Continuing Education:
Enrollment: 30
Certification Designation/s: CWT

Meetings/Conferences: Annual
Conference Chair: Grace L Jan CAE, CMP
2013 - Uncasville, CT (Mohegan Sun)/Oct. 30 - Nov. 2
2014 - Ft. Worth, TX (Fort Worth Convention Center)/ Oct. 29 - Nov. 1
2015 - Nashville, TN (Omni Nashville Hotel and Music Center)/Sept. 9 - 12
2016 - San Diego, CA (Omni San Diego Hotel)/Sept. 7 - 10

Publications:
AWT Gram; monthly
The Analyst; quarterly

Membership List Available to Non-members

The Association of Women in International Trade

204 E. St. NE
Washington, DC 20002
Tel: (202) 293-2948 *Fax:* (202) 547-6348
E-Mail: info@wiit.org
Website: wiit.org
Members: 15 Companies
Staff: 6
Annual Budget: $50-100,000

Personnel:
President: Phyllis Derrick
Secretary: Peggy Clarke
Vice President, Programs: Parva Fattahi
Vice President, Communications: Jennifer Meek
Treasurer: Hoang-Tram Tran
Vice President, Professional Development: Nancy Travis

Historical Note:
WIIT's mission is to enhance the careers of individuals in international trade by offering substantive programs pertaining to trade; providing professional development initiatives both in the public and private sectors; encouraging employment, particularly of women, in international trade; enhancing public awareness and promoting social activities among individuals employed in international trade. Membership: $75 (Individual); $45 (Students/Government); $300-900 (Corporate).

Meetings/Conferences:
Conference Chair: Parva Fattahi
Number of non-conference events/year: 5

Publications:
WIIT Newsletter; quarterly; adv.

Association of Women in the Metal Industries *(1981)*

19 Mantua Rd.
Mt. Royal, NJ 08061
Tel: (856) 423-3201 *Fax:* (856) 423-3420
E-Mail: awmi@talley.com
Website: awmi.org
Members:
900 individuals
19 corporations
Staff: 3
Annual Budget: $50-100,000

Personnel:
Executive Director: Haley J. Brust
    E-Mail: hbrust@talley.com
Director, Membership and Database contact: Monica Barnaby
    E-Mail: mbarnaby@talley.com
Administration Assistant: Linda Wright
    E-Mail: wright@talley.com

Historical Note:
AWMI is an international, professional organization dedicated to promoting and supporting the advancement of women in the metal industries. Members are women and men seeking to develop all aspects of their professional development and career advancement. Membership: $175 (Individual); $87.50 (Retiree/Sustaining Retiree).

Meetings/Conferences: Annual

Publications:
Member Directory; on-line
Metal Mail; quarterly; adv.

Association of Women Soil Scientists *(1981)*

P.O. Box 8264
Kirkland, WA 98034
Website: womeninsoils.org
Members: 200 individuals
Staff: 2
Annual Budget: Under $10,000
Tax: 501(c)(6)

Personnel:
Executive Chairperson: Wendy Greenberg
    E-Mail: wgreenberg@bemidjistate.edu

Historical Note:
AWSS' mission is to enhance communication among members, and to assist and encourage women seeking employment in the field. Membership: $20 (Professional); $10 (Student).

Meetings/Conferences: Annual

Publications:
AWSS Newsletter; quarterly
Membership Directory; on-line

Association of Women Surgeons *(1981)*

5204 Fairmount Ave.
Suite 208
Downers Grove, IL 60515
Tel: (630) 655-0392 *Fax:* (630) 493-0798
E-Mail: info@womensurgeons.org
Website: womensurgeons.org
Members: 1700 individuals
Staff: 4
Annual Budget: $100-250,000
Tax: 501(c)(6)

Personnel:
Executive Director: Katie Keel
    E-Mail: Katie@asihq.com
Executive Vice President: Judith K. Keel
    E-Mail: jkeel@asihq.com
Chief Financial Officer: Mary Moran
    E-Mail: mmoran@asihq.com

Contact, Database and Finance: Patti Perillo
  E-Mail: pperillo@asihq.com

Historical Note:
AWS's mission is to inspire, encourage, and enable women surgeons to realize their professional and personal goals. Membership: $225 (Regular); $40 (Resident); $165 (New Surgeon); $20 (Student); $5,000 (Lifetime); $200 (Associate); $500-750 (Institutional).

Meetings/Conferences: Annual
2013 - New York City, NY (New York Palace Hotel)/
  March 15 - 17

Publications:
Membership Directory; on-line

Association of Women's Business Centers (1998)
P.O. Box 1255
Camden, ME 04843
Tel: (207) 236-9753
E-Mail: info@awbc.biz
Website: awbc.biz
Staff: 2
Annual Budget: $50-100,000
Tax: 501(c)(3)

Personnel:
President and Chief Executive Officer: Ann Marie Almeida
Director, Membership Services: Susan Mpunga
  E-Mail: susan@awbc.biz

Historical Note:
The AWBC develops and strengthens a global network of women's business centers to advance the growth and success of women business owners.

Publications:
Membership Directory; on-line

Association of Women's Health, Obstetric and Neonatal Nurses (1969)
2000 L St. NW
Suite 740
Washington, DC 20036
Tel: (202) 261-2400 *Fax:* (202) 728-0575
TollFree: (800) 673-8499
E-Mail: customerservice@awhonn.org
Website: awhonn.org
Members: 23000 individuals
Staff: 6
Annual Budget: $10-25,000,000
Tax: 501(c)(3)

Personnel:
President: Rose L. Horton
Director, Publications: Carolyn Davis Cockey
  E-Mail: ccockey@awhonn.org
Ex-Officio Director: Kathleen A. Hale MS, RN
Chair, Annual Conventions: Kathleen Mahoney APN
Ex-Officio Director: Karen Peddicord
Director, Government and Media Affairs: Kerri C. Wade
  E-Mail: kwade@awhonn.org

Historical Note:
Established in 1969 within the Nurses Association of the American College of Obstetricians and Gynecologists, became an independent organization and assumed its current name in 1993. AWHONN's mission is to improve and promote the health of women and newborns and to strengthen the nursing profession through the delivery of advocacy, research, education and other professional and clinical resources to nurses and other health care professionals. Membership: $168 (Full); $144 (Associate); $192 (International); $84 (Retired/Student).

Continuing Education:
Certification Designation/s: ANCC, ICEA, NCC, ACNM, ICLA

Meetings/Conferences: Annual
2013 - Nashville, TN/June 15 - 19/11-25 exhibitors

Publications:
AWHONN News; semi-annually
AWHONN Vitals; monthly
Journal of Obstetric, Gynecologic and Neonatal
  Nursing; bi-monthly
Nursing for Women's Health; bi-monthly; adv.

Association of Woodworking and Furnishings Suppliers (1911)
500 Citadel Dr.
Suite 200
Commerce, CA 90040
Tel: (323) 838-9440 *Fax:* (323) 838-9443
TollFree: (800) 946-2937
E-Mail: info@awfs.org

Website: awfs.org
Members: 450 companies
Staff: 10
Annual Budget: $250-500,000
Tax: 501(c)(6)

Personnel:
Executive Vice President: Angelo Gangone CEM
  E-Mail: angelo@awfs.org
Contact, Fair Sales: Amy Bartz
  E-Mail: amy@awfs.org
Manager, Marketing and Membership Services: Jennifer Evans
  E-Mail: jennifer@awfs.org
Director, Education and Conferences: Nancy Fister
  E-Mail: nancy@awfs.org
Contact, Financial Services and Controller: Nancy Neely
  E-Mail: nkneely@awfs.org
Assistant Education Director: Adria Torrez
  E-Mail: adria@awfs.org
Director, Communications: Bruce Valentine
  E-Mail: bruce@awfs.org

Historical Note:
Originally a chapter of the California Furniture Manufacturers Association, it became independent as the Association of Western Furniture Suppliers in 1978. Adopted its present name in 1990 to reflect the geographic broadening of its membership and the importance of woodworking machinery suppliers to the industry. AWFS seeks to strengthen the value of the AWFS Fair for both exhibitors and attendees. Also seeks to strengthen and develop industry education. Membership: $200-1,000/year.

Meetings/Conferences:
Conference Chair: Nancy Fister
2013 - Las Vegas, NV (Las Vegas Convention Center)/
  July 24 - 27

Publications:
AWFS Member Newsletter; quarterly
E-Briefs
Membership Directory; on-line

Association of Writers and Writing Programs (1967)
Mail Stop 1E3, 4400 University Dr.
George Mason University
Fairfax, VA 22030-4444
Tel: (703) 993-4301 *Fax:* (703) 993-4302
E-Mail: awp@awpwriter.org
Website: awpwriter.org
Members: 13 colleges and 500 institutional members
Staff: 13
Annual Budget: $2-5,000,000
Tax: 501(c)(3)

Personnel:
Executive Director: David W. Fenza
Director, Publications: Supriya Bhatnagar
Manager, Advertising: Liz Gerber
Legal Council: Ronald Goldfarb
Director, Web Services and Systems Administrator: Kate McDevitt
Manager, Accounting: Roberto Perales
Director, Conferences: Christian Teresi
Director, Membership Services: Diane Zinna

Historical Note:
Formerly (2004) Associated Writing Programs. An organization of writers, teachers, students and educational institutions concerned with creative and professional writing. AWP strives to foster literary talent and achievement, to advance the art of writing as essential to a good education, and to serve the makers, teachers, students, and readers of contemporary writing. Membership: $65-110 (Individual); $40 (Students); $460-960 (Institution); $275 (Affiliate); $200 (Writer's Conference/Center).

Meetings/Conferences: Annual
Conference Chair: Christian Teresi
2013 - Boston, MA (Sheraton Boston Hotel)/March 6 -
  9/9000 attendees
2014 - Seattle, WA (Sheraton Seattle Hotel)/Feb. 26 -
  March 1/9000 attendees
2015 - Minneapolis, MN (Hilton Minneapolis)/April 8 -
  11/9000 attendees
2016 - Los Angeles, CA (JW Marriott Los Angeles L.A.
  LIVE)/March 30 - April 2/9000 attendees
2017 - Washington, DC (Washington Convention
  Center and Washington Marriott Marquis)/Feb. 8 -
  11

Publications:

AWP Newsletter
The Writer's Chronicle; adv.

Association of YMCA Professionals (1871)
Stitzer YMCA Center Second Floor
Springfield College, 263 Alden St.
Springfield, MA 01109
Tel: (413) 748-3884 *Fax:* (413) 748-3872
Website: ayponline.org
Members: 5500 individuals
Staff: 3
Annual Budget: $500-1,000,000
Tax: 501(c)(6)

Personnel:
National Executive Director and Chief Executive Officer:
  Donna French Dunn CAE
  E-Mail: donna@ayponline.org
Coordinator, Chapter and Member Programs: Lauren J.
  Anderson
  E-Mail: lauren@ayponline.org
Specialist, Communications and Digital Media: Lindsey
  Lerit
  E-Mail: lindsey@ayponline.org

Historical Note:
Formerly (1969) Association of Professional Directors of YMCAs in the United States. Assumed its current name in 2004. AYP strives to connect, inspire and advance YMCA leaders. All YMCA employees who are committed to their professional development are eligible for membership. Membership: $135/year.

Publications:
AYP eNewsletter; monthly; adv.
AYP Magazine; bi-monthly; adv.
Membership Directory; on-line

Association of Zoos and Aquariums (1924)
8403 Colesville Rd.
Suite 710
Silver Spring, MD 20910-3314
Tel: (301) 562-0777 *Fax:* (301) 562-0888
E-Mail: membership@aza.org
Website: aza.org
Members: 6,000 zoo and aquarium professionals,
  organizations and suppliers
Staff: 32
Annual Budget: $5-10,000,000
Tax: 501(c)(3)

Personnel:
President and Chief Executive Officer: Jim Maddy
Executive Director: Kristin L. Vehrs
Senior Vice President, Conservation and Education: Dr.
  Paul Boyle PhD
Senior Vice President, External Affairs: Steven Feldman
  E-Mail: sfeldman@aza.org
Vice President, Conferences and Membership: Melissa
  Howerton
Vice President, Accreditation Programs: Denny L. Lewis
Coordinator, Publications: Tim Lewthwaite MA
  E-Mail: tlewthwaite@aza.org
*Senior Vice President, Marketing, Organizational Planning
  and Operations:* Jill Nicoll
  E-Mail: jnicoll@aza.org
Vice President, Government Affairs: Steve Olson MS
  E-Mail: solson@aza.org
Membership and Database Services Coordinator: Barb
  Skewes
Vice President, Finance: Phil Wagner

Historical Note:
Formerly a branch of the American Institute of Park Executives and the National Recreation and Park Association, became an independent organization in 1971 as American Association of Zoological Parks and Aquariums; became the American Zoo and Aquarium Association in 1994; assumed its current name in 2006. AZA is dedicated to the advancement of accredited zoos and aquariums in the areas of animal care, wildlife conservation, education and science. Membership: $70-195 (Associate/Professional Affiliate/Professional Fellow); $435 (Conservation Partner Member); $1,500 (Commercial Member); $25-100 (Individual Membership Upgrade).

Continuing Education:
Certification Designation/s: CE

Meetings/Conferences:
Conference Chair: Melissa Howerton
2013 - Charleston, SC/April 7 - 12/11-25 exhibitors
2013 - Kansas City, MO/Sept. 7 - 12
2013 - Kansas City, MO/Sept. 7 - 12
2014 - Orlando, FL/Sept. 12 - 17

2015 - Salt Lake City, UT/Sept. 17 - 21
2016 - San Diego, CA/Sept. 6 - 11
Number of non-conference events/year: 1

Publications:
Connect Magazine; monthly; adv.
Membership Directory; annually; adv.

Association on American Indian Affairs (1922)
966 Hungerford Dr.
Suite 12-B
Rockville, MD 20850
Tel: (240) 314-7155 *Fax:* (240) 314-7159
E-Mail: general.aaia@indian-affairs.org
Website: indian-affairs.org
Staff: 16
Annual Budget: $500-1,000,000
Tax: 501(c)(3)

Personnel:
Executive Director: Jack F. Trope
Contact, Bookkeeper: Mike Jones
Legal Fellow: Honor Keeler
Executive Assistant and Director, Scholarship Programs:
    Lisa Wyzlic

Historical Note:
*Formerly The Eastern Association on Indian Affairs was
started in New York to assist a group of Pueblo people
who were fighting efforts to dismantle their pueblos. In
the 1920's this organization merged with a like-minded
entity, and again merged with a third entity in 1937.
In 1946, the name was changed to the Association on
American Indian Affairs. AAIA's mission is to promote
the welfare of American Indians and Alaska Natives by
supporting efforts to: sustain and perpetuate their cultures
and languages; improve their health, education, and
economic and community development.*

Publications:
AAIA Newsletter; bi-annually
Indian Affairs; bi-annually

Association on Higher Education and Disability (1977)
107 Commerce Center Dr.
Suite 204
Huntersville, NC 28078
Tel: (704) 947-7779 *Fax:* (704) 948-7779
E-Mail: ahead@ahead.org
Website: ahead.org
Members: 2500 individuals
Staff: 9
Annual Budget: $1-2,000,000
Tax: 501(c)(3)

Personnel:
Executive Director: Stephan J. Smith
    E-Mail: stephan@ahead.org
Director, Professional Development: Richard Allegra
    E-Mail: Richard@ahead.org
Manager, Operations: Tri Do
    E-Mail: Tri@ahead.org
Manager, Membership Services: Robert Plienis
    E-Mail: robert@ahead.org
Technical Advisor: Rhonda Rapp
    E-Mail: Rapp@universe.uiwtx.edu
Manager, Communications: Valerie Spears
    E-Mail: valerie@ahead.org

Historical Note:
*AHEAD is the professional association committed to full
participation of persons with disabilities in postsecondary
education. AHEAD members represent a diverse network
of professionals who actively address disability issues.
Membership: $245 (Individual); $295-895 (Institutional);
$95 (Pre-professional/Emeritus); $395-695 (Partner);
$175 (AdditionalProfessional /Associate).*

Meetings/Conferences: Annual
Conference Chair: Tri Do
2013 - Baltimore, MD (Hilton Baltimore)/July 8 - 13
2014 - Sacramento, CA/July 14 - 19

Publications:
ALERT Newsletter; bi-monthly
Journal of Postsecondary Education and Disability; on-
line
Membership Directory; on-line

Membership List Available to Non-members

The Association to Advance Collegiate Schools of Business (1916)
777 S. Harbour Island Blvd.
Suite 750

Tampa, FL 33602-5730
Tel: (813) 769-6500 *Fax:* (813) 769-6559
E-Mail: myAACSB@aacsb.edu
Website: aacsb.edu
Members: 1200 institutions
Staff: 58
Annual Budget: $10-25,000,000
Tax: 501(c)(3)

Personnel:
President and Chief Executive Officer: John J. Fernandes
coordinator, accreditation and member services: Ginger
    Ausloos
Senior Vice President and Chief Financial Officer: Neil
    Bosland
    E-Mail: neil@aacsb.edu
Secretary and Treasurer: W. Randy Boxx
Director, Business Development: Annette DeLisle
    E-Mail: annette@aacsb.edu
Senior Manager, Seminars: Robyn Hall
    E-Mail: robyn@aacsb.edu
Coordinator, Event Services: Courtney Haygood
    E-Mail: courtney@aacsb.edu
Executive Vice President and Chief Operating Officer:
    Daniel R. LeClair
    E-Mail: dan@aacsb.edu
Vice President, Human Resources: Jennifer McIntosh
    E-Mail: jennifer@aacsb.edu
Senior Manager, Information Technology: Tony Peral
    E-Mail: tperal@aacsb.edu
Director, Conference and Event Services: Kelly Warhola
    E-Mail: kelly@aacsb.edu
Coordinator, Marketing Communications: Brandy Whited
    E-Mail: brandy@aacsb.edu

Historical Note:
*AACSB's mission is to advance quality management
education worldwide through accreditation and thought
leadership. Membership: $2550 (Educational Institutions);
$2500-5000 (Partners-Non-educational members);
$10000 (Sustaining Member); $1000 (Public Sector/Not-
for-profit Organizations).*

Continuing Education:
Enrollment: 570
Certification Designation/s: BSAPA

Meetings/Conferences: Annual
Conference Chair: Courtney Haygood
2013 - Chicago, IL/April 7 - 9
Number of non-conference events/year: 4

Publications:
AACSB eNewsline; bi-monthly; adv.
BizEd Magazine; bi-monthly; adv.

ASTM International (1898)
100 Barr Harbor Dr.
P.O. Box C700
W. Conshohocken, PA 19428-2959
Tel: (610) 832-9500 *Fax:* (610) 832-9555
Website: astm.org
Members: 30000 individuals
Staff: 203
Annual Budget: $50-100,000,000

Personnel:
President: James A. Thomas
    E-Mail: jthomas@astm.org
Editor-in-Chief: Maryann Gorman
    E-Mail: mgorman@astm.org
*Vice President, Information Technology, Development and
    Applications:* Philip Lively
    E-Mail: plively@astm.org
Assistant Vice President, Business Development: Brian
    Meincke
    E-Mail: bmeincke@astm.org
Director, Technical and Professional Training: Scott
    Murphy
    E-Mail: smurphy@astm.org
Vice President, Publications and Marketing: John Pace
    E-Mail: jpace@astm.org
Director, Public Policy and International Trade: Anthony
    Quinn
    E-Mail: aquinn@astm.org
Director, Corporate Communications: Barbara Schindler
    E-Mail: bschindl@astm.org
Director, Meetings: Betty Schultz
    E-Mail: bschultz@astm.org
Manager, Member Promotion and Academic Outreach:
    Ileane Smith
    E-Mail: ismith@astm.org

Historical Note:

*ASTM International, formerly known as the American
Society for Testing and Materials (ASTM), is a globally
recognized leader in the development and delivery of
international voluntary consensus standards. ASTM's
mission is promote public health and safety, support the
protection and sustainability of the environment, and the
overall quality of life. Membership: $75 (Participating);
$400 (Organizational).*

Meetings/Conferences: Annual
Conference Chair: Betty Schultz
Number of non-conference events/year: 2

Publications:
ASTM International eNews; monthly
Membership Directory; on-line
Standardization News; bi-monthly

Membership List Available to Non-members

At-Sea Processors Association (1985)
4039 21st West
Suite 400
Seattle, WA 98199
Tel: (206) 285-5139 *Fax:* (206) 285-1841
E-Mail: apa@atsea.org
Website: atsea.org
Members: 50 participating companies
Staff: 6
Annual Budget: $1-2,000,000
Tax: 501(c)(6)

Personnel:
Executive Director: Stephanie Madsen
    E-Mail: smadsen@atsea.org
General Counsel: Paul MacGregor
    E-Mail: pmacgregor@mundtmac.com
Coordinator, Programs: Melinda Madsen Schmitt
    E-Mail: melinda@atsea.org

Historical Note:
*APA represents firms operating at-sea processing fleets
by providing regulatory and legislative advocacy. It also
strives to find ways to minimize fishing impacts on the
environment, forming cooperatives and thus using fewer
vessels and reduce incidental catches. Membership:
$500-2,000/year (Associate, based on an annual level of
economic interaction with APA members).*

Publications:
Membership Directory; annually

Atlantic Independent Union
712 Heritage Rd.
Cinnaminson, NJ 08077
Tel: (856) 303-0776
Staff: 1
Annual Budget: $100-250,000
Tax: 501(c)(5)

Personnel:
President: John W. Kerr

Atlantic intra Coastal Waterway Association (1998)
FiveA Market
Beaufort, SC 29906
Website: atlintracoastal.org
Staff: 2

Personnel:
Executive Director: Brad Pickel
    E-Mail: bpickel@seahavenconsulting.com

Historical Note:
*AIWA represents the interests of commercial and
recreational users of the waterway. It Continue to promote,
market and communicate with all organizations and
communities about the critical importance of the waterway.*

Meetings/Conferences: Annual

Atlantic Seaboard Wine Association (1973)
5222 Claridge Court
Fairfax, VA 22032-2760
Tel: (703) 323-6873 *Fax:* (703) 323-1271
E-Mail: fairfax@earthlink.net
Website: vwga.org
Members: 350 individuals
Staff: 3
Annual Budget: $50-100,000

Personnel:
President: Carl Brandhorst
    E-Mail: fairfax@earthlink.net

Historical Note:
*Formerly Vinifera Wine Growers Association, ASWA works
to advance general public wine education and appreciation.*

ASWA's mission is to advocate consumer public wine enjoyment and responsible moderate consumption as part of a healthy life style. Membership: $45/year.

ATM Industry Association *(1997)*
6905 W. Strabane Trail
Sioux Falls, SD 57106
Website: atmia.com
Members: 3500 members
Staff: 6
Annual Budget: $2-5,000,000
Tax: 501(c)(6)

Personnel:
Chief Executive Officer: Mike Lee
   E-Mail: mike@atmia.com
Executive Director: David Tente
   E-Mail: david.tente@atmia.com
Director, Conferences and Sponsorships: Dana Benson
   E-Mail: dana@atmiaconferences.com
Manager, Website Content and Social Media: Amber Howell
   E-Mail: amber@atmiaconferences.com
Global Director, Finance and Membership Services: Sharon Lane
   E-Mail: sharon@atmia.com

Historical Note:
Association representing ATM owners and operators. ATMIA's mission is to promote ATM convenience, growth and usage worldwide, protect the ATM industry's assets, interests, good name and public trust; and provide education, best practices, political voice and networking opportunities for member organizations.

Meetings/Conferences:
Conference Chair: Dana Benson
2013 - Scottsdale, AZ (Golf Club Scottsdale)/Feb. 19 - 21

Publications:
ATMIA Global Newsletter; monthly
Member Directory; on-line

ATP Tour, Inc. *(1972)*
201 ATP Tour Blvd.
Ponte Vedra Beach, FL 32082
Tel: (904) 285-8000 *Fax:* (904) 285-5966
TollFree: (800) 527-4811
Website: atpworldtour.com
Members: 800 individuals
Staff: 95
Annual Budget: $50-100,000,000
Tax: 501(c)(6)

Personnel:
Chief Executive Officer, and Chief Legal and Media Officer: Mark Young
Chief Operating Officer: Flip Galloway
Executive Vice President, Marketing and Communications: Kate Gordon

Historical Note:
Formerly Association of Tennis Professionals, assumed its current name in 1990. The goal of the association is to grow the sport and help players earn a good living. Membership: $300 (Division II Player); $1000 (Division I Player).

Publications:
Deuce Magazine; adv.

Attention Deficit Disorder Association
PO Box 7557
Wilmington, DE 19803
Tel: (800) 939-1019
TollFree: (800) 939-1019
E-Mail: info@add.org
Website: add.org
Staff: 2
Annual Budget: $100-250,000
Tax: 501(c)(3)

Personnel:
President: Evelyn Polk Green Ed, MS
Treasurer: Janet Kramer MD

Historical Note:
ADDA is the adult ADHD organization that provides information, resources and networking opportunities to help adults with Attention Deficit/Hyperactivity Disorder (AD/HD) lead better lives. Also provides hope, empowerment and connections worldwide by bringing together science and the human experience for both adults with AD/HD and professionals who serve them. Membership: $45 (Individual); $55 (Family); $150 (Professional).

Meetings/Conferences: Annual

Publications:
ADDA E-News; monthly; adv.
Membership Directory; on-line

Membership List Available to Non-members

Attorneys' Liability Assurance Society Inc. *(1987)*
311 S. Wacker Dr.
Suite 5700
Chicago, IL 60606-6629
Tel: (312) 697-6900 *Fax:* (312) 697-6901
E-Mail: info@alas.com
Website: alas.com
Members: 58000 lawyers and 232 firms
Staff: 36

Personnel:
Vice Chairman, President and Chief Executive Officer: Mark D. Nozette
Chief Administrative Officer: Kristine Aubin
Senior Vice President, Membership Services: Mark E. Gralen
Manager, Corporate Communications: Karen A. Ledger
Vice President and Director, Finance and Treasurer: David G. Ross
Chief Information Officer: Eric K. Smith
Senior Vice President, Claims and Administration: Lawrence E. Zabinski

Historical Note:
The ALAS companies were founded to provide quality law firms with a stable source of insurance coverage and a level of service that they could not find in the commercial marketplace.

Meetings/Conferences: Annual
2013 - Southampton, Bermuda (Fairmont Southampton)/June 19 - 21
2014 - Montreal, QC (Le Centre Sheraton Montreal Hotel)/June 18 - 20
2015 - Banff, AB (Fairmont Banff Springs Resort)/June 17 - 19

Publications:
E-Newsletter; on-line
Loss Prevention Journals

Audio Engineering Society *(1948)*
60 E. 42nd St.
Room 2520
New York, NY 10165-2520
Tel: (212) 661-8528 *Fax:* (212) 682-0477
TollFree: (800) 541-7299
E-Mail: hq@aes.org
Website: aes.org
Members: 14,000 members
Staff: 11
Annual Budget: $2-5,000,000

Personnel:
Executive Director: Bob Moses
Deputy Director: Roger K. Furness
   E-Mail: hq@aes.org
Treasurer, Marketing: Garry Margolis
Director, Convention Management: Chris Plunkett
   E-Mail: cwp@aes.org

Historical Note:
AES's mission is to unite persons performing professional services in the audio engineering field and its allied arts. AES is the society dealing with audio technology. Members are professionals throughout the world active in audio engineering or acoustics. Membership: $130 (Individual); $80 (Student).

Meetings/Conferences: Annual
Conference Chair: Chris Plunkett
2013 - London, United Kingdom/Feb. 6 - 8
2013 - Rome, Italy (Fontana di Trevi Conference Centre)/May 4 - 7
2013 - Murfreesboro, TN (Middle Tennessee State University)/July 25 - 27

Publications:
AES E-News Member Newsletter
AES Journal

Membership List Available to Non-members

Audio Publishers Association *(1987)*
191 Clarksville Rd.
Princeton, NJ 08550
Tel: (609) 799-6327 *Fax:* (609) 799-7032
E-Mail: info@audiopub.org
Website: audiopub.org
Members: 300 companies

Staff: 7
Annual Budget: $250-500,000
Tax: 501(c)(6)

Personnel:
Executive Director: Jennifer Thayer
   E-Mail: jthayer@audiopub.org
Executive Advisor: Jeffrey E. Barnhart
Association Coordinator: Liz Bertolotti
   E-Mail: ebertolotti@audiopub.org
Financial Director: Angie Cino
Manager, Public Relations: Kaitlin Friedmann
   E-Mail: kfriedmann@audiopub.org
Meetings Planner: Diane Galante
   E-Mail: dgalante@audiopub.org

Historical Note:
APA's mission is advocate awareness of the audiobook industry, gather and disseminate industry statistics, encourage high production standards, and represent the interests of audiobook publishers. Membership: $275-6,600 (Regular, depends on gross sales); $275-550 (Affiliate/Retailer); $275-1,650 (Affiliate/Supplier); $220 (Individual Industry Professional); $55 (Librarian/Industry Professional); $110 (Voice Talent/Industry Professional); $275 (Media).

Meetings/Conferences: Annual
Conference Chair: Diane Galante
2013 - New York City, NY (The Jacob K. Javits Convention Center)/May 29

Publications:
APA E-Newsletter; monthly

Membership List Available to Non-members

Audit Bureau of Circulations *(1914)*
48 W. Seegers Rd.
Arlington Heights, IL 60005-3913
Tel: (224) 366-6939 *Fax:* (224) 366-6949
Website: accessabc.com
Members: 4500 members
Staff: 320
Annual Budget: $10-25,000,000
Tax: 501(c)(6)

Personnel:
President and Managing Director: Michael J. Lavery
   E-Mail: michael.lavery@accessabc.com
Senior Vice President, Finance and Administration: Paul J. Fajnor
   E-Mail: paul.fajnor@accessabc.com
Vice President, Human Resources: Laura Ferraris
   E-Mail: laura.ferraris@accessabc.com
Executive Vice President, Strategic Planning, Communications: Neal Lulofs
   E-Mail: neal.lulofs@accessabc.com
Contact, Membership Services: Kristina Meinig
   E-Mail: kristina.meinig@accessabc.com
Senior Vice President, Publisher and Membership Services: Teresa Perry
   E-Mail: teresa.perry@accessabc.com
Vice President, Information Technology: Kaydene Stachelski
   E-Mail: kaydene.stachelski@accessabc.com
Vice President, Meetings: Susan Thomas
   E-Mail: susan.thomas@accessabc.com
Senior Vice President, Marketing and Sales: Mark Wachowicz
   E-Mail: mark.wachowicz@accessabc.com

Historical Note:
ABC's mission is to encourage advertisers, advertising agencies and the media they use, for the independent verification.

Meetings/Conferences: Annual
Conference Chair: Susan Thomas
Number of non-conference events/year: 4

Publications:
ABC Newsletter; on-line
Membership Directory; on-line

Membership List Available to Non-members

Authors Guild *(1912)*
31 E. 32nd St.
Seventh Floor
New York, NY 10016
Tel: (212) 563-5904 *Fax:* (212) 564-5363
E-Mail: staff@authorsguild.org
Website: authorsguild.org
Members: 8000 individuals
Staff: 18

Annual Budget: $2-5,000,000

Personnel:
Executive Director: Paul Aiken
General Counsel: Jan F. Constantine
Director, Legal Services: Anita Fore

Historical Note:
Founded as Authors League of America. Purpose is to advocate for writer's interests in effective copyright protection, fair contracts and free expression since it was founded as the Authors League of America. It provides legal assistance and a broad range of web services to its members. Membership: $90/year (Individual).

Publications:
Membership Directory; on-line
The Authors Guild Bulletin; quarterly

Auto Suppliers Benchmarking Association *(1997)*
4606 FM 1960 West
Suite 250
Houston, TX 77069
Tel: (281) 440-5044 *Fax:* (281) 440-6677
E-Mail: info@asbabenchmarking.com
Website: asbabenchmarking.com
Members: 1800 individuals
Staff: 14
Annual Budget: $1-2,000,000

Personnel:
Second Vice President and Consultant: Paul Claymore

Historical Note:
An autonomous division of The Benchmarking Network. Goal of ASBA is to provide useful benchmarking data to automotive suppliers in support of their quality program. Basic membership is available to employees of corporations whose main line of business is the manufacturing of parts, components or subassemblies for the automotive industry. No membership fee at this time, but participation in association activities is charged separately.

Meetings/Conferences:
Number of non-conference events/year: 1

Publications:
E-Benchmarking Newsletter; monthly

Automated Imaging Association *(1984)*
900 Victors Way
Suite 140
Ann Arbor, MI 48108
Tel: (734) 994-6088 *Fax:* (734) 994-3338
E-Mail: info@machinevisiononline.org
Website: visiononline.org
Members: 330 companies
Staff: 10
Annual Budget: $1-2,000,000

Personnel:
President: Jeffrey Burnstein
    E-Mail: jburnstein@robotics.org
Director, Standards Development: Jeff Fryman
    E-Mail: jfryman@robotics.org
Vice President: Dana Whalls
    E-Mail: dwhalls@robotics.org

Historical Note:
Established and managed by the Automation Technologies Council and formerly (1989) known as the Automated Vision Association, AIA seeks to promote the use of image capture and analysis technology. Members are imaging manufacturers, users or suppliers of related equipment and services for the machine vision industry. Membership: $800 (Supplier); $600 (User); $750 (System Integrator); $350 (Affiliate).

Continuing Education:
Certification Designation/s: CVP

Meetings/Conferences:
2013 - Orlando, FL (Orlando World Marriott Center)/ Feb. 20 - 22
Number of non-conference events/year: 2

Publications:
Machine Vision Industry Directory; annually; adv.
MVO e-News; bi-monthly; adv.

Automatic Fire Alarm Association *(1953)*
14 Sammy McGhee Blvd., P.O. Box 1569
Suite 103
Jasper, GA 30143
Tel: (678) 454-3473 *Fax:* (678) 454-3474
E-Mail: fire-alarm@afaa.org
Website: afaa.org
Members: 900 companies and individuals
Staff: 4

Annual Budget: $500-1,000,000
Tax: 501(c)(6)

Personnel:
President and Executive Director: Thomas P. Hammerberg CFSP, SET
    E-Mail: TomHammerberg@afaa.org
Director, Marketing and Communications: Dave Ashley
    E-Mail: DaveAshley@afaa.org
Director, Training: Michael B. Baker SET
    E-Mail: mikebaker@afaa.org
Office Manager: Jeanne Hammerberg
    E-Mail: JeanneHammerberg@afaa.org

Historical Note:
AFAA's mission is to be the foremost industry advocate organization committed to improving the quality, reliability and value of Fire and Life-Safety Systems. Members are manufacturers and installers of, and others interested in, fire alarm and detection equipment. Membership: $2,000-10,000 (Manufacturer); $200-1,000 (Corporate); $100 (Individuals).

Continuing Education:
Certification Designation/s: NICET

Meetings/Conferences: Annual
2013 - Ft. Myers, FL (Sanibel Harbour Marriott Resort and Spa)/May 1 - 4

Publications:
e-bulletin; monthly

Automatic Guided Vehicle Systems *(1979)*
8720 Red Oak Blvd., Suite 201
C/O Material Handling Industry Of America
Charlotte, NC 28217-3992
Tel: (704) 676-1190 *Fax:* (704) 676-1199
Website: mhia.org/industrygroups/agvs
Members: 14 companies
Staff: 2
Annual Budget: $25-50,000

Personnel:
Managing Executive: Gary Forger

Historical Note:
A product section of the Material Handling Industry of America. AGVS members are the Industry's leading suppliers of automatic guided vehicle systems. Mission is to promote the market growth and effective use of automatic guided vehicle systems (AGVS) in manufacturing, warehousing, distribution and other key markets.

Automatic Transmission Rebuilders Association *(1954)*
2400 Latigo Ave.
Oxnard, CA 93030
Tel: (805) 604-2000 *Fax:* (805) 604-2003
TollFree: (866) 464-2872
Website: atra.com
Members: 2000 individuals
Staff: 26
Annual Budget: $2-5,000,000

Personnel:
Chief Executive Officer: Dennis Madden
    E-Mail: dmadden@atra.com
Managing Editor: Rodger Bland
    E-Mail: rbland@atra.com
Director, Membership Services and Information Technology: Kelly Hilmer
    E-Mail: khilmer@atra.com
Manager, Seminars and Conventions: Vanessa Velasquez
    E-Mail: vvelasquez@atra.com
Technical Director: Lance Wiggins
    E-Mail: lwiggins@atra.com

Historical Note:
ATRA strives to maintain better standards in the automatic transmission repair industry for work quality, customers service and business success. Members are automatic transmission repair professionals. Membership: $50-9,600/year.

Meetings/Conferences: Annual
Conference Chair: Vanessa Velasquez
Number of non-conference events/year: 5

Publications:
GEARS Magazine; adv.

Membership List Available to Non-members

Automation Alley *(1999)*
2675 Bellingham Dr.
Troy, MI 48083-2044
Tel: (248) 457-3200 *Fax:* (248) 457-3210
TollFree: (800) 427-5100

E-Mail: info@automationalley.com
Website: automationalley.com
Members: 1000 Members
Staff: 13
Annual Budget: $5-10,000,000
Tax: 501(c)(6)

Personnel:
Executive Director: Ken Rogers
    E-Mail: rogersk@automationalley.com
Manager, Member Relations: Cheryl Buscemi
    E-Mail: buscemic@automationalley.com
Manager, Events: Jennifer Chinn
    E-Mail: chinnj@automationalley.com
Director, Finance: Maryann Daddow
    E-Mail: daddowm@automationalley.com
Director, Public Affairs: Kelly Kozlowski
    E-Mail: kozlowskik@automationalley.com
Administrative Assistant: Kim Krutsch
    E-Mail: krutschk@automationalley.com
Director, Member Services and Marketing: Andrea Oleszczak
    E-Mail: oleszczaka@automationalley.com
Administrator, Communications: Glen Sandberg
    E-Mail: sandbergg@automationalley.com
Accountant and Manager, Human Resources: John Shirk
    E-Mail: shirkj@automationalley.com

Historical Note:
Michigan's technology business association. Automation Alley is a non-profit organization that drives growth and economic development through a collaborative culture that focuses on workforce and business development initiatives.

Meetings/Conferences: Annual
Conference Chair: Cheryl Buscemi
Number of non-conference events/year: 1

Publications:
Automation Alley Newsletter
EntrepreNEWS
Member Directory; on-line
X-OLOGY Magazine; quarterly; adv.

Automotive Aftermarket Industry Association *(1999)*
7101 Wisconsin Ave.
Suite 1300
Bethesda, MD 20814-3415
Tel: (301) 654-6664 *Fax:* (301) 654-3299
E-Mail: aaia@aftermarket.org
Website: aftermarket.org
Members: 23000 companies
Staff: 37
Annual Budget: $10-25,000,000
Tax: 501(c)(6)

Personnel:
President and Chief Executive Officer: Kathleen Schmatz
    E-Mail: kathleen.schmatz@aftermarket.org
Senior Vice President, Meetings and Events: Michael E. Barratt CMP
    E-Mail: michael.barratt@aftermarket.org
Senior Director, Education: Susan Kalish
    E-Mail: sue.kalish@aftermarket.org
Chief Information Officer: Scott Luckett AAP
    E-Mail: scott.luckett@aftermarket.org
Chief Financial and Operations Officer: Susan Medick CAE, CPA
    E-Mail: susan.medick@aftermarket.org
Senior Director, Member Relations: Larry Northup
    E-Mail: larry.northup@aftermarket.org
Managing Director, Communications: Jennifer Ortiz AAP
    E-Mail: jennifer.ortiz@aftermarket.org
Office Manager: Christine Reilly
    E-Mail: christine.reilly@aftermarket.org
Senior Vice President, Marketing and Member Relations: Richard White
    E-Mail: rich.white@aftermarket.org
Senior Vice President, Regulatory and Government Affairs: Sheryl Wilkerson
    E-Mail: sheryl.wilkerson@aftermarket.org

Historical Note:
Founded as the Automotive Parts and Accessories Association, assumed its current name in 1999 and absorbed Automotive Wholesale Distributors Association in 2004. AAIA encompasses all products and services purchased for light and heavy duty vehicles after the original sale including replacement parts, accessories, lubricants, appearance products, service repairs as well as the tools and equipment necessary to make the repair. Members are manufacturers, distributors, retailers and manufacturers' representatives who market

automotive replacement parts and accessories and services. Membership: $400-8,500/year.

Meetings/Conferences: Annual
Conference Chair: Michael E. Barratt CMP
2013 - Bonita Springs, FL (Hyatt Regency Coconut Point Resort and Spa)/May 1 - 3
2013 - Phoenix, AZ (Embassy Suites Phoenix-Scottsdale)/May 14 - 16
2013 - Rosemont, IL (Hyatt Regency O'Hare)/May 21 - 22
2013 - San Francisco, CA/June 1 - 5
2013 - Dallas, TX (Omni Hotel)/Sept. 9 - 11
2013 - Las Vegas, NV (Sands Expo and Convention Center)/Nov. 5 - 7
2013 - Miami, FL/Dec. 7 - 11
2014 - Huntington Beach, CA (Hyatt Regency Huntington Beach Resort and Spa)/April 23 - 25
2014 - Boston, MA (Westin Boston Waterfront)/Sept. 3 - 5
2014 - San Diego, CA (Hyatt Regency Mission Bay Spa and Marina-San Diego)/Sept. 9 - 13
2014 - Las Vegas, NV (The Venetian)/Nov. 2 - 4
2014 - Las Vegas, NV (Sands Expo Center)/Nov. 4 - 6
Number of non-conference events/year: 26

Publications:
AAIA/BB&T Weekly Market Intelligence Update; weekly
Aftermarket Insider; bi-monthly
Capital Report newsletter.; weekly
Industry Indicators Report; monthly
Membership Directory; on-line
Smartbrief Newsletter; bi-weekly
The Digital Aftermarket Factbook
The Knowledge Center; on-line

Automotive Body Parts Association *(1980)*
1510 Eldridge Pkwy.
Suite 110-168
Houston, TX 77077
Tel: (281) 531-0809 *Fax:* (281) 531-9411
TollFree: (800) 323-5832
E-Mail: info@autobpa.com
Website: autobpa.com
Members: 170 companies
Staff: 2
Annual Budget: $500-1,000,000
Tax: 501(c)(6)

Personnel:
Executive Director: Stanley A. Rodman
   E-Mail: srodman1@sbcglobal.net
Office Manager: Myrna Rodman

Historical Note:
Formerly (1984) the Aftermarket Body Parts Distributors Association and (1990) the Aftermarket Body Parts Association. Absorbed (1997) Bumper Recycling Association of North America. ABPA is dedicated to serving the collision repair industry with quality replacement parts, backed by dependable service and fair prices. Members are companies that distribute, supply and/or manufacture automotive bumpers and other auto body crash parts for auto dealers, body shops and garages. Membership: $500-4,000 (Company, Based on number of employees); $200 (Associate).

Meetings/Conferences: Annual

Publications:
Body Language Newsletter; adv.

Automotive Communication Council *(1941)*
7101 Wisconsin Ave.
Suite 1300
Bethesda, MD 20814
Tel: (240) 333-1089 *Fax:* (301) 654-3299
E-Mail: acc@aftermarket.org
Website: acc-online.org
Members: 65 companies
Staff: 2
Annual Budget: $10-25,000

Personnel:
President: Dawn Gagne
Treasurer: Bob Zimmerman

Historical Note:
Formerly (1993) the Automotive Advertisers Council. ACC provides a sophisticated, beneficial and supportive networking forum for marketing professionals engaged in public relations, advertising, branding and other communication practices in an effort to help them manage ideas, information and resources about issues, challenges and trends impacting the automotive aftermarket

industry. Members are marketing professionals engaged in public relations, advertising, branding and other communication practices for automotive aftermarket companies. Membership: $395/year (Individual).

Meetings/Conferences: Annual

Publications:
ACC Spin; quarterly; adv.
Membership Directory; on-line

Membership List Available to Non-members

Automotive Distribution Network *(2005)*
3085 Fountainside Dr.
Suite 210
Germantown, TN 38138
Tel: (901) 682-9090 *Fax:* (901) 682-9098
E-Mail: info@networkhq.org
Website: networkhq.org
Members:
1500 affiliated auto stores
2000 affiliated service centers
Staff: 6
Annual Budget: $5-10,000,000

Personnel:
President: Mike Lambert
Vice President , Marketing and Advertising: Bob Barstow
Contributing Editor: Scott Bowden
Vice President, Information and Technology: Tom Frey

Historical Note:
The Automotive Distribution Network is the umbrella organization for Parts Plus, Independant Auto Parts of America, Auto Pride, and CMB Network.

Meetings/Conferences: Annual

Publications:
Network Magazine; quarterly; adv.

Automotive Engine Rebuilders Association *(1923)*
500 Coventry Ln.
Suite 180
Crystal Lake, IL 60014-7592
Tel: (815) 526-7600 *Fax:* (815) 526-7601
TollFree: (888) 326-2372
E-Mail: info@aera.org
Website: aera.org
Members: 3000 members
Staff: 9
Annual Budget: $1-2,000,000

Personnel:
President: Paul Hauglie
   E-Mail: paul@aera.org
Contact, Accounting Services: Yolanda Carranza
   E-Mail: yolanda@aera.org
Vice President, Operations: Jan Juhl
   E-Mail: jan@aera.org
Chief Technology Architect: Richard Rooks
   E-Mail: richard@aera.org
Contact, Membership Services: Karen Tendering
   E-Mail: karen@aera.org

Historical Note:
Formerly National Motor Regrinder and Rebuilder Association and Associated Automotive Engine Rebuilders. AERA purpose is the development and encouragement of high standards of workmanship and ethics among its members, the improvement of business conditions through the exchange of information and ideas, and the promotion of the common business interests of persons and organizations engaged in the rebuilding of internal combustion engines or basic internal components of such engines. Membership: $359-671 (Active); $394-718 (International); $428-463 (Government); $244-301 (Schools); $359-695 (Associate); $417-730 (International Associate).

Continuing Education:
Certification Designation/s: CH&EM

Publications:
A Voice in Washington
A.E.R.Aid
Engine Professional; quarterly; adv.
Membership Directory; on-line
Newsletter

Automotive Fleet and Leasing Association *(1969)*
1000 Westgate Dr.
Suite 252
St. Paul, MN 55114
Tel: (651) 203-7247 *Fax:* (651) 290-2266
E-Mail: info@aflaonline.com
Website: aflaonline.com

Members: 300 individuals
Staff: 4
Annual Budget: $500-1,000,000
Tax: 501(c)(6)

Personnel:
Executive Director: Paul Hanscom
   E-Mail: paulh@aflaonline.com
Coordinator, Events: Ashley Crunstedt
   E-Mail: ashleyc@aflaonline.com
Counsel: John Possumato
   E-Mail: possumato@carsincorporated.net
Director, Business Development: Jim Rallo
   E-Mail: jim.rallo@aflaonline.com

Historical Note:
AFLA is the forum dedicated to improving communication between sellers, buyers, fleet managers, lending institutions, fleet management companies, used vehicle marketers, and allied automotive service companies. Membership: $200 (Members); $100 (Alumni (retired)).

Continuing Education:
Certification Designation/s: CAE

Meetings/Conferences: Annual
Conference Chair: Ashley Crunstedt

Publications:
AFLA SpecSheet e-newsletter; monthly
Membership Directory; on-line

Automotive Industry Action Group *(1982)*
26200 Lahser Rd.
Suite 200
Southfield, MI 48033-7100
Tel: (248) 358-3570 *Fax:* (248) 358-3253
E-Mail: order_inquiry@aiag.org
Website: aiag.org
Members: 1200 companies
Staff: 7
Annual Budget: $10-25,000,000
Tax: 501(c)(6)

Personnel:
Executive Director: J. Scot Sharland
   E-Mail: jssharland@aiag.org
Director, Finance: Lorraine Goodrich
   E-Mail: lgoodrich@aiag.org
Vice President, Business Development: Joel Karczewski
   E-Mail: jkarczewski@aiag.org
Vice President, Commercial Development: Dave A. Lalain
   E-Mail: dlalain@aiag.org
Director, Information Technology: Russ Ortisi
   E-Mail: rortisi@aiag.org
Product Manager, Training and Certification: Stacy L. Ward
   E-Mail: sward@aiag.org
Moderator and Program Manager: Akram Yunas
   E-Mail: ayunas@aiag.org

Historical Note:
AIAG's purpose is to provide an open forum where members cooperate in developing and promoting solutions that enhance the prosperity of the automotive industry. Membership: $500-13,500 (Corporate); $1,000 (Professional Service Organizations).

Continuing Education:
Certification Designation/s: SPC, QMD, FMEA, MSA, APQP/PPAP
Meetings/Conferences:
Number of non-conference events/year: 6

Publications:
Actionline Magazine
AIAG e-News Brief; monthly
AIAG E-newsletter; monthly
Buyer's Guide; annually; adv.

Automotive Lift Institute, Inc. *(1945)*
P.O. Box 85
Cortland, NY 13045
Tel: (607) 756-7775 *Fax:* (607) 756-0888
E-Mail: info@autolift.org
Website: autolift.org
Members: 16 companies
Staff: 3
Annual Budget: $500-1,000,000
Tax: 501(c)(6)

Personnel:
President and Chief Executive Officer: R. W. O'Gorman
   E-Mail: bob@autolift.org

Historical Note:
ALI's mission is to promote public awareness of safe design, construction, installation, service, and use of

automotive lifts. ALI is an association of U.S./Canadian manufacturers and distributors of automotive lifts that are used to completely raise motor vehicles for undercarriage service.

Continuing Education:
Certification Designation/s: ALI/ETL, ANSI

Automotive Maintenance and Repair Association
(1994)
201 Park Washington Ct.
Falls Church, VA 22046
Tel: (703) 538-3557 *Fax:* (202) 318-0378
E-Mail: amra@amra.org
Website: amra.org
Members: 110 companies
Staff: 4
Annual Budget: $500-1,000,000
Tax: 501(c)(6)

Personnel:
President: Barry Soltz
Director, Administration: Joseph M. Henmueller
Program Administrator: Ben Trittipoe
  E-Mail: ben@motorist.org

Historical Note:
AMRA's mission is to strengthen the relationship between the motorist (consumer) and the automotive maintenance and repair service industry and produce communication programs that benefit consumers and automotive service providers, through its Motorist Assurance Program (MAP), MAP Participating Facility Program and MAP Qualified Technician Program. Membership: $100-25,000/year.

Meetings/Conferences: Annual
Conference Chair: Ben Trittipoe

Publications:
Directions Legislative Update; monthly
e-Directions Electronic Newsletter; monthly

Automotive Market Research Council *(1966)*
3800 Automation Dr., Suite 200
C/O BorgWarner Thermal Systems
Auburn Hills, MI 48326
Tel: (248) 754-0176
Website: amrc.org
Members: 75 companies, 250 individuals
Staff: 2
Annual Budget: $50-100,000
Tax: 501(c)(3)

Personnel:
President: Paul F. Pare
Treasurer: Frank Yezbick

Historical Note:
The AMRC is an all-volunteer organization comprised of representatives from manufacturers and suppliers of vehicles and their components. AMRC provide members information on the latest developments on the topic of market research as well as contacts at the leading suppliers of market research. Membership consists of professionals in market research, strategic planning, forecasting, sales and marketing and other various areas of expertise. Membership: $625 (OEM/Suppliers/Distibutors).

Automotive Oil Change Association *(1987)*
1701 N. Greenville Ave.
Suite 404
Richardson, TX 75081
Tel: (972) 458-9468 *Fax:* (972) 458-9539
TollFree: (800) 331-0329
E-Mail: info@aoca.org
Website: aoca.org
Members: 1,200 members
Staff: 6
Annual Budget: $1-2,000,000

Personnel:
Executive Director: Leanne Stump
  E-Mail: lstump@aoca.org
Director, Membership Services and Administration:
  Summer Beday
  E-Mail: sbeday@aoca.org
Manager, Communications: Gordon Taylor
  E-Mail: gtaylor@aoca.org

Historical Note:
Formerly (1993) National Association of Independent Lubes. AOCA is dedicated to providing its members with the business tools, resources and education to professionally and successfully deliver convenient automotive oil changes and other preventive maintenance services. Members are Fast Lube Operators and their suppliers and distributors. Membership: $375-1,200 (Fast Lube Operator); $500 (Distributor).

Meetings/Conferences: Annual

Publications:
Member Directory; on-line
Oil Changing Times; quarterly
You Auto Know; monthly

Membership List Available to Non-members

Automotive Parts Remanufacturers Association
(1941)
4460 Brookfield Corporate Dr.
Suite H
Chantilly, VA 20151-1671
Tel: (703) 968-2772 *Fax:* (703) 968-2878
E-Mail: mail@apra.org
Website: apra.org
Members: 1000 companies
Staff: 8
Annual Budget: $1-2,000,000

Personnel:
President: William C. Gager
  E-Mail: gager@BuyReman.com
Director, Financial Services: Teresa Giroux
  E-Mail: giroux@buyreman.com
Editor: Kirsten Kase
  E-Mail: kase@buyreman.com
Chief Technical Officer: Mark Kothe
  E-Mail: kothe@buyreman.com
Director, Advertising and Marketing: Morris Spector
  E-Mail: spector@buyreman.com

Historical Note:
Formerly the Automotive Parts Rebuilders Association, assumed its current name in 2004. APRA's mission is to address the needs of the automotive and truck parts remanufacturing industry and to serve its members by providing a wide range of products, services, workshops and educational information. Membership: $841-4,504.50 (Supplier); $247.25-2,195.50 (Remanufacturer/ Rebuilder Members); $478.50 (Warehouse).

Meetings/Conferences:
Conference Chair: Morris Spector

Publications:
e-Connection; weekly
Global Sourcing Directory; biennially
Membership Directory; annually; adv.
Remanufacturing Today; weekly
The APRA Global Connection; monthly

Membership List Available to Non-members

Automotive Public Relations Council *(1974)*
1301 W. Long Lake
Suite 225
Troy, MI 48098
Tel: (248) 952-6401 *Fax:* (248) 952-6404
E-Mail: info@oesa.org
Website: oesa.org/Councils-Committees/
  Automotive-Public
Members: 63 individuals
Staff: 3
Annual Budget: Under $10,000

Personnel:
Executive Director, Marketing and Communications: Greg
  Janicki
  E-Mail: gjanicki@oesa.org
Manager, Communications: Jeff Laskowski
  E-Mail: jlaskowski@oesa.org
Vice President, Sales and Membership Services: Glenn
  Stevens
  E-Mail: gstevens@oesa.org

Historical Note:
APRC operates under the management and oversight of the Original Equipment Suppliers Association (OESA) in the heart of the automotive industry and welcomes members from all aspects of automotive communications. APRC's mission is to create, develop and cultivate a network of integrated communications professionals who are dedicated to the advancement and image of the automotive industry, their professions and serving as a learning resource for the industry. Members are corporate and agency communicators. Membership: $295 (General); $495 (Affiliate); $90 (Educator).

Membership List Available to Non-members

Automotive Recyclers Association *(1943)*
9113 Church St.
Manassas, VA 20110
Tel: (571) 208-0428 *Fax:* (571) 208-0430
TollFree: (888) 385-1005
Website: a-r-a.org

Members: 1000 member companies, 2000 other
companies
Staff: 9
Annual Budget: $1-2,000,000

Personnel:
Chief Executive Officer: Michael E. Wilson
  E-Mail: michael@a-r-a.org
Contact, Membership Services: Kelly C. Badillo
  E-Mail: kelly@a-r-a.org
Accountant: John Caponiti
  E-Mail: john@a-r-a.org
Contact, Meetings and Expositions: Kim Glasscock
  E-Mail: kim@a-r-a.org
Contact, Certified Automotive Recycler Program: Chrissi
  Moyer
  E-Mail: chrissi@a-r-a.org
Director, Government Affairs: Elizabeth Vermette
  E-Mail: elizabeth@a-r-a.org

Historical Note:
Incorporated in the State of New York, formerly (1973) National Auto and Truck Wreckers Association, (1975) Association of Auto and Truck Recyclers, and (1989) Automotive Dismantlers and Recyclers. Assumed its current name in 1993. ARA aims to further the automotive recycling industry through various services and programs to increase public awareness of the industry's role in conserving the future through automotive recycling. Members are recyclers of domestic and foreign automobile, truck, and motorcycle parts. Membership: $375-1,000 (Direct); $625 (Associate/Affiliate); $2500 (Central Office); $375 (Branch); $250 (International); $375 (Canada).

Continuing Education:
Certification Designation/s: CAR, GSCARP

Meetings/Conferences: Annual
Conference Chair: Kim Glasscock

Publications:
ARA Industry Newsletter
ARA Members Directory; on-line
Automotive Recycling Magazine; bi-monthly

Automotive Safety Council *(1961)*
5518 Arbor Bay
Brighton, MI 48116
Tel: (586) 201-8653 *Fax:* (810) 225-8567
E-Mail: info@aorc.org
Website: aorc.org
Members: 50 companies
Staff: 2
Annual Budget: $250-500,000

Personnel:
President: Douglas P. Campbell
  E-Mail: dcampbell@automotivesafetycouncil.org

Historical Note:
Formerly (1977) the American Safety Belt Council and (1989) American Seat Belt Council to newest version of Automotive Safety Council. The mission of AORC is to reduce traffic deaths and injuries by providing the motoring public with reliable and effective occupant restraint systems. Membership: $50,000 (Systems Manufacturer); $6,000 (Components Manufacturer); $4,000 (Materials Manufacturer); $3,000 (Sponsoring Member).

Meetings/Conferences: Annual
2013 - Reunion, FL (Reunion Resort and Golf Club)/
  March 20 - 24

Automotive Service Association *(1951)*
8190 Precinct Line Rd.
Suite 100
Colleyville, TX 76034-7675
Tel: (817) 514-2900 *Fax:* (817) 514-0770
E-Mail: asainfo@asashop.org
Website: asashop.org
Members: 12000 Businesses and 70000
Professionals
Staff: 34
Annual Budget: $2-5,000,000
Tax: 501(c)(6)

Personnel:
President and Chief Staff Executive: Ron Pyle
  E-Mail: ronp@asashop.org
Vice President, Education and Training: Bill Haas
  E-Mail: billh@asashop.org
Vice President, Finance: Mark Hale
  E-Mail: markh@asashop.org
Vice President, Membership Services: B.J. Johnson
  E-Mail: bj@asashop.org
Manager, Information Systems and Distribution: Terri
Ruppert

E-Mail: terrir@asashop.org
Vice President, Marketing and Communications: Angie
Wilson
E-Mail: angie@asashop.org

Historical Note:
*Formed by the merger of Automotive Service Councils, Inc.
and Independent Automotive Service Association. ASA
advances professionalism and excellence in the automotive
repair industry through education, representation and
member services. Members are businesses providing
automotive service in mechanical, auto body and other
fields. Membership: Based on Sales (Regular); $495
(Associate); $50 (Educational).*

Meetings/Conferences: Annual
Number of non-conference events/year: 3

Publications:
ASA News-Network; weekly
AutoInc.; monthly; adv.
Membership Directory; on-line

Automotive Trade Association Executives *(1915)*
8400 Westpark Dr.
McLean, VA 22102
Tel: (703) 821-7072 *Fax:* (703) 556-8581
E-Mail: atae@nada.org
Website: atae.info
Members: 115 associations
Staff: 2
Annual Budget: $250-500,000
Tax: 501(c)(6)

Personnel:
Executive Director: Jennifer Colman
    E-Mail: jcolman@nada.org
Manager, Meetings: Jill Goldfine
    E-Mail: jgoldfine@nada.org

Historical Note:
*Formerly (1934) known as National Association of
Automobile Show Managers and (1984) then as National
Association of Automobile Show and Association Managers,
Automotive Trade Association Managers. ATAE provides
a forum for the exchange of information, and serves as a
clearinghouse for resources needed by member association
executives. Members are executives of state and local
automobile dealer associations. Membership : $250-750/
year.*

Meetings/Conferences: Annual
Conference Chair: Jill Goldfine

Publications:
ATAE Directory; on-line
ATAeNEWS Newsletter; bi-weekly

Automotive Training Managers Council *(1984)*
101 Blue Seal Dr. SE
Suite 101
Leesburg, VA 20175
Tel: (703) 669-6670 *Fax:* (703) 669-6126
E-Mail: dmilne@ase.com
Website: atmc.org
Members: 94 individuals
Staff: 2
Annual Budget: $25-50,000
Tax: 501(c)(6)

Personnel:
President: David Milne
    E-Mail: dmilne@atmc.org
Treasurer: Darrell Rowe

Historical Note:
*ATMC's mission is to provide a forum for the exchange
of views and opinions regarding the training needs of
the automotive trade; encourages study and research
of training effectiveness and promotes quality training.
Members are automotive aftermarket manufacturing and
distributing concerns, each represented by a training
department executive. Membership: $275 (Advisory); $425
(Corporate); $375 (Individual).*

Meetings/Conferences: Annual
2013 - Englewood, CO (Inverness Hotel and
    Conference Center)/April 15 - 17
Number of non-conference events/year: 2

Publications:
Membership Directory; on-line

Auxiliary to the National Medical Association
(1936)
8403 Colesville Rd.
Suite 920
Silver Spring, MD 20910
Tel: (301) 495-3779 *Fax:* (301) 495-0037

E-Mail: anmanationaloffice@earthlink.net
Website: anmanet.org
Staff: 5
Annual Budget: $500-1,000,000

Personnel:
President: Sharon C. Melvin
Editor: Dolores Caffey-Fleming
Treasurer: Shirley Frederick
Secretary, Financial: Judge Morris Overstreet
Co-Chair: Mae S. Walton
    E-Mail: msw213@aol.com

Historical Note:
*ANMA's mission is to create a greater interest in the
National Medical Association (NMA), aid and to encourage
the medical profession in its effort to educate and serve the
public in matters of health, and to develop and promote
a National Auxiliary Program on health, education and
legislation. Membership: $175 (Regular/Interim); $60
(Resident/Interns Spouse/Physicians).*

Meetings/Conferences: Annual
2013 - Toronto, ON/July 27 - 31

Publications:
ANMA Newsletter

Aviation Distributors and Manufacturers Association International *(1943)*
100 N. 20th St.
Suite 400
Philadelphia, PA 19103-1462
Tel: (215) 320-3863 *Fax:* (215) 564-2175
E-Mail: adma@fernley.com
Website: adma.org
Members: 90 companies
Staff: 3
Annual Budget: $100-250,000

Personnel:
Executive Director and Contact, Membership: Kristen
Olszewski
    E-Mail: kolszewski@fernley.com
Contact, Management Liaison: Trudie Bruner Rowello
    E-Mail: trowello@fernley.com
Manager, Meetings: Meg Taft
    E-Mail: mtaft@fernley.com

Historical Note:
*ADMA strives to further the development of the aviation
marketplace through the services and products produced
and distributed by members through awareness of the
advantages of the aviation marketplace. Members are
distributors and manufacturers of aviation parts, supplies
and equipment. Membership: $2,460/year (Distributor).*

Meetings/Conferences: Annual
Conference Chair: Meg Taft

Publications:
Membership Directory; annually
The Flight Plan; monthly

Aviation Industry CBT Committee *(1988)*
18608 20th Pl. NE
Shoreline, WA 98155
Tel: (253) 218-1408 *Fax:* (253) 218-1408
Website: aicc.org
Staff: 2
Annual Budget: $25-50,000

Personnel:
Chairman: Herbert Schwarz
Treasurer: Mike Sharp

Historical Note:
*The AICC's mission is to provide and promote information,
guidelines and standards that result in the effective
implementation of CBT and WBT. Membership: $2,500
(Corporate); $1,500 (Airline) $500 (Small Company).*

Publications:
eLearning Age Magazine; adv.

Membership List Available to Non-members

Aviation Insurance Association *(1976)*
400 Admiral Blvd.
Kansas City, MO 64106
Tel: (816) 221-8488 *Fax:* (816) 472-7765
E-Mail: info@aiaweb.org
Website: aiaweb.org
Members: 900 firms and individuals
Staff: 6
Annual Budget: $500-1,000,000

Personnel:
Executive Director: Mandie "Amanda" Bannwarth

E-Mail: mandie@aiaweb.org
Chief Relationship Officer: Ken Bowman
    E-Mail: kenb@robstan.com
Director, Marketing and Membership Services: Meredith
Carr
    E-Mail: meredith@robstan.com
Director, Conferences: Rosemary Hall
    E-Mail: rosemary@robstan.com
Associate Director: Casey High
    E-Mail: casey@aiaweb.org
Membership Coordinator: Tiffany Mayo
    E-Mail: tiffany@robstan.com

Historical Note:
*Founded as the Association of Independent Aviation
Insurers and assumed its current name in 1988. AIA is
committed to enhancing the aviation insurance industry
worldwide and the professional lives of those who work in
it through a variety of programs and services. Membership:
$200 (Corporate); $130 (Individual); $45 (Student).*

Continuing Education:
Certification Designation/s: CAIP

Meetings/Conferences: Annual
Conference Chair: Rosemary Hall
2013 - Orlando, FL (Hilton Bonnet Creek Resort)/May
    4 - 7

Publications:
Tailwind; monthly

Aviation Maintenance Foundation International *(1971)*
P.O. Box 456
Basin, WY 82410-0456
E-Mail: amfic@ix.netcom.com
Members:
100 companies
6000 individuals
Staff: 8
Annual Budget: $500-1,000,000

Personnel:
President and Executive Director: Richard S. Kost
    E-Mail: amfic@ix.netcom.com

Historical Note:
*Formerly (1988) the Aviation Maintenance Foundation.
Incorporated in March, 1972. Members are aviation
maintenance personnel, schools, companies and related
organizations. Membership: $40/year.*

The Aviation Security Services Association *(2002)*
B – 1780 Wemmel
Wemmel, AL 56897
Website: assa-int.org/
Staff: 1

Personnel:
Treasurer: Raj Cot

Historical Note:
*Formerly known as EASA, European Aviation Security
Association. ASSA-I is a non-profit association, composed
of the most important private security companies providing
security services for airports and airlines. It represents the
private security companies providing security services at
airports and for airlines.*

Aviation Suppliers Association *(1993)*
2233 Wisconsin Ave. NW
Suite 503
Washington, DC 20007
Tel: (202) 347-6899 *Fax:* (202) 347-6894
E-Mail: info@aviationsuppliers.org
Website: aviationsuppliers.org
Members: 400 companies
Staff: 8
Annual Budget: $1-2,000,000
Tax: 501(c)(6)

Personnel:
President: Michele Dickstein
    E-Mail: michele@aviationsuppliers.org
Coordinator, Membership Services: Dawn Carberry
    E-Mail: dawn@aviationsuppliers.org
General Counsel and Govt. Affairs Representative: Jason
Dickstein
    E-Mail: jason@washingtonaviation.com
Contact, Account Services: Diane Leeds
    E-Mail: diane@aviationsuppliers.org
Corporate Treasurer: Mitch Weinberg

Historical Note:
*Formerly (2003) Airline Suppliers Association. ASA
promotes safety, regulatory compliance and ethical business*

practices among aviation parts suppliers and throughout the aviation community. Members are companies providing materials and services to commercial airlines. Membership: $1,200-3,000 (Regular); $600 (Associate).

Meetings/Conferences: Annual
2013 - Las Vegas, NV (Four Seasons Hotel Las Vegas)/ July 9 - 11/11-25 exhibitors

Publications:
Membership Directory; on-line

Aviation Technician Education Council (1961)
2090 Wexford Ct.
Harrisburg, PA 17112
Tel: (717) 540-7121
E-Mail: info@atec-amt.org
Website: atec-amt.org
Members: 155 schools
Staff: 2
Annual Budget: $50-100,000

Personnel:
Executive Director: Dr. Richard Dumaresq EdD
E-Mail: ccdq@aol.com

Historical Note:
ATEC strives to advocate for aviation maintenance schools in the areas of curriculum improvement, technical and financial support, while promoting mutually beneficial relations with related government and industry groups. Members are FAA-approved schools training aviation maintenance technicians. Membership: $210 (International Education); $25 (Individuals); $325 (Industry) $220 (Institutional Basic); $320(Institutional Enhanced);

Meetings/Conferences: Annual
2013 - Orlando, FL/April 13 - 16

Publications:
ATEC Directory
ATEC Journal; adv.

Membership List Available to Non-members

Avko Educational Research Foundation (1974)
3084 Willard Rd.
Birch Run, MI 48415-9404
Fax: (810) 686-1101
TollFree: (866) 285-6612
Website: avko.org
Staff: 1
Annual Budget: $50-100,000

Personnel:
Research Director: Don McCabe

Historical Note:
AVKO focuses on the development and production of materials and especially techniques to teach reading and spelling, handwriting (manuscript and cursive), and keyboarding. AVKO is dedicated to the teaching everyone how to read and spell, regardless of their mild to moderate learning disabilities, dyslexia, poverty, or opportunity. Membership: $25 (Individual); $100 (Institutional).

Publications:
AVKO Newsletter; on-line

AVS: Science and Technology of Materials, Interfaces, and Processing (1953)
125 Maiden Ln.
15th Floor
New York, NY 10038
Tel: (212) 248-0200 *Fax:* (212) 248-0245
TollFree: (800) 888-1021
Website: avs.org
Members: 4500 individuals
Staff: 14
Annual Budget: $2-5,000,000

Personnel:
Manager, Exhibition and Sales: Jeannette DeGennaro
E-Mail: jeannette@avs.org
Administrator, Membership Services: Angela Klink
E-Mail: angela@avs.org
Administrator, Information Systems and Web: Keith Mitchell
E-Mail: keith@avs.org
Managing Director: Yvonne Towse
E-Mail: yvonne@avs.org

Historical Note:
Formerly known as the Committee on Vacuum Techniques, became the American Vacuum Society in 1957, and assumed its current name in 2002. AVS's aim is to enhance communication, education, networking, recommended practices, research, and the dissemination of knowledge on an international scale, in the application of vacuum and other controlled environments to understand and develop interfaces, new materials, processes, and devices through the interaction of science and technology. Membership: $95 (Individual); $25 (Student); $45 (Early Career); $500 (Corporate).

Meetings/Conferences: Annual
Conference Chair: Della Miller
2013 - San Diego, CA (San Diego Marriott Marquis and Marina)/July 28 - 31
2013 - Long Beach, CA (Long Beach Convention and Entertainment Center)/Oct. 27 - Nov. 1
2014 - Baltimore, MD (Baltimore Convention Center)/ Nov. 9 - 14
Number of non-conference events/year: 24

Publications:
AVS Corporate Members (Membership Directory); on-line
AVS Interactions; on-line
AVS President's Message; on-line
Beneath the AVS Surface; on-line
Biointerphases; quarterly; adv.
Journal of Vacuum Science & Technology B; bi-monthly; adv.
JVST A, Vacuum, Surfaces, and Films; bi-monthly; adv.
Surface Science Spectra; annually

Awards and Recognition Association (1980)
4700 W. Lake Ave.
Glenview, IL 60025
Tel: (847) 375-4800 *Fax:* (888) 374-7257
TollFree: (800) 344-2148
E-Mail: info@ara.org
Website: ara.org
Members: 4000 companies
Staff: 12
Annual Budget: $2-5,000,000
Tax: 501(c)(6)

Personnel:
Executive Director: Louise Ristau

Historical Note:
ARA's mission is to advance the capabilities and growth of businesses whose primary focus is the manufacture, distribution or sales of awards and recognition goods and services. Membership: $195 (Retail); $115 (Retailer Member's Branch/Franchise); $540-1,240 (Supplier); $595 (Affiliate/Associate); $85 (Supplier Member's Branch/Supplier Representative); $595 (Affiliate/ Associate).

Continuing Education:
Certification Designation/s: CRM, CRS

Meetings/Conferences:
2013 - Las Vegas, NV (Rio All-Suite Hotel and Casino)/ Jan. 29 - Feb. 1

Publications:
Recognition Review; monthly; adv.

BAFT-IFSA (2010)
1120 Connecticut Ave. NW
Third Floor
Washington, DC 20036
Tel: (202) 663-7575 *Fax:* (202) 663-5538
E-Mail: info@baft-ifsa.com
Website: baft-ifsa.com
Members: 200 financial institutions
Staff: 10
Annual Budget: $2-5,000,000
Tax: 501(c)(6)

Personnel:
Chief Executive Officer: Todd Burwell
Manager, Programs and Events: Colleen Kennedy
E-Mail: ckennedy@baft-ifsa.com
Manager, Training Programs: Kristi Long
Administrative Assistant: Tamika Wood
E-Mail: twood@baft-ifsa.com

Historical Note:
Founded as Banker's Association for Foreign Trade, the Association assumed the name Banker's Association for financial trade. In 2000 BAFT merged with IFSA and changed its name in 2010. It is a financial trade association whose membership represents a broad range of internationally active financial institutions and companies that provides important services throughout the global financial community. For over 87 years it has advanced the growth and evolution of international financial services. As a worldwide forum for analysis, discussion and advocacy in the international financial services community. It plays a unique role in expanding markets, shaping regulatory and legislative policy, developing business solutions and preserving the safety and soundness of the global financial system.

Continuing Education:
Enrollment: 4000
Certification Designation/s: CDCS

Meetings/Conferences: Annual
Number of non-conference events/year: 2

Publications:
The Global Voice; quarterly; adv.

Bakery, Confectionery, Tobacco Workers and Grain Millers International Union (1886)
10401 Connecticut Ave.
Kensington, MD 20895
Tel: (301) 933-8600 *Fax:* (301) 946-8452
Website: bctgm.org
Members: 120000 individuals
Staff: 38
Annual Budget: $1-2,000,000

Personnel:
International President and Editor: Frank Hurt
International Secretary, Treasurer and Director: David B. Durkee
E-Mail: ddurkee@bctgm.org

Historical Note:
BCTGM was organized in Pittsburgh and chartered by the American Federation of Labor. Merged (1969) with American Bakery and Confectionery Workers' International Union. Affiliated with AFL-CIO, CLC. Formerly (until 1978) known as the Bakery and Confectionery Workers International Union of America. Merged with the Tobacco Workers International Union in August, 1978. BCTGM's mission is to promote the material, intellectual and general welfare of all workers in the baking, confectionery, tobacco, grain milling and kindred industries by organizational action.

Publications:
BCTGM News; bi-monthly

Baking Industry Sanitation Standards Committee (1949)
P.O. Box 3999
Manhattan, KS 66505-3999
Tel: (785) 537-4750 *Fax:* (785) 537-1493
TollFree: (866) 342-4772
E-Mail: bissc@bissc.org
Website: bissc.org
Members: 100 companies
Staff: 2
Annual Budget: $50-100,000

Personnel:
Contact, Communications: Jon Anderson
E-Mail: janderson@aibonline.org
Administrative Assistant: Rosalie Wagner
E-Mail: rwagner@aibonline.org

Historical Note:
BISSC's purpose is to develop, publish and advocate the use of voluntary sanitation standards covering the design and construction of machinery and equipment used in the baking industry. Membership: $400/year (Company).

Continuing Education:
Certification Designation/s: BISSC

Publications:
ANSI / BISSC Standard Bakery Equipment-Sanitation Standard; irregular
BISSC Design Handbook for Easily Cleanable Equipment
Directory of Registered Companies; on-line

Balloon Federation of America (1961)
P.O. Box 400
1601 N. Jefferson
Indianola, IA 50125
Tel: (515) 961-8809 *Fax:* (515) 961-3537
E-Mail: bfaoffice@bfa.net
Website: bfa.net
Staff: 5
Annual Budget: $250-500,000

Personnel:
President: Troy Bradley
Contact, Website: Nancy Griffin
Treasurer: Kevin Knapp
Editor: Glen Moyer
Office Manager and Membership Contact: Sharon Ripperger
E-Mail: bfaoffice@bfa.net

Historical Note:
The BFA is a association dedicated to the advancement of the sport and science of lighter-than-air aviation, both hot

air and gas balloons. Membership: $55-65 (Associate); $1,000 (Life); $250 (Corporate); $20 (Family).

Publications:
BALLOONING Journal; bi-monthly; adv.
Membership Roster; on-line

Bank Administration Institute (1924)
115 S. LaSalle St.
Suite 3300
Chicago, IL 60603-3801
Tel: (312) 683-2464 *Fax:* (312) 683-2373
TollFree: (800) 224-9889
E-Mail: info@bai.org
Website: bai.org
Members: 1500 banks
Staff: 90
Annual Budget: $5-10,000,000
Tax: 501(c)(3)

Personnel:
President and Chief Executive Officer: Deborah L. Bianucci
    E-Mail: bianucci@bai.org
Executive Vice President, Human Resources: Ann R. Barcroft
Managing Director, Corporate Marketing: Dana Dolan
Executive Vice President and Chief Financial Officer: Thomas J. Dubnicka

Historical Note:
BAI provides information to member bankers in areas such as human resources, finance, strategic planning and marketing, accounting, corporate services, audit, taxes, retail, operations and technology, through its series of emerging issues studies, professional conferences and education programs. Members are retail banking executives and financial institutions. Membership: $1,100-22,000/year.

Continuing Education:
Certification Designation/s: CRP, AMLP, CBA

Meetings/Conferences: Annual

Publications:
BAI Banking Strategies Daily; daily

Membership List Available to Non-members

Bank Insurance and Securities Association (1981)
2025 M St. NW
Suite 800
Washington, DC 20036
Tel: (202) 367-1111 *Fax:* (202) 367-2111
E-Mail: bisa@BISAnet.org
Website: bisanet.org
Members: 410 institutions
Staff: 14
Annual Budget: $2-5,000,000
Tax: 501(c)(6)

Personnel:
Executive Director: Jim McNeil
    E-Mail: jmcneil@bisanet.org
Financial Management and Accounting Services Coordinator: Sarah Alcock
    E-Mail: salcock@bisanet.org
Senior Manager, Marketing: Kara Dress
    E-Mail: kdress@bisanet.org
Director, Operations: Anna B. Hildreth
    E-Mail: ahildreth@bisanet.org
Manager, Event Services: Melissa Huston
    E-Mail: mhuston@bisanet.org
Coordinator, Education Services: Lauren Kemp
    E-Mail: lkemp@bisanet.org
Operations Coordinator: Becky Morgan
    E-Mail: bmorgan@bisanet.org
Marketing Coordinator: Lindsay Pullen
    E-Mail: lpullen@bisanet.org
Editor and Publisher: Andrew W. Singer
    E-Mail: a.singer@verizon.net

Historical Note:
Formerly Bank Securities Association. Absorbed the Financial Institutions Insurance Association and assumed its current name in 2002. BISA's mission is to support member firms and financial professionals within depository institutions by building a community and providing forums to enhance their professionalism, knowledge, and productivity to help them best serve their clients with a broad array of financial solutions. Membership includes financial institutions, their broker/dealer and mutual fund subsidiaries, and firms providing products and/or services to support these operations. Membership: $750-9,500 (Regular); $1,500-2,500 (Associate); $25,000 (Associate-Leadership).

Meetings/Conferences: Annual
Conference Chair: Melissa Huston
2013 - Hollywood, FL (The Westin Diplomat Resort and Spa)/March 10 - 12
Number of non-conference events/year: 5

Publications:
Bank Insurance & Securities Marketing; quarterly; adv.
Benchmarking Data; monthly
Membership Directory; on-line

Baptist Communicators Association (1953)
1519 Menlo Dr.
Kennesaw, GA 30152
Tel: (770) 425-3728
E-Mail: office@baptistcommunicators.org
Website: baptistcommunicators.org
Members: 300 Members
Staff: 5
Annual Budget: $10-25,000
Tax: 501(c)(3)

Personnel:
President: Russ Rankin
    E-Mail: russ.rankin@lifeway.com
Vice President, Communications: Scott Barkley
    E-Mail: sbarkley@christianindex.org
Treasurer: Barbara L. Denman
    E-Mail: bdenman@flbaptist.org
Coordinator, Professional Development: Don Graham
Vice President, Membership Services: Stella Prather
    E-Mail: sprather@abchomes.org

Historical Note:
BCA's mission is to assist Baptist personnel in communications, professional growth and fulfillment. Membership: $60-80 (Professional); $25 (Student/Retired).

Meetings/Conferences: Annual
Conference Chair: Don Graham
Number of non-conference events/year: 1

Publications:
Baptist Communicators newsletter; on-line; adv.
Membership Directory; annually

Barre Granite Association (1889)
51 Church St.
P.O. Box 481
Barre, VT 05641
Tel: (802) 476-4131 *Fax:* (802) 476-4765
E-Mail: BGA@barregranite.org
Website: barregranite.org
Members: 81 companies
Staff: 3
Annual Budget: $100-250,000

Personnel:
Executive Director: John Castaldo

Historical Note:
BGA provides a cemetery planning assistance program designed to expand cemetery areas or establish new cemetery sections. Members are granite quarriers and manufacturers, dedicated to the production of granite monuments and other products.

Barzona Breeder's Association of America (1968)
3282 180th St.
Dexter, IA 50070
Tel: (641) 745-9170 *Fax:* (641) 743-6611
E-Mail: info@barzona.com
Website: barzona.com
Members: 80 individuals
Staff: 2
Annual Budget: $25-50,000

Personnel:
Executive Secretary: Alecia Heinz

Historical Note:
BBAA is non-profit organization established in to serve its growing number of breeders. The association provides a registry of purebred and percentage Barzona cattle and promotes the continued improvement of the Barzona breed. Members are breeders and fanciers of Barzona cattle. Membership: $75/year.

Publications:
Breeders Directory; on-line

Baseball Writers Association of America (1908)
P.O. Box 610611
Bayside, NY 11361
Tel: (718) 767-2582
E-Mail: info@bbwaa.com
Website: bbwaa.com

Members: 700 individuals
Staff: 1
Annual Budget: Under $10,000

Personnel:
Secretary and Treasurer: Jack O'Connell

Historical Note:
BBWAA's purpose is to ensure proper working conditions in press boxes and clubhouses, and to ensure its members have access to players and others in the game so members' reporting can be accurate, fair and complete. Members are sports writers on direct assignment to major league teams. Membership: $65/year (individual) (plus local dues, which vary).

Meetings/Conferences: Annual

Publications:
Membership Directory; on-line

Basic Acrylic Monomer Manufacturers (1986)
17260 Vannes Ct.
Hamilton, VA 20158
Tel: (540) 751-2093 *Fax:* (540) 751-2094
Website: bamm.net
Members: 4 manufacturers
Staff: 1
Annual Budget: $2-5,000,000

Personnel:
Executive Director: Elizabeth K. Hunt CAE
    E-Mail: e.hunt@comcast.net

Historical Note:
BAMM represents manufacturers and importers of acrylic acid and its esters. BAMM addresses health, environmental and regulatory issues concerning acrylic monomers. The association continually evaluates the information needed to assess the safety of its products and generate additional, scientifically sound studies when required, and communicate the health and safety information on the acrylic monomers to its stakeholders and the public. BAMM will anticipate regulatory trends and initiatives that could impact acrylic monomers and will develop and promote scientifically sound positions on key issues to members, regulators, legislators, stakeholders and the public.

Battery Council International (1924)
401 N. Michigan Ave.
24th Floor
Chicago, IL 60611-4267
Tel: (312) 644-6610 *Fax:* (312) 527-6640
E-Mail: info@batterycouncil.org
Website: batterycouncil.org
Members: 260 members
Staff: 4
Annual Budget: $2-5,000,000
Tax: 501(c)(6)

Personnel:
Washington Counsel: David B. Weinberg Esq.
Manager, Accounts: Ann Noll
    E-Mail: anoll@smithbucklin.com

Historical Note:
Formerly (1940) National Battery Manufacturers Association, renamed as the Association of American Battery Manufacturers in 1969 and then assumed its current name. BCI's mission is to promote the interests of the international lead-acid battery industry. Members are distributors, manufacturers and suppliers to the electrical storage battery industry. Membership: $700-55,000/year (dues based on sales volume).

Meetings/Conferences: Annual

Publications:
Battery Briefs; monthly
Best Magazine; quarterly
Regulatory and Legislative Update; monthly; adv.

BCA (1993)
55 W. 116th St.
Suite 234
New York, NY 10026
Tel: (646) 548-2949 *Fax:* (212) 283-7157
TollFree: (800) 308-8188
E-Mail: info@thebca.net
Website: bcaglobal.org
Members:
35 Colleges
500 individuals
Staff: 3
Annual Budget: $100-250,000
Tax: 501(c)(3)

Personnel:
President and Chief Executive Officer: Alex Askew

Secretary and Program Coordinator: Natividad Roman
Director, Conferences: Michael Thompson

Historical Note:
Formerly (1993) Black Culinarians Alliance; assumed current name in 2004. BCA is a national nonprofit organization that conducts networking in the foodservice, hospitality and related educational areas. Mission is to create awareness, exposure and educational opportunities for people of color in the foodservice (culinary arts) and hospitality fields and to provide a vehicle to support the professional development of young people of color who are considering culinary arts and/or hospitality as a career. Membership: $350 (Executive Management/Professional Services); $300 (Chef/Manager); $150 (Associate); $50 (College/University Student); Complimentary (High School Student Member); $1,500 (Corporate); $500 (Individual Allied); $250 (Affiliate).

Meetings/Conferences:
Conference Chair: Michael Thompson
Number of non-conference events/year: 2

Publications:
BCA Newsletter; quarterly
Membership Directory; on-line

Bearing Specialist Association *(1966)*
800 Roosevelt Rd.
Building C, Suite 312
Glen Ellyn, IL 60137-5833
Tel: (630) 858-3838 *Fax*: (630) 790-3095
E-Mail: info@bsahome.org
Website: bsahome.org
Members: 40 companies
Staff: 6
Annual Budget: $500-1,000,000

Personnel:
Executive Director: Richard W. Church
    E-Mail: dickc@cmservnet.com
Editor: Janet Arden
    E-Mail: janeta@cmservnet.com
Association Manager: Kathy Fatz
    E-Mail: kathyf@cmservices.com
Coordinator, Certification: Mary Hawkinson
    E-Mail: maryh@cmservnet.com
Legal Counsel: William C. Ives
    E-Mail: wives@nc.rr.com

Historical Note:
Formed by the merger of Anti-Friction Bearing Distributors Association and the Association of Bearing Specialists. BSA's mission is to serve and represents firms that, as authorized distributors, stock and sell factory-warranted anti-friction bearings.Membership: $1,077-$8,200 (Authorized distributors); $2,504-8,536 (Participating Manufacturer).

Continuing Education:
Certification Designation/s: CBS

Meetings/Conferences:
2013 - Atlanta, GA (Loews Atlanta Hotel)/Jan. 27 - 29
2013 - Hilton Head Island, SC (Westin Hilton Head Island Resort and Spa)/May 3 - 7
2014 - Scottsdale, AZ (Fairmont Scottsdale Princess)/May 2 - 6

Publications:
Certification Update; on-line
Membership Directory; on-line
News and Views; monthly

Beef Improvement Federation *(1968)*
North Carolina State University, Department of Animal Science
P.O. Box 7621
Raleigh, NC 27695-7621
Tel: (919) 513-0262 *Fax*: (919) 515-6884
Website: beefimprovement.org
Members: 80 organizations
Staff: 1
Annual Budget: $10-25,000

Personnel:
Executive Director: Joe Cassedy
    E-Mail: joe_cassady@ncsu.edu

Historical Note:
BIF's purpose is to standardize programs and methodology and to create greater awareness, acceptance and usage of beef cattle performance concepts. Membership, by organization, consists of groups of beef cattle breeders and state improvement associations. Membership: $100-600 (Breed Associations); $100 (State/Provincial/National Organizations/Associate); $50 (Sustaining).

Meetings/Conferences: Annual

2013 - Oklahoma City, OK/June 12 - 15

Publications:
Membership Directory; on-line

Beefmaster Breeders United *(1954)*
6800 Park Ten Blvd.
Suite 290 West
San Antonio, TX 78213
Tel: (210) 732-3132 *Fax*: (210) 732-7711
E-Mail: info@beefmasters.org
Website: beefmasters.org
Members: 7000 Beefmaster Breeders
Staff: 9
Annual Budget: $500-1,000,000
Tax: 501(c)(5)

Personnel:
Executive Vice President: Dr. Tommy Perkins
    E-Mail: tperkins@beefmasters.org
Contact, Accounting: Mary Francois
    E-Mail: mfrancois@beefmasters.org
Office Manager: Donna Henderson
    E-Mail: dhenderson@beefmasters.org
Youth Program Coordinator: Joslyn Kotzur
    E-Mail: jkotzur@beefmasters.org
Coordinator, Communications and Education: Breann Pritchard
    E-Mail: bpritchard@beefmasters.org
Contact, Member Services: Marie Zirkel
    E-Mail: mzirkel@beefmasters.org

Historical Note:
Formerly Beefmaster Breeders Universal and absorbed Foundation Beefmaster Association and assumed its current name in 1996. BBU seeks to enhance breeder's ability to raise and encourage cattle based upon the founding "Six Essentials". Member of the National Pedigree Livestock Council. Membership: $50 (Active/Associate); $30 (Junior Dues); $25 (International).

Meetings/Conferences: Annual
Conference Chair: Joslyn Kotzur
2013 - Ft. Worth, TX/Oct. 31

Publications:
Newsletter; quarterly

Beer Institute *(1986)*
122 C St. NW
Suite 350
Washington, DC 20001-2109
Tel: (202) 737-2337 *Fax*: (202) 737-7004
TollFree: (800) 379-2739
E-Mail: info@beerinstitute.org
Website: beerinstitute.org
Members: 95 brewers and suppliers
Staff: 10
Annual Budget: $5-10,000,000

Personnel:
President: Joseph S. McLain Ret., USN
President, Public Policy: Joe McClain
General Counsel: Mary J. Saunders
    E-Mail: mjsaunders@beerinstitute.org
Vice President, Communications: Chris Thorne

Historical Note:
Formerly (1941) the United States Brewers Association. BI represents the industry before Congress, state legislatures and public forums across the country. Membership is open to brewers and industry suppliers only.

Publications:
Brewers Almanac; annually
Member Directory; on-line
Newsletters

Beet Sugar Development Foundation *(1945)*
800 Grant St.
Suite 300
Denver, CO 80203
Tel: (303) 832-4460 *Fax*: (303) 832-4468
Website: bsdf-assbt.org
Members: 15 companies
Staff: 4
Annual Budget: $1-2,000,000
Tax: 501(c)(3)

Personnel:
Executive Vice President: Thomas K. Schwartz
    E-Mail: Tom@bsdf-assbt.org
Administrative Assistant: Lucy Heltzel
    E-Mail: aa@bsdf-assbt.org
Manager, Business: Rebecca Lucy
    E-Mail: becky@bsdf-assbt.org

Historical Note:
BSDF's purpose is to advance the sugarbeet production and beet sugar processing through science based research and leading educational programs. Members are U.S. and Canadian sugar beet companies and primary suppliers of sugar beet seed. Membership consists of Beet Sugar Processing Companies and Sugarbeet Seed Related Companies.

Behavior Genetics Association *(1972)*
C/O Department of Psychology
345 UCB
Boulder, CO 80309-0345
Tel: (951) 827-2430
E-Mail: treasurer@bga.org
Website: bga.org
Members: 500 individuals
Staff: 2
Annual Budget: $100-250,000
Tax: 501(c)(6)

Personnel:
President: Michael Pogue-Geile
Treasurer: Rhee Soo Hyun
    E-Mail: Treasurer@bga.org

Historical Note:
Affiliated with the International Genetics Association and American Association for the Advancement of Science (AAAS), BGA's purpose is to advocate scientific study of the interrelationship of genetic mechanisms and behavior of both animal and human. Members are persons who are engaged in teaching or research related to behavior genetics. Membership: $125 (Regular); $45 (Associate/Retired).

Meetings/Conferences: Annual
2013 - Marseille, France (Aix Marseille University)/June 28 - July 2

Publications:
Behavior Genetics; bi-monthly
Membership Directory; on-line

Membership List Available to Non-members

Belgian Draft Horse Corporation of America *(1887)*
125 Southwood Dr.
P.O. Box 335
Wabash, IN 46992
Tel: (260) 563-3205 *Fax*: (260) 563-3205
E-Mail: belgian@belgiancorp.com
Website: belgiancorp.com
Members: 5500 individuals
Staff: 2
Annual Budget: $100-250,000
Tax: 501(c)(6)

Personnel:
President: Michael R. Stone
Secretary and Treasurer: Vicki Knott
    E-Mail: belgian@belgiancorp.com

Historical Note:
Originated as the American Association of Importers and Breeders of Belgian Draft Horses and assumed its present name in 1937, BDHCA is a pedigree association for owners and breeders of Belgian Draft Horses. Membership: $100 (Individual/Partnership/Corporate/Educational Institution); $25 (Youth).

Meetings/Conferences: Annual
Number of non-conference events/year: 1

Publications:
The Belgian Newsletter; adv.

Belgian-American Chamber of Commerce *(1918)*
C/O KBC Bank
1177 Ave. of the Americas, Eighth Floor
New York, NY 10036
Tel: (212) 541-0779 *Fax*: (212) 340-6270
E-Mail: info@belcham.org
Website: belcham.org
Members: 150 companies and organizations
Staff: 2
Annual Budget: $50-100,000

Personnel:
President: Olivier Smekens
    E-Mail: olivier.smekens@belcham.org
Director and Manager, Events: Tamara Zouboff CAE, IOM
    E-Mail: tamarazouboff@belcham.org

Historical Note:
Belcham promotes trade and commerce between the United States and Belgium by providing a network of business

contacts in Belgium and the United States. Membership: $50-2500/year.

Meetings/Conferences:
Conference Chair: Tamara Zouboff CAE, IOM
Number of non-conference events/year: 5

Publications:
Membership Directory

Belt Association (1934)
C/O Dept. of Geology, Idaho State Univ.
P.O. Box 8072
Pocatello, ID 83209-8072
Tel: (208) 282-4254 Fax: (208) 282-4414
Website: idahogeology.org/DrawOnePage.asp?
  PageID = 101
Members: 24 companies
Staff: 2
Annual Budget: Under $10,000

Personnel:
Secretary: Reed Lewis
  E-Mail: reedl@uidaho.edu

Historical Note:
The Belt Association promotes and co-ordinates geologic study of the Proterozoic Belt Supergroup of the northwestern U.S.A. and the equivalent Purcell Group in southwestern Canada. Mission is to provide funds for geologic research by senior undergraduate students and graduate students working in Belt terrane.

Belted Galloway Society (1951)
C/O Hav-A-Belt Galloways
New Glarus, WI 53574
Tel: (608) 527-4811 Fax: (608) 527-4811
Website: beltie.org
Members: 900 individuals
Staff: 2
Annual Budget: $100-250,000
Tax: 501(c)(3)

Personnel:
Executive Director: Victor Eggleston DVM
  E-Mail: executivedirector@beltie.org
Editor: Leanne Fogle II
  E-Mail: beltienews@beltie.org

Historical Note:
BGS's mission is to improve cattle breed production and marketing practices and to encourage youth involvement in beef production. Membership: $550 (Lifetime); $50 (Regular); $25 (Associate); $20 (Junior).

Meetings/Conferences: Annual

Publications:
Beltie Magazine; annually
U.S. Beltie News-Newsletter; monthly; adv.

BEMA - The Baking Industry Suppliers Association (1999)
10740 Nall Ave.
Suite 230
Overland Park, KS 66210
Tel: (913) 338-1300 Fax: (913) 338-1327
E-Mail: info@bema.org
Website: bema.org
Members: 200 companies
Staff: 4
Annual Budget: $1-2,000,000

Personnel:
President and Chief Executive Officer: Kerwin Brown
  E-Mail: kbrown@bema.org
Contact, Membership Services: Deb Blaylock
  E-Mail: dblaylock@bema.org
Manager, Operations: Gay Poteet
  E-Mail: gpoteet@bema.org
Meetings and Communications Specialist: Jennifer Prusa
  E-Mail: jprusa@bema.org

Historical Note:
Founded as Bakery Equipment Manufacturers Association; later became BEMA - an International Association serving the baking and food industries before assuming its current name in 1999. BEMA's mission is to provide value to its members and their customers through communication, programs and services in the grain-based foods industry. Membership: $1,750/year (Corporate).

Meetings/Conferences: Annual
Conference Chair: Jennifer Prusa
2013 - Colorado Springs, CO (Broadmoor Resort)/June
  20 - 25

Publications:
BEMA e-Newsletter; on-line

BEMA Newsletter; quarterly
Membership Directory; annually

Benchmarking Network Association (1992)
4606 FM 1960 West
Suite 250
Houston, TX 77069
Tel: (281) 440-5044 Fax: (281) 440-6677
E-Mail: ntpo@benchmarkingnetwork.com
Website: benchmarkingnetwork.com
Members: 150000 individuals
Staff: 21
Annual Budget: $1-2,000,000

Personnel:
President: Mark T. Czarnecki
  E-Mail: mczarnecki@benchmarkingnetwork.com

Historical Note:
BNA assists in benchmarking activities and promotes communication between professionals in corporations involved in benchmarking. BNA's goal is to develop and utilize the most sophisticated technologies to provide the highest value services. Members span industries and functional expertise. BNA sponsors a number of specialty groups, including Health Care Benchmarking, Human Resources Benchmarking, Accounting and Finance Benchmarking, and International Governmental Benchmarking. Membership: Free.

Publications:
E-Benchmarking Newsletter; on-line

Beta Alpha Psi (1919)
220 Leigh Farm Rd.
Durham, NC 27707-8110
Tel: (919) 402-4044 Fax: (919) 402-4040
E-Mail: bap@bap.org
Website: bap.org
Members: 300000 members
Staff: 4
Annual Budget: $25-50,000
Tax: 501(c)(3)

Personnel:
Executive Director: Hadassah Baum
  E-Mail: hbaum@bap.org
Chapter Services Specialist: Margaret Fiorentino
  E-Mail: mfiorentino@aicpa.org
Marketing and Communications Specialist: Cortney
  Sanders
  E-Mail: csanders@aicpa.org
Planner, Meetings and Conferences: Beth Woloski
  E-Mail: bwoloski@aicpa.org

Historical Note:
BAP is an honorary, professional accounting fraternity. BAP's mission is to provide opportunities for development of technical and professional skills to complement university education; participation in community service and interaction among students, faculty and professionals. Membership: $55/year (Lifetime).

Meetings/Conferences: Annual
Conference Chair: Beth Woloski
2013 - Baltimore, MD (Marriott Baltimore Waterfront)/
  April 1
2013 - Anaheim, CA (Hyatt Regency- Orange County)/
  Aug. 8 - 10
2014 - Atlanta, GA/Aug. 7 - 9

Publications:
Beta Alpha Psi

Beta Beta Beta (1922)
University of North Alabama
UNA Box 5079
Florence, AL 35632
Tel: (256) 765-6220 Fax: (256) 765-6221
E-Mail: tribeta@una.edu
Website: tri-beta.org
Members:
200000 individuals
541 chapters
Staff: 3
Annual Budget: $250-500,000

Personnel:
President: Don Roush
  E-Mail: dhroush@una.edu
Editor: Lori Kelman
  E-Mail: lori.kelman@montgomerycollege.edu
Secretary and Treasurer: Kathy Roush
  E-Mail: tribeta@una.edu

Historical Note:

TriBeta is a society for students, particularly undergraduates, dedicated to improving the understanding and appreciation of biological study and extending boundaries of human knowledge through scientific research. Membership: $45 (Regular/Graduate/Alumnus/Honorary); $35 (Associate); $10 (Promoted).

Meetings/Conferences:
Number of non-conference events/year: 1

Publications:
BIOS; quarterly

Beta Phi Mu (1948)
C/O The iSchool at Drexel University
3141 Chestnut St.
Philadelphia, PA 19104
Tel: (215) 895-2492 Fax: (215) 895-2494
E-Mail: betaphimuinfo@admin.fsu.edu
Website: beta-phi-mu.org
Members: 35000 individuals
Staff: 3
Annual Budget: $50-100,000
Tax: 501(c)(3)

Personnel:
Executive Director: Alison M. Lewis PhD
  E-Mail: alewis@drexel.edu
Director, Programs: Erin Gabriele
  E-Mail: betaphimu@drexel.edu
Treasurer: Kathleen Inman
  E-Mail: kmi32@drexel.edu

Historical Note:
Beta Phi Mu strives to recognize and encourage scholastic achievement among library and information studies students. Membership: $85 (Individual); $100(Lifetime).

Meetings/Conferences: Annual

Publications:
Beta Phi Mu National Newsletter; on-line; adv.
The Pipeline

Beverage Media Group, Inc (1970)
152 Madison Ave.
Suite 600
New York, NY 10016
Tel: (212) 571-3232 Fax: (212) 571-4443
E-Mail: info@bevmedia.com
Website: beveragemedia.com
Staff: 1

Personnel:
Contact, Communication: Jody Slone

Historical Note:
Beverage Media Group, Inc. is dedicated to provide service to business communications system in the promotion, distribution and marketing of beverage alcohol products.

Publications:
Beverage Network
Newsletter

Bibliographical Society of America (1904)
P.O. Box 1537
Lenox Hill Station
New York, NY 10021
Tel: (212) 452-2710 Fax: (212) 452-2710
E-Mail: bsa@bibsocamer.org
Website: bibsocamer.org
Members: 500 individuals and institutions
Staff: 2
Annual Budget: $1-2,000,000
Tax: 501(c)(3)

Personnel:
Executive Director: Michele E. Randall
  E-Mail: bsa@bibsocamer.org
Treasurer: G. Scott Clemons
  E-Mail: scott.clemons@bbh.com

Historical Note:
Organized in Washington, D. C. as an outgrowth of the Bibliographical Society of Chicago. Incorporated in 1927. BSA is dedicated to the study of books and manuscripts as physical objects. Member of the American Council of Learned Societies. Membership is open to all interested in bibliographical problems and projects. Membership: $1,250 (Life); $250-265 (Sustaining); $100-115 (Contributing/ Institutional); $65-80 (Individual); $20-35 (Student).

Meetings/Conferences: Annual
2013 - New York City, NY/Jan. 25

Publications:
The Papers of the Bibliographical Society of America
  (PBSA); quarterly; adv.
Membership Directory; on-line

BICSI (1974)

8610 Hidden River Pkwy.
Tampa, FL 33637-1000
Tel: (813) 979-1991 *Fax:* (813) 971-4311
TollFree: (800) 242-7405
E-Mail: bicsi@bicsi.org
Website: bicsi.org
Members: 25000 individuals
Staff: 69
Annual Budget: $50-100,000
Tax: 501(c)(6)

Personnel:
Executive Director and Chief Executive Officer: John D.
    Clark CAE, Jr.
    E-Mail: jclark@bicsi.org
Vice President, Professional Development: Mark Coppa
    E-Mail: mcoppa@bicsi.org
Manager, Membership Services: Michael Dade
    E-Mail: mdade@bicsi.org
Vice President, Administration and Chief Financial Officer:
    Betty Eckebrecht CAE
    E-Mail: beckebrecht@bicsi.org
Manager, Information Technology: David Everett
    E-Mail: deverett@bicsi.org
Managing Editor, Technical Publications and Designs:
    Clarke Hammersley
    E-Mail: chammersley@bicsi.org
Director, Membership and Marketing: Maarja Kolberg
    E-Mail: mkolberg@bicsi.org
Director, Credentialing: Trisha Mendoza
    E-Mail: tmendoza@bicsi.org
Director, Human Resources: Ronda V. Thomas SPHR
    E-Mail: rvthomas@bicsi.org
Director, Conferences and Events: Melanie Hughes
    Younger CMP
    E-Mail: myounger@bicsi.org

Historical Note:
BICSI strives to provide training and knowledge assessment
to designers and installers of information transport systems,
including designers and installers of telecommunications
wiring. Also sponsors numerous meetings and educational
opportunities, both domestically and abroad. Membership:
$70-150/year (Individual).

Continuing Education:
Certification Designation/s: RCDD, RITP, RTPM, DCDC,
ESS, NTS, OSP, WD

Meetings/Conferences: Semi-Annual
Conference Chair: Melanie Hughes Younger CMP
2013 - Tampa, FL (Tampa Convention Center)/Jan. 20
    - 24
2013 - Las Vegas, NV (MGM Grand Hotel and
    Conference Center)/Sept. 15 - 19
2014 - Orlando, FL (Rosen Shingle Creek)/Feb. 2 - 6
2014 - Anaheim, CA (Anaheim Convention Center)/
    Sept. 28 - Oct. 2
2015 - Orlando, FL (Orlando World Center Marriott)/
    Feb. 22 - 26
2015 - Las Vegas, NV (Mandalay Bay Hotel and
    Casino)/Sept. 20 - 24
2016 - Orlando, FL (Rosen Shingle Creek)/Feb. 7 - 11
2016 - San Antonio, TX (The Henry B. Gonzalez
    Convention Center)/Sept. 11 - 16

Publications:
BICSI News Magazine; bi-monthly; adv.
STANDARDize Newsletter

Bicycle Product Suppliers Association (1940)

P.O. Box 187
Montgomeryville, PA 18936
Tel: (215) 393-3144 *Fax:* (215) 893-4872
E-Mail: bpsa@bpsa.org
Website: bpsa.org
Members: 67 companies
Staff: 3
Annual Budget: $250-500,000

Personnel:
Executive Director: Maureen Waddington
    E-Mail: bpsa@bpsa.org
Legal Counsel: George Constantine
Director, Marketing and Membership: Ray Keener

Historical Note:
Formerly (1960) Cycle Jobbers Association and (1997)
Bicycle Wholesale Distributors Association. BPSA's mission
is to provide the tools and resources that improve the
efficiency and productivity of its members in the service
they provide to the specialty bicycle retailer. Members are

suppliers and distributors who serve the independent bicycle
dealer channel of trade. Membership: $800-12,000/year.

Publications:
Membership Directory; on-line

Billiard and Bowling Institute of America (1940)

615 Six Flags Dr.
Arlington, TX 76011
Tel: (817) 385-8120 *Fax:* (817) 633-2940
TollFree: (800) 343-1329
E-Mail: answer@billiardandbowling.org
Website: billiardandbowling.org
Members: 100 manufacturers and distributors
Staff: 2
Annual Budget: $50-100,000
Tax: 501(c)(6)

Personnel:
Executive Director: Bill Supper
    E-Mail: bill@ibpsia.com

Historical Note:
BBIA, a component of the Sporting Goods Manufacturers
Association, is a not-for-profit association formed in
Chicago to serve the billiard and bowling industries. It is
also a component of the Sporting Goods Manufacturers
Association and is comprised of bowling and billiard
manufacturers, independent bowling distributors and
billiard retailers. Membership: $650 (Bowling/Billiard
Manufacturer); $425 (Bowling/Billiard Distributor/
Associate); $325 (Billiard Retailer).

Meetings/Conferences: Annual
2013 - Biloxi, MS (Beau Rivage Resort and Casino)/
    April 21 - 23

Publications:
BBIA Newsletter; quarterly
Membership Directory

Billiard Congress of America (1948)

12303 Airport Way
Suite 140
Broomfield, CO 80021
Tel: (303) 243-5070 *Fax:* (303) 243-5075
E-Mail: membership@bca-pool.com
Website: home.bca-pool.com
Members: 1300 Companies
Staff: 4
Annual Budget: $500-1,000,000
Tax: 501(c)(6)

Personnel:
Chief Executive Officer: Rob Johnson
    E-Mail: rob@bca-pool.com
Director, Trade Services: Melissa Cowan
    E-Mail: melissa@bca-pool.com
Coordinator, Membership Services and Communications:
    Shane Tyree
    E-Mail: shane@bca-pool.com

Historical Note:
BCA's mission is to enhance the success of its members and
support the game of billiards. Membership: $400-1,500
(Manufacturer/Distributor, based on annual revenues);
$200-400 (Retailer, based on number of retail locations);
$300-500 (Room Operator, based on number of locations);
$200 (Affiliate).

Meetings/Conferences: Annual
Conference Chair: Melissa Cowan
2013 - Schaumburg, IL (Schaumburg Renaissance
    Hotel and Convention Center)/July 10 - 13
Number of non-conference events/year: 1

Publications:
BCA Member Update; bi-monthly
BCA Membership Directory; on-line

Billings Ovulation Method Association of the United States (1990)

P.O. Box 2135
St. Cloud, MN 56302
Tel: (651) 699-8139 *Fax:* (320) 654-6486
E-Mail: info@boma-usa.org
Website: boma-usa.org
Members: 390 individuals
Staff: 2
Annual Budget: $500-1,000,000

Personnel:
President: Kay Ek
Executive Director: Sue Ek
    E-Mail: boma-usa@msn.com

Historical Note:

BOMA members are teachers of the Billings Ovulation
Method and others with an interest in natural family
planning. Membership: $35 (Individual/Couple in U.S.);
$45 (Canadian); $35 (Associate); $55 (Foreign Members
other than Canada).

Meetings/Conferences: Annual
Number of non-conference events/year: 2

Publications:
BOMA News

Binding Industries Association (1955)

200 Deer Run Rd.
Sewickley, PA 15143
Tel: (412) 741-6860 *Fax:* (412) 741-2311
TollFree: (800) 910-4283
E-Mail: printing@printing.org
Website: printing.org/bia
Members: 12000 companies
Staff: 1
Annual Budget: $250-500,000

Personnel:
Manager, Binding Industries Association: Justin Goldstein
    E-Mail: jgoldstein@printing.org

Historical Note:
Formerly (1971) Trade Binders and Loose Leaf Division
of PIA and (2002) Binding Industries of America. Born
out of the consolidation of PIA and GATF. BIA's mission
is to print industries of America, along with its affiliates,
delivers products and services that enhance the growth
and profitability of its members and the industry through
advocacy, education, research, and technical information.
Membership: $300 (Active); $450 (Associate).

Meetings/Conferences: Annual
Number of non-conference events/year: 19

Publications:
The Binder's Bulletin; monthly
The Binding Edge Magazine; quarterly

Membership List Available to Non-members

BioCommunications Association (1931)

220 Southwind Ln.
Hillsborough, NC 27278-7907
Tel: (919) 245-0906 *Fax:* (919) 245-0906
E-Mail: office@bca.org
Website: bca.org
Members: 300 individuals
Staff: 4
Annual Budget: $50-100,000

Personnel:
President: Susanne Loomis FBCA
    E-Mail: sloomis1@partners.org
Director, Conferences: Thomas Bednarek
    E-Mail: tbednare@utmb.edu
Editor: Karen Hensley
    E-Mail: khensley@mdanderson.org
Central Office Manager and Membership Contact: Nancy
Hurtgen

Historical Note:
Formerly Biological Photographic Association. BCA's
mission is to enhance the professional competency of its
members and to advance the profession by educating and
developing creators and users of visual communication
media in the life sciences and medicine. Members are from
health care, universities, research institutions and private
industry, and include photographers, designers, illustrators,
and videographers working in visual communications for
the life sciences. Membership: $100 (Active/Institutional);
$50 (Retired/Student).

Continuing Education:
Certification Designation/s: TBM

Meetings/Conferences: Annual
Conference Chair: Thomas Bednarek

Publications:
BCA News
Journal of Biocommunication

Membership List Available to Non-members

Bioelectromagnetics Society (1978)

2412 Cobblestone Way
Frederick, MD 21702-2626
Tel: (301) 663-4252 *Fax:* (301) 694-4948
E-Mail: office@bems.org
Website: bems.org
Members: 850 individuals
Staff: 3
Annual Budget: $250-500,000
Tax: 501(c)(3)

Personnel:
President: David Black
Treasurer: Philip Chadwick
Newsletter Editor: Janie Page

Historical Note:
Bioelectromagnetics Society is a scientific society promoting research concerned with the interaction of electromagnetic energy with biological systems. Members are biological and physical scientists, physicians and engineers interested in the interactions of non-ionizing radiation with biological systems. Membership: $105 (Full Member); $40 (Associate Member/Student Member/Emeritus Member); $1000 (Sustaining Member); $100(Charter Member).

Meetings/Conferences: Quadrennial
2013 - Thessaloniki, Greece/June 10 - 14

Publications:
BEMS Newsletter
Bioelectromagnetics; adv.

Biological Stain Commission (1922)
University of Rochester, Medical Center,
Pathology Department
P.O. Box 626, 575 Elmwood Ave.
Rochester, NY 14642-0001
Tel: (585) 275-2751 *Fax:* (585) 442-8993
E-Mail: Chad_Fagan@URMC.rochester.edu
Website: biologicalstaincommission.org
Members: 18 societies and 80 individuals
Staff: 4
Annual Budget: $100-250,000

Personnel:
President: Richard Dapson
E-Mail: dick@dapsons.com
Treasurer: Brendan Boyce
Secretary and Membership Contact: John A. Kiernan
E-Mail: jkiernan@uwo.ca

Historical Note:
Originated as a special committee of the National Research Council and later became the Commission on Biological Stains. Incorporated in New York in 1943 as the Biological Stain Commission, Inc. BSC's mission is to ensure quality of dyes, promote cooperation among manufacturers, vendors and users of dyes, educate users of biological stains and publish uses of biological staining with dyes and related techniques. Membership: $60/year.

Publications:
Biotechnic and Histochemistry; bi-monthly
Conn's Biological Stains; irregular

Membership List Available to Non-members

Biomass Thermal Energy Council (2009)
1211 Connecticut Ave. NW
Suite 600
Washington, DC 20036-2701
Tel: (202) 596-3974 *Fax:* (202) 223-5537
E-Mail: info@biomassthermal.org
Website: biomassthermal.org
Staff: 3
Annual Budget: $250-500,000
Tax: 501(c)(6)

Personnel:
Executive Director: Joseph Seymour
E-Mail: joseph.seymour@biomassthermal.org
Senior Advisor: Jeffrey A. Serfass
E-Mail: jeff.serfass@biomassthermal.org
Program Coordinator, Outreach, Education and External Affairs: Emanuel Wagner
E-Mail: emanuel.wagner@biomassthermal.org

Historical Note:
BTEC's mission is to advance the use of biomass for heat and other thermal energy applications. Membership: $12,500 (Sustaining Member); $300 (Non-Profit); $500-6500 (based on their company's expected gross annual revenues).

Publications:
BTEC Newsletter; adv.
Member Directory; on-line

Biomedical Engineering Society (1968)
8401 Corporate Dr.
Suite 1125
Landover, MD 20785-2224
Tel: (301) 459-1999 *Fax:* (301) 459-2444
TollFree: (877) 871-2637
E-Mail: info@bmes.org
Website: bmes.org
Members: 5500 individuals
Staff: 6

Annual Budget: $2-5,000,000
Tax: 501(c)(3)

Personnel:
Executive Director: Edward L. Schilling III
E-Mail: elschilling@bmes.org
Director, Communications: Doug Beizer
E-Mail: doug@bmes.org
Director, Membership Services: Jennifer Edwards
E-Mail: Jennifer@bmes.org
Director, Operations and Finance: Valerie Kolmaister
E-Mail: valerie@bmes.org
Director, Education: Michele Surricchio
E-Mail: Michele@bmes.org
Director, Meetings: Debra Tucker
E-Mail: dtuckercmp@aol.com

Historical Note:
BMES's mission is to encourage and enhance knowledge and education in biomedical engineering and bioengineering worldwide and its utilization for the health. Membership: $250 (Fellow); $200 (Member/Associate/Affiliate); $80 (Early Career); $30 (Student); $25 (Corresponding).

Meetings/Conferences: Annual
Conference Chair: Debra Tucker
2013 - Seatle, WA/Sept. 25 - 28/3000 attendees/51-100 exhibitors
2014 - San Antonio, TX/Oct. 22 - 25/3000 attendees/51-100 exhibitors
2015 - Tampa, FL/Oct. 7 - 10/3000 attendees/51-100 exhibitors
2016 - Minneapolis, MN/Oct. 5 - 8/3000 attendees/51-100 exhibitors

Publications:
Annals of Biomedical Engineering; monthly; adv.
Biomedical Engineering News; monthly; adv.
Cardiovascular Engineering and Technology; quarterly; adv.
Cellular and Molecular Bioengineering; quarterly; adv.

Membership List Available to Non-members

Biophysical Society (1957)
11400 Rockville Pike
Suite 800
Rockville, MD 20852
Tel: (240) 290-5600 *Fax:* (240) 290-5555
E-Mail: society@biophysics.org
Website: biophysics.org
Members: 9000 academics, industry, and government agencies
Staff: 15
Annual Budget: $2-5,000,000
Tax: 501(c)(3)

Personnel:
Director, Meetings and Exhibits: Dorothy Chaconas CMP
E-Mail: dchaconas@biophysics.org
Systems Director: Eric Ebene
E-Mail: eebene@biophysics.org
Executive Officer: Rosalba Kampman
E-Mail: rkampman@biophysics.org
Manager, Exhibits and Sales: Marlene Mirman
E-Mail: mmirman@biophysics.org
Director, Finance and Operations: Harris Povich
E-Mail: hpovich@biophysics.org
Coordinator, Membership Services: Bridget Swartz
E-Mail: bswartz@biophysics.org
Director, Policy and Communications: Ellen Weiss
E-Mail: eweiss@biophysics.org
Director, Publications and Membership Services: Alisha Yocum
E-Mail: ayocum@biophysics.org

Historical Note:
BPS's mission is to encourage development and dissemination of knowledge in biophysics. The Society is open to scientists who share the stated purpose of the Society and who have educational, research, or practical experience in biophysics or in an allied scientific field. Members are individuals interested in applying physical laws and techniques to the investigation of biological phenomena. Membership: $160 (Regular); $55 (Early Career); $10-25 (Student); Free (Emeritus).

Meetings/Conferences: Annual
Conference Chair: Dorothy Chaconas CMP

Publications:
Biophysical Journal; semi-monthly
Biophysical Society Newsletter; monthly
Faculty of 1000; monthly
Membership Directory; on-line
The Biophysical Society Abstracts Issue; annually

Membership List Available to Non-members

Biotechnology Industry Organization (BIO) (1993)
1201 Maryland Ave. SW.
Suite 900
Washington, DC 20024
Tel: (202) 962-9200 *Fax:* (202) 488-6301
E-Mail: info@bio.org
Website: bio.org
Members: 1100 individuals
Staff: 11
Annual Budget: Over $100,000,000
Tax: 501(c)(6)

Personnel:
President and Chief Executive Officer: Hon. James C. Greenwood
E-Mail: jgreenwood@bio.org
Senior Vice President and General Counsel: Tom DiLenge
E-Mail: tdilenge@bio.org
Chief Financial Officer and Vice President, Financial Administration: Joanne Duncan
Vice President, Corporate Development and Marketing: Amy Finan
Vice President, Communications: Jeff Joseph
Vice President, Conventions and Conferences: Robbi Lycett
Vice President, Federal Government Relations: Brent Del Monte
E-Mail: bmonte@bio.org
Chief Operating Officer: Scott Whitaker
E-Mail: swhitaker@bio.org

Historical Note:
BIO's mission is to provide advocacy, business development and communications services to its members. Membership: $45,000-170,000/Year (Corporate).

Meetings/Conferences:
Conference Chair: Robbi Lycett
2013 - Osaka, Japan (The Ritz - Carlton, Osaka)/Jan. 29 - 30
2013 - San Diego, CA/March 25 - 27
2013 - New York City, NY (Waldorf = Astoria)/Nov. 11 - 12
Number of non-conference events/year: 3

Publications:
BIO Newsletter
Membership Directory; on-line

Biscuit and Cracker Manufacturers' Association (1901)
6325 Woodside Ct.
Suite 125
Columbia, MD 21046
Tel: (443) 545-1645 *Fax:* (410) 290-8585
Website: thebcma.org
Members: 350 companies
Staff: 5
Annual Budget: $500-1,000,000
Tax: 501(c)(6)

Personnel:
President: Stacey Sharpless
E-Mail: ssharpless@thebcma.org
Manager, Education and Meetings: Kerry Kurowski
E-Mail: kkurowski@thebcma.org
Technical Advisor: Dennis Loalbo
E-Mail: dloalbo@thebcma.org
Manager, Membership Services and Student Relations: Kathy K. Phelps
E-Mail: kkinter@thebcma.org
Administrative Assistant and Manager, Entry Level Training Program: Vanessa Vial
E-Mail: vvial@thebcma.org

Historical Note:
B&CMA promotes the cookie and cracker baking industry. Absorbed the Biscuit Bakers Institute in 1965. B&CMA's mission is to bring unparalleled educational training programs and networking opportunities to members of the B&CMA. Membership: $1200/year (Allied).

Continuing Education:
Certification Designation/s: CCMC

Meetings/Conferences:
Conference Chair: Kerry Kurowski
2013 - Kansas City, MO (InterContinental Kansas City At The Plaza)/May 5 - 8
Number of non-conference events/year: 1

Publications:
Membership Directory; annually

Membership List Available to Non-members

Bituminous Coal Operators Association (1950)
801 Pennsylvania Ave. NW
Suite 612
Washington, DC 20004
Tel: (202) 783-3195 *Fax:* (202) 783-4862
Members: 19 company groups
Staff: 3
Annual Budget: $1-2,000,000

Personnel:
President: David Young
Vice President, Public Affairs: Morris D. Feibusch
Secretary, Treasurer: Charles S. Perkins III
  E-Mail: cperkinsbcoa@aol.com

Historical Note:
BCOA was formed in 1950 to represent mine operators in negotiation of the National Bituminous Coal Wage Agreement, due to the confusing situation resulting from separate company negotiations with the United Mine Workers of America. Dues are established by the Board of Directors, using tonnage produced as the basis.

BKR International (1975)
19 Fullton St.
Suite 306
New York, NY 10038
Tel: (212) 964-2115 *Fax:* (212) 964-2133
E-Mail: bkr@bkr.com
Website: bkr.com
Members: 135 companies
Staff: 5
Annual Budget: $1-2,000,000
Tax: 501(c)(6)

Personnel:
Executive Director: Maureen M. Schwartz

Historical Note:
Formerly known as the National Group of CPA Firms and (1989). BKR International is a association of independent accounting and business advisory firms. Represents the combined strength of leading-edge accounting and business advisory firms in more than 300 locations throughout the world. BKR firms offer clients the best of nationally and internationally, personalized local service and the financial expertise of a global association. Membership: $1.2-2.2/ year (Company).

Meetings/Conferences: Annual
Number of non-conference events/year: 1

Publications:
Membership Directory; on-line

Black Caucus of the American Library Association (1970)
6985 Snow Way Blvd.
Campus Box 7493
St. Louis, MO 63130-4400
Website: bcala.org
Members: 1100 individuals
Staff: 3
Annual Budget: $100-250,000
Tax: 501(c)(3)

Personnel:
President: Jerome Offord Jr.
  E-Mail: jeromeoffordjr@gmail.com
Contact, Membership Services: Rudolph Clay Jr.
  E-Mail: membership@bcala.org
Treasurer: Annie M. Ford
  E-Mail: annieford@gmail.com

Historical Note:
BCALA's mission is to serve as an advocate for the development, enhancement and improvement of library services and resources to the nation's African American community. Membership: $200 (Corporate); $60 (Institutional); $45 (Regular); $10 (Student); $20 (Library Support Staff); $500 (Lifetime); Retired membership is free.

Publications:
BCACA Newsletter; bi-monthly; adv.
BCALA Membership Directory

Black Coaches & Administrators (1987)
Pan American Plaza, 201 S. Capitol Ave.
Suite 495
Indianapolis, IN 46225
Tel: (317) 829-5600 *Fax:* (317) 829-5601
TollFree: (877) 789-1222
Website: bcasports.org
Members: 4500 individuals and institutions
Staff: 5

Annual Budget: $500-1,000,000
Tax: 501(c)(3)

Personnel:
Executive Director: Floyd A. Keith
Accounts Executive: Willis Cheaney
General Manager: Kearsten Huddleston
Director, Membership Services: Kennedy D. Wells
Director, Marketing and Events: Glenda K. Wilson

Historical Note:
BCA's purpose is to foster the growth and development of ethnic minorities at all levels of sports both nationally and internationally. Membership: $79 (Supporter); $99 (Coach/ Associate); $39 (Affiliate); $250-2500 (Institutional).

Meetings/Conferences: Annual
Conference Chair: Glenda K. Wilson
Number of non-conference events/year: 3

Publications:
BCA Newsletter

Black Data Processing Associates (1975)
9500 Arena Dr.
Suite 350
Largo, MD 20774
Tel: (301) 584-3135 *Fax:* (301) 560-8300
TollFree: (800) 727-2372
E-Mail: info@bdpa.org
Website: bdpa.org
Members:
55 Chapters
4000 Individuals
Staff: 4
Annual Budget: $10-25,000
Tax: 501(c)(6)

Personnel:
Executive Director: Donald "Don" French
  E-Mail: executivedirector@bdpamail.org
Vice President, Membership Services: Mildred Allen
  E-Mail: vpmm@bdpa.org
President Elect and Vice President, Business Management:
  Monique Berry
  E-Mail: VPBM@bdpa.org
Chief Information Officer: Milt Haynes
  E-Mail: Milt.Haynes@bdpa.org

Historical Note:
BDPA is a technology focused organization that delivers programs and services for the professional well-being of its stakeholders. Membership: $100 (Full Member); $25 (Student); $1000 (Lifetime Member).

Continuing Education:
Certification Designation/s: CISSP

Meetings/Conferences: Annual

Publications:
BDPA Journal; quarterly; adv.
BDPA Today; monthly; adv.

Black Entertainment and Sports Lawyers Association (1980)
P.O. Box 230794
New York, NY 10003
Tel: (301) 248-1818
E-Mail: beslamailbox@aol.com
Website: besla.org
Members: 600 individuals
Staff: 4
Annual Budget: $100-250,000
Tax: 501(c)(3)

Personnel:
President: Matthew J. Middleton Esq.
Treasurer: Douglas 'Tony' Brackett Esq.
Conference Chair: Tamela R. Cash-Curry Esq.
Vice President, Public Relations and Marketing: Ronda
  Robinson Kirk Esq.

Historical Note:
Formerly (1986) Black Entertainment Lawyers Association (BELA). Founded in 1979 by a group of black lawyers to encourage attorneys to develop an expertise in the fields of entertainment and sports law and related areas of specialization and to nurture and enhance individuals' aptitudes in these fields. BESLA's purpose is to provide an effective network of high- impact professional and business relationships and information-sharing. Members represent celebrities and professionals in entertainment and sports industries. Membership: $130 (Professional); $105 (Associate); $40 (Law Students); $80 (Recent Law Practitioner); $1,000 (Patron); $1,500 (Sustaining).

Meetings/Conferences: Annual
Conference Chair: Tamela R. Cash-Curry Esq.

Publications:
BESLA Newsletter

Black Farmers and Agriculturists Association (1997)
P.O. Box 61
Tillery, NC 27887
Tel: (252) 826-3017 *Fax:* (252) 826-3244
E-Mail: info@bfaa-us.org
Website: bfaa-us.org
Members: 1,500 farmers and 21 state chapters
Staff: 1

Personnel:
President: Gary R. Grant

Historical Note:
BFAA is a professional trade association created to respond to the issues and concerns of Black farmers in the U.S. and abroad.

Black Filmmaker Foundation (1978)
131 Varick St.
Suite 937
New York, NY 10013
Tel: (212) 253-1690
E-Mail: info@dvrepublic.org
Website: dvrepublic.org
Members: 2500 individuals
Staff: 3
Annual Budget: $100-250,000
Tax: 501(c)(3)

Personnel:
Founder and Chief: Warrington Hudlin
  E-Mail: hudlin@dvrepublic.org

Historical Note:
BFF's mission is to develop and administer programs that assist emerging filmmakers and builds audiences for their work. BFF hosts two online communities: dvRepublic (an online discussion forum about the intersection of media, technology, and social justice) and Cast and Crew of Color, an online professional network for people of color who work in film, TV, and the Internet. BFF also curates film series and organizes conferences, workshops. BFF is the founding member of the Media Coalition of Artists of Color.

Publications:
DV Republic Newsletter; on-line

Black Mental Health Alliance (1984)
733 W. 40th St.
Suite Ten
Baltimore, MD 21211-2107
Tel: (410) 338-2642 *Fax:* (410) 338-1771
E-Mail: bhealthall@blackmentalhealth.com
Website: blackmentalhealth.com
Staff: 17
Annual Budget: $500-1,000,000
Tax: 501(c)(3)

Personnel:
Executive Director: Tracee E. Bryant
  E-Mail: tbryant@blackmentalhealth.org

Historical Note:
BMHA's mission is to provide a forum and promote a holistic, culturally relevant approach to the development and maintenance of optimal mental health programs and services for African Americans and other people of color. Membership: $10 (Student/Senior); $50 (Individual); $150 (Professional); $1,000 (Corporate); $1,500 (Lifetime).

Publications:
Visions Newsletter

Black Psychiatrists of America (1969)
2020 Pennsylvania Ave. NW
Suite 725
Washington, DC 20006-1811
Tel: (877) 272-1967 *Fax:* (877) 272-1967
E-Mail: BPA4Info@aol.com
Website: blackpsych.org
Members: 650 individuals
Staff: 2
Annual Budget: $50-100,000

Personnel:
Secretary: Beverley Allen MD
  E-Mail: beall@aol.com
Editor: William B. Lawson DFAPA, MD, PhD
  E-Mail: wblawson@Howard.edu

Historical Note:
BPA's mission is to address issues affecting the Mental Health of African-Americans and to provide a forum for continuing education for those who provide psychiatric

care. Membership includes black psychiatrists in the United States, Canada, and the Caribbean. Membership: $200 (General); $150 (Associate); $75(Resident Physician); $25 (Student).

Meetings/Conferences:
2013 - Baltimore, MD (Baltimore Hilton Hotel)/March 22 - 23

Publications:
BPA Newsletter; monthly; adv.
Referral Directory; adv.

Black Retail Action Group *(1970)*
P.O. Box 1192
Rockefeller Center Stn.
New York, NY 10185
Tel: (212) 234-3050 *Fax:* (212) 234-3053
E-Mail: info@bragusa.org
Website: bragusa.org
Members: 300 individuals
Staff: 4
Annual Budget: $250-500,000
Tax: 501(c)(3)

Personnel:
President: Gail Monroe Perry
    E-Mail: garylampley@bragusa.org
Secretary: Laticha Brown
    E-Mail: latichabrown@bragusa.org
Vice President, Operations: Nicole Cokley
    E-Mail: nicolecokley@bragusa.org
Vice President, Finance: Shawn R. Outler
    E-Mail: shawnoutler@bragusa.org

Historical Note:
Founded by members of the former National Negro Retail Advisory Group. BRAG's purpose is to promote awareness among the corporate community of challenges facing people of color in the workplace and assisting in the selection, development and advancement of people of color. Membership: $100 (Professional); $25 (College Student); $15 (HS student).

Continuing Education:
Certification Designation/s: BRAG, CDC
Meetings/Conferences:
Number of non-conference events/year: 3

Membership List Available to Non-members

Black Theatre Network *(1986)*
8306 Bluebird Way
Suite Five
Lorton, VA 22079
Tel: (202) 274-5667 *Fax:* (850) 599-8417
E-Mail: info@blacktheatrenetwork.org
Website: blacktheatrenetwork.org
Members: 500 theater companies and subscribers
Staff: 4
Annual Budget: $10-25,000
Tax: 501(c)(3)

Personnel:
President: Artisia Green
    E-Mail: avgreen@wm.edu
Business Manager and Membership Chair: Renee Charlow
    E-Mail: thejazziediva@yahoo.com
Editor: Christina McVay
    E-Mail: cmcvay@kent.edu
Web Site Administrator: Hely Perez

Historical Note:
BTN seeks to collect, process and distribute information that supports the professional and personal development of its members and therefore nurtures the growth of Black Theatre. Network members are theatre professionals and academics. Membership: $100 (Individual); $50 (Student); $55 (Retired); $150 (Organization).

Meetings/Conferences: Semi-Annual
Conference Chair: Renee Charlow
2013 - Winston-Salem, NC (Brookstown Inn)/July 26 - 29
2013 - Winston-Salem, NC (Winston-Salem Marriott)/ July 29 - Aug. 3

Publications:
BTNews; on-line
Membership Directory; on-line

Blinded Veterans Association *(1945)*
477 H St. NW
Washington, DC 20001-2694
Tel: (202) 371-8880 *Fax:* (202) 371-8258
TollFree: (800) 669-7079

E-Mail: bva@bva.org
Website: bva.org
Staff: 9
Annual Budget: $5-10,000,000
Tax: 501(c)(3)

Personnel:
Executive Director: Al Avina
    E-Mail: aavina@bva.org
Director, Membership Services: Alyson Alt
    E-Mail: aalt@bva.org
Manager, Conventions and Operation Peer Support: Christina Hitchcock
    E-Mail: chitchcock@bva.org
Director, Administration: Brigitte Jones
    E-Mail: bjones@bva.org
Manager, Communications: Stuart Nelson
    E-Mail: snelson@bva.org
Chief Financial Officer: Kathy Ruais
    E-Mail: kruais@bva.org
Director, Government Relations: Thomas Zampieri
    E-Mail: tzampieri@bva.org

Historical Note:
BVA's mission is to promote the welfare of blinded veterans so that, not withstanding their disabilities, they may take their rightful place in the community and work with their fellow citizens toward the creation of a peaceful world. Membership: $15 (Member/Associate Member); $50-100 (Life Member/Associate Life Member).

Meetings/Conferences: Annual
Conference Chair: Christina Hitchcock

Publications:
DIALOGUE Magazine; quarterly; adv.
Membership Directory; on-line
National Resource Directory; adv.

Blue Cross Blue Shield Association *(1946)*
225 N. Michigan Ave.
Chicago, IL 60601
Tel: (312) 297-6000 *Fax:* (312) 297-6609
Website: bcbs.com
Members: 38 companies
Staff: 880
Annual Budget: Over $100,000,000
Tax: 501(c)(4)

Personnel:
President and Chief Executive Officer: Scott P. Serota
Senior Vice President, Human Resources and Administration: William J. Colbourne
Senior Vice President, Office of Policy and Representation: Alissa Fox
    E-Mail: alissa.fox@bcbsa.com
Vice President, Strategic Communications: Paul Gerrard
Senior Vice President and Chief Financial Officer: Robert Kolodgy
Senior Vice President, Operations and Chief Information Officer: Doug Porter
Vice President, Brand Strategy and Marketing Services: Jennifer Vachon
Senior Vice President, General Counsel and Corporate Secretary: Roger G. Wilson

Historical Note:
BCBSA's mission is to represent the nation's family of health benefits companies.

Publications:
Membership Directory; on-line
National Labor Office; quarterly

Blue Water Fishermen's Association *(1990)*
P.O. Box 779
Forked River, NJ 08731-5105
Tel: (609) 891-8672
Website: bwfa-usa.org
Staff: 1
Annual Budget: $100-250,000

Personnel:
Assistant Executive Director and Events Contact: Benjamin Beideman
    E-Mail: ben@bwfa-usa.org

Historical Note:
Blue Water Fishermen's Association is dedicated to the production and marketing of healthy and high-quality Atlantic sustainable swordfish and tuna seafood. Membership: $42-500/Year.

Meetings/Conferences: Annual
Conference Chair: Benjamin Beideman

Bluegrass Tourism Marketing Association *(2001)*

3493 Lansdowne Dr.
Suite Two
Lexington, KY 40517
Tel: (859) 977-7452 *Fax:* (859) 271-0607
E-Mail: infobtma@amrms.com
Website: btmaky.org
Members: 40 member entities and 100 hospitality professionals
Staff: 1

Personnel:
Managing Director: Brian Doty
    E-Mail: bdoty@btmaky.org

Historical Note:
Formerly Lexington Hospitality Sales and Marketing Association. BTMA's mission is to promote business for hotels, resorts, inns, attractions, tour companies and all other hospitality related businesses. Membership: $150/ year.

Meetings/Conferences:
Conference Chair: Brian Doty

Publications:
Newsletter; monthly

The Bluetooth Special Interest Group *(1998)*
5209 Lake Washington Blvd. NE
Suite 350
Kirkland, WA 98033
Tel: (425) 691-3535 *Fax:* (425) 691-3524
Website: bluetooth.com
Members: 16500 companies
Staff: 44
Annual Budget: $10-25,000,000

Personnel:
Executive Director: Mark Powell
Chief Marketing Officer: Suke Jawanda

Historical Note:
SIG's mission is to strengthen the bluetooth brand by empowering SIG members to collaborate and innovate, creating the preferred wireless technology to connect diverse devices. Membership: $7,500-35,000/year (Associate).

Meetings/Conferences:
2013 - Shanghai, China/April 9 - 11
Number of non-conference events/year: 3

Publications:
Memberhip Directory; on-line
SIGnature Magazine; quarterly; adv.

BMC - A Foodservice Sales and Marketing Council *(1980)*
P.O. Box 150229
Arlington, TX 76015
Tel: (682) 518-6008 *Fax:* (682) 518-6476
E-Mail: assnhqtrs@aol.com
Members: 22 food marketing companies
Staff: 2
Annual Budget: $50-100,000

Personnel:
Executive Director: Pamela L. Bess
Director, Administration: Liza L. Grove

Historical Note:
Founded as Broker Management Council; assumed its current name in 2003. BMC members are independent institutional food service brokers who specialize in institutional deli, bakery, school, hotel and restaurant food service products. BMC's purpose is to meet the challenges of the foodservice market.

Publications:
Member Directory; on-line

Board of Certified Safety Professionals *(1969)*
2301 W. Bradley Ave.
Champaign, IL 61821
Tel: (217) 359-9263 *Fax:* (217) 359-0055
E-Mail: bcsp@bcsp.org
Website: bcsp.org
Members: 22000 individuals
Staff: 24
Annual Budget: $2-5,000,000

Personnel:
Director, Human Resources and Chief Financial Officer: Dennis J. Archer PHR
    E-Mail: dennis@bcsp.org
Director, Business Development: Eddie Greer
Director, Information Technology: Sean Le
Manager, Marketing: Lisa Spencer
    E-Mail: lisa@bcsp.org

Chief Operating Officer: Treasa Turnbeaugh

Historical Note:
BCSP is the premier certification body providing domestic and international credentialing services to practitioners, technologists, technicians, supervisors, and workers through its financial strength, continuous improvement and accredited products and services by offering career advancement paths to those persons in safety, health, and environmental practitioners.

Continuing Education:
Enrollment: 22000
Certification Designation/s: CHST, CLCS, OHST, STS, CSP, ASP, GSP

Publications:
BCSP Credential Holder Directory; on-line
BCSP Newsletter; quarterly
Schools & Academic Programs Directory; on-line

Membership List Available to Non-members

Board of Registered Polysomnographic Technologists *(1978)*
8400 Westpark Dr.
Second Floor
McLean, VA 22102
Tel: (703) 610-9020 *Fax:* (703) 610-0229
E-Mail: info@brpt.org
Website: brpt.org
Members: 17000 RPSGTs
Staff: 3
Annual Budget: $1-2,000,000
Tax: 501(c)(6)

Personnel:
Executive Director: Jim Magruder
Credentialing Coordinator: Brenda Mzamo
Director, Communications: Lydia Pelliccia
    E-Mail: lpelliccia@brpt.org

Historical Note:
BRPT's mission is to provide high quality sleep technology products and to create long-term value for credential and certificate holders. BRPT administers the RPSGT certification program based on credentialing practices, which measures the knowledge, skills and abilities of technologists in the field of sleep medicine. Fosters ethical practices and requires the continued competence of those who earn the RPSGT credential. Membership: $600 (General/Honorary).

Continuing Education:
Enrollment: 1000
Certification Designation/s: CPSGT, RPSGT

Meetings/Conferences: Annual

Publications:
BRPT Insider; quarterly
Directory of RPSGTs; on-line

Membership List Available to Non-members

Board of Specialty Society *(1984)*
6300 N. River Rd.
Suite 727
Rosemont, IL 60018-4226
Tel: (847) 384-4238 *Fax:* (847) 823-0536
E-Mail: bos@aaos.org
Website: aaos.org/about/bos.asp
Members: 22 musculoskeletal specialty societies
Staff: 2

Personnel:
Chair-Elect: Steven Douglas K. Ross MD

Historical Note:
Formerly (2006) the Council of Musculoskeletal Specialty Societies. BOS's purpose is to bring together the leaders of musculoskeletal societies to address issues of mutual concern, such as advocacy, continuing medical education, research and residency and fellowship issues and is a coordinating body for professional societies in orthopaedics and related sciences.

Meetings/Conferences: Annual
2013 - Washington, DC/April 30 - May 5
2013 - Austin, TX/Oct. 16 - 20
2014 - Washington, DC/April 29 - May 4
2015 - Washington, DC/April 28 - May 3
2016 - Washington, DC/May 4 - 7
2017 - Washington, DC/April 26 - 29

Publications:
Member Listing; on-line

Board Retailers Association *(2003)*
PO Box 1170
Wrightsville Beach, NC 28480

Tel: (910) 509-0109 *Fax:* (910) 509-3181
Website: boardretailers.org
Members: 600 Board Sport Retailers with 3500 separate retail stores
Staff: 4
Annual Budget: $100-250,000
Tax: 501(c)(6)

Personnel:
President and Executive Director: Mike Duncan
    E-Mail: mike@boardretailers.org
Associate Director: Adrienne Belk
    E-Mail: adrienne@boardretailers.org
Coordinator, Communications and Events: Elizabeth Peavy
    E-Mail: elizabeth@boardretailers.org
Director, Marketing: Vicki Vasil
    E-Mail: vicki@boardretailers.org

Historical Note:
East and West Coast retailers formed the Board Retailers Association in February 2003. BRA organizes and expresses the views and concerns of independent board sport retailers to manufacturer's associations and major trade show organizations in an effort to help promote the industry and support the board sports specialty retailer. Membership: $99 (Retailer); $1,000-5,000 (Associate).

Meetings/Conferences:
Conference Chair: Vicki Vasil

Publications:
Newsletter; monthly

Boating Writers International *(1970)*
108 Ninth St.
Wilmette, IL 60091
Tel: (847) 736-4142
E-Mail: info@bwi.org
Website: bwi.org
Members: 100 supporting corporations and 350 individuals
Staff: 3
Annual Budget: $25-50,000

Personnel:
Executive Director, Secretary and Treasurer: Gregory Proteau
Editor: Alan Jones
President: John Wooldridge

Historical Note:
BWI seeks to encourage boating as a recreational and competitive sport. An organization of individuals who write about boating and allied outdoor sports for magazines, newspapers, television and radio. Members include active marine journalists across the U.S., Canada and Europe, supporting marine manufacturers and service entities, and associates in communication roles. Active members are writers, photographers, and broadcasters. Associate members are mostly public relations or communication firms. Supporting members are manufacturers or advertising agencies. Membership: $50 (Active); $60 (Associate); $175 (Supporting).

Publications:
BWI Directory; annually; adv.
BWI Newsletter
Judging Magazine

Book Industry Study Group, Inc. *(1975)*
370 Lexington Ave.
Suite 900
New York, NY 10017
Tel: (646) 336-7141 *Fax:* (646) 336-6214
E-Mail: info@bisg.org
Website: bisg.org
Members: 200 individuals and organizations
Staff: 4
Annual Budget: $500-1,000,000
Tax: 501(c)(6)

Personnel:
Executive Director: Len Vlahos
    E-Mail: len@bisg.org
Project Manager: Sara Raffel
    E-Mail: sara@bisg.org
Coordinator, Project: Nadine Vassallo
    E-Mail: nadine@bisg.org

Historical Note:
BISG's mission is to sponsor and encourage research within and about the publishing industry, to increase readership, improve distribution of books of all kinds, and expand the market for books. Members are publishers, manufacturers, suppliers, wholesalers, retailers, librarians and others engaged professionally in the development, production and dissemination of books and journals.

Membership: $625 (Individuals/Independent Consultants/ Public Libraries); $1,050-26,250 (Commercial Businesses, based on revenue); $1,050-1,695 (Non-Profits, based on revenue).

Continuing Education:
Certification Designation/s: PDCP

Meetings/Conferences: Annual
Conference Chair: Nadine Vassallo

Publications:
Book Industry Trends; annually
Consumer Attitudes Towards E-Book Reading
Digital Book Printing for Dummies
Membership Directory; on-line
U.S. Book Industry Climate Impacts and Environmental Bech Making Study
Under the Radar
Used-Book Sales

Book Manufacturers' Institute *(1933)*
Two Armand Beach Dr.
Suite 1B
Palm Coast, FL 32137-2612
Tel: (386) 986-4552 *Fax:* (386) 986-4553
E-Mail: info@bmibook.com
Website: bmibook.org
Members: 100 companies
Staff: 4
Annual Budget: $250-500,000

Personnel:
Executive Vice President: Daniel N. Bach
General Counsel: John J. Kelly Esq.
Office Manager: Dianne Morris
Coordinator, Conferences: Jackie Murray

Historical Note:
Established as the Employing Bookbinders of America; assumed its present name in 1933. Mission is to provide a forum for discussion of common intra-industry issues associated with book manufacturing. Membership: $1,500-12,500 (Active, based on sales); $2,500-5,000 (Associate-within U.S., based on sales); $1,000 (Associate, outside U.S.); $600 (Associate- Separate operating divisions/Wholly-owned subsidiaries).

Meetings/Conferences:
Conference Chair: Jackie Murray
2013 - Hilton Head Island, SC (The Westin Hilton Head Island Resort and Spa)/April 28 - 30
2013 - Marco Island, FL (Marco Island Marriott Beach Resort, Golf Club and Spa)/Nov. 1 - 6
Number of non-conference events/year: 4

Publications:
Membership Directory; on-line

The Botanical Society of America *(1893)*
4475 Castleman Ave.
P.O. Box 299
St. Louis, MO 63166-0299
Tel: (314) 577-9566 *Fax:* (314) 577-9515
E-Mail: bsa-manager@botany.org
Website: botany.org
Members: 2800 individuals
Staff: 11
Annual Budget: $2-5,000,000
Tax: 501(c)(3)

Personnel:
Executive Director: Bill Dahl
    E-Mail: bsa-manager@botany.org
Director, Information and Technology: Rob Brandt
    E-Mail: rbrandt@botany.org
Director, Membership and Subscriptions: Heather Cacanindin
    E-Mail: hcacanindin@botany.org
Director, Education: Dr. Claire Hemingway
    E-Mail: chemingway@botany.org
Administrations Officer: Wanda Lovan
    E-Mail: wlovan@botany.org
Managing Editor: Amy McPherson
    E-Mail: amcpherson@botany.org
Director, Conferences: Johanne Stogran
    E-Mail: johanne@botany.org

Historical Note:
BSA represents professional botanists, plant scientists, educators, students and amateur plant science enthusiasts around the world. BSA's purpose is to promote botany, the field of basic science dealing with the study and inquiry into the form, function, development, diversity, reproduction, evolution, and uses of plants and their interactions within the biosphere. Membership: $10-2,250/year.

Meetings/Conferences: Annual

Conference Chair: Johanne Stogran
2013 - New Orleans, LA/July 24 - Aug. 1
Publications:
American Journal of Botany; monthly
Member Directory

Bowling Proprietors' Association of America
(1932)
621 Six Flags Dr.
Arlington, TX 76011
Tel: (817) 649-5105 *Fax:* (817) 633-2940
TollFree: (800) 343-1329
Website: bpaa.com
Members:
1500 bowling centers
7000 individuals
Staff: 39
Annual Budget: $25-50,000
Tax: 501(c)(6)

Personnel:
Executive Director: Steve Johnson
  E-Mail: Steve@BPAA.com
Director, Membership Benefits: Amy Arcuri
  E-Mail: amy@bpaa.com
Director, Education: Kelly Bednar
  E-Mail: kelly@bpaa.com
Director, Finance: Judy King
  E-Mail: judy@bpaa.com
Director, Meetings and Events: Lee Ann Norton
  E-Mail: leeann@bpaa.com
Contact, Creative Services, Marketing and Production:
  Cary Richmond
  E-Mail: cary@bpaa.com
Coordinator, Communications: Ron De Roxtra
  E-Mail: ron@bpaa.com
Director, Technology: Heath Shults
  E-Mail: heath@bpaa.com

Historical Note:
*BPAA mission is to enhance the profitability of its members.
It also supports the Bowling Proprietors' Association of
America Political Action Committee. Membership: $29
(Regular Membership); $30 (Regular Direct Membership).*

Meetings/Conferences: Annual
Conference Chair: Lee Ann Norton
2013 - San Antonio, TX (Hyatt Regency Hill Country
  Resort and Spa)/Jan. 27 - 31

Publications:
BPAA Newsletter; on-line

Bowling Writers Association of America *(1934)*
621 Six Flags Dr.
Arlington, TX 76011
Tel: (817) 385-8472 *Fax:* (817) 633-2940
E-Mail: bwaa@bowlingwriters.com
Website: bowlingwriters.com
Members:
400 individuals
100 companies
Staff: 20
Annual Budget: $10-25,000
Tax: 501(c)(4)

Personnel:
President: Joan Romeo
  E-Mail: jromeo@socal.rr.com
Executive Administrator: Ron DeRoxtra
  E-Mail: ron@bpaa.com

Historical Note:
*Formerly (1931) National Bowling Writers Association.
BWAA's mission is to create a new and continuing
generation of bowling journalists dedicated to disseminating
bowling history, news, features and editorials and promotes
the circulation of material to aid writers in their work so
as to increase interest in the bowling game throughout the
nation. Membership: $30 (Professional); $20 (Associate);
$10 (Student); $100 (Corporate).*

Meetings/Conferences: Annual
Conference Chair: Ron DeRoxtra

Publications:
E-News Letter
Membership Directory; annually

BP and AMOCO Marketers Association *(1974)*
15 Lake St.
Suite 280
Savannah, GA 31411
Tel: (912) 598-7939 *Fax:* (912) 598-7949
Website: bpama.com

Members:
10000 retail locations
400 BP branded marketers
Staff: 3
Annual Budget: $250-500,000
Tax: 501(c)(6)

Personnel:
Executive Director: John Kleine
  E-Mail: jkleine@bpama.com
Contact, Meetings: Elizabethe Bogart
  E-Mail: ebogart@bpama.com
Associate Director: Tara Setter
  E-Mail: tsetter@bpama.com

Historical Note:
*Founded as the Southern Gulf Oil Distributors Association,
BPAMA works to advance the jobber channel of trade as
the preferred channel of trade within BP. Members are
marketer members, affiliate members, BP and vendors who
offer products and services to BP petroleum marketers.
Membership: $500-2000 (Jobber); $500 (Affiliate/Vendor).*

Meetings/Conferences: Annual
Conference Chair: Elizabethe Bogart

Publications:
BPAMA Membership Directory; annually

BPA Worldwide *(1931)*
100 Beard Sawmill Rd.
Sixth Floor
Shelton, CT 06484
Tel: (203) 447-2800 *Fax:* (203) 447-2900
E-Mail: info@bpaww.com
Website: bpaww.com
Members:
2700 advertiser and agency members
2600 media properties
Staff: 125
Annual Budget: $10-25,000,000

Personnel:
President and Chief Executive Officer: Glenn J. Hansen
  E-Mail: ghansen@bpaww.com
Senior Vice President, Business Development: Peter D.
  Black
  E-Mail: pblack@bpaww.com
*Senior Vice President, Human Resources, Finance and
Administration:* Doreen Castignoli
  E-Mail: dcastignoli@bpaww.com
Director, Information Services: Stacie DiNello
  E-Mail: sdinello@bpaww.com
Senior Vice President, Chief Quality Officer: Russell G.
  Haderer
  E-Mail: rhaderer@bpaww.com
Manager, Information Technology: Jim McGuire
  E-Mail: jmcguire@bpaww.com
Manager, Events Audit: John Mikstay
  E-Mail: jmikstay@bpaww.com
Manager, Communications: Glenn Schutz
  E-Mail: gschutz@bpaww.com

Historical Note:
*Formerly Controlled Circulations Audit and (1931) Business
Publications Audit of Circulation. BPA's mission is to deliver
consumer and business media audits that provide assurance
for both media owners and media buyers and also provide
advertisers, agencies and media owners with audience
insights that they can turn into competitive advantage.
Membership: $250 (Advertiser/Agency); $1,255 (Classic
Associate); $2,545 (Premium Associate).*

Publications:
Buyers Guide; on-line; adv.

Brain Injury Association of America *(1980)*
1608 Spring Hill Rd.
Suite 110
Vienna, VA 22182
Tel: (703) 761-0750 *Fax:* (703) 761-0755
TollFree: (800) 444-6443
E-Mail: familyhelpline@biausa.org
Website: biausa.org
Staff: 10
Annual Budget: $1-2,000,000

Personnel:
President and Chief Executive Officer: Susan H Connors
  E-Mail: shconnors@biausa.org
Director, Professional Services: Marianna Abashian
  E-Mail: mabashian@biausa.org
Director, Government Affairs: Amy C. Colberg
  E-Mail: acolberg@biausa.org
Director, Communications: Lissa Hurwitz

  E-Mail: lhurwitz@biausa.org
Executive Vice President and Chief Operating Officer: Mary
  S Reitter CAE
  E-Mail: mreitter@biausa.org
Coordinator, Sales and Marketing: Jenny Toth
  E-Mail: jtoth@biausa.org

Historical Note:
*An organization serving and representing individuals,
families and professionals who are affected by traumatic
brain injury (TBI).BIAA's mission is to be the voice of brain
injury, through advocacy, education and research, bringing
help, hope and healing to millions of individuals living with
brain injury, their families and the professionals who serve
them.*

Publications:
THE Challenge; quarterly

Membership List Available to Non-members

Brake Manufacturers Council *(1973)*
P.O. Box 13966
Ten Laboratory Dr.
Research Triangle Park, NC 27709-3966
Tel: (919) 549-4800 *Fax:* (919) 549-4824
E-Mail: bmc@mema.org
Website: brakecouncil.org
Members: 830000 workers, 12000 U.S. plant
locations and 29 companies
Staff: 2
Annual Budget: $100-250,000

Personnel:
Executive Director: Jack Cameron
  E-Mail: jcameron@mema.org

Historical Note:
*Formerly (1994) Brake System Parts Manufacturers
Council. A product line group of Motor and Equipment
Manufacturers Association that provides administrative
support. BMC provides members with current information
relating to the brake industry and informs its members of
legislation and regulations affecting automotive brake parts
and systems. Membership: $1750/year.*

Continuing Education:
Certification Designation/s: BEEP

Braunvieh Association of America *(1984)*
5750 Epsilon
Suite 200
San Antonio, TX 78249
Tel: (210) 561-2892 *Fax:* (210) 696-5031
E-Mail: baaoffice@braunvieh.org
Website: braunvieh.org
Members: 350 individuals
Staff: 2
Annual Budget: $250-500,000
Tax: 501(c)(5)

Personnel:
President: Jerry Jernigan
  E-Mail: jerniganfarms@yahoo.com
Manager, Operations: Patty Teeler
  E-Mail: baaoffice@braunvieh.org

Historical Note:
*BAA's mission is to support and encourage the use of
Braunvieh genetics in the global beef industry. Membership:
$50 (Associate); $25 (Junior).*

Publications:
Braunvieh World
Membership Directory; on-line

Brazilian American Chamber of Commerce
(1968)
509 Madison Ave.
Suite 304
New York, NY 10022-5501
Tel: (212) 751-4691 *Fax:* (212) 751-7692
E-Mail: info@brazilcham.com
Website: brazilcham.com
Members: 500 organizations
Staff: 5
Annual Budget: $2-5,000,000
Tax: 501(c)(6)

Personnel:
Executive Director: Roberto David de Azevedo
Treasurer: Valmor A. Bratz

Historical Note:
*Founded as the Brazilian-American Association, it
incorporated and assumed its present name in 1968.
BACC's mission is to promote bilateral trade and investment
flows between Brazil and the United States, and to forge
close ties between business communities of both countries.*

Members are Brazilian and U. S. business persons concerned with promoting trade and investment between the business communities of both nations. It is dedicated to providing each one of member firms with a personalized and tailored service to ensure they reach their business goals and make the most of this exciting time for US-Brazil relations. Membership: $500 (Member); $1,000 (Corporate); $2,000 (Contributing); $6,000 (Sponsor); $12,000 (Patron); $25,000 (Platinum).

Meetings/Conferences:
Number of non-conference events/year: 1

Publications:
Membership Directory; annually; adv.

Membership List Available to Non-members

Brazilian Studies Association (1992)
223 International Studies Building
910 S. Fifth St.
Champaign, IL 61820
Fax: (217) 244-7333
E-Mail: brasa-illinois@illinois.edu
Website: brasa.org
Members: 700 individuals
Staff: 2
Annual Budget: $10-25,000

Personnel:
Interim Executive Director: Mary Arends-Kuenning
    E-Mail: marends@illinois.edu
Editor and Translator: A. Cristina Pinto-Bailey
    E-Mail: pinto-baileyac@wlu.edu

Historical Note:
BRASA's purpose is to promote Brazilian studies and continue to build strong links between those who study Brazil and other parts of Latin America. Members are academics and others with an interest in the study of Brazil. Membership: $75-150 (Faculty); $50-75 (Independent Scholar); $30-60 (Student); $105-150 (Institution); $105-140 (Joint).

Meetings/Conferences: Annual

Publications:
BRASA-net; weekly
BRASAnotes

The Brewers Association (2005)
736 Pearl St.
Boulder, CO 80302
Tel: (303) 447-0816 *Fax:* (303) 447-2825
E-Mail: info@brewersassociation.org
Website: brewersassociation.org
Members:
1300 individuals
27000 homebrewers
Staff: 31
Annual Budget: $5-10,000,000
Tax: 501(c)(6)

Personnel:
President: Charlie Papazian
    E-Mail: charlie@brewersassociation.org
Manager, Finance Accounts: Katie Brown
Director, Finance: Tom Clark
    E-Mail: tom@brewersassociation.org
Coordinator, Human Resources and Finance: Ryan Farrell
Director, Sales and Marketing: Barbara Fusco
Coordinator, Membership Services: Erin Glass
    E-Mail: erin@brewersassociation.org
Director, Events: Nancy Johnson
    E-Mail: nancy@brewersassociation.org
Programs Manager: Pete Johnson PhD
    E-Mail: pete@brewersassociation.org
Chief Operating Officer: Robert Pease
Contact, Publisher: Kristi Switzer
    E-Mail: kristi@brewersassociation.org
Director, Information Technology: Shane Wood

Historical Note:
BA was established by the merger of the Association of Brewers (founded in 1978) and the Brewers' Association of America (founded in 1942). BA's purpose is to promote and protect small and independent American brewers, their craft beers and the community of brewing enthusiasts. Members are professional brewers at micro, regional, large and pub breweries, suppliers to the industry, and other interested individuals. Membership: $155 (Individual); $195-295 (Brewery); $495 (Allied Trade/Supplier); $295 (Craft Beer Distributor).

Meetings/Conferences: Annual
Conference Chair: Nancy Johnson
2013 - Washington, DC (Washington Convention Center)/March 26 - 29

Number of non-conference events/year: 2

Publications:
Membership Directory; on-line
The 2009-2010 North American Brewers' Resource Directory (BRD); adv.
The New Brewer; bi-monthly; adv.

Membership List Available to Non-members

Brick Industry Association (1934)
1850 Centennial Park Dr.
Suite 301
Reston, VA 20191
Tel: (703) 620-0010 *Fax:* (703) 620-3928
E-Mail: brickinfo@bia.org
Website: bia.org
Members: 200 companies
Staff: 8
Annual Budget: $5-10,000,000
Tax: 501(c)(6)

Personnel:
President and Chief Executive Officer: J. Gregg Borchelt PE
    E-Mail: borchelt@bia.org
Vice President, Engineering Services: Charles B. Clark
    E-Mail: cclark@bia.org
Vice President, Administration and Chief Financial Officer: Raymond W. Leonhard CPA
    E-Mail: rleonhard@bia.org
Director, Program Operations and Technology: Tricia Mauer
    E-Mail: tmauer@bia.org
Vice President, Marketing and Membership Services: Stephen Sears
    E-Mail: ssears@bia.org
Manager, Meetings and Membership Services: Bethany Smith CMP
    E-Mail: bsmith@bia.org
Vice President, Government Relations: Gay Westbrook
    E-Mail: gwestbrook@bia.org

Historical Note:
Founded as the Structural Clay Products Institute, became Brick Institute of America in 1972, and then merged with the National Association of Brick Distributors in 1998, assuming its current name. BIA's mission is to increase the market share of clay brick and safeguard the industry.

Continuing Education:
Certification Designation/s: CBS

Meetings/Conferences: Annual
Conference Chair: Bethany Smith CMP
2013 - Greensboro, NC (Sheraton Greensboro Hotel at Four Seasons)/Jan. 29 - 30

Publications:
Brick in Architecture; quarterly
Brick In Home Building; semi-annually
Brick News; monthly; adv.
Membership Directory; on-line
Technical Notes on Brick Construction; on-line

Bridge Grid Flooring Manufacturers Association (1985)
300 E. Cherry St.
N. Baltimore, OH 45872
Tel: (877) 257-5499 *Fax:* (419) 257-0332
E-Mail: bgfma@bgfma.org
Website: bgfma.org
Members: 4 companies, 2 associates
Staff: 1
Annual Budget: $50-100,000

Personnel:
Executive Director: Mark Kaczinski PE
    E-Mail: mkaczinski@dsbrown.com

Historical Note:
BGFMA's mission is to advocate the use of these decks through data collection, research or development and education. BGFMA will focus its efforts on demonstrating to owners and engineers the following advantages of steel grid bridge deck systems.

Meetings/Conferences: Biennial
Number of non-conference events/year: 1

Publications:
Gridline

BritishAmerican Business Inc. (1920)
52 Vanderbilt Ave.
20th Floor
New York, NY 10017-3808

Tel: (212) 661-4060 *Fax:* (212) 661-4074
E-Mail: nyinfo@babinc.org
Website: babinc.org
Members:
4500 individuals
700 companies
Staff: 8
Annual Budget: $500-1,000,000

Personnel:
Chief Executive Officer: Richard Fursland
    E-Mail: nrosier@babinc.org
Office Manager: Joyce Auker
    E-Mail: jauker@babinc.org
Associate Director, Member Relations and Programs: Tamra Eker
    E-Mail: teker@babinc.org
Director, Membership and Communications: Colleen Maloney
    E-Mail: cmaloney@babinc.org
Senior Manager, Events & Marketing: Sarah Thompson
    E-Mail: sthompson@babinc.org

Historical Note:
Founded as British-American Chamber of Commerce, BABi encourages trade and investments, and cultivates reciprocal interest in, and comity between the United States and the United Kingdom. Purpose is to provide promotional opportunities, business contacts and information services to its member companies. Membership includes the multinationals and middle-market companies, including most of the major American and European players in banking, pharmaceuticals, energy, aerospace/defense, insurance, accountancy, law, real estate, telecoms, management/business consultancies, airlines and the media. Membership: $1,600 (Corporate); $4,250 (Transatlantic Council).

Meetings/Conferences:
Conference Chair: Sarah Thompson
Number of non-conference events/year: 3

Publications:
Investment News; monthly; adv.
Issue Insight; bi-monthly; adv.
Membership Directory; annually
Network Magazine; adv.

Broadcast Cable Credit Association (1972)
550 W. Frontage Rd.
Suite 3600
Northfield, IL 60093
Tel: (847) 881-8757 *Fax:* (847) 784-8059
E-Mail: info@bccacredit.com
Website: bccacredit.com
Members: 500 stations
Staff: 8
Annual Budget: $1-2,000,000

Personnel:
President and Chief Executive Officer: Mary M. Collins
    E-Mail: mary.collins@mediafinance.org
Contact, Sales and Membership Services: Cindy Laser
    E-Mail: claser@bccacredit.com
Director, Operations: Jamie Smith
    E-Mail: jamie.smith@mediafinance.org

Historical Note:
Formerly Broadcast Cable Financial Management Association. Became the Broadcast Credit Association in 1985 and assumed its present name in 1990. BCCA's mission is to provide credit information, education, and networking opportunities which enables members to efficiently manage credit risk and increase profitability.

Meetings/Conferences: Annual
2013 - New Orleans, LA (The Roosevelt Hotel)/May 20 - 23
Number of non-conference events/year: 1

Publications:
Membership Directory; on-line
TFM: The Financial Manager; bi-monthly
UPDATE; monthly

Broadcast Education Association (1955)
1771 N St. NW
Washington, DC 20036-2891
Tel: (202) 429-5355 *Fax:* (202) 775-2981
E-Mail: beainfo@beaweb.org
Website: beaweb.org
Members: 1600 individuals and 275 Institutions
Staff: 3
Annual Budget: $1-2,000,000
Tax: 501(c)(3)

Personnel:

Executive Director: Heather Birks
 E-Mail: hbirks@nag.org
Manager, Business Operations: Traci Bailey
 E-Mail: tbailey@nab.org
Director, Sales and Marketing: J. D. Boyle
 E-Mail: jdboyle@nab.org

Historical Note:
Formerly (1973) Association for Professional Broadcasting Education. BEA focuses on the electronic media, providing a forum for issues and topics of mutual concern to educators and practitioners, to facilitate interaction between academicians and leaders in the industry. Membership: $130 (Individual); $55 (Student); $35 (Emeriti-retired professors over 65 yrs); $140-265 (Institution); $145 (Associate).

Meetings/Conferences: Annual
2013 - Las Vegas, NV (Las Vegas Hotel and Casino)/
April 7 - 10

Publications:
BEA e-Newsletter; bi-monthly
BEA Newsletter; monthly; adv.
Journal of Broadcasting & Electronic Media; quarterly
Journal of Media Education; quarterly; adv.
Journal of Radio Audio Media; semi-annually
Member Directory; on-line; adv.

Membership List Available to Non-members

Broadcast Technology Society *(1912)*
445 Hoes Ln.
Piscataway, NJ 08854
Tel: (732) 562-5407 *Fax:* (732) 981-1769
E-Mail: a.temple@ieee.org
Website: bts.ieee.org
Members: 3000 individuals
Staff: 1

Personnel:
Senior Administrator: Amanda Temple
 E-Mail: a.temple@ieee.org

Historical Note:
A technical society of the Institute of Electrical and Electronics Engineers (IEEE). roadcast Technology Society (BTS) will encompass devices, equipment, techniques, and systems related to broadcast technology, including the production, distribution, wired and wireless transmission, propagation aspects and reception. Membership: $8 (Student); $15 (Affiliate).

Meetings/Conferences: Annual

Publications:
BTS Newsletter; quarterly
Journal of Display Technology; quarterly
Membership Directory; on-line

The Broadway League *(1930)*
729 Seventh Ave.
Fifth Floor
New York, NY 10019
Tel: (212) 764-1122 *Fax:* (212) 944-2136
E-Mail: league@broadway.org
Website: broadwayleague.com
Members: 600 individuals
Staff: 62
Annual Budget: $5-10,000,000
Tax: 501(c)(6)

Personnel:
Executive Director: Charlotte St. Martin
 E-Mail: cstmartin@broadway.org
Director, Employee Benefit Funds: Chris Brockmeyer
 E-Mail: cbrockmeyer@broadway.org
Manager, Information Technology: Robert Davis
 E-Mail: rdavis@broadway.org
Director, Government Relations: Tom Ferrugia
 E-Mail: tferrugia@broadway.org
Director, Finance and Administration: Colin Gibson
 E-Mail: cgibson@brooadway.org
Director, Labor Relations: Keith Halpern
 E-Mail: khalpern@broadway.org
Director, Research: Karen Hauser
 E-Mail: khauser@broadway.org
Director, Membership Services: Ed Sandler
 E-Mail: esandler@broadway.org
Director, Communications: Elisa Shevitz
 E-Mail: EShevitz@Broadway.org
Director, Marketing: Jan Svendsen
 E-Mail: jsvendsen@broadway.org

Historical Note:
Formerly (2008) known as The League of American Theatres and Producers. BL's mission is to provide a full range of programs and services to enhance more profit. Members include theatre owners and operators, producers, presenters, and general managers in over 240 North American cities, as well as suppliers of goods and services to the theatre industry. Membership: $2200 (Associate); $1,575 (Affiliate).

Publications:
Broadway Fan Club; monthly; adv.
League Education Commitee Newsletter
Membership Directory; annually; adv.
Stage Specs; annually

Brotherhood of Locomotive Engineers and Trainmen *(1863)*
1370 Ontario St. - Mezzanine
Cleveland, OH 44113
Tel: (216) 241-2630 *Fax:* (216) 241-6516
E-Mail: PresStaff@ble-t.org
Website: ble-t.org
Members: 59000 Members
Staff: 31
Annual Budget: $10-25,000,000
Tax: 501(c)(5)

Personnel:
National President: Dennis R. Pierce
 E-Mail: pierce@ble-t.org
Editor: John Bentley
 E-Mail: bentley@ble-t.org
Director, Information Technology: Mike Hager
 E-Mail: hager@ble-t.org
Coordinator, Education and Training: Ken Kroeger
 E-Mail: kroeger@ble-t.org
Director, Research and Assistant to the Office Administrator: Gregory W. Lund
 E-Mail: Lund@ble-t.org
Director, Records Department: Louise Reich
 E-Mail: louise@ble-t.org
Director, Communications and Coordinator, Legal Affairs: Greg Ross
 E-Mail: greg@ble-t.org
National Secretary and Treasurer: William C. Walpert

Historical Note:
The Brotherhood of Locomotive Engineers and Trainmen (BLET) is a labor union founded in Marshall, Michigan, on May 8, 1863. Formerly Known as The Brotherhood of the Footboard. The Brotherhood of Locomotive Engineers merged with the International Brotherhood of Teamsters and became the BLET on January 1, 2004. BLET's mission is to promote and protect the rights, interests, and safety of its members through solidarity, aggressive representation and education.

Publications:
BLET Directory; on-line
Locomotive Engineer Newsletter; monthly
Locomotive Engineers & Trainmen Journal; semi-annually
Locomotive Engineers and Trainmen News; monthly
Locomotive Engineers Journal; quarterly
War on Workers; daily

Brotherhood of Maintenance of Way Employees Division *(1887)*
41475 Gardenbrook Rd
Novi, MI 48375-1328
Tel: (248) 662-2660 *Fax:* (248) 662-2659
E-Mail: bmwe-dc@bmwewash.org
Website: bmwe.org
Members: 60000 individuals
Staff: 964
Annual Budget: $10-25,000,000

Personnel:
President: Freddie N. Simpson
 E-Mail: fns@bmwe.org
Director, Information Systems: Rick Forbes
 E-Mail: rick@bmwe.org
Secretary and Treasurer: Perry K. Geller Sr.

Historical Note:
Formerly the Order of Railroad Trackmen, assumed its current name after merger with the Brotherhood of Teamsters in 2005. BMWE's mission is to represent the workers who build and maintain the tracks, bridges, buildings and other structures on the railroads of the United States and Canada.

Publications:
BMWED Directory; on-line
BMWED Journal; bi-monthly
Membership Directory; on-line

Brotherhood of Railroad Signalmen *(1901)*
917 Shenandoah Shores Rd.
Front Royal, VA 22630-6418
Tel: (540) 622-6522 *Fax:* (540) 622-6532
E-Mail: signalman@brs.org
Website: brs.org
Members: 10,000 members
Staff: 8
Annual Budget: $250-500,000

Personnel:
President: Willard D. Pickett
 E-Mail: wdp@brs.org
Director, Research: Mike S. Baldwin
 E-Mail: msb@brs.org
Secretary and Treasurer: Jerry C. Boles
 E-Mail: jcb@brs.org
Vice President, Headquarters: Kelly A. Haley
 E-Mail: kelly@brs.org
General Counsel: William L. Phillips Esq.
 E-Mail: wlp@brs.org

Historical Note:
Organized in the signal tower of the Altoona, Pennsylvania railroad yard in 1901 and chartered by the American Federation of Labor in 1914. Sponsors and supports the Brotherhood of Railroad Signalmen Political Action Committee. BRS represents most of the signal employees on both the freight railroads and the passenger and commuter railroads.

Meetings/Conferences:
Number of non-conference events/year: 19

Publications:
The Signalman's Journal; on-line

Membership List Available to Non-members

Brotherhood Railway Carmen/TCU *(1890)*
Three Research Pl.
Rockville, MD 20850-3279
Tel: (301) 948-4910 *Fax:* (301) 948-1369
Website: tcu6760.homestead.com
Members: 20000 individuals
Staff: 6

Personnel:
International President: Richard A. Johnson
Webmaster: Steven Pequignot

Historical Note:
BRC/TCU was formed by merger of Brotherhood of Car Repairers of North America and the Carmen's Mutual Aid Association. Merged with Transportation Communications International Union in 1986. BRC/TCU's mission is to carry out the purposes and motives of International Grand Lodge, and to further the interests of organized labor. Membership: $318/year (Individual).

The Brown Swiss Association *(1880)*
800 Pleasant St.
Beloit, WI 53511-5456
Tel: (608) 365-4474 *Fax:* (608) 365-5577
E-Mail: info@brownswissusa.com
Website: brownswissusa.com
Members: 1800 combined adult and junior members
Staff: 10
Annual Budget: $500-1,000,000

Personnel:
Executive Secretary: David Wallace
 E-Mail: dwallace@brownswissusa.com
Contact, Membership Services: Sue Basye
Co-Chair, Convention Planning: Laurie Cuevas
 E-Mail: laurie.mvc@gmail.com
Editor: Katie Henson
 E-Mail: purebredpublishing@yahoo.com
Contact, Database Access: Laura Jenson
 E-Mail: ljenson@brownswissusa.com
Director, Genetic Research: David Kendall
 E-Mail: davetmb@tds.net

Historical Note:
Formerly Brown Swiss Cattle Breeders' Association. BSA's mission is to promote and expand the Brown Swiss breed with programs that assist the membership and industry to compete favorably in the market place now and in the future.Members are breeders and fanciers of Brown Swiss dairy cattle. Membership: $25 (Individual); $10 (Junior Members Applying for Adult Membership).

Meetings/Conferences: Annual
Conference Chair: Laurie Cuevas
2013 - Waukesha, WI (Milwaukee Mariott West)/July 3 - 6

2014 - East Peoria, IL (Embassy Suites East Peoria-Hotel and RiverFront Conference Center)/June 24 - 28

Publications:
Bulletin; adv.

BSA | The Software Alliance *(1988)*
1150 18th St. NW
Suite 700
Washington, DC 20036
Tel: (202) 872-5500 *Fax:* (202) 872-5501
Website: ww2.bsa.org
Members: 41 Organisations
Staff: 52
Annual Budget: $50-100,000,000

Personnel:
President and Chief Executive Officer: Robert W. Holleyman II
   E-Mail: software@bsa.org
General Counsel and Senior Vice President, Anti-Piracy: Jodie L. Kelley
Senior Vice President, External Affairs: Matthew Reid

Historical Note:
Formerly the Business Software Alliance. BSA's mission is to advance the goals of the software industry and its hardware partners and to provide a unified voice for its members around the world.

Meetings/Conferences:
Number of non-conference events/year: 2

Publications:
de-newsletter

Builders Hardware Manufacturers Association *(1925)*
355 Lexington Ave.
15th Floor
New York, NY 10017-6603
Tel: (212) 297-2122 *Fax:* (212) 370-9047
Website: buildershardware.com
Members: 80 companies
Staff: 5
Annual Budget: $500-1,000,000
Tax: 501(c)(6)

Personnel:
Executive Director: Ralph Vasami

Historical Note:
Formerly (1961) Hardware Manufacturers Statistical Association. The organization is accredited by the American National Standards Institute (ANSI) to develop and maintain performance standards for architectural hardware. BHMA's role is ensuring the quality and performance of builders hardware. Any organization that manufactures and sells builders hardware in the United States is eligible for association membership. BHMA's mission is to protect and secure the welfare, safety and common good of the general public. Membership: $1,890-39,000 (Full); $3,150 (Associate).

Continuing Education:
Certification Designation/s: SCP

Publications:
Certified Product Directory; annually
Membership Directory; on-line

Building Commissioning Association
100 SW Main St.
Suite 1600
Portland, OR 97204
Tel: (503) 595-4446 *Fax:* (503) 227-8954
TollFree: (877) 666-2292
E-Mail: info@bcxa.org
Website: netforum.avectra.com/eweb/StartPage.aspx?S
Members: 1200 individuals
Staff: 1
Annual Budget: $250-500,000
Tax: 501(c)(6)

Personnel:
Membership and finance Coordinator: Sheri Adams
   E-Mail: sadams@bcxa.org

Historical Note:
BCA is an international non-profit organization that serves as the recognized authority and resource on commissioning. Membership: $25-600/year.

Continuing Education:
Certification Designation/s: CCP, ACP
Meetings/Conferences:
Number of non-conference events/year: 1

Publications:
The Checklist; quarterly
The NewsFlash

Building Material Dealers Association *(1915)*
1006 SE Grand Ave.
Suite 301
Portland, OR 97214
Tel: (503) 208-3763 *Fax:* (971) 255-0790
TollFree: (888) 960-6329
E-Mail: bmda@bmda.com
Website: bmda.com
Members:
850 companies
1200 individuals
Staff: 20

Personnel:
Executive Director: Gwyn Matris

Historical Note:
BMDA's mission is to assist the public in perfecting his or her lien rights. Members are companies that retail building materials. Membership: $32/year (individual); $10/year (associate); $14/year (notice).

Building Owners and Managers Association International *(1907)*
1101 15th St. NW
Suite 800
Washington, DC 20005
Tel: (202) 408-2662 *Fax:* (202) 326-6377
E-Mail: info@boma.org
Website: boma.org
Members: 19000 individuals and companies
Staff: 35
Annual Budget: $10-25,000,000
Tax: 501(c)(6)

Personnel:
President and Chief Operating Officer: Henry H. Chamberlain CAE, APR, FASAE
   E-Mail: hchamberlain@boma.org
Vice President, Education and Meetings: Amy Chisholm CAE, CMP
Program Manager: Joel Corley
   E-Mail: jcorley@boma.org
Vice President, Education and Research: Lorie Damon PhD
   E-Mail: ldamon@boma.org
Vice President, Finance, Administration and Information Technology: Brian Green CAE, CFO, CPA
   E-Mail: bgreen@boma.org
Director, Communications and Marketing: Laura Horsley
   E-Mail: lhorsley@boma.org
Director, Information Technology: Charles Longcor
   E-Mail: clongcor@boma.org
Vice President, Membership: Robert (Bob) McClure IOM
   E-Mail: rmcclure@boma.org
Vice President, Advocacy, Codes and Standards: Karen Penafiel CAE
   E-Mail: kpenafiel@boma.org
Vice President, Communications and Marketing: Lisa M. Prats CAE
   E-Mail: lprats@boma.org
Director, Administration: Marie Simeone
   E-Mail: msimeone@boma.org

Historical Note:
BOMA formerly known as National Association of Building Owners and Managers until 1968. An international federation of 91 U.S. local associations, and 14 affiliated international associations. BOMA is dedicated to sponsor and encourage innovative research, advocacy and educational activities that advance the commercial real estate industry and profession. Membership: $1,195 (Corporate National Associate); $400 (Member-At-Large).

Meetings/Conferences: Annual
Conference Chair: Lisa M. Prats CAE
2013 - Honolulu, HI (Sheraton Waikiki)/Jan. 18 - 21
2013 - San Francisco, CA (Westin St. Francis Union Square)/May 1 - 3
2013 - San Diego, CA/June 23 - 25
2014 - Washington, DC/Feb. 3 - 6
2014 - Nashville, TN (Omni Nashville Hotel)/April 30 - May 2
2014 - Orlando, FL/June 22 - 24
2015 - Los Angeles, CA/June 28 - 30
2016 - Washington, DC/June 26 - 28
Number of non-conference events/year: 3

Publications:
BOMA Magazine; irregular; adv.

Membership Directory; on-line
Membership List Available to Non-members

Building Owners and Managers Institute International *(1970)*
One Park Pl.
Suite 475
Annapolis, MD 21401
Tel: (410) 974-1410 *Fax:* (410) 974-0544
TollFree: (800) 235-2664
E-Mail: service@bomi.org
Website: bomi.org
Members: 20000 professionals
Staff: 50
Annual Budget: $2-5,000,000

Personnel:
President and Chief Executive Officer: Jeffrey A. Horn
   E-Mail: jhorn@bomi.org
Director, Education: Holly Bentley
   E-Mail: hbentley@bomi.org
Chief Operating Officer and Chief Financial Officer: Sherry Hewitt
   E-Mail: shewitt@bomi.org
Vice President, Student and Graduate Services: Amy McMonigle
   E-Mail: amcmonig@bomi.org

Historical Note:
BOMI provides course materials and professional certification for building managers (RPA-Real Property Administrator), building engineers (SMA-Systems Maintenance Administrator), and corporate facilities managers (FMA-Facilities Management Administrator). BOMI serves developers, fee managers, multinational corporations and governments in 8 countries. BOMI's mission is to be the premier international provider of educational products and services to the property and facility management industries. BOMI is not an association or society and does not have members or membership dues.

Continuing Education:
Certification Designation/s: PAC, MFE, FMC, SMC
Publications:
BOMI International Boost; on-line
Membership Directory; on-line

Building Seismic Safety Council *(1979)*
1090 Vermont Ave. NW
Suite 700
Washington, DC 20005
Tel: (202) 289-7800 *Fax:* (202) 289-1092
Website: bssc.nibs.org
Members: 77 Companies
Staff: 2
Tax: 501(c)(3)

Personnel:
Executive Director: Deke Smith FAIA
   E-Mail: dsmith@nibs.org
Vice President: Claret M. Heider
   E-Mail: cheider@nibs.org

Historical Note:
An affiliated council of National Institute of Building Sciences, which provides administrative support. Its purpose is to promote the development of training and educational courses and materials for use by design professionals, builders, building regulatory officials, elected officials, industry representatives, other members of the building community, and the public. Membership: $150 (Industry Sector); $75 (Public Interest Sector); $25 (Student); $1,000 (Sustaining Organization); $5,000 (Contributing Organization).

Meetings/Conferences: Annual

Building Service Contractors Association International *(1965)*
401 N. Michigan Ave., 22nd Floor
Suite 2200
Chicago, IL 60611-4267
Tel: (312) 321-5167 *Fax:* (312) 673-6735
TollFree: (800) 368-3414
E-Mail: info@bscai.org
Website: bscai.org
Members: 1,200 companies
Staff: 13
Annual Budget: $1-2,000,000

Personnel:
Executive Vice President and Chief Executive Officer, Government Affairs: Chris Mundschenk
   E-Mail: cmundschenk@bscai.org
Coordinator, Certifications: Sarah Kohler

E-Mail: certification@bscai.org
Coordinator, Membership Services: Meghan Miller
    E-Mail: memiller@bscai.org
Contact, Annual Conventions and Meeting Logistics:
    Megan Morrison
    E-Mail: mmorrison@bscai.org
Director, Communications and Marketing: Stephanie
    Simpson
    E-Mail: ssimpson@bscai.org
Coordinator, Publications: Kristen Weygandt
    E-Mail: kweygandt@bscai.org

Historical Note:
*Formerly (1974) National Association of Building Service
Contractors. BSCAI's mission is to provide educational
programs, publications, video training programs, seminars,
and networking opportunities, all developed specifically
for the building service contracting industry. Members
are companies offering cleaning, maintenance, security
and janitorial services, and their suppliers. Membership:
$145-750,000,000/year.*

Continuing Education:
Certification Designation/s: CSSP, CBSE, RBSM
Meetings/Conferences: Annual
Conference Chair: Megan Morrison

Publications:
BSCAI Services magazine

Building Stone Institute *(1919)*
Five Riverside Dr., Building Two
P.O. Box 419
Chestertown, NY 12817
Tel: (518) 803-4336 *Fax:* (518) 803-4338
TollFree: (866) 786-6313
E-Mail: info@buildingstoneinstitute.org
Website: buildingstoneinstitute.org
Members: 260 companies
Staff: 3
Annual Budget: $250-500,000
Tax: 501(c)(6)

Personnel:
Executive Vice President: Jane Bennett
    E-Mail: jane@buildingstoneinstitute.org
Association Services Coordinator: Kayla Carlozzi
    E-Mail: kayla@buildingstoneinstitute.org
Contact, Communications: Gina DeNardo
    E-Mail: gina@buildingstoneinstitute.org

Historical Note:
*Formerly (1955) International Cut Stone Quarrymen's
association, BSI's mission is to promote and advance the
use of natural stone. Membership is open to quarries,
fabricators, distributors, wholesalers, installers, importers,
and anyone else who has an impact on the natural stone
industry. Membership: $1000-1300 (Active); $200
(Associate/Professional).*

Continuing Education:
Certification Designation/s: DES
Meetings/Conferences: Annual
2013 - Las Vegas, NV (Mandalay Bay Convention
Center)/Jan. 27
Number of non-conference events/year: 1

Publications:
BSI Newsletter; monthly
Building Stone Magazine; quarterly; adv.
Member Directory/Buyers' Guide; annually; adv.

Building Systems Councils of the National Association of Home Builders *(1942)*
1201 15th St. NW
Washington, DC 20005
Tel: (202) 266-8200 *Fax:* (202) 266-8400
Website: nahb.org/page.aspx/category/
    sectionID = 454
Staff: 1

Personnel:
Chief Executive Officer: Gerald M. Howard

Historical Note:
*The Building Systems Councils (BSC) is the resource for
the concrete, log, modular, and panelized home building
industries. The BSC aims to educate and inspire through
consumer-friendly documents and interactive learning tools.
All members of the BSC are active members of NAHB via
their local HBA or NAHB International.*

Building Trades Association
6353 W. Rogers Cir.
Unit 3
Boca Raton, FL 33487
TollFree: (800) 326-7800

Website: buildingtrades.com
Members: 23,000 member companies
Staff: 1

Personnel:
Director, Member Services: Richard Oleck
    E-Mail: rich@buildingtrades.com

Historical Note:
*BTA is made up of companies involved in all phases of the
building and construction industries. It provides services
for its members saving them valuable time and money.
Membership: $99/year.*

Publications:
Newsletter

Builders Association *(1994)*
453 Broome St.
Suite 4C
New York, NY 10013-2669
Tel: (212) 274-0446 *Fax:* (212) 274-0529
E-Mail: info@thebuildersassociation.org
Website: thebuildersassociation.org
Staff: 2
Annual Budget: $500-1,000,000

Personnel:
Business Manager: Matthew Karges
Managing Director: Erica Laird

Historical Note:
*The Builders Association is a performance and media
company that creates original productions based on stories
drawn from contemporary life.*

Publications:
Newsletter; on-line

Bulk Carrier Conference *(1956)*
7437 Timothy's Way
Easton, MD 21061
Members: 20 companies
Staff: 1
Annual Budget: $25-50,000

Personnel:
General Manager: Reginald Mutter

Burley Tobacco Growers Cooperative Association *(1921)*
620 S. Broadway
Lexington, KY 40508
Tel: (859) 252-3561 *Fax:* (859) 231-9804
Website: burleytobacco.com
Members: 180000 individuals
Staff: 16
Annual Budget: $1-2,000,000

Personnel:
President: Roger F. Quarles
    E-Mail: roger@burleytobacco.com
General Manager: Brian Furnish
    E-Mail: brian@burleytobacco.com
Administrative Assistant, Communications: Stephanie
    Harlow
    E-Mail: stephanie@burleytobacco.com
Administrative Assistant, Operations: Kathy Sanford
    E-Mail: kathy@burleytobacco.com
Financial Manager: Donna Shields
    E-Mail: donna@burleytobacco.com

Historical Note:
*BTGCA's mission is to promote, foster and encourage the
business of marketing tobacco, to minimize speculation
and waste in the production and marketing of tobacco, to
stabilize tobacco markets, and to handle cooperatively and
collectively the problems of tobacco growers. Membership
is offered to anyone who is currently sharing in the risk of
producing Burley tobacco in the states of Indiana, Kentucky,
Missouri, Ohio and West Virginia and certifies to the
Association that they are producing at least 500 pounds of
Burley tobacco during the current crop year.*

Publications:
Burley News; quarterly

Business and Institutional Furniture Manufacturers Association International *(1973)*
678 Front Ave. NW
Suite 150
Grand Rapids, MI 49504-5368
Tel: (616) 285-3963 *Fax:* (616) 285-3765
E-Mail: email@bifma.org
Website: bifma.org
Members: 260 companies
Staff: 5

Annual Budget: $1-2,000,000

Personnel:
Executive Director: Thomas Reardon
    E-Mail: treardon@bifma.org
Contact, Publications: Roxanne DeBoer
Director, Communications and Government Affairs: Brad
    Miller
    E-Mail: bmiller@bifma.org

Historical Note:
*BIFMA's mission is to advocate, inform and develop
standards for the North American office and institutional
furniture industry. Members are manufacturers and
suppliers of goods and services to the industry.
Membership: $1,110-60,000 (Regular); $1,340-3,340
(Supplier); $2,780 (Service); $2,470 (International).*

Meetings/Conferences: Annual
2013 - Chicago, IL/June 10 - 12

Publications:
BIFMA Newsletter; quarterly; adv.

Business Council for International Understanding *(1955)*
1212 Ave. of the Americas
Tenth Floor
New York, NY 10036
Tel: (212) 490-0460 *Fax:* (212) 697-8526
Website: bciu.org
Staff: 18
Annual Budget: $2-5,000,000

Personnel:
President and Chief Executive Officer: Peter Tichansky
    E-Mail: p-tichansky@bciu.org
Assistant Vice President, Finance: Ginelle Baugh
    E-Mail: g-baugh@bciu.org
Senior Program Officer: Meghan Hagberg
    E-Mail: m-hagberg@bciu.org

Historical Note:
*BCIU facilitates dialogue and alliances between world
businesses and political leaders. Provides an ongoing forum
for senior business executives to interact with heads of
state/government, cabinet ministers, and senior government
officials.*

Meetings/Conferences: Annual
Number of non-conference events/year: 1

Publications:
BCIU Outlook Newsletter; monthly

Business Executives for National Security *(1982)*
1030 15th St. NW
Suite 200 East
Washington, DC 20005
Tel: (202) 296-2125 *Fax:* (202) 296-2490
E-Mail: bens@bens.org
Website: bens.org
Staff: 22
Annual Budget: $5-10,000,000
Tax: 501(c)(3)

Personnel:
President and Chief Executive Officer: Montgomery C.
    Meigs
Chief Operations Officer: Henry (Butch) L. Hinton Jr.
    E-Mail: hhinton@bens.org
Warrior Gateway Project Manager: Devin Holmes
    E-Mail: dholmes@bens.org
Director, Publications and Web: Clinton E. Long
    E-Mail: clong@bens.org
Chief Financial Officer: Steven W. Lowe
    E-Mail: slowe@bens.org
Communications Associate: Maggie McEvoy
    E-Mail: mmcevoy@bens.org
Vice President, Communications: Laura Keehner Rigas
    E-Mail: lrigas@bens.org
Director, Washington, D.C. Metro Region: Laura
    Willoughby
    E-Mail: lwilloughby@bens.org

Historical Note:
*BENS is a nationwide, non-partisan organization through
which senior business executives can help enhance the
nation's security. The mission of BENS is to apply best-
business practices to help government leaders implement
solutions to the most challenging problems in national
security. Membership: $100,000 (Chairman's Club);
$75,000 (Vice Chairman's Club); $50,000 (Directors
Club); $25,000 (President's Club); $10,000 (Enterprise
Club); $5,000 (Executives Club); $2,500 (Investors Club).*

Meetings/Conferences: Annual
Conference Chair: Laura Willoughby

Number of non-conference events/year: 1

Publications:
BENS Update; monthly
Membership Directory; on-line

Membership List Available to Non-members

Business for Social Responsibility (1992)
111 Sutter St.
12th Floor
San Francisco, CA 94104
Tel: (415) 984-3200 *Fax:* (415) 984-3201
Website: bsr.org
Members: 250 member companies
Staff: 92
Annual Budget: $10-25,000,000
Tax: 501(c)(3)

Personnel:
President and Chief Executive Officer: Aron Cramer
Director, Stakeholder Collaboration: Ayesha Barenblat
Director, Human Resources: Rosalind Cohen-Baruch
Director, Conference: Pamela Ellman
Director, Communications: Melanie Janin
Controller: Brenda Kahler
Director, Information Technology: Kirk Long
Chief Financial Officer: Dan Luscher

Historical Note:
BSR's mission is to work with business to create a just and sustainable world.Membership: $5000-33000 (Corporate, based on annual gross revenues); $2500 (Associate).

Meetings/Conferences: Annual
Conference Chair: Pamela Ellman
2013 - San Francisco, CA/Nov. 5 - 8
2014 - New York City, NY/Nov. 4 - 7

Publications:
BSR Insight; weekly
Membership Directory; on-line
Sustainable Investment in China; quarterly

Membership List Available to Non-members

Business Forms Management Association (1958)
1147 Fleetwood Ave.
Madison, WI 53716
Tel: (888) 367-3078 *Fax:* (937) 885-5320
E-Mail: bfma@bfma.org
Website: bfma.org
Members: 500 individuals
Staff: 2
Annual Budget: $100-250,000

Personnel:
President: Oliver J. Wischmeyer CFSP
   E-Mail: owischmeyer@metlife.com

Historical Note:
BFMA seeks to address the unique educational and networking needs of forms designers and managers. Members are form designers, analysts, systems managers and IS managers. Membership: $200 (Individual); $1,000-1,750 (Companies); $50 (Alumni/Student); $1,000 (Business); Free (Forums).

Continuing Education:
Certification Designation/s: CFSP

Meetings/Conferences: Annual

Publications:
BFMA Membership Directory; on-line
BFMA Newsletter; monthly

Membership List Available to Non-members

Business Higher Education Forum (1979)
2025 M St. NW
Suite 800
Washington, DC 20036
Tel: (202) 367-1189 *Fax:* (202) 367-2269
E-Mail: info@bhef.com
Website: bhef.com
Members: 500 CEOs, college, university
presidents and foundation leaders
Staff: 6
Annual Budget: $1-2,000,000
Tax: 501(c)(3)

Personnel:
Chief Executive Officer: Brian K. Fitzgerald
   E-Mail: brian.fitzgerald@bhef.com
Executive Assistant and Coordinator, Membership Services:
   Remy Bracey
Director, Programs and Policy Analysis: Jeanne B.
   Contardo

Manager, Business and Events: Patricia Huber
Director, External Relations: Danielle Troyan

Historical Note:
BHEF is an alliance of corporate Chief Executive Officer's and university presidents dedicated to cooperative links between higher education and corporate America. It strives to study education's relation to workplace competitiveness and other issues of mutual interest to business and education. The CRI advocates college readiness, access, and success for under-served populations, particularly in science, technology, engineering and mathematics.

Meetings/Conferences:
Conference Chair: Patricia Huber
2013 - Washington, DC/Feb. 21 - 22
2013 - Washington, DC/June 10 - 11

Publications:
BHEF Newsletter
Fortune magazine

Business History Conference (1954)
Hagley Museum and Library, 298 Buck Rd., East
P.O. Box 3630
Wilmington, DE 19807-0630
Tel: (302) 658-2400 *Fax:* (302) 655-3188
Website: thebhc.org
Members: 400 individuals
Staff: 4
Annual Budget: $50-100,000
Tax: 501(c)(3)

Personnel:
President: Kenneth Lipartito
   E-Mail: lipark@fiu.edu
Web Editor: Pat Denault
   E-Mail: pdenault@fas.harvard.edu
Secretary and Treasurer: Roger Horowitz
Editor: David Kirsch
   E-Mail: dkirsch@umd.edu

Historical Note:
BHC's mission is to stimulate all aspects of research, writing, and teaching of business history and the environment in which business operates. Membership: $60 (Regular); $75 (Regular-annual income > $75,000); $125 (Contributing); 30 (Student); $40 (Emeritus/Retired).

Meetings/Conferences: Annual
2013 - Columbus, OH (Hyatt Regency Columbus)/
   March 21 - 23
2014 - Frankfurt, Germany (Frankfurt)/March 13 - 15
2014 - Miami, FL/June 24 - 27
2015 - Miami, FL/June 24 - 27

Publications:
BEH On-Line; annually
Enterprise and Society; quarterly

Business Marketing Association (1922)
1833 Center Point Cir.
Suite 123
Naperville, IL 60563
Tel: (630) 544-5054 *Fax:* (630) 544-5055
E-Mail: info@marketing.org
Website: marketing.org
Members: 3500 individuals
Staff: 9
Annual Budget: $1-2,000,000
Tax: 501(c)(6)

Personnel:
Executive Director: Patrick Farrey
   E-Mail: pfarrey@marketing.org
Director, Communications: Chris Barry
   E-Mail: cbarry@marketing.org
Accounting Manager: Barbara Ciulla
   E-Mail: bciulla@marketing.org
Contact, Conventions and Meetings: Kriston Ewoldt
   E-Mail: kewoldt@marketing.org
Senior Vice President, Client Services: Meg Goodman
Manager, Membership Services: Lisa Schwarz
   E-Mail: lschwarz@marketing.org
Vice President, Corporate Marketing and Communications:
   George Stenitzer
Manager, Operations: Sarah Washburn
   E-Mail: swashburn@marketing.org
Managing Director and Chief Marketing Officer: Eileen
   Zicchino

Historical Note:
Formerly the Business/Professional Advertising Association, BMA works to promote better practices in the industry. BMA's mission is to advocate the quality and effectiveness of Indiana-developed business-to-business marketing

communications through the continuous proactive learning of its members. Membership: $185 (Individual); $125 (Educator); $165 (Corporate, for 4 members).

Continuing Education:
Certification Designation/s: MS/C, MS/B, MS/A

Meetings/Conferences: Annual
Conference Chair: Kriston Ewoldt

Publications:
BMA Buzz; on-line
Membership Directory; on-line

Membership List Available to Non-members

Business Products Credit Association (1875)
607 Westridge Dr.
O'Fallon, MO 63366
Tel: (636) 294-5775 *Fax:* (636) 754-0567
TollFree: (888) 514-2722
E-Mail: service@bpca.org
Website: bpca.org
Members: 341 companies
Staff: 3
Annual Budget: $500-1,000,000

Personnel:
President and Chief Executive Officer: C. David
   Schmucker
   E-Mail: dave@bpca.org

Historical Note:
Formerly (1875) Stationers and Publishers Board of Trade and (1994) Stationery and Office Equipment Board of Trade, Inc. BPCA is a credit and financial reporting bureau servicing its membership of manufacturers, factors, and wholesalers in the office products, filing supplies, office furniture, graphic arts, writing supplies, advertising specialty, janitorial and sanitary supply and forms industries. Involved in consulting with members' debtors, including out of court reorganizations and liquidations

Publications:
BPCA Bulletin; on-line

Business Professionals of America (1966)
5454 Cleveland Ave.
Columbus, OH 43231-4021
Tel: (614) 895-7277 *Fax:* (614) 895-1165
TollFree: (800) 334-2007
Website: bpa.org
Members: 51000 individuals
Staff: 8
Annual Budget: $1-2,000,000
Tax: 501(c)(3)

Personnel:
Executive Director: Kirk Lawson
   E-Mail: klawson@bpa.org
Director, Educational Services: David Coffman
   E-Mail: dcoffman@bpa.org
Finance Director and Chief Financial Officer: Richard
   Cowles
   E-Mail: rcowles@bpa.org
Specialist, Interactive Technology: Joseph Ellis
   E-Mail: jellis@bpa.org
Director, Membership Services and Events: Shawna A.
   Gfroerer
   E-Mail: sgfroerer@bpa.org

Historical Note:
Formerly (1988) Office Education Association. A career technical student organization for students pursuing careers in business management, office administration, information technology and other related career fields. BPA strives to contribute to the preparation of a world-class workforce through the advancement of leadership, citizenship, academic, and technological skills. Membership: $12 (Post-Secondary/Secondary); $9 (Associate); $8 (Middle Level); $17 (Alumni/Professional).

Continuing Education:
Certification Designation/s: ACA

Meetings/Conferences: Annual
Conference Chair: Shawna A. Gfroerer
2013 - Orlando, FL/May 8 - 12
2014 - Indianapolis, IN/April 30 - May 4
2015 - Anaheim, CA/May 6 - 10
2016 - Boston, MA/May 5 - 9
2016 - Boston, MA/May 6 - 9

Publications:
Communique; quarterly; adv.

Business Roundtable (1972)
300 New Jersey Ave. NW
Suite 800
Washington, DC 20001

Tel: (202) 872-1260 Fax: (202) 466-3509
E-Mail: info@businessroundtable.org
Website: businessroundtable.org
Members: 230 organizations
Staff: 23
Annual Budget: $10-25,000,000
Tax: 501(c)(6)

Personnel:
Vice President, Communications: Jessica Boulanger
Deputy Director, Communications and Manager, Digital Strategy: Joseph R. Crea
President and Chief Executive Officer: Hon. John M. Engler
    E-Mail: jmengler@businessroundtable.org
Senior Vice President, Communications: Tita Freeman
    E-Mail: TFreeman@BRT.org
Senior Vice President, Public Policy: Marian E. Hopkins
    E-Mail: mhopkins@businessroundtable.org
Senior Vice President: LeAnne Redick Wilson
    E-Mail: membership@brt.org

Historical Note:
An association of chief executive officers of leading corporations with a combined workforce of more than ten million employees in the U.S. The chief executives are committed to advocating public policies that foster vigorous economic growth, a dynamic global economy, and a well-trained and productive U.S. workforce essential for future competitiveness.

Business Solutions Association (1973)
5024-R Campbell Blvd.
Baltimore, MD 21236-5974
Tel: (410) 931-8100 Fax: (410) 931-8111
E-Mail: opwa@clemonsmgmt.com
Website: opwa.org
Members:
20 wholesalers
85 manufacturers
Staff: 5
Annual Budget: $250-500,000

Personnel:
Executive Vice President: Calvin K. Clemons CAE, CMP
    E-Mail: cclemons@businesssolutionsassociation.com
Association Coordinator, Meeting and Member Services: Stacey Johnson
    E-Mail: staceyj@clemonsmgmt.com
Associate Director: Paula Kreuzburg
    E-Mail: paulak@clemonsmgmt.com
Legal Counsel: Neil Kuenn
    E-Mail: nkuenn@kkrlaw.com
Financial Coordinator: Donna Liberto
    E-Mail: donnal@clemonsmgmt.com

Historical Note:
Formerly Office Products Wholesalers Association. BSA provides a forum for the development of strategic and synergistic solutions to enhance the sale and distribution of business related products and services. Membership: $750-4000 (Wholesaler, Based on sales volume of previous year); $750-4000 (Manufacturer, Based on sales volume of previous year).

Continuing Education:
Certification Designation/s: CPMR

Meetings/Conferences: Annual
Conference Chair: Calvin K. Clemons CAE, CMP
Number of non-conference events/year: 10

Publications:
Membership Directory; on-line
Office Productrs Executive Summit Magazine; annually
The BSA Record; monthly

Business Technology Association (1926)
12411 Wornall Rd.
Suite 200
Kansas City, MO 64145
Tel: (816) 941-3100 Fax: (800) 941-2829
TollFree: (800) 505-2821
E-Mail: info@bta.org
Website: bta.org
Members: 2000 companies
Staff: 6
Annual Budget: $1-2,000,000
Tax: 501(c)(6)

Personnel:
Executive Director: Brent Hoskins
    E-Mail: brent@bta.org

Manager, Membership Services Marketing: Valerie Briseno
    E-Mail: valerie@bta.org
General Counsel: Robert C. Goldberg
    E-Mail: robert.goldberg@sfnr.com
Database Administrator: Mary Hopkins
    E-Mail: mary@bta.org

Historical Note:
Founded as the National Association of Typewriter Dealers, became the National Typewriter and Office Machine Dealers Association and later National Office Machine Dealers Association, assumed its present name in 1994 after a merger with LANDA (Local Area Network Dealers Association). BTA is an international not-for-profit trade association serving independent dealers, value-added resellers, systems integrators, manufacturers and distributors in the business equipment and systems industry. Membership: $150 (Publications Associate); $1,500-2,500 (Vendor Associates); $500-950 (Service Associates); $430 (Dealer).

Continuing Education:
Certification Designation/s: CompTIA CDIA + , CompTIA PDI +
Meetings/Conferences:
Number of non-conference events/year: 7

Publications:
BTA Hotline e-newsletter; weekly; adv.
Office Technology Magazine; monthly; adv.
The Business Owner; bi-monthly

Membership List Available to Non-members

C-Port (1986)
3640-B3 N. Federal Hwy.
Suite 136
Lighthouse Point, FL 33064
Tel: (954) 261-2012
Website: cport.us
Staff: 2
Annual Budget: $100-250,000

Personnel:
Executive Director: Tina Cardone
Treasurer: Steve Winkler

Historical Note:
The Conference of Professional Operators for Response Towing is the national organization representing the marine assistance industry. Membership: $500 (Company); $300 (Organization).

Meetings/Conferences: Annual
2013 - Clearwater, FL (Hilton Clearwater Beach)/Jan. 13 - 15

Publications:
Membership Directory; on-line
Newsletter; quarterly

Cable & Telecommunications Association for Marketing (1976)
120 Waterfront St.
Suite 200
Ft. Washington, MD 20745
Tel: (301) 485-8900 Fax: (301) 560-4964
E-Mail: info@ctam.com
Website: ctam.com
Members: 5500 individuals
Staff: 40
Annual Budget: $5-10,000,000
Tax: 501(c)(6)

Personnel:
President and Chief Executive Officer: Char Beales
    E-Mail: char@ctam.com
Director, Meetings: Antoinette Allen
Director, Marketing: Rita Bowers
Vice President, Research: Claybrook Collier
Senior Vice President, Communications and Marketing: Anne Cowan
    E-Mail: anne@ctam.com
Senior Vice President, Finance and Administration: Zell Murphy
Specialist, Media Relations: Mary Shaw
Director, Information and Technology: MariAnne Woehrle

Historical Note:
Formerly Cable and Television Administration and Marketing Society, (1995) Cable and Telecommunications and assumed its current name in 1996. CTAM's mission is to help the cable business grow and to provide consumer research, an interactive executive innovation series, conferences, awards. Membership: $330/year.

Meetings/Conferences:
Conference Chair: Antoinette Allen

2013 - New Orleans, LA/Oct. 6 - 8
2014 - Boston, MA/Oct. 26 - 28
Publications:
Membership Directory; on-line

Cable and Telecommunications Human Resources Association (1993)
1717 N. Naper Blvd.
Suite 102
Naperville, IL 60563
Tel: (630) 416-1166 Fax: (630) 416-9798
E-Mail: cthra@cthra.com
Website: cthra.com
Members: 1500 individuals and 100 companies
Staff: 3
Annual Budget: $250-500,000

Personnel:
Executive Director: Pamela V. Williams CAE
    E-Mail: pwilliams@wmrhq.com
Director, Public Relations and Communications: Melissa Hicks
    E-Mail: mhicks@mosaicmarketing.com
Coordinator, Membership Services: Christine Teed
    E-Mail: cteed@cthra.com

Historical Note:
CTHRA's mission is to provide an industry specific forum and resources for HR professionals to drive organizational success. Membership: $300/year (Regular/Associate).

Publications:
CTHRA's Resource Connection; on-line
Membership Directory; on-line

Cabletelevision Advertising Bureau (1980)
830 Third Ave.
Second Floor
New York, NY 10022-7522
Tel: (212) 508-1200 Fax: (212) 832-3268
Website: thecab.tv
Members: 200 companies
Staff: 16
Annual Budget: $5-10,000,000
Tax: 501(c)(6)

Personnel:
President and Chief Executive Officer: Sean Cunningham
Contact, National Sales Initiatives: Danielle DeLauro
    E-Mail: DanielleD@cabletvadbureau.com
Contact, Public Relations: Donna Guidice
    E-Mail: donnag@cabletvadbureau.com
Contact, Publications: Nancy Lagos
    E-Mail: NancyL@cabletvadbureau.com
Contact, Public Relations: Joleen Martin
    E-Mail: JoleenM@cabletvadbureau.com
Vice President, Multicultural Sales and Emerging Market Development: Cynthia Perkins-Roberts
    E-Mail: cynthiap@cabletvadbureau.com
Contact, Accounting: Jimmie Spears
    E-Mail: jims@cabletvadbureau.com
Executive Vice President, Strategic Operations Sales and Marketing: Charles "Chuck" Thompson
    E-Mail: chuckt@cabletvadbureau.com

Historical Note:
CAB's purpose is to assist members in maximizing advertising revenues and to promote the use of cable as an advertising medium. Members include systems operators representing more than 85% of the nation's cable subscribers and virtually all ad-supported cable programming services.

Publications:
Cultural Connections

Membership List Available to Non-members

Calendar Marketing Association (1989)
214 N. Hale St.
Wheaton, IL 60187
Tel: (630) 510-4564 Fax: (630) 510-4501
E-Mail: info@CalendarAssociation.org
Website: calendarassociation.org
Members: 150 companies
Staff: 5

Personnel:
Executive Director: Mike Hansen

Historical Note:
CMA represents the interests of designers, marketers, publishers, printers and suppliers of both retail and custom calendars. Membership: $159 (Individual); $350 (Organization/Company).

Publications:
Newsletter

California Redwood Association (1916)
818 Grayson Rd.
Suite 201
Pleasant Hill, CA 94523
Tel: (925) 935-1499 *Fax:* (925) 935-1496
E-Mail: info@calredwood.org
Website: calredwood.org
Members: 6 companies
Staff: 1
Annual Budget: $500-1,000,000
Tax: 501(c)(6)

Personnel:
President: Charles Jourdain
   E-Mail: charlie@calredwood.org

Historical Note:
CRA's mission is to advocate redwood products by providing technical services to manufacturers, specifiers and builders and maintaining product quality through its Redwood Inspection Service division and educate builders and consumers on the advantages of using redwood.

CALLERLAB - International Association of Square Dance Callers (1971)
200 SW 30th St.
Suite 104
Topeka, KS 66611
Tel: (785) 783-3665 *Fax:* (785) 783-3696
TollFree: (800) 331-2577
E-Mail: info@callerlab.org
Website: callerlab.org
Members: 3000 individuals
Staff: 3
Annual Budget: $250-500,000

Personnel:
Executive Director: Dana Schirmer
   E-Mail: info@callerlab.org
Administrative Assistant: Wade Morrow

Historical Note:
CALLERLAB works to recruit, promote, and maintain the square dance activity. Members are square dance callers. It also maintains information (lists, definitions, and other information) on a variety of dance program from Basic through C-3A. Membership: $105 (New Member); $35 (Retired); $25 (Youth); $75 (Affiliate).

Continuing Education:
Certification Designation/s: CSDT

Meetings/Conferences: Annual
2013 - Cary, NC (Embassy Suites Raleigh-Durham/ Research Triangle hotel)/March 25 - 27
2014 - Reno, NV/April 14 - 16
Number of non-conference events/year: 1

Publications:
Caller Coach Directory; on-line

Calorie Control Council (1966)
1100 Johnson Ferry Rd.
Suite 300
Atlanta, GA 30342
Tel: (404) 252-3663 *Fax:* (404) 252-0774
Website: caloriecontrol.org
Members: 30 companies
Staff: 3
Annual Budget: $1-2,000,000
Tax: 501(c)(6)

Personnel:
President: Eric Allen
Media Contact: Lauren Godinez

Historical Note:
CCC is an international association of manufacturers of low-calorie and reduced fat foods and beverages that works to maintain and enhance communication between the low-calorie food and beverage industry, government and regulatory bodies, scientific and medical professionals and consumers.

Publications:
Calorie Control Commentary; quarterly

Campus Computer Resellers Alliance (1990)
500 E. Lorain St.
C/O National Association of College Stores
Oberlin, OH 44074
Tel: (800) 622-7498 *Fax:* (440) 775-4769
TollFree: (800) 622-7498
E-Mail: ccra@ccra.org

Website: nacs.org/ccra
Staff: 2

Personnel:
Director: Julie Simonson
   E-Mail: jsimonson@ccra.org
Coordinator, Membership Services: Kelly Lynch
   E-Mail: klynch@ccra.org

Historical Note:
CCRA serves as a resource and advocates for the higher education technology community. Membership: $1000/year (CorporateMember).

Meetings/Conferences: Annual
2013 - Kansas City, MO (CAMEX)/Feb. 22 - 26

Publications:
Membership Directory; on-line
The Bridge newsletter; adv.

Campus Safety, Health and Environmental Management Association (1954)
One City Centre, 120 W. Seventh St.
Suite 204
Bloomington, IN 47404-3839
Tel: (812) 245-8084 *Fax:* (812) 245-0588
E-Mail: info@cshema.org
Website: cshema.org
Members: 1000 environmental, health, and safety professionals
Staff: 5
Annual Budget: $500-1,000,000
Tax: 501(c)(3)

Personnel:
Executive Director: Jack Voorhees
   E-Mail: jvoorhee@cshema.org
Manager, Event and Corporate Sales: Tim Arth
   E-Mail: tarth@chsema.org

Historical Note:
Formerly (1995) the Campus Safety Association. CSHEMA seeks to provide information sharing opportunities, continuing education, and professional fellowship to people with environmental health and safety responsibilities in the education and research communities. Members are environmental, health, and safety professionals. Membership: $225-800 (Regular); $20 (Student); $25 (Retired); $750-1,250 (Corporate).

Meetings/Conferences: Annual
Conference Chair: Tim Arth
2013 - Orlando, FL (The Renaissance Orlando at Sea World)/July 12 - 17

Publications:
Member Directory; on-line

Membership List Available to Non-members

Can Manufacturers Institute (1938)
1730 Rhode Island Ave. NW
Suite 1000
Washington, DC 20036
Tel: (202) 232-4677 *Fax:* (202) 232-5756
E-Mail: info@cancentral.com
Website: cancentral.com
Members: 39 Companies and 22000 Members
Staff: 7
Annual Budget: $2-5,000,000
Tax: 501(c)(6)

Personnel:
President: Robert R. Budway
   E-Mail: rbudway@cancentral.com
Vice President, Marketing and Communications: Sherrie L. Rosenblatt

Historical Note:
Absorbed the Carbonated Beverage Container Manufacturers Association in 1974. Mission is to advocate common industry positions to legislative and regulatory agencies whose activities impact the metal can market, to address issues of common concern, and to promote cost-effectively the benefits of the can to protect and grow the market. Members are manufacturers, producers, sellers or distributors of cans or suppliers of goods and/or services to the can manufacturing industry. Membership: $5,000/year (Manufacturers/Suppliers).

Publications:
The Federal/State Review; monthly

Membership List Available to Non-members

Canadian-American Business Council (1987)
1900 K St. NW
Suite 100
Washington, DC 20006-1108

Tel: (202) 496-7906 *Fax:* (202) 496-7756
E-Mail: canambusco@mckennalong.com
Website: canambusco.org
Members: 130 individuals
Staff: 10
Annual Budget: $1-2,000,000

Personnel:
Programme Alliance-President: Daniele Belanger
   E-Mail: belanger_west@sympatico.ca
Treasurer: Jake Dweck
Senior Advisor: Maryscott "Scotty" Greenwood
   E-Mail: sgreenwood@mckennalong.com
Senior Advisor: Jane Moffat
   E-Mail: jmoffat@mckennalong.com
Webmaster: Debbie Phillips
   E-Mail: debbielphillips@aol.com
Executive Director: Emma C. Rigby
   E-Mail: erigby@mckennalong.com
Director, Public Relations and Special Events: Anna Velasco
   E-Mail: annavelasconyc@gmail.com

Historical Note:
Founded to represent businesses and individuals with business interests in U.S. and Canada, the Council is a non-profit, issues-oriented organization dedicated to elevating the private sector perspective on issues that affect the two nations. Membership: $25,000 (Sustaining Partner); $10,000 (Corporate Sponsor); $5,000 (Corporate); $500 (Individual).

Meetings/Conferences: Annual
Conference Chair: Anna Velasco

Cancer Immunotherapy Consortium (1953)
One Exchange Plaza
55 Broadway, Suite 1802
New York, NY 10006
Tel: (212) 688-7515 *Fax:* (212) 832-9376
E-Mail: cvc@sabin.org
Website: cancerresearch.org/programs/research/ Cancer-Im
Staff: 1

Personnel:
Chief Executive Officer and Director of Scientific Affairs: Jill O'Donnell-Tormey PhD
   E-Mail: jtormey@cancerresearch.org

Historical Note:
Members are companies who are planning a launch of potential cancer vaccines to advance their understanding of ways to achieve licensing and commercialization of this new wave of therapies. The CVC is focused on the ultimate goal of vaccine development—licensure and commercialization into a medical standard-of-care—and so is looking at advancing products through all phases of the process.

Publications:
Cancer Immunotherapy Today; monthly

Cancer Patient Education Network (1989)
154 Hansen Rd.
Suite 201
Charlottesville, VA 22911
Tel: (434) 284-4697 *Fax:* (434) 977-1856
E-Mail: info@cancerpatienteducation.org
Website: cancerpatienteducation.org
Members: 220 individuals
Staff: 2
Annual Budget: $25-50,000
Tax: 501(c)(3)

Personnel:
Treasurer: Lina Mayorga CHES, MPH
Contact, Membership Services: Alison Holcomb
   E-Mail: aholcomb@cancerpatienteducation.org

Historical Note:
CPEN's mission is to promote and provide models of excellence in the areas of patient, family and community education across the continuum of cancer care. Membership: $95/year.

Meetings/Conferences: Annual

Publications:
CPEN Newsletter; quarterly
Journal of Cancer Education
Member Directory; on-line

Canola Council of Canada
400-167 Lombard Ave.
Winnipeg, MB R3B 0T6
Tel: (204) 982-2100 *Fax:* (866) 834-4378
Website: canolacouncil.org

Staff: 7

Personnel:
President: Patti Miller
    E-Mail: millerp@canolacouncil.org
Vice President, Finance and Administration: Jason Anderson
    E-Mail: andersonj@canolacouncil.org
Director, Communications: Debbie Belanger
    E-Mail: belangerd@canolacouncil.org
Research Manager: Lisa Campbell
    E-Mail: campbell@canolacouncil.org
Accounting Assistant: Sajjad Khan
    E-Mail: khans@canolacouncil.org
Vice President, Marketing Development: Cory McArthur
    E-Mail: mcarthurc@canolacouncil.org

Historical Note:
CCC's mission is to represent the common interests of all Canola Council of Canada members and encourage the improvement, development, and expanded production.

Meetings/Conferences: Annual
2013 - Vancouver, BC/March 14 - 15

Publications:
Canola Ink e-Newsletter; bi-weekly
CanolaIndo e-Newsletter; quarterly
Hola Canola e-Newsletter; quarterly

Canon Law Society of America (1939)
The Hecker Center, 3025 Fourth St. NE
Suite 111
Washington, DC 20017-1102
Tel: (202) 832-2350 *Fax:* (202) 832-2331
E-Mail: info@clsa.org
Website: clsa.org
Members: 1600 individuals
Staff: 3
Annual Budget: $250-500,000
Tax: 501(c)(3)

Personnel:
Executive Coordinator: Sharon Euart JCD, RSM
    E-Mail: seuart@clsa.org
Treasurer: Gregory T. Bittner
Administrative and Financial Assistant: Katie Richards
    E-Mail: krichards@clsa.org

Historical Note:
CLSA's mission is to promote the pastoral ministry of the Church. It also seeks to promote the study and application of canon law in the Roman Catholic Church. Membership: $200 (Active/Associate); $100 (Student).

Meetings/Conferences: Annual
Conference Chair: Katie Richards
2013 - Sacramento, CA (Hyatt Regency Sacramento)/
    Oct. 14 - 17

Publications:
CLSA Newsletter; quarterly; adv.
Membership Directory; on-line

Membership List Available to Non-members

Cantors Assembly (1947)
55 S. Miller Rd.
Suite 201
Fairlawn, OH 44333-4168
Tel: (330) 864-8533 *Fax:* (330) 864-8343
E-Mail: caoffice@aol.com
Website: cantors.org
Members: 195 individuals
Staff: 7
Annual Budget: $500-1,000,000

Personnel:
President: Jack Chomsky
    E-Mail: cantorjc@aol.com
Executive Vice President: Stephen J. Stein
    E-Mail: caofficestein@aol.com
Account Executive: Pete Gomez
    E-Mail: PGomez@bwd.us
Editor: Joseph A. Levine
Vice President, Administration: Alisa Pomerantz-Boro
    E-Mail: hazzanapb@bethelsnj.org
Director, Placement and Human Relations: Robert Scherr
Executive Administrator and Director, Membership: Eric M. Snyder
    E-Mail: esnyder@cantors.org

Historical Note:
CA is a professional organization of cantors, members of the Jewish clergy who specialize in prayer and song. It promotes and advances the traditions of conservative Judaism. Membership: $700/year.

Meetings/Conferences: Annual

Publications:
Journal of Synagogue Music; annually

Capital Health (1997)
750 Brunswick Ave.
Trenton, NJ 08638
Tel: (609) 394-6000
Website: capitalhealth.org
Staff: 16

Personnel:
President and Chief Executive Officer: Al Maghazehe PhD, CHE
Vice President, Human Resources: J. Scott Clemmensen
Executive Vice President and Chief Operating Officer: Larry DiSanto
Vice President, Planning and Development: Dennis Dooley
Chief Financial Officer: Shane Fleming
General Counsel: Jan Gabin
Chief Information Officer: Eugene Grochala

Historical Note:
CH's mission is to provide comprehensive, quality healthcare services which improve and sustain the health status of the residents primarily in Central New Jersey and Lower Bucks County. Capital Health assures accessible, compassionate healthcare services that honor the dignity of every person. Capital Health will be a controller in defining the community's healthcare needs, in providing appropriate solutions, and developing a comprehensive continuum of care including education, prevention, disease management and restorative programs.

Publications:
Capital Living
Giving Well Newsletter

Capital Markets Credit Analysts Society (1989)
25 N. Broadway
Tarrytown, NY 10591
Tel: (914) 332-0040 *Fax:* (914) 332-1541
E-Mail: cmcas@cmcas.com
Website: cmcas.org
Members: 500 credit professionals
Staff: 3
Annual Budget: $100-250,000

Personnel:
President: Igor Shtogrin
Account Manager: Kelly Byrne
Treasurer: Henry Matthews

Historical Note:
CMCAS is a professional society whose membership consists primarily of managers and analysts in credit risk departments that directly support their employer's capital market activities. Membership: $350 (Voting Members); $90 (Independent Non-Voting Members); $65 (Non-Voting Members).

Meetings/Conferences:
Number of non-conference events/year: 1

Captive Insurance Companies Association (1972)
4248 Park Glen Rd.
Minneapolis, MN 55416-4758
Tel: (952) 928-4655 *Fax:* (952) 929-1318
E-Mail: info@cicaworld.com
Website: CICAworld.com
Members: 370 individuals
Staff: 2
Annual Budget: $500-1,000,000

Personnel:
President: Dennis P. Harwick
    E-Mail: dharwick@cicaworld.com
Account Executive: Amy Sellheim
    E-Mail: asellheim@CICAworld.com

Historical Note:
CICA is commited to providing networking, education, and advocacy for the captive insurance industry. Membership: $750 (Captive/Risk Retention Group); $2,000 (Service Provider); $300 (Affiliate Service Provider); $350 (Affiliate Captive/Risk Retention Group).

Meetings/Conferences: Annual
2013 - Palm Spring, CA (Westin Mission Hills Resort and Spa)/March 10 - 13
2014 - Scottsdale, AZ (Westin Kierland Resort and Spa)/March 9 - 11

Publications:
Captive; adv.

Car Care Council (1968)
7101 Wisconsin Ave.
Suite 1300
Bethesda, MD 20814
Tel: (240) 333-1088
E-Mail: marcella.tilli@aftermarket.org
Website: carcare.org
Staff: 15
Annual Budget: $500-1,000,000

Personnel:
President and Chief Executive Officer: Kathleen Schmatz
Executive Director: Richard White
    E-Mail: rich.white@aftermarket.org
Director, Communications: Jennifer Ortiz AAP
    E-Mail: jennifer.ortiz@aftermarket.org

Historical Note:
CCC provides public service messages on auto maintenance to radio, television, newspapers and magazines. Members are automotive aftermarket manufacturers, distributors, jobbers, service providers, associations and communications organizations. It also coordinates with the National Car Care Month each April.

Publications:
Car Care Guide
Directory of Repair Shops and Parts Stores; on-line

Cardiovascular Credentialing International (1968)
1500 Sunday Dr.
Suite 102
Raleigh, NC 27607
Tel: (919) 861-4539 *Fax:* (919) 787-4916
TollFree: (800) 326-0268
Website: cci-online.org
Staff: 5
Annual Budget: $1-2,000,000

Personnel:
Executive Director: Aaron White
    E-Mail: awhite@cci-online.org
Executive Assistant: Valerie Hunter
    E-Mail: vhunter@cci-online.org
Director, Communications: Christine Johnson
    E-Mail: cjohnson@cci-online.org
Associate Executive Director and Examination Coordinator: Jerel Noel
    E-Mail: jnoel@cci-online.org
Director, Operations: Katesha Phillips
    E-Mail: kphillips@cci-online.org

Historical Note:
CCI works to be an innovative, cost-effective organization, driven by professional ethics and integrity, through the representation of the profession(s) in providing recognized quality, competency-based examinations.

Continuing Education:
Certification Designation/s: CRAT, RCCS, RPhS, CCT, RCES, RCS, RCIS, RVS

Publications:
Pulse Newsletter; semi-annually

Care Continuum Alliance (1999)
701 Pennsylvania Ave. NW
Suite 700
Washington, DC 20004-2694
Tel: (202) 737-5980 *Fax:* (202) 478-5113
E-Mail: info@carecontinuum.org
Website: carecontinuumalliance.org
Members: 180 corporations and 50 individuals
Staff: 10
Annual Budget: $2-5,000,000
Tax: 501(c)(6)

Personnel:
President and Chief Executive Officer: Tracey Moorhead
    E-Mail: tmoorhead@carecontinuum.org
Director, Corporate Relations: Cindy DeClark
    E-Mail: cdeclark@carecontinuum.org
Director, Communications: Isabel M. Estrada-Portales
    E-Mail: iestrada-portales@carecontinuum.org
Vice President, Membership Services and Development: Lisa Gorski
    E-Mail: lgorski@carecontinuum.org
Director, Government Affairs: Victoria L. Ingenito
    E-Mail: vingenito@carecontinuum.org
Vice President, Research and Quality: Jeanette C. May PhD, MPH
    E-Mail: jmay@carecontinuum.org
Director, Research: Karen Moseley
    E-Mail: kmoseley@carecontinuum.org

Historical Note:

Formerly (2007) known as DMAA: The Care Continuum Alliance, Care Continuum Alliance works to promote population health improvement through disease and care management. Membership: $350-3000/year.

Continuing Education:
Certification Designation/s: CCP

Meetings/Conferences: Annual

Publications:
eNews; weekly; adv.
Membership Directory; on-line
Population Health Management; bi-monthly; adv.

Career Planning and Adult Development Network (1979)
P.O. Box 611930
San Jose, CA 95161-1930
Tel: (408) 272-3085 *Fax:* (408) 272-8851
E-Mail: admin@careernetwork.org
Website: careernetwork.org
Members: 1000 individuals
Staff: 1
Annual Budget: $100-250,000
Tax: 501(c)(3)

Personnel:
Executive Director and Editor: Richard L. Knowdell
    E-Mail: rknowdell@mac.com

Historical Note:
CPADN keeps its members in touch with other career counselors, career coaches, job search trainers and human resource professionals through its publications, workshops and conferences. Members are career counselors, educators and human resource specialists. Membership: $49 (Individual); $64 (Foreign).

Continuing Education:
Certification Designation/s: JCDC, CDF, CDFI, JCTC
Meetings/Conferences:
Number of non-conference events/year: 3

Publications:
NETWORK Newsletter; on-line

Cargo Airline Association (1948)
1620 L St. NW
Suite 610
Washington, DC 20036
Tel: (202) 293-1030 *Fax:* (202) 293-4377
E-Mail: info@cargoair.org
Website: cargoair.org
Members: 15 companies
Staff: 3
Annual Budget: $500-1,000,000
Tax: 501(c)(6)

Personnel:
President: Stephen A. Alterman
    E-Mail: salterman@cargoair.org
Vice President, Legislative Affairs: Gina C. Ronzello
    E-Mail: gronzello@cargoair.org
Senior Vice President and Contact, Membership Services:
    Yvette A. Rose
    E-Mail: yrose@cargoair.org

Historical Note:
Founded as Air Freight Forwarders Association; became Air Freight Association of America in 1977 and assumed its current name in 1997. Represents the industry before federal and state regulatory bodies, the United States Congress and, when necessary, in the federal and state courts. CAA acts as a resource tool for its members, publishes periodic newsletters and acts as the educational voice of the industry. Also serves as the nationwide voice for members of the all-cargo air carrier industry, and others in the air cargo marketplace that depend on these services. Membership is open to all-cargo airlines, airports and others with an interest in the all-cargo industry.

Meetings/Conferences: Annual

Publications:
CAA Newsletter
Membership Directory; on-line

Caribbean Basin Ethanol Producer Association (CBEPA)
15 Main St.
Warrenton, VA 20186
Tel: (540) 347-5283
Website: caribbeanethanolproducers.com
Members: 8 companies
Staff: 1

Personnel:
Executive Director: George Fitch

Historical Note:
A group of companies that produce ethanol at plants in the Caribbean Basin for duty free export to the United States under the Caribbean Basin Initiative or CBERA.

Caribbean Cable Communications (1983)
P. O. Box 11540
St. Thomas, VI 00801-4540
Tel: (340) 643-7595 *Fax:* (561) 952-4002
E-Mail: info@cctanet.com
Website: cctanet.com
Members: 106 members
Staff: 1

Personnel:
Executive Director: Andrea L. Martin

Historical Note:
It's mission is to advance and advocate the development of cable television service in the U.S. regions and independent nations or territories of the Caribbean.

Meetings/Conferences: Annual
2013 - Southampton, Bermuda (The Fairmont
    Southampton Hotel)/Jan. 22 - 24

Publications:
Newsletter; quarterly

Caribbean Studies Association (1974)
P.O. Box 22202
Lexington, KY 40522
Tel: (859) 257-6966 *Fax:* (859) 323-1072
Website: caribbeanstudiesassociation.org
Members: 1200 individuals
Staff: 3
Annual Budget: Under $10,000

Personnel:
Executive Director: O.R. Dathorne PhD

Historical Note:
Interdisciplinary scholarly society concerned with the Caribbean. Has no paid officers or full-time staff. Membership: $50/year (individual); $200/year (organization);$85 (Caribbean Resident); $55(Student); $160 (Non-Caribbean Resident).

The Carpet and Rug Institute (1969)
P.O. Box 2048
Dalton, GA 30722-2048
Tel: (706) 278-3176 *Fax:* (706) 278-8835
TollFree: (800) 882-8846
Website: carpet-rug.org
Members: 112 companies
Staff: 15
Annual Budget: $2-5,000,000

Personnel:
President: Werner Braun
Contact, Membership Services: Susan Newberry
    E-Mail: snewberry@carpet-rug.org
Director, Communications: Bethany Richmond
    E-Mail: brichmond@carpet-rug.org

Historical Note:
Formed by a merger of the American Carpet Institute (1928) and the Tufted Textile Manufacturers Association (1945). CRI sponsors technical conferences and other programs for floorcovering manufacturers and installers and serves its members through science-based research, customer advocacy, environmental stewardship and consensus building. Members are companies and organizations related to the carpet and rug industry. Membership: $5,000 (Carpet Manufacturer/Associate Manufacturer); $2,000-4,000 (Associate Carpet Industry); $250-1,000 (Associate SOA Service Provider).

Meetings/Conferences: Annual

Publications:
News Line

Carpet Cushion Council (1976)
23 Courtney Cir.
Bryn Mawr, PA 19010
Tel: (610) 527-3880 *Fax:* (610) 527-8535
E-Mail: carpetcushion@msn.com
Website: carpetcushion.org
Members: 32 companies and 35 individuals
Staff: 2
Annual Budget: $250-500,000
Tax: 501(c)(6)

Personnel:
Executive Director: G. William Haines
Legal Counsel: Richard H. Gimer

Historical Note:

Formerly a division of the Carpet and Rug Institute, the Council is now independent and incorporated in the District of Columbia. CCC is dedicated to encourage the use of better quality carpet cushion in all markets. Provides carpet cushion manufacturers, distributors, dealers, and installers with information that helps them understand, sell and install separate carpet cushion. Membership: $2,250-18,000/year (Manufacturing Member/Associate Member based on sales volume).

Continuing Education:
Certification Designation/s: PSCP

Membership List Available to Non-members

Caribbean Hotel and Tourism Association (1959)
2655 Le Jeune Rd
Suite 910
Coral Gables, FL 33134
Tel: (305) 443-3040 *Fax:* (305) 443-3005
Website: caribbeanhotelandtourism.com
Members: 850 hotel members and 600 supplier companies
Staff: 6

Personnel:
Director General and Chief Executive Officer: Alec
    Sanquinetti
    E-Mail: asanguinetti@chahotels.com
Director, Membership Development: George DeMercado
    E-Mail: george@caribbeanhotelandtourism.com
Manager, Marketing and Commerce: Gabi Doria
    E-Mail: gabi@caribbeanhotelandtourism.com
Director, Conference & Events: Vanessa Ledesma
    E-Mail: vanessa@caribbeanhotelandtourism.com
Coordinator, Accounting Services: Anais Saavedra
    E-Mail:
    coordinator@caribbeanhotelandtourism.com
Director, Allied Members: James G. Weitkamp MHS

Historical Note:
CHTA's mission is to facilitate the full potential of the Caribbean hotel and tourism industry by serving member needs and building partnerships in a socially responsible and sustainable manner. Membership: $250-$1,000 (Allied); $250-2,500 (Property).

Meetings/Conferences: Annual
Conference Chair: Vanessa Ledesma
2013 - San Juan, PR (Sheraton Puerto Rico Hotel and
    Casino)/May 7 - 9
Number of non-conference events/year: 3

Publications:
CHTA Monthly; monthly
CHTA Newsletter; monthly
Membership Directory; on-line

Carwash Owner's and Supplier's Association (1983)
1822 South St.
Racine, WI 53404
Tel: (262) 639-2320 *Fax:* (262) 639-4393
E-Mail: nacm@ncsc.org
Staff: 3
Annual Budget: $10-25,000

Personnel:
Director: Ed Holbus
    E-Mail: hotwax@tds.net

Historical Note:
COSA's primary objective is to raise the public image of the industry. Membership: $300/year.

Membership List Available to Non-members

Case Management Society of America (1990)
6301 Ranch Dr.
Little Rock, AR 72223
Tel: (501) 225-2229 *Fax:* (501) 221-9068
E-Mail: cmsa@cmsa.org
Website: cmsa.org
Members: 11,000 members, 20,000 subscribers,
and 75 chapters
Staff: 25
Annual Budget: $5-10,000,000
Tax: 501(c)(6)

Personnel:
Executive Director: Cheri Lattimer BSN, RN
Director, Conferences and Events: Denise Flake
    E-Mail: dflake@cm-innovators.com
Vice President, Business Development: Michael Hoehn
    E-Mail: mhoehn@acminet.com
Director, Communications: Robert Pruss MCP, MCSD
    E-Mail: rpruss@acminet.com

Senior Administrative Coordinator: Mary Beth Pruss
E-Mail: mbpruss@cm-innovators.com

Historical Note:
CMSA seeks to positively impact and improve patient well being and health care outcomes. Members are health care professionals engaged in case management on all levels. Membership: $145 (Individual); $85 (Student); $98 (Military/VA); $115 (International); $150 (Web Subscriber).

Meetings/Conferences: Annual
Conference Chair: Denise Flake

Publications:
CMSA e-newsletter; quarterly
CMSA Today; quarterly
Professional Case Management

Membership List Available to Non-members

Cashmere and Camel Hair Manufacturers Institute *(1984)*
Six Beacon St.
Suite 1125
Boston, MA 02108-3812
Tel: (617) 542-7481 *Fax:* (617) 542-2199
E-Mail: info@cashmere.org
Website: cashmere.org
Members: 21 companies
Staff: 4
Annual Budget: $100-250,000

Personnel:
President: Karl H. Spilhaus

Historical Note:
Formerly (1984) known as the Cashmere & Camel Hair Manufacturers Institute of America, assumed its current name in 1990. CCMI's goal is to maintain the integrity of cashmere and camel hair products through education, information and industry cooperation.

Publications:
Membership Directory; on-line

Casket and Funeral Supply Association of America *(1913)*
49 Sherwood Ter.
Suite Y
Lake Bluff, IL 60044-2231
Tel: (847) 295-6630 *Fax:* (847) 295-6647
E-Mail: mallen@cfsaa.org
Website: cfsaa.org
Members: 175 companies
Staff: 4
Annual Budget: $500-1,000,000

Personnel:
Executive Director: George A. Buckley CAE, J D
Contact, Meetings: Barbara Russell
E-Mail: brussell@cfsaa.org

Historical Note:
Formerly (1993) Casket Manufacturers Association of America. CFSA represents the interests of member suppliers to licensed funeral homes and licensed funeral directors. CFSA's objective is to provide useful information and perspectives on the funeral industry and the funeral supply industry to support manufacturers and suppliers of funeral goods and/or services. Members manufacture or distribute virtually every type of product used by funeral directors. Membership: Fee based on sales volume.

Meetings/Conferences: Annual
Conference Chair: Barbara Russell
2013 - New Orleans, LA (Roosevelt New Orleans, A Waldorf Astoria Hotel)/March 14 - 16

Publications:
CFSA Newsletter; monthly

Cast Iron Soil Pipe Institute *(1949)*
1064 Delaware Ave. SE
Atlanta, GA 30316
Tel: (404) 622-0073 *Fax:* (678) 973-2845
Website: cispi.org
Members: 4 foundries
Staff: 12
Annual Budget: $1-2,000,000
Tax: 501(c)(6)

Personnel:
Executive Vice President: William H. LeVan
E-Mail: blevan@mindspring.com

Historical Note:
Manufacturers of cast iron soil pipe and fittings, CISPI's purpose is to aid and improve the plumbing industry,

---

through the preparation and distribution of technical reports.

Publications:
Member Directory

Cast Stone Institute *(1927)*
813 Chestnut St.
P.O. Box 68
Lebanon, PA 17042
Tel: (717) 272-3744 *Fax:* (717) 272-5147
E-Mail: staff@caststone.org
Website: caststone.org
Members: 70 individuals
Staff: 1
Annual Budget: $100-250,000

Personnel:
Executive Director: Jan Boyer
E-Mail: jboyer@caststone.org

Historical Note:
CSI's mission is committed to developing standards and promoting the use of cast stone. CSI continually strive to increase the awareness, value and market share of cast stone relative to alternate building products. Membership: $5,000 (Producer); $500 (Associate).

Publications:
CSI Newsletter; quarterly
Memvership Directory; annually

Casting Industry Suppliers Association *(1919)*
14175 W. Indian School Rd.
Suite B4-504
Goodyear, AZ 85395
Tel: (623) 547-0920 *Fax:* (623) 536-1486
E-Mail: info@cisa.org
Website: cisa.org
Members: 70 companies
Staff: 3
Annual Budget: $250-500,000
Tax: 501(c)(6)

Personnel:
Executive Director: Roger A. Hayes
Legal Counsel: John Peterson
E-Mail: jmp@HoweHutton.com

Historical Note:
Founded in 1919, it became the Casting Industry Supplier Association in 1986. CISA is a society of executives and managers representing companies that supply equipment, materials and services to the metalcasting industry. Membership: $3,500/year.

Meetings/Conferences: Semi-Annual
2013 - Gainey Ranch, PA (Hyatt Regency Scottsdale Resort and Spa at Gainey Ranch)/May 20 - 22
2013 - Rosemont, IL (Westin O'Hare)/Nov. 6 - 7
Number of non-conference events/year: 1

Publications:
Cisa Member And Product Directory; on-line

Casualty Actuarial Society *(1914)*
4350 N. Fairfax Dr.
Suite 250
Arlington, VA 22203
Tel: (703) 276-3100 *Fax:* (703) 276-3108
E-Mail: office@casact.org
Website: casact.org
Members: 5415 members
Staff: 26
Annual Budget: $5-10,000,000
Tax: 501(c)(6)

Personnel:
Executive Director: Cynthia R. Ziegler AAI, ARM, CAE, CPCU
E-Mail: cziegler@casact.org
Director, Communications and Marketing: J. Michael Boa CAE
E-Mail: mboa@casact.org
Vice President, Marketing and Communications: Nancy A. Braithwaite
Director, Meeting Services: Kathleen R. Dean CMP
E-Mail: kdean@casact.org
Vice President, Administration: Leslie R. Marlo
Director, Finance and Operations: Todd P. Rogers CAE
E-Mail: trogers@casact.org
Manager, Publications: Elizabeth A. Smith
E-Mail: esmith@casact.org
Vice President, Professional Education: Chester John Szczepanski

---

Manager, Information Technology and Online Services: Jennifer D. Walton
E-Mail: jwalton@casact.org

Historical Note:
Formerly known as Casualty Actuarial and Statistical Society of America till 1921. The purpose of CAS is to increase the awareness of actuarial science and to contribute to the well being of society as a whole. Membership: $450 (Fellows/Associates); $225 (Affiliate).

Meetings/Conferences:
Conference Chair: Kathleen R. Dean CMP
2013 - Vancouver, BC (Westin Bayshore)/May 19 - 22
2013 - Minneapolis, MN (Hilton Minneapolis)/Nov. 2 - 6
2015 - Colorado Springs, CO (The Broadmoor)/May 17 - 20

Publications:
Actuarial Review; quarterly
E-Forum; quarterly
Future Fellows; quarterly
Membership Directory; on-line
Syllabus of Examination; annually
Variance Journal; semi-annually

Membership List Available to Non-members

Catalogue Raisonne Scholars Association *(1994)*
15 Lawrence Hall Dr.
Suite Two
Williamstown, MA 01267
Tel: (413) 597-2335
E-Mail: nancy.mowll.mathews@williams.edu
Website: catalogueraisonne.org
Members: 200 individuals
Staff: 3

Personnel:
President: Nancy Mowll Mathews
E-Mail: nancy.mowll.mathews@williams.edu
Editor: Eileen Costello
E-Mail: ecostello@mail.utexas.edu
Webmaster: Carl Schmitz
E-Mail: webmaster@catalogueraisonne.org

Historical Note:
CRSA is affiliated with College Art Association. Mission is to serve the interests of authors of catalogues raisonnes of works of art. Membership: $20/year (Individual).

Meetings/Conferences:
Number of non-conference events/year: 2

Publications:
The Journal of Catalogue Raisonne Scholars Association; quarterly

Catecholamine Club *(1968)*
Dept. of Medicine, UCSD
9500 Gilman Drive
La Jolla, CA 92093-0838
Tel: (858) 534-0626 *Fax:* (858) 534-0661
Website: catecholamineclub.org
Members: 350 individuals
Staff: 3
Annual Budget: $10-25,000

Personnel:
Club President: Daniel T. O'Connor
E-Mail: doconnor@ucsd.edu

Historical Note:
CC consists of scientists interested in all aspects of catecholamine research. Members are researchers in neuroscience interested in the properties of the ammonia-based chemical compounds known as catecholamines. Membership: $25/year.

Publications:
Catecholamine Club Chronicle; irregular
Membership Directory; on-line

Catfish Farmers of America *(1968)*
1100 Hwy. 82 E.
Suite 202
Indianola, MS 38751
Tel: (662) 887-2699 *Fax:* (662) 887-6857
Website: catfishfarmersofamerica.com
Members: 1400 farms
Staff: 3
Annual Budget: $2-5,000,000

Personnel:
President: Butch Wilson

Historical Note:

CFA represents the national farm-raised catfish industry.
Membership: $40/year.

Meetings/Conferences: Annual

Publications:
The Catfish Chronicle
The Catfish Journal; monthly

The Catfish Institute *(1986)*
6311 Ridgewood Rd.
Suite W404
Jackson, MS 39211
Tel: (601) 977-9559
E-Mail: info@catfishinstitute.com
Website: uscatfish.com
Members: 11 feed mills
Staff: 2
Annual Budget: $2-5,000,000
Tax: 501(c)(6)

Personnel:
President: Roger E. Barlow
Media Contact: Jeremy S. Robbins
   E-Mail: jrobbins@tra.net

Historical Note:
The Catfish Institute, or TCI, was formed by a group of catfish farmers and feed manufacturers to raise consumer awareness of the positive qualities of U.S. farm-raised catfish. Members are catfish farmers and processors.

Catholic Academy for Communication Arts Professionals *(1972)*
1645 Brook Lynn Dr.
Suite Two
Dayton, OH 45432-1944
Tel: (937) 458-0265 *Fax:* (937) 458-0263
E-Mail: admin@catholicacademy.org
Website: catholicacademy.org
Members: 250 individuals
Staff: 2
Annual Budget: $50-100,000

Personnel:
President: Sally Oberski
   E-Mail: soberski@toledodiocese.org
Treasurer: Sean P. Dolan
   E-Mail: sdolan@drvc.org

Historical Note:
Formerly (1972) UNDA-USA, National Catholic Association for Broadcasters/Communications. Absorbed the Catholic Broadcasters Association in 1948, assumed its current name in 2002. An affiliate of SIGNIS, the Catholic World Association. CACP's mission is to be a resource of professional service, support and education for Catholic communication arts professionals. Members are directors of communication for a diocese, religious community, health care or educational institution. Membership: $1,000 (Sponsoring); $125 (Organization/Associate); $250 (Organizational Affiliates); $210 (Individual); $125 (Associate Professional); $85 (Parish); $45 (Student); $2500 (Premier).

Meetings/Conferences: Annual

Publications:
Member Directory; on-line
Newsletter; on-line

Catholic Association of Diocesan Ecumenical and Interreligious Officers *(1972)*
1009 Stafford Ave.
Fredericksburg, VA 22401
Tel: (540) 373-6491 *Fax:* (540) 371-0251
Website: cadeio.org
Members: 200 individuals
Staff: 3
Annual Budget: $10-25,000

Personnel:
President: Fr. Don Rooney
   E-Mail: frooney@stmaryfred.org

Historical Note:
Formerly known as NADEO, the National Association of Diocesan Ecumenical Officers. CADEIO was formed to stimulate the exchange of ideas, experiences and networking among the Ecumenical Officers of the arch/dioceses in union with Rome. Members are officers in Roman Catholic dioceses responsbile for promoting Christian unity and interfaith cooperation. Has no paid officers or full-time staff. Membership: $200/year.

Publications:
CADEIO Newsletter
Membership Directory; on-line

Catholic Campus Ministry Association *(1969)*
430 Reading Rd.
Suite 400
Cincinnati, OH 45202
Tel: (513) 842-0167 *Fax:* (513) 842-0171
TollFree: (888) 714-6631
E-Mail: info@ccmanet.org
Website: ccmanet.org
Members: 1200 individuals
Staff: 6
Annual Budget: $500-1,000,000
Tax: 501(c)(3)

Personnel:
Executive Director: Martine O. Moran III
Administrator and Office Manager: Howard Binzer
   E-Mail: binzer@ccmanet.org
Director, Member Services and Communications: Chrysta Bolinger
   E-Mail: bolinger@ccmanet.org
Director, Development: Hap Durkin
   E-Mail: durkin@ccmanet.org

Historical Note:
Formerly (1968) National Newman Chaplains Association. CCMA is a national organization of individuals and groups of campus ministers who associate to foster their theological and professional growth and to promote the ministry of the Catholic Church in higher education. Membership: $125 (Individual); $105 (Team/Diocesan/Associate); $150 (Corporate Non-Profit); $250 (Corporate For-Profit).

Meetings/Conferences: Annual
2013 - Clearwater, FL (Hilton Clearwater Beach)/Jan. 8 - 11

Publications:
Crossroads Newsletter

Membership List Available to Non-members

Catholic Cemetery Conference *(1949)*
1400 S. Wolf Rd.
Building Three
Hillside, IL 60162-2197
Tel: (708) 202-1242 *Fax:* (708) 202-1255
TollFree: (888) 850-8131
E-Mail: info@catholiccemeteryconference.org
Website: ntriplec.com
Members: 1800 businesses
Staff: 4
Annual Budget: $500-1,000,000
Tax: 501(c)(3)

Personnel:
Executive Director: Dennis Fairbank
   E-Mail: dfairbank@catholiccemetryconference.org
Administrative Assistant and Bookkeeper: Beverly Ivanauski
   E-Mail:
   bivanauski@catholiccemeteryconference.org
Managing Editor: Christine Kohut
   E-Mail: cakohut@catholiccemeteryconference.org
Director, Meetings and Education: Irene K. Lazaroski
   E-Mail:
   iklazaroski@catholiccemeteryconference.org

Historical Note:
CCC provides a forum for the discussion of, and dissemination of, information concerning all phases of Catholic cemetery development, operation and maintenance. Membership is open to all Catholic cemeteries and their employees, companies that supplies any materials or services used by or in a Catholic cemetery.

Continuing Education:
Certification Designation/s: CCCE

Meetings/Conferences: Annual
Conference Chair: Irene K. Lazaroski
Number of non-conference events/year: 1

Publications:
Catholic Cemetery Magazine; monthly; adv.
Membership and Resource Directory; annually; adv.

Catholic Charities USA *(1910)*
66 Canal Center Plaza
Suite 400
Alexandria, VA 22314
Tel: (703) 549-1390 *Fax:* (703) 549-1656
TollFree: (800) 919-9338
E-Mail: info@catholiccharitiesusa.org
Website: catholiccharitiesusa.org
Members: 3000 individuals and 1700 Catholic Charities agencies

Staff: 48
Annual Budget: $10-25,000,000
Tax: 501(c)(3)

Personnel:
President: Larry Snyder
   E-Mail: lsnyder@catholiccharitiesusa.org
Senior Vice President, Administration and Chief Administrative Officer: Marla Caulk
   E-Mail: mcaulk@catholiccharitiesusa.org
Senior Director, Communications and Marketing: Roger Conner
   E-Mail: rconner@catholiccharitiesusa.org
Senior Vice President, Social Policy and Government Affairs: Candy S. Hill
   E-Mail: chill@catholiccharitiesusa.org
Vice President, Development and Communications: Patricia Hvidston
   E-Mail: phvidston@catholiccharitiesusa.org
Senior Vice President, Finance and Chief Financial Officer: John "Jack" Jackson
   E-Mail: jjackson@catholiccharitiesusa.org
Database Administrator: KC Ortiz
   E-Mail: kortiz@catholiccharitiesusa.org
Senior Director, Membership and External Services: Kristan Schlichte
   E-Mail: kschlichte@catholiccharitiesusa.org
Director, Events and Convening: Kirsten Schoenfeld
   E-Mail: kschoenfeld@catholiccharitiesusa.org
Coordinator, Human Resources: Tasha Shorter
   E-Mail: tshorter@catholiccharitiesusa.org
Conference Planner: Amy Stinger
   E-Mail: astinger@catholiccharitiesusa.org

Historical Note:
Mission is to exercise leadership in assisting its membership, particularly the diocesan Catholic Charities agencies and affiliate members, in their mission of service, advocacy and convening.

Meetings/Conferences: Annual
Conference Chair: Amy Stinger
Number of non-conference events/year: 5

Publications:
Charities USA; quarterly

Catholic Health Association of the United States *(1915)*
4455 Woodson Rd.
St. Louis, MO 63134-3797
Tel: (314) 427-2500 *Fax:* (314) 427-0029
Website: chausa.org
Members: 2000 organizations
Staff: 74
Annual Budget: $10-25,000,000

Personnel:
Senior Director, Learning Integration: Lynette Ballard
   E-Mail: lballard@chausa.org
Program Coordinator, Assembly: Paula Bommarito
   E-Mail: pbommarito@chausa.org
Senior Director, Human Resources: Cara Brouder
   E-Mail: cbrouder@chausa.org
Senior Director, Information Technology: Mary Jane Brummett
   E-Mail: jbrummett@chausa.org
Director, Meetings and Travel: Adele Gianino
   E-Mail: agianino@chausa.org
Vice President, Communications and Marketing: Ed Giganti
   E-Mail: egiganti@chausa.org
Director, Membership Relations: Kimberly Hewitt
   E-Mail: khewitt@chausa.org
Senior Vice President, Finance and Operations: Rhonda E. Mueller CMP
   E-Mail: rmueller@chausa.org
Senior Director, Finance: Kevin J. Prior
   E-Mail: kprior@chausa.org
Editorial Coordinator: Donna Grace Troy
   E-Mail: dtroy@chausa.org
Meeting Planner: Dee Walsh CMP
   E-Mail: dwalsh@chausa.org

Historical Note:
Formerly (1979) known as the Catholic Hospital Association of the United States and Canada, the association is a ministry of the Roman Catholic Church. CHA's mission is to provide resources, annual in-person educational programs and audio conferences to help members sustain their commitment to the ideals, values and vision of health care as a ministry to persons in need. Membership: $130(Joint); $190 (International).

Meetings/Conferences:
Conference Chair: Dee Walsh CMP
2013 - Anaheim, CA (Anaheim Marriott)/June 2 - 4
2014 - Chicago, IL (Chicago Marriott Downtown
   Magnificent Mile)/June 22 - 24
2015 - Washington, DC (Washington Marriott
   Wardman Park)/June 7 - 9
2016 - San Diego, CA (San Diego Marriott)/June 5 - 7
Number of non-conference events/year: 2

Publications:
Catholic Health World; semi-monthly; adv.
Health Care Ethics USA; quarterly
Health Progress; bi-monthly; adv.
Washington Update; on-line

Catholic Library Association *(1921)*
205 W. Monroe St.
Suite 314
Chicago, IL 60606-5061
Tel: (312) 739-1776 *Fax:* (312) 739-1778
TollFree: (855) 739-1776
E-Mail: cla@cathla.org
Website: cathla.org
Members: 1000 individuals and institutions
Staff: 9
Annual Budget: $100-250,000
Tax: 501(c)(3)

Personnel:
Executive Director: Jean R. Bostley

Historical Note:
CLA coordinates the exchange of ideas, provides a source of inspirational support and guidance in ethical issues related to librarianship, and offers fellowship for those who seek, serve, preserve, and share the word in all its forms. Membership: $25-175 (Individual); $125-500 (Institution); $300 (Corporate).

Meetings/Conferences: Annual
Conference Chair: Jean R. Bostley
2013 - Houston, TX (George R. Brown Convention
   Center)/April 2 - 4

Publications:
Catholic Library World; quarterly; adv.
Catholic Periodical and Literature Index; quarterly
Membership Directory/Handbook; biennially; adv.

Catholic Medical Association *(1932)*
29 Bala Ave.
Suite 205
Bala Cynwyd, PA 19004-3206
Tel: (484) 270-8002 *Fax:* (866) 666-2319
E-Mail: info@cathmed.org
Website: cathmed.org
Members: 3500 individuals
Staff: 5
Annual Budget: $500-1,000,000
Tax: 501(c)(3)

Personnel:
Executive Director: Dr. John F. Brehany PhD, STL
   E-Mail: brehany@cathmed.org

Historical Note:
Formerly the National Federation of Catholic Physicians' Guilds. CMA seeks to uphold the principles of the Catholic faith in the science and practice of medicine. Membership: $325 (Physician, Active); $175 (Physician, Retired/Non-Practicing); $125 (Allied Health Professionals/Friends/Supporters); $200 (Associate); $100 (Resident/Fellow/Clergy/Religious); $45 (Students and Seminarians).

Meetings/Conferences: Annual
2013 - Santa Barbara, CA (Fess Parker's DoubleTree
   Resort by Hilton Santa Barbara)/Oct. 24 - 26

Publications:
CMA Newsletter; quarterly
The Linacre Quarterly; quarterly; adv.

Catholic Press Association *(1911)*
205 W. Monroe St.
Suite 470
Chicago, IL 60606
Tel: (312) 380-6789 *Fax:* (312) 361-0256
E-Mail: cathjourn@catholicpress.org
Website: catholicpress.org
Members: 900 Individuals and Publications
Staff: 5
Annual Budget: $500-1,000,000

Personnel:
Executive Director: Timothy M. Walter
   E-Mail: twalter@catholicpress.org

Manager, Meetings: Sheila Lomax
   E-Mail: slomax@catholicpress.org
Operations Analyst: Barbara Mastrolia
   E-Mail: bmastrolia@catholicpress.org
Assistant Manager, Membership Services: Laura
   McDougal
   E-Mail: lmcdougal@catholicpress.org
*Manager, Communications and Production and Managing
   Editor:* Michelle M. Monckton
   E-Mail: mmonckton@catholicpress.org

Historical Note:
CPA's mission is to assist its members to serve effectively, through their words and images both in print and digital media, the social, intellectual and spiritual needs of the entire human family, and to spread and support the Kingdom of God. Membership: $426.00 (Service Members); $92.00 (Associate/Individual); $43.00 (Staff Members).

Meetings/Conferences: Annual
Conference Chair: Sheila Lomax
2013 - Denver, CO (Denver Marriott Tech Center)/June
   19 - 21

Publications:
eNewsletter; weekly; adv.
CPA Magazine; adv.

Catholic Radio Association *(1999)*
P.O. Box 587
Mauldin, SC 29662-0587
Tel: (864) 438-4801
E-Mail: info@catholicradioassociation.org
Website: catholicradioassociation.org
Staff: 2
Annual Budget: $100-250,000
Tax: 501(c)(3)

Personnel:
President: Stephen Gajdosik
   E-Mail: sgajdosik@bellsouth.net

Historical Note:
CRA's purpose is to serve the Church in its mission to bring all people to holiness in Jesus Christ by assisting and uniting Catholic radio apostolates to reach more people with efficacious programming. Membership: $295 (Full); $245 (Associate); $150 (Cleric/Religious); $100 (Individual).

Meetings/Conferences: Annual

Publications:
The Radio Active Messenger; on-line

Catholic Theological Society of America *(1946)*
John Carroll University
One John Carroll Blvd.
University Heights, OH 44118
Tel: (216) 397-4980 *Fax:* (216) 397-1804
E-Mail: mponyik@jcu.edu
Website: ctsa-online.org
Members: 1300 members
Staff: 2

Personnel:
Executive Director: Mary Jane Ponyik
   E-Mail: mponyik@jcu.edu

Historical Note:
CTSA's purpose is to promote studies and research in theology, to relate theological science to current problems, and to foster a more effective theological education, by providing a forum for an exchange of views among theologians and with scholars in other disciplines. Members are individuals engaged in scholarly research, writing, and teaching of theology in seminaries and universities. Membership: $30-120/year (Based on Income).

Meetings/Conferences: Annual
2013 - Miami, FL (Hyatt Regency)/June 6 - 9
2014 - Pittsburgh, PA (DoubleTree by Hilton Hotel and
   Suites Pittsburgh Downtown)/June 5 - 8
2015 - Milwaukee, WI (Hyatt Regency Milwaukee)/
   June 11 - 14
Number of non-conference events/year: 1

Publications:
Bulletin Board; on-line

Cattlemen's Beef Promotion and Research Board
9000 E. Nichols Ave.
Suite 215
Centennial, CO 80112
Tel: (303) 220-9890 *Fax:* (303) 220-9280
Website: beefboard.org
Members: 106 members
Staff: 5

Personnel:

Chief Executive Officer: Polly Ruhland
   E-Mail: pruhland@beefboard.org
Chief Financial Officer: Katherine Ayers
   E-Mail: kayers@beefboard.org
Operations Manager: Charlotte Coates
   E-Mail: ccoates@beefboard.org
Vice President, Communications: Lynn Heinze
   E-Mail: lheinze@beefboard.org
Administrative Assistant: Leanne Thoma
   E-Mail: lthoma@beefboard.org

Historical Note:
The Cattlemen's Beef Promotion And Research Board, usually referred to as the Cattlemen's Beef Board or CBB. Represents beef and dairy producers in each state or region.

Publications:
Checking In On The Checkoff
My Beef Checkoff News; monthly

Caucus for Producers, Writers & Directors *(1974)*
P.O. Box 11236
Burbank, CA 91510
Tel: (818) 843-7572 *Fax:* (818) 846-2159
E-Mail: info@caucus.org
Website: caucus.org
Members: 150 television producers, writers and
   program directors
Staff: 2
Annual Budget: $250-500,000
Tax: 501(c)(6)

Personnel:
Administrative Coordinator: Penny S. Rieger
   E-Mail: prieger1@aol.com
Co-Editor: Lee Miller

Historical Note:
The Caucus strives to elevate program quality in Television and New Media by promoting and protecting the artistic, intellectual and economic rights of Producers, Writers & Directors.

Meetings/Conferences: Annual

Publications:
CAUCUS CONNECTION NEWSLETTER; on-line
The Journal of the Caucus; semi-annually

Caucus for Women in Statistics *(1970)*
7732 Rydal Terrace
Rockville, MD 20855-2057
Tel: (301) 827-0170 *Fax:* (301) 827-6661
Website: caucusforwomeninstatistics.com
Members: 300 individuals
Staff: 6
Annual Budget: Under $10,000
Tax: 501(c)(3)

Personnel:
President: Lynn Palmer
   E-Mail: lpalmer@mdanderson.org
Contact, Memberships: Cathy Furlong
   E-Mail: cathy.furlong@cox.net
Contact, Website: Jenna Green
   E-Mail: jennargreen@gmail.com
Editor: Malini Iyengar
   E-Mail: m_iyengar@hotmail.com
Treasurer and Membership Contact: Anna Nevius
   E-Mail: anna.nevius@fda.hhs.gov
Contact, Communications: Jennifer Parker
   E-Mail: jdparker@cdc.gov

Historical Note:
CWIS's mission is to foster opportunities for the education, employment and advancement of women in statistics. Membership: $5 (New Member); $30-35 (Regular); $47-60 (Sustaining); $6 (Associate); $2 (Canadian Section).

Publications:
Caucus; quarterly; adv.

CBA *(1997)*
9240 Explorer Dr.
Suite 200
Colorado Springs, CO 80920
Tel: (719) 265-9895 *Fax:* (719) 272-3510
TollFree: (800) 252-1950
E-Mail: info@cbaonline.org
Website: cbaonline.org
Members: 3300 stores and companies
Staff: 40
Annual Budget: $5-10,000,000
Tax: 501(c)(6)

Personnel:
President and Chief Executive Officer: Thomas Nelson
Executive Director: Curtis Riskey
    E-Mail: criskey@cbaonline.org
Director, Meetings and Expositions: Scott E. Graham
    CMPE, MA
    E-Mail: sgraham@cbaonline.org
Contact, Events: Diane Morrow
    E-Mail: dmorrow@tbbmedia.com
Contact, Marketing: Angie Ralston
    E-Mail: aralston@cbaonline.org
Coordinator, Marketing: Lisa Ray
    E-Mail: lray@cbaonline.org
Director, Membership Services: Michael Regennitter
Contact, Media Inquiries: Robin Roth
    E-Mail: rroth@cbaonline.org
Director, Publications: Kathleen Samuelson
    E-Mail: ksamuelson@cbaonline.org

Historical Note:
Founded as Christian Booksellers Association; assumed its current name in 1997. CBA, the trade association for Christian retail, serves the interests and meets the needs of Christian retailers, publishers, music labels, and gift distributors. Membership: $250 (Retailer- Christian/ Affiliate/Prospective); $450 (Supplier/Retail Support); $350 (Auxiliary Business); $200 (Auxiliary Professional).

Meetings/Conferences: Annual
Conference Chair: Scott E. Graham CMPE, MA
2013 - St. Louis, MO (The Doubletree Hotel and
    Conference Center)/June 23 - 26
2014 - Atlanta, GA (Georgia World Congress Center)/
    June 22 - 25
2015 - Orlando, FL (Orange County Convention
    Center)/June 28 - July 1

Publications:
CBA Industry Brief E-newsletter; weekly
Membership Directory; on-line

CCIM Institute *(1954)*
430 N. Michigan Ave.
Suite 800
Chicago, IL 60611
Tel: (312) 321-4460 *Fax:* (312) 321-4530
TollFree: (800) 621-7027
E-Mail: info@cciminstitute.com
Website: ccim.com
Members: 15000 individuals
Staff: 47
Annual Budget: $10-25,000,000
Tax: 501(c)(6)

Personnel:
Executive Vice President Emeritus: Susan J. Groeneveld
Vice President, Legislation and Research: Charles A.
    Achilles
Director, Meetings and Events: Skip Barrie
    E-Mail: sbarrie@ccim.com
Senior Vice President, Operations: Gail Collins
Senior Director, Human Capital and Administration: Jodi
    Coplan
Vice President, Education: Terry Cunningham
Senior Director, Marketing: Olivia Baeza Gellman
Senior Editor: Jennifer Norbut
Chief Financial Officer: Ken Setlak
Director, Information Systems: Karen L. Smith

Historical Note:
A representative of commerical real estate brokerage professionals. Membership: $595 (Institute/Fast Track/ University Fast Track); $545 (U.S. Government Discount); $395 (Canada); $195 (International).

Continuing Education:
Certification Designation/s: CCIM

Meetings/Conferences: Semi-Annual
Conference Chair: Skip Barrie

Publications:
Commercial Investment Real Estate; bi-monthly; adv.
I-News; quarterly

Cedar Shake and Shingle Bureau *(1915)*
P.O. Box 1178
Sumas, WA 98295-1178
Tel: (604) 820-7700 *Fax:* (604) 820-0266
E-Mail: info@cedarbureau.com
Website: cedarbureau.org
Members: 450 companies
Staff: 10
Annual Budget: $1-2,000,000
Tax: 501(c)(6)

Personnel:
Director, Operations: Lynne Christensen CAE, MBA
Accountant: Barbara Enns
Coordinator, Marketing: Kelly Vaille

Historical Note:
Founded as Shingle Branch of West Coast Lumber Manufacturers Association. Incorporated as the Red Cedar Shingle Bureau in 1926. Absorbed (1963) the Red Cedar Shingle & Handsplit Shake Bureau. Adopted its present name in 1988. The Cedar Shake and Shingle Bureau is a non- profit trade association that promotes the use of Certi-label (tm) cedar roofing and sidewall products. The organization provides installation instructions, educational seminars and technical advice. Membership: $75-$1100/ year.

Meetings/Conferences: Annual

Ceilings and Interior Systems Construction Association *(1950)*
1010 Jorie Blvd.
Suite 30
Oak Brook, IL 60523
Tel: (630) 584-1919 *Fax:* (866) 560-8537
E-Mail: cisca@cisca.org
Website: cisca.org
Members: 600 firms
Staff: 5
Annual Budget: $500-1,000,000
Tax: 501(c)(6)

Personnel:
Executive Director: Shirley Wodynski
    E-Mail: shirley.wodynski@cisca.org
Contact, Accounting: Mark Kaplan
    E-Mail: mark@mgkfinancial.com
Associate, Membership and Marketing: Michele Meng
    E-Mail: michele.meng@cisca.org
Manager, Membership Services: Deborah Meyer
    E-Mail: deborah.meyer@cisca.org
Editor: Rick Reuland
    E-Mail: rmgi@comcast.net

Historical Note:
Formerly (1970) the National Acoustical Contractors Association. CISCA's mission is to recruit and retain select prominent and emerging leaders, provide relevant, effective education, develop and promote technical and installation guidelines and promote the acoustical ceilings and wall systems industry. Membership: $130-695/year.

Meetings/Conferences:
2013 - San Antonio, TX (Grand Hyatt San Antonio)/
    March 19 - 22/over 100 exhibitors
2013 - Toronto, ON (Fairmont Royal York)/Sept. 25
2014 - Las Vegas, NV (Mandalay Bay Resort and
    Casino)/March 24 - 27/over 100 exhibitors
2014 - Las Vegas, NV/March 26 - 27
2015 - Long Beach, CA (Renaissance Long Beach
    Hotel)/April 27 - 30/over 100 exhibitors
2015 - Long Beach, CA/April 29 - 30
2016 - New Orleans, LA (Hyatt Regency New Orleans)/
    April 18 - 21
2016 - New Orleans, LA/April 20 - 21
2017 - Las Vegas, NV (Mandalay Bay Resort and
    Casino)/March 20 - 23
2017 - Las Vegas, NV/March 22 - 23
2018 - Orlando, FL (Walt Disney World Resort)/March
    26 - 29
2018 - Orlando, FL/March 28 - 29
2024 - Orlando, FL/March 25 - 28

Publications:
e-newsletter; monthly
Interior Construction Magazine; adv.
Member Directory; annually

Celebrant Foundation and Institute *(2001)*
93 Valley Rd.
Second Floor
Montclair, NJ 07042
Tel: (973) 746-1792 *Fax:* (973) 746-1775
E-Mail: information@celebrantinstitute.org
Website: celebrantinstitute.org
Staff: 2
Tax: 501(c)(3)

Personnel:
Co-founder and Chief Executive Officer: Gaile Sarma
Director, Academics: Cynthia Reed

Historical Note:
The Celebrant Foundation & Institute is dedicated to educating people about the importance of ceremony and rituals marking the important transitions in life. The

---

Institute offers certificate programs in ceremonies for couples, ceremonies for funerals, healing and transition, ceremonies for families and children and ceremonies for organizations.

Continuing Education:
Certification Designation/s: CCP

Publications:
Celebrancy Today Magazine; semi-annually
Member Directory; on-line

Cellulose Insulation Manufacturers Association *(1982)*
136 S. Keowee St.
Dayton, OH 45402
Tel: (937) 222-2462 *Fax:* (937) 222-5794
TollFree: (888) 881-2462
E-Mail: info@cellulose.org
Website: cellulose.org/CIMA/
Members: 20 insulation manufacturers
Staff: 3
Annual Budget: $100-250,000
Tax: 501(c)(6)

Personnel:
Executive Director: Daniel Lea
    E-Mail: cima@cellulose.org

Historical Note:
Formerly (1992) Cellulose Industry Standards Enforcement Program. CIMA is cellulose segment of the thermal/ acoustical insulation industry. Members are manufacturers of cellulose insulation (Producers) and those who provide materials and services to manufacturers of cellulose insulation (Associate Members).

Publications:
CIMA Newsletter; on-line

Cement Employers Association *(1936)*
122 E. Broad St., Second Floor
Bethlehem, PA 18018
Tel: (610) 868-8060 *Fax:* (610) 861-2884
E-Mail: emcgehee@cementemployers.com
Members: 32 companies
Staff: 2
Annual Budget: $100-250,000
Tax: 501(c)(6)

Personnel:
Executive Director: Elton McGehee
    E-Mail: emcgehee@cementemployers.com

Historical Note:
A grouping of cement companies united to promote personnel and industrial relations.

Cement Kiln Recycling Coalition
P.O. Box 7553
Arlington, VA 22207
Tel: (703) 869-4718 *Fax:* (202) 466-5009
E-Mail: info@ckrc.org
Website: ckrc.org
Members: 19 organizations
Staff: 5
Annual Budget: $500-1,000,000
Tax: 501(c)(6)

Personnel:
Executive Director: Michael R. Benoit
Director, Government Affairs: Michelle Lusk
    E-Mail: mlusk@ckrc.org

Historical Note:
CKRC strives to represent member companies that operate facilities throughout the United States. Members are cement companies that recover energy from hazardous waste-derived fuel as well as companies involved in the collection, processing, management and marketing of such fuel for use in cement kilns.

Membership List Available to Non-members

Cemented Carbide Producers Association *(1954)*
30200 Detroit Rd.
Cleveland, OH 44145-1967
Tel: (440) 899-0010 *Fax:* (440) 892-1404
Website: ccpa.org
Members: 23 companies
Staff: 5
Annual Budget: $50-100,000
Tax: 501(c)(6)

Personnel:
Contact, Communications: Linda Hamill
    E-Mail: leh@wherryassoc.com

Historical Note:

CCPA represents manufacturers and suppliers of cemented carbide products around the world. Members are makers of sintered carbide containing tungsten.

Center for American Nurses (2003)
8515 Georgia Ave.
Suite 400
Silver Spring, MD 20910-3492
Tel: (301) 628-5022 *Fax:* (301) 628-5297
Website: centerforamericannurses.org
Staff: 2
Annual Budget: $100-250,000
Tax: 501(c)(6)

Personnel:
Executive Director: Wylecia Wiggs Harris
Executive Assistant: Valerie P. Shade
    E-Mail: valerie.shade@centerforamericannurses.org

Historical Note:
The Center for American Nurses is a national professional nursing organization that educates, equips, and empowers nurses to advocate for themselves, their profession, and their patients. The mission of the Center for American Nurses is to actively collaborate and partner with individuals and groups to create healthy work environments. Offers evidence-based solutions and powerful tools to navigate workplace challenges, optimize patient outcomes, and maximize career benefits. Membership: $96 (Associate); $36 (Subscriber).

Publications:
Center for American Nurses; monthly
Nurses First

Center for Exhibition Industry Research (1978)
12700 Park Central Dr.
Suite 308
Dallas, TX 75251
Tel: (972) 687-9242 *Fax:* (972) 692-6020
E-Mail: info@ceir.org
Website: ceir.org
Members: 350 companies
Staff: 3
Annual Budget: $250-500,000
Tax: 501(c)(6)

Personnel:
Executive Director: Cathy Breden CAE, CMP
    E-Mail: cbreden@ceir.org
President and Chief Executive Officer: Douglas L. Ducate CEM, CMP
Coordinator, Research Project: Genny Nelson
    E-Mail: gnelson@ceir.org

Historical Note:
CEIR's mission is to advance the growth, awareness and value of exhibitions and other face-to-face marketing events by producing and delivering research-based knowledge tools that enable stakeholder organizations to enhance their ability to meet current and emerging customers. Membership: $250 (Regular Member); $750 (Organization); $3,500 (Industry Council Member).

Meetings/Conferences: Annual

Publications:
CEIR Direct Newsletter; bi-monthly; adv.
CEIR Exhibition Industry Census; adv.
CEIR Index; annually; adv.
Membership Directory; on-line; adv.

Center for Research Libraries (1949)
6050 S. Kenwood Ave.
Chicago, IL 60637-2804
Tel: (773) 955-4545 *Fax:* (773) 955-4339
TollFree: (800) 621-6044
Website: crl.edu
Members: 262 Companies
Staff: 43
Annual Budget: $5-10,000,000
Tax: 501(c)(3)

Personnel:
President: Bernard Reilly
    E-Mail: breilly@crl.edu
Coordinator, Membership Services and Communications: Don Dyer
    E-Mail: ddyer@crl.edu
Human Resources: Toni Kibort
    E-Mail: tkibort@crl.edu
Financial and Exchange Assistant: Christine Matheis
    E-Mail: cmatheis@crl.edu
Controller: Raymond Sallay
    E-Mail: rsallay@crl.edu
Director, Information Systems: Patricia Xia

E-Mail: pxia@crl.edu

Historical Note:
CRL supports advanced research and teaching in the humanities, sciences, and social sciences by preserving and making available to scholars the primary source material critical to those disciplines. Membership: $1,200-5,200 (University Library); $2,000-13,000 (Global membership).

Publications:
Global Resources
Membership Directory; on-line

Center for Spiritual and Ethical Education (1898)
P.O. Box 19807
Portland, OR 97280
Tel: (503) 232-1531 *Fax:* (678) 623-5634
TollFree: (800) 298-4599
E-Mail: info@csee.org
Website: csee.org
Members: 300 schools
Staff: 5
Annual Budget: $250-500,000
Tax: 501(c)(3)

Personnel:
Executive Director: David Streight
Associate Director: Jenny Aanderud
    E-Mail: jenny@csee.org
Contact, Membership Outreach: Sue Knight
Editor: John Roberts
Business Manager: Beth Sandlin
    E-Mail: beth.sandlin@csee.org

Historical Note:
Formerly (2009) known as the Council for Spiritual and Ethical Education, CSEE works to provide resources, expert voices, and an active forum for ethical growth and spiritual development in schools. Membership: $2,000 (Century Member); $445 (International Schools-Outside U.S.); $260-1,550 (Schools).

Meetings/Conferences:
2013 - Chicago, IL (Cenacle Retreat and Conference Center)/June 23 - 28
2013 - Chicago, IL (Cenacle Retreat and Conference Center)/June 25 - 30
Number of non-conference events/year: 4

Publications:
Connections
Parenting for Moral Growth; quarterly
Religion Teacher Update; quarterly

Center for the Polyurethanes Industry (1985)
700 Second St. NE
Washington, DC 20002
Tel: (202) 249-7000 *Fax:* (202) 249-6100
E-Mail: api@plastics.org
Website: http://
  polyurethane.americanchemistry.com
Members: 60 companies
Staff: 5
Annual Budget: $5-10,000,000

Personnel:
Senior Director: Lee Salamone
    E-Mail: Lee_Salamone@americanchemistry.com

Historical Note:
Founded as the Urethane Institute (1959); The Center for the Polyurethanes Industry (CPI), formerly Alliance for the Polyurethanes Industry (API), became Society of the Plastics Industry - Polyurethane Division in 1985, and assumed its present name in 1999. Members are polyurethane chemical producers; systems formulators; machinery manufacturers; manufacturers of polyurethane flexible and rigid foams, coatings, adhesives, sealants, elastomers, and molded polyurethane products; and manufacturers of rigid polyisocyanurate foams. Membership: $1,250 (Associate); $3,500 (General); $10,000 (Steering).

Meetings/Conferences: Annual

Publications:
Technical Bulletin

Membership List Available to Non-members

Center for Waste Reduction Technologies (1991)
Three Park Ave.
New York, NY 10016-5991
Tel: (212) 591-7462 *Fax:* (212) 591-8888
E-Mail: cwrt@aiche.org
Website: awsmonline.org
Members: 20 companies
Staff: 3
Annual Budget: $500-1,000,000

Personnel:
Director: Joseph E.L. Rogers
    E-Mail: cwrt@aiche.org

Historical Note:
CWRT is an international non-profit professional organization, affiliated with the American Institute of Chemical Engineers. The Center promotes the chemical, petroleum and pharmaceutical manufacturing industries.

Centerpoint for Leaders
1400 I St. NW
Suite 800
Washington, DC 20005
Tel: (202) 244-3020
Website: centerpointforleaders.org
Staff: 1
Annual Budget: Under $10,000
Tax: 501(c)(3)

Personnel:
President and Chief Executive Officer: Sandra Trice Gray CAE
    E-Mail: sandra@centerpointforleaders.org

Historical Note:
Centerpoint for leaders is a learning community and resource for current and future executives of nonprofit organizations, board members, community volunteers, business people who volunteer or work part-time for nonprofits, and anyone involved in leading community initiatives. It offers a learning community for nonprofit and community leaders, including programs and services that respond to unmet needs identified by the nonprofit sector. The organization holds regional retreats and workshops across all subsectors of the nonprofit, business and government sectors to share and explore promising leadership practices.

Publications:
Newsletter; bi-monthly

Central Bering Sea Fisherman's Association (2009)
140 Ellerman Heights
P.O. Box 288
St. Paul Island, AK 99660
Tel: (907) 546-2597 *Fax:* (907) 546-2450
Website: cbsfa.com
Staff: 7

Personnel:
President: Phillip Lestenkof
    E-Mail: plestenkof@cbsfa.com
Office Manager: Rena J. Kudrin
    E-Mail: rkudrin@cbsfa.com
Coordinator, Community Outreach and Projects: Ray Melovidov
    E-Mail: raymelovidov@cbsfa.com
Administrative Assistant: Marva Merculief
Chief Financial Officer: Jonathan Thorpe
    E-Mail: jthorpe@cbsfa.com

Historical Note:
The fishermen's group on Saint Paul, the Central Bering Sea Fishermen's Association (CBSFA), was designated the CDQ management organization. CBSFA's mission is to develop a viable, self-sustaining, independent fisheries development organization that, on behalf of the local fishermen, and the community of St. Paul as a whole, and in cooperation with other Bering Sea Coastal Communities and CDQ groups, will ensure key participation in fishery related development in the region while exercising proper resource stewardship.

Central Conference of American Rabbis (1889)
355 Lexington Ave.
New York, NY 10017-6603
Tel: (212) 972-3636 *Fax:* (212) 692-0819
E-Mail: info@ccarnet.org
Website: ccarnet.org
Members: 1800 individuals
Staff: 15
Annual Budget: $2-5,000,000

Personnel:
Chief Executive: Steven A. Fox
    E-Mail: SFox@ccarnet.org
Director, Placement: Alan Henkin
    E-Mail: AHenkin@ccarnet.org
Manager, Publishing Technology: Daniel B. Medwin
    E-Mail: dmedwin@ccarnet.org
Director, Program and Membership Services and Director, Joint Commission on Rabbinic Mentoring: Deborah Prinz
    E-Mail: DPrinz@ccarnet.org
Contact, Membership Services: Tanya Sperling

E-Mail: tsperling@ccarnet.org

Historical Note:
CCAR enriches and strengthens the Jewish community by empowering Reform Rabbis to provide religious, spiritual and organizational leadership.

Meetings/Conferences: Annual
Conference Chair: Deborah Prinz
2013 - Long Beach, CA (Westin Long Beach)/March 3 - 7
2014 - Chicago, IL (Fairmont Chicago Millenium Park)/ March 30 - April 2
Number of non-conference events/year: 12

Publications:
CCAR Journal: The Reform Jewish; quarterly

Central Intercollegiate Athletic Association
(1912)
22 Enterprise Pkwy, Suite 210
P. O. Box 7349
Hampton, VA 23666
Tel: (757) 865-0071 *Fax:* (757) 865-8436
E-Mail: TheCIAA@aol.com
Website: theciaa.com
Members: 7,000 students
Staff: 5
Annual Budget: $5-10,000,000
Tax: 501(c)(3)

Personnel:
Director, Communications: Shera L. White
    E-Mail: swhite@theciaa.com
Financial Analyst: April Crowder
    E-Mail: acrowder@theciaa.com
Director, Compliance and External Operations: Marcus D. Grant
    E-Mail: marcusdgrant@aol.com
Assistant , Communications and External Operations: Alexxis Hutchinson
    E-Mail: ahutchinson@theciaa.com
Assistant Director, Business Operations: Marcia Robinson

Historical Note:
CIAA holds championships annually in the following sports: Men's and Women's Cross Country; Volleyball; Football; Men's and Women's Indoor and Outdoor Track; Men's and Women's Basketball; Women's Bowling; Men's and Women's Tennis; Golf; Baseball and Softball.

Central Station Alarm Association *(1950)*
8150 Leesburg Pike
Suite 700
Vienna, VA 22182
Tel: (703) 242-4670 *Fax:* (703) 242-4675
E-Mail: admin@csaaul.org
Website: csaaul.org
Members: 300 companies
Staff: 7
Annual Budget: $1-2,000,000

Personnel:
Executive Vice President and Chief Executive Officer: Stephen P. Doyle
    E-Mail: director@csaaul.org
Vice President, Membership and Programs: Becky Lane
    E-Mail: membership@csaaul.org
Vice President, Meetings and Conventions: John McDonald
    E-Mail: meetings@csaaul.org
Senior Vice President, Finance and Administration: Madeline Fullerton McMahon
    E-Mail: finance@csaaul.org
Director, Education and Training: Stephanie S. Morgan
    E-Mail: smorgan@csaaintl.org
Director, Marketing and Communications: Monique C. Talbot
    E-Mail: communications@csaaul.org

Historical Note:
Formerly (1950-1989) Central Station Electrical Protection Association. CSAA's purpose is to foster and maintain the relationship among providers, users, bureaus, and other agencies of UL-Listed and/or FM-Approved Central Station protection services, and to promote the mutual interests with public officials, the insurance industry and customers. Membership: $1,500-11,500 (North American Regular Member); $500-1,950 (Proprietary Member, based on Locations); $1,925-38,000 (Associate, based on Company Gross Revenues); $825 (International); $500 (Consultant); $300 (Press).

Meetings/Conferences: Annual
Conference Chair: John McDonald

Publications:

CSAA Dispatch newsletter; quarterly; adv.
CSAA E-Grams; annually
CSAA Signals; on-line; adv.
Membership Directory; annually

CEO Council for Growth
200 S. Broad St.
Suite 700
Philadelphia, PA 19102
Tel: (215) 545-1234
Website: selectgreaterphiladelphia.com/look/ceo_council
Members: 5,000 companies
Staff: 1

Personnel:
President and Chief Executive Officer: Thomas G. Morr

Historical Note:
The CEO Council for Growth (CEO Council) is a group of prominent business executives committed to Greater Philadelphia's growth and prosperity.

Ceramic Tile Distributors Association *(1978)*
800 Roosevelt Rd., Building C
Suite 312
Glen Ellyn, IL 60137
Tel: (630) 545-9415 *Fax:* (630) 790-3095
TollFree: (800) 938-2832
E-Mail: info@ctdahome.org
Website: ctdahome.org
Members: 600 companies
Staff: 3
Annual Budget: $500-1,000,000
Tax: 501(c)(6)

Personnel:
Executive Director: Rick Church
Legal Counsel: Bill Ives

Historical Note:
CTDA's mission is to provide educational and networking opportunities for distributors of ceramic tile and their suppliers to further the consumption of ceramic tile. Members are distributors, manufacturers and allied professionals of ceramic tile and related products. Membership: $600 (Regular/Allied Company); $600-1100 (Associate, based on annual sales); $200 (Independent Agents/Artisan).

Continuing Education:
Certification Designation/s: CCTS, PTS

Meetings/Conferences: Annual

Publications:
CTDA This Week; weekly
Floor Covering News; irregular; adv.
Floor Covering Weekly; weekly
Stone World e-Newsletter; monthly; adv.
Tile Magazine; irregular; adv.
TILE's eNewsletter
TileDealer Magazine; quarterly; adv.

Ceramic Tile Institute of America *(1957)*
12061 Jefferson Blvd.
Culver City, CA 90230-6219
Tel: (310) 574-7800 *Fax:* (310) 821-4655
E-Mail: ctioa@earthlink.net
Website: ctioa.org
Members: 150 companies
Staff: 2
Annual Budget: $100-250,000

Personnel:
Director: Thomas Brady CTC

Historical Note:
Formerly known as Ceramic Tile Institute. CTIOA strives to promote appropriate and expanded use of ceramic tile and natural stone through education. Members are installers and makers of ceramic tiles. Membership: $100/year (Non-Voting Associate Member).

Continuing Education:
Certification Designation/s: CTI, CTS

Publications:
CTIOA Report; irregular
Membership Directory; on-line

Certification Board for Urologic Nurses and Associates *(1972)*
E. Holly Ave.
P.O. Box 56
Pitman, NJ 08071-0056
Tel: (856) 256-2351 *Fax:* (856) 589-7463
TollFree: (888) 827-7862

E-Mail: suna@ajj.com
Website: suna.org
Members: 500 urologic nurses, associates, and physician's assistants
Staff: 2
Annual Budget: $50-100,000
Tax: 501(c)(3)

Personnel:
President: Valre W. Welch MSN
Treasurer: Victor P. Senese

Historical Note:
Founded as American Board of Urologic Allied Health Professionals; assumed its current name in 1996. Purpose is to improve the quality of care provided to urology patients by promoting and acknowledging the highest standards of urologic nursing practice through the certification process. SUNA is a professional organization committed to excellence in evidence-based clinical practice, research, and education of its members, patients, families, and the community. Membership: $75 (Active); $115 (Sustaining); $95 (International Active); $135 (International Sustaining); $37.50 (Student).

Continuing Education:
Certification Designation/s: CURN, CUNP, CUPA, CUCNS, CUA, CBUNA

Meetings/Conferences:
2013 - Savannah, GA (Hyatt Regency)/March 7 - 9

Publications:
Certified Directory; on-line
Membership Directory; on-line
Uro-Gram; bi-monthly
Urologic Nursing Journal; bi-monthly; adv.

Certified Auto Parts Association *(1987)*
1000 Vermont Ave. NW
Suite 1010
Washington, DC 20005
Tel: (202) 737-2212 *Fax:* (202) 737-2214
E-Mail: info@CAPAcertified.org
Website: capacertified.org
Members: 97 organizations
Staff: 1
Annual Budget: $10-25,000,000

Personnel:
Executive Director: Jack Gillis

Historical Note:
Formerly Certified Auto Parts Association. CAPA oversees a testing and inspection program that certifies the quality of automotive parts used for collision repairs. CAPA's mission is to promote price and quality competition in the collision part industry, thereby reducing the cost of crash repairs to consumers without sacrificing quality. Member organizations include collision repairers, consumer groups, distributors, and insurance companies.

Membership List Available to Non-members

Certified Claims Professional Accreditation Council *(1981)*
P.O. Box 550922
Jacksonville, FL 32255-0922
Tel: (904) 390-1506 *Fax:* (904) 390-1244
Website: ccpac.com
Members: 300 individuals
Staff: 6
Annual Budget: $10-25,000

Personnel:
Executive Director: John O'Dell HCCP
    E-Mail: jodell@landstar.com
Editor: James Cook
Legal Counselor: George Pezold
    E-Mail: george.pezold@transportlaw.com
Vice President, Certifications: Dona Vidal
    E-Mail: Dona.vidal@transplace.com
Treasurer: Jean Zimmerman CCP

Historical Note:
CCPAC's mission is to raise the professional standards of individuals who specialize in the administration and negotiation of freight claims. Membership: $75 (CCP/ HCCP/Associate); $500 (Co-Sponsor Organization); $450 (Corporate Sponsor Membership/Corporate Professional Member); $2,000 (Life).

Continuing Education:
Certification Designation/s: CCP

Publications:
Membership Directory; on-line; adv.
ProClaim Newsletter; semi-annually; adv.

Certified Contractors Network *(1996)*

6476 Sligo Mill Rd.
Takoma Park, MD 20912
Tel: (301) 891-0999 *Fax:* (866) 250-3270
E-Mail: info@contractors.net
Website: contractors.net
Members: 700 companies
Staff: 6
Annual Budget: $500-1,000,000

Personnel:
Founder: Richard Kaller
Manager, Finance: Lauren Burgess
   E-Mail: lauren@contractors.net
General Manager: Catherine Honigsberg
   E-Mail: catherine@contractors.net
Director, Membership Services: Gail McNeill
   E-Mail: gmcneill@contractors.net
Coordinator, Marketing: Megan Robinson
   E-Mail: megan@contractors.net
Office Manager: Jackie Rommel
   E-Mail: jackie@contractors.net

Historical Note:
CCN's mission is to enhance the professionalism, performance and perception of the construction industry and to promote ethics, education, leadership and innovation, so that the construction industry and the community achieve mutual benefit. Membership: $1188 (Bronze); $2388 (Silver); $3588 (Gold).

Meetings/Conferences: Semi-Annual

Publications:
Changing Times; weekly
Tool Box; monthly
Wizard Watch; weekly

Certified Milk Producers Association of America
(1908)
8300 Pine Ave.
Chino, CA 91710
Tel: (909) 393-0960 *Fax:* (415) 583-7328
Members: 6 farms
Staff: 2
Annual Budget: Under $10,000

Personnel:
President: Boyd Clarke

Historical Note:
Members are farms producing raw "certified" (pure, but unpasteurized) milk. CMPAA is affiliated with the American Association of Medical Milk Commissions. Membership fee based on production.

Cervical Spine Research Society *(1973)*
6300 N. River Rd.
Suite 727
Rosemont, IL 60018-4226
Tel: (847) 698-1628 *Fax:* (847) 823-0536
E-Mail: csrs@aaos.org
Website: csrs.org
Members: 326 individuals
Staff: 2
Annual Budget: $1-2,000,000
Tax: 501(c)(3)

Personnel:
President: Michael G. Fehlings MD, PhD
Treasurer: Darrel S. Brodke MD

Historical Note:
CSRS is a multidisciplinary organization that provides a forum for the exchange of ideas and promotes clinical and basic science research of the cervical spine. The organization values collegial interaction and strong scientific principles.

Meetings/Conferences: Annual
Number of non-conference events/year: 1

Publications:
CSRS Newsletter; annually
Membership Directory; on-line

Membership List Available to Non-members

CFA Institute *(1990)*
560 Ray C. Hunt Dr.
Charlottesville, VA 22903-2981
Tel: (434) 951-5499 *Fax:* (434) 951-5262
TollFree: (800) 247-8132
E-Mail: info@cfainstitute.org
Website: cfainstitute.org
Members: 90135 individuals and societies
Staff: 210
Annual Budget: Over $100,000,000

Tax: 501(c)(6)

Personnel:
President and Chief Executive Officer: John D. Rogers CFA
General Counsel: Jeannie Anderson JD
Managing Director, Chief Information Officer: Elaine Cheng
Managing Director, Stakeholder Services, Marketing and Communications: Raymond J. DeAngelo
Manager, Public Relations: Sarah Jane Purvis
   E-Mail: sarahjane.purvis@cfainstitute.org
Senior Managing Director: Robert R. Johnson CFA, PhD
Managing Director, Human Resources: Donna Marshall
Chief Administrative Officer and Chief Financial Officer: Timothy G. McLaughlin CFA, CPA
Managing Director, Education: Thomas R. Robinson CFA, CFP, CPA, PhD
Managing Director, Strategic Products and Technology Division: Jan Squires CFA, PhD, DBA

Historical Note:
Formed (1990) as the Association for Investment Management and Research by a merger of the Financial Analysts Federation and the Institute of Chartered Financial Analysts. CFA Institute's mission is to lead the investment profession globally by setting the standards of ethics, education, and professional excellence. Membership: $275 (CFA Institute Members); $100 (Retired).

Continuing Education:
Certification Designation/s: CFA, CIPM

Meetings/Conferences: Annual
2013 - Suntec City, Singapore (Suntec Singapore International Convention and Exhibition Centre)/ May 19 - 22
2014 - Seattle, WA/May 4 - 7
Number of non-conference events/year: 89

Publications:
Advocacy Update; bi-monthly
CFA Digest
CFA Magazine
CFA Program Newsletter; quarterly
Conference Proceedings; quarterly
Event Update; monthly
Financial Analysts Journal
Financial NewsBrief; daily
GIPS Newsletter; monthly
Investment Performance Measurement Newsletter; quarterly
Membership Directory; on-line
Private Wealth Management Newsletter; bi-monthly

CHA - Certified Horsemanship Association *(1967)*
4037 Iron Works Pkwy.
Suite 180
Lexington, KY 40511
Tel: (859) 259-3399 *Fax:* (859) 255-0726
TollFree: (800) 399-0138
E-Mail: office@cha-ahse.org
Website: cha-ahse.org
Members: 2800 individuals and organizations.
Staff: 3
Annual Budget: $250-500,000

Personnel:
Chief Executive Officer: Christy Landwehr
   E-Mail: clandwehr@cha-ahse.org
Director, Programs: Polly Haselton Barger
   E-Mail: pbarger@cha-ahse.org
Director, Membership Services: Terri Weaver
   E-Mail: office@CHA-ahse.org

Historical Note:
Formerly (1990) the Camp Horsemanship Association and The Association for Horsemanship Safety and Education (1998). Incorporated in Michigan in 1972. Members are camp owners, camp directors, colleges, stables, riding instructors and others interested in riding instruction and safety. CHA's mission is to promote excellence in safety and education for the benefit of the entire horse industry. Membership: $55 (Individual); $750 (Lifetime); $15 (Youth); $200 (Program/Business); $950 (Affiliate).

Continuing Education:
Certification Designation/s: SIC, TGC, IRDC, CITGC, SESC, VCC, DIDC

Meetings/Conferences: Annual

Publications:
The Instructor Magazine; on-line; adv.

Membership List Available to Non-members

Chain Drug Marketing Association *(1926)*
43157 W. Nine Mile Rd.

P.O. Box 995
Novi, MI 48376-0995
Tel: (248) 449-9300 *Fax:* (248) 449-9396
E-Mail: cdma@chaindrug.com
Website: chaindrug.com
Members: 101 organizations
Staff: 16
Annual Budget: $2-5,000,000

Personnel:
President: James R, Devine
   E-Mail: devine@chaindrug.com
Vice President, Membership and Trade Shows: Judy Aspinall
   E-Mail: aspinall@chaindrug.com
Vice President, Store Brand and Finance: John Devine
   E-Mail: jdevine@chaindrug.com
Communications Coordinator: Rachel Fallert
   E-Mail: fallert@chaindrug.com
Marketing Coordinator: Elaine Freeman
   E-Mail: freeman@chaindrug.com
Office Manager and Executive Assistant: Deb Hayes
   E-Mail: hayes@chaindrug.com
Administrator, Information Technology: Brett Shepherd
   E-Mail: shepherd@chaindrug.com
Event Planner and Executive Assistant: Laura Webb
   E-Mail: webb@chaindrug.com

Historical Note:
CDMA's mission is to provide products, programs, services and information that will help its members to become more profitable and efficient. Members are regional drug chains from across North America. Membership: $2500-6000/ year (Associate Member).

Meetings/Conferences:
Conference Chair: Judy Aspinall
2013 - Atlanta, GA/Feb. 23 - 25
2013 - Atlanta, GA (Hilton Atlanta)/Sept. 19 - 22
Number of non-conference events/year: 4

Publications:
Front End Focus Newsletter; quarterly
Membership Directory; on-line

Membership List Available to Non-members

Chain Link Fence Manufacturers Institute *(1960)*
10015 Old Columbia Rd.
Suite B-215
Columbia, MD 21046
Tel: (410) 290-6267 *Fax:* (410) 290-5282
E-Mail: clfmihq@aol.com
Website: associationsites.com/clfma/index.cfm
Members: 54 companies
Staff: 2
Annual Budget: $100-250,000

Personnel:
Executive Vice President: Mark Levin

Historical Note:
CLFMI provides a forum in which members can meet to be educated and exchange ideas on operations and management, promotes use of chain link fence.

Publications:
Membership Directory; on-line

Chamber Music America *(1977)*
305 Seventh Ave.
Fifth Floor
New York, NY 10001-6008
Tel: (212) 242-2022 *Fax:* (212) 242-7955
Website: chamber-music.org
Members: 8000 individuals
Staff: 11
Annual Budget: $2-5,000,000

Personnel:
Chief Executive Officer: Margaret M. Lioi
   E-Mail: mlioi@chamber-music.org
Associate, Systems: Jermaine Bowens
Director, Publications: Ellen Goldensohn
   E-Mail: egoldensohn@chamber-music.org
Manager, Conferences and Advertising: Brenden O'Hanlon
   E-Mail: bohanlon@chamber-music.org
Manager, Membership Services: Adam Reifsteck
   E-Mail: areifsteck@chamber-music.org
Manager, Conference and Events: Sherry Robinson
   E-Mail: srobinson@chamber-music.org
Director, Finance and Administration: Michael Welch
   E-Mail: mwelch@chamber-music.org
Chair, Conference Committee: Phillip Ying

Historical Note:
CMA's mission is to is to develop and strengthen an evolving chamber music community. Members are vocal and instrumental ensembles performing Western classical, jazz, contemporary, and world music, as well as individual musicians, large and small presenters, festivals and training institutions, businesses, managers, and chamber music enthusiasts. Membership: $35 (Student); $60 (Advocate); $85 (Professional Musician/Composer/Educator); $125-375 (Organization); $95 (Business).

Meetings/Conferences: Annual
Conference Chair: Phillip Ying
2013 - New York City, NY (Westin New York at Times Square)/Jan. 17 - 20
Number of non-conference events/year: 379

Publications:
Accent; weekly
Chamber Music; bi-monthly
Directory of Festivals, Schools, and Workshops; annually
Membership Directory; annually

Chamber of Shipping of America (1917)
1730 M St. NW
Suite 407
Washington, DC 20036-4517
Tel: (202) 775-4399 *Fax:* (202) 659-3795
E-Mail: info@knowships.org
Website: knowships.org
Members: 36 companies
Staff: 3
Annual Budget: $1-2,000,000
Tax: 501(c)(6)

Personnel:
President and Chief Executive Officer: Joseph J. Cox
    E-Mail: jcox@knowships.org
Administrative Assistant: Odell J. Moore

Historical Note:
Founded as American Institute of Merchant Shipping as the result of the merger of Committee of American Steamship Lines (1952), Pacific American Steamship Association (1919) and American Merchant Marine Institute (1938). Became U.S. Chamber of Shipping in 1996, and assumed its current name in 1998. CSA represents member's interests in dealings with international and domestic agencies concerned with merchant shipping. Members are companies that own or operate U.S. flag or foreign-flag ships.

Meetings/Conferences:
Number of non-conference events/year: 2

Charles Homer Haskins Society (1982)
Department of History
Ball State University
Muncie, IN 47306
Tel: (765) 285-8783 *Fax:* (765) 285-5612
Website: haskins.cornell.edu
Members: 180 individuals
Staff: 4

Personnel:
President: Bruce O'Brien
Director, Conferences: Robin Fleming
    E-Mail: robin.fleming@bc.edu
Editor and Webmaster: Steven Isaac
Treasurer: Frederick Suppe
    E-Mail: fsuppe@bsu.edu

Historical Note:
CHHS is an international scholar organization dedicated to the study of Viking Anglo-Saxon, Anglo-Norman and early Angevin history as well as the history of neighboring areas and peoples. Membership: $50-60 (Regular); $30-45 (Student); $65-90 (Sustaining).

Meetings/Conferences: Annual
Conference Chair: Robin Fleming

Publications:
Haskins Society Journal; annually
The Anglo-Norman Anonymous; quarterly

Checks Payment Systems Association (1952)
2025 M St. NW
Suite 800
Washington, DC 20036-3309
Tel: (202) 367-1144 *Fax:* (202) 367-2144
E-Mail: info@cpsa-check.org
Website: cpsa-checks.org
Members: 25 companies
Staff: 2
Annual Budget: $250-500,000
Tax: 501(c)(6)

Personnel:
Executive Director: Steven Antolick

Historical Note:
Formerly Bank Stationers Section of Lithographers and Printers National Association and the Bank Stationers Association, then became Financial Stationers Association and assumed its present name in 1999. Absorbed the Payment Systems Education Association in 1990. CPSA's mission is to be the recognized organization providing the leadership, services and programs necessary to advance the paper check and the check payment system. . Membership: $3000 (Associate); $650 (Affiliate); $685-56,595 (Regular).

Cheese Importers Association of America, Inc. (1948)
204 E St. NE
Washington, DC 20002
Tel: (202) 547-0899 *Fax:* (202) 547-6348
E-Mail: info@theciaa.org
Website: theciaa.org
Staff: 5
Annual Budget: $500-1,000,000
Tax: 501(c)(6)

Personnel:
Chief of Staff: Annette Summers
    E-Mail: asummers@theciaa.org
Legal Counsel: John W. Bode
    E-Mail: jbode@theciaa.org
Manager, Special Events: Shiela Crowley
    E-Mail: scrowley@theciaa.org
Coordinator, Membership Services: Melissa Fowler
    E-Mail: mfowler@theciaa.org

Historical Note:
The Cheese Importers Association, Inc. serves its members, the world dairy community and ultimately the end consumer by helping to facilitate the efficient import of dairy products from around the world into the United States. Membership: $2,100-8,300 (Principal Member, based on the quantity of cheese imported on a yearly basis); $1,200 (Associate Members); $2,700 (Government and Trade Association Members); $600 (Sales Broker Members).

Meetings/Conferences: Annual
Conference Chair: Shiela Crowley

Publications:
Membership Directory; on-line

Cheiron: The International Society for the History of Behavioral and Social Sciences (1968)
Earlham College
Richmond, IN 47374
E-Mail: cfaye@uakron.edu
Website: uakron.edu/cheiron
Members: 350 individuals
Staff: 3
Annual Budget: Under $10,000

Personnel:
Executive Officer: Kathy Milar
    E-Mail: kathym@earlham.edu

Historical Note:
Cheiron works to promote international cooperation and multi disciplinary studies in the history of the behavioral and social sciences. Membership: $35 (Regular); $10 (Students); $300 (Lifetime).

Meetings/Conferences: Annual

Publications:
Cheiron Newsletter
Journal of the History of the Behavioral Sciences; quarterly

Chemical Coaters Association International (1970)
P.O. Box 13
5040 Old Taylor Mill Rd.
Taylor Mill, KY 41015
Tel: (859) 356-1030 *Fax:* (859) 356-0908
TollFree: (800) 926-2848
Website: ccaiweb.com
Members: 1000 individuals and companies
Staff: 4
Annual Budget: $250-500,000

Personnel:
Executive Director: Anne Goyer
    E-Mail: aygoyer@one.net
Webmaster: Leslie Muck

Historical Note:
CCAI's mission is to raise the standards of finishing operations through educational meetings and seminars,

training manuals, certification programs, and outreach programs with colleges and universities. Provides information and training on surface coating technologies. Members are users and suppliers of industrial cleaners, paints, coatings and equipment. Membership: $95 (Individual); $150-300 (Custom Coater); $1,450-2,450 (Corporate).

Continuing Education:
Certification Designation/s: CCAI

Meetings/Conferences: Annual
2013 - Mt. Hood, OR (The Resort at the Mountain)/ June 19 - 21

Publications:
Finishing Touch; quarterly; adv.
Membership Directory; annually; adv.

Chemical Fabrics and Film Association (1927)
1300 Sumner Ave.
Cleveland, OH 44115-2851
Tel: (216) 241-7333 *Fax:* (216) 241-0105
E-Mail: cffa@chemicalfabricsandfilm.com
Website: chemicalfabricsandfilm.com
Members: 40 companies
Staff: 3
Annual Budget: $100-250,000

Personnel:
President: Jeff Post
Executive Secretary: Charles (Chuck) M. Stockinger
    E-Mail: cstockinger@thomasamc.com

Historical Note:
Established as the Pyroxylin Coated Fabric Manufacturers, CFFA became the Vinyl Fabrics Institute and assumed its present name in 1971. The Chemical Fabrics and Film Association (CFFA) is an international trade association representing manufacturers of polymer-based fabric and film products, used in the hospitality, healthcare, building and construction, automotive, fashion and other industries. Members are manufacturers of vinyl and urethane products.

Publications:
FOCUS on Sustainability

Membership List Available to Non-members

Chemical Heritage Foundation (1982)
315 Chestnut St.
Philadelphia, PA 19106-2702
Tel: (215) 925-2222 *Fax:* (215) 925-1954
TollFree: (888) 224-6006
E-Mail: info@chemheritage.org
Website: chemheritage.org
Members: 30 organizations
Staff: 57
Annual Budget: $10-25,000,000
Tax: 501(c)(3)

Personnel:
President and Chief Executive Officer: Tom Tritton
    E-Mail: ttritton@chemheritage.org
Reference Librarian and Fellowship Coordinator: Ashley Augustyniak
    E-Mail: aaugustyniak@chemheritage.org
Senior Receptionist and Human Resources Coordinator: Evelyn Bailey
    E-Mail: evelynb@chemheritage.org
Database Administrator: Joshua Balascak
    E-Mail: jbalascak@chemheritage.org
Director, Communications: Mary Ellen Burd
    E-Mail: mburd@chemheritage.org
Editor in Chief, Chemical Heritage, and Manager, Public Programming: Michal Meyer
    E-Mail: mmeyer@chemheritage.org
Outreach Coordinator: Gigi Naglak
    E-Mail: gnaglak@chemheritage.org
Vice President, Finance and Administration: Miriam Fisher Schaefer
    E-Mail: mschaefer@chemheritage.org
Manager, Events and Stewardship: Nancy Vonada
    E-Mail: nvonada@chemheritage.org

Historical Note:
Founded under the auspices of the American Chemical Society and the American Institute of Chemical Engineers, CHF is recognized as the central agency for preserving, studying and communicating the history of the chemical industry. Its mission is to advance public understanding of chemistry and related sciences.

Meetings/Conferences:
Conference Chair: Nancy Vonada
Number of non-conference events/year: 2

Publications:

Chemical Heritage Magazine; adv.

Membership List Available to Non-members

Chemical Sources Association (1972)

3301 Route 66
Suite 205, Building C
Neptune, NJ 07753
Tel: (732) 922-3038 *Fax:* (732) 922-3590
Website: chemicalsources.org
Members: 200 individuals and 80 Companies
Staff: 1
Annual Budget: $25-50,000

Personnel:
Contact, Communications: Diane Davis
    E-Mail: diane@afius.org

Historical Note:
CSA provides the flavor industry with a resource that fosters the exchange of knowledge on raw materials, current regulatory issues and patents. Membership is limited to companies that are manufacturers and/or distributors of flavoring ingredients, flavors, extracts, aromas, or related raw materials who are engaged in the business of originating, developing or selling flavoring ingredients, flavors, extracts aromas or related raw materials. Membership: $525/year (Company).

Meetings/Conferences: Annual
Number of non-conference events/year: 1

Membership List Available to Non-members

Cherry Marketing Institute (1988)

P.O. Box 30285
Lansing, MI 48909-7785
Tel: (517) 669-4264 *Fax:* (517) 669-3354
E-Mail: info@choosecherries.com
Website: choosecherries.com
Members: 1200 cherry growers
Staff: 11
Annual Budget: $2-5,000,000

Personnel:
Contact, Communications: Caitlin Solway
    E-Mail: press@choosecherries.com

Historical Note:
Cherry Marketing Institute, an organization funded by North American tart cherry growers and processors, works to increase the demand for tart cherries through promotion, market expansion, product development and research.

Publications:
E-Newsletter; on-line

Chester White Swine Record Association (1930)

P.O. Box 9758
Peoria, IL 61612-9758
Tel: (309) 691-0151 *Fax:* (309) 691-0168
E-Mail: cpspeoria@mindspring.com
Website: cpsswine.com/chester/
    chesterwhites.htm
Members: 1050 individuals
Staff: 3
Annual Budget: $250-500,000
Tax: 501(c)(5)

Personnel:
Director, Promotions: Jack Wall
Contact: Will Davis

Historical Note:
Breeders of Chester White swine. The Chester White Breed originated in Chester County, PA, in the early 19th century. Member of the National Pedigree Livestock Council. CWSRA's mission is to provide the leadership and coordination of programs, services, and activities for the betterment of members.

Publications:
Breeders Digest; monthly; adv.

Chevron and Texaco Petroleum Marketers Association

1444 N. Farnsworth Ave.
Suite 201
Aurora, IL 60505
Tel: (630) 375-5877 *Fax:* (630) 375-5854
E-Mail: ctpmadgr@sbcglobal.net
Website: ctpma.net
Members: 300 marketers and associate members
Staff: 3
Annual Budget: $250-500,000

Personnel:
Executive Director: Dave Rendall
Secretary: Bill Kent

Treasurer: Alec McBarnet

Historical Note:
Founded over 25 years ago as the Chevron Petroleum Marketers Association, became the CTPMA in 2004 with the addition of the Texaco brand. CTPMA's purpose is to help members grow and prosper in a challenging and rapidly changing marketplace. Membership: $500-1750 (Marketer); $400 (Associate).

Meetings/Conferences: Annual
Number of non-conference events/year: 2

Publications:
CTPMA News magazine; quarterly
CTPMA Newsletter; quarterly; adv.
Membership Directory; annually

Chi Eta Phi Sorority, Inc. (1932)

3029 13th St. NW
Washington, DC 20009
Tel: (202) 232-3858 *Fax:* (202) 232-3460
E-Mail: chietaphi@verizon.net
Website: chietaphi.com
Members: 8000 individuals
Staff: 3
Annual Budget: $500-1,000,000

Personnel:
Supreme Basileus: Dr. Mildred D. Fennal CNS, PhD, RN
Editor in Chief: Jamesetta A. Halley-Boyce FACHE, PhD, RN
Secretary: Priscilla Murphy

Historical Note:
Mission is to provide service for humanity and to increase interest in the nursing profession. Membership: $75/year.

Meetings/Conferences: Annual
Number of non-conference events/year: 4

Publications:
Chi Line Newsletter; semi-annually
Journal Of Chi Eta Phi Sorority; annually; adv.
Membership Directory; annually

Chief Administrators of Catholic Education (1908)

1005 N. Glebe Rd.
Suite 525
Arlington, VA 22201
Tel: (800) 711-6232 *Fax:* (703) 243-0025
Website: ncea.org
Staff: 2

Personnel:
Executive Director: William J. Campbell
    E-Mail: wcampbell@ncea.org
Administrative Assistant: Meg C. DeBoe

Historical Note:
An affiliate of the National Catholic Educational Association. CACE provides developing and supporting excellence in Catholic educational leadership by planning and approving programs and activities which address members professional and faith formation needs. CACE member representatives work closely with other NCEA school-related departments, the NCEA Department of Religious Education and the United States Conference of Catholic Bishops on the development of a national agenda for Catholic schools and catechetical programs, and to advocate for Catholic schools on public policy matters at the national level. Membership: $120.00 (Retired); $310.00 (Catholic Higher Ed. Supporting Catholic Schools/ Assistant Director Religious Education, Associate/Assistant Supt./Coordinator); $360.00 (Superintendent of Schools/ Diocesan Director of Religious Education/Vicar/Director of Total Education/Religious Congregation Director).

Meetings/Conferences: Annual

Publications:
CACE Newsletter; monthly
Membership Directory; on-line

Chief Executives Organization (1958)

7920 Norfolk Ave.
Suite 400
Bethesda, MD 20814-2507
Tel: (301) 656-9220 *Fax:* (301) 656-9221
E-Mail: info@ceo.org
Website: ceo.org
Members: 2000 chief executives and board chairmen
Staff: 34
Annual Budget: $10-25,000,000

Personnel:
Executive Director: Mike Geiger
    E-Mail: Mgeiger@ceo.org

Director, Marketing and Communications: Angie Lawry
Director, Events: Natalie Noakes

Historical Note:
Formerly (1983) Chief Executives Forum. CEO's mission is to enrich each other's lives through unique connections and enduring relationships of the community leaders. Membership: $2,600/year (by invitation only).

Meetings/Conferences:
Conference Chair: Natalie Noakes

Publications:
CEO Newsletter
CEO Upcoming; monthly
Compass; semi-annually
Events Catalog; semi-annually

Chief Officers of State Libraries Agencies (1973)

201 E. Main St.
Suite 1405
Lexington, KY 40507
Tel: (859) 514-9151 *Fax:* (859) 514-9166
Website: cosla.org
Members: 53 individuals
Staff: 3
Annual Budget: $250-500,000

Personnel:
Association Director: Laura Singler-Adams
    E-Mail: lsingler-adams@amrms.com
Database Coordinator: Diane Dougherty
    E-Mail: ddougherty@AMRms.com
Conference and Events Manager: Aaron Smither
    E-Mail: asmither@AMRms.com

Historical Note:
COSLA's mission is to identify and address issues of common concern and national interest, to further state library agency relationships with the federal government and national organizations and to initiate cooperative action for the improvement of library services to the people of the United States. Membership consists solely of these top library officers of the states and territories, variously designated as state librarian, director, commissioner or executive secretary.

Meetings/Conferences: Annual
Conference Chair: Aaron Smither

Publications:
Member Directory; on-line

Chief Petty Officers Association (1969)

5520-G Hempstead Way
Springfield, VA 22151-4009
Tel: (703) 941-0395 *Fax:* (703) 941-0397
Website: uscgcpoa.org
Members: 12000 individuals
Staff: 2
Annual Budget: $100-250,000

Personnel:
Executive Director: Randy Reid
    E-Mail: coastguardcpoa@gmail.com

Historical Note:
CPOA's mission is to assist members and their dependents who may be in urgent need, financial or otherwise, recruits for the United States Coast Guard and supports the aim and goals of the Chief Petty Officer's Academy. Membership: $400-500 (Life).

Meetings/Conferences: Annual
Conference Chair: Bill Segelken
2013 - Houston, TX/Aug. 12 - 15

Publications:
FEDweek Newsletter; weekly

Chief Warrant and Warrant Officers Association, United States Coast Guard (1929)

200 V St. SW
Washington, DC 20024
Tel: (202) 554-7753 *Fax:* (202) 484-0641
TollFree: (800) 792-8447
E-Mail: cwoauscg@verizon.net
Website: cwoauscg.org
Members: 3600 individuals
Staff: 2
Annual Budget: $50-100,000

Personnel:
Executive Director: Forrest Appelton
Treasurer: Mitzie A. Robinson

Historical Note:
Members of CWOA strive to render loyal service to superiors, subordinates and peers in every organization of which they are a member. Members are active, reserve and

retired U.S. Coast Guard warrant officers and chief warrant officers. Membership: $60/year.

Meetings/Conferences: Annual

Publications:
CWO News; bi-monthly

Child Care Aware of America *(1987)*
1515 N. Courthouse Rd.
11th floor
Arlington, VA 22201
Tel: (703) 341-4100 *Fax:* (703) 341-4101
E-Mail: info@naccrra.org
Website: naccrra.org
Members:
700 organizations
250 individuals
Staff: 30
Annual Budget: $50-100,000,000
Tax: 501(c)(3)

Personnel:
Executive Director: Ollie M. Smith
Chief, Information Technology, Sales, and Special Services:
J. Albright
   E-Mail: j.albright@naccrra.org
Chief, Business Operations: Bill Huleatt
   E-Mail: bill.huleatt@naccrra.org
Chief Financial Officer: Mike Nosil
   E-Mail: mike.nosil@naccrra.org
Chief, Policy Division and Evaluation: Grace Reef
   E-Mail: grace.reef@naccrra.org
Chief, Membership and Organizational Advancement:
Bryan Schultz
   E-Mail: bryan.schultz@naccrra.org
Senior Director, Membership Services: Jan Terhune
   E-Mail: jan.terhune@naccrra.org

Historical Note:
Formerly NACCRRA. Mission is to promote national policies and partnerships to advance the development and learning of all children and to provide vision, leadership, and support to community Child Care Resource & Referral. Membership: $55 (Child Care Provider/Student); $105 (Individual-Basic); $210 (Individual-Champion).

Meetings/Conferences:
Conference Chair: Jan Terhune
Number of non-conference events/year: 7

Publications:
Capitol Connection; on-line
Daily Parent; daily
NACCRRA in the News; on-line
NACCRRA Link
Parent Central; on-line
Parent Connection; on-line

Child Life Council *(1982)*
11821 Parklawn Dr.
Suite 310
Rockville, MD 20852-2539
Tel: (301) 881-7090 *Fax:* (301) 881-7092
TollFree: (800) 252-4515
E-Mail: clcstaff@childlife.org
Website: childlife.org
Members: 4500 individuals
Staff: 13
Annual Budget: $1-2,000,000

Personnel:
Executive Director: Dennis Reynolds CAE, MA
Staff Accountant: Lisa Crock
Director, Certification: Ame Enright
   E-Mail: certification@childlife.org
Manager, Communications and Marketing: Genevieve
Finn
Coordinator, Membership and Database: Sharon L.
Ruckdeschel
   E-Mail: membership@childlife.org
Manager, Conference and Professional Development:
Ramona Spencer CMP
   E-Mail: conference@childlife.org

Historical Note:
CLC serves child life professionals as they empower children and families to master challenging life events. Membership is composed of child life personnel, hospital school teachers, patient activity specialists, therapeutic recreation specialists, and others who use play, recreation, education, self-expression, and theories of child development to promote psychological well-being and optimum development of children, adolescents, and their families. Membership: $25 (Joining Fee-One Time); $120 (Professional); $70 (Student/Special Membership); $95 (Associate).

Continuing Education:
Certification Designation/s: CCLS

Meetings/Conferences: Annual
Conference Chair: Ramona Spencer CMP
2013 - Denver, CO (Sheraton Denver Downtown
   Hotel)/May 16 - 19
2014 - New Orleans, LA (Hilton New Orleans
   Riverside)/May 22 - 25
Number of non-conference events/year: 5

Publications:
Bulletin Newsletter; quarterly; adv.
Child Life News; monthly; adv.
Member Directory; on-line

Child Neurology Society *(1972)*
1000 W. County Rd., East
Suite 290
St. Paul, MN 55126
Tel: (651) 486-9447 *Fax:* (651) 486-9436
E-Mail:
nationaloffice@childneurologysociety.org
Website: childneurologysociety.org
Members: 223 members
Staff: 2
Annual Budget: $2-5,000,000
Tax: 501(c)(3)

Personnel:
Executive Director: Roger Larson

Historical Note:
CNS advances child neurology by providing a scientific forum for professionals in the field. Purpose is to foster the discipline of child neurology and promoting the optimal care and welfare of children with neurological and neurodevelopmental disorders. Membership: $225/year (Active).

Continuing Education:
Certification Designation/s: CME

Meetings/Conferences: Annual
2013 - Austin, TX/Oct. 30 - Nov. 2

Publications:
CNS Newsletter
Membership Directory; on-line

Child Welfare League of America *(1920)*
1726 M St. NW
Suite 500
Washington, DC 20036
Tel: (202) 688-4200 *Fax:* (202) 833-1689
Website: cwla.org
Members: 1153 individuals and 600 agencies
Staff: 51
Annual Budget: $5-10,000,000
Tax: 501(c)(3)

Personnel:
President and Chief Executive Officer: Christine James-
Brown
   E-Mail: cjamesbrown@cwla.org
Managing Editor: Rachel Adams
   E-Mail: radams@cwla.org
Chief Financial Officer: Ray Bierria
   E-Mail: rbierria@cwla.org
Director, Marketing: Karen Dunn
   E-Mail: kdunn@cwla.org
Meeting Planner: Tiffany Jefferson
   E-Mail: tjefferson@cwla.org
*Director, National Resource Center for Child Welfare Data
and Technology:* Debbie Milner
   E-Mail: dmilner@cwla.org
Director, Models of Practice and Training Development:
Donna Petras
   E-Mail: dpetras@cwla.org
Vice President, Membership Services: Cassaundra Rainey
   E-Mail: crainey@cwla.org
Vice President, Policy and Public Affairs: Linda Spears
   E-Mail: lspears@cwla.org

Historical Note:
CWLA's mission is to ensure safety, permanence, and well-being of children, youth, and their families by advancing public policy, defining and promoting practice excellence and delivering superior membership services. Membership: $25-6000/year.

Meetings/Conferences: Annual
Conference Chair: Tiffany Jefferson
2013 - Washington, DC (Hyatt Regency Crystal City at
   Reagan National Airport)/April 14 - 17
Number of non-conference events/year: 1

Publications:

Child Welfare Journal; bi-monthly; adv.
Children's Monitor; on-line
Children's Voice Magazine; bi-monthly; adv.
Membership Directory; on-line
The Link; quarterly

Membership List Available to Non-members

Children's Book Council *(1945)*
54 W. 39th St.
14th Floor
New York, NY 10018
Tel: (212) 966-1990 *Fax:* (212) 966-2073
E-Mail: cbc.info@cbcbooks.org
Website: cbcbooks.org
Members: 90 publishers
Staff: 5
Annual Budget: $500-1,000,000
Tax: 501(c)(6)

Personnel:
Executive Director: Robin Adelson
   E-Mail: robin.adelson@cbcbooks.org
Manager, Communications: Nicole Deming
   E-Mail: nicole.deming@cbcbooks.org
Manager, Events and Programs: Kelly Giordano
   E-Mail: kelly.giordano@cbcbooks.org
Associate, Programs and Membership Services: Rachel
Hoban
   E-Mail: rachel.hoban@cbcbooks.org

Historical Note:
CBC's mission is to serve the needs and advocate the interests of its members. Membership: $1,200 (Affiliate/Initiating); $400 (Associate).

Meetings/Conferences: Annual
Conference Chair: Kelly Giordano

Publications:
CBC update E-newsletter; monthly

Children's Literature Association *(1972)*
1301 W. 22nd St.
Suite 202
Oak Brook, IL 60523
Tel: (630) 571-4520 *Fax:* (708) 876-5598
E-Mail: info@childlitassn.org
Website: childlitassn.org
Members: 1050 individuals and institutions
Staff: 3
Annual Budget: $100-250,000
Tax: 501(c)(3)

Personnel:
President: Claudia Nelson
Treasurer: Jackie Stallcup

Historical Note:
ChLA's mission is to encourage standards of criticism, scholarship, research, and teaching in children's literature. Members are teachers, academics, critics, scholars, students, librarians, and institutions. Presents annual awards for excellence in children's literature. Membership: $75-105 (Individual); $50-80 (Retired); $30-60 (Student).

Meetings/Conferences: Annual
2013 - Biloxi, MS (IP Casino Resort and Spa)/June 13
   - 15

Publications:
Children's Literature: An International Journal;
   annually
ChLA Newsletter; semi-annually
ChLA Quarterly; quarterly; adv.

Membership List Available to Non-members

Chilean Avocado Importers Association (CAIA)
(2002)
717 D St. NW
Third Floor
Washington, DC 20004
Tel: (202) 626-0560 *Fax:* (202) 393-5728
Website: chileanavocados.org
Members: 39 Members
Staff: 2
Annual Budget: $2-5,000,000
Tax: 501(c)(6)

Personnel:
Executive Director and Chief Executive Officer: Xavier Fco
Equihua
   E-Mail: xfe@chileanavocados.org

Historical Note:
The Chilean Avocado Importers Association is composed of Chilean avocado importers, exporters, and producers.

Mission is to conduct market development activities and promotions to increase the consumption of Chilean Hass Avocados in the United States.

Publications:
AvoAction Newsletter

China Clay Producers Association (1978)
113 Arkwright Landing
Macon, GA 31210
Tel: (478) 757-1211 *Fax:* (478) 757-1949
E-Mail: info@georgiamining.org
Website: kaolin.com
Members: 4 companies
Staff: 1
Annual Budget: $50-100,000

Personnel:
Executive Vice President: Lee R. Lemke
   E-Mail: leelemke@georgiamining.org

Historical Note:
CCPA's mission is to promote the common business interest of producers of china clay and the development of coordinated policies which assure the industry will continue to provide jobs and contribute to the Georgia economy.

Chinese American Food Society (1975)
5735 Hitchner Hall 101A
The University of Maine
Orono, ME 04469-5735
E-Mail: cafsnet@gmail.com
Website: cafsnet.org
Members: 300 individuals
Staff: 9
Annual Budget: Under $10,000
Tax: 501(c)(6)

Personnel:
Web Communications: Haiqiang Chen
Conferences and Workshop Committee Chair: Yao-Wen Huang
   E-Mail: huang@arches.uga.edu
Secretary and Editor: Guangwei Huang
President: Yi-Cheng Su
   E-Mail: yi-cheng.su@oregonstate.edu
Membership Chair: Amos Wu
Treasurer: Dr. Vivian Wu

Historical Note:
Formerly, IFT- Chinese Association(1975) and The Association of Chinese Food Scientists and Technologists in American (1976-1977). CAFS's mission is to bring together professionals residing in North America with interests in food science and technology, as well as in Chinese culture, to provide technical consultation to industry and organizations. Membership: $20 (Active); $10 (Student); $20 (Associate); $300 (Life); $250 (Corporate Member-Payable only once).

Meetings/Conferences:
Conference Chair: Yao-Wen Huang

Publications:
CAFS Newsletter
Membership Directory; on-line

Chinese American Librarians Association (1973)
University of Arkansas Libraries
365 N. McIlroy Ave.
Fayetteville, AR 72701-4002
Website: cala-web.org
Members: 1000 individuals
Staff: 3
Annual Budget: $50-100,000
Tax: 501(c)(3)

Personnel:
Executive Director: Haipeng Li
   E-Mail: haipeng.li@oberlin.edu
Treasurer: Maria Fung
   E-Mail: maria4cala@gmail.com
Contact, Membership Services: Hong Ma
   E-Mail: hma@miami.edu

Historical Note:
Formerly Mid-West Chinese American Librarians Association. CALA's mission is to enhance communication among Chinese American librarians and American librarians, serves as a forum for the discussion of professional concerns and problems,and promotes the understanding and exchanges among librarians in the U.S. and abroad,with special emphasis in Asia and Pacific Rim countries. Membership: $30 (Regular); $15 (Student/ Non-Salaried/Overseas); $300 (Life); $100 (Institutional/ Affiliated).

Publications:

CALA E-Journal; on-line
CALA Membership Directory; annually; adv.
CALA Newsletter; semi-annually; adv.
The Journal of Library and Information Science (JLIS); semi-annually

Membership List Available to Non-members

Chinese American Medical Society (1964)
41 Elizabeth St.
Suite 403
New York, NY 10013
Tel: (212) 334-4760 *Fax:* (212) 965-1876
Website: camsociety.org
Members: 860 individuals
Staff: 1
Annual Budget: $2-5,000,000
Tax: 501(c)(3)

Personnel:
Executive Director: Hsueh-hwa Wang MD
   E-Mail: hw5@columbia.edu

Historical Note:
Formerly (1964) The American Chinese Medical Society (ACMS) and assumed its present name in 1986. CAMS's mission is to promote the scientific association of medical professionals of Chinese descent. It also seeks to advance medical knowledge and scientific research with emphasis on aspects unique to the Chinese. Membership: $200 (Regular); $25 (Resident/Associate); $2,000 (Life Member); $0 (Student).

Meetings/Conferences: Annual

Publications:
CAMS Newsletter; semi-annually
Membership Directory; annually

Chinese Language Teachers Association (1962)
C/O Dept. of Foreign Languages & Literature,
University of Wisconsin-Milwaukee
P.O Box 413
Milwaukee, WI 53201
Tel: (414) 229-2492 *Fax:* (414) 229-2741
E-Mail: clta@clta-us.org
Website: clta-us.org
Members: 800 individuals and organizations
Staff: 3
Annual Budget: $50-100,000
Tax: 501(c)(3)

Personnel:
Executive Director: Yea-Fen Chen

Historical Note:
Organization devoted exclusively to the study of Chinese language, culture and pedagogy. Acts as an advocate for and a facilitator of enhanced articulation among all Chinese language learning settings, including the integration of non-textbook- specific national standards and serves as a provider of teacher training programs. Members are mostly specialists in Chinese language, literature, linguistics and culture teaching at colleges and universities throughout the world, and also teachers of Chinese at primary and secondary schools and Chinese community schools, students of the language and other interested parties. Membership: $30-95 (Individual, based on annual income); $30 (Spouse Member at the same address); $120 (Institution); $900 (Life Member).

Meetings/Conferences: Annual

Publications:
CLTA Newsletter; quarterly
Member Directory; on-line
The Journal of the Chinese Language Teachers Association (JCLTA); quarterly

Chlorinated Paraffins Industry Association (1970)
1250 Connecticut Ave. NW
Suite 700
Washington, DC 20036
Tel: (202) 419-1500 *Fax:* (202) 659-8037
E-Mail: rfensterheim@regnet.com
Website: regnet.com/cpia
Staff: 2
Tax: 501(c)(6)

Personnel:
Executive Director: Robert J. Fensterheim CAE
   E-Mail: bobf@regnet.com

Historical Note:
CPIA works to to address the TSCA Interagency Testing Committee's recommendations for testing chlorinated paraffins. It is composed of manufacturers, distributors, and users of chlorinated paraffins, used in lubricants, plastics, and flame retardants.

Chlorine Chemistry Council (1992)
700 Second St. NE
Washington, DC 20002
Tel: (202) 249-7000 *Fax:* (202) 249-6100
Website: chlorine.americanchemistry.com
Staff: 7
Annual Budget: $5-10,000,000

Personnel:
President and Chief Executive Officer: Calvin M. Dooley
Contact, Member Communications and Marketing: Patrick Hurston
   E-Mail: Patrick_Hurston@AmericanChemistry.com
Vice President, Communications: Anne Womack Kolton
   E-Mail: Anne_Kolton@AmericanChemistry.com
Vice President, Federal Affairs: Walter Moore
Chief Financial Officer and Chief Administrative Officer: Raymond J. O'Bryan
Chief of Staff and General Counsel: Dell Perelman
Media Contact: Allyson Wilson
   E-Mail: allyson_wilson@americanchemistry.com

Historical Note:
Formerly known as the Manufacturing Chemists' Association (at its founding in 1872) and then as the Chemical Manufacturers' Association (from 1978 until 2000). ACC's mission is to deliver business value through exceptional advocacy using best-in-class member performance, political engagement, communications and scientific research. Membership: based on production/use of chlorine.

Meetings/Conferences:
2013 - Miami, FL/May 5 - 8
2013 - Colorado Springs, CO/June 3 - 5
2013 - Phoenix, AZ/Sept. 23 - 25
Number of non-conference events/year: 1

Publications:
Member Listing; on-line

Chlorine Institute (1924)
1300 Wilson Blvd.
Suite 525
Arlington, VA 22209
Tel: (703) 894-4140 *Fax:* (703) 894-4130
E-Mail: aonna@cl2.com
Website: chlorineinstitute.org
Members: 200 companies
Staff: 14
Annual Budget: $2-5,000,000

Personnel:
President: Frank Reiner
   E-Mail: freiner@CL2.com
Manager, Accounting: Peter Agnew
   E-Mail: pagnew@CL2.com
Manager, Administration: Florence Byrne
   E-Mail: fbyrne@CL2.com
Manager, Meetings and Membership Services: Autumn Onna
   E-Mail: aonna@CL2.com

Historical Note:
CI's purpose is to serve the public by fostering continuous improvements to safety and the protection of human health and the environment connected with the production, distribution and use of chlorine, sodium and potassium hydroxides, and sodium hypochlorite and the distribution and use of hydrogen chloride.

Meetings/Conferences: Annual
Conference Chair: Autumn Onna

Publications:
CI Insider e-Newsletter; on-line
Global Safety Team (GST) Newsletter; on-line
Member Directory; on-line

Chlorobenzene Producers Association (1979)
1850 M St. NW
Suite 700
Washington, DC 20036-5810
Tel: (202) 721-4100 *Fax:* (202) 296-8120
Website: socma.com
Members: 3 companies
Staff: 6
Annual Budget: $100-250,000

Personnel:
Executive Director: C. Tucker Helmes PhD
   E-Mail: helmest@socma.com
Chief Executive Officer: Larry Sloan
   E-Mail: info@socma.com

Senior Director, Membership Services and Marketing:
Dolores Alonso
E-Mail: membership@socma.com
Senior Director, Human Resources and Administration:
Charlena Patterson
E-Mail: info@socma.com
Senior Manager, Public Relations and Media: Christine
Sanchez
E-Mail: public.relations@socma.com
Director, Finance and Administration Services: Francis
Shafer

Historical Note:
An affiliate of the Synthetic Organic Chemical
Manufacturers Association, CPA was formed in 1979 to
address scientific, environmental and safety issues relating
to synthetic organic chemicals in response to federal, state,
and international regulatory activities.

Choristers Guild (1949)
12404 Park Central Dr.
Suite 100
Dallas, TX 75251-1802
Tel: (469) 398-3606 Fax: (469) 398-3611
TollFree: (800) 246-7478
E-Mail: customerservice@mailcg.org
Website: choristersguild.org
Members: 4000 individuals
Staff: 8
Annual Budget: $1-2,000,000
Tax: 501(c)(3)

Personnel:
Executive Director: Jim Rindelaub
E-Mail: jrindelaub@mailcg.org
Contact, Conferences: Eve Hehn
E-Mail: ehehn@mailcg.org
Customer Service and Distribution Operations Manager:
Brian Hehn
E-Mail: bhehn@mailcg.org
Coordinator, Membership, Chapters, Billing and Payments:
Kristin Kok
E-Mail: kkok@mailcg.org
Editor, Handbell Music: Kathy Lowrie
E-Mail: klowrie@mailcg.org
Contact, Marketing: Ellen Yost
E-Mail: eyost@mailcg.org

Historical Note:
CG's purpose is to foster a spirit of cooperation among
choirs and to enable directors to become effective vehicles
for nurturing spiritual and musical growth in young people.
Members are directors of children's and youth choirs in
churches and schools seeking to enhance the religious and
musical training of their students. Membership:$30-118/
year.

Continuing Education:
Enrollment: 62
Certification Designation/s: CGI

Meetings/Conferences:
Conference Chair: Eve Hehn

Publications:
Member Directory; on-line
The Chorister; bi-monthly; adv.

Chorus America (1977)
P.O. Box 2646
Arlington, VA 22202-0646
Tel: (202) 331-7577 Fax: (202) 331-7599
E-Mail: service@chorusamerica.org
Website: chorusamerica.org
Members: 1600 organizations and individuals
Staff: 11
Annual Budget: $1-2,000,000

Personnel:
President and Chief Executive Officer: Ann Meier Baker
E-Mail: ann@chorusamerica.org
Director, Membership Services and Operations: Catherine
Davies
E-Mail: catherine@chorusamerica.org
Director, Development: Catherine Dehoney
E-Mail: cdehoney@chorusamerica.org
Director, Communications: Robin L. Perry
E-Mail: robin@chorusamerica.org
Webmaster and Manager, Technology: Edmund Stawick
E-Mail: ed@chorusamerica.org

Historical Note:
Formerly (1987) the Association of Professional Vocal
Ensembles. Mission is to build a dynamic and inclusive
choral community so that more people are transformed
by the beauty and power of choral singing. Professional

members are choral organizations which employ a minimum
of 25% of the total ensemble membership or twelve
professional singers. Membership: $85 (Basic); $185
(Contributing); $35 (Student); $140-900 (Chorus); $300
(Business); $200 (Affiliate).

Meetings/Conferences: Annual
2013 - Seatle, WA/June 12 - 15

Publications:
eVoice; bi-weekly; adv.
Membership Directory; on-line
The American Choral Review
The Voice; quarterly; adv.

Membership List Available to Non-members

Christian Association for Psychological Studies
(2010)
PO Box 365
Batavia, IL 60510-0365
Tel: (630) 639-9478 Fax: (630) 454-3799
E-Mail: info@caps.net
Website: caps.net
Staff: 3
Annual Budget: $100-250,000

Personnel:
President: Paul Regan
E-Mail: paul.regan@caps.net
Treasurer: Jeffrey Berryhill

Historical Note:
CAPS helps in understanding the relationship between
Christianity and the behavioral sciences at both the
clinical , counseling and the theoretical and research levels

Meetings/Conferences: Annual
2013 - Portland, OR (Portland Marriott Downtown
Waterfront Hotel)/April 4 - 6

Publications:
Conversations; semi-annually
Membership Directory; on-line
The Journal of Psychology and Christianity; quarterly;
adv.

Christian Chiropractors Association (1953)
85 Franklin St.
Springville, NY 14141
Website: christianchiropractors.org
Members:
218 members
19 supplier companies
Staff: 2
Annual Budget: $100-250,000

Personnel:
President: Brian K. Scharf DC

Historical Note:
CCA seek to gather and unify Christian Doctors of
Chiropractic around the essentials of the Christian faith,
leaving minor points of doctrine to the conscience of the
individual believer. Membership: $25-195 (Doctor of
Chiropractic); $45 (Retired Doctor/Chiropractic Faculty);
$0 (Chiropractic Student/Missionary, Pastor); $50-250
(Supplier); $20 (Auxiliary).

Meetings/Conferences: Annual
2013 - Alexandria, VA (Crowne Plaza Old Town
Alexandria Hotel)/June 26 - 30

Publications:
CCA Newsletter
Membership Directory; on-line
The Christian Chiropractor

Christian College Consortium (1971)
255 Grapevine Rd.
Wenham, MA 01984
Tel: (978) 867-4802 Fax: (978) 867-4650
Website: ccconsortium.org
Members: 13 colleges
Staff: 2
Annual Budget: $100-250,000

Personnel:
President: Stan D. Gaede
E-Mail: stan.gaede@gordon.edu

Historical Note:
The consortium consists of thirteen colleges united
by regional accreditation, concentration upon liberal
arts studies, educational strengths that can be shared,
nationwide distribution and a common affirmation of faith.

Meetings/Conferences:
2013 - Beverly, MA (Wylie Inn and Conference
Center)/June 12 - 14

Publications:
Membership Directory; on-line

Christian Educators Association International
(1953)
P.O. Box 45610
Westlake, OH 44145
Tel: (440) 250-9566 Fax: (440) 250-9584
TollFree: (888) 798-1124
E-Mail: doreen@ceai.org
Website: ceai.org
Members: 7500 individuals
Staff: 20
Annual Budget: $500-1,000,000
Tax: 501(c)(3)

Personnel:
Executive Director: Finn Laursen
Contact, Publications: Judy Turpen
E-Mail: tov@ceai.org

Historical Note:
CEAI works towards serving the educational community
by encouraging and equipping Christian educators in
public and private education. Members are professional
educators (teachers, administrators and support personnel)
serving in public and private schools.CEAI's mission is to
Encourage, Equip and Empower Educators according to
Biblical Principles. Membership: $899 (Active Life Member);
$29 (Retired Educator); $379 (Retired Life Member);
$39 (Associate Member); $99 (Substitute/Part-Time
Educator); $139 (Full- Time Educator/Administrator/
Support Personnel); $199 (Husband and Wife Educators);
$25 (College Student).

Meetings/Conferences:
Number of non-conference events/year: 1

Publications:
Teachers of Vision; adv.
Washington Education Watch Newsletter; monthly

Christian Labor Association of the United States
of America (1931)
405 Centerstone Ct.
P.O. Box 65
Zeeland, MI 49464
Tel: (616) 772-9164 Fax: (616) 772-9830
TollFree: (877) 788-4252
E-Mail: michigan@cla-usa.com
Website: cla-usa.com
Members: 3000 individuals
Staff: 5
Annual Budget: $250-500,000

Personnel:
President: Clarence Merrill
Office Administrator: Jennifer Keegstra
Treasurer: Mike Van Tubergen

Historical Note:
CLA-USA's mission is to organize workers into collective
bargaining groups in order to promote justice, protect moral
and material interests and develop cooperative workplace
relationships through the application of Christian principles.

Publications:
CLA-USA Newsletter; on-line

Christian Leadership Alliance (2008)
635 Camino de los Mares
Suite 216
San Clemente, CA 92673
Tel: (949) 487-0900 Fax: (949) 487-0927
Website: christianleadershipalliance.org
Members: 6000 Individuals and 2500
Organizations
Staff: 3
Annual Budget: $1-2,000,000
Tax: 501(c)(3)

Personnel:
President and Chief Executive Officer: Tami Heim
Contact, Online Learning: Heather Martin
E-Mail: Heather.Martin@
ChristianLeadershipAlliance.org
Director, Membership Services and Contact, Events: Holly
Rosario
E-Mail: Heather.Martin@
ChristianLeadershipAlliance.org

Historical Note:
Formed by the merger of the Christian Management
Association and the Christian Stewardship Association.
CLA seeks to enhance the organizational effectiveness
of churches and para-church ministries. Membership:
$129-5,000 (Ministry-Individual/Premier/Gold/Founder

Council); $179-5,500 (Business-Individual/Premier/Gold/
Founder Council).

Meetings/Conferences: Annual
Conference Chair: Holly Rosario
2013 - Anaheim, CA (Hilton Anaheim)/April 4 - May 2
Number of non-conference events/year: 2

Publications:
Christianity Today magazine; monthly
e-Newsletter; semi-monthly; adv.
Membership Directory; annually
Outcomes magazine; quarterly; adv.

Christian Legal Society *(1961)*
8001 Braddock Rd.
Suite 302
Springfield, VA 22151
Tel: (855) 257-9800 *Fax:* (703) 642-1075
E-Mail: clshq@clsnet.org
Website: clsnet.org
Members: 4000 individuals
Staff: 13
Annual Budget: $1-2,000,000
Tax: 501(c)(3)

Personnel:
Executive Director: David Nammo
    E-Mail: dnammo@clsnet.org
Senior Legal Counsel: Kim Colby
    E-Mail: kcolby@clsnet.org
Controller: Peter Smith
    E-Mail: psmith@clsnet.org

Historical Note:
*CLS's purpose is to inspire, encourage, and equip Christian
lawyers and law students, both individually and in
community, to proclaim, love and serve Jesus Christ
through the study and practice of law, the provision of
legal assistance to the poor and needy, and the defense
of religious freedom and the sanctity of human life.
Membership: $15-200/year.*

Meetings/Conferences: Annual

Publications:
E-Devotionals; bi-weekly
Member Directory; on-line
The Christian Lawyer; monthly; adv.

Membership List Available to Non-members

Christian Management Association *(1976)*
1825 Hamilton Dr.
San Jose, CA 95125
Tel: (408) 703-6568
Website: sjcma.org
Members: 3000 individuals
Staff: 8
Annual Budget: $1-2,000,000

Personnel:
Director, Membership Services: Holly Rosario

Historical Note:
*CLA seeks to build the body of Christ by building people
and enhancing the effectiveness of Christian organizations
and large churches. Membership: $179 (Individual).*

Meetings/Conferences: Annual

Publications:
Membership Directory; on-line
Outcomes; quarterly; adv.

Christian Medical & Dental Associations *(2000)*
P.O. Box 7500
Bristol, TN 37621-7500
Tel: (423) 844-1000 *Fax:* (423) 844-1005
TollFree: (888) 230-2637
E-Mail: main@cmda.org
Website: cmda.org
Members: 17000 individuals
Staff: 47
Annual Budget: $5-10,000,000
Tax: 501(c)(3)

Personnel:
Executive Director: David Stevens MA, MD
Chief Financial Officer: Colette Davis
    E-Mail: colette.davis@cmda.org
Director, Information Technology: Michael Gregg
Manager, Meetings: Melinda Mitchell
    E-Mail: melinda.mitchell@cmda.org
Vice President, Communications: Margie Shealy
    E-Mail: communications@cmda.org
Director, Membership Services: Barbara Snapp
    E-Mail: barbara.snapp@cmda.org

Contact, Continuing Education: Sharon K. Whitmer

Historical Note:
*Founded as Christian Medical & Dental Society; assumed
its current name in 2000. Members are Christian medical
and dental personnel, some of whom serve as medical
missionaries. Membership: $0-344/year; $2,500-7,500
(Lifetime).*

Continuing Education:
Certification Designation/s: CME, CDE

Meetings/Conferences: Annual
Conference Chair: Melinda Mitchell
2013 - Ridgecrest, NC (LifeWay Ridgecrest Conference
    Center)/May 2 - 5
Number of non-conference events/year: 1

Publications:
Christian Doctor Journal; weekly
e-Pistle; monthly
GiftLegacy eNewsletter; weekly
Infusion; quarterly
Intensive Care
News & Views; bi-weekly
Progress Notes; bi-monthly
The SCAN
Today's Christian Doctor; quarterly; adv.
Weekly Devotions; weekly
Your Call; quarterly

Christian Meetings & Conventions Association
P.O. Box 350757
Westminster, CO 80035-0757
Tel: (303) 451-6678 *Fax:* (303) 252-0445
E-Mail: info@christianmeeting.org
Website: christianmeeting.org
Members: 500 individuals
Staff: 1

Personnel:
Director: Jayne Kuryluk
    E-Mail: jayne@christianmeeting.org

Historical Note:
*An association of Christian people who plan meetings and
suppliers who service them. Membership: $250/year.*

Meetings/Conferences: Annual

Publications:
Good Newsletter; quarterly
Membership Directory; on-line

Christian Schools International *(1920)*
3350 E. Paris Ave. SE
Grand Rapids, MI 49512
Tel: (616) 957-1070 *Fax:* (616) 957-5022
TollFree: (800) 635-8288
E-Mail: info@csionline.org
Website: csionline.org
Members: 500 protestant private schools
Staff: 26
Annual Budget: $2-5,000,000
Tax: 501(c)(3)

Personnel:
President and Chief Executive Officer: David Koetje
    E-Mail: DKoetje@csionline.org
Director, Membership: Jeff Blamer
    E-Mail: JBlamer@csionline.org
Administrative Assistant: Kathy Doezema
    E-Mail: KDoezema@CSIonline.org
Director, Sales: Darryl Shelton
    E-Mail: dshelton@csionline.org
Chief Financial Officer: John Wolters
    E-Mail: jwolters@csionline.org

Historical Note:
*Established as the National Union of Christian Schools,
assumed its present name in 1978. Serves Christian
schools which seek to integrate Christian faith and culture.
Purpose is to advance Christian education and support
schools in their task of teaching students to know God
and his world and to glorify him through obedient service.
Provides employee benefit programs, curriculum and
periodical publications, and services to school boards
and administrators. Membership: $160-190 (Regular/
Associate); $180-805 (Affiliate- Educational Institutions).*

Meetings/Conferences: Annual
2013 - Orlando, FL (Buena Vista Palace)/Sept. 25 - 27
Number of non-conference events/year: 7

Publications:
Christian Home and School; semi-annually; adv.
CSI's newsletters
The Christian School Teacher; semi-annually; adv.

Church and Synagogue Library Association
(1967)
10157 SW Barbur Blvd.
Suite 102C
Portland, OR 97219
Tel: (503) 244-6919 *Fax:* (503) 977-3734
TollFree: (800) 542-2752
E-Mail: csla@worldaccessnet.com
Website: cslainfo.org
Members: 1600 libraries
Staff: 3
Annual Budget: $100-250,000
Tax: 501(c)(3)

Personnel:
Administrator: Judith M. Janzen
Financial Assistant: Thomas Fountain
Editor: Jeri Zulli

Historical Note:
*CSLA's purpose is to provide counseling and guidance for
individual libraries through its library services committee
composed of experienced congregational librarians.
Membership: $50 (Individual); $55 (Individual- Canadian/
Foreign); $70 (Church/Synagogue); $75 (Church/
Synagogue - Canadian/Foreign); $100 (Affiliate); $200
(Institutional).*

Meetings/Conferences: Annual
2013 - Lake Junaluska, NC (Lake Junaluska Conference
    and Retreat Center)/July 28 - 30

Publications:
Congregational Libraries Today; quarterly; adv.

Church Music Publishers Association *(1926)*
P.O. Box 158992
Nashville, TN 37215
Tel: (615) 791-0273 *Fax:* (615) 790-8847
Website: cmpamusic.org
Members: 46 member publishers
Staff: 4
Annual Budget: $250-500,000

Personnel:
President: Casey McGinty
Executive Secretary: Diane Cobb
Legal Counsel: Rush Hicks
Secretary and Treasurer: Dale Matthews

Historical Note:
*Formerly Church and Sunday School Music Publishers
Association. CMPA is an organization of publishers of
Christian music which has a spiritual dimension to share
mutual areas of concern regarding copyright information,
education, administration and protection, facilitating
public and industry awareness in these areas, and to
develop continuing personal and professional relationships.
Membership: $450/year (Organization).*

Meetings/Conferences: Annual

Membership List Available to Non-members

CIES - The Food Business Forum *(1953)*
8455 Colesville Rd.
Suite 705
Silver Spring, MD 20910
Tel: (301) 563-3383 *Fax:* (301) 563-3386
E-Mail:
washington@theconsumergoodsforum.com
Website: ciesnet.com
Members: 400 companies
Staff: 34
Annual Budget: $10-25,000,000

Personnel:
General Manager, The Americas: Jonathan Berger
    E-Mail: j.berger@theconsumergoodsforum.com
Office Manager: Rosario Santos
    E-Mail: r.santos@theconsumergoodsforum.com

Historical Note:
*Formerly the International Association of Chain Stores -
North American Headquarters, International Center for
Companies of the Food Trade and Industry-North America
Headquarters (1989) and Food Business Forum (1996).
Provides management research on problems related to food
distribution and serves as an international forum where
food chain store executives can meet to exchange ideas and
information.*

Cigar Association of America, Inc. *(1937)*
818 Connecticut Ave. NW
Suite 200
Washington, DC 20006
Tel: (202) 223-8204 *Fax:* (202) 833-0379

E-Mail: nsharp@cigarassociation.org
Website: cmpamusic.org
Members: 60 companies
Staff: 6
Annual Budget: $2-5,000,000
Tax: 501(c)(6)

Personnel:
President and Executive Director: Craig P. Williamson
E-Mail: cwilliamson@cigarassociation.org
Comptroller and Statistician: Lita M. Conklin
E-Mail: lmconklin@cigarassociation.org
Vice President, State Relations: Chris Newbry
E-Mail: cnewbry@cigarassociation.org
President: Norman F. Sharp
E-Mail: nsharp@cigarassociation.org

Historical Note:
Established in 1937 as the Cigar Manufacturers Association of America, Inc., became the Cigar Association of America, Inc. in 1974 through a merger of the Cigar Research Council, the Cigar Manufacturers Association of America, the Cigar Institute of America and the State and Local Tax Council. CAA is the national trade organization of cigar manufacturers, importers, distributors and suppliers to the industry. It sponsors the Cigar Political Action Committee.

Publications:
Statistical Record; annually

City and Regional Magazine Association (1978)
1970 E. Grand Ave.
Suite 330
El Segundo, CA 90245
Tel: (310) 364-0193 Fax: (310) 364-0196
E-Mail: administrator@list.citymag.org
Website: citymag.org
Members: 100 companies
Staff: 4
Annual Budget: $500-1,000,000
Tax: 501(c)(6)

Personnel:
Executive Director: James C. Dowden
Editor: Barton Ortberg
E-Mail: bart.ortberg@dowdenmanagement.com

Historical Note:
CRMA's mission is to provide professional development and training opportunities, and to promote city and regional magazines as a major media market. Membership composed of ABC or BPA-audited, general news, paid subscription city and regional magazines. CRMA represents member magazines on major national and regional policy issues, encourages editorial and journalistic standards. Membership: $1,123-6,885 (Active/Affiliate); $2250 (Associate).

Meetings/Conferences: Semi-Annual

Publications:
CRMA e-Newsletter; on-line; adv.
Membership Directory; on-line

Civil Aviation Medical Association (1948)
P.O. Box 2382
Peachtree City, GA 30269-2382
Tel: (770) 487-0100 Fax: (770) 487-0080
Website: civilavmed.com
Members: 800 individuals
Staff: 5
Annual Budget: $100-250,000

Personnel:
Executive Vice President: David P. Millett MD, MPH
E-Mail: david.millett@yahoo.com
President: Hugh J. O'Neill
Vice President, Communications and Representation:
James Carpenter MD
Vice President, Education: Clayton T. Cowl MD, MS
Secretary and Treasurer: Gordon L. Ritter

Historical Note:
Established as the Airline Medical Examiners Association, assumed its present name in 1955. CAMA's mission is to promote the best methodology for assessment of the mental and physical requirements for civil aviation pilots. Membership: $100/year.

Meetings/Conferences: Annual
2013 - Orlando, FL (Renaissance Orlando Resort)/Oct. 3 - 5

Publications:
FlightPhysician; monthly

Classification Society (1969)
Univ. of Illinois, IDS Dept.

601 S. Morgan St., M/C 294
Chicago, IL 60607-7124
Tel: (312) 996-2676 Fax: (312) 413-0385
Website: classification-society.org/clsoc/
clsoc.php
Members: 200 individuals
Staff: 2
Annual Budget: $10-25,000

Personnel:
President: Rebecca Nugent PhD
E-Mail: rnugent@stat.cmu.edu
Secretary and Treasurer: Stanley L. Sclove PhD
E-Mail: slsclove@uic.edu

Historical Note:
CSNA's mission is to promote the scientific study of classification and clustering, including systematic methods of creating classifications from data, and to disseminate scientific and educational information related to its fields of interest. Members are researchers in the fields of psychology, statistics, computer science, biology, business applications, education, engineering, mathematics and sociology. Membership: $80 (Individual); $60 (Affiliate/Retired); $20 (Student).

Meetings/Conferences: Annual

Publications:
Advances in Data Analysis and Classification
Classification Society Newsletter; irregular
Journal of Classification; adv.
Journal of Classification; irregular

Membership List Available to Non-members

Clay Minerals Society (1963)
University of Illinois, W-321 Turner Hall
1102 S. Goodwin Ave.
Urbana, IL 61801
Tel: (217) 333-9636 Fax: (217) 244-7805
E-Mail: cms@clays.org
Website: clays.org
Members: 800 individuals
Staff: 3
Annual Budget: $250-500,000

Personnel:
President: Peter Komadel
E-Mail: peter.komadel@savba.sk
Treasurer: J. Reed Glasmann
E-Mail: wgsclays@yahoo.com
Editor-in-Chief: Joseph W Stucki
E-Mail: jstucki@uiuc.edu

Historical Note:
Supersedes the Committee on Clay Minerals of the National Academy of Sciences/National Research Council. CMS's purpose is to stimulate research and to disseminate information relating to all aspects of clay science and technology. Membership: $20-75/year (Member); $25 (Student).

Meetings/Conferences: Annual
2013 - Urbana, IL (University of Illinois)/Oct. 6 - 10

Publications:
Clays and Clay Minerals; on-line
Elements; bi-monthly; adv.
membership directory; on-line
Workshop Lecture Series

Clean Technology & Sustainable Industries Organization (CTSI) (2007)
3925 W. Braker Ln.
Austin, TX 78759
Tel: (512) 692-7267
Website: ct-si.org
Staff: 4
Annual Budget: $100-250,000
Tax: 501(c)(6)

Personnel:
President: Matthew Laudon
E-Mail: mlaudon@ct-si.org
Manager, Membership and Marketing: Laura Benold
E-Mail: laura@ct-si.org
Director, Technology and Operations: Regina Ramazzini
Vice President, Operations: Sarah Wenning
E-Mail: wenning@ct-si.org

Historical Note:
The Clean Technology and Sustainable Industries Organization (CTSI) runs programs design to accelerate the commercialization of emerging clean technologies. Membership: $225/year (Associate Member).

Meetings/Conferences: Annual
Conference Chair: Regina Ramazzini

Publications:
CTSI Directory
CTSI Newsletter; monthly

Cleaning Equipment Trade Association (1980)
P.O. Box 1710
Indian Trail, NC 28079
Tel: (704) 635-7362 Fax: (704) 635-7363
TollFree: (800) 441-0111
Website: ceta.org
Members: 325 companies
Staff: 1
Annual Budget: $250-500,000

Personnel:
Executive Director: Sherry Helms
E-Mail: sherry@ceta.org

Historical Note:
Formerly Cleaning Equipment Manufacturers Association and assumed its present name in 1990. CETA's mission is to increase the awareness of their products while preserving the environment. Members are manufacturers, distributors and component suppliers of powered cleaning systems. Membership: $600 (Affiliate); $390 (Distributor); $1,200 (Manufacturer); $930 (Supplier).

Continuing Education:
Certification Designation/s: CETA-MCP, CETA-DCP

Meetings/Conferences: Annual
Conference Chair: Sherry Helms

Publications:
Cleaner Times Magazine; monthly; adv.

Cleaning Management Institute (1964)
19 British American Blvd.
Latham, NY 12110-2197
Fax: (518) 783-1386
E-Mail: cmi@ntpmedia.com
Website: cminstitute.net
Members: 850 individuals
Staff: 3
Annual Budget: $250-500,000

Personnel:
Director: Matt Gallinger
E-Mail: mgallinger@ntpmedia.com
Manager, Administration: Sharon Hillis
E-Mail: shillis@ntpmedia.com
Director, Training: W. Marion Ivey
E-Mail: wmivey@comcast.net

Historical Note:
CMI is a professional society dedicated to education, training and career improvement for the facility maintenance industry. Members are individuals and companies involved in building cleaning and maintenance management. Membership: $129-319 (Domestic-USA/Canada/Mexico); $200-500 (International).

Continuing Education:
Certification Designation/s: FSCC, CSCC
Meetings/Conferences:
Number of non-conference events/year: 2

Publications:
CM/Cleaning & Maintenance Management magazine
e-newsletter; monthly
Professional Car Care e-News service; weekly

The Clearing House Association (1853)
450 W. 33rd St.
New York, NY 10001
Tel: (212) 613-0100
TollFree: (800) 875-2242
Website: theclearinghouse.org
Staff: 18

Personnel:
President and Chief Executive Officer: James Aramanda
Senior Vice President and Deputy General Counsel: Joe
Alexander
Senior Vice President, Sales and Relationship Management:
Hank Farrar
Senior Vice President, Legislative Affairs: Jill Hershey
Vice President, Communications: Erica Hurtt
E-Mail: erica.hurtt@theclearinghouse.org
Vice President and Regulatory Counsel: Eli Peterson
Vice President, Marketing and Communications: Chip
Savidge
E-Mail: chip.savidge@theclearinghouse.org
Executive Vice President, Technology and Operations: Al
Wood

Historical Note:

Formerly the New York Clearing House Association. TCH aim is to provide payment, clearing, and settlement services to its member banks and other financial institutions.

Meetings/Conferences: Annual

Publications:
Membership Directory; on-line
TCH Newsletter; weekly; adv.

Clerkship Directors in Internal Medicine *(1989)*

330 John Carlyle St.
Suite 610
Alexandria, VA 22314
Tel: (703) 341-4540 *Fax:* (703) 519-1893
E-Mail: CDIM@im.org
Website: im.org/cdim
Members:
186 physicians
182 clerkship directors and administrators
Staff: 10
Annual Budget: $250-500,000
Tax: 501(c)(3)

Personnel:
President: Heather E. Harrell MD
Treasurer: L. James Nixon MD
Vice President, Policy: Don C. Rockey MD
　E-Mail: cclayton@im.org

Historical Note:
A member organization of Alliance for Academic Internal Medicine. CDIM fosters the education of students in the core clerkship in internal medicine at accredited medical schools in the U. S. and Canada. Membership: $600 (Institutional); $125 (Individual/Associate); $500 (Affiliate).

Meetings/Conferences: Annual

Publications:
CDIM Membership Directory; on-line
Newletter

Cleveland Bay Horse Society of North America *(1885)*

PO BOX 483
Goshen, NH 03752
Tel: (903) 626-7477 *Fax:* (603) 863-5193
E-Mail: info@clevelandbay.org
Website: clevelandbay.org
Members: 150 individuals
Staff: 3
Annual Budget: Under $10,000
Tax: 501(c)(5)

Personnel:
President: Tracie Traver
　E-Mail: tratraver@aol.com
Treasurer: Anna Cohen
　E-Mail: ACohen@bayhavenfarm.com
Website Development and Maintenance: Brian Neff
　E-Mail: info@clevelandbay.org

Historical Note:
Formerly (1992) known as Cleveland Bay Horse Society of America, CBHSNA's mission is to uplift the Cleveland Bay Horse by fostering a forum for involvement and education while working with affiliates, organizations and individuals to preserve and increase the Cleveland Bay population worldwide. Membership: $55 (Individual); $70 (Family/ Overseas); $15 (Junior); $700 (Lifetime); $25 (New Junior Member).

Meetings/Conferences: Annual

Publications:
Baywatch Newsletter; bi-monthly; adv.
Member Directory; on-line; adv.

Clinical and Laboratory Standards Institute *(1968)*

950 W. Valley Rd.
Suite 2500
Wayne, PA 19087-1898
Tel: (610) 688-0100 *Fax:* (610) 688-0700
TollFree: (877) 447-1888
E-Mail: customerservice@clsi.org
Website: clsi.org
Members: 2100 organizations
Staff: 46
Annual Budget: $5-10,000,000

Personnel:
Executive Vice President: Glen Fine MBA, MS, CAE
　E-Mail: gfine@clsi.org
Director, Education: Marcy Anderson MS, MT (ASCP)
　E-Mail: manderson@clsi.org

Director, Software Products: Jim Blackwood
　E-Mail: jblackwood@clsi.org
Vice President, Marketing, Membership Services and Education: Barbara Goldsmith PhD
　E-Mail: bgoldsmith@clsi.org
Director, Membership Services and Customer Service: Kristin Hodgson CAE
　E-Mail: khodgson@clsi.org
Editor: Megan Larrisey MA
　E-Mail: mlarrisey@clsi.org
Director, Marketing: Patrick McGinn
　E-Mail: pmcginn@clsi.org
Senior Vice President, Operations: Luann Ochs MS
　E-Mail: lochs@clsi.org
Specialist, Marketing and Communications: Megan Scanlon
　E-Mail: mscanlon@clsi.org
Vice President, Standards Development and Marketing: Lois Schmidt
　E-Mail: lschmidt@clsi.org
Vice President, Finance and Administration: Marc Stormes
　E-Mail: mstormes@clsi.org

Historical Note:
Formerly (2005) NCCLS. CLSI's mission is to develop best practices in clinical and laboratory testing and enhancing their use globally using a consensus-driven process that balances the viewpoints of industry, government and the health care professions. Membership: $2,600-26,600 (Active); $875-1,350 (Consulting Firm); $1,350 (Start up Company); $4,000 (Broad Interest); $1,650 (Selected Interest); $2,150 (Mulitple Site); $300 (Education).

Publications:
e-News; monthly
Membership Directory; on-line

Clinical Immunology Society *(1986)*

555 E. Wells St.
Suite 1100
Milwaukee, WI 53202-3823
Tel: (414) 224-8095 *Fax:* (414) 272-6070
E-Mail: info@clinimmsoc.org
Website: clinimmsoc.org
Members: 750 individuals
Staff: 15
Annual Budget: $500-1,000,000
Tax: 501(c)(3)

Personnel:
Executive Director: Anne Krolikowski
　E-Mail: akrolikowski@clinimmsoc.org
Membership Assistant: Jesse Cunningham
　E-Mail: jcunningham@clinimmsoc.org
Associate Director, Programs: Michelle Roach
　E-Mail: mroach@clinimmsoc.org

Historical Note:
CIS's mission is to facilitate education, translational research and novel approaches to therapy in clinical immunology to promote excellence in the care of patients with immunologic/inflammatory disorders. Members are clinicians, investigators and trainees. Membership: $150 (Regular/Associate); $35 (Trainee).

Meetings/Conferences: Annual
Conference Chair: Michelle Roach
2013 - Miami, FL (JW Marriott Marquis)/April 25 - 28
2014 - Baltimore, MD (Hilton Baltimore)/April 10 - 13

Publications:
Clinical Immunology; monthly; adv.
Membership Directory; on-line

Membership List Available to Non-members

Clinical Laboratory Management Association *(1976)*

401 N. Michigan Ave.
Suite 2200
Chicago, IL 60611
Tel: (312) 321-5111 *Fax:* (312) 673-6927
E-Mail: info@clma.org
Website: clma.org
Members: 3000 clinical laboratory professionals
Staff: 16
Annual Budget: $10-25,000

Personnel:
Specialist, Membership Services: Liz Catalano
　E-Mail: ecatalano@clma.org
Director, Publications: Dennis Coyle
　E-Mail: DCoyle@clma.org
Senior Director, Education and Learning Services: Susan Farrell

　E-Mail: sfarrell@clma.org
Senior Director, Strategic Events: Ellie Hurley
　E-Mail: ehurley@clma.org
Director, Operations: Ruth Nelson Gallagher
　E-Mail: rnelson@clma.org
Senior Director, Marketing and Communications: Linda Schwartz
　E-Mail: lschwartz@clma.org
Director, Information Technology: Rod Stiegman
　E-Mail: rstiegman@clma.org

Historical Note:
Formerly (1976) the American Association of Clinical Laboratory Supervisors and Administrators, assumed its current name in 2002. CLMA provides leadership in the clinical laboratory industry supporting laboratory professionals at every stage of their career. Members are laboratory supervisors, managers and executives and their suppliers. Membership: $195 (General Member); $75 (Future Leader, plus any chapter dues/Emeritus Member); $450 (Bundled Member, plus any chapter dues).

Meetings/Conferences: Annual
Conference Chair: Ellie Hurley
2013 - Orlando, FL (Caribe Royale All-Suite Hotel and Convention Center)/April 7 - 10
2013 - Scottsdale, AZ (Phoenician Resort)/May 5 - 7
Number of non-conference events/year: 5

Publications:
Clinical Leadership and Management Review; quarterly
CLMA Industry Pulse; weekly
Laboratory Management Newsletter; bi-monthly; adv.
Member Directory; on-line

Membership List Available to Non-members

Clinical Ligand Assay Society *(1974)*

29003 Balmoral St.
Garden City, MI 48135
Tel: (734) 838-0422 *Fax:* (734) 838-0420
E-Mail: clas@clas.org
Website: clasnewengland.org
Members: 200 individuals
Staff: 3
Annual Budget: $100-250,000
Tax: 501(c)(3)

Personnel:
President: Eric Sigillo
　E-Mail: esigillo@novabio.com
Secretary: Janet Hurwitz
　E-Mail: jhurwitz@thepipeline.net
Treasurer: Marth Jackson
　E-Mail: MLJackson@wyeth.com

Historical Note:
Founded as the Clinical Radioassay. Assumed its present name in 1981. Later changed its name to Clinical Laboratory and Analytical Sciences, and returned again to the former. CLAS is translation of biomarkers and related technologies from discovery to clinical and analytical applications by encouraging research, educating practitioners, and fostering communication and cooperation among individuals in laboratories in medicine, academia, and industry. Membership: $160 (Regular); $180 (International); $25 (Student); $45 (International Student).

Continuing Education:
Certification Designation/s: CLAS

Publications:
CLASNews; bi-monthly
Journal of Clinical Ligand Assay; quarterly
Membership Directory; on-line

Clinical Orthopaedic Society *(1912)*

2209 Dickens Rd.
Richmond, VA 23230-2005
Tel: (804) 565-6366 *Fax:* (804) 282-0090
E-Mail: cos@societyhq.com
Website: cosociety.org
Members: 750 individuals
Staff: 3
Annual Budget: $100-250,000
Tax: 501(c)(3)

Personnel:
President: Bess E. Brackett MD
First President Elect: William C. Warner MD

Historical Note:
COS's mission is continuing medical education activity to create an interest and further study of clinical orthopaedic care. Members are orthopaedic surgeons. Membership: $300 (Regular/International); $40 (Resident/Fellow); $75 (Candidate).

Meetings/Conferences: Annual

Publications:
COS E-Newsletter; bi-annually; adv.
Journal of Surgical Orthopaedic Advances; annually
Membership Directory; annually

Membership List Available to Non-members

Clinical Social Work Association *(1971)*
P.O. Box 10
Garrisonville, VA 22463
Tel: (703) 340-1456 *Fax:* (703) 269-0707
Website: clinicalsocialworkassociation.org
Members: 11000 individuals
Staff: 2
Annual Budget: $50-100,000

Personnel:
Administrative Coordinator: Donna Dietz
   E-Mail: administrator@
   clinicalsocialworkassociation.org

Historical Note:
Formerly (1997) the National Federation of Societies for Clinical Social Work. CSWA's mission is to promote excellence in clinical social work practice through the advancement of the profession for the benefit of clients and the clinicians who serve them. CSWA works towards its goal through advocacy at the national and state level on matters related to the profession, mental health, education, and information distributed to its members. Membership consists of clinical social workers, new professionals (clinical social workers who have graduated within the last four years), emeritus members, and students. Membership: $135 (General); $85 (New Professional); $35 (Student); $60 (Emeritus).

Publications:
Clinical Social Work Journal; on-line
CSWA Newsletter; bi-annually; adv.
Membership Roster; on-line

Closure and Container Manufacturers Association *(1981)*
421 N. Northwest Hwy.
Suite 201
Barrington, IL 60010
Tel: (847) 438-2700
Website: closureandcontainer.org
Members:
43 companies
50,000 employees and 43 companies
Staff: 1
Annual Budget: $50-100,000

Personnel:
President: Candace Renwall
   E-Mail: candyr@closureandcontainer.org

Historical Note:
Founded as the Closure Committee of the Glass Packaging Institute, later became (1984) an independent affiliate of the Institute and then became independently incorporated in 2006. Most recently the Closure Manufacturers Association. CCMA helps members increase revenue, improve profits and build one-on-one industry relationships through industry standards development, annual and quarterly networking forums, research reports / statistics and public policy/regulatory/ sustainability advocacy. Membership: $0-4000/year.

Meetings/Conferences: Annual
2013 - San Francisco, CA (Grand Hyatt San Francisco)/ March 20 - 22

Publications:
CCMA Newsletter; bi-annually; adv.
Membership Directory; on-line

Clowns of America International *(1960)*
P.O. Box 1171
Englewood, FL 34295-1171
Tel: (941) 474-4351
TollFree: (877) 816-6941
E-Mail: askus@coai.org
Website: coai.org
Members: 7000 individuals
Staff: 7
Annual Budget: $100-250,000
Tax: 501(c)(6)

Personnel:
Business Manager: Tom Newton
   E-Mail: business@COAI.org

Historical Note:
Formerly (1968) known as Clown Club of America and Circus Clown Club. COAI's purpose is to share, educate, and act as a gathering place for serious minded amateurs, semiprofessionals, and professional clowns. Members are amateur, semi-professional and professional clowns. *Membership: $30- 40/year (USA); $57-91 (USA Family); $30-45 (International); $62-96 (International Family); $500 (Lifetime).*

Meetings/Conferences: Annual
Conference Chair: Tom E. King
2013 - Richmond, VA (Holiday Inn Midlothian-Richmond Koger Center)/April 16 - 21

Publications:
Membership Directory; on-line
The New Calliope; bi-monthly; adv.

Club Managers Association of America *(1927)*
1733 King St.
Alexandria, VA 22314
Tel: (703) 739-9500 *Fax:* (703) 739-0124
E-Mail: cmaa@cmaa.org
Website: cmaa.org
Members: 7000 individuals
Staff: 39
Annual Budget: $5-10,000,000
Tax: 501(c)(6)

Personnel:
Chief Executive Officer: James B. Singerling CCM, CEC
   E-Mail: Jim.Singerling@cmaa.org
Associate Editor and Manager, Communications: Kathleen Cosgrove
   E-Mail: Kathleen.Cosgrove@cmaa.org
Senior Director, Conferences, Meetings and Expositions: Guy Doria
   E-Mail: guy.doria@cmaa.org
Chief Operating Officer: Kathi Driggs
   E-Mail: kathi.driggs@cmaa.org
Director, Human Resources and Property Management: Tracy Hanafin
   E-Mail: tracy.hanafin@cmaa.org
Senior Vice President, Professional Development: Jason Koenigsfeld PhD
   E-Mail: jason.koenigsfeld@cmaa.org
Senior Director, Communications and Government Relations: Melissa Low
   E-Mail: melissa.low@cmaa.org
Chief Financial Officer: Margaret Meleney
   E-Mail: margaret.meleney@cmaa.org
Senior Vice President, Membership Operations: Kim Pasquale
   E-Mail: kim.pasquale@cmaa.org
Senior Director, Technology Operations: Chris Velo
   E-Mail: chris.velo@cmaa.org

Historical Note:
CMAA works to advance the profession of club management by fulfilling the educational and related needs of its members. Members are professional managers of private county, city, university, yacht, town and military clubs. Membership: $25-850/year.

Continuing Education:
Certification Designation/s: MCM, CCE, CCM

Meetings/Conferences: Annual
Conference Chair: Guy Doria
2013 - San Diego, CA (San Diego Convention Center)/ Feb. 7 - 11
2013 - San Diego, CA (San Diego Convention Center)/ Feb. 8 - 9

Publications:
Chapter Digest; monthly; adv.
Club Connection; weekly; adv.
Club Management Magazine; annually
CMAA NewsLine
Membership Directory; on-line; adv.
Outlook; monthly

Clydesdale Breeders of the United States *(1879)*
17346 Kelley Rd.
Pecatonica, IL 61063
Tel: (815) 247-8780 *Fax:* (815) 247-8337
Website: clydesusa.com
Members: 900 individuals
Staff: 5
Annual Budget: $250-500,000

Personnel:
Corporate Secretary: Cathy J. Behn
   E-Mail: secretary@clydesusa.com

Historical Note:
Formerly the American Clydesdale Association and Clydesdale Breeders Association of the U. S. CBUSA's mission is to collect, revise, preserve, and publish the history and pedigrees of purebred Clydesdale horses. It is also responsible for registration of eligible horses and transfer of ownership. Membership is open to people interested in the well being and advancement of the breed. *Membership: $100/year (Lifetime).*

Meetings/Conferences: Annual
Number of non-conference events/year: 1

Publications:
Breeders Directory; annually
Lead Horse Newsletter; quarterly

Coal Exporters Association of the U.S. *(1945)*
101 Constitution Ave. NW, Suite 500 East
C/O National Mining Association
Washington, DC 20001
Tel: (202) 463-2600 *Fax:* (202) 463-2666
E-Mail: cholmes@nma.org
Website: nma.org/about/cea_page.asp
Staff: 6

Personnel:
President and Chief Executive Officer: Harold P. Quinn Jr.
Contact, Government Affairs: Rich Nolan
Contact, Member Services: Moya Phelleps
Contact, Communications: Carol Raulston
Contact, Legal and Regulatory Affairs: Katie Sweeney
Contact, Legal and Regulatory Affairs: Bruce Watzman

Historical Note:
CEA is an affiliate of National Mining Association (NMA) and has the wide ranging resources of the organization available to assist in the implementation of policies and objectives of the Association. CEA was established in 1945 to promote and encourage the reliable export of quality coals from the United States.

Coal Operators and Associates *(1959)*
P.O. Box 3158
Pikesville, KY 41502
Tel: (606) 432-2161 *Fax:* (606) 432-2162
Website: miningusa.com/coa
Members: 200 Members
Staff: 3
Annual Budget: $500-1,000,000
Tax: 501(c)(3)

Personnel:
President: David A. Gooch
   E-Mail: coadavidg@se-tel.com

Historical Note:
Assistance, Insurance Benefits, Meetings & Seminars, Organization.Membership: $100-500(Associate); $50-1,000 (Coal Producers);Based upon number of employees (Non-Producers).

Publications:
COA Newsletter
Membership Directory

Coal Technology Association *(1975)*
12548 Granite Ridge Dr.
N. Potomac, MD 20878
Tel: (301) 330-2256
Website: coaltechnologies.com
Members: 20 companies
Staff: 1
Annual Budget: $100-250,000
Tax: 501(c)(3)

Personnel:
Vice President: Barbara A. Sakkestad
   E-Mail: barbarasak@aol.com

Historical Note:
CTA encourages the development and exchange of information on coal technologies through its annual international technical conference. CTA brings together the world's leading experts on cutting edge technologies each spring to Clearwater, Florida, USA.

Meetings/Conferences: Annual
2013 - Clearwater, FL (Sheraton Sand Key Resort)/June 2 - 6
Number of non-conference events/year: 1

Coal Trading Association *(1999)*
2001 Jefferson Davis
Highway Suite 1004
Arlington, VA 22202-3617
Tel: (703) 418-0392 *Fax:* (703) 416-0014
E-Mail: info@coaltrade.org
Website: coaltrade.org
Members: 40 companies
Staff: 2

Annual Budget: $50-100,000
Tax: 501(c)(6)

Personnel:
Executive Director: Robert E. McLean CAE
Treasurer: Ryan Gentil

Historical Note:
The Coal Trading Association (CTA) is the trade association committed exclusively to the needs of traders, trading managers, brokers, risk managers, sales managers and purchasing managers in the coal trading industry. Membership: $2000 (Corporate Voting); $1000 (Corporate Non-Voting); $150 (Nonprofit, Government or Academic Institution Nonvoting).

Meetings/Conferences: Annual
Number of non-conference events/year: 1

Publications:
Membership Directory; on-line

The Coalition for America's Gateways and Trade Corridors

1111 19th St. NW
Suite 800
Washington, DC 20036
Tel: (202) 828-9100 *Fax:* (202) 463-2471
Website: tradecorridors.org
Staff: 4
Annual Budget: $100-250,000
Tax: 501(c)(6)

Personnel:
Executive Director: Leslie Blakey
   E-Mail: lblakey@blakey-agnew.com
Director, Communications: Jeff Agnew
   E-Mail: jagnew@blakey-agnew.com
Director, Operations and Advocacy: Elaine Nessle
   E-Mail: enessle@blakey-agnew.com

Historical Note:
CAGTC's mission is to raise public recognition and Congressional awareness of this need and to promote sufficient funding in federal legislation for trade corridors, gateways, intermodal connectors and freight facilities. Members are state DOTs, MPOs, ports, engineering firms, and freight corridors, that have come together to improve national freight policy. Membership: $6,500/year.

Meetings/Conferences: Annual
2013 - Washington, DC/April 9 - 10

Publications:
CAGTC Newsletter; on-line
Member Directory; on-line

The Coalition for Government Procurement

(1979)
1990 M St. NW
Suite 450
Washington, DC 20036
Tel: (202) 331-0975 *Fax:* (202) 822-9788
E-Mail: info@thecgp.org
Website: thecgp.org
Members: 285 companies
Staff: 8
Annual Budget: $1-2,000,000

Personnel:
President: Roger Waldron
   E-Mail: rwaldron@thecgp.org
Executive Vice President and General Counsel: Carolyn Alston
   E-Mail: calston@thecgp.org
Executive, Membership Services: Sandy Arce
   E-Mail: sarce@thecgp.org
Director, Membership Sales: John Cissel
   E-Mail: jcissel@thecgp.org
Director, Events and Membership Support: Melissa King
Director, Business Development: Denise Mileski
   E-Mail: jberghane@thecgp.org
Director, Marketing and Events: Athena Oliff
   E-Mail: rdicharry@thecgp.org
Chief Financial Officer: Robert Rendely
   E-Mail: rrendely@thecgp.org

Historical Note:
Formerly (1988) Coalition for Common Sense in Government Procurement. CGP is an association of federal government contractors working on behalf of its members to advocate for an efficient and effective procurement system that may impact the business; Informs members in a timely manner of changes to policies and regulations that provides education on the complexities of federal procurement policy; Unite business with contracting partners to drive new opportunities. Members are firms who provide commercial goods and services to the federal government. Membership:

$1,000-5,500 (Company); $6,500 (Premier); $2,950 (Affiliate).

Meetings/Conferences: Annual
Conference Chair: Melissa King
Number of non-conference events/year: 1

Publications:
Friday Flash; weekly; adv.
Off the Shelf; monthly

Coalition for Independent Seniors

3525 Piedmont Rd.
Seven Piedmont Center, Suite 300
Atlanta, GA 30305
Tel: (202) 857-4417
TollFree: (877) 605-6393
Website: cforis.org
Staff: 2

Personnel:
Executive Director: H. West Richards

Historical Note:
The Coalition for Independent Seniors is a non-partisan, non-political, public policy coalition dedicated to preserving the opportunity for seniors to stay in their homes and protecting their ability to live financially independent lives.

Coalition for Juvenile Justice *(1984)*

1319 F St. NW
Suite 402
Washington, DC 20004
Tel: (202) 467-0864 *Fax:* (202) 887-0738
E-Mail: info@juvjustice.org
Website: juvjustice.org
Members: 1500 individuals
Staff: 7
Annual Budget: $1-2,000,000
Tax: 501(c)(3)

Personnel:
Executive Director: Nancy Gannon Hornberger
   E-Mail: nancy@juvjustice.org
Deputy Executive Director, Policy and Programs: Tara Andrews
   E-Mail: andrews@juvjustice.org
Assistant Director, Training and Technical Assistance: Franklin A. Cruz
   E-Mail: cruz@juvjustice.org
Director, Leadership and Training Programs: Mark Ferrante
   E-Mail: ferrante@juvjustice.org
Director, Communications and Operations: Idit Knaan
   E-Mail: knaan@juvjustice.org
Manager, Conferences and Member Services: Jessica Russell Murphy
   E-Mail: murphy@juvjustice.org

Historical Note:
Formerly (1994) the National Coalition of State Juvenile Justice Advisory Groups. CJJ's mission is to prevent children and youth from becoming involved in the courts and upholding the highest standards of care when youth are charged with wrongdoing and enter the justice system. Membership: $100 (Regular); $35 (Student).

Meetings/Conferences: Annual
Conference Chair: Jessica Russell Murphy

Publications:
Juvenile Justice e-Monitor; monthly; adv.

Membership List Available to Non-members

The Coalition for Transportation Productivity

(1982)
8 E St. SE
Washington, DC 20003
Tel: (202) 543-0032
Website: transportationproductivity.org
Staff: 1
Annual Budget: $250-500,000
Tax: 501(c)(6)

Personnel:
Executive Director: John Runyan

Historical Note:
The Coalition for Transportation Productivity (CTP) is a coalition of about 200 shippers and allied associations committed to increasing the federal vehicle weight limit to 97,000 pounds for vehicles equipped with an additional (sixth) axle. CTP's mission is to advocate a more efficient and productive transportation system in the United States.

The Coalition of Airline Pilots Associations *(1997)*

444 N. Capitol St.

Suite 532
Washington, DC 20001
Tel: (202) 624-3535 *Fax:* (202) 624-3536
E-Mail: capapilots@capapilots.org
Website: capapilots.org
Members: 28000 individuals
Staff: 4
Annual Budget: $250-500,000

Personnel:
Executive Vice president: Lee Collins
Executive Director: Maryanne DeMarco
   E-Mail: executivedirector@capapilots.org
President: Carl Kuwitzky
   E-Mail: ck@capapilots.org
Government Affairs Chairman: David J. Ross

Historical Note:
CAPA's mission is to address safety, security, legislative and regulatory issues affecting the professional flight deck crew member on matters of common interest to the individual member unions. Membership is comprised of the members of five airline pilots associations.

Coalition of Black Trade Unionists *(1972)*

P. O. Box 66268
Washington, DC 20035
E-Mail: cbtu1@hotmail.com
Website: cbtu.org
Members:
42 chapters
77 international unions
Staff: 3
Annual Budget: $500-1,000,000
Tax: 501(c)(3)

Personnel:
President: William Lucy

Historical Note:
CBTU seeks to fulfill the dream of Black trade unionists by achieving economic, political and social justice for every American. Members are from 77 international and national unions with 42 chapters across the country. Membership: $30 (Rank and File); $75 (Staff); $150 (International Officer); $15 (Retired Rank and File); $37.50 (Retired Staff); $75 (Retired International Officer).

Coalition of Essential Schools *(1984)*

325 Public St.
Providence, RI 02905
Tel: (401) 426-9638 *Fax:* (401) 752-2632
E-Mail: inquiries@essentialschools.org
Website: essentialschools.org
Members: 1000 schools
Staff: 2
Annual Budget: $500-1,000,000
Tax: 501(c)(3)

Personnel:
National Director: Elizabeth Jardine
   E-Mail: ejardine@essentialschools.org
Director, Publications and Communications: Jill Davidson
   E-Mail: jdavidson@essentialschools.org

Historical Note:
CES works to create academic success for every student by sharing decision-making with all those affected by the schools and deliberately and explicitly confronting all forms of inequity. Members are schools, centers, districts, and organizations. Membership: $400-500 (School/ Institutional Affiliation); $500-750 (Organizations); $10-75 (Individual Affiliation); Free (Youth).

Meetings/Conferences: Semi-Annual

Publications:
Essential Resources; bi-weekly
Horace; quarterly

Membership List Available to Non-members

Coalition of Higher Education Assistance Organizations *(1981)*

1101 Vermont Ave. NW
Suite 400
Washington, DC 20005-3586
Tel: (202) 289-3910 *Fax:* (202) 371-0197
Website: coheao.com
Members: 365 organizations
Staff: 4
Annual Budget: $100-250,000
Tax: 501(c)(6)

Personnel:
Executive Director: Harrison M. Wadsworth III
   E-Mail: hwadsworth@wpllc.net

Director, Legislative Services: Wes Huffman
  E-Mail: whuffman@wpllc.net

Historical Note:
COHEAO is a partnership of educational and commercial members that advocates access to post-secondary education. Focus is on legislative and regulatory advocacy for Federal Perkins loans and other campus-based student loan programs. Members are colleges/universities, billers and collectors of student loans. Membership: $125 (Associate); $190-545 (Institution); $3,000 (Commercial); $1,250 (Organization).

Meetings/Conferences: Annual
Conference Chair: Wes Huffman
2013 - Arlington, VA (Ritz Carlton)/Jan. 27 - 30

Publications:
The Torch; bi-monthly

Coalition of Labor Union Women (1974)
815 16th St. NW
Second Floor South
Washington, DC 20006
Tel: (202) 508-6969 *Fax:* (202) 508-6968
E-Mail: getinfo@cluw.org
Website: cluw.org
Members: 210000 individuals
Staff: 3
Annual Budget: $250-500,000

Personnel:
Executive Director: Carol Rosenblatt
  E-Mail: csrosenblatt@cluw.org
President: Karen See
  E-Mail: ksee@cluw.org

Historical Note:
CLUW's mission is to unify all union women to determine common problems and concerns and to develop action programs within the framework of unions to deal effectively with objectives. Membership: $35 (New Member); $50 (Regular/Associate); $100 (Supporting Member); $75 (Contributing); $150 (Sustaining); $15 (Retired/Student/Unemployed); $1,000 (Lifetime).

Meetings/Conferences: Annual

Publications:
CLUW Newsletter
Membership Directory; on-line

Coalition of Service Industries (1982)
1090 Vermont Ave. NW
Suite 420
Washington, DC 20005
Tel: (202) 289-7460 *Fax:* (202) 379-9864
E-Mail: csi@uscsi.org
Website: uscsi.org
Members: 65 companies
Staff: 5
Annual Budget: $1-2,000,000
Tax: 501(c)(3)

Personnel:
President: Bob Vastine
Program Associate: Andrew Jensen
Program Associate: James Lim
Director, Programs: Steve Simchak

Historical Note:
CSI is a business organization dedicated to the reduction of barriers to U.S. services exports, and to the development of constructive domestic US policies, including tax policies that enhance the global competitiveness of its members. Membership: $5,000-25,000/year.

Meetings/Conferences:
Conference Chair: Steve Simchak

Publications:
GSN Newsletter

Membership List Available to Non-members

Coalition of Visionary Resources (1996)
2051 S. Fillmore St.
Denver, CO 80210
Tel: (303) 758-0007 *Fax:* (303) 568-7713
E-Mail: info@covr.org
Website: covr.org
Members: 200 organizations and individuals
Staff: 3
Annual Budget: $25-50,000
Tax: 501(c)(6)

Personnel:
Executive Director: Justin Swanström
Assistant Executive Director: Bryce Levar
Treasurer: Kim Perkins

Historical Note:
Formerly (2002) the Coalition of Retailers of Visionary Books, Music, and Merchandise. COVR is a not-for-profit trade organization dedicated to supporting independent retailers, manufacturers, distributors, wholesalers & publishers of visionary books, music, and merchandise. Membership: $80/year.

Publications:
Inside COVR-Newsletter; monthly
New age Retailer

The Coastal and Estuarine Research Federation (1969)
P.O. Box 510
Port Republic, MD 20676-0510
Tel: (410) 326-7467 *Fax:* (410) 326-7466
E-Mail: info@erf.org
Website: erf.org
Members: 1650 individuals
Staff: 4
Annual Budget: $500-1,000,000
Tax: 501(c)(3)

Personnel:
Executive Director: Mark Wolf-Armstrong
  E-Mail: mark@erf.org
Manager, Programs: Alejandra Ally Garza
  E-Mail: ally@erf.org
Office Manager: Susan Helmrich
  E-Mail: susan@erf.org
Chair, Conferences: Steve Weisberg
  E-Mail: stevew@sccwrp.org

Historical Note:
CERF is a multidisciplinary organization of individuals who study the structure and function of estuaries, and the effect of human activities on these environments. Membership: $30-200/year.

Meetings/Conferences:
Conference Chair: Steve Weisberg
2013 - San Diego, CA (San Diego Convention Center)/ Nov. 3 - 7

Publications:
CERF Newsletter; quarterly
Coastal and Estuarine Science News; on-line
Estuaries & Coasts; quarterly
Estuaries and Coasts

Coastal Conservation Association (1977)
6919 Portwest
Suite 100
Houston, TX 77024
Tel: (713) 626-4234 *Fax:* (713) 626-5852
TollFree: (800) 201-3474
E-Mail: ccantl@joincca.org
Website: joincca.org
Members: 17 coastal state chapters
Staff: 4
Annual Budget: $10-25,000,000
Tax: 501(c)(3)

Personnel:
President: Patrick D. Murray
General Counsel: Robert G. Hayes
Federal Lobbyist: Matthew Paxton
Conservation Director and Newsroom Moderator: Ted Venker

Historical Note:
CCA's mission is to advise and educate the public on conservation of marine resources. The objective of CCA is to conserve, promote and enhance the present and future availability of these coastal resources for the benefit and enjoyment of the general public. Membership:$25-100 (Member); $15 (Associate); $200 (sponsor); $500 (Patron); $1000(Life member).

Publications:
Change of Tides
Newsletter; quarterly
Rising Tide
TIDE; bi-monthly; adv.

Coblentz Society (1954)
Department of Chemistry and Biochemistry, University of South Carolina
631 Sumter St.
Columbia, SC 29208
Tel: (803) 777-5264
Website: coblentz.org
Members: 600 individuals
Staff: 2
Annual Budget: $25-50,000

Tax: 501(c)(3)

Personnel:
President: Prof. Michael L. Myrick
  E-Mail: myrick@sc.edu

Historical Note:
CS exists to foster understanding and application of vibrational spectroscopy. CS is Affiliated with Society for Applied Spectroscopy. Membership: $20 (Regular); $10 (Student).

Meetings/Conferences: Annual

Publications:
Coblentz Society Newsletter; semi-annually

The Coca-Cola Bottlers' Association (1914)
3282 Northside Pkwy.
Suite 200
Atlanta, GA 30327
Tel: (404) 872-2258 *Fax:* (404) 872-2869
Website: ccbanet.com
Staff: 5
Tax: 501(c)(3)

Personnel:
Executive Director: W. Thomas Haynes
Chief Financial Officer: Ann Burton
Director, Customer Management Programs: Bobbie Golden
Manager, Purchasing: Brian Petersen
Treasurer: Russ Whitis

Historical Note:
The Coca-Cola Bottlers' Association Established in 1914 initially to protect members' products from sham liability claims, the 21st century finds the Association providing an ever-increasing array of products and services to its membership. CCBA's Mission is to keep the Bottlers Informed.

Publications:
Membership Directory; on-line
The Bottling Line

Cocoa Merchants' Association of America (1924)
World Financial Center
One North End Ave. -13th Floor
New York, NY 10282-1101
Tel: (212) 201-8819 *Fax:* (212) 785-5475
E-Mail: cmaa@cocoamerchants.com
Website: cocoamerchants.com
Members: 75 corporations
Staff: 1
Annual Budget: $500-1,000,000

Personnel:
Executive Director: Lori Trimarchi CAE, MEM
  E-Mail: ltrimarchi@cocoamerchants.com

Historical Note:
CMAA's purpose is to foster the trade and welfare of the cocoa industry in the United States and to obtain for its members the benefits to be secured by friendly intercourse among those engaged in importing and trading in cocoa beans. Regular members are importing dealers of cocoa beans and cocoa products. Associate membership is available for chocolate manufacturers, merchants domiciled in foreign countries, domestic commission houses, service companies and government agencies. Membership: $6500 (Regular); $3000 (Associate Trade); $1000 (Associate).

Publications:
Membership Directory; on-line

Coin Laundry Association (1960)
One S. 660 Midwest Rd.
Suite 205
Oakbrook Terrace, IL 60181
Tel: (630) 953-7920
TollFree: (800) 570-5629
E-Mail: info@coinlaundery.org
Website: coinlaundry.org
Members: 2500 individuals
Staff: 11
Annual Budget: $1-2,000,000
Tax: 501(c)(6)

Personnel:
President and Chief Executive Officer: Brian Wallace
  E-Mail: brian@coinlaundry.org
Director, Marketing and Online Development: Kim Fenolio
  E-Mail: kim@coinlaundry.org
Media Sales Coordinator and Classified Ad Sales, PlanetLaundry: Kassi Foleno
  E-Mail: kassi@coinlaundry.org
Editor: Bob Nieman

E-Mail: journal@coinlaundry.org
Director, Membership Services: Julie O'Rourke
    E-Mail: julie@coinlaundry.org

Historical Note:
Formerly the National Automatic Laundry and Cleaning Council, assumed its present name in 1983. CLA's mission is to ensure a profitable and growing retail, self-service laundry operation by providing education, products and services to laundry owners.. Members are self-service laundry and dry cleaning establishments together with manufacturers and distributors of the equipment, services and supplies they use. Membership: $260 (Potential Investor); $260-290 (Laundry Owner); $549 (Distributor); $835-4195 (Manufacturer).

Meetings/Conferences: Semi-Annual

Publications:
Membership Directory; on-line
PlanetLaundry Magazine; monthly; adv.

Membership List Available to Non-members

COLA (1988)
9881 Broken Land Pkwy.
Suite 200
Columbia, MD 21046
Tel: (800) 981-9883 Fax: (410) 381-8611
TollFree: (800) 981-9883
E-Mail: info@cola.org
Website: cola.org
Members: 7500 individuals
Staff: 86
Annual Budget: $5-10,000,000

Personnel:
Chief Executive Officer: Douglas A. Biegel
    E-Mail: dbiegel@cola.org
Specialist, Conference: Tricia Hudson
    E-Mail: thudson@cola.org
Education Specialist and Director, Symposiums: Catherine Johnson MA, MT (ASCP)
Director, Human Resources: Susan Trask
    E-Mail: strask@cola.org
Chief Operating Officer: Gerard Weiss

Historical Note:
Formerly (1997) Commission on Office Laboratory Accreditation. COLA is a physician-directed organization whose purpose is to promote laboratory medicine and patient care through a program of voluntary education, consultation and accreditation. It also sponsors programs and services including online education and national symposia, to support standards in medicine and patient care.

Continuing Education:
Certification Designation/s: QMS

Meetings/Conferences:
Conference Chair: Catherine Johnson MA, MT (ASCP)

Publications:
Insight e-newsletter

Cold-Formed Steel Engineers Institute (1994)
25 Massachusetts Ave. NW
Suite 800
Washington, DC 20001
Tel: (202) 263-4488 Fax: (202) 452-1039
E-Mail: info@cfsei.org
Website: cfsei.org
Staff: 1

Personnel:
Chairman: Nabil Rahman

Historical Note:
Formerly Light Gauge Steel Engineers Association. CFSEI's mission is to enable and encourage the efficient design of safe and cost effective cold-formed steel (CFS) framed structures. Membership: $35-$50 (Industry); $1000-$25000 (Associate); $25-$100 (General); $25 (Local); $75-$1000 (Additional).

Meetings/Conferences:
Number of non-conference events/year: 3

Publications:
newsletter; quarterly

Coleopterists Society
3009 Turnbuckle Cir.
Elk Grove, CA 95758
Tel: (916) 262-1168 Fax: (866) 783-2951
E-Mail: coleoptreas@gmail.com
Website: coleopsoc.org
Members: 570 individuals
Staff: 1
Annual Budget: $100-250,000

Tax: 501(c)(3)

Personnel:
Treasurer and Membership Secretary: Andrew R. Cline
    E-Mail: coleoptreas@gmail.com

Historical Note:
The Coleopterists Society is a professional society organized for scientific and educational purposes. Members are concerned with the study of living and fossil beetles. Membership: $40 (Individual); $150 (Institutional).

Publications:
Beetle News; on-line
Chrysomela; semi-annually
Curculio Newsletter; semi-annually
Membership Directory; on-line
Scarabs; irregular
The Coleopterists Bulletin; quarterly

Collaborative Family Healthcare Association (1993)
P.O. Box 23980
Rochester, NY 14692-3980
Tel: (585) 482-8210 Fax: (585) 482-2901
E-Mail: info@CFHA.net
Website: cfhcc.org
Staff: 4

Personnel:
Manager, Business: William Steger
    E-Mail: bill@familyenet.net

Historical Note:
CFHA's mission is to advocate a comprehensive and cost-effective model of healthcare delivery that integrates mind and body, individual and family, patients, providers and communities. Membership: $150 (Regular); $75 (Student).

Meetings/Conferences: Annual
Conference Chair: Steffani G. Blackstock CMP
2013 - Broomfield, CO (Omni Interlocken Resort)/Oct. 10 - 12

Publications:
CFHA Newsletter; monthly
Families, Systems, & Health; quarterly; adv.
Families, Systems, and Health

College and University Professional Association for Human Resources (1946)
1811 Commons Point Dr.
Knoxville, TN 37932
Tel: (865) 637-7673 Fax: (865) 637-7674
TollFree: (877) 287-2474
Website: cupahr.org
Members: 1800 colleges and universities
Staff: 29
Annual Budget: $5-10,000,000
Tax: 501(c)(3)

Personnel:
President and Chief Executive Officer: Andy Brantley
    E-Mail: abrantley@cupahr.org
Manager, Marketing: Julie Boggs
    E-Mail: jboggs@cupahr.org
Chief Corporate Relations Officer: Leah Burns
    E-Mail: lburns@cupahr.org
Director, Member Service and Human Resources: Ashleigh Dillon PHR
    E-Mail: adillon@cupahr.org
Chief Financial Officer: Wayne Everbach
    E-Mail: weverbach@cupahr.org
Director, Conferences and Meetings: Lisa Hayden
    E-Mail: lhayden@cupahr.org
Manager, Information Technology Data and Project: Jason Heydasch
    E-Mail: jheydasch@cupahr.org
Director, Communications: Gayle Kiser
    E-Mail: gkiser@cupahr.org
Managing Editor: Missy Kline
    E-Mail: mking@cupahr.org
Vice President and Chief Operating Officer: Rob Shomaker
    E-Mail: rshomaker@cupahr.org
Director, Research: Ray B. Sizemore PhD
    E-Mail: rsizemore@cupahr.org
Chief Government Relations Officer: Josh Ullman
    E-Mail: julman@cupahr.com
Director, Finance: Glee Wilson
    E-Mail: gwilson@cupahr.org

Historical Note:
Formerly (2000) College and University Personnel Association, CUPA-HR's mission is to provide leadership to the higher education human resources profession and the higher education community by delivering essential

knowledge, resources and connections that enhance individual and institutional capacity and effectiveness. Members are colleges and universities united to improve the effectiveness of their human resource management. Membership: $210-2,100 (Institutional); $1,000 (Corporate); $500 (International); $315 (Affiliate/Other-industry professional HR); $25 (Student/Retiree/Transitional).

Meetings/Conferences: Annual
Conference Chair: Lisa Hayden
2013 - Las Vegas, NV (Caesars Palace Las Vegas Hotel and Casino)/Oct. 27 - 29
2014 - San Antonio, TX (Grand Hyatt San Antonio)/Sept. 28 - 30
Number of non-conference events/year: 18

Publications:
CUPA-HR eNews; on-line; adv.
Member Directory; on-line
The Higher Education Workplace
The Higher Education Workplace; adv.

Membership List Available to Non-members

College Art Association (1911)
50 Broadway
21st Floor
New York, NY 10004
Tel: (212) 691-1051 Fax: (212) 627-2381
E-Mail: nyoffice@collegeart.org
Website: collegeart.org
Members: 14000 individuals and 2000 Institutions
Staff: 31
Annual Budget: $2-5,000,000
Tax: 501(c)(3)

Personnel:
Executive Director: Linda Downs
    E-Mail: ldowns@collegeart.org
Associate, Marketing and Communications: Helen Bayer
Staff Accountant: Onofre Beltran
Systems Administrator: Wayne Lok
Chief Financial Officer: Teresa Lopez

Historical Note:
Founded at the Cincinnati Art Museum at a meeting of the Western Drawing and Manual Training Association. CAA's missin is to promote the visual arts and their understanding through committed practice and intellectual engagement. Membership: $60-185 (Individual, based on annual income); $60 (Retired); $50 (Full-Time Student); $220 (Sustaining); $315 (Sponsoring); $525 (Patron); $375 (Institutional, Primary); $525 (Library/Department/Museum); $5,000 (Life Time); $175 (Associate); $850 (Academic/Corporate).

Meetings/Conferences: Annual
Conference Chair: Emmanuel Lemakis
2013 - Manhattan, NY (Hilton New York in midtown Manhattan)/Feb. 13 - 16
2013 - New York City, NY/Feb. 13 - 16

Publications:
Art Journal
CAA News; weekly
caa.reviews; on-line

Membership List Available to Non-members

College Athletic Business Management Association (1950)
Ricketts Hall
566 Brownson Rd.
Annapolis, MD 21402
Tel: (410) 293-8735
Website: nacda.com/cabma/nacda-cabma.html
Members: 1104 individuals and institutions
Staff: 3
Annual Budget: $100-250,000
Tax: 501(c)(3)

Personnel:
President: Chauncey Winbush
    E-Mail: winbush@usna.edu
Administrator: Pat Manak
    E-Mail: pmanak@nacda.com

Historical Note:
CABMA's mission is to assist the business management and administration of college athletic departments. Has no paid officers or full-time staff. Membership: $150 (Individual); $500 (Institution).

Meetings/Conferences: Annual
2013 - Orlando, FL (Orlando World Center Marriott)/June 10 - 13

2014 - Orlando, FL (Orlando World Center Marriott)/
June 6 - 9

Publications:
Athletics Administration

Membership List Available to Non-members

College Band Directors National Association
(1941)
Vanderbilt University, Wind Studies
2400 Blakemore Ave.
Nashville, TN 37212
Tel: (615) 322-7651 *Fax:* (615) 343-0324
Website: cbdna.org
Members: 1000 individuals
Staff: 3
Annual Budget: $100-250,000

Personnel:
Executive Secretary: Thomas Verrier
   E-Mail: thomas.verrier@vanderbilt.edu

Historical Note:
Formerly known as a committee of the Music Educators National Conference (MENC) and renamed as College Band Directors National Association in 1947. CBDNA is an inclusive organization whose members are engaged in continuous dialogue encompassing myriad philosophies and professional practices. Membership: $85 (Active); $20 (Retired/Student); $125 (Music Industry).

Meetings/Conferences: Annual
2013 - Greensboro, NC (Sheraton Greensboro at Four Seasons)/March 20 - 23
Number of non-conference events/year: 4

Publications:
CBDNA Journal; quarterly

The College Board *(1900)*
1233 20th St. NW
Suite 600
Washington, DC 20036-2304
Tel: (202) 741-4700 *Fax:* (202) 822-5920
E-Mail: govrelations@collegeboard.org
Website: collegeboard.org
Members: 5900 colleges and universities
Staff: 17

Personnel:
President: David Coleman
Vice President, Research and Development: Wayne Camara
Senior Vice President and Chief Information Officer: Diane Duggan
Chief Operating Officer: Herb Elish
Chief Financial Officer, Senior Vice President and Finance: Tom Higgins
Vice President, Communications: Peter Kauffmann
Senior Vice President, Administration and General Counsel: Neil Lane
Vice President and Chief of Staff: Kanika Lichthardt
Senior Vice President, Region and Account Services: Andrea Mainelli
Vice President, Office of Strategy Management: Steve Meyer
Senior Vice President, Relationship Development: Peter Negroni
Senior Vice President, Advanced Placement and College Readiness: Trevor Packer
Senior Vice President, Advocacy, Government Relations and Development: Tom Rudin
Vice President, Membership Services: Mary Carroll Scott
Associate Director: Eleanor M. Vogelsang
Vice President, Organizational Effectiveness: Juliet Weissman

Historical Note:
Formerly known as the College Entrance Examination Board. A membership organization of schools, colleges, universities and other educational organizations that sells standardized tests used by academically oriented post-secondary education institutions. College Board's mission is to connect students to college success and opportunity. Membership: $325/year.

Meetings/Conferences: Annual
Number of non-conference events/year: 10

Publications:
Membership Directory; on-line

College English Association *(1939)*
Nazareth College of Rochester
4245 East Ave.
Rochester, NY 14618-3790

Tel: (585) 389-2645 *Fax:* (585) 586-2452
E-Mail: cea.english@gmail.com
Website: www2.widener.edu/~cea
Members: 1525 individuals and libraries
Staff: 2
Annual Budget: $50-100,000

Personnel:
Executive Director: Charles A.S. Ernst
   E-Mail: cernst@hilbert.edu
Treasurer: Joseph Pestino
   E-Mail: jfpestin@naz.edu

Historical Note:
CEA is an organization of Teacher-Scholars dedicated to teaching English in colleges and universities. CEA's mission is to serve teacher-scholars of English in many important ways and provides a meeting ground for those interested in all areas of literature, culture, creative writing, rhetoric and composition, pedagogy and advising. Membership: $40 (Individual); $50 (Joint); $15 (Student); $25 (Retired or Part-Time); $250-450 (Lifetime).

Publications:
Membership Directory
The CEA Critic
The CEA Forum; semi-annually

College Gymnastics Association *(1950)*
1900 University Ave. SE
306 Cooke Hall
Minneapolis, MN 55455
Tel: (612) 625-9567 *Fax:* (612) 626-9922
E-Mail: cga@collegegymnastics.org
Website: collegegymnastics.org
Members: 60 individuals
Staff: 2
Annual Budget: Under $10,000

Personnel:
President: Mike Burns
   E-Mail: burns265@umn.edu

Historical Note:
Mission is to encourage participation and the pursuit of excellence in all aspects of gymnastics. CGA compiles statistics; holds competitions; maintains various coaches awards. Membership: $200 (Active/Corporate); $50 (Associate).

College Language Association *(1937)*
P.O. Box 38515
Tallahassee, FL 32315
Tel: (850) 599-3737 *Fax:* (850) 561-2976
Website: clascholars.org
Staff: 3
Annual Budget: $50-100,000

Personnel:
Treasurer: Yakini B. Kemp
   E-Mail: yakini.kemp@famu.edu

Historical Note:
CLA's mission is to fosters high professional standards for teachers of language and literature and promotes productive scholarship among its members. Membership: $80 (Regular); $55 (Student); $500 (Life); $200 (Institutional); $55 (Retire).

Meetings/Conferences: Annual
2013 - Lexington, KY/April 10 - 13

Publications:
CLA Journal; quarterly
CLA Newsletter; annually

College Media Association *(1954)*
Vanderbilt University, 2301 Vanderbilt Pl.
VU Station B 351669
Nashville, TN 37235-1669
Tel: (615) 322-6610
Website: cma.cloverpad.org
Members: 750 individuals
Staff: 3
Annual Budget: $250-500,000

Personnel:
Interim Executive Director: Chris Carroll
   E-Mail: chris.carroll@vanderbilt.edu
Interim Business Director: Jeff Breaux
   E-Mail: jeff.a.breaux@vanderbilt.edu
Interim Technology Director: Jim Hayes
   E-Mail: jim.hayes@vanderbilt.edu

Historical Note:
Established as the National Council of College Publication Advisors; assumed its present name in 1983. CMA's mission is to educate and inform advisers about their roles

in serving students and about the teaching, advising and production of collegiate media, advance the quality of the student media members advise. Membership: $50 (Active/Associate); $275 (Business/Institutional); $250 (Active-Institutional bundle).

Meetings/Conferences: Annual
2013 - New York City, NY/March 14 - 16
2013 - New Orleans, LA/Oct. 23 - 27
2014 - Philadelphia, PA/Oct. 29 - Nov. 1
2015 - Austin, TX/Oct. 28 - 31

Publications:
College Media Newsletter
Flagship journal
Membership Directory; on-line

Membership List Available to Non-members

College Music Society *(1958)*
312 E. Pine St.
Missoula, MT 59802
Tel: (406) 721-9616 *Fax:* (406) 721-9419
E-Mail: cms@music.org
Website: music.org
Members: 9500 individuals
Staff: 8
Annual Budget: $1-2,000,000
Tax: 501(c)(6)

Personnel:
Executive Director: Robby D. Gunstream
   E-Mail: execdir@music.org
Contact, Communications: Mary Catherine Anno-Murk
   E-Mail: cms@music.org
Contact, Membership Services: Shannon Devlin
   E-Mail: cmsmembership@music.org
Contact, Professional Activities: Peter S. Park
   E-Mail: profact@music.org
Director, Information Technology: David E. Schafer

Historical Note:
CMS's mission is to promote music teaching, learning, musical creativity, expression, research, dialogue, diversity and interdisciplinary interaction. Membership: $70 (Regular); $90 (Joint Regular); $35 (Retired/Full-time Student); $50 (Joint Retired/Joint Student).

Continuing Education:
Enrollment: 1

Meetings/Conferences:
2013 - Buenos Aires, Argentina (Hilton Buenos Aires)/
   June 18 - 24
2013 - Cambridge, MA (Hyatt Regency Cambridge)/
   Oct. 31 - Nov. 3
2014 - St. Louis, MO/Oct. 29 - Nov. 2

Publications:
CMS Newsletter; bi-monthly; adv.
CMS Professional Notices; on-line; adv.
College Music Symposium; quarterly; adv.
Directory of Music Faculties in Colleges & Universities,
   U.S. & Canada; on-line; adv.
The Music Vacancy List; weekly; adv.

Membership List Available to Non-members

College of American Pathologists *(1947)*
325 Waukegan Rd.
Northfield, IL 60093-2750
Tel: (847) 832-7000 *Fax:* (847) 832-8000
TollFree: (800) 323-4040
Website: cap.org
Members: 17000 individuals
Staff: 400
Annual Budget: Over $100,000,000
Tax: 501(c)(6)

Personnel:
Chief Executive Officer: Charles Roussel
Senior Director, Information Services: Marion Cook
Vice President, Education and Publication Division: Constance Filling
Vice President, Communications and Member Engagement: Sandra B Grear
   E-Mail: sgrear@cap.org
Chief Administrative and Financial Officer: Stephen Myers
Vice President, Advocacy: John H Scott
   E-Mail: jscott@cap.org

Historical Note:
Founded and incorporated on May 14, 1947. CAP's mission is to serve patients, pathologists, and the public by fostering and advocating excellence in the practice of pathology and laboratory medicine. Fellowship in the CAP is restricted to pathologists certified by the American Board of Pathology. Membership: $325/year.

Continuing Education:
Certification Designation/s: BPFT, MOC-PC, MOC-IC, MOC-PR, MOC-MK, MOC-PB, MOC-SB

Meetings/Conferences: Annual
2013 - Orlando, FL (Gaylord Palms Resort and Convention Center-Orlando)/Oct. 13 - 16/1400 attendees/over 100 exhibitors
2014 - Chicago, IL (Hyatt Regency Chicago)/Sept. 7 - 10/1400 attendees/over 100 exhibitors
2015 - Nashville, TN (The Gaylord Opryland)/Oct. 4 - 7/1400 attendees/over 100 exhibitors

Publications:
CAP TODAY; adv.
CAP@YourService - Newsletter; bi-monthly
CAP@YourService – Residents Issue; quarterly
Membership Directory; on-line
NewsPath; monthly
Pathology & Laboratory Medicine; adv.
STATLINE; bi-weekly
Tips & Tricks - e-notes; quarterly

College of Diplomates of the American Board of Orthodontics (1979)
401 N. Lindbergh Blvd.
St. Louis, MO 63141
Tel: (888) 217-2988 *Fax:* (314) 993-6843
E-Mail: TheCollege@aaortho.org
Website: cdabo.org
Members: 1800 individuals
Staff: 4
Annual Budget: $250-500,000
Tax: 501(c)(6)

Personnel:
Executive Director: Scott Cant
  E-Mail: TheCollege@aaortho.org
Editor: Dr. Irwin Kolin
  E-Mail: irwinort@hotmail.com

Historical Note:
CDABO's mission is to serve its members in their pursuit of excellence in orthodontic care by enhancing the knowledge and skills of orthodontists, advocating board certification, and educating the public and dental community on the merits of board certification by the American Board of Orthodontics. Membership: $100 (Active); $25 (Retired).

Meetings/Conferences: Annual
2013 - Whistler, BC (Fairmont Chateau Whistler Resort)/July 11 - 15
2013 - Southampton, Bermuda (Fairmont Southampton)/July 21 - 25
Number of non-conference events/year: 2

Publications:
CDABO Newsletter; semi-annually

College of Healthcare Information Management Executives (1992)
3300 Washtenaw Ave.
Suite 225
Ann Arbor, MI 48104-4250
Tel: (734) 665-0000 *Fax:* (734) 665-4922
E-Mail: staff@cio-chime.org
Website: cio-chime.org
Members: 1100 individuals
Staff: 9
Annual Budget: $2-5,000,000

Personnel:
President and Chief Executive Officer: Rich A. Correll
  E-Mail: rcorrell@cio-chime.org
Director, Meetings Planning: Susan L. Aldrich
  E-Mail: saldrich@cio-chime.org
Senior Director, Communications: Fred Bazzoli III, CAE
  E-Mail: fbazzoli@cio-chime.org
Senior Director, Advocacy Programs: Sharon Canner
  E-Mail: scanner@cio-chime.org
Vice President, Education and Communications: Keith Fraidenburg
  E-Mail: kfraiden@cio-chime.org
Director, Marketing: Melanie Hilliard
  E-Mail: mhilliard@cio-chime.org
Director, Information Technology: Tamara Kamara
  E-Mail: tkamara@cio-chime.org
Director, Education: Suzy Marzano
  E-Mail: smarzano@cio-chime.org
Senior Director, Membership Development: Anne Wizauer
  E-Mail: awizauer@cio-chime.org

Historical Note:
CHIME's mission is to serve the professional needs of healthcare Chief Information Officers and to advance the strategic application of information technology in innovative ways. Membership: $20,000 (Associate); $40,000 (Standard).

Continuing Education:
Certification Designation/s: CHCIO

Meetings/Conferences: Annual
Conference Chair: Susan L. Aldrich
2013 - New Orleans, LA (Ernest N. Morial Convention Center)/March 3 - 7
Number of non-conference events/year: 5

Publications:
CIO Connection; monthly
Member Directory; on-line

College of Optometrists in Vision Development (1971)
215 W. Garfield Rd.
Suite 200
Aurora, OH 44202
Tel: (330) 995-0718 *Fax:* (330) 995-0719
TollFree: (888) 268-3770
E-Mail: info@covd.org
Website: covd.org
Members: 1700 individuals
Staff: 5
Annual Budget: $500-1,000,000
Tax: 501(c)(3)

Personnel:
Executive Director: Pamela R. Happ CAE
  E-Mail: phapp@covd.org
Coordinator, Meetings: Jackie Cencer
  E-Mail: jcencer@covd.org
Administrative Assistant: Julie Ickes-Jefferson
  E-Mail: julie@covd.org
Editor: Dominick M. Maino FAAO, MEd
  E-Mail: dmaino@covd.org
Membership Assistant: Penny Melkerson-Kirby
  E-Mail: penny@covd.org

Historical Note:
Formed by a merger of the National Optometric Society for developmental vision care, the National Society for Vision and perception training and the southwest developmental vision society. COVD's mission is to improve lives by advancing excellence in optometric vision therapy through education and board certification. Membership: $39-390 (Associate); $42 (Optometric Vision Therapist); $0 (Student); $105 (Affiliate).

Meetings/Conferences: Annual
Conference Chair: Jackie Cencer
2013 - Orlando, FL (Rosen Shingle Creek)/Oct. 8 - 12
2014 - San Diego, CA (Four Points by Sheraton San Diego)/Oct. 21 - 25

Publications:
Optometry & Vision Development (OVD); quarterly

College Reading and Learning Association (1967)
Northern Illinois University
GA 147B
DeKalb, IL 60115
Website: crla.net
Members: 1200 individuals
Staff: 5
Annual Budget: $100-250,000

Personnel:
President: Norm Stahl
  E-Mail: stahl@niu.edu
Treasurer: Rosemarie Woodruff
  E-Mail: woodruff@hawaii.edu

Historical Note:
Formerly Western College Reading Association and Western College Reading and Learning Association. CRLA's mission is to provide college reading and learning professionals an open forum to discover and exchange the leading tools and techniques to enhance student academic success. Membership: $60/year.

Continuing Education:
Certification Designation/s: ITTPC

Meetings/Conferences: Annual
Conference Chair: Norm Stahl
2013 - Boston, MA/Nov. 6 - 9

Publications:
CRLA NewsNotes
Journal of College Reading and Learning; semi-annually

College Savings Foundation
2111 Wilson Blvd.
Suite 700
Arlington, VA 22201
Tel: (703) 351-5091 *Fax:* (703) 351-0743
E-Mail: khamor@collegesavingsfoundation.org
Website: collegesavingsfoundation.org
Members: 30 firms
Staff: 3
Annual Budget: $250-500,000

Personnel:
Executive Director: Kathy V. Hamor
  E-Mail: khamor@collegesavingsfoundation.org
Treasurer: Mary Morris
Media Contact: Lynthia Romney
  E-Mail: romneycom@aol.com

Historical Note:
Mission is to help American families achieve their education savings goals by working with public policy makers, media representatives and financial services industry executives in support of education savings programs. Members include firms that offer 529 college savings programs and/or participate in those programs as investment managers, Associate members include law firms, accounting and consulting firms, governmental and non-profit agencies and individuals who support CSF and its mission.

Membership List Available to Non-members

College Savings Plans Network (1991)
2760 Research Park Dr., P.O. Box 11910
C/O The Council Of State Governments
Lexington, KY 40578-1910
Tel: (859) 244-8175 *Fax:* (859) 244-8001
E-Mail: cspn@csg.org
Website: collegesavings.org
Members: 50 States
Staff: 3

Personnel:
Manager, Programs: Chris Hunter
  E-Mail: cspn@csg.org
Media Contact: Gretchen Steinmiller
  E-Mail: gretchen.steinmiller@fahlgren.com
Treasurer: Lynne Ward

Historical Note:
College Savings Plans Network was formed as an affiliate to the National Association of State Treasurers. CSPN works to improve 529 plans at the federal and state level and serves as a clearinghouse for information among existing programs. Membership: $500-1,500/year.

Meetings/Conferences:
Conference Chair: Chris Hunter

College Sports Information Directors of America (1957)
P.O. Box 7818
Greenwood, IN 46142-6427
Tel: (317) 490-2905
E-Mail: sportsinformation@una.edu
Website: cosida.com
Members: 2800 individuals
Staff: 5
Annual Budget: $500-1,000,000

Personnel:
President: Joe Hornstein (FIU)
  E-Mail: jhornste@fiu.edu
Secretary: Jeff Hodges
  E-Mail: sportsinformation@una.edu
Treasurer: Dave Wohlhueter
  E-Mail: dpw5@cornell.edu

Historical Note:
Originally a section of the American College Public Relations Association, became independent in 1957. CoSIDA works to help the athletic media relations and communications professionals at all levels. Membership: $115 (Active); $125 (Associate); $35 (Student).

Meetings/Conferences: Annual
2013 - Orlando, FL/June 12 - 15/26-50 exhibitors
Number of non-conference events/year: 2

Publications:
Athletics Administration Magazine; adv.
CoSIDA Directory; annually; adv.
CoSIDA E-Digest; adv.
CoSIDA E-Digests; monthly; adv.
CoSIDA E-Newsletter; monthly; adv.

Membership List Available to Non-members

College Swimming Coaches Association of America (1922)
5101 NW 21st Ave.

Suite 200
Ft. Lauderdale, FL 33309
E-Mail: cscaa@swimmingcoach.org
Website: cscaa.org
Members: 3100 Coaches and Colleges and University Swim Teams
Staff: 3
Annual Budget: $250-500,000

Personnel:
Executive Director: Joel Shinofield
  E-Mail: joel@cscaa.org
Contact, Membership Services and Liaison: Matt Hooper
  E-Mail: mhooper@swimmingcoach.org

Historical Note:
Chartered in the State of Florida on September 14, 1967. In 1984, the Women's Swim Coaches Association of America merged with the CSCAA. CSCAA's mission is to serve and provide leadership for the advancement of the sport of swimming at the collegiate level. Membership: $25/year.

Meetings/Conferences: Annual
2013 - Lake Buena Vista, FL (Walt Disney World Resort)/May 15 - 17

Publications:
CSCAA Newsletter

College Theology Society *(1953)*
Religious Studies, Cabrini College
610 King of Prussia Rd.
Radnor, PA 10987
Tel: (610) 902-8419
E-Mail: eprocariofoley@iona.edu
Website: collegetheology.org
Members: 900 individuals
Staff: 5
Annual Budget: $100-250,000

Personnel:
Secretary: Nicholas Rademacher

Historical Note:
Formerly (1967) Society of Catholic College Teachers of Sacred Doctrine. CTS provides opportunities to keep abreast of current activities in the academic study of religion, investigate the relationship of theology/religious studies to other academic disciplines and the place of religion in the total college curriculum. Membership: $50 (Associate); $25 (Student); $60 (Full Professional/Joint Professional).

Meetings/Conferences: Annual
Conference Chair: David Gentry-Akin
2013 - Omaha, NE (Creighton University)/May 30 - June 2
2014 - Latrobe, PA (Saint Vincent's College)/May 29 - June 1

Publications:
Horizons; semi-annually

Collegiate Commissioners Association *(1939)*
2201 Richard Arrington Blvd.
Birmingham, AL 35203
Fax: (205) 458-3031
Members: 32 individuals
Staff: 1
Annual Budget: $50-100,000
Tax: 501(c)(3)

Personnel:
Secretary-Treasurer: Greg Sankey

Historical Note:
Founded as National Association of Football Commissioners; became the National Association of Collegiate Commissioners in 1948 and assumed its present name in 1965. Members are commissioners and staffs of the major collegiate athletic conferences of the U.S. Publishes a number of annual handbooks for officials. Has no paid staff or permanent headquarters. Membership fee: $500/year.

Collision Industry Electronic Commerce Association *(1995)*
3149 Dundee Rd.
Suite 181
Northbrook, IL 60062
Tel: (847) 498-6945 *Fax:* (847) 897-2094
Website: cieca.com
Staff: 3
Annual Budget: $250-500,000
Tax: 501(c)(6)

Personnel:
Executive Director: Fred Iantorno
  E-Mail: fred@cieca.com

Historical Note:
CIECA's mission is to facilitate Electronic Commerce within the Collision Industry by developing technology standards and best practices that lower costs and increase efficiencies in the collision industry. Membership: $1,500 (Association Member); $750-15,000 (Corporate Non-Technology); $1,000-15,000 (Corporate Technology); $150 (Individual).

Meetings/Conferences: Semi-Annual
Conference Chair: Charley Quirt
Number of non-conference events/year: 5

Membership List Available to Non-members

Colombian American Association *(1927)*
641 Lexington Ave.
Suite 1430
New York, NY 10022
Tel: (212) 233-7776 *Fax:* (212) 233-7779
E-Mail: programs@andean-us.com
Website: colombianamerican.org
Members: 55 companies and 100 individuals
Staff: 3
Annual Budget: $50-100,000

Personnel:
Executive President and Chief Executive Officer: Maria Rosa Baquerizo
Executive Secretary: Linda A. Calvet

Historical Note:
CAA's purpose is to facilitate commerce and trade between the Republic of Colombia and the United States, foster and advance cultural relations and goodwill between the two nations, and to encourage safe and sound investments. Membership: $250 (Individual); $650 (Corporate); $2,000 (Supporting); $250 (Overseas Corporate).

Membership List Available to Non-members

The Color Association of the United States *(1915)*
33 Whitehall St.
Suite M3
New York, NY 10004
Tel: (212) 947-7774 *Fax:* (212) 594-6987
E-Mail: info@colorassociation.com
Website: colorassociation.com
Members: 1000 companies
Staff: 3
Annual Budget: $250-500,000

Personnel:
Executive Director: Leslie Harrington PhD
Director, Education: Anat Lechner PhD

Historical Note:
Formerly (1954) Textile Color Card Association of America. Mission is to capture and deliver color value to businesses and educators and empower color conscious decisions. Members are individuals in fashion, textiles, design industries and general traders in which color is a factor. Serves as the authority and arbiter of commercial colors in the US. Membership: $1,500 (Corporate); $250 (Member at large); $750 (Educator); $50 (Student).

Color Marketing Group *(1962)*
1908 Mt.Vernon Ave.
Alexandria, VA 22301
Tel: (703) 329-8500 *Fax:* (703) 329-0155
E-Mail: cmg@colormarketing.org
Website: colormarketing.org
Members: 1300 individuals
Staff: 8
Annual Budget: $500-1,000,000
Tax: 501(c)(6)

Personnel:
Executive Director: Sharon Griffis
  E-Mail: sgriffis@colormarketing.org

Historical Note:
CMG is the international association for color design professionals. CMG's mission is to create color forecast information for professionals who design and market color. Membership: $795 (Individual); $490 (Associate/ Academic); $100 (International, Country Specific); $1680 (Non-Participating); $400 (International Regional); $1000 (Company).

Meetings/Conferences: Semi-Annual
Conference Chair: Sharon Griffis
2013 - Las Vegas, NV (Mandalay Bay Convention Center)/Dec. 31/1-10 exhibitors

---

Color Pigments Manufacturers Association, Inc. *(1925)*
300 N. Washington St.
Suite 105
Alexandria, VA 22314

Tel: (703) 684-4044 *Fax:* (703) 684-1795
E-Mail: cpma@cpma.com
Website: pigments.org
Members: 20 companies
Staff: 3
Annual Budget: $1-2,000,000
Tax: 501(c)(6)

Personnel:
President: J. Lawrence Robinson CAE
  E-Mail: jlr@cpma.com

Historical Note:
Formerly (1993) Dry Color Manufacturers Association. CPMA's mission is to promote the interests of the North American color pigments and color processing industries globally.

Meetings/Conferences: Annual

Colorado Ranger Horse Association *(1938)*
1510 Greenhouse Rd.
Wampum, PA 16157
Tel: (724) 535-4841 *Fax:* (724) 535-4841
E-Mail: ridearangerhorse@yahoo.com
Website: coloradoranger.com
Members: 3100 individuals
Staff: 1
Annual Budget: $10-25,000
Tax: 501(c)(5)

Personnel:
Executive Secretary: Laurel Kosior
  E-Mail: kozyk_farm@hotmail.com

Historical Note:
Members are owners, breeders and enthusiasts of Colorado Ranger horses. Records and registers horses that can trace unbroken and direct descent from one of two foundation sires. Membership: Membership: $5-25/year.

Publications:
Rangerbred News; bi-monthly; adv.

Columbia Scholastic Press Association *(1925)*
Columbia University
Mail Code 5711
New York, NY 10027-6902
Tel: (212) 854-9400 *Fax:* (212) 854-9401
E-Mail: cspa@columbia.edu
Website: cspa.columbia.edu
Staff: 4

Personnel:
Executive Director: Edmund J. Sullivan
  E-Mail: ejs3@columbia.edu
Assistant Director, Meetings: Rebecca Castillo
  E-Mail: rc73@columbia.edu
Assistant Director, Administration: Antonio Rodriguez
  E-Mail: ar245@columbia.edu

Historical Note:
The Association unites student editors and faculty advisers working with them to produce student newspapers, magazines, yearbooks and online media. Membership: $199 (Regular); $169 (Associate); $149 (Basic).

Meetings/Conferences: Annual
Conference Chair: Rebecca Castillo
2013 - New York City, NY (Columbia University)/ March 20 - 22
2014 - New York City, NY (Columbia University)/ March 19 - 21

Publications:
Membership Directory; on-line

Columbia Sheep Breeders Association of America *(1941)*
1371 Dozier Stn. Rd.
Columbia, MO 65202
Tel: (573) 886-9419
E-Mail: columbias@centurytel.net
Website: columbiasheep.webs.com
Members: 600 individuals
Staff: 4
Annual Budget: $100-250,000
Tax: 501(c)(5)

Personnel:
President: Mary Ann Johnson
  E-Mail: hylinefarm@watchtv.net
Executive director: Ann Wehri
  E-Mail: rawehri@gmail.com

Historical Note:
CSBA strives to provide the registration of Columbia sheep and promotion of the mutual interest of the members.

Members are breeders and fanciers of Columbia sheep.
Membership: $20 (Senior); $10 (Junior).

Publications:
Breeder's Directory; annually; adv.
Speaking of Columbias; adv.

Combat Contractor's Association
P.O. Box 2667
Spotsylvania, VA 22553
Tel: (540) 710-9555
E-Mail: CombatContractors@adelphia.net
Staff: 1

Personnel:
General Manager/Owner: Dennis L. Loving
    E-Mail: CombatContractors@adelphia.net

Historical Note:
A self employed rights lobbyist and employment opportunity consulting firm.

Combat Helicopter Pilots Association (2005)
P.O. Box 42
Divide, CO 80814-0045
Tel: (719) 687-4131 *Fax:* (719) 687-4167
TollFree: (800) 832-5144
E-Mail: hq@chpa-us.org
Website: chpa-us.org
Members: 500 individuals
Staff: 4
Annual Budget: $25-50,000
Tax: 501(c)(19)

Personnel:
Vice President: Rusty Bourgoyne
    E-Mail: Membership@chpa-us.org
Executive Director: Jay Brown
    E-Mail: HQ@chpa-us.org
Secretary/Treasurer: Loren McAnally
    E-Mail: Treasurer@chpa-us.org
Vice President: Rich Miller

Historical Note:
CHPA works to organize and unify U.S. armed forces rotary wing aviators from all service branches who have flown helicopter combat missions in support of U.S. national interests. Membership: $30/year (Pilot Member); $20/year (Crew Member); $30/year as Individual or $50/year for Corporate (Friend of CHPA).

Meetings/Conferences: Annual

Publications:
Membership Directory; on-line
The Swash Plate Newsletter; monthly; adv.

The Combustion Institute (1954)
5001 Baum Blvd.
Suite 635
Pittsburgh, PA 15213-1851
Tel: (412) 687-1366 *Fax:* (412) 687-0340
E-Mail: office@combustioninstitute.org
Website: combustioninstitute.org
Members: 4000 individuals
Staff: 3
Annual Budget: $1-2,000,000
Tax: 501(c)(3)

Personnel:
President: Katharina Kohse-Höinghaus
Treasurer: Derek Dunn-Rankin

Historical Note:
CI works to promote and disseminate research in all areas of combustion science. Membership: $40 (Individual); $10 (Student).

Meetings/Conferences: Annual
2013 - Park City, UT (The Canyons Ski Resort)/May 19 - 22

Publications:
Combustion and Flame; monthly
Membership Directory; on-line
Proceedings of the Combustion Institute; biennially

COMISS Network - The Network on Ministry in Specialized Settings (1979)
2301 E. Lamar Blvd., Suite 375
P.O. Box 14
Arlington, VA 76006
Tel: (817) 385-3735 *Fax:* (817) 385-5900
E-Mail: info@comissnetwork.org
Website: comissnetwork.org
Members: 40 organizations
Staff: 2

Annual Budget: $10-25,000
Tax: 501(c)(3)

Personnel:
Treasurer: John Samb

Historical Note:
Founded as the Council on Ministry in Specialized Settings,. COMISS Network's mission is to be committed to the preparation and practice of multi-faith spiritual care through chaplaincy and pastoral counseling in specialized settings and also to promote and supports collaboration among its members. It is also a division of the American Association of Pastoral Counselors.

Meetings/Conferences: Annual

Membership List Available to Non-members

Commercial Finance Association (1944)
370 Seventh Ave.
Suite 1801
New York, NY 10001
Tel: (212) 792-9390 *Fax:* (212) 564-6053
E-Mail: info@cfa.com
Website: cfa.com
Members: 300 member companies and 16 Chapters
Staff: 14
Annual Budget: $2-5,000,000
Tax: 501(c)(6)

Personnel:
Executive Director: Michele Ocejo
    E-Mail: mocejo@cfa.com
Chief Executive Officer: Robert Trojan
Education Associate: Alana Caserta
    E-Mail: acaserta@cfa.com
Chief Operating Officer and Editor-in-Chief: Brian P. Cove
    E-Mail: bcove@cfa.com
Director, Finance and Administration: Ralph Cremone
    E-Mail: ralph@cfa.com
Co-General Counsel: Jonathan N. Helfat
Senior Editor: Eileen Wubbe
    E-Mail: ewubbe@cfa.com

Historical Note:
Founded in 1944, CFA is a trade association representing the asset-based lending and factoring industry. CFA's mission is to to make available current information on legislation and court decisions relating to asset-based financial services.

Meetings/Conferences: Annual
2013 - Los Angeles, CA (JW Marriott Los Angeles L.A. LIVE)/Nov. 13 - 17
2014 - Washington, DC (Washington Marriott Wardman Park)/Nov. 12 - 14
Number of non-conference events/year: 2

Publications:
Lender Directory; on-line
Membership Directory; on-line

Membership List Available to Non-members

Commercial Food Equipment Service Association (1963)
2216 W. Meadowview Rd.
Suite 100
Greensboro, NC 27407
Tel: (336) 346-4700 *Fax:* (336) 346-4745
Website: cfesa.com
Members: 450 companies and 450 Individuals
Staff: 5
Annual Budget: $500-1,000,000

Personnel:
Executive Director: Carla Strickland
    E-Mail: cstrickland@cfesa.com
Director, Membership Services: Heather Price
    E-Mail: hprice@cfesa.com
Administrator, Accounts: Christina Tolbert
    E-Mail: ctolbert@cfesa.com
Director, Marketing: Allison Whatley
    E-Mail: asidders@cfesa.com

Historical Note:
The Mission of CFESA is to anticipate trends and provide services and education to raise standards of performance, help its members meet the challenges of the industry and ensure customer satisfaction. Membership: $746 (Affiliate/ Associate); $115 (Voting).

Continuing Education:
Certification Designation/s: CT, CCP

Meetings/Conferences: Semi-Annual
Conference Chair: Heather Price

Publications:
eNewsletter; monthly; adv.
Membership Directory; on-line; adv.
On Target; bi-monthly; adv.

Commercial Law League of America (1895)
205 N. Michigan Ave.
Suite 2212
Chicago, IL 60601
Tel: (312) 240-1400 *Fax:* (312) 240-1408
TollFree: (800) 978-2552
E-Mail: info@clla.org
Website: clla.org
Members: 3000 individuals
Staff: 10
Annual Budget: $1-2,000,000
Tax: 501(c)(6)

Personnel:
Executive Vice President: Oliver P. Yandle CAE
    E-Mail: oyandle@clla.org
Director, Education: Megan Flesch
    E-Mail: mflesch@clla.org
Director, Membership Services: Marisa Pochter
    E-Mail: mpochter@clla.org

Historical Note:
CCLA's purpose is to act as a source of professional services in the field, to promote standards of professionalism, and to foster economic opportunities for its members in service to the credit industry. Members are commercial, insolvency and bankruptcy law professionals. Membership: $480 (General); $130 (Emerging Professional-Admitted to the bar under 6 years); $50 (Professor/Teacher/Law Clerk/Bankruptcy Section/ Creditors' Rights Section/Editors of Legal Periodicals); $25 (Law Student).

Continuing Education:
Enrollment: 2100

Meetings/Conferences:
2013 - Chicago, IL (Westin Michigan Avenue Chicago)/ April 11 - 14

Publications:
Bankruptcy & Insolvency Section Newsletter; monthly; adv.
Connections Newsletter; monthly; adv.
Debt3; bi-monthly; adv.
DePaul Business & Commercial Law Journal; quarterly
Member Directory; annually; adv.

NAIOP, The Commercial Real Estate Development Association
2201 Cooperative Way
Suite 300
Herndon, VA 22071-3034
Tel: (703) 904-7100 *Fax:* (703) 904-7942
Website: naiop.org
Members: 15000 individuals
Staff: 12
Annual Budget: $250-500,000

Personnel:
President and Chief Executive Officer: Thomas J. Bisacquino
    E-Mail: bisacquino@naiop.org
Contact, Human Resources and National Forums/NAIOP Research Foundation Administrator: Susan Bornt
    E-Mail: bornt@naiop.org
Vice President, Finance: Elizabeth R. Greene
    E-Mail: greene@naiop.org
Vice President, Marketing and Communications: Kathryn George Hamilton
    E-Mail: hamilton@naiop.org
Senior Manager, Web Site and Publications: Sandy Hudson
    E-Mail: hudson@naiop.org
Director, Information Technology: Jorge Romano
    E-Mail: romano@naiop.org
Director, Meetings: Katherine Scheuerman
    E-Mail: scheuerman@naiop.org
Vice President, Membership and Chapter Relations: Marc Selvitelli CAE
    E-Mail: selvitelli@naiop.org
Director, Research and Managing Editor: Elizabeth Sherrod
    E-Mail: sherrod@naiop.org
Vice President for Government Affairs: Aquiles F. Suarez
    E-Mail: suarez@naiop.org
Vice President, Education: James A. Tolliver
    E-Mail: tolliver@naiop.org

Vice President, Information and Research: Sheila K. Vertino
E-Mail: vertino@naiop.org

Historical Note:
Formerly known as National Association of Industrial and Office Properties. An organization for developers, owners and related professionals in office, industrial, retail and mixed-use real estate. NAIOP provides industry networking and education, and advocates for effective legislation on behalf of its members. It advances responsible, sustainable real estate development.

Meetings/Conferences:
2013 - Chicago, IL (Hilton Chicago)/April 15 - 17
2013 - Los Angeles, CA (Omni Los Angeles Hotel at California Plaza)/June 5 - 6
2013 - San Diego, CA (Manchester Grand Hyatt San Diego)/Oct. 7 - 10
2014 - Seatle, WA (Sheraton Seattle Hotel)/May 5 - 7
2014 - Jersey City, NJ (Hyatt Regency Jersey City on the Hudson)/June 12 - 13
2014 - Denver, CO (Sheraton Denver Downtown Hotel)/Oct. 27 - 30
2015 - Toronto, ON (Fairmont Royal York)/Oct. 13 - 16

Publications:
Buyers Guide; on-line
Development; quarterly; adv.
Membership Directory; on-line
NAIOP E-Newsletter; weekly; adv.

Commercial Real Estate Women Network (1989)

1201 Wakarusa Dr.
Suite C3
Lawrence, KS 66049-3803
Tel: (785) 832-1808 Fax: (785) 832-1551
E-Mail: crewnetwork@crewnetwork.org
Website: crewnetwork.org
Members: 8000 members, 58 organizations
Staff: 16
Annual Budget: $2-5,000,000
Tax: 501(c)(6)

Personnel:
Chief Executive Officer: Gail S. Ayers PhD
E-Mail: gaila@network.org
Manager, Events: Linda Bretthauer
E-Mail: lindab@crewnetwork.org
Director, Technology: Mark Brockhoff
E-Mail: markit@crewnetwork.org
Chief Financial Officer, Manager, Finance and Administration: Justin Hawkins
E-Mail: justinh@crewnetwork.org
Director, Marketing and Communications: Denise Kahler
E-Mail: denisek@crewnetwork.org
Graphic Designer and Communications Specialist: Karen Watson
E-Mail: karenw@crewnetwork.org
Manager, Membership Services: Jenny Weissenbach
E-Mail: jennyw@crewnetwork.org

Historical Note:
CREW Network is the product of a merger (1989) of Women in Commercial Real Estate National Network and Commercial Real Estate Women. Starting in 1989, known as National Network of Commercial Real Estate Women until (2001) assumed current name. CREW Network provides a national communication network for women involved in all fields of commercial real estate and assists in the formation of new local groups in cities not currently represented in the National Network. Member organizations are existing, independent, local groups with goals similar to those of the National Network. Membership: $70 (Individual); $75 (Student).

Meetings/Conferences:
Conference Chair: Linda Bretthauer
2013 - Memphis, TN (Memphis Peabody Hotel)/Jan. 31 - Feb. 1
2013 - Scottsdale, AZ (JW Marriott Camelback Inn Scottsdale Resort and Spa)/June 13 - 14

Commercial Space Flight Federation

1725 Eye St. NW
Suite 300
Washington, DC 20006
Tel: (202) 349-1121 Fax: (202) 478-5119
E-Mail: info@commercialspaceflight.org
Website: commercialspaceflight.org
Members: 40 businesses and organizations
Staff: 4

Personnel:
Executive Director: Alex Saltman

E-Mail: saltman@commercialspaceflight.org

Historical Note:
CSFF's mission is to promote the development of commercial human spaceflight, pursue ever higher levels of safety, and share best practices and expertise throughout the industry.

Publications:
Member Listing; on-line

Commercial Vehicle Safety Alliance (1982)

6303 Ivy Ln.
Suite 310
Greenbelt, MD 20770-6319
Tel: (301) 830-6143 Fax: (301) 830-6144
E-Mail: cvsahq@cva.org
Website: cvsa.org
Members: 70 agencies
Staff: 12
Annual Budget: $2-5,000,000
Tax: 501(c)(3)

Personnel:
Executive Director: Stephen A. Keppler
E-Mail: stevek@cvsa.org
Manager, Member and Program Services: Iris R. Leonard
E-Mail: irisl@cvsa.org
Manager, Meetings and Events: Claudia V. McNatt CMP
E-Mail: claudiam@cvsa.org
Deputy Executive Director: Collin Mooney
E-Mail: collinm@cvsa.org
Director, Communications and Marketing: Laura M. Zabriskie
E-Mail: laurazs@cvsa.org

Historical Note:
CVSA's mission is to promote commercial motor vehicle safety and security by providing leadership to enforcement, industry and policy makers. Membership: $950(Organization/Trade Association); $650 (Trucking/Bus Company, Safety Supplier/Vendor, Training Institution, Consultants, Insurance Company, and Others); $450 (State/Provincial Trucking Association); $225 (Small Fleet/Owner Operators).

Meetings/Conferences:
Conference Chair: Iris R. Leonard
2013 - Denver, CO (Hyatt Regency Denver at Colorado Convention Center)/Sept. 16 - 19
Number of non-conference events/year: 24

Publications:
Guardian; quarterly

Commercial Vehicle Solutions Network (2006)

3943-2 Baymeadows Rd.
Jacksonville, FL 32217
Tel: (904) 737-2900 Fax: (904) 636-9881
E-Mail: info@cvsn.org
Website: nationalwheelandrim.org
Members: 100 distributor companies with over 500 locations
Staff: 3
Annual Budget: $250-500,000

Personnel:
Executive Vice President: Angelo Volpe
E-Mail: avolpe@cvsn.org
Contact, Communications: Ramona Greene
E-Mail: rgreene@cvsn.org

Historical Note:
Formed by the merger of the Council of Fleet Specialists (CFS) and the National Wheel and Rim Association (NWRA). CVSN seeks to provide a forum to advocate advanced business practices and education for its members and their supply partners for the betterment of their businesses and the industry as a whole. Members are distributors of parts and services for heavy-duty trucks. Membership: $1,100 (Regular); $1,200-1,700 (Supplier).

Meetings/Conferences: Annual

Publications:
CVSN Insider Newsletter

The Commercial Vehicle Solutions Network (2006)

3943-2 Baymeadows Rd.
Jacksonville, FL 32217
Tel: (904) 737-2900 Fax: (904) 636-9881
E-Mail: info@cvsn.org
Website: cvsn.org
Members: 100 distributors
Staff: 2
Annual Budget: $250-500,000

Personnel:
Executive Vice President: Angelo Volpe
E-Mail: avolpe@cvsn.org
Treasurer: Dave Willis
E-Mail: crwdnw@aol.com

Historical Note:
Formerly, (1967) Council of Fleet Specialists; assumed current name on January 1, 2006, after the merger of the Council of Fleet Specialists (CFS) and the National Wheel and Rim Association (NWRA). CVSN seeks to create an industry-wide forum for professional development, legislative awareness and business opportunities by utilizing broad industry cooperation, education and the exchange of information throughout the channel. Members are distributors of parts and servicers for heavy-duty trucks. Membership: $1150/year.

Meetings/Conferences: Annual
Number of non-conference events/year: 2

Publications:
CVSN Insider Newsletter

Membership List Available to Non-members

Commercial Vehicle Training Association

7005 Backlick Ct.
Suite 100
Springfield, VA 22151
Tel: (703) 642-9444 Fax: (703) 642-3334
Website: cvta.org
Members: 44 Motor Carrier Members and Associate Members
Staff: 3
Annual Budget: $250-500,000

Personnel:
Executive Director: K. Michael O'Connell
E-Mail: mike@cvta.org
Deputy Director: Cindy Atwood
E-Mail: ccatwood@cvta.org
Webmaster, Scholarship and Certification Programs: Charlie Kim

Historical Note:
CVTA is a national trade association representing the proprietary truck driving schools in United States and Canada. Committed to promote the quality standards for commercial driver training schools. Has 49 regular member schools that operate 180 training sites in the United States. Membership: $500 (Regular).

Meetings/Conferences: Semi-Annual
Conference Chair: Cindy Atwood

Publications:
Digest Dispatch; on-line
Membership Directory; on-line

Commission on Accreditation for Law Enforcement Agencies Incorporation (1979)

13575 Heathcote Blvd.
Suite 320
Gainesville, VA 20155
Tel: (703) 352-4225 Fax: (703) 890-3126
TollFree: (800) 368-3757
E-Mail: calea@calea.org
Website: calea.org
Members: 800 law enforcement agencies
Staff: 16
Annual Budget: $2-5,000,000

Personnel:
Executive Director: Sylvester Daughtry Jr.
E-Mail: sdaughtry@calea.org
Manager, Administrative Services: Antonio T. Beatty
E-Mail: abeatty@calea.org
Associate Director: James D. Brown
E-Mail: jbrown@calea.org
Communications Specialist and E-Communique Editor: Janice Dixon
E-Mail: jdixon@calea.org
Program Manager: Christie Goddard
E-Mail: cgoddard@calea.org
Contract Specialist: Wendi Jones
E-Mail: wjones@calea.org
Coordinator, Information Technology: Linda L. Phillips
E-Mail: lphillips@calea.org

Historical Note:
Established through union of International Chiefs of Police and Black Law Enforcement Executives. Mission is to improve the delivery of public safety services, primarily by: maintaining a body of standards, developed by public safety practitioners, covering a wide range of up-to-date public safety initiatives; establishing and administering

an accreditation process; and recognizing professional excellence. Membership fee varies, based on size of agency.

Meetings/Conferences: Annual
Conference Chair: Wendi Jones
2013 - Charleston, SC/March 20 - 23
2013 - Columbus, OH/July 31 - Aug. 3
2013 - Winston-Salem, NC/Nov. 13 - 16

Publications:
CALEA News; monthly
CALEA Update Magazine

Commission on Accreditation of Allied Health Education Programs *(1994)*
1361 Park St.
Clearwater, FL 33756
Tel: (727) 210-2350 *Fax:* (727) 210-2354
E-Mail: mail@caahep.org
Website: caahep.org
Members: 70 sponsoring organizations
Staff: 4
Annual Budget: $500-1,000,000
Tax: 501(c)(3)

Personnel:
Executive Director: Kathleen Megivern
     E-Mail: megivern@caahep.org
Contact, Information and Communications: Lorna Frazier-Lindsey
     E-Mail: lorna@caahep.org
Executive Assistant and Meeting Planner: Cynthia Jackson-McNeill
     E-Mail: cynthia@caahep.org
Contact, Accreditation Services: Theresa Sisneros
     E-Mail: theresa@caahep.org

Historical Note:
Formerly known as the Committee on Allied Health Education and Accreditation till 1994. CAAHEP is a programmatic post secondary accrediting agency recognized by the Council for Higher Education Accreditation, carries out its accrediting activities in cooperation with sixteen review committees (Committees on Accreditation). Membership: $3,000 (Sponsoring Organization); $450 (Accredited Institution).

Meetings/Conferences:
2013 - Charleston, SC (Francis Marion Hotel)/April 14 - 15
Number of non-conference events/year: 12

Publications:
The Communiqué

Commission on Professionals in Science and Technology *(1953)*
1200 New York Ave. NW
Suite 113
Washington, DC 20005
Tel: (202) 326-7080 *Fax:* (202) 842-1603
E-Mail: info@cpst.org
Website: cpst.org
Members:
40 corporate
700 individuals
20 societies
Staff: 4
Annual Budget: $100-250,000
Tax: 501(c)(3)

Personnel:
Interim Executive Director: Norman L. Fortenberry
     E-Mail: nfortenb@nae.edu
Associate, Member Services: Felice Boglin
     E-Mail: fboglin@cpst.org
Manager, Publications: Carolyn Brandi
     E-Mail: cbrandi@cpst.org
Web Developer and Internet Consultant: Ernest Burkhalter
     E-Mail: service@cpst.org

Historical Note:
Formerly (1986) Scientific Manpower Commission. A private non-profit corporation formed by 14 scientific societies to collect, synthesize, analyze and disseminate reliable information about the science and engineering workforce in the United States. CPST's provides with the recruitment, training and utilization of scientific personnel by educational institutions, industry and government for the optimum benefit to the nation. Membership: $75 (Individual); $900-1,800 (Academic/Non- Profit); $1,5000-3,000 (Corporate); $150-250 (Subscription).

Meetings/Conferences:
Conference Chair: Felice Boglin
Number of non-conference events/year: 1

Publications:
A Total Human Resources Data Compendium; biennially
Salaries of Scientists, Engineers and Technicians; biennially
STEM in the States
STEM Trends

Commissioned Officers Association of the United States Public Health Service *(1947)*
8201 Corporate Dr.
Suite 200
Landover, MD 20785
Tel: (301) 731-9080 *Fax:* (301) 731-9084
TollFree: (866) 366-9593
Website: coausphs.org
Members: 7000 individuals
Staff: 7
Annual Budget: $500-1,000,000
Tax: 501(c)(6)

Personnel:
Executive Director: Gerard Farrell USN (Ret.)
     E-Mail: gfarrell@coausphs.org
Director, Administration: Teresa Hayden Foley
     E-Mail: thayden@coausphs.org
Director, Development: Brian F. McSheffrey
     E-Mail: bmcsheffrey@coausphs.org
Director, Government Relations: Judith Rensberger
     E-Mail: jrensberger@coausphs.org
Coordinator, Membership Services and Editor: Malissa Spalding
     E-Mail: mspalding@coausphs.org
Manager, Database: Donna Sparrow
     E-Mail: dsparrow@coausphs.org

Historical Note:
COA's mission is to improve and protect the public health of the United States by advocating for the commissioned corps and its officers. Membership: $85-140 (Active/Retired); $30 (Co-step/Student); $55 (Former Commissioned Officer/Associate/Civilian).

Meetings/Conferences:
Number of non-conference events/year: 1

Publications:
Frontline; irregular
Membership Directory; on-line

Committee of 200 *(1982)*
980 N. Michigan Ave.
Suite 1575
Chicago, IL 60611-7540
Tel: (312) 255-0296 *Fax:* (312) 255-0789
E-Mail: info@c200.org
Website: c200.org
Members: 494 individuals
Staff: 6
Annual Budget: $2-5,000,000
Tax: 501(c)(6)

Personnel:
Administrator, Research and Database: Miranda Ehmke
     E-Mail: mehmke@c200.org
Director, External Relations: Meghan McRae
     E-Mail: mmcrae@c200.org
Director, Membership Services: Amy O'Keeffe
     E-Mail: aokeeffe@c200.org
Chief Financial Officer: Greg Stegeman
     E-Mail: gstegeman@c200.org
Director, Programs: Judy Waak-Pearce
     E-Mail: jpearce@c200.org

Historical Note:
C200 is an international organization of business women whose mission is to foster, celebrate and advance women's leadership in business. Members are drawn from the highest ranks of women executives in successful private and public companies. Membership is by invitation only. Membership: $1,800/year (Individual).

Meetings/Conferences: Annual

Publications:
C200 Newsletter; on-line
Member Directory; on-line

Committee of Annuity Insurers *(1981)*
1455 Pennsylvania Ave. NW, Suite 1200
C/O Davis & Harman
Washington, DC 20004
Tel: (202) 347-2230 *Fax:* (202) 393-3310
E-Mail: CAI@davis-harman.com
Website: annuity-insurers.org

Members: 31 companies
Staff: 1

Personnel:
Tax Counsel: Joseph F. McKeever III
     E-Mail: jfmckeever@davis-harman.com

Historical Note:
A 30-member coalition of life insurance companies that issue annuities. Committee was formed in 1981 to address Federal legislative and regulatory issues confronting the annuity industry and to participate in the development of Federal tax policy affecting annuities.

Publications:
Membership Directory; on-line

Committee of Interns and Residents/ SEIU *(1957)*
520 Eighth Ave., Suite 1200
New York, NY 10018
Tel: (212) 356-8100 *Fax:* (212) 356-8111
TollFree: (800) 247-8877
Website: cirseiu.org
Members: 13000 residents
Staff: 80
Annual Budget: $5-10,000,000

Personnel:
Executive Director: Eric Scherzer MPH
Director, Communications: Heather Appel
     E-Mail: happel@cirseiu.org

Historical Note:
Affiliated with the Service Employees International Union (SEIU), CIR/SEIU brings together housestaff in a chapter-based organization whose purpose is to represent its doctor-members and the interests of the patients and communities they serve through the use of collective bargaining and resident advocacy. Members are interns, residents, and fellows from all member hospitals.

Publications:
CIR Vitals

Committee on History in the Classroom *(1971)*
Deptartment of History
Purdue University
West LaFayette, IN 47907-1365
Tel: (765) 494-4122 *Fax:* (765) 496-1755
Website: theaha.org/affiliates/ comt_his_classroom.htm
Members: 200 individuals
Staff: 1

Personnel:
Secretary-Treasurer: Grodon R. Mork

Historical Note:
CHC members are history teachers from both the secondary and post-secondary levels and others with an interest in the scholarship of teaching. Has no paid officers or full-time staff. Annual meetings held in conjunction with American Historical Association. Membership: $10/year (individual).

Committee on Lesbian and Gay History *(1979)*
C/O Rutgers University-Newark
Department of History, 175 University Ave.
Newark, NJ 07102
Website: clgbthistory.org
Members: 350 individuals and organizations
Staff: 6
Annual Budget: Under $10,000

Personnel:
Editor: Timothy Stewart-Winter
     E-Mail: timsw@andromeda.rutgers.edu

Historical Note:
Formerly the Committee on Lesbian and Gay History, the Committee on Lesbian, Gay, Bisexual, and Transgender History and is an affiliated society of the American Historical Association. CLGBTH seeks to prevent discrimination against gay, lesbian and transgender historians. Members are scholars from a variety of disciplines and others with an interest in the study of homosexuality in the past and present. Membership: $5-150/year.

Publications:
CLGBTH Newsletter; annually
Committee on LGBT History Newsletter; annually
Membership Directory; annually

Commodity Markets Council
1300 L St. NW
Suite 1020
Washington, DC 20005
Tel: (202) 842-0400 *Fax:* (202) 789-7223
Website: commoditymkts.org

Members: 36 Companies
Staff: 5
Annual Budget: $500-1,000,000

Personnel:
President: Sanjeev Joshipura
 E-Mail: sanjeev.joshipura@commoditymkts.org
Director, Events, Marketing and Membership: Erin E. Kelly
 Ball
 E-Mail: erin.kellyball@commoditymkts.org
Contact, Communications and Policy Associate: Meghan
 Tran
 E-Mail: meghan.tran@commoditymkts.org

Historical Note:
*Formerly known as the National Grain Trade Council;
assumed its current name in 2006. CMC advocates
open, competitive commerce by combining the expertise,
knowledge and resources of its members to develop and
support market-based policy. CMC provides the access,
forum and action for exchanges and exchange users to
take a leadership role in addressing global market and risk
management issues. Membership: $6,000 (Small); $10,000
(Medium); $18,000 (Large); $20,000 (International).*

Meetings/Conferences: Annual
Conference Chair: Erin E. Kelly Ball
2013 - Miami, FL (St. Regis Bal Harbour Resort)/Jan.
 27 - 29

Publications:
CMC Insight; monthly
CMC Newsletter; weekly

Common - A Users Group
8770 W. Bryn Mawr Ave.
Suite 1350
Chicago, IL 60631
Tel: (312) 279-0192 *Fax:* (312) 279-0227
E-Mail: common@common.org
Website: common.org
Staff: 9
Annual Budget: $2-5,000,000

Personnel:
Executive Director: Ralph Gervasi
 E-Mail: Ralph_Gervasi@common.org
Manager, Conferences and Expo: Wynn Burke
 E-Mail: wynn_burke@common.org
Representative, Membership Services and Registration:
 Kelly Burns
 E-Mail: Kelly_Burns@common.org
Project Manager, Education: Ian Cartwright
 E-Mail: ian_cartwright@common.org
Manager, Human Resources: Angela Myrick
 E-Mail: Angela_Myrick@common.org
Manager, Information Technology: Fred Pritchard
 E-Mail: Fred_Pritchard@common.org
Manager, Marketing: Manzoor Siddiqui
 E-Mail: manzoor_siddiqui@common.org

Historical Note:
*COMMON is the community of IBM midrange users
providing information, education, and networking among
users, IBM, and related third-party solution providers. The
mission is to foster leadership in the business computing
industry and provide advocacy on business computing
issues. Membership: $156 (Individual); $495 (Corporate);
$395 (Local User Group).*

Continuing Education:
Certification Designation/s: CCBCP, CBCA

Meetings/Conferences: Annual
Conference Chair: Wynn Burke
2013 - Austin, TX (Hilton Austin)/April 7 - 10

Publications:
COMMON.CONNECT; bi-monthly
Connector e-Newsletter; monthly
Membership Directory

Communications Fraud Control Association
(1985)
Four Becker Farm Rd., Fourth Floor
P.O. Box 954
Roseland, NJ 07068
Tel: (973) 871-4032 *Fax:* (973) 871-4075
E-Mail: fraud@cfca.org
Website: cfca.org
Members: 150 individuals and 150 companies
Staff: 3
Annual Budget: $100-250,000
Tax: 501(c)(6)

Personnel:
Executive Director: Roberta Aronoff

 E-Mail: raronoff@jhcohn.com
Administrative Manager: Katie Kaczorowski
 E-Mail: kkaczorowski@jhcohn.com

Historical Note:
*CFCA's mission is to support and advocate cooperation
inside and outside the communications industry regarding
communications fraud control. Membership consists of
carriers, private network owners, end-users and government
and law enforcement agencies worldwide. Membership:
$2,000-3,300 (Corporate Carrier); $1,900-2,500
(Corporate Industry); $0 (Law Enforcement); $50 (Retired).*

Continuing Education:
Certification Designation/s: CCSP

Meetings/Conferences:
2013 - New Orleans, LA (Loews New Orleans Hotel)/
 Feb. 19 - 21
2013 - Toronto, ON (Royal York Hotel)/June 4 - 6
2013 - Seatle, WA (Monaco Seattle, a Kimpton Hotel)/
 Oct. 8 - 10
Number of non-conference events/year: 1

Publications:
Membership Directory; on-line
The Communicator; quarterly

Communications Marketing Association *(1974)*
P.O. Box 5680
Lago Vista, TX 78645
E-Mail: CMAExecDirector@aol.com
Website: cma-cmc.org
Members: 400 individuals
Staff: 3
Annual Budget: $50-100,000

Personnel:
Executive Director: Karen Hollingsworth
 E-Mail: CMAExecDirector@aol.com
Chair, Sponsorship: Carroll Hollingsworth
 E-Mail: dhlago@aol.com

Historical Note:
*CMA was formed to support the relationship between
independent representatives, distributors and the
manufacturers they represent. Membership is comprised
of manufacturers, manufacturer's representatives and
distributors in the wireless communications industry.
Membership: $295 (Representative Company/Distributor
Company); $395 (Manufacturer Company).*

Meetings/Conferences: Annual
Conference Chair: Carroll Hollingsworth

Publications:
CMA Newsletter

Communications Media Management Association
(1946)
20423 State Rd Seven
Suite F6-491
Boca Raton, FL 33498
Tel: (561) 477-8100
E-Mail: cmma@cmma.org
Website: cmma.org
Members: 160 individuals
Staff: 4
Annual Budget: $250-500,000
Tax: 501(c)(6)

Personnel:
Executive Director: Jody B. Rosen APR
 E-Mail: executive.director@cmma.org
Director, Membership Services: C. Ramiro Banderas
 E-Mail: rbanderas@rollins.com
Director, Marketing: Tom Bowman
 E-Mail: tom.bowman@us.mcd.com
Director, Program: Robin Martin
 E-Mail: robin.martin@safeway.com

Historical Note:
*Formerly Industrial Audio-Visual Association and Audio
Visual Management Association. CMMA is a professional
society of individuals managing communications media
departments in business, government and education.
Membership: $350 (Active); $250 (Affiliate).*

Meetings/Conferences: Annual

Publications:
CMMA E-visions; monthly

Communications Supply Service Association
(1976)
5700 Murray St.
Little Rock, AR 72209
Tel: (501) 562-7666 *Fax:* (501) 562-7616
TollFree: (800) 252-2772

Website: cssa.net
Members: 300 companies
Staff: 27
Annual Budget: $5-10,000,000

Personnel:
Association President and Chief Executive Officer: John
 Howard Brown
Manager, Sales and Services: Sue Cabe
Director , Enterprise Sales and Technical Services: Mike
 Rew
Senior Vice President, Finance and Administration: Allison
 Richardson
Manager, Marketing: Kelly Rigby
 E-Mail: kellyr@cssa.net

Historical Note:
*CSSA is a strategic alliance of independent telephone
companies created to promote the development of rural
telephone companies and focus on distributing technology-
related products and services based on the needs of its
membership. Members are small independent telephone
companies. Membership: $100/year (Individual).*

Meetings/Conferences:
Conference Chair: Kelly Rigby

Publications:
Member Directory; on-line

Communications Workers of America *(1938)*
501 Third St. NW
Washington, DC 20001-2797
Tel: (202) 434-1100
E-Mail: cwaweb@cwa-union.org
Website: cwa-union.org
Members: 700000 Individuals
Staff: 600
Annual Budget: Over $100,000,000
Tax: 501(c)(5)

Personnel:
President: Larry Cohen
Contact, Conferences: Nancy Biagini
 E-Mail: nbiagini@cwa-union.org
Secretary and Treasurer: Annie Hill
 E-Mail: ahill@cwa-union.org
Director, Communications: Candice Johnson
 E-Mail: cjohnson@cwa-union.org
General Counsel: Mary K. O'Melveny
 E-Mail: maryo@cwa-union.org
Director, Government Affairs: Stephen Schembs

Historical Note:
*Formerly (1947) National Federation of Telephone Workers.
Joined the Congress of Industrial Organizations in 1949
and merged with Telephone Workers Organizing Committee.
Communications Workers of America holds national
affiliation with AFL-CIO. Absorbed International Union
of Electronic, Electrical, Salaried Machine and Furniture
Workers in 2001. CWA's mission is to improve the
standard of living for its current and future members and
to educate members to vote in their own interests and to
build community coalitions at the national and local levels
to support workers' rights.*

Meetings/Conferences: Annual
Conference Chair: Nancy Biagini
2013 - Pittsburgh, PA/April 22 - 23
Number of non-conference events/year: 3

Publications:
CWA News

Community Action Partnership *(1971)*
1140 Connecticut Ave. NW
Suite 1210
Washington, DC 20036
Tel: (202) 265-7546 *Fax:* (202) 265-5048
E-Mail: info@communityactionpartnership.com
Website: communityactionpartnership.com
Members: 700 agencies and 1400 individuals
Staff: 10
Annual Budget: $2-5,000,000
Tax: 501(c)(3)

Personnel:
President and Chief Executive Officer: Donald W. Mathis
 E-Mail: dmathis@communityactionpartnership.com
Director, Training and Technical Assistance: Lindley "Lil"
 Dupree
 E-Mail: ldupree@communityactionpartnership.com
Director, Fiscal Management: Linda Goff
 E-Mail: lgoff@communityactionpartnership.com
Director, Communications: Lisa Holland
 E-Mail: lholland@communityactionpartnership.com

Director, CCAP Program: Dr. James "Jim" Lopresti
Contact, Administrative and Member Services: Sranda
  Watkins
  E-Mail:
  swatkins@communityactionpartnership.com
Manager, Technical Support: Michael Weisman
  E-Mail:
  mweisman@communityactionpartnership.com
Vice President: Avril Weisman
  E-Mail:
  aweisman@communityactionpartnership.com

Historical Note:
*Founded as National Community Action Agency Executive
Directors Association; became National Association of
Community Action Agencies in 1982, and assumed its
current name in 2002. CAP's mission is to strengthen,
promote, represent and serve its network of member
agencies to assure that the issues of the poor are effectively
heard and addressed. Members are community action and
limited purpose agencies. Membership: $325-3,600/year
(varies on CSBG funding level).*

Continuing Education:
Certification Designation/s: CCAP

Meetings/Conferences: Annual
Conference Chair: Dr. James "Jim" Lopresti

Publications:
Directory of Community Action Agencies; annually
eNewsletter; weekly
The Promise; quarterly; adv.

Community Associations Institute (CAI) *(1973)*
6402 Arlington Blvd.
Suite 500
Falls Church, VA 22042
Tel: (703) 970-9220 *Fax:* (703) 970-9558
Website: caionline.org
Members: 31600 members
Staff: 49
Annual Budget: $10-25,000,000
Tax: 501(c)(6)

Personnel:
Chief Executive Officer: Thomas M. Skiba CAE
  E-Mail: tskiba@caionline.org
Director, Meetings: Holly Carson CMP
  E-Mail: hcarson@caionline.org
Vice President, Government and Public Affairs: Andrew S.
  Fortin
  E-Mail: afortin@caionline.org
Advertising Manager: Marc Ingram
  E-Mail: mingram@caionline.org
Vice President, Education: Dave Jennings CAE, SPHR
  E-Mail: djennings@caionline.org
Vice President, Communications: Frank Rathbun
  E-Mail: frathbun@caionline.org

Historical Note:
*CAI's mission is to inspire professionalism, effective
leadership and responsible citizenship. Members include
community association volunteer leaders, professional
managers, community management firms and other
professionals and companies that provide products and
services to associations. Membership: $0-10,000/year.*

Meetings/Conferences:
Conference Chair: Holly Carson CMP
2013 - San Diego, CA (Hilton San Diego Bayfront)/
  April 17 - 20/26-50 exhibitors

Publications:
CEO Insights; bi-monthly; adv.
Common Ground Magazine; bi-monthly; adv.
Community Association Law Reporter; monthly; adv.
Community Manager Newsletter; bi-monthly; adv.
Fast Tracks; adv.
Minutes; bi-monthly; adv.

Membership List Available to Non-members

Community Banking Advisors Network *(1995)*
624 Grassmere Park Dr.
Suite 15
Nashville, TN 37211
Tel: (615) 373-9880 *Fax:* (615) 377-7092
TollFree: (800) 231-2524
E-Mail: info@bankingcpas.com
Website: bankingcpas.com
Members: 30 firms
Staff: 6

Personnel:
Executive Director: Patrick Pruett
  E-Mail: patrick@the-apa.com

Historical Note:
*CBAN is an association of CPA firms that concentrate on
substantial portion of their business by providing financial
and consulting services to community banks and financial
institutions. Membership $1,695/year (Based on Territorial
Structure).*

Publications:
Memberhsip Directory; on-line

Community College Business Officers
P.O. Box 5565
Charlottesville, VA 22905-5565
Tel: (434) 293-2825 *Fax:* (434) 245-8453
E-Mail: info@ccbo.org
Website: ccbo.org
Members: 335 business operations
Staff: 3
Annual Budget: $100-250,000
Tax: 501(c)(6)

Personnel:
Managing Director: Heather Browne
  E-Mail: heather@ccbo.org

Historical Note:
*CCBO is committed to providing educational and
professional support, networking opportunities, and timely
trend and demographic information for business officers
representing community colleges and community college
system offices in the US and in Canada. Membership: $210
(Individual); $410 (Institutional); $565 (Business Partner).*

Meetings/Conferences: Annual
Conference Chair: Heather Browne
2013 - Palm Spring, CA (Westin Mission Hills Resort
  and Spa)/Sept. 28 - Oct. 1
2014 - San Antonio, TX (Crowne Plaza San Antonio
  Riverwalk)/Sept. 20 - 23
2015 - Las Vegas, NV (Treasure Island Resort and
  Casino)/Sept. 19 - 22
2016 - Orlando, FL (Disney's Contemporary Resort)/
  Sept. 24 - 27

Publications:
The Bottom Line; quarterly; adv.

Community College Journalism Association *(1968)*
20550 Wells Dr.
Woodland, CA 91364
Fax: (805) 492-9800
Website: ccjaonline.org
Members: 300 individuals
Staff: 2
Annual Budget: Under $10,000

Personnel:
President: Toni Albertson
  E-Mail: talbertson@mtsac.edu
Vice President: John Kerezy
  E-Mail: john.kerezy@tri-c.edu

Historical Note:
*Formerly the Junior College Journalism Association.
Members are journalism instructors in community and
junior colleges. Affiliated with the Association for Education
in Journalism. Membership: $40/year.*

Community Colleges Humanities Association *(1979)*
C/O Essex County College
303 University Ave.
Newark, NJ 07102
Tel: (973) 877-3577 *Fax:* (973) 877-3578
Website: ccha-assoc.org
Members: 965 colleges and individuals
Staff: 5
Annual Budget: $50-100,000
Tax: 501(c)(3)

Personnel:
Executive Director: David Berry
  E-Mail: dberry@ccha-assoc.org
Editor: Jacob Agatucci
  E-Mail: jagatucci@cocc.edu
Office Manager: Jessica DaSilva
  E-Mail: berry.ccha@earthlink.net

Historical Note:
*CCHA strives to strengthen the humanities in the
nation's community colleges.serves as a catalyst for
defining the issues which face humanities faculty and
administrators today, finding solutions to problems in
the field, and establishing a communications network for
humanists.CCHA affiliated with American Association
of Community Colleges,American Council of Learned
Societies, American Historical Association, Modern
Language Association, National Humanities Alliance
and Organization of American Historians. Members are
administrators and humanities faculty from two-year
colleges. Membership: $40 (Individual, full-time); $15
(Individual, part- time); $300-500 (Institution); $850
(Institutional Sponsor).*

Meetings/Conferences: Annual

Publications:
Member Directory; on-line
The Humanist Newsletter; adv.

Community Development Society *(1969)*
222 Gentry Hall
Columbia, MO 65211
Tel: (573) 884-0669
E-Mail: cds@assnoffice.com
Website: comm-dev.org
Members: 300 individuals
Staff: 3
Annual Budget: $50-100,000

Personnel:
President: Sharon Gulick
  E-Mail: gulicks@missouri.edu

Historical Note:
*CDS integrates knowledge from many disciplines with
theory, research, teaching, and practice as important and
interdependent functions that are vital in the public and
private sectors. Members are academics and practitioners in
community development. Membership: $65-75 (Student);
$130-150 (Regular); $200 (Library-In US); $220 (Library-
In other countries); $95-115 (Retiree).*

Meetings/Conferences: Annual
Conference Chair: Bo Beaulieu
2013 - Charleston, SC (Francis Marion Hotel)/July 20
  - 24

Publications:
Journal of the CDS; semi-annually; adv.
Vanguard Newsletter; quarterly

Community Development Venture Capital Alliance *(1993)*
424 W. 33rd St.
Suite 320
New York, NY 10001
Tel: (212) 594-6747 *Fax:* (212) 594-6717
E-Mail: cdvca@cdvca.org
Website: cdvca.org
Members: 100 corporations and organizations
Staff: 8
Annual Budget: $500-1,000,000
Tax: 501(c)(3)

Personnel:
President: Kerwin Tesdell
  E-Mail: ktesdell@cdvca.org
Managing Director: Gary Brooks
  E-Mail: gbrooks@cdvca.org
Coordinator, Programs: Eliza Chu

Historical Note:
*CDVCA promotes the field by combining advocacy,
education, communications, and best-practice dissemination
through conferences and workshops. Membership: $500/
year.*

Meetings/Conferences:
Conference Chair: Eliza Chu

Publications:
Ventures; quarterly

Membership List Available to Non-members

Community Financial Services Association of America CFSA *(1999)*
515 King St.
Suite 300
Alexandria, VA 22314
Tel: (888) 572-9329 *Fax:* (703) 684-1219
E-Mail: Info@CFSAA.com
Website: cfsaa.com
Members: 150 companies
Staff: 10
Annual Budget: $5-10,000,000

Personnel:
Chief Policy Officer: Charles Halloran
Director, Communications and Research: Amy Cantu
  E-Mail: ACantu@CFSAA.com
Manager, Communications and Public Affairs: Jacqueline
  Gilbert
  E-Mail: JGilbert@CFSAA.com

Senior Vice President, Media Relations: Steven Schlein
    E-Mail: SSchlein@Dezenhall.com

Historical Note:
CFSA provides paycheck advances and related financial services for consumers. Promotes legislation and regulation that provides payday advance customers with substantive consumer protections while preserving their access to short-term credit for millions of Americans.

Meetings/Conferences: Annual

Publications:
MembershipDirectory; on-line

Membership List Available to Non-members

Community Health Charities of America *(1940)*
1240 N. Pitt St.
Third floor
Alexandria, VA 22314
Tel: (703) 528-1007 *Fax:* (703) 528-1365
TollFree: (800) 654-0845
E-Mail: info@healthcharities.org
Website: healthcharities.org
Members: 46 Offices
Staff: 5
Tax: 501(c)(3)

Personnel:
President and Chief Executive Officer: Thomas G.
    Bognanno
Vice President, Marketing and Communications: James
    Gallisdorfer
Vice President, Finance: Molly Gravholt
Manager, Web Communications: Regina Meeks
Chief Operating Officer: Harold Samorian

Historical Note:
CHC's mission is to enhance the operations, programs and services of its member health-related charities through access to workplace giving and to provide employees at work sites access to the full range of information in order to improve the health and well-being of employees and to encourage community involvement.

Publications:
Membership Directory; on-line
Newsletter; monthly

Community Managers International Association
1007 Hemlock Farms
Lords Valley, PW 18428
Tel: (570) 775-4200 *Fax:* (570) 775-7370
E-Mail: cmiamanager@gmail.com
Website: cmiamanager.org
Staff: 3
Annual Budget: $10-25,000
Tax: 501(c)(6)

Personnel:
President: Mike Sibio
    E-Mail: msibio@excite.com

Historical Note:
CMIA's mission is to provide an environment for exchange of ideas and member services and to work with other national and state organizations to improve community association management profession. Membership: $150 (General Manager/Senior Manager/Affiliate).

Meetings/Conferences: Annual
Number of non-conference events/year: 1

Publications:
CMIA Newsletter; on-line

Community Transportation Association of America *(1989)*
1341 G St. NW
Tenth Floor
Washington, DC 20005
Tel: (800) 891-0590 *Fax:* (202) 737-9197
TollFree: (800) 891-0590
Website: ctaa.org
Members: 500 individuals and 4500 companies
and systems
Staff: 29
Annual Budget: $5-10,000,000
Tax: 501(c)(3)

Personnel:
Executive Director: Dale J. Marsico CCTM
    E-Mail: marsico@ctaa.org
Director, Communications: Scott Bogren
    E-Mail: bogren@ctaa.org
Director, Finance: Donald Browner
    E-Mail: browner@ctaa.org

Training Coordinator: Len Cahill
    E-Mail: cahill@ctaa.org
Technical Assistance Specialist: Robert Carlson
    E-Mail: carlson@ctaa.org
Director, Membership Services: Caryn R. Souza
    E-Mail: souza@ctaa.org
Director, Human Services: Chris Zeilinger
    E-Mail: zeilinger@ctaa.org

Historical Note:
CTAA is a professional association focusing on serving transit agencies in rural areas, small cities and wherever elderly, disabled or poor persons do not have access to conventional public transit. Members include transit operators, human service agencies, consultants, industry suppliers and state officials. Membership: $25-500/year.

Continuing Education:
Certification Designation/s: PASS, CCTM, CTPA, CCTS,
CCSM, PDS, VMMI, CTPA

Meetings/Conferences: Annual
Conference Chair: Len Cahill

Publications:
2011 Community Transportation Buyers Guide; on-line
Community Transportation Magazine; bi-monthly
Fast Mail
Fast Mail for RAIL
Rail Magazine; quarterly; adv.
Tappy Grams; monthly

Membership List Available to Non-members

Compact Loader/Compact Excavator Council *(1982)*
6737 W. Washington St.
Suite 2400
Milwaukee, WI 53214-5647
Tel: (414) 272-0943 *Fax:* (414) 272-1170
E-Mail: aem@aem.org
Website: aem.org/Groups/Groups/Group.asp?
    G = 14#.T1eEF8DC
Staff: 1

Personnel:
Technical and Safety Services Manager: John Wagner

Historical Note:
Facilitating information sharing and meaningful dialogue between member companies on technical, regulatory and safety issues.

Comparative and International Education Society *(1956)*
University at Albany
Albany, NY 12222
Tel: (518) 442-5083 *Fax:* (518) 442-5084
Website: cies.us
Members: 1000 institutions and individual
Staff: 4
Annual Budget: $250-500,000
Tax: 501(c)(3)

Personnel:
Secretary: Aaron Benavot
    E-Mail: abenavot@albany.edu
Treasurer: Alan Wagner
    E-Mail: awagner@uamail.albany.edu

Historical Note:
Formerly (1974) Comparative Education Society. CIES's mission is to foster cross-cultural understanding, scholarship, academic achievement and societal development through the international study of educational ideas, systems and practices. Members are comparative educators and others who work in the more applied areas of international education. Membership: $70 (Individual); $35 (Student).

Meetings/Conferences: Annual

Publications:
CIES Newsletter
Membership Directory; on-line

Competitive Carriers Association *(1992)*
805 15th St. NW
Suite 401
Washington, DC 20005
Tel: (800) 722-1872 *Fax:* (866) 436-1080
TollFree: (800) 722-1872
Website: rca-usa.org
Members: 262 members
Staff: 10
Annual Budget: $2-5,000,000
Tax: 501(c)(6)

Personnel:

President and Chief Executive Officer: Steven K. Berry
    E-Mail: president@rca-usa.org
Convention and Events Planner: Pat Holder
    E-Mail: patholder@austin.rr.com
Director, Membership Services and Operations: Suzanne
    Hord
    E-Mail
    suzanne.hord@rca-usa.org
Contact, Publications and Graphic Design: Susan Madden
    E-Mail: sclement@sti.net
General Counsel: Rebecca Thompson
    E-Mail: rebecca.thompson@rca-usa.org
Vice President, Media and Communications: Lucy Tutwiler
    E-Mail: lucy.tutwiler@rca-usa.org

Historical Note:
Formerly (2012) the Rural Cellular Association. An advocacy organization for rural and regional wireless carriers and stakeholders.

Meetings/Conferences:
Conference Chair: Pat Holder
2013 - New Orleans, LA (New Orleans Marriott)/April
    17 - 19
2013 - Las Vegas, NV/Sept. 10 - 13

Publications:
Member Directory; on-line
RCA News; monthly
The RCA Voice; bi-annually

Competitive Telecommunications Association *(1981)*
900 17th St. NW
Suite 400
Washington, DC 20006
Tel: (202) 296-6650 *Fax:* (202) 296-7585
E-Mail: info@comptel.org
Website: comptel.org
Members: 300 companies
Staff: 15
Annual Budget: $2-5,000,000

Personnel:
Chief Executive Officer: Jerry James
    E-Mail: jjames@comptel.org
Assistant General Counsel: Mary Albert
    E-Mail: malbert@comptel.org
Manager, Business Development and Marketing: Rick
    Ardalan
    E-Mail: rardalan@comptel.org
Manager, Website and Database: Anna Bayer
    E-Mail: abayer@comptel.org
Vice President, Membership and Conference Services:
    Roger Haisman
    E-Mail: rhaisman@comptel.org
Senior Vice President, Government Relations: Alan Hill
    E-Mail: ahill@comptel.org
Manager, Member Relations: Kevin Morris
    E-Mail: kmorris@comptel.org
Contact, Public Relations: Gail Norris
    E-Mail: gnorris@comptel.org
Senior Director, Meetings Services: Amy Smith
    E-Mail: asmith@comptel.org
Chief Financial Officer: Stephen D. Trotman
    E-Mail: strotman@comptel.org

Historical Note:
Formerly in 1981 as the Association of Long Distance Telephone Companies (ALTEL) and in 1984, ALTEL merged with the American Council of Competitive Telecommunications (ACCT) and the name was changed to the Competitive Telecommunications Association (COMPTEL). COMPTEL is active in state regulatory and legislative proceedings, as well as beyond U.S. borders through information submitted to the United States Trade Representative (USTR) as part of World Trade Organization (WTO) proceedings. Membership: $3,625-77,965 (Service Provider (Voting)); $3,150-17,325 (Supplier Associate); $2,625-7,350 (International); $2,625 (Professional).

Meetings/Conferences: Semi-Annual
Conference Chair: Roger Haisman
2013 - Las Vegas, NV (Aladdin Las Vegas)/March 10 -
    13
2013 - Orlando, FL (Gaylord Palms Resort and
    Convention Center-Orlando)/Sept. 23 - 26
2014 - Las Vegas, NV (Aria)/March 23 - 26
2014 - Dallas, TX (Gaylord Texan Hotel and
    Convention Center-Dallas)/Oct. 5 - 8

Publications:
Comptel CONNECTION; weekly; adv.
COMPTEL VELOCITY; quarterly; adv.
Membership Directory; on-line

Membership List Available to Non-members

Composite Can and Tube Institute (1933)
50 S. Picket St.
Suite 110
Alexandria, VA 22304-7206
Tel: (703) 823-7234 *Fax:* (703) 823-7237
E-Mail: ccti@cctiwdc.org
Website: cctiwdc.org
Members: 80 companies
Staff: 3
Annual Budget: $250-500,000
Tax: 501(c)(6)

Personnel:
Executive Vice President: Kristine J Garland
    E-Mail: ccti@cctiwdc.org
Associate Manager, Events and Publications: Janine
    Marczak
Association Counsel: B. Wayne Vance

Historical Note:
Formed in New York, NY as the National Fibre Can and Tube Institute, assumed its present name in 1970. CCTI represents the interests of manufacturers of composite paperboard cans, containers, canisters, tubes, cores, cones, fibre drums, spools, ribbon blocks, bobbins and related or similar composite products. Membership: $700-41,270 (Industry); $1,000- 2,100 (International Industry); $500 (Independent Manufactures Council); $1,800 (Self-Use Industry); $1,800 (Associate); Free (Retired); $35 (Packaging Student).

Meetings/Conferences:
Conference Chair: Janine Marczak
2013 - Myrtle Beach, SC (Myrtle Beach Marriott at
    Grande Dunes)/March 20 - 21
2013 - The Woodlands, TX (The Woodlands Resort)/
    June 6 - 8
Number of non-conference events/year: 1

Publications:
Can Tube Bulletin; bi-monthly
Industry Directory; annually
Machine Guarding Album; annually; adv.
Technical Notebook; annually
Tube and Core Recovery Brochure and Listing;
    annually

Composite Lumber Manufacturers Association (2005)
355 Lexington Ave.
15th Floor
New York, NY 10012-6603
Fax: (212) 370-9047
E-Mail: info@compositelumber.org
Website: compositelumber.org
Members: 9 Companies
Staff: 5
Annual Budget: $100-250,000

Personnel:
Executive Vice President: Ralph Vasami
    E-Mail: rvasami@kellencompany.com
General Manager: Mike Fischer
    E-Mail: mfischer@kellencompany.com

Historical Note:
Strives to advance the growth of the North American composite lumber industry through proactive technical, advocacy, and awareness efforts. Represents manufacturers and suppliers of composite lumber to the residential and commercial building construction markets. Membership: $10,000-30,000 (Regular); $2,500-5,000 (Associate); $10,000 (Affiliate); $5,000 (Contributory).

Membership List Available to Non-members

Composite Panel Association (1960)
19465 Deerfield Ave.
Suite 306
Leesburg, VA 20176
Tel: (703) 724-1128 *Fax:* (703) 724-1588
TollFree: (866) 426-6767
E-Mail: info@pbmdf.com
Website: compositepanel.org
Members: 154 Organisations
Staff: 11
Annual Budget: $2-5,000,000
Tax: 501(c)(6)

Personnel:
President: Thomas A. Julia
    E-Mail: tjulia@cpamail.org
Vice President, Government and Industry Affairs: Donald
    Bisson

E-Mail: dbisson@cpamail.org
Vice President, Membership and Administration: Jeannie
    Ervin
Regional Certification Manager: Flash Isaak
    E-Mail: fisaak@cpamail.org
Director, Marketing: Allyson O'Sullivan
    E-Mail: aosullivan@cpamail.org
Director, Certification Programs: Chris Surak
    E-Mail: csurak@cpamail.org

Historical Note:
The Composite Panel Association (CPA) is the North American trade association for producers of particleboard (PB), medium density fiberboard (MDF), hardboard (HB), decorative surfaces and other compatible products. It also brings together the complete value chain affiliated with the composite panel industry. Membership: $4,000 (General); $1,000-4,000 (Associate).

Continuing Education:
Certification Designation/s: EPP, CARB

Meetings/Conferences:
2013 - San Diego, CA (Loews Coronado Bay Resort)/
    May 5 - 7
2013 - Baltimore, MD (Hyatt Regency)/Sept. 29 - Oct.
    1

Publications:
@the edge; weekly
Membership Directory; on-line

Membership List Available to Non-members

Compressed Air and Gas Institute (1915)
1300 Sumner Ave.
Cleveland, OH 44115-2851
Tel: (216) 241-7333 *Fax:* (216) 241-0105
E-Mail: cagi@cagi.org
Website: cagi.org
Members: 49 companies
Staff: 3
Annual Budget: $250-500,000
Tax: 501(c)(6)

Personnel:
Secretary and Treasurer: John H. Addington

Historical Note:
In 1933 a group became the Compressed Air Institute and the present name was adopted in 1945. CAGI works to strengthen its role as the united voice of the compressed air industry by communicating its position on major areas of concern within the industry. Mission is to be the united voice of the compressed air industry, serving as the unbiased authority on technical, educational, promotional, and other matters that affect the industry.

Publications:
Membership Directory; on-line

Compressed Gas Association (1913)
14501 George Carter Way
Suite 103
Chantilly, VA 20151-2923
Tel: (703) 788-2700 *Fax:* (703) 961-1831
E-Mail: cga@cganet.com
Website: cganet.com
Members: 125 companies
Staff: 15
Annual Budget: $2-5,000,000

Personnel:
President and Chief Executive Officer: Michael Tiller
Manager, Meetings and Membership Services: Nancy
    Flower
    E-Mail: nflower@cganet.com

Historical Note:
CGA promotes ever-improving safe, secure, and environmentally responsible manufacture, transportation, storage, transfilling, and disposal of industrial and medical gases and their containers. Membership: $2145-9360 (Associate), $2990-5532 (Consultant).

Meetings/Conferences: Annual
Conference Chair: Nancy Flower
2013 - Scottsdale, AZ (Hyatt Regency Scottsdale Resort
    and Spa at Gainey Ranch)/April 7 - 12
Number of non-conference events/year: 2

Publications:
Compressions; quarterly
Member Directory; on-line

Computer and Communications Industry Association (1972)
900 17th St. NW
Suite 1100

Washington, DC 20006
Tel: (202) 783-0070 *Fax:* (202) 783-0534
E-Mail: ccia@ccianet.org
Website: ccianet.org
Members: 35 companies
Staff: 9
Annual Budget: $10-25,000,000
Tax: 501(c)(6)

Personnel:
Director, Media Relations: Heather Greenfield
    E-Mail: hgreenfield@ccianet.org
Vice President, Government Relations: Catherine R. Sloan
    E-Mail: csloan@ccianet.org

Historical Note:
Formerly (1976) Computer Industry Association, CCIA is a nonprofit membership organization dedicated to innovation and enhancing society's access to information and communications. It also promotes open markets, open systems, open networks and open competition in the computer, telecommunications and Internet industries. Members are manufacturers and providers of computer information processing and telecommunications- related products and services. Membership: $3,500-55,000/year (Company).

Computer Assisted Language Instruction Consortium (1983)
Texas State University
214 Centennial Hall
San Marcos, TX 78666
Tel: (512) 245-1417 *Fax:* (512) 245-9089
E-Mail: info@calico.org
Website: calico.org
Members: 780 individuals and 220 companies
Staff: 3
Annual Budget: $100-250,000
Tax: 501(c)(3)

Personnel:
President: Greg Kessler
    E-Mail: kessler@ohio.edu
Manager: Esther Horn
Editor: Mat Schulze

Historical Note:
Formerly (1991) Computer Assisted Language Learning and Instruction. CALICO strives for computer-assisted language learning (CALL) and lays an emphasis not only on language teaching and learning but also reaches out to all areas that employ the languages of the world to instruct and to learn. Members are foreign language educators, programmers, technicians, web page designers, CALL developers, CALL practitioners, novice CALL users, second language acquisition researchers. Membership: $65 (Individual); $50 (K-12/Community College); $40 (Senior/ Student); $105 (Institutional); $155 (Corporate).

Meetings/Conferences: Annual

Publications:
CALICO Journal

Membership List Available to Non-members

Computer Ethics Institute (1980)
1775 Massachusetts Ave. NW
Washington, DC 20036
Tel: (202) 797-6183 *Fax:* (202) 797-6004
E-Mail: info@computerethicsinstitute.org
Website: computerethicsinstitute.org
Members: 250 individuals
Staff: 4
Tax: 501(c)(3)

Personnel:
President: Ramon Barquin
Secretary: Stuart Allen
    E-Mail: sallen@computerethicsinstitute.org
Analyst, Information Technology: Agnes Hegyi
Treasurer: Tibor Purger

Historical Note:
Formerly known as Coalition for Computer Ethics and incorporated its current name in 1992. CEI's mission is to facilitate the examination and recognition of ethics in the development and use of computer technologies. The output of this discussion provides educational resources and governing rules.

Computer Measurement Group (1975)
P.O. Box 1124
151 Fries Mill Rd., Suite 104
Turnersville, NJ 08012
Tel: (856) 401-1700 *Fax:* (856) 401-1708
E-Mail: cmghq@cmg.org
Website: cmg.org

Members: 3000 individuals
Staff: 5
Annual Budget: $500-1,000,000

Personnel:
President: Adam Grummitt
    E-Mail: cmgpres@cmg.org
Coordinator, Conferences: Michelle Cervantes
    E-Mail: michelle@cmg.org
Senior Conference Coordinator and Office Manager:
    Barbara Flemming
    E-Mail: barbara@cmg.org
Administrative Assistant: Kathy Kinnarney
    E-Mail: kathy@cmg.org
Program Coordinator: David Troxel
    E-Mail: david@cmg.org

Historical Note:
CMG's purpose is to advocate the exchange of technical information among IT professionals through regional groups, technical publications, and an annual conference. CMG holds an international technical conference each year in the United States which consists of a technical program addressing CPE. Membership: $175/year.

Meetings/Conferences: Annual
Conference Chair: Barbara Flemming
2013 - San Diego, CA (La Jolla)/Nov. 4 - 8
2013 - Orlando, FL/Dec. 8 - 13
Number of non-conference events/year: 2

Publications:
The CMG Journal; quarterly

Computer Security Institute *(1974)*
350 Hudson St.
Suite 300
New York, NY 10014
Tel: (215) 989-4901 *Fax:* (347) 962-3931
E-Mail: csi@ubm.com
Website: gocsi.com
Members: 5000 individuals
Staff: 16
Annual Budget: $1-2,000,000

Personnel:
Director: Robert Richardson
    E-Mail: rrichardson@techweb.com

Historical Note:
CSI's mission is to provide with the resources with which to succeed both in job and in career. Also provides quality products that focus on practical, cost-effective strategies, solutions and methodologies. Membership includes data processing managers, security officers, auditors and others with an interest in computer security. Membership: $225 (Elite); $150 (Premium); $100 (Basic); $3000 (Partner).

Meetings/Conferences: Annual

Publications:
Alert
CSI Computer Crime and Security Survey; annually
Frontline End-user Awareness Newsletter; quarterly

Membership List Available to Non-members

Computerized Medical Imaging Society *(1977)*
Georgetown University Medical Center
Box 571414
Washington, DC 20057-1414
Tel: (202) 687-2121 *Fax:* (202) 687-1662
Members: 125 individuals
Staff: 1
Annual Budget: Under $10,000

Personnel:
Administrator: Sylvia Brown

Historical Note:
Formerly (1988) Computerized Radiology Society. Members are radiologists interested in using the computer to scan X-rays of selected planes of the body. Membership: $60/year.

Computing Research Association *(1972)*
1828 L St. NW
Suite 800
Washington, DC 20036-4632
Tel: (202) 234-2111 *Fax:* (202) 667-1066
E-Mail: info@cra.org
Website: cra.org
Members: 250 institutions
Staff: 11
Annual Budget: $10-25,000,000
Tax: 501(c)(3)

Personnel:
Executive Director: Andrew Bernat

    E-Mail: abernat@cra.org
Director, Government Affairs: Peter Harsha
    E-Mail: harsha@cra.org
Director, Programs: Erik Russell
    E-Mail: erik@cra.org
Senior Communications Associate and Editor: Jean E.
    Smtih
    E-Mail: jean@cra.org

Historical Note:
Formerly (1986) Computing Science Board and (1990) Computing Research Board. CRA's mission is to strengthen research and advanced education in computing and allied fields by working to influence policy that impacts computing research, encouraging the development of human resources, contributing to the cohesiveness of the professional community. Membership: $659-7,529 (Academic Department); $350-2,510 (Associate Academic Department); $1,885-15,065 (Lab and Center/Associate); $6,250- 75,000 (Professional Society) .

Meetings/Conferences:
Number of non-conference events/year: 14

Publications:
Computing Research News

Computing Technology Industry Association (CompTIA) *(1982)*
3500 Lacey Rd.
Suite 100
Downers Grove, IL 60515
Tel: (630) 678-8300 *Fax:* (630) 678-8384
E-Mail: info@comptia.org
Website: comptia.org
Members: 3,000 members and business partners
Staff: 158
Annual Budget: $50-100,000,000

Personnel:
President and Chief Executive Officer: Todd Thibodeaux
Vice President, Human Resources: Colleen Hughes
Vice President, Events and Education: Kelly Ricker
Chief Financial Officer: David Sommer
Director, Media Relations: Michael Wendy
    E-Mail: mwendy@comptia.org
Comptroller: William West

Historical Note:
Formerly (1986) Association of Better Computer Dealers and ABCD: The Microcomputer Industry Association (1993). CompTIA's mission is to facilitate the development of vendor-neutral standards in e-commerce, customer service, workforce development. Members are microcomputer resellers who provide technical assistance, training and full maintenance to customers and leading microcomputer software and hardware manufacturers and distributors. Membership: $150-20,000/year (Corporation).

Continuing Education:
Certification Designation/s: CompTIA RFID + , CompTIA Project + , CompTIA CTT + , CompTIA Server + , CompTIA Linux + , CompTIA PDI + , CompTIA CDIA + , CompTIA A + , CompTIA i-Net + , CompTIA Network +

Meetings/Conferences: Annual
Conference Chair: Kelly Ricker
Number of non-conference events/year: 6

Publications:
Connect5; weekly

Concord Grape Association *(1969)*
1100 Johnson Ferry Rd.
Suite 300
Atlanta, GA 30342-1733
Tel: (404) 252-3663 *Fax:* (404) 252-0774
E-Mail: info@concordgrape.org
Website: concordgrape.org
Members: 6 companies
Staff: 3
Annual Budget: $25-50,000

Personnel:
Coordinator: Jeannie Milewski
Contact: Donna Smith
    E-Mail: dsmith@kellencompany.com

Historical Note:
Founded as the Concord Grape Council, it became the American Concord Grape Association in 1974 and assumed its present name in 1980. Members are firms engaged in the processing of a substantial quantity of Concord grapes in North America.

Concrete Anchor Manufacturers Association *(1995)*
136, S. Main St.

Suite 2E
St. Charles, MO 63301
Tel: (314) 889-7116 *Fax:* (314) 725-6592
E-Mail: info@concreteanchors.org
Website: concreteanchors.org
Members: 25 companies and organizations
Staff: 2
Annual Budget: $25-50,000

Personnel:
Executive Director: James A. Borchers
    E-Mail: jborchers@concreteanchors.org

Historical Note:
CAMA was established to serve as an organized voice for the post- installed anchor industry. CAMA monitors issues and decisions affecting the industry and is often called upon by regulatory bodies for industry input and comment; also serves as an industry liaison and resource to state departments of transportation.

Publications:
Member Directory; on-line

Concrete Foundations Association *(1975)*
113 W. First St.
P.O. Box 204
Mt. Vernon, IA 52314-1602
Tel: (319) 895-6940 *Fax:* (320) 213-5556
E-Mail: info@cfawalls.org
Website: cfawalls.org
Members: 385 companies and individuals
Staff: 3
Annual Budget: $500-1,000,000

Personnel:
Executive Director: J. Edward Sauter
    E-Mail: esauter@cfawalls.org
Office Manager: Janette Barr
    E-Mail: jbarr1@cfawalls.org
Director, Technical Services: James Baty II
    E-Mail: jbaty@cfawalls.org

Historical Note:
Formerly (1990) Poured Concrete Wall Contractors Association of America. CFA provides promotional materials, educational seminars, networking opportunities, and technical and informative meetings for its members. Members consist primarily of foundation contractors with firm sizes ranging from six to over 100 employees. Membership: $175 (Professional); $1,000 (National Associate); $250 (Local Associate); $400-600 (Contractors).

Continuing Education:
Enrollment: 50
Certification Designation/s: CFT

Meetings/Conferences:
2013 - Las Vegas, NV (Las Vegas Convention Center)/
    Feb. 4 - 8
2013 - Albuquerue, NM (Santa Ana Pueblo)/July 10 -
    13
Number of non-conference events/year: 1

Publications:
Concrete Facts; quarterly; adv.
Membership Directory; on-line

Membership List Available to Non-members

The Concrete Industry Board
119-42 80th Rd.
Kew Gardens
New York, NY 11415-1106
Tel: (718) 459-4900 *Fax:* (718) 459-4890
E-Mail: cibnyc@earthlink.net
Website: cibofnyc.org
Staff: 2
Annual Budget: $500-1,000,000

Personnel:
Executive Director: William J. Lyons FACI, III
    E-Mail: blyons@cibofnyc.org
Treasurer: Lawrence M. Tabat PE
    E-Mail: lawrence.tabat@arcadis-us.com

Historical Note:
CIB's mission is to provide good quality design and construction of concrete structures through education, exchange and debate. Membership: $2,000 (Sustaining); $500 (Companies/Partnerships/Professional Corporations/ Government Agencies); $250 (Individual); $75 (Associate); $0 (Member Emeritus/Retired).

Continuing Education:
Certification Designation/s: CFT
Meetings/Conferences:
Number of non-conference events/year: 3

Publications:
CIB Newsletter
Concrete Industry Board Bulletin; quarterly

Concrete Plant Manufacturers Bureau (1958)
900 Spring St.
Silver Spring, MD 20910
Tel: (301) 587-1400 *Fax:* (301) 587-1605
E-Mail: nmaher@vmmb.org
Website: cpmb.org
Members: 11 companies
Staff: 4
Annual Budget: Under $10,000
Tax: 501(c)(6)

Personnel:
Executive Secretary: Robert A. Garbini PE
    E-Mail: bgarbini@cpmb.org
Contact, Government and Industry Relations: Julie Luther
    E-Mail: jluther@cpmb.org
Bureau Administrator: Nicole R. Maher
    E-Mail: nmaher@cpmb.org

Historical Note:
CPMB's purpose is to establish minimum standards for rating various components of concrete plants for the protection and assurance. Member companies are directly involved in the design, manufacture and sale of concrete plants and plant components.

Concrete Reinforcing Steel Institute (1924)
933 N. Plum Grove Rd.
Schaumburg, IL 60173-4758
Tel: (847) 517-1200 *Fax:* (847) 517-1206
E-Mail: info@crsi.org
Website: crsi.org
Members: 270 firms
Staff: 20
Annual Budget: $2-5,000,000
Tax: 501(c)(6)

Personnel:
President and Chief Executive Officer: Robert J. Risser Jr.,
    PE
    E-Mail: brisser@crsi.org
Technical Director: Anthony L. Felder
    E-Mail: afelder@crsi.org
Director, Membership Services: Aiyana Lopez
Chief Financial Officer: Kim Michael-Lee
Director, Communications: Dave Mounce
    E-Mail: dmounce@crsi.org
Controller: Susan O'Sullivan

Historical Note:
Absorbed the Associated Reinforcing Bar Producers in 1982 and the Fusion Bonded Coaters Association in 1985. CRSI's mission is to maximize the use of steel reinforcement in concrete in construction. Members are firms engaged in the production and fabrication of steel reinforcing bars and include placers of steel reinforcing bars and related products, as well as professionals who are involved in the research, design and construction of reinforced concrete. Membership: $150/year.

Meetings/Conferences:
2013 - Tempe, AZ (Tempe Mission Palms Hotel and
    Conference Center)/March 12 - 15
2013 - Scottsdale, AZ (InterContinental Montelucia
    Resort and Spa)/April 27 - 30
2013 - Chicago, IL (Swissotel Chicago)/Nov. 3 - 6
2014 - Isle of Palms, SC (Wild Dunes Resort)/April 26
    - 29
2014 - Chicago, IL (Swissotel Chicago)/Nov. 2 - 5

Publications:
CRSI E-Newsletter; on-line

Concrete Sawing and Drilling Association (1972)
13577 Feather Sound Dr.
Suite 560
Clearwater, FL 33762
Tel: (727) 577-5004 *Fax:* (727) 577-5012
E-Mail: info@csda.org
Website: csda.org
Members: 550 companies
Staff: 5
Annual Budget: $500-1,000,000
Tax: 501(c)(6)

Personnel:
Executive Director: Patrick O'Brien
    E-Mail: pat@csda.org
Associate Editor: Russell Hitchen
    E-Mail: russell@csda.org

Office Manager and Coordinator, Membership and Training:
    Aimee Pavlovich
    E-Mail: aimee@csda.org

Historical Note:
CSDA seeks to promote the use of professional sawing and drilling contractors and their methods. Members are contractors of concrete sawing and drilling and producers of diamond sawblades, drills, and equipment. Sponsors operator certification and other continuing education programs. Membership: $550-2,890 (North American Contractor, based on gross sales); $1,170-5,770 (Manufacturer, based on gross sales); $850-2,590 (Distributor, based on gross sales); $675 (Affiliate); $375 (Overseas Contractor).

Continuing Education:
Enrollment: 100
Certification Designation/s: CSDA CO

Meetings/Conferences: Semi-Annual
2013 - Duck Key, FL (Hawks Cay Island Resort)/Feb.
    28 - March 2
Number of non-conference events/year: 3

Publications:
Concrete Openings Magazine; quarterly; adv.
CSDA News
Member Directory; on-line

Membership List Available to Non-members

Conductors Guild (1975)
719 Twinridge Ln.
Richmond, VA 23235
Tel: (804) 553-1378 *Fax:* (804) 553-1876
E-Mail: guild@conductorsguild.net
Website: conductorsguild.org
Members: 1850 individuals and 120 institutions
Staff: 4
Annual Budget: $250-500,000
Tax: 501(c)(3)

Personnel:
Executive Director: Amanda Burton Winger
    E-Mail: guild@conductorsguild.org
Editor: David Leibowitz
    E-Mail: podiumnotes@conductorsguild.org
Assistant Director: Scott Winger
    E-Mail: scott@conductorsguild.org

Historical Note:
Formerly a sub-group of the American Symphony Orchestra League, the Guild became an independent entity in 1985. CG is the music service organization committed exclusively to the advancement of the art of conducting and to serving the artistic and professional needs of conductors. Guild members are conductors, students and institutions with an interest in the field. Membership: $100 (Regular/Associate/ Institution); $50 (Student/Retired); $2,000 (Life).

Meetings/Conferences: Annual
2013 - St. Louis, MO (St. Louis Union Station
    Marriott)/June 15 - 18

Publications:
Conductor Opportunities Bulletin; monthly
Journal of the Conductors Guild; semi-annually; adv.
Membership Directory; on-line
Podium Notes; quarterly; adv.

The Conference Board (1916)
845 Third Ave.
New York, NY 10022-6679
Tel: (212) 759-0900 *Fax:* (202) 980-7014
Website: conference-board.org
Staff: 240
Annual Budget: $50-100,000,000
Tax: 501(c)(3)

Personnel:
Chief Executive Officer: Jonathan Spector
Manager, Corporate Communications: Carol Courter
    E-Mail: carol.courter@conference-board.org
Executive Director, Member Engagement and Human
    Capital: Meg Gottemoeller EdD
Coordinator, Membership Services: Brandon Lawrence
Director, Office of Communications: Ralph Piscitelli
    E-Mail: ralph.piscitelli@conference-board.org
Conference Director: Leland Sandler

Historical Note:
The Conference Board works to provide the world's organizations with the practical knowledge they need to improve their performance and better serve society.

Meetings/Conferences:
Conference Chair: Meg Gottemoeller EdD

Conference Board of the Mathematical Sciences (1960)
1529 18th St. NW
Washington, DC 20036
Tel: (202) 293-1170 *Fax:* (202) 293-3412
Website: cbmsweb.org
Members: 16 professional societies
Staff: 2
Annual Budget: $250-500,000
Tax: 501(c)(3)

Personnel:
Director: Dr. Ronald C. Rosier
    E-Mail: rosier@georgetown.edu
Administrative Coordinator: Lisa R. Kolbe
    E-Mail: lkolbe@maa.org

Historical Note:
Formerly Conference Organization of the Mathematical Sciences. CBMS's purpose is to promote understanding and cooperation among these national organizations so that they work together and support each other in their efforts to promote research, improve education and expand the uses of mathematics.

Meetings/Conferences:
Number of non-conference events/year: 1

Conference for the Study of Political Thought (1967)
Department of Politics
Pitzer College
Claremont, CA 91711
Tel: (909) 607-3178 *Fax:* (909) 621-8481
Website: cspt.tulane.edu
Members: 500 individuals
Staff: 2
Annual Budget: Under $10,000

Personnel:
Contact, Editor and Membership: Eve Grace
    E-Mail: egrace@ColoradoCollege.edu
Secretary and Treasurer: Sharon N. Snowiss
    E-Mail: ssnowiss@pitzer.edu

Historical Note:
CSPT is an international, interdisciplinary organization of scholars and informed citizens concerned to promote the study of past and present political thinking especially with respect to the proper ends of political activity and the means permissible for their attainment. Members are theorists in political science, history, philosophy, the classics, language departments, sociology, and economics. Membership: $18-30 (Individual); $12 (Student); $18 (Emeritus).

Publications:
CSPT Newsletter; on-line

Conference of Business Economists
28790 Chagrin Blvd., Suite 350
Cleveland, OH 44122
Tel: (216) 464-2137 *Fax:* (216) 464-0397
E-Mail: info@nrra-usa.org
Members: 100 individuals
Staff: 5
Tax: 501(c)(6)

Personnel:
Executive Director: David L. Williams
    E-Mail: dwilliams@Admgt.com

Conference of Chief Justices (1949)
C/O Association Management
300 Newport Ave.
Williamsburg, VA 23185-4147
Tel: (757) 259-1841 *Fax:* (757) 259-1520
E-Mail: ccj@ncsc.dni.us
Website: ccj.ncsc.dni.us
Members: 58 individuals
Staff: 1
Tax: 501(c)(6)

Personnel:
President: Wallace B. Jefferson

Historical Note:
CCJ provides an opportunity for the judicial officers of the states to meet and discuss matters of importance in improving the administration of justice, rules and methods of procedure and to make recommendations to bring about improvements on such matters. Membership in the Conference of Chief Justices consists of the highest judicial officer of the fifty states, the District of Columbia, the Commonwealth of Puerto Rico, the Commonwealth of the Northern Mariana Islands, and the territories of American Samoa, Guam and the Virgin Islands.

Conference of Consulting Actuaries (1950)
3880 Salem Lake Dr.
Suite H
Long Grove, IL 60047-5292
Tel: (847) 719-6500 *Fax:* (847) 719-6506
E-Mail: conference@ccactuaries.org
Website: ccactuaries.org
Members: 1200 individuals
Staff: 7
Annual Budget: $1-2,000,000
Tax: 501(c)(6)

Personnel:
Executive Director: Rita K. DeGraaf
   E-Mail: rdegraaf@ccactuaries.org
Membership and CE Administrative Support: Catherine
   Cieck
   E-Mail: ccieck@ccactuaries.org
Manager, Information Technology and Registrar: Matthew
   D. Noncek
   E-Mail: mnoncek@ccactuaries.org
*Manager, Continuing Education Events and Special
   Projects:* Marie M. Shaw
   E-Mail: mshaw@ccactuaries.org

Historical Note:
*Formerly (1991) Conference of Actuaries in Public Practice,
CCA is a professional membership association for actuaries
working as consultants in life, health, property and casualty
insurance and in the pension planning and employee
benefits fields. Membership: $390/year.*

Meetings/Conferences: Annual
Conference Chair: Marie M. Shaw
2013 - San Antonio, TX (JW Marriott San Antonio Hill
   Country Resort and Spa)/Oct. 20 - 23
2014 - Rancho Mirage, CA (Westin Mission Hills Resort
   and Spa)/Oct. 19 - 22
Number of non-conference events/year: 20

Publications:
CCA Yearbook; annually
The Consulting Actuary; quarterly

Conference of Educational Administrators of Schools and Programs for the Deaf (1868)
P. O. Box 1778
St. Augustine, FL 32085-1778
Tel: (904) 810-5200 *Fax:* (904) 810-5525
E-Mail: nationaloffice@ceasd.org
Website: ceasd.org
Members: 800 individuals
Staff: 3
Annual Budget: $50-100,000

Personnel:
Executive Director: Joseph P. Finnegan Jr.

Historical Note:
*Formerly (1884) known as the Conference of Principals of
American Institutions for the Deaf and Dumb, and (1933)
as the Conference of Superintendents and Principals of
American Institutions for the Deaf and Dumb. In 1933,
the name Conference of Executives of American Schools for
the Deaf was adopted, and in 1980 the name was changed
to Conference of Educational Administrators Serving the
Deaf and assumed its current name in 1996. CEASD,
an association of schools for the deaf, works to promote
excellence within a continuum of equitable educational
opportunities for all children and adults who are deaf or
hard of hearing. Membership: $800-1,000 (Educational
Program); $225 (Affiliate Program); $75 (Independent
Associate); $800 (Administrative Unit Member).*

Continuing Education:
Certification Designation/s: DCC

Meetings/Conferences: Annual
2013 - Tucson, AZ/April 11 - 13

Publications:
The American Annals of the Deaf; adv.

Conference of Historical Journals (1982)
6508 Hummel Dr.
Boise, ID 83709-2055
Tel: (501) 575-5884
E-Mail: austin_bott@rmci.net
Website: uark.edu/depts/arkhist/CHJ
Members: 160 individuals
Staff: 2

Personnel:
President: David Johnson
Secretary and Treasurer: Judy Austin
   E-Mail: judyaustin40@yahoo.com

Historical Note:

*CHJ members are editors of serial publications focusing on
history and others with an interest in the field. Membership:
$25/year (individual).*

Conference of Major Superiors of Men, United States of America (1956)
8808 Cameron St.
Silver Spring, MD 20910
Tel: (301) 588-4030 *Fax:* (301) 587-4575
E-Mail: postmaster@cmsm.org
Website: cmsm.org
Members:
210 Catholic religious communities of men
19000 vowed priests
Staff: 4
Annual Budget: $250-500,000

Personnel:
Executive Director: John A. Pavlik OFM
   E-Mail: jpavlik@cmsm.org
Associate Director, Operations and Communications:
   Robert J. Bozek
   E-Mail: bbozek@cmsm.org
Director, Office of Justice & Peace: Eli S. McCarthy
   E-Mail: emccarthy@cmsm.org
Coordinator, Information and Records: Richard Oliver
   E-Mail: roliver@cmsm.org

Historical Note:
*Formerly the Conference of Major Superiors of Men's
Institutes. CMSM works to be a support to major superiors
and a resource for them in their role of leadership within
their respective institutes. Members are major superiors of
the various Roman Catholic religious orders of men in the
U.S.*

Publications:
CMSM Forum; irregular
Justice and Peace Alert; monthly
Membership Directory; annually

Conference of Minority Public Administrators (1971)
P.O. Box 10171
Jackson, MS 39206
Tel: (601) 362-4565 *Fax:* (601) 668-2518
Website: compaonline.org
Members: 500 individuals
Staff: 1
Annual Budget: $25-50,000

Personnel:
President: Aziza Zemrani

Historical Note:
*A division of the American Society for Public
Administration, COMPA members are minority ASPA
members and others concerned with the advancement of
minorities in public administration.COMPA's mission is
to advance the science, processes, technology, art and
image of public administration by providing leadership
in the elimination of discriminatory practices against all
minorities. Membership: $35/year (Individual).*

Meetings/Conferences: Annual
2013 - Long Beach, CA (Historic Queen Mary Resort
   and Hotel)/Feb. 20 - 24

Publications:
Member Directory; on-line

Conference of Minority Transportation Officials (1971)
1875 I St., NW
Suite 500
Washington, DC 20006
Tel: (703) 234-4072 *Fax:* (202) 318-0364
TollFree: (877) 782-6686
E-Mail: comto@comto.org
Website: comto.org
Members: 39 chapters encompassing
individuals, transportation agencies, academic
institutions, industry non-profits and Historically
Underutilized Businesses (HUBs).
Staff: 7
Annual Budget: $1-2,000,000
Tax: 501(c)(3)

Personnel:
President and Chief Executive Officer: Julie A.
   Cunningham
   E-Mail: jcunningham@comto.org
Director, Marketing: Bill Carney
   E-Mail: bcarney@comto.org
Director, Communications: Micki Francis
   E-Mail: mfrancis@comto.org

Manager, Convention and Event Services: Kelly Marks
   E-Mail: kmarks@comto.org
Chief Operating Officer: Cathy Vail
   E-Mail: cvail@comto.org
Coordinator, Education and Learning Services: Erica
   Weiss
   E-Mail: eweiss@comto.org

Historical Note:
*COMTO aims to ensure a level playing field and maximum
participation in the transportation industry for minority
individuals, businesses and communities of color through
advocacy, information sharing, training, education and
professional development. Membership: $25-2,000/year.*

Continuing Education:
Certification Designation/s: CEU

Meetings/Conferences: Annual
Conference Chair: Kelly Marks
2013 - Jacksonville, FL (Hyatt Regency Jacksonville
   Riverfront)/July 13 - 17

Publications:
Accelerate; quarterly
Membership Directory; on-line

Membership List Available to Non-members

Conference of Radiation Control Program Directors (1968)
1030 Burlington Ln.
Suite 4B
Frankfort, KY 40601
Tel: (502) 227-4543 *Fax:* (502) 227-7862
Website: crcpd.org
Members: 884 individuals
Staff: 11
Annual Budget: $1-2,000,000
Tax: 501(c)(3)

Personnel:
Executive Director: Ruth E. Mc Burney
   E-Mail: rmcburney@crcpd.org
Financial Manager: Jerry Bailey
   E-Mail: jbailey@crcpd.org
Administrative Assistant: Sharon Bowen
   E-Mail: sbowen@crcpd.org
Publication Editor and Manager, Mammography Programs:
   Lin Carigan
   E-Mail: lcarigan@crcpd.org
Technical Assistant: Charles R. (Russ) Meyer CHP
   E-Mail: rmeyer@crcpd.org

Historical Note:
*CRCPD's mission is to provide a forum for the exchange of
information between radiation control programs of states
and between the states and federal government. Members
are employed by state, local or foreign radiation control
programs. Membership: $55 (Associate); $130 (Director);
$95 (International); $85 (Affiliate).*

Continuing Education:
Certification Designation/s: IR

Meetings/Conferences: Annual
2013 - Portland, OR (Red Lion Hotel Jantzen)/May 20 -
   23/400 attendees
2014 - Atlanta, GA (Crowne Plaza Atlanta Perimeter at
   Ravinia)/May 19 - 22

Publications:
Directory of Personnel Responsible for Radiological
   Health Program Directors; annually; adv.
Newsbrief; irregular; adv.
Radon Bulletin; on-line
The Newsbrief

Conference of Research Workers in Animal Diseases (1920)
Colorado State University, Department of
Microbiology, Immunology & Pathology
Room A102
Ft. Collins, CO 80523-1682
Tel: (970) 491-5740 *Fax:* (970) 204-6684
Website: cvmbs.colostate.edu/mip/crwad
Members: 500 individuals
Staff: 1
Annual Budget: $100-250,000
Tax: 501(c)(3)

Personnel:
Executive Director: Robert P. Ellis
   E-Mail: robert.ellis@colostate.edu

Historical Note:
*Purpose of CRWAD is to discuss and disseminate current
research advances in animal diseases. Members are those
actively engaged in research or research administration.*

Membership: $70 (Regular); $60 (Student); $75 (Post–Doc/Resident).

Continuing Education:
Enrollment: 30
Certification Designation/s: AAVSB, RACE

Meetings/Conferences: Annual
2013 - Chicago, IL (Chicago Marriott Downtown Magnificent Mile)/Dec. 8 - 10

Publications:
Animal Health Research Reviews
CRWAD Newsletter; on-line
Member Directory; on-line

Conference of State Bank Supervisors (1902)
1129 20th St. NW
Ninth Floor
Washington, DC 20036-3403
Tel: (202) 296-2840 *Fax:* (202) 296-1928
TollFree: (800) 886-2727
Website: csbs.org
Members: 54 state regulatory organizations
Staff: 59
Annual Budget: $50-100,000,000
Tax: 501(c)(6)

Personnel:
President and Chief Executive Officer: John W. Ryan
  E-Mail: jryan@csbs.org
Vice President, Information Technology: Anthony Donfor
  E-Mail: adonfor@csbs.org
General Counsel: John S. Gorman
  E-Mail: bgorman@csbs.org
Executive Vice President, Finance and Administration: Tom Harlow CAE, CPA
  E-Mail: tharlow@csbs.org
Human Resources and Payroll Manager: Maryam Mouzount
  E-Mail: mmouzount@csbs.org
Vice President, Membership and Banker Relations: Edward Smith
  E-Mail: esmith@csbs.org
Senior Executive Vice President, Regulatory Division: Michael Stevens CEIC
  E-Mail: mstevens@csbs.org
Senior Vice President, Professional Development: Roger L. Stromberg
  E-Mail: rstromberg@csbs.org
Senior Director, Communications: Catherine Woody
  E-Mail: cwoody@csbs.org

Historical Note:
Formerly National Association of Supervisors of State Banks. CSBS assumed its current name in 1970. CSBS is the professional organization of the state bank regulators of the 50 States, Guam, Puerto Rico, the Virgin Islands, and Washington, DC that strives to protect and advance the nation's dual banking system. Membership: $249- 8,510 (Member, based on assets); $592-6,578 (International); $2,000 (Associate).

Continuing Education:
Certification Designation/s: CSMBE, CMBE, CAMLS, CCCS, CISE, CTE, ACISE
Meetings/Conferences:
Number of non-conference events/year: 30

Publications:
Examiner Newsletter; weekly

Conference of State Court Administrators (1955)
National Center for State Courts
300 Newport Ave.
Williamsburg, VA 23185-4147
Tel: (800) 877-1233 *Fax:* (757) 259-1520
TollFree: (800) 877-1233
E-Mail: cosca@ncsc.org
Website: cosca.ncsc.dni.us
Members: 56 individuals
Staff: 1
Tax: 501(c)(3)

Personnel:
Association Manager: Shelley Rockwell
  E-Mail: srockwell@ncsc.org

Historical Note:
COSCA's mission is to work to identify and study issues and, when appropriate, develop policies, principles, and standards relating to the administration of judicial systems. Members are state court administrators or equivalent officials in the fifty states, the District of Columbia, Puerto Rico, American Samoa, Guam, Northern Mariana Islands, and the Virgin Islands.

Meetings/Conferences: Annual
Number of non-conference events/year: 1

Publications:
Membership Roster; annually

Membership List Available to Non-members

Conference on Asian History (1953)
9500 Gilman Dr.
La Jolla, CA 92093
Tel: (858) 534-3401
Website: historians.org/affiliates/conf_asian_his.htm
Members: 500 individuals
Staff: 1

Personnel:
Chairman: Stefan Tanaka
  E-Mail: stanaka@ucsd.edu

Historical Note:
An affiliate of the American Historical Association, Conference members are historians specializing in the history of Asia. Membership: $10/year.

Continuing Education:
Enrollment: 400

Membership List Available to Non-members

Conference on College Composition and Communication (1949)
1111 W. Kenyon Rd.
Urbana, IL 61801-1096
Tel: (217) 328-3870 *Fax:* (217) 328-9645
TollFree: (877) 369-6283
E-Mail: cccc@ncte.org
Website: ncte.org/cccc
Members: 7500 individuals and institutions
Staff: 1
Annual Budget: $250-500,000

Personnel:
Executive Secretary and Treasurer: Kent D. Williamson

Historical Note:
CCCC's mission is to support and promote the teaching and study of college composition and communication. A subsidiary of the National Council of Teachers of English. Members are teachers of freshman English at the college level. Membership in NCTE: $40 (Individual); $20 (Student).

Meetings/Conferences: Annual
2013 - Las Vegas, NV (Hoover Dam Bypass)/March 13 - 16
2014 - Indianapolis, IN/March 19 - 22
2015 - Tampa, FL/March 18 - 21
2016 - Houston, TX/April 6 - 9
Number of non-conference events/year: 1

Publications:
College Composition and Communication; quarterly; adv.
Forum; semi-annually
Membership Directory; on-line

Conference on Consumer Finance Law (1926)
C/O Oklahoma City University School of Law
2501 N. Blackwelder Ave.
Oklahoma City, OK 73106
Tel: (405) 208-5198 *Fax:* (405) 521-5089
Website: ccflonline.org
Members: 1400 lawyers and financial institutions
Staff: 3
Annual Budget: $50-100,000
Tax: 501(c)(6)

Personnel:
Executive Director: Alvin C. Harrell
Vice President, Meetings: Robert J. Flemma Jr.

Historical Note:
Formerly (1984) Conference on Personal Finance Law. CCFL seeks to encourage research in the commercial law, banking and consumer finance fields. Members are lawyers, academics, judges, regulators, consumer advocates or financial services executives. Membership: $95/year.

Publications:
Consumer Finance Law Quarterly Report; quarterly

Conference on English Education (1965)
1111 W. Kenyon Rd.
Urbana, IL 61801-1096
Tel: (217) 328-3870 *Fax:* (217) 328-9645
TollFree: (877) 369-6283
Website: ncte.org/cee

Members: 60000 members
Staff: 1
Annual Budget: Under $10,000

Personnel:
Executive Director: Kent D. Williamson

Historical Note:
A subsidiary of the NCTE. CEE's mission is to advocate the development of literacy, the use of language to construct personal and public worlds and to achieve full participation in society, through the learning and teaching of english and the related arts and sciences of language. Members are state and local supervisors of english instruction and college english education teachers. Membership: $50 (Individual); $25 (Student); $20 (Emeritus); $600 (Lifetime).

Meetings/Conferences: Annual
2013 - Boston, MA/Nov. 21 - 24
2014 - Washington, DC/Nov. 20 - 23
2015 - Minneapolis, MN/Nov. 19 - 22
Number of non-conference events/year: 4

Publications:
CEE-GS Newsletter; semi-annually

Conference on English Leadership (1970)
1111 W. Kenyon Rd.
Urbana, IL 61801-1096
Tel: (217) 328-3870 *Fax:* (217) 328-9645
TollFree: (877) 369-6283
Website: ncte.org/cel
Members: 1800 Individuals and Institutions
Staff: 2
Annual Budget: $50-100,000

Personnel:
Administrative Liaison: Felisa Mann
  E-Mail: fmann@ncte.org
Editor: Susan L. Groenke
  E-Mail: sgroenke@utk.edu

Historical Note:
Formerly (1968) the Conference for Secondary School English Department Chairpersons. A subsidiary of the National Council of Teachers of English, to which all members of the Conference must first belong, and which provides administrative support. CEL's mission is to foster an intimate professional community dedicated to building the leadership capacity of literacy educators.CEL welcomes the involvement of all persons who wish to work with others to seek solutions to problems and to share their special insights with others. Membership: $75/year (Individual).

Meetings/Conferences: Annual
Publications:
English Leaderhip Quarterly; quarterly

Conference on Faith and History (1967)
Department of History, Huntington University
2303 College Ave.
Huntington, IN 46750
Tel: (260) 359-4242 *Fax:* (260) 359-4086
E-Mail: cfh@huntington.edu
Website: huntington.edu/cfh/default.htm
Members: 600 individuals
Staff: 4
Annual Budget: $10-25,000

Personnel:
Treasurer: Dwight D. Brautigam
  E-Mail: dbrautigam@huntington.edu
Secretary: Paul E. Michelson
  E-Mail: pmichelson@huntington.edu
Managing Editor: Jeffrey B. Webb
  E-Mail: jwebb@huntington.edu

Historical Note:
CFH seeks to encourage scholars to explore the relationship between Christian faith and historical studies. Membership: $20 (Emeriti/Undergraduate Student); $30 (Voting Member).

Meetings/Conferences: Biennial
Number of non-conference events/year: 1

Publications:
The CFH Newsletter; semi-annually

Conference on Jewish Social Studies (1933)
Stanford University, Bldg. 200, Room 11
Stanford, CA 94305-2024
Tel: (650) 725-5660 *Fax:* (650) 725-2920
E-Mail: jss@leland.stanford.edu
Members: 1400 individuals
Staff: 2
Annual Budget: Under $10,000

Personnel:

President: Steven J. Zipperstein

Historical Note:
Academics and others with an interest in Jewish social studies.

Conference on Latin American History (1926)
University of North Carolina at Charlotte
9201 University City Blvd.
Charlotte, NC 28223
Tel: (704) 687-2027 *Fax:* (704) 687-3218
E-Mail: clah@uncc.edu
Website: clah.h-net.org
Members: 850 individuals
Staff: 2
Annual Budget: $50-100,000
Tax: 501(c)(3)

Personnel:
President: Cynthia Radding
Executive Secretary: Jurgen Buchenau

Historical Note:
CLAH is devoted to encouraging the diffusion of knowledge about Latin America through fostering the study and improving the teaching of Latin American history. Membership is open to professional Latin Americanists as well as others personally interested in the region. Membership: $50 (Professionals); $25 (Students); $25 (Retirees); $700 (Lifetime).

Meetings/Conferences: Annual
2013 - New Orleans, LA/Jan. 3 - 6
2013 - New Orleans, LA (Hotel Monteleone)/Jan. 3 - 5
2014 - Washington, DC/Jan. 2 - 5
2015 - New York City, NY/Jan. 2 - 5
2016 - Atlanta, GA/Jan. 7 - 10

Publications:
CLAH Newsletter; semi-annually
Membership Directory; on-line

Congress of Chiropractic State Associations (1969)
12531 E. Meadow Dr.
Wichita, KS 67206
Tel: (316) 613-3386 *Fax:* (316) 633-4455
E-Mail: cocsa@cocsa.org
Website: cocsa.org
Members: 48 state associations
Staff: 3
Annual Budget: $100-250,000
Tax: 501(c)(6)

Personnel:
Executive Director: Amy Hardin
   E-Mail: amy4hardin@yahoo.com
Treasurer: Dr. Don Cross
   E-Mail: crosschiro@aol.com

Historical Note:
The mission of COCSA is to provide an open, nonpartisan forum for the promotion and advancement of the chiropractic profession through service to member state associations. Membership: $500 (Active Member Associations); $400 (Associate Member Associations).

Meetings/Conferences: Annual
Conference Chair: Amy Hardin

Publications:
COCSA News; on-line
Member Directory; on-line

Congress of Independent Unions (1958)
303 Ridge St.
Alton, IL 62002
Tel: (618) 462-2447
Website: ciuorg.com
Staff: 1
Annual Budget: $500-1,000,000
Tax: 501(c)(5)

Personnel:
President: R. R. Davis

Historical Note:
C.I.U. offers aid to Independent Unions which is not available elsewhere and helps such Unions in keeping their autonomy.

Congress of Lung Association Staffs (1912)
1150 18th St.
Suite 900
Washington, DC 20036
Tel: (202) 785-3355 *Fax:* (202) 452-1805
Website: lungus.org
Members: 1000 individuals

Staff: 3
Annual Budget: $100-250,000

Personnel:
Executive Director: Christine J. Pleteher
   E-Mail: cpleteher@lungusa.org

Historical Note:
Formerly National Conference of Tuberculosis Workers, and (1973) National Respiratory Disease Conference. Members are professional staff of American Lung Association offices throughout the country. Membership: $40/year (Individual).

Congress of Neurological Surgeons (1951)
10 N. Martingale Rd.
Suite 190
Schaumburg, IL 60173
Tel: (847) 240-2500 *Fax:* (847) 240-0804
E-Mail: info@1cns.org
Website: cns.org
Members: 6763 individuals
Staff: 25
Annual Budget: $10-25,000,000

Personnel:
Executive Director and Chief Executive Officer: David A Westman
President: Christopher E. Wolfla
Director, Information Technology: David C. Berg
Member Recruitment and Communications Coordinator: Jordan B Burghardt
Administrative Assistant: Cheryl. A Davidson
Manager, Human Resources: Dawn M Davis
Director, Marketing and Membership Services: Michele L Lengerman
Accounting manager: Kim . M Marcuccilli
Director, Meetings: Deanne L Starr

Historical Note:
The CNS exists to enhance health and improve lives worldwide through the advancement of education and scientific exchange. A professional society with members both from the United States and a number of foreign countries. Membership: $9- 3,430/year.

Meetings/Conferences:
Conference Chair: Deanne L Starr
2013 - San Francisco, CA/Oct. 19 - 24
2013 - San Francisco, CA/Oct. 19 - 23
2014 - Boston, MA/Oct. 18 - 23

Publications:
Clinical Neurosurgery; annually
Congress Quarterly; quarterly
Neurosurgery; monthly

Membership List Available to Non-members

Congress on Research in Dance (1965)
3416 Primm Ln.
Birmingham, AL 35216
Tel: (205) 823-5517 *Fax:* (205) 823-2760
E-Mail: ashanti@cordance.org
Website: cordance.org
Members: 1322 individuals and institutions
Staff: 3
Annual Budget: $25-50,000
Tax: 501(c)(3)

Personnel:
President: Marta Savigliano PhD
Editor: Mark Franko
   E-Mail: markfranko@earthlink.net
Treasurer: Libby Smigel

Historical Note:
Initially known as the Committee on Research in Dance, assumed its current name in 1979. CORD's mission is to provide opportunities for dance professionals from a broad range of specialties to exchange ideas, resources and methodologies through publication, international and regional conferences and workshops. Membership: $75- $85 (Regular); $40-$55 (Retired); $95 (International); $35-$50 (Student).

Meetings/Conferences:
2013 - Los Angeles, CA (University of California, Los Angeles)/April 19 - 21
2013 - Riverside, CA (Mission Inn Hotel and Spa)/Nov. 14 - 17

Publications:
Dance Research Journal; semi-annually; adv.
Membership Directory; on-line

Congressional Internet Caucus Advisory Committee
1634 I St. NW
Suite 1100
Washington, DC 20006
Tel: (202) 638-4370 *Fax:* (202) 637-0968
Website: netcaucus.org
Staff: 2
Tax: 501(c)(3)

Personnel:
Contact: Catherine Matsuda
   E-Mail: cmatsuda@netcaucus.org
Contact, Communication: Tim Lordan
   E-Mail: tlordan@netcaucus.org

Historical Note:
An organization that works to educated Congress on internet-related issues. Funded by the Internet Education Foundation. Membership is open to corporate, non-profit, and trade association organizations.

Meetings/Conferences: Annual
2013 - Washington, DC (Hyatt Regency Hotel)/Jan. 22 - 23

Congressional Legislative Staff Association (1986)
Longworth House Office Building
P.O. Box 1991
Washington, DC 20007
Tel: (202) 225-2635 *Fax:* (202) 226-4386
E-Mail: congressionalstaffers@gmail.com
Website: uscongressionalstaff.org
Members: 500 members
Staff: 2

Personnel:
President: Cory Crowly
Secretary: Trey Reffett CAE

Historical Note:
Founded as the House Legislative Assistants Association. CLSA is a nonpartisan professional organization dedicated to provide professional opportunities to the legislative staff. Serves as the public face of congressional staff and provides them with profesional opportunities. Membership: $20/year.

Connected International Meeting Professionals Association (1980)
8803 Queen Elizabeth Blvd.
Annandale, VA 22003
Tel: (512) 684-0889 *Fax:* (267) 390-5193
E-Mail: info@cimpa.org
Website: cimpa.org
Members: 3436 individuals
Staff: 6
Annual Budget: $2-5,000,000

Personnel:
President: Lida Peterson
   E-Mail: lida@cimpa.org
Director, Certification: Dr. Frances Hanson
   E-Mail: frances@cimpa.org

Historical Note:
CIMPA, an online association of meeting professionals, seeks to connect people of different cultures through meetings, travel and the internet for the purpose of promoting understanding, tolerance and friendships. Members are association executives, show organizers, meeting planners, incentive organizers, tour operators, travel agents, seminar organizers, trainers, speakers, representatives from technology companies, tourist boards, convention bureaus, hotels, airlines, car rental companies, cruise ships, tourist attractions, vendors of convention badges, portfolios and other supplies and interested persons. Membership: $295- 495 (Gold); $1,895-2,895 (Ruby); Free (Emerald).

Continuing Education:
Certification Designation/s: CGMP, CIMP, CPPM

Publications:
CIMPA Newsletter

Conservation and Preservation Charities of America
1100 Larkspur Landing Cir.
Suite 340
Larkspur, CA 94939
Fax: (415) 925-2650
TollFree: (800) 626-6685
Website: conservenow.org
Members: 86 organizations
Staff: 3
Annual Budget: $2-5,000,000
Tax: 501(c)(3)

Personnel:
President: Carl Ashley

Contact, Membership Services: Carri Harte
Treasurer: Karen Piatak

Historical Note:
The Conservation and Preservation Charities of America (CPCA) is a federation of America's national organizations working to protect and restore the Earth's natural environment and historic treasures through workplace giving campaigns.

Publications:
Membership Directory; on-line

Membership List Available to Non-members

Conservation Technology Information Center
3495 Kent Ave.
Suite J100
West LaFayette, IN 47906
Tel: (765) 494-9555 *Fax:* (765) 463-4106
E-Mail: ctic@ctic.org
Website: ctic.purdue.edu
Staff: 6
Annual Budget: $500-1,000,000
Tax: 501(c)(3)

Personnel:
Executive Director: Karen A. Scanlon
    E-Mail: scanlon@ctic.org
Director, Operations: Tammy Taylor
    E-Mail: taylor@ctic.org

Historical Note:
CTIC's mission is to champion, promote and provide information on technologies and sustainable agricultural systems that conserve and enhance soil, water, air and wildlife resources and are productive and profitable. Membership: $50-500+ (Individual); $250-1,000+ (Institutional); $500-8,500+ (Corporate).

Publications:
Member Mail; on-line
Membership Directory; on-line
Partners Magazine; quarterly; adv.

Consolidated Tape Association *(1974)*
C/O New York Stock Exchange
11 Wall St., 21st Floor
New York, NY 10005
Tel: (212) 656-2052 *Fax:* (212) 656-5848
Website: nysedata.com/cta
Members: 9 organizations
Staff: 4
Annual Budget: Under $10,000

Personnel:
Administrator: Patricia Hussey
    E-Mail: phussey@nyse.com
Investor Representative: Thomas J. Jordan
    E-Mail: tjjordan@jandj.com
Institutional Representative: Bill Lee
    E-Mail: bill.lee@morganstanley.com
Retail Representative: Richard Urian
    E-Mail: rich.urian@tdameritrade.com

Historical Note:
CTA members are stock exchanges and the National Association of Securities Dealers. CTA melds the reporting of transactions from the various stock exchanges.

Consortium for Advanced Management, International *(1972)*
6836 Bee Cave
Suite 256
Austin, TX 78746
Tel: (512) 617-6428 *Fax:* (817) 426-5799
E-Mail: admin@cam-i.org
Website: cam-i.org
Members: 100 companies and organizations
Staff: 7
Annual Budget: $1-2,000,000

Personnel:
President: Ashok Vadgama
    E-Mail: ashok@cam-i.org
Margarita Bagwell
Contact, Member Services: Nancy Thomas

Historical Note:
Founded as Computer Aided Manufacturing International; assumed the name Consortium for Advanced Manufacturing International in 1997. CAM-I's mission is to serve as a collaborative forum of thought leaders to develop practical and effective management tools, techniques and methods to advance the way organizations manage costs, processes and performance. Membership Dues: Based on annual revenue.

Meetings/Conferences:

Number of non-conference events/year: 2

Publications:
CMA Magazine
CMS Newsletter; on-line
Member Directory

Consortium for Graduate Study in Management *(1966)*
5585 Pershing Ave.
Suite 240
St. Louis, MO 63112-1795
Tel: (314) 877-5500 *Fax:* (314) 877-5505
TollFree: (888) 865-6814
Website: cgsm.org
Members:
17 schools
140 supply companies
Staff: 19
Annual Budget: $10-25,000,000
Tax: 501(c)(3)

Personnel:
Executive Director and Chief Executive Officer: Peter J. Aranda III
    E-Mail: arandap@cgsm.org
Manager, Corporate Relations: Cynthia D. Ackins
    E-Mail: ackinsc@cgsm.org
Manager, Database Operations: Jeff Farris
    E-Mail: farrisj@cgsm.org
Director, Conferences, Meetings and Events: Bridgitti Knox CMP
    E-Mail: knoxb@cgsm.org
Manager, Communications: Elizabeth Macanufo
    E-Mail: macanufoe@cgsm.org
Director, Recruiting: Corey Webb
    E-Mail: webbc@cgsm.org

Historical Note:
CGSM's mission is to enhance diversity in business education by helping to reduce the serious under representation of African Americans, Hispanic Americans and Native Americans in both member schools' enrollments and the ranks of management. The vision is to work toward the day when African Americans, Hispanic Americans and Native Americans are no longer underrepresented in management careers in the business community of the United States.

Meetings/Conferences:
Conference Chair: Bridgitti Knox CMP
Number of non-conference events/year: 3

Publications:
In Magazine

Consortium for North American Higher Education Collaboration
P.O. Box 210300
Tucson, AZ 85721-0300
Tel: (520) 621-7761 *Fax:* (520) 626-2675
E-Mail: membership@conahec.org
Website: conahec.org
Members: 45 Member
Staff: 8

Personnel:
Executive Director: Francisco J. Marmolejo
    E-Mail: fmarmole@email.arizona.edu
Administrative Associate Office, Community Relations: Gilbert Maldonado
Program Manager: Gilberto Olivas
    E-Mail: golivas@email.arizona.edu

Historical Note:
CONAHEC enhances the mutual understanding and cooperation in the North American community by fostering collaboration between institutions of higher education in Canada, Mexico, and the United States. Membership: $1,800/academic year.

Meetings/Conferences: Annual
2013 - Edmonton, AB (MacEwan University Campus)/ May 1 - 3
Number of non-conference events/year: 4

Consortium of Behavioral Health Nurses and Associates *(1987)*
1733 H St., Suite 330
PMB 1214
Blaine, WA 98230
Members: 1000 individuals
Staff: 4
Annual Budget: $10-25,000

Personnel:

Executive Director: Randy Bryson

Historical Note:
Founded as National Consortium of Chemical Dependency Nurses; assumed its current name in 2002. CBHNA members are registered and licensed practical nurses specializing in the treatment of chemical dependency. Provides certification for members. Membership: $75/year.

Consortium of College and University Media Centers *(1971)*
C/O Indiana University, Classroom Technology Services
601 E. Kirkwood Ave., Franklin Hall 0009
Bloomington, IN 47405-1223
Tel: (812) 855-6049 *Fax:* (812) 855-2103
E-Mail: ccumc@ccumc.org
Website: ccumc.org
Members:
400 libraries/media centers
750 individuals
Staff: 2
Annual Budget: $100-250,000
Tax: 501(c)(3)

Personnel:
Executive Director: Aileen Scales
    E-Mail: scales@indiana.edu

Historical Note:
Formerly known as the Consortium of University Film Centers (CUFC), assumed its current name in 1988. CCUMC's mission is to provide leadership and a forum for information exchange to the providers of media content, academic technology, and support for quality teaching and learning at institutions of higher education. Members are college and university media center managers, film/video rental librarians, film/video producers, distributors and other interested individuals and organizations. Membership: $325-795 (Institutional/Corporate, based on no. of persons); $325 (Associate); $55 (Student).

Meetings/Conferences: Annual

Publications:
College and University Media Review; annually
Membership Directory; annually
The Leader

Consortium of Forensic Science Organizations *(2000)*
120 N. Lee St.
Suite 105
Falls Church, VA 22046
Tel: (202) 577-6053
Website: thecfso.org
Members: 12,000 forensic science professionals
Staff: 1
Annual Budget: $100-250,000

Personnel:
Contact, Communication: Beth Lavach
    E-Mail: bethlavach@elsandassociates.com

Historical Note:
CFSO's mission is to speak with a single forensic science voice in matters of mutual interest to its member organizations, to influence public policy at the national level and to make a compelling case for greater federal funding for public crime laboratories and medical examiner offices.

Publications:
CFSO Newsletter; monthly

Consortium of School Networking *(1992)*
1025 Vermont Ave. NW
Suite 1010
Washington, DC 20005-3599
Tel: (202) 861-2676 *Fax:* (202) 393-2011
TollFree: (866) 267-8747
E-Mail: info@cosn.org
Website: cosn.org
Members: 600 organizations
Staff: 9
Annual Budget: $2-5,000,000
Tax: 501(c)(3)

Personnel:
Chief Executive Officer: Keith R. Krueger CAE
    E-Mail: keith@cosn.org
Director, Certification and Education: Gayle Dahlman
    E-Mail: gdahlman@cosn.org
Manager, Web and Database: Brian Foor
    E-Mail: bfoor@cosn.org
Senior Director, Conferences and Events: Juliene Heany
    E-Mail: jheaney@cosn.org
Director, Membership and Chapters: Kevin Wesolowski

E-Mail: kwesolowski@cosn.org

Historical Note:
A nonprofit education association promoting the use of information technologies and the Internet to improve primary and secondary education. CoSN's mission is to empower K-12 school district technology leaders to use technology strategically to improve teaching and learning. Membership: $250-1,000 (Institutional); $1000-4,500 (Corporate); $250 (Individual).

Meetings/Conferences: Annual
Conference Chair: Juliene Heany
2013 - San Diego, CA (Sheraton San Diego Hotel and Marina)/March 11 - 13
2014 - Washington, DC (Washington Hilton)/March 18 - 20

Publications:
CoSN Bulletin; semi-monthly
Washington Update; monthly

Consortium of Social Science Associations (1981)
1701 K St. NW
Suite 1150
Washington, DC 20006
Tel: (202) 842-3525 *Fax:* (202) 842-2788
E-Mail: cossa@cossa.org
Website: cossa.org
Members: 23 member organizations
Staff: 4
Annual Budget: $500-1,000,000
Tax: 501(c)(6)

Personnel:
Executive Director: Dr. Howard J. Silver
    E-Mail: silverhj@cossa.org
Assistant Director, Public Affairs: Gina Drioane
    E-Mail: gsdrioane@cossa.org
Assistant Director, Government Relations: La Tosha Plavnik
    E-Mail: lplavnik@cossa.org

Historical Note:
COSSA is an advocacy organization that promotes attention to and Federal funding for the social and behavioral sciences. It also serves as a bridge between the academic research community and the Washington policymaking community. Members consist of professional associations, scientific societies, universities and research centers and institutes.

Meetings/Conferences: Annual
Publications:
COSSA Washington Update; bi-weekly
Membership Directory; on-line

Consortium on Financing Higher Education (1970)
238 Main St.
Suite 402
Cambridge, MA 02142
Tel: (617) 253-5030 *Fax:* (617) 258-8280
E-Mail: cofhe@jhu.edu
Website: web.mit.edu/cofhe
Members: 31 institutions
Staff: 7

Personnel:
President: Dr. Kristine E. Dillon
Director, Information and Research Systems: Dr. Ann Birk
Office Administration: Isabel Bourelle
Assistant Director, Administration: Sydney Earle

Historical Note:
The Consortium's data collection, research, and policy analysis focus on matters pertaining to access, affordability, and assessment, particularly as they relate to undergraduate education, admissions, financial aid, and the financing of higher education.

Meetings/Conferences:
Conference Chair: Sydney Earle

Publications:
Membership Directory; on-line

Construction Financial Management Association (1981)
100 Village Blvd.
Suite 200
Princeton, NJ 08540
Tel: (609) 452-8000 *Fax:* (609) 452-0474
Website: cfma.org
Members: 6,500 members
Staff: 20
Annual Budget: $5-10,000,000

Tax: 501(c)(6)

Personnel:
President and Chief Executive Officer: Stuart Binstock
    E-Mail: sbinstock@cfma.org
Managing Editor: Kristy L. Domboski
    E-Mail: kdomboski@cfma.org
Director, Educational Services: Andrew R. Gioseffi
    E-Mail: agioseffi@cfma.org
Manager, Information Technology: Gabe Kerkuska
    E-Mail: gkerkuska@cfma.org
Director, Meeting Services: Dina M. O'Rourke
    E-Mail: dorourke@cfma.org
Manager, Human Resources: Laurel Seymour
    E-Mail: lseymour@cfma.org
Chief Operating Officer: Brian Summers
    E-Mail: bsummers@cfma.org
Director, Membership Services: Michael Verbanic
    E-Mail: mverbanic@cfma.org

Historical Note:
The purpose of CFMA is to provide resources to meet challenges of construction financial professionals. Members are accountants, controllers, financial managers and CPAs in the construction industry concerned with financial management tax, technology and risk management issues. CFMA's General Membership represents all types of contractors, including generals and subcontractors. Associate Members include the accounting, insurance, surety, software, legal, and banking specialists who serve the construction industry. Membership: $340 (General/Education); $440 (Associate); $230 (International General); $300 (International Associate); $0 (Student).

Continuing Education:
Certification Designation/s: ICCIFP

Meetings/Conferences: Annual
Conference Chair: Dina M. O'Rourke
2013 - San Diego, CA (Hilton San Diego Bayfront)/June 22 - 26
2013 - Las Vegas, NV (Caesars Palace)/Oct. 23 - 25
2014 - Las Vegas, NV (Caesars Palace)/June 7 - 11
2015 - Chicago, IL (Sheraton Chicago Hotel and Towers)/June 27 - July 1
2016 - San Antonio, TX (JW Marriott San Antonio Hill Country Resort and Spa)/June 25 - 29
2017 - Phoenix, AZ (JW Marriott Phoenix Desert Ridge Resort and Spa)/June 3 - 7
2019 - Las Vegas, NV (The Cosmopolitan Hotel)/June 1 - 5

Publications:
CFMA Building Profits; adv.

Construction Industry CPAs/Consultants Association (1989)
15011 E. Twilight View Dr.
Fountain Hills, AZ 85268
Tel: (480) 836-0300 *Fax:* (480) 836-0400
Website: cicpac.com
Members: 75 companies
Staff: 1
Annual Budget: $250-500,000

Personnel:
Executive Director: John J. Corcoran
    E-Mail: jcorcoran@cicpac.com

Historical Note:
CICPAC serves as a close-knit community for CPA firms recognized in their respective markets for providing high quality financial and consulting services to over 6,000 construction entities.

Meetings/Conferences: Annual
2013 - Chicago, IL (CICPAC Annual Conference)/July 24 - 26
Number of non-conference events/year: 7

Publications:
Member Directory; on-line

Membership List Available to Non-members

Construction Industry Round Table, Inc. (1987)
8115 Old Dominion Dr.
Suite 210
McLean, VA 22102-2325
Tel: (202) 466-6777 *Fax:* (202) 466-6767
E-Mail: cirt@cirt.org
Website: cirt.org
Members: 100 chief executive officers
Staff: 2
Annual Budget: $500-1,000,000
Tax: 501(c)(6)

Personnel:

President: Mark A. Casso
    E-Mail: mcasso@cirt.org
Director, Association Programs: Jane Bonvillain

Historical Note:
A design and construction Industry, CIRT's mission is to to be a force for positive change in the construction industry while helping members to improve the management performance of their individual companies. Members are CEOs from the leading architectural, engineering and construction firms doing business in the United States.

Meetings/Conferences: Semi-Annual
2013 - Washington, DC (Fairmont Washington)/April 30 - May 2
2013 - Chicago, IL (Park Hyatt Chicago)/Oct. 28 - 30

Publications:
CIRT News; on-line

The Construction Innovation Forum (1987)
6494 Latcha Rd.
Walbridge, OH 43465
Tel: (419) 725-3108 *Fax:* (419) 725-3079
E-Mail: info@cif.org
Website: cif.org
Staff: 1
Annual Budget: $10-25,000
Tax: 501(c)(3)

Personnel:
Chair: Timothy Alter
    E-Mail: talter@rlcos.com

Historical Note:
CIF's aim is to recognize and foster technical advances in the construction industry. Membership: $1,000 (Corporate); $250 (Associate).

Publications:
CIF Innovator

Construction Management Association of America (1982)
7926 Jones Branch Dr.
Suite 800
McLean, VA 22102-3303
Tel: (703) 356-2622 *Fax:* (703) 356-6388
E-Mail: info@cmaanet.org
Website: cmaanet.org
Members: 10000 members
Staff: 14
Annual Budget: $2-5,000,000

Personnel:
President and Chief Executive Officer: Bruce D'Agostino FCMAA, CAE
    E-Mail: bdagostino@cmaanet.org
Manager, Membership Services: Angeles Cervantes
    E-Mail: acervantes@cmaanet.org
Vice President, Professional Development: Dennis Doran
    E-Mail: ddoran@cmaanet.org
Director, Meetings and Conference Services: Mariam Ghaussy CMP
    E-Mail: mghaussy@cmaanet.org
Vice President: John J. McKeon
    E-Mail: jmckeon@cmaanet.org
Director, Certification: Nicholas Soto
    E-Mail: nsoto@cmaanet.org
Vice President, Finance and Administration: Melaine L. Sprigler CPA, MBA
    E-Mail: msprigler@cmaanet.org

Historical Note:
CMAA's mission is to promote and enhance leadership, professionalism, and excellence in managing the development and construction of projects and programs. Membership: $25-25,000/year.

Continuing Education:
Certification Designation/s: CCM

Meetings/Conferences: Semi-Annual
Conference Chair: Mariam Ghaussy CMP
2013 - New Orleans, LA (Sheraton Hotel New Orleans)/May 5 - 7
2013 - Las Vegas, NV (ARIA Resort and Casino at CityCenter)/Oct. 6 - 8/1000 attendees
2014 - Baltimore, MD (Harbor Court Baltimore)/May 4 - 6
2014 - San Francisco, CA (Marriott San Francisco Marquis)/Oct. 19 - 21/1000 attendees
2015 - Orlando, FL (Hilton Bonnet Creek Resort)/Oct. 11 - 13/1000 attendees
2016 - San Diego, CA (DoubleTree by Hilton)/Oct. 9 - 11/1000 attendees

2017 - Washington, DC (Hilton)/Oct. 8 - 10/1000 attendees
Number of non-conference events/year: 3

Publications:
CM Advisor; bi-monthly
CM eJournal; annually
CMAA NewsLine; bi-monthly

Construction Marketing Research Council *(1992)*
5420 Old Orchard Rd.
C/O Portland Cement Association
Skokie, IL 60077
Tel: (847) 966-6200 *Fax:* (847) 966-8389
E-Mail: info@c-m-r-c.com
Website: c-m-r-c.com
Members: 25 companies
Staff: 2
Annual Budget: $10-25,000

Personnel:
President: Craig Schulz

Historical Note:
CMRC is a dedicated group of global marketing professionals involved in market research, strategic planning, and forecasting in the construction and building products industry. Membership is restricted to the highest level marketing research or planning professional within a company. Associate non-voting membership is available for other individuals in different groups within the same company. Has no paid officers or full-time staff. Membership: $300/year.

Publications:
Member Listing; on-line

Construction Owners Association of America *(1994)*
5000 Austell Powder Springs Rd.
Suite 217
Austell, GA 30106
Tel: (770) 433-0820 *Fax:* (404) 577-3551
TollFree: (800) 994-2622
E-Mail: coaa@coaa.org
Website: coaa.org
Members: 475 individuals
Staff: 4
Annual Budget: $500-1,000,000
Tax: 501(c)(6)

Personnel:
Chief Executive, Education and Conferences: Lisa DeGolyer
Chief Executive, Finance and Operations: Valerie Delaney

Historical Note:
COAA is dedicated to make a significant and lasting impact on the construction industry through its leadership by creating a unified, collective voice for owners' issues in the construction process. Members include any individual, corporation, partnership, proprietorship, joint venture or any state, local or federal governmental body or agency who either regularly or from time to time engage in construction activities as the owner or developer. Membership: $350 (Owner); $1,000 (Associate/Owner- Corporate); $500 (Additional Associate); $40 (Student); $80 (Educator).

Meetings/Conferences: Semi-Annual
Conference Chair: Lisa DeGolyer
2013 - Atlanta, GA (Grand Hyatt Atlanta In Buckhead)/ May 8 - 10
2013 - San Diego, CA (Hilton Torrey Pines)/Oct. 30 - Nov. 1
Number of non-conference events/year: 2

Publications:
Membership Directory

Membership List Available to Non-members

Construction Specifications Institute *(1948)*
110 S. Union St.
Suite 100
Alexandria, VA 22314-3351
Tel: (703) 684-0300 *Fax:* (703) 236-4600
TollFree: (800) 689-2900
E-Mail: csi@csinet.org
Website: csinet.org
Members: 15000 individuals
Staff: 38
Annual Budget: Under $10,000

Personnel:
Executive Director and Chief Executive Officer: Walter T. Marlowe CAE, CSI, PE
E-Mail: wmarlowe@csinet.org

Senior Representative, Membership Services: Jordan Chatman
E-Mail: jchatman@csinet.org
Director, Professional Development: Erica Smedley Cox
E-Mail: ecox@csinet.org
Director, Communications and Web Community: Joy Davis CSI
E-Mail: jdavis@csinet.org
Senior Manager, Finance and Operations: Jing Huang
E-Mail: jhuang@csinet.org
Senior Manager, Internet Services and Web Development: Eric Kestler
E-Mail: ekestler@csinet.org
Chief Financial Officer: Shannon MacGregor
E-Mail: smacgregor@csinet.org
Senior Manager, Marketing and Communications: Christine Tanner
E-Mail: ctanner@csinet.org

Historical Note:
CSI's mission is to advance building information management and education of project teams to improve facility performance. It serves the interests of architects, specifiers, engineers, contractors, product manufacturers, and others in the construction industry. Membership: $240 (Professional); $115 (Emerging Professional); $27 (Student).

Continuing Education:
Certification Designation/s: CDT, CCCA, CCS, CCPR

Meetings/Conferences: Annual
2013 - Charlotte, NC (Charlotte Omni Hotel)/Feb. 7 - 9

Publications:
Leader Newsletter; monthly

Construction Users Roundtable *(2000)*
4100 Executive Park Dr.
Suite 210
Cincinnati, OH 45241
Tel: (513) 563-4131 *Fax:* (513) 733-9551
E-Mail: construction-users@curt.org
Website: curt.org
Members: 118 companies
Staff: 1
Annual Budget: $1-2,000,000
Tax: 501(c)(6)

Personnel:
Executive Vice President: Gregory L. Sizemore

Historical Note:
CURT's mission is to create competitive advantage for construction users by providing aggressive leadership on business issues that promote excellence in the creation of capital assets. Members include construction user/ owner,contractor,Association,Young professional.

Meetings/Conferences:
Conference Chair: Gregory L. Sizemore

Publications:
CURT Newsletter
Membership Directory; on-line
The Voice; adv.

Construction Writers Association *(1958)*
P.O. Box 14784
Chicago, IL 60614
Tel: (773) 687-8726 *Fax:* (773) 687-8627
E-Mail: info@constructionwriters.org
Website: constructionwriters.org/
Members: 300 individuals
Staff: 2
Annual Budget: $50-100,000

Personnel:
Executive Director: Deborah J. Hodges

Historical Note:
The Construction Writers Association is a non-profit, non-partisan, international organization for professional journalists, writers, editors, and publicists serving the information needs of the construction industry. CWA's mission is to provide a forum for communications professionals in all segments of the construction industry to connect with other professionals and enhance skills through education. Membership: $125 (Individual/Affiliate); $225 (Corporate).

Meetings/Conferences:
2013 - Chicago, IL/Oct. 21 - 23

Publications:
CWA e-zine; quarterly; adv.
CWA eXchange; quarterly; adv.
Membership Directory; on-line

Consultant Dietitians in Health Care Facilities *(1975)*
2219 Cardinal Dr.
Waterloo, IA 50701
Tel: (813) 474-2757 *Fax:* (319) 235-7224
E-Mail: fewalker@stellarnet.com
Website: cdhcf.org
Members: 5000 individuals
Staff: 1
Annual Budget: $100-250,000

Personnel:
Executive Coordinator: Marla Carlson

Historical Note:
A dietetic practice group of the American Dietetic Association. Membership: $30/year (individual), plus ADA membership.

Consumer Aerosol Products Council
1667 K St. NW
Suite 300
Washington, DC 20006
Tel: (202) 872-8110
E-Mail: admin@aerosolproducts.org
Website: aerosolproducts.org
Staff: 2
Annual Budget: $50-100,000
Tax: 501(c)(3)

Personnel:
President: Rick Morris
E-Mail: morris@smithharroff.com
Media Contact: Hillary VanderBand
E-Mail: hvanderband@aerosolproducts.org

Historical Note:
CAPCO is a nonprofit organization dedicated to providing accurate information about aerosol products. The purpose of the council is to educate consumers about aerosol products.

Consumer Bankers Association *(1919)*
1225 I St. NW
Suite 550
Washington, DC 20005
Tel: (202) 552-6380 *Fax:* (703) 528-1290
E-Mail: cba@cbanet.org
Website: cbanet.org
Members:
200 corporate
300 associates
Staff: 23
Annual Budget: $5-10,000,000
Tax: 501(c)(6)

Personnel:
President and Chief Executive Officer: Richard Hunt
E-Mail: rhunt@cbanet.org
Director, Information Services and Technology: Laura Armstrong
E-Mail: larmstrong@cbanet.org
Associate General Counsel: Jeffrey Bloch
E-Mail: jbloch@cbanet.org
Vice President, Congressional Affairs: Ryan Pace Bradshaw
E-Mail: pbradshaw@cbanet.org
Coordinator, Education: Matthew Brauch
Vice President, Communications and Marketing: Jean M. Bunton
Vice President, Membership and Education: Melissa J. Cabocel
E-Mail: mcabocel@cbanet.org
Coordinator, Membership Services: Stephen Congdon
Treasurer: Jayne Ellen Hunt
Manager, Communications: Deirdre Leahy
Vice President, Communications and Marketing: Marybeth Leongini
E-Mail: mleongini@cbanet.org
Conference Registrar and Database Coordinator: Tammy Morgan
Director, Exhibits and Sponsorships, Special Projects Coordinator: Erin Snyder
E-Mail: esnyder@cbanet.org
Vice President and General Counsel: Steven I. Zeisel
E-Mail: szeisel@cbanet.org

Historical Note:
Formerly (1919) Morris Plan Bankers Association. CBA's mission is to provide leadership, education, research and federal representation on retail banking issues such as privacy, fair lending, and consumer protection

legislation/regulation. *Membership:* $1,600-6,000 (Product Associate); $5,000 (National Associate).

Meetings/Conferences: Annual
Conference Chair: Jayne Ellen Hunt
Number of non-conference events/year: 4

Publications:
Membership Directory; on-line

Consumer Credit Industry Association *(1951)*
6300 Powers Ferry Rd.
Suite 600-286
Atlanta, GA 30339
Tel: (678) 858-4001 *Fax:* (312) 939-8287
Website: cciaonline.com
Members: 120 companies
Staff: 4
Annual Budget: $1-2,000,000

Personnel:
Executive Vice President: Scott J. Cipinko
    E-Mail: sjcipinko@cciaonline.com
Director, Member Services: Stephanie Brandt
    E-Mail: sbrandt@cciaonline.com
Vice President, Legislative Regulatory Counsel: Elizabeth
    (Beth) Kastigar
    E-Mail: bkastigar@cciaonline.com

Historical Note:
Formerly Consumer Credit Insurance Association. CCIA provides consumers with the financial security of knowing debt will be repaid or assets protected in the event of unexpected but foreseeable events by introducing non-insurance debt and asset protection products. Members are companies that sell or service insurance and related debt protection products provided in connection with consumer credit transactions.

Meetings/Conferences: Annual

Publications:
Membership Directory; on-line

Consumer Data Industry Association *(2000)*
1090 Vermont Ave. NW
Suite 200
Washington, DC 20005-4905
Tel: (202) 371-0910 *Fax:* (202) 371-0134
E-Mail: cdia@cdiaonline.org
Website: cdiaonline.org
Members: 250 individuals
Staff: 9
Annual Budget: $2-5,000,000

Personnel:
President and Chief Executive Officer: Stuart K. Pratt
    E-Mail: SPratt@cdiaonline.org
Contact, Membership Services: Betty Byrnes
    E-Mail: bbyrnes@cdiaonline.org
Manager, E-Commerce: Anita Popwell
    E-Mail: apopwell@cdiaonline.org
Vice President, Public Policy and Legal Affairs: Joe Rubin

Historical Note:
Formerly known as National Association of Retail Credit Agencies, became the National Association of Mercantile Agencies in 1908 and the Associated Credit Bureaus of America in 1937 and adopted its present name in the year 2000. CDIA's mission is to ensure that consumer data can be collected, maintained, and used by third parties in responsible ways by U.S. businesses to help them manage risk, create fair markets for consumers, and to increase business competition. Its consumer reporting offices dues is a tiered structure and is based on net revenue and the calculation of membership dues for the Collection Service Division is based on trade area population.

Continuing Education:
Certification Designation/s: FACTA, FCRA

Meetings/Conferences: Biennial

Consumer Electronics Association *(1996)*
1919 S. Eads St.
Arlington, VA 22202
Tel: (703) 907-7600 *Fax:* (703) 907-7675
TollFree: (866) 858-1555
E-Mail: cea@CE.org
Website: ce.org
Members: 2000 companies
Staff: 11
Annual Budget: Over $100,000,000
Tax: 501(c)(6)

Personnel:
President and Chief Executive Officer: Gary J. Shapiro
    E-Mail: gshapiro@ce.org

*Vice President, Environmental Affairs and Industry
    Sustainability:* Walter Alcorn
    E-Mail: walcorn@CE.org
Senior Director, International Trade: Sage Chandler
    E-Mail: schandler@CE.org
*Senior Vice President, Communications and Strategic
    Relations:* Jeff Joseph
*Senior Coordinator, Industry Statistics, Market Research,
    Media Contact and Wireless:* Steve Kidera
    E-Mail: skidera@ce.org
Manager, Technology and Standards: Leslie King
    E-Mail: lking@ce.org
Treasurer: Glenda MacMullin
Vice President, Congressional Affairs: Veronica O'Connell
    E-Mail: cea@ce.org
Senior Vice President, Government Affairs: Michael D.
    Petricone
    E-Mail: michaelp@ce.org
Senior Director, Publications: Cindy Stevens
    E-Mail: cstevens@ce.org
Senior Manager, Event: Sarah Szabo
    E-Mail: sszabo@CE.org

Historical Note:
CEA's mission is to grow the consumer electronics industry. Membership: $750-$30,000 (Regular depending on Annual Revenue), $350-$20,000 (Retailer/Integrator depending on Annual Revenue), $350-$10,000(Associate depending on Annual Revenue), $1,000-$30,000(Research/Analyst depending on Annual Revenue).

Continuing Education:
Certification Designation/s: MECP

Meetings/Conferences:
Conference Chair: Sarah Szabo
Number of non-conference events/year: 17

Publications:
CAE Newsletter; monthly
CE Vision; bi-monthly; adv.
Government Alert newsletter; on-line
Membership Directory; on-line
PARA Division Newsletter; monthly
Small Business Council newsletter; monthly
TechHome Division newsletter; monthly
Wireless Communications Division newsletter;
    monthly

Consumer Health Alliance *(2002)*
18715 Gibbons Dr.
Dallas, TX 75287-4045
Website: consumerhealthalliance.org
Staff: 1
Annual Budget: $500-1,000,000

Personnel:
Director, Membership Services: Marvin Migdol
    E-Mail: fmmigdol@gmail.com

Historical Note:
CHA is a discount group affiliation health care provider. CHA seeks to bring awareness and a voice to the national healthcare arena that focuses on recognizing and promoting fair and ethical business practices within the discount healthcare industry.

Consumer Healthcare Products Association *(1881)*
900 19th St. NW
Suite 700
Washington, DC 20006
Tel: (202) 429-9260 *Fax:* (202) 223-6835
Website: chpa-info.org
Members:
190 companies
190 Active and Associate members
Staff: 34
Annual Budget: $10-25,000,000
Tax: 501(c)(6)

Personnel:
President and Chief Executive Officer: Scott M. Melville
    E-Mail: melville@chpa-info.org
Vice President, Administration and Treasurer: Roman G.
    Blazauskas
    E-Mail: rblazauskas@chpa-info.org
Website Manager and Coordinator, Information Technology:
    Susan M. DiBartolo
    E-Mail: sdibartolo@chpa-info.org
Senior Director, Communications and Public Affairs:
    Elizabeth A. Funderburk
    E-Mail: efunderburk@chpa-info.org

Director, Information Technologies and Facilities: Ken W.
    Hoffman
    E-Mail: khoffman@chpa-info.org
Senior Director, Meetings: Kass Kassouf
    E-Mail: kkassouf@chpa-info.org
Manager, Human Resources: Allison A. McKee
    E-Mail: amckee@chpa-info.org
Vice President, Corporate Development: Theodore L.
    Peterson
    E-Mail: tpeterson@chpa-info.org
Vice President, Communications and Alliance Development:
    Emily Skor
    E-Mail: eskor@chpa-info.org
*Senior Vice President, Policy, and General Counsel &
    Secretary:* David C. Spangler
    E-Mail: dspangler@chpa-info.org
Manager, Membership and Corporate Development: Phyllis
    M. Taylor
    E-Mail: ptaylor@chpa-info.org

Historical Note:
CHPA was organized as the Proprietary Medicine Manufacturers and Dealers Association; became Nonprescription Drug Manufacturers Association in 1989, and assumed its present name in 1999. Purpose is to promote the role of over-the-counter medicines and nutritional supplements in America's healthcare system through science, education, and advocacy. Active members manufacture or market OTC medicines and nutritional supplements. Associate members supply goods and services to the association's Active members. Associate members include advertising agencies, national cable, radio, and television networks, contract manufacturers, executive search firms, Internet services, law firms and lawyers, logistics providers, market research firms, packaging designers and packagers. Membership fee based on sales volume.

Meetings/Conferences:
Conference Chair: Kass Kassouf
2013 - Naples, FL (Ritz-Carlton Golf Resort, Naples)/
    March 11 - 13

Publications:
Executive Newsletter; monthly
Member Directory; on-line

Consumer Mortgage Coalition *(1995)*
101 Constitution Ave. NW
Ninth Floor West
Washington, DC 20001
Tel: (202) 742-4366 *Fax:* (202) 403-3926
Staff: 1
Annual Budget: $500-1,000,000

Personnel:
Executive Director: Anne C. Canfield
    E-Mail: anne@canfieldassoc.com

Historical Note:
Represents the national residential mortgage lenders, servicers, and service providers. Its efforts are focused exclusively on lobbying in Washington, D. C. for the mortgage industry and the interests of their prime members.

Consumer Specialty Products Association *(1914)*
1667 K St. NW
Suite 300
Washington, DC 20006-2111
Tel: (202) 872-8110 *Fax:* (202) 223-2636
E-Mail: info@cspa.org
Website: cspa.org
Members: 250 Companies
Staff: 33
Annual Budget: $5-10,000,000

Personnel:
Executive Director: Susan Little
    E-Mail: slittle@cspa.org
President, Chief Executive Officer: Chris D Cathcart
    E-Mail: ccathcart@cspa.org
Director, Meetings and Conventions: Laura Mowawd Geib
Vice President, Communications: Lynne R. Harris
Director, Communications: Larry Jones
Executive Vice President, Legislative and Public Affairs:
    Philip Klein
    E-Mail: pklein@cspa.org
Vice President, General Counsel: Brigid Klein
    E-Mail: bklein@cspa.org
Director, Administrative Services and Human Resources:
    Holly Schroeder
    E-Mail: hschroeder@cspa.org
Director, Strategic Issues Advocacy: Joe Yost
    E-Mail: jyost@cspa.org

Historical Note:
Formerly the National Association of Insecticide and Disinfectant Manufacturers, became Chemical Specialties Manufacturers Association in 1948, and assumed its current name in 2001. CSPA's mission is to develop high standards to maximize the safety, performance and sustainability of its members' products. It also sponsors the CSPA Political Action Committee (CSPA-PAC).

Meetings/Conferences: Annual

Publications:
Executive Newswatch; annually; adv.
HAPPI magazine; monthly

Contact Lens Association of Ophthalmologists
(1963)
4000 Legato Rd.
Suite 700
Fairfax, VA 22033-9937
Fax: (703) 434-3003
E-Mail: eyes@clao.org
Website: clao.org
Members: 850 individuals
Staff: 3
Annual Budget: $100-250,000
Tax: 501(c)(6)

Personnel:
Executive Director: John S. Massare PhD
   E-Mail: eyes@clao.org

Historical Note:
Founded in New York, NY, by a group of members of the American Academy of Ophthalmology. CLAO seeks to provide comprehensive ophthalmologists and other eyecare professionals with education and training in contact lenses and related eye care science. Members are ophthalmologists, optometrists, and other eye care professionals. Membership: $160-295 (Regular); $245 (Affiliate); $275 (Associate); $95 (Allied Health); $595 (Group); Free (Resident/Fellow).

Publications:
Eye & Contact Lens; bi-monthly
The CLAO Journal; bi-monthly

Membership List Available to Non-members

Contact Lens Council *(1982)*
8201 Corporate Dr.
Suite 850
Landover, MD 20785
Tel: (800) 884-4252
E-Mail: clc@thecli.com
Website: mycontactlenses.org
Members: 4 organizations
Staff: 2
Annual Budget: $500-1,000,000

Personnel:
Executive Director: Edward L. Schilling III

Historical Note:
CLI members are contact lens manufacturers, producers and professional associations with an interest in the safe use of contact lenses and public education on vision correction. CLI is affiliated with and supported by the Contact Lens Institute.

Contact Lens Manufacturers Association *(1961)*
P.O. Box 29398
Lincoln, NE 68529
Tel: (402) 465-4122 *Fax:* (402) 465-4187
TollFree: (800) 344-9060
E-Mail: CLMAssociation@aol.com
Website: clma.net
Members: 110 companies
Staff: 3
Annual Budget: $500-1,000,000

Personnel:
President: Al Vaske
   E-Mail: Vaske@lensdynamics.com
Secretary and Treasurer: Jan Svochak
   E-Mail: jan_svochak@tfoptics.com
Administrative Director: Pamela B. Witham
   E-Mail: clmassociation@aol.com

Historical Note:
CLMA's mission is to increase awareness and utilization of custom manufactured contact lenses. Members are contact lens laboratories, as well as material, solution and equipment manufacturers.

Meetings/Conferences: Annual

Publications:
Membership Directory; annually
The CLMA's newsletter; bi-monthly; adv.

Contact Lens Society of America *(1955)*
441 Carlisle Dr.
Suite D
Herndon, VA 20170
Tel: (703) 437-5100 *Fax:* (703) 437-0727
TollFree: (800) 296-9776
E-Mail: clsa@clsa.info
Website: clsa.info
Members: 1500 individuals and companies
Staff: 6
Annual Budget: $500-1,000,000
Tax: 501(c)(6)

Personnel:
Executive Director: Tina M. Schott
   E-Mail: tinaschott@clsa.info
Contact, Website management: Alison Cox
Administrator, CE: Casey McPherson
Manager, Education: Teresa Miller
   E-Mail: teresamiller@clsa.info
Accounting Manager: Eugenia Mormile
   E-Mail: eugeniamormile@clsa.info
Assistant, Membership and Conventions: Rachel Reuter
   E-Mail: rachelreuter@clsa.info

Historical Note:
CLSA is dedicated to the education, evolution, and promotion of contact lens technology. Members are fitters and manufacturers, of contact lenses and companies which provide components and/or services to the contact lens industry. Membership: $145 (Regular/Affiliate); $600 (Associate/Corporate); $50 (Retired); $250 (Foundation Donation).

Meetings/Conferences: Annual
Conference Chair: Tina M. Schott
2013 - Albuquerue, NM (Hotel Albuquerue)/April 12 - 13

Publications:
CLSA Eyewitness Magazine; quarterly
Membership Directory; annually

Membership List Available to Non-members

Containerization and Intermodal Institute *(1960)*
960 Holmdel Rd.
Building Two, Suite 201
Holmdel, NJ 07733-2100
Tel: (732) 817-9131 *Fax:* (732) 817-9133
TollFree: (800) 231-8244
E-Mail: info@containerization.org
Website: containerization.org
Members: 300 companies
Staff: 3
Annual Budget: $50-100,000

Personnel:
Executive Director: Barbara Spector Yeninas
   E-Mail: execdir@containerization.org
Treasurer: Michael DiVirgilio
Contact, Media: Kimberly McCloskey
   E-Mail: kimberly@bsya.com

Historical Note:
Formerly (1960) Bulk Packaging and Containerization Institute, and (1967) The Containerization Institute. CII's mission is to promote and support the business of international trade and the intermodal container transportation community. CII is dedicated to provide educational opportunities for people interested in the intermodal container shipping industry. Serves as an information resource, providing networking opportunities, offering career guidance, arranging internships, and facilitating scholarships.

Meetings/Conferences:
Conference Chair: Barbara Spector Yeninas

Content Delivery and Security Association *(1970)*
39 N. Bayles Ave
New York, NY 11050
Tel: (516) 767-6720 *Fax:* (516) 883-5793
E-Mail: info@cdsaonline.org
Website: cdsaonline.org
Members: 450 companies
Staff: 5
Annual Budget: $1-2,000,000

Personnel:
Executive Director: Martin Porter
   E-Mail: mporter@CDSAonline.org

Historical Note:
Founded as the International Tape Association, it became (1981) the International Tape/Disc Association and then (1995) ITA - International Association of Magnetic and Optical Recording Manufacturers and then International Recording Media Association. Members are manufacturers of optical/laser, blank computer, audio and video, and recording media and equipment. Membership: Based on volume, $1000-9500/year.

Publications:
CDSA Newsletter; on-line; adv.
M&E Journal; adv.

Continental Dorset Club *(1898)*
P.O. Box 506
N. Scituate, RI 02857-0506
Tel: (401) 647-4676 *Fax:* (401) 647-4679
E-Mail: cdcdorset@cox.net
Website: dorsets.homestead.com
Members: 1893 individuals
Staff: 2
Annual Budget: $100-250,000

Personnel:
Executive Secretary and Treasurer: Debra Hopkins
   E-Mail: cdcdorset@cox.net

Historical Note:
Breeders and fanciers of Dorset sheep. Member of the National Pedigree Livestock Council. Membership: $20/ year.

Meetings/Conferences:
Number of non-conference events/year: 2

Publications:
CDC Newsletter

Continua Health Alliance
3855 SW 153rd Dr.
Beaverton, OR 97006
Tel: (503) 619-0867 *Fax:* (503) 644-6708
Website: coalitionalliance.org
Members: 220 member companies
Staff: 1
Annual Budget: $2-5,000,000

Personnel:
Executive Director: Chuck Parker

Historical Note:
Continua Health Alliance mission is to establish a system of interoperable personal telehealth solutions that fosters independence and empowers people and organizations to better manage health and wellness. Membership: $25,000 (Promoter); $6,500 (Contributor/Supporting Participant).

Meetings/Conferences: Semi-Annual
2013 - Portland, OR (Embassy Suites Portland-Downtown)/March 11 - 15
2013 - Taipei, Taiwan (Sheraton Taipei Hotel)/Oct. 7 - 11

Publications:
Continua Health Alliance Newsletter

Contract Packaging Association *(1992)*
1833 Centre Point Cir.
Suite 123
Naperville, IL 60563
Tel: (630) 544-5053 *Fax:* (630) 544-5055
E-Mail: info@contractpackaging.org
Website: contractpackaging.org
Members: 100 companies
Staff: 6
Annual Budget: $250-500,000
Tax: 501(c)(6)

Personnel:
President: Chris Nutley
   E-Mail: cnutley@midservmail.com
Vice President: John Mazelin
   E-Mail: jmazelin@accu-tec.com
Treasurer: Vicky Smitley
   E-Mail: smitleyv@rytway.com
Contact, Membership Services: Scott Thomas
   E-Mail: contractpackaging@sealedair.com

Historical Note:
Formerly Contract Manufacturing and Packaging Association; absorbed Contract Manufacturers Association in 1999. CPA strives to serve the needs of member companies through continuing education, market knowledge and customer relationships and helps its member companies lower their operating costs and improve their performance. Membership: $1,500 (Contract Packager); $2,500 (Associate).

Meetings/Conferences: Annual
Conference Chair: Vicky Smitley
2013 - Naples, FL (Waldorf Astoria Naples)/Feb. 21 - 24

Publications:
Contract Packaging Magazine; adv.
CPA Connection; monthly

Membership List Available to Non-members

Contractors Pump Bureau (1938)
6737 W. Washington St., Suite 2400
C/O Association of Equipment Manufacturers
Milwaukee, WI 53214-5647
Tel: (414) 272-0943 *Fax:* (414) 272-1170
E-Mail: aem@aem.org
Website: aem.org/Groups/Groups/Group.asp?
  G = 22
Members: 15 companies
Staff: 1
Annual Budget: Under $10,000

Personnel:
Technical Director: Ken Edwards
  E-Mail: kedwards@aem.org

Historical Note:
A group under the Association of Equipment Manufacturers (AEM), CPB promotes matters of mutual interest to contractor pump users, manufacturers, and parts and component suppliers. Members are manufacturers of contractor type pumps and manufacturers of pump engines involved in the construction industry.

Controlled Environment Testing Association (1992)
1500 Sunday Dr.
Suite 102
Raleigh, NC 27607
Tel: (919) 861-5576 *Fax:* (919) 787-4916
E-Mail: info@cetainternational.org
Website: cetainternational.org
Members: 250 individuals
Staff: 4
Annual Budget: $250-500,000
Tax: 501(c)(6)

Personnel:
Executive Director: Felicia K. Boyles
  E-Mail: fkenan@cetainternational.org
Manager, Information Technology: Brady Joyner
  E-Mail: info@cetainternational.org
Director, Membership Services: Angela Kite
  E-Mail: akite@firstpointresources.com

Historical Note:
CETA strives to promote quality assurance within the controlled environment testing industry. Membership: $177 (Individual/Corporate); $100 (Affiliate).

Continuing Education:
Certification Designation/s: CCP

Meetings/Conferences: Annual
2013 - Orlando, FL/April 12 - 16

Publications:
Performance Review; quarterly

Controlled Release Society (1973)
3340 Pilot Knob Rd.
St. Paul, MN 55121
Tel: (651) 454-7250 *Fax:* (651) 454-0766
E-Mail: crs@scisoc.org
Website: controlledrelease.org
Members: 3000 individuals
Staff: 11
Annual Budget: $1-2,000,000

Personnel:
Executive Director: Susan Kohn
  E-Mail: skohn@scisoc.org
Executive Vice President: Steve C. Nelson
  E-Mail: snelson@scisoc.org
Manager, Meeting: Leah Barna
  E-Mail: lbarna@scisoc.org
Manager, Marketing: Karen Deuschle
  E-Mail: kdeuschle@scisoc.org
Publications Director: Greg Grahek
  E-Mail: ggrahek@scisoc.org
Vice President, Operations: Amy Hope
  E-Mail: ahope@scisoc.org
Specialist, Membership Relations: Cheryl Kruchten
  E-Mail: ckruchten@scisoc.org
Vice President, Finance: Barbara Mock
  E-Mail: bmock@scisoc.org
Program Manager: Megan Pagel
  E-Mail: mpagel@scisoc.org
Technical Editor: Luca Rescigno

E-Mail: lrescigno@scisoc.org
Webmaster: Brian Simdars
  E-Mail: bsimdars@scisoc.org

Historical Note:
CRS is the international, multidisciplinary society dedicated to the science and technology of delivering bioactives. Members are firms and individuals concerned with basic and applied research on controlled release delivery systems. Maintains an office in Geneva, Switzerland, and Japan. Membership: $166 (Individual); $51 (Student); $61 (Post- Doctorate); $300 (Company).

Meetings/Conferences: Annual
Conference Chair: Leah Barna
2013 - Honolulu, HI (Hawaii Convention Center)/July
  21 - 24
2014 - Chicago, IL (The Hilton Chicago)/July 13 - 16
Number of non-conference events/year: 8

Publications:
CRS Newsletter; quarterly; adv.
Drug Delivery and Translational Research; bi-monthly
Journal of Controlled Release
Membership Directory; on-line

Convenience Caterers & Food Manufacturers Association (1965)
1205 Spartan Dr.
Madison Heights, MI 48071
Tel: (248) 982-5379 *Fax:* (248) 582-3268
E-Mail: ccfma@ymail.com
Website: mobilecaterers.com
Members: 130 companies
Staff: 1
Annual Budget: $50-100,000

Personnel:
Contact, Communications: Cori Koppal

Historical Note:
Formerly known as Mobile Industrial Caterers' Association. CCFMA is dedicated to providing every resource needed to enhance the mobile catering industry. International members are companies providing food service at job sites and similar remote locations. Membership: $350-550 (Regular, Based on Sales); $500 (Associate).

Publications:
AlaCarte newsletter; quarterly; adv.

Convention Industry Council (1949)
700 N. Fairfax St.
Suite 510
Alexandria, VA 22314
Tel: (571) 527-3116 *Fax:* (571) 527-3105
E-Mail: cichq@conventionindustry.org
Website: conventionindustry.org
Members: 103,500 individuals and 19,500 firms
Staff: 5
Annual Budget: $2-5,000,000
Tax: 501(c)(6)

Personnel:
Chief Executive Officer: Karen Kotowski CAE, CMP
  E-Mail: kkotowski@conventionindustry.org
Manager, Meetings: Amelia Ballinger
  E-Mail: aballinger@conventionindustry.org
Director, CMP Program: Christina Buck CMP
  E-Mail: cic@talley.com
Contact, Media and Public Relations: Korenna Cline
  E-Mail: korenna@epicprgroup.com

Historical Note:
Formerly (1999) Convention Liaison Council. CIC 's mission is to provide a forum for member organizations to exchange information on global trends and topics, promulgate excellence in best practices and guidelines, collaborate on industry issues and advocate the value of the meetings, conventions, exhibitions and events industry. Members are associations directly involved in the convention, exposition, trade show, meeting industry, and travel and tourism generally. Membership: $1,850-4,600/ year (Based on member organization budget).

Continuing Education:
Certification Designation/s: CMP

Meetings/Conferences: Annual
Conference Chair: Amelia Ballinger
Number of non-conference events/year: 4

Publications:
CMP Directory; on-line
Membership Directory; on-line

Converting Equipment Manufacturers Association (1984)
201 Springs St.

Ft. Mill, SC 29715
Tel: (803) 802-7820 *Fax:* (803) 802-7821
E-Mail: cema@cema-converting.org
Website: cema-converting.org
Members: 75 companies
Staff: 5
Annual Budget: $50-100,000

Personnel:
Executive Director: Craig Sheppard
Manager, Communications: Steve Bright
Event Planner: Erin Davis
Senior Administrator: Tracey Ingram
Editor-in-Chief: Mark Spaulding

Historical Note:
CEMA is a division of Association of International Metallizers, Coaters and Laminators(AIMCAL). CEMA's mission is to encourage, advance and represent the interests of converting manufacturers in the industry and markets served. CEMA provides service to the needs of Converting Equipment Manufacturers. Membership: $1,995 (Full); $935 (Trade Press); $2,495 (Premium).

Meetings/Conferences:
Conference Chair: Erin Davis
Number of non-conference events/year: 4

Publications:
Converting Quarterly; quarterly; adv.
e-Newsletter; weekly

Conveyor Equipment Manufacturers Association (1933)
5672 Strand Ct.
Suite Two
Naples, FL 34110
Tel: (239) 514-3441 *Fax:* (239) 514-3470
E-Mail: cema@cemanet.org
Website: cemanet.org
Members: 100 companies
Staff: 5
Annual Budget: $500-1,000,000
Tax: 501(c)(6)

Personnel:
Executive Vice President: Robert A. Reinfried
  E-Mail: bob@cemanet.org
Executive Secretary and Technical Contact: Philip
  Hannigan
  E-Mail: phil@cemanet.org
Contact, Publications and Labels: Karen Lampart
  E-Mail: karen@cemanet.org
Manager, Membership Services and Marketing: Kimberly
  MacLaren
  E-Mail: kim@cemanet.org
Legal Counsel: Carroll A. Weimer Jr.

Historical Note:
Formerly (1935) the Association of Conveyor and Material Preparation Equipment Manufacturers and (1945) the Conveyor Association and a member of the Machinery and Allied Products Institute. CEMA's mission is to promote, among its members and the industry, standardization of design manufacture and application on a voluntary basis. Members are North American manufacturers and designers of conveyor equipment systems and accessories. Membership: $630- 3,150 (Technical, based on no. of people) ; $3,675-12,075 (Manufacturer).

Meetings/Conferences:
Conference Chair: Karen Lampart
2013 - Phoenix, AZ (Arizona Biltmore Resort and Spa)/
  March 15 - 19
2013 - Naples, FL (La Playa Beach and Racquet)/June
  23 - 26
2013 - Chicago, IL (Hilton Chicago O'Hare Airport)/
  Sept. 17 - 18
2014 - La Quinta, CA (La Quinta Resort and Club)/
  March 14 - 18
2014 - Naples, FL (La Playa Beach and Racquet)/June
  22 - 25
2014 - Chicago, IL (Hilton Chicago O'Hare Airport)/
  Sept. 16 - 17
2015 - Naples, FL (Waldorf Astoria Naples)/March 13
  - 17
2016 - La Quinta, CA (La Quinta Resort and Club, A
  Waldorf Astoria Resort)/March 11 - 15
Number of non-conference events/year: 1

Publications:
Annual Year Book (Membership Directory); annually
CEMA Bulletin; semi-annually

Cookie and Snack Bakers Association (1970)
1128 Maple Dr. NW

Cleveland, TN 37312
Tel: (423) 472-5856
Website: casba.us
Members: 14 Baker Members and 31 Allied
Members
Staff: 2

Personnel:
Executive Director: Craig S. Parrish
    E-Mail: csparrish@worldnet.att.net

Historical Note:
*CASBA's mission is to provide association members with
an atmosphere conducive to building relationships, sharing
experiences, and exchanging information necessary to
prosper individual business and industry. Members are
bakery and snack food processors. Membership: $225/year
(Organization).*

Meetings/Conferences: Annual
2013 - Ponte Vedra Beach, FL (Ponte Vedra Inn and
    Club)/Feb. 17 - 20

Cookware Manufacturers Association (1922)
P.O. Box 531335
Birmingham, AL 35253-1335
Tel: (205) 592-0389 *Fax:* (205) 599-5598
Website: cookware.org
Members: 25 companies
Staff: 1
Annual Budget: $100-250,000
Tax: 501(c)(6)

Personnel:
Executive Director: Hugh J. Rushing
    E-Mail: hrushing@cookware.org

Historical Note:
*Formerly (until 1963) the Aluminum Wares Association
and (until 1981) the Metal Cookware Manufacturers
Association. CMA's mission is to inform and promote the
industry to its members, their customers and to the general
public. Helps develop engineering standards for the industry,
disseminates information to consumers, retailers and
manufacturers and offers forums for members to learn about
the latest advances in manufacturing, retailing, distribution
and materials. Membership: $1,100-15,000/year (Based
on sales volume).*

Publications:
Buyer's Guide; annually

Cooling Technology Institute (1950)
P.O. Box 73383
Houston, TX 77273-3383
Tel: (281) 583-4087 *Fax:* (281) 537-1721
Website: cti.org
Members: 400 corporations
Staff: 3
Annual Budget: $250-500,000

Personnel:
Administrator: Virginia A. Manser
    E-Mail: vmanser@cti.org

Historical Note:
*CTI's mission is to advocate and aid the use of
environmentally responsible Evaporative Heat Transfer
Systems (EHTS) for the benefit of the public. Promotes
improvement in technology, design, performance and
maintenance of cooling towers. Also concerned with
water and air pollution and conservation of water as a
natural resource. Membership: $600 (Corporate); $200
(Individual/Affiliate); $100 (Foreign).*

Continuing Education:
Certification Designation/s: CTI

Meetings/Conferences: Annual
2013 - Corpus Christi, TX (Omni Corpus Christi Hotel-
    Bayfront Tower)/Feb. 3 - 7
2014 - Houston, TX (Hilton Greenspoint Hotel)/Feb. 2
    - 6
Number of non-conference events/year: 1

Publications:
CTI Journal; semi-annually; adv.
Membership Directory; on-line

Cooperative Education and Internship Association (1963)
P.O. Box 42506
Cincinnati, OH 45242
Tel: (513) 793-2342 *Fax:* (513) 793-0463
E-Mail: info@ceiainc.org
Website: ceiainc.org
Members: 1200 individuals
Staff: 3
Annual Budget: $250-500,000

Tax: 501(c)(3)

Personnel:
Association Manager: Peggy Harrier

Historical Note:
*Formerly (2003) the Cooperative Education Association.
CEA provides a supportive member-driven learning
community for participating programs, students, educators
and employers. Membership: $175 (Individual); $50
(Retiree/Student); $400 (Organizational); $115 (Additional
Organization).*

Meetings/Conferences: Annual
Conference Chair: Peggy Harrier
2013 - Orlando, FL (DoubleTree by Hilton at the
    Entrance to Universal Orlando)/April 14 - 16

Publications:
Experience Magazine
Membership Directory

Coordinating Council for Women in History (1969)
C/O Northern Illinois University
715 Zulauf Hall
DeKalb, IL 60115
Tel: (815) 895-2624
E-Mail: execdir@theccwh.org
Website: theccwh.org
Members: 800 individuals
Staff: 5
Annual Budget: $10-25,000
Tax: 501(c)(3)

Personnel:
Executive Director: Sandra Dawson
    E-Mail: execdir@theccwh.org

Historical Note:
*Formerly (1995) Coordinating Committee on Women in
the Historical Profession/Conference Group on Women's
History. Affiliated with the American Historical Association,
the National Coordinating Committee for the Promotion
of History, the International Federation for Research in
Women's History, and other associations of professional
historians. CCWH's purpose is to educate men and women
on the status of women in the historical profession and to
promote research and interpretation in areas of women's
history. Membership: $75 (Individual, based on income);
$20 (Part- Time/Retired/Independent Scholar/Graduate
Student); $50 (Institutional/Full Time Employed).*

Meetings/Conferences: Annual

Publications:
CCWH Newsletter; bi-annually; adv.

Coordinating Research Council (1942)
3650 Mansell Rd.
Suite 140
Alpharetta, GA 30022
Tel: (678) 795-0506 *Fax:* (678) 795-0509
Website: crcao.org
Members: 800 Individuals and 14 Organizations
Staff: 6
Annual Budget: $5-10,000,000

Personnel:
Executive Director: Brent K. Bailey
    E-Mail: bkbailey@crcao.org
Administrative Assistant: Jane Beck
    E-Mail: jbeck@crcao.org
Accountant: Debbie Jenkins
    E-Mail: djenkins@crcao.org

Historical Note:
*CRC's mission is to encourage and advocate the arts and
sciences by directing scientific cooperative research to
develop the good possible combinations of fuels, lubricants,
and the equipment in which they are used, and to afford a
means of cooperation with the Government on matters of
national or international interest within this field. Members
are the American Petroleum Institute (API) and a group of
automobile manufacturer members.*

Meetings/Conferences: Annual
2013 - Savannah, GA (Hyatt Regency)/April 29 - May
    2
Number of non-conference events/year: 1

Copier Dealers Association (1977)
134-40 W. 26th St.
Floor Three
New York, NY 10001
Tel: (212) 741-6400
Website: cdainfo.org
Members: 80 companies
Staff: 3

Annual Budget: $100-250,000

Personnel:
President: Larry Weiss
    E-Mail: lweiss@tomorrowsoffice.com

Historical Note:
*CDA provides members with a resource network for finding
solutions to today's business challenges and for comparing
financial benchmarks on a dealer-dealer level. CDA
members are independent companies in document imaging
and copying.*

Copper and Brass Fabricators Council (1964)
3050 K St. NW
Suite 400
Washington, DC 20007-5108
Tel: (202) 833-8575 *Fax:* (202) 342-8451
E-Mail: copbrass@aol.com
Website: cbfc.us
Members: 21 companies
Staff: 2
Annual Budget: $1-2,000,000

Personnel:
Contact, Media Relations: John Arnett
    E-Mail: JArnett@kelleydrye.com

Historical Note:
*Formerly (1966) Copper & Brass Fabricators Foreign Trade
Association, Inc. The CBFC was organized to stem the flood
of unlawful imports of brass mill products, minimize the
compliance costs of federal regulations, and deal with brass
mill industry problems. Membership: dues vary according to
company size.*

Publications:
Membership Directory; on-line

Copper and Brass Servicenter Association (1951)
6734 W. 121st St.
Overland Park, KS 66209
Tel: (913) 396-0697 *Fax:* (913) 345-1006
E-Mail: cbsahq@copper-brass.org
Website: copper-brass.org
Members: 70 companies
Staff: 10
Annual Budget: $250-500,000

Personnel:
Executive Director: Susan Avery CAE
    E-Mail: savery@copper-brass.org
Graphic Designer: Bonnie Bush
    E-Mail: bbush@copper-brass.org
Manager, Marketing and Education: Wess Hudelson
    E-Mail: whudelson@copper-brass.org
Deputy Executive Director and Marketing Director: Cyndy
    Launchbaugh
    E-Mail: claunchbaugh@copper-brass.org
*Managing Editor and Director, Marketing and
    Communications:* Liz Novak
    E-Mail: lnovak@copper-brass.org
Director, Publications: Janet Thill
    E-Mail: jthill@copper-brass.org
Manager, Meetings and Finance: Laurie Warren
    E-Mail: lwarren@copper-brass.org
Coordinator, Membership Services: Randy Wilkins
    E-Mail: rwilkins@copper-brass.org

Historical Note:
*Formerly (1976) Copper and Brass Warehouse Association.
CBSA's mission is to help its member companies grow
and enhance their businesses. CBSA is composed of
wholesale distributors (Servicenters) of fabricated copper
and brass mill products; the associate members are mills
(Fabricators who manufacture such products) and metal
platers. Membership: $1,854-$5,871/year (Based on Sales
Volume).*

Meetings/Conferences: Annual
Conference Chair: Janet Thill
2013 - Amelia Island, FL/April 9 - 13

Publications:
Capsules Newsletter; monthly
CBSA Source Directory of Brass Mills and Metal Strip
    Platers; adv.
Flash Market Trend Report; monthly

Copper Development Association (1962)
260 Madison Ave.
New York, NY 10016
Tel: (212) 251-7200 *Fax:* (212) 251-7234
TollFree: (800) 232-3282
E-Mail: questions@cda.copper.org
Website: copper.org
Members: 71 companies

Staff: 27
Annual Budget: $10-25,000,000

Personnel:
President and Chief Executive Officer: Andrew G. Kireta
  Sr.
  E-Mail: andrew.kiretasr@copperalliance.org
Manager, Information Technology: Maki Isayama
  E-Mail: misayama@cda.copper.org
Principal Financial and Administrative Officer: John J.
  Kearns
  E-Mail: john.kearns@copperalliance.org
Vice President, Market Development: Andrew G. Kireta Jr.
  E-Mail: akiretajr@cda.copper.org
Senior Vice President, Technology and Technical Services:
  Harold T. Michels
  E-Mail: hmichels@cda.copper.org
Assistant, Digital Media and Market Data: Mila Milman
  E-Mail: mmilman@cda.coppeeer.org
Manager, Communications: Victoria Prather
  E-Mail: vprather@cda.copper.org
Vice President, OEM: Robert D. Weed
  E-Mail: rweed@cda.copper.org

Historical Note:
*CDA aims to influence the use of copper and copper alloys
through research, development and education, as well
as technical and end-user support. CDA is committed to
promote the proper use of copper materials in sustainable,
efficient applications for business, industry and the
home. Members are copper producers and brass mill,
wire mill and foundry fabricators of copper and copper
alloys with production facilities in the USA. Membership:
$2,500-10,000/year (Associate).*

Publications:
Building & Architecture News
Discover Copper Online; monthly
Innovations; on-line
Membership Directory; on-line

Copyright Society of the U.S.A. *(1953)*
352 Seventh Ave.
Suite 739
New York, NY 10001
Tel: (212) 354-6401 *Fax:* (212) 354-2847
Website: csusa.org
Members: 1000 individuals
Staff: 4
Annual Budget: $250-500,000
Tax: 501(c)(3)

Personnel:
President: Corey Field
Co-Editor-in-Chief: Stacey Dogan
Director, Operations and Administrator: Amy Nickerson -
  Goldstein
  E-Mail: amy@csusa.org
Treasurer: Eric Schwartz

Historical Note:
*CSUSA's mission is to advance the study and
understanding of copyright law and related rights, the scope
of rights in literature, music, art, theater, motion picture,
television, computer software, architecture. Members are
business people, lawyers in private practice and in-house,
law professors and law students who share a common
interest in copyright and related intellectual property rights.
Membership: $25-2500/year.*

Continuing Education:
Enrollment: 900
Certification Designation/s: CLE

Meetings/Conferences: Annual
2013 - Austin, TX (Omni Hotel & Resorts Downtown
  Austin)/Feb. 14 - 16
2013 - Bolton Landing, NY (Sagamore Resort)/June 9 -
  11

Publications:
CSUSA Newsletter; quarterly
Journal of the Copyright Society of the U.S.A.;
  quarterly
Membership Directory; on-line

Membership List Available to Non-members

Copywriters Council of America
P.O. Box 102
Seven Putter Ln., Department JK02
Middle Island, NY 11953-0102
Tel: (631) 924-8555 *Fax:* (631) 924-3890
E-Mail: cca4dmcopy@att.net
Website: andrewlinickdirectmarketing.com/
  CCA4U.h
Staff: 1

Personnel:
Manager and Creative Director: Susanna K. Hutcheson

Historical Note:
*Copywriters Council of America is a professional referral
organization of over 25,000 free-lance direct response
advertising copywriters and communications specialists
experienced in over 1,450 categories in business, consumer
and industrial markets.*

The Cordage Institute *(1920)*
994 Old Eagle School Rd.
Suite 1019
Wayne, PA 19087-1866
Tel: (610) 971-4854 *Fax:* (610) 971-4859
E-Mail: info@cordageinstitute.com
Website: ropecord.com
Members: 83 companies
Staff: 4
Annual Budget: $100-250,000
Tax: 501(c)(6)

Personnel:
Executive Director: Peter M. Lance
  E-Mail: pete@mmco1.com
Administrative Director: Brian Schaaf

Historical Note:
*Merged with the American Cordage and Netting
Manufacturers in 1990. CI is dedicated to the advancement
of rope and cordage products. Membership consists of
manufacturers of natural and synthetic cordage (rope,
twine and netting) and fiber and machinery suppliers.
Membership: $53-3150/year.*

Meetings/Conferences:
2013 - Dublin, Ireland/June 2 - 4

Publications:
Membership Directory; annually
Ropecord News; quarterly

CoreNet Global *(1961)*
133 Peachtree St. NE
Suite 3000
Atlanta, GA 30303
Tel: (404) 589-3200 *Fax:* (404) 589-3201
TollFree: (800) 726-8111
Website: corenetglobal.org
Members: 6500 individuals
Staff: 49
Annual Budget: $10-25,000,000

Personnel:
Chief Executive Officer: Angela Cain
  E-Mail: acain@corenetglobal.org
Director, Strategic Projects and Events: Ada Allende
  E-Mail: aallende@corenetglobal.org
Chief Operating Officer: Larry Bazrod
  E-Mail: lbazrod@corenetglobal.org
Managing Editor: Chelsie Butler
  E-Mail: cbutler@corenetglobal.org
Director, Marketing: Janet Carter
  E-Mail: jcarter@corenetglobal.org
Director, Membership Services: Kathy Godwin
  E-Mail: kgodwin@corenetglobal.org
Director, Client Relations: Fred Hernandez
  E-Mail: fhernandez@corenetglobal.org
Vice President, Strategic Communications: Richard Kadzis
  CAE
  E-Mail: rkadzis@corenetglobal.org
Director, Information Technology: David Mercurio
  E-Mail: dmercurio@corenetglobal.org
Vice President, Education: Suzanne Verity
  E-Mail: sverity@corenetglobal.org

Historical Note:
*Founded as Industrial Development Research Council;
became International Development Research Council in
1994, before merging with NACORE International and
assuming its current name in 2002. CoreNet Global's
mission is to advance the effectiveness of Corporate Real
Estate professionals and the entire industry engaged in
delivering value to corporations through the strategic
management of corporate real estate and workplace
resources. Membership: $48-921/year.*

Continuing Education:
Certification Designation/s: MCR, SLCR

Meetings/Conferences:
Conference Chair: Ada Allende
2013 - Las Vegas, NV (MGM Grand Hotel and Casino)/
  Oct. 20 - 22
Number of non-conference events/year: 8

Publications:
The Leader; bi-monthly

CNG News; bi-monthly
Info Digest; bi-monthly
Membership Directory; on-line

Corn Refiners Association, Inc. *(1913)*
1701 Pennsylvania Ave. NW
Suite 950
Washington, DC 20006-5805
Tel: (202) 331-1634 *Fax:* (202) 331-2054
E-Mail: info@corn.org
Website: corn.org
Members: 9 companies
Staff: 7
Annual Budget: $25-50,000,000
Tax: 501(c)(6)

Personnel:
President: Audrae Erickson
  E-Mail: aerickson@corn.org
Director, Communications: David Knowles
Director, Policy and Operations: Pat Saks

Historical Note:
*Formerly the Associated Manufacturers of Products from
Corn and the Corn Industries Research Foundation. CRA's
mission is to serve as a resource to the general public about
the products made from corn and represent the industry on
matters of national importance.*

Corporate Council on Africa *(1993)*
1100 17th St. NW
Suite 1100
Washington, DC 20036
Tel: (202) 835-1115 *Fax:* (202) 835-1117
E-Mail: cca@africacncl.org
Website: africacncl.org
Members: 200 American companies
Staff: 20
Annual Budget: $5-10,000,000
Tax: 501(c)(3)

Personnel:
President and Chief Executive Officer: Stephen Hayes
  E-Mail: cca@africacncl.org
Coordinator, Special Events and Marketing: Brittany Clark
Chief Financial Officer: Mbayang Diouf Diop
Director, Technology: John Jakulevicius
Director, Human Resources and Executive Assistant:
  Hillary Lucas
Vice President, Business Development: Timothy S. McCoy
  E-Mail: tmccoy@africacncl.org
Vice President, International Programs: Amb. Robert C.
  Perry
  E-Mail: rperry@africacncl.org
Director, Membership and Infrastructure: Vivienne
  Sequeira
Director, Special Projects and Events: Jennifer Wright
  E-Mail: jwright@africacncl.org

Historical Note:
*CCA assists its members identify business contacts and
trade leads in Africa. Its members work to strengthen
trade and investment ties between Africa and the United
States. Membership: $5000 (Small Companies); $10, 000
(Medium Companies); $25,000 (Large Companies).*

Meetings/Conferences: Annual
Conference Chair: Jennifer Wright

Publications:
CCA HIV/AIDS & Health Initiative Newsletter
Membership Directory; on-line

Corporate Crisis Response Officers Association
7059 Courtyard Way
Haymarket, VA 20169
Tel: (540) 630-6400 *Fax:* (503) 905-9526
E-Mail: info@ccroa.org
Website: ccroa.org
Staff: 1
Annual Budget: $50-100,000

Personnel:
National Director: Rosalie J. Wyatt
  E-Mail: rjwyatt@wyattcgi.com

Historical Note:
*CCROA's mission is to create local networks of trained
private and community sector individuals called Crisis
Response Officers ("CROs") that link to and augment the
local public sector response networks by leveraging best
practices and local resources and volunteers during the
critical first 72 hours of crisis.*

Corporate Environmental Enforcement Council
(1994)
1155 15th St. NW
Suite 500
Washington, DC 20005
Tel: (202) 289-1365 *Fax:* (202) 530-0569
E-Mail: jflatley@navista.net
Website: ceecinc.org
Members: 23 Companies
Staff: 2
Annual Budget: $100-250,000

Personnel:
Executive Director: Steve Hellem
    E-Mail: shellem@navista.net
Director, Membership Services: John Flatley
    E-Mail: jflatley@navista.net

Historical Note:
CEEC is an organization comprised of corporate counsel and environmental professionals from a wide range of industrial sectors that focus on civil and criminal environmental enforcement issues. Membership is open to companies interested in working on civil and criminal environmental enforcement issues. Membership: $11,500/ year.

Corporate Event Marketing Association (1990)
5098 Foothills Blvd.
Suite 3-386
Roseville, CA 95747
Tel: (916) 740-3623
Website: cemaonline.com
Members: 500 individuals
Staff: 2
Annual Budget: $250-500,000

Personnel:
Executive Director: Kimberley Gishler
    E-Mail: kim@cemaonline.com
Director, Membership Services: Olga Rosenbrook
    E-Mail: olga@cemaonline.com

Historical Note:
CEMA is dedicated to the needs of event professionals in the information technology industry and aims to bring together exhibit and event marketing managers, marketing communication professionals, show managers, and industry associates to partner in ways that will increase event quality and success. Membership: $295 (Corporate Event Marketer- Individual); $795 (Corporate); $475 (Industry Partner); $975 (Corporate); $325 (Independent Event Marketer).

Meetings/Conferences: Semi-Annual
Number of non-conference events/year: 1

Publications:
Member Directory; on-line
Newsletter

Membership List Available to Non-members

Corporate Facility Advisors, Inc. (1989)
103 W. Broad St.
Suite 300
Falls Church, VA 22046
Tel: (703) 532-6160 *Fax:* (703) 544-0112
E-Mail: info@corfac.com
Website: corfac.com
Members:
70 firms
1000 individuals
Staff: 3
Annual Budget: $500-1,000,000
Tax: 501(c)(6)

Personnel:
Executive Director: Susan S. Newman
    E-Mail: susan@corfac.com
Coordinator, Membership and Meetings: Sokha Ang
    E-Mail: sokha@corfac.com
Director, Education and Marketing: Alyssa Kirkman
    E-Mail: alyssa@corfac.com

Historical Note:
CORFAC's mission is to build relationships among commercial real estate professionals and among their firms.Corporate Facility Advisors, Inc. is owned by CORFAC International.

Meetings/Conferences: Annual
Conference Chair: Sokha Ang
2013 - Las Vegas, NV/April 3 - 6
Number of non-conference events/year: 1

Publications:
CORFAC Committee Profile; bi-monthly

CORFAC Newsletter; monthly

Corporate Housing Providers Association
9100 Purdue Rd.
Suite 200
Indianapolis, IN 46268
Tel: (317) 328-4631 *Fax:* (317) 280-8527
E-Mail: info@chpaonline.org
Website: chpaonline.org
Members: 220 companies
Staff: 3
Annual Budget: $500-1,000,000
Tax: 501(c)(6)

Personnel:
Chief Executive Officer: Mary Ann Passi CAE
    E-Mail: map@chpaonline.org
Director, Membership and Marketing: Amanda Cook
    E-Mail: acook@chpaonline.org
Membership and Meetings Assistant: Margie Nellinger
    E-Mail: mnellinger@chpaonline.org

Historical Note:
Founded as Association of Interim Housing Providers, assumed its current name in 2002. CHPA is a professional trade association dedicated to supporting corporate housing providers around the world. Members are professionals involved in the corporate housing industry and/or companies that supply providers with goods and services. Membership: $825-7,000 (Provider); $850 (Associate); $1,600 (President's Club).

Continuing Education:
Certification Designation/s: CCHP

Meetings/Conferences: Annual
Conference Chair: Margie Nellinger
2013 - Phoenix, AZ (Arizona Biltmore Resort and Spa)/
    Feb. 4 - 6

Publications:
CHIP; monthly
CHPA Newsletter
Membership Directory; on-line

Membership List Available to Non-members

The Corps Network (formerly the National Association of Service and Conservation Corps)
(1985)
1100 G St. NW
Suite 1000
Washington, DC 20005
Tel: (202) 737-6272 *Fax:* (202) 737-6277
E-Mail: nascc@nascc.org
Website: corpsnetwork.org
Members: 33143 corps members and
organizations
Staff: 11
Annual Budget: $1-2,000,000

Personnel:
President and Chief Executive Officer: Mary Ellen
    Ardouny
    E-Mail: mardouny@corpsnetwork.org
Manager, Member Relations: Carol Huls
    E-Mail: chuls@corpsnetwork.org
Manager, Communications: Levi Novey
    E-Mail: lnovey@corpsnetwork.org
Coordinator, Data Collection Systems: Emilie Rafal
    E-Mail: erafal@corpsnetwork.org
Director, Finance and Administration: Nancy L. Siegal
    E-Mail: nsiegal@corpsnetwork.org
National Education Coordinator: Capri St. Vil
    E-Mail: cstvil@corpsnetwork.org

Historical Note:
Formerly known as the National Association of Service and Conservation Corps. Corps Network's mission is to serve and promote civilian-military service partnerships. Membership: $625 (Start Up Corps); $775 (New Corps); $1,190-6,530 (Operating Corps).

Meetings/Conferences: Annual
2013 - Washington, DC (Washington Court Hotel)/Feb.
    12 - 15

Publications:
The Washington Update; weekly
Youth Today

Correctional Education Association (1945)
8182 Lark Brown Rd.
Suite 202
Elkridge, MD 21075
Tel: (443) 459-3080 *Fax:* (443) 459-3080
TollFree: (800) 783-1232

E-Mail: office@ceanational.org
Website: ceanational.org
Members: 3000 individuals
Staff: 15
Annual Budget: $1-2,000,000

Personnel:
Executive Director: Stephen J. Steurer
    E-Mail: ssteurer@ceanational.org
Editor: John Dowdell
    E-Mail: jdowdell@ashland.edu
Assistant Director: Erica Houser

Historical Note:
CEA is a non-profit, professional association serving educators and administrators who provide services to students in correctional settings. Members include adult and juvenile educational administrators, academic and vocational educators, correctional officers, counselors, clinicians, researchers and institution librarians. Membership: $325-450/year.

Meetings/Conferences: Semi-Annual
Number of non-conference events/year: 3

Publications:
CEA News and Notes; quarterly; adv.
Directory of Correctional Educators; annually; adv.
The Journal of Correctional Education; quarterly; adv.

Correctional Vendors Association
700 New Hampshire Ave. NW
Watergate South, Suite 409
Washington, DC 20007-5101
Tel: (202) 672-5579 *Fax:* (202) 672-5399
Members: 50 individuals
Staff: 1
Annual Budget: $250-500,000

Personnel:
President: Kate Leonard

Historical Note:
CVA supports the goals of the State & Federal Correctional Industries Inmate Work Programs, their employees, inmates and vendors who supply products and services to them. Has no paid officers or full-time staff.

Corrections, U.S.A.
P.O. Box 6912
Pueblo West, CO 81007
TollFree: (855) 469-2872
E-Mail: CUSA4EVER@aol.com
Website: cusa.org
Members: 80000 publicly employed correctional
officers
Staff: 6
Annual Budget: $250-500,000

Personnel:
Executive Director: Buffie McFadyen
    E-Mail: buffiecusa@vzw.blackberry.net
Administrator: Nina Salerno Ashford
Legislative Chairman: Tim Filson
Chairman, Membership: Richard Harcrow
Contact, Research and Information: Erik Milman
Organizer, Conferences: Lynn Witt

Historical Note:
CUSA's mission is to advance the correctional officer profession and serve as a national voice on issues of universal concern. Membership: $1 (Organizational); $10-25 (Individual).

Meetings/Conferences: Annual
Conference Chair: Lynn Witt
2013 - Las Vegas, NV (Harrah's Las Vegas Casino
    Hotel)/Feb. 4 - 6

Corrugated Polyethylene Pipe Association (1972)
105 Decker Ct.
Suite 825
Irving, TX 75062
Tel: (469) 499-1044 *Fax:* (469) 499-1063
Website: plasticpipe.org/drainage/index.html
Members: 48 individuals
Staff: 2

Personnel:
Executive Director: Tony Radoszewski
    E-Mail: inquiries@plasticpipe.org

Historical Note:
A division of the Plastics Pipe Institute, which provides administrative support. CPPA's mission is to provide information about the technology, design, specification and installation of HDPE corrugated pipe. Members are

manufacturers of polyethylene pipe for wastewater drainage and other industrial applications.

Cosmetic Executive Women *(1954)*

286 Madison Ave.
19th Floor
New York, NY 10017
Tel: (212) 685-5955 *Fax:* (212) 685-3334
E-Mail: cew@cew.org
Website: cew.org
Members: 4000 individuals
Staff: 8
Annual Budget: $2-5,000,000
Tax: 501(c)(6)

Personnel:
President: Carlotta Jackobson
  E-Mail: cjacobson@cew.org
Systems Administrator: Martin Barfield
  E-Mail: mbarfield@cew.org
Manager, Membership Services: Shari Beck
  E-Mail: sbeck@cew.org
Director, Events and Programs: Liz Bonofiglio
  E-Mail: ebonofiglio@cew.org
Vice President, Development: Lisa Klein
  E-Mail: lklein@cew.org
Director, Marketing: Randi Lloyd
  E-Mail: rlloyd@cew.org
Chief Financial Officer: Siobhan McManus
  E-Mail: smcmanus@cew.org
Office Manager: Sylvia Naismith
  E-Mail: snaismith@cew.org

Historical Note:
Formerly (1981) Cosmetic Career Women, assumed its current name in 2003 and Organized in 1954 and incorporated in New York in 1959. Membership is limited to women who have served at least 3 years in an executive capacity in business and who are presently in the cosmetic industry. The CEW Foundation, established in 1993, develops and manages cancersandcareers, an online and offline resource for women undergoing cancer treatment. Membership: $175/year.

Meetings/Conferences: Annual
Conference Chair: Liz Bonofiglio

Publications:
CEW Newsletter; on-line
Membership Directory; annually

Cosmetic Industry Buyers and Suppliers *(1948)*

830 Terry Rd.
Hauppauge, NY 11788
Tel: (516) 775-0220 *Fax:* (516) 328-9789
E-Mail: cibsmail@cibsonline.com
Website: cibsonline.com
Members: 800 individuals
Staff: 3
Annual Budget: $50-100,000
Tax: 501(c)(6)

Personnel:
President: Mario Magali
Treasurer: Laura Carey
Recording Secretary: Rafael Cruz

Historical Note:
CIBS's mission is to provide amid friendly surroundings, a meeting place where the existing and future younger element may be properly inducted into the cosmetic trade. Membership: $90 (Active/Associate); $55 (Sustaining Members over 55 years of Age).
Meetings/Conferences:
Number of non-conference events/year: 6

Costume Designers Guild *(1953)*

11969 Ventura Blvd.
First floor
Studio City, CA 91604
Tel: (818) 752-2400 *Fax:* (818) 752-2402
E-Mail: cdgia@costumedesignersguild.com
Website: costumedesignersguild.com
Staff: 6
Annual Budget: $500-1,000,000

Personnel:
Executive Director: Rachael M. Stanley
  E-Mail: rstanley@costumedesignersguild.com
Director, Sales: Dan Dodd
  E-Mail: Dan@IngleDodd.com
Administrator, Member Services: Suzanne Huntington
  E-Mail: shuntington@costumedesignersguild.com
Receptionist and Administration Assistant: Cheryl Marshall

  E-Mail: cmarshall@cdgia.com

Historical Note:
The Costume Designers Guild promotes research, artistry, and technical expertise in costume design in the field of moving pictures whether it is animation, commercial, television, motion picture, music video or any future media utilizing moving images.
Meetings/Conferences:
Number of non-conference events/year: 4

Publications:
Membership Directory; on-line
The Costume Designer; quarterly

Costume Society of America *(1973)*

390 Amwell Rd.
Suite 402
Hillsborough, NJ 08844
Tel: (908) 359-1471 *Fax:* (908) 450-1118
TollFree: (800) 272-9447
E-Mail:
national.office@costumesocietyamerica.com
Website: costumesocietyamerica.com
Members: 1800 individuals
Staff: 3
Annual Budget: $250-500,000
Tax: 501(c)(3)

Personnel:
Association Manager: Amanda Tate Speedling
  E-Mail:
national.office@costumesocietyamerica.com

Historical Note:
CSA works to advance the global understanding of all aspects of dress and appearance. Members are costume professionals and enthusiasts interested in the study, collection, preservation, presentation and interpretation of dress and appearance in societies of the past, present and future. Membership: $45-150 (Private Individual); $153 (Nonprofit/ Institutional); $150 (Business/Corporate).
Meetings/Conferences:
Number of non-conference events/year: 1

Publications:
CSA E-News; monthly
CSA News; quarterly
Membership Directory; on-line

Membership List Available to Non-members

Cottage Industry Miniaturists Trade Association *(1980)*

18453 Shaddox Hollow Ln.
Rogers, AR 72756
Tel: (479) 925-7056 *Fax:* (479) 925-2693
E-Mail: cimtainfo@aol.com
Website: cimta.org
Members: 175 handcrafters
Staff: 4
Annual Budget: $50-100,000

Personnel:
Contact, Communications: Steve Murphy

Historical Note:
CIMTA is a wholesale trade association which provides a marketplace to sell miniatures wholesale at annual trade show. CIMTA is run partially by volunteers whose regular membership is limited to handcrafters of dollhouse miniatures. Regular members of CIMTA are cottage industries, small businesses operated by an individual or group of individuals. It deals with the unique problems facing the handcrafter of miniatures within the miniature industry. Membership: $60/year.
Meetings/Conferences: Annual
Conference Chair: Steve Murphy
2013 - Las Vegas, NV (Orleans Hotel and Casino)/Jan. 28 - 30

Publications:
CIMTA Supporting Member Newsletter; semi-annually; adv.

Cotton Council International *(1956)*

1521 New Hampshire Ave. NW
Washington, DC 20036-1205
Tel: (202) 745-7805 *Fax:* (202) 483-4040
E-Mail: cottonusa@cotton.org
Website: cottonusa.org
Members: 21 companies
Staff: 16
Annual Budget: $25-50,000,000
Tax: 501(c)(6)

Personnel:

Executive Director: Allen A. Terhaar
  E-Mail: aterhaar@cotton.org
Manager, Information Technology and Member Relations: Sonia Dockery
  E-Mail: sdockery@cotton.org
Consultant, Communications: Jennifer Jackson
  E-Mail: jjackson@cotton.org
Coordinator, International Programs: Shannon Kelly
  E-Mail: skelly@cotton.org
Senior Manager, Strategic Planning and Operations: Emily Ostroman
  E-Mail: eostroman@cotton.org
Director, CCI Fiscal: Delorise Winter
  E-Mail: dwinter@cotton.org

Historical Note:
The overseas operations arm of the National Cotton Council of America. CCI's mission is to increase exports of U.S. cotton, cottonseed and U.S. manufactured cotton products through activities that affect every phase of the marketing chain.
Meetings/Conferences:
Conference Chair: Shannon Kelly
Number of non-conference events/year: 2

Publications:
Fiber Suppliers Directory; on-line
Product and Licensee Directory; on-line
Supply Chain Marketing; on-line

Cotton Growers Warehouse Association *(1957)*

P.O. Box 1378
Corpus Christi, TX 78403
Tel: (361) 882-5490 *Fax:* (361) 882-8081
Website: cottongwa.org
Members: 46 member organizations
Staff: 2

Personnel:
Executive Director: Andrew Jordan

Historical Note:
CGWA's mission is to To develop and maintain for member handlers of cotton, a high standard of efficiency in storing, handling and distribution of such cotton resulting in the highest level of membership benefits.
Meetings/Conferences: Annual

Publications:
CGWA Newsletter

Cotton Incorporated *(1970)*

6399 Weston Pkwy.
Cary, NC 27513
Tel: (919) 678-2220 *Fax:* (919) 678-2230
Website: cottoninc.com
Staff: 200
Annual Budget: $50-100,000,000
Tax: 501(c)(6)

Personnel:
President and Chief Executive Officer: Berrye Worsham
Senior Vice President, Consumer Marketing: Ric Hendee
Administrative Staff: Lynda Keys
Co-Director, Industry Public Relations: James Pruden

Historical Note:
Mission is to improve the demand for and profitability of cotton. In addition it seeks to meet the needs of the world's growing textile industry by providing agricultural, fiber and textile research, market information and technical services, advertising and public relations, fashion forecasts and retail promotions for cotton.

Meetings/Conferences: Annual
Number of non-conference events/year: 3

Publications:
Cotton LSM

Cotton Warehouse Association of America *(1969)*

316 Pennsylvania Ave. SE
Suite 401
Washington, DC 20003
Tel: (202) 544-5875 *Fax:* (202) 544-5874
E-Mail: cwaa@cottonwarehouse.org
Website: cottonwarehouse.org
Members: 125 companies
Staff: 5
Annual Budget: $100-250,000

Personnel:
Executive Director: Rebecca Davis
Executive Vice President: Hon. Larry Combest

Historical Note:

Formed in 1969 by a merger of the American and the National Cotton Compress and Cotton Warehouse Associations. CWAA is working to improve the competitiveness and marketability of U.S. cotton and to build the warehouse industry. It also supports the Cotton Warehouse Government Relations Committee. Membership: $250/year (Associate).

Meetings/Conferences: Annual
2013 - Coeur d#Alene, ID (Coeur d'Alene Resort)/June 5

Publications:
CWAA Newsletter; monthly
Membership Directory; on-line

Council for Community and Economic Research
(1961)
1700 N. Moore St.
Suite 2225, P.O. Box 100127
Arlington, VA 22210
Tel: (703) 522-4980 *Fax:* (480) 393-5098
E-Mail: info@c2er.org
Website: c2er.org
Members: 500 individuals
Staff: 10
Annual Budget: $1-2,000,000
Tax: 501(c)(6)

Personnel:
Executive Director: Dr. Kenneth E. Poole PhD
    E-Mail: kpoole@c2er.org
Chief Administrative Officer: Sean A. McNamara
    E-Mail: sam@c2er.org
Vice President, Research: Dr. Mark White PhD
    E-Mail: mwhite@c2er.org

Historical Note:
Formerly (1992) American Chamber of Commerce Research Association (ACCRA)- Association of Applied Community Researchers. Purpose is to promote excellence in community and economic research by working to improve data availability, enhance data quality, and foster learning about regional economic analytic methods. Membership: $250 (Research Member); $500 (Organization).

Continuing Education:
Certification Designation/s: CCR

Meetings/Conferences: Annual

Publications:
Journal of Applied Research in Economic Development; monthly
Membership Directory; on-line
Newsletter; monthly

Council for Adult and Experiential Learning
(1985)
55 E. Monroe St.
Suite 1930
Chicago, IL 60603-5720
Tel: (312) 499-2600 *Fax:* (312) 499-2601
E-Mail: cael@cael.org
Website: cael.org
Members: 2300 institutions and individuals
Staff: 116
Annual Budget: $5-10,000,000
Tax: 501(c)(3)

Personnel:
President and Chief Executive Officer: Pamela Tate
Associate Vice President: Diana Bamford-Rees
    E-Mail: dbamfordrees@cael.org
Director, Marketing and Communications: Beth Doyle
    E-Mail: bdoyle@cael.org
Associate Director and Student Coordinator, LearningCounts.org: Kelsey Irish
    E-Mail: kirish@cael.org
Associate Vice President, Government Services: Joel Simon
    E-Mail: jsimon@cael.org
Associate Vice President, Finance: Gloria Wagner
Vice President, Higher Education Services and Administration: Judith "Judy" Wertheim
    E-Mail: jwertheim@cael.org

Historical Note:
Established (1974) as Council for the Advancement of Experiential Learning (CAEL). Assumed its present name in 1985 to reflect changing program priorities. CAEL's mission is the advancement of experiential learning and the improvement of services to adult learners. Membership: $350-750 (Institutional); $475-575 (Organization); $50 (Student); $75 (Retiree);120 (Individual).

Continuing Education:
Certification Designation/s: PLA

Meetings/Conferences: Annual

Number of non-conference events/year: 4

Publications:
CAEL Forum & News

Membership List Available to Non-members

Council for Advancement and Support of Education *(1974)*
1307 New York Ave. NW
Suite 1000
Washington, DC 20005-4701
Tel: (202) 328-2273 *Fax:* (202) 387-4973
E-Mail: info@case.org
Website: case.org
Members:
3400 colleges, universities and K-12 private schools
64000 advancement professionals
Staff: 90
Annual Budget: $10-25,000,000
Tax: 501(c)(3)

Personnel:
President: John Lippincott
    E-Mail: lippincott@case.org
Director, Graphic Design: Wendy Bogart
    E-Mail: bogart@case.org
Vice President, Business and Finance: Donald Falkenstein
    E-Mail: falkenstein@case.org
Director, Legislative, Foundation and Recognition Programs: Brian Flahaven
    E-Mail: flahaven@case.org
Director, Educational Programs: Ed Groves
    E-Mail: groves@case.org
Vice President, Marketing, Membership, and External Relations: Ron Mattocks
    E-Mail: mattocks@case.org
Director, Human Resources: Peggy Quinn
    E-Mail: quinn@case.org
Editor-in-Chief: Liz Reilly
    E-Mail: reilly@case.org
Director, Information Systems: Adam Rosenbaum
    E-Mail: rosenbaum@case.org
Director, Communications: Pamela Russell
    E-Mail: russell@case.org
Vice President, Advancement Programs: Norma Walker
    E-Mail: walker@case.org
Director, Corporate Relations: Lori Woehrle
    E-Mail: woehrle@case.org

Historical Note:
Formed by the merger (1974) of the American College Public Relations Association and the American Alumni Council and formerly (1975) the AAC/ACPRA. CASE advances and supports educational institutions around the world by enhancing the effectiveness of the alumni relations, communications, marketing, fund raising, and other advancement professionals who serve them. Membership: $85(Professional - US and Outside UK/Europe); $25 (Student); $175 (Golden Circle Retiree).

Meetings/Conferences: Annual
Conference Chair: Norma Walker
2013 - Washington, DC (Gaylord National Hotel and Convention Center)/Jan. 13 - 15
2013 - Boston, MA (Hilton Boston Back Bay)/Jan. 15 - 17
2013 - Washington, DC (Crowne Plaza)/Feb. 6 - 8
2013 - Naples, FL (Naples Grande Beach Resort)/Feb. 25 - 27
2013 - New Orleans, LA (Omni Royal Orleans)/Feb. 27 - March 1
2013 - Atlanta, GA (Hyatt Regency Atlanta)/April 17 - 19
2013 - Denver, CO (Grand Hyatt Denver)/April 24 - 26
2013 - Newport Beach, CA (Newport Beach Marriott Hotel and Spa)/April 24 - 26
2013 - Boston, MA (Hyatt Regency Cambridge, Overlooking Boston)/April 30 - May 2
2013 - Chicago, IL (Renaissance Blackstone Hotel)/ May 1 - 3
2013 - San Francisco, CA (Hyatt Regency San Francisco)/May 6 - 8
2013 - Atlanta, GA (Westin Buckhead Atlanta)/May 8 - 10
2013 - San Francisco, CA (Hyatt Regency San Francisco)/May 8 - 9
2013 - Denver, CO (Grand Hyatt Denver)/June 5 - 7
2013 - Newport Beach, CA (Newport Beach Marriott Hotel and Spa)/June 5 - 6

2013 - San Francisco, CA (Moscone Center/San Francisco Marriott Marquis)/June 5 - 7
2013 - Atlanta, GA (Georgia Tech Hotel and Conference Center)/June 6 - 7
2013 - Newport Beach, CA (Newport Beach Marriott Hotel and Spa)/June 7
2013 - Pittsburgh, PA (Renaissance Pittsburgh Hotel)/ June 10 - 12
2013 - Indianapolis, IN (Omni Severin Hotel)/June 12 - 14
2013 - Chicago, IL (Renaissance Blackstone Hotel)/ June 19 - 21
2013 - Minneapolis, MN (Hotel Wyndham Grand)/June 19 - 21
2013 - San Francisco, CA (Embarcadero, San Francisco)/July 14 - 16

Publications:
BriefCASE e-newsletter; monthly; adv.
CASE Books; monthly
CASE Member Directory; on-line
CURRENTS; monthly; adv.
e-Headlines; weekly

Membership List Available to Non-members

Council for Affordable and Rural Housing *(1980)*
1112 King St.
Alexandria, VA 22314-3022
Tel: (703) 837-9001 *Fax:* (703) 837-8467
E-Mail: carh@carh.org
Website: carh.org
Members:
375 companies and state organizations
231 individuals
Staff: 6
Annual Budget: $1-2,000,000
Tax: 501(c)(6)

Personnel:
Executive Director: Colleen M. Fisher
    E-Mail: cfisher@carh.org
Director, Marketing: Katherine Delmonico
    E-Mail: kdelmonico@carh.org
Executive Assistant: Eppie Marecheau
    E-Mail: emarecheau@carh.org
General Counsel: Nixon Peabody
Manager, Membership Services: Tamara Schultz
    E-Mail: tschultz@carh.org
Director, Marketing and Education Programs: Anne C. Stack
    E-Mail: astack@carh.org

Historical Note:
CARH provides a respected voice for the concerns of all major participants in the affordable rural housing industry. CARH represents managers and developers of subsidized or federally- assisted housing. Membership: $600 (Basic/ Associate); $1,500 (Basic Plus); $2,000 (Associate Plus); $3,000 (Advisory Trustee).

Meetings/Conferences: Semi-Annual
2013 - Key Largo, FL (Ocean Reef Club)/Jan. 28 - 30
2013 - Arlington, VA (Ritz-Carlton, Pentagon City)/ June 9 - 11
Number of non-conference events/year: 11

Publications:
AN Express; monthly
Insights for On-Sites; quarterly

Council for Agricultural Science and Technology *(1972)*
4420 W. Lincoln Way
Ames, IA 50014-3447
Tel: (515) 292-2125 *Fax:* (515) 292-4512
E-Mail: cast@cast-science.org
Website: cast-science.org
Members:
125 institutions
550 individuals
Staff: 9
Annual Budget: $500-1,000,000
Tax: 501(c)(3)

Personnel:
Executive Vice President and Chief Executive Officer: John M. Bonner PhD
    E-Mail: jbonner@cast-science.org
Chief Operating Officer: Linda M. Chimenti
    E-Mail: lchimenti@cast-science.org
Director, Membership and Marketing: Melissa Sly
    E-Mail: msly@cast-science.org

Historical Note:
CAST strives to assemble, interpret, and communicate credible science- based information as CAST. Membership: $25-2,500/year.
Meetings/Conferences:
Number of non-conference events/year: 1

Publications:
Member Directory; on-line
Newsletter

Council for American Private Education *(1971)*
13017 Wisteria Dr.
Suite 457
Germantown, MD 20874
Tel: (301) 916-8460 *Fax:* (301) 916-8485
E-Mail: cape@capenet.org
Website: capenet.org
Members: 18 organizations
Staff: 2
Annual Budget: $250-500,000
Tax: 501(c)(3)

Personnel:
President: Irene McHenry
Treasurer: Patrice Maynard

Historical Note:
CAPE's mission is to preserve and promote educational pluralism so that parents have a choice in the schooling of their children; foster communication and cooperation within the private school community and with the public sector to improve the quality of education for all of the nation's children.

Publications:
Membership Directory; on-line
Outlook; monthly

Membership List Available to Non-members

Council for Art Education *(1984)*
P. O. Box 479
Hanson, MA 02341-0479
Tel: (781) 293-4100 *Fax:* (781) 294-0808
E-Mail: debbief@acminet.org
Website: acminet.org
Members: 4 organizations and 210 Members
Staff: 5
Annual Budget: $50-100,000

Personnel:
Executive Vice President: Deborah M. Fanning CAE
    E-Mail: debbiem@acminet.org
Director, Membership Services: Becky J. Beaudoin
Associate Director: Deborah S. Gustafson
Certification Director: Debbie J. Munroe

Historical Note:
CFAE advocates art education and school art programs, primarily through the National Youth Art Month program. It also seeks to recognize art education as a viable component in the total education curricula that develops citizens of a global society.

Continuing Education:
Certification Designation/s: ACMI
Publications:
ACMI newsletter; monthly; adv.

Council for Chemical Research, Inc. *(1979)*
1550 M St. NW, Suite 300
P.O. Box 14
Washington, DC 20005
Tel: (202) 429-3971 *Fax:* (202) 429-3976
E-Mail: info@ccrhq.org
Website: ccrhq.org
Members: 200 organizations
Staff: 4
Annual Budget: $250-500,000
Tax: 501(c)(3)

Personnel:
Executive Director: Paul Mendez
    E-Mail: pmendez@ccrhq.org
President: Seth Snyder
    E-Mail: seth@anl.gov
Treasurer: Kelly Sullivan

Historical Note:
CCR's purpose is to benefit society by advancing research in chemistry, chemical engineering, and related disciplines through leadership collaboration across discipline, institution, and sector boundaries. Members are university, government, and private industry laboratories engaged in research. Membership: $500-1,000 (Academic); $9,500 (Government Laboratory); $2,000 (Domestic Affiliates); 7,500-15,000 (Industry).

Meetings/Conferences: Annual
2013 - Arlington, VA/May 19 - 21
Publications:
CCR News; monthly
Membership Directory; on-line

Council for Children with Behavioral Disorders
P.O. Box 24246
Stanley, KS 66283
Tel: (913) 239-0550 *Fax:* (913) 239-0550
E-Mail: webmaster@ccbd.net
Website: ccbd.net
Staff: 4
Annual Budget: $100-250,000
Tax: 501(c)(3)

Personnel:
President: Kris Melloy
Webmaster: Mickey Losinski
Treasurer: Mike Paget

Historical Note:
CCBD is dedicated to supporting the professional development and enhancing the expertise of those who work on behalf of children with challenging behavior and their families. CCBD is committed to students who are identified as having emotional and behavioral disorders and those whose behavior puts them at risk for failure in school, home, and/or community. CCBD supports prevention of problem behavior and enhancement of social, emotional, and educational well-being of all children and youth. Membership: $22/year.

Meetings/Conferences: Annual
2013 - San Antonio, TX (The Henry B. Gonzalez Convention Center)/April 3 - 6

Publications:
Behavioral Disorders; quarterly; adv.
Beyond Behavior; annually
CCBD Newsletter; bi-monthly; adv.
Membership Directory; on-line

Council for Christian Colleges and Universities *(1999)*
321 Eighth St. NE
Washington, DC 20002
Tel: (202) 546-8713 *Fax:* (202) 546-8913
E-Mail: council@cccu.org
Website: cccu.org
Members: 170 institutions
Staff: 65
Annual Budget: $10-25,000,000
Tax: 501(c)(3)

Personnel:
President: Edward O. Blews Jr.
Director, Technology Services: Diana J. Allen
    E-Mail: dallen@cccu.org
Director, Conference Services: Ev Bussema
    E-Mail: ebussema@cccu.org
President Emeritus: Dr. Paul R. Corts
    E-Mail: pcorts@cccu.org
Vice President, Communications: Pamela K. Jones
    E-Mail: pjones@cccu.org
Director, Government Relations and Executive Programs:
    Shapri LoMaglio
    E-Mail: slomaglio@cccu.org
Vice President, Professional Development and Research:
    Ronald P. Mahurin
    E-Mail: rmahurin@cccu.org
Vice President, Finance and Administration: Kyle H. Royer
    E-Mail: kroyer@cccu.org
Director, Human Resources: Laura Woolsey
    E-Mail: lwoolsey@cccu.org

Historical Note:
Incorporated in the District of Columbia as Christian College Coalition in 1982, (1995) the Coalition for Christian Colleges and Universities and assumed its current title in 1999. CCCU's mission is to advance the cause of Christ-centered higher education and to help institutions transform lives by faithfully relating scholarship and service to biblical truth. Members are accredited four-year colleges and universities that apply a Christ-centered philosophy to higher education. Membership: $4,585-20,900 (Regular); $2,700 (U.S. Institutions); $1,800 (Canadian Institutions); $450 (International Institutions).

Meetings/Conferences: Annual
Conference Chair: Ev Bussema
2013 - Washington, DC/Jan. 30 - Feb. 1/11-25
    exhibitors
Number of non-conference events/year: 15
Publications:

Membership Directory; on-line

Membership List Available to Non-members

Council for Educational Diagnosticians
ENMU, Station 25
Portales, NM 88130
Tel: (575) 562-2603 *Fax:* (575) 562-2523
Website: ceds.us
Members: 1300 professionals
Staff: 4

Personnel:
President: Kathie Good
    E-Mail: Kathie.good@enmu.edu

Historical Note:
CEDS ensures the highest quality of diagnostic and prescriptive procedures involved in the education of individuals with disabilities and/or who are gifted. Council for Educational Diagnostic Services (CEDS) is a special interest division of the Council for Exceptional Children.

Publications:
Communique; quarterly

Council for Electronic Revenue Communication Advancement *(1994)*
600 Cameron St.
Suite 309
Alexandria, VA 22314
Tel: (703) 340-1655 *Fax:* (703) 340-1658
E-Mail: cerca@cerca.org
Website: cerca.org
Members: 75 companies
Staff: 4
Annual Budget: $100-250,000
Tax: 501(c)(3)

Personnel:
Executive Director: Mike Cavanagh
    E-Mail: cerca@cerca.org

Historical Note:
CERCA represents a broad cross-section of the electronic tax filing, IRS systems modernization, and state electronic revenue communities. Members are companies with an interest in advancing electronic commerce with government revenue agencies. Membership: $600-7,500 (Corporate); $250 (Government Agency-Affiliate); $1,200 (Subsidiary Companies of Full CERCA Members-Non Voting).

Publications:
Membership Directory; on-line

Council for Elementary Science International *(1920)*
One Baylor Plaza
MS: BCM411
Houston, TX 77030
Tel: (713) 798-8200
Website: cesiscience.org
Members: 1200 Members
Staff: 3
Annual Budget: $10-25,000

Personnel:
President: Barbara Tharp
    E-Mail: btharp@bcm.edu
Contact, Membership: Dee Mock
    E-Mail: mock@bcm.edu

Historical Note:
CESI's mission is to stimulate, improve, and coordinate science teaching at preschool and elementary school levels and to engage in all activities. Members are teachers, administrators and others with an interest in the teaching of science at the preschool, elementary and middle school levels. Membership: $20 (General); $10 (Retired); $18 (Student); $200 (Life).

Publications:
CESI Newsletter
Member Directory; on-line

Membership List Available to Non-members

Council for Employment Law Equity (CELE) *(2000)*
10701 Parkridge Blvd.
Suite 300
Reston, VA 20191
Tel: (703) 483-8395 *Fax:* (703) 391-7223
E-Mail: contact@cele.us.com
Website: cele.us.com
Staff: 3

Personnel:
President and Executive Director: Mark A. de Bernardo

E-Mail: mdebernardo@cele.us.com
Coordinator, Membership Services: Margo Benzekri
E-Mail: mbenzekri@cele.us.com
General Counsel: Garen Dodge
E-Mail: gdodge@cele.us.com

Historical Note:
CELE's mission is to advocate the highest standards of fair, effective, and appropriate employment practices to the employer community, before the judicial, legislative, and executive branches of government; and to the public at-large. Membership: $25,000 (Steering Committee); $10,000 (Policy Committee); $5,000 (Corporate); $1,250 (Associate).

Council for European Studies (1970)
420 W. 118th St., MC 3307
New York, NY 10027
Tel: (212) 854-4172 Fax: (212) 854-8808
E-Mail: ces@columbia.edu
Website: councilforeuropeanstudies.org
Members: 1100 individuals and institutions
Staff: 10
Annual Budget: $250-500,000
Tax: 501(c)(3)

Personnel:
Director: Siovahn A. Walker
Coordinator, Programs: Corey Fabian Borenstein
Assistant, Communications and Archives: Caroline Quinn

Historical Note:
CES's mission is to recognize and encourage excellence in European Studies. The Council produces and recognizes multidisciplinary research in European studies through a range of programs, including conferences, publications, special events and awards. Membership: $75 (Individual); $40 (Student); $450 (Institutional); $100 (Professional).

Meetings/Conferences: Annual
Conference Chair: Corey Fabian Borenstein
2013 - Amsterdam, Netherlands/June 25 - 27
2014 - Washington, DC/March 14 - 16

Publications:
Perspectives on Europe; semi-annually

Membership List Available to Non-members

Council for Exceptional Children (1922)
1110 N. Glebe Rd.
Suite 300
Arlington, VA 22201-5704
Tel: (888) 232-7733 Fax: (866) 915-5000
E-Mail: service@cec.sped.org
Website: cec.sped.org
Members: 45000 individuals
Staff: 45
Annual Budget: $5-10,000,000
Tax: 501(c)(3)

Personnel:
Executive Director: Bruce Ramirez
E-Mail: sharonr@cec.sped.org
Director, Policy and Advocacy Services: Kimberly Hymes
E-Mail: kimh@cec.sped.org
Senior Director, Policy and Advocacy: Lindsay Jones
E-Mail: lindsayj@cec.sped.org
Senior Director, Conventions, Conferences, and Meetings: Anmarie Kallas
E-Mail: aka@cec.sped.org
Manager, Marketing: Sarah Lokerson
E-Mail: sarahl@cec.sped.org
Acting Director, Publications: Kathleen McLane
E-Mail: kathleenm@cec.sped.org
Manager, Human Resources: Kathleen O'Keefe Rizza
E-Mail: kathleeno@cec.sped.org
Director, Meeting Logistics: Carol Serrano
E-Mail: carols@cec.sped.org
Chief Financial Officer: Michael Shifflett
E-Mail: michaels@cec.sped.org
Senior Director, Communications and Public Relations: Diane Shinn
E-Mail: dianes@cec.sped.org
Senior Director, Membership Services: Susan Simmons
E-Mail: susans@cec.sped.org
Director, Information Technology: David Thrower
E-Mail: dthrower@cec.sped.org

Historical Note:
CEC's mission is to improve, through advocacy, the education and quality of life for children and youth with exceptionalities and to enhance the engagement of their families.

Meetings/Conferences: Annual

Conference Chair: Carol Serrano
2013 - San Antonio, TX (The Henry B. Gonzalez Convention Center)/April 3 - 6
2014 - Philadelphia, PA/April 9 - 12
2015 - San Diego, CA/April 8 - 11
2016 - St. Louis, MO/April 13 - 16
Number of non-conference events/year: 15

Publications:
CEC Journal Gateway
CEC SmartBrief; daily
CEC Today; bi-monthly
Exceptional Children; quarterly; adv.
Inquire & Inspire
TEACHING Exceptional Children; bi-monthly

Membership List Available to Non-members

Council for Higher Education Accreditation (1996)
One Dupont Cir. NW
Suite 510
Washington, DC 20036
Tel: (202) 955-6126 Fax: (202) 955-6129
E-Mail: chea@chea.org
Website: chea.org
Members: 3000 degree granting colleges and universities
Staff: 9
Annual Budget: $2-5,000,000
Tax: 501(c)(3)

Personnel:
President: Judith S. Eaton
Vice President, Government Affairs: Jan Friis
E-Mail: Friis@chea.org
Database and Web Administrator: Ida Miggins
Coordinator, Membership and Information Services: Eric Selwyn
Director, Finance and Administration: Laura Tillett
Senior Director, Communications: Timothy Willard

Historical Note:
CHEA is an organization of colleges and universities serving as the national advocate for voluntary self-regulation through accreditation. It is supported by member institutions.

Meetings/Conferences: Annual
Number of non-conference events/year: 1

Publications:
Federal Update Newsletter; irregular

Council for International Tax Education (1984)
P.O. Box 1012
White Plains, NY 10602
Tel: (914) 328-5656 Fax: (914) 328-5757
TollFree: (800) 207-4432
E-Mail: info@citeusa.org
Website: citeusa.org
Members: 400 individuals
Staff: 4
Annual Budget: Under $10,000
Tax: 501(c)(3)

Personnel:
Executive Director: Diane Pastore

Historical Note:
Founded as FSC/DISC Tax Association; assumed its current name in 2002. CITE was formed to educate U.S. and foreign multinationals and companies engaged in international business on the tax, legal and accounting aspects of doing business overseas. Membership: $325 (Individual); $625 (Corporate).

Continuing Education:
Certification Designation/s: CLE, CPE

Meetings/Conferences: Annual
Number of non-conference events/year: 26

Publications:
Member Directory; on-line

Membership List Available to Non-members

Council for Learning Disabilities (1968)
11184 Antioch Rd.
P.O. Box 405
Overland Park, KS 66210
Tel: (913) 491-1011 Fax: (913) 491-1012
E-Mail: cldinfo@ie-events.com
Website: cldinternational.org
Members: 650 individuals
Staff: 7
Annual Budget: $100-250,000

Tax: 501(c)(3)

Personnel:
Executive Director: Linda Nease
E-Mail: lneasecld@aol.com
Editor: Diane P. Bryant, PhD
E-Mail: dpbryant@mail.utexas.edu
Director, Conferences: Mary Provost
E-Mail: mcprovost@bellsouth.net

Historical Note:
CLD is an international organization that promotes evidence-based teaching, collaboration, research, leadership, and advocacy. CLD is composed of professionals who represent diverse disciplines and are committed to enhancing the education and quality of life for individuals with learning disabilities and others who experience challenges in learning. Membership: $103 (National); $35 (Student).

Meetings/Conferences: Annual
Conference Chair: Mary Provost
Number of non-conference events/year: 1

Publications:
LD Forum; bi-monthly
Learning Disability Quarterly; quarterly; adv.
Member Directory; on-line

Membership List Available to Non-members

Council for Museum Anthropology (1975)
C/O Department of Anthropology, Coordinator of Native and Indigenous Studies
University of Connecticut, Avery Point Campus, Academic Bldg. 114A, 1084 Shennecossett Rd.
Groton, CT 06340
Tel: (860) 405-9059
Website: museumanthropology.org
Members: 450 individuals
Staff: 2
Annual Budget: $10-25,000

Personnel:
Secretary: Margaret M. Bruchac
E-Mail: margaret.bruchac@uconn.edu

Historical Note:
CMA, a section of American Anthropological Association and an Affiliate of the Professional Organization of American Association of Museums, works to foster the development of anthropology in the context of museums and related institutions. Members are anthropologists, institutions and others with an interest in the field. Membership: $25 (Professor); $20 (Student/Undergraduates).

Publications:
Museum Anthropology

Council for Near-Infrared Spectroscopy (1986)
P.O. Box 1574
Rancho Cordova, CA 95741
Tel: (770) 947-1344 Fax: (610) 255-5979
E-Mail: cnirs@idrc-chambersburg.org
Website: cnirs.org
Members: 256 individuals
Staff: 3
Tax: 501(c)(3)

Personnel:
President: Gary Ritchie
E-Mail: garyritchiems@yahoo.com
Treasurer: Susan Foulk
E-Mail: sfoulk@comcast.net.com
Secretary: Art Springsteen
E-Mail: arts@aviantechnologies.com

Historical Note:
Affiliated with the Society for Applied Spectroscopy, purpose of CNIRS is to advance the art and science of near infrared spectroscopy. Membership: $20/year (Individual).

Publications:
CNIRS Newsletter; quarterly

Council for Opportunity in Education (1981)
1025 Vermont Ave. NW
Suite 900
Washington, DC 20005-3516
Tel: (202) 347-7430 Fax: (202) 347-0786
Website: coenet.us
Members: 1,000 colleges and agencies
Staff: 30
Annual Budget: $5-10,000,000
Tax: 501(c)(3)

Personnel:
Executive Vice President: Maureen Hoyler

E-Mail: maureen.hoyler@coenet.us
President: Dr. Arnold L. Mitchem PhD
  E-Mail: arnold.mitchem@coenet.us
Vice President, Business and Finance: Susan Dorsey
  E-Mail: susan.dorsey@coenet.us
Associate Vice President, Technology: John P. Hernandez
  E-Mail: john.hernandez@coenet.us
Director, Publications: Jodi Koehn-Pike
  E-Mail: jodi.koehnpike@coenet.us
Assistant Director, Marketing and Outreach: Rheanna
  Martinez
  E-Mail: rheanna.martinez@coenet.us
Senior Vice President, Membership and Human Resources:
  Alvin K. Phillips
  E-Mail: alvin.phillips@coenet.us
Vice President, Public Policy and Communications:
  Heather Valentine
  E-Mail: heather.valentine@coenet.us
Director, New Programs and Services: Angelica
  Vialpando
  E-Mail: angelica.vialpando@coenet.us

Historical Note:
*Founded as National Council of Equal Opportunity
Associations and assumed its current name in 2000,
COE's mission is to advance and defend the ideal of equal
educational opportunity in postsecondary education.
Members are postsecondary institutions, community
agencies, corporations, and foundations that contribute to
the success of low-income students in college. Membership:
$3,000-4000 (Institution, based on no. of TRIO Programs
at an Institution).*

Meetings/Conferences: Annual
2013 - Washington, DC (Renaissance Washington,
  D.C. Downtown Hotel)/March 10 - 12
Number of non-conference events/year: 3

Publications:
COE NETworks; annually
e-News You Can Use; monthly
Equality Newsletter; quarterly
Member Directory; on-line

Council for Professional Recognition (1985)
2460 16th St. NW
Washington, DC 20009-3547
Tel: (202) 265-9090 *Fax:* (202) 265-9161
TollFree: (800) 424-4310
E-Mail: cda@cdacouncil.org
Website: cdacouncil.org
Members: 100000 individuals
Staff: 69
Annual Budget: $10-25,000,000

Personnel:
*President and Chief Executive Officer and Chairman of the
  Council:* Valora Washington
Deputy Director: Deborah Jordan
  E-Mail: cda@cdacouncil.org
Manager, Publications: Kathy Ruby
  E-Mail: kathyr@cdacouncil.org
Chief Financial Officer: David Seabrook
Director, Technology: Eric Strobel

Historical Note:
*Formerly (1987) the Child Development Associate National
Credentialing Program and (2000) the Council for Early
Childhood Professional Recognition, the Council for
Professional Recognition promotes improved performance
and recognition of professionals in the early childhood
education of children aged birth to 5 years old.*

Continuing Education:
Certification Designation/s: CDA

Publications:
CounciLINK; on-line

Council for Resource Development (1972)
One Dupont Cir. NW
Suite 365
Washington, DC 20036-1176
Tel: (202) 822-0750 *Fax:* (202) 822-5014
E-Mail: crd@crdnet.org
Website: crdnet.org
Members: 1600 individuals
Staff: 3
Annual Budget: $250-500,000

Personnel:
Executive Director: Polly Binns
  E-Mail: polly.binns@crdnet.org
Coordinator, Membership Services and Database: Yvonne
  Inniss

  E-Mail: yvonne.inniss@crdnet.org
Director, Marketing and Development: Stephanie Melvin
  E-Mail: stephanie.melvin@crdnet.org

Historical Note:
*CRD connects, educates, supports, strengthens, and
celebrates community college development professionals.
Members are presidents and development administrators of
two-year colleges. Membership: $185-285 (Individual);
$185-285 (Institution); $1100 (Affiliate); $185-285
(Associate); $185 (Emeritus).*

Meetings/Conferences: Annual
2013 - Washington, DC (Hyatt Regency Washington on
  Capitol Hill)/Nov. 4 - 11
2014 - Washington, DC (Hyatt Regency Washington on
  Capitol Hill)/Nov. 3 - 10
Number of non-conference events/year: 7

Publications:
DISPATCH; adv.

Membership List Available to Non-members

Council for Responsible Nutrition (1973)
1828 L St. NW
Suite 510
Washington, DC 20036-5114
Tel: (202) 204-7700 *Fax:* (202) 204-7701
E-Mail: ilebert@crnusa.org
Website: crnusa.org
Members: 70 companies
Staff: 10
Annual Budget: $2-5,000,000
Tax: 501(c)(6)

Personnel:
President and Chief Executive Officer: Steven M. Mister
  Esq.
  E-Mail: smister@crnusa.org
Senior Vice President, Communications: Judy Blatman
  E-Mail: jblatman@crnusa.org
Vice President, Government Relations: Mike Greene
  E-Mail: mgreene@crnusa.org
Director, Membership Development: Carl Hyland
  E-Mail: chyland@crnusa.org
Senior Director, Public Relations: Season Solorio
  E-Mail: ssolorio@crnusa.org

Historical Note:
*CRN representing dietary supplement manufacturers and
ingredient suppliers. Membership: $3,000 (Associate);
$5,000 (International); $4,000-165,000 (Voting).*

Meetings/Conferences: Annual
2013 - Park City, UT (Montage Deer Valley)/Sept. 18

Publications:
Before and After DSHEA
The Benefits of Nutritional Supplements
Vitamin and Mineral Safety

Council for the Advancement of Standards in Higher Education (1979)
One Dupont Cir. NW
Suite 300
Washington, DC 20036-1188
Tel: (202) 862-1400 *Fax:* (202) 296-3286
Website: cas.edu
Members:
100000 professionals
40 organizations
Staff: 3
Annual Budget: $100-250,000
Tax: 501(c)(3)

Personnel:
Interim Executive Director: Marybeth Drechsler Sharp
  E-Mail: executive_director@cas.edu
Editor: Dorothy I. Mitstifer
Treasurer: Pat Perfetto

Historical Note:
*Mission of CAS is to work collaboratively to develop and
promulgate standards and guidelines and to encourage
self-assessment. Members are involved in providing quality
programs and services to students to improve student
learning and development.*

Publications:
College Student Affairs Journal
Membership Directory; on-line
NASPA Journal

Membership List Available to Non-members

The Council for Trade and Economic Cooperation
445 Park Ave.

10th Floor
New York, NY 10022
Website: ctec.ru
Staff: 2

Personnel:
President and Director, Projects: Olga Lutsenko
  E-Mail: olutsenko@ctec.ru

Council of Administrators of Special Education (1952)
101 Katelyn Cir.
Suite E
Warner Robins, GA 31088
Tel: (478) 333-6892 *Fax:* (478) 333-2453
Website: casecec.org
Members: 5300 individuals
Staff: 2
Annual Budget: $500-1,000,000
Tax: 501(c)(3)

Personnel:
Executive Director: Luann Purcell
  E-Mail: lpurcell@casecec.org
Administrative Assistant: Robin Smith
  E-Mail: rsmith@casecec.org

Historical Note:
*CASE's mission is to provide leadership and support to
members by shaping policies and practices which impact
the quality of education. A division of the Council for
Exceptional Children. Membership: $60/year.*

Meetings/Conferences: Annual
Number of non-conference events/year: 2

Publications:
CASE Newsletter; bi-monthly; adv.
Journal of Special Education; adv.

Council of American Jewish Museums (1977)
University of Denver, 2000 E. Asbury Ave.
Suite 157
Denver, CO 80208-0911
Tel: (303) 871-3015
E-Mail: cajm@cajm.net
Website: cajm.net
Members: 80 institutions
Staff: 3
Annual Budget: $100-250,000

Personnel:
Executive Director: Joanne Marks Kauvar
Administrative Assistant: Mindy Humphrey
Website Manager and Editor: Amy E. Waterman

Historical Note:
*CAJM represents a broad spectrum of Jewish community
museums and galleries which recognize professional
standards of operation and programming. It works to
strengthen the Jewish museum field in North America
through training of museum staff and volunteers,
information exchange and advocacy. Membership:
$250-1,000 (Institutional); $36 (Individual, Student);
$1,000(Individual, Patron); $500 (Individual, Sustaining);
$250 (Individual, Contributing); $75 (Individual, General);
$100 (Affiliate); $250 (Business Partner).*

Meetings/Conferences: Annual
2013 - New York City, NY/March 3 - 5

Publications:
CAJM Newsletter; monthly
Member Directory; on-line

Council of American Maritime Museums (1974)
394 Taugwonk Rd.
Stonington, CT 06378
Tel: (860) 535-0786 *Fax:* (860) 535-0786
Website:
  councilofamericanmaritimemuseums.org
Members: 80 museums
Staff: 1
Annual Budget: $50-100,000
Tax: 501(c)(3)

Personnel:
President: Anne B. Brengle
  E-Mail: abrengle@cgfdn.org

Historical Note:
*CAMM works to promote professional standards in
the preservation and interpretation of maritime history.
Membership: $75/year.*

Meetings/Conferences: Annual

Publications:
Membership Directory; annually

Membership List Available to Non-members

Council of American Master Mariners *(1936)*
1760 E Littleton Ct.
Inverness, FL 34453
E-Mail: counciamm@aol.com
Website: mastermariner.org
Members: 1100 individuals
Staff: 4
Annual Budget: $50-100,000

Personnel:
President: Capt. Richard Klein
Secretary and Treasurer: David Williams

Historical Note:
CAMM's purpose is to promote nautical education to improve training standards and to support the publication of professional literature. It also serves to foster the exchange of maritime information and experience. Membership: $60/ year.

Meetings/Conferences: Annual

Publications:
Membership Directory; annually
Sidelights; bi-monthly; adv.

Council of American Overseas Research Centers *(1981)*
P.O. Box 37012
MRC178
Washington, DC 20013-7012
Tel: (202) 633-1599 *Fax:* (202) 786-2430
E-Mail: fellowships@caorc.org
Website: caorc.org
Members: 22 centers
Staff: 13
Annual Budget: $10-25,000,000
Tax: 501(c)(3)

Personnel:
Executive Director: Mary Ellen Lane
    E-Mail: lane.maryellen@caorc.org
Grants Accountant: Melissa Bradley
    E-Mail: bradley.melissa@caorc.org
Project Coordinator, Digital Library for International Research: Diane Ryan
    E-Mail: dlir@caorc.org
Project Director, Critical Language Scholarship Program: Julia Sylla
    E-Mail: sylla.julia@caorc.org

Historical Note:
Established to provide and advance higher learning and scholarly research by providing a forum for communication and cooperation among American overseas advanced research centers. CAORC develops and administers programs in collaboration with member Centers and affiliated partners.

Council of American Survey Research Organizations *(1975)*
170 N. Country Rd.
Suite Four
Port Jefferson, NY 11777
Tel: (631) 928-6954 *Fax:* (631) 928-6041
E-Mail: casro@casro.org
Website: casro.org
Members:
325 companies
32000 employees
Staff: 7
Annual Budget: $2-5,000,000
Tax: 501(c)(6)

Personnel:
President: Diane K. Bowers
Manager, Communications and Database: Meg Collins
Director, Communications: Art Flanagan
    E-Mail: aflanagan@casro.org
Vice President, Operations: Frank Petruzzo
Director, Event Planning: Nicole Kokolakis Symelidis CMP
    E-Mail: nicole@casro.org
Vice President, Membership Services and Development: Jennifer Ward

Historical Note:
CASRO is the national trade association for full-service, for profit survey research companies and their affiliated services. It promotes a code of conduct that enhances the image of survey research and protects the public's rights and privacy. Membership: $1,400 (Non-Profit Research Department); $1,125- 23,700 (Full Service Research

Company-based on U.S. Research Revenue/Commercial Research Department).

Meetings/Conferences: Annual
Conference Chair: Nicole Kokolakis Symelidis CMP
2013 - San Francisco, CA (Westin San Francisco)/ March 7 - 8/250 attendees
2013 - Westlake Village, CA (Four Seasons Hotel Westlake Village)/Oct. 7 - 10
Number of non-conference events/year: 4

Publications:
CASRO Journal; annually; adv.
CASRO Membership Directory; on-line

Membership List Available to Non-members

Council of Archives and Research Libraries in Jewish Studies *(1974)*
330 Seventh Ave.
21st Floor
New York, NY 10001
Tel: (212) 629-0500 *Fax:* (212) 629-0508
E-Mail: grants@jewishculture.org
Members: 34 institutions
Staff: 10
Annual Budget: Under $10,000

Personnel:
Executive Director: Richard A. Siegel
President and Chief Executive Officer: Elise M. Bernhardt
    E-Mail: ebernhardt@jewishculture.org
Director, Operations: Michelle Moskowitz Brown
    E-Mail: mmoskowitzbrown@jewishculture.org

Historical Note:
Founded by the National Foundation for Jewish Culture in conjunction with the National Endowment for the Humanities. CARLJS's mission is to invest in creative individuals in order to nurture a vibrant and enduring Jewish identity, culture and community. Members include the Jewish divisions of major North American municipal, university and Jewish community libraries and archives. Membership: $100/year.

Council of Better Business Bureaus *(1971)*
3033 Wilson Blvd.
Suite 600
Arlington, VA 22201
Tel: (703) 276-0100 *Fax:* (703) 525-8277
Website: bbb.org/us
Members: 450 companies and bureaus and 300000 local business members
Staff: 125
Annual Budget: $2-5,000,000

Personnel:
Interim President and Chief Executive Officer: Carrie A. Hurt
Vice President and Chief Financial Officer: Joseph E. Dillon
Director, Communications and Media Relations: Katherine R. Hutt
Senior Vice President and Chief Marketing Officer: Susan Kearney
Vice President, Human Resources: Anaise Schroeder
Vice President, General Counsel and Corporate Secretary: Richard Woods

Historical Note:
CBBB was formed by a merger of the (1971) Association of Better Business Bureaus (founded in 1921) and the National Better Business Bureau (founded in 1912). CBBB's mission is to promote the ethical relationship between businesses and the public through self-regulation, consumer and business education, and service excellence.

Membership List Available to Non-members

Council of Chief State School Officers *(1927)*
One Massachusetts Ave. NW
Suite 700
Washington, DC 20001-1431
Tel: (202) 336-7000 *Fax:* (202) 408-8072
E-Mail: info@ccsso.org
Website: ccsso.org
Members: 56 individuals
Staff: 70
Annual Budget: $25-50,000,000
Tax: 501(c)(3)

Personnel:
Executive Director: Gene Wilhoit
    E-Mail: genew@ccsso.org
Director, Education Indicators Program: Rolf Blank
    E-Mail: rolfb@ccsso.org

Chief Financial Officer: Bruce Buterbaugh
    E-Mail: bruceb@ccsso.org
Director, Communications: Kate Dando
    E-Mail: kated@ccsso.org
Chief Operating Officer, Interim Strategic Initiative Director, Information Systems and Research: Melissa Zack Johnston
Senior Director, Membership Services: Chris Minnich
Senior Meeting Planner: Madeline Morrison
    E-Mail: madelinem@ccsso.org
Manager, Human Resources: Tressa Oliver
    E-Mail: tressao@ccsso.org
Planner, Meetings: Michele Parks
    E-Mail: michelep@ccsso.org

Historical Note:
CCSSO provides leadership, advocacy, and technical assistance on major educational issues. It also seeks member consensus on major educational issues and expresses their views to civic and professional organizations, federal agencies, Congress, and the public. Members head departments of elementary and secondary education in the states, the District of Columbia, the Department of Defense Education Activity, and five U.S. extra-state jurisdictions.

Meetings/Conferences: Semi-Annual
Conference Chair: Madeline Morrison
2013 - Kohler, WI (The American Club)/July 20 - 23
2013 - Richmond, VA (Jefferson Hotel)/Nov. 14 - 17
Number of non-conference events/year: 8

Publications:
Chief Line; weekly
ELON News; monthly
Membership Directory; on-line
Teacher Quality and Improvement; bi-monthly

Council of Chiropractic Physiological Therapeutics and Rehabilitation *(1920)*
2791 Geryville Pike
Pennsburg, PA 18073
Tel: (215) 679-3419 *Fax:* (215) 679-8866
E-Mail: jsimon@rrohio.com
Website: ccptr.org
Members: 250 individuals
Staff: 7
Annual Budget: Under $10,000

Personnel:
President: Dr. George K. Petruska
    E-Mail: acrbdoc@ptd.net

Historical Note:
CCPTR works to advance education, evaluation and research in chiropractic management in rehabilitation of tissue insult. Membership: $100 (General); $50 (Student).

Meetings/Conferences: Annual
2013 - Lake Buena Vista, FL (Swan Hotel)/April 19 - 21

Publications:
Member Directory; on-line
The Journal of the North American Rehab Specialist

Council of Colleges of Acupuncture and Oriental Medicine *(1982)*
600 Wyndhurst Ave .
Suite 112
Baltimore, MD 21210
Tel: (410) 464-6040 *Fax:* (410) 464-6042
Website: ccaom.org
Members: 59 schools
Staff: 3
Annual Budget: $250-500,000
Tax: 501(c)(6)

Personnel:
Executive Director: David M. Sale JD, LLM
    E-Mail: executivedirector@ccaom.comcastbiz.net
Program Manager and Finance Administrator: Paula Diamond
    E-Mail: ccaomcnt@comcast.net

Historical Note:
CCAOM's mission is to advance acupuncture and Oriental medicine by promoting educational excellence within the field. Members are institutions of acupuncture or Oriental medicine (or acupuncture or Oriental medicine program within an accredited institution of higher education) that achieve candidacy or accreditation status with the Accreditation Commission for Acupuncture and Oriental Medicine (ACAOM). Membership: $1,250 (Accredited Schools); $625 (Candidate Schools).

Continuing Education:
Certification Designation/s: CNT

Meetings/Conferences: Biennial
2013 - Coeur d#Alene, ID (Coeur d' Alene Resort)/May 14 - 18

Publications:
CCAOM News

Council of Colleges of Arts and Sciences (1965)
C/O The College of William and Mary
P.O. Box 8795
Williamsburg, VA 23187-8795
Tel: (757) 221-1784 *Fax:* (757) 221-1776
E-Mail: ccas@wm.edu
Website: ccas.net/i4a/pages/index.cfm
Members: 1600 individuals
Staff: 2
Annual Budget: $500-1,000,000
Tax: 501(c)(3)

Personnel:
Executive Director and Secretary to the Board: Dr. Anne-Marie McCartan
 E-Mail: ammcca@wm.edu
Executive Administrative Assistant: Gayle Helmling

Historical Note:
CCAS's mission is to to provide its member institutions through a forum for discussing common problems of higher education as these relate to the Arts and Sciences and an agency to encourage, initiate, and support programs and activities to improve the intellectual stature and the public understanding of the disciplines of the Arts and Sciences and a medium for the dissemination of the results of Council deliberations and other information deemed essential to the continuing intellectual and educational strength of the Arts and Sciences.Membership includes public and private baccalaureate degree-granting colleges of arts and sciences. Membership: $375-740/year (Institution).

Meetings/Conferences: Annual
2013 - Jacksonville, FL (Hyatt Regency Jacksonville Riverfront)/Nov. 6 - 9
2014 - San Antonio, TX (San Antonio Marriott Rivercenter)/Nov. 5 - 8
2015 - Washington, DC (Washington Hilton)/Nov. 4 - 7
2016 - San Diego, CA (Manchester Grand Hyatt San Diego)/Nov. 2 - 5
2017 - Denver, CO (Sheraton Denver Downtown Hotel)/Nov. 1 - 4
Number of non-conference events/year: 1

Publications:
CCAS Newsletter; quarterly; adv.
Membership Directory; annually

Council of Communication Management (1955)
65 Enterprise
Aliso Viejo, CA 92656
Tel: (866) 463-6226 *Fax:* (949) 315-3039
E-Mail: info@thecommunicationexchange.org
Website: ccmconnection.com
Members: 500 corporations
Staff: 3
Annual Budget: $100-250,000

Personnel:
Contact, Communications: Fred Droz
 E-Mail: fred.droz@thedrozgroup.com

Historical Note:
Formerly (1955) the Industrial Communication Council. CCM provides a network through which managers, consultants and educators, who work at the policy level in organizational communication can help one another advance the practice of communication in business. Membership: $300/year.

Meetings/Conferences: Annual
2013 - Las Vegas, NV (Four Seasons Hotel Las Vegas)/ April 23 - 26

Publications:
Exchange Marketplace Directory; on-line
Member Directory; on-line

Membership List Available to Non-members

Council of Defense and Space Industry Associations (1964)
1000 Wilson Blvd., Suite 1800
Arlington, VA 22201
Tel: (703) 243-2020 *Fax:* (703) 243-8539
E-Mail: codsia@ndia.org
Website: codsia.org
Members: 7 associations
Staff: 1

Annual Budget: $50-100,000

Personnel:
Administrative Officer: Timothy M. Nunnally-Olsen
 E-Mail: codsia@ndia.org

Historical Note:
Established June 30, 1964, by industry associations having common interests in the defense and space fields, CODSIA functions as a voluntary, coordinating, non-profit, consultative body. It addresses policies, regulations, directives and procedures relating to the supplier-purchaser relationship between government and industry. Members are Aerospace Industries Association, American Electronics Association, American Shipbuilding Association, Contract Services Association, Electronic Industries Alliance, Manufacturers' Alliance for Productivity and Innovation, Professional Services Council, and National Defense Industrial Association.

Council of Development Finance Agencies (1982)
85 E. Gay St.
Suite 700
Columbus, OH 43215
Tel: (614) 224-1300 *Fax:* (614) 224-1343
E-Mail: info@cdfa.net
Website: cdfa.net
Members: 300 public, private and non-profit development entities.
Staff: 11
Annual Budget: $250-500,000

Personnel:
President and Chief Executive Officer: Toby Rittner
 E-Mail: trittner@cdfa.net
Network Administrator: Sam DeNies
 E-Mail: sdenies@dcnteam.com
Chief Financial Officer: Lori Griffin
 E-Mail: lgriffin@dcnteam.com
Director, Education and Programs: Katie Kramer
 E-Mail: kkramer@cdfa.net

Historical Note:
Formerly (1992) Council of Industrial Development Bond Issuers. CDFA's mission is to strengthen the efforts of state and local development finance agencies fostering job creation and economic growth through the use of tax-exempt and other public-private partnership finance programs. Members are state, city, and county public agencies and special authorities. Membership fee varies based on type and volume of business: $750-4,200 (State Issuer); $400-1,575 (Local Issuer); $525- 2,625 (Financial, Investment, and Legal Service Providers).

Meetings/Conferences: Annual
2013 - Washington, DC/Aug. 6 - 9

Publications:
CDFA E-Newsletter; weekly
CDFA Membership Directory; on-line
Perspectives Magazine; on-line; adv.
Site Selection; on-line

Council of Educational Facility Planners International (1921)
11445 E. Via Linda
Suite 2-440
Scottsdale, AZ 85259
Tel: (480) 391-0840 *Fax:* (480) 391-0940
Website: cefpi.org
Members: 3700 professionals
Staff: 10
Annual Budget: $1-2,000,000
Tax: 501(c)(3)

Personnel:
Executive Director and Chief Executive Officer: John K. Ramsey CAE
 E-Mail: john@cefpi.org
Director, Meetings, Conferences and Exhibits: Mike Deegan
 E-Mail: meetings@cefpi.org
Contact, Member Care: Edi Francesconi
Director, Operations and Administration: Michelle Mitchell
 E-Mail: operations@cefpi.org
Administrative Assistant and Contact, Meetings: Donna Robinson
Director, Strategic and Private Development: Barbara C. Worth

Historical Note:
Formerly (1967) the National Council on Schoolhouse Construction. CEFPI strives to be an advocate and resource for educational facilities. Members are companies and persons who plan, design, build, equip and maintain educational facilities. Membership: $40-675/year.

Continuing Education:
Enrollment: 200
Certification Designation/s: REFP

Meetings/Conferences:
Conference Chair: Mike Deegan
2013 - Overland Park, KS (Blue Valley Center for Advanced Professional Studies (CAPS))/Feb. 1 - 2
Number of non-conference events/year: 1

Publications:
CEFPI International Newsletter
Consultants Directory; annually
Creating Connections: CEFPI Guide for Educational Facility Planner
Educational Facilities Planner (EFP); quarterly; adv.
Membership Directory; annually
Space Guidelines for Institutions of Higher Education

Council of Engineering and Scientific Society Executives (1949)
P.O. Box 130656
St. Paul, MN 55113
Tel: (952) 838-3268 *Fax:* (651) 765-2890
E-Mail: info@cesse.org
Website: cesse.org
Members: 1100 individuals
Staff: 3
Annual Budget: $500-1,000,000

Personnel:
Business Manager: Corie Dacus
 E-Mail: corie@cesse.org
Managing Director, Sales and Marketing: Kevin Lewis
 E-Mail: kevin@cesse.org
Manager, Meetings: Brenda Park

Historical Note:
Formerly (1972) Council of Engineering and Scientific Society Secretaries. CESSE's mission is to share and examine successful approaches to managing engineering, scientific and technical societies while providing opportunities for networking and education of executives and senior staff of member societies. Membership: $75 (Chief Executive Officer); $35 (Staff).

Meetings/Conferences:
Conference Chair: Brenda Park
2013 - Albuquerue, NM (Hyatt Regency Tamaya Resort and Spa)/Feb. 24 - 27
2013 - Providence, RI/July 16 - 19
2013 - Providence, RI (Westin Providence)/July 16 - 18
Number of non-conference events/year: 1

Publications:
Member Directory; on-line

Council of Fashion Designers of America (1962)
65 Bleecker
Floor 11
New York, NY 10012
E-Mail: info@cfda.com
Website: cfda.com
Members: 300 individuals
Staff: 12
Annual Budget: $1-2,000,000

Personnel:
Chief Executive Officer: Steven Kolb
Director, Business Affairs: Catherine Bennett
Deputy Director, Finance and Administration: CaSandra Diggs
Director, Special Events and Public Relations: Kelly McCauley
Director, Educational Initiatives: Amy Ondocin
Deputy Director, Programs and Operations: Lisa Smilor

Historical Note:
An association of apparel manufacturers that support the American fashion and military uniform industry. CFDA is a not-for-profit trade association that leads industry-wide initiatives and whose membership consists of more than 400 of America's foremost womenswear, menswear, jewelry, and accessory designers.

Meetings/Conferences:
Conference Chair: Kelly McCauley

Publications:
CFDA Fashion Awards Journal
The CFDA and VOGUE magazine

Council of Federal Home Loan Banks (1998)
2120 L St. NW
Suite 208
Washington, DC 20037
Tel: (202) 955-0002 *Fax:* (202) 835-1144

Website: fhlbanks.com
Members: 12 FHL Banks
Staff: 3
Annual Budget: $2-5,000,000
Tax: 501(c)(6)

Personnel:
President and Chief Executive Officer: John L. von
  Seggern
  E-Mail: johnvon@cfhlb.org
General Counsel: Phil Bechtel
  E-Mail: pbechtel@cfhlb.org
Senior Manager: Keya Jackson
  E-Mail: kjackson@cfhlb.org

Historical Note:
A trade association created in 1998 which is dedicated to enhancing public awareness and understanding of the FHL Bank System.

Council of Graduate Schools *(1961)*
One Dupont Cir. NW
Suite 230
Washington, DC 20036-1173
Tel: (202) 223-3791 *Fax:* (202) 331-7157
E-Mail: general_inquiries@cgs.nche.edu
Website: cgsnet.org
Members: 500 universities in the United States
and Canada, 16 universities outside North
America
Staff: 18
Annual Budget: $2-5,000,000
Tax: 501(c)(3)

Personnel:
President: Debra W. Stewart
  E-Mail: president@cgs.nche.edu
Program Director, Best Practices and Publications: Daniel
  Denecke
  E-Mail: ddenecke@cgs.nche.edu
Vice President, Government Relations and External Affairs:
  Patricia McAllister
Director, Finance and Administration: Keith Peregonov
  E-Mail: kperegonov@cgs.nche.edu
Director, Meetings and Membership Services: Heidi Shank

Historical Note:
CGS's mission is to improve and advance graduate education in order to ensure the vitality of intellectual discovery. Membership: $2,561-7,735 (Regular); $2,301-6,844 (Associate); $1,500 (International Institutions); $25,000 (Sustaining and Corporate Partners); $5,000 (Corresponding Associates); $3,000 (Corresponding Affiliates/Global Affiliates).

Meetings/Conferences: Annual
Conference Chair: Heidi Shank
Number of non-conference events/year: 5

Publications:
CGS Communicator
CGS Newsletter; monthly
Communicator; adv.
Membership Directory; on-line

Council of Graphological Societies *(1974)*
P.O. Box 615
Hardy, AR 72542
E-Mail: graphex@copper.net
Website: handwriting.org/cogs/cogsmain.htm
Staff: 2
Annual Budget: Under $10,000

Personnel:
President: Ellen Bowers
  E-Mail: graphex@copper.net

Historical Note:
COGS serves as a coordinating council for independent graphological organizations to promote and advance the profession of graphology through dissemination of information, education, and research. Membership: $25 (Great Lakes Association of Handwriting Examiners); $35 (Handwriting Analysts International); $50 (National Society for Graphology); $5 (Special Interest Group).

Council of Hotel and Restaurant Trainers *(1970)*
P.O. Box 2835
Westfield, NJ 07091
Tel: (908) 389-9277 *Fax:* (908) 389-0767
TollFree: (800) 463-5918
E-Mail: chart@chart.org
Website: chart.org
Members: 500 members
Staff: 3
Annual Budget: $250-500,000

Tax: 501(c)(6)

Personnel:
Executive Director: Tara Davey
  E-Mail: tara@chart.org
Administrative Director: Allison Letourneau
  E-Mail: allison@chart.org
Senior Director, Marketing: Lisa Marovec
  E-Mail: lmarovec@ameritech.net

Historical Note:
CHART develops hospitality training professionals to advance industry training practices and to improve operational results by providing access to education, tools and resources. Membership: $295/year.

Meetings/Conferences: Semi-Annual
2013 - San Diego, CA (Westin San Diego)/Feb. 23 - 26
2013 - Miami, FL (InterContinental Miami)/July 20 - 23
Number of non-conference events/year: 1

Publications:
FlipCHART; monthly
FlipCHART e-Newsletter
Membership Directory; on-line
Training Flash; monthly
Training Flash e-Newsletter

Council of Independent Colleges *(1956)*
One Dupont Cir. NW
Suite 320
Washington, DC 20036-1142
Tel: (202) 466-7230 *Fax:* (202) 466-7238
E-Mail: cic@cic.nche.edu
Website: cic.edu
Members: 500 colleges
Staff: 24
Annual Budget: $25-50,000,000
Tax: 501(c)(3)

Personnel:
President: Richard Ekman
  E-Mail: cic@cic.nche.edu
Director, Conferences: Allison Blackburn
  E-Mail: ablackburn@cic.nche.edu
Manager, State Fund Programs and Web Communications:
  Christopher Dodds
  E-Mail: cdodds@cic.nche.edu
Vice President, Operations: Christoph M. Kunkel
  E-Mail: ckunkel@cic.nche.edu
Director, Print and Digital Publications: Lilia LaGesse
  E-Mail: llagesse@cic.nche.edu
Director, Finance: Cynthia Page
  E-Mail: cpage@cic.nche.edu
Director, Research Projects: Wei Song
  E-Mail: wsong@cic.nche.edu
Manager, Membership Services: Kate Webber
  E-Mail: kwebber@cic.nche.edu
Vice President, Communications: Laura A. Wilcox
  E-Mail: lwilcox@cic.nche.edu

Historical Note:
Formerly (1981) Council for the Advancement of Small Colleges. Members are independent four-year colleges of liberal arts and sciences and state, regional, and national organizations with an interest in those colleges. Sponsoring memberships are available for corporations and foundations. Purpose is to support college and university leadership, advance institutional excellence and enhance private higher education's contributions to society. Membership: $2,652-8,603 (Institutional); $900 (Associate/International); $295 (Affiliate); $665 (State Fund Member/Member Institution).

Meetings/Conferences:
Conference Chair: Allison Blackburn

Publications:
Independent Newsletter
Membership Directory; on-line

Council of Industrial Boiler Owners (CIBO)
(1978)
6801 Kennedy Rd.
Suite 102
Warrenton, VA 20187
Tel: (540) 349-9043 *Fax:* (540) 349-9850
E-Mail: cibo@cibo.org
Website: cibo.org
Members: 80 companies
Staff: 6
Annual Budget: $1-2,000,000
Tax: 501(c)(6)

Personnel:
President: Robert D. Bessette

  E-Mail: bessette@cibo.org
Consultant, Membership Services: Robert Corbin
Manager, Member and Committee Services: Candler
  Marriott
  E-Mail: cmarriott@cibo.org
Manager, Meetings and Administration: B. J. Ogden
  E-Mail: cibo@cibo.org
Administrative Support Assistant: Tiffany Woodward

Historical Note:
CIBO is a broad-based association of industrial boiler owners, architect-engineers, related equipment manufacturers and university affiliates representing 20 major industrial sectors on the full range of energy and environmental issues and technology.

Meetings/Conferences: Annual
Conference Chair: B. J. Ogden
Number of non-conference events/year: 6

Publications:
BoilerBlast News
CIBO Newsletter

Council of Infrastructure Financing Authorities
(1988)
316 Pennsylvania Ave. SE
Suite 404
Washington, DC 20003
Tel: (202) 547-7886 *Fax:* (202) 547-1867
E-Mail: cifa@navigantconsulting.com
Website: cifanet.org
Members: 96 Organizations
Staff: 1
Annual Budget: $250-500,000
Tax: 501(c)(6)

Personnel:
Executive Director: Rick Farrell
  E-Mail: cifa@madisonassoc.com

Historical Note:
CIFA is an organization of state and local agencies that have authority to assist and facilitate the issuance of debt financing for public infrastructure purposes. Membership: $1,000-5,000 (Full Member); $1,000 (Associate Member); $250 (Academic/Individual, Affiliate); $2,500 (Regional, Affiliate); $5,000 (National, Affiliate Member); $5,000 (International).

Meetings/Conferences:
Number of non-conference events/year: 1

Council of Institutional Investors *(1985)*
888 17th St. NW
Suite 500
Washington, DC 20006
Tel: (202) 822-0800 *Fax:* (202) 822-0801
E-Mail: info@cii.org
Website: cii.org
Members: 305 individuals and companies
Staff: 10
Annual Budget: $2-5,000,000
Tax: 501(c)(6)

Personnel:
Executive Director: Ann Yerger
  E-Mail: anny@cii.org
Manager, Membership Services: Adrienne Allen
Editor: Rosemary Lally
  E-Mail: rosemary@cii.org
General Counsel: Jeffrey P. Mahoney CPA
  E-Mail: jeff@cii.org
Manager, Information Technology: Michael Miller

Historical Note:
CII's mission is to educate its members, policymakers and the public about corporate governance, share owner rights and related investment issues, and to advocate on members' behalf. The Council represents approximately 115 pension funds and follows investment issues of interest to its members. Membership: $3,000-30,000 (General); $4500-15,000 (Educational Sustainers); $2,500 (International Participants).

Meetings/Conferences: Annual
2013 - Washington, DC (Capital Hilton)/April 17 - 19

Publications:
Council Governance Alert - e-newsletter; weekly
Issue Briefs
Membership Directory; on-line

The Council of Insurance Agents and Brokers
(1913)
701 Pennsylvania Ave. NW
Suite 750
Washington, DC 20004-2608

Tel: (202) 783-4400 *Fax:* (202) 783-4410
E-Mail: ciab@ciab.com
Website: ciab.com
Members: 300 corporate members
Staff: 30
Annual Budget: $5-10,000,000
Tax: 501(c)(6)

Personnel:
President: Ken A. Crerar
   E-Mail: ken.crerar@ciab.com
Associate, Human Resources and FAME Scholarships:
   Brittany Foye
   E-Mail: brittany.foye@ciab.com
Chief Financial Officer: Ce Harrison
   E-Mail: ce.harrison@ciab.com
Vice President, Meetings: Paula J. Karchner CMP
   E-Mail: paula.karchner@ciab.com
Vice President, Industry Affairs: Coletta I. Kemper ARM
   E-Mail: coletta.kemper@ciab.com
Director, Membership Development: Matt Kistler
   E-Mail: matt.kistler@ciab.com
Senior Vice President, Marketing and Communications:
   Susan Rushford
   E-Mail: susan.rushford@ciab.com
General Counsel: Scott Sinder
Associate, Database and Advertising: Jacquetta Williams
   E-Mail: jacquetta.williams@ciab.com
Senior Vice President, Government Affairs: Joel Wood
   E-Mail: joel.wood@ciab.com

Historical Note:
*Formerly (1993) the National Association of Casualty
and Surety Agents. Became The Council following a name
change in October 1993. CIAB advocates for commercial
insurance brokers on both property/casualty and employee
benefits issues.*

Meetings/Conferences:
Conference Chair: Paula J. Karchner CMP
Number of non-conference events/year: 9

Publications:
Leader's Edge Magazine; adv.
Membership Directory; on-line

Council of International Investigators (1955)
2150 N. 107th St.
Suite 205
Seattle, WA 98133-9009
Tel: (206) 361-8869 *Fax:* (206) 367-8777
TollFree: (888) 759-8884
E-Mail: office@cii2.org
Website: cii2.org
Members: 350 individuals
Staff: 3
Annual Budget: $100-250,000

Personnel:
Executive Regional Director: Galen Clements
   E-Mail: galen.clements@cii2.org
President: Brian King
   E-Mail: brian.king@cii2.org
Secretary and Treasurer: Rod Webb
   E-Mail: rod.webb@cii2.org

Historical Note:
*The purpose of CII is to encourage association among
owners and operators of investigation agencies while
developing mutual trust and respect. Membership is open
to any individual within a firm, partnership or corporation
engaged in private investigation, private patrol operation
or related security positions. Membership: $110 (Regular);
$175 (Certified); $87.50 (Affiliate).*

Continuing Education:
Certification Designation/s: CII

Meetings/Conferences: Annual
2013 - Wexford, Ireland (Riverside Park Hotel)/Sept. 17
   - 21

Publications:
The Councilor; monthly; adv.

The Council of Landscape Architectural Registration Boards (1961)
1840 Michael Faraday Dr.
Suite 200
Reston, VA 20190
Tel: (571) 432-0332 *Fax:* (571) 432-0442
E-Mail: info@clarb.org
Website: clarb.org
Members: 48 state and provincial boards
Staff: 10
Annual Budget: $2-5,000,000

Personnel:
Executive Director: Joel D. Albizo
   E-Mail: jalbizo@clarb.org
Coordinator, Information Services: Marisela Guzman
   E-Mail: mguzman@clarb.org
Accountant: Dorothy Ludwig
   E-Mail: dludwig@clarb.org
Director, Communications: Veronica Meadows
   E-Mail: vmeadows@clarb.org
Manager, Member and Stakeholder Experience: Rebecca
   Moden
   E-Mail: rmoden@clarb.org

Historical Note:
*CLARB's mission is to foster the public health, safety and
welfare related to the use and protection of the natural
and built environment affected by the practice of landscape
architecture. Members are the landscape architecture
registration boards in British Columbia and Ontario,
Puerto Rico and all of the United States except Vermont.
Membership: $1,800/year (State Board).*

Continuing Education:
Certification Designation/s: CLA, CCR

Meetings/Conferences: Annual
Conference Chair: Rebecca Moden

Publications:
Council Record Holder E-Newsletter; on-line
L.A.R.E. Connection; quarterly
Member Directory; on-line

Council of Large Public Housing Authorities (1981)
455 Massachusetts Ave. NW
Suite 425
Washington, DC 20001
Tel: (202) 638-1300 *Fax:* (202) 638-2364
E-Mail: info@clpha.org
Website: clpha.org
Members: 116 individuals, public housing
authorities
Staff: 8
Annual Budget: $1-2,000,000

Personnel:
Executive Director: Sunia Zaterman
   E-Mail: szaterman@clpha.org
Legislative Director: Gerard Holder
   E-Mail: gholder@clpha.org
Manager, Operations: Trena Mainor
   E-Mail: tmainor@clpha.org
Communications and Media Manager: Ari Romney
   E-Mail: aromney@clpha.org

Historical Note:
*CLPHA works to preserve and improve public and affordable
housing through advocacy, research, policy analysis
and public education. Members are large public housing
authorities. Membership: dues vary by number of units
managed.*

Meetings/Conferences: Annual
Conference Chair: Trena Mainor

Publications:
CLPHA Member Directory; on-line
CLPHA Newsletter; monthly
CLPHA Weekly Report; bi-weekly

Council of Literary Magazines and Presses (1967)
154 Christopher St.
Suite Three C
New York, NY 10014-9110
Tel: (212) 741-9110 *Fax:* (212) 741-9112
E-Mail: info@clmp.org
Website: clmp.org
Members: 500 literary publishers
Staff: 5
Annual Budget: $250-500,000
Tax: 501(c)(3)

Personnel:
Executive Director: Jeffrey Lependorf
   E-Mail: jlependorf@clmp.org
Director, Membership Services: Steph Opitz
   E-Mail: sopitz@clmp.org
Managing Director: Jamie Schwartz
   E-Mail: jschwartz@clmp.org
Coordinator , Website: Ira Sher
   E-Mail: webmaster@clmp.org
Development Associate and Office Manager: Tasha
   Sorenson
   E-Mail: tsorenson@clmp.org

Historical Note:
*Formerly (1990) Coordinating Council of Literary
Magazines. CLMP serves active segments of American
arts and culture: the independent publishers of fiction,
poetry and prose. Membership is open primarily to English-
language publishers. Membership: $75-750 (Regular);
$100 (Non-US Publishers).*

Meetings/Conferences: Annual

Publications:
CLMP Literary Press and Magazine Directory; annually
Membership Directory; on-line

Membership List Available to Non-members

Council of Manufacturing Associations (1907)
1331 Pennsylvania Ave. NW
Suite 600
Washington, DC 20004-1790
Tel: (202) 637-3000 *Fax:* (202) 637-3182
TollFree: (800) 814-8468
E-Mail: manufacturing@nam.org
Website: nam.org/council
Members: 225 trade associations
Staff: 5
Annual Budget: $250-500,000

Personnel:
Executive Director: Paul Hartgen
Vice President, Public Affairs: Tiffany N. Adams
   E-Mail: tiffany.n.adams@nam.org
Vice President, Information Technology: Jeff Colburn
   E-Mail: jcolburn@nam.org
Vice President, Membership Marketing: J. Cliff Johnson III
   E-Mail: jcjohnson@nam.org
Vice President, Human Resources Policy: Joe Trauger
   E-Mail: jtrauger@NAM.org

Historical Note:
*A division of National Association of Manufacturers, CMA
is composed of associations representing manufacturers
in specific industries. CMA's mission is to provide
knowledge, resources and networks to help members create
a stronger and more prosperous U.S. manufacturing sector..
Membership: $720-2,760/year, based on annual budget.*

Meetings/Conferences:
2013 - Annapolis, MD (Loews Annapolis Hotel)/Jan. 17
   - 18

Publications:
Member Focus; monthly; adv.

Council of Medical Specialty Societies (1965)
35 E. Wacker Dr.
Suite 850
Chicago, IL 60611-2106
Tel: (312) 224-2585 *Fax:* (312) 644-8557
E-Mail: mailbox@cmss.org
Website: cmss.org
Members: 20 medical societies
Staff: 4
Annual Budget: $500-1,000,000
Tax: 501(c)(3)

Personnel:
Executive Vice President and Chief Executive Officer:
   Norman B. Kahn Jr., MD
   E-Mail: nkahn@cmss.org

Historical Note:
*Founded as the Tri-College Council by the American College
of Obstetricians and Gynecologists, the American College
of Physicians and the American College of Surgeons and
as other specialty societies joined and assumed its present
name in 1967. CMSS's mission is to provide a respected
and influential voice for the medical specialty societies
and their members by working with the societies and
other medical organizations to formulate, articulate and
encourage adoption of policies that will improve the United
States healthcare system and the health of the public.
Membership: $1.50-45,000/year.*

Meetings/Conferences: Annual
2013 - Rosemont, IL (Hyatt Regency O'Hare)/May 10 -
   11
2013 - Washington, DC (Washington Court Hotel)/
   Nov. 22 - 23

Publications:
CMSS News

Council of Multiple Listing Services (1957)
2501 Aerial Center Pkwy.
Suite 103
Morrisville, NC 27560
Tel: (919) 459-2070 *Fax:* (919) 459-2075
E-Mail: info@councilofmls.com

Website: councilofmls.com
Members: 140 members
Staff: 2
Annual Budget: $250-500,000
Tax: 501(c)(6)

Personnel:
President: Greg Manship
Administrator: Sarah Carlton

Historical Note:
Formerly known (1998) Northwest Council of MLS. CMLS's mission is to advocate the exchange of ideas, office procedures and programs which lead to the continuous progress and success of CMLS and its members. Membership: $300/year (Regular/Business Partner).

Meetings/Conferences: Annual
2013 - Boise, ID/Oct. 2 - 5

Publications:
CMLS Newsletter; on-line

Council of Nephrology Nurses and Technicians
30 E. 33rd St.
New York, NY 10016-5337
Fax: (212) 689-9261
TollFree: (800) 622-9010
Website: kidney.org/professionals/CNNT/ aboutcnnt.cfm
Staff: 1

Personnel:
Chair: Danilo B. Concepcion
    E-Mail: danilo.concepcion@stjoe.org

Historical Note:
CNNT functions as a professional membership council within the framework of the National Kidney Foundation. CNNT Mission is to improve the health and well being of individuals affected with chronic kidney disease through research, patient services, national organ donor programs, and public education. Membership: $85-$95 (Nurses); $35 (Technicians); $25(Students).

Council of North American Insulation Manufacturers Association *(2010)*
44 Canal Center Plaza
Suite 310
Alexandria, VA 22314
Tel: (703) 684-0084 *Fax:* (703) 684-0427
E-Mail: insulation@naima.org
Website: naimacouncil.org
Members: 13 companies
Staff: 3

Personnel:
President and Chief Executive Officer: Kate Offringa
    E-Mail: koffringa@naima.org
Director, Government Affairs and Communications: Kevin Koonce
    E-Mail: kkoonce@ssa-dc.com
Vice President, Government and Industry Affairs: George R. Phelps

Historical Note:
The Council of NAIMA is committed to promoting legislation that will encourage and/or incentivize energy conservation and creation of North American jobs particularly in the insulation manufacturing, supply and installation fields. Membership: $125-1,000 (Individual); $100,000 (Voting Member); $50,000 (Associate Member).

Publications:
Energy Insider; bi-monthly
Topics Directory; on-line

Council of Petroleum Accountants Societies
(1961)
445 Union Blvd.
Suite 207
Lakewood, CO 80228
Tel: (303) 300-1131 *Fax:* (303) 300-3733
TollFree: (877) 992-6727
E-Mail: info@copas.com
Website: copas.org
Members: 3500 individuals and 24 participating societies
Staff: 3
Annual Budget: $500-1,000,000

Personnel:
Executive Director: Tom Wierman
    E-Mail: tom.wierman@copas.org
Administrator: Cheri McCallister
    E-Mail: cheri.mccallister@copas.org

Historical Note:

COPAS is a professional organization comprised of the oil and gas industry's accountants. It also sponsors the National Oil and Gas Accounting School with the Professional Development Institute at University of North Texas. Members are accountants involved in or closely related to the oil and gas industry. Membership: $90/year (Individual).

Publications:
ACCOUNTS; quarterly
COPAS EXTRA; on-line
Member Directory; on-line

Council of Producers & Distributors of Agrotechnology *(1975)*
1730 Rhode Island Ave.
Suite 812
Washington, DC 20036
Tel: (202) 386-7407 *Fax:* (202) 386-7409
Website: cpda.com
Members: 90 companies
Staff: 5
Annual Budget: $500-1,000,000

Personnel:
President: Dr. Susan Ferenc
    E-Mail: sferenc@cpda.com
Director, Legislative Affairs: John Boling
    E-Mail: jboling@cpda.com
Coordinator, Administration and Meeting: Melvin A. Moore-Adams
    E-Mail: mmoore@cpda.com
Director, Communications and Programs: Diane Schute
    E-Mail: dschute@cpda.com

Historical Note:
Formerly (2012) the Chemical Producers & Distributors Association. CPDA's mission is to ensure the success of its member companies by effectively managing relevant legislative and regulatory issues. Member are small to medium sized pesticide formulators, manufacturers and distributors. Membership: $3,608-75,000 (Manufacturer); $4,418-59,000 (Formulator/Distributor); $5,552-20,750 (Adjuvants and Inerts Committee); $2,150 (Associate); $1,260 (Affiliate); $150 (Retired).

Continuing Education:
Certification Designation/s: ACP

Meetings/Conferences:
Conference Chair: Diane Schute
2015 - Coeur d#Alene, ID (Coeur d'Alene Inn and Conference Center)/July 23 - 25

Publications:
Member Directory
Newsletter; quarterly

Council of Professional Associations on Federal Statistics *(1980)*
2121 Eisenhower Ave.
Suite 200
Alexandria, VA 22314
Tel: (703) 836-0404
E-Mail: copafs@aol.com
Website: copafs.org
Members: 67 organizations and affiliates
Staff: 2
Annual Budget: $500-1,000,000
Tax: 501(c)(3)

Personnel:
Executive Director: Edward J. Spar

Historical Note:
COPAFS works to increase the level and scope of knowledge about developments affecting federal statistics. Member organizations include professional associations, businesses, research institutes, and others interested in federal statistics. Membership: $2,000-15,000 (Associations); $1,000-3,000 (Other Organizations).

Meetings/Conferences: Annual

Council of Protocol Executives *(1988)*
101 W. 12th St.
Suite PH-H
New York, NY 10011
Tel: (212) 633-6934 *Fax:* (212) 633-6934
E-Mail: copeorg@aol.com
Website: councilofprotocolexecutives.org
Members: 375 individuals
Staff: 2

Personnel:
Executive Director and Treasurer: Edna Fine Greenbaum
    E-Mail: copeorg@aol.com
Contact, Membership Services: Rosanne Miskow

Historical Note:
COPE's mission is to raise the level of professionalism in the application of protocol standards for executive-level business meetings and entertainment. Membership: $250/year.

Meetings/Conferences: Annual

Publications:
COPE Newsletter; on-line
Membership Directory; on-line

Council of Real Estate Brokerage Managers
(1968)
430 N. Michigan Ave.
Suite 300
Chicago, IL 60611-4092
Tel: (800) 621-8738 *Fax:* (312) 329-8882
E-Mail: info@crb.com
Website: crb.com
Members: 6000 individuals
Staff: 7
Annual Budget: $1-2,000,000
Tax: 501(c)(6)

Personnel:
Chief Executive Officer: Ginny Shipe CAE
    E-Mail: gshipe@crb.com
Manager, Member Services: Tara Maric
    E-Mail: moc.brc@ciramt
Manager, Education and Training: Annie Snyder
    E-Mail: asnyder@crb.com

Historical Note:
Formerly (2002) the Real Estate Brokerage Managers Council and an affiliate of the National Association of Realtors. CRB's mission is to help real estate professionals adapt to the complex challenges of delivering quality service, streamlining operations, integrating new technology and innovating business strategies. Members are managers, brokers and owners. Membership: $210 (Individual, North America, plus $150 application fee); $110 (International, plus $100 application fee).

Continuing Education:
Certification Designation/s: CRB

Meetings/Conferences: Annual

Publications:
e-Connections; monthly
Membership Directory; on-line
Real Estate Business Magazine; bi-monthly; adv.

Council of Residential Specialists *(1976)*
430 N. Michigan Ave.
Chicago, IL 60611
Fax: (312) 329-8882
TollFree: (800) 462-8841
E-Mail: crshelp@crs.com
Website: crs.com
Members: 33000 individuals
Staff: 33
Annual Budget: $5-10,000,000
Tax: 501(c)(6)

Personnel:
Chief Executive Officer: Nina Cottrell
    E-Mail: ncottrell@crs.com
Director, Marketing: Eric Berkland
    E-Mail: eberkland@crs.com
Director, Education: Mary Beth Ciukaj
Manager , Information Technology: Rob Dux
Director, Communications: Michael Fenner
Director, Finance: Susan Karl
Director, Membership Services: Colleen McMahon
    E-Mail: cmcmahon@crs.com
Director, Executive and Human Resource Administration: Geri Toberman
Director, Meetings, Special Events and Facilities: Tavi Toso
    E-Mail: ttoso@crs.com
Chief Financial Officer and Chief information Officer: Keith Tristano

Historical Note:
CRS's mission is to create and provide superior educational opportunities that enhance professional competency and to provide and promote benefits which enhance the economic and other values of membership in the Council. Membership: $150/year.

Continuing Education:
Certification Designation/s: CEC

Meetings/Conferences: Annual
Conference Chair: Tavi Toso
2013 - Las Vegas, NV (Caesars Palace)/Jan. 30 - Feb. 2
Number of non-conference events/year: 3

Publications:
CRS Membership Referral Directory; on-line
Member Connect; on-line
The Residential Specialist Magazine; bi-monthly; adv.
Your Home Newsletter; monthly

Council of Science Editors (1957)
10200 W. 44th Ave.
Suite 304
Wheat Ridge, CO 80033
Tel: (720) 881-6046 *Fax:* (303) 422-8894
E-Mail: CSE@CouncilScienceEditors.org
Website: councilscienceeditors.org
Members: 1200 individuals
Staff: 5
Annual Budget: $500-1,000,000
Tax: 501(c)(3)

Personnel:
Executive Director: David L. Stumph CAE, IOM
    E-Mail: dstumph@resourcenter.com

Historical Note:
Formerly (2000) known as the Council of Biology Editors (CBE). CSE's mission is to promote excellence in the communication of scientific information. Membership consists of individuals concerned with writing, editing and publishing in the life sciences and related fields. Membership: $45-2,735/year.

Meetings/Conferences: Annual
2013 - Montreal, QC/May 3 - June 7
2013 - Montreal, QC (Fairmont The Queen Elizabeth)/
    May 3 - 6
2014 - San Antonio, TX/May 2 - 5

Publications:
Membership Directory; on-line; adv.
Science Editor; quarterly; adv.

Council of Scientific Society Presidents (1973)
PO Box 33999
Washington, DC 20033
Tel: (202) 872-4452 *Fax:* (202) 872-4079
E-Mail: cssp@acs.org
Website: thecssp.us
Members: 100 societies and 3 federations
Staff: 3
Annual Budget: $100-250,000
Tax: 501(c)(3)

Personnel:
President and Chief Executive Officer: Martin A. Apple
    PhD
    E-Mail: cssp@acs.org

Historical Note:
Formerly (1977) Committee of Scientific Society Presidents, CSSP is a leadership-development organization that exists to advocate science, improve national science policy, and focus on related issues. CSSP's mission is to develop an enduring network of past and present national leadership in science Members are past and current presidents and presidents-elect of scientific societies.

Publications:
CSSP Directory
CSSP News
The Science Leader

Council of Societies for the Study of Religion (1970)
Texas Christian University
P.O. Box 298100
Forth Worth, TX 77619
Tel: (817) 257-6448
E-Mail: cssr@rice.edu
Website: cohesion.rice.edu/CentersAndInst/
    CSSR/index
Members: 12 societies
Staff: 4
Annual Budget: $100-250,000

Personnel:
Executive Director and Editorial Board Chair: Andrew O.
    Fort
    E-Mail: a.fort@tcu.edu

Historical Note:
Formerly (1985) Council on the Study of Religion. Membership: $200-2,250 (Constituent Societies, based on number of constituents); $400 (Affiliate Society).

Publications:
Religious Studies Review (RSR); quarterly; adv.

Membership List Available to Non-members

Council of State Administrators of Vocational Rehabilitators (1940)
One Research Ct.
Suite 450
Rockville, MD 20850
Tel: (301) 519-8023 *Fax:* (301) 654-5542
Website: rehabnetwork.org
Members: 80 Agencies
Staff: 4
Annual Budget: $500-1,000,000

Personnel:
Chief Executive Officer: Steve A. Wooderson
    E-Mail: swooderson@rehabnetwork.org
Director, Government Relations: Paul J. Seifert
    E-Mail: paulseifert@rehabnetwork.org
Director, Business Relations: Kathy West-Evans
    E-Mail: kwest-evans@rehabnetwork.org

Historical Note:
CSAVR's mission is to maintain and enhance a national program of public vocational rehabilitation services which empowers individuals with disabilities to achieve employment, economic self-sufficiency, independence, inclusion and integration into communities.

Meetings/Conferences: Annual

Publications:
Membership Directory; on-line

Council of State and Territorial Epidemiologists (1986)
2872 Woodcock Blvd.
Suite 303
Atlanta, GA 30341
Tel: (770) 458-3811 *Fax:* (770) 458-8516
Website: cste.org
Members: 1050 public health epidemiologists
Staff: 24
Annual Budget: $5-10,000,000
Tax: 501(c)(6)

Personnel:
Executive Director: Pat McConnon
    E-Mail: pmcconnon@cste.org
Director, Operations: Beverly Christner
    E-Mail: bchristner@cste.org
Coordinator, Membership Services: Shundra Clinton
    E-Mail: sclinton@cste.org
Contact, Information Technology: Kevin Gibbs
    E-Mail: kgibbs@cste.org
Coordinator, Workforce and Fellowship: Amanda Masters
    E-Mail: amasters@cste.org
Business Manager: MarySue Shulin
    E-Mail: mshulin@cste.org

Historical Note:
Formerly (1986) the Conference of State and Territorial Epidemiologists. CSTE's mission is to encourage the use of epidemiologic data to guide public health practice and improve health. Membership: $50 (Active/Associate); $30 (Student).

Meetings/Conferences: Annual
2013 - Pasadena, CA/June 9 - 13

Publications:
CSTE Journal; on-line
CSTE Newsletter; quarterly
Washington Report; bi-monthly

Council of State Community Development Agencies (1974)
1825 K St. NW
Suite 515
Washington, DC 20006
Tel: (202) 293-5820 *Fax:* (202) 293-2820
E-Mail: info@coscda.org
Website: coscda.org
Members: 48 state agencies
Staff: 4
Annual Budget: $500-1,000,000
Tax: 501(c)(3)

Personnel:
Executive Director: Dianne Taylor
    E-Mail: dtaylor@coscda.org
Operations and Office Manager: Angel Billingsley
    E-Mail: abillingsley@coscda.org
Finance Manager: Michael Lightfield
    E-Mail: mlightfield@coscda.org
Senior, Advocacy and Federal Programs: Linda Thompson
    E-Mail: lthompson@coscda.org

Historical Note:

Formerly (1992) Council of State Community Affairs Agencies, the mission of COSCDA is to advocate for the common community development goals of the states, and develop policies and recommendations on community development issues. Members are employees of state community affairs agencies representing all 50 states. Membership: $1,500 (Associate-State Agencies and Non-Profit Agencies); $2,500 (Corporate).

Meetings/Conferences: Annual

Publications:
Member Updates
National Line

Council of State Governments (1933)
2760 Research Park Dr.
P.O. Box 11910
Lexington, KY 40578-1910
Tel: (859) 244-8000 *Fax:* (859) 244-8001
E-Mail: info@csg.org
Website: csg.org
Members: 5 territories, 50 states
Staff: 190
Annual Budget: $25-50,000,000
Tax: 501(c)(3)

Personnel:
Executive Director and Chief Executive Officer: David
    Adkins
    E-Mail: dadkins@csg.org
Director, Membership Services, Marketing and Media:
    Kelley Arnold
    E-Mail: karnold@csg.org
Director, Human Resources: Chip Barton
Managing Editor: Mary Branham
Director, Education Policy: Pam Goins
Chief Legal and Compliance Officer: Steven Gregory
Manager, Meeting and Marketing: Adnée Hamilton
    E-Mail: ahamilton@csg.org
Chief Financial Officer: Wade Littrell
Senior Deputy Executive Director: Mike Robinson
Manager, Information Technology: Kevin Wallace
Education Policy Analyst: Timothy Weldon

Historical Note:
Founded as the American Legislators Association and assumed its present name later. Council seeks to preserve and strengthen the role of the state in the federal system. CSG's purpose is to encourage excellence in decision making and leadership skills.

Meetings/Conferences: Annual
2013 - San Juan, PR/Dec. 6 - 9
Number of non-conference events/year: 22

Publications:
Capitol Ideas; bi-monthly; adv.
E-Newsletter; bi-monthly
The Book of the States; annually

Membership List Available to Non-members

Council of State Restaurant Associations (1935)
5024-R Campbell Blvd.
Baltimore, MD 21236
Tel: (410) 931-8100 *Fax:* (410) 931-8111
E-Mail: info@staterestaurantassociations.org
Website: staterestaurantassociations.org
Members: 200 individuals
Staff: 3
Annual Budget: $250-500,000

Personnel:
Executive Vice President: Crista LeGrand CMP, CAE
    E-Mail: cristal@clemonsmgmt.com
Financial Manager: Donna Liberto
    E-Mail: donnal@clemonsmgmt.com
Contact, Meetings and Member Services: Vince
    Mullhausen
    E-Mail: vincem@clemonsmgmt.com

Historical Note:
Formerly International Society of Restaurant Association Executives (ISRAE). CSRA's mission is to foster goodwill and promote the success of state restaurant associations and their members. Membership composed of executive staff of state and national restaurant associations.

Meetings/Conferences: Annual
Conference Chair: Vince Mullhausen
Number of non-conference events/year: 2

Publications:
Membership Directory

Council of State Retail Associations
1300 Baxter St.

Suite 360
Charlotte, NC 28204
Tel: (704) 940-7385 *Fax:* (704) 365-3678
E-Mail: info@councilsra.com
Website: councilsra.com
Staff: 2
Annual Budget: $100-250,000

Personnel:
Executive Director: Lori Harrison
    E-Mail: lori@associationoffices.com

Historical Note:
CSRA seeks to improve and advance the retail industry through close cooperation and mutual assistance among state retail association executives.

Meetings/Conferences: Annual

Publications:
Retail Connection; quarterly

Council of State Speech-Language-Hearing Association Presidents *(1975)*
700 McKnight Park Dr.
Suite 708
Pittsburgh, PA 15237
Tel: (412) 366-1177 *Fax:* (412) 366-8804
E-Mail: csap@robertcraven.com
Website: csap.org
Members: 52 states and territories
Staff: 4
Annual Budget: $50-100,000
Tax: 501(c)(6)

Personnel:
President: Molly Thompson
    E-Mail: polarspeech@yahoo.com
Business Manager: Robert Craven
    E-Mail: csap@robertcraven.com
Treasurer: Tara Gregori
    E-Mail: taragregori@bellsouth.net
Editor: Regina Lemmon

Historical Note:
The mission of CSAP is to provide leadership training for state Speech-Language-Hearing association presidents. Membership: $295/year (Organization).

Meetings/Conferences: Annual
2013 - Rockville, MD/May 17 - 18
2013 - Chicago, IL/Nov. 13
2014 - Orlando, FL/Nov. 19
2015 - Phoenix, AZ/Nov. 18
2016 - Philadelphia, PA/Nov. 16

Publications:
Slush Pile

Council of Supply Chain Management Professionals *(1963)*
333 E. Butterfield Rd.
Suite 140
Lombard, IL 60148-5617
Tel: (630) 574-0985 *Fax:* (630) 574-0989
E-Mail: cscmpadmin@cscmp.org
Website: cscmp.org
Members: 9000 individuals
Staff: 26
Annual Budget: $5-10,000,000

Personnel:
President and Chief Executive Officer: Rick Blasgen
    E-Mail: rblasgen@cscmp.org
Manager, Finance and Administration: Paul Blair
    E-Mail: pblair@cscmp.org
Director, Education and Research: Kathleen L. Hedland
    E-Mail: land@cscmp.org
Manager, Marketing and Communications: Madeleine Miller-Holodnicki
    E-Mail: mholodnicki@cscmp.org
Manager, Meetings Services: Margaret O'Connor
    E-Mail: moconnor@cscmp.org
Coordinator, Career Center: Patricia O'Rourke
    E-Mail: porourke@cscmp.org
Director, Operations: James Schulze
    E-Mail: jschulze@cscmp.org
Manager, Membership Services: Krissy Scordato
    E-Mail: kscordato@cscmp.org
Director, Membership Services and Information Technology: Janine M. Stuck
    E-Mail: jstuck@cscmp.org

Historical Note:
Formerly (1985) the National Council of Physical Distribution Management and then the Council of Logistics

Management. CSCMP's mission is to provide opportunities for supply chain professionals to communicate in order to develop and improve their supply chain management skills. Membership: $35-545/year.

Continuing Education:
Certification Designation/s: SCPro

Meetings/Conferences: Annual
Conference Chair: Margaret O'Connor
Number of non-conference events/year: 122

Publications:
CSCMP's Resource Guide; on-line
CSCMP's Supply Chain Quarterly; quarterly
Ed-Link Newsletter; semi-annually
Executive Recruiter Directory; on-line
Explores...; on-line
Global Perspectives; semi-monthly
Journal of Business Logistics; on-line
Member Directory; on-line
Roundtable Newsletter; irregular
State of Logistics Report; annually

Council of Teaching Hospitals
15850 Crabbs Branch Way
Suite 320
Rockville, MD 20850
Tel: (301) 948-9764 *Fax:* (301) 948-1928
E-Mail: coth@aacpm.org
Website: cothweb.org
Members: 200 institutions
Staff: 9
Annual Budget: $2-5,000,000

Personnel:
Chairman: Jeffrey Yung DPM

Historical Note:
COTH's mission is to foster better communication by offering educational and administrative resources to Residency Directors, coordinators and teaching faculty.

Council of the Americas *(1958)*
680 Park Ave.
New York, NY 10065
Tel: (212) 628-3200 *Fax:* (212) 517-6247
E-Mail: inforequest@as-coa.org
Website: as-coa.org
Members: 235 corporations
Staff: 18
Annual Budget: $2-5,000,000
Tax: 501(c)(3)

Personnel:
President and Chief Executive Officer: Susan L. Segal
    E-Mail: ssegal@as-coa.org
Manager, Communications: Alex Andrews
    E-Mail: aandrews@as-coa.org
Media Manager: David Gacs
Senior Director, Public Policy Programs, Corporate Relations and Membership Contact: Randy Melzi
    E-Mail: rmelzi@as-coa.org
Chief Financial Officer: Peter Reilly
Director, Information Technology: Greg Smith
    E-Mail: gsmith@as-coa.org
Editor in Chief: Carin Zissis

Historical Note:
COA members share a common commitment to economic and social development, open markets, the rule of law, and democracy throughout the Western Hemisphere. Membership consists of leading international companies representing a broad spectrum of sectors, including banking and finance, consulting services, consumer products, energy and mining, manufacturing, media, technology, and transportation. Membership: $7,500-45,000/year.

Meetings/Conferences: Annual
Conference Chair: Stephanie Davis

Publications:
Americas Quarterly; quarterly
AS/COA Newsletter; monthly
AS/COA Newsletter; weekly

Council of the Great City Schools *(1956)*
1301 Pennsylvania Ave. NW
Suite 702
Washington, DC 20004
Tel: (202) 393-2427 *Fax:* (202) 393-2400
Website: cgcs.org
Members: 65 school districts
Staff: 21
Annual Budget: $5-10,000,000
Tax: 501(c)(3)

Personnel:
Executive Director: Michael D. Casserly
    E-Mail: mcasserly@cgcs.org
Director, Management Services: Robert Carlson
Director, Communications: Henry Duvall
    E-Mail: hduvall@cgcs.org
Legislative Counsel: Julie Beth Wright Halbert
    E-Mail: jbhalbert@comcast.net
Manager, Communications: Tonya Harris
    E-Mail: tharris@cgcs.org
Director, Academic Achievement: Dr. Ricki Price-Baugh
    E-Mail: pricebaughllc@aol.com
Director, Legislative Services: Jeffrey "Jeff" Simerling
    E-Mail: jsimering@cgcs.org
Manager, Conferences: Terry Tabor
    E-Mail: ttabor@cgcs.org
Director, Finance, Administration and Conferences: Teresita T. ValeCruz
    E-Mail: tvalecruz@cgcs.org

Historical Note:
Formerly known as the Research Council for the Great Schools Improvement. CGCS's mission is to educate the nation's most diverse student body to the academic standards and prepare them to contribute to democracy and the global community.

Meetings/Conferences: Annual
Conference Chair: Teresita T. ValeCruz
2013 - Albuquerue, NM (Hyatt Regency Albuquerque)/ Oct. 30 - Nov. 3
2014 - Milwaukee, WI (Hilton Milwaukee City Center)/ Oct. 20 - 26
Number of non-conference events/year: 2

Publications:
The Urban Educator; monthly
Urban Indicator and Urban Legislator; irregular

Membership List Available to Non-members

Council of Writing Program Administrators *(1978)*
Grand Valley State University, 312 Lake Ontario Hall
Allendale, MI 49401
Tel: (616) 331-8147
Website: wpacouncil.org
Staff: 1
Annual Budget: $25-50,000
Tax: 501(c)(3)

Personnel:
Secretary: Keith Rhodes
    E-Mail: rhodekei@gvsu.edu

Historical Note:
CWPA is a national association of writing professionals with interests in developing and directing writing programs. Membership: $60 (Sustaining); $40 (Regular Tenure Track); $20 (Regular Membership for Non-Tenure Track Faculty/ Graduate Student).

Meetings/Conferences: Annual

Publications:
WPA Journal; semi-annually

Council on Anthropology and Education
Mills College
5000 MacArthur Blvd.
Oakland, CA 94613
Tel: (510) 430-3384 *Fax:* (510) 430-3379
Website: aaanet.org/sections/cae/
Staff: 4

Personnel:
President: Greg Tanaka
    E-Mail: gtanaka2@aol.com
Treasurer: Kathryn Davis
    E-Mail: davis.kathrynanne@gmail.com
Editor: Janet Hecsh
    E-Mail: jhecsh@csus.edu
Webmaster: Silvia Noguerón-Liu
    E-Mail: snoguero@uga.edu

Historical Note:
CAE's mission is to advance anti-oppressive, socially equitable, and racially just solutions to educational problems through research using anthropological perspectives, theories, methods, and findings.

Meetings/Conferences: Annual
2013 - Chicago, IL (Chicago Hilton Indian Lakes Resort)/Nov. 20 - 24
2014 - Washington, DC (Marriott Wardman Park and Omni Shoreham)/Dec. 3 - 7

2015 - Denver, CO (Colorado Convention Center)/Nov.
18 - 22

Publications:
Anthropology and Education Quarterly; quarterly
Anthropology News

Membership List Available to Non-members

Council on Botanical and Horticultural Libraries
(1969)
Auraria Library
1100 Lawrence St.
Denver, CO 80204-2095
Tel: (303) 556-2791 *Fax:* (303) 556-3528
Website: cbhl.net
Members: 240 individuals
Staff: 5
Annual Budget: $25-50,000

Personnel:
President: Robin Everly
   E-Mail: EverlyR@si.edu
Secretary: Gayle Bradbeer
   E-Mail: gayle.bradbeer@auraria.edu
Manager, Membership Services: Suzi Teghtmeyer
   E-Mail: suzirt@gmail.com

Historical Note:
*CBHL's purpose is to initiate and improve communication
and coordinate activities and programs of mutual
interest and benefit to its membership. Membership: $55
(Individual); $105 (Organization/Institutional); $35
(Student/Retiree); $150 (Commercial).*

Meetings/Conferences: Annual

Publications:
CBHL Newsletter

Membership List Available to Non-members

Council on Chiropractic Education *(1971)*
8049 N. 85th Way
Scottsdale, AZ 85258-4321
Tel: (480) 443-8877 *Fax:* (480) 483-7333
TollFree: (888) 443-3506
E-Mail: cce@cce-usa.org
Website: cce-usa.org
Members: 16 programs and institutions
Staff: 4
Annual Budget: $1-2,000,000

Personnel:
President and Chief Executive Officer: Tom Benberg
Director, Accreditation Services: S. Ray Bennett
Manger, Administration and Finance: Toshia King

Historical Note:
*CCE seeks to insure the quality of chiropractic education
in the United States by means of accreditation, educational
improvement and public information. Mission is to
establishing and encouraging standards of chiropractic
educational quality and patient-centered healthcare,
ensuring the quality of chiropractic education programs by
evaluating achievement of accepted standards, encouraging
improvement and the pursuit of excellence in chiropractic
education, advocating integrity in the governance,
administration and delivery of chiropractic education
programs, advocating scholarly activity, research and
service in chiropractic education. Informing the educational
community and public of the nature, quality and integrity of
chiropractic education.*

Meetings/Conferences: Semi-Annual
Number of non-conference events/year: 6

Publications:
Member Listing; on-line

Council on Chiropractic Orthopedics *(1967)*
4409 Sterling Ave.
Kansas City, MO 64133-1854
Tel: (816) 358-5100 *Fax:* (816) 358-6565
E-Mail: contact@ccodc.org
Website: ccodc.org
Members: 400 individuals
Staff: 2
Annual Budget: $10-25,000
Tax: 501(c)(6)

Personnel:
Treasurer: Gary L. Carver DC

Historical Note:
*A subsidiary council of the American Chiropractic
Association. CCO's mission is to preserve, promote and
protect the practice of chiropractic orthopedics for its
members and for the benefit of the patients. Members are
chiropractors with an interest in orthopedics. Membership:*

$100 (Certified/General/Supporting); $50 (Faculty/
Associate); $25 (Retired CCO / 10years +); $35 (Retired
CCO /lessthan10years); $10 (Student).

Meetings/Conferences: Annual
2013 - Las Vegas, NV (Tropicana Hotel and Casino)/
April 25 - 27

Publications:
CCO Newsletter; on-line
Membership Directory; on-line

Council on Diagnostic Imaging to the A.C.A.
(1936)
P.O. Box 190
Cheney, KS 67025
Tel: (316) 542-3400
Website: cditoday.org
Members: 1000 individuals
Staff: 3
Annual Budget: $100-250,000

Personnel:
Secretary and Treasurer: Steven Gould
   E-Mail: drgould@chc.kscoxmail.com
Editor-in-Chief: Bryan K. Hosler DACBR, DC
   E-Mail: drbkhosler@aol.com

Historical Note:
*A part of the American Chiropractic Association. Founded
as the National Council of Chiropractic Roentgenologists,
later became the Council on Roentgenography, (1964) the
American Council on Chiropractic Roentgenology, (1968)
the Council on Roentgenology to the A. C. A. and assumed
its present name in 1986. CBI's mission is to disseminate
information on diagnostic imaging to the chiropractic
profession. Membership: $80 (General); $75 (Institutional
Subscription); $25 (Radiology Residents/Student/Retired);
$100 (Institutional Subscription outside USA).*

Council on Education of the Deaf *(1930)*
Eastern Kentucky University
Wallace 245
Richmond, KY 40475
Tel: (859) 622-1043 *Fax:* (859) 622-4443
E-Mail: catalyst@kent.edu
Website: deafed.net
Members: 7 organizations
Staff: 2
Annual Budget: $25-50,000

Personnel:
Executive Director: Karen Dilka
   E-Mail: karen.dilka@eku.edu
Treasurer: Joe Finnegan

Historical Note:
*CED's mission is to promote excellence in educating deaf
and hard of hearing students.*

Continuing Education:
Certification Designation/s: CED

Council on Employee Benefits *(1961)*
1501 M St. NW
Suite 620
Washington, DC 20005
Tel: (202) 861-6025 *Fax:* (202) 861-6027
E-Mail: ccannon@ceb.org
Website: ceb.org
Members: 225 companies
Staff: 3
Annual Budget: $500-1,000,000
Tax: 501(c)(6)

Personnel:
Executive Director: Shane Canfield
   E-Mail: scanfield@ceb.org
Project Manager: Caren Cannon
   E-Mail: ccannon@ceb.org

Historical Note:
*Founded as the Federation of Employee Benefit
Associations; became the Council on Employee Benefit
Plans in 1950 and assumed its present name in 1961.
CEB's mission is to improve the administration of sound,
progressive employee benefit plans among its members, and
provides a medium for the exchange of ideas, thought and
information on the design, operation and financing of such
plans. Membership: $2,500/year.*

Meetings/Conferences: Annual
2013 - Dana Point, CA (Ritz Carlton Laguna Niquel)/
April 7 - 10

Publications:
Membership Directory; on-line

Council On Forest Engineering *(1978)*

620 SW Fourth St.
Corvallis, OR 97333
Tel: (541) 754-7558 *Fax:* (541) 754-7559
E-Mail: office@cofe.org
Website: cofe.org
Members: 360 individuals
Staff: 3
Tax: 501(c)(3)

Personnel:
Chairperson: Joe Roise
Website Contact: Dale Greene
Membership Chair: Mathew Smidt

Historical Note:
*COFE strives to foster the development of forest engineering
in industry, government, and in university teaching,
research, and extension programs. Members are individuals
with an interest in forest engineering. Membership: $15
(Individual); $5 (Student).*

Meetings/Conferences: Annual
Number of non-conference events/year: 1

Publications:
COFE Newsletter; semi-annually

Council on Foundations *(1949)*
2121 Crystal Dr.
Suite 700
Arlington, VA 22202-3706
Tel: (800) 673-9036
TollFree: (800) 673-9036
E-Mail: info@cof.org
Website: cof.org
Members: 2100 Foundations
Staff: 94
Annual Budget: $10-25,000,000
Tax: 501(c)(3)

Personnel:
President and Chief Executive Officer: Vikki Spruill
Senior Vice President and General Counsel: Janne
   Gallagher
   E-Mail: janne.gallagher@cof.org
Director, Editorial Services: David Martin
   E-Mail: martd@cof.org
Director, Communications and Marketing: Ashley Mills
   E-Mail: milla@cof.org
Vice President, Conferences and Partnerships: Rachel
   Mosher-Williams
   E-Mail: willr@cof.org
Vice President, Membership Services: Matthew Nelson
   E-Mail: Matthew.Nelson@cof.org
Vice President, Legal and Government Relations: Andrew
   Schulz
   E-Mail: andrew.schulz@cof.org

Historical Note:
*COF's mission is to commit to the public benefit and to their
philanthropic purposes and act accordingly. Membership:
$500-55,000 (Full); $500-5,000 (Associate).*

Meetings/Conferences: Annual
Conference Chair: Rachel Mosher-Williams
2013 - San Francisco, CA/Jan. 27 - 29
2013 - Chicago, IL/April 28 - 30

Publications:
COF journal
Membership Directory; on-line
Update; on-line

Membership List Available to Non-members

Council on Governmental Ethics Laws *(1978)*
P.O. Box 81237
Athens, GA 30608
Tel: (706) 548-7758 *Fax:* (706) 548-7079
E-Mail: director@cogel.org
Website: cogel.org
Members: 40 individuals and 160 companies
Staff: 1
Annual Budget: $100-250,000

Personnel:
Executive Director: L. Diane Gill CAE

Historical Note:
*Mission of COGEL is to enhance professional development
of its members in the areas of government ethics, elections,
campaign finance, lobbying, and freedom of information
and to promote government integrity throughout the world.
Membership: $445/year (Governmental/Organizational/
Educational).*

Meetings/Conferences: Annual

Publications:

COGEL Communicator
Directory; on-line
The Guardian; quarterly

Council on Governmental Relations (1948)
1200 New York Ave. NW
Suite750
Washington, DC 20005
Tel: (202) 289-6655 Fax: (202) 289-6698
E-Mail: tdecrappeo@cogr.edu
Website: cogr.edu
Members: 138 individuals
Staff: 5
Annual Budget: $1-2,000,000
Tax: 501(c)(3)

Personnel:
President: Tony DeCrappeo
    E-Mail: tdecrappeo@cogr.edu
Director, Research Compliance and Administration: Carol
    Blum
    E-Mail: cblum@cogr.edu
Director, Contracts and Intellectual Property: Robert B.
    Hardy
    E-Mail: rhardy@cogr.edu
Director, Costing Policy and Studies: David Kennedy
    E-Mail: dkennedy@cogr.edu

Historical Note:
Formerly (1995) a division of the National Association
of College and University Business Officers. COGR is an
association of research-intensive universities and affiliated
medical centers/research institutes. It is a key source of
critical information on current and emerging issues for
its members, along with agencies and organizations that
sponsor research activities.

Meetings/Conferences: Quarterly
2013 - Washington, DC (Washington Marriott)/Feb. 21
    - 23
2013 - Washington, DC (Washington Marriott)/June 6
    - 7

Council on Library-Media Technicians (1967)
28262 Chardon Rd.
P.O. Box 168
Willoughby Hills, OH 44092
Website: colt.ucr.edu
Members: 150 individuals and institutions
Staff: 2
Annual Budget: Under $10,000

Personnel:
Executive Director: Margaret R. Barron
    E-Mail: barron44101@yahoo.com

Historical Note:
Formerly (1973) Council on Library Technology, (1977)
Council on Library Technical-Assistants, and (1989)
Council on Library-Media Technical- Assistants. Affiliated
with the American Library Association. COLT's mission
is to address the issues and concerns of library and
media support staff personnel. Members are library
employees responsible for multiple tasks in circulation,
technical services and public service. Membership: $45-70
(Personal); $35 (Student); $70-95 (Institution).

Publications:
Library Mosaics
Membership Directory; annually

Council on Licensure, Enforcement and Regulation (1980)
403 Marquis Ave.
Suite 200
Lexington, KY 40502-2140
Tel: (859) 269-1289 Fax: (859) 231-1943
E-Mail: clear@mis.net
Website: clearhq.org
Members: 409 individuals and agencies
Staff: 7
Annual Budget: $500-1,000,000

Personnel:
Executive Director: Adam Parfitt
    E-Mail: aparfitt@clearhq.org
Administrative Associate: Rosa Brown
    E-Mail: rbrown@clearhq.org
Coordinator, Training: Molly Marsh
    E-Mail: mmarsh@clearhq.org
Director, Human Resources: Michelle Pedersen
    E-Mail: michelle.pedersen@dora.state.co.us
Senior Program Coordinator: Stephanie Thompson
    E-Mail: sthompson@clearhq.org

Historical Note:
Formerly (1991) National Clearinghouse on Licensure,
Enforcement and Regulation. CLEAR's mission is to
improve the quality and understanding of professional and
occupational regulation. Members include licensing boards
and agencies in the 50 states, territories and Canada.
Membership: $205-2730/year.

Continuing Education:
Certification Designation/s: NCIT

Meetings/Conferences:
Conference Chair: Stephanie Thompson
2013 - St. Louis, MO (Hyatt Regency)/Oct. 3 - 5
Number of non-conference events/year: 2

Publications:
CLEAR Exam Review; semi-annually; adv.
CLEAR News; on-line

Council on Occupational Education (1971)
7840 Roswell Rd.
Building 300, Suite 325
Atlanta, GA 30350
Tel: (770) 396-3898 Fax: (770) 396-3790
TollFree: (800) 917-2081
Website: council.org
Members: 425 institutions
Staff: 10
Annual Budget: $2-5,000,000

Personnel:
Executive Director and President: Gary Puckett
    E-Mail: puckettg@council.org
Information Specialist: Tami Maynard
    E-Mail: maynardt@council.org
Accountant: Cliff Owen
    E-Mail: owenc@council.org
Accreditation Specialist: Renee Pellom
    E-Mail: pellomr@council.org
Associate Executive Director: Cindy Sheldon
    E-Mail: sheldonc@council.org
Administrative Secretary: Kay Smarr

Historical Note:
Founded as Commission on Occupational Education
Institutions. COE's mission is to assure quality and integrity
in career and technical education. Members are postsecondary schools and institutions that are committed
to career and workforce development. Membership:
$1,245-8,320 (Institutional Accreditation); $1,245-4,160
(Programmatic Accreditation).

Meetings/Conferences: Annual
Conference Chair: Tami Maynard

Publications:
E-Councilor; irregular
Policies and Rules; annually

Membership List Available to Non-members

Council on Radionuclides and Radiopharmaceuticals
660 Pennsylvania Ave. SE
Suite 201
Washington, DC 20003
Tel: (202) 547-6582 Fax: (202) 547-4658
Website: corar.org
Members: 16 CORAR Members
Staff: 1
Annual Budget: $500-1,000,000

Personnel:
Executive Director: Michael J. Guastella
    E-Mail: michael.guastella@corar.org

Historical Note:
CORAR comprised of companies in the United States
and Canada who manufacture radionuclides and
radiopharmaceuticals primarily used in medicine and
life science research. CORAR's mission is to monitor
and participate in the legislative and regulatory process
at the federal, state, local and international levels to
ensure the appropriate treatment of radiopharmaceuticals,
radionuclides, radioactive products used in life medical
sciences, and other medical imaging agents.

Council on Renal Nutrition
30 E. 33rd St.
New York, NY 10016-5337
Tel: (800) 622-9010 Fax: (212) 689-9261
Website: kidney.org/professionals/CRN/
    aboutcrn.cfm
Staff: 2

Personnel:
Contact, Communications: Denise Dilley
    E-Mail: denise.dilley@kidney.org

Editor: Trisha Fuhrman LD, MS, RD

Historical Note:
The Council on Renal Nutrition (CRN) functions as a
professional council within the framework of the National
Kidney Foundation (NKF) and networks with other
organizations to support the National Kidney Foundation's
goal of making lives better for those with chronic kidney
disease through education, outreach and research in the
field of nutrition as it pertains to prevention, eradication and
treatment of kidney and urologic diseases.

Publications:
Journal of Renal Nutrition; quarterly

Council on Social Work Education (1952)
1701 Duke St.
Suite 200
Alexandria, VA 22314
Tel: (703) 683-8080 Fax: (703) 683-8099
E-Mail: info@cswe.org
Website: cswe.org
Members: 3500 individuals
Staff: 40
Annual Budget: $5-10,000,000

Personnel:
President: Darla Spence Coffey MSW, PhD
    E-Mail: president@cswe.org
Director, Office of Member and Communication Services:
    Deborah K. Brandt
    E-Mail: dbrandt@cswe.org
Manager, Meetings: Linda Finnerty
    E-Mail: lfinnerty@cswe.org
Associate Director, Research: Jessica Holmes
    E-Mail: jholmes@cswe.org
Manager, Educational Programs: Ashley D. Jenkins
    E-Mail: ajenkins@cswe.org
Manager, Publications: Elizabeth Simon
    E-Mail: esimon@cswe.org
Manager, Information Services: Eddie Wong

Historical Note:
A nonprofit organization committed to promoting quality
in social work education. It is the sole accrediting authority
for social work education in the U.S. and facilitates faculty
development and scholarly exchange through publications,
conferences and workshops.

Meetings/Conferences: Annual
Conference Chair: Linda Finnerty
2013 - Dallas, TX (Hilton Anatole Dallas)/Oct. 23 -
    Nov. 3
2014 - Tampa, FL (Tampa Convention Center)/Oct. 23
    - 26
2015 - Denver, CO (Sheraton Denver Downtown
    Hotel)/Oct. 15 - 18
2016 - Atlanta, GA (Atlanta Marriott Marquis)/Nov. 3
    - 6
Number of non-conference events/year: 4

Publications:
The Journal of Social Work Education; on-line

Council On State Taxation (1969)
122 C St. NW
Suite 330
Washington, DC 20001-2109
Tel: (202) 484-5222 Fax: (202) 484-5229
Website: cost.org
Members: 600 multi state corporate taxpayers
Staff: 13
Annual Budget: $2-5,000,000
Tax: 501(c)(6)

Personnel:
President and Executive Director: Douglas L. Lindholm
    E-Mail: dlindholm@cost.org
Chief Operating Officer and Senior Director: Joseph R.
    Crosby
    E-Mail: jcrosby@statetax.org
Director, Programs: Charles W. Drury Jr.
    E-Mail: cdrury@cost.org
Senior Manager, National Meetings: Karen A. Galdamez
    E-Mail: kgaldamez@cost.org
Director, Communications: Caroline B. Galleher
    E-Mail: cgalleher@cost.org
Vice President, General Counsel: Todd A. Lard
    E-Mail: tlard@cost.org
Vice President, Government Affairs: Maureen B. Riehl
    E-Mail: mriehl@cost.org
Director, Administration: Barbara A. Stanford
    E-Mail: bstanford@cost.org

Historical Note:

Organized as an advisory committee to the Council of State Chambers of Commerce, COST became separately incorporated in 1992. COST's mission is to provide educational programs and government affairs representation for its members. Members are state and local tax professionals of multistate and multinational corporate taxpayers. Membership: $3,000-7,000 (Corporate).

Meetings/Conferences: Annual
Conference Chair: Charles W. Drury Jr.
Number of non-conference events/year: 2

Publications:
COST Conscious; bi-weekly
Legislative Alert; weekly
Membership Directory; on-line
Practitioner Connection; bi-weekly

Council on Technology Teacher Education (1950)
1914 Association Dr.
Reston, VA 22091-1539
Tel: (703) 860-2100 *Fax:* (703) 860-0353
Website: ctteonline.org
Members: 900 individuals
Staff: 3
Annual Budget: $10-25,000
Tax: 501(c)(6)

Personnel:
Past President: Michael DeMiranda
    E-Mail: mdemira@cahs.colostate.edu
Editor: Chris Merrill
    E-Mail: cpmerri@ilstu.edu
President: Edward M. Reeve PhD
    E-Mail: ed.reeve@usu.edu

Historical Note:
Formerly known as the American Council on Industrial Arts Teacher Education (1986) and an affiliate of the International Technology & Engineering Educators Association and the Technology Education Collegiate Association. CTTE's mission to provide educational leadership opportunities for its members and stimulate research and scholarship related to the technology education profession. Individual membership in the ITEEA is required to be a member of the CTTE. Membership: $40 (Regular); $800 (Life); $100 (Sustaining).

Meetings/Conferences: Annual
Conference Chair: Chris Merrill

Publications:
The Journal of Technology Education; semi-annually
The Technology and Engineering Teacher

Membership List Available to Non-members

Council on the Safe Transportation of Hazardous Articles (1972)
7803 Hill House Ct.
Fairfax, VA 22039
Tel: (703) 451-4031 *Fax:* (703) 451-4207
E-Mail: mail@costha.com
Website: costha.com
Members: 150 individuals
Staff: 8
Annual Budget: $500-1,000,000

Personnel:
Director, Communications: Anne Barry
    E-Mail: anne@costha.com
Director, Marketing: Lori Buckius
    E-Mail: mail@costha.com
Administrator: Lara Mehr Currie
    E-Mail: lara@costha.com
Administrator and Chief Technical Officer: John V. Currie
Senior Technical Consultant: Tom Ferguson
    E-Mail: tom@costha.com
Association Counsel: Richard P. Schweitzer Esq.
Vice President, Member Services and Meetings Contact: Christine M. Yakush
    E-Mail: chris@costha.com

Historical Note:
COSTHA works to promote regulatory compliance and safety in the hazardous materials transportation industry. Members are shippers, carriers, manufacturers and others in the transportation industry. Membership: $1,100-3,885 (Company, based on gross revenue); $1,150 - 4,045 (Trade Association, based on number of members); $435 (Individual/Government Representative); $955 (Corporate); $510 (International Affiliate).

Meetings/Conferences: Annual
Conference Chair: Christine M. Yakush
2013 - San Diego, CA (The Westin San Diego)/April 21 - 24

Publications:

COSTHA Post; on-line
COSTHA QUARTERLY; quarterly
Member Directory; on-line

Council on Undergraduate Research (1978)
734 15th St. NW
Suite 550
Washington, DC 20005
Tel: (202) 783-4810 *Fax:* (202) 783-4811
E-Mail: cur@cur.org
Website: cur.org
Members: 4500 individuals and 600 colleges and universities
Staff: 7
Annual Budget: $2-5,000,000
Tax: 501(c)(3)

Personnel:
Executive Officer: Elizabeth Ambos
    E-Mail: eambos@cur.org
Accounting Specialist: Athenae Belton
    E-Mail: abelton@cur.org
Director, Communications and Membership Services: Lindsay Currie
    E-Mail: lcurrie@cur.org
Senior Director, Membership Services, Operations and Information Technology: Robin Howard
    E-Mail: robin@cur.org
Director, Conference and Meeting Services: MeLisa Zackery
    E-Mail: mzackery@cur.org

Historical Note:
CUR mission is to support and advocate high-quality undergraduate student-faculty collaborative research and scholarship.

Meetings/Conferences: Biennial
Conference Chair: MeLisa Zackery

Publications:
"How To" series
CUR Quarterly; quarterly; adv.
E-News
Member Directory; on-line

The Counselors of Real Estate (1953)
430 N. Michigan Ave.
Chicago, IL 60611
Tel: (312) 329-8427 *Fax:* (312) 329-8881
E-Mail: info@cre.org
Website: cre.org
Members: 1100 individuals
Staff: 10
Annual Budget: $2-5,000,000
Tax: 501(c)(6)

Personnel:
President and Chief Executive Officer: Mary Walker Fleischmann
    E-Mail: mfleischmann@cre.org
Director, Membership Development: Susan Haack
    E-Mail: shaack@cre.org
Director, Marketing and Communications: Alice L. Muncaster
    E-Mail: amuncaster@cre.org
Director, Education and Meetings: Larisa Phillips
    E-Mail: lphillips@cre.org
Chief Administrative Officer: Shea Shumpert
    E-Mail: sshumpert@cre.org

Historical Note:
Originally known as the American Society of Real Estate Counselors (ASREC). CRE's mission is to provide its members with opportunities for professional development, knowledge sharing, and networking, all grounded in a culture of camaraderie. Membership is awarded by invitation only through peer, employer and client review. Membership: $1,500/year (Individual).

Continuing Education:
Certification Designation/s: CRE

Meetings/Conferences: Annual
Conference Chair: Larisa Phillips
2013 - New York City, NY (Waldorf Astoria Hotels and Resorts)/April 28 - May 1
2013 - San Francisco, CA (Ritz Carlton Hotel)/Oct. 20 - 23

Publications:
CRE Member Directory
Membership Directory; on-line
Real Estate Issues
The Counselor
The Counselor; quarterly

Membership List Available to Non-members

Country Music Association (1958)
One Music Cir., South
Nashville, TN 37203
Tel: (615) 244-2840 *Fax:* (615) 242-4783
TollFree: (800) 788-3045
Website: cmaworld.com
Members: 6000 individuals
Staff: 47
Annual Budget: $25-50,000,000
Tax: 501(c)(6)

Personnel:
Chief Executive Officer: Steve Moore
Senior Director, Live Events and Special Projects: Chris Crawford
Vice President, Marketing: Tammy Donham
Senior Manager, Strategic Partnerships: Lara Henley
Vice President, Corporate Communications: Wendy Pearl
    E-Mail: wpearl@cmaworld.com
Senior Manager, Information Technology: Ken Sanderson
Senior Manager, Membership and Balloting: Brandi Simms
Senior Vice President, Finance and Administration: Amy Smartt
Senior Vice President, Marketing and Communications: Sheri Warnke

Historical Note:
CMA is dedicated to bringing Country Music to the world. Membership is open to any individual or organization deriving income from country music. Membership: $100 (Individual); $200-1,250 (Organization).

Meetings/Conferences: Annual
Conference Chair: Chris Crawford

Publications:
CMA Close Up; bi-monthly
CMA Directory; on-line

Country Radio Broadcasters, Inc. (1969)
819 18th Ave., S.
Nashville, TN 37203-3218
Tel: (615) 327-4487 *Fax:* (615) 329-4492
E-Mail: info@crb.org
Website: crb.org
Members: 2500 individuals
Staff: 7
Annual Budget: $1-2,000,000
Tax: 501(c)(3)

Personnel:
Executive Director: Bill Mayne
    E-Mail: bill@crb.org
Business Manager: Chasity Crouch
    E-Mail: chasity@crb.org
Meeting Planner: Dave DeBolt
    E-Mail: dave@crb.org
Contact, Brand Marketing and Strategic Partnerships: Michelle Tigard Kammerer
    E-Mail: michelle@crb.org
Director, Event Support: Kristen McRary
    E-Mail: kristen@crb.org

Historical Note:
CRB's mission is to provide ideas which will help the business of country radio to thrive, improve professionalism through education, and to sustain the country radio format as a dominant entertainment medium. Members are country radio broadcasters, music industry personnel, record label officials, publishers, songwriters and performers.

Meetings/Conferences: Annual
Conference Chair: Dave DeBolt
2013 - Nashville, TN (Nashville Convention Center)/ Feb. 27 - March 1

County Counsels' Association of California
1100 K St.
Suite 101
Sacramento, CA 95814-3941
Tel: (916) 327-7558
Website: coconet.org/conferences
Staff: 1
Annual Budget: $250-500,000

Personnel:
Contact, Conferences: Mary Penney

Historical Note:
County Counsels' Association of California holds Civil Law and Litigation Meetings annually.

Meetings/Conferences: Annual
Conference Chair: Mary Penney

2013 - Napa, CA (Silverado Resort and Spa)/Sept. 11 - 13

County Executives of America (1994)
1100 H St. NW
Suite 920
Washington, DC 20005
Tel: (202) 628-3585 *Fax:* (202) 393-3965
TollFree: (800) 296-8438
Website: countyexecutives.org
Members: 700 individuals
Staff: 8
Annual Budget: $250-500,000

Personnel:
Executive Director: Michael G. Griffin
    E-Mail: mgriffin@countyexecutives.org
Deputy Executive Director, Board Liaison, Meetings and Events, Publications, Legal: Kelly Griffin
    E-Mail: kgrif@optonline.net

Historical Note:
Founded as the National Council of Elected County Executives, assumed current name in 1997. CEA strives to help county governments serve the American people in a better way by acting as a national voice for its leaders and representing its interests on all levels of government. Members include County Executives, County Judges, Parish and Borough Presidents, City- County Mayors, Commission Presidents and Chairs, and all county leaders elected at-large by the public constituency. Membership: $10,000/year (Associate); County dues structure is population-based and can conform to annual county budget allocation.

Meetings/Conferences: Quarterly
Conference Chair: Kelly Griffin

Publications:
CEA National News Roundup; daily

Court Information Technology Officer Consortium
C/O National Center for State Courts, 300 Newport Ave.
Williamsburg, VA 23185
Tel: (757) 259-1841 *Fax:* (757) 259-1520
TollFree: (800) 616-6165
Website: citoc.org
Staff: 2

Personnel:
Vice Chair: Jim Roggero
    E-Mail: jim.roggero@courts.mo.gov
Treasurer: Jorge Basto
    E-Mail: jorge.basto@gaaoc.us

Historical Note:
Chartered in 2005 by the Joint Technology Committee. CITOC's mission is to foster the improvement of the court systems through the application of technologies to court management. Also promotes communication and the sharing of experiences among Chief Information and Chief Technology Officers in courts throughout the country. Membership: $250-500/year.

Meetings/Conferences: Annual

CPA Associates International (1957)
Meadows Office Complex
301 Route 17 North
Rutherford, NJ 07070
Tel: (201) 804-8686 *Fax:* (201) 804-9222
E-Mail: homeoffice@cpaai.com
Website: cpaai.com
Members: 158 firms
Staff: 3
Annual Budget: $500-1,000,000

Personnel:
President: James F. Flynn

Historical Note:
CPAAI's mission is to help members improve and expand their practices. Members are independent CPA and Chartered Accounting firms. Membership is limited to one firm per market area.

Meetings/Conferences: Annual
2013 - Las Vegas, NV/Oct. 27 - 30
Number of non-conference events/year: 17

Publications:
Member Newsletter
Membership Directory; on-line

CPA Auto Dealer Consultants Association (1996)
624 Grassmere Park Dr.
Suite 15
Nashville, TN 37211
Tel: (615) 373-9880 *Fax:* (615) 377-7092

TollFree: (800) 231-2524
E-Mail: info@autodealercpas.net
Website: autodealercpas.net
Members: 22 firms
Staff: 6

Personnel:
Executive Director: Patrick Pruett
    E-Mail: Patrick@TheRainmakerCompanies.com

Historical Note:
Formerly Construction Industry CPA/Consultants Association. CADCA is an association of CPA firms that concentrate a substantial portion of their business on providing financial and consulting services to auto dealers, beyond traditional tax and audit work. Members are accepted on a territorially exclusive basis. Membership: $2,400/year, based on territorial structure.

Continuing Education:
Certification Designation/s: CAFM

Publications:
CADCA Member Directory
Members E-Bulletin and News Service

CPA Manufacturing Services Association (1995)
624 Grassmere Park Dr.
Suite 15
Nashville, TN 37211
Tel: (615) 373-9880 *Fax:* (615) 377-7092
TollFree: (800) 231-2524
E-Mail: info@manufacturingcpas.com
Website: manufacturingcpas.com
Members: 13 firms
Staff: 6

Personnel:
Executive Director: Patrick Pruett
    E-Mail: patrick@the-apa.com

Historical Note:
MSA is a national association of CPA firms that provide industry specific services to manufacturers, especially CPA firms that specialize in providing accounting services beyond traditional tax and audit. MSA's mission is to provide its members with resources in education and marketing as well as foster networking among members in order to provide quality comprehensive business advisory services to the manufacturing industry. Membership: $2,400/year.

Meetings/Conferences: Annual

Publications:
Membership directory; on-line

CPA USA Network (1979)
P.O. Box 8018
Somerville, NJ 08876
E-Mail: info@cpa-usanetwork.org
Website: cpa-usanetwork.org
Members: 50 firms
Staff: 7
Annual Budget: $50-100,000

Personnel:
Executive Director: Janet Barson

Historical Note:
Formerly National Associated CPA Firms, CPA USA Network's mission is to assist in maintaining the effective management, administration, and practice developments of the member firms. It is affiliated with EPR Canada Group Inc in Canada and IEC International for global representation. Membership: 10,000/year

Meetings/Conferences: Annual
2013 - San Diego, CA (Paradise Point Hotel)/June 19 - 21

CPAmerica International (1978)
104 N. Main St., Fifth Floor
Gainesville, FL 32601
Tel: (352) 727-4070 *Fax:* (352) 727-4031
E-Mail: info@cpamerica.org
Website: cpamerica.org
Members: 2070 professionals and firms
Staff: 32
Annual Budget: $2-5,000,000

Personnel:
Director, Services: Grace Horvath
Director, Operations: Jeremy Scheer

Historical Note:
Founded as Accounting Firms Associated, assumed its present name in 1999. CPAI serves as an international network of independent public accounting firms founded to pursue and ensure excellence in accounting, financial and business consulting services.

Meetings/Conferences: Annual

Publications:
CPAConnections; monthly
Dispatch; bi-weekly

CPCU Society (1944)
720 Providence Rd.
Suite 100
Malvern, PA 19355
Tel: (610) 251-2728 *Fax:* (610) 251-2780
TollFree: (800) 932-2728
E-Mail: membercenter@cpcusociety.org
Website: cpcusociety.org
Members: 28000 individuals
Staff: 35
Annual Budget: $2-5,000,000

Personnel:
Executive Director: Kevin Brown
    E-Mail: brownk@cpcusociety.org
Chief Marketing and Communications Officer: Pi-Lan Hsu
Director, Public Relations and Communications: Stephen Young
    E-Mail: syoung@cpcusociety.org

Historical Note:
Founded as Society of Chartered Property and Casualty Underwriters and became (1995) Chartered Property Casualty Underwriters Society before assuming its current name in 2001. CPCU's mission is to meet the career development needs of a diverse membership of professionals who have earned the CPCU designation, so that they may serve others in a competent and ethical manner. Membership: $100 (Regular Retired/Disabled); $600 (Lifetime Retired).

Continuing Education:
Certification Designation/s: CPCU

Meetings/Conferences: Annual
2013 - New Orleans, LA/Oct. 26 - 29
2014 - Anaheim, CA/Sept. 20 - 23/26-50 exhibitors
2015 - Indianapolis, IN/Oct. 3 - 6
2016 - Honolulu, HI/Sept. 17 - 20
2017 - Nashville, TN/Oct. 7 - 10
Number of non-conference events/year: 3

Publications:
CPCU e-LINK; monthly
CPCU eJournal; monthly
CPCU News
Membership Directory; on-line

Membership List Available to Non-members

Craft & Hobby Association (2004)
319 E. 54th St.
Elmwood Park, NJ 07407
Tel: (201) 835-1200 *Fax:* (201) 797-0657
E-Mail: info@craftandhobby.org
Website: craftandhobby.org
Members: 3500 corporations
Staff: 21
Annual Budget: $5-10,000,000
Tax: 501(c)(6)

Personnel:
President and Chief Executive Officer: Andrej Suskavcevic
    E-Mail: andrej@craftandhobby.org
Vice President, Finance and Administration: Natalie Cohn
    E-Mail: ncohn@craftandhobby.org
Director, Marketing: Keri Cunningham
    E-Mail: kcunningham@craftandhobby.org
Director, Membership: Victor Domine
    E-Mail: vdomine@craftandhobby.org
Manager, Systems and Information Technology: William Keenan
    E-Mail: wkeenan@craftandhobby.org
Manager, Member Services and Education: Amie Kolodziej CMP
    E-Mail: akolb@craftandhobby.org
Director, Events and Expositions: Tina Lynn Mercardo CEM
    E-Mail: tmercardo@craftandhobby.org
Director, Education: Nidia Negron
    E-Mail: nnegron@craftandhobby.org
Director, Operations: Eric Waller
    E-Mail: ewaller@craftandhobby.org

Historical Note:
Formed by the merger of the Hobby Industry Association and the Association of Crafts & Creative Industries. CHA's mission is to stimulate the sales growth of the craft and hobby industry worldwide by creating consumer demand, helping members succeed and leading the industry.

Membership: $155 (Industry Professionals); $410-10,815 (Suppliers); $155-15,450 (Buyers).

Meetings/Conferences: Annual
Conference Chair: Tina Lynn Mercardo CEM
2013 - Anaheim, CA (Anaheim Convention Center)/ Jan. 11 - 15

Publications:
CHA Member News enewsletter; monthly
CHA Show Directory; annually; adv.
Marketplace Monitor; bi-weekly
Membership Directory; on-line
Portfolio Magazine; quarterly; adv.

Craft Retailers Association for Tomorrow *(2001)*
P.O. Box 293
Islamorada, FL 33036
Tel: (305) 664-3650 *Fax:* (305) 664-0199
E-Mail: info@craftonline.org
Website: craftonline.org
Members: 152 members
Staff: 4
Annual Budget: $25-50,000
Tax: 501(c)(6)

Personnel:
President: Karen Hohler
Treasurer: Randi Chervitz
Vice President, Education Projects: Donna Milstein
   E-Mail: crafts@hansongalleries.com
Administrative Assistant: Laurie Wickham

Historical Note:
Purpose of CRAFT is to promote awareness of American hand made craft through marketing, networking and communications programs. Members are galleries and shops that feature handmade craftwork of U.S. origin, and artists, partnerships, and corporations who supply a product and/or service to retailer members. Membership: $150-1,000 (Retailer/Artist); $50 (Friend/Supporter); $500 (Associate); 1,000 (Sponsor).

Meetings/Conferences: Annual

Publications:
E-mail News; weekly
Membership Directory; on-line
Newsletter

Cranberry Institute *(1951)*
P.O. Box 497
Carver, MA 02330
Tel: (508) 866-1118 *Fax:* (508) 866-1199
E-Mail: cinews@cranberryinstitute.org
Website: cranberryinstitute.org
Members: 1200 growers and handlers
Staff: 1
Annual Budget: $500-1,000,000
Tax: 501(c)(5)

Personnel:
Executive Director: Terry Humfeld CAE
   E-Mail: thumfeld@cranberryinstitute.org

Historical Note:
CI seeks to further the success of cranberry growers and the industry through health, agricultural and environmental stewardship research. Members are cranberry growers and handlers in the United States and Canada. Membership: $50-100/year (Individual); by assessment (Organization/ Company).

Publications:
Cranberry Health News; semi-annually

Crane Certification Association of America *(1984)*
28175 Haggerty Rd.
Novi, MI 48377
Tel: (248) 994-2222 *Fax:* (248) 994-2224
TollFree: (800) 447-3402
E-Mail: admin@ccaaweb.net
Website: ccaaweb.net
Staff: 3
Annual Budget: $50-100,000

Personnel:
President: Ray Feidt
Executive Officer: Joe Lane
Treasurer: Gary Lavender

Historical Note:
CCAA promotes crane safety through improvements to the certification process and participation in government forums. Membership: $525/year.

Continuing Education:
Certification Designation/s: CCS

Meetings/Conferences: Annual

Publications:
Membership Directory; on-line

Crane Manufacturers Association of America *(1955)*
8720 Red Oak Blvd., Suite 201
C/O Material Handling Industry of America
Charlotte, NC 28217-3992
Tel: (704) 676-1190 *Fax:* (704) 676-1199
Website: mhia.org/industrygroups/cmaa
Members: 35 companies
Staff: 2
Annual Budget: $25-50,000

Personnel:
President: Dave Comiono
Managing Director: Laura E. Stuber
   E-Mail: hvandiver@mhia.org

Historical Note:
Formerly (1968) Electric Overhead Crane Institute. CMAA is an affiliate of the association Material Handling Industry of America (MHIA). Mission is to deliver value to their end-users, channel partners, members and industry associates while serving the overhead material handling industry.

Meetings/Conferences: Annual

Publications:
Cranes Today Magazine; adv.
E-Newsletter; on-line
Hoist Magazine; adv.
Material Handling & Logistics Magazine; adv.
Membership Directory; on-line
Modern Materials Handling Magazine; adv.
Overhead Crane and Hoist Magazine; adv.

CRE Finance Council *(1994)*
20 Broad St.
Seventh Floor
New York, NY 10005
Tel: (212) 509-1844 *Fax:* (646) 884-7569
E-Mail: info@crefc.org
Website: crefc.org
Members: 327 corporations
Staff: 11
Tax: 501(c)(6)

Personnel:
Meetings Assistant: Megan Brandt-Meyer
   E-Mail: mbrandtmeyer@crefc.org
Vice President, Technology and Operations: Edward W. DeAngelo
   E-Mail: edeangelo@cmsaglobal.org
Managing Director, Public Relations: Kenneth Reed
   E-Mail: kreed@cmsaglobal.org

Historical Note:
A trade association dedicated to promoting the strength and liquidity of commercial real estate finance.

Meetings/Conferences:
Conference Chair: Megan Brandt-Meyer
2013 - Miami Beach, FL (Loews Miami Beach Hotel)/ Jan. 14 - 16
2013 - New York City, NY (New York Marriott Marquis)/June 10 - 12
Number of non-conference events/year: 10

Publications:
CRE Finance World
Member Directory; on-line
Weekly Briefing - Newsletter; weekly

Creative Education Foundation *(1954)*
48 N. Pleasant St.
Suite 301
Amherst, MA 01002
Tel: (508) 960-0000 *Fax:* (413) 658-0046
E-Mail: contact@creativeeducationfoundation.org
Website: creativeeducationfoundation.org
Staff: 9
Annual Budget: $500-1,000,000
Tax: 501(c)(3)

Personnel:
Finance Manager: Ann Marie Crane
Manager, Publications: Brenda Deal
Treasurer: Marion Garber
Director, Operations and Programs: Pim Vossen

Historical Note:
CEF is the center for applied imagination - helping individuals, organizations, and communities transform themselves as they confront real- world challenges.

Members share an interest in applying imagination, creative problem solving, and creative thinking. Membership: $185 (Guild Member, includes one-year subscription to the Journal of Creative Behavior); $85 (Associate).

Meetings/Conferences: Annual
Number of non-conference events/year: 2

Publications:
The Journal of Creative Behavior; quarterly

Credit Professionals International *(1930)*
10726 Manchester Rd.
Suite 210
St. Louis, MO 63122
Tel: (314) 821-9393 *Fax:* (314) 821-7171
E-Mail: creditpro@creditprofessionals.org
Website: creditprofessionals.org
Members: 450 individuals
Staff: 2
Annual Budget: $25-50,000
Tax: 501(c)(6)

Personnel:
President: Pat Evans
Treasurer: Sherry Perry

Historical Note:
Formerly (1987) known as Credit Women - International and (1990) CWI: Credit Professionals, CPI is a professional association for anyone involved in the credit or financial industries. Members are persons employed in credit or collections departments of business firms, professional offices or companies. Membership: $80/year.

Continuing Education:
Certification Designation/s: PCA, PCS, PCE, MPCE

Meetings/Conferences: Annual
2013 - San Antonio, TX (Menger Hotel)/June 13 - 16

Publications:
CPI Credit Connection; quarterly; adv.
Credit Professional Magazine; annually; adv.

Credit Research Foundation *(1949)*
1812 Baltimore Blvd.
Suite H
Westminster, MD 21157
Tel: (443) 821-3000 *Fax:* (443) 821-3627
E-Mail: crf_info@crfonline.org
Website: crfonline.org
Members: 600 corporations
Staff: 5
Annual Budget: $1-2,000,000
Tax: 501(c)(3)

Personnel:
President: Terry Callahan CCE
Manager, Customer and Member Services: Barbara Clapsadle
Manager, Communications: Tom Diana
Vice President, Research: Lyle Wallis
Secretary and Treasurer and Manager, Financial and Administrative Services: Cheryl Weaverling

Historical Note:
CRF 's mission is to conduct and carry on the work of the Foundation exclusively for educational purposes especially in the field of credit and credit practices of both domestic and foreign nature. Members are cash managers, credit executives, treasurers, and others responsible for any portion of the credit function in an organization. Sponsors research and education programs to advance the industry. Affiliated with the National Association of Credit Management. Membership: $895 (Corporate); $2,500 (Vendor); $2,000 (Premier Plus); $1,395 (Premier); $450 (International); $110 (Associate).

Meetings/Conferences:
Conference Chair: Lyle Wallis
2013 - Los Angeles, CA (Manhattan Beach Marriott)/ March 18 - 20
2013 - Minneapolis, MN (Minneapolis Marriott City Center)/Aug. 12 - 14
2013 - Ft. Lauderdale, FL (Marriott Harbor Beach Fort Lauderdale Resort and Spa)/Oct. 21 - 23
Number of non-conference events/year: 2

Publications:
Credit & Financial Management Review; quarterly
CRF News; quarterly
Membership Directory; on-line

Credit Union Executives Society *(1962)*
P.O. Box 14167
Madison, WI 53708-0167
Tel: (608) 271-2664 *Fax:* (608) 271-2303

TollFree: (800) 252-2664
E-Mail: cues@cues.org
Website: cues.org
Members: 4500 individuals
Staff: 40
Annual Budget: $5-10,000,000
Tax: 501(c)(6)

Personnel:
President and Chief Executive Officer: Fred Johnson
    E-Mail: fred@cues.org
Manager, Web and eCommerce: Lynette Van Allmen
    E-Mail: lynette@cues.org
Vice President, Publications and Social Media: Mary
    Arnold
    E-Mail: mary@cues.org
Accounting Specialist: Shannon Gherke
    E-Mail: shannon@cues.org
Editor: Lisa Hochgraf
    E-Mail: lisa@cues.org
Senior Vice President and Chief Operating Officer: Barbara
    Kachelski CAE
    E-Mail: barb@cues.org
Vice President, Membership and Product Services: Kristina
    Mattson-Erimm CAE
    E-Mail: kristina@cues.org
Senior Director, Member Relations: Greg Michlig
    E-Mail: greg@cues.org
Director, Executive Education and Meetings: Joette
    Mitchell
    E-Mail: joette@cues.org
Senior Vice President and Chief Financial Officer: Dennis
    Porter
    E-Mail: dennis@cues.org
Vice President, Finance and Technology: Jerry Saalsaa
    E-Mail: jerry@cues.org
Executive Vice President, Human Resources: LaVonne
    Stodola
    E-Mail: lavonne@cues.org

Historical Note:
Formerly (1970) CUES Managers Society. CUES's mission
is to educate and develop credit union CEOs, directors
and future leaders. Members are credit union CEOs and
other senior management personnel. Membership: $695
(Individual); $625 (Supplier member); $915 (Supplier non-
member); $110 (Retired).

Meetings/Conferences: Annual
Conference Chair: Joette Mitchell
2013 - Panama City, Panama (Riu Plaza)/June 22 - 25
Number of non-conference events/year: 10

Publications:
Credit Union Management Magazine; monthly; adv.
CUES Business Lending Edge; quarterly
CUES FYI; weekly
e-newsletters Technology Edge; monthly; adv.
Membership Directory; on-line

Credit Union National Association, Inc. (1934)
5710 Mineral Point Rd.
Madison, WI 53705-4454
Tel: (608) 231-4000 Fax: (608) 231-4263
TollFree: (800) 356-9655
E-Mail: abuse@cuna.org
Website: cuna.org
Members: 51 state credit union leagues
Staff: 310
Annual Budget: $50-100,000,000
Tax: 501(c)(6)

Personnel:
Senior Vice President, Research and Advisory Services:
    Mark Condon
Senior Vice President, Sales and Marketing: Terry Costin
Vice President, Marketing: Amy Nigrelli
    E-Mail: anigrelli@cuna.coop
Senior Vice President, Human Resources and Facilities:
    Harley Skjervem
Senior Vice President, Communications: Mark Wolff
    E-Mail: mwolff@cuna.com

Historical Note:
Formerly (1970) CUNA International Inc. CUNA is the
principal national trade association serving the nation's
12,300 credit unions through leagues in states and the
District of Columbia. CUNA's mission is to support,
protect, unifiy and advance the credit union movement.
Membership: $95-295/year (based on asset size).

Continuing Education:
Certification Designation/s: CCUE, CFSP

Publications:

Connection; quarterly
Credit Union Directors Newsletter; monthly; adv.
Credit Union Front Line Newsletter
Credit Union Magazine; adv.
E-Scan Newsletter; monthly

Cremation Association of North America (1913)
499 Northgate Pkwy
Suite 2200
Wheeling, IL 60090-2646
Tel: (312) 245-1077 Fax: (312) 321-4098
E-Mail: info@cremationassociation.org
Website: cremationassociation.org
Members: 1500 individuals
Staff: 8
Annual Budget: $500-1,000,000
Tax: 501(c)(6)

Personnel:
Executive Director: Barbara Kemmis
    E-Mail: barbara@cremationassociation.org
Coordinator, Conferences: Mia Friel
    E-Mail: mfriel@cremationassociation.org
Manager, Education: Nanette Haase
    E-Mail: nanette@cremationassociation.org
Manager, Information Technology: Denis Janis
    E-Mail: djanis@cremationassociation.org
Specialist, Membership Services: Tim Meadows
    E-Mail: tmeadows@cremationassociation.org
Managing Editor: Amie Shak
Coordinator, Marketing and Communications: Stephanie
    Webendorfer
    E-Mail: swebendorfer@cremationassociation.org

Historical Note:
Formerly (1976) Cremation Association of America.
CANA seeks to promote the modern way and the safe and
hygienic way of dealing with a dead human body and
focuses on cremation as a form of disposition. Members are
cremationists, funeral directors, funeral home operators and
owners, cemeterians, industry suppliers and consultants.
Membership: $395 (Regular/Consultant/Association/
Professional); $195 (Affiliate); $80 (Student).

Continuing Education:
Certification Designation/s: COCP

Meetings/Conferences: Annual
Conference Chair: Mia Friel
2013 - Las Vegas, NV (Signature at MGM Grand)/Feb.
    6 - 7

Publications:
CANA Newsletter; bi-monthly
Membership Directory; on-line
The Cremationist; quarterly; adv.

Cristo Rey Network (2001)
14 E. Jackson Blvd.
Suite 1200
Chicago, IL 60604
Tel: (312) 784-7200 Fax: (312) 784-7201
Website: cristoreynetwork.org
Staff: 12
Annual Budget: $2-5,000,000
Tax: 501(c)(3)

Personnel:
President and Chief Executive Officer: Rob Birdsell
    E-Mail: rbirdsell@cristoreynetwork.org
Chief Operations Officer and General Counsel: Jack J.
    Crowe
    E-Mail: jcrowe@cristoreynetwork.org
Data Manager: Beth Fuller
Chief Academic Officer: Elizabeth Stewart Goettl
    E-Mail: egoettl@cristoreynetwork.org
Director, Strategy and Finance: Nicole Hall
Advancement Officer, Media and web: Brenda Schulze
    E-Mail: bschulze@cristoreynetwork.org

Historical Note:
A national association of high schools providing Roman
Catholic college preparatory education for urban
communities.

Publications:
Cristo Rey Network E-Newsletter
Cristo Rey Network Newsletter; annually

Crop Insurance Research Bureau (1964)
201 Massachusetts Ave. NE
Suite C-5
Washington, DC 20002
Tel: (202) 544-0067 Fax: (202) 330-5255
TollFree: (888) 274-2472

Website: cropinsurance.org
Members: 32 companies
Staff: 4
Annual Budget: $500-1,000,000

Personnel:
Director, Operations: Elena Babiasz
    E-Mail: ebabiasz@cropinsurance.org
Legal Counsel: W. Kurt Henke
    E-Mail: wkh@henke-bufkin.com
Executive Vice President and Federal Affairs Representative:
    Michael K. Torrey
    E-Mail: mtorrey@torreydc.com

Historical Note:
CIRB works to improve crop insurance through unity and
leadership. Members are crop insurance and other related
companies. It also sponsors CIRB-PAC, crop insurance
industry research and provides industry liaison to the U.S.
Department of Agriculture.

Meetings/Conferences: Annual
2013 - Indian Wells, CA (Renaissance Esmeralda
    Indian Wells Resort and Spa)/Feb. 6 - 8

Publications:
CIRB Newsletter
CIRB Notes; quarterly; adv.

Crop Science Society of America (1955)
5585 Guilford Rd.
Madison, WI 53711-5801
Tel: (608) 273-8080 Fax: (608) 273-2021
E-Mail: headquarters@agronomy.org
Website: crops.org
Members: 2868 individuals
Staff: 42
Annual Budget: $2-5,000,000

Personnel:
Chief Executive Officer: Ellen G.M. Bergfeld
    E-Mail: ebergfeld@crops.org
Director, Business Development: Alexander Barton
    E-Mail: abarton@sciencesocieties.org
Director, Membership Services: Susan Chapman
    E-Mail: schapman@sciencesocieties.org
Director, Science Communications: James Giese
    E-Mail: jgiese@sciencesocieties.org
Director, Science Policy: Karl Glasener
    E-Mail: kglasener@sciencesocieties.org
Chief Financial Officer: Wes Meixelsperger
    E-Mail: wm@sciencesocieties.org
Director, Information Technology and Operations: Ian
    Popkewitz
    E-Mail: ipopkewitz@sciencesocieties.org
Director, Meetings and Conventions: Keith Schlesinger
    E-Mail: kschlesinger@sciencesocieties.org
Director, Certification Programs: Luther Smith
    E-Mail: lsmith@agronomy.org

Historical Note:
CSSA is dedicated to the conservation and use of natural
resources to produce food, feed, and fiber crops while
maintaining and improving the environment. Membership:
$95-125 (Active, US); $100-130 (Active, International);
$35 (Graduate Student- US); $40 (Graduate Student-
International); $15 (Undergraduate-US & International);
$47-62 (Emeritus-US & International).

Continuing Education:
Certification Designation/s: CPSS/CPSC, CCA, CPAg

Meetings/Conferences:
Conference Chair: Keith Schlesinger
2013 - Tampa, FL/Nov. 3 - 6
2014 - Long Beach, CA/Nov. 2 - 5
2015 - Minneapolis, MN/Nov. 15 - 18
2016 - Phoenix, AZ/Nov. 6 - 9
2017 - Tampa, FL/Oct. 22 - 25
2020 - Phoenix, AZ/Nov. 8 - 11

Publications:
Crop Science; bi-monthly; adv.
Crops & Soils; bi-monthly
Journal of Environmental Quality; quarterly; adv.
Journal of Natural Resources & Life Sciences
    Education; semi-annually; adv.
Journal of Plant Registrations; quarterly
The Plant Genome; quarterly

CropLife America (1933)
1156 15th St. NW
Suite 400
Washington, DC 20005
Tel: (202) 296-1585 Fax: (202) 463-0474
E-Mail: info@croplifeamerica.org

Website: croplifeamerica.org
Members: 97 companies
Staff: 46
Annual Budget: $10-25,000,000

Personnel:
President and Chief Executive Officer: Jay J. Vroom
    E-Mail: jvroom@croplifeamerica.org
Senior Director, Administration and Human Resources:
    Laisha C. Dismuke
    E-Mail: ldismuke@croplifeamerica.org
Executive Vice President of Government Relations and
    Public Affairs: Allen B. "Beau" Greenwood Jr.
    E-Mail: bgreenwood@croplifeamerica.org
Support Specialist, Information Technology: Brian Hayes
Director, Meetings and Events: Francesca Joyce
Executive Vice President, General Counsel and Secretary:
    Douglas T. Nelson
    E-Mail: dnelson@croplifeamerica.org
Assistant General Counsel: Josh Saltzman
    E-Mail: jsaltzman@croplifeamerica.org
Director, Communications and Marketing: Mary Emma
    Young

Historical Note:
Formerly American Crop Protection Association. CropLife
America supports safe and affordable food and fiber
production through innovative, safe and environmentally
sound crop protection technologies. Members are
major manufacturers, formulators and distributors of
crop protection and pest control products, including
bioengineered products with crop production and protection
characteristics. Member companies produce, sell and
distribute virtually all of the active compounds used in the
crop protection chemicals registered for use in the U.S.

Meetings/Conferences: Annual
Conference Chair: Francesca Joyce
Number of non-conference events/year: 1

Publications:
E- Newsletter; on-line

CROPP Cooperative / Organic Valley (1988)
One Organic Way
LaFarge, WI 54639
Fax: (608) 625-3025
TollFree: (888) 444-6455
E-Mail: organic@organicvalley.coop
Website: organicvalley.coop
Staff: 1

Personnel:
Contact, Public Relations: Elizabeth Horton
    E-Mail: elizabeth.horton@organicvalley.coop

Historical Note:
The mission of the Cooperative Regions of Organic Producer
Pools (CROPP) is to create and operate a marketing
cooperative that promotes regional farm diversity and
economic stability by the means of organic agricultural
methods and the sale of certified organic products.

Cross Country Ski Areas Association (1977)
259 Bolton Rd.
Winchester, NH 03470
Tel: (603) 239-4341 Fax: (603) 239-6387
TollFree: (877) 779-2754
E-Mail: ccsaa@xcski.org
Website: xcski.org
Members: 350 ski areas and suppliers and
retailers
Staff: 2
Annual Budget: $100-250,000
Tax: 501(c)(6)

Personnel:
President and Executive Director: Chris Frado
    E-Mail: ccsaa@xcski.org

Historical Note:
Formerly (1983) National Ski Touring Operators
Association and (1988) Cross Country Ski Areas of
America. CCSAA's purpose is to enhance the growth and
improve the quality of cross country ski operations in North
America. Members are cross country ski areas, resorts,
trail systems, guides, outfitters, and related businesses.
Membership: $350-625 (Ski Area); $350 (Supplier/
Associate); $550 (Supplier-Full); $50 (Supporting Retailer);
$200 (Supporting-Organization/Formative Ski Area); $350
(Supporting-Mail Order Catalog); $125 (Foreign Ski area
or Association).

Meetings/Conferences: Annual

Publications:
Master Skier Ski Journal; annually
Membership Directory; on-line

Nordic Network Newsletter; quarterly; adv.

Cruise Lines International Association (1875)
910 SE 17th St.
Suite 400
Ft. Lauderdale, FL 33316
Tel: (754) 224-2200 Fax: (754) 224-2250
E-Mail: info@cruising.org
Website: cruising.org
Members: 16100 agencies,cruise lines, executive
partners, suppliers, and ports
Staff: 32
Annual Budget: $10-25,000,000

Personnel:
President and Chief Executive Officer: Christine Duffy
Director, Training: Thomas Cogan
Director, Finance and Administration: Robert Fuller
Chief Financial Officer: Tom Hohman
Director, Communications: Lanie Morgenstern
Executive Vice President, Marketing and Distribution:
    Robert L. Sharak
Director, Membership Services: Gaye Stewart-Loudis
Senior Vice President, Technical and Regulatory Affairs:
    Capt. Ted Thompson (USCG Ret.)

Historical Note:
The International Council of Cruise Lines (ICCL) merged
with CLIA and adopted the CLIA name in January
2007.CLIA exists to promote all measures that foster a
safe, secure and healthy cruise ship environment, educate,
train its travel agent members, and promote and explain the
value, desirability and affordability of the cruise vacation
experience. Membership: $329 (Agency); $109 (Travel
Agent).

Continuing Education:
Certification Designation/s: ECC, MCC, CTC, CTM, CCC,
ACC, ECCS, LCS

Meetings/Conferences: Annual

Publications:
CLIA Today; on-line
Cruising Magazine; quarterly

Cryogenic Engineering Conference (1954)
917 Front St.
Suite 220
Louisville, CO 80027
Tel: (303) 499-2299 Fax: (303) 499-2599
E-Mail: cecicmc@centennialconferences.com
Website: cec-icmc.org
Members: 1000 individuals
Staff: 2
Annual Budget: Under $10,000

Personnel:
President: Melora Larson
    E-Mail: melora.e.larson@jpl.nasa.gov
Conference Chair: Al Zeller
    E-Mail: zeller@frib.msu.edu

Historical Note:
CEC's mission is to advance those areas of science and
engineering which involve cryogenics and cryo-engineering
through the education of members and non-members in
the sciences and engineering of cryogenics. Members are
scientists and engineers involved in research on extreme
cold.

Meetings/Conferences: Annual
Conference Chair: Al Zeller
2013 - Anchorage, AK (Denaina Civic and Convention
    Center)/June 17 - 21

Cryogenic Society of America (1964)
218 Lake St.
Oak Park, IL 60302-2609
Tel: (708) 383-6220 Fax: (708) 383-9337
Website: cryogenicsociety.org
Members: 607 corporate and individuals
Staff: 1
Annual Budget: $250-500,000
Tax: 501(c)(6)

Personnel:
Executive Director: Laurie Huget
    E-Mail: laurie@cryogenicsociety.org

Historical Note:
Absorbed the Helium Society in 1971. CSA works to
encourage the dissemination of information concerning low
temperature processes and techniques. Membership: $75
(Individual); $35 (Student\Retiree); $600-750 (Individual-
Lifetime); $450-7350 (Corporate Sustaining); $450
(Government/Non-Profit).

Meetings/Conferences: Annual

Number of non-conference events/year: 1

Publications:
Cold Facts; adv.
CryoChronicle; monthly
CSA Newsflashes
Member Directory; annually; adv.

CTIA - The Wireless Association (1984)
1400 16th St. NW
Suite 600
Washington, DC 20036
Tel: (202) 736-3200 Fax: (202) 785-0721
Website: ctia.org
Members: 396 companies
Staff: 100
Annual Budget: $50-100,000,000
Tax: 501(c)(6)

Personnel:
President and Chief Executive Officer: Hon. Steve Largent
Senior Vice President and General Counsel: Michael F.
    Altschul
    E-Mail: maltschul@ctia.org
Vice President, Finance and Administration: Rocco Carlitti
Vice President, Government Affairs: Jot D. Carpenter Jr.
Executive Vice President: Bobby Franklin
    E-Mail: bfranklin@ctia.org
Assistant Vice President, Marketing Operations: Heather
    Lee
Vice President, Technology and Cybersecurity: John
    Marinho
Vice President, Operations: Robert Mesirow
Assistant Vice President, External Communications and
    Public Affairs: Amy Storey
    E-Mail: astorey@ctia.org
Vice President, Public Affairs: John Walls

Historical Note:
Formerly Cellular Communications Industry
Association,Cellular Telecommunications Industry
Association, and (2004) Cellular Telecommunications and
Internet Association. Advocates on behalf of its members,
coordinates the industry's efforts to provide consumers
with choices and information regarding their wireless
products/services, operates industry trade shows, as well as
equipment testing and certification programs. Members are
providers, manufacturers, and suppliers of wireless carriers
and wireless data services and products. Membership:
$5,000 (Carrier/Supplier); $6,000 (Associate).

Continuing Education:
Certification Designation/s: CTIA

Meetings/Conferences: Annual
Number of non-conference events/year: 2

Publications:
CTIA SmartBrief (e-mail news); daily; adv.

Custom Electronic Design and Installation Association (1989)
7150 Winton Dr.
Suite 300
Indianapolis, IN 46268
Tel: (317) 328-4336 Fax: (317) 735-4012
TollFree: (800) 669-5329
E-Mail: info@cedia.org
Website: cedia.net
Members: 3000 companies
Staff: 41
Annual Budget: $10-25,000,000
Tax: 501(c)(6)

Personnel:
Chief Operating Officer: Don Gilpin
    E-Mail: dgilpin@cedia.org
Senior Director, Tradeshows and Events: Debbie Antrim
    E-Mail: debbiea@cedia.org
Manager, Finance: Dawn Cole
    E-Mail: dcole@cedia.org
Project Manager, Education Development: Lisa Duval
    E-Mail: lduval@cedia.org
Director, Membership Sales: Jody Larsen
    E-Mail: jlarsen@cedia.org
Senior Director, Human Resources and Finance: Tabatha
    O'Connor
    E-Mail: toconnor@cedia.org
Senior Director, Technology: Dave Pedigo
    E-Mail: dpedigo@cedia.org
Director, Public Policy: Darren Reaman MBA
    E-Mail: dreaman@cedia.org
Senior Director, Marketing and Public Relations: Jamie
    Riley

E-Mail: jriley@cedia.org

Historical Note:
CEDIA's mission is to develop and encourage high standards of service and conduct of designers and installers of electronic systems for the home. Members are electronic systems professionals of custom designed electronic systems. Membership: $500 (Electronic Systems Contractor/ Industry-Related Professionals); $300 (Professional Services/Sales Representatives).

Continuing Education:
Certification Designation/s: EST, CCP

Meetings/Conferences: Annual
Conference Chair: Debbie Antrim
2013 - Broadbeach, Australia (Gold Coast Exhibition Centre)/July 10 - 12
Number of non-conference events/year: 5

Publications:
CEDIA Newsletter
Membership Directory; on-line

Membership List Available to Non-members

Custom Tailors and Designers Association of America (1880)
42732 Ridgeway Dr.
Broadlands, VA 20148
Tel: (888) 248-2832 *Fax:* (866) 661-1240
TollFree: (888) 248-2832
E-Mail: info@ctda.com
Website: ctda.com
Members: 350 individuals
Staff: 1
Annual Budget: $100-250,000

Personnel:
Contact, Media Relations and advertising: Natalie Alexander

Historical Note:
Formerly the Merchant Tailors and Designers Association of America. A trade association for men's custom tailoring industry. CTDA's mission is to exchange ideas and techniques for design, pattern making, fitting, cutting and tailoring. Membership includes distinguished master tailors, designers, custom clothiers and direct sellers, who create fine custom clothing for discerning clients throughout the United States. Membership: $325/year (Merchant/ Associate).

Continuing Education:
Certification Designation/s: CTDA, MCD, CMM

Meetings/Conferences: Annual

Publications:
Membership Roster; on-line

Customer Relations Institute Global, LLC (1987)
P.O. Box 503016
San Diego, CA 92150-3016
Tel: (858) 449-9055 *Fax:* (760) 788-2024
TollFree: (800) 544-0414
E-Mail: info@criglobal.com
Website: criglobal.com
Members: 500 individuals
Staff: 12
Annual Budget: $2-5,000,000
Tax: 501(c)(3)

Personnel:
President and Chief Executive Officer: Thomas Hinton
E-Mail: tom@tomhinton.com

Historical Note:
CRI Global provides valued services to education and training programs that focus on business excellence, leadership, customer service, team building and sustainability.

Customs and International Trade Bar Association (1917)
1133 Connecticut Ave. NW
12th Floor
Washington, DC 20036
Tel: (202) 756-8383 *Fax:* (202) 756-8087
Website: citba.org
Members: 350 individuals
Staff: 3
Annual Budget: $25-50,000

Personnel:
President: James R. Cannon
E-Mail: jcannon@cassidylevy.com
Webmaster: Victor S. Mroczka
E-Mail: vmroczka@yahoo.com
Treasurer: William Sjoberg

E-Mail: sjoberg@adduci.com

Historical Note:
Formerly (1982) Association of the Customs Bar. Attorneys admitted to practice before the United States Court of International Trade (previously the United States Customs Court) and specializing in customs and international trade law in the United States. CITBA membership consist of attorneys who maintain an interest in the field of customs law, international trade law and related matters. Membership: $75 (Active); $75 (Associate); $50 (Government Employees); $25 (Retired/Student).

Publications:
CITBA Newsletter; quarterly

Czechoslovak Studies Association (1975)
Department of History, Holloway Hall 338
1101 Camden Ave., Salisbury University
Salisbury, MD 21801
Tel: (410) 543-6000 *Fax:* (410) 677-5038
E-Mail: gxference@salisbury.edu
Website: public.iastate.edu/~zarecor/CSA/ welcome.htm
Members: 140 individuals
Staff: 1
Annual Budget: Under $10,000
Tax: 501(c)(3)

Personnel:
Secretary and Treasurer: Gregory C. Ference

Historical Note:
CSA members are academics and others with an interest in the history of Czechoslovakia, its predecessor and successor states, and its historic peoples. Membership: $15 (Individual); $20 (Organization/Company); $5 (Student); $4 (Retired).

Publications:
Czechoslovak Studies Newsletter; bi-monthly

Membership List Available to Non-members

Dairy Management, Inc. (1995)
10255 W. Higgins Rd.
Suite 900
Rosemont, IL 60018-5616
Tel: (847) 803-2000 *Fax:* (847) 803-2077
TollFree: (800) 853-2479
Website: dairyinfo.com
Members: 20 member organization units
Staff: 86
Annual Budget: Over $100,000,000
Tax: 501(c)(6)

Personnel:
Director, Producer Relations: Joe Bavido

Historical Note:
Formed by the merger of the United Dairy Industry Association and the National Dairy Promotion and Research Board, DMI manages the: American Dairy Association; National Dairy Council; U.S. Dairy Export Council. DMI works with state and regional dairy promotion organizations to ensure the future success of dairy by integrating marketing; promotion; advertising; public relations; nutrition education; and nutrition, product and technology research programs.

Meetings/Conferences: Annual
2013 - Phoenix, AZ (Arizona Biltmore Resort and Spa)/ Nov. 11 - 13
2014 - Grapevine, TX (Gaylord Texan Hotel and Convention Center, Dallas Texas)/Oct. 27 - 29

Dance Critics Association (1973)
P.O. Box 1882
Old Chelsea Stn.
New York, NY 10011
E-Mail: dancecritics@hotmail.com
Website: dancecritics.org
Members: 300 Individuals
Staff: 2
Annual Budget: $25-50,000
Tax: 501(c)(3)

Personnel:
President and Interim Executive Director: Robert Abrams
Secretary: Rita Kohn

Historical Note:
DCA seeks to further the identity of dance criticism as a profession and provides the means for exchanging information and exploring fresh approaches to critical writing. Comprises of professional practitioners of dance criticism. Membership: $50(Voting/Associate); $25 (Student/Senior Voting); $75 (Institutional); $100 (Benefactor).

Meetings/Conferences: Annual

Publications:
DCA News; quarterly

Dance Educators of America (1932)
340 Fifth Ave.
P.O. Box 8607
Pelham, NY 10803-0607
Tel: (914) 636-3200 *Fax:* (914) 636-5895
TollFree: (800) 229-3868
E-Mail: dea@deadance.com
Website: deadance.com
Members: 2000 individuals
Staff: 5
Annual Budget: $1-2,000,000

Personnel:
Executive Director: Vickie Sheer

Historical Note:
DEA's promotes the education of teachers in the performing arts, including dance and stage arts. Conducts seminars and workshops to advance the theory and practice of dance education. Membership: $160/year.

Continuing Education:
Certification Designation/s: TTCP

Meetings/Conferences: Annual
Number of non-conference events/year: 29

Dance Films Association (1956)
48 W. 21st St.
Suite 907
New York, NY 10010-6989
Tel: (212) 727-0764 *Fax:* (212) 727-0764
E-Mail: info@dancefilms.org
Website: dancefilms.org
Staff: 5
Annual Budget: $100-250,000

Personnel:
Executive Director: Christy Park
E-Mail: christy@dancefilms.org
Finance Manager: Caterina Bartha
E-Mail: caterina@dancefilms.org
Communications Associate: Brighid Greene
Programming Associate: Jennifer Newman
Archivist: Melissa Silvestri
E-Mail: melissa@dancefilms.org

Historical Note:
DFA is dedicated to furthering the art of dance film. Connecting artists and organizations, fostering new works for new audiences, and sharing essential resources. Membership: $25 (Student); $50 (Individual); $85 (Organization).

Meetings/Conferences: Annual
Conference Chair: Jennifer Newman

Publications:
Dance on Camera Journal; bi-monthly
Membership Directory; on-line

Dance Masters of America, Inc. (1884)
P.O. Box 610533
Bayside, NY 11361
Tel: (718) 225-4013 *Fax:* (718) 225-4293
E-Mail: dmamann@aol.com
Website: dma-national.org
Members: 2500 individuals
Staff: 3
Annual Budget: $500-1,000,000

Personnel:
President: Phyllis R. Guy
E-Mail: pdbdance@cox.net

Historical Note:
Formerly (1926) known as the American National Association, Masters of Dancing. Mission is to provide innovative artistic experiences for the advancement of dance worldwide. Membership: $62/year.

Continuing Education:
Certification Designation/s: CMDD

Meetings/Conferences: Annual
2013 - New Orleans, LA (New Orleans Marriott)/July 14 - 20

Publications:
DMA Magazine
DMA Newsletter

Dance/USA (1982)
1111 16th St. NW
Suite 300

Washington, DC 20036
Tel: (202) 833-1717 *Fax:* (202) 833-2686
Website: danceusa.org
Members: 358 Organizations and Individuals
Staff: 10
Annual Budget: $1-2,000,000
Tax: 501(c)(3)

Personnel:
Executive Director: Amy Fitterer
    E-Mail: afitterer@danceusa.org
Director, Member Services and Board Liaison: Kellee
    Edusei
    E-Mail: kedusei@danceusa.org
Director, Government Affairs: Brandon Gryde
    E-Mail: bgryde@danceusa.org
Specialist, Communications: Laura Henning
    E-Mail: lhenning@danceusa.org
Director, Development: Vicki Kimble
    E-Mail: vkimble@danceusa.org
Contact, Events: Kim Konikow
    E-Mail: kim@artservicesandcompany.com
Director, Finance and Operations: Casey McEnelly
    E-Mail: cmcenelly@danceusa.org
Editor: Lisa Traiger

Historical Note:
*Dance/USA seeks to advance the art form of dance by
addressing the needs, concerns and interests of professional
dance. Members are ballet, modern, ethnic, jazz, culturally
specific, traditional and tap companies as well as dance
service organizations and other organizations concerned
with non- profit professional dance. Membership:
$150-350 (Agents/Artist Representatives); $150-8,700
(Dance Companies); $350-550 (Presenters); $500 (For-
profit Corporations); $350 (Not- for-profit Organizations/
Education Affiliates/Service Organizations); $150-1,000
(International Affiliates); $75 (Independent Artists/
Choreographers); $100 (Individual); $30 (Professional
Dancers/Students).*

Meetings/Conferences: Annual
Conference Chair: Kim Konikow
2013 - Philadelphia, PA/June 12 - 15

Publications:
Dance in the News; semi-monthly; adv.
eJournal; on-line
Membership Directory; on-line
The Spin; bi-weekly

Membership List Available to Non-members

Dangerous Goods Advisory Council *(1978)*
1100 H St. NW
Suite 740
Washington, DC 20005
Tel: (202) 289-4550 *Fax:* (202) 289-4074
E-Mail: info@dgac.org
Website: dgac.org
Members: 210 companies
Staff: 10
Annual Budget: $1-2,000,000

Personnel:
President: Vaughn E. Arthur
*Office Manager and Coordinator, Annual and Global
    Conferences:* Gail Cooley
Counsel: Jerry W. Cox
Specialist, Membership Services and Communications:
    Michael Steenstra
Technical Director: Frits Wybenga

Historical Note:
*Formerly (2003) Hazardous Materials Advisory Council and
incorporated in the year 1978. DGAC is an international,
non-profit, educational organization dedicated to the
promotion of the safe transportation of hazardous
materials/dangerous goods. Members are shippers, carriers
of all modes, container manufacturers and reconditioners,
emergency response and waste clean-up companies,
and other firms and associations involved in hazardous
materials transportation. Membership: $1,150-4,525/year
(Based on annual gross revenues).*

Meetings/Conferences: Annual
Conference Chair: Gail Cooley

Publications:
Membership Directory; on-line

**The Danish-American Chamber of Commerce
(USA)** *(1931)*
One Dag Hammerskjold Plaza, 885 Second Ave.
18th Floor
New York, NY 10017-2201
Tel: (917) 575-3761 *Fax:* (212) 754-1904

E-Mail: daccny@daccny.com
Website: daccny.com
Members: 160 companies
Staff: 2
Annual Budget: $50-100,000
Tax: 501(c)(3)

Personnel:
General Manager: Morten Zolde
    E-Mail: peter.frederiksen@nordea.com
Secretary: Nargis A. McGuinness
    E-Mail: nm@kelsenbisca.com

Historical Note:
*Formed through a merger of the Danish-American
Trade Council (1964) and the Danish Luncheon Club
(1931). DACC's mission is to make the business grow by
providing valuable contacts and information. Members
are concentrated in the New York city area. Membership:
$2,000 (Sustaining); $750 (Corporate); $125 (Individual).*

Data Interchange Standards Association *(1987)*
7600 Leesburg Pike
Suite 430
Falls Church, VA 22043
Tel: (703) 970-4480 *Fax:* (703) 970-4488
E-Mail: info@disa.org
Website: disa.org
Members: 450 companies
Staff: 8
Annual Budget: $1-2,000,000
Tax: 501(c)(6)

Personnel:
President: Jerry C. Connors
    E-Mail: jconnors@disa.org
Director, Membership Services and Meetings: Catherine
    McDonald
    E-Mail: cmcdonald@disa.org
Project Manager, Information Technology: Linh Nguyen
    E-Mail: lnguyen@disa.org
Manager, Publications: Lee Waggoner
    E-Mail: lwaggoner@disa.org

Historical Note:
*DISA advances the foundation of electronic trade and
commerce by supporting and promoting standards used
for business-to-business data exchange. Purpose is to
deliver best value services and solutions that help industries,
organizations and individuals improve business processes,
reduce costs and increase productivity. Membership:
$503 (Individuals); $1017 (Educational Institutions);
$1,899-4,077 (Government Agencies); $1,412-4,264
(Associations); $1,017-7,474 (Corporations & Companies/
Banks, S&Ls and Credit Unions); $3,087 (Nonprofits).*

Meetings/Conferences:
Conference Chair: Catherine McDonald
Number of non-conference events/year: 3

Publications:
Connections

Data Management Association International
(1988)
1685 Ansonborough dr
Chesterfield, MO 63017
E-Mail: info@dama.org
Website: dama.org
Members: 3000 individuals
Staff: 8
Annual Budget: $50-100,000
Tax: 501(c)(3)

Personnel:
President: Peter Aiken
    E-Mail: President@DAMA.org
Vice President, Membership Services: Lee Edwards
    E-Mail: membership@DAMA.org
Director, Program: Deborah Henderson
    E-Mail: VP_Research_and_Education@dama.org
Vice President, Financial Services: Steve Lewis
    E-Mail: VP_Financial_Services@DAMA.org
Vice President, Marketing: Lisa Nelson
    E-Mail: VP_Marketing@DAMA.org
Vice President, Conference Services: Cathy Nolan
    E-Mail: vp_conference_services@dama.org
Vice President Research, Education: Sanjay Shirude
    E-Mail: Education@dama.org
Vice President, Communications: Loretta Smith
    E-Mail: VP_Communications@DAMA.org

Historical Note:
*Founded as Data Administration Management Association
International, assumed its current name in 2002. Promotes
understanding, development, and practice of managing*

*information and data as a key enterprise asset. DAMA
is dedicated to advance the concepts and practices of
information and data management.*

Continuing Education:
Certification Designation/s: CDMP, ISP, CCP, BSDCDM,
CIDM

Meetings/Conferences:
Conference Chair: Cathy Nolan
Number of non-conference events/year: 2

Publications:
Information Management

DBA International *(1997)*
1050 Fulton Ave.
Suite 120
Sacramento, CA 95825
Tel: (916) 482-2462 *Fax:* (916) 482-2760
E-Mail: info@dbainternational.org
Website: dbainternational.org
Staff: 4
Annual Budget: $2-5,000,000

Personnel:
Executive Director: Jan Stieger
    E-Mail: jstieger@dbainternational.org
Administrative Assistant: Annette Marteeny
    E-Mail: amarteeny@dbainternational.org
Director, Governmental Affairs: David E. Reid
    E-Mail: dreid@dbainternational.org
Manager, Membership Services: Kelly Rocha
    E-Mail: krocha@dbainternational.org

Historical Note:
*Formerly, Debt Buyers' Association. DBA International
enhances the economic performance and liquidity of the
international financial services industry and supports the
ability of consumers to participate in the marketplace for
goods and services. Membership: $695/year.*

Meetings/Conferences: Annual
2013 - Las Vegas, NV (ARIA Resort and Casino Hotel)/
    Feb. 5 - 7

Publications:
Credit and Collection News
The Nilson Report

DBA International *(1997)*
1050 Fulton Ave.
Suite 120
Sacramento, CA 95825
Tel: (916) 482-2462 *Fax:* (916) 482-2760
E-Mail: info@dbainternational.org
Website: dbainternational.org
Staff: 4
Annual Budget: $2-5,000,000

Personnel:
Executive Director: Jan Stieger
    E-Mail: jstieger@dbainternational.org
Manager, Membership Services: Kelly Rocha
    E-Mail: krocha@dbainternational.org
Counsel, Media Relations: David Rubinger
    E-Mail: david@rubinger.com

Historical Note:
*Formerly the Debt Buyers' Association. Mission is to
enhance the economic performance and liquidity of the
international financial services industry and fosters the
ability of consumers to participate in the marketplace
for goods and services. Members are debt industry
professionals. Membership: $148.75-595/year.*

Meetings/Conferences: Annual
2013 - Las Vegas, NV (ARIA Resort and Casino Hotel)/
    Feb. 5 - 7/1600 attendees/over 100 exhibitors
2014 - Las Vegas, NV (ARIA Resort and Casino Hotel)/
    Feb. 4 - 6/1600 attendees/over 100 exhibitors
2015 - Las Vegas, NV (ARIA Resort and Casino Hotel)/
    Feb. 3 - 5/1600 attendees/over 100 exhibitors
2016 - Las Vegas, NV (ARIA Resort and Casino Hotel)/
    Feb. 9 - 11/1600 attendees/over 100 exhibitors

Publications:
Asset Insights; on-line; adv.
Cornerstone Quarterly
DBA the Magazine; semi-annually; adv.
Legislative Daily Updates; on-line
Legislative Insider

Decision Sciences Institute *(1968)*
75 Piedmont Ave.
Suite 340
Atlanta, GA 30303
Tel: (404) 413-7710 *Fax:* (404) 413-7714

E-Mail: dsi@gsu.edu
Website: decisionsciences.org
Members: 1000 libraries and companies, 3500
individuals
Staff: 8
Annual Budget: $500-1,000,000
Personnel:
Executive Director: Carol J. Latta
    E-Mail: clatta@gsu.edu
Supervisor, Accounting and Membership Services: Pooja K.
    Dodia
    E-Mail: pdodia1@gsu.edu
Contact, Communications and Publications Coordinator:
    Hal Jacobs
    E-Mail: hjacobs@gsu.edu
Historical Note:
Formerly American Institute for Decision Sciences. DSI's
mission is to advance the science and practice of decision
making. DSI is an international professional association
with an inclusive and cross-disciplinary philosophy, guided
by the core values of high quality, responsiveness and
professional development. Membership consists mainly of
business school faculties and management specialists who
use quantitative and behavioral techniques to apply theories
of administrative decision-making. Membership: $160
(Regular); $25 (Student); $35 (Emeritus-US/Canada); $37
(Emeritus- International).
Meetings/Conferences: Annual
2013 - Baltimore, MD (Baltimore Marriott Waterfront)/
    Nov. 16 - 19
2014 - Tampa, FL (Tampa Marriott Waterside Hotel
    and Marina)/Nov. 22 - 25
2015 - Seatle, WA (Sheraton Seattle Hotel)/Nov. 21 -
    24
Publications:
Decision Line; on-line; adv.
Decision Sciences; adv.
Decision Sciences Journal of Innovative Education; adv.
Membership Directory; on-line
Membership List Available to Non-members

Decorative Furnishings Association (1932)
61 E. 77th St.
New York, NY 10021
Website: dfa.info
Staff: 2
Annual Budget: $50-100,000
Personnel:
Executive Director: Steve Nobel
    E-Mail: snobel@nobelinks.com
Contact, Publisher: Beth Fuchs Brenner
Historical Note:
Formerly Decorative Fabrics Association, DFA's mission is
to lead the system of supply and distribution of decorative
furnishings to the interior design trade while increasing
consumer awareness and access to the trade for their home
decoration.
Publications:
Traditional Home Magazine

Decorative Plumbing and Hardware Association
401 N. Michigan Ave.
Suite 2200
Chicago, IL 60611
Tel: (312) 321-5110 Fax: (312) 673-6666
TollFree: (800) 218-8047
E-Mail: membersupport@dpha.net
Website: dpha.net
Members: 400 individuals
Staff: 13
Annual Budget: $500-1,000,000
Personnel:
Executive Director: Mark Lenhart
    E-Mail: mlenhart@dpha.net
Manager, Sales: Rebecca Baker
    E-Mail: rbaker@dpha.net
Coordinator, Education: Lauren Brosio
    E-Mail: lbrosio@dpha.net
Editorial Manager: Dennis Coyle
    E-Mail: dcoyle@dpha.net
Senior Manager, Event Services: Pat Dwyer
    E-Mail: pdwyer@dpha.net
Senior Coordinator, Operations: Tina Karamyar
    E-Mail: tkaramyar@dpha.net
Senior Director, Marketing and Communications: Linda
    Schwartz
    E-Mail: lschwartz@dpha.net

Historical Note:
DPHA's mission is to create competitive advantages for
its members and enhance their business and professional
development. Members include independent dealers,
manufacturers, representatives and others involved in the
decorative plumbing and hardware industry.
Meetings/Conferences: Annual
Publications:
Connections; monthly; adv.
Newsleak; adv.

Deep Foundations Institute (1976)
326 Lafayette Ave.
Hawthorne, NJ 07506
Tel: (973) 423-4030 Fax: (973) 423-4031
E-Mail: staff@dfi.org
Website: dfi.org
Members: 2500 individuals and organizations
Staff: 5
Annual Budget: $1-2,000,000
Tax: 501(c)(6)
Personnel:
Executive Director: Theresa Rappaport
Coordinator, Events: Katie Criqui
    E-Mail: kcriqui@dfi.org
Executive Editor: Virginia Fairweather
    E-Mail: vfairweather@dfi.org
Contact, Accounting: Barbara Octubre
    E-Mail: boctubre@dfi.org
Manager, Advertising: Karol Paltsios
    E-Mail: magads@dfi.org
Historical Note:
DFI's mission is to serve as a primary means through which
members of the institute may participate in improvement
of the planning, design and construction aspects of
deep foundations and deep excavations. Membership:
$750-2,000 (Corporate); $375 (Affiliate Corporate/Non-
Commercial Corporate); $50-95 (Individual); $50 (Student
Individual); Free (Emeritus Individual).
Continuing Education:
Enrollment: 150
Certification Designation/s: PDH
Meetings/Conferences:
Conference Chair: Katie Criqui
Publications:
Deep Foundations Magazine; quarterly; adv.
DFI Journal; biennially; adv.
Foundations Industry Desk Directory; on-line; adv.
Membership Roster; biennially

Deep Sea Fishermen's Union (1912)
5215 Ballard Ave. NW
Seattle, WA 98107
Tel: (206) 783-2922 Fax: (206) 783-5811
E-Mail: dsfu@dsfu.org
Website: dsfu.org
Staff: 2
Annual Budget: $100-250,000
Personnel:
President: Jan Standaert
Manager, Operations: Sara Chapman
    E-Mail: sara@dsfu.org
Historical Note:
An independent union and the oldest organization of
crewmen and skippers in the North Pacific. Membership:
$600 (Set-Line/Hired Skipper); $250 (Associate).
Publications:
Long Liner Newsletter

DeepStar Project
1400 Smith St.
20th Floor
Houston, TX 77002
Tel: (713) 372-2777 Fax: (713) 372-2800
Website: deepstar.org
Staff: 4
Personnel:
Director: Greg Kusinski
Accountant: Roxanne Brandy
Technology Manager: Jim Chitwood
Administrator: Janell Long
Historical Note:
DeepStar is a joint industry technology development
project focused on advancing the technologies to meet its
members' deepwater business needs to deliver increased
production and reserves. They provide a forum to execute
deepwater technology development projects and leverage
the financial and technical resources of the deepwater

industry. Membership: $6,000 (Contributor); $650,000
(Participant).

Defense Credit Union Council (1963)
601 Pennsylvania Ave. NW, South Building
Suite 600
Washington, DC 20004-2601
Tel: (202) 638-3950 Fax: (202) 638-3410
E-Mail: dcuc1@cuna.com
Website: dcuc.org
Members: 235 credit unions
Staff: 5
Annual Budget: $2-5,000,000
Personnel:
President and Chief Executive Officer: Roland A. Arteaga
    E-Mail: aarteaga@cuna.com
Specialist, Information Technology: Jennifer Hernandez
Director, Administration and Executive Assistant: Beth
    Merlo
Comptroller: Megan Mundt
Manager, Conferences: Janet Sked
    E-Mail: janetsked@dcuc.org
Historical Note:
DCUC is a niche membership association representing the
interests of credit unions operating on military installations
worldwide.
Meetings/Conferences: Annual
Conference Chair: Janet Sked
Publications:
Alert; adv.
Membership Directory; on-line

Defense Fire Protection Association (1984)
P.O. Box 1310
Falls Church, VA 22041-0310
Tel: (703) 521-3926 Fax: (703) 521-0849
E-Mail: DFPA@dfpa.org
Website: dfpa.org
Staff: 3
Tax: 501(c)(3)
Personnel:
Executive Director: Ron Fisher
Historical Note:
DFPA aids the armed services, federal agencies and the
private sector improve safety, survivability, fire, blast and
chemical biological and radiation (CBR) protection, damage
mitigation, homeland security, counter-terrorism and
emergency response programs.
Publications:
Military FireFighter Magazine

Defense Orientation Conference Association (1952)
9271 Old Keene Mill Rd.
Suite 200
Burke, VA 22015-4202
Tel: (703) 451-1200 Fax: (703) 451-1201
E-Mail: doca@doca.org
Website: doca.org
Staff: 3
Annual Budget: $500-1,000,000
Tax: 501(c)(3)
Personnel:
President: Frank M. Weinberg
Coordinator, Conference Services: Katherine Carter
Executive Vice President: David W. Morris
Historical Note:
Composed of individuals interested in national security
issues. Offers tours of defense installations in the U.S.
and overseas and provides speakers for members. DOCA
objectives are to provide a means of continuing education
of its members in matters pertaining to national security
under the jurisdiction and supervision of the Departments of
Defense and State.
Meetings/Conferences: Annual
Conference Chair: Katherine Carter

Defense Research Institute (1960)
55 W. Monroe
Suite 2000
Chicago, IL 60603
Tel: (312) 795-1101 Fax: (312) 795-0749
TollFree: (800) 667-8108
E-Mail: dri@dri.org
Website: dri.org
Members: 22000 individuals
Staff: 51

Annual Budget: $10-25,000,000

Personnel:
Executive Director: John R. Kouris
   E-Mail: johnrkouris@dri.org
Director, Education: Jennifer Cout
   E-Mail: jcout@dri.org
Director, Communications: Tim Kolly
   E-Mail: tkolly@dri.org
Director, Publications: Jay Ludlam
   E-Mail: jludlam@dri.org
Manager, Marketing Operations: Katie Malinich
   E-Mail: kmalinich@dri.org
Director, Administrative Services: Mary Ogborn
   E-Mail: mogborn@dri.org
Director, Member Services: Cheryl L. Palombizio
   E-Mail: cpalombizio@dri.org
Director, Meeting Services: Lisa M. Sykes
   E-Mail: lsykes@dri.org
Director, Information Services: Glenda F. Weaver
   E-Mail: gweaver@dri.org

Historical Note:
DRI works to enhance the skills, effectiveness, and professionalism of defense lawyers. Membership: $250 (Defense AttorneyIn-House Counsel); $160 (Government Attorney); $500 (Corporate), $130 (Young lawyer); $20 (Law Student); $50 (Senior); $65-125 (Seminar Attendee).

Meetings/Conferences: Annual
Conference Chair: Lisa M. Sykes
Number of non-conference events/year: 26

Publications:
For The Defense; quarterly; adv.
Membership Directory; on-line

Delaware Standardbred Owners Association
830 Walker Sq.
Dover, DE 19904
Tel: (302) 678-3058 *Fax:* (302) 678-8507
E-Mail: info@deharnessracing.com
Website: deharnessracing.com
Staff: 8
Annual Budget: $2-5,000,000

Personnel:
President: Andrew Markano

Historical Note:
DSOA is a non-profit organization that helps protect and promote harness racing in the State.

Publications:
Newsletter; monthly

Delta Dental Plans Association *(1954)*
1515 W. 22nd St.
Suite 400
Oak Brook, IL 60523
Tel: (630) 574-6001 *Fax:* (630) 574-6999
E-Mail: cs@ddpa.org
Website: deltadental.com
Members: 39 member companies
Staff: 19
Annual Budget: $10-25,000,000
Tax: 501(c)(6)

Personnel:
President and Chief Executive Officer: Kim E. Volk
Coordinator, Public Relations and Social Media: Bill Hupp
   E-Mail: bhupp@deltadental.com
Director, Public Relations and State Government Relations: Chris Pyle
   E-Mail: cpyle@deltadental.com

Historical Note:
DDPA's mission is to work for advancement of oral health care to its customers, partners and consumers through the dental benefits programs and philanthropic efforts of its independent member companies.

Publications:
Dental Examiner Newsletters; monthly
Grinyl e-magazine; monthly

Delta Nu Alpha *(1940)*
1720 Manistique Ave
S. Milwaukee, WI 53172
Tel: (414) 764-3063 *Fax:* (630) 499-8505
E-Mail: admin@deltanualpha.org
Website: deltanualpha.org
Members: 500 individuals
Staff: 4

Personnel:
Administrator: Laura Plizka

   E-Mail: admin@deltanualpha.org

Historical Note:
DNA provides continuing education opportunities for the work force and vigilance in communicating changes in regulations in addition to build a strong international organization. Membership: $125 (Gold); $75 (Silver); $35 (Student); $1000 (Corporate).

Meetings/Conferences: Annual

Publications:
DNA Newsletter; monthly
Journal of Transportation Management
Membership Directory

Delta Omicron *(1909)*
910 Church St.
P.O. Box 752
Jefferson City, TN 37760
Tel: (865) 471-6155 *Fax:* (865) 475-9716
Website: delta-omicron.org
Members: 26000 individuals
Staff: 4
Annual Budget: $100-250,000

Personnel:
International President: Jennifer A. Klafeta
Executive Secretary: Debbie Beckner
   E-Mail: doexecsec@att.net
Web Programmer and Technical Consultant: Whitney Mullins
Editor: Lani A. Yearicks

Historical Note:
DO's mission is to promote and support excellence in music and musicianship.

Meetings/Conferences: Triennial

Publications:
The Wheel; quarterly
The Whistle - Alumni Newsletter; annually

Delta Phi Epsilon *(1917)*
251 S. Camac St.
Philadelphia, PA 19107
Tel: (215) 732-5901 *Fax:* (215) 732-5906
E-Mail: info@dphie.org
Website: dphie.org
Members: 7000 individuals
Staff: 9
Annual Budget: $50-100,000

Personnel:
Executive Director: Nicole DeFeo
   E-Mail: ndefeo@dphie.org
Manager, Membership Services: Andrea Alhadari
   E-Mail: aalhadari@dphie.org
Chief Finance Officer, Business Manager: Angel DiRenzo
   E-Mail: adirenzo@dphie.org
Director, Communications: Stephanie Kochie
   E-Mail: skochie@dphie.org
Administrative Coordinator: Tori Saveriano
   E-Mail: tsaveriano@dphie.org

Historical Note:
Helps assure continuous development and achievement for women through individual attention and smart strategic growth. Delta Phi Epsilon was formally incorporated under laws of the State of New York during 1922.

Meetings/Conferences: Annual

Publications:
Triad

Delta Sigma Delta *(1882)*
296 15th Ave.
Nekoosa, WI 54457
Tel: (715) 325-6320 *Fax:* (715) 325-3057
TollFree: (800) 335-8744
Website: deltsig.com
Members: 28000 individuals
Staff: 1
Annual Budget: $250-500,000

Personnel:
Supreme Scribe: John H. Prey
   E-Mail: supremescribe@delstig.com

Historical Note:
DSD is a professional dental fraternity founded at the University of Michigan whose mission is to bring together the leaders of the profession to further excellence in the ethical, professional and scientific ideals of dentistry through fellowship, knowledge, strength and justice. Membership: By invitation only.

Meetings/Conferences:

Conference Chair: John H. Prey

Publications:
Desmos of Delta Sigma Delta; quarterly; adv.

Delta Sigma Pi *(1907)*
330 S. Campus Ave.
Oxford, OH 45056-2405
Tel: (513) 523-1907 *Fax:* (513) 523-7292
E-Mail: centraloffice@dspnet.org
Website: dspnet.org
Members:
300 collegiate and alumni chapters
226000 individuals
Staff: 14
Annual Budget: $10-25,000

Personnel:
Executive Director: William C. Schilling
   E-Mail: bill@dspnet.org
Administrative Assistant, Information Services and Events: Craig Cashell
   E-Mail: registration@dspnet.org
Communications Coordinator: Katy Glaccum
   E-Mail: katy@dspnet.org
Director, Information and Operational Services: Jeremy Levine
   E-Mail: jeremy@dspnet.org
Coordinator, Communications: Kellsey Miller
   E-Mail: magazine@dspnet.org
MemberShip Services Coordinator: Cindy Rathburn
   E-Mail: cindy@dspnet.org
Director, Finance and Administration: Jeanna Tipton
   E-Mail: jeanna@dspnet.org
Director, Membership Services: Heather Troyer
   E-Mail: heather@dspnet.org

Historical Note:
DSP's mission is to foster the study of business in universities, to encourage scholarship, social activity and the association of students for their mutual advancement by research and practice.

Continuing Education:
Certification Designation/s: CDL

Meetings/Conferences:
Conference Chair: Craig Cashell

Publications:
DELTASIG in the NEWS; quarterly
Deltasig Update; monthly
The DELTASIG Magazine; quarterly

Delta Theta Phi *(1900)*
Campbell University, Wiggins School of Law
225 Hillsborough St., Suite 432
Raleigh, NC 27603
Tel: (919) 865-4667
TollFree: (800) 783-2600
Website: deltathetaphi.org
Members: 136000 individuals
Staff: 3
Annual Budget: $100-250,000

Personnel:
Executive Administrator: Caroline Thatcher
   E-Mail: dtpadminnc@gmail.com
International Editor-in-Chief and Director, Alumni Relations: Vito M. Evola
   E-Mail: dtpalum.dir@gmail.com
Executive Director, Student Relations: Amy L. Goodman
   E-Mail: dtpdirector@gmail.com

Historical Note:
Formerly (1913) Delta Phi Delta. Merged with Sigma Nu Phi legal fraternity in 1989. Mission is to foster lifelong friendships and professional affiliations through legal education, international networking, and mutual respect. Members are employed in government, in business, in international affairs, on the judiciary, and in the general practice of law. Membership: $70 (One-time student initiation fee); $50 (Alumni).

Meetings/Conferences: Annual

Publications:
DTP Newsletter
Student Senate Directory; on-line
The Adelphia Law Journal

Delta Waterfowl Foundation *(1938)*
P.O. Box 3128
Bismarck, ND 58502
Tel: (701) 222-8857
TollFree: (888) 987-3695
Website: deltawaterfowl.org

Members: 46000 members and chapters
Staff: 27
Annual Budget: $5-10,000,000
Tax: 501(c)(3)

Personnel:
President: Rob Olson
Vice President, Administration and Finance: Tim Beckler
Senior Director, U.S. Policy: John Devney
Membership and Marketing Manager: Stacy Hegel
Senior Director, Human Resources: Karol Jablonski
Events Manager: Lisa Lawrence
Director, Research: Elizabeth Loos
      E-Mail: eloos@deltawaterfowl.org
Chief Operating Officer: Nick Pinizzotto
Vice President, Communications: Nigel Simms
Specialist, Information Systems: Alex Tuchscher
Editor: Paul Wait

Historical Note:
Formerly (1993) North American Wildlife Foundation. DWF provides knowledge, leaders and science-based solutions that conserve waterfowl and secure the future for waterfowl hunting. Membership: $30/year.

Meetings/Conferences:
Conference Chair: Lisa Lawrence

Publications:
Delta Waterfowl Magazine; adv.
eNewsletter; monthly; adv.

Demand Response and Smart Grid Coalition
1301 Connecticut Ave. NW
Suite 350
Washington, DC 20036
Tel: (202) 296-3636
E-Mail: info@drsgcoalition.org
Website: drsgcoalition.org
Staff: 1

Personnel:
Contact, Membership: Paul Pietsch
      E-Mail: paul.pietsch@drsgcoalition.org

Historical Note:
DRSG is a trade association for companies focused in demand response, smart meters, etc.

Publications:
DRSG Newsletter; bi-weekly
Membership Directory; on-line

Democratic Attorneys General Association
1580 Lincoln St.
Suite 1125
Denver, CO 80203
Tel: (303) 831-0100 *Fax:* (720) 570-9201
E-Mail: info@democraticags.org
Website: democraticags.org
Staff: 3

Personnel:
Executive Director: Travis Berry
Contact, Events: Stefan Chodkowski
      E-Mail: stefan@democraticags.org
Contact, Sponsorship Opportunities: Fran Katz Watson
      E-Mail: fran@democraticags.org

Historical Note:
The Democratic Attorneys General Association, (DAGA) is a national political organization formed to support the election of Democrats to the office of attorney general in all of the states and territories of the United States.

Meetings/Conferences: Semi-Annual
Conference Chair: Fran Katz Watson
Number of non-conference events/year: 3

Democratic Governors Association (1983)
1401 K St. NW
Suite 200
Washington, DC 20005
Tel: (202) 772-5600 *Fax:* (202) 772-5602
E-Mail: dga@dnc.democrats.org
Website: democraticgovernors.org
Members: 28 Governors
Staff: 5

Personnel:
Executive Director: Colm O'Comartun
Director, Events: Kelly Berens
Director, Communications: Kate Hansen
Chief Operating Officer: Ben Metcalf
Director, Operations: Donna Tappin

Historical Note:

DGA is an independent voluntary political organization organized to support Democratic governors and candidates across the nation. Membership is by contribution.

Meetings/Conferences: Annual

Democratic Lieutenant Governors' Association (DLGA) (1906)
1850 M St. NW
Suite 1100
Washington, DC 20036
Tel: (202) 724-7952 *Fax:* (202) 280-1131
E-Mail: info@dlga.org
Website: democraticltgovernors.org
Staff: 3

Personnel:
Treasurer: Lt. Gov. Tim Murray
Secretary: Lt. Gov. Elizabeth Roberts
Contact, Communications: Colleen Turrentine
      E-Mail: colleen@cmtconsulting.net

Historical Note:
The Democratic Lieutenant Governors Association (DLGA)'s mission is to support Democratic candidates and incumbents for the office of Lieutenant Governor across the country.

Dental Trade Alliance (1882)
4350 N. Fairfax Dr.
Suite 220
Arlington, VA 22203
Tel: (703) 379-7755 *Fax:* (703) 931-9429
E-Mail: info@dentaltradealliance.org
Website: dentaltradealliance.org
Members: 200 companies
Staff: 9
Annual Budget: $2-5,000,000
Tax: 501(c)(6)

Personnel:
President and Chief Executive Officer: Gary W. Price
Accountant: Anna Adelman
      E-Mail: annaadelman@dentaltradealliance.org
Manager, Membership Programs: Denise R. Bundy
Vice President, Marketing and Membership Relations: Fred A. Freedman
Coordinator, Communications and Board Activities: Amy F. Moorman
Coordinator, Meetings and Membership Services: Julie Thomas
Associate, Technology and Information: Martin Waldman

Historical Note:
Founded as American Dental Trade Association, combined with the Dental Manufacturers Association and assumed its current name in 2004. DTA strives to enhance member success and increase dental demand. Membership: $1,750-31,900 (Depending on Revenue); $1,750-2,700 (Associate Members).

Meetings/Conferences: Annual
Conference Chair: Julie Thomas
2013 - Ponte Vedra Beach, FL (Ponte Vedra Beach Resort)/Oct. 15 - 18
2014 - Indian Wells, CA (Hyatt Grand Champions Resort, Villas and Spa)/Nov. 4 - 7
Number of non-conference events/year: 10

Publications:
Regulatory Updates; on-line
Membership Directory; on-line

Department for Professional Employees - AFL-CIO (1977)
815 16th St. NW
Seventh Floor
Washington, DC 20006
Tel: (202) 638-0320 *Fax:* (202) 628-4379
E-Mail: info@dpeaflcio.org
Website: dpeaflcio.org
Members: 21 national unions
Staff: 9
Annual Budget: $500-1,000,000

Personnel:
Executive Director: David Cohen
      E-Mail: dcohen@aflcio.org
Researcher and Representative: Jennifer Dorning
      E-Mail: jdorning@dpeaflcio.org
Treasurer: Francine Lawrence

Historical Note:
The mission of this DPE is to assist its affiliated unions to achieve their objectives on behalf of professional and technical workers and it will do so by offering a forum

for discussion, collaboration, and action. It is one of six constitutional "trades" departments that are part of the AFL-CIO structure. The 23 unions affiliated with the DPE are member organizations of the Federation and represent professional and technical workers.

Publications:
DPE NewsLine; monthly

Dermatology Foundation (1964)
1560 Sherman Ave.
Suite 870
Evanston, IL 60201-4808
Tel: (847) 328-2256 *Fax:* (847) 328-0509
E-Mail: dfgen@dermatologyfoundation.org
Website: dermfnd.org
Staff: 2
Annual Budget: $5-10,000,000

Personnel:
President: Richard L. Edelson
Secretary and Treasurer: Stuart R. Lessin

Historical Note:
DF's mission is to provide research support that helps develop and retain tomorrow's teachers and researchers in dermatology, and enables advancements in patient care. Membership: $1,500 (Leaders); $750 (Scientific Society); $250 (Scholars Circle).

Meetings/Conferences: Annual
Number of non-conference events/year: 1

Publications:
Dermatology Focus; quarterly

Dermatology Nurses' Association (1982)
15000 Commerce Pkwy.
Suite C
Mt. Laurel, NJ 08054
Tel: (856) 495-7639 *Fax:* (856) 439-0525
TollFree: (800) 454-4362
E-Mail: dna@dnanurse.org
Website: dnanurse.org.
Members: 3026 individuals and local chapters
Staff: 5
Annual Budget: $1-2,000,000
Tax: 501(c)(6)

Personnel:
Executive Director: Victoria E. Elliot CAE, MBA, RPh
Director, Education: Dorothy Caputo RN, APRN, CDE
      E-Mail: edupro@ptd.net
Manager, Meetings and Exhibits: Robin Geary
Director, Membership and Administrative Services: Julianna King
Manager, Communications: Linda Woody
      E-Mail: lwoody@ahint.com

Historical Note:
DNA's mission is to advocate dermatologic care. Members are licensed registered nurses, licensed practice nurses, licensed vocational nurses and individuals involved or interested in the care of the dermatology patient. Membership: $135 (NP Society Member); $85 (Nurse Member); $75 (Associate Member); $25(Student); $3000(Corporate).

Continuing Education:
Certification Designation/s: DNC, DCNP

Meetings/Conferences: Annual
Conference Chair: Robin Geary
2013 - New Orleans, LA (Sheraton New Orleans Hotel)/April 4 - 7/26-50 exhibitors
2014 - Orlando, FL (Walt Disney World Dolphin)/May 1 - 4
Number of non-conference events/year: 3

Publications:
DNA Focus Newsletter; on-line
Journal of the Dermatology Nurses' Association; bi-monthly; adv.
Membership Directory; on-line
SmartBrief; daily; adv.

Membership List Available to Non-members

Design Management Institute (1975)
101 Tremont St.
Suite 300
Boston, MA 02108
Tel: (617) 338-6380 *Fax:* (617) 338-6570
E-Mail: dmistaff@dmi.org
Website: dmi.org
Members: 1700 members
Staff: 5
Annual Budget: $1-2,000,000

Personnel:

Systems Manager: Christopher Hancock
E-Mail: cthancock@dmi.org
Contact, Accounting: Ruth Kupfer
E-Mail: rkupfer@dmi.org
Editor, DMI Review and DMI Journal: Thomas Lockwood PhD
E-Mail: lockwood@dmi.org
Program Manager, Membership Services and Communications: Patricia Olshan
E-Mail: polshan@dmi.org
Vice President, Business Operations: John Tobin
E-Mail: jtobin@dmi.org

Historical Note:
DMI's mission is to sponsor, conduct and promote research. Members are in-house design teams and consulting design firms. Membership: $150-6400/year.

Meetings/Conferences: Semi-Annual
Number of non-conference events/year: 20

Publications:
Design Management Journal; annually; adv.
DMI News & Views; monthly; adv.
DMI Review; quarterly; adv.
Membership Directory; on-line

Membership List Available to Non-members

Design-Build Institute of America *(1993)*
1331 Pennsylvania Ave. NW
Fourth Floor
Washington, DC 20004
Tel: (202) 682-0110 *Fax:* (202) 682-5877
TollFree: (866) 692-0110
E-Mail: dbia@dbia.org
Website: dbia.org
Members: 900 companies and organizations
Staff: 22
Annual Budget: $5-10,000,000
Tax: 501(c)(6)

Personnel:
Executive Director and Chief Executive Officer: Lisa Washington CAE
E-Mail: lwashington@dbia.org
Manager, Publications and Bookstore: Patricia Carpio
E-Mail: pcarpio@dbia.org
Chief Financial Officer: Timothy J. Heck
E-Mail: theck@dbia.org
Director, Education Logistics: Mihisha Henderson
E-Mail: mhenderson@dbia.org
Managing Director, Public Relations and Information: Susan Hines
E-Mail: shines@dbia.org
Coordinator, Membership Services: Michelle R. Johnson
E-Mail: cprawdzik@dbia.org
Manager, Marketing and Creative Services: Lauren Mazanec
E-Mail: lmazanec@dbia.org
Director, Membership Development: Tucker Ophof
E-Mail: tophof@dbia.org
Manager, Web and Graphic Systems: Todd Rich CAE
E-Mail: trich@dbia.org
Vice President, Legislative Affairs: Richard Thomas
E-Mail: rthomas@dbia.org
Director, Meetings and Events: Stephenie Zvonkovich
E-Mail: szvonkovich@dbia.org

Historical Note:
DBIA promotes the value of design-build project delivery and teaches the effective integration of design and construction services to ensure success for owners and design and construction practitioners. Members include companies and individuals concerned with integrated architecture, engineering and construction services. Membership: $349 (Practitioners/Consultants); $99 (Owners); $45-99 (Students/Academia); $99 (Government/Agency/Private Facility Owner/Academic/ Non-Profit); $249 (Industry Partner-Additional Contact); $45 (Full-Time Student).

Continuing Education:
Certification Designation/s: ADBIA, PDBIA

Meetings/Conferences:
Conference Chair: Stephenie Zvonkovich
2013 - Orlando, FL (Walt Disney World Resort)/March 18 - 20
2013 - Orlando, FL (Walt Disney World Resort)/March 20 - 22

Publications:
Design-Build Insight; weekly; adv.
Directory of Design-Build Technology Solution; on-line

IQ: Integration Quarterly; quarterly; adv.
Membership Directory; on-line

Destination Marketing Association International *(1914)*
2025 M St. NW
Suite 500
Washington, DC 20036-3309
Tel: (202) 296-7888 *Fax:* (202) 296-7889
E-Mail: info@destinationmarketing.org
Website: destinationmarketing.org
Members: 550 convention and visitor bureaus
Staff: 21
Annual Budget: $5-10,000,000
Tax: 501(c)(6)

Personnel:
President and Chief Executive Officer: Michael D. Gehrisch
E-Mail: mgehrisch@iacvb.org
Vice President, Marketing and Communications: Kristen Clemens
E-Mail: kclemens@destinationmarketing.org
Senior Vice President, Professional Development and Meetings: Nancy L. Elder
E-Mail: nelder@destinationmarketing.org
Senior Vice President, Membership and Operations: Karen M. Gonzales
E-Mail: kgonzales@destinationmarketing.org
Director, Meetings and Events: Paul M. Griffin
E-Mail: pgriffin@destinationmarketing.org
Executive Vice President and Chief Operating Officer: Victoria Isley
E-Mail: visley@destinationmarketing.org
Director, Meetings: Cindy Kong
E-Mail: ckong@destinationmarketing.org
Senior Vice President, Professional Development: Doug Price CMP
E-Mail: dprice@destinationmarketing.org
Director, Operations and Destinations Showcase: Kristen White
E-Mail: kwhite@destinationmarketing.org
Chief Financial Officer: John Wooldridge
E-Mail: jwooldridge@destinationmarketing.org

Historical Note:
Formerly (1975) International Association of Convention Bureaus and then International Association of Convention and Visitors Bureaus; assumed current name in 2005. DMAI is dedicated to improving the effectiveness of professionals in marketing organizations. Represents member bureaus in over 20 countries. Membership: $45-15,000/year.

Continuing Education:
Certification Designation/s: CDME, PDM

Meetings/Conferences: Annual
Conference Chair: Paul M. Griffin
2013 - Orlando, FL/July 15 - 17
2014 - Las Vegas, NV/July 21 - 23
Number of non-conference events/year: 5

Publications:
Destination Marketing Monthly E-newsletter; monthly
DMAI Connections E-newsletter; bi-weekly
DMAI Student Newsletter; quarterly
Membership Directory; on-line
News Brief; weekly

Developmental Disabilities Nurses Association *(1992)*
P.O. Box 536489
Orlando, FL 32853-6489
Tel: (407) 835-0642 *Fax:* (407) 426-7440
TollFree: (800) 888-6733
E-Mail: ddnahq@aol.com
Website: ddna.org
Members: 1200 individuals
Staff: 1
Annual Budget: $250-500,000
Tax: 501(c)(3)

Personnel:
Executive Director: Mary Alice Willis MSN, RN
E-Mail: mawillis@ddna.org

Historical Note:
DDNA is a nursing specialty organization that is committed to advocacy, education, and care for nurses who provide services to persons with intellectual and developmental disabilities (I/DD). Members are registered, licensed practical and licensed vocational nurses with an interest in developmental disabilities nursing. Membership: $40-2,000/year.

Continuing Education:
Certification Designation/s: DDCLPN, CDDN, LVN

Meetings/Conferences: Annual
2013 - Philadelphia, PA (Double Tree by Hilton Hotel)/ April 26 - 29

Publications:
DDNA newsletter; quarterly; adv.
International Journal of Nursing in Intellectual and Developmental Disabilities (IJNIDD); adv.

Diagnostic Marketing Association
10293 N. Meridian St.
Suite 175
Indianapolis, IN 46290-1073
Tel: (317) 816-1640 *Fax:* (317) 816-1633
TollFree: (800) 278-7886
E-Mail: info@dxma.org
Website: dxma.org
Members: 300 individuals
Staff: 5
Annual Budget: $100-250,000

Personnel:
Contact, Annual Conferences: Pamela Pasakarnis

Historical Note:
Formerly known as the Biomedical Marketing Association. DxMA's mission is to serve the needs of marketing professionals in the diagnostics industry. Members are diagnostic marketers in the biomedical field. Membership: $2,500 (Service Provider); $1,150 (Business); $299 (Individual).

Meetings/Conferences:
Conference Chair: Pamela Pasakarnis
Number of non-conference events/year: 2

Publications:
Diagnostic Insight; quarterly
Membership Directory; on-line

Diamond Council of America *(1944)*
3212 W. End Ave.
Suite 400
Nashville, TN 37203
Tel: (615) 385-5301 *Fax:* (615) 385-4955
TollFree: (877) 283-5669
Website: diamondcouncil.org
Members: 297 Individuals, 4426 Stores and 3232 Students
Staff: 2
Annual Budget: $500-1,000,000
Tax: 501(c)(3)

Personnel:
President and Chief Executive Officer: Terry Chandler
Director, Operations: Lissa Roussel

Historical Note:
DCA serves as a forum to educate jewelry sales professionals about diamonds and gems. DCA's mission is to provide quality affordable education to its members' associates, enhancing their ability to sell fine jewelry with expertise, integrity and professionalism. Membership: $35-100/year (Based on number of retail stores).

Publications:
DCA Jeweler
Membership Directory; on-line

Diamond Manufacturers & Importers Association of America *(1931)*
580 Fifth Ave.
Suite 2000
New York, NY 10036
Tel: (212) 944-2066 *Fax:* (212) 202-7525
E-Mail: info@dmia.net
Website: dmia.net
Members: 150 companies
Staff: 5
Annual Budget: $50-100,000

Personnel:
Executive Director: Ben Kinzler
President: Ronald J. Friedman
Secretary: Hertz Hasenfeld
Vice President and Chief Financial Officer: Ronnie Vanderlinden

Historical Note:
Formerly the Diamond Manufacturers Association, DMIA strives to promote the standards of ethics, integrity and professionalism in the American marketplace. It also dedicated to advancing and ensuring consumer confidence in diamonds and diamond jewelry. Members are diamond manufacturers, importers, dealers and companies servicing

the diamond trade such as banks, shippers, insurers, and grading laboratories. Membership: $500/year.
Meetings/Conferences:
Number of non-conference events/year: 1

Publications:
Member Directory

Membership List Available to Non-members

Dibasic Esters Group *(1995)*
1850 M St. NW
Suite 700
Washington, DC 20036-5810
Tel: (202) 722-4100 *Fax:* (202) 296-8120
E-Mail: info@pcna.net
Members: 3 companies
Staff: 2
Annual Budget: $250-500,000

Personnel:
Senior Director: C. Tucker Helmes PhD
    E-Mail: helmest@socma.com

Historical Note:
An affiliate of the Synthetic Organic Chemical Manufacturers Association. DBE was formed to address the EPA's and Consumer Product Safety Commission's testing consent order under TSCA Section 4 for three Dibasic Esters: Dimethyl Succinate (DMS); Dimethyl Glutarate (DMG) and Dimethyl Adipate (DMA).

Diesel Technology Forum *(2000)*
5291 Corporate Dr.
Suite 102
Frederick, MD 21703
Tel: (301) 668-7230 *Fax:* (301) 668-7234
E-Mail: dtf@dieselforum.org
Website: dieselforum.org
Staff: 5
Annual Budget: $1-2,000,000

Personnel:
Executive Director: Allen R. Schaeffer
    E-Mail: aschaeffer@dieselforum.org
Director, Communications: Kristen Gifford
    E-Mail: kgifford@dieselforum.org
Manager, Membership Services and Administration: Josie Rocha
    E-Mail: jrocha@dieselforum.org

Historical Note:
A not-for-profit educational association representing the diesel industry. DTF is dedicated to raising awareness about the economic importance and essential uses of diesel engines, highlighting the continuous improvements to reduce emissions from new and existing diesel engines, and leading the way for future clean diesel technology in all applications.

Publications:
Diesel Direct newsletter

Digital Imaging Marketing Association
2282 Springport Rd.
Suite F
Jackson, MI 49202
Tel: (517) 788-8100 *Fax:* (517) 788-8371
Website: pmai.org/dima
Staff: 1

Personnel:
Secretary and Executive Director: Jim Esp

Historical Note:
DIMA is committed to exploring emerging technologies, marketing and business innovations throughout the global imaging industry and envisioning potential for its members.

Meetings/Conferences: Annual
2013 - Las Vegas, NV (Bally's Las Vegas)/Jan. 6 - 7

Digital Media Association *(1998)*
1050 17th St. NW
Suite 220
Washington, DC 20036
Tel: (202) 639-9509
E-Mail: info@digmedia.org
Website: digmedia.org
Members: 12 Members
Staff: 3
Annual Budget: $500-1,000,000
Tax: 501(c)(6)

Personnel:
Executive Director: Lee Knife
    E-Mail: lknife@digmedia.org
Consultant, Communications: Ann Brown

E-Mail: abrown@digmedia.org

Historical Note:
DiMA serves the digital media industry through representation and advocacy of Internet related issues. Encourages business and regulatory environments that support its members' growth and success, and which encourage consumers' adoption of legal digital media choices. To support the development and use of responsible measures to protect intellectual property rights underlying digital media. Members are media companies. Membership: $5,000-85,000 (Corporate Voting, varies on number of employees); $1,500-10,000 (Associate,Non-voting varies on gross revenue).

Publications:
DiMA Insider; weekly

Membership List Available to Non-members

Digital Screenmedia Association *(1936)*
13100 Eastpoint Park Blvd.
Louisville, KY 40223
Tel: (502) 489-3915 *Fax:* (502) 241-2795
Website: digitalscreenmedia.org
Members: 700 Combinations
Staff: 3
Annual Budget: $250-500,000
Tax: 501(c)(6)

Personnel:
Executive Director: David Drain
    E-Mail: davidd@digitalscreenmedia.org
Contact, Membership Services: Diana Sexson
    E-Mail: dianas@digitalscreenmedia.org

Historical Note:
Formed as a result of merger between Digital Signage Association and the Self-Service and Kiosk Association. DSA purpose is to advance the growth of the global digital signage, interactive kiosk and mobile community through advocacy, education and networking. Membership: $995-4,750 (Vendor/IntegratorAssociate); $250 (User/Deployer); $595-3,000 (Network Operator); $350-1,475 (Agency); $55 (Individual).

Publications:
DSA Quarterly; quarterly
E-Newsletter
Membership Directory; on-line

Diplomatic and Consular Officers, Retired (Dacor) *(1952)*
1801 F St. NW
Washington, DC 20006
Tel: (202) 682-0500 *Fax:* (202) 842-3295
TollFree: (800) 344-9127
E-Mail: dacor@dacorbacon.org
Website: dacorbacon.org
Members: 3000 individuals
Staff: 16
Annual Budget: $500-1,000,000

Personnel:
Executive Director: Sherry Barndollar Rock
    E-Mail: sbrock@dacorbacon.org
Program Coordinator: Brett Gold
    E-Mail: klongton@dacorbacon.org
Associate Director, Finance: Kastriot Kallushi
    E-Mail: kkallushi@dacorbacon.org
Associate Director, Operations: Kyle Longton
    E-Mail: klongton@dacorbacon.org

Historical Note:
Members are principally active and retired foreign service officers. Accepts members with overseas experience from other government agencies. Membership: $36-287/year.

Meetings/Conferences:
Conference Chair: Brett Gold

Publications:
Membership Directory; biennially

Direct Care Alliance
4 W. 43rd St.
Unit 611
New York, NY 10036
Tel: (212) 730-0741 *Fax:* (212) 302-4345
E-Mail: info@directcarealliance.org
Website: directcarealliance.org
Staff: 5
Annual Budget: $1-2,000,000
Tax: 501(c)(3)

Personnel:
Executive Director: Leonila Vega Esq.
Director, National Field: Brenda Nachtway
Director, Operations: Maureen Traverse

Historical Note:
DCA's mission is to build an empowered and valued professional direct care workforce essential to ensuring high-quality services and a life of dignity, respect, autonomy and opportunity for all to participate in community life.

Publications:
Newsletter; weekly

Direct Marketing Association *(1917)*
1120 Avenue of the Americas
New York, NY 10036-6700
Tel: (212) 768-7277 *Fax:* (212) 302-6714
E-Mail: customerservice@the-dma.org
Website: the-dma.org
Members: 3400 members
Staff: 121
Annual Budget: $25-50,000,000

Personnel:
Senior Director, Marketing: Karina Pena Garcia
    E-Mail: kpena@the-dma.org
Senior Vice President and Chief Communications Officer: Sue R.E. Geramian
    E-Mail: sgeramian@the-dma.org
Vice President, Finance, Operations and Controller: Robert "Bob" A. Greco
Vice President, Conferences and Events: Paul A. McDonnough
Vice President, Member Relations: Stephanie Miller
Vice President, Education and Professional Development: Gina Scala
Vice President, Membership Development: Andrew Somer
Senior Director, Communications and Senior Editor: Susan Taplinger

Historical Note:
Formerly (1983) Direct Mail/Marketing Association and Direct Mail Advetising Association, absorbed the Business Mail Foundation and the Mailing List Users and Suppliers Association. DMA's mission is to serve in the field of marketing and keep it economically viable, as well as maintain the flow of data that fuels multichannel marketing. DMA advocates with legislators and regulators, provides management, research and education, as well as networking and market making opportunities to improve results for the direct marketing process. Membership: $1,500 (Marketers); $3,400 (Agencies/Suppliers); $675 (Nonprofit Organization).

Meetings/Conferences:
Conference Chair: Paul A. McDonnough
Number of non-conference events/year: 2

Publications:
3D -- DMA Daily Digest; on-line
DMA Daily Digest; daily
Membership Directory; on-line
Newsstand; on-line
Politically Direct; quarterly
Quarterly Business Review; quarterly
Special Interest Council Newsletters; on-line

Direct Marketing Association Nonprofit Federation
1615 L St. NW
Suite 1100
Washington, DC 20036
Tel: (202) 955-5030
E-Mail: nonprofitfederation@the-dma.org
Website: nonprofitfederation.org
Members: 480 nonprofit members and Corporate Partners.
Staff: 4

Personnel:
Senior Vice President: Xenia "Senny" Boone
    E-Mail: SBoone@the-dma.org
Director, Conferences and Education: Jabneel "Jenny" Abreu
    E-Mail: JAbreu@the-dma.org
Director, Membership and Communications: Alicia Osgood
    E-Mail: AOsgood@the-dma.org
Regulatory Counsel: Robert Tigner

Historical Note:
Formed from the merger of The National Federation of Nonprofits and the Direct Marketing Association (New York). DMANF is the source for nonprofit marketing and fundraising professional education and industry advancement. Membership: $675/Year.

Meetings/Conferences: Semi-Annual
Conference Chair: Jabneel "Jenny" Abreu
2013 - Washington, DC (Renaissance)/Feb. 7 - 8

2013 - New York City, NY (Grand Hyatt New York)/July
17 - 18
2014 - Washington, DC (Renaissance)/Feb. 13 - 14
2014 - New York City, NY (Grand Hyatt New York)/July
16 - 17

Publications:
Journal of the DMA Nonprofit Federation; adv.

Direct Marketing Insurance and Financial Services Council
1120 Avenue of the Americas
New York, NY 10036-8096
Tel: (212) 768-7277 *Fax:* (212) 768-4546
Members: 3600 member companies
Staff: 1
Annual Budget: $100-250,000

Personnel:
Staff Contact: Kevin Thurman

Historical Note:
*DMIFSC is a council of Direct Marketing Association,
which provides administrative support. DMIFSC members
are DMA members who market insurance and financial
services.*

Direct Selling Association (1910)
1667 K St. NW
Suite 1100
Washington, DC 20006-1660
Tel: (202) 452-8866 *Fax:* (202) 452-9010
E-Mail: info@dsa.org
Website: dsa.org
Members: 200 companies
Staff: 35
Annual Budget: $5-10,000,000
Tax: 501(c)(6)

Personnel:
Executive Vice President: Adolfo Franco
E-Mail: afranco@dsa.org
Senior Vice President, Education and Meeting Services:
Melissa K. Brunton
E-Mail: mbrunton@dsa.org
Director, Membership Services: Nancy M. Burke
E-Mail: nburke@dsa.org
Communications Assistant: Molly Cox
E-Mail: mcox@dsa.org
Director, Finance and Operations: Jennifer Dunleavey
E-Mail: jdunleavey@dsa.org
Director, Marketing and Publications Services: Karen
Garrett
E-Mail: kgarrett@dsa.org
President: Joseph N. Mariano
E-Mail: jmariano@dsa.org
Senior Vice President and Chief Marketing Officer: Amy M.
Robinson APR
E-Mail: arobinson@dsa.org
*Associate Legal Counsel and Senior Director, Government
Relations:* John Webb
E-Mail: jwebb@dsa.org

Historical Note:
*DSA's mission is to protect, serve and promote the
effectiveness of member companies and the independent
business people they represent. Members are companies that
market consumer goods and services away from fixed retail
locations, primarily in homes by independent salespersons
and distributors.*

Meetings/Conferences: Annual
Conference Chair: Melissa K. Brunton
2013 - Phoenix, AZ (JW Marriott Phoenix Desert Ridge
Resort and Spa)/June 9 - 11/900 attendees
2014 - Orlando, FL (Peabody Orlando)/June 1 - 3/900
attendees
2015 - San Antonio, TX (JW Marriott San Antonio
Hill Country Resort and Spa)/May 31 - June 2/900
attendees
2017 - Orlando, FL (Peabody Orlando)/June 4 - 6/900
attendees

Publications:
Member Directory; on-line

Directed Energy Professional Society (1999)
7770 Jefferson St. NE
Suite 440
Albuquerque, NM 87109
Tel: (505) 998-4910 *Fax:* (505) 998-4917
E-Mail: office@deps.org
Website: deps.org
Members: 1,600 organizations

Staff: 7
Annual Budget: $1-2,000,000
Tax: 501(c)(3)

Personnel:
Executive Director: Samuel Blankenship
E-Mail: sam@deps.org
Business Manager and Facility Security Officer: Tiffany
Bjelke
E-Mail: tiffany@deps.org
Executive Administrator and Events Coordinator:
Cynnamon Spain
E-Mail: cynnamon@deps.org

Historical Note:
*Foster research and development of Directed Energy (DE)
technology for national defense and civil applications
through professional communication and education.*

Meetings/Conferences:
Conference Chair: Cynnamon Spain
2013 - Monterey, CA (Hyatt Regency Monterey Hotel
And Spa)/April 8 - 12
Number of non-conference events/year: 1

Publications:
Journal of Directed Energy
Wave Front

Directors Guild of America (1936)
7920 Sunset Blvd.
Los Angeles, CA 90046
Tel: (310) 289-2000 *Fax:* (310) 289-2029
TollFree: (800) 421-4173
E-Mail: jlam@dga.org
Website: dga.org
Members: 14500 individuals
Staff: 157
Annual Budget: $10-25,000,000

Personnel:
National Executive Director: Jay D. Roth
*Assistant Executive Director, Research and Strategic
Analysis:* Joyce Baron
E-Mail: joyceb@dga.org
Administrator, Membership Services: Mary Gallagher
E-Mail: maryg@dga.org
*Associate Executive Director, Government and International
Affairs:* Kathy Garmezy
E-Mail: kgarmezy@dga.org
Editor: Darrell L. Hope
E-Mail: darrell@dga.org
*Associate National Executive Director and Senior General
Counsel:* David Korduner
E-Mail: davidk@dga.org
Chief Financial Officer: Brian O'Rourke
E-Mail: briano@dga.org
Administrator, Human Resources: Moira Pittman
E-Mail: moira@dga.org
Assistant Executive Director, Communications: Morgan
Rumpf
E-Mail: morganr@dga.org

Historical Note:
*Independent labor union. DGA seeks to protect directorial
teams' legal and artistic rights, contend for their creative
freedom, and strengthen their ability to develop meaningful
and credible careers. Membership: $50/Quarter (Based on
gross earnings).*

Publications:
DGA Monthly; monthly
DGA Quarterly; quarterly
The DGA Directory of Members

Directors of Health Promotion and Education (DHPE) (1946)
1015 18th St. NW
Suite 300
Washington, DC 20036
Tel: (202) 659-2230 *Fax:* (202) 659-2339
E-Mail: info@dhpe.org
Website: dhpe.org
Members: 55 individuals
Staff: 11
Annual Budget: $2-5,000,000

Personnel:
Executive Director: Susan Goekler PhD
E-Mail: sgoekler@dhpe.org
Manager, Internship and Fellowship Program: Mariela
Alarcon-Yohe MPH
E-Mail: malarcon@dhpe.org

Director, Finance and Operations: Roosevelt Dzime-
Assison
E-Mail: roosevelt@dhpe.org
Director, Information Technology Services: Wendy Sahli
Director, Training and Marketing: Doreleena Sammons-
Posey
E-Mail: dposey@dhpe.org

Historical Note:
*Established as Conference of State and Territorial Directors
of Public Health Education; became Association of State
and Territorial Directors of Public Health Education in
1996. DHPE's mission is to conduct programs in numerous
public health areas that emphasize community-based
prevention, and health promotion/health education.
Policy, programs, training, and resources comprise the
main functions for DHPE. Membership: $50 (Associate);
$1,000 (Academic Institutions); $100 (Local Public Health
Agencies); $200 (Regular/Voting).*

Meetings/Conferences:
Conference Chair: Mariela Alarcon-Yohe MPH
Number of non-conference events/year: 3

Publications:
DHPE Newsletter; bi-monthly; adv.
Membership Directory; on-line

Disaster Preparedness and Emergency Response Association (1962)
P.O. Box 797
Longmont, CO 80502-0797
Tel: (970) 532-3362 *Fax:* (970) 532-2979
E-Mail: dera@disasters.org
Website: disasters.org
Members: 1100 individuals
Staff: 3
Annual Budget: $25-50,000
Tax: 501(c)(3)

Personnel:
Executive Director: Bascombe J. Wilson
General Counsel: Randy Helbach
Editor: Kevin J.D. Wilson

Historical Note:
*DERA's purpose is to serve as a professional association
linking professionals, volunteers, and organizations active
in all phases of emergency preparedness and management.
Members include national governments, nonprofit
associations, official agencies and departments, educational
institutions, corporations, small business concerns,
emergency management professionals, researchers, and
volunteers. Membership: $50 (Individual/General); $75
(Executive/Management Level/Non- profit Organization);
$95 (Governmental Agency); $25 (Student/Retired/
Unemployed); $125 (Small/Startup Business); $450
(Lifetime/Small Corporation); $2500 (Major Corporation);
$35 (Student/Retired/Unemployed).*

Publications:
DisasterCom Newsletter; quarterly

Disaster Recovery Contractors Association (DRCA)
300 N. Washington St.
Suite 500
Alexandria, VA 22314
Tel: (703) 683-8555 *Fax:* (703) 683-8552
Website: thedrca.org
Staff: 3
Annual Budget: $100-250,000

Personnel:
Executive Director: Rick Gill
Laurie Bendall Gravatt
Treasurer: Rashid Hallaway

Historical Note:
*Trade association comprised of private companies working
in disaster/emergency response/recovery.*

Discover America Partnership
1100 New York Ave. NW
Suite 450
Washington, DC 20005-3934
Tel: (202) 408-8422 *Fax:* (202) 408-1255
Website: discoveramericapartnership.org
Members: 46 Organizations
Staff: 2

Personnel:
Executive Director: Geoffrey Freeman
E-Mail: gfreeman@poweroftravel.org
Contact, Membership Services: Robert Bobo
E-Mail: rbobo@ustravel.org

Historical Note:

Discover America Partnership educates policymakers and opinion leaders on the economic significance of tourism and business travel to the United States. Membership: $10,000 (Steering Committee Member); $2,500 (Campaign Partner).

Distance Education and Training Council *(1926)*
1601 18th St. NW
Suite Two
Washington, DC 20009
Tel: (202) 234-5100 *Fax:* (202) 332-1386
E-Mail: detc@detc.org
Website: detc.org
Members: 100 distance educational institutions
Staff: 6
Annual Budget: $1-2,000,000
Tax: 501(c)(6)

Personnel:
Executive Director: Michael P. Lambert
    E-Mail: mike@detc.org
Specialist, Information and Accounts: Brianna Bates
    E-Mail: brianna@detc.org
Director, Media and Events: Robert Chalifoux
    E-Mail: rob@detc.org
Director, Accreditation: Nan Bayster Ridgeway
    E-Mail: nan@detc.org
Legal Counsel: Elise Scanlon
Associate Director: Sally R. Welch
    E-Mail: sally@detc.org

Historical Note:
Founded as the National Home Study Council, assumed its current name in 1994. The DETC is a voluntary, non-governmental, educational organization that operates a nationally recognized accrediting association, the DETC Accrediting Commission.

Meetings/Conferences: Annual
Conference Chair: Robert Chalifoux
2013 - San Francisco, CA (Fairmont San Francisco)/
    April 14 - 16/200 attendees
2014 - Hammock Beach, FL (Hammock Beach Resort)/
    April 6 - 8
Number of non-conference events/year: 2

Publications:
DETC News; semi-annually
Directory of Accredited Institutions; annually

Distilled Spirits Council of the United States, Inc.
(1973)
1250 Eye St. NW
Suite 400
Washington, DC 20005
Tel: (202) 628-3544 *Fax:* (202) 682-8876
Website: discus.org
Members: 12 companies
Staff: 48
Annual Budget: $10-25,000,000
Tax: 501(c)(6)

Personnel:
President and Chief Executive Officer: Dr. Peter H. Cressy
    E-Mail: pcressy@discus.org
Senior Vice President Finance and Administration: Jean Gooding
    E-Mail: jgooding@discus.org
Senior Vice President, Government Relations: Mark S. Gorman
    E-Mail: mgorman@discus.org
Senior Vice President, General Counsel and Corporate Secretary: Lynne J. Omlie
    E-Mail: lomlie@discus.org

Historical Note:
Formed by the merger of the Distilled Spirits Institute (1933), the Bourbon Institute (1958), and Licensed Beverage Industries (1946). DISCUS represents producers and marketers of distilled spirits. DISCUS's mission is to serve as the distiller's voice on policy and legislative issues in its nation's capital, state capitals and foreign capitals worldwide.

Publications:
Membership Directory; on-line

Distillers Grains Technology Council *(1945)*
University of Louisville
Lutz Hall, Room 435
Louisville, KY 40292
Tel: (502) 852-1575 *Fax:* (502) 852-1577
TollFree: (800) 759-3448
E-Mail: chstaf01@louisville.edu
Website: distillersgrains.org
Members: 30 companies

Staff: 1
Annual Budget: $100-250,000
Tax: 501(c)(6)

Personnel:
Executive Director and Chief Executive Officer: Charlie Staff
    E-Mail: chstaf01@louisville.edu

Historical Note:
Formerly (1997) Distillers Feed Research Council. DGTC strives to provide educational and technical services to member producers and users of distiller grains. Members are beverage and ethanol distillers who process by-products of the distilling process for other uses. Membership: $6,000-9,000 (Full); $1,000 (Associate).

Meetings/Conferences: Annual
2013 - Bloomington, MN (DoubleTree by Hilton Hotel Bloomington)/May 15 - 16

Publications:
Membership Directory; on-line

Membership List Available to Non-members

Distinguished Restaurants of North America
105 W. Michigan Ave.
Marshall, MI 49068
Tel: (269) 789-9316 *Fax:* (269) 789-0731
E-Mail: marketing@dirona2.com
Website: dirona.com
Members: 800 restaurants
Staff: 3
Annual Budget: $250-500,000
Tax: 501(c)(4)

Personnel:
Executive Director: Keith Kehlbeck
Manager, Membership Services and Marketing: Laura Atchison
    E-Mail: latchison@hqtrs.com

Historical Note:
DiRoNA's mission is to recognize restaurants that strive for consistent excellence, and to help consumers find their best in distinguished dining. Membership: $400/year.

Meetings/Conferences: Annual

Publications:
Signature Dish; on-line

Distributed Computing Industry Association
2838 Cox Neck Rd.,
Suite 200
Chester, MD 21619
Tel: (410) 476-7965 *Fax:* (703) 525-8277
E-Mail: info@dcia.info
Website: dcia.info
Staff: 5

Personnel:
Chief Executive Officer: Marty Lafferty
    E-Mail: marty@dcia.info
Contact, Member Service: Karen Kaplowitz
Contact, Business Affairs: Sari Lafferty
Contact, Communications: Kelly Larabee
Technology Advisor: Adam Marcus

Historical Note:
The DCIA is a voluntary, consensus organization with representation from all substantially affected sectors of the nascent distributed computing industry. DCIA participants are engaged in the development and adoption of business and technical standards-and-practices to advance the commercial development of this rapidly growing consumer-based distribution system.

Publications:
DCINFO Newsletter; weekly

Distributed Wind Energy Association
P.O. Box 1861
Flagstaff, AZ 86002
Tel: (928) 255-0214
E-Mail: info@distributedwind.org
Website: distributedwind.org
Members: 95 Companies
Staff: 1
Annual Budget: $100-250,000
Tax: 501(c)(6)

Personnel:
Executive Director: Jennifer Jenkins
    E-Mail: jjenkins@distributedwind.org

Historical Note:
DWEA's mission is to promote and foster all aspects of the American distributed wind energy industry. Membership:

$350-$2500 (Dealer / Installer / Advocate based on annual revenue); $2500-$10,000 (Manufacturer / Project Developer / Distributor based on annual revenue); $1,000-2,500 (Consultant / Vendor).

Publications:
DWEA Newsletter; monthly
Membership Directory; on-line

Distribution and LTL Carriers Association *(1956)*
950 N. Glebe Rd.
Suite 210
Arlington, VA 22203
Tel: (703) 838-1959 *Fax:* (703) 838-7994
E-Mail: bfarrell@trucking.org
Website: dltl.org
Members: 200 companies
Staff: 3
Annual Budget: $50-100,000
Tax: 501(c)(6)

Personnel:
President: Robert P. Farrell
    E-Mail: bfarrell@trucking.org
Representative, Conferences: Robert J. Kortenhaus
    E-Mail: Kathy@bilkays.co

Historical Note:
Formed in 1956 through the consolidation of the Regional and Distribution Carriers Conference and Regular Common Carrier Conference, both of which were founded in 1938. DLCA's mission is to provide the executives and owners of trucking companies with the forum to communicate, learn and improve their business management. Membership: $500 (Associate Member); $136-960 (Motor Carriers).

Meetings/Conferences:
Conference Chair: Robert J. Kortenhaus

Distribution Business Management Association
(1986)
2938 Columbia Ave.
Suite 1102
Lancaster, PA 17603
Tel: (717) 295-0033 *Fax:* (717) 299-2154
E-Mail: dbminfo@dbm-assoc.com
Website: dcenter.com
Members: 13500 individuals
Staff: 7
Annual Budget: $1-2,000,000

Personnel:
Executive Director and Editorial Director: Amy Z. Thorn
    E-Mail: athorn@dbm-assoc.com
Staff Liaison, SCFL Selection Committee: Amy Yoder
    E-Mail: ayoder@dbm-assoc.com

Historical Note:
DBM's mission is to provide educational forums and knowledge between business and academia that seek possible solutions to issues and promotes education in business areas such as supply chain and logistics. Members are companies and professional involved in warehousing and distribution, including warehouses, manufacturers of equipment, construction companies and material handling professionals and consultants.

Continuing Education:
Certification Designation/s: CAE

Meetings/Conferences: Annual
Conference Chair: Amy Yoder
Number of non-conference events/year: 1

Publications:
DBM Journal; quarterly; adv.

Distribution Contractors Association *(1961)*
101 W. Renner Rd.
Suite 460
Richardson, TX 75082-2024
Tel: (972) 680-0261 *Fax:* (972) 680-0461
E-Mail: info@dcaweb.org
Website: dcaweb.org
Members: 180 companies
Staff: 4
Annual Budget: $1-2,000,000
Tax: 501(c)(6)

Personnel:
Executive Vice President: Robert Darden CMP
Manager, Marketing and Communications: Candace Green
Manager, Membership Services and Administration: Teri M. Korson
    E-Mail: korson@dca-online.org
Manager, Meetings and Education: Melissa Leslie CMP

Historical Note:
DCA's mission is to enhance the proficiency and professionalism of members through the exchange of information. Membership: $2,000 (Regular); $750 (Associate); $375 (Industry).

Continuing Education:
Enrollment: 40
Certification Designation/s: ASC

Meetings/Conferences: Annual
Conference Chair: Melissa Leslie CMP
2013 - Miami Beach, FL (Loews Miami Beach Hotel)/ March 5 - 10
2013 - Avon, CO (Park Hyatt Beaver Creek Resort and Spa)/July 17 - 21
2014 - Cancun, QR (Ritz Carlton)/Feb. 4 - 9

Publications:
DCA Benchmark; annually
DCA Directory; annually; adv.
DCA E-News; on-line
DCA News - Newsletter; bi-monthly

Distributive Education Clubs of America (DECA)
(1946)
1908 Association Dr.
Reston, VA 20191-1594
Tel: (703) 860-5000 *Fax:* (703) 860-4013
E-Mail: info@deca.org
Website: deca.org
Members:
205000 individuals
5000 chapters
200 colleges and universities
Staff: 23
Annual Budget: $5-10,000,000
Tax: 501(c)(3)

Personnel:
Executive Director: Edward L. Davis PhD
    E-Mail: ed_davis@deca.org
Director, Corporate Affairs: Cindy Allen
    E-Mail: cindy_allen@deca.org
Project Manager, Publications: Chuck Beatty
Director, Data Management: Anne Farrell
    E-Mail: anne_farrell@deca.org
Assistant Executive Director, Corporate and External Affairs: John Fistolera
    E-Mail: john_fistolera@deca.org
Assistant Executive Director, High School Programs and Conferences: Shirlee Kyle
    E-Mail: shirlee_kyle@deca.org
Manager, Membership Services: Mike Mount
    E-Mail: michael_mount@deca.org
Director, Education: Michelle Walker
    E-Mail: michelle_walker@deca.org
Assistant Director, High School Programs and Conferences: Christopher Young
    E-Mail: christopher_young@deca.org

Historical Note:
DECA's mission is to support the development of marketing and management skills in career areas such as hospitality, finance, sales and service, business administration and entrepreneurship.

Continuing Education:
Certification Designation/s: SBE

Meetings/Conferences: Annual
Conference Chair: Cindy Allen
2013 - Orlando, FL (Disney All-Star Sports Resort)/Feb. 6 - 10
2013 - Anaheim, CA/April 24 - 27
2014 - Atlanta, GA/May 3 - 6
2015 - Orlando, FL/April 25 - 28
Number of non-conference events/year: 20

Publications:
Dimensions; quarterly

Diving Equipment and Marketing Association
(1972)
3750 Convoy St.
Suite 310
San Diego, CA 92111-3741
Tel: (858) 616-6408 *Fax:* (858) 616-6495
TollFree: (800) 862-3483
E-Mail: info@dema.org
Website: dema.org
Members: 1600 companies
Staff: 8
Annual Budget: $2-5,000,000
Personnel:

Executive Director: Tom Ingram
    E-Mail: tingram@dema.org
Coordinator, Membership Services: June French
    E-Mail: jfrench@dema.org
Accounting and Operations Manager: Laura Loomis
    E-Mail: lloomis@dema.org
Membership Services, Marketing and Communications Coordinator: Rachelle Morri
    E-Mail: rmorris@dema.org

Historical Note:
Formerly (1994) Diving Equipment Manufacturers Association. DEMA's mission is to advocate sustainable growth in safe recreational diving and snorkeling while protecting the underwater environment. Membership: $200-2525 (Manufacturers/Distributors/Diver Certification and Training Agencies/Dive Travel or Resorts); $150 (Associate).

Meetings/Conferences: Annual
2013 - Orlando, FL (Orange County Convention Center)/Nov. 6 - 9
2014 - Las Vegas, NV (Las Vegas Convention Center)/ Nov. 19 - 22
Number of non-conference events/year: 1

Publications:
DEMA Newsletter
Membership Directory; on-line

Division I-A Athletic Directors Association *(1988)*
P.O. Box 92514
Southlake, TX 76092
Tel: (817) 488-0362 *Fax:* (817) 488-4804
Website: d-1a.com
Staff: 3
Annual Budget: $500-1,000,000
Tax: 501(c)(6)

Personnel:
Executive Director: Dutch Baughman
    E-Mail: dutch@d-1a.com
Executive Administrator: Amy Hart
    E-Mail: amy@d-1a.com
Director, Affiliate Groups: Pam Overton
    E-Mail: pam@d-1a.com

Historical Note:
1A's mission is to prepare student-athletes for life as productive citizens in society.

Meetings/Conferences: Annual
2013 - Grapevine, TX/Jan. 16 - 19
2014 - San Diego, CA/Jan. 15 - 18
2015 - Washington, DC/Jan. 14 - 17
2016 - San Antonio, TX/Jan. 13 - 16
2017 - Dallas, TX/Jan. 11 - 14
2018 - Indianapolis, IN/Jan. 17 - 20
2019 - Atlanta, GA/Jan. 16 - 19

Publications:
Membership Directory; on-line

Document Security Alliance
204 E. St. NE
Washington, DC 20002
Tel: (202) 543-5552 *Fax:* (202) 547-6348
E-Mail: info@documentsecurityalliance.org
Website: documentsecurityalliance.com
Members: 75 Companies
Staff: 3
Annual Budget: $50-100,000
Tax: 501(c)(6)

Personnel:
Contact, Membership Services: Shiela Crowley
    E-Mail: smc@documentsecurityalliance.com

Historical Note:
DSA is a public/private partnership aiming to improve security documents and related security document procedures by drawing upon the knowledge and detailed technical disciplines of its members. Membership: $1,500/ year (Company).

Meetings/Conferences:
Number of non-conference events/year: 1

Publications:
Member Directory; on-line

Dog Writers' Association of America *(1935)*
173 Union Rd.
Coatesville, PA 19320-1326
Tel: (610) 384-2436
Website: dwaa.org
Members: 565 individuals
Staff: 3

Annual Budget: $25-50,000
Tax: 501(c)(6)

Personnel:
President: Carmen Battaglia
Treasurer: Marsha Pugh
Secretary: Pat Santi
    E-Mail: rhydowen@aol.com

Historical Note:
DWAA is a professional organization for writers, photographers, illustrators and others involved in creative endeavors that promote the interests of dogs. Members share ideas as well as creative and professional techniques. The organization also sponsors an annual contest. Membership: $40/year (Individual).

Continuing Education:
Enrollment: 600

Publications:
Ruff Drafts; quarterly
Writer With Dogs; on-line

Membership List Available to Non-members

Domestic Energy Producers Alliance
P.O. Box 18359
Oklahoma City, OK 73154
Tel: (405) 424-1699
Website: depausa.org
Staff: 3
Annual Budget: $1-2,000,000

Personnel:
Executive Director: Michael "Mickey" O. Thompson
Director, Governmental Affairs: Mike Cantrell
Secretary and Treasurer: Berry Mullennix

Historical Note:
DEPA's mission is to be a unified voice of independent producers and the state and national energy trade associations who represent them.

Publications:
DEPA Newsletter

Donors Forum *(1974)*
208 S. LaSalle St.
Suite 1540
Chicago, IL 60604
Tel: (312) 578-0090 *Fax:* (312) 578-0103
TollFree: (888) 578-0090
E-Mail: info@donorsforum.org
Website: donorsforum.org
Members: 182 organizations and 34 associate members
Staff: 35
Annual Budget: $2-5,000,000

Personnel:
President and Chief Executive Officer: Valerie S. Lies
    E-Mail: vlies@donorsforum.org
Senior Vice President, Member Relations: Robin Berkson
    E-Mail: rberkson@donorsforum.org
Vice President, Finance and Administration: Andreason L. Brown
    E-Mail: abrown@donorsforum.org
Manager, Database and Technology: Juan Jaimes
    E-Mail: jjaimes@donorsforum.org
Vice President, Public Policy: Laurel O'Sullivan
    E-Mail: losullivan@donorsforum.org
Vice President, External Relations: Celeste Wroblewski
    E-Mail: cwroblewski@donorsforum.org

Historical Note:
Donors Forum's mission is to provide leadership and advocacy on behalf of philanthropy and to serve its constituents by promoting an effective and informed philanthropic and nonprofit sector. Membership: Dues are based on formula.

Meetings/Conferences:
Number of non-conference events/year: 1

Publications:
Forumnotes; monthly; adv.
Membership Directory; on-line

Door and Access Systems Manufacturers Association, International *(1996)*
1300 Sumner Ave.
Cleveland, OH 44115-2851
Tel: (216) 241-7333 *Fax:* (216) 241-0105
E-Mail: dasma@dasma.com
Website: dasma.com
Members: 100 companies
Staff: 11
Annual Budget: $500-1,000,000

Tax: 501(c)(6)

Personnel:
Executive Director: John H. Addington
    E-Mail: jaddington@thomasamc.com
Controller: Melissa Allay CPA
    E-Mail: mallay@thomasamc.com
General Counsel: Naomi R. Angel Esq.
    E-Mail: nra@howehutton.com
Manager, Advertising: Ann Marie Cunningham
    E-Mail: ann@cunninghambaron.com
Technical Director: Joseph R. Hetzel
    E-Mail: jhetzel@thomasamc.com
Communications Consultant and Editor: Thomas R.
    Wadsworth
    E-Mail: daseditor@dasma.com

Historical Note:
*DASMA is collaboration of DORCMA and the NAGDM,
(2006) American Rolling Door Institute merged into
DASMA. DASMA's mission is to serve by producing better
installation procedures and safer products that provide
enhanced protection against high winds, fire, entrapment,
and injuries. Membership: $5,750/year.*

Continuing Education:
Certification Designation/s: DASMA-PCP

Meetings/Conferences: Annual

Publications:
D&AS Insider; quarterly; adv.
Door & Access Systems newsmagazine; quarterly; adv.

The Door and Hardware Institute *(1975)*
14150 Newbrook Dr.
Suite 200
Chantilly, VA 20151-2223
Tel: (703) 222-2010 *Fax:* (703) 222-2410
E-Mail: info@dhi.org
Website: dhi.org
Members: 4000 individuals
Staff: 27
Annual Budget: $2-5,000,000
Tax: 501(c)(6)

Personnel:
Chief Executive Officer: Jerry Heppes CAE, Sr.
    E-Mail: jheppes@dhi.org
Director, Finance: Kathleen Fite CPA
    E-Mail: kfite@dhi.org
Director, Business Development: Stephen R. Hildebrand
    E-Mail: shildebrand@dhi.org
Manager, Membership and Chapter Relations: Paige
    (Purdum) Horton
    E-Mail: ppurdum@dhi.org
Director, Government Relations: Bill Johnson
    E-Mail: bjohnson@dhi.org
Specialist, Human Resources and Administrative Assistant:
    Phoebe Liu
    E-Mail: pliu@dhi.org
Editor: Jesse Madden
    E-Mail: jmadden@dhi.org
*Chief Technology Officer and Director, Information
    Technology:* Chuck Molina
    E-Mail: cmolina@dhi.org
Director, Communications: Sharon Newport
    E-Mail: snewport@dhi.org
Director, Education and Certification: Keith Pardoe CDC,
    CDT
    E-Mail: kpardoe@dhi.org
Director, Meetings and Conferences: Marcia Slakie

Historical Note:
*Formerly known as National Contract Hardware
Association. Became National Builders Hardware
Association (1954). Merged with American Society of
Architectural Hardware Consultants and assumed the
current name in 1975. DHI represents the non-residential,
architectural openings industry. Members are distributors
and manufacturers of doors and builders' hardware, and
architectural hardware and certified door consultants.
Membership: $285-850/year.*

Continuing Education:
Certification Designation/s: AHC, AOC, CDC, EHC

Meetings/Conferences: Annual
Conference Chair: Marcia Slakie
Number of non-conference events/year: 1

Publications:
Doors and Hardware Magazine; monthly; adv.
IndustryWatch; bi-weekly; adv.
Membership Directory; annually; adv.
Plan Room; quarterly

Dramatists Guild of America *(1912)*
1501 Broadway
Suite 701
New York, NY 10036
Tel: (212) 398-9366 *Fax:* (212) 944-0420
Website: dramatistsguild.com
Members: 6500 individuals
Staff: 10
Annual Budget: $1-2,000,000

Personnel:
Executive Director, Business Affairs: Ralph Sevush
    E-Mail: rsevush@dramatistsguild.com
Director, Finance and Administration: Caterina Bartha
    E-Mail: cbartha@dramatistsguild.com
Director, Publications: Joey Stocks
    E-Mail: jstocks@dramatistsguild.com
Director, Education, Events and Outreach: Tari Stratton
    E-Mail: tstratton@dramatistsguild.com
Director, Membership Services: Roland Tec
    E-Mail: rtec@dramatistsguild.com

Historical Note:
*DG's mission is to protect, inform, and encourage
the interests of dramatists everywhere. Members are
playwrights, composers and lyricists. Membership: $90
(Associate); $45 (Student); $130 (Individual).*

Meetings/Conferences:
Conference Chair: Tari Stratton

Publications:
Membership Directory; on-line

Dredging Contractors of America, Inc. *(1935)*
503 D St. NW
Suite 150
Washington, DC 20001
Tel: (202) 737-2674 *Fax:* (202) 737-2677
Website: dredgingcontractors.org
Members: 33 companies
Staff: 3
Annual Budget: $1-2,000,000

Personnel:
Executive Director: Barry Holliday
    E-Mail: barryholliday@dredgingcontractors.org
Assistant Executive Director: Michael Gerhardt
    E-Mail: michaelgerhardt@dredgingcontractors.org

Historical Note:
*Formerly the National Association of Dredging Contractors.
DCA represents the industry on key issues before
Congress and is an active partner to the U.S. Army Corps
of Engineers, public port authorities, state and local
governments, as well as allied construction and maritime
organizations. DCA's mission is to improve the quality and
responsiveness of dredging service delivery to the Nation,
ensuring that America's ports, waterways, wetlands and
beaches are efficiently constructed and maintained in an
environmentally sustainable manner. Membership: Annual
dues depends on the annual sales volume.*

Meetings/Conferences:
Conference Chair: Michael Gerhardt

DRI International *(1988)*
1115 Broadway
12th Floor
New York, NY 10010
Fax: (501) 513-8026
TollFree: (866) 542-3744
E-Mail: driinfo@drii.org
Website: drii.org
Members: 3500 individuals
Staff: 9
Annual Budget: $2-5,000,000

Personnel:
President: Alan Berman
    E-Mail: aberman@drii.org
Director, Education: Kelley Okolita
    E-Mail: kokolita@drii.org
Director, Communications: Buffy Rojas
    E-Mail: broyas@drii.org
Director, Sales and Marketing: Russell Woolridge
    E-Mail: rwooldridge@drii.org

Historical Note:
*DRI administers the educational and certification programs
for those engaged in the practice of business continuity
planning and management. Members are professionals
who have got certification through DRI International.
Membership: $75-100/year.*

Continuing Education:

Certification Designation/s: CBCV, CBCA, CBCLA, ABCP,
CBCP, MBCP, CFCP
Membership List Available to Non-members

Drilling Engineering Association
C/O IADC, 10370 Richmond Ave.
Suite 760
Houston, TX 77042
Tel: (713) 292-1945 *Fax:* (713) 292-1946
Website: dea-global.org
Members: 50 companies
Staff: 2
Tax: 501(c)(6)

Personnel:
Secretary and Treasurer: Mike Killalea
    E-Mail: mike.killalea@iadc.org

Historical Note:
*DEA's mission is to present proposals for industry drilling-
related projects sponsored by members of the association for
the benefit of both members and non-members, exploring
the different levels of interest from members in potential
drilling related problems to aid in developing future industry
sponsored projects, acting as a liaison for DEA members
with universities and other research groups. Membership:
$500 (Full); $200 (Associate).*

Meetings/Conferences:
Number of non-conference events/year: 1

Publications:
Membeer Listing; on-line

Driver Employer Council of America *(1967)*
1150 17th St. NW
Suite 900
Washington, DC 20036
Tel: (202) 842-3400 *Fax:* (202) 842-0011
Website: decausa.org
Members: 25 companies
Staff: 4
Annual Budget: $50-100,000

Personnel:
Administrative Assistant: Tina Brown
    E-Mail: tlbrown@littler.com
Legal Counsel: Peter A . Susser
    E-Mail: psusser@littler.com

Historical Note:
*Formerly (1992) the Driver Leasing Council of America,
DECA's mission is to preserve and advance the interests of
driver leasing companies. Members are companies leasing
truck drivers to motor carriers.*

Meetings/Conferences:
Number of non-conference events/year: 1

Publications:
Member Directory; on-line

Driving School Association of America *(1973)*
3125 Wilmington Pike
Kettering, OH 45429
Tel: (508) 835-2333 *Fax:* (985) 649-9877
TollFree: (800) 270-3722
E-Mail: info@thedsaa.org
Website: thedsaa.org
Members: 275 firms
Staff: 4
Annual Budget: $10-25,000

Personnel:
President: Sharon Postigo Fife
Contact, Communications: Jack Varnado

Historical Note:
*DSAA seeks to advocate professionalism within the driving
school industry and to help produce safe and proficient
drivers through ethical, sound education and business
practices. Membership is composed of professional, state-
licensed driving schools in the U.S. and Canada, and
spokesmen of state associations. Membership: $125-225
(Vehicle); $1,000 (Corporate); $250 (Associate).*

Meetings/Conferences: Annual

Publications:
The Dual News; adv.

Drug & Alcohol Testing Industry Association
(1995)
1325 G St. NW, Suite 500
P. O. Box 5001
Washington, DC 20005
Tel: (800) 355-1257 *Fax:* (202) 315-3579
TollFree: (800) 355-1257
E-Mail: info@datia.org

Website: datia.org
Members: 1300 members
Staff: 5
Annual Budget: $1-2,000,000

Personnel:
Executive Director: Laura E. Shelton CMP
   E-Mail: lshelton@datia.org
Director, Membership Services: Erin Carbary
   E-Mail: membership@datia.org
Administrator, Programs: Emily Gilcher
Director, Programs: Kristina Queen
   E-Mail: kristina@datia.org

Historical Note:
DATIA's mission is to expand the workplace drug and alcohol testing market, to provide members information, resources and benefits important to their operations. DATIA represents drug and alcohol service providers, including collection sites, laboratories and testing manufactures. Membership: $249 (Regular); $500 (Corporate); $1,900 (Sustaining Corporate).

Continuing Education:
Enrollment: 5000
Certification Designation/s: NAADATP, ACF, CPC, CPCT

Meetings/Conferences: Annual
Conference Chair: Emily Gilcher
2013 - Orlando, FL (Loews Royal Pacific Resort)/May 9 - 11
2014 - Phoenix, AZ (Arizona Biltmore Resort and Spa)/ May 28 - 30
Number of non-conference events/year: 5

Publications:
DATIA eNews; weekly; adv.
DATIA Focus; quarterly
Drug & Alcohol Testing Industry Newsletter; bi-monthly
Internet Drug & Alcohol Testing Industry Directory and Buyers' Guide; on-line
Membership Directory; on-line

Drug Information Association (*1965*)
800 Enterprise Rd.
Suite 200
Horsham, PA 19044-3595
Tel: (215) 442-6100 *Fax:* (215) 442-6199
E-Mail: dia@diahome.org
Website: diahome.org
Members: 37 individuals
Staff: 110
Annual Budget: $25-50,000,000

Personnel:
Worldwide Executive Director: Paul Pomerantz CAE
   E-Mail: paul.pomerantz@diahome.org
Contact, Continuing Education: Linda Belmont
   E-Mail: linda.belmont@diahome.org
Associate, Exhibits: Jeff Korn
   E-Mail: jeff.korn@diahome.org
Worldwide Director, Human Resources: Elizabeth Lincoln MA
   E-Mail: Elizabeth.Lincoln@diahome.org
Worldwide Director, Finance: Andrew Pepito MBA
   E-Mail: Andrew.Pepito@diahome.org
Worldwide Director, Marketing and Communications: Lisa Zoks

Historical Note:
DIA strives to be a forum for sharing information that optimizes the process of drug development and lifecycle management. Members are individuals from the pharmaceutical industry, government, and academia responsible for processing and disseminating information on medicine and drugs in medicine, biology, pharmacy, and allied human/animal fields. Membership: $140/year (Individual).

Continuing Education:
Certification Designation/s: ACPE, IACET, PMI, CME

Meetings/Conferences:
Conference Chair: Jeff Korn
2013 - Amsterdam, Netherlands (Amsterdam RAI Exhibition and Convention Centre)/March 4 - 6/3000 attendees
2013 - Boston, MA (Boston Convention and Exhibition Center)/June 23 - 27/over 100 exhibitors
2014 - San Diego, CA/June 15 - 19/8000 attendees/ over 100 exhibitors
2015 - Washington, DC/June 14 - 18/8000 attendees/ over 100 exhibitors

Publications:
CSO Directory; on-line; adv.

DIA Daily; daily
DIA Dispatch; on-line
DIA Global Regulatory Activity Digest; weekly
Drug Information Journal; bi-monthly; adv.
Global Forum; bi-monthly; adv.

Drug, Chemical and Associated Technologies Association (*1890*)
One Washington Blvd.
Suite Seven
Robbinsville, NJ 08691
Tel: (609) 448-1000 *Fax:* (609) 448-1944
TollFree: (800) 640-3228
E-Mail: info@dcat.org
Website: dcat.org
Members: 350 individuals and corporates
Staff: 7
Annual Budget: $1-2,000,000
Tax: 501(c)(6)

Personnel:
Executive Director: Margaret M. Timony
   E-Mail: mtimony@dcat.org
Coordinator, Membership Services: Lauryn Kuna
   E-Mail: lkuna@dcat.org
Administrative Assistant: Jeanne Motola
   E-Mail: jeanne@dcat.org
Coordinator, Communications: Erin Sanders
   E-Mail: esanders@dcat.org

Historical Note:
Formerly (2003) Drug, Chemcial and Allied Trades Association. DCAT's mission is to provide services, programs and activities designed to support the business development objectives of its membership. Membership includes companies that manufacture, distribute or provide services to the pharmaceutical, chemical, nutritional and related industries. Membership: $1,500-3,000 (Corporate); $50 (Retirees).

Meetings/Conferences: Annual
2013 - New York City, NY (Waldorf = Astoria)/March 11 - 14
Number of non-conference events/year: 4

Publications:
DCAT Week; weekly
Membership Directory; annually

Drycleaning & Laundry Institute (*1883*)
14700 Sweitzer Ln.
Laurel, MD 20707
Tel: (301) 622-1900 *Fax:* (240) 295-0685
TollFree: (800) 638-2627
Website: ifi.org
Members: 5000 companies
Staff: 20
Annual Budget: $1-2,000,000
Tax: 501(c)(6)

Personnel:
Chief Executive Officer: Mary Scalco
   E-Mail: mscalco@ifi.org
Director, Communications: Harry A. Kimmel III
   E-Mail: hkimmel@dlionline.org
Director, Membership Services: Jon Meijer
   E-Mail: jmeijer@ifi.org

Historical Note:
Formerly International Fabricare Institute, now known as Drycleaning & Laundry Institute. DLI is a national and international association for retail/neighborhood drycleaners and launderers. Members also include manufacturers and suppliers of cleaning equipment, retailers, garment manufacturers, and others concerned with professional garment cleaning and serviceability. Membership: $427-1473(Affiliated States); $169-1595 (Non-Affiliated States); $175-249 (Drop Store/Delivery Route); $365-1950 (Allied Trade); $295 (Textile); $295-395 (Institutional); $300 (International); $190 (Retailer); $45 (Educator).

Continuing Education:
Enrollment: 300
Certification Designation/s: CED, CPW, AOE, CPD

Publications:
DLI Hot Press (e- Newsletter); weekly; adv.
Electronic Marketing Tips and Consumer Newsletter; irregular
Fabricare Magazine; bi-monthly
Fabricare Resources Journal; monthly; adv.
Heads Up; weekly
Monday Marketing Tips; weekly

Ductile Iron Pipe Research Association (*1915*)

2000 Second Ave., South
Suite 429
Birmingham, AL 35233
Tel: (205) 402-8700 *Fax:* (205) 402-8730
E-Mail: info@dipra.org
Website: dipra.org
Members: 7 companies
Staff: 22
Annual Budget: $1-2,000,000
Tax: 501(c)(6)

Personnel:
President: Gregg L. Horn PE

Historical Note:
Formerly (1928) the Cast Iron Pipe Publicity Bureau, it later became the Cast Iron Pipe Institute and the Cast Iron Pipe Research Association and assumed its present name in 1979. DIPRA strives to provide numerous services including the Regional Engineer Program, a variety of brochures, publications, representation on standards-writing committees and technical research on a variety of topics.

Ductile Iron Society (*1958*)
15400 Pearl Rd.
Suite 234
Strongsville, OH 44136
Tel: (440) 665-3686 *Fax:* (440) 878-0070
Website: ductile.org
Members: 90 companies
Staff: 2
Annual Budget: $250-500,000

Personnel:
Executive Director and Director, Technical: James N. Wood
   E-Mail: jwood@ductile.org
Treasurer: Pete Guidi

Historical Note:
The mission of DIS is to advance the technology, art and science of ductile iron production and to disseminate relevant information to the members. Members are producers of ductile iron castings, suppliers of materials, equipment or services applicable to ductile iron and research patrons who are non-producer companies. Membership: $9,600 (Foundry); $3,500 (Overseas Foundry); $2,100 (Associate); $3,600 (Research Patron).

Meetings/Conferences: Semi-Annual
Number of non-conference events/year: 1

Publications:
Ductile Iron News; on-line; adv.
Hot Topics; bi-monthly
Member Directory; on-line

Dude Ranchers' Association (*1926*)
P.O. Box 2307
1122 12th St.
Cody, WY 82414
Tel: (307) 587-2339 *Fax:* (307) 587-2776
TollFree: (866) 399-2339
E-Mail: info@duderanch.org
Website: duderanch.org
Members: 100 guest ranches
Staff: 2
Annual Budget: $250-500,000
Tax: 501(c)(6)

Personnel:
Executive Director: Colleen Hodson PhD
   E-Mail: colleen@duderanch.org

Historical Note:
DRA is the governing body of the West's Dude Ranch industry. It promotes the western ranch vacation, while continuing to build a stronger working relationship with federal and state land agencies in order to preserve and protect parks, forests, and wildlife. Membership: $1000 (Lifetime); $125 annual (Associate Ranch); $50 annual (Associate Personal Member); $250 (Supporting); $150 (Commercial and Contributing).

Meetings/Conferences: Annual
2013 - Wickenburg, AZ (Rancho de los Caballeros)/ Jan. 24 - 28

Publications:
Membership Directory; annually
Ranch Ramblings - e-newsletter; on-line; adv.

Early Care and Education Consortium (*1999*)
1313 L St. NW
Suite 120
Washington, DC 20005
Tel: (202) 408-9626
E-Mail: info@ececonsortium.org

Website: ececonsortium.org
Members: 7,500 centers
Staff: 3
Annual Budget: $500-1,000,000

Personnel:
Executive Director: Eric Karolak
    E-Mail: ekarolak@ececonsortium.org
Director, Policy: Mary Beth Salomone Testa
    E-Mail: mtesta@ececonsortium.org

Historical Note:
ECEC was formed in 1999 to create a provider voice to shape public policy in support of high-quality care and education for children and families. ECEC represents those who implement the policies created in Congress and in the states. It is engaged in the states and on the federal level in supporting strategies and advocating legislation that promotes the development and funding of high-quality early care and education.

Earthmoving & Mining Equipment Council *(1991)*
200 Nyala Farm Rd.
Westport, CT 06880
Tel: (203) 222-7170 *Fax:* (203) 222-7976
Website: aem.org/Groups/Groups/Group.asp?
  G = 28
Staff: 1

Personnel:
Chairman: Patrick Merfeld

Historical Note:
Earthmoving & Mining Equipment Council, a group of AEM, brings members together in product-focused, job-related and issues-oriented forums to address industry issues.

Earthquake Engineering Research Institute
(1948)
499 14th St.
Suite 220
Oakland, CA 94612-1934
Tel: (510) 451-0905 *Fax:* (510) 451-5411
E-Mail: eeri@eeri.org
Website: eeri.org
Members: 2425 individuals and Institutional members
Staff: 10
Annual Budget: $2-5,000,000
Tax: 501(c)(3)

Personnel:
Executive Director: Jay Berger
    E-Mail: jberger@eeri.org
Manager, Editorial and Publications: Eloise Gilland
    E-Mail: eloise@eeri.org
Coordinator, Membership Services and Publication Orders:
    Juliane Lane
    E-Mail: juliane@eeri.org
Program Associate: Maggie Ortiz
    E-Mail: maggie@eeri.org

Historical Note:
EERI's objective is to reduce earthquake risk by advancing the science and practice of earthquake engineering, improving understanding of the impact of earthquakes on the physical, social, economic, political, and cultural environment, and advocating comprehensive and realistic measures for reducing the harmful effects of earthquakes. Membership: $270 (Active); $175 (Affiliate); $135 (Retired); $25-55 (Student); $135 (Young Professional); $550 (Institutional).

Meetings/Conferences: Annual
Conference Chair: Maggie Ortiz
2013 - Seatle, WA (Grand Hyatt Seattle)/Feb. 12 - 15

Publications:
Earthquake Spectra; quarterly; adv.
EERI Newsletter; monthly; adv.

Eastern Apicultural Society of North America
(1955)
287 S. Main st.
Andover, MA 01810
E-Mail: treasurer@easternapiculture.org
Website: easternapiculture.org
Members: 1600 individuals
Staff: 3
Annual Budget: $100-250,000
Tax: 501(c)(3)

Personnel:
Web Master: Dave Meldrum
    E-Mail: webmaster@easternapiculture.org

Historical Note:

An international nonprofit for the promotion of bee culture, education of beekeepers, and excellence in bee research. Membership: $25 (Individual); $50 (State/Provincial/County/Regional Association); $250 (Lifetime).

Continuing Education:
Certification Designation/s: MBC

Meetings/Conferences: Annual
2013 - West Chester, PA (West Chester University of
    Pennsylvania)/Aug. 5 - 9
Number of non-conference events/year: 500

Publications:
EAS Journal; adv.

Ecological Farming Association *(1981)*
2901 Park Ave.
Suite D-2
Soquel, CA 95073
Tel: (831) 763-2111
E-Mail: info@eco-farm.org
Website: eco-farm.org
Staff: 3
Annual Budget: $1-2,000,000

Personnel:
Executive Director: Ken Dickerson
    E-Mail: ken@eco-farm.org
Program Coordinator: Liz Birnbaum
    E-Mail: liz@eco-farm.org
Communications Director: Joanna Dillon
    E-Mail: joanna@eco-farm.org

Historical Note:
The Ecological Farming Association nurtures healthy and just farms, food systems, communities and environment by bringing people together for education, alliance building and advocacy. EcoFarm is a educational organization funded through activities and projects, community contributions, business sponsorships, membership donations, and grants.

Meetings/Conferences: Annual
Conference Chair: Liz Birnbaum
2013 - Pacific Grove, CA (Asilomar Conference
    Grounds)/Jan. 23 - 26

Publications:
Newsletter; annually

Ecological Society of America *(1915)*
1990 M St. NW
Suite 700
Washington, DC 20036
Tel: (202) 833-8773 *Fax:* (202) 833-8775
E-Mail: esahq@esa.org
Website: esa.org
Members: 10000 individuals
Staff: 47
Annual Budget: $5-10,000,000

Personnel:
Executive Director: Katherine S. McCarter
    E-Mail: ksm@esa.org
Managing Editor: J. David Baldwin
    E-Mail: suesilver@esa.org
Chief Financial Officer: Elizabeth Biggs
    E-Mail: liz@esa.org
Manager, Marketing and Advertising: Eric Gordon
    E-Mail: eric@esa.org
Director, Administration and Meetings: Michelle Horton
    E-Mail: michelle@esa.org
Director, Public Affairs: Nadine Lymn
    E-Mail: nadine@esa.org
Director, Education: Teresa Mourad
    E-Mail: teresa@esa.org
Associate Director, Information Systems: Thet K. Oo
    E-Mail: thet@esa.org
Editor in Chief: Sue Silver
    E-Mail: suesilver@esa.org

Historical Note:
Organized in Columbus, Ohio at the annual meeting of the American Association for the Advancement of Science. ESA is a professional society of individuals interested in the study of living things in relation to their environment. It is also a member society of the American Institute of Biological Sciences. Membership: $55-106 (Regular Member); $27 (Student Member); $260 (Contributing Member); $15-85 (Developing Countries); $450-2050 (Life Member).

Continuing Education:
Certification Designation/s: ESA

Meetings/Conferences: Annual
Conference Chair: Michelle Horton

2013 - Minneapolis, MN (Minneapolis Convention
    Center)/Aug. 4 - 9
2014 - Sacramento, CA/Aug. 10 - 15
2015 - Baltimore, MD (Hilton Baltimore)/Aug. 9 - 15

Publications:
Ecological Applications
Ecological Monographs; quarterly
Ecology; monthly
Frontiers in Ecology and the Environment
Membership Directory

Econometric Society *(1930)*
Department of Economics, New York University,
19 W. Fourth St.
Sixth Floor
New York, NY 10012
Tel: (212) 998-3820 *Fax:* (212) 995-4487
E-Mail: econometrica@econometricsociety.org
Website: econometricsociety.org
Members: 7000 individuals and institutions
Staff: 3
Annual Budget: $1-2,000,000
Tax: 501(c)(3)

Personnel:
President: Jean Charles Rochet
    E-Mail: rochet@isb.uzh.ch
Editor: Daron Acemoglu
General Manager: Claire Sashi
    E-Mail: sashi@econometricsociety.org

Historical Note:
Mission is to promote studies that aim at unification of the theoretical- quantitative and empirical-quantitative approach to economic problems and that are penetrated by constructive and rigorous thinking similar to that which has come to dominate in the natural sciences. Membership: $50-90 (Member); $10-50 (Student); $500-650 (Institution).

Meetings/Conferences:
Number of non-conference events/year: 2

Publications:
Membership Directory; on-line
Monograph Series
Quantitative Economics
Quantitative Economics; adv.
Theoretical Economics
Theoretical Economics; adv.

Membership List Available to Non-members

Economic History Association *(1940)*
Santa Clara University, 500 El Camino Real
Santa Clara, CA 95053-0385
Tel: (408) 554-4348 *Fax:* (408) 554-2331
Website: eh.net/eha
Members: 3130 Institutes and individuals
Staff: 3
Annual Budget: $500-1,000,000
Tax: 501(c)(3)

Personnel:
Executive Director: Alexander J. Field
    E-Mail: afield@scu.edu
Coordinator, Meetings: Jari Eloranta
    E-Mail: elorantaj@appstate.edu
Editor: Price Fishback
    E-Mail: pfishback@eller.arizona.edu

Historical Note:
A member of the American Council of Learned Societies, EHA's mission is to encourage and advocate teaching, research, and publication on every phase of economic history, broadly defined, and to encourage and assist in the preservation and administration of the materials for research in economic history. Membership: $35 (Individual, incomes below $50,000); $60 (Individual, incomes above $50,000); $20 (Student); $52 (Student EHA/EHS); $60 (Regular EHA income over $50,000); $92 (Regular EHA/EHS income over $50,000); $67 (Regular EHA/EHS income under $50,000);

Meetings/Conferences: Annual
Conference Chair: Jari Eloranta

Publications:
Membership Directory; on-line
The Annual Newsletter of EHA; annually
The Journal of Economic History; quarterly

Membership List Available to Non-members

ECRI *(1968)*
5200 Butler Pike
Plymouth Meeting, PA 19462-1298

Tel: (610) 825-6000 *Fax:* (610) 834-1275
E-Mail: info@ecri.org
Website: ecri.org
Members: 5000 members and clients
Staff: 250
Annual Budget: $25-50,000,000
Tax: 501(c)(3)

Personnel:
President and Chief Executive Officer: Jeffrey C. Lerner PhD
    E-Mail: executiveadmins@ecri.org
Director, Risk Management Publications: Paul Anderson
    E-Mail: panderson@ecri.org
Vice President, Information Services and Health Technology Assessment: Vivian H. Coates MBA
Vice President, Finance: G. Daniel Downing MBA
Director, Public Relations and Marketing Communications: Laurie Menyo PhD
    E-Mail: lmenyo@ecri.org
Executive Vice President and General Counsel: Ronni P. Solomon JD
    E-Mail: rsolomon@ecri.org

Historical Note:
Founded as the Graduate Pain Research Institute in 1968 and assumed its present name in 1980. ECRI's mission is to benefit patient care by Lighthousepromoting the highest standards of safety, quality, and cost-effectiveness in healthcare.

Meetings/Conferences: Annual

Publications:
Exchange of Health Information Monthly Brief Newsletter; monthly
Healthcare Standards E-Newsletter; on-line
Membership Directory; on-line

Ecuadorean American Association (*1932*)
641 Lexington Ave.
Suite 1430
New York, NY 10022
Tel: (212) 233-7776 *Fax:* (212) 233-7779
E-Mail: info@andean-us.com
Website: ecuadoreanamericanassociation.org
Members:
30 companies
27 individuals
Staff: 3
Annual Budget: $10-25,000

Personnel:
Executive President and Chief Executive Officer: Maria Rosa Baquerizo
Vice President and General Manager: Evan Acosta

Historical Note:
EAA's strives to promote better knowledge and understanding of modern Ecuador. It also seeks to bring together Ecuadorean and U.S. business people, government officials, and individuals at a variety of programs. Members are international business executives, financiers, and professionals. Membership: $200 (Resident Individual); $500 (Corporate); $2,000 (Supporting).

EDA Consortium (*1989*)
111 W. Saint John St.
Suite 220
San Jose, CA 95113-1104
Tel: (408) 287-3322 *Fax:* (408) 317-3322
E-Mail: orders@edac.org
Website: edac.org
Members: 100 companies
Staff: 3
Annual Budget: $500-1,000,000

Personnel:
Executive Director: Robert Gardner
Senior Project Manager: Jennifer Cermak
Member, Technical Staff: Paul Douglas Cohen

Historical Note:
Founded as the Electronic Design Automation Consortium. EDA Consortium's mission is to encourage the health of the EDA industry, and to increase awareness of the crucial role EDA plays in today's global economy. Members are companies engaged in the development, manufacture and sale of design tools to the electronic engineering community. Membership: $250 (Individual); $5000-10,000 (Associate); $3,3000-30,000 (Voting, based on company's revenue).

Continuing Education:
Certification Designation/s: CHD

Meetings/Conferences:
Conference Chair: Jennifer Cermak

Publications:
EDA Alert; bi-weekly
EDA Confidential; weekly

Edison Electric Institute (*1933*)
701 Pennsylvania Ave. NW
Washington, DC 20004-2696
Tel: (202) 508-5000 *Fax:* (202) 508-5080
TollFree: (800) 334-4688
Website: eei.org
Members: 70 international electric companies and 200 industry suppliers
Staff: 200
Annual Budget: Over $100,000,000
Tax: 501(c)(6)

Personnel:
President: Thomas R. Kuhn
    E-Mail: tkuhn@eei.org
Vice President, General Counsel and Corporate Secretary: Edward H. Comer
    E-Mail: ecomer@eei.org
Vice President, International Programs: John J. Easton Jr.
Senior Director, Membership Relations: Brian Farrell CAE
    E-Mail: bfarrell@eei.org
Senior Vice President, Policy and Chief-of-Staff: Lynn LeMaster
    E-Mail: llemaster@eei.org
Chief Administrative Officer: Mary Miller
Contact, Conference: Tony Odett
    E-Mail: todett@eei.org
Executive Director, Membership Relations and Meeting Services: Jim Owens
    E-Mail: jowen@eei.org
Executive Vice President, Business Operations: David K. Owens
    E-Mail: dowens@eei.org
Chief Information Officer: Marc Razeghi
Executive Director, Communications: Ryan Rudominer
Chief Financial Officer: John Schlenker
    E-Mail: jschlenker@eei.org
Chief Financial Officer and Treasurer: John S. Schlenker
Executive Director, Retail Services Energy Division: Richard "Rick" Tempchin
    E-Mail: rtempchin@eei.org

Historical Note:
Association of US shareholder-owned electric companies

Meetings/Conferences: Annual
Conference Chair: Tony Odett
2013 - San Francisco, CA (San Francisco Marriott Marquis)/June 9 - 12
2013 - Orlando, FL (Orlando World Center Marriott)/Nov. 10 - 13
2014 - Las Vegas, NV (ARIA Resort and Casino Hotel)/June 8 - 11
2015 - Hollywood, FL (Westin Diplomat Resort and Spa)/Nov. 8 - 11
2016 - Phoenix, AZ (JW Marriott Desert Ridge Resort)/Nov. 6 - 9
2017 - Lake Buena Vista, FL (Walt Disney World Swan and Dolphin)/Nov. 5 - 8
Number of non-conference events/year: 25

Publications:
Electric Perspectives Magazine; bi-monthly; adv.

Edison Welding Institute (*1984*)
1250 Arthur E. Adams Dr.
Columbus, OH 43221-3585
Tel: (614) 688-5000 *Fax:* (614) 688-5001
Website: ewi.org
Members: 1,200 companies
Staff: 157
Annual Budget: $25-50,000,000
Tax: 501(c)(3)

Personnel:
President and Chief Executive Officer: Henry J. Cialone
Chief Technology Officer: Chris Conrardy
    E-Mail: cconrardy@ewi.org
Membership Sales: Leah Kohr
Vice President, Administrative Services and Chief Financial Officer: Jim Tighe
Vice President and Chief Operating Officer: Phillip Weisenbach

Historical Note:
EWI's mission is to advance the science, technology and application of welding and allied joining and cutting processes, including brazing, soldering and thermal spraying.

Meetings/Conferences:
Number of non-conference events/year: 7

Publications:
CEO Update; monthly
EWI Technical Insights; monthly
Membership Directory; on-line

Editorial Freelancers Association (*1974*)
71 W. 23rd St.
Fourth Floor
New York, NY 10010-4102
Tel: (212) 929-5400 *Fax:* (212) 929-5439
TollFree: (866) 929-5425
E-Mail: office@the-efa.org
Website: the-efa.org
Members: 1200 individuals
Staff: 4
Annual Budget: $250-500,000
Tax: 501(c)(6)

Personnel:
Editor: Barbara Magalnick
    E-Mail: pubs@the-efa.org
Contact, Education: Lisa L. Owens
    E-Mail: education@the-efa.org
Contact, Membership Services: Cassie Tuttle
    E-Mail: membership@the-efa.org

Historical Note:
Absorbed Freelance Editors Association in 2000. EFA's mission is to provide the means of developing and implementing programs of benefit to professional editorial freelancers and the publishing industry, and to support and advance the interests of both. Members are editors, writers, indexers, proofreaders, researchers, desktop publishers, translators, and others who offer a broad range of skills and specialties. Membership: $145-260 (Full); $0 (Guest).

Publications:
Membership Directory; on-line
The Freelancer; bi-monthly; adv.

Education Credit Union Council (*1972*)
P.O. Box 7558
Spanish Ft., AL 36577
Tel: (251) 626-3399 *Fax:* (251) 626-3565
E-Mail: ecuclbw@aol.com
Website: ecuc.org
Members: 350 credit unions
Staff: 1
Annual Budget: $250-500,000

Personnel:
Executive Director: Lorraine B. Zerfas

Historical Note:
ECUC works to maintain an affordable dues structure to provide opportunities for every credit union that serves educational communities. Members are credit unions serving educational institutions. Membership: $350/year (Organization).

Meetings/Conferences: Annual
2013 - Las Vegas, NV (Paris Las Vegas)/Feb. 16 - 19
2014 - New Orleans, LA (New Orleans Marriott Hotel)/Feb. 14 - 18

Publications:
ChalkTalk; bi-monthly; adv.
Membership Directory; on-line

Education Finance Council (*1993*)
1850 M St. NW
Suite 920
Washington, DC 20036
Tel: (202) 955-5510 *Fax:* (202) 955-5530
E-Mail: info@efc.org
Website: efc.org
Staff: 8
Annual Budget: $1-2,000,000
Tax: 501(c)(6)

Personnel:
President: Vince Sampson
    E-Mail: vinces@efc.org
Controller: Renee L. Burchard
    E-Mail: reneeb@efc.org
Senior Vice President and Chief Operating Officer: Gail daMota
    E-Mail: gaild@efc.org
Director, Communications and Industry Relations: Samantha DeZur
    E-Mail: samanthad@efc.org
Administrative Assistant: Caitlin Hargett
    E-Mail: caitlinh@efc.org

Director, Government Relations: Peter Warren
    E-Mail: peterw@efc.org

Historical Note:
EFC's mission is to expand access to higher education by ensuring the availability of student loan funds while striving to make paying for college easier and less expensive for all students and families. Membership comprises of non-profit and state-based student loan providers.

Meetings/Conferences:
2013 - Rancho Mirage, CA/March 7 - 8
2013 - Washington, DC (Washington Marriott at Metro Center)/July 11 - 12
Number of non-conference events/year: 2

Publications:
EFC Alert; on-line
EFC Exchange; daily
EFC Monthly Rundown; monthly
Membership Directory; on-line; adv.

Education Industry Association *(1990)*
1839 Batten Hollow Rd.
Vienna, VA 22182
Tel: (703) 938-2429 *Fax:* (703) 242-1479
TollFree: (800) 252-3280
Website: educationindustry.org
Members: 800 individuals
Staff: 3
Annual Budget: $500-1,000,000

Personnel:
Executive Director: Steven Pines
    E-Mail: spines@educationindustry.org
Coordinator, Membership Services: Clare Sladic
    E-Mail: clare@educationindustry.org

Historical Note:
Formerly (2002) known as the Association of Educators in Private Practice, became Association of Education Practitioners and Providers in 2002 and assumed its current name in 2004. EIA's aim is to prompt the public support for the education industry in order to improve educational opportunities and outcomes for all students. Members are educators working in private, corporate or other alternative settings. Membership: $250 (Emerging); $800 (Bronze); $1,250 (Silver); $2,900 (Gold); $5,800 (Platinum); $50 (Student).

Meetings/Conferences:
2013 - Washington, DC (Liasion Hotel)/Feb. 20 - 22
Number of non-conference events/year: 2

Publications:
Enterprising Educators; monthly
Member Directory

Education Law Association *(1954)*
300 College Park
Dayton, OH 45469-0528
Tel: (937) 229-3589 *Fax:* (937) 229-3845
E-Mail: ela@educationlaw.org
Website: educationlaw.org
Members: 1400 Individuals
Staff: 4
Annual Budget: $250-500,000
Tax: 501(c)(3)

Personnel:
Executive Director: Cate K. Smith J.D.
Coordinator, Member Services and Accounting: Judy Pleiman
Manager, Publications: Jody Thornburg

Historical Note:
Formerly (1996) National Organization on Legal Problems of Education, assumed its current name in 1997. ELA's mission is to promote intereste in practical knowledge, scholarship, and interdisciplinary dialogue about legal and policy issues affecting education. Membership: $160 (Individual); $100 (Retired); $50 (Student); $145 (Library Subscription).

Meetings/Conferences: Annual
2013 - Westminster, CO (Westin Westminster)/Nov. 13 - 16
2014 - San Diego, CA (Sheraton San Diego Hotel and Marina)/Nov. 8 - 11

Publications:
ELA Notes; quarterly; adv.
School Law Reporter; monthly; adv.

Education Writers Association *(1947)*
2122 P St. NW
Suite 201
Washington, DC 20037

Tel: (202) 452-9830 *Fax:* (202) 452-9837
E-Mail: ewa@ewa.org
Website: ewa.org
Members: 2000 members
Staff: 6
Annual Budget: $1-2,000,000
Tax: 501(c)(3)

Personnel:
Executive Director: Caroline W. Hendrie
    E-Mail: chendrie@ewa.org
Coordinator, Administration: Tracee Eason
    E-Mail: teason@ewa.org
Editor: Emily Richmond
    E-Mail: erichmond@ewa.org
Director, Projects: Kenneth Terrell
    E-Mail: kterrell@ewa.org

Historical Note:
Absorbed the National Council for the Advancement of Education Writing in 1975. EWA's mission is to improve the quality and quantity of education coverage through information, training, and customized support to help reporters and other communicators. Members are staff members of newspapers, magazines and broadcasting stations or freelancers. Associate members include school and college public information officers and writers who work for educational institutions and organizations. Membership: Free.

Meetings/Conferences:
Number of non-conference events/year: 2

Publications:
Education Reporter; bi-weekly
Membership Directory; on-line

Membership List Available to Non-members

Educational Association of University Centers
530 HFR
Cullowhee, NC 28723
Tel: (828) 227-3435 *Fax:* (828) 227-7081
Website: eauc.org
Staff: 1

Personnel:
Executive Director: Tom McClure
    E-Mail: mcclure@wcu.edu

Historical Note:
Represents university based economic development support organizations.

Educational Book and Media Association *(1975)*
P.O. Box 3363
Warrenton, VA 20188
Tel: (540) 318-7770 *Fax:* (202) 962-3939
E-Mail: info@edupaperback.org
Website: edupaperback.org
Members: 100 companies
Staff: 2
Annual Budget: $100-250,000

Personnel:
Executive Director: Brian Gorg
Manager, Meetings: Maureen Gelwicks

Historical Note:
formerly known as the Educational Paperback Association. EBMA's mission is to develop better techniques and procedures for the sales, marketing and distribution of paperback and prebound books in the school and library markets. Membership: $500 (Regular); $825 (Associate).

Meetings/Conferences: Annual
Conference Chair: Maureen Gelwicks
2013 - Orlando, FL (Ritz-Carlton Orlando, Grande Lakes)/Jan. 14 - 17

Publications:
Memberhip Directory; on-line

Educational Theatre Association *(1929)*
2343 Auburn Ave.
Cincinnati, OH 45219-2815
Tel: (513) 421-3900 *Fax:* (513) 421-7077
E-Mail: info@edta.org
Website: edta.org
Members: 4300 individuals, 3900 schools
Staff: 31
Annual Budget: $5-10,000,000
Tax: 501(c)(3)

Personnel:
Executive director: Julie Woffington
    E-Mail: jwoffington@schooltheatre.org
Director, Educational Programs: Nancy L. Brown
    E-Mail: nbrown@edta.org

Director, Chapter Relations: Diane Carr
    E-Mail: dcarr@edta.org
Director, Publications: Donald A. Corathers
    E-Mail: dcorathers@edta.org
Executive Administrative Assistant: Jim Flanagan
    E-Mail: jflanagan@schooltheatre.org
Director, Marketing: Christopher Hunt
    E-Mail: chunt@edta.org
Director, Membership: David LaFleche
    E-Mail: dlafleche@edta.org
Director, Development: Kristin McFadden
    E-Mail: kmcfadden@edta.org
Manager, Information Systems: Sandy Morgan
    E-Mail: smorgan@edta.org
Director, Educational Policy: James Palmarini
    E-Mail: jpalmarini@edta.org
Director, Finance: Doug Sandor
    E-Mail: dsandor@edta.org

Historical Note:
Founded as Theatre Education Association, assumed its current name in 1999. EdTA's mission is shaping lives through theatre education by: honoring student achievement in theatre and enriching their theatre education experience; supporting teachers by providing professional development, networking opportunities, resources, and recognition; and influencing public opinion that theatre education is essential and builds life skills. Membership: $75 (Professional); $50 (Affiliate Professional); $22 (Student); $65 (Thespian Troupe); $25 (Pre-professional); $50 (Emeritus).

Meetings/Conferences: Annual
Conference Chair: Diane Carr
2013 - Minneapolis, MN (Depot Renaissance Minneapolis Hotel/Sept. 26 - 30
2014 - Cincinnati, OH (Hilton Cincinnati Netherland Plaza)/July 24 - 27

Publications:
Dramatics Magazine; monthly; adv.
Teaching Theatre Journal; quarterly; adv.

Membership List Available to Non-members

Educause *(1998)*
1150 18th St.NW
Suite 900
Washington, DC 20036
Tel: (202) 872-4200 *Fax:* (202) 872-4318
E-Mail: info@educause.edu
Website: educause.edu
Members:
2267 institutions, organizations, corporations
17000 active member representatives
Staff: 79
Annual Budget: $10-25,000,000
Tax: 501(c)(3)

Personnel:
President and Chief Executive Officer: Diana G. Oblinger
    E-Mail: doblinger@educause.edu
Director, Conferences and Educational Activities: Gretchen Bliss
    E-Mail: gbliss@educause.edu
Manager, Membership Services: Tammy Burkhart
    E-Mail: tburkhart@educause.edu
Director, Hybrid and Online Meetings: Victoria B. Fanning
    E-Mail: vfanning@educause.edu
Director, Marketing Communications: Lisa Gesner
    E-Mail: lgesner@educause.edu
Director, Information Technology and Membership Services: Rebecca C. Granger
    E-Mail: rgranger@educause.edu
Editor and Manager, Publishing: Nancy Hays
    E-Mail: nhays@educause.edu
Vice President, Teaching, Learning, and Professional Development: Julie Little
    E-Mail: jlittle@educause.edu
Director, Administration and Finance: Michelle McIrvin
    E-Mail: mmcirvin@educause.edu
Chief Information Officer: Matthew Milliron
    E-Mail: mmilliron@educause.edu
Government Relations Officer: Wendy Wigen
    E-Mail: wwigen@educause.edu

Historical Note:
EDUCAUSE was formed in 1998 through a merger between CAUSE and Educom. Mission is to advance higher education by promoting the intelligent use of information technology. Has offices in Boulder, Colorado, and Washington, D.C. Membership: $1,035 (International); $2,060 (Corporate).

Meetings/Conferences:

Conference Chair: Victoria B. Fanning
2013 - Denver, CO (Sheraton Denver Downtown Hotel)/Feb. 4 - 6
2013 - Anaheim, CA/Oct. 15 - 18
2014 - Orlando, FL/Sept. 29 - Oct. 2
2015 - Indianapolis, IN/Oct. 27 - 30
Number of non-conference events/year: 52

Publications:
EDUCAUSE; quarterly; adv.
Library Journal
Member Directory; on-line

Membership List Available to Non-members

EEG and Clinical Neuroscience Society (1998)
C/O The ECNS Society, Department of Psychology
East Tennessee State University, 807 University Pkwy.
Johnson City, TN 37614
Tel: (888) 531-5335 Fax: (888) 531-5335
E-Mail: clinicaleeg@aol.com
Website: ecnsweb.com
Members: 1000 individuals and organizations
Staff: 4
Annual Budget: $50-100,000

Personnel:
President: Silvana Galderisi MD, PhD
    E-Mail: sgalderi@tin.it
Chair, Conference Planning Committee: Ivan Bodis-Wollner MD
    E-Mail: ivan.bodis-wollner@downstate.edu
Treasurer: Dr. Eric W. Sellers PhD
    E-Mail: sellers@mail.etsu.edu

Historical Note:
Founded as the American Medical Electroencephalographic Association, merged with the American Psychiatric Electrophysiology Association and assumed its current name in the year 1998. ECNS is an international scientific and educational organization dedicated to disseminating knowledge regarding the latest scientific advances in all fields of electrophysiology as they relate to the understanding, treatment, and prevention of Neurobehavioral disorders. Members are experts in neurology, psychiatry, psychology and rehabilitation involved in translational research and clinical developments in the field of behavioral neuropsychiatry. Membership: $187-207/year.

Continuing Education:
Certification Designation/s: Ph.D Cert.

Meetings/Conferences: Annual
Conference Chair: Ivan Bodis-Wollner MD

Publications:
Clinical Electroencephalography and Neuroscience; quarterly; adv.

Efficiency First
55 New Montgomery St.
Suite 802
San Francisco, CA 94105
Tel: (415) 449-0551 Fax: (415) 449-0559
E-Mail: info@efficiencyfirst.org
Website: efficiencyfirst.org
Staff: 3
Annual Budget: $500-1,000,000

Personnel:
Executive Director: Jay Murdoch
Director, Chapters and Grassroots: Coby Rudolph
Coordinator, Membership Services and Project Associate: Allison Weston

Historical Note:
Efficiency First is a national nonprofit trade association that unites the Home Performance workforce, building product manufacturers and related businesses. Membership: $50-10,000/year.

Publications:
Membership Directory; on-line

Eight Sheet Outdoor Advertising Association (1953)
P.O. Box 2680
Bremerton, WA 98310
Tel: (360) 377-9867 Fax: (360) 377-9870
TollFree: (800) 874-3387
E-Mail: ddjesoaa@comcast.net
Website: esoaa.com
Members: 130 companies
Staff: 2

Annual Budget: $25-50,000

Personnel:
Executive Director: David Jacobs
    E-Mail: davidjacobs@esoaa.com

Historical Note:
Formerly (1979) Junior Panel Outdoor Advertising Association. ESOAA's mission is to provide leadership, services, and standards to promote, protect and advance the eight sheet industry. Members are owners of eight-sheet outdoor poster panels (Jr 8 Poster Panels) which are small 6' x 12' panels used in outdoor advertising. Membership: $150-750 (Plant, based on number of panels); $250 (Supplier/Associate).

Publications:
ESOAA Newsletter
Supplier's Directory; annually

Election Technology Association
14173 Northwest Fwy.
Suite 239
Houston, TX 77040
Tel: (713) 896-9292
E-Mail: info@electiontech.org
Staff: 1
Annual Budget: Under $10,000
Tax: 501(c)(6)

Personnel:
Executive Director: David Beirne

Historical Note:
A trade association consisting of voting system providers in the United States. ETC seeks to serve as a resource for the public, election officials, and legislators to dispel mythologies regarding voting technology and to help maintain a healthy marketplace for the industry. Members are election technology providers.

Electric Drive Transportation Association (1989)
1250 Eye St. NW
Suite 902
Washington, DC 20005
Tel: (202) 408-0774 Fax: (202) 408-7610
E-Mail: info@electricdrive.org
Website: electricdrive.org
Members: 82 companies and agencies
Staff: 16
Annual Budget: $1-2,000,000
Tax: 501(c)(6)

Personnel:
President: Brian P Wynne
    E-Mail: bwynne@electricdrive.org
Director, Marketing: Benoit Colin
    E-Mail: bcolin@electricdrive.org
Vice President: Genevieve Cullen
    E-Mail: gcullen@electricdrive.org
Director, Membership Services: Kim Grever
    E-Mail: kgrever@electricdrive.org
Director, Conferences and Member Services: Michelle Harris
Coordinator, Membership and Conferences: Lynnecia Johnson
Director, Business Development and Marketing: Amy Lopez
    E-Mail: alopez@electricdrive.org
Director, Finance and Administration: Emory Oney
    E-Mail: eoney@electricdrive.org
Director, Public Relations: Christine Rogala
Manager, Marketing and Communications: Jennifer Watts

Historical Note:
Formerly (1990) Electric Vehicle Association of the Americas, assumed its current name in 2003. EDTA's mission is to advocate electric drive as the best means to achieve the highly efficient and clean use of secure energy in the transportation sector. It advances commercialization of electric vehicles in the United States, Canada and Latin America through comprehensive public information and market development programs. Membership includes vehicle and equipment manufacturers, energy providers, component suppliers and end users. Membership: $1,500 (Non- Profit/ Government Agency); $5,000 (Small Business); $8,000 (General Member); $35,000 (Board Member).

Meetings/Conferences: Annual
Conference Chair: Michelle Harris
2013 - Las Vegas, NV (Las Vegas convention)/Jan. 8 - 13
2013 - Washington, DC (Washington Marriott Wardman Park)/June 11 - 12

Publications:
Membership directory; on-line
Newsletter

World Electric Vehicle Journal

Electric Power Research Institute (1973)
3420 Hillview Ave.
Palo Alto, CA 94304
Tel: (650) 855-2121 Fax: (704) 595-2871
TollFree: (800) 313-3774
E-Mail: askepri@epri.org
Website: my.epri.com/portal/server.pt?
Members: 660 utilities
Staff: 877
Annual Budget: Over $100,000,000

Personnel:
President and Chief Executive Officer: Michael W. Howard
Vice President, General Counsel, Chief Compliance Officer and Secretary: Salvador A. Casente Jr.
Senior Vice President, Global Strategy and External Relations: Henry A. Courtright
Vice President, Chief Financial Officer and Treasurer: Pamela J. Keefe
Senior Vice President, Membership and Technical Services: Christian B. Larsen
Vice President, Marketing: Dennis Murphy
Vice President, People and Performance: Carolyn R. Shockley

Historical Note:
EPRI conducts research and development relating to the generation, delivery and use of electricity for the benefit of the public and brings together its scientists and engineers as well as experts from academia and industry to help address challenges in electricity, including reliability, efficiency, health, safety and the environment. Membership includes both publicly and privately held electric utility organizations.

Meetings/Conferences:
Number of non-conference events/year: 25

Publications:
EPRI Journal

Electric Power Supply Association (EPSA) (1997)
1401 New York Ave. NW
11th Floor
Washington, DC 20005-2110
Tel: (202) 628-8200 Fax: (202) 628-8260
E-Mail: epsainfo@epsa.org
Website: epsa.org
Members: 95 companies
Staff: 5
Annual Budget: $5-10,000,000
Tax: 501(c)(6)

Personnel:
President and Chief Executive Officer: John E. Shelk
    E-Mail: jshelk@epsa.org
Vice President, Regulatory Policy: Nancy E. Bagot
    E-Mail: nbagot@epsa.org
Vice President, Government Affairs: William S. Burlew
Vice President, Policy Research and Communication: Dan Dolan

Historical Note:
EPSA's mission is to advance the interests of its members: competitive generators, power marketers and other suppliers. Membership:$40,000 (Associate); $12,000 (Supporting); $500 (State & Regional Partners).

Publications:
Membership Directory; on-line

Electric Reliability Coordinating Council
2000 K St. NW
Suite 500
Washington, DC 20006
Tel: (202) 828-5845
Website: electricreliability.org
Staff: 1

Personnel:
Executive Director: Scott Segal
    E-Mail: scott.segal@bgllp.Com

Historical Note:
Formerly known as National Electric Reliability Coordinating Council. A coalition of six different power companies. Scott Segal serves both as outside counsel and director of the organization. It's chief mission is to provide consumers across the United States with access to reliable, affordable, and environmentally responsible power.

Publications:
Wall Street Journal; monthly

Membership List Available to Non-members

Electric Utility Fleet Managers Conference (1953)

P.O. Box 500
Williamsburg, VA 23187-0500
Tel: (757) 220-1795
Website: eufmc.com
Staff: 2
Annual Budget: $500-1,000,000

Personnel:
President: Gerald R. Owens
     E-Mail: gerald.owens@oncor.com
Director, Administration and Conference Contact: Ann C.
  Brown-Hailey
     E-Mail: abrownhailey@cox.net

Historical Note:
The Electric Utility Fleet Managers Conference (EUFMC)
is an annual meeting of fleet representatives from investor-
owned utility companies.

Meetings/Conferences: Annual
Conference Chair: Ann C. Brown-Hailey
2013 - Williamsburg, VA (Williamsburg Lodge and
  Conference Center)/June 2 - 5

Publications:
EUFMC Newsletter

Electrical and Computer Engineering Department Heads Association (1985)

233 S. Wacker Dr.
Suite 8400
Chicago, IL 60606-6338
Tel: (312) 559-3724 Fax: (312) 559-4111
E-Mail: information@ecedha.org
Website: ecedha.org
Members: 280 individuals
Staff: 3
Annual Budget: $250-500,000
Tax: 501(c)(3)

Personnel:
Executive Director: John R. Janowiak
Conference Committee Chair: Kim Simpao
     E-Mail: ksimpao@iec.org

Historical Note:
Founded as the National Electrical Engineering Department
Heads Association, assumed its current name in 2001.
ECEDHA's mission is to advance the fields of electrical and
computer engineering and contribute to the development
and dissemination of engineering knowledge in the public
interest and for the public good. Members are educators
chairing collegiate electrical and computer engineering
programs.

Meetings/Conferences: Annual
Conference Chair: Kim Simpao
2013 - Orlando, FL (Buena Vista Hotel)/March 22 - 26

Publications:
Member Directory
The ECEDHA Source E-Newsletter; quarterly

Electrical Apparatus Service Association (1933)

1331 Baur Blvd.
St. Louis, MO 63132
Tel: (314) 993-2220 Fax: (314) 993-1269
E-Mail: easainfo@easa.com
Website: easa.com
Members: 2100 firms
Staff: 17
Annual Budget: $2-5,000,000
Tax: 501(c)(6)

Personnel:
President and Chief Executive Officer: Linda J. Raynes
  CAE
     E-Mail: lraynes@easa.com
Senior Specialist, Technical Support: Thomas Bishop PE
     E-Mail: tbishop@easa.com
Manager, Product Development: Carl M. Fields
     E-Mail: cfields@easa.com
Manager, Communications: Randy Joslin
     E-Mail: rjoslin@easa.com
Manager, Meetings and Expositions: Dale W. Shuter CMP
     E-Mail: dshuter@easa.com
Manager, Finance: Richard Tutka
     E-Mail: rtutka@easa.com
Executive Secretary: Anne Vogel
     E-Mail: avogel@easa.com

Historical Note:
Established as the National Industrial Service Association;
assumed its present name in 1961. EASA's mission
is to help members enhance their performance and

achieve greater levels of success. Members are firms
selling, servicing and rebuilding electric motors,
generators, transformers and related equipment.
Membership: $540-1,625 (International Active);
$572.50-1,145(International Associate); $70 (International
Privileged); $700-1,400 (International Allied).

Meetings/Conferences: Annual
Conference Chair: Dale W. Shuter CMP
2013 - Las Vegas, NV (Mandalay Bay Resort and
  convention)/June 30 - July 2

Publications:
Currents; monthly
Membership Directory; on-line

Membership List Available to Non-members

Electrical Equipment Representatives Association (1947)

638 W. 39th St.
Kansas City, MO 64111
Tel: (816) 561-5323 Fax: (816) 561-1249
E-Mail: info@eera.org
Website: eera.org
Members: 100 companies and 99 members
Staff: 1
Annual Budget: $250-500,000
Tax: 501(c)(6)

Personnel:
Executive Director: Jane Male CAE

Historical Note:
EERA's mission is to provide a forum for industry
representatives to discuss matters pertinent to the success
of their business and to the interest of the industry.
Membership: $1,100/year.

Meetings/Conferences: Annual
2013 - New York City, NY (Grand Hyatt New York)/
  June 23 - 26

Publications:
EERA Directory; annually

Electrical Generating Systems Association (1965)

1650 S. Dixie Hwy.
Suite 400
Boca Raton, FL 33432-7462
Tel: (561) 750-5575 Fax: (561) 395-8557
E-Mail: e-mail@egsa.org
Website: egsa.org
Members: 330 companies
Staff: 10
Annual Budget: $2-5,000,000

Personnel:
Executive Director: Jalane Kellough
     E-Mail: j.kellough@egsa.org
Manager, Membership Services and Technology: Liz
  Bustamante
     E-Mail: l.bustamante@egsa.org
Manager, Communications: Peter Catalfu
     E-Mail: p.catalfu@egsa.org
Manager, Conventions and Meetings: Cara Collins
     E-Mail: c.collins@egsa.org
Director, Communications and Publications: Donald M.
  Ferreira
     E-Mail: d.ferreira@egsa.org
Manager, Marketing: Kim Giles
     E-Mail: k.giles@egsa.org
Staff Accountant: Sherry Montiel
     E-Mail: s.montiel@egsa.org
Director, Education: George Rowley
     E-Mail: g.rowley@egsa.org

Historical Note:
Founded as the Engine Generator Set Manufacturers
Association, it became the Electrical Generating Systems
Marketing Association in 1973 and assumed its present
name in 1985. EGSA's mission is to educate, provide
networking opportunities and share relevant knowledge and
trends with industry professionals including manufacturers,
distributor/dealers, engineers, manufacturer representatives,
contractor/integrators and others serving On-Site Power
consumers. Membership: $0-1025/year.

Continuing Education:
Certification Designation/s: EGSA, GTC

Meetings/Conferences: Semi-Annual
Conference Chair: Cara Collins
2013 - Sarasota, FL (Hyatt Regency Sarasota)/March
  17 - 19
2013 - Bellevue, WA (Hyatt Regency Bellevue)/Sept. 15
  - 17

Publications:

EGSA Buying Guide and Membership Directory;
  annually; adv.
Powerline; bi-monthly; adv.

Electrical Manufacturing and Coil Winding Association (1974)

P.O. Box 278
Imperial Beach, CA 91933
Tel: (619) 435-3629 Fax: (619) 435-3639
E-Mail: cthurman@emcw.org
Website: emcwa.org
Members: 300 individuals and 260 companies
Staff: 2
Annual Budget: $50-100,000

Personnel:
Executive Director: Charles E. Thurman
     E-Mail: cthurman@emcw.org

Historical Note:
Formerly the North American Council of the International
Coil Winding Association and (1993) International
Coil Winding Association. EMCWA is dedicated to
the furtherance of the conception, research, design,
manufacturing, marketing and use of electrical products.
The Association provides an array of educational
opportunities that enhance the development, knowledge,
and use of electrical technology and products. Membership:
$300 (Company-Canada, Mexico and US); $350
(Company- Other countries); $50 (Professional/Associate-
Canada,Mexico and US); $75 (Professional/Associate-
Other countries); $10 (Student).

Meetings/Conferences:
2013 - Milwaukee, WI (Frontier Airlines Center)/May 8
  - 9/over 100 exhibitors

Publications:
Membership Roster and Directory; annually

Membership List Available to Non-members

Electricity Consumers Resource Council (ELCON) (1976)

1111 19th St. NW
Suite 700
Washington, DC 20036
Tel: (202) 682-1390 Fax: (202) 289-6370
E-Mail: elcon@elcon.org
Website: elcon.org
Members:
38 member companies
7 affiliates
Staff: 5
Annual Budget: $500-1,000,000
Tax: 501(c)(6)

Personnel:
President and Chief Executive Officer: Dr. John A.
  Anderson
     E-Mail: janderson@elcon.org
Administrative Manager: Kristin Allen
Consultant, Membership Services: Lynn W. Elder
     E-Mail: elderlynn@one-eleven.net
Vice President, Technical Affairs: John P. Hughes
     E-Mail: jhughes@elcon.org
Vice President, Government and Public Affairs: Marc D.
  Yacker
     E-Mail: myacker@elcon.org

Historical Note:
ELCON's mission is to articulate and promote policies
that make it possible for buyers and sellers of electricity
to negotiate for reliable, affordable supplies in an open
market. Members are industrial consumers of electricity who
support regulatory practices that assure adequate supplies
of electricity at prices based on cost of service. Membership:
$8,000-$45,000/year, based on total consumption of
electricity (not purchased electricity) at facilities in the
United States based on each company's self-certification.

Meetings/Conferences: Annual
Number of non-conference events/year: 1

Publications:
Membership Directory; on-line

Electricity Storage Association (1991)

1155 15th St. NW.
Suite 500
Washington, DC 20005
Tel: (202) 293-0537
E-Mail: info@electricitystorage.org
Website: electricitystorage.org
Staff: 4
Annual Budget: $250-500,000

Personnel:
Executive Director: Brad Roberts
　E-Mail: b.roberts@electricitystorage.org
Director, Operations and Meetings: Becca Dietrich
　E-Mail: b.dietrich@electricitystorage.org
Chief Technical Officer: Matt Lazarewicz
Director, Membership Services and Programs: Bryan Nicholson
　E-Mail: b.nicholson@electricitystorage.org

Historical Note:
Formerly (1991) known as the Utility Battery Group (UBG).Assumed current name in 1996, was made up of eight founding utilities. International trade association comprised of utilities, manufacturers and researchers that advocate.

Meetings/Conferences: Annual
Conference Chair: Becca Dietrich
2013 - Santa Clara, CA (Santa Clara Convention Center)/May 20 - 22

Publications:
Energize Weekly; weekly
Member Directory; on-line

The Electrochemical Society *(1902)*
65 S. Main St.
Building D
Pennington, NJ 08534-2839
Tel: (609) 737-1902 *Fax:* (609) 737-2743
E-Mail: ecs@electrochem.org
Website: electrochem.org
Members: 8000 individuals
Staff: 26
Annual Budget: $5-10,000,000

Personnel:
Executive Director: Roque J. Calvo CAE
　E-Mail: roque.calvo@electrochem.org
Director, Publications: Annie Goedkoop
　E-Mail: ann.goedkoop@electrochem.org
Director, Finance: Paul Grote
　E-Mail: paul.grote@electrochem.org
Executive Administrator: Colleen B. Klepser
　E-Mail: colleen.klepser@electrochem.org
Associate Director, Sales and Marketing: Karen B. Ornstein
　E-Mail: karen.ornstein@electrochem.org
Director, Meetings and Exhibits: Stephanie Plassa
　E-Mail: stephanie.plassa@electrochem.org
Associate Director, Technical Programming: Paul Urso
　E-Mail: paul.urso@electrochem.org
Deputy Executive Director and Publisher: Mary E. Yess
　E-Mail: mary.yess@electrochem.org

Historical Note:
ECS's mission is to advance the theory and practice of electrochemistry, solid-state science, and allied subjects and to encourage research and dissemination of knowledge in these fields. Membership: $98 (Individual); $18 (Student); $1,200-5,000 (Corporate).

Meetings/Conferences: Semi-Annual
Conference Chair: Stephanie Plassa
2013 - Toronto, ON (Sheraton Centre Toronto Hotel)/May 12 - 17
2013 - San Francisco, CA (Hilton San Francisco Union Square)/Oct. 27 - Nov. 1
2014 - Orlando, FL (Hilton Bonnet Creek Resort)/May 11 - 16
2014 - Cancun, QR (Moon Palace Golf and Spa Resort)/Oct. 5 - 10

Publications:
Membership Directory; on-line
The Journal of the Electrochemical Society (JES); monthly

Electrocoat Association *(1997)*
P.O. Box 541083
Cincinnati, OH 45254-1083
Tel: (816) 496-2308 *Fax:* (513) 527-8801
TollFree: (800) 579-8806
Website: electrocoat.org
Members: 150 companies
Staff: 2
Annual Budget: $50-100,000
Tax: 501(c)(6)

Personnel:
Executive Director: Karen McGlothin
　E-Mail: kmcglothlin@electrocoat.org
Coordinator, Member Services: Anne Von Moll
　E-Mail: anne@electrocoat.org

Historical Note:
ECA's mission is to drive e-coat growth by providing access to information, education and networking with industry leaders. Membership: $500-6000 (Corporate); $50-125 (Individual); $100 (Educational Institutions); $30 (Students).

Meetings/Conferences:
Number of non-conference events/year: 1

Publications:
ECA Newsletter; bi-annually
Membership Directory; on-line

Electronic Commerce Code Management Association *(1999)*
2980 Linden St.
Suite E2
Bethlehem, PA 18017
Tel: (610) 861-5990 *Fax:* (610) 625-4657
E-Mail: info@eccma.org
Website: eccma.org
Members: 100 corporations and organizations
Staff: 10
Annual Budget: $100-250,000
Tax: 501(c)(6)

Personnel:
Executive Director and Chief Technical Officer: Peter Benson
　E-Mail: peter.benson@eccma.org
President: Sheron Koshy
　E-Mail: sheron.koshy@eccma.org
Administrative Director: Melissa Scheib
　E-Mail: melissa.scheib@eccma.org
Administrator, Membership Services: Krysten Wolf
　E-Mail: krysten.wolf@eccma.org

Historical Note:
ECCMA's mission is to provide its members with the standards and the registries necessary to measure and improve the quality of their master data.. Membership: $5,000 (Full); $350 (Associate); $50,000 (Charter).

Continuing Education:
Enrollment: 100
Certification Designation/s: MDQM

Meetings/Conferences:
Conference Chair: Melissa Scheib
Number of non-conference events/year: 2

Publications:
ECCMA Newsletter; bi-monthly
Member Directory; on-line

Electronic Components Industry Association *(2010)*
1111 Alderman Dr.
Suite 400
Alpharetta, GA 30005-4175
Tel: (678) 393-9990 *Fax:* (678) 393-9998
E-Mail: admin@nedassoc.org
Website: eciaonline.org
Members: 400 distributors and manufacturers
Staff: 6
Annual Budget: $100-250,000
Tax: 501(c)(6)

Personnel:
President: Robin B. Gray Jr.
　E-Mail: rgray@eciaonline.org
Director, Marketing and Communications: Debbie Conyers
　E-Mail: dconyers@eciaonline.org
Coordinator, Member Services: Donna Dilbeck
　E-Mail: ddilbeck@eciaonline.org
Director, Member Relations: Michelle Meyer
　E-Mail: mmeyer@eciaonline.org
Executive Vice President and Chief Technology Officer: Robert Willis
　E-Mail: rwillis@eciaonline.org
Vice President, Administration: Janet Wood
　E-Mail: jwood@eciaonline.org

Historical Note:
The National Electronic Distributors Association and the Electronic Components Association (ECA) merged (2010) to form the Electronic Components Industry Association (ECIA). ECIA supports the expanding needs and interests of the global supply chain. Membership: $1,000-20,000 (Manufacturer/Distributor, based on total annual sales volume); $1,000 (Associate).

Meetings/Conferences: Annual
Conference Chair: Michelle Meyer
2013 - Omni Hotel, TX (Omni Hotel)/March 25 - 28

2013 - Las Vegas, NV (The Cosmopolitan Hotel)/May 6 - 9
Number of non-conference events/year: 2

Publications:
EDN Magazine; adv.
Membership Directory; on-line
NEDA Headlines; monthly
The NEDA Voice; monthly; adv.

Membership List Available to Non-members

Electronic Distribution Show Corporation *(1935)*
2214 Rock Hill Rd.
Suite 170
Herndon, VA 20170-4214
Tel: (312) 648-1140 *Fax:* (312) 648-4282
E-Mail: eds@edsconnects.com
Website: edsc.org
Members: 500 companies
Staff: 5
Annual Budget: $500-1,000,000

Personnel:
Show Manager: Gretchen A. Oie
　E-Mail: gretchen@edsc.org

Historical Note:
Formerly (1996) Electronic Industry Show Corporation. Members are manufacturers who sell their products through electronics distributors. EDSC's main purpose is to conduct an annual trade show for these manufacturers. Affiliated with Electronic Industries Association, Electronic Representatives Association, and National Electronic Distributors Association.

Meetings/Conferences: Annual
Conference Chair: Gretchen A. Oie
2013 - Las Vegas, NV (The Cosmopolitan Hotel)/May 6 - 9

Publications:
Directory Advertising; on-line; adv.

Membership List Available to Non-members

Electronic Funds Transfer Association *(1977)*
4000 Legato Rd.
Suite 1100
Fairfax, VA 22030
Tel: (703) 934-6052 *Fax:* (703) 934-6058
E-Mail: eftassoc@efta.org
Website: efta.org
Members: 400 companies
Staff: 3
Annual Budget: $500-1,000,000

Personnel:
President and Chief Executive Officer: H. Kurt Helwig
　E-Mail: kurthelwig@efta.org
Senior Director, Government Relations: Dennis Ambach
　E-Mail: dennisambach@efta.org
Executive Assistant: Melanie Renner
　E-Mail: melanierenner@efta.org

Historical Note:
EFTA's mission is to give members a legislative and regulatory processes that will define their businesses far into the future. Members are financial institutions, ATM networks, owners, processors and manufactures, card companies, online payment providers, prepaid and mobile payment providers, security and technology management companies, government agencies and industry consultants. Membership: $30,000 (Sustaining Company, for companies with revenue greater than $100M); $15,000 (Sustaining Company, for companies with revenue less than $100M); $5,000 (Associate Individual); $1,250 (Government).

Meetings/Conferences:
Conference Chair: Melanie Renner
Number of non-conference events/year: 10

Publications:
Membership Directory; on-line

Electronic Retailing Association *(1990)*
607 14th St. NW
Suite 530
Washington, DC 20005
Tel: (703) 841-1751 *Fax:* (425) 977-1036
TollFree: (800) 987-6462
E-Mail: info@retailing.org
Website: retailing.org
Members: 450 companies
Staff: 12
Annual Budget: $5-10,000,000
Tax: 501(c)(6)

Personnel:

President and Chief Executive Officer: Julie Coons
  E-Mail: jcoons@retailing.org
Manager, Meetings: Christy Hopkins
  E-Mail: chopkins@retailing.org
Chief Financial Officer and Chief Operating Officer: Kevin
  Kelly
  E-Mail: kevinkelly@retailing.org
Vice President, Marketing: Dave Martin
  E-Mail: dmartin@retailing.org
Content Manager: Vi Paynich
  E-Mail: vpaynich@retailing.org
Vice President, Sales and Group Show Director: Evan
  Shubin
  E-Mail: eshubin@retailing.org
Director, Membership Recruitment: Jennifer Williamson
  E-Mail: jwilliamson@retailing.org

Historical Note:
Formerly (1994) National Infomercial Marketing
Association and (1998) NIMA International. ERA promotes
the growth, development and acceptance of the electronic
retailing industry. Members (direct response companies and
their suppliers) are involved in infomercial and short-form
commercials, television shopping channels, and internet
and multimedia marketing. Membership: $1,500-24,750
(Retailer/Marketer); $1,500-26,750 (Industry Supplier);
$750-1,500 (Media/Network/Cable); $1,500 (Latin
American); $1,900-25,000 (ERA Europe/European
Union).

Meetings/Conferences:
Conference Chair: Christy Hopkins
2013 - Miami Beach, FL (Fontainebleau Miami Beach)/
  Feb. 25 - 27
2013 - Las Vegas, NV (Wynn Las Vegas)/Sept. 24 - 26

Publications:
Electronic Retailer Magazine; monthly
Member Directory; on-line

Membership List Available to Non-members

Electronic Security Association (1948)
6333 N.State Highway 161
Suite 350
Irving, TX 75038
Tel: (972) 807-6800 Fax: (972) 807-6883
Website: esaweb.org
Members: 2800 companies
Staff: 17
Annual Budget: $2-5,000,000
Tax: 501(c)(6)

Personnel:
Executive Director: Merlin J. Guilbeau
  E-Mail: Merlin.Guilbeau@ESAweb.org
Vice President: Tony Boudreau
  E-Mail: Tony.Boudreau@ESAweb.org
Director, Government Relations: John Chwat
  E-Mail: john.chwat@chwatco.com
Director, Information Technology: Lon Crozier
  E-Mail: lonc@alarm.org
Specialist, Membership Retention and Chapter Relations:
  Mike Hampton
  E-Mail: Mike.Hampton@ESAweb.org
Director, Communications, Public Relations and Marketing:
  Laurie A. Knox
  E-Mail: Laurie.Knox@ESAweb.org
Vice President, Sales and Marketing: Shannon Murphy
  E-Mail: Shannon.Murphy@ESAweb.org
Vice President, Training and Certification: Rick Sheets
Manager, Events: Michelle H. Whitaker
  E-Mail: Michelle.Whitaker@ESAweb.org

Historical Note:
Formerly National Burglar and Fire Alarm Association.
Established in 1948, the Electronic Security Association
(ESA), a non-profit 501(c) 6 trade association, has evolved
into the largest professional trade association in the United
States with the purpose of representing and enhancing
the growth and professional development of the electronic
life safety, security, and integrated systems industry.
In cooperation with a federation of state associations,
ESA provides government advocacy and delivers timely
information, professional development tools, products and
services. Membership: $228-3,283 (Regular); $625-3,500
(Associate); $100-2,000 (Affiliate).

Continuing Education:
Certification Designation/s: CST, CSI, CSS, CAT, CFAT

Meetings/Conferences:
Conference Chair: Michelle H. Whitaker
Number of non-conference events/year: 4

Publications:
ESA Integrator; weekly; adv.

Government Insider Newsletter; adv.
Newsline; adv.
NTS News; monthly; adv.
Stay Connected; adv.

Electronic Traders Association (1990)
1101 16th St. NW
Washington, DC 20036
Tel: (202) 828-2635 Fax: (202) 828-2639
TollFree: (800) 695-5509
Website: electran.org
Members: 500 companies
Staff: 7

Personnel:
Chief Executive Officer: Jason Oxman
Director, Membership and Marketing: Del Baker
Director, Government and Industry Relations: Mary
  Bennett
Director, Education: Rori Ferensic
Chief Financial Officer: Pamela Furneaux
Contact, Meeting Exhibition and Sponsorship: Jennifer Leo
Contact, Communications: Bradford Williamson

Historical Note:
ETA is the international trade association serving the needs
of organizations offering transaction processing products
and services. Membership: $ 800-4,000 (Service Providers,
based on gross revenue); $1,250-3,500 (Financial
Institutions, based on total assets).

Continuing Education:
Certification Designation/s: CPP

Meetings/Conferences: Annual
Conference Chair: Jennifer Leo
2013 - New Orleans, LA (New Orleans Convention
  Center)/April 30 - May 2
2014 - Las Vegas, NV (Mandalay Bay)/April 8 - 10

Publications:
e-newsletter; weekly
Membership Directory; on-line
Transaction Trends; monthly; adv.

Electronic Transactions Association (1990)
1101 16th St. NW
Washington, DC 20036
Tel: (202) 828-2635 Fax: (202) 828-2639
TollFree: (800) 695-5509
E-Mail: info@electran.org
Website: electran.org
Members: 500 companies
Staff: 9
Annual Budget: $2-5,000,000
Tax: 501(c)(6)

Personnel:
Chief Executive Officer: Jason Oxman
Director, Government and Industry Relations: Mary
  Bennett
  E-Mail: bennett@electran.org
Senior Director, Research and Information: Rob
  Drozdowski
  E-Mail: rob.drozdowski@electran.org
Director, Education: Rori Ferensic
  E-Mail: rori.ferensic@electran.org
Chief Financial Officer: Pamela Furneaux
Director, Communications and Public Relations: Thomas
  D. Goldsmith
  E-Mail: thomas.goldsmith@electran.org
Contact, Meeting Exhibition and Sponsorships: Jennifer
  Leo
  E-Mail: jleo@conferencemanagers.com
Director, Membership and Marketing: Del Baker
  Robinson
  E-Mail: del.baker@electran.org
Managing Editor: Jospehine Rossi
  E-Mail: jrossi@electran.org

Historical Note:
Formerly, the Bankcard Services Association, assumed
its current name in 1996. ETA's mission is to serve its
members and advance their profession by providing
leadership through education, advocacy and the exchange
of information. Members provide a full range of services
to qualified merchants, who act as intermediaries between
merchants and settlement banks. Membership: $800-4,000
(Service Providers); $1,250-3,500 (Financial Institutions).

Meetings/Conferences: Annual
Conference Chair: Jennifer Leo
2013 - New Orleans, LA (New Orleans Convention
  Center)/April 30 - May 2

2013 - Scottsdale, AZ (Montelucia Resort and Spa)/
  Oct. 15 - 17
2014 - Las Vegas, NV (Mandalay Bay)/April 8 - 10

Publications:
ETA Currents; weekly
Membership Directory; on-line
Transaction Trends; monthly; adv.

Electronics Representatives Association (1959)
111 N. Canal St.
Suite 885
Chicago, IL 60606
Tel: (312) 527-3050 Fax: (312) 559-4566
E-Mail: info@era.org
Website: era.org
Members: 5500 companies and individuals
Staff: 7
Annual Budget: $250-500,000
Tax: 501(c)(6)

Personnel:
Executive Vice President and Chief Executive Officer:
  Thomas J. Shanahan
  E-Mail: tshanahan@era.org
Operations Manager and Executive Assistant: Karin
  Derkacz
  E-Mail: kderkacz@era.org
Web Administrator and Director, Database: Katherine
  Green
  E-Mail: kgreen@era.org
Director, Membership Services: Jim Hartranft
  E-Mail: jhartranft@era.org
Coordinator, Communications, Conferences and Chapter
  Services: Tess Hill
  E-Mail: thill@era.org
Contact, Advertising and Public Relations: Larry Kaufman
Director, Finance: William R. Warfield
  E-Mail: bwarfield@era.org

Historical Note:
Founded as the Representatives of Radio Parts
Manufacturers, became the Representatives of Electronic
Parts Manufacturers in 1942 and assumed its present
name in 1959. ERA's mission is to support its members in
optimizing the professional outsourced field sales function
in the global electronics industry by providing programs
and activities that educate, inform and advocate for
manufacturers' representatives and the manufacturers they
represent. Membership: $400-600 (National); $150-400
(Chapter).

Continuing Education:
Certification Designation/s: CPMR, CSPC

Meetings/Conferences: Annual
Conference Chair: Tess Hill

Publications:
ERA Rep Locator; on-line
The Representor Magazine; on-line

Electronics Technicians Association International
(1978)
Five Depot St.
Greencastle, IN 46135
Tel: (765) 653-4301 Fax: (765) 653-4287
TollFree: (800) 288-3824
E-Mail: eta@eta-i.org
Website: eta-i.org
Members: 6000 individuals
Staff: 16
Annual Budget: $500-1,000,000
Tax: 501(c)(6)

Personnel:
President: Teresa Maher CSS
  E-Mail: teresa@eta-i.org
New Media Director and Operations Manager: Bryan
  Allen CSS
  E-Mail: ballen@eta-i.org
Coordinator, Marketing and Sales: Chrissy Baker CSS
  E-Mail: cbaker@eta-i.org
Director, Finance: Cindy Reed CSS
  E-Mail: creed@eta-i.org
Administrator, Certification and Coordinator, Membership
  Services: Lora Roberson CSS
  E-Mail: lroberson@eta-i.org

Historical Note:
ETA strives to provide the criteria which test the knowledge
and hands-on skills needed in today's industries.
Members are involved in such fields as medical, fiber
optics, industrial, computer, and military electronics,
as well as satellite and wireless communications and

telecommunications, sound equipment and other electronic service. Membership: $15-250/year.

Continuing Education:
Certification Designation/s: ETA

Meetings/Conferences: Annual
Conference Chair: Chrissy Baker CSS

Publications:
The High-Tech News; bi-monthly; adv.

Electrostatic Discharge Association *(1982)*
7900 Turin Rd.
Building Three
Rome, NY 13440-2069
Tel: (315) 339-6937 *Fax:* (315) 339-6793
E-Mail: info@esda.org
Website: esda.org
Members: 2000 individuals
Staff: 5
Annual Budget: $1-2,000,000

Personnel:
Director, Operations: Lisa Pimpinella
   E-Mail: lpimpinella@esda.org
Program Manager, Marketing and Communications: Terry Finn

Historical Note:
Formerly known as the Electrical Overstress/Electrostatic Discharge (EOS/ESD) Association. ESDA's mission is to advance the theory and practice of electrostatic discharge (ESD) avoidance. Members are government, industry and academic organizations involved in research and development, electronic equipment manufacturers and users and manufacturers and users of ESDA effects reduction products and methods. Membership: $60 (North America, including Canada and Mexico); $70 (Other Countries).

Continuing Education:
Certification Designation/s: iNARTE, CPPM, CPDD, S20

Meetings/Conferences:
Conference Chair: Terry Finn
2013 - Las Vegas, NV (Rio All-Suite Hotel and Casino)/ Feb. 5 - 10
2013 - St. Louis, MO (Hilton St. Louis Frontenac)/June 11 - 16
2013 - Las Vegas, NV (Rio All-Suite Hotel and Casino)/ Sept. 4 - 13
2014 - Tucson, AZ (Westin La Paloma Resort and Spa)/ Feb. 11 - 16
Number of non-conference events/year: 14

Publications:
Buyer's Guide; on-line
Threshold Newsletter; bi-monthly

Membership List Available to Non-members

Embroidery Trade Association *(1990)*
P.O. Box 794534
Dallas, TX 75379-4534
Fax: (972) 755-2561
TollFree: (888) 628-2545
E-Mail: info@embroiderytrade.org
Website: embroiderytrade.org
Members: 1000 companies
Staff: 2
Annual Budget: $250-500,000

Personnel:
Executive Director: John S. Swinburn CAE
   E-Mail: john@embroiderytrade.org
Manager, Membership Services: Dolores Cheek
   E-Mail: dolores@embroiderytrade.org

Historical Note:
ETA's mission is to strengthen the commercial embroidery business through member education, business support, representation, networking, research, and consumer outreach. Members are companies and individuals involved in the embroidery industry. Membership: $195-315 (Commercial Embroidery Companies); $315 (Digitizing Companies); $370 (Corporate Vendor Companies).

Publications:
Member Minute; weekly; adv.
Membership Directory; on-line

Emdr International Association *(1995)*
5806 Mesa Dr.
Suite 360
Austin, TX 78731
Tel: (512) 451-5200 *Fax:* (512) 451-5256
E-Mail: info@emdria.org
Website: emdria.org
Staff: 6

Annual Budget: $1-2,000,000

Personnel:
Executive Director: Mark G. Doherty
   E-Mail: mdoherty@emdria.org
Administrative Assistant: Clara Bensen
   E-Mail: cbensen@emdria.org
Communications Specialist: Nicole Evans
   E-Mail: nevans@emdria.org
Coordinator, Conference and Administrative: Jennifer Olson
   E-Mail: jolson@emdria.org
Coordinator, Membership Services: Lynn Simpson
   E-Mail: lsimpson@emdria.org
Coordinator, Education and Training: Sarah Tolino
   E-Mail: stolino@emdria.org

Historical Note:
The EMDR International Association (EMDRIA) is a membership organization of mental health professionals committed to the highest standards of excellence and integrity in EMDR. Membership: $125 (Associate Member); $50 (Student); $90 (Retired Member).

Continuing Education:
Certification Designation/s: EMDR

Meetings/Conferences: Annual
Conference Chair: Jennifer Olson
2013 - Austin, TX (Renaissance Austin Hotel)/Sept. 26 - 29
2014 - Denver, CO (Hyatt Regency Denver Convention Center)/Sept. 18 - 21

Publications:
EMDRIA Newsletter; quarterly; adv.

Emergency Department Practice Management Association (EDPMA) *(1997)*
8400 Westpark Dr.
Second Floor
McLean, VA 22102
Tel: (703) 610-0314 *Fax:* (703) 995-4678
E-Mail: info@edpma.org
Website: edpma.org
Staff: 4
Annual Budget: $500-1,000,000
Tax: 501(c)(6)

Personnel:
Executive Director: Linda T. Ayers, MHCM CAE
   E-Mail: layers@edpma.org
Senior Meetings Manager: Rebecca I. Fazzari CMP
   E-Mail: rfazzari@mmgevents.com
Director, Meetings: Annette M. Suriani CMP
   E-Mail: asuriani@mmgevents.com

Historical Note:
EDPMA's mission is to advocate for emergency department physician groups and their partners to enhance quality patient care through operational excellence and financial stability. Members are Emergency Department Physician Groups, ED Billing Companies, and Supporting Organizations that make their business to deliver quality care in the ED. Membership: $1,000- 40,000 (Physician Groups and Staffing companies-based on number of patient visits); $1,000-10,000 (Billing Companies-based on number of patient visits); $1,000-10,000 (Supporting organizations-based on ED related gross revenues); $1,000 (Affiliate).

Meetings/Conferences:
Conference Chair: Rebecca I. Fazzari CMP
Number of non-conference events/year: 1

Publications:
EDPMA Member Newsletter; on-line
Government Affairs Newsletter; on-line
Memberhip Directory; on-line

Membership List Available to Non-members

Emergency Medicine Residents' Association *(1974)*
1125 Executive Cir.
Irving, TX 75038-2522
Tel: (972) 550-0920 *Fax:* (972) 692-5995
TollFree: (866) 566-2492
E-Mail: emra@emra.org
Website: emra.org
Members: 10,613 individuals
Staff: 4
Annual Budget: $1-2,000,000
Tax: 501(c)(6)

Personnel:
Executive Director: Michele Packard-Milam CAE
   E-Mail: mpackardmilam@emra.org

Contact, Financial Services: Leanne Alford
   E-Mail: lalford@acep.org
Administrative Coordinator: Chalyce Bland
   E-Mail: gachilles@emra.org
Manager, Publications and Meetings: Leah Stefanini
   E-Mail: lstefanini@emra.org

Historical Note:
EMRA strives to promote excellence in patient care through the education and development of emergency medicine residency trained physicians. Members are physicians training in the specialty of emergency medicine, and medical students interested in emergency medicine. Membership: $105 (Resident); $55 (Student); $50 (Alumni); $25 (International).

Meetings/Conferences: Annual
Conference Chair: Leah Stefanini

Publications:
EM Resident; bi-monthly; adv.
What's Up in Emergency Medicine; monthly; adv.

Membership List Available to Non-members

Emergency Nurses Association *(1970)*
915 Lee St.
Des Plaines, IL 60016-6569
Tel: (847) 460-4095 *Fax:* (847) 460-4006
TollFree: (800) 900-9659
E-Mail: execoffice@ena.org
Website: ena.org
Members: 38000 individuals
Staff: 81
Annual Budget: $10-25,000,000
Tax: 501(c)(3)

Personnel:
Executive Director: Susan M. Hohenhaus MA, RN
   E-Mail: execoffice@ena.org
Editor in Chief: Amy Carpenter Aquino
   E-Mail: aaquino@ena.org
Director, Development and Foundation: Pierre Desy
   E-Mail: pdesy@ena.org
Manager, Exhibits: Linda Moustis
   E-Mail: lmoustis@ena.org
Chief Communications Strategist: Anthony Phipps
   E-Mail: aphipps@ena.org

Historical Note:
Formerly (1974) National Emergency Department Nurses Association and (1981) the Emergency Department Nurses Association. ENA's mission is to advocate for patient safety and excellence in emergency nursing practice. Membership: $100-121 (Active); $60-81 (Senior/Affiliate); $38-50 (Nursing Student); $100 (International); $90-111 (Military).

Continuing Education:
Certification Designation/s: CATN-II, ENPC, TNCC, CEN, CFRN

Meetings/Conferences:
Conference Chair: Linda Moustis
2013 - Nashville, TN (Gaylord Hotels Resorts and Convention Centers-Nashville)/Sept. 17 - 21

Publications:
ENA Connection; adv.
ENA NewsLine; on-line
Journal of Emergency Nursing; bi-monthly; adv.

Membership List Available to Non-members

Emerging Markets Private Equity Association *(2004)*
1077 30th St. NW
Suite 100
Washington, DC 20007
Tel: (202) 333-8171 *Fax:* (202) 333-3162
E-Mail: support@empea.net
Website: empea.net
Members: 258 firms
Staff: 13
Annual Budget: $2-5,000,000
Tax: 501(c)(6)

Personnel:
President and Chief Executive Officer: Sarah E. Alexander
   E-Mail: salexander@empea.net
Director, Marketing and Communications: Holly Freedman
   E-Mail: freedmanh@empea.net
Director, Research Department: Nadiya Satyamurthy
Director, Programs and Events: Shannon Stroud
   E-Mail: delanys@empea.net
Senior Manager, Member Services: Kyoko Terada
   E-Mail: teradak@empea.net

Historical Note:
EMPEA's mission is to catalyze private equity and venture capital investment in emerging markets. Members include the leading institutional investors and private equity and venture capital fund managers across developing and developed markets. Membership: $18,000-30,000 (Leadership); $3,500-12,500 (Fund Managers); $3,500 (Associate); $5,000-10,000 (Professional); $3,000 (Institutional).

Meetings/Conferences: Annual
Conference Chair: Shannon Stroud
Number of non-conference events/year: 5

Publications:
Membership Directory; on-line
NewsWatch; weekly

Emissions Control Technology Association (ECTA)
(2004)
325 Seventh St. NW
Suite 600
Washington, DC 20004
Tel: (202) 737-8885
E-Mail: info@ectausa.com
Website: ectausa.com
Staff: 1
Annual Budget: $250-500,000

Personnel:
President: Timothy J. Regan

Historical Note:
ECTA promotes public policies aimed at achieving cleaner air by reducing mobile source emissions through the use of state-of-the-art technologies. Member companies are involved in the emissions control market for substrates, catalysts, and diesel particulate filters.

Employee Assistance Professionals Association
(1971)
4350 N. Fairfax Dr.
Suite 410
Arlington, VA 22203
Tel: (703) 387-1000 Fax: (703) 522-4585
E-Mail: info@eap-association.org
Website: eapassn.org
Members: 900 companies and 7000 individuals
Staff: 8
Annual Budget: $1-2,000,000

Personnel:
Chief Executive Officer: John Maynard CEAP, PhD
    E-Mail: j.maynard@eapassn.org
Senior Director, Finance and Operations: Chris Drake
    E-Mail: c.drake@eapassn.org
Editor, Web Services: Marina London CEAP, LCSW
    E-Mail: m.london@eapassn.org
Operations Administrator: Earl Solloway
    E-Mail: e.solloway@eapassn.org
Director, Credentialing: Shirley Springfloat
    E-Mail: s.springfloat@eapassn.org
Manager, Advertising: Joan Treece
    E-Mail: admanager@eapassn.org

Historical Note:
Formerly (1989) Association of Labor-Management Administrators and Consultants on Alcoholism. EAPA's Mission is to develop the standards of practice and the continuing development of employee assistance professionals, programs, and services. Members are individuals involved in employee assistance programs. Membership: $160 (Professional/Retired/Associate-US); $140 (Non-Professional/Retired/Associate-US); $65 (Student); $345 (Organization); $160 (Government/Agency).

Continuing Education:
Certification Designation/s: CEAP

Meetings/Conferences: Annual

Publications:
Membership Directory; on-line
The Journal of Employee Assistance; quarterly; adv.

Employee Assistance Society of North America
(1985)
2001 Jefferson Davis Hwy.
Suite 1004
Arlington, VA 22202-3617
Tel: (703) 416-0060 Fax: (703) 416-0014
E-Mail: info@easna.org
Website: easna.org
Members: 300 individuals
Staff: 1
Annual Budget: $100-250,000

Personnel:
Executive Director: Bob McLean
    E-Mail: bmclean@easna.org

Historical Note:
EASNA is an association focused on advancing knowledge, research and best practices toward achieving healthy and productive workplaces. Members are professionals involved in employee assistance. Comprised of thought leaders and change agents, EASNA is focused on ensuring that the EA field continues to grow and flourish by broadening its base of engaged and committed stakeholders. Membership: $700-3,400 (Organizational); $700 (Affiliate); $199 (Individual); $100 (Student).

Continuing Education:
Certification Designation/s: EAP

Meetings/Conferences: Annual
2013 - Chicago, IL (Hotel Sax Chicago)/May 1 - 3

Publications:
EASNA Alert
Journal of Workplace Behavioral Health

Employee Benefit Research Institute (1978)
1100 13th St. NW
Suite 878
Washington, DC 20005-4051
Tel: (202) 659-0670 Fax: (202) 775-6312
E-Mail: info@ebri.org
Website: ebri.org
Members: 148 companies
Staff: 17
Annual Budget: $2-5,000,000
Tax: 501(c)(6)

Personnel:
President and Chief Executive Officer: Dallas L. Salisbury
    E-Mail: salisbury@ebri.org
Director, Education and External Relations: Nevin Adams
    E-Mail: NAdams@ebri.org
Director, Information Technology and Research Databases: Luis Alonso
    E-Mail: alonso@ebri.org
Communications Director and Managing Editor: Stephen Blakely
    E-Mail: blakely@ebri.org
Director, Library Resources: Martha Bobbino
    E-Mail: bobbino@ebri.org
Director, Administration: Patsy D'Amelio
    E-Mail: damelio@ebri.org
Director, Health Research and Education Programs: Paul Fronstin
    E-Mail: fronstin@ebri.org
Director, Media and Public Affairs: Tracey Young
    E-Mail: young@ebri.org

Historical Note:
EBRI is a nonprofit organization committed to data dissemination, research and education on economic security and employee benefits. EBRI's mission is to contribute, encourage, and to enhance the development of sound employee benefit programs and sound public policy through objective research and education. Members are businesses, plan sponsors, consultants and others interested in employee benefit plans. Membership: $28500 (Sustaining); $15000 (Full); $7500 (Associate); $4000 (Contributing).

Meetings/Conferences:
Number of non-conference events/year: 1

Publications:
401(k) Valuations
EBRI Notes; monthly
EBRI's Washington Bulletin (when Congress is in session); semi-monthly
Facts from EBRI; monthly
Issue Briefs; monthly
Pension Investment Report

Employee Services Management Association
P.O. Box 10517
Rockville, MD 20849
Tel: (630) 559-0020 Fax: (630) 559-0025
E-Mail: esmahq@esmassn.org
Website: esmassn.org
Members:
2000 companies
20 local chapters
Staff: 4
Annual Budget: Under $10,000
Tax: 501(c)(6)

Personnel:
Executive Director: Renee M. Mula
    E-Mail: reneemula@esmassn.org

Coordinator, Marketing: Daniela Kolev
    E-Mail: danielakolev@esmassn.org
Assistant, Member Development: Dorothy McGuire
    E-Mail: dorothymcguire@esmassn.org
Editor: Christina Sanchez
    E-Mail: christinasanchez@esmassn.org

Historical Note:
The Employee Morale and Recreation Association is currently serving members of the former ESM Association and any professional or company interested in supporting employee services programs. Membership: $400 (Corporate/Senior); $210 (General); $675 (National Associate); $30 (Student); $175 (Retiree); $70 (Academic Member); $150 (Community Service).

Continuing Education:
Certification Designation/s: CESP
Meetings/Conferences:
Number of non-conference events/year: 2

Publications:
Member Directory; on-line

Employee Stock Ownership Plan Association
(1978)
1726 M St. NW
Suite 501
Washington, DC 20036
Tel: (202) 293-2971 Fax: (202) 293-7568
TollFree: (866) 366-3832
E-Mail: esop@esopassociation.org
Website: esopassociation.org
Members: 2500 companies and professionals
Staff: 10

Personnel:
President: J. Michael Keeling CAE
    E-Mail: esop@esopassociation.org
Vice President, Membership: Lisa R. Betts CAE
    E-Mail: lisa@esopassociation.org
Vice President, Meetings and Conferences: Rosemary A. Clements
    E-Mail: rose@esopassociation.org
Director, Communications: Amy E. Gwiazdowski
    E-Mail: amy@esopassociation.org
Vice President, Administration: Gwenn E. Rosenthal
    E-Mail: gwenn@esopassociation.org
Chief Financial Officer: James M. Turner III
    E-Mail: jturner@esopassociation.org

Historical Note:
The ESOP Association has represented the interests of all corporations that sponsor employee stock ownership plans. ESOP's mission is to educate and advocate about employee ownership. Membership: $ 620-4,070 (Corporate, based on the number of participants); $565 (Affiliate); $675 (Professional Individual); $155 (Educational).

Meetings/Conferences:
Conference Chair: Rosemary A. Clements
2013 - Washington, DC (Renaissance Washington Hotel)/May 9 - 10

Publications:
ESOP "Employee Owned"
ESOP Report Newsletter; monthly; adv.
Eye On. ESOPs; quarterly
Membership Directory; on-line
The ESOP Report

Employer Associations of America
N19W24400 Riverwood Dr.
Waukesha, WI 53188-1166
Tel: (262) 696-3442
Website: eaa.site-ym.com
Staff: 2
Annual Budget: $50-100,000
Tax: 501(c)(6)

Personnel:
Executive Director: Vicki Vought
    E-Mail: Vicki.Vought@mranet.org
Financial Services: Pam Estergard
    E-Mail: pame@mranet.org

Historical Note:
National organization for employer associations. Members are employees of EAA member associations.

Employers Association (1917)
401 NE Jefferson Ave.
Peoria, IL 61603-3725
Tel: (309) 637-3333 Fax: (309) 637-3300
TollFree: (800) 948-5700
E-Mail: staff@eaconnect.com

Website: chamberorganizer.com/
  charlestonchamber/mem_
Members: 630 organizations
Staff: 21

Personnel:
President and Chief Executive Officer: Mary Pille CAE,
  SPHR
  E-Mail: mpille@eaconnect.com
Manager, Membership and Business Development: Kelly
  Popadziuk
  E-Mail: kpopadziuk@eaconnect.com

Historical Note:
*Employers' Association is a not-for-profit membership
organization serving the employer community. EA shares
national affiliation with National Industrial Council -
Employer Association Group. EA's mission is to help
employers maximize their human resources and also to
provide information, guidance and training. Membership:
$436-857/year.*

Meetings/Conferences: Annual

Publications:
Connections; monthly; adv.
eConnections; weekly; adv.

Employers Council on Flexible Compensation
(1981)
1444 I St. NW
Suite 700
Washington, DC 20005
Tel: (202) 659-4300 *Fax:* (877) 747-3539
E-Mail: support@ecfc.org
Website: ecfc.org
Members: 650 companies and organizations
Staff: 9
Annual Budget: $1-2,000,000
Tax: 501(c)(6)

Personnel:
Executive Director: David Carver
  E-Mail: david@ecfc.org
Executive Director: Natasha Rankin
  E-Mail: nrankin@ecfc.org
Director, Meetings and Expositions: Julie Elfand
  E-Mail: jelfand@bostrom.com
Coordinator, Membership Services: Emily Simmons
  E-Mail: esimmons@ecfc.org

Historical Note:
*ECFC focuses to preserve, protect and defend the tax-
advantaged programs currently available to working
families through employer plan sponsors. Membership:
$295 (Individual); $495 (Associate); $995 (Plan Sponsor);
$1,925-5,900 (Industry).*

Continuing Education:
Certification Designation/s: CFCI, CFC, FCS, CAS

Meetings/Conferences: Annual
Conference Chair: Julie Elfand
2013 - Washington, DC (Hyatt Regency Washington on
  Capitol Hill)/March 6 - 8
Number of non-conference events/year: 9

Publications:
ECFC Flex Reporter; quarterly
Membership Directory; on-line

Employers of America *(1976)*
310 Meadow Ln.
Mason City, IA 50401
Tel: (641) 424-3187 *Fax:* (641) 424-3187
TollFree: (800) 728-3187
E-Mail: employer@employerhelp.org
Website: employerhelp.org
Members: 500 businesses
Staff: 5
Annual Budget: $250-500,000

Personnel:
President: Jim Collison
Executive Vice President: Rita Haxmeier Collison

Historical Note:
*Formerly Independent Small Business Employers. EofA's
mission is to provide the tools and coaching that empower
people in their work, to cut costs, boost profits in their
businesses and organizations. Membership: $149/year
(Company).*

Publications:
Empowered@Work; monthly

**EMTA - Trade Association for the Emerging
Markets** *(1990)*
360 Madison Ave.

17th Floor
New York, NY 10017
Tel: (646) 289-5410 *Fax:* (646) 289-5429
E-Mail: sortiz@emta.org
Website: emta.org
Members: 150 institutions
Staff: 8
Annual Budget: $2-5,000,000
Tax: 501(c)(6)

Personnel:
Executive Director: Michael M. Chamberlin
  E-Mail: mchamberlin@emta.org
Managing Director: Jonathan R. Murno
  E-Mail: jmurno@emta.org
Office Manager and Coordinator, Membership Services:
  Suzette Ortiz
  E-Mail: sortiz@emta.org
Administrative Assistant: Evelyn Ramirez
  E-Mail: eramirez@emta.org
General Counsel: Aviva Werner
  E-Mail: awerner@emta.org

Historical Note:
*Formerly (1992) the Emerging Markets Traders Association,
assumed its current name in 2000. The mission of EMTA
is to promote the orderly development of fair, efficient and
transparent trading markets for EM instruments and to
help integrate EM into the global capital markets. Affiliate
Members are firms that have an interest in the emerging
markets trading and investment industry. Membership:
$30,000 (Sell- Side Full Member); $5,000-10,000 (Buy-
Side Full member); $15,000 (Associate); $5,000 (Affiliate).*

Meetings/Conferences:
Conference Chair: Evelyn Ramirez

Publications:
EMTA Bulletin; quarterly

Emulsion Polymers Council *(1995)*
1250 Connecticut Ave. NW
Suite 700
Washington, DC 20036
Tel: (202) 419-1500 *Fax:* (202) 659-8037
E-Mail: epc@regnet.com
Website: regnet.com/epc
Members: 9 companies
Staff: 1
Tax: 501(c)(6)

Personnel:
Executive Director: Robert J. Fensterheim CAE

Historical Note:
*EPC is dedicated to foster product stewardship with
customers and the regulatory community. Membership fee
varies, based on production.*

Publications:
Member Listing; on-line

Enactus
1959 E. Kerr St.
Springfield, MO 65803
Tel: (417) 831-9505
E-Mail: contact@enactus.org
Website: enactus.org
Staff: 67
Annual Budget: $10-25,000,000

Personnel:
President and Chief Executive Officer: Alvin Rohrs
  E-Mail: arohrs@enactus.org
Vice President, Human Resources: Nancy Bass
  E-Mail: nbass@enactus.org
Chief Marketing Officer: Mat Burton
  E-Mail: mburton@enactus.org

Historical Note:
*Enactus's mission is to bring together the knowledge
of professional business educators and the expertise of
business leaders to focus the potential of university students
preparing for leadership roles in business.*

Endocrine Fellows Foundation *(1990)*
1310 19th St. NW
Washington, DC 20036
Tel: (877) 877-6515 *Fax:* (860) 586-7550
TollFree: (877) 877-6515
E-Mail: info@endocrinefellows.org
Website: endocrinefellows.org
Members: 600 individuals
Staff: 2
Annual Budget: $500-1,000,000
Tax: 501(c)(3)

Personnel:
Executive Director and Media Contact: Anne L. Mercer
  E-Mail: amercer@endocrinefellows.org

Historical Note:
*EFF is dedicated to fostering the careers of fellows in
endocrinology, diabetes and metabolism through education,
research funding, career guidance and mentoring.*

Meetings/Conferences: Annual
2013 - San Francisco, CA/June 15 - 18
Number of non-conference events/year: 4

Publications:
EndoTrends
Member Directory; on-line

The Endocrine Society *(1916)*
8401 Connecticut Ave.
Suite 900
Chevy Chase, MD 20815-5817
Tel: (301) 941-0200 *Fax:* (301) 941-0259
TollFree: (888) 363-6274
E-Mail: societyservices@endo-society.org
Website: endo-society.org
Members: 14000 individuals
Staff: 70
Annual Budget: $25-50,000,000
Tax: 501(c)(3)

Personnel:
Executive Director and Chief Executive Officer: Scott Hunt
  E-Mail: shunt@endo-society.org
Director, Human Resources and Administrator: Julie
  Boynton
Senior Director, Corporate Relations: Nancy Chill
  E-Mail: nchill@endo-society.org
Senior Director, Marketing and Membership Services:
  Michael Dodd
  E-Mail: mdodd@endo-society.org
Director, Information Technology: Brian Fulmer
Deputy Executive Director and Chief Operating Officer:
  John R. Heberlein
  E-Mail: jheberlein@endo-society.org
Senior Director, Meetings and Education: Wanda Johnson
  E-Mail: wjohnson@endo-society.org
Deputy Executive Officer & Chief Policy Officer: Janet B.
  Kreizman
  E-Mail: jkreizman@endo-society.org
Senior Director, Publications: Rebecca Rinehart
  E-Mail: rrinehart@endo-society.org

Historical Note:
*Founded as the Association for Study of Internal Secretions.
ES's purpose is to research on hormones and the clinical
practice of endocrinology and also works to foster a greater
understanding of endocrinology amongst the general public
and practitioners of complementary medical disciplines
and to promote the interests of all endocrinologists at the
national scientific research and health policy levels of
government. Membership: $145 (Active-US); $183 (Active-
Outside the U.S.); $13 (Trainee); $105 (Associate-US);
$113 (Associate-Outside U.S.).*

Continuing Education:
Certification Designation/s: CME

Meetings/Conferences: Annual
Conference Chair: Wanda Johnson
2013 - San Francisco, CA/June 15 - 18
2014 - Chicago, IL/June 21 - 24
2015 - San Diego, CA/March 5 - 8

Publications:
Endocrine Reviews
Endocrinology
Hormones and Cancer; bi-monthly
Membership Directory; on-line
Molecular Endocrinology
The Journal of Clinical Endocrinology & Metabolism
  (JCEM)
Translational Endocrinology & Metabolism; quarterly

Membership List Available to Non-members

Energy and Environmental Building Association
(1982)
6520 Edenvale Blvd.
Suite 112
Eden Prairie, MN 55346
Tel: (952) 881-1098 *Fax:* (952) 881-3048
E-Mail: inquiry@eeba.org
Website: eeba.org
Members: 4000 individuals
Staff: 7
Annual Budget: $1-2,000,000

Tax: 501(c)(3)

Personnel:
Interim Executive Director: Karen Thull
  E-Mail: karen@eeba.org
Director, Operations: Jackie Alexander
  E-Mail: jackie@eeba.org
Director, Programs: Nancy Bakeman
  E-Mail: nancy@eeba.org

Historical Note:
Formerly (2001) Energy Efficient Building Association. EEBA's mission is to provide education and resources to transform the residential design, development and construction industries to profitably deliver energy efficient and environmentally responsible buildings and communities. Members are architects, builders, building material suppliers, and others with an interest in energy-efficient, environmentally responsible construction.

Continuing Education:
Certification Designation/s: ABID, AIA

Meetings/Conferences: Annual
Conference Chair: Nancy Bakeman
Number of non-conference events/year: 50

Publications:
EEBA Newsletter; quarterly

Membership List Available to Non-members

Energy Bar Association *(1946)*
1990 M St. NW
Suite 350
Washington, DC 20036
Tel: (202) 223-5625 *Fax:* (202) 833-5596
E-Mail: admin@eba-net.org
Website: eba-net.org
Members: 2400 individuals
Staff: 1
Annual Budget: $1-2,000,000
Tax: 501(c)(6)

Personnel:
Executive Director: Lorna Wilson

Historical Note:
Formerly (1946) Federal Power Bar Association and (1977) Federal Energy Bar Association. EBA's mission is to promote the professional excellence and ethical integrity of its members in the practice, administration, and development of energy laws, regulations and policies. Members are lawyers and non-attorney professionals. Membership: $145 (Attorney-Private Sector); $65 (Attorney-Government/ Academic Sector); $25 (Student); $100 (Law School); $145 (Non-Attorney Professional-Private Sector); $65 (Non- Attorney Professional-Government/Academic Sector).

Meetings/Conferences:
Number of non-conference events/year: 4

Publications:
EBA Update; quarterly
EDA Membership Directory; on-line
Energy Law Journal; semi-annually; adv.

Membership List Available to Non-members

Energy Frontiers International *(1980)*
1425 K St. NW
Washington, DC 20005
Tel: (202) 587-5780
E-Mail: secretariat@energyfrontiers.org
Website: energyfrontiers.org
Members: 56 companies
Staff: 3
Annual Budget: $250-500,000
Tax: 501(c)(6)

Personnel:
President: Christopher Kidder

Historical Note:
Formerly (1996) the Council on Alternate Fuels. EFI provides technology forums, site visits and networking opportunities for companies interested in an unbiased assessment of the commercial status of important energy processes, fuels, and technologies, their commercial readiness, relative competitive position, and deployment prospects.

Meetings/Conferences: Annual

Membership List Available to Non-members

Energy Programs Consortium
1232 31st St. NW
Washington, DC 20007
Tel: (202) 333-5915
E-Mail: info@energyprograms.org

Website: energyprograms.org
Staff: 6
Annual Budget: $1-2,000,000
Tax: 501(c)(3)

Personnel:
Executive Director: Mark Wolfe
  E-Mail: mlwolfe@energyprograms.org
Contact, Legal and Tax Counsel: Elizabeth Bellis
  E-Mail: ebellis@energyprograms.org

Historical Note:
It is a joint venture of the National Association of State Community Services Programs (NASCSP), National Association of State Energy Officials (NASEO), National Association of State Regulatory Utility Commissioners (NARUC) and National Energy Assistance Directors' Association (NEADA). EPC's purpose is to foster coordination and cooperation among state and federal agencies in the areas of energy policy and program development.

Energy Recovery Council *(1991)*
1730 Rhode Island Ave. NW
Suite 700
Washington, DC 20036
Tel: (202) 467-6240 *Fax:* (202) 289-3588
E-Mail: energyrecoverycouncil.org
Website: energyrecoverycouncil.org
Members: 86 modern waste-to-energy facilities
Staff: 3
Annual Budget: $500-1,000,000
Tax: 501(c)(6)

Personnel:
President: Edward "Ted" Michaels
  E-Mail: tmichaels@energyrecoverycouncil.org

Historical Note:
Formerly the Integrated Waste Services Association and renamed as Energy Recovery Council (ERC).The Energy Recovery Council is a national trade organization representing the waste-to-energy industry and communities that own waste-to-energy facilities. Membership: $6000 (Corporate); $3000 (Business); $1000 (Small Business); $750 (Municipal).

Energy Security Council *(1981)*
2611 FM 1960 West
Suite F-121
Houston, TX 77068
Tel: (281) 587-2700 *Fax:* (281) 587-2715
E-Mail: info@energysecuritycouncil.org
Website: energysecuritycouncil.org
Members: 472 Individuals and Companies
Staff: 2
Annual Budget: $250-500,000

Personnel:
President and Chief Executive Officer: David Moore
Vice President Corporate Security: Alex de Alvarez

Historical Note:
Founded as Petroleum Industry Security Council; assumed its current name in 1999. ESC's mission is to identify serious security and operational issues and then offer practical, time-tested solutions.ESC purpose is to enhance the safety, security and business operations of its members, companies, corporations and their associates. Membership: $180 (Individual); $300 (Small Company); $600 (Medium Company); $1,500 (Large Company/Corporation).

Meetings/Conferences: Semi-Annual

Publications:
Membership Directory; on-line

Energy Solutions Center *(2003)*
400 N. Capitol St. NW
Fourth Floor
Washington, DC 20001
Tel: (202) 824-7152 *Fax:* (202) 824-7096
Website: energysolutionscenter.org
Members: 87 equipment manufacturers and energy utilities
Staff: 5
Annual Budget: $1-2,000,000
Tax: 501(c)(6)

Personnel:
Executive Director: David Weiss
  E-Mail: dweiss@escenter.org
Conference Planner: Leslie Auerbach
  E-Mail: lauerbach@escenter.org
Director, Industrial Markets: Richard Biljetina
  E-Mail: biljet@att.net
Director, Commercial and Residential Markets: Eric Burgis

E-Mail: eburgis@escenter.org
Coordinator, Contracts and Office Administration: Jennifer Couto
  E-Mail: jcouto@escenter.org

Historical Note:
ESC's mission is to accelerate the acceptance and deployment of new energy-efficient, gas-fueled technologies that enhance the operations and productivity of commercial and industrial energy users, and improve comfort and reliability for residential energy users.Membership: $1500 (Affiliate); $1000-$30,000 (Corporate based on energy utility).

Meetings/Conferences:
Conference Chair: Jennifer Couto
Number of non-conference events/year: 2

Publications:
Gas Technology Magazine
Gas Technology Magazine; quarterly; adv.
Natural Living Magazine; quarterly

Energy Storage Council
3963 Flora Pl.
Second Floor
Saint Louis, MO 63110
Tel: (314) 495-4545
E-Mail: info@energystoragecouncil.org
Website: energystoragecouncil.org
Staff: 3

Personnel:
Executive Director and Director, Publications and Communications: Jason Makansi
  E-Mail: jmakansi@pearlstreetinc.com
Staff Consultant: Septimus van der Linden
  E-Mail: brulinassoc@comcast.net
Media Director: Robert Schwieger
  E-Mail: bob@psimedia.info

Historical Note:
ESC's mission is to promote the research, development and deployment of storage technologies as well as to raise awareness of the importance of storage for the future of America's electricity supply and energy security.

Energy Telecommunications and Electrical Association *(1928)*
5005 Royal Ln.
Suite 116
Irving, TX 75063
Tel: (972) 929-3169 *Fax:* (972) 915-6040
TollFree: (888) 503-8700
E-Mail: entelec@entelec.org
Website: entelec.org
Members: 140 companies
Staff: 4
Annual Budget: $500-1,000,000

Personnel:
Executive Manager: Blaine Siske
  E-Mail: blaine@entelec.org
Coordinator, Sales and Operations: Tiffany Chase
  E-Mail: tiffany@entelec.org
Manager, Exhibits: Susan Joiner
  E-Mail: susan@entelec.org
Association Manager: Amanda Prudden
  E-Mail: amanda@entelec.org

Historical Note:
Formerly (1978) the Petroleum Industry Electrical Association. ENTELEC's purpose is to provide education for its members. Members are companies and corporations in the energy industries employing personnel having managerial, engineering or technical responsibility in the electrical, electronics, communications and allied fields. Membership: $495 (Corporate/Associate); $250 (Individual).

Meetings/Conferences: Annual
Conference Chair: Susan Joiner
2013 - Houston, TX (George R. Brown Center)/April 9 - 11
Number of non-conference events/year: 1

Publications:
ENTELEC News; on-line
Membership Directory; on-line
Supplier Directory; on-line

Energy Traffic Association *(1997)*
935 Eldridge Rd.
Suite 604
Sugar Land, TX 77478
Tel: (832) 474-3564 *Fax:* (713) 464-0702
Website: energytraffic.org

Members: 100 Companies
Staff: 1
Annual Budget: $25-50,000
Tax: 501(c)(6)

Personnel:
Executive Director and Contact, Membership Services:
Russell Powell
E-Mail: russell@energytraffic.org

Historical Note:
Formed by the merger of two former trade associations namely OSTA and SOFTA (1923) and (1941) respectively. ETA's mission is to maintain service stability and control costs in the transportation industry. Membership: $75 (Individual); $150 (Company).

Meetings/Conferences: Annual
Conference Chair: Russell Powell

Publications:
ETA Newsletter

Engineering College Magazines Associated (1920)
Institute for Mathematics and its Applications,
College of Science and Engineering
207 Church St. SE, 306 Lind Hall
Minneapolis, MN 55455
Tel: (612) 624-6066 *Fax:* (612) 626-7370
E-Mail: ecma@it.umn.edu
Website: ecmaweb.org
Members: 10 colleges of engineering
Staff: 1
Annual Budget: Under $10,000

Personnel:
Correspondent: Norma Jean MacPhee

Historical Note:
ECMA was found as a way by which engineering companies could attract engineering graduates through the publications that undergraduate engineering students produced. Grants acclaim to student engineering publications and allowes students access to many top workers in the publication industry, as well as the knowledge they possess.

Enhanced Protective Glass Automotive Association
400 Guys Run Rd.
Cheswick, PA 15024-9464
Website: epgaa.com
Staff: 3
Annual Budget: $100-250,000
Tax: 501(c)(6)

Personnel:
President: Pete Dishart
Treasurer: Chuck Butler
Contact, Public Relations: Marc Harlow
E-Mail: Marc@HarlowPR.com

Historical Note:
The Enhanced Protective Glass Automotive Association (EPGAA) is comprised of interlayer and glass providers that work to educate consumers, automakers and government officials on the benefits of laminated glass.

Enlisted Association of the National Guard of the United States (1972)
3133 Mount Vernon Ave.
Alexandria, VA 22305-2640
Tel: (703) 519-3846 *Fax:* (703) 519-3849
TollFree: (800) 234-3264
E-Mail: eangus@eangus.org
Website: eangus.org
Members: 84000 individuals
Staff: 7
Annual Budget: $1-2,000,000
Tax: 501(c)(19)

Personnel:
Executive Director: Al Garver
E-Mail: Executive-Director@eangus.org
Director, Membership Services and Chief of Staff: Bryan Birch
E-Mail: bbirch@eangus.org
Manager, Conference Operations: Brad Thomas
E-Mail: bthomas@eangus.org
Director, Government Affairs: Seth Waugh
E-Mail: seth.waugh@eangus.org

Historical Note:
National Guard Advocacy Association

Meetings/Conferences: Annual
Conference Chair: Brad Thomas

2013 - Sioux Falls, SD (Sioux Falls Convention Center)/
Aug. 18 - 21
2014 - Phoenix, AZ (Phoenix Convention Center)/Aug.
10 - 13
Number of non-conference events/year: 4

Publications:
Legislative Updates; weekly; adv.
Membership Directory; on-line
Minuteman Updates; on-line
The New Patriot; quarterly; adv.
The Signal; monthly

Enterprise Wireless Alliance (1953)
8484 Westpark Dr.
Suite 630
McLean, VA 22102
Fax: (703) 524-1074
TollFree: (800) 886-4222
Website: enterprisewireless.org
Members: 3100 licensed dealers
Staff: 30
Annual Budget: $2-5,000,000
Tax: 501(c)(6)

Personnel:
President and Chief Executive Officer: Mark E. Crosby
Senior Vice President: Andre F. Cote
E-Mail: andre@ita-relay.com
Director, Membership Development: Nancy Gruen
Vice President, Corporate Operations: Eric Hill

Historical Note:
The Enterprise Wireless Alliance (EWA), formerly ITA and AMTA, works to preserve spectrum rights and access for enterprise wireless customers. EWA's mission is to assist enterprise business users, dealers, service providers, and technology vendors and manufacturers in the deployment of wireless communications solutions that drive corporate productivity in the enterprise wireless space. Membership: $200-3000 (Business Enterprise Users); $445 (Wireless Manufacturer Representative/Distributor); $495-10000 (Wireless Sales/Service Providers); $1500-10000 (Vendor).

Meetings/Conferences: Annual

Publications:
Wireless Connections; quarterly
Wireless Insider; bi-weekly

Entertainment Merchants Association (1981)
16530 Ventura Blvd.
Suite 400
Encino, CA 91436-4551
Tel: (818) 385-1500 *Fax:* (818) 933-0910
E-Mail: ema@entmerch.org
Website: entmerch.org
Members: 200 companies
Staff: 10
Annual Budget: $2-5,000,000
Tax: 501(c)(6)

Personnel:
President and Chief Executive Officer: Crossan R. Andersen
E-Mail: bandersen@entmerch.org
Vice President, Public Affairs: Sean Devlin Bersell
E-Mail: sbersell@entmerch.org
Vice President, Marketing and Industry Relations: Carrie Dieterich
E-Mail: cdieterich@entmerch.org
Vice President, Membership Services: Frank Lucca
E-Mail: flucca@entmerch.org

Historical Note:
EMA was established through the merger of the Video Software Dealers Association (VSDA) and the Interactive Entertainment Merchants Association (IEMA). Mission is to protect the right to sell and rent entertainment products and content; promote the sale and rental of entertainment products and content. Membership comprises the full spectrum of retailers, distributors, the home video divisions of major and independent motion picture studios, video game publishers, and other related businesses that constitute and support the home entertainment industry. Membership: $500-35,000 (Retailer); $200-50,000 (Associate); $700 (Distributor); $160-5,000 (International).

Meetings/Conferences:
Conference Chair: Carrie Dieterich

Publications:
Inside; quarterly
Monthly Update; monthly

Entertainment Software Association (ESA) (1994)

575 Seventh St. NW
Suite 300
Washington, DC 20004
Tel: (202) 223-2400 *Fax:* (202) 223-2401
E-Mail: esa@theesa.com
Website: theesa.com
Members: 34 companies
Staff: 30
Annual Budget: $25-50,000,000
Tax: 501(c)(6)

Personnel:
President and Chief Executive Officer: Michael D. Gallagher
Executive Director: Danielle LaBossiere Parr
Contact, Communications: Dan Hewitt CAE
E-Mail: dhewitt@theESA.com
Coordinator, Public Relations and Membership Services: Jeannette Holder
Senior Vice President, Government Affairs: Erik V. Huey
E-Mail: ehuey@theesa.com
Director, Public Relations: Julien Lavoie

Historical Note:
ESA's mission is to support positive programs and opportunities that make a difference in the lives of America's youth. It offers a range of services to interactive entertainment software publishers including a global anti-piracy program, business and consumer research, government relations and intellectual property protection efforts. ESA also owns and operates E3.

Meetings/Conferences: Annual
2013 - Los Angeles, CA (Los Angeles Convention Center)/June 11 - 13

Publications:
ESA Newsletter; monthly
Membership Directory; on-line

Membership List Available to Non-members

Entomological Society of America (1889)
10001 Derekwood Ln.
Suite 100
Lanham, MD 20706-4876
Tel: (301) 731-4535 *Fax:* (301) 731-4538
E-Mail: esa@entsoc.org
Website: entsoc.org
Members: 6,400 members
Staff: 14
Annual Budget: $2-5,000,000
Tax: 501(c)(3)

Personnel:
Executive Director: C. David Gammel CAE
E-Mail: dgammel@entsoc.org
Assistant, Meetings and Membership Services: Mary Falcone
E-Mail: mfalcone@entsoc.org
Director, Communications and Managing Editor: Alan Kahan
E-Mail: akahan@entsoc.org
Manager, Membership Services and Member Relations: Pamela Reid
E-Mail: preid@entsoc.org
Director, Meetings: Rosina Romano
E-Mail: meet@entsoc.org
Director, Membership Services and Marketing: Debra Sutton
E-Mail: dsutton@entsoc.org
Director, Finance: Neil Willoughby
E-Mail: nwilloughby@entsoc.org

Historical Note:
Formed by the consolidation of the American Association of Economic Entomologists and the Entomological Society of America. ESA serves the professional and scientific needs of entomologists and people in related disciplines. In 1992 the American Registry of Professional Entomologists became the certification program of the ESA. Membership: $138 (Regular); $34 (Student); $210 (Family); $276 (President's Circle); $69 (Emeritus/Student Transition); $35 (Emeritus Gold); $103 (Early Professional); $500-3,000 (Sustaining Associate).

Continuing Education:
Certification Designation/s: ACE, BCE

Meetings/Conferences: Annual
Conference Chair: Mary Falcone
2013 - Austin, TX (Austin Convention Center)/Nov. 17 - 20/2500 attendees/51-100 exhibitors
2014 - Portland, OR/Nov. 16 - 19/3000 attendees/26-50 exhibitors
2015 - Minneapolis, MN/Nov. 14 - 18

Number of non-conference events/year: 1

Publications:
American Entomologist; quarterly; adv.
Annals of ESA; bi-monthly; adv.
Arthropod Management Tests; annually
eNews; on-line
Environmental Entomology; bi-monthly; adv.
Journal of Economic Entomology; bi-monthly; adv.
Journal of Integrated Pest Management; on-line; adv.
Journal of Medical Entomology; bi-monthly; adv.
Member Directory; on-line

Membership List Available to Non-members

Entrepreneurs' Organization (1987)

500 Montgomery St.
Suite 700
Alexandria, VA 22314
Tel: (703) 519-6700 Fax: (703) 519-1864
E-Mail: info@eonetwork.org
Website: eonetwork.org
Members: 8000 individuals
Staff: 50
Annual Budget: $10-25,000,000
Tax: 501(c)(3)

Personnel:
Executive Director: Bob Strader
Vice President of Membership Development: Miranda
  Barrett
  E-Mail: mbarrett@eonetwork.org
Senior Vice President, Global Membership: Brian
  Costanzo
  E-Mail: acocuzza@eonetwork.org

Historical Note:
Founded as the Young Entrepreneurs Organization;
assumed its current name in 2007. EO's mission is to help
entrepreneurs to learn and grow from each other, leading to
business success and to provides education and professional
support to businesspeople who are founders or controlling
shareholders of their businesses. Membership, by invitation
only and is restricted to executives under the age of 50
whose companies have gross annual sales of $1 million or
more.

Meetings/Conferences: Annual
Number of non-conference events/year: 4

Publications:
Membership Directory; on-line
Octane; quarterly
Overdrive e-newsletter; monthly

The Entrepreneurship Institute (1976)

3700 Corporate Dr.
Suite 145
Columbus, OH 43231
Tel: (614) 895-1153
E-Mail: info@tei.net
Website: tei.net
Staff: 1
Annual Budget: $500-1,000,000
Tax: 501(c)(3)

Personnel:
President: Jan Zupnick
  E-Mail: janz@tei.net

Historical Note:
TEI's mission is to provide unlimited opportunities for
business owners to acquire knowledge, experience and
resources needed to grow their firms and create new jobs
in their communities. Dedicated to meeting the business
information and networking needs of presidents and CEOs
leading America's small and mid-market companies.

Envelope Manufacturers Association (1933)

500 Montgomery St.
Suite 550
Alexandria, VA 22314-2530
Tel: (703) 739-2200 Fax: (703) 739-2209
Website: envelope.org
Members: 250 companies
Staff: 7
Annual Budget: $1-2,000,000

Personnel:
President and Chief Executive Officer: Maynard H.
  Benjamin CAE
  E-Mail: mhbenjamin@envelope.org
Office Manager: Margaret C. Benjamin
  E-Mail: mcbenjamin@envelope.org
Director, Member Services and GEA Administrator: Jackie
  Jordan

E-Mail: jejordan@envelope.org
Assistant Director, Industry Research and Accounting:
  Barbara M. Monson
  E-Mail: bmmonson@envelope.org
Director, Education and Meetings: Kim Moses
  E-Mail: kmoses@envelope.org

Historical Note:
EMA was formed by a merger of the American Envelope
Manufacturers Association (founded in 1909) and the
Bureau of Envelope Manufacturers (founded in 1916).
Formerly (1995) Envelope Manufacturers Association
of America. EMA seeks to share knowledge of envelope
manufacturing among the association and produce
programs to improve manufacturing efficiency. Membership:
$150 (Regular); $1,200-12,000 (Associate); $750-10,000
(International Affiliate); $2,000-20,000 (North American
Affiliate).

Meetings/Conferences:
Conference Chair: Kim Moses
2013 - Orlando, FL (Ritz-Carlton Orlando, Grande
  Lakes)/April 17 - 20

Publications:
EMA Report; on-line
Management Information Briefing; bi-monthly

Environmental and Energy Study Institute (1984)

1112 16th St. NW
Suite 300
Washington, DC 20036-4819
Tel: (202) 628-1400 Fax: (202) 204-5244
E-Mail: info@eesi.org
Website: eesi.org
Staff: 10
Annual Budget: $2-5,000,000
Tax: 501(c)(3)

Personnel:
Executive Director: Carol Werner
  E-Mail: cwerner@eesi.org
Coordinator, Communications: Amaury Laporte
  E-Mail: alaporte@eesi.org
Director, Finance and Administration: David Robison
  E-Mail: drobison@eesi.org

Historical Note:
EESI is a non-profit organization established by a
bipartisan Congressional caucus to provide timely
information and develop innovative policy solutions that set
us on a cleaner, more secure and sustainable energy path.

Publications:
Climate Change News; weekly
EESI Update
Sustainable Bioenergy, Farms, and Forests; weekly

Environmental and Engineering Geophysical Society (1992)

1720 S. Bellaire St.
Suite 110
Denver, CO 80222-4303
Tel: (303) 531-7517 Fax: (303) 820-3844
E-Mail: staff@eegs.org
Website: eegs.org
Members: 700 individuals
Staff: 3
Annual Budget: $250-500,000
Tax: 501(c)(3)

Personnel:
Executive Director: Kathie Barstnar
  E-Mail: kbarstnar@wmrdenver.com
Coordinator, Meetings and Event: Jayma File
  E-Mail: jfile@wmrdenver.com
Managing Director: Jackie Jacoby
  E-Mail: jjacoby@wmrdenver.com

Historical Note:
EEGS's mission is to promote the science of geophysics
especially as it is applied to environmental and engineering
problems and to foster common scientific interests of
geophysicists and their colleagues in other related sciences
and engineering. Members are individuals and corporations
with an interest in geophysics and applied environmental
engineering. Membership: $20-4,000/year.

Meetings/Conferences: Annual
Conference Chair: Jayma File
2013 - Denver, CO (Denver Marriott Tech Center)/
  March 17 - 21

Publications:
FastTimes; quarterly; adv.
The Journal of the Environmental and Engineering
  Geophysics; quarterly; adv.

Membership List Available to Non-members

Environmental and Water Resources Institute of the American Society of Civil Engineers (1999)

1801 Alexander Bell Dr.
Reston, VA 20191-4400
Tel: (703) 295-6380 Fax: (703) 295-6371
E-Mail: ewri@asce.org
Website: asce.org/ewri
Members: 26,000 members
Staff: 285
Annual Budget: $25-50,000,000

Personnel:
Director: Brian K. Parsons PE
Board and Meetings Specialist: Sara Hagan
Manager: Ann Rountree

Historical Note:
EWRI promotes the sustainable use, conservation, and
protection of natural resources; and promotes human well-
being. EWRI works to provide for the technical, educational
and professional needs of its members. EWRI is a civil
engineering specialty institute of the American Society of
Civil Engineers ASCE. Membership: $500 (Organizational
Membership); $85 (EWRI-Only Membership).

Meetings/Conferences:
Conference Chair: Sara Hagan
Number of non-conference events/year: 2

Publications:
E-updates; monthly
EWRI's 'Currents' newsletter; quarterly

Environmental Assessment Association

P.O. Box 879
Palm Springs, CA 92263
Tel: (760) 327-5284 Fax: (760) 327-5631
TollFree: (877) 810-5643
E-Mail: info@eaa-assoc.org
Website: eaa-assoc.org
Members: 7500 individuals
Staff: 1
Annual Budget: $1-2,000,000

Personnel:
Executive Director: Troy E. Johnson

Historical Note:
EAA is dedicated to provide members with information
and education in the environmental industry relating
to environmental inspections and testing. Members are
environmental inspectors and other professionals, primarily
in the real estate industry, involved in environmental hazard
detection and mitigation. Membership: $195/year.

Continuing Education:
Certification Designation/s: CEI, CES, CTS, CMS, CRS,
CEM, CAQS

Publications:
EAA Newsletter; on-line

Environmental Bankers Association (1994)

510 King St.
Suite 410
Alexandria, VA 22314
Tel: (703) 549-0977 Fax: (703) 548-5945
TollFree: (800) 966-7475
E-Mail: eba@envirobank.org
Website: envirobank.org
Members: 110 banks and affiliates
Staff: 5
Annual Budget: $250-500,000

Personnel:
Executive Co-Director: D. J. Telego
  E-Mail: jefftelego@envirobank.org
Executive Co-Director: Tacy Telego
  E-Mail: Tacytelego@envirobank.org
Treasurer: Scott Beckerman
  E-Mail: jsbeckerman@comerica.com
General Counsel: Dan Richardson
  E-Mail: drichardson@llw-law.com
Secretary and Communication: Stephen Richardson
  E-Mail: stephen.richardson@tdbanknorth.com

Historical Note:
EBA's mission is to protect and preserve bank net income
and assets from environmental exposure and liability
resulting from lending and trust activities through the
employment of environmental risk management in the
U.S. and worldwide. EBA voting members are banks, trust
companies, credit unions, savings and loan associations,
and other financial services organizations with an interest
in environmental risk management and related issues.
Membership: $320-1,500 (Financial Institutions);
$320-1,555 (Affiliate).

Meetings/Conferences:
2013 - New Orleans, LA (Astor Crowne Plaza)/Jan. 19 - 23
2013 - Orlando, FL/Jan. 19 - 21
2013 - San Francisco, CA/June 9 - 11

Publications:
EBA Alerts; on-line
EBA BankNotes; on-line

Environmental Council of the States (1993)
50 F St. NW
Suite 350
Washington, DC 20001
Tel: (202) 266-4920 *Fax:* (202) 266-4937
E-Mail: ecos@sso.org
Website: ecos.org
Staff: 14
Annual Budget: $2-5,000,000
Tax: 501(c)(6)

Personnel:
Executive Director: R. Steven Brown
Senior Counselor: Jim Blizzard
    E-Mail: jblizzard @ ecos.org
Office and Grants Manager: Joanne Key
    E-Mail: jkey @ ecos.org
Comptroller: Neomi Levy
    E-Mail: nlevy @ ecos.org
Senior Project Manager: Lia Parisien
Administrative Assistant: Carolyn Sistare
    E-Mail: csistare @ ecos.org

Historical Note:
ECOS's purpose is to improve the capability of state environmental agencies and their leaders to protect and improve human health and the environment of the United States of America.

Meetings/Conferences: Annual
2013 - Scottsdale, AZ (FireSky Resort and Spa)/March 4 - 6

Publications:
ECOStates Index; quarterly
ECOSWIRE; weekly

Environmental Design Research Association (1968)
1760 Old Meadow Rd.
Suite 500
McLean, VA 22102
Tel: (703) 506-2895 *Fax:* (703) 506-3266
E-Mail: edra@edra.org
Website: edra.org
Members: 700 individuals
Staff: 4
Annual Budget: $250-500,000

Personnel:
Executive Director: Kate O'Donnell
    E-Mail: kodonnell@edra.org
Manager, Resource Development: Tricia Gonzales
    E-Mail: resourcedevelopment@edra.org
Coordinator, Membership Services: Magda Halim
    E-Mail: mhalim@edra.org
Senior Events Manager: Kartraice D. Hooper CMP
    E-Mail: khooper@edra.org

Historical Note:
EDRA's mission is to advance the art and science of environmental design research, to improve understanding of the interrelationships between people and their built and natural surroundings, and to help create environments responsive to human needs. EDRA members are designers and other professionals with an interest in environmental design research. Membership: $175 (Regular); $500 (Placemaker); $300 (Wayfinder); $75 (Student/Emeritus/ Young Professional); $3000 (Lifetime).

Meetings/Conferences: Annual
Conference Chair: Kartraice D. Hooper CMP
2013 - Providence, RI (The Westin Providence Hotel)/ May 29 - June 1
Number of non-conference events/year: 8

Publications:
EDRA Reader newsletter
eDRN; weekly
Journal of Architecture and Planning Research
Journal of Environmental Planning and Management
Journal of Planning Literature
Landscape Journal

Environmental Industry Associations (1962)
4301 Connecticut Ave. NW

Suite 300
Washington, DC 20008
Tel: (202) 244-4700 *Fax:* (202) 966-4824
TollFree: (800) 424-2869
E-Mail: membership@envasns.org
Website: environmentalistseveryday.org
Members: 2000 companies
Staff: 35
Annual Budget: $5-10,000,000
Tax: 501(c)(6)

Personnel:
President and Chief Executive Officer: Sharon H. Kneiss
    E-Mail: skneiss@envasns.org
General Counsel and Director, Safety: David Biderman
    E-Mail: davidb@nswma.org
Director, Membership Services: Christine Hutcherson
    E-Mail: chutcherson@envasns.org
Director, Education: Alice Jacobsohn
    E-Mail: alicej@nswma.org
Contact, Publication Sales: Carey Lawrence
    E-Mail: clawrence@nswma.org
Manager, Meetings: Catherine Maimon
    E-Mail: cmaimon@nswma.org
Director, Communications and Public Affairs: Thom Metzger
    E-Mail: tmetzger@nswma.org

Historical Note:
Formerly (1994) National Solid Wastes Management Association. Restructured in 1994. EIA represents companies and individuals who manage solid and medical wastes, manufacture and distribute waste equipment, and provide environmental management, consulting and pollution-prevention- related services. EIA now includes the National Solid Waste Management Association (NSWMA) and the Waste Equipment Technology Association (WASTEC). Membership in EIA is open to state, county, city and district solid waste planning professionals and international companies. Membership: $150 (Affiliate, Individual); $600 (Associate, Corporate).

Meetings/Conferences:
Conference Chair: Catherine Maimon
Number of non-conference events/year: 6

Publications:
E-News; weekly; adv.
Membership Directory
Safety Monday; weekly
Waste Industry News; quarterly

The Environmental Information Association (1983)
6935 Wisconsin Ave.
Suite 306
Chevy Chase, MD 20815-6112
Tel: (301) 961-4999 *Fax:* (301) 961-3094
TollFree: (888) 343-4342
E-Mail: info@eia-usa.org
Website: eia-usa.org
Members:
280 companies
500 individuals
Staff: 5
Annual Budget: $250-500,000

Personnel:
Managing Director: Brent Kynoch
    E-Mail: bkynoch@eia-usa.org
Manager, Membership and Marketing: Kimberly Goodman
    E-Mail: kgoodman@eia-usa.org
Bookkeeper: Kelly Holston
    E-Mail: ibruce@kynoch.com
Administrative Assistant: Nehmesah Israel
    E-Mail: nisrael@eia-usa.org
Manager, Development and Communications: Kelly Rutt
    E-Mail: krutt@kynoch.com

Historical Note:
Formerly (1991) National Asbestos Council and (1993) NAC/The Environmental Information Association. The Environmental Information Association has been at the forefront in providing the environmental industry with the information needed to remain knowledgeable, responsible, and competitive in the environmental health and safety industry. EIA's mission is to generate and disseminate information concerning environmental health hazards to occupants of buildings, industrial sites and other facility operations. Membership: $165 (Individual); $650 (Organization); $35 (Student); $1,300 (Executive).

Continuing Education:
Certification Designation/s: CIER, MTR, CIES, CIEC, CIE

Meetings/Conferences: Annual
2013 - Arlington, VA (Hyatt Regency Hotel Crystal City)/March 24 - 27/26-50 exhibitors

Publications:
EIA Technical Journal
Indoor Environment Connections
Inside EIA
Membership Directory; on-line
Net News; weekly

Environmental Markets Association (1996)
529 14th St. NW
750 National Press Building, Suite 750
Washington, DC 20045
Tel: (202) 591-2465 *Fax:* (202) 223-9741
E-Mail: info@emahq.org
Website: emahq.org
Members: 270 individuals
Staff: 4
Annual Budget: $250-500,000
Tax: 501(c)(6)

Personnel:
Executive Director: Lauren Newberry
    E-Mail: Lauren@EMAhq.org
Contact, Member Services: Christina Donnelly
    E-Mail: cdonnelly@kellencompany.com
Meetings Manager: Darrel McCook
Account Controller: Lysa Robinson

Historical Note:
Formerly Emissions Markets Association. EMA is focused on promoting market-based solutions for environmental challenges through sound public policy, industry best practices, effective education and training, and member networking. Represents a diverse membership including utilities, emissions brokers and traders, exchanges, law firms, project developers, consultants, academics, NGOs and government agencies. Membership: $500-5900/year.

Meetings/Conferences: Annual
Conference Chair: Darrel McCook

Publications:
Membership Directory; on-line
E-newsletter; monthly
Environmental Finance; monthly
Environmental Markets Newsletter; daily

Environmental Mutagen Society (1969)
1821 Michael Faraday Dr.
Suite 300
Reston, VA 20190
Tel: (703) 438-8220 *Fax:* (703) 438-3113
E-Mail: emshq@ems-us.org
Website: ems-us.org
Members: 800 individuals
Staff: 3
Annual Budget: $250-500,000
Tax: 501(c)(3)

Personnel:
Executive Director: Tonia M. Masson
Contact, Conferences: Maureen Kettering
    E-Mail: mkettering@ems-us.org
Editor-in-Chief: Paul White

Historical Note:
EMS aims to encourage the study of mutagens in the human environment, particularly as they affect public health. Members are scientists working in the field of molecular genetics and mutagenesis, whether in academia, industry or government. Membership: $0-169/year.

Meetings/Conferences: Annual
Conference Chair: Maureen Kettering
2013 - Monterey, CA (Hyatt Regency Monterey Hotel And Spa)/Sept. 20 - 26
2014 - Orlando, FL (Hilton Orlando Lake Buena Vista)/ Sept. 13 - 17
2015 - New Orleans, LA (Sheraton Hotel New Orleans)/Sept. 26 - 30

Publications:
Journal- Environmental and Molecular Mutagenesis; on-line; adv.
Membership Directory; on-line; adv.
The EMS Newsletter; bi-annually; adv.

Environmental Technology Council (1982)
1112 16th St. NW,
Suite 420
Washington, DC 20036
Tel: (202) 783-0870
E-Mail: mail@etc.org

Website: etc.org
Members: 15 companies
Staff: 3
Annual Budget: $500-1,000,000
Tax: 501(c)(6)

Personnel:
Executive Director: David R. Case
Vice President, Government Relations: Scott Slesinger
   E-Mail: sslesinger@etc.org

Historical Note:
Established in Washington, DC and incorporated in Delaware. Formerly (1994) Hazardous Waste Treatment Council. ETC's mission is to promote the protection of public health and the environment through the adoption of environmentally sound procedures and technologies for recycling and detoxifying industrial wastes and by-products and properly managing and disposing of wastes and waste residues. Membership: $8,000-96,000 (Company, based on revenues); $2,500 (Firms outside the industry).

EPDM Roofing Association (2003)
7315 Wisconsin Ave.
Suite 400 East
Bethesda, MD 20814
Tel: (301) 654-5090 *Fax:* (301) 951-8041
E-Mail: info@epdmroofs.org
Website: epdmroofs.org
Members: 10 companies
Staff: 2
Annual Budget: $250-500,000

Personnel:
Associate Executive Director: Ellen Thorp
Senior Communications Consultant: George Evanko
   E-Mail: george@georgeevanko.com

Historical Note:
ERA's mission is to provide technical and research support to the public and the construction industry, offer dependable roofing solutions and communicate the longstanding attributes, consistency and the value proposition of EPDM rubber membrane roofing materials.

Publications:
Membership Directory

EPS Industry Alliance (2012)
1298 Cronson Blvd.
Suite 201
Crofton, MD 21114-2426
Tel: (410) 451-8340 *Fax:* (410) 451-8343
TollFree: (800) 944-8448
E-Mail: info@epscentral.org
Website: epspackaging.org
Members: 80 companies
Staff: 5
Annual Budget: $100-250,000

Personnel:
Executive Director: Betsy Steiner
Deputy Director: Virginia Lyle
   E-Mail: vlyle@epscentral.org

Historical Note:
Formerly Alliance of Foam Packaging Recyclers. EPS-IA facilitates the development of recycling and awareness communications and programs. Members are raw material suppliers, molders and equipment suppliers in the United States and Canada.

Meetings/Conferences: Annual
2013 - Cincinnati, OH (Hilton Cincinnati Netherland Plaza Hotel)/March 18 - 20

Publications:
Membership Directory

Epsilon Sigma Phi (1927)
450 Falls Ave.
Suite 106
Twin Falls, ID 83301
Tel: (208) 736-4495 *Fax:* (208) 736-6081
E-Mail: espoffice@espnational.org
Website: espnational.com
Members: 6000 individuals
Staff: 1
Annual Budget: $100-250,000

Personnel:
Executive Director: Bob Ohlensehlen
   E-Mail: bobnsm@cableone.net

Historical Note:
ESP is dedicated to fostering standards of excellence in the extension system and developing the extension profession and professional. Members are professional staff in U. S. land grant universities and U. S. Department of Agriculture

Extension programs. Membership: $40 (Active); $200 (Lifetime).

Meetings/Conferences: Annual
2013 - Pittsburgh, PA/Sept. 15 - 20

Equal Employment Advisory Council (1976)
1501 M St. NW
Suite 400
Washington, DC 20005
Tel: (202) 629-5650 *Fax:* (202) 629-5651
E-Mail: info@eeac.org
Website: eeac.org
Members: 300 Major Corporations
Staff: 6
Annual Budget: $2-5,000,000

Personnel:
President: Jeffrey A. Norris
Senior Counsel and Vice President, Public Policy: Michael J. Eastman
Director, Information Technology: Nicholas J. Kuriger
Administrator: Nicole McDuffie
Chief Operating Officer: G. John Tysse
General Counsel: Rae T. Vann

Historical Note:
EEAC is dedicated to provide guidance to its member companies on understanding and complying with EEO and affirmative action obligations.

Meetings/Conferences:
Number of non-conference events/year: 20

Publications:
EEAC newsletter; on-line

Equal Justice Works (1986)
1730 M St. NW
Suite 1010
Washington, DC 20036-4511
Tel: (202) 466-3686
Website: equaljusticeworks.org
Staff: 6
Annual Budget: $10-25,000,000
Tax: 501(c)(3)

Personnel:
Executive Director: David Stern
   E-Mail: dstern@equaljusticeworks.org
Senior Program Manager, Educational Debt Relief and Outreach: Isaac Bowers
   E-Mail: ibowers@equaljusticeworks.org
Director, Communications and Outreach: Sally Carlson
   E-Mail: scarlson@equaljusticeworks.org
Specialist, Member Services and Communications: Lauren Fuchs
   E-Mail: lfuchs@equaljusticeworks.org
Program Manager: Radhika Singh Miller
Director, Federal Programs and Strategic Initiatives: Kerry O'Brien
   E-Mail: kobrien@equaljusticeworks.org

Historical Note:
Formerly the National Association for Public Interest Law. Organizes, trains and supports public service-minded law students and creates summer and postgraduate public interest jobs. Student and lawyer program participants bring equal justice to millions of low-income persons and families.

Meetings/Conferences: Annual
Conference Chair: Kerry O'Brien

Publications:
Equal Justice at Work; monthly

Equipment and Tool Institute (1947)
3819 N. RT 23
Suite F
Marengo, IL 60152
Tel: (815) 520-1933
E-Mail: info@etools.org
Website: etools.org
Members: 60 companies
Staff: 3
Annual Budget: $500-1,000,000

Personnel:
Executive Manager: Charlie Gorman
   E-Mail: cgorman@etools.org
Administrative Assistant: Trisha Doornbosch
   E-Mail: trishad@etools.org
Manager, Marketing: Jessie Korosec
   E-Mail: jessiek@etools.org

Historical Note:

ETI works to advance the vehicle service industry by providing technical data and open dialogue between the manufacturers of transportation products, government regulators and the providers of tools, equipment and service information. Members are manufacturers of automotive service equipment and tools. Membership: $1,000-4,000 (Associate); $5,000-10,000 (Full).

Meetings/Conferences: Annual
Conference Chair: Jessie Korosec
2013 - San Diego, CA (Hyatt Mission Bay)/April 23 - 25
Number of non-conference events/year: 4

Publications:
News and Views; annually; adv.

Membership List Available to Non-members

Equipment Leasing and Finance Association (1961)
1825 K St. NW
Suite 900
Washington, DC 20006
Tel: (202) 238-3400 *Fax:* (202) 238-3401
Website: elfaonline.org
Members: 550 companies
Staff: 25
Annual Budget: $5-10,000,000

Personnel:
Executive Director: Kelli Nienaber
   E-Mail: knienaber@elfaonline.org
President and Chief Executive Officer: William G. Sutton CAE
   E-Mail: wsutton@elfaonline.org
Vice President, State Government Relations: Dennis Brown CAE
   E-Mail: dbrown@elamail.com
Vice President, Research and Industry Services: Bill Choi CAE
   E-Mail: bchoi@elfaonline.org
Director, Business Development and Meetings: Racquel Codling
   E-Mail: rcodling@elfaonline.org
Director, Meetings and Exhibits: Lisa Ramirez
   E-Mail: lramirez@elfaonline.org
Director, Membership and Database Services: Kesha Robinson
   E-Mail: krobinson@elfaonline.org
Vice President, Business and Professional Development: Lesley Sterling
   E-Mail: lsterling@elfaonline.org
Vice President, Finance and Administration: Paul A. Stilp
   E-Mail: pstilp@elfaonline.org
Vice President, Communications and Marketing: Amy Vogt
   E-Mail: avogt@elfaonline.org

Historical Note:
ELFA's mission is to provide member companies a forum for industry development; a platform to advocate for the industry and a principal resource for industry information and ethical standards.

Meetings/Conferences: Semi-Annual
Conference Chair: Racquel Codling
Number of non-conference events/year: 1

Publications:
Membership Directory; on-line

Equipment Marketing and Distribution Association (1950)
P.O. Box 1347
Iowa City, IA 52244
Tel: (319) 354-5156 *Fax:* (319) 354-5157
E-Mail: info@emda.net
Website: emda.net
Members: 700 companies
Staff: 5
Annual Budget: $500-1,000,000
Tax: 501(c)(6)

Personnel:
President: Marcus Kimball
Executive Vice President: Patricia Collins
Director, Membership Services: Hannah Hammontree
Manager, Conventions: Sarah Stevener

Historical Note:
Formed by the merger of AIMRA (the Agricultural & Industrial Manufacturer's Representatives Association) and FEWA (formerly the Farm Equipment Wholesalers Association). EMDA is devoted to the marketing of specialized equipments. Membership: $495-750 (Regular); $295 (Associate).

Meetings/Conferences: Annual
Conference Chair: Sarah Stevener
2013 - Indianapolis, IN (JW Marriott Indianapolis)/Oct. 22 - 25

Publications:
EMDA Membership Directory; on-line
EMDA Newsletter; monthly
Membership Directory; biennially; adv.

Equipment Service Association *(1959)*
P.O. Box 1420
Cherry Hill, NJ 08034-0054
Tel: (856) 489-0753 *Fax:* (856) 424-9248
E-Mail: esa@2esa.org
Website: 2esa.org
Members: 142 companies
Staff: 5
Annual Budget: $50-100,000

Personnel:
Executive Director: Heather Phillips
    E-Mail: hphillips@idpcreative.com
Coordinator, Membership Services and Database: Susan Dyson
    E-Mail: askus@2esa.org
Contact, Publications: Janet Hauk
Manager, Communications: Adele Kayser
    E-Mail: askus@2esa.org
Director, Operations: Donna Pollander
    E-Mail: askus@2esa.org

Historical Note:
Formerly the International Hydraulic Equipment Rebuilders Association. ESA members are engaged in the sales and service of hydraulically, pneumatically or electrically operated tools, components, and equipment. Membership: $335 (Regular); $575 (Supporting); $75 (Associate).

Meetings/Conferences:
Conference Chair: Janet Hauk

Publications:
ESA Newsletter; monthly; adv.
Membership Directory; on-line

The ERISA Industry Committee (ERIC) *(1976)*
1400 L St. NW
Suite 350
Washington, DC 20005
Tel: (202) 789-1400 *Fax:* (202) 789-1120
E-Mail: eric@eric.org
Website: eric.org
Members: 1500 benefits and human resources colleagues
Staff: 6
Annual Budget: $1-2,000,000
Tax: 501(c)(6)

Personnel:
President: Mark J. Ugoretz
    E-Mail: mugoretz@eric.org
Vice President, Administration: Deborah Chin PLC
    E-Mail: dchin@eric.org
Administrator, Membership Services: Adreanne Cooper
    E-Mail: acooper@eric.org
Director, Communications: Theodore C. Godbout
    E-Mail: tgodbout@eric.org
Senior Vice President, Health Policy: Gretchen K. Young
    E-Mail: gyoung@eric.org

Historical Note:
A non-profit association committed to the advancement of employee retirement, health, and welfare benefit plans of America's largest "Fortune 200" employers. Provides retirement, health care coverage and other economic security benefits to about 25 million active and retired workers and their families.

Publications:
Membership Directory; on-line

Esperanto-USA *(1961)*
500 Park Ave STE 134
Emeryville, CA 94608
Tel: (510) 653-0998
TollFree: (800) 377-3726
E-Mail: info@esperanto-usa.org
Website: esperanto-usa.org/
Members: 60 individuals
Staff: 2
Annual Budget: $100-250,000
Tax: 501(c)(3)

Personnel:
President: Orlando Raola

Treasurer: George Baker

Historical Note:
Esperanto-USA provides services to support Esperanto activity, including Education, Book, Subscription & Tape Services, and Publications. Members represents all ages and all levels of Esperanto experience, from beginners to fluent speakers. Membership: $20 (Youth/Limited income); $40 (Individual); $80 (Sustaining); $120 (Patron); $800 (Lifetime); $60 (Family).

Publications:
Bulteno; bi-monthly
Usona Esperantisto; bi-monthly

Membership List Available to Non-members

Espionage Research Institute International *(2001)*
4445 Corporation Ln.
Suite 291C
Virginia Beach, VA 23462
Tel: (757) 716-7353 *Fax:* (301) 292-4635
Website: erii.org
Members: 97 individuals
Staff: 3

Personnel:
Director: J. D. LeaSure
    E-Mail: JDL@erii.org

Historical Note:
Supersedes the former Business Espionage Controls and Countermeasures Association (1990-2001). The former ERI organization has been reorganized and is now ERII. ERII is dedicated to collect and promulgating information on hostile espionage activity. Members are security practitioners, businessmen and corporate executives who have security responsibilities, and newcomers to the profession. Membership: $150 (Full); $100 (Associate).

Continuing Education:
Certification Designation/s: CCISM

Meetings/Conferences: Annual
Conference Chair: J. D. LeaSure

ETAD North America *(1982)*
1850 M St. NW
Suite 700
Washington, DC 20036
Tel: (202) 721-4154 *Fax:* (202) 296-8120
Website: etad.com
Members: 9 companies
Staff: 3
Annual Budget: $250-500,000

Personnel:
Executive Director: C. Tucker Helmes PhD
    E-Mail: helmest@socma.com
Legal Counsel: W. Richard Bidstrup

Historical Note:
Founded as United States Operating Committee of ETAD, became United States Dye Manufacturers Operating Committee of ETAD in 1993 and assumed its current name in 2001. The international association, ETAD (Ecological and Toxicological Association of Dyes and Organic Pigment Manufacturers) was formed in 1974 to combine scientific and technical resources within companies in the dyestuffs industry to address ecotoxicological problems. In 1977 American companies formed the Dyes Environmental and Toxicology Organization (DETO). In 1982 most DETO members decided to join ETAD, and the two organizations were merged. ETAD North America strives to represent the interests of manufacturers and formulators of dyes in the region with regard to environmental and health hazards in the manufacture, processing, shipment, use and disposal of their products.

Ethics and Compliance Officer Association *(1992)*
411 Waverly Oaks Rd.
Suite 324
Waltham, MA 02452
Tel: (781) 647-9333 *Fax:* (781) 647-9399
Website: theecoa.org
Members: 1100 individuals
Staff: 14
Annual Budget: $2-5,000,000
Tax: 501(c)(6)

Personnel:
Executive Director: Keith T. Darcy
    E-Mail: kdarcy@theecoa.org
Assistant Director, Events: Janel Heilbrunn
    E-Mail: jheilbrunn@theecoa.org
Assistant Director, Publications: Robert Israel
    E-Mail: robert.israel@theecoa.org

Associate Director, Member Services and Education: Rebecca Rehm
    E-Mail: rebecca.rehm@theECOA.org
Assistant Director, Marketing: Bethany Senechal
    E-Mail: bethany.senechal@theecoa.org
Associate Director, Marketing and Communications: S. Maria Sonin
    E-Mail: msonin@theecoa.org
Assistant Director, Membership Development: Michelle Totilo
    E-Mail: mtotilo@theecoa.org

Historical Note:
Formerly Ethics Officer Association. ECOA purpose is to provide members with access to an unparalleled network of ethics and compliance professionals and a global forum for the exchange of ideas and strategies. Membership: $2,500-4,500 (Sponsoring Partner, based on the gross annual revenue); $750-950 (Organizations); $750-2,700 (Government).

Continuing Education:
Enrollment: 5

Meetings/Conferences: Annual
Conference Chair: Janel Heilbrunn

Publications:
ECOA Weekly Newswatch; weekly
Membership Directory; on-line

Ethylene Oxide Sterilization Association, Inc. *(1995)*
P.O. Box 33361
Washington, DC 20033
Tel: (866) 235-5030 *Fax:* (202) 557-3836
TollFree: (866) 235-5030
E-Mail: eosainfo@eosa.org
Website: eosa.org
Members: 25 companies
Staff: 4
Annual Budget: $50-100,000
Tax: 501(c)(6)

Personnel:
President: Randy Viscomi
Treasurer: Dale Stucker
Contact, Meetings: Jake Vandevort
    E-Mail: jvandevort@bc-cm.com

Historical Note:
EOSA's mission is to promote the safe use and handling of ethylene oxide for sterilization purposes. Members are persons and companies with an interest in the sterilization of medical devices, scientific instruments, and spice fumigation. It also includes contract sterilizers, sterilization equipment manufacturers, analytical equipment and systems suppliers, ethylene oxide suppliers, medical device manufacturers, and consultants. Membership: $500-7,500/year (Based on sales).

Meetings/Conferences: Annual
Conference Chair: Jake Vandevort
2013 - Anaheim, CA (Anaheim Marriott)/Feb. 11
Number of non-conference events/year: 11

Publications:
EOSA News Bulletins
Membership Directory; on-line

EUCG, Inc. *(1973)*
12100 Sunset Hills Rd
Suite 130
Reston, VA 20190
Tel: (703) 234-4143 *Fax:* (703) 435-4390
E-Mail: eucgexec@cox.net
Website: eucg.org
Members: 90 member companies
Staff: 6
Annual Budget: $500-1,000,000

Personnel:
Executive Director: Don Kaiser
    E-Mail: kaiser@eucg.org
President: George W. Sharp
    E-Mail: gwsharp@aep.com
Treasurer: Evelyn Grant
Contact, Information Technology: K. Heffelfinger
Vice President: Kathy Shirley
Director, Marketing: Stephen Thorton

Historical Note:
EUCG founded as Electric Utility Cost Group, assumed its current name in 1996. EUCG's mission is to assist its member companies to achieve better performance by providing relevant and timely information. EUCG provides members with feedback on utility and plant specific problems, to increase competitiveness and value.

Membership: $900-5,300/year, dues are dependent on the type of membership.

Meetings/Conferences: Annual
2013 - Nashville, TN (Hilton Nashville Downtown)/
April 14 - 17
Number of non-conference events/year: 1

Publications:
Membership Directory; on-line

European-American Business Council *(1989)*
919 18th St. NW
Suite 220
Washington, DC 20006
Tel: (202) 828-9104 *Fax:* (202) 828-9106
E-Mail: eabc@eabc.org
Website: eabc.org
Members: 50 companies
Staff: 6
Annual Budget: $1-2,000,000
Tax: 501(c)(6)

Personnel:
President and Chief Executive Officer: Michael C.
Maibach
E-Mail: m@mailbach.us
Membership and Media Manager: Justin Kintz
E-Mail: justin.kintz@eabc.org
Operations Manager: Dawn Nunnery
Manager, Program and Media: Hilary Sama
E-Mail: hilary@eabc.org

Historical Note:
Formerly, (1989) the European Community Chamber of Commerce and assumed its present name in 1990. A joint council of 85 multinational corporations with operations in both Europe and the U.S. to promote and sustain a healthy and open business climate worldwide. EABC's mission is to support unrestricted trade and investment between the US and the EC, promote a healthy, open and productive business environment between the two regions and provide a platform for discussion and exchange of ideas for business and government leaders in Europe and in the United States.

Publications:
Membership Directory; on-line

Evangelical Christian Publishers Association *(1974)*
9633 S. 48th St.
Suite 140
Phoenix, AZ 85044
Tel: (480) 966-3998 *Fax:* (480) 966-1944
E-Mail: info@ecpa.org
Website: ecpa.org
Members: 95 publishing houses and small press members
Staff: 10
Annual Budget: $500-1,000,000
Tax: 501(c)(6)

Personnel:
President and Chief Executive Officer: Mark W. Kuyper
E-Mail: mkuyper@ecpa.org

Historical Note:
ECPA's mission is to equip members so they can more effectively make the Christian message widely known by building industry awareness and enhancing access to markets, education, expertise, information and peers. ECPA serves the christian publishing industry by promoting excellence and professionalism, sharing relevant data, stimulating christian fellowship, raising the effectiveness of member publishing houses, and equipping them to meet the need of the changing marketplace. Membership: $1,512-15,000 (Voting Member); $600 (Small Press Member); $100-300 (International Member); $300-1,300 (Industry Affiliates); $25 (Alumni); $300 (Individual).

Meetings/Conferences:
Number of non-conference events/year: 3

Publications:
E-Link; monthly; adv.
Legal Update; on-line
Rush to Press; weekly; adv.

Evangelical Church Library Association *(1970)*
P.O. Box 353
Glen Ellyn, IL 60138-0353
Tel: (630) 375-7865 *Fax:* (847) 296-0754
Website: eclalibraries.org
Members: 350 individuals
Staff: 4
Annual Budget: $10-25,000
Tax: 501(c)(3)

Personnel:
President: Donna Waln
E-Mail: Donna@eclalibraries.org
Managing Editor: Lin Johnson
E-Mail: linjohnson@eclalibraries.org
Treasurer: Paul Trautwein
Secretary: Judi Turek
E-Mail: judi@eclalibraries.org

Historical Note:
ECLA promotes church libraries to encourage Christian growth. Membership: $40 (US Churches/Individual/Schools); $45 (Canada Churches/Individual/Schools); ; $55 (Foreign Churches/Individual/Schools); $100 (Corporate Members/Publishers).

Meetings/Conferences: Annual

Publications:
Church Libraries; quarterly; adv.

Evangelical Council for Financial Accountability *(1979)*
440 W. Jubal Early Dr.
Suite 130
Winchester, VA 22601
Tel: (540) 535-0103 *Fax:* (540) 535-0533
TollFree: (800) 323-9473
E-Mail: information@ecfa.org
Website: ecfa.org
Members: 1500 organizations
Staff: 11
Annual Budget: $2-5,000,000
Tax: 501(c)(3)

Personnel:
President: Dan Busby
E-Mail: dan@ecfa.org
Contact, Membership Services: Melinda Johnson
Head, Event Management: Marsha Miller
Vice President and Legal Counsel: John Van Drunen

Historical Note:
Accreditation agency for religious charities. ECFA is committed to helping Christian organizations earn the public's trust through developing and maintaining standards of accountability that convey religious ethical practices. Membership: $500-9,000 (Based on cash contribution); $1,000-2,000 (Based on total revenue).

Meetings/Conferences:
Conference Chair: Marsha Miller
Number of non-conference events/year: 2

Publications:
CPA Directory; on-line; adv.
Focus on Accountability; quarterly
Member List; annually
Vendor Directory; on-line; adv.

Evangelical Press Association *(1948)*
P.O. Box 28129
Crystal, MN 55428
Tel: (763) 535-4793 *Fax:* (763) 535-4794
Website: epassoc.org
Members: 425 organizations and individuals
Staff: 3
Annual Budget: $100-250,000

Personnel:
Executive Director: Doug Trouten
E-Mail: director@epassoc.org
Liaison, Member Services: Lis Trouten
Treasurer: Dwight Widaman

Historical Note:
EPA's mission is to provide inspiration, instruction, and networking to strengthen evangelical periodicals. Membership: $140-365 (Publication Membership); $70 (Student-run Campus Publication); $140 (Regional Christian Newspaper); $150 (On-line Publication); $250 (Business Affiliate); $70 (Associate Member).

Meetings/Conferences: Annual
2013 - Nashville, TN/May 1 - 3

Publications:
Membership Directory; annually
World Christian Ministries Newsletter

The Evaporative Cooling Institute *(1989)*
MSC 3ECI - NMSU
P.O. Box 30001
Las Cruces, NM 88003-8001
Tel: (505) 646-4104 *Fax:* (505) 646-2960
E-Mail: moreinfo@evapcooling.org
Website: evapcooling.org
Members:

50 individuals
15 companies
Staff: 1
Annual Budget: Under $10,000

Personnel:
Project Engineer: Robert E. Foster
E-Mail: rfoster@nmsu.edu

Historical Note:
ECI works to advance the art and science of evaporative air cooling and air-conditioning. Membership consists of manufacturers of evaporative apparatus, designers, specifiers, and users of heating, ventilating and air-conditioning systems, sales representatives, representatives of institutes of learning and governmental agencies and other interested parties. Membership: $300 (Voting); $60 (Associate/Non-Voting).

Event Planners Association *(2004)*
25432 Trabuco
Suite 207
Lake Forest, CA 92630
Tel: (866) 380-3372 *Fax:* (866) 230-3044
TollFree: (866) 380-3372
E-Mail: info@EventPlannersAssociation.com
Website: eventplannersassociation.com
Members: 4000 individuals
Staff: 3

Personnel:
President and Chief Executive Officer: Kristopher P.
Badame Esq.
Senior Vice President, Chief Marketing Officer: Kim S.
Sullivan
Vice President, Chief Financial Officer: Thomas J. Sullivan

Historical Note:
A group of professionals in the event and amusement industries. Serves as a wedding planner association, inflatable association, meeting planner association, and other event and amusement associations. Membership: $249 (Executive), $349 (Supplier), $49 (Student/Educator).

Continuing Education:
Certification Designation/s: AOSC

Event Service Professionals Association *(1988)*
191 Clarksville Rd.
Princeton Junction
Princeton, NJ 08550
Tel: (609) 799-3712 *Fax:* (609) 799-7032
E-Mail: info@acomonline.org
Website: acomonline.org
Members: 500 individuals
Staff: 4
Annual Budget: $250-500,000

Personnel:
Executive Director: Lynn McCullough
E-Mail: lmccullough@espaonline.org
Membership Services Manager and Meeting Planner:
Diane Galante
E-Mail: dgalante@acomonline.org
Manager, Public Relations: Meghan Higgins
E-Mail: mhiggins@cmasolutions.com

Historical Note:
Formerly, Association for Convention Operations Management. ESPA's mission is to advance the practice of convention services management (CSM) in the meetings industry, and to prepare CSM professionals for their critical role in the growth and success of their organizations. Membership: $250 (Individual/Allied); $225 (Meeting Professional); $25 (Student); $50 (Educational Institution) $600-3,750 (Organizational Member).

Meetings/Conferences: Annual
Conference Chair: Diane Galante
2013 - Orlando, FL (Walt Disney Swan and Dolphin
Resor)/Jan. 11 - 13

Publications:
ACOMmodate; on-line
Membership Directory; on-line

Evidence Photographers International Council *(1968)*
229 Peachtree St. NE
Suite 2200
Atlanta, GA 30303
Tel: (866) 868-3742 *Fax:* (404) 614-6406
E-Mail: csc@evidencephotographers.com
Website: evidencephotographers.com
Members: 2000 individuals
Staff: 5

Annual Budget: $50-100,000
Tax: 501(c)(3)

Personnel:
Association Director: Claire White
    E-Mail: cwerner@evidencephotographers.com

Historical Note:
EPIC's mission is to provide members with education and resources to aid in the advancement of evidence photography. Membership: $149/year.

Continuing Education:
Certification Designation/s: CEP

Meetings/Conferences: Annual
2013 - Atlanta, GA (Georgia World Congress Center)/ Jan. 19 - 22

Publications:
Evidence Magazine
Member Directory; on-line

Executive Women in Government (1974)
701 Miller Rd.
Annapolis, MD 21401
Tel: (410) 562-2552 *Fax:* (410) 263-0327
E-Mail: info@execwomeningov.org
Website: execwomeningov.org
Staff: 3
Annual Budget: $100-250,000
Tax: 501(c)(3)

Personnel:
President: Reta Jo Lewis
Treasurer: Paula Farrell
Secretary: Tanya Hodge Mottley
    E-Mail: mottley.tanya@epa.gov

Historical Note:
EWG's mission is to prepare, promote, support and mentor women for senior leadership positions in the federal government. Membership: $65 (Basic), $1000 (Lifetime).

Publications:
Membership Directory; on-line

Executive Women International (1938)
7414 S. State St.
Midvale, UT 84047
Tel: (801) 355-2800 *Fax:* (801) 355-2852
TollFree: (877) 439-4669
E-Mail: ewi@executivewomen.org
Website: executivewomen.org
Members: 3500 individuals and 3000 companies
Staff: 4
Annual Budget: $500-1,000,000
Tax: 501(c)(6)

Personnel:
Executive Director: Katie Reeder
    E-Mail: katie@ewiconnect.com
Administrator, Membership Services: Shannon Glaittli
    E-Mail: shannon@ewiconnect.com
Administrator, Marketing, Communications and Events: Brittany Jones
    E-Mail: brittany@ewiconnect.com
Office Administrator: Jordan Koehler
    E-Mail: jordan@ewiconnect.com

Historical Note:
Formerly (1978) Executives' Secretaries, Inc. EWI brings together key individuals from diverse businesses for the purpose of promoting member firms, enhancing personal and professional development, and encouraging community involvement. Members are firms, each of which is represented by individuals engaged in executive and administrative positions. Membership is by invitation only and through company representation.

Meetings/Conferences: Annual
Conference Chair: Brittany Jones

Publications:
Membership Directory; on-line

Executive Women's Golf Association (1991)
300 Ave. of the Champions
Suite 140
Palm Beach Gardens, FL 33418-3615
Tel: (561) 691-0096 *Fax:* (561) 691-0012
E-Mail: info@myewga.com
Website: ewga.com
Members: 20000 individuals
Staff: 15
Annual Budget: $2-5,000,000
Tax: 501(c)(6)

Personnel:

Chief Executive Officer: Pamela Swensen
Secretary and Treasurer: Sandra Cross CAE

Historical Note:
EWGA's mission is to connect women to learn, play and enjoy golf for business and for fun. It also serves as an advocate for positive change on issues of importance to women golfers. Membership: $400 (Executive Distinction); $155 (Classic); $75 (Young Professional); $125 (Senior/Corporate).

Meetings/Conferences: Annual
2013 - Hilton Head Island, SC (Westin Hilton Head Island Resort and Spa)/May 8 - 11

Publications:
Connections (e-newsletter); monthly
Membership Directory; on-line

The Exercise Safety Association (1978)
P.O. Box 547916
Orlando, FL 32854-7916
Tel: (407) 246-5090
E-Mail: askesa@aol.com
Website: exercisesafety.com
Members: 20000 individuals
Staff: 5

Personnel:
Executive Director: Kim Foy
    E-Mail: askesa@exercisesafety.com
Editor and Director, Education and Training: Sharon Foy
    E-Mail: askesa@exercisesafety.com

Historical Note:
ESA is a professional training organization, providing safety training and certification for fitness instructors and health facilities. Membership: $25/year.

Continuing Education:
Certification Designation/s: SSI, ESA, SEL

Publications:
ESA Newsletter

Exhibit Designers and Producers Association (1954)
Ten Norden Pl.
Norwalk, CT 06855
Tel: (203) 852-5698 *Fax:* (203) 854-6735
E-Mail: info@edpa.com
Website: edpa.com
Members: 400 companies
Staff: 5
Annual Budget: $500-1,000,000

Personnel:
Executive Director: Jeff Provost
    E-Mail: jprovost@edpa.com
Member Development Manager: Alex Chung
    E-Mail: achung@edpa.com
Marketing Project Manager: Kelly Cingari
    E-Mail: kcingari@red7media.com
Senior Financial Analyst: Kristen DelGreco
    E-Mail: kdelgreco@red7media.com
Senior Director, ACCESS Event Operations: Tracy Wakeford
    E-Mail: twakeford@accessintel.com

Historical Note:
Member of the Center for Exposition Industry Research and the International Federation of Exhibition Services (IFES). EDPA is engaged in the design, manufacture, transport, installation and service of displays and exhibits primarily for the exhibition and event industry. Members are designers, builders, and suppliers of displays for exhibits, trade shows, and events. Membership: $200-3,250 (Regular, based on annual sales); $295 (Associate/Independent Designers); $35 (Students).

Meetings/Conferences: Annual
Conference Chair: Tracy Wakeford

Publications:
EDPA Alert; monthly; adv.
Global Insights; quarterly; adv.
Membership Directory; annually; adv.

Membership List Available to Non-members

Exhibition Services and Contractors Association (1970)
5068 W. Plano Pkwy.
Suite 300
Plano, TX 75093
Tel: (972) 447-8212 *Fax:* (972) 447-8209
TollFree: (877) 792-3722
Website: esca.org
Members: 170 firms

Staff: 6
Annual Budget: $100-250,000

Personnel:
Executive Director: Larry Arnaudet
    E-Mail: larrya@augustagroup.org
Director, Membership Services: Mitt Arnaudet
    E-Mail: mitt@esca.org
Director, Finance: Harry Hieronymus
Office Manager: Tandance Lureman

Historical Note:
Formerly (2001) Exposition Service Contractors Association. ESCA is committed to the advancement of the exhibition, meeting and special events industries. It also advocates cooperation among all areas of the exhibition industry. Membership: $200 (Individual); $300-800 (Based on the service offered by the company).

Meetings/Conferences:
2013 - Carlsbad, CA (La Costa Resort and Spa)/June 23 - 26
2013 - Houston, TX (George R. Brown Convention Center)/Dec. 9
2014 - Los Angeles, CA/Dec. 8
2015 - Squaw Valley, CA (Resort at Squaw Creek)/June 28 - July 1
Number of non-conference events/year: 1

Publications:
ESCA Newsletter; bi-monthly; adv.

Exhibitor Appointed Contractors Association
2214 NW Fifth St.
Bend, OR 97701
Tel: (541) 317-8768 *Fax:* (541) 317-8749
Website: eaca.com
Staff: 1
Annual Budget: $250-500,000
Tax: 501(c)(6)

Personnel:
Executive Director: Jim Wurm

Historical Note:
Works to improve the working conditions and practices of those exhibitor appointed contractors and other individual showfloor professionals that provide exhibit services on the trade show floor. Took over management of Trade Show Exhibitors Association in 2012. Membership: $350-7500 (Bronze, Corporate Sponsor).

Publications:
Showfloor Buzz; weekly

Exotic Wildlife Association (1967)
105 Henderson Branch Rd., West
Ingram, TX 78025
Tel: (830) 367-7761 *Fax:* (830) 367-7762
E-Mail: info@myewa.org
Website: exoticwildlifeassociation.com
Members: 2500 individuals
Staff: 4
Annual Budget: $1-2,000,000
Tax: 501(c)(6)

Personnel:
Executive Director: Charly Seale
    E-Mail: charly@exoticwildlifeassociation.com

Historical Note:
Exotic Wildlife (EWA) represents breeders and producers of native and non-native hoofstock, protects the rights of private property owners. EWA's Mission is to encourage and expand the conservation of indigenous and non-indigenous hoofstock animals, and to help Members develop and strengthen the markets for their animals. Memberships: $25-1,500/year.

Meetings/Conferences: Annual
Number of non-conference events/year: 1

Publications:
Exotic Wildlife magazine; bi-monthly; adv.
Fair Safari magazine; annually; adv.
Game Ranch Directory; biennially; adv.

Expanded Shale, Clay and Slate Institute (1952)
35 E. Wacker Dr.
Suite 850
Chicago, IL 60601
Tel: (801) 272-7070 *Fax:* (312) 644-8557
E-Mail: info@escsi.org
Website: escsi.org
Members: 10 companies
Staff: 3
Annual Budget: $500-1,000,000

Personnel:

Executive Director: Abigail Gabbard
　　E-Mail: agabbard@escsi.org

Historical Note:
Founded as the Expanded Shale Institute, assumed its present name in 1955. ESCSI's mission is to promote the extensive use of rotary kiln produced lightweight aggregate in the concrete masonry, ready- mix and precast markets. Members are manufacturers of rotary kiln produced expanded shale, clay and slate lightweight aggregate.

Meetings/Conferences:
Conference Chair: Abigail Gabbard

Publications:
ESCSI E-Newsletter; on-line

Expansion Joint Manufacturers Association, Inc. (1955)

25 N. Broadway
Tarrytown, NY 10591-3201
Tel: (914) 332-0040 *Fax:* (914) 332-1541
E-Mail: inquiries@ejma.org
Website: ejma.org
Members: 9 companies
Staff: 2
Annual Budget: $50-100,000

Personnel:
Secretary: Richard C. Byrne

Historical Note:
EJMA's Technical Committee prepares industry standards. Cooperates with ASME in the development of engineering standards for metallic expansion joints for use in piping systems.

Membership List Available to Non-members

Export Institute of the United States (1964)

6901 W. 84th St.
Suite 301
Minneapolis, MN 55438
Tel: (952) 943-1505
TollFree: (800) 943-3171
E-Mail: jrj@exportinstitute.com
Website: exportinstitute.com
Members:
180 companies and other organizations
440 individuals
Staff: 8
Annual Budget: $500-1,000,000

Personnel:
President, Founder, Owner and Managing Director: John R. Jagoe
　　E-Mail: jrj@exportinstitute.com

Historical Note:
The Export Institute of the United States works to offer online export classes. Course content is updated daily to ensure that the information is always current and ready for immediate use.

Continuing Education:
Enrollment: 400
Certification Designation/s: CEM

Express Association of America

Great Falls
Great Falls, VA 22066
Tel: (703) 759-0369 *Fax:* (703) 340-7521
Website: expressamerica.org
Staff: 1
Annual Budget: $100-250,000

Personnel:
Executive Director: Michael C. Mullen
　　E-Mail: eaa_mullen@verizon.net

Historical Note:
A trade association for the express industry. The purpose of the association is to promote the political, legislative, legal, regulatory, business and educational interests of the express delivery, logistics, and freight forwarding industry.

Publications:
Membership Directory; on-line

Express Carriers Association (1991)

9532 Liberia Ave.
Suite 752
Manassas, VA 20110-1719
Tel: (703) 361-1058 *Fax:* (703) 361-5274
E-Mail: eca@expresscarriers.org
Website: expresscarriers.com
Members: 185 companies
Staff: 1
Annual Budget: $250-500,000

Personnel:
Executive Director: Fiona Morgan
　　E-Mail: fiona@expresscarriers.org

Historical Note:
ECA's mission is to foster business relationships between carriers, shippers and vendors. Membership: $600/year (Shippers/Carriers/Vendors).

Meetings/Conferences: Annual
2013 - Dallas, TX/April 9
2013 - Dallas, TX (Intercontinental Dallas)/April 9 - 11
2014 - Atlanta, GA/April 15
2014 - Atlanta, GA (Atlanta Marriott Marquis)/April 15 - 17

Publications:
Membership Directory; on-line

Express Delivery & Logistics Association (1976)

400 Admiral Blvd.
Kansas City, MO 64106
Tel: (816) 221-0254 *Fax:* (816) 472-7765
TollFree: (888) 838-0761
E-Mail: acca@aircour.org
Website:
aircour.org
expressassociation.org
Members: 100 companies
Staff: 4
Annual Budget: $100-250,000
Tax: 501(c)(6)

Personnel:
Director, Marketing: Kelly Nemec
　　E-Mail: kelly@robstan.com

Historical Note:
Formerly Air Courier Conference of America; assumed current name in 2005. XLA's mission is to encourage the business, educational and regulatory interests of the express delivery, mail and logistics industry. Members are express delivery and logistics companies. Membership: $2,500-$5000 (Industry); $1,500 (International Industry); $1,185 (Associate); $4,570 (Airline); $500 (Consultant).

Meetings/Conferences: Annual
2013 - Las Vegas, NV (Red Rock Casion)/March 10 - 13
Number of non-conference events/year: 1

Publications:
Express; quarterly
Member Directory
Xtra; monthly

Exterior Insulation and Finish Systems Industry Members Association (EIMA) (1981)

513 W. Broad St.
Suite 210
Falls Church, VA 22046-3257
Tel: (703) 538-1616 *Fax:* (703) 538-1736
TollFree: (800) 294-3462
E-Mail: eifsinfo@eima.com
Website: eima.com
Members: 400 companies
Staff: 2
Annual Budget: $1-2,000,000

Personnel:
Executive Director: David A. Johnston
　　E-Mail: djohnston@eima.com
Manager, Public Affairs: Krista Gesaman
　　E-Mail: kgesaman@eima.com

Historical Note:
Formerly (1993) the Exterior Insulation Manufacturers Association. Established for EIFS (Exterior Insulation Finish Systems) manufacturers only, EIMA includes manufacturers, suppliers, distributors, applicator/contractors, and affiliated building professionals. EIMA is a trade association representing member firms involved in the exterior insulation and finish systems (EIFS) industry. EIMA's mission is to provide a technical focus for the EIFS industry. Membership: $500 (Applicator/Contractor/Affiliate); $250 (Distributor); $3,000-75,000 (Associate).

Meetings/Conferences: Annual
2013 - San Antonio, TX (ASHRAE Convention)/June 23 - 28

Publications:
EIFS Briefs; bi-monthly
EIMA Newsletter; bi-monthly
Membership Directory; on-line

Membership List Available to Non-members

Extruded Polystyrene Foam Association

750 National Press Building
529 14th St. NW
Washington, DC 22193
Tel: (202) 591-2466 *Fax:* (202) 591-2445
TollFree: (800) 978-9772
E-Mail: office@xpsa.com
Website: xpsa.com
Members: 4 companies
Staff: 1
Annual Budget: $250-500,000
Tax: 501(c)(6)

Personnel:
Contact: Shawn Richardson
　　E-Mail: srichardson@kellencompany.com

Historical Note:
XPSA's mission is to serve, and be recognized, as the premier trade association for the extruded polystyrene foam (XPS) insulation industry.

Publications:
Membership Directory; on-line

Membership List Available to Non-members

Eye Bank Association of America (1961)

1015 18th St. NW
Suite 1010
Washington, DC 20036
Tel: (202) 775-4999 *Fax:* (202) 429-6036
E-Mail: info@restoresight.org
Website: restoresight.org
Members: 112 eye banks
Staff: 12
Annual Budget: $2-5,000,000

Personnel:
President and Chief Executive Officer: Kevin P. Corcoran
　　E-Mail: kevin@restoresight.org
Coordinator, Membership Programs: Christa Aiken
　　E-Mail: christa@restoresight.org
Director, Finance: Bernie Dellario
　　E-Mail: bernard@restoresight.org
Manager, Education Programs: Stacey Gardner
　　E-Mail: stacey@restoresight.org
Vice President, Membership Services: Molly Georgakis
　　E-Mail: molly@restoresight.org
Manager, Communications: Patricia Hardy
　　E-Mail: trish@restoresight.org
Coordinator, Operations and Programs: Carly Lawrence
　　E-Mail: carly@restoresight.org

Historical Note:
EBAA's mission is the restoration of sight through core services to its members which advance donation, transplantation and research in their communities and throughout the world. Membership: $100 (Regular); $2500 (Limited,Associate/Active).

Continuing Education:
Certification Designation/s: CEBT

Meetings/Conferences: Annual
2013 - Chicago, IL (Sheraton Chicago Hotel and Towers)/June 5 - 8
2014 - Portland, OR (Hilton Portland and Executive Tower)/June 25 - 28

Publications:
International Journal of Eye Banking; quarterly; adv.
Insight Newsletter; on-line; adv.

FAA Managers Association, Inc.

4410 Massachusetts Ave. NW
Suite 315
Washington, DC 20016
Tel: (202) 741-9415 *Fax:* (720) 920-1552
E-Mail: info@faama.org
Website: faama.org
Staff: 8
Annual Budget: $1-2,000,000
Tax: 501(c)(6)

Personnel:
Director, Membership Services: Dave Chappuies
　　E-Mail: Membership@faama.org
Director, Communications: Anita Engelmann
　　E-Mail: communications@faama.org
Director, Legislative Affairs: Tony Tisdall
　　E-Mail: TTisdall@faama.org

Historical Note:
FAAMA's mission is to promote aviation safety and efficiency, advocate for its members interests, prepare the managers of today to be the leaders of tomorrow, and support the ideals of the Federal Government. Membership

is open to Federal supervisory, managerial or non-bargaining unit staff and Federal non-supervisory, non-managerial, or bargaining unit eligible personnel who profess interest in the purpose and goals of the association. Membership: $150 (Retired Members and Nonfederal Members).

Meetings/Conferences: Annual

Publications:
Managing the Skies; bi-monthly

Fabricators & Manufacturers Association, International (1970)
833 Featherstone Rd.
Rockford, IL 61107
Tel: (815) 399-8700 *Fax:* (815) 484-7700
TollFree: (888) 394-4362
E-Mail: info@fmanet.org
Website: fmanet.org
Members: 2300 individuals
Staff: 85
Annual Budget: $10-25,000,000
Tax: 501(c)(3)

Personnel:
President and Chief Executive Officer: Ed Youdell
Director, Expositions: Mark Hoper
Director, Public Relations: Pat Lee
Director, Membership, Education, Training and Certification: Jim Warren
Director, Information Technology and Web Department: Vicki Webb

Historical Note:
Formerly the Fabricating Machinery Association,(1975) the Fabricating Manufacturers Association and assumed its present name in 1985. FMA's mission is to improve the metal forming and fabricating industry. Members are metal fabricators and manufacturers. Membership: $150 (Basic); $450 (Advantage); $1450 (Advantage Plus Training); $49 (Young Professional); $25 (Student).

Continuing Education:
Certification Designation/s: PSMO, RFOSTC

Meetings/Conferences: Annual
Conference Chair: Mark Hoper
2013 - Palm Harbor, FL (Innisbrook Golf and Spa Resort)/Feb. 27 - March 1
Number of non-conference events/year: 27

Publications:
Fabricating Update; monthly
Fabrinomics; semi-monthly
Practical Welding Today; bi-monthly; adv.
Stamping Journal; quarterly; adv.
Stamping News Brief; monthly
The Fabricator; monthly; adv.
TPJ, The Tube & Pipe Journal; bi-monthly; adv.
Tube Talk; monthly
Welding Wire; monthly

The Fair Currency Alliance
1331 Pennsylvania Ave.
Eighth Fl.
Washington, DC 20004
Website: faircurrency.org
Staff: 3

Personnel:
Executive Director: Charles Blum
E-Mail: execdir@faircurrency.org
Contact, Website: Donna Tung
Director, Communications: Lloyd Wood
E-Mail: press@faircurrency.org

Historical Note:
The Fair Currency Coalition is a group of U.S. manufacturing, service, agricultural, and labor organizations that seek an end to the practice of currency misalignment by any trading partner.

Publications:
Membership Directory; on-line

Family and Consumer Sciences Education Association (1927)
Department of Family Consumer Sciences,
Central Washington University
400 E. Eighth Ave.
Ellensburg, WA 98926-7565
Tel: (509) 963-2766 *Fax:* (509) 963-2787
E-Mail: hubbards@cwu.edu
Website: cwu.edu/~fandcs/fcsea
Members: 900 individuals
Staff: 2

Annual Budget: $25-50,000

Personnel:
Executive Director: Jan Bowers PhD
E-Mail: bowersj@cwu.edu

Historical Note:
Established as Dept. of Supervisors and Teachers of Home Economics of the National Education Association; became the Dept. of Home Economics in 1938, Home Economics Education Association in 1969, and assumed its current name in 1995. A non-governance affiliate of the NEA. FCSEA dedicated to help each individual him or herself through a better understanding and control of family and community life. FCSEA is affiliated with American Association of Family and Consumer Sciences and National Education Association. Membership: $25 (Active/Associate); $35 (Foreign); $15 (Retired/Student).

Publications:
The Educator; semi-annually

Family Firm Institute, Inc. (1986)
200 Lincoln St.
Suite 201
Boston, MA 02111
Tel: (617) 482-3045 *Fax:* (617) 482-3049
E-Mail: ffi@ffi.org
Website: ffi.org
Members: 1500 individual and organizational members
Staff: 5
Annual Budget: $1-2,000,000
Tax: 501(c)(3)

Personnel:
President: Judy L. Green
E-Mail: judy@ffi.org
Coordinator, Membership Services and Registrar, Global Education Network: Dan Frosh
E-Mail: dan@ffi.org
Coordinator, Certificate Programs: Susan Gabert
E-Mail: susan@ffi.org
Coordinator, Marketing: Brigett Owens
E-Mail: brigett@ffi.org

Historical Note:
FFI's mission is to provide educational, networking and publishing opportunities for individuals and organizations interested in issues pertinent to family-owned business and families of wealth. Members include family business advisors, consultants, researchers, educators, and other individuals who advise, study, research and consult with family-owned businesses and families of wealth. Membership: $85-3450/year.

Continuing Education:
Certification Designation/s: CFBA, CFWA

Meetings/Conferences: Annual
Conference Chair: Dan Frosh

Publications:
Conference Proceedings; annually
Directory of Consultants & Speakers; on-line
Family Business Review; quarterly; adv.
FFI On Friday; weekly
FFI Practitioner; irregular
FFI Update; on-line
Intelligence Matters; quarterly
Membership Directory; on-line

Membership List Available to Non-members

Family, Career and Community Leaders of America (1945)
1910 Association Dr.
Reston, VA 20191-1584
Tel: (703) 476-4900 *Fax:* (703) 860-2713
TollFree: (800) 234-4425
E-Mail: natlhdqtrs@fcclainc.org
Website: fcclainc.org
Members: 205000 individuals
Staff: 22
Annual Budget: $2-5,000,000

Personnel:
Executive Director: Michael L. Benjamin CAE, MPH
E-Mail: mbenjamin@fcclainc.org
Director, Conferences: Marla Burk CMP
E-Mail: mburk@fcclainc.org
Director, Education and Leadership Development: Michelle Flinton
E-Mail: mflinton@fcclainc.org
Coordinator, Marketing and Communications: Jon Giuffre
Manager, Information Systems: Chuck Hoffman
E-Mail: choffman@fcclainc.org

Chief Financial Officer: David Hunt
E-Mail: dhunt@fcclainc.org
Manager, Marketing and Membership Services: Kenatu Muleta
E-Mail: kmuleta@fcclainc.org

Historical Note:
Founded as the Future Homemakers of America, assumed its present name in 1999 and absorbed the New Homemakers of America in 1965. FCCLA's mission is to promote personal growth and leadership development through family and consumer sciences education. Members are family and consumer sciences students through grade 12. Members: $9/year.

Meetings/Conferences: Annual
Conference Chair: Marla Burk CMP
2013 - Nashville, TN/July 7 - 11
2014 - San Antonio, TX/July 6 - 10
2015 - Washington, DC/July 5 - 9
2016 - San Diego, CA/July 3 - 7
2017 - Nashville, TN/July 2 - 6
Number of non-conference events/year: 4

Publications:
Teen Times; quarterly

Farm Credit Council (1982)
50 F St. NW
Suite 900
Washington, DC 20001-1530
Tel: (202) 626-8710 *Fax:* (202) 626-8718
TollFree: (800) 525-2345
E-Mail: boscia@fccouncil.com
Website: fccouncil.com
Members: 5 district councils and farm credit banks
Staff: 12
Annual Budget: $5-10,000,000
Tax: 501(c)(6)

Personnel:
President and Chief Executive Officer: Kenneth E. Auer
E-Mail: auer@fccouncil.com
Director, Administration and Corporate Secretary and Treasurer: Kim Boscia
E-Mail: boscia@fccouncil.com
Senior Vice President and General Counsel: Charles Dana
E-Mail: dana@fccouncil.com
Senior Vice President, Policy Analysis and Development: John J. Hays
E-Mail: hays@fccouncil.com
Director, Meetings: Michele Lucas
Director, Communications: Mike Mason
Executive Vice President: Jeffry William Shipp
E-Mail: shipp@fccouncil.com

Historical Note:
FCC's mission is to provide sound and dependable credit to American farmers, ranchers, producers or harvesters of aquatic products, their cooperatives, and certain farm-related businesses.

Meetings/Conferences: Annual
Conference Chair: Michele Lucas
Number of non-conference events/year: 1

Farm Equipment Council (1919)
6737 W. Washington St.
Suite 2400
Milwaukee, WI 53214-5647
Tel: (414) 272-0943 *Fax:* (414) 272-1170
Website: aem.org/Groups/Groups/Group.asp?
G=4#.T1eC78DCn
Staff: 1

Personnel:
Chairman: Karl Klotzbach

Historical Note:
This council was originally established as the Tractor and Thresher Department in 1919. It held various names until 1990 when the current name was adopted. The focus of this council is on all types of farm-field equipment and machinery: tractors, combines, forage, tillage, etc.

Farm Labor Organizing Committee (1967)
1221 Broadway St.
Toledo, OH 43609
Tel: (419) 243-3456 *Fax:* (419) 243-5655
E-Mail: info@floc.com
Website: supportfloc.org
Staff: 2
Annual Budget: $500-1,000,000
Tax: 501(c)(5)

Personnel:
President and Founder: Baldemar Velasquez
Secretary and Treasurer: Beatriz Maya

Historical Note:
FLOC allows workers to form a union and collectively bargain with their employer is the only way to address the huge imbalance of power and provide an effective structure for self-determination.

Publications:
FLOC News

Fashion Accessories Shippers Association *(1986)*
137 W. 25th St.
Third Floor
New York, NY 10001
Tel: (212) 947-3424 *Fax:* (212) 629-0361
E-Mail: info@accessoryweb.com
Website: accessoryweb.com
Members: 225 companies
Staff: 10
Annual Budget: $2-5,000,000

Personnel:
Executive Director: Harold Sachs
    E-Mail: hsachs@geminishippers.com
Director, Government Relations and Editor: Nate Herman
    E-Mail: nherman@geminishippers.com

Historical Note:
Formerly National Handbag Association. Became National Fashion Accessories Association (NFAA). Assumed the present name in 1986. FASA seeks to promote and maintain standards of ethics, business practices and labor standards in the industry and throughout the international trade community. Membership includes handbag, belt, small leather goods, gloves, umbrella and luggage accessory business organizations.

Publications:
USTR Weekly E-Newsletter; weekly
Washington Newsline; weekly

Fashion Accessories Shippers Association/Gemini Shippers Association *(1916)*
137 W. 25th St
Third Floor
New York, NY 10001
Tel: (212) 947-3424 *Fax:* (212) 629-0361
E-Mail: info@geminishippers.com
Website: geminishippers.com
Members: 100 individuals
Staff: 10
Annual Budget: $2-5,000,000

Personnel:
President: Sara Mayes

Historical Note:
Formerly (1966) National Authority for the Ladies Handbag Industry. Added the title National Fashion Accessories Association, in 1986. Formerly (1987) National Association of Handbag Makers/National Fashion Accessories Association and National Fashion Accessories Association (2007). FASA's mission is to promote and maintain ethics, business practices and labor relations in the international trade community. Members are importers and exporters of various products as accessories, luggage, apparel, furniture, footwear, household goods, office supplies, toys and health care and includes small and medium sized companies. Membership: based on formula, if not paid by carriers on shipper's behalf.

Meetings/Conferences:
Number of non-conference events/year: 4

Publications:
Membership Directory; on-line
The Journal Of Commerce

Fashion Group International *(1931)*
Eight W. 40th St.
Seventh Floor
New York, NY 10018
Tel: (212) 302-5511 *Fax:* (212) 302-5533
E-Mail: info@fgi.org
Website: newyork.fgi.org
Members: 5000 individuals
Staff: 13
Annual Budget: $1-2,000,000

Personnel:
President: Margaret Hayes
    E-Mail: MHayes@fgi.org
Chief Technology Officer: Bruce Borner
Contact, Communications: Diane Clehane
Managing Director, Membership Services: Patricia Maffei

E-Mail: pmaffei@fgi.org
Director, Archival Liaisons and Directory Advertising Sales: Jean Meek-Barker
Manager, Special Events: Jazz Purewal

Historical Note:
FGI provides insights on major trends in person, online and in print; access to business professionals and a gateway to the influence fashion plays in the marketplace. Members are men and women executives with a minimum of three years experience representing all facets of the fashion industry including manufacturing, marketing, designing, retailing, communications and education. Includes 26 U.S. chapters and 7 overseas chapters. Membership: $210 (Executive/At-Large); $100 (Associate).

Meetings/Conferences:
Conference Chair: Jazz Purewal

Publications:
FGI Membership Directory; annually

Fashion Jewelry and Accessories Trade Association
25 Sea Grass Way
Kingston, RI 02852
Website: fjata.org
Members: 225 member companies
Staff: 2
Annual Budget: $250-500,000

Personnel:
Executive Director: Brent Cleaveland
    E-Mail: bcleaveland@fjata.org
Contact, Communication: Sheila A. Millar

Historical Note:
The Fashion Jewelry and Accessories Trade Association (FJATA) represents the interests of manufacturers, suppliers and retailers of jewelry.

Publications:
Newsletter; monthly

Fastener Industry Coalition
P.O. Box 5
Lake Zurich, OH 60047
Tel: (847) 438-8338 *Fax:* (847) 438-7580
Members: 9 associations
Staff: 1
Annual Budget: Under $10,000

Personnel:
Contact: Nancy Rich CAE, EdD, RN

Historical Note:
A coalition of regional and national fastener associations. Has no paid officers or full-time staff; administrative support provided by Mid-West Fastener Association (same address).

FBI Agents Association *(1981)*
PO Box 12650
Arlington, VA 22219
Tel: (703) 247-2173 *Fax:* (703) 247-2175
Website: fbiaa.org
Members: 12000 individual
Staff: 4
Annual Budget: $500-1,000,000
Tax: 501(c)(6)

Personnel:
President: Konrad Motyka
    E-Mail: kmotyka@fbiaa.org
National Administrator: Traci Bannon
    E-Mail: fbiaa@fbiaa.org
General Counsel: Dee Martin
    E-Mail: dee.martin@bgllp.com
Assistant National Administrator and Membership Coordinator: Glenda Whalen
    E-Mail: fbiaa@fbiaa.org

Historical Note:
A Professional, non-governmental Association for active duty FBI agents. FBIAA's purpose is to improve the bureau to ensure all FBI agents are treated in a fair manner and to ensure the best possible climate for the effective discharge of their professional duties. Membership: $130 (Active); $26 (Retired/Associate).

Meetings/Conferences:
Number of non-conference events/year: 3

Publications:
FBI AGENT Newsletter; quarterly
Membership Directory; on-line

FCIB-NACM Corporation *(1919)*
8840 Columbia 100 Pkwy.
Columbia, MD 21045-2158

Tel: (410) 423-1840 *Fax:* (410) 740-5574
TollFree: (888) 256-3242
E-Mail: fcib_info@fcibglobal.com
Website: fcibglobal.com
Members: 1000 members
Staff: 6
Annual Budget: $1-2,000,000

Personnel:
Director, North American Operations: Marta Chacon-Martinez
    E-Mail: martac@fcibglobal.com
Coordinator, Marketing Communications: Darren Rudham
    E-Mail: darrenr@fcibglobal.com
Director, Membership and Business Development: Ron Shepherd
    E-Mail: rons@fcibglobal.com

Historical Note:
A subsidiary of the National Association of Credit Management and formerly (1967) the Foreign Credit Interchange Bureau. FCIB offers unique networking and educational opportunities, enhancing professional careers and improving company competitiveness and bottom line. Membership: $100-2300/year.

Continuing Education:
Certification Designation/s: CICA, CICP, CICE

Meetings/Conferences: Annual

Federal Administrative Law Judges Conference *(1947)*
P.O. Box 1772
Washington, DC 20013
Tel: (202) 675-3065
E-Mail: faljc@comcast.net
Website: faljc.org
Members: 270 individuals
Staff: 2
Annual Budget: $50-100,000

Personnel:
Treasurer: Justice Janice Bullard
    E-Mail: janice.bullard@dm.usda.gov
President: Justice J. Jeremiah Mahoney
    E-Mail: jeremiah.mahoney@hud.gov

Historical Note:
Formerly (1973) Federal Trial Examiners Conference, FALJC's mission is to perform judicial functions within the executive branch of the government. Members are judges who preside at administrative hearings within federal agencies. Membership: $150-160 (Active); $25 (Retired Judge/Sustaining); $1,750 (Life).

Publications:
Directory of FALJC Members

Federal Bar Association *(1920)*
1220 N. Fillmore St.
Suite 444
Arlington, VA 22201
Tel: (571) 481-9100 *Fax:* (571) 481-9090
E-Mail: fba@fedbar.org
Website: fedbar.org
Members: 16000 individuals
Staff: 13
Annual Budget: $2-5,000,000
Tax: 501(c)(6)

Personnel:
Executive Director: Jack Lockridge
    E-Mail: fba@fedbar.org
Manager, Meetings and Education: Kate Faenza
Manager, Membership Services: Carlena Farrar
    E-Mail: membership@fedbar.org
Staff Accountant: April Golladay-Davis
Government Relations Counsel: Bruce L. Moyer
    E-Mail: fba@fedbar.org
Managing Editor, The Federal Lawyer: Sarah Perlman

Historical Note:
FBA is dedicated to the advancement of the science of jurisprudence and to promoting the welfare, interests, education, and professional development of all attorneys involved in federal law. Members are attorneys currently or formerly employed by the Federal Government or who have a substantial interest in federal law as evidenced by admission to practice before a federal court or agency. Membership: $75-160 (Active); $135-220 (Sustaining); $30 (Law).

Continuing Education:
Certification Designation/s: CLE

Meetings/Conferences:
Conference Chair: Kate Faenza

2013 - Washington, DC (Ronald Reagan Building and International Trade Center)/March 1

2013 - Arlington, VA (Westin Arlington Gateway)/April 4 - 6

2013 - Santa Fe, NM (Hilton Buffalo Thunder)/April 11 - 12

2013 - New Orleans, LA (Westin New Orleans Canal Place)/May 1 - 5

2013 - San Juan, PR (Caribe Hilton San Juan)/Sept. 26 - 28

2014 - Santa Fe, NM (Hilton Buffalo Thunder)/April 10 - 11

Number of non-conference events/year: 1

Publications:
Membership Directory; on-line
The Federal Lawyer; adv.

Federal Communications Bar Association (1936)
1020 19th St. NW
Suite 325
Washington, DC 20036-6101
Tel: (202) 293-4000 *Fax:* (202) 293-4317
E-Mail: fcba@fcba.org
Website: fcba.org
Members: 2800 individuals
Staff: 4
Annual Budget: $1-2,000,000
Tax: 501(c)(6)

Personnel:
Executive Director: Stanley D. Zenor
  E-Mail: stan@fcba.org
Director, Membership Services: Kerry Loughney
  E-Mail: kerry@fcba.org
Administrative Assistant: Wendy Jo Parish
  E-Mail: wendy@fcba.org

Historical Note:
FCBA is a volunteer organization of attorneys, engineers, consultants, economists, government officials and law students involved in the study, development, interpretation and practice of communications and information technology law and policy. Members are involved in the development, interpretation, implementation and practice of communications law and policy. Membership: $60-170 (Voting/Non- Voting); $75 (Paralegal); $35 (Law Student); $40 (Retired).

Publications:
FCBA Directory; annually
FCBA Newsletter; monthly
Federal Communications Law Journal; quarterly

Membership List Available to Non-members

Federal Criminal Investigators Association (1953)
P.O. Box 23400
Washington, DC 20026
Tel: (630) 969-8537 *Fax:* (800) 528-3492
E-Mail: fcianat@aol.com
Website: fedcia.org
Members: 1000 individuals
Staff: 2
Annual Budget: $10-25,000

Personnel:
President: Richard Zehme
National Secretary: RIch Ahern

Historical Note:
FCIA's mission is to promote professionalism and professional development and enhance the image of federal law enforcement officers. Membership: $50 (Regular); $25 (Retired/Student); $45 (Associate).

Publications:
Federal Investigator; semi-annually; adv.

Federal Education Association (1956)
1201 16th St. NW
Suite 117
Washington, DC 20036
Tel: (202) 822-7850 *Fax:* (202) 822-7867
E-Mail: fea@feaonline.org
Website: feaonline.org
Members: 6000 individuals
Staff: 14
Annual Budget: $1-2,000,000

Personnel:
Executive Director and General Counsel: H. T. Nguyen
President: Michael Priser
Director, Communications and Membership Development: Gary Hritz
  E-Mail: ghritz@feaonline.org

Historical Note:
FEA's mission is to advocate within the federal system for educator's rights and for quality education. Members are primarily employees of the Department of Defense Education Activity (DoDEA). Membership: $392 (Active Full Time); $199 (Active Part Time/Associate); $99.50 (Retired Lifetime/Pre Retired); Free (Student).

Publications:
FEA Journal; quarterly
NEA Magazine
Newsletter

Membership List Available to Non-members

Federal Facilities Council (1953)
500 Fifth St. NW
Washington, DC 20001
Tel: (202) 334-2400 *Fax:* (202) 334-3370
E-Mail: BICE@nas.edu
Website: nationalacademies.org/ffc
Members: 130 individuals and 25 federal agencies
Staff: 2
Annual Budget: $500-1,000,000

Personnel:
Executive Director: Lynda Stanley
  E-Mail: lstanley@nas.edu

Historical Note:
Formerly (1994) Federal Construction Council. FFC's mission is to identify and advance technologies, processes, and management practices that improve the performance of federal facilities over their life-cycles, from programming to disposal. Members are professional employees of federal agencies and members of the Board on Infrastructure and the Constructed Environment of the National Research Council.

Meetings/Conferences:
Conference Chair: Lynda Stanley

Federal Forest Resource Coalition
600 New Hampshire Ave NW, Suite 500
Washington, DC 20037
Staff: 1

Personnel:
Treasurer: jones aurg

Historical Note:
Coalition of companies and trade associations that work with Federal timber resources.

Federal Judges Association (1982)
111 W. Washington St.
Suite 1100
Chicago, IL 60602
Tel: (312) 641-1441 *Fax:* (312) 641-1288
E-Mail: fja@federaljudgesassoc.org
Website: federaljudgesassoc.org
Members: 925 individuals
Staff: 6
Annual Budget: $100-250,000
Tax: 501(c)(6)

Personnel:
President: W. Royal Furgeson Jr.
Treasurer: Catherine C. Blake
Webmaster: L. Scott Coogler
Registered Agent: Kevin M. Forde
Vice-President, Communications and Editor: Ginny Granade
Vice-President, Membership: Katharine S. Hayden

Historical Note:
Seeks to preserve the ability of the federal judiciary to attract and retain the best qualified people for judicial service and to preserve the independence of the judiciary from intrusion, intimidation, coercion or domination from any source. Membership: $200/year (individual).

Publications:
Membership Directory; on-line

Federal Law Enforcement Officers Association (1977)
1100 Connecticut Ave. NW
Suite 900
Washington, DC 20036
Website: fleoa.org
Members: 25000 individuals
Staff: 13
Annual Budget: $2-5,000,000

Personnel:
National President: Jon Adler
  E-Mail: fleoa@fleoa.org

National Executive Vice President: Nate Catura
  E-Mail: fleoa@fleoa.org
Director, Administration: Timothy Chard
National Vice President, Membership Benefits: John Ramsey
Recruitment Director: Rasheed Tahir
Vice President, Legislative Affairs: Frank Terreri

Historical Note:
FLEOA represents law enforcement officers and special agents from over sixty agencies of the federal government. FLEOA provides a legislative voice for the federal law enforcement community. Membership: $130 (Regular); $45 (Retired); $50 (Resigned); $65 (Associate/Academy).

Meetings/Conferences:
Number of non-conference events/year: 3

Federal Magistrate Judges Association
P.O. BOX 267
Scranton, PA 18501
Tel: (570) 466-3969 *Fax:* (570) 955-3075
E-Mail: info@fedjudge.org
Website: fedjudge.org
Staff: 3
Annual Budget: $100-250,000
Tax: 501(c)(6)

Personnel:
Executive Director: Deborah H. Basalyga
President: Karen Wells Roby
Treasurer: David C Keesler

Historical Note:
Federal Magistrate Judges Association is a federal trial judge appointed to serve in a United States district court for a term of eight years.

Federal Managers Association (1913)
1641 Prince St.
Alexandria, VA 22314-2818
Tel: (703) 683-8700 *Fax:* (703) 683-8707
E-Mail: info@fedmanagers.org
Website: fedmanagers.org
Members: 200000 managers, supervisors and executives
Staff: 19
Annual Budget: $500-1,000,000
Tax: 501(c)(6)

Personnel:
Executive Director: Todd V. Wells
  E-Mail: twells@fedmanagers.org
Coordinator, Membership Services: Joann Brown
  E-Mail: jbrown@fedmanagers.org
Director, Government and Public Affairs: Greg Stanford
  E-Mail: gstanford@fedmanagers.org
Office Administrator and Finance Contact: Latorea Wilson
  E-Mail: lwilson@fedmanagers.org

Historical Note:
FMA advocates public service through effective management and professionalism, as well as the active representation of its members' interests and concerns. Membership includes managers and supervisors in all federal agencies. Membership: $125 (Regular/Associate); $63 (Retired).

Continuing Education:
Certification Designation/s: FMP

Meetings/Conferences:
2013 - Washington, DC (Mayflower Renaissance Hotel)/March 3 - 6
Number of non-conference events/year: 1-10

Publications:
The Federal Manager; quarterly
The Washington Report; bi-weekly

Federal Network for Sustainability (2000)
1112 16th St. NW, Suite 240
Washington, DC 20036
Tel: (202) 628-6100 *Fax:* (202) 393-5043
E-Mail: fns@federalsustainability.org
Website: federalsustainability.org
Members: 12 agencies
Staff: 1

Personnel:
Management Executive: Christian May

Historical Note:
FNS is a consortium of government agencies organized to disseminate information about responsible energy use throughout the federal government.

Federal Physicians Association (1979)
12427 Hedges Run Dr.

Suite 104
Lake Ridge, VA 22192
Tel: (877) 222-7497 Fax: (703) 426-8400
TollFree: (800) 528-3492
E-Mail: staff@fedphy.org
Website: fedphy.org
Members: 500 individuals
Staff: 2
Annual Budget: $25-50,000
Tax: 501(c)(6)

Personnel:
Executive Director: Dennis W Boyd
    E-Mail: dennis@fedphy.org
Treasurer: Michael E. Nesemann MD
    E-Mail: nesemannme@state.gov

Historical Note:
Founded by a group of physicians concerned with the worsening situation of the physician in federal government employment. FPA improve the health of those served by federal civil service physicians and the practice of medicine within the federal government. Membership: $100 (Individual); $35 (Retired).

Publications:
Federal Physician -Newsletter; quarterly; adv.

Membership List Available to Non-members

Federal Probation and Pre-trial Officers Association (1954)

900 U.S. Courthouse, 75 Spring St.
Atlanta, GA 30303-3361
Tel: (404) 215-1989
E-Mail: info@fppoa.org
Website: fppoa.org
Members: 1000 individuals
Staff: 80
Annual Budget: $25-50,000
Tax: 501(c)(6)

Personnel:
President: Barbara Oswald
    E-Mail: barbara_oswald@ganp.uscourts.gov
Editor: Scott Hudson

Historical Note:
FPPAO strives to study and improve methods of correctional service and philosophy and advocate pre-service and in-service education. Members are federal probation and pretrial services officers. Membership: $40 (Active); $250 (Contributing); $20 (Associate); Free (Newly Appointed Officers).

Publications:
FPPOA Legislative News; on-line
FPPOA Newsletter
Member Directory; on-line

Federal Water Quality Association (1928)

P.O. Box 14303
Washington, DC 20044-4303
Tel: (202) 566-2582 Fax: (202) 566-2825
E-Mail: info@fwqa-dc.org
Website: fwqa-dc.org
Members: 175 individuals
Staff: 3
Annual Budget: $25-50,000

Personnel:
President: Adam Krantz
Secretary: Sharon Nye
Treasurer: Jim Wheeler

Historical Note:
Formerly (1961) Federal Sewage Research Association. FWQA's purpose is to promote research in sewage treatment, evaluate new technologies, and to provide technical information and assistance to Federal Agencies, municipalities, and consulting firms. Members worldwide include government executives, engineering professionals, consultants, members of the academic community, and others. Membership: $20/year.

Publications:
FWQA Newsletter; semi-annually

Federally Employed Women (FEW) (1968)

700 N. Fairfax St.
Suite 510
Alexandria, VA 22314
Tel: (202) 898-0994 Fax: (240) 266-3232
E-Mail: few@few.org
Website: few.org
Members: 100 chapters
Staff: 5

Annual Budget: $1-2,000,000

Personnel:
President: Michelle Crockett
    E-Mail: president@few.org
Vice President, Training: Suzi Inman
    E-Mail: trainingVP@few.org
Executive Vice President: Wanda Killingsworth
    E-Mail: policyplanningVP@few.org
Vice President, Membership and Chapter Organization:
    Dawn Nester
    E-Mail: membershipVP@few.org

Historical Note:
FEW's mission is to improve the quality of life for women by influencing legislative actions. Membership: $45 (Regular); $300 (Life); $500-200 (Diamond - Upgrade to Life Member).

Meetings/Conferences:
Number of non-conference events/year: 2

Publications:
News & Views; bi-monthly; adv.

Federation of American Hospitals (1966)

750 Ninth St. NW
Suite 600
Washington, DC 20001-4524
Tel: (202) 624-1500 Fax: (202) 737-6462
E-Mail: info@fah.org
Website: fah.org
Members: 1700 hospital and health care systems
Staff: 21
Annual Budget: $10-25,000,000

Personnel:
President and Chief Executive Officer: Charles N. "Chip"
    Kahn III
    E-Mail: ckahn@fah.org
Executive Vice President, Advocacy and Political Affairs:
    Jeffrey E. Cohen
    E-Mail: jcohen@fah.org
Vice President, Communications: Richard P. Coorsh
    E-Mail: rcoorsh@fah.org
Manager, Membership Services: Melody Durham
    E-Mail: mdurham@fah.org
Vice President, Quality and Health Information Technology:
    Samantha Burch Halpert
Administrative Officer: Lisa Harrison
    E-Mail: lharrison@fah.org
Executive Vice President, Management, Compliance and
    General Counsel: Jeffrey G. Micklos
    E-Mail: jmicklos@fah.org
Senior Vice President, Health Finance and Policy: Steven
    Speil JD, MPH
    E-Mail: sspeil@fah.org
Vice President, Health Finance and Policy: Elizabeth
    Ward

Historical Note:
Mission is to foster the public good through the creation and delivery of quality health care for all. The FAH members include investor-owned hospitals and other organizations involved in the delivery of health care services that share a common philosophy of providing high quality, affordable health care, through free enterprise.

Meetings/Conferences: Annual
2013 - Washington, DC (Washington Marriott
    Wardman Park)/March 3 - 5/26-50 exhibitors
2014 - Washington, DC (Washington Marriott
    Wardman Park)/March 2 - 4/26-50 exhibitors
2015 - Washington, DC (Washington Marriott
    Wardman Park)/March 1 - 3/26-50 exhibitors

Publications:
Directory of Investor-Owned Hospitals; annually

Membership List Available to Non-members

Federation of American Scientists (1945)

1725 DeSales St. NW
Sixth Floor
Washington, DC 20036
Tel: (202) 546-3300 Fax: (202) 675-1010
E-Mail: fas@fas.org
Website: fas.org
Members: 3500 Individuals
Staff: 18
Annual Budget: $2-5,000,000
Tax: 501(c)(3)

Personnel:
President: Charles D. Ferguson
    E-Mail: fas@fas.org

Director, Government Secrecy: Steven Aftergood
    E-Mail: saftergood@fas.org
Director, Communications: Monica Amarelo
    E-Mail: press@fas.org
Research Associate, Strategic Security Program and UN
    Affairs: Alicia Godsberg
    E-Mail: agodsberg@fas.org
Program Director, Learning Technologies: Melanie Ann
    Stegman
    E-Mail: mstegman@fas.org

Historical Note:
FAS is dedicated to providing rigorous, objective, evidence-based analysis and practical policy recommendations on national and international security issues connected to applied science and technology. Membership: $25 (Student); $30 (Senior); $50 (Regular); $1000 (Life Time).

Publications:
FAS Newsletter; quarterly

Membership List Available to Non-members

Federation of American Societies for Experimental Biology (1912)

9650 Rockville Pk.
Bethesda, MD 20814-3998
Tel: (301) 634-7000 Fax: (301) 634-7001
E-Mail: info@faseb.org
Website: faseb.org
Members: 26 scientific societies and 100,000
researchers
Staff: 110
Annual Budget: $10-25,000,000
Tax: 501(c)(3)

Personnel:
Executive Director: Guy Fogleman PhD
Manager, Marketing and Business Development: Stefan
    Bradham
    E-Mail: sbradham@faseb.org
Director, Financial Services: David Craven
Deputy Executive Director, Policy: Dr. Howard Garrison
    E-Mail: hgarrison@opa.faseb.org
Director, Scientific Meetings and Conferences: Marcella
    Jackson
Deputy Executive Director, Administration and Director,
    Human Resources: Maureen Murphy CMP
Deputy Executive Director, Business Development,
    Information Technology and Publications: Jennifer
    Pesanelli
Director, MARC and Professional Development Programs:
    Jacquelyn Roberts

Historical Note:
Founded in 1912, the Federation of American Societies for Experimental Biology (FASEB) was originally created by three independent scientific organizations to provide a forum in which to hold educational meetings, develop publications, and disseminate biological research results. What started as a small group of dedicated scientists has grown to be the nation's largest coalition of biomedical researchers, representing 23 scientific societies and over 100,000 researchers from around the world. FASEB is now recognized as the policy voice of biological and biomedical researchers. FASEB's mission advance health and welfare by promoting progress and education in biological and biomedical sciences through service to our member societies and collaborative advocacy.

Meetings/Conferences:
Conference Chair: Marcella Jackson

Publications:
Breakthroughs in Bioscience; semi-annually
FASEB Directory; annually
The FASEB Journal; monthly

Federation of Analytical Chemistry and Spectroscopy Societies (1972)

P.O. Box 24379
Santa Fe, NM 87502
Tel: (505) 820-1648 Fax: (505) 989-1073
E-Mail: facssc@facssc.org
Website: facss.org/facss/index.php
Members: 7 organizations
Staff: 2
Annual Budget: $250-500,000
Tax: 501(c)(3)

Personnel:
Executive Assistant: Cindi Lilly
    E-Mail: cindi@sciencemanagers.com
Treasurer: Scott McGeorge
    E-Mail: mcgeorge@transition.ca

Historical Note:

FACSS's purpose is to provide a national forum for analytical chemistry through an exhibition and technical papers. Members are the analytical division of the American Chemical Society, the Chromatography Forum of the Delaware Valley, the Coblentz Society, the Instrument Society of America, the Society for Applied Spectroscopy, the Association of Analytical Chemists, and the analytical division of the Royal Society of Chemistry.

Meetings/Conferences: Annual

Federation of Associations in Behavioral & Brain Sciences *(1980)*

750 First St. NE
Suite 905
Washington, DC 20002-4242
Tel: (202) 336-5920 *Fax:* (202) 336-6183
E-Mail: info@fabbs.org
Website: fabbs.org
Members: 23 member societies and 35 departments/divisions
Staff: 2
Annual Budget: $250-500,000
Tax: 501(c)(6)

Personnel:
Executive Director: Paula R. Skedsvold JD, PhD
    E-Mail: pskedsvold@fabbs.org
Director, Administration: Meghan McGowan MA
    E-Mail: mmcgowan@fabbs.org

Historical Note:
Formerly (2009) the Federation of Behavioral Psychological and Cognitive Sciences. FABBS promotes human potential and well-being by advancing the sciences of mind, brain, and behavior. As a coalition of scientific societies, they communicate with policy makers and the public about the importance and contributions of basic and applied research in these sciences. Membership: $12.62-14.16 (Society); $250 (Affiliate); $5,000 (Corporate).

Publications:
Member Listing; on-line

Federation of Associations of Regulatory Boards *(1974)*

1466 Techny Rd.
Northbrook, IL 60062
Tel: (847) 559-3272 *Fax:* (847) 714-9796
E-Mail: farb@farb.org
Website: farb.org
Members: 100 individuals and associations
Staff: 1
Annual Budget: $100-250,000
Tax: 501(c)(3)

Personnel:
Executive Director: Dale J. Atkinson

Historical Note:
Formerly (1985) the Federation of Associations of Health Regulatory Boards. FARB's mission is to promote excellence in regulation for public protection by providing expertise and innovation from a multi- professional perspective. Membership: $500 (Affiliate); $1,000 (Supporting); $50 (Individual).

Meetings/Conferences: Annual
2013 - San Diego, CA (Omni San Diego Hotel)/Jan. 25 - 27
Number of non-conference events/year: 1

Membership List Available to Non-members

Federation of Behavioral, Psychological and Cognitive Sciences *(1982)*

750 First St. NE
Suite 905
Washington, DC 20002-4242
Tel: (202) 336-5920 *Fax:* (202) 336-5953
E-Mail: federation@fbpcs.org
Website: fabbs.org
Staff: 2
Annual Budget: $250-500,000
Tax: 501(c)(6)

Personnel:
Executive Director: Paula R. Skedsvold JD, PhD
    E-Mail: pskedsvold@fabbs.org
Director, Administration: Meghan McGowan MA
    E-Mail: mmcgowan@fabbs.org

Historical Note:
Incorporated in 1981 and formerly (2009) known as the Federation of Behavioral, Psychological, and Cognitive Sciences, FABBS promotes human potential and well-being by advancing the sciences of mind, brain, and behavior. Membership: $250 (Affiliate Member).

Meetings/Conferences:
Conference Chair: Meghan McGowan MA

Publications:
FABBS News; on-line
Membership Directory; on-line

Federation of Defense and Corporate Counsel *(1936)*

11812 N. 56th St.
Tampa, FL 33617
Tel: (813) 983-0022 *Fax:* (813) 988-5837
Website: thefederation.org
Members: 1400 individuals
Staff: 4
Annual Budget: $50-100,000
Tax: 501(c)(3)

Personnel:
Executive Director: Martha J. Streeper
    E-Mail: mstreeper@thefederation.org
Coordinator, Membership Development: Mary Nell O'Dowd
    E-Mail: marynell@thefederation.org
Director, Finance: Michael W. Streeper
    E-Mail: mmg_mike@hotmail.com

Historical Note:
Formerly (1985) Federation of Insurance Counsel; (2001) Federation of Insurance and Corporate Counsel. FDCC's mission is to enhance knowledge, fellowship, and professionalism of its members as they pursue the course of a balanced justice system and represent those in need of a defense in civil lawsuits. Members are practicing lawyers, corporate counsel and other executives engaged in the administration or defense of claims. Membership: $250/year.

Meetings/Conferences:
2013 - San Antonio, TX (Westin La Cantera Hill Country Resort)/March 2 - 9
2013 - Colorado Springs, CO (Antlers Hilton Colorado Springs)/July 28 - Aug. 4
2014 - Marco Island, FL (Marco Island Marriott Beach Resort, Golf Club and Spa)/March 1 - 8
2014 - Napa, CA (Silverado Resort and Spa)/July 26 - Aug. 2
2015 - San Juan, PR (Waldorf Astoria El Conquistador)/Feb. 14 - March 7
2015 - Banff, AB (Fairmont Banff Springs Resort)/July 25 - Aug. 1
Number of non-conference events/year: 2

Publications:
FDCC Quarterly; quarterly
Flyer; semi-annually
Legal Services Directory; on-line
The FDCC Roster; on-line; adv.

Federation of Diocesan Liturgical Commissions *(1969)*

415 Michigan Ave. NE
Suite 70
Washington, DC 20017
Tel: (202) 635-6990 *Fax:* (202) 529-2452
E-Mail: nationaloffice@fdlc.org
Website: fdlc.org
Members: 400 individuals
Staff: 4

Personnel:
Executive Director: Lisa A. Tarker
    E-Mail: lisa@fdlc.org
Staff Assistant: Joseph Skeffington
    E-Mail: Joe@fdlc.org

Historical Note:
FDLC's mission is to promote the liturgy as the heart of Christian life-especially in the parish community. Any dues paying Diocese in the United States and its territories is eligible for membership in the FDLC. Membership entitles each Diocese to have two voting delegates at the National Meeting. Membership: $75 (Associate); $175 (Industry).

Meetings/Conferences: Annual
2013 - Erie, PA (Sheraton Bayfront)/Oct. 8 - 12

Publications:
FDLC Newsletter; bi-monthly; adv.
FDLC Online Directory

Federation of Employers and Workers of America *(1998)*

2901 Bucks Bayou Rd.
Bay City, TX 77414
Tel: (979) 245-7577 *Fax:* (979) 245-8969

Website: fewaglobal.org
Members: 7500 members
Staff: 4
Annual Budget: $1-2,000,000
Tax: 501(c)(6)

Personnel:
President: Scott Evans
General Counsel: Wesley Mathis
Business Manager: April McKinney
Office Manager: Rita Romero

Historical Note:
The Federation of Employers and Workers of America (FEWA) celebrated our seventh anniversary on December 28, 2008. The association has been hard at work "Solving America's Immigration Problems One Employer And One Worker At A Time" for members and the general business community.

Federation of Environmental Technologists, Inc. *(1982)*

W175 N11081 Stonewood Dr.
Suite 203
Germantown, WI 53022
Tel: (262) 437-1700 *Fax:* (262) 437-1702
E-Mail: info@fetinc.org
Website: fetinc.org
Members: 500 individuals and patrons
Staff: 3
Annual Budget: $250-500,000
Tax: 501(c)(3)

Personnel:
Executive Director: Barbara Hurula
    E-Mail: bhurula@fetinc.org
Treasurer: Anthony Montemurro

Historical Note:
FET's mission is to educate its members and other environmental professionals on regulatory compliance and technological developments in a cost-effective manner through training, professional development and networking. Membership: $120 (Individual); $85 (Government Employee); $40 (Student/Unemployed Professional/ Retiree); $285 (Patron Company).

Meetings/Conferences:
Conference Chair: Julie Jansett

Publications:
Environotes Newsletter

Membership List Available to Non-members

Federation of Internet Solution Providers of the Americas *(1996)*

P.O. Box 2270
Matthews, NC 28106-2270
Tel: (704) 844-2540 *Fax:* (704) 844-2728
Website: fispa.org
Members: 170 internet service providers
Staff: 3
Annual Budget: $100-250,000

Personnel:
Executive Director: Jim Hollis
    E-Mail: executive.director@fispa.org
Contact, Operations: Geri S. Armstrong Pennavaria
Contact, Accounting: Mary Anne Rayfield

Historical Note:
Formerly (1996) Florida Internet Solution Providers Association. FISPA members represent the support industry of sales, consulting, equipment, and service suppliers that enable to bring the public the right to choose superior quality, pricing, and customer support from among competing providers. Membership: $295-695 (Regular); $1,995 (Vendor).

Publications:
Membership Directory; on-line

Federation of Materials Societies *(1972)*

910 17th St. NW
Suite 800
Washington, DC 20006
Tel: (202) 296-9282
Website: materialsocieties.org
Members: 700014 individuals and societies
Staff: 1
Annual Budget: $50-100,000

Personnel:
Executive Director: Betsy Houston
    E-Mail: betsyhou@ix.netcom.com

Historical Note:

FMS's purpose is to aid the materials community in obtaining information from and exchanging information with the policy community.

Publications:
FMS News; on-line

Federation of Modern Painters and Sculptors
(1940)
113 Greene St.
New York, NY 10012
Tel: (212) 966-4864
E-Mail: info@fedart.org
Website: fedart.org
Members: 60 individuals
Staff: 4
Annual Budget: Under $10,000

Personnel:
President: Anneli Arms
Treasurer: Jon Rettich

Historical Note:
Purpose is to improve the economic and working conditions of professional artists and facilitate the exhibition of their work. Membership is concentrated within the New York area. Membership: $30/year.

Federation of Podiatric Medical Boards *(1936)*
6551 Malta Dr.
Boynton Beach, FL 33437
Tel: (561) 752-3735
Website: fpmb.org
Members: 50 states
Staff: 2
Annual Budget: $50-100,000
Tax: 501(c)(6)

Personnel:
Executive Director: Larry I. Shane
Secretary and Treasurer: Kirk M. Contento DPM

Historical Note:
FPMB's mission is to improve the quality, safety and integrity of podiatric medical health care by promoting better standards for podiatric physician licensure, regulation and practice.

Federation of Spine Associations
6300 N. River Rd.
Rosemont, IL 60018-4262
Staff: 1
Annual Budget: $50-100,000
Tax: 501(c)(3)

Personnel:
President: John R. Tongue

Federation of State Boards of Physical Therapy
(1987)
124 W. St., South
Third Floor
Alexandria, VA 22314
Tel: (703) 299-3100 *Fax:* (703) 299-3110
TollFree: (800) 881-1430
Website: fsbpt.org
Members: 400 individuals
Staff: 57
Annual Budget: $10-25,000,000
Tax: 501(c)(6)

Personnel:
Chief Executive Officer: William A. Hatherill
Quality Assurance Specialist: Holly Ball
    E-Mail: hball@fsbpt.org
Associate to Senior Staff: Maribeth C. Decker
    E-Mail: mdecker@fsbpt.org
Meeting Planner: Paul Delaney
Managing Director, Information Systems: Seif A. Mahmoud
Managing Director, Assessment: Lorin Mueller
Chief Financial Officer: Larry J. Wilkerson CPA
    E-Mail: lwilkerson@fsbpt.org

Historical Note:
FSBPT's mission is to protect the public by providing service that promote safe and competent physical therapy practice.

Meetings/Conferences: Annual
Conference Chair: Paul Delaney
2013 - San Antonio, TX (Westin Riverwalk)/Oct. 10 - 12

Publications:
Federation Forum; quarterly
Membership Directory; on-line
The NPTE Faculty Newsletter; quarterly

Federation of State Humanities Councils *(1977)*
1600 Wilson Blvd.
Suite 902
Arlington, VA 22209-2505
Tel: (703) 908-9700 *Fax:* (703) 908-9706
E-Mail: info@statehumanities.org
Website: statehumanities.org
Members: 55 state councils
Staff: 6
Annual Budget: $500-1,000,000
Tax: 501(c)(3)

Personnel:
President: Esther Mackintosh
    E-Mail: emackintosh@statehumanities.org
Vice President, Communications: Jeff Allen
    E-Mail: jallen@statehumanities.org
Manager, Meetings and Events: Shannon Loburk
    E-Mail: SLoburk@statehumanities.org
Director, Finance: Elizabeth Paine
    E-Mail: epaine@statehumanities.org
Communication and Administrative Associate: Natalie Pak
    E-Mail: npak@statehumanities.org

Historical Note:
FSHC's mission is to provide support for the state humanities councils and strives to create greater awareness of the humanities in public and private life.

Meetings/Conferences: Annual
Conference Chair: Elizabeth Paine
2013 - Birmingham, AL/Nov. 7 - 10
Number of non-conference events/year: 1

Publications:
Membership Directory; on-line

Federation of State Medical Boards of the United States *(1912)*
400 Fuller Wiser Rd.
Suite 300
Euless, TX 76039
Tel: (817) 868-4000 *Fax:* (817) 868-4099
Website: fsmb.org
Members: 70 medical and osteopathic boards
Staff: 202
Annual Budget: $25-50,000,000

Personnel:
President and Chief Executive Officer: Humayun J. Chaudhry DO, FACOI, MS, FACP
Director, Education and Legislative Services: Kelly C. Alfred MS
    E-Mail: kalfred@fsmb.org
Director, Communications: Drew Carlson
    E-Mail: dcarlson@fsmb.org
Chief Information Officer: Michael Dugan MBA
Senior Director, Marketing: David Hooper
    E-Mail: dhooper@fsmb.org
Librarian and Contact, Member Resource Center: Linda Jordan MS
    E-Mail: ljordan@fsmb.org
Vice President, Information Services: Rita H. Mohsin MBA
Chief Financial Officer: Todd Phillips
Director, Human Resources: Starr Stelivan MBA
    E-Mail: sstelivan@fsmb.org

Historical Note:
Founded as the result of a merger between the National Confederation of State Medical Examining and Licensing Boards (1891) and the American Confederation of Reciprocating Examining and Licensing Boards (1902). FSMB's mission is to promote excellence in medical practice, licensure, and regulation as the national resource and on behalf of state medical boards in their protection of the public. Membership: $2,000/year (State Board).

Meetings/Conferences:
2013 - Boston, MA (Sheraton Boston Hotel)/April 18 - 20
2014 - Denver, CO (Hyatt Regency Denver at Colorado Convention Center)/April 24 - 26
Number of non-conference events/year: 3

Publications:
FSMB eNews; bi-weekly
International Medical Education (InMedEd); quarterly
Journal of Medical Regulation; quarterly

Federation of Straight Chiropractors and Organizations *(1979)*
2276 Wassergass Rd.
Hellertown, PA 18055
Tel: (610) 838-3030 *Fax:* (610) 838-3031

TollFree: (800) 521-9856
E-Mail: fsco@straightchiropractic.com
Website: straightchiropractic.com
Members: 1200 individuals
Staff: 3
Annual Budget: $50-100,000

Personnel:
President: Shane Walker
    E-Mail: president@straightchiropractic.org
Administrative Assistant: Renee Hillman
    E-Mail: fsco@juno.com
Treasurer: Brian Mikula

Historical Note:
The International Federation of Chiropractors and Organizations (IFCO) is an international organization of chiropractors, students. IFCO's mission is to support and advance the practice of chiropractic that is exclusive for the location, analysis, and correction of vertebral subluxation because vertebral subluxation, in and of itself, is a detriment to the fullest expression of life. Membership: $50 (Non-Voting); $125-500 (Full Voting).

Meetings/Conferences: Annual

Publications:
The Anchor; quarterly; adv.

Federation of Tax Administrators *(1937)*
444 N. Capitol St. NW
Suite 348
Washington, DC 20001
Tel: (202) 624-5890 *Fax:* (202) 624-7888
Website: taxadmin.org
Members: 52 agencies
Staff: 10
Annual Budget: $2-5,000,000
Tax: 501(c)(3)

Personnel:
Executive Director: Gale Garriott
Senior Research Associate: Ronald Alt
Chief Counsel: Helen Hecht
Senior Manager, Tax Technology and Standards: Jonathan Lyon
Assistant Director and Senior Manager, Administration and Policy: Verenda Smith
    E-Mail: verenda.smith@taxadmin.org

Historical Note:
Established by the National Association of Tax Administrators, the North American Gasoline Tax Conference and the National Tobacco Tax Association. FTA subsequently absorbed all three founding organizations whose mission is to foster good tax administration. Members are the tax agencies of the 50 state governments, the District of Columbia and New York City.

Meetings/Conferences: Annual
Conference Chair: Helen Hecht
Number of non-conference events/year: 14

Publications:
TaxExPRESS; weekly

Feldenkrais Guild of North America *(1977)*
5436 N. Albina Ave.
Portland, OR 97217
Tel: (503) 221-6612 *Fax:* (503) 221-6616
TollFree: (800) 775-2118
Website: feldenkrais.com/profession/fgna/ about_fgna/
Staff: 8
Annual Budget: $500-1,000,000
Tax: 501(c)(6)

Personnel:
Executive Director: Susan Marshall
    E-Mail: executivedirector@feldenkraisguild.com

Historical Note:
Formerly (1997) Feldenkrais Guild. FGNA strives to develop, promote and protect the Feldenkrais Method by upholding the standards of practice, educating the public, in all its diversity, promoting professional development and providing service to it members. Members are practitioners and teachers of the Feldenkrais Method.

Continuing Education:
Certification Designation/s: GCFP, GCFT

Meetings/Conferences: Annual

Publications:
Feldenkrais Journal

Fellowship of United Methodists in Music and Worship Arts *(1956)*
P.O. Box 24787

Nashville, TN 37202-4787
Tel: (615) 749-6875 *Fax:* (615) 749-6874
TollFree: (800) 952-8977
E-Mail: info@fummwa.org
Website: fummwa.affiniscape.com
Members: 2200 individuals
Staff: 3
Annual Budget: $250-500,000
Tax: 501(c)(3)

Personnel:
Executive Director: David L. Bone
  E-Mail: fummwa@aol.com
Administrator: Eleanor Cobb
  E-Mail: eleanor@UMFellowship.org
Editor: Dave Wiltse

Historical Note:
Formerly (1974) National Fellowship of United Methodist Musicians, (1979) Fellowship of United Methodist Musicians, and (1995) Fellowship of United Methodists in Worship, Music and Other Arts. FUMMWA's mission is to minister, through creative gifts, in order to foster worship, which makes disciples of Jesus Christ. Membership: $45 (New); $65 (Full-time Connection); $40 (Persons over 65 years of age) $110(Sustaining Full Connection).

Meetings/Conferences: Annual
2013 - Lake Junaluska, NC/June 23 - 28
2013 - Pittsburgh, PA/July 15 - 18
2014 - Lake Junaluska, NC/June 22 - 27
Number of non-conference events/year: 3

Publications:
Music Interest Areas Newsletter; quarterly; adv.
Weekly Devotions; weekly
Worship Arts; bi-monthly; adv.

Fermenters International Trade Association (1979)
P.O. Box 1373
Valrico, FL 33595
Tel: (813) 685-4261 *Fax:* (813) 681-5625
Website: fermentersinternational.org
Members: 150 individuals
Staff: 2
Annual Budget: $10-25,000

Personnel:
Executive Director, Secretary and Treasurer: Dee Roberson
  E-Mail: droberson@fermentersinternational.org
Editor: Bill Metzger

Historical Note:
Formerly (2009) known as the Home Wine & Beer Trade Association (HWBTA), FITA works to advance the practice of the fermentation arts, such as homebrewing, winemaking, and cheesecrafting, and to expand and strengthen the industry as a whole. Members are manufacturers, distributors, retailers, and others with an interest in the home brewing and home winemaking trade. Membership: $100 (Individual Retailer); $250 (Corporate); $500 (Corporate Sponsor).

Meetings/Conferences: Annual

The Fertilizer Institute (1955)
425 Third St. SW
Suite 950
Washington, DC 20024
Tel: (202) 962-0490 *Fax:* (202) 962-0577
E-Mail: information@tfi.org
Website: tfi.org
Members: 175 individuals and organizations
Staff: 18
Annual Budget: $5-10,000,000
Tax: 501(c)(6)

Personnel:
President: Ford B. West
  E-Mail: fwest@tfi.org
Director, Administration & Finance: Carol Dorrough
  E-Mail: cdorrough@tfi.org
Vice President, Member Services: Pamela D. Guffain
  E-Mail: pguffain@tfi.org
Vice President, Public Affairs and Media Contact: Kathleen O. Mathers
  E-Mail: kmathers@tfi.org
Director, Conferences: Linda McAbee
  E-Mail: LMcAbee@tfi.org
Vice President, Government Relations: J. Clark Mica
  E-Mail: cmica@tfi.org
Director, Information Technology: Justin Sharbaugh
  E-Mail: jsharbaugh@tfi.org

Historical Note:

Product of a merger of the National Plant Food Institute (1955) and Agricultural Nitrogen Institute (1951), TFI strives to promote and protect fertilizer from the plant where it is manufactured to the plant where it is used and all points in between. Members are brokers, producers, importers, retailers and manufacturers of fertilizer and fertilizer-related equipment.

Meetings/Conferences:
Conference Chair: Linda McAbee
2013 - Orlando, FL (Hyatt Regency Grand Cypress)/ Feb. 11 - 13
2013 - Montreal, QC (Le Centre Sheraton Montreal Hotel)/Sept. 22 - 24
2013 - Tampa, FL (Tampa Marriott Waterside Hotel)/ Nov. 19 - 21
2014 - San Diego, CA (Manchester Grand)/Feb. 3 - 5
2014 - San Diego, CA (Westgate Hotel)/Sept. 7 - 9
2014 - San Francisco, CA (Westin St. Francis)/Sept. 21 - 23
2014 - Savannah, GA (Hyatt Regency)/Nov. 18 - 20
2015 - Scottsdale, AZ (Westin Kierland Resort and Spa)/Feb. 9 - 11
2016 - Hollywood, CA (Westin Diplomat Resort and Spa)/Feb. 1 - 3
2016 - San Diego, CA (Manchester Grand Hyatt San Diego)/Sept. 25 - 27
Number of non-conference events/year: 1

Publications:
TFI Newsletter; weekly

Fiber Society (1941)
North Carolina State University, College of Textiles
P.O. Box 8301, 2401 Research Dr.
Raleigh, NC 27695-8301
Tel: (919) 513-0143 *Fax:* (919) 515-3057
E-Mail: admin@thefibersociety.org
Website: thefibersociety.org
Members: 400 individuals
Staff: 5
Annual Budget: $50-100,000

Personnel:
President: Cheryl Gomes
  E-Mail: cheryl.gomes@qinetiq-na.com
Secretary: Michael Ellison
  E-Mail: ellisom@clemson.edu
Contact, Administration: Pam Gabriel
  E-Mail: psgabrie@ncsu.edu
Editor: Michael Jaffe
  E-Mail: jaffe@adm.njit.edu
Treasurer: Stephen Michielsen
  E-Mail: stephen_michielsen@ncsu.edu

Historical Note:
FS strives for the advancement of scientific knowledge pertaining to fibers, fiber based products, and fibrous materials. Members are chemists, physicists, and engineers with interests in the field of fiber science engineering and technology. Membership: $60 (Regular); $30 (Student).

Meetings/Conferences: Semi-Annual
Conference Chair: Pam Gabriel
Number of non-conference events/year: 1

Publications:
The Fiber Society Newsletter; on-line

Fiberglass Tank and Pipe Institute (1987)
11150 S. Wilcrest Dr.
Suite 101
Houston, TX 77099-4343
Tel: (281) 568-4100 *Fax:* (281) 568-9998
E-Mail: info@fiberglasstankandpipe.com
Website: fiberglasstankandpipe.com
Members: 11 companies
Staff: 1
Annual Budget: $100-250,000
Tax: 501(c)(6)

Personnel:
Executive Director: Sullivan "Sully" D. Curran PE

Historical Note:
Formerly (1995) Fiberglass Petroleum Tank and Pipe Institute. FTPI promotes and protects the interests and image of the fiberglass- reinforced thermosetting plastic tank and pipe manufacturing industry. In addition, the Institute develops, exchanges and disseminates information of benefit to its members. Members are domestic manufacturers. Membership: $4,400/year (Minimum).

Publications:
Membership Directory; on-line

Fibre Box Association (1940)
25 NW Point Blvd.
Suite 510
Elk Grove Village, IL 60007
Tel: (847) 364-9600 *Fax:* (847) 364-9639
E-Mail: fba@fibrebox.org
Website: fibrebox.org
Members: 154 companies
Staff: 7
Annual Budget: $2-5,000,000
Tax: 501(c)(6)

Personnel:
President: Dennis J. Colley
  E-Mail: dcolley@fibrebox.org
Manager, Technical: Dave Carlson
  E-Mail: dcarlson@fibrebox.org
Director, Administration and Data Services: Peggy Lacy
  E-Mail: placy@fibrebox.org
Coordinator, Marketing and Communications: Caitlin McKeown
  E-Mail: cmckeown@fibrebox.org
Legal Counsel: David Simon
  E-Mail: dsimon@foley.com

Historical Note:
FBA strives to grow, protect and enhance the overall well-being of the industry by providing member-valued programs and services. Members are makers of corrugated boxes. Membership: Minimum $975/year.

Meetings/Conferences: Annual
2013 - Miami, FL (Ritz-Carlton, South Beach)/April 8 - 10
Number of non-conference events/year: 12

Membership List Available to Non-members

Fibre Channel Industry Association (1999)
575 B Ruger St.
P.O. Box 29920
San Francisco, CA 94129-0920
Tel: (425) 359-3326 *Fax:* (415) 561-6120
TollFree: (800) 272-4618
E-Mail: info@fibrechannel.org
Website: fibrechannel.org
Members: 100 members
Staff: 1
Annual Budget: $250-500,000
Tax: 501(c)(6)

Personnel:
Executive Director: Chris Lyon
  E-Mail: clyon@fibrechannel.org

Historical Note:
FCIA strives to act as the independent technology and marketing voice of the Fibre Channel industry. Membership: $20,000 (Sponsor); $12,000 (Principal); $8,000 (Associate); $2,500 (Observer); $475 (Individual Observer).

Meetings/Conferences:
Number of non-conference events/year: 4

Publications:
FCIA Newsletter; quarterly
Membership Directory; annually

Membership List Available to Non-members

The Fiduciary and Investment Risk Management Association (1980)
P.O. Box 507
Stockbridge, GA 30281
Tel: (678) 565-6211 *Fax:* (678) 565-8788
E-Mail: info@thefirma.org
Website: thefirma.org
Members: 820 individuals
Staff: 2

Personnel:
President: Bruce K. Goldberg CPA, CTA
  E-Mail: bkgoldberg@deloitte.com
Secretary: Bradley F. Beshea CFIRS, CFP

Historical Note:
Founded as National Association of Trust Audit and Compliance Professionals, assumed its current name in 2000. FIRMA strives to educate, support and promote risk management professionals. It also strives to improve the effectiveness of risk management for the fiduciary and investment services industry. Members are audit and compliance professionals. Membership: $140 (Certified); $175 (Sustaining); $35 (Emeritus).

Meetings/Conferences:
Number of non-conference events/year: 3

Publications:
FIRMA News; on-line

Filter Manufacturers Council *(1971)*
P.O. Box 13966
Ten Laboratory Dr.
Research Triangle Park, NC 27709-3966
Tel: (919) 549-4800 *Fax:* (919) 406-1306
Website: aftermarketsuppliers.org/fmc
Members: 38 companies
Staff: 2
Annual Budget: $250-500,000

Personnel:
Executive Director: Jeremy Denton
    E-Mail: jdenton@mema.org
Meeting Contact: Liz Goad
    E-Mail: egoad@mema.org

Historical Note:
Formerly Automotive Filter Manufacturers Council till 1989. A product line council of Motor and Equipment Manufacturers Association, which provides administrative support. Membership: $2,625-13,650/year (based on annual sales).

Meetings/Conferences: Annual
Conference Chair: Liz Goad
Number of non-conference events/year: 2

Publications:
Membership Directory; on-line

Financial & Insurance Conference Planners *(1947)*
401 N. Michigan Ave.
22nd Floor
Chicago, IL 60611-4267
Tel: (312) 245-1023 *Fax:* (312) 673-6920
E-Mail: info@ficpnet.com
Website: ficpnet.com
Members: 500 professionals
Staff: 9
Annual Budget: $1-2,000,000
Tax: 501(c)(6)

Personnel:
Executive Director: Steve Bova CAE
    E-Mail: sbova@ficpnet.com
Manager, Education: Lydia Goessel
    E-Mail: lgoessel@ficpnet.com
Manager, Operations: Laura Greer
    E-Mail: lgreer@ficpnet.com
Senior Manager, Event Services: Ellie Hurley
    E-Mail: ehurley@ficpnet.com
Manager, Membership: Mark Swets
    E-Mail: mswets@ficpnet.com
Senior Manager, Marketing and Communications: Kim Walsh
    E-Mail: kwalsh@ficpnet.com

Historical Note:
Founded as Insurance Convention Planners Association, became Insurance Conference Planners Association in 1976, ICPA-An Association of Insurance and Financial Service Conference Planners in 2004, assumed its current name in 2005. FICP is an association of insurance and financial services industry-meeting planners. Mission is to promote the exchange of information on meeting management techniques and new trends. Members are meeting, conference and convention planning professionals who work for Insurance or Financial Services Companies. Membership: $375/year (Planner/Hospitality/Corporate).

Meetings/Conferences: Annual
Conference Chair: Ellie Hurley
2013 - Park City, UT (Montage Deer Valley)/June 12 - 14
2013 - Boston, MA (Sheraton Boston Hotel)/Nov. 17 - 20
2014 - Waikoloa, HI (Hilton Waikoloa Village)/Nov. 16 - 19

Publications:
NewsNet e-newsletter; monthly

Financial and Security Products Association *(1973)*
5300 Sequoia Rd. NW
Suite 205
Albuquerque, NM 87120
Tel: (505) 839-7958 *Fax:* (505) 839-0017
TollFree: (800) 843-6082
E-Mail: info@fspa1.com
Website: fspa1.com
Members: 275 dealers and manufacturers

Staff: 2
Annual Budget: $250-500,000

Personnel:
Executive Director: John M. Vrabec
    E-Mail: jv@fspa1.com

Historical Note:
Formerly (2005) National Independent Bank Equipment and Systems Association (NIBESA). FSBE is an association of independent companies involved in manufacturing, selling, installing and servicing financial security equipment for banks, credit unions and other financial institutions. Members are independent dealers, manufacturers and associates whose products and services give financial institutions an edge in performance, efficiency and economy. Membership: $395/year.

Meetings/Conferences: Annual
2013 - Scottsdale, AZ (Fairmont Scottsdale Princess Hotel and Resort)/May 30 - June 1

Publications:
FSPA Newsletter; monthly; adv.
Membership Directory; annually
The Business Owner; bi-monthly; adv.

Financial Executives International *(1931)*
1250 Headquarters Plaza
West Tower, Seventh Floor
Morristown, NJ 07960
Tel: (973) 765-1000 *Fax:* (973) 765-1018
TollFree: (877) 359-1070
E-Mail: membership@financialexecutives.org
Website: financialexecutives.org
Members: 86 chapters and 15000 individuals
Staff: 44
Annual Budget: $5-10,000,000
Tax: 501(c)(6)

Personnel:
President and Chief Executive Officer: Marie N. Hollein CTP
    E-Mail: mhollein@financialexecutives.org
Vice President and Chief Financial Officer: Paul Chase CPA
    E-Mail: pchase@financialexecutives.org
Vice President, Marketing and Communications: Lili DeVita
    E-Mail: ldevita@financialexecutives.org
Director, Conferences and Professional Development: Jim Eagen
    E-Mail: jeagen@financialexecutives.org
Editor-in-Chief: Ellen Heffes
    E-Mail: eheffes@financialexecutives.org
Director, Research: William Sinnett
    E-Mail: bsinnett@financialexecutives.org
Vice President, Information Technology and Web Services: Mark Steele
    E-Mail: msteele@financialexecutives.org
Manager, Membership Services: Angela Tise
    E-Mail: afalzarano@financialexecutives.org

Historical Note:
Mission is to provide networking, knowledge, advocacy and ethical leadership. Members are chief financial officers, treasurers, and controllers. Membership: $150 (Executive/ Associate/In-Transition).

Meetings/Conferences:
Conference Chair: Jim Eagen
2013 - Las Vegas, NV (Caesars Palace)/May 4 - 5
Number of non-conference events/year: 3

Publications:
FEI Express; weekly; adv.
FEI Membership Directory; on-line
Finance & Information Technology: Knowledge for Financial Executives; monthly
Financial Executive Magazine; monthly; adv.
Quarterly Plan Sponsor Update
What's New In Research; monthly

Financial Industry Regulatory Authority (FINRA) *(2007)*
1735 K St. NW
Washington, DC 20006-1506
Tel: (301) 590-6500
Website: finra.org
Members: 4,525 brokerage firms and 633,390 representatives
Staff: 705
Annual Budget: Over $100,000,000
Tax: 501(c)(3)

Personnel:

Chairman and Chief Executive Officer: Richard G. Ketchum
Senior Vice President and Corporate Secretary: Marcia E. Asquith
Executive Vice President and General Counsel: T. Grant Callery
Executive Vice President and Chief Technology Officer: Martin P. Colburn
Office Manager: Cassandra Cunnngham
    E-Mail: cassandra.cunningham@finra.org
Executive Vice President and Chief Financial Officer: Todd T. Diganci
Senior Vice President, Human Resources: Tracy Johnson
Executive Vice President, Corporate Communications and Government Relations: Howard M. Schloss
    E-Mail: howard.schloss@finra.org
Executive Vice President, Membership Regulation: Grace B. Vogel
President, FINRA Investor Education Foundation Vice President, FINRA Investor Education: Gerri Walsh

Historical Note:
FINRA's mission is to provide investor protection and market integrity through comprehensive regulation.

Continuing Education:
Certification Designation/s: CE

Meetings/Conferences:
2013 - Washington, DC (Renaissance Washington)/ May 20 - 22
Number of non-conference events/year: 7

Publications:
Investor Newsletter; monthly

Financial Management Association International *(1970)*
University of S. Florida, College of Business Administration
4202 E. Fowler Ave., BSN 3331
Tampa, FL 33620-5500
Tel: (813) 974-2084 *Fax:* (813) 974-3318
E-Mail: fma@coba.usf.edu
Website: fma.org
Members: 12000 individuals and institutions
Staff: 8
Annual Budget: $1-2,000,000
Tax: 501(c)(3)

Personnel:
Executive Director: Jack S. Radar
Coordinator, Membership: Linda Grimm
Editor: Betty J. Simkins
Coordinator, Special Events: Karen Wright
    E-Mail: kwright@fma.org

Historical Note:
FMA's mission is to promote the development and understanding of quality basic and applied research and of sound financial practices facilitating interaction and relationships among those who share a common interest in finance. Members are college professors of financial management, corporate and organizational financial officers. Membership: $100 (Professional); $125 (Sustaining); $30 (Ph.D./DBA Student Member).

Meetings/Conferences:
Conference Chair: Karen Wright
2013 - Napa, CA (Cakebread Cellars)/April 6
2013 - Shanghai, China (Crowne Plaza Hotel, Fudan University)/April 17 - 19
2013 - New York City, NY (St. John's University)/May 17
2013 - Luxembourg City, Luxembourg (Neumunster Abbey)/June 12 - 14
2013 - Chicago, IL (Hyatt Regency Chicago)/Oct. 16 - 19
2014 - Nashville, TN (Opryland Hotel)/Oct. 15 - 18
2015 - Orlando, FL (Hilton Orlando Bonnet Creek)/Oct. 14 - 17
2016 - Las Vegas, NV (Rio All-Suite Casino Resort)/ Oct. 19 - 22
2017 - Boston, MA (Boston Marriott Copley Place)/ Oct. 11 - 14
2018 - San Diego, CA (Hilton San Diego Bayfront Hotel)/Oct. 10 - 13
Number of non-conference events/year: 3

Publications:
Financial Management; quarterly
FMA Online; on-line
Journal of Applied Finance; irregular; adv.
Membership Directory; on-line

Financial Managers Society (1948)

100 W. Monroe St.
Suite 1700
Chicago, IL 60603-1907
Tel: (312) 578-1300 *Fax:* (312) 578-1308
TollFree: (800) 275-4367
E-Mail: info@fmsinc.org
Website: fmsinc.org
Members: 1600 individuals
Staff: 12
Annual Budget: $2-5,000,000
Tax: 501(c)(6)

Personnel:
President and Chief Executive Officer: Richard "Dick" A.
Yingst
  E-Mail: dyingst@fmsinc.org
Administrator, Human Resource and Bookkeeper:
MaryAnn Govert
  E-Mail: maryanng@fmsinc.org
Director, Professional Development: Tom King
  E-Mail: tomk@fmsinc.org
Editor: Tom Lanning
  E-Mail: toml@fmsinc.org
Administrator, Database and Information Technology:
Stacey Saunders
  E-Mail: staceys@fmsinc.org
Director, Marketing and Membership Services: Autumn
Wolfer
  E-Mail: autumnw@fmsinc.org

Historical Note:
*FMS's mission is to enhance professional development of
financial personnel within financial institutions. Members
are CFOs, controllers, CEOs, COOs, treasurers, investment
officers and internal auditors from banks, thrifts and credit
unions. Membership: $450 (Regular); $495 (Affiliate).*

Meetings/Conferences: Annual
Conference Chair: Stacey Saunders
2013 - Boston, MA (Seaport Boston Hotel)/June 16 -
18

Publications:
Financial Managers Update Newsletter; bi-weekly
Indusrty Insights; weekly
Membership and Peer Consulting Directory; on-line
Update; bi-weekly

Membership List Available to Non-members

Financial Markets Association (1991)

333 Second St. NE
Suite 104B
Washington, DC 20002
Tel: (202) 544-6327
Website: fmaweb.org
Members: 300 individuals
Staff: 1
Annual Budget: $50-100,000
Tax: 501(c)(6)

Personnel:
Managing Director: Dorcas Pearce
  E-Mail: dp-fma@starpower.net

Historical Note:
*The Financial Markets Association is specifically committed
to meeting the special and unique needs of banks and bank-
affiliated securities firms. Membership: $150 (Professional);
$75 (Regulator's Discount); $295 (Service Membership).*
Meetings/Conferences:
Number of non-conference events/year: 1

Publications:
Market Solutions; quarterly
Membership Directory; on-line

Financial Planning Association (2000)

7535 E. Hampden Ave.
Suite 600
Denver, CO 80231
Tel: (303) 759-4900 *Fax:* (303) 759-0749
TollFree: (800) 322-4237
E-Mail: fpa@fpanet.org
Website: fpanet.org
Members: 28500 individuals
Staff: 70
Annual Budget: $10-25,000,000
Tax: 501(c)(6)

Personnel:
Executive Director and Chief Executive Officer: Lauren
Schadle
  E-Mail: Lauren.Schadle@FPAnet.org

Director, Technology: Les Allen
  E-Mail: allen@fpanet.org
*Managing Director, Communications and Consumer
Services:* Lynn Brackpool
  E-Mail: lynn.brackpool@fpanet.org
Manager, Human Resources: Judy Feasby
  E-Mail: Judy.Feasby@FPAnet.org
Associate Executive Director and Chief Financial Officer:
Curt Niepoth
  E-Mail: curt.niepoth@fpanet.org
Assistant Director, Communications: Christine
Richardson
  E-Mail: Christine.Richardson@FPAnet.org
Director, Marketing and Membership: Tricia Rieple
  E-Mail: Tricia.Rieple@FPAnet.org
Director, Publications: Lance Ritchlin
  E-Mail: lance.ritchlin@fpanet.org

Historical Note:
*FPA is a resource for information and tools, connecting
consumers with financial planners who will deliver advice
using an objective, client-centered, ethical process.
Membership: $35-395/year.*

Continuing Education:
Certification Designation/s: CFP
Meetings/Conferences: Annual
2013 - Orlando, FL/Oct. 19 - 22
2014 - Seatle, WA/Sept. 27 - 30
2015 - Boston, MA/Sept. 26 - 29
Number of non-conference events/year: 2

Publications:
Membership Directory; on-line
The Capitol Update; monthly
The Journal of Financial Planning; adv.

Financial Planning Standards Board

707 17th St.
Suite 2925
Denver, CO 80202
Tel: (720) 917-0006 *Fax:* (720) 917-0001
E-Mail: info@fpsb.org
Website: fpsb.org
Members: 24 Organizations
Staff: 9
Annual Budget: $2-5,000,000

Personnel:
Chief Executive Officer: Noel Maye CAE
  E-Mail: nmaye@fpsb.org
Director, Communications: Ramey Becker
  E-Mail: rbecker@fpsb.org

Historical Note:
*FPSB association that manages, develops and operates
certification, education and related programs for financial
planning organizations, so that they may benefit the global
community by establishing, upholding and promoting
worldwide professional standards in financial planning.*

Continuing Education:
Certification Designation/s: CFP
Publications:
FPSB's Update

Financial Services Forum (2000)

601 13th St. NW
Suite 750 S.
Washington, DC 20005
Tel: (202) 457-8765 *Fax:* (202) 457-8769
Website: financialservicesforum.org
Members: 20 members
Staff: 6
Annual Budget: $2-5,000,000
Tax: 501(c)(6)

Personnel:
President and Chief Executive Officer: Robert S. Nichols
  E-Mail: rob.nichols@financialservicesforum.org
Executive Vice President, Policy: John Dearie
  E-Mail: john.dearie@financialservicesforum.org
Vice President, Communications: Laena E. Fallon
  E-Mail: laena.fallon@financialservicesforum.org
*Managing Director, Head of Government Relations and
Chief Counsel:* Courtney Geduldig
  E-Mail:
Courtney.Geduldig@financialservicesforum.org
Executive Management: Trish Horowitz
  E-Mail: trish.horowitz@financialservicesforum.org
Associate, Communications and Social Media: Jennifer
Scungio
  E-Mail: jen.scungio@financialservicesforum.org

Historical Note:
Global public policy organization.

The Financial Services Roundtable (1993)

1001 Pennsylvania Ave. NW
Suite 500 South
Washington, DC 20004
Tel: (202) 289-4322 *Fax:* (202) 628-2507
E-Mail: info@fsround.org
Website: fsround.org
Members: 100 companies
Staff: 35
Annual Budget: $10-25,000,000
Tax: 501(c)(6)

Personnel:
Chief Executive Officer: Gov. Tim Pawlenty
Executive Director and General Counsel: Richard M.
Whiting
  E-Mail: rich@fsround.org
Vice President, Meetings: Tanya Bailey
  E-Mail: tanya@fsround.org
Director, Communications: Elise Brooks
  E-Mail: elise@fsround.org
Chief Financial Officer: George Forsberg CPA
  E-Mail: george@fsround.org
Director, Membership and Information Services: Blake
Grimm
  E-Mail: blake@fsround.org
Counsel, Legal and Regulatory Affairs: Robert Hatch
  E-Mail: robert@fsround.org
Director, Research: Abby McCloskey
  E-Mail: abby@fsround.org
*Senior Vice President, Human Resources and
Administration:* Carrie Neckorcuk
  E-Mail: carrie@fsround.org
Senior Vice President, Government Affairs: Scott E.
Talbott
  E-Mail: scott@fsround.org
*President, ITAC and Senior Director, Consumer Financial
Services:* Anne Wallace

Historical Note:
*Founded as the Bankers Roundtable; the result of a merger
in 1993 of the Association of Bank Holding Companies
and the Association of Reserve City Bankers. Assumed
its current name in 1999. Acquired Financial Services
Technology Consortium in 2009. FSR's mission is to
protect and promote the economic vitality and integrity
of its members and the United States financial system.
Membership is reserved for for-profit companies delivering
integrated financial services.*

Meetings/Conferences:
Conference Chair: Tanya Bailey
Publications:
Membership Directory; on-line
Staff Directory; on-line

Finnish American Chamber of Commerce (1948)

866 United Nations Plaza
Suite 250
New York, NY 10017
Tel: (212) 821-0225 *Fax:* (212) 750-4418
E-Mail: faccnyc@verizon.net
Website: facc-ny.com
Members: 200 companies
Staff: 1
Annual Budget: $50-100,000

Personnel:
Executive Director: Kerstin E. Nordin
  E-Mail: faccnyc@verizon.net

Historical Note:
*FACC's mission is to protect, develop, encourage, promote
and foster trade, business, financial or professional interests
and commercial relations between Finland and the United
States. Membership: $80 (Individual/Young Associate);
$550 (Corporate); $1,600 (Sustaining); $30 (Student);
$300 (Small Business).*

Publications:
e-newsletter; quarterly

Finnsheep Breeders Association (1971)

P.O. Box 85
8887 Daggett Hollow Rd., C/O Lighthouse Farm
W. Clarksville, NY 14786
Tel: (585) 928-1721
E-Mail: asregistry@yahoo.com
Website: finnsheep.org
Members: 601 individuals
Staff: 2

Annual Budget: $10-25,000
Tax: 501(c)(3)

Personnel:
Secretary: Herb Tucker
   E-Mail: FBAsecretary@finnsheep.org

Historical Note:
FBA is dedicated to the promotion and preservation of Finnish Landrace Sheep, works to promote and preserve the breed and serves as a communication link for its members and others interested in the breed. Membership: $35 (New Member); $25 (Continuing Member); $10 (Youth/Associate Member); $15 (Continuing Youth/Associate Member).

Publications:
Breeders' Directory; on-line
Short Tales newsletter

Fire and Emergency Manufacturers and Services Association *(1966)*
P.O. Box 147
Lynnfield, MA 01940-0147
Tel: (781) 334-2771 *Fax:* (781) 334-2771
E-Mail: info@femsa.org
Website: femsa.org
Members: 150 companies
Staff: 3
Annual Budget: $100-250,000
Tax: 501(c)(6)

Personnel:
Administrator: Karen H. Burnham
Legal Counsel: James J. Juneau
   E-Mail: jjuneau@juneauboll.com
Secretary and Treasurer: Mike Natchipolsky
   E-Mail: mike.natchipolsky@cygnusb2b.com

Historical Note:
Formerly known as the Fire Equipment Manufacturers and Services Association (1990) incorporated in Delaware. FEMSA's mission is to coordinate the supply of fire and rescue equipment and materials to Federal, State and local authorities that oversee rescue and recovery efforts associated with natural disasters, catastrophes and terrorist attacks. Members are companies that manufacture vehicles, protective clothing, hoses and nozzles, breathing apparatus, rescue tools and other products and services used by fire fighters. Membership: $375-1500 (Active, based on number of employees); $900 (Associate).

Meetings/Conferences: Annual
Number of non-conference events/year: 36

Publications:
FEMSA News; adv.

Fire Apparatus Manufacturers' Association *(1946)*
P.O. Box 397
Lynnfield, MA 01940-0397
Tel: (781) 334-2911 *Fax:* (781) 338-2911
E-Mail: info@fama.org
Website: fama.org
Members: 124 companies
Staff: 1
Annual Budget: $100-250,000
Tax: 501(c)(6)

Personnel:
Administrator: Karen H. Burnham
   E-Mail: info@fama.org

Historical Note:
Formerly a division of the National Truck Equipment Association, became an independent organization in 1997. FAMA's purpose is to enhance the quality of the emergency service community through the manufacture and sale of safe, efficient emergency response vehicles and equipment. Membership: $1,500 (Full Assessment); $1000 (New Applicants).

Meetings/Conferences: Annual

Publications:
Buyers Directory; on-line
FAMA Flyer; quarterly

Fire Department Safety Officers Association *(1989)*
P.O. Box 149
Ashland, MA 01721-0149
Tel: (508) 881-3114 *Fax:* (508) 881-1128
E-Mail: fdsoa@fdsoa.org
Website: fdsoa.org
Members: 12000 Safety Officers, fire officers and fire fighters
Staff: 3
Annual Budget: $250-500,000

Personnel:
Executive Director: Mary McCormack
Certification Coordinator: Robert "Bob" L. Finley
   E-Mail: programs@fdsoa.org

Historical Note:
FDSOA's mission is to promote safety standards and practices in the fire, rescue and emergency services community. Membership: $85 (Active); $385 (Organizational); $500 (Sustaining).

Continuing Education:
Certification Designation/s: HSO, ISO

Meetings/Conferences: Annual
2013 - Orlando, FL (Wyndham Lake Buena Vista Resort)/Jan. 20 - 23

Publications:
Health & Safety; monthly

Fire Equipment Manufacturer's Association *(1925)*
1300 Sumner Ave.
Cleveland, OH 44115-2851
Tel: (216) 241-7333 *Fax:* (216) 241-0105
E-Mail: fema@femalifesafety.org
Website: femalifesafety.org
Members: 24 companies
Staff: 3
Annual Budget: $100-250,000

Personnel:
Specialist, Public Relations: Dana Kohlbeck
   E-Mail: dana@coalescemarketing.com

Historical Note:
Formerly (1936) the Fire Extinguisher Manufacturers' Association, Inc. FEMA provides the world with quality fire equipment and educates others about the importance of balanced fire protection. Members are companies making devices that control or extinguish fires in residential or commercial buildings. Membership: sliding scale.

Publications:
The Fire Equipment Manufacturers' Association Newsletter; quarterly

Membership List Available to Non-members

Fire Suppression Systems Association *(1982)*
5024 R Campbell Blvd.
Baltimore, MD 21236-5974
Fax: (410) 931-8111
E-Mail: fssa@clemonsmgmt.com
Website: fssa.net
Members: 94 installers and 14 manufacturers
Staff: 5
Annual Budget: $250-500,000
Tax: 501(c)(6)

Personnel:
Executive Director: Crista LeGrand CMP, CAE
   E-Mail: crista@fssa.net
Managing Director: Calvin K. Clemons CAE, CMP
Association Coordinator: Amanda Lee
   E-Mail: amandal@clemonsmgmt.com
Manager, Finance: Donna Liberto
   E-Mail: donnal@clemonsmgmt.com
Contact, Meetings and Member Services: Vince Mullhausen
   E-Mail: vincem@clemonsmgmt.com

Historical Note:
FSSA is a blend of designer, installers, manufacturers and suppliers working together to share ideas and strategies for the benefit of the fire suppression systems industry. Membership: $980 (Installer); $4000- 5,500 (Manufacturer).

Meetings/Conferences: Annual
Conference Chair: Vince Mullhausen
2013 - Bonita Springs, FL (Hyatt Regency Coconut Point Resort and Spa)/Feb. 22 - 26

Publications:
Membership Directory; on-line

Fishing Vessel Owners' Association *(1914)*
4005 - 20th Ave. West
Room 232, West Wall Building
Seattle, WA 98199-1290
Tel: (206) 284-4720 *Fax:* (206) 283-3341
Website: fvoa.org
Staff: 2

Personnel:
General Manager: Robert Alverson
Executive Assistant: Carol Batteen

Historical Note:
FVOA's mission is to promote safety at sea, ensure competitive pricing, and promote habitat-friendly gear with minimum bycatch. Members are longline fishermen. Membership: $550-330 (Active); $625 (Associate); $300 (Sustaining).

Publications:
Membership Directory; annually
The Wheel Watch-Newsletter; quarterly; adv.

Fixed Income Analysts Society *(1975)*
244 Fifth Ave.
Suite L230
New York, NY 10001
Tel: (212) 726-8100 *Fax:* (212) 591-6534
E-Mail: fiasi@fiasi.org
Website: fiasi.org
Members: 300 individuals
Staff: 5
Annual Budget: $250-500,000

Personnel:
Executive Director: Lauren Nauser

Historical Note:
FIASI's mission is to promote continuing education in all aspects of the fixed income markets. Members are individuals regularly engaged as fixed income professionals, including persons who specialize in credit research as well as those specializing in quantitative research, and belong to all disciplines (buy side, sell side, intermediaries, quants, academics), and all sectors investment grade, high yield, corporate, and structured. Membership: $160 (Individual); $25 (Student); $80 (Academic); $50 (Associate);

Publications:
Membership Directory; on-line

Flag Manufacturers Association of America *(2003)*
994 Old Eagle School Rd.
Suite 1019
Wayne, PA 19087
Tel: (610) 971-4850 *Fax:* (610) 971-4859
E-Mail: info@fmaa-usa.com
Website: fmaa-usa.com
Members: 5 Manufacturers
Staff: 2
Annual Budget: $25-50,000

Personnel:
President: Sharon K. Tannahill
   E-Mail: sharon@mmco1.com

Historical Note:
A non-profit trade association representing US flag manufacturers and suppliers, dedicated to educating and promoting the quality, variety and proper use of flags manufactured in the US. The FMAA mission is to Educate members of the general public about the United States manufactured flag industry and its significance to community, economic and social development. Membership: $11,000/year (Manufacturer Member), $1,000-2,000/year (Related Industry Member).

Continuing Education:
Certification Designation/s: CMUSA

Publications:
Newsletter; daily

Flavor and Extract Manufacturers Association *(1909)*
1620 I St. NW
Suite 925
Washington, DC 20006
Tel: (202) 293-5800 *Fax:* (202) 463-8998
Website: femaflavor.org
Members: 109 companies and 840 individuals
Staff: 20
Annual Budget: $2-5,000,000

Personnel:
Executive Director: John H. Cox
   E-Mail: jcox@vertosolutions.net

Historical Note:
Formerly the Flavoring Extract Manufacturers Association of the U.S., merged with the National Manufacturers of Beverage Flavors in 1965. FEMA strives to enhance a global environment in which the flavor industry can create, innovate and compete. Membership: $4,000 (Associates); $7,313-440,840 (Others).

Meetings/Conferences: Annual
2013 - Philadelphia, PA (Hyatt at The Bellevue)/Feb. 12 - 13
2013 - Palm Beach, FL (Ritz-Carlton)/May 5 - 8
Number of non-conference events/year: 1

Publications:
Membership Directory; on-line
Newsletter

Fleet Reserve Association *(1924)*
125 N. West St.
Alexandria, VA 22314-2754
Tel: (703) 683-1400 *Fax:* (703) 549-6610
TollFree: (800) 372-1924
E-Mail: news-fra@fra.org
Website: fra.org
Members: 1000000 individuals
Staff: 11
Annual Budget: $2-5,000,000
Tax: 501(c)(19)

Personnel:
National Executive Director: Joseph L. Barnes
   E-Mail: news-fra@fra.org
Director, Membership Development: Penny Collins
   E-Mail: penny@fra.org
Director, Legislative Programs: John R. Davis
   E-Mail: john@fra.org
Director, Administration: Alicia A. Landis
   E-Mail: adminfra@fra.org
Director, Marketing and Communications: Eileen Murphy
   E-Mail: eileen@fra.org
Finance Officer: Paul Rigby
   E-Mail: finance@fra.org

Historical Note:
A voluntary, non-profit association comprised of active duty, reserve, and retired members of the U.S. Navy, Marine Corps, and Coast Guard. Represents members before the U.S. Congress and governmental agencies with regard to pay, health care, and other benefits.

Publications:
FRA Today; monthly; adv.
OnWatch; quarterly; adv.

Fleischner Society *(1969)*
1891 Preston White Dr.
Reston, VA 20191
Tel: (703) 716-7588 *Fax:* (713) 960-0488
E-Mail: sroberts@acr.org
Website: fleischner.org
Members: 103 individuals
Staff: 2
Annual Budget: $25-50,000

Personnel:
President: David M. Hansell
Treasurer: William D. Travis MD

Historical Note:
FS's mission is to stimulate the recognition and development of chest roentgenology as a clinical specialty and to foster continuing improvement of chest radiology as an art and science. Membership is international and interdisciplinary, although the majority of members are Americans and radiologists.

Flexible Film & Bag Division *(1986)*
1667 K St. NW, Suite 1000
C/O SPI, The Plastics Industry Trade Association
Washington, DC 20006-1620
Tel: (202) 974-5200 *Fax:* (202) 296-7675
TollFree: (866) 782-7897
E-Mail: ywade@socplas.org
Website: plasticsindustry.org/IndustryGroups/
   content.cf
Members: 60 companies
Staff: 1
Annual Budget: $100-250,000

Personnel:
Director: Natha Freiburg
   E-Mail: nfreiburg@plasticsindustry.org

Historical Note:
Formerly Plastic Bag Association (1998), Film and Bag Federation. It is a committee of SPI: The Plastics Industry Trade Association. FBF's mission is to promote and preserve plastics industry on both a domestic and global basis by sharing relevant industry and economy information. It also sponsoring domestic and international trade shows, promoting new market expansion opportunities. Members are U. S. and Canadian manufacturers and suppliers of plastic retail bags.

Flexible Intermediate Bulk Container Association *(1983)*
P.O. Box 24792
Minneapolis, MN 55424

Tel: (952) 412-8867 *Fax:* (661) 339-0023
E-Mail: info@fibca.com
Website: fibca.com
Members: 50 companies
Staff: 1
Annual Budget: $100-250,000

Personnel:
Executive Director: Lewis Anderson
   E-Mail: lewis.anderson@fibca.com

Historical Note:
FIBCA's mission is to promote the use of its member's products and to serve as a source of information to its members. Members are companies manufacturing flexible intermediate bulk containers and their suppliers. Membership: $2,500/year.

Continuing Education:
Certification Designation/s: MIC

Meetings/Conferences: Semi-Annual
2013 - St. Pete Beach, FL (Lowes Don CeSar Beach
   Hotel)/April 18 - 19

Publications:
FIBC Buyers Guide; on-line
Membership Directory; on-line

Flexible Packaging Association *(1950)*
971 Corporate Blvd.
Suite 403
Linthicum, MD 21090
Tel: (410) 694-0800 *Fax:* (410) 694-0900
E-Mail: fpa@flexpack.org
Website: flexpack.org
Members: 135 companies
Staff: 6
Annual Budget: $2-5,000,000
Tax: 501(c)(6)

Personnel:
Manager, Communications: Lauren A. Kinard
   E-Mail: lkinard@flexpack.org
Vice President, Technology and Environmental Strategy:
   Ram Singhal
   E-Mail: rsinghal@flexpack.org
Director, Business and Economic Research: Bob
   Zaborowski
   E-Mail: bzaborowski@flexpack.org

Historical Note:
FPA advocates the growth of flexible packaging industry and provides industry specific information that enables its members to make educated business decisions. Members are manufacturers of flexible packaging sold to users or distributors for packaging purposes and material or equipment suppliers to the industry. Membership: $3,500-40,000 (Dues vary by sales).

Meetings/Conferences:
2013 - St. Pete Beach, FL (TradeWinds Resort)/Feb. 13
   - 15
2013 - Naples, FL (The Ritz-Carlton Golf Resort)/Feb.
   26 - 28

Publications:
Environmental Regulatory Index; quarterly
Flexible Packaging Magazine; monthly; adv.
FPA's Flexible Packaging Achievement Awards and
   Innovation Showcase; annually
FPA's Flexible Packaging Buyers Guide; semi-annually
Industry Bulletin; on-line
The FPA Membership Directory; annually

Flexographic Prepress Platemakers Association *(1997)*
2105 Laurel Bush Rd.
Suite 201
Bel Air, MD 21015
Tel: (443) 640-1045 *Fax:* (443) 640-1031
E-Mail: fppa@ksgroup.org
Website: fppa.net
Members: 100 individuals
Staff: 3
Annual Budget: $100-250,000

Personnel:
Executive Director: Diane Schafer CMP
   E-Mail: diane@ksgroup.org
Financial Director: Amy Chetelat, CAE
   E-Mail: amy@ksgroup.org

Historical Note:
FPPA's purpose is to create, promote and enhance better standards within the flexographic pre-press platemaking industry, to provide leadership through vision and direction, to strengthen education at all levels and to further the

nterests of the industry. Membership is open to businesses who are involved in or supply to the flexographic industry. Membership: $1,000 (Full); $3,500 (Associate); $1,250 (Affiliate); $500 (Affiliate Supplier); $200 (Trade Press); $100 (Academic).

Meetings/Conferences: Annual
Conference Chair: Diane Schafer CMP

Publications:
On-Target; quarterly; adv.
Wall Street Journal; on-line; adv.

Flexographic Technical Association *(1958)*
3920 Veterans Memorial Hwy.
Suite Nine
Bohemia, NY 11716
Tel: (631) 737-6020 *Fax:* (631) 737-6813
E-Mail: memberinfo@flexography.org
Website: flexography.org
Members:
1,300 companies
50,000 individuals
Staff: 7
Annual Budget: $500-1,000,000

Personnel:
President: Mark Cisternino
   E-Mail: markc@flexography.org
Director, Marketing: Sharon Cox
   E-Mail: scox@flexography.org
Director, Customer Service and Database Management:
   Carri Dodd
   E-Mail: cdodd@flexography.org
Manager, Human Resource and Accounting: Milena Flores
   E-Mail: mflores@flexography.org
Director, Membership Services and Business Development:
   Jay Kaible
   E-Mail: jkaible@flexography.org
Contact, Publications: Robert Moran
   E-Mail: rmoran@flexography.org
Director, Education: Joe Tuccitto
   E-Mail: jtuccitto@flexography.org

Historical Note:
FTA develops and advances flexographic printing technology. Members are printers, suppliers, graphic trade shops, consumer product companies, designers, end-users, consultants and educational institutions. Membership: $225 (Single Location I - up to 5 employees); $450 (Single Location II - 6-20 employees); $562.50 (Single Location III - 21-100 employees); $675 (Single Location IV - 101-250 employees); $825 (Single Location V - 250+ employees); $187 (Consumer Product Company).

Continuing Education:
Certification Designation/s: BF, FPO, AFPO, FOC

Meetings/Conferences: Annual
2013 - San Diego, CA/April 28 - May 1
2013 - Kansas City, MO/Oct. 14 - 16

Publications:
FLEXO Magazine; monthly

FlexTech Alliance
3081 Zanker Rd.
San Jose, CA 95134
Tel: (408) 577-1300 *Fax:* (408) 577-1301
E-Mail: info@flextech.org
Website: flextech.org
Staff: 10
Annual Budget: $2-5,000,000

Personnel:
President and Chief Executive Officer: Michael Ciesinski
   E-Mail: michael.ciesinski@flextech.org
Manager, Industry Events: Michelle Fabiano
Manager, Communications: Denise Rael
Office Administrator and Coordinator, Production: Krishna
   Raghunath
Chief Technology Advisor: Dr. Malcolm J. Thompson

Historical Note:
Formerly the U.S. Display Consortium. Mission is to advance the growth, profitability and success throughout the flexible, printed electronics and displays manufacturing and distribution chain Membership: $500-5,500/year.

Meetings/Conferences: Annual
Conference Chair: Michelle Fabiano
2013 - Phoenix, AZ (Phoenix Convention Center)/Jan.
   29 - Feb. 1/300 attendees

Publications:
Industry and Market Research Reports
Membership Directory; on-line

Flight Safety Foundation (1947)

801 N. Fairfax St.
Suite 400
Alexandria, VA 22314-1774
Tel: (703) 739-6700 *Fax:* (703) 739-6708
Website: flightsafety.org
Members: 1,075 individuals
Staff: 22
Annual Budget: $2-5,000,000

Personnel:
President and Chief Executive Officer: William R. Voss
  E-Mail: voss@flightsafety.org
Director, Technical Programs: James M. Burin
  E-Mail: burin@flightsafety.org
Chief Operating Officer: Capt. Kevin L. Hiatt
Director, Publications and Editor-in-Chief, AeroSafety World: Frank Jackman
  E-Mail: jackman@flightsafety.org
Senior Director, Membership and Business Development: Susan M. Lausch
  E-Mail: lausch@flightsafety.org
Director, Communications: Emily McGee
  E-Mail: mcgee@flightsafety.org
Director, Events and Seminars: Kelcey Mitchell
  E-Mail: mitchell@flightsafety.org
General Counsel and Secretary: Kenneth P. Quinn Esq.
Chief Financial Officer: Penny L. Young
  E-Mail: young@flightsafety.org

Historical Note:
FSF's mission is to promote and facilitate the global application of aviation safety assessments, standards and practices. Membership: $310-25,000/year.

Meetings/Conferences:
Conference Chair: Kelcey Mitchell
2013 - Montreal, QC (Fairmont, the Queen Elizabeth Hotel)/April 10 - 11
2014 - San Diego, CA (Sheraton San Diego Hotel and Marina)/April 15 - 17
2014 - San Antonio, TX (Grand Hyatt San Antonio)/ April 17 - 19

Publications:
Aviation Mechanics Bulletin; bi-monthly
AeroSafety World; monthly; adv.
Airport Operations; bi-monthly
Cabin Crew Safety; bi-monthly
Flight Safety Digest; monthly
Helicopter Safety; bi-monthly
Human Factors & Aviation Medicine; bi-monthly

Floor Covering Installation Contractors Association (1982)

7439 Millwood Dr.
W. Bloomfield, MI 48322-1234
Tel: (248) 661-5015 *Fax:* (248) 661-5018
Website: fcica.com
Members: 160 companies
Staff: 3
Annual Budget: $100-250,000

Personnel:
Executive Vice President: Kimberly Oderkirk
  E-Mail: keo@fcica.com

Historical Note:
FCICA's mission is to provide a network for problem solving, education and support, to enhance members businesses and the flooring industry. Members are floor covering contractors. Membership: $350-950 (Installation Contractor), $700-2,500 (Associate), $350-2,150 (Consultant).

Meetings/Conferences:
2013 - New Orleans, LA (Bourbon Orleans Hotel)/Feb. 24 - 27/11-25 exhibitors
Number of non-conference events/year: 1

Publications:
FCICA E-News; bi-weekly; adv.
Membership Directory; annually
The Flooring Contractor; quarterly; adv.

Membership List Available to Non-members

Fluid Controls Institute (1921)

1300 Sumner Ave.
Cleveland, OH 44115-2851
Tel: (216) 241-7333 *Fax:* (216) 241-0105
E-Mail: fci@fluidcontrolsinstitute.org
Website: fluidcontrolsinstitute.org
Members: 40 companies
Staff: 3

Annual Budget: $100-250,000

Personnel:
Executive Secretary: John H. Addington

Historical Note:
Established as the National Association of Steam and Fluid Specialty Manufacturers, it became the National Steam Specialty Club in 1941 and assumed its present name in 1955. FCI is an association of manufacturers of equipment for fluid (liquid or gas) control and conditioning.

Meetings/Conferences: Semi-Annual

Fluid Fertilizer Foundation (1982)

2805 Claflin Rd.
Suite 200
Manhattan, KS 66502
Tel: (785) 776-0273 *Fax:* (785) 776-8347
E-Mail: fluidfertilizer@sbcglobal.net
Website: fluidfertilizer.com
Members: 100 organizations
Staff: 2
Annual Budget: $250-500,000
Tax: 501(c)(3)

Personnel:
President: Dale Leikam
Administrative Assistant: Mary Hughes

Historical Note:
FFF is the research and education arm of the fluid fertilizer industry and the Agricultural Retailers Association. Membership: $500-5,000 (Fluid Fertilizer Dealers/ Distributors/Individual); $2,000-10,000 (National Retail Suppliers); $2,500-15,000 (Manufacturers/Suppliers of Related Products/Services); $2,500-30,000 (Producers of Nutrient Materials).

Meetings/Conferences: Annual
2013 - Scottsdale, AZ (Scottsdale Plaza Resort)/Feb. 18 - 20

Publications:
FFF Newsletter
Fluid Journal; quarterly
Membership Directory; on-line

Fluid Power Distributors Association (1974)

105 Eastern Ave.
Suite 104
Annapolis, MD 21403-3300
Tel: (410) 940-6347 *Fax:* (410) 263-1659
E-Mail: info@fpda.org
Website: fpda.org
Members: 300 companies
Staff: 12
Annual Budget: $250-500,000
Tax: 501(c)(6)

Personnel:
Executive Director: Patricia A Lilly
  E-Mail: plilly@thompsonmanagement.com
Accounting Manager: Dot Cusack
Specialist, Marketing: Beth Hiltabidle
Director, Membership Development: Amy Luckado
Office Manager: Janice Sunderland
Director, Conference and Communications: Kristin B. Thompson

Historical Note:
Membership is composed of distributors and manufacturers of hydraulic and pneumatic equipment and motion control technology. FPDA's mission is to become the professional network for fluid power, automation and motion technology providers dedicated to significantly enhancing member and channel performance by delivering indispensable networking, education and success strategies. Membership: $680-4,275/year (Distributor, Based on number of employees); $1,515-4,275 (Manufacturer, Based on number of employees).

Continuing Education:
Certification Designation/s: M + CSP

Meetings/Conferences:
Conference Chair: Kristin B. Thompson

Publications:
FPDA Express; monthly; adv.
FPDA News; bi-monthly; adv.
Membership Directory; annually; adv.

Membership List Available to Non-members

Fluid Sealing Association (1933)

994 Old Eagle School Rd.
Suite 1019
Wayne, PA 19087-1866
Tel: (610) 971-4850 *Fax:* (610) 971-4859

E-Mail: info@fluidsealing.com
Website: fluidsealing.com
Members: 60 companies
Staff: 5
Annual Budget: $250-500,000
Tax: 501(c)(6)

Personnel:
Executive Director: Robert H. Ecker
President: Edward Marchese
Administrative Director: Hope Silverman
  E-Mail: hope@fluidsealing.com

Historical Note:
Formerly Mechanical Packing Association untill 1970. FSA's mission is to influence and support the development of related standards and to provide education in the fluid sealing area. Members are manufacturers of mechanical packings, sealing devices, gaskets, rubber expansion joints, and allied products. Membership: $500 (Affiliate); $3,400-9,065 (Regular, based on annual Sales of Fluid Sealing Products).

Meetings/Conferences: Annual
2013 - San Diego, CA/Oct. 15 - 17
Number of non-conference events/year: 5

Publications:
FSA Advisor; semi-annually

Membership List Available to Non-members

Flying Physicians Association (1955)

11626 Twain Dr.
Montgomery, TX 77356
Tel: (936) 588-6505 *Fax:* (832) 415-0287
E-Mail: info@fpadrs.org
Website: fpadrs.org
Members: 795 individuals
Staff: 4
Annual Budget: $100-250,000
Tax: 501(c)(3)

Personnel:
President: Gareth A Eberle MD
Treasurer: John R. Hunt MD

Historical Note:
FPA's purpose is to promote safety, education, research and human interest projects relating to aviation. Membership: $300 (Regular); $225 (Military); $180 (Emeritus); $3600 (Annual Corporate Supporter); $125 (Associate/Resident/ intern/fellow); $40 (Medical Student Admin).

Meetings/Conferences: Annual
2013 - Milwaukee, WI (Hyatt Regency Milwaukee)/ June 23 - 27
Number of non-conference events/year: 1

Publications:
Flying Physicians Association Magazine; adv.
Membership Directory; on-line

Foil and Specialty Effects Association (1992)

2150 SW Westport Dr.
Suite 101
Topeka, KS 66614
Tel: (785) 271-5816 *Fax:* (785) 271-6404
E-Mail: fseamail@fsea.com
Website: fsea.com
Members: 350 companies
Staff: 4
Annual Budget: $250-500,000
Tax: 501(c)(6)

Personnel:
Executive Director: Jeff Peterson
  E-Mail: jeff@fsea.com
Assistant Director: Kym Conis
  E-Mail: kym@fsea.com
Director, Sales: Gayla Peterson
  E-Mail: gayla@petersonpublications.com

Historical Note:
Formerly (2009) the Foil Stamping & Embossing Association, FSEA is a non- profit international trade association of foil stampers, embossers, die cutters and industry suppliers working together for the advancement of the industry. Membership: $175-500 (Active); $250 (Associate, 1-10 employees); $750 (Associate, 11 + employees).

Meetings/Conferences:
Conference Chair: Kym Conis

Publications:
FSEA ENews; quarterly
InsideFinishing Magazine; adv.
Membership Directory
PostPress ENews; monthly

The Folk Alliance International *(1989)*
510 S. Main St.
First Floor
Memphis, TN 38103-4488
Tel: (901) 522-1170 *Fax:* (901) 522-1172
E-Mail: fa@folk.org
Website: folk.org
Members: 503 organizations and 2800 members
Staff: 5
Annual Budget: $500-1,000,000
Tax: 501(c)(3)

Personnel:
Executive Director and Director, Conferences: Louis Jay
    Meyers
Coordinator, Membership Services: Eric Garcia
    E-Mail: eric@folk.org
Contact, Administration and Media Relations: Caleb
    Sweazy

Historical Note:
*Formerly known as North American Folk Music and
Dance Alliance.FAI's mission is to to foster and promote
traditional, contemporary, and multicultural folk music
and dance and related performing arts. The Folk Alliance
seeks to strengthen and advance organizational and
individual initiatives in folk music and dance through
education, networking, advocacy, and professional and
field development. Membership: $35-500/year; $1000
(Lifetime).*

Meetings/Conferences: Annual
Conference Chair: Louis Jay Meyers
2013 - Toronto, ON (Delta Chelsea)/Feb. 20 - 24
2014 - Kansas City, MO (Westin Kansas City at Crown
    Center)/Feb. 19 - 23
2015 - Kansas City, MO (Westin Kansas City at Crown
    Center)/Feb. 18 - 22
2016 - Kansas City, MO (Westin Kansas City at Crown
    Center)/Feb. 17 - 21
2017 - Kansas City, MO (Westin Kansas City at Crown
    Center)/Feb. 15 - 19
2018 - Kansas City, MO (Westin Kansas City at Crown
    Center)/Feb. 14 - 18

Publications:
Folk Alliance International Newsletter; adv.
NewFolk Magazine; adv.

Membership List Available to Non-members

Food and Drug Law Institute *(1949)*
1155 15th St. NW
Suite 800
Washington, DC 20005-2706
Tel: (202) 371-1420 *Fax:* (202) 371-0649
TollFree: (800) 956-6293
E-Mail: comments@fdli.org
Website: fdli.org
Members: 10000 members
Staff: 21
Annual Budget: $2-5,000,000
Tax: 501(c)(3)

Personnel:
President and Chief Executive Officer: Susan C. Winckler
    Esq., RPh
    E-Mail: scw@fdli.org
Director, Information Technology: David C. Janes
    E-Mail: dcj@fdli.org
Senior Director, Membership and Marketing: Erin M.
    Jones
    E-Mail: emj@fdli.org
Vice President, Product Development and Editor-in-Chief:
    Michael Levin-Epstein
    E-Mail: mdl@fdli.org
Conference Manager: Khara L. Minter
    E-Mail: klm@fdli.org
Membership Manager: Lauren D. Roberts
    E-Mail: ldr@fdli.org
Manager, Customer Service: Michael M. Sprott
    E-Mail: mms@fdli.org
*Vice President, Finance, Administration and Information
    Technology:* Iris V. Stratton CPA
    E-Mail: ivs@fdli.org

Historical Note:
*Formerly (1965) Food Law Institute. FDLI's mission is to
provide education, training, and publications on topical
food and drug law. Members are manufacturers, suppliers,
law firms, consultants, associations, research groups,
public relations firms and others associated with the food,
drug, medical devices, cosmetics and biologics industries.
Membership: $25-12,500/year.*

Meetings/Conferences:
Conference Chair: Khara L. Minter
2013 - Washington, DC/Jan. 28 - 31
2013 - Washington, DC/April 23 - 24
Number of non-conference events/year: 5

Publications:
FDLI's E-newsletter; weekly
Food and Drug Law Journal; quarterly
Update magazine; bi-monthly

Membership List Available to Non-members

Food Distribution Research Society *(1967)*
C/O Oklahoma State University, Department of
    Agricultural Economics
114 Food & Agricultural Products Center
Stillwater, OK 74078
Tel: (405) 744-6272 *Fax:* (405) 744-6313
Website: fdrs.tamu.edu
Members: 250 individuals and companies
Staff: 6
Annual Budget: $25-50,000
Tax: 501(c)(3)

Personnel:
Vice President, Membership Services: Rodney Holcomb
    E-Mail: rodney.holcomb@okstate.edu
Secretary and Treasurer: Kellie Raper
    E-Mail: Kellie.raper@okstate.edu

Historical Note:
*Formerly (1967) Food Distribution Research Conference.
FDRS's mission is to serve the food industry, to encourage
applied research, assist with food industry education
and provide opportunities for professional development.
Membership: $15 (Junior); $45 (Professional); $65
(Library); $140 (Company/Business); $400 (Life Member);
$20 more for Non-US locations.*

Meetings/Conferences: Annual

Publications:
FDRS Newsletter; on-line; adv.
Journal of Food Distribution Research; adv.

Food Industry Association Executives *(1927)*
5657 W. 10770 North
Highland, UT 84003
Tel: (801) 599-1095 *Fax:* (815) 550-1731
Website: fiae.net
Members: 170 individuals
Staff: 2
Annual Budget: $100-250,000

Personnel:
President: Jim Olsen
    E-Mail: jolsen@fiae.net
Secretary and Treasurer: Jamie Pfuhl

Historical Note:
*Formerly (1959) the National Grocery Secretaries
Association. FIAE's mission is to provide a forum for
professional growth of the members' employees and to serve
as a vehicle for the interchange of ideas and advancement
of the food industry agenda. Members are executives of
retail grocer associations on the national, state and local
levels. Membership: $175-1,000 (Active); $500 (Affiliate).*

Publications:
FIAE Newsletter
Membership Directory; on-line

Food Industry Suppliers Association *(1968)*
1207 Sunset Dr.
Greensboro, NC 27408
Tel: (336) 274-6311 *Fax:* (336) 691-1839
Website: fisanet.org
Members: 120 companies
Staff: 2
Annual Budget: $250-500,000

Personnel:
Executive Director: Stella Jones
    E-Mail: stella@fisanet.org

Historical Note:
*FISA strives to promote distribution in the sanitary
processing industries. Members are independent distributors
and manufacturers who go to market through distribution.
Membership: $735/year (Associate Member/Manufacturer-
Regular Member/Distributor-Regular Member).*

Meetings/Conferences: Annual

Publications:
Distributor News-Newsletter; quarterly
Membership Directories; on-line
SmartBrief; on-line

The Food Institute *(1928)*
Ten Mountainview Rd.
Suite S125
Upper Saddle River, NJ 07458
Tel: (201) 791-5570 *Fax:* (201) 791-5222
E-Mail: questions@foodinstitute.com
Website: foodinstitute.com
Members:
2500 companies
5500 individuals
Staff: 16
Annual Budget: $2-5,000,000

Personnel:
President and Chief Executive Officer: Brian L. Todd
    E-Mail: btodd@foodinstitute.com
Editorial Director: Erica Dietsche
    E-Mail: edietsche@foodinstitute.com
Vice President, Member Services: Cathie Sloan
    E-Mail: cathie.sloan@foodinstitute.com

Historical Note:
*The Food Institute, also known as American Institute
of Food Distribution, strives to give current, timely and
relevant information about the food industry from farm
to fork. It also serves as a trusted source of information,
providing balanced coverage of the issues. Membership:
$795 (Individual); $455 (E- Subscription).*

Publications:
The Daily Update; daily
Today In Food; daily

Food Marketing Institute *(1977)*
2345 Crystal Dr.
Suite 800
Arlington, VA 22202-4801
Tel: (202) 452-8444 *Fax:* (202) 429-4519
E-Mail: fmi@fmi.org
Website: fmi.org
Members: 1,500 food retailers and wholesalers
Staff: 75
Annual Budget: $25-50,000,000
Tax: 501(c)(6)

Personnel:
President and Chief Executive Officer: Leslie G. Sarasin
    CAE
    E-Mail: lsarasin@fmi.org
Senior Vice President, Finance and Chief Financial Officer:
    Sam DiCarlo
    E-Mail: sdicarlo@fmi.org
*Group Vice President, Legislative and Consumer Affairs and
    Sponsor Development:* Dagmar Farr
    E-Mail: dfarr@fmi.org
Director, Media and Public Relations: Heather Garlich
    E-Mail: hgarlich@fmi.org
Contact, Events: Matt Grizzard
    E-Mail: mgrizzard@fmi.org
Senior Vice President, Government and Public Affairs:
    Jennifer L. Hatcher
    E-Mail: jhatcher@fmi.org
Vice President, Pharmacy Services: Catherine M. Polley
    E-Mail: CPolley@fmi.org
*Senior Manager, State Relations, Grassroots and Sponsor
    Development:* Gladys Swearingen
    E-Mail: gswearingen@fmi.org
*Senior Vice President, Industry Relations, Education and
    Research:* Patrick J Walsh

Historical Note:
*A non-profit association conducting programs in research,
education and public affairs. Members are food retailers
and wholesalers and their customers. Headquartered in
Arlington, VA.*

Meetings/Conferences:
Conference Chair: Matt Grizzard
2013 - Scottsdale, AZ (The Phoenician)/Jan. 20 - 22
2013 - Orlando, FL (Peabody Orlando)/April 30 - May
    2
2014 - Chicago, IL (McCormick Place)/June 10 - 13/
    over 100 exhibitors
Number of non-conference events/year: 9

Publications:
Advantage Supermarket Research; annually
International E-Newsletter; monthly
Membership Directory; on-line

Food Processing Suppliers Association *(1885)*
1451 Dolley Madison Blvd.
Suite 101

McLean, VA 22101-3850
Tel: (703) 761-2600 *Fax:* (703) 761-4334
E-Mail: info@fpsa.org
Website: fpsa.org
Members: 500 companies
Staff: 10
Annual Budget: $5-10,000,000
Tax: 501(c)(6)

Personnel:
President and Chief Executive Officer: David Seckman
  E-Mail: dseckman@fpsa.org
Coordinator, Administration and Finance: Alyssa Aiken
  E-Mail: aaiken@fpsa.org
Vice President, International Market Development: Andy Drennan
  E-Mail: adrennan@fpsa.org
Director, Membership and Communications: Adam Finney
  E-Mail: afinney@fpsa.org
Senior Advisor: George O. Melnykovich
  E-Mail: drmel@fpsa.org
Chief Financial Officer: Robyn Roche
  E-Mail: rroche@fpsa.org
Vice President, Marketing and Sales: Randy Taussig
  E-Mail: rtaussig@fpsa.org

Historical Note:
Formed in (2005) by the merger of the Food Processing Machinery Association and the International Association of Food Industry Suppliers. FPSA's mission is to provide programs and services to assist its members to be successful in marketing their products and services, and in improving their business practices. Members are suppliers to the global food, beverage, pharmaceutical, cosmetic, and related sanitary processing industries. Membership: $1,200-1,700/year (Company, based on annual revenue).

Meetings/Conferences: Semi-Annual
2013 - Scottsdale, AZ (Westin Kierland Resort & Spa)/ March 6 - 9
2013 - Chicago, IL (McCormick Place)/Nov. 3 - 6/10000 attendees

Publications:
EXPO Magazine
FPSA Bulletin; monthly

Food Sanitation Institute *(1957)*
111 blvd.
New Orleans, LA 56895
Staff: 1
Personnel:
President: Jon Rader

Food Shippers of America *(1954)*
1546 Shire Cir.
Inverness, IL 60067
Tel: (303) 319-5215
E-Mail:
nnewbourne@foodshippersofamerica.org
Website: foodshippersofamerica.org
Members: 66 companies, carriers and distributors
Staff: 2
Annual Budget: $1-2,000,000

Personnel:
Executive Director: Royce Fisk
  E-Mail: rfisk@foodshippersofamerica.org
Treasurer and Contact, Sponsorship Opportunities: Nancy Newbourne
  E-Mail: nnewbourne@foodshippersofamerica.org

Historical Note:
FSA seeks to promote improvement in supply chain efficiency. Members are carriers, distributors, and related companies serving the food industry. Membership: $150/ year (Company).

Meetings/Conferences: Annual
Conference Chair: Nancy Newbourne
2013 - Phoenix, AZ (JW Marriott Phoenix Desert Ridge Resort and Spa)/Feb. 24 - 26
2014 - Orlando, FL (JW Marriott Orlando Grande Lakes)/Feb. 23 - 25

Publications:
FSA Magazine; bi-annually; adv.
FSA Newsletter

Foodservice & Packaging Institute, Inc. *(1966)*
201 Park Washington Ct.
Falls Church, VA 22046
Tel: (703) 538-3550 *Fax:* (703) 241-5603
E-Mail: fpi@fpi.org
Website: fpi.org

Members: 215 converters, suppliers, affiliates, school districts, colleges and universities
Staff: 4
Annual Budget: $500-1,000,000
Tax: 501(c)(3)

Personnel:
President: Lynn M. Dyer
  E-Mail: ldyer@fpi.org
Vice President: Natha Freiburg
  E-Mail: nfreiburg@fpi.org
Manager, Membership Services and Meetings: Jennifer Goldman
  E-Mail: jgoldman@fpi.org

Historical Note:
FPI's mission is to expand and enhance the acceptance and marketing of all single-use food service packaging. FPI members are operators, distributors and suppliers. Membership: $4,500-35,000 (Converters/Suppliers).

Meetings/Conferences: Annual
Conference Chair: Jennifer Goldman
2013 - New York City, NY (The Conrad)/March 22 - 24

Publications:
Council Communications; quarterly
Executive Briefs; bi-weekly
FPI Newsletter; monthly
Membership Directory; on-line
Packaging Innovations & Insights; quarterly
Single Service News; semi-annually
State of the Food Service Packaging Industry; annually

Membership List Available to Non-members

Foodservice Equipment Distributors Association *(1933)*
2250 Point Blvd.
Suite 200
Elgin, IL 60123
Tel: (224) 293-6500 *Fax:* (224) 293-6505
E-Mail: feda@feda.com
Website: feda.com
Members: 290 companies
Staff: 8
Annual Budget: $500-1,000,000

Personnel:
Executive Vice President, Publisher and Editor-in-Chief: Raymond "Ray" W. Herrick CAE, II
Administration Director and Advertising Manager: Adela Ramos
Consultant, Membership Services: Amy Risinger

Historical Note:
FEDA was formerly known as Food Service Equipment Industry Inc till 1972. FEDA's mission is to provide a strong dealer advocacy voice in the food service equipment industry united for a profitable dealer-based distribution system. Membership: $595-1,805/year (Dues vary for category Class 1 to 7).

Meetings/Conferences: Annual
Conference Chair: Amy Risinger
2013 - San Antonio, TX (JW Marriott San Antonio Hill Country Resort and Spa)/April 3 - 7
2014 - Indian Wells, CA (Renaissance Esmeralda Indian Wells Resort and Spa)/March 26 - 30
2015 - Phoenix, AZ (JW Marriott Phoenix Desert Ridge Resort and Spa)/March 25 - 29
2016 - Tucson, AZ (JW Marriott Tucson Starr Pass Resort and Spa)/March 30 - April 3

Publications:
Membership Directory; annually
News and Views; bi-monthly; adv.

The Foodservice Group, Inc. *(1978)*
P.O. Box 681864
Marietta, GA 30068-0032
Tel: (770) 971-8116 *Fax:* (770) 971-1094
Website: fsgroup.com
Members: 17 companies
Staff: 1
Annual Budget: $50-100,000

Personnel:
Executive Director: Kenneth W. Reynolds
  E-Mail: kreynolds@fsgroup.com

Historical Note:
Formerly (1978) National Foodservice Marketing Associates. FSG's purpose is to create a national network of foodservice sales and marketing professionals. Members are independent food service brokers.

Meetings/Conferences:
Number of non-conference events/year: 2

Publications:
Member Listing; on-line

Membership List Available to Non-members

Foodservice Sales & Marketing Association *(1904)*
1810-J York Rd.
Suite 384
Lutherville, MD 21093
Tel: (410) 715-4084 *Fax:* (410) 997-9387
TollFree: (800) 617-1170
E-Mail: info@fsmaonline.com
Website: fsmaonline.com
Members: 800 companies
Staff: 4
Annual Budget: $1-2,000,000

Personnel:
President and Chief Executive Officer: Rick Abraham
  E-Mail: rabraham@fsmaonline.com
Vice President, Membership Services: Shannon Boyle
  E-Mail: sboyle@fsmaonline.com
Contact, Legal and Accounting Services: Barry C. Maloney
  E-Mail: bmaloney@maloneyknox.com
Manager, Membership Services and Meetings: Jessica Muffoletto
  E-Mail: jmuffoletto@fsmaonline.com

Historical Note:
FSMA was incorporated in November 2003 by firms formerly associated with the International Foodservice Brokers Association/Association of Sales & Marketing Companies. The mission of FSMA is to promote sales and marketing agencies as the preferred method for suppliers to come to market. Membership: $750-150,000/year (Corporate).

Meetings/Conferences:
Conference Chair: Shannon Boyle
2013 - Palm Spring, CA (La Quinta Resort and Club)/ Feb. 12 - 14
Number of non-conference events/year: 32

Football Bowl Association *(1892)*
c/o Law Offices of Phillip R. Hochberg
11921 Rockville Pike, #300
Rockville, MD 20852
Tel: (301) 230-6572
Website: footballbowlassociation.com
Members: 28 communities
Staff: 2
Annual Budget: $250-500,000

Personnel:
Treasurer: Bernie Olivas
  E-Mail: bolivas@sunbowl.org
Secretary: Bruce Binkowski
  E-Mail: bink@holidaybowl.com

Historical Note:
FBA's purpose is representing all post-season college football bowl games that works to build upon the tradition and increase the knowledge of the bowl experience and its benefits to college football.

Meetings/Conferences: Annual

Football Writers Association of America *(1941)*
18652 Vista del Sol
Dallas, TX 75287
Tel: (972) 713-6198
Website: sportswriters.net/fwaa
Members: 1100 individuals
Staff: 1
Annual Budget: $100-250,000

Personnel:
Executive Director: Steve Richardson

Historical Note:
FWAA works to govern areas that include game day operations, major and awards. Membership includes journalists, broadcasters and publicists as well as key executives in all the areas that involve the game. Membership: $50 (Regular); $25 (Students).

Meetings/Conferences: Annual

Publications:
Member Directory; annually
The Fifth Down - Newsletter; bi-monthly

Footwear Distributors and Retailers of America *(1944)*
1319 F St. NW
Suite 700

Washington, DC 20004
Tel: (202) 737-5660 *Fax:* (202) 645-0789
E-Mail: fdra2@aol.com
Website: fdra.org
Members: 81 companies
Staff: 5
Annual Budget: $2-5,000,000
Tax: 501(c)(6)

Personnel:
President: Matt Priest
    E-Mail: mpriest@fdra.org
Director, Finance: Faith Lewis
Vice President, Marketing and Communications:
    Stephanie Ward
    E-Mail: stephanie@fdra.org

Historical Note:
Represents footwear retailers, distributors, manufacturers, suppliers and international trade associations. FDRA's mission is to advocate its members' interests, especially in free trade, and keep its members well informed on all important issues that advance commercial interests common to the membership. Membership: $3,300-51,750 (Retailer, Based on Total Shoe Sales); $1,000-18,000 (Distributor); $5,000-25,000 (Affiliate/International Affiliate, Based on Annual Sales); $1,500 (Non-Footwear Affiliate).

Meetings/Conferences: Annual

Publications:
FDRA weekly; weekly
IFAM bulletin; monthly

Ford Motor Minority Dealers Association *(1979)*
16000 W. Nine Mile Rd.
Suite 603
Southfield, MI 48075
Tel: (248) 557-2500 *Fax:* (248) 557-2882
TollFree: (800) 247-0293
E-Mail: fmmda@fmmda.org
Website: fmmda.org
Staff: 3
Annual Budget: $250-500,000

Personnel:
Executive Director: A.V. Fleming
Manager, Public Relations and Marketing: Barbara Brazile
Dealer Consultant: Judson B. Powell

Historical Note:
Formed as part of the Ford Motor Corporation to increase and train the number of minorities who work in dealerships. FMMDA's mission is to improve the quality and quantity of FMMDA dealership through effective leadership and participation from an unified organization whose goal is parity. Membership: $50,000 (Millennium); $30,000-35,000 (Platinum); $20,000-25,000 (Gold); $10,000 (Silver); $5,000 (Bronze).

Forest History Society *(1946)*
701 William Vickers Ave.
Durham, NC 27701-3162
Tel: (919) 682-9319 *Fax:* (919) 682-2349
Website: foresthistory.org
Members: 2000 individuals
Staff: 9
Annual Budget: $500-1,000,000
Tax: 501(c)(3)

Personnel:
President and Chief Executive Officer: Steven Anderson
    E-Mail: stevena@duke.edu
Assistant, Administration and Membership Services:
    Andrea Anderson
    E-Mail: recluce2@duke.edu

Historical Note:
Formerly (1946) the Forest Products History Foundation, (1955) the American Forest History Foundation and assumed its present name in 1959. In 1984, FHS was affiliated with Duke University and moved to Durham, NC. FHS's mission is to improve natural resource management and human welfare by bringing a historical context to environmental decision-making. Membership: $0-5,000/year.

Publications:
Environmental History; quarterly; adv.
FHS Education News; on-line
Forest History Today Magazine
The Forest Timeline Newsletter; monthly

Forest Industries Telecommunications *(1947)*
1565 Oak St.
Eugene, OR 97401
Tel: (541) 485-8441 *Fax:* (541) 485-7556

E-Mail: license@landmobile.com
Website: fcclicense.org
Members: 1800 companies
Staff: 6
Annual Budget: $500-1,000,000
Tax: 501(c)(6)

Personnel:
Executive Vice President: Kenton E. Sturdevant
    E-Mail: kenton@landmobile.com

Historical Note:
Organized in 1947 to assist the forest industry in radio matters before the FCC. Recognized by the FCC as the official representative of the Forest Products Radio Service. Assists all industry and business categories with FCC licensing and frequency coordination services.

Forest Landowners Association *(1941)*
900 Cir. 75 Pkwy.
Suite 205
Atlanta, GA 30339
Tel: (404) 325-2954 *Fax:* (404) 325-2955
TollFree: (800) 325-2954
E-Mail: info@forestlandowners.com
Website: forestlandowners.com
Members: 9000 timber operators
Staff: 6
Annual Budget: $500-1,000,000
Tax: 501(c)(3)

Personnel:
Chief Executive Officer: Scott P. Jones
    E-Mail: sjones@forestlandowners.com
Coordinator, Membership Services: Katelin Baker
Director, Administration: Susan M. Johnson
    E-Mail: sjohnson@forestlandowners.com
Editor: Eddie Rider

Historical Note:
FLA's purpose is to support, through advocacy, education, and information, forest landowners' responsible management of their private property. Members include private forest landowners, consulting foresters, Timberland Investment Management Organizations (TIMOs), real estate investment trusts, forest products companies, forestry schools, professors and students, and other professionals in 48 states. Membership: $25-1,000/year.

Meetings/Conferences: Annual
Conference Chair: Susan M. Johnson
2013 - Coeur d#Alene, ID (Coeur d' Alene Resort)/June 5 - 7

Publications:
FLA Newsletter; on-line
Forest Landowner Magazine; bi-monthly; adv.
Membership Directory; on-line
The Land Report Magazine; on-line

Forest Landowners Tax Council
P.O. Box 784
Alexandria, VA 22313-0784
Tel: (703) 549-0347
E-Mail: info@fltc.net
Website: fltc.net
Staff: 1
Annual Budget: $25-50,000
Tax: 501(c)(6)

Personnel:
Executive Director: Frank Stewart
    E-Mail: director@fltc.net

Historical Note:
FLTC's mission is to provide an effective and unified voice for non-industrial, private forest (NIPF) landowners on federal tax issues. Membership is open nationwide to all individuals, associations, or organizations interested in supporting the mission of the FLTC. Membership: $1,000 (Benefactor); $500- 999 (Patron); $250-499 (Supporter); $100-249 (Contributor).

Publications:
Timber Tax newsletter

Forest Products Industry National Labor-Management Committee
P.O. Box 65175
Washington, DC 20036
Website: labormanagementcommittee.org
Staff: 1
Annual Budget: $250-500,000
Tax: 501(c)(6)

Personnel:
Director: Bill Street

Historical Note:
A coalition representing the shared policy interests of labor unions and management in the forest products industry. The Committee works to ensure that legislative, administrative, and judicial actions affecting the domestic timber supply balance environmental concerns with economic realities.

Forest Products Society *(1947)*
2801 Marshall Ct.
Madison, WI 53705-2295
Tel: (608) 231-1361 *Fax:* (608) 231-2152
Website: forestprod.org
Members: 2500 individuals
Staff: 5
Annual Budget: $500-1,000,000
Tax: 501(c)(3)

Personnel:
Executive Vice President: Stefan Bergmann
    E-Mail: stefan@forestprod.org
Database Manager and Contact, Conferences: Megan Cuccia
    E-Mail: megan@forestprod.org
Membership and Subscription Coordinator: Elaine Glowacki
Director, Conferences and Meetings: Julie Lang
    E-Mail: conferences@forestprod.org
Comptroller and Business Manager: Bruce Learmonth
    E-Mail: bruce@forestprod.org

Historical Note:
Formerly (1995) Forest Products Research Society. FPS is a not-for-profit technical association founded to provide an information network for all segments of the forest products industry. Mission is to Contribute to global stewardship by encouraging the social, economic and environmentally sustainable use of wood and other renewable cellulosic materials. Membership: $155 (Individual); $35 (Student); $400-1,200 (Corporate-Bronze/Silver/Gold); $25 (Developing Country/Retired).

Meetings/Conferences: Annual
Conference Chair: Julie Lang
2013 - Austin, TX/June 9 - 11
Number of non-conference events/year: 1

Publications:
Forest Products Journal; monthly; adv.
FPS Newsletter eUpdate; monthly; adv.
International Journal of Forest Engineering; semi-annually; adv.
Journal of Forest Products Business Research; on-line
Membership Directory; on-line
Wood Design Focus; quarterly; adv.

Forest Resources Association *(2000)*
600 Jefferson Plaza
Suite 350
Rockville, MD 20852
Tel: (301) 838-9385 *Fax:* (301) 838-9481
E-Mail: fra@forestresources.org
Website: forestresources.org
Members: 1000 companies
Staff: 12
Annual Budget: $1-2,000,000

Personnel:
President: Deborah Hawkinson
Director, Finance and Administration: Linda Gibson
    E-Mail: lrgibson@forestresources.org
Vice President, Public Affairs: Neil Ward
    E-Mail: nward@forestresources.org

Historical Note:
Founded as American Pulpwood Association; assumed its current name in 2000. Mission is to promote the interests of forest products industry members in the economical, efficient, and sustainable use of forest resources to meet the needs of the wood fiber supply chain through private enterprise. Membership: $60-100,000/year.

Meetings/Conferences: Annual
Number of non-conference events/year: 2

Publications:
Forest Operations Review
FRA Bulletin; on-line
Membership Directory; annually

Forest Stewardship Council - United States Chapter *(1995)*
212 Third Ave., North
Suite 504
Minneapolis, MN 55401
Tel: (612) 353-4511 *Fax:* (612) 208-1565
E-Mail: info@fscus.org

Website: fscus.org
Members: 120 Individuals and Organizations
Staff: 9
Personnel:
President: Corey Brinkema
   E-Mail: cbrinkema@fscus.org
Director, Finance: Bryce Denton
   E-Mail: b.denton@us.fsc.org
Director, Science and Certification: Gary Dodge
   E-Mail: gdodge@fscus.org
Director, Communications: Brad Kahn
   E-Mail: b.kahn@us.fsc.org
Chief Marketing Officer: Etienne McManus-White
   E-Mail: etienne.mw@us.fsc.org
Manager, Projects: Annika Terrana
   E-Mail: a.terrana@us.fsc.org

Historical Note:
FSC-US's mission is to coordinate the development of forest management standards throughout the different biogeographic regions of the U.S., to provide public information about certification and FSC, and to work with certification organizations to promote FSC certification in the U.S. Membership: $100 (Individual); $150-5,000 (Non-Profit Organization); $200-10,000 (For-Profit Organization).

Continuing Education:
Certification Designation/s: FSC, COC

Meetings/Conferences: Annual
Conference Chair: Annika Terrana

Publications:
FSC Newsletter; monthly
Membership Directory; on-line

Forestry Conservation Communications Association *(1944)*
122 Baltimore St.
Gettysburg, PA 17325
Tel: (717) 338-1505 *Fax:* (717) 334-5656
E-Mail: ed@fcca-usa.org
Website: fcca-usa.org
Members: 200 organizations
Staff: 3
Annual Budget: $250-500,000

Personnel:
Executive Director: Ralph Haller
   E-Mail: ed@fcca-usa.org
Counsel: Russell H. Fox
   E-Mail: rfox@mintz.com
Financial Assistant: Janet Muncy
   E-Mail: Janet.Muncy@fcca-usa.org

Historical Note:
Certified by the FCC as the radio frequency coordinator for the Forestry Conservation Radio Service. FCCA helps its members to become ambassadors for the best use of the radio frequency spectrum. Through active participation, FCCA will continue to represent public safety professionals to effect positive change.

Meetings/Conferences: Annual

Publications:
Newsletter

Forestry Equipment Council *(1975)*
6737 W. Washington St., Suite 2400
C/O Association of Equipment Manufacturers
Milwaukee, WI 53214-5647
Tel: (414) 272-0943 *Fax:* (414) 272-1170
E-Mail: aem@aem.org
Website: aem.org/Groups/Groups/Group.asp?
   G=33
Staff: 1

Personnel:
Senior Director, Technical and Safety Services: Mike Pankonin

Historical Note:
Mission is to focus on market expansion and efficiently serving the needs of the loggers and foresters, provide a forum where forestry related issues can be openly and freely discussed. Leadership of the Council is provided by a Chairman and a Vice Chairman elected from the ranks of the Council's membership.

Forging Industry Association *(1913)*
25 W. Prospect Ave.
Suite 615
Cleveland, OH 44114
Tel: (216) 781-6260 *Fax:* (216) 781-0102
E-Mail: info@forging.org

Website: forging.org
Members: 150 plants, 110 forging producers and 80 suppliers
Staff: 12
Annual Budget: $2-5,000,000
Tax: 501(c)(6)

Personnel:
Corporate Secretary, Marketing Activities: Donald "Don" Farley
   E-Mail: don@forging.org
Contact, Database and Systems Support: Mary Ann Foote
   E-Mail: maryann@forging.org
Contact, Meetings: Doug Glenn
   E-Mail: doug@forgemag.com.
General Manager: Roy W. Hardy
   E-Mail: roy@forging.org
Executive Management Support, Publications and Meetings: Billie Hurt
   E-Mail: billie@forging.org
Contact, Membership Services: Karen S. Lewis
   E-Mail: karen@forging.org
Contact, Website, Conference and Seminars: Connie Long
   E-Mail: connie@forging.org

Historical Note:
Formerly Drop Forging Association and affiliated with Forging Industry Education and Research Foundation (FIERF). FIA strives to improve members global competitiveness. Members are producers of forgings and raw materials, major equipment and supplies used in the forging industry. Membership: dues are based on a three year average of forging sales.

Meetings/Conferences:
Conference Chair: Donald "Don" Farley
2013 - Columbus, OH (Greater Columbus Convention Center)/March 26 - 28
2013 - San Diego, CA (Hotel del Coronado)/May 4 - 6
Number of non-conference events/year: 1

Publications:
FIA QuickRead; on-line
Membership Directory; on-line

Formaldehyde Council, Inc. *(2004)*
801 N. Quincy St.
Suite 700
Arlington, VA 22203
Website: formaldehyde.nclud.com
Staff: 2
Annual Budget: $1-2,000,000
Tax: 501(c)(6)

Personnel:
Executive Director: Betsy Natz
Manager, Public Affairs: Sarah Macedo
   E-Mail: smacedo@formaldehyde.org

Historical Note:
FCI's mission is to encourage accurate scientific evaluation of formaldehyde and formaldehyde-based materials and to communicate sound scientific information relating to the uses, benefits and sustainability of these products. Members are formaldehyde producers, users and associated companies.

Publications:
Membership Directory

Forming and Fabricating Community of SME
One SME Dr.
Dearborn, MI 48128
Tel: (313) 425-3000 *Fax:* (313) 425-3400
TollFree: (800) 733-4763
Website: sme.org/ffc
Staff: 1

Personnel:
Executive Director and Chief Executive Officer: Mark C. Tomlinson

Historical Note:
The Society of Manufacturing Engineers (SME) is the premier source for manufacturing knowledge, education and networking.SME's mission is to acquire and distribute manufacturing knowledge among its members and the broader manufacturing community

Meetings/Conferences: Annual
2013 - Baltimore, MD/June 2 - 4

Publications:
AeroDef Manufacturing; monthly
Daily Executive Briefing; daily
Energy Manufacturing; monthly
Journal of Manufacturing Systems (JMSY); on-line
Lean Directions; monthly

Manufacturing Engineering
Quality in Manufacturing; monthly
SME Member Newsletter
The Journal of Manufacturing Processes (JMP); on-line

Forum of Regional Associations of Grantmakers *(1940)*
2121 Crystal Dr.
Suite 700
Arlington, VA 22202
Tel: (703) 879-0812 *Fax:* (703) 879-0800
E-Mail: info@givingforum.org
Website: givingforum.org
Members: 4,000 foundations, corporations, organizations, and individual donors
Staff: 5
Annual Budget: $500-1,000,000
Tax: 501(c)(3)

Personnel:
President and Chief Executive Officer: Michael Litz
   E-Mail: mlitz@givingforum.org
Manager, Communications: Dan Brady
   E-Mail: dbrady@givingforum.org
Manager, Member Services: Courtney Moore
   E-Mail: cmoore@givingforum.org
Director, Programs: Mary ONeill
   E-Mail: moneill@givingforum.org

Historical Note:
Supports philanthropy by strengthening the ability of all regional associations to fulfill their missions; these associations promote the growth and effectiveness of philanthropy in order to improve life in their communities.

Meetings/Conferences:
Conference Chair: Courtney Moore

Publications:
Social Impact Markets; weekly
Stanford Social Innovation Review; quarterly

Foster Family-Based Treatment Association *(1988)*
294 Union St.
Hackensack, NJ 07601
Tel: (800) 414-3382 *Fax:* (201) 489-6719
TollFree: (800) 414-3382
E-Mail: ffta@ffta.org
Website: ffta.org
Members: 400 agencies
Staff: 4
Annual Budget: $500-1,000,000
Tax: 501(c)(3)

Personnel:
Executive Administrator: David Schild
Administrator: Melissa Cole
   E-Mail: mcole@ffta.org
Manager, Conference and Special Projects: Stacey Horowitz
   E-Mail: shorowitz@ffta.org

Historical Note:
FFTA works to strengthen agencies that support families caring for vulnerable children. The Association's membership is composed of agencies throughout North America currently operating treatment foster care programs. Membership: $495-2,200/year based upon the budget of the treatment foster care program.

Meetings/Conferences: Annual
Conference Chair: Stacey Horowitz
2013 - Nashville, TN (Gaylord Opryland Resort and Convention Center)/July 28 - 31

Publications:
FOCUS; adv.
FOCUS Newsletter; adv.
Membership Directory; on-line
Treatment Foster Care e-News; on-line

Foundation for Advances in Medicine and Science *(1983)*
111 Owneo Rd.
Mahwah, NJ 07430
Tel: (201) 828-9150 *Fax:* (201) 828-9077
E-Mail: tony@fams.org
Website: fams.org
Members: 350 individuals
Staff: 3
Annual Budget: Under $10,000
Tax: 501(c)(3)

Personnel:
Executive Director: Tony Bourgholtzer

E-Mail: tony@fams.org

Historical Note:
Mission of FAMS is to advance medicine and science worldwide via the exchange of knowledge and information. FAMS accomplishes this mission by sponsoring conferences, holding educational seminars and publishing books. Membership: $1,000 (Corporate); $200 (Sponsor); $50 (Individual); $30 (Student).

Foundation for International Meetings *(1983)*
1110 N. Glebe Rd., Suite 580
Arlington, VA 22201
Tel: (703) 908-0707 *Fax:* (703) 908-0709
E-Mail: info@aimc.com
Website: aimcnetwork.com
Members: 300 individuals
Staff: 2
Annual Budget: $50-100,000

Personnel:
President and Chief Executive Officer: Jack Sammis
   E-Mail: jsammis@imnsolutions.com
Contact, Membership: Graham Smith
   E-Mail: gsmit@imnsolutions.com

Historical Note:
Formerly Foundation for International Meetings. AIMC seeks to foster and promote international meetings conducted by America's trade associations and professional societies. Members are C.E.O.'s of associations and corporations which have ongoing international meeting or trade programs. Membership: $375 (Industry); $25,000 (Founding Industry); $10,000 (Contributing Industry).

Meetings/Conferences: Annual

Foundation for Russian-American Economic Cooperation *(1989)*
2601 Fourth Ave.
Suite 600
Seattle, WA 98121
Tel: (206) 443-1935 *Fax:* (206) 443-0954
Website: fraec.org
Members: 90 companies
Staff: 5
Annual Budget: $1-2,000,000
Tax: 501(c)(3)

Personnel:
Founder and President: Carol Vipperman
   E-Mail: carolv@fraec.org
Program Manager, Training and Exchanges: Curtis Cortelyou
   E-Mail: curtis@fraec.org

Historical Note:
FRAEC strives to further economic and community ties with Russia and maintains a unique focus on the Russian Far East. Membership concentrated in the Pacific Northwest, consists of businesses seeking to enter the Russian market or improve their market share in Russia. Membership: $5,000 (Executive); $2,500 (Corporate); $1,000 (Business); $500 (Individual/Non-profit).

Continuing Education:
Certification Designation/s: FRAEC

Publications:
Membership Directory; on-line

The Fragrance Foundation *(1949)*
545 Fifth Ave.
Suite 900
New York, NY 10017
Tel: (212) 725-2755 *Fax:* (212) 779-9058
E-Mail: info@fragrance.org
Website: fragrance.org
Members: 175 companies
Staff: 6
Annual Budget: $2-5,000,000

Personnel:
Executive Director: Theresa Molnar
   E-Mail: tmolnar@senseofsmell.org
Vice President: Mary Ellen Lapsansky
   E-Mail: melapsansky@fragrance.org
Director, Office Operations and Finance: Lilia Nicoletti
   E-Mail: lnicoletti@fragrance.org
Consultant, Special Projects and Events: Amy Rubin
   E-Mail: arubin@fragrance.org

Historical Note:
TFF strives to encourage the enjoyment of fragrance products through the dissemination of information on the manufacture, application and care of such products. Membership includes manufacturers, suppliers, media, advertising and public relations agencies as well as

designers, packagers and retailers. Membership: $2363-63,000 (Full); $2000 (Business Consultant); $6,300 (Media, Consulting Firm, Advertising, Designer/Retail).*

Continuing Education:
Certification Designation/s: CFSS

Meetings/Conferences:
Conference Chair: Amy Rubin
Number of non-conference events/year: 6

Publications:
Business Newsletter; quarterly
Fragrance Directory; on-line
Fragrance Forum

Fragrance Materials Association
1620 I St. NW, Suite 925
Washington, DC 20006
Tel: (202) 293-5800
Website: fmafragrance.org/
Staff: 1

Personnel:
Executive Director: Anne Steinemann

Fraternal Field Managers Association *(1935)*
1700 Farnam St.
Omaha, NE 68102
Tel: (402) 271-7250
Website: ffma.info
Members: 75 organizations
Staff: 2
Annual Budget: $25-50,000

Personnel:
Executive Secretary and Treasurer: Jim Pearson CLU, LUTCF
   E-Mail: jpearson@woodmen.org

Historical Note:
FFMA is dedicated to promote the ethical standards and professional development of the fraternal field force, fostering harmony, unity of purpose and the exchange of ideas among the member societies. Members are sales managers of fraternal life insurance societies. Membership: $50-1,000/year (Society, based on assets).

Continuing Education:
Certification Designation/s: FIC, FICF, CFFM

Meetings/Conferences: Annual

Publications:
FIC Perspective

Fraternity Executives Association *(1930)*
1750 Royalton Dr.
Carmel, IN 46032
Tel: (317) 496-2411 *Fax:* (317) 594-9299
E-Mail: fea.inc@gmail.com
Website: fea-inc.org
Members: 72 fraternities and 25 sororities
Staff: 1
Annual Budget: $250-500,000
Tax: 501(c)(6)

Personnel:
Executive Director: Sidney N. Dunn

Historical Note:
Formerly (1970) College Fraternity Secretaries Association. FEA provides for the professional development of its members while promoting the values and success of the fraternal movement. Membership: $75/year.

Meetings/Conferences: Annual
2013 - San Antonio, TX (Grand Hyatt San Antonio)/ July 6 - 10

Publications:
Membership Directory; on-line
News & Notes; monthly

Free Speech Coalition *(1992)*
P.O. Box 10480
Canoga Park, CA 91309
Tel: (866) 372-9373 *Fax:* (818) 348-8893
E-Mail: info@freespeechcoalition.com
Website: freespeechcoalition.com
Members: 3500 individuals and companies
Staff: 5
Annual Budget: $25-50,000
Tax: 501(c)(6)

Personnel:
Executive Director: Diane C. Duke
   E-Mail: diane@freespeechcoalition.com
Director, Membership Services: Joanne Cachapero
   E-Mail: joanne@freespeechcoalition.com

Treasurer: Lynn Swanson
   E-Mail: lswanson@freespeechcoalition.com

Historical Note:
The trade association for the adult entertainment industry. Membership: $100-8,000/year.

Publications:
X-Press newsletter; weekly

Freelancers Union
20 Jay St.
Suite 700
Brooklyn, NY 11201
Fax: (718) 228-9580
E-Mail: membership@freelancersunion.org
Website: freelancersunion.org
Staff: 1
Annual Budget: $5-10,000,000

Personnel:
Founder and Executive Director: Sara Horowitz

Historical Note:
Provides support for freelance and independent workers. Membership is free.

The French Film Office/UniFrance USA
424 Madison Ave.
Eighth Floor
New York, NY 10017
Tel: (212) 832-8860 *Fax:* (212) 755-0629
E-Mail: info@frenchfilm.org
Website: unifrance.org
Staff: 1

Personnel:
Executive Director: Catherine Verret

Fresh Produce and Floral Council *(1965)*
16700 Valley View Ave.
Suite 130
La Mirada, CA 90638
Tel: (714) 739-0177 *Fax:* (714) 739-0226
E-Mail: info@fpfc.org
Website: fpfc.org
Members: 1040 companies and individuals
Staff: 3
Annual Budget: $1-2,000,000
Tax: 501(c)(6)

Personnel:
President: Carissa Mace
   E-Mail: carissa@fpfc.org
Consultant, Marketing and Events: Angela Steier
   E-Mail: angela@fpfc.org
Director, Operations: Pauleen Yoshikane
   E-Mail: pauleen@fpfc.org

Historical Note:
Formerly Fresh Produce Council till 1994. FPFC is dedicated to provide members with convenient opportunities to build productive relationships, access timely market information, enhance their business skills, and pool their efforts to promote and advance the industry. Members include growers, shippers, wholesalers, brokers, distributors and retailers of produce and/or floral items. Membership: $50 (Individual); $495 (Company).

Meetings/Conferences:
Conference Chair: Pauleen Yoshikane

Publications:
Fresh DIGEST; adv.
Produce Business Magazine

Fresh Produce Association of the Americas *(1944)*
P.O. Box 848
Nogales, AZ 85628
Tel: (520) 287-2707 *Fax:* (520) 287-2948
E-Mail: info@freshfrommexico.com
Website: freshfrommexico.com
Members: 125 companies
Staff: 7
Annual Budget: $1-2,000,000
Tax: 501(c)(6)

Personnel:
President: Lance Jungmeyer
   E-Mail: lance@freshfrommexico.com
Director, Public Affairs and Contact, Membership and Conventions: Amy Adams
   E-Mail: aadams@freshfrommexico.com
Director, Events: Marlene Lopez
   E-Mail: mar@freshfrommexico.com
Communications Director: Allison Moore

E-Mail: amoore@freshfrommexico.com
Contact, Accounting and Director, Human Resources:
  Conchita Singh
    E-Mail: csingh@freshfrommexico.com

Historical Note:
Formerly West Mexico Vegetable Distributors Association.
FPAA provides a powerful voice for improvement and
sustainability, serving the needs of more than 125 North
American companies involved in the growth, harvest,
marketing, import, and distribution of Mexican produce.
Members are U.S. firms engaged in the marketing of
Mexican-grown fruits and vegetables to international
markets. Membership: $1,500/year (Associate/Distributor).

Meetings/Conferences: Annual
Conference Chair: Marlene Lopez
2013 - Toronto, ON/April 17 - 19
2013 - New Orleans, LA/Oct. 18 - 21
2013 - New Orleans, LA/Oct. 18 - 20/18000 attendees
2014 - Vancouver, BC/April 2 - 4
2014 - Anaheim, CA/Oct. 17 - 20
2014 - Anaheim, CA/Oct. 17 - 19
2015 - Atlanta, GA/Oct. 23 - 26
2015 - Atlanta, GA/Oct. 23 - 25/18000 attendees
Number of non-conference events/year: 1

Publications:
Member Directory; on-line

Friction Material Standards Institute (1948)
23 Woodland Rd.
Suite B-3
Madison, CT 06443
Tel: (203) 245-8425 Fax: (203) 245-8537
E-Mail: fmsiinc@aol.com
Website: fmsi.org
Members: 90 companies
Staff: 2
Annual Budget: $100-250,000

Personnel:
President: Patrick T. Healey
Treasurer: Rick Jamieson

Historical Note:
Formerly the Brake Lining Manufacturers Association.
FMSI strives to maintain and enhance the standardized
part numbering system for all on highway vehicles in use in
North America. Membership is open to any manufacturer
of friction and related products covered by the trademarked
FMSI and FMS part numbers. Other participants in this
industry may be eligible for licensee membership.

Publications:
Membership Directory; on-line

Friends of the National Institute of Dental and Craniofacial Research (FNIDCR) (1998)
100 S. Washington St.
Rockville, MD 20850
Tel: (240) 778-6117 Fax: (240) 778-6112
E-Mail: membership@fnidcr.org
Website: fnidcr.org
Staff: 6
Annual Budget: $100-250,000
Tax: 501(c)(3)

Personnel:
Executive Director: Peter Anas CAE
  E-Mail: peter@fnider.org
Director, Meetings and Membership Services: Laikisha
  Jeffries
    E-Mail: membership@fnidcr.org
Legislative Director: Andrew Kaffes
  E-Mail: legislative@fnidcr.org
Contact, Accounting: Marilyn Lawlor

Historical Note:
FNIDCR's mission is to educate the public and key decision
makers about the importance of investing in the NIDCR
(National Institute of Dental and Craniofacial Research).
Membership: $150-10,000 + /year.

Meetings/Conferences: Annual
Conference Chair: Laikisha Jeffries

Publications:
E-Newsletter; monthly
Legislative Updates; monthly
Oral Health Research Newsletter; quarterly

Frozen Potato Products Institute (1958)
2000 Corporate Ridge, Blvd.
Suite 1000
McLean, VA 22102
Tel: (703) 821-0770 Fax: (703) 821-1350

E-Mail: fmsiinc@aol.com
Website: affi.com
Members: 6 companies
Staff: 5
Annual Budget: $100-250,000
Tax: 501(c)(6)

Personnel:
Executive Director and Treasurer: Elise Cortina
Chief Executive Officer: Kraig R. Naasz
  E-Mail: knaasz@affi.com
Vice President, Member Services: Lucas R. Darnell
  E-Mail: ldarnell@affi.com
Vice President, Administration: Kathleen R. Greco
  E-Mail: kgreco@affi.com
Vice President, Conventions and Meetings: Jenny Mitchell

Historical Note:
A product division of American Frozen Food Institute,
which provides administrative support.

Meetings/Conferences:
Conference Chair: Jenny Mitchell

Fuel Cell and Hydrogen Energy Association (2010)
1133 19th St. NW
Ninth Floor
Washington, DC 20036-2701
Tel: (202) 261-1331 Fax: (202) 223-5537
E-Mail: info@hydrogenconference.org
Website: fchea.org
Members: 90 individuals
Staff: 4
Annual Budget: $500-1,000,000

Personnel:
President and Executive Director: Morry B. Markowitz
  E-Mail: mmarkowitz@fchea.org
Manager, External Affairs: Connor Dolan
  E-Mail: cdolan@fchea.org
Senior Technical Specialist: Karen Hall
  E-Mail: khall@fchea.org
Director, Policy and External Affairs: James Warner
  E-Mail: jwarner@fchea.org

Historical Note:
Created from the merger of the US Fuel Cell Council and
the National Hydrogen Association, FCHEA is dedicated
to the commercialization of fuel cells and hydrogen energy
technologies. Membership represents supply chain from
universities, government laboratories and agencies, trade
associations, fuel cell materials, components and systems
manufacturers, hydrogen producers and fuel distributors,
utilities and other end users. Membership : $25,000 (Tier
1); $15,000 (Tier 2); $7,000 (Tier 3); $3,000 (Tier 4).

Meetings/Conferences: Annual
2013 - Shanghai, China/Sept. 25 - 28/1500 attendees

Publications:
Fuel Cell and Hydrogen Energy Connection-
  Newsletter; monthly
Fuel Cell and Hydrogen Energy Connection; monthly
Hydrogen and Fuel Cell Safety Report; monthly
Membership Directory; on-line

Membership List Available to Non-members

Fulfillment Management Association (1948)
60 E. 42nd St.
Suite 2316
New York, NY 10165
Tel: (818) 487-2090 Fax: (818) 487-4501
E-Mail: info@fmanational.com
Website: fmanational.com
Members: 425 individuals
Staff: 3
Annual Budget: $100-250,000

Personnel:
President: Brian Knowles
  E-Mail: brian@subcoinc.com
Executive Secretary: Jo Ann Binz
  E-Mail: joann@qcs1989.com
Treasurer: Mike McCarthy
  E-Mail: mmccarthy@ebsco.com

Historical Note:
Established as the Subscription Fulfillment Managers
Association, assumed its present name in 1972. FMA's
mission is to help members keep current on important
developments in the fields of fulfillment, consumer
marketing, and customer relations by sharing ideas and
knowledge for improving service to customers. Members are
direct mail fulfillment, marketing and circulation executives.
Membership is concentrated in New York, Chicago, and
Washington, DC. Membership: $50 (Individual); $200
(Corporate).

Meetings/Conferences: Annual
Number of non-conference events/year: 1

Publications:
Membership Directory; on-line

Funeral Consumers Alliance (1963)
33 Patchen Rd.
S. Burlington, VT 05403
Tel: (802) 865-8300 Fax: (802) 865-2626
TollFree: (800) 765-0107
E-Mail: fca@funerals.org
Website: funerals.org
Members: 120 societies
Staff: 3
Annual Budget: $100-250,000
Tax: 501(c)(3)

Personnel:
Executive Director: Joshua Slocum

Historical Note:
Formerly (1995) Continental Association of Funeral
and Memorial Societies and Funeral and Memorial
Societies of America (1999). Serves as a credible source of
information for media covering death and dying. Members
are non- profit consumer groups dedicated to protect
consumer's right to choose a meaningful affordable funeral.
Membership fee varies based on group membership dues
collected.

Meetings/Conferences: Biennial

Publications:
Affiliates Directory; on-line
FCA Newsletter; quarterly; adv.

Fur Commission USA (1994)
P.O. Box 1532
Medford, OR 97501
Tel: (541) 595-8568 Fax: (541) 566-7489
E-Mail: furfarmers@aol.com
Website: furcommission.com
Members: 400 mink-farming families
Staff: 4
Annual Budget: $250-500,000

Personnel:
Executive Director: Michael Whelan

Historical Note:
Animal Welfare Coalition, Mink Farmers Research
Foundation.

Continuing Education:
Certification Designation/s: HCMA, FCUSA
Meetings/Conferences:
Number of non-conference events/year: 21

Publications:
Fur Animal Research; quarterly
Fur Farm Letter; quarterly; adv.

Fur Information Council of America (1987)
8424 A Santa Monica Blvd.
Suite 860
Hollywood, CA 90069
Tel: (323) 782-1700 Fax: (323) 651-1417
E-Mail: info@fur.org
Website: fur.org
Members: 300 individuals
Staff: 5
Annual Budget: $250-500,000
Tax: 501(c)(6)

Personnel:
Executive Director and Director, Membership Services:
  Keith Kaplan
    E-Mail: kapgrp@aol.com

Historical Note:
Provide background information and guidance on industry
developments, research market trends and consumer habits,
track and report sales and price points. Membership:
$500-1000 (Based on yearly sales); $250 (Newsletter
subscription).

Publications:
FURthermore

Furniture Manufacturers Alliance
317 W. High Ave.
High Point, NC 27260
Staff: 1

Personnel:
Chief Executive Officer: Andy Counts

Furniture Retailers of America

1150 18th St. NW, Suite 325
Washington, DC 20036
Website: furnitureretailers.interactive.biz
Staff: 1

Personnel:
Contact, Media: George Felcyn
  E-Mail: information@furnitureretailers.org

Historical Note:
The Furniture Retailers of America (FRA) was formed to protect the customers from a group of domestic furniture manufacturers who are seeking to restrict consumer access to affordable high quality wooden bedroom furniture by filing an anti-dumping petition with the U.S. International Trade Commission.

Publications:
The Wall Street Journal; on-line

Fusion Power Associates *(1979)*
Two Professional Dr.
Suite 249
Gaithersburg, MD 20879
Tel: (301) 258-0545 *Fax:* (301) 975-9869
E-Mail: fusionpwrassoc@aol.com
Website: fusionpower.org
Members:
20 companies
400 individuals
Staff: 3
Annual Budget: $100-250,000
Tax: 501(c)(3)

Personnel:
President: Stephen O. Dean PhD
  E-Mail: fusionpwrassoc@aol.com
Vice President, Communications: Mark Tillack
Vice President, Administration, Finance, Secretary and Treasurer: Ruth A. Watkins

Historical Note:
Incorporated in California in 1979, the association is concerned with the development of practical applications of fusion science and technology. The purpose of Fusion Power Associates is to ensure the timely development and acceptance of fusion as a socially, environmentally and economically attractive source of energy. Membership: $60 (Individual Affiliate); $500 (Small Business Affiliate); $1000 (Institutional Affiliate); $2,000 (Institutional Membership); $15 (Student Affiliate).

Meetings/Conferences: Annual

Publications:
Executive Newsletter; bi-monthly
Fusion Power Report; bi-monthly
Journal of Fusion Energy; bi-monthly; adv.

Futon Association International *(1995)*
P.O. Box 593730
Orlando, FL 32859
Tel: (407) 447-1706 *Fax:* (866) 595-1355
E-Mail: leasing@futon.org
Website: futonlife.com
Members: 85 manufacturers and distributors
Staff: 1
Annual Budget: $100-250,000
Tax: 501(c)(6)

Personnel:
President: Tom Tedesco
  E-Mail: s.tedesco@futon.org

Historical Note:
Formerly (1990) the Waterbed Association. Members are manufacturers, distributors, and retailers or specialty mattresses and bedding. Membership: sliding scale based on sales.

Publications:
Buyers Guide; on-line

Future Business Leaders of America - Phi Beta Lambda *(1942)*
1912 Association Dr.
Reston, VA 20191-1591
Tel: (800) 325-2946 *Fax:* (866) 500-5610
TollFree: (800) 325-2946
E-Mail: general@fbla.org
Website: fbla-pbl.org
Members: 215000 members, 11,000 college students, 20,000 student members
Staff: 13
Annual Budget: $10-25,000
Tax: 501(c)(3)

Personnel:

President and Chief Executive Officer: Jean M. Buckley
Director, Conferences: Richard Bowen
  E-Mail: conferencedir@fbla.org
Director, Marketing and Educator Relations: Greg Oliver
  E-Mail: marketing@fbla.org
Manager, Communications: Marisa Preuss
  E-Mail: communications@fbla.org
Director, Education: Barbara Small
  E-Mail: education@fbla.org
Director, Membership: Lisa Frye Smothers
  E-Mail: membershipdir@fbla.org

Historical Note:
FBLA-PBL's mission is to bring business and education together in a positive working relationship through innovative leadership and career development programs. Membership: $6 (FBLA (High School)); $4 (FBLA-Middle Level (Middle School/Jr. HS)); $10 (PBL (Postsecondary)).

Continuing Education:
Certification Designation/s: CIW

Meetings/Conferences:
Conference Chair: Richard Bowen
2013 - Anaheim, CA/June 22 - 25
2013 - Anaheim, CA/June 27 - 30
2014 - Nashville, TN/June 24 - 27
2014 - Nashville, TN/June 29 - July 2
Number of non-conference events/year: 2

Publications:
FBLA Advisers' Hotline; adv.
FBLA-Middle Level Advisers' Hotline; adv.
PBL Advisers' Hotline; adv.
PBL Business Leader; adv.
The Professional Edge; adv.
Tomorrow's Business Leader; quarterly; adv.

FutureGen Industrial Alliance, Inc.
1101 Pennsylvania Ave. NW
Sixth Floor
Washington, DC 20004
Tel: (202) 280-6019
E-Mail: info@futuregenalliance.org
Website: futuregenalliance.org
Staff: 3
Annual Budget: $10-25,000,000
Tax: 501(c)(3)

Personnel:
Chief Executive Officer: Kenneth K. Humphreys
Press Contact: Lawrence Pacheco
  E-Mail: lawrence.pacheco@fticonsulting.com
Secretary and Treasurer: Greg A. Walker

Historical Note:
The FutureGen Industrial Alliance is a consortium of 10 power producers and electric utilities from around the globe.

Futures Industry Association *(1955)*
2001 Pennsylvania Ave. NW
Suite 600
Washington, DC 20006-1823
Tel: (202) 466-5460 *Fax:* (202) 296-3184
E-Mail: info@futuresindustry.org
Website: futuresindustry.org
Members: 250 members
Staff: 18
Annual Budget: $10-25,000,000
Tax: 501(c)(6)

Personnel:
President and Chief Executive Officer: Walter Lukken
  E-Mail: wlukken@futuresindustry.org
Editor: Will Acworth
  E-Mail: wacworth@futuresindustry.org
Director, Member Services: Adoncia Boykins
  E-Mail: aboykins@futuresindustry.org
Manager, Meetings and Events: Marsha Saunders
  E-Mail: msaunders@futuresindustry.org
Senior Vice President, Chief Financial Officer and Chief Operating Officer: Guy Sheetz
  E-Mail: gsheetz@futuresindustry.org
Vice President, Communications: Tracy Wahler
  E-Mail: twahler@futuresindustry.org
Director, Human Resources: Donna Whitehead
  E-Mail: dwhitehead@futuresindustry.org
Executive Vice President and General Counsel: Barbara Wierzynski
  E-Mail: bwierzynski@futuresindustry.org
Manager, Technology Projects: David Wilson
  E-Mail: dwilson@futuresindustry.com
Chief Technology Officer: James Woods

  E-Mail: jwoods@futuresindustry.org

Historical Note:
Formerly (1975) Association of Commodity Exchange Firms and founded to represent the brokerage community, FIA serves as an effective liaison between the industry and Congress, the Commodity Futures Trading Commission and other regulators whose activities affect the derivatives markets. Membership: $1,500-50,000 (Associate).

Meetings/Conferences:
Conference Chair: Marsha Saunders
2013 - Boca Raton, FL (Boca Raton Resort and Club)/ March 12 - 15
2014 - Boca Raton, FL (Boca Raton Resort and Club)/ March 11 - 14
2015 - Boca Raton, FL (Boca Raton Resort and Club)/ March 10 - 13
2016 - Boca Raton, FL (Boca Raton Resort and Club)/ March 8 - 11
Number of non-conference events/year: 5

Publications:
eMarketBeat (on line); weekly
FI Magazine
Membership Directory; on-line

Galiceno Horse Breeders Association *(1959)*
P.O. Box 219
Godley, TX 76044-0219
Tel: (817) 389-3547
Members: 600 individuals
Staff: 1
Annual Budget: Under $10,000

Personnel:
Secretary: Chris Giles

Historical Note:
Members are owners and breeders of Galiceno horses. Membership: $20/year.

GAMA International *(1952)*
2901 Telestar Ct.
Suite 140
Falls Church, VA 22042-1205
Tel: (800) 345-2687 *Fax:* (571) 499-4302
TollFree: (800) 345-2687
E-Mail: gamamail@gama.naifa.org
Website: gamaweb.com
Members: 5000 individuals
Staff: 20
Annual Budget: $2-5,000,000
Tax: 501(c)(6)

Personnel:
Chief Executive Officer: Jeffrey R. Hughes
  E-Mail: jhughes@gamaweb.com
Director, Communications and Editor in Chief: Mary Barnes
  E-Mail: mbarnes@gamaweb.com
Coordinator, Awards and Membership: Stephanie Beattie
  E-Mail: sbeattie@gamaweb.com
Manager, Marketing: Candace Berschauer
  E-Mail: cberschauer@gamaweb.com
Senior Director, Development: Bonnie Godsman
  E-Mail: bgodsman@gama.naifa.org
Senior Director, Content and Delivery: Debra L. Grommons
  E-Mail: dgrommons@gamaweb.com
Senior Director, Communications and Executive Editor: Gina Kvitkovich
  E-Mail: gkvitkovich@gamaweb.com
Senior Director, Finance: Betty Pattison
  E-Mail: bpattison@gamaweb.com
Director, Meetings and Operations: Stacey Perry
  E-Mail: sperry@gamaweb.com
Manager, Membership Services: Michelle Pike
  E-Mail: mpike@gamaweb.com

Historical Note:
Founded as General Agents and Managers Conference of NALU, became General Agents and Managers Association in 1991, and assumed its current name in 1997. GAMA's mission is to build the leaders who build the financial services industry. Membership: $285-375 (Regular); $140-187.50 (Functional Specialist); $356-475 (Associate).

Meetings/Conferences: Annual
Conference Chair: Bonnie Godsman
2013 - San Diego, CA (Manchester Grand)/March 17 - 20
2014 - Nashville, TN (Gaylord OprylandResort and Convention Center)/March 16 - 19

2015 - Orlando, FL (Orlando World Center Marriott)/
  March 15 - 18
2016 - Las Vegas, NV (Rio Las Vegas Hotel and
  Casino)/March 20 - 23

Publications:
GAMA International Journal; bi-monthly

Game Manufacturers Association (1977)
280 N. High St.
Suite 230
Columbus, OH 43215
Tel: (614) 255-4500 *Fax:* (614) 255-4499
Website: gama.org
Members: 730 organizations
Staff: 5
Annual Budget: $250-500,000
Tax: 501(c)(6)

Personnel:
Executive Director: John Ward
  E-Mail: ed@gama.org
Coordinator, Registration and Events: Joby Miller
  E-Mail: registration@gama.org
Director, Sales: Steve Verdoliva
  E-Mail: sales@gama.org
Director, Finance: Angela Ward
  E-Mail: award@gama.org

Historical Note:
GAMA's mission is to advance the hobby games industry
and to make doing business in industry better and easier
for all professionals. Membership: $300 (Publishing/
Manufacturing); $125 (Retailer); $300 (Distributor/
Wholesaler); $50 (Communicating).

Meetings/Conferences: Semi-Annual
Conference Chair: Joby Miller
2013 - Las Vegas, NV (Bally's Las Vegas)/March 18 -
  22
2013 - Las Vegas, NV/April 8 - 11/830 attendees
2013 - Columbus, OH (Greater Columbus Convention
  Center)/June 12 - 16
2014 - Columbus, OH (Greater Columbus Convention
  Center)/June 11 - 15
2015 - Columbus, OH (Greater Columbus Convention
  Center)/June 3 - 7
Number of non-conference events/year: 4

Membership List Available to Non-members

Gamma Iota Sigma (1965)
P.O. Box 227
Norristown, PA 19404
Tel: (484) 991-4471 *Fax:* (614) 221-1989
E-Mail: grand@gammaiotasigma.org
Website: gammaiotasigma.org
Members: 14200 Alumni and current member
individuals
Staff: 1
Annual Budget: $100-250,000
Tax: 501(c)(3)

Personnel:
Executive Director: Noelle Codispoti

Historical Note:
GIS's mission is to promote, encourage, and sustain
student interest in insurance, risk management, and
actuarial science as profession; to encourage the high
moral and scholastic attainments of its members; and
to facilitate interaction of educational institutions and
industry by fostering research activities, scholarship and
improved public relations. Member of Professional Fraternity
Association. Membership: $30 (Individual/Associate)/year.

Meetings/Conferences: Annual

Publications:
The Sextant; semi-annually; adv.

Garden Centers of America (1973)
524 Springfield Ave.
Westfield, NJ 07090
Tel: (908) 232-4076 *Fax:* (908) 232-0079
Website: gardencentersofamerica.org
Staff: 2
Annual Budget: $250-500,000

Personnel:
President: David Williams
  E-Mail: williamsnursery@gmail.com

Historical Note:
GCA is dedicated to advancing information, education and
training that advocates the exchange of ideas, profitability
and positive consumer awareness of its individual member

firms. Membership: $299 (Garden Center Member);
$699(Vendor Member).

Publications:
Tour Treasures Newsletter; monthly; adv.

Garden Writers Association (1948)
10210 Leatherleaf Ct.
Manassas, VA 20111-4245
Tel: (703) 257-1032 *Fax:* (703) 257-0213
E-Mail: info@gardenwriters.org
Website: gardenwriters.org
Members: 1800 individuals
Staff: 8
Annual Budget: $500-1,000,000
Tax: 501(c)(6)

Personnel:
Executive Director: Robert C. LaGasse CAE
  E-Mail: execdir@gardenwriters.org
Director, Membership Services: Jennifer Fuchs
  E-Mail: membership@gardenwriters.org
Meeting Planner: Kathryn Nelson
  E-Mail: meetings@gardenwriters.org

Historical Note:
GWA's mission is to provide leadership and opportunities
for education, recognition, career development, and a
forum for diverse interactions for professionals in the
field of garden communication. Members are garden
professionals including book authors, staff editors,
syndicated columnists, free-lance writers, photographers,
landscape designers, television and radio personalities,
consultants, catalog publishers, extension service agents,
and more. Membership: $85 (Active/Associate); $25
(Student); $275-5,000 (Allied).

Meetings/Conferences: Annual
Conference Chair: Kathryn Nelson

Publications:
GWA Membership directory; annually; adv.
Quill & Trowel Newsletter; bi-monthly; adv.

Membership List Available to Non-members

Gas Machinery Research Council (1952)
3030 LBJ Fwy.
Suite 1300
Dallas, TX 75234
Tel: (972) 620-4026 *Fax:* (972) 620-1613
E-Mail: MemberServices@southerngas.org
Website: gmrc.org
Members: 80 companies
Staff: 3
Annual Budget: $1-2,000,000

Personnel:
President and Chief Executive Officer: Mike Grubb
  E-Mail: mgrubb@southerngas.org
Vice President: Pat "Patrick" Downey
  E-Mail: pdowney@gmrc.org
Specialist, Communications: Nicole Reilley
  E-Mail: nicole@southerngas.org

Historical Note:
A subsidiary of Southern Gas Association. Founded as
Pipeline and Compressor Research Council; assumed its
current name in 2001. GMRC provides focused, cost-
effective technology, products and services for the global
marketplace in the rapidly changing natural gas, oil
and petrochemical industries. Membership: $4000/year
(Associate).

Meetings/Conferences: Annual
Conference Chair: Pat "Patrick" Downey

Publications:
GMC Today; irregular; adv.

Gas Processors Association (1921)
6526 E. 60th St.
Tulsa, OK 74145
Tel: (918) 493-3872 *Fax:* (918) 493-3875
E-Mail: gpa@gpaglobal.org
Website: gpaglobal.org
Members: 100 companies
Staff: 8
Annual Budget: $2-5,000,000
Tax: 501(c)(6)

Personnel:
Executive Director: Mark Sutton
  E-Mail: msutton@gpaglobal.org
Director, Government Affairs: Jeff Applekamp
  E-Mail: japplekamp@gpaglobal.org
Corporate Secretary and Director, Industry Affairs: Johnny
  Dreyer CMP

  E-Mail: jdreyer@gpaglobal.org
Administrator, Publications: Judy London
  E-Mail: jlondon@gpaglobal.org
Meeting Planner: Christine Simpson CMP
  E-Mail: csimpson@gpaglobal.org

Historical Note:
Formerly (1922) Association of Natural Gasoline
Manufacturers, (1961) became Natural Gasoline
Association of America, (1974) Natural Gas Processors
Association. GPA seeks to provide local, regional and global
forums to develop standards, conduct industry research,
educate the workforce and improve operational safety.
Members produce, gather, transport and market natural
gas and natural gas liquids. Membership : $1,491-20,768
(Active Members); $1,491 (Associate); $4438 (Processor);
1,520 (International).

Meetings/Conferences: Annual
Conference Chair: Christine Simpson CMP
2013 - San Antonio, TX (San Antonio Riverwalk)/April
  7 - 10/1500 attendees
2014 - Dallas, TX (Omni Dallas Hotel)/April 13 -
  16/1500 attendees
2015 - San Antonio, TX (San Antonio Riverwalk)/April
  12 - 15
2017 - San Antonio, TX (San Antonio Riverwalk)/April
  9 - 12

Publications:
Membership Directory; annually
Newsletter-eBrief; on-line

Gas Processors Suppliers Association (1921)
6526 E. 60th St.
Tulsa, OK 74145
Tel: (918) 493-3872 *Fax:* (918) 493-3875
E-Mail: gpsa@gpaglobal.org
Website: gpsa.gpaglobal.org
Members: 350 companies
Staff: 8
Annual Budget: $250-500,000
Tax: 501(c)(6)

Personnel:
Executive Director: Mark Sutton
  E-Mail: msutton@gpaglobal.org
Director, Government Affairs: Jeff Applekamp
  E-Mail: japplekamp@gpaglobal.org
Corporate Secretary and Director, Industry Affairs: Johnny
  Dreyer CMP
Administrator, Publications: Judy London
  E-Mail: jlondon@gpaglobal.org
Executive Assistant: Piper Penny
  E-Mail: ppenny@gpaglobal.org
Meeting Planner: Christine Simpson CMP
  E-Mail: csimpson@gpaglobal.org

Historical Note:
Formerly (1928) Natural Gasoline Supply Men's
Association (NGSMA) and (1961) Natural Gas Processors
Suppliers Association, then in 1974 changed to Gas
Processors Suppliers Association. GPSA's mission is to
provide added value to the global gas processing and
gas liquids industry, from wellhead to market. GPSA is
comprised of companies that provide supplies, equipment,
or services to the gas processing industry. Members
also produce, gather, transport and market natural gas
and natural gas liquids. Membership: $2,500-50,000
(Company, based on Midstream Operational Workhours);
$3,900 (International); $3,100 (Associate).

Meetings/Conferences: Annual
Conference Chair: Christine Simpson CMP
2013 - San Antonio, TX (San Antonio Riverwalk)/April
  7 - 10
2014 - Dallas, TX (Omni Dallas Hotel)/April 13 - 16
2015 - San Antonio, TX (San Antonio Riverwalk)/April
  12 - 15
2017 - San Antonio, TX (San Antonio Riverwalk)/April
  9 - 12
Number of non-conference events/year: 1

Publications:
Member Directory; on-line

Gas Technology Institute (1941)
1700 S. Mount Prospect Rd.
Des Plaines, IL 60018-1804
Tel: (847) 768-0500 *Fax:* (847) 768-0501
E-Mail:
businessdevelopmentinfo@gastechnology.org
Website: gastechnology.org
Staff: 240
Annual Budget: $25-50,000,000

Personnel:
President and Chief Executive Officer: David C. Carroll
General Counsel and Secretary: Paul Chromek
Vice President, Finance, Treasurer and Chief Financial Officer: Chris Herman
Vice President and Chief Technology Officer: Jack Lewnard
   E-Mail: jack.lewnard@gastechnology.org
Executive Director, Business Development and Education: Rodney "Rod" Rinholm
   E-Mail: membership@gastechnology.org
Executive Director, Human Resources: Barbara Weber
Supervisor: Carol Worster
   E-Mail: publications@gastechnology.org

Historical Note:
A research and development organization, supporting the gas industry.

Continuing Education:
Certification Designation/s: RCGC, CIGC, COT, CGTP, RGDP, PIM

Meetings/Conferences:
2013 - Houston, TX/April 16 - 19/5000 attendees/over 100 exhibitors
2013 - Chicago, IL (Sheraton Chicago Hotel and Towers)/Sept. 3 - 6
2014 - Copenhagen, Denmark (Tivoli Congress Center)/Sept. 17 - 19/1000 attendees/over 100 exhibitors

Publications:
Education eNews; monthly
Gas Operations News; on-line
GTI Newsletter

Gas Turbine Association (1995)
118 Windsor Ave.
Kensington, CA 94708
Tel: (510) 705-1885
E-Mail: info@gasturbines.org
Website: gasturbine.org
Members: 15 companies
Staff: 2
Annual Budget: $100-250,000

Personnel:
Managing Director: William H. Day PhD, CAE, CMP
   E-Mail: billday3@comcast.net
Director, Government Affairs: Andy Robart
   E-Mail: awrobart@gmail.com

Historical Note:
GTA's mission is to serve as a unified voice on important matters for the gas turbine industry. The GTA leads gas turbine industry efforts to support research and development initiatives in the national interest, to assure that energy and environmental regulations are reasonable and technically sound, and to support the electric power industry in its quest to provide secure, reliable, clean and affordable electric power to the nation. Membership: $25,000 (Regular); $6,000 (Associate); $1,000 (Affiliate, Non-Profit).

Publications:
e-Newsletter; on-line
Member Directory; on-line

Gases and Welding Distributors Association (1945)
550 NW LeJeune Rd.
Miami, FL 33126
Fax: (305) 442-7451
TollFree: (877) 382-6440
E-Mail: gawda@gawda.org
Website: gawda.org
Members: 450 gases and welding supply distributors, manufacturers, Independent manufacturer's representatives and Individual members,
Staff: 5
Annual Budget: $2-5,000,000

Personnel:
Executive Director: John Ospina
   E-Mail: jospina@gawda.org
Contact, Meetings: Natasha Alexis
   E-Mail: nalexis@gawda.org
Contact, Meetings and Membership Services: Cecilia Barbier
   E-Mail: cbarbier@gawda.org
Contact, Communications: Cindy Weihl
   E-Mail: cweihl@aws.org

Historical Note:

Founded as the National Welding Supply Association, assumed its current name in 2002. GAWDA's mission is to promote the safe operation and economic vitality of distributors of industrial gases and related welding equipment and supplies. Membership: $100-10,000/year.

Meetings/Conferences:
Conference Chair: Natasha Alexis
2013 - Antonio, TX (Grand Hyatt San Antonio)/April 13 - 16
2013 - Orlando, FL/Sept. 15 - 18
2013 - Orlando, FL/Oct. 3 - 9
Number of non-conference events/year: 8

Publications:
GAWDA 2011 Directory (Membership Directory); annually
GAWDA Connection; bi-monthly
GAWDA Edge; on-line
Welding & Gases Today; quarterly; adv.

Gasification Technologies Council (1995)
4301 N. Fairfax Dr.
Suite 300
Arlington, VA 22203
Tel: (703) 276-0110 *Fax:* (703) 276-0141
E-Mail: info@gasification.org
Website: gasification.org
Members: 75 companies
Staff: 1
Annual Budget: $1-2,000,000
Tax: 501(c)(6)

Personnel:
Executive Director: Alison Kerester

Historical Note:
GTC promotes a better understanding of gasification which plays a vital role in power, chemical and refining industries with economically competitive and environmentally conscious technology. Membership: $15,000 (Regular); $10,000 (Associate); $5,000 (Affiliate).

Meetings/Conferences: Annual

Gasket Fabricators Association (1979)
994 Old Eagle School Rd.
Suite 1019
Wayne, PA 19087-1866
Tel: (610) 971-4850 *Fax:* (610) 971-4859
E-Mail: info@gasketfab.com
Website: gasketfab.com
Members: 140 companies
Staff: 5
Annual Budget: $250-500,000
Tax: 501(c)(6)

Personnel:
Executive Director: Robert H. Ecker
   E-Mail: ecker@mmco1.com

Historical Note:
GFA is a trade association of members dedicated to providing custom fabricated components and materials for use in industrial, electronic and medical applications worldwide. Its membership is composed of the foremost companies in the industry, and includes many of the smaller specialized product fabricators. Membership: $950 (Fabricator); $1,500 (Supplier).

Meetings/Conferences:
2013 - New Orleans, LA (Harrah's Hotel)/March 19 - 21
2013 - Santa Ana Pueblo, NM (Hyatt Regency Tamaya Resort and Spa)/Oct. 1 - 3
2014 - Orlando, FL (Hilton Orlando)/March 25 - 27

Publications:
Member Directory; on-line
The Gasket Fabricator; adv.

Gasoline and Automotive Service Dealers of America (1956)
One New Lebanon Ave.
Basement Apartment
Greenwich, CT 06830
Tel: (203) 327-4773 *Fax:* (203) 323-6935
Website: gasda.org
Members: 500 members and associates
Staff: 7
Annual Budget: $500-1,000,000

Personnel:
Executive Director: Michael J. Fox
   E-Mail: mike@gasda.org

Historical Note:

Formerly (1977) Gasoline Merchants. GASDA seeks to strengthen professionalism in the industry. Members are owners, operators of service stations, body shops, towing operators, and auto repair facilities. Membership: $200 (Retailer, First Location); $35 (Retailer/additional location); $300 (Associate/Vendor).

Publications:
Survivor Newsletter; quarterly
Vendor Directory; on-line

Gay and Lesbian Medical Association (1981)
1326 18th St. NW
Suite 22
Washington, DC 20036
Tel: (202) 600-8037 *Fax:* (202) 478-1500
E-Mail: info@glma.org
Website: glma.org
Members: 1000 Members
Staff: 6
Annual Budget: $500-1,000,000
Tax: 501(c)(3)

Personnel:
Executive Director: Hector Vargas
   E-Mail: hvargas@glma.org
Membership and Development Associate: Bobby Bangert
   E-Mail: bbangert@glma.org
Director, Operations and Finance: Amy Fielder
   E-Mail: afielder@glma.org
Manager, Education and Communications: Emily Kane-Lee
   E-Mail: ekanelee@glma.org
Assistant, Membership and Development: Ric Serrano
   E-Mail: rserrano@glma.org

Historical Note:
Founded as the American Association of Physicians for Human Rights. GLMA's mission is to ensure equality in health care for lesbian, gay, bisexual and transgender individuals and health care providers. Members are LGBT healthcare professionals and their allies. Membership: $100 (Health Professional); $50 (non-health professionals); $20-25 (Student); $300-5,000 (Premium Membership).

Meetings/Conferences: Annual

Publications:
LGBT Health Digest; weekly
Provider Directory; on-line

Gelatin Manufacturers Institute of America (1956)
P.O. Box 927
Sioux City, IA 51054
E-Mail: info@gelatin-gmia.com
Website: gelatin-gmia.com
Members: 6 companies
Staff: 1
Annual Budget: $50-100,000

Personnel:
President: Rob Mayberry

Historical Note:
GMIA's mission is to engage in industry wide testing and to promote the standardization of systems and methods in order to assure consumers product of consistent safety and quality.

Meetings/Conferences: Semi-Annual

Publications:
Membership Directory; on-line

Gemological Institute of America (1931)
The Robert Mouawad Campus
5345 Armada Dr.
Carlsbad, CA 92008
Tel: (760) 603-4000 *Fax:* (760) 603-4080
TollFree: (800) 421-7250
E-Mail: marketing@gia.edu
Website: gia.edu
Staff: 1078
Annual Budget: Over $100,000,000
Tax: 501(c)(3)

Personnel:
President and Chief Executive Officer: Donna M. Baker
   E-Mail: president@gia.edu
Editor-in-Chief Emeritus: Alice S. Keller
   E-Mail: akeller@gia.edu
Vice President and Chief Marketing Officer: Kathryn Kimmel
   E-Mail: vpmktgandpr@gia.edu
Director, Public Relations: Stephen B. Morisseau

Senior Vice President, GIA Laboratory and Research:
 Thomas M. Moses
  E-Mail: tmoses@gia.edu
Coordinator, Advertising: Erica Printz
  E-Mail: eprintz@gia.edu
Vice President, Human Resources: Linda Scholl
Vice President and Chief Financial Officer: David J. Tearle

Historical Note:
GIA exists to protect all purchasers of gemstones, by providing the education, laboratory services, research, and instruments needed to accurately and objectively determine gemstone quality.

Meetings/Conferences: Annual
Number of non-conference events/year: 1

Publications:
AlumConnect; quarterly
G and G eBrief; monthly
Gems and Gemology; quarterly
GIA Insider; monthly

General Aviation Manufacturers Association
(1970)
1400 K St. NW
Suite 801
Washington, DC 20005-2485
Tel: (202) 393-1500 *Fax:* (202) 842-4063
Website: gama.aero
Members: 60 manufacturers
Staff: 13
Annual Budget: $2-5,000,000

Personnel:
President and Chief Executive Officer: Col. Peter J. Bunce
  E-Mail: pbunce@GAMA.aero
Accountant: Jahan Ahmad
  E-Mail: jahmad@GAMA.aero
Vice President, Government Affairs: Paul H. Feldman
  E-Mail: pfeldman@gama.aero
Manager, Meetings and Membership Services: Bree J. Foran
  E-Mail: bforan@gama.aero
Director, Communication: Jena Longo
Director, Communications: Katie Pribyl
  E-Mail: kpribyl@gama.aero

Historical Note:
An outgrowth of the former Utility Aircraft Council of the Aerospace Industries Association. GAMA's mission is to foster and advance the general welfare, safety, interests and activities of general aviation. Members are manufacturers of general aviation aircraft equipment and components.

Meetings/Conferences: Semi-Annual
Conference Chair: Bree J. Foran

General Federation of Women's Clubs *(1890)*
1734 N St. NW
Washington, DC 20036-2990
Tel: (202) 347-3168 *Fax:* (202) 835-0246
TollFree: (800) 443-4392
E-Mail: gfwc@gfwc.org
Website: gfwc.org
Members: 100,000 members and 4000 clubs
Staff: 16
Annual Budget: $2-5,000,000
Tax: 501(c)(3)

Personnel:
Executive Director: Lisa Lopinsky CAE
  E-Mail: llopinsky@gfwc.org
Senior Director, Membership and Women's History and Resource Center: Gail Rodgers McCormick
  E-Mail: gmccormick@gfwc.org
Senior Director, Programs, Public Policy and Communications: Michele Mount
  E-Mail: mmount@gfwc.org
Manager, Meetings and Conventions: Erica Sterling
  E-Mail: ESterling@gfwc.org
Senior Director, Finance and Administration: Irina Zabello
  E-Mail: izabello@gfwc.org

Historical Note:
GFWC is an international women's organization dedicated to community improvement by enhancing the lives of others through volunteer service. Membership :$15 (GFWC members, from ages 12 to 102).

Meetings/Conferences: Annual
Conference Chair: Erica Sterling
Number of non-conference events/year: 1

Publications:
e-GFWC; bi-weekly
GFWC Clubwoman Magazine; bi-monthly

Membership Matters; quarterly
WHRC News; monthly

Membership List Available to Non-members

Generic Animal Drug Alliance
2105 Laurel Bush Rd.
Suite 200
Bel Air, MD 21015
Tel: (443) 640-1046 *Fax:* (443) 640-1086
E-Mail: info@gadaonline.org
Website: gadaonline.org
Staff: 3
Annual Budget: $100-250,000

Personnel:
Executive Director: Kathleen A. DeMarco
  E-Mail: kdemarco@gadaonline.org
Legal Counsel: Ed Allera
  E-Mail: eallera@gadaonline.org
Financial Director: Amy Chetelat, CAE
  E-Mail: amy@stringfellowgroup.net

Historical Note:
GADA represents the interests of generic animal health companies in the United States. It began following enactment of the Generic Animal Drug and Patent Term Restoration Act of 1988, and was originally affiliated with the Generic Pharmaceutical Industry Association (GPIA), before organizing separately as the Animal Drug Alliance. The organization was renamed as the Generic Animal Drug Alliance. Membership: $10,000 (Regular); $5,000 (Associate).

Meetings/Conferences: Annual

Generic Pharmaceutical Association *(1981)*
777 Sixth St. NW
Suite 510
Washington, DC 20001
Tel: (202) 249-7100 *Fax:* (202) 249-7105
E-Mail: info@gphaonline.org
Website: gphaonline.org
Members:
110 companies
40 individuals
Staff: 12
Annual Budget: $5-10,000,000

Personnel:
President and Chief Executive Officer: Ralph G. Neas
Director, Media Relations: David Belian
  E-Mail: dbelian@gphaonline.org
Senior Vice President, Finances, Planning and Special Programs: Robert Billings
  E-Mail: bbillings@gphaonline.org
Senior Vice President, Government Affairs: John M. Coster PhD, RPh
  E-Mail: jcoster@gphaonline.org
Executive Assistant to the President and Senior Manager, Membership: Cookie Cottrell CAE
  E-Mail: ccottrell@gphaonline.org
Director, Meetings and Events: Katie Dysart
Senior Director, Human Resources and Administration: Kendra L. Janevski
Vice President, Regulatory Sciences: Gordon Johnston
  E-Mail: gjohnston@gphaonline.org
Senior Director, Finance and Operations: Rachelle Kosky
  E-Mail: rkosky@gphaonline.org
Director, Meetings and Marketing: Jennifer Nguyen
  E-Mail: jnguyen@gphaonline.org
Program Manager, Legal and State Affairs: John Zoshak

Historical Note:
Founded as the Generic Pharmaceutical Industry Association, absorbed the National Pharmaceutical Alliance and the National Association of Pharmaceutical Manufacturers and assumed its current name in 2001. GPhA's core purpose is to improve the lives of consumers by providing timely access to affordable pharmaceuticals. Members are manufacturers and distributors of generic medicines, as well as the providers of technical services and goods to these firms. Membership: dues based on sales volume.

Meetings/Conferences: Annual
Conference Chair: Jennifer Nguyen
2013 - Orlando, FL (JW Marriott Orlando Grande Lakes)/Feb. 20 - 22
Number of non-conference events/year: 4

Publications:
E-Digest; weekly
GPhA Insider; monthly

Genetics Society of America *(1931)*

9650 Rockville Pike
Bethesda, MD 20814-3998
Tel: (301) 634-7300 *Fax:* (301) 634-7079
TollFree: (866) 486-4363
E-Mail: society@genetics-gsa.org
Website: genetics-gsa.org
Members: 4000 individuals
Staff: 8
Annual Budget: $2-5,000,000

Personnel:
Executive Director: Adam Fagen PhD
  E-Mail: afagen@genetics-gsa.org
Manager, Meetings: Suzy Brown
  E-Mail: sbrown@genetics-gsa.org
Director, Information Technology: Yimang Chen
  E-Mail: ychen@genetics-gsa.org
Executive Editor: Tracey DePellegrin Connelly
  E-Mail: td2p@andrew.cmu.edu
Manager, Public Relations and Communications: Phyllis Edelman
  E-Mail: pedelman@genetics-gsa.org
Director, Education and Professional Development: Elizabeth Ruedi PhD
  E-Mail: eruedi@genetics-gsa.org
Manager, Membership Services: Mary Shih
  E-Mail: mshih@genetics-gsa.org
Director, Finance and Administration: Chuck Windle
  E-Mail: cwindle@genetics-gsa.org

Historical Note:
Organized in New Orleans as an outgrowth of the Genetics Section of the American Society of Zoologists and the Botanical Society of America and incorporated in Maryland in 1984. The GSA seeks to foster a unified science of genetics and to maximize its intellectual and practical impact. Membership: $150 (Regular); $96 (Postdoctoral); $70 (Graduate Student); $25 (Undergraduate Student).

Meetings/Conferences:
Conference Chair: Suzy Brown
2013 - Pacific Grove, CA (Asilomar Conference Center)/March 12 - 17
2013 - Washington, DC (Washington Marriott Wardman Park)/April 3 - 7/2000 attendees/51-100 exhibitors
2014 - San Diego, CA (Town and Country Resort Hotel)/March 26 - 30
2015 - Chicago, IL (Hilton Chicago)/March 4 - 8
2016 - Philadelphia, PA (Philadelphia Marriott Downtown)/March 2 - 6
Number of non-conference events/year: 3

Publications:
G3: Genes, Genomes, Genetics; monthly; adv.
Genetics -Journal; monthly; adv.
GSA e-News; bi-monthly
Membership Directory; annually
The GSA Reporter - Newsletter; quarterly; adv.

Geochemical Society *(1955)*
Washington University, Department of Earth and Planetary Sciences
One Brookings Dr., CB 1169
St. Louis, MO 63130-4899
Tel: (314) 935-4131 *Fax:* (314) 935-4121
E-Mail: gsoffice@geochemsoc.org
Website: geochemsoc.org
Members: 2800 individuals
Staff: 3
Annual Budget: $250-500,000

Personnel:
Business Manager: Seth Davis
  E-Mail: seth.davis@geochemsoc.org
Administrative Assistant: Kathryn Hall
  E-Mail: kathryn.hall@geochemsoc.org
Editor: Frank Podosek
  E-Mail: fap@levee.wustl.edu

Historical Note:
GS's mission is to encourage the application of chemistry to the solution of geological and cosmological problems. Membership: $35 (Professional); $15 (Student); $20 (Senior-above 65 years of age).

Meetings/Conferences:
2013 - Florence, Italy (Firenze Fiera congress centre)/ Aug. 25 - 30/3000 attendees
2014 - Sacramento, CA (Fountain Suites Hotel)/June 9 - 13/3000 attendees/51-100 exhibitors
2015 - Prague, Czech Republic/Aug. 16 - 21/3000 attendees

Publications:

Elements Magazine; bi-monthly
G-cubed Journal; on-line
Geochemical News; quarterly
Geochimica et Cosmochimica Acta; bi-weekly

Geological Society of America (1888)

P.O. Box 9140
Boulder, CO 80301-9140
Tel: (303) 357-1000 *Fax:* (303) 357-1070
TollFree: (800) 472-1988
E-Mail: gsa@geosociety.org
Website: geosociety.org
Members: 25000 Individuals
Staff: 55
Annual Budget: $5-10,000,000

Personnel:
Executive Director: John W. Hess
  E-Mail: jhess@geosociety.org
Senior Director, Information Technology: Todd Berggren
  E-Mail: tberggren@geosociety.org
Manager, Advertising and Sponsorship: Ann Crawford
  E-Mail: acrawford@geosociety.org
Senior Director, Meetings: Melissa Cummiskey
  E-Mail: mcummiskey@geosociety.org
Controller: Thomas H. Haberthier
  E-Mail: THaberthier@geosociety.org
Director, Membership Development: Pat Kilner
  E-Mail: pkilner@geosociety.org
Senior Director, Education and Outreach: Gary Lewis
  E-Mail: glewis@geosociety.org
Senior Director, Publications: Jon Olsen
  E-Mail: jolsen@geosociety.org
Manager, Human Resources: Divya Puri
  E-Mail: dpuri@geosociety.org
Director, Communications and Marketing: Christa
  Stratton
  E-Mail: cstratton@geosociety.org

Historical Note:
Incorporated in New York (1929), GSA is a member society of the American Geological Institute. GSA strives to advance the geosciences, enhancing the professional growth of its members, and promoting the geosciences in the service to humankind and stewardship of the earth. Membership: $20-75 (Professional); $6-30 (Student/Affiliate); $20-30 (Fellow).

Meetings/Conferences: Annual
Conference Chair: Melissa Cummiskey
2013 - Denver, CO/Oct. 27 - 30
2014 - Vancouver, BC/Oct. 19 - 22
2015 - Baltimore, MD/Nov. 1 - 4
Number of non-conference events/year: 1

Publications:
Environmental & Engineering Geoscience (E&EG);
  quarterly
Geology; monthly
Geosphere; bi-monthly
GSA Bulletin; bi-monthly
GSA Today
Lithosphere; bi-monthly

Georgia Charter Schools Association (2001)

600 W. Peachtree St. NW
Suite 1555
Atlanta, GA 30308
Tel: (404) 835-8900 *Fax:* (888) 799-0837
Website: gacharters.org
Staff: 9
Annual Budget: $1-2,000,000

Personnel:
Chief Executive Officer: Tony Roberts
Administrative Assistant and Business Manager: Jeniffer
  Collins
Director, Education and Training: Elisa Falco
Director , Communications: Nina Rubin
Director, Membership and Member Business Services: Rena
  Youngblood

Historical Note:
The mission of the Georgia Charter Schools is to improve student achievement and promote educational choice by serving and advocating for public charter schools in Georgia. Membership: $ 500 (Pre-operational/Planning); $2,500 (Charter School Authorizer); $5 (Students).

Publications:
GCSA newsletters

Geoscience and Remote Sensing Society (1962)

445 Hoes Ln.

P.O. Box 6804
Piscataway, NJ 08854-6804
Tel: (732) 562-3946 *Fax:* (732) 981-1855
E-Mail: info@grss-ieee.org
Website: grss-ieee.org
Members: 2100 Individuals
Staff: 9
Tax: 501(c)(3)

Personnel:
President: Jon Benediktsson
  E-Mail: benedikt@hi.is
Vice President, Meetings and Symposia: Adriano Camps
  E-Mail: camps@tsc.upc.edu
Vice President, Publications: Wooil M. Moon
  E-Mail: wmoon@cc.umanitoba.ca

Historical Note:
GRSS seeks to advance science and technology in geoscience, remote sensing and related fields through scientific, technical and educational activities. Membership in the Society opens only to IEEE members, includes a subscription to a technical periodical in the field published by IEEE. Membership: $185 (Member); $38 (Student); $81 (Affiliate).

Meetings/Conferences: Annual
Conference Chair: Adriano Camps
2013 - Melbourne, Australia (Melbourne Convention
  and Exhibition Centre)/July 21 - 26
Number of non-conference events/year: 1

Publications:
GRSS Newsletter; monthly
Transactions on Geoscience and Remote Sensing;
  monthly

Geoscience Information Society (1965)

Science Libraries
University of Georgia Libraries
Athens, GA 30602
Tel: (706) 542-0692
Website: geoinfo.org
Members: 200 individuals
Staff: 4
Annual Budget: $10-25,000
Tax: 501(c)(3)

Personnel:
Secretary: Cynthia Prosser

Historical Note:
GSIS facilitates the exchange of information in the geosciences through cooperation among scientists, librarians, editors, cartographers, educators, and information professionals. GIS membership includes national and international representation from colleges and universities, business and industry, publishing, geological surveys, geological societies and other aspects of the field. Membership: $55 (Individual); $20 (Student/Retired); $100 (Institutional); $135 (Sustaining).

Meetings/Conferences: Annual
Number of non-conference events/year: 5

Publications:
GSIS Newsletter; bi-monthly

Geospatial Information Technology Association (1982)

P.O. Box 441170
Aurora, CO 80044
Tel: (303) 337-0513 *Fax:* (303) 337-1001
E-Mail: info@gita.org
Website: gita.org
Members: 244 organizations and 2200
individuals
Staff: 11
Annual Budget: $1-2,000,000
Tax: 501(c)(3)

Personnel:
Executive Director: Robert "Bob" M. Samborski
  E-Mail: bsamborski@gita.org
Coordinator, Education and Exhibits: Julie Eckhart
  E-Mail: jeckhart@gita.org
Senior Manager, Marketing and Development: Libby
  Hanna
  E-Mail: lhanna@gita.org
Director, Finance and Administration: Patricia Herrera
  E-Mail: pherrera@gita.org
Senior Coordinator, Education: James Sakamoto
  E-Mail: jsakamoto@gita.org

Historical Note:
GITA fosters information exchange and educational opportunities and scientific research and development

in the field of geospatial information technology. GITA's mission is to provide geospatial solutions in education, information exchange, and applied research on the use and benefits of geospatial information and technology for worldwide infrastructure. Membership: $150 (Individual); $70 (Individual Subsidized Corporate); $25 (Student); $2500 (Affiliate).

Meetings/Conferences: Annual
Conference Chair: Julie Eckhart

Publications:
Directions Magazine
E-Newsletter; on-line
Electricity Today Magazine
Intelligent Utility Magazine
Membership Directory; on-line
Pipeline & Gas Journal
Rural Electric Magazine
Underground Focus Magazine

Geosynthetic Materials Association

1801 County Rd. BW
Roseville, MN 55113-4061
Tel: (651) 225-6907 *Fax:* (651) 631-9334
TollFree: (800) 636-5042
Website: gmanow.com
Members: 80 companies
Staff: 1

Personnel:
Managing Director: Andrew Aho
  E-Mail: amaho@ifai.com

Historical Note:
GMA is a division of the Industrial Fabrics Association International (IFAI). GMA promotes the technical and economic benefits of geosynthetics to the user community and, in turn, assists in building stronger civil infrastructures in a cost-efficient manner. GMA represents the entire geosynthetics industry, including manufacturers as well as companies that test or supply materials and offer services to the industry. Membership: $385-935 (End-Product Manufacturer, Based on Sales); $1,085 (Supplier); $80-335 (Other Industry).

Publications:
Geosynthetics; adv.
Member Directory

Membership List Available to Non-members

Geothermal Energy Association (1987)

209 Pennsylvania Ave. SE
Washington, DC 20003
Tel: (202) 454-5261 *Fax:* (202) 454-5265
E-Mail: geo@geo-energy.org
Website: geo-energy.org
Members: 50 corporations
Staff: 7
Annual Budget: $1-2,000,000
Tax: 501(c)(6)

Personnel:
Executive Director: Karl Gawell
  E-Mail: karl@geo-energy.org
Business Manager: Mihaela-Daniela Antonescu
  E-Mail: daniela@geo-energy.org
Director, Outreach and Senior Editor: Leslie Blodgett
  E-Mail: leslie@geo-energy.org
Director, Marketing, Membership Services and Events:
  Kathy Kent
  E-Mail: kathy@geo-energy.org

Historical Note:
Founded as National Geothermal Association; assumed its current name in 1994. GEA is composed of U. S. companies who support the expanded use of geothermal energy and are developing geothermal resources worldwide for electrical power generation and direct heat uses. Shares administrative offices with Geothermal Resources Council. Membership: $500 (Small Business); $1,500 (Full); $5,000 (Executive); $25,000 (Board level).

Meetings/Conferences: Annual
Conference Chair: Kathy Kent
Number of non-conference events/year: 2

Publications:
Membership Directory; on-line

Geothermal Heat Pump Consortium (1960)

1050 Connecticut Ave. NW
Suite 1000
Washington, DC 20036
Tel: (202) 558-7175 *Fax:* (202) 558-6759
TollFree: (888) 255-4436
Website: geoexchange.org

Members: 15 Companies
Staff: 3
Annual Budget: $100-250,000

Personnel:
President and Chief Executive Officer: Douglas Dougherty
Manager, Outreach and Member Services: Ted Clutter
Manager, Operations: John Kelly
    E-Mail: jkelly@GeoExchange.org

Historical Note:
GEO's mission is to support members' business objectives while promoting maximum, sustainable growth of the geothermal heat pump industry through Advocacy, Partnerships, Public Outreach, and Promotion of Quality Standards.

Publications:
GEO Newsletter
Membership Directory; on-line

Geothermal Heat Pump National and International Initiative
1615 M St. NW
Suite 800
Washington, DC 20036
E-Mail: jdienna@geo-nii.org
Website: geo-nii.org
Staff: 1

Personnel:
Executive Director: Jack DiEnna
    E-Mail: jdienna@geo-nii.org

Historical Note:
Geo-nii is a collaboration between the International Ground Source Heat Pump Association (IGSHPA), the National Association of State Energy Officials (NASEO), and the Geothermal Heat Pump Consortium (GHPC). Mission is to promote geothermal heat pump technology to federal, state, and local officials, the design community, the HVAC industry, and end users in all markets.

Geothermal Resources Council (1970)
P.O. Box 1350
Davis, CA 95617-1350
Tel: (530) 758-2360 *Fax:* (530) 758-2839
Website: geothermal.org
Members: 1500 individuals
Staff: 7
Annual Budget: $1-2,000,000
Tax: 501(c)(3)

Personnel:
Interim Executive Director: Steve Ponder
    E-Mail: sponder@geothermal.org
Director, Communications and Managing Editor, GRC Bulletin: Ian Crawford
    E-Mail: grcmarketing@sbcglobal.net
Office Associate, Bulletin and Roster Advertising: Anh Lay
    E-Mail: grc_office@sbcglobal.net
Office Manager, Membership Services and Meetings: Estela M. Smith
    E-Mail: grcadmin@sbcglobal.net

Historical Note:
Mission is to encourage worldwide development of geothermal resources through the collection and timely distribution of data and technological information. Members are individuals interested in the development and production of geothermal energy. Membership: $40-2,500/year.

Meetings/Conferences: Annual
Conference Chair: Estela M. Smith
2013 - Las Vegas, NV/Sept. 29 - Oct. 2

Publications:
GRC Bulletin; bi-monthly; adv.
Membership Roster; annually; adv.
Registry of Geothermal Services & Equipment; annually; adv.

German American Business Association (1990)
1715 Villa St.
Suite G
Mountain View, CA 94041
Tel: (650) 386-5015 *Fax:* (415) 276-2375
E-Mail: info@gaba-network.org
Website: gaba-network.org
Members: 175 individuals and 125 companies
Staff: 5
Annual Budget: $100-250,000

Personnel:
Executive Director: Caroline Raynaud
Director, Membership Services: Yiman Liu
Director, Marketing: Gitta Ramakrishnan

Director, Events: Sandra Schmid
Webmaster: Martina Walther

Historical Note:
GABA is a member-driven non-profit organization that fosters transatlantic knowledge-sharing and networking among German-American and Californian business and tech communities. Members represent all facets of the international professional business community including high-tech and life science firms, trade specialists, bankers, venture capitalists, insurance, government officials, attorneys, translation firms, marketing firms, consultants and entrepreneurs. Membership: $100 (Individual); $60 (Student); $250 (Basic Corporate); $500 (Corporate); $1,500 (Premium Corporate).

Meetings/Conferences:
Conference Chair: Sandra Schmid

Publications:
GABA Newsletter; monthly
Membership Directory; on-line

German American Chamber of Commerce (1947)
75 Broad St.
21st Floor
New York, NY 10004
Tel: (212) 974-8830 *Fax:* (212) 974-8867
E-Mail: info@gaccny.com
Website: gaccny.com
Members: 2000 corporations
Staff: 64
Annual Budget: $5-10,000,000

Personnel:
President and Chief Executive Officer: Dr. Benno W. Bunse
    E-Mail: bbunse@gaccny.com
Office Manager: Kathe Dindo
    E-Mail: nmichels@gaccny.com
Director, Career Services: Thomas Dzimian
    E-Mail: tdzimian@gaccny.com
Head, Legal Services: Susanne Gellert
    E-Mail: legalservices@gaccny.com
Director, Communications: Nicola Michels
    E-Mail: nmichels@gaccny.com
Director, Marketing: Karen Vogelsang
Manager, Membership and Events: Anne Voss
    E-Mail: avoss@gaccny.com
Director, Finance, Controlling and Administration: Christine Ward
    E-Mail: cward@gaccny.com

Historical Note:
Established as a guide and liaison for U.S. and German businesses who want to practice in both the United States and Germany. Now acts as a service organization for members and non-members. Mission is to enhance the transatlantic business of German and American companies and to support them finding new business partners. GACC fosters the economic ties between Germany and America. Membership: $500 (Basic); 1,000 (Corporate); $2,000 (Blue Chip).

Meetings/Conferences: Annual
Number of non-conference events/year: 2

Publications:
e-Newsletter; monthly
German American Trade; bi-monthly; adv.
Membership Directory; annually

Gerontological Society of America (1945)
1220 L St. NW
Suite 901
Washington, DC 20005-4018
Tel: (202) 842-1275 *Fax:* (202) 842-1150
E-Mail: geron@geron.org
Website: geron.org
Members: 5000 individuals
Staff: 41
Annual Budget: $5-10,000,000
Tax: 501(c)(3)

Personnel:
Executive Director: James Appleby
    E-Mail: jappleby@geron.org
Director, Human Resources and Office Management: Kevin Brown
Senior Manager, Meetings and Education: Fay Gallagher Christenson
Manager, Meetings and Education: Jessica Clark Keim
Manager, Communications: Todd Kluss
    E-Mail: tkluss@geron.org
Manager, Marketing: Jessica Lutton
    E-Mail: jlutton@geron.org

Publications Manager: Megan McCutcheon
Meetings and Exhibits/Registration Coordinator: Jason Hawthorne Petty
Director, Information Technology: Anthony Rogers
Senior Director, Membership Services and Marketing: Paul Stearns
    E-Mail: pstearns@geron.org
Senior Director, Finance and Administration: Chris Yoder

Historical Note:
An outgrowth of the Club for Research in Aging, organized in 1939. Incorporated in New York in 1945 to promote scientific study of aging, reincorporated in Washington, D. C. in 1980. GSA is a member of the American Association for the Advancement of Science, and the International Association of Gerontology Leadership Council of Aging Organizations. GSA's mission is to promote the conduct of multi-and interdisciplinary research in aging by expanding the quantity of gerontological research and by increasing its funding resources. Members are researchers, educators and professionals in the field of aging. Membership: $25-99 (Students); $45 (Spouse); $160 (Regular Member).

Meetings/Conferences: Annual
Conference Chair: Jessica Clark Keim
2013 - New Orleans, LA/Nov. 20 - 24
2014 - Washington, DC/Nov. 5 - 9
2015 - Orlando, FL/Nov. 18 - 22
2016 - New Orleans, LA/Nov. 16 - 20
Number of non-conference events/year: 1

Publications:
Aging Means Business E-Newsletter; quarterly
Civic Engagement in an Older America E-Newsletter; bi-monthly
Gerontology & Geriatrics Education; quarterly
Journal of Aging, Humanities, and the Arts; quarterly
Journal of Gerontology: Biological Sciences
Journal of Gerontology: Medical Sciences
Journal of Gerontology: Psychological Sciences
Journal of Gerontology: Social Sciences
Membership Directory; on-line
Public Policy & Aging E-Newsletter; bi-monthly
The Gerontologist; bi-monthly

Membership List Available to Non-members

Giant Screen Cinema Association (2006)
26 Lakewood Landing Dr.
Lake Anna, VA 23024
Tel: (540) 872-3905 *Fax:* (540) 872-3906
E-Mail: info@giantscreencinema.com
Website: giantscreencinema.com
Members: 250 organizations
Staff: 3
Annual Budget: $500-1,000,000
Tax: 501(c)(3)

Personnel:
Executive Director: Tammy Thurmon
    E-Mail: Tammy@GiantScreenCinema.com
Director, Communications and Membership Services: Kelly Germain
    E-Mail: Kelly@GiantScreenCinema.com

Historical Note:
Formed from the merger of the Giant Screen Cinema Association and the Large Format Cinema Association. GSCA's mission is to advance the international business of producing and presenting educational giant screen and immersive cinema experiences globally. Membership: $850 (Corporate); $250 (Individual); $75 (Student).

Continuing Education:
Certification Designation/s: CGS

Meetings/Conferences: Semi-Annual

Publications:
E-News; irregular; adv.
Membership Directory; on-line

Gift Associates Interchange Network (1974)
1100 Main St.
Buffalo, NY 14209
Tel: (716) 887-9511 *Fax:* (716) 887-9599
TollFree: (800) 746-9428
E-Mail: info@gaingroup.com
Website: gaingroup.com
Members: 200 gift companies
Staff: 4

Personnel:
Director, Member Group Services: Donna Mosteller
    E-Mail: donna.mosteller@abc-amega.com
Representative, Member Development: Rosanne Battaglia
    E-Mail: rosanne.battaglia@abc-amega.com

Historical Note:
Formerly (1995) Giftware Associates Interchange, GAIN is an on-line credit interchange database designed by and for credit managers in giftware, greeting card, silk floral, and related industries. Members are manufacturers and importers of giftware and china. Membership: $620- 650/ year.

Meetings/Conferences: Annual
Number of non-conference events/year: 1

Publications:
GAIN Newsletter; semi-annually

Giving Institute (*1935*)
303 W. Madison St.
Suite 2650
Chicago, IL 60606-3396
Tel: (312) 981-6794 *Fax:* (312) 265-2908
E-Mail: info@givinginstitute.org
Website: givinginstitute.org
Members: 38 companies
Staff: 4
Annual Budget: $500-1,000,000

Personnel:
Executive Director: Geoffrey E. Brown CAE
    E-Mail: gbrown@givinginstitute.org
Coordinator, Membership and Operations: Sara Porter
    E-Mail: sporter@thesentergroup.com
Administrative Assistant: Thomas Radde
    E-Mail: tradde@thesentergroup.com
Senior Coordinator, Meeting and Education: Rachel Walsh CMP
    E-Mail: rwalsh@thesentergroup.com

Historical Note:
Formerly the American Association of Fundraising Counsel (AAFRC). Giving Institute strives to educate and engage members in the ethical delivery of counsel and related services to non- profits through research, advocacy, and best practices. Members are consulting firms specializing in services to nonprofit organizations.

Meetings/Conferences:
Conference Chair: Rachel Walsh CMP
2013 - Leesburg, VA (Lansdowne Resort)/July 25 - 28

Publications:
Giving USA Spotlight; quarterly

Membership List Available to Non-members

Giving USA Foundation (*1985*)
303 W. Madison St.
Suite 2650
Chicago, IL 60606-3396
Tel: (312) 981-6794 *Fax:* (312) 265-2908
E-Mail: info@givinginstitute.org
Website: givingusa.org
Staff: 4
Annual Budget: $100-250,000

Personnel:
Executive Director: Geoffrey E. Brown CAE
    E-Mail: gbrown@givinginstitute.org
Coordinator, Membership and Operations: Sara Porter
    E-Mail: sporter@thesentergroup.com
Assistant, Administration: Thomas Radde
    E-Mail: tradde@thesentergroup.com
Coordinator, Senior Meeting and Education: Rachel Walsh
    E-Mail: rwalsh@thesentergroup.com

Historical Note:
Giving Institute, formerly the American Association of Fundraising Counsel (AAFRC). Mission is to educate and engage members in the ethical delivery of counsel and related services through research, advocacy, and best practices.

Meetings/Conferences:
Number of non-conference events/year: 1

Publications:
Giving USA
Spotlight e-Newsletter; quarterly

Glass Art Society (*1971*)
6512 23rd Ave. NW
Suite 329
Seattle, WA 98117
Tel: (206) 382-1305 *Fax:* (206) 382-2630
E-Mail: info@glassart.org
Website: glassart.org
Members: 2500 individuals
Staff: 7
Annual Budget: $500-1,000,000
Tax: 501(c)(3)

Personnel:
Executive Director: Pamela Figenshow Koss
    E-Mail: pfkoss@glassart.org
Manager, Communications: Kristin Galioto
    E-Mail: kristin@glassart.org
Administrative Assistant and Registrar: Heather Kraft
    E-Mail: heather@glassart.org
Database Manager: Karen Skrinde

Historical Note:
GAS's mission is to encourage excellence in education, and to promote the appreciation and development of glass arts, and to support the worldwide community of artists who work with glass. Membership: $40- 1000/year.

Meetings/Conferences: Annual
2013 - Boston, MA/June 13 - 15

Publications:
GAS news; bi-monthly; adv.
Glass Art Society; annually; adv.
Membership Directory and Resource Guide; annually; adv.

Glass Association of North America (*1994*)
800 SW Jackson St.
Suite 1500
Topeka, KS 66612-1200
Tel: (785) 271-0208 *Fax:* (785) 271-0166
E-Mail: gana@glasswebsite.com
Website: glasswebsite.com
Members: 250 companies
Staff: 8
Annual Budget: $1-2,000,000
Tax: 501(c)(6)

Personnel:
Executive Vice President: William M. Yanek
    E-Mail: byanek@glasswebsite.com
Account Executive: Ashley M. Charest
    E-Mail: ashley@glasswebsite.com
General Counsel: Kim D. Mann Esq.
    E-Mail: kmann@scopelitis.com
Director, Marketing and Communications: Brian K. Pitman
    E-Mail: brian@glasswebsite.com
Technical Director: Urmilla Sowell PE
    E-Mail: usowell@glasswebsite.com

Historical Note:
Formed by the merger of the Flat Glass Marketing Association (1949), the Glass Tempering Association (1958), and the Laminators Safety Glass Association (1971) in 1994. Absorbed the North American Association of Mirror Manufacturers in 1999. GANA strives to provide members with premiere educational programs, publications, networking opportunities, meetings and conventions. Membership: $745-8,665 (Corporate); $190 (Affiliates); $1,270 (Multiple Divisions).

Meetings/Conferences: Annual
2013 - San Diego, CA/Jan. 21 - 25
Number of non-conference events/year: 9

Publications:
Glass Reflections - Newsletter
Human Resource Reports; irregular
Safety Bulletins; monthly

Glass Manufacturing Industry Council
600 N. Cleveland Ave.
Suite 210
Westerville, OH 43082
Website: gmic.org
Staff: 1
Annual Budget: $250-500,000
Tax: 501(c)(6)

Personnel:
Executive Director and Conference Director: Robert Weisenburger Lipetz
    E-Mail: rwlipetz@gmic.org

Historical Note:
GMIC's mission is to facilitate, organize and promote the interests and economic growth, and sustainability of the glass industry through education and cooperation in the areas of technology, productivity, innovation and the environment. Membership: $500-18,000/year.

Meetings/Conferences: Annual
Conference Chair: Robert Weisenburger Lipetz

Glass Packaging Institute (*1945*)
700 N. Fairfax St.
Suite 510
Alexandria, VA 22314

Tel: (703) 684-6359 *Fax:* (703) 299-1543
E-Mail: info@gpi.org
Website: gpi.org
Members: 45 companies and associate members
Staff: 7
Annual Budget: $2-5,000,000
Tax: 501(c)(6)

Personnel:
President: Lynn Bragg
    E-Mail: lbragg@gpi.org
Contact, Media Relations: Stacey Kerans
    E-Mail: stacey.kerans@fleishman.com

Historical Note:
Formerly (1976) the Glass Container Manufacturers Institute, Inc. GPI's purpose is to serve its member companies through legislative, public relations, promotional and technical activities. Membership: $1500-20,000/year.

Meetings/Conferences: Annual
Number of non-conference events/year: 1

Publications:
Inside Glass Packaging; monthly

Membership List Available to Non-members

Glass, Molders, Pottery, Plastics and Allied Workers International Union (*1842*)
608 E. Baltimore Pike
P.O. Box 607
Media, PA 19063-0607
Tel: (610) 565-5051 *Fax:* (610) 565-0983
E-Mail: gmpiu@gmpiu.org
Website: gmpiu.org
Members: 40000 individuals
Staff: 41
Annual Budget: $10-25,000,000

Personnel:
International Vice President: Donald Seal
President: Bruce R. Smith
Secretary and Treasurer: Randy Gould

Historical Note:
Formed in 1988 by the merger of the Glass, Pottery, Plastics and Allied Workers and the International Molders and Allied Workers Union. GMP's mission is to support the Glass, Molders, Pottery, Plastics and Allied Workers Political Education League. Members work in a range of industries such as fine china, glass and plastic containers, insulation, sanitary ware, cast metals and other products and services.

Meetings/Conferences: Quadrennial

Publications:
Horizons Magazine; bi-monthly

Global Acetate Manufacturers Association (*2000*)
355 Lexingron Ave.
15th Floor
New York, NY 10017
Website: acetateworld.com
Staff: 3
Annual Budget: $250-500,000

Personnel:
Executive Director: Alfons Westgeest
Executive Assistant: Mélanie Collot
Manager, Communication: Daniela Kolb

Historical Note:
GAMA's objective is to enhance the long-term viability of cellulose acetate and its derivative products worldwide.

Publications:
GAMA Newsletter

Global Alcohol Producers Group (*2005*)
1333 New Hampshire Ave. NW
Washington, DC 20036
E-Mail: info@globalalcoholproducersgroup.com
Website: globalalcoholproducersgroup.com
Staff: 1

Personnel:
Contact, Communication: Carol Clark

Historical Note:
GAP Group provides a channel for the World Health Organisation (WHO), member state governments and stakeholders of the WHO to engage in constructive dialogue with some of the leading alcohol beverage companies on health problems caused by harmful drinking patterns.

Global Association of Risk Professionals (*1996*)
111 Town Sq. Pl.
Suite 1215

Jersey City, NJ 07310
Tel: (201) 719-7210 *Fax:* (201) 222-5022
Website: garp.org
Members: 150000 individuals
Staff: 73
Annual Budget: $10-25,000,000

Personnel:
President and Chief Executive Officer: Richard Apostolik
  E-Mail: rich.apostolik@garp.com
Global Head, Marketing and Membership: Kathleen
  Alcorn
  E-Mail: kathleen.alcorn@garp.com

Historical Note:
GARP serves as a professional association for risk managers, managed by and for its members for the advancement of the risk profession through education, training and the promotion of practices globally. GARP's mission is to advance the risk profession through education, training and the promotion of best practices globally. Membership: $195 (Individual); $95 (Student); Free (Affiliate).

Continuing Education:
Certification Designation/s: CPE, FRM, ERP

Meetings/Conferences: Annual
2013 - New York City, NY/March 12 - 13

Publications:
E-Newsletter; monthly
Risk Professional Magazine; bi-monthly; adv.

Global Business Travel Association *(1968)*
123 N. Pitt St.
Alexandria, VA 22314
Tel: (703) 684-0836 *Fax:* (703) 684-0263
E-Mail: info@gbta.org
Website: gbta.org
Members: 5000 members
Staff: 48
Annual Budget: $2-5,000,000

Personnel:
Executive Director and Chief Operating Officer: Michael
  W. McCormick
  E-Mail: mmccormick@nbta.org
Director, Human Resources: Sallie Dietz CTE, PHR
  E-Mail: sdietz@gbta.org
Vice President, Government Relations and General Counsel:
  Patricia G. Higginbotham
  E-Mail: PHigginbotham@gbta.org
Senior Vice President, Events, Sponsorship and Advertising:
  Zane Kerby MBA
  E-Mail: zkerby@gbta.org
Director, Convention and Brand Marketing: Wendy
  Santantonio CTE
  E-Mail: wsantantonio@nbta.org
Vice President, Corporate Strategy: Hema Shah
  E-Mail: HShah@gbta.org
Senior Vice President, Operations: Edward Silver
  E-Mail: esilver@gbta.org
Vice President, Finance and Controller: Diane Young
  E-Mail: dyoung@gbta.org

Historical Note:
Formerly (2010) National Business Travel Association and (1989) National Passenger Traffic Association. GBTA connects the business travel world and promotes the value of business travel management. Members are business travel managers and business travel service and product suppliers. Membership: $1295 (Allied); $395 (Allied Umbrella); $345 (Direct); $95 (Government Direct Member).

Continuing Education:
Certification Designation/s: CCTE, CTE, GTP

Meetings/Conferences: Annual
Conference Chair: Zane Kerby MBA
2013 - San Diego, CA/Aug. 4 - 7/1400
  attendees/26-50 exhibitors

Publications:
Connecting News; monthly; adv.
Daily News Brief; daily; adv.
GBTA Business Travel; quarterly; adv.
Membership Directory; adv.

Global Cold Chain Alliance *(2007)*
1500 King St.
Alexandria, VA 22314-2730
Tel: (703) 373-4300 *Fax:* (703) 373-4301
E-Mail: email@gcca.org
Website: gcca.org
Members:
387 suppliers

1431 public refrigerated warehouse (PRW)
companies, facilities, construction companies
and transportation companies
Staff: 8

Personnel:
President and Chief Executive Officer: J.William Hudson
  E-Mail: bhudson@gcca.org
Representative, Membership Services: Trier Albanezi
  E-Mail: talbanezi@gcca.org
Director, Education and Training: Colleen Caster
  E-Mail: ccaster@gcca.org
Director, Information Systems and Communications: Tori
  Miller Liu
  E-Mail: tmiller@gcca.org
Editor: Al Rickard
  E-Mail: arickard@associationvision.com
Manager, Meetings and Events: Greg Rinck
  E-Mail: grinck@gcca.org
Manager, Marketing and Membership: James Rogers
  E-Mail: jrogers@gcca.org
Director, International Programs: Richard Tracy
  E-Mail: rtracy@gcca.org

Historical Note:
An alliance of the International Association of Refrigerated Warehouses, the World Food Logistics Organization, the International Refrigerated Transportation Association, and the International Association for Cold Storage Construction, formed in 2007. All four organizations have been retained in this merger, sharing operations and events. GCCA now acts as a platform for communication, networking and education for each link of the cold storage chain and represents the industry as a whole.

Meetings/Conferences:
2013 - Hollywood, FL (The Westin Diplomat)/May 4 -
  8
2014 - San Diego, CA (The Manchester Grand Hyatt)/
  April 26 - 30
Number of non-conference events/year: 6

Publications:
Cold Connection eNewsletter; weekly; adv.
COLD FACTS magazine; bi-monthly; adv.
Cool Designs (IACSC); monthly; adv.
Cool Moves (IRTA); monthly; adv.
e-Cold Facts (Europe); monthly
Global Cold Chain Directory; adv.

Global Health Council *(1972)*
1111 19th St. NW
Suite 1120
Washington, DC 20036
Tel: (202) 833-5900 *Fax:* (202) 833-0075
E-Mail: ghc@globalhealth.org
Website: globalhealth.org
Members:
343 organizations
3023 individuals
Staff: 41
Annual Budget: $2-5,000,000
Tax: 501(c)(3)

Personnel:
*Interim Co Chief Executive Officer and Director, Research
  and Analysis:* Susan Higman
  E-Mail: shigman@globalhealth.org
*Interim Co Chief Executive Officer and Director, Government
  Relations:* Smita Baruah
  E-Mail: sbaruah@globalhealth.org
Director, Administration and Human Resources: Karen
  Caple
  E-Mail: kcaple@globalhealth.org
Director, Publications and New Media: Annmarie
  Christensen
  E-Mail: achristensen@globalhealth.org
Director, Strategic Communications: Tina Flores
Coordinator, Membership Services: Kelly Gardner
  E-Mail: kgardner@globalhealth.org
Administrator, Member Services and Database:
  Christopher Gibbs
Administrator, Information Technology Support: Franklin
  Merritt
  E-Mail: fmerritt@globalhealth.org
Director, Annual Conference: Joanne Needham
  E-Mail: jneedham@globalhealth.org

Historical Note:
Founded as National Council for International Health, later changed its current name in 1988. Mission is to ensure that all who strive for improvement and equity in global health have the information and resources they need to succeed.

Membership: $195 (Professional); $60 (Student); $1,050
(Organizational).

Meetings/Conferences:
Conference Chair: Joanne Needham

Publications:
Global Health; quarterly
Global Health Directory; on-line
Global Health Opportunities; on-line
Malaria Chemotherapy, Control & Elimination
Policy Action Alert e-Newsletters; on-line

Membership List Available to Non-members

Global Market Development Center *(1970)*
1275 Lake Plaza Dr.
Colorado Springs, CO 80906-3583
Tel: (719) 576-4260 *Fax:* (719) 576-2661
E-Mail: info@gmdc.org
Website: gmdc.org
Members: 870 companies
Staff: 20
Annual Budget: $5-10,000,000
Tax: 501(c)(6)

Personnel:
President and Chief Executive Officer: David T. McConnell
  Jr.
  E-Mail: dmcconnell@gmdc.org
Manager, Membership Services: Vickii Barnard
  E-Mail: vbarnard@gmdc.org
Manager, Meetings: Brenda Bishop
  E-Mail: bbishop@gmdc.org
*Vice President, Business Development and Chief Marketing
  Officer:* Mark Deuschle
  E-Mail: markd@gmdc.org
Senior Director, Finance and Administration: Ann
  McConnell
  E-Mail: amcconnell@gmdc.org
Director, Industry Insights and Communications: Mark
  Mechelse
  E-Mail: markm@gmdc.org
*Vice President, Information Technology and Chief
  Technology Officer:* Michael Winterbottom
  E-Mail: mwinterbottom@gmdc.org
*Vice President, Business Development and Chief Member
  Officer:* Keith Wypyszynski
  E-Mail: kwyp@gmdc.org

Historical Note:
GMDC's mission is to enable the growth for retail and wholesale General Merchandise and Health Beauty Wellness industries through collaboration, productivity and knowledge. Membership: $2,000 (Wholesaler); $2,500 (Supplier).

Meetings/Conferences: Annual
Conference Chair: Brenda Bishop
2013 - Phoenix, AZ (JW Marriott Desert Ridge Resort)/
  Sept. 6 - 10
2014 - San Antonio, TX (JW Marriott Hill Country
  Resort & Spa)/Sept. 5 - 9
2015 - Phoenix, AZ (JW Marriott Desert Ridge Resort)/
  Sept. 18 - 22

Publications:
GMDC Insights; weekly; adv.
Membership Directory; on-line

Global Offset and Countertrade Association (GOCA) *(1986)*
818 Connecticut Ave. NW
12th Floor
Washington, DC 20006
Tel: (202) 887-9011 *Fax:* (202) 872-8324
E-Mail: goca@globaloffset.org
Website: globaloffset.org
Members: 500 individuals
Staff: 5
Annual Budget: $250-500,000
Tax: 501(c)(6)

Personnel:
Executive Director and Contact, Membership: Mary O.
  Fromyer
Secretary: Laurence Van Bockel
Deputy Director: Katy Bubolz
Treasurer: James P. Corcoran
Chairman and Chief Executive Officer: Cary F. Viktor

Historical Note:
Formed (1986) as American Countertrade Association, assumed its current name in 2005. GOCA's purpose is to promote trade and commerce between companies around the world and their foreign customers through

understanding of countertrade and offset. Membership: $450/year (Regular/Associate).

Meetings/Conferences:
2013 - Boca Raton, FL (Boca Raton Resort and Club)/ May 18 - 22

Publications:
Membership Directory; on-line

Global Semiconductor Alliance *(1994)*
12400 Coit Rd.
Suite 650
Dallas, TX 75251
Tel: (972) 866-7579 *Fax:* (972) 239-2292
E-Mail: info@gsaglobal.org
Website: gsaglobal.org
Members: 500 members
Staff: 16
Tax: 501(c)(6)

Personnel:
President: Jodi Shelton
    E-Mail: jshelton@gsaglobal.org
Manager, Events: Breanna Anderson
Director, Research: Chelsea Boone
    E-Mail: cboone@gsaglobal.org
Senior Manager, Marketing and Media Contact: Nicole Bowman
    E-Mail: nbowman@gsaglobal.org
Senior Manager, Event and Information Technology: Power Chi
    E-Mail: pchi@gsaglobal.org
Manager, Member Relations: Kate Olsen
    E-Mail: kolsen@gsaglobal.org
Chief Financial Officer: Scott Strittmatter CPA
    E-Mail: sstrittmatter@gsaglobal.org
Executive Assistant: Crystal Wang

Historical Note:
Formerly (2007) FSA, the organization adopted its new name in December 2007. GSA's mission is to accelerate the growth and increase the return on invested capital of the global semiconductor industry by fostering a more effective fabless ecosystem through collaboration, integration and innovation. Membership: $2,500-25,000 (Semiconductor); $2,500-5,500 (Supplier Partner); $5,500 (Service Partner/ Industry Partner); $3,500 (Organizations/Associations/ Government/Educational Partner).

Continuing Education:
Certification Designation/s: GASMC

Meetings/Conferences:
Conference Chair: Power Chi
Number of non-conference events/year: 2

Publications:
Global Semiconductor & Financials Tracker; quarterly
Global Semiconductor Funding, IPO and Update; monthly
GSA Forum; quarterly; adv.
GSA Semiconductor Insights: Asia; on-line
GSA Update; monthly; adv.
On the Fabless Front; quarterly
State of the Worldwide Semiconductor Industry; bi-annually

Glove Shippers Association *(1989)*
P.O. Box 1908
San Juan Capistrano, CA 92693
Tel: (949) 425-9286 *Fax:* (949) 425-9232
TollFree: (877) 877-8780
E-Mail: igcgsa@gmail.com
Members: 1100 companies
Staff: 5
Annual Budget: $100-250,000

Personnel:
Managing Director: James A. Murphy
    E-Mail: igcgsa@gmail.com

Historical Note:
Absorbed the Latex Advisors Association in 1998, GSA members are manufacturers and distributors of gloves and related medical products. Membership: $500-1,500/year.

Continuing Education:
Certification Designation/s: FOA, ASTM

Publications:
Latex Advisor; semi-annually; adv.
Medical and Latex Newsletter

Membership List Available to Non-members

Glutamate Association (United States) *(1977)*
P.O. Box 14266

Washington, DC 20044-4266
Tel: (202) 637-5926 *Fax:* (202) 637-5910
Website: msgfacts.com
Members: 9 companies
Staff: 4
Annual Budget: $100-250,000

Personnel:
Executive Director: Martin J. Hahn
    E-Mail: martin.hahn@hoganlovells.com

Historical Note:
TGA-US provides information on glutamic acid and its salts, including monosodium glutamate (MSG). Serves as a regulatory and scientific liaison for industry concerning glutamates.

Golf Coaches Association of America *(1958)*
1225 W. Main St.
Suite 110
Norman, OK 73069
Tel: (405) 329-4222 *Fax:* (405) 573-7888
TollFree: (866) 422-2669
E-Mail: info@collegiategolf.com
Website: collegiategolf.com
Members: 750 individuals
Staff: 7
Annual Budget: $500-1,000,000

Personnel:
Chief Executive Officer: Gregg Grost
    E-Mail: gregg@collegiategolf.com
Director, Business Affairs: Sharon Beery
Director, Operations: Ryan Klatt
    E-Mail: ryan@collegiategolf.com
Director, Membership Services: Katie Louis

Historical Note:
GCAA's mission is to educate, promote and recognize its members who participate in men's golf at all levels and maintains a goal of increasing awareness and the status of men's golf. Membership: $5,000 (President's Club); $2,000 (Platinum Club); $1,500 (Gold Club); $85 (Associate).

Continuing Education:
Certification Designation/s: NCAA, NAIA, NJCAA

Publications:
Membership Directory; on-line

Golf Course Builders Association of America *(1972)*
727 O St.
Lincoln, NE 68508
Tel: (402) 476-4444 *Fax:* (402) 476-4489
E-Mail: information@gcbaa.org
Website: gcbaa.org
Members: 400 companies
Staff: 4
Annual Budget: $500-1,000,000

Personnel:
Executive Director: Justin Apel
    E-Mail: justin_apel@gcbaa.org
Copy Editor: Amy Hromiak
    E-Mail: avhromiak@aol.com
Administrative Assistant, Office and Foundation: Annette Kracke
Manager, Program and Planning: Samantha Porter

Historical Note:
GCBAA's mission is to advance and and improve the profession of golf course construction while serving the interests of its member companies. Members are golf course builders and suppliers to the golf course construction industry. Membership: $550 (Builder/ Associate/International US); $200 (Independent Affiliate).

Continuing Education:
Certification Designation/s: GCBAA CP

Meetings/Conferences: Annual
Conference Chair: Samantha Porter
2013 - San Diego, CA (Hilton San Diego Bayfront)/Feb. 5 - 7

Publications:
EarthShapingNews - GCBAA newsletter; quarterly
Membership Directory; annually; adv.

Golf Course Superintendents Association of America *(1926)*
1421 Research Park Dr.
Lawrence, KS 66049-3859
Tel: (785) 841-2240 *Fax:* (785) 832-3643
TollFree: (800) 472-7878
E-Mail: infobox@gcsaa.org
Website: gcsaa.org

Members: 19000 individuals
Staff: 125
Annual Budget: $10-25,000,000
Tax: 501(c)(6)

Personnel:
Chief Executive Officer: Rhett Evans
    E-Mail: revans@gcsaa.org
Senior Director, Communications: Jeff Bollig
    E-Mail: jbollig@gcsaa.org
Associate Director, Conference Events and Meeting Planning: Jana Brown CMP
    E-Mail: jbrown@gcsaa.org
Director, Finance and Membership Solutions: Kathleen Burden
    E-Mail: kburden@gcsaa.org
Director, Professional Development: Shari Koehler
    E-Mail: skoehler@gcsaa.org
Chief Financial Officer: Cameron Oury
    E-Mail: coury@gcsaa.org
Director, Information Technology: Lambert Tomeldan
    E-Mail: ltomeldan@gcsaa.org

Historical Note:
GCSAA strives to provide education programs either in formal educational settings or at home or office through the use of videotapes, educational cassettes, and computers as well as conventional printed matter. It's mission is dedicated to serving its members, advancing their profession and enhancing the enjoyment, growth and vitality of the game of golf. Membership: $320 (Superintendent/Affiliate); $160 (Assistant Superintendent/Associate/ International Superintendent); $65 (Student/Educator); $70 (Retired); $75 (Facility Outreach).

Continuing Education:
Enrollment: 2000
Certification Designation/s: CGCS

Meetings/Conferences: Annual
Conference Chair: Jana Brown CMP
2013 - San Diego, CA (San Diego Convention Center)/ Feb. 6 - 7
2014 - Orlando, FL (Orange County Convention Center)/Feb. 5 - 6
2015 - San Antonio, TX (The Henry B. Gonzalez Convention Center)/Feb. 25 - 26
Number of non-conference events/year: 3

Publications:
Certified Golf Course Superintendent Directory; on-line
GCSAA This Week; weekly; adv.
Golf Course Management (GCM); monthly; adv.
Golf Industry Show Directory; on-line; adv.
Member Directory; on-line

Membership List Available to Non-members

Golf Range Association of America *(1992)*
P.O. Box 240
Georgetown, CT 06829
Tel: (203) 938-2720 *Fax:* (203) 938-2721
Website: golfrange.org
Members: 850 Companies and Individuals
Staff: 4
Annual Budget: $250-500,000

Personnel:
President: Steven J. DiCostanzo
    E-Mail: steve@golfrange.org
Chief Executive Officer: Rick Summers
    E-Mail: rsummers@golfrange.org
Vice President, Sales: Brian Folino
    E-Mail: bfolino@golfrange.org
Chief Operating Officer: Peter Sansone
    E-Mail: psansone@pgamagazine.com

Historical Note:
GRAA's mission is to is to harness the combined power of all golf range owners, operators and staff at all types of facilities to grow their revenues, enhance their careers and help grow the game of golf. Members are owners, operators, general manager and teaching professionals at both golf ranges and golf courses in the U.S. and Canada. Membership: $199-299 (Facility); $599 (Vendor).

Meetings/Conferences:
Number of non-conference events/year: 1

Publications:
Golf Range Magazine; bi-monthly; adv.
Golf Range Times e-Newsletter; bi-monthly
Membership Directory; on-line

Membership List Available to Non-members

Golf Writers Association of America *(1946)*
10210 Green tree Rd.

Houston, TX 77042-1232
Tel: (713) 782-6664 *Fax:* (713) 781-2575
E-Mail: golfwritersinc@aol.com
Website: gwaa.com
Members: 975 individuals
Staff: 2
Annual Budget: $100-250,000
Tax: 501(c)(6)

Personnel:
Secretary and Treasurer: Melanie Hauser
   E-Mail: mhauser806@aol.com
Contact, Membership Services: Robinson Holloway
   E-Mail: robinsonholloway@gmail.com

Historical Note:
GWAA strives to improve the press facilities at tournaments, hotel accommodations, local transportation, interviews with the players and work in concert with the Association of Golf Writers. Sponsors an annual writing contest and a number of awards, conducts a scholarship program which helps students at 17 universities around the country with scholarships and internships. Reviews new member applications only twice a year -- in January and June. Goal is to improve working conditions for the membership. Membership: $50 (Regular/Associate); $150 (Professional).

Publications:
GWAA Directory
GWAA Newsletter; monthly

Gospel Music Association (1964)
P.O. Box 22697
Nashville, TN 37202
Tel: (615) 242-0303 *Fax:* (615) 254-9755
E-Mail: info@gospelmusic.org
Website: gospelmusic.org
Members: 4000 individuals
Staff: 5
Annual Budget: $100-250,000

Personnel:
Executive Director: Jackie Patillo
   E-Mail: Jackie@gospelmusic.org
Senior Manager, Systems: Ben Cooper
   E-Mail: ben@gospelmusic.org
Manager, Events and Sponsorships: Justin Fratt
   E-Mail: justin@gospelmusic.org
Treasurer: Ed Leonard
   E-Mail: eleonard@daywind.com
Contact, Membership and Customer Services: Scott Linquist
   E-Mail: scott@gospelmusic.org

Historical Note:
GMA's mission is to support, encourage and promote the development of all kinds of gospel music. Members include recording and publishing executives, artists, church musicians, broadcasters, retailers, concert promoters, and others involved with gospel music. Membership: $25-1450/year.

Meetings/Conferences:
Conference Chair: Justin Fratt
Number of non-conference events/year: 1

Publications:
Billboard Magazine; annually; adv.
GMAil; weekly
Homecoming Magazine; bi-monthly; adv.

Government Finance Officers Association of the United States and Canada (1906)
203 N. LaSalle St.
Suite 2700
Chicago, IL 60601-1210
Tel: (312) 977-9700 *Fax:* (312) 977-4806
E-Mail: inquiry@gfoa.org
Website: gfoa.org
Members: 17400 individuals
Staff: 44
Annual Budget: $10-25,000,000
Tax: 501(c)(3)

Personnel:
Executive Director and Chief Executive Officer: Jeffrey L. Esser
   E-Mail: jesser@gfoa.org
Coordinator, Financial Administration and Distribution, Publications: Gus Corral
   E-Mail: gcorral@gfoa.org
Director, Technical Services: Stephen Gauthier
Chief Financial Officer, Financial Administration: John Jurkash
   E-Mail: jjurkash@gfoa.org

Senior Manager, Research and Consulting: Shayne Kavanagh
   E-Mail: skavanagh@gfoa.org
Manager, Communications, Operations and Marketing: Natalie Laudadio
Director, Operations and Marketing: Barbara Mollo
   E-Mail: bmollo@gfoa.org
Manager, Information Technology, Financial Administration: Dennis Podgorski Jr.

Historical Note:
Formerly (1984) the Municipal Finance Officers Association of the United States and Canada. GFOA's mission is to enhance and promote the professional management of governments for the public benefit by identifying and developing financial policies and practices and promoting them through education, training and leadership. Members are finance officers from city, county, and state governments, school, and other special districts; retirement systems and others in the U.S. and Canada interested in government finance. Membership: $ 160-4,620/year.

Continuing Education:
Certification Designation/s: CPFO

Meetings/Conferences: Annual
Conference Chair: Barbara Mollo
2013 - San Francisco, CA/June 2 - 5/over 100 exhibitors
2013 - Madison, WI (University of Wisconsin)/July 28 - Aug. 2
2014 - Minneapolis, MN/May 18 - 21/over 100 exhibitors
2015 - Philadelphia, PA/May 31 - June 3/over 100 exhibitors
2016 - Toronto, ON/May 22 - 25/over 100 exhibitors
2017 - Denver, CO/May 21 - 24/over 100 exhibitors
2018 - St. Louis, MO/May 6 - 9/over 100 exhibitors

Publications:
GAAFR Review
GFOA Newsletter; on-line
Membership Directory; on-line
Treasury Management; monthly

Government Finance Officers Association, Federal Liaison Center
203 N. LaSalle St.
Suite 2700
Chicago, IL 60601-1210
Tel: (312) 977-9700 *Fax:* (312) 977-4806
E-Mail: federalliaison@gfoa.org
Website: gfoa.org
Members: 17400 members
Staff: 44

Personnel:
Executive Director and Chief Executive Officer: Jeffrey L. Esser
Publications Distribution Coordinator: Gus Corral
Director, Technical Services: Stephen Gauthier
Chief Financial Officer: John Jurkash
Communications Manager, Operations and Marketing: Natalie Laudadio

Historical Note:
The purpose of the Government Finance Officers Association is to enhance and promote the professional management of governments for the public benefit by identifying and developing financial policies and best practices and promoting their use through education, training, facilitation of member networking, and leadership.

Continuing Education:
Certification Designation/s: CPFO

Meetings/Conferences: Annual
2013 - San Francisco, CA/June 2 - 5
2014 - Minneapolis, MN/May 18 - 21
2015 - Philadelphia, PA/May 31 - June 3
2016 - Toronto, ON/May 22 - 25
2017 - Denver, CO/May 21 - 24
2018 - St. Louis, MO/May 6 - June 9

Publications:
GFOA Newsletter; adv.
Member Directory; on-line
Treasury Management Newsletter; monthly

Government Management Information Sciences (1971)
P.O. Box 27923
Austin, TX 78755
Fax: (512) 857-7711
TollFree: (877) 963-4647
E-Mail: headquarters@gmis.org
Website: gmis.org

Members: 600 government agencies
Staff: 4
Annual Budget: $100-250,000

Personnel:
Editor: Elaine Dickey Isler
   E-Mail: isler@cityofmobile.org

Historical Note:
GMIS's mission is to provide a forum for public sector agencies to exchange information technology best practices that enhance the delivery of government services. Membership: $75-400/year (Agency, based on agency's EDP budget).

Continuing Education:
Certification Designation/s: CGCIO

Publications:
GEM Newsletter

Governmental Research Association (1914)
Room 219 Brooks Hall, Samford University
P.O. Box 292300
Birmingham, AL 35229
Tel: (205) 870-2482
Website: graonline.org
Members: 165 individuals
Staff: 3
Annual Budget: Under $10,000

Personnel:
Secretary: Kent Gardner PhD
   E-Mail: kgardner@cgr.org
Editor: Dean Michael Mead
   E-Mail: dmmead@gasb.org
Treasurer: Kriss S. Sjoblom
   E-Mail: ksjoblom@researchcouncil.org

Historical Note:
GRA's purpose is to encourage individuals and organizations to engage in governmental research in the general interest. Members work in privately sponsored government research organizations, universities, chambers of commerce and governmental agencies. Membership: $120 (Individual); $295 (Organization).

Publications:
The GRA Reporter; quarterly
The Professional Directory of Who's Who in Governmental Research

Governors' Highway Safety Association (1966)
444 N. Capitol St. NW
Suite 722
Washington, DC 20001
Tel: (202) 789-0942 *Fax:* (202) 789-0946
E-Mail: headquarters@ghsa.org
Website: statehighwaysafety.org
Members: 54 states and territories
Staff: 5
Annual Budget: $2-5,000,000
Tax: 501(c)(3)

Personnel:
Executive Director: Barbara Harsha
   E-Mail: bharsha@ghsa.org
Deputy Executive Director: Jonathan Adkins
   E-Mail: jadkins@ghsa.org
Director, Administration: Denise Alston
   E-Mail: dalston@ghsa.org
Manager, Communications: Kara Macek
   E-Mail: kmacek@ghsa.org

Historical Note:
Assumed its current name in 2002. Mission is to provide leadership and representation for the states to improve traffic safety, influence national policy and enhance program management. Members are state officials who administer the Highway Safety Act. Membership: $100 (Emeritus); $250 (Small Business); $750 (Corporate); $500 (Nonprofit).

Meetings/Conferences: Annual
2013 - San Diego, CA (Manchester Grand Hyatt San Diego)/Aug. 25 - 28
2014 - Grand Rapids, MI (Amway Grand Plaza Hotel)/Sept. 7 - 10
2015 - Nashville, TN (Omni Nashville Hotel)/Aug. 30 - Sept. 2
Number of non-conference events/year: 1

Publications:
GHSA Newsletter; quarterly

Grain Elevator and Processing Society (1930)
4248 Park Glen Rd.
Minneapolis, MN 55416

Tel: (952) 928-4640 *Fax:* (952) 929-1318
E-Mail: info@geaps.com
Website: geaps.com
Members: 3000 individuals
Staff: 10
Annual Budget: $2-5,000,000
Tax: 501(c)(6)

Personnel:
Executive Vice President and Secretary: David Krejci
  E-Mail: david@geaps.com
Manager, Marketing and Communications: Mo Dennis
  E-Mail: mo@geaps.com
Manager, Membership Services: Adrianne Fjerstad
  E-Mail: adrianne@geaps.com
Manager, Professional Development: Chuck House
  E-Mail: chuck@geaps.com
Manager, Member Services and Information: Amy
  Jorgensen
  E-Mail: amy@geaps.com
Manager, Meetings Services: Melissa Serres
  E-Mail: melissa@geaps.com
Manager, Membership Services and Publications: Jason
  Stones
  E-Mail: jasons@geaps.com

Historical Note:
*GEAPS's mission is to provide news, information, continue
education and other services to grain handling and
process operations. Regular members are individuals who
are associated directly with the grain, feed, milling and
processing industries in an operations management or
supervisory capacity. Affiliate membership is available for
academics and government officials. Associate membership
is available to suppliers of products, equipment or services
to the industry. Membership: $290 (Regular/Associate/
Affiliate); Free (Student).*

Meetings/Conferences: Annual
Conference Chair: Melissa Serres
2013 - Louisville, KY (Kentucky International
  Convention Center)/Feb. 23 - 26
2014 - Omaha, NE (Quest Center)/Feb. 22 - 25
2015 - St. Louis, MO (America's Center Convention
  Complex)/March 7 - 10
Number of non-conference events/year: 2

Publications:
In-Grain Newsletter
Member Directory; on-line
Member Newsletter; on-line

Grand Strand Business Association
P.O. Box 8082
Myrtle Beach, SC 29578-8082
Tel: (843) 421-8716
Website: grandstrandbusinessassociation.com
Staff: 2
Annual Budget: $250-500,000
Tax: 501(c)(6)

Personnel:
President: Mike Wooten
Treasurer: Shep Guyton

Historical Note:
*The mission of the Grand Strand Business Association
is to proactively support and represent businesses and
commercial interests along the Grand Strand in the political
arena.*

The Grant Professionals Association (1998)
1333 Meadowlark Ln.
Suite 105
Kansas City, KS 66102
Tel: (913) 788-3000 *Fax:* (913) 788-3398
E-Mail: info@grantprofessionals.org
Website: grantprofessionals.org
Members: 4500 individuals
Staff: 6
Annual Budget: $500-1,000,000
Tax: 501(c)(6)

Personnel:
Interim Chief Executive Officer and President: Debbie
  DiVirgilio MNM
Administrative Manager: Talitta Bell
Manager, Office and Volunteer Relations: Barb Boggs
Director, Membership Services: Kelli Romero
  E-Mail: membership@grantprofessionals.org

Historical Note:
*Formerly American Association of Grant Professionals.
GPA is a membership association, that builds and supports
an international community of grant professionals.*

Membership: $189 (National); $50 (Legacy); $79
(Student); $139 (Entry Level/Retiree).

Continuing Education:
Certification Designation/s: GPC

Meetings/Conferences: Annual
2013 - Baltimore, MD (Hyatt Regency Baltimore)/Nov.
  13 - 16

Publications:
E-Newsletters; quarterly; adv.
GPA Consultants Directory; on-line
GPA Journal; annually
Membership Directory; on-line

Graphic Artists Guild (1967)
32 Broadway
Suite 1114
New York, NY 10004-1612
Tel: (212) 791-3400 *Fax:* (212) 791-0333
E-Mail: admin@gag.org
Website: graphicartistsguild.org
Members: 1500 individuals
Staff: 2
Annual Budget: $500-1,000,000
Tax: 501(c)(5)

Personnel:
Executive Director: Patricia McKiernan
Contact, Membership and Database: Tamara Hall

Historical Note:
*GAG's mission is to promote and protect the social,
economic and professional interests of its members.
Members include illustrators, graphic designers, surface
designers, production artists, cartoonists, animators,
web designers, and digital artists. Membership: $200
(Professional); $170 (Standard Associate); $75 (Lifetime/
Retired/Student).*

Publications:
Guild News; bi-monthly
Membership Directory; on-line

Graphic Arts Sales Foundation (1983)
845 W. Chester Pike
Suite 202
W. Chester, PA 19382
Tel: (610) 431-9780 *Fax:* (610) 436-5238
E-Mail: judymiller@gasf.org
Members: 1200 individuals
Staff: 2
Annual Budget: $250-500,000
Tax: 501(c)(3)

Personnel:
Chief Executive Officer: Richard Gorelick
Administrator: Judy M. Miller

Historical Note:
*GASF is a training organization in the graphic arts industry
offering one-day, five-day and custom in-house industry-
specific education programs for C. E. O. 's, marketing
executives, sales managers, salespeople, print buyers,
customer service representatives, estimators, and production
supervisors. GASF offers a professional certification
program for graphic arts sales representatives in the graphic
arts industry (CGASR).*

Publications:
Monographs; irregular

Graphic Arts Technical Foundation (1924)
200 Deer Run Rd.
Sewickley, PA 15143-2600
Tel: (412) 741-6860 *Fax:* (412) 741-2311
TollFree: (800) 910-4283
E-Mail: printing@printing.org
Website: gain.net
Members: 13000 individuals and companies
Staff: 64
Annual Budget: $5-10,000,000
Tax: 501(c)(3)

Personnel:
President and Chief Executive Officer: Michael Makin
  E-Mail: mmakin@printing.org
Marketing Manager: Rebecca Blunt
Vice President, Research and Technology: Mark Bohan
  E-Mail: mbohan@piagatf.org
Editor: Joe Deemer
  E-Mail: jdeemer@printing.org
Executive Vice President and Executive Director: Mary
  Garnett
  E-Mail: mgarnett@piagatf.org
Conference Manager: Ned Herrick

Senior Sales Specialist: Karen Keller
Director, Educational Services: Diane Koch
  E-Mail: dkoch@piagatf.org

Historical Note:
*Formerly (1924) Lithographic Technical Foundation;
assumed current name in 1964 to reflect the Foundation's
commitment to all aspects of printing. GATF is a member
supported, nonprofit, scientific, technical, and educational
organization dedicated to the advancement of graphic
communications industries worldwide. A research and
education foundation, it produces publications, training
programs, research studies and quality control devices. Its
Print and Graphics Scholarship Foundation, established in
1956, is a nonprofit corporation that awards scholarships
to two and four year programs leading to a career in
graphic communications. In 1999, GATF consolidated with
Printing Industries of America (PIA). Membership: corporate
fee based on sales volume.*

Graphic Communications Conference of the
International Brotherhood of Teamsters (2005)
1900 L St. NW
Ninth Floor
Washington, DC 20036
Tel: (202) 462-1400 *Fax:* (202) 721-0600
Website: gciu.org
Members: 150000 individuals
Staff: 33
Annual Budget: $5-10,000,000

Personnel:
President: George Tedeschi

Historical Note:
*The Amalgamated Lithographers of America and the
International Photoengravers Union of North America
merged on September 7, 1964 to form the Lithographers
and Photoengravers International Union. This, in turn,
merged September 4, 1972 with the International
Brotherhood of Bookbinders (founded 1892) to form
the Graphic Arts International Union which merged July
1, 1983 with the International Printing and Graphic
Communications Union to form the present organization.
GCIU merged with the International Brotherhood of
Teamsters and assumed its current name in 2005. Members
are men and women who work in the printing and
publishing industry in the United States and Canada.*

Gravure Association of America (1947)
P.O. Box 25617
Rochester, NY 14625
Tel: (201) 523-6042 *Fax:* (201) 523-6048
E-Mail: gaa@gaa.org
Website: gaa.org
Members: 133 companies
Staff: 6
Annual Budget: $500-1,000,000

Personnel:
President and Chief Executive Officer: Bill Martin
  E-Mail: bmartin@gaa.org
Coordinator, Events and Administration: Michelle
  Aronowitz-Jones
  E-Mail: maronowitz-jones@gaa.org
Technical Director: Bruce Beyer
  E-Mail: bbeyer@gaa.org
Editor and Associate Publisher: Linda Casatelli
  E-Mail: lcasatelli@gaa.org
Accountant: Linda Pfingst CPA
  E-Mail: lcpfingst@gaa.org
Director, Planning and Administration: Pamela W. Schenk
  E-Mail: pwschenk@gaa.org

Historical Note:
*Formed (1988) through the merger of the Gravure
Technical Association and the Gravure Research Insitute.
Members are gravure printers, converters, suppliers,
and users. Supports the Gravure Education Foundation,
established in 1979. GAA promotes the use of the
gravure printing process for publication printing, package
printing and product (specialty) printing. Membership:
$1,130-21,800 (Domestic based on the revenue); $2,860
(International); $2,860-9,750 (Associate Supplier/
Consultant); $2,480 (Magazine Publisher/Pharmaceutical/
Packaging Buyer/Printed Electronics); $1,240 (Advertising
Agency/Retailer/Designer); $550 (Educator).*

Continuing Education:
Certification Designation/s: GAA POCP

Meetings/Conferences:
Conference Chair: Michelle Aronowitz-Jones
Number of non-conference events/year: 10

Publications:
Buyers' Guide; on-line; adv.
Gravure Magazine; on-line; adv.
Membership Directory; on-line

Greater Blouse, Skirt and Undergarment Association (1933)
87 Walker St.
New York, NY 10013
Tel: (212) 563-5052 *Fax:* (212) 563-5373
E-Mail: gbsua1333@yahoo.com
Website: greaterblouse.org
Members: 300 garment factories
Staff: 6
Annual Budget: $25-50,000

Personnel:
Executive Director: Teddy Lai

Historical Note:
Formerly (1967) Greater Blouse and Skirt Contractors Association. Members are contractors in the ladies' blouses, sportswear, underwear, and negligee industry. Membership: $85/year (Regular).

Green Hotels Association
P.O. Box 420212
Houston, TX 77242-0212
Tel: (713) 789-8889 *Fax:* (713) 789-9786
E-Mail: green@greenhotels.com
Website: greenhotels.com
Members: 325 hotels
Staff: 3

Personnel:
President and Founder: Patricia Griffin

Historical Note:
Green Hotels Association help hotels save water, energy and reduce solid waste in order to help protect beautiful destinations valued by the public. Membership: $250 (Educator); $400-500 (Environmentalists); $50 (Traveler); $400-600 (Ally, based on revenues); $200 (Partner).

Publications:
Newsletter; bi-monthly

Greeting Card Association (1941)
1133 Westchester Ave.
Suite N136
White Plains, NY 10604-3547
Tel: (914) 421-3331 *Fax:* (914) 948-1484
E-Mail: info@greetingcard.org
Website: greetingcard.org
Members: 300 companies
Staff: 8
Annual Budget: $500-1,000,000
Tax: 501(c)(6)

Personnel:
Executive Vice President: Patti Stracher
  E-Mail: pstracher@gcamail.org
Director, Membership Services: Mila Albertson
Manager, Meetings: Judy Cheris
  E-Mail: jcheris@glmshows.com
Manager, Marketing: Melissa Gray
  E-Mail: mgray@glmshows.com
Director, Communications: Kathy Krassner
  E-Mail: kkrassner@gcamail.org
Media Contact: Barbara Miller

Historical Note:
Founded as Greeting Card Association, became the National Association of Greeting Card Publishers in 1967 and assumed its current name in 1983. GCA strives to celebrate, promote and preserve the tradition of sending greeting cards, to represent the industry before government and regulatory agencies and to serve as an information service center for its members. Membership includes greeting card and stationery publishers, and allied members of the industry. Membership: $250-75,000 (Regular/Affiliate); $1,000-3,125 (Associate); $5,000 (Regular Subsidiary); $350 (International).

Meetings/Conferences: Annual
Conference Chair: Judy Cheris
2013 - Orlando, FL (The Villas of Grand Cypress)/Oct. 3 - 6

Publications:
CardTalk; on-line
Directory of Greeting Card Sales Representatives & Distributors.
Greeting Card Representatives Directory
GREETINGS etc
Party & Paper Retailer and Stationery Trends magazine; adv.

Gridwise Alliance (2003)
1155 15th St.
Suite 500
Washington, DC 20005
Tel: (202) 530-9740 *Fax:* (202) 530-0659
Website: gridwise.org
Members: 132 Companies
Staff: 6
Annual Budget: $2-5,000,000

Personnel:
Executive Director: Lee Coogan
  E-Mail: lgoogan@gridwise.org
President and Chief Executive Officer: James Morozzi

Historical Note:
Gridwise Alliance Mission is to facilitate effective collaboration among all stakeholders, and to promote, educate, and advocate for the adoption of innovative smart grid solutions that will achieve economic and environmental benefits for customers, communities, and shareholders. Membership: $5000 (Full/International); $2500 (Associate).

Grocery Manufacturers Association (GMA) (1908)
1350 Eye St. NW
Suite 300
Washington, DC 20005
Tel: (202) 639-5900 *Fax:* (202) 639-5932
E-Mail: info@gmaonline.org
Website: gmaonline.org
Members: 300 businesses
Staff: 117
Annual Budget: $25-50,000,000
Tax: 501(c)(6)

Personnel:
President and Chief Executive Officer: Pamela G. Bailey
  E-Mail: pbailey@gmaonline.org
Vice President, Membership and Meetings Services: Patrick Brookover
Executive Assistant, Policy and Strategic Planning: Emily Casto
  E-Mail: ecasto@gmabrands.com
Vice President, Industry Affairs: Elise Fennig IOM
Executive Vice President, Government Affairs: Louis Andrew Finkel
Senior Manager, Membership Services: Evie Kasper
  E-Mail: ekasper@gmaonline.org
Senior Manager, Marketing: Beth Ludwick
  E-Mail: bludwick@gmaonline.org
Vice President, Communications: Sean McBride
  E-Mail: smcbride@gmabrands.com
Senior Vice President, Chief Financial Officer and Chief Administrative Officer: Steve McCroddan CPA
Vice President, Human Resources: Carla Mitchell SPHR
  E-Mail: cmitchell@gmaonline.org
Coordinator, Legal and Meetings: Allison Conway Morgan
Vice President & General Counsel: James H. Skiles
  E-Mail: jskiles@gmaonline.org

Historical Note:
Formerly Grocery Manufacturers of America, assumed it's current name in 2005. GMA promotes sound public policy, champions initiatives that increase productivity and growth and helps to protect the safety and security of the food supply through scientific excellence. Membership: $54,000/ year (Affiliate); General membership based on sales.

Meetings/Conferences:
Conference Chair: Allison Conway Morgan
Number of non-conference events/year: 10

Publications:
BioTech Update; on-line
Emerging Chemical Contaminants Update; on-line
Executive Update; monthly
Food Safety Update; on-line
GMA Newsletter
International Update; on-line
Regulatory Update; on-line
Times and Trends; on-line

Ground Water Protection Council (1983)
13308 N. MacArthur Blvd.
Oklahoma City, OK 73142
Tel: (405) 516-4972 *Fax:* (405) 516-4973
Website: gwpc.org
Members: 13000 individuals
Staff: 7
Annual Budget: $2-5,000,000
Tax: 501(c)(6)

Personnel:
Executive Director: Mike Paque CAE
  E-Mail: mpaque@gwpc.org

Director, Technical Services: Paul Jehn
  E-Mail: pauljehn@adelphia.net
Director, Organizational Development: Daniel Yates
  E-Mail: dayates@gwpc.org

Historical Note:
GWPC's mission is to promote the protection and conservation of ground water resources for all beneficial uses, recognizing ground water as a critical component of the ecosystem. Members consist of state and federal ground water agencies, industry representatives, environmentalists and concerned citizens. Membership: $75 (Individual); $500-10,000 (Corporate Supporter).

Meetings/Conferences: Semi-Annual
Number of non-conference events/year: 1

Publications:
Membership Directory; on-line

Groundwater Management Districts Association (1975)
105 N. Lincoln Ave.
York, NE 68467
Tel: (402) 362-6601 *Fax:* (402) 362-1849
Website: gmdausa.org
Members: 140 individuals
Staff: 2
Annual Budget: Under $10,000

Personnel:
President: Linda Luebbe

Historical Note:
GMDA is a non-profit organization established to provide groundwater management districts, groundwater developers, users, owners, and other individuals and organizations concerned with the management, development, conservation and protection of groundwater, the opportunity to exchange ideas, develop or influence programs for the development, utilization, conservation, protection, management and control of groundwater. Membership includes districts, consulting organizations and individuals concerned with the management and conservation of water resources. Affiliated with the National Water Resources Association. Membership: $25 (Individual); $125 (Affiliate); $250 (Organization); $350 (District).

Meetings/Conferences: Annual

Publications:
Membership Directory; on-line

Group for the Use of Psychology in History (1971)
John Jay College - CUNY
555 W. 57th St., Suite 601
New York, NY 10019
Tel: (212) 237-8432
E-Mail: strozier2@aol.com
Website: ahaonline.org/affiliates/ group_use_psychology_his.htm
Members: 400 individuals
Staff: 1

Personnel:
Executive Officer: Charles B. Strozier
  E-Mail: strozier2@aol.com

Historical Note:
Members are academics and others with an interest in the integration of disciplines of psychology and history. Has no paid officers or full-time staff. Membership: $22/year.

Growth Energy
777 N. Capitol St. NE
Suite 805
Washington, DC 20002
Tel: (202) 545-4000 *Fax:* (202) 545-4001
Website: growthenergy.org
Members: 145 producer plants and associate members
Staff: 20
Annual Budget: $10-25,000,000

Personnel:
Chief Executive Officer: Tom Buis
  E-Mail: tbuis@growthenergy.org
Director, Government Affairs: John Fuher Conrad
Press Secretary: Michael Frohlich
Director, Membershipship Services: Bryce Jones
President and Chief Operating Officer: Jim Nussle
Vice President, Market Development: Mike O'Brien

Historical Note:
Growth Energy's mission is to provide market development, communication, advocacy, policy engagement, technical assistance and support to the members.

GSM Association (1982)
1000 Abernathy Rd.
Suite 450
Atlanta, GA 30328
Tel: (678) 281-6600 *Fax:* (678) 281-6601
Website: gsmworld.com
Staff: 5
Annual Budget: $25-50,000,000

Personnel:
Chief Executive Officer: John Hoffman
Global Director of Marketing: Dave Bailey
Chief Marketing Officer: Michael O'Hara
Chief Financial Officer and Chief Operating Officer: Jeremy
   Sewell
Chief Technology Officer: Alex Sinclair

Historical Note:
*Represents 700 GSM mobile phone operators across 218
countries. In addition, more than 200 manufacturers and
suppliers support the Association's initiatives as associate
members. Membership is based on company's annual
revenue.*

Meetings/Conferences: Annual
2013 - Shanghai, China/June 26 - 28

Guild of American Luthiers (1972)
8222 S. Park Ave.
Tacoma, WA 98408-5226
Tel: (253) 472-7853 *Fax:* (253) 472-7853
E-Mail: orders@luth.org
Website: luth.org
Members: 3400 individuals
Staff: 9
Annual Budget: $250-500,000
Tax: 501(c)(3)

Personnel:
President and Editor: Timothy L. Olsen
Contact, Membership Services: Kurt Kendall
Contact, Conventions: Deb Olsen

Historical Note:
*GAL purpose is to facilitate learning about the art, craft and
science of lutherie. Members are professional and amateur
builders and repairers of string musical instruments and
other interested individuals. Membership: $55 (U.S.); $65
(International).*

Meetings/Conferences: Annual
Conference Chair: Deb Olsen

Publications:
GAL Newsletter; on-line

Guild of Artists and Artisans (1970)
118 N. Fourth Ave.
Ann Arbor, MI 48104-1402
Tel: (734) 662-3382 *Fax:* (734) 662-0339
E-Mail: info@theguild.org
Website: theguild.org
Staff: 9
Annual Budget: $500-1,000,000
Tax: 501(c)(3)

Personnel:
Executive Director and Media Contact: Debra Clayton
   E-Mail: clayton@theguild.org
Operations Director: Alan Bogl
   E-Mail: alan@theguild.org
Senior Director, Marketing and Partnership: Karen Delhey
   E-Mail: karen@theguild.org
Membership Contact: Pamela Stoddard
   E-Mail: pam@theguild.org

Historical Note:
*A non-profit, membership organization of professional
artists in Michigan. Its mission is to promote community
awareness, understanding and appreciation of the visual
arts and to maintain a support network for artists,
which provides educational, mentoring and marketing
opportunities. Membership: $70 (Exhibiting); $120 (Joint
Exhibiting); $45 (Artist/Friends of the Guild); $60 (Joint
Artist).*

Meetings/Conferences:
Conference Chair: Alan Bogl
Number of non-conference events/year: 1

Publications:
Membership Directory; on-line
The E-Limited; monthly; adv.
Trade Magazine

Guild of Book Workers (1906)
521 Fifth Ave.
17th Floor
New York, NY 10175-0038
Tel: (212) 292-4444
Website: guildofbookworkers.org
Members: 850 individuals
Staff: 3
Annual Budget: $100-250,000
Tax: 501(c)(3)

Personnel:
President: Andrew Huot
   E-Mail: president@guildofbookworkers.org
Treasurer: Alicia Bailey
Editor: Cindy Haller
   E-Mail: newsletter@guildofbookworkers.org

Historical Note:
*GBW promotes interest in and awareness of the tradition
of the book and paper arts by maintaining high standards
of workmanship, hosting educational opportunities, and
sponsoring exhibits. Membership: $85 (U.S. Members); $10
(Canadian Postage Surcharge); $30 (Student); $15 (Other
Countries Postage Surcharge).*

Publications:
The GBW Newsletter; bi-monthly; adv.
The Guild of Book Worker's Journal; annually

Guild of Italian American Actors (1937)
Canal St. Stn.
P.O. Box 123
New York, NY 10013-0123
Tel: (201) 344-3411
E-Mail: info@giaa.us
Website: giaa.us
Members: 270 individuals
Staff: 2
Annual Budget: $10-25,000

Personnel:
President: Carlo Fiorletta
Secretary and Treasurer: Mara Lesemann

Historical Note:
*An autonomous component of the Associated Actors and
Artistes of America, which chartered it in 1938. Founded
in 1937 as Italian Actors Union; assumed its current name
in 1998. GIAA's mission is to promote positive images of
Italian Americans in the mass media and popular culture
whenever possible while keeping the Italian American
community and general public informed that actors must
sometimes accept stereotypical roles in order to "earn a
living" in a tough industry. Membership: $350/year.*

Publications:
GIAA Newsletter

Guild of Natural Science Illustrators (1968)
Ben Franklin Stn.
P.O. Box 652
Washington, DC 20044-0652
Tel: (301) 309-1514 *Fax:* (301) 309-1514
E-Mail: gnsihome@his.com
Website: gnsi.org
Members: 1000 individuals
Staff: 6
Annual Budget: $100-250,000
Tax: 501(c)(3)

Personnel:
Contact, Conventions: Kristie Bruzenak
Director, New Media: Emily Coren
   E-Mail: emilycoren@gmail.com
Secretary, Membership Services: Marlene Hill Donnelly
   E-Mail: marlenehill.donnelly@gmail.com
Webdeveloper: Britt Griswold
Director, Communications: Gail Guth
   E-Mail: guth-gnsi@comcast.net
Director, Education: Marie Metz
   E-Mail: marie.metz@ars.usda.gov

Historical Note:
*Originally formed by illustrators at the Smithsonian
Institution. Mission is to maintain and encourage standards
of competence and professional ethics by increasing
communication among its members, and assisting others
who are preparing to enter the profession. Membership: $85
(Professional); $75 (Electronic Professional).*

Meetings/Conferences: Biennial
Number of non-conference events/year: 2

Publications:
GNSI Journal; quarterly
GNSI Newsletter; monthly
Journal of Natural Science Illustration; annually
Membership Directory; on-line

Membership List Available to Non-members

Guitar and Accessories Marketing Association (1935)
875 W. 181st St.
Suite 2D
New York, NY 10033
Tel: (212) 795-3630 *Fax:* (347) 862-9238
E-Mail: assnhdqs@earthlink.net
Website: discoverguitar.com
Members: 46 companies
Staff: 2
Annual Budget: $100-250,000

Personnel:
Executive Director: Robert Sulkow

Historical Note:
*Established as the National Association of Musical
Merchandise Manufacturers, became the Guitar and
Accessory Manufacturers of America in 1963 and the
Guitar and Accessories Music Marketing Association in
1982 and assumed its present name in 1992. GAMA works
to expand the guitar industry. Members are distributors
of domestic fretted instruments and allied accessories.
Membership: $250-500/year (Regular).*

Membership List Available to Non-members

Gynecologic Oncology Group (1970)
Four Penn Center, 1600 John F. Kennedy Blvd.
Suite 1020
Philadelphia, PA 19103-2800
Tel: (215) 854-0770 *Fax:* (215) 854-0716
TollFree: (800) 225-3053
Website: gog.org
Members: 54 institutions
Staff: 32
Annual Budget: $25-50,000,000

Personnel:
Membership Administrator: Tivona McGlotten
   E-Mail: membership@gog.org
Manager, Development: Kathy Shumaker
   E-Mail: kshumaker@gog.org

Historical Note:
*The purpose of GOG is to promote quality and integrity
of clinical and basic scientific research in the field of
Gynecologic malignancies.*

Meetings/Conferences: Semi-Annual
2013 - San Diego, CA (Manchester Grand Hyatt San
   Diego)/Jan. 24 - 27
2013 - San Antonio, TX (San Antonio Marriott
   Rivercenter)/July 19 - 21
2014 - San Diego, CA (Manchester Grand Hyatt San
   Diego)/Jan. 23 - 26
2014 - Chicago, IL (Hyatt Regency)/July 18 - 20
2015 - San Diego, CA (Manchester Grand Hyatt San
   Diego)/Jan. 22 - 25
2015 - Denver, CO (Sheraton Hotel)/July 15 - 19

Publications:
The GOG Newsletter; semi-annually

Gypsum Association (1930)
6525 Belcrest Rd.
Suite 480
Hyattsville, MD 20782
Tel: (301) 277-8686 *Fax:* (301) 277-8747
E-Mail: info@gypsum.org
Website: gypsum.org
Members: 9 companies
Staff: 6
Annual Budget: $1-2,000,000
Tax: 501(c)(6)

Personnel:
Executive Director and Chief Executive Officer: Michael A.
   Gardner
   E-Mail: mgardner@gypsum.org

Historical Note:
*GA's mission is to promote the use of gypsum while
advancing the developmental growth and general welfare of
the gypsum industry in the United States and Canada on
behalf of its member companies. It also provides technical
information and assistance to the construction industry
and code enforcement community regarding gypsum board.
Members are U.S. and Canadian manufacturers of gypsum
board products.*

Continuing Education:
Enrollment: 1

Publications:
Chapter 25 – Board Talk Newsletter; on-line
Gypsumation

Halogenated Solvents Industry Alliance *(1980)*
1530 Wilson Blvd.
Suite 690
Arlington, VA 22209
Tel: (703) 875-0683 *Fax:* (703) 875-0675
E-Mail: info@hsia.org
Website: hsia.org
Members: 25 companies
Staff: 2
Annual Budget: $500-1,000,000
Tax: 501(c)(6)

Personnel:
Executive Director: Faye Graul
    E-Mail: fgraul@hsia.org
Director, Scientific Programs: Dr. Paul Dugard
    E-Mail: pdugard@hsia.org

Historical Note:
HSIA is dedicated to serving the interests of the halogenated solvents industry - interests that include solvent equipment manufacturers, and producers, distributors, and commercial users of halogenated solvents. HSIA members are producers, users, distributors and equipment manufacturers for chlorinated solvents. Membership: $100 (Solvent User/Product Formulator/Trade Association); $200 (Solvent Distributor or Recycler/Industry Consultant); $500 (Equipment Manufacturer).

Meetings/Conferences:
Conference Chair: Dr. Paul Dugard

Publications:
Membership Directory; on-line

Halon Alternatives Research Corporation *(1989)*
1001 19th St. North
Suite 1200
Arlington, VA 22209
Tel: (571) 384-7914 *Fax:* (571) 384-7959
E-Mail: harc@harc.org
Website: harc.org
Members: 50 companies
Staff: 1
Annual Budget: $100-250,000

Personnel:
Executive Director: Thomas A. Cortina
    E-Mail: cortinaec@cox.net

Historical Note:
A trade association representing producers, distributors, users of halons, and others with an interest in finding replacement agents. Membership: $7,500 (Voting); $2,500 (General).

Publications:
HARC News - Newsletter

Hand Tools Institute *(1935)*
25 N. Broadway
Tarrytown, NY 10591-3201
Tel: (914) 332-0040 *Fax:* (914) 332-1541
E-Mail: HTI@HTI.org
Website: HTI.org
Members: 60 companies
Staff: 3
Annual Budget: $250-500,000
Tax: 501(c)(6)

Personnel:
Executive Director: Richard C. Byrne

Historical Note:
Absorbed the Vise Manufacturers Association in 1969. Formerly (1973) Service Tools Institute. The Hand Tools Institute (HTI) is the trade association of North American manufacturers of non-powered hand tools and tool boxes. The objectives of the Institute are to promote and further the interests of its members relative to manufacturing, safety, standardization, international trade and government relations.

Publications:
Member Directory

The Handcrafted Soapmakers Guild *(1998)*
178 Elm St.
Saratoga Springs, NY 12866
Tel: (518) 306-6934 *Fax:* (518) 306-6935
TollFree: (866) 900-7627
Website: soapguild.org
Staff: 2
Annual Budget: $500-1,000,000
Tax: 501(c)(6)

Personnel:
Executive Director: Leigh O'Donnell

E-Mail: executivedirector@soapguild.org
Secretary: Barb De Los Santos
    E-Mail: BarbD@soapguild.org

Historical Note:
Trade association for handcrafted soapmakers. HSMG's mission is to promote the handcrafted soap industry; to act as a center of communication among soapmakers; and to circulate information beneficial to soapmakers. Members are soapmakers who make handcrafted soap and vendors who provide them with products and/or services. Membership: $80 (Associate); $500 (Professional); $100 (International/ Retired); $500-3,000 (Vendors and Suppliers); $100-500 (Benefactor).

Continuing Education:
Certification Designation/s: CS

Meetings/Conferences: Annual
2013 - Raleigh, NC (Hilton North Raleigh)/May 17 - 19

Publications:
Member Update eNews
Vendor Specials eNews; monthly

Handweavers Guild of America, Inc. *(1969)*
1255 Buford Hwy.
Suite 211
Suwanee, GA 30024
Tel: (678) 730-0010 *Fax:* (678) 730-0836
E-Mail: hga@weavespindye.org
Website: weavespindye.org
Members: 9000 individuals
Staff: 10
Annual Budget: $1-2,000,000
Tax: 501(c)(3)

Personnel:
Executive Director and Editor-in-Chief: Sandra Bowles
    E-Mail: executivedirector@weavespindye.org
Coordinator, Membership Services: Linda Campbell
    E-Mail: membership@weavespindye.org
Manager, Advertising: Dorothy Holt
    E-Mail: advertising@weavespindye.org
Eshop Manager: Judith P. Krone
    E-Mail: hgajudithk@weavespindye.org

Historical Note:
HGA's mission is to inspire creativity and encourage excellence in the fiber arts. Membership: $50 (Affiliate/ Family); $40 (Individual); $25 (Full-time Student).

Continuing Education:
Enrollment: 30
Certification Designation/s: COE

Meetings/Conferences: Biennial

Publications:
HGA Newsletter
Shuttle Spindle & Dyepot; quarterly; adv.

Membership List Available to Non-members

Hardwood Federation *(2004)*
1111 19th St. NW
Suite 800
Washington, DC 20036
Tel: (202) 463-2705 *Fax:* (202) 463-4702
E-Mail: b.ward@hardwoodfederation.com
Website: hardwoodfederation.net
Staff: 3
Annual Budget: $250-500,000

Personnel:
Executive Director: Dana Lee Cole
    E-Mail: deb.hawkinson@hardwoodfederation.com

Historical Note:
Non-profit trade association. The Hardwood Federation is the DC-based hardwood industry trade association, representing thousands of hardwood businesses and acting as the industry's advocacy voice on Capitol Hill. The Federation's mission is to Promote and represent the common business interests of and improve business conditions among members of the hardwood industry.

Publications:
HF Newsletter; monthly

Hardwood Manufacturers Association *(1935)*
665 Rodi Rd.
Suite 305
Pittsburgh, PA 15235
Tel: (412) 244-0440 *Fax:* (412) 244-9090
E-Mail: info@hardwood.org
Website: hmamembers.org
Members: 156 individuals
Staff: 4
Annual Budget: $500-1,000,000

Tax: 501(c)(6)

Personnel:
Director, Operations: Linda Jovanovich
    E-Mail: ljovanovich@hardwood.org
Contact, Conferences: Carol Belcher
    E-Mail: cbelcher@hardwood.org
Contact, Communications: Darleen Licina-Tubbs
    E-Mail: darleen@hardwood.org

Historical Note:
Formerly Southern Hardwood Producers Inc. and Southern Hardwood Lumber Manufacturers Association. Assumed present name in 1984. Southern Cypress Manufacturers Association is a division of HMA. HMA provides member companies with peer networks, state-of-the-art information, 21st Century management tools and far-reaching American hardwood encouraging campaigns.

Continuing Education:
Certification Designation/s: LEED

Meetings/Conferences: Annual
Conference Chair: Carol Belcher
2013 - Charleston, SC (Charleston Place Hotel)/March 11 - 13

Publications:
Buyers Guide and Directory; annually
HMA Link; monthly

Hardwood Plywood and Veneer Association *(1921)*
1825 Michael Faraday Dr.
Reston, VA 20190
Tel: (703) 435-2900 *Fax:* (703) 435-2537
E-Mail: hpva@hpva.org
Website: hpva.org
Members: 100 companies
Staff: 8
Annual Budget: $1-2,000,000
Tax: 501(c)(6)

Personnel:
President: Kip Howlett
    E-Mail: khowlett@hpva.org
Office Manager: Eva Mentel
    E-Mail: ementel@hpva.org
Director, Testing and Certification Programs: Brian Sause
    E-Mail: bsause@hpva.org
Manager, Membership Services and Conventions: Ketti Tyree
    E-Mail: ketti@hpva.org

Historical Note:
Established in Chicago as the Plywood Manufacturers Association and formerly known as the Plywood Manufacturing Institute, (1964) Hardwood Plywood Institute, and (1992) Hardwood Plywood Manufacturers Association, absorbed the Southern Plywood Manufacturers Association in 1953 and Fine Hardwood Veneer Association in 1998. HPVA's mission is to promote and support the use of quality, environmentally sound, decorative wood products manufactured in North America. Membership: varies, depending on sales.

Meetings/Conferences: Annual
Conference Chair: Ketti Tyree

Publications:
American National Standard for Hardwood & Decorative Plywood
Hardwood Plywood & Veneer News; weekly; adv.
Member Roster; on-line
Where to Buy Hardwood Plywood and Veneer; annually; adv.

Membership List Available to Non-members

Harness Horsemen International *(2002)*
64 State Route 33
Manalapan, NJ 07726-8301
Tel: (732) 683-1580 *Fax:* (732) 683-1578
Website: harnesslink.com
Members:
23 associations
40000 individuals
Staff: 2
Annual Budget: $10-25,000

Personnel:
President: Dominic H. Frinzi

Historical Note:
HHI represents owners, trainers, and drivers of standardbred racehorses working in the U. S. and Canada.

Harness Tracks of America *(1954)*
12025 E. Dry Gulch Pl.

Tucson, AZ 85749
Tel: (520) 529-2525 Fax: (520) 529-3235
E-Mail: info@harnesstracks.com
Website: harnesstracks.com
Members: 44 pari-mutuel harness tracks
Staff: 5
Annual Budget: $500-1,000,000

Personnel:
Executive Vice President and General Counsel: Paul J.
Estok
E-Mail: paul.estok@azbar.org
Manager, Web Development and Information Services: Jen
Foley
E-Mail: jen@harnesstracks.com
Controller: Bente Jensen

Historical Note:
HTA's mission is to obtain their economic objectives by
promoting live racing, enhancing and preserving the
integrity and image of the sport, and providing information
to members and the general public about the sport and the
significant economic impact of the industry.

Meetings/Conferences: Annual

Publications:
Membership Directory; on-line; adv.

The Harvey Society (1905)
540 First Ave.
New York, NY 10016
Tel: (212) 263-1031
Website: harveysociety.org
Members: 1700 individuals
Staff: 3
Annual Budget: $25-50,000

Personnel:
President: Ruth Lehmann PhD
Treasurer: Jessica E Treisman PhD
E-Mail: jessica.treisman@med.nyu.edu

Historical Note:
The Harvey Society sponsors a series of seven lectures
annually that are open to the public and are attended by
hundreds of scientists from New York City and environs.
The stated purpose of the Society was to forge a closer
relationship between the purely practical side of medicine
and the results of laboratory investigation.

Health and Sciences Communications Association
(1959)
P.O. Box 31323
Omaha, NE 68132
Tel: (402) 915-5373
E-Mail: hesca@hesca.org
Website: hesca.net
Members:
80 institutions
250 individuals
Staff: 2
Annual Budget: $50-100,000
Tax: 501(c)(3)

Personnel:
President: Jim Huff
E-Mail: jim.huff@ucdenver.edu
Chief Fiscal Officer: Chuck Lenosky
E-Mail: clenosky@creighton.edu

Historical Note:
HeSCA seeks to advance an international community of
professionals dedicated to promoting excellence in health
and science communications through leadership, education,
and the application of technology. Members are biomedical
scientists and health science practitioners. Membership:
$150 (Individual); $300 (Organizational Lead member);
$75 (Student); $90 (Retired); $1000 (Sustaining); $100
(Organizational Additional Member); $0.00 (Organizational
Non-Lead Member).

Meetings/Conferences: Annual

Publications:
Feedback
Journal of Biocommunication
Membership Directory; on-line

Membership List Available to Non-members

Health Care Administrators Association (1980)
1011 S.W. Emkay Dr.
Suite 209
Bend, OR 97702
Tel: (541) 312-8512
E-Mail: hcaainfo@hcaa.org
Website: hcaa.org

Members: 10 Companies
Staff: 3
Annual Budget: $500-1,000,000

Personnel:
President and Chief Executive Officer: Carolyn Jarschke
E-Mail: carolynj@qvirisk.com

Historical Note:
Formerly, Independent Administrators Association. HCAA's
mission is to improve the quality and cost effectiveness
of health care administration by promoting education,
information and the exchange of ideas. Members include
TPAs, insurance carriers, managing general underwriters,
audit firms, physician hospital organizations, broker/
agents, human resource managers and health care
consultants. Membership: $500/year.

Continuing Education:
Certification Designation/s: CSFS

Meetings/Conferences: Semi-Annual
2013 - Las Vegas, NV (Caesars Palace)/Feb. 5 - 7
2013 - Anaheim, CA (Disney's Grand Californian Hotel
and Spa)/July 10 - 12

Publications:
HCAA Newsletter; quarterly; adv.
HCAA Reports; bi-monthly; adv.

Health Care Compliance Association (1996)
6500 Barrie Rd.
Suite 250
Minneapolis, MN 55435
Tel: (952) 988-0141 Fax: (952) 988-0146
TollFree: (888) 580-8373
E-Mail: info@hcca-info.org
Website: hcca-info.org
Members: 6500 members
Staff: 26
Annual Budget: $25-50,000,000
Tax: 501(c)(6)

Personnel:
Chief Executive Officer: Roy Snell
E-Mail: roy.snell@hcca-info.org
Manager, IT Graphics: Gary DeVaan
Director, Communications and Editor: Margaret Dragon
Director, Conferences and Exhibits: Darin Dvorak
E-Mail: darin.dvorak@hcca-info.org
Director, Human Resource and Compliance Officer: Wilma
Eisenman
Managing Editor: Nancy L. Gordon
Associate Database Administrator: Patti Hoskin
E-Mail: patti.hoskin@hcca-info.org
Certification Specialist: Meg Kosowski
Chief Financial Officer: Charlie Thiem
Vice President, Membership Development: Adam
Turteltaub

Historical Note:
HCCA works to champion ethical practice and compliance
standards and to provide the necessary resources for ethics
and compliance professionals and others who share these
principles. Membership: $295 (Individual); $250 (Group);
$2,500 (Corporate); $150 (Student).

Continuing Education:
Certification Designation/s: CHRC, CHC-F, CHC, CHPC

Meetings/Conferences:
Conference Chair: Darin Dvorak
2013 - Ft. Washington, MD (Gaylord National Hotel
and Convention Center)/April 21 - 24
Number of non-conference events/year: 13

Publications:
Compliance Today; monthly
This Week In Corporate Compliance; weekly

Health Care Education Association
P.O. Box 182495
Columbus, OH 43218-2495
Tel: (614) 293-3191 Fax: (614) 293-3690
E-Mail: HCEAadmin@hcea-info.org
Website: hcea-info.org
Members: 400 individuals
Staff: 4
Tax: 501(c)(6)

Personnel:
President: Diane Moyer RN, MS
E-Mail: diane.moyer@osumc.edu

Historical Note:
Health Care Education Association (HCEA) supports and
mentors health care educators on small and large staffs,
and in rural and metropolitan settings. OHCEA provides
to a learning community for professionals committed to

improving health care and the organizations they serve
through education. Membership: $95/year (Individual);
$45/year (Student); $250/year (Patron); $1500 (Platinum
Corporate Member); $1000 (Gold Corporate Member);
$500(Silver Corporate Member).

Meetings/Conferences: Annual
Conference Chair: Wayne Neal

Publications:
HCEA Newsletter; monthly; adv.
Member Directory; on-line

Health Forum (1927)
155 N. Wacker Dr.
Suite 400
Chicago, IL 60606
Tel: (312) 893-6800 Fax: (312) 422-4500
TollFree: (800) 821-2039
Website: healthforum.com
Members: 1300 organizations and individuals
Staff: 10
Annual Budget: $5-10,000,000

Personnel:
President: Neil J. Jesuele
E-Mail: njesuele@aha.org
Editorial Director, Publication: Mary Grayson
E-Mail: mgrayson@healthforum.com
Chief Operating and Development Officer: Amy Mosser
Executive Director, Coding and Data Development:
Christine Remedios
E-Mail: cremedios@healthforum.com
Executive Director, Sales: Jerry Stoeckigt
E-Mail: jstoeckigt@healthforum.com
Executive Director, Education Programs: Laura Woodburn
E-Mail: lwoodburn@healthforum.com

Historical Note:
Founded as Association of Western Hospitals; later became
the Healthcare Forum. Absorbed the publishing and
data/information services divisions of American Hospital
Association and assumed its current name in 1998. HF
is a provider of executive education and applied research
for healthcare leaders. Mission is to enhance the capacity
of health care leaders to improve community health and
business performance. Membership: $500 (Individual);
$1,600 (Organization).

Meetings/Conferences:
2013 - Phoenix, AZ (Pointe Hilton Tapation Cliffs
Resort)/Feb. 10 - 13
2013 - San Diego, CA/July 25 - 28

Publications:
AHA News Now (afternoon news bulletin); daily; adv.
H&HN Daily; daily
Health Facilities Management; adv.
Trustee; adv.

Health Industry Business Communications
Council (1983)
2525 E. Arizona Biltmore Cir.
Suite 127
Phoenix, AZ 85016
Tel: (602) 381-1091 Fax: (602) 381-1093
E-Mail: info@hibcc.org
Website: hibcc.org
Members: 900 individuals and 300 companies
Staff: 7
Annual Budget: $1-2,000,000

Personnel:
President and Chief Executive Officer: Robert A. Hankin
PhD

Historical Note:
HIBCC is an industry-sponsored and supported nonprofit
organization. As an ANSI-accredited organization, mission
is to facilitate electronic communications by developing
appropriate standards for information exchange among
all health care trading partners. Membership: $150
(Corresponding-Individual); $2,500 (Organization).

Meetings/Conferences: Annual

Health Industry Distributors Association (1902)
310 Montgomery St.
Alexandria, VA 22314-1516
Tel: (703) 549-4432 Fax: (703) 549-6495
Website: hida.org
Members: 185 companies
Staff: 29
Annual Budget: $2-5,000,000
Tax: 501(c)(6)

Personnel:

President and Chief Executive Officer: Matthew Rowan
  E-Mail: rowan@hida.org
Senior Manager, Database and Information Services:
  Deirdre Brooks
  E-Mail: brooks@hida.org
Director, Marketing: Danielle Danko
  E-Mail: danko@hida.org
Senior Business Intelligence Analyst: Jennifer Doyle
  E-Mail: doyle@hida.org
Executive Vice President: Ian Fardy
  E-Mail: fardy@hida.org
Director, Policy and Research: Ashley Fishburn
  E-Mail: fishburn@hida.org
Senior Manager, Web Content and Marketing: Erin
  Hildreth
  E-Mail: hildreth@hida.org
Senior Vice President and Executive Director, HIDA
  Educational Foundation: Elizabeth B Hilla
  E-Mail: hilla@hida.org
Vice President, Finance and Operations: Lisa Queeney
  E-Mail: queeney@hida.org
Director, Trade Show and Sponsorships: Jessica Welch
  Shea
  E-Mail: welch@hida.org
Vice President, Policy and Research: Andrew Van Ostrand
  E-Mail: vanostrand@hida.org

Historical Note:
HIDA is dedicated to advancing the use and value of
distribution in healthcare. Members are medical products
distributors. Membership: $683-24,761 (Distributor, based
on annual sales); $5,800-25,800 (Manufacturer Associate
Program).

Continuing Education:
Certification Designation/s: AMS

Meetings/Conferences: Annual
Conference Chair: Jessica Welch Shea
2013 - Washington, DC (Gaylord National-
  Washington)/Sept. 25 - 27
2014 - Chicago, IL (Navy Pier Park)/Sept. 17 - 19
2015 - Grapevine, TX (Gaylord Texan Hotel and
  Convention Center, Dallas Texas)/Sept. 9 - 11
Number of non-conference events/year: 4

Publications:
e-Newsletter; daily
HIDA Executive Briefing; quarterly

Health Industry Representatives Association
(1978)
Eight The Meadows
Newnan, GA 30265
Tel: (303) 756-8115 Fax: (770) 683-4648
E-Mail: healthreps@comcast.net
Website: hira.org
Members: 250 companies and associates
Staff: 2
Annual Budget: $100-250,000
Tax: 501(c)(6)

Personnel:
Executive Administrator: Shannon Reddish
  E-Mail: hira@hira.org

Historical Note:
Formerly (1985) Health Associated Representatives, HIRA's
mission is to focuse on promoting the manufacturers'
representatives function within the health care industry.
Membership: $495(Allied/Service Provider); $325
(Representative).

Continuing Education:
Certification Designation/s: CPMR

Meetings/Conferences: Annual

Publications:
HIRA Membership Directory; annually

Health Information Trust Alliance (HITRUST)
6136 Frisco Square Blvd.
Suite 327
Frisco, TX 75034
Tel: (972) 330-4900 Fax: (972) 330-4901
E-Mail: info@HITRUSTalliance.net
Website: hitrustalliance.net
Staff: 3

Personnel:
Chief Executive Officer: Daniel Nutkis
Chief Information Security Officer: Dr. Bryan Cline
Director, Marketing and Corporate Communications: Mary
  Hall

Historical Note:

CSF is an information security framework that harmonizes
the requirements of existing standards and regulations,
including federal (HIPAA, HITECH), third party (PCI,
COBIT) and government (NIST, FTC). As a framework, the
CSF provides organizations with the needed structure, detail
and clarity relating to information security tailored to the
healthcare industry.

Meetings/Conferences: Annual
2013 - Grapevine, TX (Gaylord Texan Resort)/May 20
  - 22

Membership List Available to Non-members

Health Ministries Association (1989)
P.O. Box 60042
Dayton, OH 45406
Tel: (937) 558-0453 Fax: (937) 558-0453
TollFree: (800) 723-4291
E-Mail: info@hmassoc.org
Website: hmassoc.org
Members: 1300 individuals
Staff: 5
Annual Budget: $50-100,000
Tax: 501(c)(3)

Personnel:
President: Marlene Feagan BSN, MA, RN
  E-Mail: marlene.feagan@stelizabeth.com
Director, Public Relations: Sharon Becker
  E-Mail: sbecker@gshdayton.org
Director, Practice and Education: Alyson Breisch
  E-Mail: alyson.breisch@gmail.com
Chief Financial Officer and Treasurer: Craig R. Schneider
  E-Mail: CRSchnei@gshdayton.org

Historical Note:
HMA's mission is to encourage, support and empowers
leaders in the integration of faith and health in their local
communities. Membership: $105 (Active); $500 (Lifetime);
$70 (Student/Retiree).

Meetings/Conferences: Annual
2013 - Zephyr Cove, NV (Zephyr Point Presbyterian
  Conference Center)/June 10 - 12

Publications:
HMA Journal; adv.
HMA Today; monthly; adv.

Membership List Available to Non-members

Health Occupations Students of America (1976)
5555 Center Dr. Floor 2
Bay Lake, FL 32830
E-Mail: hosa@hosa.org
Website: hosa.org
Members:
120000 Individuals
6000 Students
Staff: 1
Annual Budget: $2-5,000,000

Personnel:
Chairman: Lowell Doringo
  E-Mail: ldoringo79@aol.com

Historical Note:
HOSA's Mission is to promote career opportunities in the
health care industry and to enhance the delivery of quality
health care to all people. Membership: $150 (Lifetime).

Meetings/Conferences: Annual
2013 - Nashville, TN (Gaylord Opryland Hotel)/June
  26 - 30
2014 - Orlando, FL (Disney's Coronado Springs
  Resort)/June 25 - 28
2015 - Anaheim, CA (Hilton Anaheim)/June 24 - 27
2016 - Nashville, TN (Gaylord Opryland Hotel)/June
  22 - 25

Publications:
Electronic Bulletin Boards; on-line
HOSA E-Magazine; on-line
HOSA E-Newsletter; on-line

Health Physics Society (1956)
1313 Dolley Madison Blvd.
Suite 402
McLean, VA 22101-3926
Tel: (703) 790-1745 Fax: (703) 790-2672
E-Mail: hps@burkinc.com
Website: hps.org
Members: 7000 individuals
Staff: 12
Annual Budget: $2-5,000,000
Tax: 501(c)(6)

Personnel:
President: Kathryn H. Pryor
Executive Secretary: Richard "Brett" J. Burk Jr.
Editor-in-Chief: Michael T. Ryan PhD CHP
  E-Mail: HPEditor@burkinc.com
Contact, Communications: Sandra White
  E-Mail: swhite@burkinc.com

Historical Note:
Fosters the protection of humankind and the environment
from radiation. HPS's mission is to support its members
in the practice of their profession and to promote the
science and practice of radiation safety. Affiliated with the
International Radiation Protection Association. Membership:
$0-4,700/year.

Meetings/Conferences: Semi-Annual
2013 - Scottsdale, AZ (Doubletree Paradise Valley
  Resort)/Jan. 27 - 30
2013 - Madison, WI/June 7 - 11
2013 - Madison, WI/July 7 - 11
Number of non-conference events/year: 3

Publications:
Health Physics Journal; monthly; adv.
Health Physics News; monthly; adv.
Members Directory; on-line
Operational Radiation Safety; quarterly

Healthcare Billing and Management Association
(1993)
1540 S. Coast Hwy.
Suite 203
Laguna Beach, CA 92651
Fax: (949) 376-3456
TollFree: (877) 640-4262
E-Mail: info@hbma.com
Website: hbma.org
Members: 500 individuals
Staff: 12
Annual Budget: $1-2,000,000

Personnel:
Executive Director: Bradley J. Lund
  E-Mail: brad@hbma.org
Editor: Madelon I. Berger
  E-Mail: editor@hbma.org
Associate Director, Administration and Governance:
  Michelle Botana
  E-Mail: michelle@hbma.org
Contact, Public Relations: Fran Cashen
  E-Mail: fran@hbma.org
Contact, Website and Database Management: Kris
  Cvikota
  E-Mail: kris@webteam.net
Director, Government Affairs: William A. Finerfrock
  E-Mail: bf@capitolassociates.com
Director, Education: Paul Myers
  E-Mail: paul@hbma.org
Associate Director, Finance, Certification and Membership:
  Cindy Rounds
  E-Mail: cindy@hbma.org
Director, Conference and Manager, Meetings: Gail
  Sunshine CMP
  E-Mail: gail.sunshine@hbma.org
Legal Counsel: James Wieland
  E-Mail: jbwieland@ober.com

Historical Note:
Founded as International Billing Association; assumed
its current name in 1998. HBMA's mission is to enhance
the professional image of the healthcare billing industry,
educate members, foster cooperation and networking
among HBMA members. Membership: $170 (Associate);
$1010 (Affiliate/Vendor Affiliates); $280 (Satellite Office
Member); Free (Honorary Member); $495- 1460 (Principal
Membership, based on no. of Employees).

Continuing Education:
Certification Designation/s: CHBME

Meetings/Conferences:
Conference Chair: Gail Sunshine CMP
2013 - Costa Mesa, CA (The Westin, South Coast
  Plaza)/March 5 - 7
2013 - Orlando, FL (Walt Disney Swan and Dolphin)/
  April 17 - 19
Number of non-conference events/year: 2

Publications:
Billing Newsletter
Membership Directory; on-line

Healthcare Compliance Packaging Council (1990)
22711 Buford Rd.

Suit 268
Bon Air, VA 23235-2423
Tel: (804) 338-5778 *Fax:* (888) 812-4272
Website: hcpconline.org
Members: 80 corporations and individuals
Staff: 2
Annual Budget: $250-500,000
Tax: 501(c)(3)

Personnel:
Executive Director: Walter Berghahn
    E-Mail: walterberghahn@yahoo.com
Director, Communications: Victoria Welch

Historical Note:
HCPC strives to inform and educate consumers, health professionals and policy makers about the role that compliance-prompting packaging can play in improving pharmaceutical adherence. Members are companies and individuals in the pharmaceutical packaging industry with an interest in promoting compliance packaging. Membership: $6,000 (Full Member); $3,000 (Associate/ Non-Voting).

Meetings/Conferences: Annual
2013 - Rosemont, IL (Sofitel Hotel)/April 1 - 2
2014 - Las Vegas, NV (Texas Station)/May 1 - 2
2015 - Milan, Italy (New Exhibition Center Fiera
    Milano)/May 19 - 21

Publications:
Membership Directory; on-line; adv.
Unit-Dose Alert; quarterly; adv.

Healthcare Convention and Exhibitors Association
(1930)
1100 Johnson Ferry Rd.
Suite 300
Atlanta, GA 30342
Tel: (404) 252-3663 *Fax:* (404) 252-0774
E-Mail: hcea@kellencompany.com
Website: hcea.org
Members: 600 companies
Staff: 7
Annual Budget: $1-2,000,000

Personnel:
Executive Director: Frank R. Skinner
    E-Mail: fskinner@kellencompany.com
Manager, Membership Relations: Steve Gigantiello
    E-Mail: sgigantiello@kellencompany.com
Manager, Meetings: Sean Hewitt CMP
    E-Mail: shewitt@kellencompany.com
Director, Content and Education: Jennifer Palcher-
    Silliman
    E-Mail: jpalcher@kellencompany.com

Historical Note:
Formerly (1973) Medical Exhibitors Association and (1990) Health Care Exhibitors Association. HCEA is dedicated to improve the effectiveness and quality of all healthcare conventions and congresses, medical meetings and healthcare exhibit marketing throughout the industry. Members are healthcare exhibitors, medical associations and suppliers. Membership: $595 (Regular); $299-595 (Associate); $695 (Supporting).

Meetings/Conferences: Annual
Conference Chair: Sean Hewitt CMP
2013 - Austin, TX (Hilton Hotel and Austin Convention
    Center)/June 22 - 25
Number of non-conference events/year: 1

Publications:
Directory of Healthcare Meetings/Conventions;
    annually; adv.
HCEA Edge e-Newsletter; monthly; adv.
HCEA Online Directory; on-line
Membership Directory; on-line

Healthcare Distribution Management Association
(1876)
901 N. Glebe Rd.
Suite 1000
Arlington, VA 22203
Tel: (703) 787-0000 *Fax:* (703) 812-5282
Website: healthcaredistribution.org
Members: 400 companies
Staff: 43
Annual Budget: $10-25,000,000
Tax: 501(c)(6)

Personnel:
President and Chief Executive Officer: John M. Gray
    E-Mail: jgray@hdmanet.org

Senior Director, Administration and Human Resources:
    Linda Caporaletti – Hoyt
Director, Marketing and Creative Services: Mary T.
    Coppola
Senior Director, Finance: Lonna DeBardi
*Senior Vice President, Industry Relations, Membership and
    Education:* Perry Fri
Director, Membership Services: Lisa M. Gallagher
    E-Mail: lgallagher@hdmanet.org
Vice President, Government Affairs and General Counsel:
    Elizabeth A. Gallenagh
    E-Mail: egallenagh@hdmanet.org
Director, Research and Information Services: Susan R.
    Heffner
    E-Mail: sheffner@hdmanet.org
Senior Vice President, Government Affairs: Patrick Kelly
Director, Education: Tirza N. Lofgreen
    E-Mail: tniemann@hdmanet.org
Vice President, Meetings and Conferences: Brooke N.
    Naylor
    E-Mail: bnaylor@hdmanet.org
*Vice President, Information Technology Services and
    Facilities Management:* Ted J. Pezzullo
    E-Mail: tpezzullo@hdmanet.org
Manager, Communications: Farah M. Qureshi
Publications Coordinator and Office Services Administrator:
    Heidi J. Rohrbach

Historical Note:
Established as the Western Wholesale Druggists, became National Wholesale Druggists' Association in 1881 and assumed its present name in 2002. HDMA works to protect patient safety and access to medicines through the safe and efficient distribution of healthcare products and services. Membership: $7,500 (Allied); $1,100 (International); $6000 (HBW Associate); Active membership fee varies, based on sales volume.

Meetings/Conferences: Annual
Conference Chair: Brooke N. Naylor
2013 - Tampa, FL (Tampa Marriott Waterside Hotel)/
    March 3 - 6
Number of non-conference events/year: 3

Publications:
HDMA Directory; on-line; adv.
The Weekly Digest; weekly; adv.

Healthcare Financial Management Association
(1946)
Three Westbrook Corporate Center
Suite 600
Westchester, IL 60154-5700
Tel: (708) 531-9600 *Fax:* (708) 531-0032
TollFree: (800) 252-4362
Website: hfma.org
Members: 39000 members
Staff: 80
Annual Budget: $10-25,000,000
Tax: 501(c)(6)

Personnel:
President and Chief Executive Officer: Joseph J. Fifer
Senior Editor: Carole Bolster
    E-Mail: cbolster@hfma.org
Vice President, Human Resources and Chapter Relations:
    Susan Brenkus
    E-Mail: sbrenkus@hfma.org
Director, Information Technology: Daniel Keck
Director, Marketing and Membership Services: Karen
    Metropulos
    E-Mail: kmetropulos@hfma.org
Vice President, Education: Diane Simmons
    E-Mail: dsimmons@hfma.org
Director, Membership Services: Lori Trusiak
    E-Mail: ltrusiak@hfma.org

Historical Note:
Formerly (1946) the American Association of Hospital Accountants and (1982) the Hospital Financial Management Association. HFMA's purpose is to define, realize, and advance the financial management of health care by helping members and others improve the business performance of organizations operating in or serving the healthcare field. Members are directly or indirectly associated with financial management in healthcare organizations. Membership: $50-100 (Faculty); $18-35 (Student); $67-284 (Regular).

Continuing Education:
Certification Designation/s: CHFP, HFMA, CRCR

Meetings/Conferences: Annual
2013 - Orlando, FL (Orange County Convention
    Center)/June 16 - 19

Number of non-conference events/year: 2

Publications:
HFMA Newsletter
e-Bulletin; on-line
hfm Magazine

Healthcare Information and Management Systems Society *(1961)*
33 W. Monroe St.
Suite 1700
Chicago, IL 60603-5616
Tel: (312) 664-4467 *Fax:* (312) 664-6143
E-Mail: advocacy@himss.org
Website: himss.org
Members: 23380 individuals and corporate
members
Staff: 70
Annual Budget: $50-100,000,000
Tax: 501(c)(6)

Personnel:
President and Chief Executive Officer: H. Stephen Lieber
    CAE
    E-Mail: slieber@himss.org
Vice President, Human Resources and Facilities Services:
    Brenda A. Duncan SPHR
    E-Mail: bduncan@himss.org
Senior Vice President and Chief Financial Officer: Dennis
    James
    E-Mail: djames@himss.org
Vice President, Professional Development: JoAnn W.
    Klinedinst CPHIMS, FHIMSS, PMP
    E-Mail: jklinedinst@himss.org
Senior Director, Information Technology: Jeremy Landfare
    E-Mail: jlandfare@himss.org
Director, Corporate Communications: Joyce A. Lofstrom
    E-Mail: jlofstrom@himss.org
Vice President, Meeting Services: Karen Malone
    E-Mail: kmalone@himss.org
Corporate Counsel: Racquel R. Orenick Esq.
    E-Mail: rorenick@himss.org
Executive Vice President and Chief Operating Officer: R.
    Norris Orms CAE, FACHE
    E-Mail: norms@himss.org
Vice President, Communications: Fran Perveiler
    E-Mail: fperveiler@himss.org
Vice President, Market Research: Lorren Pettit
    E-Mail: lpettit@himssanalytics.org
Senior Vice President and Chief Financial Officer: Marcia
    Zitowsky CPA, MSA
    E-Mail: mzitowsky@himss.org

Historical Note:
Formerly (1987) Hospital Management Systems Society. Absorbed CPRI- HOST, a health care information technology advocacy organization, in 2002. Mission is to serve healthcare transformation through the effective use of health information technology. HIMSS provides leadership for the optimal use of information technology (IT) and management systems for the betterment of healthcare. Membership: $160 (Individual); $30 (Online).

Continuing Education:
Certification Designation/s: CPHIMS

Meetings/Conferences: Semi-Annual
Conference Chair: Karen Malone
Number of non-conference events/year: 4

Publications:
Business Edge; monthly
Digital Office; monthly
Health IT Policy Update; weekly
HIELights; monthly
HIMSS Business Insider; monthly
HIMSS Clinical Informatics Insights; monthly
HIMSS Insider; monthly; adv.
HIMSS Weekly Insider; weekly
Journal of Healthcare Information Management (JHIM)
Membership Directory; on-line

Healthcare Leadership Council *(1990)*
750 Ninth St. NW
Suite 500
Washington, DC 20001
Tel: (202) 452-8700 *Fax:* (202) 296-9561
E-Mail: mfreeman@hlc.org
Website: hlc.org
Members: 50 individuals
Staff: 11
Annual Budget: $5-10,000,000
Tax: 501(c)(6)

Personnel:
Executive Vice President: Michael Freeman
 E-Mail: Mfreeman@hlc.org
President: Mary R. Grealy
 E-Mail: mgrealy@hlc.org
Senior Vice President: Tina Grande
 E-Mail: tgrande@hlc.org
Director, Government Relations: Amanda Uherek
 E-Mail: Auherek@hlc.org
Vice President, Finance and Administration: David
 Wiermanski
 E-Mail: dwiermanski@hlc.org

Historical Note:
Affiliated with the National Committee for Quality Healthcare, HLC aims to improve the affordability, innovation and quality of American health care. Members are physicians, health insurers, hospitals, pharmaceutical companies and medical technology firms.

Publications:
HLC Value Compendium

Healthcare Supply Chain Association (1990)
2025 M St. NW
Suite 800
Washington, DC 20036
Tel: (202) 367-1162 *Fax:* (202) 367-2162
E-Mail: info@supplychainassociation.org
Website: supplychainassociation.org
Members: 15 organizations
Staff: 11

Personnel:
President: Curtis Rooney
 E-Mail: crooney@higpa.org
Director, Operations: Mike Copps
 E-Mail: mcopps@higpa.org
Manager, Marketing and Communication: Kevin Hurley
Coordinator, Event Services: Jessica Klapstein
Accountant: Hannah Lawrence
Manager, Event Services: John Rubsamen
Coordinator, Education and Certification Services: Erica
 Weiss

Historical Note:
Formerly Health Industry Group Purchasing Association. HSCA works collaboratively with all legislative and regulatory authorities to insure fair procurement practices in an open and competitive market within the health industry. Members are organizations providing economies of scale to health care providers through group purchasing. Membership: $7,500-75,000/year (Varies based on sales).

Meetings/Conferences: Annual
Conference Chair: John Rubsamen
2013 - Washington, DC/Oct. 16 - 18

Publications:
eNews; daily
Membership Directory; on-line

Hearing Industries Association (1955)
1444 I St.
Suite 700
Washington, DC 20005
Tel: (202) 449-1090 *Fax:* (202) 216-9646
Website: hearing.org
Members: 34 companies
Staff: 4
Annual Budget: $1-2,000,000

Personnel:
Executive Director: Carole M. Rogin
 E-Mail: crogin@bostrom.com

Historical Note:
Formerly (1977) the Hearing Aid Industry Conference. HIA is the national trade association of manufacturers of hearing aids, assistive listening devices, component parts, and power sources.

Hearing Loss Association of America (1979)
7910 Woodmont Ave.
Suite 1200
Bethesda, MD 20814
Tel: (301) 657-2248 *Fax:* (301) 913-9413
E-Mail: info@hearingloss.org
Website: hearingloss.org
Staff: 20
Annual Budget: $1-2,000,000
Tax: 501(c)(3)

Personnel:
Executive Director: Brenda Battat
 E-Mail: battat@hearingloss.org

Contact, Membership and Information Technology: Kate
 Brasacchio
Business Manager: Teri Canniff
 E-Mail: tcanniff@hearingloss.org
Director, Public Policy: Lise Hamlin
 E-Mail: lhamin@hearingloss.org
Deputy Executive Director and Editor-in-Chief: Barbara
 Kelley
Director, Events and Marketing: Nancy Macklin
Coordinator, Financial Services: Sean Smith

Historical Note:
Formerly (1979) known as Self Help for Hard of Hearing People, the purpose of HLAA is to open the world of communication for people with hearing loss through information, education, advocacy and support. Membership: $35-45 (Individual); $20 (Student); $45-55 (Couple/Family); $60-75 (Professional); $50-75 (Non-Profit Organization and Libraries); $300-325 (Corporate).

Meetings/Conferences: Annual
Conference Chair: Nancy Macklin
2013 - Portland, OR (DoubleTree by Hilton)/June 27 - 30

Publications:
Hearing Loss Magazine; bi-monthly; adv.
HLAA E-News; on-line

Membership List Available to Non-members

Heart Failure Society of America (1994)
Court International - Suite 240 S
2550 University Ave W
St. Paul, MN 55114
Tel: (651) 642-1633 *Fax:* (651) 642-1502
E-Mail: info@hfsa.org
Website: hfsa.org
Staff: 5
Annual Budget: $2-5,000,000
Tax: 501(c)(3)

Personnel:
Chief Executive Officer: Michele Blair
 E-Mail: mblair@hfsa.org

Historical Note:
HFSA's mission is to provide a place for all those interested in heart function, heart failure research and patient care. The Society also serves as a resource for governmental agencies (FDA, NIH, NHLBI, CMS). Membership: $200-300 (Full); $75 (Trainee).

Meetings/Conferences: Annual
2013 - Orlando, FL (Peabody Orlando Hotel)/Sept. 22 - 25
2014 - Las Vegas, NV (Caesars Palace)/Sept. 14 - 17

Publications:
Heart Failure Society Newsletter; bi-annually
Membership Directory; on-line
The Journal of Cardiac Failure; monthly; adv.

Heart Rhythm Society (1979)
1400 K St. NW
Suite 500
Washington, DC 20005
Tel: (202) 464-3400 *Fax:* (202) 464-3401
E-Mail: info@hrsonline.org
Website: hrsonline.org
Members: 5400 physicians, scientists and
 associated professionals
Staff: 54
Annual Budget: $10-25,000,000

Personnel:
Chief Executive Officer: James H. Youngblood CAE
 E-Mail: jyoungblood@HRSonline.org
Vice President, Health Policy: Laura Blum
 E-Mail: lblum@hrsonline.org
Director, Human Resources: Dawn Godaire PHR
 E-Mail: dgodaire@HRSonline.org
*Vice President, Marketing, Communications and
 Membership Services:* Charlie Jones CAE
 E-Mail: cjones@hrsonline.org
Vice President, Education and Meeting Services: Cathy L.
 Scheck
 E-Mail: cscheck@HRSonline.org
Director, Membership Services: Jay Vegso
 E-Mail: jvegso@hrsonline.org
Director, Finance and Operations: Lisa Vienna
 E-Mail: lvienna@hrsonline.org

Historical Note:
Founded as the North American Society of Pacing and Electrophysiology; became Heart Rhythm Society in 2004. HRS's mission is to improve the care of patients

by promoting research, education and optimal healthcare policies and standards. Membership: $0-530/year.

Meetings/Conferences: Annual
Conference Chair: Cathy L. Scheck
2013 - Denver, CO (Colorado Convention Center)/May
 8 - 11
2014 - San Francisco, CA (Fairmont San Francisco)/
 May 7 - 10
2015 - Boston, MA (Boston Convention and Exhibition
 Center)/May 13 - 16

Publications:
HeartRhythm; monthly; adv.
Keeping Pace; weekly
Member Directory; on-line
Washington Reports

Hearth, Patio and Barbecue Association (2002)
1901 N. Moore St.
Suite 600
Arlington, VA 22209-2105
Tel: (703) 522-0086 *Fax:* (703) 522-0548
E-Mail: hpbamail@hpba.org
Website: hpba.org
Members: 2800 companies
Staff: 29
Annual Budget: $2-5,000,000
Tax: 501(c)(6)

Personnel:
President and Chief Executive Officer: Jack Goldman
 E-Mail: goldman@hpba.org
Director, Membership and Affiliate Relations: Jamie
 Beaulieu
 E-Mail: beaulieu@hpba.org
Director, Government Affairs: W. Allan Cagnoli
 E-Mail: cagnoli@hpba.org
Director, Finance and Operations: Catherine G. Centra
 E-Mail: centra@hpba.org
Manager, Membership, Affiliate Relations and AMS: Ian
 Glowacki
 E-Mail: iglowacki@hpba.org
PFI Executive Director: Jennifer Hedrick
 E-Mail: hedrick@hpba.org
Director, Market Research: Donald Johnson
 E-Mail: johnson@hpba.org
Director, Meetings and Expositions: Kelly Van Dermark
 E-Mail: vandermark@hpba.org
Director, Communications: Leslie G. Wheeler
 E-Mail: wheeler@hpba.org

Historical Note:
Founded (1980) as Hearth Products Association, merged (2002) with Barbecue Industry Association and assumed its current name at the same time. HPBA's purpose is to promote the interests of the hearth, barbecue and patio products industries in North America. Members include manufacturers, retailers, distributors, manufacturer's representatives, and other firms and individuals involved in these industries. Membership: $1680-39176 (Manufacturer); $225-975 (Non-Manufacturer); 150 (Associate).

Meetings/Conferences: Annual
Conference Chair: Kelly Van Dermark
2013 - Orange, FL (Orange County Convention
 Center)/March 13 - 16/12000 attendees/over 100
 exhibitors
2014 - Salt Lake City, UT/March 5 - 8/12000
 attendees/over 100 exhibitors
2015 - Nashville, FL/March 4 - 7/12000 attendees/
 over 100 exhibitors
2016 - New Orleans, LA/March 16 - 19/12000
 attendees/over 100 exhibitors

Publications:
HPBA e-Directory; annually
HPBA Journal and Bulletin; monthly
HPBA's Annual Membership Directory; annually
HPBA's Hot News; monthly

Heat Exchange Institute (1933)
1300 Sumner Ave.
Cleveland, OH 44115-2815
Tel: (216) 241-7333 *Fax:* (216) 241-0105
E-Mail: hei@heatexchange.org
Website: heatexchange.org
Members: 25 companies
Staff: 3
Annual Budget: $100-250,000
Tax: 501(c)(6)

Personnel:

Secretary and Treasurer: John H. Addington
Senior Executive, Accounts: Chris Johnson

Historical Note:
Organized primarily as a steam condenser organization. Purpose of HEI is to develop and publish standards which advance the technology, increase the efficiency, and promote the use of heat exchange and vacuum apparatus.

Heating, Airconditioning and Refrigeration Distributors International *(1947)*
3455 Mill Run Dr.
Suite 820
Columbus, OH 43026
Tel: (614) 345-4328 *Fax*: (614) 345-9161
TollFree: (888) 253-2128
E-Mail: hardimail@hardinet.org
Website: hardinet.org
Members: 890 manufacturer representatives, wholesalers and manufacturing associates
Staff: 14
Annual Budget: $2-5,000,000
Tax: 501(c)(3)

Personnel:
Executive Vice President and Chief Operating Officer:
Talbot H. Gee
   E-Mail: tgee@HARDInet.org
Coordinator, Membership Services: Sue Calvin
   E-Mail: scalvin@HARDInet.org
Consultant, Human Resources and Organizational Management: Nancye Combs
   E-Mail: NancyeCombs@aol.com
Manager, Membership Development and Services:
Stephanie Lingofelter
   E-Mail: slingofelter@HARDInet.org
Director, Marketing: Susan Little
   E-Mail: slittle@hardinet.org
Manager, Networking and Conferences: Eileen R. Mantel
   E-Mail: emantel@HARDInet.org
Director, Government Affairs: Jonathan Melchi
   E-Mail: jmelchi@hardinet.org
Director, Education and Research Foundation: Emily
Saving
   E-Mail: esaving@HARDInet.org
Coordinator, Communications and Public Relations:
Vanessa Spates
   E-Mail: vspates@hardinet.org

Historical Note:
A trade association representing distributors of HVACR equipment. HARDI was formulated by the consolidation of two long time wholesale trade organizations – Northamerican Heating, Refrigeration & Airconditioning Wholesalers (NHRAW) and Air-conditioning & Refrigeration Wholesalers International (ARWI). HARDI is the resource for marketing and distribution interests to advance the science of distributing HVACR products and supplies.

Continuing Education:
Certification Designation/s: CCS

Meetings/Conferences:
Conference Chair: Eileen R. Mantel
2013 - Dallas, TX (Hyatt Regency Dallas)/Jan. 27
2013 - Phoenix, AZ (JW Marriott Phoenix Desert Ridge Resort and Spa)/Dec. 7 - 10
2014 - San Antonio, TX (JW Marriott San Antonio Hill Country Resort and Spa)/Dec. 6 - 9
2015 - Orlando, FL (JW Marriott Orlando Grande Lakes)/Nov. 14 - 17
Number of non-conference events/year: 8

Publications:
Counterline
Member Directory; on-line
The Business Owner

Heavy Duty Brake Manufacturers Council
Ten Laboratory Dr.
P.O. Box 13966
Research Triangle Park, NC 27709-3966
Tel: (919) 549-4800 *Fax*: (919) 549-4824
E-Mail: aptaoffices@polaritytherapy.org
Website: hdma.org/Main-Menu/HDMA-Membership-Benefits/HDMA-Councils/HDBMC
Members: 15 companies
Staff: 2

Personnel:
Executive Director: Mark Iasiello
   E-Mail: miasiello@hdma.org

Historical Note:

A product line group of Motor and Equipment Manufacturers Association, HDBMC coordinates research in heavy duty brake standards and testing procedures. Membership in HDBMC is restricted to just those companies directly involved in OEM design and manufacturing of brake components and systems.

Heavy Duty Manufacturers Association *(1983)*
Ten Laboratory Dr.
P.O. Box 13966
Research Triangle Park, NC 27709-3966
Tel: (919) 549-4800 *Fax*: (919) 549-4824
E-Mail: info@hdma.org
Website: hdma.org
Members: 50 individuals
Staff: 6
Annual Budget: $50-100,000

Personnel:
President and Chief Executive Officer: Robert McKenna
   E-Mail: bmckenna@mema.org
Contact, Research: Richard Anderson
   E-Mail: randerson@mema.org
Contact, Membership Services and Support: Wayne
Fulford
   E-Mail: wfulford@mema.org
Senior Director, Marketing, Events and Membership Services: Jennifer Hjalmquist
   E-Mail: jhjalmquist@MEMA.ORG
President and Chief Operating Officer: Timothy R. Kraus
   E-Mail: tkraus@hdma.org
Manager, Communications and Membership Services:
Alison Mendys
   E-Mail: amendys@hdma.org

Historical Note:
HDMA was founded in 1983 at the International Truck Show Annual Dinner in Anaheim, California by 16 members of the Heavy Duty Business Forum, a discussion group of industry executives formed in 1978. HDMA strives to advance the image and interests of the industry and its member companies. Membership: $2000-22,000/year.

Meetings/Conferences:
Conference Chair: Jennifer Hjalmquist

Publications:
Diesel Download; weekly
HDMA Supplier Barometer; quarterly
International Diesel Download; weekly
MEMA Industry News; daily
MEMA Washington Insider; bi-weekly

Heavy Duty Representatives Association *(1973)*
C/O Wade and Partner
160 Symphony Way
Elgin, IL 60120
Tel: (847) 760-0067
Website: hdra.org
Members: 70 companies
Staff: 1
Annual Budget: $25-50,000

Personnel:
Executive Director: William Wade

Historical Note:
HDRA is a trade association of professional manufacturers representatives and the suppliers they represent. Mission is to provide full-time professional representation to the heavy duty vehicle and equipment market both OEM and after market. Associate membership open to manufacturers in the heavy-duty trucking industry. Membership: $400 (Agency); $250 (Supplier/Sponsor).

Publications:
Membership Directory; on-line

Hedge Fund Association *(1995)*
2875 NE 191 St.
Suite 900
Aventura, FL 33180
Tel: (202) 478-2000 *Fax*: (202) 478-1999
E-Mail: info@thehfa.org
Website: thehfa.org
Staff: 2
Annual Budget: $100-250,000

Personnel:
Executive Director: Lara Block
   E-Mail: lblock@thehfa.org
Media Contact: Mitch Ackles
   E-Mail: mitch.ackles@hedgefundpr.net

Historical Note:
International not-for-profit association aiming to increase awareness of the risks and benefits in hedge fund investing.

Membership: $250-1,500 (Fund Manager, Based on Assets); $100 (Investor/Student), $1,000-7,500 (Fund Professional).
Meetings/Conferences:
Number of non-conference events/year: 5

Publications:
HFA Updates; on-line; adv.

Heli Ski US Association *(1980)*
P.O. Box 1610
Cordova, AK 99574
Website: usheliskiing.com
Staff: 5

Personnel:
President: Paul Butler
   E-Mail: paul@heli-ski.com
Administrative Assistant: Jessica Quinn
   E-Mail: info@alaskaheliski.com
Secretary: Kevin Quinn
   E-Mail: info@alaskaheliski.com
Director, Membership Review Committee: Joe Royer
   E-Mail: joe@helicopterskiing.com
Treasurer: Jon Shick
   E-Mail: info@heliskijackson.com

Historical Note:
The mission of the association is to ensure and protect the future of Helicopter Skiing in the United States. Members work cooperatively to help establish the highest safety and operating standards in the helicopter skiing industry.

Publications:
Membership Directory; on-line

Helicopter Association International *(1948)*
1635 Prince St.
Alexandria, VA 22314-2818
Tel: (703) 683-4646 *Fax*: (703) 683-4745
TollFree: (800) 435-4976
Website: rotor.com
Members:
1500 organizations
1400 individuals
Staff: 47
Annual Budget: $5-10,000,000
Tax: 501(c)(6)

Personnel:
President: Matthew S. Zuccaro
   E-Mail: tailrotor@aol.com
Manager, Education Programs: Kristin Lord Anderson
   E-Mail: kristin.anderson@rotor.com
Vice President, Government Affairs: Ann Carroll
   E-Mail: ann.carroll@rotor.com
Manager, Information Systems and Web Contributor: Jay
Clark
   E-Mail: jay.clark@rotor.com
Chief Financial Officer: Kevin Cooper
   E-Mail: kevin.cooper@rotor.com
Director, Communications and Public Relations: Chris
Dancy
   E-Mail: chris.dancy@rotor.com
Executive Vice President and Corporate Secretary: Edward
F. DiCampli
   E-Mail: ed.dicampli@rotor.com
Director, Membership Services: Annette C. Duplinsky
   E-Mail: annette.duplinsky@rotor.com
Director, Human Resources and Administrative Services and Assistant Corporate Secretary: Roxanne R. Fox
   E-Mail: roxanne.fox@rotor.com
Vice President, Business Development and Expositions:
Karen Gebhart
   E-Mail: karen.gebhart@rotor.com
Director, Publications and Media: Gina Kvitkovich
   E-Mail: gina.kvitkovich@rotor.com
Manager, Administrative Services: Elaine H. Little
   E-Mail: elaine.little@rotor.com

Historical Note:
HAI is an aviation trade association dedicated to the advancement of the international helicopter community. Membership: $300-2,600 (Regular); $275-11,850 (Associate); Free (Individual- only for 1st year).

Meetings/Conferences: Annual
Conference Chair: Karen Gebhart
2013 - Las Vegas, NV (Las Vegas convention)/March 4 - 7/over 100 exhibitors

Publications:
Market Newsletters; monthly
Membership Directory; on-line
ROTOR magazine; quarterly

RotorNews; daily
The Helicopter Annual; annually; adv.

Hellenic-American Chamber of Commerce (1947)
370 Lexington Ave.
27th Floor
New York, NY 10017
Tel: (212) 629-6380 *Fax:* (212) 564-9281
E-Mail: hellenicchamber-nyc@att.net
Website: hellenicamerican.cc
Members: 250 companies
Staff: 3
Annual Budget: $500-1,000,000
Tax: 501(c)(6)

Personnel:
President: LeRoy Lambert
Executive Secretary: Stamatis A. Gikas
Executive Vice President: Michael Theodorobeakos

Historical Note:
HACC was formed over 50 years ago for the purpose of advocating and strengthening the economic and cultural ties between the United States of America and Greece. Membership: :$200 (Individual); $400 (Company).

Meetings/Conferences:
Number of non-conference events/year: 1

Publications:
HACC newsletter; annually

Help Desk Institute (1989)
102 S. Tejon
Suite 1100
Colorado Springs, CO 80903
Tel: (719) 268-0174 *Fax:* (719) 268-0184
TollFree: (800) 248-5667
E-Mail: support@thinkhdi.com
Website: thinkhdi.com
Members: 7500 members and 68 local chapters
Staff: 5
Annual Budget: $500-1,000,000

Personnel:
Executive Director, Certification and Training: Rick Joslin
    E-Mail: rjoslin@thinkhdi.com
Director, Marketing: Melanie Adamich
    E-Mail: madamich@thinkhdi.com
Director, Membership Services: Leslie Cook
    E-Mail: lcook@thinkhdi.com
Director, Events: Michelle Frilow
    E-Mail: mfrilow@thinkhdi.com
Contact, Publications: Megan Selva
    E-Mail: editor@thinkhdi.com

Historical Note:
HDI's mission is to advance the technical service and support industry by providing high-quality professional development opportunities for individuals and support centers. Members are software support sites and professionals involved in the provision of telephonic software support services. Membership: $75-6,500/year.

Continuing Education:
Certification Designation/s: SCC

Meetings/Conferences: Annual
Conference Chair: Michelle Frilow
2013 - Las Vegas, NV (Mandalay Bay Las Vegas)/April
    16 - 19/11-25 exhibitors

Publications:
Focus Series; quarterly
Industry Insider; bi-weekly
SupportWorld; bi-monthly; adv.

Hemophilia Federation of America (1994)
210 Seventh St. SE
Suite 200 B
Washington, DC 20003
Tel: (202) 675-6984 *Fax:* (202) 675-6983
TollFree: (800) 230-9797
E-Mail: info@hemophiliafed.org
Website: hemophiliafed.org
Staff: 10
Annual Budget: $1-2,000,000

Personnel:
Executive Director: Kimberly Haugstad
Office Manager: Pat Brown
Director, Technology: Matthew "Matt" Landseadel
Director, Policy: Eboni Morris
    E-Mail: e.morris@hemophiliafed.org
Manager, Communications: Rich Pezzillo

Historical Note:

The Hemophilia Federation of America (HFA) is a non-profit 501(c)3 organization incorporated in 1994 to address the evolving needs of the bleeding disorders. Membership: $25 (Individual); $50 (Family); $100 (Industry Professional).

Meetings/Conferences: Annual
2013 - Frisco, TX (Embassy Suites Dallas-Frisco/
    Hotel, Convention Center and Spa)/April 25 - 27

Publications:
Dateline Federation-Newsletter; quarterly

Herb Growing and Marketing Network (1990)
P.O. Box 245
Silver Spring, PA 17575-0245
Tel: (717) 393-3295 *Fax:* (717) 393-9261
E-Mail: herbworld@aol.com
Website: herbworld.com
Members: 1000 members
Staff: 2
Annual Budget: $100-250,000

Personnel:
Director: Maureen Rogers
    E-Mail: herbworld@aol.com

Historical Note:
HGMN is an information service for its members offering material on anything related to being in an herb business. It also helps its members grow herbs and herbal products and be an herbalist successfully. Members are growers, distributors, retailers and suppliers of materials to the industry. Membership: $225 (Corporate Sponsor); $100 (Outside North America); $95 (US, Canada, Mexico); $300 (Hosting).

Meetings/Conferences: Annual

Publications:
HerbNET; monthly; adv.

Herb Society of America (1933)
9019 Kirtland Chardon Rd.
Kirtland, OH 44094
Tel: (440) 256-0514 *Fax:* (404) 256-0541
E-Mail: herbs@herbsociety.org
Website: herbsociety.org
Staff: 6
Annual Budget: $250-500,000
Tax: 501(c)(3)

Personnel:
Executive Director: Katrinka Morgan
    E-Mail: director@herbsociety.org
Accountant: Karen Frandanisa
    E-Mail: kfrandanisa@herbsociety.org
Coordinator, Membership and Educator: Janeen Wright
    E-Mail: membership@herbsociety.org

Historical Note:
HSA focuses on educating its members and the public on the cultivation of herbs and the study of their history and uses, both past and present.HSA's mission is to promote the knowledge use and delight of herbs through educational programs, research and sharing the knowledge of its members with the community.Membership $50 (individual/ Honorary); $75 (Joint); $85 (Business); $30 (Student); $110 (International).

Meetings/Conferences: Annual

Publications:
The Herbarist; annually
The HSA Newsletter

The Herpetologists' League (1946)
Arkansas State University
Jonesboro, AR 72467
Tel: (870) 972-3111
E-Mail: herps@allenpress.com
Website: herpetologistsleague.org
Members: 1400 individuals and institutions
Staff: 5
Annual Budget: $50-100,000

Personnel:
President: Stanley E. Trauth

Historical Note:
HL supports the study of the biology of amphibians and reptiles. HL is an international organization of people committed to studying the biology of amphibians and reptiles. Membership: $75 (Regular); $125 (Contributing); $60 (Family); $35 (Student); $1,000 (Patron); $1,500 (Life).

Meetings/Conferences: Annual
2013 - Albuquerue, NM (Albuquerque Convention
    Center)/July 10 - 15
2014 - Chattanooga, TN/July 30 - Aug. 3

Publications:
Herpetologica; quarterly
Herpetological Monographs; annually
Membership Directory; annually

High Point Market (1909)
164 S. Main St.
Suite 700
High Point, NC 27260
Tel: (336) 869-1000 *Fax:* (336) 889-6999
TollFree: (800) 874-6492
Website: highpointmarket.org
Members: 2300 exhibitors
Staff: 7

Personnel:
President and Chief Executive Officer: Tom Conley
    E-Mail: tom@highpointmarket.org
Director, Registration Services: Donna Gross
    E-Mail: Donna@highpointmarket.org
Director, Marketing: Shannon Kennedy
    E-Mail: shannon@highpointmarket.org
Chief Operating Officer: Tammy Covington Nagem
Executive Assistant: Jan Wellmon
    E-Mail: Jan@highpointmarket.org

Historical Note:
Formerly (1989) the Furniture Factories' Marketing Association of the South and then International Home Furnishings Marketing Association. Acts as the introductory wholesale market for a range of finished products, including home furnishings, gift and decorative accessories, lighting, and area floor covering.

Meetings/Conferences:
Conference Chair: Donna Gross

Publications:
eNews; on-line

High Technology Crime Investigation Association
3288 Goldstone Dr.
Roseville, CA 95747
Tel: (916) 408-1751 *Fax:* (916) 408-7543
Website: htcia.org
Members: 3000 individuals
Staff: 2
Annual Budget: $500-1,000,000
Tax: 501(c)(3)

Personnel:
Executive Director: Carol Hutchings
    E-Mail: exec_secty@htcia.org
International President: Ron Wilczynski
    E-Mail: president.htcia@gmail.com

Historical Note:
HTCIA is designed to encourage, promote, aid and effect the voluntary interchange of data, information, experience, ideas and knowledge about methods, processes, and techniques relating to investigations and security in advanced technologies among its membership. Members are law enforcement professionals and corporate security with an interest in the application of technology to criminal and civil investigations. Membership: $30-70 (Dues per chapter); $25 (Student).

Meetings/Conferences: Annual

Publications:
Membership Directory; on-line

Higher Education Consortium for Special Education
University of Northern Colorado School of
Special Education
Campus Box 141
Greeley, CO 80639
Tel: (970) 351-1659 *Fax:* (970) 351-1061
Website: hecse.net
Staff: 3
Annual Budget: $50-100,000

Personnel:
President: Harvey Rude
    E-Mail: harvey.rude@unco.edu

Historical Note:
The Higher Education Consortium for Special Education (HECSE) is a national organization that represents major university programs that prepare personnel for special education leadership roles. HECSE's mission is to facilitate continuous improvement in the quality of doctoral programs offered by member institutions and to provide information to Congress, representatives of federal agencies, and others who are making policy decisions related to the preparation of special education doctoral students.Membership: $1,100 (individual).

Publications:
Newsletter; quarterly

Higher Education Consortium for Urban Affairs
(1971)
2233 University Ave., West
Suite 210
St. Paul, MN 55114
Tel: (651) 287-3300 *Fax:* (651) 659-9421
E-Mail: hecua@hecua.org
Website: hecua.org
Members: 17 liberal arts colleges, universities
and associations
Staff: 30
Annual Budget: $2-5,000,000
Tax: 501(c)(3)

Personnel:
Executive Director: Jenny Keyser
     E-Mail: jkeyser@hecua.org
Manager, Marketing and Recruitment: Mary Delorie
     E-Mail: mdelorie@hecua.org
Director, Operations: Patrick Mulvihill
     E-Mail: pmulvihill@hecua.org
Associate, Student Services: Phillip Romine
     E-Mail: promine@hecua.org

Historical Note:
*HECUA's mission is to build academic-community
partnerships for social change. Membership: $50 (Member
Institution); $75 (Non-Member Institution).*

Hinman Dental Society *(2009)*
33 Lenox Pointe NE
Atlanta, GA 30324-3172
Website: hinman.org
Staff: 6
Annual Budget: $2-5,000,000

Personnel:
Treasurer: Jon rack

Hispanic American Police Command Officers Association (HAPCOA) *(1973)*
P.O. Box 767
Cibolo, TX 78108
Tel: (210) 641-1305 *Fax:* (210) 641-1304
E-Mail: info@hapcoa.com
Website:
hapcoa.com
hapcoa.org
Staff: 2
Annual Budget: $50-100,000
Tax: 501(c)(3)

Personnel:
National Treasurer: Lee Roy Villareal
     E-Mail: villareal@hapcoa.org

Historical Note:
*HAPCOA's mission is to empower the future of law
enforcement by assisting law enforcement, criminal justice
and community organizations nationwide in their efforts to
recruit, train and promote qualified Hispanic American men
and women. Membership consists of Hispanic American
command officers from law enforcement and criminal
justice agencies at the municipal, county, state, and federal
levels. Membership: $25 (Student); $100 (Regular); $75
(Associate); 55$ (Supporting); $1,500 (Lifetime); $2500
(Organizational/Corporate).*

Meetings/Conferences: Annual

Publications:
HAPCOA Newsletter

Hispanic Association of Colleges and Universities
(1986)
8415 Data Point Dr.
Suite 400
San Antonio, TX 78229
Tel: (210) 692-3805 *Fax:* (210) 692-0823
E-Mail: hacu@hacu.net
Website: hacu.net
Members: 400 colleges and universities
Staff: 43
Annual Budget: $10-25,000,000
Tax: 501(c)(3)

Personnel:
President and Chief Executive Officer: Antonio R. Flores
PhD
     E-Mail: aflores@hacu.net
Director, Human Resources: Veronica J. Acosta-Aguilar
     E-Mail: vaguilar@hacu.net

Chief Financial Officer: Magda Gonzales
     E-Mail: mgonzalez@hacu.net
Executive Director, Student Services: Rene A. Gonzalez
     E-Mail: ragonzalez@hacu.net
Executive Director, Conferences: Silvia Kennison
     E-Mail: skennison@hacu.net
Chief Technology and Innovation Officer: Ray López
*Senior Executive Director, International Affairs and
     Membership:* Alicia Martinez
     E-Mail: amartinez@hacu.net
Executive Director, Communications and Marketing:
     Norma Jean Revilla-Garcia
     E-Mail: njgarcia@hacu.net

Historical Note:
*HACU seeks to promote the development of member colleges
and universities. HACU's mission is to improve the quality
of post-secondary educational opportunities for Hispanic
students and to meet the needs of business, industry
and government through the development and sharing
of resources, information and expertise. Membership:
$10-10,310/year.*

Continuing Education:
Certification Designation/s: HNIP

Meetings/Conferences:
Conference Chair: Silvia Kennison
2013 - San Antonio, TX (Grand Hyatt San Antonio)/
     Feb. 27 - March 1
2013 - Chicago, IL (Hilton Chicago)/Oct. 26 - 28
2014 - Denver, CO (Sheraton Denver Downtown
     Hotel)/Oct. 4 - 6
2015 - Miami Beach, FL (Fontainebleau Miami Beach)/
     Oct. 10 - 12
2016 - San Antonio, TX (Grand Hyatt San Antonio)/
     Oct. 8 - 10
2017 - San Diego, CA (Hilton San Diego Bayfront)/Oct.
     28 - 30
Number of non-conference events/year: 2

Publications:
eNewsletter; on-line
The Voice of Hispanic Higher Education magazine;
quarterly; adv.

Membership List Available to Non-members

Hispanic Association on Corporate Responsibility
(1986)
1444 I St. NW
Suite 850
Washington, DC 20005
Tel: (202) 682-4012 *Fax:* (202) 682-0086
E-Mail: hacr@hacr.org
Website: hacr.org
Staff: 6
Annual Budget: $1-2,000,000
Tax: 501(c)(3)

Personnel:
President and Chief Executive Officer: Carlos F. Orta
Office Administrator: Kevin Klich
*Director, Corporate Relations, Communications, and
     Programs Director:* Jason Leon
Managing Editor and Manager, Communications: Josh
     Silvia

Historical Note:
*HACR's mission is to advance the inclusion of Hispanics in
Corporate America at a level commensurate with economic
contributions. Membership: $15,000 (Associate); $25,000
(Generations); $50,000 (Vision).*

Meetings/Conferences: Annual
2013 - Houston, TX (Four Seasons Hotel)/April 19 - 23

Publications:
Corporate Observer; quarterly

Hispanic Dental Association *(1990)*
3085 Stevenson Dr.
Suite 200
Springfield, IL 62703
Tel: (217) 529-6517 *Fax:* (217) 529-9120
TollFree: (800) 852-7921
E-Mail: hispanicdental@hdassoc.org
Website: hdassoc.org
Members: 1500 students and professionals
Staff: 3
Annual Budget: $500-1,000,000
Tax: 501(c)(3)

Personnel:
Executive Director: Dr. C. Yolanda Bonta DMD MS MS
     E-Mail: ybonta@aol.com

Interim Associate Director: Bonnie Chandler CAE, CMP,
MPA
Editor: Tamiko Kinkade
     E-Mail: tk@tkcpsolutions.com

Historical Note:
*HDA's mission is to encourage the oral health of the
Hispanic community through improved prevention,
treatment and education. Membership: $15 (Student);
$60-150 (Professional); $350 (Institutional).*

Meetings/Conferences: Annual
2013 - Boston, MA (Boston Mariott Copley Place)/
     Sept. 27 - 29

Publications:
American Journal of Dentistry
HDA News & Reports; quarterly; adv.
Hispanic Business Magazine

Hispanic Elected Local Officials *(1976)*
1301 Pennsylvania Ave. NW
Suite 550
Washington, DC 20004-1763
Tel: (202) 626-3100 *Fax:* (202) 626-3043
E-Mail: info@nlc.org
Website: nlc.org/build-skills-networks/networks/
     constit
Members: 100 individuals
Staff: 103
Annual Budget: Under $10,000

Personnel:
Executive Director: Don Borut
     E-Mail: borut@nlc.org
Chief Finance Officer: Carlsen Griffith
Director, Member Relations: Gail Remy King
     E-Mail: remy@nlc.org
Director, Human Resource: Anna Langham
     E-Mail: langham@nlc.org
Manager, Media Relations: Gregory Minchak
     E-Mail: minchak@nlc.org
Center Director, Conferences, Education and Training:
     Janice Pauline
     E-Mail: pauline@nlc.org

Historical Note:
*NLC is committed to providing city leaders with resources
that help blaze pathways toward exceptional leadership
and professional and personal advancement. NLC offers
membership opportunities for members of the private and
non-profit sector.*

Meetings/Conferences: Annual
Conference Chair: Janice Pauline
2013 - Washington, DC (Washington Marriott
     Wardman Park)/March 9 - 13
2014 - Washington, DC (Washington Marriott
     Wardman Park)/March 8 - 12

Publications:
NLC e-newsletter; bi-weekly

Hispanic Lobbyists Association *(2006)*
P.O. Box 15429
Washington, DC 20003
Tel: (202) 448-5231 *Fax:* (202) 638-4156
Website: hispaniclobbyists.org
Staff: 2
Tax: 501(c)(6)

Personnel:
President: Cristina E. Antelo
Treasurer: Andrea Zuniga DiBitetto

Historical Note:
*Hispanic Lobbyists Association works to provide mentoring
opportunities for Hispanic youth and/or professionals
seeking to enter the profession of governmental
advocacy. HLA's mission is to organize, associate and
advocate communication, education, and bipartisanship.
Membership: $75/year.*

Hispanic National Bar Association *(1972)*
1900 L St. NW
Suite 700
Washington, DC 20036
Tel: (202) 223-4777 *Fax:* (202) 223-2324
E-Mail: info@hnba.com
Website: hnba.com
Members: 33000 individuals
Staff: 5
Annual Budget: $1-2,000,000
Tax: 501(c)(6)

Personnel:
Interim Executive Director: Antonio "Tony" Arocho Esq.

E-Mail: aarocho@hnba.com
Manager, Communications: Emily Bengtson
   E-Mail: ebengtson@hnba.com
Director, Events: Erika Lopez-Tello
   E-Mail: elopeztello@hnba.com
Manager, Membership Relations: Sarah E. Ramirez
   E-Mail: sramirez@hnba.com
Office Manager: Elizabeth Ugbomah
   E-Mail: eugbomah@hnba.com

Historical Note:
Formerly (1980) California as La Raza National Bar Association, and was re-incorporated in Washington, DC in 1983. HNBA's mission is to serve as the national voice for the concerns and opinions of Hispanics in the community generally, and in the legal profession in particular; and to promote the recruitment and retention of Hispanics in law schools and provide them with financial assistance. Membership: $20 (Affiliate/Legal Assistant/Administrator); $1,250 (Lifetime Member); $75 (Foreign Attorney).

Meetings/Conferences: Annual

Publications:
E-Noticias; adv.
Journal of Law and Policy
Noticias-Newsletter; adv.

Hispanic Organization of Latin Actors *(1975)*
107 Suffolk St.
Room 302
New York, NY 10002
Tel: (212) 253-1015 *Fax:* (212) 253-9651
E-Mail: holagram@hellohola.org
Website: hellohola.org
Members: 400 individuals
Staff: 4
Annual Budget: $100-250,000
Tax: 501(c)(3)

Personnel:
Executive Director: Manny Alfaro
Director, Special Projects: Manuel Herrera

Historical Note:
HOLA's mission is to expand the presence of Hispanic actors in both the Latino and mainstream entertainment and communications media by facilitating industry access to employing professional and emerging Hispanic actors. Membership: $125/year (Individual).

Meetings/Conferences: Annual

Publications:
La Nueva Ola E-newsletter; monthly
Membership Directory; on-line

The Histochemical Society *(1950)*
9650 Rockville Pike
Bethesda, MD 20814
Tel: (301) 634-7026 *Fax:* (301) 634-7099
E-Mail: mail@histochemcialsociety.org
Website: histochemicalsociety.org
Members: 550 individuals
Staff: 3
Annual Budget: $500-1,000,000

Personnel:
Secretary and Treasurer: Margarida Barroso
   E-Mail: barrosm@mail.amc.edu

Historical Note:
Mission is to advance the study of cell and tissue biology with molecular and morphological techniques. Members are qualified scientists who employ histochemical and cytochemical techniques in their research. Membership: $100 (Regular/Associate Members); $35 (Student).

Meetings/Conferences: Annual
2013 - Boston, MA (Boston Convention and Exposition Center)/April 20

Publications:
HCS Newsletter; semi-annually
Journal of Histochemistry & Cytochemistry; monthly

Historians Film Committee/Film & History *(1970)*
Center for the Study of Film and History
800 Algoma Blvd.
Oshkosh, WI 54901
Tel: (920) 424-0976
E-Mail: center@filmandhistory.org
Website: uwosh.edu/filmandhistory
Members: 1000 members
Staff: 2

Personnel:
Chair and Editor: Loren Baybrook
   E-Mail: baybrook@uwosh.edu

Web Coordinator: A. Bowdoin Van Riper
   E-Mail: web_coordinator@filmandhistory.edu

Historical Note:
Film & History is the peer-reviewed journal in its field, with an editorial board of international scholars from multiple disciplines in the humanities and social sciences. Affiliated with the American Historical Society. Membership: $30 (Individual); $40 (Institution).

Meetings/Conferences: Biennial

Publications:
Film & History; semi-annually; adv.

Historians of American Communism *(1884)*
400 A St. SE
Washington, CT 20003-3889
Tel: (202) 544-2422 *Fax:* (202) 544-8307
Website: historians.org/affiliates/
  hisn_am_communism.htm
Members: 165 individuals
Staff: 5
Annual Budget: Under $10,000

Personnel:
Executive Director: Jim Grossman
Manager, Marketing and Business Operations: Kelly Elmore
Manager, Databases and Information Technology: Vernon Horn
Manager, Membership: Pamela Scott-Pinkney
Director, Meetings and Administrative Operations: Sharon K. Tune

Historical Note:
AHA was incorporated for the promotion of historical studies, the collection and preservation of historical documents and artifacts, and the dissemination of historical research.Membeship Dues:$40-215(Student); $300 (Contributing);$3,500 (Life);$50(Joint spouse); $89(Associate);$72-103(K-12 Teacher).

Meetings/Conferences: Annual
2013 - New Orleans, LA (New Orleans Marriott)/Jan. 3 - 6
2014 - Washington, DC (Washington Marriott)/Jan. 2 - 5
2015 - New York City, NY (Hilton New York)/Jan. 2 - 5
2016 - Atlanta, GA (Atlanta Marriott Marquis)/Jan. 7 - 10
2020 - New York City, NY/Jan. 3 - 6

Publications:
Directory of History Dissertations
H_HOAC Journal; adv.
Perspectives on History
The American Historical Review

Membership List Available to Non-members

Historians of Islamic Art Association *(1982)*
Department of Art and Art History, The University of Texas at Austin
1 University Station D1300
Austin, TX 78712-0337
Tel: (512) 471-5851
Website: historiansofislamicart.org
Members: 230 members
Staff: 5
Annual Budget: $100-250,000

Personnel:
President: Marianna Shreve Simpson
   E-Mail: president.hiaa@gmail.com
Secretary: Ladan Akbarnia
   E-Mail: sec.hiaa@gmail.com
Treasurer: Glaire Anderson
   E-Mail: historiansofislamicart@gmail.com
Editor: Stephannie Mulder
   E-Mail: smulder@mail.utexas.edu
Interim Webmaster: Jennifer Pruitt
   E-Mail: webmaster.hiaa@gmail.com

Historical Note:
Formerly known as North American Historians of Art; assumed its present name in 2006. HIAA's mission is to promote the study and teaching of the arts and architecture of the Islamic world. Membership: $40 (Individual); $20 (Student); $60 (Joint); $100 (Institutional/Sustaining).

Meetings/Conferences: Annual

Publications:
Membership Directory; on-line
Muqarnas

Historians of Netherlandish Art *(1983)*

23 S. Adelaide Ave.
Highland Park, NJ 08904
Tel: (732) 937-8394 *Fax:* (732) 937-8394
E-Mail: info@hnanews.org
Website: hnanews.org
Members: 660 individuals, 30 institutions and businesses
Staff: 3
Annual Budget: $50-100,000

Personnel:
Administrator: Kristin Lohse Belkin
   E-Mail: kbelkin@aol.com

Historical Note:
HNA's purpose is to foster communication and collaboration among historians of Northern European art from medieval to modern times. Members comprise of academics, art professionals, publishers and book dealers. Membership: $25-200/year.

Publications:
Journal of Historians of Netherlandish Art; quarterly
Membership Directory; annually
Newsletter

History of Dermatology Society *(1973)*
1760 Market St.
Suite 301
Philadelphia, PA 19103
Tel: (215) 563-8333 *Fax:* (215) 563-3044
Website: dermato.med.br
Staff: 2

Personnel:
President: Lawrence Charles Parish MD
   E-Mail: larryderm@yahoo.com
Secretary and Treasurer: Anthony V. Benedetto FACP
   E-Mail: avb@benedettoderm.com

Historical Note:
History of Dermatology Society seeks to promote an understanding of the development of the specialty of dermatology.

Meetings/Conferences: Annual

Publications:
SKINmed; bi-monthly

History of Earth Sciences Society *(1982)*
School of Theoretical and Applied Science, Ramapo College
505 Ramapo Valley Rd.
Mahwah, NJ 07430
Tel: (201) 684-7209 *Fax:* (201) 684-7637
E-Mail: treasurer@historyearthscience.org
Website: historyearthscience.org
Members:
100 institutions
500 individuals
Staff: 3
Annual Budget: $10-25,000
Tax: 501(c)(3)

Personnel:
President: Greg Good
   E-Mail: president@historyearthscience.org
Treasurer: Emma C. Rainforth
   E-Mail: treasurer@historyearthscience.org

Historical Note:
HESS advances the study of all phases of history of the earth sciences. It also advocates and publishes historical work on all areas of the earth sciences including geology, geography, geophysics, oceanography, paleontology, meteorology, and climatology. Membership: $50-65 (Individual); $25 (Student); $80-100 (Institutions).

Publications:
Earth Sciences History; semi-annually
Member Directory; on-line

History of Economics Society *(1974)*
University of New Hampshire, McConnell Hall
15 Academic Way
Durham, NH 03824
Website: historyofeconomics.org
Members: 300 members
Staff: 4
Annual Budget: $50-100,000
Tax: 501(c)(3)

Personnel:
Treasurer: Neil B. Niman
   E-Mail: neil.niman@unh.edu
Editor: Marcel Boumans

Contact, Membership Services: Thomas Leonard
 E-Mail: tleonard@princeton.edu
Contact, Education: Sandra Peart
 E-Mail: speart@bw.edu

Historical Note:
HES's mission is to advocate the interest and inquiry into the history of economics and related parts of intellectual history. Membership: $30/year.

Meetings/Conferences: Annual
2013 - Vancouver, BC (University of British Columbia)/ June 20 - 22
Number of non-conference events/year: 1

Publications:
Journal of the History of Economic Thought; quarterly; adv.
Membership Directory; on-line

Membership List Available to Non-members

The History of Education Society (1960)
Marymount University
2807 N. Glebe Rd.
Arlington, VA 22207-4299
Tel: (703) 522-5600
E-Mail: heq@ed.uiuc.edu
Website: historyofeducation.org
Members: 600 individuals
Staff: 2
Annual Budget: $50-100,000
Tax: 501(c)(3)

Personnel:
President: Karen Graves
Meetings Contact, Secretary and Treasurer: Ralph Kidder
 E-Mail: ralph.kidder@marymount.edu

Historical Note:
HES seeks to promote and improve the teaching of the history of education in colleges and universities for the advancement of interest, study and research in the history of education. Membership: $52 (Regular); $26 (Student).

Meetings/Conferences: Annual
Conference Chair: Ralph Kidder

Publications:
History of Education Quarterly; quarterly; adv.

History of Science Society (1924)
University of Notre Dame
440 Geddes Hall
Notre Dame, IN 46556
Tel: (574) 631-1194 *Fax:* (574) 631-1533
E-Mail: info@hssonline.org
Website: hssonline.org
Members: 3500 individuals and institutions
Staff: 2
Annual Budget: $500-1,000,000
Tax: 501(c)(3)

Personnel:
Executive Director: Robert J. Malone
 E-Mail: jay@hssonline.org
Editor: Bernard V. Lightman

Historical Note:
HSS is dedicated to understanding science, technology, medicine, and their interactions with society in historical context. Membership: $106 (Individual); $33 (Student); $64 (Retired), $132 (Family).

Meetings/Conferences: Annual
2013 - Boston, MA/Nov. 21 - 24
2014 - Chicago, IL/Nov. 6 - 9

Publications:
History of Science Society Newsletter; quarterly; adv.
Isis; quarterly; adv.
Membership Directory; on-line
Osiris; annually

Hobby Manufacturers Association (2005)
P.O. Box 315
Butler, NJ 07405-0315
Tel: (973) 283-9088 *Fax:* (973) 838-7124
E-Mail: info@hmahobby.org
Website: hmahobby.org
Members: 260 companies
Staff: 3
Annual Budget: $100-250,000

Personnel:
Executive Director: Patricia S. Koziol
 E-Mail: pat.koziol@hmahobby.org
Manager, Expositions and Events: Jodi Araujo CEM
 E-Mail: jodi.araujo@hmahobby.org

Administrative Manager: Dena Botbyl
 E-Mail: dena.b@pmsa.us.com

Historical Note:
HMA seeks to stimulate the growth of the model hobby industry and to offer unique benefits to members and affiliated companies. Members include manufacturers, distributors and publishers involved in the industry. Membership: $0-1,725/year.

Meetings/Conferences: Annual
Conference Chair: Jodi Araujo CEM

Publications:
Member Directory; on-line
Membership Newsletter; monthly

Hoist Manufacturers Institute (1968)
8720 Red Oak Blvd.
Suite 201
Charlotte, NC 28217
Tel: (704) 676-1190 *Fax:* (704) 676-1199
Website: mhia.org/industrygroups/hmi
Members: 15 companies
Staff: 3
Annual Budget: $25-50,000
Tax: 501(c)(6)

Personnel:
Managing Director: Hal F. Vandiver
 E-Mail: hvandiver@mhia.org

Historical Note:
Formerly Hoist Manufacturers Association. A product section of the Material Handling Institute. HMI's mission is to deliver exceptional value to members, channel partners, consumers, end-users and industry associates, through Educational Materials, Marketing Information, Standards Development, Member and Professional Development.

Continuing Education:
Certification Designation/s: HMIC

Meetings/Conferences:
2013 - Chicago, IL (McCormick Place)/Jan. 21 - 24/30000 attendees/over 100 exhibitors

Publications:
Membership Directory; on-line

Holiday and Decorative Association (1994)
P.O. Box 420244
Dallas, TX 75342-0244
Tel: (214) 742-2747 *Fax:* (214) 742-2648
E-Mail: hda@hdanow.org
Website: hdanow.org
Staff: 1
Annual Budget: $250-500,000
Tax: 501(c)(6)

Personnel:
President: Ronald D. Poling CAE
 E-Mail: rpoling@afia.net

Historical Note:
Formerly, the American Floral Industry Association (AFIA). HDA's mission is to foster and promote all businesses within that industry and maintain a favorable business climate in North America for the use of the industry's products. Membership: $500 (Regular); $250 (Affiliate).

Meetings/Conferences: Annual

Publications:
AFIA Trends
Member Directory; on-line

Holistic Dental Association (1978)
1825 Ponce de Leon Blvd.
Suite 148
Coral Gables, FL 33134
Tel: (305) 356-7338 *Fax:* (305) 468-6359
E-Mail: info@holisticdental.org
Website: holisticdental.org
Members: 200 individuals
Staff: 2
Annual Budget: $50-100,000

Personnel:
Executive Director: Roberta Glasser
 E-Mail: director@holisticdental.org

Historical Note:
HDA provides support and guidance to practitioners of holistic and alternative dentistry, and informs the public of the benefits of holistic dentistry for their health and well-being. Members are dentists and other health professionals with an interest in a holistic approach to the practice of dentistry. Membership: $295 (Affiliate/Professional); $195 (Associate); $99 (Retired/Student).

Meetings/Conferences: Annual

2013 - Herndon, VA (Hilton Washington Dulles Airport)/April 18 - 20/1-10 exhibitors

Publications:
Membership Directory; on-line

Hollywood Radio & Television Society (1947)
13701 Riverside Dr.
Suite 205
Sherman Oaks, CA 91423
Tel: (818) 789-1182 *Fax:* (818) 789-1210
E-Mail: info@hrts.org
Website: hrts.org
Staff: 5
Annual Budget: $500-1,000,000

Personnel:
Executive Director: Dave Ferrara
Executive Assistant and Contact, Member Services: Elvia Gonzalez
 E-Mail: memberservices@hrts.org
Director, Events: Ruzzo Martinelli
Director, Operations: Jennie Nevin
Contact, Marketing and Communications: Meshack Vallesillas

Historical Note:
HRTS (Hollywood Radio & TV Society) is the entertainment industry's premier information and networking forum. HRTS gathers together leading industry executives and HRTS Network Chiefs Panel companies representing broadcast and cable networks, studios, talent and management agencies, producers, legal and financial firms, new media companies and more to address issues that are relevant to the ongoing success and future of business. Membership: $335/Year.

Meetings/Conferences:
Conference Chair: Ruzzo Martinelli

Publications:
In-Focus; monthly
Society Views; monthly; adv.
Wired Magazine

Holstein Association USA (1885)
One Holstein Pl.
P.O. Box 808
Brattleboro, VT 05302-0808
Tel: (802) 254-4551 *Fax:* (802) 254-8251
TollFree: (800) 952-5200
E-Mail: info@holstein.com
Website: holsteinusa.com
Members: 30000 individuals
Staff: 142
Annual Budget: $10-25,000,000

Personnel:
Chief Executive Officer and Executive Secretary: John M. Meyer
Chief Financial Officer and Treasurer: Barbara Casna

Historical Note:
Formerly (1988) Holstein-Friesian Association of America, assumed its current name in 1994. Mission is to provide leadership, information and services to help members and dairy producers worldwide be successful. Members are breeders of Holstein dairy cattle. Membership: $25/year.

Meetings/Conferences: Annual
2013 - Indianapolis, IN/July 8 - 11
2014 - Dubuque, IA/June 25 - 28
2015 - St. Charles, IL/June 27 - 30
Number of non-conference events/year: 1

Publications:
Journal of Dairy Science
Legislative E-Newsletter; on-line
Membership Directory; on-line
The Holstein Pulse; quarterly

Home Baking Association (1923)
2931 SW Gainsboro Rd.
Topeka, KS 66614-4413
Tel: (785) 478-3283 *Fax:* (785) 478-3024
E-Mail: hbapatton@aol.com
Website: homebaking.org
Members: 38 companies
Staff: 4
Annual Budget: $100-250,000
Tax: 501(c)(6)

Personnel:
President: Tom Payne
Contact, Educational Programs: Sharon Davis
Media Contact: Charlene Patton
 E-Mail: hbapatton@aol.com

Historical Note:
Formerly Self Rising Flour Institute and (1989) Self-Rising Flour and Corn Meal Program. HBA's mission is to promote home baking by providing tools and knowledge to perpetuate generations of home bakers. Members comprised of millers of wheat flour and corn meal, manufacturers of branded food ingredients used in home baking, and their allied trades formed for the purpose of conducting an educational program on behalf of those products. Membership: $2,000-25,600 (Corporate, sales dependent); $5,500 (Non- Profit Association Voting A); $2,000 (Non-Profit Association Voting B).

Meetings/Conferences: Annual

Publications:
Membership Directory; on-line
Newsletter
Rising Times Newsletter; monthly

Home Builders Association (2009)
111 St.
New York, NY 54785
Website: kalamazoohomepage.com
Staff: 10
Annual Budget: $1-2,000,000

Personnel:
President: Matthew Born

Home Fashion Products Association (1968)
355 Lexington Ave.
Suite 1500
New York, NY 10017-6603
Tel: (212) 297-2122 Fax: (212) 370-9047
Website: homefashionproducts.com
Members: 56 companies
Staff: 3
Annual Budget: $100-250,000
Tax: 501(c)(6)

Personnel:
Executive Director: Katie Geraghty
    E-Mail: kgeraghty@kellencompany.com
Media Contact: Katie Goshgarian
    E-Mail: kgoshgarian@kellencompany.com
Manager, Programs and Membership Services: Ellery Moses
    E-Mail: emoses@kellencompany.com

Historical Note:
Formerly (1981) National Curtain, Drapery, and Allied Products Association. Members are producers of all window and bed decor products and related accessories as included in a curtain or drapery retail assortment. HFPA serves to advance the growth of the global home fashion product industry by setting standards for excellence through technical product compliance, advocacy, and awareness efforts. Membership: $1,000-3,000/year.

Meetings/Conferences:
2013 - New York City, NY/March 18 - 21
2013 - New York City, NY/Sept. 23 - 26
2014 - New York City, NY/March 24 - 27
2014 - New York City, NY/Sept. 15 - 18

Publications:
Membership Directory; on-line; adv.

Home Furnishings Independents Association (1923)
P.O. Box 420807
Dallas, TX 75342-0807
Tel: (214) 741-7632 Fax: (214) 742-9103
TollFree: (800) 942-4663
E-Mail: info@hfia.com
Website: hfia.com
Members: 1200 companies/individuals
Staff: 6
Annual Budget: $100-250,000
Tax: 501(c)(6)

Personnel:
President: Mary Frye
    E-Mail: mary@hfia.com
Contact, Publications: Judy Thomas
    E-Mail: judy@hfia.com

Historical Note:
Formerly known as Home Furnishings International Association. HFIA offers business tools, information and solutions to help members operate profitably. Retail members are stores that stock home furnishings for resell. Associate members are consulting, design, wholesale, manufacturing, and supplier firms. Affiliate members are individuals with an interest in the industry such as manufacturer's reps, industry consultants, interior designers/decorators, retail sales persons and others.

Membership: $230-590 (Retail, Single Store-based on annual sales volume); $390 (Retail, Multi Store, minimum); $120 (Retail, Multi- Store/branch); $360 (Associate); $120 (Affiliate).

Publications:
Furniture World magazine

Membership List Available to Non-members

Home Improvement Research Institute (1981)
3922 Coconut Palm Dr.
Third floor
Tampa, FL 33619
Tel: (813) 627-6750 Fax: (813) 627-7063
E-Mail: admin@hiri.org
Website: hiri.org
Members: 84 companies
Staff: 3
Annual Budget: $500-1,000,000
Tax: 501(c)(6)

Personnel:
Managing Director: Fred Miller
    E-Mail: consumersp@aol.com
Coordinator, Administration and Conferences: Angie Angel
    E-Mail: aangel@hiri.org
Specialist, Communications: Christina Sacher-Brown
    E-Mail: csacher@hiri.org

Historical Note:
Formerly (1990) the Do-It-Yourself Research Institute. HIRI's mission is to be recognized as the primary authority for effective, useful information about home improvement products and services in North America. Members are manufacturers, retailers, wholesalers and allied organizations in the home improvement industry. Membership: $10,500 (Company); $9,500 (Associate); $2,750 (Canadian Special Interest Group).

Meetings/Conferences: Annual
Conference Chair: Angie Angel

Publications:
E-Business Tracking Study; annually
Home Improvement Activities; on-line
News Update; monthly
Remodeler Purchase Tracking Study; biennially
Size of Industry Estimates and Forecasts; semi-annually
Tracking How H/I Fits Into Internet Usage; on-line

Hop Growers of America (1956)
301 W. Prospect Pl.
P.O. Box 1207
Moxee, WA 98936
Tel: (509) 453-4749 Fax: (509) 457-8561
E-Mail: info@usahops.org
Website: usahops.org
Members: 240 growers and state associations
Staff: 1
Annual Budget: $250-500,000

Personnel:
Administrator: Ann George
    E-Mail: ageorge@wahops.org

Historical Note:
HGA provides marketing statistics, promotion, and research to U. S. hop growers, and serves as a liaison between its membership and the world brewing industry. Membership: $100 (Individual); $250 (Company).

Meetings/Conferences: Annual
2013 - Chico, CA/Jan. 22 - 25

Publications:
HGA Newsletter; monthly
U.S. Hop Merchant Directory

Hosa
6021 Morriss Rd.
Suite 111
Flower Mound, TX 75028
Tel: (972) 874-0062 Fax: (972) 874-0063
Website: hosa.org
Members: 120000 Organizations
Staff: 2

Personnel:
Executive Director: Dr. Jim Koeninger
    E-Mail: jim.koeninger@hosa.org
Director, Membership services: Jeff Koeninger
    E-Mail: jeff.koeninger@hosa.org

Historical Note:
A national student organization endorsed by the US Department of Education and the Health Science Technology Education Division of ACTE.

Meetings/Conferences: Annual
2013 - Nashville, TN (Gaylord Opryland Hotel and Convention Center Nashville, Tennessee)/June 26 - 30
2014 - Orlando, FL (Disney's Coronado Springs Resort)/June 25 - 28
2015 - Anaheim, CA (Hilton Anaheim)/June 24 - 27
2016 - Nashville, TN (Gaylord Opryland Hotel and Convention Center Nashville, Tennessee)/June 22 - 25

The Hosiery Association (1905)
7421 Carmel Executive Park
Suite 200
Charlotte, NC 28226
Tel: (704) 365-0913 Fax: (704) 362-2056
E-Mail: thainfo@hosieryassociation.com
Website: hosieryassociation.com
Members: 430 manufacturers
Staff: 8
Annual Budget: $1-2,000,000

Personnel:
President and Chief Executive Officer: Sally Kay
    E-Mail: sally.kay@hosieryassociation.com
Office Manager: Vicki Camp
Director, Finance: Sheila Simpson
    E-Mail: sheila.simpson@hosieryassociation.com

Historical Note:
Founded as the National Association of Hosiery Manufacturers, assumed its present name in 1999. THA supports and promotes leg wear manufacturers and suppliers, and serves as the information gateway to consumers, retailers, legislators and the media. The organization also works to build interest in legwear with retailers and the media on behalf of its members. Membership: $3,500-14,000/year (Hosiery/Supplier/International Member).

Meetings/Conferences:
Number of non-conference events/year: 5

Publications:
Hosiery Insider; monthly; adv.
Membership Directory; on-line

Hospice and Palliative Nurses Association (1986)
One Penn Center, West
Suite 229
Pittsburgh, PA 15276
Tel: (412) 787-9301 Fax: (412) 787-9305
E-Mail: hpna@hpna.org
Website: hpna.org
Members: 9200 individuals
Staff: 15
Annual Budget: $2-5,000,000
Tax: 501(c)(6)

Personnel:
Chief Executive Officer: Sally Welsh
    E-Mail: sallyw@hpna.org
Chief Operating Officer: Deena Butcher
    E-Mail: deenab@hpna.org
Assistant Administrator and Office Manager: Amy Killmeyer
    E-Mail: amyk@hpna.org
Director, Membership: Chad Reilly
    E-Mail: chadr@hpna.org
Director, Certification: Sandra Lee Schafer
    E-Mail: sandralees@hpna.org
Data Manager: Felicia Stratico
    E-Mail: felicias@hpna.org
Director, Education Products: Dena Jean Sutermaster
    E-Mail: denajeans@hpna.org
Director, Finance: Ginny Wingertsahn
    E-Mail: ginnyw@hpna.org

Historical Note:
Formerly (1997) the Hospice Nurses Association. Provides resources such as leadership development, education and support for advanced practice nurses, registered nurses, licensed practical nurses, and nursing assistants who care for people with life-limiting and terminal illness. HPNA members are members of the nursing team specializing in hospice and palliative care. Associate members are professionals, para- professionals, and/or volunteers engaged in or interested in palliative and hospice care.HPNA's mission is to promote excellence in the provision of palliative nursing care through leadership development, education, and the support of research in the field. Membership: $85 (RN-voting); $45 (Senior RN); $85 (Associate-non-RN); $70 (LPN/VN); $35 (Nursing Assistant); $45 (Student).

Meetings/Conferences: Annual

2013 - New Orleans, LA/March 13 - 16
2014 - San Diego, CA/March 12 - 15
2015 - Philadelphia, PA/Feb. 25 - 28
Publications:
HPNA enewsletter; on-line
Member Directory; on-line
The Journal of Hospice and Palliative Nursing; bi-monthly
The Journal of Palliative Medicine; on-line
Membership List Available to Non-members

Hospice Association of America (1985)
228 Seventh St. SE
Washington, DC 20003-4306
Tel: (202) 546-4759 *Fax:* (202) 547-9559
E-Mail: jen@nahc.org
Website: nahc.org/HAA
Members: 2800 hospices
Staff: 1
Tax: 501(c)(3)
Personnel:
Executive Director: Janet E. Neigh
    E-Mail: jen@nahc.org
Historical Note:
HAA members are hospices, related healthcare organizations, and medical professionals. The purpose of HAA is to heighten the public visibility of hospice services, to gather and disseminate data pertinent to the hospice industry, to foster, develop, and promote high standards of patient care in hospice services, to disseminate information and provide for the exchange of information with those interested in hospice services. Membership: $150/year (Individual).
Continuing Education:
Certification Designation/s: CHCE
Meetings/Conferences: Annual
Publications:
CARING; monthly
Membership Directory; on-line
NAHC Report; daily; adv.

Hospitality Financial and Technology Professionals (1952)
11709 Boulder Ln.
Suite 110
Austin, TX 78726-1832
Tel: (512) 249-5333 *Fax:* (512) 249-1533
TollFree: (800) 646-4387
E-Mail: hftp@hftp.org
Website: hftp.org
Members: 4800 individuals
Staff: 18
Annual Budget: $1-2,000,000
Personnel:
Chief Executive Officer: Frank I. Wolfe CAE
    E-Mail: frank.wolfe@hftp.org
Chief Financial Officer: Thomas J. Atzenhofer CPA
    E-Mail: Thomas.Atzenhofer@hftp.org
Programmer and Database Administrator: Gary Bourque
    E-Mail: Gary.Bourque@hftp.org
Chief Operations Officer: Lucinda Hart
    E-Mail: Lucinda.Hart@hftp.org
Director, Membership Services: Lillian Lack
    E-Mail: Lillian.Lack@hftp.org
Director, Marketing: Jennifer Lee
    E-Mail: jennifer.lee@hftp.org
Director, Communications: Eliza R. Selig
    E-Mail: Eliza.Selig@hftp.org
Director, Meetings and Special Events: Steven Stout CAE
    E-Mail: Steven.Stout@hftp.org
Director, Certification: Bryan Wood
    E-Mail: Bryan.Wood@hftp.org
Historical Note:
Formerly the National Association of Hotel Accountants, National Association of Hotel-Motel Accountants and the International Association of Hospitality Accountants. HFTP's mission is to provide continuing education and networking opportunities to its members around the world. Membership: $350/year (Individual).
Continuing Education:
Certification Designation/s: CHAE, CHTP
Meetings/Conferences: Annual
Conference Chair: Steven Stout CAE
2013 - Minneapolis, MN (Minneapolis Convention Center)/June 24 - 27
2013 - Dallas, TX (Hilton Anatole)/Oct. 16 - 19
Number of non-conference events/year: 1

Publications:
HFTP's Directory and Guide; on-line
Infoline; monthly; adv.
The Bottomline; bi-annually; adv.

Hospitality Institute of Technology and Management (1983)
670 Transfer Rd.
Suite 21A
St. Paul, MN 55114
Tel: (651) 646-7077 *Fax:* (651) 646-5984
E-Mail: info@hi-tm.com
Website: hi-tm.com
Members: 25 individuals
Staff: 1
Personnel:
President: O. Peter Snyder Jr., PhD
    E-Mail: osnyder@hi-tm.com
Historical Note:
HITM provides its clients with the latest food safety and quality information and keeps them updated on changes in regulatory standards. Members are professionals involved in all aspects of commercial and non- commercial foodservice systems. Membership: $60 (Individual); $525 (Corporation).
Continuing Education:
Certification Designation/s: HACCP
Publications:
Newsletter

Hospitality Sales and Marketing Association International (1927)
1760 Old Meadow Rd.
Suite 500
McLean, VA 22102
Tel: (703) 506-3280 *Fax:* (703) 506-3266
E-Mail: info@hsmai.org
Website: hsmai.org
Members: 7000 individuals
Staff: 12
Annual Budget: $2-5,000,000
Personnel:
President and Chief Executive Officer: Robert A. Gilbert CHME, CHA
    E-Mail: bgilbert@hsmai.org
Senior Manager, Membership and Event Services: Mandie Jorgensen
    E-Mail: mjorgensen@hsmai.org
Vice President, Communications: Jason Smith
    E-Mail: jsmith@hsmai.org
Director, Programs: Kathleen Tindell
    E-Mail: ktindell@hsmai.org
Historical Note:
Formerly (1983) Hotel Sales Management Association International and (1992) Hotel Sales and Marketing Association International. HSMAI's mission is to provide hotels and their industry partners with the most comprehensive set of resources to achieve measurable success for their businesses and for themselves. Members are sales and marketing professionals representing all segments of the hospitality industry. Membership: $365 (Regular); $395 (Partner/Supplier); $60 (Students); $90 (Faculty); $650 (Executive Elite).
Continuing Education:
Certification Designation/s: CHME, CRME, CHSE
Meetings/Conferences: Annual
Conference Chair: Mandie Jorgensen
Number of non-conference events/year: 2
Publications:
HSMAI Insights Newsletter; on-line
HSMAI Marketing Review; quarterly; adv.
HSMAI Member Update; bi-weekly
Membership List Available to Non-members

Hotel Brokers International (1959)
1420 N\W Vivion Rd.
Suite 111
Kansas City, MO 64118-4511
Tel: (816) 505-4315 *Fax:* (816) 505-4319
E-Mail: info@hbihotels.com
Website: hbihotels.com
Members: 45 firms and 145 individuals
Staff: 2
Annual Budget: $500-1,000,000
Personnel:
Managing Director: Glenda J. Webb
    E-Mail: gwebb@hbihotels.com

Historical Note:
Formerly (1984) known as the Motel Brokers of America, became (1985) the American Hotel and Motel Brokers, and later (2001) Hotel-Motel Brokers of America. HBI's mission is to provide the most comprehensive range of service and services in the lodging industry. Membership: $550 (Individual); $5,160 (Company).
Meetings/Conferences:
Number of non-conference events/year: 3
Publications:
Inside Issues; quarterly
Member Directory; on-line
TransActions by HBI; annually

Hotel Electronic Distribution Network Association (1991)
750 National Press Building
529 14th St. NW
Washington, DC 20045
Tel: (202) 204-8400 *Fax:* (202) 223-9741
E-Mail: info@hedna.org
Website: hedna.org
Members: 200 corporations
Staff: 3
Annual Budget: $500-1,000,000
Tax: 501(c)(6)
Personnel:
Executive Director: Reed Hitchcock
    E-Mail: rhitchcock@hedna.org
Staff Associate: Christina Donnelly
    E-Mail: cdonnelly@hedna.org
Historical Note:
HEDNA is an association focused on providing organizations with meaningful networking opportunities and initiatives. Members are hotels, representation companies, management companies, GDS, Internet distributors, switch companies, software providers, travel agencies, tour operators, industry consultants and educational institutions. Membership: $1,500 (Principal/Allied); $250 (Fellowship).
Meetings/Conferences: Annual
Conference Chair: Christina Donnelly
2013 - Edinburgh, United Kingdom/June 18 - 20
Publications:
HEDNA e-newsletter
Membership Directory; on-line

Housing Education and Research Association (1965)
Montana State University Extension Service, 109 Taylor Hall
P.O. Box 173580
Bozeman, MT 59717-3580
Tel: (406) 994-3451 *Fax:* (406) 994-5417
E-Mail: mvogel@montana.edu
Website: housingeducators.org
Members:
100 individuals
70 libraries
Staff: 4
Annual Budget: $10-25,000
Personnel:
Executive Director: Michael P. Vogel
Historical Note:
Formerly (2003) the American Association of Housing Educators. HERA promotes planning, development, delivery and service of decent, safe, sanitary, affordable, ecologically sound and appropriately designed housing for all people. Members are educators, researchers and policy makers. Membership: $85 (Active/Affiliate); $35 (Student); $45 (Emeritus).
Meetings/Conferences: Annual
Publications:
HERA Newsletter
Housing and Society Journal

Housing Partnership Network (1990)
160 State St.
Boston, MA 02109
Tel: (617) 720-1999 *Fax:* (617) 720-3939
E-Mail: info@housingpartnership.net
Website: housingpartnership.net
Members: 98 Members
Staff: 24
Personnel:
President and Chief Executive Officer: Thomas Bledsoe
    E-Mail: Bledsoe@housingpartnership.net
Vice President, Finance: Kathleen M. Farrell
    E-Mail: Farrell@housingpartnership.net

Vice President, Communications and Resource Development: Marcia Hertz
  E-Mail: Hertz@housingpartnership.net
Chief Financial Officer and Executive Vice President, Business Operations: Janet Saglio
  E-Mail: Saglio@housingpartnership.net
Director, Administrative Services: Julie Sweeney
  E-Mail: Sweeney@housingpartnership.net

Historical Note:
Formerly National Association of Housing Partnerships, Housing Partnership Network is a collaborative of the nation's housing and community development.

HR Policy Association *(1968)*
1100 13th St. NW
Suite 850
Washington, DC 20005
Tel: (202) 789-8670 *Fax:* (202) 789-0064
E-Mail: info@hrpolicy.org
Website: hrpolicy.org
Members: 330 corporations
Staff: 22
Annual Budget: $5-10,000,000
Tax: 501(c)(6)

Personnel:
Chief Executive Officer: Jeffrey C. McGuiness
  E-Mail: jhackett@hrpolicy.org
Director, Meetings and Events: Mara Antonio
Director, Finance: Sandy Hughes
Chief Technology Officer: Angelo Kostopoulos
  E-Mail: akostopoulos@hrpolicy.org
Vice President, Strategy and Compliance: Marisa L. Milton
  E-Mail: marisa.milton@hrpolicy.org
Media Coordinator: Marie Murphy
Vice President, Benefits and Employment Policy and Associate, General Counsel: Michael D. Peterson
  E-Mail: michael.peterson@hrpolicy.org
Director, Membership Services: Natalie Stewart
Executive Vice President: Charles G. Tharp
Senior Research Associate and Website Editor: Alec Wescott
President and General Counsel: Daniel V. Yager
  E-Mail: dan.yager@hrpolicy.org

Historical Note:
Organized in 1939; includes over 200 major U.S. companies interested in the development and implementation of the nation's human resource and labor-management relations policies; conducts extensive research and analysis of pending federal legislative issues.

Continuing Education:
Certification Designation/s: GLRP, LRP

Meetings/Conferences:
Conference Chair: Mara Antonio
Number of non-conference events/year: 2

Publications:
Membership directory; on-line

HUBZone Contractors National Council *(1997)*
P.O. Box 4041
Falls Church, VA 22044
Tel: (703) 237-3674 *Fax:* (703) 229-6425
TollFree: (888) 389-5706
E-Mail: info@hubzonecouncil.org
Website: hubzonecouncil.org
Staff: 3
Annual Budget: $100-250,000

Personnel:
Executive Director: Mark Crowley
  E-Mail: mark.crowley@hubzonecouncil.org
Secretary and Legal Counsel: David Taylor Esq.
Treasurer: Carolyn Sue Williams PhD

Historical Note:
Trade association of small businesses certified in Small The HUBZone Contractors National Council purpose is to monitor public policy and promote actions that support the well-being of the HUBZone Empowerment Contracting Program, seek public policies that support, enhance, and expand business opportunities for firms that have been certified as HUBZone firms by the U.S. Small Business Administration and reinforce relations among HUBZone firms, government agencies, and other businesses. Membership: $95-1995 (Regular member Based on Annual Gross Sale); $195-2295 (Associate/ Correspondence Based on Gross Annual sales); $375 (Non-Profit Organization); $25 (Government Employee); $6,000/ $12,000 (Regular Business/Platinum Partner); $5,000 to $20,000 (Bronze/Silver/Gold Corporate Sponsor); $950 (Government Agency Sponsor).

Meetings/Conferences: Annual

Publications:
eNewsletter

Human Anatomy and Physiology Society
251 S. L. White Blvd.
P.O. Box 2945
La Grange, GA 30241-2945
Fax: (706) 883-8215
TollFree: (800) 448-4277
E-Mail: admin@hapsweb.org
Website: hapsweb.org
Members: 1700 individuals
Staff: 4
Annual Budget: $250-500,000

Personnel:
Business Manager: Shanan Molnar
Coordinator, Membership, and Contact, and ListServe and Website Administration: Robin Hurst
Coordinator, Conference: Kebret Kebede
Co-Editor: Jenelle Malcos
  E-Mail: hapsed@hapsweb.org

Historical Note:
HAPS' mission is to promote the teaching of anatomy and physiology. Membership: $15-110/year.

Meetings/Conferences: Annual
Conference Chair: Kebret Kebede
2013 - Las Vegas, NV (Mirage Hotel and Casino)/May 25 - 30
2014 - Jacksonville, FL/May 24 - 29

Publications:
HAPS-EDucator; quarterly
Membership Directory; on-line

Membership List Available to Non-members

Human Behavior and Evolution Society *(1988)*
C/O Gretchen Walker, Center for Great Plains Studies
University of Nebraska, 1155 Q St.
Lincoln, NE 68588-0214
Tel: (402) 472-6240 *Fax:* (402) 472-9642
E-Mail: rhames@unl.edu
Website: hbes.com
Staff: 3
Annual Budget: $25-50,000

Personnel:
Treasurer: Raymond Hames
  E-Mail: rhames@unl.edu
Administrative Technician: Gretchen Walker CEOE

Historical Note:
HBES is an interdisciplinary organization founded to promote the exchange of ideas and research findings using evolutionary theory to better understand of human nature.The Society was formed to promote the exchange of ideas and research findings using evolutionary theory, including studies of animal behavior, to better understand human nature.Has no officers or full-time staff. Membership: $66 (Regular); $76 (Regular Joint); $35 (Student); $38 (Student Joint).

Meetings/Conferences: Annual
2013 - Miami Beach, FL (Loews Hotel)/July 17 - 20

Publications:
Evolution and Human Behavior
Member Directory; annually
Newsletter

Human Biology Association *(1974)*
1300 S. Second St.
Suite 300
Minneapolis, MN 55454
Tel: (612) 624-8231 *Fax:* (612) 624-0315
E-Mail: t-mcdade@northwestern.edu
Website: humbio.org
Members: 300 individuals
Staff: 3
Annual Budget: $50-100,000

Personnel:
Contact, Public Relations: Ellen W. Demerath
  E-Mail: ewd@umn.edu
Webmaster: Christopher K. Barrett PhD
  E-Mail: ckevinbarrett@gmail.com

Historical Note:
Formerly known as Human Biology Council (1995). Mission is to enhance the training of professional human biologists, and to foster a better comprehension of the scope of human biology among scientific professionals and the public and advocates education, discussion, integration and

dissemination of research on all aspects of human biological variation. Membership: $85 (Fellow/Regular); $29.40 (Student/Emeritus); $110 (Supporting and Benefactors); $35 (Spouse).

Meetings/Conferences: Annual
2013 - Knoxville, TN/April 8 - 9
2013 - Knoxville, TN (Hilton Knoxville)/April 10 - 11
2014 - Calgary, AB/April 11 - 12

Publications:
American Journal of Human Biology; bi-monthly

Human Capital Institute
205 Billings Farm Rd.
Suite Five
White River Junction, VT 05001
Tel: (866) 538-1909
TollFree: (866) 538-1909
E-Mail: support@hci.org
Website: hci.org
Members: 195000 Members
Staff: 7

Personnel:
Chief Executive Officer: Carl M. Rhodes
Vice President, Technology: Louis Calitz
Chief Learning Officer: David Forman
Executive Director, Sales: Shane Lennon
  E-Mail: shane.lennon@hci.org
Chief Financial Officer: Elizabeth Lundberg
Manager, Member Services: Barbara Sumanis
  E-Mail: barbara.sumanis@hci.org
Vice President, Marketing: Angela Young

Historical Note:
HCI's mission to help leaders achieve competitive advantage, financial success and market leadership in a global economy characterized by pervasive competition, disintermediation and change. Membership: $299 (Professional); $49-199 (Workgroup, dues depend on number of members); Free (Community).

Meetings/Conferences:
2013 - Atlanta, GA (Grand Hyatt Atlanta)/Feb. 5 - 7
2013 - Boston, MA (Boston Park Plaza)/June 10 - 12

Publications:
Membership Directory; on-line
Newsletter

Human Factors and Ergonomics Society *(1957)*
P.O. Box 1369
Santa Monica, CA 90406-1369
Tel: (310) 394-1811 *Fax:* (310) 394-2410
E-Mail: info@hfes.org
Website: hfes.org
Members: 4500 individuals
Staff: 7
Annual Budget: $1-2,000,000
Tax: 501(c)(3)

Personnel:
Executive Director: Lynn Strother CAE
  E-Mail: lynn@hfes.org
Director, Membership Services: Carlos de Falla
  E-Mail: carlos@hfes.org
Administrative Assistant: Susan Marschner
  E-Mail: susan@hfes.org
Director, Communications: Lois Smith
  E-Mail: lois@hfes.org
Managing Editor: Cameron Wile
  E-Mail: cameron@hfes.org

Historical Note:
Formerly (1957) Human Factors Society of America and then the Human Factors Society and assumed its present name in 1992. HFES's mission is to advocate the discovery and exchange of knowledge concerning the characteristics of human beings that are applicable to the design of systems and devices of all kinds. Members include psychologists, engineers, designers and scientists. Membership: $195 (Regular); $293 (Contributing); $390 (Supporting); $35 (Student); $900 (Sustaining); $70 (Emeritus).

Meetings/Conferences: Annual
2013 - San Diego, CA (Hyatt Regency Mission Bay Spa and Marina-San Diego)/Sept. 30 - Oct. 4/1500 attendees
2014 - Chicago, IL (Hyatt Regency Chicago)/Oct. 27 - 31/1500 attendees
2015 - Los Angeles, CA (JW Marriott Los Angeles L.A. LIVE)/Oct. 26 - 30/1500 attendees
2016 - Washington, DC (Washington Marriott Wardman Park)/Sept. 19 - 23/1500 attendees
2017 - Austin, TX (JW Marriott)/Oct. 9 - 13

Number of non-conference events/year: 1

Publications:

Directory of Human Factors and Ergonomics Graduate
  Programs; annually
Ergonomics in Design; quarterly; adv.
HFES Bulletin; monthly; adv.
HFES Digital Library; on-line
HFES Directory and Yearbook; annually; adv.
Human Factors; bi-monthly; adv.
Journal of Cognitive Engineering and Decision
  Making(Online); annually; adv.

Membership List Available to Non-members

Human Factors Society *(1957)*

P.O. Box 1369
Santa Monica, CA 90406-1369
Tel: (310) 394-1811 *Fax:* (310) 394-2410
E-Mail: info@hfes.org
Website: hfes.org
Members: 4500 members
Staff: 7
Tax: 501(c)(3)

Personnel:

Executive Director: Lynn Strother CAE
  E-Mail: lynn@hfes.org
Director, Member Services: Carlos de Falla
  E-Mail: carlos@hfes.org
Administrative Assistant: Susan Marschner
Director, Communications: Lois Smith
  E-Mail: lois@hfes.org
Managing Editor: Cameron Wile
  E-Mail: cameron@hfes.org

Historical Note:

*Formerly known as Human Factors Society of America and
later changed its name to Human Factors Society, Inc. In
1992 the name was again changed to the Human Factors
and Ergonomics Society. HFES is an interdisciplinary
nonprofit organization of professional people who are
involved in the human factors field. The Society's mission
is to promote the discovery and exchange of knowledge
concerning the characteristics of human beings that are
applicable to the design of systems and devices of all kinds.
Membership: $195-900 (Full/Associate/Affiliate); $35
(Student).*

Meetings/Conferences: Annual

2013 - San Diego, CA (Hilton San Diego Bayfront)/
  Sept. 30 - Oct. 4
2014 - Chicago, IL (Hyatt Regency Chicago)/Oct. 27 -
  31
2015 - Los Angeles, CA (JW Marriott Los Angeles L.A.
  LIVE)/Oct. 26 - 30
2016 - Washington, DC (Washington Hilton)/Sept. 19
  - 23
2017 - Austin, TX (JW Marriott)/Oct. 9 - 13

Publications:

Ergonomics in Design; quarterly; adv.
HFES Bulletin; monthly; adv.
HFES Directory and Yearbook; annually; adv.
Human Factors; bi-monthly
Journal of Cognitive Engineering and Decision Making;
  quarterly
Reviews of Human Factors and Ergonomics; annually

Human Milk Banking Association of North America *(1985)*

4455 Camp Bowie Blvd.
Suite 114-88
Fort Worth, TX 76107
Tel: (817) 810-9984 *Fax:* (817) 810-0087
E-Mail: info@hmbana.org
Website: hmbana.org
Staff: 3
Annual Budget: $100-250,000
Tax: 501(c)(3)

Personnel:

President: Jean Drulis
Contact, Membership Services: Emily Bartlett
  E-Mail: ebartlett@firstpointresources.com
Treasurer: Amy Vickers

Historical Note:

*HMBANA's mission is to promote, protect, and support
donor milk banking. Strives to develop guidelines
for donor human milk banking practices in North
America. Membership: $40 (Associate Institutional); $30
(Individual).*

Meetings/Conferences: Annual

Publications:

Membership Directory; on-line
Newsletter; quarterly

Human Relations Area Files *(1949)*

755 Prospect St.
New Haven, CT 06511-1225
Tel: (203) 764-9401 *Fax:* (203) 764-9404
TollFree: (800) 520-4723
Website: yale.edu/hraf
Staff: 16
Annual Budget: $1-2,000,000

Personnel:

President: Carol R. Ember
Coordinator, Membership Services: Christiane Cunnar
Office Assistant: Maureen Sacchetti

Historical Note:

*HRAF's mission is to stimulate and facilitate worldwide
comparative studies of human behavior, society, and
culture.*

Publications:

HRAF News; bi-annually

Human Resource People and Strategy *(1977)*

401 N. Michigan Ave.
Suite 2200
Chicago, IL 60611
Tel: (312) 321-6805 *Fax:* (312) 673-6944
E-Mail: info@hrps.org
Website: hrps.org
Members: 2000 individuals
Staff: 20
Annual Budget: $1-2,000,000

Personnel:

Executive Director: Mark Thorsby
  E-Mail: MThorsby@hrps.org
Contact, People and Strategy Advertising: David Perez
  Hernandez
  E-Mail: DPerez@hrps.org
Contact, Media Inquiries: Ande Leslie
  E-Mail: ALeslie@hrps.org
Director, Operations: Bridget McLaughlin
  E-Mail: BMclaughlin@hrps.org
Contact, Individual Membership Services: Maggie Shields
  E-Mail: kzapalik@hrps.org
Editor: Theresa Wojtalewicz
  E-Mail: twojtalewicz@hrps.org
Contact, Individual and Enterprise Membership Services:
  Kyle Zapalik
  E-Mail: kzapalik@hrps.org

Historical Note:

*Formerly (2008) The Human Resources Planning Society.
The new logo was unveiled at the 2009 Annual Conference
and the HR Planning Society became HR People & Strategy.
Mission is to help organizations enhance their performance
through strategic management of human resources.
Membership: $150-5000/year.*

Meetings/Conferences: Annual

2013 - Denver, CO (Denver Marriott City Center)/April
  14 - 17

Publications:

Membership Directory; on-line
People & Strategy; quarterly; adv.

Humanities Education and Research Association

P.O. Box 715
Pacifica, CA 94044-4206
Tel: (650) 359-2660 *Fax:* (616) 331-2700
E-Mail: hera.hera@att.net
Website: h-e-r-a.org
Members: 400 members
Staff: 3
Annual Budget: $10-25,000
Tax: 501(c)(3)

Personnel:

Executive Director and Chief Financial Officer: Marcia
  Green
  E-Mail: mgreen@sfsu.edu
Newsletter Editor: James Bell
  E-Mail: bellja@gvsu.edu
Webmaster: Doré Ripley
  E-Mail: dore.ripley@gmail.com

Historical Note:

*HERA is devoted to promoting the worldwide study,
teaching and understanding of the humanities across
a range of disciplines through regular conferences,
scholarship, and its journal Interdisciplinary Humanities.
Members are humanities teachers, scholars, and museum*

directors. *Membership: $90 (Individual); $130 (Joint); $45
(Student/Retired); $125 (Library).*

Meetings/Conferences: Annual

Conference Chair: Marcia Green
2013 - Houston, TX (Westin Galleria Houston)/March
  20 - 23

Publications:

HERA Newsletter
Interdisciplinary Humanities; semi-annually

Huntington College of Health Sciences *(1985)*

1204D Kenesaw
Knoxville, TN 37919-7736
Tel: (865) 524-8079 *Fax:* (865) 524-8339
TollFree: (800) 290-4226
E-Mail: studentservices@hchs.edu
Website: hchs.edu
Staff: 2

Personnel:

President: Arthur M. Presser PharmD
  E-Mail: apresser@hchs.edu
Director, Finance: Robert T. Shmaeff MPA, RPh, CAE, JD
  E-Mail: gbruno@hchs.edu

Historical Note:

*Formerly (1985) American Academy of Nutrition, assumed
its current name in 2005. HCHS's mission is to transform
lives through education by offering accessible, convenient,
affordable and comprehensive distance education in
nutrition and the health sciences.*

Continuing Education:

Certification Designation/s: CSC

Publications:

Education News And Research Reviews

Hydraulic Institute *(1917)*

Six Campus Dr.
First Floor North
Parsippany, NJ 07054-4406
Tel: (973) 267-9700 *Fax:* (973) 267-9055
E-Mail: info@pumps.org
Website: pumps.org
Members: 98 manufacturers of pumps
Staff: 13
Annual Budget: $2-5,000,000
Tax: 501(c)(6)

Personnel:

Executive Director: Robert K. Asdal
  E-Mail: rasdal@pumps.org
Administrator, Technical Affairs: Karen Anderson
  E-Mail: kandersan@pumps.org
Manager, Meetings and Events: Gabrielle Bosco
  E-Mail: gbosco@pumps.org
Contact, Publications: Susan Dunn
  E-Mail: publications@pumps.org
Administrator, Marketing and Communications: Patrick
  Maloney
  E-Mail: pmaloney@pumps.org
Technical Director: Gregg Romanyshyn
  E-Mail: gromanyshyn@pumps.org
Director, Marketing and Membership Services: Mary Silver
  E-Mail: msilver@pumps.org
Office and Committee Coordinator, Technical Affairs:
  Denielle Starr
  E-Mail: dstarr@pumps.org

Historical Note:

*HI's mission is to develop and deliver comprehensive
industry standards, and expand knowledge by providing
education and tools for the effective application, testing,
installation, operation and maintenance of pumps and
pumping systems. It also serves for the exchange of industry
information. Membership: 6,400 (Pump Manufacturer/
Systems Integrators); 8,300 (Associate).*

Meetings/Conferences:

Conference Chair: Gabrielle Bosco
2013 - Ft. Myers, FL (Sanibel Harbour Marriott Resort
  and Spa)/Feb. 7 - 12
2013 - Chicago, IL (Lincolnshire Marriott Resort)/June
  26 - 28
2013 - Baltimore, MD (Baltimore's Tremont Plaza
  Hotel)/Oct. 23 - 26
2014 - Phoenix, AZ (The Wigwam)/Feb. 6 - 11
2015 - St. Petersburg, FL (Renaissance Vinoy Resort
  and Golf Club)/Feb. 12 - 17
Number of non-conference events/year: 1

Publications:

Information & News Update; monthly
Membership Directory; annually

Pump Forum Newsletter; quarterly
Pump Standards

ICAAAA Coaches Association (1919)
3927 Benton St. NW
Washington, DC 20007
Fax: (202) 466-8987
E-Mail: golfwritersinc@aol.com
Members: 115 schools
Staff: 1
Annual Budget: Under $10,000

Personnel:
Secretary-Treasurer: Walter Krolman
   E-Mail: wjjk3927@juno.com

Historical Note:
*Track and field coaches from eastern colleges and
universities affiliated with the Intercollegiate Association of
Amateur Athletes of America (ICAAAA). Has no paid staff.
Membership: $15/year (individual).*

ICE Futures U.S. (1870)
One N. End Ave.
New York, NY 10282-1101
Tel: (212) 748-4000 *Fax:* (212) 643-4537
Website: theice.com
Members: 975 individuals
Staff: 250
Annual Budget: $50-100,000,000

Personnel:
President and Chief Operating Officer: Benjamin Jackson
Vice President, Market Regulation: Mark Fabian
Investigator and Analyst: Chris Goncalves
   E-Mail: chris.goncalves@theice.com
*Senior Vice President, Legal and Regulatory and General
   Counsel and Secretary:* Audrey H. Hirschfeld
Contact, Media Inquiries: Lee Underwood
   E-Mail: lee.underwood@theice.com

Historical Note:
*Formerly (1998) the New York Cotton Exchange and The
Coffee, Sugar and Cocoa Exchange, Inc. Oldest of the
New York commodity futures exchanges, (1966) Citrus
Associates and (1985) Finex Division. Purchased the New
York Futures Exchange, a wholly-owned subsidiary, in
1993, (2007) the New York Board of Trade (NYBOT) and
assumed its current name in 2007. Mission is to provide
global futures and options markets, as well as clearing
services, through ICE Clear U.S., its wholly owned clearing
house.*

Publications:
ICE Newsletter; monthly
Membership Directory; on-line

Ice Skating Institute (1959)
6000 Custer Rd.
Buillding Nine
Plano, TX 75023
Tel: (972) 735-8800 *Fax:* (972) 735-8815
Website: skateisi.com
Members: 60000 individuals, 3500 instructors
Staff: 8
Annual Budget: $2-5,000,000
Tax: 501(c)(6)

Personnel:
Executive Director: Peter Martell
   E-Mail: pmartell@SkateISI.org
Contact , Information Technologies: Jeff Anderson
   E-Mail: Jeff@skateisi.org
Controller: Donna Crooks
   E-Mail: donna@skateisi.org
Director, Management Programs and Services: Sean Flynn
   E-Mail: sflynn@skateisi.org
Manager, Advertising and Print Production: Carol Jackson
   E-Mail: cjackson@skateisi.org
Coordinator , Membership Services: Mary Ann Mangano
   E-Mail: maryann@skateisi.org

Historical Note:
*ISI is a non-profit trade association that represents all
aspects of the ice arena industry. Encourages participation
in ice skating as a recreational sport. Provides information
for the development and construction of ice arenas.
Produces trade and educational publications and literature.
Provides ice skating programs for skaters of all ages and
abilities. Membership: $15 (Individual); $25 (Individual
Membership - International); $150 (Professional/
Affiliate); $100 (Professional Membership - International);
$350 (Administrative); $450 (Builder/Supplier); $5 (New
Membership Card); $18-25 (Hockey).*

Continuing Education:
Certification Designation/s: JCP

Publications:
E-news; bi-weekly; adv.
ISI Directory; annually; adv.
ISI EDGE; bi-monthly; adv.
Recreational Ice Skating; quarterly; adv.

Icelandic American Chamber of Commerce (1986)
C/O Consul General of Iceland
800 Third Ave., 36th Floor
New York, NY 10022-7604
Tel: (646) 282-9360 *Fax:* (646) 282-9369
E-Mail: icecon.ny@mfa.is
Website: icelandtrade.com
Members: 110 companies
Staff: 2
Annual Budget: $25-50,000

Personnel:
General Manager: Hlynur Gudjonsson
   E-Mail: hlynur@mfa.is
Treasurer: Einar Gustavsson

Historical Note:
*Managed by the Iceland trade office at the Consulate
General of Iceland in New York. Mission is to encourage
the development of business and trade between the United
States and Iceland through membership networking events,
business conferences and other occasions in which leaders
of the business and government participate. Any company,
individual or group seeking to strengthen business and
other important relations between Iceland and The United
States of America can join as member. Membership: $60
(Individual); $200 (Company).*

Publications:
IACC Directory; on-line

ICLEI - Local Governments for Sustainability (1989)
414 13th St.
Suite 400
Oakland, CA 94612
Tel: (510) 844-0699 *Fax:* (510) 844-0698
E-Mail: iclei-usa@iclei.org
Website: iclei.org
Staff: 6

Personnel:
Corporate Treasurer: Frank Cownie
Director, Communications and Marketing: Don Knapp
Finance Officer: Dawna Liang
   E-Mail: dawna.liang@iclei.org
Director, External Affairs: Patrice Parsons
   E-Mail: patrice.parsons@iclei.org
Interim Executive Director: Michael Schmitz
   E-Mail: michael.schmitz@iclei.org
Program Officer: Amruta Sudhalkar
   E-Mail: amruta.sudhalkar@iclei.org

Historical Note:
*ICLEI's mission is to build and serve a worldwide movement
of local governments to achieve tangible improvements in
global sustainability with special focus on environmental
conditions through cumulative local actions. Membership:
$120 to $16,750/year (Full membership for Local
Government depending on Gross National Income per
Capita and population); $720 to $3,000/year (Full
membership for Association of Local Governments/Local
Government Institutesdepending on Gross National Income
per Capita and population).*

Meetings/Conferences: Annual
Number of non-conference events/year: 2

Publications:
ICLEI USA e-Newsletters; bi-monthly

ICOM, International Communications Agency Network (1950)
P.O. Box 490
Rollinsville, CO 80474-0490
Tel: (303) 258-9511 *Fax:* (303) 484-4087
E-Mail: info@icomagencies.com
Website: icomagencies.com
Members: 77 agencies
Staff: 3
Annual Budget: $500-1,000,000

Personnel:
Executive Director: Gary Burandt
   E-Mail: burandt@icomagencies.com

Historical Note:
*Founded as the National Federation of Advertising Agencies,
became the International Federation of Advertising Agencies
in 1980 and became ICOM in 1998. ICOM's mission is to
provide effective integrated communications resources for
its clients internationally. Members are non-competing local
advertising agencies, about 32% of which are American.
Membership: $1,500-5,000/year.*

Publications:
ICOM Directory.
ICOM Newsletter; monthly
Member Directory; monthly

IDEA, The Health and Fitness Association (1982)
10455 Pacific Center Ct.
San Diego, CA 92121
Tel: (858) 535-8979 *Fax:* (858) 535-8234
TollFree: (800) 999-4332
E-Mail: contact@ideafit.com
Website: ideafit.com
Members: 23000 individuals
Staff: 2

Personnel:
Executive Director: Kathie Davis
President and Chief Executive Officer: Peter Davis
   E-Mail: davisp@ideafit.com

Historical Note:
*Formerly (1990) International Dance-Exercise Association,
(1993) IDEA, The Association for Fitness Professionals,
(1997) IDEA, The International Association of Fitness
Professionals, The Health and Fitness Association and then
IDEA. IDEA committed to improving the health and fitness
of all people and focused on delivering compelling member
value by imparting knowledge, credibility, inspiration,
marketability and personal and professional growth
opportunities. Membership includes personal trainers,
program and fitness directors, business owners and
managers, and group fitness instructors. Membership:
$119 (Business/Personal Trainer/Mind-Body); $99 (Group
Fitness and Health Professional).*

Meetings/Conferences: Annual
2013 - Los Angeles, CA/Aug. 7 - 11

Publications:
IDEA Fit Tips; monthly; adv.
IDEA Fitness Journal; monthly; adv.
IDEA Fitness Manager; adv.
IDEA Pilates Today; adv.
IDEA Trainer Success; adv.
Membership Directory; on-line

Ideas America (1942)
P.O. Box 210863
Auburn HIlls, MI 48321
Tel: (248) 961-2674
E-Mail: ia@ideas-america.org
Website: ideas-america.org
Members: 400 companies
Staff: 2
Annual Budget: $25-50,000

Personnel:
Executive Director: Paula Davis
Secretary and Treasurer: Diana Allen

Historical Note:
*Formerly Employee Involvement Association. IA's purpose
is to improve employer-employee relations, to stimulate
constructive thinking on the part of both, and in general to
enhance a sympathetic understanding of mutual problems
toward making this a better working world in which to live.
Membership: $250 (Organization); $290 (Associate); $35
(Student); $70 (Individual).*

Continuing Education:
Certification Designation/s: CASS

Meetings/Conferences: Annual
2013 - Orlando, FL/Sept. 11 - 13

Publications:
Membership Directory; on-line
Newsletter

IEEE - Nuclear and Plasma Sciences Society (1949)
PPH Program Office MS D420
Los Alamos National Laboratory
Los Alamos, NM 87544
Tel: (505) 667-8214 *Fax:* (505) 665-2828
Website: ewh.ieee.org/soc/nps
Members: 3000 individuals
Staff: 3

Personnel:
President: Robert E. Reinovsky
   E-Mail: bobr@lanl.gov

Historical Note:

Formerly known as the Nuclear and Plasma Sciences Society, assumed its present name in 1999. A technical society of the Institute of Electrical and Electronics Engineers (IEEE). Membership in the Society, open only to IEEE members, includes subscription to technical periodicals in the field published by IEEE. All administrative support provided by IEEE.

Meetings/Conferences:
2013 - Marseille, France/June 24 - 27
2013 - Oxford, United Kingdom/Sept. 23 - 27
2013 - Pasadena, CA/Sept. 29 - Oct. 4
2015 - Richmond, VA/May 4 - 8
2016 - Chicago, IL/Oct. 9 - 14

Publications:
NPSS Newsletter

IEEE Aerospace and Electronic Systems Society (AESS)

445 Hoes Ln.
Piscataway, NJ 08854-4141
Tel: (732) 981-0060 *Fax:* (732) 981-0225
Website: ieee-aess.org
Members: 8500 individuals
Staff: 7

Personnel:
Executive Vice President: Robert P. Lyons Jr.
   E-Mail: lyonsrp1@earthlink.net
President: Marina Ruggieri
   E-Mail: ruggieri@uniroma2.it
Vice President, Membership: Jim Howard
   E-Mail: j.howard@ieee.org

Historical Note:
A technical society of the Institute of Electrical and Electronics Engineers (IEEE). Membership in the Society, open only to IEEE members, includes a subscription to a technical periodical in the field published by IEEE. All administrative support is provided by IEEE. Membership: $157 (U.S. Resident), $44 (U.S. Student); $63 (U.S. Resident-Affiliate).

Meetings/Conferences:
Conference Chair: Mark E. Davis
2013 - Ottawa, ON/April 29 - May 3
2013 - Schaumburg, IL/Sept. 16 - 19

Publications:
AESS Systems Magazine Tutorials; annually
IEEE Aerospace and Electronic Systems Magazine; monthly
IEEE Transactions on Aerospace and Electronic Systems; quarterly
Quarterly Email Blast; quarterly

IEEE Circuits and Systems Society

445 Hoes Ln.
Piscataway, NJ 08854
Tel: (732) 465-5821 *Fax:* (732) 981-1769
E-Mail: cas-info@ieee.org
Website: ieee-cas.org
Members: 13500 Individuals
Staff: 2
Annual Budget: $100-250,000

Personnel:
Executive Director: Heidi Zazza
   E-Mail: h.zazza@ieee.org
Administrator: L. Caruso
   E-Mail: l.caruso@ieee.org

Historical Note:
A technical society of the Institute of Electrical and Electronics Engineers (IEEE). IEEE/CAS's mission aims toward the advancement of the theory and practice of electrical, electronics, and allied branches of engineering or the related arts and science, in order to increase the professional standing of the members and affiliates. Membership is open only to IEEE members. Membership: $19 (Regular); $10 (Student).

Meetings/Conferences: Annual
2013 - Beijing, China (China National Convention Center)/May 19 - 23

Publications:
Design & Test Magazine
IEEE Circuits and Systems Magazine; quarterly
IEEE Circuits and Systems Society Newsletter; irregular
IEEE Journal on Emerging and Selected Topics in Circuits and Systems; quarterly

IEEE Communications Society (1952)

Three Park Ave.
17th Floor
New York, NY 10016

Tel: (212) 705-8900 *Fax:* (212) 705-8999
Website: comsoc.org
Members: 50000 individuals
Staff: 20
Annual Budget: $10-25,000,000

Personnel:
Executive Director: Jack Howell
   E-Mail: j.howell@comsoc.org
Director, Information and Communication Technology:
   David Alvarez
   E-Mail: d.alvarez@comsoc.org
Associate Publisher and Department Head: Joe Milizzo
   E-Mail: j.milizzo@comsoc.org
Director and Department Head, Marketing: John Pape
   E-Mail: j.pape@comsoc.org
Director, Finance, Administrator and Conferences: Bruce Worthman
   E-Mail: b.worthman@comsoc.org

Historical Note:
A subsidiary of the Institute of Electrical and Electronics Engineers, ComSoc promotes the advancement of science, technology and applications in communications and related disciplines. Purpose is to foster technological innovation and excellence for the benefit of humanity. Membership: $25 (Society); $13 (Students); $94 (Affiliate).

Continuing Education:
Certification Designation/s: IEEE-EPP

Meetings/Conferences: Annual
Conference Chair: Bruce Worthman
2013 - Las Vegas, NV/Jan. 11 - 14
2013 - Johannesburg, South Africa/March 24 - 27
2013 - Shanghai, China/April 7 - 10
2013 - Turin, Italy/April 14 - 19
2013 - Ghent, Belgium (Ghent University)/May 27 - 31
2013 - Budapest, Hungary/June 9 - 13
2013 - Taipei, Taiwan/July 8 - 11
2013 - Atlanta, GA/Dec. 9 - 13
Number of non-conference events/year: 4

Publications:
ComSoc e-News; on-line
Global Communications Newsletter; monthly
IEEE Communications Magazine; monthly; adv.
IEEE Network - The Magazine of Global Internetworking; bi-monthly; adv.
IEEE Wireless Communications; bi-monthly; adv.

IEEE Components, Packaging, and Manufacturing Technology Society (1950)

445 Hoes Ln.
Piscataway, NJ 08854
Tel: (732) 562-5529 *Fax:* (732) 465-6435
Website: cpmt.ieee.org
Members: 3900 individuals
Staff: 6

Personnel:
Executive Director: Marsha Tickman
   E-Mail: m.tickman@ieee.org
Vice President, Publications: R. Wayne Johnson
   E-Mail: johnsr7@auburn.edu
Vice President, Education: Kitty Pearsall
   E-Mail: kittyp@us.ibm.com
Vice President, Finance: Thomas G. Reynolds
   E-Mail: t.reynolds@ieee.org
Vice President, Conferences: Jean Trewhella
   E-Mail: jeanmh@us.ibm.com
Vice President, Technical Services: Jie Xue
   E-Mail: jixue@cisco.com

Historical Note:
Formerly (1996) the Components, Hybrids and Manufacturing Technology Society. A technical society of the Institute of Electrical and Electronics Engineers. CPMT is the international forum for scientists and engineers engaged in the research, design and development of revolutionary advances in microsystems packaging and manufacturing. Membership: $84.5 (Society Affiliate); $15 (Professional); $8 (Student).

Meetings/Conferences:
Conference Chair: Jean Trewhella
Number of non-conference events/year: 3

Publications:
CPMT Society Newsletter; quarterly
IEEE Spectrum Magazine

IEEE Computational Intelligence Society

9330 Scranton Rd.
San Diego, CA 92121
Tel: (858) 455-6449 *Fax:* (858) 455-1560

E-Mail: cis-info@ieee.org
Website: cis.ieee.org
Staff: 3

Personnel:
Vice President, Conferences: Gary Fogel

Historical Note:
The IEEE Computational Intelligence Society was formed as the IEEE Neural Networks Council on November 17th, 1989 with representatives from 12 different IEEE societies. On November 21, 2001, the IEEE Neural Networks Council became the IEEE Neural Networks Society, and in November of 2003 changed its name to the IEEE Computational Intelligence Society. A subsidiary of the Institute of Electrical and Electronics Engineers (IEEE). IEEE CIS is the technical society for scientists and professionals working in the area of computational intelligence. Membership: Free- $185/year (Full/Student).

Meetings/Conferences:
Conference Chair: Gary Fogel

Publications:
IEEE CI Magazine; quarterly
IEEE Transactions on Evolutionary Computation
IEEE Transactions on Fuzzy Systems; bi-monthly
IEEE Transactions on Neural Networks

IEEE Computer Society (1946)

2001 L. St. NW
Suite 700
Washington, DC 20036-4928
Tel: (202) 371-0101 *Fax:* (202) 728-9614
E-Mail: help@computer.org
Website: computer.org
Members: 85000 individuals
Staff: 6

Personnel:
Executive Director: Angela R. Burgess
   E-Mail: aburgess@computer.org
Director, Membership Development: Violet S. Doan
   E-Mail: vdoan@computer.org
Director, Marketing and Sales: Chris Jensen
Director, Information Technology and services: Ray Kahn
   E-Mail: rkahn@computer.org
Director, Finance and Accounting: John G. Miller

Historical Note:
The IEEE Computer Society is the computing professional's single, unmatched source for technology information, inspiration and collaboration.Membership: $54-123 (Professional); $40 (Student).

Continuing Education:
Certification Designation/s: CSDA, CSDP

Meetings/Conferences:
Number of non-conference events/year: 1

Publications:
Computer magazine; monthly; adv.
Computing Magazine; bi-monthly
IEEE Annals of the History of Computing; quarterly
IEEE Micro Magazine; bi-monthly
IEEE Newsletter; monthly
IEEE Smart Grid Newsletter; on-line
IEEE Software Magazine; monthly
IEEE Transactions on Parallel and Distributed Systems; monthly
Membership Directory; on-line

IEEE Consumer Electronics Society (1965)

4115 Clendenning Rd.
Gibsonia, PA 15044
Website: ewh.ieee.org/soc/ces
Members: 7000 individuals
Staff: 1
Annual Budget: $250-500,000

Personnel:
Executive Administrator: Charlotte Kobert
   E-Mail: ckobert@zbzoom.net

Historical Note:
A technical society of the Institute of Electrical and Electronics Engineers (IEEE). Strives for the advancement of the theory and practice of Electronic Engineering and of the allied arts and sciences with respect to the field of Consumer Electronics. Members are those interested in the consumer related aspects of leisure, video, and audio entertainment electronics; home information and communications systems; and interactive information and display systems. Membership in the Society, open only to IEEE members, includes a subscription to a technical periodical in the field published by IEEE. All administrative support is provided by IEEE. Membership: $15 (Regular); $8 (Student); $79.50 (Affiliate); Free (CEA Sponsored Membership for Small Businesses).

Meetings/Conferences: Annual
Conference Chair: Charlotte Kobert
2013 - Las Vegas, NV (Las Vegas Convention Center)/ Jan. 11 - 14
Number of non-conference events/year: 1

Publications:
Consumer Electronics Society Newsletter; quarterly; adv.

IEEE Control Systems Society *(1954)*
445 Hoes Ln.
P.O. Box 1331
Piscataway, NJ 08855-1331
Tel: (732) 981-0060 *Fax:* (732) 981-0225
Website: ieeecss.org
Members: 11000 individuals
Staff: 7

Personnel:
Executive Director: Mario Sznaier
   E-Mail: msznaier@coe.neu.edu
Vice President, Publication Activities: Frank Doyle
Editor: Magnus Egerstedt
   E-Mail: magnus@ece.gatech.edu
Vice President, Conference Activities: Masayuki Fujita
   E-Mail: fujita@ctrl.titech.ac.jp
Vice President, Member Activities: Shuzhi Sam Ge
   E-Mail: samge@nus.edu.sg
Vice President, Financial Activities: Pradeep Misra
   E-Mail: pradeep.misra@wright.edu

Historical Note:
A technical society of the Institute of Electrical and Electronics Engineers (IEEE). IEEE/CSS focuses on the theory, design and application of control systems. IEEE/CSS's mission is to provide the advancement of research, development, and practice in automation and control systems.. Membership in the Society, open only to IEEE members, includes a subscription to a technical periodical in the field published by IEEE. All administrative support is provided by IEEE. Membership: $10 (Student); $20 (Individual).

Meetings/Conferences: Annual
Conference Chair: Masayuki Fujita
2013 - Washington, DC (Renaissance Washington, D.C. Downtown Hotel)/June 17 - 19
2013 - Hyderabad, India/Aug. 26 - 28
2013 - Florence, Italy/Dec. 10 - 13
2014 - Los Angeles, CA/Dec. 15 - 17

Publications:
E-Letter; monthly; adv.
IEEE Control Systems Magazine; bi-monthly; adv.
Transactions on Automatic Control; monthly
Transactions on Control Systems Technology; bi-monthly

IEEE Education Society *(1963)*
164 S. Main St.
Lanesborough, MA 01237
Tel: (413) 443-6153
Website: ieee.org/edsoc
Members: 3000 individuals
Staff: 1245
Annual Budget: Over $100,000,000

Personnel:
President and Vice President, Chapter Activity: Rob Reilly EdD
   E-Mail: reilly@media.mit.edu
Vice President, Publications: Martin Llamas Nistal
   E-Mail: martin@uvigo.es

Historical Note:
IEEE Education Society, a technical society of the Institute of Electrical and Electronics Engineers (IEEE) and administrative support provided by IEEE, is dedicated to advancing technological innovation and excellence. Membership in the Society is open only to IEEE members and includes a subscription to a technical periodical in the field published by IEEE.

Meetings/Conferences:
Conference Chair: Russ Meier

IEEE Electron Devices Society *(1951)*
445 Hoes Ln.
Piscataway, NJ 08854
Tel: (732) 562-3926 *Fax:* (732) 235-1626
Website: eds.ieee.org
Members: 11,000 Individuals
Staff: 5

Personnel:
Executive Director: Christopher J. Jannuzzi

   E-Mail: c.jannuzzi@ieee.org
Coordinator, Membership: Joyce Aqara (Lombardini)
   E-Mail: j.lombardini@ieee.org
Administrator, Conferences: Jean Bae
   E-Mail: jean.bae@ieee.org
Administrator, Publications: Mariola Piatkiewicz
   E-Mail: m.piatkiewicz@ieee.org
Program Manager, Business Administration: Laura J. Riello
   E-Mail: l.riello@ieee.org

Historical Note:
A technical society of the Institute of Electrical and Electronics Engineers (IEEE). IEEE/EDS's mission is to foster professional growth of its members by satisfying their needs for easy access to and exchange of technical information, publishing, education, and technical recognition and enhancing public visibility in the field of Electron Devices. Membership in the Society, open only to IEEE members, includes subscriptions to technical periodicals in the field published by IEEE and all administrative support is provided by IEEE. Membership: $12-60/year.

Meetings/Conferences: Annual
Conference Chair: Jean Bae

Publications:
EDS roster; on-line
IEEE Electron Device Letters; monthly
IEEE Transactions on Electron Devices; monthly
Journal of Lightwave Technology
The Electron Devices Society; quarterly; adv.

IEEE Engineering in Medicine and Biology Society *(1952)*
445 Hoes Ln.
Piscataway, NJ 08855-1331
Tel: (732) 981-3433 *Fax:* (732) 465-6435
E-Mail: emb-exec@ieee.org
Website: embs.org
Members: 8085 individuals
Staff: 5

Personnel:
Executive Director: Laura J. Wolf CMM
   E-Mail: l.wolf@ieee.org
Associate Planner, Conferences: Laura Herrera
   E-Mail: laura.herrera@ieee.org
Planner, Conferences: Jessica Lotito CMP
Administrator, Society Services: Angela Martin
   E-Mail: angela.martin@ieee.org
Senior Administrator, Society Services: Alicia Tomaszewski
   E-Mail: a.tomaszewski@ieee.org

Historical Note:
A technical society of the Institute of Electrical and Electronics Engineers (IEEE). EMBS's mission is to advance the application of engineering sciences and technology to medicine and biology and promotes the profession for the benefit of its members and humanity. Membership: $103 (Affiliate Basic); $275 (Affiliate Plus); $175-213 (International).

Meetings/Conferences:
Conference Chair: Laura Herrera
2013 - San Francisco, CA (The Westin Hotel)/April 7 - 11
2013 - Osaka, Japan/July 2 - 7
2013 - Osaka, Japan (Osaka International Convention Center)/July 3 - 7
2014 - Chicago, IL/Aug. 26 - 30
2015 - Milan, Italy/Aug. 26 - 31
2016 - Orlando, FL/Aug. 30 - Sept. 4
Number of non-conference events/year: 2

Publications:
IEEE Engineering in Medicine and Biology Society Magazine; on-line; adv.
IEEE Potentials; adv.
IEEE Reviews on Biomedical Engineering (R-BME); annually
IEEE Security and Privacy Magazine; adv.
IEEE Spectrum; monthly; adv.
IEEE Transactions on Biomedical Circuits and Systems (T-BCAS); quarterly
IEEE Transactions on Biomedical Engineering; monthly
IEEE Transactions on Information Technology in Biomedicine (T-ITB); bi-monthly
IEEE Transactions on Mobile Computing; bi-monthly
IEEE Transactions on Neural Systems and Rehabilitation Engineering; quarterly
IEEE/ACM Transactions on Computational Biology and Bioinformatics (T-CBB); quarterly

The Institute; quarterly; adv.
Transactions on Biomedical Circuits and Systems (T-BCAS); quarterly
Transactions on Medical Imaging (T-MI)

IEEE - Industry Applications Society
445 Hoes Ln.
Piscataway, NJ 08854
Tel: (732) 465-6627 *Fax:* (732) 562-3881
E-Mail: ias-administrator@ieee.org
Website: ias.ieee.org
Members: 10,000 individuals
Staff: 2
Annual Budget: $500-1,000,000

Personnel:
Administrator: Lynda Bernstein

Historical Note:
IAS is a technical society of the Institute of Electrical and Electronics Engineers (IEEE). Through events and national and international conferences, the society keeps members abreast of current developments in the area of technology in electricity and electronics. Members are individuals interested in the global development, design, manufacture and application of electrical systems, apparatus, devices and controls to the processes and equipment of industry and commerce; the promotion of safe, reliable and economic installations; industry leadership in energy conservation and environmental, health and safey issues; the creation of voluntary engineering standards and recommended practices; and professional development. Membership is open only to IEEE members.

Meetings/Conferences: Biennial
Conference Chair: Lynda Bernstein
2013 - Orlando, FL (Walt Disney World Dolphin Resort)/April 14 - 18/650 attendees

Publications:
IEEE Industry Applications Magazine; bi-monthly
IEEE Transactions on Industry Applications; bi-monthly

IEEE Instrumentation and Measurement Society *(1950)*
9952 Kite Dr.
Huntington Beach, CA 92646-6540
E-Mail: r.goldberg@ieee.org
Website: ieee-ims.org
Members: 6500 individuals
Staff: 6
Annual Budget: $500-1,000,000

Personnel:
Vice President, Membership: Georg Brasseur
   E-Mail: georg.brasseur@tugraz.at
Vice president, Education: Ferdinanda Ponci
   E-Mail: FPonci@eonerc.rwth-aachen.de
Treasurer: Frank Reyes
   E-Mail: freyes210@ieee.org

Historical Note:
The IEEE Instrumentation and Measurement Society focuses on the science of developing and using electrical and electronic instruments for the purpose of measuring, monitoring or recording various physical phenomena that may or may not be of an electrical nature. This includes analog and digital electronic instruments, systems and standards for measuring and recording electrical quantities in the frequency domain (including dc) and the time domain, and transducers to give access to non-electrical quantities. Instruments with automated control and analysis functions are part of the field of interest. Membership: $28 (New Member Full Year); $15 (Student Full Year); $98 (Society affiliate); $29 (professional).

Meetings/Conferences: Annual
2013 - Milan, Italy/July 15 - 17
2013 - Wellington, New Zealand/Dec. 3 - 5
Number of non-conference events/year: 15

Publications:
IEEE Instrumentation & Measurement Magazine; bi-monthly; adv.
IEEE Transactions on Instrumentation and Measurement; monthly
IEEE/OSA Journal of Lightwave Technology; on-line

IEEE Magnetics Society *(1964)*
19803 Laurel Valley Pl.
Montgomery Village, MD 20886
Tel: (301) 527-0900 *Fax:* (301) 527-0994
Website: ieeemagnetics.org
Members: 3500 individuals
Staff: 4
Annual Budget: $500-1,000,000

Personnel:
President: Takao Suzuki
Manager, Conferences: Diane Melton
Secretary and Treasurer: Bruce D. Terris

Historical Note:
A technical society of the Institute of Electrical and Electronics Engineers (IEEE), bringing members access to the industry's most essential technical information, networking opportunities, career development tools. Members are interested in theory, design and applications of magnetic materials and devices. Membership is open only to IEEE members. Membership: $175.00 (United States); $32.00 (Student); $159.70 (Canada (incl. GST) $33.60 (Student); $170.42 (Canada (incl. HST)) $36.16 (Student); $147.00 (Africa, Europe, Middle East) $27.00 (Student); $138.00 (Latin America) $27.00 (Student); $139.00 (Asia, Pacific) $27.00 (Student).

Meetings/Conferences:
Conference Chair: Diane Melton
2013 - Denver, CO/Nov. 4 - 7

Publications:
IEEE Transactions on Magnetics; monthly
Magnetics Society Newsletter; quarterly

IEEE Microwave Theory and Techniques Society
(1992)
Eight Richard Rd.
Bedford, MA 01730
Tel: (781) 258-5494 *Fax:* (781) 275-8179
Website: mtt.org
Members: 11000 individuals
Staff: 3

Personnel:
President: Nick Kolias
E-Mail: N.Kolias@ieee.org
Treasurer: William Chappell
E-Mail: chappellw@rocketmail.com
Administrator: Richard A. Sparks
E-Mail: r.sparks@ieee.org

Historical Note:
MTT-S is a technical society of the Institute of Electrical and Electronics Engineers (IEEE) whose mission is to continue to understand and influence microwave technology. Membership: $86.50/year (Affiliate).

Meetings/Conferences: Semi-Annual
2013 - Orlando, FL/April 14 - 16
2013 - Alexandria, VA/Oct. 27 - 31
Number of non-conference events/year: 2

Publications:
IEEE Microwave and Wireless Components Letters; monthly
IEEE Microwave Magazine; quarterly; adv.
IEEE Transactions on Microwave Theory and Techniques; monthly
MTT-S e-Newsletter; monthly; adv.

IEEE Photonics Society *(1964)*
445 Hoes Ln.
Piscataway, NJ 08855-1331
Tel: (732) 562-5501 *Fax:* (732) 981-1138
Website: photonicssociety.org
Members: 7000 members
Staff: 19
Annual Budget: $2-5,000,000

Personnel:
Executive Director: Richard Linke
E-Mail: r.linke@ieee.org
Contact, Administrator, Membership and Awards: Giselle Blandin
E-Mail: g.blandin@ieee.org
Senior Conference Planner: Mary Hendrickx
E-Mail: m.hendrickx@ieee.org
Publications Manager: Linda Matarazzo
E-Mail: l.matarazzo@ieee.org
Senior Manager, Business: Douglas Razzano
E-Mail: d.razzano@ieee.org

Historical Note:
Formerly the IEEE Lasers and Electro-Optics Society (LEOS), the Photonics Society works to advance the interests of its members and the laser, optoelectronics, and photonics professional community by providing opportunities for information exchange, continuing education, and professional growth. Membership: $30 (Member Full Year); $15 (Student).

Meetings/Conferences: Annual
Conference Chair: Mary Hendrickx
2013 - Santa Fe, NM/May 5 - 8

Publications:

IEEE Photonics Journal; on-line
Journal of Quantum Electronics; monthly
Membership Directory; on-line
Photonics Technology Letters; semi-monthly
The Photonics Society News; bi-monthly; adv.

IEEE Power and Energy Society
445 Hoes Ln.
Piscataway, NJ 08854-1331
Tel: (732) 562-3883 *Fax:* (732) 562-3881
E-Mail: pes@ieee.org
Website: ieee-pes.org
Members: 25000 individuals
Staff: 10
Tax: 501 (c)(3)

Personnel:
Executive Director: Patrick P. Ryan
E-Mail: p.ryan@ieee.org
Administrator: Yuen Chan
E-Mail: y.l.chan@ieee.org
Senior Administrator, Education Services: Susan Koval
E-Mail: s.koval@ieee.org
Manager, Operations and Resource Center: Sissie Lin
E-Mail: sissie.lin@ieee.org
Administrator, Technical, Membership Services and Web Content: Steven Matarazzo
E-Mail: s.matarazzo@ieee.org
Senior Administrator, Meeting Services: D'Nese Moore
E-Mail: d.l.moore@ieee.org
Senior Administrator, Publication Services: Maria Proetto
E-Mail: m.proetto@ieee.org
Senior Manager, Membership Services: Susan Sacks
E-Mail: s.sacks@ieee.org

Historical Note:
IEEE/PES's mission is to be the provider of scientific information on electric power and energy for the betterment of society and the preferred professional development source for its members. Membership in the Society is open only to IEEE members, includes subscription to a technical periodical in the field published by IEEE. Membership: $104.50/year.

Meetings/Conferences:
Conference Chair: D'Nese Moore
2013 - Washington, DC/Feb. 24 - 28
2013 - São Paulo, Brazil/April 15 - 17
Number of non-conference events/year: 1

Publications:
eNewsUpdate; on-line; adv.
IEEE Power & Energy Magazine; bi-monthly
Membership Directory; on-line
PES Letters; monthly

IEEE Power Electronics Society *(1987)*
445 Hoes Ln.
Piscataway, NJ 08855-1331
Tel: (732) 465-6480 *Fax:* (732) 562-3881
Website: ieee-pels.org
Members: 7000 individuals
Staff: 1245
Annual Budget: Over $100,000,000
Tax: 501 (c)(3)

Personnel:
Senior Administrator: Donna M. Florek
E-Mail: d.florek@ieee.org

Historical Note:
The society shall advance the theory and practice of electrical and electronics engineering and of the allied arts and sciences and it shall promote a better level of technical excellence among its members. Membership: $94.50 (Society affiliate).

Meetings/Conferences: Annual
2013 - Champaign, IL/Feb. 22 - 23
2013 - Long Beach, CA (Long Beach Convention Center)/March 17 - 21
2013 - Chicago, IL (Westin O'Hare)/May 12 - 15
2013 - Kanazawa, Japan (Ishikawa Ongakudo)/May 26 - 30
2013 - Hamburg, Germany/Oct. 13 - 17
2014 - Ft. Worth, TX/March 16 - 20/2000 attendees
2014 - Waikoloa, HI/June 15 - 19
2014 - Pittsburgh, PA/Sept. 15 - 18
2014 - Vancouver, BC/Sept. 28 - Oct. 2
2015 - Charlotte, NC/March 15 - 19
Number of non-conference events/year: 3

Publications:
PELS Newsletter; quarterly

IEEE Signal Processing Society *(1948)*
445 Hoes Ln.
Piscataway, NJ 08854
Tel: (732) 562-3888 *Fax:* (732) 235-1627
E-Mail: sp.info@ieee.org
Website: signalprocessingsociety.org
Members: 14000 individuals
Staff: 13
Annual Budget: $5-10,000,000

Personnel:
Interim Executive Director: Rich Baseil
E-Mail: r.baseil@ieee.org
Senior Manager, Operations: Theresa Argiropoulos
E-Mail: t.argiropoulos@ieee.org
Manager, Conference Services: Lisa Schwarzbek
E-Mail: l.schwarzbek@ieee.org
Coordinator, Publications: Rebecca Wollman
E-Mail: r.wollman@ieee.org

Historical Note:
: Formerly the Acoustics, Speech and Signal Processing Society. SPS's mission is to advance and disseminate state-of-the-art scientific information and resources, educate the signal processing community, and provide a venue for people to interact and exchange ideas. Membership: $20 (Member); $10 (Student) $89.50 (Society Affiliate).

Meetings/Conferences:
Conference Chair: Lisa Schwarzbek
2013 - Vancouver, BC (Vancouver Convention and Exhibition Center)/May 26 - 31
2013 - San Jose, CA (The Fairmont Hotel)/July 15 - 19
2013 - Melbourne, Australia/Sept. 15 - 19
2014 - Florence, Italy (Firenze Fiera Congress and Exhibition Center)/May 4 - 9
2014 - Beijing, China/May 5 - 9
2014 - Chengdu, China/July 21 - 25
2014 - Paris, France/Oct. 27 - 30
2015 - Queensland, Australia (Brisbane Convention and Exhibition Centre)/April 19 - 24
2015 - Québec, QC/Sept. 28 - Oct. 1
2016 - Phoenix, AZ/Sept. 25 - 28
Number of non-conference events/year: 4

Publications:
Content Gazette; monthly
IEEE Journal of Selected Topics in Signal Processing; quarterly
IEEE MultiMedia Magazine; quarterly; adv.
IEEE Sensors Journal; monthly
IEEE Signal Processing Letters; monthly
IEEE Signal Processing Magazine; bi-monthly; adv.
IEEE Transactions in Computing in Science and Engineering; monthly; adv.
IEEE Transactions on Affective Computing; quarterly
IEEE Transactions on Audio, Speech and Language Processing; bi-monthly
IEEE Transactions on Image Processing; monthly
IEEE Transactions on Information Forensics and Security; quarterly
IEEE Transactions on Medical Imaging; monthly
IEEE Transactions on Mobile Computing; monthly
IEEE Transactions on Multimedia; bi-monthly
IEEE Transactions on Signal Processing; monthly
IEEE Transactions on Smart Grid; quarterly
IEEE Transactions on Wireless Communications; bi-monthly; adv.
Inside Signal Processing eNewsletter; monthly
Membership Directory; annually

IEEE Society on Social Implications of Technology
C/O University of Connecticut, Computer Science and Engineering
One University Pl.
Stamford, CT 06901-2315
Tel: (215) 898-8534
Website: ieeessit.org
Members: 2000 individuals
Staff: 2

Personnel:
President: Gerald Engel
E-Mail: gengel64@aol.com

Historical Note:
IEEE-SSIT focuses on environmental, health, and safety implications of technology; engineering ethics and professional responsibility and the history of electrotechnology. Membership: $101.50/year (Affiliate).

Meetings/Conferences: Annual
Publications:

e-News Update
IEEE Technology and Society Magazine; quarterly; adv.

IEEE Technology Management Council (1950)
445 Hoes Ln.
Piscataway, NJ 08854-4141
Tel: (732) 981-0060
Website: ieeetmc.org
Members: 8500 individuals
Staff: 6

Personnel:
President: Tuna Tarim
Editor: Paul Bergey
   E-Mail: pkbergey@ncsu.edu
Vice President, Operations: Irving Engelson
Vice President, Publications: Gerard H. (Gus) Gaynor
   E-Mail: i.engelson@ieee.org
Treasurer: Dilip Kotak
Vice President, Conferences: Robert A. Shapiro

Historical Note:
Formed through the merger of the professional Group on Engineering Management of the IRE and the Engineering Management Committee of the AIEE, in 2008, the EMS transitioned to become the Technology Management Council (TMC). IEEE Technology Management Council provides information and services to IEEE members and the worldwide audience of practitioners and researchers engaged in the profession of engineering, technology, and innovation management. As a council, TMC has fourteen member societies but no individual members.

Meetings/Conferences: Annual
Conference Chair: Robert A. Shapiro
2013 - Hague, Netherlands/June 24 - 26

IEEE Ultrasonics, Ferroelectrics and Frequency Control Society (1985)
Pennsylvania State University Ceramics Science & Engineering
151 Materials Research Laboratory
University Park, PA 16802
Tel: (732) 981-0060 *Fax:* (732) 562-6380
TollFree: (800) 678-4333
E-Mail: contactcenter@ieee.org
Website: ieee-uffc.org
Members: 2300 Individuals
Staff: 1
Annual Budget: $250-500,000

Personnel:
Executive Director: E. James Pendergrast

Historical Note:
A technical society of the Institute of Electrical and Electronics Engineers (IEEE). Membership in the Society, open only to IEEE members, includes a subscription to a technical periodical in the field published by IEEE. All administrative support is provided by IEEE. UFFCS' mission is to seek the ideas and help of its Society members to support both technical programs and its administrative activities. Membership: $20 (Member Full Year); $10 (Member Half Year); $10 (Student Full Year); $5 (Student Half Year).

Meetings/Conferences: Annual
2013 - Prague, Czech Republic (Prague Congress Centre)/July 21 - 25

Publications:
Transactions; quarterly; adv.
UFFC-S Newsletter; irregular

IFCA International (1930)
3520 Fairlane Ave. SW
P.O. Box 810
Grandville, MI 49418-1536
Tel: (616) 531-1840 *Fax:* (616) 531-1814
E-Mail: office@ifca.org
Website: ifca.org
Members: 28 bible Colleges, home mission agencies, and church planting agencies and1000 individuals
Staff: 2
Tax: 501 (c)(3)

Personnel:
Executive Director: Dr. Les Lofquist
Director, Finance and Operations: Tom Olson
   E-Mail: olson@ifca.org

Historical Note:
IFCA International is a Fellowship of churches and Christian workers committed to biblical ministry. Mission is to glorify God by providing an arena for independent churches and organizations to participate interdependently in the common cause of advancing authentic, dynamic, compassionate Christianity to all people groups. Membership: $75/year (Vocational Worker/Lay).

Meetings/Conferences: Annual
2013 - Miami, FL (DoubleTree by Hilton)/June 24 - 28

Publications:
Chera; quarterly
Harvester's Letter; on-line
IFCA NEWS Connection; monthly
IFCA YouthLine; monthly
VOICE Magazine; bi-monthly; adv.

IFIA Americas Committee Inc. (1998)
3942 N. Upland St.
Arlington, VA 22207
Tel: (703) 533-9539 *Fax:* (703) 533-1612
E-Mail: ifianac@aol.com
Website: ifia-federation.org/content/sector-committees/
Staff: 2

Personnel:
Director General: Roger Brockway
   E-Mail: roger.brockway@ifia-federation.org
Executive Director: Milton M. Bush JD, CAE
   E-Mail: lfianac@aol.com

Historical Note:
The purpose of IFIA-AC is to promote internationally accepted standards in methods, documentation and qualification of companies and personnel. Membership: $2,750/year.

Continuing Education:
Certification Designation/s: CPI

Publications:
IFIA Newsletter
Membership Directory; on-line

IGAF Polaris (1977)
3235 Satellite Blvd.
Buliding 400, Suite. 300
Duluth, GA 30096
Tel: (678) 417-7730 *Fax:* (678) 999-3959
E-Mail: info@accountants.org
Website: accountants.org
Members: 53000 staff and professionals
Staff: 5
Annual Budget: $100-250,000

Personnel:
President and Chief Executive Officer: Kevin Mead
   E-Mail: kmead@igafworldwide.org
Manager, Technology and Support Services: Sara Folk
   E-Mail: sfolk@igafworldwide.org
Chief Financial Officer: Anne Hampson
   E-Mail: ahampson@igafworldwide.org
Director, Marketing: Debra Helwig
   E-Mail: dhelwig@igafworldwide.org
Manager, Member Services: Donna Munday

Historical Note:
Formerly PrimeGlobal. Founded as International Group of Accounting Firms; assumed its current name in 2011. IGAF Polaris' mission is to provide member firms with the tools and resources they need to furnish a broad spectrum of efficient, cost- effective accounting, auditing, and management services to clients around the globe. Members are full-service public accountants and chartered accountants.

Meetings/Conferences:
2013 - Newport Beach, CA (Island Hotel Newport Beach)/Jan. 6 - 9

Publications:
Membership Directory; on-line

Membership List Available to Non-members

Illuminating Engineering Society of North America (1906)
120 Wall St.
17th Floor
New York, NY 10005-4001
Tel: (212) 248-5000 *Fax:* (212) 248-5017
E-Mail: ies@ies.org
Website: ies.org
Members: 8000 individuals
Staff: 26
Annual Budget: $5-10,000,000

Personnel:
Executive Vice President: William H. Hanley CAE
   E-Mail: whanley@ies.org

Manager, Marketing: Clayton Gordon
   E-Mail: cgordon@ies.org
Director, Technology: Rita Harrold
   E-Mail: rharrold@ies.org
Director, Public Policy: Robert Horner
Director, Membership Services: Valerie Landers
   E-Mail: vlanders@ies.org
Controller: Bruce Sohl
Editor and Associate Publisher: Paul Tarricone
   E-Mail: ptarricone@ies.org

Historical Note:
Organized in February 13, 1906, with 178 charter members and incorporated in New York in 1907. IES seeks to improve the lighted environment by bringing together those with lighting knowledge and by translating that knowledge into actions that benefit the public. Members are lighting designers, architects, interior designers, government, utility personnel, engineers, contractors, manufacturers, distributors, researchers and educators throughout the United States, Canada, Mexico and around the world. Membership: $20-15,000/year.

Meetings/Conferences: Annual
2013 - Phoenix, AZ (JW Marriott Phoenix Desert Ridge Resort and Spa)/Sept. 8 - 11
2013 - Huntington Beach, CA (Hyatt Regency Huntington Beach Resort and Spa)/Oct. 27 - 29

Membership List Available to Non-members

Illustrator's Partnership of America (1998)
845 Moraine St.
Marshfield, MA 02050
Website: illustratorspartnership.org
Staff: 1

Personnel:
Director, Operations: Ken Dubrowski
   E-Mail: info@illustratorspartnership.org

Historical Note:
Educate artists on how to protect and manage their intellectual property rights. Membership: $200(General/ Supporting); $50(Student); $400 (Educational Institutional).

Publications:
Illustrators News

IMAGE Society (1987)
P.O. Box 6221
Chandler, AZ 85246-6221
E-Mail: image@asu.edu
Website: image-society.org
Members:
40 corporate
500 individuals
Staff: 1
Annual Budget: $100-250,000

Personnel:
President: Eric G. Monroe PhD
   E-Mail: image@asu.edu

Historical Note:
Members are individuals concerned with visual and related simulation technologies and applications. $50 (Individual (U.S.)); $65 (Individual (Non-U.S.)); $25 (Student (U.S.)); $40 (Student (Non-U.S.)).

Meetings/Conferences: Annual
2013 - Scottsdale, AZ/June 3 - 6

Imaging and Perimetry Society (1974)
University of Iowa
Department of Ophthalmology and Visual Sciences
Iowa City, IA 52242-1091
Tel: (319) 356-2864 *Fax:* (319) 356-0363
Website: perimetry.org
Members: 150 individuals
Staff: 2
Annual Budget: $25-50,000

Personnel:
President: Chris Johnson PhD
   E-Mail: chris-a-johnson@uiowa.edu

Historical Note:
Formerly International Perimetric Society. Changed name to Imaging and Perimetry Society (IPS) in 2008. IPS promotes the study of normal and abnormal visual function in the entire visual field, development of new methods and instruments, establishes standards for recording and classification of visual field defects, equipment and nomenclature and liaison with other international organizations. Members are ophthamologists and other professionals working in the area of visual field testing.

Membership: $75 (Regular); $50 (Students/ Technicians/ Research Assistants).

Meetings/Conferences: Annual

Imaging Supplies Coalition (1994)
1435 E. Venice Ave.
Suite 104, MBN 249
Venice, FL 34292
Tel: (941) 961-7897
E-Mail: info@isc-inc.org
Website: isc-inc.org
Members: 9 companies
Staff: 1
Annual Budget: $100-250,000

Personnel:
President: Allen D. Westerfield
   E-Mail: iscwesterfield@aol.com

Historical Note:
ISC is dedicated to educating, empowering and protecting consumers to combat counterfeiting and fraud in the imaging supplies industry. ISC is comprised of original equipment manufacturers (OEMs) of consumable imaging supplies (ribbons, toner, inks, cartridges, etc.) and equipment that have joined together to protect their customers by combating illegal activities in the imaging supplies industry. The mission of the ISC is to protect its members' customers from misrepresented products and services by seeking the worldwide protection of intellectual property and related assets of the Imaging Supplies Industry's distributors, suppliers, and manufacturers.

Meetings/Conferences: Annual

Immigration and Ethnic History Society (1965)
Waubonsee Community College, Division of
Social Science and Education
Route 47, Waubonsee Dr.
Sugar Grove, IL 60554-9454
Tel: (630) 466-7900
Website: iehs.org
Members: 800 individuals
Staff: 4
Annual Budget: Under $10,000

Personnel:
Secretary: Timothy D. Draper
   E-Mail: tdraper@waubonsee.edu

Historical Note:
IEHS was founded as the Immigration History Group and renamed the Immigration History Society in 1972. In 1998, it changed its name to the Immigration and Ethnic History Society. IEHS's mission is to promote the study of the history of immigration to the United States and Canada from all parts of the world. Membership: $45-90 (Individual); $25-70 (Student); $35-80 (New member); $245-330 (Institutional).

Publications:
Ethnic History Newsletter; semi-annually
Journal of American Ethnic History; quarterly
Membership Directory; on-line

In-Plant Printing and Mailing Association (1964)
105 S. Jefferson
Suite B-4
Kearney, MO 64060
Tel: (816) 903-4762 Fax: (816) 902-4766
E-Mail: ipmainfo@ipma.org
Website: ipma.org
Members: 600 individuals
Staff: 3
Annual Budget: $250-500,000

Personnel:
Executive Director: Carma Goin
   E-Mail: cgoin@ipma.org
Office Assistant and Financial Coordinator: Jenece
   Saunders
   E-Mail: jsaunders@ipma.org
Assistant, Communications and Membership Services: Deb
   Svoboda
   E-Mail: dsvoboda@ipma.org

Historical Note:
Formerly (1982) the In-Plant Printing Management Association, (1996) the IPMA-A Graphic Communications Management Association and (1994) the In-Plant Management Association. IPMA exists to provide corporate publishing and distribution professionals the resources to attain greater productivity and cost effectiveness through education, certification and information exchange. Members are corporate publishing (creation, production, distribution) professionals who work for educational

institutions, government, and private industry. Membership: $300-1500/year.

Continuing Education:
Certification Designation/s: CMM, CGCM

Meetings/Conferences: Annual
2013 - San Mateo, CA (San Mateo Marriott San Francisco Airport)/June 2 - 5

Publications:
Bulletin; weekly
Inside Edge; bi-weekly

Membership List Available to Non-members

iNARTE, Inc. (1982)
600 N. Plankinton Ave.
Suite 301
Milwaukee, WI 53201
Fax: (414) 765-8661
TollFree: (888) 722-2440
E-Mail: narte@narte.org
Website: narte.com
Members: 5200 individuals
Staff: 4
Annual Budget: $250-500,000
Tax: 501(c)(6)

Personnel:
President and Chief Executive Officer: Peter Holtmann
   E-Mail: pholtmann@rabqsa.com
Executive Director: Brian Lawrence
   E-Mail: lawrence@inarte.us
Director, Global Operations: Adam Maxwell
   E-Mail: amaxwell@rabqsa.com
Operations Administrator, iNARTE Certification and other
   iNARTE Business: Jeameeka White
   E-Mail: jeameeka@inarte.us

Historical Note:
Founded (1982) as National Association of Radio and Telecommunications Engineers; assumed its current name in 2002. NARTE became iNARTE, International Association for Radio, Telecommunications and Electromagnetics in 2007. iNARTE is a non-profit certification agency, formed by telecommunication industry leaders concerned about potential proliferation of pseudo-qualified engineers and technicians that could result as a by-product of Federal deregulation. Membership: $25-75/year.

Continuing Education:
Certification Designation/s: PSEC, UWSIC, EMI, PSEC, PSTC, iNAE, WIE, WIT, iNAT, ESD, EMC, FCC-COLE

Publications:
iNARTE Newsletter

Incentive Federation, Inc. (1984)
805 15th St. NW
Suite 100
Washington, DC 20005
E-Mail: incentivefed@cox.net
Website: incentivefederation.org
Members: 150 companies
Staff: 3
Annual Budget: $100-250,000

Personnel:
Executive Director: George B. Delta Esq., CMP
   E-Mail: gdelta@deltalaw.net

Historical Note:
IFI works to promote, protect and research the incentive field, encompassing recognition, promotional products and related promotions. Regular members are national incentive marketing trade associations and professional societies. Membership: $5,000 (Platinum); $2,500 (Gold); $1,000 (Silver); $500 (Corporate); $100 (Business Individual).

Publications:
Membership Directory
Washington Newsletter
Washington Quarterly Review; quarterly

Incentive Manufacturers & Representatives Alliance (1963)
1601 N. Bond St.
Suite 303
Naperville, IL 60563
Tel: (630) 369-7786 Fax: (630) 369-3773
Website: imraonline.org
Members: 325 companies
Staff: 3
Annual Budget: $250-500,000

Personnel:
Executive Director: Karen Renk CAE
   E-Mail: karen@incentivemarketing.org

Accountant: Sheryl Patterson
   E-Mail: Sheryl@associationenterprise.org
Administrative Director: Nicole Sweigart
   E-Mail: nicole@incentivemarketing.org

Historical Note:
Formerly (1977) National Premium Manufacturers Representatives, Inc. IMRA's purpose is to promote professional standards of interaction between representative and manufacturer members thereby contributing to growth, understand and excellence of the incentive Industry. Members are incentive marketing specialists. Membership: $250 (Representative/International/Manufacturers/ Suppliers/NMC/Press/Technology/Resource Provider/ Partner); $125 (Associate).

Publications:
Inside IMRA; bi-monthly
Member Directory; on-line

Incentive Marketing Association (1956)
1601 N. Bond St.
Suite 303
Naperville, IL 60563
Tel: (630) 369-7780 Fax: (630) 369-3773
E-Mail: ContactUs@incentivemarketing.org
Website: incentivemarketing.org
Members: 400 companies
Staff: 4
Annual Budget: $500-1,000,000
Tax: 501(c)(6)

Personnel:
Executive Director: Karen Renk CAE
   E-Mail: karen@incentivemarketing.org
Administrative and Education Support: Tracy Hodge
   E-Mail: tracy@incentivemarketing.org
Director, Membership Services: Susan Peterson
   E-Mail: sue@incentivemarketing.org
Administrative Director: Nicole Sweigart
   E-Mail: nicole@incentivemarketing.org

Historical Note:
Formerly (1990) the National Premium Sales Executives and (2000) Association of Incentive Marketing, IMA's purpose is to increase corporate America's use of incentives. Members are professional premium/incentive marketing executives. Membership: $600 (Company); $125 (Affiliate); $250 (International).

Continuing Education:
Certification Designation/s: CPIM

Meetings/Conferences: Annual

Publications:
IMA Newsletter; monthly
Membership Directory; on-line; adv.
Return on Performance; quarterly; adv.

Membership List Available to Non-members

Incorporated Research Institutions for Seismology (1984)
1200 New York Ave. NW
Suite 400
Washington, DC 20005
Tel: (202) 682-2220 Fax: (202) 682-0633
Website: iris.edu
Staff: 63
Annual Budget: $25-50,000,000
Tax: 501(c)(3)

Personnel:
President: David Simpson
   E-Mail: simpson@iris.edu
Meeting Planner: Mary Baranowski
   E-Mail: maryb@iris.edu
Director, Information Technology: Rob Casey
   E-Mail: rob@iris.washington.edu
Manager, Accounting Services: David Fillebrown
   E-Mail: davidf@iris.edu
Human Resources and Administration Generalist: April
   Jones
   E-Mail: april@iris.edu
Executive Assistant: Leslie Linn
   E-Mail: leslie@iris.edu
Chief Financial Officer: Candy Shin
   E-Mail: candy@iris.edu
EPO Director: John Taber
   E-Mail: taber@iris.edu

Historical Note:
Facilitates and conducts geophysical investigations of seismic sources and Earth properties using seismic and other geophysical methods. IRIS is comprised of United States educational and not-for-profit institutions with a major commitment to research in seismology and

related fields. IRIS programs contribute to scholarly research, education, earthquake hazard mitigation, and the verification of a Comprehensive Test Ban Treaty.

Meetings/Conferences:
Conference Chair: Mary Baranowski

Publications:
DMS Newsletter; quarterly
EarthScope onSite; quarterly
IRIS Newsletter

Membership List Available to Non-members

INDA, Association of the Nonwoven Fabrics Industry *(1968)*
P.O. Box 1288
Cary, NC 27512-1288
Tel: (919) 233-1210 *Fax:* (919) 233-1282
E-Mail: info@inda.org
Website: inda.org
Members: 300 Companies
Staff: 20
Annual Budget: $5-10,000,000

Personnel:
President: David Rousse
Director, Finance: Annette Balint CPA
　E-Mail: abalint@inda.org
Associate Director, Sales and Membership: Marilyn Bellinger
　E-Mail: mbellinger@inda.org
Director, Government Affairs: Jessica E. Franken
　E-Mail: jfranken@inda.org
Coordinator, Publications, Website and Database: Cindy Garcia
　E-Mail: cgarcia@inda.org
Manager, Education and Statistics: Deanna Lovell
　E-Mail: dlovell@inda.org
Director, Statistical, Technical, Education, Publications: Steve Ogle
　E-Mail: sogle@inda.org
Director, Marketing: Phil Pitt
　E-Mail: ppitt@inda.org
Director, Administration, Human Resources, Information Technology, Meetings and Trade Shows: Lori Reynolds
　E-Mail: lreynolds@inda.org

Historical Note:
Formerly (1972) the Disposables Association and (1977) the International Nonwovens and Disposables Association. INDA seeks to promote the value and profitability of the global nonwovens and engineered fabrics industry to benefit the members. Membership: $1,300-23,500 (Corporate); $120 (Academic); $500 (Associate Consultant/Association); $1,000 (Research Agency).

Meetings/Conferences:
Conference Chair: Deanna Lovell
2013 - Miami, FL (Miama Beach resort and Spa)/April 12 - 14
2013 - Miami, FL (Miama Beach resort and Spa)/April 23 - 25
2013 - Denver, CO (Grand Hyatt Denver)/Sept. 30 - Oct. 3
2013 - Chicago, IL (Navy Pier Park)/Nov. 19 - 21

Publications:
e-Filter Newsletter; on-line
INDA's On-line International Nonwovens Directory; on-line
Journal of Engineered Fibers and Fabrics; on-line

Membership List Available to Non-members

Independent Armored Car Operators Association *(1971)*
8000 Research Forest Dr.
Suite 115-155
The Woodlands, TX 77382
Tel: (281) 292-8208 *Fax:* (281) 292-9308
Website: iacoa.com
Members: 127 companies
Staff: 3
Annual Budget: $100-250,000

Personnel:
President: Jack Elder
　E-Mail: jack.elder@ibiarmored.com
Administrator and Secretary: John Margaritis
　E-Mail: jmiacoa@yahoo.com
Legal Counsel and Treasurer: Richard C. Otter
　E-Mail: ottwill@bellsouth.net

Historical Note:

IACOA works to bring together armored carriers from throughout the United States to pool knowledge and attack problems faced by the industry. Membership: $500/year (Regular).

Meetings/Conferences: Annual

Publications:
IACOA Industry Newsletter; quarterly; adv.
Membership Directory; on-line

Independent Association of Accredited Registrars
3942 N. Upland St.
Arlington, VA 22207
Tel: (703) 533-9539 *Fax:* (703) 533-1612
E-Mail: info@iaar.org
Website: iaar.org
Staff: 2
Annual Budget: $100-250,000

Personnel:
Executive Director: Milton M. Bush JD, CAE
Secretary and Treasurer: Gary Bogan

Historical Note:
The IAAR promotes management system assessment by acting as a resource for organizations developing their own management assessment based programs and works with industry groups, government agencies and other organizations to provide guidance in the appropriate use of international standards, the accreditation process and reliance on accredited registrars. Membership: $3500 (Full member); $2400 (Affiliate Members).

Publications:
Membership Directory; on-line

Independent Automotive Damage Appraisers Association *(1964)*
P.O. Box 12291
Columbus, GA 31917-2291
Fax: (888) 423-2669
TollFree: (800) 369-4232
E-Mail: admin@iada.org
Website: iada.org
Members: 300 companies
Staff: 2
Annual Budget: $500-1,000,000

Personnel:
Executive Vice President: John Williams

Historical Note:
Formerly (1947) the Independent Appraisal Plan. IADA's mission is to set the standard for vehicle appraising and to provide a forum for exchange of ideas and solutions to common problems in automotive appraisal and repair.

Meetings/Conferences: Annual
Conference Chair: John Williams

Publications:
IADA News; irregular
IADA Newsletter
IADA Service Directory; annually; adv.

Independent Bakers Association *(1968)*
Georgetown Station
P.O. Box 3731
Washington, DC 20027-0231
Tel: (202) 333-8190 *Fax:* (202) 337-3809
E-Mail: independentbaker@yahoo.com
Website: independentbaker.net
Members: 400 wholesale bakeries
Staff: 4
Annual Budget: $10-25,000,000

Personnel:
President: Nicholas A. Pyle
　E-Mail: napyle@gmail.com
Administrator: Alexis Fobes
Meeting Planner and Legislative Contact: Brandon Van Hoff
　E-Mail: independentbaker@yahoo.com
Legal Counsel: Ellen S. Pyle

Historical Note:
Independent Bankers is a trade association that informs, educates and connects community banks by keeping them in tune with industry trends. Membership: $425-2,200 (Baker, Based on Bakery Sales); $275-1,100 (Allied, Based on Company Sales).

Meetings/Conferences:
Conference Chair: Brandon Van Hoff

Publications:
IBA Newsletter; monthly

The Independent Book Publishers Association *(1983)*
1020 Manhattan Beach Blvd.
Suite 204
Manhattan Beach, CA 90266
Tel: (310) 546-1818 *Fax:* (310) 546-3939
E-Mail: info@IBPA-online.org
Website: pma-online.org
Members: 4200 publishers
Staff: 6
Annual Budget: $2-5,000,000

Personnel:
President: Florrie Binford Kichler
　E-Mail: Florrie@ibpa-online.org
Executive Director and Secretary: Terry Nathan
　E-Mail: Terry@ibpa-online.org
Contact, Vendor Relations, Marketing and Advertising: Chris Kahn
　E-Mail: Chris@ibpa-online.org
General Counsel: Jonathan Kirsch
　E-Mail: jk@jonathankirsch.com

Historical Note:
Formerly (1983) the Publishing Marketing Association and PMA, the Independent Book Publishers Association, assumed its present name in 2009. IBPA is a non-profit trade association of independent publishers who cooperatively market their titles to the trade. Membership: $129-435 (Publisher Member); $185-615 (Non-Publisher Member).

Publications:
IBPA E-Newsletter; bi-weekly
IBPA Independent; monthly; adv.
IBPA Membership Directory; on-line
Publishers Weekly Magazine; weekly; adv.

Membership List Available to Non-members

Independent Community Bankers of America *(1930)*
1615 L St. NW
Suite 900
Washington, DC 20036
Tel: (202) 659-8111 *Fax:* (202) 659-3604
TollFree: (800) 422-8439
E-Mail: info@icba.org
Website: icba.org
Members: 7000 community banks and members
Staff: 186
Annual Budget: $25-50,000,000

Personnel:
President and Chief Executive Officer: Camden R. Fine
　E-Mail: camden.r.fine@icba.org
Director, Human Resources: Janet Blank
　E-Mail: janet.blank@icba.org
Vice President, Marketing: Andrea Bona
Senior Vice President, Publications: Timothy P. Cook
　E-Mail: tim.cook@icba.org
Vice President, Legislative Counsel: Brian D. Cooney
　E-Mail: brian.cooney@icba.org
Senior Executive Vice President, Chief Financial Officer and Chief Operating Officer, ICBA Services: Patricia Hopkins
　E-Mail: tricia.hopkins@icba.org
Vice President, Accounting and Capital Policy: James Kendrick
　E-Mail: james.kendrick@icba.org
Executive Vice President and Chief Marketing Officer: Chris Lorence
　E-Mail: chris.lorence@icba.org
Executive Vice President, Sauk Centre Operations and Education: Greg Martinson
　E-Mail: greg.martinson@icba.org
Senior Vice President, Conventions and Meetings: Jan Meyer
　E-Mail: jan.meyer@icba.org
Executive Vice President and Chief Information Officer: Dewite North
　E-Mail: dewite.north@icba.org
Director, Member Data: LuAnne A. Roelike
　E-Mail: luanne.roelike@icba.org
Senior Executive Vice President, Government Relations and Public Policy: Karen M. Thomas
　E-Mail: karen.thomas@icba.org
Vice President and Regulatory Counsel: Lilly Thomas
　E-Mail: lilly.thomas@icba.org

Historical Note:

Founded as the Independent Bankers Association of America and assumed its present name in 1999. ICBA's mission is to create and promote an environment where community institutions flourish. Membership: $1,495-4,995 (Corporate Associate).

Meetings/Conferences: Annual
Conference Chair: Jan Meyer

Publications:
ICBA Independent Banker; monthly; adv.
ICBA NewsWatch Today; daily
ICBA Washington Report
Member Access; bi-weekly
Membership Directory; on-line

Membership List Available to Non-members

Independent Cosmetic Manufacturers and Distributors *(1974)*
21925 Field Pkwy.
Suite 205
Deer Park, IL 60010
Tel: (847) 991-4499 *Fax:* (847) 991-8161
TollFree: (800) 334-2623
E-Mail: info@icmad.org
Website: icmad.org
Members: 650 individuals and companies
Staff: 5
Annual Budget: $500-1,000,000
Tax: 501(c)(6)

Personnel:
President and Chief Executive Officer: Pamela Jo Busiek
Contact, Accounting Services: Cathy Caramusa
Contact, Membership Services: Lisa Lopofsky
Associate, Marketing and Communications: Marilyn Mages
Vice President, Operations: Sheila Sebor

Historical Note:
ICMAD represents, educates and fosters the growth and profitability of entrepreneurial companies in the cosmetic and personal care industries worldwide. Membership: $495-2,500/year.

Meetings/Conferences: Annual

Publications:
ICMAD Digest; annually; adv.
Mini-Digest; quarterly
Trade Directories; annually

Independent Distributors Association *(1958)*
3030 LBJ Fwy.
Suite 700
Dallas, TX 75234-5771
Tel: (972) 241-1124 *Fax:* (214) 722-7658
E-Mail: info@idaparts.org
Website: idaparts.org
Members: 450 companies
Staff: 2
Annual Budget: $1-2,000,000
Tax: 501(c)(6)

Personnel:
President: Russ LeRoy
Vice President: Pete Smith

Historical Note:
Formerly (1987) Associated Independent Distributors. IDA seeks to enhance, develop, and strengthen a worldwide organization for independent construction machinery rebuilders, parts suppliers, and manufacturers and strives to promote the cooperation, communication and unity among its members. Members are manufacturers and distributors of replacement parts for construction equipment. Membership: $450 (Regular-U.S/Canada/Mexico); $500 (Outside U.S/Canada/Mexico); $450 (Associate).

Meetings/Conferences: Annual

Publications:
Member Directory; on-line
Universal Magazine

Independent Distributors of Electronics Association
6312 Darlington Ave.
Buena Park, CA 90621
Tel: (714) 670-0200 *Fax:* (714) 670-0201
E-Mail: info@idofea.org
Website: idofea.org
Staff: 1
Annual Budget: $100-250,000
Tax: 501(c)(6)

Personnel:
General Manager: Debra Eggeman

E-Mail: deggeman@idofea.org

Historical Note:
IDEA's mission is to promote the independent distribution industry through a media advocacy campaign, to improve the quality of products and services through a quality certification program, educational seminars, and conferences, and to promote the study, development, and implementation of techniques and methods designed to improve the business of independent distributors. Members are companies that sell electronic components. Membership: $3,000-8,500/year (General/Associate).

Continuing Education:
Certification Designation/s: ICE

Publications:
IDEA Newsletter; monthly
Member Directory; on-line

Membership List Available to Non-members

Independent Educational Consultants Association *(1976)*
3251 Old Lee Hwy.
Suite 510
Fairfax, VA 22030
Tel: (703) 591-4850 *Fax:* (703) 591-4860
E-Mail: info@iecaonline.com
Website: iecaonline.com
Members: 1300 affiliates and 875 individuals
Staff: 9
Annual Budget: $1-2,000,000
Tax: 501(c)(6)

Personnel:
Executive Director: Mark H Sklarow
    E-Mail: msklarow@iecaonline.com
Manager, Membership Services: Janice Berger
    E-Mail: janice@iecaonline.com
Manager, Communications: Sarah Brachman
    E-Mail: sarah@iecaonline.com
Manager, Conferences: Rachel Diamond King
    E-Mail: rachel@iecaonline.com
Administrative Assistant: Sheila Kirk
    E-Mail: Sheila@IECAonline.com
Accounting Specialist: Mary Patrick
    E-Mail: Mary@IECAonline.com
Manager, Education Programs: Valerie Vasquez-Guzman
    E-Mail: Valerie@IECAonline.com

Historical Note:
IECA offers information to students and their families regarding school selection issues and works to ensure that those in the profession adhere to better ethical and business standards. Membership: $600 (Professional Member); $300 (Associate Member); $60 (Student).

Meetings/Conferences: Semi-Annual
Conference Chair: Rachel Diamond King
2013 - Atlanta, GA/April 10 - 13
2013 - San Diego, CA/Nov. 13 - 16

Publications:
Conference Directory; semi-annually
Information Bulletin; quarterly
Insights; bi-monthly; adv.
Membership Directory; on-line

Membership List Available to Non-members

Independent Electrical Contractors *(1957)*
4401 Ford Ave.
Suite 1100
Alexandria, VA 22302
Tel: (703) 549-7351 *Fax:* (703) 549-7448
TollFree: (800) 456-4324
E-Mail: info@ieci.org
Website: ieci.org
Members: 3700 companies and 60 chapters
Staff: 16
Annual Budget: $250-500,000

Personnel:
Executive Vice President & Chief Executive Officer: Thayer Long
    E-Mail: tlong@ieci.org
Vice President, Training and Development: Robert "Rob" W. Baird
    E-Mail: bbaird@ieci.org
Vice President, Public Affairs: Joseph Cephas
    E-Mail: jcephas@ieci.org
Director, Education: Lysa Egly
    E-Mail: legly@ieci.org
Vice President, Finance: Vernice L. Howard MBA
    E-Mail: vhoward@ieci.org

Senior Vice President, Meetings and Membership Services: Tim Welsh
    E-Mail: twelsh@ieci.org

Historical Note:
Formerly (1981) the Associated Independent Electrical Contractors of America. IEC's mission is to enhance the independent electrical contractor's success by developing a workforce, communicating clearly with government, promoting business practices, and providing leadership for the electrical industry. Membership: $195 (Individual); $100 (Company).

Meetings/Conferences: Annual
Conference Chair: Tim Welsh

Publications:
Insights Magazine
Membership Directory; annually

Independent Equipment Dealers Association *(2002)*
P.O Box 403
Victor, NY 14564
Tel: (585) 869-9002 *Fax:* (585) 486-3484
TollFree: (877) 710-0995
E-Mail: globalnetwork@iedagroup.com
Website: iedaorg.point2agent.com
Members: 59 Companies
Staff: 2
Annual Budget: $100-250,000
Tax: 501(c)(6)

Personnel:
Executive Director: Kristen Williams
    E-Mail: Kristen@iedagroup.com
Treasurer: Mark Dyer
    E-Mail: acatmantoo@aol.com

Historical Note:
IEDA's mission is to promote free enterprise and entrepreneurialism through the advocacy of the independent equipment dealer as the distribution method of choice. Membership: $1,000 (Regular/International); $1,500 (Associate).

Meetings/Conferences:
Number of non-conference events/year: 1

Publications:
The Independent; quarterly

Independent Film and Television Alliance *(1980)*
10850 Wilshire Blvd.
Ninth Floor
Los Angeles, CA 90024-4321
Tel: (310) 446-1000 *Fax:* (310) 446-1600
E-Mail: info@ifta-online.org
Website: ifta-online.org
Members: 150 companies
Staff: 30
Annual Budget: $10-25,000,000
Tax: 501(c)(6)

Personnel:
President and Chief Executive Officer: Jean M. Prewitt
    E-Mail: jprewitt@ifta-online.org
Director, Membership Services: Natasha Berechko
    E-Mail: nberechko@ifta-online.org
Vice President, Marketing and Membership Services: Robin Burt
    E-Mail: rburt@ifta-online.org
Vice President and General Counsel: Susan Cleary
    E-Mail: scleary@ifta-online.org
Vice President, Communications: Jennifer Garnick
    E-Mail: jgarnick@ifta-online.org
Director, Human Resources and Administration: Portia McGrew
    E-Mail: pmcgrew@ifta-online.org
Vice President, Finance and Accounting: Robert Newman
    E-Mail: rnewman@ifta-online.org

Historical Note:
Founded as American Film Marketing Association; became AFMA in 1997 and assumed its current name in 2004. IFTA's purpose is to protect and strengthen its member's ability to finance, produce, distribute, market and distribute independent films and television programs in an ever-changing and challenging global marketplace. Membership: $6,000 (Associate/Voting); $4,000 (Affiliate)

Publications:
Membership Directory; on-line

Membership List Available to Non-members

Independent Filmmaker Project *(1979)*
68 Jay St.

Room 425
Brooklyn, NY 11201
Tel: (212) 465-8200 *Fax:* (212) 465-8525
Website: ifp.org
Members: 10000 filmmakers
Staff: 6
Annual Budget: $1-2,000,000

Personnel:
Executive Director: Joana Vincente
Manager, Finance: Armando M. Gil
National Advertising Manager: Folayo Lasaki
   E-Mail: flasaki@ifp.org
Editor: Scott Macaulay
*Coordinator, Communications, Membership and
   Programming:* Dan Schoenbrun
   E-Mail: dschoenbrun@ifp.org
Senior Director, Programming: Milton Tabbot

Historical Note:
*IFP is a not-for-profit membership and advocacy
organization that supports and serves the independent
film community by connecting creative talent and the film
industry. Members are independent feature film directors
and producers. Membership: $35-3000/year.*

Meetings/Conferences: Annual
Number of non-conference events/year: 2

Publications:
Filmmaker Magazine

Independent Free Papers of America *(1980)*
107 Hemlock Dr.
Rio Grande, NJ 08242
Tel: (609) 408-8000 *Fax:* (609) 889-8359
TollFree: (800) 639-9753
E-Mail: Gary@IFPA.com
Website: ifpa.com
Members: 347 free newspapers
Staff: 4
Annual Budget: $250-500,000

Personnel:
Executive Director: Gary Rudy
   E-Mail: gary@ifpa.com
Director: Dwight Bitokofer
   E-Mail: bitikofer@timesnewspapers.com

Historical Note:
*IFPA's mission is to help Independent Publishers compete in
fast changing world. Membership: $150/year (Associate/
Individual).*

Meetings/Conferences: Annual

Publications:
Membership Application; on-line
T.I.P; monthly

Independent Fuel Terminal Operators Association
901 15th St. NW
Washington, DC 20005-2301
Tel: (202) 371-6000
Staff: 1

Personnel:
President: Jon S. Matsumura MD

Historical Note:
*The Independent Fuel Terminal Operators Association
is an organization composed of 16 companies, each of
which operates at least one deepwater terminal. Specifically,
members operate 56 deepwater and 40 barge oil terminals
along the East Coast from Maine to Florida.*

Independent Hardee's Franchisee Association
(1997)
638 Independence Pkwy.
Suite 100
Chesapeake, VA 23320
Tel: (757) 497-7297 *Fax:* (757) 473-9897
E-Mail: IHFA@IHFA.com
Website: ihfa.com
Members: 95 companies
Staff: 2

Personnel:
Executive Liaison: Cathy Crossfield
Contact, Meetings and Conventions: Brooke Goodwin
   E-Mail: Meetings@IHFA.com

Historical Note:
*IHFA's mission is to represent all franchisees in the
Hardee's system by protecting and enhancing the economic
investments of the franchisees. Membership: $100
(Franchisee); $1,000-25,000 (Associate).*

Meetings/Conferences: Annual

Conference Chair: Brooke Goodwin
2013 - Charleston, SC (Embassy Suites Hotel Airport
   and Convention Center)/Oct. 8 - 10

Publications:
The INSIGHT; quarterly; adv.
Vendor Directory; on-line

Independent Insurance Agents & Brokers of America, Inc. *(1896)*
127 S. Peyton St.
Suite 300
Alexandria, VA 22314
Tel: (703) 706-5443 *Fax:* (703) 683-7556
TollFree: (800) 221-7917
E-Mail: info@iiaba.org
Website: iiaba.net
Members: 300,000 agents and brokers
Staff: 75
Annual Budget: $25-50,000,000
Tax: 501(c)(6)

Personnel:
President and Chief Executive Officer: Robert A. Rusbuldt
   E-Mail: Bob.Rusbuldt@iiaba.net

Historical Note:
*Founded as the National Local Association of Fire
Insurance Agents, underwent name change to the National
Association of Insurance Agents in 1913. Became the
Independent Insurance Agents of America in 1975.
Assumed its present name in 2002. IIABA provides
members with a sustainable competitive advantage.*

Meetings/Conferences: Annual
2013 - Antonio, TX (Grand Hyatt San Antonio)/Sept.
   25 - 29
2014 - Grand Rapids, MI (Amway Grand Plaza Hotel)/
   Sept. 10 - 14
2015 - New Orleans, LA (Roosevelt New Orleans
   Hotel)/Sept. 30 - Oct. 4

Publications:
IA Magazine; monthly
Insurance News & Views; weekly
Life-Health Leads
Smart Agency

Independent Laboratory Distributors Association *(1988)*
P.O. Box 438
North Versailles, PA 15137
Tel: (412) 829-5190 *Fax:* (412) 829-5191
TollFree: (888) 878-4532
Website: ilda.org
Members: 94 companies
Staff: 1
Annual Budget: $100-250,000
Tax: 501(c)(6)

Personnel:
Association Manager: Kathi Bretcko
   E-Mail: kbretcko@ilda.org

Historical Note:
*An association of independent laboratory product
distributors and their suppliers. ILDA is committed
to providing a forum for networking and educating
its members and for promoting the association to the
laboratory market. Membership: $1,000 (Distributor/
Resource/Manufacturers Representative); $2,000-3,000
(Associate).*

Meetings/Conferences: Semi-Annual
Conference Chair: Kathi Bretcko

Publications:
Member Directory; on-line

Independent Lubricant Manufacturers Association *(1948)*
400 N. Columbus St.
Suite 201
Alexandria, VA 22314
Tel: (703) 684-5574 *Fax:* (703) 836-8503
E-Mail: ilma@ilma.org
Website: ilma.org
Members: 310 companies
Staff: 6
Annual Budget: $2-5,000,000
Tax: 501(c)(6)

Personnel:
Executive Director: Celeste M. Powers CAE
   E-Mail: cpowers@ilma.org
Manager, Communications: Brenda Gillinson CAE
   E-Mail: bgillinson@ilma.org

Associate Director: Martha Jolkovski
   E-Mail: mjolkovski@ilma.org

Historical Note:
*Formerly (1980) known as the Independent Oil
Compounders Association. ILMA's mission is to serve and
be an advocate for Independent Lubricant Manufacturers in
a global marketplace. Members are independent blenders
and compounders of lubricants, metalworking fluids, and
greases. Membership: $2,300/year.*

Meetings/Conferences: Semi-Annual
Conference Chair: Martha Jolkovski
2013 - Carlsbad, CA (Park Hyatt Aviara Resort)/April
   18 - 20
2013 - San Antonio, TX (Hyatt Regency Hill Country
   Resort and Spa)/Oct. 5 - 8
2014 - Indian Wells, CA (Hyatt Grand Champions
   Resort, Villas and Spa)/March 18 - 21
2014 - Aventura, FL (Turnberry Isle Aventura)/April 9
   - 12
2015 - Boca Raton, FL (Boca Raton Resort and Club)/
   Oct. 17 - 20

Publications:
Compoundings; monthly; adv.
FlashPoint; weekly; adv.
Membership Directory; on-line; adv.

Membership List Available to Non-members

Independent Medical Distributors Association *(1978)*
5204 Fairmount Ave.
Downers Grove, IL 60515
Tel: (866) 463-2937 *Fax:* (630) 493-0798
TollFree: (866) 463-2937
E-Mail: imda@imda.org
Website: imda.org
Members: 70 companies
Staff: 8
Annual Budget: $100-250,000
Tax: 501(c)(6)

Personnel:
Executive Director: Katie Keel
   E-Mail: kswamrtz@asihq.com
Executive Vice President: Judith K. Keel
Legal Counsel: Mitchell Kramer
Chief Financial Officer: Mary Moran
Senior Administrator: Patti Perillo
Director, Communications and Editor: Mark Thill
   E-Mail: markthill@thillcommunications.com

Historical Note:
*IMDA's mission is to advance the business interests of
independent medical sales and marketing companies.
Members are specialty sales and marketing companies that
distribute innovative medical technologies. Membership:
$1,200-5,200 (Based on product sales).*

Meetings/Conferences: Annual
2013 - Orlando, FL (Loews Royal Pacific Resort)/June 9
   - 11

Publications:
IMDA Update Newsletter; monthly
Membership Directory; on-line

Independent Office Products and Furniture Dealers Association *(1904)*
301 N. Fairfax St.
Suite 200
Alexandria, VA 22314
Tel: (703) 549-9040 *Fax:* (703) 683-7552
TollFree: (800) 542-6672
E-Mail: pmiller@iopfda.org
Website: iopfda.org
Members: 1200 companies
Staff: 7
Annual Budget: $500-1,000,000

Personnel:
President: Chris Bates
   E-Mail: cbates@iopfda.org
*Director, Communications and Marketing and Editor, Office
   Furniture Dealer:* Alicia Ellis
   E-Mail: aellis@nopanet.org
Manager, Membership Data Services: Mary Tucker Grady
   E-Mail: mgrady@nopanet.org
Director, Government Affairs: Paul Miller PLC
Representative, Membership Development: Molly Murray
   E-Mail: mmurray@iopfda.org
Director, Research and Standards: Billie Zidek
   E-Mail: bzidek@iopfda.org

Historical Note:
Formerly the Business Products Industry Association, IOPFDA is the trade association for independent dealers of office products and office furniture. Mission is to provide independent dealers with the information, tools and knowledge they need to help them to be successful in an evolving business environment. Membership: 495/year.

Meetings/Conferences: Annual
Conference Chair: Billie Zidek
Number of non-conference events/year: 8

Publications:
iDealer; monthly; adv.
Membership Directory; on-line
NOPA Connecting eNewsletter; weekly; adv.
OF Dealer; monthly; adv.
OFDA Connecting eNewsletter; weekly; adv.

Independent Petroleum Association of America *(1929)*
1201 15th St. NW
Suite 300
Washington, DC 20005
Tel: (202) 857-4722 *Fax:* (202) 857-4799
Website: ipaa.org
Members: 5500 companies
Staff: 26
Annual Budget: $5-10,000,000
Tax: 501(c)(6)

Personnel:
President and Chief Executive Officer: Barry Russell
  E-Mail: brussell@ipaa.org
Vice President, Public Affairs and Communications: Jeffrey Eshelman
  E-Mail: jeshelman@ipaa.org
Director, Information Technology and Webmaster: Kirk Friedman
Vice President, Government Relations: Lee O. Fuller
  E-Mail: lfuller@ipaa.org
Vice President, Meetings: Tina Hamlin
  E-Mail: thamlin@ipaa.org
Vice President, Business Development, Capital Markets and Membership: Bob Jarvis
  E-Mail: bjarvis@ipaa.org
Vice President, Economics and International Affairs: Frederick Lawrence
  E-Mail: flawrence@ipaa.org
Vice President, Administration and Membership Services: Therese McCafferty
  E-Mail: tmccafferty@ipaa.org
Director, Education: Doris Richardson
  E-Mail: drichardson@ipaa.org

Historical Note:
IPAA is dedicated to ensuring a strong, viable domestic oil and natural gas industry, recognizing that an adequate and secure supply of energy is essential to the national economy. Membership: $450-60,000/year.

Meetings/Conferences:
Conference Chair: Tina Hamlin
2013 - Toronto, ON (The Ritz-Carlton)/June 11
2013 - Laguna Nigel, CA (The Ritz-Carlton)/June 24 - 25
2013 - San Antonio, TX (Hyatt Regency Hill Country Resort and Spa)/Nov. 7 - 9
Number of non-conference events/year: 17

Publications:
IPAA Access Magazine; adv.
IPAA Washington Report; weekly
Membership Directory

Independent Photo Imagers *(1982)*
2518 Anthem Village Dr.
Suite 104
Henderson, NV 89052
Tel: (702) 617-1141 *Fax:* (702) 617-1181
E-Mail: ipimemberinfo@ipiphoto.com
Website: ipiphoto.com
Members: 650 individuals
Staff: 7

Personnel:
President and Executive Director: Brent Bowyer
  E-Mail: brent@ipiphoto.com
Director, Accounting & Administration: Fran Bowyer
Director, Operations and Membership Services: Brenda DiVincenzo
  E-Mail: brenda@ipiphoto.com
Director, Marketing: Erin von Holdt
  E-Mail: erin@ipiphoto.com

Director, Member Services and Supplying Partners: Ron Mohney
  E-Mail: ron@ipiphoto.com
Executive Administrative Assistant: Whitney Solomon
  E-Mail: whitney@ipiphoto.com

Historical Note:
IPI provides opportunities for revenue growth and profitability increases through privileged pricing, information exchange, and education. Membership: $1,200/year (Individual).

Meetings/Conferences: Annual

Publications:
Innovative Imager; monthly
Innovative Imager; weekly

Independent Pilots Association *(1993)*
3607 Fern Valley Rd.
Louisville, KY 40219-1916
Tel: (502) 968-0341 *Fax:* (502) 968-0470
TollFree: (800) 285-4472
Website: ipapilot.org
Staff: 2
Annual Budget: $10-25,000,000
Tax: 501(c)(5)

Personnel:
President: Robert Travis
  E-Mail: President@IPApilot.org
Media Contact: Brian Gaudet
  E-Mail: brian.gaudet@gmail.com

Historical Note:
IPA's mission is is dedicated to providing for the well being of children and their basic needs with a focus on making life changing differences for children with exceptional medical requirements.

Independent Professional Painting Contractors Association of America *(1982)*
C/O Heinz K. Hoffmann, P.O. Box 1759
Huntington, NY 11743-0630
Tel: (631) 423-3654
Members: 45 companies
Staff: 1
Annual Budget: Under $10,000

Personnel:
Executive Director: Heinz K. Hoffmann

Historical Note:
Founded to fill the need for an independent painting contractors association, IPPA represents open-shop painting contractors only. Has no paid officers or full-time staff. Membership concentrated in the New York/Long Island metropolitan area. Membership: $125/year (full member); $85/year (associate); $45/year (outside New York metro area).

Independent Professional Representatives Organization *(1988)*
34157 W. Ninth Mile Rd.
Farmington Hills, MI 48335
Tel: (248) 514-4418 *Fax:* (248) 474-0522
TollFree: (800) 420-4268
E-Mail: ray@avreps.org
Website: avreps.org
Members:
70 companies
70 individuals
Staff: 1
Annual Budget: $50-100,000
Tax: 501(c)(6)

Personnel:
Executive Director: Ray Wright
  E-Mail: ray@avreps.org

Historical Note:
Established and incorporated in Missouri. IPRO's mission is to conduit to manage relationships and sales performance through education and ethical conduct. Members are independent manufacturers' representatives of audio- visual specialty products. Membership: $350-1,200/year.

Meetings/Conferences: Annual
Conference Chair: Ray Wright

Publications:
The IPRO Newsletter
The Virtual Representative

Independent Research Libraries Association *(1972)*
C/O Virginia Historical Society, 428 North Blvd.
P.O. Box 7311

Richmond, VA 23221-0311
Tel: (804) 342-9656 *Fax:* (804) 355-2399
E-Mail: cbryan@vahistorical.org
Website: irla.lindahall.org
Members: 20 institutions
Staff: 1
Annual Budget: Under $10,000

Personnel:
President: Dr. Charles F. Bryan Jr.
  E-Mail: cbryan@vahistorical.org

Historical Note:
IRLA is established to address the future of independent, privately- supported research libraries. Members are independently-supported research libraries that are not part of a larger institution (e.g., a university).

Publications:
Membership Directory

Independent Sealing Distributors *(1992)*
105 Eastern Ave.
Suite 104
Annapolis, MD 21403-3300
Tel: (410) 940-6344 *Fax:* (410) 263-1659
E-Mail: info@isd.org
Website: isd.org
Members: 170 companies
Staff: 10
Annual Budget: $100-250,000
Tax: 501(c)(6)

Personnel:
Executive Director: Debbie Mitchell Jr.
Accounting Manager: Dorothy Cusack
Director, Membership: Amy Luckado
Manager, Certifications: Colleen McDonough
Director, Communications and Conferences: Kristin B. Thompson
General Manager: Joseph M. Thompson Jr.
Manager, Communications: Nicole Weber
  E-Mail: nweber@isd.org

Historical Note:
ISD is an international trade association representing distributors and manufacturers of mechanical and hydraulic seals and gaskets and other fluid sealing devices. ISD is a member of the National Association of Wholesaler Distribution (NAW). Purpose is to enhance the success of professional sealing distributors through information, education and interaction. Membership: $525-2095/year(Associate/Affiliate, Based on Number of Employees); $475-2045 (Distributor, Based on Number of Employees).

Meetings/Conferences:
Conference Chair: Kristin B. Thompson
Number of non-conference events/year: 3

Publications:
ISD Insider; quarterly
Membership Directory

Independent Sector *(1980)*
1602 L St. NW
Suite 900
Washington, DC 20036
Tel: (202) 467-6100 *Fax:* (202) 467-6101
E-Mail: info@independentsector.org
Website: independentsector.org
Members: 600 institutions
Staff: 41
Annual Budget: $10-25,000,000
Tax: 501(c)(3)

Personnel:
President and Chief Executive Officer: Diana Aviv
  E-Mail: diana@independentsector.org
Executive Marketing Producer: Darcy Corcoran
  E-Mail: darcyc@independentsector.org
Director, Conference and Event Management: Elizabeth Culkin
  E-Mail: lizc@independentsector.org
Senior Director, Human Resources: Mitchell Eisman
  E-Mail: mitche@independentsector.org
Vice President, Public Policy and Government Affairs: Lois Fu
  E-Mail: loisf@independentsector.org
Chief Development Officer: Michael Goff
  E-Mail: michaelg@independentsector.org
Chief Finance Officer and Senior Vice President: Teresa O'Brien
  E-Mail: terrio@independentsector.org
Project Director, Database and Information Technology: Monique Riviere

E-Mail: moniquer@independentsector.org
Vice President, Communications and Marketing: Lorraine Snebold
E-Mail: lorraines@independentsector.org
Editorial Director and Grant Writer: Susan Drake Swift
E-Mail: susands@independentsector.org

Historical Note:
Formed by a merger of the Coalition of National Voluntary Organizations and the National Council on Philanthropy. IS's mission is to advance the common good by strengthening, and mobilizing the charitable community. Membership: $350-17,500/year.

Meetings/Conferences: Annual
Conference Chair: Elizabeth Culkin
2013 - New York City, NY (Hilton New York)/Sept. 29 - Oct. 1
2014 - Seatle, WA (Sheraton Seattle Hotel)/Nov. 16 - 18

Publications:
IS CONNECT; monthly
Membership Directory; on-line

Independent Staffing Alliance (1962)
525 SW Fifth St.
Suite A
Des Moines, IA 50309
Tel: (515) 282-8192 Fax: (515) 282-9117
Website: independentstaffingalliance.com
Members: 14 Organisations
Staff: 1
Annual Budget: $10-25,000

Personnel:
President and Chief Executive Officer: Kate Banasiak
E-Mail: kate@assoc-mgmt.com

Historical Note:
Formerly (1999) the Independent Office Services Institute. ISA seeks to recruit the independently owned staffing firms across the nation to best serve national client base. Equipped with knowledge of the staffing industry, strives to set themselves apart from national staffing firms.

Continuing Education:
Certification Designation/s: WBE

Independent Telephone and Telecommunications Alliance (1994)
1101 Vermont Ave. NW
Suite 501
Washington, DC 20005
Tel: (202) 898-1514 Fax: (202) 898-1589
Website: itta.us
Members: 30 million customers
Staff: 3
Annual Budget: $1-2,000,000
Tax: 501(c)(6)

Personnel:
President: Genevieve Morelli
E-Mail: gmorelli@itta.us
Vice President, Legislative Affairs: Paul Raak
E-Mail: praak@itta.us

Historical Note:
ITTA provides wireline and wireless voice, data, Internet and video telecommunications services.

Publications:
Membership Directory; on-line

Membership List Available to Non-members

Independent Terminal Operators Association
901 15th St. NW
Washington, DC 20005-2301
Staff: 1

Personnel:
President: Steve Jackson

Independent Time and Labor Management Association (1978)
1244 State St.
Suite 358
Lemont, IL 60439
Tel: (630) 243-0430 Fax: (203) 724-4375
E-Mail: info@itlma.org
Website: itlma.org
Members: 350 manufacturers
Staff: 4
Annual Budget: $25-50,000
Tax: 501(c)(6)

Personnel:

Executive Secretary: Ron Henricksen
E-Mail: ron.henricksen@itlma.org

Historical Note:
ITLMA's purpose is to assist the time equipment and labor management dealers in implementing their business plans more professionally. Membership: $149 (Direct Member-Voting); $349 (Associate Member-Non- Voting); $69 (Subscription Member-Non-Voting).

Meetings/Conferences: Annual
2013 - Grapevine, TX (Gaylord Texan Resort and Convention Center)/May 7 - 9

Publications:
Marking Time; quarterly

Independent Turf and Ornamental Distributors Association (1990)
174 Crestview Dr.
Bellefonte, PA 16823-8516
Tel: (877) 326-5995 Fax: (814) 355-2452
E-Mail: info@itoda.org
Website: itoda.org
Members: 70 companies
Staff: 1
Annual Budget: $50-100,000

Personnel:
Executive Director: Patricia E. Heuser
E-Mail: pat@heusergroup.com

Historical Note:
ITODA's purpose is to foster the trade, commerce and interests of those independently-owned businesses engaged in the business of servicing and marketing products for the turf and ornamental landscaping industries. Membership: $850 (Premiere/Associate); $250 (Training).

Meetings/Conferences: Annual
2013 - Clearwater, FL (Clearwater Beach Marriott Suites on Sand Key)/Feb. 27 - March 1
Number of non-conference events/year: 8

Publications:
Member Directory; on-line

Indian Arts and Crafts Association (1974)
4010 Carlisle NE
Suite C
Albuquerque, NM 87107
Tel: (505) 265-9149 Fax: (505) 265-8251
E-Mail: info@iaca.com
Website: iaca.com
Members: 750 companies and craftpersons
Staff: 4
Annual Budget: $100-250,000
Tax: 501(c)(6)

Personnel:
Executive Director: Gail E. Chehak (Klamath)
E-Mail: gchehak@iaca.com
Contact, Membership Services and Marketing: Brian Lush (Yankton Sioux)
E-Mail: blush@iaca.com
Assistant, Information Services and Research: Robert Meek
Treasurer: Kathi Ouellet
E-Mail: kathi@rivertradingpost.com

Historical Note:
IACA's mission is to promote, protect, and preserve native American Indian arts and crafts. Membership: $35 (Student); $130 (Sustaining); $70-90 (Collector); $105 (Associate Organization); $75 (Museum); $235 (Wholesale/Retail/Tribal Enterprise, Coop, Guild); $70 (Subsequent Location); $80 (Artist/Craftsperson).

Meetings/Conferences: Annual

Publications:
IACA Bulletin; semi-annually; adv.
IACA Newsletter; on-line
Membership Directory; annually; adv.

Indian Dental Association (USA) (1983)
140 Tulip Ave.
Floral Park, NY 11001
Tel: (516) 345-8244
E-Mail: idausamemberservices@gmail.com
Website: ida-usa.org
Members: 275 individuals
Staff: 2
Annual Budget: $50-100,000

Personnel:
Executive Director: Chad P. Gehani
Treasurer: Deepak Bhagat

Historical Note:
IDA (USA)'s mission is to encourage the art and science of dentistry. Members are dentists of Asian-Indian heritage. Membership: $75 (Active); $25 (Associate); $10 (Student); $250 (Life Time) $50(Annual).

Publications:
IDA Newsletter Sampark; monthly; adv.

Indian Diamond and Colorstone Association (1984)
56 W. 45th St.
Suite 705
New York, NY 10036
Tel: (212) 921-4488 Fax: (212) 768-7935
E-Mail: info@idcany.org
Website: idcany.org
Members: 300 companies
Staff: 2
Annual Budget: $25-50,000

Personnel:
President: Nimish Mehta
Treasurer: Gopal Agrawal

Historical Note:
IDCA's purpose is to promote, support, maintain, protect and increase the business of diamonds and precious stones, pearls, jewelry etc., to promote a code of conduct and high standards of ethics in the trade among members. Membership : $450 (Associate/Individual): $200 (Affiliate Company).

Meetings/Conferences: Annual

Publications:
Member Directory; on-line

Indian Educators Federation (1967)
2309 Renard Pl. SE
Suite 202
Albuquerque, NM 87106
Tel: (505) 243-4088 Fax: (505) 243-4098
TollFree: (888) 433-2382
E-Mail: ief@ief-aft.org
Website: ief-aft.org
Members: 800 individuals
Staff: 2
Annual Budget: $100-250,000

Personnel:
President: Verna Tallsalt
E-Mail: president@ief-aft.org
Secretary: June Lano
E-Mail: secretary@ief-aft.org

Historical Note:
Formerly the National Council of BIA Educators. IEFW members are teachers in schools operated by the Bureau of Indian Affairs. Affiliated with the American Federation of Teachers.

Indoor Tanning Association (1999)
2025 M St. NW
Suite 800
Washington, DC 20036
Tel: (888) 377-0477 Fax: (202) 367-2142
TollFree: (888) 377-0477
E-Mail: admin@theita.com
Website: theita.com
Members: 150 Companies
Staff: 2
Annual Budget: $1-2,000,000

Personnel:
Executive Director: John Overstreet
E-Mail: joverstreet@theita.com

Historical Note:
Founded to protect the freedom of individuals to acquire a suntan, via natural or artificial light. ITA also strives to strengthen and advance the position through research and education efforts and by partnering with other organizations whose efforts further the ITA's mission. Membership: $1,000-150,000 (Non-Salon); $300 (Salon); $500 (Associate).

Publications:
ITA Newsletter; quarterly
Membership Directory; on-line

Industrial Asset Management Council (2002)
6625 Corners Pkwy.
Suite 200
Norcross, GA 30092
Tel: (770) 325-3461 Fax: (770) 263-8825
E-Mail: info@iamc.org
Website: iamc.org

Members: 367 individuals
Staff: 10
Annual Budget: $2-5,000,000
Tax: 501(c)(6)

Personnel:
Executive Director: Ronald Starner
    E-Mail: ron.starner@conway.com
Director, Marketing: Rya Hobart Hazelwood
    E-Mail: rya.hobart@iamc.org
Contact, Publications: Scott Larsen
    E-Mail: scott.larsen@conway.com
Information Manager: Mike O'Connor MBA
    E-Mail: mike.oconnor@conway.com
Director, Conference Programs And Leadership
    Development: Hazel J. Pankey
    E-Mail: hazel.pankey@iamc.org
Director, Research and Education: Joel Parker
    E-Mail: joel.parker@conway.com
Director, Membership Development: Cathy Pierce
    E-Mail: cathy.pierce@iamc.org
Administrative Assistant: Michelle Roy
    E-Mail: michelle.roy@iamc.org

Historical Note:
Represents asset management and corporate real estate executives, their suppliers and service providers, and economic developers. IAMC's mission is to provide strategic insights, educational resources and exclusive networking opportunities for the leaders of the manufacturing and industrial asset management industry. Membership: $795 (First Member from Active Member Company); $295 (Additional Member from an Active Member Company); $1495 (Associate); $100 (Retired); $50 (Students); 100 (Faculty).

Continuing Education:
Certification Designation/s: BCIR

Meetings/Conferences: Semi-Annual
Conference Chair: Hazel J. Pankey

Publications:
IAMC Dispatch; monthly
IAMC Notes; monthly; adv.
Membership Directory; on-line
Site Selection; adv.

Industrial Designers Society of America *(1944)*
555 Grove St.
Suite 200
Herndon, VA 20170-4728
Tel: (703) 707-6000 *Fax:* (703) 787-8501
E-Mail: idsa@idsa.org
Website: idsa.org
Members: 3400 individuals
Staff: 19
Annual Budget: $2-5,000,000

Personnel:
Manager, Publications: Tim Adkins
    E-Mail: tima@idsa.org
Contact, Administration and Finance and Membership
    Services: Bridget Brooks
    E-Mail: bridgetb@idsa.org
Contact, Marketing: Kaycee Childress
    E-Mail: kayceec@idsa.org
Contact, Education: Ben Chisholm
    E-Mail: benc@idsa.org
Contact, Press and Media and Public Relations: Roxann
    Henze
    E-Mail: roxannh@idsa.org
Contact, Membership Services: Jill Richardson
    E-Mail: jillr@idsa.org
Contact, National Conference and Education Symposium:
    Kristyn Rivellese
    E-Mail: kristynr@idsa.org
FIDSA Legal Issues: Brian Vogel
    E-Mail: execdir@idsa.org

Historical Note:
The product of a merger of American Society of Industrial Designers (1944), Industrial Designers Institute (1938) and Industrial Design Education Association. IDSA serves the industrial design profession, advancing the quality and positive impact of design. Mission is to inspire design quality and responsibility through professional development and education. Membership: $375 (Professional/Affiliate/International); $125-250 (Young Professional); $50 (Student).

Meetings/Conferences: Annual
Conference Chair: Kristyn Rivellese

Publications:
designBytes; weekly
e-newsletter; monthly

Innovation; quarterly; adv.
Membership Directory; on-line

Industrial Diamond Association of America *(1946)*
P.O. Box 29460
Columbus, OH 43229
Tel: (614) 797-2265 *Fax:* (614) 797-2264
Website: superabrasives.org
Members: 190 individuals
Staff: 2
Annual Budget: $100-250,000

Personnel:
Executive Director: Terry M. Kane
    E-Mail: tkane-ida@insight.rr.com

Historical Note:
IDA works to promote the use, application and development of superabrasive materials to advance the growth of the superabrasives industry. Members are concerned with industrial diamonds, either as material suppliers, importers, dealers or manufacturers of diamond tools. Membership: $52-3,990/year.

Meetings/Conferences: Annual
Conference Chair: Terry M. Kane
2013 - Baltimore, MD (Hyatt Regency)/May 6 - 8
Number of non-conference events/year: 3

Publications:
Finer Points Magazine; quarterly; adv.

Industrial Electronics Society *(1974)*
Electrical and Computer Engineering Department
Auburn University
Auburn, AL 36849-5201
Website: ieee-ies.org
Members: 5000 individuals
Staff: 3
Annual Budget: $500-1,000,000

Personnel:
President Elect: John Hung
    E-Mail: hugjoh@auburn.org

Historical Note:
The Industrial Electronics Society through its members encompasses a diverse range of technical activities devoted to the application of electronics and electrical sciences for the enhancement of industrial and manufacturing processes.

Publications:
IEEE Industrial Electronics Magazine; on-line
IEEE Industrial Electronics Newsletter; on-line

Industrial Energy Consumers of America
1155 Fifteenth St. NW
Suite 500
Washington, DC 20005
Tel: (202) 223-1661 *Fax:* (202) 530-0659
Website: ieca-us.com
Staff: 3
Annual Budget: $500-1,000,000
Tax: 501(c)(6)

Personnel:
President: Paul N. Cicio
    E-Mail: pcicio@carbonleaf.net
Administrator Assistant: Traci Bush
Manager, Government Affairs: Marnie Satterfield
    E-Mail: msatterfield@ieca-us.org

Historical Note:
The Voice of the industrial Energy Consumers.

Industrial Fabrics Association International *(1912)*
1801 Count Rd. B, West
Roseville, MN 55113-4061
Tel: (651) 222-2508 *Fax:* (651) 631-9334
TollFree: (800) 225-4324
E-Mail: generalinfo@ifai.com
Website: ifai.com
Members: 2000 companies
Staff: 53
Annual Budget: $5-10,000,000
Tax: 501(c)(6)

Personnel:
President and Chief Executive Officer: Mary J. Hennessy
    E-Mail: mjhennessy@ifai.com
Director, Membership Services and Safety and Technical
    Products: Andrew M. Aho
    E-Mail: amaho@ifai.com
Director, Human Resources: Pam Egan-Blahna

    E-Mail: peblahna@ifai.com
Director, Marketing: Bonnie J. Hanson
    E-Mail: bjhanson@ifai.com
Vice President, Conference Management: Todd V.
    Lindemann
    E-Mail: tvlindemann@ifai.com
Publisher: Susan R. Niemi
    E-Mail: srniemi@ifai.com
Vice President, Finance and Administration and Chief
    Financial Officer: Steven C. Rider CITP, CMA, CPA
    E-Mail: scrider@ifai.com

Historical Note:
Founded as the National Canvas Goods Manufacturers Association, became the Canvas Products Association International in 1956 and assumed its present name in 1980. IFAI invests its revenue to advance the industry and subsidize member programs. Membership: $385-935 (End Product Manufacturer); $1,085 (Supplier); $335 (Sponsoring); $235 (Affiliate), $180 (Individual); $80 (Student).

Continuing Education:
Certification Designation/s: IFM, MFC

Meetings/Conferences: Annual
Conference Chair: Todd V. Lindemann
Number of non-conference events/year: 8

Publications:
Fabric Architecture; bi-monthly; adv.
Fabric Graphics; bi-monthly; adv.
Geosynthetics; bi-monthly; adv.
IFAI Worldwide; on-line
InTents; bi-monthly; adv.
Marine Fabricator; bi-monthly; adv.
Membership Directory; annually
Specialty Fabrics Review; monthly; adv.
Upholstery Journal

Industrial Fasteners Institute *(1931)*
6363 Oak Tree Blvd.
Independence, OH 44131
Tel: (216) 241-1482 *Fax:* (216) 241-5901
E-Mail: orders@indfast.org
Website: indfast.org
Members: 230 individuals and companies
Staff: 7
Annual Budget: $2-5,000,000
Tax: 501(c)(6)

Personnel:
Managing Director: Robert J. Harris
    E-Mail: rharris@indfast.org
Director, Engineering Technology: Joe Greenslade
    E-Mail: jgreenslade@indfast.org

Historical Note:
IFI's mission is to serve its suppliers, customers, the government and the public at large to advance the competitiveness of the member companies in a global marketplace. Members are comprised of North American manufacturers of bolts, nuts, screws, rivets and all types of special formed parts. Membership: $4,500-19,500 (Associate).

Continuing Education:
Certification Designation/s: DoDSMC

Publications:
IFI Technology Connection; annually

Industrial Foundation of America *(1960)*
402 E. San Antonio Ave.
Boerne, TX 78006
Tel: (830) 249-7899 *Fax:* (800) 628-2397
TollFree: (800) 592-1433
E-Mail: ifasmith@gvtc.com
Website: ifa-america.com
Members: 800 organizations
Staff: 1
Annual Budget: $500-1,000,000
Tax: 501(c)(6)

Personnel:
Executive Director: Bill Smith

Historical Note:
IFA strives to represent different construction, trucking, oil drilling, retail interests, and medically related services throughout the United States. Membership: $125/year.

Industrial Heating Equipment Association *(1929)*
5040 Old Taylor Mill Rd.
P.O. Box 13
Taylor Mill, KY 41015
Tel: (859) 356-1575 *Fax:* (859) 356-0908

E-Mail: ihea@ihea.org
Website: ihea.org
Members: 57 companies
Staff: 6
Annual Budget: $100-250,000

Personnel:
Executive Vice President: Anne Goyer
    E-Mail: anne@goyermgt.com
Legal Counsel: David Goch

Historical Note:
Formerly (1954) Industrial Furnace Manufacturers
Association. IHEA's mission is to provide services
to member companies that will enhance member
company capabilities to serve end users in the industrial
heat processing industry and improve the member
company's business performance as well. Members are
manufacturers of industrial furnaces, ovens, combustion
equipment, induction and dielectric heaters. Membership:
$2,000-8,500 (Manufacturing); $3,500 (Professional
Services).

Publications:
IHEA Newsletter; quarterly; adv.
Membership Directory; on-line

Industrial Metal Containers and Wire Decking Product Section
8720 Red Oak Blvd.
Suite 201
Charlotte, NC 28217-3992
Tel: (704) 676-1190 Fax: (704) 676-1199
Website: mhia.org/learning/glossary/i
Members: 10 companies
Staff: 2

Personnel:
Managing Director: Allan M. Howie
    E-Mail: ahowie@mhia.org

Historical Note:
A product section of the Material Handling Industry
Association that provides administrative support.

Industrial Minerals Association -- North America
(2002)
2011 Pennsylvania Ave. NW
Suite 301
Washington, DC 20006
Tel: (202) 457-0200 Fax: (202) 457-0287
E-Mail: info@ima-na.org
Website: ima-na.org
Members: 80 companies
Staff: 4
Annual Budget: $1-2,000,000
Tax: 501(c)(6)

Personnel:
President: Mark G. Ellis
    E-Mail: markellis@ima-na.org
Vice President, Government Affairs: Christopher K.
    Greissing
    E-Mail: chrisgreissing@ima-na.org
Financial Assistant: Paige Huggins
    E-Mail: paigehuggins@ima-na.org
Executive Vice President: Darrell K. Smith
    E-Mail: darrellsmith@ima-na.org

Historical Note:
IMA-NA seeks to advance the interests of North American
companies that mine or process minerals used throughout
the manufacturing and agricultural industries. IMA-
NA's mission is to promote best practices in health,
safety, operations, and the environment Membership:
$10,000-12,500 (Producer Member); $2,500-7,500
(Associate Member).

Publications:
IMA-NA e-Newsletter

Industrial Perforators Association (1961)
6737 W. Washington St.
Suite 1300
Milwaukee, WI 53214
Tel: (414) 389-8618 Fax: (414) 276-7704
E-Mail: info@iperf.org
Website: iperf.org
Members: 18 companies
Staff: 2
Annual Budget: $100-250,000

Personnel:
Executive Manager: Jane A. Svinicki CAE
    E-Mail: iperf@iperf.org
Coordinator: Jenny Rodriguez
    E-Mail: iperf@iperf.org

Historical Note:
Mission is to to perpetuate and increase the market for
perforated materials. Members are companies making
perforated metal products. The IPA conducts studies,
research on applications, handles trade inquiries.

Industrial Research Institute (1938)
2200 Clarendon Blvd.
Suite 1102
Arlington, VA 22201
Tel: (703) 647-2580 Fax: (703) 647-2581
E-Mail: information@iriweb.org
Website: iriweb.org
Members: 200 companies
Staff: 13
Annual Budget: $2-5,000,000

Personnel:
President: Edward Bernstein
    E-Mail: bernstein@iriweb.org
Junior Associate, Programs: Genevieve Borello
Junior Associate, Operations and Member Recruitment:
    Elizabeth Kalmus
    E-Mail: kalmus@iriweb.org
Junior Associate, Publications: Diana Schipper
    E-Mail: schipper@iriweb.org
Manager, Information Technology and Operations:
    Abhilasha Singh
    E-Mail: singh@iriweb.org
Vice President, Resource Distribution: Michele Taussig
    E-Mail: taussig@iriweb.org
Vice President, Membership Relations: Erika Toman
    E-Mail: toman@iriweb.org
Vice President, Operations: Ludita Vallarta

Historical Note:
IRI's mission is to enhance the effectiveness of technological
innovation by networking the world's best practitioners
and thought leaders to seek, share learn and create.
Membership: $11,800 (Company).

Meetings/Conferences: Annual
2013 - Washington, DC (Omni Shoreham Hotel,
    Washington D.C.)/May 21 - 23
Number of non-conference events/year: 7

Publications:
Innovation News Newsletter; monthly
Member Directory; on-line
Research Technology Management; bi-monthly; adv.

Membership List Available to Non-members

Industrial Truck Association (1951)
1750 K St. NW
Suite 460
Washington, DC 20006
Tel: (202) 296-9880 Fax: (202) 296-9884
E-Mail: indtrk@earthlink.net
Website: indtrk.org
Members: 82 associated firms and manufacturers
Staff: 5
Annual Budget: $2-5,000,000
Tax: 501(c)(6)

Personnel:
Executive Director: Brian Feehan
    E-Mail: bjfeehan@earthlink.net

Historical Note:
Founded as the Electric Industrial Truck Association,
assumed its present name in 1951. Members are
manufacturers of powered and non-powered lift trucks
as well as their major component suppliers. Membership:
$1,500 (Associate/Regular).

Meetings/Conferences: Semi-Annual
2013 - Washington, DC (Four Seasons Hotel
    Washington, D.C.)/March 11 - 13
2013 - White Sulphur Springs, WV (Greenbrier)/Sept.
    23 - 25

Publications:
Membership Directory; on-line

Industrial/Agricultural Mower Manufacturers Council (1981)
6737 W. Washington St.
Suite 2400
Milwaukee, WI 53214-5647
Tel: (414) 272-0943 Fax: (414) 272-1170
Website: aem.org/Groups/Groups/Group.asp?
    G=38
Staff: 1

Personnel:
Chairman: John Fisher

Historical Note:
Originally formed under the Industrial and Construction
Equipment Division (ICED) of FIEI, the council was
established as the IAMMC in 1981. The IAMMC, an
international group of manufacturers of industrial and
agricultural mowers, focuses on a variety of national/
international standards, safety related programs and
liaisons with several regulatory agencies.

Industry Council on Tangible Assets (1983)
P.O. Box 1365
Severna Park, MD 21146-8365
Tel: (410) 626-7005 Fax: (410) 626-7007
Website: ictaonline.org
Members: 450 firms
Staff: 2
Annual Budget: $250-500,000
Tax: 501(c)(6)

Personnel:
Executive Director: Eloise Ullman
    E-Mail: eloise.ullman@ictaonline.org

Historical Note:
ICTA's mission is to promote the interests of those
individuals, partnerships, firms, associations and
corporations who are engaged in the business of
manufacturing, importing, distributing or selling at retail
any tangible asset, including any precious metal, coin,
antique or art object. ICTA works to prevent laws and
regulations that would interfere with the ability to do
business and/or are excessively burdensome. Membership:
$300-25000 minimum (based on sales volume).

Infectious Diseases Society of America (1963)
1300 Wilson Blvd.
Suite 300
Arlington, VA 22209
Tel: (703) 299-0200 Fax: (703) 299-0204
E-Mail: info@idsociety.org
Website: idsociety.org
Members: 8400 individuals
Staff: 56
Annual Budget: $10-25,000,000

Personnel:
Chief Executive Officer: Mark A. Leasure
    E-Mail: mleasure@idsociety.org
Vice President, Public Policy and Government Relations:
    Robert J. Guidos J D
    E-Mail: rguidos@idsociety.org
Vice President, Meetings and Education: Sandra Vura
    Harwood CMP
    E-Mail: sharwood@idsociety.org
Senior Education Officer: Kathleen Matikonis
    E-Mail: kmatikonis@idsociety.org
Vice President, Communications: Diana Olson
    E-Mail: dolson@idsociety.org
Vice President, Administration and Finance: Donna Wilds
    E-Mail: dwilds@idsociety.org

Historical Note:
IDSA's mission is to improve the health of individuals,
communities, and society by promoting excellence in patient
care, education, research, public health and prevention
relating to infectious diseases. Membership: $25-295/year.

Meetings/Conferences: Annual
Conference Chair: Sandra Vura Harwood CMP

Publications:
Clinical Infectious Diseases; bi-weekly
HIVMA e-News; on-line
IDSA News; monthly
Journal of Infectious Disease; bi-weekly
Membership Directory; on-line

Membership List Available to Non-members

Inflatable Advertising Dealers Association
P.O. Box 502
Tipp City, OH 45371
Tel: (937) 222-1024 Fax: (937) 222-5794
E-Mail: info@inflatableads.com
Website: inflatableads.com
Members: 125 individuals
Staff: 3
Annual Budget: $25-50,000
Tax: 501(c)(6)

Personnel:
President: Chris Austin
Secretary and Treasurer: Bruce Cohen
Association Executive: Daniel Lea
    E-Mail: dlea@woh.rr.com

Historical Note:

IADA's purpose is to provide and promote a better understanding of the functions of inflatable advertising and its values. Members are companies engaged in the business of designing, manufacturing, selling, renting, installing or servicing inflatable advertising shapes, helium products and related products and other visual promotion devices. Membership: $225/year (Dealer Member).

Meetings/Conferences: Annual

Publications:
IADA Newsletter; quarterly
Membership Directory; on-line

Inflatable Boat Manufacturers Association (2006)
231 S. LaSalle St.
Suite 2050
Chicago, IL 60604
Tel: (312) 946-6200
Website: nmma.org/affiliates/ibma/default.aspx
Members: 9 individuals
Staff: 1

Personnel:
Director, Affiliates: Bernice McArdle
    E-Mail: bmcardle@nmma.org

Historical Note:
The Inflatable Boat Manufacturers Association is dedicated to serving the inflatable boat sector of the marine industry by creating, promoting and protecting an environment where members can achieve financial success through excellence in manufacturing and customer satisfaction.

InfoComm International (1939)
11242 Waples Mill Rd.
Suite 200
Fairfax, VA 22030
Tel: (703) 273-7200 Fax: (703) 278-8082
TollFree: (800) 659-7469
E-Mail: customerservice@infocomm.org
Website: infocomm.org
Members:
5000 companies
600 associates
Staff: 101
Annual Budget: $10-25,000,000

Personnel:
Chief Executive Officer: David Labuskes
Director, Public and Government Relations: Betsy Jaffe
    E-Mail: bjaffe@infocomm.org
General Counsel: Stephen D. Strauss Esq.
Staff Instructor: Bill Thomas
    E-Mail: bthomas@infocomm.org

Historical Note:
InfoComm International is the nonprofit association serving the professional AV communications industry worldwide. The association offers industry expertise and market research serving press and others seeking information about the industry. Membership: $500 (Commercial AV); $300-500 (Organization); $175 (Associate).

Continuing Education:
Certification Designation/s: CTS, CTS-I, CTS-D

Meetings/Conferences:
2013 - Beijing, China (China National Convention Center)/April 10 - 12
2013 - Orlando, FL (Orange County Convention Center)/June 8 - 14
2013 - Mumbai, India/Sept. 17 - 19
Number of non-conference events/year: 4

Publications:
e-news; quarterly
InfoComm Executive Updates; on-line
InfoComm News and Information Network; on-line
iQ Online AV Buyers Guide; on-line
Membership Directory; on-line

Information Storage Industry Consortium (1991)
12396 World Trade Dr.
Suite 201
San Diego, CA 92128
Tel: (858) 279-7230 Fax: (858) 279-8591
E-Mail: insic@insic.org
Website: insic.org
Members: 70 companies and organizations
Staff: 3
Annual Budget: $250-500,000
Tax: 501(c)(6)

Personnel:
Executive Director: Paul D. Frank
    E-Mail: paul@insic.org

Historical Note:
Founded as National Storage Industry Consortium, assumed current name in 2002. INSIC's mission is to enhance the growth and technical vitality of the information storage industry and to advance the state of information storage technology. Members are computer data storage manufacturers and other companies, universities and government laboratories with an interest in research in the field. Membership: $5,000 (Limited Member); $11,000-55,000 (Corporate, based on revenue); $500 (Associate).\; $5,000-22,000 (New Govt Agency).

Meetings/Conferences: Annual
2013 - Denver, CO/Nov. 4 - 8
2014 - Honolulu, HI/Nov. 3 - 7

Information Systems Audit and Control Association (1969)
3701 Algonquin Rd.
Suite 1010
Rolling Meadows, IL 60008
Tel: (847) 253-1545 Fax: (847) 253-1443
E-Mail: info@isaca.org
Website: isaca.org
Members: 100,000 constituents
Staff: 116
Annual Budget: $25-50,000,000

Personnel:
Chief Executive Officer and Corporate Secretary: Susan M. Caldwell
    E-Mail: scaldwell@isaca.org
Contact, Marketing: Amanda Beto
Contact, Membership Services: Bevin Callan
Contact, Virtual Conferences: Connie Djerrouf
Certification Coordinator: Diane Gabel
Editor: Jen Hajigeorgiou
    E-Mail: jhajigeorgiou@isaca.org
Contact, Media Relations: Deborah Vohasek
Contact, Research: Linda Wogelius

Historical Note:
Formerly (1994) EDP Auditors Association, ISACA is engaged in the development, adoption and use of globally accepted, industry knowledge and practices for information systems. Membership: $135 (Association); $51 (Student).

Continuing Education:
Certification Designation/s: CRISC, CGEIT, CISA, CISM

Meetings/Conferences: Annual
Conference Chair: Connie Djerrouf

Publications:
@ISACA; bi-weekly; adv.
ISACA Journal; bi-monthly

Information Systems Security Association (1984)
9220 SW Barbur Blvd.
Suite 119-333
Portland, OR 97219
Tel: (206) 388-4584 Fax: (206) 299-3366
TollFree: (866) 349-5818
Website: issa.org
Members: 13500 individuals
Staff: 10
Annual Budget: $1-2,000,000
Tax: 501(c)(6)

Personnel:
President: Kevin Richards
Editor: Thom Barrie
    E-Mail: editor@issa.org
Contact, Member and Chapter Services: Sarah Bellet
    E-Mail: sarah.bellet@issa.org
Director, Educational Programs and Partner Relations: Kate Kanapeaux
    E-Mail: katek@issa.org
Manager, Web Services: Dana Paulino
    E-Mail: dpaulino@issa.org
Controller: Doug Pease
    E-Mail: dougp@issa.org
Manager, Events and Communications: Kris Tanaka
    E-Mail: krist@issa.org
Managing Director: Lyn Trainer
    E-Mail: ltrainer@issa.org
Manager, Vendor Relations and Sponsorship: Justin Valdivia
    E-Mail: justinv@issa.org
Manager, Communications, Membership Development and Educational Programs: Anna Vembu
    E-Mail: apvembu@issa.org

Historical Note:
ISSA's mission is to promote the education and expand the knowledge and skills of its members in the interrelated fields of information systems security and information data processing. Members are professionals responsible for the protection of information databases. Membership: $95 (General); $995 (Executive); $90 (Organization); $30 (Student).

Continuing Education:
Certification Designation/s: CISM, CISA

Meetings/Conferences: Annual
Conference Chair: Kris Tanaka
Number of non-conference events/year: 25

Publications:
Directory; on-line
ISSA E-News; on-line
ISSA Journal; monthly; adv.

Information Technology Alliance (2010)
23940 N. 73rd Pl.
Scottsdale, AZ 85255-3425
Tel: (480) 363-1170 Fax: (602) 294-2399
Website: italliance.com
Staff: 2
Annual Budget: $500-1,000,000

Personnel:
Incoming President: Stan Mork
Treasurer: Lissa Johnsen CMC

Historical Note:
The mission ITA is to provide a collaborative environment where leading IT professionals share information and build relationships that significantly enhance the way they, and their clients, do business.

Meetings/Conferences: Biennial
2013 - St. Petersburg, FL (Vinoy Renaissance)/April 28 - 30
2013 - Salt Lake City, UT (The Grand America)/Dec. 8 - 10

Information Technology Industry Council (1916)
1101 K St. NW
Suite 610
Washington, DC 20005
Tel: (202) 737-8888 Fax: (202) 638-4922
E-Mail: info@itic.org
Website: itic.org
Members: 56 companies
Staff: 38
Annual Budget: $5-10,000,000

Personnel:
President and Chief Executive Officer: Dean C. Garfield
Manager, Human Resources and Facilities: Janelle Blackwood
    E-Mail: jblackwood@itic.org
Communications Associate: Meghan Fletcher
    E-Mail: mfletcher@itic.org
Director, Standards Programs: Jennifer Garner
    E-Mail: jgarner@itic.org
Senior Vice President, Public Policy: Robert Hoffman
    E-Mail: rhoffman@itic.org
Counsel: Ronald M. Jacobs
Director, Global Cybersecurity Policy: Danielle Kriz
    E-Mail: dkriz@itic.org
Executive Assistant and Event Planner: Anthony Lucas
    E-Mail: alucas@itic.org

Historical Note:
Formerly (1962) Office Equipment Manufacturers Institute, Business Equipment Manufacturers Association ((1973)), and Computer and Business Equipment Manufacturers Association (1994), ITI represents providers of computers, business and telecommunications equipment, software and services. It acts on domestic and international issues that affect the high-technology industry and also serves as the Secretariat for the American National Standards Institute Committee, Information Technology (X3). ITI engages in a broad range of issues, some of which include: corporate tax reform, trade, telecommunications, cybersecurity, energy efficiency, workforce and STEM initiatives, regulatory compliance, accessibility and environmental sustainability.

Meetings/Conferences:
Conference Chair: Anthony Lucas

Publications:
Cyber Specs; monthly

Information Theory Society
Three Park Ave.
17th Floor
New York, NY 10016-5997
Website: itsoc.org/
Members: 5700 individuals
Staff: 4

Annual Budget: $500-1,000,000

Personnel:
President: Muriel Medard
  E-Mail: medard@mit.edu
Editor: Tara Javidi

Historical Note:
A technical society of the Institute of Electrical and Electronics Engineers (IEEE). Membership in the Society, open only to IEEE members, includes a subscription to a technical periodical in the field published by IEEE. All administrative support is provided by IEEE. ITS's mission is to focus on the processing, transmission, storage, and use of information, and the foundations of the communication process.

Meetings/Conferences:
Conference Chair: Bruce Hajek
Number of non-conference events/year: 1

Publications:
IEEE Transactions on Information Theory; monthly
IT Society Newsletter; quarterly

Infrared Data Association (1994)
P.O. Box 3883
Walnut Creek, CA 94598
Tel: (925) 943-6546 *Fax:* (925) 943-5600
E-Mail: information@irda.org
Website: irda.org
Members: 80 companies
Staff: 2
Annual Budget: $100-250,000

Personnel:
Executive Director: Daphne Terrell
  E-Mail: daphne@irda.org
Executive Director, Marketing and Business Plans: Midori Miller

Historical Note:
IRDA is a consortium of companies united to develop and promote interoperable, low-cost infrared data connection standards that support a broad range of appliances, computers, and communication devices. Membership: $1,500-4,000 (Corporate, based on gross annual revenue); $8,000 (Executive).

Meetings/Conferences:
Conference Chair: Daphne Terrell

Publications:
IrDA Frontline
IrDA Insider; adv.

Infusion Nurses Society (1973)
315 Norwood Park South
Norwood, MA 02062
Tel: (781) 440-9408 *Fax:* (781) 440-9409
TollFree: (800) 694-0298
E-Mail: ins@ins1.org
Website: ins1.org
Members: 5700 indivduals
Staff: 22
Annual Budget: $2-5,000,000
Tax: 501(c)(3)

Personnel:
Chief Executive Officer: Mary Alexander CAE, CRNI, MA, RN, FAAN
  E-Mail: mary.alexander@ins1.org
Director, Membership and Marketing Services: Jason Beal
  E-Mail: jason.beal@ins1.org
Manager, Accounting: Michaelle Frost
  E-Mail: michaelle.frost@ins1.org
Executive Vice President: Christopher Hunt
  E-Mail: chris.hunt@ins1.org
Manager, Publications: Dorothy Lohmann
  E-Mail: dorothy.lohmann@ins1.org
Manager, Education: Kathy Marinucci BSN, CRNI, RN
  E-Mail: kathy.marinucci@ins1.org
Manager, Meetings: Heather Sampson CMP
  E-Mail: heather.sampson@ins1.org
Certification Manager: Julie Smiley
  E-Mail: julie.smiley@incc1.org

Historical Note:
Formerly the National Intravenous Therapy Association, assumed its current name in 2001. INS's mission is to set the standard for infusion nursing by developing and disseminating standards of practice and providing professional development opportunities and quality education of the nurses. Membership consists primarily of Registered Nurses involved in the clinical practice of infusion therapies. Membership: $90/year.

Continuing Education:
Enrollment: 5800

Certification Designation/s: CRNI

Meetings/Conferences:
Conference Chair: Heather Sampson CMP
2013 - Charlotte, NC/May 18 - 23/1200 attendees
2013 - Boston, MA/Nov. 8 - 10/600 attendees

Publications:
INS Connection; quarterly; adv.
INS Newsbrief; bi-monthly
INS Newsline; bi-monthly; adv.
Journal of Infusion Nursing; bi-monthly; adv.

Inland Marine Underwriters Association (1930)
14 Wall St.
Floor Eight
New York, NY 10005
Tel: (212) 233-0550 *Fax:* (212) 227-5102
Website: imua.org
Members: 400 companies
Staff: 3
Annual Budget: $500-1,000,000
Tax: 501(c)(6)

Personnel:
President and Chief Executive Officer: Kevin O'Brien
  E-Mail: kobrien@imua.org
Vice President and Secretary: Lillian Colson
  E-Mail: lcolson@imua.org
Specialist, Education Training: Eileen Monreale
  E-Mail: emonreal@imua.org

Historical Note:
IMUA addresses problems of common concern to companies underwriting Inland Marine and transportation insurance. Provides its members with education, research and communications services that support the inland marine underwriting discipline. Members include U.S. licensed insurers or reinsurers writing inland marine business and associate members who are vendors, brokers, law firms or any business that relates to the inland marine industry. Membership: $3,500 (Regular, minimum); $1,750 (Associate).

Meetings/Conferences: Annual

InsideNGO
1221 Post Rd., East
Suite 302
Westport, CT 06880
Tel: (203) 226-3650 *Fax:* (203) 226-3652
E-Mail: info@insidengo.org
Website: insidengo.org
Members: 270 members
Staff: 19
Annual Budget: $2-5,000,000
Tax: 501(c)(3)

Personnel:
Executive Director: Alison N. Smith
  E-Mail: asmith@insidengo.org
Contact, Marketing and Communications: Pat Bryant
  E-Mail: pbryant@insidengo.org
Contact, Program, Human Resources, Information Technology and Legal: Marie McNamee
  E-Mail: mmcnamee@insidengo.org
Contact, Event Registration and Financial Management: Sophia Rakowsky
  E-Mail: srakowsky@insidengo.org
Contact, Program, Finance, Grants, Contracts, Membership and Industry Partners: Bonnie Ricci
  E-Mail: bricci@insidengo.org

Historical Note:
InsideNGO is a collaborative community that strengthens the operational and management capacity of the international development and relief non-profit community in the pursuit of global development.

Meetings/Conferences: Annual
Conference Chair: Sophia Rakowsky
Number of non-conference events/year: 47

InSight
401 N. Michigan Ave.
Suite 2200
Chicago, IL 60611
Tel: (312) 321-6839 *Fax:* (312) 673-6721
E-Mail: info@InSight-net.org
Website: insight-net.org
Staff: 21
Annual Budget: $500-1,000,000

Personnel:
Executive Director: Brian Langerman
  E-Mail: blangerman@insight-net.org

Coordinator, Event Services: Dana Almdale
  E-Mail: dalmdale@insight-net.org
Manager, Marketing: Vickie Crews-Anderson
  E-Mail: Vcrews-A@insight-net.org
Education Program, Senior Manager: Julie Ferry
  E-Mail: jferry@smithbucklin.com
Association Associate: Jacqueline Hill
  E-Mail: jhill@insight-net.org
Operation Manager: Erin Thornburg
  E-Mail: ethornburg@insight-net.org

Historical Note:
Founded as the Technology and Information Management Education Society, assumed its present name in 1999. Aims to provide industry's main source of customer led advocacy, communication and education for McKesson Provider Technologies. Membership: $120 (Outsourced /Consultant Membership); $1,500 (Affiliate Business Partner), $125 (Individual).

Meetings/Conferences: Annual
Conference Chair: Dana Almdale
2013 - Orlando, FL (Orange County Convention Center)/Sept. 24 - 27

Publications:
e-Newsletter
Membership Directory; on-line

Institute for Briquetting and Agglomeration (1949)
P. O. Box 205
Portersville, PA 16051
E-Mail: iba@charter.net
Website: agglomeration.org
Members:
150 companies
225 individuals
Staff: 3
Annual Budget: $25-50,000
Tax: 501(c)(6)

Personnel:
Executive Director: Bob Hinkle
  E-Mail: iba@agglomeration.org

Historical Note:
Formerly (1967) International Briquetting Association, IBA is a group of business and technical people interested and involved in the research, development and production of briquets, pellets and other densified products and the equipment to produce them in the advance and mutual interests of its membership. Membership: $95 (Individual); $125 (Consultant).

Meetings/Conferences: Biennial

Publications:
Agglomerate and Communicate; quarterly
Membership Roster; on-line

Membership List Available to Non-members

Institute for Business & Home Safety (1977)
4775 E. Fowler Ave.
Tampa, FL 33617
Tel: (813) 286-3400 *Fax:* (813) 286-9960
E-Mail: info@ibhs.org
Website: disastersafety.org
Members: 486 Associate members
Staff: 40
Annual Budget: $5-10,000,000
Tax: 501(c)(3)

Personnel:
President and Chief Executive Officer: Julie Rochman
  E-Mail: jrochman@ibhs.org
General Counsel and Senior Vice President, Public Policy: Debra T. Ballen
  E-Mail: dballen@ibhs.org
Research Director: Anne D. Cope PE, PhD
Director, Finance: Susan Baxter Gibson
Director, Public Affairs: Candace Iskowitz
Manager, Media Relations: Joseph King
Senior Manager, Office Systems: Ricardo Paiva
Director, Human Resources: Deborah Perricone
  E-Mail: dperricone@ibhs.org
Senior Vice President, Research and Chief Engineer: Timothy A. Reinhold PhD
Director, Member Relations: Joy Whaley
  E-Mail: jwhaley@ibhs.org

Historical Note:
IBHS's mission is to conduct objective, scientific research to identify and advocate effective actions that strengthen homes, businesses, and communities against natural disasters and other causes of loss. Members are insurers

and reinsurers that conduct business in the United States.
Membership: $200-25,000(Associate).

Continuing Education:
Certification Designation/s: DHS

Institute for Certification of Computing Professionals (1973)
2400 E. Devon Ave.
Suite 281
Des Plaines, IL 60018
Tel: (847) 299-4227 Fax: (847) 299-4280
TollFree: (800) 843-8227
E-Mail: office2@iccp.org
Website: iccp.org
Members: 27 associations
Staff: 4
Annual Budget: $250-500,000

Personnel:
Executive Director: Kewal Dhariwal CCP, ISP
  E-Mail: office2@iccp.org
Director, Finance and Administration: Cindy Blaese
  E-Mail: cablaese@aol.com
Director, Membership Services: Suford Lewis
Director, Certification: John Whitehouse CCP, Jr.
  E-Mail: vitriol@cox.net

Historical Note:
ICCP's mission is to establish high professional standards
for the computer industry and promote these standards
by offering the broadly applicable and internationally
recognized certification program in the profession.
Membership: $22,500 (Consultant/Associate); $105
(Student).

Continuing Education:
Certification Designation/s: CITCP, CITC, CDMP, CCP,
ACP, ISA, CBIP, CDP, ISP
Meetings/Conferences:
Number of non-conference events/year: 2

Publications:
ICCP Certification News; quarterly; adv.
ICCP Newsletter; semi-annually
Membership Directory; on-line

Institute for Credentialing Excellence (1977)
2025 M St. NW
Suite 800
Washington, DC 20036-3309
Tel: (202) 367-1165 Fax: (202) 367-2165
E-Mail: info@credentialingexcellence.org
Website: credentialingexcellence.org
Members: 300 organizations
Staff: 8
Annual Budget: $1-2,000,000
Tax: 501(c)(3)

Personnel:
Executive Director: B. Denise Roosendaal
Staff Accountant: Sarah Alcock
Manager, Operations: Elizabeth Grater
Senior Manager, Education and Program Services: Delicia
  Hurdle
Senior Manager, Conferences: Melissa Huston
Senior Manager, Marketing and Creative Services:
  Amanda Wood

Historical Note:
Formerly known as National Organization for Competency
Assurance. Assumed its present name in 2009. ICE
advances credentialing through education, standards,
research, and advocacy to ensure competence across
professions and occupations. Accredited by the American
National Standards Institute as a Standards Developer.
Membership: $670 (Organization); $2,785 (Sustaining
Members); $1,340 (Affiliate); $340 (Individual).

Meetings/Conferences: Annual
Conference Chair: Melissa Huston
2013 - Amelia Island, FL (Omni Amelia Island
  Plantation Resort)/Nov. 11 - 14/11-25 exhibitors

Publications:
ICE News; quarterly; adv.
Membership Directory; on-line

Membership List Available to Non-members

Institute for Operations Research and the Management Sciences (1952)
7240 Pkwy. Dr.
Suite 300
Hanover, MD 21076-1310
Tel: (443) 757-3500 Fax: (443) 757-3515
TollFree: (800) 446-3676

E-Mail: informs@informs.org
Website: informs.org
Members: 10000 individuals
Staff: 54
Annual Budget: $5-10,000,000
Tax: 501(c)(3)

Personnel:
Executive Director: Melissa Moore
  E-Mail: melissa.moore@informs.org
Director, Marketing: Gary Bennett
  E-Mail: gary.bennett@informs.org
Director, Finance: Randy Chandler
  E-Mail: randy.chandler@informs.org
Director, Meetings: Teresa V. Cryan
  E-Mail: terry.cryan@informs.org
Director, Information Technology: Rose Futchko
  E-Mail: Rose.Futchko@informs.org
Director, Communications: Barry List
  E-Mail: barry.list@informs.org
Contact, Human Resources: Gina Lloyd
Director, Membership Services, Subdivisions and
  International Activities: Mary T. Magrogan
  E-Mail: mary.magrogan@informs.org
Director, Publications: Miranda Walker

Historical Note:
Formerly Operations Research Society of America, merged
with The Institute of Management Sciences and assumed
its current name in 1995. INFORMS's mission is to
advance the practice, research, methods, and applications
or OR/MS by encouraging, facilitating, and rewarding
excellence; serves the scientific and professional needs
of O.R. educators, investigators, scientists, students,
managers and consultants, as well as the organizations
they serve. Members are dedicated to applying scientific
methods to help improve decision-making, management,
and operations. Membership: $148 (Regular); $37 (Retired/
Student).

Meetings/Conferences:
Conference Chair: Teresa V. Cryan
2013 - Santa Fe, NM (Eldorado Hotel and Spa)/Jan. 6
  - 8
2013 - Steamboat Springs, CO (Sheraton Steamboat
  Resort,)/Feb. 7 - 10
2013 - San Antonio, TX (The Grand Hyatt San
  Antonio)/April 7 - 9
2013 - Istanbul, Turkey (Swissôtel The Bosphoru)/July
  11 - 13
2013 - San Jose, Costa Rica (Marriott Costa Rica)/July
  14 - 17
2013 - Minneapolis, MN (Hilton Minneapolis)/Oct. 6 -
  9
2014 - Seatle, WA (University of Washington)/June 19
  - 21
2014 - San Francisco, CA (Hilton San Francisco Union
  Square)/Nov. 16 - 19
Number of non-conference events/year: 1

Publications:
Analytics; bi-monthly
Decision Analysis; quarterly
Information Systems Research (ISR)
INFORMS Transactions on Education; on-line
Interfaces; bi-monthly
Journal on Computing; quarterly
Management Science
Management Science; monthly
Manufacturing & Service Operations Management
  (M&SOM); quarterly
Marketing Science; bi-monthly
Mathematics of Operations Research; quarterly
Membership Directory; on-line
Operations Research
Operations Research; bi-monthly
OR/MS Today; bi-monthly
OR/MS Tomorrow; semi-annually
Organization Science
PubsOnLine Suite; on-line
Transportation Science; quarterly

Institute for Professionals in Taxation (1976)
600 Northpark Town Center
1200 Abernathy Rd., Suite L-2
Atlanta, GA 30328-1040
Tel: (404) 240-2300 Fax: (404) 240-2315
E-Mail: ipt@ipt.org
Website: ipt.org
Members: 4000 members
Staff: 16
Annual Budget: $2-5,000,000

Tax: 501(c)(3)

Personnel:
Executive Director: Billy D. Cook
  E-Mail: bcook@ipt.org
Manager, Education and Certification Programs: Christina
  Akin
  E-Mail: cakin@ipt.org
Manager, Finance and Member Services: Margaret
  Dickson
  E-Mail: mdickson@ipt.org
Administrative Assistant: Jennifer Goodwin
  E-Mail: jgoodwin@ipt.org

Historical Note:
Formerly Institute of Property Taxation, IPT strives to
educate, certify and establish strict codes of conduct for
state and local income, property and sales and use tax
professionals who represent taxpayers. Members are
corporate sales/property income tax representatives and
attorneys, accountants and other professionals representing
corporate clients in these fields. Membership: $175
(Regular/Affiliate Member, Special Offer); $138 (Associate,
Special Offer)

Continuing Education:
Enrollment: 965
Certification Designation/s: CMI

Meetings/Conferences: Annual
2013 - Orlando, FL (Renaissance Orlando at
  SeaWorld)/June 23 - 26
2013 - Monterey, CA (Hyatt Regency Monterey Hotel
  And Spa)/Sept. 29 - Oct. 2
2013 - Indian Wells, CA (Hyatt Grand Champions
  Resort, Villas and Spa)/Nov. 3 - 6
2014 - Phoenix, AZ (JW Marriott Phoenix Desert Ridge
  Resort and Spa)/June 29 - July 2
2014 - Ft. Lauderdale, FL (Harbor Beach Marriott
  Resort and Spa)/Nov. 9 - 12
Number of non-conference events/year: 4

Publications:
Membership Directory; on-line
Tax Report; monthly

Institute for Responsible Housing Preservation (1989)
401 Ninth St. NW
Suite 900
Washington, DC 20004
Tel: (202) 585-8739 Fax: (202) 585-8080
E-Mail: irhp@aol.com
Website: housingpreservation.org
Members: 70 companies
Staff: 1
Annual Budget: $250-500,000
Tax: 501(c)(6)

Personnel:
Executive Director: Linda D. Kirk

Historical Note:
IRHP members are owners and managers of Low Income
Housing Preservation and Resident Housing Act (1990)
housing and ELIHPA housing and concerned professionals.
Membership: $5/unit/year.

Publications:
IRHP Newsletter; on-line
Member Directory; on-line

Institute for Supply Management (1915)
P.O. Box 22160
Tempe, AZ 85285-2160
Tel: (480) 752-6276 Fax: (480) 752-7890
TollFree: (800) 888-6276
Website: ism.ws
Members: 40000 individuals
Staff: 75
Annual Budget: $10-25,000,000

Personnel:
Chief Executive Officer: Thomas W. Derry
Contact, Information Technology: Joe Boudrie
  E-Mail: jboudrie@ism.ws
Director, Accounting: Sheri George
  E-Mail: sgeorge@ism.ws
Manager, Public Relations: Jean McHale
  E-Mail: jmchale@ism.ws
Manager, Meetings and Events: Terry Pizzano CMP
  E-Mail: tpizzano@ism.ws
Contact, Human Resource: Sue Roswurm
  E-Mail: sroswurm@ism.ws
Vice President, Education: Scott Sturzl APP, CPM, CPSM
  E-Mail: ssturzl@ism.ws

Vice President, Editor-in-Chief: Terri Tracey CAE
  E-Mail: ttracey@ism.ws
Vice President, Marketing and Sales: Cindy Urbaytis
  E-Mail: curbaytis@ism.ws

Historical Note:
*Formerly National Association of Purchasing Agents,
(1968) National Association of Purchasing Management
and assumed its current name in 2001. ISM's mission is to
guide supply management profession. Membership: $160
(Regular plus affiliate dues); $190 (Direct); $50 (Direct
Member for Defense Employees); $100-200 (International).*

Continuing Education:
Certification Designation/s: CPSM

Meetings/Conferences: Annual
Conference Chair: Terry Pizzano CMP
2013 - New Orleans, LA/Feb. 5 - 7
2013 - Grapevine, TX/April 28 - May 1
2014 - Las Vegas, NV/May 5 - 7
2015 - Phoenix, AZ/May 3 - 6
2016 - Indianapolis, IN/May 16 - 18
Number of non-conference events/year: 69

Publications:
eSide Supply Management; bi-monthly; adv.
Inside Supply Management; monthly; adv.
ISM eDigest; quarterly
ISM Member's Edge Newsletter; on-line; adv.
ISM Newsline Newsletter; monthly
ISM Supply Line 2055: Certification Update; quarterly
Just in ETime Newsletter; on-line; adv.
Membership Directory; on-line
Supply IN Demand; annually; adv.
The Journal of Supply Chain Management; quarterly

Institute Management Accountants *(1919)*
10 Paragon Dr.
Suite One
Montvale, NJ 07645-1718
Tel: (201) 573-9000 *Fax:* (201) 474-1600
TollFree: (800) 638-4427
E-Mail: ima@imanet.org
Website: imanet.org
Members: 60000 Individuals
Staff: 60
Annual Budget: $50-100,000
Tax: 501(c)(3)

Personnel:
President and Chief Executive Officer: Jeffrey C. Thomson
  E-Mail: jthomson@imanet.org
Director, Communications and Public Relations: Marc
  Gerrone
  E-Mail: mgerrone@imanet.org
Senior Vice President, Certification: Dennis Whitney
  E-Mail: dwhitney@imanet.org

Historical Note:
*Established as National Association of Cost Accountants
changed to National Association of Accountants in 1957
and assumed its current name in 1991. IMA's mission
is to provide a forum for research, practice development,
education, knowledge sharing, and the advocacy of the
highest ethical and best business practices in management
accounting and finance. Membership: $195 (Professional/
International); $130 (Young Professional); $39 (Student);
$98 (Academic/Retired); $65 (Associate).*

Continuing Education:
Certification Designation/s: CMA

Meetings/Conferences:
2013 - Los Angeles, CA (New Orleans)/June 22 -
26/11-25 exhibitors
Number of non-conference events/year: 1

Publications:
Campus Connection
Campus Connection; quarterly
Career Connection; quarterly
CMA Connection; quarterly
IMA Educational Case Journal (on-line); quarterly
IMA Online News; weekly; adv.
Management Accounting Quarterly; quarterly
Research Connection; annually
Small Business Update; monthly; adv.
Strategic Finance; monthly; adv.
Strategic TechNotes; semi-monthly

Membership List Available to Non-members

Institute of Behavioral and Applied Management
600 Hoyt St.
P.O. Box Ten
Peru, NE 68421

Tel: (402) 872-2421
Website: ibam.com
Members: 150 individuals
Staff: 3
Annual Budget: $10-25,000

Personnel:
President: Rebecca Herman PhD, SPHR
  E-Mail: Rebecca.herman.ibam@gmail.com
Treasurer: Sheri A. Grotrian
  E-Mail: sgrotrian@peru.edu

Historical Note:
*IBAM provides a forum for management educators, business
practitioners, and students to share their ideas, research,
and experiences in a friendly and supportive environment.
IBAM members are educators and other professionals
interested in organizational behavior and management
theory. Membership: $50/year.*

Meetings/Conferences: Annual

Publications:
Journal of Behavioral and Applied Management; on-
line

Institute of Business Appraisers *(1978)*
1111 Brickyard Rd.
Suite 200
Salt Lake City, UT 84106
Tel: (954) 584-1144 *Fax:* (866) 353-5406
TollFree: (800) 299-4130
E-Mail: hqiba@go-iba.org
Website: go-iba.org
Members: 2000 individuals
Staff: 9
Annual Budget: $1-2,000,000

Personnel:
Executive Director: Howard A. Lewis
  E-Mail: hlewis@go-iba.org

Historical Note:
*IBA is committed to provide the good quality of service to
its members by assisting them in a journey to professional
excellence in the field of business appraisal. Membership:
$495 (Appraisal Practitioner/Business Broker); $295
(Academician); $195 (Student).*

Continuing Education:
Certification Designation/s: CBA, BVAL, ABAR, MCBA

Meetings/Conferences: Annual
Number of non-conference events/year: 1

Publications:
IBA Business Appraisal Practice; quarterly
IBA Newsletter; bi-monthly; adv.

Institute of Career Certification International
(1994)
618 Church St.
Suite 220
Nashville, TN 37219
Tel: (615) 250-7789 *Fax:* (615) 254-7047
E-Mail: info@careercertification.org
Website: careercertification.org
Members: 325 individuals
Staff: 5
Annual Budget: $25-50,000
Tax: 501(c)(6)

Personnel:
Executive Director: Edward C. Witherell
Manager, Accounts: Sharon Barkmeier
  E-Mail: sbarkmeier@xmi-amc.com
Contact, Communication: Devin Anna Bradford
Editor: Marilyn Stika CMP
Chief Financial Officer: Laurence J. Stybel

Historical Note:
*Founded as Outplacement Institute, became International
Board for Career Management Certification in 1999 and
assumed its present name in 2003. ICC International is the
international, not-for-profit, and independent certifying
body for career services professionals.*

Continuing Education:
Certification Designation/s: CMF, CMP, CMA

Publications:
ICC Global Update; bi-monthly
ICCI Newsletter; bi-monthly

Institute of Caster and Wheel Manufacturers
(1933)
8720 Red Oak Blvd.
Suite 201
Charlotte, NC 28217-3992

Tel: (704) 676-1190 *Fax:* (704) 676-1199
Website: mhia.org/industrygroups/icwm
Members: 40 companies
Staff: 2
Annual Budget: $50-100,000
Tax: 501(c)(6)

Personnel:
President: Bill LeMeur
Contact: Allan M. Howie
  E-Mail: ahowie@mhia.org

Historical Note:
*Formerly (1990) Caster and Floor Truck Manufacturers
Association; (2002) Institute of Caster Manufacturers, an
affiliate of Material Handling Industry of America, which
provides administrative support. Members are suppliers
of casters, wheels, bearings, and industrial trailer trucks,
platform trucks and towline trucks. They supply caster and
wheel solutions worldwide and in virtually every major
manufacturing and distribution sector.*

Publications:
ENewsletter; on-line
Membership Directory; on-line

Institute of Certified Business Counselors *(1975)*
18831 Willamette Dr.
W. Linn, OR 97068
Fax: (503) 292-8237
TollFree: (877) 422-2674
E-Mail: inquiry@i-cbc.org
Website: i-cbc.org
Members: 160 individuals
Staff: 2
Annual Budget: Under $10,000
Tax: 501(c)(6)

Personnel:
President: Monty W. Walker
  E-Mail: mwalker@waa-online.com
Administrator: Mary Ann Gray

Historical Note:
*ICBC works to be an association of business transfer,
planning and support professionals through the team
application of integrated disciplines designed to meet
the needs of business owners, their employees and
other stakeholders. Members are primarily professional
intermediaries specializing in assisting clients in
the operation of the sale or purchase of businesses,
accountants, attorneys, appraisers, bankers and I-Bankers,
business valuations experts, estate planners, M & A
Intermediaries and tax experts. Membership: $350/year.*

Continuing Education:
Certification Designation/s: MCBC, CBC

Meetings/Conferences: Annual
2013 - Miami, FL (Hilton Miami Downtown)/Jan. 14 -
17

Publications:
I-CBC Newsletter; on-line
Membership Directory; on-line

Membership List Available to Non-members

Institute of Certified Professional Managers
(1974)
James Madison University
MSC 5504
Harrisonburg, VA 22807
Tel: (540) 568-3247 *Fax:* (540) 801-8650
TollFree: (800) 568-4120
E-Mail: icpmcm@jmu.edu
Website: icpm.biz
Members: 11000 managers
Staff: 4
Annual Budget: $250-500,000
Tax: 501(c)(3)

Personnel:
Executive Director: Lynn S. Powell MBA
  E-Mail: powellls@jmu.edu
Manager, Customer Relations: Melody Branner
Manager, Assessment and Technology: Drew Koch
  E-Mail: kochas@jmu.edu
Instructional Designer: Jonathan Lutz

Historical Note:
*ICPM's mission is to raise competency & professionalism
in the field of management through certification and
continuing professional development. Certified Manager
(CM) certificants gain use of the "CM" professional
credential which is recognized worldwide as a sign of
managerial competency. CM certificants benefit from
enhanced levels of performance and possess a competitive
edge for employment and advancement.*

Continuing Education:
Enrollment: 1000
Certification Designation/s: CMAR, CM

Meetings/Conferences: Annual
Conference Chair: Lynn S. Powell MBA

Publications:
Management World; bi-monthly
The Certified Letter; biennially

Institute of Certified Records Managers *(1975)*
403 E. Taft Rd.
Syracuse, NY 13212
Tel: (315) 234-1904 *Fax:* (315) 474-1784
TollFree: (877) 244-3128
E-Mail: admin@icrm.org
Website: icrm.org
Members: 2000 individuals
Staff: 9
Annual Budget: $250-500,000
Tax: 501(c)(6)

Personnel:
Editor: Linda Buss
Regent, Public Relations and Professional Development:
  Rae Lynn Haliday CRM, MBA
  E-Mail: haliday@stlzoo.org
Coordinator, Public Relations: Peter A. Kurilecz CA, CRM
  E-Mail: pakurilecz@gmail.com

Historical Note:
Developed by the American Records Management Association (1966), incorporated in 1975. ICRM's mission is to certify RIM professionals as Certified Records Managers (CRM) and administer a certification maintenance program.Membership: $200 (Active CRM); $15 (Retired).

Continuing Education:
Certification Designation/s: CRM

Meetings/Conferences:
Conference Chair: Daniel McGlynn CRM

Publications:
ICRM Newsletter; on-line
Membership Directory; on-line

Institute of Clean Air Companies *(1960)*
2025 M St. NW
Suite 800
Washington, DC 20036
Tel: (202) 367-1114
E-Mail: icacinfo@icac.com
Website: icac.com
Members: 100 corporations
Staff: 6
Annual Budget: $500-1,000,000
Tax: 501(c)(6)

Personnel:
Executive Director: Betsy Natz
  E-Mail: bnatz@icac.com
Coordinator, Accounting Services: Sarah Alcock
  E-Mail: SAlcock@icac.com
Director, Government Affairs: Doug Austin
  E-Mail: Daustin@icac.com
Senior Associate: Laura Somerville
  E-Mail: LSomerville@icac.com
Director, Marketing and Communications: Amanda Wood
  E-Mail: AMWood@icac.com
Senior Coordinator, Events: Alexandra Zapple
  E-Mail: AZapple@icac.com

Historical Note:
Formed as the Industrial Gas Cleaning Institute (IGCI) and established as Institute of Clean Air Companies (ICAC) in 1991. Members are manufacturers of industrial air pollution control and monitoring equipment for stationary sources. Influences federal, regional, and state clean air policy, works constructively with government, business, public and private groups to ensure that the industry and its products are properly represented, and offers information for the media about their work. Membership: $5,000-32,000 (Regular, based on sales revenue); $1,500-5,000 (Associate, based on sales revenue).

Continuing Education:
Certification Designation/s: QEP

Meetings/Conferences: Annual
Conference Chair: Alexandra Zapple
2013 - Naples, FL (Waldorf Astoria Naples)/April 25 - 27
Number of non-conference events/year: 2

Publications:
ICAC Newsletter; weekly
Membership Directory; on-line; adv.

Institute of Diving *(1977)*
17314 Panama City Beach Pkwy.
Panama City, FL 32413
Tel: (850) 235-4101
E-Mail: info@maninthesea.org
Website: maninthesea.org/about.php
Members: 500 individuals and companies
Staff: 2
Annual Budget: $25-50,000

Personnel:
Contact, Communications: Michael DeGroote

Historical Note:
Members are sports, commercial and military divers, individuals, organizations and corporations interested in diving and diving-related activities. Supports the Museum of Man in the Sea. Membership: $35 (Individual); $1000 (Lifetime).

Publications:
Newsletter

Institute of Electrical and Electronics Engineers (IEEE) *(1884)*
Three Park Ave.
17th Floor
New York, NY 10016-5997
Tel: (212) 419-7900 *Fax:* (212) 752-4929
E-Mail: ieeeusa@ieee.org
Website: ieee.org
Members: 400000 individuals
Staff: 1245
Annual Budget: Over $100,000,000

Personnel:
Executive Director: E. James Prendergast
Staff Executive, Human Resources: Elizabeth (Betsy) Davis
Staff Executive, Publications: Anthony J. Durniak
Managing Director, Educational Activities: Doug Gorham
General Counsel and Chief Compliance Officer: Eileen M. Lach
Staff Executive, Corporate Strategy and Communications: Matthew S. Loeb
  E-Mail: m.loeb@ieee.org
Chief Marketing Officer: Patrick Mahoney
Staff Executive, Information Technology and Chief Information Officer: Alexander Pasik
Chief Financial Officer: Thomas Siegert

Historical Note:
Merger (1963) of the American Institute of Electrical Engineers (1884) and Institute of Radio Engineers (1912). IEEE's mission is to promote the practice and expansion of effective and responsible philanthropy to improve the health and vitality of its region. Membership: $183 (United States); $163.90 (Canada GST); $177.94 (Canada HST); $151 (Africa, Europe, Middle East); $142 (Latin America); $143 (Asia, Pacific); $32 (Student, United States); $33.60 (Student, Canada GST); $36.16 (Student, Canada HST); $27 (Student- Africa,Europe,Middle East/Latin America/ Asia, Pacific).

Continuing Education:
Certification Designation/s: CBP, CSDA, CSDP, WCET

Meetings/Conferences: Annual
2013 - Maui, HI/Jan. 11 - 14

Publications:
IEEE Spectrum; monthly; adv.
The Institute; monthly; adv.

Institute of Environmental Sciences and Technology *(1953)*
Arlington Pl. One, 2340 S. Arlington Heights Rd.
Suite 100
Arlington Heights, IL 60005-4516
Tel: (847) 981-0100 *Fax:* (847) 981-4130
E-Mail: information@iest.org
Website: iest.org
Members: 1600 individuals
Staff: 9
Annual Budget: $500-1,000,000
Tax: 501(c)(3)

Personnel:
Executive Director and Managing Editor: Roberta Burrows
  E-Mail: executive@iest.org
Coordinator, Membership Services and Accounting: Mara Douvris
  E-Mail: membershipdept@iest.org
Administrative Assistant: Pam Farmer
  E-Mail: customerservice@iest.org

Director, Communications and Programs: Diana Granitto
  E-Mail: director@iest.org
Coordinator, Marketing and Meetings: Heather Wooden
  E-Mail: marketing@iest.org

Historical Note:
Formed by a merger of the Institute of Environmental Engineers (1955) and the Society of Environmental Engineers. Absorbed the American Association for Contamination Control in 1973. IEST's mission is to serve its members and the industries they represent (simulating, testing, controlling, and teaching the environments of earth and space) through education and the development of recommended practices and standards. Members are engineers, scientists, and educators of environmental sciences and technology. Membership: $195 (Individual); $90 (Young Professional); $30 (Student).

Meetings/Conferences:
Conference Chair: Heather Wooden
2013 - Orlando, FL (Rosen Shingle Creek Resort)/Jan. 28 - 31
2013 - San Diego, CA (San Diego Marriot Del Mar)/ April 29 - May 2
Number of non-conference events/year: 1

Publications:
Buyer's Guide; on-line
Journal of the IEST; on-line

The Institute of Financial Operations *(2011)*
615 E. Colonial Dr.
Orlando, FL 32803
Tel: (407) 351-3322 *Fax:* (407) 895-5031
TollFree: (877) 885-4277
Website: financialops.org
Members: 5000 individuals
Staff: 9
Tax: 501(c)(6)

Personnel:
Executive Director: Jo E. LaBorde
  E-Mail: jo.laborde@financialops.org
Vice President, Event Services: Ken Brown
  E-Mail: en.brown@financialops.org
Editor-in-Chief and Vice President, News and Publications: Laureen Crowley
  E-Mail: laureen.crowley@financialops.org
Administrator: Jennifer Garner
  E-Mail: jennifer.garner@financialops.org
Vice President, Business Development: Josh Gold
  E-Mail: josh.gold@financialops.org
Web and Database Administrator: Princess Stephens
  E-Mail: princess.stephens@financialops.org
Chief Financial Officer: Brandie Tapscott
  E-Mail: brandie.tapscott@financialops.org
Vice President, Membership and Communications: Isabel Vermeer
  E-Mail: isabel.vermeer@financialops.org
Vice President, Professional Development: Elizabeth Wagonseller
  E-Mail: elizabeth.wagonseller@financialops.org

Historical Note:
An umbrella organization comprising of four affiliates for finance professionals: International Accounts Payable Professionals (IAPP), International Accounts Receivable Professionals (IARP), the National Association of Purchasing and Payables (NAPP), and The Association for Work Process Improvement (TAWPI). IFO is a membership-based professional association serving the financial operations ecosystem, with a particular focus on the accounts payable and accounts receivable disciplines and the related fields of information management and data capture. Membership: $245 (Premium); $145 (Virtual).

Continuing Education:
Certification Designation/s: CAPA, CAPP

Meetings/Conferences:
Conference Chair: Ken Brown
2013 - Orlando, FL (Disney's Coronado Springs Resort)/May 19 - 23

Publications:
AP Matters (IAPP); quarterly
AR Matters (IARP); quarterly
Financial Operations Matters; bi-monthly; adv.
Membership Directory; on-line
Today (TAWPI); quarterly

Institute of Food Technologists *(1939)*
525 W. Van Buren
Suite 1000
Chicago, IL 60607
Tel: (312) 782-8424 *Fax:* (312) 782-8348

TollFree: (800) 438-3663
E-Mail: info@ift.org
Website: ift.org
Members: 22000 individuals
Staff: 80
Annual Budget: $10-25,000,000

Personnel:
Executive Vice President and Ex Officio Member: Barbara
    Byrd Keenan CAE
    E-Mail: bbkeenan@ift.org
Chief Administrative Officer: Kelley Ahuja
    E-Mail: kahuja@ift.org
Chief Financial Officer: Mark Barenie
    E-Mail: mbarenie@ift.org
Vice President, Information Technology: Marc Bernstein
    E-Mail: mjbernstein@ift.org
Vice President, Communications and Media Relations:
    Jerry M. Bowman
    E-Mail: jmbowman@ift.org
Vice President, Science and Policy Initiatives: Will Fisher
    E-Mail: wfisher@ift.org
Manager, Human Resources: Susan Harris
    E-Mail: sharris@ift.org
Vice President, Meetings and Business Partnerships:
    Christine M. Klein CMP
Director, Membership: Sharon Kneebone CAE
    E-Mail: skneebone@ift.org
Director, Marketing: Jennifer London
    E-Mail: jalondon@ift.org
Vice President, Knowledge and Learning Experiences: Bob
    Moore CAE, MA
    E-Mail: bmoore@ift.org
Director, Publications and Editor-In-Chief: Bob Swientek
    E-Mail: bswientek@ift.org
Director, Media Relations: Mindy Weinstein
    E-Mail: mweinstein@ift.org

Historical Note:
IFT's mission is to advance the science and technology of
food through the exchange of knowledge, and by doing
so, to bring sound science to the public discussion of food
issues. Members work in food science, technology and
related professions in academia, government and industry.
Membership: $190(Regular/Professional); $50 (Student);
$25 (Emeritus).

Meetings/Conferences: Annual
Conference Chair: Christine M. Klein CMP
2013 - Rosemont, IL (InterContinental Chicago
    O'Hare)/March 27 - 28
2013 - Chicago, IL/July 13 - 16
2014 - Las Vegas, NV/June 21 - 24
2015 - Chicago, IL/July 11 - 14
Number of non-conference events/year: 1

Publications:
Eat Your Words; monthly
Express Connect; monthly
Food Technology Magazine; bi-monthly; adv.
IFT Weekly Newsletter; weekly
Membership Directory; on-line
Nutraceutical Newsletter; monthly
Special Edition Newsletters

Institute of General Semantics (1938)
72-11 Austin St.
Suite 233
Forest Hills, NY 11375
Tel: (212) 729-7973 Fax: (718) 793-2527
Website: generalsemantics.org
Members: 700 individuals
Staff: 5
Annual Budget: Under $10,000
Tax: 501(c)(3)

Personnel:
President and Editor: Martin H. Levinson
Secretary: Vanessa Biard-Schaeffer
Webmaster: Ben Hauck
Editor: Bill Petkanas
Treasurer: Jacqueline J. Rudig

Historical Note:
International Society for General Semantics (ISGS) merged
with the Institute of General Semantics(IGS) in 2003. IGS
promotes a scientific approach to understanding human
behavior, especially that related to symbol systems and
language, and the application of proven principles that
guide advancements in critical thinking, rational behavior,
and general sanity. Membership: $50 (Individual); $25
(Student); $40 (Gift Membership); $100-1000 (Exclusive).

Meetings/Conferences: Annual

Publications:
ETC: A Review of General Semantics; quarterly; adv.
General Semantics Bulletin (GSB); annually
Time-Bindings - Newsletter; semi-annually; adv.

Institute of Hazardous Materials Management
(1984)
11900 Parklawn Dr.
Suite 450
Rockville, MD 20852-2624
Tel: (301) 984-8969 Fax: (301) 984-1516
E-Mail: info@ihmm.org
Website: ihmm.org
Members: 15000 individuals
Staff: 8
Annual Budget: $1-2,000,000
Tax: 501(c)(6)

Personnel:
Executive Director: Jeffrey H. Greenwald CAE, P E
    E-Mail: jgreenwald@ihmm.org
Recertification Assistant and Contributing Editor: M.
    Patricia Buley
    E-Mail: pbuley@ihmm.org
Director, Certification: Ginger L. Harrison
    E-Mail: gharrison@ihmm.org
Accounting Manager: Kim L. Smith
    E-Mail: KSmith@ihmm.org

Historical Note:
IHMM's mission is to develop and advocate professional
standards for certification and to administer credible
certification programs for individuals who practice in
disciplines involving the general management of hazardous
materials and related areas. Annual maintenance fee:
$125/year.

Continuing Education:
Certification Designation/s: CHMM, CHMP

Publications:
IHMM Credentials Directory; on-line
IHMM Today; on-line

Institute of Industrial Engineers (1981)
3577 Pkwy. Ln.
Suite 200
Norcross, GA 30092
Tel: (770) 449-0460 Fax: (770) 441-3295
TollFree: (800) 494-0460
E-Mail: cs@iienet.org
Website: iienet.org
Members: 15000 individuals
Staff: 20
Annual Budget: $250-500,000
Tax: 501(c)(3)

Personnel:
Chief Executive Officer: Don H. Greene CAE, P E
    E-Mail: dgreene@iienet.org
Director, Continuing Education and Program Development:
    Larry Aft PE
    E-Mail: training@iienet.org
Director, Membership: Heather Bradley
    E-Mail: membership@iienet.org
Director, Communications: Monica Elliott
    E-Mail: editor@iienet.org
Managing Editor: Michael Hughes
Director, Finance and Information Technology: J. J. Koran
Manager, Sponsorships, Exhibits and Advertising Sales:
    Michelle Lorusso RN
    E-Mail: advertising@iienet.org
Senior Vice President, Continuing Education: James E.
    Moore
    E-Mail: jmoore@usc.edu

Historical Note:
Founded as the American Institute of Industrial Engineers,
assumed its present name in 1981, a member of the
Accreditation Board for Engineering and Technology
and the Council of Engineering Examiners, absorbed the
Industrial Management Society in 1982. IIE's mission is
to provide knowledge, training, networking opportunities
and recognition to enhance the skills and effectiveness of
the industrial engineering profession and those individuals
involved with improving quality and productivity.
Membership: $149 (Professional/Senior); $74.50 (Retired/
Life/First-Year Graduating); $35 (Student).

Continuing Education:
Certification Designation/s: SSBBC, SSGBC, LSSGB,
LSSFC, HCCP, LECP, IEPSCP, SSCP, LEMPCP, EMCP

Meetings/Conferences:
Conference Chair: Michelle Lorusso RN

2013 - San Juan, PR (Caribe Hilton San Juan)/May 18
    - 22
Number of non-conference events/year: 3

Publications:
IIE Transactions; monthly
IIE Transactions on Healthcare Systems Engineering
Industrial Engineer; monthly
Industrial Management; bi-monthly
Journal of Enterprise Transformation
Membership Directory; on-line
The Engineering Economist; quarterly

The Institute of Inspection, Cleaning and
Restoration Certification (1972)
2715 E. Mill Plain Blvd.
Vancouver, WA 98661
Tel: (360) 693-5675 Fax: (360) 693-4858
TollFree: (800) 835-4624
E-Mail: info@iicrc.org
Website: iicrc.org
Members:
4600 certified firms
46000 certified technicians
Staff: 3
Annual Budget: $2-5,000,000
Tax: 501(c)(6)

Personnel:
President: Patrick Winters
Executive Administrator: Tom Hill
    E-Mail: tom@iicrc.org

Historical Note:
Formerly (1993) the International Institute of Carpet and
Upholstery Certification, IICRC serves as an independent
certification body to advance communication and technical
proficiency within the inspection, cleaning and restoration
service industries. Members are firms and individuals
concerned with fabric restoration.

Continuing Education:
Certification Designation/s: ASD, RRT, SCI, SMT, UFT,
WLFI, CTI, RFI, WDRT, MSI, JFSRT, CRRT, JCT, CCT,
UFCT, OCT, CCRT, FCT, HST, LCT, RFMT, FSDRT, RCT,
SCT, JWDRT, MSFRT, MWDRT, MTC, ASDT, AMRT,
CCMT, SMCTC, ISSI

Publications:
IICRC e-Newsletter; bi-monthly

The Institute of Internal Auditors (1941)
247 Maitland Ave.
Altamonte Springs, FL 32701-4201
Tel: (407) 937-1100 Fax: (407) 937-1101
Website: theiia.org
Members: 160000 individuals
Staff: 100
Annual Budget: $25-50,000,000
Tax: 501(c)(6)

Personnel:
President and Chief Executive Officer: Richard F.
    Chambers
    E-Mail: richard.chambers@theiia.org
Vice President, Governance and Communication: Judy
    Burke
    E-Mail: judy.burke@theiia.org
Director, Human Resources: JoAnn Clayton
    E-Mail: joann.clayton@theiia.org
Vice President, Global Relations and Development: Sylvia
    Gonner
Vice President, Professional Guidance: Susan B. Lione
    E-Mail: slione@theiia.org
Editorial Director: Anne Millage
    E-Mail: anne.millage@theiia.org
Vice President, Research: Bonnie Ulmer
    E-Mail: bonnie.ulmer@theiia.org

Historical Note:
IIA's mission is to provide dynamic leadership for the global
profession of internal auditing. Membership: $70-2100/
year (US/Canada).

Continuing Education:
Certification Designation/s: CFSA, CCSA, CIA, CGAP,
CRMA

Meetings/Conferences: Semi-Annual
Conference Chair: Judy Burke
Number of non-conference events/year: 2

Publications:
IIA Insight; on-line; adv.
IIA Newsletter; on-line; adv.
IIA Today; on-line
Internal Auditor Magazine; adv.

Institute of International Bankers (1966)

299 Park Ave.
17th Floor
New York, NY 10171
Tel: (212) 421-1611 *Fax:* (212) 421-1119
E-Mail: iib@iib.org
Website: iib.org
Members: 230 banks
Staff: 7
Annual Budget: $2-5,000,000
Tax: 501(c)(6)

Personnel:
Chief Executive Officer: Sarah "Sally" Miller
    E-Mail: smiller@iib.org
Manager, Government Relations: Paul Begey
General Counsel: Richard Coffman
    E-Mail: rcoffman@iib.org
Director, Communications: William Goodwin
    E-Mail: wgoodwin@iib.org
Coordinator, Membership Services and Events Registration:
    Andy Lebron
    E-Mail: alebron@iib.org
Manager, Information Technology: James S. Strype
    E-Mail: jstrype@iib.org

Historical Note:
IIB's mission is to help resolve the many special legislative, regulatory and tax issues confronting internationally headquartered financial institutions that engage in banking, securities and/or insurance activities in the United States. Membership consists of banking/financial organizations headquartered outside the United States.

Meetings/Conferences: Annual
Conference Chair: Andy Lebron
2013 - Washington, DC (Four Seasons Hotel
    Washington, D.C.)/March 3 - 5
Number of non-conference events/year: 3

Publications:
Bulletin; weekly
Global Survey of Regulatory and Market
    Developments; annually
International Banking Focus/Institute News; bi-
    monthly
Membership Directory; on-line

Institute of International Container Lessors
(1971)
1990 M St. NW
Suite 650
Washington, DC 20036-3417
Tel: (202) 223-9800 *Fax:* (202) 223-9810
E-Mail: info@iicl.org
Website: iicl.org
Members: 12 companies
Staff: 3
Annual Budget: $1-2,000,000

Personnel:
President and Secretary: Steven R. Blust
Director, Technical Services: Gary Danback
    E-Mail: gdanback@iicl.org
Director, Marketing and Administration: Eliseo Mena Jr.
    E-Mail: emena@iicl.org

Historical Note:
IICL's membership engages in leasing marine cargo containers and chassis to ship operators and others on a broad international basis.The institute is active in governmental, regulatory, customs, tax, educational, technological and environmental areas.

Continuing Education:
Certification Designation/s: CIC

Publications:
Newsletter

Membership List Available to Non-members

Institute of International Finance (1983)
1333 H St. NW
Suite 800E
Washington, DC 20005-4770
Tel: (202) 857-3600 *Fax:* (202) 775-1430
E-Mail: info@iif.com
Website: iif.com
Members: 375 financial institutions
Staff: 96
Annual Budget: $25-50,000,000

Personnel:
Managing Director: Charles H. Dallara

Historical Note:

IIF's mission is to support the financial industry in prudently managing risks, including sovereign risk; in developing best practices and standards; and in advocating regulatory, financial, and economic policies that are in the broad interest of its members and foster global financial stability. Members include commercial banks, development banks, trading companies, export credit agencies and multinational corporations.

Meetings/Conferences: Annual
2013 - Paris, France/June 25 - 27
Number of non-conference events/year: 4

Institute of Judicial Administration (1952)
New York University School of Law
139 MacDougal St., Room 116
New York, NY 10012
Tel: (212) 998-6149 *Fax:* (212) 995-4657
Website: law.nyu.edu/index.htm
Members: 1600 individuals
Staff: 3
Annual Budget: $500-1,000,000

Personnel:
Executive Director: Torrey L. Whitman
    E-Mail: torrey.whitman@nyu.edu

Historical Note:
Founded by Arthur T. Vanderbilt at the New York University School of Law. IJA's purpose is to improve the administration of justice in the federal and state courts. Membership: $75 (Judicial/Academic/Court Administrator); $150 (Regular, Non-Judicial, Non-Academic); $500 (Contributing); $750 (Sponsoring).
Meetings/Conferences:
Number of non-conference events/year: 16

Membership List Available to Non-members

Institute of Makers of Explosives (1913)
1120 19th St. NW
Suite 310
Washington, DC 20036-3605
Tel: (202) 429-9280 *Fax:* (202) 293-2420
E-Mail: info@ime.org
Website: ime.org
Members: 32 companies
Staff: 8
Annual Budget: $1-2,000,000
Tax: 501(c)(6)

Personnel:
President: Christopher J. Ronay
    E-Mail: jcronay@ime.org
Executive Vice President: Cynthia Hilton
    E-Mail: chilton@ime.org
Office Manager: Cindy Lopez
    E-Mail: clopez@ime.org
Associate, Government Affairs and Meeting Planner:
    Lauren Nilssen
    E-Mail: lnilssen@ime.org
Manager, Technical Services: Lon Santis
    E-Mail: ldsantis@ime.org
Secretary and General Counsel: Gilbert P. Sperling
Manager, Human Resources and Finance: Suzanne
    Swanhorst
    E-Mail: sjs@ime.org

Historical Note:
IME develops recommendations and guidelines for all facets of explosives operations from manufacture to use and disposal. Mission is to provide accurate information and comprehensive recommendations concerning commercial explosive materials.

Meetings/Conferences:
Conference Chair: Lauren Nilssen

Publications:
2010 State Explosives License/Permit and Fee
    Directory; annually
Safety Publications; irregular

Institute of Management Consultants USA (1968)
2025 M St. NW
Suite 800
Washington, DC 20036-3309
Tel: (202) 367-1134 *Fax:* (202) 367-2134
E-Mail: office@imcusa.org
Website: imcusa.org
Members: 2000 individuals
Staff: 3
Annual Budget: $500-1,000,000
Tax: 501(c)(6)

Personnel:
Executive Director: Gail R. McCauley

    E-Mail: gail@imcusa.org
Administrator, Certifications: Kimberly Lauer
    E-Mail: kimberly@imcusa.org
Legal Counsel: Alex W. Zabrosky Esq.

Historical Note:
IMC USA's mission is to promote excellence and ethics in management consulting through certification, education and professional resources. Members are individual management consultants. Membership: $95 (Student); $495 (Affiliate); $325 (Professional).

Continuing Education:
Certification Designation/s: CMC

Meetings/Conferences: Annual

Publications:
Connector; monthly; adv.
Membership Directory; on-line

Institute of Mathematical Statistics (1935)
P.O. Box 22718
Beachwood, OH 44122
Tel: (216) 295-2340 *Fax:* (216) 295-5661
TollFree: (877) 557-4674
E-Mail: ims@imstat.org
Website: imstat.org
Members: 4000 individuals
Staff: 2
Annual Budget: $2-5,000,000
Tax: 501(c)(3)

Personnel:
Executive Director: Elyse R. Gustafson
    E-Mail: erg@imstat.org
Coordinator, Advertising: Audrey Weiss

Historical Note:
Established during the joint meeting of the American Mathematical Society and the Mathematical Association of America in Ann Arbor. IMS seeks to foster the development and dissemination of the theory and applications of statistics and probability. Also a member of the Conference Board of the Mathematical Sciences. Membership: $36-516/year.

Meetings/Conferences: Annual
2013 - Varanasi, India (Banaras Hindu University)/Jan.
    6 - 10
2013 - Orlando, FL (Orlando World Center)/March 10
    - 13
2013 - Amsterdam, Netherlands (VU University)/June
    10 - 14
2013 - Ithaca, NY/July 15 - 26
2013 - Boulder, CO/July 29 - Aug. 2
2013 - Montreal, QC (Palais Des Congres de
    Montreal)/Aug. 3 - 8
2013 - Basel-Stadt, Switzerland/Oct. 15 - 16
2013 - Hong Kong, China/Dec. 20 - 23
2014 - Baltimore, MD (Baltimore Convention Center)/
    March 16 - 19
2014 - Sydney, Australia/July 7 - 11
2014 - Boston, MA (Boston Convention and Exhibition
    Center)/Aug. 2 - 7
2015 - Seatle, WA (Washington State Convention and
    Trade Center)/Aug. 8 - 13
2016 - Chicago, IL (McCormick Place)/July 30 - Aug. 4
2017 - Baltimore, MD (Baltimore Convention Center)/
    July 29 - Aug. 3
2018 - Vancouver, BC/July 28 - Aug. 2
Number of non-conference events/year: 12

Publications:
e-Bulletins; monthly
IMS Bulletin; annually; adv.

Membership List Available to Non-members

Institute of Medicine (1970)
500 Fifth St. NW
Washington, DC 20001
Tel: (202) 334-2000 *Fax:* (202) 334-1694
E-Mail: iomwww@nas.edu
Website: iom.edu
Members: 1713 individuals
Staff: 150
Annual Budget: $10-25,000,000

Personnel:
Executive Director and Chief Operating Officer: Judith A.
    Salerno
    E-Mail: jsalerno@nas.edu

Historical Note:
IOM's mission is to advance the nation's health and serve as adviser to the nation to improve health. It works outside

of government to provide unbiased and authoritative advice to decision makers and the public.

Continuing Education:
Certification Designation/s: PPT

Meetings/Conferences: Annual
Number of non-conference events/year: 13

Publications:
IOM News; monthly

Membership List Available to Non-members

Institute of Nautical Archaeology (1973)

P.O. Drawer HG
College Station, TX 77841-5137
Tel: (979) 845-6694 *Fax:* (979) 847-9260
E-Mail: info@inadiscover.com
Website: inadiscover.com
Members: 1398 individuals
Staff: 26
Annual Budget: $1-2,000,000
Tax: 501(c)(3)

Personnel:
President: Deborah L. Carslon PhD
Secretary and General Counsel: James Goold

Historical Note:
Formerly known as The American Institute of Nautical Archaeology, INA's mission is to conduct significant archaeological research that will increase knowledge of the evolution of civilizations through the location and excavation of submerged or buried ships, submerged ruins, and their associated artifacts, and dissemination of the knowledge gained therefrom. It does its research in association with the Nautical Archaeology Program at Texas A&M University. Membership: $25-5000/year.

Meetings/Conferences: Annual

Publications:
INA Quarterly; quarterly; adv.
The INA Annual; annually

Institute of Navigation (1945)

8551 Rixlew Ln.
Suite 360
Manassas, VA 20109
Tel: (703) 366-2723 *Fax:* (703) 366-2724
E-Mail: membership@ion.org
Website: ion.org
Members: 4000 individuals
Staff: 6
Annual Budget: $2-5,000,000
Tax: 501(c)(3)

Personnel:
Executive Director: Lisa Beaty
Technical Director: Carl Andren

Historical Note:
ION's mission is advancement of the art and science of positioning, navigation and timing (PNT). ION offers advancement of the art and science of navigation. Members are individuals interested in advancing the science of space, land, air, and marine navigation. Corporate members include corporations, civil and military government agencies, private scientific and technical institutions, universities and training academies, and consulting firms. Membership: $160-180 (Premium); $75-95 (Professional), $50-70 (Retired); $40-60 (Student); $400-800 (Corporate).

Meetings/Conferences:
2013 - San Diego, CA (Catamaran Resort Hotel and Spa)/Jan. 28 - 30
2013 - Orlando, FL (Renaissance Orlando at SeaWorld)/June 10 - 13/11-25 exhibitors
2013 - Nashville, TN (Nashville Convention Center)/ Sept. 16 - 20
2014 - San Diego, CA (Catamaran Resort Hotel and Spa)/Jan. 27 - 29
2014 - Orlando, FL (Renaissance Orlando at SeaWorld)/June 16 - 19
2014 - Tampa, FL (Tampa Convention Center)/Sept. 8 - 14
2015 - Tampa, FL (Tampa Convention Center)/Sept. 14 - 18

Publications:
ION Newsletter; quarterly; adv.
Membership Directory; on-line
Navigation; quarterly

Institute of Noise Control Engineering (1971)

9100 Purdue Rd.
Suite 200

Indianapolis, IN 46268
Tel: (317) 735-4063 *Fax:* (317) 280-8527
E-Mail: ibo@inceusa.org
Website: inceusa.org
Members: 1107 individuals and companies
Staff: 5
Annual Budget: $250-500,000

Personnel:
Office Director: Amy Herron
E-Mail: ibo@inceusa.org
Manager, Advertising and Exposition: Richard J. Peppin

Historical Note:
Incorporated in Washington, DC. INCE's mission is to promote engineering solutions to environmental, product, machinery, industrial and other noise problems. Membership: $50 (USA); $115 (Domestic & Foreign); Free (Student).

Meetings/Conferences: Annual
Conference Chair: Richard J. Peppin
2013 - Denver, CO (Marriott Denver City Center downtown)/Aug. 26 - 28
2013 - Innsbruck, Austria (Congress Innsbruck)/Sept. 15 - 18
2014 - Melbourne, Australia (Melbourne Convention and Exhibition Centre)/Nov. 16 - 19
Number of non-conference events/year: 2

Publications:
Membership Directory; on-line
Noise Control Engineering Journal; bi-monthly; adv.
Noise News International; quarterly; adv.

Institute of Nuclear Materials Management (1958)

111 Deer Lake Rd.
Suite 100
Deerfield, IL 60015
Tel: (847) 480-9573 *Fax:* (847) 480-9282
E-Mail: inmm@inmm.org
Website: inmm.org
Members: 800 individuals
Staff: 6
Annual Budget: $500-1,000,000
Tax: 501(c)(6)

Personnel:
Executive Director: Jodi Metzgar
E-Mail: jmetzgar@inmm.org
Administrator: Anne Czeropski
E-Mail: aczeropski@inmm.org
Manager, Advertising: Jill Hronek
E-Mail: jhronek@inmm.org
Administrator, Membership Services: Jake Livsey
E-Mail: jlivsey@inmm.org
Manager, Meetings and Exhibitions: Lyn Maddox
E-Mail: lmaddox@inmm.org
Marketing, Communications and Web Site Manager and Managing Editor: Patricia Sullivan
E-Mail: psullivan@inmm.org

Historical Note:
INMM's mission is to help combine on-the-job training and the exchange of ideas in the field of nuclear materials management and to encourage the advancement of nuclear materials management, promotion of research in the field of nuclear materials management. Members are individuals and companies concerned with the managing and safeguarding of nuclear materials. Membership: $50 (Regular); $20 (Student); $250-750 (Organization-Sustaining, based on no. of employees); $20 (Emeritus); $50 (Fellow/Senior).

Meetings/Conferences:
Conference Chair: Lyn Maddox
2013 - Palm Desert, CA (JW Marriott Desert Springs Resort and Spa)/July 14 - 18/11-25 exhibitors
2014 - Atlanta, GA (Market Center Inforum)/July 19 - 24/11-25 exhibitors
2015 - Las Vegas, NV (JW Marriott Las Vegas Resort and Spa)/July 12 - 16/11-25 exhibitors
Number of non-conference events/year: 3

Publications:
INMM Communicator
Journal of Nuclear Materials Management; quarterly; adv.
Membership Directory; annually

Membership List Available to Non-members

Institute of Nuclear Power Operations (1979)

700 Galleria Pkwy. SE
Suite 100

Atlanta, GA 30339-5943
Tel: (770) 644-8000 *Fax:* (770) 644-8549
Website: inpo.info
Members: 28 members and participants
Staff: 347
Annual Budget: Over $100,000,000
Tax: 501(c)(3)

Personnel:
President and Chief Executive Officer: Robert "Bob" F. Willard

Historical Note:
INPO's mission is to promote safe and reliability in the operation of nuclear electric generating plants. Members are electric utilities owning a share in a nuclear power plant, operating one, or holding a license to construct one.

Institute of Packaging Professionals (1989)

1833 Center Point Cir.
Suite 123
Naperville, IL 60563
Tel: (630) 544-5050 *Fax:* (630) 544-5055
TollFree: (800) 432-4085
E-Mail: info@iopp.org
Website: iopp.org
Members: 7000 individuals
Staff: 13
Annual Budget: $1-2,000,000
Tax: 501(c)(3)

Personnel:
Executive Director: Patrick Farrey
E-Mail: pfarrey@iopp.org
Director, Communications: Chris Barry
E-Mail: cbarry@iopp.org
Manager, Membership Services and Certification Programs: Barb Dykes
E-Mail: bdykes@iopp.org
Director, Education: Jim George
E-Mail: jimg@iopp.org
Business Manager: Michael Greskiewicz
E-Mail: michaelg@iopp.org
Manager, Finance: Perla Kohoutek
E-Mail: perla@iopp.org
Program Coordinator: Donna Levy
E-Mail: dlevy@iopp.org
Manager, Awards and Events: Carole Schiller
E-Mail: cschiller@iopp.org
Operations Manager: Sarah Washburn
E-Mail: swashburn@iopp.org

Historical Note:
Formed as a merger of the Packaging Institute International (1939) and the Society of Packaging Professionals (1946). IoPP is dedicated to creating networking and educational opportunities that help packaging professionals succeed. Membership: $175 (Professional); $17.50 (Student); $25 (Retired), $1,500 (Corporate Sponsor Program); $10,000 (Benefactor Program).

Continuing Education:
Certification Designation/s: CPP, CPIT

Meetings/Conferences: Annual
Conference Chair: Carole Schiller

Publications:
IoPP Journal of Packaging; on-line
IoPPupdate Newsletter; bi-monthly
Membership Directory; on-line
Who's Who in Packaging; annually

Institute of Public Utilities (1965)

Michigan State University
W157 Owen Graduate Hall
East Lansing, MI 48825-1109
Tel: (517) 355-1876 *Fax:* (517) 355-1854
E-Mail: ipu@msu.edu
Website: ipu.msu.edu
Members: 28 companies
Staff: 2
Annual Budget: $250-500,000
Tax: 501(c)(3)

Personnel:
Director: Janice A. Beecher
E-Mail: beecher@msu.edu
Administrative Assistant: Ligita Nelson
E-Mail: ligita@msu.edu

Historical Note:
IPU's mission is to provide the regulatory policy community integrative and interdisciplinary educational programs and applied research on the institutions, theory, and practice

of modern utility regulation. *Membership: $12,000/year (Company).*

Meetings/Conferences: Annual
Number of non-conference events/year: 3

Membership List Available to Non-members

Institute of Real Estate Management (1933)
430 N. Michigan Ave.
Chicago, IL 60611-4090
Tel: (312) 329-6000 *Fax:* (800) 338-4736
TollFree: (800) 837-0706
E-Mail: custserv@irem.org
Website: irem.org
Members: 18000 individuals, 535 firms and 93
U.S. and international chapters
Staff: 60
Annual Budget: $100-250,000

Personnel:
Executive Vice President and Chief Executive Officer:
Russell C. Salzman
E-Mail: rsalzman@irem.org
Chief Legislative and Research Officer: Charles A. Achilles
E-Mail: charles@irem.org
Vice President, Leadership Services: Phyllis Coneset
E-Mail: pconeset@irem.org
Vice President, Membership Services and Marketing: Lynn
M. Disbrow
E-Mail: ldisbrow@irem.org
Vice President Global Service and Chief Strategy Officer:
Nancye J. Kirk
E-Mail: nkirk@irem.org
Director, Governance and Executive Office: Diane Miller
E-Mail: dcole@irem.org
Chief Financial Officer: Kenneth M. Paul
E-Mail: kpaul@irem.org
Vice President, Technology and Communications: Manuel
Rodriguez
E-Mail: mrodriguez@irem.org
Contact, Publishing: Mariana Toscas
E-Mail: mtoscas@irem.org

Historical Note:
*IREM's mission is to serve the needs of real estate
management professionals worldwide. Membership:
$490 (CPM); $80 (ARM; $75 (ACoM); $425 (AMO);
$205 (Associate) $195 (Academic); $40 (Student); $60
(International Student).*

Continuing Education:
Certification Designation/s: CPM, ARM, AMO, ACoM

Meetings/Conferences: Semi-Annual
Conference Chair: Phyllis Coneset
2013 - Scottsdale, AZ (Westin Kierland Resort and
Spa)/Oct. 15 - 19
2014 - Orlando, FL (Hilton Orlando Bonnet Creek)/Oct.
14 - 18
2015 - Washington, DC (Omni Shoreham Hotel)/April
11 - 15
2015 - Salt Lake City, UT (Grand America Hotel)/Oct.
20 - 24
2016 - San Diego, CA (Hilton San Diego Bayfront)/Oct.
18 - 22
Number of non-conference events/year: 5

Publications:
Directory of Volunteers; on-line
eNotes; monthly
FYI Flash; on-line
Journal of Property Management; bi-monthly; adv.
Legislative Bulletin; on-line
Membership Directory; on-line

Institute of Scrap Recycling Industries, Inc. (1987)
1615 L St. NW
Suite 600
Washington, DC 20036-5610
Tel: (202) 662-8500 *Fax:* (202) 626-0900
E-Mail: isri@isri.org
Website: isri.org
Members: 1600 companies
Staff: 40
Annual Budget: $10-25,000,000
Tax: 501(c)(6)

Personnel:
President: Robin K. Wiener
E-Mail: robinwiener@isri.org
Vice President, Meeting and Membership Services: Chuck
Carr

E-Mail: chuckcarr@isri.org
Advertising Sales Director: Bob Emery
E-Mail: bobemery@scrap.org
Vice President, Government Relations and General Counsel:
Scott J. Horne
E-Mail: scotthorne@isri.org
Publisher and Editor-in-Chief: Kent Kiser
E-Mail: kentkiser@scrap.org
Director, Communications: Kevin Lawlor
E-Mail: kevinlawlor@isri.org
Director, Information Technology: Dawn Moore
E-Mail: dawnmoore@isri.org
Vice President, Human Resource and Office Administration:
Sheryl Pursch
E-Mail: sherylpursch@isri.org
Meetings Planner: Nancy Reynolds
E-Mail: nancyreynolds@isri.org
Vice President, Finance: Edward M. Szrom
E-Mail: edszrom@isri.org

Historical Note:
*ISRI's mission is to promote public awareness of the
value and importance of recycling to the production of
the world's goods and services, along with the positive
environmental benefits derived from scrap recycling.
Membership: $1,224-37,391 (Active); $1,118-5,952
(Consumer); $500 (Affiliate Individual Associate); $2,091
(International Associate); $2,081 (National).*

Meetings/Conferences: Annual
Conference Chair: Nancy Reynolds
2013 - Orlando, FL (Orange County Convention
Center)/April 9 - 13
2014 - Las Vegas, NV (Mandalay Bay Resort and
Casino)/April 6 - 10
2015 - Vancouver, BC (Vancouver Convention Center)/
April 14 - 18
2016 - Las Vegas, NV (Mandalay Bay Resort and
Casino)/April 3 - 7
Number of non-conference events/year: 2

Publications:
Membership Directory; on-line
Scrap Magazine; adv.

Institute of Shortening and Edible Oils (1932)
1319 F St. NW
Suite 600
Washington, DC 20004
Tel: (202) 783-7960 *Fax:* (202) 393-1367
E-Mail: contactus@iseo.org
Website: iseo.org
Members: 19 companies
Staff: 3
Annual Budget: $500-1,000,000

Personnel:
President: Robert L. Collette
E-Mail: r.collette@iseo.org
Office Administrator: Diana L. Stare
E-Mail: dstare@iseo.org

Historical Note:
*Formerly the Institute of Shortening Manufacturers. ISEO
serves the refiners of edible fats and oils in the United
States. Members represent approximately 90-95% of
the edible fats and oils produced domestically, which are
used in numerous foods including margarine, shortening,
cooking and salad oils, confections and toppings and used
as ingredients in a wide variety of foods.*

Publications:
Food Fats and Oils; irregular
Membership Directory; on-line

Institute of Store Planners (1961)
25 N. Broadway
Tarrytown, NY 10591
Tel: (914) 332-1806 *Fax:* (914) 332-1541
TollFree: (800) 379-9912
E-Mail: info@retaildesigninstitute.org
Website: retaildesigninstitute.org
Members: 1100 individuals
Staff: 2
Annual Budget: $250-500,000

Personnel:
President: Andrew R. McQuilkin
E-Mail: amcquilkin@retaildesigninstitute.org
Treasurer: Luanne Perry

Historical Note:
*Retail Design Institute (RDI) was formerly (2008) known
as Institute of Store Planners (ISP). RDI promotes the
advancement and collaborative practice of creating selling
environments. Each Chapter is required to hold at least*

four *Continuing Education meetings each year. It holds
design Competition and Store Design Awards every
year. Members are store planners and designers, visual
merchandisers, educators, as well as contractors and
suppliers to the industry. Membership: $200 (professional),
$100 (associate); $500 (trade); $10 (student); $25
(educator/life).*

Meetings/Conferences: Annual

Publications:
Membership Directory; on-line

Membership List Available to Non-members

Institute of Tax Consultants (1980)
7500 - 212th SW
Suite 205
Edmonds, WA 98026
Tel: (425) 774-3521 *Fax:* (425) 672-0461
Website: taxprofessionals.homestead.com
Staff: 3
Tax: 501(c)(3)

Personnel:
Registrar: Carol Kraemer
E-Mail: carol_kraemer@comcast.net
Treasurer: Jim Warberg
Editor: David Williams

Historical Note:
*ITC's mission is to provide tax practitioners with the
opportunity to upgrade their professionalism through
certification. Conducts educational programs and
certification examinations.*

Continuing Education:
Certification Designation/s: CTP, CTPS

Publications:
Regent - Newsletter

Institute of Transportation Engineers (1930)
1627 Eye St. NW
Suite 600
Washington, DC 20006
Tel: (202) 785-0060 *Fax:* (202) 785-0609
E-Mail: ite_staff@ite.org
Website: ite.org
Members: 17000 individuals
Staff: 34
Annual Budget: $5-10,000,000

Personnel:
Executive Director and Chief Executive Officer: Thomas
W. Brahms
E-Mail: tbrahms@ite.org
Public Information Manager: Michelle S. Birdsall
E-Mail: mbirdsall@ite.org
Deputy Executive Director, Technical Programs: Philip J.
Caruso
E-Mail: pcaruso@ite.org
Contact, Membership Services and Conference Services:
Sallie C. Dollins
E-Mail: sdollins@ite.org
Deputy Executive Director, Finance and Administration:
Peter W. Frentz
E-Mail: pfrentz@ite.org
Senior Director, Marketing and Membership Services:
Christina Garneski
E-Mail: cgarneski@ite.org
*Senior Director, Meetings and Executive Assistant to the
Executive Director:* Carol A. MacDougall
E-Mail: cmacdougall@ite.org
Senior Director, Operations and Management: Douglas E.
Noble PE, PTOE
E-Mail: dnoble@ite.org
Senior Director, Media Production: Marianne Saglam
E-Mail: msaglam@ite.org
Contact, Professional Development Training: Nicola
Tavares
E-Mail: ntavares@ite.org
Contact, Publications: Kenneth L. Wallington
E-Mail: kwallington@ite.org

Historical Note:
*ITE's mission is to enhance professional collaboration
and advance the technical body of knowledge through
communities of common interests. Members are individual
professionals responsible for planning, designing, and
operating surface transportation facilities. Membership:
$225 (Member); $255 (Fellow); $20 (Student); $160
(Institute Affiliate); $112.50 (Retired).*

Continuing Education:
Certification Designation/s: PTOE, TOPS, PTP, TSOS

Meetings/Conferences:

Conference Chair: Carol A. MacDougall
2013 - San Diego, CA (Sheraton San Diego Hotel and
   Marina)/March 3 - 6
2013 - Boston, MA (Sheraton Boston and Hynes
   Convention Center)/Aug. 4 - 7
2014 - Miami, FL (Hyatt Regency Miami)/March 9 - 12
2014 - Seatle, WA (Washington State Convention
   Center)/Aug. 10 - 13
2015 - Tucson, AZ (Westin La Paloma Resort and Spa)/
   March 29 - April 1
2015 - Hollywood, FL (Westin Diplomat Resort and
   Spa)/Aug. 2 - 5
2016 - Anaheim, CA (Anaheim Convention Center)/
   Aug. 14 - 17
2017 - Toronto, ON (Sheraton Centre Toronto Hotel)/
   July 30 - Aug. 2

Publications:
Certification Directory; on-line
ITE e-newsletter; monthly
ITE Journal; monthly; adv.
Journal of Transportation of the Institute of
   Transportation Engineers
Transportation Products and Services Yellow Pages!;
   on-line

Membership List Available to Non-members

Institute on Religion in an Age of Science (1954)
744 DuBois Dr.
Baton Rouge, LA 70808
Website: iras.org/Welcome.html
Members: 400 individuals
Staff: 2
Annual Budget: $50-100,000

Personnel:
Contact, Membership and Publications: Michael
   Cavanaugh
Contact, Conference Registration: Joan Hunter
   E-Mail: jbh_11@verizon.net

Historical Note:
*IRAS's mission is to promote creative efforts leading to
the formulation, in the light of contemporary knowledge,
of effective doctrines and practices for human welfare.
Membership: $70 (Individual); $80 (Joint); $100
(Organization); $40 (Student).*

Meetings/Conferences: Annual
Conference Chair: Joan Hunter

Publications:
IRAS Newsletter; on-line
Zygon: Journal of Religion & Science; on-line

Institutional Life Markets Association
925 15th St. NW
Suite 500
Washington, DC 20005
Tel: (202) 552-2788 *Fax:* (202) 342-0650
E-Mail: info@lifemarketsassociation.org
Website: lifemarketsassociation.org
Members: 18 Companies
Staff: 2
Annual Budget: $500-1,000,000

Personnel:
Managing Director: Jack A. Kelly
   E-Mail: jkelly@mcphersongroup.us
Contact, Membership: Katherine Houston
   E-Mail: khouston@mcphersongroup.us

Historical Note:
*ILMA's mission is to expand and apply capital market
solutions in life insurance, educate consumers that their
insurance may be a valuable asset, expand consumer
choices about how to manage it, and support the
responsible growth and regulation of the industry.*

Publications:
Membership Directory; on-line

Instructional Technology Council (1977)
426 C St. NE
Washington, DC 20002-5839
Tel: (202) 293-3110 *Fax:* (202) 822-5014
Website: itcnetwork.org
Members: 500 institutions
Staff: 4
Annual Budget: $100-250,000

Personnel:
Executive Director: Christine Mullins
   E-Mail: cmullins@itcnetwork.org
Contact, Conventions and Meetings: Kimberley Maddox

   E-Mail: kimberley.maddox@conferencedirect.com
Coordinator, Membership Services: Amy Weinfurter
   E-Mail: aweinfurter@itcnetwork.org

Historical Note:
*An affiliated council of the American Association of
Community Colleges and formerly the Instructional
Telecommunications Consortium and then the Instructional
Telecommunications Council, in 1993, the association
was renamed as Instructional Technology Council.
ITC's mission is to provide exceptional leadership and
professional development to its network of eLearning
experts by advocating, collaborating, researching, and
sharing exemplary, innovative practices and potential
in learning technologies. Members are educators and
organizations involved in higher education instructional
telecommunications and distance learning. Membership:
$200-450 (Institution); $750 (Corporate).*

Meetings/Conferences: Annual
Conference Chair: Kimberley Maddox
2013 - San Antonio, TX (Grand Hyatt San Antonio)/
   Feb. 17 - 20
Number of non-conference events/year: 20

Publications:
ITC Newsletter; quarterly; adv.

Instrumentation Testing Association (1984)
P.O. Box 2428
Pensacola, FL 32513
Tel: (702) 568-1445 *Fax:* (702) 568-1446
TollFree: (877) 236-1256
E-Mail: ita.instrument@earthlink.net
Website: instrument.org
Members: 97 agencies
Staff: 2
Annual Budget: $100-250,000
Tax: 501(c)(3)

Personnel:
President: Saeed Assef

Historical Note:
*Formerly (1988) Instrumentation Testing Service. ITA's
mission is to advance the performance and reliability
of instrumentation and automation technologies used
in water and wastewater treatment facilities. Members
are public and private agencies. Membership: $95
(Individual); $255-3,800 (Public Utilities); $820-1,580
(Industrial); $315-2,530 (Consultant and Manufacturer
Representatives); $950-8,855 (Manufacturers); $275
(Academic/Non profit); $1100 (Regulatory).*

Publications:
ITA Enews; on-line

Insulated Cable Engineers Association (1925)
P.O. Box 1568
Carrollton, GA 30112
Tel: (770) 830-0369 *Fax:* (770) 830-8501
E-Mail: support@ICEA.NET
Website: icea.net
Staff: 2
Annual Budget: $100-250,000

Personnel:
President: Frank Kupta
Communications Officer: Jim Ryan

Historical Note:
*The Insulated Cable Engineers Association (ICEA) is
a professional organization dedicated to developing
cable standards for the electric power, control, and
telecommunications industries.Since 1925, the objective has
been to ensure safe, economical, and efficient cable systems
utilizing proven state-of-the-art materials and concepts.*

Insulating Concrete Form Association (1995)
1298 Cronson Blvd.
Suite 201
Crofton, MD 21114
Tel: (410) 451-0825 *Fax:* (410) 451-8343
TollFree: (888) 864-4232
E-Mail: info@forms.org
Website: forms.org
Members: 400 individuals
Staff: 3
Annual Budget: $100-250,000
Tax: 501(c)(6)

Personnel:
Executive Director: Betsy Steiner
   E-Mail: emsteiner@epscentral.org

Historical Note:
*ICFA's mission is to encourage the use of ICFs, and to help
its members to overcome industry obstacles. Represents
manufacturers and marketers of concrete form systems*

for building construction. Membership: $2,500-5,000
(Sustaining); $500-3,000 (Associate); $250-1,500
(Contractor/Distributor/Professional, based on volume of
ICF products).*

Continuing Education:
Certification Designation/s: AIA

Publications:
ICFA Dialogue; quarterly
ICFA Informer; on-line; adv.

Insulation Contractors Association of America
(1977)
1321 Duke St.
Suite 303
Alexandria, VA 22314
Tel: (703) 739-0356 *Fax:* (703) 739-0412
E-Mail: icaa@insulate.org
Website: insulate.org
Members: 300 companies
Staff: 2
Annual Budget: $500-1,000,000
Tax: 501(c)(6)

Personnel:
Executive Director: Michael Kwart
   E-Mail: icaaconv@insulate.org

Historical Note:
*ICAA works to assist its members by developing and
executing programs which keep them on the edge of
valuable information and knowledge in the rapidly
changing world of insulation. Members are residential
and commercial insulation contractors and suppliers.
Membership: $620-3,125 (General/Provisional/Associate
Contractor); $625-5,200 (Associate Industry Member);
$775 (Associate Other Member); $325 (Corresponding
Associate Member).*

Meetings/Conferences: Annual

Publications:
ICAA Magazine; adv.
ICAA Online Contractor Locator and Buyers' Guide
   (Membership Directory); on-line
Insulation Contractors Report; bi-monthly

Membership List Available to Non-members

Insurance Accounting and Systems Association
(1928)
131 N. Clinton St.
Park Ridge, IL 60068
Tel: (847) 823-2868 *Fax:* (919) 489-1994
E-Mail: info@iasa.org
Website: iasa.org
Members: 1700 companies
Staff: 8
Annual Budget: $2-5,000,000
Tax: 501(c)(3)

Personnel:
Executive Director: Joseph Pomilia
Director, Operations: Gina Jolly
   E-Mail: gjolly@iasa.org
Vice President, Conference and Events: Margaret McKeon
   E-Mail: mmckeon@iasa.org
Vice President, Business Development: Mark Roth
   E-Mail: mroth@iasa.org
Manager, Membership Services: Tricia Stillman
   E-Mail: tstillman@iaas.org

Historical Note:
*Formerly (1983) Insurance Accounting and Statistical
Association. IASA's mission is to initiate and facilitate
the exchange of educational information and ideas among
insurance related professionals to enhance the effectiveness
of these individuals, their employers and the financial
services industry. Membership includes insurance companies
of all types. Membership: $525 (Regular); $1,575
(Affiliate).*

Meetings/Conferences: Annual
Conference Chair: Margaret McKeon
2013 - Washington, DC (Gaylord National Hotel and
   Convention Center)/June 2 - 5
2014 - Indianapolis, IN (Indianapolis Convention
   Center)/June 8 - 11
2015 - Las Vegas, NV (Mandalay Bay Resort and
   Casino)/June 7 - 10
2016 - San Antonio, TX (San Antonio Convention
   Center)/June 12 - 15
2017 - Orlando, FL (Marriott Orlando World Center)/
   June 4 - 7

Publications:
The Interpreter Magazine; quarterly

Insurance Consumer Affairs Exchange (1976)

P.O. Box 746
Lake Zurich, IL 60047
Tel: (847) 991-8454
E-Mail: info@icae.com
Website: icae.com
Members: 151 companies and individuals
Staff: 3
Annual Budget: $50-100,000
Tax: 501(c)(6)

Personnel:
Executive Director: Nancy Brebner
    E-Mail: nbrebner@icae.com
Treasurer: Carol Crosson
    E-Mail: carol_crosson@glic.com
Web Technology: Mitch Wilson
    E-Mail: mitchw@ohioinsurance.org

Historical Note:
ICAE's mission is to promote professionalism and shape the standards of behavior in relationships between insurance organizations, regulators and customers through proactive dialogue, research, communication and education.
Membership: $250 (Individual); $500 (Organization).

Meetings/Conferences: Semi-Annual

Publications:
Catalyst Newsletter; on-line
Membership Directory; on-line

Insurance Information Institute (1959)

110 William St.
New York, NY 10038
Tel: (212) 346-5500 Fax: (212) 732-1916
TollFree: (800) 942-4242
E-Mail: info@iii.org
Website: iii.org
Members: 87 Groups
Staff: 36
Annual Budget: $5-10,000,000

Personnel:
President: Dr. Robert P. Hartwig CPCU
Vice President, Media Relations: Michael Barry
    E-Mail: michaelb@iii.org
Executive Vice President: Cary M. Schneider
    E-Mail: carys@iii.org
Vice President, Publications and Information Services:
    Madine Singer
    E-Mail: madines@iii.org
Vice President, Communications: Loretta Worters

Historical Note:
I.I.I.'s mission is to build public understanding of insurance-what it does and how it works-primarily through the media. Membership is available to property/casualty, life/health and reinsurance companies. Membership dues are based on a company's direct written premiums.

Publications:
Financial Services Fact Book; annually
Insurance Daily; daily
International Insurance Facts; annually

Membership List Available to Non-members

Insurance Institute for Highway Safety (1959)

1005 N. Glebe Rd.
Suite 800
Arlington, VA 22201-4751
Tel: (703) 247-1500 Fax: (703) 247-1588
E-Mail: iihs@highwaysafety.org
Website: iihs.org
Staff: 70
Annual Budget: $10-25,000,000
Tax: 501(c)(3)

Personnel:
President: Adrian K. Lund PhD
Director, Insurer Relations: Brenda O'Donnell
    E-Mail: bodonnell@iihs.org
Senior Vice President, Communications: Russ Rader
    E-Mail: rrader@iihs.org
Executive Assistant, Legal Affairs: Shelley Shelton
    E-Mail: sshelton@iihs.org

Historical Note:
IIHS's mission is to reduce the losses, deaths, injuries and property damage from crashes on the nation's highways. Institute members are property-casualty insurers.

Publications:
Membership Directory; on-line
Status Report Newsletter

Insurance Loss Control Association (1931)

P.O. Box 346
Morton, IL 61550
Tel: (309) 696-2551
E-Mail:
administration@insurancelosscontrol.org
Website: insurancelosscontrol.org
Members: 350 individuals
Staff: 2
Annual Budget: Under $10,000

Personnel:
President: Kevin Matthews

Historical Note:
Formerly (1968) Association of Mutual Fire Insurance Engineers, (1980) and then Association of Mutual Insurance Engineers. ILCA strives to provide education and knowledge sharing opportunities that improve the loss control capabilities of its members, and to raise awareness of the benefits of professional loss control practices.
Membership: $75/year.

Meetings/Conferences: Annual

Publications:
ILCA's Newsletter (eNews); on-line; adv.
Vendor Directory; on-line

Membership List Available to Non-members

Insurance Marketing Communications Association (1923)

1140 Schneider St.,
Oak Park, IL 60302
E-Mail: info@imcanet.com
Website: imcanet.com
Members: 171 Associate Members and companies
Staff: 2
Annual Budget: $100-250,000
Tax: 501(c)(6)

Personnel:
Executive Director: Tom Wetzel
    E-Mail: twetzel@imcanet.com
Vice President, Corporate Communications: Linda J.
    Collins

Historical Note:
Formerly (1984) the Insurance Advertising Conference, IMCA's mission is to deliver marketing and communication techniques that help to maximize business outcomes of its members. Membership includes the insurance and financial services industries throughout the U.S., Canada, Mexico and Bermuda and members represent mutual, stock and direct writer, property and casualty insurance companies.
Membership: $360-1,270 (Based on Number of member).

Meetings/Conferences: Annual
2013 - Philadelphia, PA/June 23 - 26

Publications:
Quarterly Newsletter; quarterly; adv.

Insured Retirement Institute (1991)

1101 New York Ave. NW
Suite 825
Washington, DC 20005
Tel: (202) 469-3000 Fax: (202) 469-3030
E-Mail: iri@irionline.org
Website: irionline.org
Members: 300 Companies
Staff: 21
Annual Budget: $2-5,000,000
Tax: 501(c)(6)

Personnel:
President and Chief Executive Officer: Catherine J.
    Weatherford
    E-Mail: cweatherford@irionline.org
Director, Administration and Operations: Julie Benson
Vice President, Communications, Marketing and Research:
    Danielle Holland
Vice President, Membership Services: Barbara Hume
Director, Meetings and Conferences: Elizabeth Maddox
Senior Vice President, Operations and Technology:
    Christopher McDaniel
Chief Operating Officer: Claudia Mansfield Sutton
    E-Mail: CSutton@irionline.org

Historical Note:
Formerly the National Association for Variable Annuities (NAVA). IRI's mission is to: encourage industry adherence to ethical principles; promote better understanding of the insured retirement value proposition; to improve value delivery; and to advocate before public policy makers on critical issues affecting insured retirement strategies.
Membership: $30,000-85,000 (Insurer); $1,500-40,000

(Distributor); $10,000-40,000 (Asset Managers);
$5,000-10,000 (Solution Provider).

Meetings/Conferences:
Conference Chair: Elizabeth Maddox
2013 - Washington, DC (Washington Hilton)/Feb. 16 - 19
2013 - Chicago, IL (Fairmont Chicago, Millennium Park)/Sept. 22 - 24
2014 - New York City, NY (Hilton New York)/Feb. 7 - 13

Publications:
Government Affairs Updates; weekly
IRI e-Wire; bi-weekly
IRI Fact Book; annually
IRI Insight; bi-monthly
Newsletter; quarterly

The Integrated Ocean Drilling Program (2003)

1001 Connecticut Ave. NW
Suite 504
Washington, DC 20036
Tel: (202) 465-7500 Fax: (202) 955-8363
Website: iodp.org
Staff: 6
Annual Budget: $10-25,000,000

Personnel:
President and Chief Executive Officer: Kiyoshi Suyehiro
Data and Publications Manager: Jamus Collier
    E-Mail: jcollier@iodp.org
Director, Finance and Administration: John Emmitte
    E-Mail: jemmitte@iodp.org
Operations Manager: Yoshi Kawamura
    E-Mail: ykawamura@iodp.org
Manager, Outreach and Communications: Miyuki Otomo
    E-Mail: motomo@iodp.org
Contact, Communications: Matthew Wright
    E-Mail: mwright@oceanleadership.org

Historical Note:
IODP is an international scientific research program supported by 26 countries that works to advance scientific understanding of the earth by monitoring, drilling, sampling, and analyzing sub seafloor environments.

Publications:
IODP E-News Newsletter; on-line
Scientific Drilling Journal; semi-annually

Intellectual Property Owners Association (1972)

900 19th St. NW
Suite 1150
Washington, DC 20006
Tel: (202) 507-4500 Fax: (202) 507-4501
E-Mail: info@ipo.org
Website: ipo.org
Members: 200 companies and 12000 individuals
Staff: 14
Annual Budget: $2-5,000,000
Tax: 501(c)(6)

Personnel:
Deputy Executive Director: Jessica K. Landacre
    E-Mail: jessica@ipo.org
Executive Director: Herbert C. Wamsley
    E-Mail: herb@ipo.org
Manager, Operations: Nicholas W. Evans
    E-Mail: nevans@ipo.org
Director, Meetings and Events: Megan Griggs
    E-Mail: mgriggs@ipo.org
Chief Operating Executive: Samantha Grover Jakhelln
    E-Mail: samantha@ipo.org
Manager, Meetings and Events: Clara Li Stanfield
    E-Mail: cstanfield@ipo.org
Government Relations Counsel: Kirsten E. Zewers
    E-Mail: kzewers@ipo.org

Historical Note:
IPO serves all intellectual property owners in all industries and all fields of technology. Membership: $600-24,325 (Corporate); $1,500-6,875 (Law Firm); $175-350 (Individual).

Meetings/Conferences: Annual
Conference Chair: Megan Griggs
2013 - Boston, MA (Sheraton Boston Hotel)/Sept. 15 - 17/11-25 exhibitors
2014 - Vancouver, BC (Vancouver Convention Centre)/ Sept. 7 - 9/11-25 exhibitors
2015 - Chicago, IL (Hyatt Regency)/Sept. 27 - 29/11-25 exhibitors

Publications:
IPO Daily News; daily

Intelligent Transportation Society of America (1991)

1100 17th St. NW
Suite 1200
Washington, DC 20036
Tel: (202) 484-4847 *Fax:* (202) 484-3483
TollFree: (800) 374-8472
E-Mail: info@itsa.org
Website: itsa.org
Members: 450 member organizations
Staff: 25
Annual Budget: $5-10,000,000
Tax: 501(c)(3)

Personnel:
President and Chief Executive Officer: Scott F. Belcher
   E-Mail: sbelcher@itsa.org
Manager, Information Technology: Sharon Alexander
   E-Mail: salexander@itsa.org
Director, Meetings: Sandra Collier
   E-Mail: scollier@itsa.org
Vice President, Administration, Finance, Information Technology and Chief Financial Officer: Thomas V. Cox CPA
   E-Mail: tcox@itsa.org
Director, Communications: Cherie Gibson
Coordinator, Membership Services: Jennifer Harrison
   E-Mail: jharrison@itsa.org
Manager, Member Services: Charlie Tennyson
   E-Mail: ctennyson@itsa.org

Historical Note:
ITS America fosters the use of advanced technologies in surface transportation systems. Membership: $60-2,850/year.

Meetings/Conferences: Annual
Conference Chair: Sandra Collier

Publications:
Membership Directory; on-line
Transportation Technology News; weekly

Inter-American Bar Association (1940)

1211 Connecticut Ave. NW
Suite 202
Washington, DC 20036
Tel: (202) 466-5944 *Fax:* (202) 466-5946
E-Mail: iaba@iaba.org
Website: iaba.org
Members:
44 bar associations
2500 individuals
Staff: 5
Annual Budget: $250-500,000
Tax: 501(c)(6)

Personnel:
Secretary General: Dante Figueroa
Treasurer: Paulo de Miranda
Secretary: Roanne Peña
President: Rafael A. Veloz

Historical Note:
IABA in alliance with LatPro, offers members the ability to receive a Full Annual Membership in the LatPro employment website. IABA represents a permanent forum for the exchange of professional views and information for lawyers to promote the Rule of Law and protect the democratic institutions in the Americas. IABA's mission is to promote and defend the rule of law as the foundation of a just and free society in the Western Hemisphere. Membership: $160 (Junior); $200 (Senior); $50 (Student); $290 (Contributing); $3,500 (Life).

Publications:
IABA E-Newsletter; on-line
IABA Law Review; on-line
Member Directory; on-line

Inter-Company Marketing Group (2010)

44335 Premier Plaza
Suite 125
Ashburn, VA 20147
Tel: (703) 729-7701 *Fax:* (888) 220-5492
E-Mail: info@icmg.org
Website: icmg.org
Staff: 2
Annual Budget: $250-500,000

Personnel:
Executive Director: Audrey S. Wittenburg
Treasurer: Richard S. Katz ChFC, CLU

Historical Note:

ICMG's Mission is to provide a networking and educational forum for member insurance and financial services organizations to develop strategic alliances and business relationships.

Meetings/Conferences: Annual
2013 - St. Petersburg, FL (Marriott Vinoy Renaissance Resort and Golf Club)/Jan. 29 - 31
2014 - Phoenix, AZ (Talking Stick Resort)/Feb. 4 - 6

Publications:
E-Newsletter; on-line; adv.
Membership Directory; on-line

Inter-Industry Conference on Auto Collision Repair (1979)

5125 Trillium Blvd.
Hoffman Estates, IL 60192
Tel: (847) 590-1198 *Fax:* (800) 590-1215
TollFree: (800) 422-7872
Website: i-car.com
Members: 100 individuals
Staff: 549
Annual Budget: $10-25,000,000

Personnel:
President and Chief Executive Officer: John Van Alstyne
Technical Director: Jason Bartanen
Director, Business Development: Joyce Kasmer
   E-Mail: joyce.kasmer@i-car.com
Specialist, Marketing Communications: Kelly McNalis
   E-Mail: kelly.mcnalis@i-car.com
Director, Human Resources: Shirley Pincus
   E-Mail: shirley.pincus@i-car.com

Historical Note:
I-CAR is an international not-for-profit organization dedicated to training the collision inter-industry. Members are major auto manufacturers, insurance companies, auto collision repair shops, tool, equipment, and supply manufacturers and related industry and trade associations. Membership: $500 (Individual/Educational Partner); $2,500 (Corporate); $5,000 (Sustaining).

Publications:
I-CAR E-newsletter; bi-weekly

Inter-National Association of Business Industry & Rehabilitation (1985)

P.O. Box 15242
Washington, DC 20003
Tel: (202) 543-6353
Website: inabir.org
Members: 120 organization members
Staff: 2
Annual Budget: $50-100,000

Personnel:
Executive Director: Charles W. Harles
Treasurer: Lynn Van Vactor

Historical Note:
I-NABIR's mission is to promote national and international collaboration, facilitate networking and information exchange, and strengthen partnerships between employers, labor unions, and service providers. Members include major international corporations, local rehabilitation service organizations, state and regional programs, labor organizations, state rehabilitation agencies, and organizations which provide services to people with disabilities who are seeking competitive employment.

Inter-Society Color Council (1931)

11491 Sunset Hills Rd.
Reston, VA 20190
Tel: (703) 318-0263 *Fax:* (703) 318-0514
E-Mail: isccoffice@cs.com
Website: iscc.org
Members:
25 organizations
860 individuals
Staff: 3
Annual Budget: $25-50,000
Tax: 501(c)(6)

Personnel:
President: Dr. Frank O'Donnell
   E-Mail: fxodonnell@sherwin.com
Office Manager: Cynthia Sturke

Historical Note:
Established December 29, 1931 at the Museum of Science and Industry in New York City. ISCC's aim is to stimulate and coordinate the work being done by the various members leading to the description and specification of color by those members. Membership: $75 (Individual); $10 (Student); $750 (Sustaining); $10 (Retired); $75 (Overseas); $200 (Member Body)

Meetings/Conferences: Annual
Number of non-conference events/year: 2

Publications:
ISCC Newsletter; bi-monthly

InterAction (American Council of Voluntary International Action)

1400 16th St. NW
Suite 210
Washington, DC 20036
Tel: (202) 667-8227 *Fax:* (202) 667-8236
E-Mail: ia@interaction.org
Website: interaction.org
Members: 190 members
Staff: 62
Annual Budget: $5-10,000,000

Personnel:
President and Chief Executive Officer: Sam Worthington
   E-Mail: sworthington@interaction.org
Chief Technology Officer and the Director, Information Technologies: Allen Abtahi
System Administrator: Hernan Cibello
Executive Vice President, Policy and Communications: Lindsay Coates
   E-Mail: lcoates@interaction.org
Accountant and Senior Associate, Human Resources: Mariam Ehsanyar
   E-Mail: mehsanyar@interaction.org
Policy Coordinator, Humanitarian Affairs: Natalie Eisenbarth
   E-Mail: neisenbarth@interaction.org
Vice President, Finance and Administration: Peter R. Engebretson
Coordinator, Marketing: Zoe Plaugher
Senior Director, Communications: Sue Pleming
   E-Mail: SPleming@Interaction.org
Vice President, Membership and Standards: Barbara Wallace

Historical Note:
InterAction, an alliance of more than 160 U.S.-based international development and humanitarian nongovernmental organizations, works to eliminate extreme poverty, uphold human rights, safeguard a sustainable planet and ensure human dignity for poor and vulnerable populations worldwide by elevating and advancing the goals of the U.S.-based international nonprofit community. Membership: $2,000-46,000/year.

Meetings/Conferences:
Number of non-conference events/year: 35

Publications:
Associate Member Directory; on-line
InterAction Newsletter
Member Directory; on-line
Monday Developments; monthly

Interactive Advertising Bureau (1996)

116 E. 27th St.
Seventh Floor
New York, NY 10016
Tel: (212) 380-4700 *Fax:* (212) 380-4702
E-Mail: greg@iab.net
Website: iab.net
Members: 375 companies
Staff: 37
Annual Budget: $10-25,000,000
Tax: 501(c)(6)

Personnel:
President and Chief Executive Officer: Randall Rothenberg
Director, Professional Development: Jennifer Deutsch
Executive Vice President and Chief Operating Officer: Patrick Dolan
Senior Vice President and Chief Marketing Officer: David Doty
Senior Director, Finance and Administration: Mark Goldman
Manager, Finance and Human Resources: Andrew Kao
Vice President, Events: Lisa Milgram
Senior Director, Events: Virginia Rollet Moore
Director, Technical Standards: Brendan Riordan-Butterworth
Vice President, Training and Development: Michael Theodore

Historical Note:
Formerly (2003) Internet Advertising Bureau, merged with Internet Local Advertising and Commerce Association in 1998. IAB evaluates and recommends standards and practices for online advertising and sponsors research on

behalf of its members. Membership: $5,000/year (Startup/ Associate/General).

Continuing Education:
Certification Designation/s: IAC

Meetings/Conferences:
Conference Chair: Virginia Rollet Moore
Number of non-conference events/year: 7

Publications:
IAB Informer; monthly
IAB SmartBrief; daily

Membership List Available to Non-members

Interactive Audio Special Interest Group *(1994)*
P.O. Box 3173
La Habra, CA 90632-3173
Tel: (714) 736-9774 *Fax:* (714) 736-9775
E-Mail: info@iasig.org
Website: iasig.org
Members: 150 individuals
Staff: 1

Personnel:
Managing Director: Tom White

Historical Note:
Formerly the Association of Interactive Audio and Music Professionals. IA-SIG is an autonomous organization sponsored by the MIDI Manufacturers Association. IA-SIG's mission is to improve the performance of interactive applications by influencing hardware, software, and tool design. Members are companies and individuals involved in interactive audio development. Membership: $50 (Individual); $250-2500 (Corporate, depends upon revenue).

Publications:
The Interactive Audio Journal

Interactive Gaming Council Canada *(1996)*
175-2906 W. Broadway
Vancouver, BC V6K 2G8
Tel: (604) 732-3833 *Fax:* (604) 677-5785
Website: igcouncil.org
Staff: 1

Personnel:
Chief Executive: John K. FitzGerald
E-Mail: john.fitzgerald@igcouncil.org

Historical Note:
The Interactive Gaming Council (IGC) is an international trade organisation based in Canada but which operates worldwide. The IGC champions initiatives that address the multi-various challenges and opportunities facing the Internet gambling industry, in order to ensure an environment of fair and responsible gambling.

Publications:
Newsletter

Interactive Media Entertainment & Gaming Association *(2007)*
2325 Dulles Corner Blvd.
Suite 500
Herndon, VA 20171
Tel: (703) 788-6845
E-Mail: info@imega.org
Website: imega.org
Staff: 2
Annual Budget: $500-1,000,000
Tax: 501(c)(6)

Personnel:
Chairman and Chief Executive Officer: Joseph Brennan Jr.
Contact, Media Relations: Elizabeth Phillips

Historical Note:
iMEGA's mission is to foster cooperation between the online industry and government at all levels, and to promote innovation, openness and freedom on the Internet.

Publications:
iMEGA Newsletter; on-line

Interactive Multimedia and Collaborative Communications Alliance *(1998)*
P.O. Box 756
Syosset, NY 11791-0756
Tel: (516) 818-8184 *Fax:* (516) 922-2170
Website: imcca.org
Members: 2000 individuals
Staff: 1
Annual Budget: $100-250,000

Personnel:
Executive Director: Carol Zelkin
E-Mail: czelkin@IMCCA.org

Historical Note:
Founded as the International Teleconferencing Association, absorbed the National Telecommuting and Telework Association in 1994, assumed its current name in 2000. IMCCA's mission is to foster and promote people-to-people communications and learning throughout the industry. Membership: $750-6,250 (Vendor).

Meetings/Conferences: Annual
Conference Chair: Carol Zelkin
2013 - Amsterdam, Netherlands/Jan. 29 - 31/over 100 exhibitors

Publications:
IMCCA Newsletter
Membership Directory; on-line

Interactive Travel Services Association *(1998)*
1250 Connecticut Ave. NW
Suite 825
Washington, DC 20036
Tel: (202) 557-4180
E-Mail: JRubin@InteractiveTravel.org
Website: interactivetravel.org
Staff: 2
Annual Budget: $500-1,000,000
Tax: 501(c)(6)

Personnel:
Executive Director: Joe Rubin
E-Mail: JRubin@InteractiveTravel.org

Historical Note:
ITSA promotes consumer choice, access, confidence, protection and information in the rapidly growing world of online travel. Seeks to develop consensus among industry, consumer organizations and policy makers on issues related to consumer use of the Internet to meet their travel needs. Represents companies in the online travel industry.

Publications:
Membership Directory; on-line

Membership List Available to Non-members

Interagency Communications Interoperability Joint Powers Authority *(2003)*
613 E. Broadway
Suite 200
Glendale, CA 91206-4391
Tel: (818) 548-4844 *Fax:* (818) 547-6740
E-Mail: DWright@ci.glendale.ca.us
Website: icisradio.org
Staff: 2

Personnel:
Executive Director: Don Wright
E-Mail: DWright@ci.glendale.ca.us
Business Manager: Bob Elliot

Historical Note:
The association is a joint powers authority formed to allow the Interagency Communications Interoperability System to govern itself and to perform its day to day business.

InterAmerican College of Physicians and Surgeons *(1979)*
2020 Pennsylvania Ave. NW
Suite 695
Washington, DC 20006
Tel: (202) 467-4756 *Fax:* (212) 267-5394
TollFree: (866) 291-7544
E-Mail: contact@icps.org
Website: icps.org
Staff: 3
Annual Budget: $500-1,000,000

Personnel:
President: Rene F. Rodriguez MD
E-Mail: rodriguez@icps.org
Program Administrator: Jack Ienna
E-Mail: icps@icps.org
Treasurer: Ramon E. Ravelo MD

Historical Note:
A national Hispanic medical association representing Hispanic physicians in the U.S. and Puerto Rico. Works to increase the number of Hispanics in the medical profession and to advocate equitable health care policy legislation and health care services for Hispanic Americans. Headquartered in New York, NY. Announced plans to move offices in 2003. ICPS's mission states that health is a fundamental human value and the basis for the achievement of any other values.Membership:$60 (Physician < 62 yrs); $40 (Physician > 62 Yrs); $175-300 (Life member); $25 (Medical Students/ Residents).

Publications:
Médico de Familia; on-line

Medico Interamericano; on-line

Intercoiffure America/Canada *(1933)*
1303 Campbell Rd.
Houston, TX 77055
Tel: (713) 987-8800 *Fax:* (713) 935-4409
TollFree: (800) 442-3007
E-Mail: intercoiffure@creativeage.com
Website: intercoiffure.us
Members: 350 companies
Staff: 3
Annual Budget: $1-2,000,000
Tax: 501(c)(6)

Personnel:
President: Lois Christie
E-Mail: lois@intercoiffure.us
Membership Chair: Maryanne McCormack
E-Mail: maryanne@visiblechanges.com
Coordinator, Events: April Menendz
E-Mail: amenendz@creativeage.com

Historical Note:
Formerly (1966) the International des Coiffures de Dames and later (2003) Intercoiffure America. ICA's mission is to bring together the members of the hairdressing profession to exchange ideas and information and to set standards for the beauty profession to emulate. Members are beauty salon owners/licensed cosmetologists. Membership: $1250/year.

Meetings/Conferences: Annual
Conference Chair: April Menendz
Number of non-conference events/year: 1

Publications:
ICA Newsletter; on-line
Membership directory; on-line

Intercollegiate Broadcasting System *(1940)*
367 Windsor Hwy.
New Windsor, NY 12553-7900
Tel: (845) 565-0003 *Fax:* (845) 565-7446
E-Mail: ibs@ibsradio.org
Website: ibsradio.org
Members: 1011 stations
Staff: 6
Annual Budget: $50-100,000
Tax: 501(c)(3)

Personnel:
Chief Operating Officer: Raghav Gupta
Vice President, Information Services: Jeff Tellis

Historical Note:
IBS is an organization of non- profit, education-affiliated radio stations (and webcasters). Members are high school, college and university radio and webcasting stations. Membership: $125/year.

Meetings/Conferences:
2013 - New York City, NY (New York's Hotel Pennsylvania)/March 8 - 10
Number of non-conference events/year: 6

Publications:
IBS Radio Newsletter

Intercollegiate Men's Choruses, an International Association of Male Choruses *(1915)*
The University of Virginia, 1503 S. St. NW
Washington, DC 20009
Tel: (202) 986-5867
E-Mail: cparr@depaul.edu
Website: imci.us
Members: 70 choruses
Staff: 3
Annual Budget: Under $10,000

Personnel:
President: Frank Albinder
E-Mail: FSAlbinder@pobox.com

Historical Note:
Formerly (1988) the Intercollegiate Musical Council, The National Association of Male Choruses. Promotes research, publication and production of quality music for male choruses. Inactive during and after World War II, the Council was revived in 1952; annual seminars have been held since 1954. Membership is made up of Male Choruses \Glee Clubs of the nation's universities, colleges, and secondary schools. Membership: $170 (College/University); $40 (Secondary Schools/Supporting Individuals).

Meetings/Conferences: Annual

Publications:
QUODLIBET

Intercollegiate Tennis Association *(1956)*

---

174 Tamarack Cir.
Skillman, NJ 08558-2021
Tel: (609) 497-6920 *Fax:* (609) 497-9766
E-Mail: ita@itatennis.com
Website: itatennis.com
Members: 22000 coaches and collegiates
Staff: 12
Annual Budget: $500-1,000,000

Personnel:
Executive Director: David A. Benjamin
    E-Mail: dbenjamin@itatennis.com
Director, Communications: Daniel Jankowski
    E-Mail: djankowski@itatennis.com
Manager, Membership Services: Rachel Kushma
    E-Mail: rkushma@itatennis.com
Administrator and Assistant to the Exec. Director: Tondi
  Rice
    E-Mail: itatondi2@aol.com
Technical Support, Information Technology: Michael Sing
    E-Mail: msing@itatennis.com
Manager, Communications: Nick Snow
    E-Mail: nsnow@itatennis.com
Manager, Events and Championships: Troy Venechanos
    E-Mail: tvenechanos@itatennis.com

Historical Note:
*Formerly (1958) National Collegiate Tennis Coaches
Association and (1992) the Intercollegiate Tennis Coaches
Association. ITA is the governing body of collegiate tennis.
ITA's mission is to foster and encourage the playing
of intercollegiate tennis in accordance with the highest
tradition of sportsmanship and consistent with the general
objectives of higher education. Membership: $25-295/year.*

Meetings/Conferences: Annual
Conference Chair: Troy Venechanos
Number of non-conference events/year: 18

Publications:
ITA e-Newsletter; bi-monthly; adv.
Membership Directory; on-line

Interim Ministry Network (2009)
5740 Executive Dr.
Suite 212
Baltimore, MD 21228
Tel: (410) 719-0777 *Fax:* (410) 719-0795
Website: imnedu.org
Staff: 3
Annual Budget: $500-1,000,000

Personnel:
Executive Director: Cynthia Huheey CAE
    E-Mail: President@imnedu.org
Manager, Education and Membership: Ellen Goudy
    E-Mail: Ellen@imnedu.org
Manager, Finance: Crystal Wells
    E-Mail: Crystal@IMNedu.org

Historical Note:
*IMN's mission is to introduce basic theories that are
foundational to interim ministry. Membership: $105/year.*

Meetings/Conferences: Annual
2013 - Indianapolis, IN (Sheraton Hotel)/June 3 - 6

Publications:
IMN Newsletter; quarterly

Interior Design Educators Council (1963)
9100 Purdue Rd.
Suite 200
Indianapolis, IN 46268
Tel: (317) 328-4437 *Fax:* (317) 280-8527
E-Mail: info@idec.org
Website: idec.org
Members: 600 individuals
Staff: 4
Annual Budget: $250-500,000

Personnel:
Executive Director: Jeffrey Beachum CAE
    E-Mail: jbeachum@idec.org
Coordinator, Marketing and Membership Communications:
  Rachel Daeger
    E-Mail: rdaeger@idec.org
Event Planner: Christine Saricos
    E-Mail: csaricos@idec.org

Historical Note:
*IDEC's mission is the advancement of interior design
education, scholarship and service. Membership: $255
(Industry Affiliate); $250 (Associate); $305 (Professional);
$95 (Graduate/Retired).*

Meetings/Conferences: Annual

Conference Chair: Christine Saricos
2013 - Indianapolis, IN (JW Mariott)/Feb. 17 - 19

Publications:
eNews; monthly; adv.
eRecord; quarterly
Journal of Interior Design; on-line
Membership Directory; on-line

Membership List Available to Non-members

Interior Design Society (1973)
164 S. Main St.
Suite 404
High Point, NC 27260
Tel: (336) 884-4437 *Fax:* (336) 885-3291
TollFree: (888) 884-4469
E-Mail: info@interiordesignsociety.org
Website: interiordesignsociety.org
Members: 4000 individuals and companies
Staff: 7
Annual Budget: $250-500,000

Personnel:
Chapter Coordinator: Abbie Emms
    E-Mail: aemms@interiordesignsociety.org
Coordinator, Membership Services: Jessica Fondario
    E-Mail: jfondario@interiordesignsociety.org
Office Manager: Snoa Garrigan
    E-Mail: shuffman@interiordesignsociety.org
Representative, Membership Services: Bonnie Hair
    E-Mail: bhair@interiordesignsociety.org

Historical Note:
*A division of National Home Furnishings Association,
which provides administrative support. IDS's mission
is to strengthen and grow the Interior Design Society
by providing its members with education, resources,
programs, and services to aid them in their path to
professionalism in residential interior design. Membership:
$299 (Professional); $225 (Associate); $175 (Affiliate);
$35 (Student); $75 (Home Furnishing Sales Specialist);
$60 (Sales/Manufacturer's Representative).*

Continuing Education:
Certification Designation/s: CQRID

Meetings/Conferences: Annual

Publications:
Portfolio; quarterly

Interlocking Concrete Pavement Institute (1993)
13921 Park Center Rd.
Suite 270
Herndon, VA 20171
Tel: (703) 657-6900 *Fax:* (703) 657-6901
TollFree: (800) 241-3652
E-Mail: icpi@icpi.org
Website: icpi.org
Members: 1,100 members
Staff: 10
Annual Budget: $2-5,000,000
Tax: 501(c)(6)

Personnel:
Executive Director: Charles A. McGrath CAE
    E-Mail: cmcgrath@icpi.org
Manager, Administration and Communications: Alison
  Brosius
Director, Marketing and Membership: Jessica Chase
Manager, Education: Jackie Conklin
Advertising Director: Amanda Daniel
Manager, Meetings: Laura Garcia
Finance Director: Wavel Joseph
Director, Technical Services: David R. Smith

Historical Note:
*ICPI's mission is to increase the use of segmental concrete
pavement systems in North American commercial,
institutional, governmental, industrial and residential
markets. Members are producers, suppliers, contractors,
design professionals and consultants. Membership:
$262.50-26,250/year.*

Continuing Education:
Enrollment: 18000
Certification Designation/s: CCPI

Meetings/Conferences: Annual
Conference Chair: Laura Garcia
2013 - Indianapolis, IN/Jan. 11 - 15

Publications:
Activities Update; biennially
ICPI Tech Specs; annually
Interlocking Concrete Pavement Magazine; quarterly;
  adv.
Membership Directory; annually; adv.

The Paver Express; weekly; adv.

Membership List Available to Non-members

Intermarket Agency Network (1967)
5307 S. 92nd St.
Hales Corners, WI 53130
Tel: (414) 425-8800 *Fax:* (414) 425-0021
E-Mail: bille@nonbox.com
Website: intermarketnetwork.com
Members: 22 companies
Staff: 1
Annual Budget: $10-25,000

Personnel:
Executive Director: Bill Eisner

Historical Note:
*Founded as Intermarket Association of Advertising
Agencies; assumed its current name in 2001. IAN members
are small and mid-size advertising agencies, averaging
$2-30 million in billings annually. Membership: $1,750/
year.*

Membership List Available to Non-members

Intermediaries and Reinsurance Underwriters Association (1967)
971 Route 202 North
Branchburg, NJ 08876
Tel: (908) 203-0211 *Fax:* (908) 203-0213
E-Mail: info@irua.com
Website: irua.com
Members: 40 member companies
Staff: 2
Annual Budget: $250-500,000

Personnel:
Executive Director: Amy Barra
    E-Mail: abarra@irua.com

Historical Note:
*Formerly (1998) Independent Reinsurance Underwriters
Association. IRU's mission is to promote professionalism
and to provide service for the useful exchange of ideas
among member companies. Membership: $5,000/year
(Regular/Affiliate).*

Meetings/Conferences: Semi-Annual
2013 - Southampton, Bermuda (Fairmont
  Southampton)/April 21 - 23
Number of non-conference events/year: 5

Publications:
Member Directory; on-line
The Journal of Reinsurance; quarterly

Intermodal Association of North America (1991)
11785 Beltsville Dr.
Suite 1100
Calverton, MD 20705
Tel: (301) 982-3400 *Fax:* (301) 982-4815
E-Mail: info@intermodal.org
Website: intermodal.org
Members: 900 companies
Staff: 22
Annual Budget: $5-10,000,000

Personnel:
President and Chief Executive Officer: Joanne "Joni" F.
  Casey
    E-Mail: iana@intermodal.org
Vice President, Policy and Communications: Thomas J.
  Malloy
    E-Mail: tom.malloy@intermodal.org
Manager, Publications and Production: Maggie Miller
    E-Mail: maggie.miller@intermodal.org
Manager, Conferences and Meetings: Angie Mogensen
    E-Mail: angie.mogensen@intermodal.org
Assistant Vice President, Membership Services: James R.
  Morrow
    E-Mail: james.morrow@intermodal.org
Director, Information Technology: Tom Parson
    E-Mail: tparson@intermodal.org

Historical Note:
*Formed by the merger of the Intermodal Transportation
Association with the Intermodal Marketing Association
and the National Railroad Intermodal Association in
1991. IANA seeks to promote the benefits of inter modal
freight transportation and encourages its growth through
innovation and dialogue. Members are motor, rail and
water transportation companies and allied services.
Associate (non-voting) members include shippers,
academic institutions, government entities and non- profit
associations. Membership: $350-15,000 (Corporate-Voting
Member); $125 (At-Large Member).*

Meetings/Conferences: Annual
Conference Chair: Angie Mogensen
Number of non-conference events/year: 4

Publications:
Intermodal Insights; monthly
Membership Directory; on-line

International Academy for Child Brain Development (1984)
8801 Stenton Ave.
Wyndmoor, PA 19038
Tel: (215) 233-2050 Fax: (215) 233-9312
E-Mail: institutes@iahp.org
Website: iahp.org/jp/index.php?id = 194
Members: 300 individuals
Staff: 115
Annual Budget: Under $10,000

Personnel:
Director: Janet Doman
    E-Mail: institutes@iahp.org

Historical Note:
The goal of the institutes is to raise the intellectual, physical, and social abilities of all children. IACBD members are physicians, psychologists and other professionals with an interest in child brain development.

International Academy of Behavioral Medicine, Counseling and Psychotherapy (1979)
6750 Hillcrest Plaza Dr.
Suite 221
Dallas, TX 75230-1425
Tel: (972) 407-6833 Fax: (214) 615-0291
E-Mail: info@iabmcp.net
Website: iabmcp.net
Members: 1000 individuals
Staff: 1
Annual Budget: $25-50,000

Personnel:
Diplomat, IABMCP: Charles D. Spielberger PhD

Historical Note:
Formerly (1988) the American Academy of Behavioral Medicine. IABMCP seeks to promote the standards of professional excellence in the areas of Behavioral Medicine, Counseling, Psychotherapy, Chemical Dependency Counseling and Coaching. Members are psychologists, psychiatrists and others interested in the general field of behavioral medicine and health care. Membership: $90 (Diplomate Status/Student); $75 (Clinical); $60 (Associate).

Meetings/Conferences: Biennial
Number of non-conference events/year: 4

Publications:
Newsletter; monthly

International Academy of Compounding Pharmacists (1991)
4638 Riverstone Blvd.
Suite 100
Missouri City, TX 77459
Tel: (281) 933-8400 Fax: (281) 495-0602
TollFree: (800) 927-4227
E-Mail: iacpinfo@iacprx.org
Website: iacprx.org
Members: 1900 individuals
Staff: 9
Annual Budget: $1-2,000,000
Tax: 501(c)(6)

Personnel:
Executive Vice President and Chief Executive Officer: David G. Miller
    E-Mail: davidmiller@iacprx.org
Director, Marketing and Communications: Dagmar Climo
    E-Mail: dagmar@iacprx.org
Vice President, Government Affairs: Sarah Dodge
    E-Mail: sarahdodge@iacprx.org
Director, Events and Education: Meridyth Garcia
    E-Mail: meridyth@iacprx.org
Manager, Accounting and Human Resources: Michelle McMahan
    E-Mail: michelle@iacprx.org
Vice President, Operations and Development: Elizabeth Proctor
    E-Mail: elizabeth@iacprx.org
Director, Membership Services: Lindsey Turnau
    E-Mail: lindsey@iacprx.org

Historical Note:

IACP members are state-licensed pharmacists who provide and promote compounding services utilizing their knowledge and skill in the art of preparing, mixing, assembling, packaging, or labeling drugs/devices. Membership: $35 (Student); $65 (Professor/Retired Pharmacist/Technician); $300 (International Pharmacist); $500 (U.S. Pharmacist).

Meetings/Conferences: Annual
Conference Chair: Meridyth Garcia

Publications:
e-link; bi-monthly
The Link; quarterly

International Academy of Gnathology - American Section (1964)
1322 Ave. D
Suite A
Snohomish, WA 98290
E-Mail: mansueto@uthscsa.edu
Website: gnathologyusa.org
Members: 500 individuals
Staff: 3
Annual Budget: $100-250,000

Personnel:
Secretary and Treasurer: Thomas E. Cyr
    E-Mail: smileman47@comcast.net

Historical Note:
International Academy of Gnathology - American Section, the parent organization of IAG, provides an international brotherhood of dental professionals practicing and teaching the disciplines of Gnathology. Members are dentists. Membership: $450 (Local); $675 (International); $425 (Full-Time Faculty); $360 (Full Time International); $100 (Retired); $525(International faculty); $575 (USA Member).

Meetings/Conferences: Biennial
Conference Chair: Michael A. Mansueto

International Academy of Oral Medicine and Toxicology (1984)
8297 Champions Gate Blvd.
Suite 193
Championsgate, FL 33896
Tel: (863) 420-6373 Fax: (863) 419-8136
E-Mail: info@iaomt.org
Website: iaomt.org
Members: 700 individuals
Staff: 2
Annual Budget: $250-500,000
Tax: 501(c)(3)

Personnel:
Executive Director: Kym Smith

Historical Note:
IAOMT members are dentists and other medical professionals with an interest in the biocompatibility of materials. The mission of the International Academy of Oral Medicine and Toxicology is to advocate the health of the public at large. Membership: $15 (Student); $395 (Retired).

Meetings/Conferences: Biennial
2013 - Charleston, SC (Wild Dunes Resort)/March 14 - 16
2013 - Las Vegas, NV (JW Marriott Resort and Spa)/ Sept. 5 - 7

Publications:
IAOMT Newsletter
In Vivo Newsletter; quarterly
International Chapter Directory; on-line
Membership Directory; semi-annually

International Academy of Television Arts and Sciences (1969)
25 W. 52nd St.
New York, NY 10019
Tel: (212) 489-6969 Fax: (212) 489-6557
E-Mail: iemmys@iemmys.tv
Website: iemmys.tv
Members: 50 countries and 500 companies
Staff: 9
Annual Budget: $2-5,000,000

Personnel:
Senior Vice President and Executive Director: Camille Bidermann-Roizen
Manager Events and Partnership: Aurelie Dauphin-Fletcher
    E-Mail: Aurelie.Dauphin@iemmys.tv
Coordinator, Web and Marketing: Zoë Dyck
    E-Mail: Zoe.Dyck@iemmys.tv
Coordinator Membership and Office: Max Newman

    E-Mail: Max.Newman@iemmys.tv
Director, Communications: Eva Obadia
    E-Mail: Eva.Obadia@iemmys.tv

Historical Note:
The Academy was chartered with a mission to recognize excellence in television programming produced outside of the United States. Membership: $1,000 (Individual).

Meetings/Conferences: Annual

Publications:
International Emmy Almanac; annually
Newsletter

International Academy of Trial Lawyers (1954)
2575 E. Camelback Rd.
Phoenix, AZ 85016
Tel: (602) 530-8181 Fax: (602) 530-8500
E-Mail: iatl@llmsi.com
Website: iatl.net
Members: 500 active trial lawyers
Staff: 3
Annual Budget: $1-2,000,000
Tax: 501(c)(6)

Personnel:
President: Patrick J. McGroder

Historical Note:
The purpose of IATL is to promote reforms in the law, facilitate the Administration of Justice, promote the Rule of Law internationally, and elevate the standards of integrity, honor and courtesy in the legal profession. Fellowship is by invitation only, and trial lawyers are invited to become Fellows only after an extremely careful vetting process. Membership: $600/year (Individual).

Meetings/Conferences: Annual
2013 - Newport Beach, CA (Pelican Hill)/April 3 - 7
2013 - Chicago, IL (Trump International Hotel)/July 17 - 21

Publications:
Member Directory; on-line

International Advertising Association (1930)
275 Madison Ave.
Suite 2102
New York, NY 10016
Tel: (212) 557-1133 Fax: (212) 983-0455
E-Mail: iaa@iaaglobal.org
Website: iaaglobal.org
Members: 4000 individuals and 143 companies, organizations and chapters
Staff: 7
Annual Budget: $500-1,000,000

Personnel:
Chief Executive Officer and Executive Director: Deborah Malone
Chairman and President: Alan Rutherford
Manager, Information Systems: Karl Kam
Coordinator, Education: Nubia Martinez
Director, Membership Services: Marie J. Scotti
    E-Mail: marie.scotti@iaaglobal.org
Corporate Communications: Pat Sloan
Corporate Counsel: Eric Vaughn-Flam

Historical Note:
Formerly (1954) Export Advertising Association. IAA's mission is to promote and facilitate excellence in the communications industry. It also seeks to use global network as a platform for sharing knowledge on industry issues, best practices and insights in a rapidly changing business environment. Membership: $100-200 (Individual Member); $50 (Academic); $4,000-10,000 (Corporate Member); $405 (Organizational Member); $20 (Young Professional Member).

Publications:
EU insights; monthly
EU News; monthly

The International Air Cargo Association (1994)
P.O. Box 661510
Miami, FL 33266-1510
Tel: (786) 265-7011 Fax: (786) 265-7012
E-Mail: secgen@tiaca.org
Website: tiaca.org
Members: 335 individuals
Staff: 9
Annual Budget: $100-250,000
Tax: 501(c)(6)

Personnel:
Treasurer: Vincent Carrodeguas
Director, sales: Reha Erman

Secretary General: Daniel C. Fernandez
E-Mail: secgen@tiaca.org

Historical Note:
Mission of TIACA is to promote innovation among its members and to provide industry-specific information, analysis and knowledge. TIACA members include all major components of the industry - air and surface carriers, forwarders, shippers, vendors, manufacturers, airports, countries, financial institutions and consultants. TIACA also represents regional, national and city air cargo associations, service providers to the industry and educational institutions and their students involved in air cargo training. Membership: $1,000 (Trustee/Corporate); $100 (Affiliate); $300(Forwarder).

Meetings/Conferences: Annual

Publications:
Member Directory; on-line
TIACA TIMES Magazine
TIACA Times newsletter

International Air Transport Association (1945)
601 Pennsylvania Ave. NW
Suite 300
Washington, DC 20004
Tel: (202) 628-9292 Fax: (202) 628-9448
Website: iata.org
Staff: 3

Personnel:
Director General and Chief Executive Officer: Tony Tyler
Head, Congressional Affairs: Matthew Jennings

Historical Note:
IATA's mission is to represent, lead and serve the airline industry. It is the prime vehicle for inter-airline cooperation in promoting safe, reliable, secure and economical air services - for the benefit of the world's consumers. Membership:1,500-15,000/Year.

Continuing Education:
Certification Designation/s: IATA

Meetings/Conferences: Annual
2013 - Cape Town, South Africa (Cape Town's International Convention Centre)/June 2 - 4
Number of non-conference events/year: 16

Publications:
Airlines International; bi-monthly
Newsletter

The International Alliance for Women (1980)
1760 Old Meadow Rd.
Suite 500
McLean, VA 22102
Tel: (866) 533-8429 Fax: (905) 305-1548
TollFree: (866) 533-8429
E-Mail: info@tiaw.org
Website: tiaw.org
Members: 50000 individuals
Staff: 2
Annual Budget: $100-250,000
Tax: 501(c)(3)

Personnel:
Executive Director: Maxine Westaway
E-Mail: mwestaway@TIAW.org

Historical Note:
TIAW's aim is to encourage, develop, fund and implement programs that foster economic empowerment and advancement for women around the world. Alliance members are executive and professional women. Membership: $165 (Individual); $300 (Supporting); $500 (Sustaining); $750-5,500 (Association); $2,500-15,000 (Corporate); 1500 (Lifetime)

Publications:
Alliance Newsletter; irregular; adv.
eBulletins; on-line
eConnections; monthly
Membership Directory; on-line

International Alliance for Women in Music (1975)
3290 Darley Ave.
Boulder, CO 80305-6412
Website: iawm.org
Members: 500 individuals
Staff: 3
Annual Budget: $10-25,000
Tax: 501(c)(3)

Personnel:
President: Hsiao-Lan Wang
E-Mail: hlwang2000@gmail.com

Treasurer: Julie Cross
Editor-in-Chief: Eve R. Meyer

Historical Note:
Formed by the merger of the International Congress for Women in Music (1979), the American Women Composers (1976) and the International League of Women Composers (1975). Aim is to establish a network of support and encouragement for female musicians; to gain status and recognition for female musicians and to provide a forum for the interchange of ideas through workshops, meetings, and performances. Membership: $30 (Student); $55 (Individual/Institutional); $80 (Joint); $1,000 (Lifetime); $45 (Senior); $85 (Supporting); $1500 (Joint Lifetime).

Meetings/Conferences: Annual

Publications:
IAWM Journal; semi-annually; adv.
Women and Music Journal; semi-annually

Membership List Available to Non-members

International Alliance of Technology Integrators (1998)
1100 College St.
Northfield, MN 55057-2835
Tel: (507) 664-9548 Fax: (786) 551-2952
E-Mail: sdavis@iati.org
Website: iati.org
Members: 15 Companies
Staff: 4
Annual Budget: $10-25,000,000

Personnel:
Executive Director: Scott Davis
E-Mail: sdavis@iati.org

Historical Note:
IATI's mission is to leverage collective skills and experiences to improve the practice and results of technology integration. Memebrship: $3588/year (Company).

Publications:
Membership Directory; on-line

International Alliance of Theatrical Stage Employees, Moving Picture Technicians, Artists and Allied Crafts of the U.S., Its Territories and Canada (1893)
1430 Broadway
20th Floor
New York, NY 10018
Tel: (212) 730-1770 Fax: (212) 730-7809
E-Mail: iatsepac@iatse-intl.org
Website: iatse-intl.org
Members: 113000 individuals
Staff: 15
Annual Budget: $2-5,000,000

Personnel:
International President: Matthew D. Loeb
Department Director, Communications: Emily Tao
Department Director, Education and Training: Patricia White

Historical Note:
Originally chartered by the American Federation of Labor as the National Alliance of Theatrical Stage Employees in 1893 and in 1899, with the acceptance of two Canadian locals, the words "and Canada" were added, in 1902 "International" was substituted for "National" and in 1995 the current name was accepted. IATSE is a labor union representing technicians, artisans and craftspersons in the entertainment industry, including live theatre, motion picture and television production, and trade shows. Members include stage hands and projectionists and other craftspersons in the various branches of the entertainment industry, including motion picture and television production, product demonstration and industrial shows, conventions, facility maintenance, casinos, audio visual, and computer graphics. Membership: $480 (President's Club); $240 (Leader's Club); $120 (Activist's Club).

Meetings/Conferences: Annual
Number of non-conference events/year: 1

Publications:
Official Bulletin; quarterly
The Organizer; quarterly

International Allied Printing Trades Association (1896)
1900 L St. NW, Eighth Floor
Washington, DC 20036
Tel: (202) 434-1235 Fax: (202) 721-0641
Website: alliedlabel.org/
Members: 2 labor unions
Staff: 1

Tax: 501(c)(5)

Personnel:
Secretary-Treasurer: Robert Lacey

Historical Note:
Exercises jurisdiction throughout the United States and Canada in regard to the Allied Printing Trades Label. Member unions are the Graphic Communications Conference/IBT and the Printing, Publishing & Media Workers Sector of the C.W.A. Adopted and owned by the Association, the label designates the products of the labor of its members.

International Aloe Science Council (1981)
8630 Fenton St.
Suite 918
Silver Spring, MD 20910
Tel: (301) 588-2420 Fax: (301) 588-1174
E-Mail: info@iasc.org
Website: iasc.org
Members: 275 Companies
Staff: 3
Annual Budget: $250-500,000

Personnel:
Executive Director: Devon Powell
E-Mail: dpowell@iasc.org
Coordinator, Certification Program: Rosie Ysasi
E-Mail: rysasi@iasc.org

Historical Note:
Formerly known as the National Aloe Science Council (1990). The International Aloe Science Council is a non-profit trade organization for the Aloe Vera industry world-wide. Serves as a liaison and source of information for research, development and promotion of Aloe Vera and associated products. Membership includes aloe growers, processors, finished goods manufacturers, marketing companies, insurance companies, equipment suppliers, printers, sales organizations, physicians, scientists and researchers. Membership: $1,100-7,500/year (Organization/Company).

Continuing Education:
Certification Designation/s: IASC

Publications:
Inside Aloe Online; quarterly
Membership Directory; on-line

International and American Associations of Clinical Nutritionists (1983)
15280 Addison Rd.
Suite 130
Addison, TX 75001
Tel: (972) 407-9089 Fax: (972) 250-0233
E-Mail: ddc@clinicalnutrition.com
Website: iaacn.org
Staff: 5
Annual Budget: $250-500,000

Personnel:
Executive Director: Kevin P. Henry
Secretary: Heidi Zappone

Historical Note:
Merged with International Academy of Nutrition and Preventive Medicine in 1997. IAACN is a professional association of practicing clinical nutritionists in many health care professions who strive to attain better standards of competency and practice. Membership: $395 (Professional Individual); $360 (Professional Associate); $300 (Associate); $45 (Student); $900 (Corporate).

Continuing Education:
Certification Designation/s: CCN, CEP

Publications:
IAACN eNewsletter; weekly
IAACN Insight; semi-annually; adv.
Journal of Applied Nutrition; adv.
Journal Of Applied Nutrition; annually; adv.

International Andalusian and Lusitano Horse Association
101 Carnoustie North
P.O. Box 200
Birmingham, AL 35242
Tel: (205) 995-8900 Fax: (205) 995-8966
E-Mail: infoShare@ialha.org
Website: ialha.org
Members: 1900 individuals
Staff: 6
Annual Budget: $250-500,000
Tax: 501(c)(5)

Personnel:
President: Julie Alonzo

E-Mail: president@ialha.org

Historical Note:
*IALHA is devoted to Iberian horses and related interests.
Membership: $1500 (Lifetime Full); $35-160/year.*

Publications:
Andalusian Magazine; adv.
IALHA Member Handbook & Directory; annually
Membership Directory; on-line

International Anesthesia Research Society (1922)
100 Pine St.
Suite 230
San Francisco, CA 94111-5104
Tel: (415) 296-6900 *Fax:* (415) 296-6901
E-Mail: info@iars.org
Website: iars.org
Members: 15000 individuals
Staff: 12
Annual Budget: $10-25,000,000
Tax: 501(c)(3)

Personnel:
Executive Director: Thomas A. Cooper
    E-Mail: tcooper@iars.org
Director, Administration: Julie Bradaric
    E-Mail: jbradaric@iars.org
Director, Membership Services: Laura J. Kuhar
    E-Mail: lkuhar@iars.org
Director, Marketing, Meetings and Education: Julie
    McGrath
    E-Mail: jmcgrath@iars.org
Director, Publishing and Strategic Partnerships: Steven
    Sayre
    E-Mail: ssayre@iars.org

Historical Note:
*IARS's mission is to encourage, stimulate, and fund the
ongoing anesthesia-related research projects that will
enhance and advance the specialty and to disseminate
current, basic and clinical research data in all areas of
clinical anesthesia, including perioperative medicine, critical
care, and pain management. Members are physicians,
physician residents, and others with doctoral degrees, as
well as health professionals in anesthesia-related practice.
Membership: $140 (Full Member); $25 (In-Training); $210
(Joint IARS/SCA).*

Meetings/Conferences: Annual
Conference Chair: Julie McGrath
2013 - San Diego, CA (Sheraton San Diego Hotel and
    Marina)/May 4 - 7
2014 - Montreal, QC (Fairmont The Queen Elizabeth)/
    March 17 - 20
2015 - Honolulu, HI (Hilton Hawaiian Village Waikiki
    Beach Resort)/March 21 - 24

Publications:
Anesthesia & Analgesia; monthly; adv.

Membership List Available to Non-members

International Anti-Counterfeiting Coalition
(1979)
1730 M St. NW
Suite 1020
Washington, DC 20036
Tel: (202) 223-6667 *Fax:* (202) 223-6668
E-Mail: iacc@iacc.org
Website: iacc.org
Members: 208 companies
Staff: 4

Personnel:
President: Robert C. Barchiesi
    E-Mail: bbarchiesi@iacc.org
Director, Marketing and Membership Development: Kim
    Handzo
Vice President and Director, Legislative Affairs and Policy:
    Travis D. Johnson
    E-Mail: tjohnson@iacc.org
Associate Counsel and Director, Special Projects: Kristina
    Montanaro

Historical Note:
*IACC's mission is to combat counterfeiting and piracy by
promoting laws, regulations and directives designed to
render the theft of intellectual property undesirable and
unprofitable. Membership: $1,750-4,600 (Investigative
Firms); $4600-8000 (IP Owners/Law Firms/Trade
Associations); $150 (Government Officials)*

Meetings/Conferences:
2013 - Dallas, TX/May 1 - 3
2013 - Scottsdale, AZ/Oct. 16 - 18
2014 - Hong Kong, China/May 7 - 9

Publications:
Get Real
IACC Update; monthly

International Association for Business and Society (1990)
C/O Kim Rodela, BYU Romney Institute
770 TNRB
Provo, UT 84602
Tel: (202) 994-2536 *Fax:* (202) 994-8113
Website: iabs.net
Members: 300 individuals
Staff: 3
Annual Budget: $50-100,000
Tax: 501(c)(3)

Personnel:
President: Jamie Hendry
    E-Mail: jhendry@bucknell.edu
IABS, Operations Manager: Kim Rodela
    E-Mail: kimrodela@iabs.net
Editor: Duane Windsor

Historical Note:
*IABS is a learned society devoted to research and teaching
about the relationships between business, government and
society. Its research domain covers the various aspects of
the interface between management and the social political
dynamics of the surrounding society. Membership: $100
(Faculty/Professional); $50 (Doctoral Student).*

Meetings/Conferences: Annual
2013 - Portland, OR (Marriott Downtown Waterfront
    Hotel)/June 6 - 9

Publications:
Business and Society; quarterly
IABS Newsletter; quarterly

International Association for Cold Storage Construction (1978)
1500 King St., Suite 201
C/O Global Cold Chain Alliance
Alexandria, VA 22314-2730
Tel: (703) 373-4300 *Fax:* (703) 373-4301
E-Mail: email@iacsc.org
Website: gcca.org/iacsc
Staff: 3

Personnel:
Treasurer: Mark Barrett
Chairman: Janet Madden Charles
Contact, Membership and Marketing: James Rogers
    E-Mail: jrogers@gcca.org

Historical Note:
*Became a part of the Global Cold Chain Alliance in 2007,
which now represents its membership providing all of
its operational support. IACSC represents contractors and
suppliers in the cold storage construction industry. IACSC
provides a forum for innovative ideas, promotes standards
of practice, hosts professional education programs, and
promotes the interests of the industry in political, legal and
regulatory arenas. Membership: $550-850/year.*

Meetings/Conferences: Annual

Publications:
COLD FACTS magazine; bi-monthly; adv.
Cool Designs; bi-monthly
Membership Directory; adv.

International Association for Colon Hydrotherapy
(1989)
P.O. Box 461285
San Antonio, TX 78246-1285
Tel: (210) 366-2888 *Fax:* (210) 366-2999
E-Mail: homeoffice@i-act.org
Website: i-act.org
Members: 1000 individuals
Staff: 4
Annual Budget: $250-500,000
Tax: 501(c)(3)

Personnel:
Executive Director: A.R. "Dick" Hoenninger PhD
Secretary And Treasurer: Millie Campbelll
President Elect And Vice-president: Gail Naas
    E-Mail: gailnaasiacted@aol.com

Historical Note:
*Formerly (1995) the American Colon Therapy
Association. I-ACT heightens the awareness of the
colon hydrotherapy profession, ensures continuing and
progressive education in the field of colon hydrotherapy
and implements professionalism beyond reproach. Members
are colon hygiene therapists and other health care
professionals. Membership: $250 (Affiliate- Groups/*

---

*Organizations/Companies); $150 (Full-Professional Colon
Hydrotherapist); $35 (Donating-Clients/Health Care
Practitioners/Family/Friends); $75 (Patron).*

Continuing Education:
Certification Designation/s: I-ACT

Meetings/Conferences: Annual

Publications:
I-ACT Quarterly Newsletter; quarterly; adv.

International Association for Computer Information Systems (1960)
220 College of Business, Oklahoma State
University
Stillwater, OK 74078
Tel: (405) 744-8632 *Fax:* (405) 744-5180
Website: iacis.org
Members: 750 individuals and organizations
Staff: 4
Annual Budget: $100-250,000

Personnel:
Managing Director: G. Daryl Nord
    E-Mail: daryl.nord@okstate.edu
Director, Publications: Jeretta Horn Nord
    E-Mail: Jeretta.Nord@IACIS.org

Historical Note:
*Formerly (1987) the Society for Data Educators and
(1990) the Association for Computer Educators. IACIS's
mission is to improve information systems and the education
of information systems and computer professionals.
Members are individuals with a particular interest in all
levels of computers. Membership: $95 (Individual); $395
(Institution).*

Meetings/Conferences: Annual
2013 - San Juan, PR (San Juan Marriott Resort and
    Stellaris Casino)/Oct. 2 - 5

Publications:
Issues in Information Systems; semi-annually
ournal for Computer Information Systems (JCIS);
    quarterly

International Association for Continuing Education and Training (1968)
1760 Old Meadow Rd.
Suite 500
McLean, VA 22102
Tel: (703) 506-3275 *Fax:* (703) 506-3266
E-Mail: info@iacet.org
Website: iacet.org
Members: 700 organizations
Staff: 9
Annual Budget: $500-1,000,000
Tax: 501(c)(3)

Personnel:
Executive Director: Sara Meier MSEd, CAE
    E-Mail: smeier@iacet.org
Manager, Creative Services: Jessica Conyers
Coordinator, Membership Services: Judson Lineberger
    E-Mail: jlineberger@iacet.org
Senior Director, Programs: Khunteang Pa
    E-Mail: kpa@iacet.org
Manager, Events: Mary Katherine Saladino
Associate Vice President, Public Relations: Andy Schwartz

Historical Note:
*Formerly (1990) the Council on the Continuing
Education Unit. IACET's mission is to promote and
enhance quality in continuing education and training
through research, education, and the development and
continuous improvement of IACET criteria, principles, and
standards. Members are educational institutions, hospitals,
professional societies and others providing continuing
education. Membership: $110/year (Individual).*

Continuing Education:
Enrollment: 700
Certification Designation/s: ANSI

Meetings/Conferences:
Conference Chair: Mary Katherine Saladino
Number of non-conference events/year: 1

Publications:
Membership Directory; on-line

International Association for Corporate and Professional Recruitment (1976)
327 N. Palm Dr.
Suite 201
Beverly Hills, CA 90210
Tel: (310) 550-0304 *Fax:* (206) 202-4838
E-Mail: office@iacpr.org

Website: iacpr.org
Members: 250 individuals
Staff: 3
Annual Budget: $250-500,000

Personnel:
Executive Director: Kay Kennedy
Associate Director: Agnes Gomes-Koizumi

Historical Note:
Formerly (1991) the National Association of Corporate and Professional Recruiters and (1995) International Association of Corporate and Professional Recruiters. IACPR's mission is to provide the senior-level recruitment community with opportunities to network, share practices and build cutting-edge expertise within a collaborative environment. Members are professionals with at least ten years experience in the recruiting of executives. Membership: $500/year (Individual).

Meetings/Conferences: Annual

International Association for Correctional and Forensic Psychology (1954)
897 Oak Park Blvd.
Suite 124
Pismo Beach, CA 93449
Tel: (805) 489-0665 Fax: (805) 499-0871
E-Mail: jg@ia4cfp.org
Website: ia4cfp.org
Members: 250 individuals
Staff: 3
Annual Budget: $250-500,000

Personnel:
Executive Director: John L. Gannon PhD
E-Mail: jg@ia4cfp.org

Historical Note:
IACFP, an affiliate of the American Correctional Association, works to promote the development of psychological practice in criminal justice and law enforcement settings. Membership: $75 (IACFP Annual Membership); $25 (Student); $125 (IACFP Two-Year Membership, Joint Annual FMHAC and IACFP Membership); $90 (Joint Annual ICCA and IACFP Membership).

Meetings/Conferences:
Number of non-conference events/year: 8

Publications:
Criminal Justice and Behavior; monthly; adv.
The Correctional Psychologist; quarterly; adv.

International Association for Dental Research (1920)
1619 Duke St.
Alexandria, VA 22314-3406
Tel: (703) 548-0066 Fax: (703) 548-1883
E-Mail: research@iadr.org
Website: dentalresearch.org
Members: 12000 members
Staff: 17
Annual Budget: $2-5,000,000
Tax: 501(c)(3)

Personnel:
Executive Director: Christopher H. Fox
E-Mail: cfox@iadr.org
Senior Manager, Membership Benefits: Marissa E. Naspinski
Director, Government Affairs: Jonathan Nurse
Manager, Program: Emily Sidla
Senior Director, Marketing, Membership Services and Publications: Denise S. Streszoff
Manager, Marketing and Communications: Ingrid L. Thomas
Senior Director, Finance and Information Technology: R. Darin Walsh
Director, Meetings: Leslie Zeck

Historical Note:
IADR's mission is to advance research and increase knowledge for the improvement of oral health worldwide, to support and represent the oral health research community and to facilitate the communication and application of research findings. Membership: $48-120 (Individual); $35 (Student).

Meetings/Conferences: Annual
Conference Chair: Leslie Zeck
2013 - Seatle, WA/March 20 - 23
2014 - Cape Town, South Africa/June 25 - 28
2015 - Boston, MA/March 11 - 14
Number of non-conference events/year: 1

Publications:
Global Research Update; monthly

IADR Reports; annually
Journal of Dental Research

International Association for Energy Economics (2010)
28790 Chagrin Blvd.
Suite 350
Cleveland, OH 44122
Tel: (216) 464-5365 Fax: (216) 464-2737
E-Mail: iaee@iaee.org
Website: iaee.org
Members: 3,800 members
Staff: 8
Annual Budget: $500-1,000,000

Personnel:
Executive Director: David L. Williams
Vice President, Academic Affairs: Edmar Luiz de Almeida
E-Mail: edmar@ie.ufrj.br
Vice President, Conferences: Gürkan Kumbaroglu
E-Mail: gurkank@boun.edu.tr
Vice President, Communications: Roberto Malaman
E-Mail: rmalaman@autorita.energia.it
Vice President, Publications: Jacques Percebois
E-Mail: jacques.percebois@univ-montp1.fr

Historical Note:
IAEE is a non-profit membership organization for business, government, academic and other professionals concerned with energy and related issues in the international community. Mission is to advance the knowledge, understanding and application of economics across all aspects of energy and foster communication amongst energy concerned professionals. Membership: $50-2,500/year.

Meetings/Conferences:
Conference Chair: Gürkan Kumbaroglu
2013 - Lagos, Nigeria/April 22 - 23
2013 - Daegu, Republic of Korea (South Korea) (Hotel Inter-Burgo EXCO)/June 16 - 20
2013 - Anchorage, AK (Hotel Captain Cook)/July 28 - 31
2014 - Prague, Czech Republic (4-star Diplomat)/June 15 - 18

Publications:
Economics of Energy and Environmental Policy; semi-annually
Energy Forum; quarterly
Membership Directory; on-line
The Energy Journal; quarterly

International Association for Food Protection (1911)
6200 Aurora Ave.
Suite 200W
Des Moines, IA 50322-2864
Tel: (515) 276-3344 Fax: (515) 276-8655
TollFree: (800) 369-6337
E-Mail: info@foodprotection.org
Website: foodprotection.org
Members: 3400 individuals
Staff: 15
Annual Budget: $2-5,000,000

Personnel:
Executive Director: David W. Tharp
E-Mail: dtharp@foodprotection.org
Director, Membership Services: Julie A. Cattanach
E-Mail: jcattanach@foodprotection.org
Senior Accountant: Donna Gronstal
E-Mail: dgronstal@foodprotection.org
Administrative Assistant: Laurie Hews
E-Mail: lhews@foodprotection.org
Contact, Advertising: Dave Larson
E-Mail: larson6@mchsi.com

Historical Note:
Founded as the International Association of Dairy and Milk Inspectors, (1932) International Association of Milk Sanitarians, (1949) the International Association of Milk and Food Sanitarians, International Association of Milk, (1966) Food and Environmental Sanitarians and assumed its present name in 2000. IAFP's mission is to provide food safety professionals worldwide with a forum to exchange information on protecting the food supply. Membership: $27.50-5,000/year.

Meetings/Conferences: Annual
2013 - Charlotte, NC (Charlotte Convention Center)/July 28 - 31
2014 - Indianapolis, IN (Indiana Convention Center)/Aug. 3 - 6
2015 - Portland, OR (Oregon Convention Center)/July 26 - 29

Number of non-conference events/year: 2

Publications:
Food Protection Trends; on-line; adv.
IAFP Report; monthly
Journal of Food Protection; monthly; adv.
Membership Directory; on-line

International Association for Healthcare Security and Safety (1968)
P.O. Box 5038
Glendale Heights, IL 60139
Tel: (630) 529-3913 Fax: (630) 529-4139
TollFree: (888) 353-0990
E-Mail: info@iahss.org
Website: iahss.org
Members: 1600 individuals
Staff: 5
Annual Budget: $1-2,000,000

Personnel:
Executive Director: Evelyn F. Meserve CHPA
E-Mail: evelyn@iahss.org
Executive Assistant: Nancy Felesena
E-Mail: Nancy@IAHSS.org

Historical Note:
Formerly (1991) the International Association for Hospital Security and an affiliate of the American Hospital Association. IAHSS strives to promote excellence in healthcare security and safety worldwide. Membership: $150 (Partner); $125 (Senior); $50 (Associate).

Continuing Education:
Certification Designation/s: CHPA(F), CHPA, CHSO, CAHSO

Meetings/Conferences: Annual
2013 - Myrtle Beach, SC (Hilton)/May 5 - 9
Number of non-conference events/year: 2

Publications:
IAHSS Directions; on-line
Journal of Healthcare Protection Management; quarterly
Member Directory; on-line

International Association for Human Resource Information Management (1980)
P.O. Box 1086
Burlington, MA 01803
Tel: (781) 791-9488 Fax: (781) 998-8011
TollFree: (800) 804-3983
E-Mail: information@ihrim.org
Website: ihrim.org
Members: 2000 individuals
Staff: 7
Annual Budget: $1-2,000,000
Tax: 501(c)(6)

Personnel:
President and Chief Executive Officer: Lynne Mealy
E-Mail: lmealy@ihrim.org
Manager, Membership Services, Marketing and Vendor Relations: Jean Andrews
E-Mail: jandrews@ihrim.org
Manager, Marketing and Communications: Laurie Carantit
E-Mail: lcarantit@ihrim.org
Manager, Education and Special Programs: Michelle Czosek
E-Mail: mczosek@ihrim.org
Contact, Publications: Tom Faulkner
E-Mail: tomf@futurapublishing.com
Manager, Membership Programs: Karen Murray
E-Mail: kmurray@ihrim.org
Manager, Expositions: Blaine Siske
E-Mail: bsiske@mpire-group.com

Historical Note:
Formerly known as the Association of Human Resource System Professionals (HRSP), HRSP unified with its Canadian counterpart (CHRSP) in 1996 and assumed its current name. IHRIM's mission is to provide knowledge, education and solutions supporting the human resource information management community. Membership: $295 (Regular New); $80 (Faculty); $35 (Student), $324 (Regular New Membership including WSR); $500 (Regular Two Year New).

Continuing Education:
Certification Designation/s: HRIP

Meetings/Conferences: Annual
Conference Chair: Lynne Mealy
2013 - Orlando, FL (Disney's Contemporary Resort)/June 2 - 5

Publications:
IHRIM Wire; monthly
Membership Directory; on-line
Workforce Solutions Review; bi-monthly

Membership List Available to Non-members

International Association for Hydrogen Energy
(1975)
5794 SW 40th St.
Suite 303
Miami, FL 33155
Tel: (305) 284-4666 *Fax:* (305) 284-2580
E-Mail: info@iahe.org
Website: iahe.org
Members: 2600 individuals
Staff: 4
Annual Budget: $100-250,000

Personnel:
President and Editor in Chief: T. Nejat Veziroglu PhD
   E-Mail: veziroglu@miami.edu
Comptroller: Ayfer Veziroglu
   E-Mail: ayfer@iahe.org
Editor-in-Chief: Emre A. Veziroglu
   E-Mail: emrev1@cox.net

Historical Note:
IAHE strives to advance the day when hydrogen energy will become the principal means by which the world will achieve its long- sought goal of abundant clean energy for mankind. Members, hailing from 86 countries, are scientists and engineers professionally involved in the development of hydrogen energy. Membership: $95-170 (Individual); $75-115 (Associate); $45-85 (Emeritus).

Meetings/Conferences: Biennial
2014 - Gwangju, Republic of Korea (South Korea) (Kimdaejung Convention Center)/June 15 - 20/over 100 exhibitors
Number of non-conference events/year: 3

Publications:
IAHE eNewsletter; quarterly
International Journal of Hydrogen Energy; quarterly; adv.

International Association for Identification
(1915)
2131 Hollywood Blvd.
Suite 403
Hollywood, FL 33020
Tel: (954) 589-0628 *Fax:* (954) 589-0657
E-Mail: iaisecty@theiai.org
Website: theiai.org
Members: 6000 individuals
Staff: 8
Annual Budget: $2-5,000,000
Tax: 501(c)(3)

Personnel:
Chief Operations Officer: Glen Calhoun
Coordinator, Education: Jim Gettemy
Legal Counsel: Phyllis Karasov
Editor: Alan McRoberts
Conference Planner: Candace Murray
   E-Mail: conference@theiai.org

Historical Note:
Organized in Oakland, CA as the International Association for Criminal Identification. Assumed its present name in 1920. Absorbed the International Association for Voice Identification in 1981. IAI promotes research in forensic sciences. Membership consists of persons engaged in forensic identification, investigation and scientific examination of physical evidence. Membership: $7-70/year.

Continuing Education:
Certification Designation/s: FC, FAC, CSC, TFC, LPC, FPC, BPEC

Meetings/Conferences: Annual
Conference Chair: Candace Murray
2013 - Providence, RI/Aug. 4 - 10
2014 - Minneapolis, MN/Aug. 10 - 16

Publications:
Journal of Forensic Identification; bi-monthly; adv.
Membership Directory; on-line

International Association for Impact Assessment
(1980)
1330 23rd St., South
Suite C
Fargo, ND 58103-3705
Tel: (701) 297-7908 *Fax:* (701) 297-7917
E-Mail: info@iaia.org

Website: iaia.org
Members: 2500 individuals
Staff: 8
Annual Budget: $500-1,000,000

Personnel:
Chief Executive Officer: Rita R. Hamm
Specialist, Publications and Meetings: Jennifer Howell
Specialist, Marketing and Financial Services: Bridget John
Member Liaison and Conference Registrar: Shelli LaPlante
Web Developer and Administrator: Jeff Torreson

Historical Note:
IAIA's mission is to advance innovation and communicate better practice in all forms of impact assessment so as to further the development of local, regional, and global capacity in impact assessment. Members are corporate planners and managers, public interest advocates, government planners and managers, private consultants and policy analysts, and university teachers and students. Membership: $55-1,000/year.

Meetings/Conferences: Annual
Conference Chair: Jennifer Howell
2013 - Calgary, AB/May 13 - 16

Publications:
IAIA Newsletter; quarterly; adv.
Impact Assessment and Project Appraisal; quarterly
Membeship Directory; on-line

Membership List Available to Non-members

International Association for Insurance Law - United States Chapter (1963)
P.O. Box 9001
Mt. Vernon, NY 10552
Tel: (914) 966-3180 *Fax:* (914) 966-3264
Website: aidaus.org
Members: 700 individuals
Staff: 2
Annual Budget: $50-100,000

Personnel:
Managing Director: Stephen C. Acunto
   E-Mail: sa@cinn.com
Contact, Membership Services: Alessia Sciullo
   E-Mail: asciullo@cinn.com

Historical Note:
AIDA-US's mission is to bring together lawyers and executives from companies, law firms, brokers and related businesses, as well as academics, to share perspectives and develop opportunities in the insurance and reinsurance fields. Members are insurance and reinsurance attorneys in private practice and in companies, regulators and academics. Membership: $100/year (Individual).

International Association for Language Learning Technology (1965)
2020 E. Maple St.
North Canton, OH 44720
Tel: (330) 490-7453
Website: iallt.org
Members:
300 institutions
500 individuals
Staff: 2
Annual Budget: $10-25,000
Tax: 501(c)(3)

Personnel:
President: Ute S Lahaie

Historical Note:
Founded as the National Association of Language Lab Directors, it became the National Association Learning Laboratories and later (1982) became the International Association for Learning Laboratories. IALLT is a professional organization whose members provide leadership in the development, integration, evaluation and management of instructional technology for the teaching and learning of language, literature and culture. It is also affiliated with the American Council on the Teaching of Foreign Languages and the Computer Assisted Language Learning Consortium. Membership: $50 (Educational Member Individual); $200 (Commercial Member); $25 (Student/Retired).

Publications:
IALLT Journal of Language Learning Technologies; semi-annually; adv.
IALLT newsletters; on-line

International Association for Mathematical Geosciences (1968)
5868 Westheimer Rd.
Suite 537
Houston, TX 77057

Tel: (832) 380-8833 *Fax:* (800) 983-1346
E-Mail: support@iamgmembers.org
Website: iamg.org
Members: 500 individuals
Staff: 4
Annual Budget: $100-250,000
Tax: 501(c)(3)

Personnel:
Treasurer: David Collins

Historical Note:
Founded at the XXIII International Geological Congress, Prague, Czechoslovakia in 1968. The aim of IAMG is to promote international cooperation in the application and use of mathematics in geological research and technology. Membership: $12-3,500/year.

Meetings/Conferences: Annual
2013 - Hong Kong, China/Aug. 25 - 30
2013 - Madrid, Spain/Sept. 2 - 6
2014 - New Delhi, India (Jawaharlal Nehru University of New Delhi)/Oct. 17 - 20

Publications:
Computers & Geosciences; semi-annually; adv.
Mathematical Geosciences; adv.
Natural Resources Research; adv.

International Association for Modular Exhibitry
(1987)
155 West St., Unit Three
Wilmington, MA 01887-3064
Tel: (978) 988-1100 *Fax:* (978) 988-1128
Members: 47 companies
Staff: 7
Annual Budget: $100-250,000

Personnel:
Executive Director: Irving Sacks
   E-Mail: isacks6421@aol.com

Historical Note:
IAME members are companies with an interest in promoting the use of modular exhibits for trade shows and museums.

International Association for Near Death Studies, Inc. (1981)
2741 Campus Walk Ave.
Building 500
Durham, NC 27705-8878
Tel: (919) 383-7940 *Fax:* (919) 383-7940
E-Mail: services@iand.org
Website: iands.org
Members: 1200 individuals
Staff: 3
Annual Budget: $100-250,000
Tax: 501(c)(3)

Personnel:
Business Manager and Assistant Editor: Rhonda Bailey
Editor: Bruce Greyson MD
Contact, Marketing and support: Marybeth Maranuk BA

Historical Note:
Formerly (1978) known as the Association for the Scientific Study of Near-Death Phenomena, IANDS' mission is to build global understanding of NDE's through research, education and support. Membership: $40-1,000/year.

Publications:
Journal of Near-Death Studies; quarterly
Vital Signs; quarterly

International Association for Orthodontics (1961)
750 N. Lincoln Memorial Dr.
Suite 422
Milwaukee, WI 53202
Tel: (414) 272-2757 *Fax:* (414) 272-2754
E-Mail: worldheadquarters@iaortho.org
Website: iaortho.org
Members: 4200 individuals
Staff: 5
Annual Budget: $500-1,000,000
Tax: 501(c)(6)

Personnel:
Executive Director: Detlef B. Moore
   E-Mail: director@iaortho.org
Coordinator, Membership Services: Jenn Baker-Batterman
   E-Mail: jennba@iaortho.org
Managing Editor: Mary Byers
   E-Mail: marybyers@comcast.net
Coordinator, Association Services: Jenny Fisher
   E-Mail: jenny@iaortho.org

Historical Note:
Formerly International Academy of Orthodontics. IAO's purpose is to promote an exchange of ideas and experiences based on a biomechanical approach, between the various fields of dentistry related to orthodontics. Membership: $114-259 (Doctor, developed countries); $109 (Doctor, developing countries); $25 (Dental Student); $50 (Auxiliary); $100 (Vendor).

Continuing Education:
Certification Designation/s: ACI

Meetings/Conferences: Annual
Conference Chair: Jenny Fisher
2013 - Universal City, CA (Sheraton Universal Hotel)/
   April 11 - 14

Publications:
International Journal of Orthodontics (IJO); quarterly
Membership Directory; on-line
Straight Talk

International Association for Philosophy and Literature *(1976)*
Stony Brook University, Department of Philosophy
Stony Brook, NY 11794-3750
Tel: (631) 331-4598 *Fax:* (631) 331-0142
Website: iapl.info
Members: 3000 individuals
Staff: 5
Annual Budget: $10-25,000

Personnel:
Executive Director and Program Coordinator: Hugh J. Silverman
   E-Mail: hugh.silverman@stonybrook.edu
Coordinator, Membership Services and Registrations: Claire C. Goberman
   E-Mail: iaplmembers@woh.rr.com
Coordinator, Conference On-Site Registration: Taylor Hammer
Coordinator, Book Exhibits: Aaron Krempa
Designer, Web and Online Processing: Vaibhav Shrivastava

Historical Note:
IAPL is dedicated to the exchange of ideas and scholarly research within the humanities. Members are scholars and educators interested in interdisciplinary approaches to philosophy and literature. Membership: $95 (Regular); $60 (Retired/Student); $700-900 (Lifetime/Supporting); $1,500 (Institutional).

Meetings/Conferences: Annual
Conference Chair: Taylor Hammer
2013 - Singapore, Singapore/June 3 - 9

Publications:
Membership DIrectory; on-line

International Association for the Study of Cooperation in Education *(1979)*
11 South Rd.
Readfield, ME 04355
Tel: (207) 685-3171 *Fax:* (207) 685-4455
Website: iasce.net
Members: 1000 individuals
Staff: 4
Annual Budget: $25-50,000

Personnel:
Treasurer: Kathryn Markovchick
   E-Mail: kathrynm@maine.edu
Editor, Newsletter: Lalita Agashe
   E-Mail: lalitaagashe@gmail.com
Editor: George M. Jacobs
   E-Mail: george@vegetarian-society.org
Secretary: Yael Sharan
   E-Mail: yaelshar@015.net.il

Historical Note:
IASCE supports development and dissemination of research, particularly educator research and inquiry that foster the understanding of cooperative learning. Members are educators and other professionals with an interest in the use of cooperative activities in education. Membership: $20-50 (Individual); $35-95 (Institutional).

Meetings/Conferences: Annual
2013 - Scarborough, United Kingdom (The University of Hull)/July 4 - 6
Number of non-conference events/year: 2

Publications:
IASCE Newsletter
Membership Directory; on-line

International Association for the Study of Dreams *(1983)*
1672 University Ave.
Berkeley, CA 94703
Tel: (209) 724-0889 *Fax:* (209) 724-0889
E-Mail: office@asdreams.org
Website: asdreams.org
Members: 800 individuals
Staff: 5
Annual Budget: $100-250,000

Personnel:
Scott: G. Scott Sparrow
   E-Mail: gssparrow@utpa.edu
Contact, Research Grants, Conference Chair: Robert J. Hoss
   E-Mail: robertjhoss@aol.com
Treasurer: David L. Kahn
   E-Mail: lucidreverie3@gmail.com
Chair, Publicity Committee: Wendy Pannier
   E-Mail: dreamwendy@verizon.net
Director, Operations and Contact, Website: Richard Wilkerson

Historical Note:
IASD was formerly Association for the Study of Dreams (ASD). IASD was established as a multidisciplinary organization to promote the scientific research into the study of dreams and to provide an educational forum for the interdisciplinary exchange of such information among the scientific and professional community and the general public. ASD's mission is to promote an awareness and appreciation of dreams in both professional and public arenas. Members are individuals with serious interests in dreams. Membership: $100 (Individual); $65 (Student/ Limited Income); $150 (Couple/Patron); $150- $300 (Affiliate Organization).

Meetings/Conferences: Semi-Annual
Conference Chair: Robert J. Hoss
2013 - Virginia Beach, VA (Virginia Beach Resort Hotel)/June 21 - 25

Publications:
Dream News; monthly
Dream Time; monthly; adv.
Dreaming; quarterly; adv.

International Association for the Study of Organized Crime *(1984)*
Department of Law, Police Science and Criminal Justice Administration
899 Tenth Ave., Suite 422-17
New York, NY 10019
Tel: (212) 237-8249
E-Mail: iasoc_office@yahoo.com
Website: iasoc.net
Members: 350 individuals
Staff: 2
Annual Budget: Under $10,000

Personnel:
Executive Director: Sharon Melzer
President: Klaus von Lampe

Historical Note:
IASOC's mission is to encourage understanding and research about organized crime in all its manifestations. Members are criminologists, researchers, working professionals, teachers, and students. Membership: $25/ year.

Meetings/Conferences: Annual

International Association for the Study of Pain *(1973)*
111 Queen Anne Ave. North
Suite 501
Seattle, WA 98109-4955
Tel: (206) 283-0311 *Fax:* (206) 283-9403
E-Mail: iaspdesk@iasp-pain.org
Website: iasp-pain.org
Members: 8,000 members in 129 countries, 87 national chapters, and 19 Special Interest Groups
Staff: 14
Annual Budget: $10-25,000,000
Tax: 501(c)(3)

Personnel:
Executive Director: Kathy Kreiter
   E-Mail: kreiter@iasp-pain.org
Director, Finance and Administration: Elena Bespalova
   E-Mail: elina.bespalova@iasp-pain.org
Coordinator, Membership Services: Marleda C. Di Pierri
   E-Mail: members@iasp-pain.org

Director, Publications: Ivar Nelson
   E-Mail: ivar.nelson@iasp-pain.org
Manager, Meetings and Education: Terry Onustack
   E-Mail: terry.onustack@iasp-pain.org
Manager, Web Marketing: Sarah Reebs
   E-Mail: sarah.reebs@asp-pain.org
Director, Membership, Marketing and Communications: Karen Smaalders
   E-Mail: karen.smaalders@iasp-pain.org

Historical Note:
IASP works to bring together scientists, clinicians, health care providers and policymakers to stimulate and support the study of pain, and to translate that knowledge into improved pain relief worldwide. Membership includes physicians, dentists, psychologists, nurses, physical therapists, pharmacists and other health professionals working in the pain field. Membership: $40-200 (Regular); $40-130 (Trainee/Retired); $1,000 (Affiliate).

Meetings/Conferences:
Conference Chair: Terry Onustack

Publications:
IASP Newsletter; quarterly
Membership Directory; on-line
Pain; monthly; adv.
Pain: Clinical Updates; monthly

Membership List Available to Non-members

International Association for Truancy and Dropout Prevention *(1911)*
1718 River Shore Dr.
Knoxville, TN 37914
Tel: (865) 546-4958
Website: iatdp.org
Members: 500 individuals and libraries
Staff: 4
Annual Budget: $10-25,000

Personnel:
Executive Director: Jimmie Thacker
   E-Mail: brendajimt@comcast.net
Contact, Meetings: Brenda Vallee
   E-Mail: bfvallee@bellsouth.net

Historical Note:
Founded as National League to Promote School Attendance; became International Association of Pupil Personnel Workers in 1957, and assumed its current name in 2004. IATDP's mission is to create a partnership which facilitates the dissemination of information, emerging practices and research designed to support learning and increase high school graduation rates. IATDP members are pupil personnel workers, social workers, educators, government officials, stakeholders and others concerned with school attendance. Membership: $50 (Regular); $30 (Student/ Retired); $400 (Life); $40 (Library).

Meetings/Conferences: Annual
Conference Chair: Brenda Vallee

Publications:
IATDP Journal; semi-annually
Membership Directory; annually

International Association of Accident Reconstruction Specialists *(1980)*
1804 Thornhill Pass SE
Conyers, GA 30013-6321
Tel: (770) 918-0973
Website: iaars.org
Members: 130 individuals
Staff: 2

Personnel:
President: Fred Rice
   E-Mail: fred.rice@isp.idaho.gov
Secretary: Ralph Cunningham
   E-Mail: ralph.cunningham@att.net

Historical Note:
IAARS is a professional association of civilian and law enforcement personnel who are involved in the field of accident reconstruction. Composed of members and associates from 38 states, as well as abroad. Membership comprised of law enforcement officers and civilian personnel. Membership: $50/year (Individual Member/ Member with Diplomate Status/Member with Fellow Status).

Publications:
Membership Directory; on-line
The SOARce; on-line

International Association of Addictions and Offender Counselors *(1972)*
Argosy University - Atlanta

980 Hammond Dr. Suite 100
Atlanta, GA 30328
Tel: (770) 407-1177
E-Mail: info@iaaoc.org
Website: iaaoc.org
Members: 958 individuals
Staff: 3

Personnel:
President: Geneva M. Gray LPC, NCC, PhD
    E-Mail: geneva_gray@yahoo.com

Historical Note:
Formerly (1990) Public Offenders Counselors Association. IAAOC's mission is to provide leadership in the advancement of the fields of addictions and offender counseling. A division of the American Counseling Association. Membership: $48 (Professional/Regular); $30 (New Professional/Student).

Meetings/Conferences: Annual

Publications:
IAAOC News Newsletter; quarterly; adv.
Journal of Addictions and Offender Counseling; biennially

Membership List Available to Non-members

International Association of Administrative Professionals (1942)

10502 NW Ambassador Dr.
Kansas City, MO 64153
Tel: (816) 891-6600 *Fax:* (816) 891-9118
Website: iaap-hq.org
Members: 22000 individuals and affiliates
Staff: 29
Annual Budget: $2-5,000,000
Tax: 501(c)(6)

Personnel:
Executive Director: Jay Donohue
    E-Mail: jay.donohue@iaap-hq.org
Manager, Communications and Publications: Emily Allen
    E-Mail: eallen@iaap-hq.org
Information Specialist: Creig Cooper
    E-Mail: ccooper@iaap-hq.org
Membership Project Specialist: Lisa Hicks
    E-Mail: lisa.hicks@iaap-hq.org

Historical Note:
Formerly (1981) National Secretaries Association (International). Incorporated in the State of Missouri. IAAP's mission is to enhance the success of career-minded administrative professionals by providing opportunities for growth through education, community building and leadership development. Membership: $83 (Professional); $50 (Student); $180 (Associate).

Continuing Education:
Certification Designation/s: CAP

Meetings/Conferences:
2013 - Anaheim, CA (Hilton Anaheim)/March 17 - 20
2013 - Anaheim, CA (Anaheim Marriott)/July 27 - 31
2014 - Milwaukee, WI (Milwaukee Convention Center)/July 26 - 30
2015 - Louisville, KY (Kentucky Internat'l Convention Center)/July 25 - 29

Publications:
IAAP Connections; monthly
OfficePRO
OfficePro Express (e-newsletter); monthly

Membership List Available to Non-members

International Association of Airport and Seaport Police (1968)

Port PD 425 S. Palos Verdes St.
San Pedro, CA 90731
Tel: (202) 595-9111 *Fax:* (202) 595-2035
E-Mail: info@InterPortPolice.org
Website: interportpolice.org
Staff: 7

Personnel:
President: Ronald J. Boyd

Historical Note:
InterPort Police comprised of jurisdictions serving their communities and nations around the world to ensure public safety of passengers, the supply chain, transnational crime and prevention of terrorism at airports, seaports and the transport system. Membership: $225.00-10,000 (Agency Member, depending on the no. of members); $200.00 (Former Official); $75.00 (Retired); $130.00-1,950 (Partner).

Publications:
IPASS White Paper

International Association of Airport Duty Free Stores (1966)

2025 M St. NW
Suite 800
Washington, DC 20036-3309
Tel: (202) 367-1184 *Fax:* (202) 429-5154
E-Mail: iaadfs@iaadfs.org
Website: iaadfs.org
Members: 500 companies
Staff: 6
Annual Budget: $2-5,000,000

Personnel:
Executive Director: Michael L. Payne
Associate Executive Director: Steven Antolick
Manager, Conventions: Christie Frey
Legal Counsel: Allan Hillman
Government Relations Coordinator: Jonathan Kent
Coordinator: Renee Lurker

Historical Note:
IAADFS's mission is to promote the airport duty free industry as an important segment of the international business community. Membership: $450/year (Company).

Meetings/Conferences: Annual
Conference Chair: Christie Frey
2013 - Orlando, FL (Orlando Convention Center)/April 7 - 11

Publications:
Membership Directory; on-line
Show News; daily; adv.

International Association of Amusement Parks and Attractions(IAAPA) (1918)

1448 Duke St.
Alexandria, VA 22314
Tel: (703) 836-4800 *Fax:* (703) 836-6742
E-Mail: iaapa@iaapa.org
Website: iaapa.org
Members: 4500 facility, supplier, and individual members
Staff: 36
Annual Budget: $10-25,000,000

Personnel:
Chief Executive Officer: James Chip Cleary
    E-Mail: ccleary@iaapa.org
Vice President, Exhibitor Marketing and Sales: Pete Barto
    E-Mail: pBarto@iaapa.org
Director, Publications: Amanda Charney
    E-Mail: acharney@iaapa.org
Senior Vice President, Safety & Advocacy: Randall "Randy" P. K. Davis
    E-Mail: rdavis@iaapa.org
Vice President, Education, Professional Development and Training Services: John Henderson
    E-Mail: jhenderson@iaapa.org
Vice President, Communications Services: David Mandt
    E-Mail: dmandt@iaapa.org
Incoming Chief Executive Officer: Paul Noland
Vice President, Membership and Marketing Services: Stephanie Robert
    E-Mail: sRobert@iaapa.org
Vice President, Exhibitions, Conferences, and Sales: Ryan Strowger
    E-Mail: rStrowger@iaapa.org
Director, Meetings and Events: Diane Williams
    E-Mail: dwilliams@iaapa.org

Historical Note:
Formed by merger of the National Association of Amusement Parks and the American Association of Pools and Beaches. Became (1964) the International Association of Amusement Parks; assumed its present name in 1972. Absorbed the National Water Slide Association in 1982. IAAPA's mission is to serve the membership by promoting safe operations, global development, professional growth, and commercial success of the amusement parks and attractions industry. Membership: $49 (Student); $432 (Individual); $463 (Manufacturer/Supplier/Consultant); $576-2,038 (Amusement Facilities); -2,038/year.

Continuing Education:
Certification Designation/s: CAM, CAP, CAE

Meetings/Conferences: Annual
Conference Chair: Diane Williams
2013 - Singapore, Singapore (Marina Bay Sands Casino)/June 4 - 7/4500 attendees/over 100 exhibitors
Number of non-conference events/year: 3

Publications:
Funworld; monthly; adv.

Membership Directory; on-line
Membership List Available to Non-members

International Association of Approved Basketball Officials, Inc. (1923)

P.O. Box 355
Carlisle, PA 17013-0355
Tel: (717) 713-8129 *Fax:* (717) 718-6164
Website: iaabo.org
Members: 16000 individuals
Staff: 2
Annual Budget: $500-1,000,000

Personnel:
Executive Director: Tommy Lopes
    E-Mail: tlopes@iaabo.org

Historical Note:
IAABO is a recruiting and training association for basketball officials. IAABO is a nonprofit service and professional organization managed by and for basketball referees. IAABO's purpose is to promote the welfare of the game basket ball. IAABO officials need to earn their membership by successful completion of training which includes written and practical testing. Membership: $40 (Individual); $35 (Renewal); $35 (Honorary/New/Provisional); $5 (Dual); $0 (Life).

Publications:
Sportorials; irregular

International Association of Aquatic and Marine Science Libraries and Information Centers (1975)

Oregon State Univ., Hatfield Marine Science Center
2030 S. Marine Science Dr.
Newport, OR 97365
Tel: (541) 867-0108 *Fax:* (541) 867-0105
Website: iamslic.org
Members: 350 libraries and information center
Staff: 4
Annual Budget: Under $10,000

Personnel:
President: Maria Kalentsits
Contact, Membership Services: Kristen L. Metzger
    E-Mail: kmetzger@conshelf.com
Contact, Communications: Janet Webster
    E-Mail: janet.webster@oregonstate.edu

Historical Note:
Formerly (1975) the Marine Science Library Association. Became the International Association of Marine Science Libraries and Information Centers and assumed its present name in 1978. IAMSLIC provides a forum for exchange and exploration of ideas and issues of mutual concern. Membership: $50 (Prospective members from high-income countries); $20 (Prospective members from low and middle income countries/Retired).

Meetings/Conferences: Annual
2013 - Dania Beach, FL/Oct. 20 - 24

Publications:
IAMSLIC Newsletter; on-line
Membership Directory; on-line

International Association of Arson Investigators (1949)

2111 Baldwin Ave.
Suite 203
Crofton, MD 21114
Tel: (410) 451-3473 *Fax:* (410) 451-9049
E-Mail: iaai@firearson.com
Website: firearson.com
Members: 5,000 fire investigation professionals
Staff: 7
Annual Budget: $1-2,000,000
Tax: 501(c)(3)

Personnel:
Executive Director: Deborah Neitch
    E-Mail: deborah.neitch@firearson.com
Director, Governmental Relations: Stephen P. Austin
    E-Mail: steveaustin@earthlink.net
Regional Training Director: Deb Bell
    E-Mail: deb.bell@firearson.com
Contact, Certification and Membership: Christine Burt
    E-Mail: chris.burt@firearson.com
Legal Counsel: William A. LeMire
    E-Mail: walemire@arthurchapman.com
Manager, Finance and Accounts: Debra Miller
    E-Mail: debra.miller@firearson.com
Director, Administration: Gloria Gaemsey Ryan
    E-Mail: gloria.ryan@firearson.com

Historical Note:
IAAI is committed to suppress the crime of arson through professional fire investigation. Members are private investigators, law enforcement officers, fire service personnel, attorneys, researchers, educators, and insurance industry representatives. Membership: $75 (Active/ Associate); $25 (Retired/Student).

Continuing Education:
Certification Designation/s: FIT, ECT, CI, CFI

Meetings/Conferences: Annual
2013 - Orlando, FL (Rosen Centre Hotel)/May 5 - 10
Number of non-conference events/year: 2

Publications:
Membership Directory; on-line
The Fire and Arson Investigator; quarterly; adv.

International Association of Art Critics (1949)
London Terrace Stn.
P.O. Box 20533
New York, NY 10011
E-Mail: board@aicausa.org
Website: aicausa.org
Members:
64 member nations
4000 art critics
Staff: 2
Annual Budget: $25-50,000

Personnel:
President: Marek Bartelik
Vice President, Membership: Christopher French

Historical Note:
The U. S. branch of the international organization, headquartered in Paris, France. Each year, AICA USA presents museums, galleries and alternative spaces with Best Show awards. Award excellence in museum and gallery exhibitions. Has no paid officers or full-time staff. Membership: $60 (Initial); $45 (Renewal).

Meetings/Conferences:
Number of non-conference events/year: 1

Publications:
AICA E-Newsletter; on-line

International Association of Assessing Officers (1934)
314 W. Tenth St.
Kansas City, MO 64105-1616
Tel: (816) 701-8100 *Fax:* (816) 701-8149
TollFree: (800) 616-4226
Website: iaao.org
Members: 7300 individuals
Staff: 22
Annual Budget: $2-5,000,000
Tax: 501(c)(3)

Personnel:
Executive Director: Lisa Daniels MPA
    E-Mail: daniels@iaao.org
Director, Publications and Marketing: Christopher Bennett
    E-Mail: bennett@iaao.org
Director, Administration: Angela Blazevic AAS
    E-Mail: blazevic@iaao.org
Director, Professional Development: Larry Clark CAE
    E-Mail: clark@iaao.org
Accounting Manager: Mary Ann Deming
    E-Mail: deming@iaao.org
Director, Meetings: Aubrey Moore
    E-Mail: moore@iaao.org
Director, Membership Services: Robin Parrish
    E-Mail: parrish@iaao.org
Technology and Data Coordinator: Aaron Weatherford
    E-Mail: weatherford@iaao.org

Historical Note:
Formerly (1959) the National Association of Assessing Officers. IAAO's mission is to promote innovation and excellence in property appraisal, assessment administration, and property tax policy through professional development, education, research, and technical assistance. Members are professionals involved in the administration of property assessments. Membership: $175 (Regular); $180 (Associate).

Continuing Education:
Certification Designation/s: RES, PPS, CAE, AAS, CMS

Meetings/Conferences: Annual
Conference Chair: Aubrey Moore
2013 - Grand Rapids, MI/Aug. 25 - 28
2014 - Sacramento, CA/Aug. 24 - 27
2015 - Indianapolis, IN/Sept. 13 - 16
2016 - Tampa, FL/Aug. 28 - 31

Number of non-conference events/year: 6

Publications:
Fair & Equitable; monthly; adv.
IAAO On-line Vendor & Consultants Directory; on-line; adv.
Journal of Property Tax Assessment & Administration; quarterly; adv.

Membership List Available to Non-members

International Association of Attorneys and Executives in Corporate Real Estate (1990)
20106 S. Sycamore Dr.
Frankfort, IL 60423
Tel: (815) 464-6019 *Fax:* (815) 464-8334
E-Mail: lcarreras@aecre.org
Website: aecre.org
Members: 155 members
Staff: 2
Annual Budget: $50-100,000
Tax: 501(c)(6)

Personnel:
Executive Vice President and Director: Lisa Carreras
    E-Mail: lcarreras@aecre.org

Historical Note:
AECRE provides a collegial forum for real estate executives and attorneys to explore corporate real estate issues of common interest. It also sponsors educational programs, including workshops. Membership is sponsored and by invitation only. Membership: $380 (Regular); $200 (Add-on, members from organizations with one current member enrolled at the regular rate); $190 (Retired/Non-Profit/ Academic).

Meetings/Conferences: Annual
2013 - Washington, DC/April 25 - 27

Publications:
Corporate Real Estate and The Law; on-line; adv.
Membership Directory; on-line

International Association of Audio Information Services (1977)
P.O. Box 847
Lawrence, KS 66044
Tel: (416) 422-4222 *Fax:* (785) 864-5278
TollFree: (800) 280-5325
E-Mail: info@iaais.org
Website: iaais.org
Members: 140 reading services
Staff: 3
Annual Budget: $50-100,000
Tax: 501(c)(3)

Personnel:
President: Kim Walsh
    E-Mail: kwalsh@wdetfm.org
Vice President, Public Affairs: Stuart Holland
    E-Mail: stuart.holland@state.mn.us
Chair, Membership Committee and Administrative Assistant: Lori Kesinger
    E-Mail: lrk@ku.edu

Historical Note:
Formerly (1999) known as the Association of Radio Reading Services. IAAIS strives to encourage and support the establishment and maintenance of audio information services that provide access to printed information for individuals who cannot read conventional print because of blindness or any other visual, physical or learning disability. Membership open to audio information services for blind and other print-handicapped persons. Membership: $200 (Full/Sustaining); $50 (Satellite); $100 (Associate).

Meetings/Conferences: Annual
Conference Chair: Stuart Holland

Publications:
IAAIS Directory; annually
The IAAIS Report; monthly

Membership List Available to Non-members

International Association of Audio Visual Communicators (1957)
1339 Shell Canyon Rd.
P.O. Box 250
Ocotillo, CA 92259-0250
Tel: (760) 358-7000 *Fax:* (760) 358-7569
Website: iaavc.org/
Members: 5200 individuals
Staff: 4
Annual Budget: $500-1,000,000

Personnel:
Executive Director: Philip N. Shug

Historical Note:
Founded as Industry Film Producer Association; later became Information Film Producers of America. Became (1985) Association of Visual Communicators, and assumed its current name in 1997. Members are audio- visual professionals using the media of film, video, the internet and interactive media to communicate information. Membership: $100/year (individual), $20/year (full-time student); $275 - $1,000 (3 - 20 members).

Meetings/Conferences:
Number of non-conference events/year: 2

Membership List Available to Non-members

International Association of Auto Theft Investigators (1952)
P.O. Box 223
Clinton, NY 13323-0223
Tel: (315) 853-1913 *Fax:* (315) 883-1310
Website: iaati.org
Members: 3,604 individuals
Staff: 2
Annual Budget: $250-500,000

Personnel:
Executive Director: John V. Abounader
    E-Mail: jvabounader@iaati.org
Treasurer: Robert C. Hasbrouck

Historical Note:
IAATI is dedicated to developing and encouraging the professional standards of conduct among auto theft investigators, and strives to eliminate all factors interfering with the administration of the auto theft suppression effort. Affiliate members are from the insurance industry, car rental firms, and various automobile associations. Membership: $45 (New); $40 (Renewal).

Meetings/Conferences: Annual

Publications:
APB; quarterly; adv.
E-News; bi-monthly; adv.
Membership Directory; on-line

International Association of Baptist Colleges and Universities (1949)
8120 Sawyer Brown Rd.
Suite 108
Nashville, TN 37221-1410
Tel: (615) 673-1896 *Fax:* (615) 662-1396
Website: baptistschools.org
Members: 52 member schools
Staff: 3
Annual Budget: $100-250,000
Tax: 501(c)(3)

Personnel:
Executive Director: Michael Arrington
    E-Mail: marrington@baptistschools.org
Associate Director: Tim Fields
    E-Mail: tim_fields@baptistschools.org

Historical Note:
Incorporated as the Southern Association of Baptist Colleges and Schools in 1949, changed its name to the Association of Southern Baptist Colleges and Schools and assumed its current name in 2006. IABCU's mission is to help students find the right school and find the resources needed to make education possible. Members are presidents and chief academic officials of Baptist colleges, universities, Bible schools and academies.

Meetings/Conferences: Annual

Publications:
The Baptist Educator Online; on-line

International Association of Bedding and Furniture Law Officials (1936)
6758 Crump Dr.
Mechanicsville, VA 23111
Tel: (860) 713-6123
Website: abflo.info
Members: 30 individuals
Staff: 2
Annual Budget: Under $10,000

Personnel:
Treasurer: Margaret Davis

Historical Note:
Founded as ABFLO (Association of Bedding and Furniture Law Officials), assumed its current name in 2003. IABFLO strives and actively promotes uniformity in laws, terminology, test methods, and enforcement procedures within the various state programs. Members are state officials who are responsible for the enforcement of consumer oriented bedding and furniture laws in their

respective states. *Membership: $50 (Regular); $150 (Associate).*

Meetings/Conferences: Annual
2013 - Williamsburg, VA (Williamsburg Lodge)/April
    10 - 11

Publications:
IABFLO Newsletter

International Association of Black Professional Fire Fighters *(1970)*
1020 N. Taylor Ave.
St. Louis, MO 63113
Tel: (513) 226-6940 *Fax:* (314) 558-4132
TollFree: (877) 213-2170
E-Mail: office@iabpff.org
Website: iabpff.org
Members: 5100 individuals and 90 chapters
Staff: 8
Annual Budget: $100-250,000

Personnel:
Executive Director: Jeff Harris
Treasurer: Sam Aubrey

Historical Note:
IABPFF's mission is to create a community of black firefighters globally and advocate on their behalf. Members are black firefighters and related professionals. Membership: $30 (Individual/Organization); $350 (Corporation). A member in good standing in their local chapter who retires from active duty (fire service) shall pay a one-time membership fee of $100.00 to the IABPFF.

Continuing Education:
Certification Designation/s: EDI

International Association of Bridge, Structural, Ornamental and Reinforcing Iron Workers *(1896)*
1750 New York Ave. NW
Suite 400
Washington, DC 20006
Tel: (202) 383-4800 *Fax:* (202) 638-4856
E-Mail: iwmagazine@iwintl.org
Website: ironworkers.org
Members: 120000 individuals
Staff: 70
Annual Budget: $10-25,000,000

Personnel:
President: Walter Wise
Political and Legislative Representative: David L. Kolbe
    E-Mail: dkolbe@iwintl.org

Historical Note:
Formerly (1896) the International Association of Bridge and Structural Iron Workers, Chartered by the American Federation of Labor in 1903, (1917) the International Association of Bridge, Structural and Ornamental Iron Workers and Pile Drivers and (1997) International Association of Bridge, Structural and Ornamental Iron Workers. IABSORIW's mission is to ensure that all workers who possess ironworker skills, through the efforts of organization, gain the benefits and protection of union affiliation.

Meetings/Conferences: Annual
Number of non-conference events/year: 2

Publications:
Membership Directory; on-line
The Ironworker; monthly

International Association of Broadcast Monitors *(1981)*
7604 Big Bend Blvd.
Suite D
St. Louis, MO 63119
Tel: (314) 646-7984 *Fax:* (314) 504-1044
E-Mail: info@iabm.com
Website: iabm.com
Members: 110 companies
Staff: 2
Tax: 501(c)(6)

Personnel:
Secretary and Treasurer: Jack McCarthy
    E-Mail: jmccarthy@iabm.com

Historical Note:
IABM's purpose is to foster the exchange of goodwill among its members; encourage the exchange and dissemination of industry information among its members; act as the spokesperson for the broadcast monitoring industry and secure co-operative action in advancing common purposes to the members of the association. Membership: $199

(Monitoring Company Members/Associate Members); $50 (Affiliate); $395 (Supporting Members).

Meetings/Conferences: Annual
2013 - Las Vegas, NV (Las Vegas Convention Center)/
    April 6 - 11/11-25 exhibitors

International Association of Business Communicators *(1970)*
601 Montgomery St.
Suite 1900
San Francisco, CA 94111
Tel: (415) 544-4700 *Fax:* (415) 544-4747
TollFree: (800) 776-4222
Website: iabc.com
Members: 15000 business communication
professionals
Staff: 34
Annual Budget: $5-10,000,000
Tax: 501(c)(6)

Personnel:
Executive Director: Chris Sorek
Senior Software Engineer: Isaac Chapman
Vice President, Professional Development: Michele
    Cushnie PhD
Senior Vice President, Education: Chris Grossgart
Senior Vice President and Chief Information Officer: Chris
    Hall
    E-Mail: chall@iabc.com
Director, Conferences and Events: Charles Herrick
    E-Mail: cherrick@iabc.com
Vice President, Finance and Human Resource: Maureen
    Lennon
    E-Mail: mlennon@iabc.com
Executive Editor: Natasha Nicholson
    E-Mail: nspring@iabc.com
*Senior Vice President, Global Membership Marketing and
    Development:* Lee Anne Snedeker
    E-Mail: lasnedeker@iabc.com
Vice President Marketing and Communication: Paige
    Wesley

Historical Note:
IABC is the product of a merger (1970) of the International Council of Industrial Editors (1941) and the American Association of Industrial Editors (1938). Absorbed Corporate Communicators Canada (1942) in 1974. The purpose of IABC is to provide products, services, activities and networking opportunities to help people and organizations achieve excellence in public relations, employee communication, marketing communication, public affairs and other forms of communication. Members are communication and public relations professionals. Membership: $163-324/year; $10-65 (Chapter/Regional).

Meetings/Conferences:
Conference Chair: Charles Herrick
2013 - New York City, NY (Hilton New York)/June 23 -
    26
2014 - Toronto, ON (Sheraton Centre Toronto Hotel)/
    June 8 - 11
2015 - San Francisco, CA (San Francisco Marriott
    Marquis)/June 14 - 17
2016 - New Orleans, LA (Hilton New Orleans
    Riverside)/June 5 - 8
Number of non-conference events/year: 4

Publications:
Communication World; adv.
CW Bulletin; monthly

International Association of Campus Law Enforcement Administrators *(1958)*
342 N. Main St.
Hartford, CT 06117-2507
Tel: (860) 586-7517 *Fax:* (860) 586-7550
E-Mail: info@iaclea.org
Website: iaclea.org
Members:
2600 institutions
1700 individuals
Staff: 10
Annual Budget: $1-2,000,000

Personnel:
Chief Staff Officer: Peter J. Berry CAE
    E-Mail: pberry@iaclea.org
Director of Corporate Relations: Susan Koczka
    E-Mail: skoczka@iaclea.org
Director, Accreditation and LEMAP Programs: John
    Leonard
    E-Mail: jleonard@iaclea.org
Director, Meetings and Events: Elizabeth Pillsworth CMP

E-Mail: epillsworth@iaclea.org
Coordinator , Membership Services: Deborah Rondeau
    E-Mail: drondeau@iaclea.org

Historical Note:
Formerly National Association of College and University Security Directors, (1980) International Association of College and University Security Directors. IACLEA advances public safety for educational institutions by providing educational resources, advocacy, and professional development services. Membership: $100 (Professional/ Affiliate); $60 (Associate); $300 (Supporting); $30 (Retired); $250-425 (Institutional).

Meetings/Conferences: Annual
Conference Chair: Elizabeth Pillsworth CMP
2013 - Louisville, KY (Kentucky International
    Convention Center)/June 28 - July 2
2014 - Montreal, QC/June 20 - 24
2015 - Nashville, TN/June 29 - July 3
Number of non-conference events/year: 1

Publications:
The Campus Law Enforcement Journal; bi-monthly;
    adv.

International Association of Career Consulting Firms *(1987)*
C/O Champion Career Consultants
5550 Wild Rose Ln. Suite 400
Des Moines, IA 50266
Tel: (515) 661-6184
TollFree: (800) 736-8840
Website: iaccf.org
Members: 14 firms
Staff: 2
Annual Budget: $25-50,000

Personnel:
President: Kaye Jones
Secretary: Judy Alexander

Historical Note:
Founded as National Association of Career Development Consultants; assumed its current name in 1992. IACCF's mission is to establish and enforce a code of self-regulating ethics in the advertising, marketing and delivery of consulting practices for client success and satisfaction. Has no paid officers or full-time staff. Membership: $50 (IACCF member); $500(non IACCF member).

Continuing Education:
Certification Designation/s: RCC

International Association of Certified Thermographers *(2006)*
38 Raft Island Dr. NW
Gig Harbor, WA 98335
Tel: (253) 509-3742
E-Mail: info@iactthermography.org
Website: iactthermography.org
Staff: 2

Personnel:
Secretary: Chris Troutt
    E-Mail: condir@iactthermography.org
Treasurer: Scott Woods

Historical Note:
IACT's mission is to build consumer awareness of the importance of infrared thermography in all three areas of focus (building sciences, condition monitoring, and medical applications) and to enhance the professionalism of current and future thermographers. Membership: $125 (Certified Individual); $300 (Non-Certified Individual); $750- 1,000 (Associate).

Publications:
Newsletter

Membership List Available to Non-members

International Association of Chiefs of Police *(1893)*
515 N. Washington St.
Alexandria, VA 22314-2340
Tel: (703) 836-6767 *Fax:* (703) 836-4543
TollFree: (800) 843-4227
E-Mail: information@theiacp.org
Website: theiacp.org
Members: 20000 individuals
Staff: 132
Annual Budget: $10-25,000,000

Personnel:
Executive Director: Daniel N. Rosenblatt
    E-Mail: rosenblatt@theiacp.org
Program Manager: Carolyn Cockroft
    E-Mail: cockroftc@theiacp.org

Manager, Membership Services: Christian D. Faulkner
    E-Mail: faulkner@theiacp.org
Coordinator, Advertising: B. J. Hendrickson
    E-Mail: hendrickson@theiacp.org
Chief Financial Officer: Michele Henry CFE, CPA
    E-Mail: henrym@theiacp.org
Contact, Education and Training: Charles Higginbotham
    E-Mail: higginboth@theiacp.org
Contact, Conferences: Mara Johnston
    E-Mail: johnstonm@theiacp.org
Manager, Legislative and Media Affairs: Meredith Mays
    E-Mail: mays@theiacp.org
Senior Program Manager, Communications and Technology:
    David J. Roberts
    E-Mail: Roberts@theiacp.org
Managing Editor: Kerry Sullivan
    E-Mail: sullivan@theiacp.org
Legal Officer and Director, State Associations of Chiefs of
    Police: Gene Voegtlin
    E-Mail: voegtling@theiacp.org
Manager, Legislative and Media Affairs: Meredith Ward
    E-Mail: WardM@theiacp.org

Historical Note:
Formerly (1895) the National Chiefs of Police Union,
(1898) the National Association of Chiefs of Police, (1902)
the Chiefs of Police of the United States and Canada.
IACP's purpose is to advance the science and art of
police services and to develop and disseminate improved
administrative, technical and operational practices and
promote their use in police work. Membership consists of
the operating chief executives of international, federal, state
and local agencies of all sizes. Membership: $120/year
(Active/Associate).

Meetings/Conferences: Annual
Conference Chair: Mara Johnston
2013 - Philadelphia, PA/Oct. 19 - 23/51-100 exhibitors
2014 - Orlando, FL/Oct. 25 - 29/over 100 exhibitors

Publications:
Police Chief; monthly; adv.

International Association of Clerks, Recorders, Election Officials and Treasurers (1971)
2400 Augusta Dr.
Suite 250
Houston, TX 77057-0296
Tel: (713) 725-1982 Fax: (713) 789-1897
TollFree: (800) 890-7368
Website: iacreot.com
Members: 2000 individuals and companies
Staff: 5
Annual Budget: $250-500,000

Personnel:
Executive Director: Tony J. Sirvello III
    E-Mail: tjsthree@msn.com
Chair, Education and Training: Judith Beaudreau
    E-Mail: judithbeaudreau@gmail.com
Director, Trade Shows: Margaret "Peggy" Sparks
    E-Mail: pegysparks@att.net

Historical Note:
IACREOT's mission is to provide a forum for the exchange
of information among government officials, to improve
the standards of operation that will best serve the public,
to encourage the passage of uniform laws governing the
operation of state and local offices, and to provide a unified
voice on matters of importance to governmental officials.
Membership: $195 (Full/Member-At-Large/Life First Year),
$145 (Deputies/Deputy of Corporate), $500 (Corporate);
$20 (Life).

Continuing Education:
Certification Designation/s: CCP

Meetings/Conferences: Semi-Annual
Conference Chair: Tony J. Sirvello III
2013 - Savannah, GA (The Mulberry Inn)/Jan. 10 - 15
2013 - Louisville, KY/June 27 - July 1

Publications:
Enewsletter; monthly

International Association of Clothing Designers and Executives (1911)
835 NW 36th Ter.
Oklahoma City, OK 73118
Tel: (405) 602-8037 Fax: (405) 602-8038
E-Mail: newyorkiacde@cox.net
Website: iacde.net
Members: 400 individuals
Staff: 2
Annual Budget: $50-100,000

Personnel:

President: Joachim Hensch
Treasurer: Dr. Heino , Freudenberg

Historical Note:
Founded as the National Association of Clothing Designers,
changed its name in 1919 to International Association
of Clothing Designers, and assumed present name in
1994. IACDE functions as a forum for the discussion
of professional problems encountered by duly accredited
members of the IACDE. Membership figure includes both
designers and industrial members. Membership: $400
(Manufacturing Executives/Retail Tailoring Directors/
Executives/Designer/Education); $700 (Industrial).

Publications:
Newsletter

International Association of Color Manufacturers (1972)
1620 I St. NW
Suite 925
Washington, DC 20006
Tel: (202) 293-5800 Fax: (202) 463-8998
E-Mail: info@iacmcolor.org
Website: iacmcolor.org
Members: 15 companies
Staff: 5
Annual Budget: $100-250,000

Personnel:
President and Treasurer: Joseph D. Kern
Director, Communications: Mathew Gulick
    E-Mail: mgulick@vertosolutions.net

Historical Note:
Manufacturers of certified colors for food, drugs,
and cosmetics. Formerly (1993) the Certified Color
Manufacturers Association. The mission of the IACM is
to actively represent the interests of the regulated color
industry by demonstrating the safety of color additives,
and to promote the industry's economic growth by actively
participating in new color approvals and regulatory and
legislative issues that affect the industry worldwide.

Publications:
Member Directory; on-line

International Association of Commercial Collectors (2010)
4040 W. 70th St.,
Minneapolis, MN 55435
Tel: (952) 925-0760 Fax: (952) 926-1624
E-Mail: iacc@commercialcollector.com
Website: commercialcollector.com
Staff: 1
Annual Budget: $100-250,000

Personnel:
Executive Director: Tammy Schoenberg
    E-Mail: schoenberg@commercialcollector.com

Historical Note:
IACC's mission is to contribute to the growth and
profitability of its members by delivering essential
educational and professional tools and services in a highly
collaborative and participatory environment.

Meetings/Conferences: Annual
2013 - Miami Beach, FL (Eden Roc Renaissance Miami
    Beach)/Jan. 16 - 18

Publications:
Membership Directory; on-line
Scope Newsletter

International Association of Conference Center Administrators (1976)
P.O. Box 298
Church Hill, MD 21623
Tel: (443) 282-5858
E-Mail: admin@iacca.org
Website: iacca.org
Members: 285 individuals
Staff: 2
Annual Budget: $50-100,000

Personnel:
President: Pam Harris
    E-Mail: pam@runriver.net
Secretary and Treasurer: Rex Miller

Historical Note:
IACCA provides a supportive community that facilitates the
sharing of knowledge and experience and the addressing
of common challenges. Membership: $245 (Executive/
Associate); $95 (Business Associate); $25 (Student); $70
(Affiliate); $340-465 (Member Center, based on executive
and associate members).

Continuing Education:

Certification Designation/s: CCCP

Meetings/Conferences: Annual

Publications:
Member Directory; on-line

International Association of Conference Centers (1981)
243 N. Lindbergh Blvd.
St. Louis, MO 63141
Tel: (314) 993-8575 Fax: (314) 993-8919
E-Mail: info@iacconline.org
Website: iacconline.org
Members:
300 organizations
128 individuals
Staff: 5
Annual Budget: $500-1,000,000
Tax: 501(c)(6)

Personnel:
Executive Vice President: Tom Bolman CAE
    E-Mail: tbolman@iacconline.ORG
Director, Marketing and Public Relations: James Mahon
    E-Mail: jmmahon@aol.com
Director, Administration: Michele Schurk
    E-Mail: mschurk@iacconline.org
Director, Education and Technology: Jerry L. White
    E-Mail: jwhite@iacconline.ORG

Historical Note:
IACC's mission is to assist its members in providing the
most productive meeting facilities around the world.
Member facilities represent prominent venues available to
meeting professionals on a global basis. IACC also collects
and distributes information on the industry and its trends.
Membership: $600-3750/year.

Meetings/Conferences: Annual
2013 - Chicago, IL/March 19 - 22
Number of non-conference events/year: 1

Publications:
CenterLines
IACC Around the Globe
Membership Directory; annually

International Association of Correctional Training Personnel (1974)
P.O. Box 473254
Aurora, CO 80047
Tel: (877) 884-2287 Fax: (719) 738-9969
TollFree: (877) 884-2287
E-Mail: iactp@correctionsmail.com
Website: iactp.org
Members: 450 individuals
Staff: 6
Annual Budget: Under $10,000
Tax: 501(c)(6)

Personnel:
Editor: Linda Dunbar
    E-Mail: LSdunbar@embarqmail.com
Secretariat: Ed Wolahan

Historical Note:
Formerly (1992) the American Association of Correctional
Training Personnel. Formed in Carbondale, IL to improve
the quality of correctional training. IACTP's mission is to
enhance public safety and the fair and humane treatment
of offenders by promoting organizational and individual
excellence in the profession of training. Membership: $50
(Individual/Library); $35 (Full-Time Student); $200-1200
(Agency).

Continuing Education:
Certification Designation/s: TC, CTCC

Meetings/Conferences: Annual
Conference Chair: Terry Satterfield

Publications:
Membership Directory; on-line
The Correctional Trainer; quarterly; adv.

Membership List Available to Non-members

International Association of Counseling Services (1972)
101 S. Whiting St.
Suite 211
Alexandria, VA 22304
Tel: (703) 823-9840 Fax: (703) 823-9843
E-Mail: iacsinc@earthlink.net
Website: iacsinc.org
Members: 83 Organizations
Staff: 2

Annual Budget: $100-250,000
Tax: 501(c)(3)

Personnel:
Executive Director: Nancy E. Roncketti MS
    E-Mail: acsinc@earthlink.net
Administrative Assistant: Rattana Thanagosol
    E-Mail: iacsadmin@earthlink.net

Historical Note:
IACS's mission is to encourage and aid counseling services throughout the United States and to foster communication among counseling services operating in a variety of settings. Membership: $1000/year (Company).

Publications:
IACS Newsletter

International Association of Counselors and Therapists *(1990)*
8852 SR 3001
Laceyville, PA 18623
Tel: (570) 869-1021 *Fax:* (570) 869-1249
TollFree: (800) 553-6886
E-Mail: info@iact.org
Website: iact.org
Members:
5000 individuals
140 classrooms
Staff: 11
Annual Budget: $50-100,000

Personnel:
Executive Director: Linda Otto
Membership Services Coordinator: Christie Boecker
Contact, Information Technology: Steve Latimer
Liaison, Conference: Christa Otto
President and Chief Executive Officer: Robert Otto
    E-Mail: rfotto@epix.net
Administrative Assistant: Joann Wright

Historical Note:
IACT is an association for holistic practitioners that provides a forum for its members to exchange ideas, information, techniques and methodologies. Members includes Medical practitioners, psychologists, clinical social workers, stress consultants, NLP practitioners, clergy, licensed massage therapists, hypnotherapists, biofeedback specialists, nutritionists, educators, Mental health therapists, substance abuse counselors and others in the helping, healing arts. Membership: $95/year (Individual/Associate).

Continuing Education:
Certification Designation/s: CMT

Meetings/Conferences: Annual
Conference Chair: Christa Otto
2013 - Daytona Beach, FL (Daytona Hilton)/May 17 - 19

Publications:
Ask The Professional; monthly
Member Directory; on-line
Unlimited Human! Magazine; annually; adv.

International Association of Credit Portfolio Managers *(2001)*
360 Madison Ave.
17th Floor
New York, NY 10017-7111
Tel: (646) 289-5430 *Fax:* (646) 289-5429
E-Mail: dara@iacpm.org
Website: iacpm.org
Members: 86 financial institutions
Staff: 6
Annual Budget: $2-5,000,000

Personnel:
Executive Director: Som-lok Leung
    E-Mail: somlok@iacpm.org
Manager, Administration and Meetings Planner: Debbie Devine
    E-Mail: debbie@iacpm.org
Research: Juliane Sarry Littman
    E-Mail: juliane@iacpm.org
Director, Membership Services: Argie Simon
    E-Mail: argie@iacpm.org

Historical Note:
The IACPM is an industry association established to further the practice of credit exposure management by providing an active forum for its member institutions to exchange ideas on topics of common interest. Membership is open to all types of financial institutions managing portfolios of credit assets including banks, non-banks, regional entities and asset managers. Membership: $18000(Full); $9000 (Affiliate); $9000 (Associate).

Continuing Education:
Certification Designation/s: CFA

Meetings/Conferences:
Conference Chair: Debbie Devine
Number of non-conference events/year: 5

Publications:
IACPM Smartbrief; weekly
Membership Directory; on-line

International Association of Culinary Professionals *(1978)*
1221 Avenue of the Americas
42nd floor
New York, NY 10020
Tel: (646) 358-4957 *Fax:* (866) 358-2524
TollFree: (866) 358-4951
E-Mail: info@iacp.com
Website: iacp.com
Members: 3000 individuals
Staff: 11
Annual Budget: $1-2,000,000
Tax: 501(c)(6)

Personnel:
Executive Director: Meredith Deeds
    E-Mail: meredith@iacp.com
Associate, Member Engagement: Laura Atkinson
    E-Mail: communications@iacp.com
Director, Marketing: Margaret Bradley-Foley
    E-Mail: iacp.partners@gmail.com
Director, Communications and Content: Martha Holmberg
    E-Mail: communications@iacp.com
Director, Operations: Judith Klinger
    E-Mail: partnerprogram@iacp.com

Historical Note:
Formerly Association of Cooking Schools; became (1985) International Association of Cooking Schools; (1988) International Association of Cooking Professionals and assumed its current name in 1990. IACP provides continuing education and development for its members who are engaged in the areas of culinary education, communication, or in the preparation of food and drink. Membership: $85-1,005/year.

Continuing Education:
Certification Designation/s: CCP

Meetings/Conferences: Annual
Conference Chair: Judith Klinger
2013 - San Francisco, CA (Hyatt Embarcadero Hotel)/ April 6 - 9

Publications:
Frontburner; monthly
Membership Directory; on-line; adv.

International Association of Defense Counsel *(1920)*
303 W. Madison
Suite 925
Chicago, IL 60606
Tel: (312) 368-1494 *Fax:* (312) 368-1854
E-Mail: info@iadclaw.org
Website: iadclaw.org
Members: 2500 individuals
Staff: 10
Annual Budget: $2-5,000,000
Tax: 501(c)(6)

Personnel:
Executive Director: Mary Beth Kurzak
    E-Mail: mkurzak@iadclaw.org
Administrative Assistant: Liz Anderson
    E-Mail: landerson@iadclaw.org
Senior Manager, Membership Services: Carmela Balice
    E-Mail: cbalice@iadclaw.org
Managing Editor: Bob Greenlee Esq.
    E-Mail: rgreenlee@iadclaw.org
Director, Professional Development: Amy O'Maley Esq.
    E-Mail: aomaley@iadclaw.org
Coordinator, Communications: Elizabeth Okoro
    E-Mail: eokoro@iadclaw.org
Director, Meetings: Rebecca Zurcher
    E-Mail: rzurcher@iadclaw.org

Historical Note:
Formerly (1986) International Association of Insurance Counsel. IADC is dedicated to serve and benefit members, the legal profession, and the civil justice system by enhancing the development of skills, professionalism, and camaraderie in the practice of law. Members are defense attorneys and insurance and corporate counsel; membership is by invitation only. Membership: $580/year.

Meetings/Conferences:
Conference Chair: Rebecca Zurcher
2013 - Boca Raton, FL (Boca Raton Resort and Club)/ Feb. 9 - 14
2013 - Maui, HI (Grand Waila Resort)/July 7 - 12
2013 - Stanford, CA (Stanford Law School)/July 25 - Aug. 2
2014 - Carlsbad, CA (Four Seasons Hotels and Resorts)/Feb. 18 - 23
2014 - Vienna, Austria (Hilton Vienna)/July 5 - 10
2015 - Marco Island, FL (Marriot Marco Island)/Feb. 14 - 19
2015 - Colorado Springs, CO (The Broadmoor)/July 5 - 10
2016 - Pebble Beach, CA (Lodge at Pebble Beach)/Feb. 20 - 25
Number of non-conference events/year: 4

Publications:
Committee Newsletters; weekly
Defense Counsel Journal; quarterly

International Association of Diecutting and Diemaking *(1972)*
651 W. Terra Cotta Ave.
Suite 132
Crystal Lake, IL 60014
Tel: (815) 455-7519 *Fax:* (815) 455-7510
TollFree: (800) 828-4233
E-Mail: staff@iadd.org
Website: iadd.org
Members: 1002 individuals and firms
Staff: 3
Annual Budget: $500-1,000,000
Tax: 501(c)(6)

Personnel:
Chief Executive Officer: Cindy Crouse CAE
    E-Mail: cccrouse@iadd.org
Assistant, Chapters and Meetings: Nikki Faul
    E-Mail: nfaul@iadd.org
Contact, Membership Services and Desktop Publishing Assistant: Jenny Holliday
    E-Mail: jholliday@iadd.org

Historical Note:
Formerly (1980) Diemakers and Diecutters Association, (1991) the National Association of Diemakers and Diecutters. IADD seeks to be the definitive resource for the diecutting converting industry, bringing together and serving people who convert soft to semi-rigid materials into various cut parts. Members are firms involved in diemaking, diecutting and related equipment and supply areas. Membership: $849 (Patron); $469 (Company); $339 (Affiliate); $49-199 (Individual); $139 (Associate).

Meetings/Conferences: Annual
Conference Chair: Nikki Faul

Publications:
Membership Directory; on-line
The Cutting Edge; monthly; adv.

International Association of Dive Rescue Specialists *(1979)*
P.O. Box 877
Vero Beach, FL 32961-0877
Tel: (970) 482-1562 *Fax:* (234) 564-2377
TollFree: (800) 423-7791
Website: iadrs.org
Members: 1000 individuals
Staff: 2
Annual Budget: $50-100,000
Tax: 501(c)(3)

Personnel:
Executive Director: Blades Robinson
    E-Mail: brobinson@iadrs.org
Director, Communications: David Owens
    E-Mail: owens082962@gmail.com

Historical Note:
IADRS's mission is to help water rescue professionals stay informed about advances in training, equipment, and life saving techniques. Membership: $25 (Individual); $40 (Canadian and Foreign Member); $18-20 (Team).

Meetings/Conferences: Annual
Conference Chair: David Owens

Publications:
IADRS Newsletter; bi-monthly

International Association of Drilling Contractors *(1940)*
P.O. Box 4287

Houston, TX 77210-4287
Tel: (713) 292-1945 *Fax:* (713) 292-1946
E-Mail: info@iadc.org
Website: iadc.org
Members: 1300 companies
Staff: 44
Annual Budget: $10-25,000,000
Tax: 501(c)(6)

Personnel:
President and Chief Executive Officer: Stephen A. Colville
Senior Director, Finance: Dean Gant
Vice President, Membership and Publications: Jason McFarland
Coordinator, Operations: Leslie Packard
Vice President, Conferences: Leesa Teel
Senior Vice President, Business Development: Thomas T. Terrell

Historical Note:
Formerly (1972) American Association of Oilwell Drilling Contractors. IADC's mission is to improve industry health, safety and environmental practices, advance drilling and completion technology. It is dedicated to enhancing interests of oil-and-gas and geothermal drilling and completion industry worldwide. Members includes oil-and-gas producers, manufacturers and suppliers. Membership: $300-30,000 (Contractor Membership); $ 500-3,000 (Producer Membership); $ 200-2000 (Associate Membership).

Meetings/Conferences:
Conference Chair: Leesa Teel
2013 - Houston, TX (Omni Houston Hotel Westside)/ May 16
2013 - Istanbul, Turkey (Hilton Istanbul)/June 19 - 20
2013 - Galveston, TX (Galveston Moody Gardens)/ Aug. 20 - 21
2013 - Amsterdam, Netherlands (Movenpick Hotel)/ Sept. 25 - 26
2013 - San Antonio, TX (The Westin La Cantera Resort)/Oct. 23 - 24
2013 - Bangkok, Thailand (Conrad Hotel)/Nov. 20 - 21
Number of non-conference events/year: 5

Publications:
DRILLBITS; monthly
Drilling Contractor
Membership Directory

International Association of Eating Disorders Professionals (1985)
P.O. Box 1295
Pekin, IL 61555-1295
Fax: (800) 800-8126
TollFree: (800) 800-8126
E-Mail: iaedpmembers@earthlink.net
Website: iaedp.com
Members: 38 organizations and 800 individuals
Staff: 5
Annual Budget: Under $10,000
Tax: 501(c)(3)

Personnel:
Managing Director: Bonnie Harken
    E-Mail: Iaedpmembers@earthlink.net
Coordinator, Membership Services: Rebecca Albertini
    E-Mail: ralbertini@premierebusinesssolutions.com
Director, Membership and Chapter: Alice Gibson
Director, Certifications: Julie Holland
    E-Mail: jholland@crchealth.com
Director, Media Relations and Assistant Managing Director: Blanche Williams
    E-Mail: blanche@blanchewilliams.com

Historical Note:
IAEDP's mission is to promote a high level of professionalism among practitioners who treat those suffering from eating disorders by promoting ethical and professional standards, offering education and training in the field, certifying those who have met prescribed requirements, promoting public and professional awareness of eating disorders and assisting in prevention efforts. Membership: $195 (Individual); $75 (Student/ Retired).

Continuing Education:
Certification Designation/s: CEDA, CEDS, CEDAN, CEDSN, CEDRD

Meetings/Conferences:
2013 - Henderson, NV (Westin Lake Las Vegas Resort and Spa)/March 21 - 24

Publications:
Clinical Newsletter
IAEDP Newsletter; on-line
Membership directory; on-line

The Journal of Treatment and Prevention
Membership List Available to Non-members

International Association of Electrical Inspectors (1928)
P.O. Box 830848
Richardson, TX 75080-0848
Tel: (972) 235-1455 *Fax:* (972) 235-6858
TollFree: (800) 786-4234
E-Mail: customerservice@iaei.org
Website: iaei.org
Members: 26000 individuals
Staff: 15
Annual Budget: $2-5,000,000
Tax: 501(c)(5)

Personnel:
Chief Executive Officer and Executive Director: David E. Clements
    E-Mail: dclements@iaei.org
Director, Administrative Services: Natalie Coleman
    E-Mail: ncoleman@iaei.org
Contact, Administrative Professional, Seminar and Education: Barbara Eastwood
    E-Mail: beastwood@iaei.org
Bookkeeper: Cathy Higgs
    E-Mail: chiggs@iaei.org
Director, Publishing and Marketing and Managing Editor: Kathryn P. Ingley
Director, Education, Codes and Standards: L. Keith Lofland
    E-Mail: klofland@iaei.org
Director, Membership and Customer Service: Annette Thomas
    E-Mail: athomas@iaei.org

Historical Note:
IAEI's purpose is to formulate standards for safe installation and use of electrical materials, devices, and appliances. Membership: $102 (Inspector/Associate); $78 (Student); $105 (Section); $525 (National/International); $204 (Inspection Agency).

Continuing Education:
Enrollment: 6000
Certification Designation/s: CEI-R, NCPCCI, CEI-M

Meetings/Conferences:
Conference Chair: Barbara Eastwood

Publications:
1&2 Family Electrical Systems; irregular; adv.
Ferm's Fast Finder Index; irregular; adv.
IAEI Magazine
IAEI News; bi-monthly; adv.
Membership Directory; annually; adv.
Soares Grounding; irregular; adv.

International Association of Electronic Keyboard Manufacturers (1963)
c/o Korg USA
316 S. Service Rd.
Melville, NY 11747-3201
Tel: (631) 390-6500 *Fax:* (631) 390-6501
Website: iaekm.org
Members: 20 companies
Staff: 1
Annual Budget: $10-25,000

Personnel:
President: Joe Castronovo

Historical Note:
Founded as the National Association of Electronic Organ Manufacturers; became the National Association of Electronic Keyboard Manufacturers in 1983 and assumed its present name in 1990. Affiliated with the American Music Conference. Membership: $100/year.

International Association of Emergency Managers (1952)
201 Park Washington Ct.
Falls Church, VA 22046-4527
Tel: (703) 538-1795 *Fax:* (703) 241-5603
E-Mail: info@iaem.com
Website: iaem.com
Members: 5000 individuals
Staff: 11
Annual Budget: $2-5,000,000
Tax: 501(c)(3)

Personnel:
Chief Executive Officer: Elizabeth B. Armstrong CAE, MAM
    E-Mail: armstrong@iaem.com

Policy Advisor and Staff Liaison, Government Affairs: Martha Braddock
    E-Mail: braddock@iaem.com
Manager, Meetings: Susan A. Denston
Manager, Membership Services and Registrar: Sharon L. Kelly
Manager, Accounting and Finance: Hui-Ling Liang
Manager, Communications and Director, Scholarship Programs: Dawn M. Shiley-Danzeisen
    E-Mail: shiley@iaem.com
Editor: Karen Thompson
    E-Mail: thompson@iaem.com
Administrator and Manager, Certification Programs: Kate Walker
    E-Mail: kwalker@iaem.com

Historical Note:
Founded as United States Civil Defense Council, became National Coordinating Council on Emergency Management in 1983, and assumed its current name in 1998. IAEM's mission is to serve its members by providing information, networking and professional opportunities and to advance the emergency management profession. Membership: $170 (Individual); $795 (Affiliate); $25 (Student); $50 (International).

Continuing Education:
Certification Designation/s: CEM, AEM

Meetings/Conferences: Annual
Conference Chair: Susan A. Denston
2013 - Reno, NV (Silver Legacy Resort Casino)/Oct. 25 - 30
2014 - San Antonio, TX (Grand Hyatt San Antonio)/ Nov. 14 - 19

Publications:
IAEM Bulletin Newsletter; monthly; adv.
IAEM Membership Directory; on-line

Membership List Available to Non-members

International Association of Equine Dentists (1987)
P.O. Box 1141
Seguin, TX 78156
Tel: (202) 470-3245
E-Mail: ask@iaedonline.com
Website: iaedonline.com
Staff: 2

Personnel:
Executive Director: Will Phillips
Treasurer: Jennifer Wittman
    E-Mail: jwittman07302@yahoo.com

Historical Note:
IAED's mission is to provide and engage in educational, scientific research and services programs to benefit the equine species. Membership: $225 (Regular); $150 (Student); $50 (Supporting Member).

Meetings/Conferences: Annual
2013 - Tempe, AZ (Fiesta Inn Resort)/Feb. 15 - 17

Publications:
IAED Newsletter; on-line
Membership Directory; on-line

International Association of Exhibitions and Events (1928)
12700 Park Central Dr.
Suite 308
Dallas, TX 75251-1313
Tel: (972) 458-8002 *Fax:* (972) 458-8119
E-Mail: news@iaee.com
Website: iaee.com
Members:
1300 Organizations
8000 Individuals
Staff: 22
Annual Budget: $1-2,000,000
Tax: 501(c)(6)

Personnel:
President: David DuBois CMP, CAE, FASAE, CTA
Coordinator, Digital Marketing: Julie Ballard
    E-Mail: jballard@iaee.com
Chief Operating Officer: Cathy Breden CAE, CMP
    E-Mail: cbreden@iaee.com
Vice President, Marketing and Communications: Susan Brower CCP, CMM
    E-Mail: sbrower@iaee.com
Director, Conventions and Events: Scott Craighead CEM
    E-Mail: scraighead@iaee.com
Director, Learning Experiences: Shawntay Skjoldager MBA, MS

E-Mail: sskjoldager@iaee.com
Chief Financial Officer: Scott Stanton
    E-Mail: sstanton@iaee.com
Senior Manager, Communications and Public Relations:
    Mary Tucker
    E-Mail: mtucker@iaee.com
Director, Membership Services and Chapter Relations:
    Tanisha Ward
    E-Mail: tward@iaee.com

Historical Note:
*Formerly (2000) the National Association of Exhibit
Managers and (2007) the International Association for
Exhibition Management. IAEE promotes the value of
exhibitions and other events that bring buyers and sellers
together such as road shows, conferences with an exhibition
component, and proprietary corporate exhibitions. Members
are managers of shows, exhibits and exhibitions and
industry suppliers. Membership: $35-40,530/year.*

Continuing Education:
Certification Designation/s: CEM

Meetings/Conferences: Annual
Conference Chair: Scott Craighead CEM
2013 - Houston, TX (George R. Brown Convention
    Center)/Dec. 10 - 13
Number of non-conference events/year: 28

Publications:
E2: Exhibitions and Events; monthly; adv.
IAEE Insider; adv.
IAEE News and Industry Report; weekly; adv.

International Association of Fairs and Expositions
(1885)
3043 E. Cairo St.
Springfield, MO 65802
Tel: (417) 862-5771 *Fax:* (417) 862-0156
TollFree: (800) 516-0313
E-Mail: iafe@fairsandexpos.com
Website: fairsandexpos.com
Members: 1300 Individuals
Staff: 14
Annual Budget: $2-5,000,000
Tax: 501(c)(6)

Personnel:
President and Chief Executive Officer: Jim Tucker
    E-Mail: jimt@fairsandexpos.com
Director, Education: Marla Calico CFE
    E-Mail: marlac@fairsandexpos.com
Managing Editor: Rebekah Lee
    E-Mail: rebekahl@fairsandexpos.com
Director , Technology: Rachel Mundhenke
    E-Mail: rachelm@fairsandexpos.com
*Director, Membership Services, Sponsorships and Trade
    Show:* Steve Siever
    E-Mail: steves@fairsandexpos.com
Manager, Web Communications: Lindsey Steiro
    E-Mail: lindseys@fairsandexpos.com
Meeting Planner and Registrar: Kate Turner
    E-Mail: katet@fairsandexpos.com
*Chief Financial Officer, Chief Operating Officer and
    Director, Meetings and Publications:* Max Willis
    E-Mail: maxw@fairsandexpos.com

Historical Note:
*IAFE is a voluntary, non-profit corporation, organizing
state, provincial, regional, and county agricultural fairs,
shows, exhibitions, and expositions. IAFE represents and
facilitate the interests of agricultural fairs, exhibitions and
show associations. Membership consists of individual
agricultural fairs and regional associations of agricultural
fairs. Membership: $100-1,600 (Active Member); $195
(Associate); $50 (Alumni Association/Affiliate).*

Meetings/Conferences: Annual
Conference Chair: Max Willis
2013 - West Palm Beach, FL (West Palm Beach
    Marriott)/April 25 - 28
2013 - Las Vegas, NV (Paris Hotel)/Dec. 8 - 12
Number of non-conference events/year: 7

Publications:
Fairs and Expositions; bi-monthly; adv.
IAFE eNewsletter; on-line
Membership Directory; on-line; adv.

International Association of Financial Crimes
Investigators (1968)
1020 Suncast Ln.
Suite 102
El Dorado Hills, CA 95762
Tel: (916) 939-5000 *Fax:* (916) 939-0395
E-Mail: admin@iafci.org

Website: iafci.org
Members: 3900 individuals
Staff: 4
Annual Budget: $1-2,000,000

Personnel:
Executive Director: Janis Moffett CMP
    E-Mail: jan@iafci.org

Historical Note:
*Founded as International Association of Credit Card
Investigators, assumed its current name in 1996. IAFCI
promotes the establishment of effective international card
and cheque security programs, the suppression of fraudulent
use of cards and travelers cheques and the detection and
apprehension of those responsible. Membership: $120
(Regular/Annual); $70 (Law Enforcement).*

Continuing Education:
Certification Designation/s: CFCI
Meetings/Conferences:
Number of non-conference events/year: 1

Publications:
IAFCI News; quarterly
Membership Directory

International Association of Fire Chiefs (1873)
4025 Fair Ridge Dr.
Suite 300
Fairfax, VA 22033-2868
Tel: (703) 273-0911 *Fax:* (703) 273-9363
E-Mail: membership@iafc.org
Website: iafc.org
Members: 13000 individuals
Staff: 77
Annual Budget: $10-25,000,000
Tax: 501(c)(3)

Personnel:
Chief Executive Officer and Executive Director: Mark W.
    Light MPA, CAE
    E-Mail: mlight@iafc.org
Senior Advisor, Government Relations and Policy: Alan
    Caldwell
    E-Mail: acaldwell@iafc.org
Director, Administration and Finance: Robert Duke CAE
    E-Mail: rduke@iafc.org
Editor and Communications Manager: Jacqueline Garnier
    E-Mail: jgarnier@iafc.org
Junior Director, Government Relations and Policy: Ken
    LaSala
    E-Mail: klasala@iafc.org
Director, Conferences and Education: Pamela Magnani
    E-Mail: pmagnani@iafc.org
Director, Membership Services and External Relations:
    Terry Monroe
    E-Mail: tmonroe@iafc.org
Manager, Marketing: Kate Ruhe
    E-Mail: kruhe@iafc.org

Historical Note:
*Formerly (1926) National Association of Fire Engineers.
IAFC's mission is to promote, enhance and improve value-
centered human relationships. Membership: $25-234/year.*

Meetings/Conferences: Annual
Conference Chair: Pamela Magnani

Publications:
Fire Chief
FireRescue; monthly
Membership Directory; on-line
On Scene

International Association of Fire Fighters (1918)
1750 New York Ave. NW
Suite 300
Washington, DC 20006-5395
Tel: (202) 737-8484 *Fax:* (202) 737-8418
Website: iaff.org
Members: 300,000 professional fire fighters and
paramedics
Staff: 110
Annual Budget: $10-25,000,000
Tax: 501(c)(5)

Personnel:
General President: Harold A. Schaitberger
    E-Mail: pr@iaff.org
Director, Communications: Jane Blume
    E-Mail: jblume@iaff.org
Director, Public Affairs and Media Relations: William
    Glanz
    E-Mail: bglanz@iaff.org
Director, Conferences and Event Planning: Dawn Iacino

E-Mail: diacino@iaff.org
Director, Governmental Affairs: Barry Kasinitz
    E-Mail: bkasinitz@iaff.org
Director, Human Resources: Jim Larkin
    E-Mail: jlarkin@iaff.org
Chief, Operations: Jim Lee
*Assistant to General President, Membership Services,
    Technical Assistance and Information Resources:* Lori
    Moore-Merrell
    E-Mail: lmoore@iaff.org
Director, Education: Kevin Rader
    E-Mail: krader@iaff.org
Legal Counsel: Baldwin Robertson
    E-Mail: brobertson@iaff.org
Director, Web Operations: Bentley Westfield
    E-Mail: bwestfield@iaff.org

Historical Note:
*IAFF's mission is to organize all fire fighters and emergency
medical or rescue workers; secure just compensation for
their services and equitable settlement of their grievances;
promote the establishment of just and reasonable working
conditions and promote the research and treatment of burns
and other related health problems common to fire fighters.*

Meetings/Conferences: Annual
Conference Chair: Dawn Iacino
2013 - Halifax, NS/July 28 - 31
Number of non-conference events/year: 8

Publications:
International Fire Fighter Magazine; adv.

International Association of Flight And Critical
Care Paramedics (1986)
4835 Riveredge Cove
Snellville, GA 30039
Tel: (770) 979-6372 *Fax:* (770) 979-6500
E-Mail: info@flightparamedic.org
Website: iafccp.org
Members: 1200 individuals
Staff: 1
Annual Budget: $50-100,000

Personnel:
Executive Director: Monica Newman
    E-Mail: m.newman@flightparamedic.org

Historical Note:
*Formerly the National Flight Paramedics Association
and later known as International Association of Flight
Paramedics. IAFCCP's mission is to maintain an
organization of paramedics which support and coordinate
educational and research activities relating to its members
and the flight paramedic industry. Members are involved in
transporting critical care patients by airplane, helicopter,
and ground ambulance. Membership: $80 (Individual-
Active/Associate); $65 (International).*

Meetings/Conferences: Semi-Annual
Number of non-conference events/year: 2

Publications:
Air Medical Journal; bi-monthly
FP News; quarterly; adv.
Government & Legislative Affairs Committee
    Newsletter; quarterly
Membership Directory; on-line

International Association of Forensic Nurses
(1992)
1517 Ritchie Hwy.
Suite 208
Arnold, MD 21012-2323
Tel: (410) 626-7805 *Fax:* (410) 626-7804
E-Mail: info@iafn.org
Website: iafn.org
Members: 3100 individuals
Staff: 9
Annual Budget: $1-2,000,000
Tax: 501(c)(6)

Personnel:
Chief Executive Officer: Carey Goryl
    E-Mail: careygoryl@iafn.org
Manager, Communications and Membership: Alexander
    Cooper
    E-Mail: acooper@iafn.org
Meetings and Events Planner: Carol Dunn
    E-Mail: caroldunn@iafn.org
Coordinator, Education and Certification: Marcia
    Tomaselli
    E-Mail: mtomaselli@iafn.org

Historical Note:

IAFN seeks to provide leadership in forensic nursing practice by developing, promoting, and disseminating information internationally about forensic nursing science. Members are registered nurses, assault nurse examiners, clinical trauma nurses, correctional nurse specialists, including all nursing roles defined as forensic practice. Membership: $129 (Regular); $100 (Associate); $70 (Student).

Continuing Education:
Enrollment: 800
Certification Designation/s: SANE-A, SANE-P

Meetings/Conferences: Annual
Conference Chair: Carol Dunn

Publications:
Journal of Forensic Nursing; quarterly
Monthly Update; monthly
On the Edge; quarterly

Membership List Available to Non-members

The International Association of Forensic Toxicologists (1963)
NMS Labs
3701 Welsh Rd.
Willow Grove, PA 19090
E-Mail: info@tiaft.org
Website: tiaft.org
Members: 1400 individuals
Staff: 3

Personnel:
President: Alain G. Verstraete
    E-Mail: alain.verstraete@ugent.be
Secretary: Daniel S. Isenschmid DABFT, PhD
    E-Mail: disensch@co.wayne.mi.us

Historical Note:
TIAFT's mission is to promote cooperation and coordination of efforts among members and to encourage research in forensic toxicology. Has no paid officers or full-time staff. Membership: $40/year.

Meetings/Conferences: Annual
2013 - Funchal, Portugal/Sept. 2 - 6
2015 - Florence, Italy/Aug. 30 - Sept. 4
Number of non-conference events/year: 1

Publications:
Bulletin
Membership Directory; on-line

Membership List Available to Non-members

International Association of Geophysical Contractors (1971)
1225 N. Loop West
Suite 220
Houston, TX 77008
Tel: (713) 957-8080 Fax: (713) 957-0008
TollFree: (866) 558-1756
E-Mail: iagc@iagc.org
Website: iagc.org
Members: 235 companies
Staff: 5
Annual Budget: $1-2,000,000
Tax: 501(c)(6)

Personnel:
President: G.C. Chip Gill
Director, Communications, Marketing, and Public Relations: William "Bill" Ainsworth
Database Administrator: Timothy Fransioli
    E-Mail: tim.fransioli@iagc.org
Office Manager: Criss Rennie
Vice President, Marine Environment: Sarah Lindsay Tsoflias

Historical Note:
IAGC's mission is to optimize the business climate and commercial health of the geophysical industry, and to promote the conduct of business in a professional, safe, and environmentally responsible manner. Membership: based on annual revenue and a formula (Core Member-Company); $350-33,500 (Supporting-based on annual revenues).

Meetings/Conferences: Annual
2013 - Houston, TX (Norris Conference Center)/Feb. 21

Publications:
IAGC Newsletter; on-line; adv.

International Association of Golf Administrators (1968)
2974 Sproul Rd.
Suite 400
Broomall, PA 19008

Tel: (610) 687-2340 Fax: (610) 687-2082
E-Mail: iaga@aol.com
Website: iaga.org
Members: 180 individuals
Staff: 1
Annual Budget: $100-250,000

Personnel:
Managing Director: Jan Garber
    E-Mail: jgarber@gapgolf.org

Historical Note:
IAGA seeks to conserve the best interests and the true spirit of the game of golf as embodied in its ancient and honorable traditions and serves as a medium for golf administrators to exchange information, techniques and other data relating to the game of golf and establish channels of communication among all of the world's golfing fraternities. Membership: $150/year (Associate/Affiliate).

Publications:
Membership Directory; on-line

International Association of Healthcare Central Service Materiel Management (1958)
213 W. Institute Pl.
Suite 307
Chicago, IL 60610
Tel: (312) 440-0078 Fax: (312) 440-9474
TollFree: (800) 962-8274
Website: iahcsmm.com
Members: 12000 individuals
Staff: 13
Annual Budget: $2-5,000,000

Personnel:
Executive Director: Betty Hanna
    E-Mail: betty@iahcsmm.org
Manager, Administrative Services: Susan Adams
    E-Mail: SAdams@IAHCSMM.org
Director, Government Affairs: Josephine Colacci
    E-Mail: jo@iahcsmm.org
Manager, Advertising: Lisa Gosser
    E-Mail: lisa@iahcsmm.org
Director, Education: Natalie Lind
    E-Mail: natalie@iahcsmm.org
Coordinator, Membership Services: Loretta Short
    E-Mail: loretta@iahcsmm.org
Contact, Publications and Merchandise Ordering: Elnora Underwood
    E-Mail: elnora@iahcsmm.org
Office Manager: Jeff Warren
    E-Mail: jeff@iahcsmm.org
Manager, Media Relations: Julie Williamson
    E-Mail: Julie@iahcsmm.org

Historical Note:
Formerly (1969) the National Association of Hospital Central Service Personnel and the International Association of Hospital Central Service Management (1989). IAHCSMM's mission is to provide organized educational opportunities, professional development, a forum for information exchange, member services in response to member identified needs and priorities. Active members are managers, supervisors, and technicians of Central Service departments in the U.S. and worldwide. Membership: $40/year (Active/Associate).

Continuing Education:
Enrollment: 2000
Certification Designation/s: CIS, CHL, CRCST

Meetings/Conferences: Annual
Conference Chair: Jeff Warren
2013 - San Diego, CA (Town and Country Resort Hotel)/May 5 - 8/11-25 exhibitors
2014 - Columbus, OH (Columbus Convention Center)/ May 4 - 7/11-25 exhibitors
2015 - Ft. Lauderdale, FL (Broward Country Convention Center)/May 3 - 6

Publications:
Membership Directory; on-line

International Association of Healthcare Practitioners
11211 Prosperity Farms Rd.
Suite D-325
Palm Beach Gardens, FL 33410-3487
Tel: (561) 622-8273 Fax: (561) 622-4771
E-Mail: iahp@iahp.com
Website: iahp.com
Members: 100,000 therapists
Staff: 1

Personnel:
Contact, Communication: Cliff Korn

Historical Note:
The IAHP serves as a global directory for bodyworkers and their clients; and supports the Upledger Institute, Chikly Institute and the Barral Institute alumni. Membership: $100 (Individual).

Publications:
Newsletter

International Association of Heat and Frost Insulators and Asbestos Workers (1903)
9602 M. L. King Jr. Hwy.
Lanham, MD 20706
Tel: (301) 731-9101 Fax: (301) 731-5058
E-Mail: IIIATF@insulators.org
Website: insulators.org
Members: 21000 individuals
Staff: 15
Annual Budget: $10-25,000

Personnel:
General President: James A. Grogan
General Secretary and Treasurer: James "Bud" McCourt

Historical Note:
Chartered in 1904 by the American Federation of Labor as the National Association of Heat, Frost, General Insulators and Asbestos Workers of America. The word 'International' was adopted after the acceptance of Canadian citizens into the association in 1910. The objective of the union is to assist its membership in securing employment, and by education and cooperation, raise them to a higher position in society. Affiliated with the AFL-CIO Building Trades Department and the Canadian Labour Congress.

Publications:
Journal; quarterly

International Association of Home Staging Professionals (1999)
2420 Sand Creek Rd.
C-1, Suite 263
Brentwood, CA 94513
Fax: (925) 665-0322
TollFree: (800) 392-7161
Website: iahsp.com
Staff: 4
Annual Budget: $10-25,000

Personnel:
Chairwoman and Founder: Barb Schwarz
    E-Mail: DirectorOfOperations@IAHSP.com
Treasurer: Kirk Bohrer
Director, Membership and Meeting: Joan Inglis
Director, Operations: BJ Johnson

Historical Note:
IAHSP's mission is to advance the art and education of the professional stager who prepare homes for sale by facilitating Home Stager business development opportunities. Membership: $150 (Individual); $400 (Corporate).

Meetings/Conferences: Annual
Conference Chair: Joan Inglis

Publications:
IAHSP Newsletter
Membership Directory; on-line

Membership List Available to Non-members

International Association of Homes and Services for the Ageing (1994)
2519 Connecticut Ave. NW
Washington, DC 20008-1520
Tel: (202) 508-9468 Fax: (202) 220-0041
E-Mail: iahsa@aahsa.org
Website: iahsa.net
Staff: 2
Annual Budget: $100-250,000

Personnel:
President and Chief Executive Officer: William "Larry" Minnix Jr.
    E-Mail: lminnix@aahsa.org
Executive Director: Katie Smith Sloan
    E-Mail: ksloan@iahsa.net

Historical Note:
A division of the American Association of Homes and Services for the Aging, which provides administrative support. IAHSA's mission is to enhance the quality of life for the ageing. Membership: $550 (Multi System Organization/Government/Association/NGO/Industry Partners); $200 (Single Site Facility); $100 (University/ Individual).

Meetings/Conferences: Biennial
2013 - Shanghai, China/Nov. 17 - 20

Publications:
Alliance-newsletter; monthly

International Association of Hygienic Physicians
(*1978*)
4620 Euclid Blvd.
Youngstown, OH 44512-1633
Tel: (330) 788-0526 *Fax:* (330) 788-0093
Website: iahp.net
Members: 50 individuals
Staff: 1
Annual Budget: $10-25,000

Personnel:
*Secretary and Treasurer and Contact, Membership and
   Website:* Mark A. Huberman
   E-Mail: mhuberman@zoominternet.net

Historical Note:
*Founded as International Association of Professional
Natural Hygienists, assumed its current name in 1995.
IAHP's mission is to promote clinical advancement of its
profession, ethical responsibility, certification of other
professionals, accreditation of schools or training programs
and the health freedom of its membership. Provides
service to primary care physicians specializing in fasting
supervision as an integral part of Hygienic Care. Members
are limited to primary care doctors specializing in the
supervision of fasting as an integral part of natural Hygienic
care. Membership: $50 (Regular); $200 (Fasting Institute
Supplement); $10 (Graduate Student).*

Continuing Education:
Certification Designation/s: PC

Publications:
Newsletter; quarterly

International Association of Ice Cream Vendors
(*1969*)
5024-R Campbell Blvd.
Baltimore, MD 21236
Tel: (410) 931-8100 *Fax:* (410) 931-8111
E-Mail: info@iaicdv.org
Website: iaicdv.org
Members: 130 companies
Staff: 4
Annual Budget: $100-250,000

Personnel:
Executive Director: Crista LeGrand CMP, CAE
   E-Mail: crista@iaicdv.org
Associate Director: Taylor Dubord
   E-Mail: taylor@iaicdv.org
Manager, Finance: Donna Liberto
   E-Mail: donna@iaicdv.org
Contact, Membership Services: Shannon Stamm
   E-Mail: shannon@iaicdv.org

Historical Note:
*Formerly (2008) National Association of Ice Cream Vendors
(NAICV). IAICDV promotes and enhances a quality
image for safe ice cream vending and the success of the
industry. Membership includes suppliers, manufacturers,
and anyone engaged in the selling or marketing of ice cream
novelty products. Membership: $1,500-2,000 (Supplier);
$495-1,250 (Operator); $1000 (Broker).*

Meetings/Conferences: Annual

Publications:
Chimes Newsletter; monthly
IAICDV Directory; annually

International Association of Independent Tanker
Owners (*1970*)
801 N. Quincy St.
Suite 200
Arlington, VA 22203
Tel: (703) 373-2269
Website: intertanko.com
Members: 250 members
Staff: 2

Personnel:
Managing Director: Katharina Stanzel
Director, Regulatory Affairs and the Americas: Joseph
   Angelo
   E-Mail: joe.angelo@intertanko.com

Historical Note:
*NTERTANKO provides leadership to the Tanker Industry in
serving the world with the safe, environmentally sound and
efficient seaborne transportation of oil, gas and chemical
products. Membership: $5,985-72,675/year.*

Publications:
INTERTANKO Newsletter; on-line

International Association of Industrial Accident
Boards and Commissions (*1914*)
5610 Medical Cir.
Suite 24
Madison, WI 53719-1295
Tel: (608) 663-6355 *Fax:* (608) 663-1546
Website: iaiabc.org
Members: 200 members and regulatory
government agencies
Staff: 11
Annual Budget: $500-1,000,000

Personnel:
Executive Director: Greg Krohm
   E-Mail: gkrohm@iaiabc.org
Events and Office Administrator: Christina Klein
   E-Mail: cklein@iaiabc.org
Manager, Membership and Marketing: Heather Lore
   E-Mail: hlore@iaiabc.org

Historical Note:
*IAIABC is dedicated to promoting the advancement of
workers' compensation systems throughout the world
through education, research, and resource management.
Members are governmental units, companies and others
interested in improving workers compensation laws and
their administration. Membership: $1500-9,000 (U.S.
Jurisidictional, per congressional district); $950 (Non-
U.S. Jurisdictional); $1000 (Associate Corporate); $500
(Associate Individual).*

Meetings/Conferences: Annual
Conference Chair: Christina Klein
2013 - San Diego, CA (Westin Gaslamp Quarter, San
   Diego)/Sept. 30 - Oct. 3
Number of non-conference events/year: 4

Publications:
IAIABC Journal; semi-annually; adv.
IAIABC Newsletters; bi-monthly

International Association of Infant Massage
(*1986*)
P.O. Box 6370
Ventura, CA 93006
Tel: (805) 644-8524 *Fax:* (805) 830-1729
TollFree: (800) 248-5432
E-Mail: iaim4us@aol.com
Website: iaim.ws
Members: 3000 individuals
Staff: 3
Annual Budget: $100-250,000
Tax: 501(c)(3)

Personnel:
*Chief Executive Officer and Contact, Finance and
   Administration:* Susan Campbell
   E-Mail: SRCwinc@me.com
Contact, Marketing and Communication: Andrea Kelly

Historical Note:
*IAIM's mission is to foster a renaissance of various nations'
traditions of infant massage and promote the field through
training, education, and research. Membership: $85
(Regular); $65 (Supporting).*

Continuing Education:
Certification Designation/s: CIMI, IAIMI, IAIM

Publications:
Newsletter

International Association of Insurance Receivers
(*1991*)
11401 Century Oaks Terrace
Suite 310
Austin, TX 78758
Tel: (512) 404-6555 *Fax:* (512) 404-6530
E-Mail: mcs@thebeaumontgroup.com
Website: iair.org
Members: 400 individuals
Staff: 4
Annual Budget: $100-250,000
Tax: 501(c)(6)

Personnel:
Executive Director: Palomar Financial
   E-Mail: slhiroms@palomarfin.com
Director: Mary Cannon Veed
   E-Mail: mcveed@arnstein.com

Historical Note:
*IAIR's mission is to promote a uniform code of professional
standards for insurance receivers and develop educational
and training programs to enhance the qualifications of
persons working in the field of insurance receiverships.*

Membership: $375 (Profit-Entities); $175 (Not-For-Profit
Entities).

Continuing Education:
Certification Designation/s: AIR, CIR

Meetings/Conferences: Annual
Number of non-conference events/year: 1

Publications:
Member Directory; on-line
The Insurance Receiver; quarterly

International Association of Jewish Vocational
Services (*1939*)
1845 Walnut St.
Suite 640
Philadelphia, PA 19103-4701
Tel: (215) 854-0233 *Fax:* (215) 854-0212
Website: iajvs.org
Members: 28 national and international human
service agencies
Staff: 3
Annual Budget: $500-1,000,000
Tax: 501(c)(3)

Personnel:
Executive Director: Genie Cohen
   E-Mail: coheng@iajvs.org
Executive Assistant and Contact, Conferences and Meetings:
   Karen Rosen
   E-Mail: rosenk@iajvs.org

Historical Note:
*Formerly (1976) known as the Jewish Occupational Council
and (1990) National Association of Jewish Vocational
Services, IAJVS works to provide its membership with
services that strengthen local capacity. Members are
voluntary Jewish vocational guidance, employment, training
and rehabilitation organizations in the U.S., Canada and
Israel. It is funded through individual agency memberships,
volunteer campaign contributions, and federal grants.*

Meetings/Conferences: Annual
Conference Chair: Karen Rosen

Publications:
E-Lights; quarterly

International Association of Law Enforcement
Firearms Instructors, Inc. (*1981*)
25 Country Club Rd.
Suite 707
Gilford, NH 03249-6909
Tel: (603) 524-8787 *Fax:* (603) 524-8856
E-Mail: info@ialefi.com
Website: ialefi.com
Members: 8000 individuals
Staff: 3
Annual Budget: $250-500,000

Personnel:
Executive Director and Treasurer: Robert D. Bossey
   E-Mail: ialefi@lr.net

Historical Note:
*IALEFI's mission is to encourage the development and
operation of training programs to firearms instructors
among law enforcement, security, criminal justice, and
investigative agencies and organizations. Members are
certified firearms instructors from police departments,
security agencies, criminal justice, and investigative
personnel. Membership: $55 (Active/Associate); $550
(Corporate).*

Meetings/Conferences:
Number of non-conference events/year: 1

Publications:
IALEFI Newsletter; on-line
Membership Directory; on-line

International Association of Law Enforcement
Intelligence Analysts (*1980*)
P.O. Box 13857
Richmond, VA 23225
Fax: (804) 565-2059
E-Mail: admin@ialeia.org
Website: ialeia.org
Members: 1650 individuals
Staff: 6
Annual Budget: $100-250,000
Tax: 501(c)(3)

Personnel:
President: Jennifer J. Johnstone
   E-Mail: johnstone@ialeia.org
Treasurer: Jennifer S. Dauzier
   E-Mail: dauzier@ialeia.org

Director, Membership and Outreach: George Gelman-Kipnis
  E-Mail: gelman@ialeia.org
Director, Professional Development: Merle Manzi
  E-Mail: manzi@ialeia.org
Director, Communications: Lynn A. McCloskey
  E-Mail: mccloskey@ialeia.org
Administrator: Christy Taylor

Historical Note:
Affiliated with the Australian Institute of Professional Intelligence Officers. ALEIA is a professional organization representing law enforcement analysts. Members are presently or formerly employed in a specialized law enforcement intelligence capacity, sworn or civilian, by a government entity. Membership: $50 (Regular/Associate); $25 (Student); $1000 (Corporate); $10 (Members from developing countries).

Continuing Education:
Certification Designation/s: CICA

Meetings/Conferences: Annual
2013 - Chicago, IL (Swissotel Chicago)/April 8 - 12

Publications:
IALEIA Journal; semi-annually
Intelscope; adv.
Member Directory; on-line; adv.

International Association of Lighting Designers
(1969)
440 N. Wells St.
Suite 210
Chicago, IL 60654
Tel: (312) 527-3677 *Fax:* (312) 527-3680
E-Mail: iald@iald.org
Website: iald.org
Members: 700 individuals
Staff: 10
Annual Budget: $2-5,000,000
Tax: 501(c)(6)

Personnel:
Executive Vice President: Marsha L. Turner CAE
  E-Mail: marsha@iald.org
Manager, Meetings and Professional Relations: Kelly Ashmore
  E-Mail: kelly@iald.org
Coordinator, Marketing and Communications: Jessica Burke
  E-Mail: jessica@iald.org
Legal Counsel: Pamela Beck Danner
  E-Mail: pbdanner@ideamatics.net
Accountant: Douglas Gustafson
  E-Mail: doug.gustafson@sbcglobal.net
Director, Integrated Communications and Technology: Jennifer Jones
  E-Mail: jennifer@iald.org
Administrative Assistant: Sharonda Kennedy
  E-Mail: sharonda@iald.org
Manager, Membership Services: Armando Ramirez
  E-Mail: armando@iald.org

Historical Note:
Mission is to serve the IALD worldwide membership by promoting the visible success of its members in practicing lighting design. Membership: $20-260/year.

Meetings/Conferences:
Conference Chair: Kelly Ashmore

Publications:
IALD Directory; on-line
Reflections; monthly; adv.

International Association of Lighting Management Companies *(1952)*
1255 SW Prairie Trail Pkwy.
Ankeny, IA 50023-7068
Tel: (515) 243-2360 *Fax:* (515) 334-1173
E-Mail: director@nalmco.org
Website: nalmco.org
Members: 120 individuals
Staff: 4
Annual Budget: $500-1,000,000

Personnel:
Executive Director: Heather Tamminga CAE
  E-Mail: director@nalmco.org
Meeting Planner: Kim Johnson
  E-Mail: meetings@nalmco.org
Director, Administration and Membership Services Assistant: Kelly Kipping
  E-Mail: memberservice@nalmco.org

Director, Technology and Web Site Coordinator: Darcy Watson
  E-Mail: technology@nalmco.org

Historical Note:
Formerly (until 1978) the National Association of Lighting Maintenance Contractors and (1987) International Association of Lighting Maintenance Contractors. NALMCO's mission is to deliver services, information and industry relationships for the benefit of its members and their customers. Members are companies that clean, repair, maintain and manage commercial and industrial lighting fixtures. Offers members tradeshows and conventions, various educational products, videos, certification programs and seminars. Membership: $750-2,600/year.

Continuing Education:
Certification Designation/s: CALT, CSLT, CLMC

Meetings/Conferences: Annual
Conference Chair: Kim Johnson

Publications:
LM&M Magazine; quarterly; adv.
Membership Directory; annually; adv.

International Association of Machinists and Aerospace Workers *(1888)*
9000 Machinists Pl.
Upper Marlboro, MD 20772-2687
Tel: (301) 967-4500 *Fax:* (301) 967-4588
Website: goiam.org
Members: 730000 individuals
Staff: 23
Annual Budget: $2-5,000,000

Personnel:
President: Thomas R. Buffenbarger
Director, Government Employees: Frank Carelli
  E-Mail: fcarelli@iamaw.org
General Counsel: Christopher T. Corson
Controller: David Cramer
Director, Membership Services: Kathy Delio
General Secretary and Treasurer: Warren L. Mart
Director, Information Systems: Brad Schmelzer
Director, Communications: Richard S. Sloan
  E-Mail: rsloan@iamaw.org

Historical Note:
Formerly the Order of United Machinists and Mechanical Engineers, became the National Association of Machinists in 1889 and the International Association of Machinists in 1891, absorbed the Industrial Union of Marine and Shipbuilding Workers of America in 1988 and assumed its present name in 1964. On October 1, 1991 the Pattern Makers' League of North America was merged with IAMAW and in 1994 IAMAW merged with the International Woodworkers of America - U.S. Aims to professionally negotiate contracts that guarantee secure, well-paying jobs which members can perform in safe workplaces where they would be free from harassment or intimidation. Sponsors and supports the International Association of Machinists and Aerospace Workers Political Action Committee. Membership: $326/year minimum (Individual).

Publications:
IAM Journal; quarterly
iMail; on-line
vMail; weekly

International Association of Marriage and Family Counselors *(1989)*
C/O Texas A&M University - Corpus Christi,
College of Education
6300 Ocean Dr.
Corpus Christi, TX 78412
Tel: (361) 825-2307 *Fax:* (361) 825-2732
TollFree: (800) 347-6647
Website: iamfconline.com
Members: 8000 individuals
Staff: 3
Annual Budget: $50-100,000
Tax: 501(c)(4)

Personnel:
Executive Director: Dr. Robert L. Smith PhD
  E-Mail: director@iamfc.org
Administrator, Web Site: Michael Lambert
  E-Mail: webmaster@iamfc.org
Administrative Assistant: Betty Zinna
  E-Mail: betty.zinna@selu.edu

Historical Note:
IAMFC was formed to meet the need to focus on the problems connected with marital and family issues. Members are ACA members whose primary work-related responsibilities or interests are in the area of marriage and family, specifically marriage counseling, marital therapy,

divorce counseling, mediation and family counseling or therapy. Membership: $44 (Student/Retired/Individual); $60 (Professional/Regular).

Publications:
The Family Digest - Newsletter
The Family Journal; quarterly

Membership List Available to Non-members

International Association of Medical Equipment Remarketers and Servicers (IAMERS) *(1993)*
85 Edgemont Pl.
Teaneck, NJ 07666-1603
Tel: (201) 357-5400 *Fax:* (201) 833-2021
TollFree: (877) 304-2637
E-Mail: info@iamers.org
Website: iamers.org
Members: 130 organizations
Staff: 6

Personnel:
President: Diana Upton
  E-Mail: dupton@optonline.net
Events Chairman: Bob Feldman
Treasurer and Legislative Chairman: James Goldner
Marketing Chairman: Rob Manetta
Membership Chairman: Rick Stockton

Historical Note:
IAMERS is an organization of Medical Equipment Remarketing and Servicing. Membership: $1530-4995/year.

Meetings/Conferences: Annual
Conference Chair: Bob Feldman

Publications:
IAMERS Newsletter; monthly
Membership Directory; on-line

International Association of Microfinance Investors *(2008)*
355 Lexington Ave.
15th Floor
New York, NY 10017
Tel: (212) 297-2137
E-Mail: info@iamfi.com
Website: iamfi.com
Staff: 3
Annual Budget: $100-250,000
Tax: 501(c)(6)

Personnel:
Executive Director: Joan Trant
  E-Mail: jtrant@iamfi.com
Program Associate: Jordan Filko

Historical Note:
IAMFI's mission is to help current and potential commercially oriented investors in microfinancing to achieve their financial and social goals.

Publications:
IAMFI Journal
Member Directory; on-line

International Association of Milk Control Agencies *(1935)*
New York Department of Agriculture and Markets
Ten B Airline Dr.
Albany, NY 12235-1715
Tel: (518) 457-5731 *Fax:* (518) 485-5816
E-Mail: charley.huff@agmkt.state.ny.us
Website: state.me.us/agriculture/mmc/iamca/index
Members: 26 agencies
Staff: 2
Annual Budget: $25-50,000

Personnel:
President: Charlie Huff
  E-Mail: charlie.huff@aqmkt.state.ny.us
Counsel: Larry Swartz

Historical Note:
IAMCA's mission is to improve the effectiveness and uniformity of regulation among the economic regulatory agencies. It also seeks to provide a forum for exchange of information and provide a unique forum for understanding and reacting to the ever-changing milk industry. Members are duly constituted governmental milk marketing regulatory agencies, parties involved with the dairy industry and any group or organization that has an interest in improving the dairy industry. Membership: $150 (Regular); $50 (Associate).

Publications:
IAMCA Newsletter

Membership directory; on-line

International Association of Movers (1962)
5904 Richmond Hwy.
Suite 404
Alexandria, VA 22303
Tel: (703) 317-9950 *Fax:* (703) 317-9960
E-Mail: info@iamovers.org
Website: iamovers.org
Members: 2000 companies
Staff: 8
Annual Budget: $2-5,000,000
Tax: 501(c)(6)

Personnel:
President: Terry R. Head
    E-Mail: terry.head@iamovers.org
General Manager: Belvian Carrington
    E-Mail: b.carrington@iamovers.org
Administrative Assistant: Lanee Johnson
    E-Mail: lanee.johnson@iamovers.org
Manager, Operations: Jamila Kenney
    E-Mail: jamila.kenney@iamovers.org
Manager, Programs: Brian Limperopulos
    E-Mail: brian.limperopulos@iamovers.org
Manager, Membership Services: Julia O'Connor
    E-Mail: julia.oconnor@iamovers.org
Director, Communications and Membership Engagement:
    Janet Cave Seely
    E-Mail: janet.seely@iamovers.org
Director, Military and Government Relations: Charles
    (Chuck) White
    E-Mail: charles.white@iamovers.org

Historical Note:
*IAM's mission is to provide the service and expertise
necessary to advance global commerce. IAM comprises of
auditing, forwarding, moving, and shipping companies that
provide services to its customers. Membership: $25-3000/
year.*

Meetings/Conferences: Annual
Conference Chair: Brian Limperopulos
2013 - Vancouver, BC (Vancouver Convention Center)/
    Oct. 7 - 10

Publications:
IAM e-Newsletter; on-line
Membership Directory; annually
The Portal magazine; bi-monthly

International Association of Music Libraries, United States Branch (1931)
8551 Research Way
Suite 180
Middleton, WI 53562
Tel: (608) 836-5825 *Fax:* (608) 831-8200
E-Mail: mla@areditions.com
Website: musiclibraryassoc.org
Members: 200 individuals and libraries
Staff: 5
Annual Budget: Under $10,000

Personnel:
President: Jerry L. McBride
    E-Mail: jerry.mcbride@stanford.edu
Administrative Officer: Linda W. Blair
    E-Mail: lblair@esm.rochester.edu
Web Site Editor: Michelle Oswell
    E-Mail: moswell@rci.rutgers.edu
Editor, Copyright Music Librarians: Tammy Ravas
    E-Mail: copyright@musiclibraryassoc.org
Director, Sales and Marketing: James L. Zychowicz
    E-Mail: james.zychowicz@areditions.com

Historical Note:
*MLA is the professional association for music libraries
and librarianship in the United States.MLA provides
a professional forum for librarians, archivists, and
others who support and preserve the world's musical
heritage. Membership: $60-230 (Personal,US/Non-
US); $50-70 (Student,US/Non-US); $105-155
(Institutional,US/Non-US); $460-770(Corporate,US/Non-
us); $110-120(Subscribers,US/Non-US).*

Meetings/Conferences: Annual
2013 - San Jose, CA/Feb. 27 - March 3
2014 - Atlanta, GA/Feb. 24 - March 2

Publications:
Membership directory; on-line
MLA Newsletter; quarterly
Notes; quarterly

International Association of Natural Resource Pilots (1972)
222 Seven Oaks Rd.
Glenwood Springs, CO 81601
Tel: (970) 618-9483
Website: ianrp.org
Members: 225 individuals
Staff: 3

Personnel:
President: Jeff Faught
    E-Mail: jfaught@nd.gov
Treasurer: Larry Gepfert
    E-Mail: larry.gepfert@state.co.us
Webmaster: Jason Jensen
    E-Mail: jason.jensen@juno.com

Historical Note:
*IANRP is a group of pilots who utilize aircraft in the field
of renewable resources. Members are pilots and aircrew
employed by federal, state and provincial natural resource/
conservation agencies in the United States and Canada.
Membership: $15 (Student); $35 (Regular).*

Publications:
Membership Directory; annually

International Association of Official Human Rights Agencies (1949)
444 N. Capitol St. NW
Suite 536
Washington, DC 20001
Tel: (202) 624-5410 *Fax:* (202) 624-8185
E-Mail: iaohra@sso.org
Website: iaohra.org
Members: 160 agencies
Staff: 3
Annual Budget: $50-100,000
Tax: 501(c)(3)

Personnel:
Acting Director: Shannon Bennett
Treasurer: Lonnie Douglas
Office Manager and Web Master: Lisa Sims

Historical Note:
*IAOHRA's mission is to foster human and intergroup
relations and provide opportunities and forums for the
exchange of ideas and information among human rights
advocates. Any official human rights agency or private
organization dedicated to the purposes and objectives of the
association can become a member of IAOHRA after meeting
membership requirements. Membership: $50-600/year.*

Continuing Education:
Certification Designation/s: CFHI

Meetings/Conferences: Annual

Publications:
Membership Directory; on-line
Tennessee Human Rights Commission Newsletter

Membership List Available to Non-members

International Association of Operative Millers (1896)
10100 W. 87th St.
Suite 306
Overland Park, KS 66212
Tel: (913) 338-3377 *Fax:* (913) 338-3553
E-Mail: info@iaom.info
Website: iaom.info
Members: 1500 individuals
Staff: 4
Annual Budget: $500-1,000,000
Tax: 501(c)(6)

Personnel:
Executive Vice President: Melinda Farris
Administrative Assistant: Dannell (Danni) Altman
Director, Meetings and Exhibits: Shannon Henson
    E-Mail: shannon.henson@iaom.info
Director, Professional Development: Carol Shankel

Historical Note:
*Formerly, the Association of Operative Millers, was renamed
as International Association of Operative Millers (IAOM),
in 2003. IOAM strives for the advancement of technology
in the flour milling, cereal grain and seed processing
industries. Members are millers, superintendents, engineers,
plant managers, and others in the flour milling, cereal
milling, and grain and seed industry. Membership: $195
(Active/Associate); $30 (Junior Active).*

Meetings/Conferences: Annual
Conference Chair: Shannon Henson

2013 - Niagara Falls, ON (Hilton Hotel and Suites
    Niagara Falls/Fallsview)/April 29 - May 3/800
    attendees
2014 - Omaha, NE (Hilton Omaha)/May 19 - 23/800
    attendees
Number of non-conference events/year: 1

Publications:
International Miller; quarterly; adv.
Membership Directory; annually; adv.

International Association of Oral and Maxillofacial Surgeons (1962)
17 W. 220 22nd St.
Suite 420
Oakbrook Terrace, IL 60181-4480
Tel: (630) 833-0945 *Fax:* (630) 833-1382
Website: iaoms.org
Members: 5800 individuals
Staff: 9
Annual Budget: $1-2,000,000
Tax: 501(c)(3)

Personnel:
Executive Director: Barbara Morrison CAE, IOM
IT Consultant: Jeff Jarzabek
Membership Associate: Lisa Markovic
Director: Susan A. Nowicki
    E-Mail: snowicki@iaoms.org
Assistant Executive Director/Newsletter Editor: Dr. Alexis
    B. Olsson
Professional Conference Organizer: Haydee Pampel
Administrative Assistant: Jan Vorel

Historical Note:
*Founded in 1962 by Sir Terence Ward (United Kingdom)
and Fred A. Henny, (USA) as the International Association
of Oral Surgeons. IAOMS' mission is to elevate the quality
of healthcare worldwide through the advancement of the art
and science of oral and maxilofacial surgery. Membership
$195 (Fellow/Associate); $ 85 (Fellow, reduced - residents
of selected countries)*

Meetings/Conferences: Annual
Conference Chair: Haydee Pampel
Number of non-conference events/year: 10

Publications:
International Association of Oral and Maxillofacial
    Surgeons Newsletter; adv.
International Journal of Oral and Maxillofacial Surgery
    (IJOMS); monthly; adv.
Membership Directory; on-line

International Association of Outsourcing Professionals (2005)
2600 South Rd.
Suite 44-240
Poughkeepsie, NY 12601
Tel: (845) 452-0600 *Fax:* (845) 452-6988
E-Mail: info@iaop.org
Website: iaop.org
Members: 120000 individuals and corporations
worldwide
Staff: 6

Personnel:
Managing Director, Certification: Jagdish Dalal
Director, Member Services Operations: Michael Forbes
    E-Mail: memberservices@iaop.org
PULSE Editor-in-Chief: Sandy Frinton
    E-Mail: sandy.frinton@iaop.org
Senior Managing Director: Deborah L. Hamill
    E-Mail: debi.hamill@iaop.org
Manager, Media and Communications: Kate Hammond
    E-Mail: kate.hammond@iaop.org
Public Relations Contact: Julie Huson
    E-Mail: julie.huson@iaop.org.

Historical Note:
*IAOP brings together outsourcing customers, providers
and advisors to exchange thoughts on leadership, share
best practices and network to maximize their effectiveness
in using outsourcing as a management tool. Membership:
$345 (Professional); $50 (Student); $5,000 (Corporate);
$15,000 (Corporate Provider/Advisor Full).*

Continuing Education:
Certification Designation/s: COP, COS

Meetings/Conferences: Annual
2013 - Phoenix, AZ (JW Marriott Phoenix Desert
    Ridge)/Feb. 18 - 20

Publications:
Globalization Today; adv.
IAOP Newsletter; monthly

Membership Directory; on-line
PULSE Magazine; monthly; adv.

International Association of Personal Protection Agents (1989)
711 Main
Grandview, MO 64030
Tel: (816) 765-5551
E-Mail: info@iappa.net
Website: iappa.net
Members:
600 individuals
30 countries
Staff: 3
Annual Budget: $10-25,000

Personnel:
Executive Director: Dr. Stephen R. Barnhart
   E-Mail: srb@iappa.net
Director, Operations and Training: Charles Mallice

Historical Note:
Founded as International Bodyguard Association, assumed its current name in 1996. IAPPA's purpose is to promote information about the protective service agent and also help its members in reaching specialized security services in particular close protection operations. Membership: $100 (Regular); $50 (Associate); $450 (Corporate).

Continuing Education:
Certification Designation/s: CPPA, CCPA

Publications:
Membership Directory; on-line

International Association of Personnel in Employment Security (1913)
1801 Louisville Rd.
Frankfort, KY 40601
Tel: (502) 223-4459 *Fax:* (502) 223-4127
TollFree: (888) 898-9960
E-Mail: iawp@iawponline.org
Website: iawponline.org
Members: 13000 members
Staff: 2

Personnel:
Director, Administration and Conference Planning: Mary Riddell
   E-Mail: maryr2@bellsouth.net
Contact, Membership Services: Paige Stodghill
   E-Mail: paige2@bellsouth.net

Historical Note:
IAWP is a professional association for members who work in public and private workforce development programs. Membership: $50 (Chapter-affiliated); $150 (Non-chapter affiliated).

Continuing Education:
Certification Designation/s: CWS

Meetings/Conferences:
Conference Chair: Mary Riddell
2013 - Chicago, IL/July 7 - 10

Publications:
Membership Directory; on-line

International Association Of Pet Cemeteries and Crematories (1971)
4991 Peachtree Rd.
Atlanta, GA 30341
Tel: (678) 892-6942 *Fax:* (770) 457-8160
E-Mail: iaopc@aol.com
Website: iaopc.com
Members: 165 cemeteries
Staff: 5
Annual Budget: $50-100,000

Personnel:
President: Debra Bjorling
Editor: Angie Hansen
Director, National Marketing and Promotion: Scott Hunter
Executive Secretary: Donna Shugart-Bethune
Treasurer: Barbara Wells

Historical Note:
Founded in Chicago as the National Association of Pet Cemeteries, it assumed its present name in 1978. IAOPCC's mission is to advance pet cemeteries everywhere through public awareness programs. Membership: $250 (Regular/ Affiliate); $300 (Supplier).

Meetings/Conferences:
Number of non-conference events/year: 1

Publications:
Membership Directory; on-line
News & Views; bi-monthly; adv.

International Association of Physicians in AIDS Care (1995)
123 Madison St.
Suite 1704
Chicago, IL 60602
Tel: (312) 795-4930 *Fax:* (312) 795-4938
E-Mail: iapac@iapac.org
Website: iapac.org
Members: 17000 individuals
Staff: 8
Annual Budget: $1-2,000,000
Tax: 501(c)(3)

Personnel:
President and Chief Executive Officer: Jose M. Zuniga MPH, PhD
Senior Program and Research Manager: Angela Knudson
Manager, Finance: Cathy Patterson
Director, Finance: Sonia Reynolds
   E-Mail: sreynolds@iapac.org

Historical Note:
IAPAC works to craft and implement global educational and advocacy strategies to improve the quality of care provided to all people living with HIV/AIDS. Membership: $75-200/ year.

Meetings/Conferences: Annual
2013 - Miami, FL/June 2 - 4

Publications:
Journal of the International Association of Physicians in AIDS Care; bi-monthly; adv.

Membership List Available to Non-members

International Association of Plastics Distributors (1956)
6734 W. 121 St.
Overland Park, KS 66209
Tel: (913) 345-1005 *Fax:* (913) 345-1006
E-Mail: iapd@iapd.org
Website: iapd.org
Members: 450 companies
Staff: 15
Annual Budget: $1-2,000,000

Personnel:
Executive Director: Susan E. Avery CAE
   E-Mail: savery@iapd.org
Graphic Designer: Bonnie Bush
   E-Mail: bbush@iapd.org
Manager, Marketing and Education: Wess Hudelson
   E-Mail: whudelson@iapd.org
Managing Editor: Mia Katz
   E-Mail: mkatz@iapd.org
Director, Advertising and Sales: Helen Muntean
   E-Mail: hmuntean@iapd.org
Managing Editor and Director, Marketing and Communications: Liz Novak
   E-Mail: lnovak@iapd.org
Manager, Meetings and Finance: Laurie Warren
   E-Mail: lwarren@iapd.org
Coordinator, Membership Services: Randy Wilkins
   E-Mail: rwilkins@iapd.org

Historical Note:
Formerly United Plastics Distributors Association and then (1970) National Association of Plastics Distributors. IAPD's mission is to expand the market for distributed plastics through collaboration, education and a commitment to sustainability. Membership: $752-6,269/year.

Continuing Education:
Certification Designation/s: IAPDPCP

Meetings/Conferences: Annual
Conference Chair: Laurie Warren

Publications:
Designing With Plastics; monthly; adv.
IAPD Magazine; bi-monthly; adv.
Membership Directory; on-line; adv.

International Association of Plumbing and Mechanical Officials (1926)
4755 E. Philadelphia St.
Ontario, CA 91761
Tel: (909) 472-4100 *Fax:* (909) 472-4150
E-Mail: iapmo@iapmo.org
Website: iapmo.org
Members: 3700 individuals
Staff: 120
Annual Budget: $10-25,000,000

Personnel:
Chief Executive Officer: G. P. Russ Chaney

   E-Mail: tricia.schwenke@iapmo.org
Senior Writer, Marketing, Communications and Editor: Geoff Bilau
   E-Mail: geoff.bilau@iapmo.org
General Counsel: Neil Bogatz Esq.
   E-Mail: neil.bogatz@iapmo.org
Administrator, Human Resources: Catalina Burks
   E-Mail: cathy.burks@iapmo.org
Staff Writer and Editor: Tim denHartog
   E-Mail: tim.denhartog@iapmo.org
Executive Assistant: Leticia Gallegos
   E-Mail: leticia.gallegos@iapmo.org
Director, Marketing and Communications: Duane Huisken
   E-Mail: duane.huisken@iapmo.org
Director, Program Development: Kathleen Mihelich
   E-Mail: kathleen.mihelich@iapmo.org
Director, Finance: Cesar Monzon
   E-Mail: cesar.monzon@iapmo.org
Director, Information Technology: Mitchell Morris
   E-Mail: mitch.morris@iapmo.org
Director, Travel and Events: Tina Rice
   E-Mail: tina.rice@iapmo.org
Director, Membership Services: Alan Wald
   E-Mail: alan.wald@iapmo.org

Historical Note:
Formerly (1966) Western Plumbing Officials Association. IAPMO strives to protect public's health and safety by working in concert with government and industry to implement comprehensive plumbing and mechanical systems around world. Members are government officials, agencies, industries and others interested in promotion of Uniform Plumbing and Mechanical Codes. Membership: $15-425 (IAPMO); $50-4500 (RPA).

Continuing Education:
Enrollment: 5000
Certification Designation/s: IAPMO

Meetings/Conferences: Annual
Conference Chair: Tina Rice
Number of non-conference events/year: 3

Publications:
Directory of Listed Plumbing Products; monthly
Directory of Listed Plumbing Products for Manufactured Housing & RVs; monthly
Directory of Water Conserving Products; monthly
Green e-Newsletter; monthly; adv.
IAPM online; weekly
Newsletter -I-Connection; monthly
Official Magazine; bi-monthly; adv.
Uniform Mechanical Code
Uniform Plumbing Codes
Uniform Solar Energy Code
Uniform Swimming Pool, Spa & Hot Tub Code

International Association of Printing House Craftsmen (1919)
PO Box 2549
Maple Grove, MN 55311-7549
E-Mail: headquarters@iaphc.org
Website: iaphc.org
Members: 6500 individuals
Staff: 2
Annual Budget: $100-250,000
Tax: 501(c)(6)

Personnel:
President: Kevin P. Keane
   E-Mail: kkeane1069@aol.com

Historical Note:
IAPHC works for the individuals in the printing and graphic arts industry for the purpose of their self development, their companies' success and the enhancement of the printing and graphic arts industry in society. Membership is open to persons employed in or retired from the graphic arts industry. Membership: $100/year.

Meetings/Conferences:
Number of non-conference events/year: 2

Publications:
E-Newsletter

International Association of Privacy Professionals (2000)
75 Rochester Ave.
Suite Four
Portsmouth, NH 03801
Tel: (603) 427-9200 *Fax:* (603) 427-9249
TollFree: (800) 266-6501
E-Mail: information@privacyassociation.org
Website: privacyassociation.org
Members: 10000 members

Staff: 43
Annual Budget: $5-10,000,000
Tax: 501(c)(6)

Personnel:
President and Chief Executive Officer: J. Trevor Hughes
    E-Mail: jthughes@privacyassociation.org
Director, Publications: Tracey Bentley
    E-Mail: tracey@privacyassociation.org
Global Director, Strategic Sales: Wills Catling CIPP
    E-Mail: wills@privacyassociation.org
Vice President: Brad Clark
    E-Mail: bclark@privacyassociation.org
Manager, Events: Rebecca Faherty
    E-Mail: rebecca@privacyassociation.org
Communications Manager: Alison Forman CIPP
    E-Mail: alison@privacyassociation.org
Manager, Membership and Customer Relations: Nicholas Lanzer
    E-Mail: nicholas@privacyassociation.org
Director, Information Technology: Jeff Northrop
    E-Mail: jeff@privacyassociation.org
Certification Director: Dick Soule
    E-Mail: dsoule@privacyassociation.org

Historical Note:
IAPP's mission is to define, promote and improve the privacy profession globally. Also provides a forum for privacy professionals to share best practices, track trends, advance privacy management issues, standardize the designations for privacy professionals, and provide education and guidance on opportunities in the field of information privacy. Membership: $50-20,000 /year.

Continuing Education:
Certification Designation/s: CIPP/IT, CIPP/C, CIPP, CIPP/G, CIPP/E

Meetings/Conferences: Annual
Conference Chair: Rebecca Faherty
2013 - Washington, DC/March 6 - 8

Publications:
Membership Directory; on-line
The Daily Dashboard; daily; adv.
The Peppers & Rogers; monthly

International Association of Professional Security Consultants *(1984)*
575 Market St.
Suite 2125
San Francisco, CA 94105
Tel: (415) 536-0288 *Fax:* (415) 764-4915
E-Mail: iapsc@iapsc.org
Website: iapsc.org
Members: 120 individuals
Staff: 4
Annual Budget: $50-100,000

Personnel:
Executive Director: Kerry Parker CAE
Manager, Accounting: Kam Choy
Administrative Coordinator: Alison Corley
Manager, Meetings: Chezka Solon

Historical Note:
IAPSC's mission is to establish and maintain better standards of professionalism and ethical conduct in the industry. Members are independent, non-product affiliated, security management technical and forensic consultants. Membership: $395/year (Active/Associate/Internal Consultant).

Continuing Education:
Certification Designation/s: CSC

Meetings/Conferences: Annual
Conference Chair: Chezka Solon
2013 - Napa, CA (The Meritage Resort and Spa)/April 21 - 24

Publications:
IAPSC eNewsletter; on-line
Membership Directory; on-line
The Independent Security Consultant; quarterly

Membership List Available to Non-members

International Association of Protocol Consultants *(2002)*
P.O. Box 6150
McLean, VA 22106-6159
Tel: (202) 631-5713
E-Mail: email@choosingcivility.org
Website: protocolconsultants.org
Members: 500 Organizations
Staff: 2
Annual Budget: Under $10,000

Tax: 501(c)(6)

Personnel:
President: Cherlynn Conetsco
Executive Director: Alinda Lewris

Historical Note:
A volunteer-driven, all-inclusive, nonprofit membership organization. IAPC's mission is to represent all areas of protocol, etiquette, and civility. Offers educational programs in leadership, country-specific do's and taboos, and international protocol.

Continuing Education:
Certification Designation/s: CPO, CPC

Publications:
Protocol Today

International Association of Railway Operating Officers *(1892)*
C/O Ted Hagemo
6645 MacArthur Dr.
Missoula, MT 59808
Tel: (406) 370-6977
Website: iaroo.org
Members: 500 individuals
Staff: 2
Annual Budget: $25-50,000

Personnel:
President: Kim Kautzman
    E-Mail: Kim.Kautzman@MontanaRail.com
Secretary and Treasurer: Ted Hagemo
    E-Mail: 2070cooper@msn.com

Historical Note:
Formerly Traveling Engineers Association. Merged with International Fuel Association in 1936 to form the Railway Fuel & Traveling Engineers Association. Became Railway Fuel and Operating Officers Association in 1956 and adopted the current name in 1988. IAROO's mission is to provide its members with pertinent operating and technical information that will allow them to provide better railroad management for the future. Membership: $30 (US); $35 (International).

Meetings/Conferences: Annual

Publications:
Manifest Bulletin; bi-monthly

International Association of Refrigerated Warehouses
1500 King St.
Suite 201
Alexandria, VA 22314
Staff: 16
Annual Budget: $2-5,000,000
Tax: 501(c)(6)

Personnel:
President and Chief Executive Officer: J. William (Bill) Hudson
    E-Mail: bhudson@gcca.org

Historical Note:
A division of the Global Cold Chain Alliance (see seperate listing). IARW promotes best practices in temperature-controlled warehousing and logistics industry through research, industry benchmarking, networking, and education.

International Association of Rehabilitation Professionals *(1977)*
1926 Waukegan Rd.
Suite One
Glenview, IL 60025-1770
Tel: (847) 657-6964 *Fax:* (847) 657-6963
TollFree: (888) 427-7722
Website: rehabpro.org
Members: 2800 individuals
Staff: 5
Annual Budget: $500-1,000,000
Tax: 501(c)(6)

Personnel:
Executive Director: Carl A. Wangman CAE
    E-Mail: carlw@tcag.com
Manager, Communications: Bruce Adams
    E-Mail: bruce@tcag.com
Manager, Conferences: Marcie McGlynn
    E-Mail: marciem@tcag.com
Manager, Education: Pat Sistler
    E-Mail: pats@tcag.com
Director, Marketing and Technology: Brett Wangman
    E-Mail: brettw@tcag.com

Historical Note:

Formerly (2000) the National Association of Rehabilitation Professionals in the Private Sector. IARP's aim is to promote multidisciplinary rehabilitation, disability management, and return-to- work services on behalf of persons with disabilities and the economically disadvantaged. Members are individuals in private sector companies or non-profit organizations that provide rehabilitation services. Membership: $167 (Individual); $125 (Associate); $25 (Student).

Meetings/Conferences: Annual
Conference Chair: Marcie McGlynn
Number of non-conference events/year: 1

Publications:
Journal of Life Care Planning (JLCP); adv.
Membership Directory; on-line
The Rehabilitation Professional; adv.

International Association of Round Dance Teachers *(1976)*
176 S. Cole Rd.
Boise, ID 83709-0932
Tel: (208) 377-1232 *Fax:* (208) 377-1236
TollFree: (800) 346-7522
E-Mail: roundalab@roundalab.org
Website: roundalab.org
Members: 1400 individuals
Staff: 1
Annual Budget: $100-250,000

Personnel:
Executive Administrator: Al Shaw

Historical Note:
ROUNDALAB's purpose is to provide a framework for standardizing various aspects of the activity such as dance figures, cue terms, cue sheet format and teaching methodology. Membership: $70 (International, per Renewal Teaching Unit); $60 (U.S.); $65 (Canada).

Meetings/Conferences: Annual
Conference Chair: Al Shaw
2013 - Oklahoma City, OK (Meridian Convention Center)/June 23 - 26

Publications:
Membership Directory; on-line

International Association of School Librarianship *(1971)*
65 E. Wacker Pl.
Suite 1900
Chicago, IL 60601-7246
Fax: (312) 419-8950
Website: iasl-online.org
Members: 700 individuals
Staff: 5
Annual Budget: $25-50,000
Tax: 501(c)(3)

Personnel:
Webmaster: Karen Bonanno
Executive Secretary and Publications Contact: Carla Funk

Historical Note:
IASL provides an international forum for people interested in promoting school library media programs as viable instruments in the educational process. It also provides guidance and advice for the development of school library programs and the school library profession. Membership: $10-30 (Student); $40-200 (Association/Institution); $2,000 (Life); $15- 2000 (Personal).

Meetings/Conferences: Annual

Publications:
IASL Newsletter
School Libraries Worldwide; bi-annually

International Association of Skateboard Companies *(1995)*
22431 Antonio Pkwy.
Suite B160-412
Rancho Santa Margarita, CA 92688
Tel: (949) 455-1112 *Fax:* (949) 455-1712
E-Mail: info@skateboardiasc.org
Website: skateboardiasc.org
Members: 50 companies
Staff: 2
Annual Budget: $100-250,000
Tax: 501(c)(6)

Personnel:
Executive Director: Josh Friedberg

Historical Note:
IASC's mission is to promote skateboarding, increase participation, save its members money and educate. Members are companies with products or goods and

services within the skateboard marketplace. Membership: $250-7,500/year.

Meetings/Conferences: Annual
Number of non-conference events/year: 2

Publications:
IASC Newsletter; monthly
Membership Directory; on-line

International Association of Speakers Bureaus
(1986)
3933 S. McClintock Dr.
Suite 505
Tempe, AZ 85282
Tel: (480) 839-1423 *Fax:* (480) 603-4141
E-Mail: info@iasbweb.org
Website: iasbweb.org
Members: 160 speakers bureaus and agencies
Staff: 2
Annual Budget: $100-250,000
Tax: 501(c)(6)

Personnel:
Executive Vice President: Marie Fredette CAE
Treasurer: Karen Harris

Historical Note:
Formerly (1991 known as International Group of Agents and Bureaus; became (2001) International Group of Agencies & Bureaus. IASB's mission is to raise the awareness of speakers bureaus to meeting planners and to educate members on accepted practices. It also seeks to provide leadership to the bureau industry through education, resources and partnerships. Represents speakers bureaus and agencies worldwide. Membership: $600/year.

Meetings/Conferences: Annual

Publications:
Bureau Directory; on-line; adv.
Bureau Talk; semi-monthly; adv.
Speaker Directory; on-line; adv.

International Association of Special Investigation Units *(1984)*
3230 Maiden Ln., Suite Five
P.O. Box 26
Manchester, MD 21102
Tel: (443) 507-6500 *Fax:* (443) 507-6519
E-Mail: info@iasiu.org
Website: iasiu.org
Members: 4600 individuals
Staff: 10
Annual Budget: $500-1,000,000

Personnel:
Executive Director: Dawn R. Lipsey

Historical Note:
IASIU's mission is to promote a coordinated effort within the industry to combat insurance fraud. Membership : $25-100/year.

Continuing Education:
Enrollment: 4200
Certification Designation/s: CIFI

Meetings/Conferences: Annual
Conference Chair: Dawn R. Lipsey
2013 - Atlanta, GA (Atlanta Marriott Marquis)/Sept. 8 - 11
Number of non-conference events/year: 2

Publications:
SIU Today; quarterly; adv.

International Association of Structural Movers
(1983)
P.O. Box 2637
Lexington, SC 29071-2637
Tel: (803) 951-9304 *Fax:* (803) 951-9314
Website: iasm.org
Members: 385 Companies
Staff: 3
Annual Budget: $250-500,000

Personnel:
Staff Executive: N. Eugene Brymer APR, CAE
E-Mail: gbrymer@windstream.net

Historical Note:
Members are movers of heavy structural products, trusses, barns, houses, machinery, bridges, ships, and other structures, or in the manufacturing of products used in this work. Membership: $350-750 (Company); $175 (Retired/ Company Representative).

Meetings/Conferences: Annual

2013 - Ontario, CA (DoubleTree by Hilton)/March 20 - 24

Publications:
Membership Directory; on-line; adv.
The Structural Mover Magazine; quarterly; adv.

International Association of Tool Craftsmen
(1953)
3710 Kasper St.
Racine, WI 53402-3542
Tel: (309) 782-5776
Members: 200 individuals
Staff: 1
Annual Budget: $10-25,000

Personnel:
Secretary: Michael Kubarth

Historical Note:
Independent labor union.

International Association of Tour Managers - North American Region *(1961)*
9500 Rainier Ave., South, Suite 603
Seattle, WA 98118
Website: tourmanager.org
Members: 1000 individuals
Staff: 3
Annual Budget: $500-1,000,000

Personnel:
Chair: Scott McGraw

Historical Note:
Affiliated with American Society of Travel Agents, European Tour Operators Association, National Federation of Tourist Guide Associations, Professional Association of Tour Managers; membership: $125/year ($65/year for students); associate membership available to tour operators.

International Association of Used Equipment Dealers *(2001)*
214 Edgewood Dr.
Suite 100
Wilmington, DE 19809-3255
Tel: (302) 765-3571 *Fax:* (302) 765-3571
E-Mail: info@iaued.org
Website: iauedadmin.bluestep.net
Members: 50 dealers
Staff: 1
Annual Budget: $100-250,000
Tax: 501(c)(6)

Personnel:
President: Darryl D. McEwen
E-Mail: darryl@iaued.org

Historical Note:
IAUED is an association representing the used capital equipment industry, as well as firms that supply services to truckers, riggers, leasing companies, etc. Members buy, sell and appraise used metalworking, plastics, woodworking, materials handling, electrical, medical, construction, food and chemical processing, and other types of equipment. Membership: $250 (Regular/Associate); $125 (Branch Membership).

Meetings/Conferences: Annual
Number of non-conference events/year: 4

Publications:
Membership Directory; on-line

Membership List Available to Non-members

International Association of Venue Managers
(1924)
635 Fritz Dr.
Suite 100
Coppell, TX 75019-4422
Tel: (972) 906-7441 *Fax:* (972) 906-7418
TollFree: (800) 935-4226
Website: iavm.org
Members:
400 Allied companies
3500 individuals
Staff: 18
Annual Budget: $2-5,000,000

Personnel:
President and Chief Executive Officer: Vicki Hawarden
E-Mail: vicki.hawarden@iavm.org
Director, Knowledge and Meetings: Margot Angles
E-Mail: Margot.Angles@iavm.org
Editor: R. V. Baugus
E-Mail: rv.baugus@iaam.org

Director, Membership Services: Gina Brydson
E-Mail: gina.brydson@iavm.org
Manager, Marketing Communications: Susan Ferraro
E-Mail: susan.ferraro@iavm.org
Chief Operating Officer: Steve Flamm
E-Mail: steve.flamm@iavm.org
Legal Counsel: Turner Madden Esq.
E-Mail: tdmadden@verizon.net
Accounting Specialist: Maria Selgado
E-Mail: maria.selgado@iavm.org
Director, Information Technology and Operations: Ramesh Vodoor
E-Mail: ramesh.vodoor@iavm.org
Director, Marketing: Kris Williams
E-Mail: kris.williams@iaam.org
Vice President, Education: Rodney Williams MBA, PhD
E-Mail: rodney.williams@iavm.org

Historical Note:
Formerly International Association of Assembly Managers (2010) and International Association of Auditorium Managers (1996). IAVM's mission is to educate, advocate, and inspire public assembly venue professionals worldwide. Membership: $75-590/year.

Continuing Education:
Certification Designation/s: CFE

Meetings/Conferences:
Conference Chair: Margot Angles
2013 - New Orleans, LA/July 26 - 30

Publications:
Facility Manager; adv.
IAAM News; bi-monthly; adv.
Membership Directory; on-line
Venue Safety and Security; monthly

Membership List Available to Non-members

International Association of Wildland Fire *(1983)*
1418 Washburn St.
Missoula, MT 59801
Tel: (406) 531-8264 *Fax:* (205) 823-2760
TollFree: (888) 440-4293
E-Mail: iawf@iawfonline.org
Website: iawfonline.org
Members: 700 individuals
Staff: 3
Annual Budget: $100-250,000
Tax: 501(c)(3)

Personnel:
Executive Director: Mikel Robinson
E-Mail: execdir@iawfonline.org
Exhibitor and Fundraising Coordinator: Michelle Ekstrom
E-Mail: exhibits@iawfonline.org
Public Affairs Officer: Paula Nelson
E-Mail: publicaffairs@iawfonline.org

Historical Note:
IWAF's purpose is to facilitate communication and provide leadership for the wildland fire community. Members are academics and professionals with an interest in wildland fires. Membership: $60 (Individual); $25 (Student); $75 (Library/Organization); $250 (Corporate 5); $600 (Agency); $1100 (Corporate 25).

Meetings/Conferences: Semi-Annual
Conference Chair: Michelle Ekstrom
2013 - Raleigh, NC/Feb. 18 - 22
2013 - St. Petersburg, Russia/July 1 - 4
Number of non-conference events/year: 2

Publications:
IAWF Newsletter; monthly
International Journal of Wildland Fire
Membership Directory; on-line
WildFire Magazine; adv.

Membership List Available to Non-members

International Association of Women in Fire and Emergency Services *(1982)*
4025 Fair Ridge Dr.
Suite 300
Fairfax, VA 22033
Tel: (703) 896-4858 *Fax:* (703) 273-9363
E-Mail: info@wfsi.org
Website: i-women.org
Members:
250 organizations
820 individuals
Staff: 3
Annual Budget: $25-50,000
Tax: 501(c)(3)

Personnel:
President: Jeanne Pashalek
Vice President and Treasurer: Laura Baker
Manager, Association and Programs: Sharon Baroncelli
    E-Mail: staff@i-women.org

Historical Note:
*Formerly known as Women in the Fire Service; (1989)
Women in Fire Suppression. WFS is dedicated to improving
the fire service through the involvement and success of
women. Membership: $25 (Full Time Student/Volunteer
Emergency Responder/Wildland); $45 (Associate); $50
(Career Emergency Responder); $100 (Chief Officer); $150
(Department).*

Meetings/Conferences: Annual
Conference Chair: Sharon Baroncelli

Publications:
iWomen Newsletter; monthly; adv.

International Association of Women Ministers
(1919)
579 Main St.
Stroudsburg, PA 18360
Tel: (412) 734-2263
E-Mail: iawmpage@aol.com
Website: womenministers.org
Members: 350 individuals
Staff: 5
Annual Budget: $10-25,000
Tax: 501(c)(3)

Personnel:
Co President: Linda B. Brebner
President: Dr. Eunice B. Poethig
    E-Mail: iawm-president@womenministers.org
Editor: LaVonne Althouse
    E-Mail: iawm-editor@womenministers.org
Treasurer: Carol S. Brown
Website Editor: Jean Henderson
    E-Mail: iawm-webeditor@womenministers.org

Historical Note:
*IAWM's mission is to support and develop relationships
with women in ministry around the world. Membership:
$350 (Lifetime); $5-40 (Based on Proportionate to Income).*

Meetings/Conferences: Annual

Publications:
The Women's Pulpit; quarterly

International Association of Women Police
(1915)
P.O. Box 11038
Denver, CO 80211-0038
Tel: (720) 256-7498 *Fax*: (720) 913-0058
E-Mail: iawp@iawp.org
Website: iawp.org
Members: 3000 individuals
Staff: 15
Annual Budget: $100-250,000
Tax: 501(c)(6)

Personnel:
Treasurer: Kim Covert
    E-Mail: kimcovert95029@msn.com
Contact, Meetings: Julia Jaeger
Editor: Simon C. Townsley
    E-Mail: scmtownsley@blueyonder.co.uk
Business Manager: Wendy Wilson
    E-Mail: wjw4905@aol.com

Historical Note:
*Originally founded as the International Policewoman's
Association (1915) and disbanded in 1932; reorganized
under its present name in 1956. IAWP's mission is
to strengthen, unite and raise the profile of women in
criminal justice internationally. Members are full-time law
enforcement officers with powers of arrest. Membership:
$25-500/year.*

Meetings/Conferences: Annual
Conference Chair: Julia Jaeger
2013 - Durban, South Africa/Sept. 21 - 26
2014 - Winnipeg, MB/Sept. 28 - Oct. 2

Publications:
Woman Police Magazine; quarterly; adv.

International Association of Workforce
Professionals (IAWP) *(1913)*
1801 Louisville Rd.
Frankfort, KY 40601-3922
Tel: (502) 223-4459 *Fax*: (502) 223-4127
TollFree: (888) 898-9960
E-Mail: iawp@iawponline.org

Website: iawponline.org
Members: 13000 individuals
Staff: 3
Annual Budget: $250-500,000
Tax: 501(c)(6)

Personnel:
Director, Administration and Conference Planning: Mary
    Riddell
    E-Mail: maryr@iawponline.org
Coordinator, Membership Services: Paige Stodghill
    E-Mail: paige2@bellsouth.net

Historical Note:
*Formerly International Association of Public Employment
Services and then International Association of Personnel
in Employment Security, assumed current name in 2003.
IAWP is dedicated to advance in the the field of workforce
development through education, research, legislative action,
financial support, international networking, and useful
publications. Members are involved in unemployment
compensation and job placement in local, state and federal
agencies. Membership: $50 (International, Chapter-
Affiliated); $150 (Non Chapter-Affiliated).*

Continuing Education:
Certification Designation/s: CWS, WPDP

Meetings/Conferences:
2013 - Chicago, IL (Fairmont Chicago Millenium Park)/
    July 7 - 10
2014 - Portland, OR (Red Lion Hotel)/June 22 - 25
2015 - Savannah, GA (Hyatt Regency Savannah)/June
    14 - 17

Publications:
Chapter Activity Countdown; monthly
Membership Directory; on-line
Workforce Professional; quarterly

International Atherosclerosis Society *(1979)*
6535 Fannin
M.S. A-601
Houston, TX 77030
Tel: (713) 797-0401 *Fax*: (713) 796-8853
E-Mail: athero@bcm.edu
Website: athero.org
Members: 13329 individuals
Staff: 3
Annual Budget: $100-250,000
Tax: 501(c)(3)

Personnel:
Executive Director: Ann Stephens Jackson
    E-Mail: ias@bcm.edu
Editor-in-Chief: Scott M. Grundy
    E-Mail: scott.grundy@utsouthwestern.edu

Historical Note:
*IAS advocates, at an international level, the advancement of
science, research and teaching in the field of atherosclerosis.
Members are physicians, scientists and other health
professionals. Membership: $10 (Individual); $3
(Organization/Company).*

Meetings/Conferences: Annual

Publications:
Atherosclerosis - Journal; monthly
E-literature; monthly
E-newsletter; monthly

International Aviation Ground Support
Association *(2003)*
201 Park Washington Ct.
Falls Church, VA 22046-4527
Tel: (703) 533-0251 *Fax*: (703) 241-5603
E-Mail: info@iagsa.org
Website: iagsa.org
Staff: 3

Personnel:
Executive Director: Clay D. Tyeryar CAE, MAM
Director, Communications: Karen Thompson
    E-Mail: karen@shadyvale.com
Coordinator, Membership Services: Kristina Wise

Historical Note:
*IAGSA aims to unite support equipment manufacturers and
suppliers and associations that represent the industry's
customers. Membership: $500 (Annual Sales under $2
million); $1000 (Annual Sales $2 million or more).*

International Aviation Women's Association
(1988)
P.O. Box 1088
Edgewater, MD 21037
Tel: (410) 571-1990

E-Mail: info@iawa.org
Website: iawa.org
Members: 150 individuals
Staff: 7
Annual Budget: $100-250,000

Personnel:
Contact, Administration: Karen Griggs
    E-Mail: karengriggs@iawa.org
Vice President, Public Relations and Communications:
    Diana Gurfel

Historical Note:
*IAWA is dedicated to promote advancement of women
in industry and serves as an information exchange and
resource to professional women. It brings together women
of achievement in aviation industry and promotes their
advancement internationally through establishment
of a worldwide network of aviation professional
contacts. Membership: $200/year; $175 (Government
Representatives/Employees).*

Continuing Education:
Enrollment: 10
Certification Designation/s: CLE

Meetings/Conferences: Annual
Conference Chair: Karen Griggs

Publications:
IAWA News and Views

International Balloon Association *(1989)*
1600 Lynnhurst Ave.
Wichita, KS 67212
Tel: (316) 943-7223 *Fax*: (316) 941-4097
TollFree: (866) 413-7358
Website: ibaonline.net
Staff: 2
Annual Budget: $25-50,000

Personnel:
Executive Director: Marty Fish
    E-Mail: Marty@ibaonline.net
Treasurer: Jeff Manke
    E-Mail: Jeff@msrballoons.com

Historical Note:
*IBA's mission is to increase the communication within
the industry and to continue to seek other services for
productive benefit of the membership. Membership: $450
(Distributor); $1500 (Balloon Manufacturers/Helium
Manufacturers); $700 (Accessories Manufacturers/Helium
Suppliers/Support Services).*

Meetings/Conferences:
2013 - St. Louis, MO (St. Louis Airport Marriott Hotel)/
    Jan. 27 - 30
2013 - Long Beach, CA (Hilton Long Beach & Executive
    Meeeting Center)/July 25 - 28
2014 - Denver, CO/March 26 - 30

Publications:
What's Up? Newsletter

International Banana Association *(1983)*
1901 Pennsylvania Ave. NW
Suite 1100
Washington, DC 20006
Tel: (202) 303-3400 *Fax*: (202) 303-3433
E-Mail: info@eatmorebananas.com
Website: eatmorebananas.com
Members: 7 companies
Staff: 2
Annual Budget: $500-1,000,000
Tax: 501(c)(6)

Personnel:
Executive Director: Tim Debus
    E-Mail: tdebus@uffva.org

Historical Note:
IBA ia a trade association of the banana industry.

International Beverage Dispensing Equipment
Association *(1971)*
3837 Naylors Ln.
Baltimore, MD 21208
Tel: (410) 602-0616 *Fax*: (410) 486-6799
E-Mail: ibdea@cornerstoneassoc.com
Website: ibdea.org
Members: 250 companies and 200 individuals
Staff: 2
Annual Budget: $250-500,000

Personnel:
Executive Director: Marvin "Marv" Howard

Historical Note:

Established as the National Soda Dispensing Equipment Association; became National Beverage Dispensing Equipment Association in 1982 and assumed its current name in 1996. IBDEA is a non-profit trade association representing companies that sell, lease, rent, manufacture and service beverage dispensing equipment and supplies. Members are companies which sell, rent or service beverage dispensing equipment. Membership: $325-925 (Regular); $625 (Associate).

Continuing Education:
Enrollment: 20
Certification Designation/s: BOC

Meetings/Conferences: Annual
2013 - Weston, FL (Hyatt Regency Bonaventure Conference Center and Spa)/March 7 - 12
Number of non-conference events/year: 5

Publications:
IBDEAReport - Newsletter; quarterly
Membership Directory; on-line

International Biometric Industry Association
(1998)
919 18th St. NW
Suite 901
Washington, DC 20006
Tel: (202) 587-4855 *Fax:* (202) 587-4888
E-Mail: ibia@ibia.org
Website: ibia.org
Members: 28 Organizations
Staff: 1
Annual Budget: $100-250,000

Personnel:
Managing Director: Tovah LaDier
    E-Mail: tladier@ibia.org

Historical Note:
IBIA's mission is to promote the effective and appropriate use of technology to determine identity and enhance security, privacy, productivity, and convenience for individuals, organizations, and governments. Membership: $200 (Individual); $500 (Colleges/Universities); $1,000 (Nonprofit organizations); $1,000-20,000 (Companies, depending on the Annual worldwide sales).

Publications:
Membership Directory; on-line

International Biometric Society *(1947)*
1444 First St. NW
Suite 700
Washington, DC 20005-6542
Tel: (202) 712-9049 *Fax:* (202) 216-9646
E-Mail: ibs@bostrom.com
Website: tibs.org
Members: 6500 individuals
Staff: 3
Annual Budget: $500-1,000,000
Tax: 501(c)(3)

Personnel:
President: John Hinde
Executive Director: Claire Shanley

Historical Note:
The Biometric Society was founded at Woods Hole, MA in September 1947 as a result of a report at the First International Biometric Conference. Became the International Biometric Society in 1994. Promotes the application of mathematical and statistical methods and applications in pure and applied biological sciences. Membership: $60 (Individual); $300 (Organization/ Company).

Meetings/Conferences:
Number of non-conference events/year: 20

Publications:
Biometric Bulletin; quarterly; adv.
Biometrics; quarterly
Journal of Agricultural, Biological, and Environmental Statistics; quarterly

International Bluegrass Music Association *(1985)*
Two Music Cir., South
Suite 100
Nashville, TN 37203
Tel: (615) 256-3222 *Fax:* (615) 256-0450
TollFree: (888) 438-4262
E-Mail: info@ibma.org
Website: ibma.org
Members: 1000 individuals
Staff: 5
Annual Budget: $500-1,000,000
Tax: 501(c)(6)

Personnel:
Executive Director: Nancy Cardwell
    E-Mail: nancyc@ibma.org
Administrative and Media Assistant: Katherine Coe
Director, Member and Convention Services: Jill Crabtree
    E-Mail: jill@ibma.org
Director, Publications Editor and Special Projects: Caroline Wright

Historical Note:
IBMA's mission is to work together for standards of professionalism, a greater appreciation for member music, and the success of the worldwide bluegrass community. Members are musicians, broadcasters, record manufacturers, distributors, writers and event promoters. Membership: $75 (Professional Individual); $205 (Professional Organization); $40 (Grass Roots Club); $15 (Youth); $1,000 (Individual, Lifetime); $2,500 (Organization, Lifetime).

Meetings/Conferences: Annual
Conference Chair: Jill Crabtree
Number of non-conference events/year: 1

Publications:
International Bluegrass
Membership Directory; on-line

International Bone and Mineral Society *(1960)*
401 N Michigan Ave.
Suite 2200
Chicago, IL 60611
Tel: (312) 321-5113 *Fax:* (312) 673-6934
E-Mail: info@ibmsonline.org
Website: ibmsonline.org
Staff: 6
Annual Budget: $1-2,000,000

Personnel:
Executive Director: Kevin Baliozian
    E-Mail: kbaliozian@ibmsonline.org
Education Coordinator: Nicole Anderson
Editor in Chief: Serge Ferrari
Association Manager: Janene Chan Powers
    E-Mail: jchanpowers@ibmsonline.org
Director, Development: Jeanette Ruby
    E-Mail: jruby@ibmsonline.org
Meetings Coordinator: Alexandra Zapple

Historical Note:
The International Bone and Mineral Society was originally constituted as the Parathyroid Conferences. IBMS is the international organization that facilitates the generation and dissemination of knowledge of bone and mineral metabolism through communication, community, training, and multi-disciplinary meetings throughout the world.Membership: $135-$175 (Individual); $100(Member-in-Training); $12,500 (Corporate).

Meetings/Conferences:
Conference Chair: Alexandra Zapple
2013 - Kobe, Japan (Kobe Convention Center and Kobe Portopia Hotel)/May 28 - June 1
2013 - Miami, FL/Nov. 7 - 9

Publications:
Bone Journal
Membership Directory; on-line

International Bottled Water Association *(1958)*
1700 Diagonal Rd.
Suite 650
Alexandria, VA 22314
Tel: (703) 683-5213 *Fax:* (703) 683-4074
TollFree: (800) 928-3711
E-Mail: info@bottledwater.org
Website: bottledwater.org
Members: 640 members
Staff: 12
Annual Budget: $5-10,000,000
Tax: 501(c)(6)

Personnel:
President: Joseph Doss
    E-Mail: jdoss@bottledwater.org
Director, Conventions, Trade Shows and Meetings: Michele Campbell
    E-Mail: mcampbell@bottledwater.org
Manager, Membership Services: Dennis N. Carpenter
    E-Mail: dcarpenter@bottledwater.org
Vice President, Government Relations: Daniel Felton
    E-Mail: dfelton@bottledwater.org
Manager, Publications and Special Projects: Sabrina Hicks
    E-Mail: shicks@bottledwater.org
Vice President, Education, Science and Technical Relations: Robert R. Hirst

    E-Mail: rhirst@bottledwater.org
Vice President, Communications: Christopher Hogan
    E-Mail: chogan@bottledwater.org
Chief Financial Officer: Michelle S. Tiller
    E-Mail: mtiller@bottledwater.org

Historical Note:
Established as American Bottled Water Association, assumed its present name in 1982. Represents the bottled water industry. IBWA provides service to all bottled water industry and related business issues. Mission is to expand the use of bottled water through consumer awareness, government relations, technical and Scientific expertise, and other appropriate activities. Membership consists of owners and operators of bottled water plants, dealers, distributors and industry suppliers. Membership: $1,093-384,580/ year.

Meetings/Conferences:
Conference Chair: Michele Campbell
2013 - Cocoa Beach, FL (Holiday Inn Express Hotel and Suites Cocoa Beach)/Jan. 28 - 31

Publications:
e-Newsletter; weekly
Membership Directory

International Bowling Pro Shop and Instructors Association *(1990)*
P.O. Box 6574
Arlington, TX 76005-6574
Tel: (817) 649-0079 *Fax:* (817) 633-2940
TollFree: (800) 659-9444
Website: ibpsia.com
Members:
630 retailers
96 manufacturers
Staff: 6
Annual Budget: $100-250,000

Personnel:
Executive Director and Managing Director: Bill Supper
    E-Mail: bill@ibpsia.com
Director, Member Benefits: Amy Arcuri
    E-Mail: amy@bpaa.com
Director, Information Technology and General Services: Rich Cairns
    E-Mail: rich@ibpsia.com
Director, Communications: Ron DeRoxtra
    E-Mail: ron@bpaa.com
Director, Finance: Judy King
    E-Mail: judy@bpaa.com
Director, Meetings and Events: Lee Ann Norton
    E-Mail: leeann@bpaa.com

Historical Note:
Formerly the International Bowling Pro Shop Association (1994). IBPSIA's mission to assist pro shops and instruction professionals to become successful and more profitable by providing education, benefits and industry standardization.. IBPSIA members are retailers, manufacturers and interested individuals. Membership: $250 (U.S., Mexican and Canadian Retailers, Regular/ Affiliate, Associate Branch); $450 (U.S., Mexican and Canadian Associates); $275 (Foreign Retailer); $475 (Foreign Associates); $150 (Regular Branch) $125 (Foreign Regular/Regular Branch); $275 (Foreign Affiliate).

Continuing Education:
Certification Designation/s: HOTS

Meetings/Conferences:
Conference Chair: Lee Ann Norton
Number of non-conference events/year: 1

Publications:
IBPSIA E-Net News; weekly
Merchandising Trends- Newsletter; monthly

International Boxing Federation *(1983)*
899 Mountain Ave.
Suite 2C
Springfield, NJ 07081
Tel: (973) 564-8046 *Fax:* (973) 564-8751
Website: ibf-usba-boxing.com
Staff: 12
Annual Budget: $1-2,000,000

Personnel:
President: Daryl J. Peoples
    E-Mail: dpeoples@ibfboxing.com
Administrative Assistant: Arnold D. Peoples
Director, Public Relations: Jeanette Salazar
    E-Mail: jsalazar@ibfboxing.com

Historical Note:
The International Boxing Federation, or IBF, is one of four major organizations recognized by IBHOF which sanction

world championship boxing bouts, alongside the WBA, WBC and WBO. Membership: $200/year.

Meetings/Conferences: Annual

Publications:
Membership Directory; on-line

International Brain Injury Association (1993)
P.O. Box 1804
Alexandria, VA 22313
Tel: (703) 960-6500 *Fax:* (703) 960-6603
E-Mail: info@internationalbrain.org
Website: internationalbrain.org
Staff: 1
Annual Budget: $500-1,000,000
Tax: 501(c)(3)

Personnel:
Executive Director, Administration: Margaret Roberts
    E-Mail: mjroberts@aol.com

Historical Note:
Underwent merger with the International Association for the Study of Brain Injury in 1998. IBIA is dedicated to the development and support of multidisciplinary medical and clinical professionals, advocates, policy makers, consumers and others who work to improve outcomes and opportunities for persons with brain injury. Membership: $250/year.

Publications:
Brain Injury
International NeuroTrauma Letter; quarterly

Membership List Available to Non-members

International Brangus Breeders Association (1949)
5750 Epsilon
San Antonio, TX 78249
Tel: (210) 696-8231 *Fax:* (210) 696-8718
E-Mail: info@int-brangus.org
Website: gobrangus.com
Members: 2500 individuals
Staff: 10
Annual Budget: $1-2,000,000
Tax: 501(c)(5)

Personnel:
Executive Vice President: Joseph M. Massey
    E-Mail: joemassey@int-brangus.org
Manager, Information Technology: Jim Bulger
    E-Mail: jim_bulger@gps-beef.com
Coordinator, Communications: Brittni Drennan
    E-Mail: brittni@int-brangus.org
Director, Marketing Programs: Ben Spitzer
    E-Mail: ben@int-brangus.org
Contact, Registry: Rosanne Sralla
    E-Mail: rosanne_sralla@int-brangus.org
Contact, Accounts: Patti Teeler
    E-Mail: patti@gps-beef.com

Historical Note:
Association of breeders and merchandisers of Brangus beef cattle. The purpose of IBBA is to empower members to advance the quality, reliability and value of Brangus and Brangus influenced cattle; and also provides innovative programs and services which enhance the economic well-being of members and commercial customers. Membership: $125 (Senior); $25 (Associate/Junior).

Meetings/Conferences: Annual
Conference Chair: Rosanne Sralla

Publications:
Brangus Journal; bi-monthly; adv.
FRONTLINE Beef Producer; quarterly; adv.
Semen Directory; on-line

International Bridge, Tunnel and Turnpike Association (1932)
1146 19th St. NW
Suite 600
Washington, DC 20036
Tel: (202) 659-4620 *Fax:* (202) 659-0500
E-Mail: info@ibtta.org
Website: ibtta.org
Members: 250 companies and organizations
Staff: 9
Annual Budget: $2-5,000,000
Tax: 501(c)(6)

Personnel:
Executive Director and Chief Executive Officer: Patrick D. Jones
    E-Mail: pjones@ibtta.org

Manager, Conference Logistics and Administrator, Membership Database: Kathleen Davis
    E-Mail: kdavis@ibtta.org
Manager, Marketing: Cari Dellinger
    E-Mail: cdellinger@ibtta.org
Director, Government affairs: Neil A. Gray
    E-Mail: neilgray@ibtta.org
Office Manager and Meeting Registrar: Harry Smith
    E-Mail: hsmith@ibtta.org

Historical Note:
Founded as the American Toll Bridge Association, became the American Bridge, Tunnel and Turnpike Association in 1948 and assumed its present name in 1964. IBTTA's purpose is to provide a forum for sharing knowledge and ideas to promote and enhance toll-financed transportation services. Membership consists of public agencies, private companies, and support organizations operating toll facilities. Membership: $4,800 (Associate); $9,000 (Sustaining).

Meetings/Conferences: Annual
Conference Chair: Kathleen Davis
2013 - Vancouver, BC (Fairmont Hotel Vancouver)/
    Sept. 22 - 25
2014 - Austin, TX (Hilton Austin)/Sept. 14 - 17
Number of non-conference events/year: 10

Publications:
IBTTA Membership Directory; on-line
Tollways; semi-annually; adv.

International Brotherhood of Boilermakers, Iron Shipbuilders, Blacksmiths, Forgers and Helpers (1893)
753 State Ave.
Suite 570
Kansas City, KS 66101
Tel: (913) 371-2640 *Fax:* (913) 281-8101
E-Mail: ibb_dga@boilermakers.org
Website: boilermakers.org
Members: 70000 individuals
Staff: 150
Annual Budget: $25-50,000,000

Personnel:
International President: Newton B. Jones
    E-Mail: ipjones@boilermakers.org
Coordinator, Research, Education and Training: Tyler Brown
    E-Mail: tbrown@boilermakers.org
International Secretary and Treasurer: William Creeden
    E-Mail: ist@boilermakers.org
Coordinator, Employer Outreach: Kathy Duran
    E-Mail: kduran@bnf-kc.com
Manager, Membership Services: Stephanie Joyce
Director, Communications and Managing Editor: Mike Linderer
    E-Mail: mlinderer@boilermakers.org
Chief of Staff and Director, Administrative Affairs of the International President: James A. Pressley
Director, Information Technology Services: Curtis Smith
    E-Mail: csmith@boilermakers.org

Historical Note:
National Boilermaker and Helpers Protective and Benevolent Union merged with the National Brotherhood of Boilermakers in 1893 to form the International Brotherhood of Boilermakers and Iron Ship Builders of America. Became the International Brotherhood of Boilermakers, Iron Ship Builders and Helpers of America in 1912 and then merged in 1951 with the International Brotherhood of Blacksmiths, Forgers and Helpers, adopting the current name. Merged with United Cement, Lime, Gypsum and Allied Workers International Union (1984); Stove, Furnace and Allied Appliance Workers and Western Energy Workers (1994); and the Metal Polishers, Buffers, Platers and Allied Workers International Union in 1997. Affiliated with AFL-CIO. Members perform work in construction, shipbuilding, railroad, manufacturing, and service industries.

Meetings/Conferences: Annual

Publications:
The Boilermaker Reporter; quarterly

International Brotherhood of Correctional Officers
159 Burgin Pkwy.
Quincy, MA 02169-4213
Tel: (617) 376-0220 *Fax:* (617) 376-0285
TollFree: (866) 412-7762
Website: ibco.org
Members: 297 members
Staff: 2

Personnel:

President: David J. Holway
Secretary: Barbara Osgood

Historical Note:
A unit of the National Association of Government Employees, IBCO offers direct access to professional negotiators on staff, ready to help local negotiate the best contract possible.

International Brotherhood of Electrical Workers (1891)
900 Seventh St. NW
Washington, DC 20001
Tel: (202) 833-7000 *Fax:* (202) 728-7676
E-Mail: journal@ibew.org
Website: ibew.org
Members: 725000 individuals
Staff: 250
Annual Budget: $5-10,000,000
Tax: 501(c)(5)

Personnel:
International President: Edwin D. Hill
Director, Political and Legislative Affairs: Brian Baker
    E-Mail: ibewpoliticaldept@ibew.org
Director, Information Technology: Darren DeMarco
    E-Mail: IT@ibew.org
Director, Construction Organizing and Membership Development: Scott Hudson
    E-Mail: MembershipDev@ibew.org
Director, Education: Jan Schwingshakl
    E-Mail: education@ibew.org
Director, Media Department: James "Jim" Spellane
    E-Mail: JournalDept@ibew.org
Director, Human Services: Carolyn Williams
    E-Mail: humanservices@ibew.org

Historical Note:
Mission is to organize all workers in the entire electrical industry in the United States and Canada, including all those in public utilities and electrical manufacturing, into local unions.

Meetings/Conferences: Annual
2013 - Naples, FL (The Naples Beach Hotel and Golf Club)/Jan. 31 - Feb. 1

Publications:
IBEW Journal; monthly; adv.

International Brotherhood of Electrical Workers #98
1701 Spring Garden St.
Philadelphia, PA 19130
Tel: (215) 563-5592 *Fax:* (215) 561-2168
Website: ibew98.org
Staff: 427
Annual Budget: Over $100,000,000

Personnel:
President: Brian Burrows
Business Manager: John J. Dougherty
Treasurer: Todd Neilson
Financial Secretary: Francis Walsh

Historical Note:
IBEW is a law firm. Local 98 members work in the electrical, telecommunications and broadcast industries in Philadelphia and the surrounding counties.

Publications:
Newsletter

International Brotherhood of Magicians (1922)
13 Point West Blvd.
St. Charles, MO 63301-4431
Tel: (636) 724-2400 *Fax:* (636) 724-8566
E-Mail: office@magician.org
Website: magician.org
Members: 12357 individuals and local groups
Staff: 11
Annual Budget: $500-1,000,000
Tax: 501(c)(3)

Personnel:
Executive Secretary: Sindie Richison
    E-Mail: sindie@magician.org
Legal Advisor: John R. Browne III
Contact, Electronic Communications: Kirk De Weese
Contact, Membership Services: Terry Richison
    E-Mail: magictwr@charter.net
Contact, Annual Conferences: David Sandy
Editor: Samuel Patrick Smith
Chairman, Conventions: Michael Stratman

Historical Note:

Members are professional and amateur magicians and their suppliers. Membership: $30-65/year.

Meetings/Conferences:
Conference Chair: David Sandy
2013 - Phoenix, AZ (Hyatt Regency and Phoenix Convention Center)/July 17 - 20
Number of non-conference events/year: 3

Publications:
Linking Ring; monthly; adv.

International Brotherhood of Police Officers
159 Burgin Pkwy.
Quincy, MA 02169
Tel: (617) 376-0220 Fax: (617) 984-5695
TollFree: (866) 412-7762
Website: ibpo.org
Staff: 4
Annual Budget: $100-250,000

Personnel:
President: David J. Holway
Treasurer: James Farley
Director, Communications: Stephanie Zaiser
    E-Mail: szaiser@nage.org

Historical Note:
A division of the National Association of Government Employees. IBPO members reach out to help people in their communities who are elderly or disabled, or who need temporary assistance.

Continuing Education:
Certification Designation/s: IBPO-SP

International Brotherhood of Teamsters (1903)
25 Louisiana Ave. NW
Washington, DC 20001
Tel: (202) 624-6800 Fax: (202) 624-6918
Website: teamster.org
Members: 140000 individuals
Staff: 300
Annual Budget: Over $100,000,000
Tax: 501(c)(5)

Personnel:
President: James P. Hoffa
Legislative Director: Frederick P. McLuckie Jr.
    E-Mail: fmcluckie@teamster.org

Historical Note:
Established in Niagara Falls, New York as the International Brotherhood of Teamsters through the merger of the Teamsters National Union (founded in 1902) and the Team Drivers International Union (founded in 1899). Became the International Brotherhood of Teamsters, Chauffeurs, Warehousemen and Helpers of America in 1940 and assumed its present name in 1991.

Meetings/Conferences: Annual

Publications:
Bakery & Laundry
Brewery & Soft Drink
Building Material and Construction Trade
Carhaul
Dairy
Food Processing
Freight
Human Rights Commission
Industrial Trades
Motion Picture
Newspaper, Magazine and Electronic Media
Public Services
Rail Teamster
Retirees
Solid Waste
Tankhaul
Teamster Leader
Teamster Magazine; monthly
Teamster Women
Trade Show & Convention Centers
UPS Teamster
Warehouse

International Brotherhood of Teamsters - Airline Division
25 Louisiana Ave. NW
Washington, DC 20001
Tel: (202) 624-6848
TollFree: (800) 635-3961
Website: teamster.org/content/airline-division
Members: 80,000 airline employee
Staff: 2

Personnel:

President: James P. Hoffa
General Secretary and Treasurer: Ken Hall

Historical Note:
A union that represents workers in the airline industry. Mission of Airline Division is to focus on raising airline industry standards, promoting safety, educating members, fighting outsourcing and securing the careers of its members.

Publications:
Teamster Magazine; quarterly

International Buckskin Horse Association (1971)
P.O. Box 268
Shelbyville, IN 46377
Tel: (219) 552-1013
E-Mail: ibhainc@sbcglobal.net
Website: ibha.net
Members: 3500 individuals
Staff: 4
Annual Budget: $100-250,000

Personnel:
Executive Secretary: Richard E. Kurzeja

Historical Note:
A member body of the American Youth Horse Council. IBHA's mission is to record and preserve the pedigree of Buckskin, Dun, Red Dun, and Grulla horses registered with the association while maintaining the integrity of the association. Membership: $15 (Youth/Amateur); $30 (Individual); $250 (Life).

Meetings/Conferences: Annual
Conference Chair: Richard E. Kurzeja
2013 - Milwaukee, WI (Wyndham Milwaukee Airport Hotel and Convention Center)/March 14 - 16
Number of non-conference events/year: 1

International Builders Exchange Executives/ Builders Exchange Network (1948)
Rochester Builders Exchange
Rochester, NY 14625
E-Mail: info@ibeeonline.com
Website: ibeeonline.com
Members: 78 builders exchanges, construction associations and organizations
Staff: 2
Annual Budget: $100-250,000
Tax: 501(c)(6)

Personnel:
President: Aaron Hilger

Historical Note:
Branded itself as the Builders Exchange Network (BXNet/ BXNetwork) in 2003, IBEE works to support and enhance builders exchanges and construction associations by providing networking, educational and affinity opportunities to their members. Members are executive heads of local building trade associations in the United States and Canada. Membership: $1,000 (Executive); $2,500 (Corporate); $5,000 (Affiliate).

Meetings/Conferences:
2013 - Marco Island, FL (Hilton Marco Island Beach Resort and Spa)/Feb. 6 - 8
2013 - Broomfield, CA (Omni Interlocken Resort)/June 12 - 14
Number of non-conference events/year: 1

Publications:
Membership Directory; annually

International Business Brokers Association (1983)
3525 Piedmont Rd. NE
Building Five, Suite 300
Atlanta, GA 30305
Fax: (404) 240-0998
E-Mail: admin@ibba.org
Website: ibba.org
Members: 1500 individuals
Staff: 13
Annual Budget: $1-2,000,000

Personnel:
Executive Director: Karl Kirsch
    E-Mail: kkirsch@ibba.org
President: Steve Bova
    E-Mail: sbova@ibba.org
Director, Finance: Jennifer Buzalski
    E-Mail: jbuzalski@smithbucklin.com
Director, Events: Shannon Cavanaugh
    E-Mail: scavanaugh@ibba.org
Director, Information Technology: Denis Janis

    E-Mail: djanis@ibba.org
Education and Certification Manager: Maggie Nicholson
    E-Mail: mnicholson@ibba.org
Membership and Communications Senior Coordinator:
    Simone Shahdadi
    E-Mail: sshahdadi@ibba.org
Director, Operations: Lynne Weil
    E-Mail: lweil@ibba.org

Historical Note:
IBBA is a trade association of business brokers providing education, conferences, professional designations and networking opportunities. Members are individuals specializing in the sales of businesses of all sizes. Membership: $449 (Regular/Associate); $249 (International); $169 (Student); $495 (M&A Source).

Continuing Education:
Certification Designation/s: CBI

Meetings/Conferences: Semi-Annual
Conference Chair: Shannon Cavanaugh

Publications:
IBBA Quarterly; quarterly; adv.
Membership Directory; on-line

International Business Music Association (1971)
1213 Priest Dr.
Ballwin, MO 63021
Tel: (636) 825-6360
E-Mail: bwaters@ibma.net
Website: ibma.net
Members: 94 businesses
Staff: 8
Annual Budget: $10-25,000

Personnel:
Executive Director and President: Bud Waters
    E-Mail: bwaters@ibma.net
Treasurer: Randy Johnson
    E-Mail: rj@soundsolutionsinc.com

Historical Note:
IBMA provides a forum for the members of the business music industry. Membership: $200 (Regular); $250 (Associate).

Publications:
IBMA Newsletter; on-line

International Cadmium Association (1980)
9222 Jeffery Rd.
Great Falls, VA 22066
Tel: (703) 759-7400 Fax: (703) 759-7003
Website: cadmium.org
Members: 30 companies
Staff: 2
Annual Budget: $250-500,000

Personnel:
Senior Consultant: Hugh Morrow
    E-Mail: icdamorrow@aol.com

Historical Note:
Formerly a committee of the Zinc Institute, the association is the marketing, research and promotional arm of the cadmium industry. The International Cadmium Association (ICdA) was formed by the merger of the Cadmium Council (North America) and the Cadmium Association (Europe). ICdA represents the interests of a large number of industrial companies which, in the course of their operations, extract, smelt, refine, process, use and recycle cadmium, cadmium compounds, and their products. Members are producers and consumers of cadmium. Membership fee based on annual cadmium production or consumption.

International Card Manufacturers Association (1990)
191 Clarksville Rd.
Princeton, NJ 08550
Tel: (609) 799-4900 Fax: (609) 799-7032
E-Mail: info@icma.com
Website: icma.com
Members: 220 companies
Staff: 7
Annual Budget: $1-2,000,000

Personnel:
Executive Director: Jeffrey E. Barnhart
    E-Mail: Jbarnhart@icma.com
Manager, Communications and Editor: Kaitlin Friedmann
    E-Mail: kfriedmann@icma.com
Manager, Public Relations: Meghan Higgins
    E-Mail: mhiggins@icma.com
Coordinator, Membership Services: Elizabeth Roe
    E-Mail: eroe@icma.com
Technical Representative: David Tushie

E-Mail: dtushie@magellan-consulting.com
Contact, Advertising, Sponsorship and Exhibit Sales:
Diane Webster
E-Mail: Dwebster@icma.com

Historical Note:
ICMA is a non-profit trade association of plastic card manufacturers and personalizers, supported by suppliers and other industry participants. ICMA promotes the plastic card industry and the value of its products and services providing an independent forum to speak for the industry. Membership: $1,000-7,000/year.

Meetings/Conferences: Annual
Conference Chair: Diane Webster
2013 - Washington, DC (Washington Marriott Wardman Park)/June 4 - 7/11-25 exhibitors

Publications:
Card Manufacturing Magazine; on-line; adv.
Membership Directory; on-line

International Cargo Gear Bureau (1954)
321 W. 44th St.
New York, NY 10036
Tel: (212) 757-2011 *Fax:* (212) 757-2650
E-Mail: incargear@aol.com
Website: icgb.com
Members: 35 companies
Staff: 9
Annual Budget: $1-2,000,000

Personnel:
President and Chairman: Charles G. Visconti
Manager, Financial Records: S. Luciano
General Counsel and Assistant Secretary: Todd L. Platek Esq.
Staff Assistant, Certification Services: David E. Zielinski

Historical Note:
Members are makers and users of material handling equipment ashore and afloat. ICGB provides recognized registration, inspection, certification, documentation, design evaluation, and consultation services throughout the world.

International Cargo Security Council (1969)
2300 N St. NW
Suite 710
Washington, DC 20037
Tel: (202) 452-1200 *Fax:* (202) 833-3636
Members: 1200 companies and individuals
Staff: 2
Annual Budget: $25-50,000

Personnel:
Executive Director: Graham Hauck
E-Mail: director@cargosecuirty.com
Director, Meetings and Member Services: Brian Mandrier
E-Mail: bmandrier@hauck.com

Historical Note:
Formerly National Cargo Security Council, assumed its current name on January 1, 2005, ICSC's mission is to enhance the integrity and efficiency of the supply chain through the development and dissemination of security practices. Membership: $2,000-4,000 (Corporate); $300 (Individual); Free (Affiliate).

Meetings/Conferences:
Conference Chair: Brian Mandrier

International Carwash Association (1946)
401 N. Michigan Ave.
Suite 2200
Chicago, IL 60611
Tel: (312) 321-5199 *Fax:* (312) 245-1085
TollFree: (888) 422-8422
E-Mail: info@carwash.org
Website: carwash.org
Members: 2000 companies
Staff: 16
Annual Budget: $2-5,000,000

Personnel:
Chief Executive Officer: Eric Wulf CAE
E-Mail: ewulf@carwash.org
Director, Operations: Megan Clark
E-Mail: mclark@carwash.org
Director, Conventions: Keri Cote
E-Mail: kcote@carwash.org
Director, Education: Ariane Daniels
E-Mail: adaniels@carwash.org
Director, Sales: Carrie North
E-Mail: cnorth@carwash.org
Director, Membership: Greta Weber
E-Mail: gweber@carwash.org

Historical Note:
ICA comprised of operators, manufacturers, and suppliers, serves its members and the global car wash community by providing products and services to ensure its success. Membership: $275 (Operator/Provisional); $325 (Vendor).

Meetings/Conferences: Annual
Conference Chair: Keri Cote
2013 - Las Vegas, NV (Sands Expo and Convention Center)/April 22 - 24

Publications:
CAR WASH magazine; quarterly; adv.
ICA Newsletter; monthly

International Cast Polymer Alliance (1974)
3033 Wilson Blvd.
Suite 420
Arlington, VA 22201
Tel: (703) 525-0511 *Fax:* (703) 525-0743
E-Mail: icpa@icpa-hq.org
Website: icpa-hq.org
Members: 300 companies
Staff: 21

Personnel:
Director, Marketing and Communications: Mary Johnson
E-Mail: mjohnson@acmanet.org
Director, Communications: Steven Joseph
E-Mail: abrown@acmanet.org
Director, Finance and Administration: Judy Norton
E-Mail: jnorton@acmanet.org
Director, Conventions and Education: Heather Rhoderick CMP
E-Mail: hrhoderick@acmanet.org

Historical Note:
ICPA represents over 300 manufacturers, suppliers, fabricators, and installers of cultured marble, cultured granite, cultured onyx, and solid surface kitchen and bath products. Membership: $525-20130 (Manufacturers); $1,570-30,130 (Suppliers/Distributors); $160-1000(Affiliates).

Continuing Education:
Certification Designation/s: CCT-CP, CCT-SS

Meetings/Conferences: Annual
2013 - Orlando, FL (Orange County Convention Center)/Jan. 29 - 31
2014 - San Antonio, TX/Feb. 18 - 20
2015 - Las Vegas, NV/Feb. 2 - 5

Publications:
Composites Manufacturing; adv.

International Cast Polymer Association (1974)
3033 Wilson Blvd.
Suite 420
Arlington, VA 22201
Tel: (703) 525-0511 *Fax:* (703) 525-0743
E-Mail: icpa@icpa-hq.org
Website: icpa-hq.com
Members: 300 companies
Staff: 18
Annual Budget: Under $10,000

Personnel:
Chief Staff Executive: Thomas Dobbins
E-Mail: tdobbins@acmanet.org
Manager, Certification and Education: Anne Ashurst
E-Mail: aashurst@acmanet.org
Manager, Conferences and Education: Caitlin Felker
E-Mail: cfelker@acmanet.org
Director, Marketing and Communications: Mary Johnson
E-Mail: mjohnson@acmanet.org
Director, Finance and Administration: Judy Norton
E-Mail: jnorton@acmanet.org
Director, Conventions and Education: Heather Rhoderick CMP
E-Mail: hrhoderick@acmanet.org
Manager, Composites Growth Initiatives: Jonathan Roberts
E-Mail: jroberts@acmanet.org

Historical Note:
Formerly (1993) Cultured Marble Institute. Manufacturers and suppliers of polyester resin-based synthetic marble, onyx and granite-densified products. ICPA promotes quality in the cast polymer products industry. Membership: $350-21,140 (Manufacturer/Distributor), $1,650-31,635 (Suppliers); $160-1,000 (Affiliate).

Meetings/Conferences: Annual
Conference Chair: Caitlin Felker

2013 - Orange, FL (Orange County Convention Center)/Jan. 29 - 31/3500 attendees/over 100 exhibitors
2014 - San Antonio, TX/Feb. 18 - 20
2015 - Las Vegas, NV/Feb. 2 - 5

Publications:
MasterCast; on-line
Product Directory; on-line

International Castor Oil Association (1957)
24 Burton Ave.
Woodmere, NY 11598
Tel: (516) 978-0629 *Fax:* (516) 569-6940
E-Mail: icoa@icoa.org
Website: icoa.org
Members: 34 companies and 52 individuals
Staff: 1
Annual Budget: $50-100,000

Personnel:
Administrative Assistant and Membership Contact: Donna Bialor

Historical Note:
ICOA strives to improve the agronomic conditions of castor beans, the development of new applications for castor oil and its derivatives and the dissemination of information to its members and the industries they serve. Membership: $1,000/year (Company).

Meetings/Conferences: Annual
Conference Chair: Donna Bialor
Number of non-conference events/year: 1

Publications:
Membership Directory; on-line

International Casual Furnishings Association (2008)
317 W. High Ave.
Tenth Floor
High Point, NC 27260
Tel: (336) 884-5400 *Fax:* (336) 884-5303
Website: icfanet.org
Members: 258 companies
Staff: 2
Annual Budget: $250-500,000

Personnel:
Executive Director: Joseph P. Logan
E-Mail: jlogan@ahfa.us
Executive Assistant: Rhonda Craven
E-Mail: rcraven@ICFAnet.org

Historical Note:
The ICFA's predecessor organization was the Summer and Casual Furniture Manufacturers Association (SCFMA). It is composed of manufacturers/importers, retailers, designers, sales representatives and associate members in the outdoor and casual furnishing industry. In 2008, the Casual Furniture Retailers Association merged into ICFA. Membership: $300-2,500 (Retailer); $100 (Designer/ Sales Representative); $100 (Associate); $1,200-44,675 (Manufacturer); $750-3,000 (Supplier).

Meetings/Conferences: Semi-Annual
2013 - Chicago, IL (Merchandise Mart)/July 16 - 18
2013 - Chicago, IL (Merchandise Mart)/Sept. 17 - 20
2014 - Chicago, IL (Merchandise Mart)/July 15 - 17
2014 - Chicago, IL (Merchandise Mart)/Sept. 16 - 19
2015 - Chicago, IL (The Merchandise Mart)/July 14 - 16
2015 - Chicago, IL (The Merchandise Mart)/Sept. 16 - 19
2016 - Chicago, IL (The Merchandise Mart)/July 12 - 14
2016 - Chicago, IL (The Merchandise Mart)/Sept. 20 - 23
2017 - Chicago, IL (The Merchandise Mart)/July 11 - 13
2017 - Chicago, IL (The Merchandise Mart)/Sept. 12 - 15
Number of non-conference events/year: 5

Publications:
ICFA Newsletter; quarterly
Member Directory; on-line

International Cemetery, Cremation and Funeral Association (1887)
107 Carpenter Dr.
Suite 100
Sterling, VA 20164-4468
Tel: (703) 391-8400 *Fax:* (703) 391-8416
TollFree: (800) 645-7700

E-Mail: hq@iccfa.com
Website: iccfa.com
Members: 7500 cemeteries, funeral homes, crematories, memorial designers and related businesses worldwide
Staff: 14
Annual Budget: $50-100,000

Personnel:
Executive Director and General Counsel: Robert M. Fells
    E-Mail: rfells@iccfa.org
Director, Operations: Nadira E. Baddeliyanage
    E-Mail: nadira@iccfa.com
Director, Communications and Membership Services: Linda R. Budzinski
    E-Mail: lindab@iccfa.com
Manager, Membership Services: Sheila J. Cephas
Office Administrator and Associations Liaison: Brenda Clough
Meeting Planner: Karen R. Gray
Managing Editor: Susan J. Loving

Historical Note:
Formerly (1944) the Association of American Cemetery Superintendents, (1945) and (1996) the American Cemetery Association, added "Cremation" to its name in 2006, merged with the National Association of Cemeteries in 1980 and absorbed the Pre-Arrangement Association of American in 1996. ICCFA serves and supports members through a host of benefits designed to increase their management proficiency and improve their businesses such as regular updates on government and legal issues, and educational meetings. Membership includes memorial designers and related businesses worldwide. Membership: $245 (Regular-Voting/Supplier-Professional); $35 (College Student/Faculty).

Continuing Education:
Certification Designation/s: CCFE, CSE, CCrE, CFuE, CCE, CPLP

Meetings/Conferences:
Conference Chair: Nadira E. Baddeliyanage
2013 - Tampa, FL (Tampa Convention Center)/April 10 - 13/over 100 exhibitors
Number of non-conference events/year: 2

Publications:
ICCFA Buyer's Guide and Membership Directory
ICCFA Magazine; adv.
ICCFA Wireless E-Newsletter; bi-weekly

Membership List Available to Non-members

International Center for Study of Psychiatry and Psychology (1971)
2711 Sunrise Point Rd.
Las Cruces, NM 88011
Tel: (575) 522-8371 Fax: (575) 635-4331
E-Mail: agalves2003@comcast.net
Website: psychintegrity.org
Staff: 5
Annual Budget: $50-100,000
Tax: 501(c)(3)

Personnel:
International Executive Director and Contributing Editor: Albert Galves PhD
    E-Mail: agalves2003@yahoo.com
Director, Membership: Carolyn Crowder
    E-Mail: crowdercz@netzero.com
Director, Continuing Education and Conferences: Michael Gilbert PsyD
    E-Mail: docgilbert@hotmail.com
Director, Newsletter: Jill Littrell
    E-Mail: littrell@gsu.edu
Website Administration: Maria Mangicaro
    E-Mail: mangicaro829@aol.com

Historical Note:
Formerly ICSPP, ISEPP's is a network of professionals and individuals concerned with the impact of mental health theories on public policy, and the effects these theories have on therapeutic practices, individual well-being, personal freedom, and family and community values. Members are psychiatrists, psychologists, professional clinical counselors, academic researchers, educators, lawyers, psychiatric survivors, concerned family members, other mental health professionals and advocates. Membership: $100 (US Residents, includes Newsletters and a One Year Subscription to EHPP); $110 (International, includes Newsletters and a One Year's Subscription to EHPP); $15 (Students/Individuals with hardship situations, includes Newsletters but not EHPP); $60 (U.S. if International Address, includes Newsletters but not EHPP); $50 (U.S. Membership, includes Newsletters but not EHPP).

Meetings/Conferences: Annual

Conference Chair: Michael Gilbert PsyD

Publications:
Ethical Human Psychology and Psychiatry; adv.
The ISEPP Bulletin

International Ceramic Association (1958)
17098 Pheasant Meadow Ln. SW
Prior Lake, MN 55372
Tel: (952) 447-6421
E-Mail: info@ceramic-ica.org
Website: ceramic-ica.com
Members: 3000 companies
Staff: 1
Annual Budget: $10-25,000

Personnel:
Treasurer: Helen Daum

Historical Note:
Incorporated in the State of Illinois in August, 1958 as the National Ceramics Association, assumed its present name in 1982. Maintains the International Ceramics Association Educational Foundation. Mission is to make the association a source of information for the industry. ICA's main purpose is education and judging program. Members are suppliers of raw materials, manufacturers, distributors and teachers of ceramics. Membership fee varies, $25-100/year.

Meetings/Conferences: Annual

Publications:
Newsletter; quarterly

International Chemical Workers Union Council/UFCW (1944)
1655 W. Market St.,
Akron, OH 44313
Tel: (330) 926-1444 Fax: (330) 926-0816
E-Mail: icwucreg3@aol.com
Website: icwuc.org
Members: 35000 individuals
Staff: 7
Annual Budget: $100-250,000

Personnel:
President: Frank Cyphers
    E-Mail: fcyphers@icwuc.org
Office Manager: Dan Ardelian
    E-Mail: dardelian@icwuc.org
Organizer: Jerry Hurocy
    E-Mail: jhurocy@icwuc.org
Director, Data Processing: Sandy Noble
    E-Mail: snoble@icwuc.org
Administrative Assistant: Kim Schmidt
    E-Mail: kschmidt@icwuc.org
Counsel: Randy Vehar
    E-Mail: rvehar@icwuc.org
Secretary and Treasurer: Greg Villanova
    E-Mail: gvillannova@icwuc.org

The International Childbirth Education Association (1960)
1500 Sunday Dr.
Suite 102
Raleigh, NC 27607
Tel: (919) 863-9487 Fax: (919) 787-4916
TollFree: (800) 624-4934
E-Mail: info@icea.org
Website: icea.org
Members: 8000 individuals
Staff: 7
Annual Budget: $100-250,000
Tax: 501(c)(3)

Personnel:
Executive Director: David Feild
Director, Meeting Planning Services: Heather S. Blanken CMP, MBA
Director, Certification and Membership Services: Ryan Couch
Director, Accounting Services: Ellen Gioielli
Director, Information Technology: Brad Joyner

Historical Note:
Association concerned with family-centered maternity care with minimal medical intervention. ICEA's mission is to support educators and other health care providers who believe in freedom to make decisions based on knowledge of alternatives in family-centered maternity and newborn care. ICEA membership is predominantly concentrated in the U.S. Membership: $75 (Individual); $100 (Supporting).

Continuing Education:
Certification Designation/s: CEC, ECEC, DC, TCEC, PEC, PFEC

Meetings/Conferences: Annual
Conference Chair: Heather S. Blanken CMP, MBA
2013 - Ft. Lauderdale, FL (Royal Caribbean's Liberty of the Seas)/Nov. 9 - 14

Publications:
ICEA E-Newsletter; monthly
International Journal of Childbirth Education (IJCE); quarterly; adv.
Membership Directory; on-line

International Chiropractic Pediatric Association (1986)
327 N. Middletown Rd.
Media, PA 19063
Tel: (610) 565-2360 Fax: (610) 565-3567
Website: icpa4kids.com
Staff: 12
Annual Budget: $1-2,000,000

Personnel:
Executive Director: Jeanne Ohm DC
Head, Membership: Elizabeth Kirchhoff
    E-Mail: membership@icpa4kids.com

Historical Note:
ICPA's mission is to provide education, training, and support research on chiropractic care in pregnancy and throughout childhood because all children need chiropractic care. Members are chiropractic doctors and students around the world. Membership: $229 (US and Canada); $195 (International); $129 (First Year D.C./Associate DC); $279 (Married Couple); $79 (Student); $179 (State Affiliate D.C.); $195 (International D.C.); $95 (International First Year D.C./International Associate DC); $245 (International Married Couple); $65 (International Student).

Continuing Education:
Certification Designation/s: C.A.C.C.P.

Publications:
Family Wellness First
Find a Chiropractor (Membership Directory)
Pathways to Family Wellness Magazine; quarterly; adv.
PedEx e-Newsletter
Research Newsletter

International Chiropractors Association (1926)
6400 Arlington Blvd.
Suite 800
Falls Church, VA 22042
Tel: (703) 528-5000 Fax: (703) 528-5023
TollFree: (800) 423-4690
E-Mail: chiro@chiropractic.org
Website: chiropractic.org
Members: 8000 practitioners, students, chiropractic assistants, educators and lay persons
Staff: 10
Annual Budget: $1-2,000,000

Personnel:
Executive Director: Bob Photos
President: Gary Walsemann
    E-Mail: drwalsemann@comcast.net

Historical Note:
Established as the Chiropractic Health Bureau, assumed its present name in 1941. ICA's mission is to advance chiropractic throughout the world as a distinct health care profession predicated upon its unique philosophy, science, and art. Membership: $0-5000/year.

Publications:
Membership Directory; on-line
The Chiropractic Choice; bi-monthly; adv.
The ICA Review; quarterly; adv.

Membership List Available to Non-members

International Cinema Technology Association (1971)
770 Broadway
Seventh Floor
New York, NY 10003-9595
Tel: (212) 493-4097 Fax: (212) 257-6428
Website: internationalcinematechnologyassociation.com
Members: 180 companies
Staff: 2
Annual Budget: $250-500,000

Personnel:
Executive Director: Robert H. Sunshine
Legal Counsel: David P. Wilson

Historical Note:

Formed as a result of the merger of Theatre Equipment Dealers Association and the Supply Manufacturers Association, as the Theatre Equipment and Supply Manufacturers Association. Became the International Cinema Technology Association (ICTA) in 2006. ICTA's mission is to serve and support the theater industry. Membership: $375 (Active); $200 (Associate).

Meetings/Conferences:
2013 - Los Angeles, CA/Jan. 14 - 16

Publications:
ICTA Newsletter; on-line
Membership Directory; on-line
NATO In Focus; on-line

Membership List Available to Non-members

International City/County Management Association (1914)
777 N. Capitol St. NE
Suite 500
Washington, DC 20002-4201
Tel: (202) 289-4262 *Fax:* (202) 962-3500
TollFree: (800) 745-8780
E-Mail: customerservices@icma.org
Website: icma.org
Members: 8300 individuals
Staff: 120
Annual Budget: $25-50,000,000
Tax: 501(c)(3)

Personnel:
Executive Director: Robert J. O'Neill
    E-Mail: roneill@icma.org
Director, Public Information: Michele Frisby
    E-Mail: mfrisby@icma.org
Director, Publications: Ann Mahoney
    E-Mail: amahoney@icma.org

Historical Note:
Founded as the International City Managers Association, it became the International City Management Association in 1969 and assumed its present name in 1991. Also known as ICMA - The Professional Local Government Management Association. ICMA's mission is to create excellence in local governance by advocating and developing the professional management of local government worldwide. Membership dues vary.

Continuing Education:
Certification Designation/s: CM

Meetings/Conferences: Annual
Conference Chair: Ann Mahoney
2013 - Boston, MA (Massachusetts State House)/Sept. 22 - 25
2014 - Charlotte, NC (Charlotte Marriott SouthPark)/ Sept. 14 - 17
2015 - Seatle, WA (King County)/Sept. 27 - 30
2016 - Kansas City, MO (InterContinental Kansas City At The Plaza)/Sept. 25 - 28
2017 - San Antonio, TX (Bexar County)/Sept. 10 - 13

Publications:
ICMA Newsletter; adv.

International Claim Association (1909)
1155 15th St. NW
Suite 500
Washington, DC 20005
Tel: (202) 452-0143 *Fax:* (202) 530-0659
Website: claim.org
Members: 298 corporations, 21 individuals
Staff: 2
Annual Budget: $500-1,000,000
Tax: 501(c)(6)

Personnel:
Executive Director: Christopher M. Murphy
    E-Mail: cmurphy@claim.org
Manager, Membership and Events: Darci Chuba
    E-Mail: dchuba@claim.org

Historical Note:
ICA's mission is to provide a forum for information exchange and a program of education tailored to the needs of its member life and health insurance companies, reinsurers, managed care companies, TPAs, and Blue Cross and Blue Shield organizations worldwide. Members are life and health insurance companies represented by claims employees and officers. Membership: $1,250 (Corporate); $800 (Individual).

Meetings/Conferences:
Conference Chair: Darci Chuba
2013 - Chicago, IL (Chicago Marriott Downtown Magnificent Mile)/Oct. 13 - 16

2014 - New Orleans, LA (New Orleans Marriott)/Sept. 21 - 24
2015 - Las Vegas, NV (Mirage Hotel and Casino)/Sept. 27 - 30
Number of non-conference events/year: 4

Publications:
ICA News; quarterly
Membership Directory; on-line

International Clarinet Association (1990)
14070 Proton Rd.
Suite 100 LB9
Dallas, TX 75244
Tel: (972) 233-9107 *Fax:* (972) 490-4219
E-Mail: membership@clarinet.org
Website: clarinet.org
Members: 3700 individuals
Staff: 3
Annual Budget: $250-500,000
Tax: 501(c)(3)

Personnel:
Executive Director: Madeleine Crouch

Historical Note:
ICA strives to provide opportunities for exchange of ideas, materials, and information among its members. Members include teachers, manufacturers, amateur musicians and others with an interest in clarinet. Membership: $50 (Regular/Institutional); $25 (Student).

Meetings/Conferences: Annual
Conference Chair: Piero Vincenti
2013 - Assisi, Italy/July 24 - 28
2014 - Baton Rouge, LA (Campus of Louisiana State University)/July 30 - Aug. 3

Publications:
Membership Directory
The Clarinet Journal; quarterly; adv.

International Coach Federation (1995)
2365 Harrodsburg Rd.
Suite A325
Lexington, KY 40504
Tel: (859) 219-3580 *Fax:* (859) 226-4411
TollFree: (888) 423-3131
E-Mail: icfheadquarters@coachfederation.org
Website: coachfederation.org
Members: 19000 individuals
Staff: 17
Annual Budget: $2-5,000,000

Personnel:
Executive Director: Magda Mook
Communications Coordinator: Lindsay Bodkin
    E-Mail: lindsay.bodkin@coachfederation.org
Manager, Marketing: Ann Jarvis
    E-Mail: ann.jarvis@coachfederation.org
Director, Research and Education: Mark Ruth
Director, Meetings and Events: Denise Stenzel
Director, Membership: Don Whittle

Historical Note:
ICF is dedicated to advancing the coaching profession by setting high standards, providing independent certification, and building a worldwide network of credentialed coaches. Membership: $195/year.

Meetings/Conferences: Annual
Conference Chair: Denise Stenzel

Publications:
Coaching Research Newsletter
Coaching World Newsletter; monthly; adv.
Membership Directory

International College of Applied Kinesiology (1976)
6405 Metcalf Ave.
Suite 503
Shawnee, KS 66202-3929
Tel: (913) 384-5336 *Fax:* (913) 384-5112
E-Mail: icak@dci-kansascity.com
Website: icakusa.com
Members: 600 individuals
Staff: 6
Annual Budget: $250-500,000
Tax: 501(c)(3)

Personnel:
Manager, Conferences: Angela Capra
    E-Mail: acapra@dci-kansascity.com
Coordinator, Membership Services and Publications: Cheryl Whelan

E-Mail: cwhelan@dci-kansascity.com

Historical Note:
International College of Applied Kinesiology-U.S.A. (ICAK-U.S.A.) founded by a group of doctors. ICAK's mission is to provide leadership in applied kinesiology through individual professional development and to advance education in health care. Membership: $135-400 (Doctor), based on month of joining; $200 (Retired); $25 (Student).

Meetings/Conferences:
Conference Chair: Angela Capra
2013 - Cairns, Australia (Cairns Convention Center)/ April 19 - 21

Publications:
ICAK's Newsletter; quarterly
Membership Directory; annually

International College of Cranio-Mandibular Orthopedics (1979)
P.O. Box 1491
Cannon Beach, OR 97110
Tel: (206) 633-4355 *Fax:* (206) 633-4352
TollFree: (866) 379-3656
E-Mail: info@iccmo.org
Website: iccmo.org
Staff: 2
Annual Budget: $100-250,000

Personnel:
Executive Director: Tracy Abel
    E-Mail: tracy@iccmo.org
International Treasurer: Barry Cooper DDS
    E-Mail: tmjbcooper@aol.com

Historical Note:
ICCMO is a society of health care professionals who have a common interest in the anatomy and physiology of occlusion, jaw function and orthopedics dysfunction with resultant symptoms in the head and neck.ICCMO's mission is to alleviate the widespread human suffering of those afflicted with the varied symptomatology of head and neck pain and dysfunction (TMD). Members are doctors and other health professionals. Membership: $450/year.

Meetings/Conferences:
2013 - Munich, Germany (Four Seasons Munich)/Oct. 10 - 12
Number of non-conference events/year: 1

Publications:
Membership Directory; on-line

International College of Dentists, U.S.A. Section (1928)
51 Monroe St.
Suite 1400
Rockville, MD 20850-2412
Tel: (301) 251-8861 *Fax:* (240) 499-8975
E-Mail: reg-sg@icd.org
Website: usa-icd.org
Members: 6500 individuals
Staff: 4
Annual Budget: $250-500,000

Personnel:
Office Manager: Mary Webster
Editor: Richard J. Galeone
    E-Mail: rjgdds59@comcast.net
Administrative Assistant: Jennifer Greenville
Public Relations Specialist: Paula W. Rinaudo

Historical Note:
ICD-USA's mission is to advance the science and art of dentistry for the health and welfare of the public, to bring together the world's outstanding members of the dental profession for the exchange of dental knowledge. It also encourages the growth of the profession and promote cordial relations among dentists worldwide.

Meetings/Conferences: Semi-Annual

Publications:
Key; annually; adv.
KEY-Mail; monthly
Keynotes; semi-annually
Membership Roster; on-line
The College Today; quarterly
The Globe; annually

International College of Surgeons (1935)
1516 N. Lakeshore Dr.
Chicago, IL 60610-1607
Tel: (312) 642-3555 *Fax:* (312) 787-1624
TollFree: (800) 766-3427
E-Mail: info@icsglobal.org
Website: icsglobal.org

Members: 8000 individuals
Staff: 5
Annual Budget: $500-1,000,000

Personnel:
Executive Director: Max C. Downham
  E-Mail: max@icsglobal.org
Director, Membership Services: Patricia V. Binfa
  E-Mail: Patricia@icsglobal.org
Controller: Jennifer Tran
  E-Mail: jennifer@icsglobal.org

Historical Note:
Founded in Geneva, Switzerland and incorporated in the District of Columbia in 1940. ICS's mission is to improve the lives of patients through the development and education of their members and the advancement of the medical field. Membership: $195/year.

Meetings/Conferences: Biennial

Publications:
International Surgery; quarterly; adv.

International Communication Association (1950)
1500 21st St. NW
Washington, DC 20036
Tel: (202) 955-1444 *Fax:* (202) 955-1448
E-Mail: icahdq@icahdq.org
Website: icahdq.org
Members: 3,500 members
Staff: 6
Annual Budget: $1-2,000,000
Tax: 501(c)(3)

Personnel:
Executive Director: Michael L. Haley
  E-Mail: mhaley@icahdq.org
Assistant, Administrative and Accounts Payable: Colleen
  Brady
  E-Mail: cbrady@icahdq.org
Director, Communications: John Paul Gutierrez
  E-Mail: jpgutierrez@icahdq.org
*Coordinator, Conferences, Membership and Accounts
  Receivable:* Emily Karsnak
  E-Mail: ekarsnak@icahdq.org
Director, Member Services: Sam Luna
  E-Mail: sluna@icahdq.org
Publications Manager and Newsletter Editor: Michael J.
  West
  E-Mail: mwest@icahdq.org

Historical Note:
ICA's purpose is to provide an international forum to enable the development, conduct, and critical evaluation of communication research. Membership: $150 (Regular); $75 (Student); $415 (Sustaining); $5,000 (Life).

Meetings/Conferences: Annual
Conference Chair: Emily Karsnak
2013 - London, United Kingdom/June 15 - 19
2013 - London, United Kingdom/June 17 - 21
2014 - Seatle, WA/May 22 - 26
2015 - San Juan, PR/May 21 - 25
2016 - Fukuoka, Japan/June 9 - 13

Publications:
Human Communication Research; bi-weekly
ICA Newsletter; monthly
Journal of Computer-Mediated Communication;
  monthly
The Journal of Communication; on-line

Membership List Available to Non-members

International Community Corrections Association (1964)
2100 Stella Ct.
Columbus, OH 43215
Tel: (614) 420-4966 *Fax:* (614) 252-7987
E-Mail: staff@iccalive.org
Website: iccaweb.org
Members: 1500 community corrections programs
Staff: 1
Annual Budget: $250-500,000
Tax: 501(c)(3)

Personnel:
Executive Director: Mary Shilton
  E-Mail: mshilton@iccaweb.org

Historical Note:
Formerly (1989) the International Halfway House Association and (1995) the International Association of Residential and Community Alternatives. ICCA's primary goal is the successful reintegration of the client into the community. Members are public and private agencies

involved in providing community based correctional programming and services. Membership: $50-5000/year.

Meetings/Conferences: Annual
Number of non-conference events/year: 2

Publications:
Doing What Works; monthly
ICCA Journal on Community Corrections; quarterly;
  adv.

The International Compressor Remanufacturers Association (1965)
1505 Carthage Rd.
Lumberton, NC 28358
Tel: (910) 301-7060 *Fax:* (910) 738-6994
E-Mail: info@icracomp.com
Website: icracomp.com
Members: 113 individuals and companies
Staff: 2
Annual Budget: $25-50,000

Personnel:
Contact, Membership Services: Sandra Walker

Historical Note:
ICRA's mission is to promote good standards of quality remanufacturing, ethical business practice and in providing education and training to its members for their benefit. Membership: $500/year (Active/Associate/Allied).

Publications:
Membership Directory; on-line

International Computer Music Association (1974)
1819 Polk St.
Suite 330
San Francisco, CA 94109
Tel: (734) 878-3310 *Fax:* (734) 878-3031
E-Mail: icma@umich.edu
Website: computermusic.org
Members: 700 individuals
Staff: 8

Personnel:
President: Tae Hong Park
  E-Mail: park@tulane.edu
Vice President, membership: Tom Erbe
Webmaster: Toine Heuvelmans
Contact, Accounts: DeVera Long
Editor: Scott McLaughlin
Secretary and Treasurer: Chryssie Nanou
Administrative Assistant: Sandra Neal
Vice President, Conferences: Margaret Schedel

Historical Note:
ICMA serves composers, computer software and hardware developers, researchers, and musicians who are interested in the integration of music and technology. Membership: $63.52 (Individual); $105.32 (Sustaining/Student Chapter); $37.40 (Senior); $208.50 (Nonprofit Institutional); $311.50 (Corporate); $26.95 (Student).

Meetings/Conferences:
Conference Chair: Tae Hong Park

Publications:
Computer Music Journal
Journal of New Music Research
Membership Directory
Organised Sound

International Concatenated Order of Hoo-Hoo (1892)
207 Main St.
P.O. Box 118
Gurdon, AR 71743
Tel: (870) 353-4997 *Fax:* (870) 353-4151
TollFree: (800) 979-9950
E-Mail: info@hoo-hoo.org
Website: hoo-hoo.org
Members: 4000 individuals
Staff: 1
Annual Budget: $50-100,000
Tax: 501(c)(7)

Personnel:
Executive Secretary: Beth Thomas

Historical Note:
HHI's mission is to provide welfare and promotion of the forest products industry.

Meetings/Conferences: Semi-Annual

Publications:
Catnips
Indonesia Club Newsletter
Log & Tally; adv.

Nine Lives- JIV's Roving Cat Report
Rameses Ramblings Newsletter
The Purrer

International Concrete Repair Institute (1988)
10600 W. Higgins Rd.
Suite 607
Rosemont, IL 60018
Tel: (847) 827-0830 *Fax:* (847) 827-0832
Website: icri.org
Members: 1400 companies and individuals
Staff: 5
Annual Budget: $1-2,000,000

Personnel:
Executive Director: Kelly Page
  E-Mail: kelly.page@icri.org
Technical Director: Mark Hughes PE
  E-Mail: mark.hughes@icri.org
Manager, Marketing and Chapters: Dale Regnier
  E-Mail: dale.regnier@icri.org

Historical Note:
Formerly (1993) International Association of Concrete Repair Specialists. ICRI's mission is to improve the quality of concrete restoration, repair and protection, through education of, and communication among, the members and those who use their services. Members are contractors, manufacturers, engineers. Membership: $195-3,125 (Supporting Member Company); $10-160 (Individual).

Meetings/Conferences:
Conference Chair: Susan Adams
2013 - St. Pete Beach, FL (TradeWinds Island Resort)/
  March 20 - 22
2013 - Chicago, IL (Fairmont Chicago Millenium Park)/
  Nov. 13 - 15
Number of non-conference events/year: 1

Publications:
Concrete Repair Bulletin; bi-monthly; adv.
Membership Directory; on-line; adv.
Who's Who in Concrete Repair; annually; adv.

International Conference of Funeral Service Examining Boards (1903)
1885 Shelby Ln.
Fayetteville, AR 72704
Tel: (479) 442-7076 *Fax:* (479) 442-7090
E-Mail: info@theconferenceonline.org
Website: theconferenceonline.org
Members: 211 individuals, school members and
  states
Staff: 10
Annual Budget: $1-2,000,000

Personnel:
Executive Director: Dalene Paull
  E-Mail: director@theconferenceonline.org
Coordinator, Examination Services: Eric Forsbach
  E-Mail: exams@theconferenceonline.org
Coordinator, Public Relations: Sarah Gill
  E-Mail: admin@theconferenceonline.org
Coordinator, Information Services: Dustin Wardlow
  E-Mail: info@theconferenceonline.org

Historical Note:
ICFSEB's mission is to provide examination services, information and regulatory support to the death care profession. Members are executive secretaries and board members of state and provincial agencies, licensing embalmers and funeral directors in the U.S. and Canada. Associate members are mortuary science schools accredited by the American Board of Funeral Service. Membership: $250/year (Organization/Company).

Meetings/Conferences: Annual
2013 - Henderson, NV (Westin Lake Las Vegas Resort
  and Spa)/Feb. 27 - 28

Publications:
The Conference Report; semi-annually

International Conference of Police Chaplains (1973)
P.O. Box 5590
Destin, FL 32540-5590
Tel: (850) 654-9736 *Fax:* (850) 654-9742
E-Mail: icpc@icpc.gccoxmail.com
Website: icpc4cops.org
Members: 2600 individuals
Staff: 2
Annual Budget: $500-1,000,000
Tax: 501(c)(3)

Personnel:

President: Keoki Awai
    E-Mail: kmbc205@hotmail.com
Executive Administrator: Ruby Kinlaw
    E-Mail: admin@icpc.gccoxmail.com

Historical Note:
*ICPC is dedicated to serving all law enforcement chaplains
and developing professional chaplains through dynamic
education and support. Membership: $125/year.*
Meetings/Conferences:
Number of non-conference events/year: 1
Publications:
ICPC Journal; quarterly
Membership Roster; monthly

International Conference of Symphony and Opera Musicians (1962)
1609 Tammany Dr.
Nashville, TN 37206
Tel: (615) 227-2379 *Fax:* (615) 259-9140
Website: icsom.org
Members: 4000 individuals
Staff: 9
Annual Budget: $100-250,000
Tax: 501(c)(5)

Personnel:
President: Brian Rood
    E-Mail: brianfrood@sbcglobal.net
Editor: Richard Levine
    E-Mail: senza@richlevine.com
Treasurer: Michael Moore
    E-Mail: treasurer@atlantabrass.com
Webmaster: Charles Noble
    E-Mail: icsom.webmaster@gmail.com
Secretary: Laura Ross
    E-Mail: lar2vln@comcast.net

Historical Note:
*ICSOM's mission is to facilitate communication between its
member orchestras and their delegates to the Conference,
the Governing Board, and other members of the greater
musical community, offering support and assistance
wherever needed. Members are professional symphony,
opera and ballet musicians united to encourage the welfare
of and make more rewarding the livelihood of the orchestral
performer and to disseminate inter-orchestra information
through correspondence and a newsletter. Affiliated with the
American Federation of Musicians. Membership: fees vary.*

Publications:
ICSOM bulletins; bi-monthly; adv.
ICSOM Directory; annually; adv.
Senza Sordino
Senza Sordino; bi-monthly; adv.

International Congress of Oral Implantologists (1972)
248 Lorraine Ave.
Upper Montclair, NJ 07043-1454
Tel: (973) 783-6300 *Fax:* (973) 783-1175
TollFree: (800) 442-0525
E-Mail: icoi@dentalimplants.com
Website: icoi.org
Members: 10000 individuals
Staff: 8
Annual Budget: $5-10,000,000

Personnel:
Executive Director: R. Craig Johnson
    E-Mail: rcjohnson1228@sbcglobal.net
Director, Membership Services: Jennifer Berg
    E-Mail: berg@icoi.org
Editor-in-Chief: Morton L. Perel DDS, MScD
    E-Mail: implantsmp@aol.com
Advertising Manager: Angela Santelli
    E-Mail: icoi@dentalimplants.com

Historical Note:
*ICOI's mission is to serve the needs of the dental implant
industry. It works to provide members with quality
education to better serve their patients. Members are
dentists, oral surgeons, research personnel and others
involved in oral implant procedures. Membership:
$50-350/year.*
Continuing Education:
Certification Designation/s: ADA, CERP
Meetings/Conferences:
Conference Chair: Angela Santelli
2013 - Las Vegas, NV/May 16 - 18
Number of non-conference events/year: 3
Publications:
ICOI World News; quarterly; adv.

Implant Dentistry; on-line; adv.
Membership List Available to Non-members

International Consumer Product Health and Safety Organization (1993)
7044 S. 13th St.
Oak Creek, WI 53154
Tel: (414) 908-4930 *Fax:* (414) 768-8001
E-Mail: customercare@icphso.org.
Website: icphso.org
Staff: 2
Annual Budget: $500-1,000,000
Tax: 501(c)(3)

Personnel:
Executive Director: Ross Koeser
    E-Mail: rkoeser@icphso.org
Association Manager: Paul Rossmann
    E-Mail: p.rossmann@icphso.org

Historical Note:
*ICPHSO's purpose is to address health and safety
issues related to consumer products marketed globally.
Membership: $300 (Business); $100 (Non-Business
Member); $75 (Non-Conference Member); $150
(Additional).*
Meetings/Conferences: Annual
2013 - Arlington, VA (Hyatt Regency Crystal City at
Reagan National Airport)/Feb. 26 - March 1/500
attendees
Publications:
ICPHSO Newsletter; quarterly
Membership Directory; on-line

International Contact Center Benchmarking Consortium (1998)
4606 FM 1960 West
Suite 250
Houston, TX 77069
Tel: (281) 440-5044 *Fax:* (281) 440-6677
E-Mail: info@iccbc.org
Website: iccbc.org
Members: 3700 individuals
Staff: 14
Annual Budget: $1-2,000,000

Personnel:
Senior Consultant: Paul Claymore

Historical Note:
*An autonomous division of The Benchmarking Network,
ICCBC members are individuals and companies operating
customer service or information call centers. Provides
information on industry best practices to members.*
Meetings/Conferences:
Number of non-conference events/year: 1

International Contrast Ultrasound Society (2008)
300 N. LaSalle Dr.
Suite 100
Chicago, IL 60654
Tel: (888) 555-1212
TollFree: (888) 555-1212
E-Mail: info@icus-society.org
Website: icus-society.org
Staff: 2
Annual Budget: $10-25,000

Personnel:
President: Steven B. Feinstein
Treasurer: Michael Main

Historical Note:
*ICUS's mission is to promote the safe and efficacious use
of contrast-enhanced ultrasound ("CEUS") in patients with
diverse medical profiles and disease states and provide a
global inter-disciplinary forum to foster education, research,
and development of CEUS applications.*
Publications:
ICUS Weekly News Monitors; weekly

International Copper Association (1960)
260 Madison Ave.
16th Floor
New York, NY 10016-2401
Tel: (212) 251-7240 *Fax:* (212) 251-7245
E-Mail: info@copperalliance.org
Website: copperalliance.org
Members: 11 associate members and 43
companies
Staff: 20
Annual Budget: $10-25,000,000

Personnel:
President: John J. Holland
Director, Communications and Membership Relations:
    Steve L. Kukoda
    E-Mail: skukoda@copper.org
Director, Technology: Hal Stillman

Historical Note:
*In 2011, the ICA Network adopted a branding campaign
referred to as Copper Alliance. ICA's mission is to defend
and grow markets for copper based on its superior technical
performance and its contribution to a higher quality of life
worldwide.*
Publications:
Membership Directory; on-line

International Corrugated Packaging Foundation (1985)
113 S. West St.
Alexandria, VA 22314
Tel: (703) 549-8580 *Fax:* (703) 549-8670
E-Mail: info@icpfbox.org
Website: icpfbox.org
Staff: 2
Annual Budget: $2-5,000,000
Tax: 501(c)(3)

Personnel:
President: Richard M. Flaherty
Treasurer: A. Steven Young

Historical Note:
*ICPF's mission is to generate a stream of increasingly
qualified students to enter the corrugated industry, now and
into the future.*

International Cost Estimating and Analysis Association effective (1990)
8221 Old Courthouse Rd.
Suite 106
Vienna, VA 22182
Tel: (703) 938-5090 *Fax:* (703) 938-5091
E-Mail: scea@sceaonline.org
Website: sceaonline.org
Members: 1500 individuals
Staff: 4
Annual Budget: $250-500,000
Tax: 501(c)(6)

Personnel:
Certification Program Administrator: Sharon Burger
    E-Mail: sharon@sceaonline.org
Information Technology Support: Don Clarke
    E-Mail: don@sceaonline.org
Executive Director: Erin Whittaker
    E-Mail: erin@sceaonline.org
Coordinator, Membership Services: Erica Wilkening
    E-Mail: erica@sceaonline.org

Historical Note:
*Formed (1990) by a merger of the National Estimating
Society (1966) and the Institute of Cost Analysis (1980),
SCEA's mission is to seek further effectiveness and efficiency
of cost estimating and analysis and related disciplines in
the public and private sectors by enhancing the competence
and achievements of its professional members. Members are
professionals engaged primarily in the field of government
contract estimating and pricing. Membership: $55
(Individual); 550 (Lifetime).*
Continuing Education:
Enrollment: 50
Certification Designation/s: CCEA
Meetings/Conferences: Annual
Number of non-conference events/year: 1
Publications:
Journal of Cost Analysis and Parametrics; irregular
SCAF Newsletter; on-line
The National Estimator; semi-annually; adv.

International Council for Health, Physical, Education, Recreation, Sport and Dance (1958)
1900 Association Dr.
Reston, VA 20191-1598
Tel: (703) 476-3462 *Fax:* (703) 476-9527
E-Mail: ichper@aahperd.org
Website: ichpersd.org
Members: 145 countries
Staff: 3

Personnel:
Honorary President: Dr. Dong Ja Yang
    E-Mail: djyang@erols.com
Administrative Associate: Carmella Gilpin

Historical Note:
An outgrowth of an idea conceived in 1950 by the Board of the American Association for Health, Physical Education, and Recreation (see listing for AAHPER). ICHPER.SD's mission is fostering the essence of education in HPERSD fields through international understanding and goodwill, safeguarding peace, freedom, and respect for human dignity. Membership: $300-2,700 (National); $200 (Institution); $40-60 (Individual); $1,500 (Life); $300 (International); $100 (Library); $1000 (Contributing).

Meetings/Conferences: Annual
2013 - Charlotte, NC/April 23 - 27

Publications:
ICHPER-SD Journal of Research (JR); semi-annually

International Council for Machinery Lubrication
1943 W. Concord Cir.
Broken Arrow, OK 74012
Tel: (918) 259-2950 *Fax:* (918) 259-0177
E-Mail: info@lubecouncil.org
Website: lubecouncil.org
Staff: 3
Annual Budget: $250-500,000

Personnel:
Executive Director: Suzy Jamieson

Historical Note:
A vendor-neutral, nonprofit organization founded to facilitate growth and development of machine lubrication as a technical field of endeavor. Membership: $60 (Individual); $2,000 (Sustaining).

Continuing Education:
Certification Designation/s: MLA, MLT, LLA

Publications:
Membership Directory; on-line
Newsletter; quarterly

International Council for Small Business (1955)
GWU School of Business
2201 G. St. NW, Funger Hall, Suite 315
Washington, DC 20052
Tel: (202) 994-0704 *Fax:* (202) 994-4930
E-Mail: icsb@gwu.edu
Website: icsb.org
Members: 1800 individuals
Staff: 3
Annual Budget: $250-500,000
Tax: 501(c)(3)

Personnel:
Executive Director: Ayman El Tarabishy
    E-Mail: aymanelt@icsb.org
Manager, Operations: Michael Battaglia
Editor: George T. Solomon PhD
    E-Mail: gsolomon@gwu.edu

Historical Note:
Formerly (1977) National Council for Small Business Management Development. ICSB is devoted to the advancement of management development practices for potential entrepreneurs and existing small business owner/managers through education, research, and the free exchange of ideas. Membership: $125 (Regular/ Individual}; $250 (Organization); $75 (Student); $25-65 (International).

Meetings/Conferences: Annual
2013 - Ponce, PR/June 20 - 23

Publications:
E-Alerts; on-line
Journal for Small Business Management; quarterly
Membership Directory; on-line
The Bulletin; quarterly

International Council of Air Shows (1968)
750 Miller Dr. SE
Suite F-3
Leesburg, VA 20175
Tel: (703) 779-8510 *Fax:* (703) 779-8511
E-Mail: icas@airshows.aero
Website: airshows.aero
Members: 900 companies and organizations
Staff: 5
Annual Budget: $1-2,000,000
Tax: 501(c)(6)

Personnel:
President: John Cudahy
    E-Mail: cudahy@airshows.org
Director, Financial Services: Karen Dolan
    E-Mail: kadolan@airshows.org
Director, Administrative Services and Membership Services: Marcia Lowry

E-Mail: lowry@airshows.org
Advertising Sales Representative, Air Shows Magazine: Mary Ann McManamay
    E-Mail: mcmanamay@airshows.aero
Director, Meeting Services: Mary Quigg
    E-Mail: mary.quigg@conferencedirect.com

Historical Note:
ICAS works to maintain safety and serves as an information resource on air show issues for those within and outside the industry. Provides for the training and continuing education needs of it's members and air show professionals generally and promotes the air show industry to the media, Corporate North America and the general public. Members are air show event organizers from the United States, Canada and the rest of the world. Membership: $295/year.

Meetings/Conferences: Annual
Conference Chair: Mary Quigg

Publications:
Air Shows Magazine; quarterly; adv.
Fast Facts e-mail newsletter; semi-monthly; adv.
Operations Bulletin e-mail newsletter; semi-monthly

International Council of Employers of Bricklayers and Allied Craftworkers (1987)
P.O. Box 21462
Washington, DC 20009
Tel: (202) 457-9040 *Fax:* (202) 457-9051
E-Mail: info@icebac.org
Website: icebac.org
Members: 10000 signatory contractors
Staff: 3
Annual Budget: $100-250,000
Tax: 501(c)(6)

Personnel:
Executive Director: Matthew S. Aquiline
    E-Mail: maquiline@icebac.org
Director, Advocacy: Laina M. Aquiline
    E-Mail: laquiline@icebac.org

Historical Note:
ICE's purpose is to engage in labor relations matters in dealing with the International Union of Bricklayers and Allied Craftworkers and its constituent local unions located in the United States and Canada. Members are contractors who are signatory to collectively-bargained labor agreements with the International Union of Bricklayers and Allied Craftworkers.

Continuing Education:
Certification Designation/s: IMICC

Publications:
ICE Voice Newsletter; quarterly
Membership Directory; on-line

International Council of Fine Arts Deans (1964)
P.O. Box 110168
Bradenton, FL 34211
Tel: (941) 753-0080 *Fax:* (813) 974-2091
Website: icfad.org
Members: 400 individuals
Staff: 2
Annual Budget: $100-250,000
Tax: 501(c)(3)

Personnel:
Executive Director: Liz Cole
    E-Mail: colee@icfad.org
Business Manager: Carl H. Koenig
    E-Mail: carlkoenig@icfad.org

Historical Note:
ICFAD's mission is to foster the standards in leadership for the fine arts, and encourage global understanding and cooperation in the field. Membership: $450 (Institutional); $150 (Associate); $200 (Affiliate).

Meetings/Conferences: Annual
2013 - New Orleans, LA (Hotel Monteleone)/Oct. 23 - 26/200 attendees
2014 - Kansas City, MO/Oct. 22 - 25

Publications:
Membership Directory; on-line
Newsletter; weekly

International Council of Library Association Executives (1975)
50 E Huron St.
Chicago, IL 60611
Tel: (800) 545-2433
Members: 30 individuals
Staff: 1
Annual Budget: Under $10,000

Personnel:
Contact: John Lawrence Adams

Historical Note:
Formerly Council of Library Association Executives, the Council assumed its present name in 1983. Members are executive directors, or equivalent, of state, provincial and regional library associations. Membership: $10/year.

International Council of Psychologists (1941)
Eight Althea St.
St. Augustine, FL 32084
Tel: (904) 461-3382
Website: icpweb.org
Members: 1200 individuals
Staff: 2
Annual Budget: $25-50,000
Tax: 501(c)(3)

Personnel:
President: Ludwig Lowenstein
Treasurer: Dr. Gerald L. Gamache
    E-Mail: drjerrygamache@bellsouth.net

Historical Note:
Established as National Council of Women Psychologists in the U. S. A. Became (1947) International Council of Women Psychologists, and (1959) International Council of Psychologists. ICP's mission is to advance psychology and the application of its scientific findings throughout the world. Membership: $25-100 (Individual, based on Country of residence); $25 (Student).

Meetings/Conferences: Annual

Publications:
International Psychologist; quarterly
Membership Directory; on-line

International Council of Shopping Centers (1957)
1221 Avenue of the Americas
41st Floor
New York, NY 10020-1099
Tel: (646) 728-3800 *Fax:* (732) 694-1755
E-Mail: government@icsc.org
Website: icsc.org
Members: 50000 individuals
Staff: 159
Annual Budget: $50-100,000,000

Personnel:
President and Chief Executive Officer: Michael P. Kerchval
    E-Mail: mkercheval@icsc.org
Staff Vice President, Finance and Controller: Glen Hale
    E-Mail: ghale@icsc.org
Senior Staff Vice President, Communications and External Relations: Malachy Kavanagh
    E-Mail: mkavanagh@icsc.org
Senior Vice President, Global Public Policy: Betsy Laird
    E-Mail: blaird@icsc.org
Director, Communications and Public Relations, Global Public Policy: Stephanie Lockwood
    E-Mail: slockwood@icsc.org
Staff Vice President, Human Resources and Office Services: Fran Marmer
    E-Mail: fmarmer@icsc.org
Staff Vice President: Lorraine Mazza
    E-Mail: lmazza@icsc.org
President and Executive Director, Projects: Gregg A. McCort
    E-Mail: gmccort@icsc.org
Staff Vice President and Chief Information Officer: Michael J. Merrick
    E-Mail: mmerrick@icsc.org
Director, Publications: Patricia Montagni
    E-Mail: pmontagni@icsc.org
Senior Staff Vice President, Programs and Services: Marvin Morrison
    E-Mail: mmorrison@icsc.org
Manager, Membership Records: Eddie Ong
    E-Mail: eong@icsc.org
Staff Vice President, General Counsel: Gregory Peterson
    E-Mail: gpeterson@icsc.org
Senior Staff Vice President and Chief Global Marketing Officer: Jay Starr
    E-Mail: jstarr@icsc.org

Historical Note:
Formerly known as the International Association of Shopping Centers. ICSC strives to advance the development of the shopping center industry and to establish the individual shopping center as a major institution in the community. Members are shopping center owners, developers, managers, marketing specialists, investors, lenders, retailers and other professionals as well as

academics and public officials. *Membership:* $800 (Regular/Associate); $100 (Affiliate/Public/Academic); $50 (Public/Academic Affiliate/Student).

Continuing Education:
Certification Designation/s: CMD, ASM, SCSM, AMD, CLS, CSM, SCMD, CDP

Meetings/Conferences:
Conference Chair: Lorraine Mazza
2013 - Whistler, BC/Jan. 27 - 29
2013 - London, United Kingdom/May 15 - 17
2013 - Las Vegas, NV (Las Vegas Convention Center)/ May 19 - 22
Number of non-conference events/year: 9

Publications:
ICSC AsiaBrief; weekly
ICSC EuroBrief; weekly
ICSC IndiaBrief; weekly
ICSC Middle East Brief; weekly
ICSC SmartBrief
ICSC Voice; quarterly
International Outlet Journal; quarterly; adv.
Member Directory; on-line
Resumen Iberoamericano; weekly
Resumen Mexicano; weekly
Retail Law Strategist; quarterly
SCTWeek; weekly
Shopping Center Legal Update
Shopping Centers Today; monthly; adv.
Shopping Centers Today Latinoamérica
Value Retail News; quarterly; adv.

International Council on Education for Teaching
(1953)
C/O National-Louis University, 1000 Capitol Dr.
Wheeling, IL 60090-7201
Tel: (847) 899-5622 *Fax:* (847) 899-5622
E-Mail: contact@icet4u.org
Website: icet4u.org
Members: 500 individuals
Staff: 4
Annual Budget: $10-25,000
Tax: 501(c)(3)

Personnel:
President and Director, Research: James O'Meara
E-Mail: president@icet4u.org

Historical Note:
ICET's mission is to foster international cooperation in improving the quality of preparation of teachers, administrators and other education specialists through the development of national, regional and international networks. Membership is open to individuals, institutions, associations and government agencies that are willing to share their educational expertise with counterparts around the world. Membership: $50 (Individual); $400 (Life); $300 (Institutions).

Meetings/Conferences: Annual
2013 - Nonthaburi, Thailand/June 25 - 28

Publications:
Newsletter; quarterly

Membership List Available to Non-members

International Council on Hotel, Restaurant and Institutional Education *(1946)*
2810 N. Parham Rd.
Suite 230
Richmond, VA 23294
Tel: (804) 346-4800 *Fax:* (804) 346-5009
Website: chrie.org
Members: 2500 individuals
Staff: 5
Annual Budget: $1-2,000,000
Tax: 501(c)(3)

Personnel:
Chief Executive Officer: Kathy McCarty
E-Mail: kmccarty@chrie.org
Vice President, Operations: Kevin Anderson
E-Mail: kanderson@chrie.org
Manager, Publications: Amie Garrett Grayson
E-Mail: agrayson@chrie.org
Manager, Membership Services: Mia Williamson
E-Mail: membership@chrie.org

Historical Note:
Founded as the National Council on Hotel and Restaurant Education, assumed its present name in 1959. ICHRIE's mission is to provide programs and services to continually improve the quality of global education, research, service, and business operations in the hospitality and tourism industry. Membership: $1,000 (Premium); $105-205

(Individual-Educator); $365-565 (Institution); $565 (Corporate).

Meetings/Conferences: Annual
2013 - Macau, China/May 21 - 24
2013 - St. Louis, MO/July 24 - 27

Publications:
CHRIE Communique; monthly; adv.
Hosteur; on-line; adv.
Journal of Hospitality and Tourism Education; quarterly; adv.
Journal of Hospitality and Tourism Research; quarterly; adv.
Membership Directory; on-line
Pioneers of the Hospitality Industry

International Council on Systems Engineering
(1990)
7670 Opportunity Rd.
Suite 220
San Diego, CA 92111-2222
Tel: (858) 541-1725 *Fax:* (858) 541-1728
TollFree: (800) 366-1164
E-Mail: info@incose.org
Website: incose.org
Members:
60 companies
7500 individuals
Staff: 4
Annual Budget: $1-2,000,000
Tax: 501(c)(6)

Personnel:
Managing Executive: Holly Witte
E-Mail: holly.witte@incose.org
Associate Director, Events: Jonas Andersson
E-Mail: jonas.andersson@incose.org
Manager, Operations: Christine Kowalski
E-Mail: christine@univmgmt.com
Associate Director, Technical Operations: Dick Wray
E-Mail: richard.wray@incose.org

Historical Note:
The International Council on Systems Engineering (INCOSE) is a not-for-profit membership organization founded to develop and disseminate the interdisciplinary principles and practices that enable the realization of successful systems. Membership: $135 (Regular Member); $35 (Student); $75 (Senior).

Continuing Education:
Enrollment: 500
Certification Designation/s: CSEP, ESEP, ASEP

Meetings/Conferences: Annual
Conference Chair: Jonas Andersson
2013 - Herzliya, Israel (the Daniel hotel)/March 4 - 6
Number of non-conference events/year: 2

Publications:
eNote; monthly; adv.
Insight Newsletter; quarterly; adv.
Journal of Systems Engineering; quarterly; adv.
Membership Directory; on-line

International Crystal Federation
P.O. Box 6250
Avon, CO 81620-6250
Tel: (970) 949-5651
Website: internationalcrystalfederation.org
Members: 80 individuals
Staff: 1
Annual Budget: $50-100,000
Tax: 501(c)(6)

Personnel:
Executive Director: Craig Boreiko

Historical Note:
The ICF is a not-for-profit international organization of manufacturers, distributors and suppliers of crystal. ICF's mission is to serve as an advocate for the crystal industry in the areas of governmental relations, trade relations and consumer education.

International Customer Service Association
(1981)
1110 S. Ave.
Suite 50
Staten Island, NY 10314
Tel: (347) 273-1303 *Fax:* (347) 273-1403
E-Mail: info@icsatoday.org
Website: icsatoday.org
Members: 3200 individuals
Staff: 7

Annual Budget: $100-250,000
Tax: 501(c)(6)

Personnel:
President: Bill Gessert
Administrative Director: Lisa Gessert
Director, Membership Services: Betty McCorkle
Director, Communications: Don Yager

Historical Note:
ICSA's mission is to advance, strengthen, and promote the industry of Professional Customer Service. Members are customer service management professionals. Membership: $295/year (Individual).

Continuing Education:
Certification Designation/s: ICSA

Meetings/Conferences: Annual
Number of non-conference events/year: 1

Publications:
ICSAToday Newsletter; weekly
Membership Directory; on-line

Membership List Available to Non-members

International Cut Flower Growers Association
(1937)
P.O. Box 99
Haslett, MI 48840
Tel: (517) 655-3726 *Fax:* (517) 655-3727
E-Mail: icfg@voyager.net
Members: 300 individuals
Staff: 4
Annual Budget: $10-25,000

Personnel:
Executive Secretary: Jay Stawarz
E-Mail: icfg@voyager.net

Historical Note:
Founded as Roses Incorporated assumed its current name in 2000. ICFG's mission is to provide support through publications, research and educational programs. Membership: $500 (Growers and Suppliers); $300 (Associates).

International Dairy Foods Association *(1990)*
1250 H St. NW
Suite 900
Washington, DC 20005
Tel: (202) 737-4332 *Fax:* (202) 331-7820
E-Mail: membership@idfa.org
Website: idfa.org
Members: 550 companies
Staff: 35
Annual Budget: $2-5,000,000
Tax: 501(c)(6)

Personnel:
President and Chief Executive Officer: Connie Tipton
E-Mail: ctipton@idfa.org
Vice President, Communications: Peggy Armstrong
E-Mail: parmstrong@idfa.org
Director, Board and Employee Relations: Tracy Boyle
Vice President, Meetings and Educational Services: Diana Carmenates CAE, CMP
E-Mail: dcarmenates@idfa.org
Director, Membership Services: Cindy Cavallo
E-Mail: ccavallo@idfa.org
Meetings Assistant and Registrar: Patrick Crosson
E-Mail: pcrosson@idfa.org
Senior Group Vice President and General Counsel: Clayton L. Hough
E-Mail: chough@idfa.org
Senior Vice President, Finance, Administration and Trade Shows: Neil Moran
E-Mail: nmoran@idfa.org
Senior Vice President, Legislative Affairs & Economic Policy: Jerry D. Slominski
E-Mail: jslominski@idfa.org

Historical Note:
IDFA's mission is to provide strategic leadership to association members, government officials, customers and other audiences to promote full and open markets to maximize sales. It is a trade association that works with legislators, regulators and the public on issues affecting the dairy processing industry and is committed to facilitate growth of the industry.

Meetings/Conferences: Semi-Annual
Conference Chair: Diana Carmenates CAE, CMP
2013 - Orlando, FL (JW Marriott Orlando Grande Lakes)/Jan. 27 - 30
2013 - Scottsdale, AZ (The Boulders)/May 4 - 6
2013 - Chicago, IL (McCormick Place)/Nov. 3 - 6

Number of non-conference events/year: 7

Publications:
Dairy Facts; annually; adv.
IDFA Membership Directory; annually; adv.
IDFA SmartBrief e-newsletter; on-line; adv.
News Update; weekly

Membership List Available to Non-members

International Dairy-Deli-Bakery Association
(1964)
P.O. Box 5528
Madison, WI 53705-0528
Tel: (608) 310-5000 *Fax:* (608) 238-6330
E-Mail: iddba@iddba.org
Website: iddba.org
Members: 1458 companies
Staff: 24
Annual Budget: $10-25,000,000
Tax: 501(c)(6)

Personnel:
Executive Director: Carol L. Christison
    E-Mail: cchristison@iddba.org
Director, Membership Services, Registration and Exhibits:
    Lucie Arendt
    E-Mail: larendt@iddba.org
Contact, Communications: Jessica Hughes
    E-Mail: jhughes@iddba.org
Editor: Mary Kay O'Connor
    E-Mail: mcconnor@iddba.org
Contact, Training and Certification: Karen Peckham
    E-Mail: kpeckham@iddba.org

Historical Note:
Formerly (1985) the International Cheese and Deli Association and International Dairy-Deli Association (1991). IDDBA's mission is to promote the growth and development of dairy, deli, and bakery sales in the food industry. Members are companies involved in the production, processing or selling of deli, dairy and bakery products. Membership: $450 (Corporate); $200 (Retail); $250 (DSD Distributor).

Meetings/Conferences: Annual
Conference Chair: Lucie Arendt
2013 - Orlando, FL (Orange County Convention
    Center)/June 2 - 4
2014 - Denver, CO/June 1 - 3
2015 - Atlanta, GA/June 7 - 9
2016 - Houston, TX/June 5 - 8
2016 - Houston, TX/June 5 - 7

Publications:
Dairy·Deli·Bake Digest; monthly
Dairy·Deli·Bake Wrap-Up; quarterly
IDDBA & YOU; monthly
IDDBA Legis-Letter; monthly

International Decorative Artisans League (1984)
1100-H Brandywine Blvd.
Zanesville, OH 43701-7303
Tel: (740) 452-4541 *Fax:* (740) 452-2552
E-Mail: office@decorativeartisans.org
Website: decorativeartisans.org
Staff: 5
Tax: 501(c)(3)

Personnel:
Executive Director: Penny Sitler
    E-Mail: psitler@offinger.com
Contact, Conventions and Expositions: Denise Brosie
    E-Mail: convention@decorativeartisans.org
Editor: Pat Ganino
    E-Mail: artisphere@decorativeartisans.org
Treasurer and Contact, Membership Services: Ed
    Mattingly
    E-Mail: membership@decorativeartisans.org
Contact, Marketing: Anthony Pinkston
    E-Mail: marketing@decorativeartisans.org

Historical Note:
IDAL's mission is to promote and preserve the art of stenciling and related decorative painting. Membership provides opportunities for artistic and professional growth through: education, certification, public awareness, and networking. Membership: $32 (Student); $60 (Individual); $82 (Home Based Business); $107 (Professional); $202-500 (Business Partner).

Continuing Education:
Certification Designation/s: CMS, CMST, CST, CSA, CS

Meetings/Conferences: Annual
Conference Chair: Denise Brosie

2013 - Indianapolis, IN (Sheraton Indianapolis Hotel at
    Keystone Crossing)/Oct. 8 - 12

Publications:
Artisphere Online; quarterly; adv.
IDAL E-Newsletter; monthly; adv.
Membership Directory; on-line

Membership List Available to Non-members

International Desalination Association (1973)
94 Central St., Suite 200
P.O. Box 387
Topsfield, MA 01983
Tel: (978) 887-0410 *Fax:* (978) 887-0411
E-Mail: info@idadesal.org
Website: idadesal.org
Members: 6400 core members and worldwide
members
Staff: 6
Annual Budget: $1-2,000,000
Tax: 501(c)(6)

Personnel:
Secretary General: Patricia A. Burke
    E-Mail: paburke@idadesal.org
Manager, Special Technical Programs: Beth M. Bodo
    E-Mail: bbodo@idadesal.org
Manager, Administrative Services: Leslie J. Merrill
    E-Mail: lmerrill@idadesal.org
Manager, Special Projects and Finance: Nancy T. Pagels
    E-Mail: npagels@idadesal.org
Manager, Conferences and Technical Programs: Darlene
    A. Seta
    E-Mail: dseta@idadesal.org

Historical Note:
Established as the National Water Supply Improvement Association, became the Water Supply Improvement Association in 1982, and assumed its present name in 1985 on merging with the International Desalination and Environmental Association. IDA is committed to development and promotion of the appropriate use of desalination and desalination technology globally in water supply, water reuse, water pollution control, water purification, water treatment and other water sciences and technology. Membership: $75-120 (Individual); $1050 (Corporations/Utilities); $700 (Small Companies); $25 (Full-time Students /Non-profit Libraries/ Least Developed Countries).

Meetings/Conferences: Annual
Conference Chair: Darlene A. Seta

Publications:
Desalination and Water Reuse Quarterly; quarterly
IDA Newsletter; on-line
The IDA Journal On Desalination And Water Reuse

International Digital Enterprise Alliance (1966)
1600 Duke St.
Suite 420
Alexandria, VA 22314
Tel: (703) 837-1070 *Fax:* (703) 837-1072
E-Mail: info@idealliance.org
Website: idealliance.org
Members: 200 companies and organizations
Staff: 10
Annual Budget: $2-5,000,000
Tax: 501(c)(3)

Personnel:
President and Chief Executive Officer: David J. Steinhardt
    E-Mail: dsteinhardt@idealliance.org
Vice President of Operations and Managing Director:
    Frank Balser
    E-Mail: fbalser@idealliance.org
Executive Vice President, Marketing: Steve Bonoff
    E-Mail: sbonoff@idealliance.org
Vice President, Print Media: Joe Fazzi
    E-Mail: jfazzi@idealliance.org
Director, Training and Systems Integration: Illeny Maaza
    E-Mail: imaaza@idealliance.org
Director, Events and Membership Services: Georgia
    Volakis
    E-Mail: gvolakis@idealliance.org
Manager, Information Systems: Johnny White
    E-Mail: jwhite@idealliance.org

Historical Note:
Organized as Graphic Communications Computer Association, became Graphic Communications Association in 1966, and assumed its present name in 2001. Merged with IPA - The Association of Graphic Solutions Providers in 2010. IDEA's mission is to provide a user-driven, cross-industry, and open environment in which its members can

strategize, innovate, standardize, and implement solutions to real business challenges in eMedia-based publishing. Membership: $1,300-27,500 (Sales Volume/Budget).

Continuing Education:
Certification Designation/s: OPPSC, eMPC, CMPC, G7C, JDFEC, G7SC, PSC, DPC

Meetings/Conferences: Annual
Conference Chair: Georgia Volakis
Number of non-conference events/year: 5

Publications:
IDEA Newsletter; bi-monthly

International Disaster Recovery Association
(1989)
P.O. Box 4515
C/O BWT Associates
Shrewsbury, MA 01545
Tel: (508) 845-6000 *Fax:* (508) 842-9003
E-Mail: bwt@bwt.com
Website: idra.com
Staff: 1

Personnel:
Executive Director: Benjamin W. Tartaglia CSP, MBA

Historical Note:
IDRA works to maintain adequate voice, data and image telecommunication services during periods of extraordinary activity and interruptions in normal operations. Membership: $100 (Associate/Professional); $1,500 (Corporate); $2,500 (Sponsoring); $5,000 (Sustaining).

Meetings/Conferences: Annual

Publications:
ACK-NAK News; quarterly; adv.

International Disk Drive Equipment and Materials Association (1986)
1226 Lincoln Ave.
Suite 100
San Jose, CA 95125
Tel: (408) 294-0082 *Fax:* (408) 294-0087
E-Mail: info@idema.org
Website: idema.org
Members:
600 companies
100 individuals
Staff: 2
Annual Budget: $1-2,000,000

Personnel:
Chairman: Mark Geenen
Manager, Office: Trudy Gressley
    E-Mail: tgressley@idema.org

Historical Note:
IDEMA's mission is to provide measurable value and leadership to all levels of the global HDD infrastructure. Membership: $5,000-30,000 (Industry Leader); $6,250-12,500 (Core Technology Provider); $1,000-2,000 (Partner/Customer); $300 (University/Individual); $5,000-10,000 (Solid- State Drive Supplier/New).

Meetings/Conferences:
Conference Chair: Trudy Gressley

Publications:
Membership Directory; on-line

International District Energy Association (1909)
24 Lyman St.
Suite 230
Westborough, MA 01581-2841
Tel: (508) 366-9339 *Fax:* (508) 366-0019
E-Mail: idea@districtenergy.org
Website: districtenergy.org
Members: 1500 individuals
Staff: 12
Annual Budget: $2-5,000,000
Tax: 501(c)(6)

Personnel:
President and Chief Executive Officer: Robert P. Thornton
    E-Mail: rob.idea@districtenergy.org
General Counsel: Joel Greene
    E-Mail: jgreene@jsslaw.com
Office Manager and Executive Assistant to the President:
    Cheryl Jacques
    E-Mail: cheryl.idea@districtenergy.org
Director, Sales and Marketing: Tanya Kozel
    E-Mail: tanya.idea@districtenergy.org
Director, Business Development: Leonard A. Phillips
    E-Mail: len.idea@districtenergy.org
Conference and Meeting Planner: Anne Picillo

E-Mail: apicillo@custommademeetings.com
Legislative Director: Mark Spurr
E-Mail: mspurr@fvbenergy.com

Historical Note:
Formerly (1969) National District Heating Association, (1985) International District Heating Association, and (1994) International District Heating and Cooling Association, absorbed North American District Heating and Cooling Institute in 1988. IDEA's mission is to promote energy efficiency and environmental quality through the advancement of district heating, district cooling and cogeneration. Membership: $50-25,000/year.

Meetings/Conferences: Semi-Annual
Conference Chair: Tanya Kozel
2013 - San Diego, CA (Sheraton San Diego Hotel and Marina)/Feb. 18 - 22
2013 - Miami, FL (Hyatt Regency Miami)/June 23 - 26
2014 - Atlanta, GA (Atlanta Marriott Marquis)/Feb. 17 - 21
2014 - Seattle, WA (Washington State Convention Center)/June 8 - 11
Number of non-conference events/year: 6

Publications:
District Energy; quarterly; adv.
IDEA's Membership Directory; on-line

Membership List Available to Non-members

International Documentary Association (1982)
1201 W. Fifth St.
Suite M270
Los Angeles, CA 90017-1461
Tel: (213) 534-3600 *Fax:* (213) 534-3610
E-Mail: administration@documentary.org
Website: documentary.org
Members: 2800 individuals
Staff: 11
Annual Budget: $2-5,000,000
Tax: 501(c)(3)

Personnel:
Executive Director: Michael Lumpkin
E-Mail: michael@documentary.org
Office Manager and Manager, Membership Services: Jon Curry
E-Mail: jon@documentary.org
Director, Technology and Webmaster: Mark Dischler
E-Mail: mark@documentary.org
Program Manager, Fiscal Sponsorships: Amy Halpin
E-Mail: amy@documentary.org
Manager, Programs and Events: Amy Jelenko
E-Mail: amy.j@documentary.org
Manager, Advertising and Sales: Jodi Pais Montgomery
E-Mail: jodi@documentary.org
Editor: Thomas White
E-Mail: tom@documentary.org

Historical Note:
IDA promotes nonfiction filmmakers, and is dedicated to increase public awareness for the documentary genre. Membership consists of foreign as well as American members and includes producers, directors, writers, editors, camera operators, musicians, researchers, technicians, journalists, broadcast and cable programmers, academics, distributors and members of the general public. Membership: $45-15,000/year.

Meetings/Conferences:
Conference Chair: Amy Jelenko

Publications:
Documentary Magazine; quarterly; adv.
Membership Directory; on-line

International Door Association (1995)
P.O. Box 246
W. Milton, OH 45383-0246
Tel: (937) 698-8042 *Fax:* (937) 698-6153
TollFree: (800) 355-4432
E-Mail: info@longmgt.com
Website: doors.org
Members: 1600 Individuals
Staff: 10
Annual Budget: $2-5,000,000
Tax: 501(c)(6)

Personnel:
Managing Director: Christopher S. Long
E-Mail: chrislong@longmgt.com
Manager, Marketing: Shawn Hicks
E-Mail: shicks@longmgt.com
Manager, Publications: Art Komorowski
E-Mail: artk@longmgt.com

Manager, Meetings and Expositions: Roe Long-Wagner
E-Mail: roelong@longmgt.com
Administrative Assistant: Deb Schwan
E-Mail: dschwan@longmgt.com
Accounting Manager: Steve Smith
E-Mail: ssmith@longmgt.com
Manager, Membership Services and Affiliate Relations: Jane Treiber
E-Mail: jtreiber@longmgt.com

Historical Note:
The International Door Association was created in 1995 with the merger of the Door and Operator Dealers Association (est. 1968) and the Far Western Garage Door Association (est. 1964). IDA's mission is to attain a better level product and installation quality. International Door Association strives for quality creation and control by providing helpful programs and services to those who sell, install, and service the products. Members are producers and installers of garage door systems. Membership: $350 (Dealer); $100 (Subscribing Dealer); $100 (Subscribing Associate).

Meetings/Conferences: Annual
Conference Chair: Roe Long-Wagner

Publications:
IDA News Alert; irregular; adv.
International Door & Operator Industry; on-line; adv.
Membership Directory; on-line; adv.

International Double Reed Society (1971)
2423 Lawndale Rd.
Finksburg, MD 21048-1401
Tel: (410) 871-0658 *Fax:* (410) 871-0659
Website: idrs.org
Members: 4400 individuals
Staff: 5
Annual Budget: $250-500,000
Tax: 501(c)(3)

Personnel:
President: Martin Schuring
E-Mail: M.Schuring@asu.edu
Conference Coordinator: Mark Fink
E-Mail: mdfink@facstaff.wisc.edu
Advertising Coordinator: Wayne Gaver
E-Mail: waynegaveridrs@msn.com
Executive Secretary and Treasurer: Norma R. Hooks
E-Mail: norma4idrs@verizon.net
Editor: Yoshiyuki Ishikawa

Historical Note:
IDRS is dedicated to the dissemination of information related directly to double reed performance, pedagogy, and research. Members are performers, teachers, students and manufacturers of double reed instruments (e.g., bassoon, oboe). Membership: $35-400/year.

Meetings/Conferences: Annual
Conference Chair: Mark Fink
2013 - Redlands, CA (University of Redlands)/June 25 - 29

Publications:
Double Reed; quarterly; adv.
Member Directory; on-line; adv.

Membership List Available to Non-members

International Downtown Association (1954)
1025 Thomas Jefferson St. NW
Suite 500W
Washington, DC 20007
Tel: (202) 393-6801 *Fax:* (202) 393-6869
E-Mail: question@ida-downtown.org
Website: ida-downtown.org
Members: 600 individuals
Staff: 5
Annual Budget: $1-2,000,000
Tax: 501(c)(6)

Personnel:
President and Chief Executive Officer: David T. Downey CAE
E-Mail: ddowney@ida-downtown.org
Coordinator, Membership Services: Rebecca Bishophall
E-Mail: rbishophall@ida-downtown.org
Director, Development and Exhibits: Tracie D. Clemmer
E-Mail: tclemmer@ida-downtown.org
Director, Information and Research: Rowena Gono
E-Mail: rgono@ida-downtown.org
Director, Finance and Administration: Patricia Stephenson
E-Mail: pstephenson@ida-downtown.org

Historical Note:

Formerly (1986) International Downtown Executives Association. Mission is to accomplish good combination of learning and information resources to its members. Members are downtown development organizations or city, county or state agencies or and individuals and corporations with an interest in downtown development. Membership: $310 (Individual/Academic); $310-2,650 (Organization/Agency/Corporate, based on the size of operating budget or gross revenue); $55 (Student); $105 (International).

Meetings/Conferences:
Conference Chair: Tracie D. Clemmer

Publications:
Braintrust
IDAdvantage; monthly
Jobs/RFPs eReport; bi-weekly
Membership Directory; on-line
Next American City; quarterly
Parking Today; daily

Membership List Available to Non-members

International Dyslexia Association (1949)
40 York Rd.
Fourth Floor
Baltimore, MD 21204-5202
Tel: (410) 296-0232 *Fax:* (410) 321-5069
E-Mail: info@interdys.org
Website: interdys.org
Members: 8000 individuals
Staff: 15
Annual Budget: $2-5,000,000
Tax: 501(c)(3)

Personnel:
Executive Director: Lee Grossman
E-Mail: lgrossman@interdys.org
Development Director: Kristi Bowman
E-Mail: kbowman@interdys.org
Editor: Denise Douce
E-Mail: ddouce@interdys.org
Manager, Membership Services: Jill Eagan
E-Mail: jeagan@interdys.org
Director, Marketing, Membership Services and Communications: Michael J. Hayes
E-Mail: mhayes@interdys.org
Director, Professional Services: Elisabeth Liptak
E-Mail: eliptak@interdys.org
Director, Operations: Linda Marston
E-Mail: lmarston@interdys.org
Manager, Publications: Diane Nies
E-Mail: dnies@interdys.org
Director, Conferences: Kristen Penczek
E-Mail: kpenczek@interdys.org

Historical Note:
Formerly (1997) The Orton Dyslexia Society. IDA seeks to pursue and provide the most comprehensive range of information and services that address the full scope of dyslexia and related difficulties in learning to read and write. Members are individuals with dyslexia and their families, educators, school administrators, researchers, physicians, psychologists, and policy makers. Membership: $45 (Parent); $80 (Advocate); $95 (Educational/Allied Professional); $135 (Family); $2500 (Lifetime); $60 (Senior/Retired/Student); $395 (Educational Institution); $495 (Corporate/Business).

Meetings/Conferences: Annual
Conference Chair: Kristen Penczek
2013 - New Orleans, LA (Ernest N. Morial Convention Center)/Nov. 6 - 9
2014 - San Diego, CA (Hilton San Diego Bayfront)/Nov. 12 - 15
2015 - Grapevine, TX (Gaylord Texan Hotel and Convention Center-Grapevine)/Oct. 28 - 31

Publications:
Annals of Dyslexia; bi-annually
E-Newsletter; on-line
Perspectives on Language and Literacy; quarterly; adv.

Membership List Available to Non-members

International Economic Development Council (2001)
734 15th St. NW
Suite 900
Washington, DC 20005
Tel: (202) 223-7800 *Fax:* (202) 223-4745
Website: iedconline.org
Members: 4500 individuals
Staff: 46
Annual Budget: $5-10,000,000

Tax: 501(c)(3)

Personnel:
Senior Associate, Managing Editor: Louise Anderson
   E-Mail: landerson@iedconline.org
Coordinator, Administration: Kelly Bielen
   E-Mail: kbielen@iedconline.org
Conferences Coordinator: Matt Buccelli
   E-Mail: mbuccelli@iedconline.org
Director, Meetings: Jaclyn Kerper Gibson
   E-Mail: jgibson@iedconline.org
Vice President, Marketing: Paul L. Kelley
   E-Mail: pkelley@iedconline.org
Senior Government Affairs Associate: Matthew Mullin
   E-Mail: mmullin@iedconline.org
*Vice President, Knowledge Management and Economic
   Development Practice:* Liz Thorstensen
   E-Mail: ethorstensen@iedconline.org

Historical Note:
*Established in 2001 through the merger of the Council for
Urban Economic Development (CUED) and the American
Economic Development Council (AEDC). AEDC strives to
provide leadership and excellence in economic development
for its communities, members, and partners. Membership:
$1,075 (Corporate development partner); $145 (Additional
Individual Member); $60 (Student); $475 (International);
$95 (Member in Transition/Retired); $5,000 (Economic
Development Research Partner); $345-1,075 (Public
Agency/Non-profit/Consultant/Utility).*

Continuing Education:
Certification Designation/s: CEcD

Meetings/Conferences:
Conference Chair: Jaclyn Kerper Gibson
2013 - Philadelphia, PA (Philadelphia Marriott
   Downtown)/Oct. 6 - 9
2014 - Ft. Worth, TX (Ft. Worth Convention Center)/
   Oct. 19 - 22
Number of non-conference events/year: 2

Publications:
Economic Development America; quarterly
Economic Development Journal
Economic Development Now; bi-monthly
Membership Directory

Membership List Available to Non-members

The International Ecotourism Society *(1990)*
P.O. Box 96503
Suite 34145
Washington, DC 20090-6503
Tel: (202) 506-5033 *Fax:* (202) 789-7279
E-Mail: info@ecotourism.org
Website: ecotourism.org
Members: 520 Organization and 1100 Individual
Staff: 4
Annual Budget: $500-1,000,000
Tax: 501(c)(3)

Personnel:
Director, Communications: Ayako Ezaki
   E-Mail: media@ecotourism.org
Manager, Events: Mercedes Hunt
   E-Mail: events@ecotourism.org
Director, Membership and Operations: Ferdinand Weps
   E-Mail: fweps@ecotourism.org

Historical Note:
*TIES's mission is Create an international network of
individuals, institutions and the tourism industry, Educate
tourists and tourism professionals, Influence the tourism
industry, public institutions and donors to integrate the
principles of ecotourism into their operations and policies.
Membership: Free (Traveler/Student); $0-1,250/year.*

Meetings/Conferences:
Conference Chair: Mercedes Hunt

Publications:
Ecotourism; on-line
TIESNewsletter

InterNational Electrical Testing Association
(1972)
3050 Old Centre Ave.
Suite 102
Portage, MI 49024
Tel: (269) 488-6382 *Fax:* (269) 488-6383
TollFree: (888) 300-6382
E-Mail: neta@netaworld.org
Website: netaworld.org
Members: 1100 individuals and companies
Staff: 6
Annual Budget: $1-2,000,000

Tax: 501(c)(6)

Personnel:
Executive Director: Jayne M. Tanz
   E-Mail: jtanz@netaworld.org
Director, Marketing: Jill Howell
   E-Mail: jhowell@netaworld.org
Coordinator, Membership Services: Kristie Mulder
   E-Mail: kmulder@netaworld.org
Coordinator, Administration and Publications: James Noel
   E-Mail: jnoel@netaworld.org
Manager, Finance and Business: Melissa Richard
   E-Mail: mrichard@netaworld.org
Director, Technical Services: Kristen Wicks
   E-Mail: kschmidt@netaworld.org

Historical Note:
*Formerly (2005) National Electrical Testing Association.
International Electrical Testing Association is an accredited
standards developer for the American National Standards
Institute. NETA's mission is to serve the electrical
testing industry by establishing standards, publishing
specifications, accrediting independent testing companies,
certifying test technicians, and promoting the professional
services of its members. Membership: $250 (International
Associate); $135 (Affiliate); $775 (Gold Affiliate).*

Continuing Education:
Certification Designation/s: ETT

Meetings/Conferences: Annual
2013 - New Orleans, LA (Sheraton New Orleans
   Hotel)/Feb. 18 - 21

Publications:
NETA World Journal; quarterly; adv.

Membership List Available to Non-members

International Electronic Article Surveillance Manufacturers Association
1800 K St. NW
Suite 718
Washington, DC 20006
Tel: (202) 466-4214 *Fax:* (202) 466-7414
E-Mail: info@ieasma.net
Website: ieasma.org
Members: 12 companies
Staff: 7
Annual Budget: $250-500,000

Personnel:
Executive Vice President: Randy Dyer CAE
Meeting Coordinator: Elvie Lou

Historical Note:
*IEASMA is an association of manufacturers and suppliers of
Electronic Article Surveillance (EAS) anti-theft equipment.
Mission is to encourage and support International
Standardisation. Membership: varies, based on gross sales.*

International Electronic Commerce Association
1560 SW Eighth Ave.
Boca Raton, FL 33486
Tel: (954) 650-1266 *Fax:* (801) 729-9921
E-Mail: info@inteca.org
Staff: 1

Personnel:
Contact Person: Chris Williams

Historical Note:
*The Association offers a mutual help forum to assist all
merchants in dealing with the problems of trading on a
worldwide stage.*

International Electronic Manufacturing Initiative
2214 Rock Hill Rd.
Suite 110
Herndon, VA 20170-4214
Tel: (703) 834-0330 *Fax:* (703) 834-2735
Website: inemi.org
Members: 80 electronics manufacturers
Staff: 10

Personnel:
Chief Executive Officer: Bill Bader
   E-Mail: bill.bader@inemi.org
Director, Communications: Cynthia Williams
   E-Mail: cwilliams@inemi.org

Historical Note:
*Formerly The National Electronics Manufacturing Initiative
(NEMI). iNEMI forecast and accelerate improvements in
the electronics manufacturing industry for a sustainable
future. Membership: $5,000- 75,000 (Corporations, based
on Corporate Sales); $10,000 (Government laboratory/
research institution); $5,000 (University).*

Publications:

iNEMI Environmental Newsletter; quarterly
iNEMI Newsletter; monthly

International Embryo Transfer Society *(1974)*
1800 S. Oak St.
Suite 100
Champaign, IL 61820-6974
Tel: (217) 398-4697 *Fax:* (217) 398-4119
E-Mail: iets@assochq.org
Website: iets.org
Members: 1100 individuals
Staff: 2
Annual Budget: $250-500,000
Tax: 501(c)(3)

Personnel:
President: Gabriel A. Bo DVM, PhD
   E-Mail: gabrielbo@iracbiogen.com.ar

Historical Note:
*IETS seeks to further science of animal embryo transfer by
promoting more effective research, disseminating scientific
and educational information, fostering standards of
education, maintaining standards of ethics, and cooperating
with other organizations having similar objectives. Active
members are persons interested in the technology of embryo
transfer with a veterinary, master's or doctorate degree in a
field related to embryo transfer. Membership: $150 (Full/
Associate); $70 (Student); $75 (Emeritus).*

Meetings/Conferences: Annual
2013 - Hanover, Germany (Hanover Congress
   Centrum)/Jan. 19 - 22
2014 - Reno, NV (John Ascuaga's Nugget Hotel Resort
   Casino)/Jan. 11 - 14

Publications:
Embryo Transfer Newsletter; adv.
IETS Newsletters; quarterly
Membership Directory; on-line
Reproduction, Fertility and Development (RFD)

International Emissions Trading Association *(1999)*
1730 Rhode Island Ave. NW
Suite 802
Washington, DC 20036
Tel: (202) 629-5980 *Fax:* (202) 629-5999
E-Mail: ietadc@ieta.org
Website: ieta.org
Staff: 5
Annual Budget: $500-1,000,000

Personnel:
DC Representative: Tom Lawler
Director, United States Policy: David Hunter
   E-Mail: hunter@ieta.org
Program Manager: Ben McCarthy
   E-Mail: mccarthy@ieta.org

Historical Note:
*IETA is a nonprofit business organization created to
establish a functional international framework for trading in
greenhouse gas emission reductions.*

Meetings/Conferences: Annual
Conference Chair: Ben McCarthy

Publications:
IETA Newsletter; monthly
Membership Directory; on-line

International Energy Credit Association *(1923)*
15000 Commerce Pkwy.
Suite C
Mt. Laurel, NJ 08054
Tel: (856) 380-6854 *Fax:* (856) 439-0525
Website: ieca.net
Members: 1300 individuals
Staff: 3
Annual Budget: $1-2,000,000

Personnel:
Executive Director: Michelle Biordi
   E-Mail: mbiordi@ahint.com
Meeting Manager: Caitlin Dougherty
   E-Mail: cdougherty@ahint.com
Membership Coordinator: Ryan Harkins
   E-Mail: rharkins@ahint.com

Historical Note:
*Founded as Petroleum Refiners Bureau of the National
Association of Credit Men (NACM), changed to American
Petroleum Credit Association in 1946 and became the
American Petroleum Credit Association, Inc. in 1979.
Name changed to the International Petroleum Credit
Association in 1992. The present name was adopted in*

1998. IECA's mission is to promote the professionalism of its members by providing continuing education and a forum for the exchange of ideas relevant to credit and financial management of the energy industry. Membership: $325 (Individual); $275 (Corporate 5 or more members).

Meetings/Conferences:
Conference Chair: Caitlin Dougherty
2013 - Stateline, NV (Harveys Lake Tahoe)/March 17 - 19
2013 - Orlando, FL (JW Marriott Orlando Grande Lakes)/Sept. 29 - Oct. 2
2014 - San Antonio, TX (Westin La Cantera Hill Country Resort)/April 6 - 8
2014 - Palm Desert, CA (JW Marriott Desert Springs Resort)/Oct. 6 - 9

Publications:
IECA Journal; adv.
Membership directory; annually; adv.

International Engineering Consortium (1944)
233 S. Wacker Dr.
Suite 8400
Chicago, IL 60606-6338
Tel: (312) 283-8457 Fax: (312) 559-4111
E-Mail: info@iec.org
Website: iec.org
Members: 73 universities
Staff: 50
Annual Budget: Under $10,000

Personnel:
Executive Vice President: Roger Plummer

Historical Note:
Formerly (1974) National Electronics Conference and (1993) National Engineering Consortium. IEC's mission is to provide quality continuing education, research, publications, and service programs for the international information industry. Membership: Based on annual gross revenue of the organizations, $7,000-40,000 (Manufacturer); $5,000-20,000 (Service Provider); $5,000-20,000 (Consultant/Analyst); $7,500 (Venture Capitalist); $3,000 (Non-Profit).

Meetings/Conferences:
Number of non-conference events/year: 6

Publications:
Membership Directory; on-line

International Engraved Graphics Association (1911)
305 Plus Park Blvd.
Nashville, TN 37217
Tel: (615) 366-1094 Fax: (615) 366-4192
TollFree: (800) 821-3138
E-Mail: engraved1@earthlink.net
Website: iega.org
Members: 80 companies
Staff: 2
Annual Budget: $50-100,000

Personnel:
President: Baird Conner
Manager: Harris B. Griggs

Historical Note:
Formerly National Association of Steel and Copper Plate Engravers, became Engraved Stationery Manufacturers Association in 1938 and assumed its present name in 2000. IEGA is dedicated to help designers, brand image managers and purchasers find reliable information and sources for fine engraving.

Meetings/Conferences: Annual

Publications:
ESMA Newsletter; quarterly

International Entertainment Buyers Association (1970)
600 12th Ave. South
Suite 513
Nashville, TN 37203
Tel: (615) 679-9601 Fax: (615) 866-0116
E-Mail: info@ieba.org
Website: ieba.org
Members: 800 individuals
Staff: 2
Annual Budget: $250-500,000
Tax: 501(c)(6)

Personnel:
Executive Director: Tiffany Davis
Manager, Operations and Events: Candice Davis

Historical Note:

IEBA provides networking, showcasing and educational opportunities to strengthen relationships, foster growth and increase revenue for the live entertainment industry. Members are talent buyers, concert promoters, agents, managers, artists and other related entertainment professionals. Membership: $125 (Professional); $25 (Student).

Meetings/Conferences: Annual
Conference Chair: Candice Davis
Number of non-conference events/year: 1

Publications:
Encore; weekly
Member Directory; on-line
The Rider; quarterly; adv.

International Erosion Control Association (1972)
3401 Quebec St.
Suite 3500
Denver, CO 80207
Tel: (303) 640-7554 Fax: (866) 308-3087
TollFree: (800) 455-4322
E-Mail: ecinfo@ieca.org
Website: ieca.org
Members: 3000 companies and 3500 individuals
Staff: 8
Annual Budget: $1-2,000,000
Tax: 501(c)(3)

Personnel:
Executive Director: Russel "Russ" Adsit
E-Mail: russ@ieca.org
Manager, Marketing and Contact, Media Relations: Katie Laurin
E-Mail: katie@ieca.org

Historical Note:
IECA's mission is to connect, educate and develop the worldwide erosion and sediment control community. Landscape contractors, architects, engineers, and suppliers, as well as government officials concerned about soil erosion. Membership: $25-2500/year.

Meetings/Conferences: Annual
2013 - San Diego, CA (Town and Country Resort and Convention Center)/Feb. 10 - 13/2000 attendees/ over 100 exhibitors

Publications:
E-Update; monthly; adv.
Environmental Connection; quarterly; adv.
Membership Directory; annually; adv.

Membership List Available to Non-members

International Executive Association
P.O. Box 328
Edison, NJ 08818
Tel: (732) 983-0599 Fax: (440) 551-7503
E-Mail: sales@ieausa.org
Website: ieausa.org
Members: 15,000 members
Staff: 5

Personnel:
President and Chief Executive Officer: Wilson Lu
Vice President, Membership: John Hill
Vice President, Training and Seminar: Helen Kwang
Vice President, Event and Conference: Allen Stevenson
Executive Vice President and Chief Technology Officer: Linjun Zhang

Historical Note:
IEA is a membership organization that focuses on programs that increases the effectiveness of leaders within member organizations through certified education, promotion of ethical practices, and availability of Information.

Meetings/Conferences:
Conference Chair: Allen Stevenson

Publications:
Membership Directory; on-line
Newsletter; monthly

International Executive Housekeepers Association (1930)
1001 Eastwind Dr.
Suite 301
Westerville, OH 43081-3361
Tel: (614) 895-7166 Fax: (614) 895-1248
TollFree: (800) 200-6342
E-Mail: excel@ieha.org
Website: ieha.org
Members:
5000 individuals
3500 organizations

Staff: 7
Annual Budget: $500-1,000,000

Personnel:
Executive Director and Chief Executive Officer: Beth B. Risinger
E-Mail: brisinger@ieha.org
Contact, Chapter and Membership Services: Tremaine Chubb
Contact, Education Services: Jessica Chubb
Manager, Conventions: Tina Chubb
EHT Editor and Advertising Sales: Leah Driscoll
Coordinator, Membership and Accounting: Jody Thomas

Historical Note:
Formerly (1996) National Executive Housekeepers Association. IEHA provides members with an array of channels such as leadership opportunities, resource materials, educational designation, networking, an annual convention and trade show through which they can achieve personal and professional growth. Membership: $160/Year (Individual).

Continuing Education:
Enrollment: 500
Certification Designation/s: CEH, REH, CFAP

Meetings/Conferences: Annual
Conference Chair: Tina Chubb
2013 - Houston, TX (Omni Houston Hotel)/Feb. 11 - 13
Number of non-conference events/year: 1

Publications:
Executive Housekeeping Today; monthly

International Facility Management Association (1980)
One E. Greenway Plaza
Suite 1100
Houston, TX 77046-0104
Tel: (713) 623-4362 Fax: (713) 623-6124
E-Mail: ifma@ifma.org
Website: ifma.org
Members:
127 chapters
22,655 individuals
Staff: 65
Annual Budget: $10-25,000,000

Personnel:
President and Chief Executive Officer: Anthony J. Keane CAE
E-Mail: tony.keane@ifma.org
Director, Membership and Councils: Lowell Aplebaum
E-Mail: lowell.aplebaum@ifma.org
Manager, Conferences: Ann Burton
E-Mail: ann.burton@ifma.org
Director, Marketing: Stewart Dallas
E-Mail: stewart.dallas@ifma.org
Director, Information Systems: Lindy Daniels
E-Mail: lindy.daniels@ifma.org
Director, Government Relations: Jeffery Johnson
E-Mail: jeffrey.johnson@ifma.org
Vice President, Education: Cathy Pavick
E-Mail: cathy.pavick@ifma.org
Director, Communications and Editor-in-Chief, Facility Management Journal: Andrea E. Sanchez
E-Mail: andrea.sanchez@ifma.org
Senior Director, Finance and Administration: Christeen Seymour
E-Mail: christeen.seymour@ifma.org

Historical Note:
Founded as the National Facility Management Association, assumed its present name in 1982. Regular membership is open to any individual who is an in-house member or manager of a department responsible for facility planning, design, or management; and to those providing products or services. Membership: $383 (Premium Professional, Associate); $303 (Premium Young Professional); $259 (Premium Retired); $132 (Premium Student) $179 (Basic Professional, Associate); $100 (Basic Retired); $10 (Basic Student).

Continuing Education:
Certification Designation/s: FMP, CFM

Meetings/Conferences: Semi-Annual
Conference Chair: Ann Burton
2013 - Los Angeles, CA/April 2 - 4
2013 - Philadelphia, PA/Oct. 2 - 4
2014 - New Orleans, LA/Sept. 16 - 18

Publications:
Facility Management Journal; bi-monthly; adv.
FM Resource Guide; annually; adv.
The Wire; on-line

International Family Recreation Association
(1982)
P.O. Box 520
Gonzalez, FL 32560-0520
Tel: (850) 937-8354
Website: funoutdoors.com/node/view/785
Members: 9500 individuals
Staff: 5
Annual Budget: $100-250,000
Personnel:
Executive Director: K.W. Stephens
Historical Note:
IFRA is an association of commercial and individual advocates of family recreation that supports recommendations and legislations advantageous to recreation, leisure and travel. Membership: $49 (Family/Individual); $100 (Commercial).

International Federation for Artificial Organs
(1977)
10 W. Erie St.
Suite 200
Painesville, OH 44077-3270
Tel: (440) 358-1102 *Fax:* (440) 358-1104
Website: ifao.org
Members: 1000 individuals
Staff: 3
Annual Budget: $25-50,000
Personnel:
President: Joerg Vienken
Treasurer: Takeshi Nakatani, MD, PhD
  E-Mail: tnakatan@res.ncvc.go.jp
Historical Note:
Formerly (1977) International Society for Artificial Organs; assumed current name in 2004. IFAO's mission is to encourage knowledge, research, and education regarding artificial organs. Members are involved in the research, development or application of artificial organs. Membership: $180/year.
Publications:
Artificial Organs; monthly; adv.

International Federation for Choral Music *(1982)*
Dept. of Theatre and Music, College of
Architecture and the Arts
1040 W. Harrison St., Rm. L018, MC-255
Chicago, IL 60607-7130
Tel: (312) 996-8744 *Fax:* (512) 551-0105
E-Mail: info@ifcm.net
Website: ifcm.net
Members: 2700 organizations and individuals
Staff: 3
Annual Budget: $1-2,000,000
Tax: 501(c)(3)
Personnel:
Executive Director: Jean Sturm
President: Michael J. Anderson
Managing Editor: Andrea Angelini
Historical Note:
IFCM's mission is to strengthen cooperation between national and international organizations and individuals interested in all aspects of choral music. Membership: $42-84 (Individual); $62-105 (Family); $90-181 (Choir); $163-269 (Institution); $269-449 (Business).
Meetings/Conferences:
Number of non-conference events/year: 4
Publications:
Membership Directory; on-line
The International Choral Bulletin; quarterly; adv.
The World Choral Census; on-line

International Federation of Accountants *(1977)*
529 Fifth Ave.
Sixth Floor
New York, NY 10017
Tel: (212) 286-9344 *Fax:* (212) 286-9570
E-Mail: Communications@ifac.org
Website: ifac.org
Members: 167 members and associates
Staff: 5
Annual Budget: $10-25,000,000
Tax: 501(c)(6)
Personnel:
Chief Executive Officer: Ian Ball
Technical Director: Stephenie Fox
Executive Director, Quality and Member Relations: Russell Guthrie

Executive Director, Governance and Operations: Alta Prinsloo
Director, Quality and Member Relations: Sylvia Wei Yen Tsen
Historical Note:
IFAC is dedicated to serving the public interest by strengthening the profession and contributing to the development of strong international economies.
Publications:
IFAC Newsletter; quarterly
Membership Directory; on-line

International Federation of Fertility Societies
(1951)
19 Mantua Rd.
Mt. Royal, NJ 08061
Tel: (856) 423-7222 *Fax:* (856) 423-3420
E-Mail: secretariat@iffs-reproduction.org
Website: iffs-reproduction.org
Members: 40000 specialists
Staff: 5
Annual Budget: $250-500,000
Personnel:
President: Joe Leigh Simpson
Editor-in-Chief: Gabriel de Candolle
  E-Mail: secretariat@iffs-reproduction.org
Director, Medical Education: Paul Devroey
Secretary General: Richard Kennedy
Treasurer: Edgar Mocanu MD
Historical Note:
IFFS's purpose is to stimulate basic and applied research and the dissemination of knowledge in all aspects of reproduction and fertility.
Meetings/Conferences: Annual
2013 - Boston, MA (Boston Marriot)/Oct. 12 - 17
2014 - Honolulu, HI (Hawaii Convention Center)/Oct. 18 - 24
Publications:
British Journal of Obstetrics and Gynaecology; adv.
IFFS Newsletter; semi-annually
Journal of Obstetrics and Gynaecology
Membership Directory; on-line
The International Journal of Andrology; adv.

International Federation of Leather Guilds
(1966)
Ten Park Pl.
Mansfield, TX 76063
Tel: (817) 453-2386
Website: ifolg.org
Members: 700 individuals
Staff: 3
Annual Budget: Under $10,000
Personnel:
Executive Director: David Smith
  E-Mail: saddlesmith@sbcglobal.net
Historical Note:
IFoLG is an umbrella organization made up of guilds whose memberships include both hobbyists and professionals with skill levels ranging from beginner to master. Membership: $1/member (Guild).
Meetings/Conferences: Annual
Publications:
Member Directory; on-line
Newsletter

International Federation of Nurse Anesthetists
(1989)
3600 Market St.
Suite 400
Philadelphia, PA 19104-2651
Tel: (215) 222-8454 *Fax:* (215) 622-0425
E-Mail: info@cgfns.org
Website: ifna-int.org
Members: 34 country members
Staff: 3
Personnel:
Executive Director: Pascal Rod
  E-Mail: ifna.rod@wanadoo.fr
Treasurer: Zorica Kardos
Historical Note:
IFNA represents and promotes nurse anesthetists internationally through the education activities and continuing education programs.

International Federation of Pharmaceutical Wholesalers *(1977)*
10569 Crestwood Dr.
Manassas, VA 20109
Tel: (703) 331-3714 *Fax:* (703) 331-3715
E-Mail: info@ifpw.org
Website: ifpw.com
Members: 50 companies
Staff: 1
Annual Budget: $500-1,000,000
Personnel:
President: Mark W. Parrish
Historical Note:
IFPW promotes efficient delivery of pharmaceuticals to hospitals, physicians, and pharmacists; seeks to increase public awareness of the role played by members in the health care system. Facilitates cooperation and exchange of information among members; represents members' commercial and regulatory interests; sponsors educational and promotional programs. Membership: $3,000-18,000/year.
Meetings/Conferences:
2013 - Tampa, FL (Tampa Marriott Waterside Hotel)/March 3 - 6
Number of non-conference events/year: 1
Publications:
FOCUS; bi-weekly
MEMBERSHIP DIRECTORY; on-line

International Federation of Professional and Technical Engineers *(1918)*
501 Third St. NW
Suite 700
Washington, DC 20001
Tel: (202) 239-4880 *Fax:* (202) 239-4881
E-Mail: generalinfo@ifpte.org
Website: ifpte.org
Members: 80000 individuals
Staff: 18
Annual Budget: $5-10,000,000
Tax: 501(c)(5)
Personnel:
President: Gregory J. Junemann
  E-Mail: gjunemann@ifpte.org
Legislative and Political Director: Matthew Biggs
  E-Mail: mbiggs@ifpte.com
General Counsel: Julia A. Clark
  E-Mail: jclark@ifpte.org
Coordinator, Membership Services: Kristina Morgan
  E-Mail: kmorgan@ifpte.org
Director, Communications and Coordinator, Conventions: Candace M. Rhett
  E-Mail: crhett@ifpte.org
Secretary and Treasurer: Paul Shearon
  E-Mail: pshearon@lfpte.org
Historical Note:
Founded in Washington, DC, as the International Federation of Draftsmen's Unions. Became the International Federation of Technical Engineers' Architects' and Draftsmen's Unions (1919), the American Federation of Technical Engineers (1953) and assumed its present name in 1973. IFPTE's mission is to advance the issues that affect working families and to assist candidates for government who advance those concerns unique to its membership. Members includes women and men in professional, technical, administrative and associated occupations. Membership: $12/year (Associate).
Meetings/Conferences:
Conference Chair: Candace M. Rhett
Publications:
Outlook Magazine; quarterly

International Federation of the Phonographic Industry
IFPI Latin America, Inc.
3470 NW 82nd Ave.
Doral, FL 33122
Tel: (305) 567-0861 *Fax:* (305) 567-0871
Website: ifpi.org
Members: 1400 members
Staff: 5
Personnel:
Regional Director: Javier Asensio
Coordinator, Regional Internet Antipiracy: Paulo Batimarchi
Assistant, Administration and Finance: Natalia Echeverri
Director, Administration: Armando Lugo

Director, Legal Affairs: Juan Luis Marturet

Historical Note:
IFPI is affiliated with the Recording Industry Association of America (RIAA). IFPI's mission is to promote the value of recorded music, safeguard the rights of record producers and expand the commercial uses of recorded music in all markets where its members operate.

International Festivals and Events Association
(1956)
2603 W. Eastover Terrace
Boise, ID 83706
Tel: (208) 433-0950 *Fax:* (208) 433-9812
Website: ifea.com
Members: 2000 individuals
Staff: 8
Annual Budget: $500-1,000,000
Tax: 501(c)(6)

Personnel:
President and Chief Executive Officer: Steven Wood Schmader CFEE
    E-Mail: schmader@ifea.com
Director, Partnership Marketing, Advertising Sales and Expo Booking: Sylvia Allen
    E-Mail: sylvia@allenconsulting.com
Vice President and Director, Marketing and Communications: Nia Hovde
    E-Mail: nia@ifea.com
Director, Finance and Coordinator, CFEE Program: Bette Monteith
    E-Mail: bette@ifea.com
Director, Membership Services: Beth Petersen
    E-Mail: beth@ifea.com
Director, Creative and Publications: Craig Sarton
    E-Mail: craig@ifea.com

Historical Note:
IFEA's mission is to inspire and enable those in the industry to realize their dreams, build community and sustain success through celebration. Members are primarily individuals employed by the administrations of community and civic festivals and events, along with event suppliers, chamber of commerce, municipalities, corporations and more. Membership: $180-1250 (Organizational-based on gross annual revenue); $110-125 (Individual); $25 (Student).

Continuing Education:
Certification Designation/s: CFEE

Meetings/Conferences: Annual
Conference Chair: Sylvia Allen

Publications:
Affiliate Connection Newsletter; on-line
ie - The Business of International Events Magazine; quarterly; adv.
IFEA Weekly Update (e-mail broadcast); weekly
Membership Directory; on-line; adv.
The Event Insider; weekly

Membership List Available to Non-members

International Fine Print Dealers Association
(1987)
250 W. 26th St.
Suite 405
New York, NY 10001-6737
Tel: (212) 674-6095 *Fax:* (212) 674-6783
E-Mail: info@ifpda.org
Website: ifpda.org
Members: 168 elected members
Staff: 6
Annual Budget: $1-2,000,000
Tax: 501(c)(6)

Personnel:
Executive Director: Michele T. Senecal
    E-Mail: msenecal@ifpda.org
Manager, Public Relations and Marketing: Laura Beth Gencarella

Historical Note:
IFPDA's mission is to ensure the ethical standards and quality among fine print dealers, and to promote greater appreciation of fine prints among art collectors and the general public.

Meetings/Conferences: Annual
2013 - San Francisco, CA (Fort Mason Center)/Jan. 18 - 20
Number of non-conference events/year: 1

Publications:
Membership Directory; on-line

Membership List Available to Non-members

International Fire Marshals Association *(1906)*
One Batterymarch Park
C/O National Fire Protection Association
Quincy, MA 02169-7471
Tel: (617) 770-3000 *Fax:* (617) 770-0700
E-Mail: ifma@nfpa.org
Website: nfpa.org/ifma
Members: 1800 individuals
Staff: 3

Personnel:
Executive Secretary: Steven F. Sawyer
    E-Mail: ssawyer@nfpa.org

Historical Note:
Founded as Fire Marshals Association of North America, and reorganized as a section of the National Fire Protection Association in 1927, assumed its current name in 2000. IFMA's mission is to promote and provide leadership in the prevention or mitigation of fire, explosions, and other related hazardous conditions. Members are fire marshals, fire prevention officers or similar government officials charged with investigating or preventing fires.

Publications:
Fire Marshals; quarterly
Fire Marshals Directory; annually
IFMA Quarterly; quarterly; adv.

International Fire Photographers Association
(1964)
401 Seneca Manor Dr.
Suite 1603
Rochester, NY 14621-1650
Tel: (585) 300-5527
E-Mail: ifpadave@frontier.com
Website: ifpafirephotos.org
Members: 200 individuals
Staff: 6
Annual Budget: Under $10,000

Personnel:
President: Stephen J. Walsh
    E-Mail: stephenwalsh1030@msn.com
Contact, Public Relations: Chuck Clougherty Jr.
    E-Mail: chuck1rwn@live.com
Journal Editor: Joshua Smith
    E-Mail: Journal@IFPAFirePhotos.org
Contact, Membership Services: David B. Weimer Jr.
    E-Mail: ifpadave@rochester.rr.com

Historical Note:
IFPA's mission is the advancement of emergency service visual journalism, creation, practice, training, editing and distribution in all emergency service media. Membership: $20 (Individual-U.S.); $22.50 (Individual-Canadian); $25 (Individual-Overseas).

Publications:
IFPA Journal; bi-monthly

International Firestop Council *(1990)*
2931 Tumbleweed Ln.
Ft. Collins, CO 80526
Tel: (877) 241-3769 *Fax:* (978) 250-9788
E-Mail: info@firestop.org
Website: firestop.org
Members: 32 companies
Staff: 3
Annual Budget: $100-250,000

Personnel:
Executive Director: Sean DeCrane
President: Jim Stahl Jr.
Treasurer: Tim Mattox

Historical Note:
IFC's mission is to promote the technology of fire and smoke containment in modern building construction through research, education and development of safety standards and code provisions. Membership: $$5,250-21,525 (Voting); $750 (Associate); $250 (Industry Advocate).

Meetings/Conferences: Semi-Annual

Publications:
IFC Newsletters; quarterly
Member Listing; on-line

International Fitness Professionals Association
(1994)
14509 University Point Pl.
Tampa, FL 33613
Tel: (813) 979-1925 *Fax:* (813) 979-1978
E-Mail: info@ifpa-fitness.com
Website: ifpa-fitness.com
Staff: 1

Personnel:
Founder and Chief Executive Officer: James T. Bell PhD

Historical Note:
IFPA is devoted to offering quality learning experiences to individuals aiming to improve their lifestyles. Serves as a lifelong exercise and training resource to the entire fitness community and offers practical and scientifically based health and fitness information.

Continuing Education:
Certification Designation/s: AWMI, CKS, CKAS, CLSMDS, CPECS, CPFWS, CPI, CS (4 Types), CSMS, CSBTC, CTRS, CTEC, GFIC, IFPACFCSC, AEM, SPS, YSFI, YFI, IFPA PTC, APFTC, MPFTS, FPMNSM, FMTS, IFPSAEPC, MFS, MLPS, PFT, PSRS, PPNC, PDS, SFS, SCS, SNS, SBTS, STS, WFS, ABCASC, BSESC, CEMS, CHPAS, APESCS, AFS, AFTC, ASNC, ICC, CLFC:R, LS

Publications:
FitBits; monthly

International Flight Services Association *(1965)*
1100 Johnson Ferry Rd. NE
Suite 300
Atlanta, GA 30342
Tel: (404) 252-3663 *Fax:* (404) 252-0774
E-Mail: ifsa@kellencompany.com
Website: ifsanet.com
Members: 400 businesses
Staff: 6
Annual Budget: $500-1,000,000

Personnel:
Executive Director: Jim Fowler CAE
    E-Mail: jfowler@kellencompany.com
Executive Administrator: Pam Chumley
    E-Mail: pchumley@kellencompany.com
Specialist, Membership Services: Caitlin Ellery
    E-Mail: cellery@kellencompany.com
Meetings Manager: Linda Jobes
    E-Mail: ljobes@kellencompany.com
Manager, Communications: Jacqueline Petty
    E-Mail: jpetty@kellencompany.com

Historical Note:
IFSA's mission is to develop and represent the global business interests of the onboard services industry. Members are domestic and international airlines personnel, inflight and rail caterers and their suppliers. Membership: $360 (Airlines/Rail); $820 (Caterers/Suppliers).

Meetings/Conferences: Annual
Conference Chair: Linda Jobes
Number of non-conference events/year: 1

Publications:
Membership Directory; on-line
Onboard IFSA E-newsletter; monthly

The International Fluid Power Society *(1957)*
P.O. Box 1420
Cherry Hill, NJ 08034-0054
Tel: (856) 489-8983 *Fax:* (856) 424-9248
TollFree: (800) 308-6005
E-Mail: Askus@ifps.org
Website: ifps.org
Members: 4000 individuals
Staff: 8
Annual Budget: $500-1,000,000
Tax: 501(c)(3)

Personnel:
Executive Director: Donna Pollander
    E-Mail: dpollander@ifps.org
Administrative Assistant: Beth Borodziuk
Coordinator, Membership Services: Sue Dyson
    E-Mail: sdyson@ifps.org
Manager, Website and Communications: Adele Kayser
    E-Mail: akayser@ifps.org
Bookkeeper: Diane McMahon
    E-Mail: dmcmahon@ifps.org
Manager, Meetings Planner and Certification: Sue Tesauro
    E-Mail: stesauro@ifps.org

Historical Note:
IFPS's mission is to pursue and promote the application of Fluid Power technology through certification, standardization and education essential to professional growth. Members are individuals dedicated to enhance the quality of certifications, educational opportunities, technology evolution, and professionalism within the fluid power and motion control industry. Membership: $75 (Professional); $35 (Student/Active Military/Retired / Disabled).

Continuing Education:
Certification Designation/s: FPE, FPCC, FPCM, FPCT, FPS

Meetings/Conferences: Semi-Annual
Conference Chair: Sue Tesauro
2013 - San Antonio, TX/Feb. 27 - March 2
2013 - Chicago, IL (Chicago Marriott O'Hare)/Nov. 27 - 29

Publications:
Fluid Power Journal; adv.
IFPS E-Newsletter; monthly; adv.

International Food Additives Council *(1980)*
1100 Johnson Ferry Rd. NE
Suite 300
Atlanta, GA 30342
Tel: (404) 252-3663 *Fax:* (404) 252-0774
E-Mail: ifac@assnhq.com
Website: ifacmem.org
Members: 11 companies
Staff: 3
Annual Budget: $250-500,000

Personnel:
President: Lyn O'Brien Nabors

Historical Note:
Information clearing house concerning the use in food and safety of food additives. Members are companies engaged in the manufacture, sale, reformulation and commercial use of food additives. Serves as a regulatory and scientific liaison for industry concerning food additives.

International Food & Beverage Association (IFBA)
(1963)
1218 Grand Saconnex
Geneva, AL 12345
Website: ifballiance.org
Staff: 1

Personnel:
Treasurer: Alan jone

Historical Note:
A trade association representing major international food and beverage industries. Headquartered in Switzerland.

The International Food & Beverage Forum
(1993)
44487 Little Lake Rd.
P.O. Box 2401
Mendocino, CA 95460-2401
Tel: (707) 937-1368 *Fax:* (707) 202-0234
Website: foodandbeverageforum.com
Members: 50 individuals
Staff: 2
Annual Budget: $100-250,000
Tax: 501(c)(3)

Personnel:
Founder and President: Kurt H. Fischer
E-Mail: kurth@kurthfisher.com
Executive Vice President: Claude Peiffer

Historical Note:
Formerly the Hotel Food and Beverage Forum. IFBF strives to enhance global dialogue, knowledge, viable creativity and to foster the education of young hospitality professionals. Membership is by invitation only. Membership: $300-1,000 (Individual); $1,000-5,000 (Benefactor).

Meetings/Conferences: Annual

International Food Service Executives' Association
(1901)
4955 Miller St.
Suite 107
Wheat Ridge, CO 80033
Tel: (775) 825-2665 *Fax:* (775) 825-6411
TollFree: (800) 893-5499
E-Mail: hq@ifsea.com
Website: ifsea.com
Members: 2000 individuals
Staff: 2
Annual Budget: $250-500,000

Personnel:
Coordinator: Michelle Hackman
E-Mail: Michelle@ifsea.com

Historical Note:
Formerly (1957) International Stewards' and Caterers' Association and (1977) Food Service Executives' Association, Inc. IFSEA's mission is to serve the industry as a membership based organization promoting people, programs, businesses, and services that consistently raise the level of professionalism within foodservice and hospitality. Membership: $30-150/year.

Continuing Education:
Certification Designation/s: CFE, CFM

Meetings/Conferences: Annual
2013 - Dallas, TX (Hyatt Regency Dallas at Reunion)/ April 11 - 14

Publications:
Hotline Magazine
Infusion Newsletter; monthly

International Food, Wine and Travel Writers Association *(1956)*
1142 S. Diamond Bar Blvd.
Suite 177
Diamond Bar, CA 91765-2203
Tel: (909) 860-6914 *Fax:* (909) 396-0014
TollFree: (877) 439-8929
E-Mail: admin@ifwtwa.org
Website: ifwtwa.org
Members: 465 individuals
Staff: 4
Annual Budget: $50-100,000
Tax: 501(c)(6)

Personnel:
Executive Director: Patricia A. Anis
Newsletter Editor: Marilyn Green
E-Mail: mgreenjournalist@yahoo.com
Webmaster: Timothy W. Lack
E-Mail: twlack@tppm.com
Secretary and Treasurer: Sherrie A. Wilkolaski

Historical Note:
IFWTWA is a global network of journalists who cover the hospitality and lifestyle fields, and the people who promote them. Members are freelance and/or staff writers, editors, and photographers specializing in food, wine and/or travel writing. Membership: $75 (Student); $235 (Associate); 150 (Regular); 120 (Regular International).

Meetings/Conferences: Annual
2013 - Honolulu, HI (Hilton Hawaiian Village Waikiki Beach Resort)/May 23 - 27

Publications:
Global Writes; on-line; adv.
Membership Directory; on-line
Press Pass; monthly

International Foodservice Distributors Association *(1956)*
1410 Spring Hill Rd.
Suite 210
McLean, VA 22102
Tel: (703) 532-9400 *Fax:* (703) 538-4673
Website: ifdaonline.org
Members: 700 distribution facilities
Staff: 18
Annual Budget: $5-10,000,000

Personnel:
President and Chief Executive Officer: Mark S. Allen
E-Mail: mallen@ifdaonline.org
Director, Education and Research: Toni Rae Brotons
E-Mail: tbrotons@ifdaonline.org
Director, Communications and Marketing: Chris Caldwell
E-Mail: ccaldwell@ifdaonline.org
Director, Conferences: Kathy Devey
E-Mail: kdevey@ifdaonline.org
Senior Vice President, Government Relations: Jonathan B. Eisen
E-Mail: jeisen@ifdaonline.org
Vice President, Finance and Administration: Theresa Kessler
Manager, Member Communications: Tom Moran
Director, Member Retention and Recruitment: Heidi Weiss

Historical Note:
Formed by food distributors from the Northeast and Midwest, NWGA merged with the American Wholesale Grocers' Association and then it was renamed as National-American Wholesale Grocers' Association. NAWGA merged with the U.S. Wholesale Grocers Association and that organization's "Institutional Food Distributors of America (IFDA)" became NAWGA's foodservice division. As IFDAs membership expanded outside of the U.S., the name was changed to the International Foodservice Distributors Association. IFDA began operations as an independent entity on January 1, 2003. Mission is to advance the interests of foodservice distributors through government relations, industry relations, education, and research. Membership: $975-161,825 (Distributor); $5,000-15,000 (Allied); $2,500-7,500 (Associate).

Meetings/Conferences:
Conference Chair: Kathy Devey

2013 - Boston, MA (Boston Marriott Long Wharf)/July 21 - 23
2013 - Orlando, FL (Marriott World Center)/Oct. 14 - 16
Number of non-conference events/year: 4

Publications:
IFDA Newsletters

International Foodservice Editorial Council
(1956)
Seven Point Pl.
P.O. Box 491
Hyde Park, NY 12538-0491
Tel: (845) 229-6973 *Fax:* (845) 229-6973
E-Mail: ifec@ifeconline.com
Website: ifeconline.com
Members: 250 individuals
Staff: 2
Annual Budget: $250-500,000

Personnel:
Executive Director: Carol Lally
Contact, Administration and Accounts: Gabrielle Fredette

Historical Note:
IFEC is a non-profit organization dedicated to improving the quality of business-to-business communication within the foodservice industry and to encouraging high professional and aesthetic standards among those working in and with the foodservice media. Members include foodservice editors, publicists, marketers, educators, representatives of multi-unit operations, foodservice home economists, consultants and others active in foodservice communications. Membership: $295/year.

Meetings/Conferences: Annual
Conference Chair: Carol Lally
Number of non-conference events/year: 1

Publications:
IFEC Newsletter; on-line
Member Directory; on-line

International Foodservice Manufacturers Association *(1952)*
Two Prudential Plaza, 180 N. Stetson Ave.
Suite 4400
Chicago, IL 60601
Tel: (312) 540-4400 *Fax:* (312) 540-4401
E-Mail: ifma@ifmaworld.com
Website: ifmaworld.com
Members: 600 companies
Staff: 14
Annual Budget: $5-10,000,000
Tax: 501(c)(6)

Personnel:
President and Chief Executive Officer: Larry Oberkfell
E-Mail: larry@ifmaworld.com
Director, Meetings and Events: Christina Burke
E-Mail: christina@ifmaworld.com
Vice President, Sales and Membership Services: Anthony R. DePaolo
E-Mail: tony@ifmaworld.com
Associate Director, Information Services: Eric Donaldson
E-Mail: eric_donaldson@ifmaworld.com
Director, Integrated Marketing: Lisa Ptak
E-Mail: lisa@ifmaworld.com
Chief Financial Officer: Jennifer Tarulis
E-Mail: Jennifer@ifmaworld.com

Historical Note:
Founded as the Institutional Food Manufacturers of America; became the Institutional Food-Service Manufacturers Association in 1964 and assumed its present name in 1970. IFMA's mission is to shape the future of foodservice by creating an environment for positive change and actionable solutions benefiting manufacturers and their foodservice channel partners. Members are manufacturers of food, equipment and supplies for the away-from-home feeding market. Membership: $2,550-27,997 (Regular); $2,750 (Associate); $1,000 (International).

Meetings/Conferences: Annual
Conference Chair: Christina Burke
Number of non-conference events/year: 8

Publications:
IFMA World; on-line
Membership Directory; on-line

International Formalwear Association *(1973)*
244 E. Main
Galesburg, IL 61401
Tel: (309) 721-5450 *Fax:* (309) 342-5921
E-Mail: admin@formalwear.org

Website: formalwear.org
Members: 325 companies
Staff: 2
Annual Budget: $100-250,000
Tax: 501(c)(6)

Personnel:
President: Rod Benbroo

Historical Note:
Formerly a division of the Menswear Retailers of America, became autonomous in 1981 as the American Formalwear Association. Assumed its present name in 1987. IFA is an alliance of all industry segments worldwide. IFA's purpose is to promote and stimulate recognition, use and acceptance of men's formalwear. Members are specialists, suppliers, wholesalers and consultants. Membership: $499 (Supplier); $149-649 (Specialist); $249-649 (Wholesaler).

Publications:
IFP Newsletter

International Formula Council *(1988)*

1100 Johnson Ferry Rd.
Suite 300
Atlanta, GA 30342
Tel: (404) 252-3663 *Fax:* (404) 252-0774
E-Mail: info@infantformula.org
Website: infantformula.org
Members: 5 companies
Staff: 4
Annual Budget: $2-5,000,000
Tax: 501(c)(6)

Personnel:
Executive Vice President: Mardi K. Mountford

Historical Note:
Formed through the merger of Infant Formula Council (1970) and Enteral Nutrition Council (1983). IFC is an international association of formulated nutrition products, infant formula and adult nutritionals.

Publications:
Infant Feeding & Nutrition News

International Foundation for Telemetering *(1964)*

8337 W. Sunset Rd.
Suite 250
Las Vegas, NV 89113
Tel: (877) 462-1916 *Fax:* (575) 524-4744
E-Mail: admin@telemetry.org
Website: telemetry.org
Staff: 2
Annual Budget: $500-1,000,000
Tax: 501(c)(6)

Personnel:
Executive Coordinator: Lena Moran
   E-Mail: admin@telemetry.org

Historical Note:
The International Foundation for Telemetering (IFT) is a nonprofit organization dedicated to serve the professional and technical interests of the "Telemetering Community".

Meetings/Conferences: Annual
Conference Chair: Lena Moran

International Foundation of Employee Benefit Plans *(1954)*

P.O. Box 69
Brookfield, WI 53008-0069
Tel: (262) 786-6700 *Fax:* (262) 786-8670
TollFree: (888) 334-3327
E-Mail: pr@ifebp.org
Website: ifebp.org
Members: 35000 individuals
Staff: 143
Annual Budget: $25-50,000,000

Personnel:
Chief Executive Officer: Michael Wilson CMPE, MBA
Senior Director, Publications: Dee Birschel
Contact, Meetings: Kathryn Gleesing
   E-Mail: kathryng@ifebp.org
Director, Public Relations and Advertising: Stacy Van Alstyne
   E-Mail: stacyv@ifebp.org

Historical Note:
Formerly (1973) National Foundation of Health, Welfare and Pension Plans. IFEBP's mission is to be an objective and independent global source of employee benefits, compensation, and financial literacy education and information. Membership consists of individuals working

in the field of employee benefits and compensation. Membership: $715 (Organization); $295 (Individual).

Continuing Education:
Certification Designation/s: AMP, TMP, ATMS, CAPPP

Meetings/Conferences: Annual
Conference Chair: Dorothy Ellis MD
2013 - Las Vegas, NV/Oct. 20 - 23
2014 - Boston, MA/Oct. 12 - 15
2015 - Honolulu, HI/Nov. 8 - 11
2016 - Miami, FL/Nov. 13 - 16
2017 - Las Vegas, NV/Oct. 22 - 25
2018 - New Orleans, LA/Oct. 14 - 17
2019 - San Diego, CA/Oct. 20 - 23
2020 - Honolulu, HI/Nov. 15 - 18

Publications:
Benefits Magazine; monthly
Benefits Quarterly; quarterly
Canadian Benefits & Compensation Digest; bi-monthly
Membership Directory; on-line

International Fragrance Association North America *(1979)*

1001 19th St. North
Suite 1200
Arlington, VA 22209
Tel: (571) 346-7580 *Fax:* (571) 384-7959
E-Mail: info@ifrana.org
Website: ifrana.org
Members: 47 companies
Staff: 5
Annual Budget: $500-1,000,000

Personnel:
Executive Director: Jennifer Abril
   E-Mail: jabril@ifrana.org
General Counsel: John Cox
   E-Mail: jcox@vertosolutions.net
Manager, Industry Affairs: Amy Reuter
   E-Mail: areuter@ifrana.org
Director, Communications: Elena Solovyov
   E-Mail: esolovyov@ifrana.org
Director, Government Affairs: Jane Wishneff
   E-Mail: jwishneff@ifrana.org

Historical Note:
Ensure the safety of fragrance materials through a dedicated science program.

Meetings/Conferences: Annual
2013 - Teaneck, NJ (Teaneck Marriott at Glenpointe)/ Jan. 11
Number of non-conference events/year: 4

Publications:
IFRA Newsletter; on-line

International Franchise Association *(1960)*

1501 K St. NW
Suite 350
Washington, DC 20005
Tel: (202) 628-8000 *Fax:* (202) 628-0812
E-Mail: ifa@franchise.org
Website: franchise.org
Members: 32000 companies
Staff: 39
Annual Budget: $10-25,000,000

Personnel:
President and Chief Executive Officer: Stephen J. Caldeira
   E-Mail: scaldeira@franchise.org
Senior Director, Education and Diversity: Miriam Brewer
   E-Mail: mbrewer@franchise.org
Manager, Certification Program: Rose DuPont
   E-Mail: rdupont@franchise.org
Senior Director, Marketing and Digital Communications: Dan Gibson
Vice President, Public Affairs and Chief of Staff to the President: Matthew Haller
   E-Mail: mhaller@franchise.org
Senior Vice President, Communications and Marketing: Alisa Harrison
   E-Mail: aharrison@franchise.org
Vice President, Operations: Debra A. Moss
   E-Mail: dmoss@franchise.org
Senior Director, Meetings: Anne Poodiack
   E-Mail: apoodiack@franchise.org
Director, Development and Membership Services: Paul Rocchio
   E-Mail: procchio@franchise.org
Director, Finance: Virgie Sison
   E-Mail: vsison@franchise.org

Senior Vice President, Government Relations & Public Policy: Judith Thorman
   E-Mail: jthorman@franchise.org
Director, Information Systems: Jason Yusko
   E-Mail: jyusko@franchise.org

Historical Note:
IFA protects, enhances, and promotes franchising. It also sponsors and supports the Franchising Political Action Committee and the IFA Educational Foundation. Membership consists of companies franchising the distribution of their goods or services, unit owners (franchisees) and companies supplying products and services to franchise businesses. Membership: $2,900 (Supplier); $100-500 (Franchisee); $500 (Organizational).

Continuing Education:
Enrollment: 400
Certification Designation/s: CFE

Meetings/Conferences:
Conference Chair: Anne Poodiack
2013 - Las Vegas, NV (MGM Grand Garden Arena)/ Feb. 17 - 20/over 100 exhibitors
2013 - Washington, DC (JW Marriott Washington, D.C.)/May 5 - 7
2013 - Washington, DC (OW Marriott)/May 7 - 8
2014 - New Orleans, LA (New Orleans Morial Convention Center)/Feb. 22 - 25/over 100 exhibitors
2014 - Chicago, IL (Chicago Marriott Downtown Magnificent Mile)/May 4 - 6
2014 - Chicago, IL (Chicago Marriott Downtown Magnificent Mile)/May 6 - 7
2015 - Las Vegas, NV (MGM Grand Garden Arena)/ Feb. 15 - 18/over 100 exhibitors
2015 - Chicago, IL (Chicago Marriott Downtown Magnificent Mile)/May 3 - 5
2016 - Washington, DC (JW Marriott Washington, D.C.)/May 15 - 17
Number of non-conference events/year: 4

Publications:
Franchising World Magazine; monthly; adv.
IFA Insider Newsletter; weekly
IFA Smart Brief Email; adv.
SmartBrief; weekly

International Frozen Food Association *(1974)*

2000 Corporate Ridge
Suite 1000
McLean, VA 22102
Tel: (703) 821-0770 *Fax:* (703) 821-1350
E-Mail: info@affi.com
Website: affi.org
Members: 40 companies and associations
Staff: 2
Annual Budget: $10-25,000
Tax: 501(c)(6)

Personnel:
Director General: Kraig R. Naasz
Vice President, Administrator: Kathleen R. Greco
   E-Mail: kgreco@affi.com

Historical Note:
Affiliated with the American Frozen Food Institute, IFFA is a federation of associations and companies involved in distribution, production or marketing of frozen food for international markets.

International Fruit Tree Association *(1958)*

16020 Swingley Ridge Rd.
Suite 300
Chesterfield, MO 63017
Tel: (636) 449-5083 *Fax:* (636) 449-5051
E-Mail: dungey@ifruittree.org
Website: ifruittree.org
Staff: 1
Annual Budget: $250-500,000

Personnel:
Executive Director: Rick Dungey
   E-Mail: dungey@ifruittree.org

Historical Note:
IFTA's mission is to promote an understanding of the nature and use of dwarf fruit trees through research, education and dissemination of information. Membership: $100/year (Individual).

Meetings/Conferences: Annual
2013 - Boston, MA/Feb. 23 - 28
Number of non-conference events/year: 1

Publications:
Compact Fruit Tree Journal; quarterly
IFTA Newsletter

Member Directory; on-line

International Function Point Users Group *(1984)*
191 Clarksville Rd.
Princeton, NJ 08550
Tel: (609) 799-4900 *Fax:* (609) 799-7032
E-Mail: ifpug@ifpug.org
Website: ifpug.org
Members: 1200 members
Staff: 5
Annual Budget: $250-500,000
Tax: 501(c)(6)

Personnel:
Executive Director: Connie Holden
   E-Mail: cholden@cmasolutions.com

Historical Note:
IFPUG's mission is to promote and encourage the effective management of application software development and maintenance activities through the use of Function Point Analysis and other software measurement techniques. Members are companies and individuals employing the function point measurement process for business management. Membership: $185 (Individual); $625 (Corporate); $3,750 (Corporate, worldwide); $50 (Student); $1,850 (Affiliate I); $675 (Affiliate II).

Continuing Education:
Certification Designation/s: CEP, CSMS, CFPS

Meetings/Conferences: Annual

Publications:
Membership Directory; on-line
Newsletter

International Furnishings and Design Association
(1947)
610 Freedom Business Center
Suite 110
King of Prussia, PA 19406
Tel: (610) 992-0011 *Fax:* (610) 992-0021
E-Mail: info@ifda.com
Website: ifda.com
Members: 2000 individuals
Staff: 2
Annual Budget: $100-250,000

Personnel:
Executive Director: Martha A. Heinze CMP
   E-Mail: martha@ifda.com

Historical Note:
Formerly National Home Fashions League. Serves as the professional alliance of leaders representing the diverse industries that constitute the universe of residential and commercial furnishings and design. IFDA is the driving force, through its programs and services, to enhance the professionalism and stature of the industry worldwide. Membership: $0-225/year.

Meetings/Conferences:
Number of non-conference events/year: 26

Publications:
IFDA Network Newsletter; quarterly
Membership Directory; on-line
Window Fashion Vision

International Furniture Rental Association
(1967)
5229 College Hill Rd.
Woodstock, VT 05091
Website: ifra.org
Staff: 2
Annual Budget: Under $10,000

Personnel:
President: Bill Swets

Historical Note:
IFRA is the industry association devoted exclusively to furniture rental and leasing. Membership: $ 365-1,450/ year (depending on the no, of showrooms).

Meetings/Conferences: Annual

Publications:
Membership Directory
Newsletter

International Furniture Transportation and Logistics Council *(1926)*
282 N. Ridge
Brooklyn, MI 49230
Fax: (517) 467-9056
E-Mail: admin@iftlc.org
Website: iftlc.org
Members: 150 individuals

Staff: 2
Annual Budget: $25-50,000

Personnel:
Managing Director: Russ Matthews
   E-Mail: Russ111@comcast.net

Historical Note:
Founded as National Furniture Traffic Conference; assumed its current name in 2000. Members are logistics and shipping professionals employed in the various segments of the furniture industry. Membership: $225/year.

Meetings/Conferences: Annual

Publications:
Furniture Transporter

International Game Developers Association
(1995)
19 Mantua Rd.
Mt. Royal, NJ 08061
Tel: (856) 423-2990 *Fax:* (856) 423-3420
E-Mail: contact@igda.org
Website: igda.org
Members: 2500 individuals
Staff: 5
Annual Budget: $500-1,000,000

Personnel:
Interim Executive Director: Dustin Clingman
   E-Mail: Dustin@igda.org
Coordinator, Operations: James Baldwin
   E-Mail: ops@igda.org
Media Contact: Robert Brown
   E-Mail: Robert@bohle.com
Events Manager: Alexandra Springer
   E-Mail: alex@igda.org

Historical Note:
IGDA's mission is to advance the careers and enhance the lives of game developers by connecting members with their peers, promoting professional development, and advocating on issues that affect the developer community. Membership: $25 (Individual); $30 (Students); $48 (Professional); $600 (Lifetime).

Meetings/Conferences:
Conference Chair: Alexandra Springer

Publications:
Member Directory; on-line
Newsletter

International Gay and Lesbian Travel Association
(1983)
1201 NE 26th St.
Suite 103
Ft. Lauderdale, FL 33305
Tel: (954) 630-1637 *Fax:* (954) 630-1652
E-Mail: iglta@iglta.org
Website: iglta.org/
Members: 2200 members
Staff: 8
Annual Budget: $500-1,000,000

Personnel:
President and Chief Executive Officer: John Tanzella
   E-Mail: john@iglta.org
Contact, Membership Support: Emilio Collyer
   E-Mail: emilio@iglta.org
Manager, Media Relations: LoAnn Halden
   E-Mail: loann@iglta.org
Vice President, Marketing: Deborah Sas
   E-Mail: deborah@iglta.org
Administrative Assistant: Antonia Serrano
   E-Mail: antonia@iglta.org

Historical Note:
Founded with 25 founding members, IGLTA's mission is to connect businesses in the LGBT tourism industry. Membership: $300-960 (General Business); $90 (Associate).

Meetings/Conferences: Annual
2013 - Chicago, IL/May 2 - 4

Publications:
Member Directory; on-line

International Glove Association *(1902)*
P.O. Box 146
Brookville, PA 15825
Tel: (814) 328-5208 *Fax:* (814) 328-2308
E-Mail: gloves@windstream.net
Website: iga-online.com
Members: 75 companies
Staff: 3

Annual Budget: $50-100,000
Tax: 501(c)(6)

Personnel:
Executive Director: Carol Burdge
   E-Mail: gloves@windstream.net

Historical Note:
Formerly known as Work Glove Institute, and (1967) Work Glove Manufacturers Association and then (1991) International Hand Protection Association, and (2003) National Industrial Glove Distributors Association. IGA's mission is to further build an association that improves manufacturing and distribution of hand protection. Members are manufacturers of work gloves and related workplace safety material. Membership: $595-1,345/year (Based on annual gross sales).

Continuing Education:
Certification Designation/s: IGA

Meetings/Conferences:
Number of non-conference events/year: 1

Publications:
Glove Brand Directory; on-line
Membership Directory; on-line

International Golf Associates
1040 Genter St.
suite 103
La Jolla, CA 92037-5550
Tel: (858) 546-4737 *Fax:* (619) 615-2083
Website: iga-golf.com
Staff: 1

Personnel:
President: Roberto Tronchetti

Historical Note:
IGA's mission is to enable members to have a regular opportunity to play golf.

International Graphic Arts Education Association
(1923)
1899 Preston White Dr.
Reston, VA 20191-4367
E-Mail: igaea@npes.org
Website: igaea.org
Members: 800 individuals
Staff: 5
Annual Budget: $50-100,000
Tax: 501(c)(3)

Personnel:
Contact, Conference Planning: John Leininger

Historical Note:
Founded in 1936 as the National Graphic Arts Education Association. Adopted the present name in 1950 and was incorporated in 1969. IGAEA is an association of educators in partnership with industry, dedicated to share theories, principles, techniques and processes relating to graphic communications and imaging technology. Members are teachers of printing, photography and the graphic arts. Membership: $50 (Individual); $20 (Retiree); $10 (Student); $20 (Library); $50-500 (Sustaining).

Meetings/Conferences: Annual
Conference Chair: John Leininger
2013 - Menomonie, WI (University of Wisconsin-Stout)/July 21 - 25

Publications:
The Communicator; adv.
Visual Communications Journal; semi-annually; adv.

International Graphoanalysis Society *(1929)*
842 Fifth Ave.
New Kensington, PA 15068
Tel: (724) 472-9701 *Fax:* (509) 271-1149
Website: igas.com
Members: 15000 individuals
Staff: 1
Annual Budget: $250-500,000

Personnel:
President: Greg Greco
   E-Mail: greg@igas.com

Historical Note:
Absorbed the American Institute of Grapho Analysis in 1949. IGAS supports a worldwide network of thousands of certified handwriting analysts through International Graphoanalysis Society and its associated chapters. Membership: $90/year.

Continuing Education:
Certification Designation/s: CGA
Meetings/Conferences:
Number of non-conference events/year: 1

Publications:
IGAS Newsletter

International Grooving & Grinding Association
(1972)
12573 Route Nine West
W. Coxsackie, NY 12192-1709
Tel: (518) 731-7450 *Fax:* (518) 731-7490
Website: igga.net
Members: 37 companies
Staff: 3
Annual Budget: $500-1,000,000

Personnel:
Executive Director: John H. Roberts
Office Manager: Michele Rivenburg
    E-Mail: mrivenburg@pavement.com
Director, Engineering and Research: Larry Scofield
    E-Mail: lscofield@pavement.com

Historical Note:
IGGA's mission to promote the increased and proper use of diamond grinding and grooving on all pavement surfaces as well as the preservation and restoration of PCC pavement. Members include Associates, Concrete construction material manufacturers and suppliers, Concrete sawing & cutting equipment manufacturers, Consultants, Contractors, Diamond blade manufacturers, Honorary life members.

Publications:
Membership Directory; on-line

International Ground Source Heat Pump Association *(1987)*
1201 S. Innovation Way
Suite 400
Stillwater, OK 74074
Tel: (405) 744-5175 *Fax:* (405) 744-5283
TollFree: (800) 626-4747
E-Mail: igshpa@okstate.edu
Website: igshpa.okstate.edu
Members: 2800 individuals
Staff: 12
Annual Budget: $500-1,000,000

Personnel:
Executive Director: Jim Bose PhD PE
    E-Mail: jim.bose@okstate.edu
Coordinator, Conference and Membership Services: Shelly
    Fitzpatrick
    E-Mail: shelly.fitzpatrick@okstate.edu
Senior Assistant, Administrative Support: Brenda James
    E-Mail: brenda.james@okstate.edu
Specialist, Communications: Jeanne Knobbe
    E-Mail: jeanne.knobbe@okstate.edu
Accounting Specialist: Jo Lynne Stephens
    E-Mail: jo.l.stephens@okstate.edu

Historical Note:
Members are manufacturers, distributors and installers of ground service heat pumps, which utilize the earth as the heat exchanges. IGHSPA promotes the use of ground source heat pump technology worldwide through education and communication. Membership: $26-10,500/year.

Continuing Education:
Certification Designation/s: CGD

Meetings/Conferences: Annual
Conference Chair: Shelly Fitzpatrick

Publications:
Buyers Guide; annually; adv.
GeoOutlook Magazine; quarterly; adv.

International Guards Union of America *(1948)*
420 Hardwicke Dr.
Knoxville, TN 37923
Tel: (865) 256-2386 *Fax:* (865) 531-4703
Website: theigua.org
Members: 1800 individuals
Staff: 20
Annual Budget: $100-250,000

Personnel:
International President: Randy Lawson
    E-Mail: iguapresident@tds.net

Historical Note:
Originally affiliated with the Building Services Employees International Union, IGUA became an independent union in 1948. IGUA Guards, watchmen and others hired to protect personnel and property.

International Guild of Candle Artisans *(1965)*
1426 E. 111th Pl.
Northglenn, CO 80233

Tel: (443) 305-2501
E-Mail: contact@igca.net
Website: igca.net
Members: 200 companies and individuals
Staff: 4
Annual Budget: $10-25,000

Personnel:
President: Larry Houseman
Contact, Web site issues: Clint Bradford
Treasurer: Jim Ellis
Secretary and Membership Contact: Jackie Weber
    E-Mail: secretary@igca.net

Historical Note:
IGCA's purpose is to raise and maintain the standards of candlemaking. IGCA seeks to instruct and train members, to encourage good will, cooperation, fellowship and exchange of educational ideas. Members are individuals and companies with an interest in candle making. Membership: $50 (Individual); $10 (Associate).

Meetings/Conferences: Annual

Publications:
Candlelighter Newsletter; bi-monthly; adv.
Member Directory; annually

International Guild of Symphony, Opera and Ballet Musicians *(1985)*
12724 19th Ave. NE
Seattle, WA 98125
Tel: (206) 524-7050 *Fax:* (206) 524-7015
E-Mail: info@igsobm.org
Website: igsobm.org
Members: 400 individuals
Staff: 4
Tax: 501(c)(5)

Personnel:
President: Matthew Kocmieroski
    E-Mail: mkocmieroski@hotmail.com
Treasurer: Betty Agent

Historical Note:
IGSOBM is an independent labor union. Members are musicians, music librarians, and others who work in not-for-profit music organizations, including regional symphonies and orchestras. Membership Dues : $50/year.

Publications:
Newsletter

International Hard Anodizing Association *(1989)*
P.O. Box 579
Moorestown, NJ 08057-0579
Tel: (856) 234-0330 *Fax:* (856) 727-9504
Website: ihanodizing.com
Members: 40 companies
Staff: 3
Annual Budget: $10-25,000
Tax: 501(c)(6)

Personnel:
Executive Director and Secretary: Denise Downing CMP
    E-Mail: Denise@NeffDowning.com

Historical Note:
IHAA is an organization of companies which are engaged in the production of hard anodized finishes on aluminum components, either for customers or for their own products. Mission is to promote the common interests of its members and the progress and growth of the hard anodizing industry. Membership: $400/year (Corporate).

Meetings/Conferences: Annual

Membership List Available to Non-members

International Health, Racquet and Sportsclub Association *(1981)*
70 Fargo St.
Boston, MA 02210
Tel: (617) 951-0055 *Fax:* (617) 951-0056
TollFree: (800) 228-4772
E-Mail: info@ihrsa.org
Website: ihrsa.org
Members:
740 companies
9750 clubs
570 supplier companies
10000 club members
Staff: 54
Annual Budget: $10-25,000,000
Tax: 501(c)(6)

Personnel:
President and Chief Executive Officer: Joe Moore

E-Mail: jmoore@ihrsa.org
Executive Vice President, Public Policy: Helen Durkin J D
Vice President, Meetings and Trade Shows: William
    Dussor
Publications, Business Development: Will Finn
Senior Manager, Meetings and Education: Marc Gagnon
Chief Operating Officer: Anita Horne-Lawlor
    E-Mail: ahl@ihrsa.org
Administrator, Membership: Debbi Kellner
*Vice President, International Operations, Global
    Membership Division:* Catherine Masterson McNeil
Vice President, Human Resources: Regina Satagaj Orrock
Coordinator, Public Policy Communications: Lilly Prince
Manager, Research: Melissa Rodriguez
    E-Mail: mr@ihrsa.org
Senior Marketing Manager: Alba Valentin
Senior Editor: Kristen Walsh
    E-Mail: kwalsh@ihrsa.org
Assistant Vice President, Business and Finance: Michelle
    Young MBA

Historical Note:
Formed as International Racquet Sports Association as the result of a merger between the National Court Clubs Association and the National Tennis Association; became IRSA- The Association of Quality Clubs in 1991, and assumed its current name in 1995. IHRSA's mission is to grow, protect and promote the health and fitness industry, and to provide its members with benefits that will help them be successful. Members are commercial, for profit health, racquet and sport clubs, as well as manufacturers and suppliers. Membership fee varies, based on annual revenues. Membership: $250-500 (Club, minimum); $995-1,070 (Club Developer); $825 (Associate); $199 (Individual); $50 (Student).

Meetings/Conferences: Annual
Conference Chair: William Dussor
2013 - Los Angeles, CA (Los Angeles Convention
    Center)/Jan. 19 - 20
2013 - Bologna, Italy (Fiera di Bologna)/Feb. 21 - 23
2013 - Hilton Head Island, SC (Westin Hilton Head
    Island Resort and Spa)/March 18 - 22/6000
    attendees/over 100 exhibitors
2013 - Las Vegas, NV (Mandalay Bay)/March 19 - 22
2013 - Taipei, Taiwan (TWTC Nangang Hall)/March 19
    - 22
2013 - Cologne, Germany/April 11 - 14
2013 - Sydney, Australia (Sydney Convention and
    Exhibition Centre- Darling Harbour)/April 19 - 21
2014 - San Diego, CA (San Diego Convention Center)/
    March 12 - 15
2015 - Los Angeles, CA (Los Angeles Convention
    Center)/March 11 - 14
Number of non-conference events/year: 6

Publications:
Capitol Report (e-newsletter); weekly
Club Business Europe; quarterly; adv.
Club Business for Entrepreneurs; quarterly
Club Business International; monthly; adv.
Fitness Business Latin America; bi-monthly; adv.
Get Active!; quarterly; adv.
Health E-Review; bi-weekly
Membership Directory; on-line
The International Health, Racquet & Sportsclub
    Association E-Newsletter; monthly; adv.
The Link; monthly
The Pulse; monthly

International Hearing Society *(1951)*
16880 Middlebelt Rd.
Suite Four
Livonia, MI 48154
Tel: (734) 522-7200 *Fax:* (734) 522-0200
Website: ihsinfo.org
Members: 3000 individuals
Staff: 9
Annual Budget: $1-2,000,000
Tax: 501(c)(6)

Personnel:
Executive Director: Kathleen Mennillo MBA
    E-Mail: kmennillo@ihsinfo.org
Communications Specialist: Sandra den Boer
    E-Mail: sdenboer@ihsinfo.org
Coordinator, Membership Services: Bernadette "Bennie"
    Demicoli
    E-Mail: bdemicoli@ihsinfo.org
Bookkeeper: Rosalie Francis
    E-Mail: rfrancis@ihsinfo.org
Editor and Manager, Strategic Alliances: Kara Nacarato

E-Mail: knacarato@ihsinfo.org
Manager, Marketing: Fran Vincent
    E-Mail: fvincent@ihsinfo.org
Director, Education: Joy Wilkins
    E-Mail: jwilkins@ihsinfo.org

Historical Note:
Founded as Society of Hearing Aid Audiologists, became
National Hearing Aid Society in 1966 and assumed its
current name in 1992. IHS's mission is to promote and
maintain the possible standards for its members in the best
interest of the hearing impaired it serves. Membership:
$275 (Professional); $125 (Professional-International);
$50 (Associate/Affiliate); $35 (Student).

Meetings/Conferences: Annual
Number of non-conference events/year: 5

Publications:
Member Directory; on-line
The Hearing Professional; bi-monthly; adv.

International Herb Association (1985)
61247 Rt 415
Avoca, NY 14809
Website: iherb.org
Members: 200 individuals
Staff: 3
Annual Budget: $25-50,000
Tax: 501(c)(3)

Personnel:
President: Matthias Reisen

Historical Note:
Formerly (1994) International Herb Growers and Marketers
Association. IHA's purpose is to enhance herbs and unite
herb professionals for growth through encouragement
and education. Membership: $100 (Individual); $50
(Educator/Non-profit organization/Small Business Start-
up); $100-200 (Affiliate); $100 (Business Professional);
$25 (Full-time Student); $500 (Sponsor).

Meetings/Conferences: Annual

Publications:
Herb of the Year; annually
IHA Newsletter; quarterly
Membership Directory; on-line

Membership List Available to Non-members

International Home Furnishings Representatives Association (1934)
P.O. Box 670
High Point, NC 27261
Tel: (336) 889-3920 Fax: (336) 802-1959
E-Mail: ihfra@ihfra.org
Website: IHFRA.org
Members:
26 chapters
1500 individuals
Staff: 3
Annual Budget: $100-250,000
Tax: 501(c)(6)

Personnel:
Executive Director: Kathy Parks
    E-Mail: kparks@ihfra.org
Secretary and Treasurer: Frank Lorenzo
    E-Mail: fjlfurnitures@msn.com
Membership Coordinator: Jennifer Sova
    E-Mail: jsova@ihfra.org

Historical Note:
Formerly (1967) National Wholesale Furniture Salesmens'
Association and (1972) National Home Furnishings
Representatives Association. A federation of local home
furnishings representatives associations. IHFRA's mission
is to provide education, professional standards and
services, legislative advocacy and communications for the
membership to remain a viable, responsive and financially
secure organization. Membership: $160/year (Affiliate).

Continuing Education:
Certification Designation/s: CHR

Publications:
IHFRAmation; monthly

International Horn Society (1970)
P.O. Box 630158
Lanai City, HI 96763-0158
Tel: (808) 565-7273 Fax: (808) 565-7273
E-Mail: exec-secretary@hornsociety.org
Website: hornsociety.org
Members: 3500 individuals
Staff: 5
Annual Budget: $100-250,000

Tax: 501(c)(3)

Personnel:
Manager, Website: Dan Phillips
    E-Mail: manager@hornsociety.org
Executive Secretary: Heidi Vogel
    E-Mail: exec-secretary@hornsociety.org

Historical Note:
IHS members are professional players, instructors
and students of the French horn. IHS is dedicated to
the performance, teaching, composition, research,
preservation, and promotion of the horn as a musical
instrument. Provides information concerning future and
past international, regional, and area workshops/symposia,
events, and competitions, and supports research concerning
the history, literature, and pedagogy of the horn in a variety
of ways. Membership: $45 (Regular); $30 (Student); $750
(Life); $120 (Three-year).

Meetings/Conferences: Annual
2013 - Memphis, TN/July 29 - Aug. 3

Publications:
IHS Online; on-line
Member Directory; on-line
The Horn Call; adv.
The HornZone

International Hot Rod Association (1970)
Nine 1/2 E. Main St.
Norwalk, OH 44857
Tel: (419) 663-6666 Fax: (419) 663-4472
E-Mail: comments@ihra.com
Website: ihra.com
Members: 17500 individuals
Staff: 18
Annual Budget: $2-5,000,000

Personnel:
President: Aaron Polburn
    E-Mail: fpeaco@feldinc.com
Director, Competition and Technical Services: Mike Baker
    E-Mail: mbaker@feldinc.com
Director, Media Relations: Larry Crum
    E-Mail: lcrum@feldinc.com
Manager, Membership Services and Points: Donna Harper
    E-Mail: dharper@feldinc.com
Managing Editor, Drag Review: Pam Marchyshyn
    E-Mail: pmarchyshyn@feldinc.com
Vice President, Marketing: Jim Marchyshyn
    E-Mail: jmarchyshyn@feldinc.com
Director, Operations: Sharon Ramlow
    E-Mail: sramlow@feldinc.com

Historical Note:
IHRA is a division of Feld Entertainment, promotes
professional, semi- professional and local level racing
opportunities for drivers at all levels. Members are drivers
and their sponsors, tracks, and spectators. Membership:
$50-60/year.

Meetings/Conferences:
Number of non-conference events/year: 9

Publications:
IHRA Inside Nitro Newsletter; on-line

Membership List Available to Non-members

International Housewares Association (1938)
6400 Shafer Ct.
Suite 650
Rosemont, IL 60018-4929
Tel: (847) 292-4200 Fax: (847) 292-4211
Website: housewares.org
Members: 1700 companies
Staff: 51
Annual Budget: $10-25,000,000

Personnel:
President: Philip J. Brandl
    E-Mail: pbrandl@housewares.org
Manager, Membership Services, Sales and Marketing:
  Ginny Costello
    E-Mail: gcostello@housewares.org
Vice President, Finance and Information Technology: Dean
  Kurtis
    E-Mail: dkurtis@housewares.org
Vice President, Trade Shows: Mia Rampersad
    E-Mail: mrampersad@housewares.org
Vice President, Marketing and Trade Development: Perry
  Reynolds
    E-Mail: preynolds@housewares.org
Manager, Media Relations and Communications: Deborah
  Teschke
    E-Mail: dteschke@housewares.org

Historical Note:
Formerly National Housewares Manufacturers Association,
assumed its current name in 2002. IHA's mission is to
assist its members throughout the year by offering global
opportunities in the international arena, by providing
business solutions for operating more profitably and
by developing reliable industry resources for growing
the business. Membership: $400-700 (Regular); $450
(Associate).

Meetings/Conferences: Annual
Conference Chair: Mia Rampersad
2013 - Chicago, IL (McCormick Place)/March 2 -
  5/60000 attendees/over 100 exhibitors
2014 - Chicago, IL (McCormick Place)/March 15 -
  18/60000 attendees/over 100 exhibitors
2015 - Chicago, IL (McCormick Place)/March 7 -
  10/60000 attendees/over 100 exhibitors
2016 - Chicago, IL (McCormick Place)/March 5 -
  8/60000 attendees/over 100 exhibitors

Publications:
BusinessWatch; monthly
Housewares SmartBrief; daily
IHA Reports; bi-monthly
MarketWatch; quarterly
Membership Directory; on-line

International Housewares Representatives Association (1994)
1755 Lake Cook Rd.
Suite 318
Highland Park, IL 60035
Tel: (847) 748-8269 Fax: (847) 748-8273
TollFree: (800) 315-7430
E-Mail: info@ihra.org
Website: ihra.org
Members: 250 companies
Staff: 3
Annual Budget: $50-100,000

Personnel:
Executive Director: William Weiner
Administrative Assistant: Stephanie Baron
Financial Director : Myra Weiner

Historical Note:
IHRR seeks to bring together its members and
manufacturers seeking performance-proven sales agencies
- and to promote, protect and improve the field sales
professional function. Members are manufacturer
representatives, multiple-line, field sales professionals
servicing the home, housewares, gourmet and consumer
hardware industries in the Americas and many International
markets. Membership: $147.50/year (Regular).

Meetings/Conferences: Annual
2013 - Chicago, IL/March 2 - 5

Publications:
IHRA Newsletter; monthly; adv.

Membership List Available to Non-members

International Hunter Education Association (1949)
2727 W. 92nd Ave.
Suite 103
Federal Heights, CO 80260
Tel: (303) 430-7233 Fax: (303) 430-7236
E-Mail: info@ihea.com
Website: ihea-usa.org
Members: 750,000 students
Staff: 3
Annual Budget: $250-500,000
Tax: 501(c)(3)

Personnel:
President: Mark Birkhauser
Executive Director: Wayne East
Treasurer: Megan Wisecup

Historical Note:
IHEA's mission is to provide leadership, and establish
standards in the development of hunters to be safe,
responsible, knowledgeable and involved. It involves
thousands of dedicated instructors across the country, plus
cooperators in the shooting sports industry, conservation
organizations. Membership: $25 (Volunteer Instructor);
$100 (Instructor Association).

Meetings/Conferences: Annual
2013 - San Antonio, TX (Hyatt Regency Hill Country
  Resort and Spa)/April 2 - 6

Publications:
Hunter Education Journal

International Hydrofoil Society (1970)

P.O. Box 51
Cabin John, MD 20818
Tel: (202) 267-1676
Website: foils.org
Members: 240 individuals
Staff: 1
Annual Budget: Under $10,000

Personnel:
President: Mark Bebar

Historical Note:
IHS's mission is to provide a source of authoritative education and advice on hydrofoil history, technology, and application. Membership: $30 (Regular); $10 (Student); $250 (Sustaining).

Publications:
IHS Newsletter; quarterly

Membership List Available to Non-members

International Hydrolized Protein Council *(1976)*
P.O. Box 14266
Washington, DC 20044-4266
Tel: (202) 637-5926 *Fax:* (202) 637-5910
Members: 20 companies
Staff: 2
Annual Budget: $50-100,000

Personnel:
General Counsel: Martin J. Hahn

Historical Note:
Members are companies producing or using hydrolized proteins.

International Hyperbaric Medical Association, Inc.
8210 Cinder Bed Rd.
Suite C-3
Lorton, VA 22079-1135
Website: hyperbaricmedicalassociation.org
Staff: 1
Annual Budget: Under $10,000
Tax: 501(c)(4)

Personnel:
Executive Director: Ken Locklear

Historical Note:
The American Association for Health Freedom (AAHF) is leading a campaign to reform the Food and Drug Administration (FDA). IHMA's mission is to improve public health by: implementing high ethical and scientific standards for hyperbaric medicine; promoting sound hyperbaric research and treatment protocols; educating the medical community, the general public, decision makers and policy experts about the benefits of hyperbaric medicine and adjunctive therapies; and working to make hyperbaric medicine more universally available and affordable. Membership: $ 25 (Friends); $200 (Professional); $ 100 (Allied Health Professional); $ 750 (Corporate); $2,500 (Platinum); $1,000 (Medical Practice).

Publications:
Newsletter

International Ice Cream Association *(1900)*
1250 H St. NW
Suite 900
Washington, DC 20005-3952
Tel: (202) 737-4332 *Fax:* (202) 331-7820
Website: idfa.org/about-idfa/boards--
  committees/interna
Members: 60 companies
Staff: 35
Annual Budget: $1-2,000,000
Tax: 501(c)(6)

Personnel:
Executive Vice President and Vice Chairman: Brian Perry
Director, Membership Services: Cindy Cavallo
Vice President, Marketing: Rachel Kyllo

Historical Note:
IICA's mission is to provide strategic leadership to association members, government officials, customers and other audiences to promote full and open markets to maximize sales and reduce government intervention in commercial markets. Represents manufacturers, distributors, and marketers of ice cream, frozen yogurt and other frozen desserts. IICA's activities range from legislative and regulatory advocacy to market research, industry training and education. Administrative support provided by International Dairy Foods Association. Membership fee based on volume.

International Imaging Industry Association
(1946)
401 Edgewater Pl.

Suite 600
Wakefield, MA 01880
Tel: (914) 285-4933 *Fax:* (949) 645-1443
E-Mail: i3ainfo@i3a.org
Website: i3a.org
Members: 60 companies
Staff: 4
Annual Budget: $500-1,000,000
Tax: 501(c)(6)

Personnel:
President: Lisa A. Walker
   E-Mail: i3ainfo@i3a.org
Contact, Marketing Communications: Donna Cohn
   E-Mail: donnac@i3a.org
Contact, Membership Development: Noel Mareno
   E-Mail: noelm@i3a.org
Media Contact: Judith Vanderkay
   E-Mail: jvanderkay@virtualmgmt.com

Historical Note:
Formerly (1997) National Association of Photographic Manufacturers and (2001) Photographic and Imaging Manufacturers Association. I3A's mission is to enable the use of imaging to simplify and enrich people's lives through visual experiences that connect generations, communities, information and services. Membership: $1,875-11,900 (Associate); $5,000- 32,500 (Regular); $25,000-80,000 (Strategic) fee varies, based on annual sales.

Publications:
Eye on Imaging; monthly; adv.

Membership List Available to Non-members

International Imaging Technology Council *(2000)*
3157 N. Rainbow
Suite 340
Las Vegas, NV 89108
Tel: (702) 838-4279 *Fax:* (702) 838-3695
Website: i-itc.org
Staff: 2
Annual Budget: $100-250,000

Personnel:
Executive Director: Tricia Judge
   E-Mail: exec@i-itc.org
Contact, Publications: Richelle Lambert
   E-Mail: richelle@i-itc.org

Historical Note:
Int'l ITC's mission is to advance product improvement through industry testing standards and other product enhancement programs and educating the members on business and technology issues.Membership: $275 (Dealer); $550 (Executive); $825 (Supporter); $1,650 (Benefactor).

Publications:
Global Service Directory; on-line
Imaging Spectrum; monthly; adv.
Int'l ITC Newsletter; on-line; adv.

International Institute for Energy Conservation
(1984)
10005 Leamoore Ln.
Suite 100
Vienna, VA 22181
Tel: (703) 281-7263 *Fax:* (703) 938-5153
E-Mail: iiecdc@iiec.org
Website: iiec.org
Staff: 2
Annual Budget: $1-2,000,000

Personnel:
President: Nitin Pandit
   E-Mail: iiecdc@iiec.org
Manager,Finance: Scott Knusden

Historical Note:
IIEC's mission is to accelerate the global adoption of energy efficiency, transport and environmental policies, technologies and practices to enable economic and environmentally sustainable development.

Publications:
e-Notes Newsletter; on-line; adv.

International Institute for Lath and Plaster
(1976)
P.O. Box 1663
Lafayette, CA 94549
Tel: (925) 283-5160 *Fax:* (925) 283-5161
Website: iilp.org
Members:
20 organizations
52 individuals
Staff: 2

Annual Budget: $25-50,000

Personnel:
Secretary: Frank E. Nunes

Historical Note:
Formed by the merger of the Associated Institute for Lath and Plaster and the International Council for Lathing and Plastering (founded 1952 and formerly the National Bureau for Lathing and Plastering). Purpose is dedicated to the promotion of the lathing and plastering trades.

International Institute of Ammonia Refrigeration
(1971)
1001 N. Fairfax St.
Suite 503
Alexandria, VA 22314
Tel: (703) 312-4200 *Fax:* (703) 312-0065
E-Mail: iiar_request@iiar.org
Website: iiar.org
Members: 1400 members
Staff: 6
Annual Budget: $2-5,000,000
Tax: 501(c)(6)

Personnel:
President: Bruce Badger

Historical Note:
IIAR's mission is to provide advocacy, education, standards, and information for the benefit of the ammonia refrigeration industry worldwide. Members includes manufacturers, contractors, consulting engineers, wholesalers, and end users of ammonia refrigeration products. Membership: $50-1200/year.

Meetings/Conferences: Annual
2013 - Colorado Springs, CO/March 17 - 20
Number of non-conference events/year: 28

Publications:
Condenser; quarterly; adv.
Membership Directory; monthly
NH3 News; on-line

International Institute of Connector and Interconnection Technology *(1958)*
Emerson Connectivity
3000 Lakeside Dr., Suite 308N
Bannockburn, IL 60015
Tel: (847) 739-0352 *Fax:* (941) 739-6544
E-Mail: info@iicit.org
Website: iicit.org
Members:
140 companies
2500 individuals
Staff: 4
Annual Budget: $250-500,000

Personnel:
President: Dale Reed
   E-Mail: dale.reed@emerson.com
Secretary: Doug Parker
   E-Mail: dparker@tempo.textron.com
Treasurer: Anthony Romeo
   E-Mail: arromeo@iicit.org
Vice President: Dave Ryan
   E-Mail: PMXdfr@aol.com

Historical Note:
Formerly (1988) the Electronic Connector Study Group, IICIT's mission is to foster critical thinking, to encourage innovation, to provide clarity to issues that match end user needs to product attributes, and to promote personal and professional growth for its members. Membership includes engineers, manufacturers, sales representatives and any other people involved with any type of connector or interconnection application. Membership: $35 (Individual); $1200 (National Corporate).

Meetings/Conferences: Annual

Membership List Available to Non-members

International Institute of Fisheries Economics and Trade *(1982)*
Department of Agricultural and Resource Economics
Oregon State University
Corvallis, OR 97331-3601
Tel: (541) 737-1416 *Fax:* (541) 737-2563
E-Mail: iifet@oregonstate.edu
Website: oregonstate.edu/dept/IIFET
Members: 400 individuals
Staff: 2

Personnel:
Executive Director: Ann L. Shriver

E-Mail: ann.l.shriver@oregonstate.edu
Assistant, IIFET: Kara Keenan
E-Mail: iifet@oregonstate.edu

Historical Note:
IIFET was found for interaction and exchange between people from all countries and professional disciplines about marine resource economics and trade issues. IIFET's goal is to facilitate cooperative research and data exchange. Membership: $80 (Regular, Individual); $500 (Corporate/Institutional); $30 (Student/Developing Country); $200 (Library).

Meetings/Conferences:
Conference Chair: Ann L. Shriver

Publications:
IIFET Newsletter; annually
Membership Directory; on-line

International Institute of Forecasters (1981)
53 Tesla Ave.
Medford, MA 02155
Tel: (781) 234-4077 *Fax:* (509) 357-5530
Website: forecasters.org
Members: 500 individuals
Staff: 4
Annual Budget: $250-500,000
Tax: 501(c)(6)

Personnel:
President: Mohsen Hamoudia
E-Mail: mohsen.hamoudia@orange.com
Marketing Director: Kim Leonard
E-Mail: kimleonard@forecasters.org
Director, Business: Pamela Stroud
E-Mail: forecasters@forecasters.org
Editor: Len Tashman
E-Mail: lentashman@forecasters.org

Historical Note:
IIF is dedicated to developing and furthering the generation, distribution, and use of knowledge on forecasting. IIF's mission is to develop and unify forecasting as a multidisciplinary field of research drawing on management, behavioral sciences, social sciences, engineering, and other fields. Members are decision makers, forecasters and researchers involved with forecasting in the management, social, engineering and behavioral sciences. Membership: $145 (Regular); $55 (Student); $795 (Corporate).

Continuing Education:
Certification Designation/s: CF

Meetings/Conferences: Annual
Conference Chair: Pamela Stroud
2013 - Seoul, Republic of Korea (South Korea)/June 23 - 26
2014 - Rotterdam, Netherlands/June 29 - July 2

Publications:
FORESIGHT: The International Journal of Applied Forecasting; quarterly; adv.
The International Journal of Forecasting; quarterly; adv.
The Oracle; on-line; adv.

Membership List Available to Non-members

International Institute of Municipal Clerks (1947)
8331 Utica Ave.
Suite 200
Rancho Cucamonga, CA 91730
Tel: (909) 944-4162 *Fax:* (909) 944-8545
TollFree: (800) 251-1639
E-Mail: hq@iimc.com
Website: iimc.com
Members: 10000 individuals
Staff: 9
Annual Budget: $1-2,000,000
Tax: 501(c)(6)

Personnel:
Executive Director: Chris Shalby
E-Mail: Chriss@iimc.com
Director, Membership Services: Janis Daudt
E-Mail: janis@iimc.com
Coordinator ,Communication: Emily Maggard
E-Mail: emily@iimc.com
Finance Specialist: Janet Pantaleon
E-Mail: janetp@iimc.com
Education Analyst: Jennifer Ward
E-Mail: jward@iimc.com

Historical Note:
Founded in 1947 at French Lick, Indiana as the National Institute of City and Town Clerks. Became the National Institute of Municipal Clerks in 1949 and the International

Institute of Municipal Clerks in 1960. The Mission of IIMC is professionalism in local government through education. Membership consists of persons serving as clerks, secretaries or recorders at the state, provincial, county or local level of government. Awards the CMC (Certified Municipal Clerk) designation. Membership: $125- 225 (Full,varies by population); $50 (Outside North America/Overseas Associate); $75 (Additional Full Member/Associate); $25 (Retired); $600 (Corporate).

Continuing Education:
Certification Designation/s: CMC, MMC

Meetings/Conferences: Annual
2013 - Atlantic City, NJ/May 19 - 23
2014 - Milwaukee, WI/May 18 - 22
2015 - Hartford, CT/May 17 - 20
2016 - Omaha, NE/May 22 - 25

Publications:
Membership Directory; on-line

International Institute of Synthetic Rubber Producers (1960)
2077 S. Gessner Rd.
Suite 133
Houston, TX 77063
Tel: (713) 783-7511 *Fax:* (713) 783-7253
E-Mail: info@iisrp.com
Website: iisrp.com
Members: 50 companies
Staff: 4
Annual Budget: $1-2,000,000
Tax: 501(c)(6)

Personnel:
Managing Director and Chief Executive Officer: James L. McGraw
E-Mail: jlmcgraw@iisrp.com
Manager, Accounts Services: Robin Boyd
E-Mail: RBoyd@IISRP.com
Executive Assistant and Event Coordinator: Sue Flynn
E-Mail: flynn@iisrp.com

Historical Note:
Mission is to promote the synthetic rubber industry and its benefits to society, stressing its history of innovation, technology improvement and its contributions to an improved quality of life. Membership: $19,000/year (Organization/Company).

Meetings/Conferences:
Conference Chair: Sue Flynn

Publications:
Synthetic Rubber Manual; irregular
Worldwide Rubber Statistics; annually

Membership List Available to Non-members

International Insurance Society (1965)
101 Murray St.
New York, NY 10007-2165
Tel: (212) 815-9291 *Fax:* (212) 815-9297
E-Mail: jeastmond@iisonline.org
Website: iisonline.org
Members: 900individual and companies
Staff: 6
Annual Budget: $2-5,000,000
Tax: 501(c)(3)

Personnel:
President and Chief Executive Officer: Michael J. Morrissey

Historical Note:
IIS's mission is to facilitate international understanding, the transfer of ideas and innovations, and the development of personal networks across insurance markets through a joint effort of leading executives and academics on a worldwide basis and also provides global exchange of ideas and initiates practical, original research addressing critical issues facing the industry. Membership: $100 (Academic), $400 (Individual); $3,500 (Corporate); $9,500 (Global).

Publications:
Global Insurance Directory
Global NewsLink; daily
IIS Newsletter; daily
IIS Research Review; monthly

International Interior Design Association (1994)
222 Merchandise Mart Plaza
Suite 567
Chicago, IL 60654
Tel: (312) 467-1950 *Fax:* (312) 467-0779
TollFree: (888) 799-4432
E-Mail: iidahq@iida.org
Website: iida.org

Members: 13000 individuals
Staff: 23
Annual Budget: $2-5,000,000
Tax: 501(c)(6)

Personnel:
Executive Vice President and Chief Executive Officer: Cheryl Durst
E-Mail: cdurst@iida.org
Managing Director, Education Services and Programs: Michael Ancheta
E-Mail: mancheta@iida.org
Manager, Industry Relations and Special Events: Erin Cook
E-Mail: ecook@iida.org
Communications Intern: Victoria Guerrero
E-Mail: vguerrero@iida.org
Manager, Information Technology: Jessica Leung
E-Mail: jleung@iida.org
Senior Director, Government and Regulatory Affairs: Allison Levy
E-Mail: alevy@iida.org
Director, Finance: Ella McHugh
E-Mail: emchugh@iida.org
Marketing Coordinator: Charissa Tolentino
E-Mail: ctolentino@iida.org
Senior Director, Membership Services: Lisa Toth
E-Mail: ltoth@iida.org

Historical Note:
Formed (1994) by the merger of Council of Federal Interior Designers, Institute of Business Designers, and International Society of Interior Designers. IIDA provides a forum to demonstrate design professionals' impact on the health, safety, well being and virtual soul of the public, balancing passion for good design and strategy for best business practices. Members are professionals from various facets of the interior design industry. Membership: $50-8000/year.

Meetings/Conferences: Annual
Conference Chair: Erin Cook
Number of non-conference events/year: 1

Publications:
Custom; quarterly
DesignMatters; bi-weekly
GRAction Newsletter; on-line
Member Directory; on-line
Perspective; quarterly; adv.
Quad; quarterly

International Iridology Practitioners Association (1982)
2101 Magnolia Ave.
Suite 100A
Birmingham, AL 35205
Tel: (205) 226-3522
TollFree: (888) 682-2208
E-Mail: iipacentraloffice@iridologyassn.org
Website: iridologyassn.org
Members: 500 individuals
Staff: 2
Annual Budget: $25-50,000
Tax: 501(c)(3)

Personnel:
President: Betty Sue O'Brian
Treasurer: Rebecca Thomas

Historical Note:
Formerly National Iridology Research Association, assumed its present name in year 2000. IIPA strives to promote art and science of iridology. It also provides a forum for exchange of information and research with goal of promoting excellence in international Iridology standards. Membership: $99 (Certified); $49 (Associate).

Continuing Education:
Certification Designation/s: CI

Meetings/Conferences: Annual
2013 - Las Vegas, NV (Hilton Garden Inn)/Feb. 22 - 24
Number of non-conference events/year: 1

Publications:
Insights into Health newsletter; monthly
Member Directory; on-line

International Isotope Society (1986)
CEO IICH Inc.
P.O. Box 6986
Leawood, KS 66206
Tel: (913) 488-5028
E-Mail: iis@intl-isotope-soc.org
Website: intl-isotope-soc.org
Members: 650 individuals

Staff: 3
Annual Budget: $10-25,000

Personnel:
President: Dr. Alexander Susan
   E-Mail: Alex.iichkansas@gmail.com

Historical Note:
The International Isotope Society is a chartered, international organization independent of special interests groups or companies. It is run entirely by the enthusiastic and unselfish dedicated volunteer work of its members. IIS members are academics and researchers involved in the study and application of chemical isotopes. Has no paid officers or full-time staff. Membership: $50/year (regular member); $350/year (associate).

Publications:
IIS Newsletter
The Journal of Labeled Compounds and
   Radiopharmaceuticals; adv.

International Jelly and Preserve Association
(1898)
750 National Press Building
529 14th St. NW
Washington, DC 20045
Tel: (202) 785-3232 *Fax:* (202) 223-9741
E-Mail: jpa@kellencompany.com
Website: jelly.org
Staff: 1

Personnel:
Executive Director: Carol Freysinger

Historical Note:
The International Jelly & Preserve Association was organized as the National Preservers Association. It now operates under the umbrella of the Juice Products Association, as its Fruit Spread Section. Its purpose is to establish and keep current standards of excellence for the preserve industry and to promote and protect the interests of both consumers and manufacturers in the industry. Section members produce the majority of jams, jellies, preserves and fruit spreads annually in the United States.

International Kitchen Exhaust Cleaning Association *(1989)*
100 N. 20th St.
Suite 400
Philadelphia, PA 19103-1462
Tel: (215) 320-3876 *Fax:* (215) 564-2175
E-Mail: information@ikeca.org
Website: ikeca.org
Members: 170 companies
Staff: 5
Annual Budget: $250-500,000
Tax: 501(c)(6)

Personnel:
Executive Director: Sarah Hagy
   E-Mail: shagy@fernley.com
Administrative Director: Lisa Chester
Director, Membership Services: Jason Harbonic
   E-Mail: jharbonic@fernley.com
Manager, Meetings: Tina Phelan
   E-Mail: tphelan@fernley.com

Historical Note:
IKECA is committed to serve and represent the interests of the commercial kitchen exhaust cleaning industry by promoting the highest cleaning and ethical standards. Also provides education and certification opportunities. Membership: $50-2,000/year.

Continuing Education:
Certification Designation/s: CECS, CECT, CESI

Meetings/Conferences: Annual
Conference Chair: Tina Phelan
2013 - Naples, FL (Hilton Naples)/April 17 - 20
Number of non-conference events/year: 1

Publications:
IKECA Journal; quarterly; adv.
Membership Directory; on-line
Newsletter; quarterly

International Labor Communications Association *(1955)*
815 16th St. NW
Four North
Washington, DC 20006
Tel: (202) 637-5068 *Fax:* (202) 318-9133
E-Mail: ILCA@aflcio.org
Website: ilcaonline.org
Members: 400 individuals
Staff: 3

Annual Budget: $100-250,000
Tax: 501(c)(5)

Personnel:
President: David Katzman
Secretary: Kathy Cummings
Treasurer: Mike Henneberry

Historical Note:
Formerly (1984) International Labor Press Association. Formed by the merger of the International Labor Press of America (1911) and the CIO Editors and Public Relations Conference (1940). ILCA's mission is to build the power of labor journalism by providing a place for labor's communication professionals to exchange ideas, share their stories, learn the latest in both technology and storytelling and recognize the talent within the community. Full members are union publications, websites etc. Membership: $55 (Full-minimum, based on circulation or membership); $10-1,000 (Associate).

Publications:
ILCA newsletter; monthly
ILCA Reporter; irregular; adv.
Insider e-newsletter; weekly
Member Directory; on-line

International Labor Rights Forum *(1986)*
1634 I St. NW
Suite 1001
Washington, DC 20006
Tel: (202) 347-4100 *Fax:* (202) 347-4885
E-Mail: laborrights@ilrf.org
Website: laborrights.org
Staff: 10
Annual Budget: $1-2,000,000
Tax: 501(c)(3)

Personnel:
Executive Director: Judy Gearhart
Director, Policy and Legal Programs: Brian Campbell
Director, Operations: Vonetta Faulkner
Research Associate: Adeline Lambert
Associate, Development and Communications: Jacqueline
   Starr

Historical Note:
ILRF represents human rights and labor rights and it's mission is to achieve just and humane treatment for workers worldwide.

International Lactation Consultant Association *(1985)*
2501 Aerial Center Pkwy.
Suite 103
Morrisville, NC 27560
Tel: (919) 861-5577 *Fax:* (919) 459-2075
TollFree: (888) 452-2478
E-Mail: info@ilca.org
Website: ilca.org
Members: 4600 individuals
Staff: 7
Annual Budget: $2-5,000,000
Tax: 501(c)(3)

Personnel:
Executive Director: Natalie Sroka
   E-Mail: natalie@ilca.org
Manager, Administration: Erin Barnette
   E-Mail: erinb@uslca.org
Contact, Media Requests: Cathy Carothers
   E-Mail: cathycarothers@ilca.org
Coordinator, Publications: Lisa Joncich
   E-Mail: lisa@ilca.org
Director, Conferences: Amanda Joslin
   E-Mail: amanda@ilca.org
Coordinator, Education: Judith Lauwers BA, IBCLC
   E-Mail: judi@ilca.org
Coordinator, Membership Services: Glenna Thurston
   E-Mail: glenna@ilca.org

Historical Note:
ILCA's mission is to advance the profession of lactation consulting worldwide through leadership, advocacy, professional development, and research. Membership: $182 (Contributing Professional); $150 (Standard); $205 (Contributing Professional-Canada); $170 (Standard-Canada).

Meetings/Conferences: Annual
Conference Chair: Amanda Joslin
2013 - Melbourne, Australia (Melbourne Convention
   Centre)/July 25 - 28
2014 - Phoenix, AZ (JW Marriott Desert Ridge Resort)/
   July 23 - 26

2015 - Washington, DC (Washington Marriott
   Wardman Park)/July 22 - 25
2016 - Chicago, IL (Sheraton Chicago Hotel and
   Towers)/July 20 - 23
Number of non-conference events/year: 1

Publications:
Inside Track
Membership Directory; on-line
The Journal of Human Lactation (JHL); quarterly; adv.

International Laser Display Association *(1986)*
7062 Edgeworth Dr.
Orlando, FL 32819
Tel: (407) 797-7654 *Fax:* (503) 344-3770
E-Mail: mail@laserist.org
Website: laserist.org
Members: 153 companies and individuals
Staff: 1
Annual Budget: $50-100,000

Personnel:
Executive Director: Patrick Murphy

Historical Note:
ILDA's mission is to advance the use of laser displays in the fields of art, entertainment and education. Membership: $50-125 (Non-Profit/Individual); $50 (Student); $150-1000 (Corporate).

Continuing Education:
Certification Designation/s: ILDAP

Publications:
Membership Directory; on-line
The Laserist; quarterly; adv.

International Law Students Association *(1960)*
25 E. Jackson Blvd.
Suite OMB1051
Chicago, IL 60604
Tel: (312) 362-5025 *Fax:* (312) 362-5073
E-Mail: ilsa@ilsa.org
Website: ilsa.org
Staff: 1
Annual Budget: $500-1,000,000

Personnel:
Executive Director: Lesley A. Benn

Historical Note:
ILSA's mission is to educate students and lawyers around the world in the principles and purposes of international law, international organizations and institutions, and comparative legal systems, through activities that include academic conferences, the publication of books, magazines, and other academic resources, the global coordination of student chapter organizations. $12.50 (U.S. Residents); $15 (Non-U.S.).

Publications:
FOJ Newsletter; monthly
ILA Journal; irregular
ILSA magazine; quarterly

International Lead Zinc Research Organization *(1958)*
1822 E. NC Hwy. 54 East
Suite 120
Durham, NC 27713-3210
Tel: (919) 361-4647 *Fax:* (919) 361-1957
Website: ilzro.org
Members: 45 companies
Staff: 8
Annual Budget: $5-10,000,000
Tax: 501(c)(6)

Personnel:
President: Stephen Wilkinson
Vice President, Materials Sciences: Frank Goodwin
   E-Mail: fgoodwin@ilzro.org
Director, Communications: Rob Putnam
   E-Mail: rputnam@ilzro.org

Historical Note:
Established in New York and incorporated in North Carolina. Members are miners and refiners of lead and zinc. ILZRO manages environment, health, sustainable development and product-related research programs on behalf of the International Lead Association (ILA) and the International Zinc Association (IZA).

International League of Electrical Associations *(1936)*
39 Harmon Rd.
P.O. Box 24
Churchville, NY 14428

Tel: (585) 538-6350 Fax: (585) 538-6166
E-Mail: info@ileaweb.org
Website: ileaweb.org
Members: 31 organizations
Staff: 3
Annual Budget: $250-500,000

Personnel:
Executive Director: Kirstie Steves
    E-Mail: kirstie@ileaweb.org
Treasurer: Barbette Cejalvo
Manager, Conference: Skip Morris

Historical Note:
Formerly known as International Association of Electrical
Leagues, assumed its current name in 1979. ILEA's mission
is to promote, advance and unify the electrical industry by
strengthening its representative organizations. Members are
manufactures, distributors, contractors and suppliers in the
electrical industry. Membership: $250-400/year.

Meetings/Conferences: Annual
Conference Chair: Skip Morris

Publications:
Compensation Survey; annually
Membership Directory; annually
Salary Survey; annually
Watt's New; monthly

International League of Professional Baseball Clubs (1884)
55 S. High St.
Suite 202
Dublin, OH 43017
Tel: (614) 791-9300 Fax: (614) 791-9009
E-Mail: office@ilbaseball.com
Website: ilbaseball.com
Members: 14 clubs
Staff: 3
Annual Budget: $1-2,000,000
Tax: 501(c)(6)

Personnel:
President and Treasurer: Randy A. Mobley

Historical Note:
Membership includes baseball clubs.

International Legal Fraternity of Phi Delta Phi (1869)
1426 21st St. NW
Washington, DC 20036
Tel: (202) 223-6801 Fax: (202) 223-6808
TollFree: (800) 368-5606
E-Mail: info@phideltaphi.org
Website: phideltaphi.org
Members: 200000 individuals
Staff: 3
Annual Budget: $250-500,000
Tax: 501(c)(6)

Personnel:
Executive Director: Tim Wheat
Director, Membership Services and Development: Regina
Yun
    E-Mail: ryun@pdp.org

Historical Note:
PDP is dedicated to the promotion of legal ethics and
academic distinction in the law schools and the profession
at large. Membership: $75 (Active); $475 (Active Life).

Publications:
Membership Directory; on-line
The Headnoter; adv.

Membership List Available to Non-members

International Licensing Industry Merchandisers' Association (1985)
350 Fifth Ave.
Suite 4019
New York, NY 10118
Tel: (212) 244-1944 Fax: (212) 563-6552
E-Mail: info@licensing.org
Website: licensing.org
Members: 1000 companies
Staff: 8
Annual Budget: $2-5,000,000

Personnel:
President: Charles M. Riotto
    E-Mail: criotto@licensing.org
Director, Marketing: Christina Attardo
    E-Mail: cattardo@licensing.org
General Counsel: Gregory J. Battersby

Senior Vice President, Membership and New Business
Development: Adam Berg
    E-Mail: aberg@licensing.org
Senior Vice President, Industry Relations and Information:
Marty Brochstein
    E-Mail: mbrochstein@licensing.org
Vice President, Member Relations: Louise Q. Caron
    E-Mail: louise@licensing.org
Director, Finance and Administration: Leah R. Hunter
    E-Mail: lhunter@licensing.org
Director, Operations: Mary Verdegaal
    E-Mail: mverdegaal@licensing.org

Historical Note:
Formed by the merger of Licensing Industry Association
(founded March 1980) and Licensed Merchandisers'
Association (founded April 1983). LIMA's mission is to
foster the growth and expansion of licensing. Membership:
$750-3,750/year.

Continuing Education:
Certification Designation/s: CLS

Meetings/Conferences: Annual
2013 - Hong Kong, China (Grand Hall and Grand
Foyer, Hong Kong Convention and Exhibition
Centre)/Jan. 7 - 9/16000 attendees/over 100
exhibitors
2013 - Las Vegas, NV (Mandalay Bay Convention
Center)/June 18 - 20/18000 attendees/over 100
exhibitors
Number of non-conference events/year: 110

Publications:
LIMA Bottomline Newsletter
Membership Directory; on-line

Membership List Available to Non-members

International Life Sciences Institute (1978)
1156 15th St. NW
Suite 200
Washington, DC 20005
Tel: (202) 659-0074 Fax: (202) 659-3859
E-Mail: info@ilsi.org
Website: ilsi.org
Members: 37 companies
Staff: 16
Annual Budget: $2-5,000,000
Tax: 501(c)(3)

Personnel:
Executive Director: Eric Hentges PhD
    E-Mail: ehentges@ilsi.org
Chief Financial Officer: Beth-Ellen Berry
    E-Mail: bberry@ilsi.org
Assistant Manager, Communications and Membership:
Jackie Bessette
Senior Project Manager: Heather Steele
    E-Mail: hsteele@ilsi.org
Deputy Executive Director: Sharon Weiss CAE, MS

Historical Note:
ILSI's mission is to improve public health and well-being by
engaging academic, government and industry scientists in
a neutral forum to advance scientific understanding in the
areas related to nutrition, food safety, risk assessment, and
the environment.

Meetings/Conferences:
Conference Chair: Heather Steele
2013 - Miami, FL (InterContinental Miami)/Jan. 18 - 23
Number of non-conference events/year: 10

Publications:
ILSI News; quarterly
Nutrition Reviews; adv.

International Light Transportation Vehicle Association, Inc. (1984)
Two Ravinia Dr.
Suite 1200
Atlanta, GA 30346
Tel: (770) 394-7200 Fax: (770) 454-0138
E-Mail: info@ ILTVA.org
Website: iltva.org
Staff: 1
Annual Budget: $100-250,000
Tax: 501(c)(6)

Personnel:
Secretary and General Counsel: Fred L. Somers Jr.
    E-Mail: somersf@abanet.org

Historical Note:
Formerly National Golf Car Manufacturers Association,
Inc. ILTVA's mission is to promote the common business

interest of its members; to improve business conditions for
its members of one or more of their lines of business to
encourage the use of their vehicles by implementing market
development; to work for the enactment of laws to advance
the common business interests of its members.

International Liquid Terminals Association (1974)
1005 N. Glebe Rd.
Suite 600
Arlington, VA 22201
Tel: (703) 875-2011 Fax: (703) 875-2018
E-Mail: info@ilta.org
Website: ilta.org
Members: 83 companies
Staff: 7
Annual Budget: $1-2,000,000
Tax: 501(c)(6)

Personnel:
President: E. David Doane
    E-Mail: ddoane@ilta.org
Manager, Travel and Meetings: Cynthia A. Carroll
    E-Mail: ccarroll@ilta.org
Director, Meetings and Information Services: Renita Gross
Manager, Regulatory Analysis and Education Programs:
Katie Vassalli
Director, Regulatory Compliance and Safety: Robert
"Peter" Weaver

Historical Note:
ILTA provides its members with essential informational
tools to facilitate regulatory compliance and improve
operations, safety and environmental performance. Member
companies operate for-hire and proprietary terminals.
Membership: $4,017-14,729 (Terminal Member -Voting);
$2,009-7,365 (Terminal Member -International); $450
(Supplier Member).

Meetings/Conferences:
Conference Chair: Renita Gross
2013 - Houston, TX (Hilton Americas-Houston)/June 3
- 5
2014 - Houston, TX (Hilton Americas-Houston)/June 3
- 4
Number of non-conference events/year: 5

Publications:
ILTA Newsletter; monthly
Member Directory; on-line

International Listening Association (1979)
P.O. Box 164
Belle Plaine, MN 56011
Tel: (952) 594-5697
E-Mail: info@listen.org
Website: listen.org
Members: 400 individuals
Staff: 1
Annual Budget: $25-50,000
Tax: 501(c)(3)

Personnel:
Executive Director: Nanette Johnson-Curiskis
    E-Mail: nanette.johnson-curiskis@mnsu.edu

Historical Note:
ILA's purpose is to advance the practice, teaching, and
research of listening throughout the world. Members will
exchange information by sharing teaching objectives,
learning activities, promotional methods and materials,
and additional professional experience. Membership: $115
(Regular); $650 (Organizational); $57.50 (Student/
Emeritus); $1500 (Lifetime).

Continuing Education:
Certification Designation/s: CLP

Meetings/Conferences: Annual
2013 - Montreal, QC/June 20 - 23

Publications:
International Journal of Listening; semi-annually
Listening Education; on-line
Listening Post
Listening Professional; on-line
Member Directory; on-line

International Liver Transplantation Society (1990)
15000 Commerce Pkwy.
Suite C
Mt. Laurel, NJ 08054
Tel: (856) 439-0500 Fax: (856) 439-0525
E-Mail: ilts@ahint.com
Website: ilts.org
Members: 900 individuals

Staff: 5
Annual Budget: $2-5,000,000
Tax: 501(c)(3)

Personnel:
Executive Director: Diann Stern MS
    E-Mail: dstern@ahint.com
Manager, Meetings and Exhibits: Shannon Fagan
    E-Mail: sfagan@ahint.com
Director, Membership Services: Priscilla Rodriguez
    E-Mail: prodriguez@ahint.com

Historical Note:
ILTS's mission is to promote and disseminate multidisciplinary scientific advances in liver transplantation worldwide. Membership: $190 (Regular); $95 (Non-Physician); $75 (Trainee); $40 (Web Subscriber).

Meetings/Conferences: Annual
Conference Chair: Shannon Fagan
Number of non-conference events/year: 1

Publications:
Liver Transplantation Journal; monthly
Membership Directory; on-line

International Longshore and Warehouse Union (1937)
1188 Franklin St.
Fourth Floor
San Francisco, CA 94109
Tel: (415) 775-0533 *Fax:* (415) 775-1302
E-Mail: info@ilwu.org
Website: ilwu.org
Members: 59500 individuals
Staff: 25
Annual Budget: $5-10,000,000
Tax: 501(c)(5)

Personnel:
President: Robert McEllrath
Director, Research and Education: Russ Bargmann
Office Manager and Executive Secretary: Linda Kuhn
    E-Mail: linda.kuhn@ilwu.org
Director, Communication and Senior Editor: Craig
    Merrilees
    E-Mail: craig@ilwu.org

Historical Note:
The International Longshore and Warehouse Union (ILWU) is a labor union which primarily represents dock workers on the West Coast of the United States, Hawaii and Alaska, and in British Columbia, Canada and aims to unite all workers within the jurisdiction.

Publications:
The Dispatcher; monthly

International Longshoremen's Association, AFL-CIO (1892)
5000 W. Side Ave.
N. Bergen, NJ 07047
Tel: (212) 425-1200 *Fax:* (212) 425-2928
Website: ilaunion.org
Members: 65000 longshoremen
Staff: 30
Annual Budget: $25-50,000

Personnel:
President: Harold J. Daggett
    E-Mail: hdagg01@ila-ports.com

Historical Note:
Established in Detroit in 1892 as the National Longshoremen's Association of the United States. Became the International Longshoremen's Association in 1895 and was chartered by the American Federation of Labor in 1896. Expelled for corruption and racketeering by the AFL in 1953, the ILA was an independent union until 1959, when it re-affiliated with AFL-CIO.

Meetings/Conferences:
Number of non-conference events/year: 7

Publications:
Membership Directory; on-line
News Report; quarterly

International Magnesium Association (1943)
1000 N. Rand Rd.
Suite 214
Wauconda, IL 60084
Tel: (847) 526-2010 *Fax:* (847) 526-3993
E-Mail: info@intlmag.org
Website: intlmag.org
Members: 120 companies
Staff: 2
Annual Budget: $500-1,000,000

Tax: 501(c)(6)

Personnel:
Interim Executive Vice President: Joyce Mandel
    E-Mail: jmandel@tso.net
Contact, Membership Services: Ann Scheible

Historical Note:
IMA's mission is to promote the use of the metal magnesium in material selection and encourage innovative applications of the versatile metal. Regular membership is open to organizations or individuals directly engaged in the production, manufacture or marketing of metallic magnesium in some product form; and those supplying materials, equipment or services to the industry. Membership: $3,450 (Regular); $3,450 (Associate); $500 (University); $25 (Student).

Meetings/Conferences: Annual
2013 - Xi'an, China (Not decided)/May 19 - 22
Number of non-conference events/year: 1

Publications:
Buyers Guide; on-line
IMA Newsletter; weekly

International Magnetics Association (1959)
Eight S. Michigan Ave.
Suite 1000
Chicago, IL 60603
Tel: (312) 456-5590 *Fax:* (312) 580-0165
E-Mail: ima@gss.net
Website: intl-magnetics.org
Members: 35 companies
Staff: 2
Annual Budget: $50-100,000

Personnel:
President: Lowell Bosley
Secretary, Treasurer and Chair, Finance Committee: Paul B.
    Oberbeck

Historical Note:
Established as the Permanent Magnet Producers Association; became Magnetic Materials Producers Association in 1967 and assumed its current name in 2002. Absorbed Magnetics Distributors and Fabricators Association in 2003. Mission is to promote the worldwide growth, understand and use of magnetic materials and devices. IMA develops, maintains, and distributes industry standards, educates magnet users through presentations on materials and contemporary applications, and conducts statistical surveys to gather market information on materials and to ebenchmark key industry business indicators. Membership: $1,000 (Full-Producer/Distributor/Fabricator); $500 (Full- Supplier/User/Publications/Other Media/University); $250 (Affiliate).

Continuing Education:
Certification Designation/s: SPC

Publications:
Membership Directory; on-line

International Maintenance Institute (1960)
P.O. Box 751896
Houston, TX 77275-1896
Tel: (281) 481-0869 *Fax:* (281) 481-8337
TollFree: (888) 207-1773
E-Mail: iminst@swbell.net
Website: imionline.org
Members: 2500 individuals
Staff: 12
Annual Budget: $25-50,000

Personnel:
Executive Secretary: Joyce Rhoden
    E-Mail: iminst@swbell.net

Historical Note:
Organization made up of decision making maintenance leaders as well as related sales and service professionals dedicated to keeping the nation's infrastructure operating smoothly. Mission is to professionalize the maintenance function by helping maintenance managers to work smarter through the exchange of ideas and education. Membership: $50 (Senior/Technical); $100 (Associate); $10 (Student); $750 (Corporate).

Continuing Education:
Certification Designation/s: CMT, CMP, CMM, CWWMT
Meetings/Conferences:
Number of non-conference events/year: 1

Publications:
Maintenance Journal; adv.
The IMI News; bi-monthly; adv.

International Manganese Institute
17 rue Duphot
Paris 75001

Website: manganese.org
Staff: 1

Personnel:
Treasurer: Jone Hall

Historical Note:
A non-profit industry association that represents manganese ore and alloy producers, manufacturers of manganese-based products, traders, industry service providers, and universities and research organizations world-wide.

International Map Trade Association (1981)
23052 - H Alicia Pkwy.
Suite 602
Mission Viejo, CA 92692
Tel: (949) 458-8200 *Fax:* (949) 458-0300
E-Mail: info@imtamaps.org
Website: imtamaps.org
Members: 800 companies and organizations
Staff: 4
Annual Budget: $100-250,000

Personnel:
Executive Director: Sanford J. Hill
    E-Mail: imta@maptrade.org
Director, Programs: Linda Hill

Historical Note:
Formerly (1993) The International Map Dealers Association. IMTA's mission is to stimulate the sale and use of maps and related material, to promote better standards of professional competence, conduct, and ethics, and to foster communication and cooperation among publishers, wholesalers, retailers, and others in the map industry. Members are retail stores featuring maps, distributors, manufacturers, wholesalers, and publishers. Membership: $180-550 (General); $100 (Associate).

Meetings/Conferences: Annual
Conference Chair: Linda Hill
2013 - Cambridge, MA (Hyatt Regency Cambridge)/
    Sept. 8 - 10

Publications:
Membership directory; on-line
The IMTA Report Newsletter; bi-monthly; adv.

International Maple Syrup Institute (1975)
555 Route 78
Swanton, VT 05488
Tel: (802) 868-7244 *Fax:* (802) 868-4113
Website: internationalmaplesyrupinstitute.com
Members: 15000 individuals
Staff: 3
Annual Budget: $5-10,000,000

Personnel:
Executive Director: Dave Chapeskie
    E-Mail: agrofor@ripnet.com
Editor: Roy Hutchison
Treasurer: Steve Selby
    E-Mail: steve@businessamericaservices.com

Historical Note:
IMSI's mission is to promote the use of pure maple syrup and protect the integrity of the product while encouraging cooperation among all persons or groups involved in any aspect of the maple industry. Membership: $25 (Individual); $200-1000 (Packer).

Meetings/Conferences: Annual

Publications:
Maple Digest Newsletter

International Marine Minerals Society (1987)
C/O University of Hawaii
1000 Pope Rd., MSB 303
Honolulu, HI 96822
Tel: (808) 956-6036 *Fax:* (808) 956-9772
Website: immsoc.org
Members: 160 individuals
Staff: 3
Annual Budget: $25-50,000
Tax: 501(c)(6)

Personnel:
President: Georgy Cherkashov
Administrative Officer: Karynne Chong Morgan
    E-Mail: karynnem@hawaii.edu
Treasurer: John C. Wiltshire

Historical Note:
IMMS's mission is to promote and improve the understanding of marine mineral deposits within the province of the global ocean. Membership: $35 (Regular); Free (Student).

Meetings/Conferences: Annual

Publications:
Member Directory; on-line
Soundings; monthly

International Marking and Identification Association *(1910)*
P.O. Box 49649
Charlotte, NC 28277
Tel: (704) 847-0064 *Fax:* (704) 847-0211
E-Mail: office@marking-id.org
Website: marking-id.org
Members: 300 companies
Staff: 1
Annual Budget: $100-250,000

Personnel:
Executive Director: Steve Hewitt
    E-Mail: e-steve@marking-id.org

Historical Note:
Formerly known as the International Stamp Manufacturers Association. Became International Marking Device Association in 2002. IMIA is an association of companies engaged in the manufacture and/or distribution of marking and identification products such as rubber stamps, polymer hand stamps, pre-inked rubber stamps, self-inking rubber stamps, seals, inks, stencils, metal stamping tools, name plates, identification badges, signage and other related products. Members are manufacturers of embossing seals, notary seals, rubber and metal stamps, plates, signs, and other hand-held marking devices. Membership: $249-499 (Regular); $199-1375 (Premier); $2175-3175 (Sustaining).

Meetings/Conferences: Annual

Publications:
IMIA E-Newsletter; on-line
IMIA Membership Directory; annually
Marking Industry Magazine; on-line
Update; bi-monthly

International Masonry Institute *(1970)*
The James Brice House
42 E. St.
Annapolis, MD 21401
Tel: (410) 280-1305 *Fax:* (301) 261-2855
TollFree: (800) 803-0295
E-Mail: masonryquestions@imiweb.org
Website: imiweb.org
Staff: 170
Annual Budget: $25-50,000,000
Tax: 501(c)(6)

Personnel:
President: Joan Baggett Calambokidis
Chief of Staff: Cristina Morse
Director, Communications: Hazel Bradford
Administrative Manager: Elena Johnson
Manager, Marketing: Dawn Lafey
National Director, Industry Development: David Sovinski

Historical Note:
A Labor/Management Trust established between the International Union of Bricklayers and Allied Craftsmen and contractors who employ BAC members. IMI offers training for craftworkers, professional education for masonry contractors and free technical assistance to the design and construction communities.

Continuing Education:
Certification Designation/s: ICP, SCP

Meetings/Conferences:
Number of non-conference events/year: 38

Publications:
IMI Today; monthly

International Memorialization Supply Association *(1955)*
P.O. Box 425
W. Bend, WI 53095-0425
TollFree: (800) 375-0335
E-Mail: info@imsa-online.com
Website: imsa-online.com
Members: 102 companies
Staff: 8
Annual Budget: $10-25,000
Tax: 501(c)(6)

Personnel:
Contact, Membership Services: Eric Robuck
    E-Mail: Eric@VastDataConcepts.com

Historical Note:
IMSA was formerly (until 1980) known as the Cemetery and Funeral Supply Association and (until 1994) the International Cemetery Supply Association. The member

companies of the IMSA are dedicated to servicing the needs of death care professionals worldwide. Membership: $135/year (Individual).

Publications:
IMSA NewsLetter; quarterly

International Metal Decorators Association *(1934)*
9574 Deereco Rd.
Timonium, MD 21093
Tel: (410) 252-5205 *Fax:* (410) 628-8079
E-Mail: info@metaldecorators.org
Website: metaldecorators.com
Members: 850 individuals
Staff: 2
Annual Budget: $250-500,000

Personnel:
Executive Director: Michael Masenior
    E-Mail: ampmgt@aol.com

Historical Note:
IMDA aims to foster and encourage improvements and advances in the art of metal decorating and the industrial progress of the metal decorating trade by all lawful means. Members are individuals in firms that apply decoration and supplies and services to metal surfaces through lithography or rollercoating. Membership: $75/year, plus $50 application fee.

Meetings/Conferences: Annual
Conference Chair: Michael Masenior

Publications:
International Metal Decorator
Membership Directory; annually

International Microelectronics and Packaging Society - IMAPS *(1967)*
611 Second St. NE
Washington, DC 20002-4909
Tel: (202) 548-4001 *Fax:* (202) 548-6115
E-Mail: imaps@imaps.org
Website: imaps.org
Members:
300 companies
4000 individuals
Staff: 6
Annual Budget: $1-2,000,000
Tax: 501(c)(3)

Personnel:
Executive Director: Michael O'Donoghue
    E-Mail: modonoghue@imaps.org
Manager, Marketing and Communications: Ann Bell
    E-Mail: abell@IMAPS.org
Director, Membership and Chapter Programs: Steven Greene
    E-Mail: sgreene@imaps.org
Manager, Meetings: Elizabeth Keller
    E-Mail: ekeller@imaps.org
Manager, Technical Program Development: Jackki Morris
    E-Mail: jmorris@imaps.org
Director, Program Development and Technology: Brian Schieman
    E-Mail: bschieman@imaps.org

Historical Note:
Formed in 1996 by the merger of the International Society for Hybrid Microelectronics and the International Electronic Packaging Society. IMAPS's mission is to provide means of communication, education and interaction at all levels. Membership: $75 (Individual); $600 (Corporate); $2,500 (Corporate Premier); $40 (Unemployed); $5 (Retired/Student).

Meetings/Conferences: Annual
Conference Chair: Elizabeth Keller
Number of non-conference events/year: 6

Publications:
Advancing Microelectronics; bi-monthly; adv.
Journal of Microelectronics and Electronic Packaging; quarterly; adv.

International Microwave Power Institute *(1966)*
P.O. Box 1140
Mechanicsville, VA 23111
Tel: (804) 559-6667 *Fax:* (804) 559-4087
E-Mail: info@impi.org
Website: impi.org
Members: 300 individuals
Staff: 2
Annual Budget: $100-250,000
Tax: 501(c)(3)

Personnel:
Executive Director: Molly Poisant
    E-Mail: molly.poisant@impi.org
Editorial Assistant: Alexandra Cornwell

Historical Note:
IMPI's mission is to provide a global community in which researchers, academia and business professionals have the opportunity for open exchange on existing and potential non-communications uses of microwave energy. Members are engineers, educators, home economists and scientists interested in non-communication aspects of microwave power. Membership: $170 (Professional); $2,800 (Deluxe Corporate); $1,800 (Corporate); $50 (Student).

Meetings/Conferences: Annual
Number of non-conference events/year: 2

Publications:
IMPI News
Journal of Microwave Power and Electromagnetic Energy; quarterly

Membership List Available to Non-members

International Military Community Executives Association *(1972)*
P.O. Box 7286
Alexandria, VA 22307-0286
Tel: (571) 207-8893 *Fax:* (866) 369-2435
E-Mail: imcea@imcea.com
Website: imcea.com
Members: 950 individuals
Staff: 4
Annual Budget: $100-250,000
Tax: 501(c)(3)

Personnel:
Executive Director: Arthur J. Myers
    E-Mail: art@imcea.org
Director, Communications: Toni Shortsleeve
    E-Mail: toni@imcea.org
Director, Finance and Member Services: John Walker
    E-Mail: john@imcea.org

Historical Note:
Formerly (1989) the International Military Club Executives Association. IMCEA exists to advance the professional development of military MWR/Services program managers. It provides a forum for military community executives to exchange viewpoints and ideas, and share better business practices. Membership is open to all personnel involved in morale, welfare and recreation, (MWR) activities, including clubs, bowling and golf managers. Membership: $225 (Position); $30 (Regular); $350 (Lifetime); $50 (Retired/Inactive/Affiliate); $525 (Associate).

Continuing Education:
Certification Designation/s: CMCE

Meetings/Conferences: Annual
Conference Chair: Dave Pruka
2013 - Las Vegas, NV (Mirage Resort and Casino)/
    March 10 - 13

Publications:
Connections; monthly

International Miniature Cattle Breeders Society *(1984)*
25204 156th Ave. SE
Covington, WA 98042
Tel: (253) 631-1911 *Fax:* (253) 631-5774
E-Mail: info@minicattle.com
Website: minicattle.com
Members: 4534 individuals
Staff: 4

Personnel:
Founding Director: Emeritus Richard Gradwohl

Historical Note:
IMCBS represents breeders and ranchers of 24 breeds of mini- and mid-size miniature cattle. Membership: $100/year.

Publications:
IMCBS Newsletter; adv.

International Molded Fibre Association *(1997)*
1425 W. Mequon Rd.
Suite C-D
Mequon, WI 53092
Tel: (262) 241-0522 *Fax:* (262) 241-3766
E-Mail: info@imfa.org
Website: imfa.org
Staff: 2
Annual Budget: $50-100,000

Personnel:

Executive Director: Joseph Grygny
Assistant Director: Cassandra Niesing

Historical Note:
IMFA seeks to advocate the products and services of its supporting membership and to expand the markets for renewable molded fiber products. Members are product manufacturers, marketers, as well as governmental agencies, universities and specific organizations. Membership: $5,000 (Charter); $2,500 (Premier); $1,850 (Affiliate); Free (Customers, Universities, Trade Groups, Government).

Publications:
Newsletter; monthly

International Motor Press Association *(1962)*
P.O. Box 146
Harrington Park, NJ 07640
Tel: (201) 750-3533 *Fax:* (201) 750-2010
E-Mail: info@impa.org
Website: impa.org
Members: 500 individuals
Staff: 3
Annual Budget: $100-250,000

Personnel:
President: Fred Chieco
    E-Mail: fred.chieco@abc.com
Editor: Rachel Geylin
    E-Mail: rsg@kgpr.com
Treasurer: Mike Geylin
    E-Mail: mgeylin@kgpr.com

Historical Note:
IMPA consists of writers and editors producing auto articles for the press, radio or TV. Concentrated in the New York area, IMPA is the U.S. Chapter of the International Federation of Automotive Journalists. Membership: $60/year.

Meetings/Conferences:
Number of non-conference events/year: 2

Publications:
IMPACT Newsletter; on-line

International Multimedia Telecommunications Consortium *(1994)*
Bishop Ranch Six
2400 Camino Ramon, Suite 375
San Ramon, CA 94583
Tel: (925) 275-6600 *Fax:* (925) 275-6691
Website: imtc.org
Members: 61 corporations
Staff: 3
Annual Budget: $250-500,000
Tax: 501(c)(6)

Personnel:
Executive Director: John Ehrig
    E-Mail: jehrig@inventures.com
Vice President, Industry Relations: Rouzbeh Farhoumand
    E-Mail: rouzbeh.farhoumand@huawei.com
Treasurer: Markus Hanhisalo
    E-Mail: markus.hanhisalo@nokia.com

Historical Note:
IMTC's mission is to foster and facilitate the development and use of interoperable, real-time, telecommunications products and services based on open international standards. Members include Internet application developers and service providers, teleconferencing hardware and software suppliers, telecommunications companies and equipment vendors, end users, educational institutions, government agencies and non-profit corporations. Membership: $8,500 (Full Voting); $1000 (Non Profit/University).

Meetings/Conferences: Semi-Annual
2013 - Porto, Portugal (Porto Palatio)/April 26 - May 4
2013 - Porto, Portugal/Oct. 8 - 10

Publications:
IMTC Newsletters
Membership Directory; on-line

International Municipal Lawyers Association *(1935)*
7910 Woodmont Ave.
Suite 1440
Bethesda, MD 20814
Tel: (202) 466-5424 *Fax:* (202) 785-0152
E-Mail: info@imla.org
Website: imla.org
Members:
1500 cities and counties
2500 members

Staff: 9
Annual Budget: $1-2,000,000

Personnel:
Executive Director and General Counsel: Charles W. Thompson Jr.
    E-Mail: cthompson@imla.org
Associate Director, Events: Trina Shropshire-Paschal
    E-Mail: trina@imla.org
Senior Associate Counsel: Sophia M. Stadnyk
    E-Mail: sstadnyk@imla.org
Associate Director, Membership Services: Brandi Teel
    E-Mail: bteel@imla.org

Historical Note:
Formerly known as the National Institute of Municipal Law Officers (NIMLO) till 1995. IMLA's mission is to serve local government lawyers and to advance the interests of local government law locally, nationally, and internationally. Membership: $125-6160/year.

Continuing Education:
Certification Designation/s: CLE

Meetings/Conferences: Annual
Conference Chair: Trina Shropshire-Paschal
2013 - San Francisco, CA/Sept. 29 - Oct. 2
2014 - Baltimore, MD/Sept. 8 - 14
Number of non-conference events/year: 2

Publications:
IMLA's Magazine; monthly

International Municipal Signal Association *(1896)*
165 E. Union St.
P.O. Box 539
Newark, NJ 14513-0539
Tel: (315) 331-2182 *Fax:* (315) 331-8205
TollFree: (800) 723-4672
E-Mail: info@imsasafety.org
Website: imsasafety.org
Members: 12000 individuals
Staff: 14
Annual Budget: $1-2,000,000

Personnel:
Executive Director: Marilyn Lawrence
    E-Mail: mel@imsasafety.org
Contact, Technical Training: Lori Blaisdell
    E-Mail: lmb@imsasafety.org
Director, Education and Assistant Editor: Sharon Earl
    E-Mail: sne@imsasafety.org
Coordinator, Membership Records: Sharon Prutsman
    E-Mail: slp@imsasafety.org
Contact, Certification Seminar: Amanda Santell
    E-Mail: ais@IMSAsafety.org.

Historical Note:
Formerly International Association of Fire and Police Telegraph Superintendents. In 1900 the organization changed its name to the "International Association of Municipal Electricians" (I.A.M.E.) and In the 1920's to New England Municipal Signal Association. In September 1937, the organization name was officially changed to the "International Municipal Signal Association" (I.M.S.A.). IMSA is dedicated to providing quality certification programs for the safe installation, operation and maintenance of public safety systems. Members are government employees and municipal contractors involved in public safety operations. Membership: $80 (Active/Associate); $70 (Public Agency); $35 (Student); $400 (Sustaining).

Continuing Education:
Enrollment: 6500
Certification Designation/s: IMSA

Meetings/Conferences: Annual
Conference Chair: Amanda Santell
2013 - Scottsdale, AZ (Westin Kierland Resort and Spa)/July 18 - 25

Publications:
IMSA Journal; bi-monthly; adv.
Membership Directory; on-line

Membership List Available to Non-members

International Museum Theatre Alliance *(1990)*
C/O Museum of Science and Industry
57th St. and lake Shore Dr.
Chicago, IL 60637
Website: imtal.org
Members: 150 individuals
Staff: 5
Annual Budget: Under $10,000

Personnel:
President: Jillian Finkle

    E-Mail: president@imtal.org
Officer, Membership Services: Heather Barnes
    E-Mail: membership@imtal.org
Website Contact and Secretary: Elizabeth Keaney
Treasurer: Simone Mortan
    E-Mail: Treasurer@imtal.org
Publications Officer: Marcos Stafne

Historical Note:
IMTAL works to inspire and support the use of theatre and theatrical technique to cultivate emotional connections, provoke action, and add public value to the museum experience. It became an Affiliate Group of the American Association of Museums in 1994, and combined with the Professional Interest Council (PIC) of AAM in 2002. Membership: $35 (Student); $55 (Individual); $110 (Business/Institution).

Meetings/Conferences: Annual
2013 - Washington, DC (Smithsonian Institution)/Oct. 6 - 10

Publications:
INSIGHTS; quarterly
Member Directory; annually

International Nanny Association *(1985)*
P.O. Box 12347
Wilmington, NC 28405
Tel: (888) 878-1477 *Fax:* (508) 638-6462
E-Mail: info@nanny.org
Website: nanny.org
Members: 700 individuals
Staff: 3
Annual Budget: $100-250,000
Tax: 501(c)(3)

Personnel:
Executive Director: Michelle LaRowe
    E-Mail: admin@nanny.org
Treasurer: Sandra Costantin
    E-Mail: sandyc108@aol.com
Operations Manager: Rachel Lawrence

Historical Note:
INA's mission is to serve the in-home child care industry by providing information, education and guidance to the public and to industry professionals. Members are nannies, nanny placement agencies and others with an interest in the field. Membership: $35 (Individual); $125 (Independent Supporter); $215 (Standard); $315 (Supporting).

Meetings/Conferences: Annual
2013 - Louisville, KY/April 12 - 15

Publications:
INAVision newsletter
Membership Directory; on-line

International Natural Sausage Casing Association *(1964)*
12339 Carroll Ave.
Rockville, MD 20852-1867
Tel: (301) 231-8383 *Fax:* (301) 231-4871
Website: insca.org
Members: 250 companies
Staff: 4
Annual Budget: $500-1,000,000

Personnel:
Executive Director: Amy DeAvegno
Legal Counsel: Shirley A. Coffield
Accountant: Tina Moore

Historical Note:
Formerly (1965) Natural Casing Institute. Members include producers, suppliers and brokers of natural casing products. Membership: $1,500 (Regular); $750 (Associate/Affiliate).

International Network of Merger and Acquisition Partners *(1971)*
6000 Cattleridge Dr.
Suite 300
Sarasota, FL 34232
Tel: (941) 894-4259 *Fax:* (941) 378-5505
E-Mail: info@imap.com
Website: imap.com
Members: 50 companies
Staff: 3
Annual Budget: $50-100,000

Personnel:
Chairman and Chief Executive Officer: Sevket Basev
    E-Mail: sevket.basev@imap.com
President: Mark Esbeck
    E-Mail: mark.esbeck@imap.com
Treasurer: Scott Eisenberg

Historical Note:
Formerly (1982) National Association of Merger and Acquisition Consultants, (1995) International Association of Merger and Acquisition Professionals, and (2005) International Merger and Acquisition Professionals. IMAP unites a select group of professional organizations active in international transactions into a seamless global partnership. Members are specialists in selling, buying, and merging medium-sized public and private businesses.
Meetings/Conferences:
Number of non-conference events/year: 1

International Neural Network Society *(1987)*
2424 American Ln.
Madison, WI 53704
Tel: (608) 443-2461 *Fax:* (608) 443-2474
E-Mail: inns@reesgroupinc.com
Website: inns.org
Members: 2000 individuals
Staff: 4
Annual Budget: $100-250,000

Personnel:
Vice President, Membership: Irwin King
  E-Mail: king@cse.cuhk.edu.hk

Historical Note:
INNS is the organization for individuals interested in a theoretical and computational understanding of the brain and applying that knowledge to develop new and more effective forms of machine intelligence. Members are neural network scientists and other professionals interested in neurocomputing and theoretical neuroscience. Membership: $25-125/year.

Meetings/Conferences: Annual
Conference Chair: Danil Prokhorov
Number of non-conference events/year: 5

Publications:
Membership Directory; on-line
Natural Intelligence Magazine
Neural Networks

Membership List Available to Non-members

International Neuropsychological Society *(1967)*
The Ohio State University, Department of Psychiatry
1670 Upham Dr., Room 130F
Columbus, OH 43210
Tel: (614) 293-4774 *Fax:* (614) 293-4667
Website: the-ins.org
Members: 4500 individuals
Staff: 2
Annual Budget: $500-1,000,000

Personnel:
Executive Secretary: Robert A. Bornstein PhD
  E-Mail: bornstein.1@osu.edu

Historical Note:
INS's mission is to promote the international and interdisciplinary study of brain-behavioral relationships throughout the lifespan. Dedicated to enhancing communication among the scientific disciplines which contribute to the understanding of brain-behavior relationships. Membership: $120 (Regular); $60 (Associate).

Meetings/Conferences: Semi-Annual
2013 - Waikoloa, HI (Hilton Waikoloa Village)/Feb. 6 - 9
2013 - Amsterdam, Netherlands/July 10 - 13
2014 - Seatle, WA/Feb. 12 - 15

Publications:
Journal of the International Neuropsychological Society (JINS)
Membership Directory; on-line

International Newspaper Group *(1974)*
4335 NW 36th Terr.
Gainesville, FL 32605
Tel: (941) 378-2182
Website: azcentral.org
Members: 250 individuals
Staff: 1
Annual Budget: $50-100,000

Personnel:
Secretary-Treasurer: Martin Donner
  E-Mail: mdonner2@cox.net

Historical Note:
ING members are executives responsible for newspaper production and operations, and suppliers to the industry.

International Newspaper Marketing Association *(1930)*
P.O. Box 740186
Dallas, TX 75374
Tel: (214) 373-9111 *Fax:* (214) 373-9112
E-Mail: inma@inma.org
Website: inma.org
Members: 5000 members
Staff: 9
Annual Budget: $1-2,000,000
Tax: 501(c)(6)

Personnel:
Executive Director and Chief Executive Officer: Earl J. Wilkinson
  E-Mail: wilkinson@inma.org
Event Manager: Bridgette Joye
Bookkeeper: Andrea Loubier
Membership and Operations Manager: Kris Williams

Historical Note:
Formerly (1967) National Newspaper Promotion Association. Became International Newspaper Promotion Association and assumed its current name in 1987. INMA's mission is to provide newspapers with professional leadership and assistance in creating effective marketing of the total newspaper. Membership is composed of members from more than 40 countries including the United States and Canada. Membership: $695 (Individual); $2,995 (Company Membership); $1000 (Group Membership per unit).

Meetings/Conferences:
Number of non-conference events/year: 5

Publications:
Ideas Magazine; monthly; adv.
INMA e-Newsletter; weekly

International Nubian Breeders Association *(1956)*
5124 FM 1940
Franklin, TX 77856
Tel: (979) 828-4158
Website: i-n-b-a.org
Members: 400 individuals
Staff: 11
Annual Budget: Under $10,000

Personnel:
President: Marshall Losey
  E-Mail: president@i-n-b-a.org
Editor: Kathy Goodin
  E-Mail: editor@i-n-b-a.org
Secretary and Treasurer: Caroline Lawson
  E-Mail: secretary@i-n-b-a.org

Historical Note:
INBA's mission is to monitor and propose revisions to the breed standard, awards outstanding animals and breeders, and provide a forum for breeders to learn about, advertise, and encourage their breed. Membership: $10 (Individual); $20 (Family); $5 (Youth).

Publications:
Newsletter; adv.

Membership List Available to Non-members

International Nurses Society on Addititions *(1975)*
P.O. Box 14846
Lenexa, KS 66285-4846
Fax: (913) 895-4652
TollFree: (877) 646-8672
E-Mail: intnsa@intnsa.org
Website: intnsa.org
Members: 700 individuals
Staff: 4
Annual Budget: $100-250,000

Personnel:
Executive Director: Monica Evans-Lombe
  E-Mail: mevanslombe@goamp.com
Director, Governmental Affairs: Wade Delk
  E-Mail: wdelk@goamp.com
Administrative Assistant: Patricia (Pat) Payne
  E-Mail: patricia.payne@goamp.com
Meeting Planner: Barbara Tanner
  E-Mail: tonja.britt@goamp.com

Historical Note:
Formerly (1983) the National Nurses Society on Alcoholism, assumed its current name in 2000. IntNSA's mission is to help nurses provide comprehensive, quality nursing care for addicted patients and their families. Membership: $75-170/year.

Continuing Education:
Certification Designation/s: CARN-AP, CARN

Meetings/Conferences: Annual
Conference Chair: Barbara Tanner
2013 - Washington, DC (Madison Hotel)/Oct. 9 - 12
2014 - Washington, DC (Madison Hotel)/Oct. 15 - 18
Number of non-conference events/year: 6

Publications:
Counseling Points
IntNSA Today; quarterly
Journal of Addictions Nursing; quarterly
Membership Directory; on-line

International Oil Mill Superintendents Association *(1894)*
940 Mesa Vista Dr.
Crowley, TX 76036
Tel: (817) 297-4668 *Fax:* (817) 297-6016
E-Mail: general@iomsa.org
Website: iomsa.org
Members: 400 individuals
Staff: 2
Annual Budget: $50-100,000
Tax: 501(c)(6)

Personnel:
Secretary and Treasurer: Linda Paukert
  E-Mail: paukert.linda@sbcglobal.net

Historical Note:
Formerly Oil Mill Superintendents Association of Texas. Absorbed the International Oil Seed Superintendents Association and the Tri-States Oil Mill Superintendents Association in 1996. IOMSA is an organization serving the needs of superintendents of these mills. Membership: $100/year (Domestic/Foreign).

Meetings/Conferences: Annual
2013 - Denver, CO/June 16 - 18

Publications:
Member Directory; on-line
Oil Mill Gazetteer; monthly; adv.

International Oil Scouts Association *(1924)*
363 N. Sam Houston Pkwy. East
Suite 2020
Houston, TX 77060
Tel: (281) 847-6023
Website: oilscouts.com
Members: 100 individuals
Staff: 5
Annual Budget: Under $10,000
Tax: 501(c)(6)

Personnel:
Vice President, Membership Services: Don Grimm
  E-Mail: dgrimm@newfield.com

Historical Note:
Formerly (1960) the National Oil Scouts and Landmen's Association. IOSA's mission is to promote scouting and petroleum industry. Membership: $100/year.

Meetings/Conferences: Annual
Conference Chair: Pam Florek

International Ombudsman Association *(2005)*
390 Amwell Rd.
Suite 402
Hillsborough, NJ 08844
Tel: (908) 359-0246 *Fax:* (908) 842-0376
E-Mail: info@ombudsassociation.org
Website: ombudsassociation.org
Members: 600 individuals
Staff: 2
Annual Budget: $500-1,000,000
Tax: 501(c)(6)

Personnel:
President: Nicholas Diehl
  E-Mail: diehln@usa.redcross.org
Treasurer: Wayne Blair
  E-Mail: wblair@unc.edu

Historical Note:
Formed by the merger of the University and College Ombuds Association (UCOA) and The Ombudsman Association (TOA). IOA's mission is to support and advance the global organizational ombudsman profession and ensure that practitioners work to the highest professional standards. Membership: $195 (Regular); $160 (Associate); $135 (Affiliate); $45 (Retiree).

Continuing Education:
Certification Designation/s: CO-OP

Meetings/Conferences: Annual

2013 - Miami, FL (Hyatt Regency Miami)/April 21 - 24

Publications:
Journal of the International Ombudsman Association; on-line
Membership Directory; on-line
The Independent Voice

International Order of the Golden Rule (1928)
6405 Hwy.
90
Milton, FL 32570
Tel: (850) 623-2243 Fax: (850) 623-6345
E-Mail: info@ogr.org
Website: ogr.org
Members: 1000 funeral homes
Staff: 13
Annual Budget: $1-2,000,000
Tax: 501(c)(6)

Personnel:
President: Michael S. Lewis
E-Mail: mslewis1952@yahoo.com

Historical Note:
OGR's mission is to promote the image of the independent funeral home and provides resources and services through its for-profit Golden Services Group subsidiary. Members are locally-and family-owned and operated funeral homes, located throughout North America, and several overseas. Membership: $35 (Student); $150 (Auxiliary Member); $50 (Educator).

Continuing Education:
Enrollment: 300
Certification Designation/s: CEU

Meetings/Conferences: Annual
2013 - Memphis, TN (The Peabody Memphis)/April 25 - 28
Number of non-conference events/year: 1

Publications:
The Independent; quarterly; adv.
The Independent Brief; on-line

International Organization of Masters, Mates and Pilots (1887)
700 Maritime Blvd.
Suite B
Linthicum, MD 21090-1953
Tel: (410) 850-8700 Fax: (410) 850-0973
E-Mail: iommp@bridgedeck.org
Website: bridgedeck.org
Members: 6800 individuals
Staff: 50
Annual Budget: $5-10,000,000
Tax: 501(c)(5)

Personnel:
President: Timothy A. Brown
E-Mail: president@bridgedeck.org
Treasurer and Secretary: Donald Marcus
Director, Communications: Lisa Rosenthal
E-Mail: lrosenthal@bridgedeck.org

Historical Note:
MM&P is affiliated with the AFL-CIO, supports the Maritime Institute for Research and Industrial Development, member of the AFL-CIO's Transportation Trades Department (TTD) and Maritime Trades Department (MTD), and is very active with the International Transport Workers' Federation (ITF). MM & P is involved in the creation and enforcement of safe and humane standards for vessel safety on third world flag-of- convenience registered vessels whose crews have few advocates for their well-being.

Meetings/Conferences: Annual

Publications:
Master, Mate & Pilot; bi-monthly
Wheelhouse Weekly email; weekly

International Oxygen Manufacturers Association (1943)
1025 Thomas Jefferson St. NW
Suite 500 East
Washington, DC 20007
Tel: (202) 521-9300 Fax: (202) 833-3636
E-Mail: ioma@iomaweb.org
Website: iomaweb.org
Members: 140 companies
Staff: 2
Annual Budget: $250-500,000
Tax: 501(c)(6)

Personnel:

Executive Director: David A Saunders

Historical Note:
IOMA's members are the manufacturers of all of the industrial and medical gases (oxygen, nitrogen, argon, acetylene, carbon dioxide, hydrogen, etc.) or of equipment and supplies (plants, cylinders, valves, tanks, etc.) used by the industrial gas companies.

Meetings/Conferences: Annual

International Ozone Association-Pan American Group Branch (1973)
P.O. Box 28873
Scottsdale, AZ 85255
Tel: (480) 529-3787 Fax: (480) 473-9068
E-Mail: info3zone@io3a.org
Website: io3a.org
Members: 970 individuals and companies
Staff: 2
Annual Budget: $100-250,000
Tax: 501(c)(3)

Personnel:
Executive Director: Paul Overbeck
E-Mail: pauloverbeck@io3a.org

Historical Note:
Formerly (1978) the International Ozone Institute, Inc. IOA-PAGB is an educational association which performs its information-sharing functions through sponsorship of international symposia, seminars, publications, and the development of personal relationships among ozone specialists throughout the world. Membership: $50-825/year.

Meetings/Conferences: Annual

Publications:
Membership Directory; on-line

International Packaged Ice Association (1917)
P.O. Box 1199
Tampa, FL 33601-1199
Tel: (813) 258-1690 Fax: (813) 251-2783
TollFree: (800) 742-0627
Website: packagedice.com
Members: 400 companies
Staff: 5
Annual Budget: $500-1,000,000

Personnel:
Executive Director: Jane McEwen
E-Mail: jane@packagedice.org

Historical Note:
IPIA's mission is to provide the retailer and consumer with a safe, quality, consumable food product. Members are manufacturers and distributors of ice and their suppliers. Membership: $350 (Industry Member); $1,000-2,000 (Associate).

Meetings/Conferences: Annual

Publications:
Ice World Journal; quarterly
Membership Directory; annually

International Paralegal Management Association (1984)
P.O. Box 659
Avondale Estates, GA 30002-0659
Tel: (404) 292-4762 Fax: (404) 521-4233
E-Mail: info@paralegalmanagement.org
Website: paralegalmanagement.org
Members: 700 individuals
Staff: 2
Annual Budget: $250-500,000
Tax: 501(c)(6)

Personnel:
Executive Director: Michael J. Mazur Jr.
Director, Membership and Conferences Services: Ashley J. Mahaffey
E-Mail: ashley@theipma.org

Historical Note:
Formerly, Legal Assistant Management Association (LAMA) and was renamed as International Paralegal Management Association (2005). IPMA's mission is to promote the development, professional standing and visibility of paralegal management professionals. Membership: $250 (Regular); $225 (Associate); $175 (Academic); $150 (Govt./Non-profit); $50 (Emeritus); $1,400 (Corporate Sustaining); $350 (Individual Sustaining).

Meetings/Conferences: Annual
Conference Chair: Ashley J. Mahaffey
2013 - Orlando, FL (Hyatt Regency Grand Cypress)/Oct. 16 - 19

Publications:
IPMA at a Glance; monthly
Membership Directory; on-line
Paralegal Management Magazine; quarterly; adv.

International Parking Institute (1962)
P.O. Box 7167
Fredericksburg, VA 22404-7167
Tel: (540) 371-7535 Fax: (540) 371-8022
E-Mail: ipi@parking.org
Website: parking.org
Members: 1300 organizations
Staff: 11
Annual Budget: $2-5,000,000
Tax: 501(c)(6)

Personnel:
Executive Director: Shawn D. Conrad
E-Mail: conrad@parking.org
Executive Assistant and Associate, Publications: Aisha Adams
E-Mail: duckworth@parking.org
Finance Administrator: Faith Altman
E-Mail: altman@parking.org
Director, Membership Services: T. J. Cantwell
E-Mail: cantwell@parking.org
Certification Administrator: Lauri A. Chudoba
E-Mail: chudoba@parking.org
Editor: Kim Fernandez
E-Mail: fernandez@parking.org
Director, Convention and Meeting Services: Michelle W. Jones CMP
E-Mail: mjones@parking.org
Communications Counsel: Helen Sullivan
E-Mail: sullivan@parking.org
Vice President, Sales and Marketing: Bonnie L. Watts
E-Mail: watts@parking.org

Historical Note:
Formerly International Municipal Parking Congress and (1995) Institutional and Municipal Parking Congress. Until 1962 IPI was a branch of the National League of Cities that strives to provide leadership, information and education. IPI's mission is to provide leadership, information and education. Members are cities, colleges, hospitals, airports, port authorities, civic centers, state and federal government agencies, commercial parking operators and others concerned with parking, as well as suppliers and consultants. Membership: $595 (Regular); $298 (International); $50 (Student/Scholar); $100 (Transitional/Retiree).

Continuing Education:
Certification Designation/s: CAPP

Meetings/Conferences: Annual
Conference Chair: Michelle W. Jones CMP
2013 - Ft. Lauderdale, FL/May 19 - 22
2013 - Ft. Lauderdale, FL/May 19 - July 22/over 100 exhibitors
2014 - Grapevine, TX/June 1 - 4
2015 - Las Vegas, NV/June 29 - July 2
2016 - Nashville, TN/May 22 - 25

Publications:
IPI Parking Buyers Guide and Consultants Directory; annually; adv.
IPInsider; bi-weekly; adv.
The Parking Professional; monthly; adv.
Who's Who in Parking (Membership Directory); annually

International Pediatric Nephrology Association (1974)
General Clinical Research Center
10833 Le Conte Ave., 27-066 CHS
Los Angeles, CA 90095-1697
Tel: (310) 206-9295 Fax: (310) 206-9440
Website: ipna-online.org
Members: 1500 individuals
Staff: 3
Annual Budget: $1-2,000,000

Personnel:
Secretary General: Isidro B. Salusky MD
Membership and Subscriptions: Suzanne Conley
E-Mail: Suzanne@ipna-online.org

Historical Note:
IPNA is comprised of roughly 1500 pediatric nephrologists and allied professionals representing 89 countries around the world. Members are physicians specializing in pediatric kidney disease. Membership: $175/year.

Meetings/Conferences: Annual

Publications:

European Journal of Pediatrics
International Urology and Nephrology Journal
IPNA Currents
Member Directory; on-line
Pediatric Nephrology

International Pediatric Transplant Association
15000 Commerce Pkwy.
Suite C
Mt. Laurel, NJ 08054
Tel: (856) 439-0500 *Fax:* (856) 439-0525
E-Mail: info@iptaonline.org
Website: iptaonline.org
Members: 700 individuals
Staff: 3
Annual Budget: $500-1,000,000

Personnel:
Executive Director: Theresa "TC" Field
    E-Mail: tfield@ahint.com
Membership Coordinator: Caitlin Frontino
    E-Mail: cfrontino@ahint.com
Manager, Meetings: Meredith Weiner
    E-Mail: mweiner@ahint.com

Historical Note:
IPTA's purpose is to advance the science and practice of pediatric transplantation worldwide in order to improve the health of all children who require such treatment. It also dedicated to promoting technical and scientific advances in pediatric transplantation and to advocating for the rights of all children who need transplantation. Membership: $195 (Regular); $50 (Regular-Emerging Economy); $100 (Allied Professional); $50 (Allied Professional-Emerging Economy); $100 (Trainee); Free (Emeritus).

Meetings/Conferences: Annual
Conference Chair: Meredith Weiner

Publications:
IPTA Newsletter; on-line
Pediatric Transplantation; adv.

Membership List Available to Non-members

International Pet and Animal Transportation Association (1979)
2129 S. FM 2869
Suite Four
Hawkins, TX 75765
Tel: (903) 769-2267 *Fax:* (903) 769-2867
E-Mail: inquiries@ipata.com
Website: ipata.com
Members: 320 companies
Staff: 3
Annual Budget: $100-250,000
Tax: 501(c)(6)

Personnel:
Association Director: Cherie Derouin
    E-Mail: cherie@ipata.com
President: Sally Smith
Treasurer: Simon Jackson

Historical Note:
IPATA's mission is to strive for the safe and humane transport of pets and other animals. Members are companies providing animal transportation services. Membership: $375/year (Active/Associate).

Meetings/Conferences: Annual
2013 - Las Vegas, NV (Paris Las Vegas Hotel and
    Casino)/Nov. 2 - 5
Number of non-conference events/year: 2

Publications:
Membership Directory; quarterly

International Pharmaceutical Aerosol Consortium
1500 K St. NW
Suite 1100
Washington, DC 20005-1209
Tel: (202) 842-8465
E-Mail: comments@ipacmdi.com
Website: ipacmdi.com
Staff: 1

Personnel:
Secretary and Legal Counsel: Maureen Donahue
    Hardwick
    E-Mail: maureen.hardwick@dbr.com

Historical Note:
IPAC is committed to meeting the treatment needs of patients who suffer from asthma and chronic obstructive pulmonary disease (COPD) and represents manufacturers of metered-dose inhalers (MDIs).

International Pharmaceutical Excipients Council of the Americas (1991)
1655 N. Ft. Myer Dr.
Suite 700
Arlington, VA 22209
Tel: (703) 875-2127 *Fax:* (703) 525-5157
E-Mail: ipecamer@aol.com
Website: ipecamericas.org
Members: 60 U.S. companies
Staff: 5
Annual Budget: $1-2,000,000

Personnel:
Executive Director: Kimberly Beals CAE
    E-Mail: ipecamer@aol.com
Office Manager: Tammy Kramer
Treasurer: Alan M Mercill
Event Manager, Excipient Fest, Inc.: Marisol Perez
    E-Mail: marisol.perez@excipientfest.com
Information Systems Specialist, IPEC-Americas
    Administrator and Secretary and Treasurer: Valeria
    Stewart

Historical Note:
IPEC aims to develop, implement, and promote voluntary guidance and other programs for the world pharmaceutical industry. Members are companies with an interest in the otherwise inert chemicals used as vehicles for medicines. Membership: $8,400-28,000 (Full); $25 (Graduate Student); $100 (Academic); $350 (Individual Consultants and Companies, Pharmaceutical Industry Associations); $200 (Not for Profit Scientific Organization); $2000 (Distributors/Providers of Specialized Research Services). Affiliate member dues are 3/4 of the Full Member's annual dues)

Meetings/Conferences:
Conference Chair: Marisol Perez
Number of non-conference events/year: 2

Publications:
Journal of Excipients and Food Chemicals (JEFC);
    quarterly
Membership Directory
The Weekly Insider; weekly

Membership List Available to Non-members

International Physical Fitness Association (1960)
415 W. Court St.
Flint, MI 48503
Tel: (810) 239-2166 *Fax:* (810) 239-9390
TollFree: (877) 520-4732
E-Mail: contact@ipfa.us
Website: ipfa.us
Members: 1200 fitness centers
Staff: 2
Annual Budget: $10-25,000

Personnel:
President: Jerry Kahn
Secretary and Treasurer: Don Hudson

Historical Note:
Formerly (1975) Universal Gym Affiliates. IPFA coordinates reciprocity for its member gyms and clubs, allowing member facilities to offer access to sister fitness clubs worldwide. Membership: $125/year (Individual).

Meetings/Conferences: Annual

Publications:
Membership Directory; on-line

International Planetarium Society (1970)
P.O. box 4451
Hilo, HI 96720
Tel: (808) 969-9735 *Fax:* (808) 969-9748
Website: ips-planetarium.org
Members: 700 individuals
Staff: 3
Annual Budget: $50-100,000
Tax: 501(c)(6)

Personnel:
Treasurer and Membership Chair: Shawn Laatsch
    E-Mail: slaatsch@imiloahawaii.org

Historical Note:
Until 1976 known as the International Society of Planetarium Educators. Purpose is to encourage the sharing of ideas among its members through conferences, publications, networking and members become better planetarians. Membership: $65 (Individual); $250 (Institution); $450 (Corporate).

Meetings/Conferences: Biennial
2014 - Beijing, China (Beijing Planetarium)/June 23 -
27

Publications:
IPS News
Membership Directory; on-line
The; quarterly; adv.

International Plant Nutrition Institute (1935)
3500 Pkwy. Ln.
Suite 550
Norcross, GA 30092-2844
Tel: (770) 447-0335 *Fax:* (770) 448-0439
E-Mail: info@ipni.net
Website: ipni.net
Members:
16 companies
7 Affliate members
Staff: 5
Annual Budget: $10-25,000,000
Tax: 501(c)(6)

Personnel:
President: Dr. Terry L. Roberts
    E-Mail: TRoberts@ipni.net
Vice President, Administration: Steve Couch
    E-Mail: SCouch@ipni.net
Manager, Information Technology: Brian Green
    E-Mail: BGreen@ipni.net
Contact, Statistics and Accounting Services: Brenda Rose
    E-Mail: BRose@ipni.net
Editor: Gavin D. Sulewski
    E-Mail: GSulewski@ipni.net

Historical Note:
IPNI's mission is to develop and promote scientific information about the responsible management of plant nutrition for the benefit of the human family. Members are basic producers of one or more of the major plant nutrients (nitrogen, phosphate, potash, and sulfur) for agricultural purposes and large retail organizations.

Continuing Education:
Certification Designation/s: CCA

Publications:
Better Crops with Plant Food; quarterly
IPNI Insights; on-line

International Plant Propagators Society (1951)
Four Hawthorn Ct.
Carlisle, PA 17015-7930
Tel: (717) 243-7685 *Fax:* (717) 243-7691
E-Mail: secretary@ipps.org
Website: ipps.org
Members: 2100 individuals
Staff: 1
Annual Budget: $50-100,000

Personnel:
International Secretary and Treasurer: Patricia E. Heuser
    E-Mail: secretary@ipps.org

Historical Note:
IPPS's mission is to advance the art and science of growing plants, and to disseminate knowledge throughout the global community from and to those engaged in plant production. Membership includes those with an interest in ornamental horticulture, vegetable and fruit plant production, floriculture, silviculture, plantation crop production, amenity horticulture, and all other fields related to the production of plants for public use. Membership: $70-110/year (vary with the format of the association's journal the members prefer to receive).

Meetings/Conferences: Annual

Publications:
Combined Proceedings; annually
Propagation of Ornamental Plants; quarterly

International Plate Printers, Die Stampers and Engravers Union of North America (1893)
906 Dennis Ave.
Silver Spring, MD 20901
Tel: (301) 681-7052
Website: dpeaflcio.org/about/affiliates/
    internationa
Members: 200 individuals
Staff: 2
Annual Budget: $25-50,000

Personnel:
President: Daniel Bradley
Secretary and Treasurer: James L. Kopernick

Historical Note:
Organized in Boston in 1892 as the National Steel and Cooper Plate Printers of the United States of America and affiliated with the American Federation of Labor in 1898. Accepted Canadian members in 1901 and became the

International Plate Printers and Die Stampers Union of North American in 1921. A merger with the International Steel and Copper Plate Engravers League in 1925 resulted in adoption of the present title. Members are employed in the printing of U.S. and Canadian currency as well as stocks, bonds and foreign currency.

International Police Mountain Bike Association
(1991)
583 Frederick Rd.
Suite 5B
Baltimore, MD 21228
Tel: (410) 744-2400 *Fax:* (410) 744-5504
E-Mail: info@ipmba.org
Website: ipmba.org
Members: 3000 individuals
Staff: 5
Annual Budget: $250-500,000
Tax: 501(c)(3)

Personnel:
Executive Director: Maureen Becker
    E-Mail: maureen@ipmba.org
Coordinator, Membership: James Englert
    E-Mail: membership@ipmba.org
Treasurer: Kurt Feavel
    E-Mail: treasurer@ipmba.org
Coordinator, Conference: Tom Harris
    E-Mail: conferences@ipmba.org
Director, Education: Mitch Trujillo
    E-Mail: education@ipmba.org

Historical Note:
A non-profit educational organization providing resources, networking opportunities, and complete training for public safety bicyclists. Membership: $55 (Individual); $750 (Corporate).

Continuing Education:
Enrollment: 1200
Certification Designation/s: IPMBA-PCC, IPMBA-EMS, IPMBA-PSC, IPMBA-MOC, IPMBA-SCC, IPMBA-IC

Meetings/Conferences: Annual
Conference Chair: Tom Harris
2013 - Baton Rouge, LA/April 27 - May 4
2014 - Tampa, FL/May 16 - 23

Publications:
IPMBA News; quarterly; adv.

Membership List Available to Non-members

International Precious Metals Institute *(1976)*
5101 N. 12th Ave.
Suite C
Pensacola, FL 32504
Tel: (850) 476-1156 *Fax:* (850) 476-1548
E-Mail: mail@impi.org
Website: ipmi.org
Members: 1000 individuals and185 companies
Staff: 3
Annual Budget: $500-1,000,000
Tax: 501(c)(3)

Personnel:
Executive Director: J. P. Rosso
Administrative Assistant: Sandra T. Arrants
Legal Advisor: Peter L. Costas

Historical Note:
IPMI's mission is to provide a forum for the exchange of technical, financial, economic, environmental and other industry relevant information and an international networking opportunity for all delegates in attendance. Membership: $20-2000/year.

Meetings/Conferences: Annual
2013 - Phoenix, AZ (JW Marriott Phoenix Desert Ridge Resort and Spa)/June 22 - 25
2014 - Orlando, FL (JW Marriott Orlando Grande Lakes)/June 7 - 10

Publications:
Conference Proceedings; annually
IPMI Membership Directory; annually; adv.
Precious Metals News; monthly

International Premium Cigar and Pipe Retailers
(1933)
Four Bradley Park Ct.
Suite 2-H
Columbus, GA 31904-3637
Tel: (706) 494-1143 *Fax:* (706) 494-1893
E-Mail: info@ipcpr.org
Website: rtda.org
Members: 3000 tobacco retailers

Staff: 5
Annual Budget: $2-5,000,000

Personnel:
Chief Executive Officer: William S. Spann

Historical Note:
Formerly RTDA. IPCPR is a trade association representing and assisting premium retail tobacconists and their suppliers.The association provides its members with assistance to fight draconian and onerous tobacco legislation, and brings retailers and manufacturers together in mutually advantageous business relationships. Membership: $295 (Domestic (US) Retailer/International Retailer/International Distributor/Broker/Supplier); $600-2500 (Associate based on gross sales).

Meetings/Conferences: Annual

Publications:
IPCPR E-Newsletter; weekly
IPCPR Report; quarterly
Smokeshop
Tobacconist

International Private Infrastructure Association
(2004)
Two Wisconsin Cir.
Suite 700
Chevy Chase, MD 20815
Tel: (240) 235-6060 *Fax:* (240) 235-6061
E-Mail: assocmail@aol.com
Website: ipia.us
Staff: 1

Personnel:
Executive Director: Jay McCrensky PhD

Historical Note:
Founded as International Private Energy Association; assumed its current name in 2004. IPIA aims to establish, finance and administer Payment Contingency Funds and to support the Contingency Funds with tiers of reinsurance enabling an insurance wrap resulting in AAA bond ratings for the client infrastructure projects. Membership: $5000 (Sponsoring Member); $2500 (Basic Corporate); $500 (Individual).

International Professional Groomers *(1988)*
123 Manley Ave.
Greensboro, NC 27407
Tel: (336) 852-9867 *Fax:* (336) 299-7164
E-Mail: info@ipgicmg.com
Website: ipgicmg.com
Members: 800 individuals
Staff: 5
Annual Budget: Under $10,000

Personnel:
Executive Director: Hayley Keyes
    E-Mail: hayley@ipgicmg.com

Historical Note:
IPG is an organization for certification and continued education of dog groomers in the United States. IPG's mission is to provide a quality, personalized, convenient grooming service and also provides International industry standards for the professional pet groomer based upon the countries breed standards of perfection. Membership: $90/year.

Continuing Education:
Enrollment: 200
Certification Designation/s: ICMG

Meetings/Conferences:
Conference Chair: Hayley Keyes
Number of non-conference events/year: 10

Publications:
Directory of IPG Certified Groomers; annually; adv.
IPG Guidelines; adv.
IPG Newsletter; quarterly; adv.

International Professional Rodeo Association
(1957)
P.O. Box 83377
Oklahoma City, OK 73148
Tel: (405) 235-6540 *Fax:* (405) 235-6577
E-Mail: info@iprarodeo.com
Website: ipra-rodeo.com
Members: 3500 individuals
Staff: 5
Annual Budget: $1-2,000,000

Personnel:
National Director: Lisa Lance
    E-Mail: lisalance@coxinet.net
IFR Tradeshow Coordinator: Tammie Hiatt
    E-Mail: okropegirl1@att.net

Contact, CES, Insurance, Fines and Membership Services: Pam Queen
    E-Mail: pam@iprarodeo.com
General Manager, Sponsorships and IFR Marketing: Dale Yerigan
    E-Mail: dale@iprarodeo.com

Historical Note:
Formerly Interstate Rodeo Association (1963) and the International Rodeo Association (1983), IPRA is a governing body for professional rodeo that promotes the positive image of rodeo, preserve the Western Heritage, and maintains a better regard for the livestock. Membership: 275/year.

Meetings/Conferences: Annual
Conference Chair: Tammie Hiatt
2013 - Oklahoma City, OK/Jan. 18 - 20

Publications:
Rodeo News

International Psycho-Oncology Society *(1984)*
C/O Custom Management Group
154 Hansen Rd., Suite 201
Charlottesville, VA 22911
Tel: (434) 293-5350 *Fax:* (434) 977-1856
E-Mail: info@ipos-society.org
Website: ipos-society.org
Members: 325 individuals
Staff: 7
Annual Budget: $100-250,000
Tax: 501(c)(3)

Personnel:
Executive Director: Elliott Graham
    E-Mail: egraham@ipos-society.org
Director, Education: Jennifer Alluisi MA, Ed
    E-Mail: jalluisi@ipos-society.org
Manager, Membership Services: Laruen Baur
    E-Mail: lbaur@ipos-society.org
Accountant: Patricia Cuthbert
    E-Mail: pcuthbert@ipos-society.org
Program Director: Alison Holcomb
    E-Mail: aholcomb@ipos-society.org
Manager, Membership Services: Kendyl Kradz
    E-Mail: kkvad@ipos-society.org
Director, Publications and Website Services: Marilla Owens
    E-Mail: mowens@ipos-society.org

Historical Note:
The mission of IPOS is to be the international multi-disciplinary organization dedicated to fostering the science of psychosocial and behavioral oncology and improving the care of cancer patients and their families throughout the world. Membership: $45-95/year.

Meetings/Conferences: Annual
Conference Chair: Alison Holcomb

Publications:
Journal of Cancer Survivorship; quarterly
Palliative and Supportive Care; quarterly; adv.
Psycho-Oncology; monthly; adv.

Membership List Available to Non-members

International Psychogeriatric Association *(1982)*
550 Frontage Rd.
Suite 3759
Northfield, IL 60093
Tel: (847) 501-3310 *Fax:* (847) 501-3317
E-Mail: membership@ipa-online.org
Website: ipa-online.org
Members: 1400 individuals
Staff: 1
Annual Budget: $500-1,000,000
Tax: 501(c)(3)

Personnel:
Executive Director: Susan M. Oster CAE
    E-Mail: soster@ipa-online.org

Historical Note:
IPA' mission is to improve the mental health of older people everywhere through education, research, professional development, advocacy, health promotion, and service development. Members are health care professionals and academics with an interest in developments in mental health care related to the elderly. Membership: $40-120 (Physician); $25-75 (Non- Physician); $25-55 (Student/Retiree/Government Employee).

Meetings/Conferences:
2013 - Seoul, Republic of Korea (South Korea)/Oct. 1 - 4
Number of non-conference events/year: 1

Publications:
International Psychogeriatrics
IPA Bulletin
IPA Newsletter

International Psychohistorical Association (1977)
266 Monroe Ave.
Wyckhoff, NJ 07481-1915
Website: psychohistory.us
Members: 250 individuals
Staff: 3
Annual Budget: $10-25,000

Personnel:
President: Denis J. O'Keefe
   E-Mail: djo212@nyu.edu
Treasurer: Lloyd de Mause
   E-Mail: psychhst@gmail.com
Membership Secretary: Henry W. Lawton
   E-Mail: hwlipa@gmail.com

Historical Note:
IPA's goal is to further the study and teaching of psychohistory. Membership is open to scholars from all disciplines who are interested in advancing the study and practice of psychohistory. Membership: $40 (Individual); $1,000 (Lifetime).

Meetings/Conferences: Annual
Conference Chair: Henry W. Lawton

Publications:
Membership Directory; on-line
Psychohistory News

International Public Management Association for Human Resources (1906)
1617 Duke St.
Alexandria, VA 22314
Tel: (703) 549-7100 *Fax:* (703) 684-0948
E-Mail: ipma@ipma-hr.org
Website: ipma-hr.org
Members: 10000 individuals and 1300 agencies
Staff: 9
Annual Budget: $2-5,000,000
Tax: 501(c)(3)

Personnel:
Executive Director: Neil E. Reichenberg
   E-Mail: nreichenberg@ipma-hr.org
Senior Director, Government Affairs and Communications:
   Christina Chiappetta
   E-Mail: cchiapp@ipma-hr.org
Manager, Professional Development and Research:
   Heather Corbin
   E-Mail: hcorbin@ipma-hr.org
Chief Operating Officer: Sima Hassassian
   E-Mail: shassassian@ipma-hr.org
Director, Publications: Elizabeth Kirkland
   E-Mail: ekirkland@ipma-hr.org
Research Associate: Andrey Pankov
   E-Mail: apankov@ipma-hr.org
Manager, Accounting Services: Joanne Sisson
   E-Mail: jsisson@ipma-hr.org

Historical Note:
Formerly (1906) Civil Service Assembly of the United States and Canada, (1957) Public Personnel Association, then (1973) consolidated with Society for Personnel Administration to form International Personnel Management Association and assumed its current name in 2003. IPMA-HR strives to provide human resource leadership and advocacy, professional development, information and services to enhance organizational and individual performance in the public sector. Membership: $149 (Standard Individual); $50 (Entry-Level Professional); $105 (Online); $77 (Emeritus); $37 (Student).

Continuing Education:
Enrollment: 1000
Certification Designation/s: IPMA-CP, IPMA-HR, IPMA-CS

Meetings/Conferences: Annual
2013 - Las Vegas, NV (Tropicana Las Vegas)/Sept. 21 - 25
Number of non-conference events/year: 4

Publications:
HR Bulletin; weekly; adv.
HR News Magazine; monthly; adv.

International Radio and Television Society Foundation Inc. (1952)
1697 Broadway
Tenth Floor
New York, NY 10019
Tel: (212) 867-6650 *Fax:* (212) 867-6653

E-Mail: membership@irts.org
Website: irtsfoundation.org
Members: 1000 individuals
Staff: 6
Annual Budget: $1-2,000,000
Tax: 501(c)(3)

Personnel:
President and Chief Executive Officer: Joyce M. Tudryn
General Counsel and Secretary: Stuart Shorenstein

Historical Note:
Formerly (1962) Radio and Television Executives Society. Originally formed by a merger in 1952 of the Radio Executives Club (1939) and the American Television Society (1940). IRTS's mission is to build future media leaders via access, education and diversity. Members are professionals in radio, television, cable, advertising, and related areas, as well as interested members of the general public. Membership: $50-99 (Friend); $75-99 (Associate); $100-149 (Sponsor); $150-499 (Patron); $500-999 (Benefactor); $1,000-2,499 (Pacesetter); $2,500 (Legacy).

Meetings/Conferences:
Number of non-conference events/year: 2

International Reading Association (1956)
800 Barksdale Rd.
P.O. Box 8139
Newark, DE 19711
Tel: (302) 731-1600 *Fax:* (302) 731-1057
TollFree: (800) 336-7323
E-Mail: irawash@reading.org
Website: reading.org
Members: 70000 individuals
Staff: 6
Annual Budget: $250-500,000

Personnel:
Chief Executive Officer: Mark Mullen
   E-Mail: exec@reading.org
Executive Director: Marcie Craig Post
   E-Mail: exec@reading.org
Director, Budget and Finance: Deborah Harris
   E-Mail: dharris@reading.org
Director, Research and Professional Development: Gail
   Keating
   E-Mail: gkeating@reading.org
Director, Publications: Dan Mangan
   E-Mail: dmangan@reading.org

Historical Note:
Founded through a merger of the International Council for the Improvement of Reading Instruction and the National Association for Remedial Teaching. IRA's mission is to promote reading by continuously advancing the quality of literacy instruction and research worldwide. Members are classroom teachers, reading specialists, consultants, administrators, supervisors, college teachers, researchers, psychologists, and librarians. Membership: $39 (Individual); $24 (Student/Emeritus); $138-318 (Institutional).

Meetings/Conferences: Annual
2013 - San Antonio, TX/April 19 - 22

Publications:
Inspire e-newsletter; monthly
Journal of Adolescent & Adult Literacy; adv.
Reading Online; on-line
Reading Research Quarterly; quarterly; adv.
Reading Today; bi-monthly; adv.
The Reading Teacher; adv.

Membership List Available to Non-members

International Real Estate Federation - American Chapter (1949)
103 W. Broad St.
Suite 320
Falls Church, VA 22046
Tel: (703) 536-4279 *Fax:* (703) 991-6256
E-Mail: info@fiabci-usa.com
Website: fiabci-usa.com
Members: 347 members
Staff: 3
Annual Budget: Under $10,000
Tax: 501(c)(6)

Personnel:
President: Sharon K. Young
Treasurer: Edward Alford
Secretary General: Bill Endsley
   E-Mail: bill@fiabci-usa.com

Historical Note:
Headquartered in Paris, IREF-USA seeks to open the international community to its members on a local,

national, and international level, so that they may develop a broad base of real estate contacts that will translate into increased business opportunities and ultimately financial success. Members are real estate professionals and those in related fields. Membership: $605 (Young); $895 (Special); $845 (Regular) $1000 (Patron).

Meetings/Conferences: Annual
Number of non-conference events/year: 12

Publications:
Membership Directory; on-line; adv.

Membership List Available to Non-members

International Real Estate Institute (1975)
P.O. Box 879
Palm Springs, CA 92263
Tel: (760) 327-5284 *Fax:* (760) 327-5631
E-Mail: support@assoc-hdqts.org
Website: irei-assoc.org
Members: 5000 Individuals
Staff: 16
Annual Budget: $1-2,000,000

Personnel:
Executive Director: Robert G. Johnson

Historical Note:
Formerly (1984) the International Institute of Valuers. The primary objective of IREI is to provide professional recognition and a method to easily network with real estate professionals both internationally as well as within the United States. Members represent the area of real estate valuation, finance investment and development and management on an international level. Membership: $95-275/year.

Publications:
Membership Directory; annually
Newsletter; irregular

International Reciprocal Trade Association (1979)
524 Middle St.
Portsmouth, VA 23704
Tel: (757) 393-2292 *Fax:* (757) 257-4014
Website: irta.com
Members: 180 organizations
Staff: 2
Annual Budget: $250-500,000
Tax: 501(c)(6)

Personnel:
Executive Director: Ron Whitney
   E-Mail: ron@irta.com

Historical Note:
Formerly (1994) the International Association of Trade Exchanges. IRTA's mission is to provide all industry members with an ethically based global organization dedicated to the advancement of Modern Trade and Barter and other Alternative Capital Systems, through the use of education, self regulation, better standards and government relations. Membership: $250-5,000/year.

Continuing Education:
Certification Designation/s: CTB, RTB
Meetings/Conferences:
Number of non-conference events/year: 1

Publications:
Membership Directory; on-line
Newsletter

International Regional Magazine Association (1960)
P.O. Box 252
Montpelier, VT 05601-0252
Tel: (802) 522-6531 *Fax:* (888) 806-1533
E-Mail: irma@airpost.net
Website: regionalmagazines.org
Members: 41 publications
Staff: 1
Annual Budget: $100-250,000
Tax: 501(c)(6)

Personnel:
Executive Director: Andrew Jackson

Historical Note:
Formerly (1994) Regional Publishers Association. IRMA's purpose is to promote and support regional publishing generally and to encourage the free flow of information among member magazines. Membership: $995/year.

Meetings/Conferences: Annual

Publications:
The eSignature; on-line

International Reprographic Association (1927)

Seven First Ave.
Suite 1-04
Boston, MA 02116
Tel: (857) 334-4108 *Fax:* (312) 673-6724
TollFree: (800) 833-4742
E-Mail: info@irga.com
Website: irga.com
Members: 500 companies
Staff: 7
Annual Budget: $500-1,000,000
Tax: 501(c)(6)

Personnel:
Managing Director: Joel Salus

Historical Note:
Formerly (1973) the International Association of Blue Print and Allied Industries and (1980) as the International Reprographic Blueprint Association. IRgA's mission is to serve its member firms by providing services, benefits and information which improve member profitability and the industry image, and provide a forum for the exchange of information. Membership consists of wide format digital printing companies and reprographics equipment manufacturers and suppliers, focusing primarily on the construction industry. Membership: $395-2,295 (Reprographer); $695- 1,775 (Vendor).

Publications:
Membership Directory; on-line
News Digest; monthly; adv.

International Right of Way Association (1934)

19210 S. Vermont Ave., Bldg. A
Suite 100
Gardena, CA 90248
Tel: (310) 538-0233 *Fax:* (310) 538-1471
E-Mail: info@irwaonline.org
Website: irwaonline.org
Members: 10000 individuals
Staff: 21
Annual Budget: $2-5,000,000
Tax: 501(c)(6)

Personnel:
Executive Vice President: Mark Rieck
    E-Mail: rieck@irwaonline.org
Vice President, Publisher and Editor-in-Chief: Barbara Billitzer
    E-Mail: billitzer@irwaonline.org
Education Chief: Valerie J. Fries
    E-Mail: fries@irwaonline.org
Assistant Controller, Member Services: Bonnie Gray
    E-Mail: gray@irwaonline.org
Finance, Controller and Personal Manager: Rakhshan Mazarei
    E-Mail: rmazarei@irwaonline.org
Vice President and Chief Financial Officer: Fred Nasri CAE, CPA
    E-Mail: nasri@irwaonline.org
Vice President, Field Operations: Daniel Stekol
    E-Mail: stekol@irwaonline.org
Manager, Meetings and Events: Jade Yoong
    E-Mail: yoong@irwaonline.org
Computer Services Senior Manager: Sergey Yushkevich
    E-Mail: yushkevich@irwaonline.org

Historical Note:
Formerly the Southern California Right of Way Association. IRWA's mission is to be the central authority for the Right of Way profession, providing the tools members need to build and advance in their careers. Members include multi-disciplined professionals employed by private industry and government agencies Membership: $102.50-205 (U.S.).

Meetings/Conferences: Annual
Conference Chair: Jade Yoong

Publications:
Membership Directory; on-line
Right of Way Magazine; bi-monthly; adv.

International Road Federation (1948)

500 Montgomery St.
Fifth Floor
Alexandria, VA 22314
Tel: (703) 535-1001 *Fax:* (703) 535-1007
E-Mail: info@irfnews.org
Website: irfnet.org
Members: 750 companies and government agencies
Staff: 8
Annual Budget: $1-2,000,000
Tax: 501(c)(6)

Personnel:
President and Chief Executive Officer: Patrick C Sankey

Historical Note:
IRF's mission is to promote the education and understanding of the social, economic and environmental benefits which are derived from developing modern road networks, road transport systems and road traffic control. Encourage and promote the improvement of road safety. The IRF has a major role to play in all aspects of road policy and development worldwide. Membership: $800 (Universities/Colleges/Research Institutes); $1,900-18,000 (Governments); $2,100-10,000 (National Road Associations/Other Industry Related Organizations); $2,000-31,000 (Companies).

Meetings/Conferences:
2013 - Marrakech, Morocco (The Pullman Marrakech Palmeraie Resort & Spa)/March 19 - 20
2013 - Riyadh, Saudi Arabia/Nov. 9 - 13
2014 - Cheltenham, United Kingdom/May 18 - 21
Number of non-conference events/year: 2

Publications:
IRF Bulletin
IRF Newsletters
World Highways; monthly

International Rural Sociology Association (1976)

Ohio State University, International Program in Agriculture
2120 Fyffe Rd.
Columbus, OH 43085
Tel: (614) 292-7252 *Fax:* (614) 292-1757
Website: irsa-world.org
Members: 6 regional associations
Staff: 2
Annual Budget: Under $10,000
Tax: 501(c)(3)

Personnel:
President: Reidar Almas
    E-Mail: Reidar.almas@bygdeforskning.ntnu.no

Historical Note:
IRSA seeks to foster the development of rural sociology and to further the application of sociological inquiry to the improvement of the quality of rural life and provide a mechanism whereby rural sociologists can generate dialogue and useful exchange. Membership: $100-4000 (Regional Organization); $200-600 (Associate Organization); $20 (Individual).

International Safe Transit Association (1948)

1400 Abbott Rd.
Suite 160
East Lansing, MI 48823-1900
Tel: (517) 333-3437 *Fax:* (517) 333-3813
E-Mail: ista@ista.org
Website: ista.org
Members: 800 companies
Staff: 6
Annual Budget: $1-2,000,000
Tax: 501(c)(6)

Personnel:
President: Edward A. Church
    E-Mail: echurch@ista.org
Director, Special Events: Lisa Bonsignore
    E-Mail: lisa@ista.org
Manager, Business and Accounting Services: Barbara Church
    E-Mail: bchurch@ista.org
Vice President, Membership: Meredith Dougherty
    E-Mail: meredith@ista.org
Vice President ,Technical Services: A.J. Gruber
    E-Mail: ajgruber@ista.org
Director, Communications: Kathy A. Joneson
    E-Mail: kjoneson@ista.org

Historical Note:
Formerly (1974) National Safe Transit Committee, Inc. Became (1992) the National Safe Transit Association and (1994) National/International Safe Transit Association. ISTA's mission is to be focused on the specific concerns of transport packaging. Members are shippers, carriers, manufacturers, packagers, package designers, and testing laboratories interested in reducing damage to goods in transit. Membership: $600 (Carrier/Shipper/Supplier, without a Laboratory); $800-900 (Carrier/Shipper/Supplier, with a Laboratory); $100 (AssociateAdditional Location); $150 (Individual); $10-30 (Student).

Continuing Education:
Enrollment: 200
Certification Designation/s: CPLP

Meetings/Conferences: Semi-Annual
Conference Chair: Lisa Bonsignore

Publications:
i-News; adv.
ista views; adv.
Member Directory; on-line

International Safety Equipment Association (ISEA) (1933)

1901 N. Moore St.
Suite 808
Arlington, VA 22209-1762
Tel: (703) 525-1695 *Fax:* (703) 528-2148
E-Mail: isea@safetyequipment.org
Website: safetyequipment.org
Members: 80 companies
Staff: 6
Annual Budget: $1-2,000,000
Tax: 501(c)(6)

Personnel:
President: Daniel K. Shipp
    E-Mail: dshipp@safetyequipment.org
Office Assistant and Meeting Planner: Sabra L. Decker
    E-Mail: sdecker@safetyequipment.org
Director, Membership and Technical Services: Cristine Z. Fargo
    E-Mail: cfargo@safetyequipment.org
Public Affairs Director: Daniel I. Glucksman
    E-Mail: dglucksman@safetyequipment.org
Advisor, Marketing Communications: Joseph L. Walker III
    E-Mail: jwalker@safetyequipment.org

Historical Note:
ISEA's mission is to support and promote the common business interests of its member companies. Member companies are united in the goal of protecting the health and safety of people worldwide exposed to hazardous and potentially harmful environments. Members are manufacturers of personal protective equipments and clothing for workers.

Continuing Education:
Enrollment: 75

Meetings/Conferences: Annual
Conference Chair: Sabra L. Decker

Publications:
Market Intelligence Digest; weekly
Membership Directory; on-line
Protection Update; quarterly; adv.
Washington Report; semi-monthly

International SalonSpa Business Network (ISBN)

207 E. Ohio St.
Suite 361
Chicago, IL 60611
Tel: (866) 444-4272 *Fax:* (866) 444-5139
TollFree: (866) 444-4272
Website: salonspanetwork.org
Staff: 1
Annual Budget: $250-500,000

Personnel:
Manager, Business Development: Margie Melaniphy
    E-Mail: margie@salonspanetwork.org

Historical Note:
Formerly known as the International Chain Salon Association. ISBN is dedicated to help its members grow their businesses, effect positive change politically, provide a forum for members to share their views and ideas and interface with the professional beauty industry on behalf of the chain salons and spas. Membership: $895-1495/Year; $2000(Affiliate).

Meetings/Conferences: Annual
2013 - San Antonio, TX (Hyatt Hill Country Resort)/ May 19 - 21

International Sanitary Supply Association (1923)

7373 N. Lincoln Ave.
Lincolnwood, IL 60712-1799
Tel: (847) 982-0800 *Fax:* (847) 982-1012
TollFree: (800) 225-4772
E-Mail: info@issa.com
Website: issa.com
Members: 5500 companies
Staff: 36
Annual Budget: $10-25,000,000
Tax: 501(c)(6)

Personnel:
Executive Director: John Garfinkel
Director, Conventions and Meetings: Kimberly Althoff

E-Mail: kim@issa.com
Director, Environmental Services and Legislative Affairs:
  Bill Balek
  E-Mail: bill@issa.com
Manager, Marketing: Lauren Ketchum
  E-Mail: lauren@issa.com
Manager, Education: Martha Reynoso
  E-Mail: martha@issa.com
Director, Industry Outreach: Dianna Steinbach
  E-Mail: diannab@issa.com
Financial Manager: Donna Tode
  E-Mail: donna@issa.com
Director, Media Communications and Publications: Lisa
  Veeck
  E-Mail: lisav@issa.com
Manager, Operations: Tracy Weber
  E-Mail: tracy@issa.com
Director, Technology Services: Lori Zarling
  E-Mail: lori@issa.com

Historical Note:
*Formerly National Sanitary Supply Association and later
assumed its present name International Sanitary Supply
Association in the year 1966.ISSA's mission is to facilitate
ongoing networking, communications, and commercial
opportunities for the members, Provide members with the
highest quality, industry-specific, relevant information.*

Continuing Education:
Certification Designation/s: CIMS

Meetings/Conferences:
Conference Chair: Kimberly Althoff
2013 - Mexico City, DF/March 6 - 8
2013 - Mexico City, DF (World Trade Center)/March 13
  - 15
2013 - Las Vegas, NV (Las Vegas Convention Center)/
  Nov. 18 - 21
2014 - Amsterdam, Netherlands/May 6 - 9
2014 - Orlando, FL/Nov. 4 - 7
2015 - Las Vegas, NV/Oct. 20 - 23
2016 - Chicago, IL/Oct. 25 - 28
2017 - Las Vegas, NV/Oct. 17 - 20

Publications:
Buyers' Guide; on-line
CleanScene e-Newsletter; monthly; adv.
Exhibit Zone
ISSA Formulator News; on-line
ISSA Times e-newsletter; monthly
ISSA Today; bi-monthly; adv.
ISSAlerts; annually
Legislative and Regulatory Update Newsletter; monthly
Membership Directory; on-line
Sanitation Canada

International Saw and Knife Association *(1965)*
12880 Bel-Red Rd.
Bellevue, WA 98005
Tel: (425) 454-7627 *Fax:* (425) 454-4274
Website: iska.org
Members: 200 companies
Staff: 3
Annual Budget: $25-50,000

Personnel:
Membership Chair: Mike Lindsay
  E-Mail: mikel@eastsidesaw.com

Historical Note:
*Formerly the National Association of Saw Shops, assumed
its present name in 1983. ISKA's mission is to further
the interests of individuals, partnerships and corporations
in the saw works business by improving the prestige
of the industry and by working for the betterment of
educational and other measures fulfilling the purpose
of this corporation. Members are companies repairing,
selling, manufacturing or servicing large band and circular
saws, paper knives, shear blades, circular slitters and
metal cutting bands. Membership: $125 (Regular); $225
(Associate).*

Meetings/Conferences:
Conference Chair: Mike Lindsay
Number of non-conference events/year: 24

Publications:
Cutting Times- Newsletter; quarterly

International Sculpture Center *(1960)*
19 Fairgrounds Rd.
Suite B
Hamilton, NJ 08619
Tel: (609) 689-1051 *Fax:* (609) 689-1061
Website: sculpture.org
Staff: 20

Annual Budget: $1-2,000,000

Personnel:
Executive Director: Johannah Hutchison
  E-Mail: johannah@sculpture.org
Manager, Membership Services: Julie Hain
  E-Mail: julie@sculpture.org
Editor: Glenn Harper
  E-Mail: gharper@sculpture.org
Web and Portfolio Manager: Karin Jervert
  E-Mail: karin@sculpture.org
Office Manager: Denise Jester
  E-Mail: denise@sculpture.org
Development Manager: Candice Lombardi
  E-Mail: candice@sculpture.org
Advertising Sales Manager: Brenden O'Hanlon
  E-Mail: advertising@sculpture.org
Coordinator, Conferences and Events: Samantha
  Rauscher
  E-Mail: samantha@sculpture.org

Historical Note:
*ISC's mission is to expand public understanding and
appreciation of sculpture internationally and promote
a supportive environment for sculpture and sculptors.
Membership: $100-120 (Individual); $200-220
(Organizations).*

Meetings/Conferences:
Conference Chair: Samantha Rauscher
Number of non-conference events/year: 1

Publications:
Sculpture; monthly; adv.
The Insider Newsletter

International Security Management Association *(1983)*
P.O. Box 623
Buffalo, IA 52728-0623
Tel: (563) 381-4008 *Fax:* (563) 381-4283
E-Mail: isma3@aol.com
Website: isma.com
Members: 400 individuals
Staff: 3
Annual Budget: $1-2,000,000

Personnel:
Deputy Administrator: Liz Chamberlin
  E-Mail: liz@isma.com
Treasurer: Zack Lowe
Consulting Business Manager: Susan W. Pohlmann
  E-Mail: isma3@aol.com

Historical Note:
*ISMA's mission is to provide and support an international
forum of selected security executives whose combined
expertise will be utilized in a synergistic manner in
developing, organizing, assimilating, and sharing
knowledge within security disciplines for the ultimate
purpose of enhancing professional and business standards.
Members are corporate security directors and executives of
full service security service firms. Membership: $1,500/
year.*

Publications:
Membership Directory; on-line

International Shippers Association *(1999)*
5904 Richmond Hwy.
Suite 404
Alexandria, VA 22303
Tel: (703) 317-9950 *Fax:* (703) 317-9960
E-Mail: info@isaship.org
Website: isaship.org
Staff: 7

Personnel:
Director: Terry R. Head
  E-Mail: terry.head@iamovers.org

Historical Note:
*ISA's purpose is to provide its membership with the lowest
comparative rates (FCL & LCL) and best service for the
movement of household goods throughout the world
by establishing volume-induced discounts through ISA
preferred vendors. Membership: $200 (IAM Members);
$400 (Non IAM Members).*

Continuing Education:
Certification Designation/s: FCL, LCL

Publications:
Membership Directory; on-line

Membership List Available to Non-members

International Sign Association *(1944)*
1001 N. Fairfax St.

Suite 301
Alexandria, VA 22314
Tel: (703) 836-4012 *Fax:* (703) 836-8353
TollFree: (866) 949-7446
E-Mail: info@signs.org
Website: signs.org
Members: 2300 manufacturers, suppliers and
distributors
Staff: 18
Annual Budget: $5-10,000,000
Tax: 501(c)(6)

Personnel:
President and Chief Executive Officer: Lori Anderson
  E-Mail: lori.anderson@signs.org
Executive Vice President: Rich Gottwald
  E-Mail: rich.gottwald@signs.org
Director, Education and Communications: Tracey Cook
  E-Mail: tracey.cook@signs.org
Director, Technical and Regulatory Affairs: Bill Dundas
  E-Mail: bill.dundas@signs.org
Vice President, Government Relations: David T. Hickey
  E-Mail: david.hickey@signs.org
Director, Meetings and Events: Iain Mackenzie
  E-Mail: iain.mackenzie@signs.org
*Program Manager, Education and Professional
  Development:* Denise Miller
  E-Mail: denise.miller@signs.org
Director, Education: Matthew Rumbaugh
  E-Mail: matt.rumbaugh@signs.org
Director, Marketing: Sarah Singleton
  E-Mail: sarah.singleton@signs.org
Vice President, Finance: Bill Winslow
  E-Mail: bill.winslow@signs.org

Historical Note:
*ISA is strives to support, promote and improve the sign
industry through government advocacy, education and
training programs, technical resources, stakeholder outreach
and industry networking events. Represents sign users,
sign supply distributors, product manufacturers, and sign
companies manufacturing on-premise signs. Membership:
$100-1,650/year.*

Meetings/Conferences:
Conference Chair: Iain Mackenzie
2013 - Las Vegas, NV (Mandalay Bay Convention
  Center)/April 3 - 6/over 100 exhibitors
Number of non-conference events/year: 2

Publications:
ISA Directory; on-line; adv.
ISA Insider; monthly
ISA Signals; bi-monthly
ISA Smartbrief; weekly; adv.
Signline; annually; adv.

Membership List Available to Non-members

International Silo Association *(1907)*
E106 Church Rd.
Luxemburg, WI 54217
Tel: (920) 655-3301
E-Mail: info@silo.org
Website: silo.org
Members: 14 companies
Staff: 1
Annual Budget: $50-100,000

Personnel:
President: Leroy Shefchik

Historical Note:
*Formerly (1956) the National Association of Silo
Manufacturers and (1990) the Feed Automation
Association. Members manufacture crop storage facilities.*

International Sled Dog Racing Association *(1966)*
22702 Rebel Rd.
Merrifield, MN 56465
Tel: (218) 765-4297 *Fax:* (218) 765-3246
Website: isdra.org
Members: 750 individual members
Staff: 1
Annual Budget: $50-100,000

Personnel:
Executive Director: Dave Steele
  E-Mail: dsteele@brainerd.net

Historical Note:
*ISDRA's mission is to advocate public interest in the sport,
encourage cooperation between race organizations, create
and maintain standardized race management procedures,
advocate the highest standards of animal welfare for
canine athletes and aid in sponsor relations for ISDRA*

members and ISDRA sanctioned events. Membership: $40 (Individual); $20 (Family Members); $30 (Associate); $110 (Club/RGO).

Publications:
Dog and Driver Magazine; bi-monthly; adv.
Dog and Driver Newsletter

International Sleep Products Association (1915)
501 Wythe St.
Alexandria, VA 22314-1917
Tel: (703) 683-8371 Fax: (703) 683-4503
E-Mail: info@sleepproducts.org
Website: sleepproducts.org
Members: 700 companies
Staff: 21
Annual Budget: $2-5,000,000
Tax: 501(c)(6)

Personnel:
President: Ryan T. Trainer
    E-Mail: rtrainer@sleepproducts.org
Vice President, Sales: Kerri Bellias
    E-Mail: kbellias@sleepproducts.org
Chief Financial Officer: Bob Bobowski CPA
    E-Mail: bbobowski@sleepproducts.org
Director, Marketing and Member Services: Deb Chapman
    E-Mail: dchapman@sleepproducts.org
Vice President, Government Relations & Policy:
    Christopher Hudgins
    E-Mail: chudgins@sleepproducts.org
Senior Vice President, Finance, Meetings and Exhibitions:
    Catherine Lyons
    E-Mail: clyons@sleepproducts.org
Director, Communications: Karin Mahoney
    E-Mail: kdillner@sleepproducts.org
Manager, Database and Website Operations: Deborah
    Nicholas
    E-Mail: dnicholas@sleepproducts.org
Manager, Member Services: Jane Oseth
    E-Mail: joseth@sleepproducts.org
Chief Editor: Julie Palm
    E-Mail: jpalm@sleepproducts.org
Vice President, Membership and Communications: Mary
    Helen Uusimaki
    E-Mail: mhuusimaki@sleepproducts.org

Historical Note:
Formerly (1986) National Association of Bedding Manufacturers and affiliate organizations include the Better Sleep Council and the Sleep Products Safety Council. ISPA is dedicated to protecting and enhancing the growth, profitability and stature of the mattress industry. Members are mattress manufacturers and bedding component, machinery and service suppliers. Membership: $600-4000/year.

Meetings/Conferences:
Conference Chair: Catherine Lyons
2013 - Orlando, FL (Disney's Grand Floridian Resort and Spa)/March 6 - 7
2013 - Cologne, Germany/May 13 - 16/over 100 exhibitors
2014 - New Orleans, LA (New Orleans Morial Convention Center)/March 26 - 29
2016 - Orlando, FL/March 16 - 19
Number of non-conference events/year: 1

Publications:
BedTimes Supplies Guide; on-line
ISPA Advocacy Connection; monthly
ISPA Insider; weekly
Membership Directory; on-line
Sleep Savvy magazine; on-line

International Slurry Surfacing Association (1963)
Three Church Cir.
P.O. Box 250
Annapolis, MD 21401
Tel: (410) 267-0023 Fax: (410) 267-7546
Website: slurry.org
Members: 200 companies
Staff: 3
Annual Budget: $500-1,000,000

Personnel:
Executive Director: Mike Krissoff
    E-Mail: krissoff@slurry.org
General Counsel: David H. Baker
    E-Mail: david.baker@dhbakerlaw.com
Director, Member Services: Lisa Cerone
    E-Mail: cerone@slurry.org

Historical Note:

Formerly known as the International Slurry Seal Association (1990). ISSA is an international non-profit trade association comprised of contractors, equipment manufacturers, public officials, research personnel, consulting engineers and other industry professionals, working together to promote the concept of pavement preservation. ISSA promotes the standards of ethics and quality while providing its members with information, technical assistance and ongoing opportunities for networking and professional development. Membership: $100-3,000/year.

Meetings/Conferences: Annual
2013 - Indian Wells, CA (Renaissance Esmeralda Indian Wells Resort and Spa)/Feb. 19 - 23
Number of non-conference events/year: 2

Publications:
ISSA Report - Newsletter; quarterly; adv.
Membership Directory; annually

Membership List Available to Non-members

International Snowmobile Manufacturers Association (1995)
1640 Haslett Rd.
Suite 170
Haslett, MI 48840
Tel: (517) 339-7788 Fax: (517) 339-7798
E-Mail: ismasue@aol.com
Website: snowmobile.org
Members: 4 manufacturers
Staff: 2
Annual Budget: $500-1,000,000
Tax: 501(c)(6)

Personnel:
President: Edward J. Klim ScD

Historical Note:
Formerly (1995) the International Snowmobile Industry Association. Organized and incorporated in Michigan. ISMA serves the interests of the snowmobile manufacturing industry as well as recreational snowmobiling.

Publications:
E-Newsletter

International Society for Adolescent Psychiatry and Psychology (1984)
P.O. Box 570218
Dallas, TX 570218
Tel: (972) 686-6166 Fax: (972) 754-2197
E-Mail: adpsych@aol.com
Website: isapp.org
Members: 500 individuals
Staff: 1
Annual Budget: $10-25,000

Personnel:
Administrative Officer: Frances Roton Bell
    E-Mail: frda1@airmail.net

Historical Note:
ISAPP's purpose is to provide a forum for intellectual exchange among professionals concerned with disturbed adolescents. Members are psychiatrists, psyschologists, and allied professionals working with disturbed adolescents in several parts of the world. Membership: $75/year (Individual).

Meetings/Conferences:
Number of non-conference events/year: 1

Publications:
ISAPP Newsletter; semi-annually
Member Directory; on-line

International Society for Advancement Cytometry
9650 Rockville Pike
Bethesda, MD 20814-3998
Tel: (301) 634-7435 Fax: (301) 634-7099
E-Mail: isac@isac-net.org
Website: isac-net.org
Members: 1900 individuals
Staff: 2
Annual Budget: $1-2,000,000

Personnel:
Interim Executive Director: Joan R. Goldberg
    E-Mail: toddp@isac-net.org
Treasurer: Paul K. Wallace
    E-Mail: pkw@rpciflow.org

Historical Note:
Formerly International Society for Analytical Cytology. ISAC is a scientific and educational organization that leads the way in development of cytometry, transfer of new methodologies, and exchange of cutting-edge scientific and technical information in quantitative cell sciences. Members

are scientists interested in the study of the cell. Membership: $10 (Emeritus); $5-304 (Student); $126 (Full Member).

Publications:
Cytometry; monthly

Membership List Available to Non-members

International Society for Antiviral Research (1987)
2025 M St. NW
Suite 800
Washington, DC 20036
Tel: (202) 973-8690 Fax: (202) 331-0111
E-Mail: isar@courtesyassoc.com
Website: isar-icar.com
Members: 414 individuals
Staff: 2
Annual Budget: $250-500,000

Personnel:
President: Phillip Furman
Treasurer: Dale Barnard

Historical Note:
ISAR is an internationally recognised organization for scientist involved in basic, applied, and clinical aspects of antiviral research. Membership: $150/year.

Meetings/Conferences: Annual
2013 - San Francisco, CA (Hyatt Regency Embarcadero Hotel)/May 11 - 15

Publications:
ISAR News; bi-annually
Membership Directory; on-line

International Society for Astrological Research (1960)
P.O. Box 771430
Lakewood, OH 44107
Website: isarastrology.com
Staff: 4

Personnel:
President: Gisele Terry
Secretary, Membership: Marguerite Dar Boggia
Operations Manager and Journal Publisher: Richard Smoot

Historical Note:
ISAR is dedicated to encouraging the highest standards of quality in astrology.by offering a certification program that emphasizes ethics awareness, competence in techniques and interpretation, and consulting skills, by networking with other organizations to provide the best astrological educational services possible. Membership: $49 (Individual).

Continuing Education:
Certification Designation/s: CAP

Meetings/Conferences: Annual

Publications:
e-newsletter; weekly
ISAR's International Astrologer; adv.
Membership Directory; on-line

International Society for Clinical Densitometry (1993)
306 Industrial Park Rd.
Suite 208
Middletown, CT 06457
Tel: (860) 259-1000 Fax: (860) 259-1030
E-Mail: iscd@iscd.org
Website: iscd.org
Members: 6000 individuals
Staff: 8
Annual Budget: $2-5,000,000
Tax: 501(c)(3)

Personnel:
Executive Director: Peter Brown
    E-Mail: pbrown@iscd.org
Director, Education: Sue Alexander
    E-Mail: salexander@iscd.org
Administrative Coordinator: Anabela Coyne
    E-Mail: acoyne@iscd.org
Legislative Counsel: Donna M. Fiorentino
    E-Mail: dfiorentino@iscd.org
Manager, Meetings and Educational Programs: Meghan
    Girard
    E-Mail: mgirard@iscd.org
Web and Technology Manager: Tim Kiefer
    E-Mail: tkiefer@iscd.org
Director, Operations and Certification: Mary Saier
    E-Mail: msaier@iscd.org

Educational Programs and Publications Assistant: Amy Scrivens
E-Mail: ascrivens@iscd.org

Historical Note:
ISCD works to advance excellence in the assessment of skeletal health by promoting education and a broader understanding of the clinical applications of bone mass measurement and other skeletal health assessment technologies. Membership: $300 (Full - Clinician/Scientist/Researcher); $85-130 (Technologist); $65-110 (Associate/Retired); $65-220 (International).

Continuing Education:
Enrollment: 13581
Certification Designation/s: CBDT, CCD, CDT

Meetings/Conferences: Annual

Publications:
Certification Registry; on-line
Journal of Clinical Densitometry; quarterly; adv.
Members Online Directory; on-line
News You Can Use E-Newsletter; monthly
OsteoFlash; on-line
SCAN Newsletter; quarterly

Membership List Available to Non-members

International Society for Computational Biology
9500 Gilman Dr.
MC 0505
La Jolla, CA 92093-0505
Tel: (858) 822-0852 *Fax*: (760) 888-0313
E-Mail: admin@iscb.org
Website: iscb.org
Members: 3000 members
Staff: 3
Annual Budget: $1-2,000,000
Tax: 501(c)(3)

Personnel:
Executive Officer: BJ Morrison McKay
E-Mail: bj@iscb.org
Administrative Support: Suzi Smith
E-Mail: admin@iscb.org

Historical Note:
A scholarly society dedicated to advancing the scientific understanding of living systems through computation.

International Society for Computerized Electrocardiology (1984)
11495 Emmanuel Way
Suite 518
Solomons, MD 20688-3031
Tel: (410) 394-3216 *Fax*: (410) 394-3219
E-Mail: isceoffice@comcast.net
Website: isce.org
Staff: 3
Annual Budget: $100-250,000

Personnel:
President: Rory W. Childers MD
Treasurer: Denis W. Drew MD
Contact, Conference and Membership Services: Martha R. Horton
E-Mail: marthahorton@comcast.net

Historical Note:
ISCE is devoted to the advancement of electrocardiology through the application of computer methods. It promotes the dissemination of research results through publication of conference proceedings and provision of a venue for validating computer programs and development of databases for such validation. Membership: $250/year.

Meetings/Conferences: Annual
Conference Chair: Martha R. Horton
2013 - San Jose, CA (Dolce Hayes Mansion)/April 17 - 21

International Society for Developmental Psychobiology (1967)
8181 Tezel Rd.
Suite 10269
San Antonio, TX 78250
Tel: (830) 796-9393 *Fax*: (830) 796-9394
TollFree: (866) 377-4416
E-Mail: isdp@isdpcentraloffice.org.
Website: isdp.org
Members: 300 individuals
Staff: 5
Annual Budget: $100-250,000
Tax: 501(c)(3)

Personnel:
President: Scott Robinson

Conference Coordinator: Julien Gross
E-Mail: jules@psy.otago.ac.nz
Treasurer: Jane Herbert
E-Mail: j.s.herbert@sheffield.ac.uk
Program Director: Susan Swithers
E-Mail: swithers@purdue.edu
Webmaster: Marianne Van Wagner
E-Mail: isdp@isdpcentraloffice.org

Historical Note:
ISDP's mission is to foster the application of valid findings of research on human affairs in a way beneficial to mankind, and to encourage research on the development of behavior in all organisms including man, with special attention to the effects of biological factors operating at any level of organization. Membership: $120 (Postdoctoral); $170 (Regular); $90 (Student).

Meetings/Conferences: Annual
Conference Chair: Julien Gross

Publications:
Developmental Psychobiology Journal; on-line; adv.
ISDP Newsletter
Membership Directory; on-line; adv.

International Society for Ecological Economics (1989)
15 River St.
Suite 204
Boston, MA 02108
E-Mail: secretariat@ecoeco.org
Website: ecoeco.org
Members: 1000 individuals
Staff: 2
Annual Budget: $50-100,000
Tax: 501(c)(3)

Personnel:
Managing Editor and Executive Secretary: Anne Carter Aitken
E-Mail: accarter@bu.edu

Historical Note:
ISEE is a not-for-profit, member-governed, organization dedicated to advancing understanding of the relationships among ecological, social, and economic systems for the mutual well-being of nature and people. Members are researchers, academics, and other professionals who study the impact of economic models and policies on the environment. The Society assists its members and ecological economists, regional societies of ecological economics, related societies, and other organizations in such matters of common concern which can be dealt with effectively by united action. Membership: $7.50-70/year.

Meetings/Conferences: Biennial

Publications:
Ecological Economics; adv.
ISEE Newsletter; bi-annually

International Society for Ecological Modelling-North American Chapter (1975)
550 M Ritchie Hwy.
P.O. Box 255
Severna Park, MD 21146
Website: isemna.org
Members: 150 individuals
Staff: 3
Annual Budget: Under $10,000

Personnel:
President: Sven E. Jørgensen
Webmaster: Jonathan Clough
E-Mail: webmaster@isemna.org
Treasurer: David A Mauriello

Historical Note:
ISEM promotes the international exchange of general knowledge, ideas and scientific results in the area of the application of systems analysis and simulation to ecology, environmental science and natural resource management using mathematical and computer modelling of ecological systems. Membership: $10 (Student); $20 (Regular); $100 (Institutional).

Meetings/Conferences: Biennial
2013 - Toulouse, France (Toulouse University)/Oct. 28 - 31

Publications:
ECOMOD; irregular

International Society for Educational Planning (1970)
2903 Ashlawn Dr.
Blacksburg, VA 24060-8101
Website: isep.info

Members: 350 individuals
Staff: 3
Annual Budget: $50-100,000
Tax: 501(c)(3)

Personnel:
Secretary and Treasurer: Dr. Glen I. Earthman
E-Mail: earthman@vt.edu

Historical Note:
ISEP's mission is to improve education through the application of planning processes. Members are school administrators and school district executives. Membership: $125 (Professional/Institutional); $50 (Student).

Meetings/Conferences: Annual
Conference Chair: Linda Lemasters

Publications:
Educational Planning; quarterly; adv.

International Society for Heart and Lung Transplantation (1981)
14673 Midway Rd.
Suite 200
Addison, TX 75001
Tel: (972) 490-9495 *Fax*: (972) 490-9499
E-Mail: ishlt@ishlt.org
Website: ishlt.org
Members: 2500 Members
Staff: 5
Annual Budget: $2-5,000,000

Personnel:
Executive Director: Amanda W. Rowe
E-Mail: amanda.rowe@ishlt.org
Director, Meetings: Lisa Edwards
E-Mail: lisa.edwards@ishlt.org
Director, Membership Services: Phyllis Glenn
E-Mail: phyllis.glenn@ishlt.org
Director, Operations: Lee Ann Mills
E-Mail: leeann.mills@ishlt.org
Managing Editor and Webmaster: Susie Newton
E-Mail: susie.newton@ishlt.org

Historical Note:
Formerly (1991) International Society for Heart Transplantation, ISHLT is a multidisciplinary, professional organization that strives to improve the care of patients with advanced heart or lung disease through transplantation, mechanical support and innovative therapies via research, education and advocacy. Membership: $310 (Regular); $155 (Student/Resident).

Meetings/Conferences: Annual
Conference Chair: Lisa Edwards
2013 - Montreal, QC (Palais Des Congres de Montreal)/April 24 - 27
2014 - San Diego, CA (Manchester Grand)/April 9 - 12

Publications:
ISHLT Links Newsletter; monthly
Membership Directory; on-line
Monograph Series; annually
The Journal of Heart and Lung Transplantation; monthly; adv.

International Society for Infectious Diseases (1986)
Nine Babcock St.
Third Floor
Brookline, MA 02446
Tel: (617) 277-0551 *Fax*: (617) 278-9113
E-Mail: info@isid.org
Website: isid.org
Members: 55000 individuals
Staff: 9
Annual Budget: $2-5,000,000

Personnel:
Executive Director: Norman R. Stein
Coordinator, Program and Membership: Amy Galblum
Editor: Larry Madoff
Administrative Assistant: Laurence Mialot
Conference Manager: Doris Steinbach
Program Director: Eric F. Summers
Manager, Information Technology: Drew Tenenholz

Historical Note:
ISID strives to increase the knowledge base of infectious diseases through research and enhance the professional development of individuals in this discipline. Membership: $40/year.

Meetings/Conferences: Annual
Conference Chair: Eric F. Summers
2013 - Vienna, Austria (Hilton Vienna)/Feb. 15 - 18

Publications:

International Journal of Infectious Diseases
ISID NEWS; quarterly

International Society for Magnetic Resonance in Medicine (1994)
2030 Addison St.
Seventh Floor
Berkeley, CA 94704
Tel: (510) 841-1899 *Fax:* (510) 841-2340
E-Mail: info@ismrm.org
Website: ismrm.org
Members: 8500 individuals
Staff: 17
Annual Budget: $5-10,000,000
Tax: 501 (c)(3)

Personnel:
Executive Director: Roberta A. Kravitz
    E-Mail: roberta@ismrm.org
Director, Finance: Mariam Barzin
    E-Mail: mariam@ismrm.org
Director, Education: Jacob Coverstone
    E-Mail: jacob@ismrm.org
Director, Meetings: Sandra Daudlin
    E-Mail: sandra@ismrm.org
Director, Publications: Mary Keydash
    E-Mail: mary@ismrm.org
Director, Electronic Communications: Sally Moran
    E-Mail: sally@ismrm.org
Director, Membership and Study Groups: Jerusha Rich
    E-Mail: jerusha@ismrm.org

Historical Note:
Formed as a merger of the Society for Magnetic Resonance Imaging and the Society of Magnetic Resonance in Medicine in 1994, assumed its current name in 1996. ISMRM's mission is to enhance communication, research, development and applications in the field of magnetic resonance in medicine and biology and other related topics and to develop and provide channels and facilities for continuing education in the field. Membership: $235-395 (Full Member), $30-240 (Student); $30 (Associate); $80 (Technologist).

Continuing Education:
Certification Designation/s: ABMP, ARR

Meetings/Conferences: Annual
Conference Chair: Sandra Daudlin
2013 - Salt Lake City, UT (Salt Palace Convention Center)/April 20 - 26
2014 - Milan, Italy/May 10 - 16
2015 - Toronto, ON/May 30 - June 5
2016 - Singapore, Singapore/May 7 - 13

Publications:
Journal of Magnetic Resonance Imaging; monthly; adv.
Magnetic Resonance in Medicine; monthly; adv.
Membership Directory; on-line

International Society for Medical Publication Professionals (2005)
Three Hillcrest Dr.
P.O. Box 2523
Briarcliff Manor, NY 10510
Fax: (914) 618-4453
E-Mail: ismpp@ismpp.org
Website: ismpp.org
Staff: 5
Annual Budget: $1-2,000,000
Tax: 501 (c)(6)

Personnel:
Executive Director: Kimberly Goldin
    E-Mail: kgoldin@ismpp.org
Director, Projects and Technical Services: Michele Kantrowitz
    E-Mail: mkantrowitz@ismpp.org
Treasurer: Rosie Lynch
Manager, Membership and Logistics: Sue Marek
    E-Mail: smarek@ismpp.org
Director, Credentialing: Danita Sutton
    E-Mail: jciafullo@ismpp.org

Historical Note:
ISMPP's purpose is to advance the medical publication profession through education and advocacy. Membership: $195/year.

Continuing Education:
Certification Designation/s: CMPP

Meetings/Conferences: Annual
Conference Chair: Michele Kantrowitz
2013 - London, United Kingdom (Etc Venues)/April 22 - 23

Publications:
Member Directory; on-line
The map; quarterly

The International Society for Minimally Invasive Cardiothoracic Surgery (1997)
500 Cummings Center
Suite 4550
Beverly, MA 01915
Tel: (978) 927-8330 *Fax:* (978) 524-8890
Website: ismics.org
Staff: 4
Annual Budget: $1-2,000,000

Personnel:
Executive Director: Aurelie M. Alger JD
    E-Mail: aurelie@prri.com
Editor: Ralph J. Damiano Jr., MD
Treasurer: Gregory P. Fontana

Historical Note:
ISMICS's mission is to create a forum of discussion for the development and verification of new MICS procedures and instrumentation designed to facilitate use, to create a safe and effective delivery of such cardiovascular care with principles as well as provide educational and research opportunities for members. Membership: $300 (Active); $100 (Candidate-Fellows/Residents/Medical Students).

Continuing Education:
Enrollment: 793
Certification Designation/s: CME

Meetings/Conferences:
2013 - Prague, Czech Republic (Hilton Prague Hotel)/ June 12 - 15

Publications:
Innovation; bi-monthly
ISMICS Newsletter; annually
Membership Directory; on-line

International Society for Molecular Plant Microbe Interactions (1990)
3340 Pilot Knob Rd.
St. Paul, MN 55121-2097
Tel: (651) 454-7250 *Fax:* (651) 454-0766
TollFree: (800) 481-2698
E-Mail: ismpmiinfo@scisoc.org
Website: ismpminet.org
Members: 400 individuals
Staff: 7
Annual Budget: $25-50,000

Personnel:
President: Sophien Kamoun
    E-Mail: sophien.kamoun@tsl.ac.uk
Treasurer: Peter Dodds
    E-Mail: peter.dodds@csiro.au
Contact, Publications: Greg Grahek
Contact,: Amy Hope
    E-Mail: ahope@scisoc.org
Business Executive: Steve Nelson
    E-Mail: snelson@scisoc.org
Contact, Membership Services: Cindy Scheller
    E-Mail: cscheller@scisoc.org

Historical Note:
IS-MPMI is comprised of members from over 30 countries.IS-MPMI's mission is to research the molecular aspects of microorganisms' interactions with plants and the consequences of such interactions. Membership: $50 (Regular); $35 (Post-Doc); $20 (Student).

Continuing Education:
Certification Designation/s: SPDC

Publications:
Molecular Plant-Microbe Interactions; monthly; adv.
IS-MPMI Reporter; bi-monthly; adv.
Member Directory; on-line

International Society for Neuronal Regulation
1350 Beverly Rd., Suite 115
P.O. Box 114
McLean, VA 22101-3633
Tel: (703) 848-1994 *Fax:* (703) 848-1994
E-Mail: office@isnr.org
Website: isnr.org
Staff: 2
Tax: 501 (c)(3)

Personnel:
Executive Director: Cindy A. Yablonski
    E-Mail: cyablonski@isnr.org

Historical Note:
ISNR aims to promote excellence in clinical practice, educational applications, and research in applied neuroscience in order to better understand and enhance brain function. Membership includes many health professionals, researchers, educators and other individuals who work with neurofeedback. Membership: $225 (Individuals); $80 (Students); $125 (Post-Doc and Interns); $175 (Retirees); $550 (Corporate).

Continuing Education:
Certification Designation/s: BCIA

Meetings/Conferences: Annual
Conference Chair: Ann Marie Horvat
2013 - Addison, TX (Intercontinental Dallas Hotel)/ Sept. 18 - 22

Publications:
Membership Directory; on-line
The Journal of Neurotherapy; semi-annually

International Society for Performance Improvement (1962)
1400 Spring St.
Suite 400
Silver Spring, MD 20910-2753
Tel: (301) 587-8570 *Fax:* (301) 587-8573
E-Mail: info@ispi.org
Website: ispi.org
Members: 2500 individuals
Staff: 6
Annual Budget: $1-2,000,000
Tax: 501 (c)(3)

Personnel:
Executive Director: April Davis CAE
    E-Mail: april@ispi.org
Director, Certification and Industry Relations: Gay E. Bruhn CPT, EdD
    E-Mail: gaybruhn@ispi.org
Administrative Assistant: Jessica Charles
    E-Mail: jessicac@ispi.org
Director, Information Technology: Craig Grimm
    E-Mail: craigg@ispi.org
Director, Meetings: Ellen Kaplan CMP
    E-Mail: ellenk@ispi.org
Manager, Membership and Programs: Robin Stimson
    E-Mail: robins@ispi.org

Historical Note:
Formerly (1973) National Society for Programmed Instruction and then (1995) National Society for Performance and Instruction, ISPI's mission is to develop and recognize the proficiency of its members and advocate the use of Human Performance Technology. Membership: $75-5000/year; $1,750 (Lifetime).

Continuing Education:
Enrollment: 842
Certification Designation/s: CPT

Meetings/Conferences: Annual
Conference Chair: Ellen Kaplan CMP
2013 - Reno, NV (Silver Legacy Resort Casino)/April 12 - 17

Publications:
Membership Directory; on-line
Performance Improvement Journal (PIJ); monthly; adv.
Performance Improvement Quarterly (PIQ); quarterly
Performance Xpress; monthly; adv.

Membership List Available to Non-members

International Society for Pharmaceutical Engineering (1980)
600 N. Westshore Blvd.
Suite 900
Tampa, FL 33609
Tel: (813) 960-2105 *Fax:* (813) 264-2816
E-Mail: ASK@ispe.org
Website: ispe.org
Members: 22,000 members
Staff: 61
Annual Budget: $5-10,000,000

Personnel:
President and Chief Executive Officer: Nancy Berg
    E-Mail: nberg@ispe.org
Director, Event Operations: Kindra Bess
    E-Mail: kbess@ispe.org
Director, Publications and Editor: Gloria Hall
    E-Mail: ghall@ispe.org
Manager, Communications: Danielle Hould
    E-Mail: dhould@ispe.org
Vice President, Member Relations: Karleen Kos
    E-Mail: kkos@ispe.org

Director, Business Initiatives: Scott Ludlum
   E-Mail: sludlum@ispe.org
Director, Information Systems: Chris Muratore
   E-Mail: cmuratore@ispe.org
Director, Human Resources: Wendy Perez
   E-Mail: wperez@ispe.org
Director, Professional Certification: Michael Phelan
   E-Mail: mphelan@ispe.org
Director, International Sales: John Phillips
   E-Mail: jphillips@ispe.org
Director, Marketing Communications: Marny Reed
   E-Mail: mreed@ispe.org
Manager, Continuing Education Program: Julianne Rill
   E-Mail: jrill@ispe.org
Vice President, Administration and Chief Financial Officer:
   Victoria Smoke
   E-Mail: vsmoke@ispe.org

Historical Note:
Founded in 1980, ISPE has worldwide headquarters in Tampa, Florida, USA; Brussels, Belgium, and an office in Singapore to serve Asia-Pacific. ISPE's Mission is to educate and advance pharmaceutical manufacturing professionals and their industry. Members are pharmaceutical manufacturing professionals. ISPE provides an environment for experts, technologists, regulators, consultants and students to exchange ideas and practical experience. Membership: US $239 (Industry); $75 (Regulatory Authority/Government/Academic/Emerging Economy/Young Professionals); $20 (Student).

Continuing Education:
Certification Designation/s: CPIP

Meetings/Conferences: Annual
Conference Chair: Kindra Bess
2013 - Washington, DC (Washington Marriott
   Wardman Park)/Nov. 3 - 6
2014 - San Diego, CA (San Diego Marriott Marquis and
   Marina)/Nov. 9 - 12
Number of non-conference events/year: 20

Publications:
ISPE E-Letters; quarterly; adv.
ISPE Informer; monthly; adv.
ISPEAK; bi-monthly; adv.
Membership Directory; on-line
Pharmaceutical Engineering; bi-monthly; adv.

International Society for Pharmacoeconomics and Outcomes Research *(1995)*
505 Lawrence
Square Blvd South
Lawrenceville, NJ 08648
Tel: (609) 586-4981 *Fax:* (609) 586-4982
TollFree: (800) 992-0643
E-Mail: info@ispor.org
Website: ispor.org
Members: 4300 individuals
Staff: 22
Annual Budget: $5-10,000,000
Tax: 501(c)(3)

Personnel:
Founding Executive Director: Marilyn Dix Smith PhD
   E-Mail: mdsmith@ispor.org
Senior Director, Meetings: Sue Capon
   E-Mail: scapon@ispor.org
Director, Meetings and Member Services: Jennifer Casillas
   E-Mail: jcasillas@ispor.org
Director, Education Services and International Development:
   Jerusha Harvey
   E-Mail: jharvey@ispor.org
Director, Publications and Communications: Stephen
   Priori
   E-Mail: spriori@ispor.org

Historical Note:
Founded as Association for Pharmacoeconomics and Outcomes Research; absorbed International Society for Economic Evaluation of Medicines and assumed its current name in 1998. ISPOR's mission is to increase the efficiency, effectiveness, and fairness of health care resource use to improve health. ISPOR promotes the science of pharmacoeconomics (health economics) and outcomes research (the scientific discipline that evaluates the effect of health care interventions on patient well-being including clinical outcomes, economic outcomes, and patient-reported outcomes). Membership: $140-275 (Regular); $35-120 (Student).

Meetings/Conferences: Annual
Conference Chair: Sue Capon
2013 - New Orleans, LA (Sheraton Hotel New
   Orleans)/May 18 - 22

2014 - Montreal, QC (Palais Des Congres de
   Montreal)/May 31 - June 4
2015 - Philadelphia, PA (Philadelphia Marriott
   Downtown)/May 16 - 20
2016 - Washington, DC/May 21 - 25

Publications:
E-Bulletin; monthly
ISPOR Connections; bi-monthly
ISPOR Student News
Medical Device and Diagnostic News
Value in Health

Membership List Available to Non-members

International Society for Pharmacoepidemiology
5272 River Rd.
Suite 630
Bethesda, MD 20816
Tel: (301) 718-6500 *Fax:* (301) 656-0989
E-Mail: ispe@paimgmt.com
Website: pharmacoepi.org
Members: 500 individuals
Staff: 6
Annual Budget: $1-2,000,000
Tax: 501(c)(3)

Personnel:
Executive Secretary: Mark H. Epstein ScD
   E-Mail: mepstein@paimgmt.com
Assistant, Membership Services: Rene Atkinson
   E-Mail: Membership@paimgmt.com
Controller: Thomas O'Hora CPA
   E-Mail: tohora@paimgmt.com
Staff Accountant: Scott A. Recht
   E-Mail: srecht@paimgmt.com

Historical Note:
ISPE members are scientists and researchers using epidemiologic approaches to study the use, effectiveness, value and safety of pharmaceuticals. ISPC's mission is to advance the health of the public by providing a forum for the open exchange of scientific information and for the development of policy, education, and advocacy for the field of pharmacoepidemiology, including pharmacovigilance, drug utilization research, and therapeutic risk management. Membership: $240 (Regular); $440 (Fellow); $85 (Student/Retiree); $25 (Special); $500-100,000 (Corporate, based on the type of organization).

Meetings/Conferences: Annual
2013 - Munich, Germany (Hilton Munich City)/April 11
   - 13
2013 - Montreal, QC (Montreal Convention Centre)/
   Aug. 25 - 28
Number of non-conference events/year: 2

Publications:
Member Directory; on-line
Official Journal of the International Society for
   Pharmacoepidemiology; on-line
SCRIBE; bi-annually

Membership List Available to Non-members

International Society for Philosophical Enquiry
(1974)
700 Terrace Heights
Suite 60
Winona, MN 55987
Tel: (202) 293-9300 *Fax:* (202) 293-9350
Website: thethousand.com
Members: 600 individuals
Staff: 10
Tax: 501(c)(3)

Personnel:
President: Patrick M. O'Shea
   E-Mail: oshea@ispe-1000.org
Comptroller: Roger Brown
   E-Mail: rbrown@ispe-1000.org
Webmaster: Stevan Damjanovic
   E-Mail: stevan@damjanovic.org
General Counsel: Stephen Levin Esq.
   E-Mail: slevin@ispe-1000.org
Public Relations Officer: Michael Perilstein
   E-Mail: peril@ispe-1000.org
Recruiting Officer: Cindy Smith
   E-Mail: cms@smith.org
Treasurer: Mark Van Vuuren
   E-Mail: mark.vv@telkomsa.net

Historical Note:
Formerly The Thousand. ISPE's mission is to encourage written communications between members with similar interests and intellectual levels of ability, for the purpose of

exchanging thoughts, ideas, and discoveries. Membership: $50 (Regular); $37.50 (Senior); $65 (Family).

Publications:
Telicom - Journal
The Thousander - Newsletter; monthly

International Society for Plastination *(1986)*
University of Toledo, Department of
Neurosciences
3000 Arlington Ave., Mail Stop 1007
Toledo, OH 43614-2591
Tel: (419) 383-4283 *Fax:* (419) 383-3008
Website: isp.plastination.org
Members: 200 individuals
Staff: 2

Personnel:
President: Carlos A.C. Baptista MD, PhD
   E-Mail: carlos.baptista@utoledo.edu

Historical Note:
ISP strives to provide and maintain an international association for individuals and institutions who perform plastination techniques, or are interested in plastination preservation methods. Members are professionals with an interest in the use of curable polymers in the preparation of biological specimens. Membership: $75 (Individual).

Meetings/Conferences: Biennial

Publications:
Journal of Plastination

Membership List Available to Non-members

International Society for Prenatal Diagnosis
(1996)
154 Hansen Rd.
Suite 201
Charlottesville, VA 22911
Tel: (434) 979-4773 *Fax:* (434) 977-1856
E-Mail: info@ispdhome.org
Website: ispdhome.org
Staff: 5
Annual Budget: $500-1,000,000
Tax: 501(c)(3)

Personnel:
Executive Director: Elliott Graham
   E-Mail: egraham@ispdhome.org
Director, Programs: Allison Ball
   E-Mail: aball@ispdhome.org
Accountant: Patricia Cuthbert
   E-Mail: pcuthbert@ispdhome.org
Coordinator, Membership Services: Cory McCann
   E-Mail: cmccann@ispdhome.org
Director, Website Services: Marilla Owens
   E-Mail: mowens@ispdhome.org

Historical Note:
ISPD's mission is to advance the art and science of all aspects of fetal diagnosis, including pre-implantation diagnosis, fetal imaging, fetal chromosome analysis and DNA diagnosis, prenatal screening, fetal therapy, ethical and psychosocial issues and the provision of prenatal diagnostic services. Membership: $225 (Professional); $75 (Student).

Meetings/Conferences: Annual

Publications:
Membership Directory; on-line
Prenatal Diagnosis

International Society for Preventive Oncology
(1980)
University of Massachusetts Medical School, 365
Plantation St.
Suite 175
Worcester, MA 01605-2398
Tel: (508) 856-1822 *Fax:* (508) 856-1824
E-Mail: editor@cancerprev.org
Website: cancerprev.org
Members: 600 individuals
Staff: 6
Annual Budget: $10-25,000

Personnel:
Secretary General and Editor-in-Chief: Herbert E.
   Neiburgs MD
   E-Mail: editor@cancerprev.org

Historical Note:
ISPO is the forum of an international membership committed to the study of interactive etiologic factors in cancer development and their impact on prevention, detection, and management of neoplastic diseases. ISPO's mission is to support primary prevention of cancer

through identification and control of cancer causes, and identification of high risk individuals, secondary prevention through detection and management of occult cancer and precursor lesions. ISPO members are medical doctors, scientists and other professionals who are actively involved in preventive oncology. ISPO encourages continuing education in molecular biology of carcinogenesis, immunovirology, genetics and environmental influences. Membership: $135/year.

Publications:
Cancer Detection & Prevention; bi-monthly

International Society for Prosthetics and Orthotics - United States (1970)
P.O. Box 3188
Dublin, OH 43016
Tel: (614) 659-0197 Fax: (614) 336-8596
E-Mail: administrator@usispo.org
Website: usispo.org
Members: 2800 individuals and National Member Societies
Staff: 2
Annual Budget: $50-100,000

Personnel:
Contact, Administrative Services: Dianne Farabi
E-Mail: dfarabi@columbus.rr.com

Historical Note:
Established in Copenhagen, Denmark and incorporated in Dover, Delaware. ISPO's mission is to promote improvements in the care of all persons with neuromuscular and skeletal impairments. Members are those engaged in prosthetics, orthotics and rehabilitation engineering, including research, education, clinical practice and other significant aspects of prosthetics and/or orthotics and those with an interest in supporting the objectives of ISPO. Membership: $195 (Regular); $520 (Institutional); $90 (Student).

Meetings/Conferences: Biennial
2013 - Hyderabad, India (HICC)/April 4 - 7
2014 - Waikoloa, HI (Waikoloa Beach Marriott Resort and Spa)/Jan. 26 - 29/1-10 exhibitors
Number of non-conference events/year: 2

Publications:
US IPSO Highlights

International Society for Quality of Life Research
555 E. Wells St.
Suite 1100
Milwaukee, WI 53202
Tel: (414) 918-9797 Fax: (414) 276-3349
E-Mail: info@isoqol.org
Website: isoqol.org
Staff: 3
Annual Budget: $500-1,000,000

Personnel:
Executive Director: Rebecca Brandt CAE
E-Mail: rbrandt@isoqol.org
Editor: Ana Popielnicki BA

Historical Note:
ISOQOL's mission is to advance the scientific study of health-related quality of life and other patient-centered outcomes to identify interventions, enhance the quality of health care and promote the health of populations. Membership: $42-10,000/year.

Meetings/Conferences: Annual
2013 - Miami, FL/Oct. 9 - 12

Publications:
Membership Directory; on-line
Quality of Life Research; semi-annually

International Society for Quality-of-Life Studies (1995)
1800 Kraft Dr.
Suite 111
Blacksburg, VA 24060-6351
Fax: (540) 961-4162
E-Mail: isqols@vt.edu
Website: isqols.org
Members: 300 individuals
Staff: 5
Annual Budget: Under $10,000

Personnel:
Executive Director: M. Joseph Sirgy
E-Mail: sirgy@vt.edu
Vice President, Publications: Laura Camfield
E-Mail: laura.camfield@qeh.ox.ac.uk
Vice President, Finance: Andrew Clarke
E-Mail: andrew.clark@ens.fr

Vice President, Publicity and Membership Services: Denis Huschka
E-Mail: dhuschka@ratswd.de
Vice President, Professional Affairs: Eduardo Wills-Herrera
E-Mail: ewills@uniandes.edu.co

Historical Note:
ISQOLS's mission is to provide an organization through which all academic and professional researchers interested in QOL studies may coordinate their efforts to advance the field of QOL studies within various disciplines. Membership: $75 (Regular); $220 (Institutional); $50 (Full-time Student/Retired); $300 (New Charter Lifetime).

Continuing Education:
Certification Designation/s: CIRP

International Society for Research on Aggression (1972)
420 Deleware St. SE, Department of Pediatrics
University of Minnesota, Mayo Mail Code 486
Minneapolis, MN 55455-0323
Website: israsociety.com
Members: 250 individuals
Staff: 4
Annual Budget: $25-50,000

Personnel:
President: John F. Knutson
Treasurer: Eric Dubow
Executive Secretary: Michael Potegal
E-Mail: poteg001@umn.edu

Historical Note:
ISRA is a society of scholars and scientists interested in the scientific study of aggression and violence. ISRA members are academics, scientists and other professionals with an interest in the field of aggression. Membership: $60-$65 (Fellow/Associate); $65-$70 (Dual); $30-$35 (Student).

Meetings/Conferences: Biennial
2014 - Atlanta, GA/July 15 - 19

Publications:
Membership Directory; on-line
Newsletter

International Society for Respiratory Protection
P.O. Box 580
South Park, PA 15129-0580
Website: isrp.com.au
Members: 12 corporations
Staff: 5
Annual Budget: $25-50,000
Tax: 501(c)(3)

Personnel:
President: Andy Capon
Webmaster: Torbjorn Lundmark
Secretary and Treasurer: Bill Newcomb
Manager, Education Program: Simon Smith
Editor: Ziqing Zhuang PhD
E-Mail: JISRP-EDITOR@ATT.NET

Historical Note:
ISRP advocates the health and safety of users of respiratory protection devices and all aspects of respiratory care. Membership: $60 (Individual); $600 (Corporate).

Meetings/Conferences: Biennial
2014 - Prague, Czech Republic (Hilton Prague Old Town hotel)/Sept. 21 - 25

Publications:
The Journal of the ISRP (JISRP)

International Society for Technology in Education (1979)
1710 Rhode Island Ave. NW
Suite 900
Washington, DC 20036
Tel: (202) 861-7777 Fax: (202) 861-0888
E-Mail: iste@iste.org
Website: iste.org
Members: 13000 individuals, corporate and organizational affiliate members
Staff: 78
Annual Budget: $10-25,000,000
Tax: 501(c)(3)

Personnel:
Chief Executive Officer: Brian Lewis CAE
Senior Corporate Relations Officer: Stephen "Steve" R. Abbott
Senior Government Affairs Officer: Hilary Goldmann
E-Mail: hgoldmann@iste.org
Senior Officer, Strategic Initiatives: Lynn Nolan

E-Mail: lnolan@iste.org

Historical Note:
Formed by the merger of the International Council for Computers in Education and the International Association for Computing in Education in 1979 . Merged with the National Educational Computing Association in 2002. ISTE is engaged in improving learning and teaching by advancing the effective use of technology in PK-12 and teacher education. Members include individuals, affiliate organizations, and corporations. Membership: $39-5,000/year.

Continuing Education:
Certification Designation/s: GCSAS

Meetings/Conferences: Annual
Conference Chair: Donella Evoniuk
2013 - San Antonio, TX/June 23 - 26/20000 attendees/over 100 exhibitors
2014 - Atlanta, GA/June 29 - July 2/20000 attendees/over 100 exhibitors
2015 - Philadelphia, PA/June 28 - July 1/over 100 exhibitors
Number of non-conference events/year: 1

Publications:
Learning & Leading with Technology (L&L); adv.
ISTE Update; monthly; adv.
Journal for Computing Teachers; semi-annually
Journal of Digital Learning in Teacher Education; quarterly
Journal of Research on Technology in Education; quarterly

Membership List Available to Non-members

International Society for the Comparative Studies of Civilizations (1961)
Western Michigan University
Haworth College of Business
Kalamazoo, MI 49008
Tel: (269) 387-5710 Fax: (269) 387-5710
Website: wmich.edu/iscsc
Members: 500 individuals and institutions
Staff: 3
Annual Budget: $10-25,000

Personnel:
President: Dr. Andrew Targowski
E-Mail: targowski@wmich.edu
Treasurer: Betsy Drummer
E-Mail: betsy.drummer@wmich.edu
Chair, Conferences: William McGaughey
E-Mail: 2wmcg@earthlink.net

Historical Note:
Established in Salzburg, Austria, ISCSC moved its headquarters to the U.S. in 1970 and was reconstituted over a two-year period. ISCSC's mission is to provide a forum for collaboration among all persons interested in the advancement of the comparative study of civilizations. Membership: $75 (Joint); $60 (Institutional/Individual); $50 (Retiree); $40 (Student).

Meetings/Conferences: Annual
Conference Chair: William McGaughey

Publications:
Comparative Civilizations Review; semi-annually
ISCSC Newsletter; annually

International Society for the Performing Arts (1949)
630 Ninth Ave.
Suite 213
New York, NY 10036-4752
Tel: (212) 206-8490 Fax: (212) 206-8603
E-Mail: info@ispa.org
Website: ispa.site-ym.com
Members:
600 executives and directors
50 Countries
Staff: 4
Annual Budget: $10-25,000
Tax: 501(c)(3)

Personnel:
Chief Executive Officer: David Baile
E-Mail: dbaile@ispa.org
Manager, Membership and Administration: Taylor S. Harris
E-Mail: tharris@ispa.org
Bookkeeper: Melanie Hopkins
E-Mail: mhopkins@ispa.org
Administrative Coordinator: Nicole Merritt
E-Mail: nmerritt@ispa.org

Historical Note:
ISPA's goal is to provide the best possible support, information and opportunities for collegial exchange to members throughout the world. Membership:$995-$1,835 (Star Member); $600-1,095 (Full Member); $290 (Affiliate); $50 (Student).

Publications:
Member Organizations Directory
Network e-newsletter; monthly

International Society for the Study of Dissociation
(1983)
8400 Westpark Dr.
Second Floor
McLean, VA 22102
Tel: (703) 610-9037 *Fax:* (703) 610-0234
E-Mail: info@isst-d.org
Website: isst-d.org
Staff: 3
Annual Budget: $500-1,000,000

Personnel:
Executive Director: Thérèse O. Clemens
　E-Mail: tclemens@isst-d.org
Manager, Program and Membership Services: Jennifer Randall
　E-Mail: jrandall@isst-d.org

Historical Note:
ISSTD seeks to advance clinical, scientific, and societal understanding about the prevalence and consequences of chronic trauma and dissociation. Membership: $187 (Regular/Full Member); $91 (Student Member); $84 (Retired Member); $93 (Affiliate Member).

Meetings/Conferences: Annual
Conference Chair: Jennifer Randall
2013 - Baltimore, MD (Hilton Baltimore Hotel)/Nov. 16 - 18

Publications:
ISSTD Newsletter; quarterly; adv.
Journal of Trauma and Dissociation; quarterly; adv.
Membership Directory; on-line; adv.

International Society for the Study of Subtle Energies and Energy Medicine *(1989)*
2770 Arapaho Rd.
Suite 132
Lafayette, CO 80026
Tel: (303) 425-4625 *Fax:* (866) 269-0972
E-Mail: info@issseem.org
Website: issseem.org
Members: 1450 individuals
Staff: 5
Annual Budget: $250-500,000

Personnel:
President: Jacob Liberman DSc, PhD
Office Administrator: Linda Block CHt
　E-Mail: linda@issseem.org
Manager, Member Services: Lysa Rodriguez
Treasurer: Lynn Van Buren
Editor: Bernard O. Williams PhD

Historical Note:
ISSSEEM's mission is to promote understanding, exploration, research and application of the energies of consciousness. Members are interested in integrating traditional knowledge about subtle energies and the healing process with modern scientific method and theory. Membership: $45 (Associate); $100 (Full); $1,000 (Lifetime); $200 (Organization & Company).

Publications:
Bridges; adv.
Membership Directory
Subtle Energies and Energy Medicine Journal; adv.

International Society for the Study of Trauma and Dissociation *(1984)*
8400 Westpark Dr.
Second Floor
McLean, VA 22102
Tel: (703) 610-9037 *Fax:* (703) 610-0234
E-Mail: info@isst-d.org
Website: isst-d.org
Members: 1500 individuals
Staff: 3
Annual Budget: $250-500,000
Tax: 501(c)(3)

Personnel:
Executive Director: Therese O. Clemens
　E-Mail: tclemens@isst-d.org

Manager, Programs and Membership Services: Jennifer Randall
　E-Mail: jrandall@isst-d.org

Historical Note:
Formerly (1994) International Society for the Study of Multiple Personality and Dissociation. ISSTD's mission is to advance clinical, scientific, and societal understanding about the prevalence and consequences of chronic trauma and dissociation. Members are professionals in psychology, psychiatry, medicine, nursing, sociology, social work, anthropology, philosophy, theology and other disciplines seriously involved in the study and treatment of multiple psychological processes. Membership: $187 (Regular); $91 (Student); $84 (Retired); $93 (Affiliate).

Meetings/Conferences: Annual
Conference Chair: Jennifer Randall
2013 - Baltimore, MD (Hilton Baltimore Hotel)/Nov. 16 - 18

Publications:
ISSTD News; adv.
Journal of Trauma and Dissociation
Membership Directory; on-line; adv.

Membership List Available to Non-members

International Society for Third-Sector Research
(1992)
3400 N. Charles St.
559 Wyman Park Building
Baltimore, MD 21218-2688
Tel: (410) 516-4678 *Fax:* (410) 516-4870
E-Mail: istr@jhu.edu
Website: istr.org
Members: 700 individuals and institutions
Staff: 2
Annual Budget: $250-500,000
Tax: 501(c)(3)

Personnel:
Executive Director: Margery Berg Daniels
Program Administration: Robin Wehrlin
　E-Mail: istr_pa@jhu.edu

Historical Note:
ISTR's mission is to promote the development of quality research and education internationally on third sector related issues, theories, and policies and to enhance the dissemination and application of knowledge about the third sector as widely as possible throughout the world. Membership: $100-2,000/year.

Meetings/Conferences: Annual
Conference Chair: Robin Wehrlin

Publications:
Inside ISTR Newsletter; on-line
ISTR Annual Report; annually
ISTR Reports; on-line
Membership Directory; on-line
Voluntas Journal; quarterly; adv.

Membership List Available to Non-members

International Society for Traumatic Stress Studies
(1985)
111 Deer Lake Rd.
Suite 100
Deerfield, IL 60015
Tel: (847) 480-9028 *Fax:* (847) 480-9282
E-Mail: istss@istss.org
Website: istss.org
Members: 2500 individuals
Staff: 9
Annual Budget: $1-2,000,000
Tax: 501(c)(3)

Personnel:
Executive Director: Rick Koepke
　E-Mail: rkoepke@istss.org
Manager, Marketing and Communications: Lindsay Arends
　E-Mail: larends@istss.org
Director, Administration: Krista Baran
　E-Mail: kbaran@istss.org
Accountant: John Herfkens
　E-Mail: jherfkens@istss.org
Specialist, Membership Services: Tajuanna Laws
　E-Mail: tlaws@istss.org
Manager, Education: Kismet Saglam
　E-Mail: ksaglam@istss.org
Manager, Conferences: Jacky Schweinzger
　E-Mail: jschweinzger@istss.org

Historical Note:

Formerly (1991) Society for Traumatic Stress Studies. Established in Washington and incorporated in Ohio. ISTSS's mission is to promote advancement and exchange of knowledge about severe stress and trauma. Society members include psychiatrists, psychologists, social workers, nurses, counselors, researchers, administrators, advocates, journalists, clergy and others with an interest in the study and treatment of traumatic stress. Membership: $180-200 (Regular); $80-100 (Student); $144-164 (Affiliate Regular); $64-84 (Affiliate Student).

Meetings/Conferences: Annual
Conference Chair: Jacky Schweinzger
2013 - Philadelphia, PA (Philadelphia Marriott Downtown)/Nov. 7 - 9/1300 attendees/1-10 exhibitors
2014 - Miami, FL (InterContinental)/Nov. 6 - 8/1-10 exhibitors

Publications:
Membership Directory; on-line
Traumatic StressPoints; bi-monthly; adv.
Traumatic StressPoints Newsletter; bi-monthly; adv.

International Society of Air Safety Investigators
(1964)
107 E. Holly Ave.
Suite 11
Sterling, VA 20164
Tel: (703) 430-9668 *Fax:* (703) 430-4970
E-Mail: isasi@erols.com
Website: isasi.org
Members: 1462 individuals and companies
Staff: 3
Annual Budget: $100-250,000

Personnel:
International Office Manager: Ann Schull
　E-Mail: isasi@erols.com

Historical Note:
Formerly (1977) the Society of Air Safety Investigators. ISASI seeks to promote air safety by the exchange of ideas, experiences and information about aircraft accident investigations and to aid in the advancement of flight safety to promote technical advancement in procedures. Membership: $125-165 (Associate/Affiliate); $45-80 (Student); $600 (Corporate); $50 (Fellow).

Meetings/Conferences: Annual

Publications:
FORUM; quarterly

International Society of Applied Intelligence
(1993)
C/O Department of Computer Science, Texas State University, San Marcos
601 University Dr.
San Marcos, TX 78666-4616
Tel: (512) 245-8050 *Fax:* (512) 245-8750
E-Mail: ma04@txstate.edu
Website: isai.cs.txstate.edu
Members: 500 individuals
Staff: 4
Annual Budget: $50-100,000
Tax: 501(c)(3)

Personnel:
President: Moonis Ali PhD
Treasurer: Tim Hendlass
Contact, Conferences: He Jiang
　E-Mail: jianghe@dlut.edu.cn
Secretary: Kishan Mehrotra

Historical Note:
ISAI's purpose is to conduct scientific literacy and educational activities. Members are academics, computer scientists and others with an interest in the applications of artificial intelligence. Membership: $125 (Individual); $50 (Student); $545 (Institution).

Meetings/Conferences: Annual
Conference Chair: He Jiang
Number of non-conference events/year: 2

Publications:
Newsletter
The International Journal of Artificial Intelligence

International Society of Appraisers *(1979)*
303 W. Madison St.
Suite 2650
Chicago, IL 60606
Tel: (312) 981-6778 *Fax:* (312) 265-2908
TollFree: (866) 481-1689
E-Mail: isa@isa-appraisers.org
Website: isa-appraisers.org

Members: 1400 individuals
Staff: 5
Annual Budget: $500-1,000,000
Tax: 501(c)(6)

Personnel:
Executive Director: Joseph M. Jackson CAE
    E-Mail: jjackson@thesentergroup.com
Coordinator, Membership Services and Operations: Sara
    Porter
    E-Mail: sporter@thesentergroup.com
Administrative Assistant: Thomas Radde
    E-Mail: tradde@thesentergroup.com
Director, Meetings and Education: Moria Twitty
    E-Mail: mtwitty@thesentergroup.com

Historical Note:
*ISA's mission is to advance the professionalism and
effectiveness of personal property appraisers. Members
are appraisers, specializing in fine arts, gems, and jewelry,
antiques and collectibles, household items, and machinery
and equipment. Membership: $450/year.*

Meetings/Conferences: Annual
Conference Chair: Moria Twitty
2013 - Chicago, IL (J.W. Marriott Hotel)/April 12 - 15

Publications:
ISA News; on-line

International Society of Arboriculture *(1924)*
P.O. Box 3129
Champaign, IL 61826-3129
Tel: (217) 355-9411 *Fax:* (217) 355-9516
TollFree: (888) 472-8733
E-Mail: isa@isa-arbor.com
Website: isa-arbor.com
Members: 20000 individuals
Staff: 39
Annual Budget: $5-10,000,000
Tax: 501(c)(5)

Personnel:
Executive Director: Jim Skiera
    E-Mail: jskiera@isa-arbor.com
Director, Finance and Operations: Mark Bluhm
    E-Mail: mbluhm@isa-arbor.com
Manager, Sales and Customer Relations: Lisa Butler
    E-Mail: lbutler@isa-arbor.com
Administrative Services Manager: Jessica Carroll
    E-Mail: jcarroll@isa-arbor.com
Manager, Human Resource: Cindy Harris
    E-Mail: charris@isa-arbor.com
Manager, Corporate Communications: Janet Huber
    E-Mail: jhuber@isa-arbor.com
Director, Marketing and Member Services: Samantha
    Koon
    E-Mail: skoon@isa-arbor.com
Manager, Information Technology: Ernie Noa
    E-Mail: enoa@isa-arbor.com
Director, Certification: Marya Ryan
    E-Mail: mryan@isa-arbor.com
Manager, Meetings and Events: Kara Stachowiak
    E-Mail: kstachowiak@isa-arbor.com
Editorial and Production Manager: Amy Theobald
    E-Mail: atheobald@isa-arbor.com

Historical Note:
*Formerly (1976) International Shade Tree Conference.
ISA's mission is to promote the professional practice of
arboriculture and to foster public awareness of the benefits
of trees through research, technology, and education.
Membership: $125 (Professional); $45 (Student/Senior);
$1250 (Life).*

Continuing Education:
Certification Designation/s: ISA

Meetings/Conferences:
Conference Chair: Kara Stachowiak
2013 - Toronto, ON/Aug. 3 - 7
2014 - Milwaukee, WI/Aug. 2 - 6
2015 - Orlando, FL/Aug. 8 - 12
2016 - Ft. Worth, TX/Aug. 13 - 17

Publications:
Arboriculture & Urban Forestry; bi-monthly
Arborist News; bi-monthly; adv.
CERT Today; quarterly
ISA Today; monthly
Planting Seeds e-Newsletter; quarterly

International Society of Arthroscopy, Knee Surgery and Orthopaedic Sports Medicine *(1997)*
2678 Bishop Dr.
Suite 250

San Ramon, CA 94583-2338
Tel: (925) 807-1197 *Fax:* (925) 807-1199
E-Mail: isakos@isakos.com
Website: isakos.com
Members: 1700 individuals
Staff: 7
Annual Budget: $2-5,000,000

Personnel:
Executive Director: Michele C. Johnson
    E-Mail: isakos@isakos.com
Project Manager, Congress Programs: Katie Anderson
Manager, Finance: Donna Festo
Membership and Congress Registrar: Morgan Huffy
Project Manager, Congress Exhibit Manager: Hilary
    Matthews
Marketing and Communications Manager: Kathleen Reyes
Administrative Support and Member Services: April
    Warden

Historical Note:
*An international society of surgeons established to advance
the worldwide exchange and dissemination of education,
research and patient care in arthroscopy, knee surgery
and orthopaedic sports medicine. Membership: $275/year
(Associate/Active); $200.00 (AANA).*

Meetings/Conferences: Annual
Conference Chair: Hilary Matthews
Number of non-conference events/year: 3

Publications:
Arthroscopy Journal; monthly; adv.
ISAKOS Newsletter; bi-annually
Membership Directory; on-line

International Society of Automation *(1945)*
67 T.W. Alexander Dr.
P.O. Box 12277
Research Triangle Park, NC 27709
Tel: (919) 549-8411 *Fax:* (919) 549-8288
E-Mail: info@isa.org
Website: isa.org
Members:
60 companies
30000 individuals
Staff: 53
Annual Budget: $10-25,000,000
Tax: 501(c)(3)

Personnel:
Executive Director and Chief Executive Officer: Patrick
    Gouhin
    E-Mail: pgouhin@isa.org
Executive Office Manager: Debbie Eby
    E-Mail: deby@isa.org
Director, Products and Services: Timothy Feldman
    E-Mail: tfeldman@isa.org
*Director, Finance Administration, Customer Service and
    Facility Operations:* Kenneth R. Hilgers
    E-Mail: khilgers@isa.org
Contact, Membership Services: Stacey Peterson
    E-Mail: speterson@isa.org
Contact, Accreditation: Dalton Wilson
    E-Mail: dwilson@isa.org

Historical Note:
*ISA's mission is to certify industry professionals; providing
education and training; publishing books and technical
articles; hosting conferences and exhibitions for automation
professionals; and developing standards for industry.
Membership: $100 (Individual); $10 (Student); $50
(Country Member); $50 (Affiliate Member); $5 (Virtual
Student).*

Continuing Education:
Enrollment: 75
Certification Designation/s: CAP, CCST

Meetings/Conferences: Annual
Conference Chair: Timothy Feldman
2013 - New Orleans, LA (Astor Crowne Plaza Hotel)/
    Aug. 11 - 13
Number of non-conference events/year: 7

Publications:
CAPacity
InTech; bi-monthly; adv.
ISA Directory of Automation; on-line
ISA Transactions; quarterly

International Society of Barristers *(1965)*
802 Legal Research Building
University of Michigan Law School
Ann Arbor, MI 48109-1215
Tel: (734) 763-0165 *Fax:* (734) 764-8309

E-Mail: info@internationalsocietyofbarristers.org
Website: isob.com
Members: 800 individuals
Staff: 3
Annual Budget: $500-1,000,000

Personnel:
President: Michael A. Kelly
Administrative Secretary and Editor: Donald Beskind
    E-Mail: beskind@law.duke.edu
Secretary and Treasurer: Rutledge R. Liles

Historical Note:
*ISOB is committed to preserving trial by jury, the adversary
system and an independent judiciary Membership: $650/
year.*

Meetings/Conferences: Annual
2013 - Punta Mita, NA (Four Seasons)/March 10 - 16
Number of non-conference events/year: 1

Publications:
Journal of the International Society of Barrister;
    quarterly

International Society of Bassists *(1967)*
14070 Proton Rd.
Suite 100
Dallas, TX 75244
Tel: (972) 233-9107 *Fax:* (972) 490-4219
E-Mail: info@isbworldoffice.com
Website: isbworldoffice.com
Members: 3000 individuals
Staff: 4
Annual Budget: $250-500,000
Tax: 501(c)(3)

Personnel:
President: John Kennedy
Editor: Jeremy Baguyos
General Manager: Madeleine Crouch
Director, Meetings: Miloslav Jelinek
    E-Mail: jelinekmilos@volny.cz

Historical Note:
*ISB serves as a forum for communication among bassists
throughout the world and across a wide variety of musical
styles. Mission is to stimulate public interest in the double
bass and to improve performance standards. Members are
teachers, students, reseachers and manufacturers of the
double bass. Membership: $30-175/year.*

Meetings/Conferences: Annual
Conference Chair: Miloslav Jelinek
2013 - Rochester, NY/June 2 - 8

Publications:
Bass Line newsletter; semi-annually; adv.
Bass World; adv.
E-Newsletter; on-line; adv.
Journal of Bass Research; on-line; adv.

International Society of Beverage Technologists *(1953)*
14070 Proton Rd.
Suite 100, LB Nine
Dallas, TX 75244-3601
Tel: (972) 233-9107 *Fax:* (972) 490-4219
E-Mail: office@bevtech.org
Website: bevtech.org
Members: 1000 individuals
Staff: 2
Annual Budget: $250-500,000
Tax: 501(c)(3)

Personnel:
Executive Director: Larry Hobbs
    E-Mail: larry_hobbs@comcast.net
Treasurer: Stefanie Ringo
    E-Mail: stefanie_ringo@cargill.com

Historical Note:
*Formerly (1995) Society of Soft Drink Technologists,
ISBT is a professional society of individuals engaged
in the beverage industry. Membership is open to any
person engaged in the science, technology or production
of soft drinks or beverages, including those suppliers
to the beverage industry whose principle occupation is
substantially technical in nature. Membership: $200/year.*

Meetings/Conferences: Annual
Number of non-conference events/year: 1

Publications:
IndiaLive; on-line
ISBT Newsletter; on-line
Who's Who in Beverage Technology; on-line

International Society of Certified Electronics Technicians (1970)
3608 Pershing Ave.
Fort Worth, TX 76107-4527
Tel: (817) 921-9101 *Fax:* (817) 921-3741
TollFree: (800) 946-0201
E-Mail: info@iscet.org
Website: iscet.org
Members: 2000 individuals
Staff: 4
Annual Budget: $100-250,000

Personnel:
Executive Director: Mack Blakely
    E-Mail: mack@iscet.org
Associate, Membership Services and Testing: Patricia
    Bohon
    E-Mail: patricia@iscet.org
Director, Communications and Information Technology:
    Sheila Fredrickson
    E-Mail: sheila@nesda.com
Administrative Assistant: Margaret Vazquez
    E-Mail: margaret@iscet.org

Historical Note:
*ISCET's mission is to advocate technical certification
worldwide, and provides a place for certified technicians
to band together for professional advancement. Tests for
and awards the CET (Certified Electronics Technician)
designation. Publishes technical information, conducts
technical training and product serviceability inspections.
Only CETs are eligible for membership. Membership: $70
(Individual); $35 (Retired); $25 (Student); $425 (Life).*

Continuing Education:
Certification Designation/s: CET, ESA, MST, NASTeC

Meetings/Conferences: Annual
2013 - Tunica, MS (Harrah's Veranda Hotel)/July 29 -
    Aug. 2

Publications:
ISCET Update; annually
ProService; bi-monthly; adv.

International Society of Certified Employee Benefit Specialists (1981)
18700 W. Bluemound Rd.
P.O. Box 209
Brookfield, WI 53008-0209
Tel: (262) 786-8771 *Fax:* (262) 786-8650
E-Mail: iscebs@iscebs.org
Website: iscebs.org
Members: 37000 individuals
Staff: 4
Annual Budget: $10-25,000

Personnel:
Director: Sandra L. Becker
    E-Mail: sandyb@iscebs.org
Assistant, Administration: Kathy Frank
    E-Mail: kathyf@iscebs.org
Manager, Member Services: Jennifer Mathe
    E-Mail: jenniferm@iscebs.org

Historical Note:
*An affiliate of the International Foundation of Employee
Benefit Plans. ISCEBS is an interactive community providing
educational resources, innovative thinking and collective
wisdom to help members excel and prosper in their careers.
Membership: $175 (Graduate); $85 (CEBS Member/
Student); $50 (Unemployed/Retired).*

Continuing Education:
Certification Designation/s: CEBS, CMS, GBA, RPA

Meetings/Conferences: Annual
2013 - Boston, MA (Westin Copley Place Boston)/Sept.
    22 - 25

Publications:
Benefits Quarterly; quarterly; adv.
Membership Directory; on-line
Newsbriefs; bi-monthly

International Society of Chemical Ecology (1983)
Department of Entomology
University of California
Riverside, CA 92521
Website:
chemecol.org
chemecol.org
Members:
600 individuals
450 members
Staff: 3

Annual Budget: $25-50,000
Tax: 501(c)(3)

Personnel:
President: Ring Carde
    E-Mail: president@chemecol.org

Historical Note:
*ISCE's purpose is to promote the understanding of
interactions between organisms and their environment
that are mediated by naturally occurring chemicals.
Membership: $15-35 (Regular); $10-15 (Student); $1,000
(Corporate Associate).*

Meetings/Conferences: Annual
2013 - Melbourne, Australia (Melbourne Convention
    and Exhibition Centre)/Aug. 19 - 22
Number of non-conference events/year: 4

Publications:
Journal of Chemical Ecology; monthly; adv.
ISCE Newsletters; adv.
Membership Directory; on-line

International Society of Communication Specialists (1984)
201 Blue Sky Dr.
Marietta, GA 30068-3511
Tel: (770) 973-0662 *Fax:* (770) 973-1410
E-Mail: ecs91@aol.com
Website: iscs.cc
Members: 70 companies
Staff: 1
Annual Budget: $100-250,000

Personnel:
Executive Director: Ed Sanner

Historical Note:
*ISCS members are companies that represent on-location
audio and video recording services for the association
community. Membership: $275/year (company).*

International Society of Copier Artists (1982)
759 President St., Suite 2H
Brooklyn, NY 11215
Tel: (718) 638-3264
E-Mail: isca4art2b@aol.com
Members:
26 museums and libraries
125 individuals
Staff: 1
Annual Budget: Under $10,000
Tax: 501(c)(3)

Personnel:
Director: Louise Neaderland
    E-Mail: isca4art2b@aol.com

Historical Note:
*Founded to promote the use of the copier as a creative tool.
Membership: $30/year (contributing artist); $90-110/year
(supporting member).*

International Society of Crime Prevention Practitioners (1978)
P.O. Box 476
Simpsonville, SC 29681-0476
Tel: (864) 884-8466
Website: iscpp.org
Members: 1300 individuals
Staff: 3
Annual Budget: $10-25,000
Tax: 501(c)(3)

Personnel:
Executive Director: Richard Cannady
Coordinator, Membership Services: Christine Donnelly
    MS
Treasurer: Bruce Wall

Historical Note:
*Absorbed National Crime Prevention Institute in 1997.
ISCPP's mission is to establish and support a permanent
network of crime prevention practitioners who can provide
leadership, foster cooperation, encourage information
exchange, and extend and improve crime prevention
education and programs internationally. Membership: $35/
year (Individual).*

Continuing Education:
Certification Designation/s: ICPS

Meetings/Conferences: Annual

Publications:
ISCPP E-News; semi-monthly
The Practitioner; quarterly

International Society of Explosives Engineers (1974)
30325 Bainbridge Rd.
Cleveland, OH 44139-2295
Tel: (440) 349-4400 *Fax:* (440) 349-3788
E-Mail: isee@isee.org
Website: isee.org
Members: 4600 individuals
Staff: 9
Annual Budget: $1-2,000,000

Personnel:
Executive Director: Winston J. Forde
Program Director, SEE Education Foundation: Arlene
    Chafe
    E-Mail: chafe@isee.org
Coordinator, Publications: Lauren Creneti
    E-Mail: creneti@isee.org
Manager, Meetings and Conferences: Lynn Mangol CMP
    E-Mail: mangol@isee.org
Director, Communications: Dede Manross
    E-Mail: explo@comcast.net
Coordinator, Membership Services: Ruth Schaefer CAE,
    IOM
    E-Mail: schaefer@isee.org
Office Manager: Mary Spena-Bosch
    E-Mail: spena@isee.org
Manager, Marketing: Bill Wahl
    E-Mail: wahl@isee.org

Historical Note:
*ISEE's mission is to advance the science and art of
explosives engineering. Membership: $80 (Individual/
Associate); $395 (Corporate); $20 (Full-time Student).*

Continuing Education:
Enrollment: 3000
Certification Designation/s: ISEECP

Meetings/Conferences: Annual
Conference Chair: Lynn Mangol CMP
2013 - Ft. Worth, TX (Omni Fort Worth Hotel)/Feb. 10
    - 13
Number of non-conference events/year: 1

Publications:
Journal of Explosives Engineering; bi-monthly; adv.
Membership Directory; on-line

Membership List Available to Non-members

International Society of Exposure Science (1990)
C/O JSI Research and Training Institute
44 Farnsworth St.
Boston, MA 02201
Tel: (617) 482-9485 *Fax:* (617) 482-0617
E-Mail: iseamail@jsi.com
Website: isesweb.org
Members: 390 individuals
Staff: 1
Annual Budget: $100-250,000
Tax: 501(c)(3)

Personnel:
Secretariat: Carol Rougvie

Historical Note:
*Formerly known as International Society of Exposure
Analysis. ISES represents a variety of professionals
with an interest in the statistical analysis of risk factors,
environmental exposure, and related issues. Has no
paid officers or full-time staff. Membership:$145/year
(International); $40/year (Student); $40/year (Emeritus).*

Meetings/Conferences: Annual
2013 - Basel, Switzerland (Congress Center)/Aug. 20 -
    23

Publications:
Journal of Exposure Science and Environmental
    Epidemiology
Membership Directory

International Society of Fire Service Instructors (1960)
14001C Saint Germain Dr.
Suite 128
Centreville, VA 20121
Tel: (800) 435-0005 *Fax:* (800) 435-0005
TollFree: (800) 435-0005
E-Mail: info@isfsi.org
Website: isfsi.org
Members: 7300 individuals and companies
Staff: 16
Annual Budget: $100-250,000
Tax: 501(c)(3)

Personnel:
President: Doug Cline

Historical Note:
Founded as International Society of Fire Service Instructors. Became Alliance for Fire and Emergency Management (1995). Resumed its original name in 1997. ISFSI's mission is to contribute to the fire service through the education and support of fire service instructors everywhere. Members are individuals responsible for the training of fire, police, ambulance and rescue personnel, and the public. Membership: $125 (Individual). $40 (Student); $45-875 (Department).

Publications:
ISFSI Newsletter; on-line
Membership Directory; on-line

International Society of Hair Restoration Surgery
(1993)
303 W. State St.
Geneva, IL 60134
Tel: (630) 262-5399 *Fax:* (630) 262-1520
TollFree: (800) 444-2737
E-Mail: info@ishrs.org
Website: ishrs.org
Members: 900 individuals
Staff: 8
Annual Budget: $1-2,000,000
Tax: 501(c)(3)

Personnel:
Executive Director: Victoria Ceh MPA
Manager, Integrated Communications: Matt Batt
Managing Editor, Graphic Design, and Contact, Advertising Sales: Cheryl Duckler
Contact, Finance, Accounting, Investments: Patrick Melvin
Contact, Database and Technical Support: Jeffrey Miller
Head Quarters and Administrative Manager: Kimberly Miller
Manager, Membership Services: Liz Rice-Conboy
Manager, Meetings and Exhibits: Jule Uddfolk CMP

Historical Note:
ISHRS's mission is to achieve excellence in patient outcomes by promoting member education, international collegiality, research, ethics, and public awareness. The International Society encourages continuing quality improvement and education for professionals in the field of medical hair restoration surgery. Membership: $600 (Physician/ Adjunct); $185 (Resident); $125 (Surgical Assistant); $0 (Emeritus).

Meetings/Conferences: Annual
Conference Chair: Jule Uddfolk CMP
2013 - San Francisco, CA/Oct. 23 - 27
2013 - San Francisco, CA/Oct. 23 - 27
Number of non-conference events/year: 10

Publications:
Dermatologic Surgery
Drugs in Dermatology
Hair Transplant Forum International; bi-monthly; adv.
Human Trichology
Membership Directory; on-line; adv.

Membership List Available to Non-members

International Society of Hospitality Consultants
(1988)
411 Sixth St., South
Suite 204
Naples, FL 34102
Tel: (239) 436-3915 *Fax:* (239) 436-3916
E-Mail: ishc@ishc.com
Website: ishc.com
Members: 200 individuals
Staff: 3
Annual Budget: $250-500,000

Personnel:
Executive Director: Lori E. Raleigh
E-Mail: lraleigh@ishc.com
Director, Membership Services: Andrea Belfanti
E-Mail: abelfanti@ishc.com

Historical Note:
ISHC provides networking and professional support to principals and management at consulting firms in the hospitality industry. Membership is by invitation only.

Meetings/Conferences: Annual

Publications:
Membership Directory; on-line

International Society of Hotel Association Executives *(1946)*

374 Marlborough St.
Boston, MA 02115
Tel: (360) 701-3474 *Fax:* (360) 866-4176
E-Mail: admin@ishae.org
Website: ishae.org
Members: 75 individuals
Staff: 1
Annual Budget: $50-100,000
Tax: 501(c)(6)

Personnel:
Executive Director: Christina Pappas
E-Mail: cpappas@ishae.org

Historical Note:
Formerly (1974) American Hotel Trade Association Executives. Affiliated with the American Hotel and Lodging Association. The purpose of ISHAE is to provide professional development and networking opportunities for lodging association executives. Members include CEOs of hotel and lodging associations in the US, Canada and the Caribbean. Membership: $200/year.

Meetings/Conferences: Annual

Publications:
ISHAE Newsletter
Membership Directory; on-line

International Society of Managing and Technical Editors *(2008)*
1107 Mantua Pike
Suite 701, Room 122
Mantua, NJ 08051
Tel: (856) 292-8512 *Fax:* (856) 292-8513
E-Mail: ismteoffice@gmail.com
Website: ismte.org
Staff: 1
Annual Budget: $50-100,000

Personnel:
Executive Director: Leslie McGeoch

Historical Note:
ISMTE's mission is to is to enhance the professionalism of scholarly journals' editorial office staff by providing networking and training infrastructure, establishing and providing resources for best practices, and studying, benchmarking and reporting on editorial office practices. Membership: $135/year (Individual).

Meetings/Conferences: Annual

Publications:
ISMTE Newsletter; monthly

International Society of Meeting Planners *(1981)*
P.O. Box 879
Palm Springs, CA 92263
Tel: (760) 327-5284 *Fax:* (760) 327-5631
TollFree: (877) 743-6802
E-Mail: support@assoc-hdqts.org
Website: ismp-assoc.org
Members: 2800 individuals
Staff: 6

Personnel:
General Manager: Brent Felstead

Historical Note:
ISMP serves as a medium for meeting planners to communicate not only on a national basis, but on an international basis as well. Membership: $175 (Affiliate); $210 (Registered Meeting Planner/Certified Event Planner/ Certified Destination Specialist/Certified Entertainment Manager).

Publications:
Global Connections
Membership Directory; on-line

International Society of Nurses in Genetics
461 Cochran Rd.
P.O. Box 246
Pittsburgh, PA 15228
Tel: (412) 344-1414 *Fax:* (412) 344-0599
E-Mail: isongHQ@msn.com
Website: isong.org
Staff: 2
Annual Budget: $50-100,000
Tax: 501(c)(6)

Personnel:
Executive Director: Beth Kassalen MBA
E-Mail: isonghq@msn.com
Treasurer: Marie Twal PhD, RN
E-Mail: metwal@auxmail.iup.edu

Historical Note:

ISONG's mission is to foster the scientific, professional, and personal development of members in the management of genomic information. Caring for people's genetic and genomic health. Membership: $125 (Full); $75 (Student/ Retired/Affiliate).

Continuing Education:
Certification Designation/s: GCC

Meetings/Conferences: Annual

Publications:
ISONG newsletter; adv.
Membership Directory; on-line

International Society of Offshore and Polar Engineers *(1989)*
495 N. Whisman Rd.
Suite 300
Mountain View, CA 94043-5711
Tel: (650) 254-1871 *Fax:* (650) 254-2038
Website: isope.org
Staff: 1
Annual Budget: $500-1,000,000
Tax: 501(c)(3)

Personnel:
Executive Director: Prof. Jin S. Chung

Historical Note:
ISOPE seeks to advance the arts and sciences and promote and improve technological progress in the interdisciplinary fields of offshore, ocean and polar engineering and related technologies through international cooperation and participation. Membership is open equally to all with a B.S. degree and up who are interested in promoting engineering and scientific progress in the fields of offshore and polar engineering. Membership: $100 (Fellow/Associate); $50 (Student).

Meetings/Conferences: Annual
2013 - Anchorage, AK (Anchorage Convention Center)/ June 30 - July 4

Publications:
International Journal of Offshore and Polar Engineering; quarterly
ISOPE EUROMS Proceedings; irregular
ISOPE IDOT proceedings; irregular
ISOPE OMS proceedings; bi-annually
ISOPE PACOMS proceedings; bi-annually
Proceedings of the Annual International Offshore and Polar Engineering Conference; annually

International Society of Political Psychology
(1978)
Virginia Commonwealth University, 923 W. Franklin St.
P.O. Box 842028
Richmond, VA 23284-2028
Tel: (804) 828-1989
E-Mail: ispp@vcu.edu
Website: ispp.org
Members: 900 individuals
Staff: 4
Annual Budget: $250-500,000

Personnel:
Executive Director: Severine Bennett
Treasurer: Andrea Grove
News Editor: Melinda Jackson
Editor: Alex Mintz

Historical Note:
ISPP is an interdisciplinary organization representing all fields of inquiry concerned with exploring the relationships between political and psychological processes. Members include psychologists, political scientists, psychiatrists, historians, sociologists, economists, anthropologists, journalists, government officials and others. Membership: $30-1700/year.

Meetings/Conferences: Annual
Conference Chair: Alex Mintz
2013 - Herzliya, Israel/July 8 - 11
2014 - Rome, Italy (Ergife Palace Hotel)/July 7 - 10
Number of non-conference events/year: 2

Publications:
ISPPNews; semi-annually
Political Psychology

International Society of Protistologists *(1947)*
Sea Education Association
P.O. Box 6
Woods Hole, MA 02543
Tel: (902) 494-2753
Website: uga.edu/protozoa
Members: 970 individuals

Staff: 6
Annual Budget: $50-100,000

Personnel:
President: Sina Adl
E-Mail: sadl@dal.ca
Editor in Chief: Roberto Docampo
E-Mail: jeukmic@uga.edu
Information Officer: Andrea Habura
E-Mail: amh09@health.state.ny.us
Treasurer: Denis Lynn
E-Mail: editor@jeukmic.com
Secretary: Michaela Strueder-Kypke
E-Mail: mstruede@uoguelph.ca
Membership Secretary: Erik R. Zettler
E-Mail: ezettler@sea.edu

Historical Note:
Founded as an international scientific society. Member of the World Federation of Parasitologists. ISOP promotes the presentation and discussion of new or important facts and problems in protistology, and works to provide resources for the promotion and advancement of this science. Membership: $80-87 (Regular); $40-43 (Student/ Emeritus); $26 (Corresponding).

Meetings/Conferences: Annual
2013 - Steamboat Springs, CO (Steamboat Grand Resort)/July 7 - 12
2013 - Vancouver, BC (The Westin Bayshore - Vancouver)/July 29 - Aug. 2
Number of non-conference events/year: 1

Publications:
Stentor: The ISOP Newsletter; on-line
The Journal of Eukaryotic Microbiology; bi-monthly; adv.

Membership List Available to Non-members

International Society of Psychiatric Consultation Liaison Nurses (1986)
2424 American Ln.
Madison, WI 53704-3102
Tel: (608) 443-2463 *Fax:* (608) 443-2474
TollFree: (866) 330-7227
E-Mail: info@ispn-psych.org
Website: ispn-psych.org/html/ispcln.html
Members: 250 individuals
Staff: 4
Annual Budget: $25-50,000

Personnel:
Editor: Beverly G. Hart
Division Director: Susan L.W. Krupnick
E-Mail: skrupnick@charter.net

Historical Note:
The International Society of Psychiatric Consultation Liaison Nurse (ISPCLN), a division of ISPN, promotes mental health of individuals and families (across the life span) who are experiencing physical illness(es) and or injury. Membership: $125 (Full Member); $60 (Retiree/ Student Member).

Meetings/Conferences: Annual
2013 - San Antonio, TX (Hyatt Regency Hill Country Resort and Spa)/April 16 - 20

Publications:
Archives of Psychiatric Nursing
Connections; quarterly
Journal of Child and Adolescent Psychiatric Nursing
Membership Directory; on-line
Perspectives in Psychiatric Care; quarterly; adv.

International Society of Psychiatric-Mental Health Nurses (1971)
University of North Carolina at Chapel Hill
Carrington Hall 426, CB 7460
Chapel Hill, NC 27599
Tel: (919) 843-8587 *Fax:* (608) 443-2474
E-Mail: info@ispn-psych.org
Website: ispn-psych.org
Members: 850 individuals
Staff: 2
Annual Budget: $100-250,000
Tax: 501(c)(3)

Personnel:
President: Victoria Soltis- Jarrett
E-Mail: vsoltis@email.unc.edu

Historical Note:
Founded as Alliance of Psychiatric and Mental Nurses; assumed its current name in 1999. ISPN's mission is to unite and strengthen the presence and the voice of specialty psychiatric-mental health nursing. It also influences

health care policy to boost equitable, evidence-based and effective treatment and care for individuals, families and communities. Membership: $125 (Full Membership/Higher Income Nations); $60 (Student/Retired/Military/ Lower Middle and Low Income Nations); $25 (Associate Student).

Meetings/Conferences: Annual
2013 - San Antonio, TX (Hyatt Regency Hill Country Resort and Spa)/April 16 - 20

Publications:
Archives of Psychiatric Nursing
Connections; quarterly
Journal of Child and Adolescent Psychiatric Nursing
Member ENews; on-line
Perspectives in Psychiatric Care
The Journal of Child and Adolescent Psychiatric Nursing and Perspectives in Psychiatric Care

International Society of Refractive Surgery of the American Academy of Ophthalmology (1940)
655 Beach St.
P.O. Box 7424
San Francisco, CA 94109-1336
Tel: (415) 561-8581 *Fax:* (415) 561-8575
E-Mail: member_services@aao.org
Website: aao.org/isrs
Members: 3500 individuals
Staff: 7

Personnel:
Contact, Web Master: Annamarie Hastings
E-Mail: ahastings@aao.org
Contact, Sponsorship: Todd Lyckberg
E-Mail: tlyckberg@aao.org
Editor-in-Chief: J. Bradley Randleman MD

Historical Note:
Formerly (2009) known as the ISRS/AAO, ISRS, a partner of AAO, promotes research, education, and exchange to advance the ethical practice of refractive surgery. Membership:$210 (U.S./ International/Associate); $95 (Members in Training).

Meetings/Conferences: Annual
Conference Chair: Todd Lyckberg

Publications:
Journal of Refractive Surgery; monthly; adv.
Refractive Surgery Outlook; monthly

International Society of Transport Aircraft Trading (1983)
401 N. Michigan Ave.
Suite 2200
Chicago, IL 60611
Tel: (312) 321-5169 *Fax:* (312) 673-6579
E-Mail: istat@istat.org
Website: istat.org
Members: 2600 individuals
Staff: 13
Annual Budget: $2-5,000,000

Personnel:
Executive Director: Ron Pietrzak
E-Mail: rpietrzak@istat.org
Senior Coordinator, Operations: Ben Barclay
E-Mail: bbarclay@istat.org
Senior Manager, Event Services: Cynthia Cortis
E-Mail: ccortis@istat.org
Senior Manager, Marketing: Marcia Daudelin
E-Mail: Mdaudelin@istat.org
Manager, Information Technology: Meredith Halperin
E-Mail: mhalperin@istat.org
Senior Manager, Financial Management: Jason Roe

Historical Note:
ISTAT provides a communications medium and promotes standards for those engaged in the purchase, sale, financing, appraisal or insuring of transport category aircraft. Serves as the official voice for the entire commercial transport aircraft secondary marketplace. Members are airline, airframe, engine and aviation equipment executives, banking and leasing officials, appraisers, insurers, consultants, attorneys and brokers. Membership: $400 (Individual/Individual-Airline); $1,750 (Corporate); $200 (Additional Corporate Member).

Continuing Education:
Certification Designation/s: AC, SAC

Meetings/Conferences: Annual
Conference Chair: Cynthia Cortis
2013 - Orlando, FL (JW Marriott Orlando Grande Lakes)/March 10 - 12

Publications:
Jetrader; bi-monthly; adv.
Member Directory; annually

International Society of Travel and Tourism Educators (1980)
23220 Edgewater
St. Clair Shores, MI 48082
Tel: (586) 294-0208 *Fax:* (586) 294-0208
Website: istte.org
Members: 150 individuals
Staff: 7
Annual Budget: $50-100,000
Tax: 501(c)(3)

Personnel:
Executive Director: Joanne Bruss
E-Mail: joannb@istte.org
Contact, Workshop and Presentations: A. Dawn Aitken
Contact, Media Relations: Anna Kulinski
E-Mail: annak@istte.org

Historical Note:
Formerly (1977) known as Society of Travel and Tourism Educators. ISTTE is a nonprofit international organization dedicated to improving the quality of education and research in the travel, tourism and hospitality industries by promoting the exchange of information, ideas, and outstanding service to members. Members are teachers and administrators of programs that offer degrees in the areas of travel and tourism. Membership: $75-400/year.

Meetings/Conferences: Annual
Conference Chair: A. Dawn Aitken

Publications:
ISTTE News and Views Quarterly; quarterly; adv.
Journal of Teaching in Travel & Tourism; quarterly

International Society of Weekly Newspaper Editors (1955)
C/O Institute of International Studies, Missouri
Southern State University
3950 E. Newman Rd.
Joplin, MO 64801-1595
Tel: (417) 625-9736 *Fax:* (417) 659-4445
Website: iswne.org
Members: 253 individuals
Staff: 2
Annual Budget: $10-25,000

Personnel:
Executive Director: Chad D. Stebbins
E-Mail: stebbins-c@mssu.edu
President: Cheryl Wormley
E-Mail: indepublisher@tomcast.net

Historical Note:
ISWNE's purpose is to help those involved in the weekly press to improve standards of editorial writing and news reporting and to encourage strong, independent editorial voices. Encourages and promotes wise and independent editorial comment, news content and leadership in community newspapers throughout the world. Membership: $50 (Regular); $100 (Sustaining).

Meetings/Conferences: Annual
2013 - De Pere, WI (St. Norbert College)/June 10 - 14
2014 - Durango, CO (Fort Lewis College)/June 25 - 29
2015 - Columbia, MO/June 24 - 28

Publications:
Grassroots Editor; quarterly
ISWNE Newsletter
Member Directory; on-line

International Society of Weighing and Measurement (1916)
13017 Wisteria Dr.
Suite 341
Germantown, MD 20874
Tel: (240) 753-4397 *Fax:* (866) 285-3512
E-Mail: staff@iswm.org
Website: iswm.org
Members: 700 individuals
Staff: 3
Annual Budget: $100-250,000

Personnel:
Executive Director: Karen Hutchison
E-Mail: karen@iswm.org

Historical Note:
Formerly (1985) National Men's Scale Association. ISWM's mission is to commit to the technical advancements created by and for the weighing and measurement industry. Members include manufacturers, distributors, government officials, end users, scale purchasers, and suppliers to the industry. Membership: $285 (Dealer/Distributor/End User); $500 (Manufacturer); $52 (Individual Affiliate of a Corporate Membership) $52 (Government/Retired); $130 (Independent).

Continuing Education:
Certification Designation/s: CWS, CWT, CWP
Meetings/Conferences: Annual
2013 - Atlantic City, NJ (Trump Plaza Hotel and
   Casino)/March 13 - 15
Number of non-conference events/year: 1
Publications:
ISWM News; quarterly
Membership Directory; on-line

International Society on Thrombosis and Hemostasis (1969)
610 Jones Ferry Rd.
Suite 205
Carrboro, NC 27510
Tel: (919) 929-3807 *Fax:* (919) 929-3935
E-Mail: info@isth.org
Website: isth.org
Members: 3000 members
Staff: 6
Annual Budget: $5-10,000,000
Tax: 501(c)(3)
Personnel:
Executive Director: Thomas "Tom" Reiser
   E-Mail: tom_reiser@isth.org
Director, Meetings: Lisa Astorga
   E-Mail: lisa_astorga@isth.org
Manager, Program and Technology: Robert Cary Clark
   E-Mail: cary_clark@isth.org
Coordinator, Membership Services: Sharon Overcash
   E-Mail: membership@isth.org
Coordinator, Program: Allison Peacock
   E-Mail: allison_peacock@isth.org
Director, Corporate Relations: Margo Price
   E-Mail: margo_price@isth.org
Historical Note:
*ISTH works for the advancement of understanding,
prevention, diagnosis and treatment of thrombotic and
bleeding disorders. Membership: $160 (Regular); $35
(Associate/Reach-the-World/Nurse/Allied Health
Professional).*
Meetings/Conferences: Annual
Conference Chair: Margo Price
2013 - Amsterdam, Netherlands (Amsterdam RAI)/
   June 29 - July 4
2014 - Milwaukee, WI/June 23 - 26
2015 - Toronto, ON/June 20 - 25
Publications:
2011 ISTH Membership Directory; on-line
Enewsletter; on-line
Journal of Thrombosis and Haemostasis; monthly; adv.

International Spa Association (1991)
2365 Harrodsburg Rd.
Suite A325
Lexington, KY 40504-4326
Tel: (859) 226-4326 *Fax:* (859) 226-4445
TollFree: (888) 651-4772
E-Mail: ispa@ispastaff.com
Website: experienceispa.com
Members: 3200 companies
Staff: 14
Annual Budget: $2-5,000,000
Tax: 501(c)(6)
Personnel:
President: Lynne Walker McNees
   E-Mail: lynne.mcnees@ispastaff.com
Vice President , Operations: Laura Beiting
   E-Mail: laura.beiting@ispastaff.com
Vice President, Membership Services and Marketing:
   Crystal Ducker
   E-Mail: crystal.ducker@ispastaff.com
Manager, Member Relations: Carrie Fay
   E-Mail: carrie.fay@ispastaff.com
Manager, Public Relations: Allie Hembree
   E-Mail: allie.hembree@ispastaff.com
Director, Marketing: Kerri Keefer
   E-Mail: kerri.keefer@ispastaff.com
Editor: Mae Manacap-Johnson
   E-Mail: mae.manacap-johnson@ispastaff.com
Director, Events and Education: Melissa Riley
   E-Mail: melissa.riley@ispastaff.com
Historical Note:
*ISPA's mission is to advance the spa industry by providing
educational and networking opportunities, promoting
the value of the spa experience. Members include club
spas, cruise ship spas, day spas, destination spas, resort/*

*hotel spas, medical spas and mineral spring spas, as
well as suppliers to the industry. Membership: $92-130
(Individual); $569-1129 (Spa); $649-1129 (Resource
Partner).*
Continuing Education:
Certification Designation/s: CSS
Meetings/Conferences: Annual
Conference Chair: Melissa Riley
2013 - Las Vegas, NV (Mandalay Bay)/Oct. 21 - 23
2014 - Kissimmee, FL (Gaylord Palms Resort and
   Convention Center-Kissimmee)/Oct. 27 - 29
Publications:
LiveSpa Magazine; adv.
Membership Directory; on-line
Pulse Magazine; adv.
Touch Points e-newsletter; monthly

International Special Events Society (1987)
401 N. Michigan Ave.
Suite 2200
Chicago, IL 60611-4267
Tel: (312) 321-6853 *Fax:* (312) 673-6953
TollFree: (800) 688-4737
E-Mail: info@ises.com
Website: ises.com
Members: 7200 individuals
Staff: 4
Annual Budget: $1-2,000,000
Tax: 501(c)(6)
Personnel:
Executive Director: Kevin Hacke
   E-Mail: khacke@smithbucklin.com
Associate, Membership Services: Tom McCurrie
   E-Mail: tmccurrie@smithbucklin.com
Coordinator, Education: Lauren Rini
   E-Mail: lrini@smithbucklin.com
Historical Note:
*ISES's mission is to educate, advance and promote the
special events industry and its network of professionals
along with related industries. Members are caterers,
decorators, special event producers, meeting planners,
destination management companies, rental companies, hotel
sales managers, convention center managers, and other
professionals. Membership: $399 (Individual/Corporate-
Primary); $299 (Corporate-Additional/Non-Profit); $35
(Student).*
Continuing Education:
Enrollment: 500
Certification Designation/s: CSEP, CMP
Meetings/Conferences: Annual
Number of non-conference events/year: 1
Publications:
Membership Directory; on-line
Special Events Magazine; monthly; adv.

Membership List Available to Non-members

International Sport Show Producers Association (1970)
P.O. Box 480084
Denver, CO 80248-0084
Tel: (303) 892-6800 *Fax:* (303) 892-6322
Website: sportshow.org
Members: 15 companies
Staff: 3
Annual Budget: Under $10,000
Personnel:
President: Jeff Haughton
   E-Mail: haughton@iei-expos.com
Executive Secretary: Debbie Hathorne
   E-Mail: dhathorne@iei-expos.com
Historical Note:
*Members are producers of sports and vacation shows
serving major North American markets. Membership:
$1000/year (New Member).*
Publications:
Membership Directory; on-line

International Sports Heritage Association (1971)
P.O. Box 2384
Florence, OR 97439
Tel: (541) 991-7315 *Fax:* (541) 997-3871
E-Mail: info@sportsheritage.org
Website: sportsheritage.org
Members: 130 organizations
Staff: 2
Annual Budget: $25-50,000
Personnel:

Executive Director: Karen Bednarski
   E-Mail: kbednarski@sportsheritage.org
Treasurer: Ben Sapp
   E-Mail: bens@gshf.org
Historical Note:
*Formerly, Association of Sports Museums and Halls of Fame
(ASHMHF), later renamed to International Association
of Sports Museums and Hall of Fame and assumed its
current name in 2006. ISHA's purpose is to educate,
stimulate and support organizations and individuals
engaged in the celebration of sports heritage. Membership:
$185-450 (Regular-Depending on the Annual Budget of
Organization); $185-275 (Associate-Depending on the
Profit of the Organization).*
Meetings/Conferences: Annual
Publications:
Honoring our Heroes
ISHA Newsletter; quarterly; adv.
Membership Directory; annually; adv.

Membership List Available to Non-members

The International Stability Operations Association (2001)
1634 I St. NW
Suite 800
Washington, DC 20006
Tel: (202) 464-0721 *Fax:* (202) 464-0728
E-Mail: ISOA@stability-operations.org
Website: stability-operations.org
Members: 57 companies
Staff: 7
Annual Budget: $500-1,000,000
Tax: 501(c)(6)
Personnel:
President: Doug Brooks
   E-Mail: dbrooks@ipoaonline.org
Manager, Membership and Business Development: Jason
   Kennedy
   E-Mail: jkennedy@stability-operations.org
Associate, Publications: Alaina Monismith
Director, Programs and Operations: Jessica Mueller
Associate, Communications and Outreach: Eric Shaw
Research Associate: Hanna Streng
   E-Mail: Programs@stability-operations.org
Associate, Government and Legal Affairs: Varun Vira
Historical Note:
*IPOA's mission is to promote operational and ethical
standards of firms active in the peace and stability
operations industry. Membership comprises of international
'contingency contractors' utilized to support stability and
peacekeeping operations and disaster relief efforts globally.
Membership: $6,000-15,000/year (Companies).*
Meetings/Conferences: Annual
Conference Chair: Jason Kennedy
Number of non-conference events/year: 2
Publications:
ISOA Weekly Digest; weekly; adv.
Journal of International Peace Operations; bi-monthly;
   adv.
Membership Directory; on-line

Membership List Available to Non-members

International Staple, Nail and Tool Association (1966)
512 W. Burlington Ave.
Suite 203
La Grange, IL 60525-2245
Tel: (708) 482-8138 *Fax:* (708) 482-8186
E-Mail: isanta@ameritech.net
Website: isanta.org
Members: 21 companies
Staff: 2
Annual Budget: $250-500,000
Tax: 501(c)(6)
Personnel:
Executive Vice President: John Kurtz
Historical Note:
*Founded as the Industrial Stapling Manufacturer's Institute,
became the Industrial Stapling and Nailing Technical
Association in 1972 and assumed its present name in
1982. ISANTA is an international organization of power
fastening companies involved in the design, manufacturing,
and sales of pneumatic and cordless tools and the fasteners
they drive.*
Publications:
Membership Directory; on-line

International Stress Management Association - USA (1973)
c/o Wesley E. Sime, University of Nebraska
135 Mable Lee Hall
Lincoln, NE 68588-0229
E-Mail: info@isma-usa.org
Website: isma-usa.org
Members: 100 individuals
Staff: 4
Annual Budget: Under $10,000

Personnel:
Chairperson: Marigold A. Edwards PhD
E-Mail: mae@pitt.edu
Special Events: Camille Frey PhD
E-Mail: Isma2004usa@yahoo.ca
Secretary: Carolyn S. Massello
Treasurer: N. Blithe Runsdorf PhD
E-Mail: brunsdorf@hotmail.com

Historical Note:
Formerly (1980) American Association for the Advancement of Tension Control and (1992) International Stress and Tension Control Association. ISMA members are individuals with an interest in the dissemination and acquisition of scientific knowledge for stress management, related disorders and tension control strategies. Membership: $65/year.

Meetings/Conferences:
Conference Chair: Camille Frey PhD

Membership List Available to Non-members

International Studies Association (1959)
324 Social Sciences
University of Arizona
Tucson, AZ 85721
Tel: (520) 477-2050 Fax: (520) 621-5780
E-Mail: isa@isanet.org
Website: isanet.org
Members: 5300 individuals
Staff: 12
Annual Budget: $2-5,000,000
Tax: 501(c)(3)

Personnel:
Executive Director: Thomas J. Volgy
E-Mail: volgy@isanet.org
Director, Administrative Support: Lyn Brabant
E-Mail: embrabant@isanet.org
Director, Online and Membership Services: Joel Davis
E-Mail: joeldavis@isanet.org
Director, Technical Services: Miguel Escalante
E-Mail: mescalan@isanet.org
Director, Academic Development: Andrea K. Gerlak
E-Mail: agerlak@isanet.org
Finance and Travel Grant Manager: Brittany John
E-Mail: BrittanyJohn@isanet.org
Director, Operations: Dana B. Larsen
Manager, Finance: Vanessa Malkin
E-Mail: vmalkin@isanet.org
Manager, Marketing and Advertising: Suela Mustafa
E-Mail: suelamustafa@isanet.org
Coordinator, Communications: Angelica Robison
E-Mail: arobison@isanet.org
Director, Conventions and Meetings: Jeanne White
E-Mail: jeannewhite@isanet.org

Historical Note:
ISA's mission is to provide opportunities for communications among educators, researchers, and practitioners in order to continually share intellectual interests and meet the challenges of a changing global environment. Membership concerned with the communication of national, international, and transnational issues, concerns, and ideas. Membership: $25-35 (Student); $1,350 (Institutional); $40-120 (Faculty, income dependent); $20 (Family).

Continuing Education:
Enrollment: 5300

Meetings/Conferences: Annual
Conference Chair: Jeanne White
2013 - San Francisco, CA (Hilton San Francisco Union Square)/April 3 - 6/5000 attendees
2014 - Toronto, ON (Sheraton Centre Toronto Hotel)/March 26 - 29/5000 attendees
2015 - New Orleans, LA (Hilton New Orleans Riverside)/Feb. 18 - 21
2016 - Atlanta, GA (Atlanta Marriott Marquis)/March 16 - 19
2017 - Baltimore, MD (Hilton Baltimore)/Feb. 22 - 25

2018 - San Francisco, CA (San Francisco Hotels)/April 4 - 7
2019 - Toronto, ON (Sheraton Centre Toronto Hotel)/March 27 - 30
2020 - Honolulu, HI (Hilton Hawaiian Village Waikiki Beach Resort)/March 25 - 28
Number of non-conference events/year: 3

Publications:
Foreign Policy Analysis; quarterly
International Interactions; quarterly
International Political Sociology; quarterly
International Studies Perspectives; quarterly
International Studies Quarterly; quarterly
International Studies Review; quarterly
ISA Newsletter; monthly
Membership Directory; on-line

Membership List Available to Non-members

International Superyacht Society (1989)
757 SE 17th St.
Suite 744
Ft. Lauderdale, FL 33316
Tel: (954) 525-6625 Fax: (954) 525-4325
E-Mail: info@superyachtsociety.org
Website: superyachtsociety.org/home-page.aspx
Staff: 4
Annual Budget: $250-500,000

Personnel:
Executive Director: Amy Halsted
E-Mail: seagourmet@toad.net
President: Ken Hickling
E-Mail: iyp.uk@akzonobel.com
Member And Treasurer: Bransom Bean
E-Mail: bbean@finefocusing.com
Administrator: Vanessa Stuart

Historical Note:
The International Superyacht Society is a not-for-profit organization serving and representing the large yacht industry worldwide. ISS's mission is to build alliances worldwide with regional associations and to serve as communications conduit for issues affecting the marketplace, owners, crew and industry members. Society members are individuals and companies who have been recognized for their leadership and dedication to raising the standards of design construction, maintenance, repair and operation of large yachts. Individual, professional, crew, vessel, company memberships are available. Membership: $150 (Crew); $200 (Individual); $300 (Professional); $600 (Corporate/Industry Association/Vessel) $1500(Supporting).

Publications:
Membership Directory; on-line

International Surface Fabricators Association
165 N. 1330 West
Suite A3
Orem, UT 84057
Tel: (801) 341-7360 Fax: (801) 341-7361
TollFree: (877) 464-7732
E-Mail: info@isfanow.org
Website: isfanow.org
Staff: 6
Annual Budget: $500-1,000,000

Personnel:
Director, Communications: Kevin Cole
E-Mail: kevin@isfanow.org
Director, Education: Mike Nolan
E-Mail: mike@isfanow.org
Administrative Assistant and Registrar: Meg Pettingill
E-Mail: meg@isfanow.org
Sales Representative: Paul Wisnefski
E-Mail: wisnefski@sbcglobal.net

Historical Note:
ISFA's mission is to help ISFA members become more profitable in their businesses by Promoting ISFA members and the products they offer, Educating ISFA members to help them become better craftsmen and business people, and Improving the industry through professionalism and honesty. Membership: $200-400 (Fabricator); $100 (Individual); $249-7500 (Associate).

Continuing Education:
Certification Designation/s: ISFA CP

Publications:
CAS magazine; quarterly

International Swaps and Derivatives Association (1985)
360 Madison Ave.

16th Floor
New York, NY 10017
Tel: (212) 901-6000 Fax: (212) 901-6001
E-Mail: isda@isda.org
Website: isda.org
Members: 835 member institutions
Staff: 50
Annual Budget: $25-50,000,000

Personnel:
Chief Executive Officer: Robert G. Pickel
Chief Operating Officer: Mary Cunningham
General Counsel and Head of Equity, FX and Interest Rate Legal: Katherine Tew Darras
E-Mail: kdarras@isda.org
Head of Finance: Huzefa Deesawala
E-Mail: hdeesawala@isda.org
Head of Human Capital Management: Corrinne Greasley
Senior Director and Head, U.S. Public Policy: Mary Johannes
E-Mail: mjohannes@isda.org
Global Head, Strategy and Communications: Steven Kennedy
Director, Information Technology: Dillon Miller
Global Head, Conferences: Kelly Sanderson
Head, Membership Services: Liz Zazzera
E-Mail: lzazzera@isda.org

Historical Note:
Founded as International Swap Dealers Association; assumed its current name in 1993. ISDA's mission is to encourage the prudent and efficient development of the privately negotiated derivatives business by promoting practices conducive to the efficient conduct of the business, including the development and maintenance of derivatives documentation and promoting the development of sound risk management practices.

Meetings/Conferences:
Conference Chair: Liz Zazzera
Number of non-conference events/year: 12

Publications:
ISDA in Review; monthly
Membership Directory; on-line

Membership List Available to Non-members

International Tax Institute (1961)
C/O Holland & Knight LLP
31 W. 52nd St.
New York, NY 10019
Tel: (212) 513-3555 Fax: (212) 385-9010
Website: internationaltaxinstitute.org
Members: 75 individuals
Staff: 2
Annual Budget: $50-100,000
Tax: 501(c)(3)

Personnel:
President: Mark Stone
Vice President and Treasurer: William H. Green

Historical Note:
Formerly (1971) Institute on U.S. Taxation of Foreign Income. ITI is a professional organization of tax executives, lawyers and accountants concerned with taxation of international business income. ITI's mission is to provide first rate speakers and Government panelists for timely programs of interest to the international tax professional. Membership: $600 (Corporate); $195 (Individual).

International Technology and Engineering Educators Association (1939)
1914 Association Dr.
Suite 201
Reston, VA 20191-1539
Tel: (703) 860-2100 Fax: (703) 860-0353
E-Mail: iteea@iteea.org
Website: iteaconnect.org
Members: 35,000 secondary technology and engineering educators
Staff: 10
Annual Budget: $1-2,000,000
Tax: 501(c)(3)

Personnel:
Executive Director: Kendall N. Starkweather DTE, PhD
E-Mail: iteea@iteea.org
Coordinator, Communications and Publications: Katie De La Paz
E-Mail: kdelapaz@iteea.org
Coordinator, Computer Operations: Catherine James
E-Mail: cjames@iteea.org
Coordinator, Publications: Tamara MacDonald

E-Mail: tmacdonald@iteea.org
Director, Membership and Marketing: Christine Maggio
    E-Mail: cmaggio@iteea.org
Coordinator, Meeting Planning: Susan Perry
    E-Mail: susan@perry-group.com
Accountant: Puja Tucker
    E-Mail: ptucker@iteea.org
Director, Membership and Marketing: Maureen Wiley
    E-Mail: mwiley@iteea.org

Historical Note:
ITEEA's mission is to advance technological capabilities for all people and to nurture and promote the professionalism of those engaged in these pursuits. ITEEA seeks to meet the professional needs and interests of members as well as to improve public understanding of technology, innovation, design, and engineering education and its contributions. Membership: $240 (Institutional/Museum); $160 (Elementary School); $80 (Professional); $40 (Advocate/Student); $65 (Electronic); $100 (Joint); $400 (Corporate).

Meetings/Conferences: Annual
Conference Chair: Susan Perry
2013 - Columbus, OH/March 7 - 9

Publications:
ITEEA's Newsletter; on-line
Journal of Technology Education; quarterly
Membership Directory; on-line
STEM Connections; on-line; adv.
Technology and Children; quarterly; adv.
Technology and Engineering Teacher; on-line

Membership List Available to Non-members

International Technology Law Association (1971)
401 Edgewater Pl.
Suite 600
Wakefield, MA 01880-6200
Tel: (781) 876-8877 *Fax:* (781) 224-1239
E-Mail: office@itechlaw.org
Website: itechlaw.org
Members: 2200 individuals
Staff: 3
Annual Budget: $500-1,000,000

Personnel:
President: John P Beardwood
    E-Mail: president@itechlaw.org
Secretary: Jenna Karadbil
    E-Mail: secretary@itechlaw.org
Treasurer: Sajai Singh
    E-Mail: treasurer@itechlaw.org

Historical Note:
Formerly known as the Computer Law Association (CLA) assumed its present name in 2006. ITechLaw's mission is to create unparalleled opportunities for international networking and exchanging knowledge and experience with experts and colleagues around the world. It represents lawyers in the technology sector. Membership: $16.67-$5000/year. .

Meetings/Conferences: Tri-annual
2013 - Phoenix, AZ (Westin Kierland Resort and Spa)/
    May 1 - 3
2014 - New York City, NY/May 1
2015 - San Diego, CA/May 1
2016 - Miami, FL/May 1

Publications:
ITechLaw eBulletin; quarterly
ITechLaw eNews; monthly
Membership Directory; annually

Membership List Available to Non-members

International Test and Evaluation Association (1980)
4400 Fair Lakes Ct.
Suite 104
Fairfax, VA 22033-3801
Tel: (703) 631-6220 *Fax:* (703) 631-6221
E-Mail: itea@itea.org
Website: itea.org
Members: 1700 individuals and 100 Companies
Staff: 7
Annual Budget: $1-2,000,000
Tax: 501(c)(3)

Personnel:
Executive Director: James M. Gaidry CAE
    E-Mail: jgaidry@itea.org
Manager, Corporate Development and Sales: Bill Dallas
    E-Mail: wdallas@itea.org
Editor in Chief: Rita Janssen
    E-Mail: rjanssen@allenpress.com

Director, Events: Eileen G. Redd
    E-Mail: eredd@itea.org
Manager, Chapter and Membership Support: Bonnie
    Schendell
    E-Mail: bschendell@itea.org
Director, Education: Jay Weaver
    E-Mail: jweaver@itea.org

Historical Note:
ITEA's mission is to advance the field of Test and Evaluation worldwide in government, industry and academia. Membership: $60 (U.S Individual); $80 (International); $25 (Full time Student); $500-1,000 (Corporate).

Meetings/Conferences:
Conference Chair: Eileen G. Redd
2013 - Denver, CO/Sept. 16 - 20
Number of non-conference events/year: 3

Publications:
Corporate Capabilities Directory; annually
ITEA Journal; quarterly; adv.

International Textile and Apparel Association (1944)
P.O. Box 70687
Knoxville, TN 37938-0687
Tel: (865) 992-1535 *Fax:* (916) 722-8149
E-Mail: info@itaaonline.org
Website: itaaonline.org
Members: 1000 individuals
Staff: 2
Annual Budget: $100-250,000
Tax: 501(c)(3)

Personnel:
Executive Director: Nancy Rutherford PhD
    E-Mail: executivedirector@itaaonline.org

Historical Note:
Formerly (1991) Association of College Professors of Textiles and Clothing. ITAA's mission is to promote the discovery, dissemination, and application of knowledge and is a primary resource for its members in strengthening leadership and service to society. Membership: $35-300/year.

Meetings/Conferences: Annual
2013 - New Orleans, LA (Sheraton New Orleans
    Hotel)/Oct. 15 - 18
2014 - Charlotte, NC (Hilton Charlotte Center City)/
    Nov. 11 - 17

Publications:
Clothing and Textiles Research Journal (CTRJ); on-line
ITAA eNews; on-line
ITAA Newsletter; bi-monthly; adv.
Membership Directory; on-line

International Thermographers Association (1973)
38 Raft Island Dr. NW
Gig Harbor, WA 98335
Members: 84 companies
Staff: 1
Annual Budget: $100-250,000

Personnel:
Treasurer: Scott Wood

Historical Note:
A section of the Printing Industries of America, composed of members who specialize in thermography (heat-raised printing). Membership: $140-660/year.

International Ticketing Association (1980)
One College Park, 8910 Purdue Rd.
Suite 480
Indianapolis, IN 46268
Tel: (212) 629-4036 *Fax:* (212) 629-8532
E-Mail: info@intix.org
Website: intix.org
Members: 1100 ticketing, sales, technology, finance, and marketing professionals
Staff: 5
Annual Budget: $500-1,000,000
Tax: 501(c)(3)

Personnel:
President and Chief Executive Officer: Jena L. Hoffman
    E-Mail: jhoffman@intix.org
Manager, Meetings: Kathy Foreman
    E-Mail: kforeman@ontrackevents.com
Associate, Membership Services: Tiffany Kelham
Accounting Associate: Mary Leaton
Sales Manager: Kevin McDonnell

    E-Mail: kmcdonnell@townsend-group.com

Historical Note:
INTIX is committed to lead the entertainment ticketing industry. Represents ticketing, sales, technology, finance, and marketing professionals who work in arts, sports, and entertainment as well as a full range of public venues and institutions. Membership: $108-540 (Organization); $108-614 (Vendors); $24-516 (Individuals).

Meetings/Conferences: Annual
Conference Chair: Kathy Foreman
2013 - Orlando, FL (Walt Disney World Resort)/Jan. 29
    - 31
2014 - Chicago, IL (Sheraton Chicago Hotel and
    Towers)/Jan. 28 - 30

Publications:
INTIX News; monthly; adv.
Membership Directory; annually

International Titanium Association (1984)
11674 Huron St.
Suite 100
Northglenn, CO 80234
Tel: (303) 404-2221 *Fax:* (303) 404-9111
E-Mail: ita@titanium.org
Website: titanium.org
Members: 2195 individualsa and companies
Staff: 4
Annual Budget: $1-2,000,000
Tax: 501(c)(6)

Personnel:
Executive Director: Jennifer Simpson
    E-Mail: jsimpson@titanium.org
Administrator, Member Services: Stacey Blicker
    E-Mail: sblicker@titanium.org
Sales: Carolyn Smith
    E-Mail: csmith@titanium.org
Contact, Accounting and Registration: Andrea White
    E-Mail: awhite@titanium.org

Historical Note:
Founded as Titanium Development Association; assumed its current name in 1995. ITA's mission to help facilitate the expanded use of titanium based products in existing and new market sectors and applications by enlarging the knowledge about Titanium through promoting at trade shows and distribution of collateral materials. Membership: $500-80,000 (Producer/User); $1,000-4,500 (Consumer); $500 (Academic); $800 (Vendor/Consultant); $1,000 (Not-for-Profit); 4,500 (Supplier).

Meetings/Conferences: Annual
Conference Chair: Stacey Blicker

Publications:
Titanium Update Newsletter; on-line; adv.

International Trade Commission Trial Lawyers Association (1984)
P.O. Box 6186
Benjamin Franklin Stn.
Washington, DC 20004
Tel: (202) 508-6331
E-Mail: admin@itctla.org
Website: itctla.org
Members: 350 individuals
Staff: 5
Annual Budget: $50-100,000
Tax: 501(c)(6)

Personnel:
Secretary: Sarah Hamblin
    E-Mail: Hamblin@adduci.com

Historical Note:
ITCTLA's mission is to improve the administration of Section 337 as a remedy to prevent the importation of infringing goods at the border. Members are attorneys in good standing of the bar of any State or of the District of Columbia who possess an interest in practice before the United States International Trade Commission and persons authorized to practice before a foreign court or agency exercising authority in areas of interest to the United States International Trade Commission, or otherwise have an interest in practice before the United States International Trade Commission, or students. Membership: $95 (Attorneys); $35 (Government Attorneys) $25 (Students).

Meetings/Conferences:
Number of non-conference events/year: 10

Publications:
Membership Directory
The 337 Reporter

International Trademark Association (1878)

655 Third Ave.
Tenth Floor
New York, NY 10017-5617
Tel: (212) 642-1700 *Fax:* (212) 768-7796
E-Mail: info@inta.org
Website: inta.org
Members: 5,900 trademark owners, professionals
and academics
Staff: 60
Annual Budget: $10-25,000,000
Tax: 501(c)(6)

Personnel:
Executive Director: Alan C. Drewsen
    E-Mail: executivedirector@inta.org
Director, Human Resources and Association Governance:
    Maria Bachman
Senior Planner, Exhibits and Sponsorship: Paula Lee
    E-Mail: plee@inta.org
Director, External Relations: Bruce MacPherson
    E-Mail: bmacpherson@inta.org
Director, Information Technology: Steven Merzon
Counsel: Michael Metteauer
Director, Publications: Randi Mustello
Director, Finance and Administration: Lisa Paulen

Historical Note:
*Formerly The United States Trademark Association.
Incorporated in the state of New York January 8, 1887.
INTA's mission is to protect and promote the rights of
trademark owners, to secure useful legislation and to give
aid and encouragement to all efforts for the advancement
and observance of trademark rights. Membership: $950
(Regular); $650 (Regular Reduced/Supplementary); $850
(Associate); $600 (Non-profit); $75 (Professor); $25
(Student); $100 (Student Bridging).*

Meetings/Conferences: Annual
Conference Chair: Paula Lee
2013 - Dallas, TX (Dallas Convention Center)/May 4 -
    8
2014 - Hong Kong, China/May 10 - 14
2015 - San Diego, CA (Hilton San Diego Bayfront)/May
    2 - 6
2016 - Orlando, FL/May 21 - 25
2017 - Los Angeles, CA (Los Angeles Convention
    Center)/April 29 - May 3
2018 - Vienna, Austria/May 5 - 9
2019 - Boston, MA (Boston Convention and Exhibition
    Center)/May 18 - 22
2020 - Seatle, WA (Washington State Convention
    Center)/May 16 - 20
2021 - San Francisco, CA/April 24 - 28
2021 - San Diego, CA/May 17 - 21
2022 - Toronto, ON/May 21 - 25
2025 - San Diego, CA/May 17 - 21
Number of non-conference events/year: 4

Publications:
INTA Bulletin; quarterly; adv.
Membership Directory; annually; adv.
The Trademark Reporter; bi-monthly

Membership List Available to Non-members

The International Transactional Analysis
Association (1958)
2843 Hopyard Rd.
Suite 155
Pleasanton, CA 94588
Tel: (925) 600-8110 *Fax:* (925) 600-8112
E-Mail: itaa@itaa-net.org
Website: itaa-net.org
Members: 1600 individuals
Staff: 3
Annual Budget: $250-500,000
Tax: 501(c)(3)

Personnel:
Chief Financial Officer: Ken Fogleman
    E-Mail: ken@itaa-net.org
Coordinator, Training and Certification: Janet Chin
    E-Mail: tc.admin@itaa-net.org
Managing Editor: Robin Fryer
    E-Mail: robinfryer@aol.com

Historical Note:
*Founded in 1950-51 as the San Francisco Social Psychiatry
Seminars, Inc and became International Transactional
Analysis Association, Inc. in 1964. ITAA is a scientific
organization that strives to investigate and promote the
use of transactional analysis (TA) in psychotherapy,
education, business and other fields of human interaction.
Professional membership includes individuals from the
fields of psychotherapy, business, education, religion,*

medicine and industry. Associate membership is available
*for those whose interest is not related to their profession.
Membership: $80 (Student/Associate); $130 (Regular/
Certified Transactional Analyst); $200 (Teaching).*

Continuing Education:
Certification Designation/s: STA, TSTA, CTA, TTA

Meetings/Conferences: Annual

Publications:
Directory of TA Practitioners; on-line
Membership Directory; on-line
The Script Newsletter; adv.
Transactional Analysis Journal; quarterly; adv.

International Transplant Nurses Society (1992)
4700 W. Lake Ave.
Glenview, IL 60025
Tel: (847) 375-6340 *Fax:* (847) 375-6341
E-Mail: itns@msn.com
Website: itns.org
Members: 1400 individuals
Staff: 5
Annual Budget: $500-1,000,000
Tax: 501(c)(3)

Personnel:
Executive Director: Beth Kassalen MBA
President: Chris Shay-Downer
    E-Mail: shayc@ccf.org
Director, Education: Michelle James CNS, MS, RN
    E-Mail: mjames2@fairview.org
Director, Marketing: Patrice Pfeiffenberger BSN, CCTC,
    RN
    E-Mail: pfeiffep@uphs.upenn.edu
Treasurer: Karla Weis BSN, CCTC, RN
    E-Mail: Weis.Karla@mayo.edu

Historical Note:
*ITNS is committed to the promotion of excellence in
transplant clinical nursing by providing educational
and professional growth opportunities, interdisciplinary
networking and collaborative activities and transplant
nursing research. Membership: $75 (Active); $50
(Associate).*

Continuing Education:
Certification Designation/s: CCTC, CCTN

Meetings/Conferences: Annual
Number of non-conference events/year: 4

Publications:
E-Updates; on-line
ITNS Newsletter; quarterly

International Transplant-Skin Cancer
Collaborative (2001)
555 E. Wells St.
Suite 1100
Milwaukee, WI 53202-3823
Tel: (414) 918-3191 *Fax:* (414) 276-3349
E-Mail: info@itscc.org
Website: itscc.org
Staff: 1
Annual Budget: $10-25,000
Tax: 501(c)(3)

Personnel:
Executive Director: Kim Schardin CAE, MBA
    E-Mail: kschardin@itscc.org

Historical Note:
*ITSCC's mission is to integrate and support basic scientific
and clinical research to address the special needs of
transplant recipients with skin cancer in order to improve
quality of care and to educate patients, scientists, primary
care doctors and specialist physicians on the unique needs
and clinical care issues in the transplant patients.*

Continuing Education:
Enrollment: 1

Meetings/Conferences: Annual
2013 - Miami, FL/Feb. 28

International Travel Writers and Editors
Association (1972)
1224 N. Nokomis Ave. NE
Alexandria, MN 56308
E-Mail: ismp@iami.org
Website: iami.org/ismp
Members: 3000 individuals
Staff: 3
Annual Budget: $500-1,000,000

Personnel:
Executive Director: Robert G. Johnson

Historical Note:
Membership: $85/year (individual).

International Truck Parts Association (1974)
1720 Tenth Ave. South, Suite Four
P.O. Box 199
Great Falls, MD 20817-4909
Tel: (202) 544-3090 *Fax:* (800) 895-4654
TollFree: (866) 346-5692
E-Mail: info@itpa.com
Website: itpa.com
Members: 125 companies
Staff: 2
Annual Budget: $100-250,000

Personnel:
Editor and Contact, Meetings: Scott Tetz
    E-Mail: scott@itpa.com

Historical Note:
*ITPA's mission is to exchange information and to improve
and advance the truck parts aftermarket. ITPA is a revenue
sharing partner of HDAW (Heavy Duty Aftermarket Week).
Works to promote and foster relationships among sellers
and buyers of trucks and truck surplus products. Members
are dealers in used and rebuilt parts for heavy duty trucks.
Membership: $450/year.*

Meetings/Conferences: Annual
Conference Chair: Scott Tetz
2013 - Las Vegas, NV (Mirage)/Jan. 21 - 24

Publications:
ITPA Casting Number Directory; on-line

Membership List Available to Non-members

International Trumpet Guild (1974)
P.O. Box 2688
Davenport, IA 52809-2688
Tel: (563) 676-2435 *Fax:* (413) 403-8899
E-Mail: treasurer@trumpetguild.org
Website: trumpetguild.org
Members: 6000 individuals
Staff: 5
Annual Budget: $250-500,000
Tax: 501(c)(3)

Personnel:
President: Kim Dunnick
    E-Mail: president@trumpetguild.org
Executive Director, Web Site: Michael Anderson
    E-Mail: website@trumpetguild.org
Treasurer and Contact, Membership Services: Dixie
    Burress
    E-Mail: treasurer@trumpetguild.org
General Counsel: Mark Haynie
Editor: Gary Mortenson
    E-Mail: editor@trumpetguild.org

Historical Note:
*ITG's purpose is to promote communications among
trumpet players around world and to improve artistic
level of performance, teaching, and literature associated
with trumpet. ITG members are professional and amateur
trumpet players and teachers of trumpet. Membership:
$50-60 (Regular); $30-35 (Student/Senior); $100
(Library); $30-60 (Sponsor).*

Meetings/Conferences: Annual
2013 - Grand Rapids, MI/June 11 - 15
Number of non-conference events/year: 26

Publications:
ITG Journal; quarterly; adv.
ITG Newsletter

International Tuba-Euphonium Association
(1973)
P.O. Box 50867
Kalamazoo, MI 49005
Tel: (903) 319-4744 *Fax:* (888) 331-4832
Website: iteaonline.org
Members: 2700 individuals
Staff: 5
Annual Budget: $50-100,000
Tax: 501(c)(3)

Personnel:
Executive Director: Adam McFarlin
    E-Mail: adam@iteaonline.org
President: Deanna Swoboda
    E-Mail: deanna.swoboda@wmich.edu
Editor: Jason Roland Smith
    E-Mail: editor@iteaonline.org
Conferences Coordinator: Kenyon Wilson
    E-Mail: kenyon-wilson@utc.edu

Historical Note:
Founded as Tubists Universal Brotherhood Association; assumed its current name in 2001. ITEA is dedicated to promoting and advancing the tuba and euphonium instruments. Members are performers, educators, students, and amateurs of all backgrounds. Membership: $28 (Student Group-Five or more students); $50 (Professional/Amateur/Business); $35 (Student/Retired); $56 (Secondary School Music Educator); $940 (Lifetime); $32 (E-Member).

Meetings/Conferences: Annual
Conference Chair: Kenyon Wilson

Publications:
ITEA Journal; quarterly; adv.
ITEA Journal E-Newsletters; on-line
Membership Directory; on-line

International Turfgrass Society (1969)
C/O University of Florida, FLREC
3205 College Ave.
Ft. Lauderdale, FL 33314-7799
Tel: (954) 577-6336 *Fax:* (954) 475-4125
E-Mail: jlci@ufl.edu
Website: turfsociety.com
Members: 325 individuals
Staff: 3
Annual Budget: Under $10,000
Tax: 501(c)(3)

Personnel:
Treasurer and Membership Contact: John Cisar
    E-Mail: jlci@ufl.edu
President: Liebao Han

Historical Note:
ITS seeks to encourage research and education in turfgrass science, and to promote personal communication among the international community of turfgrass researchers by organizing international conferences to present turfgrass research and information on all phases of turfgrass production and use. Membership: $300 (Regular); $1,000 (Sustaining); $150 (Student).

Meetings/Conferences: Quadrennial
2013 - Beijing, China (Beijing Friendship Hotel)/July 14 - 19

Publications:
ITS Newsletter
ITS Research Journal

International Union of Bricklayers and Allied Craftworkers (1865)
620 F St. NW
Washington, DC 20004
Tel: (202) 783-3788 *Fax:* (202) 393-0219
TollFree: (888) 880-8222
E-Mail: askbac@bacweb.org
Website: bacweb.org
Members: 90,000 masonry-trowel trades craftworkers
Staff: 248
Annual Budget: $25-50,000,000

Personnel:
President: James Boland
Executive Vice President: Gerard Scarano

Historical Note:
Aim of BAC is to improve its members quality of life on and off the job through access to fair wages, good benefits, safe working conditions and solidarity among members.

Meetings/Conferences: Annual

Publications:
BAC Journal

Membership List Available to Non-members

International Union of Electronic, Electrical, Salaried, Machine, and Furniture Workers-CWA (1949)
2701 Dryden Rd.
Dayton, OH 45439
Website: iue-cwa.org
Members: 300000 members
Staff: 75
Annual Budget: $10-25,000,000

Personnel:
President: Jim Clark
Assistant to the President: Laure Asplen
General Counsel: Peter Mitchell
Director, Region 7: Willie Thorpe

Historical Note:
Founded as the International Union of Electrical, Radio and Machine Workers (AFL-CIO), it became the International

Union of Electronic, Electrical, Technical, Salaried and Machine Workers (AFL-CIO) in 1983, and assumed its present name in 1987. Merged with Communication Workers of America (CWA) in 2001. IUE-CWA's mission is to build a better life for all union members and their families.

International Union of Elevator Constructors (1901)
7154 Columbia Gateway Dr.
Columbia, MD 21046
Tel: (410) 953-6150 *Fax:* (410) 953-6169
E-Mail: contact@iuec.org
Website: iuec.org
Members: 25000 individuals
Staff: 11
Annual Budget: $10-25,000,000
Tax: 501(c)(5)

Personnel:
General President: Dana A. Brigham
General Secretary and Treasurer: Kevin P. Stringer

Historical Note:
Established in Pittsburgh July 18, 1901 as the National Union of Elevator Constructors, became the International Union of Elevator Constructors in 1903 and received a charter from the American Federation of Labor. IUEC's mission is to maintain an elevator constructor's school for instructing and teaching the practical applications of the elevator industry.

Publications:
Elevator Constructor Journal

International Union of Journeymen and Allied Trades (1874)
93 Lake Ave.
Suite 103
Danbury, CT 06810
Tel: (203) 205-0101 *Fax:* (203) 205-0006
E-Mail: info@iujat.org
Website: iujat.org
Members: 57224 individuals
Staff: 22
Annual Budget: $2-5,000,000

Personnel:
International President: Steven R. Elliott
Director, Communications: Jacqueline Elliot
Secretary and Treasurer: William Sweeney

Historical Note:
Formerly (2000) International Union of Journeymen Horseshoers of the United States and Canada. IUJAT provides training and information on efficient, proper and humane horseshoes to the professional and amateur horseman as well as working to obtain equitable wages for horseshoers. Membership: $720/year (Individual).

Publications:
IUJAT Newsletter; on-line

International Union of Operating Engineers (1896)
1125 17th St. NW
Washington, DC 20036
Tel: (202) 429-9100 *Fax:* (202) 778-2613
Website: iuoe.org
Members: 400000 individuals
Staff: 160
Annual Budget: $50-100,000,000
Tax: 501(c)(5)

Personnel:
General Secretary and Treasurer: Christopher Hanley
    E-Mail: chanley@iuoegpp.org
Director, Department of Politics, Corporate and Government Affairs: Timothy P. James
Co-General Counsel: Elizabeth A. Nadeau
    E-Mail: lnadeau@iuoe.org

Historical Note:
Established in Chicago, IL in 1896 as the National Union of Steam Engineers and received a charter from the American Federation of Labor the following year, became the International Union of Steam Engineers (1898) following the acceptance of Canadian locals, renamed as the International Union of Steam and Operating Engineers, which in 1927 merged with the International Brotherhood of Steam Shovel and Dredgemen, assumed its present name in 1928 and absorbed the United Welders International Union (1969). IUOE's mission is to ensure protections of prevailing wages on public projects, to alleviate healthcare costs through coalition building, to improve its contractors' competitiveness. Members are operating engineers, stationary engineers, nurses, other health industry workers and public employees.

Publications:
IUOE Magazine; on-line

International Union of Painters and Allied Trades (1887)
7234 Pkwy. Dr.
Hanover, MD 21076
Tel: (410) 564-5900
E-Mail: mail@iupat.org
Website: iupat.org
Members: 140000 individuals
Staff: 5
Annual Budget: $25-50,000,000
Tax: 501(c)(5)

Personnel:
General Secretary and Treasurer: George Galis
Manager, Communications: Gavin McDonald
    E-Mail: gmcdonald@iupat.org
Executive General Vice President: Kenneth E. Rigmaiden

Historical Note:
Formerly (1887) the Brotherhood of Painters and Decorators, (1890) Brotherhood of Painters, Decorators and Paperhangers of America, (1969) International Brotherhood of Painters and Allied Trades, Absorbed the United Scenic Artists, the National Paperhangers Association and the National Union of Sign Painters. Merged with the Amalgamated Glass Workers International Association in 1915 and assumed its present name in 1999. IUPAT's mission is to fight for fair and equal representation in the workplace as the core of the labor movement. Members work in finishing trades as painters, drywall finishers, wallcoverers, glaziers, glass workers, floor covering installers, sign makers, display workers, convention and show decorators.

Publications:
EXHIBITOR Magazine
General Constitution
Painters and Allied Trades Journal

International Union of Police Associations, AFL-CIO (1979)
1549 Ringling Blvd.
Sixth Floor
Sarasota, FL 34236
Tel: (941) 487-2560 *Fax:* (941) 487-2570
E-Mail: iupa@iupa.com
Website: iupa.org
Members: 80000 individuals
Staff: 22
Annual Budget: $5-10,000,000
Tax: 501(c)(5)

Personnel:
International President: Sam A. Cabral
    E-Mail: iupa@iupa.com
President: Samuel A. Cabral
    E-Mail: sam@iupa.org
International Executive Vice President: John O'Keefe
Chief of Staff: Thomas Jordan
Marketing Director: Michael Keene
General Counsel: Aaron Nisenson
    E-Mail: gcounsel@iupa.org
International Secretary and Treasurer: Timothy A. Scott
Legislative Liaison: Dennis J. Slocumb
    E-Mail: iupa@iupa.com

Historical Note:
The International Union of Police Associations (IUPA or I.U.P.A.) is a trade union in the United States chartered for law enforcement, corrections. IUPA's mission is to support law enforcement and corrections officers in addition to support personnel.

Meetings/Conferences: Annual
Number of non-conference events/year: 5

Publications:
Membership Directory; on-line
Newsletter

International Union of Toxicology (1980)
James L. Winkle College of Pharmacy, University of Cincinnati
3225 Eden Ave.
Cincinnati, OH 45267
Tel: (513) 558-3326
E-Mail: iutoxhq@iutox.org
Website: iutox.org
Members: 20047 individuals and national/regional society members
Staff: 2
Annual Budget: $100-250,000

Personnel:
President: Daniel Acosta Jr., CAE
   E-Mail: Daniel.Acosta@uc.edu

Historical Note:
IUTOX's mission is to improve human health through the science and practice of toxicology world-wide. IUTOX achieves its vision by supporting international scientific cooperation for the global acquisition and utilization of knowledge in toxicology for the improvement of human health. Membership: $200-6000/year (Based on members).

Meetings/Conferences: Annual
2013 - San Antonio, TX (The Henry B. Gonzalez Convention Center)/March 10 - 14
2014 - Phoenix, AZ (Phoenix Convention Center)/ March 23 - 27
2015 - San Diego, CA (San Diego Convention Center)/ March 22 - 26

Publications:
IUTOX Newsletter

International Utility Efficiency Partnerships
2000 L St. NW
Suite 805
Washington, DC 20036
Tel: (202) 293-7992 *Fax:* (202) 478-2525
E-Mail: contact@iuep.org
Website: iuep.org
Staff: 1
Annual Budget: $250-500,000

Personnel:
President and Executive Director: Ronald C. Shiflett Jr.
   E-Mail: ronalsee@eei.org

Historical Note:
The IUEP's objective is to sponsor the projects that prove real potential to reduce emissions in the atmosphere, thereby facilitating the creation of actual 'tons of reductions on the table, and the development of strong partnerships between the developing world and U.S. manufacturers, developers, and electricity providers.

International Vessel Operators Dangerous Goods Association *(1972)*
Ten Hunter Brook Ln.
Queensbury, NY 12804
Tel: (518) 761-0263 *Fax:* (518) 792-7781
E-Mail: mail@ivodga.com
Website: ivodga.com
Members: 29 ocean carriers
Staff: 5
Annual Budget: $100-250,000

Personnel:
Administrator and Chief Technical Officer: John V. Currie
   E-Mail: jack@ivodga.com
Director, Communications: Anne Barry
   E-Mail: mail@ivodga.com
Director, Marketing: Lori Buckius
   E-Mail: mail@ivodga.com
Administrator: Lara Mehr Currie
   E-Mail: lara@vohma.com
Vice President, Membership Services: Christine M. Yakush
   E-Mail: chris@ivodga.com

Historical Note:
Formerly (2010) known as the International Vessel Operators Hazardous Materials Association (VOHMA). IVODGA's primary focus is to foster the safe handling of hazardous materials in shipment by sea, and to offer the expertise of the ocean carriers in forging regulatory development. It also provides a variety of services and benefits to its members, ranging from discounts on technical and educational publications and programs, opportunities and network to share information. Membership: $2,800 (Associate); $3,750-5,550 (Based on TEUs).

Meetings/Conferences:
Conference Chair: Anne Barry

Publications:
email newsletter; bi-monthly
Membership Directory; on-line

International Veterinary Academy of Pain Management *(2003)*
618 Church St.
Suite 220
Nashville, TN 37219
Fax: (615) 254-7047
E-Mail: ivapm@xmi-amc.com
Website: ivapm.org

Staff: 2
Annual Budget: $100-250,000

Personnel:
Treasurer: Kathy Morris-Stilwell

Historical Note:
IVPAM's mission is to provide forums for communication among all interested parties of knowledge concerning the biology and treatment of animal pain, provide continuing education in the area of pain recognition and treatment. Membership: $120 (Veterinarians/Medical Doctors/ Dentist/PhDs/Physical Therapists); $60 (Veterinary Nurses/Technicians); $30 (Students/Graduates Students/ Residents); $40 (Retired Professionals).

Continuing Education:
Certification Designation/s: CVPP, CAPP

Publications:
IVAPM Newsletter
Membership Directory; on-line

International Veterinary Acupuncture Society *(1974)*
1730 S. College Ave.
Suite 301
Ft. Collins, CO 80525
Tel: (970) 266-0666 *Fax:* (970) 266-0777
E-Mail: office@ivas.org
Website: ivas.org
Members: 1,900 Individuals
Staff: 4
Annual Budget: $500-1,000,000

Personnel:
Executive Director: Vikki Weber MBA
   E-Mail: vikki.weber.mba@ivas.org

Historical Note:
IVAS's mission is to provide, advocate and support veterinary acupuncture and related treatment modalities through quality basic, advanced and continuing education. It offers educational programs and accreditation examinations. Membership: $100 (Active/Associate); $85 (Affiliate); $75 (Institutional); $40 (Retired).

Continuing Education:
Certification Designation/s: BVA, CVCHM, VAC

Publications:
The Point; quarterly; adv.

International Visual Literacy Association *(1968)*
St. Joseph's University
5600 City Ave.
Philadelphia, PA 19131
E-Mail: treasurer@ivla.org
Website: ivla.org
Members: 350 individuals
Staff: 2
Annual Budget: Under $10,000

Personnel:
President: Nicos Valanide
   E-Mail: nichri@ucy.ac.cy
Executive Treasurer: Teri Sosa
   E-Mail: tsosa@sju.edu

Historical Note:
Affiliated with the Association for Educational Communications and Technology. IVLA's mission is to provide a multidisciplinary forum for exploration, presentation, and discussion of visual communication; to serve as an organizational base for professionals interested in visual literacy projects, programs, and research. Membership: $60 (Full); $30 (Retired/Student); $500 (Lifetime).

Meetings/Conferences: Annual

Publications:
Journal of Visual Literacy; bi-annually
The Review; quarterly

International Warehouse Logistics Association *(1891)*
2800 S. River Rd.
Suite 260
Des Plaines, IL 60018
Tel: (847) 813-4699 *Fax:* (847) 813-0115
TollFree: (800) 525-0165
E-Mail: email@iwla.com
Website: iwla.com
Members: 500 companies
Staff: 13
Annual Budget: $2-5,000,000

Personnel:
President and Chief Executive Officer: Joel Anderson

   E-Mail: janderson@iwla.com
IWLA Convention and Meetings Consultant: Scott Brewster
   E-Mail: sbrewster@iwla.com
Database Coordinator: Ben Fairbank
   E-Mail: bfairbank@IWLA.com
Marketing and Communications Coordinator: Camille Golden
   E-Mail: cgolden@iwla.com
Senior Coordinator, Accounting and Finance: Rocio Lemke
   E-Mail: rlemke@IWLA.com
Manager, Administrative and Personnel Services: Sheresa McClain
   E-Mail: smcclain@iwla.com
Washington Representative: Pat O'Connor
   E-Mail: patoconnor@kentoconnor.com
Director, Media and Industry Relations: David Sparkman
   E-Mail: dsparkman@iwla.com
Director, Membership, Marketing and Business Development: Jay Strother
   E-Mail: jstrother@IWLA.com
Manager, Education: Liz Whitney
   E-Mail: lwhitney@IWLA.com

Historical Note:
Formed from a merger of the Canadian Association of Warehousing and Distribution Services (CAWDS) with the American Warehouse Association (AWA) in 1997. IWLA works for warehousing and logistics industry, representing third-party logistics (3PL) and warehousing service providers. Mission is to help members run high-quality, profitable warehouse logistics businesses. Members are committed to warehousing and protecting the free flow of products across international borders.

Continuing Education:
Enrollment: 69
Certification Designation/s: CLP

Meetings/Conferences: Annual
Conference Chair: Scott Brewster
2013 - Orlando, FL (Loews Portofino Bay Hotel at Universal Orlando)/March 10 - 12
Number of non-conference events/year: 4

Publications:
3PL America; quarterly; adv.
This Week @ IWLA; on-line; adv.

Membership List Available to Non-members

International Waterlily and Water Gardening Society *(1984)*
P.O. Box 546
Greenville, VA 24440
Tel: (540) 337-4507 *Fax:* (540) 337-0738
E-Mail: info@iwgs.org
Website: iwgs.org
Members: 500 individuals
Staff: 3
Annual Budget: $50-100,000

Personnel:
Executive Director: Larry Nau
   E-Mail: execdirector@iwgs.org
Editor: Tim Davis
   E-Mail: timgod555@hotmail.com

Historical Note:
Formerly (1985) the Water Lily Society and (1998) International Water Lily Society. Established and incorporated at Lilypons, MD. IWGS is concerned with all aspects of water gardening. Mission is to promote knowledge, leadership, and standards of excellence in water gardening and related aquatic plant areas. Membership: $0-5,000/year.

Meetings/Conferences: Annual
Number of non-conference events/year: 1

Publications:
Aquatic Resources Directory; on-line
IWGS Journal; quarterly
Membership Directory; on-line

Membership List Available to Non-members

International Webmasters Association *(1996)*
119 E. Union St.
Suite F
Pasadena, CA 91103
Tel: (626) 449-3709 *Fax:* (626) 449-8308
TollFree: (866) 607-1773
Website: iwanet.org
Members: 22000 individuals
Staff: 4
Annual Budget: $50-100,000

Tax: 501(c)(6)

Personnel:
Executive Director: Richard S. Brinegar
Contact, Membership Services: Claudia Garcia

Historical Note:
IWA's mission is to provide and foster professional advancement opportunities among individuals dedicated to or pursuing a web career, and to work diligently to enhance their effectiveness, image, and professionalism as they attract and serve their clients and employers. Members are webmasters, web site developers, graphic designers, multimedia specialists and others who participate in the development, monitoring and management of web site. Membership: $49 (Individual Full Regular); Free (Individual Trial Member).

Continuing Education:
Certification Designation/s: WSC, CWP

Publications:
IWA Newsletter; monthly
Member Directory; on-line

International Weed Science Society *(1975)*
University of Arkansas, Department of Crop, Soil, and Environmental Sciences
1366 W. Altheimer Dr.
Fayetteville, AR 72704
Tel: (479) 575-3984 *Fax:* (479) 575-3975
E-Mail: secretary@iwss.info
Website: iwss.info
Members: 610 individuals and institutions
Staff: 3
Annual Budget: Under $10,000

Personnel:
Vice President: Nilda R. Burgos
    E-Mail: vice-president@iwss.info

Historical Note:
IWSS encourages, promotes, and assists development of global weed science and weed control technology. Membership: $30 (Individual); $100 (Associate); $300 (Lifetime).

Meetings/Conferences:
Number of non-conference events/year: 2

Publications:
IWSS Newsletter; bi-annually
Membership Directory; on-line
Weed Science Journal

International Wild Rice Association *(1969)*
5213 Lake Washburn Rd. NE
Outing, MN 56662
Tel: (218) 792-5722 *Fax:* (218) 792-5723
E-Mail: iwra@brainerd.net
Website: wildrice.org
Members:
22 Individuals and Organisations
31 Companies
Staff: 2
Annual Budget: $10-25,000

Personnel:
President: Larry Payne
Secretary/Treasurer: Walt Oilar

Historical Note:
IWRA is dedicated to the exchange of generic information and ideas relevant to wild rice production, processing and marketing for the overall benefit of its members. Membership: $150 (Regular); $75 (Associate).

Meetings/Conferences: Annual

Publications:
IWRA Newsletter; annually
Membership Directory; on-line

Membership List Available to Non-members

International Wildlife Management Consortium
1470 Heather Ridge Blvd.
Unit 104
Dunedin, FL 34698
Tel: (727) 734-4949 *Fax:* (727) 734-4949
E-Mail: iwmc@iwmc.org
Website: iwmc.org
Staff: 1

Personnel:
Vice President: Dr. Janice Henke

Historical Note:
IWMC mission is to promote Sustainable Use of wild resources, terrestrial and aquatic as a conservation mechanism.

Publications:
Sustainable eNews; monthly

International Window Cleaning Association *(1989)*
400 Admiral Blvd.
Kansas City, MO 64106
Tel: (816) 471-4922 *Fax:* (816) 472-7765
TollFree: (800) 875-4922
E-Mail: iwca@robstan.com
Website: iwca.org
Members: 700 companies
Staff: 5
Annual Budget: $250-500,000
Tax: 501(c)(6)

Personnel:
Executive Director: Ken Bowman
    E-Mail: kenb@robstan.com
Director, Conferences: Rosemary Hall
    E-Mail: rosemary@robstan.com
Director, Membership Services: Casey High
    E-Mail: casey@robstan.com

Historical Note:
IWCA's mission is to educate and assist its members in developing professionalism, ethics and standards of safety and to promote the welfare of the industry through advocacy, education, training and community involvement. Members are firms engaged in the provision of window cleaning services, or those engaged in the manufacturing, converting or supplying of products or services for the same. Membership: $250-800 (Professional); $350-1,000 (Associate); $225 (Corresponding).

Continuing Education:
Certification Designation/s: IWCASC, CRR, CCG, CRDS, CSS, CHRS

Meetings/Conferences: Annual
Conference Chair: Rosemary Hall
2013 - St. Pete Beach, FL (TradeWinds Island Resort)/ Feb. 13 - 16/400 attendees

Publications:
Membership Directory; on-line

Membership List Available to Non-members

International Window Film Association *(1991)*
P.O. Box 3871
Martinsville, VA 24115-3871
Tel: (276) 666-4932 *Fax:* (276) 666-4933
E-Mail: admin@iwfa.com
Website: iwfa.com
Members: 800 individuals
Staff: 3
Annual Budget: $1-2,000,000
Tax: 501(c)(6)

Personnel:
Executive Director: Darrell K. Smith CIH, PhD
    E-Mail: Admin@IWFA.com
Administrative Assistant: Laura McGee
    E-Mail: Laura@IWFA.com
Clerical Assistant: Dolly Whisonant
    E-Mail: Dolly@IWFA.com

Historical Note:
The mission of the IWFA is to provide value-added services to the membership, to help sustain and grow the member's businesses, and to partner with the manufacturers and other members to increase consumer awareness and demand for all types of professionally-installed window film products. Membership: $100-&175175 (U.S. Dealer); $100-$135 (International and Canadian Dealer); $2,500 (Distributor, U.S. and Canadian); $375 (International); $10,000 (Manufacturer); $2,000 (Supplier, Raw Materials); $500 (Supplier, Equipment and Accessories/Sub-Distributor); $2,000 (International Chapter).

Meetings/Conferences: Annual

Publications:
IWFA Newsletter; quarterly

International Women's Writing Guild *(1976)*
317 Madison Ave.
Suite 1704
New York, NY 10017
Tel: (212) 737-7536 *Fax:* (212) 737-9469
E-Mail: iwwg@iwwg.org
Website: iwwg.org
Members: 3200 individuals
Staff: 3
Annual Budget: $100-250,000
Tax: 501(c)(3)

Personnel:

Founder: Hannelore Hahn
    E-Mail: dirhahn@iwwg.org
Executive Director: Cynthia Fritts Stillwell
Contact, Communications: Elizabeth Julia Stoumen
    E-Mail: elizabethjulia88@aol.com

Historical Note:
IWWG's mission is to provide an unfiltered, non-commercial space in which creative people and the public can connect in a meaningful, productive way through artists' projects, critical writing, fiction, poetry, visual essays, interviews and music. Membership: $55-65 (Adult); $30-40 (Youth).

Meetings/Conferences: Annual
Number of non-conference events/year: 2

Publications:
Membership Directory; on-line
Network; quarterly

Membership List Available to Non-members

The International Wood Products Association *(1956)*
4214 King St. West
Alexandria, VA 22302
Tel: (703) 820-6696 *Fax:* (703) 820-8550
E-Mail: info@iwpawood.org
Website: iwpawood.org
Members: 220 companies
Staff: 4
Annual Budget: $25-50,000
Tax: 501(c)(6)

Personnel:
Executive Vice President: Brent J. McClendon CAE
    E-Mail: brent@iwpawood.org
Manager, Government and Public Affairs: Ashley Amidon
Manager, Membership Services and Marketing: Lance Clark
Director, Finance and Administration: Annette Ferri

Historical Note:
Represents companies that import wood and wood products. IWPA's mission is advancing international trade in wood products through education and leadership in business, environmental and public affairs. Membership: $1,890-8,295 (Voting); $1,365 (Associate); $1,130 (Overseas).

Meetings/Conferences: Annual
2013 - Vancouver, BC (Westin Bayshore)/April 17 - 19/300 attendees

Publications:
IHPA Industry Standards; irregular
International Wood (IW) Magazine; adv.
International Wood: The Guide to Applications, Sources, and Trends; on-line; adv.
IWPA eNews; on-line
Membership Directory; on-line

International Writing Centers Association *(1983)*
West Virginia University
English Department
Morgantown, WV 26505
Tel: (304) 293-9731
E-Mail: meodice@ou.edu
Website: writingcenters.org
Members: 400 individuals
Staff: 3
Annual Budget: $10-25,000
Tax: 501(c)(3)

Personnel:
President: Nathalie Singh-Corcoran
    E-Mail: Nathalie.Singh-Corcoran@mail.wvu.edu
Contact, Meetings: Ginny Ryan
    E-Mail: vryan@mun.ca

Historical Note:
The National Writing Centers Association, which would later become the International Writing Centers Association, had its origins in the East Central Writing Centers Association in an effort led by Nancy McCracken and others. IWCA is an affiliate of National Council of Teachers of English whose mission is to foster communication among writing centers and to provide a forum for concerns. Members are writing center directors and staff members. Membership: $30/year.

Meetings/Conferences: Annual
Conference Chair: Ginny Ryan
Number of non-conference events/year: 1

Publications:
Membership Directory; on-line
The Writing Center Journal; semi-annually

Writing Lab Newsletter; monthly; adv.

International Zinc Association-America (1990)
1750 K. St. NW
Suite 700
Washington, DC 20006
Tel: (202) 223-2478 *Fax:* (202) 223-2479
E-Mail: info@zinc.org
Website: zinc.org
Members: 240 companies
Staff: 1
Annual Budget: $500-1,000,000

Personnel:
Stephen Wilkinson

Historical Note:
IZA's mission is to promote the general welfare of the zinc industry, to serve as a spokesgroup and information center for zinc and monitor environmental and other issues pertinent to the zinc industry. Members are producers of zinc metal, oxide and dust selling in the United States and consumers of zinc.

Meetings/Conferences: Annual

Publications:
Membership Directory; on-line
Zinc in Fertilizers-Newsletter

Internet Alliance (1982)
1615 L St. NW
Suite 1100
Washington, DC 20036-5624
Tel: (202) 861-2407
E-Mail: info@internetalliance.org
Website: internetalliance.org
Members: 70 states and companies
Staff: 5
Annual Budget: $250-500,000

Personnel:
Executive Director: Tammy Cota
   E-Mail: tammy@internetalliance.org
Press Secretary and Administration Lobbyist: Robert Sherman

Historical Note:
Founded as Interactive Services Association, merged with the National Association for Interactive Services in 1994, and assumed its current name in 1998. The IA's mission is to advocate confidence and trust in the Internet so it can reach its potential as the most dynamic market medium of this century.Membership consists of companies developing mass market electronic information and transaction services and all other components of the industry. Membership: $20,000/year (Company).

Publications:
IA Newsletter; on-line

Internet Commerce Association (f/k/a Internet Traffic Association)
1155 F St. NW
Washington, DC 20004
Staff: 1
Annual Budget: $100-250,000

Personnel:
Counsel: Philip S. Corwin

Historical Note:
Trade association for domain name investors and developers.

Internet Marketing Association (2001)
Ten Mar Del Rey
San Clemente, CA 92673
Tel: (949) 443-9300 *Fax:* (949) 443-2215
E-Mail: info@imanetwork.org
Website: imanetwork.org
Members: 650,000 members
Staff: 9

Personnel:
Executive Director: Tyler Holliday
   E-Mail: tyler@imanetwork.org
Director, Government Relations: Bill Brough
Contact, Creative Designer and Web Master: Lei Lani Fera
Internet Marketing Director: Hesam Rasoulzadeh
Director, Administration: Ana Rotar
   E-Mail: ana@imanetwork.org
Director, Finance: Vince Walden
   E-Mail: vince@imanetwork.org

Historical Note:
A professional organization that, since its inception in 2001, has accrued more than 650,000 members in various

fields including sales, marketing, business ownership, programming and creative development. IMA mission is to provide a knowledge-sharing platform for business professionals where proven Internet marketing strategies are demonstrated and shared in an effort to increase each member's value to their organization.

Continuing Education:
Certification Designation/s: CIM

Meetings/Conferences: Annual

Membership List Available to Non-members

Internet Security Alliance (2000)
2500 Wilson Blvd.
Arlington, VA 22201
Tel: (703) 907-7090 *Fax:* (703) 907-7093
E-Mail: info@isalliance.org
Website: isalliance.org
Staff: 4
Annual Budget: $1-2,000,000
Tax: 501(c)(6)

Personnel:
President and Chief Executive Officer: Larry Clinton
   E-Mail: lclinton@isalliance.org
Associate Vice President: Stephanie Schaffer
   E-Mail: sschaffer@isalliance.org

Historical Note:
Formed from a collaboration between the Electronic Industries Alliance, CyLab at Carnegie Mellon University and various trade associations. ISA's mission is to integrate advancements in technology with pragmatic business needs and enlightened public policy to create a sustainable system of cyber security. Membership comprises of cross-sectoral industry leaders in the U.S. and international markets. Membership: $25,000 (Full); $5,000 (Associate/Wholesale); $70,000 (Sponsor).

Publications:
Memship directory; on-line

Internet Society (1992)
1775 Wiehle Ave.
Suite 201
Reston, VA 20190-5108
Tel: (703) 439-2120 *Fax:* (703) 326-9881
E-Mail: isoc@isoc.org
Website: internetsociety.org
Members: 100 organisation, 44,000 individual and 80 Chapters
Staff: 62
Annual Budget: $25-50,000,000
Tax: 501(c)(3)

Personnel:
President and Chief Executive Officer: Lynn St. Amour
   E-Mail: st.amour@isoc.org
Regional Director, North America: Paul Brigner
   E-Mail: brigner@isoc.org
Senior Manager, Events: Kevin Craemer
   E-Mail: craemer@isoc.org
Chief Internet Technology Officer: Leslie Daigle
   E-Mail: daigle@isoc.org
Director, Online Marketing Programs: Dan Graham
   E-Mail: dan.graham@isoc.org
Chief Financial Officer: Greg Kapfer
   E-Mail: kapfer@isoc.org
Human Resources and Internal Policy: Linda Klieforth
   E-Mail: klieforth@isoc.org
Vice President, Public Policy: Markus Kummer
   E-Mail: kummer@isoc.org
Senior Director, Membership and Services: Ted Mooney
   E-Mail: mooney@isoc.org
Staff Accountant: Sabina Nabi
   E-Mail: nabi@isoc.org
Chief Operating Officer: Walda W. Roseman
   E-Mail: roseman@isoc.org
Director, Finance: Sandy Spector
   E-Mail: spector@isoc.org
Director, Communications Operations and Planning: Greg Wood
   E-Mail: wood@isoc.org

Historical Note:
ISOC's mission is to promote the open development, evolution, and use of the Internet for the benefit of all people throughout the world. Also provides leadership in Internet related standards, education, and policy. Members are technologists, developers, educators, researchers, government representatives, business people and others with an interest in internet technologies and applications. Membership: $75 (Sustaining); $50,000-100,000 (Platinum Member); $25,000- 50,000 (Gold Member); $12,500-25,000 (Silver Member); $5,000-10,000

(Executive Member); $2,500-5,000 (Professional Member); $1,250-2,500 (Small Business Member).

Meetings/Conferences: Annual
Conference Chair: Kevin Craemer
Number of non-conference events/year: 2

Publications:
e-OTI; on-line
IETF Journal
Internet Society Monthly Newsletter; monthly

Intersocietal Accreditation Commission (1990)
6021 University Blvd.
Suite 500
Ellicott City, MD 21043
Tel: (800) 838-2110 *Fax:* (866) 663-5663
TollFree: (800) 838-2110
Website: intersocietal.org
Members: 5000 laboratories
Staff: 36
Annual Budget: $5-10,000,000
Tax: 501(c)(6)

Personnel:
Chief Executive Officer: Sandra L. Katanick CAE
   E-Mail: katanick@intersocietal.org
Manager, Creative Design: Kellie Bair
   E-Mail: bair@intersocietal.org
Chief Operations Officer: Patricia Catalano
   E-Mail: catalano@intersocietal.org
Chief Information Officer: Kenneth Kirby
   E-Mail: kirby@intersocietal.org
Director, Finance: Bonnie Miller
   E-Mail: miller@intersocietal.org
Director, Marketing and Communications: Tamara Sloper
   E-Mail: sloper@intersocietal.org
Chief Compliance Officer , Accreditation and QA Monitor: Cindy Weiland
   E-Mail: weiland@intersocietal.org

Historical Note:
IAC provides accreditation programs for Vascular Testing, Echocardiography, Nuclear/PET, MRI, CT/Dental and Carotid Stenting. IAC's mission is to improve health care through accreditation.The IAC is comprised of six member divisions, each ensuring quality patient care and promoting health care within a specific medical specialty, all dedicated to one common mission.

Publications:
IAC Newsletter; monthly

Intersociety Council For Pathology Information (1957)
9650 Rockville Pike
Bethesda, MD 20814-3993
Tel: (301) 634-7200 *Fax:* (301) 634-7990
E-Mail: icpi@asip.org
Website: pathologytraining.org
Members: 5 societies
Staff: 2
Annual Budget: $250-500,000
Tax: 501(c)(3)

Personnel:
Executive Officer: Mark E. Sobel MD, PhD
   E-Mail: mesobel@asip.org
Administrator and Managing Editor: Donna Stivers
   E-Mail: dstivers@asip.org

Historical Note:
Incorporated in 1968. ICPI's mission is to serve as a source of information about pathology in the practice of medicine, in medical research, and to provide literature about pathology as a career. Membership: $100/year (Associate).

Continuing Education:
Certification Designation/s: CP

Publications:
Directory of Pathology Training Programs; annually

Interstate Council on Water Policy (1959)
25 State Police Dr.
West Trenton, NJ 08628-0360
Tel: (609) 883-9500
E-Mail: icwp2005@yahoo.com
Website: icwp.org
Members: 70 agencies and businesses and associations
Staff: 4
Annual Budget: $100-250,000
Tax: 501(c)(3)

Personnel:

Secretary and Treasurer: Bob Tudor
E-Mail: robert.tudor@drbc.state.nj.us

Historical Note:
Formerly (1990) The Interstate Conference on Water Policy. ICWP's mission is to provide means for its members to exchange information, ideas, and experience and to work with federal agencies which share water management responsibilities. Members are state and regional agencies concerned with conservation, development and administration of water and land-related resources. Membership: $5,000 (Large State/Agency, population over 5 million); $3,500 (Small State, population less than 5 million); $1,500 (Affiliate).

Meetings/Conferences: Annual

Publications:
Membership Directory; on-line

Interstate Natural Gas Association of America (1944)
20 F St. NW
Suite 450
Washington, DC 20001
Tel: (202) 216-5900
Website: ingaa.org
Members: 39 companies
Staff: 26
Annual Budget: $10-25,000,000
Tax: 501(c)(6)

Personnel:
President and Chief Executive Officer: Donald F. Santa Jr.
E-Mail: dsanta@ingaa.org
Senior Vice President, Environment, Safety and Operations: Terry D. Boss
E-Mail: tboss@ingaa.org
Office Manager and Manager, Information Technology: Marvel Colliet
Vice President and General Counsel: Joan Dreskin
E-Mail: jdreskin@ingaa.org
Vice President, Legislative Affairs: Martin E. Edwards III
E-Mail: medwards@ingaa.org
Executive Director, INGAA Foundation: Richard Hoffmann
Director, Communications: Catherine J. Landry
Executive Assistant and Meeting Planner: Nichole Willison

Historical Note:
Formerly Independent Natural Gas Association of America. Assumed its present name in 1974. INGAA advocates regulatory and legislative positions of importance to the natural gas pipeline industry in North America. INGAA represents interstate natural gas transmission pipeline companies operating in the U.S., as well as in Canada and Mexico.

Meetings/Conferences: Annual
Conference Chair: Nichole Willison

Interstate Oil and Gas Compact Commission (1935)
P.O. Box 53127
Oklahoma City, OK 73152-3127
Tel: (405) 525-3556 Fax: (405) 525-3592
E-Mail: iogcc@iogcc.state.ok.us
Website: iogcc.state.ok.us
Members: 37 International Affliates and states
Staff: 4
Annual Budget: $1-2,000,000

Personnel:
Executive Director: Michael Smith
Coordinator, Member Benefits: Laurel Baird
Manager, Communications: Carol Booth
E-Mail: carolbooth@iogcc.state.ok.us
Manager, Federal Projects: Amy Childers

Historical Note:
Formerly (1991) the Interstate Oil and Gas Compact Commission. IOGCC's mission is to promote the conservation and efficient recovery of domestic oil and natural gas resources while protecting health, safety and the environment. Any oil or gas producing state is entitled to become a regular member of the Commission by executing the Compact in the manner provided. Any state desiring to be an associate member may make an application to the Commission in writing, signed by its governor.

Meetings/Conferences:
2013 - Point Clear, AL (Grand Hotel Marriott Resort, Golf Club and Spa)/May 20 - 22
2013 - Long Beach, CA (Renaissance Long Beach Hotel)/Nov. 4 - 6
Number of non-conference events/year: 2

Publications:
IOGCC Newsletter; irregular
Membership Directory; on-line

Membership List Available to Non-members

Interstate Renewable Energy Council (1982)
P.O. Box 1156
Latham, NY 12110-1156
Tel: (518) 458-6059
E-Mail: info@irecusa.org
Website: irecusa.org
Staff: 4
Annual Budget: $2-5,000,000
Tax: 501(c)(3)

Personnel:
Executive Director and Contact, Workforce Development Program: Jane Weissman
E-Mail: jane@irecusa.org
Coordinator, Administrative Services: Maryteresa Colello
E-Mail: mt@irecusa.org
Contact, Credentialing Programs: Patricia Fox
E-Mail: patfox@irecusa.org
Contact, Communications: Jane Pulaski
E-Mail: janep@irecusa.org

Historical Note:
IREC strives to accelerate the sustainable utilization of renewable energy sources and technologies in and through state and local government and community activities. Members include state energy offices, city energy offices, other municipal and state agencies, national laboratories, solar and renewable organizations and companies, and individual members. Membership: $500 (State Government Agencies/Local and County Government Agencies/Federal Government Agencies/Corporate Members); $250 (Non-Profit Organizations); $100 (Community Members); $75 (Individual Members); $1,000 (Corporates, with more than 25 employees); $1,500 (Sustaining Members).

Continuing Education:
Certification Designation/s: ISPQ

Meetings/Conferences: Annual

Publications:
Connecting to the Grid:; monthly
Small Wind Energy Newsletter; quarterly
The IREC Report; monthly
The ISPQ Insider; monthly
The SITN Quarterly; quarterly

Intersure, Ltd. (1966)
Three Hotel St.
Warrenton, VA 20186
Tel: (540) 349-0969 Fax: (540) 349-0971
E-Mail: info@intersurepartners.com
Website: intersurepartners.com
Members: 45 insurance agencies
Staff: 2
Annual Budget: $50-100,000

Personnel:
Contact, Communications: Millie Curtis

Historical Note:
Formerly (1985) Association of International Insurance Agents. Purpose is to promote the principles of a free exchange of ideas and mutual cooperation based on the standards of integrity, confidentiality and trust.

Meetings/Conferences: Semi-Annual

Intertribal Monitoring Association on Indian Trust Funds (1990)
2309 Renard SE
Suite 212
Albuquerque, NM 87106
Tel: (505) 247-1447 Fax: (505) 247-2013
E-Mail: itma@itmatrustfunds.org
Website: itmatrustfunds.org
Members: 65 Organisations
Staff: 3

Personnel:
Executive Director: Mary Zuni Chalan
Legal Counsel: Brian Gunn Esq.
Administrative Assistant and Records Manager and Technical Support: Daniel Little

Historical Note:
ITMA's mission is to focus on trust fund and asset management initiatives as developed by tribal participants.

Meetings/Conferences: Annual

Publications:
ITMA Newsletter

Intertribal Timber Council (1976)
1112 NE 21st Ave.
Suite Four
Portland, OR 97232-2114
Tel: (503) 282-4296 Fax: (503) 282-1274
E-Mail: itc1@teleport.com
Website: itcnet.org
Staff: 2
Annual Budget: $500-1,000,000
Tax: 501(c)(3)

Personnel:
Program Manager: Laura Alvidrez
Technical Specialist: Don Motanic

Historical Note:
Intertribal Timber Council works to pursue and promote the the conservation and development of Indian forest resources for the benefit and advancement of Indian people. Membership: $250 (General); $25 (Associate).

Meetings/Conferences: Annual
2013 - Keshena, WI/June 10 - 13

Publications:
ITC Newsletter
Membership Directory

Investigative Reporters and Editors (1975)
141 Neff Annex
Missouri School of Journalism
Columbia, MO 65211
Tel: (573) 882-2042 Fax: (573) 884-5544
E-Mail: info@ire.org
Website: ire.org
Members: 5200 individuals
Staff: 18
Annual Budget: $1-2,000,000

Personnel:
Executive Director: Mark Horvit
E-Mail: mhorvit@ire.org
Coordinator, Membership Services: John Green
E-Mail: jgreen@ire.org
Financial Officer: Heather Feldmann Henry
E-Mail: heather@ire.org
Web Editor: Coulter Jones
E-Mail: coulter@ire.org
Managing Editor: Megan Luther
E-Mail: megan@ire.org
Senior Coordinator, Conferences: Stephanie Sinn
E-Mail: stephanie@ire.org
Senior Contributing Editor: Steve Weinberg
E-Mail: weinbergs@missouri.edu

Historical Note:
IRE's mission is to foster service in investigative journalism, which is essential to a free society. Members are individuals involved or concerned with investigative journalism. Membership: $70 (Professional/Academic/Associate/Retiree); $25 (Student).

Meetings/Conferences:
Conference Chair: Stephanie Sinn
2013 - Louisville, KY (Hyatt Regency Louisville)/Feb. 28 - March 3
2013 - San Antonio, TX (San Antonio Marriott Rivercenter)/June 20 - 23
Number of non-conference events/year: 12

Publications:
Quick Hits; on-line; adv.
The IRE Journal; on-line; adv.
Timely Tips; bi-weekly
Uplink; on-line; adv.

Investment Adviser Association (1937)
1050 17th St. NW
Suite 725
Washington, DC 20036-5514
Tel: (202) 293-4222 Fax: (202) 293-4223
E-Mail: info@investmentadviser.org
Website: investmentadviser.org
Members: 500 SEC and non-SEC-registered investment advisory firms.
Staff: 14
Annual Budget: $2-5,000,000
Tax: 501(c)(6)

Personnel:
Executive Director and Executive Vice President: David G. Tittsworth
E-Mail: david.tittsworth@investmentadviser.org
General Counsel: Karen L. Barr
E-Mail: karen.barr@investmentadviser.org

Director, Meetings and Events: Lisa Gillette
   E-Mail: lisa.gillette@investmentadviser.org
Manager, Membership Services: Garrett Honea
   E-Mail: garrett.honea@investmentadviser.org
Director, Finance and Operations: Linda Mackey
   E-Mail: linda.mackey@investmentadviser.org
Vice President for Government Relations: Neil A. Simon
   E-Mail: neil.simon@investmentadvisor.org

Historical Note:
Formerly known as Investment Counsel Association of America, assumed its present name in 2005. IAA's is the trade association for the Investment Adviser Profession. It represents the profession in the development, formulation, and enactment of legislation, rules, and regulations relating to investment advisers. IAA's mission is to provide effective, quality representation of the investment advisory profession with respect to the development, formulation, and enactment of legislation, rules, and regulations relating to investment advisers. Members are firms that manage assets for a variety of institutional and individual clients, including pension plans, trusts, investment companies, endowments, foundations, and corporations. Membership: $2,675-18,775 (Firm, based on assets under management); $1,500 (Associate).

Continuing Education:
Enrollment: 295
Certification Designation/s: CIC

Meetings/Conferences: Annual
Conference Chair: Lisa Gillette
2013 - Arlington, VA (Crystal Gateway Marriott)/
   March 7 - 8
Number of non-conference events/year: 8

Publications:
Activity Report; semi-annually
Directory of Firm Personnel; on-line
Evolution Revolution, A Profile of the Investment
   Adviser Profession; annually
IAA Alerts
IAA Newsletter; annually
Investment Management Compliance Testing Survey
   Report; semi-annually
Membership Directory; on-line
Service Provider Directory; on-line

Investment Casting Institute *(1953)*
136 Summit Ave.
Montvale, NJ 07645-1720
Tel: (201) 573-9770 *Fax:* (201) 573-9771
E-Mail: ici@investmentcasting.org
Website: investmentcasting.org
Members: 200 companies
Staff: 5
Annual Budget: $1-2,000,000
Tax: 501(c)(6)

Personnel:
Executive Director: Michael C. Perry
   E-Mail: mperry@investmentcasting.org
Meetings Planner: Carol Cammisa
   E-Mail: ccammisa@investmentcasting.org
Editor: Leland D. Martin
   E-Mail: incast@investmentcasting.org

Historical Note:
ICI's purpose is to promote quality standards, collect and disseminate information about the industry, and provide industry education opportunities to members. Members are companies employing the precision, investment casting process and suppliers to the industry. Membership: $850-5,100 (Casting, Associate); $950-5,700 (Casting, Regular); $425-1,487.50 (Affiliate, Associate); $475-1,662.50 (Affiliate, Regular); $75 (Alumni- Casting/ Supplier).

Continuing Education:
Certification Designation/s: ICS

Meetings/Conferences: Annual
Conference Chair: Carol Cammisa
Number of non-conference events/year: 1

Publications:
INCAST Magazine; monthly; adv.
Membership Directory; on-line

Membership List Available to Non-members

Investment Company Institute *(1940)*
1401 H St. NW, 12th Floor
Suite 1200
Washington, DC 20005-2148
Tel: (202) 326-5800
Website: ici.org
Members: 9300 mutual funds

Staff: 167
Annual Budget: $50-100,000,000
Tax: 501(c)(6)

Personnel:
Chief Public Communications Officer: F. Gregory Ahern
   E-Mail: greg.ahern@ici.org
Chief Government Affairs Officer and Co-Head: Donald C.
   Auerbach
Associate Counsel: Karen Gibian
   E-Mail: kgibian@ici.org
General Counsel: Karrie McMillan
Media Contact: Mike McNamee
   E-Mail: mike.mcnamee@ici.org
President: Paul Schott Stevens
   E-Mail: paul.stevens@ici.org

Historical Note:
Formerly (1961) National Association of Investment Companies. Absorbed the Association of Mutual Fund Plan Sponsors in 1973, the Unit Investment Trust Association in 1985, and the Association of Publicly Traded Investment Funds in 1987. Members are open-end and closed-end investment companies registered under the Investment Company Act of 1940, and their advisers and principal underwriters, as well as unit investment trust sponsors. ICI's mission is to encourage adherence to ethical standards by all industry participants; advancing the interests of funds, their shareholders, directors, and investment advisers; and promoting public understanding of mutual funds and other investment companies.

Meetings/Conferences:
Number of non-conference events/year: 1

Publications:
Investment Company Service Directory; adv.
Membership Directory; on-line
The Wall Street Journal

Investment Management Consultants Association *(1985)*
5619 DTC Pkwy.
Suite 500
Greenwood Village, CO 80111
Tel: (303) 770-3377 *Fax:* (303) 770-1812
E-Mail: imca@imca.org
Website: imca.org
Members: 8000 individuals
Staff: 31
Annual Budget: $10-25,000,000
Tax: 501(c)(6)

Personnel:
Executive Director and Chief Executive Officer: Sean
   Walters CAE
   E-Mail: swalters@imca.org
Deputy Executive Director, Certification: Gary
   Diffendaffer
   E-Mail: gdiffendaffer@imca.org
Director, Conferences: Stephanie Lifland Lasser CMP
   E-Mail: slasser@imca.org
Chief Financial Officer: Angie Lutterman CPA
   E-Mail: alutterman@imca.org
Deputy Executive Director, Operations: Ian MacKenzie
   E-Mail: imackenzie@imca.org
Managing Editor: Debbie Nochlin
   E-Mail: dnochlin@imca.org
Manager, Membership, Marketing and Communications:
   Jamie Parrish
   E-Mail: jparrish@imca.org
Manager, Information Systems: Bryant Strickland
   E-Mail: bstrickland@imca.org

Historical Note:
IMCA's mission is to deliver better investment consulting and wealth management credentials and world-class educational offerings. Membership: $395/year (Individual).

Continuing Education:
Enrollment: 1000
Certification Designation/s: CPWA, CIMA, CIMC, CIS

Meetings/Conferences: Annual
Conference Chair: Stephanie Lifland Lasser CMP
2013 - New York City, NY (New York Marriott
   Marquis)/Feb. 4 - 5
2013 - Seatle, WA (Washington State Convention
   Center)/April 29 - May 1
2013 - Chicago, IL (Marriott Michigan Avenue)/Oct. 7
   - 8
2014 - New York City, NY (New York Marriott
   Marquis)/Feb. 10 - 11
2014 - Boston, MA (John B. Hynes Veterans Memorial
   Convention Center)/May 5 - 7

2015 - Las Vegas, NV (ARIA Resort and Casino Hotel)/
   April 27 - 29

Publications:
IMCA eNews; semi-monthly
IMCA Legislative Intelligence; on-line
IMCA Research Quarterly; quarterly
Investments & Wealth Monitor; bi-monthly
Membership Directory; on-line
The Journal of Investment Consulting; semi-annually

Investment Program Association *(1985)*
P.O. Box 480
Ellicott City, MD 21041-0480
Tel: (212) 812-9799
Website: ipa.com
Members: 150 companies
Staff: 6
Annual Budget: $2-5,000,000

Personnel:
Chief Executive Officer and President: Kevin Hogan
   E-Mail: kevin@theipaonliner.org
Coordinator, Events: Jenna Erickson
   E-Mail: jerickson@ipa.com
Office Administrator: Angela Handy
   E-Mail: ahandy@ipa.com
Director, Communications: Dawn Jacobsen
   E-Mail: djacobsen@ipa.com
Associate Director: Tracy Mesterharm
   E-Mail: tracy@theipaonline.org
Director, Education: Ken Montgomery
   E-Mail: kmontgomery@ipa.com

Historical Note:
Formerly (1991) Investment Partnership Association. IPA's mission is to provide objective input to Federal and state authorities for the development of rules, regulations and guidance that govern the industry. Membership: $5,000 (Associate); $10,000-50,000 (Sponsor, dues based on capital raised).

Meetings/Conferences:
Conference Chair: Jenna Erickson
2013 - Washington, DC (Capital Hilton)/May 8 - 9
2013 - Dallas, TX (The Fairmont)/Nov. 5 - 7
2014 - Washington, DC/April 2 - 3
2014 - Phoenix, AZ (Arizona Grand Hotel)/Oct. 28 - 30

Publications:
IPA Newsletter; on-line

Investment Recovery Association *(1981)*
P.O. Box 419264
Kansas City, MO 64141
Tel: (816) 561-5323 *Fax:* (816) 561-1991
TollFree: (800) 728-2272
E-Mail: info@invrecovery.org
Website: invrecovery.org
Members: 300 companies
Staff: 1
Annual Budget: $250-500,000
Tax: 501(c)(6)

Personnel:
Executive Director: Jane Male CAE
   E-Mail: jmale@swassn.com

Historical Note:
IR is the professional organization for managers of surplus and idle assets and a diverse group of suppliers to the industry. IR is the practice of recouping the value of assets no longer needed by a company by identifying and reusing or disposing of surplus assets. Membership: $400 (Individual); $550 (Associate).

Continuing Education:
Certification Designation/s: CMIR

Meetings/Conferences: Annual
2013 - Memphis, TN/March 24 - 27

Publications:
Investment Recovery Business Journal; semi-annually;
   adv.
Membership Directory; on-line

Membership List Available to Non-members

IPC - Association Connecting Electronics Industries *(1957)*
3000 Lakeside Dr.
Suite 309 South
Bannockburn, IL 60015
Tel: (847) 615-7100 *Fax:* (847) 615-7105
Website: ipc.org
Members: 2700 companies and 3,300 members

Staff: 90
Annual Budget: $10-25,000,000

Personnel:
President and Chief Executive Officer: John W. Mitchell
Director, Membership Services: Neal Bender
    E-Mail: bendne@ipc.org
Application Director: Mark Duris
    E-Mail: durima@ipc.org
Vice President, Industry Programs: Anthony Hilvers
    E-Mail: hilvan@ipc.org
Director, Meetings and Special Events: Tracy Riggan
    E-Mail: riggtr@ipc.org
Director, Market Research: Sharon Starr
    E-Mail: starsh@ipc.org
Vice President, Marketing and Communications: Kim
    Sterling
    E-Mail: sterki@ipc.org

Historical Note:
*Formerly the Institute of Printed Circuits(1957); became
the Institute for Interconnecting and Packaging Electronic
Circuits in 1978 (commonly known as IPC). Assumed
its current name in 1999. IPC is dedicated to furthering
the competitive excellence and financial success of its
members, who are participants in the electronics industry.
Membership: $1,050 (Primary Site); $625 (Company, with
revenues under $5 million/Consultant); $275 (Government
Agency/Not-for- profit organization).*

Continuing Education:
Certification Designation/s: CIS, CID, CIT, CEPM

Meetings/Conferences:
Conference Chair: Tracy Riggan
Number of non-conference events/year: 18

Publications:
IPC Review; monthly
Membership Directory; on-line

Membership List Available to Non-members

IPC - Surface Mount Equipment Manufacturers Association *(1987)*
3000 Lakeside Dr.
309 South
Bannockburn, IL 60015
Tel: (847) 615-7100 *Fax:* (847) 615-7105
Website: ipc.org/ContentPage.aspx?pageid = IPC-
    Management
Members: 3021 Combinations
Staff: 55
Annual Budget: $50-100,000

Personnel:
President and Chief Executive Officer: John W. Mitchell
    E-Mail: JohnMitchell@ipc.org
Director, Membership: Neal Bender
    E-Mail: NealBender@ipc.org
Director, Applications: Mark Duris
    E-Mail: MarkDuris@ipc.org
Director, Industry Programs: Susan Filz
    E-Mail: SusanFilz@ipc.org
Director, Marketing and Communications: Anna Garrido
    E-Mail: AnnaGarrido@ipc.org
*Vice President, Finance and Administration and Chief
    Operating Officer:* Art Huenecke
    E-Mail: ArtHuenecke@ipc.org
Director, Meetings and Special Events: Tracy Riggan
Controller: Jennifer Sandahl
    E-Mail: JenniferSandahl@ipc.org
Chief Marketing Officer: Kim Sterling
    E-Mail: KimSterling@ipc.org

Historical Note:
*Founded as Surface Mount Equipment Manufacturers
Association; became part of IPC and assumed its current
name in 1999. IPC-SMEMA's objectives are to develop
and promote standards for the interface and operation
of equipment; to assure users that each machine in their
production line will interface effectively and smoothly
with others; to advance the technology; and to investigate
areas where the association may act to the benefit of
all its members. Members are companies manufacturing
equipment or producing software for surface mount board
production (a process of placing and securing electrical
components on printed circuit boards). Membership: $1050
(primary); $275-625 (Government, educational and not-
for-profit organizations).*

Continuing Education:
Certification Designation/s: CEPM

Meetings/Conferences: Annual
Conference Chair: Tracy Riggan
2013 - San Diego, CA (San Diego Convention Center)/
    Feb. 19 - 21/over 100 exhibitors

Membership List Available to Non-members

IPC Washington Office *(1957)*
3000 Lakeside Dr., 309 S
Bannockburn, IL 60015
Tel: (847) 615-7100 *Fax:* (847) 615-7105
Website: ipc.org
Staff: 45

Personnel:
President and Chief Executive Officer: John W. Mitchell
    E-Mail: JohnMitchell@ipc.org
Director, Membership Services: Neal Bender
    E-Mail: bendne@ipc.org
Technical Publications Manager: Eva Combes
    E-Mail: EvaCombes@ipc.org
Director, Marketing and Communications: Anna Garrido
    E-Mail: AnnaGarrido@ipc.org
*Vice President, Finance and Administration and Chief
    Operating Officer:* Art Huenecke
    E-Mail: huenar@ipc.org
Webmaster: Sarajoy Pickholtz
    E-Mail: SarajoyPickholtz@ipc.org
Director - Meetings and Special Events: Tracy Riggan
    E-Mail: riggtr@ipc.org
Chief Marketing Officer: Kim Sterling
    E-Mail: sterki@ipc.org

Historical Note:
*An association connecting electronics industries.
Headquartered in Northbrook, IL. IPC's mission is
to furthering the competitive excellence and financial
success of its members, who are participants in the
electronics industry. Membership: $1,050-1,890 (Primary);
$275-495 (Government agencies, academic institutions,
nonprofit organizations); $850-1,530 (Additional facility);
$625-1,125 (Consultant/Companies with an annual
revenue of less than $5,000,000).*

Meetings/Conferences:
Conference Chair: Tracy Riggan
2013 - Budapest, Hungary/Feb. 6 - 7

Publications:
IPC Newsletter
Member Directory; on-line

Iranian American Community of Northern California
721 San Luis Rd.
Berkeley, CA 94707
Website: iacnorcal.com
Staff: 1

Personnel:
Executive Director: Ahmad Moein

Historical Note:
*Association of Iranian-American citizens in U.S. who
support democratic change in Iran.*

Meetings/Conferences: Annual

Ireland Chamber of Commerce in the United States *(1988)*
556 Central Ave.
New Providence, NJ 07974
Tel: (908) 286-1300 *Fax:* (908) 286-1200
E-Mail: info@iccusa.org
Website: iccusa.org
Members: 750 individuals
Staff: 5
Annual Budget: $250-500,000
Tax: 501(c)(6)

Personnel:
President and Chief Executive Officer: Maurice A. Buckley
Executive Director: Larry A. Handeli
    E-Mail: larryh@iccusa.org
Director, Events: Padma Kondapeta

Historical Note:
*ICCUSA is a corporate and professional membership
organization promoting the interests of Ireland and
expanding trade opportunities between the U.S. and Ireland.
Membership: $10,000 (Founding Charter Member); $1,000
(Corporate Member); $500 (Professional Member); $250
(Individual Member); $125 (Young Professional Member).*

Meetings/Conferences: Annual
Conference Chair: Padma Kondapeta
Number of non-conference events/year: 3

Publications:
The Ireland Chamber Magazine; on-line

Irish Blacks Cattle Society *(1971)*
25377 WCR 17

Johnstown, CO 80534
Tel: (970) 412-3658 *Fax:* (970) 587-2252
Website: irishblacks.com
Members: 150 individuals
Staff: 1
Annual Budget: Under $10,000

Personnel:
President: Maurice W. Boney
    E-Mail: mmboney@webtv.net

Historical Note:
*Members are breeders of Irish Black cattle. Has no paid
officers or full- time staff.*

Iron Casting Research Institute *(1939)*
2802 Fisher Rd.
Columbus, OH 43204
Tel: (614) 275-4201 *Fax:* (614) 275-4203
E-Mail: icri@ironcasting.org
Website: ironcasting.org
Members: 17 companies
Staff: 4
Annual Budget: $500-1,000,000

Personnel:
Executive Director: Bruce T. Blatzer
    E-Mail: icri@ironcasting.org
Technical Director: Robert H. Bigge
Manager, Membership Services: Susan J. Lambert
    E-Mail: icri@ironcasting.org

Historical Note:
*Formerly (1982) Gray Iron Research Group. ICRI's mission
is to provide means by which each member can become
more technically proficient in producing low cost, high
quality iron castings. Membership: $20,000/year (One
Foundry); 15% of the annual dues every year for each
additional foundry listed.*

Publications:
Member Listing; on-line

Iroquois Healthcare Alliance
17 Halfmoon Executive Park Dr.
Clifton Park, NY 12065-5631
Tel: (518) 383-5060 *Fax:* (518) 383-2616
Website: iroquois.org
Members: 53 hospitals and health systems
Staff: 23
Annual Budget: $500-1,000,000

Personnel:
President: Gary J. Fitzgerald
    E-Mail: gfitzgerald@iroquois.org
Specialist, Meeting and Coordinator, Business: Mary
    Brisson
    E-Mail: mbrisson@iroquois.org
Vice President, Membership and Advocacy: Stacy Connors
    E-Mail: sconnors@iroquois.org
Senior Vice President and Chief Financial Officer: Debbie
    Dennis
    E-Mail: ddennis@iroquois.org
Coordinator, Information: Denise Foeder
    E-Mail: dfoeder@iroquois.org

Historical Note:
*IHA's mission is to serve as a resource and leader to
support their members and the communities they serve
through advocacy, education, information, cost-saving
initiatives and business solutions.*

Publications:
Iroquois News

Irrigation Association *(1949)*
6540 Arlington Blvd.
Falls Church, VA 22042
Tel: (703) 536-7080 *Fax:* (703) 536-7019
E-Mail: info@irrigationshow.org
Website: irrigation.org
Members: 1600 companies
Staff: 21
Annual Budget: $500-1,000,000
Tax: 501(c)(6)

Personnel:
Executive Director: Deborah M. Hamlin CAE, FASAE
    E-Mail: DeborahHamlin@irrigation.org
Director, Finance: Rebecca J. Bayless
    E-Mail: RebeccaBayless@irrigation.org
Manager, Membership Services: Marcia E. Cram
    E-Mail: MarciaCram@irrigation.org
Government Affairs Director: John R. Farner Jr.
    E-Mail: JohnFarner@irrigation.org
Manager, Communications: Erin N. Fisher

E-Mail: ErinFisher@irrigation.org
Senior Manager, Trade Show and Meetings: Sandy V. Fridy
E-Mail: SandyFridy@irrigation.org
Director, Marketing: Kathleen Markey
E-Mail: KathleenMarkey@irrigation.org
Director, Certification and Operations: Sherrie Schulte
E-Mail: SherrieSchulte@irrigation.org
Director, Education: Robert D. von Bernuth CID, PE, PhD
E-Mail: BobVonBernuth@irrigation.org
Senior Manager, Information Technology: Keith A. Williams
E-Mail: KeithWilliams@irrigation.org

Historical Note:
Formerly the Sprinkler Irrigation Association, adopted its present name in 1976 and absorbed the Drip Irrigation Association in 1979. IA's mission is to promote efficient irrigation and works to improve industry proficiency, advocates sound water management, and grow demand for water-efficient products and services. Members are manufacturers, designers, suppliers, consultants, and contractors of all irrigation systems. Membership: $30 (Student); $300-16,000 (Company); $300-8,000 (Associate); $75 (Retired); $300 (Retired Lifetime); $125 (Technical); $500 (Technical Lifetime); $75 (Unemployed).

Continuing Education:
Certification Designation/s: CLWM, CAWM, CIC, CAIS, CGIA, CID, CLIA

Meetings/Conferences: Annual
Conference Chair: Sandy V. Fridy

Publications:
IA Times; on-line; adv.
Irrigation Foundation E-Newsletter; on-line
Member Update; semi-annually; adv.
Newsletter
Smart Tips for Smart Irrigation Month; on-line; adv.

ISA -The Association of Learning Providers (1978)
12427 Hedges Run Dr.
Suite 120
Lake Ridge, VA 22192
Tel: (703) 730-2828 *Fax:* (703) 730-2857
TollFree: (877) 533-4914
E-Mail: info@isaconnection.org
Website: isaconnection.org
Members: 150 companies
Staff: 2
Annual Budget: $500-1,000,000
Tax: 501(c)(6)

Personnel:
Executive Director: Pamela J. Schmidt
E-Mail: pschmidt@isaconnection.org
Manager, Finance and Administration: Lois Donovan
E-Mail: ldonovan@isaconnection.org

Historical Note:
ISA's mission is to build, enhance and share success among members in the business of training and performance development. Members are training industry firms which produce generic and/or custom-designed training programs or consult for business and industry. Membership: $6,975/year (Firm).

Meetings/Conferences: Annual
Conference Chair: Lois Donovan
2013 - Scottsdale, AZ (Marriott's Camelback Inn Resort)/March 17 - 20
Number of non-conference events/year: 3

Publications:
Membership Directory; on-line
Newswire

ISEH Society for Hematology and Stem Cells (1972)
401 N. Michigan Ave.
Suite 2200
Chicago, IL 60611
Tel: (312) 321-5114 *Fax:* (312) 673-6923
E-Mail: iseh@dc.sba.com
Website: iseh.org
Members: 800 individuals and 14 corporate
Staff: 6
Annual Budget: $1-2,000,000
Tax: 501(c)(3)

Personnel:
Executive Director: Kevin Baliozian
E-Mail: kbaliozian@iseh.org
Managing Editor: Carolina Abramovich
E-Mail: exphem@iseh.org

Editor, Connections Newsletter: Dennis Coyle
E-Mail: editor@iseh.org
Manager, Operations: Kimberly Eskew
E-Mail: keskew@iseh.org
Membership Associate: Robin L. Rosenstein
E-Mail: RRosenstein@iseh.org
Director, Development: Jeanette Ruby
E-Mail: jruby@iseh.org

Historical Note:
Formerly (2006) International Society for Experimental Hematology. ISEH's mission is to advance the scientific knowledge and clinical application of basic hematology, immunology, stem cell research, cell and gene therapy and related aspects of research through publications, discussions, scientific meetings and the support of young investigators. Members are clinicians and researchers involved in the field of experimental hematology. Membership: $175 (Active); $65 (Associate/Member in Training); $7,500 (Corporate).

Meetings/Conferences: Annual
Conference Chair: Jeanette Ruby
2013 - Vienna, Austria (Imperial Riding School Renaissance Hotel)/Aug. 22 - 25
Number of non-conference events/year: 2

Publications:
Connections e-Newsletter; bi-monthly
Experimental Hematology

Islamic Medical Association of North America (1967)
101 W. 22nd St.
Suite 106
Lombard, IL 60148
Tel: (630) 932-0000 *Fax:* (630) 932-0005
E-Mail: hq@imana.org
Website: imana.org
Members: 3000 individuals
Staff: 4
Annual Budget: $1-2,000,000
Tax: 501(c)(3)

Personnel:
Executive Director: Rasheed Ahmed
Specialists, Communications: Jessica Censotti
Operations Administrator: Akrama Hashmi

Historical Note:
IMANA's mission is to provide a forum and resource for Muslim physicians and other health care professionals. Members are Muslim physicians and health professionals. Membership: $0-3,000/year.

Meetings/Conferences: Annual
2013 - Vancouver, BC/Aug. 17 - 21
Number of non-conference events/year: 1

Publications:
Journal of the Islamic Medical Association of North America; quarterly
Membership Directory; on-line
The IMA Newsletter; bi-monthly

IT Financial Management Association (1988)
P.O. Box 30188
Santa Barbara, CA 93130
Tel: (805) 687-7390 *Fax:* (805) 687-7382
E-Mail: info@itfma.com
Website: isfma.com
Members: 950 individuals
Staff: 1
Annual Budget: $100-250,000

Personnel:
President and Director: Terence A. Quinlan

Historical Note:
Formerly (1996) the Financial Management for Data Processing and (2001) IS Financial Management Association, assumed its current name in 2002. ITFMA's mission is to promote professional development and personal advancement. Members are those involved with any aspect of the financial management of Information Technology (IT) organizations. Membership: $100 (Individual); $500 (Corporate-Upto 15 Members).

Continuing Education:
Enrollment: 450
Certification Designation/s: ITIL, FPBR, PMB, AM, GFM, CABC, FMA, TFM, FMC

Meetings/Conferences: Semi-Annual

Publications:
IT Financial Management; adv.
Journal of IT Financial Management; adv.
Membership Directory; on-line
Newsletter

Italian American Studies Association (1966)
C/O The John D. Calandra Italian American Institute
25 West, 43rd St., 17th Floor
New York, NY 10036
Website: italianamericanstudies.net
Members: 800 individuals
Staff: 4
Annual Budget: $10-25,000

Personnel:
President: George Guida
E-Mail: gguida@citytech.cuny.edu
Contact, Membership Services: Teresa Cerasuola
E-Mail: TeresaCerasuola@aol.com,
Treasurer: Dawn Esposito
E-Mail: espositd@stjohns.edu

Historical Note:
IASA's purpose is interdisciplinary study of the culture, history, literature, sociology, demography, folklore, and politics of Italians in America. Membership: $40 (Regular Individual); $25 (Senior); $20 (Student); $60 (Family per Couple); $80 (Institutional); $800 (Life).

Meetings/Conferences: Annual

Publications:
Executive Council Minutes; bi-annually
Newsletters; bi-annually

Italy-America Chamber of Commerce (1887)
730 Fifth Ave.
Suite 600
New York, NY 10019
Tel: (212) 459-0044 *Fax:* (212) 459-0090
E-Mail: info@italchamber.org
Website: italchamber.org
Members: 1200 individuals
Staff: 4
Annual Budget: $500-1,000,000

Personnel:
Secretary General: Franco De Angelis
E-Mail: deangelis@italchamber.org
Coordinator, Membership and Events: Alice Biagini

Historical Note:
Formerly American Chamber of Commerce for Trade with Italy. IACC represents the interests of companies that have, or that are interested in establishing business and commercial relations between the United States and Italy. Membership: $900 (General); $2,500 (Sustaining); $3,000 (Senior Sustaining).

Meetings/Conferences:
Conference Chair: Alice Biagini

Publications:
IACCInform; monthly; adv.

JAWS Society
1103 E. Montclair St.
Springfield, MO 65807
Tel: (417) 887-8800 *Fax:* (417) 886-3685
E-Mail: CenterAdmin@association-resources.com
Website: jawssociety.org
Members: 105 Individuals
Staff: 2

Personnel:
President: Susan Rust

Historical Note:
JAWS Society's mission is to promote the professional development of the Oral and Maxillofacial Surgery Administrators and Managers through peer interaction and educational programs. Membership: $200/year.

Meetings/Conferences: Annual
2013 - Grapevine, TX (Gaylord Texan Hotel and Convention Center, Dallas Texas)/April 14 - 17

Publications:
JAWS Society Newsletter

Jean Piaget Society (1970)
1960 East West Rd.
Biomed T 311
Honolulu, HI 96822
Tel: (808) 956-7343
Website: piaget.org
Members: 600 individuals
Staff: 5
Annual Budget: $100-250,000
Tax: 501(c)(3)

Personnel:

Vice President, Communications: Saba Ayman-Nolley
E-Mail: S-Ayman-Nolley@neiu.edu
Treasurer: Ashley Maynard
E-Mail: amaynard@hawaii.edu
Vice President, Program Planning: Larry Nucci

Historical Note:
JPS's mission is to provide an open forum, through symposia, books, journal and other publications, for the presentation and discussion of scholarly work on issues related to human knowledge and its development. Members are researchers and practitioners in the fields of psychology, education, philosophy and psychiatry who are interested in the nature of human knowledge. Membership: $140 (Regular); $95 (Student/Postdoc-with journal); $65 (Student/Postdoc-without journal).

Meetings/Conferences: Annual
Conference Chair: Larry Nucci

Publications:
Cognitive Development; quarterly; adv.
Membership Directory; on-line
The Genetic Epistemologist; annually; adv.

Membership List Available to Non-members

Jesuit Association of Student Personnel Administrators (1954)
St. Joseph's University, 5600 City Ave.
Philadelphia, PA 19131-1308
Tel: (610) 660-1045 Fax: (610) 660-1069
Website: jaspa.creighton.edu
Members: 28 institutions
Staff: 4
Annual Budget: Under $10,000

Personnel:
President: Cissy Petty
E-Mail: mlpetty@loyno.edu
Secretary: Robert D. Kelly
E-Mail: rkelly@seattleu.edu

Historical Note:
Formerly (1954) known as the Conference of Jesuit Student Personnel Administrators (CJSPA), assumed its current name in 1981. JASPA works to promote the mission of Jesuit higher education. Members of JASPA represent the 28 Jesuit Colleges and Universities in the United States and also include affiliate members from other institutions. Membership: Based on a sliding scale.

Meetings/Conferences: Annual

Publications:
Membership Directory; on-line

Membership List Available to Non-members

Jesuit Secondary Education Association (1970)
1016 16th St. NW
Suite 200
Washington, DC 20036
Tel: (202) 667-3888 Fax: (202) 387-6305
E-Mail: jsea@jsea.org
Website: jsea.org
Members: 48 schools
Staff: 6
Annual Budget: $100-250,000
Tax: 501(c)(3)

Personnel:
President: James A. Stoeger SJ
E-Mail: stoegerj@jsea.org
Manager, Communications: Kathreja A. Mills
E-Mail: sarfatik@jsea.org
Administrative Assistant: Ellen S. Palmer
E-Mail: palmere@jsea.org

Historical Note:
Formerly, with the Association of Jesuit Colleges and Universities, a part of the Jesuit Education Association. It works with Jesuit leadership on planning and caring for the apostolate of Jesuit education. JSEA's mission is to initiate programs and provide services that enable its member schools to sustain their Ignatian vision and Jesuit mission in the formation of young men and women of competence, conscience and compassion.

Publications:
AJCU/JSEA Directory; annually
JSEA-Bulletin
MAGISine; annually

Jewelers Board of Trade (1884)
95 Jefferson Blvd.
Warwick, RI 02888-1046
Tel: (401) 467-0055 Fax: (401) 467-6070
E-Mail: jbtinfo@jewelersboard.com
Website: jewelersboard.com

Members: 3200 businesses
Staff: 58
Annual Budget: $2-5,000,000

Personnel:
President and Chief Executive Officer: Dione D. Kenyon
Manager, Membership Services and Education: Brenda Gamba
E-Mail: bgamba@jewelersboard.com

Historical Note:
JBT seeks to promote the welfare of its membership and the jewelry industry overall by obtaining and delivering accurate and reliable credit information, effective collection services and education in credit related matters. Members include manufacturers, wholesalers and other suppliers of jewelry or related products. Membership: $900 (U.S. and Canada, USVI); $1,110 (All other companies).

Publications:
Weekly Alert; weekly

Membership List Available to Non-members

Jewelers of America (1906)
52 Vanderbilt Ave.
19th Floor
New York, NY 10017-3827
Tel: (646) 658-0246 Fax: (646) 658-0256
TollFree: (800) 223-0673
E-Mail: info@jewelers.org
Website: jewelers.org
Members: 11000 stores
Staff: 22
Annual Budget: $500-1,000,000

Personnel:
President and Chief Executive Officer: Matthew A. Runci
E-Mail: matt@jewelofam.org
Manager, Information Technology: Marcin Bielawski
E-Mail: mbielawski@jewelers.org
Incoming Chief Executive Officer: David Bonaparte
Director, Finance and Administration: Annie Doresca
E-Mail: adoresca@jewelers.org
Director, Marketing and Membership: Molly Fallon
E-Mail: mfallon@jewelers.org
Director, Communications: Amanda Gizzi
E-Mail: agizzi@jewelers.org
Director, Education and Industry Relations: David Peters
E-Mail: dpeters@jewelers.org
Associate, Office and Human Resources: Madeline Rivera
E-Mail: mrivera@jewelers.org

Historical Note:
JA's mission is to improve consumer confidence in the jewelry industry by advocating professionalism, including high ethical, social and environmental standards and developing initiatives that will benefit the retail jewelry marketplace. Membership: $115-1960 (Retailer, based on number of stores); $390-3,350 (Supplier, based on Annual Sales Volume).

Continuing Education:
Certification Designation/s: CSP, CBJT, CSSP, CBJ, CMBJ, CSBJ, CMP

Publications:
Membership Directory; on-line
The JA Report; monthly

Jewelers Shipping Association (1956)
125 Carlsbad St.
Cranston, RI 02920
Tel: (401) 943-6020 Fax: (401) 943-1490
TollFree: (800) 688-4572
Website: jewelersshipping.com
Members: 115 companies
Staff: 14
Annual Budget: $5-10,000,000

Personnel:
Managing Director: David Roche
Office Manager: Kathy Roche
Sales and Rate Manager: Michael D. Silva

Historical Note:
Founded as the Jewelers Shipping Service and incorporated under its present name in 1962. JSA's mission is to provide its members with a better quality of service possible at an economical price. Membership: $10/year.

Jeweler's Vigilance Committee (1917)
25 W. 45th St.
Suite 1406
New York, NY 10036
Tel: (212) 997-2002 Fax: (212) 997-9148
TollFree: (800) 564-6582

E-Mail: Jvcquestions@aol.com
Website: jvclegal.org
Members: 1300 companies
Staff: 5
Annual Budget: $1-2,000,000
Tax: 501(c)(6)

Personnel:
President, Chief Executive Officer and General Counsel: Cecilia L. Gardner
E-Mail: clg@jvclegal.org
Director, Marketing and Development: Amy Greenbaum
E-Mail: amy@jvclegal.org
Director, Membership Services: Jeff Mercado
E-Mail: jmercadojvc@aol.com

Historical Note:
JVC is the legal arm and guardian of the jewelry industry, advocating legal compliance and ethical practices. It also monitors legislation, provides government agency liaison, trade liaison, and consumer dispute resolution services. Membership: $425-6,375 (Distributor/Manufacturer/Wholesaler, based on no of employees); $195-6,900 (Retailers).

Meetings/Conferences:
Conference Chair: Cecilia L. Gardner
2013 - Tucson, AZ (Tucson Convention Center)/Feb. 5 - 10

Publications:
eNews & Views; on-line
JVC Member Database (Membership Directory); on-line

Jewelers' Security Alliance of the United States (1883)
Six E. 45th St.
New York, NY 10017
Tel: (212) -687-032 Fax: (212) 808-9168
TollFree: (800) 537-0067
E-Mail: jsa2@jewelerssecurity.org
Website: jewelerssecurity.org
Members: 21000 jewelry businesses
Staff: 6
Annual Budget: $1-2,000,000
Tax: 501(c)(6)

Personnel:
President: John J. Kennedy
E-Mail: jsa2@jewelerssecurity.org
Manager, Membership Services: Helen M. Buck
E-Mail: jsa2@jewelerssecurity.org

Historical Note:
JSA's mission is to inform and alert jewelers about crime through frequent email crime alerts and print publication, a web site, seminars and consulting activities. Membership: $180-830 (Regular, depending on number of employees); $250-2750 (Retail Chain); $600 (Associate); Free (Law Enforcement).

Jewelry Industry Distributors Association (1946)
230 Homewood Dr.
Butler, PA 16001
Tel: (973) 762-2222 Fax: (973) 762-7767
E-Mail: info@jida.info
Website: jida.info
Members: 135 companies
Staff: 4
Annual Budget: $25-50,000
Tax: 501(c)(6)

Personnel:
Contact: Daniel Weinglass PhD
E-Mail: dan@newarkjewelers.com

Historical Note:
Formerly (1984) the Watch Material and Jewelry Distributors Association of America. Its purpose is to oster and establish standards of service and to facilitate the exchange of information among members in order to improve business, maximize opportunities and minimize risks, and maintain and encourage friendly relations among individuals engaged in the industry. Membership: $495/year (Associate).

Membership List Available to Non-members

Jewish Book Council (1925)
520 Eighth Ave.
Fourth Floor
New York, NY 10018
Tel: (212) 201-2920 Fax: (212) 532-4952
E-Mail: jbc@jewishbooks.org
Website: jewishbookcouncil.org
Members: 100 organizations

Staff: 8
Annual Budget: $1-2,000,000
Tax: 501(c)(3)

Personnel:
Director: Carolyn Starman Hessel
Director, Program: Miri Pomerantz Dauber
Director, Web and Publications: Naomi Firestone
E-Mail: naomi@jewishbooks.org

Historical Note:
JBC's mission is to advocate the reading, writing, publishing and distribution of quality Jewish content books in English.

Publications:
Jewish Book World Magazine; quarterly; adv.

Membership List Available to Non-members

Jewish Communal Service Association of North America (1899)
25 Broadway
Suite 1700
New York, NY 10004
Tel: (212) 284-6945 *Fax:* (212) 284-6566
E-Mail: info@jcsana.org
Website: jcsana.org
Members: 127 member agencies
Staff: 4
Annual Budget: $250-500,000

Personnel:
Executive Director: Brenda Gevertz
Treasurer: Jeremy Bandler
Program Coordinator: Layah Blacksberg
Journal Editor: Gail Chalew

Historical Note:
Formerly known as The National Conference of Jewish Charities (NCJC), JCSA's mission is to connect practitioners and leadership and provide opportunities to share knowledge and collaborate across fields of service. Membership: $75 (General); $50 (Transitional/Retiree); $15 (Full Time Student); $25 (Adjuct); $125 (Supporting).

Publications:
JCSA Newsletter; monthly
Journal of Jewish Communal Service; quarterly

Jewish Community Centers Association of North America (1921)
520 Eighth Ave.
New York, NY 10018
Tel: (212) 532-4949 *Fax:* (212) 481-4174
E-Mail: info@jcca.org
Website: jcca.org
Members: 350 agencies
Staff: 66
Annual Budget: $10-25,000,000
Tax: 501(c)(3)

Personnel:
President and Chief Executive Officer: Allan Finkelstein
E-Mail: jccal@jcca.org
Senior Vice President and Chief Marketing Officer: Robin Ballin
E-Mail: robin@jcca.org
Vice President, Professional Leadership: Alan Goldberg
E-Mail: gold@jcca.org
Manager, Human Resources: Irina Khomina
E-Mail: ikhomina@jcca.org
Senior Vice President and Chief Financial Officer: Bob Kimsal
E-Mail: bkimsal@jcca.org
Assistant Vice President, Health, Wellness Services and Membership Recruitment Consultant: Anthony Slayen
E-Mail: anthonys@jcca.org
Executive Vice President and Chief Operating Officer: Jerry Wische
E-Mail: jwische@jcca.org
Manager, Information Technology: Andy Zhang
E-Mail: andy@jcca.org

Historical Note:
Founded as the National Jewish Welfare Board, merged with the Council of Young Men's Hebrew and Kindred Associations in 1921, assumed the name JWB in 1977 and its present name in 1990. JCCA supports Jewish early childhood centers and Jewish summer camps in North America. JCC is a U. S. government accredited agency for serving the religious and social needs of Jewish military personnel through JWB Jewish Chaplains Council.

Meetings/Conferences: Annual
2013 - Orlando, FL (Rosen Plaza Hotel)/March 3 - 6
Number of non-conference events/year: 26

Publications:

JCC Circle

Jewish Education Service of North America (1939)
318 W. 39th St.
Fifth Floor
New York, NY 10018
Tel: (212) 284-6950 *Fax:* (212) 284-6951
E-Mail: info@jesna.org
Website: jesna.org
Members: 2000 individuals
Staff: 37
Annual Budget: $2-5,000,000

Personnel:
President: Donald A. Sylvan PhD
Managing Director, Communications: Joe Berkofsky
E-Mail: joe.berkofsky@jewishfederations.org
Vice President, Programs and Organizational Learning: Leora Isaacs
E-Mail: lisaacs@jesna.org
Chief Marketing Officer: Rika Levin-Reisman MBA
E-Mail: rlevin@jesna.org
Associate, Human Resources: Kris Marin-Pilgrim
E-Mail: kmarin-pilgrim@jesna.org
Chief Financial Officer: Ralia Wagner
E-Mail: rwagner@jesna.org

Historical Note:
Formerly (1981) the American Association for Jewish Education, JESNA is dedicated to building a strong Jewish future where learners of all ages lead Jewish lives infused with purpose and meaning. Membership: $75 (Professionals); $50 (Students/Retirees).

Publications:
JESNA E-Newsletter; on-line

Jewish Educators Assembly (1951)
Broadway and Locust Ave.
P.O. Box 413
Cedarhurst, NY 11516
Tel: (516) 569-2537 *Fax:* (516) 295-9039
E-Mail: jewisheducators@jewisheducators.org
Website: jewisheducators.org
Members: 500 individuals
Staff: 3
Annual Budget: $100-250,000
Tax: 501(c)(5)

Personnel:
Executive Director and Placement Advisor: Edward Edelstein
E-Mail: Jewisheducators@aol.com

Historical Note:
JEA's mission is to promote excellence among educators committed to Conservative Jewish education by advancing professionalism, encouraging leadership, pursuing lifelong learning and building community. Members are Jewish education professionals and educational administrators who identify with the Conservative Movement. Membership is based upon 7% of salary. $50 (Student/Israeli Educators/Retired); $75 (Teachers); $150 (Academic/Supporter); $210-840 (Regular).

Meetings/Conferences: Annual

Publications:
JEA Newsletter

Jewish Funeral Directors of America (1932)
107 Carpenter Dr.
Suite 100
Sterling, VA 20164
Fax: (703) 391-8416
TollFree: (888) 477-5567
E-Mail: info@jfda.com
Website: jfda.org
Members: 100 firms
Staff: 2
Annual Budget: $100-250,000

Personnel:
Treasurer: Marc Benjamin

Historical Note:
JFDA's purpose is to preserve the traditions and customs of the Jewish funeral service as recognized and practiced by those of the Jewish faith to enrich and strengthen the association as an exemplar of Jewish values, to formulate and advocate the highest principles, ideals and ethics of the funeral profession.

Publications:
Funeral Etiquette
Member Directory; annually

The Jewish Funeral in Contemporary Life
The Ultimate Kindness

The Jockey Club (1894)
40 E. 52nd St.
New York, NY 10022
Tel: (212) 371-5970 *Fax:* (212) 371-6123
TollFree: (800) 444-8521
E-Mail: contactus@jockeyclub.com
Website: jockeyclub.com
Members: 100 individuals
Staff: 14
Annual Budget: $10-25,000,000
Tax: 501(c)(5)

Personnel:
President and Chief Operating Officer: James L. Gagliano
Executive Vice President and Executive Director: Matt F. Iuliano
Executive Vice President and Chief Financial Officer: Laura Barillaro

Historical Note:
A service organization to the racing industry which encourages the development of thoroughbred horses, establishes regulations governing them and sets the foundation for rules adopted by all racing states. Members are individual owners/breeders and others connected with the racing industry.

The Jockeys' Guild (1940)
103 Wind Haven Dr.
Suite 200
Nicholasville, KY 40356
Tel: (859) 523-5625 *Fax:* (859) 219-9892
TollFree: (866) 465-6257
E-Mail: info@jockeysguild.com
Website: jockeysguild.com
Members: 800 individuals
Staff: 11
Annual Budget: $2-5,000,000
Tax: 501(c)(3)

Personnel:
National Manager: Terence J. Meyocks
E-Mail: tmeyocks@jockeysguild.com
Contact, Mount Fees, Media Rights and Special Events: Jamie Carter
E-Mail: jamie@jockeysguild.com
Legal Counsel: Mindy L. Coleman
E-Mail: mcoleman@jockeysguild.com
Contact, Accounts Receivable and Payable, Invoicing: Tina Linville
E-Mail: Tina@jockeysguild.com
Contact, Membership Services and Newsletter and Web Site Administration: Jennifer Ray
E-Mail: jray@jockeysguild.com

Historical Note:
Established as the Jockey's Community Fund and Guild, assumed its present name in 1946. JG represents thoroughbred horse racing and American quarter horse professional jockeys. Members are licensed flat riding jockeys.

Meetings/Conferences:
Conference Chair: Jamie Carter

Publications:
JG Newsletter; irregular
Membership Directory; on-line

Joint Council of Allergy, Asthma and Immunology (1975)
50 N. Brockway St.
Suite 3-3
Palatine, IL 60067
Tel: (847) 934-1918 *Fax:* (847) 934-1820
E-Mail: info@jcaai.org
Website: jcaai.org
Members:
4200 Allergists/Immunologists
2 organizations
Staff: 3
Annual Budget: $500-1,000,000
Tax: 501(c)(6)

Personnel:
President: James L. Sublett

Historical Note:
The Mission of JCAAI is to act on behalf of the specialty of Allergy/Immunology and the patients it serves; and to provide a unified voice in medical socio-economics which will enable patients to receive the highest quality Allergy/

Immunology care. Membership: $175 (Physician); $20-50 (Fellow in Training); $25 (Associate-Non-Physician).

Publications:
JCAAI newsletter

Joint Electron Device Engineering Council (1941)
3103 N. Tenth St.
Suite 240-S
Arlington, VA 22201-2107
Fax: (703) 907-7583
Website: jedec.org
Members: 300 companies
Staff: 10
Annual Budget: $1-2,000,000

Personnel:
President: John Kelly
E-Mail: johnk@jedec.org
Senior Coordinator, Membership Services: Arlene Collier
Director, Marketing and Communications: Emily Desjardins
E-Mail: emilyd@jedec.org
Director, Administration and Finance: Lorraine Hurlbutt
E-Mail: lorraineh@jedec.org
Senior Website Administrator: Arnaud Lebegue
Director, Events: Donna McEntire
E-Mail: donnam@jedec.org

Historical Note:
Affiliated with the Electronic Industries Association. JEDEC is the semiconductor engineering standardization body of the Electronic Industries Alliance (EIA), a trade association that represents all areas of the electronics industry. Members are manufacturers and users of semiconductor components and others allied to the field. Membership: $2,500-15,000/year (Individual).

Meetings/Conferences: Annual
Conference Chair: Donna McEntire
Number of non-conference events/year: 7

Publications:
JEDEC SmartBrief; on-line

Joint National Committee for Languages (1976)
4646 40th St. NW
Suite 310
Washington, DC 20016
Tel: (202) 966-8477 Fax: (202) 966-8310
E-Mail: info@languagepolicy.org
Website: languagepolicy.org
Members: 60 national and regional organizations
Staff: 3
Annual Budget: $100-250,000
Tax: 501(c)(3)

Personnel:
Policy Analyst: Crystal B. Goldie
E-Mail: cgoldie@languagepolicy.org
Office Manager: Walter Martinez
E-Mail: info@languagepolicy.org

Historical Note:
In 1976, the Joint National Committee for Languages began as an informal coalition of eight national language teaching associations. JNCL is an member-funded nonprofit education policy association.

Joint National Committee for Languages-National Council for Languages and International Studies (1988)
4646 40th St. NW
Suite 310
Washington, DC 20016
Tel: (202) 966-8477 Fax: (202) 966-8310
E-Mail: info@languagepolicy.org
Website: languagepolicy.org
Members:
300000 professionals
60 organizations
Staff: 4

Personnel:
Executive Director: Dr. William P. Rivers
E-Mail: wrivers@languagepolicy.org
Treasurer: Dr. Peter Krawutschke
E-Mail: peter.krawutschke@wmich.edu
Program Manager: Ashley L. Lenker
Office Manager: Walter Martinez
E-Mail: info@languagepolicy.org

Historical Note:
JNCL-NCLIS is a membership organization that aims for all Americans to have the opportunity to learn and use English and at least one other language.

Joint Review Committee on Education in Radiologic Technology (1969)
20 N. Wacker Dr.
Suite 2850
Chicago, IL 60606-3182
Tel: (312) 704-5300 Fax: (312) 704-5304
E-Mail: mail@jrcert.org
Website: jrcert.org
Staff: 3
Annual Budget: $2-5,000,000

Personnel:
Chief Executive Officer: Leslie F. Winter MS, RT (R)
E-Mail: lwinter@jrcert.org
Manager, Finance and Computer Services: Teresa Cruz
E-Mail: tcruz@jrcert.org
Administrative Assistant: Joanne Sauter
E-Mail: jsauter@jrcert.org

Historical Note:
JRCERT promotes excellence in education and elevates the quality and safety of patient care through the accreditation of educational programs in radiography, radiation therapy, magnetic resonance, and medical dosimetry.

Continuing Education:
Certification Designation/s: ARRT
Meetings/Conferences:
Number of non-conference events/year: 12

Journalism Education Association (1924)
Kansas State University
103 Kedzie Hall
Manhattan, KS 66506-1505
Tel: (785) 532-5532 Fax: (785) 532-5563
TollFree: (866) 532-5532
E-Mail: jea@spub.k-state.edu
Website: jea.org
Members: 2100 individuals
Staff: 4
Annual Budget: $500-1,000,000

Personnel:
Executive Director: Kelly Furnas
E-Mail: furnas@ksu.edu
Developer, Web and Database: Arthi Subramanian
E-Mail: arthis@k-state.edu
Editor: Bradley Wilson
E-Mail: bradleywilson08@gmail.com

Historical Note:
Established as National Association of Journalism Directors (1924), became a division of National Education Association (1937); assumed its present name in 1963. JEA mission is to support free and responsible scholastic journalism by providing resources and educational opportunities, by advocating professionalism, by encouraging and rewarding student excellence and teacher achievement, and by supporting an atmosphere. Members are principally secondary school journalism teachers and advisers. Membership: $55 (Teacher/Adviser); $75 (Associate/Institutional); $25 (College Student); $60 (Affiliate Organization); $30 (Emeritus Teacher/Adviser); $600 (Lifetime).

Continuing Education:
Certification Designation/s: CJE, MJE
Meetings/Conferences: Semi-Annual
2013 - San Francisco, CA (San Francisco Marriott Marquis)/April 25 - 28
2013 - Boston, MA/Nov. 14 - 18
2013 - Boston, MA/Nov. 14 - 17
2014 - San Diego, CA/April 10 - 13
2014 - Washington, DC/Nov. 6 - 9
2015 - Denver, CO/April 16 - 19
2015 - Orlando, FL/Nov. 12 - 16

Publications:
Communication: Journalism Education Today; quarterly; adv.
Membership Directory; on-line

Judge Advocates Association (1943)
P.O. Box 30380
Alexandria, VA 22310
Tel: (202) 318-9122 Fax: (202) 318-9122
E-Mail: execdir@jaa.org
Website: jaa.org
Members: 400 individuals
Staff: 1
Annual Budget: $25-50,000

Personnel:
Executive Director: Christopher Santoro
E-Mail: execdir@jaa.org

Historical Note:
JAA seeks to advocate improvement of military legal and judicial system. Members are lawyers who serve or have served in the Armed Forces or who practice before the U.S. Court of Appeals for the Armed Forces and U.S. Courts of Appeals for Veterans Cause and holds National affiliate with American Bar Association (ABA). Membership: $50 (Senior); $30 (Junior/Associate Member); $20 (Law Student); $350-500 (Life Member).

Meetings/Conferences: Annual
Publications:
The Military Advocate; bi-annually

Juice Products Association (1957)
529 14th St. NW
750 National Press Building
Washington, DC 20045
Tel: (202) 785-3232 Fax: (202) 223-9741
E-Mail: jpa@kellencompany.com
Website: juiceproducts.org
Members: 130 companies and 60 associates
Staff: 7
Annual Budget: $1-2,000,000
Tax: 501(c)(6)

Personnel:
Executive Director: Carol Freysinger
President: Richard E. Cristol
Director, Technical: Pat Faison
Manager, Meetings: Darrel McCook
Media Contact: Stephanie Meyering
E-Mail: smeyering@kellencompany.com
Legal Counsel: Richard S. Silverman

Historical Note:
JPA was previously known as the National Association of Citrus Juice Processors and became the National Orange Juice Association in 1960. In 2003, the National Juice Products Association and Processed Apples Institute consolidated to form the Juice Products Association, Inc. JPA's mission is to promote standards of quality for juice and fruit products and to promote research. Membership: $500/year (Regular/Associate).

Meetings/Conferences: Annual
Conference Chair: Darrel McCook
2013 - Miami, FL (Ritz Carlton Key Biscayne)/April 12 - 17
2013 - Austin, TX (Four Seasons Hotel Austin)/Oct. 15 - 16

Publications:
JPA Newsletter
Member Directory

Just Plain Folks Songwriting/Musician Networking Organization
5327 Kit Dr.
Indianapolis, IN 46237
E-Mail: JPFolksPro@aol.com
Website: jpfolks.com
Members: 51500 members
Staff: 1

Personnel:
Founder: Brian Austin Whitney

Historical Note:
JPF is created to provide a network of cooperation and inclusion for musicians. Members are songwriters, recording artists, music publishers, record labels, performing arts societies, educational institutions, recording studios and engineers, producers, legal professionals, publicists and journalists, publications, music manufacturers and retailers.

Publications:
Just Plain Notes; on-line

Justice Research and Statistics Association (1974)
777 N. Capitol St. NE
Suite 801
Washington, DC 20002
Tel: (202) 842-9330 Fax: (202) 842-9329
E-Mail: cjinfo@jrsa.org
Website: jrsa.org
Members: 300 individuals and institutions
Staff: 19
Annual Budget: $2-5,000,000

Personnel:
Executive Director: Joan C. Weiss MSW
Director, Finance and Administration: Sandra Dayton CPA
E-Mail: sdayton@jrsa.org
Director, Membership Services: Karen F. Maline
E-Mail: kmaline@jrsa.org

Director, Publications: Nancy Michel
  E-Mail: nmichel@jrsa.org
Director, Research: Stan Orchowsky PhD
  E-Mail: sorchows@jrsa.org

Historical Note:
JRSA is funded primarily by Justice Department grants.
JRSA's purpose is to promote exchange of information
among the Statistical Analysis Centers (SACs), enabling
them to work towards common goals, and as a liaison
between the state agencies and the Justice Department.
Members include directors of state criminal justice statistics
analysis centers and individuals engaged in applied
statistical analysis in criminal and juvenile justice agencies
and academia. Membership: $75 (Individual); $400
(Institution); $40 (Student).

Meetings/Conferences: Annual
Conference Chair: Karen F. Maline

Publications:
JRP Digest; on-line
JRSA E-News; monthly
The JRSA Forum; quarterly

Juvenile Products Manufacturers Association
(1959)
15000 Commerce Pkwy.
Suite C
Mt. Laurel, NJ 08054
Tel: (856) 638-0420 Fax: (856) 439-0525
E-Mail: jpma@jpma.org
Website: jpma.org
Members: 250 companies
Staff: 8
Annual Budget: $1-2,000,000
Tax: 501(c)(6)

Personnel:
Executive Director: Michael Dwyer CAE
  E-Mail: mdwyer@ahint.com
Certification Administrative Director: Megan Capie
  E-Mail: mcapie@ahint.com
Director, Communications: Amy Chezem
  E-Mail: achezem@ahint.com
Director, Meetings, Exhibits, and Trade Shows: Clare
  MacNab
  E-Mail: cmacnab@ahint.com
Coordinator, Marketing: Ashley Scherer
  E-Mail: ascherer@ahint.com
Coordinator, Membership: Evan Wallace
  E-Mail: ewallace@ahint.com

Historical Note:
JPMA's mission is to promote the industry and the
safe use of juvenile products. JPMA exists to advance
the interest, growth and well being of North American
prenatal to preschool product manufacturers, importers,
and distributors marketing under their own brands to
consumers. Members are companies which manufacture,
import, and/or distribute infant products such as cribs, car
seats, strollers, bedding, lamps, accessories and decorative
items. Membership: $990-33,415 (Regular); $3,000-
8,000 (Affiliate);$1,000-7,500 (Associate).

Continuing Education:
Certification Designation/s: JPMA

Meetings/Conferences: Annual
Conference Chair: Clare MacNab

Publications:
Connections; semi-annually
Directory of Certified Products; on-line
e-Bulletins; monthly
Manufacturer's Directory; on-line
Member Directory; on-line
Retail Rattle; quarterly

JWB Jewish Chaplains Council (1917)
520 Eighth Ave.
New York, NY 10018
Tel: (212) 532-4949 Fax: (212) 481-4174
E-Mail: info@jcca.org
Website: jcca.org/jwb
Members: 16 rabbis
Staff: 2
Annual Budget: Under $10,000

Personnel:
Director: Rabbi Harold Robinson
  E-Mail: hlrobinson@jcca.org
Deputy Director: Barry Baron
  E-Mail: bbaron@jcca.org

Historical Note:
Founded in 1917 as the Chaplains' Committee of the JWB,
renamed the Committee for Army and Navy Religious

Affairs (CANRA) during World War II, and later retitled
the Commission on Jewish Chaplaincy. The Jewish Welfare
Board, a division of JCC Association, is a government
accredited agency providing for the religious, educational,
and morale needs of Jewish military personnel, their
families, and patients in Veterans Affairs hospitals.
Members are Jewish chaplains in the Army, Air Force, and
Department of Veterans Affairs. Membership: $10/year.

Meetings/Conferences:
Number of non-conference events/year: 50

Publications:
Membership Directory

Kamut Association of North America (1990)
333 Kamut Ln.
Big Sandy, MT 59520
Tel: (406) 378-3105 Fax: (406) 378-3106
Website: kamut.com
Members: 90 individuals
Staff: 4
Annual Budget: $25-50,000

Personnel:
President: Robert M. Quinn
  E-Mail: bob.quinn@kamut.com
Managing Director: Mark Callebert

Historical Note:
Formed in 1990, KANA members are growers, processors
and distributors of kamut grain. KANA's mission is to
promote organic agriculture and support organic farmers,
to increase diversity of crops and diets and to protect the
heritage of a quality, delicious ancient grain for the benefit
of this and future generations.

Publications:
KAMUT Nesletter; quarterly

Kappa Delta Epsilon (1933)
619 34th Ave., East
Tuscaloosa, AL 35404-3321
Tel: (205) 556-2120
Website: kappadeltaepsilon.org
Members: 40000 individuals
Staff: 3
Annual Budget: $50-100,000

Personnel:
President: Patricia C. Clark
  E-Mail: sealark7@aol.com

Historical Note:
KDE is an honorary educational fraternity which supports
the cause of education by fostering a spirit of fellowship,
standards of scholastic attainment and professional
ideals among its members. Membership: $35 (initial new
member), $15 (alumni per member per year).

Meetings/Conferences: Biennial

Publications:
The Current

Kappa Delta Pi (1911)
3707 Woodview Trace
Indianapolis, IN 46268-1158
Tel: (317) 871-4900 Fax: (317) 704-2323
TollFree: (800) 284-3167
E-Mail: admin@kdp.org
Website: kdp.org
Members: 45000 members
Staff: 20
Annual Budget: $250-500,000
Tax: 501(c)(3)

Personnel:
Executive Director: Faye Snodgress CAE
  E-Mail: faye@kdp.org
Director, Publications and Managing Editor: Kathie-Jo
  Arnoff
  E-Mail: kathiejo@kdp.org
Director, Finance: Patti Bontempo
  E-Mail: patti@kdp.org
Director, Membership and Chapter Services: Rachelle J.
  Merkel
  E-Mail: rachelle@kdp.org
Manager, Programs: Carol A. Paddock
  E-Mail: carol@kdp.org
Web Facilitator: Erin Sanders
  E-Mail: erin@kdp.org
Director, Marketing and Communications: Ulrike Steinert
  E-Mail: ulrike@kdp.org
Coordinator, Information Technology: Todd Tompkins
  E-Mail: todd@kdp.org

Historical Note:

The mission of KDP is to sustain an honored community of
diverse educators by promoting excellence and advancing
scholarship, leadership, and service. Members are education
professionals. Membership: $42 (Regular); $23 (Retiree);
$13 (Emeritus Gold); $750 (Lifetime); $64 (Family).

Meetings/Conferences: Biennial
Conference Chair: Carol A. Paddock

Publications:
KDP News; monthly
Membership Directory; on-line
New Teacher Advocate; quarterly; adv.
Novice Notes; quarterly
ProPointers; quarterly
Resource Roundup; on-line
The Leader; semi-monthly

Kappa Kappa Iota-National (1921)
1875 E. 15th St.
Tulsa, OK 74104-4610
Tel: (918) 744-0389 Fax: (918) 744-0578
TollFree: (800) 678-0389
E-Mail: kappa@galstar.com
Website: nationalkappakappaiota.org
Members: 7000 individuals
Staff: 2
Annual Budget: $100-250,000
Tax: 501(c)(3)

Personnel:
Executive Director: Radious Guess

Historical Note:
KKI is an organization established in Stillwater and
Oklahoma, the name was changed to Kappa Kappa Iota.
In April 1949, Kappa Kappa Iota was nationalized. KKI's
mission is to encourage the advancement of education by
providing an effective network for the exchange of education
and teaching practices by educators. Membership: $20
(Individual); $300 (Life).

Meetings/Conferences: Annual
2013 - Omaha, NE (DoubleTree by Hilton Hotel Omaha
  Downtown)/June 25 - 30
Number of non-conference events/year: 4

Kappa Psi Pharmaceutical Fraternity, Inc. (1879)
2060 N. Collins Blvd.
Suite 128
Richardson, TX 75080-2657
Tel: (972) 479-1879
E-Mail: centraloffice@kappapsi.org
Website: kappapsi.org
Members:
80000 graduate members
5000 collegiate members
Staff: 3
Annual Budget: $100-250,000

Personnel:
Executive Director: Johnny W. Porter MBA, RPh
  E-Mail: jporterky@aol.com

Historical Note:
Founded at Russell Military Academy, New Haven, CT.,
Kappa Psi is a professional fraternity in pharmacy whose
mission is to conduct a professional fraternal organization
for the mutual benefit of its members. It also develops
industry, sobriety, and fellowship. Membership: $5-40
(Capita Grand Council); $150 (Graduate Chapter); $50
(Voluntary Graduate Brother).

Meetings/Conferences: Biennial
2013 - St. Pete Beach, FL (Trade Winds Resort)/July 30
  - Aug. 4
Number of non-conference events/year: 2

Publications:
Membership Directory

Keyboard Teachers Association International
(1963)
11111 Maricopa Ln.
Dewey, AZ 86327
E-Mail: sontina@futureone.com
Website: areaweb.com/516/music/mtai/
Members: 250 individuals
Staff: 1
Annual Budget: Under $10,000

Personnel:
President and Secretary-Treasurer: Elfriede Evans-Richey

Historical Note:
Formerly the Keyboard Teachers Association
International,Inc.; (1979) National Association of Organ
Teachers, Inc. and (1986) International Association of
Organ Teachers USA. MTAI is an international association

of music teachers and students dedicated to the study and practical development of musical instruction and performance. *Membership: $25/year (individual); variable fee for organizations.*

Kidney Care Partners (2003)
2550 M St. NW
Washington, DC 20037
Tel: (703) 830-9192
Website: kidneycarepartners.org
Staff: 1
Annual Budget: $1-2,000,000
Personnel:
Contact, Communications: Susan Murdock
    E-Mail: susan@murdockinc.com
Historical Note:
Coalition of providers, suppliers, and support organizations for individuals with end stage renal disease. Mission is to involve patient advocates, care professionals, providers and manufacturers.

Kitchen Cabinet Manufacturers Association
(1955)
1899 Preston White Dr.
Reston, VA 20191-5435
Tel: (703) 264-1690 *Fax:* (703) 620-6530
E-Mail: info@kcma.org
Website: kcma.org
Members: 400 manufacturers
Staff: 4
Annual Budget: $1-2,000,000
Tax: 501(c)(6)
Personnel:
Executive Vice President: C. Richard Titus
    E-Mail: dtitus@kcma.org
Director, Accounting: Karen Kazmark
    E-Mail: kkazmark@kcma.org
Director, Membership Services and Marketing: Janet Titus
    E-Mail: jtitus@kcma.org
Director, Certifications: Terry W. Zinn
    E-Mail: tzinn@kcma.org
Historical Note:
Formerly National Institute of Wood Kitchen Cabinets, became the National Kitchen Cabinet Association in 1962 and assumed its present name in 1990 and absorbed the Decorative Laminate Products Association in 1995. KMCA works to advance the industry through advocacy, setting standards, sponsoring research, and providing management tools and educational programs. Members are manufacturers of assembled prefinished kitchen cabinets. Membership: $535/year (Minimum, based on member company's sales volume).
Continuing Education:
Certification Designation/s: ANSI/KCMA
Meetings/Conferences: Annual

The Kite Trade Association International (1983)
P.O. Box 443
Otis, OR 97368
Tel: (541) 994-9647 *Fax:* (503) 419-4369
TollFree: (800) 243-8548
E-Mail: exdir@kitetrade.org
Website: kitetrade.org
Members: 300 companies
Staff: 2
Annual Budget: $10-25,000
Tax: 501(c)(6)
Personnel:
Executive Director: Maggie Vohs CAE
    E-Mail: exdir@kitetrade.org
Secretary/Treasurer: Jim Christianson
Historical Note:
KTAI's mission is to support and promote the manufacturing, distributing and retailing of kites and wind related products. Members consist of wholesalers, retailers and other interested parties from around the world. Membership: $150 (Regular); $250 (Patron); $500 (Benefactor).
Meetings/Conferences: Annual
Conference Chair: Maggie Vohs CAE
2013 - Las Vegas, NV (Texas Station)/Jan. 28 - 31
Number of non-conference events/year: 1
Publications:
Email Updates; monthly
Membership Directory; on-line

The Knitting Guild Association (1984)
1100-H Brandywine Blvd.

Zanesville, OH 43701-7303
Tel: (740) 452-4541 *Fax:* (740) 452-2552
E-Mail: tkga@tkga.com
Website: tkga.com
Members: 10,000 members
Staff: 3
Annual Budget: $250-500,000
Personnel:
Executive Director: Penny Sitler
    E-Mail: psitler@offinger.com
Coordinator, Programs and Events: Debby Johnston
    E-Mail: djohnston@offinger.com
Managing Editor and Advertising Sales: Jane Miller
    E-Mail: jmiller@offinger.com
Historical Note:
Founded as Knitting Guild of America, assumed its current name in 2003. TKGA is an organization of knitters dedicated to promoting knitting as a worthwhile and enjoyable hobby. Membership: $30-54 (Individual/Designer); $54-1000 (Corporate).
Continuing Education:
Enrollment: 300
Certification Designation/s: TKGA
Meetings/Conferences: Semi-Annual
Conference Chair: Debby Johnston
Number of non-conference events/year: 2
Publications:
Cast On Magazine; quarterly; adv.
Membership Directory; on-line
Swatches eNewsletter; quarterly

Knowledge Alliance (1997)
One Saint Matthew's Ct. NW
Washington, DC 20036
Tel: (202) 518-0847
E-Mail: info@nekia.org
Website: nekia.org
Members: 35 companies
Staff: 4
Annual Budget: $500-1,000,000
Tax: 501(c)(6)
Personnel:
President and Chief Executive Officer: James W. Kohlmoos
    E-Mail: jim@knowledgeall.net
Policy Director: Kathryn Bannan
    E-Mail: bannan@knowledgeall.net
Director, Operations: John Waters
    E-Mail: waters@knowledgeall.net
Historical Note:
Founded as Council for Educational Development and Research; changed its name in April 2007 from NEKIA to Knowledge Alliance. Mission is to improve k-12 education by widely expanding the development and use of research-based knowledge in policy and practices. Membership: $10,000-30,000/year (Varies according to the size of the Organization).
Meetings/Conferences:
Number of non-conference events/year: 1
Publications:
Knowledge-able Source; weekly

Korean American Spine Society
One Barnes Plaza
W. Pavilion Suite 11300
St. Louis, MO 63110
Tel: (630) 681-1040
Website: kassmd.org
Staff: 3
Annual Budget: $100-250,000
Personnel:
Contact, Exhibition: Kate Laney
    E-Mail: klaney@broad-water.com
Treasurer: K. Daniel Riew MD
Historical Note:
It is the Mission of KASS to improve the quality of scientific knowledge, patient care, and clinical practice among professionals in the field of spinal disorders and promote social and cultural interaction between Korean American Spine Specialists.
Meetings/Conferences: Annual
Conference Chair: Kate Laney
2013 - Boston, MA (Hyatt Regency Boston)/June 27 - 29
Publications:
Membership Directory; on-line

Korean Drycleaners-Laundry Association (1982)
14909 Crenshaw Blvd.
Suite 201
Gardena, CA 90249
Fax: (310) 679-6890
E-Mail: kdla@kdla.org
Website: kdla.org
Members: 2000 members
Staff: 2
Annual Budget: $50-100,000
Personnel:
President: Paul Choe
    E-Mail: paulcchoe@gmail.com
Secretary: Jin Ki Han
    E-Mail: kdla@kdla.org
Historical Note:
The purpose of KDLA is to promote mutual benefits for the members and communities at large where members operate their business through education of members and community, exchanging information as to cleaning skills and research results, and other related activities.

KWPN of North America (1983)
609 E. Central
P.O. Box O
Sutherlin, OR 97479
Tel: (541) 459-3232 *Fax:* (541) 459-2967
E-Mail: office@kwpn-na.org
Website: kwpn-na.org
Members: 1350 individuals
Staff: 5
Annual Budget: $250-500,000
Tax: 501(c)(5)
Personnel:
President: Dan Ruediger
    E-Mail: dan@sonnenberg.us
Treasurer: Susan M. Taylor
    E-Mail: staylor@claybrookfarms.com
Historical Note:
Formerly the Dutch Warmblood Studbook/North America. KWPN-NA's mission is to establish, maintain and operate a non-profit association of breeders, owners and other interested individuals for the encouragement and preservation of the registered (KWPN) Dutch warmblood horse in North America. Membership: $85 (Full); $50 (Associate); $35 (Youth); $850 (Lifetime).
Meetings/Conferences: Annual
2013 - Chesapeake City, MD (Hassler Dressage)/ March 14 - 16
Number of non-conference events/year: 1
Publications:
KWPN-NA Newsletter; quarterly; adv.
Stallion Directory; annually; adv.

Label Printing Industries of America (1976)
200 Deer Run Rd.
Sewickley, PA 15143
Tel: (412) 741-6860 *Fax:* (412) 741-2311
TollFree: (800) 910-4283
E-Mail: printing@printing.org
Website: printing.org/lpia
Members: 50 companies
Staff: 6
Annual Budget: $100-250,000
Personnel:
President and Chief Executive Officer: Michael Makin
    E-Mail: mmakin@printing.org
Manager, Marketing: Lisa Erdner
    E-Mail: lerdner@printing.org
Section Manager: Justin Goldstein
    E-Mail: jgoldstein@printing.org
Assistant, Meetings: Teresa Rees
    E-Mail: trees@piagatf.org
Director, Special Interest Groups: Laurie Reynolds
    E-Mail: lreynolds@printing.org
Chief Financial Officer: Nicholas G. Stratigos CAE
Historical Note:
An affiliate of Printing Industries of America, which provides administtrative support. LPIA delivers products and services that enhance the growth, efficiency, and profitability of its members and the industry through advocacy, education, research, and technical information. Membership: $750- 5,500/year (Based on Sales Volume).
Meetings/Conferences:
Conference Chair: Teresa Rees
Number of non-conference events/year: 2
Publications:

Newsletter; quarterly

Labor and Employment Relations Association
(1947)
University of Illinois at Urbana-Champaign
121 LER Building, 504 E. Armory Ave.
Champaign, IL 61820
Tel: (217) 333-0072 *Fax:* (217) 265-5130
E-Mail: LERAoffice@illinois.edu
Website: leraweb.org
Members: 3000 individuals
Staff: 3
Annual Budget: $250-500,000
Tax: 501(c)(3)

Personnel:
Executive Director: Paula D. Wells
   E-Mail: pdwells@illinois.edu
Editor: Mike Lillich
   E-Mail: lillich@illinois.edu

Historical Note:
LERA is a member of Allied Social Science Associations. LERA's mission is to promote constructive dialogue and action on issues of policy, practice, theory and research that lie at the intersection of the interests of labor, management, government, neutrals and scholars, in the airline industry. Membership: $185 *(Regular);* $95 *(Emeritus);* $25 *(Fulltime Student);* $300 *(Contributing);* $200-250 *(Institutional/Library Subscription).*

Meetings/Conferences:
2013 - San Diego, CA (La Meridian)/Jan. 6 - 8
2013 - St. Louis, MO (Crowne Plaza Hotel)/June 6 - 9

Publications:
Labor and Employment Law Newsletter; monthly
LERA Newsletter; quarterly; adv.
Members Directory; on-line
Perspectives on Work; bi-annually; adv.

Membership List Available to Non-members

Labor Council for Latin American Advancement (LCLAA) *(1972)*
815 16th St. NW
Fourth Floor
Washington, DC 20006
Tel: (202) 508-6919 *Fax:* (202) 508-6922
E-Mail: headquarters@lclaa.org
Website: lclaa.org
Staff: 2
Annual Budget: $500-1,000,000
Tax: 501(c)(3)

Personnel:
Executive Vice President: Aida Garcia
Secretary and Treasurer: Maria Portalatin

Historical Note:
A Hispanic trade union association representing about 40 unions in 80 chapters throughout the country. Linked to the AFL-CIO in working for voter registration, education and participation by Hispanic workers.Membership $5 *(Student);* $10 *(retiree);* $20*(Associate/Union).*

Publications:
LCLAA Magazine
LCLAA Newsletter; monthly

Laboratory Animal Management Association
(1984)
7500 Flying Cloud Dr.
Suite 900
Eden Prairie, MN 55344
Tel: (952) 253-6235 *Fax:* (952) 835-4774
E-Mail: lama@associationsolutionsinc.com
Website: lama-online.org
Members: 500 individuals
Staff: 4
Annual Budget: $250-500,000
Tax: 501(c)(6)

Personnel:
Executive Director: Jim Manke CAE
   E-Mail: jrmanke@associationsolutionsinc.com
*Manager, Membership Development and Review
   Coordinator:* Judy Hansen
   E-Mail: jhansen@associationsolutionsinc.com
Manager, Meetings: Kathi Schlieff
   E-Mail: kschlieff@associationsolutionsinc.com

Historical Note:
Formerly the Laboratory Animal Manager Association. LAMA is dedicated to enhancing the quality of management and care of laboratory animals throughout the world. Members are managers of laboratory animal facilities.

Membership: $100 *(Domestic);* $120 *(International);* $250 *(Institutional).*

Continuing Education:
Certification Designation/s: CM, CMAR, CMP II

Meetings/Conferences: Annual
Conference Chair: Kathi Schlieff
2013 - Clearwater, FL (Hilton Clearwater Beach Resort)/April 24 - 26
Number of non-conference events/year: 10

Publications:
THE LAMA; monthly
The LAMA Review; quarterly; adv.

Laboratory Products Association *(1918)*
P.O. Box 428
Fairfax, VA 22038
Tel: (703) 836-1360 *Fax:* (703) 836-6644
E-Mail: info@lpanet.org
Website: lpanet.org
Members: 125 companies
Staff: 2
Annual Budget: $500-1,000,000

Personnel:
President: Clark Mulligan CAE
   E-Mail: cmulligan@lpanet.org
*Director, Membership Services, Marketing and
   Communications:* Lauren Hefner

Historical Note:
LPA's mission is to enable its members to constantly improve their global and commercial success by providing them with unique opportunities in networking, market information, and education. Members are manufacturers and distributors of lab products and services such as glass and plasticware, chemicals, equipment and supplies used in scientific research and applied science and life science worldwide. Membership: $1,985-21,425 *(Regular, based on annual sales);* $2,500 *(Associate Publisher).*

Meetings/Conferences: Annual
Conference Chair: Lauren Hefner
Number of non-conference events/year: 1

Publications:
LPA Newsletter
Membership directory; on-line

Laborers International Union of North America
(1903)
905 16th St. NW
Washington, DC 20006
Tel: (202) 737-8320 *Fax:* (202) 737-2754
E-Mail: membermail@liuna.org
Website: liuna.org
Members: 500,000 men and women
Staff: 150
Annual Budget: $50-100,000,000
Tax: 501(c)(5)

Personnel:
General President: Terence M. O'Sullivan
Legislative and Political Director: Bevin Albertani
   E-Mail: balbertani@liuna.org
General Counsel: Michael Bearse
Representative, Member Benefits: Madonna Brennan
Director, Strategic Communications: Richard Greer
   E-Mail: rgreer@liuna.org
Director, Education: Kevin O'Sullivan
General Secretary and Treasurer: Armand E. Sabitoni

Historical Note:
Formerly the International Hod Carriers and Building Laborers' Union of America and chartered by the AFL-CIO, (1912) the International Hod Carriers' and Common Laborers' Union of America, the International Hod Carriers', Building and Common Laborers' Union of America, merged in 1918 with the Compressed Air and Foundation Workers' International Union and in 1929 with the Tunnel and Subway Constructors' International Union and assumed its present name in September 20, 1965. Sponsors and supports the Laborers' Political League, Laborers' Health and Safety Fund on North America, Laborers-Employers Cooperation and Education Trust, Laborers-ACG-Education and Training Fund.

Publications:
The Laborer; semi-annually

Laborers-Employers Cooperation & Education Trust
905 16th St. NW
Washington, DC 20006
Tel: (202) 393-7344 *Fax:* (202) 347-1721
TollFree: (800) 562-1181

E-Mail: info@lecet.org
Website: lecet.org
Staff: 14
Annual Budget: $10-25,000,000
Tax: 501(c)(5)

Personnel:
Executive Director: Christopher P. Engquist
Manager, Computer Services: Katey Bailey
   E-Mail: katey@lecet.org
Researcher: Frank DiBitetto
Director, Government Affairs: Leo J. Gannon
   E-Mail: leo@lecet.org
Accounting Manager: Linda Priscilla
Manager, Communications: Edward Rehfeld
Coordinator, Publications: Louiza Sokaris

Historical Note:
LECET's mission is to help Laborers' Local Unions and the contractors with whom they work win projects and jobs.

Meetings/Conferences: Annual

Ladies Professional Golf Association *(1950)*
100 International Golf Dr.
Daytona Beach, FL 32124-1092
Tel: (386) 274-6200 *Fax:* (386) 274-1099
E-Mail: feedback@lpga.com
Website: lpga.com
Members: 1600 professional golfers
Staff: 84
Annual Budget: $50-100,000,000
Tax: 501(c)(6)

Personnel:
Executive Director: Nancy Henderson
   E-Mail: nancy.henderson@lpga.com
President, LPGA Foundation: Carol Corcoran
Coordinator, Human Resources: Barbara Dodds
   E-Mail: barbara.dodds@lpga.com
Senior Vice President and Chief Financial Officer: Kathy
   Milthrope
   E-Mail: kathy.milthrope@lpga.com
*Senior Vice President, Project Development and Membership
   Services:* Mindy Moore
Chief Marketing Officer: Jon Podany

Historical Note:
LPGA's mission is to aid economic empowerment for its members. Members are golf teachers, coaches, golf professionals and facility managers. Membership: $150/ *year.*

Publications:
LPGA Anti-Doping Newsletter; quarterly

Lake Carriers Association *(1880)*
20325 Center Ridge Rd.
Suite 720
Rocky River, OH 44116
Tel: (440) 333-4444 *Fax:* (440) 333-9993
E-Mail: info@lcaships.com
Website: lcaships.com
Members: 17 companies
Staff: 4
Annual Budget: $1-2,000,000
Tax: 501(c)(6)

Personnel:
President: James H.I. Weakley
Administrative Assistant: Katie Gumeny
General Counsel: Harold W. Henderson
Vice President: Glen G. Nekvasil

Historical Note:
The successor organization to Cleveland Vessel Owners Association (1880) and Lake Carriers' Association of Buffalo (1885). Members are U.S. -Flag Great Lakes vessel operators engaged in transportation of iron ore, coal, grain, limestone, cement and petroleum products. LCA's mission is to facilitate a broad-based understanding of U.S.-Flag shipping on the Great Lakes and its role in the nation's economy.

Lamaze International *(1960)*
2025 M St.
Suite 800
Washington, DC 20036-3309
Tel: (202) 367-1128 *Fax:* (202) 367-2128
TollFree: (800) 368-4404
E-Mail: info@lamaze.org
Website: lamaze.org
Members: 3000 individuals
Staff: 15
Annual Budget: $2-5,000,000

Tax: 501(c)(3)

Personnel:
Executive Director and Chief Executive Officer: Linda L. Harmon MPH
E-Mail: lharmon@lamaze.org
Program Associate: Mary Kate Heisler
E-Mail: mheisler@lamaze.org
Manager, Client Information Technology: Denis Janis
E-Mail: djanis@smithbucklin.com
Associate Executive Director and Chief Operating Officer: Jeanne Mendelson
E-Mail: jmendelson@lamaze.org
Manager, Accounting: Russell Nuzum
E-Mail: RNuzum@smithbucklin.com
Director, Education and Programs: Chris Peck
E-Mail: cpeck@smithbucklin.com
Associate, Membership Services: Janna Royer
E-Mail: jroyer@lamaze.org
Senior Manager, Marketing and Communications: Amanda Wood 'McLafferty'
E-Mail: amwood@smithbucklin.com

Historical Note:
Formerly (1998) the American Society for Psychoprophylaxis in Obstetrics. Lamaze International's mission is to promote a natural, healthy and safe approach to pregnancy, childbirth and early parenting. It also serve as a resource for information about what to expect and what choices are available during the childbearing years. Membership: $75 (Birth Advocates); $85-115 (Regular).

Continuing Education:
Certification Designation/s: LCEC, LCCE

Meetings/Conferences: Annual
Conference Chair: Mary Kate Heisler
2013 - New Orleans, LA (Astor Crowne Plaza Hotel)/ Oct. 11 - 13

Publications:
Membership Directory; annually
The Journal of Perinatal Education; quarterly; adv.

Membership List Available to Non-members

Lambda Kappa Sigma (1913)
P.O. Box 570
Muskego, WI 53150-0570
Tel: (888) 557-1913 *Fax:* (262) 679-4558
E-Mail: lks@lks.org
Website: lks.org
Members: 22000 individuals
Staff: 3
Annual Budget: $100-250,000

Personnel:
Executive Director: Joan E. Rogala CAE, IOM
E-Mail: joanrogala@msn.com

Historical Note:
LKS's mission is to promote the profession of pharmacy among women. Represents undergraduate and graduate pharmacy students and practicing pharmacists. LKS educational programs enhance professional development in the field of pharmacy, with an emphasis placed on women's health issues. Membership: $90 (Alumni); $75 (Graduate Students/Retirees); $75 (New Initiates); $60 (Returning Student).

Meetings/Conferences: Annual

Publications:
Alumni News; quarterly
LinKS
Membership Directory; on-line

Membership List Available to Non-members

Land Improvement Contractors of America (1951)
3080 Ogden Ave.
Suite 300
Lisle, IL 60532
Tel: (630) 548-1984 *Fax:* (630) 548-9189
E-Mail: nlica@aol.com
Website: licanational.com
Members: 2200 companies
Staff: 3
Annual Budget: $250-500,000

Personnel:
Chief Executive Officer: Gerald J. Biuso Sr.
E-Mail: gbiusosr@earthlink.net
Publisher: Eileen Levy
E-Mail: nlica@aol.com
Director, Government Relations: John Peterson
E-Mail: jwpeterson@cox.net

Historical Note:
Mission is to promote, perpetuate and improve the proper use of renewable natural resources. LICA is engaged in the conservation of soil and clean water. Membership: $300 (National Associate); $195 (Member-At-Large).

Continuing Education:
Certification Designation/s: CCP

Meetings/Conferences:
2013 - Savannah, GA (Savannah Marriott Riverfront)/ Feb. 5 - 10
Number of non-conference events/year: 15

Publications:
Land and Water Magazine; bi-monthly; adv.
LICA Contractor; quarterly; adv.
LICA News; bi-monthly; adv.

Land Mobile Communications Council (1967)
8484 Westpark Dr.
Suite 630
McLean, VA 22102-5117
Tel: (703) 528-5115 *Fax:* (703) 524-1074
Website: lmcc.org
Members: 20 organizations
Staff: 2
Annual Budget: $10-25,000
Tax: 501(c)(6)

Personnel:
Secretary and Treasurer: Mark E. Crosby
E-Mail: mark.crosby@enterprisewireless.org

Historical Note:
The LMCC is a nonprofit association of organizations that represent the wireless communications interests of public safety, critical infrastructure, business, industrial, transportation, private and common carriers, and manufacturers of wireless communications equipment. LMCC membership represents telecommunications sectors such as public safety, industrial/land transportation, private radio, specialized mobile radio and critical infrastructure.

Publications:
Membership Directory; on-line

Land Trust Alliance (1982)
1660 L St. NW
Suite 1100
Washington, DC 20036
Tel: (202) 638-4725 *Fax:* (202) 638-4730
E-Mail: lta@lta.org
Website: landtrustalliance.org
Members: 2057 organizations and individuals
Staff: 60
Annual Budget: $5-10,000,000
Tax: 501(c)(3)

Personnel:
President: Rand Wentworth
E-Mail: rwentworth@lta.org
Director, Communications: Rob Aldrich
E-Mail: raldrich@lta.org
Chief Financial Officer and Chief Operating Officer: Marilyn Ayres
E-Mail: mayres@lta.org
Manager, Communications and Marketing: Peshie Chaifetz
E-Mail: pressroom@lta.org
Director, Education: Renee Kivikko
E-Mail: rkivikko@lta.org
Manager, Training and Conferences: Pam Nicholls
E-Mail: training@lta.org
Manager, Office and Human Resources: Dee Perkins
E-Mail: lperkins@lta.org
Director, Public Policy: Russell Shay
E-Mail: rshay@lta.org
Editor: Chris Soto
E-Mail: csoto@lta.org
Manager, Information Technology: Andy Weaver
E-Mail: aweaver@lta.org
Coordinator, Membership Services: Bart Zerfas
E-Mail: bzerfas@lta.org

Historical Note:
Formerly (1991) Land Trust Exchange, LTA is dedicated for land conservation professionals, volunteers and supporters - to quickly, effectively and permanently save valued natural resource across America. Members are local and regional non- profit land conservation groups and other concerned organizations and individuals. Membership: $35-999 (Individual); $225-2,500 (Organization, based on operating expenses).

Continuing Education:
Certification Designation/s: LCLP

Meetings/Conferences: Annual
Conference Chair: Pam Nicholls
2013 - New Orleans, LA/Sept. 17 - 19
Number of non-conference events/year: 1

Publications:
Stay Informed; quarterly

Membership List Available to Non-members

Large Public Power Council (1987)
1050 Thomas Jefferson St. NW
Seventh Floor
Washington, DC 20007-3877
Tel: (202) 430-0101 *Fax:* (843) 278-8351
E-Mail: lppc@lppc.org
Website: lppc.org
Members: 26 Companies
Staff: 1
Annual Budget: $2-5,000,000

Personnel:
Executive Director: Missy Mandell

Historical Note:
A consortium of 21 state and local government-owned utilities in Arizona, California, Colorado, Florida, Georgia, Nebraska, South Carolina, Tennessee, Texas, Washington State, and Puerto Rico, including the municipal power departments of New York City and Los Angeles.

Publications:
Membership Directory; on-line

Large Urology Group Practice Association (LUGPA) (2008)
1100 E. Woodfield Rd.
Suite 520
Schaumburg, IL 60173
Tel: (847) 517-7225 *Fax:* (847) 517-7229
E-Mail: info@lugpa.org
Website: lugpa.org
Members: 1800 urologists
Staff: 2
Annual Budget: $1-2,000,000
Tax: 501(c)(6)

Personnel:
Executive Director: Liz Schumacher JD
Contact, Publications: Ruth A. Gottmann MBA
E-Mail: ruth@wjweiser.com

Historical Note:
LUGPA was established to enhance communication between large groups, allowing for benchmarking of operations, promotion of quality clinical outcomes, development of new business opportunities, and enhanced advocacy in the legislative and regulatory arenas.

Publications:
Eblasts; on-line
LUGPA Informant

Laser and Electro-Optics Manufacturers' Association (1986)
123 Kent Rd.
Pacifica, CA 94044
Tel: (650) 738-1492 *Fax:* (650) 738-1592
E-Mail: Info@leoma.com
Website: leoma.com
Members: 40 companies
Staff: 1
Annual Budget: $100-250,000

Personnel:
Executive Director: C. Breck Hitz
E-Mail: breck@leoma.com

Historical Note:
Formerly (1991) Laser Association of America. Members are companies with an interest in laser technology. Membership: $200-22, 000/year.

Laser Institute of America (1968)
13501 Ingenuity Dr.
Suite 128
Orlando, FL 32826
Tel: (407) 380-1553 *Fax:* (407) 380-5588
TollFree: (800) 345-2737
E-Mail: lia@laserinstitute.org
Website: lia.org
Members: 2000 individuals, companies and institutions
Staff: 18
Annual Budget: $2-5,000,000
Tax: 501(c)(3)

Personnel:
Executive Director: Peter M. Baker
  E-Mail: pbaker@lia.org
Director, Education: Gustavo Anibarro
  E-Mail: ganibarro@lia.org
Coordinator, Marketing: David Evans
  E-Mail: devans@lia.org
Chief Financial Officer: Jeannette Gabay
  E-Mail: cfo@lia.org
Director, Conferences: Gail Loiacono
  E-Mail: gloiacono@lia.org
Director, Marketing: James Naugle
  E-Mail: jnaugle@lia.org

Historical Note:
Established in February 1968 in California as the Laser Industry Association by a group of laser pioneers, inventors, and industry leaders, the name was changed to Laser Institute of America in 1972. LIA's mission is to foster lasers, laser applications, and laser safety worldwide. Membership: $110 (Individual); $400-995 (Corporation); $1,100 (Individual-Lifetime); $55 (Retired/Student).

Meetings/Conferences: Annual
Conference Chair: Gail Loiacono
2013 - Houston, TX (Hilton Houston North)/Feb. 12 - 13
Number of non-conference events/year: 3

Publications:
Corpoarte Membership Directory; annually
Individual Directory; on-line
Journal Laser Applications; adv.
LIA Connection; monthly; adv.
LIA Today; bi-monthly; adv.

Latin American Studies Association *(1965)*
416 Bellefield Hall, University of Pittsburgh
Pittsburgh, PA 15260
Tel: (412) 648-7929 *Fax:* (412) 624-7145
E-Mail: lasa@pitt.edu
Website: lasa.international.pitt.edu
Members: 7000 members
Staff: 5
Annual Budget: $1-2,000,000

Personnel:
Executive Director: Milagros Pereyra-Rojas
Operation Manager, Congress Coordinator: Pilar Rodriguez Blanco
Special Projects Coordinator: Maria Soledad Cabezas
Specialist, Communications: Ryan Lincoln
Membership Coordinator: Israel R. Perlov

Historical Note:
LASA's mission is to foster intellectual discussion, research, and teaching on Latin America, the Caribbean, and its people throughout the Americas, promote the interests of its diverse membership, and encourage civic engagement through network building and public debate. Members are both teachers and scholars concerned with the promotion of Latin American Studies. Membership: $45-$125 (Regular Membership); $30 (Student); $36(joint); $30-$60(Latin American Resident); $2,500/$1000 (Life Member); $85-$300(Institutional member);

Meetings/Conferences:
Number of non-conference events/year: 9

Publications:
The Latin American Research Review (LARR); on-line

Membership List Available to Non-members

Latin Business Association *(1976)*
120 S. San Pedro St.
Suite 530
Los Angeles, CA 90012
Tel: (213) 628-8510 *Fax:* (213) 628-8519
E-Mail: info@lbausa.com
Website: lbausa.com
Members: 2000 individuals
Staff: 5
Annual Budget: $250-500,000
Tax: 501(c)(6)

Personnel:
Executive Director: Larissa Ordaz
  E-Mail: Lordaz@lbausa.com
Coordinator, Membership Services: Melissa LeSane
  E-Mail: membership@lbausa.com

Historical Note:
LBA's mission is to build economic wealth and opportunity for Latino business entrepreneurs. It provides innovative programs and services that enhance the success, growth and advancement of Latino and Minority businesses, and

the community at large. Membership: $250-500 (Business); $250 (Associate).

Continuing Education:
Certification Designation/s: LBAI

Meetings/Conferences:
Conference Chair: Melissa LeSane
Number of non-conference events/year: 3

Publications:
LBA eNewsletter; monthly; adv.
Member Directory; on-line

Latino Hotel Association
2600 S. Shore Blvd.
Suite 300
League City, TX 77573
Tel: (281) 668-9165 *Fax:* (281) 668-9199
Website: latinhospitality.org
Staff: 1
Annual Budget: Under $10,000

Personnel:
President and Chief Executive Officer: Angela Gonzalez-Rowe

Historical Note:
Formerly known as Hispanic Hotel Owners Association. LHA's mission is to increase opportunities for Latinos to own, develop and operate hotels; as well as advance Latino suppliers serving the hotel industry. Membership: $1,000 (Allied/Individual Property/Multi Unit Owner); $5,000 (Corporate); $500 (Developer/Investor); $300 (Faculty); $25 (Student); $2000 (Life time); $150 (Restaurant Operator/Hotel Operator);

Continuing Education:
Certification Designation/s: CLM, CHA

Meetings/Conferences: Annual

Publications:
LHA News; on-line

Law and Society Association *(1964)*
380 S.1400 East
Suit 320
Salt Lake City, UT 84112
Tel: (413) 545-4617 *Fax:* (413) 577-3194
E-Mail: lsa@lawandsociety.org
Website: lawandsociety.org
Members: 1500 individuals
Staff: 5
Annual Budget: $500-1,000,000
Tax: 501(c)(3)

Personnel:
Executive Officer: Ronald M. Pipkin
  E-Mail: pipkin@lawandsociety.org
Coordinator, Administration: Lissa Ganter
  E-Mail: ganter@lawandsociety.org
Editor, Review: Kathleen Hull
  E-Mail: hull@umn.edu
Coordinator, Subscription and Newsletter: Mary McClintock
  E-Mail: mcclintock@lawandsociety.org
Coordinator, Membership Services: Judy Rose
  E-Mail: rose@lawandsociety.org

Historical Note:
LSA fosters the development of academic programs in law and society around the world. Members are social science and legal professionals and others interested in exploring the relationships between law and society. Membership: $37-196 (Individual); 37 (Student); $22 (Special International Member).

Meetings/Conferences: Annual
Conference Chair: Lissa Ganter
2013 - Boston, MA (Sheraton Boston Hotel)/May 30 - June 2
2014 - Minneapolis, MN (Hilton Minneapolis)/May 29 - June 1
2015 - Seattle, WA (Weston Seattle)/May 28 - 31

Publications:
Association Newsletter; on-line
Law and Society Newsletter
Law and Society Review; quarterly; adv.
Member Directory; on-line

Membership List Available to Non-members

Law Enforcement Alliance of America *(1990)*
5538 Port Royal Rd.
Springfield, VA 22151
Tel: (703) 847-2677 *Fax:* (703) 556-6485
Website: leaa.org
Members: 75000 members

Staff: 4
Annual Budget: $1-2,000,000
Tax: 501(c)(4)

Personnel:
President: John Chapman
  E-Mail: leaa.steve@erols.com
Executive Director: James J. Fotis
  E-Mail: leaa.steve@erols.com
Treasurer: Capt. William F. Seaman Jr.

Historical Note:
LEAA seeks criminal justice reform which "puts victims' rights above criminals' rights" and opposes what it considers to be "restrictive" gun control legislation which infringes the Second Amendment rights of law-abiding citizens. It is a non-profit, non-partisan membership association comprised of law enforcement professionals, victims of crime and other private citizens. Membership: $200 (Life Member); $26 (Annual Member); $34 (Family Member).

Publications:
LEAA Advisor
Shield Magazine (production of Shield is indefinitely suspended)

Lawn and Garden Dealers' Association *(1986)*
5616 S. 122nd E. Ave.
Suite N
Tulsa, OK 74146
Tel: (800) 752-5296 *Fax:* (918) 254-0713
TollFree: (800) 752-5296
E-Mail: info@lgda.com
Website: lgda.com
Members: 2000 companies
Staff: 5
Annual Budget: $500-1,000,000

Personnel:
Contact, Exhibitors: Polly Moter
  E-Mail: polly@promoterinc.com
Owner: Kirk K. Nellis

Historical Note:
LGDA works to help small businesses in the outdoor industries. Members are in the professional lawn and garden industry and include lawn equipment dealers, nurseries, small engine repair, and landscape and irrigation companies. Membership: $45/year.

Meetings/Conferences: Annual
Conference Chair: Polly Moter

The Lawn Institute *(1955)*
Two E. Main St.
Dundee, IL 60018
Tel: (847) 649-5555 *Fax:* (847) 649-5678
E-Mail: info@thelawninstitue.org
Website: thelawninstitute.org
Staff: 4
Annual Budget: $25-50,000

Personnel:
Executive Director: Kirk Hunter

Historical Note:
LI's mission is to assist and encourage through research and education the improvement of lawns and sports turf. Membership includes growers of improved turfgrasses as well as distributor groups, associations and suppliers such as fertilizer, chemical and equipment companies. It is administered by Turfgrass Producers International.

Publications:
e-newsletter; quarterly

Lawyers Committee on Nuclear Policy *(2010)*
866 UN Plaza
Suite 4050
New York, NY 10017-1830
Tel: (212) 818-1861 *Fax:* (212) 818-1857
Website: lcnp.org
Staff: 2
Annual Budget: $100-250,000

Personnel:
Executive Director: John Burroughs
Treasurer: Charles J. Moxley Jr.

Historical Note:
LCNP serves as the UN office of the International Association of Lawyers Against Nuclear Arms to provide legal and policy analysis to national and international policymakers, civil society, and media.

Publications:
Newsletters

Leading Jewelers Guild *(1958)*

P.O. Box 64609
Los Angeles, CA 90064
Tel: (310) 820-3386 *Fax:* (310) 820-3530
Website: leadingjewelersguild.org
Members: 27 companies and 150 stores
Staff: 10

Personnel:
Executive Director: James West
   E-Mail: JimmyWest@aol.com

Historical Note:
LJG is a coalition of independent jewelers and jewelry retailers. LJG's mission is to Provide cooperative purchasing and marketing programs to its members and administers a number of registered trademarks on their behalf, including Love Story Diamonds.

LeadingAge (American Association of Homes and Services for the Aging) (1961)
2519 Connecticut Ave. NW
Washington, DC 20008-1520
Tel: (202) 783-2242 *Fax:* (202) 783-2255
E-Mail: info@aahsa.org
Website: leadingage.org
Members:
5700 organizations
25000 individuals
Staff: 76
Annual Budget: $10-25,000,000
Tax: 501(c)(3)

Personnel:
President and Chief Executive Officer: William "Larry" Minnix Jr.
   E-Mail: lminnix@LeadingAge.org
Vice President and Senior Editor: Deborah Cloud
   E-Mail: dcloud@aahsa.org
Vice President, Education and Leadership Development: Julieta Holguin
   E-Mail: jholguin@leadingage.org
Vice President, Human Resources and Administration: Cheryl Jackson
   E-Mail: cjackson@LeadingAge.org
Vice President, Information Technology: Chris Kasmark
   E-Mail: ckasmark@leadingage.org
Senior Vice President, Advocacy: Dr. Cheryl Phillips
   E-Mail: cphillips@leadingage.org
Vice President, Communications: Lauren Shaham
   E-Mail: lshaham@LeadingAge.org
Vice President, Conferences and Sales: Sharon Sullivan
   E-Mail: ssullivan@leadingage.org
Director, Sales: Margaret Wanca-Daniels
   E-Mail: mwanca-daniels@aahsa.org

Historical Note:
Formerly (2010) American Association of Homes and Services for the Aging and (1994) American Association of Homes for the Aging. Mission is to serve the aging, nursing homes, assisted independent housing, continuing care retirement communities and senior housing. Membership: annual dues vary.

Continuing Education:
Certification Designation/s: EDDA, CME

Meetings/Conferences: Annual
Conference Chair: Sharon Sullivan
2013 - Washington, DC (Washington Marriott Wardman Park)/March 18 - 20
2013 - Dallas, TX/Oct. 27 - 30
2014 - Washington, DC (Washington Marriott Wardman Park)/March 17 - 19
2014 - Nashville, TN/Oct. 19 - 22
2015 - Boston, MA/Nov. 1 - 4
2016 - Indianapolis, IN/Oct. 30 - Nov. 2
2017 - New Orleans, LA/Oct. 29 - Nov. 1
2018 - Philadelphia, PA/Oct. 28 - 31
Number of non-conference events/year: 5

Publications:
LeadingAge magazine; bi-monthly
Membership Directory; on-line

Leafy Greens Council (1976)
33 Pheasant Ln.
St. Paul, MN 55127
Tel: (651) 484-7270 *Fax:* (651) 484-1098
Website: leafy-greens.org
Members: 100 companies and 100 individuals
Staff: 1
Annual Budget: $25-50,000
Tax: 501(c)(6)

Personnel:

Executive Director: Ray L. Clark Jr.

Historical Note:
Founded as the National Spinach Association. Became the Leafy Greens Council in 1977. Mission is to improve the marketing and increase consumption and educate consumers about the nutritional values of leafy greens through media campaigns and provide networking opportunities for members. Membership includes growers, shipper, brokers, terminal market operators, and suppliers. Membership: $100-600 (Affiliate, based on annual sales volume); $600 (Supplier).

Publications:
Membership Directory; on-line

League for Innovation in the Community College (1968)
1333 S. Spectrum Blvd.
Suite 210
Chandler, AZ 85286
Tel: (480) 705-8200 *Fax:* (480) 705-8201
Website: league.org
Members: 750 institutions
Staff: 23
Annual Budget: $2-5,000,000
Tax: 501(c)(3)

Personnel:
President and Chief Executive Officer: Gerardo E. de los Santos
   E-Mail: delossantos@league.org
Specialist, Technology: Yuyi Chen
   E-Mail: chen@league.org
Staff Editor: Kelly Dooling
   E-Mail: dooling@league.org
Chief Financial Officer: Anthony Guiterman
   E-Mail: guiterman@league.org;
Specialist, Partnership and Marketing: Chris Hennessey
   E-Mail: hennessey@league.org
Vice President, Services and Programs and Director, STEMtech: Edward J. Leach
   E-Mail: leach@league.org
Executive Vice President and Chief Operating Officer and Director, Innovations: Stella Perez
   E-Mail: perez@league.org
Specialist, Membership Services: LaRita Phillips
   E-Mail: phillips@league.org
Meeting Planner: Robin Piccirilli
   E-Mail: piccirilli@league.org
Vice President, Learning and Research and Director, Learning College Summit: Cynthia Wilson
   E-Mail: wilson@league.org

Historical Note:
League for Innovation in the Community College, a national consortium of 20 districts established to stimulate innovation in community college education, assists its members in experimenting in teaching, learning, student services and other aspects of community college operation, and in sharing the results of these experiments. The association catalyzes the community college movement. Membership: $825-1,350 (Full-Time Student Equivalent/Alliance); $2,825-5,850 (Alliance Advantage); $250 (Individual).

Meetings/Conferences: Annual
Conference Chair: Edward J. Leach
2013 - Dallas, TX (Hilton Anatole Dallas)/March 10 - 13
2013 - Atlanta, GA (Sheraton Atlanta Hotel)/Oct. 27 - 30
2014 - Anaheim, CA (Anaheim Marriott)/March 2 - 5

Publications:
League Connections; monthly

League of American Orchestras (1942)
33 W. 60th St, fifth Floor
New York, NY 10023
Tel: (212) 262-5161 *Fax:* (212) 262-5198
E-Mail: hnoonan@americanorchestras.org
Website: americanorchestras.org
Staff: 33

Personnel:
President and Chief Executive Officer: Jesse Rosen
   E-Mail: jrosen@americanorchestras.org
Director, Advertising and Meeting: Stephen Alter
   E-Mail: salter@americanorchestras.org
Vice President, Marketing and Membership Development: Russell Jones
   E-Mail: rjones@americanorchestras.org
Vice President, Learning and Leadership Development: Polly Kahn

   E-Mail: pkahn@americanorchestras.org
Vice President, Strategic Communications: Judith Kurnick
   E-Mail: jkurnick@americanorchestras.org
Senior Manager, Government Affairs and Education Advocacy: Najean Lee
   E-Mail: najeanl@ccsso.org
Chief Operating Officer: Stephen Lisner
   E-Mail: slisner@americanorchestras.org
Director, Finance: Marc Martin
   E-Mail: mmartin@americanorchestras.org
Vice President, Advocacy: Heather C. Noonan
   E-Mail: hnoonan@americanorchestras.org
Editor-in-Chief,: Robert Sandla
   E-Mail: rsandla@americanorchestras.org
Web Manager: Sam Sundaram
   E-Mail: ssundaram@americanorchestras.org
Director, Marketing: Melanie Thibeault
Director, Member Services: Rebecca Vierhaus
   E-Mail: rvierhaus@americanorchestras.org

Historical Note:
Formerly (2007) known as American Symphony Orchestra League, this is the national service organization for the 1,800 symphony and chamber orchestras in America. Founded in 1942 and chartered by Congress in 1962, the League works to ensure the artistic and financial strength of American orchestras. It provides professional training, management consulting, publications, artistic resources, and public policy information for orchestra management and volunteers and maintains an information center to respond to public inquiries.

Meetings/Conferences: Annual
Conference Chair: Stephen Alter
2013 - St. Louis, MO/June 17 - 20

Publications:
Member Directory; on-line
Symphony Magazine; on-line
The League of American Orchestras Newsletter; on-line

League of Historic American Theatres (1976)
2105 Laurel Bush Rd.
Suite 200
Bel Air, MD 21015
Tel: (443) 640-1058 *Fax:* (443) 640-1031
E-Mail: info@lhat.org
Website: lhat.org
Members: 500 individuals
Staff: 3
Annual Budget: $250-500,000
Tax: 501(c)(3)

Personnel:
Executive Director: Ken Stein
Director, Membership Services: Colleen Poehlman
   E-Mail: cpoehlman@lhat.org

Historical Note:
LHAT is a network of national resources designed to help its more than 300 member theatres throughout North America improve their historic venues, their businesses and their communities. Recognizing the issues and challenges unique to operating historic theatres, LHAT facilitates information exchange among its members through peer interaction, conferences, and collaborative projects. Membership: $325-1250 (Theatres); $600-1250 (Allied Members); $150 (Subscribers); $75 (Student Subscribers).

Meetings/Conferences: Annual
Number of non-conference events/year: 3

Publications:
inLEAGUE; monthly
Membership Directory; on-line; adv.

Membership List Available to Non-members

League of Resident Theatres (1965)
1501 Broadway
Suite 2401
New York, NY 10036
Tel: (212) 944-1501 *Fax:* (212) 768-0785
Website: lort.org
Members: 75 theatres
Staff: 3

Personnel:
President: Tim Shields
Management Associate: Stephanie Drotar
   E-Mail: stephanie@lort.org
Treasurer: Buzz Ward

Historical Note:
LORT serves as a forum for sharing information regarding all aspects of theatre and promotes the general welfare of

resident Theatres in the United States and its territories. Members are professional resident theatres.

Publications:
Membership Directory; on-line

The Learning Disabilities Association (1964)
4156 Library Rd.,
Pittsburgh, PA 15234-1349
Tel: (412) 341-1515 *Fax:* (412) 344-0224
E-Mail: info@LDAAmerica.org
Website: ldanatl.org
Staff: 48
Annual Budget: $1-2,000,000

Personnel:
Executive Director: Mary Clare Reynolds
    E-Mail: mcreynolds@ldaamerica.org
Manager, Accounting: Heather Nicklow
    E-Mail: hnicklow@ldaamerica.org
Director, Program Committee Support: Andrea
    Turkheimer
    E-Mail: aturkheimer@ldaamerica.org
Coordinator, Membership Services: Jayme Vertullo
    E-Mail: jvertullo@ldaamerica.org

Historical Note:
Provided understanding and support to people with learning disabilities. LDA's mission is to create opportunities for success for all individuals affected by learning disabilities and to reduce the incidence of learning disabilities in future generations. Membership: $25 (Student); $30-$50 (Annual).

Meetings/Conferences: Annual
Conference Chair: Andrea Turkheimer
2013 - San Antonio, TX (Grand Hyatt San Antonio
    Hotel)/Feb. 13 - 16
2014 - Anaheim, CA/Feb. 19 - 22
2015 - Chicago, IL/Feb. 25 - 28

Publications:
HCP E-Newsletter; on-line
Learning Disabilities: A Multidisciplinary Journal

Learning Forward (1978)
17330 Preston Rd.
Suite 106-D
Dallas, TX 75252
Tel: (972) 421-0900 *Fax:* (972) 421-0899
E-Mail: nsdcoffice@nsdc.org
Website: nsdc.org
Members: 10000 individuals
Staff: 34
Annual Budget: $5-10,000,000

Personnel:
Executive Director: Stephanie Hirsh
    E-Mail: stephanie.hirsh@learningforward.org
Publications Editor: Anthony Armstrong
    E-Mail: anthony.armstrong@learningforward.org
Manager, Marketing: Mary Catherine Burford
    E-Mail: mary.burford@learningforward.org
Director, Learning: Carol Francois
    E-Mail: carol.francois@learningforward.org
Assistant Director, Conferences and Meetings: Carrie
    Freundlich
    E-Mail: carrie.freundlich@learningforward.org

Historical Note:
Formerly (2010) National Staff Development Council. An association of learning educators focused on increasing student achievement through more effective professional learning. Membership: $299(Organization); $149 (Comprehensive); $99 (Standard); $69 (Digital).

Meetings/Conferences: Annual
Conference Chair: Carrie Freundlich

Publications:
JSD; bi-monthly; adv.
Teachers Teaching Teachers; on-line

Learning Resources Network (1974)
P.O. Box 9
River Falls, WI 54022
Tel: (715) 426-9777 *Fax:* (989) 671-1127
TollFree: (800) 678-5376
E-Mail: info@lern.org
Website: lern.org
Members: 4000 Individuals
Staff: 21
Annual Budget: $2-5,000,000

Personnel:
President: William A. Draves CAE, IV
    E-Mail: draves@lern.org

Editor: Jason Coates
    E-Mail: jason@lern.org
Vice President, Information Services: Julie Coates
    E-Mail: coates@lern.org
Director, Membership Services: Heather Dimitt
    E-Mail: heather@lern.org
Director, Marketing: Suzanne Kart
    E-Mail: kart@lern.org
Coordinator, Administrative and Customer Service: Leslie
    Kowalczyk
    E-Mail: leslie@lern.org
Director, Contract Training: Julia King Tamang
    E-Mail: KingTamang@lern.org

Historical Note:
LERN is an international association of lifelong learning programming, offering information and resources to providers of lifelong learning programs. Membership: $195 (Non U.S./Canadian based organizations); $295 (Museums, Botanical Gardens, Libraries); $395 (Canada based Organizations, Churches, Government (including Military), Public Schools, Recreation Departments, other Non-Profits); $495 (Associations and Health Care organizations); $595 (Community Colleges, Technical College, Universities, For-Profit Private Industry).

Continuing Education:
Certification Designation/s: CFD, COI, CeP

Meetings/Conferences: Annual
Conference Chair: Paul Franklin

Publications:
E-LERN; on-line
LERN Magazine

Leather Apparel Association (1990)
4705 Center Blvd.
Suite 806
Long Island City, NY 11109
Tel: (718) 606-0767 *Fax:* (718) 606-6345
E-Mail: info@leatherapparelassociation.com
Website: leatherapparelassociation.com
Members: 100 companies
Staff: 2
Annual Budget: $10-25,000

Personnel:
Executive Director: Richard Harrow
    E-Mail: fharrow@leatherassociation.com
Contact, Communications: Mina Behar
    E-Mail: mbehar@leatherapparelassociation.com

Historical Note:
LAA strives to promote the sale of leather garments through publicity, education, and business support services. Members are retailers, manufacturers, tanners, cleaners and suppliers of leather apparel. Membership: based on annual gross domestic sales.

Leather Industries of America (1917)
3050 K St. NW
Suite 400
Washington, DC 20007
Tel: (202) 342-8497 *Fax:* (202) 342-8583
E-Mail: info@leatherusa.com
Website: leatherusa.com
Members: 62 companies
Staff: 3
Annual Budget: $500-1,000,000
Tax: 501(c)(6)

Personnel:
Director, Finance and Administration: Deborah Hodges
    E-Mail: deborah@leatherusa.com
Chief Financial Officer: Maggie Gustavson
    E-Mail: maggie@leatherusa.com

Historical Note:
Formerly the Tanners' Council of America. LIA provides environmental, technical, education, statistical and marketing services to its membership and to the benefit of the leather industry.

Meetings/Conferences: Annual
Conference Chair: Maggie Gustavson

Publications:
Membership Directory & Buyer's Guide; annually

Legal Marketing Association (1985)
401 N. Michigan Ave.
Suite 2200
Chicago, IL 60611-6610
Tel: (312) 321-6898 *Fax:* (312) 673-6894
E-Mail: headquarters@legalmarketing.org
Website: legalmarketing.org
Members: 2500 individuals

Staff: 8
Annual Budget: $2-5,000,000
Tax: 501(c)(6)

Personnel:
Executive Director: Betsi Roach
    E-Mail: broach@legalmarketing.org
Director, Education: Julie Ferry CAE, MPA
    E-Mail: jferry@legalmarketing.org
Contact, Membership Services: Sara Giacalone
    E-Mail: sgiacalone@legalmarketing.org
Manager, Information Technology: Meredith Halperin
    E-Mail: mhalperin@legalmarketing.org
Director, Finance and Accounting: Jay Schommer CPA
    E-Mail: jschommer@legalmarketing.org
Coordinator, Meetings: Aldi Stripnieks
    E-Mail: astripnieks@legalmarketing.org
Director, Marketing and Communications: Marcie Valerio
    E-Mail: mvalerio@legalmarketing.org
Editorial Coordinator: Theresa Wojtalwicz
    E-Mail: twojtalewicz@legalmarketing.org

Historical Note:
Formed as the National Association of Law Firm Marketing Administrators; became (1990) National Law Firm Marketing Association and assumed its present name in 1999. LMA serves the needs of and maintains professional standards for those involved in marketing for the legal profession. Membership: $425 (Full); $250 (Limited); $300 (Full, Outside U.S.); $250 (Limited, Outside U.S.); $125 (Affiliate-U.S. and International); $35 (Student); $100 (New Member Initiation Fee).

Meetings/Conferences: Annual
Conference Chair: Aldi Stripnieks
2013 - Las Vegas, NV (ARIA Resort and Casino Hotel)/
    April 8 - 10
Number of non-conference events/year: 8

Publications:
e-newsletter; monthly
Strategies – The Journal of Legal Marketing

Membership List Available to Non-members

Legal Netlink Alliance
330 N. Wabash Ave.
Suite 1700
Chicago, IL 60611
Tel: (312) 755-3166
E-Mail: info@sprat.org
Website: legalnetlink.net
Members: 50 U.S. law firms
Staff: 1

Personnel:
Director: Jay A. Frank
    E-Mail: jfrank@agdglaw.com

Historical Note:
LNA is a global alliance of selected, midsized, general practice, independent law firms. Firms are selected for membership because they represent a high level of quality and integrity. The Alliance also pursues cooperative arrangements with other non-legal networks.

Meetings/Conferences: Annual
2013 - Madrid, Spain/Jan. 25 - 26
2013 - Chicago, IL/May 9 - 10
2013 - Bucharest, Romania/June 28 - 29
2013 - Minneapolis, MN/Sept. 26 - 28

Liability Insurance Research Bureau (1990)
3025 Highland Pkwy.
Suite 800
Downers Grove, IL 60515-1291
Tel: (630) 724-2250 *Fax:* (630) 724-2260
TollFree: (888) 711-7572
E-Mail: lirb@lirb.org
Website: lirb.org
Members: 252 insurance companies
Staff: 35
Annual Budget: $500-1,000,000

Personnel:
Vice President and General Counsel: Paul C. Dispensa
    E-Mail: pdispensa@lirb.org

Historical Note:
Spun off from Property Loss Research Bureau. Provides legal research, consulting, and educational services in auto liability and CGL lines. LIRB's mission is to promote education and new and beneficial developments within the property and casualty insurance industry. Members are stock and mutual insurance companies. Membership: $1,190-$86,324 + $1 per million (Based on premium writings); $925 (Affiliate); $45,000 (Franchisor).

Meetings/Conferences: Annual

2013 - Boston, MA/March 17 - 20
2013 - Philadelphia, PA/April 7 - 10
2014 - Indianapolis, IN/March 16 - 19

Publications:
E-Newsletter; weekly
Membership Directory; on-line

Liaison Committee of Cooperating Oil and Gas Associations (1957)
800 SW Jackson St.
Suite 1400
Topeka, KS 66612
Tel: (316) 263-7297 *Fax:* (316) 263-3021
E-Mail: kiogaed@swbell.com
Members: 25 associations
Staff: 2
Annual Budget: Under $10,000

Personnel:
Secretary-Treasurer: Edward P. Cross
Project Manager: Kristy Hawthorne

Historical Note:
The Liaison is a network organization of state and regional trade associations that represent the independent oil and gas exploration and production industry in the United States. Liaison members meet to coordinate issue advocacy and exchange views of mutual interest. The committee was established to facilitate communication among state and regional oil and gas associations. Has no paid or full-time staff.

Library and Information Technology Association (1966)
50 E. Huron St.
Chicago, IL 60611-2795
Fax: (312) 280-3257
TollFree: (800) 545-2433
E-Mail: lita@ala.org
Website: ala.org/lita/
Members: 3500 individuals
Staff: 3
Annual Budget: $250-500,000
Tax: 501(c)(3)

Personnel:
Executive Director: Mary C. Taylor
     E-Mail: mtaylor@ala.org
Coordinator, Programs: Valerie A. Edmonds
     E-Mail: vedmonds@ala.org
Specialist, Programs and Marketing: Melissa Prentice
     E-Mail: mprentice@ala.org

Historical Note:
A division of the American Library Association. Formerly Information Science and Automation Division. Adopted its current name in 1978. LITA educates, serves, and reaches out to its members, other ALA members and divisions, and the entire library and information community through its publications, programs, and other activities designed to promote, develop, and aid in the implementation of library and information technology. Membership: $125 (Personal); $60 (Individual); $90 (Organization); $25 (Student).

Meetings/Conferences:
Conference Chair: Valerie A. Edmonds
Number of non-conference events/year: 2

Publications:
Information Technology and Libraries; quarterly
Membership Directory; on-line

Membership List Available to Non-members

Library Binding Institute (1935)
4440 PGA Blvd.
Suite 600
Palm Beach Gardens, FL 33410
Tel: (561) 745-6821 *Fax:* (561) 472-8401
E-Mail: info@lbibinders.org
Website: lbibinders.org
Members: 76 companies
Staff: 1
Annual Budget: $100-250,000
Tax: 501(c)(6)

Personnel:
Executive Director: Debra S. Nolan CAE
     E-Mail: dnolan@hardcoverbinders.org

Historical Note:
The mission of LBI is to maintain and encourage support for the quality standards for Certified Library Binders and to promote their benefits to libraries. Members are firms binding books for libraries, their suppliers and certain libraries with an in-house binding capacity. Membership:

$100 (Institutional); $995-3,500 (Active); $395 (Active International); $500 (Associate/Non Profit).

Continuing Education:
Certification Designation/s: CIM, CLB

Meetings/Conferences: Annual

Publications:
Endpaper; monthly
Membership Directory; annually
ShelfLife; quarterly

Library Copyright Alliance
21 Dupont Cir. NW
Washington, DC 20036
Tel: (212) 296-2296
Website: librarycopyrightalliance.org
Members: 300000 professionals
Staff: 4

Personnel:
Executive Director: Charles B. Lowry
     E-Mail: clowry@arl.org
Coordinator, Communications and Project: Tricia Donovan
     E-Mail: tricia@arl.org
Publications Program Officer: Lee Anne George
     E-Mail: leeanne@arl.org
Director, Information Technology: Gary Roebuck
     E-Mail: gary@arl.org

Historical Note:
The Library Copyright Alliance (LCA) consists of three major library associations, the American Library Association, the Association of Research Libraries, and the Association of College and Research Libraries. LCA's mission is to foster global access and fair use of information for creativity, research, and education.

Library Leadership and Management Association (1957)
50 E. Huron St.
Chicago, IL 60611-2795
Tel: (312) 280-5036 *Fax:* (312) 280-2169
TollFree: (800) 545-2433
E-Mail: llama@ala.org
Website: ala.org/llama
Members: 5000 individuals
Staff: 2
Annual Budget: $250-500,000

Personnel:
Executive Director: Kerry Ward
     E-Mail: kward@ala.org
Program Officer, Continuing Education: Fred Reuland
     E-Mail: freuland@ala.org

Historical Note:
Founded as Library Administration Division of the American Library Association, it remains a division of the ALA. LLAMA's mission is to encourage and nurture current and future library leaders, and to develop and promote better leadership and management practices. Membership: $50 (Personal Member); $15 (Student); $65 (Corporate/Organizational); $35 (New Member).

Meetings/Conferences:
Conference Chair: Fred Reuland
Number of non-conference events/year: 1

Publications:
Library Leadership & Management; quarterly

Licensing Executives Society (1965)
1800 Diagonal Rd.
Suite 280
Alexandria, VA 22314
Tel: (703) 836-0026 *Fax:* (703) 836-3107
E-Mail: info@les.org
Website: lesi.org
Members: 10000 individuals
Staff: 14
Annual Budget: $2-5,000,000

Personnel:
Executive Director: Kenneth Schoppmann
     E-Mail: schoppk@les.org
Treasurer: James Sobieraj
     E-Mail: jsobieraj@usebrinks.com

Historical Note:
LES is engaged in the transfer, use, development, manufacture and marketing of intellectual property. Membership: $290 (Active); $35 (Student).

Continuing Education:
Certification Designation/s: CLP, PDS, LES, BIO, TTS

Meetings/Conferences:

2013 - Brisbane, Australia/March 14 - 16
2013 - Rio de Janeiro, Brazil/April 5 - 12
2014 - Moscow, Russia/May 21 - 23
2015 - Brussels, Belgium/April 12 - 15
Number of non-conference events/year: 1

Publications:
les Nouvelles quarterly journal of the LESI; quarterly

Life Insurance Settlement Association (1995)
1011 E. Colonial Dr.
Suite 500
Orlando, FL 32803
Tel: (407) 894-3797 *Fax:* (407) 897-1325
Website: thevoiceoftheindustry.com
Members: 183 companies
Staff: 5
Annual Budget: $1-2,000,000
Tax: 501(c)(6)

Personnel:
Executive Director: Darwin Bayston
     E-Mail: darwin@lisassociation.org
Director, Education and Marketing: Wesley Costa
     E-Mail: wcosta@lisa.org
Business Manager: Will Menezes
Director, Member Services and Sales: Tisha Williams
     E-Mail: twilliams@lisa.org

Historical Note:
Founded as Viatical Association of America; Later known as the Viatical and Life Settlement Association. Assumed its current name in 2008. LISA seeks to advance the development, integrity and reputation of the life settlement industry and to promote a competitive market for the people it serves. Members are companies who purchase life insurance policies from people with terminal illnesses. Works to establish reasonable regulation for the industry. Membership: $7,000 (Law/Accounting Firm/General-Voting/Associate); $2,000 (Provisional).

Continuing Education:
Certification Designation/s: CCP
Meetings/Conferences:
Number of non-conference events/year: 3

Publications:
LISA e-Newsletter; on-line
Member Directory; on-line

Life Insurers Council (1910)
2300 Windy Ridge Pkwy.
Suite 600
Atlanta, GA 30339-8443
Tel: (770) 984-3720 *Fax:* (770) 984-6422
TollFree: (800) 275-5662
E-Mail: infoctr@loma.org
Website: loma.org/lic
Members: 62 companies and 38 associates
Staff: 2
Annual Budget: $100-250,000

Personnel:
Executive Director: Jeffrey S. Shaw ChFC, CLU
     E-Mail: jshaw@limra.com
Administrative Assistant: Rose Hoyt

Historical Note:
LIC encourages the exchange of ideas between members, strives to maintain high standards of business conduct, and represents its members in connection with legislative, regulatory, and consumer matters. Affiliate membership is available to non-insurance companies which provide a service or product to the life insurance industry. LIC membership is open to any insurer. Membership: $1,500-3,000 (Individual, based on salary); $650 (Affiliate/International Member); $1950-$3900 (Company).

Meetings/Conferences:
2013 - New Orleans, LA (Omni Royal Orleans Hotel)/
     April 23 - 25
Number of non-conference events/year: 2

Publications:
LIC Directory; on-line
LIC Newsletter; monthly

Membership List Available to Non-members

Lift Manufacturers Product Section - Material Handling Institute (1990)
8720 Red Oak Blvd.
Suite 201
Charlotte, NC 28217-3992
Tel: (704) 676-1190 *Fax:* (704) 676-1199
E-Mail: acunningham@mhia.org

Website: mhia.org/industrygroups/lmps
Members: 8 companies
Staff: 28
Annual Budget: $10-25,000

Personnel:
Chief Executive Officer: George Prest
    E-Mail: gprest@mhia.org
Meeting and Event Services Planner: Kay Clark
    E-Mail: kclark@mhia.org
Member Services Assistant: Amy Gray Cunningham
    E-Mail: acunningham@mhia.org
Web Developer: Joey Holt
    E-Mail: jholt@mhia.org
Vice President, Finance: Michael Laurent
    E-Mail: mlaurent@mhia.org
Vice President, Marketing and Communications: Carol
    Miller
    E-Mail: cmiller@mhia.org
Director, Educational Services: Ray Niemeyer
    E-Mail: rniemeyer@mhia.org
Vice President, Educational and Technical Services: Mike
    Ogle
    E-Mail: mogle@mhia.org

Historical Note:
MHIA seeks to deliver exceptional value to its member
companies, their customers and other industry constituents
in order to promote growth and prosperity of their
organizations and its industry. Members are material
handling and logistics equipment, systems and software
manufacturers, consultants, systems integrators and
simulators.

Meetings/Conferences:
Conference Chair: Kay Clark
2013 - Chicago, IL (McCormick Place)/Jan. 21 - 24/
    over 100 exhibitors
2013 - Charlotte, NC (Charlotte Marriott City Center)/
    April 7 - 10
2013 - Orlando, FL (Florida Hotel and Conference
    Center)/Sept. 30 - Oct. 3
2014 - Atlanta, GA (Georgia World Congress Center)/
    March 17 - 20
Number of non-conference events/year: 1

Publications:
Industry News; on-line
Member Directory; on-line
On The Mhove; quarterly

Light Aircraft Manufacturers Association (1984)
2001 Steamboat Ridge Ct.
Daytona Beach, FL 32128-6918
Tel: (651) 592-7565 Fax: (651) 226-1825
E-Mail: info@lama.bz
Website: lama.bz
Members: 500 individuals and companies
Staff: 5
Annual Budget: $10-25,000

Personnel:
Chairman and President: Dan Johnson
    E-Mail: danjohnson@lama.bz

Historical Note:
LAMA is a trade association for manufacturers of
light aircraft, engines, avionics, parts/subassemblies,
suppliers and distributors.LAMA's mission is to represent
government, associations, and other entities and to
Participate in voluntary consensus standards, quality
assurance audits, and other technical services. Members are
manufacturers of light and ultralight aircraft and suppliers
of parts. LAMA participates in voluntary consensus
standards, quality assurance audits, and other technical
services, provides representation to government and
promotes member products. It also works to improve the
business condition of light aviation and highlight the role of
light aviation in the national economy. Membership: $500/
year.

Publications:
LAMA Membership Directory; on-line
LAMA Newsletter; irregular

Lighter Association (1986)
1700 Pennsylvania Ave. NW
Suite 400
Washington, DC 20006
E-Mail: info@lighterassociation.org
Website: lighterassociation.org
Members: 10 companies
Staff: 1
Annual Budget: $100-250,000
Tax: 501(c)(6)

Personnel:
General Counsel: David H. Baker
    E-Mail: dhbakerlaw@aol.com

Historical Note:
LA represents the industry's interests before federal and
state regulatory bodies and the U.S. Congress. Also
partners with other non- profit and charitable organizations
to produce public service announcements, news articles
and other media promoting the safe usage of lighters.
Members are manufacturers, suppliers and distributors of
lighters. Membership: $4000-48000 (Manufacturers and
Distributors); $1000 (Suppliers); $3000 (Affiliate); $100
(Associate).

Publications:
Membership Directory; on-line

Membership List Available to Non-members

Lightning Protection Institute (1955)
25475 Magnolia Dr.
P.O. Box 99
Maryville, MO 64468
Tel: (800) 488-6864 Fax: (660) 582-0430
TollFree: (800) 488-6864
E-Mail: lpi@lightning.org
Website: lightning.org
Members: 100 companies
Staff: 1
Annual Budget: $250-500,000
Tax: 501(c)(6)

Personnel:
Executive Director: Harold "Bud" VanSickle III

Historical Note:
LPI's mission is to design and develop information resources
on complete lightning protection systems for consumers &
specifiers. The organization markets education products to
members for use in the construction industry. It also focuses
to develop the total market for lightning protection through
promotion of National Standards with supporting loss data,
experience from past design, and new information from
research. Membership: $750 (Dealers/Contractors); $500
(Affiliate); $75 (Individual).

Continuing Education:
Certification Designation/s: MIC, DIS, MID

Meetings/Conferences: Annual
Number of non-conference events/year: 1

Publications:
LPI Newsletter; quarterly
Membership Directory; on-line

Lignite Energy Council (1974)
1016 E. Owens Ave.
P.O. Box 2277
Bismarck, ND 58502-2277
Tel: (701) 258-7117 Fax: (701) 258-2755
TollFree: (800) 932-7117
E-Mail: lec@lignite.com
Website: lignite.com
Members: 355 companies
Staff: 9
Annual Budget: $2-5,000,000
Tax: 501(c)(6)

Personnel:
President and Chief Executive Officer: John W. Dwyer
    E-Mail: johndwyer@lignite.com
Director, Administration and Information Technology:
    Dave Allard
    E-Mail: daveallard@lignite.com
Vice President, Research and Development: Michael Jones
    E-Mail: mikejones@lignite.com
Vice President, Government Affairs: Sandi Tabor
    E-Mail: sanditabor@lignite.com
Vice President, Communications: Steve Van Dyke
Director, Member Services and Education: Renee Walz
    E-Mail: reneewalz@lignite.com

Historical Note:
LEC's mission is to maintain a viable lignite coal industry
and enhance the development of the region's lignite
coal resources for use in generating electricity, synthetic
natural gas and valuable byproducts. Members include
mining companies, major users that use lignite to generate
electricity, synthetic natural gas and other valuable
byproducts and businesses that provide goods and services
to the lignite industry. Membership: $5,170 (Major
Supplier); $2,345 (Sustaining); $1,175 (Investor); $590
(Associate).

Continuing Education:
Enrollment: 120
Certification Designation/s: GC
Meetings/Conferences:

Number of non-conference events/year: 2

Publications:
Newsletter; bi-monthly

Linguistic Association of Canada and the United States (1974)
Center for the Study of Languages, MS-36
Rice University
Houston, TX 77251-1892
Tel: (713) 348-2820 Fax: (713) 348-5846
E-Mail: lchen@rice.edu
Website: lacus.weebly.com
Members: 700 individuals and institutions
Staff: 6
Annual Budget: Under $10,000
Tax: 501(c)(3)

Personnel:
President: Alan Melby
Archivist: Lilly Lee Chen
Program Chair: Douglas Coleman
    E-Mail: douglas.coleman@utoledo.edu
Secretary and Treasurer: Rennie Gonsalves
    E-Mail: renniegons@yahoo.com
Contact, Publications and Website Services: Dan Mailman
Director, Publications: William J. Sullivan
    E-Mail: wjsiii@uni.wroc.pl

Historical Note:
Established and incorporated in Illinois, LACUS is an
educational and scientific organization that promotes the
objective study of language and to create a forum for the
free flow of ideas and discussion on communication going
beyond traditional grammatical studies in the various
traditional modes. Membership: $50 (Professional); $30
(Student); $40 (Emeritus); $600 (Life).

Meetings/Conferences: Annual
Conference Chair: Douglas Coleman

Publications:
LACUS Forum; annually; adv.

Linguistic Society of America (1924)
1325 18th St. NW
Suite 211
Washington, DC 20036-6501
Tel: (202) 835-1714 Fax: (202) 835-1717
E-Mail: lsa@lsadc.org
Website: lsadc.org
Members: 5000 individuals
Staff: 4
Annual Budget: $500-1,000,000
Tax: 501(c)(3)

Personnel:
Executive Director: Alyson W. Reed
    E-Mail: areed@lsadc.org
Executive Assistant: Rita M. Lewis
    E-Mail: rlewis@lsadc.org
Director, Membership Services and Meetings: David
    Robinson
    E-Mail: drobinson@lsadc.org
Editor-in-Chief: Dieter Stein
    E-Mail: stein@phil-fak.uni-duesseldorf.de

Historical Note:
Formerly known as the American Museum of Natural
History, a constituent member of the American Council of
Learned Societies, an affiliate of Permanent International
Committee of Linguistics (CIPL) and a founding member of
the Consortium of Social Science Associations (COSSA),
LSA is dedicated to the advancement of the scientific study
of language. Membership: $40-1900/year.

Continuing Education:
Enrollment: 1000

Meetings/Conferences: Annual
Conference Chair: David Robinson
2013 - Boston, MA (Boston Marriott Copley Place)/Jan.
    3 - 6/1000 attendees
2014 - Minneapolis, MN (Hilton Minneapolis)/Jan. 2 -
    5/1000 attendees
2015 - San Francisco, CA (Hilton San Francisco Union
    Square)/Jan. 8 - 11/1000 attendees
2016 - Washington, DC (Washington Marriott
    Marquis)/Jan. 7 - 10/1000 attendees
Number of non-conference events/year: 1

Publications:
eLanguage; on-line
Language; quarterly; adv.
Membership Directory; on-line

Membership List Available to Non-members

Lipizzan Association of North America (1992)

74 Trinity Pl.
Suite 1800
New York, NY 10006
Tel: (765) 215-6798 *Fax:* (765) 641-1208
E-Mail: info@lipizzan.org
Website: lipizzan.org
Members: 175 individuals
Staff: 9
Annual Budget: $25-50,000
Tax: 501(c)(3)

Personnel:
Chairman: Dr. Delphi Toth
   E-Mail: Delphi@lipizzan.org
Legal Counsel and Registrar: John Nicholas Iannuzzi
   E-Mail: Iannuzzi@lipizzan.org

Historical Note:
Formerly (1980) the Royal International Lipizzan Club. In (1992) the Lipizan Association of America assumed this name following a merger with the Lipizan Society of North America. Members own and breed Lipizzan horses. LANA's mission is to provide members with accessible, verifiable pedigree information from America and oversees breeders. Membership: $55 (Full, Individual/Family/Corporation); $25 (Friend of Lipizzan).

Publications:
Haute École; quarterly; adv.
Membership Directory; on-line

Membership List Available to Non-members

Literacy Research Association (1950)

7044 S. 13th St.
Oak Creek, WI 53154
Tel: (414) 908-4924 *Fax:* (414) 768-8001
Website: nrconline.org
Members: 1100 individuals
Staff: 2
Annual Budget: $250-500,000

Personnel:
Executive Director: Christopher Roper
   E-Mail: c.roper@nrconline.org
Association Manager: Elisa Nelsen-Oyervides
   E-Mail: elisa@Literacyresearchassociation.org

Historical Note:
Formerly the National Reading Conference. LRA's mission is dedicated to promote research that enriches the knowledge, understanding, and development of lifespan literacies in a multicultural and multilingual world. LRA is committed to ethical research that is rigorous, methodologically diverse, and socially responsible. Membership: $110 (Regular); $60 (Second Member/Same Household); $75 (Emeritus); $40 (Student).

Meetings/Conferences: Annual
2013 - Dallas, TX/Dec. 4 - 7

Publications:
Journal of Literacy Research; annually; adv.
Membership Directory; on-line
NRC Newsletter; semi-annually

Literary Managers and Dramaturgs of the Americas (1985)

20985, P.A.C.C.
P.O. Box 36
New York, NY 10129
TollFree: (800) 680-2148
E-Mail: lmdanyc@gmail.com
Website: lmda.org
Members: 600 individuals
Staff: 4
Annual Budget: $25-50,000

Personnel:
President: Danielle Mages Amato
   E-Mail: dmagesamato@gmail.com
Vice President, Programs: Stephen Colella
   E-Mail: programs@lmda.org
Vice President, Publications: D.J. Hopkins
   E-Mail: dhopkins@mail.sdsu.edu
Vice President, Communications: Janine Sobeck
   E-Mail: communications@lmda.org

Historical Note:
Formerly (1990) Literary Managers and Dramaturgs of America. LMDA's mission is to expand the possibilities of the field to other media and institutions, and to cultivate, develop and promote the function of dramaturgy and literary management. Membership: $25 (Student/Intern); $60 (Individual); $200 (Institutional); $500 (Spotlight Sponsor Institutional).

Meetings/Conferences:
Conference Chair: Stephen Colella

Publications:
LMDA Newsletter; quarterly
Membership Directory; on-line
The LMDA Review; on-line

Livestock Marketing Association (1947)

10510 NW Ambassador Dr.
Kansas City, MO 64153-1278
Tel: (816) 891-0502 *Fax:* (816) 891-7926
TollFree: (800) 821-2048
E-Mail: lmainfo@lmaweb.com
Website: lmaweb.com
Members: 800 livestock marketing business members
Staff: 35
Annual Budget: $1-2,000,000
Tax: 501(c)(6)

Personnel:
Chief Executive Officer: Mark Mackey
Coordinator, Membership and Information Technology: Cathy Collet
Director, Human Resources: Melanie Harris
Media Contact: John J. McBride
   E-Mail: jmcbride@lmaweb.com
Chief Financial Officer: Vincent Nowak
Vice President, Membership Services: Kristen Parman
   E-Mail: kparman@lmaweb.com
Contact, Legal Assistance: Ernest H. VanHooser

Historical Note:
Formerly National Livestock Auction Association. LMA's mission is to support and protect the local livestock auction markets and the livestock marketing industry.

Publications:
Membership Directory; on-line

Livestock Publications Council (1974)

910 Currie St.
Fort Worth, TX 76107
Tel: (817) 336-1130 *Fax:* (817) 232-4820
Website: livestockpublications.com
Members: 175 publications
Staff: 1
Annual Budget: $100-250,000

Personnel:
Executive Director: Diane E. Johnson
   E-Mail: diane@livestockpublications.com

Historical Note:
LPC provides a forum through which members can obtain information on how to improve their overall effectiveness and value to both readers and advertisers. Members are magazines, newspapers and other periodicals devoting at least 50% of their average content to the livestock industry. Membership: $150 (Service); $175 (Publication); $35 (Student); $50 (Alumni).

Publications:
LPC Directory of Members; on-line
LPC Newsletter; monthly; adv.

Loading Dock Equipment Manufacturers

8720 Red Oak Blvd.
Suite 201
Charlotte, NC 28217-3992
Tel: (704) 676-1190 *Fax:* (704) 676-1199
Website: mhia.org/industrygroups/lodem
Members: 9 companies
Staff: 7
Annual Budget: Under $10,000

Personnel:
Chief Executive Officer: George Prest
   E-Mail: gprest@mhia.org
Director, Sales: Greg Baer
   E-Mail: gbaer@mhia.org
Manager, Human Resources Services: Loretta Barter
   E-Mail: lbarter@mhia.org
Managing Director: Allan Howie
   E-Mail: ahowie@mhia.org
Vice President, Finance: Michael Laurent
   E-Mail: mlaurent@mhia.org
Vice President, Marketing and Communications Services: Carol Miller
   E-Mail: cmiller@mhia.org
Vice President, Educational and Technical Services: Mike Ogle
   E-Mail: mogle@mhia.org

Historical Note:

LODEM's mission is to develop and advocate standard nomenclature and to collect and disseminate reliable industry statistics. It is a product section of the Material Handling Industry of America, and of the Material Handling Industry Association that provides administrative support.

Continuing Education:
Certification Designation/s: CAMH

Publications:
e-Mhove; monthly
On The Mhove; quarterly

Loan Syndication & Trading Association (1995)

366 Madison Ave.
15th Floor
New York, NY 10017
Tel: (212) 880-3000 *Fax:* (212) 880-3040
Website: lsta.org
Members: 326 member institutions
Staff: 17
Annual Budget: $10-25,000,000

Personnel:
Executive Director: Bram Smith
   E-Mail: bsmith@lsta.org
Administrator, Membership and Marketing: Clara Colon
   E-Mail: ccolon@lsta.org
Manager, Special Projects and Events: Lorena DeLuca
   E-Mail: ldeluca@lsta.org
Vice President, Operations: Ellen Hefferan
   E-Mail: ehefferan@lsta.org
Senior Vice President and Deputy General Counsel: Bridget Marsh
   E-Mail: bmarsh@lsta.org
Website Administrator: Christine Ramos
   E-Mail: cramos@lsta.org
Executive Vice President Communication, Marketing Membership and Education: Alicia Sansone
   E-Mail: asansone@lsta.org
Manager, Finance and Compliance: John Sol
   E-Mail: jsol@lsta.org

Historical Note:
A trade association for the loan syndication industry. LSTA undertakes a wide variety of activities to foster the development of policies and market practices designed to advocate just and equitable marketplace principles and to encourage cooperation and coordination with firms facilitating transactions in loans and related claims.

Meetings/Conferences: Annual
Conference Chair: Lorena DeLuca
Number of non-conference events/year: 1

Publications:
Membership Directory; on-line
Service Provider Directory; on-line

Local Media Association (1971)

116 Cass St.
Traverse City, MI 49684
Tel: (231) 932-2971 *Fax:* (231) 932-2985
TollFree: (888) 486-2466
E-Mail: sna@suburban-news.org
Website: suburban-news.org
Members: 2000 newspapers and companies
Staff: 8
Annual Budget: $500-1,000,000
Tax: 501(c)(3)

Personnel:
President: Nancy Lane
   E-Mail: nancylanesna@aol.com
Vice President, Operations: Al Cupo
   E-Mail: al.cupo@localmedia.org
Manager, Membership Services: Valerie Donn
   E-Mail: valerie.donn@localmedia.org
Director, Information Technology: David Lee
   E-Mail: david.lee@suburban-news.org
Director, Sales and Classified Avenue: Deanna Lewis
   E-Mail: deanna.lewis@localmedia.org
Director, Communications: Jamie Mork
   E-Mail: jamie.mork@suburban-news.org
Director, Accounting and Financial Services: Janice Norman
   E-Mail: janice.norman@localmedia.org
Editor, Suburban publisher: Deb Shaw
   E-Mail: debshawlma@gmail.com

Historical Note:
Formerly the Suburban Newspapers of America, formed by a merger of Accredited Home Newspapers of America, the Suburban Press Foundation and the Suburban Section of the National Newspaper Association. SNA's mission is to support the community newspaper industry and

related online media through leadership, education, innovation, promotion, research and the advancement of high standards. Membership: $8,395-11,595 (Corporate); $550-4,295 (Regular); $659 (Associate); $99 (Individual/ Professional).

Continuing Education:
Certification Designation/s: BPC, AOSC, MSMC

Meetings/Conferences: Annual
2013 - New Orleans, LA (Roosevelt New Orleans)/Feb. 18 - 20

Publications:
Membership Directory; on-line; adv.
Suburban Publisher; monthly; adv.

Local Search Association (fka Yellow Pages Association) *(1988)*
400 Connell Dr.
Suite 1100
Berkeley Heights, NJ 07922-2747
Tel: (908) 286-2380 *Fax:* (908) 286-0620
Website: ypassociation.org
Members: 400 companies
Staff: 39
Annual Budget: $10-25,000,000

Personnel:
President: Negley Norton
    E-Mail: Neg.Norton@ypassociation.org
Chief Financial Officer: Donna Borowicz
    E-Mail: Donna.Borowicz@ypassociation.org
Vice President, Communications: Stephanie Hobbs
    E-Mail: stephanie.hobbs@ypassociation.org
Human Resources Manager: Lori Ross Melton
    E-Mail:
    Lori.RossMelton@localsearchassociation.org

Historical Note:
Formerly Yellow Pages Publishers Association, the result of the merger of American Association of Yellow Pages Publishers and National Yellow Pages Service Association, (2001) Yellow Pages Integrated Media Association, (2004) Yellow Pages Association and assumed current name in 2011. LSA's mission is to lead, serve, grow and advocate for the Yellow Pages Industry. Members are companies publishing yellow pages and other specialty directories. Membership: $1500 (Domestic Publisher); $15,000 (Industry Partner Silver); $2,500 (Industry Colleague); $1,000 (Industry Affiliate); $7,500 (Industry Partner); $25,000 (Industry Partner Gold); $40,000 (Industry Partner Platinum).

Meetings/Conferences:
Conference Chair: Stephanie Hobbs
2013 - Las Vegas, NV (Planet Hollywood Resort and Casino)/April 13 - 16

Publications:
Advertising Specifications; quarterly
Billing List; monthly
CMR Contact List publications; annually
Flash Newsletter; monthly
Membership Directory; on-line

Log Home Builders Association of North America *(1965)*
14241 NE Woodinville-Duvall Rd.
Suite 335
Woodinville, WA 98072-8564
E-Mail: info@loghomebuilders.org
Website: loghomebuilders.org
Members: 16900 companies and 45000 members
Staff: 4
Annual Budget: $500-1,000,000

Personnel:
Contact, Membership Services: Mike Wilder

Historical Note:
Formerly known as Log House Association of North America (1976). LHBANA's purpose is to preserve the "true-and-pure" craft of log home building, to disseminate information about log homes, to pass the craft on to future generations, and to teach people how to "build" or "buy" the best log homes for the least amount of money. Membership: $795/year (Life).

Log Homes Council *(1985)*
1201 15th St.
Washington, DC 20005
Tel: (800) 368-5242 *Fax:* (202) 266-8141
TollFree: (800) 368-5242
Website: loghomes.org
Members: 41 manufacturer members
Staff: 3

Personnel:
Chairman: Nicole Robinson
President: James Young
Secretary: Gregg Caldwell

Historical Note:
LHC is part of the Building Systems Councils, a council of the National Association of Home Builders. Council members are log home manufacturers and producers who have united to develop and promote quality building systems and ethical business practices by participation in both mandatory and voluntary council programs designed to benefit log home customers. Membership: $200-1,350/ year.

Publications:
LHC Membership Directory; annually

LOMA *(1966)*
2300 Windy Ridge Pkwy.
Suite 600
Atlanta, GA 30339-8443
Tel: (770) 951-1770 *Fax:* (770) 984-0441
TollFree: (800) 275-5662
E-Mail: askloma@loma.org
Website: loma.org
Members: 1200 companies
Staff: 160
Annual Budget: $10-25,000,000

Personnel:
President and Chief Executive Officer: Robert A. Kerzner ChFC, CLU
Vice President, Human Resources: Michele LaBouff
Vice President, Marketing: Carol Larco-Murzyn PhD
Vice President, Education and Training: Kathy Milligan ACS, FLMI
Chief Information Officer: Jake Star
Associate Vice President, Marketing: Paul Wilson
    E-Mail: wilsonp@loma.org

Historical Note:
Formerly Life Office Management Association till 1996. Mission is to sponsor education, training, employee development programs, networking, and research to promote effective management in life and health insurance companies and other related organizations. Membership: $2,265-5,050 (Affiliate); $1,950-6,500 (International Associate); $1,900-6,000 (International Affiliate); $850 (International Academic).

Continuing Education:
Certification Designation/s: ARA, FFSI, PCS, AIAA, ACS, FLMI, AIRC, AIAF, AAPA

Meetings/Conferences: Annual
2013 - Orlando, FL (Hyatt Regency Grand Cypress)/ Sept. 8 - 10
2014 - San Francisco, CA (Hyatt Regency San Francisco)/Sept. 7 - 9
Number of non-conference events/year: 14

Publications:
LOMA e-News; monthly
Membership Directory; on-line
Resource; monthly; adv.

Lpga Tournament Owners Association *(2010)*
801 International Pkwy., Fifth Floor
Lake Mary, FL 32746
Tel: (401) 562-1140
Website: lpgatoa.org
Staff: 1
Annual Budget: $250-500,000

Personnel:
President: Gail Graham
    E-Mail: Gail@lpgatoa.org

Historical Note:
LPGA Tournament Owners Association (TOA) originally came into existence under the name of the LPGA Tournament Sponsors Association (TSA) in the late 1970's, TSA was renamed Tournament Owners Association in 2005. The Mission of the Tournament Owners Association is to enhance the ability of its membership to develop formulas for success and long-term sustainability.

Lutheran Education Association *(1942)*
7400 Augusta St.
River Forest, IL 60305
Tel: (708) 209-3343 *Fax:* (708) 209-3458
E-Mail: lea@lea.org
Website: lea.org
Members: 3500 individuals
Staff: 4
Annual Budget: $1-2,000,000

Tax: 501(c)(3)

Personnel:
Executive Director: Jonathan C. Laabs EdD
    E-Mail: laabsjc@lea.org
Director, Publications and Communications: Edward "Ed" Grube LLD
    E-Mail: ed.grube@lea.org

Historical Note:
LEA links, equips, and affirms educators and workers in ministries for the purpose of building up the body of Christ. Membership: $109-255 (Individual); $135-330 (Husband/Wife); $60-150 (Retired/Student); $85-210 (Retired Husband/Wife); $60 (Student).

Meetings/Conferences: Annual
Number of non-conference events/year: 3

Publications:
LEAnews; weekly
Lutheran Education Journal
Shaping the Future; quarterly

Lutheran Educational Conference of North America *(1910)*
2601 S. Minnesota Ave., Suite 105
P.O. Box 377
Sioux Falls, SD 57105-4750
Tel: (605) 271-9894 *Fax:* (605) 271-9895
E-Mail: info@lutherancolleges.org
Website: lutherancolleges.org/lecna
Members:
40 colleges and universities
2 church bodies
Staff: 3
Annual Budget: $250-500,000

Personnel:
President: William E. Hamm
    E-Mail: hamm@lutherncolleges.org
Director, Marketing: Laurie Brill
    E-Mail: brill@lutherancolleges.org
Director, Business Operations: Wendy Hoyne
    E-Mail: hoyne@lutherancolleges.org

Historical Note:
Formerly (until 1967) National Lutheran Educational Conference. LECNA's mission is to proclaim the traditions and values of Lutheran higher education and to adhere to the standards of integrity and ethics in all matters. Members are Lutheran colleges, and church boards of higher education. Membership: $500-3,000/year (Based on type of Institution).

Meetings/Conferences: Annual
2013 - Amelia Island, FL (The Ritz-Carlton, Amelia Island)/Feb. 9 - 11

Publications:
Lutheran Higher Education Directory; on-line
Member Directory; on-line

Lyrasis *(2009)*
1438 W. Peachtree St. NW
Suite 200
Atlanta, GA 30309
Fax: (404) 892-7879
TollFree: (800) 999-8558
Website: lyrasis.org
Members: 1700 members
Staff: 110
Annual Budget: Over $100,000,000

Personnel:
Chief Executive Officer: Kate Nevins
    E-Mail: kate.nevins@lyrasis.org
Contact, Membership: Tim Cherubini
    E-Mail: membership@lyrasis.org
Chief Financial Officer: Vern Ritter
    E-Mail: vern.ritter@lyrasis.org
Director, Human Resources: Paquita Wright
    E-Mail: paquita.morris@lyrasis.org

Historical Note:
Formed through the merger of PALINET (established in 1936 in Philadelphia and serving libraries in the Mid-Atlantic) and SOLINET (established in 1973 to serve libraries in the Southeast). LYRASIS partners with member libraries to create, access and manage information, while building and sustaining collaboration, enhancing library and technology operations, and increasing buying power. Membership: $450-1,525 (Institution).

Meetings/Conferences: Annual

Publications:
LYRASIS News; semi-monthly

Machine Knife Association (1933)
30200 Detroit Rd.
Cleveland, OH 44145-1967
Tel: (440) 899-0010 *Fax:* (440) 892-1404
E-Mail: djh@wherryassoc.com
Website: machineknife.org
Members: 9 companies
Staff: 2
Tax: 501(c)(6)

Personnel:
Executive Secretary: Jeffrey J. Wherry
   E-Mail: jjw@wherryassoc.com
Contact, Communications: Donna Haders
   E-Mail: djh@wherryassoc.com

Historical Note:
Formerly (1991) Machine Knife Manufacturers Association, the Machine Knife Association was founded in order to promote wider uses and markets for the machine knife industry and to collect and provide information relating to the industry to the member companies as well as to end users of machine knives. Regular members are individuals, firms or corporations actively and substantially engaged for at least one year in the manufacture of machine knives and/or metal cutting knives in North America. Membership dues include the cost of one statistical survey with the opportunity to participate in several surveys.

Meetings/Conferences: Annual
Number of non-conference events/year: 1

Publications:
Membership Directory; on-line

Machinery Dealers National Association (1941)
315 S. Patrick St.
Alexandria, VA 22314-3501
Tel: (703) 836-9300 *Fax:* (703) 836-9303
TollFree: (800) 872-7807
E-Mail: office@mdna.org
Website: mdna.org
Members: 400 individuals
Staff: 5
Annual Budget: $500-1,000,000
Tax: 501(c)(6)

Personnel:
Executive Vice President: Mark Robinson
   E-Mail: mark@mdna.org

Historical Note:
MDNA is an international trade association dedicated to the promotion of the used machinery industry. Membership: $900/year.

Meetings/Conferences: Annual

Publications:
MDNA News; bi-monthly
MDNA News Bi-Weekly; bi-weekly
The Trucker's & Riggers Directory; annually
Used Machinery Buyer's Guide; annually

Magic Dealers Association (1946)
P.O. Box 7670
Auburn, CA 95604
Tel: (530) 823-7077 *Fax:* (530) 823-7078
E-Mail: mda@sterlingmagic.com
Website: magicdealers.com
Members: 67 companies
Staff: 1
Annual Budget: Under $10,000

Personnel:
International Treasurer: John T. Nightingale
   E-Mail: mda@sterlingmagic.com

Historical Note:
MDA's mission is to assist networking magic-related businesses and to provide a common bond of integrity. Members consist of retailers, wholesalers, jobbers, publishers, and inventors who develop, manufacture and sell magic-related products. Membership: $75/year (Associate/ Full).

Publications:
MAGIC Magazine; bi-monthly
MDA newsletter; quarterly

Magnet Schools of America (1960)
1012 14th St. NW
Suite 203
Washington, DC 20005
Tel: (202) 824-0672 *Fax:* (202) 737-0100
Website: magnet.edu
Members: 4,000 Magnet and theme-based schools

Staff: 6
Annual Budget: $1-2,000,000

Personnel:
Legislative and Communications Manager: John Laughner
Administrative Assistant, Membership Services: Bunmi Omo-Dare
   E-Mail: membership@magnet.edu
Coordinator, Events: Judy Shen
   E-Mail: events@magnet.edu

Historical Note:
Provides leadership for innovative instructional programs that advocate equity, diversity, and academic excellence for all students. Membership: $60-125 (Individual); $225 (Institution); $3,000-5,000 (District).

Meetings/Conferences: Annual
Conference Chair: Judy Shen
2013 - Washington, DC (The Hamilton Crowne Plaza Hotel)/Feb. 3 - 6
2013 - Tulsa, OK/May 5 - 8

Publications:
Newsletter; quarterly

Membership List Available to Non-members

Mail Systems Management Association (1981)
P.O. Box 1145
N. Riverside, IL 60546-1145
Tel: (708) 442-8589 *Fax:* (708) 853-0471
TollFree: (800) 714-6762
Website: msmanational.org
Members: 2000 individuals
Staff: 7
Annual Budget: $50-100,000

Personnel:
Vice President, Membership Services: Linda Henry CMDSM
   E-Mail: linda.henry@insperity.com
Director, Certification Services: Jane Patton CMDSM
   E-Mail: jane.patton@tgslc.org
Vice President, Education: Erik Warner CMDSM
   E-Mail: erik.j.warner@gmail.com

Historical Note:
MSMA's mission is to provide a professional organization for people involved in the management, supervision, and support of mail systems in business, industry, government and institutions. Membership: $100 (Individual); $200 (Corporate).

Continuing Education:
Certification Designation/s: CMDSM, CMDSS

Meetings/Conferences: Annual
2013 - Atlantic City, NJ (Tropicana Grand Exhibition Center)/April 28 - May 1

Publications:
MAIL Magazine; adv.
Postscript; irregular

Major Cities Chiefs Association (1960)
P.O Box 145497
Salt Lake City, UT 84114-5497
Tel: (801) 799-3802 *Fax:* (410) 433-9010
Website: majorcitieschiefs.org
Members: 90 Police Departments
Staff: 2
Annual Budget: $250-500,000
Tax: 501(c)(3)

Personnel:
Executive Director: Darrel W. Stephens
   E-Mail: dstephens@carolina.rr.com
Director, Conferences: Patricia Williams

Historical Note:
MCC is a professional organization of police executives representing the largest cities in the United States and Canada. MCC's mission is to provides a unique forum for urban police, sheriffs and other law enforcement chief executives to discuss common problems, to share information and problem-solving strategies. MCC articulates the public safety needs of large cities in the formulation of criminal justice policy. Membership is comprised of the Chiefs of the sixty-three largest police departments in the United States and Canada.

Meetings/Conferences:
Conference Chair: Patricia Williams
Number of non-conference events/year: 3

Major County Sheriffs' Association
1450 Duke St.
Alexandria, VA 22314-3490
Tel: (804) 445-9539 *Fax:* (804) 445-9023

Website: mcsheriffs.com
Members: 73 Counties
Staff: 1
Annual Budget: $100-250,000
Tax: 501(c)(6)

Personnel:
Executive Director: Joseph R. Wolfinger
   E-Mail: jrwolfinger@mcsheriffs.com

Historical Note:
MCSA is a professional law enforcement association of elected sheriffs representing counties or parishes with 500,000 population or more. Works to promote a understanding of law enforcement strategies to address futures problems and identify law enforcement challenges facing the members of the organization.

Meetings/Conferences: Annual

Publications:
Membership Directory; on-line

Major Indoor Soccer League (1984)
1715 N. Westshore Blvd.
Suite 825
Tampa, FL 33607
Tel: (813) 963-3909 *Fax:* (813) 963-3807
E-Mail: info@misl.net
Website: misl.net
Members: 10 clubs
Staff: 9

Personnel:
Chief Executive Officer: Alec Papadakis
   E-Mail: alec.papadakis@uslsoccer.com
Controller: Brad Freeman
   E-Mail: brad.freeman@uslsoccer.com
National Technical Director: Peter Mellor
   E-Mail: peter.mellor@uslsoccer.com
Director, Communications: Jay Preble
   E-Mail: jay.preble@uslsoccer.com

Historical Note:
Founded as National Professional Soccer League; assumed its current name in 2001. MISL actively pursues corporate sponsorships and provides a variety of promotional opportunities at the local, regional, and national levels.

Major League Baseball Players Association (1966)
12 E. 49th St.
24th Floor
New York, NY 10017
Tel: (212) 826-0808 *Fax:* (212) 752-4378
E-Mail: feedback@mlbpa.org
Website: mlbplayers.mlb.com
Members: 1200 individuals
Staff: 48
Annual Budget: $25-50,000,000
Tax: 501(c)(5)

Personnel:
Executive Director: Michael Weiner
Director, Communications: Greg Bouris
Chief Administrative Officer: Martha Child
Special Counsel: Steve Fehr
Chief Operating Officer: Gene Orza
Chief Labor Counsel: David Prouty

Historical Note:
The Major League Baseball Players Association (or MLBPA) is the union of professional major-league baseball players.

Continuing Education:
Certification Designation/s: MLBPA

Major League Soccer (1996)
420 Fifth Ave.
Seventh Floor
New York, NY 10018
Tel: (212) 450-1200 *Fax:* (212) 450-1300
E-Mail: feedback@mlsnet.com
Website: mlssoccer.com
Members: 10 teams
Staff: 6

Personnel:
President: Mark Abbott
Executive Vice President, Communications: Dan Courtemanche
   E-Mail: dan.courtemanche@mlsnet.com
Chief Marketing Officer: Howard Handler
Executive Vice President, Human Resources and Administration: JoAnn Neale
Senior Vice President and General Counsel: Bill Ordower

Chief Financial Officer: Sean Prendergast

Historical Note:
MLS's mission is to advocate the sport of soccer in general and serves as the central administrative office for its member franchises.

Meetings/Conferences: Annual

Publications:
MLS W.O.R.K.S.; monthly

Membership List Available to Non-members

Malaysian Rubber Export Promotion Council (USA) (2000)
3516 International Ct. NW
Washington, DC 20008
Tel: (202) 572-9771 Fax: (202) 572-9787
E-Mail: info@mrepc.com
Website: mrepc.com
Staff: 8

Personnel:
Senior Executive Officer: Donny Chan
    E-Mail: mrepcusa1@aol.com
Manager, Finance and Administration: Ilyana Sudani Z ahari
    E-Mail: ilyana@mrepc.com
Director, Industry Relations and Public Affairs: Brandon Chan Siew Hon
    E-Mail: brandon@mrepc.com
Contact, Public Relations: Julisa Joehari
    E-Mail: julisa@mrepc.com
Director, marketing and Development: Low Yoke Kiew
    E-Mail: lykiew@mrepc.com
Head, Information Technology: Kevin Cheah Kal Lok
    E-Mail: kevincheah@mrepc.com

Historical Note:
MREPC's mission is to facilitate and promote the export of quality rubber products.

Malignant Hyperthermia Association of the United States (1981)
P.O. Box 1069
Sherburne, NY 13460
Tel: (607) 674-7901
Website: mhaus.org
Staff: 4
Annual Budget: $500-1,000,000

Personnel:
Executive Director: Dianne Daugherty
    E-Mail: dianne@mhaus.org
Contact, Accounts and Finance: Elaina Morgan
    E-Mail: Elaina@mhaus.org
Database Administrator: Nicole Viera
    E-Mail: nicole@mhaus.org
Coordinator, Public Relations and Project: Michael Wesolowski
    E-Mail: michael@mhaus.org

Historical Note:
MHAUS Mission is to promote optimum care and scientific understanding of Malignant Hyperthermia and related disorders.

Publications:
MHAUS e-Newsletter; bi-monthly
The Communicator; quarterly

Man and Cybernetics Systems Society
Three Park Ave.
17th Floor
New York, NY 10016-5997
Tel: (212) 419-7900 Fax: (212) 752-4929
Website: ieeesmc.org
Members: 4200 individuals
Staff: 12

Personnel:
President: C. Philip Chen
    E-Mail: Philip.Chen@ieee.org
Vice President, Planning and Finance: Irv Engelson
    E-Mail: i.engelson@ieee.org
Vice President, Membership and Student Activities: Loi Lei Lai
Vice President, Membership Services: Loi Lei Lai
    E-Mail: l.l.lai@city.ac.uk
Vice President, Conferences and Meetings: Seong-Whan Lee
Vice President, Conferences and Meetings: Seong-Whan Lee
    E-Mail: swlee@image.korea.ac.kr
Editor-in-Chief: Witold Pedrycz

    E-Mail: wpedrycz@ualberta.ca
Secretary: Rodney Roberts
Vice President, Publications: Ljiljana Trajkovic
Vice President, Publications: Ljiljana Trajkovic
    E-Mail: ljilja@cs.sfu.ca
Treasurer: Robert Woon
Treasurer: Robert Woon
    E-Mail: rpwoon@gmail.com

Historical Note:
A technical society of the Institute of Electrical and Electronics Engineers (IEEE). Membership in the Society, open only to IEEE members, includes a subscription to a technical periodical in the field published by IEEE. All administrative support provided by IEEE. Mission is to serve the interests of its members and the community at large by promoting the theory, practice, and interdisciplinary aspects of systems science and engineering, human-machine systems, and cybernetics.

Meetings/Conferences: Annual
Conference Chair: Seong-Whan Lee
2013 - Manchester, United Kingdom (Ramada Manchester Piccadilly Hotel)/Oct. 13 - 16
2014 - San Diego, CA/Oct. 5 - 8

Publications:
IEEE Transactions on Systems, Man, and Cybernetics; monthly
SMCS e-Newsletter; quarterly; adv.

Managed Funds Association (1991)
600 14th St. NW
Suite 900
Washington, DC 20005
Tel: (202) 730-2600
E-Mail: hq@mfainfo.org
Website: managedfunds.org
Members: 146 Organizations
Staff: 31
Annual Budget: $10-25,000,000
Tax: 501(c)(6)

Personnel:
President and Chief Executive Officer: Hon. Richard H. Baker
    E-Mail: rbaker@mfainfo.org
Coordinator, Membership Services: Roscoe Butler
    E-Mail: rbutler@managedfunds.org
Executive Vice President and Managing Director, Chief Operating Officer: Marc T. Charon
    E-Mail: marc@managedfunds.org
Executive Vice President and Managing Director, Marketing and Communications: D. Brooke Harlow
    E-Mail: bharlow@managedfunds.org
Federal Lobbyist: Roger Hollingsworth
    E-Mail: rhollingsworth@managedfunds.org
Executive Vice President and General Counsel: Stuart J. Kaswell
    E-Mail: skaswell@managedfunds.org
Director, Conferences and Events: Annette Ott-Barnett
    E-Mail: aott-barnett@managedfunds.org
Manager, Information Technology: Jake Stratton
    E-Mail: jstratton@managedfunds.org

Historical Note:
Formerly Managed Futures Association, assumed its present name in 1999. MFA's mission is to enhance the image and understanding of the alternative investments industry through media relations initiatives. Members include Fund managers and Service Providers. Membership: $250-40,000/year.

Meetings/Conferences: Annual
Conference Chair: Annette Ott-Barnett
2013 - Biscayne, FL (The Ritz-Carlton, Miami Key)/Jan. 28 - 30

Publications:
Membership Directory; on-line
MFA Reporter; bi-monthly
The Week in Review; weekly

Membership List Available to Non-members

Management Association for Private Photogrammetric Surveyors (1982)
1856 Old Reston Ave.
Suite 205
Reston, VA 20190
Tel: (703) 787-6996 Fax: (703) 787-7550
E-Mail: info@mapps.org
Website: mapps.org
Members:
180 companies

150 individuals
Staff: 5
Annual Budget: $500-1,000,000
Tax: 501(c)(6)

Personnel:
Executive Director: John M. Palatiello
    E-Mail: john@mapps.org
Manager, Finance and Administration: Margaret Bulas
Contact, Member Services: Tammy Joslyn
    E-Mail: tammy@mapps.org
Assistant Executive Director, External Affairs: Nick Palatiello
    E-Mail: nick@mapps.org
Meeting Planner: Sally Palatiello
    E-Mail: sally@mapps.org

Historical Note:
MAPPS' primary objective is to develop strength and unity on matters affecting the interests of its member firms. Its membership spans the entire spectrum of the geospatial community, including member firms engaged in satellite and airborne remote sensing, surveying, photogrammetry, aerial photography, LIDAR, hydrography, bathymetry, charting, aerial and satellite image processing, GPS, and GIS data collection and conversion services. It also includes associate member firms, which are companies that provide hardware, software, products and services to the geospatial profession in the United States and other firms from around the world. Independent Consultant members are sole proprietors engaged in consulting in or to the geospatial profession, or provides a consulting service of interest to the geospatial profession. Membership: $250-1,000 (Sustaining Member); $1,085-7,520 (Regular); $1,340-3,245 (Associate); $500 (Independent Consultant); $100 (Emeritus).

Meetings/Conferences:
Conference Chair: Sally Palatiello
2013 - Sunny Isles Beach, FL (Trump Hotel)/Jan. 27 - 31

Publications:
Capitol Coverage; bi-weekly; adv.
Flightline Newsletter; bi-monthly; adv.
Membership Directory; on-line

Manufactured Housing Association for Regulatory Reform (1985)
1331 Pennsylvania Ave. NW
Suite 508
Washington, DC 20004
Tel: (202) 783-4087 Fax: (202) 783-4075
E-Mail: mharrdg@aol.com
Members: 40 companies
Staff: 2
Annual Budget: $250-500,000
Tax: 501(c)(6)

Personnel:
President: Daniel D. Ghorbani
    E-Mail: DANNYGHORBANI@AOL.COM

Historical Note:
Formerly the Association for Regulatory Reform. MHARR represents the interests and views of producers of federally regulated manufactured housing. Dedicated to the reform of unnecessary regulation of American housing industry and to make housing affordable for moderate and low income American families.

Meetings/Conferences:
Number of non-conference events/year: 2

Manufactured Housing Institute (1936)
2111 Wilson Blvd.
Suite 100
Arlington, VA 22201-3040
Tel: (703) 558-0400 Fax: (703) 558-0401
E-Mail: info@mfghome.org
Website: manufacturedhousing.org
Members: 300 companies
Staff: 9
Annual Budget: $2-5,000,000
Tax: 501(c)(6)

Personnel:
President and Chief Executive Officer: Richard Jennison
    E-Mail: rjennison@mfghome.org
Vice President, Government Affairs: Jason Boehlert
    E-Mail: jboehlert@mfghome.org
Director, Business Development: Cheryl Langley
    E-Mail: cheryl@mfghome.org
Director, Database and Membership Administration: Megan O'Kane
    E-Mail: mokane@mfghome.org
Vice President, Education: Ann Parman
    E-Mail: aparman@mfghome.org

Historical Note:
Established as Trailer Coach Manufacturers Association. Became Mobile Homes Manufacturers Association in 1956 and the Manufactured Housing Institute in 1975. Absorbed the National Manufactured Housing Federation in 1991 and the National Manufactured Housing Finance Association in 1992. MHI is the national trade organization representing all segments of the factory-built housing industry. MHI serves its membership by providing industry research, promotion, education and government relations programs, and by building and facilitating consensus within the industry. Membership: $575-11,500/year.

Continuing Education:
Certification Designation/s: PHC, ACM

Meetings/Conferences:
Conference Chair: Cheryl Langley
2013 - Las Vegas, NV (Paris Hotel)/April 16 - 18
2013 - San Diego, CA (La Costa Spa)/Sept. 29 - Oct. 1
2014 - Las Vegas, NV (Paris Hotel)/April 15 - 17
2015 - Las Vegas, NV (Paris Hotel)/April 14 - 16
2016 - Las Vegas, NV (Caesars Palace)/May 3 - 5
2017 - Las Vegas, NV (Caesars Palace)/May 2 - 4
Number of non-conference events/year: 25

Publications:
Membership Directory; on-line
MH Newswire; monthly
Week in Review; weekly

Manufacturers Alliance/MAPI Inc. *(1933)*
1600 Wilson Blvd.
11th Floor
Arlington, VA 22209-2594
Tel: (703) 841-9000 *Fax:* (703) 841-9514
E-Mail: mapi@mapi.net
Website: mapi.net
Members: 525 manufacturing companies
Staff: 17
Annual Budget: $10-25,000,000
Tax: 501(c)(6)

Personnel:
President and Chief Executive Officer: Stephen V. Gold
  E-Mail: sgold@mapi.net
Director, Technology: Noah Cohrssen
  E-Mail: ncohrssen@mapi.net
Director, Communications: James F. Engelhardt
  E-Mail: jengelhardt@mapi.net
Editor: Andrea J. Goodwin
  E-Mail: agoodwin@mapi.net
Director, Finance: Roger R. Harrison
  E-Mail: rharrison@mapi.net
Vice President and Council Director: Tracy Hollingsworth
  E-Mail: thollingsworth@mapi.net
Associate General Counsel and Council Director: Rae Ann S. Johnson
Director, Member Services: Caroline M. Mack
  E-Mail: cmack@mapi.net
Vice President, Sales and Marketing: Cameron L. Mackey
  E-Mail: cmackey@mapi.net
Senior Attorney: Leslie D. Miller
Vice President, General Counsel and Secretary: Frederick T. Stocker
  E-Mail: fstocker@mapi.net

Historical Note:
Formerly (1989) the Machinery and Allied Products Institute, became (1996) the Manufacturers Alliance for Productivity and Innovation/MAPI before assuming its current name. MAPI's mission is to provide manufacturers with the competitive intelligence to make them more effective, the knowledge to make them best-in-class firms, and the cutting edge research to assist them in maximizing their resources in a global landscape that changes daily, and, often, dramatically. Membership: $1,950-3,950/year (Council).

Continuing Education:
Enrollment: 250

Manufacturers Elevating and Work Platform Council
6737 W. Washington St.
Suite 2400
Milwaukee, WI 53214-5647
Website: aem.org/Groups/Groups/Group.asp?
  G = 45#.T1eD4MDCnIY
Staff: 1

Personnel:
Consultant, Technical Standards and Safety Services: Dan Moss

Historical Note:

The Manufacturers of Mobile Elevating Work Platforms Council (MEWPC) Engineering Committee is comprised of manufacturers of scissor-type, boom-type and personnel-type work platforms.MEWPC's mission is to promote and further the interests of the manufacturers of elevating work platforms on issues related to safety, standards and regulations, statistics and market data, education, public policy and the improvement of the overall industry's image.

Publications:
Membership Directory; on-line

Manufacturers of Emission Controls Association *(1976)*
2020 N. 14th St.
Suite 220
Arlington, VA 22201
Tel: (202) 296-4797
E-Mail: info@meca.org
Website: meca.org
Members: 46 companies
Staff: 4
Annual Budget: $1-2,000,000

Personnel:
Executive Director: Joseph E. Kubsh
  E-Mail: jkubsh@meca.org
Contact, Communications: Antonio Santos
  E-Mail: asantos@meca.org

Historical Note:
MECA is a non-profit association that provides solid technical information on emission control technology for motor vehicles. Members include manufacturers of a variety of emission control equipment for automobiles, trucks, buses, off-road vehicles and stationary sources.

Publications:
Membership Directory

Manufacturers Representatives of America, Inc. *(1978)*
P.O. Box 150229
Arlington, TX 76015
Tel: (682) 518-6008 *Fax:* (682) 518-6476
E-Mail: assnhqtrs@aol.com
Website: mra-reps.com
Members: 250 sales and marketing companies
Staff: 2
Annual Budget: $50-100,000
Tax: 501(c)(6)

Personnel:
Executive Director: Pamela L. Bess

Historical Note:
MRA's purpose is to promote the function of the independent manufacturers representative to go to market and to provide the necessary products, services, and support to help develop their capabilities to become proactive participants in the janitorial, paper, plastics, and disposables markets. Members are manufacturers' representatives in the paper, plastic, packaging, and sanitary supply fields. Membership: $505- 770 (Representative); $650 (Manufacturer); $515 (Associate).

Meetings/Conferences:
Number of non-conference events/year: 1

Publications:
Member Directory; on-line
MRA Newsline Newsletter

Manufacturers Standardization Society of the Valve and Fitting Industry, Inc. *(1924)*
127 Park St. NE
Vienna, VA 22180-4602
Tel: (703) 281-6613 *Fax:* (703) 281-6671
E-Mail: info@mss-hq.org
Website: mss-hq.org
Staff: 1

Personnel:
Executive Director: Robert O'Neill
  E-Mail: boneill@mss-hq.org

Historical Note:
Develops and publishes standards/specifications for industry products, including valves, valve acuators, flanges, pipe fittings, pipe hangers and associated seals. Membership: $1,900/year

Meetings/Conferences: Annual
2013 - Marco Island, FL (Marco Island beach Resort)/ April 23 - May 3

Publications:
Membership Directory; on-line

Manufacturers Standardization Society of the Valve and Fittings Industry *(1924)*
127 Park St. NE
Vienna, VA 22180-4602
Tel: (703) 281-6613 *Fax:* (703) 281-6671
E-Mail: info@mss-hq.org
Website: mss-hq.org
Members: 85 companies
Staff: 3
Annual Budget: $500-1,000,000

Personnel:
Executive Director: Robert O'Neill

Historical Note:
MSS's mission is to provide the means to develop engineering standard practices for the use and benefit of the industry. Members are manufacturing companies. Membership: $1,900/year.

Meetings/Conferences: Annual

Manufacturers' Agents Association for the Foodservice Industry *(1949)*
1199 Euclid Ave.
Atlanta, GA 30307
Tel: (404) 214-9474 *Fax:* (404) 522-0132
E-Mail: info@mafsi.org
Website: mafsi.org
Members:
2,000 sales and marketing professionals and manufacturing executives
490 professional trade association and independent sales agencies
Staff: 3
Annual Budget: $500-1,000,000

Personnel:
Executive Director: Alison Cody
  E-Mail: acody@mafsi.org
Manager, Marketing and Programs: Amanda Ambrus
  E-Mail: aambrus@mafsi.org
Director, Membership Services: Suzanne G. Fraga
  E-Mail: sfraga@mafsi.org

Historical Note:
Formerly (1993) Marketing Agents for Food Service Industry, MAFSI's purpose is to elevate the business and ethical practices of their members. Membership: $730 (Associate); $435-1,975 (Agent, based on total personnel).

Continuing Education:
Certification Designation/s: CPMR, MTC

Meetings/Conferences: Biennial
2014 - Palm Beach Gardens, FL (PGA National Resort and Spa)/Jan. 15 - 18
Number of non-conference events/year: 6

Publications:
MAFSI E-News; on-line
Member Directory; on-line
OutFront; quarterly; adv.

Manufacturers' Agents National Association *(1947)*
16 A Journey
Suite 200
Aliso Viejo, CA 92656-3317
Tel: (949) 859-4040 *Fax:* (949) 855-2973
TollFree: (877) 626-2776
E-Mail: mana@manaonline.org
Website: manaonline.org
Members: 6600 companies
Staff: 10
Annual Budget: $1-2,000,000
Tax: 501(c)(6)

Personnel:
President and Chief Executive Officer: Charles Cohon
  E-Mail: ccohon@manaonline.org
Executive Vice President: Helen Degli-Angeli
  E-Mail: helen@manaonline.org
Coordinator, Membership Services: Lisa Ball
  E-Mail: lball@manaonline.org
Editor: Jack Foster
  E-Mail: jfoster@manaonline.org
Contact, Advertising Services: Pam Hamlin
  E-Mail: phamlin@manaonline.org
Director, Publications and Art: Alane LaPlante
  E-Mail: alaplante@manaonline.org
Vice President and General Manager: Jerry Leth
  E-Mail: jleth@manaonline.org
Conference and Event Planner and Management Assistant: Linda McKee

E-Mail: lmckee@manaonline.org
Accounting Manager, Secretary and Treasurer: Susan
Strouse
E-Mail: sstrouse@manaonline.org

Historical Note:
MANA is the association of interdependent manufacturers
and representatives dedicated to educating, protecting
and encouraging the multi-line, outsourced sales
function.MANA's mission is,it is the association of
interdependent manufacturers and representatives
dedicated to educating, protecting and promoting the
multi-line, outsourced sales function. Membership: $259
(Regular, US and Canada); $349 (Regular, Foreign); $514
(Manufacturers).

Continuing Education:
Certification Designation/s: MTC

Meetings/Conferences: Annual
Conference Chair: Linda McKee

Publications:
Agency Sales Magazine; monthly
Directory of Manufacturer's Sales Agencies; weekly;
adv.
MANA Newsletter

Manufacturing Jewelers and Suppliers of America
(1903)
57 John L. Dietsch Sq.
Attleboro Falls, MA 02763
Tel: (401) 274-3840 Fax: (401) 274-0265
TollFree: (800) 444-6572
E-Mail: info@mjsa.org
Website: mjsa.org
Members: 1400 companies
Staff: 11
Annual Budget: $1-2,000,000
Tax: 501(c)(3)

Personnel:
President and Chief Executive Officer: David W. Cochran
E-Mail: david.cochran@mjsa.org
Director, Sales and Business Development: Corrie Silvia
Berry
E-Mail: corrie.silvia@mjsa.org
Assistant Controller and Information Technology
Coordinator: Dawn Britland
E-Mail: dawn.britland@mjsa.org
Representative, Membership Services: Marie Goncalves
E-Mail: marie.goncalves@mjsa.org
Operations Manager: Kristin Kopaz
E-Mail: kristin.kopaz@mjsa.org
Chief Operating Officer and Chief Financial Officer: James
K. McCarty
E-Mail: james.mccarty@mjsa.org
Coordinator, Membership: Travis Searle
E-Mail: travis.searle@mjsa.org
Editor-in-Chief: Tina Wojtkielo Snyder
Chief Communications Officer & Publisher: Rich Youmans
E-Mail: rich.youmans@mjsa.org

Historical Note:
Established as the New England Manufacturing Jewelers
Association; became Manufacturing Jewelers and
Silversmiths of America in 1956. A trade association for
all segments of the American jewelry manufacturing and
supply industry. MJSA's mission is to provide services that
help jewelry manufacturers and designers compete and
prosper. Membership includes American, foreign and retail
companies and anyone connected to the manufacture or sale
of jewelry. Membership: $125 (Artisan/Custom Jeweler);
$250 (Standard); $215 (School); $65 (Student).

Continuing Education:
Certification Designation/s: SCOP

Meetings/Conferences: Annual
2013 - New York City, NY (Hilton New York)/March 10
- 12/over 100 exhibitors
Number of non-conference events/year: 2

Publications:
Member Directory; on-line
MJSA Custom Jeweler; quarterly
MJSA Journal; monthly

Membership List Available to Non-members

Manuscript Society *(1948)*
P.O. Box 84686
Baton Rouge, LA 70884
E-Mail: manuscrip@cox.net
Website:
manuscript.org
manuscript.org
Members: 1200 individuals

Staff: 3
Annual Budget: $100-250,000
Tax: 501(c)(3)

Personnel:
Executive Director: Dr. Shirley J. Sands
E-Mail: sands@manuscript.org
Editor: David Chesnutt
E-Mail: dchesnutt@earthlink.net

Historical Note:
Formerly (1953) National Society of Autograph Collectors.
MS is devoted to the collection, preservation, use, and
enjoyment of autographs and manuscripts. Members
are dealers, curators, collectors and others interested in
original manuscripts, autographs, letters and documents.
Membership: $65 (North America); $90 (International);
$100 (Contributing); $500-750 (Benefactor); $250
(Sustaining); $1,000 (Patron).

Meetings/Conferences: Annual

Publications:
Manuscript Society Digest; monthly
Manuscripts; quarterly; adv.
The Manuscript Society News; quarterly

Maple Flooring Manufacturers Association *(1897)*
111 Deer Lake Rd.
Suite 100
Deerfield, IL 60015
Tel: (847) 480-9138 Fax: (847) 480-9282
TollFree: (888) 480-9138
E-Mail: mfma@maplefloor.org
Website: maplefloor.org
Members: 195 companies
Staff: 4
Annual Budget: $500-1,000,000
Tax: 501(c)(6)

Personnel:
Executive Director: Daniel Heney
E-Mail: dheney@maplefloor.org
Manager, Conferences: Madhuri Carson
E-Mail: mcarson@maplefloor.org
Director, Marketing and Communications: Heather
Gagnon
E-Mail: hgagnon@maplefloor.org
Technical Director: Daniel Krupa
E-Mail: dkrupa@maplefloor.org

Historical Note:
MFMA establishes product quality, performance and
installation guidelines; educates end users about safety,
performance and maintenance issues; and promotes the
use of maple, beech and birch flooring products worldwide.
Membership consists of manufacturers, installation
contractors, distributors and allied product. Membership:
$550 (Distributor/Sport Floor Contractor); $1,550 (Allied
Manufacturer).

Continuing Education:
Enrollment: 80
Certification Designation/s: AI

Meetings/Conferences: Annual
Conference Chair: Madhuri Carson

Publications:
Buyers Guide; on-line; adv.
E-Blast; on-line
Membership Directory; on-line

Marble Institute of America *(1944)*
28901 Clemens Rd.
Suite 100
Cleveland, OH 44145-1166
Tel: (440) 250-9222 Fax: (440) 250-9223
E-Mail: miainfo@marble-institute.com
Website: marble-institute.com
Members: 1800 companies
Staff: 9
Annual Budget: $1-2,000,000
Tax: 501(c)(6)

Personnel:
Executive Vice President and Chief Executive Officer: Garis
F. Distelhorst CAE
E-Mail: gdistelhorst@marble-institute.com
Director, Communications: Garen P. Distelhorst
E-Mail: gpdistelhorst@marble-institute.com
Director, Meetings and Special Events: Helen Distelhorst
E-Mail: hdistelhorst@marble-institute.com
Manager, Membership Relations: Jeff Handley
E-Mail: jhandley@marble-insitute.com
Manager, Industry Research and Information Services:
Michael W. Loflin

E-Mail: Mloflin@marble-institute.com
Director, Technical Services: Charles Muehlbauer
E-Mail: Miainfo@marble-institute.com

Historical Note:
Absorbed the National Association of Marble Dealers
in 1962. MIA's mission is to serve and support the
dimensional natural stone industry by providing an
array of services, products, and authoritative information
important to, and valued by, industry members.
Members include producers, exporters/importers,
distributors, fabricators, finishers, installers, restoration
and maintenance contractors, industry suppliers and
consultants. Membership: $850 (Regular/Associate
Members–North America); $925 (Regular/Associate
Members–International); $125 (Branch Members).

Continuing Education:
Enrollment: 25
Certification Designation/s: ANSF

Meetings/Conferences: Annual
Conference Chair: Helen Distelhorst
2013 - Jaipur, India (Centre for Development of
Stones)/Jan. 31 - Feb. 3
2013 - Atlanta, GA (Georgia World Congress Center)/
April 29 - May 2
2013 - London, United Kingdom/April 30 - May 2
2013 - Nuremberg, Germany (Exhibition Centre
Nuremberg)/May 29 - June 1

Publications:
Cutting Edge; monthly; adv.
Dimension Stone Design Manual
Membership Directory; annually; adv.
StoneDimensions; semi-annually; adv.

Marine Corps Association *(1913)*
715 Broadway St.
Quantico, VA 22134
Tel: (877) 469-6223 Fax: (703) 640-0823
TollFree: (800) 336-0291
E-Mail: mcaf@mca-marines.org
Website: mca-marines.org
Staff: 18
Annual Budget: $10-25,000,000
Tax: 501(c)(19)

Personnel:
President and Chief Executive Officer: MajGen Edward
Usher USMC (Ret.)
E-Mail: e.usher@mca-marines.org
Director, Finance: Johnna Ebel
E-Mail: j.ebel@mca-marines.org
Chief Operating Officer: Tom Esslinger
E-Mail: t.esslinger@mca-marines.org
Editor - Leatherneck: Walt Ford
E-Mail: w.ford@mca-marines.org
Director, Information Technology and Webmaster: Bradley
Kirkland
E-Mail: b.kirkland@mca-marines.org
Director, Membership Services: Lisa Pappas
E-Mail: l.pappas@mca-marines.org
Director, Marketing and Membership Services: Robert
Rubrecht
E-Mail: r.rubrecht@mca-marines.org
Director, Human Resource: Faith Woods
E-Mail: f.woods@mca-marines.org

Historical Note:
MCA's mission is the development and recognition of
professional excellence and expanding awareness of the
rich traditions, history, and esprit of the United States
Marine Corps. A membership organization for marines.
Membership: $35-70 year (Individual).

Publications:
Corps Daily News; daily
Leatherneck; monthly
Marine Corps Gazette; adv.
Membership Directory; on-line

Marine Corps Aviation Association *(1972)*
P.O. Box 296
715 Broadway St.
Quantico, VA 22134
Tel: (703) 630-1903 Fax: (703) 630-2713
TollFree: (800) 280-3001
Website: flymcaa.org
Staff: 3
Annual Budget: $500-1,000,000

Personnel:
Executive Director: LTCOL Raul A. Sifuentes USMC
(Ret.)
Contact, Editor and Advertising Sales: Roxanne Kaufman

Office Manager: Pam Lawrence

Historical Note:
The Marine Corps Aviation Association's mission is to promote and recognize professional excellence in Marine aviation, support the fraternal bond of its membership, preserve Marine aviation heritage and safeguard the future of Marine aviation through awards programs, events and publications. Membership: $35/Year.

Meetings/Conferences: Annual
2013 - Reno, NV (Grand Sierra Hotel & Casino)/May 15 - 18

Publications:
MCAA Journal Magazine; adv.
The Yellow Sheet; adv.

Marine Corps League *(1923)*
P.O. Box 3070
Merrifield, VA 22116-3070
Tel: (703) 207-9588 *Fax:* (703) 207-0047
TollFree: (800) 625-1775
E-Mail: mcl@mcleague.org
Website: mcleague.com
Members: 76000 individuals
Staff: 6
Annual Budget: $100-250,000
Tax: 501(c)(4)

Personnel:
Executive Director and Executive Editor: Michael A. Blum
     E-Mail: execdir@mcleague.org
Chief Technology Officer: Richard Blum
     E-Mail: CTO@MCLeague.org
Managerial Assistant: Jeanette Eshoo
     E-Mail: JEshoo@MCLeague.org
Manager, Membership: Johanna Hill
     E-Mail: JHill@MCLeague.org
Director, Government Affairs: LTGEN Stephen G. Olmstead
     E-Mail: SOLmstead@MCLeague.org
Support Staff: Beth Snider

Historical Note:
The Marine Corps League works to preserve the traditions and promote the interests of the United States Marine Corps. Membership includes Marines, former Marines, and qualified Navy FMF Corpsmen. Membership: $30 (Member-at-Large/Associate); $150-500 (Life, based on age)

Meetings/Conferences: Annual
2013 - Falls Church, VA (Fairview Park Marriott)/Feb. 7 - 9
2013 - Grand Rapids, MI (Amway Grand Plaza Hotel)/ Aug. 4 - 9

Publications:
Semper Fi; bi-monthly; adv.
Update; semi-monthly

Marine Corps Reserve Association *(2003)*
8626 Lee Hwy.
Suite 205
Fairfax, VA 22031-2135
Tel: (703) 289-1204 *Fax:* (703) 289-1206
E-Mail: hqs@usmcra.org
Website: usmcra.org
Members: 5000 individuals
Staff: 3
Annual Budget: $25-50,000
Tax: 501(c)(3)

Personnel:
Executive Director: Vernon Leubecker
Vice-President, Communications: Thomas LPM Howlett
Vice President, Membership Services: Gary Schroeder

Historical Note:
Founded as Marine Corps Reserve Officers Association, assumed its current name in 2003. MCRA's mission is to stimulate the advancement of the professional knowledge of its members and to advocate the interest of the members. MCRA serves to support the Marine Corps, its Reserve Component, and Marine Reservists. Members are active, former and retired Marine Corps Reservists. Membership: $15-100 (Individual); $300-600 (Life).

Continuing Education:
Certification Designation/s: PME

Publications:
MCRA e-Newsletter; on-line
Membership Directory; on-line

Membership List Available to Non-members

Marine Engineers Beneficial Association *(1875)*

444 N. Capitol St. NW
Suite 800
Washington, DC 20001
Tel: (202) 638-5355 *Fax:* (202) 638-5369
E-Mail: mebahq@d1meba.org
Website: d1meba.org
Members: 35000 full and affiliate members
Staff: 10
Annual Budget: $5-10,000,000

Personnel:
President: Mike Jewell
Director, Communications: Marco Cannistraro
     E-Mail: mcannistraro@d1meba.org
Director, Government and Legal Affairs: William Doyle
     E-Mail: wdoyle@d1meba.org
Executive Secretary: Ann Holmes
Chief Information Officer: Jeff F. Merrifield
Secretary and Treasurer: William Van Loo

Historical Note:
MEBA's mission is to provide each of today's professional marine engineers, deck officers, and related industry professionals with internationally recognized, state of the art training and experience that enhances the safety, reliability, and profitability of their vessels and equipment, while preserving and protecting the natural environment. MEBA holds national affiliation with AFL-CIO

Publications:
Marine Officer; on-line
MEBA TELEX TIMES
Member Directory; on-line

Marine Fabricators Association
1801 County Rd. B West
Roseville, MN 55113-4061
Tel: (651) 225-6952 *Fax:* (651) 631-9334
TollFree: (800) 209-1810
E-Mail: info@marinecanvas.com
Website: marinecanvas.com
Members:
320 marine fabricator members
320 companies
Staff: 1
Annual Budget: $50-100,000

Personnel:
Managing Director: Beth L. Hungiville
     E-Mail: blhungiville@ifai.com

Historical Note:
MFA is a division of the Industrial Fabrics Association International (IFAI). MFA's purpose is to provide resources and programs for marine fabricators and establish standards for business practices, products and craftsmanship. Membership: $385-935 (End Product Manufacturing Company, based on Manufacturer's Annual Sales); $1,085 (Supplier); $335 (Sponsor); $235 (Affiliate); $180 (Individual); $80 (Student).

Continuing Education:
Certification Designation/s: CC, IFM, MFC

Meetings/Conferences: Annual
2013 - Cape Coral, FL (Resort at Marina Village)/Jan. 18 - 20

Publications:
Marine Fabricator Magazine; on-line; adv.
Membership Directory; on-line
MFA News
MFA newsletter; bi-monthly
Specialty Fabrics Review; adv.

Membership List Available to Non-members

Marine Preservation Association *(1990)*
8777 N. Gainey Center Dr.
Suite 165
Scottsdale, AZ 85258
Tel: (480) 991-5500 *Fax:* (480) 991-6085
E-Mail: mpa@mpaz.org
Website: mpaz.org
Members: 150 companies
Staff: 2
Annual Budget: $10-25,000,000
Tax: 501(c)(6)

Personnel:
President, Secretary and Chief Executive Officer: Brett Drewry
Treasurer and Assistant Secretary: Leon Crites

Historical Note:
In 1990 the Oil Pollution Act (OPA 90) was enacted and the Marine Preservation Association (MPA) was created for the sole purpose of addressing problems caused by oil

spills on water. MPA ensures that members have direct and immediate access to MSRC, so that clean-up can begin right away.

Marine Retailers Association of America *(1972)*
P.O. Box 725
Boca Grande, FL 33921
Tel: (941) 964-2534 *Fax:* (941) 531-6777
E-Mail: mraa@mraa.com
Website: mraa.com
Members: 3000 companies
Staff: 4
Annual Budget: $250-500,000
Tax: 501(c)(6)

Personnel:
Editor: Pat Lucas

Historical Note:
MRAA aims to provide a common source of information concerting all aspects of marine retailing, to stimulate a continuing exchange of ideas among its members. Membership: $300 (Retail); $400(Associate) $500(Marine Trades Associations), $1,500(Partner Members),

Continuing Education:
Certification Designation/s: MIC, SCSP

Publications:
Bearings; monthly
MRAA Newsletter
Washington Watch; on-line

Marine Technology Society *(1963)*
1100 H St. NW
Suite LL-100
Washington, DC 20005
Tel: (202) 717-8705 *Fax:* (202) 347-4302
E-Mail: membership@mtsociety.org
Website: mtsociety.org
Members: 3000 individuals
Staff: 9
Annual Budget: $2-5,000,000
Tax: 501(c)(3)

Personnel:
Executive Director: Richard Lawson
     E-Mail: rich.lawson@mtsociety.org
Director, Meetings and Professional Development: Chris Barrett
     E-Mail: chris.barret@mtsociety.org
Manager, Membership and Marketing: Jeanne Glover
     E-Mail: jeanne.glover@mtsociety.org
Treasurer and Vice President, Budget and Finance: Debra Kill
     E-Mail: debbi.kill@ise.bc.ca
Vice President, Publications: Donna Kocak
     E-Mail: dkocak@harris.com
Contact, Communications, Newsletters and Press Releases: MaryBeth Loutinsky
     E-Mail: mbloutinsky@gmail.com
Vice President, Government and Public Affairs: Justin Manley
     E-Mail: justin.manley@liquidr.com
Vice President, Industry and Technology: Ray Toll
     E-Mail: RAYMOND.F.TOLL.JR@saic.com
Vice President, Education and Research: Jill Zande
     E-Mail: jzande@mpc.edu

Historical Note:
MTS's mission is to promote and improve marine technology and related educational programs. Membership: $75 (Individual/Associate); $25 (Student); $100 (Patron); $40 (Emeritus); $1000 (Life/Corporate); $2000 (Fortune 500); $550 (Small Business/ Institutional).

Meetings/Conferences:
Conference Chair: Chris Barrett
2013 - New Orleans, LA (Morial Convention Center)/ Jan. 15 - 17
2013 - Bergen, Norway (Grieghallen Culture & Convention Center)/June 10 - 13
2013 - San Diego, CA/Sept. 23 - 27
2014 - St. John's, NF/Sept. 14 - 19

Publications:
Education & Training Programs in Oceanography & Related Fields; irregular
Marine Technology Society Journal; bi-monthly; adv.

Maritime Fire and Safety Association *(1983)*
200 SW Market St.
Suite 190
Portland, OR 97201
Tel: (503) 220-2055 *Fax:* (503) 295-3660

Website: mfsa.com
Members: 23 Organizations
Staff: 5
Annual Budget: $2-5,000,000
Tax: 501(c)(6)

Personnel:
Executive Director: Liz Wainwright
　E-Mail: wainright@pdxmex.com
Senior Administrator: Marisa Chilafoe
　E-Mail: allen@pdxmex.com
Communications and Systems Administrator: Jim Harrison
　E-Mail: meere@pdxmex.com

Historical Note:
Maritime Safety Association (TMSA), combining the Delaware River and Bay Marine Fire Fighting Task Force (MFFTF) & Tri-state Search And Rescue.

Meetings/Conferences:
Conference Chair: Marisa Chilafoe

Maritime Law Association of the U.S. (1899)
Mosely Prichard Parrish Knight And Jones
501 W. Bay St.
Jacksonville, FL 32202
Tel: (904) 421-8436 *Fax:* (904) 421-8437
Website: mlaus.org
Members: 3000 individuals
Staff: 3
Annual Budget: $500-1,000,000

Personnel:
President: Robert B. Parrish
　E-Mail: BPARRISH@MPPKJ.COM

Historical Note:
Represents U.S. in the Comite Maritime Internationale. MLA's mission is to unify and improve maritime law, and to educate members in the field. Membership: $135/year (Individual).

Continuing Education:
Certification Designation/s: CLE

Meetings/Conferences: Annual
2013 - New York City, NY/April 30 - May 2
Number of non-conference events/year: 1

Publications:
Membership Directory; on-line
MLA Proceedings; irregular
MLA Reports; semi-annually

Market Technicians Association (1971)
61 Broadway
Suite 514
New York, NY 10006
Tel: (646) 652-3300 *Fax:* (646) 652-3322
Website: mta.org
Members: 4,100 members
Staff: 9
Annual Budget: $2-5,000,000

Personnel:
Executive Director and Chief Executive Officer: Tim Licitra
　E-Mail: tim@mta.org
Manager, Communications: Tyshawn Jenkins
　E-Mail: tyshawn@mta.org
Office Assistant: Angel Montemayor
　E-Mail: angel@mta.org
Director, Member Services: Marie Penza
　E-Mail: marie@mta.org
Manager, Accounting: Diana Perez
　E-Mail: diana@mta.org
Director, Technology: Shane Skwarek
　E-Mail: shane@mta.org
Director, Marketing: Tyler Wood
　E-Mail: tyler@mta.org
CMT Program Director: Jeanette Young
　E-Mail: jeanette@mta.org

Historical Note:
he MTA's main objectives involve the education of the public, the investment community and its membership in the theory, practice and application of technical analysis. MTAE's mission is to educate the public and the investment community of the value and universality of technical analysis.

Continuing Education:
Certification Designation/s: CMT

Meetings/Conferences: Annual
2013 - New York City, NY (Sentry Centers)/April 4 - 5

Publications:
CMT Newsletter

Marketing Agencies Association Worldwide (1969)
89 Woodland Cir.
Minneapolis, MN 55424
Tel: (952) 922-0130 *Fax:* (760) 437-4141
Website: maaw.org
Members: 85 agencies
Staff: 1
Annual Budget: $250-500,000

Personnel:
Executive Director: Keith McCracken
　E-Mail: keith.mccracken@maaw.org

Historical Note:
Formerly (1995) the Council of Sales Promotion Agencies, (2003) the Association of Promotion Marketing Agencies Worldwide. MAAW is dedicated solely to the CEOs, presidents, managing directors and principals of top marketing services agencies to give them and their agencies an unfair advantage. Members are entrepreneurs and forward-thinking executives, who together create an extraordinary opportunity for likeminded people to meet with their peers, share global knowledge, raise their company profile on both a national and a global platform, and to influence the future of the industry. 50% of MAAW membership is foreign. Membership: $3,700 (Full); $1,000 (Associate).

Marketing and Advertising Global Network (1946)
1017 Perry Hwy.
Suite Five
Pittsburgh, PA 15237
Tel: (412) 366-6850 *Fax:* (412) 366-6840
E-Mail: mxdirector@verizon.net
Website: magnetglobal.org
Members: 836 companies and clients
Staff: 1
Annual Budget: $100-250,000

Personnel:
Executive Director: Cheri D. Gmiter
　E-Mail: mxdirector@verizon.net

Historical Note:
Founded as the Midwestern Advertising Agency Network; later became Mutual Advertising Agency Network and assumed its present name in 1999. MAGNET's mission is to provide ways for its member agencies to share their experience, knowledge and ideas with other agencies in other parts of the world. Members are independently owned advertising agencies in major markets throughout the world. Membership: $6,500 (Corporate); $2,500 (Initiation).

Meetings/Conferences:
Number of non-conference events/year: 1

Publications:
MAGNET Newsletter; weekly; adv.
Membership Directory; annually

Membership List Available to Non-members

Marketing Association of Credit Unions (1986)
1575 Spinnaker Dr.
Suite 205
Ventura, CA 93001
E-Mail: mac@hp-assoc.com
Website: macnetwork.org
Members: 350 individuals
Staff: 2
Annual Budget: $100-250,000

Personnel:
Contact, Membership: Laura Parsons

Historical Note:
Founded as Marketing Association of California, assumed its current name in 2000. MAC supports the needs of its members and provides them with educational opportunities to improve their technical and management skills. Membership: $299-399 (Individual); $199-299 (Credit Union/Associate).

Meetings/Conferences: Annual
2013 - Las Vegas, NV/May 29 - 31

Marketing Education Association (1982)
Department of Marketing, Campus Box 79
P.O. Box 173362
Denver, CO 80217
Tel: (303) 556-2114 *Fax:* (303) 556-3307
E-Mail: mea@nationalmea.org
Website: marketingeducators.org
Members: 600 individuals
Staff: 4
Annual Budget: $50-100,000

Tax: 501(c)(6)

Personnel:
President: Susan Cadwallader
　E-Mail: scadwallader@fullerton.edu
Marketing Director: David Ackerman
　E-Mail: david.s.ackerman@csun.edu
Secretary and Treasurer: Clay Daughtrey
　E-Mail: daughtre@mscd.edu
Webmaster: Lars Perner
　E-Mail: perner@marshall.usc.edu

Historical Note:
Formed by a merger of the Council of Distributive Teacher Educators, National Association of Distributive Education Local Supervisors, National Association of Distributive Education Teachers and National Association of State Supervisors of Distributive Education. Formerly (1985) known as Marketing and Distributive Education Association and then (1989) National Marketing and Distributive Education Services Center. MEA's mission is to foster the development and expansion of education for and about marketing as a profession. Membership: $30 (First Year); $56 (Professional); $15 (Student); $111 (Executive); $20 (Loyalty).

Meetings/Conferences: Annual
2013 - Portland, OR (Nines Hotel)/April 18 - 20

Publications:
Journal of Marketing Education
Membership Directory; on-line

Marketing Research Association (1954)
1111 16th St. NW
Suite 120
Washington, DC 20036
Tel: (202) 800-2545 *Fax:* (888) 512-1050
E-Mail: membership@marketingresearch.org
Website: marketingresearch.org
Members: 3000 individuals
Staff: 22
Annual Budget: $2-5,000,000

Personnel:
Chief Executive Officer: David Almy
　E-Mail: david.almy@marketingresearch.org
Senior Manager, Education and Events: Jennifer Cattel
　E-Mail: jennifer.cattel@marketingresearch.org
Director, Government Affairs: Howard Fienberg
　E-Mail: howard.fienberg@marketingresearch.org
General Counsel: LaToya Rembert Lang
　E-Mail: latoya.lang@marketingresearch.org
Director, Development: Lisa Lockwood
　E-Mail: lisa.lockwood@marketingresearch.org
Director, Technology: Mary-Jo Machel
　E-Mail: maryjo.machel@marketingresearch.org
Director, Communications: Ann Morgan
　E-Mail: maryjo.machel@marketingresearch.org
Director, Administration: Linda Pylant
　E-Mail: linda.pylant@marketingresearch.org
Editor: Amy Shields
　E-Mail: amy.shields@marketingresearch.org

Historical Note:
Formed in 1954 as an outgrowth of the Trade Problem Discussion Group of the American Marketing Association's (AMA) New York Chapter. Formerly (1971) Marketing Research Trade Association. Merged with Council for Marketing and Opinion Research (2008). Mission of MRA is to support and advocate for its members professional growth and success. Membership: $315-15,000 (Company); $350 (Individual); $200 (Government); $95 (Educator); $55 (Student).

Continuing Education:
Certification Designation/s: PRC

Meetings/Conferences: Annual
Conference Chair: Jennifer Cattel
2013 - Orlando, FL (Walt Disney World Swan)/June 10 - 12/600 attendees
Number of non-conference events/year: 1

Publications:
Alert Magazine; monthly
MRA News; daily
MRA Update Newsletter; bi-weekly; adv.

Marketing Science Institute (1961)
1000 Massachusetts Ave.
Cambridge, MA 02138-5396
Tel: (617) 491-2060 *Fax:* (617) 491-2065
E-Mail: msi@msi.org
Website: msi.org
Members: 71 Companies
Staff: 7

Annual Budget: $2-5,000,000
Tax: 501(c)(3)

Personnel:
Executive Director: John Deighton
    E-Mail: jdeighton@msi.org
Editorial Director: Susan Keane
    E-Mail: skeane@msi.org
Director, Finance and Administration: Brian Kostantin
    E-Mail: bkostantin@msi.org
Director, Conferences: Donna Peck
    E-Mail: dpeck@msi.org
Director, Systems and Member Services: Michele
    Rainforth
    E-Mail: mrainforth@msi.org
Research Director: Ross Rizley
    E-Mail: ross@msi.org
Chief Marketing Officer: Earl Taylor
    E-Mail: etaylor@msi.org

Historical Note:
*MSI's mission is to provide intellectual leadership in
marketing and its allied fields, with the goal of improving
and influencing business thinking and practice. membership:
$37,500 (individual).*

Meetings/Conferences: Annual
Conference Chair: Donna Peck
2013 - Boston, MA (Taj Hotel)/April 11 - 12

Publications:
Insights from MSI
MSI Review

MASINT Association *(1999)*
701 Pennsylvania Ave. NW
Suite 900
Washington, DC 20004
Tel: (571) 214-2415
E-Mail: mastassoc@earthlink.net
Website: masint.org
Staff: 4
Annual Budget: $250-500,000

Personnel:
Chairman: Robert Chiralo
    E-Mail: robert.chiralo@sri.com
Associate Executive Director: Phil Edson
Secretary and Treasurer: Brian Gore
    E-Mail: brian.j.gore@boeing.com
Executive Director: Jim Longley
    E-Mail: jblongley@aol.com

Historical Note:
*Supports the development of the use of Measurement and
Signatures Intelligence technologies.*
Meetings/Conferences:
Number of non-conference events/year: 2

Membership List Available to Non-members

Mason Contractors Association of America *(1950)*
1481 Merchant Dr.
Algonquin, IL 60102
Tel: (224) 678-9709 *Fax:* (224) 678-9714
TollFree: (800) 536-2225
E-Mail: info@masoncontractors.org
Website: masoncontractors.org
Members: 1000 individuals
Staff: 6
Annual Budget: $500-1,000,000

Personnel:
President and Chief Executive Officer: Jeff Buczkiewicz
Director, Membership Services: Bob Birdsell
    E-Mail: bbirdsell@masoncontractors.org
Publisher: John Llewellyn
    E-Mail: llewellyn@lionhrtpub.com
*Director, Marketing, Education and Information
    Technology:* Timothy "Tim" W. O'Toole
Administrative Assistant and Controller: Ann Trownsell

Historical Note:
*MCAA is a national trade association representing masonry
contractors and suppliers in national legislative and political
affairs, codes and standards composition, workforce
development, education, market promotion and general
industry advocacy. Members are masonry contractors and
suppliers and are represented by officers who are elected by
the membership every two years. Membership: $560-3,000
(Contractors); $300-2,000 (Associate).*

Continuing Education:
Certification Designation/s: NMC

Meetings/Conferences:
2013 - Las Vegas, NV/Feb. 3 - 8

2014 - Las Vegas, NV/Jan. 19 - 24
Publications:
Buyers Guide; on-line
e-mail newsletter; on-line
MASONRY Magazine; monthly; adv.
MCAA Newsletter; quarterly
Membership Directory; on-line

The Masonry Heater Association of North America
(1986)
2180 S. Flying Q Ln.
Tucson, AZ 85731
Tel: (520) 883-0191 *Fax:* (480) 371-1139
Website: mha-net.org
Members: 80 individuals
Staff: 1
Annual Budget: $100-250,000
Tax: 501(c)(6)

Personnel:
Executive Director: Richard (Dick) Smith
    E-Mail: execdir@mha-net.org

Historical Note:
*MHA is an association of builders, manufacturers and
retailers of masonry heaters whose purpose is to advocate
the industry, sponsor research and development, shape
regulations, standards and codes and further the expertise
and professionalism of its membership. Membership: $275
(Voting); $150 (Affiliate).*

Publications:
Member Directory; on-line

Membership List Available to Non-members

Masonry Institute of America *(1957)*
22815 Frampton Ave.
Torrance, CA 90501
Tel: (310) 257-9000 *Fax:* (310) 257-1942
TollFree: (800) 221-4000
Website: masonryinstitute.org
Staff: 1
Annual Budget: $25-50,000

Personnel:
Executive Director: Bill McEwen

Historical Note:
*Formerly Masonry Research. The Masonry Institute of
America is primarily supported by Southern California
union signatory masonry contractors through a labor
management contract between unions and contractors. The
Masonry Institute of America is active in the development
and distribution of seminars and publications that enhance
the use of masonry.*

The Masonry Society *(1977)*
105 S. Sunset St.
Suite Q
Longmont, CO 80501-6172
Tel: (303) 939-9700 *Fax:* (303) 541-9215
E-Mail: info@masonrysociety.org
Website: masonrysociety.org
Members:
50 organizations
660 individuals
Staff: 2
Annual Budget: $500-1,000,000
Tax: 501(c)(3)

Personnel:
Secretary and Treasurer: Jerry M. Painter

Historical Note:
*TMS is dedicated to the advancement of scientific,
engineering, architectural and construction knowledge of
masonry. The Society stimulates research and education
and disseminates information on masonry materials,
design and construction. Membership: $165 (Professional/
Associate); $35 (Student); $425 (Affiliate Organization);
$65 (Junior, below or equal to 28 years of age); $1400
(Sustaining Organization).*

Meetings/Conferences: Annual
2013 - Vancouver, BC/May 31 - June 3
2013 - Vancouver, BC/May 31 - June 2
2013 - Vancouver, BC/June 2 - 5
Number of non-conference events/year: 2

Publications:
TMS e-Newsletter; bi-monthly
TMS Journal; annually
TMS News; quarterly; adv.
TMS Sustainabilty E-News; bi-monthly; adv.

Masonry Veneer Manufacturers Association
(2006)
750 National Press Building
529 14th St. NW
Washington, DC 20045
Tel: (202) 591-2438 *Fax:* (202) 591-2445
E-Mail: info@masonryveneer.org
Website: masonryveneer.org
Members: 35 Companies
Staff: 6
Annual Budget: $250-500,000

Personnel:
Executive Vice President: Ralph Vasami
Administrative Manager: Penny Alston
Director, Communications: Dan Fernandez
General Manager: John Ferraro
Director, Industry Affairs: Mike Fischer
Staff Associate: Kelly Franklin
    E-Mail: kfranklin@kellencompany.com

Historical Note:
*MVMA's mission is to advance the growth of the
manufactured masonry veneer products industry through
proactive technical, advocacy, and awareness efforts.
Membership: $10,000-40,000 (Regular); $2,500-5,000
(Associate); $10,000 (Affiliate).*

Meetings/Conferences:
2013 - Las Vegas, NV (Las Vegas Convention Center)/
Jan. 22 - 25
2013 - Las Vegas, NV (Las Vegas Convention Center)/
Feb. 5 - 8

Publications:
MVMA Foundations

Membership List Available to Non-members

Mass Finishing Job Shops Association *(1981)*
808 13th St.
P.O. Box 795
East Moline, IL 61244-1628
Tel: (309) 755-1101 *Fax:* (309) 755-1121
E-Mail: apexmetalfinishing@msn.com
Website: mfjsa.com
Members: 43 companies
Staff: 1
Annual Budget: Under $10,000

Personnel:
Executive Director: Terry Larson

Historical Note:
*MFJSA's mission is to promote and encourage Job Shops for
the deburring, cleaning, surface finishing, etc. of metal and
other parts by tumbling, vibratory and other Mass Finishing
methods. Members are companies providing advanced metal
finishing services. Membership: $350/year.*

Meetings/Conferences: Annual
Publications:
Membership Directory; on-line

Mass Marketing Insurance Institute *(1969)*
400 Admiral Blvd.
Kansas City, MO 64106
Tel: (816) 221-7575 *Fax:* (816) 472-7765
E-Mail: gregc@robstan.com
Website: mi2.org
Members: 300 companies
Staff: 2
Annual Budget: $100-250,000

Personnel:
Executive Director: Gregory Carlile
    E-Mail: grege@robstan.com

Historical Note:
*MI2 provides a forum for professionals engaged in
marketing, sales and administration of voluntary benefits.
Membership: $749/year (manufacturers/administrators/
vendors); $299/year (producers/brokers).*

Master Brewers Association of the Americas
(1887)
3340 Pilot Knob Rd.
St. Paul, MN 55121-2097
Tel: (651) 454-7250 *Fax:* (651) 454-0766
E-Mail: mbaa@mbaa.com
Website: mbaa.com
Members: 2300 individuals
Staff: 10
Annual Budget: $1-2,000,000

Personnel:
Executive Vice President: Steve C. Nelson

E-Mail: snelson@scisoc.org
Director, Membership Services: Michelle Bjerkness
   E-Mail: mbjerkness@scisoc.org
Director, Publications: Karen Cummings
   E-Mail: kcummings@scisoc.org
Manager, Marketing: Karen Deuschle
Coordinator, Meetings and Education: Beth Elliott
   E-Mail: belliott@scisoc.org
Director, Publications: Greg Grahek
   E-Mail: ggrahek@scisoc.org
Vice President, Operations: Amy Hope
   E-Mail: ahope@scisoc.org
Representative, Membership Services: Cheryl Kruchten
   E-Mail: ckruchten@scisoc.org
Vice President, Finance: Barbara Mock
   E-Mail: bmock@scisoc.org

Historical Note:
Formerly Master Brewers Association of America, gained its current name in 1979. MBAA's mission is to provide technical and practical knowledge that assists the brewing industry to continuously improve product, procedures, and processes from raw materials through consumption. Membership: $139 (Professional); $41 (Student); $0-40 (Districts).

Continuing Education:
Certification Designation/s: BPTC

Meetings/Conferences: Biennial
Conference Chair: Beth Elliott
2013 - Austin, TX (Hilton Austin)/Oct. 23 - 26
Number of non-conference events/year: 3

Publications:
Membership Directory; on-line
Technical Quarterly; quarterly; adv.
The MBAA Communicator; bi-weekly; adv.

Master Pools Guild, Inc. *(1962)*
9601 Gayton Rd.
Suite 101
Richmond, VA 23238
Tel: (804) 741-7081 *Fax:* (804) 741-7091
TollFree: (800) 392-3044
E-Mail: mpg@masterpoolsguild.com
Website: masterpoolsguild.com
Members: 110 elite custom builders
Staff: 1

Personnel:
Executive Director: Dick Covert
   E-Mail: dick@masterpoolsguild.com

Historical Note:
MPG's mission is to Provide a forum for members to share building techniques, technology and creative design ideas in their continuous pursuit of building the world's finest pools.

Publications:
Member Builder; on-line

Membership List Available to Non-members

Material Handling Equipment Distributors Association *(1954)*
201 U.S. Hwy. 45
Vernon Hills, IL 60061-2398
Tel: (847) 680-3500 *Fax:* (847) 362-6989
E-Mail: connect@mheda.org
Website: mheda.org
Members: 600 companies
Staff: 9
Annual Budget: $2-5,000,000
Tax: 501(c)(6)

Personnel:
Executive Vice President: Liz Richards
   E-Mail: lrichards@mheda.org
Manager, Membership Services: Kathy Cotter
   E-Mail: kcotter@mheda.org
Manager, Education: Susan Freibrun
   E-Mail: sfreibrun@mheda.org
Coordinator, Networking and Communications: Rebecca Hein
   E-Mail: rhein@mheda.org
Manager, Marketing: Anna Mariae Kendall
   E-Mail: akendall@mheda.org
Coordinator, Membership Services: Joanne Piacenza
   E-Mail: jpiacenza@mheda.org
Manager, Finance: Shirley Robinson
   E-Mail: srobinson@mheda.org

Historical Note:
MHEDA's mission to improve the proficiency of the material handling equipment distributors and to be a resource to all industry stakeholders. Membership: $715- 3,905

(Distributor/Factory-Owned Branch /Manufacturer Representative); $1,215- 3,925 (Supplier/Associate).

Meetings/Conferences: Annual
Conference Chair: Susan Freibrun
2013 - Palm Desert, CA (JW Marriott Desert Springs Resort and Spa)/May 4 - 8
2014 - Orlando, FL (Loews Portofino Bay Resort)/May 3 - 7
Number of non-conference events/year: 2

Publications:
Membership Directory; annually; adv.
MHEDA Connection; semi-monthly; adv.
MHEDA Journal; quarterly

Material Handling Industry of America *(1945)*
8720 Red Oak Blvd.
Suite 201
Charlotte, NC 28217-3992
Tel: (704) 676-1190 *Fax:* (704) 676-1199
Website: mhia.org
Members: 800 companies
Staff: 30
Annual Budget: $5-10,000,000

Personnel:
Chief Executive Officer: George Prest
   E-Mail: gprest@mhia.org
Manager, Human Resource Services: Loretta Barter
   E-Mail: lbarter@mhia.org
Director, Meetings and Executive Assistant to Chief Executive Officer: Kay Clark
   E-Mail: vwheeler@mhia.org
Senior Vice President, Professional Development: Gary Forger
   E-Mail: gforger@mhia.org
Web Developer: Joey Holt
   E-Mail: jholt@mhia.org
Vice President, Finance: Michael Laurent
   E-Mail: mlaurent@mhia.org
Vice President, Marketing and Communications: Carol Miller
   E-Mail: cmiller@mhia.org
Director, Educational Services: Ray Niemeyer
   E-Mail: rniemeyer@mhia.org
Vice President, Academic and Technical: Mike Ogle
   E-Mail: mogle@mhia.org
Executive Vice President , Business Development and Operations: Jeff Woroniecki
   E-Mail: jworoniecki@mhia.org

Historical Note:
Formerly (1995) Material Handling Institute, and Material Handling Industry Association (2002). MHIA's mission is to deliver exceptional value to its member companies, their customers and other industry constituents in order to promote the growth and prosperity of their organizations and industry. Membership: $2,000/year (Company).

Continuing Education:
Certification Designation/s: CAMH, PCMH, CICMHE

Meetings/Conferences: Semi-Annual
Conference Chair: Kay Clark
2013 - Charlotte, NC (Charlotte Marriott City Center)/ April 7 - 10
2013 - Orlando, FL (Florida Hotel and Conference Center)/Sept. 30 - Oct. 3

Publications:
e-Mhove; monthly
On The Mhove; quarterly

Membership List Available to Non-members

Materials and Methods Standards Association *(1962)*
4125 LaPalma Ave.
Suite 250
Anaheim, CA 92807
Tel: (203) 393-0015 *Fax:* (713) 688-2448
Website: mmsa.ws
Members: 40 companies
Staff: 2
Annual Budget: $10-25,000

Personnel:
President: Jim Whitfield
Secretary and Treasurer: Steven Fine
   E-Mail: sbfine@laticrete.com

Historical Note:
MMSA was formerly incorporated as the Mortar Manufacturers Standards Association, became Methods and Materials Standards Association in 1977 and assumed its present name in 1984. Purpose is to establish standards

of quality and performance of materials and methods for installation and use in the ceramic tile and dimensional stone industries. Membership is composed of manufacturers of ceramic tile and its installation products. Membership: $500/year (Company).

Meetings/Conferences: Annual
Number of non-conference events/year: 1

Materials Handling and Management Society *(1947)*
8720 Red Oak Blvd.
Suite 201
Charlotte, NC 28217-3992
Tel: (704) 676-1190 *Fax:* (704) 676-1199
Website: mhia.org
Members: 1500 individuals
Staff: 10
Annual Budget: $50-100,000

Personnel:
Chief Executive Officer: George Prest
   E-Mail: gprest@mhia.org
Director, Sales: Greg Baer
   E-Mail: gbaer@mhia.org
Manager, Human Resources: Loretta Barter
   E-Mail: lbarter@mhia.org
Senior Vice President, Exhibitions: Tom Carbott
   E-Mail: tcarbott@mhia.org
Senior Vice President, Professional Development: Gary Forger
   E-Mail: gforger@mhia.org
Vice President, Finance: Michael Laurent
   E-Mail: mlaurent@mhia.org
Vice President, Marketing and Communications Services: Carol Miller
   E-Mail: cmiller@mhia.org
Membership Services Assistant: Cathy Moose
   E-Mail: cmoose@mhia.org
Vice President, Educational and Technical Services: Mike Ogle
   E-Mail: mogle@mhia.org
Executive Vice President, Business Development and Operations: Jeff Woroniecki
   E-Mail: jworoniecki@mhia.org

Historical Note:
Founded as the American Material Handling Society, it became the International Material Management Society in 1966 and assumed its present name in 1991. A professional society of individuals interested in advancing the theory and practice of the management and handling of all types of material. MHMS mission is to provide career development and recognition for material handling professionals. Membership: $2000/year.

Meetings/Conferences: Annual
Conference Chair: Tom Carbott
2013 - Chicago, IL (McCormick Place)/Jan. 21 - 24/ over 100 exhibitors
2014 - Atlanta, GA (Georgia World Congress Center)/ March 17 - 20/over 100 exhibitors

Publications:
DC Velocity Magazine; monthly; adv.
e-Mhove Newsletter; monthly; adv.

Materials Marketing Associates *(1963)*
106 Summerlea Rd.
C/O Chemroy Canada, Inc.
Brampton, ON L6T 4X3
Tel: (905) 789-0701 *Fax:* (905) 789-7170
E-Mail: email@mma4u.com
Website: mma4u.com
Members: 15 companies
Staff: 3
Annual Budget: $50-100,000

Personnel:
Vice President: John Graham
   E-Mail: j.graham@chemroy.ca

Historical Note:
MMA's mission is to exchange knowledge and operational expertise between member firms while developing opportunities to share resources, increase awareness and promote the value of regional independent distributors. Members are chemical distributors representing manufacturers marketing chemical raw material specialties to makers of coatings, inks, pharmaceuticals, adhesives, cosmetics, plastics, soaps, detergents, etc. Membership: $2000/year (Organization/Company).

Publications:
Membership Directory; on-line

Materials Properties Council (1966)
P.O. Box 1942
New York, NY 10156
Tel: (216) 658-3847 Fax: (216) 658-3854
E-Mail: mpc@forengineers.org
Website: foreng1.securesites.net/mpc
Members: 850 individuals and organizations
Staff: 3
Annual Budget: $250-500,000

Personnel:
Executive Director: Dr. Martin Prager PhD
E-Mail: mprager@forengineers.org

Historical Note:
Formerly (1986) it was The Metal Properties Council and an outgrowth of the ASTM-ASME Joint Committee on the Effect of Temperature on the Properties of Metals, MPC's mission is to serve as an international focus identifying major needs for reliable data on the engineering properties and performance of materials.

Materials Research Society (1973)
506 Keystone Dr.
Warrendale, PA 15086-7537
Tel: (724) 779-3003 Fax: (724) 779-8313
E-Mail: info@mrs.org
Website: mrs.org
Members: 15000 individuals
Staff: 40
Annual Budget: $10-25,000,000
Tax: 501(c)(3)

Personnel:
Executive Director: Todd Osman
E-Mail: osman@mrs.org
Director, Finance and Administration: J. Ardie (Butch) Dillen
E-Mail: dillen@mrs.org
Principal Development Editor: Elizabeth Fleischer
E-Mail: fleischer@mrs.org
Administrator, Payroll and Human Resources: Sandy Forrest
E-Mail: forrest@mrs.org
Technical Support Analyst: Frank Gordon
E-Mail: gordon@mrs.org
Contact, Membership Services and Order Processing: Elaine Gross
E-Mail: gross@mrs.org
Manager, Information Systems and Development: Jeff Hamidi
E-Mail: hamidi@mrs.org
Director, Meeting Activities: Patricia A. Hastings
E-Mail: hastings@mrs.org
Manager, Accounting and Operations: Gopi Kalavar
E-Mail: kalavar@mrs.org
Program Coordinator, Meetings: Paula Mahar
E-Mail: mahar@mrs.org
Manager, Marketing and Communications: Anita Miller
E-Mail: amiller@mrs.org
Director, Communications: Eileen Kiley Novak
E-Mail: enovak@mrs.org
Manager, Education and Outreach: Richard Souza
E-Mail: souza@mrs.org
Director, Membership Development: Sandra DeVincent Wolf

Historical Note:
MRS is an organization of materials researchers from academia, industry, and government that promotes communication for the advancement of interdisciplinary materials research to improve the quality of life. Members are individuals adopting a multi-disciplinary approach towards the problems of research on materials. Membership: $115 (Regular); $30 (Student/Unemployed/Retired).

Meetings/Conferences: Semi-Annual
Conference Chair: Patricia A. Hastings
2013 - San Francisco, CA (Moscone Center)/April 1 - 5
2013 - Boston, MA (Hynes Convention Center)/Dec. 1 - 6
2014 - San Francisco, CA/April 21 - 25
2014 - Boston, MA/Nov. 30 - Dec. 5
Number of non-conference events/year: 2

Publications:
Journal of Materials Research
Membership Directory; on-line
MRS Bulletin Energy Quarterly; quarterly
MRS Communications

Materials Technology Institute (1977)
1215 Fern Ridge Pkwy.
Suite 206
St. Louis, MO 63141-4405
Tel: (314) 576-7712 Fax: (314) 576-6078
E-Mail: mtiadmin@mti-global.org
Website: mti-global.org
Members: 56 companies
Staff: 11
Annual Budget: $1-2,000,000
Tax: 501(c)(6)

Personnel:
Director, Operations: Debby Ehret
E-Mail: dehret@mti-global.org

Historical Note:
The mission of MTI is to sponsor projects focused on both developing new technology and transferring existing knowledge to day-to-day practice. Practical, generic, nonproprietary studies are conducted on the selection, design, fabrication, testing, inspection, and performance of materials of construction used in the process industries. Each members investment in MTI is multiplied 10 to 15 times in terms of technical product output. Membership: Based on annual sales.

Publications:
Communications Newsletter; semi-annually; adv.
Membership Directory; on-line

Mathematical Association of America (1915)
1529 18th St. NW
Washington, DC 20036-1358
Tel: (202) 387-5200 Fax: (202) 265-2384
TollFree: (800) 741-9415
E-Mail: maahq@maa.org
Website: maa.org
Members:
500 institutions
22000 individuals
Staff: 43
Annual Budget: $25-50,000
Tax: 501(c)(3)

Personnel:
Executive Director: Michael Pearson
E-Mail: mpearson@maa.org
Assistant Director, Membership and Marketing: Carrie Adams
Director, Supporting Underrepresented Minorities Mathematical Achievement (SUMMA) Program: Bill Hawkins PhD
E-Mail: bhawkins@maa.org
Director, Publications and Communications: Ivars Peterson
E-Mail: ipeterson@maa.org
Director, Meetings and Facilities: Peter Smith
E-Mail: psmith@maa.org
Chief Financial Officer: Sharon L. Tryon
E-Mail: stryon@maa.org
Director, Information Technology: John Wyatt
E-Mail: jwyatt@maa.org

Historical Note:
MAA promotes the teaching of mathematics, especially on the collegiate level. A constituent member of the Conference Board of the Mathematical Sciences. Membership: $190-266 (Regular); $64-140 (Graduate Student); $95-171 (Retired); $64-140 (Unemployed).

Meetings/Conferences: Annual
Conference Chair: Peter Smith
2013 - San Diego, CA (San Diego Convention Center)/ Jan. 9 - 12/7200 attendees
2013 - Hartford, CT/Aug. 1 - 3
2014 - Baltimore, MD/Jan. 15 - 18
2014 - Portland, OR/Aug. 7 - 9
2015 - San Antonio, TX/Jan. 10 - 13
2015 - Washington, DC/Aug. 5 - 8
2016 - Seattle, WA/Jan. 6 - 9
2017 - Atlanta, GA/Jan. 4 - 7

Publications:
MAA FOCUS; bi-monthly
MAA Math Alert; monthly
Mathematics Magazine; on-line
The American Mathematical; monthly
The College Mathematics Journal; on-line

Membership List Available to Non-members

Meals on Wheels Association of America (1973)
203 S. Union St.
Alexandria, VA 22314-3355
Tel: (703) 548-5558 Fax: (703) 548-8024
E-Mail: mowaa@mowaa.org
Website: mowaa.org
Members: 1300 members
Staff: 22
Annual Budget: $10-25,000,000
Tax: 501(c)(3)

Personnel:
President and Chief Executive Officer: Enid A. Borden
E-Mail: enid@mowaa.org
Fiscal Officer: Elizabeth Z. Doyle
E-Mail: liz@mowaa.org
Vice President, Educational Programming: Magda Hageman-Apol
Vice President and General Counsel: Robert T. Herbolsheimer
Executive Vice President: Peggy Ingraham
E-Mail: peggy@mowaa.org
Chief Financial Officer: Tom Marullo
Assistant Vice President, Membership Services and Communications: Mary McNamara
Director, Membership Services: Emily Persson
Vice President and Chief Marketing Officer: Marley Rave
E-Mail: marley@mowaa.org
Chief Accountability Officer: Larry Tomayko

Historical Note:
MOWAA's mission is to provide national leadership to end senior hunger. Members are organizations providing meals, particularly to the elderly, disabled and homebound. Membership: $150 (Principal Member). Additional member dues are $50 and affiliate membership is free.

Meetings/Conferences: Annual
Number of non-conference events/year: 1

Publications:
Membership Directory; on-line
MOWAA News; monthly

Measurement, Control and Automation Association (1940)
P.O. Box 3698
Williamsburg, VA 23187-3698
Tel: (757) 258-3100 Fax: (757) 258-3100
E-Mail: mcaa@measure.org
Website: measure.org
Members: 120 companies
Staff: 5
Annual Budget: $250-500,000
Tax: 501(c)(6)

Personnel:
President: Cynthia A. Esher
E-Mail: esher@measure.org
Administrator, Revenue Services: Christine Cottingham
E-Mail: cottingham@measure.org
Manager, Membership Development: Michael R. Robertson
E-Mail: robertson@measure.org
Manager, Membership Services: Teresa L. Sebring
E-Mail: sebring@measure.org
Administrative Assistant: Tahitia Whitby
E-Mail: whitby@measure.org

Historical Note:
MCAA helps the management teams of process and factory automation product and solution providers run and grow successful businesses by offering timely, unique and highly specialized resources acquired from shared management benchmarks and strategies where proprietary company information is secure. MCAA disassociated from the SAMA Group of Associations in 1994. Membership is open to companies which provide (manufacturers and distributors) instrumentation, systems and software used in industrial process control, field measurement and factory automation, engineering firms and systems integrators and suppliers of services to such companies. Membership: $1,720-11,470 (Manufacturers); $7,990-14,820 (Corporate); $1,235-1,965 (Channel Partners); $1,000-2,655 (Consultants/Partners).

Meetings/Conferences: Annual
Conference Chair: Christine Cottingham
2013 - Las Vegas, NV (Monte Carlo Las Vegas Resort and Casino)/May 19 - 21

Publications:
Measuring Markets; quarterly; adv.
Processing magazine; on-line; adv.

Meat Importers Council of America (1962)
1910 Association Dr.
Terrace Level
Reston, VA 20191
Tel: (703) 522-1910 Fax: (703) 524-6039

Website: micausa.org
Members: 160 companies
Staff: 2
Annual Budget: $500-1,000,000

Personnel:
Executive Director and Secretary: Laurie I. Bryant
E-Mail: lauriebryant@micausa.org
Legal Counsel: Matthew T. McGrath
E-Mail: mmcgrath@brc-dc.com

Historical Note:
Formerly Meat Importers' Council, Inc. In 1969 the name of the Corporation was amended to the Meat Importers Council of America. MICA's mission is to advance the trade, commerce and interests of importers, exporters, foreign suppliers, end-users, and processors of fresh, frozen, cured, cooked, canned imported meats. Membership: $4,500 (Corporate); $3,500 (Major importers and End-users); $2,500 (Medium Importers and End-users); $2,000 (Small Importers and End-users); $1,250 (Exporters and Associations); $1,000 (Ancillary).

Meetings/Conferences: Annual

Publications:
MICA Newsletter

Meat Industry Suppliers Alliance (1948)
1451 Dolley Madison Blvd.
Suite 101
McLean, VA 22101-3850
Tel: (703) 761-2600 Fax: (703) 761-4334
Website: fpsa.org/meat-industry-suppliers-alliance-misa
Members: 30 companies
Staff: 2
Annual Budget: $100-250,000

Personnel:
Contact, Communications and Senior Advisor: George O. Melnykovich
E-Mail: drmel@fpsa.org

Historical Note:
Formerly (1981) known as Meat Industry Supply and Equipment Association. Absorbed the Meat Machinery Manufacturers Institute and the Food Machinery Service Institute in 1984. Merged with the Meat, Poultry and Seafood Council of the Food Processing Machinery Association and assumed its current name in 2003. A non-profit council of the Food Processing Suppliers Association (FPSA) that is dedicated to the missions and goals of its supplier members and the industries they serve. MISA is committed to advancing hygienic equipment design validation and machinery safety initiatives. Members are suppliers to the meat, poultry and seafood packing and processing industries.

Publications:
MISA e-Newsletter; on-line

Mechanical Association Railcar Technical Services (1901)
2146 Windsor Ave. SW
Roanoke, VA 24015
Tel: (540) 343-8991 Fax: (540) 343-2410
E-Mail: admin@marts-rail.org
Website: marts-rail.org
Members: 500 companies and individuals
Staff: 2
Annual Budget: Under $10,000
Tax: 501(c)(3)

Personnel:
Secretary and Treasurer: John Robertson
E-Mail: j.w.robertson@cox.net

Historical Note:
Founded as Chief Interchange Car Inspectors' and Car Foremen's Association, became the Railway Car Department Officers Association the same year, the Master Car Builders Association in 1926, Car Department Officers Association in 1928, and assumed its present name in 1999. MARTS' mission is to provide a forum for sharing railcar customer maintenance needs through new technology, practical experience and practices with the purpose to improve profitable industry share. Membership: $20 (Individual); $100 (Company).

Meetings/Conferences: Annual

Publications:
Membership Directory; annually

Mechanical Power Transmission Association (1933)
6724 Lone Oak Blvd.
Naples, FL 34109
Tel: (239) 514-3441 Fax: (239) 514-3470

Website: mpta.org
Members: 28 companies
Staff: 2
Annual Budget: $50-100,000
Tax: 501(c)(6)

Personnel:
Executive Director: Robert A. Reinfried
E-Mail: bob@mpta.org

Historical Note:
Formerly (1961) Multiple V-Belt Drive and Mechanical Power Transmission Association. MPTA's mission is to promote the manufacture and sale of mechanical power transmission equipment while increasing the public awareness and knowledge of such equipment. Membership: $250-3,850/year.

Meetings/Conferences:
2013 - Litchfield Park, AZ (The Wigwam Resort)/April 7 - 10

Mechanical Service Contractors of America (1971)
1385 Piccard Dr.
Rockville, MD 20850
Tel: (301) 869-5800 Fax: (301) 990-9690
TollFree: (800) 556-3653
Website: msca.org
Members: 1200 mechanical system contractor members
Staff: 24
Annual Budget: $10-25,000,000

Personnel:
Executive Director: Barbara A. Dolim
E-Mail: bdolim@mcaa.org
Contact, Conventions: Sobeida Orantes
E-Mail: saorantes@mcaa.org

Historical Note:
Formerly (1990) National Mechanical Equipment Services and Maintenance Bureau (SMB). A department of the Mechanical Contractors Association of America, MSCA promotes the interests of service contractors by acting as a clearinghouse for information and by providing liaison between the contractor and the UA. Members are employers of United Association of Journeymen and Apprentices of the Plumbing and Pipe Fitting Industry of the United States and Canada labor who are involved in service and maintenance work in the heating, ventilating, air conditioning and process piping industries.

Continuing Education:
Certification Designation/s: MSCA STAR, UA STAR

Meetings/Conferences: Annual
Conference Chair: Sobeida Orantes
Number of non-conference events/year: 1

Publications:
MSCA Dateline; monthly

Membership List Available to Non-members

Media Communications Association International (1970)
C/O MCA-I Madison Chapter
P.O. Box 5135
Madison, WI 53705-0135
Tel: (608) 836-0722 Fax: (888) 862-8150
TollFree: (888) 899-6224
Website: mca-i.org
Members: 3000 individuals
Staff: 2
Annual Budget: $100-250,000
Tax: 501(c)(6)

Personnel:
Executive Director: Connie Terwilliger
E-Mail: connie@voiceover-talent.com
Co-Executive Director: Lois Weiland
E-Mail: loiswei@aol.com

Historical Note:
Founded in 1968 as the National Industrial Television Association. Merged in 1973 with the Industrial Television Society to become the International Industrial Television Association. Became International Television Association in 1978 and assumed its current name in 2001. MCA-I provides opportunities for networking, forums for education and resources for information. Membership: $40-1,500 (Individual); $300-400 (Group).

Meetings/Conferences:
Conference Chair: Connie Terwilliger

Publications:
E-News; adv.
Membership Directory; on-line

Media Credit Association (1903)
919 Third Ave., 22nd Floor
New York, NY 10022
Tel: (212) 752-0055 Fax: (212) 888-4623
E-Mail: jmitchell@magazine.org
Members: 850 magazines
Staff: 3
Annual Budget: $100-250,000

Personnel:
Vice President: Vaughn Benjamin
Coordinator, Records: Janice Mitchell
E-Mail: jmitchell@magazine.org

Media Financial Management Association (1961)
550 W. Frontage Rd.
Suite 3600
Northfield, IL 60093
Tel: (847) 716-7000 Fax: (847) 716-7004
E-Mail: info@mediafinance.org
Website: mediafinance.org
Members: 1280 individuals
Staff: 8
Annual Budget: $1-2,000,000
Tax: 501(c)(6)

Personnel:
President and Chief Executive Officer: Mary M. Collins
E-Mail: mary.collins@mediafinance.org
Manager, Administration: Debi Borden
E-Mail: debi.borden@mediafinance.org
Sales Account Executive: Cindy Laser
E-Mail: claser@bccacredit.com
Manager, Membership Services and Sales: Arcelia Pimentel
E-Mail: arcelia.pimentel@mediafinance.org
Director, Operations: Jamie L. Smith
E-Mail: jamie.smith@mediafinance.org
Editor: Janet Stilson
E-Mail: jstilson@nyc.rr.com
Coordinator, Conferences and Financial Consultant: Charlie Warner
E-Mail: charlie.warner@mediafinance.org

Historical Note:
Formerly known as Broadcasting Cable Financial Management Association. Became the Broadcast Financial Management Association (1977) and Broadcast Cable Financial Management Association (1990). Adopted the present name in 2007. Combined with Interactive and Newsmedia Financial Executives in 2009. MFM's mission is to provide information, education, and networking opportunities assisting its members to efficiently manage credit risk and increase profitability. Membership: $195-395 (Industry) $195 (Academic); $220-445 (Associate); $100 (Retired/Student) $3,700-52,000 (Corporate).

Continuing Education:
Certification Designation/s: CPE

Meetings/Conferences:
Conference Chair: Charlie Warner
2013 - Ft. Lauderdale, FL (Atlantic Hotel)/Feb. 21 - 22
2013 - New Orleans, LA (The Roosevelt Hotel)/May 20 - 22
Number of non-conference events/year: 5

Publications:
Membership Directory; annually; adv.
MFM e-letter; on-line
Monthly Update; monthly
The Financial Manager; irregular; adv.

Media Rating Council (1964)
420 Lexington Ave.
Suite 343
New York, NY 10170
Tel: (212) 972-0300 Fax: (212) 972-2786
E-Mail: staff@mediaratingcouncil.org
Website: mediaratingcouncil.org
Members: 122 organizations
Staff: 4
Annual Budget: $1-2,000,000

Personnel:
Chief Executive Officer: George W. Ivie
E-Mail: givie@mediaratingcouncil.org

Historical Note:
Formerly (1983) Broadcast Rating Council and (1997) Electronic Media Rating Council. MRC was established by broadcast industry, trade groups and major networks to maintain industry confidence in the integrity of broadcast rating services. MRC's mission is to secure the media

industry and related users audience measurement that is valid, reliable, and effective. Conducts an accreditation system involving regular audits by professional CPA firms of all aspects of the operation of the independent companies which produce radio, TV, cable and print ratings.

Continuing Education:
Certification Designation/s: MEP

Medicaid Health Plans of America
1150 18th St. NW
Suite 1010
Washington, DC 20036
Tel: (202) 857-5720 Fax: (202) 857-5731
E-Mail: info@mhpa.org
Website: mhpa.org
Staff: 7
Annual Budget: $1-2,000,000

Personnel:
President and Chief Executive Officer: Thomas L. Johnson
Director, Membership Services and Development: Leanne Cardwell
Coordinator, Events and Membership Services: Thanh Duong
Manager, Marketing and Communications: Joe Reblando
Director, Finance and Administration: Terri Wallace

Historical Note:
The mission of MHPA is to develop and advance public policy that controls costs and stimulate access and delivery of quality health care to Medicaid members. Membership: $7,000-45,000/ Year.

Meetings/Conferences: Annual
Conference Chair: Thanh Duong

Publications:
Industry NewsBrief Newsletter; bi-weekly; adv.

Medical Device Manufacturers Association (1992)
1333 H St. NW
Suite 400 West
Washington, DC 20005
Tel: (202) 354-7171 Fax: (202) 349-7176
E-Mail: mdmainfo@medicaldevices.org
Website: medicaldevices.org
Members: 250 individuals
Staff: 7
Annual Budget: $2-5,000,000

Personnel:
President and Chief Executive Officer: Mark B. Leahey Esp.
    E-Mail: mleahey@medicaldevices.org
Vice President, Public Affairs: Brendan Benner
Director, Operations and Executive Assistant to the President: Sheri DeVinney
Vice President, Government Relations: Thomas C. Novelli
    E-Mail: tnovelli@medicaldevices.org
Administrative Assistant: Elliott Warren

Historical Note:
MDMA's mission is to promote public health and improve patient care through the advocacy of innovative, research-driven medical device technology. Represents manufacturers of medical devices, diagnostic products, and health care information systems. Membership: $500-4,460 (Active); $1,000-3,000 (Allied).

Meetings/Conferences: Annual
2013 - Washington, DC (JW Marriott Hotel - Washington)/May 21 - 23

Publications:
BioWorld Today; daily
MDMA Newsletter; monthly
MDMA Q Review; quarterly; adv.
MDMA Update; weekly
Medical Device and Diagnostic Industry; monthly
Medical Product Outsourcing
The Gray Sheet; weekly

Medical Fitness Association (1991)
1905 Huguenot Rd.
Suite 203
Richmond, VA 23235-8026
Tel: (804) 897-5701 Fax: (804) 897-5704
E-Mail: info@medicalfitness.org
Website: medicalfitness.org
Staff: 9
Annual Budget: $250-500,000
Tax: 501(c)(6)

Personnel:
Executive Director: Ken Germano
Director, Business Development: Jim Gallagher

E-Mail: jim.gallagher@medicalfitness.org
Director, Membership Services: Stephanie Marquart
Manager, Education: Abbe Voigt
    E-Mail: education@medicalfitness.org

Historical Note:
MFA's mission is to foster opportunities for the development and operational success of medically integrated fitness centers. Membership: $225 (Individual Professional); $575 (Physician); $1200 (Facility); $95 (Student); $3,500 (Patron); $8,500 (Preferred Patron).

Continuing Education:
Certification Designation/s: MFFC, WCC

Meetings/Conferences: Annual

Publications:
ACSM Health & Fitness Journal; bi-monthly; adv.
Benchmarks for Success; semi-annually
Membership Directory; on-line
MFA e-Newsletter; bi-monthly; adv.

Membership List Available to Non-members

Medical Imaging and Technology Alliance
1300 N. 17th St.
Suite 1752
Arlington, VA 22209
Tel: (703) 841-3200 Fax: (703) 841-3392
Website: medicalimaging.org
Staff: 3

Personnel:
Executive Director: Gail Rodriguez
    E-Mail: lmorris@medicalimaging.org
Manager, Administration and International Programs: Zach Helzer
    E-Mail: zhelzer@medicalimaging.org

Historical Note:
The Medical Imaging & Technology Alliance (MITA), a division of the National Electrical Manufacturers Association (NEMA). MITA's mission is to increase awareness and understanding of the value of medical imaging and Improve regulatory harmonization of the global market for medical imaging products. Membership: $1,000-$4000 (Industrial Suppliers); $500-$4000 (Associate Enterprises); $750-$3000 (WholeSale Trade);

Publications:
FierceMedicalImaging Newsletter; weekly

Medical Imaging Contrast Agent Associations (1999)
660 Pennsylvania Ave. SE
Suite 201
Washington, DC 20003
Tel: (202) 547-1831 Fax: (202) 547-4658
E-Mail: micaa@micaa.org
Website: micaa.org
Members: 6 Companies
Staff: 1
Annual Budget: $250-500,000

Personnel:
Contact: James D. Massie
    E-Mail: micaa@micaa.org

Historical Note:
Membership comprised of manufacturers and developers of contrast agents used in the fields of medicine and life sciences. Acts as a voice for the medical imaging industry and pursue appropriate reimbursement, regulation, and review of contrast agents.

Medical Library Association (1898)
65 E. Wacker Pl.
Suite 1900
Chicago, IL 60601-7246
Tel: (312) 419-9094 Fax: (312) 419-8950
E-Mail: info@mlahq.org
Website: mlanet.org
Members: 4000 health professionals
Staff: 16
Annual Budget: $250-500,000
Tax: 501(c)(3)

Personnel:
Executive Director: Carla J. Funk
    E-Mail: funk@mlahq.org
Director, Professional Development: Kathleen Combs
    E-Mail: mlapd1@mlahq.org
Director, Membership, Research and Information Systems: Kate E. Corcoran
    E-Mail: mlamis@mlahq.org
Coordinator, Membership Services: Tomi Gunn
    E-Mail: mlams2@mlahq.org

Director, Publications: Elizabeth Lund
    E-Mail: mlacom1@mlahq.org
Director, Financial and Administrative Services: Ray Naegele
    E-Mail: naegele@mlahq.org

Historical Note:
Formerly (1907) known as the Association of Medical Librarians and incorporated in Maryland in 1934. MLA provides lifelong educational opportunities, supports a knowledgebase of health information research, and works with a global network of partners to promote the importance of quality information for improved health to the health care community and the public. Membership: $195 (Regular); $295-695 (Institution); $130 (International/Introductory); $70 (Emeritus); $50 (Student); $120 (Affiliate).

Continuing Education:
Enrollment: 1000
Certification Designation/s: AHIP

Meetings/Conferences: Annual
2013 - Boston, MA (Sheraton Boston Hotel)/May 3 - 8
2014 - Chicago, IL/May 16 - 21
2015 - Austin, TX/May 15 - 20

Publications:
Journal of the MLA; quarterly; adv.
MLA News; monthly; adv.
MLA-FOCUS; bi-monthly

Membership List Available to Non-members

Medical Marketing Association (1965)
575 Market St., Suite 2125
San Francisco, CA 94105
Tel: (415) 927-5732 Fax: (415) 927-5734
TollFree: (800) 551-2173
E-Mail: mma@mmanet.org
Website: mmanet.org
Members: 1100 individuals
Staff: 1
Annual Budget: $500-1,000,000

Personnel:
Executive Director: Sheri Thomas

Historical Note:
MMA is a professional association comprised of over 1, 000 medical marketers from the pharmaceutical, device, diagnostic, and marketing/advertising industries. Membership: $199/year (individual).

Medical Mycological Society of the Americas (1966)
C/O Annette Fothergill
7703 Floyd Curl Dr.
San Antonio, TX 78229
Tel: (210) 567-6074 Fax: (210) 567-4076
E-Mail: info@mycologicalsociety.org
Website: mycologicalsociety.org
Members: 350 individuals
Staff: 1

Personnel:
Secretary, Treasurer and Technical Director: Annette W. Fothergill MA, MBA
    E-Mail: fothergill@uthscsa.edu

Historical Note:
MMSA seeks to provide recognition to medical mycology as a flourishing and distinct division of medical microbiology. Membership: $20/year.

Meetings/Conferences: Annual
Number of non-conference events/year: 1

Publications:
Membership Directory; on-line
MMSA Newsletter

Medical Transcription Industry Association (MTIA) (1993)
4230 Kiernan Ave.
Suite 130
Modesto, CA 95356
Tel: (209) 527-9620 Fax: (209) 527-9633
TollFree: (800) 543-6842
E-Mail: cdia@cdiaweb.org
Website: mtia.com
Members: 100 Companies
Staff: 2
Annual Budget: $500-1,000,000

Personnel:
President and Chief Executive Officer: Linda Yaniszewski
Treasurer: Maria Thomas-French

Historical Note:

CDIA, formerly known as Medical Transcription Industry Association (MTIA). CDIA's mission is to ensure content clarity of electronic patient information for physicians, patients and payers, by setting and promoting measurable process management standards for clinical documentation excellence. Membership: $10,000 (Gold), $5,000 (Silver), $2,000 (Bronze).

Meetings/Conferences:
Number of non-conference events/year: 1

Publications:
Member Directory; on-line

Membership List Available to Non-members

Medical-Dental-Hospital Business Associates
(1939)
350 Poplar Ave.
Elmhurst, IL 60126
Tel: (630) 941-8100 *Fax:* (630) 359-4274
E-Mail: info@mdhba.org
Website: mdhba.org
Members: 70 companies
Staff: 2
Annual Budget: $50-100,000

Personnel:
Executive Director: Michael J. Bandy
   E-Mail: mbandy@mdhba.org

Historical Note:
Founded as the Medical-Dental-Hospital Bureaus of America, assumed its current name in 1996. MDHBA's mission is to service association of select, quality accounts receivable management companies working together to provide educational programs and quality services for its members and the health care industry. Members are owners/general managers of collection bureaus, credit bureaus and accounts receivable management agencies. Membership: $650-1,025 /year.

Continuing Education:
Certification Designation/s: CHC, CPBE, CHBA, CPAS

Meetings/Conferences: Annual
Number of non-conference events/year: 1

Publications:
Membership Directory; on-line
News & Views; irregular

Medieval Academy of America *(1925)*
104 Mt. Auburn St.
Fifth Floor
Cambridge, MA 02138
Tel: (617) 491-1622 *Fax:* (617) 492-3303
E-Mail: info@themedievalacademy.org
Website: medievalacademy.org
Members:
1800 libraries and institutions
3900 individuals
Staff: 5
Annual Budget: $2-5,000,000
Tax: 501(c)(3)

Personnel:
Executive Director and Editor: Eileen Gardiner
   E-Mail: egardiner@themedievalacademy.org
Coordinator, Membership Services and Communications:
   Christopher Cole
   E-Mail: ccole@themedievalacademy.org

Historical Note:
MAA's mission is to support research, publication and teaching in medieval art, archaeology, history, law, literature, music philosophy, religion, science, social and economic institutions, and all other aspects of the Middle ages. Member of American Council of Learned Societies. Members are scholars with an interest in the period 500-1500 AD. Membership: $30-275/year.

Continuing Education:
Certification Designation/s: SF, BBF

Meetings/Conferences: Annual
2013 - Knoxville, TN (University of Tennessee)/April 4 - 6
2014 - Los Angeles, CA (UCLA campus)/April 10 - 12
2015 - Notre Dame, Australia (University of Notre Dame)/March 12 - 14
2016 - Boston, MA/March 31 - April 2
Number of non-conference events/year: 3

Publications:
Medieval Academy News
Speculum; quarterly; adv.

Meeting Professionals International *(1972)*
3030 Lyndon B. Johnson Fwy.
Suite 1700

Dallas, TX 75234-2759
Tel: (972) 702-3000 *Fax:* (972) 702-3070
E-Mail: feedback@mpiweb.org
Website: mpiweb.org
Members:
24000 members
68 chapters
Staff: 72
Annual Budget: $10-25,000,000
Tax: 501(c)(3)

Personnel:
Editor-in-Chief: David R. Basler
   E-Mail: dbasler@mpiweb.org
Vice President, Events and Certification: Danya Casey
Chief Operating Officer and Interim Chief Staff Officer:
   Cynthia D'Aoust
Developer, Information Technology: Damon Davies
Director, Strategic Communications: Theresa Davis
   E-Mail: tdavis@mpiweb.org
Accountant: Ken Gilliam
Director, People and Performance: Diane M. Hawkins
   SPHR
   E-Mail: dhawkins@mpiweb.org
Vice President, Sales and Marketplace: Junior Tauvaa
   E-Mail: jtauvaa@mpiweb.org

Historical Note:
Formerly (1994) Meeting Planners International, MPI members manage meetings and related activities for associations, corporations, and educational institutions. Membership: $375 (Corporate Meeting Professional/ Association/Non Profit Meeting Professional/Government Meeting Professional/Planners); $195 (Faculty); $40 (Student); $500 (Suppliers).

Continuing Education:
Certification Designation/s: CMM, CMP

Meetings/Conferences: Annual

Publications:
Membership Directory; annually; adv.
One + Magazine; monthly
The Pulse; weekly

MEMA Information Services Council *(1972)*
P.O. Box 13966
Research Triangle Park, NC 27709-3966
Tel: (919) 549-4800 *Fax:* (919) 549-4824
E-Mail: info@miscouncil.org
Website: aftermarketsuppliers.org
Members: 50 companies
Staff: 3
Annual Budget: $10-25,000

Personnel:
President and Chief Operating Officer: Steve Handschuh
   E-Mail: shandschuh@mema.org
Senior Director, Marketing and Communications: Margaret
   Beck
   E-Mail: mbeck@mema.org
Vice President, Programs and Member Services: Chris
   Gardner
   E-Mail: cgardner@mema.org

Historical Note:
A peer group within the Motor and Equipment Manufacturers Association. Formerly the MEMA Information Services Council (MIS Council) and (2011) Mema Technology Council. ATC serves as a medium for industry interaction, education and idea exchange regarding matters of common interest to Information Technology (IT) and E-commerce professionals in the automotive aftermarket industry. Membership: $900-19,000 (Suppliers); $3,000 (Affiliate); $600-775 (Associate); $1,200 (Divisional/Product Line).

Meetings/Conferences: Annual

Publications:
AASA OAC Global Report; monthly
AASA Top 100; annually
e-News; weekly
MEMA Industry News; daily
OptiCat News; monthly
Replacement Rates Report; annually
Status Report; annually
Washington Insider; bi-weekly
World Motor Vehicle Market Report; annually

Men of Reform Judaism *(1923)*
633 Third Ave.
New York, NY 10017
Tel: (212) 650-4100 *Fax:* (212) 650-4189
TollFree: (800) 765-6200

E-Mail: Mrj@Urj.Org
Website: menrj.org
Staff: 3

Personnel:
Executive Director: Douglas E. Barden
Director Membership Services: Richard A. Fishkin
Treasurer: Bob Ingrum

Historical Note:
Formerly National Federation of Temple Brotherhoods is changed to Men of Reform Judaism. MRJ's mission is to Promote the establishment of affiliated brotherhoods and other local organized men's groups in congregations affiliated with URJ and Stimulate men's fellowship, interest in Jewish worship, Jewish studies, tikkun olam, and service to the congregation, Jewish Community and the Community at large.

Meetings/Conferences:
2013 - Ft. Lauderdale, FL (Ft Lauderdale Westin Beach Resort)/June 27 - 30

Publications:
Achim
Newsletter; monthly

Mental Health America *(1909)*
2000 N. Beauregard St.
Sixth Floor
Alexandria, VA 22311
Tel: (703) 684-7722 *Fax:* (703) 684-5968
TollFree: (800) 969-6642
Website: nmha.org
Members: 1300 individuals and affiliates
Staff: 29
Annual Budget: $2-5,000,000
Tax: 501(c)(3)

Personnel:
President and Chief Executive Officer: Wayne Lindstrom
Senior Director, Government Affairs: Julio Abreu
   E-Mail: jabreu@nmha.org
Director, Public Education: Erica Ahmed MA, MS
   E-Mail: eahmed@mentalhealthamerica.net
Vice President, Finance and Human Resources: Julie
   Nicholson Burke
   E-Mail: jburke@mentalhealthamerica.net
Pro Bono General Counsel: Joseph N. de Raismes III JD
   E-Mail: jderaismes@mentalhealthamerica.net
Senior Vice President, Operations: Dianne Felton
   E-Mail: dfelton@mentalhealthamerica.net
Vice President, Affiliate Services: Kate Gaston
   E-Mail: kgaston@mentalhealthamerica.net
Senior Director, Office Services and Meeting Planning:
   Michael King
   E-Mail: mking@mentalhealthamerica.net
Associate, Publication Sales and Office Services:
   Antionette Means
   E-Mail: ameans@mentalhealthamerica.net
Manager, Resource Development: Taylor Rhodes
   E-Mail: trhodes@mentalhealthamerica.net
Senior Director, Media Relations: Steve Vetzner
   E-Mail: svetzner@mentalhealthamerica.net

Historical Note:
Formed by the merger of the National Committee for Mental Hygiene, the National Mental Health Foundation and the Psychiatric Foundation and formerly (1978) the National Association for Mental Health and (1980) the National Mental Health Association, assumed its present name in 2006. MHA is dedicated to promote mental health, preventing mental and substance use conditions and achieving victory over mental illnesses and addictions through advocacy, education, research and service. Membership: $50 (Individual); $75 (Family); $150 (Organizational).

Meetings/Conferences: Annual
Conference Chair: Michael King
Number of non-conference events/year: 1

Publications:
Bell; quarterly
Legislative Alert

Messenger Courier Association of the Americas
(1987)
750 National Press Building
529 14th St. NW
Washington, DC 20045
Tel: (202) 591-2460 *Fax:* (202) 223-9741
E-Mail: info@mcaa.com
Website: mcaa.com
Members: 400 companies
Staff: 7

Annual Budget: $1-2,000,000
Tax: 501(c)(6)

Personnel:
Executive Director: Robert DeCaprio
E-Mail: bdecaprio@mcaa.com
Director, Meetings: Linda Arcangeli-Story
E-Mail: larcangeli@mcaa.com
Coordinator, Membership: Mary Donovan
Staff Coordinator: Tara McLaughlin
E-Mail: tmclaughlin@mcaa.com
Media Contact: Andrea Obston
E-Mail: aobston@aomc.com
Director, Government Affairs: Shawn J. Swearingen

Historical Note:
MCAA's mission is to promote and advance the common interests of those engaged in the delivery and logistics industry worldwide through education and advocacy. Membership:$ 820-9,310(Regular); $600 (Affiliate); $500 (International); $150(Shipper).

Meetings/Conferences: Semi-Annual
Conference Chair: Linda Arcangeli-Story
2013 - New Orleans, LA (Sheraton Hotel New Orleans)/May 8 - 11
2013 - Kansas City, MO (The Westin Crown Center)/ Oct. 10 - 12
2014 - Scottsdale, AZ (The Westin Kierland)/May 14 - 17
2014 - Austin, TX (Hyatt Regency Lost Pines Resort and Spa)/Sept. 18 - 20
2015 - Orlando, FL (The Swan and Dolphin)/May 6 - 9
2015 - Denver, CO (The Sheraton Downtown)/Oct. 1 - 3
Number of non-conference events/year: 1

Publications:
Government Affairs Newsletter
Member Directory
Time Critical Journal; quarterly; adv.

Metal Building Contractors and Erectors Association (2002)
P.O. Box 499
Shawnee, KS 66201
Tel: (913) 432-3800 Fax: (913) 432-3803
TollFree: (800) 866-6722
E-Mail: mbcea@kc.rr.com
Website: mbcea.org
Members: 325 companies
Staff: 12
Annual Budget: $50-100,000

Personnel:
Executive Director: Angela M. Walsh CAE
E-Mail: angela@mbcea.org

Historical Note:
Founded as Metal Building Dealers; became Systems Builders Association in 1984, and assumed its current name in 2002. MBCEA's mission is to support the professional advancement of metal building contractors, erectors, and its industry. Membership: $182-365 (Contractor); $247-495 (National/Regional Industry Member).

Publications:
MBCEA Newsletter; on-line
Membership Directory; on-line

Metal Building Manufacturers Association (1956)
1300 Sumner Ave.
Cleveland, OH 44115-2851
Tel: (216) 241-7333 Fax: (216) 241-0105
E-Mail: mbma@mbma.com
Website: mbma.com
Members:
96 companies
12000 Individuals
Staff: 6
Annual Budget: $1-2,000,000
Tax: 501(c)(6)

Personnel:
General Manager: Charles (Chuck) M. Stockinger
E-Mail: cstockinger@thomasamc.com
Director, Research and Engineering: Lee w Shoemaker PhD PE
E-Mail: mbma@mbma.com
Technical Engineer: Dan J. Walker P E

Historical Note:
Merged with Metal Roofing Systems Association in 1998. MBMA's mission is to enhance the collective interests of the Metal Building Systems industry and to promote the design

and construction of metal building systems in the low-rise, non-residential building marketplace. MBMA is a trade association representing building systems manufacturers, roofing systems manufacturers and suppliers to the industry.
Meetings/Conferences:
Number of non-conference events/year: 2

Publications:
IMPACT Newsletter; quarterly
Member Directory

Membership List Available to Non-members

Metal Construction Association (1983)
4700 W. Lake Ave.
Glenview, IL 60025
Tel: (847) 375-4718 Fax: (847) 375-6488
E-Mail: mca@metalconstruction.org
Website: metalconstruction.org
Members: 100 companies
Staff: 8
Annual Budget: $1-2,000,000

Personnel:
Executive Director: Mark Engle
E-Mail: mengle@connect2amc.com
Legal Counsel: John Kelly
Technical Affairs: Scott Kriner
E-Mail: skriner1@verizon.net
Manager, Meetings: Jodi Lehrfeld
Editor: June Pinyo
Manager, Marketing: Cathy Szmurlo
E-Mail: cszmurlo@connect2amc.com
Manager, Certification: Alice Taylor

Historical Note:
MCA's mission is to enhance the use of metal in construction. Initiatives include market development, educational programs, issue and product awareness campaigns, and publication of technical guidelines and specifications manuals. Membership: $ 20000-25000 (Manufacturer); $25,000 (Coil Coater/Metal Producer); $11,000 (Distributor/Equipment Manufacturer/Insulation Manufacturer/Accessories); $3000 (Associate/MCM F abricator/Fabricator/Publication); $5,000 (Affiliate); $8,000 (Onsite Rollformer & Regional Pre-Engineered Metal Buildings).

Continuing Education:
Certification Designation/s: MRCP
Meetings/Conferences:
Conference Chair: Jodi Lehrfeld
2013 - Rancho Mirage, CA (Rancho Las Palmas)/Jan. 27 - 29
2013 - Raleigh, NC (The Umstead)/June 24 - 26
2013 - Atlanta, GA/Oct. 1 - 3
2014 - Denver, CO/Oct. 1 - 3

Publications:
Membership Directory; on-line
Newsletter; semi-annually

Metal Findings Manufacturers Association (1930)
30-R Houghton St.
Providence, RI 02904
Tel: (401) 861-4667 Fax: (401) 861-0429
E-Mail: info@mfma.net
Website: mfma.net
Members: 60 companies
Staff: 1
Annual Budget: Under $10,000

Personnel:
Executive Officer: John Augustyn

Historical Note:
Makers of metal parts and fittings used in the assembly of jewelry. Has no paid staff or permanent address. Officers change every two years. Membership: $200/year (organization/company).

Metal Framing Manufacturers Association (1981)
401 N. Michigan Ave.
Chicago, IL 60611-4267
Tel: (312) 644-6610 Fax: (312) 321-4098
E-Mail: mfma@sba.com
Website: metalframingmfg.org
Members: 7 companies
Staff: 2
Annual Budget: $10-25,000

Personnel:
Executive Director: Mark Thorsby
Contact, Communications: Amanda Frjelich
E-Mail: mfma@sba.com

Historical Note:

MFMA focuses on the manufacture of ferrous and nonferrous metal framing (continuous slot metal channel systems) which consist of channels with in- turned lips and associated hardware for fastening to the channels (Strut) at random points. Membership: $1,600/year.

Publications:
Membershp Directory; on-line

Membership List Available to Non-members

Metal Injection Molding Association
105 College Rd., East
Princeton, NJ 08540
Tel: (609) 452-7700 Fax: (609) 987-8523
E-Mail: info@mpif.org
Website: mimaweb.org
Members: 26 companies
Staff: 1
Tax: 501(c)(6)

Personnel:
Administrator: James R. Dale
E-Mail: jdale@mpif.org

Historical Note:
A constituent association of the Metal Powder Industries Federation, the objectives of MIMA are to improve and promote the products of the MIM industry by promoting investigation, research, and interchange of ideas among members.

Meetings/Conferences: Annual
2013 - Orlando, FL (Hilton Orlando Lake Buena Vista)/ March 4 - 6
Number of non-conference events/year: 1

Publications:
MPIF Management Digest; monthly; adv.

Metal Powder Industries Federation (1944)
105 College Rd., East
Princeton, NJ 08540-6692
Tel: (609) 452-7700 Fax: (609) 987-8523
E-Mail: info@mpif.org
Website: mpif.org
Members: 275 companies
Staff: 15
Annual Budget: $2-5,000,000

Personnel:
Executive Director and Chief Executive Officer: C. James Trombino CAE
E-Mail: jtrombino@mpif.org
Director, Technical Services: James P. Adams
E-Mail: jadams@mpif.org
Vice President, Member and Industry Relations: James R. Dale
Systems Administrator: Stacy M. Kalokitis
E-Mail: skalokitis@mpif.org
Manager, Meetings and Conferences: Sandra E. Leatherman
E-Mail: sleatherman@mpif.org
Coordinator, Publications: Peggy LeBedz
E-Mail: plebedz@mpif.org
Director, Communications: Donni Magid
E-Mail: dmagid@mpif.org
Vice President, Finance and Administration: Jillaine K. Regan
E-Mail: jregan@mpif.org

Historical Note:
Represents the international trade, commercial and technological interests of the metal powder producing and consuming industries. The Federation consists of the following constituent associations: The Powder Metallurgy Parts Association, Metal Powder Producers Association, Powder Metallurgy Equipment Association, Refractory Metals Association, Isostatic Pressing Association and Metal Injection Molding Association. MPIF's Mission is to be the international trade association serving the global interests of the North American PM and contiguous industries. Membership: Varies from several hundred dollars to several thousand dollars depending upon the company's involvement in powder metallurgy.

Meetings/Conferences: Annual
Conference Chair: Sandra E. Leatherman
2013 - Chicago, IL/June 23 - 26
2013 - Chicago, IL (Chicago Sheraton Hotel and Towers)/June 24 - 27
2014 - Orlando, FL (Lake Buena Vista Resort Village and Spa)/May 18 - 22
Number of non-conference events/year: 2

Publications:
Advances in PM and Particulate Materials; annually
Newsbytes; weekly

Metal Powder Producers Association
105 College Rd. East
Princeton, NJ 08540-6692
Tel: (609) 452-7700 *Fax:* (609) 987-8523

Personnel:
Administrative Director: James Adams
    E-Mail: jadams@mpif.org

Metal Treating Institute (1933)
504 Osceola Ave.
Jacksonville, FL 32250
Tel: (904) 249-0448 *Fax:* (904) 249-0459
E-Mail: info@heattreatonline.com
Website: heattreatonline.com
Members: 500 companies
Staff: 18
Annual Budget: $500-1,000,000
Tax: 501(c)(6)

Personnel:
Chief Executive Officer: Tom Morrison
    E-Mail: tom@callmti.com
Director, Meetings, Communications and Member Relations:
    Niki Mann
    E-Mail: niki@callmti.com
Contact, Technical Questions: David Pye
    E-Mail: davidpye@pyemet.com
Chief Administrative Officer: Carla Quimby
    E-Mail: carla@callmti.com

Historical Note:
MTI's mission is to enhance the image and profitability of the heat treating industry. Represents the network of commercial heat treaters in the world. It also represents manufacturers with in-house heat treating operations and suppliers who serve both commercial and captive heat treaters. Membership: $1,200-2,500 (Commercial Heat Treater); $3,000 (Associate Member); $300 (International); $243.50 + $3 Per Employee in Heat Treating (Associate/ Captive Member).

Meetings/Conferences: Semi-Annual
Conference Chair: Niki Mann
2013 - Ft. Lauderdale, FL (Harbor Beach Marriott Resort and Spa)/April 18 - 20
2013 - Las Vegas, NV (Mirage)/Oct. 10 - 12
2014 - Nashville, TN (Renaissance Nashville Hotel)/ Oct. 7 - 8
2015 - Orlando, FL (Disney's Yacht Club Resort)/April 9 - 11
2016 - Nashville, TN (Renaissance Nashville Hotel)/ Oct. 4 - 5
Number of non-conference events/year: 2

Publications:
Heat Treat Magazine; quarterly; adv.
Hot Enews; weekly
Industry News; weekly
Membership Directory; on-line
MTI Insight; monthly
News Fax; bi-weekly

Metals Service Center Institute (1907)
4201 Euclid Ave.
Rolling Meadows, IL 60008
Tel: (847) 485-3000 *Fax:* (847) 485-3001
E-Mail: info@msci.org
Website: msci.org
Members: 400 companies
Staff: 13
Annual Budget: $5-10,000,000
Tax: 501(c)(6)

Personnel:
President and Chief Executive Officer: Bob Weidner
    E-Mail: bweidner@msci.org
Vice President, Marketing: Ann D'Orazio
    E-Mail: adorazio@msci.org
Vice President, Finance and Administration: Jonathan Kalkwarf
    E-Mail: jkalkwarf@msci.org
Vice President, Membership Services and Events: Rose Manfredini
    E-Mail: rmanfredini@msci.org
Vice President, Research and Technology: Chris Marti
    E-Mail: cmarti@msci.org
Vice President, Education: Ann Zastrow
    E-Mail: azastrow@msci.org

Historical Note:
Formerly (1907) American Iron and Steel and Heavy Hardware Association; (1932) American Steel and Heavy Hardware Association; (1959) American Steel Warehouse

Association, Inc. and then Steel Service Center Institute; assumed its current name in 2002. MSCI's mission is to promote the profitability and well-being of the metals industry and its role in the North American manufacturing value chain.

Meetings/Conferences:
Conference Chair: Rose Manfredini
2013 - Colorado Springs, CO (Broadmoor)/May 15 - 17
2013 - Schaumburg, IL (Marriott Renaissance Schaumburg Hotel and Convention Center)/Sept. 9 - 10
2013 - Schaumburg, IL (Renaissance Schaumburg Convention Center Hotel)/Sept. 10 - 11
2014 - Scottsdale, AZ (Fairmont Scottsdale Princess)/ May 4 - 6
Number of non-conference events/year: 5

Publications:
Advocacy Newsletter; monthly
Membership Directory; on-line

Metaphysical Society of America (1950)
Gonzaga University
A.D. Box 47, 502 E. Boone Ave.
Spokane, WA 99258
Tel: (509) 313-5885
Website: metaphysicalsociety.org
Members: 600 individuals
Staff: 2
Annual Budget: Under $10,000

Personnel:
President and Meeting Contact: May Sim
    E-Mail: msim@holycross.edu
Secretary and Treasurer: Brian G. Henning
    E-Mail: henning@gonzaga.edu

Historical Note:
MSA promotes the consideration of fundamental philosophical issues from a wide range of historical and contemporary perspectives. A member of the American Council of Learned Societies. Membership: $200 (Benefactor); $50 (Sustaining); $25 (Regular); Free (Student/Emeritus).

Meetings/Conferences: Annual
Conference Chair: May Sim
2013 - Worcester, MA (The College of the Holy Cross)/ April 11 - 13

Publications:
MSA-L

Membership List Available to Non-members

Methacrylate Producers Association (1987)
17260 Vannes Ct.
Hamilton, VA 20158-3163
Tel: (540) 751-2093 *Fax:* (540) 751-2094
Website: mpausa.org
Members: 4 manufacturers
Staff: 2
Annual Budget: $1-2,000,000
Tax: 501(c)(6)

Personnel:
Executive Director: Elizabeth "Betty" Hunt CAE
    E-Mail: e.hunt@comcast.net

Historical Note:
Members are manufacturers of basic methacrylate monomers. MPA serves to pool health, safety and environmental information; to sponsor testing when appropriate; and to communicate the industry's views on regulatory matters.

Methanol Institute (1989)
124 S. West St.
Suite 230
Alexandria, VA 22314
Tel: (703) 248-3636 *Fax:* (703) 248-3997
TollFree: (888) 275-0768
E-Mail: mi@methanol.org
Website: methanol.org
Members: 30 corporations
Staff: 4
Annual Budget: $1-2,000,000
Tax: 501(c)(6)

Personnel:
Executive Director Americas / Europe: Gregory A. Dolan
Manager, Government Affairs: Matthew Roberts
    E-Mail: mroberts@methanol.org

Historical Note:

Supports the use of clean reformulated gasoline and encourages the development of emerging methanol-powered fuel cell technology.

Meetings/Conferences: Annual

Publications:
Methanol in the News; on-line

Mexican-American Grocers Association (1977)
405 N. San Fernando Rd.
Los Angeles, CA 90031
Tel: (323) 227-1565 *Fax:* (323) 227-6935
E-Mail: maga727@sbcglobal.net
Website: maga.org
Members: 14000 individuals
Staff: 10
Annual Budget: $250-500,000
Tax: 501(c)(6)

Personnel:
Executive Vice President: Jack Sinclair

Historical Note:
MAGA's mission is to serve the grocery industry across the United States and Mexico. Members are food store owners, manufacturers, processors, brokers, distributors and service providers who cater to the Hispanic market in the United States. Membership: varies according to membership classification.

Continuing Education:
Certification Designation/s: MALDEF

Meetings/Conferences: Annual
Number of non-conference events/year: 1

Mexico-U.S. Business Committee, U.S. Council
1310 G St. NW, Suite 690
Washington, DC 20005-3000
Tel: (202) 639-0724 *Fax:* (202) 639-0794
E-Mail: smiller@as-coa.org
Website: counciloftheamericas.org
Staff: 1

Personnel:
Executive Director: Jennifer Fernandez
    E-Mail: smiller@as-coa.org

Historical Note:
A binational business organization dedicated to increasing trade and investment between Mexico and the United States.

MGMA-ACMPE (1926)
104 Inverness Ter., East
Englewood, CO 80112-5306
Tel: (303) 799-1111 *Fax:* (303) 643-4439
TollFree: (877) 275-6462
E-Mail: support@mgma.com
Website: mgma.com
Members: 22,500 members and 13,600 organizations
Staff: 145
Annual Budget: $25-50,000,000
Tax: 501(c)(6)

Personnel:
President and Chief Executive Officer: Susan L. Turney MD
Chief Information Officer: Gary C. Fox
    E-Mail: support@mgma.com
Vice President, Membership Services, Marketing and Communication: Dana Guilfoyle
Vice President, Human Resources: Marion Pfaff

Historical Note:
MGMA's mission is to improve the performance of medical group practice professionals and the organizations they represent. Membership: $460 (Regular); $35 (Student).

Continuing Education:
Enrollment: 250
Certification Designation/s: ACMPE, CMPE, FACMPE

Meetings/Conferences: Annual

Publications:
Inside Access; on-line
Member Directory; on-line
MGMA Connexion Magazine; adv.
MGMA e-Source; on-line; adv.
Staff Directory; on-line

Membership List Available to Non-members

Microanalysis Society (1968)
P.O. Box 502
Fairport, NY 14550-0502
Tel: (585) 586-4985
E-Mail: microbeam@williamthompsoncpa.com

Website: microbeamanalysis.org
Members: 1660 individuals and companies
Staff: 4
Annual Budget: $50-100,000

Personnel:
Society Accountant: William S. Thompson
    E-Mail: microbeam@williamthompsoncpa.com

Historical Note:
Formerly (1973) Electron Probe Analysis Society of America
and Microbeam Analysis Society. MAS's purpose is to
advance and diffuse knowledge concerning the principles
and applications of microbeam instruments or related
instrumentation, and to provide continuity, advanced
planning, and a financing mechanism for annual meetings.
Membership: $40 (Regular); $10 (Emeritus/Student).

Meetings/Conferences: Annual
2013 - Indianapolis, IN/Aug. 4 - 8
2014 - Hartford, CT/Aug. 3 - 7
2014 - Hartford, CT/Aug. 8 - 11
2015 - Portland, OR/Aug. 2 - 6
2016 - Columbus, OH/July 24 - 28

Publications:
Membership Directory; on-line
Microscopy and Microanalysis

Microscopy Society of America (1942)
12100 Sunset Hills Rd.
Suite 130
Reston, VA 20190
Tel: (703) 234-4115 Fax: (703) 435-4390
TollFree: (800) 538-3672
E-Mail:
associationmanagement@microscopy.org
Website: microscopy.org
Members: 4000 individuals
Staff: 2
Annual Budget: $1-2,000,000
Tax: 501(c)(3)

Personnel:
Managing Director: Peter Doherty
    E-Mail: pdoherty@drohanmgmt.com
Manager, Meetings: Nicole Guy
    E-Mail: nicoleguy@conferencemanagers.com

Historical Note:
Formerly (1992) the Electron Microscopy Society of
America. Established as the Electron Microscope Society
of America at the Second National Chemical Exposition in
Chicago and incorporated in Delaware. MSA is dedicated
to the promotion and advancement of techniques and
applications of microscopy and microanalysis in all relevant
scientific disciplines. Membership: $60 (Regular-US); $78
(Regular-International), $20 (Student-US); $38 (Student-
International); $400 (Sustaining Member-US); $418
(Sustaining Member-International).

Continuing Education:
Certification Designation/s: CEMT

Meetings/Conferences: Annual
Conference Chair: Nicole Guy
2013 - Indianapolis, IN/Aug. 4 - 8
2014 - Hartford, CT/Aug. 3 - 7
2015 - Portland, OR/Aug. 3 - 7
2016 - Columbus, OH/July 25 - 28

Publications:
Membership Directory; on-line
Microscopy and Microanalysis
Microscopy Today; bi-monthly; adv.
MSA E-Newsletter; on-line

Middle East Librarians' Association (1972)
UCLA
P.O. Box 951575
Los Angeles, CA 90095-1575
Tel: (773) 702-8425 Fax: (773) 753-0569
Website: mela.us
Members: 250 individuals and institutions
Staff: 4
Annual Budget: Under $10,000
Tax: 501(c)(3)

Personnel:
President: David G. Hirsch
    E-Mail: dhirsch@library.ucla.edu
Secretary and Treasurer: William Kopycki
    E-Mail: secretary@mela.us

Historical Note:
MELA's mission is to facilitate communication among
members through meetings and publications and to improve
the quality of area librarianship through the development of
standards for the profession and education of Middle East

library specialists. Members are librarians and others who
support the study or dissemination of information about
the Middle East. Has no paid officers or full-time staff.
Membership: $30 (Individual/Institutional/Foreign); $600
(Lifetime).

Meetings/Conferences: Annual
2014 - Washington, DC (Washington Marriott)/Nov. 22
    - 25
2015 - Denver, CO (Sheraton Denver Downtown
    Hotel)/Nov. 21 - 24
2017 - Washington, DC (Washington Marriott)/Nov. 18
    - 21
Number of non-conference events/year: 4

Publications:
MELA Notes; annually; adv.

Middle East Studies Association of North America (1966)
University of Arizona
1219 N. Santa Rita Ave.
Tucson, AZ 85721
Tel: (520) 621-5850 Fax: (520) 626-9095
E-Mail: SBS-MESA@email.arizona.edu
Website: mesa.arizona.edu
Members: 3000 individuals
Staff: 6
Annual Budget: $500-1,000,000

Personnel:
Executive Director and Treasurer: Amy W. Newhall
    E-Mail: newhall@u.arizona.edu
Graduate Student Representative: Ziad M. Abu Rish
    E-Mail: ziadaburish@gmail.com
Editor, Newsletter and Coordinator, Film Fest: Nadia
Hlibka
    E-Mail: nhlibka@u.arizona.edu
Assistant Director and Meeting Planner: Mark J. Lowder
    E-Mail: mlowder@email.arizona.edu
Executive Assistant: Shirley Nellson
    E-Mail: snellson@email.arizona.edu
Manager, Membership Services: Sara L. Palmer
    E-Mail: palmers@email.arizona.edu

Historical Note:
Organized by a group of U. S. and Canadian scholars
concerned with the study of the Middle East, from Morocco
to Pakistan, Turkey to the Sudan. MESA is a non-political
association that fosters the study of the Middle East,
promotes high standards of scholarship and teaching,
and encourages public understanding of the region and its
peoples through programs, publications and services that
enhance education, further intellectual exchange, recognize
professional distinction, and defend academic freedom.
Membership: $65-210 (Full/Associate); $55 (Student); $70
(Retired); $500 (Institutional); $2,000 (Life Membership);
$25 (Joint).

Meetings/Conferences: Annual
Conference Chair: Mark J. Lowder
2013 - New Orleans, LA (Sheraton Hotel New
    Orleans)/Oct. 10 - 13
2014 - Washington, DC (Washington Marriott
    Wardman Park)/Nov. 22 - 25
2015 - Denver, CO (Sheraton Denver Downtown
    Hotel)/Nov. 21 - 24
2016 - Boston, MA (Boston Marriott Copley Place)/
    Nov. 17 - 20
2017 - Washington, DC (Washington Marriott
    Wardman Park)/Nov. 18 - 21
2018 - Antonio, TX (Grand Hyatt San Antonio)/Nov. 15
    - 18

Publications:
Annual Meeting Program; annually; adv.
International Journal of Middle East Studies (IJMES);
    quarterly
MESA Newsletter; quarterly; adv.
Review of Middle East Studies; semi-annually; adv.

Membership List Available to Non-members

MIDI Manufacturers Association (1984)
P.O. Box 3173
La Habra, CA 90632-3173
Tel: (714) 736-9774 Fax: (714) 736-9775
E-Mail: info@midi.org
Website: midi.org
Members: 80 companies
Staff: 1
Annual Budget: $50-100,000

Personnel:
President and Chief Executive Officer: Tom White

Historical Note:
MMA's mission is to insure interoperability of MIDI
products through an open standards process with
broad industry participation. Members are companies
involved in the design and manufacture of MIDI (Musical
Instrument Digital Interface) hardware or software and
the application of audio technology to a wide variety of
fields including stage and theater, performance, recording,
multimedia computing, film and broadcast. Establishes
MIDI specifications as an open standard. Membership:
$475-6000/year (Company, based on sales).

Meetings/Conferences: Annual

Publications:
Newsletter

Membership List Available to Non-members

Midwest Dairy Coalition
1301 Hancock Ave.
Alexandria, VA 22301
E-Mail: info@midwestdairycoalition.com
Website: midwestdairycoalition.com
Members: 11,000 Dairy Farmers
Staff: 1

Personnel:
Coordinator: Steve Etka
    E-Mail: steveetka@gmail.com

Historical Note:
A database and news site on issues and progress around the
Trans-Pacific Partnership (TPP) free trade agreeemnt.

Publications:
Membership Directory; on-line

Midwest Free Community Papers
P.O. Box 1350
Iowa City, IA 52244-1350
Tel: (319) 341-4352 Fax: (319) 341-4358
TollFree: (800) 248-4061
Website: mfcp.org
Members: 120 free papers
Staff: 3

Personnel:
Executive Director: Brian Gay
    E-Mail: brian@mfcp.org
Office Manager: Jori Hendon
    E-Mail: jori@mfcp.org
Treasurer: Robin Noth
    E-Mail: robin.noth@lee.net

Historical Note:
MFCP's mission is to improve member publications through
education, exchanging of ideas and information.

Meetings/Conferences: Semi-Annual

Publications:
Member Directory

Midwives Alliance of North America (1982)
611 Pennsylvania Ave. SE
Suite 1700
Washington, DC 20003-4303
Fax: (503) 523-4296
TollFree: (888) 923-6262
E-Mail: info@mana.org
Website: mana.org
Members: 1200 individuals
Staff: 6
Annual Budget: $250-500,000
Tax: 501(c)(3)

Personnel:
Executive Director: Geradine Simkins
    E-Mail: executivedirector@mana.org
Coordinator, Conferences: Camille Abbe
    E-Mail: conferencecoordinator@mana.org
Secretary: Sarita Bennett
    E-Mail: secretary@mana.org
Director, Administrative Section: Melissa Cheyney CPM,
LM, PhD
    E-Mail: research@mana.org
Press Officer: Jana Studelska
Editor: Tina Williams
    E-Mail: newsletter@mana.org

Historical Note:
MANA is a member of the International Confederation
of Midwives and participates in the North American
Registry of Midwives. MANA seeks to unify and strengthen
the profession of midwifery and to improve the quality
of health care for women, babies and communities
to expand communication and support among North
American midwives. Members are midwives and student

midwives, supportive healthcare providers in complementary professions, and consumers. Membership: $95-185 (Midwife-Voting); $55 (Student/Affiliate/Apprentice).

Continuing Education:
Certification Designation/s: CPM

Meetings/Conferences: Annual
Conference Chair: Camille Abbe
2013 - Nashua, NH (Holiday Inn)/March 1 - 3
Number of non-conference events/year: 6

Publications:
MANA News; quarterly

Military Chaplains Association of the U.S. (1925)
P.O. Box 7056
Arlington, VA 22207
Tel: (703) 533-5890 *Fax:* (703) 533-5890
E-Mail: chaplains@mca-usa.org
Website: mca-usa.org
Staff: 1
Annual Budget: $100-250,000
Tax: 501(c)(3)

Personnel:
Executive Director: Chaplain Robert Certain
E-Mail: chaplains@mca-usa.org

Historical Note:
A professional support and Veterans Service Organization. Dedicated to the religious freedom and spiritual welfare of Armed Services members, Veterans, their families, and their survivors. Membership: $25 (new regular/associate); $50 (renewal per year); $400-600 (life/associate life depending on age).

Publications:
The Military Chaplain; adv.

Military Chaplains Association of the United States (1925)
P.O. Box 7056
Arlington, VA 22207-7056
Tel: (703) 533-5890
E-Mail: chaplains@mca-usa.org
Website: mca-usa.org
Members: 1875 individuals
Staff: 1
Annual Budget: $100-250,000
Tax: 501(c)(3)

Personnel:
Executive Director: Gary R. Pollitt CHC, USN

Historical Note:
Formerly (1925) known as the Army Chaplains Association. In 1940 known as the Army and Navy Chaplains Association and the present name was adopted in 1948. MCA's purpose is dedicated to the religious freedom and spiritual welfare of armed services members, veterans, their families and survivors. Membership: $25 (Introductory); $50 (Regular/Associate); $400- 600 (Life/Associate Life).

Publications:
Membership Directory; on-line

Military Impacted Schools Association (1986)
19650 Chandler St.
Gretna, NE 68028
Tel: (402) 293-4005 *Fax:* (402) 291-7982
TollFree: (800) 291-6472
E-Mail: cbellevue@aol.com
Website: militaryimpactedschoolsassociation.org
Members: 55 school districts
Staff: 2
Annual Budget: $2-5,000,000

Personnel:
Chief Executive Director: John Deegan
Executive Director: Kyle Fairbairn
E-Mail: kykef@hotmail.com

Historical Note:
MISA's mission is to serve school districts with a high concentration of military children. MISA is composed of school districts that serve children from military installations. Members are school districts with military personnel.

Meetings/Conferences: Annual
2013 - St. Louis, MO/June 23 - 25

Military Officers Association of America (MOAA) (1929)
201 N. Washington St.
Alexandria, VA 22314
Tel: (800) 234-6622 *Fax:* (703) 549-2311

TollFree: (800) 234-6622
E-Mail: msc@moaa.org
Website: moaa.org
Members: 370000 individuals
Staff: 95
Annual Budget: $50-100,000,000
Tax: 501(c)(19)

Personnel:
President: VADM Norbert R. Ryan Jr., USN (Ret.), VADM
E-Mail: norbryan@moaa.org
Director, Public Relations: Col. Marvin J. Harris USAF (Ret.)
E-Mail: marvh@moaa.com
Director, Contract Services and Marketing: Col. Michael Jordan USAF (Ret.)
Director, Print and Digital Media: COL Warren C. Lacy USA-Ret.
E-Mail: warrenl@moaa.org
Director, Council and Chapter Affairs: Col. Lee Lange USMC (Ret.)
E-Mail: leel@moaa.org
General Counsel and Corporate Secretary: MGEN Joseph G. Lynch USAF (Ret.)
E-Mail: JoeL@moaa.org
Chief Financial Officer: James O'Brien
E-Mail: jimo@moaa.org
Director, Member Service Center: Col. Ana R. Smythe USMC (Ret.)
E-Mail: anas@moaa.org
Director, Public Relations: Susan Stalder
Col. Steven P. Strobridge USAF (Ret.)
Executive Assistant to the President and Director, Meetings and Conferences: Suzanne Walker
Director, Information Technology: James "Rusty" Woolfolk

Historical Note:
Formerly known as the TROA, assumed its current name in 2003. MOAA serves by providing career transition assistance, improved member products, military benefits counseling, educational assistance to children of military families and strong involvement in military professionalism activities. Membership: $17 (Active); $34 (Regular); $31 (Auxiliary).

Meetings/Conferences: Annual
Conference Chair: Suzanne Walker
Number of non-conference events/year: 2

Publications:
Military Officer; monthly; adv.
MOAA Newsletter; daily; adv.

Membership List Available to Non-members

Military Operations Research Society (1966)
1703 N. Beauregard St.
Suite 450
Alexandria, VA 22311
Tel: (703) 933-9070 *Fax:* (703) 933-9066
E-Mail: morsoffice@mors.org
Website: mors.org
Members: 2000 individuals
Staff: 6
Annual Budget: $1-2,000,000

Personnel:
Chief Executive Officer: Susan K. Reardon
E-Mail: susan@mors.org
Director, Events: Jill Clark
E-Mail: Jill@mors.org
Director, Membership Services and Security: Eric Hamp
E-Mail: Eric@mors.org
Director, Marketing and Communications: Paul Laporte
E-Mail: Paul@mors.org
Coordinator, Administrative and Registration Services: Liz Marriott
E-Mail: Jenna@mors.org

Historical Note:
MORS's mission is to enhance the quality and effectiveness of military operations research. Membership: $75 (Member); $25 (Student); $100 (International Member); $35 (International Student).

Meetings/Conferences: Annual
Conference Chair: Jill Clark
2013 - West Point, NY (United States Military Academy)/June 17 - 20

Publications:
Membership Directory; on-line
Military Operations Research; annually; adv.
Phalanx; quarterly; adv.

Membership List Available to Non-members

Milking Machine Manufacturers Council (1946)
6737 W. Washington St., Suite 2400
C/O Association of Equipment Manufacturers
Milwaukee, WI 53214-5647
Tel: (414) 272-0943 *Fax:* (414) 272-1170
Website: aem.org/Groups/Groups/Group.asp?
 G = 54
Staff: 2

Personnel:
Vice President, Market Information, Technical and Member Services: Charlie O'Brien
Member Services Manager: Anita Sennett

Historical Note:
Formerly (1963) Dairy Equipment Department. Mission is to provide member manufacturers a forum to address issues effecting the dairy industry and the manufacture of milking equipment and related products. To promote the interests of member manufacturers regarding standards, market statistics and other subjects relating to the dairy industry.

Million Dollar Round Table (1927)
325 W. Touhy Ave.
Park Ridge, IL 60068-4265
Tel: (847) 692-6378 *Fax:* (847) 518-8921
E-Mail: info@mdrt.org
Website: mdrt.org
Members: 36000 individuals
Staff: 74
Annual Budget: $25-50,000,000

Personnel:
Chief Executive Officer: Stephen P. Stahr CAE
E-Mail: sstahr@mdrt.org
Contact, Senior Program Analyst: Vic Bianchini
E-Mail: vbianchini@mdrt.org
Director, Marketing and Communications: Pamela Brown
E-Mail: pbrown@mdrt.org
Director, Human Resources: Jacqueline F. Campa
E-Mail: jcampa@mdrt.org
Director, Membership Services: Thomas Ensign
E-Mail: tensign@mdrt.org
Executive Assistant: Gina Fadin
E-Mail: gfadin@mdrt.org
Director, Human Resources: Laura Good
E-Mail: lgood@mdrt.org
Editor: Kathryn F. Keuneke
E-Mail: kkeuneke@mdrt.org
Director, Meeting Services: Ray Kopcinski
E-Mail: rayk@mdrt.org
Accounting Manager: Laura McGrady
E-Mail: lmcgrady@mdrt.org
Manager, Marketing: Donald Noverini
E-Mail: dnoverini@mdrt.org
Director, Finance: Geraldine Smrcina

Historical Note:
MDRT's mission in to be a valued, member-driven, international network of leading insurance and investment financial services professionals/advisors who serve their clients by exemplary performance and the highest standards of ethics, knowledge, service and productivity. Membership: $450/year (Individual).

Meetings/Conferences: Annual
Conference Chair: Ray Kopcinski
2013 - Philadelphia, PA/June 9 - 13
2013 - Philadelphia, PA/June 9 - 12
2013 - Scottsdale, AZ/Oct. 9 - 12
2014 - Toronto, ON/June 8 - 12
Number of non-conference events/year: 2

Publications:
MDRT e-Newsletter; monthly
Membership Directory
Round the Table

Membership List Available to Non-members

Mine Safety Institute of America (1912)
319 Paintersville Rd.
Hunker, PA 15139
Tel: (724) 925-5150
E-Mail: sikora.lisa@dol.gov
Website: miningorganizations.org/index.php/ msia-
Members: 400 individuals
Staff: 3
Annual Budget: Under $10,000

Personnel:
President: Frank Linkous

Secretary and Treasurer: Gerald E. Davis
Assistant Secretary and Treasurer: Lisa Sikora
E-Mail: sikora.lisa@dol.gov

Historical Note:
Founded as Mine Inspectors' Institute of America; assumed its current name in 1998. MSIA promotes safety in the mines through the exchange of ideas, technology and experience. Members are state, provincial and federal mine inspectors in the United States and Canada. Has no paid officers or full-time staff.

Mineral Economics and Management Society
(1991)
1600 Arapahoe
Golden, CO 80401
Tel: (303) 273-3321 Fax: (303) 273-3314
E-Mail: registrar@minecon.com
Members: 200 individuals
Staff: 1
Annual Budget: $10-25,000

Personnel:
Registrar: Melody Francisco
E-Mail: mfrancis@mines.edu

Historical Note:
The purpose of the organization is to further the application of economics, management, finance, and policy analysis to the issues of the minerals and materials industries, including resource, energy, and environmental issues. Membership: $60/year (individual); $30/year (student).

Mineralogical Society of America (1919)
3635 Concorde Pkwy.
Suite 500
Chantilly, VA 20151-1110
Tel: (703) 652-9950 Fax: (703) 652-9951
E-Mail: business@minsocam.org
Website: minsocam.org
Members: 2500 individuals
Staff: 3
Annual Budget: $2-5,000,000
Tax: 501(c)(3)

Personnel:
Executive Director: Dr. J. Alexander Speer PhD
E-Mail: jaspeer@minsocam.org
Administrative Assistant: Michael Harris
E-Mail: mharris@minsocam.org
Coordinator, Accounts: Everett L. Johnson
E-Mail: ejohnson@minsocam.org

Historical Note:
MSA's mission is to encourage fundamental research about natural materials and support the teaching of mineralogical concepts and procedures. It also attempts to raise the scientific literacy of society with respect to issues involving mineralogy. It is a professional society of mineralogists, petrologists, geochemists, crystallographers and others interested in the study of minerals. Member society of the American Geological Institute. Membership: $70 (Regular); $220 (Sustaining); $10 (Student).

Meetings/Conferences: Annual
2013 - Denver, CO/Oct. 27 - 30
2014 - Johannesburg, South Africa (Sandton Convention Center)/Aug. 30 - Sept. 5
2014 - Vancouver, BC/Oct. 19 - 22

Publications:
American Mineralogist; bi-monthly
Elements; bi-monthly; adv.
GMR Journal
Membership Directory; on-line
Monographs and Textbooks; annually
Reviews in Mineralogy and Geochemistry; annually

Minerals, Metals and Materials Society (1871)
184 Thorn Hill Rd.
Warrendale, PA 15086-7514
Tel: (724) 776-9000 Fax: (724) 776-3770
TollFree: (800) 759-4867
E-Mail: tmsgeneral@tms.org
Website: tms.org
Members: 11000 individuals
Staff: 43
Annual Budget: $5-10,000,000

Personnel:
Executive Director: James J. Robinson
E-Mail: robinson@tms.org
Senior Manager, Membership and Marketing: Michael Bazzy
E-Mail: mbazzy@tms.org

Senior Manager, Editorial, Content and Communications: Maureen Byko
E-Mail: mbyko@tms.org
Director, Finance and Operations: Adrianne Carolla
E-Mail: acarolla@tms.org
Accountant: Peter DeLuca
E-Mail: deluca@tms.org
Awards and Recognition Specialist: Deborah Price
E-Mail: price@tms.org
Specialist, Accounting and Human Resources: Marleen Schrader
E-Mail: mschrader@tms.org
Senior Manager, Events, Programming, and Sales: Louise Wallach CMP
E-Mail: lwallach@tms.org
Manager, Information Technology: Paul Zappas
E-Mail: zappas@tms.org

Historical Note:
From 1957-1988, it was known as The Metallurgical Society. The Society was separately incorporated in 1985. TMS's mission is to promote the global science and engineering professions concerned with minerals, metals, and materials. Membership: $0-115/year; $1,725 (Life Membership).

Continuing Education:
Certification Designation/s: EMC

Meetings/Conferences: Annual
Conference Chair: Louise Wallach CMP
2013 - San Antonio, TX (The Henry B. Gonzalez Convention Center)/March 3 - 7/4000 attendees/ over 100 exhibitors
2013 - Salt Lake City, UT (Salt Lake Marriott Downtown at City Creek)/July 7 - 11
Number of non-conference events/year: 7

Publications:
JOM: THE MEMBER'S JOURNAL
The Journal of Electronic Materials (JEM); monthly
TMS e-News; monthly

Membership List Available to Non-members

Miniature Book Society (1983)
702 Rosecrans St.
San Diego, CA 92106-3013
TollFree: (877) 627-1983
Website: mbs.org
Members: 320 individuals and companies
Staff: 4
Annual Budget: $25-50,000
Tax: 501(c)(6)

Personnel:
President: Mark Palkovich
Editor: Joan Boring
E-Mail: joan_boring@yahoo.net
Coordinator, Exhibit Services: Jim Brogan
E-Mail: jbrogan1@verizon.net
Treasurer, Coordinator, Website and Membership Chair: Karen Nyman
E-Mail: karennyman2@cox.net

Historical Note:
MBS's mission is to provide a forum for the exchange of ideas and to serve as a clearing house for information about miniature books. Members are artisans, publishers of miniature-format books, curators and collectors. Has no paid officers or full-time staff. Membership: $40-55 (Personal); $50-65 (Business/Institutions).

Meetings/Conferences:
Conference Chair: Jim Brogan

Publications:
MBS Newsletter; quarterly
Membership Directory; annually

Membership List Available to Non-members

Mining and Metallurgical Society of America
(1908)
P.O. Box 810
Boulder, CO 80306-0810
Tel: (303) 444-6032
E-Mail: contactmmsa@mmsa.net
Website: mmsa.net
Members: 114 charter members
Staff: 3
Annual Budget: $100-250,000
Tax: 501(c)(6)

Personnel:
Executive Director: Betty L. Gibbs
President: Mark Jorgensen

Treasurer: Paul C. Jones

Historical Note:
MMSA seeks to promote and improve understanding and appreciation of the role of the U.S. Mining Industry. Membership: $100 (Regular); $150 (Qualified Professional/ Regular Qualified Professional); $50 (Senior).

Meetings/Conferences: Annual
2013 - Denver, CO/Feb. 24 - 25

Publications:
Newsletter; quarterly

Minor League Baseball (1901)
P.O. Box A
St. Petersburg, FL 33731
Tel: (727) 822-6937 Fax: (727) 821-5819
E-Mail: admin@minorleaguebaseball.com
Website: milb.com
Members: 20 minor leagues
Staff: 37

Personnel:
President and Chief Executive Officer: Pat O'Conner
Senior Assistant Director, Exhibition Services and Sponsorships: Noreen Branter
E-Mail: noreenbrantner@minorleaguebaseball.com
Director, Finance and Accounting: Sean Brown
E-Mail: sbrown@milb.com
Director, Information Technology: Rob Colamarino
E-Mail: robcolamarino@minorleaguebaseball.com
Executive Director, Communications: Steve Densa
E-Mail: stevedensa@minorleaguebaseball.com
Vice President, Business Development: Tina Gust
E-Mail: tina@milb.com
Vice President, Sales and Marketing: Rod Meadows
E-Mail: rodmeadows@minorleaguebaseball.com
Vice President, Legal Affairs: Scott Poley

Historical Note:
National Association of Professional Baseball Leagues, now known as Minor League Baseball. MiLB's goal is to provide up-to-date informative and comprehensive source of Minor League Baseball information on the Web. Membership: $25 (Basic); $35 (Affiliate); $500 (Lifetime-basic); $700 (Lifetime-affiliate).

Meetings/Conferences: Annual
Conference Chair: Noreen Branter
2013 - Orlando, FL (Walt Disney World Swan And Dolphin)/Dec. 9 - 12/3000 attendees/over 100 exhibitors
Number of non-conference events/year: 6

Publications:
Baseball News; on-line; adv.
Minor League Baseball Information; annually; adv.

Missouri Fox Trotting Horse Breed Association
(1948)
P.O. Box 1027
Ava, MO 65608
Tel: (417) 683-2468 Fax: (417) 683-6144
E-Mail: foxtrot@mfthba.com
Website: mfthba.com
Members: 8000 individuals
Staff: 5
Annual Budget: $250-500,000

Personnel:
Events Coordinator and Show Director: Donna Watson
E-Mail: donnawatson@mfthba.com
Contact, Membership Services: Cathy Lansdown
E-Mail: cathylansdown@mfthba.com
Contact, Journal Advertising and Articles: Donna Nagel
E-Mail: journaleditor@mfthba.com

Historical Note:
MFTHBA seeks to promote the horse through membership participation in expositions, fairs, horse shows, trail rides and other venues. Members are owners and breeders of Missouri Fox Trotting horses. Membership: $40 (Regular/ Internationa); $50 (Corporate); $500 (Lifetime); $15 (Youth, 17 and under).

Meetings/Conferences:
Conference Chair: Donna Watson

Publications:
Fox Trotter Newsletter
MFTHBA Journal; monthly; adv.
Show Catalog; annually

Membership List Available to Non-members

Mobile Air Conditioning Society Worldwide
(1981)
P.O. Box 88

Lansdale, PA 19446
Tel: (215) 631-7020 *Fax:* (215) 631-7017
E-Mail: info@macsw.org
Website: macsw.org
Members: 1600 companies
Staff: 10
Annual Budget: $1-2,000,000
Tax: 501(c)(6)

Personnel:
President and Chief Operating Officer: Elvis L. Hoffpauir
    E-Mail: elvis@macsw.org
Vice President, Accounting and Human Resources: Lynn Fee
    E-Mail: lynn@macsw.org
Contact, Member Services: Kathy Huney
    E-Mail: kathy@macsw.org
Vice President, Sales and Marketing: Marion J. Posen
    E-Mail: marion@macsw.org
Manager, Events: Pam Smith
    E-Mail: pam@macsw.org
Editor: Jim Taylor
    E-Mail: jt@macsw.org

Historical Note:
MACS's mission is to provide training, education and compliance programs for the mobile air conditioning and heat transfer industry. Membership: $400 (Distribution); $700 (Manufacturer/Supplier); $200 (Service/Installer); $140 (Educational/Associate/Individual).

Continuing Education:
Certification Designation/s: MACS

Meetings/Conferences: Annual
Conference Chair: Pam Smith
2013 - Orlando, FL (Caribe Royale All Suite Hotel and Convention Center)/Feb. 7 - 9
2014 - New Orleans, LA (Sheraton New Orleans Hotel)/Jan. 16 - 18

Publications:
Action magazine
MACS Service Reports; monthly
Membership Directory; on-line

Membership List Available to Non-members

Mobile Marketing Association *(2000)*
P.O. Box 3963
Bellevue, WA 98009-3963
Tel: (425) 635-4600 *Fax:* (303) 499-0952
Website: mmaglobal.com.
Members: 700 member companies
Staff: 13
Annual Budget: $2-5,000,000

Personnel:
Chief Executive Officer: Greg Stuart
    E-Mail: greg.stuart@mmaglobal.com
Chief Financial Officer: Carol Basile
    E-Mail: carol.basile@mmaglobal.com

Historical Note:
Formerly Wireless Advertising Association (WAA). In 2003, the WAA and the European-based Wireless Marketing Association (WMA) joined to form Mobile Marketing Association. MMA's mission is to establish mobile as an indispensible part of the marketing mix. Members include agencies, advertisers, hand held device manufacturers, wireless operators and service providers, retailers, software and services providers, as well as any company focused on the potential of marketing via the mobile channel. Membership: $7500-25000 (Global); $2500-10000 (Regional); $1000 (Individual); $400-1000 (Academic)

Continuing Education:
Certification Designation/s: MMC

Publications:
International Journal of Mobile Marketing; bi-annually
Memberhip Directory; on-line
Mobile Messenger newsletter; monthly

Modern Greek Studies Association *(1968)*
P.O. Box 945
Brunswick, ME 04011
Tel: (207) 406-2567 *Fax:* (330) 672-4025
E-Mail: mgsa@kent.edu
Website: mgsa.org
Members: 400 individuals
Staff: 1
Annual Budget: $25-50,000
Tax: 501(c)(3)

Personnel:
Executive Director: Prof. S. Victor Papacosma
    E-Mail: spapacos@kent.edu

Historical Note:
MSGA is dedicated to the promotion of Modern Greek Studies in the United States and Canada and conversant internationally on all issues, historical and contemporary, which pertain to Greek matters. MGSA holds affiliation with American Council on the Teaching of Foreign Languages, American Historical Association, American Philological Association, International Studies Association, Modern Language Association. Membership: $60 (Regular); $30 (Student); $95 (Institutional); $750 (Life Member).

Meetings/Conferences: Biennial

Publications:
Bulletin of Modern Greek Studies; annually
Directory; on-line
The Journal of Modern Greek Studies; bi-annually

Membership List Available to Non-members

Modern Language Association *(1883)*
26 Broadway
Third Floor
New York, NY 10004-1789
Tel: (646) 576-5000 *Fax:* (646) 458-0030
Website: mla.org
Members: 30000 individuals
Staff: 122
Annual Budget: $10-25,000,000

Personnel:
Executive Director: Rosemary G. Feal
Associate Executive Director and Director, Publishing Operations: Judy Goulding
Director, Financial Operations: Amilde Hadden
Director, Marketing and Sales: Kathleen M. Hansen
Director, Convention Programs: Maribeth T. Kraus
    E-Mail: mkraus@mla.org
Director, Research and ADE: David E. Laurence
Manager, Membership and Customer Services: Leonard J. Moreton
    E-Mail: membership@mla.org
Manager, Information Technology Center: Kinglen L. Wang

Historical Note:
Incorporated in 1900. MLA strives to provide opportunities for its members to share their scholarly findings and teaching experiences with colleagues and to discuss trends in the academy. Members are college-level teachers of modern languages. Membership:$21-289/year.

Meetings/Conferences: Annual
Conference Chair: Maribeth T. Kraus
2013 - Boston, MA/Jan. 3 - 6/11-25 exhibitors
2014 - Chicago, IL/Jan. 9 - 12
Number of non-conference events/year: 1

Publications:
JIL
MLA International Bibliography; annually
MLA Newsletter; on-line
PMLA; quarterly; adv.
Profession; annually

Modular Building Institute *(1983)*
944 Glenwood Stn. Ln.
Suite 204
Charlottesville, VA 22901-1480
Tel: (434) 296-3288 *Fax:* (434) 296-3361
TollFree: (888) 811-3288
E-Mail: info@modular.org
Website: modular.org
Members: 210 individuals and 325 companies
Staff: 6
Annual Budget: $1-2,000,000
Tax: 501(c)(6)

Personnel:
Executive Director: Tom Hardiman CAE
    E-Mail: tom@modular.org
Director, Membership Services: Aileen Holland
    E-Mail: aileen@modular.org
Marketing Specialist and Graphic Designer: Joni Lane
    E-Mail: joni@modular.org
Manager, Communications: Erin Whitt
    E-Mail: erin@modular.org
Director, Operations: Steven Williams
    E-Mail: steven@modular.org

Historical Note:
MBI's mission to expand the use of offsite construction through construction practices, outreach and education to the construction community and customers. Members are manufacturers, contractors, and dealers in two distinct segments of the industry - permanent modular construction (PMC) and relocatable buildings (RB). Membership:

$1,000-4,500 (Associate); $1,000-15,000 (Dealer/Contractor/Manufacturer).

Continuing Education:
Certification Designation/s: AIA

Meetings/Conferences: Annual
Conference Chair: Steven Williams
2013 - Scottsdale, AZ (Westin Kierland Resort and Spa)/March 16 - 19

Publications:
E-link; bi-weekly
Member Connection; quarterly; adv.
Membership Directory; on-line; adv.

Modular Building Systems Council *(1942)*
1201 15th St. NW
Washington, DC 20005
Tel: (202) 266-8200 *Fax:* (202) 266-8559
TollFree: (800) 368-5242
Website: arcat.com/arcatcos/cos37/arc37423.html
Staff: 2
Annual Budget: $100-250,000

Personnel:
President and Chief Executive Officer: Gerald M. Howard
Vice President, Media and Publications: Donna Reichle
    E-Mail: dreichle@nahb.org

Historical Note:
A division of the Building Systems Councils of the National Association of Home Builders. MBSC aims to guide the way in increasing awareness of the inherent quality of modular home building. Membership: $540-2,100/year (Based on Annual Sales Volume).

Publications:
Building Women Magazine; quarterly; adv.
Education Insider; quarterly
Eye on the Economy; bi-weekly
Land Development Magazine; quarterly; adv.
Membership Directory; on-line
NAHB HouseKeys; quarterly
ReNews; monthly; adv.
Subscribe to Sales + Marketing Ideas (SMI) Magazine; bi-monthly; adv.
Systems-Built Advantage; bi-monthly
Washington Hotline; monthly

Membership List Available to Non-members

Mohair Council of America *(1966)*
233 W. Twohig Ave.
San Angelo, TX 76903
Tel: (325) 655-3161 *Fax:* (325) 655-4761
TollFree: (800) 583-3161
E-Mail: mohair@mohairusa.com
Website: mohairusa.com
Members: 10500 individuals
Staff: 3
Annual Budget: $100-250,000
Tax: 501(c)(6)

Personnel:
Executive Director: Judy Hyde
Contact, Accounting and Finance: Debbie Carr
    E-Mail: debbie@mohairusa.com
Contact, Bookkeeping Services: Natasha Wahoski-Hufford

Historical Note:
MCA members are Angora goat breeders.

Money Management Institute *(1997)*
1737 H St. NW
Fifth Floor
Washington, DC 20006
Tel: (202) 822-4949 *Fax:* (202) 822-5188
E-Mail: info@mminst.org
Website: moneyinstitute.com
Members: 65 organizations
Staff: 9
Annual Budget: $2-5,000,000

Personnel:
President: Christopher L. Davis
    E-Mail: cdavis@mminst.org
Director, Special Events and Marketing: Elizabeth Bontrager
    E-Mail: ebontrager@mminst.org
Vice President, Industry Operations: Gary Jones
    E-Mail: gjones@mminst.org
Vice President, Membership Development: Arlen Oransky
    E-Mail: aoransky@mminst.org

Vice President, Administration: Laura Payne
  E-Mail: lpayne@mminst.org

Historical Note:
Formerly Forum for Investor Advice and merged into the Money Management Institute (MMI) on October 18, 2007, the Money Management Institute (MMI) is the national organization for the managed account solutions industry, representing portfolio manager firms and sponsors of investment consulting programs. Membership comprises firms that offer comprehensive financial consulting services to individual investors, foundations, retirement plans and trusts.

Meetings/Conferences: Annual
Conference Chair: Elizabeth Bontrager
Number of non-conference events/year: 2

Publications:
Member Directory; on-line

Monorail Manufacturers Association (1933)
8720 Red Oak Blvd.
Suite 201
Charlotte, NC 28217-3992
Tel: (704) 676-1190 *Fax:* (704) 676-1199
Website: mhia.org/industrygroups/mma
Members: 16 companies
Staff: 5

Personnel:
President: Brian Reh
Managing Director: Laura E. Stuber
  E-Mail: hvandiver@mhia.org

Historical Note:
The Monorail Manufacturers Association, Inc is an independent incorporated trade association affiliated with the Material Handling Industry. MMA's mission is to deliver real value to members, channel partners, consumers, and users by driving demand for products and services and delivering education and professional development programs. Membership: $2,500/year.

Continuing Education:
Certification Designation/s: MMA-C

Montadale Sheep Breeders Association (1945)
3321 Piney Creek Dr.
Elkhorn, NE 68022-4422
Tel: (402) 884-7555 *Fax:* (402) 763-2252
E-Mail: info@montadale.com
Website: montadales.com
Members: 300 individuals
Staff: 2
Annual Budget: Under $10,000

Personnel:
Executive Secretary: Mildred E. Moore

Historical Note:
Members are breeders and fanciers of Montadale sheep. Membership: $20-30 (Senior); $10-15 (Junior); $35 (Booster).

Publications:
Breed Directory; on-line
Montadale Mover

Monument Builders of North America (1906)
C/O Murphy Granite Carving
320 Maple Ave. SE, P.O. Box 40
Richmond, MN 56368
Tel: (320) 597-3070 *Fax:* (320) 597-3080
TollFree: (800) 233-4472
E-Mail: info@monumentbuilders.org
Website: monumentbuilders.org
Members: 840 companies
Staff: 7
Annual Budget: $500-1,000,000

Personnel:
President: Donald (Don) B. Calhoun
  E-Mail: don@murphygranite.com

Historical Note:
Formed by a merger of the Monument Builders of America (formerly Memorial Craftsmen of America, founded in 1906) and the Canadian Granite and Marble Dealers. MBNA's purpose is to serve its members for the betterment of their customers and to safeguard the consumer. Members are manufacturers, retailers, wholesalers and suppliers of cemetery markers and monuments. Membership: $195 (Associate); $120 (Branch); $375 (Retailer/Division).

Continuing Education:
Certification Designation/s: CM

Meetings/Conferences: Annual
2013 - Cincinnati, OH/Feb. 8 - 10

Publications:

Membership Directory; on-line

Moroccan American Business Council
1085 Commonwealth Ave.
Suite 194
Boston, MA 02215
Tel: (508) 230-5985 *Fax:* (508) 230-9943
E-Mail: info@usa-morocco.org
Website: usa-morocco.org
Staff: 1
Tax: 501(c)(3)

Personnel:
Contact, Communication: Susan Saliba

Historical Note:
MABC's mission is to bring together, the Moroccan and American communities, provide educational, cultural, social and business services.

Publications:
MABC Newsletter

Mortgage Bankers Association of America (1914)
1717 Rhode Island Ave. NW
Suite 400
Washington, DC 20036-3023
Tel: (202) 557-2700 *Fax:* (202) 833-1305
E-Mail: info@mortgagebankers.org
Website: mbaa.org
Members: 2400 member companies
Staff: 135
Annual Budget: $50-100,000,000
Tax: 501(c)(6)

Personnel:
President and Chief Executive Officer: David H. Stevens
Chief Economist and Senior Vice President, Research and Economics: Jay Brinkmann PhD
  E-Mail: jbrinkmann@mortgagebankers.org
Senior Vice President, Conferences and Meetings: Marcia Davies
Vice President and Deputy, Membership, Marketing and Communications: Sarah Tinsley Demarest
  E-Mail: stinsley@mortgagebankers.org
Vice President, Public Policy: Josh Denney
  E-Mail: jdenney@mortgagebankers.org
Vice President, Financial Accounting and Public Policy: Jim Gross
  E-Mail: jgross@mortgagebankers.org
Vice President, Meetings and Conferences, Corporate Relations: Elaine Howard
Senior Vice President, Legislative and Political Affairs: William Killmer
  E-Mail: bkillmer@mortgagebankers.org
Senior Vice President, Chief Financial Officer: Angela Lazear
Vice President, Communications, Membership and Marketing: John T. Mechem
  E-Mail: jmechem@mortgagebankers.org
Vice President, Human Resources: Gene D. Neill SPHR
  E-Mail: gneill@mortgagebankers.org
Senior Vice President, Public Policy and Industry Relations: Steve O'Connor
  E-Mail: soconnor@mortgagebankers.org
Senior Vice President and General Counsel, Human Resources and Legal Affairs: Phyllis K. Slesinger
  E-Mail: pslesinger@mortgagebankers.org
Senior Vice President, Communications and Marketing: Barbera Van Allen
  E-Mail: barbara@vanallen.org

Historical Note:
Absorbed National Home Equity Mortgage Association in 2006. Formed to promote growth and excellence in the real estate finance industry, MBA seeks to create an environment that enables its members to invest in communities and achieve their business objectives through sound business practices. Members include mortgage companies, commercial banks, thrifts, life insurance companies, and other institutions. Membership: $2,750-11,000/year (Associate).

Meetings/Conferences: Annual
Conference Chair: Elaine Howard
2013 - San Diego, CA (Manchester Grand Hyatt San Diego)/Feb. 3 - 6
2013 - Dallas, TX (Gaylord Texan Hotel and Convention Center-Dallas)/Feb. 19 - 22
2013 - Hollywood, FL (Westin Diplomat Resort)/April 14 - 17
2013 - New York City, NY (New York Marriott Marquis)/May 5 - 8
2013 - Boca Raton, FL (Boca Raton Hotel)/May 19 - 22

2013 - Phoenix, AZ (Arizona Biltmore Resort and Spa)/ May 19 - 22

Publications:
MBA Commercial/Multifamily NewsLink; weekly
MBA NewsLink; daily
Membership Directory; on-line
Mortgage Banking Magazine; quarterly; adv.
Products & Services Online Catalog; annually

Mortgage Insurance Companies of America (1973)
1425 K St. NW
Suite 210
Washington, DC 20005
Tel: (202) 682-2683 *Fax:* (202) 842-9252
Website: privatemi.com
Members: 6 companies
Staff: 6
Annual Budget: $10-25,000,000
Tax: 501(c)(6)

Personnel:
Executive Vice President: Suzanne C. Hutchinson
Director, Legislative and Regulatory Relations: Susan B. Ironfield
Media Contact: Chris Robichaux
  E-Mail: chris@micadc.com
Editorial Contact: Gaye L. Torrance
  E-Mail: lgtorrance@torranceco.com

Historical Note:
MICA represents the private mortgage insurance industry and provides information on related legislative and regulatory issues, and strives to enhance understanding of the vital role PrivateMI plays in housing Americans.

Publications:
PrivateMI Perspective; quarterly

Motion Picture Association of America (MPAA) (1922)
1600 Eye St. NW
Washington, DC 20006
Tel: (202) 293-1966 *Fax:* (202) 296-7410
E-Mail: info@mpaa.com
Website: mpaa.org
Members: 8 companies
Staff: 247
Annual Budget: $25-50,000,000

Personnel:
Chairman and Chief Executive Officer: Hon. Christopher J. Dodd
Director, Strategic Communications: Kate Bedingfield
Senior Executive Vice President and Global General Counsel: Henry Hoberman
Vice President, Regulatory Affairs: Linda Kinney
Senior Executive Vice President Global Policy and External Affairs: Michael O'Leary
  E-Mail: moleary@mpaa.org
Senior Vice President and Associate General Counsel: Dan Robbins
Vice President, Senior Content Protection Counsel: Karen Thorland
  E-Mail: karen_thorland@mpaa.org

Historical Note:
MPAA strives to serve and advocate of the American motion picture, home video and television industries.

Motor and Equipment Manufacturers Association (1904)
Ten Laboratory Dr.
P.O. Box 13966
Research Triangle Park, NC 27709-3966
Tel: (919) 549-4800 *Fax:* (919) 549-4824
E-Mail: info@mema.org
Website: mema.org
Members: 700 companies
Staff: 70
Annual Budget: $25-50,000,000
Tax: 501(c)(6)

Personnel:
President and Chief Executive Officer: Robert Bob McKenna
  E-Mail: bmckenna@mema.org
Senior Director, Marketing and Communications: Margaret Beck
  E-Mail: mbeck@mema.org
Vice President, Secretary and Chief Financial Officer: Wendy Earp

E-Mail: wearp@mema.org
Vice President, Human Resources and Administration: Jo
  Anne Farr SPHR
  E-Mail: jfarr@mema.org
Senior Director, Market Research: Frank Hampshire
Senior Vice President, Government Affairs: Ann Wilson
  E-Mail: awilson@mema.org

Historical Note:
*MEMA serves as an association management service
for other associations and manufacturers of automotive
aftermarket and original equipment used on, in or for
the servicing of cars, trucks and buses. Membership:
$900-17,000/year, based on sales volume.*
Meetings/Conferences:
Number of non-conference events/year: 6

Publications:
Diesel Download; weekly
MEMA Industry News; daily
Washington Insider; bi-weekly

Motorcycle Industry Council, Inc. (1914)
Two Jenner St.
Suite 150
Irvine, CA 92618-3806
Tel: (949) 727-4211 *Fax:* (949) 727-3313
Website: mic.org
Members: 310 Manufacturers
Staff: 10
Annual Budget: $2-5,000,000
Tax: 501(c)(6)

Personnel:
President: Tim Buche
  E-Mail: tbuche@mic.org
Manager, Aftermarket Membership Services: David Kopf
  E-Mail: dkopf@mic.org
Executive Business Assistant: Wendy Larkin
  E-Mail: wlarkin@mic.org
Director, Communications: Sheryl Van der Luen
  E-Mail: svanderluen@mic.org
Senior Coordinator, Events: Mia MacDougall
  E-Mail: mmacdougall@mic.org
Senior Manager, Communications: Mike Mount
  E-Mail: mmount@mic.org
Manager, Membership Recruitment: Danielle Reaves
  E-Mail: dreaves@mic.org
Research Systems Administrator: Steve Smith
  E-Mail: ssmith@mic.org

Historical Note:
*Liaison with federal and state governments on behalf
of manufacturers and distributors of motorcycles and
motorcycle parts and accessories, and of some members of
allied trades.*
Meetings/Conferences:
Conference Chair: Mia MacDougall

Publications:
Membership Directory; on-line

Motorcycle Safety Foundation (1973)
Two Jenner St.
Suite 150
Irvine, CA 92618-3806
Tel: (949) 727-3227 *Fax:* (949) 727-4217
Website: online2.msf-usa.org/msf/Default.aspx
Members: 10 companies
Staff: 40
Annual Budget: $10-25,000,000
Tax: 501(c)(3)

Personnel:
President and Chief Executive Officer: Tim Buche

Historical Note:
*MSF's mission is to make motorcycling safer and more
enjoyable by ensuring access to lifelong quality education
and training for current and prospective riders and by
advocating a safer riding environment. Membership: Dues
are based on market share.*
Publications:
The Journal of Educational Research

Motorist Information and Services Association (1988)
1500 Liberty St. SE
Suite 150
Salem, OR 97302
Tel: (503) 373-0864 *Fax:* (503) 378-6282
E-Mail: info@misaonline.org
Website: misaonline.org
Members: 125 individuals

Staff: 1
Annual Budget: $25-50,000

Personnel:
Executive Director: Annie Von Domitz
  E-Mail: annie@oregontic.com

Historical Note:
*MISA purpose is to provide a forum for free and open
discussion of developments in motorist information
and services systems. Membership: $100 (Government
Agency/Employee); $125 (Individual); $250 (Business/
Association).*

Publications:
Membership Directory; on-line
Newsletter

Mountain Rescue Association (1959)
P.O. Box 880868
San Diego, CA 92168-0868
Tel: (858) 229-4295 *Fax:* (619) 374-7072
E-Mail: info@mra.org
Website: mra.org
Members:
2500 members
86 accredited units
Staff: 4
Annual Budget: $50-100,000
Tax: 501(c)(3)

Personnel:
Executive Secretary: Kayley Bell
  E-Mail: info@mra.org

Historical Note:
*MRA's mission is to save lives through rescue and
mountain safety education and to promote standards,
mutual aid response, research and education programs.
Membership: $150 (Regular/Associate, based on no.
of team members); $250-500 (Corporate, Summit
Club); $1,000 (Corporate, Patron); $2,000 (Corporate,
Benefactor).*

Meetings/Conferences: Annual

Publications:
Meridian Newsletter; quarterly
Team Newsletters

Mounted Breakers Manufacturers Bureau
6737 W. Washington St.
Suite 2400
Milwaukee, WI 53214-5647
Tel: (414) 272-0943 *Fax:* (414) 272-1170
E-Mail: aem@aem.org
Website: aem.org/Groups/Groups/Group.asp?
  G=56
Staff: 1

Personnel:
Senior Advisor: Ken Edwards
  E-Mail: kedwards@aem.org

Historical Note:
*MBMB's major focus has been the development, through
a technical subcommittee, of an AEM Tool Energy Rating
for hydraulic breakers. It is exploring interfacing issues with
excavator manufacturers and other issues, such as noise
abatement, safety labeling and statistical programs.*

Movement Disorder Society (1985)
555 E. Wells St.
Suite 1100
Milwaukee, WI 53202-3823
Tel: (414) 276-2145 *Fax:* (414) 276-3349
E-Mail: info@movementdisorders.org
Website: movementdisorders.org
Members: 2300 individuals
Staff: 5
Annual Budget: $5-10,000,000

Personnel:
Executive Director: Anne McGhiey CAE
  E-Mail: amcghiey@movementdisorders.org
Senior Manager, Membership and Communications:
  Elizabeth Laur
  E-Mail: elaur@movementdisorders.org
Manager, Meetings and Education: Jennifer Peterson
  E-Mail: jpeterson@movementdisorders.org
Associate Director, Meetings: Jenny Quebbeman
  E-Mail: jquebbeman@movementdisorders.org
Director, Education: Kirk Terry
  E-Mail: kterry@movementdisorders.org

Historical Note:
*MDS seeks to advance the neurological sciences
pertaining to Movement Disorders and to encourage*

research. Members are clinicians, scientists, and
other healthcare professionals who are interested in
Parkinson's disease, related neurodegenerative and
neurodevelopmental disorders, hyperkinetic movement
disorders and abnormalities in muscle tone and motor
control. Membership: $300 (Regular); $100-175 (Junior/
Health Professional); $10 (Student).*
Meetings/Conferences: Annual
Conference Chair: Jennifer Peterson

Publications:
MDS E-Newsletter; monthly
Membership Directory; annually
Movement Disorders; monthly; adv.
Moving Along; quarterly; adv.

Membership List Available to Non-members

MPA - The Association of Magazine Media (1987)
810 Seventh Ave.
24th Floor
New York, NY 10019
Tel: (212) 872-3700 *Fax:* (212) 888-4217
TollFree: (888) 567-3228
E-Mail: mpa@magazine.org
Website: magazine.org
Members: 220 companies
Staff: 36
Annual Budget: $10-25,000,000

Personnel:
President and Chief Executive Officer: Mary G. Berner
Senior Vice President, Systems and Technology: Myra
  Barcan
Director, Marketing: Patty Bogie
*Executive Vice President and General Manager, Finance and
  Administration:* Frank J. Costello
Director, Communications and Platforms: Cristina Dinozo
  E-Mail: cdinozo@magazine.org
Senior Vice President, Research: Wayne Eadie
  E-Mail: weadie@magazine.org
Program Coordinator, Publications: Nina Fortuna
  E-Mail: nfortuna@magazine.org
Director, Events: Sarah Hansen
  E-Mail: shansen@magazine.org
Chief Marketing and Digital Officer: Christopher
  Kevorkian
  E-Mail: ckevorkian@magazine.org
*Director, IMAG, Consumer Marketing, Membership and
  Education Services:* Suzette Kraemer
*Executive Vice President, Communications, Platforms and
  Events:* Howard Polskin
  E-Mail: mpa@magazine.org

Historical Note:
*Formerly the National Association of Periodical Publishers,
(1920) National Publishers Association, (1947) National
Association of Magazine Publishers, (1952) Magazine
Publishers Association, (1987) Magazine Publishers of
America. MPA is a non-profit organization representing
magazine media, print and digital. Membership: $2,750
(International- National only publisher/National-only non-
publisher); $3,250 (International-Multinational publisher);
$2,500-15,000 (Associate).*
Meetings/Conferences: Annual
Conference Chair: Sarah Hansen
Number of non-conference events/year: 6

Publications:
International Newsletter; weekly
Membership Directory; on-line
MPA Newsletter; on-line

MTM Association for Standards and Research (1951)
1111 E. Touhy Ave.
Suite 280
Des Plaines, IL 60018
Tel: (847) 299-1111 *Fax:* (847) 299-3509
E-Mail: lburns@mtm.org
Website: mtm.org
Members: 1000 individuals and 200 corporations
Staff: 4
Annual Budget: $250-500,000
Tax: 501(c)(3)

Personnel:
Executive Director: Dirk Rauglas
Administration Assistant: Lillian Burns

Historical Note:
*Mission is to be a good provider of management systems,
training, and services to the manufacturing, government,
and service industries that increases profitability for its
clients. Membership consists of industrial psychologists,*

industrial engineers, academicians and corporate members. Conducts research and training on the efficiency of human motion. Also known as Methods Time Measurement Association for Standards and Research. *Membership: $40/year (Individual); $750/year (Company).*

Mu Phi Epsilon (1903)
4705 N. Sonora Ave.
Suite 114
Fresno, CA 93722-3947
Tel: (559) 277-1898 *Fax:* (559) 277-2825
TollFree: (888) 259-1471
E-Mail: ExecutiveOffice@MuPhiEpsilon.org
Website: muphiepsilon.org
Members: 70000 individuals
Staff: 4
Annual Budget: $100-250,000

Personnel:
Fraternity President: Rosemary Ames
   E-Mail: president@muphiepsilon.org
International Executive Secretary and Treasurer: Gloria Debatin
   E-Mail: executiveoffice@muphiepsilon.org
International Editor: Melissa Eddy
   E-Mail: editor@muphiepsilon.org

Historical Note:
Mu Phi Epsilon's mission is to advance music in the community, nation, and throughout the world; to promote musicianship, scholarship, therapy, and education, with emphasis on service through music and to enhance loyalty to the Alma Mater and develop true bonds of friendship. Membership is open to music majors or minors enrolled in schools where chapters exist. Concert artists, teachers, composers and other music leaders are also included. Membership: $65/Year (Allied).

Meetings/Conferences: Annual

Publications:
The Triangle; quarterly

Mulch and Soil Council (1972)
10210 Leatherleaf Ct.
Manassas, VA 20111-4245
Tel: (703) 257-0111 *Fax:* (703) 257-0213
E-Mail: info@mulchandsoilcouncil.org
Website: mulchandsoilcouncil.org
Members: 104 companies
Staff: 5
Annual Budget: $250-500,000
Tax: 501(c)(6)

Personnel:
Executive Director: Robert C. LaGasse CAE
   E-Mail: execdir@mulchandsoilcouncil.org
Coordinator, Membership Services: Jennifer Gillette
   E-Mail: membership@mulchandsoilcouncil.org

Historical Note:
Formerly (1988) National Bark Producers Association and (2001) became National Bark and Soil Producers Association in 1988, the mission of MSC is to define quality products and promote a fair and open marketplace. Members are manufacturers of bark and soil products and industry suppliers. Membership: $900-15,000 (Regular); $1,500 (Affiliate); $1,000 (Associate); $500 (Foreign); $295 (Non-Profit).

Continuing Education:
Certification Designation/s: MSC

Meetings/Conferences: Annual
Number of non-conference events/year: 1

Publications:
News, Notes & Quotes Newsletter; monthly; adv.

Multi-Housing Laundry Association (1959)
1500 Sunday Dr.
Suite 102
Raleigh, NC 27607
Tel: (919) 861-5579 *Fax:* (919) 787-4916
TollFree: (800) 380-3652
E-Mail: nshore@mla-online.com
Website: mla-online.com
Members: 20 companies
Staff: 3
Annual Budget: $250-500,000
Tax: 501(c)(6)

Personnel:
Executive Director: Dave Feild
   E-Mail: dfeild@firstpointresources.com
General Counsel: Reid Chambers
   E-Mail: rchambers@sonosky.com
Contact, Membership Services: Steve Kerrigan

E-Mail: srk1953@aol.com

Historical Note:
Formerly (1982) National Association of Coin Laundry Equipment Operators. Members provide professional laundry services for the multi-housing industry. MLA's mission is to work for a favorable legislative and regulatory climate for the industry, facilitate the exchange of technical and business information among members, and demonstrate the value of the industry to target markets.

Meetings/Conferences: Annual

Publications:
MLA News; irregular

Multi-Level Marketing International Association (1985)
119 Stanford Ct.
Irvine, CA 92612
Tel: (949) 854-0484 *Fax:* (949) 854-7687
E-Mail: info@mlmia.com
Website: mlmia.com
Members: 5000 individuals
Staff: 2
Annual Budget: $250-500,000

Personnel:
CO-Founder, President Emeritus: Doris Wood

Historical Note:
MLMIA works to strengthen network marketing around the world while bringing professionalism and credibility to the industry. Members are companies which market their products and services directly to consumers through distributors, suppliers to the industry. Membership: $1,200-12,000 (Corporate, based on number of distributors); $600-1,000 (Support, based on industry billing); $60-90 (Distributor, based on number of people).

Meetings/Conferences:
Number of non-conference events/year: 1

Publications:
Corporate Directory; on-line

Membership List Available to Non-members

Municipal Waste Management Association (1982)
1620 Eye St. NW
Washington, DC 20006
Tel: (202) 293-7330 *Fax:* (202) 293-2352
Website: usmayors.org/mwma
Members: 200 local government organizations
Staff: 4
Annual Budget: $50-100,000

Personnel:
Managing Director: Jubi Headley
   E-Mail: jheadley@usmayors.org

Historical Note:
Formerly (1991) the National Resource Recovery Association. MWMA is the the environmental affiliate of The United States Conference of Mayors. MWMA's mission is to promote operational efficiencies, facilitates information, fosters innovation and promotes legislative advocacy around Superfund, Brownfields redevelopment, clean air, clean water and waste to energy regulations. Active members are local government organizations; associate members are from the private sector. Membership: $510-6,120 (Active, varies by population); $310-1,020 (Associate, varies by number of employees).

Publications:
Membership Directory; on-line
Municipal News Headlines; weekly
The Public Place; semi-annually

Musculoskeletal Tumor Society (1977)
P.O. Box 320062
Alexandria, VA 22320
Tel: (703) 548-2112 *Fax:* (703) 548-4882
E-Mail: info@msts.org
Website: msts.org
Members: 180 individuals
Staff: 2
Annual Budget: $500-1,000,000
Tax: 501(c)(3)

Personnel:
Executive Director: Barbara Rapp
Treasurer: Richard Terek
   E-Mail: richard_terek@brown.edu

Historical Note:
MSTS mission is to advance the science of orthopaedic oncology and to promote standards of patient care. It does this through excellence in education and research and through advocacy on behalf of patients and orthopaedic oncologists.

Meetings/Conferences: Annual

Publications:
MSTS Newsletter

Museum Education Roundtable (1969)
P.O. Box 15727
Washington, DC 20003
Tel: (202) 547-8378 *Fax:* (202) 547-8345
E-Mail: info@mer-online.org
Website: museumeducation.info
Members: 1000 individuals
Staff: 3
Annual Budget: $10-25,000
Tax: 501(c)(3)

Personnel:
President: Jill Orr
Treasurer: Matt Hill
Secretary: Carole Krucoff

Historical Note:
MER dedicated to promote the role of museums and other cultural institutions as primary resources for life-long learning. Members are museum educators, teachers, museums and schools. Membership: $40 (Individual); $120 (Institution); $30 (Retired/Student); $60 (Library); $1-99 (Donor-Contributor); $100-199 (Donor-Patron); $200-499 (Donor-Sponsor); $500 (Donor-Benefactor).

Meetings/Conferences:
Number of non-conference events/year: 1

Publications:
Journal of Museum Education; on-line

Museum Store Association (1955)
4100 E. Mississippi Ave.
Suite 800
Denver, CO 80246-3055
Tel: (303) 504-9223 *Fax:* (303) 504-9585
E-Mail: info@museumstoreassociation.org
Website: museumdistrict.com
Members: 3000 museums and companies
Staff: 12
Annual Budget: $1-2,000,000

Personnel:
Executive Director: Beverly Barsook
   E-Mail: bbarsook@museumstoreassociation.org
Coordinator, Conference and Expo Services: Jennifer Anderson
   E-Mail: janderson@msaweb.org
Communications Editor: Kathy Cisar
   E-Mail: kcisar@museumstoreassociation.org
Senior Manager, Membership and Program: Bridget Dummett
   E-Mail: bdummett@museumstoreassociation.org
Communications and Office Assistant: Sybil Faurer
   E-Mail: sfaurer@museumstoreassociation.org
Database Administrator: Adriana Herald
   E-Mail: aherald@museumstoreassociation.org
Senior Manager, Communications: Stephanie Peters
   E-Mail: speters@museumstoreassociation.org

Historical Note:
A professional organization affiliated with the American Association of Museums. MSA's purpose is to enhance the success of cultural commerce and of the professionals engaged in it. Membership: $190-470 (Museum Member); $605 (Commercial Affiliate); $345 (Exhibitor Affiliate); $1,575 (Tradeshow Organizer); $320 (Allied); $105 (Emeritus); $115 (Individual); $125 (Individual Affiliate).

Meetings/Conferences: Annual
Conference Chair: Jennifer Anderson
2013 - Los Angeles, CA (Los Angeles Convention Center)/April 13 - 15

Publications:
Member Directory; on-line
Museum Store; quarterly; adv.
Museum Store Marketplace; on-line

Museum Trustee Association (1971)
1776 I St. NW
Ninth Floor
Washington, DC 20006
Tel: (202) 756-4832 *Fax:* (202) 756-1301
TollFree: (888) 264-2688
E-Mail: office@mta-hq.org
Website: mta-hq.org
Members:
150 institutions
75200 individuals and museum trustees
Staff: 6

Annual Budget: $100-250,000
Tax: 501(c)(3)

Personnel:
President: James L. McCreight
   E-Mail: president@mta-hq.com
Treasurer: Murray R Tarnapoll

Historical Note:
Founded as a Committee of the American Association of Museums, MTA was separately incorporated as the Museum Trustee Committee for Research and Development and assumed its current name in 1986. MTA's mission to provide ongoing board education programs, services and resources for the special needs of museum trustees. Membership: $200- 1,000 (Institutional, based on annual operating budget); $1,000 (Patron); $1,500 (Dual Patron); $100 (Friend); $250 (Contributor); $500 (Donor).

Meetings/Conferences:
Number of non-conference events/year: 2

Publications:
Membership Directory; on-line
MTA Briefings; quarterly
MTA E-News; monthly

Membership List Available to Non-members

Music and Entertainment Industry Educators Association (1979)
1900 Belmont Blvd.
Nashville, TN 37212-3757
Tel: (615) 460-6946
E-Mail: office@meiea.org
Website: meiea.org
Members: 650 individuals
Staff: 5
Annual Budget: $50-100,000
Tax: 501(c)(3)

Personnel:
Executive Director: Dave Tough
   E-Mail: toughd@mail.belmont.edu
Director, Student Relations: Cutler Armstrong
   E-Mail: csarmstr@butler.edu
Director, Membership Services: Kristél Pfeil Kemmerer
   E-Mail: membership@meiea.org
Editor: Bruce Ronkin
   E-Mail: b.ronkin@neu.edu

Historical Note:
Formerly (1986) Music Industry Educators Association. MEIEA's mission is to facilitate an exchange of information between educators and practitioners in order to prepare students for careers in the music and entertainment industries. Members are individuals, educational institutions and companies concerned with music and recording industry. Membership: $60 (Active); $180-590 (Institutional); $18 (Student).

Meetings/Conferences:
Number of non-conference events/year: 1-10

Publications:
e-Blast; monthly
MEIEA eZine; on-line
MEIEA Journal; annually

Music Critics Association of North America (1956)
722 Dulaney Valley Rd.
Suite 259
Baltimore, MD 21204-5109
Tel: (410) 435-3881 Fax: (410) 435-3881
E-Mail: info@mcana.org
Website: mcana.org
Members: 230 individuals
Staff: 3
Annual Budget: $10-25,000

Personnel:
President: Donald Rosenberg
Treasurer: Susan Elliott
Managing Director and Web Page Editor: Robert H. Leininger
   E-Mail: musiccritics@aol.com

Historical Note:
Added "of North America" to its name in 1994. MCANA's mission is to seek to improve the caliber of music criticism and to promote an interest in music in the U.S. and Canada. Members are classical music critics from the various communications media. Membership: $125 (Active Critics/Journalists/ Editors/Book Authors/Program Annotators/Retired MCANA Members); $50 (Student).

Publications:
MCANA Newsletter
Membership Directory; on-line

Music Distributors Association (1939)
14070 Proton Rd.
Suite 100 LB Nine
Dallas, TX 75244-3601
Tel: (972) 233-9107 Fax: (972) 490-4219
E-Mail: office@musicdistributors.org
Website: musicdistributors.org
Members: 125 companies
Staff: 2
Annual Budget: $25-50,000
Tax: 501(c)(6)

Personnel:
Executive Director: Madeleine Crouch

Historical Note:
Formerly (1977) the National Association of Musical Merchandise Wholesalers, MDA is an international, non-profit trade association. MDA's mission is to represent and serve manufacturers, wholesalers, importers and exporters of musical instruments and accessories, sound reinforcement products and published music. Two-thirds of member companies are domestic, one-third are overseas. Membership: $675 (Domestic); $350 (International).

Meetings/Conferences: Annual
Conference Chair: Madeleine Crouch

Publications:
Membership Directory; on-line

Music Industry Conference (1923)
1806 Robert Fulton Dr.
Reston, VA 20191
Tel: (703) 860-4000 Fax: (703) 860-1531
Website: musiced.nafme.org
Members: 500 companies
Staff: 46
Annual Budget: $25-50,000

Personnel:
Executive Director: Michael A. Butera
   E-Mail: michaelb@nafme.org
Chief Financial Officer: Paul Baker
   E-Mail: paulb@nafme.org
Senior Manager, Member Services: Betty Cook
   E-Mail: bettyc@nafme.org
Manager, Editor: Roz Fehr
   E-Mail: rozf@nafme.org
Communications and Production Coordinator: Michelle Mathews
   E-Mail: michellem@nafme.org
IT Associate: Robert Nguyen
   E-Mail: robertn@nafme.org

Historical Note:
MIC strives to serve as a launching ground for intellectual and creative networking, as well as to nurture career growth and to contribute to building professional relationships.

Meetings/Conferences:
2013 - Hartford, CT/April 4 - 7
2014 - St. Louis, MO (Hilton St. Louis Frontenac)/April 10 - 12

Publications:
General Music Today; on-line
Journal of Music Teacher Education; on-line
Journal of Research in Music Education; on-line
MENC Collegiate; monthly
MENC Mariachi; monthly
Music Educators Journal; on-line

Music Library Association (1931)
8551 Research Way
Suite 180
Middleton, WI 53562
Tel: (608) 836-5825 Fax: (608) 831-8200
E-Mail: mla@areditions.com
Website: musiclibraryassoc.org
Members: 3 individuals and institutions
Staff: 5
Annual Budget: $500-1,000,000
Tax: 501(c)(3)

Personnel:
President: Jerry L. McBride
   E-Mail: jerry.mcbride@stanford.edu
Development Officer: James P. Cassaro
Manager, Conventions: Laura Gayle Green
   E-Mail: laura.gayle.green@gmail.com
Advertising Manager: Anne Shelley
   E-Mail: ashelley@umn.edu
Placement Officer: Alisa Rata Stutzbach
   E-Mail: placementofficer@musiclibraryassoc.org

Historical Note:
MLA provides a professional forum for librarians, archivists, and others who support and preserve the world's musical heritage. Membership: $50- 770/year.

Meetings/Conferences:
Conference Chair: Laura Gayle Green
2013 - San Jose, CA/Feb. 27 - March 3
2014 - Atlanta, GA/Feb. 24 - March 2

Publications:
MLA Newsletter; quarterly; adv.

Music Publishers Association of the United States (1895)
243 Fifth Ave.
Suite 236
New York, NY 10016
Tel: (212) 327-4044
E-Mail: admin@mpa.org
Website: mpa.org
Members: 75 music publishers
Staff: 4
Annual Budget: $100-250,000

Personnel:
President: Kathleen Marsh
Legal Counsel: Katie Baron
Treasurer: Bryndon Bay
Secretary: Todd Vunderink

Historical Note:
MPA is the music trade organization in the United States, fostering communication among publishers, dealers, music educators, and all ultimate users of music. It serves as a forum for publishers to address the music industry's vital issues. Membership: $50-1,500/year.

Meetings/Conferences: Annual
Number of non-conference events/year: 3

Publications:
Directory of Music Publishers; on-line
Directory of Publisher Imprints

Music Teachers National Association (1876)
441 Vine St.
Suite 3100
Cincinnati, OH 45202-3004
Tel: (513) 421-1420 Fax: (513) 421-2503
TollFree: (888) 512-5278
E-Mail: mtnanet@mtna.org
Website: mtna.org
Members: 24000 individuals
Staff: 13
Annual Budget: $10-25,000
Tax: 501(c)(3)

Personnel:
Executive Director and Chief Executive Officer: Gary L. Ingle
   E-Mail: gingle@mtna.org
Associate, Member Development: Melissa Curtice
   E-Mail: mcurtice@mtna.org
Director, Membership Processing: Elaine Donaldson
   E-Mail: edonaldson@mtna.org
Director, Publishing and Managing Editor: Marcie Gerrietts Lindsey
   E-Mail: mlindsey@mtna.org
Meetings Associate: Tonya Schauer
   E-Mail: tschauer@mtna.org
Marketing and Public Relations Associate: Chad Schwalbach
   E-Mail: cschwalbach@mtna.org
Deputy Executive Director and Chief Operations Officer: Brian Shepard
   E-Mail: bshepard@mtna.org

Historical Note:
Founded by Theodore Presser in Delaware, Ohio on December 26, 1876 with 62 charter members.The mission of Music Teachers National Association is to advance the value of music study and music making to society and to support the professionalism of music teachers. Membership: $68 (Active); $51 (Active Member with Senior discount); $16 (Collegiate); $68 (International); $75 (Patron); $200 (Corporate/Institutional); $34 (Retired).

Continuing Education:
Certification Designation/s: MTNAPC, NCTM

Meetings/Conferences: Annual
Conference Chair: Tonya Schauer
2013 - Anaheim, CA (Disneyland Hotel)/March 9 - 13/2000 attendees
2014 - Chicago, IL (Marriott Chicago Downtown)/ March 22 - 26

Publications:
American Music Teacher; bi-monthly; adv.
MTNA e-journal

Membership List Available to Non-members

Mutual Fund Education Alliance *(1971)*
2345 Grand Blvd.
Suite 1750
Kansas City, MO 64108
Tel: (816) 454-9422 *Fax:* (816) 454-9322
E-Mail: mfea@mfea.com
Website: mfea.info
Members: 40 companies
Staff: 5
Annual Budget: $500-1,000,000
Tax: 501(c)(6)

Personnel:
Director: Brian M. Smith
   E-Mail: bmsmith@mfea.com
Director, Operations: Kimber L. Lintz
   E-Mail: klintz@mfea.com
Associate Director: Michelle A. Smith
   E-Mail: masmith@mfea.com

Historical Note:
Formerly No-Load Mutual Fund Association; assumed its present name in 1989. MFEA is an association for investment companies who market their shares directly to the public and provides investor education and data, including on its web site. MFEA's mission is to educate individual investors about mutual funds and the benefits of long-term investing. Members are committed to investor education and dedicated to helping investors understand mutual funds and the benefits of long-term investing. Membership: $5000-20000 (Individual, based on Mutual Fund Assets).

Publications:
Membership Directory; on-line

Mycological Society of America *(1932)*
P.O. Box 7065
Lawrence, KS 66044
Tel: (785) 843-1234 *Fax:* (785) 843-6153
TollFree: (800) 627-0326
E-Mail: msa@allenpress.com
Website: msafungi.org
Members: 1400 individuals
Staff: 2
Annual Budget: $250-500,000

Personnel:
Association Manager: Kay Rose
   E-Mail: krose@allenpress.com

Historical Note:
Founded as an outgrowth of the Microbiological Section of the Botanical Society of America, and incorporated in 1966 in the District of Columbia. A scientific society dedicated to advancing mycology, the study of fungi of all kinds including mushrooms, truffles, yeasts, plant pathogens, and medically important fungi. Members are individuals interested in the study of fungi. Membership: $98 (Regular, Individual); $20 (Additional Family Member); $50 (Student); $50 (Associate); $278 (Sustaining); $1,500 (Life).

Meetings/Conferences: Annual
2013 - Austin, TX/Aug. 10 - 14
Number of non-conference events/year: 4

Publications:
Inoculum - Newsletter; bi-monthly
Membership Directory; on-line
Mycologia; bi-monthly; adv.

Membership List Available to Non-members

Mystery Shopping Providers Association *(1998)*
455 S. Fourth st.
Suite 650
Louisville, KY 40202
Tel: (502) 574-9033 *Fax:* (502) 589-3602
E-Mail: info@mysteryshop.org
Website: mysteryshop.org
Members: 275 companies
Staff: 3
Annual Budget: $10-25,000
Tax: 501(c)(6)

Personnel:
President: Stan Hart
Conference Committee Chair: Stefan Doomanis
Treasurer: Carl Phillips

Historical Note:

Mystery Shopping Providers Association is dedicated to improving service quality using anonymous resources. Membership includes marketing research and merchandising companies, private investigation firms, training organizations and companies that specialize in providing mystery shopping services. Membership: $550-950 (Regular); $1,200 (Associate); $250 (Affiliate).

Continuing Education:
Certification Designation/s: MSPA

Meetings/Conferences: Annual
Conference Chair: Stefan Doomanis

Publications:
This Just In; monthly

Mystery Writers of America *(1945)*
1140 Broadway
Suite 1507
New York, NY 10001
Tel: (212) 888-8171 *Fax:* (212) 888-8107
E-Mail: mwa@mysterywriters.org
Website: mysterywriters.org
Members: 2800 individuals
Staff: 2
Annual Budget: $1-2,000,000

Personnel:
Administrative Manager: Margery L. Flax
Contact, Public Relations: Meryl Zegarek

Historical Note:
MWA's mission is to promote higher regard for crime writing and recognition and respect for those who write within the genre. Members are professional writers of crime and mystery stories and novels. Unpublished writers are affiliate members; publishers and agents are associate members. Membership: $95/year.

NABIM - the International Band and Orchestral Products Association *(1920)*
P.O. Box 757
New York, NY 10033
Tel: (212) 795-3630 *Fax:* (212) 795-3630
E-Mail: assnhdqs@earthlink.net
Website: nabim.org
Members: 34 companies
Staff: 2
Annual Budget: $25-50,000

Personnel:
Executive Vice President: Robert Sulkow
   E-Mail: assnhdqs@earthlink.net

Historical Note:
Formerly (2003) National Association of Band Instrument Manufacturers. Membership: $500-$3000/year (fee varies by sales).

NACE International *(1943)*
1440 S. Creek Dr.
Houston, TX 77084-4906
Tel: (281) 228-6223 *Fax:* (281) 228-6300
TollFree: (800) 797-6223
E-Mail: firstservice@nace.org
Website: nace.org
Members: 25,000 individuals
Staff: 100
Annual Budget: $25-50,000,000
Tax: 501(c)(3)

Personnel:
Executive Director: Bob Chalker
Manager, Membership Services: Heather Butler
Manager, Marketing: Lisa Copeland
Director, Technical Activities: Linda Goldberg
Program Manager, Conferences and Exhibits: Jackie Hune
Director, Publications: Gretchen Jacobson
Director, Education: Pat Kutt
Manager, Human Resources: Jeff Magee
Director, Quality Management and Information Services: John Perry
   E-Mail: john.perry@nace.org
Senior Director, Membership Services, Public Affairs, and Standards: Helena Seelinger
   E-Mail: helena.seelinger@nace.org
Senior Director, Finance and NACE Foundation: Calvin Tang
   E-Mail: calvin.tang@nace.org

Historical Note:
Originally known as The National Association of Corrosion Engineers (1943). NACE International provides education and communicates information to protect people, assets, and the environment from the effects of corrosion. Membership: $0-65 (Individual); $500-5000 (Corporate).

Continuing Education:
Enrollment: 8000
Certification Designation/s: CP, CIP

Meetings/Conferences: Annual
Conference Chair: Jackie Hune
2013 - Orlando, FL (Orange County Convention Center)/March 17 - 21/11-25 exhibitors
2014 - San Antonio, TX/March 9 - 13
2015 - Dallas, TX (Dallas Convention Center)/March 15 - 19
Number of non-conference events/year: 28

Publications:
CoatingsPro; bi-monthly; adv.
CorrDefense; quarterly; adv.
Corrosion - The Journal of Science and Engineering; monthly; adv.
InspectThis!; on-line; adv.
Materials Performance Magazine; monthly
Membership Directory; on-line
NACE Access; on-line; adv.
NACE Advocate; quarterly
SprayFoam; bi-monthly; adv.
Stay Current; semi-annually; adv.

NACHA - The Electronic Payments Association *(1974)*
13450 Sunrise Valley Dr.
Suite 100
Herndon, VA 20171
Tel: (703) 561-1100 *Fax:* (703) 787-0996
E-Mail: info@nacha.org
Website: nacha.org
Members: 10000 financial institutions
Staff: 48
Annual Budget: $10-25,000,000

Personnel:
President and Chief Executive Officer: Janet O. Estep
Senior Director and Group Manager, Membership Services: Anne Andrews
   E-Mail: aandrews@nacha.org
Managing Director, ACH Network Rules: Michael Herd
   E-Mail: mherd@nacha.org
Senior Director, Healthcare Payments: Priscilla C. Holland CCM, AAP
   E-Mail: pholland@nacha.org
Senior Vice President, Association Services: Scott Lang AAP
   E-Mail: slang@nacha.org
Contact, Sponsorship, Exhibiting and Advertising: Joshua Maze
   E-Mail: jmaze@nacha.org
Senior Director, Communications and Marketing: Colleen Morrison
   E-Mail: cmorrison@nacha.org
Senior Director, Network Services: Deborah L. Shaw
   E-Mail: dshaw@nacha.org

Historical Note:
Founded as National Automated Clearing House Association; assumed its current name in 2000. NACHA's mission is to promote the development of electronic solutions that improve the payments system for the benefit of its members and their customers. NACHA forms the cooperative foundation for the automated clearing house (ACH) payments system through a network of 21 ACH associations nationwide. Also works to establish the rules for the exchange of ACH transactions between financial institutions and provides marketing and educational support to the banking industry.

Meetings/Conferences: Annual
Conference Chair: Priscilla C. Holland CCM, AAP
2013 - San Diego, CA (San Diego Convention Center)/ April 21 - 24/11-25 exhibitors
Number of non-conference events/year: 4

Publications:
NACHA's Risk Management News

NADCA: The HVAC Inspection, Maintenance and Restoration Association *(1989)*
15000 Commerce Pkwy.
Suite C
Mt. Laurel, NJ 08054
Tel: (856) 380-6810 *Fax:* (856) 439-0525
TollFree: (855) 466-2322
E-Mail: info@nadca.com
Website: nadca.com
Members: 1000 companies
Staff: 6
Annual Budget: $1-2,000,000

Tax: 501(c)(6)

Personnel:
Executive Director: Jodi Araujo CEM
    E-Mail: jaraujo@ahint.com
Coordinator, Membership and Certification: Jacqueline
    Hargrave
    E-Mail: jhargrave@ahint.com
Director, Meetings: Clare MacNab
    E-Mail: cmacnab@ahint.com

Historical Note:
*Formerly the National Air Duct Cleaners Association.
NADCA's mission is to include the representation
of qualified companies engaged in the assessment,
cleaning, and restoration of HVAC systems, and to assist
its members in providing high quality service to their
customers. Membership: $825 (Regular/Associate); $250
(Supplemental).*

Continuing Education:
Certification Designation/s: VSMR, ASCS, CVI

Meetings/Conferences: Annual
Conference Chair: Clare MacNab
2013 - New Orleans, LA/March 15 - 18
Number of non-conference events/year: 1

Publications:
Buyer's Guide; annually; adv.
DucTales magazine; bi-monthly; adv.
Membership Directory; annually

NAFA Fleet Management Association *(1957)*
125 Village Blvd.
Suite 200
Princeton, NJ 08540
Tel: (609) 720-0882 *Fax:* (609) 452-8004
E-Mail: info@nafa.org
Website: nafa.org
Members: 3900 individuals
Staff: 13
Annual Budget: $2-5,000,000

Personnel:
Executive Director: Phillip E. Russo CAE
    E-Mail: prusso@nafa.org
Senior Manager, Marketing: Christine Hamershock
    E-Mail: chamershock@nafa.org
Accounting Manager: Richard Kadash
    E-Mail: kadash@nafa.org
Director, Marketing and Communications: Joanne Marsh
    E-Mail: jmarsh@nafa.org
Director, Meetings and Education: Jayne Ratyniak
    E-Mail: jratyniak@nafa.org
Assistant, Education: Kate Shelko
    E-Mail: kshelko@nafa.org
Administrator, Database and Membership Services:
    Maureen Smith
    E-Mail: msmith@nafa.org
Manager, Communications: Gary Wien
    E-Mail: gwien@nafa.org

Historical Note:
*Formerly known as the National Association of Fleet
Administrators, Individual membership professional society
serving members who manage fleets of automobiles,
SUVs, trucks, vans and a wide range of specialized mobile
equipment for organizations across the globe. NAFA's
mission is to promote professional management of vehicles,
enabling all members to improve their ability to contribute
to an employer's success. Members are individuals
responsible for administration of a fleet of 25 or more motor
vehicles not for hire commercially. Membership: $475
(U.S./Canadian Full); $385 (U.S./Canadian Associate);
$725 (International Full); $635 (International Associate);
$45 (U.S./Canadian Student).*

Continuing Education:
Certification Designation/s: CAFM, CAFS

Meetings/Conferences: Annual
Conference Chair: Jayne Ratyniak
2013 - Atlantic City, NJ/April 20 - 23
2013 - Atlantic City, NJ (Atlantic City Convention
    Center)/April 23 - 26/11-25 exhibitors
2014 - Minneapolis, MN (Minneapolis Convention
    Center)/April 8 - 11

Publications:
Fleet Perspectives; quarterly
FleetFOCUS; bi-weekly
FLEETSolutions; bi-monthly; adv.
Legislative Updates; monthly
NAFA's Professional Online Directory; on-line

NAFSA: Association of International Educators *(1948)*
1307 New York Ave. NW
Eighth Floor
Washington, DC 20005-4701
Tel: (202) 737-3699 *Fax:* (202) 737-3657
TollFree: (800) 836-4994
E-Mail: inbox@nafsa.org
Website: nafsa.org
Members: 10000 individuals
Staff: 87
Annual Budget: $10-25,000,000
Tax: 501(c)(3)

Personnel:
Executive Director and Chief Executive Officer: Marlene
    M. Johnson
    E-Mail: marlenej@nafsa.org
*Deputy Executive Director, Communications and
    Engagement Services:* Frank Doyle
    E-Mail: frankd@nafsa.org
Database Administrator: Peter Kehoe
    E-Mail: peterk@nafsa.org
Director of Marketing: Robin Little
    E-Mail: robinl@nafsa.org
Marketing Manager: Khalilah Long
    E-Mail: khalilahl@nafsa.org
Senior Director, Publications: Christopher Murphy
    E-Mail: chrism@nafsa.org
Director, Media Relations and Strategic Communications:
    Ursula Oaks
    E-Mail: ursulao@nafsa.org
*Deputy Executive Director, Membership Services and
    Organizational Advancement:* Christie Philips
Deputy Executive Director: Betty Soppelsa
    E-Mail: bettys@nafsa.org
Deputy Executive Director, Conference Planning: Elizabeth
    F. Soppelsa
    E-Mail: bettys@nafsa.org
Senior Adviser, Planning and Service Development: Robert
    Stableski
    E-Mail: bobs@nafsa.org
Deputy Executive Director, Public Policy: Jill Welch
Chief Financial Officer: Joseph A. Zillo
    E-Mail: joez@nafsa.org

Historical Note:
*Founded in 1948 as National Association of Foreign
Student Advisors. Mission is to work in the field of
international education and exchange. NAFSA serves
international educators and their institutions and
organizations by setting standards of good practice,
providing training and professional development
opportunities, providing networking opportunities, and
advocating for international education. Membership: $370
(Regular); $123 (Associate).*

Meetings/Conferences: Annual
Conference Chair: Elizabeth F. Soppelsa
2013 - Louisville, KY (Kentucky Exposition Center)/
    May 26 - 31
2014 - San Diego, CA (Convention Center)/May 25 -
    30
2015 - Boston, MA (Four Seasons Hotels and Resorts)/
    May 24 - 29
2016 - Denver, CO (Denver Metro Convention and
    Visitors Bureau)/May 29 - June 3
2017 - San Francisco, CA/May 28 - June 2
2018 - Philadelphia, PA/May 27 - June 1
2019 - Washington, DC/May 26 - 31
Number of non-conference events/year: 1

Publications:
International Educator; bi-monthly; adv.
Journal of Studies in International Education
NAFSA Adviser's Manual Online; on-line
NAFSA Directory; on-line
NAFSA.news; weekly
Policy Briefs; on-line

NAGMR Consumer Product Brokers *(1949)*
C/O MANA, 16A Journey
Suite 200
Aliso Viejo, CA 92656
Tel: (949) 859-4040 *Fax:* (949) 855-2973
E-Mail: lball@manaonline.org
Website: nagmr.com
Members: 32 firms
Staff: 2
Annual Budget: $25-50,000

Personnel:
President: Ken Laner
    E-Mail: klaner@6ideas.com

Treasurer: Jordan Stone
    E-Mail: jordan@healthsourcemarketing.com

Historical Note:
*Formerly (1976) National Association of Drug
Manufacturer's Representatives, (1978) National
Association of Diversified Manufacturers' Representatives,
(1998) National Association General Merchandise
Representatives. NAGMR is a professional association
representing manufacturers to the drug, mass merchandise,
and food trade. Membership: $500 first year membership
dues (plus $250 for each Satellite Office); $250 (Satellite
Offices).*

Publications:
The Representative; on-line

NAIR -- International Association of Bowling Equipment Specialists *(1973)*
5806 W. 127th St.
Alsip, IL 60803
Tel: (708) 371-8237 *Fax:* (708) 371-8283
E-Mail: nairbowllanecare@email.msn.com
Website: nairbowl.com
Members: 55 companies
Staff: 1

Personnel:
Executive Secretary: Nancy Surprenant
    E-Mail: nairbowlanecare@msn.com

Historical Note:
*Founded as National Association of Independent
Resurfacers and assumed its current name in 2001. Purpose
of NAIR is to provide an environment that is conducive
to learning and exchanging ideas openly. Members are
companies engaged in the installation and refinishing,
injecting and repairing of bowling lanes.*

Meetings/Conferences: Annual

Publications:
Membership Directory; on-line
NAIR Newsletter

National Association of Independent Review Organizations
100 W. Main St.
Suite 310
Lansdale, PA 19446
Website: nairo.org
Staff: 2

Personnel:
Executive Director: Gib Smith JD
Treasurer: Joyce Muller

Historical Note:
*NAIRO) was formed by the majority of URAC-accredited
independent review organizations (IRO). NAIRO's mission
is to protect the integrity of the independent medical peer
review processes. Utilizing the expertise of hundreds
of board-certified clinicians throughout the country,
NAIRO members embrace an evidence-based approach
to independent medical peer review, in order to resolve
coverage disputes between enrollees and their health plans.
Membership: $3000 (Full Member); $2500 (Associate
Member).*

NALP - The Association for Legal Career Professionals *(1971)*
1220 19th St. NW
Suite 401
Washington, DC 20036-2405
Tel: (202) 835-1001 *Fax:* (202) 835-1112
E-Mail: info@nalp.org
Website: nalp.org
Members:
1100 law schools and employers
2400 total individuals
Staff: 13
Annual Budget: $2-5,000,000
Tax: 501(c)(6)

Personnel:
Executive Director: James G. Leipold
    E-Mail: jleipold@nalp.org
Director, Member Professional Development: Mary Beal
    E-Mail: mbeal@nalp.org
Director, Meetings and Membership Services: Christopher
    Brown
    E-Mail: cbrown@nalp.org
Manager, Communications and Marketing: John S. Chen
    E-Mail: jchen@nalp.org
Administrator, Finance: Julie P. Hamre
    E-Mail: jhamre@nalp.org

Director, Technology and Electronic Information Systems:
Lisa Quirk
E-Mail: lisa@nalp.org
*Associate Director, Membership and Conference Services
and Manager, Operations:* Jay Richards
E-Mail: jrichards@nalp.org
Director, Communications: Janet E. Smith
E-Mail: jsmith@nalp.org
Deputy Director: Fred E. Thrasher
E-Mail: fthrasher@nalp.org

Historical Note:
*NALP is dedicated to facilitating legal career counseling and
planning, recruitment and retention, and the professional
development of law students and lawyers. Membership
includes virtually every ABA-approved law school in the
US, Canadian law schools and hundreds of legal employers
from both the public and private sectors. Membership:
$225-920/year.*

Meetings/Conferences: Annual
Conference Chair: Christopher Brown
2013 - Jacksonville, FL/Feb. 28 - March 2
2013 - Tampa, FL (Grand Hyatt Tampa Bay)/April 24 -
27
2014 - Seattle, WA (Washington State Convention
Center)/April 9 - 12
2015 - Chicago, IL (Sheraton Chicago Hotel and
Towers)/April 22 - 25
2016 - Boston, MA (Hynes Convention Center)/April
13 - 16
Number of non-conference events/year: 3

Publications:
Member Handbook and Membership Directory;
annually; adv.
NALP Canadian Directory of Legal Employers; on-line
NALP Directory of Law Schools; annually
NALP Directory of Legal Employers; annually
NALPnow; bi-weekly
News Digest; weekly
The Bulletin; monthly

Membership List Available to Non-members

NALS (1929)
8159 E. 41st St.
Tulsa, OK 74145
Tel: (918) 582-5188 *Fax:* (918) 582-5907
E-Mail: info@nals.org
Website: nals.org
Members: 6000 individuals
Staff: 6
Annual Budget: $500-1,000,000
Tax: 501(c)(3)

Personnel:
Executive Director: Tammy Hailey CAE
E-Mail: hailey@nals.org
Manager, Membership Services: Saundra Bates
E-Mail: bates@nals.org
Manager, Meetings: Jennifer King CMP
E-Mail: king@NALS.org
Manager, Communications: Jay Moore
E-Mail: moore@nals.org
Manager, Education and Certifications: Diana Price
E-Mail: price@nals.org

Historical Note:
*Established as the California Association of Legal
Secretaries, it became Legal Secretaries, Inc. in 1940,
National Association of Legal Secretaries in 1950, and
assumed its present name in 2003. NALS's mission is to
enhance the competencies and contributions of members
in the legal services profession. It offers professional
development by providing continuing legal education,
certifications, information, and training to those choosing
the legal services industry as their career. Members include
paralegals and legal assistants to legal administrators and
office managers. Membership: $175 (International); $143
(New); $19 (Student); $53 (Associate/Retired).*

Continuing Education:
Certification Designation/s: ALS, PP, PLS

Meetings/Conferences: Annual
Conference Chair: Jennifer King CMP
2013 - Oklahoma City, OK (DoubleTree Warren Place)/
Feb. 27 - March 2
2013 - Atlanta, GA (Atlanta Marriott Perimeter Center)/
Oct. 17 - 20
Number of non-conference events/year: 1

Publications:
e-Learn; monthly; adv.
E-News; bi-weekly; adv.
Leading the Way; bi-monthly

The NALS Docket; monthly; adv.

Membership List Available to Non-members

NAMM - The International Music Products Association (1901)
5790 Armada Dr.
Carlsbad, CA 92008-4391
Tel: (760) 438-8001 *Fax:* (760) 438-7327
TollFree: (800) 767-6266
E-Mail: info@namm.org
Website: namm.org
Members: 9,000 manufacturers and retailers of
musical instruments and sound products
Staff: 7
Annual Budget: $10-25,000,000
Tax: 501(c)(6)

Personnel:
President and Chief Executive Officer: Joe Lamond
E-Mail: joel@namm.org
Associate Director, Trade Show Sales: Dominique Agnew
E-Mail: dominiquea@namm.org
Manager, Public Relations and Social Media: Kymberly
Drake
Director, Public Affairs and Government Relations: Mary
Luehrsen
E-Mail: maryl@namm.org
Associate Director, Trade Show Sales: Dan Moylan
E-Mail: danielm@namm.org
Director, Public Relations and Social Media: Scott
Robertson
E-Mail: scottr@namm.org

Historical Note:
*Founded as National Association of Music Merchants and
assumed its current name in 1997. NAMM's mission is
to unify, lead and strengthen the global music products
industry and to increase active participation in music
making. Membership: $195 (Manufacturers of Musical
Instruments/Products, Distributors, Import/Export and
Publishers); $600 (Service Provider Member/Others).*

Meetings/Conferences:
Conference Chair: Dan Moylan
2013 - Anaheim, CA (Anaheim Convention Center)/
Jan. 24 - 27/11-25 exhibitors

Publications:
Membership Directory; on-line
Mix Magazine
PLAYback Magazine; quarterly
UpBeat Daily; daily; adv.

NANDA International (1982)
P.O. Box 157
Kaukauna, WI 54130-0157
Tel: (215) 545-8105 *Fax:* (215) 564-2175
TollFree: (800) 647-9002
E-Mail: info@nanda.org
Website: nanda.org
Members: 500 individuals
Staff: 10
Annual Budget: $250-500,000

Personnel:
Executive Director: T. Heather Herdman PhD, RN
E-Mail: execdir@nanda.org
Contact, Communications: Susan Finco
E-Mail: sfinco@LFpublicrelations.com

Historical Note:
*Formerly North American Nursing Diagnosis Association,
assumed its current name in 2002. NANDA-I's mission is
to develop, refine and promote terminology that accurately
reflects nurses' clinical judgments. Members are registered
nurses and other health professionals with an interest in
nursing diagnosis. Membership: $105 (Regular/Associate/
Student); $65 (Retired).*

Meetings/Conferences: Annual

Publications:
International Journal of Nursing Terminologies and
Classifications; quarterly; adv.
NANDA-I News; quarterly
Online Member Directory; on-line

NanoBusiness Alliance
8045 Lamon Ave.
Skokie, IL 60077
Tel: (312) 224-8319
Website: nanobusiness.org
Staff: 2
Annual Budget: $100-250,000
Tax: 501(c)(6)

Personnel:
Executive Director: Vincent Caprio
E-Mail: vincentcaprio@nynanobusiness.org
Senior Coordinator: Alisa Kronshage

Historical Note:
*The NanoBusiness Commercialization Association was
formed in 2011 as the next- generation iteration of the
former NanoBusiness Alliance. The Alliance's mission is to
create a collective voice of the emerging small tech industry
and develop a range of initiatives to support and strengthen
the nanotechnology business community, through public
policy efforts, events, research, and through the creation of
partnerships. Membership: $100/Year.*

Meetings/Conferences:
Conference Chair: Alisa Kronshage

Publications:
NanoBusiness Alliance Newsletter

Napa Valley Vintners Association (1944)
P.O. Box 141
St. Helena, CA 94574
Tel: (707) 963-3388 *Fax:* (707) 963-3488
E-Mail: reception2@napavintners.com
Website: napavintners.com
Members: 420 Members
Staff: 24
Annual Budget: $2-5,000,000

Personnel:
Executive Director: Linda Reiff
Manager, Membership Services: Connor Best
Managing Director, Marketing and Promotions: Stacey
Dolan Capitani
Office Manager: Aram Chakerian
Director, Communications: Terry Hall
Manager, Special Events: Mike Jackson
Manager, Information Technology: Joe Thrift
Director, Finance and Administration: Steve Tradewell

Historical Note:
*Association of grape growers and wine makers in Napa,
California. Its mission is to advocate, protect and enhance
the Napa Valley appellation and its wines. Membership:
$500-1,500 (General);$1,200-2,400(Fixed);$420
(Sustaining).*

Publications:
Member Directory

NARSA-The International Heal Transfer Association (1954)
3000 Village Run Rd.
Suite 103, No. 221
Wexford, PA 15090-6315
Tel: (724) 799-8415 *Fax:* (724) 799-8416
E-Mail: info@narsa.org
Website:
narsa.org
narsa.org
Members: 1500 individuals
Staff: 10
Annual Budget: $500-1,000,000
Tax: 501(c)(6)

Personnel:
Executive Director: Wayne Juchno
E-Mail: wjuchno@narsa.org
Manager, Sales and New Business Development: Douglas
P. Shymoniak
E-Mail: dshymoniak@narsa.org

Historical Note:
*NARSA's mission is to promote the interests of radiator
repair shop owners and to promote educational practices
and improving procedures, fostering and promoting business
friendships, conducting research, providing educational,
technical, safety and marketing programs and solutions for
the industry's issues. Membership: $700 (Associate); $325
(Regular).*

Meetings/Conferences: Semi-Annual
Number of non-conference events/year: 1

Publications:
Heating & Cooling Exchange eNewsletter; monthly;
adv.
Membership Directory; annually; adv.
NARSA eNewsletter; monthly; adv.
Radiator Report
The Cooling Journal; monthly; adv.

Nashville Songwriters Association, International (1967)
1710 Roy Acuff Pl.
Nashville, TN 37203

Tel: (615) 256-3354
TollFree: (800) 321-6008
Website: nashvillesongwriters.com
Members: 5000 Members
Staff: 16
Annual Budget: $1-2,000,000
Tax: 501(c)(6)

Personnel:
Executive Director: Bart Herbison
Manager, Membership Services: Tali Giles
   E-Mail: tali@nashvillesongwriters.com
Director, Information Technology: Todd Givens
   E-Mail: todd@nashvillesongwriters.com
Director, Events: Dave Petrelli
   E-Mail: davidpetrelli@nashvillesongwriters.com
Director, Finance: Jennifer Purdon-Turnbow
   E-Mail: jennifer@nashvillesongwriters.com
Chief Operation Officer: Erika Wollam-Nichols
   E-Mail: erika@nashvillesongwriters.com

Historical Note:
NSAI consists of a body of creative minds, including songwriters from all genres of music, professional and amateur, who are committed to protecting the rights and future of the profession of songwriting and to educate, elevate, and celebrate the songwriter and to act as a unifying force within the music community and the community at large. Membership: $200 (Active); $100 (Student/Professional); $150 (FAN).

Meetings/Conferences:
Conference Chair: Dave Petrelli

Publications:
Member E-News; on-line
NSAI Newsletter

National Association of Student Personnel Administrators *(1919)*
111 K St. NE
Tenth Floor
Washington, DC 20002
Tel: (202) 265-7500 *Fax:* (202) 898-5737
E-Mail: office@naspa.org
Website: naspa.org
Members: 13,000 members
Staff: 33
Annual Budget: $5-10,000,000

Personnel:
Executive Director: Gwendolyn J. Dungy
   E-Mail: gdungy@naspa.org
Director, Member Services: Rhoda Chari
   E-Mail: rchari@naspa.org
Director, Publications: Melissa Dahne
   E-Mail: mdahne@naspa.org
Senior Director, Professional Development: Stephanie Gordon
   E-Mail: sgordon@naspa.org
Senior Director, Accounting and Human Resources: Olivia Jones
   E-Mail: ojones@naspa.org
Senior Director, Marketing and Communications: Kaaryn Keller
   E-Mail: kkeller@naspa.org
Senior Director, Information Technology: John Kennedy
   E-Mail: jkennedy@naspa.org
Senior Director, Meetings: Arlene Kidwell
   E-Mail: akidwell@naspa.org

Historical Note:
Established as the National Association of Deans and Advisers of Men by a group of Midwestern deans, (1951) Became National Association of Student Personnel Administrators. NASPA's mission is to serve as a source for leadership, scholarship, professional development, and advocacy for student affairs. Membership: $26-693/year.

Meetings/Conferences: Annual
Conference Chair: Arlene Kidwell
2013 - Orlando, FL (Orlando World Center Marriott)/ March 16 - 20/11-25 exhibitors
2014 - Baltimore, MD/March 15 - 19
2015 - New Orleans, LA/March 21 - 25
2016 - Indianapolis, IN/March 12 - 16
Number of non-conference events/year: 6

Publications:
Journal of College and Character
Journal of Student Affairs Research and Practice
Leadership Exchange; quarterly; adv.
NASPA Almanac; semi-annually
NASPA Forum; monthly
NASPA Journal About Women in Higher Education

NetResults; bi-monthly

NaSPA: Networks and Systems Professional Association *(1986)*
7044 S. 13th St.
Oak Creek, WI 53154
Tel: (414) 908-4945 *Fax:* (414) 768-8001
E-Mail: customercare@naspa.com
Website: naspa.com
Members:
10000 companies
29000 individuals
Staff: 22
Annual Budget: $2-5,000,000

Personnel:
President and Chairman: Leo A. Wrobel
Treasurer: Raymond Hall
Secretary: Kiesha Robinson

Historical Note:
Founded as National Systems Programmers Association; became (1994) NaSPA: the Association for Corporate Computing Professionals, and assumed its current name in 1997. NaSPA's mission is to enhance the status and promote the advancement of all network and systems professionals; nurture members' technical and managerial knowledge and skills. NaSPA members are technical professionals in corporate computing environments. Membership: Free (Gold/Individual); $995 (Life).

Publications:
NaSPA E-News; bi-weekly; adv.
Technical Support magazine
Virtualize! magazine

NASTD - Technology Professionals Serving State Government *(1978)*
P.O. Box 11910
Lexington, KY 40578-1910
Fax: (859) 244-8001
Website: nastd.org
Members: 1000 individuals
Staff: 4
Annual Budget: $500-1,000,000

Personnel:
Executive Director: Mark McCord
   E-Mail: mmccord@csg.org
Technology Analyst: Paul Czarnecki
   E-Mail: pczarnecki@csg.org
Manager, Meetings and Member Services: Pam Johnson
   E-Mail: pjohnson@csg.org
Vice President and Program Chair: Dan Oehmke
   E-Mail: dan.oehmke@state.mn.us

Historical Note:
Founded as the National Association of State Telecommunications Directors, assumed its current name in 2005. NASTD's purpose is to advance and promote the use of information technology and services to improve the operation of state government. Members are information technology professionals. Membership: $3,500 (State/Corporate Affiliate); $500 (Associate); $1,500 (Small/Micro Business Affiliate).

Meetings/Conferences: Annual
Conference Chair: Pam Johnson

Publications:
Membership Directory

Natco-The Organization for Transplant Professionals *(1980)*
P.O. Box 15384
Lenexa, KS 66285-5384
Tel: (913) 895-4612 *Fax:* (913) 895-4652
E-Mail: natco-info@goamp.com
Website: natco1.org
Members: 2141 individuals
Staff: 6
Annual Budget: $1-2,000,000

Personnel:
Executive Director: Janene Dawson MBA
Association Manager: Raven Hardin BA
Meeting Planner, Annual Conference and Conventions: Debbie Jennings
Director, Education: Christie Ross CAE
Managing Editor: Rebecka Ryan

Historical Note:
NATCO is committed to the advancement of organ and tissue donation and transplantation. Members are health professionals involved in obtaining and distributing human organs and tissues for transplant or working with transplant recipients.

Meetings/Conferences: Annual
Conference Chair: Christie Ross CAE
2013 - Miami, FL (Loews Miami Beach Hotel)/Feb. 1 - 3
2013 - San Diego, CA (Manchester Grand Hyatt San Diego)/Aug. 11 - 14
2014 - San Antonio, TX (Grand Hyatt San Antonio)/ Aug. 10 - 13
Number of non-conference events/year: 2

Publications:
In Touch Newsletter; quarterly
Membership Directory
Progress In Transplantation; quarterly; adv.

National Abortion Federation *(1977)*
1660 L St. NW
Suite 450
Washington, DC 20036
Tel: (202) 667-5881 *Fax:* (202) 667-5890
TollFree: (800) 772-9100
E-Mail: naf@prochoice.org
Website: prochoice.org
Members: 500 institutions and individuals
Staff: 35
Annual Budget: $2-5,000,000
Tax: 501(c)(3)

Personnel:
President and Chief Executive Officer: Vicki A. Saporta
   E-Mail: vsaporta@prochoice.org
Vice President and General Counsel: Cathleen M. Mahoney

Historical Note:
NAF is the professional association of abortion providers and works to ensure safe, legal, and accessible abortion care to promote health and justice for women. Members include clinics, doctors and hospitals.

Continuing Education:
Certification Designation/s: CME

Publications:
Act for Choice Alerts; irregular
Choice
Clinical Policy Guidelines; annually
Clinicians for Choice E-Newsletter; quarterly
Providing Early Options; on-line

National Abstinence Education Association *(2007)*
1701 Pennsylvania Ave. NW
Suite 300
Washington, DC 20006
Tel: (202) 248-5420 *Fax:* (866) 935-4850
E-Mail: info@theNAEA.org
Website: abstinenceassociation.org
Staff: 2
Annual Budget: $100-250,000
Tax: 501(c)(4)

Personnel:
Executive Director: Valerie Huber
   E-Mail: valerie.huber@theNAEA.org
Media Contact: Sandy Estep
   E-Mail: sestep@theNAEA.org

Historical Note:
NAEA exists to serve, support and represent individuals and organizations in the practice of abstinence education. Membership: $5,000 (Platinum Lifetime); $1,000 (Gold); $500 (Silver); $350 (Bronze); $100 (Individual).

Continuing Education:
Certification Designation/s: SRAS

Publications:
Newsletter; weekly

National Academic Advising Association *(1979)*
Kansas State University, 2323 Anderson Ave.
Suite 225
Manhattan, KS 66502-2912
Tel: (785) 532-5717 *Fax:* (785) 532-7732
E-Mail: nacada@ksu.edu
Website: nacada.ksu.edu
Members: 10750 individuals
Staff: 16
Annual Budget: $2-5,000,000
Tax: 501(c)(3)

Personnel:
Executive Director: Charlie L. Nutt AA, BSEd, EdD, MEd
   E-Mail: cnutt@ksu.edu
Assistant Director, Annual Conferences: Rhonda Baker

E-Mail: baker@ksu.edu
Manager, Information Technology Systems: Gary Cunningham AA, BS, MS
E-Mail: gcunning@ksu.edu
Managing Editor and Coordinator, Educational Programming: Leigh Cunningham
E-Mail: leigh@ksu.edu
Manager, Marketing: Bev Martin
E-Mail: bmartin@ksu.edu
Senior Administrative Assistant, Membership and Finance: Cathy Swartz
E-Mail: swartz@ksu.edu
Manager, Membership, Database Management and Accounts Receivable: Judy Weyrauch
E-Mail: weyrauch@ksu.edu

Historical Note:
NACADA seeks to promote and support quality academic advising in institutions of higher education to enhance the educational development of students and provide a forum for discussion, debate, and the exchange of ideas pertaining to academic advising through its activities and publications. Membership: $20 (Student); $55 (Individual/ General/Professional/Allied); $75 (Individual/Associate); $30 (Retiree); $200 (Institutional).

Meetings/Conferences: Annual
Conference Chair: Rhonda Baker
2013 - Salt Lake City, UT (Salt Palace Convention Center)/Oct. 6 - 9
2014 - Minneapolis, MN (Minneapolis Convention Center)/Oct. 8 - 11
2015 - Las Vegas, NV (Caesars Palace)/Oct. 4 - 7
Number of non-conference events/year: 5

Publications:
Academic Advising Today; quarterly
Membership Directory; on-line
NACADA Highlights; on-line
NACADA Journal; bi-annually

Membership List Available to Non-members

National Academies of Practice *(1981)*
1501 Euclid Ave., Suite 310
C/O The Center for Community Solutions
Cleveland, OH 44115
Tel: (216) 781-2944 *Fax*: (216) 781-2988
E-Mail: naphdq@comcast.net
Website: napractice.org
Members: 700 individuals
Staff: 5
Annual Budget: $100-250,000
Tax: 501(c)(3)

Personnel:
Conference Planner: Rosyln Miller

Historical Note:
NAP is dedicated to quality health care for all by serving as the nation's distinguished, interdisciplinary policy forum that addresses public policy, education, research and inquiry. NAP is a nonprofit professional organization composed of elected, distinguished representatives from ten different health professions. Membership: $100/year (Distinguished Practioner and Fellow/Distinguished Scholar and Fellow/Distinguished Public Policy Fellow).

Meetings/Conferences: Annual
Conference Chair: Rosyln Miller
Number of non-conference events/year: 1

Publications:
5 Things You Need to Know this Week; weekly
Member Directory; on-line
NAP Academy

National Academy of Arbitrators *(1947)*
One N. Main St.
Suite 412
Cortland, NY 13045
Tel: (607) 756-8363 *Fax*: (888) 317-1729
E-Mail: naa@naarb.org
Website: naarb.org
Members: 660 individuals
Staff: 3
Annual Budget: $500-1,000,000

Personnel:
President: Sara Adler
Executive Secretary and Treasurer: David A Petersen

Historical Note:
Founded in Chicago on September 14, 1947 to upgrade the professionalism of those engaged in the arbitration of labor-management disputes. The purpose of NAA is to establish and foster the standards of integrity, competence, honor,

and character among those engaged in the arbitration of labor-management disputes on a professional basis.

Meetings/Conferences: Annual
2013 - Vancouver, BC (The Fairmont Hotel Vancouver)/June 5 - 8
2013 - St. Louis, MO (Hilton St. Louis Frontenac)/Oct. 18 - 20
2014 - Chicago, IL (Fairmont Chicago, Millennium Park)/May 21 - 24

National Academy of Building Inspection Engineers *(1989)*
P.O. Box 860
Shelter Island, NY 11964
Tel: (631) 749-8870
TollFree: (800) 294-7729
E-Mail: director@nabie.org
Website: nabie.org
Members: 165 individuals
Staff: 1
Annual Budget: $25-50,000
Tax: 501(c)(6)

Personnel:
Executive Director: Michael L. Stotts
E-Mail: director@nabie.org

Historical Note:
NABIE's mission is to protect the integrity of the home and building inspection industry and the general public. Membership: $200 (Professional/Intern/Correspondent/ International/Student); $250 (Executive); $300 (Diplomate/Fellow).

Continuing Education:
Certification Designation/s: BIECI

Publications:
Member Directory; on-line
The EXAMINER; quarterly

National Academy of Clinical Biochemistry *(1976)*
1850 K St. NW
Suite 625
Washington, DC 20006
Tel: (800) 892-1400 *Fax*: (202) 887-5093
Website: aacc.org/members/nacb
Members: 575 individuals
Staff: 3
Annual Budget: $25-50,000

Personnel:
Executive Director: Penelope Jones
President: Stanley Lo
Treasurer: William Clarke

Historical Note:
NACB is the official Academy of the American Association for Clinical Chemistry (AACC) and membership in AACC is required to join the Academy. NACB's purpose is to advance the science and practice of laboratory medicine through scientific research and educational programs. Membership: $60/year.

Publications:
NACB Newsletter

National Academy of Education *(1965)*
500 Fifth St. NW
Suite One
Washington, DC 20001
Tel: (202) 347-9530 *Fax*: (202) 334-2350
E-Mail: info@naeducation.org
Website: naeducation.org
Members: 150 Institutions
Staff: 3
Annual Budget: $1-2,000,000
Tax: 501(c)(3)

Personnel:
Executive Director: Gregory White
E-Mail: gwhite@naeducation.org
Program Officer: Judie Ahn
E-Mail: jahn@naeducation.org
Director, Membership Services and Professional Development Programs: Jennifer Tinch
E-Mail: jtinch@naeducation.org

Historical Note:
The National Academy of Education (NAEd) works to advance better quality education research and its use in policy formation and practice. Membership: $150/year (Regular).

Meetings/Conferences: Annual
Number of non-conference events/year: 2

Publications:

Academy Notes-Newsletter; quarterly
Membership List Available to Non-members

National Academy of Elder Law Attorneys, Inc. *(1987)*
1577 Spring Hill Rd.
Suite 220
Vienna, VA 22182
Tel: (703) 942-5711 *Fax*: (703) 563-9504
E-Mail: naela@naela.org
Website: naela.org
Members: 4200 attorneys
Staff: 8
Annual Budget: $2-5,000,000
Tax: 501(c)(6)

Personnel:
Executive Director: Peter G. Wacht CAE
E-Mail: pwacht@naela.org
Manager, Member Services: Laura Munley
E-Mail: lmunley@naela.org
Administrative Specialist: Amelia (Amy) Seaton
E-Mail: aseaton@naela.org
Senior Director, Planning and Programs: Kirsten Brown Simpson
E-Mail: kbrownsimpson@naela.org
Senior Director, Communications and Publications: Nancy M. Sween
E-Mail: nsween@naela.org
Manager, Meetings and Education: Pam Yanni
E-Mail: pyanni@naela.org

Historical Note:
NAELA is dedicated to improve the quality of legal services provided to seniors and people with special needs. Membership is comprised of attorneys in the private and public sectors, as well as judges, professors of law, and students. Membership: $425 (Attorney); $345 (Law Professor/Judge); $225 (LSC Program/Title III/New Bar Admittees); $35 (Law Students, Full Time).

Continuing Education:
Certification Designation/s: CELA

Meetings/Conferences:
Conference Chair: Pam Yanni
2013 - Grapevine, TX (Embassy Suites Dallas)/Jan. 18 - 20
2013 - Washington, DC (Omni Shoreham Hotel, Washington D.C.)/Nov. 5 - 9
Number of non-conference events/year: 3

Publications:
Membership Directory; annually
NAELA eBulletin; weekly
NAELA Journal; semi-annually
NAELA News; bi-monthly

National Academy of Engineering of the United States of America *(1964)*
500 Fifth St. NW
Washington, DC 20001
Tel: (202) 334-3200 *Fax*: (202) 334-2290
Website: nae.edu
Members: 2115 individuals
Staff: 38
Annual Budget: $10-25,000,000
Tax: 501(c)(3)

Personnel:
President: Charles M. Vest
E-Mail: cvest@nae.edu
Editor: Carol Arenberg
E-Mail: carenber@nae.edu
Director, Membership Services: Mary Lee Berger-Hughes
E-Mail: mhughes@nae.edu
Senior Program Officer: Catherine Didion
E-Mail: cdidion@nae.edu
Senior Director, Development: Radka Z. Nebesky
E-Mail: rnebesky@nae.edu
Director: Proctor Reid
E-Mail: preid@nae.edu
Director, Finance: Mary Resch
E-Mail: mresch@nae.edu

Historical Note:
NAE's mission is to promote the technological welfare of the nation by marshalling the expertise and insights of eminent members of the engineering profession. Membership: $1,943 (Active); $238 (Emeritus); $188 (Foreign Associate).

Meetings/Conferences: Semi-Annual
Conference Chair: Proctor Reid
Number of non-conference events/year: 5

Publications:
Membership Directory
The Bridge; quarterly

National Academy of Neuropsychology (1975)
7555 E. Hampden Ave.
Suite 525
Denver, CO 80231
Tel: (303) 691-3694 *Fax:* (303) 691-5983
E-Mail: office@nanonline.org
Website: nanonline.org
Members: 3300 individuals
Staff: 5
Annual Budget: $500-1,000,000

Personnel:
Executive Director: William Perry PhD
  E-Mail: wperry@ucsd.edu

Historical Note:
Formerly (1989) National Academy of Neuropsychologists. NAN's mission is to advance neuropsychology as a science and health profession, to promote human welfare, and to generate and disseminate knowledge of brain- behavior relationships. Members are neurophsychologists and other individuals who have interests in brain behavior relationships and neurophyschology as a science and profession. Membership: $150 (Professional/Associate/ Affiliate); $75 (Postdoctoral Fellows); $50 (Student/Special Category).

Meetings/Conferences: Annual
2013 - San Diego, CA (Manchester Grand)/Oct. 16 - 19
2014 - Fajardo, PR (El Conquistador Resort, The Waldorf Astoria Collection)/Nov. 12 - 16

Publications:
Archives of Clinical Neuropsychology; bi-monthly; adv.
NAN Bulletin

Membership List Available to Non-members

National Academy of Opticianry (1963)
8401 Corporate Dr.
Suite 605
Landover, MD 20785
Tel: (800) 229-4828 *Fax:* (301) 577-3880
TollFree: (800) 229-4828
E-Mail: info@nao.org
Website: nao.org
Members: 5300 individuals
Staff: 6
Annual Budget: $500-1,000,000

Personnel:
Director, Education: Brian Iciek
  E-Mail: brian.iciek@nao.org
Contact, Membership Services: Erin Staples
  E-Mail: estaples@nao.org
Director, Membership and Marketing: Cindy Tucker
  E-Mail: ctucker@nao.org

Historical Note:
NAO is dedicated solely to education and training for ALL opticians. Members are individual opticians who are state licensed or nationally certified. Membership: $75 (Fellows and Associates); $10 (Student).

Continuing Education:
Certification Designation/s: CEC
Meetings/Conferences:
Number of non-conference events/year: 2

Publications:
NAO Newsletter; on-line

National Academy of Public Administration (1967)
900 Seventh St. NW
Suite 600
Washington, DC 20001
Tel: (202) 347-3190 *Fax:* (202) 393-0993
E-Mail: academy@napawash.org
Website: napawash.org
Members: 680 Fellows
Staff: 5
Annual Budget: $5-10,000,000
Tax: 501(c)(3)

Personnel:
President and Chief Executive Officer: Dan G. Blair
  E-Mail: dblair@napawash.org
General Counsel: Allison Fahrenkopf Brigati
  E-Mail: abrigati@napawash.org
Chief Financial Officer: Tom Reidy
  E-Mail: treidy@napawash.org

Senior Research Associate: Matt Thomas
  E-Mail: mthomas@napawash.org
Director, Human Resources: Victoria Wickert
  E-Mail: vwickert@napawash.org

Historical Note:
NAPA mission is to evaluate the structure, administration, operation, and program performance of governments; anticipate, identify, and analyze significant problems; and suggest timely corrective action.

National Academy of Recording Arts and Sciences (1957)
3030 Olympic Blvd.
Santa Monica, CA 90404
Tel: (310) 392-3777 *Fax:* (310) 399-3090
E-Mail: washingtondc@grammy.com
Website: grammy.com
Members: 20000 individuals
Staff: 149
Annual Budget: $50-100,000,000

Personnel:
President: Neil Portnow
Chief Operating Officer: Wayne Baruch
Vice President, West Region: Angelia Bibbs-Sanders
Senior Vice President, Executive Director: Enrique Fernandez
Chief Financial Officer: Susan Leary
Senior Director, Communications and Media Relations: Lourdes Lopez
Vice President, Member Services: Kristen Madsen
Vice President, Business Development: Mitch Roth
Vice President, South Region: Nancy Shapiro
Senior Vice President, Awards: Diane Theroit

Historical Note:
NARAS presents the annual "Grammy" awards for outstanding recordings and grants the "Grammy Lifetime Achievement" to those who have contributed to the world of music during their lifetime. Members are singers, musicians, engineers, composers, arrangers and others engaged in producing commercial recordings. Membership: $100-420 (Voting);

National Academy of Sciences (1863)
500 Fifth St. NW
Washington, DC 20001
Tel: (202) 334-2000 *Fax:* (202) 334-1684
E-Mail: webmailbox@nas.edu
Website: nasonline.org
Members: 2,200 members and 400 foreign associates
Staff: 45
Annual Budget: Over $100,000,000
Tax: 501(c)(3)

Personnel:
Executive Director: Kenneth R. Fulton
  E-Mail: kfulton@nas.edu

Historical Note:
NAS works to serve as an advisor to the federal government on questions of science and technology. Conducts studies in disciplines of natural and social sciences and engineering, with emphasis on science advisory role in public policy issues. Members are elected to the National Academy of Sciences in recognition of their distinguished and continuing achievements in original research.

Meetings/Conferences:
Conference Chair: Pamela Wimmer

Publications:
Biographical Memoirs
Issues in Science and Technology; quarterly
Letter to Members
Membership Directory; on-line
Proceedings of the National Academy of Sciences (PNAS); weekly; adv.

Membership List Available to Non-members

National Academy of Television Arts and Science (1955)
1697 Broadway
Suite 1001
New York, NY 10019
Tel: (212) 586-8424 *Fax:* (212) 246-8129
Website: emmyonline.org
Members: 13000 individuals
Staff: 7
Annual Budget: $2-5,000,000

Personnel:
Executive Director: Brent Stanton

Chief Operating Office and Chief Financial Officer: Carolyn Grippi
Senior Manager, Information Technology Services: Robert Lazo
President and Chief Executive Officer: Peter O. Price
Director, Special Events: Lauren Saverine

Historical Note:
NATAS's purpose is to advance the arts and sciences of television and the promotion of creative leadership for artistic, educational and technical achievements within the television industry. Maintains an archival program library on the campus of UCLA. Members are writers, engineers, editors, musicians and others engaged in the creative aspects of the television industry.

Meetings/Conferences:
Conference Chair: Lauren Saverine

Publications:
The National Online; on-line

National Accounting and Finance Council (1941)
950 N Glebe Rd.
Suite 210
Arlington, VA 22203-4181
Tel: (703) 838-1915 *Fax:* (703) 838-1701
E-Mail: nafc@trucking.org
Website: truckline.com/Federation/Councils/ NAFC/
Members: 1000 individuals
Staff: 4
Annual Budget: $250-500,000

Personnel:
Executive Director: David Hershey
Technical Director: David Salerno
  E-Mail: dsalerno@trucking.org

Historical Note:
NAFC's mission is to create value for its members through advocacy, education, research and technical assistance regarding finance, accounting, tax, and risk management issues impacting the trucking industry. NAFC is a member organization of chief financial officers within the trucking industry and is a part of the American Trucking Association.

Meetings/Conferences: Annual

National Action Council for Minorities in Engineering (NACME) (1974)
440 Hamilton Ave.
Suite 302
White Plains, NY 10601-1813
Tel: (914) 539-4010 *Fax:* (914) 539-4032
E-Mail: info@nacme.org
Website: nacme.org
Members: 20000 alumni
Staff: 13
Annual Budget: $2-5,000,000

Personnel:
President and Chief Executive Officer: Irving Pressley McPhail
  E-Mail: saustin@nacme.org
Senior Vice President, Operations: Saundra Johnson Austin
  E-Mail: saustin@nacme.org
Director, Research, Evaluation and Policy: Dr. Lisa Frehill PhD
  E-Mail: lfrehill@nacme.org
Director, Communications: Brenda O. Krulik
  E-Mail: bkrulik@nacme.org
Manager, Corporate and Foundation Relations: Susanna Miller
  E-Mail: smiller@nacme.org
Vice President, Administration & Chief Financial Officer.: Michael T. Pan
Director, Information Technology: Carolina Sanchez
  E-Mail: csanchez@nacme.org

Historical Note:
NACME works to insure American competitiveness in a flat world by leading and supporting the national effort to expand U.S. capability through increasing the number of successful African American, American Indian, and Latino women and men in science, technology, engineering and mathematics (STEM) education and careers.

Meetings/Conferences: Annual
Number of non-conference events/year: 1

Publications:
NACME Now; on-line

National Active and Retired Federal Employees Association *(1921)*

606 N. Washington St.
Alexandria, VA 22314
Tel: (703) 838-7760 *Fax:* (703) 838-7785
TollFree: (800) 456-8410
E-Mail: hq@narfe.org
Website: narfe.org
Members: 320000 individuals
Staff: 60
Annual Budget: $25-50,000

Personnel:
National President: Joseph A. Beaudoin
   E-Mail: natpres@narfe.org
Legislative Director: Dan C. Adcock
   E-Mail: dadcock@narfe.org
Director, Membership Services: Bridget A. Boel
Director, Communications: Margaret Carter
Director, Information Technology: Fred Hamidzada
Director, Marketing and Meeting Planning: Juliet Harding
   E-Mail: jharding@narfe.org
Director, Human Resources: Linda Parsons
   E-Mail: lparsons@narfe.org
Director, Retirement Benefits Services: David Snell
National Treasurer: Richard G. Thissen

Historical Note:
Formerly (1971) National Association of Retired Civil Employees. Sponsors and supports the National Active and Retired Federal Employees Association Political Action Committee. NAFRE's mission is to protect the earned rights and benefits of America's active and retired federal workers. Membership includes retirees, active employees, spouses, former employees and former spouses legally entitled to a federal survivor annuity. Membership: $40/year (Individual).

Meetings/Conferences:
Conference Chair: Juliet Harding

Publications:
Membership Directory; on-line
NARFE Magazine; monthly; adv.
NARFE Newsletter; monthly

National Adult Day Service Association *(1979)*

1421 E. Broad St.
Suite 425
Fuquay Varina, NC 27526
Tel: (877) 745-1440 *Fax:* (919) 825-3945
E-Mail: info@nadsa.org
Website: nadsa.org
Members: 3500 adult day centers
Staff: 2

Personnel:
Managing Director: Sara Myers
Director, Communications: Teresa Johnson
   E-Mail: tj.ccadc@mindspring.com

Historical Note:
Formally (1995) National Institute on Adult Daycare. Mission is to enhance the success of its members through advocacy, education, technical assistance, research and communications services. It represents community-based group programs that provide care services for seniors in a non-residential setting. Membership: $299 (Center); $1,000 (Vendor Partner); $300 (State Association Partners); $79 (Associate/Individual); $49 (Associate).

Meetings/Conferences: Annual
2013 - Louisville, KY/Sept. 15 - 21

Publications:
Member Directory
Newsletter; quarterly

National Adult Education Professional Development Consortium *(1990)*

444 N. Capitol St. NW
Suite 422
Washington, DC 20001
Tel: (202) 624-5250 *Fax:* (202) 624-1497
E-Mail: lmclendon@naepdc.org
Website: naepdc.org
Members: 55 state and territorial agencies
Staff: 1
Annual Budget: $250-500,000

Personnel:
Executive Director: Dr. Lennox McLendon
   E-Mail: lmclendon@naepdc.org

Historical Note:

NAEPDC's mission is to coordinate, develop, and conduct programs of professional development for state adult education staffs.

Publications:
News, Views, and Clues; monthly

National Aeronautic Association *(1905)*

One Reagan National Airport Hngr Seven
Suite 202
Washington, DC 20001-6015
Tel: (703) 416-4888 *Fax:* (703) 416-4877
E-Mail: naa@naa.aero
Website: naa.aero
Members: 3000 individuals and 10 Organization
Staff: 4
Annual Budget: $500-1,000,000
Tax: 501(c)(3)

Personnel:
President: Jonathan Gaffney
   E-Mail: jgaffney@naa.aero
Contact, Awards and Events: Cassandra Bosco
   E-Mail: cbosco@naa.aero
General Counsel: George U. Carneal
Director, Administration: Nancy Sack
   E-Mail: nsack@naa.aero

Historical Note:
NAA's mission is the advancement of the art, sport, and science of aviation and space flight by fostering opportunities to participate fully in aviation activities and by promoting public understanding of the importance of aviation and space flight to the United States. Membership: $39 (Bronze Level); $125 (Silver Level); $250 (Gold Level); $1000 (Platinum (Life) Level).

Meetings/Conferences: Annual
Conference Chair: Cassandra Bosco
Number of non-conference events/year: 3

Publications:
Aero; bi-monthly; adv.
Air & Space; adv.
Membership Directory; on-line
The NAA Record; monthly

National Aerosol Association *(1986)*

P.O. Box 5510
Fullerton, CA 92838
Tel: (714) 525-1518 *Fax:* (714) 526-1295
E-Mail: naa@nationalaerosol.com
Website: nationalaerosol.com
Members: 30 companies and 30 individuals
Staff: 2
Annual Budget: $50-100,000

Personnel:
Executive Director: Mary Metzner
   E-Mail: info@waib.org
Newsletter Publisher: Sharon Rowson

Historical Note:
NAA is dedicated to the promotion and protection of the aerosol package. It also encourages expanded use of aerosol products through pro-active public relations that enumerate the merits of the aerosol package, such as being environmentally desirable, economical, hygienic, tamper-proof, and highly efficient. Membership: $1,250-5,000 (Corporate); $500 (Professional); $250 (Affiliate).

Meetings/Conferences: Annual
Conference Chair: Mary Metzner
2013 - San Antonio, TX (Marriott San Antonio Riverwalk Hotel)/March 5 - 7

Publications:
NAA Aerosol News; quarterly

National Affordable Housing Management Association *(1990)*

400 N. Columbus St.
Suite 203
Alexandria, VA 22314
Tel: (703) 683-8630 *Fax:* (703) 683-8634
Website: nahma.org
Members: 2500 individuals
Staff: 9
Annual Budget: $1-2,000,000
Tax: 501(c)(6)

Personnel:
Executive Director: Kris Cook CAE
   E-Mail: kris.cook@nahma.org
Director, Finance and Administration: Rajni Agarwal
   E-Mail: rajni.agarwal@nahma.org

Coordinator, Education Programs and Special Projects: Timothy H. Bishop
   E-Mail: tim.bishop@nahma.org
Director, Government Affairs: Michelle L. Kitchen
   E-Mail: michelle.kitchen@nahma.org
Director, Meetings and Membership: Brenda Moser
   E-Mail: brenda.moser@nahma.org

Historical Note:
Formerly the National Assisted Housing Management Association, formed through a merger of the former National Advisory Council of HUD Management Agents and the National Federation of Associations of HUD Management Agents. NAHMA's mission is to support legislative and regulatory policy that promotes the development and preservation of decent and safe affordable housing. Members are owners and managers of affordable housing and multifamily housing communities subject to the regulations of federal agencies. Membership: $1,150-2,900 (Executive); $1,400 (Associate); $900 (Affiliate).

Continuing Education:
Certification Designation/s: NAHP, NAHP-e, FHC, NAHMT, NAHMS, CGPM, CPO, SHCM

Meetings/Conferences:
Conference Chair: Brenda Moser
Number of non-conference events/year: 1

Publications:
Membership Directory; annually
NAHMA News; bi-monthly
NAHP Update; quarterly

National After School Association

8400 Westpark Dr., Second Floor
Suite 200
McLean, VA 22102
Tel: (703) 610-9002 *Fax:* (703) 610-9003
E-Mail: info@naaweb.org
Website: naaweb.org
Members:
9000 individuals
36 institutional
Staff: 4
Annual Budget: $1-2,000,000

Personnel:
Executive Director: Gina Warner
   E-Mail: gwarner@naaweb.org
Manager, Accreditation: Susan Knight
   E-Mail: slnknight@bellsouth.net

Historical Note:
Formerly National School-Age Care Alliance (NSACA). Affiliate Organizations are found for this Association. NAA is dedicated to development, education, and care of children and youth during their out of school hours. Membership: $70 (Full Member); $35 (Associate Member); $395 (Supplier).

Meetings/Conferences: Annual
2013 - Indianapolis, IN (Indianapolis Convention Center)/April 7 - 10

Publications:
AfterSchool Today; quarterly
NAA E-News; bi-weekly; adv.
NAA Standards
New Directions for Youth Development; quarterly

National Agri-Marketing Association *(1956)*

11020 King St.
Suite 205
Overland Park, KS 66210
Tel: (913) 491-6500 *Fax:* (913) 491-6502
E-Mail: agrimktg@nama.org
Website: nama.org
Members: 2500 individuals
Staff: 6
Annual Budget: $1-2,000,000

Personnel:
Executive Vice President and Chief Executive Officer: Jenny Pickett
   E-Mail: jennyp@nama.org
Manager, Chapter and Membership Services: Debbie Brummel
   E-Mail: debbieb@nama.org
Manager, Programs and Information Services: Jan Cichello
   E-Mail: janc@nama.org
Administrative Assistant: Penny Graham
   E-Mail: pennyg@nama.org
Manager, Accounting Services: Sherry Pfaff
   E-Mail: sherryp@nama.org

Historical Note:

Originated as the Chicago Area Agricultural Advertising Association. Became (1963) National Agricultural Advertising and Marketing Association, assumed its present name in 1973. NAMA is a professional association for professionals in marketing and agribusiness. Mission is to bring together all aspects of the industry for the betterment of all in its business. Membership: $175/year (Individual-Average).

Meetings/Conferences: Semi-Annual
Conference Chair: Jan Cichello
2013 - Kansas City, MO (Sheraton Crown Center)/April 17 - 19

Publications:
Membership Directory; annually
NAMA e-Newsletter; on-line

National Agricultural Alumni and Development Association
1000 Westgate Dr.
Suite 252
St. Paul, MN 55114
Tel: (651) 203-7246 *Fax:* (651) 290-2266
E-Mail: naadahq@aol.com
Website: naada.org
Staff: 9
Annual Budget: $100-250,000

Personnel:
President: Jillian Stevenson
   E-Mail: jstevenson@psu.edu
Contact, Finance and Accounting: Jane Bernier
   E-Mail: janeb@ewald.com
Contact, Conference Management: Carissa Broderick
   E-Mail: carissab@naada.org
Contact, Marketing and Communications: Janey Duntley
   E-Mail: janeyd@naada.org
Contact , Finance and Sponsorship: Bill McCloskey
   E-Mail: billb.mccloskey@ky.gov
Contact, Membership Services: Chris Swanson
   E-Mail: memberservices@naada.org
Contact, Publications and Projects Competition: Jill Tyson
   E-Mail: tyson.46@osu.edu
Contact, Education: Tina Veal
   E-Mail: vealt@illinois.edu

Historical Note:
NAADA's mission is to provide education, support and recognition for individuals dedicated to expanding resources for land-grant and other colleges of agricultural sciences and related programs. Membership: $500-1500 (Institution, Based on number of staff); $350 (Organization); $500 (Corporate Silver); $1000 (Corporate Gold); $2500 (Corporate Platinum); $25 (Associate).

Meetings/Conferences: Annual
Conference Chair: Carissa Broderick
2013 - Alexandria, VA (Crowne Plaza Old Town Alexandria Hotel)/June 16 - 19

Publications:
Connections; monthly
Membership Directory; on-line

National Agricultural Aviation Association (1966)
1005 E St. SE
Washington, DC 20003-2847
Tel: (202) 546-5722 *Fax:* (202) 546-5726
E-Mail: information@agaviation.org
Website: agaviation.org
Members: 1600 members
Staff: 6
Annual Budget: $1-2,000,000
Tax: 501(c)(6)

Personnel:
Executive Director: Andrew D. Moore
   E-Mail: admoore@agaviation.org
Manager, Communications: Jay Calleja
Director, Education and Safety: Kenneth W. Degg
Manager, Government and Public Relations: Danna Kelemen

Historical Note:
Formerly (1971) National Aerial Applicators Association. NAAA represents the interests of small business owners and pilots licensed as commercial applicators that use aircraft to enhance food, fiber and bio-fuel production, protect forestry and control health-threatening pests. Membership: 85-1,000/year.

Meetings/Conferences: Annual
2013 - Reno, NV/Dec. 9 - 12
2015 - Savannah, GA/Dec. 7 - 10

Publications:
Membership Directory; on-line

NAAA eNewsletter; adv.

National Air Carrier Association (1962)
1000 Wilson Blvd.
Suite 1700
Arlington, VA 22209
Tel: (703) 358-8060 *Fax:* (703) 358-8070
Website: naca.cc
Members: 25 companies
Staff: 3
Annual Budget: $500-1,000,000

Personnel:
President: A. Oakley Brooks
   E-Mail: obrooks@naca.cc
Director, Government Affairs: Paul Doell
   E-Mail: pauldoell51@yahoo.com
Director, Technical Services: Ty Prettyman
   E-Mail: ty.prettyman@naca.cc

Historical Note:
NACA is an aviation trade association promoting the national and international interests of its members and represent their interests before the Congress of the United States and the Government agencies. Sustaining members are airlines that hold operating certificates under 14 CFR 121.

Publications:
Air Currents; weekly; adv.

National Air Filtration Association (1980)
P.O. Box 68639
Virginia Beach, VA 23471
Tel: (757) 313-7400 *Fax:* (757) 497-1895
E-Mail: nafa@nafahq.org
Website: nafahq.org
Members:
180 companies
20 individuals
Staff: 7
Annual Budget: $250-500,000
Tax: 501(c)(6)

Personnel:
Executive Director: Alan C Veeck CAFS
Contact, Conventions: Terry Driscoll
   E-Mail: nafa@nafahq.org

Historical Note:
NAFA's mission is to conduct education and certification programs for members and end-user personnel. Members include air filter and component manufacturers, sales and service companies, and HVAC and indoor air quality professionals across the United States and in several foreign countries. Membership: $520 (Active); $945 (Associate); $200 (Supplemental); $75 (Affiliate); $125 (Professional/General); $25 (Student); $25 (application processing fee).

Continuing Education:
Certification Designation/s: NCT, NCT II, CAFS

Meetings/Conferences: Annual
Conference Chair: Terry Driscoll
2013 - Savannah, GA (The Westin Savannah Harbor Golf Resort & Spa)/Sept. 25 - 27

Publications:
Membership Directory
NAFA Air Media magazine; quarterly

National Air Traffic Controllers Association (1987)
1325 Massachusetts Ave. NW
Washington, DC 20005
Tel: (202) 628-5451 *Fax:* (202) 628-5767
TollFree: (800) 266-0895
Website: natca.org
Members: 20000 individuals
Staff: 43
Annual Budget: $50-100,000

Personnel:
Executive Director: Barry Krasner
   E-Mail: bkrasner@natcadc.org
Director, Government Affairs: Jose Ceballos
   E-Mail: jceballos@natcadc.org
Director, Communications: Doug Church
   E-Mail: dchurch@natcadc.org
General Counsel: Marguerite L. Graf
   E-Mail: mgraf@natcadc.org
Director, Labor Relations: Anna Jancewicz
   E-Mail: ajancewicz@natcadc.org
Manager, Outreach and Special Events: Kelly Richardson
   E-Mail: krichardson@natcadc.org
Manager, Information Technology: Phil Yanchulis

E-Mail: pyanchulis@natcadc.org
Director, Membership and Marketing: Lew Zietz

Historical Note:
NATCA is committed to ensure the safety of every flight. It serves its membership and also strives to further the public's interest in safe and efficient air transportation. Members are controllers, engineers and other safety-related professionals. Membership: $25-250 (Associate), $500-1,250 (Corporate).

Meetings/Conferences:
Conference Chair: Kelly Richardson

Publications:
NATCA Insider; weekly
The Air Traffic Controller; bi-monthly

National Air Transportation Association (1974)
4226 King St.
Alexandria, VA 22302-1507
Tel: (703) 845-9000 *Fax:* (703) 845-8176
TollFree: (800) 808-6282
E-Mail: info@nata.aero
Website: nata.aero
Members: 2000 air carriers and airport service organizations
Staff: 26
Annual Budget: $5-10,000,000
Tax: 501(c)(6)

Personnel:
President and Chief Executive Officer: Tom Hendricks
Vice President, Government and Industry Affairs: Eric R Byer
   E-Mail: ebyer@nata.aero
Director, Marketing and Communications: Shannon Chambers
Director, Meetings and Conventions: Diane Gleason
Director, Membership Services and Business Development: Daniel Gurley
   E-Mail: dgurley@nata.aero
Vice President, Finance: Timothy Heck
   E-Mail: theck@nata.aero
Director, Safety and Training: Amy B Koranda
   E-Mail: akoranda@nata.aero
Comptroller: Johanna OToole
   E-Mail: jotoole@nata.aero
Director, Technology Initiative: David Vernon
   E-Mail: dvernon@nata.aero

Historical Note:
Public policy group representing the interests of aviation businesses

Meetings/Conferences:
Conference Chair: Diane Gleason
Number of non-conference events/year: 10

Publications:
ASC Monthly Update; monthly; adv.
Aviation Business Journal; quarterly; adv.
Membership Directory; on-line
NATA News; weekly; adv.

National Aircraft Finance Association (1969)
P.O. Box 1570
Edgewater, MD 21037
Tel: (410) 571-1740 *Fax:* (410) 571-1780
E-Mail: info@nafa.aero
Website: nafa.aero
Members: 70 lending institutions
Staff: 3
Annual Budget: $250-500,000

Personnel:
Executive Director: Karen Griggs
   E-Mail: karengriggs@nafa.aero
Treasurer: Tobias Kleitman
General Counsel: David Warner

Historical Note:
NAFA strives to promote the general welfare of individuals and organizations providing aircraft financing and loans secured by aircraft. Members are lending institutions involved in aircraft financing. Membership: $600/year (Full/Associate).

Meetings/Conferences: Annual
Number of non-conference events/year: 21

Publications:
Membership Directory; on-line
NAFA Newsletter

National Aircraft Resale Association
P.O. Box 3860

Grapevine, TX 76099
Tel: (866) 284-4744 *Fax:* (866) 447-1777
Website: nara-dealers.com
Members: 105 companies
Staff: 2
Annual Budget: $500-1,000,000

Personnel:
President: Susan L. Sheets
    E-Mail: slsheets@nara-dealers.com
Association Director: Devri Pitts
    E-Mail: dpitts@nara-dealers.com

Historical Note:
NARA's mission is to create a competitive advantage for members and their customers by leveraging a global collective knowledge and maintaining the highest professional standards. NARA members are brokers and resellers specializing in pre-owned aircraft. Associate membership is available for firms who supply services or materials to the industry.

Meetings/Conferences: Annual
Conference Chair: Devri Pitts
2013 - Amelia Island, FL (Amelia Island Ritz-Carlton)/
    April 3 - 5

Membership List Available to Non-members

National Alarm Association of America *(1984)*
P.O. Box 3409
Dayton, OH 45401-3409
Tel: (800) 283-6285 *Fax:* (937) 866-5098
TollFree: (800) 283-6285
E-Mail: info@naaa.org
Website: naaa.org
Members: 300 companies and 50 associate companies
Staff: 2
Annual Budget: $10-25,000
Tax: 501(c)(6)

Personnel:
President: Gene Riddlebaugh
    E-Mail: gdridd@aol.com

Historical Note:
Purpose is to promote the welfare of members through free exchange of ideas and the dissemination of information concerning trade practices, business conditions, technical developments within the industry and any related subject of concern to the security industry. Members are small alarm dealers. Membership: $100 (Regular/Associate); $50 (Electronic Security Association - ESA).

Publications:
Membership Directory; on-line

National Alcohol Beverage Control Association *(1938)*
4401 Ford Ave.
Suite 700
Alexandria, VA 22302-1473
Tel: (703) 578-4200 *Fax:* (703) 820-3551
E-Mail: nabca.info@nabca.org
Website: nabca.org
Members: 195 companies
Staff: 40
Annual Budget: $5-10,000,000

Personnel:
President and Chief Executive Officer: James M. Sgueo
    E-Mail: jsgueo@nabca.org
Director, Finance and Human Resources: Carmen Ford
General Counsel: James M. Goldberg
Contact, Membership Services: Dixie Jamison
    E-Mail: djamison@nabca.org
Senior Vice President, Administration and Chief Financial Officer: Patricia K. LaCava
Senior Vice President, Public Policy and Communications: Steven L. Schmidt
    E-Mail: sschmidt@nabca.org
Coordinator, Database: Dionne Thompson
Manager, Meetings: Lorrie Zimecki

Historical Note:
NABCA's mission is to support alcohol control systems by providing resources, compiling research and fostering relationships to address policy for the responsible sale and consumption of alcoholic beverages. Members include control jurisdictions, supplier members and industry trade associations. Membership: $750 (Broker/Allied); $1,500 (Association); $500 (Governmental).

Meetings/Conferences: Semi-Annual
Conference Chair: Lorrie Zimecki

Publications:

NABCA Online Directory; on-line

National ALEC Association/ Prepaid Communications Association
2001 Pennsylvania Ave. NW
Suite 400
Washington, DC 20006-1851
Tel: (202) 862-3773 *Fax:* (202) 296-6518
E-Mail: info@nala-pca.org
Website: nala-pca.org
Staff: 1

Personnel:
Office Administrator: Torian Meals

Historical Note:
NALA/PCA represents local exchange carriers, long distance distributors, and other companies.

National Alfalfa Alliance
4630 Churchill St.
Suite One
St. Paul, MN 55126
Tel: (651) 484-3888 *Fax:* (651) 638-0756
E-Mail: nafa@comcast.net
Website: alfalfa.org
Staff: 7
Annual Budget: $250-500,000

Personnel:
President: Beth Nelson
Director, Communications: Jenna Knoblauch
Coordinator, Events: Chelsea Russell

Historical Note:
NAFA's mission is to ensure the ability of all segments of the alfalfa and forage industry to compete effectively and profitably, domestically and abroad. Membership: $100 (Industrial Producer); $500 (Associate); $1,500-20,000 (Silver/Gold/Platinum/Diamond).

Meetings/Conferences: Annual
Conference Chair: Chelsea Russell

Publications:
e Hay Weekly; weekly
Hay & Forage Grower; adv.
Winter Survival, Fall Dormancy, & Pest Resistance Ratings for Alfalfa Varieties Leadlet; annually

National Alfalfa and Forage Alliance *(2006)*
4630 Churchill St.
Suite One
St. Paul, MN 55126
Tel: (651) 484-3888 *Fax:* (651) 638-0756
E-Mail: nafa@comcast.net
Website: alfalfa.org
Members: 1500 individuals and companies
Staff: 8
Annual Budget: $250-500,000

Personnel:
President: Beth Nelson
Executive Secretary: Rod Christensen
Education Director: Shane Johnson
Director, Communications: Jenna Knoblauch
Director, Information Technology: Sherry Liu
Publications Director: Sheri Nolan
Coordinator, Events: Chelsea Russell

Historical Note:
Formerly (2003) National Alfalfa Alliance. Supersedes Alfalfa Council (1953-2003). NAFA's mission is to ensure the ability of all segments of the alfalfa and forage industry to compete effectively and profitably, domestically and abroad. It also provide a forum for consensus building among stakeholders and is a political advocate on behalf of the industry. Membership: $100-20,000/year.

Meetings/Conferences:
Conference Chair: Chelsea Russell

Publications:
Hay and Forage

National Alliance for Accessible Golf *(2001)*
1733 King St.
Alexandria, VA 22314
Tel: (703) 299-4296 *Fax:* (703) 739-0124
E-Mail: info@accessgolf.org
Website: accessgolf.org
Staff: 3
Annual Budget: $100-250,000

Personnel:
President: Betsy Clark PhD
    E-Mail: bclark.dbcc@gmail.com
Board Director: Andrew Brockman

    E-Mail: andrew.brockman@accessgolf.org
Treasurer: Stephen Jubb
    E-Mail: sjubb@pgahq.com

Historical Note:
The mission of the Alliance is to increase participation of people with disabilities in the game of golf.

Membership List Available to Non-members

National Alliance for Advanced Transportation Batteries
122 S. Michigan Ave.
Suite 1700
Chicago, IL 60603
Tel: (312) 588-0477
Website: naatbatt.org
Staff: 5

Personnel:
Executive Director: Jim Greenberger
Chief Technology Officer: Ralph Brodd
Chief Financial Officer: Sanford Kane
Head, Communications: Michael Lew
Director, Operations and Development: Elena Pitt

Historical Note:
Promotes the domestic manufacture of lithium-ion batteries.NAATBatt's misson is to accelerate the development and domestic manufacture of large format advanced technology batteries in the United States for transportation and large scale energy storage applications consistent with the national goals of enhancing energy security and increasing carbon-free electricity generation.membership: $7500 (Platinum members); $5000(Gold members); $2500(Silver members); $500(Academic members).

Meetings/Conferences: Annual
2013 - Austin, TX (Renaissance Austin Hotel)/Jan. 16 - 18

Publications:
NAATBatt Advanced Battery Weekly; weekly

National Alliance for Hispanic Health *(1973)*
1501 16th St. NW
Washington, DC 20036-1401
Tel: (202) 387-5000 *Fax:* (202) 797-4353
E-Mail: alliance@hispanichealth.org
Website: hispanichealth.org
Members: 1200 organizations and individuals
Staff: 100
Annual Budget: $5-10,000,000
Tax: 501(c)(3)

Personnel:
President and Chief Executive Officer: Dr. Jane L. Delgado PhD, MS
    E-Mail: jdelgado@hispanichealth.org
Vice President, Science and Policy: Adolph P. Falcon MPP
    E-Mail: afalcon@hispanichealth.org
Chief Financial Officer: Hazel E. Moss
Senior Program Manager: Edgar Gil Rico
Media Contact: Adam Segal
    E-Mail: media@hispanichealth.org

Historical Note:
Formerly National Coalition of Hispanic Mental Health and Human Services Organizations, became National Coalition of Hispanic Health and Human Services Organizations in 1986 and assumed its current name in 2000. NAHH's mission is to improve the health of Hispanic communities and work with others to secure health for all. Membership: $75 (Professional); $25 (Student/Retired); $12 (Consumer); $500-10,000 (Organization).

Meetings/Conferences: Annual
Number of non-conference events/year: 10

Publications:
Newsletter; on-line

National Alliance for Hospice Access
1220 N. Fillmore St.
Suite 400
Arlington, VA 22201
Website: hospiceaccess.com
Staff: 1

Personnel:
Treasurer: Ran Millan

Historical Note:
The National Alliance for Hospice Access (NAHA) is a non-profit grassroots .

National Alliance for Media Arts and Culture *(1980)*

145 Ninth St.
Suite 102
San Francisco, CA 94103
Tel: (415) 431-1391 *Fax:* (415) 431-1392
E-Mail: namac@namac.org
Website: namac.org
Members: 350 media arts centers
Staff: 4
Annual Budget: $250-500,000

Personnel:
Executive Director: Jack Walsh
 E-Mail: jack@namac.org
Online Community Manager: Rachel Allen
 E-Mail: rachel@namac.org
Manager, Program and Membership Services: Aggie
 Ebrahimi Bazaz
 E-Mail: aggie@namac.org
Coordinator, Conferences: Kathy Harr
 E-Mail: kathy@namac.org

Historical Note:
*Formerly (1992) the National Alliance of Media Arts
Centers, NAMAC fosters and fortifies the culture and
business of independent media arts. Members include
community-based media production centers and facilities,
university-based programs, museums, media presenters and
exhibitors, film festivals, distributors, film archives, youth
media programs, community access television, digital arts
and online groups, and policy-related centers. Membership:
$75-450 (Institutional); $75 (Independent Professional);
$40 (Student).*

Meetings/Conferences:
Conference Chair: Kathy Harr

Publications:
eBulletin; monthly; adv.

National Alliance for Musical Theatre *(1985)*
520 Eighth Ave.
Suite 301
New York, NY 10018
Tel: (212) 714-6668 *Fax:* (212) 714-0469
E-Mail: info@namt.org
Website: namt.org/
Members: 150 theatres and organizations
Staff: 9
Annual Budget: $500-1,000,000
Tax: 501(c)(3)

Personnel:
Executive Director: Betsy King Militello
 E-Mail: betsy@namt.org
Interim Office Coordinator: Marvin Avila
 E-Mail: kimberly@namt.org
Director, Membership Services: Adam Grosswirth
 E-Mail: adam@namt.org

Historical Note:
*NAMT's mission is to provide service for sharing of
resources and information relating to professional
musical theatre through communications, networking and
programming. Members are theatres and professional
drama organizations with an interest in the development of
stage musicals. Membership: $525-2,600 (Organizational);
$350 (Associate).*

Meetings/Conferences: Annual
Conference Chair: Adam Grosswirth
2013 - Chicago, IL (Chicago Shakespeare Theater)/
 April 4 - 6

Publications:
E-News; weekly
Membership Directory; on-line
New Works Newsletter; monthly

National Alliance for Specialty Healthcare Programs *(2003)*
222 S. First St.
Suite 303
Louisville, KY 40202
Tel: (502) 403-1122 *Fax:* (502) 403-1129
Website: nasho.org
Members: 32 organizations
Staff: 2

Personnel:
Executive Director: Julian Roberts
 E-Mail: jroberts@nasho.org
Manager, Membership Services: Pat Ciresi
 E-Mail: pciresi@nasho.org

Historical Note:
*NASHO is an American Association of Preferred Providers
(AAPPO) partner association, launched in January 2003*

to advance and evolve specialty healthcare delivery in the
United States.

Publications:
Membership Directory; on-line

National Alliance for Youth Sports *(1981)*
2050 Vista Pkwy.
W. Palm Beach, FL 33411
Tel: (561) 684-1141 *Fax:* (561) 684-2546
TollFree: (800) 729-2057
E-Mail: nays@nays.org
Website: nays.org
Members: 150000 individuals
Staff: 44
Annual Budget: $2-5,000,000
Tax: 501(c)(3)

Personnel:
President and Chief Executive Officer: Fred C. Engh
 E-Mail: Fengh@nays.org
Vice President, Communications: Greg Bach
 E-Mail: gbach@nays.org
Chief Operating Officer: John Engh
 E-Mail: Jengh@nays.org
Vice President, Membership Programs: Emmy Martinez
 E-Mail: Emartinez@nays.org
Chief Financial Officer: Yolanda Williams
 E-Mail: ywilliams@nays.org

Historical Note:
*Formerly (1997) National Youth Sport Coaches
Association. NAYS seeks to make the sports experience
safe, fun and healthy for all children and also promotes the
value and importance of sports and physical activities in
the emotional, physical, social and mental development of
youth.*

Meetings/Conferences: Annual
2013 - San Diego, CA (San Diego Convention Center)/
 Nov. 21 - 23

Publications:
SportingKid Magazine; quarterly; adv.

National Alliance of Black School Educators *(1970)*
310 Pennsylvania Ave. SE
Washington, DC 20003
Tel: (202) 608-6310 *Fax:* (202) 608-6319
TollFree: (800) 221-2654
E-Mail: info@nabse.org
Website: nabse.org
Members: 4000 individuals
Staff: 4
Annual Budget: $1-2,000,000

Personnel:
Executive Director: Quentin R. Lawson
 E-Mail: qlawson@nabse.org
Accountant: Fistume Andeberhan
 E-Mail: Fistume@nabse.org
Director, Membership and Conferences: Ed Potillo
 E-Mail: epotillo@nabse.org

Historical Note:
*Formerly (1970) the National Alliance of Black School
Superintendents, assumed its current name in 1973.
NABSE's mission is to promote and facilitate the education
of all students, with a particular focus on African American
students. Membership: $20-2000/year.*

Meetings/Conferences: Annual
Conference Chair: Ed Potillo
Number of non-conference events/year: 2

Publications:
NewsBriefs; annually
The Journal of the Alliance of Black School Educators

National Alliance of Community Economic Development Associations *(2006)*
P.O. Box 12192
Washington, DC 20005
Tel: (202) 518-2660
E-Mail: info@naceda.org
Website: naceda.org
Members: 4000 community-based organizations
Staff: 2
Annual Budget: $250-500,000
Tax: 501(c)(3)

Personnel:
Director: Frank Woodruff

Historical Note:
*NACEDA is a national organization created to support
the work of community economic development (CED)*

associations, local Community Development corporations
(CDCs) and practitioners nationwide. NACEDA's mission is
to lead the community development field and its partners in
shaping and influencing strategies that advance community
prosperity. Membership: $500-1,500 (Voting); $100-750
(Affiliate); $75 (Individual); $25 (Student).

Publications:
Newsletters; monthly

National Alliance of Forest Owners *(2008)*
122 C St. NW, Suite 630
Washington, DC 20001
Tel: (202) 747-0759 *Fax:* (202) 824-0770
E-Mail: info@nafoalliance.org
Website: nafoalliance.org
Members: 61 companies and associations
Staff: 6
Annual Budget: $2-5,000,000
Tax: 501(c)(6)

Personnel:
President and Chief Executive Officer: David Tenny
 E-Mail: dtenny@nafoalliance.org
Manager, Operations and Government Relations: Amy
 Castellano
 E-Mail: acastellano@nafoalliance.org
Vice President, Policy and General Counsel: Chip Murray
 E-Mail: cmurray@nafoalliance.org
Vice President, Communications: Gretchen Schaefer
 E-Mail: gschaefer@nafoalliance.org

Historical Note:
*NAFO's mission is to protect and enhance the economic
and environmental values of privately-owned forests
through targeted policy advocacy at the national level.*

National Alliance of Independent Crop Consultants *(1978)*
349 E. Nolley Dr.
Collierville, TN 38017
Tel: (901) 861-0511 *Fax:* (901) 861-0512
Website: naicc.org
Members: 500 individuals
Staff: 1
Annual Budget: $250-500,000
Tax: 501(c)(6)

Personnel:
Executive Vice President: Allison Jones
 E-Mail: JonesNAICC@aol.com

Historical Note:
*NAICC is an outgrowth of the Southern Alliance of
Independent Crop Consultants. NAICC is a professional
society that represents the nation's crop production
and research consultants. Membership: $225 (Voting/
Associate/Provisional); $175 (Additional Members); $10
(Student); $65 (Retired); $750-2,500 (Company).*

Continuing Education:
Certification Designation/s: CPCC

Meetings/Conferences: Annual
2013 - Jacksonville, FL (Hyatt Regency Jacksonville
 Riverfront)/Jan. 23 - 26

Publications:
Membership Directory; on-line
NAICC News; monthly; adv.

Membership List Available to Non-members

National Alliance of Medicare Set-Aside Professionals, Inc. *(2005)*
2851 S. Parker Rd.
Suite 560
Aurora, CO 80014
Tel: (877) 389-4803 *Fax:* (407) 629-2502
E-Mail: info@namsap.org
Website: namsap.org
Staff: 2
Annual Budget: $100-250,000
Tax: 501(c)(6)

Personnel:
President: Michael E. Westcott
 E-Mail: mwestcott@ringlerassociates.com
Treasurer: David J. Korch

Historical Note:
*NAMSAP's mission is to foster the standards of
integrity and competence among Medicare Set-Aside
professionals and those they serve. Membership: $175/year
(Professional/Associate).*

Continuing Education:
Certification Designation/s: CHCC, MSCC

Meetings/Conferences: Annual

2013 - Baltimore, MD (Hyatt Regency Baltimore)/April
25 - 26

Publications:
NAMSAP E-Newsletter; quarterly

National Alliance of Postal and Federal Employees
(1913)
1628 11th St. NW
Washington, DC 20001
Tel: (202) 939-6325 *Fax:* (202) 939-6389
E-Mail: NAPFEFCU@napfe.org
Website: napfe.com
Members: 35000 individuals
Staff: 51
Annual Budget: $2-5,000,000
Tax: 501(c)(5)

Personnel:
President: James M. McGee
    E-Mail: jmcgee@napfe.org
Secretary: Noel V.S. Murrain
Editor: Ernestine Watts-Taylor
    E-Mail: etaylor@napfe.org

Historical Note:
*Formerly National Alliance of Postal Employees with the
purpose of preventing elimination of blacks from railway
mail service, became the first industrial Union in the U.S.
in 1923 and assumed its present name in 1965. Supports
the National Alliance for Political Action and is dedicated to
working together to eliminate discrimination and injustice
in the federal service. Members are people who serve the
Nation as rank and file employees in the federal and or
postal service.*

Publications:
Credit Union Newsletter; quarterly
National Alliance Magazine; monthly
President's Newsletter; monthly

National Alliance of Preservation Commissions
(1983)
P.O. Box 1605
Athens, GA 30603
Tel: (706) 542-4731 *Fax:* (706) 369-5864
E-Mail: napc@uga.edu
Website: napc.uga.edu/
Members: 2400 commissions and individuals
Staff: 1
Annual Budget: $100-250,000
Tax: 501(c)(3)

Personnel:
Director, Programs: Paul Trudeau
    E-Mail: ptrudeau@uga.edu

Historical Note:
*NAPC's mission is to build strong local preservation
programs through education, advocacy, and training.
Members are local historic district commissions and
architectural review boards across the country. Membership:
$35-130/year (Individual/Commissions, based on budget).*

Continuing Education:
Certification Designation/s: CLG, CEE

Meetings/Conferences:
Conference Chair: Paul Trudeau
Number of non-conference events/year: 1

Publications:
The Alliance Review; bi-monthly

National Alliance of State and Territorial AIDS
Directors *(1992)*
444 N. Capitol St. NW
Suite 339
Washington, DC 20001
Tel: (202) 434-8090 *Fax:* (202) 434-8092
E-Mail: NASTAD@NASTAD.org
Website: nastad.org
Members: 59 individuals
Staff: 32
Annual Budget: $5-10,000,000
Tax: 501(c)(3)

Personnel:
Executive Director: Julie M. Scofield
    E-Mail: jscofield@NASTAD.org
Director, Finance and Accounting Services: Eric Booth
    E-Mail: ebooth@NASTAD.org
Director, Human Resources and Administration: Kelly
    Campagne
    E-Mail: kcampagne@NASTAD.org
*Director, Membership Services and Leadership
    Development:* Lynne Greabell

    E-Mail: lgreabell@NASTAD.org
Manager, Meetings, Travel and Membership Services:
    Jermaine Ivy
    E-Mail: jivy@NASTAD.org

Historical Note:
*NASTAD's mission is to strengthen state and territory-
based leadership, expertise and advocacy and bring them
to bear in reducing the incidence of HIV and viral hepatitis
infections and on providing care and support to all who live
with HIV/AIDS and viral hepatitis. Members are nation's
chief state health agency staff.*

Meetings/Conferences:
Conference Chair: Jermaine Ivy

Publications:
Membership Directory; on-line

National Alliance of State Broadcast Associations
2333 Wisconsin St. NE
Albuquerque, NM 87112
Tel: (505) 881-4444 *Fax:* (505) 881-5353
Website: nasbaonline.net/
Staff: 2
Annual Budget: $250-500,000

Personnel:
President: Sharon Tinsley
Secretary and Treasurer: Kent Cornish

Historical Note:
*NASBA's mission is to strive for promotion and
representation of television and broadcasting industry.*

National Alliance of State Pharmacy Associations
(1927)
2530 Professional Rd.
Suite 202
Richmond, VA 23235
Tel: (804) 285-4431 *Fax:* (804) 612-6555
Website: naspa.us
Members:
56 associate member companies
103 individuals
Staff: 9
Annual Budget: $1-2,000,000

Personnel:
Executive Vice President and Chief Executive Officer:
    Rebecca P. Snead
    E-Mail: rsnead@naspa.us
Secretary and Treasurer: Joni Cover
*Vice President, Membership Services, Meetings and
    Corporate Affairs:* Janie Severance
    E-Mail: janie@naspa.us

Historical Note:
*Formerly (2007) National Council of State Pharmacy
Association Executives and (1993) National Council of
State Pharmaceutical Association Executives. NASPA's
mission is to enhance the professional management of state
pharmacy associations and to facilitate communication
and activities related to issues of common concern among
state association members. Membership: $2500 (For Profit
Company); $1000 (Not For Profit company).*

Meetings/Conferences:
Conference Chair: Janie Severance
2013 - Los Angeles, CA/March 1 - 3
2013 - Orlando, FL/Oct. 12 - 13
Number of non-conference events/year: 1

Publications:
Membership directory; on-line

National Alliance of State Science and
Mathematics Coalitions *(1994)*
2200 Wilson Blvd.
Suite 102-166
Arlington, VA 22201-3324
Tel: (703) 516-5973
E-Mail: info@nassmc.org
Website: nassmc.org
Staff: 4
Annual Budget: $50-100,000

Personnel:
Executive Director: Kenneth W. Heydrick EdD
    E-Mail: kheydrick@nassmc.org

Historical Note:
*NASSMC is an umbrella organization for state coalitions
of business, education and public policy leaders united
for systemic change in science, technology, engineering
and mathematics (STEM) education for all students. In
August, 2002, NASSMC moved its office to Arlington from
Washington. Membership: $300/Year; $5000 (Sponsors).*

Meetings/Conferences: Annual
Publications:
NASSMC News Bulletin; monthly

National Alliance to Save Native Languages
(2006)
1455 Pennsylvania Ave. NW
Suite 400
Washington, DC 20004
Tel: (206) 420-4638 *Fax:* (202) 659-1340
Website: savenativelanguages.org
Staff: 1

Personnel:
President: Ryan Wilson
    E-Mail: r_lakota@hotmail.com

Historical Note:
*National Alliance to Save Native Languages purpose is
promoting the revitalization of Native Languages.*

National AMBUCS *(1922)*
P.O. Box 5127
High Point, NC 27262
Tel: (336) 852-0052 *Fax:* (336) 852-6830
TollFree: (800) 838-1845
E-Mail: ambucs@ambucs.org
Website: ambucs.org
Members: 5500 individuals
Staff: 10
Annual Budget: $1-2,000,000
Tax: 501(c)(3)

Personnel:
Executive Director: J. Joseph Copeland
    E-Mail: joec@ambucs.org
Coordinator, Membership Services and Scholarships:
    Janice Blankenship
    E-Mail: janiceb@ambucs.org
Director, Marketing and Communications: Marianna
    Bryce
    E-Mail: mariannab@ambucs.org
Director, Communications: Semaj Marsh
    E-Mail: semajm@ambucs.org

Historical Note:
*Founded as National Association of American Business
Clubs. AMBUCS is dedicated to creating mobility and
independence for people with disabilities. Programs include
community service projects, scholarships for therapists,
and Amtryke, the therapeutic tricycle for children with
disabilities. Currently, there more than 5,500 AMBUCS
members spread throughout more than 130 chapters in over
30 states.*

Meetings/Conferences:
2013 - Ft. Worth, TX/July 24 - 27

Publications:
AMBUCS Magazine; quarterly; adv.
The Leader Newsletter

National AMBUCS, Inc *(1922)*
P.O. Box 5127
High Point, NC 27262
Tel: (800) 838-1845 *Fax:* (336) 852-6830
E-Mail: ambucs@ambucs.org
Website: ambucs.org
Members: 5835 members and chapters
Staff: 10
Annual Budget: $1-2,000,000

Personnel:
Executive Director: J. Joseph Copeland
    E-Mail: joec@ambucs.org
Coordinator, Membership Services and Scholarship: Janice
    Blankenship
    E-Mail: janiceb@ambucs.org
Director, Marketing and Communications: Marianna
    Bryce
    E-Mail: mariannab@ambucs.org
Contact, Sales and Membership Services: Dannell
    Copeland
    E-Mail: dannell@ambucs.org

Historical Note:
*Formerly National Association of American Business Clubs.
AMBUCS's mission is creating mobility and independence
for people with disabilities.*

Meetings/Conferences: Annual
2013 - Ft. Worth, TX/July 24 - 27

Publications:
AMBUCS Magazine; quarterly; adv.
The Leader; monthly

National American Indian Court Judges Association (1969)
3300 Arapahoe Ave.
Suite 206
Boulder, CO 80303
Tel: (303) 449-4112 *Fax:* (303) 449-4038
E-Mail: info@naicja.org
Website: naicja.org
Members: 150 individuals
Staff: 1
Annual Budget: $250-500,000
Tax: 501(c)(3)

Personnel:
Executive Director: Tina M. Farrenkopf

Historical Note:
NAICJA mission is to strengthen and enhance tribal justice systems. Membership: $75/year.

Meetings/Conferences: Annual

Publications:
NAICJA News

National American Indian Housing Council (1974)
900 Second St. NE
Suite 107
Washington, DC 20002
Tel: (202) 789-1754 *Fax:* (202) 789-1758
TollFree: (800) 284-9165
E-Mail: housing@naihc.net
Website: naihc.net
Members: 734 members and agencies
Staff: 18
Annual Budget: $2-5,000,000
Tax: 501(c)(3)

Personnel:
Executive Director: Mellor C. Willie
    E-Mail: mwillie@naihc.net
Coordinator, Membership Services: Bernadette BC EchoHawk
Manager, Communications: April Hale
Director, Governmental Affairs: Shawn Pensoneau
Finance Officer: Barbara Renshof
Contact, Web and Information Technology: Burke Sampson
    E-Mail: bsampson@naihc.net

Historical Note:
NAIHC's mission is to promote and support American Indians, Alaska Natives and native Hawaiians in their self-determined goal to provide culturally relevant and quality affordable housing for native people.

Meetings/Conferences: Annual
Number of non-conference events/year: 3

Publications:
Membership Directory; on-line

National American Legion Press Association (1923)
P.O. Box 334
W. Seneca, NY 14224-0334
Tel: (716) 675-0560 *Fax:* (716) 674-2817
Website: nalpa.org
Members: 2000 individuals
Staff: 5
Annual Budget: Under $10,000

Personnel:
Executive Director: Michael P. Duggan
    E-Mail: mdug1015@roadrunner.com
Public Relations Officer: Debra Murrell
    E-Mail: pr@legion.org
Webmaster: Mike Phelps
    E-Mail: mike_phelps@att.net
Finance: Joe Porempski

Historical Note:
Formerly (1973) American Legion Press Association. NALPA is an association of editors, writers, business managers, historians, public relations officers and individuals who are members of The American Legion, the Sons of The American Legion, the American Legion Auxiliary, and other subsidiary organizations. Encourages the exchange of ideas, promotes the development of local newsletters and public relations activities. Membership: $10/year.

Publications:
NALPA Newsletter; semi-annually; adv.

National Animal Control Association (1978)
P.O. Box 480851

Kansas City, MO 64148-0851
Tel: (913) 768-1319 *Fax:* (913) 768-1378
E-Mail: naca@nacanet.org
Website: nacanet.org
Members: 9800 individuals and animal care centers
Staff: 3
Annual Budget: $500-1,000,000
Tax: 501(c)(3)

Personnel:
Executive Director: John W. Mays

Historical Note:
NACA's mission is to define and promote professionalism in the animal protection care and humane law enforcement field by providing quality services, education, training, and support. Members are animal shelters, public health organizations, government officials, humane societies, and individuals concerned with animal care and control. Membership: $35-50 (Individual); $125-150 (Agency/Exhibitor).

Meetings/Conferences: Annual
2013 - Atlanta, GA (Atlanta Marriott Marquis)/Sept. 5 - 6
Number of non-conference events/year: 5

Publications:
NACA News; bi-monthly; adv.

National Animal Supplement Council (2001)
P.O. Box 2568
Valley Center, CA 92082
Tel: (760) 751-3360
Website: nasc.cc
Members: 125 companies
Staff: 4
Annual Budget: $250-500,000

Personnel:
President: Karen Howard
    E-Mail: k.howard@nasc.cc
Vice President: Dale Metz
    E-Mail: dmetz@foodsciencecorp.com
Federal lobbyist: William Bookout
    E-Mail: b.bookout@nasc.cc
Secretary and Treasurer: Ryan Cargo
    E-Mail: r.cargo@nasc.cc

Historical Note:
NASC's mission is to work cooperatively with state, federal and international government officials to create a legislative and regulatory environment that provides a framework that is Consistent.

Meetings/Conferences: Annual
2013 - St. Pete Beach, FL (TradeWinds Island Grand)/May 14 - 16

Publications:
NASC newsletter

National Antique and Art Dealers Association of America (1954)
220 E. 57th St.
New York, NY 10022
Tel: (212) 826-9707 *Fax:* (212) 832-9493
E-Mail: inquiries@naadaa.org
Website: naadaa.org
Members: 85 individuals and companies
Staff: 3
Annual Budget: $10-25,000

Personnel:
President: James McConnaughy
Director: Anthony Blumka
Treasurer: Steven J. Chait

Historical Note:
Formerly New York Antique and Art Dealers Association, Inc. NAADAA seeks to promote the interests of the antique art trade to sponsor and organize antique art exhibitions and to promote honorable and ethical trade practices.

Publications:
Membership Directory; on-line

National Apartment Association (1939)
4300 Wilson Blvd.
Suite 400
Arlington, VA 22203
Tel: (703) 518-6141 *Fax:* (703) 248-9440
E-Mail: info@naahq.org
Website: naahq.org
Members:
170 state and local affiliates
32000 individuals

Staff: 51
Annual Budget: $10-25,000,000
Tax: 501(c)(6)

Personnel:
President and Chief Executive Officer: Doug Culkin CAE
    E-Mail: doug@naahq.org
Business Development Manager, National Lease Program: Justin Barker
    E-Mail: justin@naahq.org
Director, Communications: Paul Bergeron
    E-Mail: paul@naahq.org
Staff Writer: Lauren Boston
    E-Mail: lauren@naahq.org
Vice President, Government Affairs: Gregory Brown
    E-Mail: greg@naahq.org
Manager, Human Resources: Nancy Carbone
    E-Mail: nancycarbone@naahq.org
Vice President and Chief Financial Officer: Melissa Cecchine CPA
    E-Mail: melissa@naahq.org
Senior Vice President, Meetings, Communications and Sales: Jeremy Figoten CAE
    E-Mail: jeremy@naahq.org
Director, Membership and Affiliate Services: Valerie Hairston
    E-Mail: valerie@naahq.org
Director, Information Technology: Michael Jones
    E-Mail: mikej@naahq.org
Paralegal and Research Assistant: Lauren Kelly
    E-Mail: laurenk@naahq.rg
Executive Vice President, Education: Maureen Lambe CAE
    E-Mail: maureen@naahq.org
General Counsel: John J. McDermott
    E-Mail: jmcdermott@naahq.org

Historical Note:
Established as National Apartment Owners Association, it assumed its present name in 1967. NAA's mission is to serve the interests of multifamily housing owners, managers, developers and suppliers and maintain a high level of professionalism in the multifamily housing industry to better serve the rental housing needs of the public. Members are local and state associations of owners, builders, investors and managers of rental property. Membership: $125/year (Regular/Associate).

Continuing Education:
Certification Designation/s: CAS, CAMT, CAPS

Meetings/Conferences: Annual
Conference Chair: Jeremy Figoten CAE
2013 - San Diego, CA (San Diego Convention Center)/June 20 - 22
2014 - Denver, CO (Colorado Convention Center)/June 19 - 21
2015 - Las Vegas, NV (Mandalay Bay Resort and Casino)/June 25 - 27
2016 - San Francisco, CA (Moscone Center)/June 9 - 11
2017 - Miami, FL (Celebrity Cruises)/June 22 - 24
2018 - San Diego, CA (San Diego Convention Center)/June 14 - 16
2019 - Denver, CO (Colorado Convention Center)/June 27 - 29
Number of non-conference events/year: 4

Publications:
HotSheet; monthly
NAA Affiliate Directory; on-line
NAA/NMHC Issue Fact Sheets
State and Local Policy Outlook; quarterly
The Industry Insider; weekly
Units; monthly; adv.

National Appliance Parts Suppliers Association (1966)
4015 W. Marshall Ave.
C/O APCO
Longview, TX 75604
Tel: (903) 759-3983
E-Mail: board06@napsaweb.org
Website: napsaweb.org
Members: 250 companies
Staff: 4
Annual Budget: Under $10,000

Personnel:
Vice President and Treasurer: Sherry Harrell

Historical Note:
NAPSA is a wholesale distributors of appliance parts and accessories and provides members and their suppliers with

a forum for the mutual exchange of information and ideas. *Membership:* $300 (Member Distributor); $400 (Member Distributor Plus); $450 (Member Distributor Deluxe); $50 (Member Branch); $100(Member Branch Plus/Vendor Rep); $250 (Vendor Member).

Publications:
Membership Directory

National Appliance Service Association (1949)
3407 Williams Dr.
P.O. Box 2514
Kokomo, IN 46904
Tel: (765) 453-1820 *Fax:* (765) 453-1895
E-Mail: nasahq@sbcglobal.net
Website: nasa1.org
Members: 200 companies
Staff: 1
Annual Budget: $10-25,000

Personnel:
Executive Director: Carrie Giannakos

Historical Note:
NASA's mission is to promote the interests of the domestic/ commercial appliance and electromechanical service industry. Members are owners of portable small appliance repair centers, appliance manufacturers and industry suppliers. Membership: $250/year.

Publications:
Membership Directory; annually
NASA News; monthly

National Aquaculture Council
PO Box 1146
Booragoon, WA 56954
Staff: 1

Personnel:
Treasurer: glyn jone

Historical Note:
A division of the National Fisheries Institute, NAC members are farmers, food processors, and food distributors with an interest in aquaculture.

National Arab-American Medical Association (1975)
801 S. Adams Rd.
Suite 208
Birmingham, MI 48009
Tel: (248) 646-3661 *Fax:* (248) 646-0617
E-Mail: naama@naama.com
Website: naama.com
Staff: 3
Annual Budget: $500-1,000,000
Tax: 501(c)(3)

Personnel:
Executive Director: Renee Ahee APR
    E-Mail: rahee@naama.com

Historical Note:
NAAMA's mission is to encompass a wide range of professional, educational, charitable, humanitarian and cultural activities. Membership: $200 (Active); $100 (Affiliate); $35 (Associates).

Continuing Education:
Enrollment: 800
Certification Designation/s: CME

Meetings/Conferences: Annual

Publications:
Al Hakeem; on-line; adv.
Membership Directory; on-line
NAAMA Chapter Newsletter; on-line
NAAMA eNewsletter; on-line

Membership List Available to Non-members

National Armored Car Association (1929)
9532 Stevebrook Rd.
Fairfax, VA 22032
Tel: (703) 426-1976 *Fax:* (703) 666-9085
E-Mail: lsabbath@nationalarmoredcar.com
Website: nationalarmoredcar.com
Members: 4 companies
Staff: 1
Annual Budget: $100-250,000
Tax: 501(c)(6)

Personnel:
Executive Director: Lawrence E. Sabbath
    E-Mail: lsabbath@nationalarmoredcar.com

Historical Note:
Absorbed the Armored Transportation Institute in 1993. Membership: annual dues vary based on company size.

National Art Education Association (1947)
1806 Robert Fulton Dr.
Suite 300
Reston, VA 20191
Tel: (703) 860-8000 *Fax:* (703) 860-2960
TollFree: (800) 299-8321
E-Mail: info@arteducators.org
Website: arteducators.org
Members: 45000 students
Staff: 12
Annual Budget: $2-5,000,000
Tax: 501(c)(3)

Personnel:
Executive Director: Deborah B. Reeve EdD
    E-Mail: dreeve@arteducators.org
Manager, Visual Communications and Marketing: Krista Brooke
    E-Mail: kbrooke@arteducators.org
Manager, Membership Services: Christie Castillo
    E-Mail: ccastillo@arteducators.org
Executive Services, Convention and Programs Manager: Kathy Duse
    E-Mail: kduse@arteducators.org
Manager, Publications: Lynn Ezell
    E-Mail: lezell@arteducators.org

Historical Note:
Founded by the merger of Eastern Arts Association, Pacific Arts Association, Southeastern Arts Association and Western Arts Association with the Art Department of the National Education Association. NAEA's mission is to advance visual arts education to fulfill human potential and promote global understanding. Membership: $65 (Active/ Associate); $55 (First Year Professional); $45 (Retired); $35 (Student); $185 (Institutional).

Meetings/Conferences: Annual
Conference Chair: Kathy Duse
2013 - Ft. Worth, TX (Fort Worth Convention Center)/ March 7 - 10/over 100 exhibitors

Publications:
Art Education; bi-monthly; adv.
NAEA News; bi-monthly; adv.
Translations; bi-annually

NAMTA - National Art Materials Trade Association (1950)
20200 Zion Ave.
Cornelius, NC 28031
Tel: (704) 892-6244
E-Mail: info@namta.org
Website: namta.org
Members: 900 companies
Staff: 5
Annual Budget: $500-1,000,000
Tax: 501(c)(6)

Personnel:
Executive Director: Reggie Hall
    E-Mail: rhall@namta.org
Administrative Assistant: Karen Brown
    E-Mail: kbrown@namta.org
Contact, Accounting Services: Susan Cohen
    E-Mail: scohen@namta.org
Director, Meetings: Rick Munisteri
    E-Mail: rmunisteri@namta.org
Contact, Membership Services and Foundation: Leah Siffringer
    E-Mail: lsiffringer@namta.org

Historical Note:
NAMTA seeks to provide its art/creative materials industry members with the products, services and information they need to grow and prosper. Members are retailers, suppliers, sales reps and associates. Membership: $105-735 (Retailers); $210-2,625 (Suppliers); $262.50 (Manufacturer's Reps); $315 (Associate).

Meetings/Conferences: Annual
Conference Chair: Rick Munisteri
2013 - Minneapolis, MN (Minneapolis Convention Center)/May 1 - 3/over 100 exhibitors
2014 - Pittsburgh, PA/April 30 - May 2
Number of non-conference events/year: 1

Publications:
Membership Directory
NAMTA Notes; weekly; adv.
NAMTA's e-Newsletter; bi-weekly
News and Views; quarterly; adv.

Membership List Available to Non-members

National Asian Pacific American Bar Association (1988)
1612 K St. NW, Suite 1400
Washington, DC 20006
Tel: (202) 775-9555 *Fax:* (202) 775-9333
Website: napaba.org
Staff: 5
Annual Budget: $2-5,000,000
Tax: 501(c)(6)

Personnel:
Executive Director: Tina Matsuoka
    E-Mail: tmatsuoka@napaba.org
Director, Policy: Emily Chatterjee
    E-Mail: echatterjee@napaba.org
Administrator: Andre Harrison
    E-Mail: aharrison@napaba.org

Historical Note:
NAPABA advocates for the legal needs and interests of the Asian Pacific American community. Members are Asian Pacific American (APA) attorneys, judges, law professors, and law students. Membership:$25-500/year.

Meetings/Conferences: Annual

Publications:
Member Directory; on-line
The NAPABA Lawyer; quarterly

National Asphalt Pavement Association (1955)
5100 Forbes Blvd.
Suite 200
Lanham, MD 20706-4407
Tel: (301) 731-4748 *Fax:* (301) 731-4621
TollFree: (888) 468-6499
E-Mail: napa@hotmix.org
Website: asphaltpavement.org
Members: 1200 companies
Staff: 23
Annual Budget: $5-10,000,000

Personnel:
President: Mike Acott
    E-Mail: macott@hotmix.org
Vice President, Marketing and Public Affairs: Margaret B. Cervarich
Manager, Membership Services: Joanie Frykman
Vice President, Conventions and Meetings: Nancy Lawler CMP
Director, Environmental and Regulatory Affairs: Howard Marks PhD, JD, MPH
    E-Mail: hmarks@hotmix.org
Director, Communications: T. Carter Ross
    E-Mail: cross@asphaltpavement.org
Vice President, Finance and Operations: Carolyn Wilson

Historical Note:
Represents the interests of the asphalt pavement material producer and paving contractor on the national level with Congress, government agencies, and other national trade and business organizations. Membership: $675-5600/year.

Meetings/Conferences: Annual
Conference Chair: Nancy Lawler CMP
2013 - Scottsdale, AZ (The Phoenician)/Feb. 9 - 13

Publications:
ActionNews; weekly
Asphalt Pavement magazine; adv.
HMAT Magazine; bi-monthly
NAPA Directory

National Assembly of State Arts Agencies (1968)
1029 Vermont Ave. NW
Second Floor
Washington, DC 20005
Tel: (202) 347-6352 *Fax:* (202) 737-0526
E-Mail: nasaa@nasaa-arts.org
Website: nasaa-arts.org
Members: 56 states and jurisdictions
Staff: 16
Annual Budget: $2-5,000,000
Tax: 501(c)(3)

Personnel:
Chief Executive Officer: Jonathan Katz
    E-Mail: jonathan@nasaa-arts.org
Chief Program and Planning Officer: Kelly J. Barsdate
    E-Mail: kelly@nasaa-arts.org
Legislative Counsel: Isaac Brown
    E-Mail: IBrown@edwardswildman.com
Controller: W. Dennis Dewey
    E-Mail: dennis.dewey@nasaa-arts.org
Director, Meetings and Events: Sharon Gee

E-Mail: sharon.gee@nasaa-arts.org
Manager, Development and Membership: Dora Shick
E-Mail: dora.shick@nasaa-arts.org
Chief Advancement Officer: Laura Smith CFRE
E-Mail: laura.smith@nasaa-arts.org
Manager, Communications: Sue Struve
E-Mail: sue.struve@nasaa-arts.org
Manager, Arts and Education Program: Kim Willey
E-Mail: kim.willey@nasaa-arts.org

Historical Note:
Founded in June 1968 as the North American Assembly of State and Provincial Arts Agencies and affiliated with the Associated Councils of the Arts. The organization became independent and assumed its present name in 1976. NASAA's purpose is to strengthen state arts agencies. Members are state agencies receiving appropriations from their states and designated by federal legislation to receive funding from the National Endowment for the Arts.

Meetings/Conferences: Annual
Conference Chair: Sharon Gee

Publications:
e-NOTES - newsletter; on-line
Membership Directory; on-line

National Association for Ambulatory Care *(1973)*
5395 Ashcroft Rd.
Minnetonka, MN 55345
E-Mail: info@nafac.com
Website: nafac.com
Members: 1700 clinics
Staff: 1
Annual Budget: $500-1,000,000

Personnel:
President: William H. Wenmark

Historical Note:
Founded as National Association of Centers for Urgent Treatment; became (1982) National Association of Freestanding Emergency Centers and (1984) National Association for Ambulatory Care. Assumed its current name in 2001 NAFAC represents the operational, economic, and legislative interests of 8, 500 ambulatory care centers (ACC) in the United States; and provides services and information to individuals and corporations planning to open ambulatory care centers. Membership: $150 (individual); $350 (corporate).

National Association for Armenian Studies and Research *(1955)*
395 Concord Ave.
Belmont, MA 02478-3049
Tel: (617) 489-1610 *Fax:* (617) 484-1759
E-Mail: hq@naasr.org
Website: naasr.org
Members: 1200 individuals
Staff: 11
Annual Budget: $250-500,000

Personnel:
Director, Academic Affairs: Marc A. Mamigonian
Administrative Director: Catherine Minassian

Historical Note:
NAASR's mission is to foster and promote Armenian Studies through scholarship, research, and publication. Membership: $35-1,000/year.

Meetings/Conferences: Annual

Publications:
Journal of Armenian Studies
NAASR Newsletter

National Association for Behavioral Health *(2006)*
1101 Pennsylvania Ave. NW
Suite 600
Washington, DC 20004
Tel: (202) 379-2949 *Fax:* (985) 369-4461
Website: thenabh.com
Staff: 2
Annual Budget: $250-500,000

Personnel:
Executive Director: Donna Newchurch
E-Mail: donna@newchurchassoc.com

Historical Note:
NABH's mission is to to promote Partial Hospital and Outpatient Programs as an essential sector of behavioral healthcare to provide advocacy for these beneficial programs.

Publications:
Behavioral Healthcare Magazine
NABH Newsletter; weekly

National Association for Bilingual Education *(1975)*
8701 Georgia Ave.
Suite 611
Silver Spring, MD 20910
Tel: (240) 450-3700 *Fax:* (240) 450-3799
E-Mail: nabe@nabe.org
Website: nabe.org
Members: 5000 individuals
Staff: 2
Annual Budget: $500-1,000,000
Tax: 501(c)(3)

Personnel:
National Interim Executive Director: Santiago V. Wood EdD
Senior Specialist, Membership Services: Celia Torres-Sobers
E-Mail: c_torres@nabe.org

Historical Note:
NABE's mission is to advocate for nations Bilingual and English Language Learners and families and to cultivate a multilingual multicultural society by supporting and promoting policy, programs, pedagogy, research, and professional development that yields academic success. NABE represents the interests of non-English background children and families. Membership: $60 (Individual); $125 (Institutional); $30 (College/University Student/ Paraprofessional/Parent); $1000 (Lifetime); $55 (State Affiliate).

Meetings/Conferences: Annual
2013 - Orlando, FL (Walt Disney World Swan And Dolphin)/Feb. 5 - 9
2013 - Lake Buena Vista, FL (Coronado Springs Resort)/Feb. 7 - 9/2000 attendees
2014 - San Diego, CA/Feb. 12 - 15
2014 - San Diego, CA (San Diego Convention Center)/ Feb. 13 - 15
2015 - Reno, NV/March 4 - 6

Publications:
Bilingual Research Journal
NABE News; adv.

National Association for Biomedical Research *(1979)*
818 Connecticut Ave. NW
Suite 900
Washington, DC 20006
Tel: (202) 857-0540 *Fax:* (202) 659-1902
E-Mail: info@nabr.org
Website: nabr.org
Members: 300 organizations
Staff: 6
Annual Budget: $5-10,000,000
Tax: 501(c)(6)

Personnel:
President: Frankie L Trull

Historical Note:
Founded as the Research Animal Alliance; became (1981) Association for Biomedical Research before absorbing the National Society for Medical Research and assuming its present name in 1985. Advocating sound public policy that recognizes the vital role of humane animal use in biomedical research, higher education, and product safety testing. NABR works to safeguard the future of biomedical research. Members are institutions, professional societies and companies that use animals in biomedical research and testing. The association's purpose is to keep members informed of legislative and regulatory activity in the field. Membership: $600-2,400 (Nonprofit Institutions); $600-40,000 (Industry).

Publications:
NABR Alerts
NABR Update; bi-weekly

National Association for Black Geologists and Geophysicists *(1981)*
4212 San Felipe
Suite 420
Houston, TX 77027-2902
Tel: (479) 575-6603
E-Mail: nabgg_us@hotmail.com
Website: nabgg.com
Members: 250 individuals
Staff: 3
Tax: 501(c)(3)

Personnel:
President: Michael Carroll
E-Mail: mcarroll@huntoil.com

Treasurer: Walter Doyle
Secretary: Geraldine Grant
E-Mail: Geraldine_Grant@oxy.com

Historical Note:
NABGG informs students of career opportunities that exist in the field of Geosciences, encourages them to take advantage of scholarship programs, grants, loans, etc., that are established for minority students, gives financial support to students pursuing degrees in Geology and Geophysics. NABGG members are geologists and geophysicists employed by major and independent oil companies, academics, students and others with an interest in the organization's goals. Membership: $50 (Professional/Associate), $25 (Teacher/Emeritus); $10 (Student).

Publications:
Member Directory; on-line
Prism; bi-annually

National Association for Business Economics *(1959)*
1233 20th St. NW
Suite 505
Washington, DC 20036-2304
Tel: (202) 463-6223 *Fax:* (202) 463-6239
E-Mail: nabe@nabe.com
Website: nabe.com
Members: 2500 individuals
Staff: 8
Annual Budget: $1-2,000,000
Tax: 501(c)(6)

Personnel:
Executive Director: Tom Beers
E-Mail: tbeers@nabe.com
Associate Director, Programs: Colette Brissett
E-Mail: nabe@nabe.com
Coordinator ,Events: Suzanne Clegg
E-Mail: stclegg2@gmail.com
Editor: Pam Ginsbach
E-Mail: pamg@nabe.com
Associate Director, Communications and Analysis: Chris Jonas
E-Mail: chris@nabe.com
Associate Director, Education and Professional Development: Tara Munroe
E-Mail: TMunroe@nabe.com

Historical Note:
Founded as National Association of Business Economists. Assumed its current name in 2000. NABE's mission is to provide leadership in the use and understanding of economics. Membership: $150 (Individual); $100 (Retiree Member); $160 (International Member); $30 (Student Member); $600 (Institutional Class A); $1200 (Institutional Class B); $1800 (Institutional Class C); $2400 (Institutional Class D).

Meetings/Conferences: Semi-Annual
Conference Chair: Colette Brissett
2013 - Washington, DC (Washington Court Hotel)/ March 3 - 5
2013 - San Francisco, CA (San Francisco Hyatt Regency)/Sept. 7 - 10
Number of non-conference events/year: 3

Publications:
Business Economics; quarterly; adv.
Membership Directory; on-line
NABE News; quarterly
NABE NewsDigest; weekly; adv.

National Association for Business Teacher Education *(1927)*
1914 Association Dr.
Reston, VA 20191-1596
Tel: (703) 860-8300 *Fax:* (703) 620-4483
E-Mail: nbea@nbea.org
Website: nabte.org
Staff: 5

Personnel:
President: Diane J. Fisher
E-Mail: diane.fisher@usm.edu
Editor: Ginny Richerson
E-Mail: vricherson@murraystate.edu
Secretary: James R. Smith
E-Mail: jimmy_smith@ncsu.edu
Research Coordinator: Dr. Lisa Gueldenzoph Snyder
E-Mail: gueldenzoph@att.net
Executive Director: Janet M. Treichel
E-Mail: jtreichel@nbea.org

Historical Note:

NABTE is the institutional division of NBEA. NABTE's mission is to promote business teacher education by providing national leadership and services to its member institutions and business teacher educators. It is a division of the National Business Education Association. Membership is open only to such colleges and universities that offer business teacher education curriculums approved by their respective State Departments of Education for the certification of business teachers. Membership: $200 (Institutional); $30 (Associate).

Meetings/Conferences: Annual

Publications:
Business Teacher Education Journal; annually
NABTE Newsletter; on-line

National Association for Campus Activities (1960)
13 Harbison Way
Columbia, SC 29212
Tel: (803) 732-6222 *Fax:* (803) 749-1047
TollFree: (800) 845-2338
E-Mail: info@naca.org
Website: naca.org
Members: 950 college and university members and 500 associate members
Staff: 22
Annual Budget: $2-5,000,000
Tax: 501(c)(4)

Personnel:
Executive Director: Alan B. Davis
    E-Mail: aland@naca.org
Director, Finance and Administration: Brenda Baker
    E-Mail: brendab@naca.org
Manager, Education and Research: Dionne Ellison
Content Editor: Glenn Farr
    E-Mail: glennf@naca.org
Manager, Information Technology: Mark Sury
    E-Mail: marks@naca.org
Director, Membership, Marketing and Events: Dawn Thomas
    E-Mail: dawnt@naca.org
Manager, Marketing and Communications: Latrice Williams

Historical Note:
NACA advances campus activities in higher education through a business and learning partnership, creating educational and business opportunities for its school and professional members. Members are artists, lecturers and performers. Membership: $250-388 (Affiliate); $575-758 (Associate); $421-986 (School).

Meetings/Conferences: Annual
Conference Chair: Dawn Thomas
2013 - Nashville, TN (Nashville Convention Center)/ Feb. 16 - 20/2000 attendees

Publications:
Professional Staff; bi-weekly
Associate Newsletter; bi-weekly
Campus Activities Programming Magazine
Event Newsletter; bi-weekly
Membership Directory; on-line

National Association for Chicana and Chicano Studies (1972)
P.O. Box 720052
San Jose, CA 95172-0052
Tel: (408) 924-5310 *Fax:* (408) 920-0711
E-Mail: naccs@naccs.org
Website: naccs.org
Staff: 4

Personnel:
Executive Director: Julia E. Curry Rodriguez PhD
    E-Mail: Executive_Director@naccs.org
Secretary: Cynthia Duarte PhD
    E-Mail: cynthia@naccs.org
Conference Chair: Jaime Garcia PhD
    E-Mail: jaime@naccs.org
Treasurer: Rhonda Rios Kravitz
    E-Mail: rhonda@naccs.org

Historical Note:
Formerly (1995) known as National Association for Chicano Studies. NACCS's mission is to encourage, promote, and assist the development of Chicana and Chicano studies centers, programs, and departments. Members are academics with an interest in the study of Chicano culture. Membership: $45-125 (Regular, based on income); $30 (Undergraduate Student); $40 (Graduate Student); $60 (Retired); $85 (Library); $250 (Institution); $250 (Life).

Meetings/Conferences: Annual

Conference Chair: Jaime Garcia PhD
2013 - Colonnade, TX (Omni San Antonio Hotel)/ March 20 - 23

Publications:
Membership Directory; on-line
Noticias de NACCS - Newsletter; quarterly; adv.

Membership List Available to Non-members

National Association for Children's Behavioral Health (NACBH)
1025 Connecticut Ave. NW
Suite 1012
Washington, DC 20036
Tel: (202) 857-9735 *Fax:* (202) 362-5145
E-Mail: info@nacbh.org
Website: nacbh.org
Staff: 2
Annual Budget: $250-500,000
Tax: 501(c)(6)

Personnel:
Executive Director: Joy Midman
    E-Mail: nacbh@verizon.net
Director: Pat Johnston

Historical Note:
Formerly, the National Association of Psychiatric Treatment Centers for Children. Works for the availability of comprehensive treatment services for persons under the age of 21 with emotional and behavioral problems and their families through active lobbying, public policy development, education and political action. Membership: $5,735-12,280 (Based on annual revenues for Board-Eligible Members, Association Members) and $15,225 (for Multi-Facility System Members with $3,300 annually for each additional participant).

Publications:
Membership Directory

National Association for College Admission Counseling (1937)
1050 N. Highland St.
Suite 400
Arlington, VA 22201
Tel: (703) 836-2222 *Fax:* (703) 243-9375
TollFree: (800) 822-6285
E-Mail: info@nacacnet.org
Website: nacacnet.org
Members: 7050 individuals and 3095 organizations
Staff: 59
Annual Budget: $10-25,000,000
Tax: 501(c)(3)

Personnel:
Chief Executive Officer: Joyce E. Smith
    E-Mail: ceo@nacacnet.org
Director, Information Systems: Joe Brentzel
    E-Mail: is@nacacnet.org
Director, Finance and Administration: Joan Burdette
    E-Mail: fa@nacacnet.org
Director, Membership Services and Affiliate Relations: Heather Caldwell
    E-Mail: member@nacacnet.org
Director, Conference and Meetings: Bethany Blue Chirico CMP
    E-Mail: meetings@nacacnet.org
Director, Education and Training: Don Fraser
    E-Mail: pd@nacacnet.org
Director, Public Policy and Research: David A Hawkins
    E-Mail: legislative@nacacnet.org
Director, Communications, Publications and Technology: Shanda Thomas Ivory
    E-Mail: sivory@nacacnet.org

Historical Note:
NACAC supports and advances the work of counseling and enrollment professionals. Membership: $12.50-455 (Institutional); $ 12.50-215 (Individual); $315 (Organization: Voting); $375 (Organization: Non-voting).

Meetings/Conferences: Annual
Conference Chair: Bethany Blue Chirico CMP
2013 - Toronto, ON/Sept. 19 - 21
2014 - Indianapolis, IN/Sept. 18 - 20
2014 - Indianapolis, IN/Sept. 19 - 21
2015 - San Diego, CA/Oct. 1 - 3
Number of non-conference events/year: 45

Publications:
Journal of College Admission; quarterly; adv.
NACAC Bulletin; semi-monthly
NACAC Membership Directory; on-line; adv.

Steps to College; on-line

Membership List Available to Non-members

National Association for Community Mediation (1994)
1959 S. Power Rd.
Suite 103-279
Mesa, AZ 85206
Tel: (602) 633-4213
E-Mail: admin@nafcm.org
Website: nafcm.org
Members: 260 community mediation centers, and 525 individuals
Staff: 4
Annual Budget: $50-100,000
Tax: 501(c)(3)

Personnel:
Executive Director: Justin R. Corbett
    E-Mail: corbett@nafcm.org

Historical Note:
NAFCM supports the maintenance and growth of community-based mediation program and processes; presents a compelling voice in appropriate policy- making, legislative, professional, and other arenas; and encourages the development and sharing of resources for these efforts. Members are community mediation programs, volunteer mediators, and other organizations and individuals that support community mediation. Membership: $50 (Individual); $100-400 (Program)

Meetings/Conferences:
Number of non-conference events/year: 1

Publications:
Member Directory; on-line
NAFCM's newsletter; on-line

Membership List Available to Non-members

National Association of County Community and Economic Development (1978)
2025 M St. NW
Suite 800
Washington, DC 20036-3309
Tel: (202) 367-1149 *Fax:* (202) 367-2149
E-Mail: info@nacced.org
Website: nacced.org
Members: 120 individuals
Staff: 5
Annual Budget: $250-500,000
Tax: 501(c)(3)

Personnel:
Executive Director: John C. Murphy
    E-Mail: jmurphy@nacced.org
Associate, Marketing and Communications: Holly Beck
    E-Mail: hbeck@smithbucklin.com
Associate, Conference Registration: Brittany Boykin
    E-Mail: bboykin@smithbucklin.com
Manager, Education and Programs: Delicia Hurdle
    E-Mail: dhurdle@smithbucklin.com
Staff Accountant: Victor Lee
    E-Mail: vlee@smithbucklin.com

Historical Note:
NACCED, created as an affiliate of the National Association of Counties (NACo), strives to assist in developing the technical capacity of county agencies. Membership: $275 -3,850/year.

Meetings/Conferences: Annual
Conference Chair: Brittany Boykin
2013 - Tucson, AZ/Oct. 18 - 23

Publications:
NACCED Insights; quarterly
Membership Directory; on-line

National Association for Court Management (1985)
National Center for State Courts
300 Newport Ave.
Williamsburg, VA 23185-4147
Tel: (757) 259-1841 *Fax:* (757) 259-1520
TollFree: (800) 616-6165
E-Mail: nacm@ncsc.org
Website: nacmnet.org
Members: 2000 members
Staff: 4
Annual Budget: $1-2,000,000
Tax: 501(c)(3)

Personnel:
President: Pamela Q. Harris
    E-Mail: pam@nacmnet.org

Contact, Publications: Peter Coolsen
    E-Mail: pecools@cookcountygov.com
Secretary and Treasurer: Stephanie Hess
    E-Mail: stephanie@nacmnet.org
Contact, Conferences: Stacey Smith

Historical Note:
NACM's purpose is to develop and improve leadership in the judicial system and the leadership qualities of court managers. Members are clerks of court, court administrators and others serving in a court management capacity. Membership: $125 (Regular/Associate); $350 (Sustaining); $35 (Student); $50 (Retired).

Meetings/Conferences:
Conference Chair: Stacey Smith
2013 - Los Angeles, CA (Westin Bonaventure Hotel and Suites, Los Angeles)/Feb. 10 - 12
2013 - San Antonio, TX (San Antonio Marriott Rivercenter)/July 14 - 18
2014 - Savannah, GA (Hyatt Regency Savannah)/Feb. 9 - 11
2014 - Scottsdale, AZ (Westin Kierland Resort and Spa)/July 13 - 17
2015 - Louisville, KY (Louisville Marriott Downtown)/July 12 - 16

Publications:
Court Express; quarterly; adv.
Court Manager; quarterly; adv.

National Association for Developmental Education *(1976)*
San Jacinto College
4624 Fairmont Pkwy., Suite 203
Pasadena, TX 77504-3398
Tel: (281) 459-7667 *Fax:* (281) 998-6130
E-Mail: office@nade.net
Website: nade.net
Members: 3000 individuals
Staff: 5
Annual Budget: $500-1,000,000
Tax: 501(c)(3)

Personnel:
President: Rebecca Goosen EdD, MS
    E-Mail: rebecca.goosen@sjcd.edu

Historical Note:
NADE's mission is to improve the theory and practice of developmental education at all levels of the educational spectrum, the professional capabilities of developmental educators, and the design of programs to prepare developmental educators. Membership: $60 (Individual); $30 (Student); $25 (Retiree); $400 (Institutional/Program).

Continuing Education:
Certification Designation/s: NADE Cert.

Meetings/Conferences: Annual
2013 - Denver, CO (Sheraton Denver Downtown Hotel)/Feb. 27 - March 2
2014 - Dallas, TX (Hilton Anatole Dallas)/March 5 - 8

Publications:
NADE Digest; semi-annually; adv.
NADE Newsletter; on-line
The Journal of Developmental Education (JDE)

National Association for Drama Therapy *(1979)*
44365 Premier Plaza
Suite 220
Ashburn, VA 20147
Tel: (888) 416-7167 *Fax:* (571) 223-6440
TollFree: (888) 416-7167
E-Mail: nadt.office@nadt.org
Website: nadt.org
Members: 400 individuals
Staff: 4
Annual Budget: $100-250,000

Personnel:
Editor: Meredith Dean
Treasurer: Mary Mary Caligiure, MA, RDT, LCAT
    E-Mail: treasurer@nadt.org
Editor: Christine Mayor
President: Nisha Sajnani, PhD, RDT
    E-Mail: president@nadt.org

Historical Note:
NADT works to establish and uphold rigorous standards of professional competence for drama therapists. Members are professionals trained in theatre arts, psychology and psychotherapy making use of drama/theatre processes to achieve therapeutic goals. Membership: $55 (Allied Professional); $35 (Student); $100 (Organization/School); $45-55 (Member); $95 (Professional RDT); $115 (Professional RDT/BCT).

Continuing Education:
Certification Designation/s: RDT, BCT

Meetings/Conferences: Annual
Number of non-conference events/year: 5

Publications:
Behind the Scenes; on-line
Dramascope
Membership Directory; annually
The Dramascope

National Association for Environmental Management *(1990)*
1612 K St. NW
Suite 1102
Washington, DC 20006
Tel: (202) 986-6616 *Fax:* (202) 530-4408
TollFree: (800) 391-6236
E-Mail: programs@naem.org
Website: naem.org
Members: 1200 individuals
Staff: 11
Annual Budget: $500-1,000,000

Personnel:
Executive Director: Carol Singer Neuvelt
    E-Mail: programs@naem.org
Manager, Information Technology: Sadaqat Ahmad
Research Analyst: Fletcher Fields
    E-Mail: fletcher@naem.org
Manager, Marketing and Sales: Brent Hendrix
    E-Mail: brent@naem.org
Program Director: Mike Mahanna
    E-Mail: mike@naem.org
Manager, Interactive Media and Communications: Elizabeth Ryan
    E-Mail: elizabeth@naem.org
Manager, Member Services and Administration: Briana Warner

Historical Note:
Formerly the National Association for Environmental Management. NAEM's mission is to advance the integration of EHS into business as a value driver and promote the growth and implementation of EHS management systems worldwide. Membership: $195 (Individual); $900-5,000 (Corporate, based on gross revenues/Government/Nonprofit); $1,000-3,000 (Affiliate, based on annual revenues); $50 (Student).

Meetings/Conferences:
2013 - Charlotte, NC (Charlotte Convention Center)/Oct. 23 - 25
2014 - Austin, TX (Hilton Austin)/Oct. 22 - 24
Number of non-conference events/year: 2

Publications:
NAEM Network News; bi-weekly
Newsletter; quarterly

National Association for Equal Opportunity in Higher Education *(1969)*
209 Third St. SE
Washington, DC 20003-1904
Tel: (202) 552-3300 *Fax:* (202) 552-3330
Website: nafeo.org
Members: 150 institutions
Staff: 2
Annual Budget: $2-5,000,000
Tax: 501(c)(3)

Personnel:
President and Chief Executive Officer: Dr. Lezli Baskerville JD
    E-Mail: baskerville@nafeo.org
Senior Vice President, Governmental and International Affairs: Dr. Napoleon Moses
    E-Mail: nmoses@nafeo.org

Historical Note:
NAFEO serves along with the nation's Historically Black Colleges and Universities (HBCUs) and Predominantly Black Institutions (PBIs). NAFEO serves to advocate for preservation and enhancement of African Americans in higher education. Membership: $10,000/year (Organization).

Continuing Education:
Certification Designation/s: NAFEO

National Association for Ethnic Studies *(1972)*
Department of Ethnic Studies, Colorado State University
1790 Campus Delivery
Ft. Collins, CO 80523-1790

Tel: (970) 491-3927 *Fax:* (970) 491-2717
E-Mail: NAES@ethnicstudies.org
Website: ethnicstudies.org/
Members:
300 institutions
225 individuals
Staff: 3
Annual Budget: $25-50,000

Personnel:
President and Editor: Ron Scapp
Vice President: Carleen D. Sanchez
    E-Mail: csanchez@ethnicstudies.org
Treasurer: Irene Vernon

Historical Note:
Formerly, the National Association of Interdisciplinary Ethnic Studies. Assumed its current name in 1985. NAES's mission is to promote the activities and scholarship in the field of ethnic studies. NAES serves as a forum to its members for promoting research, study, curriculum design, and publications. Membership: $35-85 (Individual, based on annual income); $40 (Student/Associate/Retiree); $65 (Library/Institution); $150 (Patron); $1000 (Lifetime); $3,000 (Institutional Lifetime).

Meetings/Conferences: Annual
2013 - Ft. Collins, CO (Colorado State University)/April 12 - 13

Publications:
Ethnic Studies Review; bi-annually
The Ethnic Reporter; bi-annually

National Association for Family and Community Education *(1936)*
4250 County Rd C
Dighton, KS 67839-8801
E-Mail: nafcehq@fuse.net
Website: nafce.org
Members: 20000 individuals
Staff: 5
Annual Budget: $100-250,000
Tax: 501(c)(3)

Personnel:
President: Judy Fullmer
    E-Mail: jfullmer@st-tel.net

Historical Note:
NAFCE's mission is to strengthening individuals, families and communities through continuing education, developing leadership and community action. Membership: $50 (Individual); $100 (Corporate).

Meetings/Conferences:
Conference Chair: Judy Fullmer
2013 - Fargo, ND (Holiday Inn of Fargo)/July 18 - 21

Publications:
Membership Directory; on-line

National Association for Family Child Care *(1982)*
1743 W. Alexander St.
Salt Lake City, UT 84119
Tel: (801) 886-2322 *Fax:* (801) 886-2325
E-Mail: nafcc@nafcc.org
Website: nafcc.org
Members: 8000 child care organizations
Staff: 12
Annual Budget: $250-500,000
Tax: 501(c)(6)

Personnel:
Executive Director: Linda Geigle
    E-Mail: LGeigle@nafcc-mail.org
Director, Accreditations: Eva Daniels
    E-Mail: EDaniels@nafcc-mail.org
Affiliate Member Specialist: Tracy Halverson
Financial Specialist: Patricia K. Price
    E-Mail: PPrice@nafcc-mail.org
Director, Special Projects: Barbara Sawyer
    E-Mail: BSawyer@nafcc-mail.org

Historical Note:
Formerly the National Association for Family Day Care and present name was incorporated in 1994, NAFCC strives to promote quality child care by strengthening the profession of family child care. Members are providers and users of family child care services. Membership: $35 (Provider/Advocate/Parent); $70 (Association); $140 (Agency).

Meetings/Conferences: Annual
Conference Chair: Barbara Sawyer
2013 - Scottsdale, AZ (Fairmont Scottsdale Princess Hotel)/July 18 - 20

Publications:
Member Mailings; on-line; adv.

The National Perspective; quarterly; adv.

National Association for Fixed Annuities *(1998)*
2300 E. Kensington Blvd.
Milwaukee, WI 53211
Tel: (414) 332-9306 *Fax:* (888) 884-6232
Website: nafa.com
Members: 200000 Agents
Staff: 5
Annual Budget: $500-1,000,000
Tax: 501(c)(6)

Personnel:
President and Chief Executive Officer: Kim O'Brien CFP, MBA
General Legal Counsel: Pamela M. Heinrich
Director, Education and Conferences: W. Scott Hinds
    E-Mail: scott@nafa.com
Director, Membership: Theresa Meyer
    E-Mail: theresa@nafa.com
Operations Coordinator: Bailey Sorensen
    E-Mail: bailey@nafa.com

Historical Note:
National trade association representing the fixed annuity industry. Membership: $275-375 (Annuity Professional/ Preferred Producer).

Meetings/Conferences:
Conference Chair: W. Scott Hinds
Number of non-conference events/year: 5

National Association for Gifted Children
1331 H St. NW
Suite 1001
Washington, DC 20005
Tel: (202) 785-4268 *Fax:* (202) 785-4248
E-Mail: nagc@nagc.org
Website: nagc.org
Members: 8000 members
Staff: 12
Annual Budget: $1-2,000,000
Tax: 501(c)(3)

Personnel:
Executive Director: Nancy Green CAE
    E-Mail: ngreen@nagc.org
Director, Finance and Administration: Andrew Bassett
    E-Mail: abassett@nagc.org
Director, Public Education: Jane Clarenbach J D
    E-Mail: janec@nagc.org
Director, Professional Development and Meetings: Robin Feldman
    E-Mail: rfeldman@nagc.org
Editor: Jennifer Jolly PhD
    E-Mail: jollyphp@gmail.com
Manager, Membership Services: Adriane Wiles
    E-Mail: awiles@nagc.org
Senior Director, Marketing and Membership Services: Karen Yoho CAE
    E-Mail: kyoho@nagc.org

Historical Note:
NAGC's mission is to support and develop policies and practices that encourage and respond to the diverse expressions of gifts and talents in children and youth. NAGC is an organization of parents, teachers, educators, other professionals, and community leaders Membership: $99 (Individual); $30 (Parent Associate); $59 (Graduate Student); $1000 (Lifetime).

Meetings/Conferences: Annual
Conference Chair: Robin Feldman
2013 - Indianapolis, IN/Nov. 6 - 10
2014 - Baltimore, MD/Nov. 13 - 16

Publications:
Gifted Child Quarterly; quarterly; adv.
Parenting for High Potential; quarterly; adv.
Teaching For High Potential; quarterly; adv.

Membership List Available to Non-members

National Association for Girls and Women in Sport *(1899)*
1900 Association Dr.
Reston, VA 20191-1598
Tel: (703) 476-3453 *Fax:* (703) 476-4566
TollFree: (800) 213-7193
E-Mail: nagws@aahperd.org
Website: aahperd.org/nagws
Members: 4000 individuals
Staff: 3
Annual Budget: $250-500,000

Personnel:

Executive Director: Pamela Nokes
    E-Mail: pnoakes@aahperd.org
Program Manager: Chandelle Schulte
    E-Mail: cschulte@aahperd.org

Historical Note:
A member association of the American Alliance for Health, Physical Education, Recreation and Dance (AAHPERD), NAGWS is dedicated to advocacy, education and the promotion of girls and women in sport.

Meetings/Conferences: Annual
Conference Chair: Chandelle Schulte
Number of non-conference events/year: 12

Publications:
GWS News; on-line; adv.
NAGWS Gazette; on-line
Women in Sport and Physical Activity Journal; on-line

National Association for Government Training and Development *(1980)*
Montana Dept of Transportation
2701 Prospect Ave.
Helena, MT 59620-1001
Tel: (406) 444-7477
E-Mail: gotonagtad@gmail.com
Website: nagtad.org
Members: 78 individuals
Staff: 4
Annual Budget: Under $10,000
Tax: 501(c)(3)

Personnel:
President: Angel Molyneaux
    E-Mail: amolyneaux@mt.gov

Historical Note:
Founded as National Association of Government Training and Development Directors, assumed its current name in 1998. NAGTAD is a resource for public sector training and development professionals in the United States. Membership: $30(Professional/Individual); $100 (Entity).

Publications:
e-Learn Magazine; on-line

National Association for Health and Fitness *(1979)*
C/O Be Active New York State
65 Niagara Sq., Room 607
Buffalo, NY 14202
Tel: (716) 851-4052 *Fax:* (716) 851-4309
E-Mail: wellness@city-buffalo.org
Website: physicalfitness.org
Members: 50 members
Staff: 1
Annual Budget: Under $10,000
Tax: 501(c)(3)

Personnel:
Executive Director: Philip Haberstro

Historical Note:
Founded as National Association of Governors Councils on Physical Fitness and Sports; assumed its current name in 2000. NAHF's purpose is to improve quality of life for individuals in United States through promotion of physical fitness, sports and healthy lifestyles. Membership: $175 (Gov Council/State Coalition); $140 (Corporate/Business); $100 (Non Profit/Public Sector); $50 (Individual).

Membership List Available to Non-members

National Association for Health Care Recruitment *(1975)*
P.O. Box 14385
Lenexa, KS 66285-4385
Tel: (913) 895-4627 *Fax:* (913) 895-4652
E-Mail: nahcr@goamp.com
Website: nahcr.com
Members: 1000 individuals
Staff: 5
Annual Budget: $500-1,000,000

Personnel:
Executive Director: Sheila O'Neal
    E-Mail: soneal@goamp.com
Association Manager: Raven Hardin BA
    E-Mail: rhardin@goAMP.com
Administrative Assistant: Tressie Nootz
    E-Mail: tnootz@goAMP.com
Director, Education: Jody Shelton CAE, EdD
    E-Mail: jody.shelton@goAMP.com
Meeting Planner: Barbara Tanner
    E-Mail: barbara.tanner@goamp.com

Historical Note:

Established in 1975 as National Association for Nurse Recruiters; assumed its current name in 1984. NAHCR provides leadership and support for the health care recruiting profession. A recruiter or human resources professional in any organization providing direct health care (hospital, long term/subacute care, home health, military, HMO) can become a member. Membership: $135 (Active); $185 (Associate); $1,100 (Institutional).

Continuing Education:
Certification Designation/s: CHCR

Meetings/Conferences: Annual
Conference Chair: Barbara Tanner
2013 - Minneapolis, MN (Hyatt Regency Minneapolis)/ July 16 - 19/250 attendees/26-50 exhibitors

Publications:
Current : e-newsletter; monthly
NAHCR Directions - Newsletter; bi-monthly; adv.
The Who's Who - Membership and Resource Directory; annually; adv.

Membership List Available to Non-members

National Association for Healthcare Quality *(1976)*
4700 W. Lake Ave.
Glenview, IL 60025-1485
Tel: (847) 375-4720 *Fax:* (847) 375-6320
TollFree: (800) 966-9392
E-Mail: info@nahq.org
Website: nahq.org
Members: 7100 institutions and individuals
Staff: 9
Annual Budget: $2-5,000,000

Personnel:
Executive Director: Stacy Sochacki BA, MS
    E-Mail: ssochacki@nahq.org
Manager, Marketing and Membership: Angelisa Belden
    E-Mail: abelden@nahq.org
Contact, Public Relations: Marlyne Campbell
Senior Manager, Meetings: Vanessa Mobley CMP
    E-Mail: vmobley@nahq.org
Senior Manager, Education: Jacki Van Oort
    E-Mail: jvanoort@nahq.org
Managing Editor: June Pinyo

Historical Note:
Formerly (1992) National Association of Quality Assurance Professionals. NAHQ's purpose is to improve healthcare quality across all points of care through education, certification, and advocacy. Membership: $150 (Individual); $500 (Institutional); $75 (Emeritus).

Continuing Education:
Certification Designation/s: CPHQ

Meetings/Conferences: Annual
Conference Chair: Vanessa Mobley CMP
2013 - Louisville, KY (Kentucky International Convention Center)/Oct. 6 - 9
2014 - Nashville, TN (Music City Convention Center, Omni Hotel and Resort)/Sept. 7 - 10

Publications:
Journal for Healthcare Quality; on-line
Membership Directory; annually
NAHQ E-News; monthly; adv.

National Association for Home Care and Hospice *(1982)*
228 Seventh St. SE
Washington, DC 20003-4306
Tel: (202) 547-7424 *Fax:* (202) 547-3540
E-Mail: exec@nahc.org
Website: nahc.org
Members: 4000 agencies
Staff: 46
Annual Budget: $10-25,000,000

Personnel:
President: Val J. Halamandaris
    E-Mail: vjh@nahc.org
Director, Conventions and Meetings: Sandy J. Antor CMP
    E-Mail: sja@nahc.org
Director, Certification and Accreditation: Marcia L. Barnette
    E-Mail: mb@nahc.org
Director, Human Resources and Administration: Trenell Bradley
Director, Arts: Gerette Braunsdorf
    E-Mail: ggb@nahc.org
Vice President, Technology Policy: Richard D. Brennan Jr., MA
    E-Mail: rdb@nahc.org

Director, Center for Health Care Law and Vice President, Law: William A. Dombi
    E-Mail: wad@nahc.org
Vice President, Exhibits: Ron Everly
Systems Manager: Suzanne D. Ewing
    E-Mail: sde@nahc.org
Director, Membership: Gail Gronlund
Education Associate: Craig L. Kelly
    E-Mail: clk@nahc.org
Director, Sales: Tom Murphy
Chief Operating Officer: Janet E. Neigh
    E-Mail: jen@nahc.org
Contact, Public Relations: Megan Rose
    E-Mail: mrose@gcjpr.com

Historical Note:
Formed (1982) through the merger of the National Association for Home Health Agencies (NAHHA) and the Council of Home Health Agencies/Community Health Services (CHHA/CHS). NAHCH's mission is to preserve the solidarity of families, the fundamental building block of society. Members are home care agencies, hospices, home care aide organizations, and medical equipment suppliers. Membership: $8,925-73,500/year.

Continuing Education:
Certification Designation/s: CHCE

Meetings/Conferences: Annual
Conference Chair: Sandy J. Antor CMP
Number of non-conference events/year: 1

Publications:
Caring; monthly; adv.
Membership Directory; on-line
NAHC Report; daily

National Association for Information Destruction, Inc.
1951 W. Camelback Rd.
Suite 350
Phoenix, AZ 85015
Tel: (602) 788-6243 *Fax:* (480) 658-2088
E-Mail: info@naidonline.org
Website: naidonline.org
Staff: 9
Annual Budget: $2-5,000,000

Personnel:
Chief Executive Officer: Robert J. Johnson
    E-Mail: rjohnson@naidonline.org
Director, Communications: Kristina Carlberg
    E-Mail: kcarlberg@naidonline.org
Chief Information Officer: Marley Day
    E-Mail: mday@naidonline.org
Chief Financial Officer: Kathy Goldman
    E-Mail: kgoldman@naidonline.org
Director, Certification Operations: Katie Mahoney
    E-Mail: kmahoney@naidonline.org
Director, Member Services: Jena Robinson
    E-Mail: jrobinson@naidonline.org
Director, Events and Programs: Jamie Steimer
    E-Mail: jsteimer@naidonline.org
Manager, Sales: Tracy Tarlton
    E-Mail: ttarlton@naidonline.org

Historical Note:
NAID's mission is to promote the information destruction industry and the standards and ethics of its member companies. Members are document shredding firms and manufacturers of related equipment. Suppliers of products, equipment and services to destruction companies are also eligible for membership. Membership: $600-5,720 (Active); $300-5,720 (International Active/Franchise).

Continuing Education:
Certification Designation/s: CPP

Meetings/Conferences: Semi-Annual
Conference Chair: Jamie Steimer
2013 - Sydney, Australia (Sheraton on the Park)/Feb. 19
2013 - Nashville, TN (The Gaylord Opryland)/March 22 - 24
Number of non-conference events/year: 2

Publications:
Membership Directory; on-line
NAID Direct; bi-weekly; adv.
NAID News; quarterly; adv.

National Association for Interpretation (1988)
P.O. Box 2246
Ft. Collins, CO 80522
Tel: (970) 484-8283 *Fax:* (970) 484-8179
TollFree: (888) 900-8283

E-Mail: naiexec@aol.com
Website: interpnet.com
Members: 5300 individuals and organizations
Staff: 8
Annual Budget: $1-2,000,000
Tax: 501(c)(3)

Personnel:
Executive Director: Tim Merriman
Administrative Assistant: Sheila Caputo
Interim Executive Director: Paul Caputo
    E-Mail: pcaputo@interpnet.com
Manager, Membership Services: Jamie King
    E-Mail: jking@interpnet.com
Specialist, Certification Programs: Carrie Miller
    E-Mail: cmiller@interpnet.com
Manager, Events: Deb Tewell
    E-Mail: dtewell@interpnet.com

Historical Note:
Formed by a merger of the Association of Interpretive Naturalists and the Western Interpreter's Association. NA's mission is to advance heritage interpretation as a profession. Members are naturalists, historians, park rangers, educators, museum technicians and curators, administrators, recreation specialists, and others. Membership: $1,500 (Life); $69 (Regular); $49 (Senior); $25 (Student); $125 (Institutional); $150 (Commercial).

Continuing Education:
Certification Designation/s: CIG, CIT, CHI, CIHT, CIM, CIP

Meetings/Conferences: Annual
Conference Chair: Deb Tewell
2013 - Las Vegas, NV/Nov. 6 - 9
2014 - Denver, CO/Nov. 18 - 22
2017 - Reno, NV/Nov. 8 - 11
2019 - Denver, CO/Nov. 19 - 23
Number of non-conference events/year: 7

Publications:
Journal of Interpretation Research; adv.
Legacy; bi-monthly; adv.
Membership Directory; annually
NAI e-Newsletter; monthly
NAI e-Newsletter; semi-monthly
NAI Quarterly Newsletter; quarterly
The Interpreter magazine; bi-monthly; adv.

National Association for Kinesiology in Higher Education (1978)
53 Shore Ave.
Quincy, MA 02169
Website: nakhe.org
Members: 500 individuals
Staff: 1
Annual Budget: $25-50,000

Personnel:
Executive Director: Carrie Sampson Moore
    E-Mail: clsmoore@mit.edu

Historical Note:
Formerly, National Association for Kinesiology and Physical Education in Higher Education (NAKPEHE). NAKHE is the result of a merger between the National Association for Physical Education of College Women and the National College Physical Education Association for Men (founded in 1907). NAKHE's purpose is to foster leadership in teaching, administration, policy, preparation for the professions and scholarship. Membership: $80 (Professional); $40 (Associate Professional); $30 (NAK Concurrent Professional/Emeritus); $20 (Student Professional).

Meetings/Conferences: Annual
2013 - Ft. Lauderdale, FL (Hilton Fort Lauderdale Marina Hotel)/Jan. 2 - 5

Publications:
Chronicle of Kinesiology and Physical Education in Higher Education; adv.
Quest; quarterly; adv.

National Association for Medical Direction of Respiratory Care
8618 Westwood Center Dr.
Suite 210
Vienna, VA 22182
Tel: (703) 752-4359 *Fax:* (703) 752-4360
E-Mail: execoffice@namdrc.org
Website: namdrc.org
Members: 700 individuals
Staff: 3
Annual Budget: $250-500,000

Personnel:
Executive Director: Phillip Porte

E-Mail: phil@namdrc.org
Associate Executive Director: Karen Liu RN, MS
    E-Mail: karen@namdrc.org
Director, Membership Services: Vickie Parshall
    E-Mail: vickie@namdrc.org

Historical Note:
Formerly (1994) National Association of Medical Directors of Respiratory Care. NAMDRC's mission is to educate its members and address regulatory, legislative and payment issues that relate to the delivery of healthcare to patients with respiratory disorders. Members are physicians who work in in respiratory care departments and critical/intensive care units. Membership: $350 (Individual); $275 (Group); $50 (Voluntary Assessment).

Meetings/Conferences: Annual
2013 - San Diego, CA (US Grant Hotel)/March 21 - 23

Publications:
Current Controversies; irregular; adv.
The Presidential Update; semi-annually
Washington Watchline; monthly; adv.

National Association for Multi-Ethnicity in Communications (1980)
320 W. 37th St.
Eighth Floor
New York, NY 10018
Tel: (212) 594-5985 *Fax:* (212) 594-8391
E-Mail: info@namic.com
Website: namic.com
Members: 2000 individuals
Staff: 8
Tax: 501(c)(6)

Personnel:
President and Chief Executive Officer: Nicol Turner-Lee PhD
    E-Mail: nicol.turner-lee@namic.com
Manager, Chapter and Membership Services: Stana Fields
    E-Mail: stana.fields@namic.com
Manager, Meetings and Events: Sandra Girado
    E-Mail: sandra.girado@namic.com
Vice President, Education Programs: James C. Jones
    E-Mail: jim.jones@namic.com
Vice President, Marketing and Communications: Daphne Leroy
    E-Mail: daphne.leroy@namic.com
Manager, Research and Publications: Susan Waldman
    E-Mail: susan.waldman@namic.com
Manager, Operations: Monique Wells
    E-Mail: monique.wells@namic.com

Historical Note:
Founded as National Association of Minorities in Cable, became National Association of Minorities in Communications in 1999, and assumed its current name in 2003. NAMIC works for the cause of diversity in the telecommunications industry. Membership: $275 (Platinum); $150 (Gold); $75 (Silver); $40 (Student).

Meetings/Conferences: Annual
Conference Chair: Sandra Girado

Publications:
Cultural Lens; quarterly
Diversity Scoop; bi-weekly
InTouch; bi-monthly
Member Directory; on-line

National Association for Multicultural Education (1990)
2100 M St.
Suite 170-245
Washington, DC 20037
Tel: (202) 679-6263 *Fax:* (214) 602-4722
E-Mail: name@nameorg.org
Website: nameorg.org
Staff: 1
Annual Budget: $500-1,000,000
Tax: 501(c)(3)

Personnel:
Executive Director: Bette Tate-Beaver
    E-Mail: bette@nameorg.org

Historical Note:
NAME's mission is to advance and advocate for equity and social justice through multicultural education. Membership: $65-100 (Individual); $125-1000 (Institutional); $2000 (Lifetime).

Meetings/Conferences: Annual
2013 - Berkeley, CA (University Of California, Berkeley)/Jan. 12

Publications:

Multicultural Perspectives; quarterly; adv.
NAMENews; adv.

The National Association for Music Education (Formerly MENC) (1907)
1806 Robert Fulton Dr.
Reston, VA 20191
Tel: (703) 860-4000 *Fax:* (703) 860-1531
TollFree: (800) 336-3768
Website: musiced.nafme.org
Members: 110000 individuals
Staff: 57
Annual Budget: $5-10,000,000
Tax: 501(c)(3)

Personnel:
Executive Director and Chief Executive Officer: Michael A. Butera
    E-Mail: michaelb@nafme.org
Chief Financial Officer: Paul Baker
    E-Mail: paulb@nafme.org
Deputy Executive Director and Chief Operating Officer: Michael Blakeslee
    E-Mail: mikeb@nafme.org
Manager, Membership Services: Betty Cook
    E-Mail: bettyc@nafme.org
Chief Technology Officer: Trinh Hoang
    E-Mail: trinhh@nafme.org
Assistant Executive Director, Members Center and Constituency Relations: Elizabeth W. Lasko
    E-Mail: elizabethl@nafme.org
Director, Government Relations and Advocacy Communications: Nancy Townes
    E-Mail: nancyt@nafme.org

Historical Note:
Formerly (1934) the Music Supervisors National Conference. A professional organization of music teachers, administrators and students. MENC's mission is to advance music education by encouraging the study and making of music by all. Membership: $89-126 (Active); $39-60 (Retired); $23-39 (Collegiate).

Meetings/Conferences: Biennial
Conference Chair: Adriane Darvishian
2014 - St. Louis, MO (St. Louis Union Station Marriott)/April 10 - 12

Publications:
General Music Today
Journal of Music Teacher Education; semi-annually
Journal of Research in Music Education; quarterly
Music Educators Journal; quarterly; adv.
Teaching Music; bi-monthly; adv.
UPDATE: Applications of Research in Music Education; semi-annually

Membership List Available to Non-members

National Association for Oilheat Research and Education
183 Madison Ave.
New York, NY 10016
Tel: (212) 695-1380
Staff: 1
Annual Budget: $100-250,000

Personnel:
Treasurer: John Maniscalcony

Historical Note:
Education & Training .

National Association for Olmsted Parks (1980)
1111 16th St. NW
Suite 310
Washington, DC 20036
Tel: (202) 223-9113 *Fax:* (202) 223-9112
E-Mail: info@naop.org
Website: olmsted.org
Staff: 3
Annual Budget: $250-500,000

Personnel:
Executive Director: Iris Gestram
Office and Membership Coordinator: Joanne Martonik
Director, Development and Membership: Emily Walton

Historical Note:
NAOP is a coalition of design and preservation professionals, historic property and park managers, scholars, municipal officials, citizen activists and representatives of numerous Olmsted organizations around the United States. NAOP advances Olmsted principles and legacy of irreplaceable parks and landscapes that revitalize communities and enrich people's lives.

Meetings/Conferences:
2014 - Washington, DC (National Building Museum)/ March 27 - 28

Publications:
Field Notes; quarterly

National Association for PET Container Resources (1987)
P.O. Box 1327
Sonoma, CA 95476-1327
Tel: (707) 996-4207 *Fax:* (707) 935-1998
E-Mail: information@napcor.com
Website: napcor.com
Members: 29 companies (corporate)
Staff: 4
Annual Budget: $500-1,000,000

Personnel:
Executive Director: Dennis Sabourin
    E-Mail: dsabourin@napcor.com
Director, Public Policy: Resa Dimino
    E-Mail: rdimino@napcor.com
Director, Communications: Kate Eagles
    E-Mail: keagles@napcor.com
Director, Technical Services: Michael F. Schedler
    E-Mail: mschedler@napcor.com

Historical Note:
NAPCOR is the trade association for the PET plastic packaging industry in the United States and Canada. NAPCOR facilitates the economical recovery of plastic containers with emphasis on PET plastic bottles and assists communities in promoting PET recycling and publicizes PET as an environmentally sound packaging material. Members are polyethylene terephthalate (PET) resin producers and container manufacturers.

Publications:
PET Projects; on-line
Resource Recycling

Membership List Available to Non-members

National Association for Poetry Therapy (1981)
256 McCaslin Blvd.
Suite 100
Louisville, CO 80027
Tel: (616) 363-6352 *Fax:* (888) 361-5540
TollFree: (888) 498-1843
E-Mail: naptadmin@poetrytherapy.org
Website: poetrytherapy.org
Members: 200 individuals
Staff: 5
Annual Budget: $50-100,000
Tax: 501(c)(3)

Personnel:
President: Catherine Conway CADC, CPT
Administrator: Diana K. McLean
    E-Mail: naptadmin@poetrytherapy.org
Vice President, Conferences: Rob Merritt PhD
    E-Mail: conference@poetrytherapy.org
Contact, Publications: Karen vanMeenen CPT, MA
    E-Mail: publications@poetrytherapy.org

Historical Note:
NAPT is a world-wide community of poets, writers, journal keepers, helping professionals, health care professionals, educators, and lovers of words who recognize and appreciate the healing power of language. Membership: $80-250/year.

Meetings/Conferences: Annual
Conference Chair: Rob Merritt PhD
2013 - Chicago, IL (Cenacle Retreat and Conference Center)/April 11 - 14

Publications:
e-Newsletter; monthly
Journal of Poetry Therapy; quarterly; adv.
Membership Directory; annually
Museletter; quarterly; adv.

Membership List Available to Non-members

National Association for Practical Nurse Education and Service (1941)
1940 Duke St.
Suite 200
Alexandria, VA 22314
Tel: (703) 933-1003 *Fax:* (703) 940-4089
Website: napnes.org
Members: 10000 individuals
Staff: 3
Annual Budget: $100-250,000
Tax: 501(c)(3)

Personnel:
Executive Director and Editor: Helen M. Larsen JD, LPN
Director, Education: Mary Eyles PhD, RN

Historical Note:
NAPNES is dedicated to promote and defend the practice, education and regulation of Licensed Practical Nurses (LPN), Licensed Vocational Nurses (LVN), Practical Nursing Educators, Practical Nursing Schools, and Practical Nursing Students. Membership: $75 (Regular); $10 (Student); $100 (Agency); $35 (Associate, Retirees); $125 (Council); $500 (Life Member); $35-125 (Faculty Member).

Continuing Education:
Certification Designation/s: NCP, IVT, CLTC

Publications:
Journal of Practical Nursing; adv.

National Association for Printing Leadership (2005)
One Meadowlands Plaza
Suite 1511
East Rutherford, NJ 07073
Tel: (201) 634-9600 *Fax:* (201) 634-0234
TollFree: (800) 642-6275
E-Mail: info@napl.org
Website: napl.org
Members: 3000 companies
Staff: 31
Annual Budget: $2-5,000,000

Personnel:
President and Chief Executive Officer: Joseph P. Truncale CAE
    E-Mail: jtruncale@napl.org
Administrator, Benefits: Mary Canda
Vice President, Member Relations: Dean D'Ambrosi
Senior Director, Communications: Dawn A. Lospaluto
    E-Mail: dlospaluto@napl.org
Coordinator, Marketing and Information Technology: Carol Rocke

Historical Note:
Established as the National Association of Photo-Lithographers in 1933, became the National Association of Printers and Lithographers in 1972, and assumed its present name in 1999, absorbed the Research and Engineering Council of the Graphic Arts in 2002, and merged with the National Association of Quick Printers in 2005. NAPL works to increase printers' profitability via a full range of management and educational services for its worldwide membership. Its services cover aspects of profitable printing management including cost and finance, human resources, sales and marketing, quality, desktop, economics, the environment and more. Membership: $795-1200 (Company, based on number of employees); $1200-3500 (Associate, based on number of employees); $250 (Educational Member); $750 (International Internet).

Meetings/Conferences:
Number of non-conference events/year: 1

Publications:
[P]REVIEW
NAPL Business Review
Printing Business Conditions; on-line
Twenty:10; on-line

National Association for Program Information and Performance Measurement
1133 19th St. NW
Suite 400
Washington, DC 20036
Tel: (202) 682-0100 *Fax:* (202) 682-0100
Website: napipm.org
Members: 50 individuals
Staff: 3

Personnel:
President: Suzanne H. Connolly PA
    E-Mail: SConnolly@state.pa.gov
Treasurer: Susan M. Becktold
    E-Mail: Susan.M.Becktold@state.or.us
Web Master: Collins Greer
    E-Mail: Collins.Greer@arkansas.gov

Historical Note:
Formerly (1998) National Association of Human Service Quality Control Directors. An affiliate unit of the Association of Public Welfare Association which provides administrative support.NAPIPM's mission is to assist professional government staff and other interested individuals in assessing and improving public assistance program performance and performance data collection. Members are Public or Private Human Services employees. No dues or membership fee required beyond the fee paid as membership to APHSA.

Meetings/Conferences: Annual
Publications:
Membership Directory; on-line
NAPIPM Newsletter

National Association for Proton Therapy (1990)
1301 Highland Dr.
Silver Spring, MD 20910
Tel: (301) 587-6100
Website: proton-therapy.org
Members: 12 medical centers and proton centers
Staff: 1
Annual Budget: $100-250,000
Tax: 501(c)(3)

Personnel:
Executive Director: Leonard Arzt
    E-Mail: lenarzt@proton-therapy.org

Historical Note:
NAPT promotes the therapeutic benefits of proton therapy for cancer treatment in the U.S. and abroad. Members are universities and/or medical centers with a proton beam radiation facility treating thousands of cancer patients with proton therapy.

Meetings/Conferences: Annual
2013 - Washington, DC (The Washington Marriott Hotel)/Feb. 11 - 14

National Association of Public Health Statistics and Information Systems (1933)
962 Wayne Ave.
Suite 701
Silver Spring, MD 20910
Tel: (301) 563-6001 *Fax:* (301) 563-6012
E-Mail: hq@naphsis.org
Website: naphsis.org
Members: 300 individuals
Staff: 7
Annual Budget: $2-5,000,000
Tax: 501(c)(3)

Personnel:
Executive Director: Patricia Potrzebowski PhD
    E-Mail: ppotrzebowski@naphsis.org
Project Manager: Rose Trasatti
    E-Mail: rtrasatti@naphsis.org
Director, Communications and Training: Will Whitman
    E-Mail: wwhitman@naphsis.org

Historical Note:
Formerly (1958) known as the American Association of Registration Executives, became (1995) the American Association for Vital Records and Public Health Statistics and (1997) Association for Public Health Statistics and Information Systems. NAPHSIS's mission is to provide national leadership and advocacy on behalf of its members to ensure the quality, security, confidentiality and utility of vital records and health statistics. Membership: $50/year.

Meetings/Conferences: Annual
Conference Chair: Rose Trasatti

Publications:
Executive Director's Newsletter; on-line
Member Directory; on-line

National Association for Pupil Transportation (1974)
1840 Western Ave.
Albany, NY 12203
Tel: (518) 452-3611 *Fax:* (518) 218-0867
TollFree: (800) 989-6278
E-Mail: info@napt.org
Website: napt.org
Members: 1651 individuals and 149 companies
Staff: 5
Annual Budget: $500-1,000,000
Tax: 501(c)(6)

Personnel:
Executive Director: Michael J. Martin
    E-Mail: mike.martin@napt.org
Specialist, Education: Josh Bresett
    E-Mail: josh.bresett@napt.org
Manager, Trade Shows: Bill Loshbough
    E-Mail: execuwest@aol.com
Specialist, Marketing and Communications: Lynn M. Martin
    E-Mail: lynn.martin@napt.org
Specialist, Member Services: Brianne L. Peck
    E-Mail: brianne.peck@napt.org

Historical Note:

NAPT's mission is to generate world-class professionals who provide safe and efficient pupil transportation for children. Membership: $100 (Individual); $1,400 (Business Partner); $2,500 (State Association); $750 (Affiliate).

Continuing Education:
Certification Designation/s: CSPT, CDPT, CPTS, CPTDI
Meetings/Conferences: Annual
Conference Chair: Bill Loshbough

Publications:
Membership Directory; annually
News & Views from NAPT; monthly
Newsletter; weekly
The NAPT Dispatch

National Association for Rehabilitation Leadership
633 S. Washington St.
Alexandria, VA 22314
Tel: (703) 836-0850 *Fax:* (703) 836-0848
E-Mail: info@nilausa.org
Website: prosites-nraa.homestead.com/
Members: 1000 individuals
Staff: 3

Personnel:
President: Lori Bruch
Editor: Carl Flowers
Treasurer: Adrian Johnson

Historical Note:
Founded as National Rehabilitation Administration Association; assumed its current name in 2003. A professional division of the National Rehabilitation Association. Members are non-profit rehabilitation administrators, state agency vocational rehabilitation administrators and private rehabilition administrators. NRAA supports professional training sessions on the state and regional levels and encourages professional development of rehabilitation administrators. Membership: $150 (Member); $48 (Student); $700 (Organizational); $108 (Professional/Affiliate).

National Association for Relationship and Marriage Education (2010)
P.O. Box 14946
Tallahassee, FL 32317
Website: narme.org
Staff: 1
Annual Budget: $100-250,000

Personnel:
Treasurer: Richard Albertson
    E-Mail: richard@livethelife.org

Historical Note:
NARME's mission is to foster education for healthy marriages, responsible fathers, and strong families in America. Membership: $50 - 4,000 (individuals, based on annual budget); $5,000 (Association Sponsors); $25 (Friends).

Meetings/Conferences: Annual
2013 - Anaheim, CA (Anaheim Marriott)/June 22 - 27

Publications:
Membership List; on-line
Newsletter; monthly

National Association for Research in Science Teaching (1928)
12100 Sunset Hills Rd.
Suite 130
Reston, VA 20190-3221
Tel: (703) 234-4138 *Fax:* (703) 435-4390
E-Mail: info@narst.org
Website: narst.org
Members: 1500 individuals
Staff: 2
Annual Budget: $500-1,000,000

Personnel:
Executive Director: William C. Kyle Jr.
    E-Mail: bill_kyle@umsl.edu
Editor: Joseph Krajcik
    E-Mail: krajcik@umich.edu

Historical Note:
Affiliated with the National Science Teachers Association. NARST's mission is to encourage and support the application of diverse research methods and theoretical perspectives from multiple disciplines to the investigation of teaching and learning in science, communicating science education research findings to researchers, practitioners, and policy makers. Membership: $110-$120 (Regular); $15-$55 (Student/Non-collegiate Educator); $45-$55 (Emeritus); $40-$50 (UNDP).

Meetings/Conferences: Annual
2013 - Rio Grande, Puerto Rico (Wyndham Rio Mar)/ April 6 - 9
2015 - Pittsburgh, PA/March 30 - April 2
Number of non-conference events/year: 3

Publications:
e-NARST News; semi-annually
Journal of Research in Science Teaching; monthly
Membership Directory; on-line
The International Journal of Science Education

Membership List Available to Non-members

National Association for Retail Marketing Services (1995)
2095 W. Sixth Ave.
Suite 213
Broomfield, CO 80020
Tel: (720) 442-9011
E-Mail: admin@narms.com
Website: narms.com
Members: 522 companies
Staff: 6
Annual Budget: $1-2,000,000
Tax: 501(c)(6)

Personnel:
Executive Director: Tom Caddell
    E-Mail: tcaddell@narms.com
Senior Director, Marketing and Trade Relations: Rhonda Bauer
    E-Mail: rbauer@narms.com
Office Administration Manager: Cynthia Davis
    E-Mail: cdavis@narms.com
Director, Member Relations and Communication: Fiona Lipscomb CMP
    E-Mail: flipscomb@narms.com
Director, Accounting: Susan Witkowski CAE

Historical Note:
Absorbed Fluid Marketing Services Association in 2002. NARMS is a not-for-profit trade association dedicated to driving, promoting, expanding, and fostering the business of providing retail merchandising and marketing services, and sales marketing services to all classes of trade. Membership: $595-6,000 (Company; Depending on Revenue); $1,500 (Manufacturers/Retailers/Associate); $250 (Divisions/ Subsidiaries/Offices of existing NARMS Members).

Meetings/Conferences: Annual
2013 - Scottsdale, AZ (Scottsdale Plaza Resort)/April 27 - 30

Publications:
Competitive Edge Newsletter; adv.
Membership Directory; on-line
NARMS Today; quarterly; adv.
NewsFeed

National Association for Rural Mental Health (1977)
300 33rd Ave., South
Suite 101
Waite Park, MN 56387
Tel: (320) 202-1820 *Fax:* (320) 202-1833
TollFree: (800) 809-5879
E-Mail: info@narmh.org
Website: narmh.org
Members: 500 individuals
Staff: 1
Annual Budget: $50-100,000

Personnel:
Manager: LuAnn Rice

Historical Note:
NARMH works to develop and enhance rural mental health and substance abuse services and to support mental health providers in rural areas. Members include social workers, psychiatrists, psychologists and others who work in rural community mental health settings. Membership: $65 (Individual); $175 (Organizational); $350 (Large Group); $1,000 (Sponsor); $30 (Retired/Student/Consumer).

Meetings/Conferences: Annual
Conference Chair: LuAnn Rice
2013 - San Antonio, TX (Hyatt Regency San Antonio)/ July 31 - Aug. 3

Publications:
Journal of Rural Mental Health; on-line
NARMH Newsletter; on-line

National Association for Search and Rescue (1974)
P.O. Box 232020

Centreville, VA 20120-2020
Tel: (703) 222-6277 *Fax:* (703) 222-6277
TollFree: (877) 893-0702
E-Mail: info@nasar.org
Website: nasar.org
Members: 14000 individuals
Staff: 4
Annual Budget: $250-500,000
Tax: 501(c)(3)

Personnel:
Executive Director: Megan Riccardi Bartlett
    E-Mail: meganr@nasar.org
Director, Education Services: Janet Adere
Chief Financial Officer: Ross Robinson
    E-Mail: rossr@nasar.org
Manager, Customer Care Services: Ellen Wingerd
    E-Mail: ellenw@nasar.org

Historical Note:
Established as the National Association of Search and Rescue Coordinators, assumed its present name in 1975. Members belong to various emergency medical, fire or survival rescue services. NASAR provides advancing professional, literary, and scientific knowledge in fields related to search and rescue. Membership: $74-1,250/year.

Continuing Education:
Certification Designation/s: CAR, CDR, SARTECH II, SARTECH I, SARTECH III

Meetings/Conferences:
Conference Chair: Megan Riccardi Bartlett

Publications:
NASAR Newsletter

Membership List Available to Non-members

National Association for Sport and Physical Education *(1974)*
1900 Association Dr.
Reston, VA 20191-1598
Tel: (703) 476-3410 *Fax:* (703) 476-8316
TollFree: (800) 213-7193
E-Mail: naspe@aahperd.org
Website: aahperd.org/naspe/index.cfm
Members: 15000 individuals
Staff: 15
Annual Budget: $100-250,000

Personnel:
Executive Director: Charlene R. Burgeson
    E-Mail: cburgeson@aahperd.org
Senior Director, Programs: Carly Braxton
    E-Mail: cbraxton@aahperd.org
Director, Communications: Paula K. Kun
    E-Mail: pkun@aahperd.org
Manager, Publications: Joe McGavin
    E-Mail: jmcgavin@aahperd.org
Senior Director, Programs: Cheryl Richardson
    E-Mail: CRichardson@aahperd.org
Senior Manager, Professional Services: Susan Schoenberg
    E-Mail: sschoenberg@aahperd.org

Historical Note:
Created from the merger of the Division of Men's Athletics and the Physical Education Division of the American Association for Health, Physical Education, Recreation and Dance. NASPE is one of the AAHPERD's five autonomous affiliates whose mission is to enhance knowledge, improve professional practice, and increase support for quality physical education, sport, and physical activity programs through research, development of standards, and dissemination of information. Membership: $50 (Undergraduate/Graduate); $135 (Graduating Senior/ Professional); $200 (Institutional); $45 (Retired).

Continuing Education:
Certification Designation/s: DPA

Meetings/Conferences:
Conference Chair: Cheryl Richardson
Number of non-conference events/year: 3

Publications:
Academy Scoops; monthly
International Electronic Journal of Health Education; on-line
Journal of Coaching Education; semi-annually
Journal of Physical Education, Recreation & Dance
Member Directory; on-line
NASPE News; adv.
Strategies-A Journal for Physical and Sport Educators; bi-monthly; adv.

Membership List Available to Non-members

National Association for State Community Services Programs *(1968)*
444 N. Capitol St. NW
Suite 846
Washington, DC 20001
Tel: (202) 624-5866 *Fax:* (202) 624-8472
E-Mail: nascsp@nascsp.org
Website: nascsp.org
Members: 52 states and Puerto Rico and the District of Columbia
Staff: 29
Annual Budget: $2-5,000,000
Tax: 501(c)(6)

Personnel:
Executive Director: Timothy R. Warfield
    E-Mail: warfield@nascsp.org
Director, Research: Tabitha Beck
    E-Mail: tbeck@nascsp.org
Communications Assistant: Payten Carroll
    E-Mail: pcarroll@nascsp.org
Director, Operations: Joan D. Harris
    E-Mail: jharris@nascsp.org
Director, Government Relations: Arley Johnson
    E-Mail: ajohnson@nascsp.org
Director, Membership Services: Terry Joyner
    E-Mail: tjoyner@nascsp.org
Policy Director, Communications: Gretchen Knowlton
    E-Mail: gknowlton@nascsp.org
General Counsel: Brad A. Penney
    E-Mail: bpenney@nascsp.org
Director, Program Services: Jovita Tolbert
    E-Mail: jtolbert@nascsp.org

Historical Note:
NASCSP's mission is to asssist states in responding to poverty issues. Members are state administrators of federal Community Services Block Grant (CSBG) and Weatherization Assistance Programs (WAP).

Meetings/Conferences: Semi-Annual
Conference Chair: Jovita Tolbert
Number of non-conference events/year: 12

Publications:
NASCSP Newsletter; monthly

National Association for Surface Finishing *(1955)*
1155 15th St. NW
Suite 500
Washington, DC 20005
Tel: (202) 457-8404 *Fax:* (202) 530-0659
E-Mail: info@namf.org
Website: nasf.org
Members: 2600 individuals and companies
Staff: 5
Annual Budget: $1-2,000,000
Tax: 501(c)(6)

Personnel:
Manager, Membership Services: Philip Assante
    E-Mail: passante@nasf.org
Director, Events: Cheryl Clark
    E-Mail: cclark@nasf.org
Deputy Executive Director and Executive Director, Foundation: Carrie Hoffman
    E-Mail: choffman@nasf.org
Executive Vice President: Christian Richter
    E-Mail: crichter@thepolicygroup.com
Coordinator, Education and Communications: Luke Zorich
    E-Mail: lzorich@nasf.org

Historical Note:
NASF was Created by reorganizing and bringing together the members of the American Electroplaters and Surface Finishers Society (AESF), the Metal Finishing Suppliers Association (MFSA) and the National Association of Metal Finishers (NAMF). NAMF was a product of merger of the National Federation of Metal Finishers and the National Association of Plating. NASF's mission is to promote and advance the North American Surface Finishing Industry Globally. Members are executives of firms engaged in all methods of finishing metal, plastic and organic surfaces. Membership: $1,100-11,000 (Corporate Supplier-U.S.); $880-8,800 (Corporate Supplier-Foreign); $1,100-11,000 (Corporate Domestic); $880 (Job shop-domestic); $1,100 (Job Shop- Foreign/Associate); $150 (Individual- Domestic); $125 (Individual- Foreign); $75 (Student/Retired).

Continuing Education:
Certification Designation/s: CEF/MSF

Meetings/Conferences: Annual
Conference Chair: Cheryl Clark

2013 - San Juan, PR (InterContinental Hotel)/March 11 - 15
Number of non-conference events/year: 2

Publications:
NASF Newsletter; monthly
NASF Weekly Bulletin; weekly
Plating and Surface Finishing; monthly; adv.
The Journal of Applied Surface Finishing (JASF)

National Association for the Advancement of Orthotics and Prosthetics *(1987)*
1501 M St. NW
Seventh Floor
Washington, DC 20005-1700
Tel: (202) 624-0064 *Fax:* (202) 785-1756
TollFree: (800) 622-6740
E-Mail: info@naaop.org
Website: naaop.org
Staff: 3
Annual Budget: $100-250,000
Tax: 501(c)(6)

Personnel:
Executive Director: George W. Breece
    E-Mail: george@breece.com
Treasurer: Jim Rogers
General Counsel: Peter W. Thomas

Historical Note:
NAAOP's mission is to be an unifying advocate, representing the interests of the O&P patient and practice communities specifically championing causes concerning patient access, funding, and outcomes through leadership in national and state policy formation. Members are orthotics and prosthetics professionals who advocate for better education better quality and more advanced technology to assist employees and others with physical disabilities. Membership: $250 (Individual Practitioner); $500 (Educational/Research Institution); $150 (Fitters/ Technicians/Assistants); $50 (Student/Resident); $1000 (Independent); $100 (Friend).

National Association for the Advancement of Psychoanalysis *(1972)*
80 Eighth Ave.
Suite 1501
New York, NY 10011
Tel: (212) 741-0515 *Fax:* (212) 366-4347
E-Mail: naap@naap.org
Website: naap.org
Members: 1500 individuals and 33 organizations
Staff: 3
Annual Budget: $100-250,000
Tax: 501(c)(6)

Personnel:
Executive Director: Margery Quackenbush
    E-Mail: mq@naap.org
Editor: Kirsty Cardinale
    E-Mail: naapnews@naap.org

Historical Note:
NAAP works to establish educational standards for psychoanalytic training institutes seeking accreditation. Membership: $275 (Psychoanalyst); $125 (Associate); $75 (Affiliate/Research and Mental Health Affiliate/Friend/ Retired); $450 (Organizational).

Continuing Education:
Enrollment: 1900
Certification Designation/s: NCPA

Meetings/Conferences: Annual

Publications:
Membership Directory; on-line
NAAP News; quarterly; adv.
NAAP's e-Bulletin; weekly

Membership List Available to Non-members

The National Association for the Dually Diagnosed *(1983)*
132 Fair St.
Kingston, NY 12401-4802
Tel: (845) 331-4336 *Fax:* (845) 331-4569
TollFree: (800) 331-5362
E-Mail: info@thenadd.org
Website: thenadd.org
Members: 1500 individuals
Staff: 5
Annual Budget: $500-1,000,000
Tax: 501(c)(3)

Personnel:

Founder and Chief Executive Officer: Robert J. Fletcher
DSW
   E-Mail: rfletcher@thenadd.org
Conference Meeting Planner: Lisa Christie
   E-Mail: lchristie@thenadd.org
Manager, Information Technology: William Hicks
Office Manager: Michelle Jordan
   E-Mail: mjordan@thenadd.org

Historical Note:
*Founded as the National Association for the Dually
Diagnosed Mental Illness/Mental Retardation. NADD's
mission is to advance mental wellness for persons with
developmental disabilities through the promotion of
excellence in mental health care. Membership: $60-1,440/
year.*

Meetings/Conferences: Annual
Conference Chair: Lisa Christie
2013 - Baltimore, MD/Oct. 23 - 25
Number of non-conference events/year: 1

Publications:
Journal of Mental Health Research in Intellectual
   Disabilities (JMHRID)
Membership Directory
NADD Bulletin; bi-monthly

Membership List Available to Non-members

National Association for the Education of Young Children *(1926)*
1313 L St. NW
Suite 500
Washington, DC 20005
Tel: (202) 232-8777 *Fax:* (202) 328-1846
TollFree: (800) 424-2460
E-Mail: naeyc@naeyc.org
Website: naeyc.org
Members: 80000 individuals
Staff: 100
Annual Budget: $10-25,000,000
Tax: 501(c)(3)

Personnel:
Executive Director: Jerlean Daniel
   E-Mail: jdaniel@naeyc.org
Director, Meetings and Conferences: Monique Cabiness
   E-Mail: mcabiness@naeyc.org
Senior Director, Human Resources: Terri Carter
   E-Mail: tcarter@naeyc.org
Senior Director, Information Technology and Data Services:
   Khalid Chaudhry
   E-Mail: kchaudhry@naeyc.org
Associate Director, Sales and Development: Kathleen
   Donato
   E-Mail: kdonato@naeyc.org
Chief Accounting Officer: Richard Holly
   E-Mail: rholly@naeyc.org
Director, Marketing and Communications: Bruce Holmes
   E-Mail: bholmes@naeyc.org
Editor In Chief: Derry Koralek
   E-Mail: DKoralek@naeyc.org
*Senior Director, Higher Education Accreditation and
   Program Support:* Alison Lutton
   E-Mail: alutton@naeyc.org
General Counsel: Theresa Myers
   E-Mail: tmyers@naeyc.org
Deputy Executive Director, Policy & Public Affairs: Adele
   Robinson
   E-Mail: arobinson@naeyc.org
Director, Association Services: Valerie Sheehan
   E-Mail: vsheehan@naeyc.org
Manager, Marketing Projects: Melanie White
   E-Mail: mwhite@naeyc.org

Historical Note:
*Established as the National Association for Nursery
Education, assumed its present name in 1964, NAEYC
strives to improve the well-being of all young children.
Members are administrators and teachers in schools for
children (birth through age 8). Membership: $90-135
(Comprehensive); $55-85 (Regular); $25-65 (Student);
$80-332.25 (International).*

Meetings/Conferences: Annual
Conference Chair: Monique Cabiness

Publications:
Early Childhood Research Quarterly; quarterly
Membership Directory; on-line
NEXT for TYC
Teaching Young Children; adv.
Young Children; bi-monthly; adv.

Membership List Available to Non-members

National Association for the Practice of Anthropology *(1983)*
2200 Wilson Blvd.
Suite 600
Arlington, VA 22201-3357
Tel: (703) 528-1902 *Fax:* (703) 528-3546
Website: practicinganthropology.org
Staff: 3

Personnel:
President: Tim Wallace
   E-Mail: tmwallace@mindspring.com
Editor: Satish Kedia
   E-Mail: skkedia@memphis.edu
Treasurer: John Massad
   E-Mail: jpnmassad@gmail.com

Historical Note:
*A section of the American Anthropological Association.
NAPA's mission is to promote the practice of anthropology
and the interests of practicing anthropologists, and to
further the practice of anthropology as a profession. To join
NAPA, one must be a member of AAA. Membership: $35
(Professional); $20 (Student).*

Meetings/Conferences: Annual
Number of non-conference events/year: 1

Publications:
NAPA Newsletter; on-line; adv.

National Association for the Self-Employed *(1981)*
325 Seventh St. NW
Suite 250
Washington, DC 20004
Tel: (202) 466-2100 *Fax:* (202) 466-2123
Website: nase.org
Members: 250000 individuals
Staff: 21
Annual Budget: $2-5,000,000
Tax: 501(c)(6)

Personnel:
President and Chief Executive Officer.: Kristie L. Arslan
   E-Mail: kdarien@nase.org
General Counsel: Michael Beene
   E-Mail: mike.beene@nase.org
Federal Lobbyist: Kristin Oberlander
   E-Mail: koberlander@naseadmin.org
Federal Lobbyist: Katie Vlietstra

Historical Note:
*NASE's mission is to promote small business growth and
entrepreneurship. It represents entrepreneurs and micro-
businesses. Membership: $120/year.*

Publications:
Membership Directory; on-line
NASE Newsletter; on-line
Self-Employed Magazine; bi-monthly
SelfInformed; monthly
Washington Watch; weekly

National Association for the Specialty Food Trade *(1952)*
136 Madison Ave.
12th Floor
New York, NY 10016
Tel: (212) 482-6440 *Fax:* (212) 482-6459
TollFree: (800) 627-3869
E-Mail: customerservice@nasft.org
Website: specialtyfood.com
Members: 2700 companies
Staff: 66
Annual Budget: $10-25,000,000

Personnel:
President: Ann Daw
   E-Mail: adaw@nasft.org
Manager, Programs and Events: Jennifer Carney
Senior Vice President, Media: Chris Crocker
Director, Education Programs: Laura Lozada
   E-Mail: llozada@nasft.org
Senior Director and Editor: Denise Purcell
Chief Marketing Director: Ken Seiter
Senior Director, Finance and Administration: Meryl Skyler
Director, Chief Information Technology: Lisa Stefanoff
*Vice President, Communications, Education, Government
   and Industry Relations:* Ron Tanner

Historical Note:
*Absorbed Speciality Food Distributors and Manufacturers
Association in 2002. NASFT's mission is to foster trade,
commerce and interest in the specialty food industry, in*

*addition to providing business- building programs, services
and networking opportunities. Members are manufacturers,
importers, distributors, chefs, caterers, catalogers, gift stores
of specialty gourmet foods, beverages and confections.
Membership: $100-600 (Company); $100 (Brokers); $200
(Government Entities, Domestic/Foreign).*

Continuing Education:
Certification Designation/s: FD

Meetings/Conferences: Semi-Annual
Conference Chair: Jennifer Carney
2013 - San Francisco, CA/Jan. 20 - 22/1-10 exhibitors
2013 - New York City, NY/June 30 - July 2/1-10
   exhibitors
2014 - San Francisco, CA/Jan. 19 - 21
2014 - New York City, NY/June 29 - July 1/1-10
   exhibitors

Publications:
Official Show Directory; annually; adv.
Specialty Food Magazine; adv.
Specialty Food Newsletter; daily; adv.

National Association for the Support of Long Term Care *(1989)*
1050 17th St. NW
Suite 500
Washington, DC 20036-5558
Tel: (202) 803-2385
E-Mail: membership@nasl.org
Website: netforum.avectra.com/eweb/
   startpage.aspx?site = nasl
Members: 120 companies
Staff: 4
Annual Budget: $500-1,000,000
Tax: 501(c)(6)

Personnel:
Executive Vice President: Cynthia Morton CAE
   E-Mail: cynthia@nasl.org
Director, Administrative Services: Laura de la Calzada
   E-Mail: lauradlc@nasl.org
Director, Government Relations: Andrea R. Price-Carter
   FACHE
   E-Mail: andrea@nasl.org

Historical Note:
*NASL represent providers and suppliers on healthcare
policy and advocate for cost-effective care. Members are
providers to the long term care industry. Membership:
$1,700 (Associate); $27,500 (Board of Governors, based
on revenue); $4,200 (Bronze, based on revenue); $15,750
(Gold, based on revenue); $8,150 (Silver, based on
revenue).*

Meetings/Conferences: Annual
Conference Chair: Laura de la Calzada

Publications:
Individual Directory; on-line
Membership Directory; on-line

National Association for Uniformed Services *(1968)*
5535 Hempstead Way
Springfield, VA 22151-4094
Tel: (703) 750-1342 *Fax:* (703) 354-4380
TollFree: (800) 842-3451
E-Mail: naus@naus.org
Website: naus.org
Members: 200000 members
Staff: 12
Annual Budget: $2-5,000,000

Personnel:
President and Chief Executive Officer: Jack W. Klimp
   E-Mail: jklimp@naus.org
Chief Financial Officer and Director, Membership Services:
   Windora Bradburn
   E-Mail: wbradburn@naus.org
Managing Editor: William "Tommy" Campbell
   E-Mail: tcampbell@naus.org
Manager, Membership: Toni Cimini
   E-Mail: tcimini@naus.org
Director, Marketing: Steve Hein
   E-Mail: shein@naus.org
Director, Legislation: Richard A. Jones
   E-Mail: rjones@naus.org
Administration, Director: Vicki Sumner
   E-Mail: vsumner@naus.org

Historical Note:
*NAUS's mission is to protect and enhance the earned
benefits of uniformed servicemembers, retirees, veterans,
and their families and survivors, while maintaining a strong
defense, and to foster esprit de corps among uniformed*

services personnel and veterans of the United States, through nonpartisan advocacy on Capitol Hill and with other government officials. Membership: $25-95 (Single Member); $45-160 (Joint (Member & Spouse); $19-69 (Widower);

Meetings/Conferences: Annual

Publications:
Uniformed Services Journal; bi-monthly; adv.

National Association for Year-Round Education
(1972)
P.O. Box 711386
San Diego, CA 92171-1386
Tel: (619) 276-5296 *Fax:* (858) 571-5754
E-Mail: info@nayre.org
Website: nayre.org
Members: 130 institutions and 1570 individuals
Staff: 5
Annual Budget: Under $10,000
Tax: 501(c)(3)

Personnel:
Executive Director: Samuel J. Pepper
  E-Mail: spepper@nayre.org
Contact, Member Services: Shirley Jennings

Historical Note:
Formerly called as the National Council on Year-Round Education (1986). NAYRE is a professional association of individuals with an interest in the concept of year round education and provides leadership and service to individuals and organizations on all aspects of time and learning. The association encourages research, produces publications, provides consultants to schools and districts, and conducts yearly conferences regionally and nationally to provide the most up-to-date information available to educators and community members. Members include educators, policy makers, journalists, business leaders and parents. Schools and school districts compose NAYRE's institutional membership. Membership: $45 (Individual); $350-750 (Institution-varies by enrollment); $200 (Commercial); $250 (Lifetime); $25 (Retired).

Publications:
Year-Rounder Newsletter; bi-monthly

National Association of Medical Staff Services
(1978)
2025 M St. NW
Suite 800
Washington, DC 20036
Tel: (202) 367-1196 *Fax:* (202) 367-2196
E-Mail: info@namss.org
Website: namss.org
Members: 4500 medical staff and credentialing services professionals
Staff: 19
Annual Budget: $2-5,000,000

Personnel:
Executive Director: Megan Cohen CAE, MPA
  E-Mail: mcohen@namss.org
Senior Manager, Membership and Education Services: Stacey Barnes
  E-Mail: sbarnes@namss.org
Senior Manager, Marketing and Communications: Kara Dress
  E-Mail: kdress@namss.org
Manager, Conventions and Tradeshows: Kelly Marks
  E-Mail: meetings@namss.org
Senior Director, Education and Learning Services: Chris Murphy Peck
  E-Mail: cpeck@namss.org
Director, Accounting and Financial Management: Russ Nuzum
Director, Government Relations: John Richardson

Historical Note:
NAMSS strives to advance a healthcare environment that maximizes the patient experience through the delivery of quality services. Members are medical staff and credentialing services professionals from medical group practices, hospitals, managed care organizations, and CVOs. Membership: $215 (Active Member); $110 (Affiliate Member).

Continuing Education:
Certification Designation/s: CPMSM, CPCS

Meetings/Conferences: Annual
Conference Chair: Kelly Marks
2013 - Hollywood, FL (Westin Diplomat Resort and Spa)/Sept. 21 - 25/11-25 exhibitors
2014 - New Orleans, LA (Hilton New Orleans Riverside)/Sept. 27 - Oct. 1/11-25 exhibitors

Publications:

Membership Directory; annually
NAMSS e-Newsletter; monthly; adv.
Synergy; bi-monthly; adv.

National Association of Academic Advisors for Athletes *(1975)*
1500 South University Parks Dr.
Waco, TX 76706
Tel: (254) 710-3790
E-Mail: info@nfoura.org
Website: nfoura.org
Members: 1000 individuals
Staff: 4
Annual Budget: $250-500,000

Personnel:
President: Bart Byrd
  E-Mail: bart_byrd@baylor.edu
Division Director, Membership Services: Tierra Barber
  E-Mail: tierra_barber@baylor.edu

Historical Note:
N4A's mission is to promote the integrity of their profession by providing guiding principles and quality services to support one another as they share information, resources and expertise in their efforts to empower student-athletes to become more productive individuals through educational and personal development. Members are academic support and student services personnel who are committed to enhancing the opportunities for academic, athletic and personal success for collegiate student-athletes. Membership: $50 (Student); $125 (Professional/Affiliate).

Continuing Education:
Certification Designation/s: N4A

Meetings/Conferences: Annual
2013 - Jacksonville, FL (Hyatt Regency Jacksonville Riverfront)/June 6 - 9

Publications:
The Academic Athletic Journal; on-line
The N4A News; annually

Membership List Available to Non-members

National Association of Academies of Science
(1926)
49 Mountain Meadow Rd.
Warren, NH 03279
Tel: (603) 764-5284
Website: academiesofscience.org/naas
Members: 44 academies
Staff: 4
Annual Budget: $100-250,000

Personnel:
Executive Director: Ed Brogie
Webmaster: Michael Eckhoff
  E-Mail: michael.eckhoff@academiesofscience.org
Newsletter Editor: Dr. Don M. Jordan
  E-Mail: djordan@sc.edu
Treasurer: Amy Strong
  E-Mail: amy.strong@wichita.edu

Historical Note:
Before 1919 various academies were informally associated with the American Association for the Advancement of Science (AAAS). In 1920, they were given the right of representation on the AAAS council and became known as the Affiliated Academies. In 1926, they became a more organized group known as the Academy Conference, and in 1969 became known as the Association of Academies of Science. Affiliated with AAAS. Until 1979, known as the Association of Academies of Science. Membership: $250/year (maximum).

Meetings/Conferences: Annual
2013 - Boston, MA/Feb. 13 - 17

Publications:
NAAS Newsletter

National Association of Active Investment Managers *(1989)*
6732 W. Coal Mine Ave.
Suite 446
Littleton, CO 80123
Fax: (303) 979-2192
TollFree: (888) 261-0787
E-Mail: info@naaim.org
Website: naaim.org/
Members: 200 firms
Staff: 1
Annual Budget: $250-500,000

Personnel:
Administrator: Susan Truesdale

Historical Note:
Represents registered investment advisors who provide active money management services to their clients, in order to produce favorable risk-adjusted returns as an alternative to more passive, buy and hold strategies.

Meetings/Conferences: Annual
Conference Chair: Susan Truesdale
2013 - Denver, CO (Westin Denver Downtown)/April 28 - May 1
Number of non-conference events/year: 1

Publications:
Active Manager Newsletter; bi-monthly
NAAIM Membership Directory; on-line
NAAIM News; on-line

National Association of Activity Professionals
(1982)
1327 E. Central Ave.
P.O. Box 277
LaFollette, TN 37766
Tel: (865) 429-0717 *Fax:* (865) 453-9914
E-Mail: thenaap@aol.com
Website: thenaap.com
Members: 1800 individuals
Staff: 5
Annual Budget: $100-250,000
Tax: 501(c)(6)

Personnel:
Executive Director: Irene Taylor ACC, MS
  E-Mail: thenaap@aol.com

Historical Note:
NAAP's mission is to provide excellence in support services to activity professionals through education, advocacy, technical assistance, promotion of standards, fostering of research, and peer and industry relations. Membership is open to anyone interested in working within a geriatric setting. Membership: $59 (Active); $39 (Associate/Retired/International); $49 (Student/Corporate).

Meetings/Conferences: Annual
2013 - Las Vegas, NV (The Tropicana Las Vegas Hotel)/April 24 - 27
Number of non-conference events/year: 1

Publications:
NAAP Newsletter; bi-monthly

National Association of Addiction Treatment Providers *(1978)*
313 W. Liberty St.
Suite 129
Lancaster, PA 17603-2748
Tel: (717) 392-8480 *Fax:* (717) 392-8481
Website: naatp.org
Members: 250 members
Staff: 4
Annual Budget: $250-500,000
Tax: 501(c)(6)

Personnel:
President and Chief Executive Officer: Michael E. Walsh CAP, MS
  E-Mail: MWalsh@naatp.org
Contact, Meetings: Sherry Anderson
  E-Mail: sanderson@naatp.org

Historical Note:
NAATP's mission is to promote, assist and enhance the delivery of ethical, effective, research-based treatment for alcoholism and other drug addictions. Members are for-profit and non-profit treatment centers for alcoholism and drug dependency. Membership: $12,360/year (Associate).

Continuing Education:
Enrollment: 300
Certification Designation/s: CEU

Meetings/Conferences: Semi-Annual
Conference Chair: Sherry Anderson
2013 - San Antonio, TX (Westin La Cantera Hill Country Resort)/May 18 - 21
Number of non-conference events/year: 1

Publications:
CEO Forecast; monthly
Visions Newsletter; monthly; adv.

National Association of Advisors for the Health Professions *(1974)*
P.O. Box 1518
Champaign, IL 61824-1518
Tel: (217) 355-0063 *Fax:* (217) 355-1287
E-Mail: naahpja@aol.com
Website: naahp.org

Members: 1200 individuals
Staff: 7
Annual Budget: $500-1,000,000

Personnel:
Administrative Assistant and Membership: Aliesha Dennis
    E-Mail: adennis@naahp.org
Manager, National Office and Marketing: Theron R. Sands
    E-Mail: tsands@naahp.org
Bookkeeper: Pamela Smith
    E-Mail: psmith@naahp.org

Historical Note:
NAAHP is dedicated to the needs of the health professions advisor and to serve as a resource for the professional development of health professions advisors. Membership includes pre-health advisors in many of the country's undergraduate colleges and universities, who counsel students on careers in the health professions, and also includes representatives of national health associations and deans of professional schools' admissions/student affairs departments. Membership: $85-110 (Advisor); $350 (Full Patron); $175 (Patron Associate); $20 (Emeritus).

Meetings/Conferences: Biennial
2014 - San Francisco, CA (Hilton San Francisco Union Square)/June 25 - 29

Publications:
Advisor; quarterly; adv.
NAAHP-NET Newsletter; monthly

National Association of Affordable Housing Lenders *(1990)*
1667 K St. NW
Suite 210
Washington, DC 20006
Tel: (202) 293-9850 *Fax:* (202) 293-9852
E-Mail: naahl@naahl.org
Website: naahl.org
Members: 80 organizations
Staff: 4
Annual Budget: $500-1,000,000
Tax: 501(c)(6)

Personnel:
President and Chief Executive Officer: Judith A. Kennedy
    E-Mail: naahl@naahl.org
Chief Operating Officer: Paul Haaland
Administrative Assistant: Kristen Schott

Historical Note:
NAAHL strives to increase private capital lending and investment in low and moderate income communities. Members are the key executives of private sector lenders and investors in affordable housing and community economic development: banks, thrifts, insurance companies, community development corporations, mortgage companies, loan consortia, financial intermediaries, pension funds, foundations, local and national nonprofits, and public agencies. Membership: $1,000-5,000 (General); $500-1,000 (Organization); $500 (Associate).

Meetings/Conferences:
Conference Chair: Kristen Schott

Publications:
Washington Update; irregular

National Association of African American Studies and Affiliates *(1992)*
P.O. Box 6670
Scarborough, ME 04070-6670
Tel: (207) 839-8004 *Fax:* (207) 839-3776
E-Mail: natlaffiliates@earthlink.net
Website: naaas.org
Members: 376 individuals and organizations
Staff: 3
Annual Budget: $100-250,000

Personnel:
Executive Director: Dr. Lemuel Berry Jr., PhD

Historical Note:
NAAAS's mission is to serve as a resource for scholars in the field who desire information and support for research related to the African and African American, Hispanic, Latino(a) and Chicano(a), Native American and Asian experiences. Membership: $3,000 (Life); $500 (Institutional); $100 (Student/Sustaining); $125 (Individual).

Meetings/Conferences: Annual
2013 - Baton Rouge, LA (Crowne Plaza Executive Center Baton Rouge)/Feb. 11 - 16
Number of non-conference events/year: 2

Publications:
Journal of Intercultural Disciplines; annually

NAAAS Newsletter; quarterly
Membership List Available to Non-members

National Association of Agricultural Educators *(1948)*
300 Garringus Bldg.
University of Kentucky
Lexington, KY 40546-0215
Tel: (859) 257-2224 *Fax:* (859) 323-3919
TollFree: (800) 509-0204
Website: naae.org
Members: 7650 individuals
Staff: 10
Annual Budget: $1-2,000,000
Tax: 501(c)(3)

Personnel:
NAAE Executive Director: William Jay Jackman CAE, PhD
    E-Mail: jjackman.NAAE@uky.edu
Meeting Planner: Miranda Chaplin
    E-Mail: mchaplin.naae@uky.edu
Coordinator, Communications and Marketing: Julie Fritsch
    E-Mail: jfritsch.naae@uky.edu

Historical Note:
The National Association of Agricultural Educators (NAAE) is a organization for school-based agricultural educators in the United States.

Meetings/Conferences: Annual
2013 - Las Vegas, NV/Dec. 3 - 7
2014 - Nashville, TN/Nov. 18 - 22

Publications:
News & Views; bi-monthly; adv.
Advocacy in Action

Membership List Available to Non-members

National Association of Agricultural Fair Agencies *(1966)*
1156 15th St. NW
Suite 1020
Washington, DC 20005
Tel: (202) 296-9680 *Fax:* (202) 296-9686
E-Mail: nasda@nasda.org
Website: nasda.org/cms/7195/8878/13177.aspx
Members: 35 agencies
Staff: 6
Annual Budget: Under $10,000

Personnel:
Chief Executive Officer: Stephen Haterius
    E-Mail: stephen@nasda.org
Director, Trade Shows & Grants Management: DeWitt Ashby
    E-Mail: dewitt@nasda.org
Director, Legislative and Regulatory Affairs: Nathan Bowen
    E-Mail: nathan@nasda.org
Secretary and Treasurer: Greg Ibach
Program Director: Charlie Ingram
    E-Mail: charlie@nasda.org
Controller: Debra Talbott
    E-Mail: debra@nasda.org

Historical Note:
U.S. and Canadian representatives of state/provincial agencies that are responsible for the support of educational and agricultural fairs. Affiliated with the National Association of State Departments of Agriculture. Membership: $35/year.

Meetings/Conferences: Annual
2013 - New Orleans, LA (The Roosevelt Hotel)/June 9 - 13
2013 - Medora, ND/June 20 - 24
2013 - Asheville, NC (Inn On Biltmore Estate)/Sept. 8 - 13
Number of non-conference events/year: 3

National Association of Agriculture Employees *(1954)*
9080 Torrey Rd.
Willis, MI 48191
Tel: (734) 942-9005 *Fax:* (734) 942-7691
Website: aginspectors.org
Members: 750 individuals
Staff: 3
Annual Budget: $50-100,000

Personnel:
President: Sarah Rehberg
    E-Mail: sarahrehberg1@yahoo.com

Legal Counsel: Kim Mann
Treasurer: James Triebwasser
    E-Mail: triebwas2000@yahoo.com

Historical Note:
Formerly (1981) the Federal Plant Quarantine Inspectors National Association. NAAE is an independent federal labor union which represents employees working for the U.S. Dept. of Agriculture, Animal and Plant Health Inspection Service, Plant Protection and Quarantine. Members are professional employees with college degrees in Biological Sciences.

Publications:
NAAE Newsletter

National Association of Air Medical Communication Specialists *(1989)*
1235 E Cherokee
Springfield, MO 65804
Tel: (417) 820-9651 *Fax:* (417) 820-8623
Website: naacs.org
Members: 200 individuals
Staff: 3
Annual Budget: $25-50,000

Personnel:
President: Clayton Hummer
    E-Mail: ckhummer@sbcglobal.net

Historical Note:
Formerly (2000) National Association of Air Communications Specialists. NAACS seeks to enhance the professionalism of the Air Medical communications specialists through education, recognition, and standardization. Members are air medical communications specialists. NAACS's mission is to provide representation of Air Medical Communications Specialists on a National level. Membership: $35 (Individual/Program); $25 (Associate).

Continuing Education:
Certification Designation/s: CFC, OCS

Publications:
NAACS Newsletter; quarterly

National Association of Aircraft and Communication Suppliers
P.O. Box 190
Camarillo, CA 93011-0190
Tel: (202) 237-0505 *Fax:* (210) 924-4901
E-Mail: info@naacs.com
Website: naacs.com
Members: 120 small businesses
Staff: 1

Personnel:
Chair, Membership: Ed Wilk

Historical Note:
NAACS protects and represents the interests of the military surplus aircraft parts industry. Membership: $500 (Basic); $1,000 (Sustaining); $2,000 (Founder's Circle).

Continuing Education:
Certification Designation/s: EUC

National Association for Alcoholism and Drug Abuse Counselors *(1972)*
1001 N. Fairfax St.
Suite 201
Alexandria, VA 22314
Tel: (703) 741-7686 *Fax:* (800) 377-1136
TollFree: (800) 548-0497
E-Mail: naadac@naadac.org
Website: naadac.org
Members:
44 state affiliates
75000 members, addiction counselors, educators and other addiction-focused health care professionals
Staff: 11
Annual Budget: $1-2,000,000
Tax: 501(c)(3)

Personnel:
Executive Director: Cynthia Moreno Tuohy SAP
    E-Mail: cmoreno@naadac.org
Director, Government Relations: Christopher C. Campbell MA
    E-Mail: ccampbell@naadac.org
Lead Administrative Coordinator: Latressa Cross
    E-Mail: lcross@naadac.org
Coordinator, Certification and Education: Donna Croy
    E-Mail: dcroy@naadac.org

*Director, Certification and Education and National
    Certification Commission Staff Liaison:* Shirley Beckett
    Mikell SAP
    E-Mail: sbeckettmikell@naadac.org
Director, Training and Professional Development: Misti
    Storie MS
    E-Mail: mstorie@naadac.org

Historical Note:
*NAADAC's mission is to lead, unify and empower addiction
focused professionals to achieve excellence through
education, advocacy, knowledge, standards of practice,
ethics, professional development and research. Membership:
$85 (Full/Professional Member); $64 (Associate Member);
$32.50 (Student).*

Continuing Education:
Certification Designation/s: CSCHAPF, TAS, SAP, ASE,
MAC, NCAC I, NCAC II, CRRCP

Meetings/Conferences: Annual
2013 - Atlanta, GA (InterContinental Buckhead
Atlanta)/Oct. 11 - 14

Publications:
Addiction Professional magazine; on-line; adv.
Directory of Education and Training; annually; adv.
NAADAC newsletters; bi-monthly; adv.

National Association of Animal Breeders (1946)
P.O. Box 1033
Columbia, MO 65205-1033
Tel: (573) 445-4406 *Fax:* (573) 446-2279
E-Mail: naab-css@naab-css.org
Website: naab-css.org
Members: 23 organizations
Staff: 4
Annual Budget: $1-2,000,000

Personnel:
President: Dr. Gordon A Doak PhD
    E-Mail: gdoak@naab-css.org
Contact, Meetings: Marcia Clarahan
    E-Mail: mclarahan@naab-css.org
Technical Director: Jere R Mitchell
    E-Mail: jmitchel@naab-css.org
Administrator, Genetic Programs: Dr. Kent Weigel
    E-Mail: kweigel@facstaff.wisc.edu

Historical Note:
*Formerly the National Association of Artificial Breeders.
NAAB seeks to unite those individuals and organizations
engaged in the artificial insemination of cattle and other
livestock into an affiliated federation operating under self-
imposed standards of performance and to conduct and
promote the mutual interest and ideals of its members.
Members are farmer co-ops and others interested in
livestock improvement. Membership: $100 (Regular); $125
(Associate).*

Meetings/Conferences: Semi-Annual
Conference Chair: Marcia Clarahan

Publications:
Newsletter; adv.

National Association of Architectural Metal Manufacturers (1938)
800 Roosevelt Rd.
Building C, Suite 312
Glen Ellyn, IL 60137
Tel: (630) 942-6591 *Fax:* (630) 790-3095
E-Mail: info@naamm.org
Website: naamm.org
Members: 112 companies
Staff: 4
Annual Budget: $500-1,000,000
Tax: 501(c)(6)

Personnel:
Executive Vice President: Jeff Church
    E-Mail: jeffc@cmservices.com

Historical Note:
*NAAMM is involved in developing, maintaining, publishing
and distributing technical information on metal products
for building construction which includes specifications,
manuals and other information for building design
professionals. Comprised of six divisions: Architectural
Metal Products,Detention Equipment Manufacturers,
Expanded Metal, Expanded Metal Lath, Hollow Metal
Doors and Frames, and Metal Bar Grating. Membership:
$1,220-3,640 (Corporate); $1,220 (Affiliate).*

Meetings/Conferences:
2013 - San Antonio, TX (Hyatt Regency San Antonio)/
April 19 - 21

Publications:
Membership Directory; on-line

National Association of Area Agencies on Aging (1974)
1730 Rhode Island Ave. NW
Suite 1200
Washington, DC 20036
Tel: (202) 872-0888 *Fax:* (202) 872-0057
E-Mail: info@n4a.org
Website: n4a.org
Members: 885 agencies
Staff: 31
Annual Budget: $2-5,000,000

Personnel:
Chief Executive Officer: Sandy Markwood
    E-Mail: smarkwood@n4a.org
Associate Director, Communications: Joanetta Bolden
    E-Mail: JBolden@n4a.org
Information Specialist, Eldercare Locator: Carlos Dávila
Manager, Marketing and Special Projects: Mark Fetterhoff
    E-Mail: mfetterhoff@n4a.org
Senior Director, Public Policy and Advocacy: Amy E.
    Gotwals
    E-Mail: AGotwals@n4a.org
Senior Manager, Programs: Jo Reed
    E-Mail: jreed@n4a.org
Contact, Membership Services and Executive Assistant:
    Rhoda Seay
    E-Mail: rseay@n4a.org

Historical Note:
*N4A's mission is to promote a national policy that
enhances the ability of older Americans to remain
independent in their communities and homes. Members
include Area Agencies on Aging and Title VI - Native
American Aging Programs. Membership: $125-7,000/year,
based on total annual budget of agency.*

Meetings/Conferences: Annual
Number of non-conference events/year: 3

Publications:
Advocacy Alert; on-line; adv.
e-Newsletter; weekly

National Association of Arms Shows
P.O. Box 290
Kaysville, UT 84037-0290
Website: naasgunshows.com
Staff: 1
Annual Budget: $50-100,000

Personnel:
President: Robert Templeton
    E-Mail: bobandlynntempleton@msn.com

Historical Note:
*NAAS's mission is dedicated to creating a more positive
image of firearm shows, to support and encourage members
in efforts to produce quality shows and encourage the
legal, safe and ethical trading of firearms and related
items.Membership: $500-3000 (Based on the number of
show produced per calendar year); $100 (Individuals).*

Publications:
The Big Show Journal

National Association of Assistant United States Attorneys (1993)
12427 Hedges Run Dr.
Suite 104
Lake Ridge, VA 22192
Tel: (800) 455-5661 *Fax:* (800) 528-3492
TollFree: (800) 455-5661
E-Mail: info@naausa.org
Website: naausa.org
Members: 5400 AUSAs
Staff: 2
Annual Budget: $100-250,000
Tax: 501(c)(6)

Personnel:
Executive Director: Dennis W Boyd
    E-Mail: Dennis@naausa.org
Counsel and Washington Representative: Bruce L. Moyer
    E-Mail: brumoyer@verizon.net

Historical Note:
*NAAUSA is a professional association dedicated to
promote, protect and serve the common interests of nation's
criminal and civil attorneys. Membership: $143 (AUSA for
5 years or more); $84.50 (AUSA for less than 5 years);
$25 (Former Assistant U.S. Attorneys).*

Publications:
NAAUSA News; bi-monthly; adv.

National Association of Athletic Development Directors (1993)
24651 Detroit Rd.
Westlake, OH 44145
Tel: (440) 892-4000 *Fax:* (440) 892-4007
Website: nacda.com/naadd/nacda-naadd.html
Members: 500 individuals
Staff: 6
Annual Budget: $250-500,000
Tax: 501(c)(6)

Personnel:
Assistant Secretary and Assistant Treasurer: Jason
    Galaska
    E-Mail: jgalaska@nacda.com
Director, Membership Services: Brian Horning
    E-Mail: bhorning@nacda.com
Senior Staff Administrator: Pat Manak
    E-Mail: pmanak@nacda.com
Assistant Executive Director, Communications: Julie Work

Historical Note:
*NAADD strives to bring together individuals with a mutual
interest in collegiate athletics development so they can
educate and network with fellow development professionals.
Membership: $450 (College/University); $125 (Active/
Affiliate); $25 (Student); $250 (Commercial).*

Publications:
Membership Directory; on-line
NAADD E-Newsletter; monthly

National Association of Attorneys General (1907)
2030 M St. NW
Eighth Floor
Washington, DC 20036
Tel: (202) 326-6000 *Fax:* (202) 331-1427
Website: naag.org
Members: 56 individuals
Staff: 40
Annual Budget: $2-5,000,000

Personnel:
Executive Director: James McPherson
Director, Finance: Theresia Heller
Director, Web and New Media Services: Lisa Jeter
Meeting Planner: Erin McManimon
Director, Communications: Marjorie Tharp
Associate General Counsel and Congressional Liaison:
    Blair Tinkle
Deputy Executive Director: Christopher Toth

Historical Note:
*NAAG's mission is to facilitate interaction among Attorneys
General as peers and to facilitate the enhanced performance
of Attorneys General and their staffs. Members are the
Attorneys General of the 50 states, 5 territorial jurisdictions
and the Corporation Counsel of the District of Columbia.*

Meetings/Conferences:
Conference Chair: Erin McManimon
Number of non-conference events/year: 2

Publications:
Bankruptcy Bulletin
Consumer Protection Report; semi-monthly
Cybercrime E-Newsletter
Electronic Discovery Bulletin; monthly
Naagazette; monthly
Supreme Court Report

National Association of Bankruptcy Trustees (1982)
One Windsor Cove
Suite 305
Columbia, SC 29223
Tel: (803) 252-5646 *Fax:* (803) 765-0860
TollFree: (800) 445-8629
E-Mail: info@nabt.com
Website: nabt.com
Members: 1200 individuals
Staff: 3
Annual Budget: $1-2,000,000
Tax: 501(c)(6)

Personnel:
Executive Director: Christina Hicks
    E-Mail: christina@jee.com
Executive Liaison: Nancy H. Cooper
    E-Mail: ncooper@usit.net
Treasurer: Lynne F. Riley

Historical Note:
*NABT's purpose is to improve the administration of
bankruptcy by promoting professionalism, education and by*

providing open exchange of ideas among its members and other members of the bankruptcy community. Membership: $350 (Trustee/Associate/Auctioneer/Presidential Circle); $75 (Trustee Assistant/Governmental); $150-350 (Supplier).

Meetings/Conferences: Annual
2013 - White Sulphur Springs, WV (Greenbrier)/Aug. 8 - 11
2014 - Salt Lake City, UT (Grand America Hotel)/Sept. 10 - 14
Number of non-conference events/year: 2

Publications:
Journal of the National Association of Bankruptcy Trustees; quarterly

Membership List Available to Non-members

National Association of Baptist Professors of Religion *(1927)*
900 College St.
UMHB Box 8374
Belton, TX 76513
E-Mail: DMynatt@umhb.edu
Website: nabpr.org
Members: 350 individuals
Staff: 3
Annual Budget: $10-25,000

Personnel:
President: Rosalie Beck
    E-Mail: rosalie_beck@baylor.edu
Executive Secretary and Treasurer: Daniel S. Mynatt
    E-Mail: DMynatt@umhb.edu
Senior Editor: R. Scott Nash
    E-Mail: nash_rs@mercer.edu

Historical Note:
Formerly (1983) the Association of Baptist Professors of Religion. NABPR is a community of teaching scholars.NABPR purpose is to promote communication and cooperation among professors of religion, to provide opportunities for consideration of methods, techniques, and procedures in the teaching of religion, to aid in the sharing of curricular concepts, and to exchange new approaches in the study of religion. Members are not required to be related to any Baptist group or denomination. Membership: $20-50 (Varies with salary levels).

Meetings/Conferences:
Conference Chair: Rosalie Beck

Publications:
NABPRNews; quarterly
Perspectives in Religious Studies; quarterly

National Association of Bar Executives *(1941)*
C/O ABA Division for Bar Services
321 N. Clark St.
Chicago, IL 60654
Tel: (312) 988-6008 *Fax:* (312) 988-5492
E-Mail: nora.warens@americanbar.org
Website: nabenet.org
Members: 250 state, local and national bar associations
Staff: 4
Annual Budget: $500-1,000,000
Tax: 501(c)(6)

Personnel:
Associate Director: Pamela Robinson
    E-Mail: pamela.robinson@americanbar.org
Administrator, Finance and Business: Tondanisha Nevels
    E-Mail: tondanisha.tomlinson@americanbar.org
Manager, Meetings and Project: Leticia Spencer
Coordinator, Membership: Nora Warens
    E-Mail: nora.warens@americanbar.org

Historical Note:
NABE was founded to serve the management staff of bar associations and law-related organizations. The mission of the National Association of Bar Executives is to enhance the skills and enrich the professional lives of bar association executives. Membership: (Based on the size of bar association) $125-800/year.

Meetings/Conferences: Semi-Annual
Conference Chair: Leticia Spencer
2013 - Dallas, TX (Hilton Anatole)/Feb. 5 - 7
2013 - San Francisco, CA/Aug. 6 - 8
2014 - Chicago, IL/Feb. 4 - 6
2014 - Boston, MA/Aug. 5 - 7

Publications:
Member Directory; on-line

National Association of Bar-Related Title Insurers *(1948)*
1430 Lee St.
Des Plaines, IL 60018
Tel: (847) 298-8300 *Fax:* (847) 298-8388
Website: nabrti.com
Members: 26 Regional Members
Staff: 1
Annual Budget: $25-50,000

Personnel:
Executive Vice President: Joanne P. Elliott
    E-Mail: joanne@elliottlaw.com

Historical Note:
The purpose of NABRTI is to promote the use of Bar-Related title insurance to best serve the public's interest, to cooperate and lend assistance to the formation of Bar-Related organizations in areas where they are not available, and to further the Bar-Related movement to maintain the role of the real estate lawyer.

Publications:
TitlePLUS Tips

National Association of Barber Boards of America *(1926)*
2703 Pine St.
Arkadelphia, AR 71923
Tel: (501) 682-2806 *Fax:* (501) 682-5073
E-Mail: nabba@att.net
Website: nationalbarberboards.com
Members:
110 members
50 state licensing boards
Staff: 1
Annual Budget: $50-100,000

Personnel:
Executive Director: Charles Kirkpatrick
    E-Mail: nabba@att.net

Historical Note:
Formerly (1986) National Association of Boards of Barbers Examiners of America. NABBA's mission is to promote the exchange of information between state barber boards and state agencies examining licensing and gulating the barber industry and to develop standards and procedures for examining barbers. Members are state licensing boards for barbers. Active membership is open to State Board Members, officers, and administrators and related industry partners. Membership: $200 (State); $150 (Delegate).

Meetings/Conferences:
Number of non-conference events/year: 1

Publications:
NABBA Newsletter; on-line

National Association of Basketball Coaches *(1927)*
1111 Main St.
Suite 1000
Kansas City, MO 64105-2136
Tel: (816) 878-6222 *Fax:* (816) 878-6223
Website: nabc.org
Members: 5000 individuals
Staff: 12
Annual Budget: $5-10,000,000
Tax: 501(c)(6)

Personnel:
Executive Director: James A. Haney
Manager, Conventions: Janelle Guidry
    E-Mail: janellenabc@yahoo.com
Director, Internal Operations: Carol Haney
Director, Public Relations: Rick Leddy
    E-Mail: ricknabc@gmail.com
Director, Membership Services: Rose Tate
Director, Finance: Stephanie Whitcher
    E-Mail: stephanie@nabc.com

Historical Note:
Formerly (1998) known as National Association of Basketball Coaches of the United States. NABC works to further the interests of the game of basketball as well as the players and coaches who participate in the sport. Lobbies on the behalf of college coaches and serves as a resource for coaches. Membership: $70-350/year (Individual).

Meetings/Conferences: Annual
Conference Chair: Janelle Guidry

Publications:
NABC Newsletter; on-line
Time-Out Magazine; weekly; adv.

Membership List Available to Non-members

National Association of Beverage Importers Inc. *(1934)*
529 14th St. NW
Suite 1183
Washington, DC 20045
Tel: (202) 393-6224 *Fax:* (202) 393-6595
Website: bevimporters.org
Members: 60 companies
Staff: 2
Annual Budget: $500-1,000,000
Tax: 501(c)(6)

Personnel:
President: William T. Earle
Vice President, Assistant Treasurer and Corporate Secretary: Bernadeen Emamali

Historical Note:
Formerly (until 1979) known as the National Association of Alcohol Beverage Importers, Inc. NABI's mission is to help the importer members operate their businesses more efficiently and profitably by providing timely information, aggressive representation, and thoughtful advice on technical and political matters. Membership: $2,000/year (Associate).

National Association of Biology Teachers *(1938)*
1313 Dolley Madison Blvd.
Suite 402
McLean, VA 22101
Tel: (703) 264-9696 *Fax:* (730) 790-2672
TollFree: (800) 501-6228
E-Mail: office@nabt.org
Website: nabt.org
Members: 7500 individuals
Staff: 5
Annual Budget: $250-500,000
Tax: 501(c)(3)

Personnel:
Executive Director: Jaclyn Reeves-Pepin
    E-Mail: jreevespepin@nabt.org
Business Office Manager: David A. Drupa
    E-Mail: ddrupa@nabt.org
Coordinator, Membership Services: Jill Drupa
    E-Mail: jdrupa@nabt.org
Accountant: Philip Phan
    E-Mail: pphan@nabt.org
Coordinator, Meetings: Lori Strong
    E-Mail: lstrong@nabt.org

Historical Note:
Incorporated in Illinois in 1956. NABT's mission is to empower educators to provide the best possible biology and life science education for all students. Members are biology educators and administrators in elementary schools, middle and junior high schools, high schools and colleges. Membership: $25-1,750/year.

Meetings/Conferences: Annual
Conference Chair: Lori Strong
2013 - Atlanta, GA (Hyatt Regency Atlanta)/Nov. 20 - 23

Publications:
News and Views; bi-weekly
The American Biology Teacher; adv.

Membership List Available to Non-members

National Association of Black Accountants, Inc. *(1969)*
7474 Greenway Center Dr.
Suite 1120
Greenbelt, MD 20770
Tel: (301) 474-6222 *Fax:* (301) 474-3114
E-Mail: nabaoffice@nabainc.org
Website: nabainc.org
Members: 5500 individuals
Staff: 20
Annual Budget: $2-5,000,000

Personnel:
Executive Director: Guillermo L. Hysaw
Coordinator, Information Technology and Web: Jason Allen
Manager, Membership Operations: Dennis Carpenter
Associate Director, Communications: Trineka Greer
Manager, Program Development: Rochelle Jones
    E-Mail: rjones@nabainc.org
Vice President, Operations: Manuel Torres

Historical Note:
NABA's mission is to expand the influence of minority professionals in the fields of accounting and finance.

Membership: $120 (Regular Professional); $20 (Student); $65 (Academia or senior 65 years or older).

Meetings/Conferences: Annual
2013 - Nashville, TN (Gaylord Opryland Resort and Convention Center)/June 5 - 8
Number of non-conference events/year: 1

Publications:
Achieve; bi-annually
NewsPlus; quarterly; adv.
Spectrum Magazine; annually; adv.

National Association of Black County Officials
(1975)
1090 Vermont Ave. NW
Suite 1290
Washington, DC 20005
Tel: (202) 350-6696 *Fax:* (202) 350-6699
E-Mail: nobco@nobcoinc.org
Website: blackcountyofficials.com
Members: 3000 Members
Staff: 3
Annual Budget: $250-500,000

Personnel:
President: Arlanda J. Williams
Treasurer: Andrea Harrison
General Counsel: Patrick Jefferson

Historical Note:
NABCO's mission is to promote the sharing of knowledge and methods to improve government operations. Members are black county officials who review, share and develop responses to local and national issues. The National Association of Counties provides its administrative support. Membership: $100 (Regular); $40 (Associate).

Publications:
Member Directory; annually

National Association of Black Journalists *(1975)*
1100 Knight Hall
Suite 3100
College Park, MD 20742
Tel: (301) 405-0248 *Fax:* (301) 314-1714
Website: nabj.org
Members: 4000 individuals
Staff: 9
Annual Budget: $2-5,000,000

Personnel:
Executive Director: Maurice Foster
  E-Mail: mfoster@nabj.org
Manager, Finance: Nathaniel Chambers
  E-Mail: nchambers@nabj.org
Manager, Membership Services: Veronigue Dodson
  E-Mail: vdodson@nabj.org
Consultant, Communications: Aprill O. Turner
  E-Mail: aturner@nabj.org
Program Manager: Irving Washington
  E-Mail: iwashington@nabj.org

Historical Note:
Founded by a group of journalists covering the Third National Institute for Black Elected Officials in Washington, DC. NABJ seeks to strengthen ties among black journalists and increase the number of black journalists in management positions and encourage black journalists to become entrepreneurs. Membership: $75-3,000 (Associate); $1,500 (Corporate). $150 (Premium Full); $35-40 (Student); $79 (Emeritus/Retired Full).

Meetings/Conferences: Annual
Conference Chair: Irving Washington
2013 - Orlando, FL (Gaylord Palms Resort and Convention Center-Orlando)/July 31 - Aug. 4
Number of non-conference events/year: 4

Publications:
Membership Directory; on-line
NABJ E-News; weekly
NABJ Journal

Membership List Available to Non-members

National Association of Black Professors *(1974)*
P.O. Box 526
Crisfield, MD 21817
Tel: (410) 968-2393
Members: 135 individuals
Staff: 1

Personnel:
President: S. Miles Woods PhD

Historical Note:

NABP was formed to foster communication among Black professors and to sponsor activities to help minority students go on for advanced education.

National Association of Black Social Workers
(1968)
2305 Martin Luther King Ave. SE
Washington, DC 20020
Tel: (202) 678-4570 *Fax:* (202) 678-4572
E-Mail: harambee@nabsw.org
Website: nabsw.org
Members: 130 membership chapters, university and college student chapters
Staff: 3
Annual Budget: $250-500,000
Tax: 501(c)(3)

Personnel:
President: Joe Benton

Historical Note:
NABSW strives to enhance the quality of life and empower people of African ancestry through advocacy, human services delivery and research. Membership: $100 (Individual); $400 (Organization plus $25 per capita).

Meetings/Conferences: Annual
2013 - Jacksonville, FL (Hyatt Regency Jacksonville Riverfront)/April 2 - 6
Number of non-conference events/year: 1

Publications:
NABSW Newsletter; quarterly; adv.
The Black Caucus Journal; bi-annually

National Association of Black Suppliers *(1987)*
P.O. Box 441243
Detroit, MI 48244-1243
Tel: (248) 872-2216 *Fax:* (734) 547-5119
Website: nabssf.org
Staff: 2
Annual Budget: $50-100,000
Tax: 501(c)(3)

Personnel:
Business Manager and Secretary: Rhonda A. Glover
  E-Mail: rglover@nabssf.org
Treasurer: Cassie N. Stafford

Historical Note:
Formerly National Association of Black Automotive Suppliers. An advocacy association serving black automotive suppliers and automotive manufacturers. NABS is affiliated with the Michigan Black Chamber of Commerce.

Meetings/Conferences: Annual

Publications:
Newsletter

National Association of Black Women Entrepreneurs *(1978)*
1 Ford Pl.
Detroit, MI 48202
Tel: (313) 874-6284
E-Mail: info@nabwe.org
Members: 5500 individuals
Staff: 7
Annual Budget: Under $10,000
Tax: 501(c)(3)

Personnel:
President: Dolores Ratcliffe

Historical Note:
Provides professional support and networking to members.

National Association of Black-Owned Broadcasters *(1976)*
1201 Connecticut Ave. NW
Suite 200
Washington, DC 20036
Tel: (202) 463-8970 *Fax:* (202) 429-0657
E-Mail: nabobinfo@nabob.org
Website: nabob.org
Members: 240 radio and 20 television stations and 102 companies
Staff: 3
Annual Budget: $500-1,000,000

Personnel:
President: Bennie L. Turner
Executive Director and General Counsel: James L. Winston
  E-Mail: jwinston@rwdhc.com
Treasurer: Karen E. Slade

Historical Note:

Incorporated in the District of Columbia in 1977. NABOB's goal is to improve and increase the opportunities for success for black and minority owners in the broadcast industry. Membership: $500-5,000 (Standard based on billing); $50-2,000 (Associate).

Meetings/Conferences: Annual

Publications:
Membership Directory; on-line

National Association of Blacks in Criminal Justice
(1974)
106 Whiting Criminal Justice Building, 1801 Fayetteville St.
P.O. Box 20011-C
Durham, NC 27707
Tel: (919) 683-1801 *Fax:* (919) 683-1903
TollFree: (866) 846-2225
E-Mail: office@nabcj.org
Website: nabcj.org/
Members: 5000 individuals
Staff: 5
Annual Budget: $250-500,000
Tax: 501(c)(3)

Personnel:
President: Carlyle I. Holder
  E-Mail: ceocmcg@aol.com
Legal Advisor: Keith Branch
  E-Mail: keith.branch@att.net
National Office Manager: Deborah Burwell
  E-Mail: office@nabcj.org
Director, Membership Services: Jeffrey E. Carson
  E-Mail: ellisjcarson@gmail.com
Chief Financial Officer: Eddie Pearson
  E-Mail: eddie.pearson@vadoc.virginia.gov

Historical Note:
NABCJ is a multi-racial, non-partisan, non-profit association of criminal justice professionals and community leaders dedicated to improving the administration of justice. NABCJ's mission is to promote equal justice for all. The association was founded as a vehicle by which criminal justice practitioners could initiate positive changes from within, while increasing opportunities for the average citizen to better understand the nature and the operation of the local, state, and federal criminal justice processes. Membership and participation in the activities of the association are open to all, irrespective of race, creed, or country of national origin. Membership: $50 (Active); $15 (Full- time Student); $300 (Agency); $750 (Lifetime).

Meetings/Conferences:
Conference Chair: Carlyle I. Holder
2013 - Little Rock, AR (The Peabody Hotel)/July 21 - 25

Publications:
NABCJ Conference Program Journal; adv.
The College Connection
The Commitment; quarterly

National Association of Blacks In Government
(1975)
3005 Georgia Ave. NW
Washington, DC 20001-3807
Tel: (202) 667-3280 *Fax:* (202) 667-3705
E-Mail: bignational@bignet.org
Website: bignet.org
Staff: 8

Personnel:
National President: J. David Reeves
  E-Mail: jdavid.reeves@bignet.org
Account Executive: Sylin Bynoe
  E-Mail: sbynoe@talley.com
Meeting Manager: Erika Davis
  E-Mail: edavis@talley.com
National Treasurer: Lenora Grable-Grant
  E-Mail: treasurer@bignet.org
Office Manager: Susan Harmon
  E-Mail: sharmon@talley.com
Membership Specialist: Sharon Odle
  E-Mail: membership.inquiries@bignet.org
Director, Office Staff: James Wilson

Historical Note:
Incorporated in 1976. BIG's mission is to enable all present and future Black employees in Local, State, and Federal governments to have the ability to maximize their career opportunities and provide a mechanism for inclusion, growth and advocacy. Membership: $20-300/year.

Meetings/Conferences:
Conference Chair: Erika Davis

Publications:
BIG Magazine; quarterly

BIG Newsletters

National Association of Blind Merchants
1837 S. Nevada Ave.
P.O.Box 243
Colorado Springs, CO 80905
Tel: (719) 527-0488
TollFree: (866) 543-6808
Website: blindmerchants.org
Staff: 1
Annual Budget: $100-250,000
Personnel:
Executive Director: Kevan Worley
   E-Mail: kevanworley@blindmerchants.org
Historical Note:
*NABM's mission to serve as an active division of the
National Federation of the Blind; to function as a
mechanism through which blind entrepreneurs and
interested sighted persons can come together in local, state
and national meetings to plan and carry out programs
to improve business opportunities and quality of life for
the blind; to provide a means of collective action for blind
business people. Membership: $10/year.*
Meetings/Conferences: Annual
2013 - Indianapolis, IN (Indianapolis Marriott
   Downtown)/May 20 - 23
Publications:
Merchant Messenger; quarterly

National Association of Blind Teachers (1971)
1025 Ree way
Knoxville, TN 37909
Tel: (865) 692-4888
E-Mail: info@acb.org
Website: blindteachers.net
Members: 185 individuals
Staff: 1
Annual Budget: $10-25,000
Personnel:
Contact, Membership Services: John Buckley
   E-Mail: johnbuckley25@comcast.net
Historical Note:
*An association of blind and visually impaired teachers with
members teaching on all levels from elementary to graduate
school in subjects ranging from rehabilitation to physics,
special ed. to history, and music to foreign language.
Members teach both blind and sighted students. The
primary purpose of the organization is to provide support to
members and other blind and visually impaired teachers or
students.Affiliated with the American Council of the Blind,
which provides administrative support. Membership: $25
(Teachers); $20 (Non-Teachers); $10 (Students).*
Publications:
The Blind Teacher; adv.
The Braille Forum; monthly

National Association of Boards of Examiners of Long Term Care Administrators
1444 I St. NW
Suite 700
Washington, DC 20005-6542
Tel: (202) 712-9040 *Fax:* (202) 216-9646
E-Mail: nab@nabweb.org
Website: nabweb.org
Members: 50 states and the District of Columbia
licensing boards/agencies
Staff: 5
Annual Budget: $1-2,000,000
Personnel:
President and Chief Executive Officer: Randy Lindner CAE
   E-Mail: rlindner@bostrom.com
Director of Meetings: Julie Elfand
   E-Mail: jelfand@bostrom.com
Director of Marketing: Heidi Lapka
   E-Mail: hlapka@bostrom.com
Director of Administration: Jason Silberberg
   E-Mail: jsilberberg@bostrom.com
Historical Note:
*NAB strives to enhance the effectiveness of state boards
of long term care administrators in meeting their statutory
and regulatory duties and responsibilities to protect the
health, safety, and welfare of the public. Membership: $70
(Associate/Subscribing).*
Meetings/Conferences: Semi-Annual
Conference Chair: Julie Elfand

National Association of Boards of Pharmacy
(1904)

1600 Feehanville Dr.
Mt. Prospect, IL 60056
Tel: (847) 391-4405 *Fax:* (847) 391-4502
E-Mail: custserv@nabp.net
Website: nabp.net
Members: 66 states or jurisdictions
Staff: 86
Annual Budget: $25-50,000,000
Tax: 501(c)(3)
Personnel:
President: Michael A. Burleson RPh
Executive Director and Secretary: Carmen A. Catizone
   DPh, MS, RPh
   E-Mail: exec-office@nabp.net
Historical Note:
*NABP is the independent, international, and impartial
association that assists its member boards and jurisdictions
in developing, implementing, and enforcing uniform
standards for the purpose of protecting the public health.
Membership: $250/year (State Board).*
Continuing Education:
Certification Designation/s: NAPLEX, FPGEC, FPGEE,
MPJE
Meetings/Conferences: Annual
2013 - St. Louis, MO (Hyatt Regency St. Louis at The
   Arch)/May 18 - 21
2014 - Phoenix, AZ (Sheraton Phoenix Downtown
   Hotel)/May 17 - 20
Publications:
NABP E-News; on-line
NABP Newsletter
National Pharmacy Compliance News; quarterly
State Newsletters; quarterly
Survey of Pharmacy Law; annually
The Model Act

National Association of Boat Manufacturers
(1945)
231 S La Salle St Ste 2050
Chicago, IL 60604
Tel: (312) 346-6220
Members: 1325 boat manufacturers
Staff: 36
Annual Budget: $100-250,000
Personnel:
Treasurer: Steven Josh
Historical Note:
*Members are makers of pleasure boats. A partner affiliate of
National Marine Manufacturers association, which provides
administrative support.*

National Association of Bond Lawyers (1979)
601 Thirteenth St. NW
Suite 800 South
Washington, DC 20005-3875
Tel: (202) 503-3300 *Fax:* (202) 637-0217
E-Mail: governmentalaffairs@nabl.org
Website: nabl.org
Members: 3000 individuals
Staff: 11
Annual Budget: $2-5,000,000
Tax: 501(c)(6)
Personnel:
Chief Operating Officer: Linda H. Wyman
   E-Mail: lwyman@nabl.org
Manager, Membership Services: Karen Michael
   E-Mail: kmichael@nabl.org
Manager, Marketing and Communications: Beth Walkos
   E-Mail: bwalkos@nabl.org
Director, Education and Membership Services: Susan
   Zelner
   E-Mail: szelner@nabl.org
Historical Note:
*NABL's mission is to provide members with the resources,
information, and leadership that enable them to provide
services in a professional manner to benefit the public
as well as employers and clients. Members are lawyers
specializing in the legal problems of debt obligations of the
various states and their political subdivisions. Membership:
$245-395 (Regular); $50 (Retired); $80 (Paralegal).*
Meetings/Conferences:
Conference Chair: Susan Zelner
Number of non-conference events/year: 4
Publications:
Membership Directory; on-line
NABL NEWS; monthly
The Bond Lawyer; quarterly

The Weekly Wrap; weekly

National Association of Broadcast Employees and Technicians-Communications Workers of America, AFL-CIO (NABET-CWA) (1934)
501 Third St. NW
Sixth Floor
Washington, DC 20001-2797
Tel: (202) 434-1100 *Fax:* (202) 434-1426
E-Mail: nabet-cwa@cwa-union.org
Website: nabetcwa.org
Members:
8900 Workers
10000 individuals
Staff: 3
Annual Budget: $500-1,000,000
Personnel:
Sector President: James Joyce
   E-Mail: jjoyce@cwa-union.org
Interim Assistant to the President: Jodi Fabrizio-Clontz
   E-Mail: jfabrizi@cwa-union.org
Technical Assistant: Anthony Grigsby
   E-Mail: tgrigsby@cwa-union.org
Historical Note:
*Organized as a company union in 1934 by the National
Broadcasting Company under the title, Association of
Technical Employees. Broke away from NBC in 1940 and
changed its name to the National Association of Broadcast
Engineers and Technicians. Chartered as an industrial union
in 1951 by the Congress of Industrial Organizations under
the name, National Association of Broadcast Employees
and Technicians. Merged with the Communications Workers
of America, AFL-CIO, January 1, 1994. Membership:
1.666% of gross wages.*
Publications:
CWA Newsletter; quarterly

National Association of Broadcasters (1922)
1771 N St. NW
Washington, DC 20036-2891
Tel: (202) 429-5300
E-Mail: nab@nab.org
Website: nab.org
Members: 8300 radio, tv stations and associates
Staff: 175
Annual Budget: $50-100,000,000
Tax: 501(c)(6)
Personnel:
Chief Executive Officer: Hon. Gordon Smith
*Senior Vice President, Conventions and Business
   Operations:* Chris Brown
   E-Mail: cabrown@nab.org
Senior Vice President, Science and Technology: Lynn D.
   Claudy
   E-Mail: lclaudy@nab.org
Vice President, Communications: Ann Marie Cumming
   E-Mail: amcumming@nab.org
Executive Vice President and Chief Technology Officer:
   Kevin Gage
Executive Vice President, Government Relations: Laurie
   Knight
Chief Operating and Strategy Officer: Christopher D.
   Ornelas
Associate General Counsel: Lawrence Walke
   E-Mail: lwalke@nab.org
Executive Vice President, Media Relations: Dennis
   Wharton
   E-Mail: dwharton@nab.org
*Chief Financial Officer and Executive Vice President,
   Finance:* Joy Whitlow
Historical Note:
*NAB's mission is to improve the quality and profitability
of broadcasting, encourages content and technology
innovation, spotlights the important stations serve their
communities. Membership: $500-3,500 (Associate
Member); $500 (International Broadcast Member).*
Continuing Education:
Enrollment: 10
Meetings/Conferences:
Conference Chair: Chris Brown
2013 - Las Vegas, NV (Las Vegas Convention Center)/
   April 6 - 11
Number of non-conference events/year: 2
Publications:
NAB Pulse; weekly
NAB@Work; weekly
Radio TechCheck; weekly

TV TechCheck; weekly

National Association of Business Owners and Entrepreneurs
21732 Brink Meadow Ln.
Germantown, MD 20876
Tel: (301) 873-1475
Website: naboe.org
Members: 256 employees
Staff: 1

Personnel:
Executive Director: Ronald K. Wills

Historical Note:
NABOE serves the independent business community and works closely with media to help promote its businesses, team leaders and partners.

Publications:
Magazine

National Association of Business Political Action Committees *(1977)*
101 Constitution Ave. NW
Suite L-110
Washington, DC 20001
Tel: (202) 341-3780 *Fax:* (202) 478-0342
E-Mail: contact@nabpac.org
Website: nabpac.org
Members:
300 PAC and government affairs professionals
168 corporations and associations
Staff: 2
Annual Budget: $500-1,000,000
Tax: 501(c)(6)

Personnel:
Executive Director: Geoff C. Ziebart

Historical Note:
NABPAC provides a forum for improving PAC management, solicitation and contributions. Lobbies on campaign finance legislation. NABPAC provides membership services to PAC and grassroots professionals through continuing educational workshops, annual conferences, informative publications and peer-to-peer advising. Offers services ranging from free legal compliance support to regular PAC Rap Sessions, members have unlimited access to the latest PAC tools and information available. Membership: $2000-5,000/year (Organization-based on PAC Revenues).

Meetings/Conferences: Biennial
Publications:
Electronic Newsletter; bi-weekly

National Association of Business Travel Agents *(1980)*
3699 Wilshire Blvd., Suite 700
Los Angeles, CA 90010-2726
Tel: (213) 382-3335 *Fax:* (213) 480-7712
E-Mail: sjfaber@sbcglobal.net
Members: 1600 individuals
Staff: 6

Personnel:
Director: Stuart J. Faber

Historical Note:
Travel agents who specialize in servicing corporate and business accounts and provide travel services for businesses and organizations holding out-of-town meetings and conventions. Promotes members' awareness of practical methods of servicing and increasing their accounts. Prepares detailed descriptions of convention facilities, hotels, restaurants, tour operators, and tourist attractions for members. Organizes family trips for members to visit destinations and view convention facilities. Members are travel agents specializing in corporate and business travel.

National Association of Casino Party Operators *(1990)*
P.O. Box 5626
San Francisco, CA 94083
Tel: (650) 802-8075 *Fax:* (650) 583-1736
TollFree: (888) 922-0777
E-Mail: info@casinoparties.com
Website: nactpo.com
Members: 50 companies
Staff: 1
Annual Budget: $25-50,000

Personnel:
Executive Secretary: Connie Hegre

Historical Note:
Founded as Casino and Theme Party Operators Association, assumed its current name in 2001. NACPO works to

provide better possible products, services, and assistance to achieve the objectives of those for whom they work. Members are casino and theme party operators, planners, suppliers and others with an interest in the industry. Membership: $395/year (Organization/Company).

Meetings/Conferences: Annual

Publications:
Membership Directory; on-line
NACPO Newsletter; quarterly
Suppliers and Manufacturers Directory; irregular

National Association of Catastrophe Adjusters *(1976)*
P.O. Box 821864
N. Richland Hills, TX 76182
Tel: (817) 498-3466 *Fax:* (817) 498-0480
E-Mail: naca@nacatadj.org
Website:
nacatadj.info/naca/html
nacatadj.org
Members: 457 individuals and business
associates
Staff: 3
Annual Budget: $100-250,000
Tax: 501(c)(6)

Personnel:
President: Wanda Hogan
    E-Mail: wicked44@aol.com
Secretary and Treasurer: John Postava
    E-Mail: john.postava@catadjuster.com
Executive Administrator: Lori Ringo

Historical Note:
NACA's mission is to provide a professional organization focused on catastrophe insurance adjusting for members through education, shared resources, and technology. Membership: $400 (Business Associate); $200 (Individual-General/Associate/Apprentice).

Meetings/Conferences: Annual
Conference Chair: Lori Ringo
2013 - Houston, TX (Omni Houston Galleria Hotel)/
    Jan. 20 - 24

Publications:
Membership Roster; on-line
NACA News; quarterly; adv.

National Association of Catering and Events *(1958)*
9891 Broken Land Pkwy.
Suite 301
Columbia, MD 21046
Tel: (410) 290-5410 *Fax:* (410) 290-5460
Website: nace.net
Members: 3500 individuals
Staff: 7
Annual Budget: $50-100,000

Personnel:
Executive Director: Bonnie Fedchock
    E-Mail: bfedchock@nacenet.org
Administrative Assistant: Sylvia Buell
    E-Mail: sbuell@nace.net
Director, Membership and Marketing: Kim Grimm
    E-Mail: kgrimm@nacenet.org
Director, Education and Certifications: Leslie Jones
    E-Mail: ljones@nace.net
Coordinator, Marketing and Communications: Joanne Kim
    E-Mail: jkim@nacenet.org

Historical Note:
Founded as the Banquet Managers Guild in New York City on June 3, 1958, assumed its present name in 1980. NACE offers members, partners, and the public a variety of resources that support, promote and enhance the catering and special events industries. Membership: $50-500/year.

Continuing Education:
Certification Designation/s: CPCE
Meetings/Conferences: Annual
2013 - Denver, CO (Hyatt Regency Denver at Colorado
    Convention Center)/Sept. 15 - 16

Publications:
catersource Magazine; irregular
Consumer Directory; on-line
Membership Directory; on-line
NACE e-News; monthly
NACE Trends Report; irregular

National Association of Catholic Chaplains *(1965)*
4915 S. Howell Ave.
Suite 501

Milwaukee, WI 53207
Tel: (414) 483-4898 *Fax:* (414) 483-6712
E-Mail: info@nacc.org
Website: nacc.org
Members: 2578 individuals
Staff: 9
Annual Budget: $500-1,000,000
Tax: 501(c)(3)

Personnel:
Executive Director: David A. Lichter Dmin
    E-Mail: dlichter@nacc.org
Specialist, Administration, Education and Renewal of Certification: Jeanine Annunziato
    E-Mail: jannunziato@nacc.org
Editor: Laurie Hansen Cardona
    E-Mail: vision@nacc.org
Coordinator, Certification and Education: Susanne Chawszczewski PhD
    E-Mail: schaw@nacc.org
Specialist, Administration, Information Technology and Special Projects: Philip Paradowski
    E-Mail: pparadowski@nacc.org
Specialist, Administration and Membership Services: Mary T. Pawicz
    E-Mail: mpawicz@nacc.org
Specialist, Administration and Finance: Sue Walker
    E-Mail: swalker@nacc.org

Historical Note:
NACC advocates for the profession of spiritual care and educates, certifies, and supports chaplains, clinical pastoral educators, and all members who continue the healing ministry of Jesus in the name of the Church. Members are Catholic priests, sisters, permanent deacons, and laity engaged in professional health care and related institutional and parish ministries. Membership: $50-340/year.

Continuing Education:
Certification Designation/s: CAS, CC, CCPES

Meetings/Conferences: Annual
Conference Chair: Jeanine Annunziato
2013 - Pittsburgh, PA (Sheraton Station Square Hotel)/
    April 13 - 16

Publications:
Membership Directory; on-line
NACC Now; bi-weekly; adv.
Vision; bi-monthly; adv.

Membership List Available to Non-members

National Association of Catholic School Teachers *(1978)*
1700 Sansom St.
Suite 903
Philadelphia, PA 19103
Tel: (215) 665-0993 *Fax:* (215) 568-8270
E-Mail: nacst@mail.idt.net
Website: nacst.com
Members: 5000 individuals
Staff: 1
Annual Budget: $100-250,000
Tax: 501(c)(5)

Personnel:
President: Rita C. Schwartz
    E-Mail: nacst.nacst@verizon.net

Historical Note:
NACST works to promote the interests of Catholic school teachers. Members are teachers in Catholic schools. Membership: $60/year (Individual).

Publications:
NACST Newsletter

National Association of Certified Professional Midwives
243 Banning Rd.
Putney, VT 05346
Tel: (207) 522-6043
Website: nacpm.org
Staff: 3
Annual Budget: $100-250,000

Personnel:
Executive Director: Mary Lawlor CPM
    E-Mail: executivedirector@nacpm.org

Historical Note:
NACPM's purpose is to contribute to a new era in maternity care by inspiring and engaging CPMs to be an organized force for change. Membership: $25 (Student); $85 (National/State Organization); $50 (Chapter); $125 (Basic); $35 (Auxiliary); $75 (Family income less than 35K).

Publications:
Newsletter

National Association of Certified Valuation Analysts (1990)
1111 Brickyard Rd.
Suite 200
Salt Lake City, UT 84106-5401
Tel: (801) 486-0600 *Fax:* (801) 486-7500
TollFree: (800) 677-2009
E-Mail: nacva1@nacva.com
Website: nacva.com
Members: 7000 individuals
Staff: 35

Personnel:
Executive Director: Pam Bailey
  E-Mail: pamb1@nacva.com
Manager, Marketing: Kirk Bowden
  E-Mail: kirkb1@nacva.com
Director, Project Management: Melissa Cardwell
  E-Mail: melissac1@nacva.com
Media and Public Relations Officer: Dave Dix
  E-Mail: daved1@nacva.com
Director, Education and Conferences: Brien Jones
  E-Mail: brienj1@nacva.com
Senior Financial Officer: Steve Marston
  E-Mail: stevem1@nacva.com
Director, Membership Services: Sheila Travis
  E-Mail: sheilat1@nacva.com

Historical Note:
NACVA supports the users of business and intangible asset valuation services and financial forensic services, including damages determinations of all kinds and fraud detection and prevention, by training and certifying financial professionals in these disciplines. Membership: $485 (Practitioner); $215 (Professional/Academician); 125 (Government Employee/ Associate/Student).

Continuing Education:
Certification Designation/s: CVA, AVA

Meetings/Conferences: Annual
Conference Chair: Brien Jones
2013 - Washington, DC/June 5 - 8

Publications:
The Association News; on-line
The Value Examiner; bi-monthly

National Association of Chain Drug Stores (1933)
413 N. Lee St.
P.O. BOX 1417-DR49
Alexandria, VA 22314-2301
Tel: (703) 549-3001
E-Mail: info@nacds.org
Website: nacds.org
Members: 39,000 pharmacies
Staff: 84
Annual Budget: $25-50,000,000

Personnel:
President and Chief Executive Officer: Steven C. Anderson CAE
  E-Mail: sanderson@nacds.org
Director, Pharmacy Programs: Alex Adams
  E-Mail: aadams@nacds.org
Senior Vice President, Legal Affairs and General Counsel: Don L. Bell
  E-Mail: dbell@nacds.org
Director, Communications: Lisa Boylan
Vice President, Finance and Accounting: David Fitzsimmons
  E-Mail: dfitzsimmons@nacds.org
Executive Vice President and Chief Financial Officer: James R. Huber
  E-Mail: jhuber@nacds.org
Senior Vice President, Government Affairs and Public Policy: Carol A. Kelly
  E-Mail: ckelly@nacds.org
Vice President, Membership Services: Rhoda L. Kelly
  E-Mail: rkelly@nacds.org
Vice President, Legal Affairs and Associate General Counsel: Mary Ellen Kleiman
  E-Mail: mkleiman@nacds.org
Vice President, Media Relations: Chrissy Kopple
  E-Mail: ckopple@nacds.org
Senior Vice President, Marketing, Communications and Media Relations: Christopher Krese
  E-Mail: ckrese@nacds.org
Vice President, Conference Services: Larry Lotridge
  E-Mail: llotridge@nacds.org

Assistant General Counsel: Nicki Robins
  E-Mail: nrobins@nacds.org
Executive Assistant, Legal Affairs: Corrine Sanders
  E-Mail: csanders@nacds.org
Senior Vice President, Membership Programs and Services: Jim A. Whitman
  E-Mail: Jwhitman@nacds.org

Historical Note:
NACDS's mission is to provide a wide range of services to meet the needs of the chain drug industry in accordance with its goals and objectives. Members are retail chain drugstore companies with four or more stores. Membership: $1,500 (Chain Member); $2,760-9,960 (Associate); $2,500 (International Associate); $1,500-2,500 (International Chain).

Meetings/Conferences: Annual
Conference Chair: Larry Lotridge
2013 - Palm Beach, FL (The Breakers)/April 20 - 23
Number of non-conference events/year: 5

Publications:
CEO Update; weekly
Membership Directory; on-line

National Association of Chain Manufacturers (1933)
P.O. Box 89014
Tucson, AZ 85752-9014
Tel: (520) 886-0695 *Fax:* (520) 886-0695
E-Mail: NACMoffice@nacm.info
Website: nacm.info
Members: 7 companies
Staff: 1
Annual Budget: $25-50,000

Personnel:
Executive Director: Donald Sayenga
  E-Mail: dsayenga@aol.com

Historical Note:
NACM represents domestic manufacturers of welded and weldless chain. Members provide a wide range of chain products such as stainless steel chain, galvanized chain, decor chain, double loop chain, Grade 80 and Grade 100 chain, and tow chain.

Membership List Available to Non-members

National Association of Chapter Thirteen Trustees (NACTT) (1965)
One Windsor Cove
Suite 305
Columbia, SC 29223
Tel: (803) 252-5646 *Fax:* (803) 765-0860
TollFree: (800) 445-8629
E-Mail: info@nactt.com
Website: nactt.com
Members: 1000 Members
Staff: 2
Annual Budget: Under $10,000

Personnel:
Executive Director: Courtney L.C Waldrup
  E-Mail: courtney@jee.com
Treasurer: D. Sims Crawford

Historical Note:
NACTT's Mission is to establish and implement professional standards and participate in the national legislative and administrative processes while promoting the highest ethical principles. Members are staff, lawyers, debtor and creditor attorneys, judges, CPA's, students, insolvency specialists, and other related professionals. Membership: $250 and $100 (Chapter 13 Trustee and Educational Fee); $150 (Associate Member).

Meetings/Conferences: Annual
2013 - New York City, NY (New York Marriott Marquis)/Aug. 3 - 6
2014 - Chicago, IL (Chicago Marriott Downtown Magnificent Mile)/July 16 - 19

Publications:
NACTT Quarterly; quarterly

National Association of Charter School Authorizers (2000)
105 W. Adams St.
Suite 3500
Chicago, IL 60603-6253
Tel: (312) 376-2300 *Fax:* (312) 376-2400
E-Mail: loreleic@qualitycharters.org
Website: qualitycharters.org
Members: 5,000 charter schools
Staff: 20

Annual Budget: $2-5,000,000

Personnel:
President and Chief Executive Officer: Greg Richmond
  E-Mail: gregr@qualitycharters.org
Director, Knowledge: Parker Baxter
  E-Mail: parkerb@qualitycharters.org
Manager, Communications: Courtney Leigh Beisel
  E-Mail: courtneyb@qualitycharters.org
Chief Financial Officer: Michael R. Cernauskas
  E-Mail: mikec@qualitycharters.org
Coordinator, Communications and Member Services: Courtney Smith
  E-Mail: courtneys@qualitycharters.org
Manager, Finance and Administration: Mary Zawaski
  E-Mail: maryz@qualitycharters.org

Historical Note:
NACSA's mission to develop the quality authorizing environments that result in a greater number of quality charter schools.

Meetings/Conferences: Annual

Publications:
Authorizing Matters; quarterly
Member Notes; weekly
Membership Directory; on-line

National Association of Charterboat Operators (1991)
P.O. Box 2990
Orange Beach, AL 36561
Tel: (251) 981-5136 *Fax:* (251) 981-8191
TollFree: (866) 981-5136
E-Mail: info@nacocharters.org
Website: nacocharters.org
Members: 3600 individuals
Staff: 4
Annual Budget: $100-250,000

Personnel:
Editor and Executive Director: Bobbi M. Walker
President: Captain Bob Zales, II
  E-Mail: bobzales@att.net
Treasurer: Capt. Ron Maglio
  E-Mail: ronmaglio@msn.com

Historical Note:
NACO members are operators of sport fishing, diving and small excursion vessels. NACO provides group charterboat insurance and a drug testing consortium. Membership: $50/year (Individual).

National Association of Chemical Distributors (1971)
1555 Wilson Blvd.
Suite 700
Arlington, VA 22209
Tel: (703) 527-6223 *Fax:* (703) 527-7747
E-Mail: nacdpublicaffairs@nacd.com
Website: nacd.com
Members: 400 companies
Staff: 12
Annual Budget: $2-5,000,000
Tax: 501(c)(6)

Personnel:
President: Christopher L. Jahn
  E-Mail: cjahn@nacd.com
Associate Manager, Meetings and Membership: Sophia S. Bezas
  E-Mail: sbezas@nacd.com
Director, Meetings and Exhibits: Roselle Foley CMP
  E-Mail: rfoley@nacd.com
Vice President, Government Affairs: Jennifer C. Gibson
  E-Mail: jgibson@nacd.com
Director, Member Advancement and Strategic Communications: Matthew T. Glaser
  E-Mail: mglaser@nacd.com
Director, Information Services: Randy Schlegel
  E-Mail: rschlegel@nacd.com
Vice President, Marketing and Member Programs: Lucinda A. Schofer
  E-Mail: lschofer@nacd.com

Historical Note:
NACD seeks to enhance and communicate the professionalism and stewardship of the chemical distribution industry. Members are chemical distributor companies that purchase and take title of chemical products from manufacturers. Membership: $2,020-44,420 (Distributor); $1,680-6,300 (Affiliate)

Meetings/Conferences: Annual
Conference Chair: Roselle Foley CMP

Number of non-conference events/year: 5

Publications:
ChemBytes; weekly
Chemical Distributor; bi-monthly; adv.
Membership Directory; on-line
NACD News Briefs; bi-weekly

National Association of Chiefs of Police *(1967)*
6350 Horizon Dr.
Titusville, FL 32780
Tel: (321) 264-0911 *Fax:* (321) 264-0033
E-Mail: policeinfo@aphf.org
Website: nacoponline.org
Members: 11000 individuals
Staff: 20
Annual Budget: $1-2,000,000
Tax: 501(c)(3)

Personnel:
Chief Executive Officer: Donna M. Shepherd
    E-Mail: dshepherd@aphf.org
Executive Director: Barry Shepherd
    E-Mail: bshepherd@aphf.org
Chief Financial Officer: Debra Chitwood
    E-Mail: dchitwood@aphf.org
Executive Editor: Peter Connolly
    E-Mail: peterc@aphf.org
Director, Communications: Jamie Shepherd
    E-Mail: jshepherd@aphf.org
Director, Operations: Brent Shepherd

Historical Note:
Formerly National Police Museum. NACOP's mission is to support and promote the law enforcement profession. Membership: $60/year (Regular); $500 (Lifetime).

Continuing Education:
Certification Designation/s: CLES

Publications:
The Chief of Police Magazine; quarterly

National Association of Child Care Professionals *(1984)*
C/O Child Care Systems of America, Inc.
5100 Stoneleigh Cir.
Brentwood, TN 37027
E-Mail: admin@naccp.org
Website: naccp.org
Members: 1500 individuals
Staff: 14
Annual Budget: $500-1,000,000
Tax: 501(c)(3)

Personnel:
President: Bobette Thompson
    E-Mail: director@naccp.org

Historical Note:
NACP, a professional association for supervisors and administrators of child care facilities, is committed to strengthen the skills of owners, directors, administrators, emerging leaders and other professionals who are dedicated to early care and education. Membership: $130 (Individual); $100-130 (Multi-site); $85 (Affiliate); $40 (Career in Caring).

Meetings/Conferences: Annual
2013 - Nashville, FL/April 24 - 26

Publications:
Executive Excerpts for Excellence; monthly
Legal Insights; monthly; adv.
Member Directory; on-line
NAC for Excellence; monthly
Professional Connections Newsletter; quarterly; adv.
Teamwork Newsletter; quarterly; adv.

Membership List Available to Non-members

National Association of Children's Hospitals and Related Institutions
401 Wythe St.
Alexandria, VA 22314
Tel: (703) 684-1355 *Fax:* (703) 684-1589
E-Mail: mbrsvcs@nachri.org
Website: childrenshospitals.net
Members: 223 children's hospitals
Staff: 104
Annual Budget: $10-25,000,000
Tax: 501(c)(3)

Personnel:
President and Chief Executive Officer: Mark Wietecha
Associate, Sponsorship and Corporate Relationships:
    Nicolette Daleske

    E-Mail: ndaleske@nachri.org
Senior Vice President: Mary Gorman
    E-Mail: mgorman@nachri.org
Contact, Conferences: Carrie Hoover
    E-Mail: meetings@nachri.org
Chief Financial Officer: Brian Humphreys
Vice President, Public Policy: James Kaufman
    E-Mail: jkaufman@nachri.org
Vice President, Human Resources: Mark Riley
Chief Information Officer: Richard Stepanek
Director, Communications: Sallie Strang
    E-Mail: sstrang@nachri.org
Contact, Membership Services: Carolyn Walker
    E-Mail: cwalker@nachri.org

Historical Note:
Formerly National Association Of Children's Hospital Inc. NACHRI advocates for public policies that support the ability of children's hospitals to fulfill their missions of clinical care, education, research, and advocacy to advance health care for all children. Members are free standing hospitals.

Meetings/Conferences: Annual
Conference Chair: Carrie Hoover
2013 - New Orleans, LA (Marriott New Orleans)/Oct. 13 - 16
2014 - Palm Desert, CA (JW Marriott Desert Springs Resort and Spa)/Oct. 11 - 14
Number of non-conference events/year: 2

Publications:
Child Advocacy Bulletin; monthly
Children's Hospitals This Week; weekly
Children's Hospitals Today; quarterly; adv.
Grants Alert; monthly
The Policy Monitor; monthly

National Association of Chronic Disease Directors *(1988)*
2872 Woodcock Blvd.
Suite 220
Atlanta, GA 30341
Tel: (770) 458-7400 *Fax:* (770) 458-7401
Website: chronicdisease.org
Members: 3000 members
Staff: 9
Annual Budget: $5-10,000,000
Tax: 501(c)(3)

Personnel:
Executive Director: John W. Robitscher MPH
    E-Mail: jrobitscher@chronicdisease.org
Director, Finance and Operations: Schwanna C. Lakine
    E-Mail: slakine@chronicdisease.org
Director, Communications and Membership Services: John Patton
    E-Mail: jpatton@chronicdisease.org
Event Planner: Jillian Smith
    E-Mail: jsmith@chronicdisease.org

Historical Note:
Founded as Association of State and Territorial Chronic Disease Program Directors. NACDD works to reduce the impact of chronic diseases and their risk factors on states and communities nationwide. Membership: $50-20,000/ year.

Meetings/Conferences: Annual
Conference Chair: Jillian Smith
Number of non-conference events/year: 1

Publications:
Chronic Disease Chronicles; semi-annually
Chronic Disease Directors eBulletin; monthly
Membership Directory; on-line
NACDD Newsletter

National Association of Church Business Administration *(1957)*
100 N. Central Expy.
Suite 914
Richardson, TX 75080-5326
Tel: (972) 699-7555 *Fax:* (972) 699-7617
TollFree: (800) 898-8085
E-Mail: info@nacba.net
Website: nacba.net
Members: 2700 individuals
Staff: 6
Annual Budget: $1-2,000,000
Tax: 501(c)(3)

Personnel:
Chief Executive Officer: Simeon May CAE, CCA, CPA
    E-Mail: simeon@nacba.net

Manager, Conferences: Ernestine Haas
    E-Mail: ernestine@nacba.net
Associate, Education: Rose Ella McCleary
    E-Mail: rose.ella@nacba.net
Associate, Administrative: Tammy Mirau
    E-Mail: tammy@nacba.net
Associate, Membership Services: Ruth Swingle
    E-Mail: ruth@nacba.net

Historical Note:
NACBA's mission is to serve the Church by advancing professional excellence in individuals serving Christ through administration in local churches. Membership: $180 (Active); $180 (Associate/Affiliate); $275 (Business); $50 (Student); $130 (Additional member from the same organization).

Continuing Education:
Certification Designation/s: FCBA

Meetings/Conferences: Annual
Conference Chair: Ernestine Haas
2013 - Charlotte, NC (Holiday Inn Charlotte-Center City)/July 11 - 15
2014 - Nashville, TN (Gaylord Opryland Hotel and Convention Center Nashville, Tennessee)/July 14 - 18
2015 - Orlando, FL (Gaylord Palms Resort and Convention Center-Orlando)/July 7 - 11
2016 - Dallas, TX (Gaylord Texan Hotel and Convention Center-Dallas)/July 6 - 10
2017 - Washington, DC (Gaylord National-Washington)/July 3 - 7

Publications:
MultiBrief; weekly
NACBA Gram; monthly; adv.
NACBA Ledger; quarterly; adv.

Membership List Available to Non-members

National Association of Church Food Service *(1990)*
P.O. Box 43694
Birmingham, AL 35243
Tel: (205) 970-5176 *Fax:* (404) 240-8276
E-Mail: nacfs.ceo@gmail.com
Website: nacfs.org
Members: 225 individuals
Staff: 2
Annual Budget: $25-50,000

Personnel:
Conference Chair: Marjorie Savage

Historical Note:
NACFS's mission is to promote the advancement of the science of church food service and to provide a basis for a network to meet and exchange ideas both in technology and ministry. Members are persons who are currently active in church food service or retired from church food service. Membership: $50 (New Member); $85 (Membership Renewal); $25 (Retired); $45 (Additional); $200 (Associate/Business Member).

Continuing Education:
Certification Designation/s: CFSA, CFSD

Meetings/Conferences: Annual
Conference Chair: Marjorie Savage

Publications:
Membership Directory; on-line
NACFS Newsletter; monthly

National Association of Church Personnel Administrators *(1971)*
100 E. Eighth St.
Cincinnati, OH 45202-2129
Tel: (513) 421-3134 *Fax:* (513) 421-3085
E-Mail: nacpa@nacpa.org
Website: nacpa.org
Members: 1200 individuals
Staff: 6
Annual Budget: $500-1,000,000

Personnel:
Executive Director: Mary Jo Moran PhD, SPHR
    E-Mail: mjmoran@nacpa.org
Administrative Assistant: Charlene Sanders
    E-Mail: nacpa@nacpa.org

Historical Note:
NACPA's mission is to promote the development of just personnel practices rooted in gospel values. Formed by the National Federation of Priests' Councils at the University of Notre Dame. Members include clergy, religious, lay men and women. Membership: $160 (Individual); $600 (Group); $100 (Additional member over five-Group) .

Meetings/Conferences: Annual
Number of non-conference events/year: 1-10

Publications:
Newsnotes - Newsletter; bi-monthly

National Association of City and County Health Officials *(1960)*
1100 17th St. NW
Seventh Floor
Washington, DC 20036
Tel: (202) 783-5550 *Fax:* (202) 783-1583
E-Mail: info@naccho.org
Website: naccho.org
Members: 2700 local health departments
Staff: 152
Annual Budget: $25-50,000,000

Personnel:
Executive Director: Robert M. Pestronk MPH
    E-Mail: rpestronk@naccho.org
Director, Media and Public Affairs: Alisa Blum
    E-Mail: ablum@naccho.org
*Senior Director, Membership Services and State
    Partnerships:* Anne-Marie Burton
    E-Mail: aburton@naccho.org
Administrative Assistant: Janet Carr
    E-Mail: jcarr@naccho.org
Director, Publications: Caren Clark
    E-Mail: cclark@naccho.org
Chief, Government and Public Affairs: Laura Hanen
    E-Mail: lhanen@naccho.org
Director, Meetings and Events: Laura Harrison CMP,
    MTA
    E-Mail: lharrison@naccho.org
Chief Financial Officer: John Mericsko
    E-Mail: jmericsko@naccho.org
Communications Specialist: Katie Miller
    E-Mail: kmiller@naccho.org
Senior Director, Information Technology: Dennis Small
    E-Mail: dsmall@naccho.org
Senior Director, Human Resources: Lee Snowden
    E-Mail: lsnowden@naccho.org

Historical Note:
*NACCHO's mission is to be a leader, partner, catalyst, and
voice for local health departments in order to ensure the
conditions that promote health and equity, combat disease,
and improve the quality and length of all lives. Membership:
$25-3,988/year.*

Meetings/Conferences: Annual
Conference Chair: Laura Harrison CMP, MTA
2013 - Washington, DC (Omni Shoreham Hotel)/July
    10 - 12

Publications:
Journal of Public Health Management and Practice; bi-
    monthly
NACCHO Connect; monthly

National Association of Clean Air Agencies
444 N. Capitol St. NW
Suite 307
Washington, DC 20001
Tel: (202) 624-7864 *Fax:* (202) 624-7863
E-Mail: 4cleanair@4cleanair.org
Website: 4cleanair.org
Staff: 7
Annual Budget: $2-5,000,000
Tax: 501(c)(3)

Personnel:
Executive Director: William Becker
    E-Mail: 4cleanair@4cleanair.org
Administrative Assistant: Monique Faye

Historical Note:
*Formerly STAPPA/ALAPCO. NACAA serves to encourage
the exchange of information among air pollution control
officials, to enhance communication and cooperation among
federal, state, and local regulatory agencies, and to promote
good management of air resources. Represents air pollution
control agencies in 53 states and territories and over 165
major metropolitan areas across the United States.*

Publications:
Member Directory; on-line
Washington Update; weekly

Membership List Available to Non-members

National Association of Clean Water Agencies *(1970)*
1816 Jefferson Pl. NW
Washington, DC 20036-2505

Tel: (202) 833-2672 *Fax:* (888) 267-9505
E-Mail: info@nacwa.org
Website: nacwa.org
Members: 340 agencies
Staff: 19
Annual Budget: $5-10,000,000
Tax: 501(c)(6)

Personnel:
Executive Director: Ken Kirk
    E-Mail: kkirk@nacwa.org
Director, Membership Development: Kelly Brocato
    E-Mail: kbrocato@nacwa.org
Deputy Executive Director: Paula Dannenfeldt
    E-Mail: pdannenfeldt@nacwa.org
Director, Marketing and Print Management: Robin Davis
    E-Mail: rdavis@nacwa.org
Director, Information Systems: Gunnar Gehrmann
    E-Mail: ggehrmann@nacwa.org
Associate, Legal and Government Affairs: Thea Graybill
    E-Mail: tgraybill@nacwa.org
Senior Director, Regulatory Affairs: Chris Hornback
    E-Mail: chornback@nacwa.org
Manager, Human Resources and Property Management:
    Sharon Powell
    E-Mail: spowell@nacwa.org
Managing Director, Finance: Meredith Ristic
    E-Mail: mristic@nacwa.org
Director, Social Media and Communications: Elizabeth
    Striano
    E-Mail: estriano@nacwa.org

Historical Note:
*Founded as Association of Metropolitan Sewerage Agencies,
incorporated in the District of Columbia in 1970, assumed
its current name in 2005. NACWA's mission is to develop
and implement scientifically-based, technically- sound and
cost-effective environmental programs. Membership consists
of sewerage agencies. Membership: $1,200-55,370 (Public
Agency); $1,090-5,820 (Collection and Conveyance
System/Stormwater Management Agency); $1,051-5,598
(Public Affiliate); $1,040-15,600 (Corporate Private
Affiliate); $1,100-7,680 (Legal Private Affiliate); $1,000
(Supporting Affiliate), $1,040 (Academic/Non-Profit
Organization).*

Meetings/Conferences: Semi-Annual
2013 - Miami, FL (Hyatt Regency Miami)/Feb. 3 - 6
2013 - Cincinnati, OH (Hilton Cincinnati Netherland
    Plaza)/July 14 - 17
Number of non-conference events/year: 3

Publications:
Competitive Management Publications; adv.
Legal Publications; adv.
Security & Emergency Preparedness Publications; adv.

National Association of Clinical Nurse Specialists *(1995)*
100 N. 20th St.
Fourth Floor
Philadelphia, PA 19103
Tel: (215) 320-3881 *Fax:* (215) 564-2175
E-Mail: info@nacns.org
Website: nacns.org
Members: 2500 individuals
Staff: 2
Annual Budget: $500-1,000,000
Tax: 501(c)(6)

Personnel:
Executive Director: Melinda Mercer Ray
Managing Director: Ethan Gray

Historical Note:
*NACNS strives to enhance and promote the contribution
of the clinical nurse specialist to the health and well-
being of individuals, families, groups, and communities.
Membership: $125 (Regular); $80 (Student); $62.50
(Senior).*

Continuing Education:
Certification Designation/s: CNS

Meetings/Conferences: Annual
2013 - San Antonio, TX (Hyatt Regency San Antonio)/
    March 7 - 9

Publications:
Clinical Nurse Specialist
NACNS eNewsletter; quarterly
NACNS Newsletter; irregular

National Association of College and University Attorneys *(1960)*
One Dupont Cir. NW

Suite 620
Washington, DC 20036
Tel: (202) 833-8390 *Fax:* (202) 296-8379
E-Mail: nacua@nacua.org
Website: nacua.org
Members: 660 colleges and universities
Staff: 14
Annual Budget: $2-5,000,000
Tax: 501(c)(3)

Personnel:
Chief Executive Officer: Kathleen C. Santora
    E-Mail: Ksantora@nacua.org
Administrator, Accountant and Benefits: Linda P. Beza
    E-Mail: LBeza@nacua.org
Director, Information Services: John R. Bishop
    E-Mail: jbishop@nacua.org
Director, Legal Resources: Karl F. Brevitz
    E-Mail: kbrevitz@nacua.org
Manager, Membership and Outreach Services: Haleema
    M. Burton
    E-Mail: hburton@nacua.org
Meetings and Events Planner: Meredith L. McMillan
    E-Mail: mmcmillan@nacua.org
Services Assistant, Office and Publications: Michelle J.
    Parker
    E-Mail: mparker@nacua.org

Historical Note:
*NACUA's mission is to advance the effective practice
of higher education attorneys for the benefit of the
colleges and universities they serve. Membership: $710
(International Members); $755 (Associate Individual);
$1330 (Associate Institutional).*

Meetings/Conferences:
Conference Chair: Meredith L. McMillan
2013 - New Orleans, LA (Hotel Monteleone)/Jan. 11 -
    12
2013 - Philadelphia, PA (Philadelphia Marriott
    Downtown)/June 19 - 22
2014 - Denver, CO (Hyatt Regency Denver at Colorado
    Convention Center)/June 22 - 25
Number of non-conference events/year: 1

Publications:
The Journal of College and University Law (JCUL)

Membership List Available to Non-members

National Association of College and University Business Officers *(1956)*
1110 Vermont Ave. NW
Suite 800
Washington, DC 20005
Tel: (202) 861-2500 *Fax:* (202) 861-2583
TollFree: (800) 462-4916
Website: nacubo.org
Members: 2500 colleges and universities
Staff: 55
Annual Budget: $10-25,000,000
Tax: 501(c)(3)

Personnel:
President and Chief Executive Officer: John Walda
    E-Mail: john.walda@nacubo.org
Manager, Human Resources: Candice Deans
    E-Mail: candice.deans@nacubo.org
Chief Technology Officer: David DeLorenzo
    E-Mail: david.delorenzo@nacubo.org
Executive Vice President: Bill "William" Dillon
    E-Mail: bill.dillon@nacubo.org
Vice President, Professional Development: Marta Perez
    Drake
Senior Vice President, Advocacy and Issues Analysis:
    Matthew Hamill
    E-Mail: matt.hamill@nacubo.org
Director, Annual Meetings and Logistics: Earla Jones
    E-Mail: earla.jones@nacubo.org
Associate Director, Communications: Lisa Jordan
    E-Mail: lisa.jordan@nacubo.org
Administrative Coordinator: Maryanne Laager
Director, Marketing and Membership Services: Juliet
    Mason
    E-Mail: jmason@nacubo.org
Vice President, Business Operations: Elbert Ouzts
    E-Mail: elbert.ouzts@nacubo.org
Manager, Membership Services: Kristin Witters
    E-Mail: kristin.witters@nacubo.org

Historical Note:
*Formerly (1962) National Federation of College and
University Business Officers Association, NACUBO
represents accredited, non-profit institutions of higher*

learning approved for membership by a regional business officers association. Members represent approximately two-thirds of all institutions of higher learning in the U.S. Membership: $99 (Student/Retiree); $1,636 (For-Profit Higher Education Organizations); $670-1,640 (Business Partner); $759 (Affiliate); $1,314 (International/Governing Boards/Systems Office); $1,314 (Associate); $1,592-7,697 (Higher Education Institutions).

Continuing Education:
Certification Designation/s: CPES

Meetings/Conferences: Annual
Conference Chair: Earla Jones
2013 - Indianapolis, IN/July 13 - 16
2014 - Seatle, WA/July 19 - 22
2015 - Nashville, TN/July 18 - 21
2016 - Montreal, QC/July 16 - 19
Number of non-conference events/year: 10

Publications:
Business Officer Magazine; monthly; adv.
Campus Business Portal; annually
E-Bulletin; on-line
Membership Directory; on-line

Membership List Available to Non-members

National Association of College and University Food Services (1958)
2525 Jolly Rd.
Suite 280
Okemos, MI 48864-3680
Tel: (517) 332-2494 Fax: (517) 332-8144
Website: nacufs.org
Members:
3000 individuals
1100 educational institutions and industry members
Staff: 13
Annual Budget: $2-5,000,000

Personnel:
Executive Director: Joseph H. Spina CAE, PhD
    E-Mail: jspina@nacufs.org
Financial Coordinator: Trish Collier
Specialist, Membership Development: Majel Maes CAE
    E-Mail: mmaes@nacufs.org
Director, Education: Lori Mason
    E-Mail: lmason@nacufs.org
Senior Administrative Assistant: Karen Ruthenberg
    E-Mail: kruthenberg@nacufs.org
Project Manager, National Conferences: Sandra L. Smith
    E-Mail: ssmith@nacufs.org
Director, Communications and Marketing: Rachel Warner
    E-Mail: rwarner@nacufs.org

Historical Note:
NACUFS's mission is to foster campus dining programs for food and service and by leadership in education, professional development, networking, information exchange, and innovation in a culture of volunteerism. NACUFS provides members with a full-range of educational programs, publications, technical assistance, industry information, research, management services, and networking opportunities. Membership: $25-600/year.

Meetings/Conferences: Annual
Conference Chair: Sandra L. Smith
2013 - Minneapolis, MN/July 10 - 13
2014 - Baltimore, MD/July 9 - 12
2014 - Baltimore, MD/July 9 - 14
2015 - Indianapolis, IN/July 22 - 25
Number of non-conference events/year: 3

Publications:
Campus Dining Today; bi-annually; adv.
NACUFS e-Newsletter; weekly; adv.
NACUFS Membership Directory; annually

Membership List Available to Non-members

National Association of College Auxiliary Services (1973)
P.O. Box 5546
Charlottesville, VA 22905-5546
Tel: (434) 245-8425 Fax: (434) 245-8453
E-Mail: info@nacas.org
Website: nacas.org
Members: 908 U.S., Canadian and overseas Institutions
Staff: 12
Annual Budget: $1-2,000,000
Tax: 501(c)(3)

Personnel:
Chief Executive Officer: Bob Hassmiller CAE

    E-Mail: bob@nacas.org
Director, Business Partner Services: Heather W. Brown CEM
    E-Mail: heather@nacas.org
Controller: Herman "Trace" Gaskins III
    E-Mail: trace@nacas.org
Director, Education and Membership Services: Anne P. Munson MEd
    E-Mail: anne@nacas.org
Executive Administrative and Accounting Assistant NACAS Conference Registrar: Marcia Oakley
    E-Mail: marcia@nacas.org
Associate Executive Director: Abby Tammen
    E-Mail: abby@nacas.org
Director, Marketing and Technology: Caleb Welty
    E-Mail: caleb@nacas.org
Director, Education and Certification: Kim Wilbur
    E-Mail: kim@nacas.org

Historical Note:
Founded as the Association of College Auxiliary Services; assumed its present name in 1973. NACAS's mission is to provide professional development and leadership opportunities necessary for its members to be successful as they support higher education through auxiliary and campus services in an ever-changing environment. Members are directors of college auxiliary services such as book stores, laundries, food services, housing, vending, printing, etc. Membership: $255-1,050 (Institutional); $480 (Overseas); $640 (Business Partners); $125 (Retired/Subscribers); $95 (Additional Official Representatives).

Meetings/Conferences: Annual
Conference Chair: Abby Tammen
2013 - Anaheim, CA (Anaheim Marriott)/Oct. 27 - 30/51-100 exhibitors
2014 - Montreal, QC (Palais Des Congres de Montreal)/Oct. 5 - 8/51-100 exhibitors
2015 - Indianapolis, IN (JW Marriott Indianapolis)/Oct. 9 - 12
2015 - Antonio, TX (Grand Hyatt San Antonio)/Nov. 1 - 4/51-100 exhibitors
2017 - Colorado Springs, CO (The Broadmoor)/Nov. 5 - 8
2018 - Orlando, FL (Rosen Shingle Creek)/Oct. 14 - 17
Number of non-conference events/year: 4

Publications:
College Services; quarterly; adv.
Membership Directory; on-line
NACAS Conference e-Newsletter; on-line; adv.
NACAS Quarterly; quarterly; adv.

Membership List Available to Non-members

National Association of College Stores (1923)
500 E. Lorain St.
Oberlin, OH 44074-1294
Tel: (440) 775-7777 Fax: (440) 775-4769
TollFree: (800) 622-7498
Website: nacs.org
Members: 3,000 collegiate retailers and 1,000 associate members
Staff: 233
Annual Budget: $25-50,000,000

Personnel:
Chief Executive Officer: Brian Cartier CAE
    E-Mail: bcartier@nacs.org
Chief Technology Officer: Dan Bell
    E-Mail: dbell@nacs.org
Vice President, Meetings and Expositions: Hugh Easley
    E-Mail: heasley@nacs.org
Chief Human Resources Officer: Sheila Giano SPHR
    E-Mail: sgiano@nacs.org
Director, Government Relations: Richard Hershman
    E-Mail: rhershman@nacs.org
Vice President, Marketing and Membership Services: Wendy Holliday
    E-Mail: wholliday@nacs.org
Director, Marketing Communications: Anne Mendenhall
    E-Mail: amendenhall@nacs.org
Director, Finance: Jane Nizza CPA
    E-Mail: jnizza@nacs.org
Director, Publications: Cindy Ruckman
    E-Mail: cruckman@nacs.org
Director, Public Relations: Charlie Schmidt
    E-Mail: cschmidt@nacs.org
Chief, Planning and Research: Julie Traylor
    E-Mail: jtraylor@nacs.org

Historical Note:
NACS ensures the health and vitality of higher education retailers through education and research, the provision

of critical programs and services, and the development of strategic partnerships that enable members to better serve their customers. Membership: $50-2300/year.

Continuing Education:
Enrollment: 20
Certification Designation/s: CCR

Meetings/Conferences:
Conference Chair: Hugh Easley

Publications:
Campus Marketplace; weekly; adv.
CM Scan Newsletter; weekly; adv.
NACS Directory of Colleges and College Stores; annually
The Bridge Newsletter; monthly; adv.
The College Store Magazine; bi-monthly; adv.
Torchlight E-newsletter; quarterly

Membership List Available to Non-members

National Association of College Wind and Percussion Instructors (1951)
Division of Fine Arts
Truman State University, 308 Hillcrest Dr.
Kirksville, MO 63501
Tel: (660) 785-4442 Fax: (660) 785-7463
Website: nacwpi.org
Members: 1400 individuals
Staff: 2
Annual Budget: $10-25,000
Tax: 501(c)(3)

Personnel:
Executive Secretary and Treasurer: Richard K. Weerts
    E-Mail: dweerts@sbcglobal.net

Historical Note:
NACWPI's mission is to encourage and develop more effective teaching of wind and percussion instruments on the college level and provide efficient interchange of information, ideas and materials among members. Membership: $35 (Regular/Associate/Canadian); $25 (Student); $15 (Retired).

Meetings/Conferences: Annual

Publications:
NACWPI Journal; quarterly

National Association of Colleges and Employers (1956)
62 Highland Ave.
Bethlehem, PA 18017-9085
Tel: (610) 868-1421 Fax: (610) 868-0208
TollFree: (800) 544-5272
Website: naceweb.org
Members: 3000 colleges and employers
Staff: 9
Annual Budget: $5-10,000,000
Tax: 501(c)(4)

Personnel:
Executive Director: Marilyn F. Mackes PhD
Director, Communications: Mimi Collins
    E-Mail: mcollins@naceweb.org
Representative, Member Services: Cindy Corpora
    E-Mail: ccorpora@naceweb.org
Manager, Membership Services: Diane Giglio
    E-Mail: dgiglio@naceweb.org
Associate Editor: Pattie Giordani
    E-Mail: pgiordani@naceweb.org
Coordinator, Meetings and Events: Maria Kaczmar
    E-Mail: mkaczmar@naceweb.org
Executive Assistant: Cecelia M. Nader
    E-Mail: cnader@naceweb.org

Historical Note:
Formerly (1953) the Association of School and College Placement and (1995) the College Placement Council, NACE's mission is to facilitate the employment of the college educated. Membership: $400 (Organizational); $95 (e-Membership).

Meetings/Conferences: Annual
Conference Chair: Maria Kaczmar
2013 - Orlando, FL (Marriott World Center)/June 4 - 7
2014 - San Antonio, TX (San Antonio Marriott Riverwalk)/June 8 - 11
2015 - Anaheim, CA (Anaheim Marriott)/June 2 - 5
Number of non-conference events/year: 3

Publications:
Job Choices; annually
Member News; monthly
Membership Directory; on-line
NACE Journal; quarterly
Spotlight E-mail Newsletter; bi-weekly

National Association of Collegiate Directors of Athletics (1965)
24651 Detroit Rd.
Westlake, OH 44145
Tel: (440) 892-4000 *Fax:* (440) 892-4007
Website: nacda.com
Members: 7700 institutions and individuals
Staff: 13
Annual Budget: $1-2,000,000
Tax: 501(c)(6)

Personnel:
Executive Director: Bob Vecchione
   E-Mail: bvecchione@nacda.com
Manager, Communications: Erin Dengler
   E-Mail: edengler@nacda.com
Director, Membership Services: Brian Horning
   E-Mail: bhorning@nacda.com
Exhibits Manager: Denise Manak
   E-Mail: dmanak@nacda.com

Historical Note:
NACDA serves as the professional association for those in the field of intercollegiate athletics administration, provides educational opportunities and serves as a vehicle for networking, the exchange of information, and advocacy on behalf of the profession. Members are directors of athletics and athletic staff members at two- and four-year institutions. Membership: $125-375 (Individuals, based on NCAA division and size of school); $275-$1,750 (Group, based on NCAA division and size of school).

Meetings/Conferences: Semi-Annual
Conference Chair: Denise Manak
2013 - Marco Island, FL (Hilton Marco Island Beach Resort and Spa)/Jan. 25 - 28
2013 - Orlando, FL (Orlando World Center Marriott)/ June 13 - 16
2014 - Marco Island, FL (Hilton Marco Island Beach Resort and Spa)/Jan. 24 - 27
2014 - Orlando, FL (Orlando World Center Marriott)/ June 9 - 12
2015 - Marco Island, FL (Hilton Marco Island Beach Resort and Spa)/Jan. 23 - 26
2015 - Orlando, FL (Orlando World Center Marriott)/ June 15 - 18
2016 - Marco Island, FL (Hilton Marco Island Beach Resort and Spa)/Jan. 29 - Feb. 1
2016 - Dallas, TX (Hilton Anatole Dallas)/June 13 - 16
2017 - Marco Island, FL (Hilton Marco Island Beach Resort and Spa)/Jan. 27 - 30
2017 - Orlando, FL (Orlando World Center Marriott)/ June 12 - 15
2018 - Marco Island, FL (Hilton Marco Island Beach Resort and Spa)/Jan. 26 - 29
2019 - Orlando, FL (Orlando World Center Marriott)/ June 10 - 13
2021 - Orlando, FL (Orlando World Center Marriott)/ June 14 - 17
Number of non-conference events/year: 9

Publications:
Athletics Administration; bi-monthly
Membership Directory; on-line
NACDA Daily Review; daily

National Association of Collegiate Marketing Administrators (1989)
24651 Detroit Rd.
Westlake, OH 44145
Tel: (440) 892-4000 *Fax:* (440) 892-4007
E-Mail: bhorning@nacda.com
Website: nacda.com/nacma/nacda-nacma.html
Members: 1200 individuals
Staff: 13
Annual Budget: $250-500,000
Tax: 501(c)(6)

Personnel:
Executive Director: Bob Vecchione
   E-Mail: bvecchione@nacda.com
Assistant Executive Director: Jason Galaska
   E-Mail: jgalaska@nacda.com
Director, Membership Services: Brian Horning
Assistant Executive Director, Communications: Julie Work
   E-Mail: jwork@nacda.com

Historical Note:
An affiliate of National Association of Collegiate Directors of Athletics, which provides administrative support, NACMA strives to promote a standard of ethics and provides professional support to members. Members are public relations and marketing professionals in college

and university athletics departments. Membership: $125 (Active); $25 (Student); $200 (Corporate); $375 (Institutional); $500 (Group Corporate).

Meetings/Conferences: Annual
2013 - Marco Island, FL (Hilton Marco Island Beach Resort and Spa)/Jan. 25 - 28
2013 - Orlando, FL (Orlando World Center Marriott)/ June 10 - 13
2014 - Marco Island, FL (Hilton Marco Island Beach Resort and Spa)/Jan. 24 - 27
2014 - Orlando, FL (Orlando World Center Marriott)/ June 6 - 9
2015 - Marco Island, FL (Hilton Marco Island Beach Resort and Spa)/Jan. 23 - 26
2015 - Orlando, FL (Orlando World Center Marriott)/ June 15 - 18
2016 - Marco Island, FL (Hilton Marco Island Beach Resort and Spa)/Jan. 29 - Feb. 1
2016 - Dallas, TX (Hilton Anatole Dallas)/June 13 - 16
2017 - Marco Island, FL (Hilton Marco Island Beach Resort and Spa)/Jan. 27 - 30
2017 - Orlando, FL (Orlando World Center Marriott)/ June 12 - 15
2018 - Marco Island, FL (Hilton Marco Island Beach Resort and Spa)/Jan. 26 - 29
2019 - Orlando, FL (Orlando World Center Marriott)/ June 10 - 13
2021 - Orlando, FL (Orlando World Center Marriott)/ June 14 - 17

Publications:
Athletics Administration; adv.

National Association of Collegiate Women Athletic Administrators (1979)
2000 Baltimore
Suite 100
Kansas City, MO 64108
Tel: (816) 389-8200 *Fax:* (816) 389-8220
E-Mail: nacwaa@nacwaa.org
Website: nacwaa.org
Members: 2000 individuals
Staff: 5
Annual Budget: $250-500,000
Tax: 501(c)(3)

Personnel:
Chief Executive Officer: Patti Phillips
   E-Mail: pphillips@nacwaa.org
Director, National Events: Ashley Broockerd
   E-Mail: abroockerd@nacwaa.org
Director, Marketing: Laura Lewis
   E-Mail: llewis@nacwaa.org
Director, Membership Services and Educational Programming: Shannon Myers
   E-Mail: smyers@nacwaa.org

Historical Note:
Formerly, Council of Collegiate Women Athletic Administrators. Assumed it's present name in 1992. NACWAA's mission is to empower, develop and advance the success of women throughout the profession. Provides educational programs, professional and personal development opportunities, information exchange, and support services to enhance college athletics and to promote the growth, of women as athletics administrators, professional staff, coach, and student athletes. Membership: $150 (Active); $100 (Associate);$250 (Corporate); $35 (Retiree/Student/Intern).

Meetings/Conferences: Annual
Conference Chair: Ashley Broockerd
Number of non-conference events/year: 2

Publications:
Membership Directory; on-line
NACWAA Newsletter; annually
Weekly Update; weekly

The National Association of Colored Women's Club, Inc. (1896)
1601 R St. NW
Washington, DC 20009
Tel: (202) 667-4080 *Fax:* (202) 667-2574
Website: nacwc.org
Members: 1000 organizations
Staff: 3
Annual Budget: $50-100,000

Personnel:
President: Evelyn Rising
   E-Mail: erising@usw.edu
Executive Secretary: Carole A. Early
   E-Mail: cearly@nacwcya.org

Treasurer: Sandra Lewis

Historical Note:
Formed through a merger of the National Colored Women's League and the National Federation of Afro-American Women. NACWC's mission is to promote the education of women and youth through the work of departments, promote the economic, moral, religious and social welfare of women and youth and increase inter-racial understanding. Membership: $75 (Regular); $100 (Associate); $1000 (Life).

Meetings/Conferences: Annual

Publications:
NACWC Newsletter

National Association of Commissions for Women (1970)
555 Northgate Dr.
Suite 250
San Rafael, CA 94903
Tel: (415) 492-4420 *Fax:* (415) 454-0102
E-Mail: info@nacw.org
Website: nacw.org
Members: 220 commissions
Staff: 2
Annual Budget: $50-100,000

Personnel:
President: Cecilia Zamora
   E-Mail: latinocoun@aol.com

Historical Note:
NACW is the national advocate for government commissions for women. It also plays a role in national policy and legislative development. Membership: $50-350/ year.

Meetings/Conferences: Annual

Publications:
NACW Newsletter

Membership List Available to Non-members

National Association of Community Health Centers (1971)
7501 Wisconsin Ave.
Suite 1100W
Bethesda, MD 20814
Tel: (301) 347-0400 *Fax:* (301) 347-0459
TollFree: (800) 685-2272
Website: nachc.com
Members: 1200 community health centers
Staff: 97
Annual Budget: $25-50,000,000

Personnel:
President and Chief Executive Officer: Thomas Van Coverden
   E-Mail: tvancoverden@nachc.com
Coordinator, Communications: Yvette Crenshaw
   E-Mail: ycrenshaw@nachc.com
Associate Vice President, Membership and Marketing: Maurice Denis
   E-Mail: mdenis@nachc.com
Associate Vice President , Meetings and Exhibits: Cynthia (Cindy) Gady
Executive Vice President, Communications: Claudia Gibson
Director, Information Technology: Jason Gump
Senior Vice President, Finance and Administration: Mary Hawbecker CPA
   E-Mail: mhawbecker@nachc.com
Vice President, Policy Research and Analysis: Daniel R. Hawkins Jr.
   E-Mail: dhawkins@nachc.com
Director, Communications: Amy Simmons
   E-Mail: asimmons@nachc.com
Manager, Human Resources: Kelly Stanford

Historical Note:
Formerly (1971) National Association of Neighborhood Health Center Directors and Administrators and (1977) National Association of Neighborhood Health Centers. NACHC's mission is to promote the provision of quality, comprehensive and affordable health care. Membership: $65 (Individual); $5,000 (Corporate); $750 (Associate).

Meetings/Conferences:
Number of non-conference events/year: 3

Publications:
Community Health Forum; adv.
PCA Updates
Prep Tips
Programs and Policy Update
Washington Update; weekly

National Association of Composers, USA (1933)

Barrington Stn.
P.O. Box 49256
Los Angeles, CA 90049
E-Mail: nacusa@music-usa.org
Website: music-usa.org/nacusa
Members: 600 individuals
Staff: 6
Annual Budget: Under $10,000
Tax: 501(c)(3)

Personnel:
Treasurer: Joe L. Alexander
Media Broadcast Coordinator and Secretary: Sylvia
   Constantinidis
Coordinator, Membership Services: Michael Robert Conti
   E-Mail: contimic@msu.edu
Webmaster: John Winsor

Historical Note:
NACUSA is devoted to the promotion and performance
of American concert hall music. Members are composers,
conductors and performers of music, and interested
individuals. Membership: $30 (Regular); $15 (Students/
Seniors/Newsletter Subscriber); $250 (Life); Free (National,
Seniors age 80 +); $30 -250 (Chapter)..

Publications:
ComposerUSA; on-line; adv.

National Association of Computerized Tax Processors (1969)

101 Arthur Andersen Pkwy
Suite 340
Sarasota, FL 34232
Tel: (941) 343-7708
E-Mail: email@nactp.org
Website: nactp.org
Members: 70 companies
Staff: 3
Annual Budget: $10-25,000

Personnel:
President: Todd Goldberg
Treasurer: Rebecca McCaulley
Webmaster: Sanford Schmidt

Historical Note:
NACTP's mission is to provide expertise in and knowledge
of software systems to assist government agencies in
implementing new technologies. Members are companies
developing products and services for the tax industry. Has
no paid officers or full-time staff. Membership: $750/year.

Publications:
Membership Directory; on-line

National Association of Concessionaires (1944)

35 E. Wacker Dr.
Suite 1816
Chicago, IL 60601
Tel: (312) 236-3858 Fax: (312) 236-7809
E-Mail: info@naconline.org
Website: naconline.org
Members: 1000 companies
Staff: 4
Annual Budget: $500-1,000,000
Tax: 501(c)(6)

Personnel:
Executive Director: Dan Borschke
   E-Mail: dborschke@NAConline.org
Manager, Membership Services: Barbara Aslan
   E-Mail: baslan@NAConline.org
Director, Communications: Susan M. Cross
   E-Mail: scross@naconline.org

Historical Note:
NAC's mission is to provide its members with information
and services that maintain and enhance the standards of
excellence and professionalism within the recreation and
leisure time food, beverage and related services industry.
Membership: $545 (Full/Associate/Supplier/Equipment
Manufacturer/Wholesaler/Jobber/Distributor/Broker);
$180 (New Membership); $75 (Associate); $265-750
(Concession Operators)

Continuing Education:
Certification Designation/s: CMC, CCM, ECM, FSC, ACE,
CPFMC

Meetings/Conferences: Annual
2013 - New Orleans, LA (Hilton Riverside Hotel)/Aug.
   6 - 9

Publications:
Concession Profession; bi-annually; adv.
Concessionworks; semi-annually

Membership List Available to Non-members

National Association of Congregational Christian Churches (1955)

8473 S Howell Ave.
PO Box 288
Oak Creek, WI 53154
Fax: (414) 764-0319
TollFree: (800) 262-1620
Website: naccc.org
Staff: 10
Tax: 501(c)(3)

Personnel:
Chief Financial Officer: Dan Drea
   E-Mail: ddrea@naccc.org
Coordinator, Technical Services: Rebecca Moore
   E-Mail: rmoore@naccc.org

Historical Note:
NACCC is designed to allow local congregations to consult
and advise together as churches upon matters of common
concern to them, both temporal and spiritual, without
infringing on their self-government.

Meetings/Conferences: Annual
2013 - Orlando, FL (Hilton Lake Buena Vista)/June 22
   - 25

Publications:
Congregational Communicator
NACCC News; bi-monthly
The Congregationalist; quarterly

National Association of Conservation Districts (1946)

509 Capitol Ct. NE
Washington, DC 20002-4937
Tel: (202) 547-6223 Fax: (202) 547-6450
E-Mail: washington@nacdnet.org
Website: nacdnet.org
Members: 20000 individuals and districts
Staff: 27
Annual Budget: $2-5,000,000

Personnel:
Chief Executive Officer: John Larson
Senior Advisor: Rich Duesterhaus
   E-Mail: rich-duesterhaus@nacdnet.org
Director, Finance and Administration: Arthur Ganta
   E-Mail: arthur-ganta@nacdnet.org
Director, Communications: Bethany Shively
   E-Mail: bethany-shively@nacdnet.org
Director, Legislative Affairs: Laura Wood

Historical Note:
Formerly (1970) National Association of Soil and Water
Conservation Districts. NACD's mission is to serve
conservation districts by providing national leadership for
natural resource conservation. Membership: $50 (Steward);
$100 (Champion); $1000 (Lifetime); $15 (Student).

Meetings/Conferences: Annual
2013 - San Antonio, TX (Marriott Rivercenter Hotel)/
   Jan. 27 - 30
Number of non-conference events/year: 3

Publications:
eNotes; weekly
Forestry Notes; monthly
The Resource; quarterly

National Association of Consumer Advocates (1995)

1730 Rhode Island Ave. NW
Suite 710
Washington, DC 20036
Tel: (202) 452-1989 Fax: (202) 452-0099
E-Mail: info@naca.net
Website: naca.net
Members: 1500 consumer advocates and
attorneys
Staff: 12
Annual Budget: $1-2,000,000
Tax: 501(c)(6)

Personnel:
Executive Director: Ira Rheingold
   E-Mail: ira@naca.net
Director, Operations: Patty Budka
Legislative Director: Delicia Reynolds Hand
Director, Development and Marketing: Jetheda Hernandez
Manager, Education and Development: Chelsea Langston
Coordinator, Membership Services: Maxine McIntosh
Manager, Member Services: Cynthia Reddersen

Historical Note:
NACA's mission is to promote justice for all consumers
by maintaining a forum for communication, networking,
and information sharing among consumer advocates
across the country, particularly regarding legal issues, and
by serving as a voice for its members and consumers in
the ongoing struggle to curb unfair or abusive business
practices that affect consumers. Membership: $37.50-150
(Private Attorney); $25-100 (Public Interest Attorneys);
$25-50 (Legal Services and Law Students); $2,500-25,000
(Bronze/Silver/Gold/Platinum Member); $1,500
(Benefactor); $1,000 (Patron); $500 (Advocate).

Meetings/Conferences: Annual

Publications:
Find an Attorney (Membership Directory); annually
The Consumer Advocate

National Association of Consumer Agency Administrators (1976)

P.O. Box 40542
Nashville, TN 37204
Tel: (615) 498-1563
E-Mail: eowen@nacaa.net
Website: nacaa.net
Members: 160 government agencies, 50
corporate consumer offices.
Staff: 2
Annual Budget: $100-250,000
Tax: 501(c)(3)

Personnel:
Executive Director: Elizabeth Owen

Historical Note:
NACAA's mission is to promote consumer education,
consumer rights and needed consumer legislation. It
also seeks to encourage corporate participation and seek
their advice. Members are municipal, county or state
supported consumer affairs agencies. Qualified individuals.
Membership: $100-450 (Varies by agency budget); $750
(Corporate Member).

Publications:
Membership Directory; on-line
NACAA Newsletter; weekly

Membership List Available to Non-members

National Association of Consumer Bankruptcy Attorneys (1992)

20310 Chagrin Blvd
Suite 3A
Cleveland, OH 44122
Tel: (216) 491-6770 Fax: (866) 571-3560
Website: nacba.org
Members: 4,000 members
Staff: 6
Annual Budget: $2-5,000,000

Personnel:
Executive Director: Barbara Andelman
   E-Mail: barbara.andelman@nacba.org
Administrative Assistant: Rachael Hodgen
   E-Mail: rachael.hodgen@nacba.org

Historical Note:
NACBA is the only national organization dedicated to
serving the needs of consumer bankruptcy attorneys and
protecting the rights of consumer debtors in bankruptcy.
Membership: $200-$500 (Member); $125 (Active
Member); $200 (Bankruptcy); $125 (Attorneys).

Meetings/Conferences: Annual
2013 - San Diego, CA/April 25 - 28
2014 - New York City, NY/April 9 - 13
Number of non-conference events/year: 1

Publications:
Membership Directory; on-line
Newsletter; monthly

National Association of Consumer Credit Administrators (1935)

P.O. Box 20871
Columbus, OH 43220-0871
Tel: (614) 326-1165 Fax: (614) 326-1162
E-Mail: nacca2007@sbcglobal.net
Website: naccaonline.org
Members: 55 individuals
Staff: 2
Annual Budget: $50-100,000

Personnel:
Executive Director: Raymond J. Sasala
   E-Mail: nacca2007@sbcglobal.net
Secretary and Treasurer: Mike Larsen

Historical Note:
Formerly Association of Small Loan Administrators and National Association of Small Loan Supervisors. NACCA seeks to improve the personal financial literacy of young adults. Membership: $350/year.

Meetings/Conferences: Annual
2013 - San Antonio, TX (The Hyatt Regency San Antonio)/June 11 - 14
Number of non-conference events/year: 2

National Association of Consumer Shows (1987)
147 SE 102nd Ave.
Portland, OR 97216
Tel: (503) 253-0832 Fax: (503) 253-9172
TollFree: (800) 728-6227
E-Mail: info@publicshows.com
Website: publicshows.com
Members: 400 individuals
Staff: 3
Annual Budget: $100-250,000

Personnel:
President: Lesli Gray
   E-Mail: lgray@ncboatshows.com
Treasurer: Jim Fricke
   E-Mail: jim@gardeningcolorado.com
Associate Director: Megan Tomlinson CEM
   E-Mail: mtomlinson@paconvention.com

Historical Note:
NACS's mission is to further the growth and professionalism of those involved in the production of consumer shows. Membership: $260/year (Regular/Associate).

Meetings/Conferences: Annual
2013 - Chicago, IL (Hilton Chicago Hotel)/May 8 - 10

Publications:
Membership Directory; annually
Show Producer Newsletter; bi-monthly

National Association of Container Distributors (1925)
800 Roosevelt Rd.
Building C-312
Glen Ellyn, IL 60137
Tel: (630) 942-6585 Fax: (630) 790-3095
E-Mail: info@nacdmeetings.org
Website: nacd.net
Staff: 2
Annual Budget: $500-1,000,000

Personnel:
First Vice President and Contact, Public Relations and Advertising: Mary Dahl
   E-Mail: mdahl@northpak.com
Membership Contact: Mary Von Qualen
   E-Mail: mvonqualen@nacd.net

Historical Note:
The National Association of Container Distributors (NACD) is a professional association of rigid packaging distributors who supply bottles, tubes, pumps, sprayers and other closure systems. Mission is to advocate the concept that wholesale distribution is the most effective and efficient channel to bring packaging components to the manufacturers of consumer and industrial products.

Meetings/Conferences: Annual
2013 - Austin, TX (Barton Creek Resort & Spa)/April 16 - 20

Publications:
Member Directory; on-line

National Association of Convenience Stores (1961)
1600 Duke St.
Seventh Floor
Alexandria, VA 22314-3436
Tel: (703) 684-3600 Fax: (703) 836-4564
TollFree: (800) 966-6227
E-Mail: nacs@nacsonline.com
Website: nacsonline.com
Members: 80400 retail companies and outlets
Staff: 65
Annual Budget: $25-50,000,000

Personnel:
President and Chief Executive Officer: Henry Armour
   E-Mail: harmour@nacsonline.com
Director, Meetings and Convention Services: Amy Ashley-Burke
   E-Mail: aburke@nacsonline.com
Coordinator, Information Technology: Jeffrey Attoh

   E-Mail: jattoh@nacsonline.com
Senior Vice President, Government Relations: Lyle Beckwith
   E-Mail: lbeckwith@nacsonline.com
Senior Vice President and Chief Financial Officer: Kimmel Brian
   E-Mail: bkimmel@nacsonline.com
Vice President, Membership Services: Michael Davis
   E-Mail: mdavis@nacsonline.com
Vice President, Industry Advocacy: Jeff Lenard
   E-Mail: jlenard@nacsonline.com
Vice President, Human Resources: Tom Monday
   E-Mail: tmonday@nacsonline.com
Vice President, Publishing: Erin Pressley
   E-Mail: epressley@nacsonline.com
Vice President, Marketing: Doug Reed
   E-Mail: dreed@nacsonline.com
Director, Education and Programming: Carolyn Schnare
   E-Mail: cschnare@nacsonline.com

Historical Note:
Mission of NACS is to serve the convenience and petroleum retailing industry by providing industry knowledge, connections and advocacy to ensure the competitive viability of its members' businesses. Membership: $200-20,000 (Domestic Retailer); $250-2,500 (International Retailer); $15,000-65,000 (Supplier).

Meetings/Conferences:
Conference Chair: Amy Ashley-Burke
2013 - Miami Beach, FL (Fontainebleau Miami Beach)/Feb. 11 - 13
2013 - Chicago, IL (InterContinental Chicago O'Hare)/April 9 - 11
Number of non-conference events/year: 61

Publications:
Membership and Services Directory; annually
NACS Daily; daily; adv.
NACS Magazine; monthly; adv.

National Association of Corporate Directors (1977)
2001 Pennsylvania Ave. NW
Suite 500
Washington, DC 20006
Tel: (202) 775-0509 Fax: (202) 775-4857
E-Mail: info@nacdonline.org
Website: nacdonline.org
Members: 17500 members
Staff: 55
Annual Budget: $10-25,000,000
Tax: 501(c)(3)

Personnel:
President and Chief Executive Officer: Kenneth Daly
   E-Mail: kennethdaly@NACDonline.org
Senior Manager, Human Resources: Donna Crum
Membership Services Development Officer: Kelly Dodd
Director, Education: Erin Essenmacher
Editor and Research Manager: Suzanne Meyer
   E-Mail: slmeyer@nacdonline.org
Director, Member and Chapter Relations: Susan Paley
Chief Information Officer: Michael Pantaleone
Director, Strategic Communications and Partnerships: Doreen Kelly Ruyak
Chief Marketing Officer: Henry Stoever
Senior Manager, Conferences and Events: Donna L Vaught
General Counsel, Secretary and Director, Board Advisory Services: Steven Walker

Historical Note:
NACD's mission is to advance exemplary board leadership - for directors, by directors. Membership: $575 (Individual); $3,000 (Corporate); $2,500 (Associate).

Continuing Education:
Certification Designation/s: CE

Meetings/Conferences: Annual
Conference Chair: Donna L Vaught
Number of non-conference events/year: 7

Publications:
NACD Directors Daily
NACD Directorship; bi-monthly; adv.

National Association of Corporate Treasurers (1982)
12100 Sunset Hills Rd.
Suite 130
Reston, VA 20190-3221
Tel: (703) 437-4377 Fax: (703) 435-4390
E-Mail: nact@nact.org

Website: nact.org
Members: 825 individuals
Staff: 6
Annual Budget: $250-500,000
Tax: 501(c)(6)

Personnel:
Executive Director: Kathy Hoskins
   E-Mail: khoskins@drohanmgmt.com
Director, Finance: Glenn Beales
   E-Mail: Gbeales@drohanmgmt.com
Administrative Assistant: Challee Blackwelder
   E-Mail: cblackwelder@drohanmgmt.com
Director, Communications: Micki Francis
   E-Mail: mfrancis@drohanmgmt.com
Manager, Program: Laura Yarborough
   E-Mail: lyarborough@drohanmgmt.com

Historical Note:
Established in Blacksburg, Virginia and incorporated in Washington, DC. NACT's purpose is to facilitate the exchange of information beneficial to the management of corporate treasury operations.NACT members are corporate chief financial officers, treasurers, or assistant treasurers. Membership: $500/year.

Meetings/Conferences: Annual
Conference Chair: Laura Yarborough
2013 - New York City, NY (Westin Times Square Hotel)/May 29 - 31

Publications:
Membership Directory; on-line

National Association of Councils on Developmental Disabilities (2002)
1660 L St. NW, Suite 700
Suite 600
Washington, DC 20036
Tel: (202) 506-5813 Fax: (202) 506-5846
E-Mail: info@nacdd.org
Website: nacdd.org
Members: 55 councils
Staff: 6
Annual Budget: $1-2,000,000
Tax: 501(c)(3)

Personnel:
Director, Training and Technical Assistance: Hillary Spears
Conference Planner and Office Manager: Pat Brown
   E-Mail: pbrown@nacdd.org
Manager, Administrative Operations: Marshall Jones
   E-Mail: mjones@nacdd.org
Senior Manager, Council Services, Training and Technical Assistance: Sheryl Matney
   E-Mail: smatney@nacdd.org

Historical Note:
Founded as National Conference on Developmental Disabilities, became National Association of Developmental Disabilities Councils in 1978, and assumed its current name in 2002. NACDD's mission is to provide support and assistance to member Councils in order to promote a consumer and family centered system of services and supports for individuals with developmental disabilities.

Meetings/Conferences: Annual
Conference Chair: Pat Brown
Number of non-conference events/year: 1

Publications:
NACDD Newsletter; on-line

National Association of Counsel for Children (1977)
13123 E. 16th Ave.
Suite B390
Aurora, CO 80045
Tel: (303) 864-5324 Fax: (303) 864-5351
TollFree: (800) 828-6222
Website: naccchildlaw.org
Members: 2500 individuals
Staff: 7
Annual Budget: $500-1,000,000
Tax: 501(c)(3)

Personnel:
President and Chief Executive Officer: Maureen Farrell-Stevenson JD
   E-Mail: maureen.farrell-stevenson@childrenscolorado.org
Director, Membership Services: Janis McCubbrey
   E-Mail: janis.mccubbrey@childrenscolorado.org
Development and Events Administrator: Taylor Stockdell
   E-Mail: taylor.stockdell@childrenscolorado.org

Director, Certifications: Daniel Trujillo
  E-Mail: daniel.trujillo@childrenscolorado.org
Manager, Business and Operations: Sara Whalen
  E-Mail: sara.whalen@childrenscolorado.org

Historical Note:
NACC's mission is to improve the lives of children and families through legal advocacy. Members are lawyers, judges, mental health professionals, social services professionals and others with an interest in the legal status of children. Membership: $100 (Regular); $0 (Student); $150 (Supporting); $175 (Sustaining); $300 (Patron); $2,500 (Lifetime).

Continuing Education:
Enrollment: 150
Certification Designation/s: CWLS

Meetings/Conferences: Annual
Conference Chair: Taylor Stockdell

Publications:
Children's Legal Rights Journal; quarterly
Membership Directory; on-line
The Guardian; quarterly; adv.

National Association of Counties *(1935)*
25 Massachusetts Ave. NW
Suite 500
Washington, DC 20001
Tel: (202) 393-6226 *Fax:* (202) 393-2630
TollFree: (888) 407-6226
Website: naco.org
Members: 3,068 counties
Staff: 85
Annual Budget: $10-25,000,000
Tax: 501(c)(4)

Personnel:
Executive Director: Matthew Chase
Director, Research: Jacqueline Byers
  E-Mail: jbyers@naco.org
Director, Membership and Marketing: Andrew Goldschmidt CAE
  E-Mail: agoldschmidt@naco.org
Director, Finance and Administration: David Keen
  E-Mail: dkeen@naco.org
Director, Education and Training: Ruth Nybro
  E-Mail: rnybro@naco.org
Director, Legislative Affairs: Edwin S. Rosado
  E-Mail: erosado@naco.org
Executive Editor, County News: Beverly Schlotterbeck
Director, Conferences and Meetings: Kim Struble
  E-Mail: kstruble@naco.org
Managing Director and Chief Executive Officer, Financial Services Corporation: Steve Swendiman
  E-Mail: sswendiman@naco.org

Historical Note:
Formerly National Association of County Officials. Founded in 1935, The National Association of Counties (NACo) provides services to the nation's 3,066 counties. NACo represents its members before the federal government and assists counties in finding and sharing innovative solutions through education and research.

Meetings/Conferences: Annual
Conference Chair: Kim Struble
2013 - Ft. Worth, TX (Fort Worth Convention Center)/ July 19 - 22
2014 - New Orleans, LA (New Orleans Morial Convention Center)/July 11 - 14
2015 - Charlotte, NC (Charlotte Convention Center)/ July 10 - 13

Publications:
Criminal Justice Newsletter

National Association of County Administrators *(1961)*
777 N. Capitol St. NE, Suite 500
C/O ICMA
Washington, DC 20002-4201
Tel: (202) 289-4262 *Fax:* (202) 962-3500
E-Mail: naca@icma.org
Website: icma.org/en/na
Members: 450 individuals
Staff: 3
Annual Budget: $25-50,000

Personnel:
Managing Editor: Robert "Bob" McEvoy
  E-Mail: rmc@albany.edu
Contact, Membership Services: Rita Ossolinski
  E-Mail: rossolinski@icma.org

Historical Note:

An affiliate of the National Association of Counties that provides administrative support. NACA is the professional association of county administrators. NACA advances and encourages professional development for county administrators and strives to improve the management of county government. Membership: $75-175 (Corporate); $35 (Associate); $1,500 (Affiliate).

Publications:
Journal of County Administration; bi-monthly
Membership Directory; on-line

National Association of County Aging Programs *(1978)*
440 First St. NW, Eighth Floor
Washington, DC 20001
Tel: (202) 393-6226 *Fax:* (202) 393-2630
Website: naco.org
Members: 350 individuals
Staff: 1
Annual Budget: $10-25,000

Personnel:
Director, County Services: Edward E. Ferguson
  E-Mail: eferguso@naco.org

Historical Note:
Composed of county elected and appointed officials with an interest or direct responsibility for the delivery of aging services. Develops policy position on aging issues, highlights and disseminates information on aging and offers training to its members.

National Association of County Agricultural Agents *(1915)*
6584 W. Duroc Rd.
Maroa, IL 61756
Tel: (217) 794-3700 *Fax:* (217) 794-5901
Website: nacaa.com
Members: 4500 individuals
Staff: 3
Annual Budget: $500-1,000,000
Tax: 501(c)(6)

Personnel:
President: Paul Craig
Executive Director and Editor: Scott Hawbaker
  E-Mail: exec-dir@nacaa.com
Treasurer: Parman Green
  E-Mail: greenp@missouri.edu

Historical Note:
Mission NACAA, an organization of professional extension educators, is to further the professional improvement of its members, communication and cooperation among all extension educators and provide for enhancement of the image of extension and the development of personal growth opportunities for extension professionals. Membership: $50/ year.

Meetings/Conferences: Annual
2013 - Pittsburgh, PA/Sept. 15 - 20
2014 - Mobile, AL/July 20 - 24
2015 - Sioux Falls, SD/July 12 - 16

Publications:
Journal of the NACAA
The County Agent; quarterly

Membership List Available to Non-members

National Association of County and City Health Officials *(1960)*
1100 17th St. NW
Seventh Floor
Washington, DC 20036
Tel: (202) 783-5550 *Fax:* (202) 783-1583
E-Mail: info@naccho.org
Website: naccho.org
Members:
1450 local health departments
10000 individuals
Staff: 105
Annual Budget: $25-50,000,000
Tax: 501(c)(3)

Personnel:
Executive Director: Robert M. Pestronk MPH
  E-Mail: rpestronk@naccho.org
Director, Media and Public Relations: Alisa Blum
  E-Mail: ablum@naccho.org
Media Advocacy Specialist: Ashley Bowen MA
  E-Mail: abowen@naccho.org
Director, Government Affairs: Eli Briggs
  E-Mail: ebriggs@naccho.org
Senior Director, Membership service and State Partnerships: Anne-Marie Burton

  E-Mail: aburton@naccho.org
Director, Publications: Caren Clark
  E-Mail: cclark@naccho.org
Director, Meetings and Events: Laura Harrison CMP, MTA
  E-Mail: lharrison@naccho.org
Chief Financial Officer: John Mericsko
  E-Mail: jmericsko@naccho.or
Senior Director, Information Technology: Dennis Small
  E-Mail: dsmall@naccho.org
Senior Director, Human Resources: Lee Snowden
  E-Mail: lsnowden@naccho.org

Historical Note:
Formerly (1994) National Association of County Health Officials. NACCHO's mission is to promote health and equity, combat disease, and improve the quality and length. NACCHO is governed by a 27-member Board of Directors, comprising local and tribal health officials from across the country, and including ex officio members representing the National Association of Counties, of which NACCHO is an affiliate, and the U.S. Conference of Mayors.Membership: $55-3,530 (Local Public Health Departments); $25 (Student); $50 (Retiree/Alumni); $110 (Other Individual Affiliates); $340 (Non-profit/Govt.Organization); $2,425 (Profit Organization).

Meetings/Conferences: Annual
Number of non-conference events/year: 4

Publications:
MRC: In Focus; quarterly
NACCHO Connect e-newsletter; bi-monthly; adv.
NACCHO Exchange; quarterly

National Association of County Behavioral Health and Developmental Disability Directors *(1996)*
25 Massachusetts Ave. NW
Suite 500
Washington, DC 20001
Tel: (202) 661-8816
Website: nacbhdd.org
Members: 320 individuals
Staff: 3
Annual Budget: $250-500,000

Personnel:
Executive Director: Ron Manderscheid PhD
  E-Mail: rmanderscheid@nacbhd.org
Manager, Advocacy and Operations: Melissa Stein
  E-Mail: mstein@nacbhd.org

Historical Note:
Formerly (1997) National Association of County Mental Health Directors. NACBHD's mission is to assure that national policy and funding recognizes and supports county and other local government authorities that are responsible for the development and management of publicly funded systems of care for people affected by mental illness, addiction, and developmental disabilities.

Publications:
Membership Directory; on-line
NACBHDD Newsletter; monthly

National Association of County Civil Attorneys *(1935)*
25 Massachusetts Ave. NW
Suite 500
Washington, DC 20001
Tel: (202) 393-6226 *Fax:* (202) 393-2630
TollFree: (888) 407-6226
Website: naco.org
Members: 240 individuals
Staff: 70
Annual Budget: Under $10,000

Personnel:
President: Chris Rodgers
Contact, Communications: Tom Goodman
  E-Mail: tgoodman@naco.org
Executive Assistant to CEO: Karen McRunnel
  E-Mail: kmcrunne@naco.org
Senior Policy Advisor: Donald Murray
  E-Mail: dmurray@naco.org

Historical Note:
NACCA is an affiliate organization of the National Association of Counties (NACo). National organization that represents county governments in the United States. NACCA improves the public's understanding of county government, assists counties in finding and sharing innovative solutions through education and research, and provides value-added services to save counties and taxpayers money.

Meetings/Conferences: Annual

2013 - Ft. Worth, TX (Fort Worth Convention Center)/
July 19 - 22

Publications:
NACo e-News; bi-weekly

National Association of County Engineers *(1956)*
25 Massachusetts Ave. NW
Suite 580
Washington, DC 20001
Tel: (202) 393-5041 *Fax:* (202) 393-2630
E-Mail: nace@naco.org
Website: countyengineers.org
Members: 1900 Members
Staff: 4
Annual Budget: $500-1,000,000

Personnel:
Executive Director: Brian C. Roberts
Senior Legislative Director: Robert Fogel
    E-Mail: bfogel@naco.org
Office Manager: Constantine "Connie" Radoulovitch
Assistant Executive Director: Bonnie M. West

Historical Note:
NACE's mission is to promote the use of recognized engineering standards for the design, construction, and maintenance of public works; to promote the spirit of cooperation between local, state and federal agencies; and, by the exchange of ideas, to give all counties, in each state, the advantage of qualified professional engineering services in all phases of public works.Members are county engineering professionals or road management authorities. NACE is an affiliate of the National Association of Counties. Membership: $130 (Individual); $500-5,000 (Organization/Company).

Meetings/Conferences: Annual
Conference Chair: Bonnie M. West
2013 - Des Moines, IA (Des Moines Marriott
    Downtown)/April 21 - 25
2014 - Baton Rouge, LA (Hilton Baton Rouge Capitol
    Center)/April 13 - 17
2015 - Daytona Beach, FL (Hilton Daytona Beach
    Resort/Ocean Walk Village)/April 19 - 23
Number of non-conference events/year: 7

Publications:
E-News; bi-weekly
NACE News; monthly

National Association of County Health Facility Administrators *(1978)*
P.O. Box 603
Powers, MI 49874-0603
Tel: (906) 497-5244 *Fax:* (906) 497-5005
E-Mail: pmcf0001@pinecrestmcf.org
Members: 240 individuals
Staff: 2
Annual Budget: Under $10,000

Personnel:
President: Gerald Betters
    E-Mail: pmcf0001@pinecrestmcf.org
Staff Liaison: Paul Beddoe
    E-Mail: pbeddoe@naco.org

Historical Note:
An affiliate of the National Association of Counties, which provides administrative support. NACHFA works to improve the quality of healthcare available from county nursing homes and other long-term care institutions. Membership: $25/year (individual); $250/year (organization).

National Association of County Human Services Administrators *(1935)*
440 First St. NW
Suite 800
Washington, DC 20001
Tel: (202) 393-6226 *Fax:* (202) 393-2630
Website: nachsa.org
Members: 600 counties
Staff: 4
Annual Budget: $50-100,000

Personnel:
President: J. Glenn Osborne
Editor: Kelly Andrisano JD
Treasurer: Bob Suver

Historical Note:
Formerly (1981) National Association of County Welfare Directors and also a national affiliate of the National Association of Counties that provides administrative support, NACHSA's mission is to support the professional development of administrators committed to delivering quality services to county residents in need. Membership:

$130-1,310 (County/State, based on population);
$1,310 (Statewide Association of County Human Services
Administrators).

Publications:
NACHSA Networker

National Association of County Information Officers *(1965)*
25 Massachusetts Ave. NW
Washington, DC 20001
Tel: (202) 393-6226 *Fax:* (202) 393-2630
Website: nacio.org
Members: 325 individuals
Staff: 2
Annual Budget: $10-25,000
Tax: 501(c)(4)

Personnel:
Secretary: Terri Graham

Historical Note:
An affiliate of the National Association of Counties, which provides administrative support. NACIO offers comprehensive services and support to help its members grow professionally and in their understanding of the relationship between public official and those they serve. Members are county public information officers and staff. Membership: $75 (Individual); $100 (State Association Staff); $175 (Non-County Governments); $250 (Corporate).

Meetings/Conferences: Annual

Publications:
NACIO Newsletter; semi-annually; adv.
The Art of Communication; semi-annually; adv.

Membership List Available to Non-members

National Association of County Information Technology Administrators
25 Massachusetts Ave.
Suite 500
Washington, DC 20001
Tel: (202) 393-6226 *Fax:* (202) 393-2630
Members: 2000 individuals
Staff: 8

Personnel:
IT Manager: Jerryl Guy

Historical Note:

National Association of County Intergovernmental Relations Officials *(1966)*
25 Massachusetts Ave.,NW
Washington, DC 20001
Tel: (202) 393-6226 *Fax:* (202) 942-4281
E-Mail: dharris@naco.org
Website: naco.org
Members: 100 individuals
Staff: 15
Annual Budget: Under $10,000

Personnel:
Executive Director: Matthew D. Chase
    E-Mail: mchase@naco.org
President: Edith Stewart
    E-Mail: stewarte@hillsboroughcounty.org
Director, Research: Jacqueline Byers
    E-Mail: jbyers@naco.org
Manager, Conferences and Meetings: Amanda Clark
    E-Mail: aclark@naco.org
Director, Marketing: William E. Cramer
    E-Mail: bcramer@naco.org
Secretary: Mary Beth Davidson
    E-Mail: mary.davidson@co.hennepin.mn.us
Director, Membership and Marketing: Andrew
    Goldschmidt
    E-Mail: agoldschmidt@naco.org
Manager, Information Technology: Jerryl Guy
    E-Mail: jguy@naco.org
Vice President and Treasurer: Frank Johnson
    E-Mail: fjohnson@ccg.carr.org
Director, Administration and Finance: David Keen
    E-Mail: dkeen@naco.org
Manager, Media Relations: Jim Philipps
    E-Mail: jphilipps@naco.org
Executive Editor: Beverly Schlotterbeck
    E-Mail: bschlott@naco.org
Director, Human Resource: Deborah Stoutamire
    E-Mail: dstoutamire@naco.org
Director , Conferences and Meetings: Kim Struble
Administrative Assistant: Gail Yates
    E-Mail: gyates@naco.org

Historical Note:
Established in 1966 as the National Association of County Development Coordinators to satisfy the need for a greater exchange of ideas in coordinating federal and state aid programs at the county level; became (1975) National Association of Counties Council of Intergovernmental Coordinators; assumed current name in 1991. An affiliate of the National Association of Counties.

Meetings/Conferences:
Conference Chair: Kim Struble

Publications:
County News; bi-weekly; adv.
NACo e-News; bi-weekly

National Association of County Park and Recreation Officials *(1964)*
P.O. Box 74
Marienville, PA 16239
Tel: (814) 927-8212 *Fax:* (814) 927-6659
E-Mail: nacpro.office@gmail.com
Website: nacpro.org
Members: 250 individuals
Staff: 3
Annual Budget: $25-50,000

Personnel:
President: Mark Denny
    E-Mail: markdenny@ocparks.com
Executive Director: Dan Gooch
    E-Mail: rdangooch@aol.com
Manager, Association: Brenda Adams-Weyant
    E-Mail: brenda@nacpro.org

Historical Note:
NACPRO's purpose is to provide members with opportunities for networking, sharing resources, and professional development and to advance official policies that support county parks and recreation systems. An affiliate of the National Association of Counties and the National Recreation and Park Association (NRPA). Members are professionals in the field of parks, recreation and leisure-related services. Membership: $80-100 (Professional, depending on the Counties' population); $200 (Corporate).

Meetings/Conferences:
2013 - Vancouver, BC/June 10 - 15
2013 - Houston, TX/Oct. 8 - 10

Publications:
NACPRO News; quarterly; adv.

National Association of County Recorders, Election Officials and Clerks *(1949)*
2501 Aerial Center Pkwy.
Suite 103
Morrisville, NC 27560
Tel: (919) 459-2080 *Fax:* (919) 459-2075
TollFree: (800) 497-5128
E-Mail: info@nacrc.org
Website: nacrc.org
Members: 765 individuals
Staff: 2
Annual Budget: $100-250,000

Personnel:
Executive Director: Whitney Bertram
    E-Mail: whitney@imiae.com

Historical Note:
Formerly the National Association of County Recorders and Clerks. An affiliate of the National Association of Counties. NACRC is a professional organization of elected and appointed county administrative officials, who network on a national level to share information and ideas. Members include county officials who are responsible for administration of land/property records, courts and elections. Membership: $55-250 (County, based on the population); $35 (Associate); $500 (Corporate/ Business Membership/National Association); $350 (State Association); $50 (Deputy/Director of Association/Deputy of Corporate); $55 (New, first year public official).

Continuing Education:
Certification Designation/s: NACRC

Meetings/Conferences: Annual
2013 - Washington, DC (Washington Marriott)/March
    2 - 3
Number of non-conference events/year: 4

Publications:
Membership Directory; annually
NACRC Bulletin; quarterly

Membership List Available to Non-members

National Association of County Surveyors

P.O. Box 1188
Gainesville, FL 32602
Tel: (352) 374-5245 *Fax:* (352) 337-6243
Website: uscounties.org/nacs/index.htm
Staff: 2

Personnel:
President: Robert W. Wigglesworth
    E-Mail: Rwigglesworth@alachuacounty.us

Historical Note:
An affiliate of the National Association of Counties which provides administrative support. Membership: $50 (Voting); $25 (Associate); $100 (Affiliate); $250 (Corporate).

Publications:
NACS Newsletters; quarterly

National Association of Credential Evaluation Services, Inc. *(1987)*
P.O. Box 514070
Milwaukee, WI 53203-3470
Tel: (414) 289-3400 *Fax:* (414) 289-3411
E-Mail: naces@ierf.org
Website: naces.org
Members: 16 firms
Staff: 1
Annual Budget: Under $10,000

Personnel:
Membership Committee Past Chairman: James S. Frey

Historical Note:
NACES's mission is to promote excellence and committed to setting the standards for the profession. Members are companies specializing in the evaluation of foreign educational credentials for further education, professional licensure, employment, or immigration. Has no paid officers or full-time staff.

National Association of Credit Management *(1896)*
8840 Columbia 100 Pkwy.
Columbia, MD 21045-2158
Tel: (410) 740-5560 *Fax:* (410) 740-5574
E-Mail: nacm_national@nacm.org
Website: nacm.org
Members: 25000 individuals
Staff: 55
Annual Budget: $2-5,000,000
Tax: 501(c)(6)

Personnel:
President and Chief Operating Officer: Robin Schauseil
    CAE
    E-Mail: robins@nacm.org
Director, Information Technology: Ben Anawalt
    E-Mail: bena@nacm.org
Director, Marketing and Design: Dan LaRusso
    E-Mail: danl@nacm.org
Director, Meetings: Jill Leimbach
    E-Mail: jilll@nacm.org
Editorial Director: Caroline Zimmerman
    E-Mail: caroline@nacm.org

Historical Note:
NACM serves as a resource for credit and financial management information and education, delivering products and services, which improve the management of business credit and accounts receivable. Plays an active part in legislative issues pertaining to business credit and corporate bankruptcy. Members of NACM are credit and financial executives, primarily representing manufacturers, wholesalers, financial institutions, and varied service organizations.

Continuing Education:
Certification Designation/s: CCE, CBF, CBA

Meetings/Conferences:
Conference Chair: Jill Leimbach
2013 - Las Vegas, NV (Rio Hotel)/May 19 - 22

Publications:
Business Credit; adv.
Credit Managers' Index; monthly
NACM eNews; weekly

National Association of Credit Specialists
5 Leather Bark Ct.
Stafford, VA 22554
Tel: (919) 875-4852
Website: nacsfsa.net
Staff: 1
Annual Budget: $50-100,000

Personnel:
President: Joe Austin

E-Mail: Joe.Austin@nc.usda.gov

Historical Note:
A credit and banking association. Membership: $120/year.

Publications:
National newsletter

National Association of Credit Union Chairmen *(1976)*
P.O. Box 160
Del Mar, CA 92014-0160
Tel: (858) 792-3883 *Fax:* (858) 792-3884
TollFree: (888) 987-4247
E-Mail: nacuc@nacuc.org
Website: nacuc.org
Members: 165 members
Staff: 2
Annual Budget: $100-250,000
Tax: 501(c)(6)

Personnel:
Executive Director: Celeste A. Shelton
    E-Mail: celeste@nacuc.org

Historical Note:
Formerly (1993) the National Association of Credit Union Presidents. Also known as The Chairmen's Group. NACUC's mission is to provide credit union chairmen with unique educational forums and networking opportunities designed to develop and improve their leadership skills and expertise. Membership: $350/year.

Meetings/Conferences:
Number of non-conference events/year: 2

Publications:
Exchange Newsletter; on-line
Membership Directory; on-line

National Association of Credit Union Service Organizations *(1985)*
11338 Harbor Breeze Dr.
Montgomery, TX 77356
Tel: (713) 208-0989 *Fax:* (832) 442-5517
E-Mail: info@nacuso.org
Website: nacuso.org
Members: 412 individuals
Staff: 5
Annual Budget: $500-1,000,000

Personnel:
President and Chief Executive Officer: Jack M. Antonini
    E-Mail: jantonini@aol.com

Historical Note:
NACUSO works to help credit unions explore the use of CUSOs and the delivery of non-traditional products and services. Membership is open to credit unions without established CUSOs. Membership: $750 (Primary Voting Member); $1,250 (Contributory Member); $10,000 (Gold Partner); $20,000 (Platinum Partner).

Meetings/Conferences: Annual
Conference Chair: Shawna Luna
2013 - Las Vegas, NV (Encore Las Vegas Resort)/April
    16 - 19
Number of non-conference events/year: 1

Publications:
Information/eNEWs

National Association of Credit Union Supervisory and Auditing Committees *(1985)*
P.O. Box 160
Del Mar, CA 92014-0160
Tel: (800) 287-5949 *Fax:* (858) 792-3884
E-Mail: nacusac@nacusac.org
Website: nacusac.org
Members: 500 individuals
Staff: 3
Annual Budget: $100-250,000

Personnel:
Executive Director: Celeste Shelton
Associate Director: Lauren Clark

Historical Note:
NACUSAC is an organization of, by and for credit union supervisory and audit committee members. It seeks to provide leadership, support and education to enhance the capability of credit union supervisory and auditing committee members to fulfill their responsibilities. Membership : $400 (Regular); $500 (Associate).

Meetings/Conferences: Annual
2013 - Savannah, GA (Hilton Savannah DeSoto Hotel)/
    June 12 - 15

Publications:
E-Newsletter; on-line

Membership Directory; on-line
NACUSAC Newsletter

The National Association of Crime Victim Compensation Boards *(1977)*
P.O. Box 16003
Alexandria, VA 22302
Tel: (703) 780-3200 *Fax:* (703) 780-3261
E-Mail: nacvcb@aol.com
Website: nacvcb.org
Members: 52 state government programs
Staff: 1
Annual Budget: $100-250,000
Tax: 501(c)(3)

Personnel:
Executive Director: Dan Eddy
    E-Mail: dan.eddy@nacvcb.org

Historical Note:
NACVCB's mission is to provide leadership, professional development, and collaborative opportunities to members to strengthen their capacity to improve services to crime victims and survivors. They strive to ensure that every victim compensation program is fully funded, optimally staffed, and functioning effectively to help victims cope with the costs of crime. Members are professionals working in state and territory crime victim compensation programs.

Meetings/Conferences: Annual
Number of non-conference events/year: 50

Publications:
Crime Victim Compensation; quarterly
Membership Directory; on-line

National Association of Criminal Defense Lawyers *(1958)*
1660 L St. NW
12th Floor
Washington, DC 20036
Tel: (202) 872-8600 *Fax:* (202) 872-8690
E-Mail: assist@nacdl.org
Website: nacdl.org
Members:
11000 direct members and 35000 members
95 state, local, and international affiliate
organizations
Staff: 33
Annual Budget: $5-10,000,000

Personnel:
Executive Director: Norman L. Reimer
    E-Mail: norman@nacdl.org
Director, Sales and Marketing: James Bergmann
    E-Mail: jbergmann@nacdl.org
Editor: Quintin Chatman
    E-Mail: quintin@nacdl.org
Director, Membership Services: Michael Connor
    E-Mail: michaelc@nacdl.org
Director, State Legislative Affairs: Angelyn Frazer
    E-Mail: afrazer@nacdl.org
Manager, Meetings and Education: Tamara Kalacevic
    E-Mail: tkalacevic@nacdl.org
Associate Executive Director, Programs: Gerald Lippert
    E-Mail: gerald@nacdl.org
Manager, Information Services: Steven Logan
    E-Mail: steven@nacdl.org
Associate Executive Director for Policy: Kyle O'Dowd
    E-Mail: kyle@nacdl.org
Special Assistant to the Executive Director: Daniel Weir
    E-Mail: daniel@nacdl.org

Historical Note:
Formerly (1972) National Association of Defense Lawyers in Criminal Cases, NACDL's purpose is to assure justice and due process for persons accused of crime or wrongdoing. Membership: $290 (Regular); $165 (New Lawyer/International); $55 (Law Student); $175 (Associate/Judge); $150 (Law Professor/Military Lawyers); $5,000 (Life Time); $125 (Federal Public Defender/State Public Defender).

Continuing Education:
Enrollment: 4

Meetings/Conferences: Annual
Conference Chair: Tamara Kalacevic
2013 - San Francisco, CA (Westin San Francisco)/July
    24 - 27

Publications:
Membership Directory; on-line
NACDL E-News; monthly
The Champion; adv.

National Association of Crop Insurance Agents
111 W. St.
Memphis, TN 54587
Staff: 1

Personnel:
Treasurer: Hon Mate

Historical Note:
A representative of crop insurance agents on federal crop insurance issues.

National Association of Cruise Oriented Agencies
(1985)
7378 Atlantic Blvd.
Suite 115
Margate, FL 33063-4214
Tel: (305) 663-5626 *Fax:* (866) 816-7143
E-Mail: nacoafl@aol.com
Website: nacoaonline.com
Members: 800 agencies
Staff: 3
Annual Budget: $250-500,000

Personnel:
President: Donna Kaye Esposito MCC
Vice President and Treasurer: Sandra Perdue MCC

Historical Note:
Formerly National Association of Cruise Only Agencies (1998). NACOA's mission is to promote cruise vacations, unite cruise retailers, provide educational programs and create a forum for cruise agents and cruise lines. Members are travel agencies specializing in cruise ship bookings. Allied membership is available for cruise lines, suppliers to the industry, trade publications and other entities with an interest in the industry. Membership: $75/year (Individual).

Publications:
NACOA Newsletter; on-line; adv.

National Association of Decorative Fabric Distributors *(1968)*
1010 W. 2610 South
Salt Lake City, UT 84119
Tel: (801) 972-6770 *Fax:* (801) 972-5005
E-Mail: info@nadfd.com
Website: nadfd.com
Members: 60 companies
Staff: 2
Annual Budget: $50-100,000
Tax: 501(c)(6)

Personnel:
President: Ted Sargetakis
    E-Mail: ted@silverstatetextiles.com

Historical Note:
Formerly (1975) National Association of Upholstery Fabric Distributors. NADFD is dedicated to provide education and network opportunities to promote its member's growth and profitability. Membership: $900/year (Regular/Associate).

Meetings/Conferences: Annual
2013 - Loretto, NM (The Inn and Spa)/Aug. 7 - 9
Number of non-conference events/year: 1

Publications:
Membership Directory; on-line

National Association of Dental Assistants *(1974)*
900 S. Washington St.
Suite G13
Falls Church, VA 22046-4020
Tel: (703) 237-8616 *Fax:* (703) 533-1153
Members: 3000 individuals
Staff: 4
Annual Budget: $50-100,000

Personnel:
Director: Ruth Ludeman

Historical Note:
NADA's purpose is to assist its members in achieving their career goals by keeping them informed of advances and/or changes in their chosen professions, by offering continuing education opportunities, and by promoting the free exchange of ideas with their peers. Membership is open to anyone employed by a dentist, including office personnel. Membership: $30; $55 (For 2 years).

Publications:
The Explorer; adv.

Membership List Available to Non-members

National Association of Dental Laboratories
(1951)
325 John Knox Rd.

Suite L103
Tallahassee, FL 32303
Tel: (850) 205-5626 *Fax:* (850) 222-0053
TollFree: (800) 950-1150
E-Mail: nadl@nadl.org
Website: nadl.org
Members: 2000 individuals and 9000 Certified Technicians
Staff: 10
Annual Budget: $1-2,000,000

Personnel:
Chief Staff Executive: Bennett E. Napier CAE
    E-Mail: bennett@nbccert.org
Director, Technology: Amy Bean
Editor: Cassie Corcoran
Meeting Planner: Jill Jackson CMP
Director, Membership Services: William Lessley
Deputy Director, Certification: Adrienne Segundo

Historical Note:
A federation of state laboratory associations formed by a merger of the Dental Laboratory Institute of America and the American Dental Laboratory Association. From 1968-71 it was known as the National Association of Certified Dental Laboratories. Affiliated with the National Board for Certification in Dental Laboratory Technology, granting the Certified Dental Technician (CDT) designation and the National Board for Certification of Dental Laboratories, granting the Certified Dental Laboratory (CDL) designation. NADL supports dentistry and servs the public interest by promoting high standards. Membership: $350 (Laboratory/Education); $400 (Supplier/Component); $85 (Technician).

Continuing Education:
Certification Designation/s: RET, RG, CDT

Meetings/Conferences: Annual
Conference Chair: Jill Jackson CMP
2013 - Las Vegas, NV (Caesars Palace)/Jan. 17 - 19

Publications:
Membership Directory; on-line
The Journal of Dental Technology

National Association of Dental Plans *(1989)*
12700 Park Central Dr.
Suite 400
Dallas, TX 75251
Tel: (972) 458-6998 *Fax:* (972) 458-2258
E-Mail: info@nadp.org
Website: nadp.org
Members: 80 companies
Staff: 8
Annual Budget: $1-2,000,000
Tax: 501(c)(6)

Personnel:
Executive Director: Evelyn F. Ireland CAE
    E-Mail: eireland@nadp.org
Director, Research and Information: Jerry Berggren
    E-Mail: jberggren@nadp.org
Director, Membership and Communications: Rene Chapin
    E-Mail: rchapin@nadp.org
Director, Government Relations: Kristen Hathaway
    E-Mail: khathaway@nadp.org
Office Administrator: Shayne Leatherwood
    E-Mail: sleatherwood@nadp.org
Assistant, Education and Meetings: Sopha Lim
    E-Mail: slim@nadp.org

Historical Note:
NADP's mission is to promote and advance the dental benefits industry to improve consumer access to affordable, quality dental care. Members include major commercial carriers, regional and single state companies, as well as companies organized as non-profit organizations. Membership: $3,080-41,025/Year.

Meetings/Conferences: Annual
Conference Chair: Sopha Lim

Publications:
Monthly byte-; monthly
SmartBrief; weekly

National Association of Development Companies
(1981)
6764 Old McLean Village Dr.
McLean, VA 22101
Tel: (703) 748-2575 *Fax:* (703) 748-2582
E-Mail: info@nadco.org
Website: nadco.org
Members: 350 companies
Staff: 6
Annual Budget: $1-2,000,000

Tax: 501(c)(6)

Personnel:
President and Chief Executive Officer: Christopher L. Crawford
    E-Mail: chris@nadco.org
Director, Communications and Outreach: Merril Levesque
    E-Mail: merril@nadco.org
Manager, Events and Education: Becky Marrs
    E-Mail: becky@nadco.org
Administrative Assistant: Thu Nguyen
    E-Mail: thu@nadco.org
Director, Marketing and Outreach: Terri Tackett
    E-Mail: terri@nadco.org
Manager, Membership Services: Brianne Tolson
    E-Mail: brianne@nadco.org

Historical Note:
Members provide lending services to small businesses under several Small Business Administration guarantee programs. NADCO represents the membership before Congress and government agencies and provides education, research, industry communications and insurance services to members.

Meetings/Conferences: Annual
Conference Chair: Becky Marrs
2013 - Coronado, CA (Hotel del Coronado)/May 15 - 18
2014 - Colorado Springs, CO (Broadmoor)/April 30 - May 3
Number of non-conference events/year: 3

Publications:
NADCO newsletter; monthly

National Association of Development Organizations *(1967)*
400 N. Capitol St. NW
Suite 390
Washington, DC 20001
Tel: (202) 624-7806 *Fax:* (202) 624-8813
E-Mail: info@nado.org
Website: nado.org
Members: 540 organizations
Staff: 8
Annual Budget: $1-2,000,000
Tax: 501(c)(4)

Personnel:
Executive Director: Matthew Chase
    E-Mail: mchase@nado.org
Director, Government Relations and Legislative Affairs: Deborah Cox
    E-Mail: dcox@nado.org
Manager, Communications: Zanetta Doyle
    E-Mail: zdoyle@nado.org
Director, Meetings and Membership Services: Vicki Glass
    E-Mail: vglass@nado.org
Deputy Executive Director: Laurie Thompson
    E-Mail: lthompson@nado.org

Historical Note:
NADO's mission is to provide advocacy, education, networking and research for regional development organizations primarily serving small metropolitan and rural regions. Members are multi-county regional development organizations, mainly in small metropolitan and rural areas. Membership: $500 (Associate); $1,000 (Sustaining Associate); $2,000 (General); $3,000 (Sustaining); $4,000 (Platinum); $6000 (Platinum Plus).

Meetings/Conferences: Annual
Conference Chair: Vicki Glass
2013 - Greenville, SC (Hyatt Regency Greenville)/April 23 - 25
2013 - Greenville, SC (Hyatt Regency Greenville)/April 24 - 26
2013 - San Francisco, CA (Hilton San Francisco Union Square)/Aug. 24 - 27
2014 - Arlington, VA (Crystal Gateway Marriott)/ March 24 - 26
Number of non-conference events/year: 3

Publications:
Membership Directory; on-line

National Association of Diaconate Directors
(1976)
7625 N. High St.
Columbus, OH 43235
Tel: (614) 985-2276
E-Mail: naddinfo@nadd.org
Website: nadd.org
Members: 350 individuals

Staff: 2
Annual Budget: $100-250,000
Tax: 501(c)(3)

Personnel:
Executive Director: Deacon Thomas MPS R. Dubois MPS
    E-Mail: exec@nadd.org
Secretary and Treasurer: Deacon Michael Jelley
    E-Mail: sec@nadd.org

Historical Note:
Founded as National Association of Permanent Diaconate Directors; assumed its current name in 1995.NADD's mission to support diaconate directors, associate directors, and their staffs in their mission to enable deacons, candidates, aspirants, their wives and families to utilize their gifts in the service to the Church following the model of Jesus Christ. Membership: $550 (Diocesan); $150 (Each Additional Full Membership); $125 (Each Additional Associate Non-Voting Membership).

Meetings/Conferences: Annual
Conference Chair: Deacon Thomas MPS R. Dubois MPS
2013 - Albuquerue, NM (Albuquerque Marriott Pyramid North)/April 10
2014 - Atlanta, GA (Archdiocese of Atlanta)/April 21 - 25
2015 - Minneapolis, MN (Archdiocese of St. Paul)/April 13 - 17
2016 - Houston, TX (Archdiocese of Galveston)/April 4 - 8
Number of non-conference events/year: 1

Publications:
Deacon Digest (Abbey Press - Publisher); bi-monthly; adv.
Membership Directory; on-line
NADD Newsletter; quarterly
National Diaconate Directory; annually

National Association of Directors of Nursing Administration in Long Term Care (1986)
11353 Reed Hartman Hwy.
Suite 210
Cincinnati, OH 45241
Tel: (513) 791-3679 Fax: (513) 791-3699
TollFree: (800) 222-0539
E-Mail: info@nadona.org
Website: nadona.org
Members: 3400 members
Staff: 4

Personnel:
Executive Director: Sherrie Dornberger
    E-Mail: sherrie@nadona.org
Membership Assistant: Cheryl Hecker
    E-Mail: cheryl@nadona.org
Treasurer: Neal Larson BC, RN
    E-Mail: nlarson4@midco.net
Coordinator, Membership Services: Jan Ward
    E-Mail: jan@nadona.org

Historical Note:
NADONA/LTC is an educational organization dedicated to nursing and administration professionals in the Long Term Care and Assisted Living professions. Membership: 100 (Associate); $500 (Patron Member); $5,000 (Corporate Patron).

Continuing Education:
Enrollment: 3400
Certification Designation/s: CALN, LPN-CLTC, CDON/LTC

Meetings/Conferences: Annual
Conference Chair: Jan Ward
2013 - Las Vegas, NV (Caesar\'s Palace)/June 8 - 12
Number of non-conference events/year: 1

Publications:
E-newsletter; monthly
The Director Journal; quarterly; adv.
The NCCDP Newsletter; quarterly

National Association of Disability Evaluating Professionals (1984)
13801 Village Mill Dr.
Midlothian, VA 23113
Tel: (804) 378-7275
Website: nadep.com
Members: 1000 individuals
Staff: 2
Annual Budget: $250-500,000

Personnel:
Director: Virgil Robert May III

Historical Note:

NADEP purpose is to develop the art and science of disability evaluation, enhance public awareness about disability evaluation and improve professional recognition for disability evaluation practitioners. Members are lawyers, medical doctors and other professionals involved in the evaluation and rehabilitation of persons with disabilities resulting from work or personal injuries. Membership: $50 (Full/Associate); $25 (Staff/Retiree); $200-500 (Corporate).

National Association of Disability Examiners
(1963)
701 Pike St.
Suite 1000
Seattle, WA 98101
Tel: (213) 736-7088 Fax: (206) 553-0013
TollFree: (888) 737-1762
Website: nade.org
Members:
2000 individuals
18 Corporate Members
Staff: 6
Annual Budget: $25-50,000

Personnel:
President: Richard Todd Deshong
    E-Mail: richard.deshong@ssa.gov
Contact, Conferences: Laura Dunipace
    E-Mail: Laura.Dunipace@ssa.gov

Historical Note:
Established as a division of the National Rehabilitation Association, NADE became autonomous in 1978. Members are doctors and examiners engaged in judging social security disability claims. NADE's mission is to encourage disability evaluation as a science and a profession. Membership: $50 (Full/Associate); $25 (Retiree/Full Support Staff); $200 (Organization); $500 (Gold Corporate); $350 (Silver Corporate).

Continuing Education:
Certification Designation/s: EC, SP, MC

Meetings/Conferences:
Conference Chair: Laura Dunipace

Publications:
Membership Directory; on-line
The NADE Advocate; quarterly; adv.

National Association of Disability Representatives
(2000)
P.O. Box 96503
Suite 30550
Washington, DC 20090-6503
Tel: (202) 822-2155 Fax: (972) 245-6701
Website: nadr.org
Staff: 3

Personnel:
President: Trisha Cardillo
    E-Mail: trisha@ssdisabilityassistance.com
Administrator: Eva Sirman
    E-Mail: eva@nadr.org
Treasurer: Caitlin Thomas
    E-Mail: caitlinthomas@comcast.net

Historical Note:
Represents professional Social Security claimant representatives. Membership: $295 (Individual).

Meetings/Conferences: Annual
2013 - Seatle, WA (Grand Hyatt Seattle)/May 1 - 4

Publications:
NADR newsletter; quarterly

National Association of Division Order Analysts
(1974)
P.O. Box 1718
Helena, MT 59624
E-Mail: administrator@nadoa.org
Website: nadoa.org
Members: 1300 individuals
Staff: 3
Annual Budget: $250-500,000

Personnel:
President: Betty Davidson
    E-Mail: bdavidson@cima-energy.com
Treasurer: Sandi Rupprecht
    E-Mail: srupprecht@enerplus.com
Board Advisor: Noemi Taylor
    E-Mail: ntaylor@concho.com

Historical Note:
NADOA is dedicated to promote the degree of professionalism, technical expertise and ethical standards. Members are petroleum and gas company employees or

independent consultants responsible for royalty, working interest and overriding royalty payments. Membership: $75/year (Active/Associate).

Continuing Education:
Certification Designation/s: CDOA

Meetings/Conferences: Annual
Number of non-conference events/year: 1

Publications:
Annual Institute Journal; annually
Directory; annually; adv.
NADOA Newsletter; quarterly; adv.

National Association of Document Examiners
(1979)
9126 Raeford Dr.
Dallas, TX 75243
TollFree: (866) 569-0833
E-Mail: documentexam@earthlink.net
Website: documentexaminers.org
Members: 165 individuals
Staff: 4
Annual Budget: $25-50,000

Personnel:
President: Linda James CDE
    E-Mail: lcj@handwriting-examiner.com
Treasurer: Susan Abbey
    E-Mail: susanabbey@sbcglobal.net
Contact, Website: Ginger Collins
Editor in Chief: Jacqueline A. Joseph
    E-Mail: jjoseph@jjhandwriting.com

Historical Note:
NADE's mission is to promote the interests of forensic document examiners specializing in handwriting identification through seminars, publications, and a certification program for professional members. Members are private forensic handwriting or document examiners. Membership: $100/year (Individual).

Continuing Education:
Certification Designation/s: CDE

Meetings/Conferences: Annual
2013 - Omaha, NE/April 25 - 27

Publications:
Journal of the National Association of Document Examiners
Membership Directory; on-line

The National Association of Dog Obedience Instructors (1965)
P.O. Box 1439
Socorro, NM 87801
Tel: (505) 850-5957
Website: nadoi.org
Members: 450 individuals
Staff: 3

Personnel:
Executive Director: Jan Gribble
Treasurer: Gwen Chaney
Administrator, Membership: Linda Lundgren
    E-Mail: membership@nadoi.org

Historical Note:
NADOI's mission is to certify dog obedience instructors of the highest caliber, to provide continuing education and learning resources to those instructors, and to continue to promote humane, effective training methods and competent instruction. Membership: $70/year (Individual).

Meetings/Conferences: Annual

Publications:
ForwarD; quarterly; adv.
Nadoi Notes; on-line

National Association of Drug Court Professionals
(1994)
1029 N. Royal St.
Suite 201
Alexandria, VA 22314
Tel: (703) 575-9400 Fax: (703) 575-9402
TollFree: (877) 266-1374
Website: nadcp.org
Members: 3882 drug courts and problem-solving courts
Staff: 24
Annual Budget: $5-10,000,000
Tax: 501(c)(3)

Personnel:
Chief Executive Officer: C. West Huddleston
    E-Mail: whuddleston@nadcp.org

Senior Director, Public Policy: Jennifer Columbel
    E-Mail: jcolumbel@nadcp.org
Director, Communications: Christopher Deutsch
    E-Mail: cdeutsch@nadcp.org
Director, Membership: Robert Foster
    E-Mail: rfoster@nadcp.org
Chief Operating Officer and Chief Counsel: Carson Fox
    E-Mail: cfox@nadcp.org
Coordinator, Training: Clifford Jacobs
    E-Mail: cjacobs@nadcp.org
Director, Meetings: Jennifer Lubold
    E-Mail: jlubold@nadcp.org
Chief Financial Officer: Janet McCuller
    E-Mail: jmcculler@nadcp.org
Manager, Human Resources: Meisha Moody
    E-Mail: mmoody@nadcp.org

Historical Note:
A non-profit organization that works to reduce substance abuse, crime and recidivism through funding and utilizing resources to provide training and support to its association members. Members work to improve the justice system by using a combination of judicial monitoring and effective treatment to compel drug-using offenders to change their lives. Members are public, Drug Court, DWI Court, and Mental Health Court professionals, including justice system, alcohol and drug treatment, and mental health treatment professionals. Membership: $60 (Individual); $60- 500 (Organization); $3,500-25,000 (Corporate); $25 (Drug Court Graduate).

Meetings/Conferences: Annual
Conference Chair: Jennifer Lubold
2013 - Ft. Washington, MD (Gaylord National Resort and Convention Center-National Harbor)/July 14 - 17
2014 - Anaheim, CA (Anaheim Convention Center)/ May 28 - 31
2015 - Ft. Washington, MD (Gaylord National Resort and Convention Center-National Harbor)/July 19 - 22

Publications:
All Rise Magazine; quarterly; adv.
Membership Directory; on-line

Membership List Available to Non-members

National Association of Ecumenical and Interreligious Staff *(1940)*
766 John St.
Suite B
Seattle, WA 98109
Tel: (206) 625-9790
E-Mail: info@naeis.org
Website: naeis.org
Members: 375 individuals
Staff: 2
Annual Budget: $50-100,000

Personnel:
President: Rev. C. Dana Krutz
Treasurer: Alice M. Woldt

Historical Note:
Formerly (1971) Association of Council Secretaries and (1997) National Association of Ecumenical & Interreligious Staff. NAEIS is the product of a merger of the Employed Council Officers Association and the Association of Executive Secretaries. Mission is to serve the professional development and personal enrichment of its members, empowering them to do their work more effectively and faithfully. Membership: $75 (Executive (Head of Staff)/ Denominational Ecumenical or Interreligious Officer); $50 (Executive of Organization with budgets less than $100,000/Program Staff of Ecumenical/Interreligious Agency); $25 (Introductory for Executives and Staff); $250 (Group membership).

Publications:
NAEIS News; on-line

National Association of Educational Office Professionals *(1934)*
P.O. Box 12619
Wichita, KS 67277-2619
Tel: (316) 942-4822 *Fax:* (316) 942-7100
E-Mail: naeop@naeop.org
Website: naeop.org
Members: 4800 individuals
Staff: 7
Annual Budget: $250-500,000

Personnel:
Executive Director: Angela Meyer
    E-Mail: angela@naeop.org
Secretary and Treasurer: Theresa Cote

Membership Coordinator: Linda Hopper
    E-Mail: membership@naeop.org
Coordinator, Affiliates: Jennifer Jackson
    E-Mail: affiliates@naeop.org
Accounting Coordinator: Jenny Olson
    E-Mail: accounting@naeop.org
Editor: Linda Sockwell
    E-Mail: linda.sockwell@risd.org
President: Lola Young CEOE
    E-Mail: lyoung5@unl.edu

Historical Note:
Formerly (1979) the National Association of Educational Secretaries and (1995) National Association of Office Personnel. Mission is to provide professional growth opportunities, leadership, and service for employees in education through a specifically-designed certification program, quality training, a network for sharing information and ideas, recognition of achievements, and fellowship. Members are office personnel in educational institutions. Membership: $50 (Active/Associate); $30 (Retired); $85 (Institutional); $60 (Corporate).

Continuing Education:
Certification Designation/s: CEOE

Meetings/Conferences: Annual
Conference Chair: Jennifer Jackson
2013 - Alexandria, VA/July 21 - 26

Publications:
Keeping Affiliates Active Newsletter; irregular
Membership Directory; on-line
NAEOP State and Local Affiliate Newsletter; irregular

Membership List Available to Non-members

National Association of Educational Procurement, Inc. *(1920)*
5523 Research Park Dr.
Suite 340
Baltimore, MD 21228
Tel: (443) 543-5540 *Fax:* (443) 543-5550
Website: naepnet.org
Members: 1900 institutions
Staff: 11
Annual Budget: $1-2,000,000
Tax: 501(c)(3)

Personnel:
Chief Executive Officer: Doreen Murner
    E-Mail: dmurner@naepnet.org
Manager, Education and Training: Melanie Freeman
    E-Mail: mfreeman@naepnet.org
Coordinator, Marketing and Volunteer: Jackie Harget
    E-Mail: jharget@naepnet.org
Editor-in-Chief: Neil Markee
    E-Mail: ndm11777@aol.com
Senior Manager, Technology: Mark Polakow
    E-Mail: mpolakow@naepnet.org
Director, Finance and Administration: Paul Ravenscroft
    E-Mail: pravenscroft@naepnet.org
Administrator, Membership Services: Shaunte Shelton-Slappy
    E-Mail: sshelton@naepnet.org
Director, Membership Services, Marketing and Technology: Toni Valenti
    E-Mail: tvalenti@naepnet.org

Historical Note:
Founded as the Educational Buyers Association, it became the National Association of Educational Buyers in 1947, and assumed its current name in 2007. NAEP's mission is to facilitate the development, exchange and practice of ethical procurement principles and techniques within higher education and associated communities, through continuing education, networking, public information and advocacy. Members are college and university purchasing directors and purchasing staff. Membership: $440-2,980 (Voting Member); $550 (Associate).

Continuing Education:
Certification Designation/s: CPPO, CPSM, CPPB

Meetings/Conferences:
2013 - Orlando, FL (Disney's Contemporary Resort)/ April 7 - 10
2014 - Louisville, KY (Louisville Marriott Downtown)/ May 18 - 21
2015 - Atlanta, GA (Atlanta Hyatt)/April 12 - May 15
2016 - San Antonio, TX (Grand Hyatt San Antonio)/ May 22 - 25
2017 - Reno, NV (Peppermill Resort Spa Casino)/ March 26 - 29
2018 - Orlando, FL (Walt Disney World Resorts)/April 8 - 11

Publications:

Educational Procurment Journal; quarterly
Membership Directory; on-line
Purchasing Link; annually

Membership List Available to Non-members

National Association of Electrical Distributors *(1908)*
1181 Corporate Lake Dr.
St. Louis, MO 63132
Tel: (314) 991-9000 *Fax:* (314) 991-3060
TollFree: (888) 791-2512
Website: naed.org
Members: 470 Companies
Staff: 41
Annual Budget: $5-10,000,000
Tax: 501(c)(6)

Personnel:
President and Chief Executive Officer: Tom Naber
    E-Mail: tnaber@naed.org
Vice President, Membership: Anita Bauer
    E-Mail: abauer@naed.org
Senior Director, Meetings and Conferences: Becky Burgess
    E-Mail: becky.burgess@naed.org
Data Manager: Kathy Dailey
    E-Mail: kdailey@naed.org
Vice President, Finance: Tim Dencker
    E-Mail: tdencker@naed.org
Educational Program Manager: John Kiso
    E-Mail: jkiso@naed.org
Office and Executive Manager: Sheila Logan
    E-Mail: slogan@naed.org
Vice President, Government Affairs: Ed Orlet
    E-Mail: eorlet@naed.org
Publisher: Craig Riley
    E-Mail: criley@naed.org
Senior Manager, Marketing and Communications: Linda Thurman
    E-Mail: lthurman@naed.org

Historical Note:
Formerly (1928) Electrical Supply Jobbers Association and (1949) National Electric Wholesalers Association. NAED serves as a resource for electrical distributors to gain business opportunities, education, industry knowledge, and information. Membership: $645-27,735 (Distributor); $1,142-28,550 (Associate/Allied Partner, varies with sales through distribution).

Continuing Education:
Certification Designation/s: CEP, CSP

Meetings/Conferences: Annual
Conference Chair: Becky Burgess
2013 - Boston, MA (Boston Marriott Copley Place)/ May 4 - 7
2014 - San Francisco, CA (San Francisco Marriott Marquis)/April 26 - 29
Number of non-conference events/year: 8

Publications:
EPEC Newsletters
NAED Online Member Directory; on-line
tED magazine; adv.

National Association of Elementary School Principals *(1921)*
1615 Duke St.
Alexandria, VA 22314-3483
Tel: (703) 684-3345 *Fax:* (703) 549-5568
TollFree: (800) 386-2377
E-Mail: naesp@naesp.org
Website: naesp.org
Members: 30000 individuals
Staff: 52
Annual Budget: $5-10,000,000
Tax: 501(c)(6)

Personnel:
Executive Director: Gail Connelly
    E-Mail: gconnelly@naesp.org
Deputy Executive Director: Michael L. Schooley
    E-Mail: mschooley@naesp.org
Senior Associate Executive Director, Membership Services, Marketing and Communications: Deborah Bongiorno
    E-Mail: dbongiorno@naesp.org
Associate Executive Director, Membership Development, Affiliate Relations and Business Alliances: Christine Dolan
    E-Mail: cdolan@naesp.org
Director, Marketing and Business Development: Ann Henley
    E-Mail: ahenley@naesp.org

Associate Executive Director, Research and Development:
Christine Mason
E-Mail: cmason@naesp.org
Associate Executive Director, Administration and Related Resources: Patrick Murphy
E-Mail: pmurphy@naesp.org
Associate Executive Director, Advocacy, Policy and Special Projects: Kelly Duquin Pollitt
E-Mail: kpollitt@naesp.org
Development Specialist: Carol Riley
E-Mail: criley@naesp.org
Managing Editor: Kaylen Tucker
E-Mail: ktucker@naesp.org
Director, Convention and Meetings: Deborah Young
E-Mail: dyoung@naesp.org

Historical Note:
Founded in 1921 as a division of the National Education Association, it became autonomous in 1972. Mission is to support for elementary and middle level principals and other education leaders in their commitment for all children. Membership: $235 (Active); $280 (Institutional Active); $80 (Aspiring Principal); $135(Associate); $165 (International Associate); $150 (Institutional Subscription); $118 (Emeritus); $60(Retired).

Continuing Education:
Certification Designation/s: NPMCP

Meetings/Conferences: Annual
Conference Chair: Deborah Young
2013 - Baltimore, MD (Baltimore Convention Center)/ July 11 - 13
Number of non-conference events/year: 11

Publications:
Communicator; monthly; adv.
E-Newsletter; adv.
Membership Directory; on-line
Principal; adv.
Principal's Bookshelf; monthly; adv.
Staff Directory; on-line

National Association of Elevator Contractors
(1950)
1298 Wellbrook Cir.
Suite A
Conyers, GA 30012
Tel: (770) 760-9660 *Fax:* (770) 760-9714
TollFree: (888) 847-7530
E-Mail: info@naec.org
Website: naec.org
Members: 735 companies
Staff: 8
Annual Budget: $1-2,000,000
Tax: 501(c)(6)

Personnel:
Executive Director: Teresa M. Shirley
E-Mail: teresa@naec.org
Coordinator, Education: Kathy Bell
Manager, Tradeshow and Publication: Patti Bonner
E-Mail: patti@naec.org
Manager, Member Services: Shawn Cowden
E-Mail: shawn@naec.org
Manager, Marketing and Meetings: Kerrie Rebmann
E-Mail: kerrie@naec.org
Office Assistant: Stacey Snipes
E-Mail: stacey@naec.org

Historical Note:
NAEC is an association of elevator contractors and suppliers serving primarily the interests of independent elevator contractors and independent suppliers of products and services; encouraging safe and reliable elevator, escalator and short-range transportation and enhancing excellence in the management of member companies. Membership: $525 (Contractor/Associate Contractor/ Supplier/Professional); $625 (Non-U. S. Contractor/ Associate Contractor/Supplier).

Continuing Education:
Certification Designation/s: CAT, CET

Meetings/Conferences: Semi-Annual
Conference Chair: Patti Bonner
2013 - Dana Point, CA (Ritz Carlton Laguna Niquel)/ April 13 - 16
2013 - Tampa, FL (Tampa Bay Convention Center)/ Sept. 23 - 26
2014 - Ft. Myers, FL (Sanibel Harbour Resort and Spa)/ March 29 - April 1
2014 - San Antonio, TX (Hyatt Regency Hill Country Resort and Spa)/Sept. 8 - 11
2015 - Honolulu, HI (Sheraton Waikiki)/April 18 - 21
2015 - Boston, MA (Boston College)/Sept. 28 - Oct. 1

Number of non-conference events/year: 8

Publications:
Mainline Newsletter
Membership Directory; annually

National Association of Elevator Safety Authorities International *(1969)*
6957 Littlerock Rd. SW
Suite A
Tumwater, WA 98512
Tel: (360) 292-4968 *Fax:* (360) 292-4973
TollFree: (800) 746-2372
E-Mail: info@naesai.org
Website: naesai.org
Members: 2200 individuals
Staff: 3
Annual Budget: $250-500,000

Personnel:
Executive Director: Dotty Stanlaske
E-Mail: dotty@naesai.org
Administrative Assistant: Felicity Wilkinson
E-Mail: felicity@naesai.org

Historical Note:
NAESA International's mission is to promote current codes and standards, teach and educate stakeholders, certify inspectors, and assist the populace in enhancing elevator safety and understanding new elevator technology. Members are manufacturers, installers, services and inspectors of elevators. Membership: $75 (AHJ Inspector/Private Inspector); $125 (Professional); $350 (Organizational).

Continuing Education:
Certification Designation/s: QEI
Meetings/Conferences:
Number of non-conference events/year: 3

Publications:
Membership Directory; on-line
The Progress - e-newsletter; monthly; adv.

National Association of Emergency Medical Technicians *(1975)*
P.O. Box 1400
Clinton, MS 39060-1400
Tel: (601) 924-7744 *Fax:* (601) 924-7325
TollFree: (800) 346-2368
E-Mail: info@naemt.org
Website: naemt.org
Members: 32000 individuals
Staff: 7
Annual Budget: $1-2,000,000
Tax: 501(c)(6)

Personnel:
Executive Director: Pamela Lane
E-Mail: pamela.lane@naemt.org
Assistant Executive Director: Lisa Lindsay
E-Mail: lisa.lindsay@naemt.org
Manager, Education: Corine Curd
E-Mail: corine.curd@naemt.org
Coordinator, Membership Services: Tammie W. Patterson
E-Mail: tammie.patterson@naemt.org
Assistant Business Manager: Keshia Robinson
E-Mail: keshia.robinson@naemt.org
Manager, Communications: Rebecca Dinan Schneider
E-Mail: rebecca.dinan@naemt.org

Historical Note:
NAEMT's mission is to represent and serve emergency medical services personnel through advocacy, educational programs and research. Members are state certified and/ or nationally registered emergency medical technicians (EMTs), paramedics, and other professionals working in prehospital emergency medicine. Membership: $40 (Full); $30 (Affiliate); $25 (Military/Student); $600 (Lifetime); $400 (Squad).

Continuing Education:
Certification Designation/s: PHTLS, AMLS, EPC

Meetings/Conferences: Annual

Publications:
NAEMT News; quarterly

National Association of EMS Educators *(1995)*
250 Mount Lebanon Blvd.
Suite 209
Pittsburgh, PA 15234
Tel: (412) 343-4775 *Fax:* (412) 343-4770
E-Mail: naemse@naemse.org
Website: naemse.org
Staff: 7
Annual Budget: $500-1,000,000

Tax: 501(c)(3)

Personnel:
Executive Director: Joann Freel
E-Mail: joann.freel@naemse.org
Coordinator, Communications: Brandon Ciampaglia
E-Mail: brandon.ciampaglia@naemse.org
Coordinator, Education: Laurie Davin
E-Mail: laurie.davin@naemse.org
Coordinator, Membership Services: Holly Dubiel
E-Mail: holly.dubiel@naemse.org
Administrative Assistant: Larissa Kocelko
E-Mail: larissa.kocelko@naemse.org
Business Manager: Stephen Perdziola
E-Mail: stephen.perdziola@naemse.org

Historical Note:
NAEMSE's mission is inspire excellence in EMS education and lifelong learning within the global community. Membership: $85 (Individual).

Continuing Education:
Certification Designation/s: NEMSEC, NCEE

Meetings/Conferences: Annual
2013 - Washington, DC (Omni Shoreham Hotel)/Aug. 5 - 10
Number of non-conference events/year: 7

Publications:
EMS Magazine
Membership Directory; on-line
Prehospital Emergency Care

National Association of EMS Physicians *(1984)*
P.O. Box 19570
Lenexa, KS 66285
Tel: (913) 895-4611 *Fax:* (913) 895-4652
TollFree: (800) 228-3677
E-Mail: info-naemsp@goamp.com
Website: naemsp.org
Members: 1250 individuals
Staff: 5
Annual Budget: $1-2,000,000

Personnel:
Executive Director: Jerrie Lynn Kind
E-Mail: jlkind@goamp.com
Administrative Assistant: Diane Conner
E-Mail: diane.conner@goAMP.com
Manager, Meetings: Megan Finnell
E-Mail: megan.finnell@goAMP.com

Historical Note:
NAEMSP's mission is to provide leadership and foster excellence in out of hospital emergency medical services. NAEMSP members are designated, medically-legally responsible medical directors of municipal and state emergency medical systems and programs, as well as key associates, including state directors, administrative heads, regular EMS personnel and legal experts from the United States and Canada. Membership: $325 (Physician); $130 (Resident Physician); $160 (International/Professional/ Fellow); $100 (Medical Student).

Meetings/Conferences: Annual
Conference Chair: Megan Finnell
2013 - Bonita Springs, FL (Hyatt Regency Coconut Point Resort and Spa)/Jan. 10 - 12
2014 - Tucson, AZ (JW Marriott Tucson Starr Pass Resort and Spa)/Jan. 16 - 18
Number of non-conference events/year: 1

Publications:
Membership Directory; on-line
NAEMSP® E-News; monthly; adv.
NAEMSP® News; quarterly; adv.
Prehospital Emergency Care (PEC) Journal; quarterly; adv.

National Association of Energy Service Companies
(1983)
1615 M St. NW
Suite 800
Washington, DC 20036
Tel: (202) 822-0950 *Fax:* (202) 822-0955
E-Mail: info@naesco.org
Website: naesco.org
Members: 140 companies
Staff: 4
Annual Budget: $1-2,000,000
Tax: 501(c)(6)

Personnel:
President: Donald Gilligan
Executive Director: Terry E. Singer
E-Mail: tes@dwgp.com

Senior Program Manager: Nina K. Lockhart
Director, Membership and Communications: Meghan Morrison

Historical Note:
Trade association to promote the benefits of the widespread use of energy efficiency. Membership: $250 (Public Sector); $2000 (International); $3500 (Associate Affiliate); $7000 (Affiliate); $7000-15000 (Full).

Meetings/Conferences: Annual
Conference Chair: Nina K. Lockhart

Publications:
Membership Directory; on-line
Newsletter; quarterly

National Association of Enrolled Agents *(1978)*
1120 Connecticut Ave. NW
Suite 460
Washington, DC 20036
Tel: (202) 822-6232 *Fax:* (202) 822-6270
TollFree: (855) 880-6232
E-Mail: info@naea.org
Website: naea.org
Members: 11,000 independent, licensed tax professionals
Staff: 13
Annual Budget: $2-5,000,000
Tax: 501(c)(6)

Personnel:
Executive Vice President: Michael S. Nelson CAE
　　E-Mail: mnelson@naea.org
Director, Finance and Operations: William Grutzkuhn
　　E-Mail: bgrutzkuhn@naea.org
Database Manager: Eli Hernandez
　　E-Mail: shernandez@naea.org
Senior Director, Communications and Marketing: Virginia 'Gigi' Jarvis
　　E-Mail: vjarvis@naea.org
Director, Education and Meetings: Holli Jones
　　E-Mail: hjones@naea.org
Senior Director, Government Relations: Robert Kerr
　　E-Mail: rkerr@naea.org
Deputy Director, Membership Services: Sam Matlick CAE
　　E-Mail: smatlick@naea.org
Managing Editor: Margaret Mitchell
　　E-Mail: mmitchell@naea.org

Historical Note:
Formed (1972) as the Association of Enrolled Agents, assumed its current name in 1978. NAEA's mission is to foster the professionalism and growth of its members and be an advocate of taxpayer rights. Membership: $185/year.

Meetings/Conferences: Annual
Conference Chair: Holli Jones

Publications:
E@lert; weekly; adv.
EA Journal; bi-monthly; adv.

National Association of Environmental Professionals *(1975)*
P.O. Box 460
Collingswood, NJ 08108
Tel: (856) 283-7816 *Fax:* (856) 210-1619
E-Mail: naep@bowermanagementservices.com
Website: naep.org
Members: 1600 individuals
Staff: 2
Annual Budget: $250-500,000

Personnel:
Contact, Communications: Tim Bower CAE
Conference Coordinator: Donna Carter

Historical Note:
NAEP is dedicated to developing the highest standards of ethics and proficiency in the environmental professions. Members reflect a diversity of employers, including government, industry, academia, consulting firms, and the private sector in the U.S. and abroad. Membership: $40-750/year.

Meetings/Conferences: Annual
Conference Chair: Donna Carter
2013 - Los Angeles, CA (JW Marriott Los Angeles L.A. LIVE)/April 1 - 5

Publications:
Environmental Practice; on-line; adv.
Membership Directory; on-line
National eNews; bi-monthly; adv.

National Association of Epilepsy Centers *(1987)*
600 Maryland Ave. SW, Suite 835 West

Washington, DC 20024
Tel: (202) 484-1100 *Fax:* (202) 484-1244
E-Mail: info@naec-epilepsy.org
Website: naec-epilepsy.org
Members: 170 Epilepsy Centers
Staff: 2
Annual Budget: $250-500,000
Tax: 501(c)(6)

Personnel:
President: David M. Labiner MD
Secretary and Treasurer: Susan T. Herman MD

Historical Note:
NAEC's mission is to make high quality healthcare available and affordable for epilepsy patients across the country. Membership: $2000 (Epilepsy Center); $100 (Individual).

Publications:
Membership Directory; on-line

National Association of Episcopal Schools *(1954)*
815 Second Ave.
Suite 819
New York, NY 10017
Tel: (212) 716-6134 *Fax:* (212) 286-9366
TollFree: (800) 334-7626
E-Mail: info@episcopalschools.org
Website: episcopalschools.org
Members: 1200 schools
Staff: 5
Annual Budget: $1-2,000,000
Tax: 501(c)(3)

Personnel:
Executive Director: Daniel R. Heischman Dmin
　　E-Mail: drh@episcopalschools.org
Director, Operations: Linda A. Glad CMP, CAE
　　E-Mail: lag@episcopalschools.org
Assistant, Membership Services: Erin J. Neary
　　E-Mail: ejn@episcopalschools.org
Coordinator, Communications and Events: David J. Schnabel CAE
　　E-Mail: djs@episcopalschools.org

Historical Note:
Founded as Episcopal School Association (1954); incorporated as NAES in 1965. NAES's mission is to serve those who serve Episcopal schools. Members are Episcopal schools. Membership: $150-5,249/year; $500-750 (Corporate) $225 (School Exploration Committee).

Meetings/Conferences:
Conference Chair: David J. Schnabel CAE
2013 - Tampa, FL (Berkeley Preparatory School)/Feb. 7 - 9
2014 - Anaheim, CA (Anaheim Marriott)/Nov. 20 - 22

Publications:
Membership Directory; on-line; adv.

National Association of Equipment Leasing Brokers *(1990)*
455 S. Fourth St.
Suite 650
Louisville, KY 40202
Fax: (877) 875-4750
TollFree: (800) 996-2352
E-Mail: info@naelb.org
Website: naelb.org
Members: 800 companies
Staff: 2
Annual Budget: $250-500,000
Tax: 501(c)(6)

Personnel:
Executive Administrator: Monica Harper
　　E-Mail: mharper@hqtrs.com
Coordinator, Membership: Leah McCollum
　　E-Mail: lmccollum@hqtrs.com

Historical Note:
NAELB works to promote the interests of equipment leasing brokers through education, advocacy, improved communication with funders and programs designed to upgrade the professionalism and profitability of brokers, funders and others engaged in the business of equipment lease financing. Membership: $165-865/year.

Meetings/Conferences: Annual
2013 - Las Vegas, NV (Tropicana Las Vegas Hotel and Casino)/April 18 - 20
Number of non-conference events/year: 3

Publications:
Membership Directory; on-line
NAELB Newsletter.

National Association of Estate Planners and Councils *(1962)*
1120 Chester Ave.
Suite 470
Cleveland, OH 44114
Fax: (216) 696-2582
TollFree: (866) 226-2224
E-Mail: admin@naepc.org
Website: naepc.org
Staff: 3
Annual Budget: $250-500,000

Personnel:
President: Clark B. McCleary ChFC, CLU, MSFS
Treasurer: Joanna Averett CFP, MBA
Administrator: Eleanor M. Spuhler

Historical Note:
NAEPC's mission is to promote the multi-disciplinary approach to estate planning by supporting local estate planning councils and their members and by encouraging the formation of new councils. Membership: $125-400 (Council); $80 (Individual).

Continuing Education:
Certification Designation/s: AEP, EPLS

Meetings/Conferences: Annual
2013 - Las Vegas, NV (Cosmopolitan of Las Vegas)/ Nov. 20 - 22/1-10 exhibitors
2014 - San Antonio, TX (Marriott Rivercenter Hotel)/ Nov. 5 - 7

Publications:
AEP Alert; on-line
Membership Directory; on-line
NAEPC Journal of Estate and Tax Planning; quarterly; adv.
NAEPC News; bi-monthly
Technical Newsletter; monthly

Membership List Available to Non-members

National Association of Exclusive Buyer Agents *(1995)*
1481 N Elesio Felix Jr. Way
Suite 223
Avondale, AZ 85323-1216
Tel: (623) 932-0098 *Fax:* (623) 932-0212
TollFree: (888) 623-2211
E-Mail: naeba@naeba.info
Website: naeba.org
Staff: 2
Annual Budget: $250-500,000
Tax: 501(c)(6)

Personnel:
Executive Director: Kimberly Kahl CAE
　　E-Mail: kkahl@naeba.info
Coordinator, Membership Services: Kirt Myers
　　E-Mail: kmyers@naeba.info

Historical Note:
NAEBA is an organization of real estate professionals who have dedicated their business lives to representing only buyers of real estate. NAEBA's mission is to give today's home-buying consumers the level of service they deserve. Membership: $400 (Service Provider Affiliate); $350 (Master Brokerage/International Affiliate).

Continuing Education:
Certification Designation/s: CEBA

Meetings/Conferences: Annual

Publications:
Member Directory; on-line
NAEBAHood News

National Association of Export Companies *(1963)*
P.O. Box 3949
Grand Central Station
New York, NY 10163
Fax: (646) 349-9628
TollFree: (877) 291-4901
E-Mail: director@nexco.org
Website: nexco.org
Members: 300 companies
Staff: 3
Annual Budget: $25-50,000
Tax: 501(c)(3)

Personnel:
President: Barney Lehrer
Treasurer: Valerie Oakes-Locascio
Vice President, Marketing: Lisa Wallerstein

Historical Note:

Formerly (1983) National Association of Export Management Companies. NEXCO's purpose is to provide educational seminars and webinars on global issues to the international community. Members are importers, exporters, manufacturers, export management companies, international trade service vendors, and other international trade companies. Membership: $95 (Basic); $395 (Corporate); $1,000 (Sponsor).

Meetings/Conferences:
Number of non-conference events/year: 1

Publications:
Membership Directory; on-line
NEXCO Newsletter

Membership List Available to Non-members

National Association of Extension 4-H Agents
(1946)
20423 State Rd. Seven
Suite F6-491
Suite F6-491, FL 33498
Tel: (561) 477-8100
E-Mail: execdir@nae4ha.com
Website: nae4ha.com
Members: 3300 individuals
Staff: 7
Annual Budget: $500-1,000,000

Personnel:
Executive Director: Jody Rosen
    E-Mail: execdir@nae4ha.com
Vice President, Marketing and Outreach: Linda Aldridge
    E-Mail: laldridge@purdue.edu
Vice President , Finance and Operations: Tony Carrell
    E-Mail: tcarrell@purdue.edu
Contact, Conference Services: Kay Chelena
    E-Mail: kay@themanagementoffice.com
Contact, Publications: Joseph Donaldson
    E-Mail: jldonaldson@tennessee.edu
Vice President, Membership Services: Kim Gressley
    E-Mail: gressley@ag.arizona.edu
Vice President, Professional Development: Christy Price
    E-Mail: mcprice@wsu.edu

Historical Note:
Established as the National Association of County Club Agents, it became the National Association of County 4-H Club Agents and in 1969 assumed its present name. NAE4-HA's mission is to provide professional development an inclusive and supportive network integration of scholarship, research and practice. Membership: $70/year.

Meetings/Conferences: Annual
Conference Chair: Kay Chelena

Publications:
Journal of Youth Development; semi-annually
News & Views

National Association of Farm Broadcasting
(1944)
1100 Platte Falls Rd.
P.O. Box 500
Platte City, MO 64079
Tel: (816) 431-4032 Fax: (816) 431-4087
E-Mail: info@nafb.com
Website: nafb.com
Members: 600 individuals
Staff: 5
Annual Budget: $1-2,000,000
Tax: 501(c)(6)

Personnel:
Executive Director: Tom Brand
    E-Mail: tom@nafb.com
Director, Member Service: Aaron Corbet
    E-Mail: aaron@nafb.com
Director, News Service: Stacia Cudd
    E-Mail: stacia@nafb.com
Director, Marketing and Communications: Becki Rhoades
    E-Mail: becki@nafb.com
Manager, Operations: Susan Tally
    E-Mail: susan@nafb.com

Historical Note:
Founded as National Association of Radio Farm Directors (NARFD); became the National Association of Television-Radio Farm Directors in 1956 and assumed its present name in 2005. NAFB is dedicated to serving the interest of the agricultural community and creating value for its Broadcast member stations and networks. Membership: $100 (Management and Sales Council); $200 (Allied Industry Council); $25 (Student).

Meetings/Conferences: Annual

Publications:

eChats; monthly
Membership Directory; on-line

National Association of Farm Service Agency County Office Employees (1949)
P.O. Box 59
Norvelt, PA 15674
Tel: (662) 647-8857 Fax: (662) 647-5673
E-Mail: nascoemembership@bellsouth.net
Website: nascoe.org
Members: 10000 individuals
Staff: 2
Annual Budget: $250-500,000

Personnel:
President: John Lohr
    E-Mail: john.lohr@pa.usda.gov

Historical Note:
Formerly (1995) the National Association of ASCS County Office Employees and (1997) the National Association of FSA County Office. NASCOE seeks to assist and assure successful operation of the Farm Service Agency, to cooperate with common interest groups and organizations to conserve and improve nation's natural resources, secure equitable salaries, working conditions, and retirement provisions for all county office employees, and to promote professionalism of workers. Members are county office employees of the U. S. Department of Agriculture's Farm Service Agency. Membership: $40/year (Individual).

Meetings/Conferences:
Number of non-conference events/year: 1

Publications:
Legislative Activity Reports; monthly
NASCOE Newsletter; on-line

National Association of Farmer Elected Committees (NAFEC) (1965)
P.O. Box 666
Matador, TX 79244
Tel: (806) 269-0610 Fax: (806) 347-2974
E-Mail: nafec@jminsuredirect.om
Website: fsacountycommittees.org
Members: 8000 members
Staff: 2
Annual Budget: $25-50,000

Personnel:
President: Craig Turner
    E-Mail: turner_and_turner@yahoo.com

Historical Note:
National Association of Farmer Elected Committee members work to promote and improve the farmer elected committee system for the local administration of farm programs. Members are farmers. Membership: $35 (County Committee); $20 (Associate).

Publications:
NAFEC Newsletter

National Association of Farmers Market Nutrition Programs (1992)
P.O. Box 9080
Alexandria, VA 22304
Tel: (703) 837-0451 Fax: (919) 471-0137
E-Mail: info@nafmnp.org
Website: nafmnp.org
Staff: 1
Annual Budget: $100-250,000
Tax: 501(c)(3)

Personnel:
Executive Director: Phil A. Blalock
    E-Mail: phil@triangleassociatesinc.com

Historical Note:
NAFMNP's mission is to cultivate opportunities for consumers to buy fresh produce from local growers. Membership: $10 (Supporting); $20 (Sustaining); $30 (Leadership); $50 (National).

Meetings/Conferences: Annual

Publications:
NAFMNP Newsletter

National Association of Federal Credit Unions
(1967)
3138 Tenth St. North
Third Floor
Arlington, VA 22201-2149
Tel: (703) 522-4770 Fax: (703) 524-1082
TollFree: (800) 336-4644
E-Mail: membership@nafcunet.org
Website: nafcu.org

Members: 804 federal credit unions
Staff: 71
Annual Budget: $10-25,000,000

Personnel:
President and Chief Executive Officer: Fred R. Becker Jr.
    E-Mail: fbecker@nafcu.org
Executive Vice President, Government Affairs: B. Daniel Berger
    E-Mail: dberger@nafcu.org
Director, Public Relations: Patty Briotta
    E-Mail: pbriotta@nafcu.org
Managing Editor, News and Web Services: Susan Broaddus
    E-Mail: sbroaddus@nafcu.org
Director, Human Resources and Administration: Irene E. Cardon PHR
    E-Mail: icardon@nafcu.org
Director, Events and Education: Lisa Cox
    E-Mail: lcox@nafcu.org
General Counsel and Vice President, Regulatory Affairs: Carrie Hunt Esq.
    E-Mail: chunt@nafcu.org
Director, Finance: Gregory Johns
    E-Mail: gjohns@nafcu.org
Director, Information Technology: Eric Miller
    E-Mail: emiller@nafcu.org
Director, Membership Services: Chris Anne Sanyer
    E-Mail: csanyer@nafcu.org
Regulatory Affairs Counsel: Tessema Tefferi Esq.
    E-Mail: ttefferi@nafcu.org
Senior Vice President, Marketing and Communications: Karen Tyson
    E-Mail: ktyson@nafcu.org

Historical Note:
Provides its members with representation, information, education, and assistance to meet the challenges that cooperative financial institutions face in today's economic environment. Membership: dues vary according to a formula based on asset size.

Meetings/Conferences: Annual
Conference Chair: Lisa Cox
2013 - Austin, TX (Sheraton Austin Hotel at the Capitol)/Feb. 26 - 28
2013 - New Orleans, LA (Hyatt French Quarter)/March 12 - 14
2013 - Sonoma, CA (Fairmont Sonoma Mission Inn and Spa)/April 24 - 26
2013 - Asheville, NC (Renaissance Asheville Hotel)/ May 15 - 17
2013 - Boston, MA (Sheraton Boston Hotel)/July 9 - 13
Number of non-conference events/year: 18

Publications:
BSA Blast; quarterly
NAFCU Today; daily
NAFCU's Compliance Monitor; monthly
The Federal Credit Union; bi-monthly; adv.
Update; weekly

National Association of Federal Education Program Administrators (1975)
125 David Dr.
Sutter Creek, CA 95685
Tel: (916) 669-5102 Fax: (888) 487-6441
Website: nafepa.org
Members:
24 state affiliates
3600 individuals
Staff: 2
Annual Budget: $250-500,000
Tax: 501(c)(3)

Personnel:
President: Rick Carder
    E-Mail: rickc@sia-us.com

Historical Note:
Formerly (1984) the National Association of Administrators of State and Federal Education Programs and (1985) the National Association of Administrators of Federal Education Programs. Organized in 1975 to represent those professional educators employed by local and intermediate school districts, state departments of education, non-public schools, and education-product suppliers who have responsibility for supervising, coordinating or administering federally funded education programs. Membership: $100/ year (Individual).

Meetings/Conferences: Annual
Conference Chair: Debra Baros

Publications:

Membership Directory; on-line

National Association of Federal Veterinarians
(1918)
1910 Sunderland Pl. NW
Washington, DC 20036-1608
Tel: (202) 223-4878 Fax: (202) 223-4877
E-Mail: nafv@nafv.org
Website: nafv.net
Members: 1000 members
Staff: 3
Annual Budget: $100-250,000
Tax: 501(c)(5)

Personnel:
Executive Vice President: Michael Gilsdorf
    E-Mail: mgilsdorf@nafv.org
Secretary and Treasurer: John Sanders

Historical Note:
Affiliated with the American Veterinary Medical
Association. NAFV strives to serve both veterinarians and
the agencies they work for by facilitating communication,
making suggestions for improvements and working
collaboratively to address issues of concern. It also supports
the National Association of Federal Veterinarians Political
Action Committee. Membership: $59-234/year.

Publications:
Federal Veterinarian newsletter

National Association of Federally Impacted
Schools (1973)
444 N. Capitol St. NW
Suite 419
Washington, DC 20001
Tel: (202) 624-5455 Fax: (202) 624-5468
E-Mail: nafis@nafisdc.org
Website: nafisdc.org
Members: 600 school districts
Staff: 5
Annual Budget: $1-2,000,000
Tax: 501(c)(4)

Personnel:
Executive Director: John B. Forkenbrock
    E-Mail: johnfork@nafisdc.org
Director, Government Affairs: Jocelyn Bissonnette
    E-Mail: jocelyn@nafisdc.org
Director, Communications: Bryan Jernigan
    E-Mail: bryan@nafisdc.org
Director, Information Systems: Lynn Watkins
    E-Mail: lynn@nafisdc.org

Historical Note:
NAFIS educates congress on the importance of impact aid.
It works to ensure that the needs of federally connected
children are met with adequate federal funds. Membership:
$350/year.

Meetings/Conferences:
2013 - Washington, DC (Hyatt Regency Bethesda, near
    Washington, D.C.)/March 3 - 5
Number of non-conference events/year: 2

Publications:
Blue Book; annually
IMPACT; bi-monthly
Impact!Insider; irregular

National Association of Federally Licensed
Firearms Dealers (1972)
2620 Alamanda Ct.
Ft. Lauderdale, FL 33301
Tel: (954) 467-9994 Fax: (954) 463-2501
Website: amfire.com
Members: 25000 individuals
Staff: 11

Personnel:
President: Andrew Molchan
    E-Mail: km@400bellsouth.net

Historical Note:
NAFLFD members are individuals licensed to sell firearms.
Membership: $35/year.

Publications:
American Firearms Industry Magazine; monthly; adv.
Andy Molchan's E-Newsletter; on-line

National Association of Field Training Officers
2554 Ordinance Rd.
Santa Rosa, CA 95403
Tel: (707) 579-7760
Website: nafto.org

Staff: 2
Annual Budget: $50-100,000

Personnel:
Executive Director: Sgt. Kimber Williams
    E-Mail: KWILLIAM@sonoma-county.org

Historical Note:
NAFTO's mission is to promote and foster mutual
cooperation between Field Training Officers, other
members of their agencies, private industry and the public.
Membership: $40 (Annual); $520-2,400 (Agency).

Meetings/Conferences: Annual
Number of non-conference events/year: 1

National Association of Fire Equipment
Distributors (1963)
122 S. Michigan Ave.
Suite 1040
Chicago, IL 60603
Tel: (312) 461-9600 Fax: (312) 461-0777
Website: nafed.org
Members: 1200 companies
Staff: 6
Annual Budget: $1-2,000,000

Personnel:
Executive Director, Operations: Danny Harris
    E-Mail: dharris@nafed.org
Office Manager: Socorro Garcia
    E-Mail: socorrog@nafed.org
Executive Director, Technical: Norbert W. Makowka
    E-Mail: norbm@nafed.org
Communications Coordinator and Editor: Tamara
    Matthews
    E-Mail: tamaram@nafed.org

Historical Note:
NAFED's mission is to continuously improve the economic
environment, business performance and technical
competence in the fire protection industry. Membership:
$395 (Distributor); $550 (Supplier); $250 (Affiliate).

Continuing Education:
Certification Designation/s: FK, FN, FE

Meetings/Conferences:
2013 - Chicago, IL (Swissotel Chicago)/May 23 - 24
Number of non-conference events/year: 2

Publications:
Firewatch; quarterly; adv.
Firewire; quarterly
Membership Directory; annually

National Association of Fire Investigators (1961)
857 Tallevast Rd.
Sarasota, FL 34243
Tel: (941) 359-2800 Fax: (941) 351-5849
TollFree: (877) 506-6234
E-Mail: nafi_info@yahoo.com
Website: nafi.org
Members: 4200 individuals
Staff: 2
Annual Budget: $250-500,000
Tax: 501(c)(6)

Personnel:
President: John Kennedy

Historical Note:
NAFI's purpose is to increase the knowledge and improve
the skills of persons engaged in the investigation and
analysis of fires/explosions or in the litigation which ensues
from such investigations. Membership: $45 (Regular); $55
(Certified).

Continuing Education:
Certification Designation/s: CFII, CFEI, CVFI

Meetings/Conferences: Annual

Publications:
Membership Directory; on-line
NAFI Newsletter; on-line

National Association of Flavors and Food-
Ingredient Systems (1917)
3301 Route 66
Building C, Suite 205
Neptune, NJ 07753
Tel: (732) 922-3218 Fax: (732) 922-3590
E-Mail: info@naffs.org
Website: naffs.org
Members: 140 companies
Staff: 5
Annual Budget: $50-100,000

Personnel:

Executive Director: Bob Bauer
    E-Mail: bobbauer@naffs.org
Associate Director: Diane Davis
Treasurer: Pia Henzi

Historical Note:
Formerly (1974) National Fruit and Syrup Manufacturers
Association and (2003) National Association of Fruits,
Flavors and Syrups. NAFFS's mission is to provide a
forum for the exchange of technology and marketing
information. Members are manufacturers, processors and
suppliers of fruits, flavors, syrups, stabilizers, emulsifiers,
colors, sweeteners, cocoa and related food ingredients and
companies that serves food industry. Membership: $500/
year.

Meetings/Conferences: Annual
Number of non-conference events/year: 1

Publications:
Flavor & Ingredients Industry Report; annually
Membership Directory; annually

National Association of Flight Instructors (1967)
730 Grand St.
Allegan, MI 49010
Tel: (866) 806-6156 Fax: (920) 426-6865
TollFree: (866) 806-6156
E-Mail: nafi@nafinet.org
Website: nafinet.org
Members: 5000 individuals
Staff: 4
Annual Budget: $500-1,000,000
Tax: 501(c)(6)

Personnel:
Executive Director: Jason Blair
    E-Mail: jblair@eaa.org
Director, Sponsorships and Advertising: John Gibson
    E-Mail: jgibson@nafinet.org
Editor: David Hipschman
    E-Mail: editor@nafinet.org
Coordinator, Programs: John Niehaus
    E-Mail: jniehaus@nafinet.org

Historical Note:
NAFI's mission is to raise the professional standards for
flight instruction through education and organization.
Members are flight instructors certified by the Federal
Aviation Administration and others who support flight
instruction. Membership: $49/year.

Meetings/Conferences:
Conference Chair: John Niehaus

Publications:
FLYING Magazine
eMentor; bi-monthly; adv.
Mentor Magazine; monthly; adv.

National Association of Flood and Stormwater
Management Agencies (1978)
1333 H St. NW
West Tower, Tenth Floor
Washington, DC 20005
Tel: (202) 289-8625 Fax: (202) 530-3389
E-Mail: info@nafsma.org
Website: nafsma.org
Members: 102 agencies
Staff: 4
Annual Budget: $100-250,000
Tax: 501(c)(6)

Personnel:
Executive Director: Susan E. Gilson
    E-Mail: sgilson@nafsma.org

Historical Note:
Formerly the National Association of Urban Flood
Management Agencies; assumed its present name in
1989. Mission of NAFSMA is to advocate public policy,
encourage technologies and conduct education programs
that facilitate the achievement of the public service function
of its members. Members are public agencies and include
state, county and municipal organizations concerned with
the management of water resources in metropolitan areas.
Membership: $1,000- 9,000 (Regular-Local and State
Agencies, based on service population); $1,500-3,500
(Associate); $1,500-2,500 (Subscribing).

Meetings/Conferences:
Number of non-conference events/year: 1

Publications:
Flood and Stormwater Management Update; semi-
    monthly
Membership Directory; on-line

National Association of Flour Distributors (1919)

5350 Woodland Pl.
Canfield, OH 44406
Tel: (330) 718-6563 *Fax:* (877) 573-1230
Website: thenafd.com
Members:
104 Distributors, suppliers, and flour mills.
181 individuals
Staff: 3
Annual Budget: $100-250,000

Personnel:
Association Executive: G. Timothy Dove
    E-Mail: timdove51@gmail.com

Historical Note:
NAFD's mission is to serve the interests of the members who are engaged in the flour industry and those companies allied there to provide educational, professional and networking opportunities. Members are brokers, distributors, manufacturers and other professionals allied with the flour industry. Membership: $250/year.

Meetings/Conferences: Annual
2013 - Scottsdale, AZ (The Phoenician)/May 15 - 19
2014 - Naples, FL (The Ritz Carlton)/May 14 - 18
Number of non-conference events/year: 1

Publications:
Membership Directory; annually
The Flour Distributor; semi-annually

National Association of Foreign Trade Zones
(1973)
1001 Connecticut Ave. NW
Suite 350
Washington, DC 20036
Tel: (202) 331-1950 *Fax:* (202) 331-1994
E-Mail: info@naftz.org
Website: naftz.org
Members: 800 organizations
Staff: 5
Annual Budget: $1-2,000,000
Tax: 501(c)(6)

Personnel:
President: Daniel T. Griswold
Manager, Education and Meetings: Victoria Cartwright
Manager, Financial and Administrative Affairs: Matthew S. Dougherty
Manager, Communications and Member Relations: Brian Picone

Historical Note:
NAFTZ works to promote and improve FTZs and their use. Operator/User members are private companies that operate a zone or subzone, or benefits from the use of FTZ procedures. Membership: $300-1200/year.

Meetings/Conferences: Annual
Conference Chair: Victoria Cartwright
2013 - Charleston, SC (DoubleTree by Hilton)/May 12 - 13
Number of non-conference events/year: 1

Publications:
Membership Directory; on-line
Newsletter; on-line

National Association of Forensic Economics
(1986)
P.O. Box 394
Mt. Union, PA 17066
Tel: (814) 542-3253 *Fax:* (814) 542-3253
TollFree: (866) 370-6233
Website: nafe.net
Members: 855 individuals and organizations
Staff: 3
Annual Budget: $100-250,000

Personnel:
Executive Director: Jim Rodgers
    E-Mail: jdr@psu.edu
President: Steven J. Shapiro
    E-Mail: sshapiro@analyticresources.com
Contact, Membership Services and Publications: Nancy Eldredge
    E-Mail: nancy@nafe.net

Historical Note:
Formerly (1992) National Association of Forensic Economists. NAFE's mission is to foster research and education in the application of economics to litigation. Members are economists, accountants, finance and business professionals, vocational counselors, lawyers, and actuaries engaged in such fields as business valuation, commercial litigation, employment litigation, and personal injury and

wrongful death torts. Membership: $165 (Individual/Institutional); $80 (Student).

Meetings/Conferences: Annual
Number of non-conference events/year: 3

Publications:
Journal of Forensic Economics; bi-annually
NAFE Membership Directory; biennially
NAFE Newsletter; quarterly

National Association of Foster Grandparent Program Directors *(1971)*
3107 SW 21st St.
Topeka, KS 66604
Website: nafgpd.org
Members: 325 individuals
Staff: 2
Annual Budget: $100-250,000
Tax: 501(c)(3)

Personnel:
Treasurer: Connie Stewart
    E-Mail: connie.stewart@kni.ks.gov

Historical Note:
NAFGPD's purpose is to provide a means for communication between the Foster Grandparent Programs, related organizations and agencies and to explore areas of general interest affecting older adults. Membership: $100 (Professional); $65 (Supporting); $150 (Sponsor).

Meetings/Conferences: Annual
2013 - Kansas City, MO (THE EMBASSY SUITES HOTEL)/April 7 - 10

Publications:
Membership Directory; on-line
NAFGPD Update; irregular

National Association of Fraternal Insurance Counsellors *(1950)*
211 Canal Rd.
Waterloo, WI 53594
Tel: (920) 478-9586 *Fax:* (920) 478-9586
TollFree: (866) 478-3880
E-Mail: office@nafic.org
Website: nafic.org
Members: 4700 individuals
Staff: 2
Annual Budget: $250-500,000

Personnel:
Executive Director: Anna Maenner

Historical Note:
Formerly (1966) Fraternal Insurance Counsellors Association and an affiliate of the Fraternal Field Managers Association, NAFIC's mission is to serve the Fraternal Insurance Agent who has achieved the Fraternal Insurance Counsellor (FIC) or Fraternal Insurance Counsellor Fellow (FICF) designation. Membership: $95/year.

Meetings/Conferences: Annual
2013 - Savannah, GA (Hilton Savannah DeSoto)/May 6 - 8

Publications:
The FIC Perspective

National Association of Free Clinics *(2001)*
1800 Diagonal Rd.
Suite 600
Alexandria, VA 22314
Tel: (703) 647-7427 *Fax:* (866) 875-3827
E-Mail: info@freeclinics.us
Website: nafcclinics.org
Members: 1200 free clinics
Staff: 3
Annual Budget: $1-2,000,000
Tax: 501(c)(3)

Personnel:
Executive Director: Nicole D. Lamoureux
    E-Mail: nlamoureux@freeclinics.us
Manager, Outreach and Operations: Ariana Gordillo
Manager, Membership Office: Lau'ren Thornton

Historical Note:
NAFC provides research, education and resources to promote, strengthen and advocate for member organizations and the communities they serve. Membership: $100-3,500/year (Based on Current Operating Budget).

Meetings/Conferences: Annual

Publications:
NAFC E-Newsletter; on-line

National Association of Fundraising Ticket Manufacturers *(1983)*
335 Atrium Office Bldg.
1295 Bandana Blvd.
St. Paul, MN 55108
Tel: (651) 644-4710 *Fax:* (651) 644-5904
Website: naftm.org
Members: 5 manufacturers
Staff: 2
Annual Budget: $100-250,000
Tax: 501(c)(6)

Personnel:
Legal Counsel: Mary Magnuson
    E-Mail: marymagnuson@naftm.org

Historical Note:
NAFTM's mission is to keep its members informed of ever-changing product standards, gaming laws, regulations, and enforcement practices. Members are companies that manufacture pull tabs, bingo paper, and related supplies for the North American charitable gaming industry.

National Association of Geoscience Teachers *(1938)*
C/O Carleton College, B-SERC
One N. College St.
Northfield, MN 55057
Tel: (507) 222-5634 *Fax:* (507) 222-5175
Website: nagt.org
Members: 1400 individuals
Staff: 10
Annual Budget: $250-500,000
Tax: 501(c)(3)

Personnel:
Executive Director: Cathryn Manduca
    E-Mail: cmanduca@carleton.edu
Contact, General Inquiries: Linda Goozen
    E-Mail: lgoozen@carleton.edu
Editor-in-Chief: Julie Libarkin
    E-Mail: jge@msu.edu

Historical Note:
Founded as the Association of College Geology Teachers, dropped "College" from name in 1946, became the National Association of Geology Teachers in 1958 and assumed its present name in 1996. NAGT is a member society of the American Geological Institute that works to emphasize the cultural significance of the earth sciences and to disseminate knowledge in this field to the general public. Members are K-12 teachers, college and university faculty as well as educators working with the general public through outlets such as museums and science centers. Membership: $20 (Student Domestic); $45 (Regular Domestic); $57 (Regular International); $35 (K-12 Teacher Domestic); $47 (K-12 Teacher International); $30 (Retired Domestic); $42 (Retired International); $20 (Student Domestic); $32 (Student International).

Meetings/Conferences: Annual

Publications:
e-News Magazine; quarterly; adv.
In the Trenches; quarterly; adv.
Journal of Geoscience Education; quarterly; adv.

National Association of Government Archives and Records Administrators *(1984)*
1450 Western Ave.
Suite 101
Albany, NY 12203
Tel: (518) 694-8472 *Fax:* (518) 463-8656
E-Mail: nagara@caphill.com
Website: nagara.org
Members: 398 individuals and state agencies
Staff: 1
Annual Budget: $50-100,000

Personnel:
Coordinator, Membership Services and Publications: Steve Grandin
    E-Mail: nagara@caphill.com

Historical Note:
NAGARA's mission is to serve for the effective use and management of government information and to publicly recognize their efforts and accomplishments. It also seeks to promote the availability of documentary legacy by improving the quality of records and information management at all levels of government. Membership: $75 (Individual); $1,200 (Federal); $600 (State/Combined Programs); $300 (State/Separate); $150 (Local Government Programs).

Meetings/Conferences: Semi-Annual

Publications:

Clearinghouse; quarterly; adv.
Crossroads; on-line
Membership Directory; on-line
NAGARA Talk; adv.

Membership List Available to Non-members

National Association of Government Communicators (1976)
201 Park Washington Ct.
Falls Church, VA 22046-4527
Tel: (703) 538-1787 *Fax:* (703) 241-5603
E-Mail: info@nagconline.org
Website: nagc.com
Members: 500 individuals
Staff: 6
Annual Budget: $100-250,000

Personnel:
Executive Director and Secretary: Elizabeth B. Armstrong CAE, MAM
    E-Mail: armstrong@nagconline.org
Meetings Registrar and Membership Services: Mary Ackleson
    E-Mail: ackleson@nagconline.org
Manager, Financial Services: Hui-Ling Liang
    E-Mail: hliang@asmii.net
Manager, Communications: Dawn M. Shiley-Danzeisen
    E-Mail: shiley@nagconline.org
Manager, Website Content: Karen Thompson
    E-Mail: thompson@nagconline.org
Director, Professional Development: John S. Verrico
    E-Mail: john.verrico@dhs.gov

Historical Note:
Product of a merger of the Federal Editors Association, the Government Information Organization, and the Armed Forces Writers' League. NAGC is a network of federal, state and local government employees who disseminate information within and outside the government. Members are editors, writers, graphic artists, video professionals, broadcasters, photographers, information specialists and agency spokespersons. It is also a member of the Council of Communication Societies. Membership: $125 (Active); $495 (Organization/Agency); $250 (Affiliate); $1,000 (Affiliate Group-five individuals); $50 (Retired); $35 (Student); $60 (Military).

Meetings/Conferences: Annual
Conference Chair: Mary Ackleson
2013 - Arlington, VA (Sheraton Pentagon City Hotel)/ April 16 - 19

Publications:
Membership Directory; on-line
NAGC News; quarterly

National Association of Government Defined Contribution Administrators (1980)
201 E. Main St.
Suite 1405
Lexington, KY 40507
Tel: (859) 514-9161 *Fax:* (859) 514-9188
E-Mail: InfoNAGDCA@AMRms.com
Website: nagdca.org
Members: 275 government agency companies
Staff: 3
Annual Budget: $500-1,000,000
Tax: 501(c)(6)

Personnel:
Association Director: Tracy Tucker
    E-Mail: ttucker@amrms.com
Director, Conferences and Events: Joy Kirchner
    E-Mail: jkirchner@amrms.com

Historical Note:
Founded as National Association of Government Deferred Compensation Administrators, assumed its current name in 2000. NAGDCA's mission is to unite representatives from state and local governments along with private sector organizations that service and support defined contribution plans. Membership: $300 (Government; New Member); $600 (Government; Existing); $900 (Industry); $400 (Associate Industry).

Continuing Education:
Certification Designation/s: CRASM, CRC, INFRE

Meetings/Conferences: Annual
Conference Chair: Joy Kirchner
2013 - Louisville, KY (Kentucky Exposition Center)/ Sept. 7 - 11
2014 - San Antonio, TX (Grand Hyatt San Antonio)/ Sept. 6 - 10
2015 - Indianapolis, IN (JW Marriot Indianapolis)/ Sept. 25 - Oct. 1

Publications:
Membership Directory; on-line
NAGDCA Newsletter; quarterly

National Association of Government Employees (1961)
159 Burgin Pkwy.
Quincy, MA 02169
Tel: (617) 376-0220 *Fax:* (617) 472-7566
TollFree: (866) 412-7762
E-Mail: nage@erols.com
Website: nage.org
Members: 200000 individuals
Staff: 100
Annual Budget: $10-25,000

Personnel:
President: David J. Holway
Director, Membership Services: Sheila Anderson
    E-Mail: membership@nage.org
Treasurer: James Farley
    E-Mail: jfarley@nage.org
Director, Communications: Stephanie Zaiser
    E-Mail: szaiser@nage.org

Historical Note:
NAGE is a labor union, represents civilian government employees, which includes the National Association of Nurses, National Association of Health Care Workers, International Brotherhood of Correctional Officers, and International Brotherhood of Police Officers, sponsors and supports the Government Employees' Political Research Institute and the National Association of Government Employees Political Action Committee.

National Association of Government Guaranteed Lenders (NAGGL)
215 E. Ninth Ave.
Stillwater, OK 74076
Tel: (405) 377-4022 *Fax:* (405) 377-3931
Website: naggl.org
Staff: 9
Annual Budget: $2-5,000,000

Personnel:
President and Chief Executive Officer: Anthony R. Wilkinson
    E-Mail: twilkinson@naggl.org
Assistant Vice President, Marketing: Jennifer Brake
Executive Vice President: Jane Butler
    E-Mail: jbutler@naggl.org
Assistant Vice President, Meeting Planning: Pam Nichols
Vice President, Education: Susanne Queen
Member Relations and Support Services Specialist: Casady Sisco
Chief Operations Officer: Jennifer Sterrett-O'Neill
    E-Mail: joneill@naggl.org
Vice President, Convention Services: Cheryl Stone

Historical Note:
NAGGL serves the needs and represent the interests of the small business lending community that utilizes SBA and other government guaranteed loan programs. Membership: $2,625 (Sustaining); $495-2,095 (Regular); $700 (Associate); $875 (Indirect Lender).

Meetings/Conferences: Annual
Conference Chair: Jane Butler

Publications:
E-Newsletter; monthly
Member Directory; on-line

National Association of Government Labor Officials (1914)
P.O. Box 504
Jefferson City, MO 65102
Tel: (573) 751-3978 *Fax:* (573) 751-4135
Website: naglo.org
Members: 50 individuals
Staff: 3
Annual Budget: $50-100,000

Personnel:
President: Lawrence (Larry) G. Rebman
    E-Mail: larry.rebman@labor.mo.gov
Secretariat: Jeannine Konieczny
    E-Mail: jeannine.konieczny@dol.state.ga.us

Historical Note:
Founded as the International Association of Governmental Labor Officials; assumed its present name in 1979. NAGLO's mission is to improve the protection of worker's rights, and to promote safe and healthy workplaces. Members are directors and commissioners of state labor

departments. *Membership: $1,500 (Active); $1,000 (Associate Government/International); 2,000 (Affiliate).*

Publications:
NAGLO Newsletter; irregular

National Association of Graduate Admissions Professionals (1987)
P.O. Box 14605
Lenexa, KS 66285-4605
Tel: (913) 895-4616 *Fax:* (913) 895-4652
E-Mail: info@nagap.org
Website: nagap.org
Members: 1500 individuals
Staff: 5
Annual Budget: $1-2,000,000
Tax: 501(c)(3)

Personnel:
Executive Director: Monica Evans-Lombe
    E-Mail: mevanslombe@goamp.com
Manager, Meetings: Debbie Jennings , CMP
    E-Mail: djennings@goamp.com
Association Manager: Dana VanMeerhaeghe
    E-Mail: dana.vanmeerhaeghe@goamp.com

Historical Note:
Founded as New England Association of Graduate Admissions Professionals. NAGAP's mission is to support, advance, and engage graduate enrollment professionals by promoting integrity, excellence, and collaboration through education and professional development. Provides an opportunity to network with professional colleagues at all sizes and types of institutions. Membership: $225 (Single); $450 (Affiliate); $50 (Retired).

Meetings/Conferences: Annual
2013 - Orlando, FL (Gaylord Palms Resort and Convention Center-Orlando)/April 24 - 27
2014 - San Diego, CA (Manchester Grand Hyatt San Diego)/April 30 - May 3
Number of non-conference events/year: 2

Publications:
E-Newsletter
Graduate Fairs Calendar; on-line
Membership Directory; on-line

Membership List Available to Non-members

National Association of Graduate-Professional Students
P.O. Box 96503,
Suite 36821
Washington, DC 20090-6503
Tel: (202) 643-8043
E-Mail: office@nagps.org
Website: nagps.org
Members: 60 universities and colleges
Staff: 6
Annual Budget: $50-100,000

Personnel:
President and Chief Executive Officer: Matt Cooper
    E-Mail: president@nagps.org
Executive Director: Jackie Tyson
Director, Communications: Zach Aman
    E-Mail: communications@nagps.org
Director, Finance: Sophie Ni
    E-Mail: finance@nagps.org
Director, Administration: Rosario Michelle Ramirez
    E-Mail: administration@nagps.org
Director, Relations: Jared Voskuhl
    E-Mail: relations@nagps.org

Historical Note:
A non-profit organization for improving the quality of graduate and professional student life in the United States of America. Membership: $12,500 (Legacy, Lifetime); $75-750/year.

Meetings/Conferences: Annual

Publications:
Membership Directory; on-line

National Association of Graphic and Product Identification Manufacturers (1951)
1300 Sumner Ave.
Cleveland, OH 44115-2851
Tel: (216) 241-7333 *Fax:* (216) 241-0105
E-Mail: gpistaff@thomasamc.com
Website: gpionline.org
Members: 80 companies
Staff: 12
Annual Budget: $100-250,000

Personnel:
President: Randy White
Chief Financial Officer: Steve Doerfler

Historical Note:
Formerly Metal Etching and Fabricating Association. Became National Association of Metal Name Plate Manufacturers (1967), then National Association of Name Plate Manufacturers (1979). Assumed its current name in 1994. GPI's mission is to support member's business in the form of business and technical programs, promote the general welfare of the industries that manufacture and sell identification and related products and promoting communications from suppliers on new materials, equipment and processes. Membership: $1300-2,800 (Corporate-Voting, based on no. of employees); $1,049.00(annual), $1,574.00 (9 months), $2,623.00(15 months) for Associate-Non Voting.

Meetings/Conferences: Semi-Annual
2013 - La Jolla, CA (The Lodge at Torrey Pines)/April 9 - 12
2013 - Denver, CO (The Sheraton Downtown)/Sept. 22 - 24

Publications:
Membership Directory; on-line
The Communiqué

National Association of Health and Educational Facilities Finance Authorities
P.O. Box 906
Oakhurst, NJ 07755
Fax: (888) 414-5713
TollFree: (888) 414-5713
E-Mail: info@whefa.com
Website: naheffa.com
Members: 41 member associations
Staff: 6

Personnel:
President and Director: Pamela Lenane
Director, Operations: Nichole Doxey
   E-Mail: ndoxey@naheffa.com
Conference Coordinator: Douglas Mitchell
   E-Mail: mitchdorf@gmail.com
Contact, Sponsorship Program: Larry Nines
   E-Mail: info@whefa.com
Treasurer and Director: Don Templeton

Historical Note:
Created from the merger of the National Council of Health Facilities Finance Authorities and the National Association of Higher Educational Facilities Authorities. NAHEFFA's mission is to provide assistance and support to its member higher education authorities through education, communication, advocacy and leadership development.

Meetings/Conferences: Annual
Conference Chair: Douglas Mitchell
2013 - Pensacola, FL (Hilton Pensacola Beach Gulf Front)/April 15 - 17

Publications:
Membership Directory; on-line
NAHEFFA Newsletter; quarterly

National Association of Health Data Organizations
(1986)
448 E. 400 South
Suite 301
Salt Lake City, UT 84111
Tel: (801) 532-2299 *Fax:* (801) 532-2228
E-Mail: info@nahdo.org
Website: nahdo.org
Members: 46 organizations
Staff: 4
Annual Budget: $500-1,000,000
Tax: 501(c)(3)

Personnel:
Executive Director: Denise Love
   E-Mail: dlove@nahdo.org
Meeting Coordinator: Carly Barrell
   E-Mail: cbarrell@nahdo.org
Membership Coordinator: Erin Eppler
   E-Mail: eeppler@nahdo.org

Historical Note:
NAHDO is a non-profit membership and educational association dedicated to improving health care data collection and use. Members are federal and state health data organizations, software developers, consultants, hospital associations, health series researchers, insurers, managed care firms, cost containment companies, and health trade groups. Membership: $3,000 (Public Organization); $3,500 (Non-for-Profit); $4,000 (For Profit); $1,000 (Individual).

Meetings/Conferences: Annual
Conference Chair: Carly Barrell

Membership List Available to Non-members

National Association of Health Education Centers
(1989)
1533 N. RiverCenter Dr.
Milwaukee, WI 53212-3913
Tel: (414) 390-2188 *Fax:* (414) 390-2199
E-Mail: nahec@nahec.org
Website: nahec.org
Staff: 1
Annual Budget: $50-100,000

Personnel:
Executive Director: David Midland

Historical Note:
NAHEC's mission is to make health education broadly accessible, effective, and sustainable. Membership: $500-2,000 (based on Annual Operating Budget of the member institution).

Meetings/Conferences: Annual

Publications:
eNAHEC; monthly
Member directory

National Association of Health Services Executives
(1968)
1050 Connecticut Ave. NW
Tenth Floor
Washington, DC 20036
Tel: (202) 772-1030 *Fax:* (202) 772-1072
E-Mail: nahsehq@nahse.org
Website: nahse.org
Members: 1700 individuals
Staff: 2
Annual Budget: $500-1,000,000
Tax: 501(c)(3)

Personnel:
President and Chief Executive Officer: Andrea R. Price-Carter FACHE

Historical Note:
NAHSE's mission is to ensure greater participation of African Americans and minority groups in the health care field while elevating the quality of health care services rendered to African Americans, minorities and other underserved communities. Members are African-American health care executives. Membership: $1,500 (Institutional); $200 (Personal); $50 (Student Type I); $100 (Student Type II); $500 (Associate).

Publications:
Membership Directory; on-line
NAHSE Newsletter; on-line

National Association of Health Unit Coordinators
(1980)
1947 Madron Rd.
Rockford, IL 61107-1716
Tel: (815) 633-4351 *Fax:* (815) 633-4438
TollFree: (888) 226-2482
E-Mail: office@nahuc.org
Website: nahuc.org
Members: 1900 individuals
Staff: 5
Annual Budget: $100-250,000

Personnel:
President: Juliann Olsen
   E-Mail: juliann.olsen@imail.org
Association Manager: Patricia N. Rice
Director, Membership Services: Sara Brown
   E-Mail: sbtx53@hotmail.com
Director, Communications: Nadine Stratford
   E-Mail: nadine.stratford@imail.org
Director, Education Board: Linda R. Winslow
   E-Mail: winslow.linda@gmail.com

Historical Note:
Formerly (1990) National Association of Health Unit Clerks/Coordinators. NAHUC is dedicated to promoting health unit coordinating as a profession through education and certification, complying with the NAHUC Standards of Practice, Standards of Education, and Code of Ethics. Members are coordinators of non-clinical nursing unit activities, educators, supervisors, students and graduates in the field. Membership: $20-75/year.

Continuing Education:
Certification Designation/s: NAHUC

Meetings/Conferences: Annual
2013 - Orlando, FL (Rosen Plaza Hotel)/Aug. 7 - 10

2014 - Bloomington, MN (Hilton MSP Airport/Mall of America)/Aug. 6 - 9
2015 - Savannah, GA (Hilton Savannah DeSoto)/Aug. 5 - 8

Publications:
The Coordinator; quarterly; adv.

Membership List Available to Non-members

National Association of Healthcare Access Management *(1974)*
2025 M St. NW
Suite 800
Washington, DC 20036
Tel: (202) 367-1125 *Fax:* (202) 367-2125
E-Mail: info@naham.org
Website: naham.org
Members: 1700 individuals
Staff: 13
Annual Budget: $1-2,000,000
Tax: 501(c)(6)

Personnel:
Executive Director: Mike Copps
   E-Mail: mcopps@naham.org
Manager, Education and Learning Services: Stacey Barnes
   E-Mail: sbarnes@naham.org
Senior Associate, Membership Affairs and Certification Services: Belle McFarland
   E-Mail: bmcfarland@naham.org
Senior Director, Public Policy: Frank Moore
   E-Mail: fmoore@smithbucklin.com
Coordinator, Marketing and Communications: Lindsay Pullen
   E-Mail: lpullen@naham.org
Conference Planner: Alex Zapple
   E-Mail: azapple@naham.org

Historical Note:
Formerly (1990) the National Association of Hospital Admitting Managers. NAHAM provides quality educational programs and interaction for professionals engaged in the management of patient access services in healthcare delivery (patient scheduling, admissions, registration, and revenue cycle management). Membership: $165 (Active); $1,500 (Business Partner); $0 (Honorary, granted upon recommendation of the board of directors); $60 (Associate).

Continuing Education:
Enrollment: 1700
Certification Designation/s: CHAA, CHAM

Meetings/Conferences: Annual
Conference Chair: Alex Zapple
2013 - Atlanta, GA (Hyatt Regency Atlanta)/May 15 - 18
2014 - Ft. Lauderdale, FL (Westin Diplomat Resort and Spa)/May 13 - 16
Number of non-conference events/year: 5

Publications:
CertAlert
Connections; quarterly
Membership Directory; on-line
NAHAM Access Management Journal; quarterly
Weekly NAHAM Newsbrief; weekly

Membership List Available to Non-members

National Association of Healthcare Education Centers *(1910)*
7044 S. 13th St.
Oak Creek, WI 53154
Tel: (414) 908-4953 *Fax:* (414) 768-8001
E-Mail: info@nationalahec.org
Website: nationalahec.org
Members:
235 centers
56 AHEC programs
120 medical schools and 600 nursing and allied health schools
Staff: 1
Tax: 501(c)(3)

Personnel:
Executive Director: Robert M. Trachtenberg MS

Historical Note:
AHEC works to enhance access to quality health care, particularly primary and preventive care, by improving the supply and distribution of healthcare professionals through community/academic educational partnerships. Members are governmental agencies, educational institutions, nonprofit organizations and businesses professionally affiliated with local or state level AHEC organizations and medallion members are organizations, institutions,

businesses, or individual donors that provide annual financial support to NAO with or without current local or state affiliation with an AHEC. *Membership: $640-1760 (Basic Organizational); $2,000-3,000 (Medallion Organizational); $25 (Student); $250 (Affiliate).*

Meetings/Conferences: Annual

Publications:
Journal of the National AHEC Organization; quarterly; adv.
Membership Directory; on-line
NAO Quarterly e-news; quarterly

National Association of Heavy Equipment Training Schools
P.O. Box 50682
Henderson, NV 89016
Tel: (702) 518-4702 *Fax:* (702) 644-9316
TollFree: (888) 879-9492
E-Mail: admin@nahets.com
Website: heavy-equipment-school.com
Members: 5 schools
Staff: 6

Personnel:
Executive Director: Matt Klabacka
    E-Mail: mattk@nahets.com
Chief Operating Officer: Robert A. Albano
Corporate Counsel: Garry Hayes
Contact, Payroll and Human Resources: Julie Johnson
Director, Finance: Jenene Olsen
Technology Director: Brian Thornton

Historical Note:
NAHETS provides advanced heavy equipment operator training and education whose mission is to improve standardized heavy equipment and crane training for today's modern operators.

Continuing Education:
Certification Designation/s: OPCAT

National Association of Hispanic and Latino Studies (1992)
P.O. Box 6670
Scarborough, ME 04070-6670
Tel: (207) 839-8004 *Fax:* (207) 839-3776
E-Mail: natlaffiliates@earthlink.net
Website: naaas.org/nahls.html
Members: 176 individuals,2 organizations
Staff: 3
Annual Budget: $100-250,000

Personnel:
Executive Director: Dr. Lemuel Berry Jr., PhD
    E-Mail: naaasconference@earthlink.net

Historical Note:
In 1996, the National Association of Hispanic and Latino Studies became an affiliate of NAAAS. The National Association of Native American Studies and the International Association of Asian Studies became affiliates in 1998.NAAAS goals are to To serve as a resource for scholars in the field who desire information and support for research related to the African and African American, Hispanic, Latino(a) and Chicano(a), Native American and Asian experiences. Membership: $3,000 (Life Membership); $500 (Institutional Membership); $125 (Individual Membership); $100 (Student Membership/ Sustaining Donor).

Meetings/Conferences: Annual
2013 - Baton Rouge, LA (Crowne Plaza Executive Center Baton Rouge)/Feb. 11 - 16

Publications:
Affiliate News
Journal of Intercultural Disciplines

National Association of Hispanic Federal Executives (1980)
P.O. Box 23270
Washington, DC 20026-3270
Tel: (202) 315-3942 *Fax:* (202) 478-0806
Website: nahfe.org
Members: 30 national Hispanic organizations
Staff: 4
Annual Budget: $50-100,000
Tax: 501(c)(3)

Personnel:
President: Al Gallegos
    E-Mail: president@nahfe.org
General Counsel: Gilberto Garcia Jr.
    E-Mail: garciajr.gilberto@dol.gov
Secretary: Dafna Silberfeld
    E-Mail: dafna@nahfe.org

Senior Policy Advisor: Ed Valenzuela PhD
    E-Mail: dredv@aol.com

Historical Note:
NAHFE's purpose is to help identify, encourage, prepare and promote the advancement of hispanics into the SES ranks. Membership: $50/year.

National Association of Hispanic Firefighters (1995)
1220 L St. NW
Suite 100-199
Washington, DC 20005
Tel: (877) 342-6243 *Fax:* (855) 759-6243
TollFree: (877) 342-6243
E-Mail: info@nahf.org
Website: nahf.org
Staff: 2
Annual Budget: $25-50,000

Personnel:
President and Chief Executive Officer: Daniel Valenzuela
    E-Mail: D.Valenzuela@nahf.org
Executive Vice President, Communications: Randy Rodriquez
    E-Mail: R.Rodriquez@nahf.org

Historical Note:
NAHF's goal is to encourage fire departments to take a proactive approach to prevent harm through bilingual fire and life safety programs to reduce the loss of life and property. Membership: $30 (Individual); $24 (Retired); $1,000 (Corporate Member); $500 (Friend).

Publications:
NAHF On-Line Newletter; on-line; adv.

National Association of Hispanic Journalists (1984)
1050 Connecticut Ave. NW
Tenth Floor
Washington, DC 20036
Tel: (202) 662-7145 *Fax:* (202) 662-7144
TollFree: (888) 346-6245
E-Mail: nahj@nahj.org
Website: nahj.org
Members: 1500 members
Staff: 9
Annual Budget: $1-2,000,000

Personnel:
Interim Executive Director: Anna Lopez Buck
    E-Mail: alopez@nahj.org

Historical Note:
NAHJ is dedicated to the recognition and professional advancement of Hispanics in the news industry. Membership: $75 (Regular/Associate/Academic); $20 (Student); $110 (Individual); $2,000 (Corporate), $50 (Professionals).

Meetings/Conferences:
Number of non-conference events/year: 1

Publications:
Membership Directory; on-line
NAHJ Noticias Newsletter

National Association of Hispanic Nurses (1975)
1455 Pennsylvania Ave. NW
Suite 400
Washington, DC 20004
Tel: (202) 387-2477 *Fax:* (202) 483-7183
E-Mail: info@thehispanicnurses.org
Website: thehispanicnurses.org
Members: 3000 Members
Staff: 2
Annual Budget: $500-1,000,000
Tax: 501(c)(3)

Personnel:
Executive Director and Chief Executive Officer: Celia Trigo Besore CAE, MBA
    E-Mail: cbesore@thehispanicnurses.org
Administrative Associate: Margaret Farrell
    E-Mail: mfarrell@thehispanicnurses.org

Historical Note:
NAHN's mission is to advance the health in Hispanic communities and to lead, promote and advocate the educational, professional, and leadership opportunities for Hispanic nurses. Membership: $100-225 (Full/Associate); $50-75 (Affiliate/International); $75-90 (Retired); $30-40 (Student); $5,000 (Corporate).

Meetings/Conferences: Annual
2013 - New Orleans, LA (Astor Crowne Plaza Hotel)/ Aug. 6 - 9

Publications:
Hispanic Health Care International; quarterly
Membership Directory; on-line
NAHN Newsletters; irregular

National Association of Hispanic Publications (1982)
529 14th St. NW
Suite 1126
Washington, DC 20045
Tel: (202) 662-7250 *Fax:* (202) 662-7251
E-Mail: info@nahp.org
Website: nahp.org
Members: 234 Publication Members
Staff: 3
Annual Budget: $250-500,000
Tax: 501(c)(6)

Personnel:
Executive Director: Amy Hinojosa
    E-Mail: ahinojosa@nahp.org
Vice President, Membership: Jose Luis B. Garza
    E-Mail: pepebgarza@yahoo.com
Vice President, Marketing: Fanny Miller
    E-Mail: Fanny.miller@ellatino.net

Historical Note:
NAHP's mission is to further the excellence, recognition and usage of Hispanic publications by providing access to professional development opportunities to better serve and empower Hispanic communities. Membership is open to Spanish language and Hispanic owned newspapers, magazines and related media as well as businesses that offer products and services to this market throughout the United States. Membership: $1,000-10,000 (Partner); $300-1,600 (Associate/General, based on circulation); $50 (Student); $75 (Professor); $100 (Creative); $150 (Author); $200 (Consultant).

Meetings/Conferences: Annual

Publications:
The NAHP Membership Directory

National Association of Hispanic Real Estate Professionals (1999)
5414 Oberlin Dr.
Suite 230
San Diego, CA 92121
Tel: (858) 622-9046
Website: nahrep.org
Members: 18000 individuals
Staff: 4
Annual Budget: $25-50,000
Tax: 501(c)(6)

Personnel:
Co-Executive Director: Gary Acosta
    E-Mail: gacosta@nvam.net
Senior Manager, Operations: Marisa Calderon
    E-Mail: mcalderon@nahrep.org
Membership Services: Yadira Jimenez
    E-Mail: membership@nahrep.org
Director, Communications: Mary Mancera
    E-Mail: mary@phasetwocommunications.com

Historical Note:
NAHREP's mission is to increase the rate of sustainable Hispanic homeownership by empowering the real estate professionals that serve the community and accomplishes this by providing educational tools and a networking forum, and through the power of advocacy. Members are real estate agents, brokers, loan officers, mortgage brokers, title officers, escrow officers, appraisers, insurance agents. NAHREP has 60 affiliates in 18 states. Membership: $199 (Platinum); $99 (Full,vary depending on chapter pricing); $1000-10,000 (Corporate); $0 (Associate).

Continuing Education:
Certification Designation/s: CTC

Publications:
Membership Directory; on-line
NAHREP News Update; irregular

National Association of Home and Workshop Writers (1973)
P.O. Box 12
Baker, NV 89311
Tel: (775) 234-7167 *Fax:* (775) 234-7361
Website: nahww.org
Members: 100 individuals
Staff: 4
Annual Budget: Under $10,000

Personnel:
President: Monte Burch

Newsletter Editor: Rich Day
Membership Contact, Secretary and Treasurer: Susan Geary
    E-Mail: Geary775@mwpower.net
Webmaster: Dan Ramsey

Historical Note:
The NAHWW is a group of friends with a common interest in helping others learn how to do things through instructions. Membership: $36 (Active/Associate); $220 (Supporting).

Publications:
Membership, Directory; on-line
NAHWW Newsletter; on-line

Membership List Available to Non-members

National Association of Home Builders (1942)
1201 15th St. NW
Washington, DC 20005
Tel: (202) 266-8200 *Fax*: (202) 266-8400
TollFree: (800) 368-5242
E-Mail: info@nahb.org
Website: nahb.org
Members: 160,000 members
Staff: 307
Annual Budget: $50-100,000,000
Tax: 501(c)(6)

Personnel:
Chief Executive Officer: Gerald "Jerry" M. Howard
    E-Mail: jhoward@nahb.com
Staff Counsel: Jeffrey Augello
    E-Mail: jaugello@nahb.org
Operations Manager: Jessi Boyce
Program Assistant: Tara Burnett
    E-Mail: tburnett@nahb.org
Senior Counsel: Amy Chai
    E-Mail: achai@nahb.org
Director, Legal Research: David Crump
    E-Mail: dcrump@nahb.org
Deputy General Counsel: Diane Djordjevic
    E-Mail: ddjordevic@nahb.org
Senior Vice President and General Counsel: Daniel Durden
    E-Mail: ddurden@nahb.org
Vice President, Construction Liability and Legal Research: David Jaffe
    E-Mail: djaffe@nahb.org
Legislative Director: Scott Meyer
    E-Mail: smeyer@nahb.org
Assistant Association Counsel: John Ritchie
    E-Mail: jritchie@nahb.org
Contact, Publications and Affinity Programs: Christy Ronaldson
    E-Mail: cronaldson@nahb.org
Legal Assistant: Lavon Roxbury
    E-Mail: lroxbury@nahb.org
Contact, Information Technology: Asim Shafiq
    E-Mail: ashafiq@nahb.org
Vice President, Legal Services and Litigation: Thomas Ward
    E-Mail: tward@nahb.org
Staff Counsel: Felicia Watson
    E-Mail: fwatson@nahb.org

Historical Note:
Absorbed the National Association of Home Manufacturers in 1981 and the North American Log Homes Council in 1987. NAHB represents the building industry by serving its members who are involved in all aspects of a diversified building industry, create jobs for millions of people and contribute significantly to the economic activity of their community, the nation and the world. Membership: $500/Year (International Associate/International Builder).

Meetings/Conferences: Annual
2013 - Las Vegas, NV/Jan. 22 - 25
2013 - Las Vegas, NV/Jan. 22 - 24
2014 - Las Vegas, NV/Feb. 4 - 7
2015 - Las Vegas, NV/Jan. 20 - 23
2016 - Las Vegas, NV/Jan. 19 - 22
2017 - Orlando, FL/Jan. 11 - 14
2018 - Orlando, FL/Feb. 22 - 25
2019 - Las Vegas, NV/Feb. 19 - 22
2020 - Las Vegas, NV/Jan. 21 - 24

Publications:
50 + Housing Online Magazine; on-line
Building Women Magazine; quarterly; adv.
Eye on the Economy; bi-weekly
Land Development Magazine; quarterly; adv.
NAHB E-Newsletters; on-line

Nation's Building News Online; bi-weekly
Sales and Marketing Ideas Magazine; adv.

Membership List Available to Non-members

National Association of Home Builders Research Center (1964)
400 Prince George's Blvd.
Upper Marlboro, MD 20774
Tel: (301) 249-4000 *Fax*: (301) 430-6180
TollFree: (800) 638-8556
Website: nahbrc.com/index.aspx
Staff: 3

Personnel:
President, Chief Executive Officer: Michael Luzier
Vice President and Chief Operating officer: Terre Belt
Vice President, Engineering & Research: Thomas Kenney P E

Historical Note:
In 1964 as a subsidiary of the National Association of Home Builders (NAHB), and since then have provided clients with an unrivaled depth of understanding of the housing industry and access to its business leaders. It develop a strong core of research capabilities to respond to the changing needs of the home building industry

Publications:
Building Women Magazine; quarterly; adv.
Business of Building eSource; monthly; adv.
Land Development Magazine; quarterly; adv.
Monday Morning Briefing; weekly; adv.
Nation's Building News Online; bi-weekly; adv.

National Association of Home Inspectors (1987)
4426 Fifth St., West
Bradenton, FL 34207
Tel: (941) 462-4265 *Fax*: (952) 929-1318
TollFree: (800) 448-3942
E-Mail: info@nahi.org
Website: nahi.org
Members: 2300 individuals
Staff: 4
Annual Budget: $250-500,000

Personnel:
Executive Director: Claude McGavic
    E-Mail: Claude@nahi.org
Director,Membership: Jeannie Flynn
    E-Mail: Jeannie@nahi.org
Director, Marketing: Judi McGavic
    E-Mail: Judi@nahi.org

Historical Note:
NAHI seeks to promote and develop certified and licensed home inspectors in the professional home inspection industry. Members are home inspectors. The National Association of Home Inspectors strives to promote excellence and professionalism in the Home Inspection industry; to provide a home inspector standards of practice and a code of ethics for home inspectors in the USA. Membership: $405 (Regular/Associate Members); $305 (Regular/Associate Multiple Members).

Continuing Education:
Certification Designation/s: NAHI CRI

Publications:
NAHI Forum Magazine; quarterly; adv.

National Association of Hospital Hospitality Houses (1986)
P. O. Box 1439
Gresham, OR 97030-4271
Tel: (503) 328-9294
TollFree: (800) 542-9730
E-Mail: helpinghomes@nahhh.org
Website: nahhh.org
Members: 200 organizations
Staff: 2
Annual Budget: $100-250,000

Personnel:
Executive Director: Karylinn Echols MA

Historical Note:
NAHHH's mission is to support homes that help and heal to be more effective in their service to their patients and families. Membership: $425 (House); $275 (Provisional/Affiliate).

Publications:
Inside Hospitality
Member Directory; on-line

National Association of Housing and Redevelopment Officials (1933)

630 Eye St. NW
Washington, DC 20001-3736
Tel: (202) 289-3500 *Fax*: (202) 289-8181
TollFree: (877) 866-2476
E-Mail: nahro@nahro.org
Website: nahro.org
Members: 23050 individual members, associates and agency members
Staff: 38
Annual Budget: $5-10,000,000
Tax: 501(c)(3)

Personnel:
Chief Executive Officer: Saul N. Ramirez Jr.
Senior Director, Congressional Relations, Public Affairs and Field Operations: John Bohm
    E-Mail: jbohm@nahro.org
Director, Marketing and Conferences: Lori Myers-Carpenter
    E-Mail: lmcarpenter@nahro.org
Director, Professional Development: Sharon Sherrill
    E-Mail: ssherrill@nahro.org
Manager, Exhibition and Vendor Relations: Freda Stewart
    E-Mail: fstewart@nahro.org
Membership Assistant: Lynetta Tolliver

Historical Note:
Formerly (1953) National Association of Housing Officials. NAHRO's mission is to create affordable housing and safe, viable communities that enhance the quality of life for the countrymen, particularly those having low/moderate income. Membership: $25-16,000/year.

Continuing Education:
Certification Designation/s: CMPO, NCC, CSO - HCV, CSI - HQS, CSI - UPCS, CSSO - HCV, CMMO, CSO - PH, CSSO - PH, CME, CMVO, CS-PHM

Meetings/Conferences: Annual
Conference Chair: Freda Stewart
Number of non-conference events/year: 2

Publications:
Journal of Housing and Community Development; bi-monthly
Membership Directory; on-line
NAHRO Newsletter; quarterly

National Association of Housing Cooperatives (1960)
1444 I St. NW
Suite 700
Washington, DC 20005-6542
Tel: (202) 737-0797 *Fax*: (202) 216-9646
E-Mail: info@nahc.coop
Website: coophousing.org
Members: 1000 coops and professional firms
Staff: 5
Annual Budget: $250-500,000
Tax: 501(c)(3)

Personnel:
Executive Director: Mitchell Dvorak CAE, MS
Membership Manager: Mik Bauer
Chairman: Ralph J. Marcus
Accounting Manager: Ben McDonnell
Communications Manager: Kelly Wixson

Historical Note:
NAHC is a federation of regional or specialized associations of cooperatives. NAHC's mission is to support and educate existing and new cooperative housing communities as the economical form of homeownership. Membership: $30 (Housing Cooperatives); $350 (Professional); $1,750 (Supporting); $75 (Individual).

Meetings/Conferences: Annual

Publications:
NAHC Newsletter; on-line

National Association of Housing Information Managers (1992)
134 S. 13th St.
Suite 701
Lincoln, NE 68508-1901
Tel: (402) 476-9424 *Fax*: (402) 477-3407
TollFree: (800) 379-3807
E-Mail: nahimexec@aol.com
Website: nahim.org
Members: 130 public housing authorities
Staff: 2
Annual Budget: $10-25,000

Personnel:
Executive Director: John E. Mooring
    E-Mail: nahimexec@aol.com

Historical Note:
NAHIM seeks to serve as non-profit trade and educational association for public housing authority computer specialists. Membership: $50-125 (Depending Upon the Size of the PHA); $250 (Associate).

National Association of Independent Brokers Dealers *(1979)*
191 Clarksville Rd.
Princeton, NJ 08550
Tel: (609) 799-6253 *Fax:* (609) 799-7032
E-Mail: naibd@naibd.com
Website: naibd.com
Members: 12150 members
Staff: 1

Personnel:
Contact, Communications: Kaitlin Friedmann
E-Mail: kfriedmann@naibd.org

Historical Note:
Formerly the California Association of Independent Broker/ Dealers. NAIBD serves as a forum to discuss areas of common interest such as Due Diligence, Compliance and Regulation. Members are firms and industry vendors throughout the United States. Membership: $300 (Broker/ Dealer); $2,500 (Industry Associate Member).

Meetings/Conferences: Annual
2013 - Ft. Lauderdale, FL (Manchester Grand Hyatt)/ May 8 - 10
Number of non-conference events/year: 2

Publications:
Member Directory; on-line

National Association of Independent Colleges and Universities *(1976)*
1025 Connecticut Ave. NW
Suite 700
Washington, DC 20036-5405
Tel: (202) 785-8866 *Fax:* (202) 835-0003
E-Mail: geninfo@naicu.edu
Website: naicu.edu
Members: 1000 members
Staff: 20
Annual Budget: $5-10,000,000
Tax: 501(c)(3)

Personnel:
President: David L. Warren
E-Mail: david@naicu.edu
Director, Finance and Administration: Linda S. Allison
E-Mail: linda@naicu.edu
Vice President, Research and Policy Analysis: Frank Balz
E-Mail: frank@naicu.edu
Vice President, Government Relations and Policy: Sarah A. Flanagan
E-Mail: sarah@naicu.edu
System Administrator: Cheryl L. Frisby
E-Mail: cheryl@naicu.edu
Vice President, Public Affairs: Roland H. King
E-Mail: roland@naicu.edu
Director, Communications: Tony Pals
E-Mail: tony@naicu.edu
Director, Member Relations and Conference Planning: Deborah Sykes Reilly
E-Mail: deborah@naicu.edu

Historical Note:
Founded as Federation of State Associations of Colleges and Universities, a lobbying group for the Association of American Colleges, it became the National Council of Independent Colleges and Universities in 1971, and assumed independence under its present name in 1976. NAICU is committed to celebrating and protecting the diversity of the nation's private colleges and universities. Members include traditional liberal arts colleges, major research universities, church- and faith-related institutions, historically black colleges and universities, women's colleges, performing and visual arts institutions, two-year colleges, and schools of law, medicine, engineering, business, and other professions.

Meetings/Conferences:
Conference Chair: Deborah Sykes Reilly
2013 - Washington, DC (Hyatt Regency Bethesda, near Washington, D.C.)/Feb. 3 - 6
2013 - Washington, DC (Washington Court Hotel)/ Nov. 13 - 15
2014 - Washington, DC (Hyatt Regency Bethesda, near Washington, D.C.)/Feb. 2 - 5

Publications:
Membership Directory; on-line
Newsletter

National Association of Independent Fee Appraisers *(1961)*
401 N. Michigan Ave.
Suite 2200
Chicago, IL 60611
Tel: (312) 321-6830 *Fax:* (312) 673-6652
E-Mail: info@naifa.com
Website: naifa.com
Members: 3000 individuals
Staff: 16
Annual Budget: $500-1,000,000

Personnel:
Executive Vice President: Kevin Hacke
E-Mail: kevin_hacke@naifa.com
Marketing Manager: Dennis Coyle
E-Mail: Dennis_Coyle@naifa.com
Director, Operations and Education: Susan Lane
E-Mail: susan_lane@naifa.com
Senior Associate, Education and Membership Services: Lee Ann Searight
E-Mail: leeann_searight@naifa.com

Historical Note:
NAIFA's mission is to support its members, for a service of trust and integrity, that benefits its members, the profession and the general public. Members are self-employed appraisers specializing in the appraisal of real estate. Membership: $375 (Associate-Appraiser/Reinstatement-Appraiser); $195 (Associate-Affiliate); $245 (Professional Business Partner Corporate); $475 (IFA/IFAA/IFAC/IFAS).

Continuing Education:
Certification Designation/s: IFAA, IFAS, IFAC, IFA

Meetings/Conferences: Annual
2013 - Atlantic City, NJ (Golden Nugget Hotels and Casinos)/April 10 - 11

Publications:
Appraiser's Voice; quarterly
Capital Updates; monthly
Membership Directory; annually
NAIFA News; bi-weekly

National Association of Independent Housing Professionals
601 Pennsylvania Ave. NW
South Building, Suite 900
Washington, DC 20004
Tel: (202) 587-9300 *Fax:* (304) 267-9046
E-Mail: info@naihp.org
Website: naihp.org
Staff: 2

Personnel:
President: Marc Savitt
E-Mail: msavitt@naihp.org
Secretary and Treasurer: Kate Crawford

Historical Note:
NAIHP is strictly a legislative and regulatory organization, leaving education and other such issues to trade associations with individual interests. Membership: $50 (Annual).

National Association of Independent Insurance Adjusters *(1937)*
P.O. Box 807
Geneva, IL 60134
Tel: (630) 208-5002 *Fax:* (630) 208-5020
E-Mail: naiia@hilltek.com
Website: naiia.com
Members: 300 companies
Staff: 3
Annual Budget: $250-500,000
Tax: 501(c)(6)

Personnel:
Executive Vice President: David F. Mehren

Historical Note:
NAIIA correlates the activities of the association in the interest of the insurance adjusting profession and the public which it serves. Members are independently-owned property and casualty claims adjusting companies. Membership: $200/year (Individual).

Meetings/Conferences: Annual
Number of non-conference events/year: 2

Publications:
The Blue Book; on-line

National Association of Independent Insurance Auditors and Engineers *(1963)*
C/O Charles E. Hock

P.O. Box 794
Clifton Park, NY 12065
Tel: (800) 773-9323 *Fax:* (616) 957-8972
TollFree: (800) 232-2342
E-Mail: service@c-hock.com
Website: naiiae.com
Members: 18 organizations
Staff: 1
Annual Budget: $100-250,000

Personnel:
Treasurer: Charles Hock

Historical Note:
NAIIAE's mission is to provide the insurance industry on a nationwide basis with the best and most reliable audit, inspection and safety engineering services. Members are independent companies providing audits, underwriting surveys, loss control services and other related services to the insurance industry. Has no paid staff; officers change annually. Membership: $250-1,500/year.

Publications:
NAIIAE Directory; annually; adv.
NAIIAE Newsletter

National Association of Independent Life Brokerage Agencies *(1981)*
11325 Random Hills Rd.
Suite 110
Fairfax, VA 22030
Tel: (703) 383-3081 *Fax:* (703) 383-6942
E-Mail: info@nailba.org
Website: nailba.org
Members: 350 agencies
Staff: 9
Annual Budget: $2-5,000,000
Tax: 501(c)(6)

Personnel:
Chief Executive Officer: Jack Chiasson CFA, CAE
E-Mail: jchiasson@nailba.org
Director, Membership and the Foundation: Kathy Allison
E-Mail: kallison@nailba.org
Deputy Executive and Director, Meetings and Communications: Susan Grimes
Director, Business Development: Susan D. Haning CEM, CMP
E-Mail: shaning@nailba.org
Manager, Meetings and Education: Rachel Marineau CMP
E-Mail: rschmidt@nailba.org
Manager, Exhibits, Sponsorships and Advertising: Sarah O'Hanley
E-Mail: sohanley@nailba.org
Director, Administration and Operations: John Tong
E-Mail: jtong@nailba.org
Director, Government Affairs: Mark Valentini MPP
E-Mail: mvalentini@nailba.org

Historical Note:
NAILBA represents the independent wholesale life brokerage agencies of United States and Canada. Membership: $1,495/year.

Meetings/Conferences: Annual
2013 - Dallas, TX (Gaylord Texan Hotel and Convention Center-Dallas)/Nov. 21 - 23
2014 - Hollywood, FL (Westin Diplomat Resort and Spa)/Nov. 20 - 22
2015 - Orlando, FL (JW Marriott Orlando Grande Lakes)/Nov. 19 - 21
2016 - Dallas, TX (Gaylord Texan Hotel and Convention Center-Dallas)/Nov. 17 - 19
2017 - Hollywood, FL (Westin Diplomat Resort and Spa)/Nov. 16 - 18
2018 - Orlando, FL (JW Marriott Orlando Grande Lakes)/Nov. 15 - 17
2019 - Dallas, TX (Gaylord Texan Hotel and Convention Center-Dallas)/Nov. 14 - 16
Number of non-conference events/year: 2

Publications:
NAILBA Now!; bi-weekly; adv.
Perspectives; bi-monthly; adv.

National Association of Independent Lighting Distributors *(1977)*
2207 Elmwood Ave.
Suite B
Buffalo, NY 14216-1009
Tel: (716) 875-3670 *Fax:* (716) 875-0734
TollFree: (800) 205-6210
E-Mail: info@naild.org

Website: naild.org
Members: 180 companies
Staff: 3
Annual Budget: $250-500,000

Personnel:
Administrator: Linda M. Daniel
    E-Mail: lmd@naild.org
Administrative Assistant and Coordinator, Marketing and
    Membership Services: Megan Lambright
    E-Mail: megan@naild.org

Historical Note:
NAILD strives to increase the effectiveness and profitability of the specialized lighting distributor through educational programs and provides information to members pertaining to the distribution of lighting products. Membership in the association is made up of Specialty Lighting Distributors and Vendor/Manufacturers of lighting goods & supplies used in the operation of specialized lighting distributors. Membership: $1,100 (Distributor); $5,070 (Vendor); $7,070 (Associate Vendor).

Continuing Education:
Certification Designation/s: LS I, LS II

Meetings/Conferences: Annual
Conference Chair: Megan Lambright
2013 - Scottsdale, AZ (Hilton Scottsdale Resort and
    Villas)/March 17 - 20
Number of non-conference events/year: 2

Publications:
NAILD Membership Directory; annually; adv.
Today's Lighting Distributor; irregular; adv.

National Association of Independent Public Finance Advisors *(1989)*
P.O. Box 304
Montgomery, IL 60538-0304
Tel: (630) 896-1292 *Fax:* (209) 633-6265
TollFree: (800) 624-7321
E-Mail: rhoban@naipfa.com
Website: naipfa.com
Members:
63 firms
71 individuals
Staff: 1
Annual Budget: $100-250,000

Personnel:
Executive Director: Roseanne M. Hoban
    E-Mail: rhoban@naipfa.com

Historical Note:
NAIPFA's mission is to promote common interests of independent advisory firm members. Initially, efforts will build credibility and recognition by implementing public relations and marketing plan to champion the professional, independent image of the member firms.Membership: $750-4,000 (Firm); $500 (Associate); $95 (Academic).

Continuing Education:
Enrollment: 10
Certification Designation/s: CIPFA

Meetings/Conferences: Annual

Publications:
NAIPFA Newsletters

National Association of Independent Publishers Representatives *(1989)*
111 E.14th St.
P.O. Box 157
New York, NY 10003-4103
Tel: (267) 546-6561 *Fax:* (800) 416-2586
TollFree: (888) 624-7779
E-Mail: robert.rooney@naipr.org
Website: naipr.org
Members:
450 companies
350 individuals
Staff: 2
Annual Budget: $50-100,000

Personnel:
Executive Director: Robert Rooney
    E-Mail: robert.rooney@naipr.org
Legal Counsel: Steven M. Sack Esq.
    E-Mail: stevensack54@hotmail.com

Historical Note:
NAIPR's mission is to educate the publishing community at large about sales issues and practices related to field sales promotion and independent bookselling. Members are individuals and companies acting as sales representatives for one or more independent publishers on contractual basis. Membership: $50/year.

Publications:
NAIPR Newsletter; monthly

National Association of Independent Schools
(1962)
1129 20th St. NW
Suite 800
Washington, DC 20036-3425
Tel: (202) 973-9700 *Fax:* (202) 973-9790
E-Mail: info@nais.org
Website: nais.org
Members: 1400 schools and 96 associations
Staff: 60
Annual Budget: $10-25,000,000
Tax: 501(c)(3)

Personnel:
President: Patrick F. Bassett
    E-Mail: bassett@nais.org
Director, Annual Conferences: Amy Ahart
    E-Mail: ahart@nais.org
Vice President, Leadership Education and Diversity: Gene
    Batiste
    E-Mail: batiste@nais.org
Director, Human Resources: Duawwonna Bell
    E-Mail: bell@nais.org
Vice President, Government and Community Relations:
    Jefferson G. Burnett
    E-Mail: burnett@nais.org
Managing Director, Member Services: Vivian Dandridge
    Charles
    E-Mail: dandridge@nais.org
Chief Financial Officer: Corey McIntyre
    E-Mail: mcintyre@nais.org
Chief Operating Officer: Donna Orem
    E-Mail: orem@nais.org
Vice President, Communications: Nancy Raley
    E-Mail: raley@nais.org
Vice President, Information Technology: John Rodrigues
    E-Mail: rodrigues@nais.org
Vice President, Marketing: Zoe Sherlick
    E-Mail: sherlick@nais.org
Director, Publications: Kitty Thuermer
    E-Mail: thuermer@nais.org
Director, Academic Research: Amada Torres
    E-Mail: torres@nais.org
Legal Counsel: Debra Wilson
    E-Mail: wilson@nais.org

Historical Note:
The result of a merger in 1962 of the National Council of Independent Schools and the Independent Schools Education Board. Represents independent schools and associations in the United States, and affiliates with independent schools abroad as well. NAIS's mission is serve the independent schools and the center for collective action on their behalf. Members are independent elementary and secondary schools, K-12, day, boarding and a combination of both. Membership: $1,420 (School Subscriber); $1,470 (Corporate/Nonprofit).

Meetings/Conferences: Annual
Conference Chair: Amy Ahart
2013 - Philadelphia, PA (Pennsylvania Convention
    Center)/Feb. 27 - March 1
Number of non-conference events/year: 1

Publications:
Directory; annually; adv.
Independent School; quarterly; adv.
Membership Directory; on-line
NAIS e-Bulletin; monthly

Membership List Available to Non-members

National Association of Industrial and Technical Teacher Educators *(1937)*
Illinois State University
298 W. Jefferson St.
El Paso, IL 61738
Tel: (309) 438-5874 *Fax:* (309) 438-8626
Members: 300 individuals
Staff: 2
Annual Budget: $10-25,000

Personnel:
Membership Chair: Ed Livingston
    E-Mail: eclivin@ilstu.edu
Editor: Klaus Schmidt
    E-Mail: kschmid@ilstu.edu

Historical Note:
NAITTE advances and promotes excellence in industrial and technical teacher education and training in all settings.

It has no paid officers or full-time staff. Membership: $50 (Regular); $15 (Student); $60 (International); $150 (Institutional).

Meetings/Conferences:
Number of non-conference events/year: 1

Publications:
Industrial Teacher Education Directory; quarterly
The News and Views Newsletter; quarterly

National Association of Industrial Bankers *(1967)*
60 S. 600 East
Suite 150
Salt Lake City, UT 84102
Tel: (801) 355-2821 *Fax:* (801) 328-3388
Website: industrialbankers.org
Staff: 2
Annual Budget: $25-50,000

Personnel:
Executive Director: Frank Pignanelli
Contact, Administration: Aimee McConkie
    E-Mail: aimee@uafs.net

Historical Note:
NAIB's mission is to provide service to expand access to credit, guarantee consumer choice, and providing unique banking services to Americans.

National Association of Insurance and Financial Advisors *(1890)*
2901 Telestar Ct.
P.O. Box 12012
Falls Church, VA 22042-1205
Tel: (703) 770-8100
TollFree: (877) 866-2432
Website: naifa.org
Members:
600 state and local associations
200,000 members
Staff: 65
Annual Budget: $10-25,000,000
Tax: 501(c)(6)

Personnel:
Chief Executive Officer, Government Relations: Dr. Susan
    B. Waters CAE
    E-Mail: swaters@naifa.org
Senior Vice President, Government Relations: William R.
    Anderson
    E-Mail: wanderso@naifa.org
Senior Director, Strategic Communications: Mark Briscoe
    E-Mail: mbriscoe@naifa.org
Executive Administrator: Jennifer Corcoran
    E-Mail: jcorcoran@naifa.org
General Counsel: Michael Gerber
    E-Mail: mgerber@naifa.org
Director, Strategic Membership and Communications:
    Ernie Halal
    E-Mail: ehalal@naifa.org
Senior Vice President, Federal Relations: Michael L.
    Kerley
    E-Mail: mkerley@naifa.org
Vice President, Communications and Marketing: Sheila
    Owens
    E-Mail: sowens@naifa.org
Senior Counsel, State Government Relations: Roland L.
    Panneton FLMI
    E-Mail: rpanneton@naifa.org
Vice President, Professional Development and Education:
    Diane Powers
    E-Mail: dpowers@naifa.org
Director, Conventions and Meetings: Diane Ramos
    E-Mail: dramos@naifa.org
Vice President, Finance and Facilities: Paul C. Wessel
    E-Mail: pwessel@naifa.org

Historical Note:
Founded as National Association of Life Underwriters; assumed its current name in 2000. NAIFA's mission is to advocate for a positive legislative and regulatory environment, enhance business and professional skills, and promote the ethical conduct of its members. Sponsors and supports the NAIFA Political Action Committee. Membership: $300/year.

Meetings/Conferences: Annual
Conference Chair: Diane Ramos
2013 - San Antonio, TX/Sept. 28 - Oct. 1
2014 - San Diego, CA/Sept. 6 - 9
2015 - New Orleans, LA/Oct. 3 - 6

Publications:
Advisor Today; bi-monthly; adv.

Connections; weekly; adv.
GovTalk; bi-weekly
GovWatch; irregular
Membership Directory; on-line
YAT Chat; monthly; adv.

National Association Of Insurance and Financial Advisors(NAIFA) (1890)

2901 Telestar Ct.
Falls Church, VA 22042-1205
Tel: (703) 770-8100 *Fax:* (703) 770-8201
E-Mail: ahia@naifa.org
Website: naifa.org
Members: 4000 individuals
Staff: 5
Annual Budget: $1-2,000,000

Personnel:
Executive Vice President: Diane R. Boyle
     E-Mail: dboyle@naifa.org
Manager, Association Services: Carey Engle
     E-Mail: cengle@naifa.org
AHIA Federal Counsel: Michael L. Kerley
     E-Mail: mkerley@naifa.org
Coordinator, Marketing: Caitlin Kubler
     E-Mail: ckubler@naifa.org

Historical Note:
Formerly (2002) Association of Health Insurance Agents, AHIA is the NAIFA health and employee benefits advocate that strives to protect the role of the advisor in offering affordable choices in a competitive marketplace.NAIFA's mission is to advocate for a positive legislative and regulatory environment, enhance business and professional skills, and promote the ethical conduct of their members. Membership: $120/year.

Continuing Education:
Certification Designation/s: CLTC

Publications:
Advisor Today Magazine; adv.
Member Directory; on-line
The CalSurance Connector; monthly; adv.

National Association of Insurance Commissioners (1871)

444 N. Capitol St. NW
Suite 701
Washington, DC 20001
Tel: (202) 471-3990 *Fax:* (816) 460-7493
TollFree: (866) 470-6242
E-Mail: prodserv@naic.org
Website: naic.org
Members: 55 state officials
Staff: 18
Annual Budget: $50-100,000,000
Tax: 501(c)(3)

Personnel:
Chief Executive Officer: Therese M. Vaughan PhD
     E-Mail: tvaughan@naic.org
Senior Manager, Meetings: Brian Arscott
     E-Mail: barscott@naic.org
Chief Operating Officer and Chief Legal Officer: Andrew Beal
     E-Mail: abeal@naic.org
Director, Communications: Scott Holeman
     E-Mail: sholeman@naic.org
Chief Financial Officer and Business Strategy Officer: Brady Kelley
     E-Mail: bkelley@naic.org
Director, Technical Services: Frosty Mohn
     E-Mail: fmohn@naic.org
Statistical Analyst: Sara Pankow
     E-Mail: spankow@naic.org
Senior Manager, Education and Training: Jennifer Passariello
     E-Mail: jpassari@naic.org
Director, Membership Services: Trish Schoettger
     E-Mail: tschoett@naic.org

Historical Note:
Formerly National Conference of Insurance Commissioners. NAIC's mission is to assist state insurance regulators, individually and collectively, in serving the public interest and achieving the following fundamental insurance regulatory goals in a responsive, efficient and cost effective manner, consistent with the wishes of its members.

Meetings/Conferences:
Conference Chair: Brian Arscott
2013 - Houston, TX (Hilton Americas-Houston)/April 6 - 9

2013 - Indianapolis, IN (JW Marriott Indianapolis)/ Aug. 24 - 27
2013 - Washington, DC (Washington Marriott)/Oct. 28 - 31

Publications:
NAIC News; on-line

National Association of Insurance Women (International) (1940)

9343 E. 95th Ct., South
Tulsa, OK 74133
Tel: (918) 294-3700 *Fax:* (918) 294-3711
TollFree: (800) 766-6249
E-Mail: joinnaiw@naiw.org
Website: naiw.org
Members: 13500 individuals
Staff: 6
Annual Budget: $500-1,000,000
Tax: 501(c)(6)

Personnel:
Executive Vice President: Mark Adams
Director, Products and Education: Brandi Capps
Director, Communications and Editor: Melissa Cobbs
     E-Mail: editor@naiw.org
Director, Membership Services: John McColloch
     E-Mail: membership@naiw.org

Historical Note:
NAIW is an association of insurance professionals dedicated to the development of leaders in the insurance and risk management industries through education, networking and industry alliance. It offers education programs through 400 local chapters in the United States, Western Canada, and Puerto Rico and offers the Certified Professional Insurance Woman/Man (CPIW/CPIM) designation. Members are agents/brokers, adjusters, underwriters, claims professionals, risk managers, producers, insurance educators, customer service representatives, agency owners and automation specialists. Membership: $86 (Local Association); $113.50 (Member-At- Large).

Continuing Education:
Certification Designation/s: DAE, CPIW/M

Meetings/Conferences: Annual
2013 - Orlando, FL (Caribe Royale All Suites Resort)/ June 5 - 8
Number of non-conference events/year: 59

Publications:
NAIW Connections; adv.

National Association of Intercollegiate Athletics (1937)

1200 Grand Blvd.
Kansas City, MO 64106-2304
Tel: (816) 595-8000 *Fax:* (816) 595-8200
Website: naia.org
Members: 300 member colleges and universities, 650,000 students, 23 national championships.
Staff: 40
Annual Budget: $5-10,000,000

Personnel:
President and Chief Executive Officer: James Carr
     E-Mail: jcarr@naia.org
Director, Technology and Operations: Tony Bybee
     E-Mail: tbybee@naia.org
Manager, Information Technology: Charles Davenport
     E-Mail: cdavenport@naia.org
Vice President, Administration and Finance: Kevin Dee
     E-Mail: kdee@naia.org
Director, Legislative Services: Matt Hanson
     E-Mail: mhanson@naia.org
Director, Marketing and Public Relations: Kay Hawes
     E-Mail: khawes@naia.org
Director, Membership Resources: Sue Robinson
     E-Mail: srobinson@naia.org
Manager, Marketing Services and Conventions: Amy Stover
     E-Mail: astover@naia.org
Senior Vice President for Membership and Character Initiatives: Lori Thomas
     E-Mail: lthomas@naia.org
Vice President, Marketing and Communications: Lori Joseph Wiles
     E-Mail: lwiles@naia.org

Historical Note:
Formerly (1952) National Association of Intercollegiate Basketball. NAIA's mission is to promote the education and development of students through intercollegiate athletics participation. Members are colleges and universities. Membership: $6,300/year.

Meetings/Conferences: Annual
Conference Chair: Amy Stover
2013 - Kansas City, MO (Sheraton Kansas City Hotel at Crown Center)/April 19 - 23

Publications:
Statistical Newsletter

National Association of Investigative Specialists (1984)

P.O. Box 82148
Austin, TX 78708
Tel: (512) 719-3595 *Fax:* (512) 719-3594
E-Mail: rthomas007@aol.com
Website: pimall.com/nais/nais.j.html
Members: 5000 individuals
Staff: 5
Annual Budget: $100-250,000

Personnel:
Director: Ralph D. Thomas
     E-Mail: RThomas007@mac.com

Historical Note:
NAIS promotes the private investigative profession, focuses on marketing investigative services, provides training programs for those in practice or those wishing to enter the field, and develops positive media coverage of the profession, acting as a center for case referrals and positive publicity referrals to members. Members are private investigative professionals. Membership: $85/year.

Continuing Education:
Certification Designation/s: NAISC

Publications:
Membership Directory; on-line
PI Bites
PI Daily; daily

National Association of Investment Companies (1971)

1300 Pennsylvania Ave. NW
Suite 700
Washington, DC 20005
Tel: (202) 204-3001 *Fax:* (202) 204-3022
E-Mail: info@naicpe.com
Website: naicvc.com
Members: 47 companies
Staff: 2
Annual Budget: $1-2,000,000

Personnel:
President and Chief Executive Officer: Ed Dandridge
Secretary: Lloyd Metz

Historical Note:
NAIC is the financial industry association for private equity firms that invest in an ethnically diverse marketplace.NAIC's mission is to promote the development of successful private equity investment firms that invest in businesses significantly owned by ethnic individuals. Membership: $4,000- 12,000 (Full members, based on fund size); $5,000 (Affiliate); $1,00 (Funds in Formation).

Meetings/Conferences: Annual

Publications:
E-News Updates; on-line
Journal of EDM Finance; bi-annually

National Association of Investment Professionals (1996)

12664 Emmer Pl.
Suite 201
St. Paul, MN 55124
Tel: (651) 621-3825
Website: naip.com
Members: 100 individuals
Staff: 2
Annual Budget: Under $10,000
Tax: 501(c)(6)

Personnel:
President and Founder: Tom Sheridan O'Keefe
     E-Mail: tokeefe@naip.com

Historical Note:
NAIP's mission is to provide accurate, quick, and easily assessable information that will help protect and/or grow the business of members. Members are individuals (stockbrokers, registered sales assistants, traders, investment advisors) and companies who provide financial planning services to individuals. Membership: $39/year (New).

Publications:
Newsletter

National Association of Investors Corporation (1951)

711 W. 13 Mile Rd.
Madison Heights, MI 48071
Tel: (248) 654-3056 *Fax:* (248) 583-4880
Website: betterinvesting.org
Staff: 2
Annual Budget: $5-10,000,000
Tax: 501(c)(3)

Personnel:
Contact, Media: Brenda Gayle
    E-Mail: mediacenter@betterinvesting.org
Director, Corporate Relations: Derwin A. Wallace
    E-Mail: derwinw@betterInvesting.org

Historical Note:
BetterInvesting's mission is to provide a program of sound investment information, education, and support that helps create successful lifetime investors.

Publications:
BetterInvesting Magazine

National Association of Jai Alai Frontons (1977)

5701 Lee St. NE
St. Petersburg, FL 33703
Website: national-jai-alai.com/
Members: 11 frontons
Staff: 2
Annual Budget: Under $10,000

Personnel:
Computer Technician/Web Maintenance: Michael Berry

Historical Note:
Established January 1, 1977 and incorporated in Florida. NAJAF represents the interests of fronton (venue) operators. Has no paid officers or full-time staff.

National Association of Japan-America Societies (1979)

1819 L St. NW
Suite 200
Washington, DC 20036
Tel: (202) 429-5545 *Fax:* (202) 429-0027
E-Mail: contact@us-japan.org
Website: us-japan.org
Members: 40 independent Japan-related organizations
Staff: 2
Annual Budget: $1-2,000,000
Tax: 501(c)(3)

Personnel:
President: Peter Kelley
Treasurer: Celso Mataac

Historical Note:
The mission of the NAJAS is to strengthen cooperation and understanding between the peoples of Japan and the United States by providing programs, services, and information to and facilitating cooperation among its member societies throughout North America.

Meetings/Conferences:
Number of non-conference events/year: 3

Publications:
Membership Directory; on-line

National Association of Jewelry Appraisers (1981)

P.O. Box 18
Rego Park, NY 11374-0018
Tel: (718) 896-1536 *Fax:* (718) 997-9057
E-Mail: office@najaappraisers.com
Website: najaappraisers.com
Members: 750 individuals
Staff: 5
Annual Budget: $100-250,000

Personnel:
Executive Director: Gail Brett Levine GG

Historical Note:
NAJA seeks to promote the trademark and professional designations earned by its members and to make available continuing educational materials. Members include jewelers, jewelry appraisers, importers, brokers and other professionally interested trade members. Membership: $195 (Individual-US); $235 (Individual- Canada/International).

Continuing Education:
Enrollment: 125
Certification Designation/s: CM, CSM, CMA

Meetings/Conferences: Semi-Annual
2013 - Tucson, AZ (Tucson Convention Center)/Feb. 3 - 4

2013 - Pittsburgh, PA/Aug. 10 - 14
Publications:
Membership Directory; annually
The Jewelry Appraiser; quarterly

National Association of Jewish Legislators (1977)

P.O. Box 42442
Washington, DC 20015
Tel: (202) 494-7991 *Fax:* (202) 318-8189
E-Mail: najleg@aol.com
Website: jewishlegislator.org
Staff: 2

Personnel:
President: Mark Weprin
Director and Counsel: Jeffrey M Wice
    E-Mail: najleg@aol.com

Historical Note:
Comprised of Jewish state legislators, city council members, county legislators, and other non-federal elected officials and non-Jewish legislators who support NAJL's goals.

National Association of Judiciary Interpreters and Translators (1978)

1901 Pennsylvania Ave. NW
Suite 804
Washington, DC 20006
Tel: (202) 293-0342 *Fax:* (202) 293-0495
E-Mail: headquarters@najit.org
Website: najit.org
Members:
1000 individuals
200 organizations and companies
Staff: 2
Annual Budget: $100-250,000
Tax: 501(c)(3)

Personnel:
Executive Director: Robin Lanier

Historical Note:
Formerly the Court Interpreters and Translators Association. NAJIT's purpose is to promote professional standards of performance and integrity, to achieve wider recognition for the profession of judiciary interpreting and translating and to advocate policies for the training and certification of interpreters through competent and reliable methodologies. Members are interpreters and translators working in federal, state or local courts, or in other capacities within the legal profession. Membership: $10-300/year.

Continuing Education:
Enrollment: 40
Certification Designation/s: SIT

Meetings/Conferences: Annual
2013 - St. Louis, MO (Clayton Sheraton)/May 17 - 19
Number of non-conference events/year: 17

Publications:
Membership Directory; on-line
Proteus; quarterly; adv.

Membership List Available to Non-members

National Association of Junior Auxiliaries

P.O. Box 1873
Greenville, MS 38702-1873
Tel: (662) 332-3000 *Fax:* (662) 332-3076
E-Mail: najanet@bellsouth.net
Website: najanet.org
Members: 14830 individuals
Staff: 5
Annual Budget: $500-1,000,000
Tax: 501(c)(3)

Personnel:
Executive Director: Merrill Greenlee
    E-Mail: najanet@bellsouth.net
Contact, Accounting and Clerical Services: Kathy Dunavant
    E-Mail: kdunavant@najanet.org
Contact, Scholarship and Membership Services: Missy Lee
    E-Mail: mlee@najanet.org

Historical Note:
NAJA strives to provide support, resources, and educational, leadership, cultural, and healthcare training for NAJA members in order to optimize community service by NAJA chapters.

Meetings/Conferences: Annual

Publications:
The Crownlet; semi-annually; adv.

National Association of Latino Elected and Appointed Officials (1976)

1122 W. Washington Blvd.
Third Floor
Los Angeles, CA 90015
Tel: (213) 747-7606 *Fax:* (213) 747-7664
E-Mail: info@naleo.org
Website: naleo.org
Members: 6000 individuals
Staff: 32
Annual Budget: $100-250,000
Tax: 501(c)(4)

Personnel:
Executive Director: Arturo Vargas
    E-Mail: avargas@naleo.org
Senior Director, Programs and Communications: Erica Bernal
    E-Mail: ebernal@naleo.org
Executive Assistant, Development: Jeanine Cavicchia
    E-Mail: jcavicchia@naleo.org
Manager, Special Events: Maria Fernandez
    E-Mail: mfernandez@naleo.org
Senior Director, Policy, Research, and Advocacy: Rosalind Gold
    E-Mail: rgold@naleo.org
Senior Director, Finance: Juan C. Vargas
    E-Mail: jvargas@naleo.org
Manager, Information Systems: Rene Vasquez
    E-Mail: rvasquez@naleo.org
Director, Human Resources and Administration: Angela Weimer
    E-Mail: aweimer@naleo.org

Historical Note:
Organization of the nation's elected and appointed Latino officials. NALEO is a non-profit, non-partisan civic affairs research organization which works to initiate public policies responsive to the Hispanic community and to inform that community of issues affecting them. Membership: $1,000 (Lifetime); $100 (Member).

Meetings/Conferences: Semi-Annual
Conference Chair: Maria Fernandez
Number of non-conference events/year: 1

Publications:
e-Newsletter; on-line; adv.

Membership List Available to Non-members

National Association of Latino Independent Producers

P.O. Box 1247
Santa Monica, CA 90406
Tel: (310) 395-8880 *Fax:* (310) 395-8811
E-Mail: info@nalip.org
Website: nalip.org
Staff: 3
Annual Budget: $1-2,000,000

Personnel:
Executive Director: Bienvenida Matias
Membership Coordinator: Icela Nahyr Bracamontes
    E-Mail: membership@nalip.org
Director, Conference: Octavio Marin
    E-Mail: octavio@nalip.org

Historical Note:
NALIP's mission is to promote the advancement, development and funding of Latino/Latina film and media arts in all genres. Membership: $50-125 (Individual); $150-275 (Professional / Executive); $20 (Student); $25 (International); $10 (International Student); $25 (Associate); $110 (Joint w/ IDA); $200 (Organizational); $1000 (Lifetime Membership).

Meetings/Conferences: Annual
Conference Chair: Octavio Marin

Publications:
Latinos In The Industry; bi-weekly

National Association of Legal Assistants (1975)

1516 S. Boston
Suite 200
Tulsa, OK 74119
Tel: (918) 587-6828 *Fax:* (918) 582-6772
E-Mail: nalanet@nala.org
Website: nala.org
Members: 6397 individuals, state and local associations
Staff: 9
Annual Budget: $1-2,000,000
Tax: 501(c)(6)

Personnel:
Executive Director: Marge Dover CAE
 E-Mail: mdover@nala.org
Director, Administrative Services and Certification: Marie Greninger
 E-Mail: mgreninger@nala.org
Contact, Membership Services and CP Recertification: Staci Shannon
 E-Mail: sshannon@nala.org
Contact, Convention and Educational Programs: Vanessa Williamson
 E-Mail: vwilliamson@nala.org

Historical Note:
NALA seeks to lead the paralegal profession by providing a voluntary certification program, continuing legal education, and professional development programs for all paralegals. Members are professional legal assistants. Membership: $100 (Associate); $125 (Active/Charter); $70 (Sustaining); $50 (Student).

Continuing Education:
Certification Designation/s: CLA, CP, APC

Meetings/Conferences: Annual
Conference Chair: Vanessa Williamson
2013 - Portland, OR (Hilton Portland and Executive Tower)/July 10 - 13
Number of non-conference events/year: 3

Publications:
Career Chronicle; annually
Facts & Findings; quarterly; adv.
National Utilization and Compensation Survey Report; biennially
Vendor Directory; annually; adv.

National Association of Legal Investigators
(1967)
235 N. Pine St.
Lansing, MI 48933
Tel: (517) 702-9835 *Fax:* (517) 372-1501
TollFree: (866) 520-6254
E-Mail: info@nalionline.org
Website: nalionline.org
Members: 700 professional legal investigators
Staff: 3
Annual Budget: $50-100,000
Tax: 501(c)(6)

Personnel:
Contact, Membership Services: Larry Julian
 E-Mail: larry@julianvail.com

Historical Note:
NALI's primary focus is to educate and advance the art and science of legal investigation and to ensure the standard of professional ethics. Membership is open to all professional legal investigators who are actively engaged in negligence investigations for the plaintiff and/or criminal defense. Membership: $175/year.

Continuing Education:
Certification Designation/s: CLI

Meetings/Conferences: Annual
2013 - Memphis, TN (The Peabody Memphis)/Feb. 14 - 16
2013 - New Orleans, LA/June 13 - 15
Number of non-conference events/year: 2

Publications:
Membership Directory; on-line
The Legal Investigator; quarterly

National Association of Legal Search Consultants
(1984)
1525 N. Park Dr.
Suite 102
Weston, FL 33326
Tel: (954) 349-8081 *Fax:* (954) 349-1979
TollFree: (866) 902-6587
E-Mail: info@nalsc.org
Website: nalsc.org
Members: 170 firms
Staff: 4
Annual Budget: $100-250,000
Tax: 501(c)(6)

Personnel:
Executive Director: Joseph Ankus Esq.
 E-Mail: info@ankusconsulting.com
Account Executive: Stephanie Ankus

Historical Note:
Originally organized to establish a code of ethics for the legal recruiting industry. NALSC is dedicated to enhancing the image of the legal search profession through national public relations. Provides education and information on trends and issues in the marketplace. NALSC members are legal recruiters in United States and Canada as well as international locations. Membership: $150-1,000/year.

Meetings/Conferences: Annual
2013 - Coronado, CA (Hotel del Coronado)/April 18 - 20
Number of non-conference events/year: 1

Publications:
NALSC Code of Ethics
NALSC Member Directory; annually
Newsletter; quarterly

National Association of Letter Carriers *(1889)*
100 Indiana Ave. NW
Washington, DC 20001-2144
Tel: (202) 393-4695 *Fax:* (202) 737-1540
E-Mail: nalcinf@nalc.org
Website: nalc.org
Members: 312790 individuals
Staff: 160
Annual Budget: Over $100,000,000
Tax: 501(c)(5)

Personnel:
Executive Vice President: Timothy C. O'Malley
President: Fredric V. Rolando
Secretary and Treasurer: Jane E. Broendel
Director, Communications and Media Relations: Philip Dine
 E-Mail: dine@nalc.org
Director, Legislative and Political Affairs: Jennifer Warburton
 E-Mail: warburton@nalc.org

Historical Note:
The National Association of Letter Carriers (or NALC) is an American labor union, representing non-rural letter carriers employed by the United States Postal Service. Membership: $17.50/year (National).

Meetings/Conferences: Biennial
2014 - Philadelphia, PA (Pennsylvania Convention Center)/July 21 - 25
2016 - Los Angeles, CA (The Los Angeles Convention Center)/Aug. 15 - 19

Publications:
NALC Bulletin; on-line
The Postal Record

National Association of Litho Clubs *(1945)*
3268 N. 147th Ln.
Goodyear, AZ 85395
Tel: (650) 592-4347
Website: graphicarts.org
Members: 1000 individuals
Staff: 3
Annual Budget: $10-25,000

Personnel:
National Secretary: Blair Dreyfus
 E-Mail: evpblair@yahoo.com

Historical Note:
NALC's purpose is to function as a forum for the interchange of information relative to the operation of the Litho Clubs, graphic arts job skills, technical developments and processes and trends in the graphic arts industry. Club members are supervisory personnel in lithographic plants, company owners and suppliers. Membership: $12/year (Individual).

Publications:
Litho Tips

National Association of Local Boards of Health *(1992)*
1840 E. Gypsy Lane Rd.
Bowling Green, OH 43402
Tel: (419) 353-7714 *Fax:* (419) 352-6278
E-Mail: nalboh@nalboh.org
Website: nalboh.org
Members: 840 members,22000 individuals
Staff: 12
Annual Budget: $1-2,000,000
Tax: 501(c)(3)

Personnel:
Interim Chief Executive Officer: Ned Baker
 E-Mail: ned@nalboh.org
Manager, Publications: Mark Schultz
 E-Mail: mark@nalboh.org
Director , Operations: Tracy Schupp
 E-Mail: tracy@nalboh.org

Director, Membership and Affiliate Relations: Tim Tegge BS
 E-Mail: tim@nalboh.org

Historical Note:
NALBOH is dedicated to preparing and strengthening boards of health, empowering them to promote and protect the health of their communities through education, training, and technical assistance.The mission of NALBOH is to strengthen and improve public health governance. Membership: $135-225 (Institutional); $75 (Associate); $20 (Retired/Student); $100-1,000(Sponsor).

Meetings/Conferences: Annual
2013 - Salt Lake City, UT/Aug. 14 - 16

Publications:
NALBOH NEWSBRIEF; quarterly

National Association of Local Government Auditors *(1989)*
449 Lewis Hargett Cir.
Suite 290
Lexington, KY 40503-3590
Tel: (859) 276-0686 *Fax:* (859) 278-0507
E-Mail: memberservices@governmentauditors.org
Website: governmentauditors.org
Members:
2000 Individual members
300 organizations
Staff: 3
Annual Budget: $250-500,000

Personnel:
President: Drummond Kahn
 E-Mail: drummond.kahn@portlandoregon.gov
Contact, Membership Services and Publications: Fay Kurkjy
 E-Mail: fkurkjy@nasact.org
Manager, Conference: Donna Maloy CMP
 E-Mail: dmaloy@nasact.org

Historical Note:
ALGA was formed to bring together professional local government auditors to provide opportunities for the free exchange of information, to offer pertinent education and training. To improve the quality of auditing in local government, to provide a forum for local government auditing issues and to encourage and uphold the highest quality standards of professional ethics. Membership: $180-910 (Organization); $325 (Individual/Association).

Meetings/Conferences: Annual
Conference Chair: Donna Maloy CMP

Publications:
ALGA Quarterly; quarterly
Member Directory

National Association of Local Government Environmental Professionals *(1993)*
1101 Connecticut Ave.
Suite 405
Washington, DC 20036
Tel: (202) 337-4503 *Fax:* (202) 429-5290
E-Mail: nalgep@spiegelmcd.com
Website: nalgep.org
Members: 200 members
Staff: 4
Annual Budget: $100-250,000
Tax: 501(c)(3)

Personnel:
Executive Director: Ken Brown
 E-Mail: kenbrown318@gmail.com
Coordinator, Projects: Kristina Byrne
 E-Mail: kbyrne@securityandsustainabilityforum.org

Historical Note:
NALGEP is a national organization representing local government professionals responsible for environmental compliance and the development of local environmental policy. Membership: $175-225 (New, based on population); $400 (Associate).

Meetings/Conferences: Annual

Publications:
News Flash; bi-weekly

National Association of Local Housing Finance Agencies *(1982)*
2025 M St. NW
Suite 800
Washington, DC 20036-3309
Tel: (202) 367-1197 *Fax:* (202) 367-2197
TollFree: (800) 321-3010

E-Mail: info@nalhfa.org
Website: nalhfa.org
Members: 275 organizations
Staff: 8
Annual Budget: $500-1,000,000

Personnel:
Executive Director: John C. Murphy
   E-Mail: jmurphy@nalhfa.org
Coordinator, Marketing: Holly Beck
   E-Mail: hbeck@smithbucklin.com
Staff Accountant: Jonathan Hutchins
   E-Mail: jhutchins@courtesyassoc.com
Senior Associate, Education and Certification: Lauren
   Kemp
   E-Mail: lkemp@smithbucklin.com
Coordinator, Conventions: Jessica Klapstein
   E-Mail: JKlapstein@smithbucklin.com

Historical Note:
NALHFA's mission is to provide leadership in the field of
affordable housing finance and to deliver quality services to
its members. Members are city and county agencies, nonprofits, and private firms, such as underwriters, consultants,
financial advisors, bond counsels, and rating agencies.
Membership: $850-2,550 (Regular); $3,150 (Sustaining);
$550 (Nonprofit Member); $800-8,000 (Affiliate).

Meetings/Conferences: Annual
Conference Chair: Jessica Klapstein
2013 - New Orleans, LA (InterContinental New
   Orleans)/April 4 - 6

Publications:
Housing Finance Update; monthly; adv.
NALHFA Membership Directory; annually

National Association of Long Term Care Administrator Boards (1970)
1444 I St. NW
Washington, DC 20005-2210
Tel: (202) 712-9040 Fax: (202) 216-9646
E-Mail: nab@nabweb.org
Website: nabweb.org
Members: 102 licensing boards and individuals
Staff: 5
Annual Budget: $2-5,000,000
Tax: 501(c)(3)

Personnel:
President and Chief Executive Officer: Randy Lindner CAE
   E-Mail: rlindner@bostrom.com
Program Coordinator, NCERS: Eric Bernard
   E-Mail: ebernard@bostrom.com
Director, Meetings: Julie Elfand
   E-Mail: jelfand@bostrom.com
Manager, Marketing: Heidi Lapka
   E-Mail: hlapka@bostrom.com
Director, Administration: Jason Silberberg
   E-Mail: jsilberberg@bostrom.com

Historical Note:
NAB strives to enhance the effectiveness of state boards
of long term care administrators in meeting their statutory
and regulatory duties and responsibilities to protect the
health, safety, and welfare of the public. Regular members
are licensing boards. Associate members are individuals,
subscribing members are non- profit organizations and
educational institutions. Membership: $70/year (Associate/
Subscribing).

Continuing Education:
Certification Designation/s: NHA, NCERS, RCAL

Meetings/Conferences: Annual
Conference Chair: Julie Elfand

Publications:
NAB Newsletter
NAB NHA Study Guide
NAB RC/AL Study Guide

National Association of Managed Care Physicians
(1991)
4435 Waterfront Dr.
Suite 101
Glen Allen, VA 23060
Tel: (804) 527-1905 Fax: (804) 747-5316
TollFree: (800) 722-0376
E-Mail: info@namcp.org
Website: namcp.org
Members: 1000 individuals
Staff: 2
Tax: 501(c)(6)

Personnel:
President: Thomas Morrow

Editor-in-Chief: Dexter W. Shurney MBA, MD, MPH

Historical Note:
NAMCP's mission is to improve patient outcomes by
providing educational material, evidence-based tools and
resources to medical directors from purchasers, plans and
provider systems. Membership: $149/year (Physician).

Meetings/Conferences: Annual
Number of non-conference events/year: 1

Publications:
Genomics Biotech eNews; weekly; adv.
Journal of Managed Care Medicine; quarterly
Managed Care eNews; weekly; adv.

National Association of Managed Care Physicians
(1991)
4435 Waterfront Dr.
P.O. Box 4765, Suite 101
Glen Allen, VA 23058-4765
Tel: (804) 527-1905 Fax: (804) 747-5316
E-Mail: info@namcp.org
Website: namcp.org
Members: 15000 individuals
Staff: 16
Annual Budget: $5-10,000,000
Tax: 501(c)(6)

Personnel:
Vice President, Education: Katie Eads
   E-Mail: keads@namcp.org
Publisher: Jack F. Klose
   E-Mail: jklose@namcp.org
Director, Communications: Jeremy Williams
   E-Mail: jwilliams@namcp.org

Historical Note:
NAMCP's mission is to improve patient outcomes by
providing educational material, evidence-based tools and
resources to medical directors from purchasers, plans and
provider systems. Membership: $149 (Physician); $25
(Resident/Student); $195 (Associate); $5000-15,000
(Corporate).

Continuing Education:
Certification Designation/s: CMCN

Meetings/Conferences: Annual

Publications:
Genomics & Biotech; quarterly
Journal of Managed Care Medicine; annually; adv.

Membership List Available to Non-members

National Association of Manufacturers (1895)
1331 Pennsylvania Ave. NW
Suite 600
Washington, DC 20004-1790
Tel: (202) 637-3000 Fax: (202) 637-3182
TollFree: (800) 814-8468
E-Mail: manufacturing@nam.org
Website: nam.org
Members: 11000 companies
Staff: 164
Annual Budget: $25-50,000,000
Tax: 501(c)(6)

Personnel:
President and Chief Executive Officer: Jay W. Timmons
   E-Mail: jtimmons@nam.org
Vice President, Information Technology: Jeff Colburn
Vice President, Tax and Domestic Economic Policy:
   Dorothy Coleman
   E-Mail: dcoleman@nam.org
Senior Vice President, Communications: Maureen
   Davenport
   E-Mail: mdavenport@nam.org
Senior Director, International Business Policy: Stephen
   Jacobs
Vice President, Membership and Marketing: J. Cliff
   Johnson III
Senior Vice President, Chief Financial Officer and Treasurer:
   Richard I. Klein
Vice President, Human Resources Policy: Jeri Kubicki
   E-Mail: jgillespie@nam.org
Vice President, Energy and Resources Policy: Keith McCoy
   E-Mail: kmccoy@nam.org
Senior Vice President, Government Relations and Policy:
   Aric Newhouse
   E-Mail: Aric.A.Newhouse@nam.org
Vice President, Litigation and Deputy General Counsel:
   Quentin Riegel
   E-Mail: qriegel@nam.org
Senior Vice President, Communications: Erin Streeter

Vice President, International Economic Affairs: Franklin J.
   Vargo
   E-Mail: fvargo@nam.org

Historical Note:
NAM's mission is to inform legislators, the administration,
the media, policy influencers and the public about
manufacturing's vital leadership in innovation, job
opportunity, technological progress and economic security.
Membership: $720-2,760/year (Based on annual budget).

Continuing Education:
Certification Designation/s: SCS

Publications:
Capital Briefing; weekly
Dispatch from the front; on-line
Manufacturers in the Courts; on-line
Member Focus; monthly
Monday Economic Report; weekly

National Association of Margarine Manufacturers
(1936)
529 14th St. NW
Suite 750
Washington, DC 20045
Tel: (202) 591-2438 Fax: (202) 223-9741
E-Mail: namm@kellencompany.com
Website: margarine.org
Members: 5 companies
Staff: 3
Annual Budget: $100-250,000
Tax: 501(c)(6)

Personnel:
President: Richard E. Cristol
   E-Mail: rcristol@kellencompany.com

Historical Note:
The National Association of Margarine Manufacturers
(NAMM) is a non- profit trade association formed in 1936.
Association serving health conscious consumers and the
margarine industry. Represents the manufacturers and
distributors of margarine products and suppliers to the
industry. Members are manufacturers and distributors of
margarine industry products.

National Association of Marine Laboratories
1080 Shennecossett Rd.
Groton, CT 06340
Fax: (860) 445-2969
Website: naml.org
Members: 120 members
Staff: 2

Personnel:
President: Ivar G. Babb
   E-Mail: ivar.babb@uconn.edu

Historical Note:
NAML member laboratories provide a variety of academic,
research, and public service programs.

National Association of Marine Services (1951)
5458 Wagon Master Dr.
Colorado Springs, CO 80917
Tel: (719) 573-5946 Fax: (719) 573-5952
E-Mail: nams@namsshipchandler.com
Website: namsshipchandler.com
Members: 60 firms
Staff: 2
Annual Budget: $100-250,000
Tax: 501(c)(6)

Personnel:
Executive Director: William L. Robinson

Historical Note:
Established as Associated Ship Chandlers, changed name
to National Associated Marine Suppliers and assumed its
present name in 1969. NAMS works to further the growth
and profitability of all segments of the ship supply industry
through the promotion of harmonious relationships between
ship suppliers and manufacturers. Members are purveyors of
supplies and equipment to ocean- going commercial vessels.

Meetings/Conferences: Annual

Publications:
NAMS Newlsetter; quarterly

The National Association of Marine Surveyors, Inc. (1962)
P.O. Box 9306
Chesapeake, VA 23321-9306
Tel: (757) 638-9638 Fax: (757) 638-9639
TollFree: (800) 822-6267
E-Mail: office@namsglobal.org

Website: namsglobal.org
Members: 400 individuals
Staff: 4
Annual Budget: $100-250,000
Tax: 501(c)(6)

Personnel:
President: Steven P. Weiss
Treasurer: James A. Neville
National Secretary: Edward L. Shearer
Editor: Gregory B. Weeter

Historical Note:
NAMS strives to develop and improve the competence and professional ethics of its members and to provide a means for marine surveyors to obtain professional certification by engaging in a rigorous accreditation program, as well as continuing education opportunities. Membership is made up of surveyors specializing in different aspects of the maritime and transportation industries. Membership: $450 (Full/Certified); $250 (Associate); $125 (Apprentice).

Continuing Education:
Certification Designation/s: NAMS-CMS

Meetings/Conferences: Annual
3013 - San Diego, CA (Catamaran Resort Hotel and Spa)/March 3 - 5

Publications:
NAMS eNews; bi-monthly
Technical Journal

National Association of Media and Technology Centers *(1979)*
P.O. Box 9844
Cedar Rapids, IA 52409-9844
Tel: (319) 654-0608 *Fax:* (319) 654-0609
Website: namtc.org
Members: 260 individuals
Staff: 2
Annual Budget: $25-50,000
Tax: 501(c)(3)

Personnel:
Executive Director: Betty Gorsegner Ehlinger
    E-Mail: bettyge@namtc.org
Treasurer: Geoff Craven

Historical Note:
NAMTC is an organization committed to promoting leadership among its membership through networking, advocacy, and support activities that will enhance the equitable access to media, technology, and information services to educational communities. Membership: $30 (Retired); $150 (Institutional/Individual); $360 (Corporate).

Meetings/Conferences: Annual
2013 - San Antonio, TX (San Antonio Hill Country Resort)/Dec. 3 - 4

Publications:
Corporate Directory; annually
NAMTC Newsletter; on-line

Membership List Available to Non-members

National Association of Media Brokers *(1985)*
2910 Electra Dr.
Colorado Springs, CO 80906-1073
Tel: (719) 630-3111
E-Mail: vpepper@wcsr.com
Website: nambonline.com
Members: 60 firms
Staff: 2
Annual Budget: $50-100,000

Personnel:
President: Jody McCoy
    E-Mail: jbmccoy@mediaservicesgroup.com
Treasurer: Glenn Serafin
    E-Mail: gserafin@tampabay.rr.com

Historical Note:
NAMB's mission is to strive to address issues of concern within the broadcast brokerage community, and to advocate with the Federal Communications Commission for the economic and business interests of its clients. Members are media brokerage firms.

National Association of Medicaid Directors *(1979)*
444 N. Capitol St.
Suite 524
Washington, DC 20001
Tel: (202) 403-8620 *Fax:* (202) 403-8627
Website: medicaiddirectors.org
Staff: 7

Annual Budget: $250-500,000
Tax: 501(c)(3)

Personnel:
Executive Director: Matt Salo
    E-Mail: matt.salo@namd-us.org
Director, Federal Policy and Strategy: Andrea Maresca
    E-Mail: andrea.maresca@namd-us.org
Chief Operating Officer: Tess Moore
    E-Mail: tess.moore@namd-us.org

Historical Note:
Formerly, National Association of State Medicaid Directors (NASMD). NAMD's mission is to provide a focused, coordinated voice for the Medicaid program in national policy discussion and to meet the needs of the member states.

Meetings/Conferences: Annual

Publications:
Membership Directory; on-line
Public Newsletter

National Association of Medical Examiners *(1966)*
31479 Arrow Ln.
Marceline, MO 64658
Tel: (660) 734-1891 *Fax:* (888) 370-4839
E-Mail: name@thename.org
Website: thename.org
Members: 900 individuals
Staff: 2
Annual Budget: $500-1,000,000
Tax: 501(c)(6)

Personnel:
Executive Director: Denise D. McNally
    E-Mail: name@thename.org
Meeting Planner: Mary Fran Ernst
    E-Mail: ernstmf@slu.edu

Historical Note:
NAME's mission to improve the quality of death investigation nationally and to recognize excellence in death investigation systems. Membership is open to all physicians, investigators and administrators who are active in medicolegal death investigation. Membership: $152 (Resident); $85-237 (Affiliates).

Meetings/Conferences: Annual
Conference Chair: Mary Fran Ernst

Publications:
The American Journal of Forensic Medicine and Pathology; quarterly; adv.

National Association of Medical Minority Educators, Inc. *(1975)*
1500 Sunday Dr.
Suite 102
Raleigh, NC 27607
Tel: (919) 573-1309 *Fax:* (919) 573-1310
TollFree: (855) 201-6247
E-Mail: fkboyles@nammenational.org
Website: nammenational.org
Staff: 1
Annual Budget: $100-250,000
Tax: 501(c)(3)

Personnel:
Executive Director: Felicia Kenan Boyles
    E-Mail: fkboyles@nammenational.org

Historical Note:
NAMME is a national organization dedicated to developing and sustaining productive relationships as well as action-oriented programs among national, state, and community stakeholders working to ensure racial and ethnic diversity in all of the health professions. Membership is comprised of educators, administrators, practitioners and students representing the following professions: allied health, allopathic medicine, chiropractic, dentistry, nursing, optometry, osteopathic medicine, pharmacy, podiatry, public health and veterinary medicine. Membership: $130 (Regular); $40 (Student).

Meetings/Conferences: Annual
Conference Chair: Felicia Kenan Boyles

Publications:
Member Directory; on-line
Newsletter

National Association of Mental Health Planning Advisory Council *(1986)*
2000 N. Beauregard St.
Sixth Floor
Alexandria, VA 22311

Tel: (703) 797-2595
Website: namhpac.org
Staff: 2
Annual Budget: Under $10,000

Personnel:
Executive Director: Judy Stange PhD
    E-Mail: judy@namhpac.org
Manager, Program: Tiffani Pullen MSW
    E-Mail: tpullen@nmha.org

Historical Note:
NAMHPAC's mission is to provide support, policy development, knowledge products, and technical assistance to the nation's State-based mental health planning and advisory councils. Membership includes members form each State and Territory mental health planning council.

Meetings/Conferences:
Conference Chair: Tiffani Pullen MSW

Publications:
Membership Directory; on-line
NAMHPAC Newsletter; monthly

National Association of Minority and Women Owned Law Firms *(2001)*
732 N. Water St.
Suite 1205
Milwaukee, WI 53202
Tel: (414) 227-1139 *Fax:* (414) 831-2285
E-Mail: contact@namwolf.org
Website: namwolf.org
Staff: 10
Annual Budget: $500-1,000,000
Tax: 501(c)(6)

Personnel:
Chief Executive Officer and General Counsel: David Askew
    E-Mail: david_askew@namwolf.org
Senior Director, Events and Marketing: Jane Kalata
    E-Mail: jane_kalata@namwolf.org
Coordinator, Communications and Membership: Samantha Surillo
    E-Mail: samantha_surillo@namwolf.org

Historical Note:
Promotes diversity in the legal profession by fostering the development of long lasting relationships between preeminent minority and women owned law firms and private/public entities.

Meetings/Conferences: Annual

Publications:
Newsletter; semi-annually

National Association of Minority Automobile Dealers *(1980)*
9475 Lottsford Rd.
Suite 150
Largo, MD 20774
Tel: (301) 306-1614 *Fax:* (301) 306-1493
Website: namad.org
Members: 650 individuals
Staff: 4
Annual Budget: $1-2,000,000
Tax: 501(c)(3)

Personnel:
President: Damon Lester
    E-Mail: damon.lester@namad.org

Historical Note:
NAMAD is committed to increase opportunities for ethnic minorities in all aspects of the automotive industry. It seeks to ensure the presence of a meaningful, representative number of minority entrepreneurs and employees in the retail sales, supplier and service sectors, and the manufacturing ranks. Membership: $500 (Premier); $5,000 (Regular); $150 (Dealer Candidate).

Meetings/Conferences: Annual

Publications:
NAMAD News; on-line
Vendor Directory; on-line

National Association of Minority Contractors *(1969)*
1300 Pennsylvania Ave. NW
Suite 700
Washington, DC 20004
Tel: (202) 204-3093 *Fax:* (202) 789-7349
E-Mail: info@namcnational.org
Website: namcnational.org
Members: 1200 individuals and/or firms
Staff: 2
Annual Budget: $100-250,000

Tax: 501(c)(3)

Personnel:
President: Gloria Shealey
    E-Mail: president@namcnational.org

Historical Note:
Established in Washington, DC in 1969 and incorporated the same year. Purpose is to provide education and training to minority contractors in building and construction trades. Membership consists of, but is not limited to, general contractors, subcontractors, construction managers, manufacturers, suppliers, local minority contractor associations, funded technical assistance organizations, state and local government agencies, attorneys and accountants. Membership: $400-1,600 (Individual/National, Based on Annual Gross Revenue).

Continuing Education:
Enrollment: 100
Certification Designation/s: GA
Meetings/Conferences:
Number of non-conference events/year: 2

Publications:
Building Concerns; irregular; adv.
Chapter Information; on-line

National Association of Miscellaneous, Ornamental and Architectural Products Contractors *(1969)*
10382 Main St., Suite 200
P.O. Box 280
Fairfax, VA 22038
Tel: (703) 591-1870 *Fax:* (703) 591-1895
Members: 950 companies
Staff: 3
Annual Budget: $100-250,000

Personnel:
Executive Vice President: Fred H. Codding

Historical Note:
Members are companies fabricating and installing decking systems, ornamental iron, steel and aluminum sheathing and architectural motifs on building exteriors.

National Association of Mortgage Bankers
7900 Westpark Dr.
Suite T307
McLean, VA 22102
Staff: 147
Annual Budget: $250-500,000

Personnel:
President: Donald J. Frommeyer

National Association of Mortgage Brokers *(1973)*
2701 W. 15th St.
Suite 536
Plano, TX 75075
Tel: (972) 758-1151 *Fax:* (530) 484-2906
E-Mail: membership@namb.org
Website: namb.org
Members: 25000 individuals
Staff: 8
Annual Budget: $500-1,000,000

Personnel:
Director, Membership service and Marketing: Jessica Savitz
    E-Mail: jsavitz@namb.org
Chief Lobbyist: Roy DeLoach
    E-Mail: roydeloach@dcstrategies.us
Media Contact: Eric C. Peck

Historical Note:
NAMB promotes the industry through programs and services such as education, professional certification and government affairs representation. Membership: $120 (Platinum); $50 (Silver).

Continuing Education:
Certification Designation/s: GMA, CRMS, CMC

Meetings/Conferences: Annual

Publications:
National Mortgage Professional Magazine; monthly; adv.

National Association of Multicultural Engineering Program Advocates *(1979)*
341 N. Maitland Ave.
Suite 130
Maitland, FL 32751
Tel: (407) 647-8839 *Fax:* (407) 629-2502
E-Mail: namepa@namepa.org
Website: namepa.org

Members: 450 individuals
Staff: 11
Annual Budget: $100-250,000

Personnel:
Executive Vice President: Phil Pyster CAE
    E-Mail: phil@crowsegal.com
Assistant Director: Latisha Moore
    E-Mail: latisha@crowsegal.com

Historical Note:
NAMEPA's mission is to provide quality services, information, and tools for stakeholders to produce a diverse pool of engineers and scientists, and achieve equity and parity in the nation's workforce. Membership: $300 (Individual); $600 (Institution); $5,000 (Corporate/Government Agency); $20 (Student).

Meetings/Conferences: Annual

Publications:
Membership Directory; on-line
NAMEPA Newsletter; bi-annually

National Association of Multicultural Media Executives *(1990)*
7950 Jones Branch Dr.
McLean, VA 22107
Tel: (703) 854-7178 *Fax:* (703) 854-7181
Website: namme.org
Members: 350 individuals
Staff: 2
Annual Budget: $100-250,000

Personnel:
Executive Director: Toni F. Laws
    E-Mail: tlaws@namme.org
Administrator: Nancy Osborn

Historical Note:
NAMME members are minority media executives working in the mainstream media. Provides executive development opportunities for its members and works to improve minority representation among executives in print, broadcast, and emerging media. Membership: $300 (Senior Executive); $5000 (Corporate); $7,500 (Life); $3,000 (Affiliate); $500 (Educational); $200 (Mid-Career Executive); $100 (Junior Executive).

National Association of Mutual Insurance Companies *(1895)*
3601 Vincennes Rd.
P.O. Box 68700
Indianapolis, IN 46268
Tel: (317) 875-5250 *Fax:* (317) 879-8408
E-Mail: govaff@namic.org
Website: namic.org
Members: 1400 companies
Staff: 82
Annual Budget: $2-5,000,000
Tax: 501(c)(6)

Personnel:
President and Chief Executive Officer: Charles M. Chamness
Chief Operating Officer and General Counsel: Gregg Dykstra
Director, Communications - State and Policy Affairs: Lisa Floreancig
    E-Mail: lfloreancig@namic.org
Meeting Designer and Project Manager: Crista Hassett CMP
Meeting Planner: Susan Morgan
Director, Web Services: Lisa Rodgers
Vice President, Member Development: Kristen Sizelove
    E-Mail: ksizelove@namic.org
Director, Human Resources: Megan Trainor

Historical Note:
NAMIC benefits member companies through government relations, educational services, and insurance and employee benefit programs. Membership consists of property and casualty mutual insurance companies. Sponsors and supports the NAMIC Political Action Committee. Membership: $3,850-56,000/year.

Meetings/Conferences: Annual
Conference Chair: Susan Morgan
2013 - Seatle, WA (Sheraton Seattle Hotel)/Sept. 22 - 25/1700 attendees/over 100 exhibitors
2014 - Ft. Washington, MD/Sept. 21 - 24/1700 attendees/over 100 exhibitors
Number of non-conference events/year: 11

Publications:
IN Magazine; quarterly
NAMIC Advocacy Update; on-line

NAMIC dailyLead; on-line
The Farm Mutual Forum; monthly

National Association of Native American Studies *(1992)*
PO Box 6670
Scarborough, ME 04070-6670
Tel: (207) 839-3776 *Fax:* (207) 839-8004
E-Mail: natlaffiliates@earthlink.net
Website: naaas.org/
Staff: 1

Personnel:
Executive Director: Dr. Lemuel Berry Jr., PhD
    E-Mail: naaasconference@earthlink.net

Historical Note:
The National Association of African American Studies and Affiliates (NAAAS) a non-profit organization founded in 1992. The overarching goal of the organization was directed toward providing faculty and students an opportunity to engage in scholarly endeavors. This goal has been expanded and the following goals are the foundation from which the organization derives its directions and actions.

Meetings/Conferences: Annual
2013 - Baton Rouge, LA (Crowne Plaza Executive Center Baton Rouge)/Feb. 11 - 16

Publications:
Journal of Intercultural Disciplines
NAAAS & Affiliates Monograph Series; annually

Membership List Available to Non-members

National Association of Negro Business and Professional Women's Clubs *(1935)*
1806 New Hampshire Ave. NW
Washington, DC 20009
Tel: (202) 483-4206 *Fax:* (202) 462-7253
E-Mail: info@nanbpwc.org
Website: nanbpwc.org
Members: 10380 individuals and clubs
Staff: 6
Annual Budget: $250-500,000
Tax: 501(c)(3)

Personnel:
Executive Director: Jennifer Bryant
    E-Mail: executivedirector@nanbpwc.org
President: Marie E. Castillo
    E-Mail: NationalPresident@nanbpwc.org
Meeting Planner: Joanne E. Braxton
    E-Mail: meetingplanner@nanbpwc.org
Director, Membership Services: Hazel Briceno
    E-Mail: membership@nanbpwc.org
Director, Education: Annie Lucas
    E-Mail: education@nanbpwc.org
Accounting Assistant: Robin Waley
    E-Mail: admin@nanbpwc.org

Historical Note:
NANBPWC holds affiliation with NCNW, BWA, and UN. NANBPWC's mission is to promote and protect the interests of African American business and professional women; to serve as a bridge for young people seeking to enter business and the professions; to improve the quality of life in the local and global communities; and to foster good fellowship. Membership: $75 (Members-at-Large); $50 (Associate).

Meetings/Conferences: Annual
Conference Chair: Joanne E. Braxton
2013 - Baltimore, MD (Hyatt Regency Baltimore)/Aug. 12 - 18
Number of non-conference events/year: 2

Publications:
Membership Directory; on-line

Membership List Available to Non-members

National Association of Neighborhoods *(1975)*
1300 Pennsylvania Ave. NW
Suite 700
Washington, DC 20004
Tel: (202) 332-7766 *Fax:* (202) 789-7349
E-Mail: info@nanworld.org
Website: nanworld.org
Members: 2500 Members
Staff: 4
Annual Budget: $100-250,000
Tax: 501(c)(3)

Personnel:
Executive Director: Ricardo C Byrd
    E-Mail: ricardo@nanworld.org

National Association of Neonatal Nurses

Historical Note:
NAN's mission is to improve the quality of life in the nation's neighborhood communities. Membership: $25 (Individual); $50 (Organization).

Meetings/Conferences: Annual

National Association of Neonatal Nurses (1984)
4700 W. Lake Ave.
Glenview, IL 60025-1485
Tel: (847) 375-3660 *Fax:* (847) 375-6491
TollFree: (800) 451-3795
E-Mail: info@nann.org
Website: nann.org
Members: 7000 individuals
Staff: 14
Annual Budget: $2-5,000,000
Tax: 501(c)(6)

Personnel:
Executive Director: Catherine Underwood CAE, MBA
    E-Mail: cunderwood@connect2amc.com
Senior Manager, Marketing: Erin Abbey
Director, Education: Steve Biddle MEd
    E-Mail: sbiddle@nann.org
Operations Manager: Laura Feldt
    E-Mail: lfeldt@nann.org
Senior Manager, Professional Relations: Brian Fitzgerald CEM
    E-Mail: bfitzgerald@nann.org
Senior Manager, Membership Development and Component Relations: Carrie Gremer
    E-Mail: cgremer@nann.org
Managing Editor: Katie Macaluso
    E-Mail: kmacaluso@nann.org
Senior Manager, Meetings: Darlene Somers CMP
    E-Mail: dsomers@nann.org

Historical Note:
NANN strives to shape neonatal nursing through excellence in practice, education, research and professional development. Regular members are nurses specializing in neonatal care and memberships are also available to companies and individuals interested in neonatal care. Membership: $40-2500/year.

Meetings/Conferences: Annual
Conference Chair: Darlene Somers CMP
2013 - Nashville, TN (Nashville Convention Center)/
Oct. 2 - 5

Publications:
Advances in Neonatal Care; bi-monthly
Member Directory; on-line
NANN Central; quarterly; adv.

National Association of Nephrology Technologists and Technicians (1982)
P.O. Box 2307
Dayton, OH 45401-2307
Tel: (937) 586-3705 *Fax:* (937) 586-3699
TollFree: (877) 607-6268
E-Mail: nant@meinet.com
Website: dialysistech.net
Members: 1000 individuals
Staff: 3
Annual Budget: $250-500,000

Personnel:
Executive Director: Francine "Fran" W. Rickenbach CAE, IOM
Manager, Meetings: Doug Conrad
Administrator, Membership: Roxy West

Historical Note:
Added Technicians to their title in 1993. NANT's mission is to promote the highest quality of care for Chronic Kidney Disease (CKD) patients through education and professionalism. Membership: $50 (Full/Associate); $35 (Student).

Meetings/Conferences: Annual
Conference Chair: Doug Conrad
Number of non-conference events/year: 1

Publications:
NANT News; bi-monthly

National Association of Noise Control Officials (1978)
53 Cubberley Rd.
W. Windsor, NJ 08550-3400
Tel: (609) 586-2684 *Fax:* (609) 588-5253
Members: 70 individuals
Staff: 1

Personnel:

Administrator: Edward J. Di Polvere

Historical Note:
Incorporated in the State of New Jersey. Members are employees of the federal or state governments, consultants, scientists and students concerned with acoustical control of the environment. NANCO is an affiliate of the National Environmental Health Association.

National Association of Nonprofit Accountants & Consultants
624 Grassmere Park Dr.
Suite 15
Nashville, TN 37211
Tel: (615) 373-9880 *Fax:* (615) 377-7092
TollFree: (800) 231-2524
E-Mail: info@nonprofitcpas.com
Website: nonprofitcpas.com
Staff: 2

Personnel:
Executive Director: Patrick Pruett
    E-Mail: patrick@enterpriseworldwide.org
Secretary: Harvey Hoskins
    E-Mail: hhoskins@hoskinscpas.com

Historical Note:
A nationwide affiliation of independently owned accounting firms that work with nonprofit organizations. An affiliate of the Alliance of Professional Associations. Membership: $2,400/year (based on territorial structure); $1,500 (one-time enrollment fee).

National Association of Nuclear Pharmacies (1984)
C/O College of Pharmacy MSC09 5369, One University of New Mexico
Albuquerque, NM 87131-0001
Tel: (505) 272-8101
Website: nanp.net
Members: 400 pharmacies
Staff: 2
Annual Budget: $50-100,000

Personnel:
Executive Director and Chairman: Jeffrey P. Norenberg
    E-Mail: jpnoren@unm.edu

Historical Note:
NANP's mission is to focus on the specific business, regulatory, and professional issues that affect nuclear pharmacies. Membership includes chain, independent, and academic/institutional nuclear pharmacies.

Publications:
NANP Newsletter; quarterly

National Association of Nurse Massage Therapists (1992)
P.O. Box 232
W. Milton, OH 45383
Tel: (937) 698-4128 *Fax:* (937) 698-6153
TollFree: (855) 366-2668
E-Mail: info@nanmt.org
Website: nanmt.org
Members: 91 individuals
Staff: 3
Annual Budget: $25-50,000
Tax: 501(c)(6)

Personnel:
Executive Director: Roe Long-Wagner
    E-Mail: roelong@longmgt.com
Manager, Marketing: Shawn Hicks
    E-Mail: shicks@longmgt.com
Manager, Membership Services: Peggy Sanders
    E-Mail: psanders@longmgt.com

Historical Note:
NANMT's mission is to promote recognition of therapeutic touch within nursing practice, and acts as a source of information for members of nursing profession. Members are licensed nurses who practice touch and massage therapy. Membership: $100 (Active); $55 (Student); $300 (Institutional); $75 (Supporting); $65 (Elder).

Publications:
Membership Directory; on-line
Newsletter

National Association of Nurse Practitioners in Women's Health (1980)
505 C St. NE
Washington, DC 20002
Tel: (202) 543-9693
E-Mail: info@npwh.org
Website: npwh.org

Members: 3500 individuals
Staff: 5
Annual Budget: $2-5,000,000
Tax: 501(c)(3)

Personnel:
Chief Executive Officer: Gay Johnson
    E-Mail: gjohnson@npwh.org
Contact, Communications and Health Policy: Emily Longvall
Director, Education: Susan Rawlins MS, NP
    E-Mail: srawlins@gmail.com
Office Administrator and Coordinator, Membership Services: Carol Wiley
    E-Mail: cwiley@npwh.org

Historical Note:
Founded as the National Association of Nurse Practitioners in Reproductive Health, assumed its present name in 1999. NPWH's mission is to assure the provision of quality health care to women of all ages by nurse practitioners. NPWH defines quality health care to be inclusive of an individual's physical, emotional, and spiritual needs. Membership: $95 (Active/Associate); $55 (Retired/Student); $175 (Supporting); $85 (Members of ARHP).

Meetings/Conferences: Annual

Publications:
The Monthly Cycle; monthly
Women's Health Care

Membership List Available to Non-members

National Association of Nutrition and Aging Services Programs (1977)
1612 K St. NW
Suite 400
Washington, DC 20006
Tel: (202) 682-6899 *Fax:* (202) 223-2099
TollFree: (800) 999-6262
Website: nanasp.org
Members: 1000 individuals
Staff: 4
Annual Budget: $100-250,000

Personnel:
Executive Director: Robert B. Blancato
    E-Mail: rblancato@matzblancato.com
President: Paul Downey
Contact, Finance and Operations: Scott Carlson
    E-Mail: scarlson@nanasp.org
Contact, Membership Services and Education: Pamela Carlson
    E-Mail: pcarlson@nanasp.org

Historical Note:
NANASP seeks to strengthen through advocacy and education those who help older Americans. Members are individuals and organizations involved with direct service provision under the Older Americans Act. Membership: $165 (Non-Profit); $300 (Corporate/Profit); $0 (Additional membership with a Non-Profit or Corporate Member).

Meetings/Conferences: Annual

Publications:
Congressional Directory; on-line
Membership Directory; on-line

National Association of Ordnance and Explosive Waste Contractors (1995)
720 Brooker Creek Blvd.
Suite 204
Oldsmar, FL 34677
Tel: (813) 343-6354 *Fax:* (813) 343-6355
Website: naoc.org
Members: 68 Organizations
Staff: 4

Personnel:
President: Victoria Kantsios
Membership Contact: Kornelia 'Connie' Berner
    E-Mail: cbirner@usatampa.com
Treasurer: John Chionchio

Historical Note:
The National Association of OEW Contractors (NAOC) represents and promotes the interests of its members and the public in all aspects of military munitions response services and provide a source of current information on all matters relating to trends or current activities of interest to the industry. Membership: $3850 (Large Business); $2750 (Small Business); $1375 (Small Business With Less than $5M in Annual Revenue).

Meetings/Conferences: Annual

Publications:
NAOC Newsletter; semi-annually; adv.

National Association of Older Worker Employment Services (1980)
300 Third St. SW
Suite 801
Washington, DC 20024
Tel: (202) 479-1200 *Fax:* (202) 479-0735
Website: ncoa.org
Staff: 1

Personnel:
Vice President, Workforce Development Division: Donald L. Davis
   E-Mail: donald.davis@ncoa.org

Historical Note:
An organization of the National Council on the Aging. Promotes expansion of voluntary placement programs to increase job opportunities for older adults.

National Association of Optometrics and Opticians (1959)
P.O. Box 459
Marblehead, OH 43440
Tel: (419) 798-2031 *Fax:* (419) 798-8548
Website: aoa.org
Members: 15500 individuals
Staff: 2
Annual Budget: $100-250,000

Personnel:
Secretary and Treasurer: Franklin D Rozak
   E-Mail: fdrozak@cros.net

Historical Note:
Formerly the National Optical Association. NAOO carries out continuing educational and public affairs programs of mutual importance to members and serves as a clearing house for retail optical information. Membership: $500/year (individual); $1,000 minimum/year (organization/company).

National Association of Optometrists and Opticians
P.O. Box 459
Marblehead, OH 43440
Tel: (419) 798-2031
Staff: 1
Annual Budget: $100-250,000

Personnel:
Contact, Communications: Robin Mohr

Historical Note:
Association of optometrists, opticians, and corporations in the retail optical industry

National Association of Orthopedic Nurses (1980)
401 N. Michigan Ave.
Suite 2200
Chicago, IL 60611
Fax: (312) 673-6941
TollFree: (800) 289-6266
E-Mail: naon@smithbucklin.com
Website: orthonurse.org
Members: 6000 individuals
Staff: 13
Annual Budget: Under $10,000
Tax: 501(c)(6)

Personnel:
Executive Director: Kaye Englebrecht CAE
   E-Mail: kenglebrecht@smithbucklin.com
Associate, Membership Services: Jenny Bohrman
Education Associate: Katie DenHollander
   E-Mail: kdenhollander@smithbucklin.com
Senior Manager, Marketing and Communications: Kara Dress
Show Coordinator: Linda Trummel

Historical Note:
NAON's mission is to advance the specialty of orthopaedic nursing through excellence in research, education and nursing practice. Members are licensed registered nurses, LVNs or LPNs, and students associated with all facets of orthopaedic patient care. Membership: $110 (General); $157 (Extended General); $100 (Associate); $40-50 (Student).

Continuing Education:
Certification Designation/s: ONC, APN

Meetings/Conferences: Annual
Conference Chair: Linda Trummel

Publications:
Membership Directory; on-line
NAON News; bi-monthly

Orthopaedic Nursing journal; bi-monthly

National Association of Orthopaedic Technologists (1982)
8365 Keystone Crossing
Suite 107
Indianapolis, IN 46240
Tel: (317) 205-9484 *Fax:* (317) 205-9481
E-Mail: naot@hp-assoc.com
Website: naot.org
Members: 1000 individuals
Staff: 6
Annual Budget: $250-500,000

Personnel:
Executive Director: Bruce Davis
   E-Mail: bdavis@np-assoc.com
Manager, Meeting and Membership: Julie Schafer
   E-Mail: naot@hp-assoc.com

Historical Note:
NAOT's mission is to work for the continued education of orthopaedic technologists, and other related allied health care professionals, who specialize in casting, splinting and bracing and the general public. Membership: $100 (Full); $50 (Military); $30 (Student/Associate).

Continuing Education:
Certification Designation/s: OTC

Meetings/Conferences: Annual
Conference Chair: Bruce Davis
2013 - New Orleans, LA (Hyatt Regency)/July 31 - Aug. 3

Publications:
Membership Directory; on-line
Orthotech Professional; bi-monthly

National Association of Osteopathic Foundations (1897)
142 E. Ontario St.
Chicago, IL 60611-2864
Tel: (312) 202-8000 *Fax:* (312) 202-8200
TollFree: (800) 621-1773
E-Mail: corules@aol.com
Website: osteopathic.org
Members: 78,000 osteopathic physicians
Staff: 2

Personnel:
Executive Director: John B. Crosby JD
Treasurer: Karen J. Nichols

Historical Note:
The American Osteopathic Association was founded with the goal of uniting the efforts of individual physicians and colleges to advance the osteopathic medical profession. Originally called the American Association for the Advancement of Osteopathy, the name changed to the American Osteopathic Association in 1901. The primary objects of the organization are, in the broadest sense, to work toward and attain all things that will truly tend to the "advancement of Osteopathy," and the rounding of it into its destined proportions as the eternal truth and vital principle of therapeutic science. Membership:$0-683/year.

Meetings/Conferences: Annual
2013 - Chicago, IL/July 16 - 21

Publications:
Predoc e-Newsletter
The Journal of the American Osteopathic Association; monthly; adv.

National Association of Parliamentarians (1930)
213 S. Main St.
Independence, MO 64050-3808
Tel: (816) 833-3892 *Fax:* (816) 833-3893
TollFree: (888) 627-2929
E-Mail: hq@nap2.org
Website: parliamentarians.org
Members: 4000 individuals
Staff: 3
Annual Budget: $500-1,000,000
Tax: 501(c)(3)

Personnel:
Executive Director: Leonard M. Young
   E-Mail: len@nap2.org
Administrative Assistant: Debbie Montavy
   E-Mail: debbie@nap2.org

Historical Note:
NAP is dedicated to educate leaders throughout the world in effective meeting management through the use of parliamentary procedure. Membership: $75/year.

Continuing Education:

Enrollment: 50
Certification Designation/s: RP, PRP

Meetings/Conferences: Annual
2013 - Portland, OR (Hilton Portland and Executive Tower)/Sept. 6 - 9

Publications:
Membership Directory; on-line
NAP President Newsletter; quarterly
National Parliamentarian Magazine; quarterly

National Association of Partners in Education (1988)
209 Madison St.
Suite 401
Alexandria, VA 22314
Tel: (703) 836-4880 *Fax:* (703) 836-6941
Website: napehq.org
Members: 400,000 partnerships
Staff: 1
Annual Budget: $1-2,000,000

Personnel:
President, Chief Executive Director: Daniel W. Merenda

Historical Note:
Formed as a result of a merger of the National School Volunteer Program and National Symposium on Partnerships in Education, NAPE. To provide leadership in the formation and growth of effective partnerships that ensure success for all students.

Publications:
Newsletter; monthly

National Association of Passports and Visa Services (2004)
1417 Highland Dr.
Silver Spring, MD 20910
Tel: (301) 650-2321
Website: napvs.org
Members: 1000 companies, federal and state government agencies, and international nonprofit organizations
Staff: 1

Personnel:
Executive Director: Robert L. Smith Jr.
   E-Mail: rsmith@napvs.org

Historical Note:
Mission of NAPVS is to represent the interests of the U.S. passport and visa service industry and to increase consumer and business confidence in using passport and visa services to obtain expedited passports. Membership: $650-18,000/year (Based on total annual revenue).

Publications:
Membership Directory; on-line

National Association of Pastoral Musicians (1976)
962 Wayne Ave.
Suite 210
Silver Spring, MD 20910-4461
Tel: (240) 247-3000 *Fax:* (240) 247-3001
E-Mail: npmsing@npm.org
Website: npm.org
Members: 8900 individuals
Staff: 10
Annual Budget: $1-2,000,000
Tax: 501(c)(3)

Personnel:
President: J. Michael McMahon
   E-Mail: npmpres@npm.org
Director, Continuing Education: Rev. Paul H. Colloton OP
   E-Mail: npmpaul@npm.org
Director, Membership Services: Kathleen Haley
   E-Mail: haley@npm.org
Manager, Advertising: Karen Heinsch
   E-Mail: npmkaren@npm.org
Director, Convention Operations: Peter Maher
   E-Mail: npmpeter@npm.org
Senior Editor: Dr. Gordon E. Truitt
   E-Mail: npmedit@npm.org
Contact, Finance: Anthony Worch
   E-Mail: laworch@aol.com

Historical Note:
NPM nurtures the art of musical liturgy. Membership: $70 (Individual); $33 (Youth); $118 (Regular-Parish); $85 (Single-Parish); $37 (Retired/Senior).

Continuing Education:
Enrollment: 40
Certification Designation/s: ICC, BCC, SPC, CDMM, CAEO

Meetings/Conferences: Annual
Conference Chair: Karen Heinsch
2013 - Washington, DC (Marriott Wardman Park Hotel)/July 29 - Aug. 3/1-10 exhibitors
Number of non-conference events/year: 3

Publications:
Pastoral Music Magazine; bi-monthly; adv.
Pastoral Music Notebook newsletter
The Liturgical Singer; quarterly

Membership List Available to Non-members

National Association of Pediatric Nurse Practitioners (1973)
20 Brace Rd.
Suite 200
Cherry Hill, NJ 08034-2634
Tel: (856) 857-9700 Fax: (856) 857-1600
TollFree: (877) 662-7627
E-Mail: info@napnap.org
Website: napnap.org
Members: 7500 members
Staff: 21
Annual Budget: $2-5,000,000
Tax: 501(c)(6)

Personnel:
Chief Executive Officer: Sandra Vassos MPA
Director, Practice, Education and Research: Dolores C. Jones CAE, EdD, RN
    E-Mail: djones@napnap.org
Director, Membership, Chapters and Communications: Felicia K. Taylor BA
    E-Mail: ftaylor@napnap.org
Director, Human Resource, Finance and Administration: Catherine Van Horn

Historical Note:
NAPNAP's mission is to promote optimal health for children through leadership, practice, advocacy, education and research.

Meetings/Conferences: Annual
Conference Chair: Dolores C. Jones CAE, EdD, RN
2013 - Orlando, FL (Hilton Orlando)/April 17 - 20/1500 attendees/11-25 exhibitors
2014 - Boston, MA (John B. Hynes Veterans Memorial Convention Center)/March 11 - 14/1500 attendees/11-25 exhibitors
2015 - Las Vegas, NV (Caesars Palace)/March 11 - 14/1500 attendees/11-25 exhibitors

Publications:
Membership Directory; annually
The Journal of Pediatric Health Care; bi-monthly; adv.
The Pediatric Nurse Practitioner; bi-monthly; adv.

Membership List Available to Non-members

National Association of Personal Financial Advisors (1983)
3250 N. Arlington Heights Rd.
Suite 109
Arlington Heights, IL 60004
Tel: (847) 483-5400 Fax: (847) 483-5415
TollFree: (800) 366-2732
E-Mail: info@napfa.org
Website: napfa.org
Members: 2400 members
Staff: 14
Annual Budget: $2-5,000,000
Tax: 501(c)(6)

Personnel:
Chief Executive Officer: Ellen Turf
    E-Mail: turfe@napfa.org
Managing Editor: Kevin Adler
    E-Mail: kadler2@earthlink.net
Coordinator, Membership Services: Anthony Aloy
    E-Mail: aloya@napfa.org
Manager, Education and Conference: Robin Gemeinhardt
    E-Mail: gemeinhardtr@napfa.org
Manager, Communications and Marketing: Ben Lewis
    E-Mail: ben@bdlpr.com
Manager, Public Policy and Advocacy: Karen Nystrom
    E-Mail: nystromk@napfa.org
Manager, Conferences: Margery Wasserman

Historical Note:
NAPFA is dedicated to the advancement of fee-only financial planning. Members are financial planners who are compensated only by fees, meaning commissions are not accepted. Membership: $575 (NAPFA- Registered Financial Advisor/Provisional); $150 (Sustaining/Academic Affiliate); $350 (Financial Services Affiliate); $100 (Student Affiliate).

Meetings/Conferences: Annual
Conference Chair: Margery Wasserman
2013 - San Diego, CA (Manchester Grand)/April 29 - May 4/800 attendees/over 100 exhibitors
2013 - Las Vegas, NV (Paris Las Vegas Hotel and Casino)/May 8 - 10
2014 - Chicago, IL (Hilton Chicago)/May 12 - 17/800 attendees
2015 - San Diego, CA (Manchester Grand)/May 11 - 15
Number of non-conference events/year: 4

Publications:
Advisor Magazine; adv.
Membership Directory; on-line
Planning Prespectives; quarterly
Resource Partner Directory; on-line
What's New At NAPFA; monthly

National Association of Personnel Services (1961)
6625 Hwy. 53 East
Suite 410-201
Dawsonville, GA 30534
Tel: (706) 531-0060 Fax: (866) 739-4750
E-Mail: info@recruitinglife.com
Website: recruitinglife.com
Members: 1100 companies
Staff: 3
Annual Budget: $250-500,000

Personnel:
President: John Sacerdote
    E-Mail: jsacerdote@recruitinglife.com
Office Manager: Carolyn Boyer

Historical Note:
Formerly (1992) the National Association of Personnel Consultants. Mission is to serve, protect, inform, and represent all facets of the personnel services industry regarding federal legislation and regulatory issues by providing education, certification, and member services which enhance the ability to conduct business with integrity and competence. Membership: $4800 (Corporate/Single shop); $240 (Individual); $360 (Sole Proprietor/Firm); 600 (Firm-Sole Proprietor).

Continuing Education:
Certification Designation/s: CTS, NAF, CPC, CERS, PRC, NRCSIP

Meetings/Conferences: Annual

Publications:
Inside NAPS Newsletter
Membership Directory; on-line
The Credential Newsletter; bi-monthly
The Fordyce Newsletter

National Association of Photo Equipment Technicians (1973)
2282 Springport Rd.
Jackson, MI 49202
Tel: (517) 788-8100 Fax: (517) 788-8371
TollFree: (800) 762-9287
Website: pmai.org/Napet
Members: 20000 individuals
Staff: 2
Annual Budget: $10-25,000

Personnel:
President: Raymond J. Heinbokel Jr.
Staff Liaison: Nick Shaver

Historical Note:
A division (1976) of the Photo Marketing Association International. NAPET has reintroduced its Manufacturer Service Support Award. NAPET bridges together independent camera repair businesses and photo manufacturers for increased communication and improved services offered by photographic equipment repair businesses. Membership $25 (Individual); $95 (Company).

Publications:
Membership Directory; on-line

National Association of Physician Nurses (1973)
900 S. Washington St., Suite G-13
Falls Church, VA 22046-4020
Tel: (703) 237-8616 Fax: (703) 533-1153
Members: 2000 individuals
Staff: 3
Annual Budget: $100-250,000

Personnel:
Director, Membership: S. Young

Historical Note:
Membership: $31/year.

Membership List Available to Non-members

National Association of Physician Recruiters (1984)
222 S. Westmonte Dr.
Suite 101
Altamonte Springs, FL 32714
Tel: (407) 774-7880 Fax: (407) 774-6440
TollFree: (800) 726-5613
E-Mail: napr@napr.org
Website: napr.org
Members: 300 companies
Staff: 14
Annual Budget: $100-250,000
Tax: 501(c)(6)

Personnel:
Executive Vice President: Bill Kautter CAE
    E-Mail: bkautter@napr.org
Director, Membership Services: Martha Dunn
    E-Mail: mdunn@napr.org
Planner, Meetings: Marna Krot
    E-Mail: mkrot@napr.org
Director, Communications and Marketing: Elaine York PhD
    E-Mail: eyork@napr.org

Historical Note:
NAPR is a professional organization representing recruiters who are dedicated in serving the healthcare industry. Members are physician recruiting organizations, hospitals, medical groups, individuals and vendor organizations. Membership: $475 (Active); $275 (Institutional); $490 (Vendor).

Meetings/Conferences: Annual
Conference Chair: Marna Krot
2013 - Orlando, FL (Disney's Contemporary Resort)/ April 10 - 12

Publications:
Membership Directory
The Pulse e-Newsletter; quarterly; adv.

National Association of Pipe Coating Applicators (1965)
1000 Louisiana
Suite 3400
Houston, TX 77002
Tel: (713) 276-5306 Fax: (713) 276-6206
Website: napca.com
Members: 145 companies
Staff: 2
Annual Budget: $250-500,000
Tax: 501(c)(6)

Personnel:
Managing Director and General Counsel: Merritt B. Chastain III
    E-Mail: mchastain@gardere.com

Historical Note:
NAPCA's purpose is to promote the growth of its industry and to provide its members, their customers and the international public with better standards of quality and workmanship necessary to protect the world's pipeline infrastructure. Membership includes most U.S. applicators of protective coatings for pipe used in the construction of gas distribution and transmission and oil transportation pipelines. Membership: $50-1,500/year.

Meetings/Conferences:
2013 - Indian Wells, CA (Renaissance Esmeralda Indian Wells Resort and Spa)/April 24 - 28
2014 - Bonita Springs, FL (Hyatt Regency Coconut Point Resort and Spa)/April 23 - 26
2016 - Ft. Lauderdale, FL (Marriott Harbor Beach Resort & Spa)/April 13 - 16
Number of non-conference events/year: 1

Publications:
Membership Directory; on-line
Newsletter

National Association of Pipe Fabricators (1977)
2887 Goat Creek Rd.
P.O. Box 242
Kerrville, TX 78028
Tel: (888) 798-1924 Fax: (800) 860-5700
E-Mail: info@napf.com
Website: napf.com
Members: 40 individuals
Staff: 2
Annual Budget: $50-100,000

Personnel:
Executive Director: Tom Brakefield

Legal Counsel: David Houghton

Historical Note:
NAPF's mission is to serve the ductile iron pipe industry. Members are fabricators of ductile iron pipe used in water and waste water treatment plants. Membership: $2,500/year (Company).

Meetings/Conferences: Annual

Publications:
Member Directory
Newsletter; quarterly

National Association of Pizzeria Operators (1982)
908 S. Eighth St.
Suite 200
Louisville, KY 40203
Tel: (502) 736-9500 Fax: (502) 736-9531
TollFree: (800) 489-8324
E-Mail: info@polppay.org
Website: napo.com
Members: 1600 companies and 40,000 pizzeria professionals
Staff: 5
Annual Budget: $500-1,000,000

Personnel:
President and Publisher: Pete Lachapelle
    E-Mail: plachapelle@pizzatoday.com
Vice President, Meetings and Conferences: Bruce Allar
    E-Mail: ballar@pizzatoday.com
Membership Director: Angela Hoskins
Executive Vice President: Bill Oakley
    E-Mail: boakley@pizzatoday.com
Editor-in-Chief: Jeremy White
    E-Mail: jwhite@pizzatoday.com

Historical Note:
Formerly (2003) National Association of Pizza Operators. Pizza equipment manufacturers, industry suppliers, franchise and independent pizza operators and frozen pizza producers. Provides liaison between pizza industry and governmental agencies. Researches industry data and statistics. Membership: $99/year (retail), $1000/year (Corporate).

Meetings/Conferences: Annual
Conference Chair: Bill Oakley
2013 - Las Vegas, NV (Las Vegas Convention Center)/ March 19 - 21/over 100 exhibitors

Publications:
Buyers' Guide; on-line; adv.
Pizza Today magazine; monthly; adv.
Vendor Directory; on-line

National Association of Planning Councils (1990)
11118 Ferndale Rd.
Dallas, TX 75238
Tel: (214) 341-3657
TollFree: (888) 298-7459
E-Mail: napc@communityplanning.org
Website: communityplanning.org
Members: 24 organizations and 18 members
Staff: 1
Tax: 501(c)(3)

Personnel:
Coordinator and Website Manager: Sharon Clark
    E-Mail: sharonclark@communityplanning.org

Historical Note:
NAPC's mission is to improve the human condition through encouraging research-based community planning and action. Membership Dues: $150-350 (Member Organization, dues determined by annual budget); $100 (Individual); $25 (Student); $500 (Supporting); $750 (Contributing); $1,000 (Memberplus); $1,500 (Sustaining).

Meetings/Conferences: Annual
2013 - Alexandria, VA (Embassy Suites Alexandria-Old Town)/April 5 - 7

Publications:
NAPC e-newsletter; on-line

National Association of Plant Patent Owners (1939)
1000 Vermont Ave. NW
Suite 300
Washington, DC 20005-4903
Tel: (202) 789-2900 Fax: (202) 789-1893
Members: 70 individuals
Staff: 2
Annual Budget: $10-25,000
Tax: 501(c)(6)

Personnel:

President: Steve Hutton
Senior Director, Government Relations: Craig J. Regelbrugge
    E-Mail: cregelbrugge@anla.org

Historical Note:
NAPPO is a trade association dedicated to promoting the development, protection, production and distribution of new and improved plant varieties. Members are owners of patents on newly propagated flowers, trees and plants. Affiliated with American Nursery and Landscape Association. It is administered by the ANLA. Membership meetings are held in January and July. Active member dues are based on the number of patents owned. Associate membership is open to any individual or business interested in plant breeding, introduction, and intellectual property protection. Membership: $100/year (Associate); $100-$800/year (Active).

National Association of Police Athletics/Activities Leagues, Inc.
658 W. Indiantown Rd.
Suite 201
Jupiter, FL 33458
Tel: (561) 745-5535 Fax: (561) 745-3147
Website: nationalpal.org
Members: 400 member chapters
Staff: 6
Annual Budget: $2-5,000,000

Personnel:
Executive Director: Mike Dillhyon
Legal Counsel: Dan Akel
Treasurer: Leslee Brimer
Chief, Officials: Robert Nicholson
Contact, Marketing and Website Development: David Roose
Manager, Events, Training and Membership: Eric Widness
    E-Mail: ewidness@nationalpal.org

Historical Note:
National PAL work to prevent juvenile crime and violence by building the bond between cops and kids. Membership: $400/year.

Meetings/Conferences: Annual
Conference Chair: Eric Widness
Number of non-conference events/year: 2

Publications:
Membership Directory; on-line

National Association of Police Organizations (1978)
317 S. Patrick St.
Alexandria, VA 22314-3501
Tel: (703) 549-0775 Fax: (703) 684-0515
TollFree: (800) 322-6276
E-Mail: info@napo.org
Website: napo.org
Members: 241000 law enforcement personnel
Staff: 9
Annual Budget: $1-2,000,000
Tax: 501(c)(6)

Personnel:
Executive Director: William J. Johnson
Director, Government Affairs: Rachel Hedge
    E-Mail: rhedge@napo.org
Treasurer: Sean Smoot

Historical Note:
NAPO is a coalition of police unions and associations from across the United States that serves to advance the interests of America's law enforcement officers through legislative and legal advocacy, political action and education. Members are law enforcement officers. Membership: $1.75-4 (Group, based on no. of members,minimum $200; $2.75 (Retired); $25 (Individual).

Meetings/Conferences: Annual
2013 - Nashville, TN (Millennium Maxwell House Hotel)/July 20 - 24
Number of non-conference events/year: 3

Publications:
Legislative Updates; on-line
Membership Directory; on-line
Washington Report; monthly

National Association of Portable X-Ray Providers
2584 W. Village Terrace
Springfield, MO 65810
Tel: (417) 234-5801
TollFree: (800) 533-9729
Website: napxp.org
Staff: 2

Annual Budget: $100-250,000

Personnel:
President: Ken Andrews
    E-Mail: kandrews@kaxray.com

Historical Note:
The National Association of Portable X-Ray Providers is a national affiliation whose members supply portable x-ray and EKG services to nursing homes. NAPXP's mission is to protect industry from unwarranted cuts in funding and fees. Membership: $3,000 (Active); $ 2,500 (Associate).

Publications:
Membership Directory; on-line

National Association of Postal Supervisors (1908)
1727 King St.
Suite 400
Alexandria, VA 22314-2753
Tel: (703) 836-9660 Fax: (703) 836-9665
E-Mail: napshq@naps.org
Website: naps.org
Members: 28000 members
Staff: 7
Annual Budget: $2-5,000,000
Tax: 501(c)(5)

Personnel:
Executive Vice President: James F. Killackey III
    E-Mail: naps.jk@naps.org
President: Louis M. Atkins
    E-Mail: naps.la@naps.org
Contact, Membership: Jovan Duncan
    E-Mail: naps.jd@naps.org
Legislative Counsel: Bruce Moyer
    E-Mail: brumoyer@verizon.net

Historical Note:
NAPS strives to promote, through appropriate and effective action, the welfare of its members, and to cooperate with USPS and other agencies of the federal government. Sponsors the Supervisors Political Action Committee. Membership: $78/year (Individual).

Meetings/Conferences: Annual
Number of non-conference events/year: 8

Publications:
Legislative Newsletter; on-line
Membership Directory; on-line

National Association of Postmasters of the United States (1898)
Eight Herbert St.
Alexandria, VA 22305-2600
Tel: (703) 683-9027 Fax: (703) 683-6820
E-Mail: napusinfo@napus.org
Website: napus.org
Members: 85,000 individuals, other Postmasters, officers-in-charge and retired Postmasters.
Staff: 5
Annual Budget: $2-5,000,000
Tax: 501(c)(6)

Personnel:
Executive Director: Charles Moser
    E-Mail: cmoser@napus.org
Director, Government Relations: Robert Levi
    E-Mail: blevi@napus.org
Director, Membership Services: Nick Somers
    E-Mail: membership@napus.org

Historical Note:
NAPUS's mission is to represent, promote and protect postmasters. Members are active and retired postmasters. It also sponsors and supports the Political Education for Postmasters Political Action Committee and a Free Life Insurance of $10,000 is given to the newly appointed postmaster. Membership: $42-386 (Active Individual).

Meetings/Conferences: Semi-Annual
2013 - Arlington, VA (Crystal Gateway Marriott)/ March 16 - 21
2013 - Bellevue, WA (Hyatt Regency Bellevue)/Aug. 17 - 22
Number of non-conference events/year: 3

Publications:
E-NAPUS Legislative Newsletter; bi-monthly
Membership Directory; on-line
The Postmasters Gazette; monthly; adv.

National Association of Power Engineers (1882)
One Springfield St.
Chicopee, MA 01013-2624
Tel: (413) 592-6273 Fax: (413) 592-1998
E-Mail: nape@powerengineers.com

Website: powerengineers.com
Members: 2000 individuals
Staff: 3
Annual Budget: $100-250,000

Personnel:
President: Ted Ross
    E-Mail: Ted@tedrossconsulting.com
Assistant Editor: Adele Gamelli
    E-Mail: nape@onecommail.com
Secretary and Treasurer: David Grinder
    E-Mail: dcfdpower@verizon.net

Historical Note:
Formerly, National Association of Stationary Engineers. NAPE is dedicated to the purpose of education. Members include those in power plant operation and maintenance responsible for supplying industry and service establishments with process power, heat, air conditioning, lighting, ventilation and related building and plant services. *Membership:* $100 (Individual); $500 (Corporation).

Meetings/Conferences: Annual
2013 - Williamsburg, VA (The Woodlands Inn and Suites)/June 19 - 23

Publications:
National Engineer; bi-monthly; adv.

National Association of Principals of Schools for Girls (1921)
23490 Caraway Lakes Dr.
Bonita Springs, FL 34135-8441
Tel: (239) 947-6196 *Fax:* (855) 390-3245
E-Mail: napsg@mac.com
Website: napsg.org
Members: 625 heads and administrators
Staff: 1
Annual Budget: $250-500,000
Tax: 501(c)(3)

Personnel:
Executive Director: Bruce W. Galbraith
    E-Mail: napsg@mac.com

Historical Note:
NAPSG's mission is to further the professional growth of its members by providing a forum in which issues pertinent to the education of girls and young women are presented and discussed. *Membership:* $300 (Principal/Associate); $50 (College); $25 (Affiliate, Employed); $10 (Affiliate, Retired); $70-150 (Affiliate Lifetime).

Meetings/Conferences: Annual
2013 - Ponte Vedra Beach, FL (Ponte Vedra Inn and Club)/Feb. 24 - 26
2014 - Orlando, FL/Feb. 23 - 25

National Association of Printing Ink Manufacturers (1916)
581 Main St.
Suite 520
Woodbridge, NJ 07095-1104
Tel: (732) 855-1525 *Fax:* (732) 855-1838
E-Mail: napim@napim.org
Website: napim.org
Members: 123 ink companies and suppliers
Staff: 7
Annual Budget: $500-1,000,000

Personnel:
Executive Director: Brad Bergey
    E-Mail: bbergey@napim.org
Administrative Assistant: Janet Ciravolo
    E-Mail: jciravolo@napim.org
Director, Regulatory Affairs and Technology: George Fuchs
    E-Mail: gfuchs@napim.org

Historical Note:
Established as the National Association of Printing Ink Makers; assumed its present name in 1967. NAPIM provides information and assistance to its members to better manage their businesses, and represents the printing ink industry in the United States. It also seeks to sponsor the National Printing Ink Research Institute.

Meetings/Conferences: Annual

National Association of Private Special Education Centers (1971)
601 Pennsylvania Ave. NW
S. Building, Suite 900
Washington, DC 20004
Tel: (202) 434-8225 *Fax:* (202) 434-8224
E-Mail: napsec@aol.com
Website: napsec.org

Members: 300 schools
Staff: 4
Annual Budget: $250-500,000
Tax: 501(c)(4)

Personnel:
Executive Director and Chief Executive Officer: Sherry L. Kolbe
    E-Mail: napsec@aol.com
Administrative Assistant: Candice Battle
Coordinator, Communications: Alison Figi
Coordinator, Membership Services: Ryan Norton

Historical Note:
NAPSEC's mission is to improve educational opportunities for individuals with disabilities and to promote private special education. *Membership:* $567-2,260 (School Budget); $2,435-5,796 (Sustaining/ Contributing/Friend of NAPSEC/Gold/Platinum); $550 (Affiliate).

Meetings/Conferences: Annual
2013 - Phoenix, AZ/Jan. 27 - 30
2013 - Phoenix, AZ (Camelback Inn)/March 27 - 30

Publications:
Membership Directory; on-line; adv.

National Association of Private, Nontraditional Schools and Colleges (1974)
182 Thompson Rd.
Grand Junction, CO 81503
Tel: (970) 243-5441 *Fax:* (970) 242-4392
E-Mail: director@napnsc.org
Website: napnsc.org
Members: 4 institutions
Staff: 2
Annual Budget: $10-25,000

Personnel:
Executive Director: H. Earl Heusser EdD
Office Manager: Irene L. Heusser PsyD

Historical Note:
Formerly (1977) National Association of Schools and Colleges. Later (1998) National Association of Private, Nontraditional Schools and Colleges. Its Accrediting Commission for Higher Education is the only national institutional accrediting body which has developed criteria, standards and guidelines expressly for private, nontraditional or alternative education at all secondary and postsecondary levels. Several categories of membership are available such as Correspondent, Candidate Accrediton etc.

National Association of Produce Market Managers (1947)
P.O. Box 291284
Columbia, SC 29229
Tel: (803) 333-9421
Website: napmm.org
Members: 110 individuals
Staff: 3

Personnel:
President: Ben Vitale
Treasurer: Deb Churchill
Administrator, Marketing and Communications: Gwen Tillisch
    E-Mail: gtillisch@gmail.com

Historical Note:
NAPMM strives to help market managers improve facilities and increase services while encouraging cooperation and exchange of ideas between members and partners.Their mission is to improve and strengthen the economic health and vitality of year-round, permanent, wholesale produce markets, retail farmer's markets, and public markets. *Membership:* $75 (Executive); $300 (Commercial); $75 (Associate); $20 (Retired). Honorary members are selected by Board of Directors and no fee is applicable to them.

Continuing Education:
Certification Designation/s: CPMM

Publications:
Membership Directory; on-line
The GreenSheet Newslette

National Association of Professional Asian American Women (1987)
304 Oak Knoll Terrace
Rockville, MD 20850
Tel: (301) 785-8585
E-Mail: napaw.conference@comcast.net
Website: napaw.org
Staff: 3
Tax: 501(c)(3)

Personnel:
National Chair: Vivian C. Kim MA

Chief, Financial Operations: Rosemarie Leung
Executive Secretary: Hanna Yun

Historical Note:
NAPAW's mission is to promote the social status of Asian American professional women by providing better educational and training opportunities and to enhance leadership skills, development, and occupational and business opportunities. *Membership:* Free

Meetings/Conferences: Annual

National Association of Professional Background Screeners (2003)
12100 Sunset Hills Rd.
Suite 130
Reston, VA 20190
Tel: (703) 234-4066 *Fax:* (703) 435-4390
E-Mail: info@napbs.com
Website: napbs.com
Members: 722 members
Staff: 4
Annual Budget: $1-2,000,000

Personnel:
Executive Director: Carol Wynne
Contact, Events: Audrey Molinari
    E-Mail: amolinari@drohanmgmt.com
Contact, Membership and Accreditation: Pam Owens
    E-Mail: powens@drohanmgmt.com

Historical Note:
NABPS mission is to promote ethical business practices, promote compliance with the Fair Credit Reporting Act and foster awareness of issues related to consumer protection and privacy rights within the background screening industry. *Membership:* $500-6,000 (Regular); $150 (Affiliate); $500 (Associate-Provider); $350 (International).

Continuing Education:
Certification Designation/s: DATIA

Meetings/Conferences: Annual
Conference Chair: Audrey Molinari
2013 - Scottsdale, AZ (JW Marriott Phoenix Desert Ridge Resort and Spa)/Sept. 15 - 17
2014 - Denver, CO (Hyatt Regency Denver at Colorado Convention Center)/Sept. 7 - 9

Publications:
NAPBS Journal; bi-monthly; adv.
Vendor Directory; on-line

National Association of Professional Band Instrument Repair Technicians (1976)
2026 Eagle Rd.
P.O. Box 51
Normal, IL 61761-0051
Tel: (309) 452-4257 *Fax:* (309) 452-4825
E-Mail: napbirt@napbirt.org
Website: napbirt.org
Members: 1300 individuals
Staff: 2

Personnel:
Executive Director: Bill Mathews
Administrative Manager: Ross Watkins

Historical Note:
NAPBIRT's mission is to promote possible standards of musical instrument repair service by providing members with a central agency for the exchange of information and continued education through the administration of programs that benefit its membership. *Membership:* $100 (Apprentice/Student); $140 (Professional/Associate).

Meetings/Conferences: Annual
2013 - Portsmouth, VA (Renaissance Portsmouth Hotel and Waterfront Conference Center)/April 5 - 8
2014 - Portland, OR (DoubleTree by Hilton)/April 4 - 7

Publications:
TechniCom Magazine; bi-monthly; adv.

National Association of Professional Baseball Leagues (1901)
P.O. Box A
St. Petersburg, FL 33731
Tel: (727) 822-6937 *Fax:* (727) 821-5819
Website: minorleaguebaseball.com
Staff: 66
Annual Budget: $2-5,000,000

Personnel:
President and Chief Executive Officer: Pat O'Conner
    E-Mail: admin@minorleaguebaseball.com
Senior Assistant Director, Event Services: Kelly Butler
    E-Mail: kellybutler@minorleaguebaseball.com
Director, Information Technology: Rob Colamarino

E-Mail: robcolamarino@minorleaguebaseball.com
Executive Director, Communications: Steve Densa
E-Mail: stevedensa@minorleaguebaseball.com
Vice President, Sales and Marketing: Rod Meadows
E-Mail: rodmeadows@minorleaguebaseball.com
Senior Vice President, Finance: David Nunes
E-Mail: davidnunes@minorleaguebaseball.com
Senior Vice President, Legal Affairs: Scott Poley

Historical Note:
Formerly National Association of Professional Baseball Leagues. MiLB purpose is the running of Baseball's annual Winter Meetings, the convention of professional baseball, in conjunction with the Commissioner's Office.

Meetings/Conferences: Annual
Conference Chair: Kelly Butler

Publications:
Baseball News; adv.

National Association of Professional Employer Organizations *(1984)*
707 N. Saint Asaph St.
Alexandria, VA 22314
Tel: (703) 836-0466 *Fax*: (703) 836-0976
E-Mail: info@napeo.org
Website: napeo.org
Members: 350 PEO members
Staff: 15
Annual Budget: $2-5,000,000

Personnel:
President and Chief Executive Officer: Patrick J. Cleary
E-Mail: pcleary@napeo.org
Editor, PEO Insider: Stephanie Oetjen
E-Mail: soetjen@napeo.org
Administrator, Member and Database Services: Marion Powell
E-Mail: mpowell@napeo.org
General Counsel: William J. Schilling
E-Mail: wschilling@napeo.org
Director, Meetings and Conference Services: Robin Schlesinger
E-Mail: rschlesinger@napeo.org
Director, Communications: Kerry Marshall Schmit
Director, Membership Services: Catherine Schmutz
E-Mail: cschmutz@napeo.org
Vice President, Government Affairs: Tim Tucker
E-Mail: ttucker@napeo.org
Senior Vice President, Chief Operating Officer: Melissa Viscovich
E-Mail: mviscovich@napeo.org

Historical Note:
NAPEO's mission is to advance the professional employer organization industry by promoting a set of professional standards that address financial, legal and ethical performance.

Meetings/Conferences: Annual
Conference Chair: Robin Schlesinger
Number of non-conference events/year: 1

Publications:
Membership Directory; on-line
Monthly Legal Reviews; monthly
NAPEO E-News; weekly

National Association of Professional Geriatric Care Managers *(1985)*
3275 W. Ina Rd.
Suite 130
Tucson, AZ 85741-2198
Tel: (520) 881-8008 *Fax*: (520) 325-7925
Website: caremanager.org
Members: 2000 individuals
Staff: 6
Annual Budget: $500-1,000,000
Tax: 501(c)(6)

Personnel:
Executive Director: Kaaren Boothroyd
E-Mail: kboothroyd@napgcm.org
Meeting Planner: Pamela "Pam" Carlson
E-Mail: meetings@napgcm.org
Contact, Membership Services, Database and Products: Sarah Garcia
E-Mail: sgarcia@napgcm.org
Contact, Technology, Membership Services and Organizational Support: Amanda Mizell
E-Mail: amizell@napgcm.org
Contact, Operations, Publications and Registrar: Julie Wagner

E-Mail: jwagner@napgcm.org

Historical Note:
Formerly (1994) known as the National Association of Private Geriatric Care Managers. NAPGCM's mission is to advance professional geriatric care management through education, collaboration, and leadership. Membership: $85-495/year.

Continuing Education:
Certification Designation/s: CMC, CCM, C-ASWCM, C-SWCM

Meetings/Conferences: Annual
Conference Chair: Pamela "Pam" Carlson
2013 - Philadelphia, PA (DoubleTree by Hilton Philadelphia Center City)/April 17 - 20

Publications:
eFlash Enewsletter; on-line
Inside GCM
Inside GCM; adv.
Membership Directory; on-line; adv.
The NAPGCM Journal; semi-annually

Membership List Available to Non-members

National Association of Professional Insurance Agents *(1931)*
400 N. Washington St.
Alexandria, VA 22314
Tel: (703) 836-9340 *Fax*: (703) 836-1279
E-Mail: info@pianet.org
Website: pianet.com
Members: 160000 individuals
Staff: 15
Annual Budget: $2-5,000,000
Tax: 501(c)(6)

Personnel:
Chief Executive Officer: Ronald Von Haden
Senior Vice President, Communications and Public Relations: Ted Besesparis
E-Mail: tedbe@pianet.org
Senior Vice President, Government and Regulatory Affairs: Patricia A. Borowski
E-Mail: patbo@pianet.org
Executive Assistant and Meetings Contact: Roxanne Johnson
E-Mail: roxannejo@pianet.org
Administrative Assistant and Membership Coordinator: Teresa Lewis
E-Mail: teresale@pianet.org
Vice President, Finance: Loan Nguyen
E-Mail: loanng@pianet.org
Vice President, Marketing and Affiliate Relations: Alexi Papandon
E-Mail: alexipa@pianet.org

Historical Note:
Formerly (1976) the National Association of Mutual Insurance Agents. PIA's mission is to promote, protect and defend the integrity of members, the value of their profession and the success of their businesses. Supports the Professional Insurance Agents Political Action Committee. Members are independent insurance agents/brokers and their employees. Membership: $200 (Active); $25 (Retired).

Meetings/Conferences: Annual
Conference Chair: Roxanne Johnson

Publications:
Connection Marketplace; on-line; adv.
PIA Connection; adv.

National Association of Professional Mortgage Women *(1964)*
P.O. Box 451718
Garland, TX 75045
TollFree: (800) 827-3034
E-Mail: napmw1@aol.com
Website: napmw.org
Members: 3400 individuals
Staff: 3
Annual Budget: $25-50,000

Personnel:
President: Candace M. Smith
E-Mail: president@napmw.org

Historical Note:
NAPMW helps its members to advance in business, personal and leadership development. Members are professionals who engage in the mortgage/banking industry. Membership: $86-319 (Individual); $100 (Basic); $107 (Bronze); $152 (Silver); $242 (Gold).

Continuing Education:
Certification Designation/s: CME, CMI

Meetings/Conferences: Annual

Publications:
Membership Directory; on-line
Notes and Deeds; adv.

National Association of Professional Organizers *(1983)*
15000 Commerce Pkwy.
Suite C
Mt. Laurel, NJ 08054
Tel: (856) 380-6828 *Fax*: (856) 439-0525
E-Mail: napo@napo.net
Website: napo.net
Members: 4,200 professional organizers
Staff: 3
Annual Budget: $500-1,000,000
Tax: 501(c)(3)

Personnel:
President: Angela Wallace
Director, Professional Development: Elizabeth Hagen
Editor: Eileen Koff

Historical Note:
NAPO strives to develop and promote professional organizers and the organizing industry. Members are professional organizers. Membership: $200 (Industry Member Provisional); $230-280 (Industry Member); $125-150 (Employee of Industry Member); $50 (Emeritus); $615 (Corporate Associate); $2,065 (Corporate Partner); $6,565 (Premier Corporate Partner).

Continuing Education:
Certification Designation/s: BCPO, CPO

Meetings/Conferences: Annual
2013 - New Orleans, LA (Sheraton Hotel New Orleans)/April 17 - 20
2014 - Phoenix, AZ (Westin Kierland Resort and Spa)/ May 28 - 31
2015 - Los Angeles, CA (Westin Bonaventure Hotel and Suites, Los Angeles)/April 15 - 18
2016 - Atlanta, GA (Sheraton Atlanta Hotel)/May 18 - 21

Publications:
NAPO News; bi-monthly; adv.
Press release; monthly
Professional Organizer Directory; on-line

National Association of Professional Pet Sitters *(1989)*
15000 Commerce Pkwy.
Suite C
Mt. Laurel, NJ 08054
Tel: (856) 439-0324 *Fax*: (856) 439-0525
TollFree: (800) 296-7387
E-Mail: NAPPS@petsitters.org
Website: petsitters.org
Members: 2000 companies
Staff: 4
Annual Budget: $250-500,000
Tax: 501(c)(6)

Personnel:
Executive Director: Felicia Lembesis
E-Mail: flembesis@ahint.com
Director, Administration: Cathe Delaney
E-Mail: cdelaney@ahint.com
Manager, Trade Show and Exhibits: Caitlin Dougherty
E-Mail: cdougherty@ahint.com

Historical Note:
Formerly (1994) National Association of Pet Sitters. Mission of NAPPS is to provide tools and support to foster the success of members' businesses and to promote the value of pet setting to the public. Members are owners of pet-care services offering in- home pet care. Membership: $160 (Company); $75 (Individual); $500 (Professional/ Nonprofit-Associate); $2,000 (Platinum Associate); $100 (Individual-Associate); $1,000 (Gold Associate); $50 (Individual).

Continuing Education:
Certification Designation/s: CPS

Meetings/Conferences: Annual
Conference Chair: Caitlin Dougherty
2013 - San Antonio, TX (Hyatt Regency & Hilton)/Feb. 8 - 10

Publications:
Member Directory; on-line
The NAPPS Network; quarterly; adv.

Membership List Available to Non-members

National Association of Professional Process Servers (1982)

P.O. Box 4547
Portland, OR 97208-4547
Tel: (503) 222-4180 *Fax:* (503) 222-3950
TollFree: (800) 477-8211
E-Mail: administrator@napps.org
Website: napps.org
Members: 1800 individuals
Staff: 3
Annual Budget: $500-1,000,000
Tax: 501(c)(6)

Personnel:
Administrator: Gary A. Crowe
    E-Mail: administrator@napps.org

Historical Note:
NAPPS's mission is to form a nationwide organization to fight proposed federal legislation adverse to the process serving industry. Membership is based on an individual basis allowing members to be screened adequately ensuring that they have not been convicted of any felonies and that they adhere to the ethical standards. Membership: $175/ year.

Meetings/Conferences: Annual
2013 - Phoenix, AZ (Hyatt Regency Phoenix)/April 18 - 20

Publications:
Membership Directory; bi-annually
NAPPS Supplement; monthly
The Docket Sheet; on-line; adv.

The National Association of Professional Receptionists

P.O. Box 104
College Park, MD 20741
Tel: (301) 220-1613
TollFree: (877) 709-5051
Website: receptionists.us
Staff: 1

Personnel:
Executive Director: Rosalind Redrick
    E-Mail: rredrick@receptionservices.com

Historical Note:
NAPR's mission is to promote the value of a Professional Receptionist, setting standards for professionalism through certification, providing a voice in communication with management. Membership : $960 (Corporate); $120 (Individual); $29.99 (Trail).

Continuing Education:
Certification Designation/s: CPR
Meetings/Conferences:
Number of non-conference events/year: 1

Publications:
Member Directory; on-line

National Association of Professional Surplus Lines Offices, Ltd. (1975)

200 NE 54th St.
Suite 200
Kansas City, MO 64118
Tel: (816) 741-3910 *Fax:* (816) 741-5409
E-Mail: info@napslo.org
Website: napslo.org
Members: 2000 firms
Staff: 8
Annual Budget: $5-10,000,000

Personnel:
Executive Director: Brady Kelley
Director, Communications and Technology: Mike Ardis
    E-Mail: mike@napslo.org
Director, Meetings and Conventions: Debbie Hill
    E-Mail: debbie@napslo.org
Director, Education: Randall D. Jones
Director, Government Relations: Keri Kish
Manager, Accounting and Membership Services: Kathy Reid
    E-Mail: kathy@napslo.org

Historical Note:
NAPSLO represents the surplus lines industry and the wholesale insurance marketing system. Membership: $1,000-7,125/year.

Meetings/Conferences: Annual
Conference Chair: Debbie Hill
2013 - San Diego, CA/Sept. 30 - Oct. 3
Number of non-conference events/year: 2

Publications:

E-News; on-line
Membership Directory; on-line
NAPSLO News; bi-monthly
Membership List Available to Non-members

National Association of Professors of Hebrew (1950)

University of Wisconsin-Madison
1346 Van Hise Hall, 1220 Linden Dr.
Madison, WI 53706-1558
Tel: (608) 262-2997 *Fax:* (608) 262-9417
E-Mail: naph@mailplus.wisc.edu
Website: vanhise.lss.wisc.edu/naph
Members: 400 individuals
Staff: 4
Annual Budget: $50-100,000

Personnel:
Executive Vice President: Gilead Morahg
    E-Mail: gmorahg@wisc.edu

Historical Note:
NAPH is a professional organization of professors and instructors in colleges, universities and seminaries who specialize in Hebrew language and literature of the ancient, medieval and modern periods. Membership: $60 (Regular); $30 (Retired); $20 (Student).

Meetings/Conferences: Annual
Conference Chair: Zafrira Lidovsky Cohen
2013 - New York City, NY/June 24 - 26
Number of non-conference events/year: 1

Publications:
Hebrew Higher Education
Hebrew Studies
Iggeret; annually

Membership List Available to Non-members

National Association of Property Tax Representatives - Transportation, Energy, Communications (1963)

175 E. Houston, Room 8-H-40
San Antonio, TX 78205
Tel: (210) 351-2425 *Fax:* (210) 351-3960
Members: 200 individuals
Staff: 7
Annual Budget: Under $10,000

Personnel:
President: Bill Ware

Historical Note:
Formerly National Association of Railroad and Public Utilities Tax Representatives; assumed its present name in 1999. Has no paid staff or permanent address; officers change annually. Membership: $25/year.

National Association of Psychiatric Health Systems (1933)

900 17th St. NW
Suite 420
Washington, DC 20006-2507
Tel: (202) 393-6700 *Fax:* (202) 783-6041
E-Mail: naphs@naphs.org
Website: naphs.org
Members: 700 hospitals and behavioral systems of care
Staff: 6
Annual Budget: $2-5,000,000
Tax: 501(c)(6)

Personnel:
President and Chief Executive Officer: Mark J. Covall
Senior Project Manager: Frieda Eastmann
Director, Quality and Regulatory Affairs: Kathleen McCann RN, PhD
Director, Administration and Membership Services: Maria Merlie
    E-Mail: maria@naphs.org
Director, Operations and Communications: Carole Szpak
    E-Mail: comm@naphs.org
Director, Congressional Affairs: Nancy R. Trenti JD
    E-Mail: ntrenti@naphs.org

Historical Note:
Formerly (1993) the National Association of Private Psychiatric Hospitals. Mission is to encompass all organizations serving people with psychiatric and substance abuse disorders. NAPHS serves specialty psychiatric healthcare organizations for the treatment of mental illness, alcohol, and drug dependencies, works to promote quality mental health and substance abuse care. Membership: $1,000/year (Individual).

Meetings/Conferences: Annual

Conference Chair: Maria Merlie
2013 - Washington, DC (Mandarin Oriental Washington D.C.)/March 11 - 13
Number of non-conference events/year: 12

Publications:
Behavioral Health Updates; monthly; adv.
CEO Forecast; weekly; adv.
Hot Topics; quarterly
Membership Directory; annually; adv.
NAPHS Purchasing Directory for Behavioral Healthcare Decision-makers; annually; adv.

Membership List Available to Non-members

National Association of Public Child Welfare Administrators (1983)

1133 19th St. NW
Suite 400
Washington, DC 20036
Tel: (202) 682-0100 *Fax:* (202) 204-0071
E-Mail: napcwa@aphsa.org
Website: napcwa.org
Members: 700 individuals
Staff: 10
Annual Budget: $250-500,000
Tax: 501(c)(3)

Personnel:
Deputy Executive Director, Policy and Programs: Anita Light
    E-Mail: anita.light@aphsa.org
Administrative Assistant: Robin Henderson
    E-Mail: robin.wallace@aphsa.org
Senior Associate, Programs: Bertha Levin
    E-Mail: bertha.levin@aphsa.org
Research Assistant: Angela You
    E-Mail: angela.you@aphsa.org

Historical Note:
A constituent unit of the American Public Human Services Association, NAPCWA's mission is to be recognized as the national leader in promoting better public policy, model programs and practices, and critical capacity building resources needed to achieve positive outcomes for children and families. Members are state or local administrators responsible for public child welfare agencies that provide child protective services, foster care, adoption, and family preservation services. Membership: $85 (Individual); $95 (Sustaining); $110 (Century Club); $25 (Retiree/ Student,Full-time Only); $285 (APHSA).

Meetings/Conferences:
Conference Chair: Robin Henderson
Number of non-conference events/year: 8

Publications:
NAPCWA Weekly Update; weekly
Policy & Practice; bi-monthly
Public Human Services Directory; on-line

National Association of Public Hospitals and Health Systems (1980)

1301 Pennsylvania Ave. NW
Suite 950
Washington, DC 20004
Tel: (202) 585-0100 *Fax:* (202) 585-0101
E-Mail: info@naph.org
Website: naph.org
Members: 110 hospitals and hospital systems
Staff: 34
Annual Budget: $5-10,000,000

Personnel:
President and Chief Executive Officer: Bruce Siegel
    E-Mail: bsiegel@naph.org
Manager, Human Resources: Kellie Burke
    E-Mail: kburke@naph.org
Director, Information Technology: Mark Campbell
    E-Mail: mcampbell@naph.org
Vice President, Education: Betsy Carrier
    E-Mail: bcarrier@naph.org
Vice President, Policy and Advocacy: Beth Feldpush
Senior Associate, Education: Josel Bernardo Fritz CHES, MPH
    E-Mail: jfritz@naph.org
Vice President, Finance and Administration: Rhonda Gold
    E-Mail: rgold@naph.org
Assistant Vice President, Communications: Carl Graziano
    E-Mail: cgraziano@naph.org
Web Writer and Publications Editor: Sandy Laycox
    E-Mail: slaycox@naph.org
Coordinator, Membership Services: Maeceon Lewis
    E-Mail: mlewis@naph.org

Manager, Meetings: Nneka St. Gerard
   E-Mail: nstgerard@naph.org
Manager, Marketing: Katie Zimmerman
   E-Mail: kzimmerman@naph.org

Historical Note:
Formerly (1996) National Association of Public Hospitals. NAPH's mission is to provide national, regional and local advocacy on behalf of public and other hospitals and health systems, conduct research and analysis, and provide a host of related services needed by its members. Members provide primary care and public health services. Membership: $45,200/year.

Meetings/Conferences: Annual
Conference Chair: Nneka St. Gerard
Number of non-conference events/year: 5

Publications:
Data Brief
IssueBrief
Membership Directory; on-line
PolicyBrief
Research Brief

National Association of Public Insurance Adjusters *(1951)*
21165 Whitfield Pl.
Suite 105
Potomac Falls, VA 20165
Tel: (703) 433-9217 *Fax:* (703) 433-0369
E-Mail: info@napia.com
Website: napia.com
Members: 120 companies
Staff: 5
Annual Budget: $500-1,000,000

Personnel:
Executive Director: David W. Barrack
   E-Mail: david@napia.com
Manager, Events and Membership Services: Jessica Elleman
Counsel: Brian S. Goodman Esq.
   E-Mail: BGoodman@HPKLegal.com
Director, Communications and Events: Marjorie Musick

Historical Note:
NAPIA aims at improving and maintaining the professional standards of the public insurance adjuster through a rigid code of professional conduct and ethics. It unites public insurance adjusters in U.S. for their mutual benefit and protection, and for the benefit and protection of the general public. Membership: $1,000 (Regular), $435 (Associate), $220 (Independent Contractor); $1,440 (Vendor/Supplier); $720 (Individual/State Association).

Continuing Education:
Certification Designation/s: CPPA, SPPA

Meetings/Conferences: Semi-Annual
Conference Chair: Jessica Elleman
2013 - San Antonio, TX (The Westin La Cantera Resort)/June 19 - 22
2013 - Las Vegas, NV (Encore)/Dec. 5 - 7

Publications:
Membership Directory; annually; adv.
NAPIA Bulletin; quarterly; adv.
Newsletter

National Association of Publicly Traded Partnerships *(1983)*
4350 N. Fairfax Dr.
Suite 815
Arlington, VA 22203
Tel: (703) 822-4995 *Fax:* (703) 842-8333
Website: naptp.org
Members: 109 companies
Staff: 2
Annual Budget: $1-2,000,000
Tax: 501(c)(6)

Personnel:
Executive Director: Mary S. Lyman
   E-Mail: mlyman@naptp.org
Treasurer: Carl A. Luna

Historical Note:
Formerly known as Coalition of Publicly Traded Partnerships. Managed and represented by Navigant & Consulting Inc. NAPTP's mission is to promote the common interest of public policy traded partnerships. Membership: $16,000 (Large Associations); $11,000 (Small Associations).

National Association of Publishers' Representatives *(1950)*
1901 N. Roselle Rd.

Suite 920
Schaumburg, IL 60195
Tel: (847) 885-2410 *Fax:* (847) 885-8393
E-Mail: napr@napronline.org
Website: napronline.org
Members: 360 individuals
Staff: 4
Annual Budget: $25-50,000

Personnel:
President: Ian Mc Donald
   E-Mail: ian@roymcdonald.com
Vice President and Treasurer: William D. Farmakis
   E-Mail: bill@jlfarmakis.com
General Counsel: Herbert W. Solomon
Secretary: Jan Zeman
   E-Mail: jzeman@repswest.com

Historical Note:
Formerly (1982) the Association of Publishers' Representatives. NAPR's objectives are to create a better understanding between publishers and representatives, to raise the level of the profession, and to improve selling efficiency. Membership: $200/year.

Meetings/Conferences: Annual

Publications:
Membership Directory; on-line; adv.
NAPR Newsletter; monthly

National Association of Puerto Rican-Hispanic Social Workers *(1983)*
P.O. Box 651
Brentwood, NY 11717
Tel: (631) 864-1536 *Fax:* (631) 864-1536
E-Mail: naprhsw@aol.com
Website: naprhsw.com
Members: 350 individuals
Staff: 2
Annual Budget: $25-50,000
Tax: 501(c)(3)

Personnel:
President: Pauline Velazquez MSW
Treasurer and Editor, Newsletter and Website: Sonia Palacio-Grottola LCSW

Historical Note:
NAPRHSW's mission is to organize social workers and other human service professionals to strengthen, develop and improve the resources and services that meet the needs of Puerto Rican/Hispanic families. Membership: $20-250/year.

Meetings/Conferences: Annual
Number of non-conference events/year: 3

Publications:
NAPRHSW Newsletter; adv.

National Association of Pupil Services Administrators *(1966)*
P.O. Box 113
Williamsport, PA 17701
Tel: (570) 323-2050 *Fax:* (570) 323-2051
E-Mail: napsa@comcast.net
Website: napsa.com
Members: 800 individuals
Staff: 3
Annual Budget: $50-100,000
Tax: 501(c)(3)

Personnel:
Executive Director: Wayne D. Fausnaught
   E-Mail: napsa@comcast.net
Legislative Liaison: Ted Kozlik
   E-Mail: tkozlikjr@gmail.com

Historical Note:
Formerly the National Association of Pupil Personnel Administrators, the group assumed its present name in 1989. NAPSA's mission is to serve and focus on the development of administrators and programs designed to serve the academic, social, emotional and physical needs of all students. Membership: $145 (Regular); $500 (Institutional); $65 (Student); $25 (Honarary/Retired).

Meetings/Conferences: Annual

Publications:
Legislative Update; on-line
Membership Directory; on-line
NAPSA News; quarterly

National Association of Railroad Passengers *(1967)*
505 Capitol Ct. NE
Suite 300

Washington, DC 20002-7706
Tel: (202) 408-8362 *Fax:* (202) 408-8287
E-Mail: narp@narprail.org
Website: narprail.org
Members: 20,000 individual members.
Staff: 5
Annual Budget: $1-2,000,000
Tax: 501(c)(3)

Personnel:
President and Chief Executive Officer: Ross B. Capon
   E-Mail: narp@narprail.org
Vice President: Sean Jeans-Gail

Historical Note:
NARP's mission is to work for a modern, customer-focused national passenger train network that provides a travel choice Americans want. Membership: $35 (Individual); $45 (Family); $20 (Student); $25 (Senior).

Meetings/Conferences: Annual
2013 - Alexandria, VA (Hilton Alexandria Old Town Hotel)/April 22 - 24

Publications:
Newsletter

National Association of Railroad Trial Counsel *(1954)*
1430 E. Missouri Ave.
Suite B200
Phoenix, AZ 85014
Tel: (602) 265-2700 *Fax:* (602) 265-2705
E-Mail: info@nartc.org
Website: nartc.org
Members: 1100 individuals
Staff: 2
Annual Budget: $500-1,000,000
Tax: 501(c)(6)

Personnel:
Executive Director: Michelle Miller Thorpe

Historical Note:
NARTC serves as a support, resource, and continuing education center for rail carriers and their counsel. Members get updates about the latest developments in the law affecting railroad litigation, and comprise of leading trial attorneys who defend railroads and their subsidiary companies. Membership: $310 (Individual); $125-225 (In Practice).

National Association of Real Estate Appraisers *(1966)*
P.O. Box 879
Palm Springs, CA 92263
Tel: (760) 327-5284 *Fax:* (760) 327-5631
TollFree: (877) 815-4172
E-Mail: info@narea-assoc.org
Website: narea-assoc.org
Members: 23500 individuals
Staff: 23
Annual Budget: $2-5,000,000

Personnel:
Manager, Membership Services: Lisa Slam

Historical Note:
NAREA provides standards, guidelines, regulations, education, training, appraisal leads and recognition in the field of residential and commercial real estate valuation. It also provides representation on local, state and national legislative issues. Members are expert witnesses, review appraisers, educators and published authors and primarily specialize in residential appraisals. New members must have two years of experience in the field, submit two appraisal reports and pass an appraisal certification examination. Awards the Certified Real Estate Appraiser (CREA) and Certified Commercial Real Estate Appraiser (CCRA) designations. Mandatory continuing education/recertification of 60 hours every 5 years required. Membership: $155-295/year (New).

Continuing Education:
Certification Designation/s: CREA, CCRA, RTA, RPM

Publications:
Membership Directory; on-line
NAREA Newsletter

National Association of Real Estate Brokers *(1947)*
9831 Greenbelt Rd.
Suite 309
Lanham, MD 20706
Tel: (301) 552-9340 *Fax:* (301) 522-9216
E-Mail: info@nareb.com
Website: nareb.com

Members: 13000 individuals
Staff: 5
Annual Budget: $500-1,000,000

Personnel:
Treasurer: Lawrence Butler
General Counsel: Gerald Neal

Historical Note:
NAREB's mission is to bring together the nation's minority professionals in the real estate industry to promote exchange of ideas about business and how to serve clientele. Membership consists principally of minority real estate brokers. It certifies qualified members to use the title, "Realtists" and gives members license to use Realtist symbol. Membership: $349/year (Broker). Subscriber membership is free.

Meetings/Conferences:
Number of non-conference events/year: 1

Publications:
Membership Directory; on-line

National Association of Real Estate Editors
(1929)
1003 NW Sixth Terr.
Boca Raton, FL 33486-3455
Tel: (561) 391-3599 *Fax:* (561) 391-0099
Website: naree.org
Members: 650 individuals
Staff: 1
Annual Budget: $100-250,000
Tax: 501(c)(6)

Personnel:
Executive Director: Mary Doyle-Kimball
   E-Mail: madkimba@aol.com

Historical Note:
Founded as National Conference of Real Estate Editors; assumed its current name in 1936. NAREE's mission is to serve the interest of real estate journalists, including writers and editors, from all forms of media. Active membership benefits include one free entry in the real estate journalism competition. Membership: $75 (Active); $195 (Associate).

Meetings/Conferences:
2013 - Las Vegas, NV/Jan. 22 - 24
Number of non-conference events/year: 1

Publications:
NAREE Network; annually
NAREE News; irregular

National Association of Real Estate Investment Managers *(1990)*
400 N. Michigan Ave.
Suite 1215
Chicago, IL 60611
Tel: (312) 884-5180
Website: nareim.org
Members: 80 corporate members
Staff: 2
Annual Budget: $1-2,000,000
Tax: 501(c)(6)

Personnel:
President and Chief Executive Officer: Gunnar Branson
   E-Mail: gbranson@nareim.org
Director, Administration and Meetings: Monica Lockhart
   E-Mail: mlockhart@nareim.org

Historical Note:
NAREIM seeks to advance the profession and performance of real estate investment managers. Membership: $9,500 (Organization/Company); $5,000-15,000 (U.S. and Canada).

Meetings/Conferences: Annual
Conference Chair: Monica Lockhart
2013 - Irving, TX (Four Seasons Resort and Club)/Jan. 24 - 25
Number of non-conference events/year: 1

Publications:
Membership Directory; on-line

Membership List Available to Non-members

National Association of Real Estate Investment Trusts (NAREIT) *(1960)*
1875 I St. NW
Suite 600
Washington, DC 20006
Tel: (202) 739-9400 *Fax:* (202) 739-9401
TollFree: (800) 362-7348
Website: reit.com
Members: 2000 REITS, 1500 affiliated individuals
Staff: 48

Annual Budget: $10-25,000,000
Tax: 501(c)(6)

Personnel:
President and Chief Executive Officer: Steven A. Wechsler
   E-Mail: swechsler@nareit.com
Vice President, Publications: Matthew Bechard
   E-Mail: mbechard@nareit.com
Vice President, Meetings: Pamela Coleman
   E-Mail: pcoleman@nareit.com
Senior Vice President, Government Relations: Robert Dibblee
   E-Mail: rdibblee@nareit.com
Executive Vice President and General Counsel: Tony M. Edwards
   E-Mail: tedwards@nareit.com
Senior Vice President, Industry and Membership Affairs: Bonnie Gottlieb
   E-Mail: bgottlieb@nareit.com
Executive Vice President, Finance and Operations: Sheldon M. Groner
   E-Mail: sgroner@nareit.com
Vice President, Marketing: Jeff Henriksen
   E-Mail: jhenriksen@nareit.com
Director, Human Resources and Operations: Mackenzie Kilcawley
   E-Mail: mkilcawley@nareit.com
Vice President, Communications: Ron Kuykendall
   E-Mail: rkuykendall@nareit.com
Senior Vice President, Investment Affairs and Investor Education: Kurt Walten
   E-Mail: kwalten@nareit.com
Senior Vice President, Financial Standards: George Yungmann
   E-Mail: gyungmann@nareit.com

Historical Note:
Formerly National Association of Real Estate Investment Funds, assumed its present name in 1972, NAREIT's purpose is to represent the REIT and publicly owned real estate industry before Congress and the Executive branch. It also provides education and information about the industry to the investment community and the financial media. Membership is open to qualified REITs and publicly traded real estate companies and other organizations and individuals in related fields such as law, accounting, financial advising, mortgage and investment banking, teaching and real estate services. Membership: $295-850/year (Individual).

Meetings/Conferences: Semi-Annual
Conference Chair: Pamela Coleman
2013 - La Quinta, CA (La Quinta Resort and Club, A Waldorf Astoria Resort)/March 20 - 22
2013 - San Francisco, CA (San Francisco Marriott Marquis)/Nov. 13 - 15
2014 - Boca Raton, FL (Boca Raton Resort and Club)/April 2 - 4
Number of non-conference events/year: 8

Publications:
Compensation Surveys; annually
Membership Directory; annually
NAREIT NewsBrief; monthly
Real Estate Investment SmartBrief; daily
REIT; bi-monthly
REIT Magazine; bi-monthly; adv.
REIT Story; on-line

National Association of Realtors *(1908)*
430 N. Michigan Ave.
Chicago, IL 60611-4087
Tel: (312) 329-8200 *Fax:* (312) 329-8576
TollFree: (800) 874-6500
E-Mail: infocentral@realtors.org
Website: realtor.org
Members: 1000000 members
Staff: 300
Annual Budget: Over $100,000,000
Tax: 501(c)(6)

Personnel:
Chief Executive Officer: Dale A. Stinton CAE
Director, Leadership Development and Outreach: Bobbie Albrecht
   E-Mail: balbrecht@realtors.org
Senior Editor: Wendy Cole
   E-Mail: wcole@realtors.org
Director, NAR Human Resource Services: Donna Garcia
   E-Mail: dgarcia@realtors.org
Vice President, Information Technology Services: Keith Garner
   E-Mail: kgarner@realtors.org

Senior Vice President, Marketing, Business Development and Commercial Services: Bob Goldberg
Vice President, Conventions: Sue Gourley
Director, Digital Engagement: Nobu Hata
Manager, Professional Development: Renee Holland
   E-Mail: rholland@realtors.org
General Counsel: Laurene K. Janik
Vice President and Director, Editorial: Pamela Geurds Kabati
Senior Vice President, Publications: Frank Sibley

Historical Note:
Formerly (1916) National Association of Real Estate Exchanges; (1974) National Association of Real Estate Boards. NAR provides a forum for professional development, research and the exchange of information among its members, and to the public and government for the purpose of preserving the free enterprise system and the right to own real property. Members are realtors who are involved in residential and commercial real estate as brokers, salespeople, property managers, appraisers, counselors and others engaged in all aspects of the real estate industry.

Continuing Education:
Certification Designation/s: SFR, RSPS, ABR, SRES, BPOR, E-PRO, AHWD, RAA, RCE

Meetings/Conferences:
Conference Chair: Sue Gourley
2013 - Washington, DC/May 15 - 17
2013 - San Francisco, CA/Nov. 8 - 11
2014 - Washington, DC/May 14 - 16
2014 - New Orleans, LA/Nov. 7 - 10
2015 - Washington, DC/May 13 - 15
2015 - San Diego, CA/Nov. 13 - 16
2016 - Washington, DC/May 11 - 13
2016 - Orlando, FL/Nov. 4 - 7
2017 - Washington, DC/May 17 - 19
2017 - Chicago, IL/Nov. 3 - 6
2018 - Washington, DC/May 16 - 18
2018 - Boston, MA/Nov. 2 - 5
2019 - Washington, DC/May 15 - 17
2019 - San Francisco, CA/Nov. 8 - 11
Number of non-conference events/year: 25

Publications:
Member Guide; annually
Realtor Magazine; bi-monthly; adv.

National Association of Recording Merchandisers (NARM) *(1958)*
Nine Eves Dr.
Suite 120
Marlton, NJ 08053-3138
Tel: (856) 596-2221 *Fax:* (856) 596-3268
Website: narm.com
Members: 500 companies
Staff: 8
Annual Budget: $1-2,000,000
Tax: 501(c)(6)

Personnel:
President: Jim Donio
   E-Mail: donio@narm.com
Executive Director, Scholarship Foundation and Meeting Planner: Pat Daly
   E-Mail: daly@narm.com
Manager, Membership Services: Evelyn Dichter
   E-Mail: dichter@narm.com
Manager, Information Systems: Vincent Goffin
   E-Mail: goffin@narm.com
Director, Communications: Nicole Hennessey
   E-Mail: hennessey@narm.com

Historical Note:
Mission is to advance the promotion, marketing, distribution, and sale of music and entertainment by providing its members with a forum for diverse meeting and networking opportunities, information, and education to support their businesses, as well as advocating for their common interests. Members include music and other entertainment retailers, wholesalers, distributors, record labels, multimedia suppliers, and suppliers of related products and services, as well as individual professionals and educators in the music business field. Membership: $300-39,750 (Retailer.); $595-39,750 (Wholesaler/Distributor/Supplier of Related products and services); $8,995-17,995 (Entertainment Service Provider, based on the total U.S. sales volume); $160 (Individual); $30 (Student).

Meetings/Conferences: Annual
Conference Chair: Pat Daly

National Association of Regional Councils *(1967)*

777 N. Capitol St. NE
Suite 305
Washington, DC 20002
Tel: (202) 986-1032 *Fax:* (202) 986-1038
E-Mail: nykwest@narc.org
Website: narc.org
Members: 250 councils
Staff: 7
Annual Budget: $2-5,000,000
Tax: 501(c)(3)

Personnel:
Executive Director: Fred Abousleman
   E-Mail: fred@narc.org
Director, Policy Affairs: Beverly C. Nykwest
   E-Mail: nykwest@narc.org
Deputy, Communications: Lindsey Riley
   E-Mail: lindsey@narc.org

Historical Note:
Established by the National League of Cities and the National Association of Counties. NARC's mission is to provide research and analysis of key national issues and developments that impact its members and advocate effectively for the role of regional councils in the coordination, planning and delivery of current and future federal programs. Membership: $1000-12500/year.

Meetings/Conferences: Annual
Conference Chair: Lindsey Riley
2013 - Washington, DC/Feb. 10 - 12
Number of non-conference events/year: 3

Publications:
eRegions; bi-weekly
Membership Directory; on-line

National Association of Regulatory Utility Commissioners *(1889)*
1101 Vermont Ave. NW
Suite 200
Washington, DC 20005
Tel: (202) 898-2200 *Fax:* (202) 898-2213
E-Mail: admin@naruc.org
Website: naruc.org
Members: 360 individuals
Staff: 29
Annual Budget: $5-10,000,000
Tax: 501(c)(4)

Personnel:
Executive Director: Charles D Gray
   E-Mail: cgray@naruc.org
Manager, Human Resources and Payroll: Sheryl Herrod-Jeter
   E-Mail: shjeter@naruc.org
Director, Grants and Research: Miles Keogh
   E-Mail: mkeogh@naruc.org
Director, Meetings: Michelle Malloy CAE, CMP
   E-Mail: mmalloy@naruc.org
Director, Legislative: Chris Mele
   E-Mail: cmele@naruc.org
Chief Financial Officer: Andre Parraway
   E-Mail: aparraway@naruc.org
General Counsel: James Bradford Ramsay
   E-Mail: jramsay@naruc.org
Executive Assistant: Deborah Scott
   E-Mail: dscott@naruc.org
Director, Communications: Robert Julius Thormeyer
   E-Mail: rthormeyer@naruc.org

Historical Note:
State and Federal regulatory commissioners. Formerly (1918) National Association of Railway Commissioners; (1923) National Association of Railroad and Utilities Commissioners and (1967) National Association of Regulatory Utility Commissioners. NARUC's mission is to serve the public interest by improving the quality and effectiveness of public utility regulation.

Meetings/Conferences: Annual
Conference Chair: Michelle Malloy CAE, CMP
2013 - Orlando, FL (Hilton Orlando Bonnet Creek)/ Nov. 17 - 20
2014 - San Francisco, CA (San Francisco Marriott Marquis)/Nov. 16 - 19
Number of non-conference events/year: 7

Publications:
Membership Directory; on-line

Membership List Available to Non-members

National Association of Rehabilitation Providers and Agencies *(1978)*
701 Eighth St. NW

Suite 500
Washington, DC 20001
Tel: (813) 855-9168 *Fax:* (813) 855-6449
E-Mail: nara@naranet.org
Website: naranet.org
Members: 15000 healthcare professionals
Staff: 3
Annual Budget: $100-250,000

Personnel:
Executive Director: Christie Sheets
Treasurer: Ted Botens

Historical Note:
Formerly (2001) National Association of Rehabilitation Agencies. NARA provides a multitude of skilled rehabilitation therapy services to individuals in a variety of settings including inpatient, outpatient, skilled care, assisted living, educational systems, industry/occupational health. Members are government-certified rehabilitation agencies, non-certified rehabilitation agencies, multidisciplinary rehabilitation companies, and rehabilitation vendors. Membership: $5,000 (Elite); $3,000 (Gold); $975- $3100 (Active); $600 (Associate).

Meetings/Conferences: Annual

Publications:
NARA eAlerts

National Association of Rehabilitation Research and Training Centers
3630 Sinton Rd,
Suite 103
Colorado Springs, CO 80907-5072
Website: narrtc.org/
Staff: 2
Annual Budget: $50-100,000

Personnel:
President: Dr. Jana Burke
   E-Mail: jburke@mtc-inc.com

Historical Note:
To improve the quality of life.NARRTC members are current projects funded through the National Institute on Disability and Rehabilitation Research.NARRTC's mission is to promote the full inclusion of persons with disabilities in American society through applied research and training.Membership Dues: $150-650 (Based on Project Budget).

Meetings/Conferences: Annual

Publications:
NARRTC News; quarterly

National Association of Reinforcing Steel Contractors *(1969)*
P.O. Box 280
Fairfax, VA 22038
Tel: (703) 591-1870 *Fax:* (703) 591-1895
E-Mail: info@narsc.com
Website: narsc.com
Members: 425 companies
Staff: 3
Annual Budget: $50-100,000
Tax: 501(c)(6)

Personnel:
First Vice President: Keith LePage

Historical Note:
NARSC supply vital safety training and information and provides practical assistance that helps businesses grow. Members are involved with the placing and installation of reinforcing steel end post-tensioning in commercial, bridge, highway, industrial and public projects.

Meetings/Conferences: Annual
2013 - Palm Beach, Aruba (Westin Aruba Resort)/ March 1 - 8

Publications:
Newsletter

National Association of Resale & Thrift Shops *(1984)*
P.O. Box 80707
St. Clair Shores, MI 48080-5707
Tel: (586) 294-6700 *Fax:* (586) 294-6776
TollFree: (800) 544-0751
E-Mail: info@narts.org
Website: narts.org
Members: 1100 individuals
Staff: 3
Annual Budget: $250-500,000
Tax: 501(c)(6)

Personnel:

Executive Director: Adele R. Meyer
   E-Mail: adele@narts.org
Director, Membership Services: Gail A. Siegel
   E-Mail: gail@narts.org

Historical Note:
NARTS's mission is to provide members with professional development, educational opportunities, communication within the industry and member services. Members are owners, managers, professionals and other individuals who represent both profit and non-profit resale and thrift shops. Membership: $120 (Primary/Provisional); $84 (Secondary); $36 (Associate).

Meetings/Conferences: Annual
2013 - San Diego, CA (Westin Gaslamp Quarter, San Diego)/June 28 - July 1
Number of non-conference events/year: 2

Publications:
Membership Directory; on-line
YOUR NARTS Network - Newsletter; monthly

National Association of Residential Property Managers *(1988)*
638 Independence Pkwy.
Suite 100
Chesapeake, VA 23320
Tel: (800) 782-3452 *Fax:* (866) 466-2776
E-Mail: info@narpm.org
Website: narpm.org
Members: 3000 individuals
Staff: 4
Annual Budget: $1-2,000,000
Tax: 501(c)(6)

Personnel:
Executive Director: Gail S. Phillips CAE
   E-Mail: executivedirector@narpm.org
Coordinator, Conferences and Conventions: Carla Earnest CMP
   E-Mail: conventioninfo@narpm.org
Administrative Assistant: Cher Leadbeater
   E-Mail: cleadbeater@narpm.org
Director, Governmental Affairs: Andrew Sinclair
   E-Mail: asinclair@narpm.org

Historical Note:
NARPM seeks to promote professionalism through education and publications for the single-family residential property manager. Members are real estate agents, brokers, managers and their employees. Membership: $245 (Professional/Affiliate); $125 (Support Specialist).

Continuing Education:
Certification Designation/s: CSS, CRMC, MPM, RMP

Meetings/Conferences: Annual
Conference Chair: Carla Earnest CMP
2013 - San Diego, CA (Hyatt Regency La Jolla)/Oct. 15 - 18
2014 - Minneapolis, MN (Hyatt Regency)/Oct. 22 - 24
Number of non-conference events/year: 5

Publications:
Membership Directory; on-line; adv.
Residential Resource; adv.

National Association of Resource Conservation and Development Councils *(1988)*
444 N. Capitol St. NW
Suite 345
Washington, DC 20001
Tel: (202) 434-4780 *Fax:* (202) 434-4783
E-Mail: narcdc@rcdnet.org
Website: rcdnet.org
Members:
375 Resource Conservation and Development (RC&D) Councils
39 applicant Councils
Staff: 5
Annual Budget: $500-1,000,000

Personnel:
Executive Director and Counsel: Andrew Gordon
   E-Mail: agordon@sso.org
Program Manager: Peter Costolanski
   E-Mail: pcostlanski@sso.org

Historical Note:
The National Association of Resource Conservation and Development Councils (NARC&DC) serves as an advocate for local RC&D Councils.

Meetings/Conferences: Triennial
Conference Chair: Andrew Gordon
Number of non-conference events/year: 1

Publications:

Membership Directory; on-line
National Catalyst Newsletter; quarterly

National Association of Retail Collection Attorneys (1993)

601 Pennsylvania Ave. NW
Suite 900, South
Washington, DC 20004
Tel: (202) 861-0706 *Fax:* (240) 559-0959
TollFree: (800) 633-6069
E-Mail: narca@narca.org
Website: narca.org
Members: 700 law firms
Staff: 5
Annual Budget: $2-5,000,000
Tax: 501(c)(6)

Personnel:
Executive Vice President: Diane Darrow
   E-Mail: diane@narca.org
Contact, Exhibit Sales: Dorothea Heck
   E-Mail: narca_exhibits@gomeeting.com
Director, Communications: Debbie Lewis
   E-Mail: debbie@narca.org
Manager, Meetings: Lisa Linke
Director, Government and Public Affairs: Eric
   Rosenkoetter
   E-Mail: eric@narca.org

Historical Note:
NARCA's mission is to educate the public and members of the credit and collection industry as to all aspects of the consumer collection industry. Membership: $750 (Regular/Vendor); $375 (Associate).

Meetings/Conferences:
Conference Chair: Diane Darrow
2013 - Las Vegas, NV (Caesars Palace Las Vegas Hotel and Casino)/May 8 - 11
2013 - Washington, DC (Washington, DC, Renaissance Hotel)/Oct. 16 - 19
2014 - Miami, FL (Loews Miami Beach Hotel)/May 12 - 15
Number of non-conference events/year: 2

Publications:
Membership Directory; on-line
NARCA Newsletter; weekly

Membership List Available to Non-members

National Association of Retired and Senior Volunteer Program Directors (1976)

P. O. Box 852
Athens, AL 35612
Tel: (256) 232-7207 *Fax:* (256) 232-8842
Website: narsvpd.com
Members: 800 individuals
Staff: 1
Annual Budget: $50-100,000
Tax: 501(c)(3)

Personnel:
President: Betty M. Ruth
   E-Mail: bruth@al-rsvp.com

Historical Note:
NARSVPD's mission is to provide visibility and advocacy for RSVP and to create a network of communication among RSVP directors and projects. Serves as a vehicle for expression of majority opinion on behalf of RSVP and older Americans to the corporation for national and community service. Membership: $100 (Professional); $50 (Associate); $125 (Organization).

Publications:
Grand Magazine; adv.
Membership Directory; on-line
Newsletter; quarterly

National Association of Reunion Managers (1986)

P.O. Box 335428
Las Vegas, NV 89033-5428
Fax: (702) 649-1154
TollFree: (800) 654-2776
E-Mail: info@reunions.com
Website: reunions.com
Members: 60 companies
Staff: 3
Annual Budget: $10-25,000

Personnel:
President: Cyndi Clamp
   E-Mail: cyndi@varsityreunions.com
Executive Director: Sherri Lokken
   E-Mail: sherri@reunions.com

Treasurer: Mike Silva
   E-Mail: michael@greatreunions.com

Historical Note:
Formerly (1994) National Association of Reunion Planners. NARM's purpose is to serve the reunion planning industry. Membership: $450/year (Corporate).

National Association of Review Appraisers and Mortgage Underwriters (1975)

P.O. Box 879
Palm Springs, CA 92263
Tel: (760) 327-5284 *Fax:* (760) 327-5631
TollFree: (877) 743-6805
E-Mail: info@naramu.org
Website: naramu.org
Members: 8000 individuals
Staff: 12
Annual Budget: $1-2,000,000

Personnel:
Executive Director: Robert G. Johnson

Historical Note:
NARAMU is dedicated to maintain professional standards and promoting ongoing education in the fields of appraisal review and mortgage underwriting. Members representing international corporations, banks, thrifts, insurance companies, accounting firms, law firms, and private real estate lenders. Membership: $195/year.

Continuing Education:
Certification Designation/s: CRA

Publications:
Membership Directory; on-line
NARA/MU Newsletter

National Association of Royalty Owners (1980)

15 W. Sixth St.
Suite 2626
Tulsa, OK 74119
Tel: (918) 794-1660 *Fax:* (918) 794-1662
TollFree: (800) 558-0557
E-Mail: naro@naro-us.org
Website: naro-us.org
Members: 5000 individuals
Staff: 3
Annual Budget: $500-1,000,000
Tax: 501(c)(3)

Personnel:
Executive Director: Jerry Simmons

Historical Note:
NARO's mission is to promote exploration and production of minerals in the U. S. while preserving, protecting, advancing and representing the interests and rights of mineral and royalty owners through education, advocacy and assistance to members, to NARO chapter organizations, to government bodies and to the public. Membership: $150 (Basic); $550 (All American/Business/Corporate/Institutional); $300 (Family Trust); $500 (National Legislative Council); $1,500(Foundation Eagles).

Meetings/Conferences: Annual

Publications:
Member Directory; on-line
Rocky Mountain Oil Journal; weekly; adv.

National Association of Rural Health Clinics

Two E. Main St.
Fremont, MI 49412
Fax: (888) 907-7890
TollFree: (866) 306-1961
E-Mail: info@narhc.org
Website: narhc.org
Staff: 3
Annual Budget: $250-500,000

Personnel:
Director, Finance: Chris Christoffersen
   E-Mail: christoffersen@hsagroup.net
Director, Meeting Planning and Office Operations: Rhondi Davis
   E-Mail: meetings@narhc.org

Historical Note:
NARHC's mission is to improve the delivery of quality, cost-effective health care in rural under served areas through the Rural Health Clinics (RHC) Program. Membership: $250 (New RHC Clinic); $450 (Independent RHC/Provider-based RHC); $130 (Each Additional Clinic); $400 (Governmental/Association); $550 (Corporate Non-Voting/Consultant).

Meetings/Conferences: Annual
Conference Chair: Rhondi Davis

2013 - San Antonio, TX (Crowne Plaza San Antonio Riverwalk)/March 13 - 15

Publications:
Membership Directory
NARHC News; quarterly; adv.
The NARHC Legislative Update and FASTMAIL

National Association of RV Parks and Campgrounds (1966)

9085 E. Mineral Cir.
Suite 200
Centennial, CO 80112
Tel: (303) 681-0401 *Fax:* (303) 681-0426
TollFree: (800) 395-2267
Website: arvc.org
Members: 3700 RV Parks and Campgrounds
Staff: 7
Annual Budget: $1-2,000,000
Tax: 501(c)(6)

Personnel:
President and Chief Executive Officer: Paul Bambel
   E-Mail: pbambei@arvc.org
Director, Finance and Accounting: Lynn Clouse
   E-Mail: lclouse@arvc.org
Coordinator, Events and Advertising: Rochelle Paulet
   E-Mail: rpaulet@arvc.org
Editor: Evanne Schmarder
   E-Mail: roadabode@earthlink.net
Senior Director, Marketing Communications and Partnerships: Jennifer Schwartz
   E-Mail: jschwartz@arvc.org
Director, Membership and Government Affairs: Jeff Sims
   E-Mail: jsims@arvc.org
Senior Director, Membership and Education: Barb Youmans
   E-Mail: byoumans@arvc.org

Historical Note:
Formerly (1992) the National Campground Owners Association. ARVC promotes growth of RV parks, campgrounds and the Outdoor Hospitality industry. Members are campground owners and operators, manufacturers and suppliers of campground products and services. Membership: $100 (Associate, Individual); $135-458 (RV Park/Campground).

Continuing Education:
Certification Designation/s: OHA, OHG, OHP, OHE

Meetings/Conferences: Annual
Conference Chair: Rochelle Paulet
2013 - Knoxville, TN (Knoxville Convention Center)/Nov. 6 - 8
2014 - Las Vegas, NV (Rio All-Suite Hotel and Casino)/Dec. 3 - 6
Number of non-conference events/year: 2

Publications:
ARVC Report; monthly

Membership List Available to Non-members

National Association of Sales Professionals (1991)

555 Friendly St.
Bloomfield Hills, MI 48302
Fax: (248) 254-6757
TollFree: (866) 365-1520
E-Mail: info@nasp.com
Website: nasp.com
Members: 3000 companies
Staff: 5
Annual Budget: $100-250,000

Personnel:
President and Chief Operating Officer: Idris Grant
Chairman and Chief Executive Officer: Rod Hairston
Director, Sales: Brooke Dukes
Director, Business Operations, Partner Relations and Program Development: Tonia Revere
Director, Membership Services and Advisor: Amanda Ritz

Historical Note:
NASP's mission is to reach out to all individuals and organizations interested in building professional sales to attain the highest heights of professionalism, integrity, and value to societies and peoples worldwide. It creates an online resource for Sales Professionals with Lead Exchange, Job Board, Training, Sales Library, Conferences, Forums, Webinars, and Certification Levels. Membership: $75/year.

Continuing Education:
Certification Designation/s: CPSP

National Association of School Music Dealers (1962)

14070 Proton Rd.
Suite 100
Dallas, TX 75244
Tel: (972) 233-9107 *Fax:* (972) 490-4219
E-Mail: office@nasmd.com
Website: nasmd.com
Members: 300 dealers and manufacturers
Staff: 3
Annual Budget: $250-500,000
Tax: 501(c)(6)

Personnel:
President: Joel Menchey
Executive Secretary: Madeleine Crouch

Historical Note:
Formed by a charter group of music dealers during the Trade Show in Chicago. NASMD is dedicated to serve the school music market and helping school music students make music. Represents retailers, manufacturers, and service providers. Membership: $250-350 (Dealer, based on number of storefronts); $350 (Associate); $125 (Emeritus).

Meetings/Conferences: Annual
2013 - San Antonio, TX (Hyatt Riverwalk)/March 13 - 16

Publications:
Membership Directory; on-line
NASMD Newsletter

National Association of School Nurses *(1968)*
8484 Georgia Ave.
Suite 420
Silver Spring, MD 20910
Tel: (240) 821-1130 *Fax:* (301) 585-1791
TollFree: (866) 627-6767
E-Mail: nasn@nasn.org
Website: nasn.org
Members: 14000 individuals
Staff: 29
Annual Budget: $2-5,000,000
Tax: 501(c)(3)

Personnel:
Executive Director: Donna J. Mazyck MS, RN
Director, Research: Martha Dewey Bergren
    E-Mail: mbergren@nasn.org
Chief Financial Officer: Christopher Cephas
    E-Mail: ccephas@nasn.org
Director, Information Technology: Sharon Conley
    E-Mail: sconley@nasn.org
Director, Membership: Jenelle Cooper
    E-Mail: jcooper@nasn.org
Meeting Planner: Devin Dinkel
    E-Mail: ddinkel@nasn.org
Director, Government Affairs: Mary Louise Embrey
    E-Mail: membrey@nasn.org
Manager, Communications: Kenny Lull
    E-Mail: klull@nasn.org
Specialist, Publications and Billing: Aisha Pyles
    E-Mail: apyles@nasn.org

Historical Note:
Originally established by the National Education Association as the Department of School Nurses (DSN), NASN became a separate entity in 1978. NASN's mission is to improve the health and education of children and youth by developing and providing leadership to advance school nursing practice by specialized registered nurses. Membership: $102.50 (Retired); $145.50 (Active/ Associate/Member-at-large).

Continuing Education:
Certification Designation/s: SNC

Meetings/Conferences: Annual
Conference Chair: Devin Dinkel

Publications:
Journal of School Nursing; bi-monthly; adv.
Membership Directory; on-line
NASN School Nurse; bi-monthly; adv.
Weekly Digest; weekly

Membership List Available to Non-members

National Association of School Psychologists
(1969)
4340 EW Hwy.
Suite 402
Bethesda, MD 20814
Tel: (301) 657-0270 *Fax:* (301) 657-0275
TollFree: (866) 331-6277
Website: nasponline.org
Members: 26000 individuals

Staff: 30
Annual Budget: $5-10,000,000
Tax: 501(c)(6)

Personnel:
Executive Director: Susan Gorin CAE
    E-Mail: sgorin@naspweb.org
Director, Research: Jeffrey L. Charvat
    E-Mail: jcharvat@naspweb.org
Director, Communications: Kathy Cowan
    E-Mail: kcowan@naspweb.org
Director, Publications: Denise Ferrenz
    E-Mail: dferrenz@naspweb.org
Director, Membership Services and Marketing: Wendy Finn
    E-Mail: wfinn@naspweb.org
Director, Technical Services: Alex Hyman
    E-Mail: ahyman@naspweb.org
Director, Human Resources: Glenda Kornegay
    E-Mail: gkornegay@naspweb.org
Director, Meetings and Conventions: Glenn M. Reighart CAE, CMP
    E-Mail: greighart@naspweb.org
Director, Financial Operations: Holly Sullivan
    E-Mail: hsullivan@naspweb.org
Manager, Marketing: Meg Thurgood
    E-Mail: mthurgood@naspweb.org
Director, Government Relations: Kelly Vaillancourt
    E-Mail: kvaillancourt@naspweb.org

Historical Note:
NASP provides educationally and psychologically healthy environments for all children and youth by implementing research-based programs that prevent problems, enhance independence, and provide optimal learning. It seeks to empower school psychologists to ensure that all children and youth attain optimal learning and mental health. Represents school psychology and supports school psychologists. Membership: $55-175/year.

Continuing Education:
Certification Designation/s: NCSP

Meetings/Conferences: Annual
Conference Chair: Glenn M. Reighart CAE, CMP
2013 - Seatle, WA (Sheraton Seattle Hotel)/Feb. 12 - 16
2014 - Washington, DC (Marriott Wardman Park/Omni Shoreham)/Feb. 18 - 23
2015 - Orlando, FL (Walt Disney World Swan & Dolphin Resort)/Feb. 17 - 21
2016 - New Orleans, LA (New Orleans Marriot & Sheraton)/Feb. 10 - 13
2017 - San Antonio, TX (The Henry B. Gonzalez Convention Center)/Feb. 21 - 24
2018 - Chicago, IL (Hyatt Regency)/Feb. 13 - 16
Number of non-conference events/year: 5

Publications:
Membership Directory; on-line
School Psychology Forum; adv.
School Psychology Review; quarterly; adv.

Membership List Available to Non-members

National Association of School Resource Officers
(1989)
2020 Valleydale Rd.
Suite 207A
Hoover, AL 35244
Tel: (205) 739-6060 *Fax:* (205) 536-9255
TollFree: (888) 316-2776
Website: nasro.org
Members: 6000 individuals
Staff: 6
Annual Budget: $500-1,000,000
Tax: 501(c)(3)

Personnel:
Executive Director: Mo Canady
    E-Mail: mo.canady@nasro.org
Administrative Assistant: Janet Hyatt
    E-Mail: janet.hyatt@nasro.org
President, Media Relations and Public Information Officer: Kevin Quinn
    E-Mail: kevin.quinn@nasro.org
Editor: Jennifer L. Thornton
    E-Mail: jennifer.thornton@nasro.org
Treasurer: Deb Van Velzen
    E-Mail: deb.vanvelzen@nasro.org

Historical Note:
NASRO promotes a safe and secure learning environment. Its members are school police, security officers, administrators and others law enforcement professionals

with an interest in police-student relations. Membership: $40/year.

Meetings/Conferences: Annual
Conference Chair: Jennifer L. Thornton

Publications:
Journal of School Safety; quarterly; adv.

National Association of School Safety and Law Enforcement Officers *(1970)*
3841 West St. Paul Ave.
Milwaukee, WI 53208
Tel: (414) 345-6638 *Fax:* (414) 345-6609
E-Mail: nassleo@nassleo.org
Website: nassleo.org
Members: 350 individuals
Staff: 3
Annual Budget: $25-50,000

Personnel:
Director, Training: Jay Navone
    E-Mail: training@nassleo.org

Historical Note:
Founded (1970) as the National Association of School Security Directors. NASSLEO's mission is to bring together people that are joined in a common effort to make its schools safe for its students and staff. Members are persons engaged in school security and school policy operations. Membership: $50/year.

Meetings/Conferences: Annual
Conference Chair: James Ream

Publications:
NASSLEO Newsletter; on-line; adv.

National Association of Schools of Art and Design
(1944)
11250 Roger Bacon Dr.
Suite 21
Reston, VA 20190-5248
Tel: (703) 437-0700 *Fax:* (703) 437-6312
E-Mail: info@arts-accredit.org
Website: nasad.arts-accredit.org
Members: 322 art and design schools
Staff: 10
Annual Budget: $500-1,000,000
Tax: 501(c)(3)

Personnel:
Executive Director: Samuel Hope
    E-Mail: shope@arts-accredit.org
Programming and Editorial Associate: Chira Kirkland
    E-Mail: ckirkland@arts-accredit.org
Associate, Data and Records: Jenny Kuhlmann
    E-Mail: jkuhlmann@arts-accredit.org
Management Associate, Finance and Operations: Tracy Maraney
    E-Mail: tmaraney@arts-accredit.org
Executive Assistant, Associate Director and Meetings Associate: Lisa A. Ostrich
    E-Mail: lostrich@arts-accredit.org
Projects Associate and Webmaster: Willa J. Shaffer
    E-Mail: wshaffer@arts-accredit.org

Historical Note:
Established as the National Conference of Schools of Design, became (1948) National Association of Schools of Design and then (1961) National Association of Schools of Art before assuming its present name in 1981. NASAD's purpose is to improve educational practices and maintain professional standards in art and design education. Membership: $75/year (Individual); $1,556-$2,571(Institutional).

Meetings/Conferences: Annual
Conference Chair: Chira Kirkland
2013 - St. Louis, MO (Hyatt Regency St. Louis at The Arch)/Oct. 10 - 12
2014 - Minneapolis, MN (Hyatt Regency Minneapolis)/ Oct. 16 - 18

Publications:
Handbook; biennially
NASAD Briefing Letter; weekly
NASAD Directory; annually

Membership List Available to Non-members

National Association of Schools of Dance *(1981)*
11250 Roger Bacon Dr.
Suite 21
Reston, VA 20190-5248
Tel: (703) 437-0700 *Fax:* (703) 437-6312
E-Mail: info@arts-accredit.org
Website: nasd.arts-accredit.org

Members: 70 schools of dance
Staff: 12
Annual Budget: $50-100,000
Tax: 501(c)(3)

Personnel:
Executive Director: Samuel Hope
  E-Mail: shope@arts-accredit.org
Coordinator, Accreditation: Teresa Kabo
  E-Mail: tricciardi@arts-accredit.org
Programming and Editorial Associate: Chira Kirkland
  E-Mail: ckirkland@arts-accredit.org
Data and Records Associate: Jenny Kuhlmann
  E-Mail: jkuhlmann@arts-accredit.org
Management Associate, Finance and Operations: Tracy
  Maraney
  E-Mail: tmaraney@arts-accredit.org
Office Manager: Stacy McMahon
  E-Mail: smcmahon@arts-accredit.org

Historical Note:
*NASD works to establish a national forum to stimulate
the understanding and acceptance of the educational
disciplines inherent in the creative arts in higher education
in the United States. The Association also provides
information to the public. It produces statistical research,
provides professional development for leaders of dance
schools, and engages in policy analysis. Membership:
$549 (Independent Community and Precollegiate Schools);
$824 (Postsecondary Professional Non-Degree-Granting
Institutions); $979 (Institutions with Graduate Degrees);
$824 (All Other Institutions); $75 (Individual).*

Meetings/Conferences: Annual
Conference Chair: Chira Kirkland
2013 - St. Pete Beach, FL (Don CeSar Beach Hotel)/
  Sept. 11 - 13

Publications:
The NASD Directory; annually

Membership List Available to Non-members

National Association of Schools of Music *(1924)*
11250 Roger Bacon Dr.
Suite 21
Reston, VA 20190-5248
Tel: (703) 437-0700 *Fax:* (703) 437-6312
E-Mail: info@arts-accredit.org
Website: nasm.arts-accredit.org
Members: 644 music schools
Staff: 12
Annual Budget: $2-5,000,000

Personnel:
Executive Director: Samuel Hope
  E-Mail: shope@arts-accredit.org
Associate, Programming and Editorial: Chira Kirkland
  E-Mail: ckirkland@arts-accredit.org
Management Associate, Finance and Operations: Tracy
  Maraney
  E-Mail: tmaraney@arts-accredit.org
Projects Associate, Editor and Webmaster: Willa J. Shaffer
  E-Mail: wshaffer@arts-accredit.org

Historical Note:
*NASM's purpose is to provide a national forum for the
discussion and consideration of concerns relevant to the
preservation and advancement of standards in the field of
music, particularly in higher education. Membership: $65
(Individual); $737- 2,642 (Institutional).*

Meetings/Conferences: Annual
Conference Chair: Chira Kirkland
2013 - Hollywood, FL (Westin Diplomat Resort)/Nov.
  22 - 26
2014 - Scottsdale, AZ (Westin Kierland Resort and
  Spa)/Nov. 21 - 25
2015 - St. Louis, MO (Hyatt Regency at the Arch
  Hotel)/Nov. 20 - 24
2016 - Dallas, TX (Omni Dallas Hotel)/Nov. 18 - 22

Publications:
Handbook; biennially
NASM Briefing Letter; quarterly
NASM Directory; annually

Membership List Available to Non-members

National Association of Schools of Public Affairs and Administration *(1970)*
1029 Vermont Ave. NW
Suite 1100
Washington, DC 20005-3517
Tel: (202) 628-8965 *Fax:* (202) 626-4978
E-Mail: naspaa@naspaa.org
Website: naspaa.org

Members: 253 institutions
Staff: 9
Annual Budget: $1-2,000,000
Tax: 501(c)(3)

Personnel:
Executive Director: Laurel McFarland
  E-Mail: mcfarland@naspaa.org
Chief Accreditation Officer: Crystal Calarusse
  E-Mail: calarusse@naspaa.org
Director, Finance: Peter Green
  E-Mail: green@naspaa.org
Director, Communications and Public Affairs: Stuart
  Heiser
  E-Mail: heiser@naspaa.org
*Coordinator, Conferences and National Director, Pi Alpha
  Alpha:* Jackie Lewis
  E-Mail: jlewis@naspaa.org
Director, Web Services and Office Manager: Monchaya
  Wanna
  E-Mail: wanna@naspaa.org

Historical Note:
*NASPAA is an institutional membership organization which
exists to promote excellence in public service education.
Membership includes U.S. university programs in public
affairs, public policy, public administration and nonprofit
management. Membership: $834-5701 (Institutional
depending on Number of students); $600 (Associate).*

Continuing Education:
Certification Designation/s: COPRA

Meetings/Conferences: Annual
Conference Chair: Jackie Lewis
Number of non-conference events/year: 3

Publications:
Journal of Policy Analysis and Management
Journal of Public Administration Research and Theory
Journal of Public Affairs Education; quarterly; adv.
Newsletter

National Association of Schools of Theatre *(1965)*
11250 Roger Bacon Dr.
Suite 21
Reston, VA 20190-5248
Tel: (703) 437-0700 *Fax:* (703) 437-6312
E-Mail: info@arts-accredit.org
Website: nast.arts-accredit.org
Members: 162 schools
Staff: 12
Annual Budget: $250-500,000

Personnel:
Executive Director: Samuel Hope
Management Associate, Finance and Operations: Tracy
  Maraney
  E-Mail: tmaraney@arts-accredit.org
Executive Assistant and Meetings Associate: Lisa Ostrich
  E-Mail: lostrich@arts-accredit.org
Accreditation and Research Assistant: Andrea Plybon
  E-Mail: aplybon@arts-accredit.org
Projects Associate and Webmaster: Willa J. Shaffer
  E-Mail: wshaffer@arts-accredit.org

Historical Note:
*NAST's purpose is to establish a national forum to
stimulate the understanding and acceptance of the
educational disciplines inherent in the creative arts in higher
education in the United States. It is the national accrediting
agency for theatre and theatre-related disciplines.
Membership: $75 (Individual); $1,491(Institutions with
Graduate Degrees); $1,242 (All Other Institutions).*

Meetings/Conferences: Annual
Conference Chair: Lisa Ostrich
2013 - Cambridge, MA (Royal Sonesta Hotel)/March 21
  - 23
2014 - Chicago, IL (Swissôtel Chicago)/March 20 - 22
Number of non-conference events/year: 1

Publications:
Directory of Member Institutions; annually

Membership List Available to Non-members

National Association of Science Writers *(1934)*
P.O. Box 7905
Berkeley, CA 94707
Tel: (510) 647-9500 *Fax:* (858) 793-1144
Website: nasw.org
Members: 2552 individuals
Staff: 3
Annual Budget: $100-250,000

Personnel:

Executive Director and Meeting Contact: Tinsley Davis
  E-Mail: director@nasw.org
Editor: Lynne Friedmann
  E-Mail: LFriedmann@nasw.org
Treasurer: Ron Winslow

Historical Note:
*Organized by twelve science reporters, incorporated
in the state of New York in 1955. NASW fosters the
dissemination of accurate information regarding science
through all media normally devoted to informing the
public. Members are journalists and others who convey
information about scientific developments to the public.
Membership: $85 (Regular- US); $90 (Regular-Canada);
$100 (Regular-International); $35 (Student-US); $40
(Student-International).*

Meetings/Conferences: Annual
Conference Chair: Tinsley Davis
2013 - Gainesville, FL/Nov. 1 - 5

Publications:
ScienceWriters Magazine; quarterly; adv.

National Association of Scientific Materials Managers *(1974)*
Macalester College
Olin-Rice Science Center, 382d
St. Paul, MN 55105
Tel: (651) 696-6484 *Fax:* (651) 696-6432
Website: naosmm.org
Members: 500 individuals
Staff: 5
Annual Budget: $100-250,000
Tax: 501(c)(3)

Personnel:
President: Heather McCollor
  E-Mail: mccollor@macalester.edu
Manager, Newsline Advertising: Tiffany Clark
  E-Mail: tclark01@siu.edu
Newsline Managing Editor: Barbara Neff
  E-Mail: bneff@sju.edu
Treasurer: Virginia Sari
  E-Mail: vasari@princeton.edu
Internet Chair and Webmaster: Philip A. Waite
  E-Mail: waite@denison.edu

Historical Note:
*NAOSMM's mission is to educate and assist in the
professional development of its members. Members are
laboratory and stockroom managers, supervisors and other
support personnel, mainly in university, industry, and
commercial research laboratories, who purchase scientific
equipment. Membership: $75 (Regular); $175 (Corporate);
$100 (Associate).*

Continuing Education:
Certification Designation/s: CSMM

Meetings/Conferences: Annual
2013 - Niagara Falls, NY/July 29 - Aug. 2
2014 - Indianapolis, IN/July 25 - 29

Publications:
Membership Directory; on-line
Newsline; quarterly; adv.

Membership List Available to Non-members

National Association of Secondary School Principals *(1916)*
1904 Association Dr.
Reston, VA 20191-1537
Tel: (703) 860-0200 *Fax:* (703) 476-5432
TollFree: (800) 253-7746
Website: nassp.org
Members: 30000 individuals
Staff: 116
Annual Budget: $10-25,000,000
Tax: 501(c)(3)

Personnel:
Executive Director: JoAnn Bartoletti
  E-Mail: bartolettij@nassp.org
Associate Director, Human Resources: Barbara Beasley
  E-Mail: beasleyb@nassp.org
Chief Financial Officer: John N. Dripps CAE
  E-Mail: dripps@nassp.org
Senior Director, Communications and Development: Robert
  Farrace
  E-Mail: farraceb@nassp.org
Senior Director, Leadership Programs and Services: Dick
  Flanary
  E-Mail: flanaryd@nassp.org
Director, Membership Services: Kathy Greenaway
  E-Mail: greenawayk@nassp.org

Director of Government Relations: Amanda Karhuse
  E-Mail: karhusea@nassp.org
Senior Director, Marketing, Diversity and Sales: Jeanne
  Leonard CAE
  E-Mail: leonardj@nassp.org
Interim Deputy Executive Director: Nancy Riviere
  E-Mail: rivieren@nassp.org
Graphic Designer: Lisa Schnabel
  E-Mail: schnabell@nassp.org
Associate Editor: Sharon Teitelbaum
  E-Mail: teitelbaums@nassp.org

Historical Note:
*NASSP's mission is to promote excellence in middle
level and high school leadership through research-based
professional development, resources, and advocacy so
that every student can be prepared for postsecondary
learning opportunities and be workforce ready. Membership:
$250 (Individual/Institutional); $85 (Associate); $115
(International); $50 (Retired).*

Meetings/Conferences: Annual
Conference Chair: Nancy Riviere
2013 - Ft. Washington, MD (Gaylord National Resort
  and Convention Center-National Harbor)/Feb. 28 -
  March 2
Number of non-conference events/year: 1

Publications:
AP Insight; bi-monthly; adv.
Leadership for Student Activities; monthly; adv.
Membership Directory; on-line
Middle Level Leader; monthly; adv.
NASSP Bulletin; quarterly
NewsLeader; monthly
Principal Leadership; monthly; adv.
Principal's Update; weekly; adv.
Principals Research Review; bi-monthly

Membership List Available to Non-members

National Association of Secretaries of State
(1904)
444 N. Capitol St. NW
Suite 401
Washington, DC 20001
Tel: (202) 624-3525 *Fax:* (202) 624-3527
E-Mail: nass@sso.org
Website: nass.org
Members: 54 individuals
Staff: 5
Annual Budget: $500-1,000,000

Personnel:
Executive Director: Leslie Reynolds
  E-Mail: sfisher@sso.org
Executive Assistant and Event Manager: Stacy Dodd
  E-Mail: sfisher@sso.org
Director, Communications and Special Projects: Kay
  Stimson
  E-Mail: nass@sso.org

Historical Note:
*Established at the St. Louis World's Fair as the Association
of American Secretaries of State and assumed its present
name in 1921. NASS serves as a medium for the
exchange of information and fosters cooperation between
states governments in the development of public policy.
Membership: assessed by state population and tied to the
CPI.*

Meetings/Conferences: Semi-Annual
Conference Chair: Stacy Dodd
2013 - Washington, DC (JW Marriott Hotel -
  Washington)/Jan. 24 - 27
2014 - Baltimore, MD (Hilton Baltimore)/July 13 - 16

Publications:
Membership Directory; on-line

National Association of Securities Professionals
(1985)
727 N.W 15th St.
Suite 750
Washington, DC 20005
Tel: (202) 371-5535 *Fax:* (202) 371-5536
E-Mail: info@nasphq.org
Website: nasphq.org
Members: 450 individuals
Staff: 3
Annual Budget: $100-250,000
Tax: 501(c)(6)

Personnel:
Executive Director: Orim Graves
  E-Mail: ograves@nasphq.org

Director Communications and Program Development:
  Farzin A. Khan
  E-Mail: FKhan@nasphq.org
Manager, Conferences: Tonya Bessillieu Williams
  E-Mail: tonya@tbwconsultinggroup.com

Historical Note:
*NASP serves as a resource for the minority community at
large and for minority professionals within the securities
and investments industry, by providing opportunities to
share information about the securities markets, functioning
as a repository for information regarding current trends,
facilitating fundamental educational seminars, and creating
networking opportunities. Members are minority and
women securities professionals. Membership: $125-325
(Individual); $75 (Associate); $25 (Student).*

Meetings/Conferences: Annual
Conference Chair: Tonya Bessillieu Williams
Number of non-conference events/year: 1

Publications:
Member Directory; on-line

National Association of Security Companies (NASCO) *(1972)*
444 N. Capitol St. NW
Suite 345
Washington, DC 20001
Tel: (202) 347-3257 *Fax:* (202) 393-7006
E-Mail: info@nasco.org
Website: nasco.org
Members: 17 companies
Staff: 3
Annual Budget: $250-500,000

Personnel:
Executive Director: Jeff Flint
Federal Legislative Counsel: Stephen D. Amitay
  E-Mail: steve@amitayconsulting.com
Deputy Executive Director: Roy Rahn

Historical Note:
*Formerly (1993) the Committee of National Security
Companies. Incorporated in New York. NASCO's mission
is to promote standards and professionalism for private
security officers and within the contract security industry.
Members are major contract security guard firms concerned
with industry standards, legislation and public education.
Membership: Varies for different categories.*

Meetings/Conferences: Annual

Publications:
Membership Directory; on-line
NASCO e-Newsletter; on-line

National Association of Self-Instructional Language Programs *(1971)*
University of Arizona , 1717 E. Speedway Blvd.
Suite 3312
Tucson, AZ 85721-0151
Tel: (520) 626-5258 *Fax:* (520) 626-8205
E-Mail: nasilp@u.arizona.edu
Website: nasilp.net
Members: 110 Institutions
Staff: 3
Annual Budget: $50-100,000

Personnel:
President: Craig Christy
  E-Mail: tcchristy@una.edu
Executive Director: Alexander Dunkel
  E-Mail: adunkel@u.arizona.edu
Treasurer: Louis A. Wagner
  E-Mail: lwagner@allegheny.edu

Historical Note:
*NASILP is an organizational affiliate of JNCL and NCLIS.
Mission is to fostering study of less commonly taught
languages through self-instructional principles utilizing
a prochievement modality developed for an academic
setting.Membership: $200/year (Institutional).*

Meetings/Conferences: Annual

National Association of Service Managers *(1955)*
P.O. Box 250796
Milwaukee, WI 53225
Tel: (414) 466-6060 *Fax:* (414) 466-0840
Website: nasm.com
Members: 200 individuals
Staff: 3
Annual Budget: $25-50,000
Tax: 501(c)(6)

Personnel:
President: David Jones

  E-Mail: davidejones@eaton.com
Contact, Meetings: Angela Antinucci
Treasurer: Ken Cook
  E-Mail: kencook@kencook.com

Historical Note:
*NASM is an organization dedicated to providing
professional leadership and education to the service
executive, while developing their managerial expertise
in the business and organizations that they represent.
Membership: $225 (Regular/Associate); $112.50
(Chapter).*

Continuing Education:
Enrollment: 50
Certification Designation/s: CSE, ASE, CSM

Meetings/Conferences: Annual
Conference Chair: Angela Antinucci

Publications:
NASM Newsletter; quarterly; adv.

National Association of Service Providers in Private Rehabilitation
633 S. Washington St.
Alexandria, VA 22314
Tel: (703) 836-0850 *Fax:* (703) 836-0848
TollFree: (888) 258-4295
Website: nationalrehab.org/cwt/external/
  wcpages/divisions/nasppr.aspx
Staff: 5

Personnel:
Executive Director: Beverlee Stafford
  E-Mail: Beverlee@nationalrehab.org
Director, Membership: Brian Coupe
  E-Mail: Membership@nationalrehab.org
Office Manager: Veronica Hamilton
  E-Mail: vhamilton@nationalrehab.org
Director, Governmental Affairs: Patricia Leahy
  E-Mail: patricia@nationalrehab.org
Administrative Assistant: Sandra Mulliner
  E-Mail: sandra@nationalrehab.org

Historical Note:
*A professional division of the National Rehabilitation
Association, which provides it administrative support.
Members include rehabilitation counselors, nurses,
placement specialists, physical therapists, occupational
therapists, vocational evaluators, job developers, employers,
speech pathologists, insurance adjusters, administrators,
managers/supervisors, educators, attorneys, physicians
and students. Memberships available to all service
providers in private rehabilitation and others enhancing
the rehabilitation opportunities of people with disabilities.
Membership: $30 (Professional and Affiliate); $5
(students).*

Meetings/Conferences: Annual

National Association of Seventh-Day Adventist Dentists *(1943)*
P.O. Box 101
Loma Linda, CA 92354-0101
Tel: (909) 558-8187 *Fax:* (909) 558-0209
E-Mail: nasdad@llu.edu
Website: nasdad.org
Members: 600 individuals
Staff: 4
Annual Budget: $50-100,000
Tax: 501(c)(3)

Personnel:
President: Ken W. Pierson DDS
Secretary and Treasurer: Sharon Boggs RDH
Editor: William H. Heisler DDS
Vice President and Coordinator, Conventions: Doyle Nick
  DDS, MS

Historical Note:
*Affiliated with the American Dental Association. NASDAD
seeks to promote professional competence, spiritual
endeavors, family relationships, and community outreach.
Membership: $58 (RDH Member/1st year post-grad DDS);
$115 (DDS Member); Free (Current Missionaries/Dental/
Hygiene Student).*

Meetings/Conferences: Annual
Conference Chair: Doyle Nick DDS, MS
2013 - Palm Spring, CA/Oct. 24 - 27
Number of non-conference events/year: 1

Publications:
Member Directory; on-line
NASDAD News

National Association of Sewer Service Companies
(1976)

11521 Cronridge Dr.
Suite J
Owings Mills, MD 21117
Tel: (410) 486-3500 *Fax:* (410) 486-6838
E-Mail: director@nassco.org
Website: nassco.org
Members: 250 companies
Staff: 4
Annual Budget: $500-1,000,000

Personnel:
Executive Director: Ted DeBoda PE
   E-Mail: director@nassco.org
Technical Assistant: Diego Calderon
   E-Mail: diego@nassco.org
Administrative Assistant and Program Coordinator: Dawn Jaworksi
   E-Mail: dawn@nassco.org
Manager, Operations: Heather Myers
   E-Mail: heather@nassco.org

Historical Note:
NASSCO's mission is to improve the success rate of everyone involved in the pipeline rehabilitation industry through education, technical resources, and industry advocacy. Membership: $450 (Contractor/Manufacturer); $250 (Professional/Municipal); $75 (Individual).

Continuing Education:
Certification Designation/s: ITCP, MACP, LACP, PACP

Meetings/Conferences: Annual
2013 - Duck Key, FL (Hawks Cay Island Resort)/Feb. 13 - 16

Publications:
Membership Directory; on-line; adv.
NASSCO Pipeline; on-line; adv.
NASSCO Times; quarterly; adv.

National Association of Shareholder and Consumer Attorneys (1988)
818 Connecticut Ave. NW
Suite 1100
Washington, DC 20006
Tel: (215) 988-9548 *Fax:* (215) 988-9885
Website: nascat.org
Staff: 3
Annual Budget: $500-1,000,000

Personnel:
President: Ira Schochet
Executive Administrator: Lara McDermott
Treasurer: Karen Hanson Riebel

Historical Note:
NASCAT is a trade organization and public policy voice for lawyers interested in a better system of federal and state legal protections for investors and consumers.

Meetings/Conferences: Annual

Publications:
Class Act Newsletter; weekly

National Association of Shell Marketers (1974)
P.O. Box 658
Garrisonville, VA 22463-0658
Tel: (703) 582-8478 *Fax:* (540) 720-0320
Website: https://netforum.avectra.com/eWeb/DynamicPage.asp
Staff: 2
Annual Budget: $250-500,000
Tax: 501(c)(6)

Personnel:
President: Jennifer Richards
   E-Mail: jsr@nasmonline.com

Historical Note:
NASM's mission is to promote shell brand, maintain a dialogue with shell on behalf of its members and provide shell marketers with access to valuable services and information. Membership: $598-1,500 (Wholesale Marketer, based on annual gallons of Shell Petroleum products sold); $360 (Subjobber/Supplier Associate); $575-1,500 (Lubricant Marketer).

Meetings/Conferences: Annual
Conference Chair: Jennifer Richards

Publications:
@NASM; monthly; adv.
Membership Directory; on-line
Supplier Associate Directory; on-line

National Association of Sign Supply Distributors (1991)
1001 N. Fairfax St.

Suite 301
Alexandria, VA 22314
Tel: (703) 836-4012 *Fax:* (703) 836-8353
E-Mail: nassd@clemonsmgmt.com
Website: nassd.org
Members: 58 distributors and manufacturers
Staff: 3
Annual Budget: $100-250,000

Personnel:
Executive Director: Brandon Hensley
Meeting and Member Services Manager: Taylor Flynn
   E-Mail: taylorf@clemonsmgmt.com
Legal Counsel: Neil Kuenn
   E-Mail: nkuenn@kkrlaw.com

Historical Note:
NASSD is a non-profit trade association dedicated to promoting the common interests and value that full service, sign supply distribution and manufacturing provides to the Sign Industry. Members are persons, firms and corporations engaged in the sign and graphics distribution industry in North America who conduct full-service wholesale distribution of sign and graphics products and also those firms engaged in the manufacture or supply of commercial, neon and/or electrical sign products who distribute such products through sign supply distributors and who demonstrate an interest in furthering the goals and objectives of NASSD. Membership : $1,500-2,000 (Distributors, based on no. of locations); $2,000 (Associate).

Meetings/Conferences: Annual
Conference Chair: Taylor Flynn

Publications:
NASSD Membership Directory; on-line

National Association of Small Business Contractors
700 12th St. NW
Suite 700
Washington, DC 20005
Tel: (888) 861-9290
E-Mail: supportteam@nabc.org
Website: nasbc.org
Staff: 2
Tax: 501(c)(6)

Personnel:
Chief Executive Officer: Terry Williams
President: Cris Young

Historical Note:
NASBC's mission is to support and advance the interests of small business contractors. Membership: $395/year (Small Business).

Continuing Education:
Certification Designation/s: CFGS
Meetings/Conferences:
Number of non-conference events/year: 1

Publications:
Membership Directory; on-line

National Association of Small Trucking Companies (1989)
104 Stuart Dr.
Hendersonville, TN 37075
Tel: (615) 451-4555 *Fax:* (615) 451-0041
TollFree: (800) 264-8580
E-Mail: info@nastc.com
Website: nastc.com
Members: 3000 Companies
Staff: 4

Personnel:
President: David Owen
   E-Mail: david@nastc.com
Vice President, Operations: Dana Campbell
Contact, Information Technology And Marketing: Keith Owen
   E-Mail: keith.owen@nastc.com
Vice President, Sales and Marketing: Hunter Owen
   E-Mail: hunter.owen@nastc.com

Historical Note:
NASTC's mission is to help small trucking companies control their costs through managed purchasing, analysis, consultation and advocacy and to level the competitive playing field allowing member companies to grow, prosper and remain a significant force in the transportation industry. Membership: $850 (Associate Vendor); $150 (Best Broker).

Meetings/Conferences: Annual

Publications:
Best Broker Directory; annually
NASTC Newsletter; quarterly

National Association of Social Workers (1955)
750 First St. NE
Suite 700
Washington, DC 20002-4241
Tel: (202) 408-8600 *Fax:* (202) 336-8311
TollFree: (800) 742-4089
E-Mail: aofosu@naswdc.org
Website: naswdc.org
Members: 145,000 members
Staff: 127
Annual Budget: $10-25,000,000
Tax: 501(c)(3)

Personnel:
Executive Director: Elizabeth J. Clark PhD, ACSW, MPH, II
   E-Mail: bclark@naswdc.org
Director, Human Resources and International Affairs: Luisa Lopez
General Counsel: Carolyn I. Polowy

Historical Note:
Formed by the merger of the American Association of Group Workers, the American Association of Medical Social Workers, the American Association of Psychiatric Social Workers, the American Association of Social Workers, Association for the Study of Community Organization, the National Association of School Social Workers and the Social Work Research Group. NASW's mission is to enhance the professional growth and development of its members, to create and maintain professional standards, and to advance sound social policies. Membership: $125-190 (Regular); $48-143 (Student); $190 (Associate).

Continuing Education:
Certification Designation/s: CE, ACSW, DCSW, QCSW

Publications:
Children & Schools
Health & Social Work
NASW News; daily
Practice Perspectives
Social Work; quarterly
Social Work Abstracts; quarterly
Social Work Research

Membership List Available to Non-members

National Association of Spine Specialists (1999)
7075 Veterans Blvd.
Burr Ridge, IL 60527
Tel: (630) 230-3600 *Fax:* (630) 230-3700
TollFree: (866) 960-6277
Website: spine.org
Members: 6500 Members
Staff: 6
Annual Budget: $500-1,000,000
Tax: 501(c)(6)

Personnel:
Executive Director: Eric Muehlbauer CAE
Senior Manager, Exhibits and Corporate Relations: Rick Bacon
   E-Mail: rbacon@spine.org
Director , Education Council: Jeffrey Wang MD
Director, Administration Council: F. Todd Wetzel

Historical Note:
The National Association of Spine Specialists brings together spine care providers and patients as a unified voice in the fight for sound health policy. Membership: $0-595/year..

Meetings/Conferences: Annual
Conference Chair: Rick Bacon
2013 - New Orleans, LA/Oct. 9 - 12
2014 - San Francisco, CA/Nov. 12 - 15
2015 - Chicago, IL/Oct. 14 - 17
2016 - Boston, MA/Oct. 26 - 29

Publications:
Leadership Directory; on-line
Membership Directory; on-line
SpineLine; bi-monthly; adv.
The Spine Journal; monthly; adv.

National Association of Sporting Goods Wholesalers (1953)
1833 Centre Point Cir.
Suite 123
Naperville, IL 60563
Tel: (630) 596-9006 *Fax:* (630) 544-5055
E-Mail: nasgw@nasgw.org
Website: nasgw.org
Members: 4,500 employees and salespeople

Staff: 7
Annual Budget: $1-2,000,000
Tax: 501(c)(6)

Personnel:
Executive Director: Patrick Farrey
   E-Mail: pfarrey@nasgw.org
Director , Marketing and Communications: Chris Barry
   E-Mail: cbarry@nasgw.org
Manager, Accounts: Barbara Ciulla
   E-Mail: bciulla@nasgw.org
President and Secretary: Maurice A. Desmarais
   E-Mail: mdesmarais@nasgw.org
Contact, Member Services: Laura Hallen
   E-Mail: lhallen@nasgw.org
Manager, Events and Awards: Meg Pawelski
   E-Mail: mpawelski@nasgw.org
Manager, Operations: Sarah Washburn
   E-Mail: swashburn@nasgw.org

Historical Note:
*Organized in 1953 and incorporated in 1954. Formerly the
Sporting Goods Jobbers Association. NASGW's mission is
to serve as a liaison with other sporting goods associations.
Membership includes wholesalers of primarily fishing
and shooting sports equipment, and manufacturers and
representative groups of this equipment. Membership:
$2,000 (Wholesalers); $850 (Manufacturers/Importers);
$500 (International Manufacturer); $250 (Manufacturer's
Representative); $195 (Service/ Suppliers); $100 (Trade
Press/Publishers).*

Meetings/Conferences: Annual
Conference Chair: Meg Pawelski
2013 - Grapevine, TX (Gaylord Texan Resort)/Oct. 29
   - Nov. 1
2014 - Little Rock, AR (Little Rock Convention Center)/
   Oct. 14 - 17

Publications:
InSight e-Newsletter; irregular
Membership directory; on-line
NASGW Newsletter; on-line

Membership List Available to Non-members

National Association of Sports Commissions
(1992)
9916 Carver Rd.
Suite 100
Cincinnati, OH 45242
Tel: (513) 281-3888 *Fax:* (513) 281-1765
E-Mail: NASC@SportsCommissions.org
Website: sportscommissions.org
Members: 600 organizations
Staff: 3
Annual Budget: $500-1,000,000

Personnel:
Executive Director: Don Schumacher
   E-Mail: Don@SportsCommissions.org
Director, Membership Services: Elizabeth Chaney
   E-Mail: Elizabeth@SportsCommissions.org
Director, Meetings and Events: Beth Hecquet
   E-Mail: Beth@SportsCommissions.org

Historical Note:
*NASC's mission is to deliver quality education, networking
opportunities and event management. Membership: $795
(Active/Allied); $100 (Rights Holder).*

Continuing Education:
Certification Designation/s: CSEE

Meetings/Conferences: Annual
Conference Chair: Beth Hecquet
2013 - Louisville, KY (Louisville Marriott Downtown)/
   April 22 - 25
2014 - Oklahoma City, OK (Oklahoma City Convention
   and Visitors Bureau)/March 31 - April 3
2015 - Milwaukee, WI (Visit Milwaukee)/April 27 - 30

Publications:
Membership Directory; on-line
NASC News and Notes; irregular; adv.

National Association of Sports Officials *(1980)*
2017 Lathrop Ave.
Racine, WI 53405
Tel: (262) 632-5448 *Fax:* (262) 632-5460
E-Mail: cservice@naso.org
Website: naso.org
Members: 18,000 officials
Staff: 21
Annual Budget: $1-2,000,000
Tax: 501(c)(3)

Personnel:

President and Publisher: Barry Mano
   E-Mail: bmano@naso.org

Historical Note:
*NASO's mission is to serve as the source of officiating
information, programs and services and improve officiating
performance through educational programs and training
materials. Membership: $103/year.*

Meetings/Conferences: Annual
2013 - Grand Rapids, MI/July 28 - 30

Publications:
It's Official Newsletter; monthly
NASO LockerRoom e-newsletter; monthly
Referee Magazine; monthly

National Association of Sports Public Address Announcers
4424 NW Wildwood Dr.
Gladstone, MO 64116
Tel: (816) 305-6293 *Fax:* (720) 302-6293
Website: naspaa.net
Staff: 2
Tax: 501(c)(3)

Personnel:
Executive Director and President: Brad Rumble
   E-Mail: brumble@naspaa.net
Legal Counsel: Tom Busch

Historical Note:
*NASPAA's mission is to raise the level of professionalism
of public address announcing by serving as a resource for
training, education and professional development for those
individuals who provide their services to sports events at all
levels nationwide. Membership: $20- 30 (Individual); $69
(School).*

Continuing Education:
Certification Designation/s: NASPAA, CPAA

Publications:
NASPAA E-newsletter
The Voice; quarterly

National Association of State Administrators and Supervisors of Private Schools *(1971)*
P.O. Box 025250
Suite 60017
Miami, FL 33102-5250
Website: nasasps.org
Members: 50 individuals
Staff: 2
Annual Budget: $25-50,000

Personnel:
President: John Ware
Treasurer: Lane Goodwin

Historical Note:
*NASASPS's mission is to improve and enhance effective
state regulation of private postsecondary education.
Membership: $495 (Regular/Partnership); $795
(Associate).*

Meetings/Conferences: Annual
2013 - Sacramento, CA (Hilton Sacramento Arden
   West)/April 21 - 24
Number of non-conference events/year: 1

National Association of State Agencies for Surplus Property *(1947)*
1924 S. 10 - 1/2 St.
Springfield, IL 62703
Tel: (217) 785-6903 *Fax:* (217) 785-6905
Website: nasasp.org
Members: 56 state agencies
Staff: 3
Annual Budget: $250-500,000

Personnel:
Executive Director: Scott E. Pepperman
   E-Mail: nasaspexecdir@aol.com
Director, Associate Membership: Tina Rodriguez
   E-Mail: tina.rodriguez@nasasp.org

Historical Note:
*NASASP's mission is to save taxpayer dollars. Members
are surplus property agencies in the states and territories.
Membership: $39 (Associate); $200 (Corporate).*

Publications:
e-Newsletter; on-line

National Association of State Alcohol and Drug Abuse Directors (NASADAD) *(1971)*
1025 Connecticut Ave. NW
Suite 605

Washington, DC 20036
Tel: (202) 293-0090 *Fax:* (202) 293-1250
E-Mail: dcoffice@nasadad.org
Website: nasadad.org
Members: 57 state and territorial agencies
Staff: 14
Annual Budget: $2-5,000,000
Tax: 501(c)(3)

Personnel:
Executive Director: Robert Morrison
   E-Mail: rmorrison@nasadad.org
Director, Public Policy: Michelle Dirst
   E-Mail: mdirst@nasadad.org
Director, Research and Program Applications: Rick
Harwood
   E-Mail: rharwood@nasadad.org
Meeting Planner and Administrative Assistant: Fachon
James-Simpson
   E-Mail: fsimpson@nasadad.org
Director, Finance: Hollis McMullen
   E-Mail: hmcmullen@nasadad.org

Historical Note:
*Formerly (until 1978) known as the National Association
of State Drug Abuse Program Coordinators. NASADAD's
purpose is to foster and support the development of effective
alcohol and other drug abuse prevention and treatment
programs throughout every state. Membership: dues based
on size of state.*

Meetings/Conferences: Annual
Conference Chair: Fachon James-Simpson

Publications:
Prevention Newsletter; monthly

National Association of State & Local Equity Funds *(1994)*
1970 Broadway
Suite 250
Oakland, CA 94612
Tel: (510) 444-1101 *Fax:* (703) 435-4390
E-Mail: info@naslef.org
Website: naslef.org
Staff: 1
Annual Budget: $250-500,000
Tax: 501(c)(6)

Personnel:
Executive Director: Julie Sontag
   E-Mail: jsontag@merrittcap.org

Historical Note:
*NASLEF's mission is to promote a greater understanding of
the Low Income Housing Tax Credit (LIHTC) and encourage
the professional development of its member organizations.
Membership: $2,000/year (Active Member/Corporate
Member).*

Meetings/Conferences: Annual

Publications:
Membership Directory; on-line
NASLEF Newsletters

Membership List Available to Non-members

National Association of State Archaeologists
(1978)
C/O Connecticut State Museum of Natural
History & Connecticut Archaeology Center, Univ.
of Connecticut, Unit 1023
2019 Hillside Rd.
Storrs, CT 06269-1023
Tel: (860) 486-5248 *Fax:* (860) 486-0827
E-Mail: cmcgimsey@crt.state.la.us
Website: uiowa.edu/ ~ osa/nasa
Members: 58 individuals
Staff: 4
Annual Budget: Under $10,000

Personnel:
President: Nicholas Bellantoni
   E-Mail: nicholas.bellantoni@uconn.edu
Editor: Hester Davis
   E-Mail: hadavis@comp.uark.edu
Secretary and Treasurer: Arthur E. Spiess
   E-Mail: arthur.spiess@maine.gov

Historical Note:
*NASA's mission is to facilitate communication among
state archaeologists. Membership is limited to the official
State Archaeologist of each state in the United States.
Membership: $25/year (Individual).*

Publications:
NASA Directory; on-line

National Association of State Auditors, Comptrollers and Treasurers (1915)
449 Lewis Hargett Cir.
Suite 290
Lexington, KY 40503-3590
Tel: (859) 276-1147 *Fax:* (859) 278-0507
E-Mail: nasactdc@sso.org
Website: nasact.org
Members: 170 individuals
Staff: 12
Annual Budget: $1-2,000,000
Tax: 501(c)(3)

Personnel:
Executive Director: R. Kinney Poynter CPA
    E-Mail: kpoynter@nasact.org
Manager, Communications: Glenda G. Johnson
    E-Mail: gjohnson@nasact.org
Manager, Conferences: Donna Maloy CMP
    E-Mail: dmaloy@nasact.org
Manager, Information Technology and Web Services:
    Adrian Puryear
    E-Mail: apuryear@nasact.org

Historical Note:
NASACT's mission is to assist state leaders in enhancing and promoting effective and efficient management of government resources. It has three affiliates that share office space in Lexington and at the Office of Federal Relations in Washington, D.C., which handles lobbying efforts in Congress and the federal agencies. Affiliates are the National State Auditors Association (NSAA), the National Association of State Comptrollers (NASC) and the National Association of State Treasurers (NAST). Membership consists of three individuals from each state who serve in the capacity of auditors, comptrollers and treasurers of each state.

Meetings/Conferences: Annual
Conference Chair: Donna Maloy CMP
Number of non-conference events/year: 6

National Association of State Aviation Officials (1931)
Washingtion National Airport, Hangar Seven
Suite 218
Washington, DC 20001
Tel: (703) 417-1880 *Fax:* (703) 417-1885
E-Mail: info@nasao.org
Website: nasao.org
Members: 51 states and territories
Staff: 4
Annual Budget: $500-1,000,000
Tax: 501(c)(4)

Personnel:
Manager, Member Relations and Administration: Bridgette
    Bailey
    E-Mail: bbailey@nasao.org
Director, Operations: A. Kathryn Solee
    E-Mail: ksolee@nasao.org

Historical Note:
NASAO's mission is to promote and develop a safe and responsive air transportation system for the public benefit. Membership: $1500/year (Corporations/Associations/Individuals)

Meetings/Conferences: Annual

Publications:
Membership Directory; on-line
State Aviation Directory; on-line

National Association of State Boards of Accountancy (1908)
150 Fourth Ave., North
Suite 700
Nashville, TN 37219-2417
Tel: (615) 880-4200 *Fax:* (615) 880-4290
TollFree: (866) 696-2722
E-Mail: cbtcpa@nasba.org
Website: nasba.org
Members: 55 state boards
Staff: 265
Annual Budget: $25-50,000,000

Personnel:
President and Chief Executive Officer: Ken L. Bishop
Senior Meetings Planner: Katie Bodiford
    E-Mail: kbodiford@nasba.org
Senior Vice President and Chief Financial Officer: Michael
    R. Bryant
Director, Legislative Affairs: John W. Johnson

Historical Note:

Formerly (1967) Association of Certified Public Accountant Examiners. NASBA's mission is to enhance the effectiveness of state boards of accountancy. Membership: $100/year (Individual/Organization).

Continuing Education:
Certification Designation/s: SCC, CNMI, IQEX, CPA

Meetings/Conferences: Annual
Conference Chair: Katie Bodiford
2013 - Maui, HI/Oct. 27 - 30

Publications:
ALD News; on-line
CPE Monitor; on-line

National Association of State Boards of Education (1959)
2121 Crystal Dr.
Suite 350
Arlington, VA 22202
Tel: (703) 684-4000 *Fax:* (703) 836-2313
TollFree: (800) 368-5023
E-Mail: boards@nasbe.org
Website: nasbe.org
Members: 750 board members
Staff: 21
Annual Budget: $2-5,000,000
Tax: 501(c)(3)

Personnel:
Chief Executive Officer: James W. Kohlmoos
    E-Mail: jimk@nasbe.org
Senior Manager, Communications and Managing Editor:
    Steve Berlin
    E-Mail: steveb@nasbe.org
Director, Conventions and Meetings and Membership
    Associate: Doris J. Cruel
Director, Information Technology: Jason Gentili
    E-Mail: jasong@nasbe.org
Director, Government and Public Affairs: David Griffith
    E-Mail: davidg@nasbe.org
Director, Publications and Chief Knowledge Officer: David
    Kysilko
    E-Mail: davidk@nasbe.org
Chief Financial Officer: Jeff Pollard III
    E-Mail: jeffp@nasbe.org
Director, Government Affairs: Tony Shivers
    E-Mail: tonys@nasbe.org

Historical Note:
NASBE's mission is to promote policy frameworks that are clearly recognizable as scholarly, student-focused, nonpartisan and adaptable to state by state implementation. NASBE also strives to strengthen State Boards as the educational policy making bodies for students and citizens. Composed of state board of education members from the U.S. and U.S Territories. Membership: $75/year (Associate).

Meetings/Conferences: Annual
Conference Chair: Doris J. Cruel

Publications:
Headline Review; weekly
Healthline Review
Monthly Mailing; monthly
SmartBrief; weekly
State Education Standard

National Association of State Boards of Geology (1991)
P.O. Box 11591
Columbia, SC 29211-1591
Tel: (803) 739-5676 *Fax:* (803) 739-8874
E-Mail: asbog@asbog.org
Website: asbog.org
Members: 29 boards
Staff: 4
Annual Budget: $250-500,000

Personnel:
Executive Director: S. G. 'Sam' Christiano
    E-Mail: asbog@asbog.org
Administrative Assistant: Barbara A. Chavis
Media Relations: Gloria N. Hicks
Treasurer: William S. Schenck

Historical Note:
NASBG's mission is to serve as a connective link among the individual state geologic registration licensing boards for the planning and preparation of uniform procedures and the coordination of geologic protective measures for the general public. Members are state boards of geology.

Meetings/Conferences: Annual
2013 - Seattle, WA/Nov. 2

2014 - Indianapolis, IN/Nov. 15
Publications:
Journal of Geoscience Education

National Association of State Boating Law Administrators (1959)
1500 Leestown Rd.
Suite 330
Lexington, KY 40511-2047
Tel: (859) 225-9487 *Fax:* (859) 231-6403
E-Mail: info@nasbla.org
Website: nasbla.org
Members: 150 associations, states and territories
Staff: 11
Annual Budget: $2-5,000,000
Tax: 501(c)(3)

Personnel:
Executive Director and Chief Executive Officer: John K.
    Johnson
    E-Mail: john@nasbla.org
Director, Education: Pam Dillon
    E-Mail: pam@nasbla.org
Director, Law Enforcement: John Fetterman
    E-Mail: john.fetterman@nasbla.org
Director, Finance and Administration: Tom Hayward
    E-Mail: tom@nasbla.org
Editor: Kimberly Jenkins
    E-Mail: kim@nasbla.org
Director, Membership Services: Sam Lynch
    E-Mail: sam@nasbla.org
Director, Training: Kristy Moore
    E-Mail: kristy@nasbla.org
Deputy Director: Ron Sarver CAE
Director, Government Affairs: Charlie Sledd
    E-Mail: charlie@nasbla.org

Historical Note:
NASBLA's mission is to strengthen the ability of the state and territorial boating authorities to reduce death, injury and property damage associated with recreational boating and ensure a safe, secure and enjoyable boating environment. Members are recreational boating authorities all 50 states and the U.S. territories. Membership: $300 (Non-Profits); $1,000 (Other Organizations).

Meetings/Conferences: Annual
2013 - Boise, ID/Sept. 15 - 18
Number of non-conference events/year: 15

Publications:
Et Cetera; monthly
Membership Directory; annually
Small Craft Advisory; bi-monthly; adv.

National Association of State Budget Officers (1945)
444 N. Capitol St. NW
Suite 642
Washington, DC 20001-1551
Tel: (202) 624-5382 *Fax:* (202) 624-7745
E-Mail: nasbo-direct@nasbo.org
Website: nasbo.org
Members: 160 individuals
Staff: 5
Annual Budget: $1-2,000,000
Tax: 501(c)(3)

Personnel:
Executive Director: Scott D. Pattison
    E-Mail: spattison@nasbo.org
Manager, Membership Relations and Conferences: Lauren
    Cummings
    E-Mail: lcummings@nasbo.org
Administrative Coordinator: Brukie Gashaw
    E-Mail: bgashaw@nasbo.org
Fiscal Policy Analyst: Michael Streepey
    E-Mail: mstreepey@nasbo.org

Historical Note:
Affiliated with the National Governors Association, NASBO strives to improve the quality and availability of information to state budget offices. NASBO's mission is to provide opportunities to share practices across states and provide training and research information through publications and seminars.

Meetings/Conferences: Semi-Annual
Conference Chair: Lauren Cummings
2013 - Santa Ana Pueblo, NM (Hyatt Regency Tamaya
    Resort and Spa)/April 25 - 27
2013 - Anchorage, AK (Hotel Captain Cook)/July 21 -
    24
Number of non-conference events/year: 1

Publications:
Health Care Issues Update
Membership Directory; on-line
NASBO News Flash Archives
State Budget Press Clips
The Fiscal Survey of States; bi-annually
Washington Report & NASBO News
Weekly ARRA Updates; weekly

National Association of State Catholic Conference Directors (1968)
P.O. Box 29260
Washington, DC 20017
Tel: (301) 853-5342 *Fax:* (301) 853-7671
Website: nasccd.org
Members: 43 member state agencies and individuals
Staff: 1
Annual Budget: Under $10,000

Personnel:
Executive Director: Ronald G. Jackson

Historical Note:
NASCCD seeks to facilitate and encourage the exchange of information among its members pertaining to the activities, programs, and organization of the conferences. Members are executive directors of state Catholic conferences and affiliate diocesan agencies.

National Association of State Charity Officials (1978)
C/O Elizabeth Grant, Oregon Department of Justice
1515 SW Fifth Ave., Suite 410
Portland, OR 97201
Website: nasconet.org
Members: 100 individuals
Staff: 1
Annual Budget: Under $10,000
Tax: 501(c)(3)

Personnel:
Assistant Attorney General: Elizabeth Grant
E-Mail: Elizabeth.Grant@doj.state.or.us

Historical Note:
NASCO is an association of state offices charged with oversight of charitable organizations and charitable solicitation in the United States. Members are state government officers responsible for the regulation of charities. Has no paid officers or full-time staff.

Meetings/Conferences: Annual

Publications:
Membership Directory; on-line
NASCO Newsletter; on-line

National Association of State Chief Administrators (1976)
P.O. Box 708
Lexington, KY 40588
Tel: (515) 321-4139
E-Mail: nasca@csg.org
Website: nasca.org
Members: 37 states
Staff: 4
Annual Budget: $50-100,000
Tax: 501(c)(3)

Personnel:
Executive Director: Ray Walton
E-Mail: rwalton@nasca.org
Research Analyst: Michael Snyder
E-Mail: msnyder02@qub.ac.uk
Director, Operations: Marcia Stone
E-Mail: mstone@csg.org
Association Manager: Shawn Vaughn
E-Mail: svaughn@AMRms.com

Historical Note:
Formerly (1999) National Association of State Directors of Administration and General Services. NASCA is a National affiliate of Council of State Governments. NASCA's mission is to provide a forum for state chief administrators and those who partner with them to easily share information regarding the diverse issues they work to solve every day. Members are governor appointed administrators charged with the administration of state general services and corporate partners. Membership: $2,000/year.

Publications:
NASCA Newsletter; quarterly

National Association of State Chief Information Officers (1969)

C/O AMR Management Services, 201 E. Main St.
Suite 1405
Lexington, KY 40507
Tel: (859) 514-9156 *Fax:* (859) 514-9166
E-Mail: nascio@amrms.com
Website: nascio.org
Members: 50 states
Staff: 9
Annual Budget: $2-5,000,000
Tax: 501(c)(3)

Personnel:
Executive Director: Doug Robinson
E-Mail: drobinson@amrms.com
Coordinator, Programs: Alison Keller
E-Mail: akeller@AMRms.com
Coordinator, Membership Services and Communications: Shawn Vaughn
E-Mail: svaughn@AMRms.com
Director, Government Affairs: Pam Walker
E-Mail: pwalker@amrms.com

Historical Note:
Formerly (2001) National Association for State Information Resource Executives. NASCIO's mission is to foster government excellence through business practices, information management, and technology policy. Members are state chief information officers and information technology executives and managers. Membership: $8000 (Corporate Member); $500 (Federal/Local/International/ Non-Profit Organizations/Academic/Tribal Government); $2,000 (Territory).

Meetings/Conferences: Semi-Annual
Conference Chair: Alison Keller
2013 - Washington, DC (Capital Hilton)/April 28 - May 1
2013 - Philadelphia, PA (Philadelphia Marriott Downtown)/Oct. 13 - 16
2014 - Nashville, TN (Omni Nashville Hotel)/Sept. 28 - Oct. 1

Publications:
Membership Directory; on-line
NASCIO Connections; monthly
Newsbrief; weekly

Membership List Available to Non-members

National Association of State Controlled Substances Authorities (1984)
72 Brook St.
Quincy, MA 02170
Tel: (617) 472-0520 *Fax:* (617) 472-0521
E-Mail: kathykeough@nascsa.org
Website: nascsa.org
Staff: 1
Annual Budget: $250-500,000
Tax: 501(c)(3)

Personnel:
Executive Director: Katherine Keough
E-Mail: kathykeough@nascsa.org

Historical Note:
NASCSA's primary purpose is to provide a continuing mechanism through which state and federal agencies, as well as others can work to increase the effectiveness and efficiency of state and national efforts to prevent and control drug diversion and abuse and to provide an educational forum to further this purpose. Members are state, commonwealth and territory government agencies responsible for implementing and administering controlled substance scheduling, regulation and diversion control. Membership: $200/year (Regular/Associate/Associate Individual).

Meetings/Conferences: Annual
2013 - Kansas City, MO/Oct. 22 - 25
2014 - Savannah, GA/Oct. 21 - 24

Publications:
NASCSA e-Newsletter

National Association of State Credit Union Supervisors (1965)
1655 N. Ft. Myer Dr.
Suite 300
Arlington, VA 22209
Tel: (703) 528-8351 *Fax:* (703) 528-3248
TollFree: (800) 728-7927
E-Mail: offices@nascus.org
Website: nascus.org
Members: 900 individuals
Staff: 7
Annual Budget: $1-2,000,000
Tax: 501(c)(6)

Personnel:
President and Chief Executive Officer: Mary Martha Fortney
E-Mail: marymartha@nascus.org

Historical Note:
NASCUS's mission is to enhance state credit union supervision and advocate for a safe and sound credit union system. Membership: $0-12,000/year.

Continuing Education:
Enrollment: 200
Certification Designation/s: CSCUES, CASCUE, CSCUE

Meetings/Conferences: Annual
Conference Chair: Tammy Gentilini
2013 - San Antonio, TX (Omni San Antonio Hotel)/ March 19 - 20

Publications:
NASCUS Profile of State Credit Union Regulatory Agencies; biennially
Facts from Washington; bi-weekly
NASCUS Profile of State Credit Union Regulatory Agencies; bi-annually
Stateline; quarterly

National Association of State Departments of Agriculture (1915)
1156 15th St. NW
Suite 1020
Washington, DC 20005-1711
Tel: (202) 296-9680 *Fax:* (202) 296-9686
E-Mail: nasda@nasda.org
Website: nasda.org
Members: 54 departments
Staff: 10
Annual Budget: $500-1,000,000
Tax: 501(c)(3)

Personnel:
Chief Executive Officer: Stephen Haterius
E-Mail: stephen@nasda.org
Director, Trade Shows and Grants Management: DeWitt Ashby
E-Mail: dewitt@nasda.org
Senior Director, Legislative and Regulatory Affairs: Amy Hendrickson
E-Mail: amy@nasda.org
Director, Programs: Charles W. Ingram
E-Mail: charlie@nasda.org

Historical Note:
NASDA's mission is to represent the state departments of agriculture in the development, implementation, and communication of sound public policy and programs which support and promote the American agricultural industry, while protecting consumers and the environment.

Meetings/Conferences: Annual
Conference Chair: DeWitt Ashby
2013 - Chicago, IL (McCormick Place)/May 18 - 21
2014 - Chicago, IL (McCormick Place)/June 10 - 13
Number of non-conference events/year: 1

Publications:
Member Directory; on-line
NASDA News; semi-monthly

National Association of State Directors of Career Technical Education Consortium (1920)
8484 Georgia Ave.
Suite 320
Silver Spring, MD 20910
Tel: (301) 588-9630 *Fax:* (301) 588-9631
Website: careertech.org
Members:
50 state agencies
200 members
Staff: 8
Annual Budget: $500-1,000,000

Personnel:
Executive Director: Kimberly A. Green
E-Mail: kgreen@careertech.org
Manager, Public Policy: Nancy Conneely
E-Mail: nconneely@careertech.org
Research and Policy Manager: Kara Herbertson
E-Mail: kherbertson@careertech.org
Manager, Membership Services: Ramona Schescke
E-Mail: rschescke@careertech.org
Manager, Communications and Marketing: Erin Uy
E-Mail: euy@careertech.org

Historical Note:
NASDCTEC's purpose is to provide leadership for career technical education's role in education, workforce

preparation and economic development. Membership comprises of 59 career and technical education agency heads, and business, labor and education officials who are committed to quality occupational education at the secondary, post-secondary and adult levels. Membership: $1,500 (Organization, for 3 Employees); $100 (Associate Non-State Employee); $75 (Associate State Employee).

Meetings/Conferences: Biennial
Number of non-conference events/year: 1

Publications:
Membership Directory; on-line

National Association of State Directors of Developmental Disabilities Services, Inc. (1964)
113 Oronoco St.
Alexandria, VA 22314
Tel: (703) 683-4202 Fax: (703) 684-1395
Website: nasddds.org
Members: 50 states and the District of Columbia
Staff: 9
Annual Budget: $2-5,000,000

Personnel:
Executive Director: Nancy Thaler
   E-Mail: nthaler@nasddds.org
Director, Federal Policy: Dan Berland
   E-Mail: dberland@nasddds.org
Director, Technical Assistance: Robin Cooper
   E-Mail: rcooper@nasddds.org
Director, Administrative Services: Katherine Karol Snyder
   E-Mail: ksnyder@nasddds.org

Historical Note:
NASDDDS's mission is to assist member state agencies in building person-centered systems of services and supports for people with developmental disabilities and their families. Membership: $525 (Individuals).

Meetings/Conferences: Annual

Publications:
Community Services Reporter; monthly
Federal Perspectives; monthly
Membership Directory; on-line

National Association of State Directors of Migrant Education (1968)
1001 Connecticut Ave. NW
Suite 915
Washington, DC 20036
Tel: (202) 462-7444 Fax: (202) 775-7784
E-Mail: mlap@mlap.org
Website: nasdme.org
Members: 51 individuals
Staff: 2
Annual Budget: $250-500,000
Tax: 501(c)(3)

Personnel:
President: Robin Lisboa
Secretary and Treasurer: Dr. Myrna Toney

Historical Note:
NASDME encourages interstate coordination and cooperation to further the education of children whose parents are migrant agriculture farm workers. Members are the persons in each state education agency who bear the responsibility for Chapter One Migrant Education Program operation.

Meetings/Conferences: Annual
2013 - Orlando, FL/April 28 - May 1/1500 attendees

Publications:
NASDME Newsletter; on-line

National Association of State Directors of Special Education (1938)
225 Reinekers Ln.
Suite 420
Alexandria, VA 22314
Tel: (703) 519-3800 Fax: (703) 519-3808
Website: nasdse.org
Members: 100 individuals
Staff: 15
Annual Budget: $2-5,000,000

Personnel:
Executive Director: Bill East
Policy Analyst, Government Relations: Amanda Lowe
   E-Mail: Lowe@nasdse.org
Contact, Financial Services and Operations: Carla Burgman Meade
Manager, Publications: Nancy Tucker
   E-Mail: nancy.tucker@nasdse.org

Historical Note:

NASDSE seeks to promote and support education programs and related services for children and youth with disabilities in the United States and outlying areas. Members are state directors of special education in all 50 states, the District of Columbia, the Department of Defense, the Bureau of Indian Education, the federal territories and the Freely Associated States. Membership: $100 /year (Affiliate).

Meetings/Conferences: Annual

Publications:
NASDSE Works!; quarterly

Membership List Available to Non-members

National Association of State Directors of Teacher Education and Certification (1928)
1629 K St. NW
Suite 300
Washington, DC 20006
Tel: (202) 204-2208 Fax: (202) 204-2210
Website: nasdtec.org
Members:
20 stake holders
260 government agencies, colleges and universities
Staff: 2
Annual Budget: $250-500,000
Tax: 501(c)(3)

Personnel:
Executive Director: Dr. Phillip Rogers
   E-Mail: philrogers@nasdtec.com

Historical Note:
NASDTEC is dedicated to licensing well-prepared, safe and wholesome educators for the nation's schools. Represents professional standards boards, commissions and state departments of education in all 50 states, the District of Columbia, the Department of Defense Educational Activity, the U.S. Territories, and the Canadian provinces of Alberta, British Columbia, and Ontario. Members are government agencies, schools and companies involved with the preparation and certification of professional school personnel. Membership: $400/year (Associate).

Meetings/Conferences: Semi-Annual
2013 - Austin, TX (Omni Austin Hotel Downtown)/June 6 - 9
2013 - Boise, ID (Grove Hotel)/Oct. 23 - 25

Publications:
Communicator; on-line
KnowledgeBase; on-line
Member Directory; on-line

National Association of State Directors of Veterans Affairs (1973)
107 S. West St.
Suite 550
Alexandria, VA 22314
Tel: (503) 373-2000 Fax: (503) 373-2362
Website: nasdva.us
Members: 56 individuals
Staff: 2
Annual Budget: $50-100,000
Tax: 501(c)(3)

Personnel:
President: Jim Willis
Treasurer: Clayton Clark

Historical Note:
NASDVA's mission is to provide professional support to the administrators of each State's respective office for veteran affairs. Has no paid officers or full-time staff. Membership: $400/year.

National Association of State Election Directors (1989)
12543 Westella
Suite 100
Houston, TX 77077-3929
Tel: (281) 752-6200 Fax: (281) 293-0453
E-Mail: services@nased.org
Website: nased.org
Members: 50 individuals
Staff: 3
Annual Budget: $100-250,000
Tax: 501(c)(3)

Personnel:
Legislative Advisor and President-Elect: Chris Thomas

Historical Note:
NASED's purpose is to share among its members information about their duties, responsibilities, methods of operation, suggestions and proposals for improvement of election laws and their administration and the

administrative support is provided by the Council of State Governments. Membership: $400/year (Individual).

Continuing Education:
Certification Designation/s: NASEDVSC

Meetings/Conferences:
2013 - Washington, DC (JW Marriott Hotel - Washington)/Jan. 24 - 26

Publications:
Membership Directory

National Association of State Emergency Medical Services Officials (1980)
201 Park Washington Ct.
Falls Church, VA 22046-4527
Tel: (703) 538-1799 Fax: (703) 241-5603
E-Mail: info@nasemso.org
Website: nasemso.org
Members: 250 state EMS officials
Staff: 12
Annual Budget: $1-2,000,000
Tax: 501(c)(3)

Personnel:
Executive Vice President: Elizabeth B. Armstrong CAE, MAM
   E-Mail: Armstrong@nasemso.org
Executive Director: Dia Gainor
   E-Mail: dia@nasemso.org
Manager, Meetings and Exhibits: Susan A. Denston
   E-Mail: denston@nasemso.org
Coordinator, Membership and Executive Assistant: Sharon L. Kelly
Program Manager: Kathy Robinson
   E-Mail: robinson@nasemso.org
Director, Communications and Marketing: Dawn M. Shiley CAE, MAM
   E-Mail: dshiley@asmii.net
Manager, Web Site Contents: Karen S. Thompson
   E-Mail: thompson@nasemso.org

Historical Note:
NASEMSO's mission is to support its members in developing EMS policy and oversight, as well as in providing vision and resources in the development and improvement of state, regional and local EMS and emergency care systems. Membership: $250 (Associate); $2,000 (Corporate); $450-1,200 (State).

Meetings/Conferences: Annual
Conference Chair: Susan A. Denston
Number of non-conference events/year: 2

Publications:
Membership Directory; on-line
NASEMSO Notes; quarterly
Prehospital Emergency Care; quarterly
Professional Journal; quarterly
Washington Update; semi-monthly

Membership List Available to Non-members

National Association of State Energy Officials (1992)
1414 Prince St.
Suite 200
Alexandria, VA 22314-2853
Tel: (703) 299-8800 Fax: (703) 299-6208
E-Mail: energy@naseo.org
Website: naseo.org
Members: 56 officials and administrators
Staff: 11
Annual Budget: $5-10,000,000
Tax: 501(c)(3)

Personnel:
Executive Director: David Terry
   E-Mail: dterry@naseo.org
Director, Accounting and Administration: Donna Brown
   E-Mail: donna@naseo.org
General Counsel: Jeffrey C. Genzer
   E-Mail: jcg@dwgp.com
Manager, Grants and Programs: Shemika Spencer
   E-Mail: sspencer@naseo.org

Historical Note:
NASEO provides leadership on oil, gas, coal, electricity and alternative fuels and guiding regional, state and federal government officials toward a deeper understanding of energy's pivotal role in the economy and environment, and informing them about the specific energy priorities and concerns of the states and territories. Membership includes the governor-designated energy officials from each state and territory. Membership: $5000 (For-profit

Corporation); $2500 (Not-for-profit association or educational institution).

Meetings/Conferences:
2013 - Washington, DC (Fairmont Hotel)/Feb. 5 - 8
2013 - Denver, CO (Curtis Hotel)/Sept. 15 - 18
2014 - Washington, DC (Fairmont Hotel)/Feb. 4 - 7
Number of non-conference events/year: 2

National Association of State Facilities Administrators (1987)
P.O. Box 11910
Lexington, KY 40578-1910
Tel: (859) 244-8181 *Fax:* (859) 244-8001
E-Mail: nasfa@nasfa.net
Website: nasfa.net
Members: 1265 individuals, corporate affiliates and states
Staff: 2
Annual Budget: $100-250,000

Personnel:
Executive Director: Marcia Stone
    E-Mail: mstone@csg.org

Historical Note:
NASFA's mission is to provide leadership in the development and implementation of state facility administration practices. It is affiliated with Council of State Governments. Membership: $1,800 (State/Corporate Affiliate); $1,000 (Other Governmental).

Meetings/Conferences: Annual
2013 - San Diego, CA/June 9 - 12

Publications:
Membership Directory; on-line
NASFA News; monthly
State Facilities Quarterly Newsletter; quarterly

National Association of State Farm Agents
7044 S. 13th St.
Oak Creek, WI 53154
Tel: (414) 908-4959 *Fax:* (414) 768-8001
E-Mail: info@nasfa.com
Website: nasfa.com
Staff: 9
Annual Budget: $250-500,000

Personnel:
Executive Director: Preston Sherer
    E-Mail: p.sherer@nasfa.com

Historical Note:
NASFA, a professional association of State Farm independent contractor agents, endeavors to provide timely and insightful information to members to foster a spirit of camaraderie and professional fellowship and work tirelessly to maintain the Independent Contractor. Membership: $300 (Regular); $348 (Gold/Retired Gold); $540 (Platinum); $126 (Retired).

Meetings/Conferences: Annual
Conference Chair: Denver Kennedy

Publications:
NASFAX; semi-monthly
The Mirror; quarterly

National Association of State Fire Marshals (1989)
P.O. Box 671
Cheyenne, WY 82003
Tel: (202) 737-1226 *Fax:* (202) 393-1296
E-Mail: info@firemarshals.org
Website: firemarshals.org
Members: 51 fire marshals
Staff: 4
Annual Budget: $1-2,000,000
Tax: 501(c)(6)

Personnel:
Executive Director: James Narva
    E-Mail: jnarva@narvaassociates.com
Executive Assistant: Erin Friel
    E-Mail: EFriel@firemarshals.org
National Program Director and Trainer: Phil Oakes
    E-Mail: POakes@narvaassociates.com

Historical Note:
NASFM's mission is to protect human life, property and the environment from fire. Members are state fire marshals and private industry supporters. Membership: $400 (Principal); $250 (Associate); $100 (Affiliates) $2,500-15,000 (Corporate and Association).

Meetings/Conferences: Annual
Number of non-conference events/year: 1

Publications:

Newsletter

National Association of State Foresters (1920)
444 N. Capitol St. NW
Suite 540
Washington, DC 20001
Tel: (202) 624-5258 *Fax:* (202) 624-5407
E-Mail: nasf@stateforesters.org
Website: stateforesters.org
Members: 54 jurisdictions
Staff: 14
Annual Budget: $2-5,000,000
Tax: 501(c)(5)

Personnel:
Executive Director: Jay Farrell
Manager, Educational Materials: Warren Boyette
Chief Financial Officer: LouAnn Gilmer
Director, Communications: Sarah McCreary

Historical Note:
Formerly Association of State Foresters in 1920 and a successor to the Association of Eastern Foresters (1911), NASF assumed its present name in 1964. Through public-private partnerships, NASF seeks to discuss, develop, sponsor and promote programs and activities which will advance the practice of sustainable forestry, the conservation and protection of forest lands and associated resources and the establishment and protection of forests in the urban environment. Membership: $3,500/year (State).

Meetings/Conferences:
Number of non-conference events/year: 2

Publications:
Membership Directory; on-line
NASF Washington Weekly Report; weekly

National Association of State Head Injury Administrators (1990)
PO Box 878
Waitsfield, VT 05673
Tel: (802) 498-3349 *Fax:* (773) 945-2341
Website: nashia.org
Staff: 3
Annual Budget: $50-100,000
Tax: 501(c)(3)

Personnel:
Executive Director: Lorraine Wargo RN
    E-Mail: execdirector@nashia.org
Bookkeeper: Donna Huckestein
    E-Mail: finance@nashia.org

Historical Note:
NASHIA's mission is to plan, implement, and administer public programs and services for individuals with brain injury and their families. Membership: $1000 (State Agency); $200 (Individual); $175 (Retiree); $125 (Associate); $50 (Student); $500-1,500 (Supporting); $2,000 (Benefactor).

Publications:
Defense Centers of Excellence

National Association of State Land Reclamationists (1973)
C/O Anna Harrington Caswell
SIUC Coal Research Center
Carbondale, IL 62901-4623
Tel: (618) 536-5521 *Fax:* (618) 453-7346
Website: crc.siu.edu/naslr.htm
Members: 140 individuals
Staff: 2
Annual Budget: Under $10,000
Tax: 501(c)(6)

Personnel:
Secretary, Treasurer and Webmaster: Anna Harrington Caswell
    E-Mail: aharring@siu.edu

Historical Note:
NASLR's mission is to bring together state reclamation officials for activities of mutual interest and to promote cooperation between the states, private mining groups and the federal government on matters affecting the reclamation of mined lands. NASLR advocates the use of research, new technology and professional discourse to foster the restoration of lands and waters affected by mining related activities. Membership: $10 (Individual/Associate); $100 (Corporate Sponsor); $200 (State).

Meetings/Conferences: Annual

Publications:
NASLR Newsletter; quarterly

National Association of State Mental Health Directors (1959)
66 Canal Center Plaza
Suite 302
Alexandria, VA 22314
Tel: (703) 739-9333 *Fax:* (703) 548-9517
Website: nasmhpd.org
Members: 55 Individuals
Staff: 23
Annual Budget: $50-100,000
Tax: 501(c)(3)

Personnel:
Executive Director: Robert W. Glover PhD
    E-Mail: bob.glover@nasmhpd.org
Coordinator, Consumer Affairs: Tonier Cain
    E-Mail: tonier.cain@nasmhpd.org
Chief Financial Officer: Jay Meek CPA, MBA
    E-Mail: jay.meek@nasmhpd.org
Director, Human Resources & Administration: Kathy Parker MA
    E-Mail: kathy.parker@nasmhpd.org
Director, Operations: Roy Praschil
    E-Mail: roy.praschil@nasmhpd.org
Technical Assistance: Timothy Tunner
    E-Mail: timothy.tunner@nasmhpd.org

Historical Note:
NASMHPD serves as the national representative and advocate for state mental health agencies and their directors and supports effective stewardship of state mental health systems.

Meetings/Conferences: Annual

Publications:
Member Directory; on-line

National Association of State Mental Health Program Directors (1959)
66 Canal Center Plaza
Suite 302
Alexandria, VA 22314-1591
Tel: (703) 739-9333 *Fax:* (703) 548-9517
E-Mail: info@nasmhpd.org
Website: nasmhpd.org
Members: 50 states and 4 territories
Staff: 26
Annual Budget: $10-25,000,000
Tax: 501(c)(3)

Personnel:
Executive Director: Robert W. Glover PhD
    E-Mail: bob.glover@nasmhpd.org
Network Manager: Shina Animasahun
    E-Mail: shina.animasahun@nasmhpd.org
Chief Financial Officer: Jay Meek CPA, MBA
    E-Mail: jay.meek@nasmhpd.org
Director, Human Resources and Administration: Kathy Parker MA
    E-Mail: kathy.parker@nasmhpd.org
Director, Public Policy: Elizabeth Prewitt MA
    E-Mail: elizabeth.prewitt@nasmhpd.org
Administrative Program Associate: Melanie Sutherland
    E-Mail: melanie.sutherland@nasmhpd.org

Historical Note:
NASMHPD's mission is to serve the national representative and advocate for state mental health agencies and their directors and support effective stewardship of state mental health systems. NASMHPD holds affiliation with NRI, NAC/SMHA and NCMHDI.

Meetings/Conferences: Annual

Publications:
Membership Directory; on-line
NASMHPD Newsletter

National Association of State Outdoor Recreation Liaison Officers (1967)
105 H, ABNR Building
University of Missouri
Columbia, MO 65211
Tel: (573) 353-2702 *Fax:* (573) 882-9526
E-Mail: nasorlo@embarqmail.com
Website: nasorlo.org
Members: 56 state and territorial representatives
Staff: 1
Annual Budget: $25-50,000

Personnel:
Executive Director: Doug Eiken

Historical Note:

NASORLO's mission is to provide a liaison to Congress and the Department of Interior for the administration of matching funds to state and local governments for outdoor recreation. Members are governor-appointed state administrators of outdoor recreational grant programs funded under the federal Land and Water Conservation Act. *Membership: $950 (State/Territory); $20 (Associate); Free (Affiliate/Honorary).*

Meetings/Conferences: Annual

National Association of State Park Directors
(1962)
8829 Woodyhill Rd.
Raleigh, NC 27613
Tel: (919) 676-8365 *Fax:* (919) 676-8365
Website: naspd.org
Members:
50 states
1 territory (Puerto Rico)
Staff: 3
Annual Budget: $500-1,000,000
Tax: 501(c)(6)

Personnel:
Executive Director: Philip K. McKnelly
   E-Mail: naspd@me.com
Coordinator, Event: Dannie Jones
   E-Mail: dannie.jones@state.nm.us

Historical Note:
NASPD's mission is to promote and advance the state park systems of America for their own significance as well as important contributions to the nation's environment, heritage, health and economy. Members are chief administrative officers of each state park agency. Membership: $1,400/year (State).

Meetings/Conferences: Annual
Conference Chair: Dannie Jones

National Association of State Personnel Executives *(1977)*
P.O. Box 11910
Lexington, KY 40578-1910
Tel: (859) 244-8182 *Fax:* (859) 244-8001
E-Mail: lscott@csg.org
Website: naspe.net
Members: 150 individuals
Staff: 1
Annual Budget: $250-500,000

Personnel:
Director: Leslie Scott
   E-Mail: lscott@csg.org

Historical Note:
NASPE was established to enhance communication and the exchange of information among state government personnel executives across the country. An affiliate of the Council of State Governments which provides administrative support. Purpose is to provide educational resources for its members and a forum to share practices in state human resource management through meetings, publications, surveys, and online discussion forums. Membership: $1,500/year (State).

Meetings/Conferences: Annual
2013 - Washington, DC (The Dupont Circle Hotel)/ Jan. 25 - 27

Publications:
Inside NASPE; monthly
NASPE Executive; weekly

Membership List Available to Non-members

National Association of State Procurement Officials *(1947)*
201 E. Main St.
Suite 1405
Lexington, KY 40507
Tel: (859) 514-9159 *Fax:* (859) 514-9166
E-Mail: naspo@amrms.com
Website: naspo.org
Members: 128 individuals
Staff: 6
Annual Budget: $5-10,000,000
Tax: 501(c)(3)

Personnel:
Association Director: Jack Gallt
   E-Mail: jgallt@amrms.com
Coordinator, Marketing and Communications: Melanie Bowzer
   E-Mail: mbowzer@AMRms.com
Deputy Director and Program Manager: Lee Ann Pope
   E-Mail: lpope@AMRms.com

Coordinator, Programs and Education Coordinator: Lisa Thompson
   E-Mail: lthompson@AMRms.com

Historical Note:
Formerly National Association of State Purchasing Officials. NASPO's mission is to serve as primary liaison for small vendors seeking procurement opportunities. Membership: $500/year (Associate).

Meetings/Conferences: Annual
Number of non-conference events/year: 1

Publications:
NASPO Newsletter; monthly

Membership List Available to Non-members

National Association of State Retirement Administrators *(1956)*
P.O. Box 842
Essex, CT 06426-0842
Tel: (225) 757-7452 *Fax:* (270) 918-6177
Website: nasra.org
Members: 247 associate members and individuals
Staff: 5
Annual Budget: $1-2,000,000
Tax: 501(c)(6)

Personnel:
Executive Director: Linda R. Savitsky
   E-Mail: lindasavitsky@nasra.org
Director, Research: Keith Brainard
   E-Mail: keithb@nasra.org
Manager, External Affairs: Ady Dewey

Historical Note:
NASRA represents the administrators of various public-sector retirement programs, providing legislative advocacy and public and professional education. Membership: $2,900 (Member); $3,100 (Associate).

Meetings/Conferences: Annual
Conference Chair: Linda R. Savitsky
2013 - Portland, OR (Portland Marriott Downtown Waterfront)/Aug. 2 - 7
2014 - Asheville, NC (Grove Park Inn)/Aug. 1 - 6

Publications:
Members Directory; on-line
NASRA Newsletter; bi-annually

National Association of State Student Grant and Aid Programs
603 E. 12th St.
Fifth Floor
Des Moines, IA 50319
Tel: (515) 725-3420 *Fax:* (515) 725-3401
E-Mail: nassgap@nassgap.org
Website: nassgap.org
Staff: 2
Annual Budget: $50-100,000

Personnel:
President: Julie Leeper
   E-Mail: julie.leeper@iowa.gov

Historical Note:
The National Association of State Student Grant and Aid Programs (NASSGAP) is dedicated to the promotion, strengthening, encouragement and enhancement of better standards in the administration and operation of state grant and aid programs so that these programs shall be available to students in all states to expand and further post secondary educational opportunities.

Meetings/Conferences: Annual
2013 - Washington, DC (Hilton Garden Inn)/Oct. 15 - 18

Publications:
Member Directory; on-line

National Association of State Technology Directors *(1978)*
2760 Research Park Dr.
Lexington, KY 40511-8482
Tel: (859) 244-8187
Website: nastd.org
Staff: 3
Annual Budget: $500-1,000,000
Tax: 501(c)(3)

Personnel:
Executive Director: Mark McCord
Analyst, Technology: Paul Czarnecki
Manager, Meetings and Member Services: Pam Johnson

Historical Note:

A member-driven organization whose purpose is to advance and promote the effective use of information technology and services to improve the operation of state government. *Membership: $3500 (State/Corporate affiliate); $500(Associate); $1500 (Small/micro business affiliate).*

Meetings/Conferences: Annual
2013 - Charleston, SC (Charleston Marriott)/Aug. 26 - 30
2014 - Coeur d#Alene, ID (Coeur d'Alene Hotel)/Aug. 24 - 28

National Association of State Treasurers *(1976)*
P.O. Box 11910
Lexington, KY 40578-1910
Tel: (859) 244-8175 *Fax:* (859) 244-8053
E-Mail: nast@csg.org
Website: nast.net
Members: 50 individuals
Staff: 8
Annual Budget: $2-5,000,000
Tax: 501(c)(6)

Personnel:
Executive Director: Jonathan Lawniczak
Office Manager: Wanda Birch

Historical Note:
NAST's mission is to promote education and exchange of ideas among its members who are state treasurers, their deputies and staff. Membership: $3,000 (Principal Member); $1,000 (Subsidiary Member); $1,500-2,000 (Associate).

Meetings/Conferences: Annual
2013 - Asheville, NC (Grove Park Inn)/Oct. 6 - 9

Publications:
Membership Directory; on-line

National Association of State Utility Consumer Advocates (NASUCA) *(1979)*
8380 Colesville Rd.
Suite 101
Silver Spring, MD 20910
Tel: (301) 589-6313 *Fax:* (301) 589-6380
E-Mail: nasuca@nasuca.org
Website: nasuca.org
Members: 44 consumer advocates
Staff: 2
Annual Budget: $250-500,000

Personnel:
Executive Director: Charles A. Acquard
   E-Mail: charlie@erols.com

Historical Note:
NASUCA provides a forum to exchange ideas, improves consumer representation at the state and federal levels, and encourages greater consumer participation in the regulatory process. Members are designated by the laws of their respective jurisdictions to represent the interests of utility consumers before state and federal regulators and in the courts.

Meetings/Conferences: Semi-Annual
2013 - Seatle, WA/June 9 - 11
2013 - Orlando, FL/Nov. 17 - 20

Publications:
Member Directory

National Association of State Veterans Homes *(1953)*
100 Patriots Rd.
Stony Brook, NY 11790
Tel: (631) 444-8606 *Fax:* (631) 444-8575
E-Mail: info@nasvh.org
Website: nasvh.org
Members: 137 facilities
Staff: 2
Annual Budget: $100-250,000

Personnel:
President: Fred Sganga
   E-Mail: fsganga@notes.cc.sunysb.edu
Secretary and Treasurer: Robert Graham

Historical Note:
NASVH's mission is to insure that each and every eligible U.S. veteran receives the benefits, services, long term health care and respect which they have earned by their service and sacrifice. Membership is comprised of the administrators and staff representing the state operated veterans homes throughout the 50 states of the union, its districts and commonwealths. Membership: $800/year minimum (State Veterans Home-based on the number of authorized beds).

Meetings/Conferences: Annual
2013 - Alexandria, VA (Embassy Suites Alexandria-Old Town)/Feb. 24 - March 1

National Association of State Workforce Agencies
(1937)
444 N. Capitol St. NW
Suite 142
Washington, DC 20001-1512
Tel: (202) 434-8020 *Fax:* (202) 434-8033
E-Mail: naswa@naswa.org
Website: workforceatm.org
Members: 53 state agencies
Staff: 19
Annual Budget: $2-5,000,000
Tax: 501(c)(4)

Personnel:
Executive Director: Richard A. Hobbie PhD
  E-Mail: rhobbie@naswa.org
Director, Technology: Lou Ansaldi
  E-Mail: lansaldi@naswa.org
Chief Financial Officer and Fiscal and Administrative Director: James Black
  E-Mail: jblack@naswa.org
Director, Center for Employment Security Education and Research: Yvette Chocolaad
  E-Mail: ychocolaad@naswa.org
Director, Congressional and Intergovernmental Public Affairs: Marc Katz
  E-Mail: mkatz@naswa.org
Manager, Office and Membership Services: Martina L. Pass
  E-Mail: mpass@naswa.org
Director, Workforce Development and Deputy Executive Director: Bob Simoneau
  E-Mail: bsimoneau@naswa.org
Operations Manager: Charlie Terrell
  E-Mail: bsimoneau@naswa.org

Historical Note:
Founded as the Interstate Conference of Unemployment Compensation Agencies became the Interstate Conference of Employment Security Agencies in 1939, and assumed its current name in 2000. NASWA's mission is to provide a cost-effective national employment system that improves labor market efficiency and reflects nation's diverse workforce. Members are administrators of state agencies responsible for employment and training programs, unemployment insurance and labor market information. Membership: $1000/year (Affiliate).

Meetings/Conferences: Annual
Conference Chair: Charlie Terrell
Number of non-conference events/year: 2

Publications:
NASWA Bulletin; on-line

National Association of States United For Aging and Disabilities *(1964)*
1201 15th St. NW
Suite 350
Washington, DC 20005-2842
Tel: (202) 898-2578 *Fax:* (202) 898-2583
E-Mail: info@nasua.org
Website: nasuad.org
Members:
57 state and territorial agencies
57 individuals
Staff: 13
Annual Budget: $2-5,000,000
Tax: 501(c)(3)

Personnel:
Executive Director: Martha Roherty
  E-Mail: mroherty@nasuad.org
Coordinator, Conferences and Outreach: Kimberly Fletcher
  E-Mail: kfletcher@nasuad.org
Chief Operating Officer: Eric Risteen
  E-Mail: eristeen@nasuad.org

Historical Note:
NASUAD works to design, improve, and sustain state systems delivering home and community based services and supports for people who are older or have a disability, and their caregivers.

Meetings/Conferences: Annual
Conference Chair: Kimberly Fletcher
Number of non-conference events/year: 1

Publications:
Friday Updates; weekly

National Association of Steel Pipe Distributors
(1975)
1501 E. Mockingbird Ln.
Suite 307
Victoria, TX 77904
Tel: (361) 574-7878 *Fax:* (832) 201-9479
E-Mail: info@naspd.com
Website: naspd.com
Members: 250 companies
Staff: 3
Annual Budget: $500-1,000,000

Personnel:
Executive Director: Susannah F. Porr
Office Administrator: Gail Belcik
Contact, Editor and Advertising Sales: Linda Key

Historical Note:
Trade Association organized in San Antonio, TX, and incorporated in the same state. NASPD's mission is to provide a participative environment and forum for members to network, communicate, educate and promote the steel pipe and tube industry. Membership: $950-1,200 (Regular); $1,050-1,300 (Associate/Professional Affiliate); $100 (Continuing Member).

Continuing Education:
Certification Designation/s: NCEES-RCEP

Meetings/Conferences:
2013 - Las Vegas, NV (Wynn Las Vegas and Encore Resort)/Feb. 21 - 23
2013 - Toronto, ON (Hyatt Regency Toronto)/June 6 - 8
2013 - Nashville, TN (Hilton Nashville Downtown)/ Sept. 19 - 21
Number of non-conference events/year: 1

Publications:
Membership Directory; on-line
Pipeline Magazine; adv.

National Association of Stock Plan Professionals
(1993)
P.O. Box 21639
Concord, CA 94521-0639
Tel: (925) 685-9271 *Fax:* (925) 930-9284
E-Mail: naspp@naspp.com
Website: naspp.com
Members: 6000 Members
Staff: 7

Personnel:
Executive Director: Barbara Baksa
Director, Programs: Jennifer Baehr
Manager, Administration and Member Services: Vicki Brill
Contact, Exhibiting and Sponsorship Opportunities: Gary Hill
  E-Mail: gary@naspp.com
Editorial Director: Jennifer Namazi
Director, Membership Services: Broc Romanek
Director, Education: Robyn Shutak

Historical Note:
NASPP mission's is to provide services to its members that will enrich their professional skills, further their professional knowledge and, in general, enhance the stock plan profession at every level. Membership: $525 (Individual); $130 (Single Corporate Member); $675(Corporate, up to three Individuals).

Meetings/Conferences: Annual
Conference Chair: Jennifer Baehr

Publications:
Membership Directory; on-line
The NASPP Advisor; bi-monthly

National Association of Street Schools *(1996)*
PO Box 140069
Denver, CO 80214
Website: streetschoolnetwork.org
Members: 33 Schools
Staff: 4
Annual Budget: $100-250,000
Tax: 501(c)(3)

Personnel:
President: Tom Tillapaugh
  E-Mail: TomT@StreetSchoolNetwork.org
Vice President, Education: Todd Goble
  E-Mail: ToddG@StreetSchoolNetwork.org

Historical Note:
Formerly National Association of Street Schools. The goal of the StreetSchool Network is to provide services that help network schools develop and thrive as they seek to assist high need students living in at-risk environments

in becoming productive, contributing members of society through educational and spiritual intervention.

Publications:
Newsletter

National Association of Student Affairs Professionals *(1954)*
Claflin University, 400 Magnolia St.
Corson Hall, Suite 106
Orangeburg, SC 29115
Tel: (478) 825-6291 *Fax:* (229) 430-6398
Website: nasap.net
Members: 150 individuals
Staff: 15
Annual Budget: $10-25,000

Personnel:
Treasurer: Denver L. Malcom
  E-Mail: dmalcom@claflin.edu

Historical Note:
Formerly (1994) National Association of Personnel Workers. NASAP seeks to promote excellence in the area of Student Affairs. Members are student affairs personnel in the fields of teaching, housing, financial aid and social services. Membership: $300 (Institutional); $40 (Professional/Associate); $12 (Student).

Meetings/Conferences: Annual
2013 - Jackson, MS (Jackson State University)/Jan. 31 - Feb. 2

Publications:
NASAP Focus Newsletter
NASAP Journal

National Association of Student Councils *(1931)*
1904 Association Dr.
Reston, VA 20191
Tel: (703) 860-0200 *Fax:* (703) 476-5432
TollFree: (800) 253-7746
E-Mail: nasc@nasc.us
Website: nasc.us
Staff: 1

Personnel:
Co-Chair: Shannon Porter

Historical Note:
NASC represents middle level and high school councils nationwide. It seeks to provide a valuable leadership partnership between students and their school. Membership: $95/year.

Continuing Education:
Certification Designation/s: CSL

Meetings/Conferences: Annual
2013 - Las Vegas, NV (Sunrise Mountain High School)/ June 22 - 24

Publications:
Leadership for Student Activities Magazine; monthly; adv.
Membership Directory; on-line
NASC E-Bulletin; on-line

National Association of Student Financial Aid Administrators *(1966)*
1101 Connecticut Ave. NW
Suite 1100
Washington, DC 20036-4303
Tel: (202) 785-0453 *Fax:* (202) 785-1487
Website: nasfaa.org
Members: 18,000 student financial assistance professionals and 2,800 institutions
Staff: 26
Annual Budget: $10-25,000,000
Tax: 501(c)(3)

Personnel:
President: Justin Draeger
  E-Mail: draegerj@nasfaa.org
Senior Director, Legislative and Regulatory Analysis: Joan Berkes
  E-Mail: berkesj@nasfaa.org
Director, Communications: Haley Chitty
  E-Mail: chittyh@nasfaa.org
Editor: Linda Conard
  E-Mail: conardl@nasfaa.org
Vice President, Membership, Marketing and Programs: Mindy Kaplan Eline
  E-Mail: elinemk@nasfaa.org
Vice President, Training and Professional Development: Barbara Gordon
  E-Mail: gordonb@nasfaa.org

Director, Exhibits and Advertising: Jennifer L. Jackson
E-Mail: jacksonj@nasfaa.org
Director, Professional Assessment, Training, and Regulatory Assistance: Connie McCormick
E-Mail: mccormickc@nasfaa.org
Associate Director, Member Services: Beth Spenard
E-Mail: spenardb@nasfaa.org
Chief Financial Officer: Janet Wessling
E-Mail: wesslingj@nasfaa.org
Director, Information Technology and Services: Roland Zizer
E-Mail: zizerr@nasfaa.org

Historical Note:
NASFAA ia a non-profit corporation of post secondary institutions, individuals, agencies, and students interested in promoting the effective administration of student financial aid in the U.S. Membership: $770 (Affiliate); $1,420-6,745 (Constituent); $125 (Student); $100 (Retiree).

Meetings/Conferences: Annual
Conference Chair: Jennifer L. Jackson
2013 - Las Vegas, NV/July 14 - 17
2014 - Nashville, TN/June 29 - July 2
2015 - New Orleans, LA/July 19 - 22
2016 - Washington, DC/July 10 - 13
Number of non-conference events/year: 1

Publications:
Journal of Student Financial Aid; adv.
NASFAA Online Membership Directory; on-line; adv.
Student Aid Transcript Magazine; adv.
Today's News; daily

Membership List Available to Non-members

National Association of Subrogation Professionals *(1998)*
6600 Steubenville Pike
Three Robinson Plaza, Suite 130
Pittsburgh, PA 15205
Tel: (412) 706-8000 *Fax:* (412) 706-7164
TollFree: (800) 574-9961
Website: subrogation.org
Staff: 6
Annual Budget: $1-2,000,000
Tax: 501(c)(6)

Personnel:
Executive Director: Leslie S. Wiernik
E-Mail: leslie.wiernik@subrogation.org
Coordinator, Membership Services: Joanne Corcoran
E-Mail: joanne.corcoran@subrogation.org
Event Planner: Rita Swanson
E-Mail: rita@premierplanningservices.com
Accountant: MaryLou Sydor
E-Mail: marylou.sydor@subrogation.org
Coordinator, Publications: Elle Wiernik
E-Mail: elle.wiernik@subrogation.org

Historical Note:
NASP's mission is to enhance the stature and effectiveness of subrogation and recovery professionals through education, training and the exchange of information.

Continuing Education:
Certification Designation/s: CSRP

Meetings/Conferences:
2013 - San Diego, CA (Hilton San Diego Bayfront)/Nov. 3 - 6
2014 - Orlando, FL (Rosen Shingle Creek)/Nov. 8 - 11
2015 - Reno, NV (Peppermill Resort and Casino)/Nov. 8 - 11
Number of non-conference events/year: 1

Publications:
Subrogator magazine

National Association of Supervisors for Business Education *(1965)*
Three Capitol Mall
Suite 404
Little Rock, AR 72201
Tel: (501) 682-1809 *Fax:* (501) 682-1501
Website: nasbe.us
Members: 125 individuals
Staff: 4
Annual Budget: Under $10,000

Personnel:
Editor and Webmaster: H. Roger Fulk
E-Mail: roger.fulk@wright.edu
Treasurer: Sandra Porter
E-Mail: sandra.porter@arkansas.gov

Historical Note:
Formerly (1981) National Association of State Supervisors of Business and Office Education. NASBE's mission is to develop and increase the effectiveness of educational opportunities in the area of Business Education commensurate to the needs and abilities of all individuals in the American society. Members are state supervisors of business education programs. Membership: $20/year (Individual).

Publications:
Membership Directory; annually
NASBE Newsletter; quarterly; adv.

Membership List Available to Non-members

National Association of Supervisors of Agricultural Education *(1962)*
300 Garrigus Bldg., University of Kentucky
Lexington, KY 40546-0215
Tel: (859) 257-2224 *Fax:* (859) 323-3919
TollFree: (800) 509-0204
E-Mail: jjackman.naae@uky.edu
Website: ffa.org/thecouncil/nasae/Pages/index.html
Members: 7650 individuals
Staff: 1
Annual Budget: $25-50,000

Personnel:
Executive Treasurer: Jay Jackman
E-Mail: jjackman.naae@uky.edu

Historical Note:
NASAE was established to provide members with information essential for planning and conducting quality agricultural education programs. The general goals of the organization are to professionally represent and support advancement of school-based agricultural education. Membership: $50-60 (Active); $35 (Associate); $420 (Associate Life); $720 (Active Life Member).

Meetings/Conferences: Annual
Conference Chair: Jay Jackman
2013 - Louisville, KY/Oct. 28 - 30
2014 - Louisville, KY/Oct. 27 - 29
2015 - Louisville, KY/Oct. 26 - 28
2016 - Indianapolis, IN/Oct. 17 - 19
2017 - Indianapolis, IN/Oct. 23 - 25
2018 - Indianapolis, IN/Oct. 22 - 24

National Association of Surety Bond Producers *(1942)*
1140 19th St. NW
Suite 800
Washington, DC 20036-5104
Tel: (202) 686-3700 *Fax:* (202) 686-3656
E-Mail: info@nasbp.org
Website: nasbp.org
Members: 5000 surety agents and brokers
Staff: 11
Annual Budget: $2-5,000,000

Personnel:
Chief Executive Officer: Mark McCallum
E-Mail: mmccallum@nasbp.org
Manager, Membership Services: Dasha Y. Brock
E-Mail: dbrock@nasbp.org
Director, Technology: David Golden
E-Mail: dgolden@nasbp.org
Director, Communications: Kathy J. Mapes Hoffman
E-Mail: khoffman@nasbp.org
Director, Meeting Services: Bethany H. Jones
E-Mail: bjones@nasbp.org
Managing Director, Operations, Finance and Membership Services: Koula Korson
E-Mail: kkorson@nasbp.org
Managing Director, Professional Development and Education: Ann Latham
E-Mail: alatham@nasbp.org
Director, Government Relations: Lawrence E. LeClair
E-Mail: lleclair@nasbp.org

Historical Note:
NASBP is solely dedicated to the needs and interests of surety bond producers. Members are independent insurance agencies and brokerage firms that specialize in providing surety bonding and insurance programs to construction contractors. Membership: open only to firms who have produced a minimum of $200,000 in total surety premiums in one calendar year for more than one company.

Meetings/Conferences: Annual
Conference Chair: Bethany H. Jones
2013 - San Francisco, CA (Fairmont San Francisco)/April 21 - 24

2014 - San Antonio, TX (JW Marriott San Antonio Hill Country Resort and Spa)/April 27 - 30
2015 - San Diego, CA (Manchester Grand Hyatt San Diego)/April 19 - 22
2016 - Colorado Springs, CO (The Broadmoor)/May 15 - 18

Publications:
Membership Directory; on-line
NASBP SmartBrief; weekly
Pipeline; bi-monthly

National Association of Swine Records *(1954)*
1769 U.S. Hwy. 52 West
P.O. 2417
West LaFayette, IN 47996-2417
Tel: (765) 463-3594 *Fax:* (765) 497-2959
E-Mail: jjackman.naae@uky.edu
Members: 8 companies and 8 associations
Staff: 2
Annual Budget: $100-250,000

Personnel:
Chairman: Mike Paul

National Association of Tax Professionals *(1979)*
P.O. Box 8002
Appleton, WI 54912-8002
Tel: (800) 558-3402 *Fax:* (800) 747-0001
E-Mail: natp@natptax.com
Website: natptax.com
Members: 20,000 individuals
Staff: 71
Annual Budget: $5-10,000,000
Tax: 501(c)(3)

Personnel:
Chief Executive Officer: Kathy Stanek
E-Mail: skath@natptax.com
Director, Finance and Administration: Matt Bone CPA
Director, Membership Services, Business Development and Government Relations: Paul Cinquemani CPA
E-Mail: pcinquemani@natptax.com
Director, Marketing and Communications: Susan Lucius
E-Mail: susanl@natptax.com
Meeting Planner: Jan Rogers
Coordinator, Information Technology: Jerry Sparkman
Editor: Cindy Van Beckum
E-Mail: vcindyvb@natptax.com
Director, Tax Knowledge Center: Greta Zeimetz

Historical Note:
NATP's mission is to serve its members by providing the support, education, products, and services they need to work in the tax profession. Members include individual practitioners, enrolled agents, accountants, CPAs, attorneys, and financial planners. Membership: $176 (Individual); $115 (Academic/International).

Meetings/Conferences: Annual
Conference Chair: Jan Rogers
2013 - Phoenix, AZ (JW Marriott Desert Ridge Resort)/July 8 - 11
Number of non-conference events/year: 1

Publications:
Chapter Weekly; weekly
TAXPRO Journal; quarterly
TAXPRO Monthly; monthly
TAXPRO Weekly; weekly

National Association of Teacher Educators for Family Consumer Sciences *(1949)*
Western Kentucky University
1906 College Heights Blvd., Suite 11037
Bowling Green, KY 42101-1037
Tel: (270) 745-3997 *Fax:* (270) 745-3999
Website: natefacs.org
Members: 150 individuals
Staff: 2
Annual Budget: $10-25,000

Personnel:
President: Kathy Croxall
E-Mail: Kathy.Croxall@wku.edu
Treasurer and Membership Chairperson: Mari Borr
E-Mail: Mari.Borr@ndsu.edu

Historical Note:
Formerly (1995) National Association of Teacher Educators for Vocational Home Economics. NATEFACS's mission is to improve and strengthen teacher education in family and consumer sciences. Members are individuals engaged in pre-service and/or in-service education of Family

and Consumer Sciences teachers. *Membership: $20 (Professional); $15 (Graduate Students/Retired).*

Publications:
Journal of Family and Consumer Sciences Education; semi-annually
Membership Directory; on-line

National Association of Teachers of Singing (*1944*)
9957 Moorings Dr.
Suite 401
Jacksonville, FL 32257
Tel: (904) 992-9101 *Fax:* (904) 262-2587
E-Mail: info@nats.org
Website: nats.org
Members: 7000 individuals
Staff: 5
Annual Budget: $500-1,000,000

Personnel:
Executive Director and Publisher: Allen Henderson
    E-Mail: allen@nats.org
Coordinator, Advertising and Administrative Assistant: Joan Adams
    E-Mail: joan@nats.org
Coordinator, Membership Services: Susan R. Grizzard
    E-Mail: susan@nats.org
Director, Operations and Managing Editor: Deborah L. Guess
    E-Mail: deborah@nats.org
Assistant, Special Events: Mandy Ruddock

Historical Note:
NATS's mission is to encourage better standards of the vocal art and of ethical principles in the teaching of singing and to promote vocal education and research at all levels, both for the enrichment of the general public and for the professional advancement of the talented. Membership: $52 (U.S. Full/Professional Singer or Coach/Associate/Affiliate); $56 (International).

Meetings/Conferences: Biennial
Conference Chair: Mandy Ruddock
2014 - Boston, MA (Boston Marriott Copley Place)/July 5 - 9/11-25 exhibitors
Number of non-conference events/year: 4

Publications:
Journal of Singing; adv.

National Association of Teachers' Agencies (*1914*)
797 Kings Hwy.
Fairfield, CT 06825
Tel: (203) 333-0611 *Fax:* (203) 334-7224
E-Mail: info@jobsforteachers.com
Website: jobsforteachers.com
Members: 22 agencies
Staff: 1
Annual Budget: Under $10,000

Personnel:
Secretary: Mark King

Historical Note:
Members are private employment agencies concentrating on the placement of teachers and administrators serving public and private schools. Absorbed the Association of Southern Teacher Agencies (1909). Membership: $225/year (organization).

National Association of Telecommunications Officers and Advisors (*1981*)
3213 Duke St.
Suite 695
Alexandria, VA 22314
Tel: (703) 519-8035 *Fax:* (730) 997-7080
E-Mail: info@natoa.org
Website: natoa.org
Members: 800 agencies and individuals
Staff: 5
Annual Budget: $500-1,000,000
Tax: 501(c)(4)

Personnel:
President: Joanne Hovis
    E-Mail: jhovis@CTCnet.us
Deputy Director: Tonya Rideout
    E-Mail: trideout@natoa.org
Executive Director, Government Relations: Steve Traylor
    E-Mail: straylor@natoa.org

Historical Note:
NATOA's mission is to support and serve the communications interests and needs of local governments. Membership: $440 (Individual); $470-1,105 (Agency,

based on population); $410 (Associate, Non-Profit); $1025 (Associate, Profit); $30 (Student).

Meetings/Conferences: Annual

Publications:
Membership Directory; on-line; adv.
NATOA Journal; quarterly
NATOA's Newsletter; monthly; adv.

National Association of Television Program Executives (*1964*)
5757 Wilshire Blvd.
Penthouse Ten
Los Angeles, CA 90036-3681
Tel: (310) 453-4440 *Fax:* (310) 453-5258
E-Mail: info@natpe.org
Website: natpe.org
Members: 4000 corporations
Staff: 24
Annual Budget: $5-10,000,000

Personnel:
Chief Executive Officer: Rod Perth
Senior Vice President, Marketing: Beth Braen
    E-Mail: bbraen@natpe.org
Chief Financial Officer: Jon Dobkin
    E-Mail: JD@natpe.org
Director, Faculty and Student Programs: Greg Pitts
    E-Mail: gpitts@gmail.com
Vice President, Event Programming: Jordan Ryder
    E-Mail: jordan@natpe.org
New Media Producer and Digital Content Manager: Jack Sullivan
    E-Mail: jsullivan@natpe.org

Historical Note:
NATPE is dedicated to the creation, development and distribution of televised programming in all forms across all mature and emerging media platforms. Membership: $95 (Educational); $195 (Professional); $600 (Exhibitor).

Meetings/Conferences: Annual
Conference Chair: Jordan Ryder
2013 - Miami, FL (Fontainebleau Resort)/Jan. 28 - 30
2013 - Budapest, Hungary (Sofitel Chain Bridge Hotel)/June 25 - 27
Number of non-conference events/year: 1

Publications:
NATPE News; monthly; adv.
NATPE Online Directory; on-line
New Media Minute; weekly; adv.

National Association of Temple Administrators (*1941*)
5808 NW 209th St.
P.O. Box 936
Ridgefield, WA 98642
Fax: (866) 767-3791
E-Mail: nataoffice@natanet.org
Website: natanet.org
Members: 400 individuals
Staff: 2
Annual Budget: $250-500,000
Tax: 501(c)(3)

Personnel:
President: Livia Thompson FTA
    E-Mail: Livia@censyn.org
Association Manager: Kathy Small
    E-Mail: nataoffice@natanet.org

Historical Note:
Established as the National Association of Temple Secretaries, assumed its present name in 1959. NATA's mission is to support its members by providing education and training activities. Members are synagogue executive directors in the Reform Jewish movement. Membership: $260- 1,560 (Regular/Senior Members); $36 (Retired); $260 (Courtesy).

Continuing Education:
Certification Designation/s: FTA

Meetings/Conferences: Annual
2013 - Dallas, TX/Oct. 19 - 23
2014 - New Orleans, LA/Nov. 8 - 12
Number of non-conference events/year: 1

Publications:
Membership Directory; on-line
NATA Journal; semi-annually

National Association of Temple Educators (*1955*)
633 Third Ave.
New York, NY 10017-6778

Tel: (212) 452-6510 *Fax:* (212) 452-6512
E-Mail: nateoff@aol.com
Website: natenet.org
Members: 950 individuals
Staff: 2
Annual Budget: $100-250,000
Tax: 501(c)(3)

Personnel:
Executive Director: Rabbi Stan Schickler RJE
    E-Mail: sschickler@natenet.org

Historical Note:
NATE seeks to promote and encourage the professional growth of its members and also provide the advocating for the profession of Jewish education by improving the context in which educators work. Affiliated with the Union of American Hebrew Congregations. Members are educational leaders associated with the Reform Jewish movement in the United States, Canada, England, Israel, Australia and South Africa. Membership: $50 (LESS than $5,000/Overseas Resident); $36 (Full-Time Student/ECE-RJ Member); $75 (FROM $5,000 to $10,000); $72 (Sustaining Active); $18 (Ziknay NATE (Retired)); $100 (Central Agency Employee/Youth Worker/HUC-JIR Employee/URJ Employee).

Continuing Education:
Certification Designation/s: RJE, CEO

Meetings/Conferences: Semi-Annual

Publications:
NATE News
Ziknay NATE Newsletter; quarterly

National Association of Test Directors (*1985*)
Cincinnati Public Schools
P.O. Box 5381
Cincinnati, OH 45201-5381
Tel: (513) 363-0171
Website: natd.org
Members: 300 individuals
Staff: 2
Annual Budget: Under $10,000
Tax: 501(c)(3)

Personnel:
Treasurer: Dr. Elizabeth Holtzapple
    E-Mail: holtzae@cps-k12.org

Historical Note:
NATD's mission is to share information and to encourage the appropriate use of testing in educational settings; to improve the applications of measurement to students and educational programs and to encourage research in the area of elementary and secondary school testing and measurement. Membership: $20/year (Individual).

Meetings/Conferences: Annual
Number of non-conference events/year: 1

Publications:
Membership Directory; on-line
Newsletters

National Association of the Remodeling Industry (*1983*)
P.O. Box 4250
Des Plaines, IL 60016
Tel: (847) 298-9200 *Fax:* (847) 298-9225
TollFree: (800) 611-6274
E-Mail: info@nari.org
Website: nari.org
Members: 60 chapters and 8200 companies
Staff: 12
Annual Budget: $2-5,000,000
Tax: 501(c)(6)

Personnel:
Executive Vice President: Mary Busey Harris CAE
    E-Mail: mharris@nari.org
Manager, Marketing and Communications: Nikki Golden
    E-Mail: ngolden@nari.org
Chief Operations Officer: Elsie Iturralde
    E-Mail: eiturralde@nari.org,
Director, Education: Dan Taddei
    E-Mail: dtaddei@nari.org
Director, National Membership Services and Business Development: Don Vossburg
    E-Mail: dvossburg@nari.org

Historical Note:
The result of a merger (1983) between the National Remodelers Association and the National Home Improvement Council. NARI's purpose is to advance and promote the remodeling industry's professionalism, product & vital public purpose. Membership: $260/year (Individual).

Meetings/Conferences: Annual
2013 - Boston, MA (Boston Marriott Copley Place)/
    May 28 - June 1
Number of non-conference events/year: 90

Publications:
Membership Directory; on-line
Remodelers Journal; bi-monthly; adv.
Tuffin' It Out e-newsletter; weekly; adv.

National Association of Theatre Owners (1948)
750 First St. NE
Suite 1130
Washington, DC 20002
Tel: (202) 962-0054 *Fax:* (202) 962-0370
E-Mail: nato@natodc.com
Website: natoonline.org
Members: 600 companies
Staff: 11
Annual Budget: $10-25,000,000
Tax: 501(c)(6)

Personnel:
Executive Director: Kathy Conroy
    E-Mail: kmc@natodc.com
Deputy Director, Membership Services: David E. Binet
Director, Media and Research: Patrick Corcoran
    E-Mail: pfc@natoca.com
President and Chief Executive Officer: John Fithian
    E-Mail: jf@natodc.com
Deputy Director, Government Affairs: Todd R. Halstead
Vice President and General Counsel: Gary J. Klein

Historical Note:
Formerly Theatre Owners of America and (1966) Absorbed Allied Theatre Owners of America. NATO represents its members in the heart of the nation's capital as well as the center of the entertainment industry.

Meetings/Conferences: Annual
2013 - Las Vegas, NV (Caesars Palace Las Vegas Hotel
    and Casino)/April 15 - 18/51-100 exhibitors
2014 - Las Vegas, NV (Caesars Palace)/March 24 - 27
2015 - Las Vegas, NV (Caesars Palace)/April 20 - 23
Number of non-conference events/year: 5

Publications:
Boxoffice Magazine; monthly; adv.
Encyclopedia of Exhibition; on-line; adv.

National Association of Therapeutic Schools and Programs (NATSAP) (1999)
5272 River Rd.
Suite 600
Bethesda, MD 20816
Tel: (301) 986-8770 *Fax:* (301) 986-8772
E-Mail: info@natsap.org
Website: natsap.org
Members: 115 individual professional members
Staff: 7
Annual Budget: $500-1,000,000
Tax: 501(c)(3)

Personnel:
Executive Director: Clifford M. Brownstein
Director, Government Relations and Membership:
    Claiborne Guy
    E-Mail: claiborne@natsap.org
Director, Conferences and Administration: Melissa
    Lawson

Historical Note:
NATSAP serves as an advocate and resource for innovative organizations to provide care and education of struggling young people and their families. Membership is comprised of therapeutic schools, residential treatment programs, wilderness programs, outdoor therapeutic programs, young adult programs, and home-based residential programs. Membership: $750 (Affiliate/Business Partner); $85 (Individual Professional).

Meetings/Conferences: Annual
Conference Chair: Melissa Lawson
2013 - Irvine, CA (Hyatt Regency Irvine)/Feb. 7 - 9
2014 - Henderson, NV (Green Valley Ranch)/Feb. 6 - 8

Publications:
NATSAP 2011 Directory
NATSAP Journal

National Association of Ticket Brokers (1994)
214 N. Hale St.
Wheaton, IL 60187
Tel: (630) 510-4594 *Fax:* (630) 510-4501
E-Mail: info@natb.org
Website: natb.org

Members: 193 companies
Staff: 4
Annual Budget: $250-500,000

Personnel:
Executive Director: Terry Stevenson

Historical Note:
NATB represents the interest of legitimate ticket brokers by promoting consumer protection and educating the public about the industry. Members must abide by the NATB code of ethics. Membership: $1075 (1 to 3 Employees); $1,400 (4 to 6 Employees); $1,725 (7 + Employees).

Meetings/Conferences: Annual

Publications:
Membership Directory; annually; adv.
NATB Newsletter; quarterly; adv.

National Association of Tower Erectors (1995)
Eighth Second St. SE
Watertown, SD 57201-3624
Tel: (605) 882-5865 *Fax:* (605) 886-5184
TollFree: (888) 882-5865
E-Mail: nate@natehome.com
Website: natehome.com
Members: 500 companies
Staff: 5
Annual Budget: $2-5,000,000
Tax: 501(c)(6)

Personnel:
Executive Director: Todd Schlekeway
    E-Mail: todd@natehome.com
Senior Staff Associate: Carol Coughlin
    E-Mail: carol@natehome.com
Administrative Assistant: Chelsea Hlavacek
    E-Mail: chelsea@natehome.com
Contact, Conventions and Publications: Corene Iverson
    E-Mail: corene@natehome.com
Director, Operations: Paula Nurnberg
    E-Mail: paula@natehome.com

Historical Note:
An association that pursues and formulates uniform standards of safety to ensure the well-being of tower personnel, and to educate the general public, applicable government agencies and clients on continued progress toward safer industry standards. Provides members with uniform safety standards, improved communications, and a unified voice. Membership: $1000-7000 (Voting); $1500-3500 (Non-Voting); $1,250-2,500 (Manufacturer/Construction/Affiliate/Associate, dues vary on gross annual revenue).

Meetings/Conferences: Annual
Conference Chair: Paula Nurnberg
2013 - Ft. Worth, TX/Feb. 18 - 21

Publications:
Membership Directory; on-line
Tower Times; monthly; adv.

National Association of Town Watch (1981)
One Wynnewood Rd., Suite 102
P.O. Box 303
Wynnewood, PA 19096
Tel: (610) 649-7055 *Fax:* (610) 649-5456
E-Mail: info@natw.org
Website: nationaltownwatch.org
Staff: 1
Annual Budget: $1-2,000,000
Tax: 501(c)(3)

Personnel:
Executive Director: Matt Peskin

Historical Note:
NATW's mission is to develop and promote organized, law enforcement-affiliated crime and drug prevention programs. Membership: $50 (Contributor); $25 (Basic).

Publications:
New Spirit Newsletter

National Association of Towns and Townships (NATAT) (1976)
1130 Connecticut Ave. NW
Suite 300
Washington, DC 20036
Tel: (202) 454-3950 *Fax:* (202) 331-1598
TollFree: (866) 830-0008
E-Mail: info@natat.org
Website: natat.org
Members: 13000 local governments
Staff: 5
Annual Budget: $250-500,000

Tax: 501(c)(4)

Personnel:
President: Jim Fisher
    E-Mail: jfisher@rangenet.com
Secretary and Treasurer: Matthew DeTemple
    E-Mail: detemple@ohiotownships.org
Deputy Federal Director: Andy Seth III
    E-Mail: aseth@tfgnet.com
Director, Policy: Matt Ward
    E-Mail: mward@tfgnet.com

Historical Note:
NATaT has developed a proactive federal agenda to ensure that the needs and interests of small communities are reflected in all major federal statutory, regulatory, funding, and policy decisions. Business consulting and government relations.

Publications:
Washington Report

National Association of Trade Exchanges (1987)
926 Eastern Ave.
Malden, MA 02148
Tel: (781) 388-9200
E-Mail: gary@natebarter.com
Website: natebarter.com
Members: 80 individuals
Staff: 4
Annual Budget: $50-100,000
Tax: 501(c)(6)

Personnel:
President: Gary Oshry
    E-Mail: gary@natebarter.com

Historical Note:
NATE is a nonprofit, non-stock corporation that helps its members network with new trading partners across the U.S. and Canada. NATE provides marketing solutions, opportunities, sales training, and annual conventions that are informative. Its members trade exclusively through The BANC (Barter Association National Currency). Membership: $495/year (Organization).

Continuing Education:
Certification Designation/s: RTB, CTB
Meetings/Conferences:
Number of non-conference events/year: 1

Publications:
Membership Directory

National Association of Traffic Accident Reconstructionists and Investigators (1984)
P.O. Box 2588
W. Chester, PA 19382
Tel: (610) 696-1919
E-Mail: natari@natari.org
Website: natari.org
Members: 200 individuals
Staff: 1
Annual Budget: $25-50,000

Personnel:
President: William C. Camlin
    E-Mail: wccamlin@comcast.net

Historical Note:
NATARI aims to provide a source of information to be shared among accident professionals on a national basis. Membership is open to professionals who constitute three levels of experience and training. Membership: $60/year.

Meetings/Conferences: Annual
Number of non-conference events/year: 1

Publications:
Member Directory
NATARI Newsletter; quarterly

National Association of Trailer Manufacturers (1987)
1320 SW Topeka Blvd.
Topeka, KS 66612-1817
Tel: (785) 272-4433 *Fax:* (785) 272-4455
E-Mail: natmhq@natm.com
Website: natm.com
Members: 210,000 American workers
Staff: 11
Annual Budget: $1-2,000,000
Tax: 501(c)(6)

Personnel:
Executive Director: Pam O'Toole
    E-Mail: pamo@natm.com
Executive Assistant: Linda Brink

E-Mail: Linda.Brink@natm.com
Technical Director: Clint Lancaster
   E-Mail: clint@natm.com
Director, Membership Services: Allison Malmstrom
   E-Mail: allisonm@natm.com
Director, Marketing: Shannon Miller
   E-Mail: shannon@natm.com

Historical Note:
*Formerly (1992) National Association of Livestock Trailer
Manufacturers. NATM's mission is to unify the light and
medium duty trailer manufacturing industry by improving
trailer safety and performance. Membership: $840
(Regular/International Regular); $240 (Branch Member/
International Branch Member); $720 (Associate); $135
(Associate Branch Member).*

Meetings/Conferences: Annual
Conference Chair: Linda Brink
2013 - North Charleston, SC (Charleston Area
   Convention Center)/Feb. 20 - 23/26-50 exhibitors

Publications:
Membership Directory; annually; adv.
Tracks; bi-monthly; adv.

National Association of Tribal Historic Preservation Officers (1998)
1785 Massachusetts Ave. NW
P.O. Box 19189
Washington, DC 20036-9189
Tel: (202) 628-8476 *Fax:* (202) 628-2241
E-Mail: info@nathpo.org
Website: nathpo.org
Staff: 1
Annual Budget: $250-500,000

Personnel:
President: D. Bambi Kraus
   E-Mail: bambi@nathpo.org

Historical Note:
*NATHPO's purpose is to support the preservation,
maintenance and revitalization of the culture and traditions
of Native peoples of the United States. Regular Membership
is restricted to Tribal Historic Preservation Officers who are
officially designated by a federally-recognized Indian tribe
or Alaska Native group to direct a program approved by
the National Park Service. Tribal Associate Membership is
open to officials directing tribal preservation programs who
are either seeking or who are considering seeking National
Park Service approval, as well as officials directing tribal
programs dedicated to or actively supporting the purposes
of NATHPO. Membership: $250/year (Associate).*

Meetings/Conferences: Annual

Publications:
Membership Directory

National Association of Truck Stop Operators(NATSO) (1960)
1737 King St.
Suite 200
Alexandria, VA 22314
Tel: (703) 549-2100 *Fax:* (703) 684-4525
TollFree: (888) 275-6287
Website: natso.com
Members: 1202 travel plazas and truckstops
Staff: 22
Annual Budget: $2-5,000,000

Personnel:
President and Chief Executive Officer: Lisa J. Mullings
   E-Mail: lmullings@natso.com
Vice President, Government Affairs: Holly Alfano
   E-Mail: halfano@natso.com
Manager, Information and Research: Taryn Brice-
   Rowland
   E-Mail: tbrice-rowland@natso.com
Vice President, Strategic Partnerships: Pamela Hayes
   E-Mail: phayes@natso.com
Specialist, Member Care: Kimberly Roberts
   E-Mail: kroberts@natso.com
Chief, Operations: Christine K. Schoessler
   E-Mail: cschoessler@natso.com
Vice President, Membership Services: Darren Schulte
Senior Director, Marketing and Design: Amy "Carle"
   Toner
   E-Mail: atoner@natso.com
Senior Director, Public Affairs: Tiffany Wlazlowski
   E-Mail: twlazlowski@natso.com

Historical Note:
*NATSO serves the needs of truckstops, travel plazas and
their suppliers by serving as the source of information on
the diverse industry. It also serves the industries on Capitol*

Hill and regulatory agencies such as the Environmental
Protection Agency, the Department of Transportation,
the Department of Labor and the Department of Energy.
Membership: $730-2430 (Truckstop/Travel Plaza, based
on number of gallons of diesel fuel pumped per year at your
location); $1300-14000 (Allied); $700 (Associate).*

Meetings/Conferences: Annual
Conference Chair: Pamela Hayes
2013 - Savannah, GA (Westin Savannah Harbor Golf
   Resort and Spa)/Feb. 2 - 6
Number of non-conference events/year: 3

Publications:
NATSO News Weekly; weekly
NATSO Truckers News Magazine
NATSO's Membership Directory and the Buyer's
   Guide; on-line
Online Buyers Guide
Stop Watch; bi-monthly; adv.

National Association of Unclaimed Property Administrators (1962)
C/O NAST, 2760 Research Park Dr.
P.O. Box 11910
Lexington, KY 40578-1910
Tel: (859) 244-8150 *Fax:* (859) 244-8053
E-Mail: naupa@csg.org
Website: unclaimed.org
Members: 53 state offices
Staff: 2
Annual Budget: $100-250,000

Personnel:
President: Carolyn Atkinson
Secretary and Treasurer: Kristi Carlow

Historical Note:
*Formerly (1980) the Association of Unclaimed Property
Administrators. NAUPA's mission is to promote and support
excellence and professionalism among those individuals
charged with the responsibilities of unclaimed property
administration and compliance. NAUPA members are state
officials who administer escheat and unclaimed property
programs. Membership: $200/year.*

Publications:
Membership Directory; on-line

National Association of Underwater Instructors (1959)
9030 Camden Field Pkwy.
Riverview, FL 33578
Tel: (813) 628-6284 *Fax:* (813) 628-8253
TollFree: (800) 553-6284
E-Mail: nauihq@naui.org
Website: naui.org
Members: 10500 individuals
Staff: 9
Annual Budget: $1-2,000,000
Tax: 501(c)(6)

Personnel:
President and Manager, Accounting Services: Jim Bram
   E-Mail: jbram@naui.org
Manager, Operations: Kathy Brownlow
   E-Mail: kbrownlow@naui.org
Vice President, Training and Product Development: Jed
   Livingstone
   E-Mail: jlivingstone@naui.org
Editor, Sources Magazines and Editorial Submissions:
   Peter Oliver
   E-Mail: poliver@naui.org
Chief Information Officer: James R. Yaufman II
   E-Mail: jyaufman@naui.org

Historical Note:
*Formerly, National Diving Patrol. NAUI, a certified
instructor of basic, advanced, and specialized courses
in underwater diving. NAUI's mission is to promote,
through education, the techniques necessary for the general
public to participate safely in underwater activities while
preserving the underwater environment. Offers instructor
certification programs and training programs. Affiliated
with the National Safety Council, National Boating Council,
American Red Cross and Underwater Society of America.
Membership: $75-145 (Instructor, Active/Sustaining/
Emeritus); $75-90 (Divemaster and Skin Diving Instructor,
Active/Sustaining/Emeritus); $75-90 (Assistant Instructor,
Active/Emeritus).*

Continuing Education:
Certification Designation/s: ICC, TDC, DM, ITC, TIC, SDI,
AI

Publications:
Newsletter

National Association of Uniform Manufacturers and Distributors (1933)
6800 Jericho Tnpk.
Suite 120W
Syosset, NY 11791
Tel: (516) 393-5838 *Fax:* (516) 393-5878
Website: naumd.com
Members: 475 companies
Staff: 5
Annual Budget: $500-1,000,000

Personnel:
President and Chief Executing Officer: Richard J. Lerman
   CCM
   E-Mail: rjlerman@naumd.com
Director, Marketing and Member Relations: Miranda
   Brock
   E-Mail: mbrock@naumd.com
*Manager, Membership Information Services and
   Bookkeeper:* Tervia Metzner
   E-Mail: tmetzner@naumd.com
Director, Communications: Jackie Rosselli -Verrico
   E-Mail: jarosselli@naumd.com

Historical Note:
*A trade association that represents the uniform industry.
Members are manufacturers of uniforms, mills, fibre
producers, and dealers. Membership: $995-3,500
(Manufacturer/ Associate, Based on Yearly Volume);
$395-1,500 (Dealer/Distributor, Based on Yearly Volume).*

Meetings/Conferences: Annual
2013 - Orlando, FL (The Renaissance Orlando at Sea
   World)/April 4 - 7/51-100 exhibitors

Publications:
Membership Directory & Resource Guide; annually;
   adv.
NAUMD eConvention Dailies
NAUMD Industry News
NAUMD UniformMarket News

National Association of University Fisheries and Wildlife Programs (1991)
University of Florida, Department of Wildlife
Ecology and Conservation
P.O. Box 110200
Gainesville, FL 32611-0200
Tel: (352) 392-1784 *Fax:* (352) 392-4965
Website: naufwp.org
Members: 55 university programs
Staff: 2
Annual Budget: $10-25,000
Tax: 501(c)(3)

Personnel:
President: Dr. John Hayes
   E-Mail: hayes@ufl.edu
Secretary and Treasurer: Dr. Kenneth Wilson
   E-Mail: kenneth.wilson@colostate.edu

Historical Note:
*NAUFWP represents member institutions in their collective
dealings with government entities, natural resources
organizations, commodity and industry groups, educational
and scientific organizations, and the public. Members
are administrators of fisheries and wildlife programs in
colleges/universities. Membership: $600 (Full Members-
Institution); $200 (New Member).*

National Association of University Forest Resources Programs (1981)
P.O. Box 2004
3325 Rose Ln.
Falls Church, VA 22042
Fax: (703) 538-1135
Website: naufrp.org
Members: 100 Members
Staff: 4
Annual Budget: $100-250,000
Tax: 501(c)(3)

Personnel:
President: Tim White
Executive Liaison: Terri Bates
   E-Mail: naufrp@verizon.net
Secretary and Treasurer: Barry Goldfarb

Historical Note:
*Formerly known as the National Association of Professional
Forestry Schools and Colleges. NAUFRP's purpose is to
advance the health, productivity, and sustainability of
America's forests by providing university-based natural
resource education, research, science, extension and
international programs.*

Publications:
Membership Directory; on-line
NAUFRP Newsletter
Washington Update

National Association of University Women (1924)
1001 E St. SE
Washington, DC 20003
Tel: (202) 547-3967 *Fax:* (202) 547-5226
E-Mail: info@nauw1910.org
Website: nauw1910.org
Staff: 1
Annual Budget: $500-1,000,000
Tax: 501(c)(3)

Personnel:
President: Dolores Y. Owens

Historical Note:
NAUW works to help women, youth and disadvantaged communities in developing countries by addressing issues in education and women's rights, and strategically partnering with allied organizations. Members are women holding a bachelor's or higher degree from an accredited college, university or scientific school listed by the United States Department of Education. Membership: $80/year.

Meetings/Conferences: Annual

National Association of Urban Hospitals (1993)
21351 Gentry Dr.
Suite 210
Sterling, VA 20166
Tel: (703) 444-0989 *Fax:* (703) 444-3029
E-Mail: info@nauh.org
Website: nauh.org
Members: 47 Member Organizations
Staff: 5
Annual Budget: $100-250,000
Tax: 501(c)(6)

Personnel:
Executive Director: Ellen J. Kugler Esq.
   E-Mail: ellen@nauh.org
Legislative Director: Kate Finkelstein
Contact, Data Analysis and Policy Development Activities:
   James A. Tomkins

Historical Note:
Formerly (1998) known as National Association of Urban Critical Access Hospitals, NAUH is an association that focuses on the interests of urban hospitals and advocates on behalf of the needs of these hospitals before the congress and the administration. Membership: $12,000 (Full); $5,000 (Associate).

Publications:
Member Directory; on-line

National Association of Vertical Transportation Professionals (1990)
15600 NE Eighth St.
Suite B1, PMB 153
Bellevue, WA 98008
Tel: (425) 732-3328 *Fax:* (425) 957-0834
Website: iaec.org
Members: 100 companies
Staff: 3
Annual Budget: $100-250,000

Personnel:
Executive Director: Gordon J. Ernst
   E-Mail: gernst@iaec.org
President: Jay A Popp
   E-Mail: jay.popp@lerchbates.com
Treasurer: John L Donnelly
   E-Mail: john.l.Donnelly@att.net

Historical Note:
Formerly National Association of Vertical Transportation Professionals. IAEC's mission is to bring together qualified professionals so as to improve the general function of the industry in all its phases, and to create a forum for professionals in the vertical transportation industry to exchange ideas, reports, innovations and regulations, all of which are designed to improve the vertical transportation industry. Members are engineers and other professionals specializing in elevator and escalator design. Membership: $300/year.

Meetings/Conferences: Annual
2013 - San Antonio, TX (San Antonio Marriott Riverwalk)/April 29 - May 1
Number of non-conference events/year: 1

Publications:
IAEC Newsletter

National Association of Veterans Affairs Physicians and Dentists (1975)
P.O. Box 15418
Arlington, VA 22215-0418
Tel: (866) 836-3520 *Fax:* (540) 972-1728
E-Mail: service@navapd.org
Website: navapd.org
Members: 2000 individuals
Staff: 2
Annual Budget: $250-500,000

Personnel:
President: Samuel V. Spagnolo MD
   E-Mail: navapd@aol.com
Executive Director and PAC Director: C. William Booher Jr.

Historical Note:
In 1989, NAVAP welcomed VA dentists into the organization and NAVAP became NAVAPD. NAVAPD's mission is to improve and maintain the quality of patient care within the veterans administration, also improve and maintain an optimum professional environment for the VA physician in order to provide first-class medical care. Membership: $160 (Physicians/ Dentists-Full time); $100 (Physicians/ Dentists-Half time); $80 (Retired); $45 (Residents/Fellows); $1,500 (Lifetime); $13 (Professionals).

Publications:
Membership Directory; on-line
NAVAPD Newsletters

National Association of Veterans Program Administrators (1975)
2020 Pennsylvania Ave. NW
Suite 1975
Washington, DC 20006-1846
Tel: (203) 392-6822 *Fax:* (203) 392-6813
E-Mail: info@navpa.org
Website: navpa.org
Members: 1050 individuals, universities and colleges
Staff: 3
Annual Budget: $100-250,000
Tax: 501(c)(3)

Personnel:
President: Dorothy Gillman
Treasurer: Josie Adams
Secretary: Jennifer Matteson

Historical Note:
NAVPA's purpose is to promote professional competency and efficiency through an association of members and others associated with and involved in veterans education assistance programs. Members are coordinators of veterans programs on college campuses. Membership: $200 (Institutional/Individual/Associate); $25 (Auxiliary).

Meetings/Conferences: Annual
Number of non-conference events/year: 1

Membership List Available to Non-members

National Association of Veterans Research and Education Foundations (1992)
5480 Wisconsin Ave.
Suite 214
Chevy Chase, MD 20815
Tel: (301) 656-5005 *Fax:* (301) 656-5008
E-Mail: navref@navref.org
Website: navref.org
Members: 85 organizations
Staff: 2
Annual Budget: $250-500,000
Tax: 501(c)(3)

Personnel:
Executive Director: Barbara F. West
   E-Mail: bwest@navref.org
Director, Programs: Angela Murakami
   E-Mail: amurakami@navref.org

Historical Note:
NAVREF's mission is to advance the success of the VA-affiliated research and education corporations and promoting research partnerships to improve veterans' health. Membership: $100-15,000/year (Organization, based on Revenues).

Continuing Education:
Enrollment: 84

Meetings/Conferences: Annual
Conference Chair: Angela Murakami
2013 - San Francisco, CA (Hilton San Francisco Financial District)/Sept. 14 - 17

2014 - Washington, DC (Washington Marriott Wardman Park)/Sept. 14 - 17
Number of non-conference events/year: 1

Publications:
Member Directory; on-line

Membership List Available to Non-members

National Association of Video Distributors (1982)
6548 Waterford Pl.
Owensboro, KY 42303
Tel: (270) 280-0100 *Fax:* (270) 280-0010
Website: navdonline.org
Members: 35 companies
Staff: 2
Annual Budget: $50-100,000

Personnel:
Executive Director: Bill Burton
General Counsel: Elroy H. Wolf

Historical Note:
NAVD represents the US and Canadian distributors of all forms of pre-recorded video product as well as their content suppliers, the home video divisions of the major Hollywood studios and other major and independent movie producers. Members are wholesale distributors of home video software; associate members are manufacturers of such goods.

Meetings/Conferences: Annual

Publications:
Membership Directory; on-line

National Association of Vision Care Plans
222 S. First St.
Suite 330
Louisville, KY 40202
Tel: (502) 403-1122 *Fax:* (502) 403-1129
E-Mail: info@navcp.org
Website: navcp.org
Members: 33 primary and allied members
Staff: 3
Annual Budget: $250-500,000

Personnel:
Executive Director: Julian Roberts
Secretary and Treasurer: Aspasia Shappet

Historical Note:
NAVCP's mission is to improve quality in managed care and to provide input and perspective concerning standards and credentials.

Publications:
NAVCP Newsletter; on-line

National Association of Vision Professionals (1976)
C/O Prevention of Blindness Society Washington Area, 1775 Church St. NW
Washington, DC 20036
Tel: (202) 234-1010 *Fax:* (202) 234-1020
E-Mail: contact@visionpros.org
Website: visionpros.org
Members: 100 individuals
Staff: 3

Personnel:
Treasurer and Contact, Membership: Michelle D. Hartlove
   E-Mail: mhartlove@usa.net

Historical Note:
Formerly (1985) the National Association of Vision Program Consultants. NAVP is an organization concerned with prevention, detection and follow- up of vision services for pre-school and school-aged children and adults. Members are Ophthalmologists, optometrists, vision teachers, nurses, industrial safety personnel, screening technicians, para-professionals, volunteers and others concerned with vision health. Membership: $35/year.

Meetings/Conferences: Annual
Conference Chair: Michelle D. Hartlove

Publications:
NAVP Newsletter

National Association of Wastewater Transporters (1985)
P.O. Box 220
1720 Maple Lake Dam Rd
Three Lakes, WI 54562
Fax: (715) 546-3786
TollFree: (800) 236-6298
E-Mail: info@nawt.org
Website: nawt.org
Members: 600 individuals

Staff: 2
Annual Budget: $100-250,000
Tax: 501(c)(6)

Personnel:
Executive Director: Courtney Peterson
Treasurer: Ralph Macchio
    E-Mail: rgmacchio@aol.com

Historical Note:
NAWT aims at unifying the sanitary liquid waste management industry and increasing its professionalism and public image. It does so through educating industry members and the public, and developing national representation of individual, state, and regional chapters. Membership: $150 (Individual); $300 (Company/ Associate).

Publications:
NAWT News; quarterly
Pumper Magazine

National Association of Water Companies (NAWC)
(1895)
2001 L St. NW
Suite 850
Washington, DC 20036
Tel: (202) 833-8383 *Fax:* (202) 331-7442
E-Mail: info@nawc.com
Website: nawc.org
Members: 225 companies
Staff: 8
Annual Budget: $2-5,000,000
Tax: 501(c)(6)

Personnel:
Executive Director: Michael Deane
    E-Mail: michael@nawc.com
Director, Administration and Membership Services: Michael J. Horner
    E-Mail: mike@nawc.com
Director, Government Relations: Petra M. Smeltzer
    E-Mail: petra@nawc.com
Manager, Information Technology and Membership Services: Carlos Villanueva
    E-Mail: carlos@nawc.com

Historical Note:
Established as the Pennsylvania Water Works Association became the Eastern Water Company Conference in 1959, and in 1963 the National Water Company Conference. Adopted its present name in 1971. NAWC's mission is to promote the value of the private sector as the provider of quality, sustainable, water services and innovative solutions. Membership: $450/year (Associate).

Meetings/Conferences: Annual
Conference Chair: Carlos Villanueva

Publications:
NewsFlow; semi-monthly

National Association of Waterfront Employers
(1933)
919 18th St. NW
Suite 901
Washington, DC 20006
Tel: (202) 587-4800 *Fax:* (202) 587-4888
E-Mail: mto@nawe.us
Website: nawe.us
Members: 15 companies
Staff: 5
Annual Budget: $1-2,000,000
Tax: 501(c)(6)

Personnel:
Executive Director: Charles "Chuck" T. Carroll Jr.
General Counsel: F.E. Win Froelich
Editor: Meg Kane
Office Manager and Meetings Coordinator: Elaine Tendler

Historical Note:
Formerly (1993) National Association of Stevedores, NAWE's mission is to promote marine cargo efficiency, security, safety and health, clean environment, international trade and economic growth through advocacy, education and industry cooperation.

Publications:
Membership Directory; on-line

Membership List Available to Non-members

National Association of Waterproofing and Structural Repair Contractors *(1981)*
8015 Corporate Dr.
Suite A
Baltimore, MD 21236

Tel: (410) 931-3332 *Fax:* (410) 931-2060
TollFree: (800) 245-6292
E-Mail: info@nawsrc.org
Website: nawsrc.org
Members: 180 companies
Staff: 2
Annual Budget: $100-250,000

Personnel:
Executive Director: Claudia J. Clemons
    E-Mail: nawsrc@managementalliance.com
Secretary and Treasurer: Brandon Smith

Historical Note:
Formerly (2000) National Association of Waterproofing Contractors. NAWSRC's purpose is to promote ethical business standards and to improve communication in the waterproofing and structural repair industry. Membership: $795/year.

Continuing Education:
Certification Designation/s: CWS, CAWS, CSRS

Publications:
NAWSRC Foundation News; monthly; adv.

National Association of Wheat Growers *(1950)*
415 Second St. NE
Suite 300
Washington, DC 20002-4993
Tel: (202) 547-7800 *Fax:* (202) 546-2638
E-Mail: wheatworld@wheatworld.org
Website: wheatworld.org
Members: 25000 individuals
Staff: 6
Annual Budget: $1-2,000,000
Tax: 501(c)(6)

Personnel:
Chief Executive Officer: Dana Peterson
    E-Mail: dpeterson@wheatworld.org
Accountant: Delver Charlery
    E-Mail: finance@wheatworld.org
Contact, Membership Services: Katrina Custer
    E-Mail: kcuster@wheatworld.org
Director, Government Affairs for Research and Technology: Jane DeMarchi
    E-Mail: jdemarchi@wheatworld.org
Director, Communications: Melissa George Kessler
    E-Mail: mgeorge@wheatworld.org
Director, Government. Affairs: Eric Steiner
    E-Mail: esteiner@wheatworld.org

Historical Note:
NAWG's mission is to unite the wheat growers to create beneficial policies for wheat growers; effective relationships with industry; and profitable opportunities through research and technology. Membership: $50 (Individual); $2,000 (Company).

Meetings/Conferences: Annual
Conference Chair: Katrina Custer
Number of non-conference events/year: 1

Publications:
Membership Directory; on-line
NAWG News; monthly

Membership List Available to Non-members

National Association of Wholesaler-Distributors
(1970)
1325 G St. NW
Suite 1000
Washington, DC 20005-3100
Tel: (202) 872-0885 *Fax:* (202) 785-0586
E-Mail: naw@naw.org
Website: naw.org
Members: 40166 companies and associations
Staff: 23
Annual Budget: $2-5,000,000

Personnel:
President: Dirk Van Dongen
    E-Mail: dvandongen@nawd.org
Communications Assistant: Samantha Ager
    E-Mail: sager@naw.org
Senior Vice President, Corporate Relations: Carl Farr
    E-Mail: cfarr@naw.org
Senior Vice President, Strategic Direction: Ron Schreibman CAE
    E-Mail: rschreibman@naw.org
Contact, Business Services: George Valiga
    E-Mail: gvaliga@naw.org
Senior Vice President-Government Relations: Jade West
    E-Mail: jwest@nawd.org

Administrative Assistant, Corporate Relations and Manager, Membership Services: Keisha Wilson
    E-Mail: kwilson@naw.org

Historical Note:
Formerly the National Association of Wholesalers, assumed its present name in 1970. NAW's mission is to support the Wholesaler-Distributor Political Action Committee (WDPAC) and maintain the Distribution Research and Education Foundation and the NAW Service Corporation. Membership: $815-39,785 (Direct Member); $1,750 (Associate).

Meetings/Conferences: Annual
Conference Chair: Keisha Wilson
2013 - Washington, DC (Fairmont Washington)/Jan. 29 - 31
Number of non-conference events/year: 30

Publications:
Membership Directory; on-line
Warehousing Tips PLUS Warehousing Forum newsletter; monthly

National Association of Women Artists *(1889)*
80 Fifth Ave.
Suite 1405
New York, NY 10011
Tel: (212) 675-1616 *Fax:* (212) 675-8257
E-Mail: office@thenawa.org
Website: thenawa.org
Members: 800 individuals
Staff: 4
Annual Budget: $100-250,000
Tax: 501(c)(3)

Personnel:
Executive Director: Susan G. Hammond
    E-Mail: sgh35mm@comcast.net
Treasurer: Charles (Chip) Fears
Contact, Administration: Amanda Kopp

Historical Note:
Formerly (1941) known as the Women's Art Club of the City of New York. NAWA provides a forum for women artists to share ideas and to exhibit their work. The purpose of the Association is to promote culture and education in the visual arts through exhibitions of its member's works, lectures, art demonstrations, scholarships, awards and other educational programs. Membership: $180 (Individual); $50 (Junior/Student); $60 (Associate).

Meetings/Conferences: Annual

Publications:
ART TIMES; bi-monthly; adv.

National Association of Women Business Owners
(1976)
601 Pennsylvania Ave. NW
South Building, Suite 900
Washington, DC 20004
Tel: (800) 556-2926 *Fax:* (202) 403-3788
TollFree: (800) 556-2926
E-Mail: national@nawbo.org
Website: nawbo.org
Members: 9000 individuals
Staff: 6
Annual Budget: $1-2,000,000
Tax: 501(c)(6)

Personnel:
President and Chief Executive Officer: Diane Lenegham Tomb

Historical Note:
Established as the Association of Women Business Owners, assumed its present name in 1976. NAWBO's mission is strengthening the wealth creating capacity of its members and promoting economic development within the entrepreneurial community. Membership: $150 (Student/ Emerging Business Owner); $200 (Supporting/Established Business Owner); $350 (Sustaining); $220 (At-Large Member).

Meetings/Conferences:
Number of non-conference events/year: 3

Publications:
Membership Directory; on-line
NAWBO Focus; monthly; adv.
NAWBO SmartBrief; bi-weekly; adv.

National Association of Women Highway Safety Leaders, Inc. *(1967)*
2743 N. Albany
Chicago, IL 60647
Tel: (773) 278-8476 *Fax:* (773) 278-7135
Website: nawhsl.org

Members: 100000 individuals
Staff: 2
Annual Budget: $10-25,000
Tax: 501(c)(3)

Personnel:
Executive Director and Director, Region V: Judy Keippel
   E-Mail: judikeippel@yahoo.com

Historical Note:
NAWHSL's mission is to disseminate systematic information
and educational programs to promote safe behavior
among high risk groups, and to assure vigorous, effective
public policy programs to reduce highway crashes and
crash severity. Promotes safety belt usage, alcohol and
drug education, child passenger seats, car care, gasoline
saving tips, motorcycle safety, police enforcement, highway
environment, traffic court improvement, mature driver
safety, and high school driver education.

Meetings/Conferences:
Conference Chair: Judy Keippel

National Association of Women in Construction
(1955)
327 S. Adams St.
Fort Worth, TX 76104
Tel: (817) 877-5551 *Fax:* (817) 877-0324
TollFree: (800) 552-3506
E-Mail: nawic@nawic.org
Website: nawic.org
Members:
170 chapters
5000 individuals
Staff: 7
Annual Budget: $500-1,000,000
Tax: 501(c)(6)

Personnel:
President: Judy DeWeese
Communications Designer: Paul Barton
   E-Mail: paulb@nawic.org
Editor: Autumn Daughetee
   E-Mail: autumnd@nawic.org

Historical Note:
NAWIC encourages women to pursue and establish
careers in the construction industry and helps promote
their education in the field of construction. Members
hold diverse positions within the construction industry,
including as architects, owners, estimators, accountants
and tradeswomen. Membership: $223 (Active/Associate/
Member-At-Large); $298 (Corporate); $47 (Student); $50
(Retired); $38 (Student-At-Large); $152 (International).

Meetings/Conferences: Annual
2013 - Bellevue, WA/Aug. 28 - 31
2014 - Indianapolis, IN/Sept. 3 - 6
2015 - Nashville, TN/Sept. 2 - 5

Publications:
The Connection; monthly; adv.
The Nawic Image; adv.

National Association of Women Judges *(1979)*
1341 Connecticut Ave. NW
Suite 4.2
Washington, DC 20036-1834
Tel: (202) 393-0222 *Fax:* (202) 393-0125
E-Mail: nawj@nawj.org
Website: nawj.org
Members: 1200 individuals
Staff: 3
Annual Budget: $1-2,000,000
Tax: 501(c)(3)

Personnel:
Executive Director: Marie Komisar
   E-Mail: mkomisar@nawj.org
Assistant, Programs and Publication: Lavinia Cousin
   E-Mail: lcousin@nawj.org
Director, Finance and Administration: Craig A. Evans

Historical Note:
NAWJ's mission is to promote the judicial role of protecting
the rights of individuals under the rule of law through
strong, committed, diverse judicial leadership, fairness
and equality in the courts, and equal access to justice.
Members are judicial clerks, attorneys and law students.
Membership: $3000 (Life); $200 (Sitting Judge); $175
(Associate Member/Retired Judge/Amicus Judicii); $50
(Law Clerk); $25 (Law Student).

Meetings/Conferences: Semi-Annual
Conference Chair: Lavinia Cousin

Publications:
counterbalance; irregular
Membership Directory; on-line

Monthly Update; monthly

National Association of Women Lawyers *(1899)*
American Bar Center, 321 N. Clark St.
Mail Stop 21.1
Chicago, IL 60654
Tel: (312) 988-6186 *Fax:* (312) 988-5100
TollFree: (800) 285-2221
E-Mail: nawl@nawl.org
Website: nawl.org
Members: 2000 individuals
Staff: 4
Annual Budget: $500-1,000,000
Tax: 501(c)(6)

Personnel:
Executive Director: Vicky DiProva
   E-Mail: diprovav@nawl.org
Coordinator, Programs: Jonathan Becks
   E-Mail: becksj@nawl.org
Editor: Deborah S. Froling
   E-Mail: froling.deborah@arentfox.com
Coordinator, Membership Services and Systems: Georgette
Johnson
   E-Mail: johnsong@nawl.org

Historical Note:
Founded as the Women Lawyers Club. Reorganized in
1911 as the National Association of Women Lawyers.
NAWL continues to support and advance the interests of
women in and under the law, and in so doing, supports
and advances the social, political, and professional
empowerment of women. Membership: $250-500
(Corporate Legal Department); $0-1,500 (Individual); $55
(Law Association); $350-1500 (Law Firm); $450 (Law
School); $100 (Bar Association), $1500 (Life).

Meetings/Conferences: Annual
Conference Chair: Jonathan Becks
2013 - Orlando, FL (Walt Disney World Grand
Floridian Resort)/Feb. 14 - 16
Number of non-conference events/year: 21

Publications:
NAWL's e-Newsletter; monthly
The Women Lawyers Journal (WLJ); quarterly; adv.

National Association of Workforce Boards (NAWB) *(1979)*
1133 19th St. NW
Suite 400
Washington, DC 20036
Tel: (202) 857-7900 *Fax:* (202) 857-7955
E-Mail: nawb@nawb.org
Website: nawb.org
Members: 650 councils
Staff: 9
Annual Budget: $2-5,000,000
Tax: 501(c)(3)

Personnel:
Chief Executive Officer: Ron Painter
   E-Mail: painterr@nawb.org
Special Assistant, Professional and Project Development:
Tim Aldinger
   E-Mail: aldingert@nawb.org
Manager, Operations: Aisha Alexander
   E-Mail: alexandera@nawb.org
Event Planner: Marti Balcom
   E-Mail: marti@thebalcomgroup.com
Director, Membership and Board Relations: Josh Copus
   E-Mail: copusj@nawb.org
Media Requests: Celina Shands-Gradijan
   E-Mail: celina@fullcapacitymarketing.com

Historical Note:
Founded as National Association of Private Industry
Councils, it assumed its current name in 1999. NAWB's
mission is to support members through advocacy, training
and technical assistance, communication, and the
promotion of strategic partnerships for the advancement of
American workforce. Members are private industry councils
and private employers concerned with employment and
training policies in the context of economic development and
education. Membership: $650-1000 (Full Member); $750
(Associate).

Meetings/Conferences: Annual
Conference Chair: Marti Balcom
Number of non-conference events/year: 2

Publications:
Member Directory; on-line
Workforce Alert; on-line
Workforce Boards in Action; quarterly
Workforce Brief; on-line

National Association of Workforce Development Professionals *(1989)*
1133 19th St. NW
Fourth Floor
Washington, DC 20036
Tel: (202) 589-1790 *Fax:* (202) 589-1799
E-Mail: nawdp@aol.com
Website: nawdp.org
Members: 4500 individuals
Staff: 3
Annual Budget: $500-1,000,000
Tax: 501(c)(6)

Personnel:
Executive Director: Bridget Brown
   E-Mail: bridget@nawdp.org
Coordinator, Membership: Linh Hoang
   E-Mail: Linh@NAWDP.org
Secretary and Treasurer: Patti Meldrum CWDP, MS
   E-Mail: gammpm@marktwain.net

Historical Note:
NAWDP is a national association for individual
practitioners who work in workforce development programs.
NAWDP's mission is to be the national voice for the
profession and meet the individual professional development
needs of its membership. Administers and endorses the
CWDP program as a way to certify the skills, knowledge,
experience and training of individual workforce development
practitioners. Membership: $50 (Individual); $50 minimum
(Agency/Organization-5 or more staff from the same
organization); $75 (Annual); $500 (Lifetime).

Continuing Education:
Enrollment: 1400
Certification Designation/s: CWDP

Meetings/Conferences: Annual
2013 - Minneapolis, MN/May 19 - 22
2014 - Denver, CO/May 4 - 6
Number of non-conference events/year: 1

Publications:
eVantage Electronic Newsletter; monthly; adv.
The Advantage Newsletter; monthly; adv.
The Journal of Workforce Development; bi-annually

Membership List Available to Non-members

National Associations of State Directors of Pupil Transportation Services *(1968)*
P.O. Box 5446
Steamboat Springs, CO 80477
Tel: (970) 871-1784
Website: nasdpts.org
Members: 22 associations
Staff: 3
Annual Budget: $100-250,000

Personnel:
Executive Director: Bob Riley
   E-Mail: execdir@nasdpts.org
Contact, Membership Services: Mary Jo Major
   E-Mail: memberservices@nasdpts.org
Contact, Administrative Services: Rodney McKnight
   E-Mail: adminservices@nasdpts.org

Historical Note:
NASDPTS's mission is to provide safe, secure, efficient,
economical, and quality transportation to school children
on their trips to and from school and school-related
activities. Membership is comprised of state and national
leaders in school bus transportation, local school
transportation administrators, suppliers of products and
services, as well as grassroots practitioners. Membership:
$150-29,000/year.

Meetings/Conferences: Annual
2013 - Reno, NV/July 22

Publications:
NASDPTS Newsletter

National Athletic Trainers Association *(1950)*
2952 Stemmons Fwy.
Suite 200
Dallas, TX 75247-6916
Tel: (214) 637-6282 *Fax:* (214) 637-2206
TollFree: (888) 491-8833
Website: nata.org
Members: 30000 individuals
Staff: 42
Annual Budget: $5-10,000,000

Personnel:
Executive Director: Eve Becker-Doyle CAE
   E-Mail: ebd@nata.org
Manager, Human Resources: Michael Anto

E-Mail: michael@nata.org
Associate Executive Director, Policy and Advocacy: Cate Brennan CAE
    E-Mail: cate@nata.org
Manager, Membership Services: Kelly Carlin
    E-Mail: kellyc@nata.org
Manager, Information Technology: Damon Eason
    E-Mail: damone@nata.org
Director, Member Services and Business Development: John Honaman
    E-Mail: johnh@nata.org
Manager, Knowledge Initiatives: Anita James
    E-Mail: anitaj@nata.org
Director, Meetings Management: Lori Marker
    E-Mail: lorim@nata.org
Coordinator, Marketing and Public Relations: Kathryn Moore
    E-Mail: kathrynm@nata.org
Manager, Public Relations: Ellen Satlof
    E-Mail: ellens@nata.org

Historical Note:
NATA's mission is to enhance the quality of health care provided by certified athletic trainers and to advance the athletic training profession. Membership: $80-240 (Professional); $53-85 (Student).

Continuing Education:
Certification Designation/s: CAT

Meetings/Conferences: Annual
Conference Chair: Lori Marker
2013 - Las Vegas, NV/June 24 - 27
2014 - Indianapolis, IN/June 25 - July 28
2015 - St. Louis, MO/June 23 - 26
2016 - Baltimore, MD/June 22 - 25

Publications:
e-zine; weekly
Journal of Athletic Training; bi-monthly
NATA News; monthly

National Auctioneers Association *(1949)*
8880 Ballentine St.
Overland Park, KS 66214-1985
Tel: (913) 541-8084 *Fax:* (913) 894-5281
TollFree: (888) 541-8084
E-Mail: support@auctioneers.org
Website: auctioneers.org
Members: 5870 individuals
Staff: 14
Annual Budget: $2-5,000,000
Tax: 501(c)(6)

Personnel:
Chief Executive Officer: Hannes Combest CAE
    E-Mail: hcombest@auctioneers.org
Director, Education: Michael Avery
    E-Mail: mavery@auctioneers.org
Administrator, Information Technology: Steve Jackson
    E-Mail: sjackson@auctioneers.org
Deputy Executive Director: Chris Longly
    E-Mail: clongly@auctioneers.org
Manager, Conferences and Shows: Joyce Peterson
    E-Mail: joyce@auctioneers.org
Specialist, Membership Services: Heather Rempe
    E-Mail: hrempe@auctioneers.org
Director, Publications and Trade Show: Bryan Scribner
    E-Mail: bscribner@auctioneers.org
Director, Finance and Administrative Services: Rhonda Truitt
    E-Mail: rtruitt@auctioneers.org

Historical Note:
Absorbed Auction Marketing Institute in 2003. NAA's mission is to promote the auction method of marketing and enhancing the professionalism of its members through education and technology. Membership: $500 (Affiliate); $225 (Associate/Online); $300 (Regular); $450 (Spouse); $25 (Auxillary).

Continuing Education:
Certification Designation/s: MPPA, ATS, AARE, CES, CAI, GPPA-M, BAS, GPPA

Meetings/Conferences:
Conference Chair: Joyce Peterson
2013 - Kansas City, MO (Embassy Suites Kansas City)/ March 4 - 5
2013 - Indianapolis, IN (JW Marriott Indianapolis)/July 16 - 20

Publications:
Auction E-News; semi-monthly; adv.
Auctioneer Magazine; monthly; adv.
Membership Directory; on-line

National Auto Auction Association *(1948)*
5320 Spectrum Dr.
Suite D
Frederick, MD 21703
Tel: (301) 696-0400 *Fax:* (301) 631-1359
E-Mail: naaa@naaa.com
Website: naaa.com
Members: 321 auto auctions
Staff: 7
Annual Budget: $2-5,000,000

Personnel:
Chief Executive Officer: Frank Hackett
    E-Mail: hackett@naaa.com
Manager, Meetings: Tom Dozier
    E-Mail: dozier@naaa.com
Manager, Legislative and Information: Tricia Heon
    E-Mail: theon@naaa.com
General Counsel: Thomas E. Lynch
    E-Mail: tlynch@naaa.com
Chief Financial Officer: Steve McConnaughey
    E-Mail: mcconn@naaa.com
Communications and Web Manager: Laurie Oakman
    E-Mail: oakman@naaa.com
Membership and Database Manager: Beth Weber
    E-Mail: bweber@naaa.com

Historical Note:
NAAA represents auto auctions both domestic and international. Mission is to provide a unified voice for the auto auction industry and to protect and promote the interests of its members. Members are dealers auto auctions, held in a permanent location on a regular weekly schedule. Membership: $800-2,200/year (Organization/Company).

Meetings/Conferences: Semi-Annual
Conference Chair: Tom Dozier
2013 - Las Vegas, NV (Caesars Palace)/March 6 - 7
2013 - Indianapolis, IN (JW Marriott Indianapolis)/ Sept. 3 - 6
2014 - Las Vegas, NV (Caesars Palace)/March 5 - 6
2014 - Boston, MA (Sheraton Boston Hotel)/Sept. 23 - 26
2015 - Las Vegas, NV (Caesars Palace)/March 4 - 5

Publications:
Auction Industry History
Industry Standards
Membership Directory; annually; adv.
On the Block; quarterly

National Automatic Merchandising Association *(1936)*
20 N. Wacker Dr.
Suite 3500
Chicago, IL 60606-3102
Tel: (312) 346-0370 *Fax:* (312) 704-4140
TollFree: (888) 337-8363
Website: vending.org
Members: 2500 companies
Staff: 22
Annual Budget: $5-10,000,000
Tax: 501(c)(6)

Personnel:
President and Chief Executive Officer: Carla Balakgie CAE, FASAE
    E-Mail: cbalakgie@vending.org
Chief Financial Officer and Assistant Secretary and Treasurer: Patrick Caffarelli CCS
    E-Mail: pcaffarelli@vending.org
Director, Public Relations: Jackie Clark
    E-Mail: jclark@clarkcommunicationsonline.com
Director, Membership Services: Dawn Gary
    E-Mail: dgary@vending.org
Vice President, Sales and Service: Dean R. Gilland CCS
    E-Mail: dgilland@vending.org
Senior Director and Counsel, Government Affairs: Sandra Larson
    E-Mail: slarson@vending.org
Executive Vice President and Chief Operating Officer: Dan Mathews
    E-Mail: dmathews@vending.org
Manager, Meeting Services: Barbara M. Moll
    E-Mail: bmoll@vending.org
Vice President, Marketing and Public Relations: Roni Moore
    E-Mail: rmoore@vending.org
Senior Director, One Show and Education: Lynae Schleyer CMP
    E-Mail: lschleyer@vending.org

Historical Note:
Mission is to collectively advance and promote the automatic merchandising and coffee service industries. NAMA operates programs in health, safety and standards, public relations, employee relations and training, education, accounting, and statistics. Members are makers and operators of automatic vending equipment, contract food service management, and office coffee service industry in collaboration with the providers of products and services to the vending industry. Membership: $600-2,100 (Broker/Distributor, based on annual total gross sales volume); $500 (Sustaining); $1,650-28000 (Supplier); $3000-28000 (Machine Manufacturer); $450-675 (International Subscriber).

Continuing Education:
Certification Designation/s: QCCP, TTP, NCE, RDCP

Meetings/Conferences: Annual
Conference Chair: Barbara M. Moll
2013 - Las Vegas, NV (Venetian Resort Hotel Casino)/ April 24 - 26
Number of non-conference events/year: 3

Publications:
InTouch; quarterly
Membership Directory; on-line
NAMA Legislative Alert; on-line
Staff Directory; on-line

National Automobile Dealers Association *(1917)*
8400 Westpark Dr.
McLean, VA 22102
Tel: (703) 821-7000 *Fax:* (703) 821-7075
TollFree: (800) 252-6232
E-Mail: nadainfo@nada.org
Website: nada.org
Members:
17,000 new car and truck dealers
37,500 franchises
Staff: 94
Annual Budget: $25-50,000,000

Personnel:
Interim President, Chief Operating Officer and Chief Financial Officer: Joseph L. Cowden
    E-Mail: jcowden@nada.org
Vice President and Chief Public Affairs Officer: David F. Hyatt
    E-Mail: dhyatt@nada.org
Vice President and General Counsel: Andrew D. Koblenz
Vice President and Chief Information Officer: Richard E. Malaise
Vice President, Conventions and Expositions: Stephen R. Pitt
    E-Mail: expo@nada.org
Vice President, Legislative Affairs: David W. Regan
    E-Mail: dregan@nada.org
Executive Director, Publications: Marc H. Stertz
    E-Mail: mstertz@nada.org
Director, Legislative Affairs and Communications: A. Bailey Wood Jr.
    E-Mail: bwood@nada.org

Historical Note:
NADA's mission is to conduct training and service programs to improve dealership business operations, sales and service practices. Membership: $190-925 (Franchised Car Dealer, based on new retail vehicle sales volume); $110-420 (Franchised New Heavy and Medium Duty Truck Dealers in the 50 US states only); $315-455 (International Dealer Affiliate); $275 (Sustaining Member).

Continuing Education:
Certification Designation/s: SASP

Meetings/Conferences: Annual
Conference Chair: Stephen R. Pitt
2013 - Orange, FL (Orange County Convention Center)/Feb. 8 - 11
2013 - Orlando, FL/Feb. 9 - 11
2014 - New Orleans, LA/Jan. 24 - 27
2015 - San Francisco, CA/Jan. 23 - 26
2016 - Las Vegas, NV/April 1 - 4
Number of non-conference events/year: 40

Publications:
ATD Insider; weekly
Director's Column; on-line
NADA DATA; annually
NADA Headlines; daily
NADA Weekly; weekly
NADA's AutoExec
Regulatory Review; quarterly

National Automotive Finance Association *(1996)*

7250 Pkwy. Dr.
Suite 510
Hanover, MD 21076-1343
Tel: (410) 712-4036 *Fax:* (410) 712-4038
TollFree: (800) 463-8955
E-Mail: information@nafassociation.com
Website: nafassociation.com
Members: 85 companies and individuals
Staff: 2
Annual Budget: $250-500,000
Tax: 501(c)(6)

Personnel:
Executive Director: Jack Tracey CAE
Counsel: Tom Hudson

Historical Note:
NAF serves the below-prime auto financing industry and supports its members and the industry with programs and education. Membership: $1,500 (Full-Dealer); $1,250 (Associate); $1,500-5,000 (Full - Based on Financing Source).

Meetings/Conferences: Annual

Publications:
Non-Prime Times; bi-monthly; adv.

National Ballroom and Entertainment Association (1947)
2799 Locust Rd.
Decorah, IA 52101-7600
Tel: (563) 382-3871
E-Mail: nbea@q.com
Website: nbea.com
Members:
66 member ballrooms
400 individuals
Staff: 1
Annual Budget: $10-25,000
Tax: 501(c)(6)

Personnel:
Executive Director: John Matter

Historical Note:
Founded in 1941 as the Midwestern Ballroom Operators Association, it became the National Ballroom Operators Association in 1947. In 1970 the name was changed to the Entertainment Operators of America and the present name was adopted in 1976. NBEA advocates social dancing as a life-long activity that contributes to the physical, mental and social well-being of individuals. Members include band leaders, agents and dance instructors. Membership: $125 (Active); $90 (Entertainment); $25 (Associate).

Meetings/Conferences: Annual

National Band Association (1960)
6947 Conservation Dr.
Springfield, VA 22153
Tel: (703) 455-2323
E-Mail: info@nationalbandassociation.org
Website: nationalbandassociation.org
Members: 3000 individuals
Staff: 2
Annual Budget: $100-250,000
Tax: 501(c)(3)

Personnel:
President: Roy Holder
E-Mail: roy.holder@fcps.edu

Historical Note:
NBA's mission is to encourage musical and educational significance of bands and is dedicated to the attainment of a high level of excellence for bands and band music. Members are band directors, music teachers, musical instrument makers and others interested in band development. Membership: $15-200/year.

Meetings/Conferences:
Number of non-conference events/year: 1

Publications:
The NBA Journal
Membership Directory; on-line
The Instrumentalist; monthly

National Bankers Association (1927)
1513 P St. NW
Washington, DC 20005
Tel: (202) 588-5432 *Fax:* (202) 588-5443
Website: nationalbankers.org
Members: 52 banks
Staff: 3
Annual Budget: $500-1,000,000
Tax: 501(c)(6)

Personnel:
President: Michael A. Grant
E-Mail: mgrant@nationalbankers.org
Chief Administrative Officer: Evonne Holliday
E-Mail: eholliday@nationalbankers.org

Historical Note:
Formerly (1951) National Negro Bankers Association, NBA's purpose is to serve as an advocate for the nation's minority and women owned banks on legislative and regulatory matters concerning and affecting its members and the communities they serve. Members are minority and women's banking institutions, minority individuals employed by majority banks and majority institutions. Membership: $250 (Associate); $2,000 (Affiliate).

Meetings/Conferences: Annual
Number of non-conference events/year: 1

National Bar Association (1925)
1225 11th St. NW
Washington, DC 20001
Tel: (202) 842-3900 *Fax:* (202) 289-6170
Website: nationalbar.org
Members: 20,000 lawyer, judges, educators and law students.
Staff: 7
Annual Budget: $2-5,000,000

Personnel:
Executive Director: Demetris W. Cheatham
E-Mail: dcheatham@nationalbar.org
Manager, Membership Services: Teka Miller
E-Mail: tmiller@nationalbar.org
Communications Coordinator: Erika Owens
E-Mail: eowens@nationalbar.org
Chief Financial Officer: Sedric Roberts MBA
E-Mail: sroberts@nationalbar.org
Advocacy and Legislative Counsel: Kimberly Tignor
E-Mail: ktignor@nationalbar.org

Historical Note:
NBA's mission is to advance the science of jurisprudence and to improve the administration of justice. Membership: $15-6,000/year.

Meetings/Conferences: Annual
Number of non-conference events/year: 7

Publications:
The NBA Magazine; semi-annually; adv.

National Barbecue Association (1991)
455 S. Fourth St.
Suite 650
Louisville, KY 40202
Tel: (512) 454-8626 *Fax:* (502) 589-3602
TollFree: (888) 909-2121
E-Mail: nbbqa@hqtrs.com
Website: nbbqa.org
Members: 2,000 members
Staff: 6
Annual Budget: $100-250,000
Tax: 501(c)(6)

Personnel:
Executive Director: Jeff Allen
E-Mail: jallen@hqtrs.com
Contact, Marketing and Communications: Michael Alderson
E-Mail: malderson@hqtrs.com
Coordinator, Membership Services: Laura Atchison
E-Mail: latchison@hqtrs.com
Contact, Finance and Operations: John Bunker
E-Mail: jbunker@hqtrs.com
Contact, Public Relations and Digital Media: Andrea Parr
E-Mail: jbunker@hqtrs.com
Contact, Event Services: Peg Plaut
E-Mail: pplaut@hqtrs.com

Historical Note:
NBBQA represents manufacturers of barbecue equipment, products, and supplies, as well as professional barbecuer, food industry professionals in barbecue, and barbecue enthusiasts. NBBQA's mission is to share and expand the diverse culture of barbecue through networking and education. Membership: $0 (Friend Member); $50 (Enthusiast); $175 (Operator); $200 (Trade Partner).

Meetings/Conferences: Annual
Conference Chair: Peg Plaut
2013 - Mobile, AL (Renaissance Mobile Riverview Plaza Hotel)/Feb. 20 - 23

Publications:
BIB E-Newsletter; monthly; adv.

National Barley Growers Association (1989)
P.O. Box 131
Soda Springs, ID 83276
E-Mail: tjones@idahograin.org
Website: nationalbarley.com
Members: 18 Members
Staff: 4
Annual Budget: $100-250,000

Personnel:
President: Scott Brown
E-Mail: swb0203@msn.com

Historical Note:
NBGA's mission is to enhance and maintain the profitability of the U.S. barley industry.

National Barrel Horse Association (1992)
P.O. Box 1988
Augusta, GA 30903
Tel: (706) 722-7223 *Fax:* (706) 823-3700
E-Mail: nbha@nbha.com
Website: nbha.com
Members: 23000 Members
Staff: 6

Personnel:
Executive Director: Sherry Fulmer
E-Mail: sherry.fulmer@morris.com
Director, Membership Services: Rick Hardy
Accountant: Tranis Harper
E-Mail: tranis.harper@morris.com
Coordinator, Events: Renee Jenkins
E-Mail: renee.jenkins@nbha.com

Historical Note:
NBHA introduced the divisional format to the barrel racing industry, which allows riders of all skill levels a chance to win money and prizes in barrel racing competitions. Membership: $62 (Regular); $48 (Charter); $52 (Adult); $37 (Child).

Meetings/Conferences:
Conference Chair: Renee Jenkins
Number of non-conference events/year: 1

Publications:
Barrel Horse News; monthly

National Basketball Association (1946)
645 Fifth Ave.
15th Floor
New York, NY 10022
Tel: (212) 407-8000 *Fax:* (212) 754-6414
Website: nba.com
Members: 29 clubs
Staff: 800
Annual Budget: $5-10,000,000

Personnel:
Commissioner: David Stern
E-Mail: bmcintyre@nba.com
Executive Vice President, Events and Attractions: Ski Austin
Senior Vice President, Marketing and Communications: Michael Bass
Executive Vice President and General Counsel: Richard W. Buchanan
Executive Vice President, Human Resources: Kerry D. Chandler
Senior Vice President, Legal and Business Affairs: David Denenberg
Senior Vice President and Chief Information Officer: Michael S. Gliedman

Historical Note:
NBA's mission is to administer the principal professional basketball league in the United States.

Meetings/Conferences:
Conference Chair: Ski Austin

Publications:
HOOP Magazine
Membership Directory; on-line
NBA All-Access Europe Newsletter; on-line
NBA Daily; daily
NBA Offers; on-line
NBA Top 5; weekly
NBA.com Fantasy Basketball; weekly

National Basketball Athletic Trainers Association (1974)
C/O Rollin Mallernee
400 Colony Sq., Suite 1750
Atlanta, GA 30361

Tel: (404) 892-8919 Fax: (404) 892-8560
Website: nbata.com
Members: 57 individuals
Staff: 1
Annual Budget: $100-250,000

Personnel:
General Counsel: Rollin E. Mallernee II
    E-Mail: rmallernee@mallernee-branch.com

Historical Note:
NBATA is dedicated to enhance professional stability of its members by maintaining an atmosphere of trust, support, motivation and involvement.

Publications:
Membership Directory; on-line

National Basketball Players Association (1954)
310 Lenox Ave.
New York, NY 10027
Tel: (212) 655-0880 Fax: (212) 655-0881
TollFree: (800) 955-6272
E-Mail: info@nbpa.com
Website: nbpa.com
Members: 420 individuals
Staff: 20
Annual Budget: Over $100,000,000
Tax: 501(c)(5)

Personnel:
Executive Director: G. William Hunter
General Counsel: Gary Hall
Director, Special Events and Sponsorships: Megan Inaba
    E-Mail: megan.inaba@nbpa.org
Director, Finance: Theresa Clark Messer
Director, Career Development Program: Deborah
    Rothstein Murman
Director, Communications: Dan Wasserman
    E-Mail: danw@nbpa.org
Director, Operations: Pamela Wheeler

Historical Note:
Independent labor union. Purpose of the association is to ensure that the rights of NBA players are protected, and that everything possible is being done to help players maximize their opportunities and achieve their goals on and off the court. Membership: $5,000/year.

Meetings/Conferences:
Conference Chair: G. William Hunter

National Basketball Referees Association (1977)
1455 Pennsylvania Ave. NW
Suite 225,The Willard Offices
Washington, DC 20004
Tel: (202) 638-5090 Fax: (202) 638-5564
E-Mail: lmcmorris@nbra.net
Website: nbra.net
Members: 60 referees
Staff: 5
Annual Budget: $250-500,000
Tax: 501(c)(3)

Personnel:
Executive Director: Lamell J. McMorris
    E-Mail: lmcmorris@nbra.net
Media Contact: Lloyd Pierson
    E-Mail: media@nbra.net

Historical Note:
Formerly (1973) National Basketball Officials Association, (1977) National Association of Basketball Referees. NBRA's mission is to support and promote its member's charitable and educational goals.

Publications:
Member Directory; on-line

Membership List Available to Non-members

National Beauty Culturists' League (1919)
25 Logan Cir. NW
Washington, DC 20005-3725
Tel: (202) 332-2695 Fax: (202) 332-0940
E-Mail: nbcl@bellsouth.net
Website: nbcl.org
Members: 10000 individuals
Staff: 1
Annual Budget: $100-250,000

Personnel:
President: Dr. Katie B. Catalon

Historical Note:
NBCL's mission is to promote goodwill and cooperative effort among all beauticians, manufacturers, and persons engaged in related fields and to promote the general

welfare and raise the public image of those engaged in the beauty culture field. Membership: $100 (Individual); $200 (Sustaining); $50 (Beauty School Student); $500 (Corporate).

Continuing Education:
Certification Designation/s: PBA, PMA, DPC

Meetings/Conferences: Annual
Conference Chair: Dr. Katie B. Catalon
2013 - Alexandria, VA (Hilton Alexandria Mark
    Center)/July 27 - Aug. 3
Number of non-conference events/year: 1

Publications:
Membership Directory; on-line

National Beer Wholesalers Association (1938)
1101 King St.
Suite 600
Alexandria, VA 22314-2944
Tel: (703) 683-4300 Fax: (703) 683-8965
TollFree: (800) 300-6417
E-Mail: info@nbwa.org
Website: nbwa.org
Members: 3,300 licensed, independent beer
distributors
Staff: 26
Annual Budget: $10-25,000,000

Personnel:
President: Craig A. Purser CAE
    E-Mail: cpurser@nbwa.org
Executive Vice President and Chief Advocacy Officer:
    Michael W. Johnson
    E-Mail: mjohnson@nbwa.org
Contact, Media Relations: Kathleen Joyce
    E-Mail: kjoyce@nbwa.org
Chief Financial Officer: Kim McKinnish
    E-Mail: kmckinnish@nbwa.org
Senior Vice President, Industry Affairs and General Counsel:
    Paul Pisano
    E-Mail: ppisano@nbwa.org
Vice President, Membership Services and Meetings: Patti
    Rouzie
    E-Mail: prouzie@nbwa.org
Vice President, Public Affairs and Chief Communications
    Officer: Rebecca Spicer
    E-Mail: rspicer@nbwa.org

Historical Note:
NBWA works to strengthen the state-based system of alcohol regulation that facilitates an orderly marketplace; creates a transparent and accountable system of alcohol distribution that protects American consumers; and promotes responsibility in the manufacture, distribution, sale and consumption of alcohol. Membership: $100,000/year (Distributor).

Meetings/Conferences:
Conference Chair: Patti Rouzie
2013 - Las Vegas, NV (Caesars Palace)/Sept. 29 - Oct.
    2
2014 - New Orleans, LA (Hyatt Regency New Orleans)/
    Sept. 28 - Oct. 1
Number of non-conference events/year: 2

Publications:
Membership Directory; on-line
NBWA Newsletter; monthly
The Beer Route; bi-weekly
The Daily Brew; daily

Membership List Available to Non-members

National Bicycle Dealers Association (1946)
3176 Pullman St.
Suite 117
Costa Mesa, CA 92626
Tel: (949) 722-6909 Fax: (949) 722-1747
E-Mail: info@nbda.com
Website: nbda.com
Members: 1200 dealers
Staff: 3
Annual Budget: $500-1,000,000
Tax: 501(c)(6)

Personnel:
Executive Director: Fred Clements
    E-Mail: fred@nbda.com
Director, Marketing and Communications: Mike Baker
    E-Mail: mike@nbda.com
Managing Editor: John Francis
    E-Mail: john@nbda.com

Historical Note:

NBDA represents speciality bicycle retailers in America. Membership: $150 (Dealer); $360 (Associate Member 'A'); $150 (Associate Member 'C'); $50 (Informational).

Meetings/Conferences: Annual
Number of non-conference events/year: 2

Publications:
The Outspokin; monthly; adv.

National BioDiesel Board
1331 Pennsylvania Ave. NW
Suite 512
Washington, DC 20004
Tel: (202) 737-8801
Website: biodiesel.org
Staff: 20
Annual Budget: $10-25,000,000

Personnel:
Chief Executive Officer: Joe Jobe
Director, Communications: Jessica Robinson
Vice President, Federal Affairs: Anne Steckel
Director, Information Technology: Scott Tremain
Director, Operations: Doug Whitehead
Chief Financial Officer: April Yaeger

Historical Note:
National trade association representing the biodiesel industry in the United States.

Meetings/Conferences: Annual
2013 - Las Vegas, NV (The Mirage Casino- Hotel)/Feb.
    4 - 7

Publications:
BEN Newsletter
Biobased Solutions-Newsletter
Biodiesel Magazine; monthly; adv.

National Biosolids Partnership
601 Wythe St.
Alexandria, VA 22314-1994
Tel: (703) 684-2438 Fax: (703) 684-2492
Website: wef.org/biosolids
Staff: 1

Personnel:
Biosolids Program Director: Jim Cox
    E-Mail: jcox@wef.org

Historical Note:
NBP's mission is to advance the understanding and adoption of effective practices in biosolids management and offer education, training and technical assistance.

Continuing Education:
Certification Designation/s: BMP

Publications:
NBP Newsletter

National Bison Association
8690 Wolff Ct.
Suite 200
Westminster, CO 80031
Tel: (303) 292-2833 Fax: (303) 845-9081
Website: bisoncentral.com
Members: 1500 individuals
Staff: 4
Annual Budget: $250-500,000
Tax: 501(c)(5)

Personnel:
Executive Director: Dave Carter
    E-Mail: david@bisoncentral.com
Bookkeeper: Vicky Vlaanderen
    E-Mail: vicky@bisoncentral.com
Editor: Marilyn Wentz
    E-Mail: marilyn.wentz@tds.net

Historical Note:
Formerly (1965) the National Buffalo Association and (1975) American Bison Association. Absorbed National Buffalo Association in 1994. NBA's purpose is to promote and preserve the American Bison. Membership: $3,000 (Life); $200 (Active); $250 (Allied Industry); $50 (Junior/ Friend); $200 (Student).

Meetings/Conferences: Annual
2013 - Denver, CO (Renaissance Denver Hotel)/Jan. 23
    - 26

Publications:
Bison World; quarterly; adv.
Membership Directory; on-line
Weekly Update; weekly; adv.

Membership List Available to Non-members

National Black Association for Speech, Language and Hearing (1978)
700 McKnight Park Dr.
Suite 708
Pittsburgh, PA 15237
Tel: (412) 366-1177 *Fax:* (412) 366-8804
E-Mail: NBASLH@nbaslh.org
Website:
nbaslh.org
nbaslh.org
nbaslh.org
Members: 400 individuals
Staff: 3
Annual Budget: $50-100,000
Tax: 501(c)(3)

Personnel:
Secretary: Kellie E. Ingram CCC-SLP, MA
    E-Mail: kellie0502@gmail.com
Editor: Dr. Ronald Jones CCC-A, COI, PhD
    E-Mail: rjones@nsu.edu
Treasurer: Dr. Linda McCabe Smith CCC-SLP, PhD
    E-Mail: lsmith@siu.edu

Historical Note:
NBASLH aims to maintain a viable mechanism through which the needs of Black professionals, students and individuals with communication disorders can be met. Members are individuals working in the area of speech, language and/or hearing, students in training in the field, consumer or any other persons showing interest in the speech, language and hearing problems of Black people. Membership: $75 (Professional); $50 (Associate); $25 (Student).

Meetings/Conferences: Annual
2013 - Washington, DC (L'Enfant Plaza Hotel)/April 18 - 21

Publications:
ECHO; on-line
Resound

National Black Caucus of Local Elected Officials (1970)
1301 Pennsylvania Ave. NW
Suite 550
Washington, DC 20004
Tel: (202) 626-3000 *Fax:* (202) 626-3043
E-Mail: info@nlc.org
Website: nlc.org/build-skills-and-networks/
    networks/con
Members: 1500 African American officials
Staff: 4

Personnel:
President: Deborah Denard Delgado
Secretary: Louvenia Mathison
Senior Assistant, Constituency Group Programs and Contact, Membership: Marsena Mitchell
    E-Mail: mitchell@nlc.org

Historical Note:
A division of National League of Cities that provides administrative support, NBC-LEO's purpose is to increase African American participation on the NLC's steering and policy committees to ensure that policy and program recommendations reflect African American concerns and benefit their communities. Membership: $50 (Voting Member from an NLC Member City); $75 (Non Voting Member from a Non Member City); $100 (Non Voting Member from an NLC Member or Non Member City).

Meetings/Conferences: Annual

Publications:
Membership Directory
NBC-LEO Newslines; quarterly

National Black Caucus of State Legislators (1977)
444 N. Capitol St. NW
Suite 622
Washington, DC 20001
Tel: (202) 624-5457 *Fax:* (202) 508-3826
E-Mail: staff@nbcsl.com
Website: nbcsl.org
Members:
600 African American state legislators and representatives
120 Representatives from Corporations and Labor Unions
Staff: 6
Annual Budget: $2-5,000,000
Tax: 501(c)(3)

Personnel:

Executive Director: LaKimba De Sadier Walker
    E-Mail: lakimba@nbcsl.org
Policy Director: Ajenai S. Clemmons
    E-Mail: ajenai@nbcsl.org
Associate, Communications: Mori Diane
    E-Mail: mori@nbcsl.org
Communications and Research Associate: Lauren Williams
    E-Mail: lauren@nbcsl.org

Historical Note:
NBCSL's primary mission is to develop, conduct and promote educational, research and training programs designed to enhance the effectiveness of its members, as they consider legislation and issues of public policy which impact, either directly or indirectly upon "the general welfare" of African American constituents within their respective jurisdictions. Annual Membership: $100 (Legislative); $10,000 (Private Sector).

Publications:
Directory of African American State Legislators (Membership Directory)
Legislator Magazine; adv.
The Legislator

National Black Chamber of Commerce (1993)
1350 Connecticut Ave. NW
Suite 405
Washington, DC 20036
Tel: (202) 466-6888 *Fax:* (202) 466-4918
E-Mail: info@nationalbcc.org
Website: nationalbcc.org
Members: 100175 Black owned businesses and chapters and affiliates
Staff: 2
Annual Budget: $500-1,000,000
Tax: 501(c)(3)

Personnel:
President and Chief Executive Officer: Harry C. Alford Jr.
    E-Mail: halford@nationalbcc.org
Senior Vice President and Co-founder: Kay DeBow Alford
    E-Mail: kdebow@nationalbcc.org

Historical Note:
NBCC is dedicated to economically empowering and sustaining African American communities through entrepreneurship and capitalistic activity within the U.S. via interaction with the black diaspora. Membership: $300-35,000/year.

Meetings/Conferences: Annual
Conference Chair: Kay DeBow Alford

Publications:
Chamber Report; quarterly
Convention Journal

National Black Farmers Association (1995)
68 Wind Rd.
Baskerville, VA 23915
Tel: (434) 447-3444
Website: blackfarmers.org
Members: 80000 individuals
Staff: 1

Personnel:
President: John W. Boyd Jr.
    E-Mail: johnwesleyboydjr@gmail.com

Historical Note:
Helps small and disadvantaged farmers in gaining access to resources of state and federal programs administered by the United States Department of Agriculture. Membership: $100/year.

Publications:
Newsletter; quarterly

National Black MBA Association (1970)
180 N. Michigan Ave.
Suite 1400
Chicago, IL 60601
Tel: (312) 236-2622 *Fax:* (312) 236-0390
E-Mail: mail@nbmbaa.org
Website: nbmbaa.org
Members: 7500 individuals
Staff: 25
Annual Budget: $50-100,000
Tax: 501(c)(3)

Personnel:
President and Chief Executive Officer: Kimberly Corbin
Director, Chapters, Membership Services, and University Relations: Elizabeth Liz Hope

Director, Development and Marketing Communications: Vera Lewis
Vice President, Finance and Legal Affairs and Chief Financial Officer: Cecil B. Lucy CPA, JD
Director, Information Technology: Fred J. Phillips III
    E-Mail: fred.phillips@nbmbaa.org
Vice President, Strategy Program Initiatives: Kim R. Wilson
Director, Human Resources: Reniece R. Wright

Historical Note:
NBMBAA's mission is to provide innovative programs to stimulate intellectual and economic growth; build partnerships with key stakeholders who help facilitate this growth and increase awareness and facilitate access to graduate management education programs and career opportunities in management fields. Membership: $125 (Full/Associate); $50 (Full/Associate- International); $60 (Student); $35 (Collegiate Student).

Meetings/Conferences: Annual
Conference Chair: Kim R. Wilson
Number of non-conference events/year: 3

Publications:
Access E-Newsletter; monthly; adv.
Black Enterprise; monthly
Black MBA; adv.
BusinessWeek; weekly
Conference Daily E-Newsletter

National Black Nurses Association (1971)
8630 Fenton St.
Suite 330
Silver Spring, MD 20910-3803
Tel: (301) 589-3200 *Fax:* (301) 589-3223
TollFree: (800) 575-6298
E-Mail: contact@nbna.org
Website: nbna.org
Members: 150000 nurses
Staff: 5
Annual Budget: $10-25,000
Tax: 501(c)(3)

Personnel:
Executive Director: Millicent Gorham
    E-Mail: millicent@nbna.org
Coordinator, Membership Services and Advertising: Patricia Gray
    E-Mail: patgray@nbna.org
Manager, Membership Services: Estella Lazenby
    E-Mail: elazenby@nbna.org
Manager, Conference Services: Dianne Mance
    E-Mail: dmance@nbna.org
Contact, Administration: Frederick George Thomas
    E-Mail: fthomas@nbna.org

Historical Note:
NBNA strives to improve the quality of life of persons who share the African American heritage and other ethnic groups. Members are African American registered, licensed vocational/practical nurses, nursing students and retired nurses throughout the United States. Membership: $2,000 (Lifetime); $150 (RN/LPN/LVN); $35 (Student); $75 (1st Year Graduate); $75 (Retired).

Meetings/Conferences: Annual
Conference Chair: Dianne Mance
2013 - New Orleans, LA (Hyatt Regency New Orleans)/ July 31 - Aug. 4
Number of non-conference events/year: 3

Publications:
Journal of The NBNA (JNBNA); semi-annually; adv.
NBNA News; quarterly; adv.

National Black Police Association (1972)
3100 Main St.
Suite 256
Dallas, TX 75226
Tel: (855) 879-6272
E-Mail: nbpanatofc@worldnet.att.net
Website: blackpolice.org
Members: 130 associations
Staff: 2
Annual Budget: $100-250,000

Personnel:
Fiscal Officer: Donna Ross
    E-Mail: dross@blackpolice.org

Historical Note:
NBPA's mission is to increase the awareness of the community, to be the conscience of the Criminal Justice System, and to enhance the quality of life in the African American Community. Membership: $100 (Individual); $200 (Organization).

Publications:
Membership Directory; on-line
NBPA Advocate Newsletter; quarterly; adv.

National Black Public Relations Society (1987)
14636 Runnymede St.
Van Nuys, CA 91405
TollFree: (888) 976-0005
Website: nbprs.org
Members:
5 chapters
2500 individuals
Staff: 3
Annual Budget: $25-50,000
Tax: 501(c)(3)

Personnel:
President: Deborah Hyman
 E-Mail: deborah.hyman@nbprs.org
Contact, Membership Services: Chanda Johnson
 E-Mail: chanda.johnson@nbprs.org

Historical Note:
NBPRS aims to serve as an advocate for black professionals in the public relations, media relations, corporate communications, investor relations, government affairs, community relations and related fields. NBPRS strives to nurture, enlighten and inform its membership about new technologies and techniques, and goal is to empower entrepreneurs and practitioners to network and succeed. Membership: $99 (Professional); $25 (Student).

Meetings/Conferences: Annual

Membership List Available to Non-members

National Blacksmiths and Weldors Association
(1875)
P.O. Box 123
Arnold, NE 69120
Website: arcat.com/arcatcos/cos40/
 arc40213.html
Members: 250 individuals
Staff: 4
Annual Budget: Under $10,000

Personnel:
President: Mark Knapp
Editor: Helen Hart
 E-Mail: dhart@ndsupernet.com
Information Officer: James E. Holman
Contact, Membership Services: Terry Rodman

Historical Note:
Formerly (1875) known as Horseshoers Association. In 1895 the Horseshoers and Blacksmiths joined together to form one association. In 1892 the National Blacksmiths and Weldors Association was chartered. NBWA's mission is to organize and offer assistance to state organizations for the advancement of their members with education and guiding measures for the present and future prospects of the trade. Membership principally in the Midwest. Membership: $40/year.

National Block and Bridle Club (1919)
IFAS - Dept. of Animal Sciences, University of Florida
P.O. Box 110910
Gainesville, FL 32611-0910
Tel: (352) 392-7560 *Fax:* (352) 392-7652
Website: blockandbridle.org
Members: 87 active chapters
Staff: 4
Annual Budget: Under $10,000

Personnel:
Editor: Joel V. Yelich
 E-Mail: yelich@ufl.edu

Historical Note:
Professional fraternity of men and women working in animal husbandry. NBBC's mission is to promote a higher scholastic standard and a more complete understanding of Animal Science among student members. NBBC shares national affiliation with American Society of Animal Science.

Meetings/Conferences: Annual

Publications:
Newsletter

National Board for Certification in Occupational Therapy, Inc.
12 S. Summit Ave.
Suite 100
Gaithersburg, MD 20877
Tel: (301) 990-7979 *Fax:* (301) 869-8492

E-Mail: info@nbcot.org
Website: nbcot.org
Staff: 2
Annual Budget: $10-25,000,000
Tax: 501(c)(6)

Personnel:
President and Chief Executive Officer: Paul Grace CAE, MS
 E-Mail: paul.grace@nbcot.org
Director, Credentialing Services: Shaun Conway OTR

Historical Note:
NBCOT is a credentialing agency that provides certification for the occupational therapy profession. Serves the public interest by developing, administering and continually reviewing a certification process that reflects current standards of competent practice in occupational therapy.NBCOT's mission is to serve the public interest. NBCOT provides a world-class standard for certification of occupational therapy practitioners.

Continuing Education:
Certification Designation/s: COTA, OTR

Publications:
Report To The Profession; quarterly

National Board for Certified Clinical Hypnotherapists (1991)
1110 Fiddler Ln.
Suite 1218
Silver Spring, MD 20910
Tel: (301) 608-0123 *Fax:* (301) 588-9535
TollFree: (800) 449-8144
E-Mail: admin@natboard.com
Website: natboard.com
Members: 2900 individuals
Staff: 5
Annual Budget: $100-250,000

Personnel:
Executive Director, Administration: Ron Klein
Executive Director, Certification: Judy Pearson PhD
 E-Mail: judy@engagethepower.com
Office Manager: Elaine Garson
 E-Mail: admin@natboard.com
Deputy Director and Editor: Sandy Silbermann
 E-Mail: ssilbes@aol.com

Historical Note:
NBCCH mission is to improve the quality of hypnotherapeutic services rendered to the public. Membership: $65/year.

Continuing Education:
Certification Designation/s: NBCCH, NBCDCH, NBCFCH, NBCFCH-PS, NBCCH-PS, NBCDCH-PS

Publications:
Interlink Newsletter; irregular
Membership Directory; on-line

National Board for Certified Counselors (1982)
Three Terrace Way
Greensboro, NC 27403-3660
E-Mail: nbcc@nbcc.org
Website: nbcc.org
Members: 42000 counselors
Staff: 66
Annual Budget: $5-10,000,000

Personnel:
Director, Human Resources: Katrina Gooch
Manager, Information Technology: Bob Henegar

Historical Note:
NBCC is an independent not-for-profit credentialing body for counselors that works to establish and monitor a national certification system, to identify those counselors who have voluntarily sought and obtained certification, and to maintain a register of those counselors. It also serves as a certification organization that provides testing and credentialing to professionals in counseling and mental health care.

Continuing Education:
Certification Designation/s: NCGC, NCCC, CCMHC, NCSC, NCC, MAC

Meetings/Conferences: Annual

Publications:
The National Certified Counselor; adv.

National Board for Professional Teaching Standards (NBPTS) (1987)
1525 Wilson Blvd.
Suite 500
Arlington, VA 22209

Tel: (703) 465-2700 *Fax:* (703) 465-2715
TollFree: (800) 228-3224
Website: nbpts.org
Staff: 116
Annual Budget: $50-100,000,000

Personnel:
President and Chief Executive Officer: Ronald Thorpe
Media Contact: April Jones
 E-Mail: ajones@nbpts.org

Historical Note:
NBPTS is dedicated to advance quality teaching and learning. A nonprofit organization focusing on educational reform and advancing the quality of teaching and learning by maintaining rigorous standards for accomplished teachers, providing a national voluntary system certifying teachers who meet these standards and advocating related education reforms to integrate National Board Certification in American education and to capitalize on the expertise of National Board Certified Teachers.

Continuing Education:
Certification Designation/s: NBCT

National Board for Respiratory Care (1960)
18000 W. 105th St.
Olathe, KS 66061-7543
Tel: (913) 895-4900 *Fax:* (913) 895-4650
TollFree: (888) 341-4811
E-Mail: nbrc-info@nbrc.org
Website: nbrc.org
Staff: 9
Annual Budget: $5-10,000,000

Personnel:
President: Kerry E. George MEd, RRT
Chief Executive Officer and Executive Director: Gary L. Smith
Chief Financial Officer: Scott M. Hermansen CPA

Historical Note:
NBRC'S mission is to provide high quality voluntary credentialing examinations for practitioners of respiratory therapy and pulmonary function technology, establish standards to credential practitioners to work under medical direction. American Registry of Inhalation Therapists (ARIT) was incorporated as a not-for-profit corporation. This organization has responded to the growth of the profession through the years and has evolved as the current NBRC. Applied Measurement Professionals, Inc. (AMP), is a wholly-owned subsidiary of the NBRC.

Publications:
Newsletter

National Board of Boiler and Pressure Vessel Inspectors (1919)
1055 Crupper Ave.
Columbus, OH 43229-1183
Tel: (614) 888-8320 *Fax:* (614) 888-0750
E-Mail: information@nationalboard.org
Website: nationalboard.org
Members: 60 jurisdictions
Staff: 70
Annual Budget: $10-25,000,000
Tax: 501(c)(4)

Personnel:
Executive Director: David A. Douin
Assistant Executive Director, Administration: Richard L. Allison
Director, Public Affairs: Paul Brennan
 E-Mail: pbrennan@nationalboard.org
Manager, Training: Kimberly Miller
 E-Mail: kmiller@nationalboard.org
Editor: Wendy Witherow
Assistant Executive Director, Technical: Chuck Withers
 E-Mail: cwithers@nationalboard.org

Historical Note:
NBIC promotes greater safety to life and property through uniformity in the construction, installation, repair, maintenance, and inspection of pressure equipment. Members are the chief boiler inspectors.

Meetings/Conferences: Annual
2013 - Miami, FL (Hyatt Regency Miami)/May 13 - 17
2014 - Bellevue, WA (Hyatt Regency Bellevue)/May 12 - 16
2015 - Colorado Springs, CO (The Broadmoor)/April 27 - May 1
2016 - Orlando, FL (Gaylord Palms Resort and Convention Center-Orlando)/May 9 - 13

Publications:
Manufacturer and Repair Directory; on-line
Pressure Relief Device Certifications; monthly

National Board of Medical Examiners (1915)
3750 Market St.,
Philadelphia, PA 19104-3102
Tel: (215) 590-9500
Website: nbme.org
Staff: 1
Annual Budget: Over $100,000,000

Personnel:
President: Donald E. Melnick

Historical Note:
National Board of Medical Examiners (NBME) is an independent, not-for-profit organization that serves the public through its high- quality assessments of healthcare professionals.

Publications:
NBME Examiner

National Book Critics Circle (1974)
160 Varick St
11th Floor
New York, NY 10013
E-Mail: info@bookcritics.org
Website: bookcritics.org
Members: 650 individuals
Staff: 6
Annual Budget: $25-50,000
Tax: 501(c)(3)

Personnel:
Vice President, Awards and Media Contact: Barbara Hoffert
   E-Mail: hoffer@reedbusiness.com

Historical Note:
NBCC's mission is to honor outstanding writing and supports a national conversation about reading, criticism and literature. Membership: $15 (Non-voting Student); $25 (Non-voting Associate); $40-75 (Voting); $30 (Regular Voting); $500 (Lifetime Voting).

Publications:
NBCC Newsletter; on-line
Critical Mass blog; on-line
NBCC's Newswire; on-line; adv.

National Border Patrol Council (1967)
P.O. Box 47208
Tampa, FL 33647
Tel: (813) 390-1339
E-Mail: nbpc-info@nbpc.net
Website: nbpc.net
Members: 17,000 Border Patrol Agents
Staff: 8
Annual Budget: $1-2,000,000
Tax: 501(c)(3)

Personnel:
President: George McCubbin III

Historical Note:
NBPC is a professional labor union representing border patrol agents and support staff.

National Braille Association (1945)
95 Allens Creek Rd.
Building One, Suite 202
Rochester, NY 14618
Tel: (585) 427-8260 *Fax:* (585) 427-0263
Website: nationalbraille.org
Staff: 1
Annual Budget: $250-500,000

Personnel:
Executive Director: David Shaffer

Historical Note:
Formerly (1964) National Braille Club. NBA is dedicated to providing continuing education to those who prepare braille, and to providing braille materials to persons who are visually impaired. Mission is to provide continuing education to those who prepare braille, and to provide braille materials to persons who are visually impaired. Membership: $50-55 (Regular); $60 (Sustaining); $150 (Patron).

Meetings/Conferences:
2013 - Washington, DC (Hilton Washington DC North/ Gaithersburg)/April 18 - 20

Publications:
Bulletin/Journal; quarterly; adv.

The National Building Granite Quarries Association (1917)
1220 L St. NW

Suite 100-167
Washington, DC 20005
Tel: (800) 557-2848
TollFree: (800) 557-2848
Website: nbgqa.com
Members: 10 companies
Staff: 2
Annual Budget: $10-25,000

Personnel:
Secretary: Kurt M. Swenson

Historical Note:
Members are producers of granite blocks and slabs for architectural applications. NBGDA provides current quarrying and fabrication specifications for member quarries. Membership fee varies, based on sales volume.

National Bulk Vendors Association (1950)
1202 E. Maryland Ave.
Suite One K
Phoenix, AZ 85014
Tel: (480) 302-5998 *Fax:* (480) 302-5108
TollFree: (888) 628-2872
Website: nbva.org
Members: 300 Companies
Staff: 4
Annual Budget: $100-250,000
Tax: 501(c)(6)

Personnel:
President: Steve Schechner
Administrator: Amy Contre
Treasurer: Judi Heston
Co-chair, Conference: Diane Olson

Historical Note:
Founded as the National Vendors Association; assumed its present name in 1977. NBVA is dedicated to addressing the needs of its members, ensuring the stability of the industry as a whole by promoting individual growth and success. Members are makers and operators of bulk vending equipment and supplies. Membership:$100-$1500

Meetings/Conferences:
Conference Chair: Diane Olson
2013 - Las Vegas, NV (Las Vegas Convention Center)/ March 20 - 22

Publications:
NBVA Newsletter; quarterly

Membership List Available to Non-members

National Business Association (1982)
5151 Beltline Rd.
Suite 1150
Dallas, TX 75254
Tel: (972) 458-0900 *Fax:* (972) 960-9149
TollFree: (800) 456-0440
E-Mail: info@nationalbusiness.org
Website: nationalbusiness.org
Members: 30000 individuals
Staff: 11
Annual Budget: $2-5,000,000
Tax: 501(c)(6)

Personnel:
President: Raj Nisankarao
   E-Mail: raj.n@nationalbusiness.org

Historical Note:
NBA is a national nonprofit organization that assists the self-employed and small business community in achieving their professional and personal goals. Members are small-business owners, entrepreneurs, and professionals. Membership: $144 (Select); $420 (Premium).

Publications:
NBA Newsletter; on-line

National Business Aviation Association (1947)
1200 18th St. NW
Suite 400
Washington, DC 20036-2527
Tel: (202) 783-9000 *Fax:* (202) 331-8364
TollFree: (800) 394-6222
E-Mail: info@nbaa.org
Website: nbaa.org
Members: 8000 companies
Staff: 74
Annual Budget: $25-50,000,000

Personnel:
President and Chief Executive Officer: Edward M. Bolen
   E-Mail: ebolen@nbaa.org
Senior Vice President, Conventions and Forums: Kathleen Blouin

   E-Mail: kblouin@nbaa.org
Chief Operating Officer: Steven J. Brown
   E-Mail: sbrown@nbaa.org
Chief People Officer: Holly Clark
Chief Financial Officer: Marc Freeman
Senior Vice President, Communications: Dan Hubbard
   E-Mail: dhubbard@nbaa.org
Vice President, Operational Excellence and Professional Development: Mike Nichols
   E-Mail: mnichols@nbaa.org
Vice President, Exhibit Services: Linda A. Peters
   E-Mail: lpeters@nbaa.org
Senior Vice President, Government Affairs: Lisa Piccione
   E-Mail: lpiccione@nbaa.org
Senior Vice President, Marketing and Member Services: Chris Strong
   E-Mail: cstrong@nbaa.org
Manager, Human Resources: Michele Terner
   E-Mail: mterner@nbaa.org

Historical Note:
NBAA's mission is to serve members by promoting the aviation interests of organizations utilizing general aviation aircraft for business purposes in the United States and worldwide. Represents interests of the business aviation community. Membership: $45-280 (Corporate/Business Member); $440-2,225 (Associate Member).

Continuing Education:
Certification Designation/s: SEBA, CAM, PDP

Meetings/Conferences:
Conference Chair: Linda A. Peters
2013 - Austin, TX/Feb. 12 - 13
2013 - Geneva, Switzerland/May 14 - 16
2013 - Las Vegas, NV/Oct. 22 - 24
2014 - Geneva, Switzerland/May 13 - 15
2014 - Orlando, FL/Oct. 21 - 23
2015 - Geneva, Switzerland/May 19 - 21
Number of non-conference events/year: 12

Publications:
Business Aviation Insider; bi-monthly; adv.
Membership Directory; on-line
NBAA Exhibitor Update; on-line; adv.
NBAA Update; weekly; adv.

National Business Education Association (1946)
1914 Association Dr.
Reston, VA 20191-1596
Tel: (703) 860-8300 *Fax:* (703) 620-4483
E-Mail: nbea@nbea.org
Website: nbea.org
Members: 11000 individuals
Staff: 4
Annual Budget: $1-2,000,000
Tax: 501(c)(3)

Personnel:
Executive Director: Janet M. Treichel
   E-Mail: nbea@nbea.org
Director, Conventions and Meetings: Laura Sutherland
   E-Mail: lsutherland@nbea.org

Historical Note:
Founded as United Business Education Association through a merger of the Department of Business Education of the National Education Association and the National Council for Business Education. Absorbed the National Business Teachers Association and assumed its present name in 1962. The National Association for Business Teacher Education is a division of NBEA. NBEA is committed to the advancement of the professional interest and competence of its members and provides programs and services that enhance members' professional growth and development. Membership: $80 (Professional); $110 (Professional/ International Society for Business Education); $40 (Student); $50 (Retired); $95-115 (Associate).

Meetings/Conferences: Annual
Conference Chair: Laura Sutherland
2013 - Atlanta, GA (Atlanta Marriott Century Center)/ April 16 - 20
2014 - Los Angeles, CA (JW Marriott Los Angeles L.A. LIVE)/April 15 - 19
2015 - Chicago, IL (Chicago Marriott Downtown Magnificent Mile)/March 31 - April 4
2019 - Chicago, IL (Chicago Marriott Downtown Magnificent Mile)/April 16 - 20

Publications:
Keying In Newsletter; on-line
The Business Education Forum Journal; quarterly; adv.

National Business Group on Health (1974)
20 F St. NW

Suite 200
Washington, DC 20001-6700
Tel: (202) 558-3000 *Fax:* (202) 628-9244
E-Mail: info@businessgrouphealth.org
Website: businessgrouphealth.org
Staff: 34
Annual Budget: $10-25,000,000
Tax: 501(c)(3)

Personnel:
President and Chief Executive Officer: Helen Darling
    E-Mail: darling@businessgrouphealth.org
Vice President, Membership Services: Pamela J. Kalen
    E-Mail: kalen@businessgrouphealth.org
Vice President, Public Policy: Steve Wojcik
    E-Mail: wojcik@businessgrouphealth.org

Historical Note:
A national non-profit organization exclusively devoted to representing the perspective of large employers and providing practical solutions to its' members' most important health care problems. Business Group members, typically Fortune 500 and large public sector employers, provide health coverage for more than 39 million U.S. workers, retirees, and their families.

Meetings/Conferences: Annual

Publications:
Membership Directory; on-line

National Business Incubation Association (1985)
20 E. Cir. Dr.
Suite 37198
Athens, OH 45701-3571
Tel: (740) 593-4331 *Fax:* (740) 593-1996
E-Mail: info@nbia.org
Website: nbia.org
Members: 1900 individuals
Staff: 33
Annual Budget: $1-2,000,000
Tax: 501(c)(3)

Personnel:
Acting Chief Executive Officer: Tracy Kitts
Director, Marketing and Advertising: Kim Barlag
Director, Development: Sheila Buckley
Manager, Membership and Administrative Services: Mary
    Ann Gulino
    E-Mail: mgulino@nbia.org
Director, Policy Analysis and Research: Linda Knopp
    E-Mail: lknopp@nbia.org
Director, Publications: Bridget Lair
Director, Membership Services: Randy Morris
    E-Mail: rmorris@nbia.org
Director, Events and International Programs: Tom
    Strodtbeck
    E-Mail: tstrodtbeck@nbia.org

Historical Note:
NBIA's advances the business creation process to increase entrepreneurial success and individual opportunity, strengthening communities worldwide. Membership: $119 (Emeritus/Student); $329 (Individual Faculty); $525 (Silver); $1,500 (Corporate); $695 (Gold); $995 (Platinum); $750 (Consultant/Vendor/Service Provider).

Continuing Education:
Certification Designation/s: IMCP

Meetings/Conferences: Annual
Conference Chair: Tom Strodtbeck
2013 - Boston, MA (Sheraton)/April 7 - 10

Publications:
Membership Directory; on-line
NBIA Memberabilia
NBIA Review

National Cable & Telecommunications Association (1952)
25 Massachusetts Ave. NW
Suite 100
Washington, DC 20001-1413
Tel: (202) 222-2300
Website: ncta.com
Members: 3189 cable systems and associates
Staff: 85
Annual Budget: $50-100,000,000
Tax: 501(c)(6)

Personnel:
President and Chief Executive Officer: Michael Powell
Senior Vice President, Finance and Administration: Bruce
    Carnes
Senior Vice President, Science and Technology: William
    Check

E-Mail:
    scienceandtechnologydepartment@ncta.com
Vice President, Communications: Brian Dietz
    E-Mail: bdietz@ncta.com
Contact, Meetings: Pamela Ford
    E-Mail: pford@ncta.com
Senior Vice President, Government Relations: Rita M.
    Lewis
    E-Mail: governmentrelationsdepartment@ncta.com
Senior Vice President, Communications and Public Affairs:
    Rob Stoddard
    E-Mail: rstoddard@ncta.com

Historical Note:
Formerly National Cable Television Association, NCTA's mission is to provide its members with a strong national presence by providing a single, unified voice on issues affecting the cable and telecommunications industry. Members are cable TV systems and associate members are manufacturers, distributors, suppliers of hardware, programmers and other services. Membership: $1,575-29, 418 (Associate); $1734-82,112 (Programmer); $1050 (Affiliate).

Meetings/Conferences: Annual
Conference Chair: Pamela Ford
2013 - Washington, DC/June 10 - 12

Publications:
NCTA Newsletter; monthly

The National Campus Ministry Association (1964)
13339 Bolingbrook Ln.
Charlotte, NC 28273-0955
Tel: (704) 588-0183
E-Mail: ncma.info@gmail.com
Website: campusministry.net
Members: 350 individuals
Staff: 1
Annual Budget: $25-50,000

Personnel:
President: Paul Walley

Historical Note:
NCMA's mission strives to be a professional organization educating, encouraging, and equipping those engaged in the practice of ministry in higher education. Membership: $25-120/year.

Meetings/Conferences: Annual

Publications:
Membership Directory; on-line
NCMA Newsletter; quarterly

National Cancer Registrars Association (1974)
1340 Braddock Pl.
Suite 203
Alexandria, VA 22314
Tel: (703) 299-6640 *Fax:* (703) 299-6620
E-Mail: info@ncra-usa.org
Website: ncra-usa.org
Members: 5000 individuals
Staff: 8
Annual Budget: $1-2,000,000
Tax: 501(c)(6)

Personnel:
Executive Director: Lori Swain
    E-Mail: lswain@ncra-usa.org
Manager, Operations: Nancy Allen
    E-Mail: narmel@ncra-usa.org
Manager, Membership: Janice Ford
    E-Mail: jford@ncra-usa.org
*Coordinator, Continuing Education and Membership
    Services:* Robin Havens
    E-Mail: ce@ncra-usa.org
Director, Membership Services and Credentialing: Michael
    Hechter
    E-Mail: mhechter@ncra-usa.org
Manager, Education Programs: Mary Maul
    E-Mail: mmaul@ncra-usa.org
Coordinator, Marketing: Paula Spitler
    E-Mail: pspitler@ncra-usa.org
Administrative Assistant: Angel Valant

Historical Note:
Formerly (1993) National Tumor Registrars Association. NCRA's mission is to improve lives through quality cancer data management. NCRA represents Cancer Registrars who capture a complete summary of patient history, diagnosis, treatment, and status for every cancer patient in the United States. Membership: $105 (Active); $50 (Inactive); $200 (Sustaining); $90 (Associate); $65 (International); $40 (Student).

Continuing Education:

Certification Designation/s: CTR

Meetings/Conferences: Annual
Conference Chair: Nancy Allen
2013 - San Francisco, CA/May 29 - June 1/26-50
    exhibitors
2013 - San Francisco, CA (Hilton Union Square)/May
    30 - June 2
2014 - Nashville, TN/May 14 - 17/26-50 exhibitors

Publications:
Journal of Registry Management; quarterly; adv.
Membership Directory; on-line
The Connection; quarterly; adv.

Membership List Available to Non-members

National Candle Association (1974)
529 14th St. NW
Suite 750
Washington, DC 20045
Tel: (202) 393-2210 *Fax:* (202) 331-2714
E-Mail: info@candles.org
Website: candles.org
Members: 90 candle manufacturers and suppliers
Staff: 6
Annual Budget: $500-1,000,000
Tax: 501(c)(6)

Personnel:
President: Bob Nelson
Director, Membership Services: Mila Albertson
contact, media: Barbara Miller CCC-SLP, MA

Historical Note:
NCA represents the candle industry to promote the safe use and enjoyment of candles, monitor and respond to issues impacting the industry, and advance the industry as a whole. It maintains a technical committee, providing research on topics relevant to the industry. Membership: $2,310-48,510 (Regular); $2,888-11,550 (Associate/ Affiliate).

Meetings/Conferences: Annual
2013 - Hollywood, FL/July 8 - 11

National Cannabis Industry Association (2010)
P.O. Box 78062
Washington, DC 20013
Tel: (202) 379-4861 *Fax:* (202) 232-0442
E-Mail: Info@TheCannabisIndustry.org
Website: thecannabisindustry.org
Members: 60 companies
Staff: 2
Annual Budget: $25-50,000
Tax: 501(c)(6)

Personnel:
Executive Director: F. Aaron Smith

Historical Note:
NCIA advocates for and represents the interests of the cannabis industry and its consumers . Members are businesses involved in the cannabis industry. Mission is to promote the growth of a responsible and legitimate cannabis industry and to work for a favorable social, economic and legal environment for that industry in the United States. Membership is comprised of the leading businesses and organizations in America's emerging cannabis industry. Membership: $1,000 (Regular); $2,500 (Sponsoring); $5,000 (Sustaining).

National Career Development Association (1913)
305 N. Beech Cir.
Broken Arrow, OK 74012
Tel: (918) 663-7060 *Fax:* (918) 663-7058
TollFree: (866) 367-6232
Website: associationdatabase.com/aws/NCDA/
    pt/sp/Home
Members: 4500 individuals
Staff: 5
Annual Budget: $100-250,000

Personnel:
Executive Director: Deneen Pennington
    E-Mail: dpennington@ncda.org
Director, Conventions and Education: Bobbi Carter
    E-Mail: bcarter@ncda.org
Director, Membership Services and Publications: Natalie
    Scrimsher
    E-Mail: nscrimsher@ncda.org

Historical Note:
Founded as the National Vocational Guidance Association. Assumed its present name in 1985. NCDA is a division of the American Counseling Association (ACA). NCDA's mission is to inspire and empower the achievement of career and life goals by providing professional development,

resources, standards, scientific research, and advocacy. Members are counselors and career development professionals who work in education, business/industry, community agencies, military installations and private practice. Membership: $65 (Regular); $28 (New Professional/Student); $40 (Retired).

Meetings/Conferences: Annual
Conference Chair: Bobbi Carter
2013 - Boston, MA (Westin Boston Waterfront)/July 8 - 10

Publications:
Career Convergence; monthly
Career Development Quarterly; quarterly; adv.
Career Developments; quarterly
Membership Directory; on-line
NCDA Newsletter; on-line; adv.

Membership List Available to Non-members

National Cargo Bureau (1952)
17 Battery Pl.
Suite 1232
New York, NY 10004-1110
Tel: (212) 785-8300 Fax: (212) 785-8333
E-Mail: ncbnyc@natcargo.org
Website: natcargo.org
Members: 205 businesses
Staff: 135
Annual Budget: $10-25,000,000

Personnel:
President: Ian J. Lennard
Chief, Technical Department: Philip I. Anderson
Chief Financial Officer: Richard Nagle

Historical Note:
Formed by the merger of the Bureau of Inspection of the Board of Underwriters of New York (founded in 1820) and the Board of Marine Underwriters of San Francisco (founded in 1886). Purpose is to promote the safe loading, stowage, securing and unloading of cargo on all vessels.

National Cartoonists Society (1946)
341 N. Maitland Ave.
Suite 130
Maitland, FL 32751
Tel: (407) 647-8839 Fax: (407) 629-2502
E-Mail: info@reuben.org
Website: reuben.org
Members: 500 individuals
Staff: 5
Annual Budget: $100-250,000

Personnel:
President: Tom Richmond
Secretary: John Kovaleski
Contact, Communications: Phil Pyster CAE
E-Mail: phil@crowsegal.com
Treasurer: Jerry Van Amerongen

Historical Note:
NCS seeks to advance professional cartooning standards and ideals, and to promote a social, cultural and intellectual interchange among professional cartoonists of all types. Members are professional cartoonists, individuals who work as professionals in the cartooning industry.

Publications:
Members Directory; on-line

National Catholic Band Association (1953)
Office of Music Activities, Villanova University
800 E. Lancaster Ave.
Villanova, PA 19085
E-Mail: info@catholicbands.org
Website: catholicbands.org
Members: 150 individuals
Staff: 2
Annual Budget: Under $10,000
Tax: 501(c)(3)

Personnel:
President: Rick Mlynarski
Chair, Conferences: George Pinchock
E-Mail: george.pinchock@villanova.edu

Historical Note:
Formerly (1993) National Catholic Bandmasters' Association. NCBA works for the development of Catholic School Band. Members are qualified band directors who teach in a Catholic grammar school, high school or college, and to woodwind, brass or percussion instructors in a Catholic band program. Membership: $40/year.

Meetings/Conferences: Annual
Conference Chair: George Pinchock
Number of non-conference events/year: 2

Publications:
Membership Directory; annually
NCBA Newsletter; bi-monthly

National Catholic College Admission Association (1959)
P.O. Box 267
New Albany, OH 43054
Tel: (614) 633-5444 Fax: (614) 839-9232
E-Mail: masek@nationalccaa.org
Website: catholiccollegesonline.org
Staff: 1
Annual Budget: $250-500,000
Tax: 501(c)(3)

Personnel:
Executive Director: Joyce Masek
E-Mail: masek@nationalccaa.org

Historical Note:
National CCAA is a non-profit organization of Catholic colleges and universities committed to promoting the value of Catholic higher education and serving students in the transition to college.

National Catholic Development Conference (1968)
86 Front St.
Hempstead, NY 11550-3667
Tel: (516) 481-6000 Fax: (516) 489-9287
TollFree: (888) 879-6232
Website: ncdc.org
Members: 500 organizations
Staff: 6
Annual Budget: $500-1,000,000

Personnel:
President and Chief Executive Officer: Georgette Lehmuth OSF
E-Mail: glehmuth@ncdc.org
Associate Director, Membership Communications: John D. Baldwin
E-Mail: jbaldwin@ncdc.org
Associate Director, Finance and Information Management: Robert E. (Bob) Cupo
E-Mail: bcupo@ncdc.org
Associate Director, Programming and Publicity: Rachel Donofrio
E-Mail: rdonofrio@ncdc.org

Historical Note:
NCDC's mission is to lead Catholic organizations toward excellence in their development ministries by providing opportunities for growth in leadership and excellence through conferences and networking. Members are religious fund raising organizations including development officers and key fund raisers of charitable institutions and agencies, religious orders, dioceses and educational institutions. Membership: $400-4,400 (Active); $500-1,700 (Associate); $500-1,500 (Corporate/Diocese).

Continuing Education:
Certification Designation/s: CFRE

Meetings/Conferences: Annual

Publications:
Breaking News; on-line; adv.
Conference; on-line
Dimensions; on-line; adv.
E-News; on-line
E-ssentials; on-line
Jobs E-bulletin; on-line
Membership Directory; on-line; adv.
Newswire; on-line
Workshops/Program Announcements; on-line

Membership List Available to Non-members

National Catholic Educational Association (1904)
1005 N. Glebe Rd.
Suite 525
Arlington, VA 22201
Tel: (800) 711-6232 Fax: (703) 243-0025
TollFree: (800) 711-6232
E-Mail: nceaadmin@ncea.org
Website: ncea.org
Members: 24000 individuals and institutions
Staff: 31
Annual Budget: $5-10,000,000
Tax: 501(c)(3)

Personnel:
Executive Director: Regina M. Haney EdD
E-Mail: haney@ncea.org
President: Karen M. Ristau EdD

E-Mail: president@ncea.org
Membership Service Representative: Quitina Armstead
E-Mail: qabrown@ncea.org
Director, Information Technology: Cedric Bernescut
E-Mail: bernescut@ncea.org
Director, Events: Amy Durkin CEM
E-Mail: ADurkin@ncea.org
Director, Communications: Barbara A. Keebler
E-Mail: keebler@ncea.org
Associate Chief Operating Officer: Wade Marshall
E-Mail: marshall@ncea.org
Director, Public Policy and Educational Research: Sr. Dale McDonald PBVM, PhD
E-Mail: mcdonald@ncea.org
Director, Marketing: Kate Reich

Historical Note:
Formerly Catholic Education Association. NCEA includes the Association of Catholic Colleges and Universities (ACCU), Chief Administrators of Catholic Education and the National Association for Parish Coordinators and Directors of Religion Education (NPCD). NCEA provides leadership, direction and service to fulfill the evangelizing, catechizing and teaching mission of the Church. Membership: $165 (Individual); $80 (Student); $120-360 (Chief Administrators Department); $50-350 (Religious Education Department); $165-750 (Seminary Department); $200-335 (Board of Education); $240-645 (Elementary School Membership); $155 (Early Childhood); $300-1080 (Secondary School).

Meetings/Conferences: Annual
Conference Chair: Amy Durkin CEM
2013 - Houston, TX (George R. Brown Convention Center)/April 2 - 4/1-10 exhibitors
Number of non-conference events/year: 3

Publications:
Membership Directory; annually
Momentum; bi-monthly; adv.
NCEA Notes

National Catholic Educational Exhibitors (1950)
1005 N. Glebe Rd.
Suite 525
Arlington, VA 22201
Tel: (800) 711-6232 Fax: (703) 243-0025
Website: ncea.org
Members:
350 companies
500 individuals
Staff: 9
Annual Budget: $25-50,000

Personnel:
Executive Director: Regina M. Haney
Director, Information Technology: Cedric Bernescut
E-Mail: network@ncea.org
Director, Conventions and Meeting: Amy Durkin CEM
E-Mail: adurkin@ncea.org
Editor: Brian Gray
E-Mail: momentum@ncea.org
Director, Communications: Barbara A. Keebler
E-Mail: keebler@ncea.org
Director, Administrative and Member Services: Wade Marshall
E-Mail: marshall@ncea.org
Director, Public Policy and Educational Research: Sister Dale McDonald
E-Mail: mcdonald@ncea.org
Administrative Assistant: Jessica Randazzo
Director, Finance: Philip Reilly

Historical Note:
NCEE represents companies and individuals who exhibit at Catholic shows, and aims to help them develop better quality and confidence in their exhibited products and services. Associate members are 150 Catholic school superintendents and administrators. Membership: $150 (Corporate); $10 (Associate).

Meetings/Conferences: Annual
Conference Chair: Amy Durkin CEM
2013 - Houston, TX (George R. Brown Convention Center)/April 2 - 4
2014 - Pittsburgh, PA/April 22 - 24
2015 - Orlando, FL/April 7 - 9
Number of non-conference events/year: 1-10

Publications:
Momentum; quarterly
NCEE Directory; annually
NCEE News; quarterly

National Cattlemen's Beef Association (1898)

9110 E. Nichols Ave.
Suite 300
Centennial, CO 80112
Tel: (303) 694-0305 *Fax:* (303) 694-2851
TollFree: (866) 233-3872
Website: beefusa.org
Members: 36000 individuals and 130 associations
Staff: 193
Annual Budget: $50-100,000,000
Tax: 501(c)(6)

Personnel:
Chief Executive Officer: Forrest Roberts
  E-Mail: froberts@beef.org
Chief Financial Officer: Douglas L. Evans
  E-Mail: devans@beef.org
Executive Director, Conventions and Meetings: Debbie Kaylor
  E-Mail: dkaylor@beef.org
Vice President, Association Marketing: Marvin Kokes
  E-Mail: mkokes@beef.org
Senior Vice President, Research and Education: James Reagan
  E-Mail: jreagan@beef.org
Coordinator, Administration and Membership Services: Sheryl Slagle
  E-Mail: sslagle@beef.org

Historical Note:
Formed as National Cattlemen's Association as the result of a merger of American National Cattlemen's Association and National Livestock Feeders Association (founded 1943). Absorbed National Livestock Tax Committee in 1978. NCBA's mission is to provide unified efforts on behalf of the beef industry to increase market share and provide quality meat. Membership: $50 (Student); $150 (Business); $100 (Individual); $100- 750 (Producer).

Meetings/Conferences: Annual
Conference Chair: Debbie Kaylor
2013 - Tampa, FL (Tampa Bay Convention Center)/Feb. 6 - 9/6000 attendees
2014 - Nashville, TN (Gaylord Hotels Resorts and Convention Centers-Nashville)/Feb. 4 - 7/6000 attendees
2015 - San Antonio, TX (San Antonio Convention Center)/Feb. 4 - 7/6000 attendees
2017 - Nashville, TN/Feb. 1 - 4
Number of non-conference events/year: 2

Publications:
Beltway Beef newsletter
Daily News; daily
eUpdate newsletter; on-line
National Cattlemen

National Caves Association (1965)
92 Hidden Dr.
Camdenton, MO 65020
Tel: (573) 836-2256
E-Mail: caveinfo@cavern.com
Website: cavern.com
Members: 95 cave operators
Staff: 2
Annual Budget: $100-250,000
Tax: 501(c)(6)

Personnel:
General Manager and Vice President: Steve Thompson
  E-Mail: steve@bridalcave.com

Historical Note:
NCA is a non-profit organization which sets and maintains standards for show caves throughout the country. Membership: $300-650/year.

Meetings/Conferences:
Conference Chair: Diane Thompson

Membership List Available to Non-members

National Center for Asia-Pacific Economic Cooperation
500 Union St.
Suite 300
Seattle, WA 98101
Tel: (206) 441-9022 *Fax:* (206) 441-1006
E-Mail: info@ncapec.org
Website: ncapec.org
Members: 21 members
Staff: 7
Annual Budget: $2-5,000,000

Personnel:
Executive Vice President: Robert Modarelli III

President: Monica Hardy Whaley
Administrator, Human Resources and Finance: Marilou Christiansen
Director, Finance, Operations and Programs: Linda Eng

Historical Note:
The National Center for APEC is a member-driven business organization focused exclusively on facilitating American private sector input to the APEC process.

Meetings/Conferences: Annual

Publications:
APEC Insights; quarterly

National Center for Assisted Living
1201 L St. NW
Washington, DC 20005
Tel: (202) 842-4444 *Fax:* (202) 842-3860
E-Mail: sosborne@ncal.org
Website: ncal.org
Staff: 3

Personnel:
President and Chief Executive Officer: Mark Parkinson
Director, Public Affairs: Lisa Gelhaus
  E-Mail: lgelhaus@ncal.org
Contact, Communications: Shane Osborne
  E-Mail: sosborne@ncal.org

Historical Note:
The National Center for Assisted Living (NCAL) is the assisted living voice of the American Health Care Association (AHCA). NCAL is dedicated to serving the needs of the assisted living community through national advocacy, education, networking, professional development, and quality initiatives.NCAL aims to to help assisted living professionals, serving its members through consumer education, network opportunities, public affairs and professional development.

Meetings/Conferences: Annual
2013 - Ft. Lauderdale, FL (Westin Beach Resort and Spa)/March 12 - 13

Publications:
AHCA Notes; monthly
NCAL Connections
NCAL Focus; monthly
Provider; monthly

National Center for Employee Ownership (1981)
1736 Franklin St.
Eighth Floor
Oakland, CA 94612-3445
Tel: (510) 208-1300 *Fax:* (510) 272-9510
E-Mail: customerservice@nceo.org
Website: nceo.org
Members: 3000 members
Staff: 10
Annual Budget: $1-2,000,000
Tax: 501(c)(3)

Personnel:
Executive Director: Loren Rodgers
  E-Mail: LRodgers@nceo.org
Assistant, Meeting, Marketing, and Membership Services: Becky Chavez
  E-Mail: RChavez@nceo.org
Administrative Assistant: Monica Dozier-Brame
  E-Mail: MDozier@nceo.org
Director, Research: Camille Kerr
  E-Mail: CKerr@nceo.org
Director, Conference: Deborah Krant CMP
  E-Mail: DKrant@nceo.org
Director, Publishing and Information Technology: Scott Rodrick
  E-Mail: SRodrick@nceo.org

Historical Note:
NCEO's mission is to provide the most objective and reliable information possible on employee ownership at the most affordable price possible. Membership: $90 (Associate, in U.S.); $100 (Associate, outside U.S.); $350 (Referral Service); $40 (Academic); $50 (Academic, outside the U.S.).

Meetings/Conferences: Annual
Conference Chair: Deborah Krant CMP
2013 - Seattle, WA (Westin Seattle)/April 24 - 26
Number of non-conference events/year: 1

Publications:
Membership Directory; on-line
NCEO Newsletter; bi-monthly

National Center for Homeopathy (1974)
101 S. Whiting St.

Suite 315
Alexandria, VA 22304
Tel: (703) 548-7790 *Fax:* (703) 548-7792
TollFree: (877) 624-0613
E-Mail: info@nationalcenterforhomeopathy.org
Website: nationalcenterforhomeopathy.org
Members: 6000 individuals
Staff: 6
Annual Budget: $500-1,000,000

Personnel:
Executive Director: Sharon Stevenson
Director, Communications: Peter Gold
Managing Editor: Mitzi Lebensorger

Historical Note:
Formerly associated with the American Foundation for Homoeopathy, but now independent. Mission is to promote health through homeopathy. Membership: $49.00 (new members)

Publications:
Homeopathy Today; quarterly; adv.
NCH Newsletter; monthly

National Center for Housing Management (1972)
333 N. First St.
Suite 305
Jacksonville Beach, FL 32250
Tel: (800) 368-5625 *Fax:* (866) 571-5660
TollFree: (800) 368-5625
Website: nchm.org
Staff: 3
Annual Budget: $2-5,000,000

Personnel:
President: Glenn W. Stevens
Chief Operating Officer: Martha Abrams-Bell
Trainer, Certifications: Shane Knutson

Historical Note:
NCHM's mission is to provide objective and independent leadership at the national level in helping meet the Nation's housing management and training needs.

Continuing Education:
Certification Designation/s: COS, HMOC

Publications:
Housing Management Update; monthly
NCHM eNews; on-line

National Center for Manufacturing Sciences (1986)
3025 Boardwalk
Ann Arbor, MI 48108
Fax: (734) 995-0380
TollFree: (800) 222-6267
E-Mail: info@ncms.org
Website: ncms.org
Staff: 3
Annual Budget: $10-25,000,000
Tax: 501(c)(3)

Personnel:
Manager, Membership Services: Alissa Roath
  E-Mail: alissar@ncms.org

Historical Note:
NCMS's mission is to provide project management for collaborative R&D and has evolved with manufacturers now to provide products, services, and initiatives designed to further the overall goal of improving competitiveness in the global market.

Publications:
Membership directory; on-line

National Center for Simulation (1993)
3039 Technology Pkwy.
Orlando, FL 32826
Tel: (407) 384-6111 *Fax:* (407) 384-0043
Website: simulationinformation.com
Staff: 1

Personnel:
President and Executive Director: Thomas L. Baptiste USAF(Ret.)
  E-Mail: tbaptiste@simulationinformation.com

Historical Note:
The vision for NCS is to be the internationally recognized leader in supporting and expanding the modeling and simulation community. Membership: $25/year (Student).

Publications:
Member Directory
The Simulator Newsletter; adv.

National Center for State Courts (1971)

300 Newport Ave.
Williamsburg, VA 23185
Tel: (800) 616-6164 *Fax:* (757) 220-0449
TollFree: (800) 616-6164
Website: ncsc.org
Staff: 140
Annual Budget: $25-50,000,000
Tax: 501(c)(3)

Personnel:
President: Mary Campbell McQueen
Executive Vice President and General Counsel: Robert N Baldwin
E-Mail: rbaldwin@ncsc.org
Vice President, Research and Technology: Thomas M Clarke
E-Mail: tclarke@ncsc.org
Director, Knowledge and Information Services: Carol R Flango
E-Mail: cflango@ncsc.org
Director , Association and Conference Services: Jennifer Haire
E-Mail: jhaire@ncsc.org
Director, Human Resources: Deborah A Mason
E-Mail: dwhite@ncsc.org
Vice President, External Affairs: Jesse Rutledge
E-Mail: jrutledge@ncsc.org
Chief Financial Officer and Vice President, Finance and Administration: Gwen W Williams
E-Mail: gwilliams@ncsc.org

Historical Note:
NCSC's mission is to improve the administration of justice through leadership and service to state courts, as well as courts around the world.

Continuing Education:
Certification Designation/s: CMP, CEDP

Meetings/Conferences:
Conference Chair: Jennifer Haire

Publications:
e-Newsletters

National Certification Commission (1993)

P.O. Box 15282
Chevy Chase, MD 20825-0282
Tel: (301) 847-0104 *Fax:* (301) 847-0103
E-Mail: certification@usa.com
Website: associationcertification.org
Members:
150 associations
100 individuals
Staff: 3
Annual Budget: $100-250,000

Personnel:
Executive Director: Richard C. Jaffeson ACA, AICP

Historical Note:
NCC provides information and assistance to national associations on development and improvement of certification programs with designations in numerous professions and occupations. Members are associations and individuals with interests in certification policies and procedures. NCC also offers the Advanced Certification Administrator (ACA), Basic Certification Administrator (BCA), Certification Committee Administrator (CCA) and Distinguished Certification Administrator (DCA) designations, and national accreditation of certification programs. Membership: $100 (association/Accreditation); $40-60(Designations);$35(individuals).

Continuing Education:
Enrollment: 100
Certification Designation/s: ACA, BCA, CCA, DCA

Publications:
Career Captions; on-line
Member Directory; on-line

National Certification Commission for Acupuncture and Oriental Medicine (1982)

76 S. Laura St.
Suite 1290
Jacksonville, FL 32202
Tel: (904) 598-1005 *Fax:* (904) 598-5001
E-Mail: info@nccaom.org
Website: nccaom.org
Staff: 20
Annual Budget: $2-5,000,000
Tax: 501(c)(6)

Personnel:
Chief Executive Officer: Kory Ward-Cook CAE, PhD

Director, Administration: Irene Basore
Deputy Director, Media Inquiries, Public Relations and Regulatory Affairs: Mina Larson MS
E-Mail: publicrelations@nccaom.org
Manager, Certification Services: Sheila Lusis
E-Mail: applications@nccaom.org
Manager, Information Technology: Paul May
Specialist, Regulatory Affairs and Research: Stephanie Mills
Director, Finance: Neel Tenali

Historical Note:
NCCAOM's mission is to establish, assess, and promote recognized standards of competence and safety in acupuncture and Oriental medicine for the protection and benefit of the public.

Continuing Education:
Certification Designation/s: ABT

Meetings/Conferences:
Conference Chair: Mina Larson MS

Publications:
Diplomate News You Can Use; on-line
The Diplomate; on-line

Membership List Available to Non-members

National Certification Council for Activity Professionals (1986)

P.O. Box 62589
Virginia Beach, VA 23466-2589
Tel: (757) 552-0653 *Fax:* (757) 552-0491
E-Mail: info@nccap.org
Website: nccap.org
Members: 6600 individuals
Staff: 3
Annual Budget: $250-500,000
Tax: 501(c)(6)

Personnel:
Executive Director: Cindy Bradshaw ACC, BS
E-Mail: nccapexec111@aol.com

Historical Note:
NCCAP is a credentialing body that exclusively certifies activity professionals who work with the elderly. Mission is to directly provide opportunities for and/or information about educational offerings thereby enabling its members and potential members to pursue professional development.

Continuing Education:
Certification Designation/s: ACC, ADC, AAC, ADPC

Publications:
NCCAP News; quarterly; adv.

National Certified Pipe Welding Bureau (1944)

1385 Piccard Dr.
Rockville, MD 20850-4340
Tel: (301) 869-5800 *Fax:* (301) 990-9690
TollFree: (800) 556-3653
Website: mcaa.org/ncpwb
Members: 600 companies
Staff: 2
Annual Budget: $250-500,000

Personnel:
Executive Director: Dariush "Nick" Nikpourfand
E-Mail: nnikpourfard@mcaa.org
Contact, Government Relations: John McNerney
E-Mail: jmcnerney@mcaa.org

Historical Note:
The National Certified Pipe Welding Bureau (NCPWB) is a subsidiary of the Mechanical Contractors Association of America, that was established to keep contractors informed about welding and brazing technology and to simplify welding and brazing qualification practices. Membership: $475/year, plus local chapter fees if applicable.

Continuing Education:
Certification Designation/s: CW

Publications:
Member Directory

National Cheese Institute (1927)

1250 H St. NW
Suite 900
Washington, DC 20005
Tel: (202) 737-4332 *Fax:* (202) 331-7820
Website: idfa.org/about-idfa/boards--committees/national-cheese-institute
Members: 75 manufacturers, distributors and producers
Staff: 24
Annual Budget: $1-2,000,000

Personnel:
President and Chief Executive Officer: Jon Davis
Assistant Director, Membership Services: Cindy Cavallo
E-Mail: membership@idfa.org
President and Chief Operating Officer, Operations: Ron Dunford
Senior Vice President, Supply Chain and Corporate Affairs: Mike Reidy
Vice President, Policy and Legislative Affairs: Ruth Saunders
Senior Vice president, Legislative Affairs and Economic Policy: Jerry Slominski
E-Mail: jslominski@idfa.org

Historical Note:
NCI's mission is to provide information on dairy-related issues for members and the media, and to collaborate with dairy industry partners to protect and enhance the image of dairy. Members are manufacturers, processors and distributors of natural and processed cheese and cheese products.

Meetings/Conferences: Annual
2013 - Orlando, FL (JW Marriott Orlando Grande Lakes)/Jan. 27 - 30/over 100 exhibitors

Publications:
IDFA e-newsletter; weekly
Membership Directory; on-line

Membership List Available to Non-members

National Chemical Credit Association (1938)

1100 Main St.
Buffalo, NY 14209-2356
Tel: (716) 887-9547 *Fax:* (716) 878-0479
E-Mail: robert.gagliardi@abc-amega.com
Website: ncca1.org
Members: 100 companies
Staff: 3
Annual Budget: $250-500,000

Personnel:
Director, Member Group Services: Robert Gagliardi
E-Mail: robert.gagliardi@abc-amega.com

Historical Note:
A national organization of credit professionals. NCCA's mission is to empower its members to make individual credit decisions and to foster education in the profession. NCCA Credit interchange allows members to exchange customer payment experience using a safe, secure, and private web site available only to members of the NCCA. Members are major producers of basic chemicals and allied products.

Meetings/Conferences: Semi-Annual
2013 - Ft. Lauderdale, FL (The Westin Beach Resort)/ Feb. 16 - 17
2013 - Charlotte, NC (Omni Charlotte Hotel)/May 16 - 17
2013 - Houston, TX (Magnolia Hotel)/Nov. 21 - 22
Number of non-conference events/year: 4

National Cherry Growers and Industries Foundation (1948)

2667 Reed Rd.
Hood River, OR 97031
Tel: (541) 386-5761 *Fax:* (541) 386-3191
Website: nationalcherries.com
Members: 1500 growers and industries
Staff: 2
Annual Budget: $100-250,000
Tax: 501(c)(6)

Personnel:
Director, Marketing: Cheryl Kroupa
E-Mail: cheryl@pentel.net

Historical Note:
NCGIF represents the processed cherry industry to lobby against excessive cherry imports. NCGIF was formed for the purpose of having a unified effort from the processed cherry industry to lobby against excessive cherry imports.

National Chicken Council (1954)

1015 15th St. NW
Suite 930
Washington, DC 20005-2622
Tel: (202) 296-2622 *Fax:* (202) 293-4005
E-Mail: ncc@chickenusa.org
Website: nationalchickencouncil.com
Members: 225 companies
Staff: 10
Annual Budget: $2-5,000,000

Personnel:
President: Michael J. Brown

E-Mail: mbrown@chickenusa.org
Vice President, Government Relations: Mary Colville
    E-Mail: mcolville@chickenusa.org
Senior Director, Meetings and Member Communications:
    Margaret Ernst
    E-Mail: mernst@chickenusa.org
Manager, Membership and Information Systems: Wade R.
    Parker
    E-Mail: wparker@chickenusa.org
Vice President, Science and Technology: Ashley Peterson
    PhD
    E-Mail: apeterson@chickenusa.org
Senior Vice President and Chief Economist: William P.
    Roenigk
    E-Mail: wroenigk@chickenusa.org
Vice President, Communications: Tom Super
    E-Mail: tsuper@chickenusa.org

Historical Note:
*Formerly (1954) known as the National Broiler Council
and assumed the current name in 1998. NCC promotes
and protects the interests of the chicken industry and is
the industry's voice before Congress and federal agencies.
Member companies include chicken producer/processors,
poultry distributors, and allied industry firms. Membership:
Processors - fee based on liveweight production; Allied -
supplies to broiler trade industry $2,500 (Basic); $11,500
(Leader); $275 (Distributor).*

Meetings/Conferences: Annual
Conference Chair: Margaret Ernst
Number of non-conference events/year: 4

Publications:
Chicken Scoop
NCC's weekly newsletter; weekly

National Chief Petty Officers' Association (1988)
Six Saint Thomas Ct.
Stafford, VA 22556-3649
Tel: (703) 232-7328
E-Mail: ncpoahays@aol.com
Website: goatlocker.org/ncpoa
Members: 2900 individuals
Staff: 2
Tax: 501(c)(19)

Personnel:
National President and Coordinator, Membership Services:
    Jerry L. Sweeney
    E-Mail: jerrylsweeney@gmail.com

Historical Note:
*NCPOA's purpose is to generate worldwide awareness of
the importance of Regular and Reserve Chief Petty Officers
in the U.S. Navy and Coast Guard of the past, present
and future; to encourage young sailors to appreciate the
importance of study and advancement within the various
ratings of these services and to promote reunions of
members. Membership: $60-330 (Life Membership, based
on age); $15 (New Member).*

Meetings/Conferences: Annual

Publications:
Membership Roster; on-line
NCPOA Newsletter
Netchiefs Roster; on-line

National Child Care Association (1987)
1325 G St. NW
Suite 500
Washington, DC 20005
Tel: (866) 536-1945
E-Mail: info@nccanet.org
Website: nccanet.org
Members: 5000 company sites
Staff: 6
Annual Budget: $250-500,000
Tax: 501(c)(3)

Personnel:
President: Linda Kostantenaco

Historical Note:
*NCCA strives to promote the growth and safeguard the
interest of quality early childhood care and education
focusing on licensed, private providers of these services.
Membership: $88 (Center); $93 (Individual); $35 (Student/
At-Large Members); $405 (Associate).*

Continuing Education:
Certification Designation/s: CCP, NAC
Meetings/Conferences:
Number of non-conference events/year: 2

Publications:
E-Magazine; on-line
NCCA Voice; monthly

Week @ A Glance; weekly; adv.

National Child Support Enforcement Association
(1952)
1760 Old Meadow Rd.
Suite 500
McLean, VA 22102
Tel: (703) 506-2880 *Fax:* (703) 506-3266
E-Mail: ncsea@ncsea.org
Website: ncsea.org
Members: 1972 individual, state, county and
international agencies
Staff: 5
Annual Budget: $500-1,000,000

Personnel:
Executive Director: Colleen Delaney Eubanks CAE
    E-Mail: ColleenEubanks@ncsea.org
Manager, Resource Development: Shaughna Giracca
    E-Mail: sgiracca@ncsea.org
Coordinator, Member Services and Communications: Kristy
    Loftus
    E-Mail: KristyLoftus@ncsea.org
Manager, Association Programs: Ann Marie Ruskin
    E-Mail: AnnMarieRuskin@ncsea.org
Director, Public Relations: Andy Schwartz
    E-Mail: aschwarz@ncsea.org

Historical Note:
*Formerly (1984) the National Conference on Uniform
Reciprocal Enforcement of Support and National Reciprocal
and Family Support Enforcement Association. NCSEA
seeks to serve child support professionals, agencies,
and strategic partners worldwide through professional
development, communications, public awareness, and
advocacy to enhance the financial, medical, and emotional
support that parents provide for their children. Members
are child support professionals at all levels of government.
Membership: $100 (Individual); $315-3,000 (Agency);
$315 (NonProfit); $5,015 (Premier Education and Training
Package).*

Meetings/Conferences: Annual
Conference Chair: Ann Marie Ruskin
2013 - Baltimore, MD (Baltimore Omni Inner Harbor)/
    Aug. 5 - 7
2014 - Portland, OR (Hilton Portland and Executive
    Tower)/Aug. 11 - 13
2015 - Milwaukee, WI (Hilton Milwaukee City Center)/
    Aug. 10 - 12

Publications:
Child Support Quarterly (CSQ)
Child Support CommuniQue; monthly

National Chimney Sweep Guild (1977)
2155 Commercial Dr.
Plainfield, IN 46168
Tel: (317) 837-1500 *Fax:* (317) 837-5365
E-Mail: office@ncsg.org
Website: ncsg.org
Members: 1100 service companies and 45
additional companies
Staff: 10
Annual Budget: $500-1,000,000
Tax: 501(c)(6)

Personnel:
Executive Director: Mark McSweeney CAE
    E-Mail: mmcsweeney@ncsg.org
Program Coordinator: Sharon Anderson
    E-Mail: sanderson@ncsg.org
Director, Finance: Candice Bradbury
    E-Mail: cbradbury@ncsg.org
Coordinator, Membership Development: Debbie Cornelius
    E-Mail: dcornelius@ncsg.org
Director, Education: Ashley Eldridge COI, CPP
    E-Mail: ashley@ncsg.org
Director, Communications and Marketing: Melissa Heeke
    CAE
    E-Mail: mheeke@ncsg.org
Certification, Coordinator: Donna Lee Kasmer
    E-Mail: dkasmer@ncsg.org
Office Manager: Megan McMahon
    E-Mail: mmcmahon@ncsg.org

Historical Note:
*NCSG's mission is to promote the success of its members by
providing progressive services, encouraging professionalism
and accountability, and advancing the chimney and venting
industry through public awareness of the trade. Members
are professional chimney service companies and their
suppliers. Membership: $459 (Voting); $239 (Affiliate/
International); $139 (Senior); $689 (Supplier).*

Continuing Education:
Certification Designation/s: CSIA

Meetings/Conferences: Annual
Conference Chair: Donna Lee Kasmer
2013 - Branson, MO (Chateau on the Lake Resort Spa
    and Convention Center)/April 4 - 7

Publications:
Membership Directory; on-line
Sweeping: The Journal of Chimney & Venting
    Technology; monthly; adv.

National Christian College Athletic Association
(1968)
302 W. Washington St.
Greenville, SC 29601
Tel: (864) 250-1199 *Fax:* (864) 250-1141
E-Mail: info@thenccaa.org
Website: thenccaa.org
Members: 105 colleges
Staff: 5
Annual Budget: $1-2,000,000
Tax: 501(c)(3)

Personnel:
Executive Director: Dan Wood
    E-Mail: dwood@thenccaa.org
Office Manager: Jill Hancock
    E-Mail: Jhancock@thenccaa.org
Coordinator, Media and Communications: Allie Johns
    E-Mail: Ajohns@thenccaa.org
Director, Membership Relations: Jerry Malone
    E-Mail: jmalone@thenccaa.org
Director, Community Relations: Kelly Wood
    E-Mail: kwood@thenccaa.org

Historical Note:
*NCCAA mission is to use athletic competition as an integral
component of education, evangelism and encouragement.
Members are evangelical Christian colleges. Membership:
$500 (Associate-Christian Liberal Arts College, Division I);
$400 (Associate-Bible College, Division II).*

Meetings/Conferences: Annual
2013 - St. Paul, MN (Northwestern College)/May 30 -
    June 1
Number of non-conference events/year: 2

Publications:
Membership Directory; annually
The Pursuit; semi-annually

National Christian School Association (1980)
P.O. Box 11000
Oklahoma City, OK 73136
Tel: (405) 425-5520
Website: nationalchristian.org
Staff: 2
Annual Budget: $100-250,000

Personnel:
President: Dr. Philip Patterson
    E-Mail: president@nationalchristian.org
Treasurer: Melanie Semore

Historical Note:
*Formerly (1988) Partners in Christian education. The
National Christian School Association is an educational
association of more than 120 secondary schools in 30
states serving more than 40,000 students.*

Meetings/Conferences: Annual
2013 - Oklahoma City, OK/March 6 - 9

National Christmas Tree Association (1955)
16020 Swingley Ridge Rd.
Suite 300
Chesterfield, MO 63017
Tel: (636) 449-5070 *Fax:* (636) 449-5051
E-Mail: info@realchristmastrees.org
Website: christmastree.org
Members: 1200 individuals
Staff: 6
Annual Budget: $500-1,000,000

Personnel:
Executive Director: DeLaine Bender
    E-Mail: dbender@AMRms.com
Contact, Public Relations: Rick Dungey
    E-Mail: rdungey@AMRms.com

Historical Note:
*Formerly (1974) the National Christmas Tree Growers'
Association. NCTA's mission is to promote the traditions
and memories of celebrating Christmas with a Real Tree.
Membership: $199 (General); $254-1,029 (Premier); $220
(Related Industry).*

Meetings/Conferences: Annual
Number of non-conference events/year: 7

Publications:
American Christmas Tree Journal; quarterly
Membership Directory; annually
NCTA Intelligencer; semi-annually
NCTA Newsletter; on-line
Section Newsletters; adv.
Tradition Makers; semi-annually

Membership List Available to Non-members

National Church Goods Association *(1907)*
800 Roosevelt Rd.
Building C, Suite 312
Glen Ellyn, IL 60137
Tel: (630) 942-6599 *Fax:* (630) 790-3095
E-Mail: ncga@ncgaweb.com
Website: ncgaweb.com
Members: 300 companies
Staff: 1
Annual Budget: $100-250,000
Tax: 501(c)(6)

Personnel:
Executive Director: Jeff Church

Historical Note:
NCGA provides a forum for its member dealers and suppliers of church goods, religious articles and published materials to effectively, ethically and creatively serve the institutional and retail markets.

National Church Library Association *(1958)*
275 S.Third St.
Suite 204
Stillwater, MN 55082-4987
Tel: (651) 430-0770
E-Mail: info@churchlibraries.org
Website: churchlibraries.org
Members: 1925 individuals and church libraries
Staff: 2
Annual Budget: $50-100,000

Personnel:
Executive Director and Editor: Susan Benish
   E-Mail: suebenish@churchlibraries.org

Historical Note:
Formerly the Lutheran Church Library Association. Became the National Church Library Association in 2004. NCLA's mission is to further the Gospel through Church Libraries. Membership: $55 (Basic); $99 (Corporate); $100-5,000 + (Supporting).

Publications:
Libraries Alive; quarterly

National Civic League *(1894)*
1889 York St.
Denver, CO 80206
Tel: (303) 571-4343
E-Mail: ncl@ncl.org
Website: ncl.org
Members: 36 individuals
Staff: 4
Annual Budget: $250-500,000
Tax: 501(c)(3)

Personnel:
President: Gloria Rubio-Cortes
   E-Mail: gloriarc@ncl.org
Chief Information Officer and Senior Editor: Michael McGrath

Historical Note:
NCL's mission is to strengthen democracy by increasing the capacity of groups and individuals to participate fully in and build healthy and prosperous communities. Membership: $100 (Individual/Nonprofit/Local Government); $50 (Student/Senior); $250-1000 (Corporate/Sustaining Membership).

Publications:
Civic Action e-newsletter
National Civic Review; quarterly

National Classification Management Society *(1964)*
994 Old Eagle School Rd.
Suite 1019
Wayne, PA 19087-1866
Tel: (610) 971-4856 *Fax:* (610) 971-4859
E-Mail: info@classmgmt.com
Website: classmgmt.com
Members: 3000 individuals

Staff: 1
Annual Budget: $1-2,000,000
Tax: 501(c)(6)

Personnel:
Executive Director: Sharon K. Tannahill
   E-Mail: sharont@mmco1.com

Historical Note:
NCMS seeks to advance the practice of classification management in the disciplines of industrial security, information security, government designated unclassified information, and intellectual property and to foster security professionalism among its members. Members are information security professionals concerned with identifying and assigning a security classification to information and materials needing protection in the national interest. Membership: $90 (Regular); $105 (Outside U.S.); $2,000 (Associate).

Continuing Education:
Certification Designation/s: ISP

Meetings/Conferences: Annual
2013 - Chicago, IL (Palmer House Hilton Hotel)/June 25 - 27
Number of non-conference events/year: 8

Publications:
Membership Directory; on-line
NCMS BULLETIN; bi-monthly; adv.

National Clay Pipe Institute *(1944)*
P.O. Box 759
Lake Geneva, WI 53147
Tel: (262) 248-9094 *Fax:* (360) 242-9094
E-Mail: info@ncpi.org
Website: ncpi.org
Members: 8 companies
Staff: 2
Annual Budget: $250-500,000
Tax: 501(c)(6)

Personnel:
President: Michael VanDine PE
   E-Mail: mjvandine@ncpi.org
Vice President, Technical Services: Jeff Boschert PE
   E-Mail: jeffboschert@sbcglobal.net

Historical Note:
Formerly National Clay Pipe Manufacturers. NCPI is a not-for-profit technical resource for design, installation and operation of vitrified clay pipe (VCP) gravity sewer systems. Members are makers of vitrified clay sewer pipes and fittings.

Continuing Education:
Certification Designation/s: SMART

Publications:
NCPI Newsletter

Membership List Available to Non-members

National Cleaners Association *(1946)*
252 W. 29th St.
New York, NY 10001-5201
Tel: (212) 967-3002 *Fax:* (212) 967-2240
TollFree: (800) 888-1622
E-Mail: info@nca-i.com
Website: nca-i.com
Members: 4200 companies
Staff: 12
Annual Budget: $1-2,000,000

Personnel:
Executive Director: Nora Nealis
   E-Mail: ncaiclean@aol.com
Contact, Membership Services: Simon Bai
   E-Mail: simon@nca-i.com
Contact, Information Technology: Leonard Weiss CMP
   E-Mail: lenny@nca-i.com

Historical Note:
Formerly Neighborhood Cleaners Association, assumed current name in 2004. NCA provides the welfare of well-groomed consumers and the professional cleaners and suppliers who serve them. Membership: $459-1,595/year.

Continuing Education:
Certification Designation/s: DEC
Meetings/Conferences:
Number of non-conference events/year: 4

Publications:
NCA Membership Magazine
NCA Newsletter

National Club Association *(1961)*
1201 15th St. NW
Suite 450

Washington, DC 20005
Tel: (202) 822-9822 *Fax:* (202) 822-9808
TollFree: (800) 625-6221
E-Mail: info@nationalclub.org
Website: nationalclub.org
Members: 1000 private clubs
Staff: 11
Annual Budget: $1-2,000,000
Tax: 501(c)(6)

Personnel:
President and Chief Executive Officer: Susanne R. Wegrzyn
   E-Mail: wegrzyn@nationalclub.org
Manager, Communications: Jaclyn Abrams
   E-Mail: abrams@nationalclub.org
Director, Marketing and Membership Services: Sharlyn Moore
   E-Mail: moore@nationalclub.org
Vice President, Government Relations and General Counsel: Brad D. Steele Esq.
   E-Mail: steele@nationalclub.org
Senior Director, Knowledge Management and Publisher: Cindy Vizza
   E-Mail: vizza@nationalclub.org

Historical Note:
NCA's mission is to defend, protect and advance the interests and well-being of private, social and recreational clubs. Members are private golf, country, city, tennis, and yacht clubs. Membership: $900-3,800 (Club); $1,050 (Associate).

Meetings/Conferences: Annual

Publications:
Club Director; quarterly; adv.
Membership Directory; annually; adv.
NCAConnect; monthly; adv.
SmartBrief; weekly
Washington Weekly Update; weekly; adv.

The National Coal Council
1730 M St. NW
Suite 907
Washington, DC 20036
Tel: (202) 223-1191 *Fax:* (202) 223-9031
Website: nationalcoalcouncil.org
Members: 116 members
Staff: 2
Annual Budget: $500-1,000,000

Personnel:
Executive Vice President and Chief Operating Officer: Robert A. Beck
   E-Mail: RABeck@nationalcoalcouncil.org
General Counsel: Larry B. Grimes
   E-Mail: larrygrimes@cox.net

Historical Note:
NCC provides advice and guidance on a continuing basis as requested by the Secretary of Energy on the general policy matters relating to coal.

Publications:
NCC Newsletter

National Coal Transportation Association
4 W. Meadow Lark Ln.
Suite 100
Littleton, CO 80127-5718
Tel: (303) 979-2798 *Fax:* (303) 973-1848
Website: nationalcoaltransportation.org
Members: 150 members
Staff: 2
Annual Budget: $500-1,000,000

Personnel:
Executive Director: Thomas C. Canter
   E-Mail: tom@nationalcoaltransportation.org
Director, Communications and Editor: Pat Scherzinger
   E-Mail: scherzinger@nationalcoaltransportation.org

Historical Note:
NCTA seeks to provide education and facilitation for the resolution of coal transportation issues in order to serve the needs of the general public, industry, and all modes of transportation. Membership is open to producers or consumers of coal produced in North America and other entities which are interested in its transportation and related issues. Membership: $1,250/year.

Meetings/Conferences:
2013 - Tucson, AZ (Westin La Paloma Resort and Spa)/ April 14 - 17

2013 - Kansas City, MO (InterContinental at the Plaza)/June 11 - 13
Number of non-conference events/year: 5
Publications:
Coal Transporter; semi-annually; adv.

National Coalition for Assistive and Rehab Technology
161 Huxley Dr.
Buffalo, NY 14226
Tel: (716) 839-9728 *Fax:* (716) 839-9624
E-Mail: info@ncart.us
Website: ncartcoalition.org
Members: 54 companies
Staff: 1
Annual Budget: $500-1,000,000
Tax: 501(c)(6)

Personnel:
Executive Director: Don Clayback
    E-Mail: dclayback@ncart.us

Historical Note:
NCART's mission is to promote the interests of the Rehab and Assistive Technology industry and ensure adequate consumer access to appropriate technology and services while creating a stable business environment for providers and manufacturers of rehab and assistive technology. Membership: $3,000-25,000 (Manufacturer, based on annual revenue); $1,000- 20,000 (Provider/Friend, based on annual revenue).

National Coalition of African American Owned Media
264 S. La Cienega Blvd.
Suite 1091
Beverly Hills, CA 90211
Tel: (310) 218-0460
Website: ncaaom.tv
Staff: 1

Personnel:
President and Chief Executive Officer: Stanley E. Washington

Historical Note:
NCAAOM has the responsibility of ensuring that African American owned media companies are given the same opportunities as their non-African American.

National Coalition of Alternative Community Schools *(1978)*
P.O. Box 1451
Ann Arbor, MI 48106
Tel: (734) 483-7040 *Fax:* (734) 482-7436
E-Mail: office@ncacs.org
Website: ncacs.org
Members: 250 schools
Staff: 1
Annual Budget: Under $10,000
Tax: 501(c)(3)

Personnel:
Chairperson: Olivia C. Loria
    E-Mail: olivia@purplemtn.com

Historical Note:
NCACS's mission is to unite and organize a grassroots movement of learners and learning communities dedicated to participant control, liberation from all forms of oppression, and the pursuit of freedom. Membership includes individuals, schools, home schools, foreign schools and resources supporting alternatives to traditional educational systems including educating children at home and developing tools and skills to work for social justice. Membership: $75 (Individual/Family/Less than 50 students); $150-250 (Student, dues vary based on number); $65 (Independent Associate); $20 (Affiliated Associate).

Publications:
Home Education Magazine; bi-monthly; adv.
National Coalition News; bi-annually; adv.

National Coalition of Black Meeting Planners *(1983)*
4401 Huntchase Dr.
Bowie, MD 20720
Tel: (301) 860-0200 *Fax:* (301) 860-0500
E-Mail: ncbmp.hq@verizon.net
Website: ncbmp.com
Members: 1200 individuals
Staff: 4
Annual Budget: $250-500,000

Personnel:

Executive Director: Ozzie Jenkins-Gibson CMP
Treasurer: John Crump CMP, CAE
    E-Mail: jcrumpnba@aol.com

Historical Note:
Formerly (1984) the National Black Meeting Planners Coalition. NCBMP's mission is to train needs of African American meeting planners. Members include meeting planners from numerous business, civil rights, church and fraternal organizations. Membership: $225 (Meeting Planner/Association Executive/Academic Professional); $400 (Supplier/Third Party Planner/Affiliate).

Meetings/Conferences: Annual
Conference Chair: Ozzie Jenkins-Gibson CMP

Publications:
NCBMP Newsletter; quarterly

National Coalition of Creative Arts Therapies Associations *(1979)*
C/O American Music Therapy Association
8455 Colesville Rd., Suite 1000
Silver Spring, MD 20910
Tel: (301) 589-3300 *Fax:* (301) 589-5175
E-Mail: info@namt.com
Website: nccata.org
Members:
15000 individual members
6 creative arts therapies associations
Staff: 1

Personnel:
Virtual Assistant and Recording Secretary: Donna Betts ATR-BC, PhD
    E-Mail: donnabettsatrbc@aol.com

Historical Note:
NCCATA is an alliance of professional associations dedicated to the advancement of the arts as therapeutic modalities and is a coalition of membership organizations.

National Coalition of Girls' Schools *(1991)*
50 Leonard St.
Suite C
Belmont, MA 02478
Tel: (617) 489-0013 *Fax:* (617) 489-0024
E-Mail: ncgs@ncgs.org
Website: ncgs.org
Members: 90 schools
Staff: 6
Annual Budget: $500-1,000,000
Tax: 501(c)(3)

Personnel:
Executive Director: Megan Murphy
    E-Mail: mmurphy@ncgs.org
Director,Programs and Communications: Leslie Coles
    E-Mail: lcoles@ncgs.org
Deputy Director, Senior Director , Operations and Development: Emilie Liebhoff
    E-Mail: eliebhoff@ncgs.org
Director, Member and Administrative Services: Ann Parke

Historical Note:
NCGS conducts research, supports public outreach activities, with a focus on girls and learning. It serves its member schools as they prepare young women to be the visionaries and leaders who will make the world a better one for all. Represents boarding, day, public and private schools for girls in the U. S., Canada, and Australia. Membership: $1,795-6,757 (Schools); $825 (School with less than 100 students).

Meetings/Conferences: Annual
Number of non-conference events/year: 2

Publications:
NCGS e-Newsletter; monthly
NCGS News; on-line
The Girls' School Advantage

National Coalition of Public Safety Officers
2804 Gateway Oaks Dr.
Suite 150
Sacramento, CA 95833
Tel: (916) 921-4500
E-Mail: jdoran@cwa-union.org
Website: ncpso-cwa.org
Members: 16000 public safety officers
Staff: 1

Personnel:
Liaison and Director: John Doran
    E-Mail: jdoran@cwa-union.org

Historical Note:

NCPSO is the public safety division of CWA, representing police officers, deputies, state police, correctional officers and probation officers.

Publications:
Union Plus E-News; monthly

National Coffee Association of the U.S.A. *(1911)*
45 Broadway
Suite 1140
New York, NY 10006
Tel: (212) 766-4007 *Fax:* (212) 766-5815
E-Mail: info@ncausa.org
Website: ncausa.org
Members: 185 companies
Staff: 11
Annual Budget: $1-2,000,000

Personnel:
President and Chief Executive Officer: Robert F. Nelson
    E-Mail: rfnelson@ncausa.org
Director, Marketing, Membership and Events: Jim Bell
Director, External Membership Relations and Communications: Joe DeRupo
    E-Mail: jfderupo@ncausa.org
Director, Knowledge Management: Graham Hill
    E-Mail: grhill@ncausa.org
Director, Administration: Donna Pacheco
    E-Mail: djpacheco@ncausa.org
Manager, Membership Relations: Leigh Price
    E-Mail: ljprice@ncausa.org

Historical Note:
Mission is to serve the well-being of the US coffee industry within the context of the world coffee community. NCA membership is composed of coffee producers, exporters, importers, roasters, wholesalers/distributors, retailers and allied trade professionals. Formerly (1939) Associated Coffee Industries of America. Membership dues depend on the sub-categories. Membership: $300-89,050/year.

Meetings/Conferences: Annual
Conference Chair: Jim Bell
2013 - San Francisco, CA (Palace Hotel-San Francisco)/March 21 - 23

Publications:
Coffee Trax; quarterly
Membership Directory; on-line
The Coffee Reporter; monthly

Membership List Available to Non-members

National Coil Coating Association *(1962)*
1300 Sumner Ave.
Cleveland, OH 44115-2851
Tel: (216) 241-7333 *Fax:* (216) 241-0105
E-Mail: ncca@coilcoating.org
Website: coilcoating.org
Members: 89 companies
Staff: 4
Annual Budget: $500-1,000,000
Tax: 501(c)(6)

Personnel:
Executive Director: John H. Addington
    E-Mail: cjohnson@thomasamc.com
Contact, Communications: Leslie Schraff
    E-Mail: lschraff@thomasamc.com

Historical Note:
Formerly (2000) National Coil Coaters Association. NCCA is dedicated to the growth of coil coated products. Members are manufacturers of continuously coated metal coil and suppliers of materials or services used in coil coating. Membership: 1,250-9,350/year.

Meetings/Conferences:
2013 - Orlando, FL (Loews Portofino Bay Hotel)/April 22 - 24
2013 - Baltimore, MD (Baltimore Marriott Waterfront)/ Sept. 23 - 25
2015 - Tucson, AZ (Loews Ventana Canyon Resort)/ April 20 - 22
2016 - Orlando, FL (Loews Portofino Bay Hotel)/April 18 - 20
Number of non-conference events/year: 3

Publications:
Membership Directory; on-line
NCCA e-Newsletter; on-line

National Collaboration for Youth
1101 14th St. NW
Suite 600
Washington, DC 20005
Tel: (202) 347-2080 *Fax:* (202) 393-4517

Website: collab4youth.org
Members: 100 organizations and 50 members
Staff: 10

Personnel:
Project Director: Pam Garza

Historical Note:
Can be contacted through The National Human Services Assembly, of which it is an affinity group. SparkAction is an online journalism and advocacy center by and for the child and youth field. Its mission is to provide a united voice as advocates for youth to improve the conditions of young people in America, and to help young people reach their full potential.

Publications:
Membership Directory; on-line

National College of Probate Judges (1968)
300 Newport Ave.
Williamsburg, VA 23185-4147
Tel: (757) 259-1841
E-Mail: ncpj@ncsc.org
Website: ncpj.org
Staff: 3
Annual Budget: $100-250,000
Tax: 501(c)(3)

Personnel:
Specialist, Association Management: Shelley Rockwell

Historical Note:
NCPJ promotes efficient, fair and just judicial administration in the probate courts and provides opportunities for continuing judicial education for probate judges and related personnel. Membership: $150 (Regular/Professional/Judicial Position); $75 (Retired/Associate); $1,000 (Life).

Meetings/Conferences: Semi-Annual

Publications:
Member Directory; on-line
NCPJ Journal; on-line

National Collegiate Athletic Association (1906)
700 W. Washington St.
P.O. Box 6222
Indianapolis, IN 46206-6222
Tel: (317) 917-6222 *Fax:* (317) 917-6888
TollFree: (877) 262-1492
E-Mail: pmr@ncaa.org
Website: ncaa.org
Members: 1060 institutions and organizations
Staff: 350
Annual Budget: Over $100,000,000
Tax: 501(c)(3)

Personnel:
President: Mark A. Emmert
Assistant Coordinator: Becky Cooper
  E-Mail: bcooper@ncaa.org
Managing Director, Government Relations: Abe L. Frank
  E-Mail: afrank@ncaa.org
Vice President, Communications: Bob Williams

Historical Note:
Officially constituted as Intercollegiate Athletic Association of the United States (IAAUS) in March 31, 1906, assumed its present name in1910. NCAA's purpose is to govern competition in a fair, safe, equitable and sportsmanlike manner, and to integrate intercollegiate athletics into higher education so that the educational experience of the student-athlete is paramount. Members are colleges, universities and related educational athletic organizations. Membership: $25,000 (Exploratory Member); $225 (Affiliates).

Continuing Education:
Certification Designation/s: NCAA AC

Meetings/Conferences: Annual
Conference Chair: Becky Cooper
2013 - Grapevine, TX/Jan. 16 - 19
2014 - San Diego, CA/Jan. 15 - 18
2015 - Washington, DC/Jan. 14 - 17
2016 - San Antonio, TX/Jan. 13 - 16
2017 - Dallas, TX/Jan. 11 - 14
2018 - Indianapolis, IN/Jan. 17 - 20
2019 - Atlanta, GA/Jan. 16 - 19
Number of non-conference events/year: 9

Publications:
Membership Directory; on-line

National Collegiate Baseball Writers Association (1962)
5201 N. O'Connor Blvd.
Suite 300
Irving, TX 75039

Tel: (214) 774-1351 *Fax:* (214) 496-0055
Website: sportswriters.net/ncbwa
Staff: 3

Personnel:
Executive Director: Bo Carter
  E-Mail: bo.carter@ncbwa.com
Associate Executive Director: Russ Anderson
  E-Mail: rdanderson@c-usa.org
Webmaster: Ted Gangi
  E-Mail: ted.gangi@sportswriters.net

Historical Note:
NCBWA is dedicated to the advancement of college baseball. Membership is open to writers, broadcasters and publicists of baseball. Membership: $20/year.

Publications:
NCBWA Directory; on-line
NCBWA Newsletter; on-line; adv.

National Collegiate Honors Council (1966)
1100 Neihardt Residence Center
University of Nebraska - Lincoln, 540 N. 16th St.
Lincoln, NE 68588-0627
Tel: (402) 472-9150 *Fax:* (402) 472-9152
E-Mail: nchc@unl.edu
Website: nchchonors.org
Members: 944 institutions and individuals
Staff: 5
Annual Budget: $1-2,000,000

Personnel:
Executive Director: Cynthia M. Hill
  E-Mail: chill2@unl.edu
Director, Membership Services: Carolee Martin Brink
Contact, Finance: Teri King
  E-Mail: tking5@unl.edu
Contact, Conferences: Kristi Smith
  E-Mail: nchcassist@unl.edu
Manager, Technology: Trish Souliere
  E-Mail: psouliere2@unl.edu

Historical Note:
NCHC provides support for institutions and individuals developing, implementing, and expanding Honors education through curriculum development, program assessment, teaching innovation, national and international study opportunities, internships, service and leadership development, and mentored research. Membership: $100-600 (Institutional/Professional); $350 (Non-Institutional Professional); $35 (Student); $50 (Affiliate).

Meetings/Conferences: Annual
Conference Chair: Kristi Smith

Publications:
E-newsletter; monthly
Honors in Practice; semi-annually
Journal of the National Collegiate Honors Council; semi-annually
Membership Directory; on-line

Membership List Available to Non-members

National Collegiate Wrestling Association (1997)
13111 N. Central Expwy.
Fifth Floor
Dallas, TX 75243
Tel: (214) 378-8700 *Fax:* (469) 533-6030
Website: ncwa.net
Members: 140 College and Universities, 3000 College Wrestlers and 240 Officials
Staff: 6
Annual Budget: $25-50,000
Tax: 501(c)(3)

Personnel:
Executive Director: Jim Giunta
  E-Mail: jim@ncwa.net
Executive Treasurer: Lelan Brotherman
  E-Mail: lelan@ncwa.net
Webmaster: David Mathews
  E-Mail: webmaster@ncwa.net

Historical Note:
NCWA's mission is to provide both College and High school wrestling programs with the top choices in professional officiating and to provide Officials with the tools to improve themselves in the profession of choice and to open doors for officials to use their talents by linking them with top notch College and High School teams that need their services.

Meetings/Conferences:
Number of non-conference events/year: 10

Publications:
Newsletter

National Committee for Quality Assurance (1979)
1100 13th St. NW
Suite 1000
Washington, DC 20005
Tel: (202) 955-3500 *Fax:* (202) 955-3599
TollFree: (888) 275-7585
E-Mail: customersupport@ncqa.org
Website: ncqa.org
Staff: 150
Annual Budget: $25-50,000,000
Tax: 501(c)(3)

Personnel:
President: Margaret E. O'Kane
  E-Mail: okane@ncqa.org
General Counsel: Sharon King Donohue
  E-Mail: donohue@ncqa.org
Assistant Vice President, Physician Recognition Programs: Mina Harkins
  E-Mail: harkins@ncqa.org
Chief Financial Officer: Scott Hartranft MBA
  E-Mail: hartranft@ncqa.org
Chief Information Officer: Rick Moore
  E-Mail: moore@ncqa.org
Vice President, Research and Analysis: Sarah Hudson Scholle
Vice President, Public Policy and Communications: Sarah Thomas
  E-Mail: thomas@ncqa.org
Vice President, Strategic and Quality Solutions: Phyllis Torda
  E-Mail: torda@ncqa.org

Historical Note:
Founded as a subdivision of Group Health Association of America, became an autonomous organization in 1990. NCQA's mission is to improve the quality of health care.

Continuing Education:
Certification Designation/s: CVO, DM, PO, UM/CR, PHQ, HIP, OC-UM/CR

Meetings/Conferences: Annual
Number of non-conference events/year: 13

Publications:
NCQA Update; irregular
Quality Matters Newsletters; irregular
Recognition Notes Newsletter; irregular

Membership List Available to Non-members

National Commodity Supplemental Food Program Association
31 Evans Terminal Rd.
Hillside, NJ 07205
Tel: (908) 355-3663 *Fax:* (908) 355-0979
Website: ncsfpa.org
Staff: 3
Annual Budget: $50-100,000

Personnel:
Treasurer: Donald Farrell
  E-Mail: Dfarrell@njfoodbank.org

Historical Note:
NCSFPA's mission is to provide leadership in program advocacy, accountability, delivery of healthy foods and nutrition education. Membership: $50 (State Agency/Associate); $50-500 (Local Agency).

Meetings/Conferences: Annual

Publications:
NCSFPA Newsletters and E-Newsletters; on-line

National Communication Association (1914)
1765 N St. NW
Washington, DC 20036
Tel: (202) 464-4622 *Fax:* (202) 464-4600
E-Mail: inbox@natcom.org
Website: natcom.org
Members: 7700 educators, practitioners, and students
Staff: 14
Annual Budget: $2-5,000,000
Tax: 501(c)(3)

Personnel:
Chief of Staff: Mark Fernando
  E-Mail: mfernando@natcom.org
Director, Membership Services: Joseph Burak
  E-Mail: jburak@natcom.org
Communications Associate: Jennifer Glicoes
  E-Mail: jglicoes@natcom.org
Executive Director: Nancy Kidd

E-Mail: nkidd@natcom.org
Associate Director, Educational Initiatives: Brad Mello
PhD
E-Mail: bmello@natcom.org
Senior Manager, Convention and Meetings: Michelle
Randall CMP
E-Mail: mrandall@natcom.org
Interim Chief Financial Officer: Thomas Rhine
E-Mail: trhine@natcom.org
Director, Public Affairs and Public Information: Arlyn G.
Riskind
E-Mail: ariskind@natcom.org
Director, Publications: Rachel Hartigan Shea
E-Mail: rshea@natcom.org
Senior Manager, Information Technology: Terry Wilson
E-Mail: twilson@natcom.org

Historical Note:
*Founded as the National Association of Academic Teachers
of Public Speaking. Became the National Association of
Teachers of Speech in 1923, the Speech Association of
America in 1946, the Speech Communication Association
in 1970, and the National Communication Association
in 1998. Incorporated in Missouri in 1950. NCA's
mission is to promote communication scholarship and
education. Members are teachers at all levels and in all
aspects of communication arts and sciences, media and
communications consultants, students, libraries, and
persons in theatre production. Membership: $165 (Regular);
$60 (Student); $265 (Patron); $150 (Departmental).*

Meetings/Conferences: Annual
Conference Chair: Michelle Randall CMP

Publications:
Communication and Critical/Cultural Studies;
quarterly
Communication Education; quarterly
Communication Monographs; quarterly
Communication Teacher; quarterly
Critical Studies in Media Communication
Journal of Applied Communication Research; quarterly
Journal of International and Intercultural
Communication; quarterly
Quarterly Journal of Speech; quarterly
Text and Performance Quarterly; quarterly
The Review of Communication; quarterly

Membership List Available to Non-members

National Community Development Association
(1968)
522 21st St. NW
Suite 120
Washington, DC 20006
Tel: (202) 293-7587 *Fax:* (202) 887-5546
E-Mail: ncda@ncdaonline.org
Website: ncdaonline.org
Members: 550 local governments
Staff: 3
Annual Budget: $500-1,000,000
Tax: 501(c)(3)

Personnel:
Executive Director: Cardell Cooper
E-Mail: ccooper@ncdaonline.org
Manager, Operations: Karen Parker
E-Mail: karen@ncdaonline.org
Director, Legislative: Vicki Watson

Historical Note:
*Formerly (1977) National Model Cities Community
Development Directors Association. NCDA strives to secure
better housing and community development programs for
local governments. Members are community development
program administrators. Membership: $550-3,430
(Entitlement Members - Depending on Population); $375
(Non-Entitlement Members); $2500 (Affiliate Members);
$450 (Alumni Members); $375 (Subscriber Members); $50
(Student).*

Publications:
Newsletter

National Community Pharmacists Association
(1898)
100 Daingerfield Rd.
Third Floor
Alexandria, VA 22314-2888
Tel: (703) 683-8200 *Fax:* (703) 683-3619
TollFree: (800) 544-7447
E-Mail: info@ncpanet.org
Website: ncpanet.org
Members: 36000 individuals
Staff: 40

Annual Budget: $10-25,000,000
Tax: 501(c)(6)

Personnel:
Chief Executive Officer: B. Douglas Hoey MBA, RPh
E-Mail: doug.hoey@ncpanet.org
Director, Membership Services: Colleen Agan
E-Mail: colleen.agan@ncpanet.org
Vice President, Publications: Mike Conlan
E-Mail: mike.conlan@ncpanet.org
Director, Sales and Marketing: Nina Dadgar
E-Mail: nina.dadgar@ncpanet.org
Senior Director, Meetings and Conventions: Patrick
Dougherty
E-Mail: patrick.dougherty@ncpanet.org
Vice President, Policy and Regulatory Affairs: Ronna
Hauser
E-Mail: ronna.hauser@ncpanet.org
Senior Vice President and Chief of Staff: Beverly Martin
E-Mail: beverly.martin@ncpanet.org
Manager, Information Systems: Michael Miller
E-Mail: michael.miller@ncpanet.org
Vice President, Public Affairs: Kevin Schweers
E-Mail: kevin.schweers@ncpanet.org

Historical Note:
*Formerly the National Association of Retail Druggists,
adopted its acronym (NARD) as its official name in
1987 before assuming its current name in 1996. NCPA
is dedicated to the continuing growth and prosperity of
independent community pharmacy in the United
States. Membership: $95-295 (Active/Sustaining);
$3,500-1,01,000 (Multiple Location); $75 (Pharmacy
Technician); $100 (Retired); $175 (Staff Pharmacist); $35
(Student).*

Continuing Education:
Certification Designation/s: CAALLTC, DCCP, RCCP,
OCCP, TSFC, TFCCP

Meetings/Conferences: Annual
Conference Chair: Patrick Dougherty
2013 - Orlando, FL (Walt Disney World Swan And
Dolphin)/Oct. 12 - 16
2014 - Austin, TX (Austin Convention Center)/Oct. 18
- 22
2015 - Washington, DC (Gaylord National Harbor)/
Oct. 10 - 14
Number of non-conference events/year: 4

Publications:
America's Pharmacist
NCPA eNews; weekly
NCPA Executive Update; weekly
The NCPA Digest

National Comprehensive Cancer Network *(1995)*
275 Commerce Dr.
Suite 300
Ft. Washington, PA 19034
Tel: (215) 690-0300 *Fax:* (215) 690-0260
Website: nccn.org
Members: 21 member Institutions
Staff: 89
Annual Budget: $25-50,000,000

Personnel:
Chief Executive Officer: William T. McGivney
Communications Specialist: Katie Kiley Brown
Executive Vice President and Chief Operating Officer:
Patricia J. Goldsmith
Senior Vice President, Finance and Chief Financial Officer:
Lisa G. Kimbro
Senior Vice President, Clinical Information and Publications:
Joan S. McClure
Director, Marketing: Jennifer Tredwell

Historical Note:
*NCCN's mission is to develop treatment guidelines for
cancer, and conducts research to improve the quality of care
provided to patients whom they serve.*

Continuing Education:
Certification Designation/s: CME/CE

Meetings/Conferences: Annual
Conference Chair: Jennifer Tredwell
2013 - Hollywood, FL (Westin Diplomat Resort and
Spa)/March 13 - 17/1700 attendees
2014 - Hollywood, FL (Westin Diplomat Resort and
Spa)/March 12 - 16
Number of non-conference events/year: 3

Publications:
NCCN eBulletin; adv.
The Journal of the National Comprehensive Cancer
Network; adv.

National Concrete Burial Vault Association *(1930)*
P.O. Box 917525
Longwood, FL 32791-7525
Tel: (888) 886-2282 *Fax:* (407) 774-6751
TollFree: (888) 886-2282
E-Mail: ncbva@ncbva.org
Website: ncbva.org
Members: 350 companies
Staff: 5
Annual Budget: $100-250,000

Personnel:
Executive Director: Thomas A. Monahan CAE
E-Mail: tom@camco.biz
Legal Counsel: J. Scott Calkins
E-Mail: youngscott@aol.com
Account Executive: Sylvia Heidemann
E-Mail: sylvia@camco.biz
Director, Publications: Jan Monahan
E-Mail: jan@camco.biz

Historical Note:
*NCBVA's mission is to provide a unified voice for the
concrete burial vault industry regardless of product
affiliation, brand recognition or location. Members are
companies seeking recognition and uniformity in the
industry. Membership: $225-700 (Manufacturer); $300
(Associate); $1000 (Franchise Group).*

Meetings/Conferences: Annual
2013 - Orlando, FL (Gaylord Palms Resort and
Convention Center-Orlando)/Feb. 23 - 25

Publications:
Bulletin; bi-monthly; adv.
Membership Directory; on-line

National Concrete Masonry Association *(1918)*
13750 Sunrise Valley Dr.
Herndon, VA 20171-4662
Tel: (703) 793-1900 *Fax:* (703) 713-1910
E-Mail: ncma@ncma.org
Website: ncma.org
Members: 400 companies
Staff: 26
Annual Budget: $2-5,000,000

Personnel:
President: Robert D. Thomas
E-Mail: rthomas@ncma.org
Manager, Communications: Mary Arnston-Terrell
E-Mail: mterrell@ncma.org
Publications and Administrative Assistant: Mahsheed
Rouhani Ferdowsyan
E-Mail: mrouhani@ncma.org
Manager, Support Operations: Rich Gemelaris
E-Mail: rgemelaris@ncma.org
Director, Technical Publications: Dennis W. Graber
E-Mail: dgraber@ncma.org
Executive and Education Administrator: Brittaney R.
Kamhong Thompson
E-Mail: bkamhong@ncma.org
Vice President, Finance and Administration: Larry J.
Medley
E-Mail: lmedley@ncma.org
Director, Meetings and Conventions: Deborah W. Morris
E-Mail: dmorris@ncma.org
Director, Government Affairs: William H. Plenge
E-Mail: bplenge@ncma.org
Manager, Membership Services: Heidi Weiss
E-Mail: hweiss@ncma.org

Historical Note:
*NCMA's mission is to advance and protect the common
interests of professionals in the concrete masonry industry.
Membership: $250-23,000/year.*

Continuing Education:
Certification Designation/s: CCMT, CEF, PQC, CSIP

Meetings/Conferences: Semi-Annual
Conference Chair: Deborah W. Morris
2013 - Indianapolis, IN (Indiana Convention Center)/
Jan. 11 - 13
Number of non-conference events/year: 2

Publications:
Concrete Masonry Designs; bi-monthly
e-news Brief; weekly; adv.
Membership Directory; on-line

Membership List Available to Non-members

National Confectioners Association *(1884)*
1101 30th St. NW
Suite 200

Washington, DC 20007
Tel: (202) 534-1440 *Fax:* (202) 337-0637
E-Mail: info@candyusa.com
Website: candyusa.com
Members: 69 confectionery manufacturing firms
Staff: 23
Annual Budget: $10-25,000,000
Tax: 501(c)(6)

Personnel:
President: Lawrence T. Graham
   E-Mail: Larry.Graham@candyusa.com
Senior Director, Expositions and Membership Services:
   Theresa Anthony
   E-Mail: theresa.anthony@CandyUSA.com
Executive Vice President: Alison Bodor
   E-Mail: alison.bodor@candyusa.com
Director, Trade Communications and Marketing: Jenn Ellek
   E-Mail: Jenn.Ellek@CandyUSA.com
Vice President, Finance and Administration: Linda Jamie
   E-Mail: linda.jamie@candyusa.com
Director, Technology: Reginald Meyer
   E-Mail: reggie.meyer@candyusa.com
Executive Assistant to the President and Administrator,
   Human Resources: Barbara E. O'Brien
   E-Mail: barbara.obrien@CandyUSA.com
Vice President, Government Affairs: Elizabeth Reilly
Senior Vice President, Communications and Outreach:
   Susan S. Smith
   E-Mail: susan.smith@candyusa.com
Vice President, Membership Services and Meetings: Libby
   Taylor
   E-Mail: libby.taylor@candyusa.com
Vice President, Communications: Susan Fussell
   Whiteside
   E-Mail: susan.whiteside@CandyUSA.com

Historical Note:
Manufacturers of confectionery products and their suppliers. NCA is connected with the National Confectioners Association of the United States Political Action Committee. NCA's aim is to encourage the interests of the confectionery industry and its consumers. Membership: $1545-66,300 (Domestic/International Manufacturer); $1,200-2,150 (Supplier); $845-3,250 (Confectionery Broker/Supplier).

Meetings/Conferences:
Conference Chair: Libby Taylor
2013 - Miami, FL (Fontainebleau Resort)/Feb. 24 - 27
2013 - Chicago, IL (McCormick Place)/May 21 - 23/
   over 100 exhibitors

Publications:
Candy & Snack TODAY; daily; adv.
Membership Directory; on-line

National Confectionery Sales Association *(1899)*
Spitfire House, 3135 Berea Rd.
Cleveland, OH 44111
Tel: (216) 631-8200 *Fax:* (216) 631-8210
E-Mail: info@candyhalloffame.org
Website: candyhalloffame.org/NCSA
Members: 365 individuals
Staff: 2
Annual Budget: $100-250,000

Personnel:
President: Mark Antonucci
Treasurer: Morton B. Gleit

Historical Note:
Formerly (1912) the National Confectionery Salesmen's Association of America, incorporated in 1912, sponsors the Candy Hall of Fame, established in 1971. NCSA's mission is to further positive growth and acceptance of confectionery and allied products by education, open and frank dialogue and recognition of peers' notable accomplishments. Membership: $100/year (Individual).

Meetings/Conferences: Annual

National Conference of Appellate Court Clerks
(1973)
Supreme Court of Appeals of West Virginia State
Capitol, Room E-317
1900 Kanawha Blvd., East
Charleston, WV 25305
Tel: (304) 558-2601
E-Mail: inquiries@appellatecourtclerks.org
Website: appellatecourtclerks.org
Members: 230 individuals
Staff: 3
Annual Budget: $100-250,000
Tax: 501(c)(3)

Personnel:
President: Rory Perry
   E-Mail: rory.perrty@courtswv.gov

Historical Note:
NCACC's mission is to promote and improve the contribution of the offices of appellate court clerks within the area of effective court administration. Members are clerks, assistant clerks or deputy clerks or people holding similar positions or title. Membership: $150 (Regular); $25 (Retired).

Meetings/Conferences: Annual

Publications:
NCACC Newsletter; on-line

National Conference of Bankruptcy Judges
(1926)
241 Aristides Dr.
Irmo, SC 29063
Tel: (803) 749-4115 *Fax:* (803) 749-4116
Website: ncbj.org
Members: 350 individuals
Staff: 1
Annual Budget: $1-2,000,000
Tax: 501(c)(6)

Personnel:
Executive Director: Christine J. Molick
   E-Mail: cjmolick@sc.rr.com

Historical Note:
NCBJ's mission is to provide continuing legal education to judges, lawyers and other involved professionals, to promote cooperation among the Bankruptcy Judges, to secure quality and uniformity in the administration of the bankruptcy system and to improve the practice of law in the bankruptcy courts of the United States.

Meetings/Conferences: Annual
Conference Chair: Christine J. Molick
2013 - Atlanta, GA/Oct. 30 - Nov. 2
2014 - Chicago, IL/Oct. 8 - 11
2015 - Miami, FL/Sept. 27 - 30
2016 - San Francisco, CA/Oct. 26 - 29

Publications:
American Bankruptcy Law Journal; quarterly

National Conference of Bar Examiners *(1931)*
302 S. Bedford St.
Madison, WI 53703-3622
Tel: (608) 280-8550 *Fax:* (608) 280-8552
E-Mail: contact@ncbex.org
Website: ncbex.org
Staff: 3
Annual Budget: $10-25,000,000
Tax: 501(c)(3)

Personnel:
President: Erica Moeser
Chief Justice: Debra Martin
   E-Mail: dmartin@ncbex.org

Historical Note:
NCBE mission is to work with other institutions to develop, maintain, and apply reasonable and uniform standards of education and character for eligibility for admission to the practice of law.

Continuing Education:
Certification Designation/s: MBE, MPT, MEE, MPRE

Publications:
The Bar Examiner Magazine

National Conference of Bar Foundations *(1977)*
C/O ABA Division for Bar Services
321 N. Clark St., Suite 2000
Chicago, IL 60654
Tel: (312) 988-5344 *Fax:* (312) 988-5492
E-Mail: ncbf.info@ncbf.org
Website: ncbf.org
Members: 80 bar foundations
Staff: 4
Annual Budget: $50-100,000
Tax: 501(c)(3)

Personnel:
Program Assistant: Kira Baltutis
Secretary: Elizabeth Lynch
   E-Mail: elynch@massbar.org

Historical Note:
NCBF's mission is to promote the integral role of bar foundations in advancing law-related philanthropy to the organized bar, the larger legal community, and the philanthropic community. Membership: $150-350 (Organizational); $100 (Individual).

Meetings/Conferences:
2013 - Dallas, TX (Hilton Anatole)/Feb. 7 - 9
2013 - San Francisco, CA/Aug. 8 - 10
2014 - Chicago, IL/Feb. 6 - 8
2014 - Boston, MA/Aug. 7 - 9
2015 - Houston, TX/Feb. 5 - 7
2015 - Chicago, IL/July 30 - Aug. 1

Publications:
Bar Leader Magazine
Membership Directory; on-line
NCBF Newsletter; bi-monthly

Membership List Available to Non-members

National Conference of Bar Presidents *(1950)*
C/O ABA Division for Bar Services
321 N. Clark St., 16th Floor
Chicago, IL 60654-7598
Tel: (312) 988-5353 *Fax:* (312) 988-5492
Website: ncbp.org
Members: 420 bar associations and individuals
Staff: 3
Annual Budget: $250-500,000
Tax: 501(c)(3)

Personnel:
Coordinator, Membership Services: Chrishelle M. Thomas
   E-Mail: thomasc@staff.abanet.org
Coordinator, Communications: Kimberly Vann
   E-Mail: VannK2@staff.abanet.org

Historical Note:
NCBP's purpose is to provide high-quality programming to current bar leaders at two meetings held each year contemporaneously with the annual and midyear meetings of the ABA. Membership: $140-315 (Organization/ Company, depending on number of members); $35 (Individual Fellow); $100 (Sustaining Fellow/Sustaining Life Fellow); $1,000 (Life Fellow).

Meetings/Conferences: Annual
2013 - Dallas, TX (Hilton Anatole Hotel)/Feb. 7 - 9

Publications:
President's Forum; quarterly

National Conference of Black Lawyers *(1968)*
P.O. Box 998
New York, NY 10024
Tel: (212) 864-4000 *Fax:* (212) 222-2680
TollFree: (866) 266-5091
Website: ncbl.org
Members: 1500 individuals
Staff: 1
Annual Budget: $10-25,000

Personnel:
Co-Chair: Mark Fancher

Historical Note:
NCBL serves as the legal arm of the movement for Black Liberation, to analyze and study problems of Black attorneys in the United States in their legal practices, to encourage Black youth to study law, to work for the elimination of racism in the law and to give attention to the root problems of the Black community. Members are lawyers, scholars, judges, legal workers, law students and legal activists. Membership: $1,000 (Life); $500 (Sustaining); $20-175 (Individual); $50 (Affiliate).

Meetings/Conferences: Annual

National Conference of Black Mayors *(1974)*
191 Peachtree St. NE, Building 191
Suite 849
East Point, GA 30303
Tel: (404) 765-6444 *Fax:* (404) 765-6430
E-Mail: info@ncbm.org
Website: ncbm.org
Members: 600 individuals
Staff: 8
Annual Budget: $500-1,000,000
Tax: 501(c)(3)

Personnel:
Executive Director: Vanessa R. Williams
Director, Operations: Wynona Singleterry

Historical Note:
Formerly as the Southern Conference of Black Mayors, it changed to its present name in January, 1977. NCBM's mission is to enhance the executive management capacity of its member mayors and provides technical and management assistance through cutting-edge research.

Publications:
Convention Program and Journal; annually; adv.
E-newsletter; on-line

National Conference of Black Political Scientists
(1969)
14000 Hwy. 82 W
MVSU 5098
Itta Bena, MS 38941-1400
Tel: (601) 750-7318 *Fax:* (662) 254-3130
E-Mail: info@ncobps.org
Website: ncobps.org
Members: 400 individuals
Staff: 2
Annual Budget: $25-50,000

Personnel:
Interim Executive Director and Treasurer: Kathie Stromile
   Golden
Editor: Michael Mitchell
   E-Mail: Michael.Mitchell@asu.edu

Historical Note:
*NCOBPS's mission is to study and promote the political
aspirations of people of African descent in the U.S. and
around the world, and to resolve the challenges they face.
Membership: $65 (Professional); $40 (Student); $500
(Institutional).*

Meetings/Conferences: Annual
2013 - Oak Brook, IL (Doubletree Hotel Chicago)/
   March 14 - 16
2014 - Wilmington, DE/March 12 - 15

Publications:
NCOBPS E-Newsletter; monthly
The National Political Science Review (NPSR); annually

National Conference of Commissioners on Uniform State Laws *(1892)*
111 N. Wabash Ave.
Suite 1010
Chicago, IL 60602
Tel: (312) 450-6600 *Fax:* (312) 450-6612
Website: uniformlaws.org
Members: 335 individuals
Staff: 8
Annual Budget: $1-2,000,000

Personnel:
Executive Director: John A. Sebert
   E-Mail: john.sebert@uniformlaws.org
Chief Administrative Officer: J. Elizabeth Cotton-Murphy
   E-Mail: ecotton@uniformlaws.org
Senior Accounting and Finance Officer: Elizabeth
   Cunneen
   E-Mail: lcunneen@uniformlaws.org
Director, Legislative and Legal Counsel: Michael R. Kerr
   E-Mail: michael.kerr@nccusl.org
Deputy Legislative Director and Communications Officer:
   Katie Robinson
   E-Mail: katie.robinson@uniformlaws.org
Manager, Publications: Kristina Shidlauski
   E-Mail: kshidlauski@uniformlaws.org
Manager, Membership and Meetings: Leang K. Sou
   E-Mail: lsou@uniformlaws.org
Director, Development: Melissa Walls
   E-Mail: melissa.walls@nccusl.org

Historical Note:
*Provides states with non-partisan, well-conceived and well-
drafted legislation that brings clarity and stability to critical
areas of state statutory law.*

Meetings/Conferences:
Conference Chair: Leang K. Sou

Publications:
ULC Bulletin e-Newsletter; on-line

National Conference of CPA Practitioners *(1979)*
22 Jericho Tnpk.
Suite 110
Mineola, NY 11501
Tel: (516) 333-8282 *Fax:* (516) 333-4099
TollFree: (888) 488-5400
E-Mail: office@nccpap.org
Website: nccpap.org
Members: 1000 firms
Staff: 3
Annual Budget: $100-250,000

Personnel:
Executive Director: Holly Coscetta
Treasurer: Sarah Jansen CPA
President: Lana Kupferschmid CPA

Historical Note:
*NCCPAP's mission is to promote the exchange of ideas
and information among members. Provides a means for*
*members to develop and maintain skills necessary to
be successful in the competitive business environment.
Membership: $230 (Sole Practitioner); $260 (CPA Firm);
$420-745 (CPA, non- member firm).*

Publications:
Membership Directory; on-line
National newsletter
The Journal of the CPA Practitioner

National Conference of Diocesan Vocation Directors *(1962)*
440 W. Neck Rd.
Huntington, NY 11743
Tel: (631) 645-8210 *Fax:* (631) 812-0249
E-Mail: office@ncdvd.org
Website: ncdvd.org
Members: 688 individuals and organizations
Staff: 3
Tax: 501(c)(3)

Personnel:
Executive Director: Rosemary C. Sullivan
   E-Mail: eventsNCDVD@aol.com

Historical Note:
*NCDVD's mission is to promote diocesan priesthood,
providing resources for the formation, support, and
advocacy of diocesan vocation directors as they work within
the Catholic Church to foster a culture of vocations, raising
up new priests for the Body of Christ.*

Meetings/Conferences: Annual
2013 - Dallas, TX/Sept. 23 - 27

National Conference of Executives of The ARC *(1964)*
1825 K St.
Suite 1200
Washington, DC 20006
Tel: (800) 433-5255 *Fax:* (202) 534-3731
E-Mail: info@thearc.org
Website: thearc.org
Members: 450 individuals
Staff: 11
Annual Budget: $100-250,000
Tax: 501(c)(3)

Personnel:
Chief Executive Officer: Peter Berns
   E-Mail: berns@thearc.org
Chief Research and Innovations Office: Ann Cameron
   Caldwell
   E-Mail: caldwell@thearc.org
Project and Information Specialist: Leigh Ann Davis
   E-Mail: ldavis@thearc.org
Director, Chapter Organizing and Advocacy: Dee Dee
   Eberle
   E-Mail: eberle@thearc.org
Project Specialist: Kate Hull
   E-Mail: hull@thearc.org
Chief Development and Marketing Officer: Trudy R.
   Jacobson
   E-Mail: jacobson@thearc.org
Chief Operating Officer: Darcy Littlefield
   E-Mail: littlefield@thearc.org
Director, Communications: Kristen McKiernan
   E-Mail: mckiernan@thearc.org
Human Resources Manager: Rhonda Schaver
   E-Mail: schaver@thearc.org
Administrative Assistant: Brenda Walker
   E-Mail: walker@thearc.org
Finance Manager: Feng Zhang
   E-Mail: zhang@thearc.org

Historical Note:
*Formerly the National Conference of Executives of
Associations for Retarded Citizens. The Arc promotes and
protects the human rights of people with intellectual and
developmental disabilities and actively supports their full
inclusion and participation in the community throughout
their lifetimes. Membership: $35 (Self-Advocate); $50
(Individual); $125 (Family).*

Meetings/Conferences: Annual
2013 - Bellevue, WA (Hyatt Regency Bellevue)/Aug. 2
   - 5

Publications:
Arc E-Newsletter; bi-monthly; adv.
Empower; quarterly

National Conference of Federal Trial Judges
(1972)
321 N. Clark St.
Chicago, IL 60654-7598
Tel: (312) 988-5709
Website: americanbar.org/groups/judicial/
   conferences/fe
Members: 4000 individuals
Staff: 4
Annual Budget: $25-50,000

Personnel:
Meetings Manager: Kris Berliant
   E-Mail: Kris.Berliant@americanbar.org
Manager: Denise Jimenez
   E-Mail: denise.jimenez@americanbar.org
Director, Chief Counsel: Peter Koelling
   E-Mail: Peter.Koelling@americanbar.org
Specialist, Member Communications: Jo Ann Saringer
   E-Mail: JoAnn.Saringer@americanbar.org

Historical Note:
*NCFTJ's mission is to meet the needs of the federal judiciary
and to offer opportunities for interaction among federal
trial judges through educational, networking and social
programs.*

Meetings/Conferences:
Conference Chair: Kris Berliant

Publications:
Judges' Journal
Judicial Division Record; on-line

National Conference of Insurance Legislators
(1969)
385 Jordan Rd.
Troy, NY 12180
Tel: (518) 687-0178 *Fax:* (518) 687-0401
E-Mail: info@ncoil.org
Website: ncoil.org
Members: 36 states
Staff: 7
Annual Budget: $500-1,000,000

Personnel:
Executive Director: Susan F. Nolan
Coordinator, Operations: Simone Smith

Historical Note:
*Added "National" to its name in 1987. Liasons with the
National Association of Insurance Commissioners. NCOIL
represents state legislators in Washington to counter federal
initiatives to preempt state insurance regulation. It educates
state legislators on current and perennial insurance issues
to improve the quality of insurance regulation. Membership:
$10,000/year (State).*

Meetings/Conferences:
2013 - Washington, DC (Hyatt Regency Washington on
   Capitol Hill)/March 8 - 10
2013 - Philadelphia, PA (Philadelphia Marriott
   Downtown)/July 11 - 14
2013 - Nashville, TN (Hilton Nashville Downtown)/
   Nov. 21 - 24
2014 - Savannah, GA (Hyatt Regency)/March 6 - 9
2014 - Boston, MA (Boston Park Plaza)/July 10 - 13
2014 - San Francisco, CA (Grand Hyatt in Union
   Square)/Nov. 20 - 23
Number of non-conference events/year: 1

Publications:
NCOIL NEWSLETTER; monthly

National Conference of Local Environmental Health Administrators *(1938)*
1010 S. Third St.
Dayton, WA 99328
Tel: (509) 382-2181 *Fax:* (509) 382-2942
Website: depts.washington.edu/clehaweb
Members: 300 individuals
Staff: 2
Annual Budget: Under $10,000

Personnel:
Chair: David Riggs
   E-Mail: David_Riggs@co.columbia.wa.us

Historical Note:
*Formerly (1966) the Conference of Municipal Public Health
Engineers and (1983) Conference of Local Environmental
Health Administrators. NCLEHA's purpose is to provide
a professional organization for environmental health
administrators, focused on the issues and problems of
local environ-mental health programs. Members are
administrator or supervisor of local environmental health
programs. Membership: $25/year.*

Publications:
NCLEHA Newsletter

National Conference of Personal Managers
(1942)
P.O. Box 50008
Henderson, NV 89016-0008
Tel: (702) 837-1170 *Fax:* (610) 366-7117
E-Mail: askncopm@ncopm.com
Website: ncopm.com
Members: 220 individuals
Staff: 6
Annual Budget: $10-25,000

Personnel:
President: Clinton Ford Billups Jr.
    E-Mail: president@ncopm.com

Historical Note:
NCOPM is committed to the advancement of member personal managers and their clients. A personal manager advises and counsels talent and personalities in the entertainment industry. Members have experience and expertise in concerts, motion pictures, publishing, radio, recordings, television, and theatre. Membership: 180/year.

Publications:
The Personal Manager

National Conference of Specialized Court Judges
(1969)
321 N. Clark St.
19th Floor
Chicago, IL 60654-7598
Tel: (312) 988-5697 *Fax:* (312) 988-5709
TollFree: (800) 238-2667
Website: americanbar.org/groups/judicial/
    conferences/sp
Members: 900 individuals
Staff: 11

Personnel:
Justice Center Director and Chief Counsel: Peter Koelling
    E-Mail: Peter.Koelling@americanbar.org
Meetings Manager, Justice Center: Kris Berliant
    E-Mail: Kris.Berliant@americanbar.org
Specialist, Member Communications and Editor: Jo Ann Saringer
    E-Mail: JoAnn.Saringer@americanbar.org
Program Associate: Gena Taylor
    E-Mail: Gena.Taylor@americanbar.org

Historical Note:
Represents judges of limited and special jurisdiction from around the country. NCSCJ's mission is to represent special court judges in relation to the legal profession and to the public; to promote a representative, educated and sensitive judiciary providing equal justice under the law; and to assist judges in meeting challenges facing the judiciary. Members include traffic court, probate, district, county, military, immigration and municipal court judges.

Meetings/Conferences: Annual
Conference Chair: Jo Ann Saringer

Publications:
Judicial Division Record; quarterly
The Judges' Journal; quarterly

Membership List Available to Non-members

National Conference of State Fleet Administrators
(1987)
301 W. High St.
Room 760
Jefferson City, MO 65101
Tel: (301) 519-0535 *Fax:* (301) 519-0536
E-Mail: info@ncsfa.net
Website: ncsfa.net
Members: 350 fleet professionals
Staff: 2
Annual Budget: $100-250,000
Tax: 501(c)(3)

Personnel:
Treasurer: Cindy Dixon
    E-Mail: cindy.dixon@oa.mo.gov
President: Chris Hoffman
    E-Mail: chris.hoffman@okstate.edu

Historical Note:
NCSFA provides its members with proactive networking and political forum, bringing State Fleet representatives together to educate, inform, problem solve and instruct members on current fleet management policies, procedures and exchange of ideas, solutions and technology. Members are state government administrators responsible for vehicle fleet management. Membership: $200-250 (Government); $350-3,000 (Corporate); $299 (Associate); Free (Retiree).

Continuing Education:

Certification Designation/s: CAFM, CAFS

Meetings/Conferences: Annual

Publications:
Fleet Administration News Newsletter; quarterly
Membership Roster; on-line
NCSFA Corporate Committee News - Newsletter;
    quarterly

National Conference of State Historic Preservation Officers
(1969)
444 N. Capitol St. NW
Suite 342
Washington, DC 20001
Tel: (202) 624-5465 *Fax:* (202) 624-5419
Website: ncshpo.org
Members: 59 states and territories
Staff: 3
Annual Budget: $2-5,000,000
Tax: 501(c)(3)

Personnel:
Executive Director: Nancy Schamu
    E-Mail: schamu@sso.org
Director, Government Relations: Elizabeth Hebron
    E-Mail: belleville@sso.org
Business Manager: Sharon Smith
    E-Mail: smith@sso.org

Historical Note:
NCSHPO acts as a communications vehicle among the SHPO (State Historic Preservation Officer) and their staffs and represents the SHPO with federal agencies and national preservation organizations.

Meetings/Conferences: Annual

Publications:
Member Directory; on-line

National Conference of State Legislatures *(1975)*
7700 E. First Pl.
Denver, CO 80230
Tel: (303) 364-7700 *Fax:* (303) 364-7800
E-Mail: info@ncsl.org
Website: ncsl.org
Members:
50 state legislatures
37000 individuals
Staff: 200
Annual Budget: $10-25,000,000

Personnel:
Executive Director: William T. Pound
    E-Mail: bill.pound@ncsl.org
Director, Revenue and Sales: LeAnn Hoff
    E-Mail: leann.hoff@ncsl.org

Historical Note:
Formed by a merger of the National Legislative Conference (founded in 1947), the National Conference of State Legislative Leaders (founded 1959) and the National Society of State Legislators (founded in 1965). NCSL's mission is to improve the quality and effectiveness of state legislatures and to promote policy innovation and communication among state legislatures.

Meetings/Conferences:
Number of non-conference events/year: 8

Publications:
Budget and Revenue Newsletter; weekly
Capitol To Capitol; weekly
Child Care and Early Education Legislative Network;
    monthly
Child Welfare Legislative Policy Newsletter; monthly
E-Bulletin: Sentencing and Corrections Policy Updates;
    quarterly
Foundation for State Legislatures e-Newsletter;
    monthly
HITCH eBulletin; monthly
LED Committee Report; monthly
LegisBrief
National Association of Legislative Information
    Technology (NALIT) Newsletter; semi-annually
NLPES News
Public Health Herald; quarterly
RACSS Newsletter; quarterly
State Budget and Tax Notes; irregular
State Legislatures Magazine; monthly; adv.
The Canvass: States and Election Reform
The Legislative Lawyer
The Legislative Research Librarians Newsline;
    quarterly
Transport Report; monthly

Transportation Coordination Quarterly Newsletter;
    quarterly
Women's Legislative Network News; semi-annually
Youth Legislative Policy Network; monthly

Membership List Available to Non-members

National Conference of State Liquor Administrators *(1934)*
543 Long Hill Rd.
Gurnee, IL 60031
Tel: (847) 721-6410
Website: ncsla.org
Members: 41 government and state agencies
Staff: 1
Annual Budget: $250-500,000
Tax: 501(c)(4)

Personnel:
Executive Director: Pamela Frantz
    E-Mail: pfrantz@ncsla.org

Historical Note:
NCSLA's purpose is to encourage enactment of effective and equitable state alcoholic beverage control laws, and to enhance balance in the administration of alcoholic beverage control laws among several states. Membership: dues vary with nature, scope and size of the organization. Membership: $300-5000/year.

Meetings/Conferences: Annual
2013 - Honolulu, HI (Sheraton Waikiki)/June 24 - 26
Number of non-conference events/year: 1

Publications:
Membership Directory; on-line
NCSLA Newsletter; on-line

National Conference of State Social Security Administrators *(1952)*
C/O Colorado Public Employees Social Security Section
633 17th St. Seventh Floor
Denver, CO 80202-2117
Tel: (303) 318-8061 *Fax:* (303) 318-8069
E-Mail: info@ncsssa.org
Website: ncsssa.org
Members: 115 individuals
Staff: 2
Annual Budget: $25-50,000

Personnel:
President: Angie Dowdy
    E-Mail: president@ncsssa.org
Treasurer: Rick Beckstead
    E-Mail: treasurer@ncsssa.org

Historical Note:
Formerly (1963) Conference of State Social Security Administrators. NCSSSA aims at promoting economic security for American individuals through shaping and managing national social security programs. Membership: $125/year (Organization).

Meetings/Conferences: Annual
2013 - Philadelphia, PA (Sheraton Society Hill Hotel)/
    July 28 - 31
2014 - New Orleans, LA (Bourbon Orleans Hotel)/July
    27 - 30

Publications:
NCSSSA- Today; quarterly

National Conference of Women's Bar Associations *(1981)*
P.O. Box 82366
Portland, OR 97282-0366
Tel: (503) 775-4396 *Fax:* (503) 775-6525
E-Mail: info@ncwba.org
Website: ncwba.org
Members: 35000 women lawyers
Staff: 1
Annual Budget: $10-25,000,000
Tax: 501(c)(6)

Personnel:
Executive Director: Diane Rynerson
    E-Mail: diane@ncwba.org

Historical Note:
NCWBA's mission is to promote and assist the growth of local and statewide women's bar associations and ideas among women's bar associations and women's bar sections of local and statewide bar associations. Members are state and local women's bar associations, sections, special interest groups and individuals. Membership: $100-500 (Individual); $75-350 (based upon Bar Association).

Publications:

NCWBA e-Newsletter; quarterly
Membership List Available to Non-members

National Conference of Yeshiva Principals (1947)
160 Broadway
New York, NY 10038
Tel: (212) 227-1000 *Fax:* (212) 406-6934
E-Mail: umesorah@aol.com
Members: 380 individuals
Staff: 2
Annual Budget: $25-50,000

Personnel:
Executive Vice President: A. Moshe Possick

Historical Note:
Affiliated with the National Society for Hebrew Day Schools.

National Conference on Public Employee Retirement Systems (1941)
444 N. Capitol St. NW
Suite 630
Washington, DC 20001
Tel: (877) 202-5706 *Fax:* (202) 624-1439
TollFree: (877) 202-5706
E-Mail: info@ncpers.org
Website: ncpers.org
Members:
550 organizations
1300 individuals
Staff: 5
Annual Budget: $2-5,000,000
Tax: 501(c)(4)

Personnel:
Executive Director and Counsel: Hank H. Kim Esq.
   E-Mail: hank@ncpers.org
Administrative Assistant: Alexander Bunte
   E-Mail: Alexander@ncpers.org
Director, Communications: Ryan R. Francis
   E-Mail: ryan@ncpers.org
Director, Membership Services: Tenikka Greene
   E-Mail: tenikka@ncpers.org
Director, Meetings and Expositions: Cassandra T. Smoot CMP
   E-Mail: cassandra@ncpers.org

Historical Note:
NCPERS is a national, nonprofit public pension advocate representing administrators and trustees of public pension funds. NCPERS was founded to protect public employees from an action by the federal government that would have wiped out public pension systems by requiring Social Security coverage for non-covered state and local government employees. Membership: $150-600 (Fund/ Union Member, based on number of members); $6,000 (Corporate).

Meetings/Conferences:
Conference Chair: Cassandra T. Smoot CMP
2013 - Washington, DC (Capital Hilton Hotel)/Jan. 27 - 29
2013 - Honolulu, HI (Hilton Hawaiian Village Waikiki Beach Resort)/May 19 - 23
2013 - Rancho Mirage, CA/Oct. 6 - 9
Number of non-conference events/year: 4

Publications:
NCPERS News Clips; weekly
Persist
The Monitor

National Conference on Research in Language and Literacy (1932)
University of Wisconsin La Crosse
235 Morris Hall, 1725 State St.
La Crosse, WI 54601
Tel: (608) 785-8160
E-Mail: mmjuzwik@msu.edu
Website: ncrll.org
Members: 450 individuals
Staff: 3
Annual Budget: $25-50,000

Personnel:
Treasurer: Margaret J. Finders PhD
Chair, Publications: Mary Juzwik
   E-Mail: mmjuzwik@msu.edu
Chair, Membership and Elections: Rebecca Rogers
   E-Mail: rogersrl@umsl.edu

Historical Note:
Formerly the National Conference on Research in English (1996). NCRLL strives to stimulate and encourage

research in the teaching and learning of language and literacy. Members are teachers and researchers in english. Membership: $100/year (Lifetime).

National Conference on Weights and Measures (1905)
1135 M St.
Suite 110
Lincoln, NE 68508
Tel: (402) 434-4880 *Fax:* (402) 434-4878
E-Mail: info@ncwm.net
Website: ncwm.net
Members: 3500 individuals
Staff: 4
Annual Budget: $500-1,000,000

Personnel:
Executive Director: Don Onwiler
Office Manager: LuAnne Groenjes
Associate, Membership Services: Robert Murnane Jr.

Historical Note:
NCWM mission is to advance a healthy business and consumer climate through the development and implementation of uniform and equitable weights and measures standards using a consensus building process. Members are weights and measures enforcement officials from federal, state, county and local governments. Membership: $75 (Government); $90 (Industry).

Continuing Education:
Certification Designation/s: NTEP

Meetings/Conferences: Annual
2013 - Charleston, SC/Jan. 27 - 30
2013 - Louisville, KY/July 14 - 18
2014 - Albuquerque, NM/Jan. 19 - 22
2014 - Detroit, MI/July 12 - 17

Publications:
Member Directory; on-line
NCWM News; quarterly; adv.

National Congress of Inventor Organizations (1977)
8306 Wilshire Blvd.
Suite 391
Beverly Hills, CA 90211
Tel: (323) 878-6952
TollFree: (800) 458-5624
E-Mail: ncio@inventionconvention.com
Website: inventionconvention.com/ncio
Staff: 1

Personnel:
Executive Director: Stephen Paul Gnass

Historical Note:
NCIO is the central organization representing inventors groups and collegiate inventors programs in the U.S. Membership: $75 (Individual); $200 (Organization); $600 (Company).

Publications:
Newsletter; on-line

National Constables Association (1973)
302 E. Carson Ave.
Fifth Floor
Las Vegas, NV 89155-2110
Tel: (251) 463-1489 *Fax:* (251) 776-6609
Website: nationalconstablesassociation.com
Members: 15000 individuals
Staff: 3
Annual Budget: $10-25,000

Personnel:
President: Daniel Palazzo
   E-Mail: palazzod@co.clark.nv.us

Historical Note:
Founded as the National Police Constables Association and incorporated in Pennsylvania (1976). Formerly National Constables Association (NCA). Purpose is to maintain a close and positive relationship with all other law enforcement agencies. Membership: $60 (Regular), $600 (Lifetime).

Meetings/Conferences: Annual

National Consumers League (1899)
1701 K St. NW
Suite 1200
Washington, DC 20006
Tel: (202) 835-3323 *Fax:* (202) 835-0747
E-Mail: info@nclnet.org
Website: nclnet.org
Staff: 15

Annual Budget: $2-5,000,000
Tax: 501(c)(3)

Personnel:
Executive Director: Sally Greenberg
   E-Mail: sallyg@nclnet.org
Vice President, Public Policy, Telecommunications and Fraud: John Breyault
Director, Life Smarts Program: Lisa Hertzberg
   E-Mail: lisah@nclnet.org
Vice President, Communications: Carol McKay
   E-Mail: carolm@nclnet.org

Historical Note:
NCL's mission is to protect and promote social and economic justice for consumers and workers in the United States and abroad. It represents consumers and workers on such issues as healthcare, e-commerce, fair labor standards, privacy, food and drug safety, technology, telecommunications, and fraud.

Publications:
NCL e-newsletter; on-line

National Contract Management Association (1959)
21740 Beaumeade Cir.
Suite 125
Ashburn, VA 20147
Tel: (571) 382-0082 *Fax:* (703) 448-0939
TollFree: (800) 344-8096
Website: ncmahq.org
Members: 21000 Individuals
Staff: 28
Annual Budget: $5-10,000,000
Tax: 501(c)(6)

Personnel:
Executive Director: Neal J. Couture CPCM
   E-Mail: couture@ncmahq.org
Director, Education: Susan Esprella Colon
   E-Mail: esprella@ncmahq.org
Director, Meetings: Jennifer Coy
   E-Mail: jreece@ncmahq.org
Director, Marketing: Jessica Friedman
   E-Mail: jfriedman@ncmahq.org
Chief Editor: Kerry McKinnon
   E-Mail: kmckinnon@ncmahq.org
Manager, Information Technology: Wyatt Miedema
   E-Mail: wmiedema@ncmahq.org
Chief Financial Officer: Sam Smith CPA
   E-Mail: ssmith@ncmahq.org
Director, Certification: Chuck Woodside
   E-Mail: cwoodside@ncmahq.org

Historical Note:
Formed (1965) by merger of two associations National Association of Professional Contracts Administrators and Government Contract Management Association. NCMA's mission is to enhance organizational performance through effective contract management. Members are concerned with various forms of contracting with federal, state and local governments and industry. Membership: $150 (Individual); $65 (Associate); $55 (Retired); $1,000 (Life); $25 (Student).

Continuing Education:
Certification Designation/s: CPCM, CCCM, CFCM

Meetings/Conferences: Semi-Annual
Conference Chair: Jennifer Coy
2013 - Las Vegas, NV (Planet Hollywood Resort and Casino)/Jan. 18 - 19
2013 - San Diego, CA (Westin San Diego)/March 14 - 15
2014 - Las Vegas, NV (Planet Hollywood Resort and Casino)/Jan. 17 - 18

Publications:
Contract Management Magazine; monthly
Contract Management News; bi-monthly
Journal of Contract Management

Membership List Available to Non-members

National Cooperative Business Association (1985)
1401 New York Ave. NW
Suite 1100
Washington, DC 20005
Tel: (202) 638-6222 *Fax:* (202) 638-1374
E-Mail: ncba@ncba.coop
Website: ncba.coop
Members: 261 Companies and 385 Individuals
Staff: 35
Annual Budget: $10-25,000,000

Tax: 501(c)(6)

Personnel:
President and Chief Executive Officer: Mike Beall
Director, Communications: Andrea Cumpston
    E-Mail: acumpston@ncba.coop
Chief Financial Officer: John Gillespie
Editor and Specialist, Communications: Andrew McLeod
Assistant Editor: Gabriel Rivin
    E-Mail: grivin@ncba.coop
Vice President, Public Affairs and Membership Services:
    Adam Schwartz
    E-Mail: aschwartz@ncba.coop

Historical Note:
NCBA was known as the Cooperative League of America until 1922 and as the Cooperative League of the USA (CLUSA) until 1985. Mission is dedicated to developing, advancing and protecting cooperatives. It works for cooperatives, helping them compete in a changing economic and political environment. Membership: $52 (Individual); $105 (Individual- Twin Pines); $525 (Individual-Lifetime, based on sales, revenue, income, assets, housing units, number of members).

Meetings/Conferences: Semi-Annual

Publications:
Cooperative Business Journal; bi-monthly; adv.
eNEWS; monthly

National Coordinating Committee for Multiemployer Plans *(1974)*
815 16th St. NW
Washington, DC 20006
Tel: (202) 737-5315 *Fax:* (202) 737-1308
E-Mail: nccmp@nccmp.org
Website: nccmp.org
Staff: 4
Annual Budget: $2-5,000,000
Tax: 501(c)(4)

Personnel:
Executive Director: Randy G. DeFrehn
    E-Mail: rdefrehn@nccmp.org
Director, Communications: Patricia Douglas
    E-Mail: nccmp@nccmp.org
Deputy Executive Director, Research and Education: Josh
    Shapiro
Coordinator, Membership Services: Margaret M. Tobin

Historical Note:
NCCMP's mission is to assure an environment in which multiemployer plans can continue in their vital role in providing benefits to working Americans with a minimum of regulatory or other interference. Membership: $25000 (Contributing/Sustaining); $3000-7500 (Regular); $5000 (Associate).

Meetings/Conferences: Annual

National Corn Growers Association *(1957)*
632 Cepi Dr.
Chesterfield, MO 63005
Tel: (636) 733-9004 *Fax:* (636) 733-9005
E-Mail: corninfo@ncga.com
Website: ncga.com
Members: 37447 individuals
Staff: 37
Annual Budget: $10-25,000,000
Tax: 501(c)(5)

Personnel:
Chief Executive Officer: Richard S. Tolman
    E-Mail: tolman@ncga.com
Director, Communications: Ken Colombini
    E-Mail: colombini@ncga.com
Manager, Marketing: Joe Hodes
    E-Mail: hodes@ncga.com
Director, Administration: Rodger Mansfield
    E-Mail: mansfield@ncga.com
Specialist, Association and Membership Services: Mike
    Shelby
    E-Mail: shelby@ncga.com
Vice President, Marketing: Fred O. Stemme
    E-Mail: stemme@ncga.com

Historical Note:
NCGA's mission is to create and increase opportunities for corn growers. Members are farmers. Membership: $20-50/year (varies by state).

Meetings/Conferences: Annual

Publications:
Corn Action News; weekly
Corn Grower Update; quarterly

National Correctional Industries Association *(1941)*
1202 N. Charles St.
Baltimore, MD 21201
Tel: (410) 230-3972 *Fax:* (410) 230-3981
E-Mail: info@nationalcia.org
Website: nationalcia.org
Members: 8000 individuals
Staff: 7
Annual Budget: $500-1,000,000
Tax: 501(c)(3)

Personnel:
Executive Director: Gina Honeycutt
    E-Mail: gina@nationalcia.org
Director, Operations and Grant Manager: Wil Heslop
    E-Mail: wil@nationalcia.org
Systems Coordinator: Farrah Marriott
    E-Mail: farrah@nationalcia.org
Accounting Manager: Julio Nacario
    E-Mail: julio@nationalcia.org
Manager, Sales and Marketing: Rebekah Zinno
    E-Mail: rebekah@nationalcia.org

Historical Note:
NCIA is an international nonprofit professional association whose members represent all 50 state correctional industry agencies, Federal Prison Industries, foreign correctional industry agencies and city/county jail industry programs. Mission is to promote excellence and credibility in correctional industries through professional development and innovative business solutions. Membership: $775-3,500 (Agency, based on number of employees); $500 (Jail Industries and Correctional Institution); $25-45 (Individual); $45-1200 (Corporate).

Meetings/Conferences: Annual
2013 - Charlotte, NC (Westin Charlotte)/March 24 - 27

Publications:
NCIA Directory; annually; adv.
NCIA News; quarterly; adv.

National Corrugated Steel Pipe Association *(1956)*
14070 Proton Rd.
Suite 100, LB Nine
Dallas, TX 75244
Tel: (972) 850-1907 *Fax:* (972) 490-4219
E-Mail: info@ncspa.org
Website: ncspa.org
Members: 90 manufacturers
Staff: 3
Annual Budget: $250-500,000
Tax: 501(c)(6)

Personnel:
President: Patrick Collings
Chief Engineer: Michael McGough
    E-Mail: mmcgough@ncspa.org
Association Management Services: Becky Tiemann
    E-Mail: btiemann@ncspa.org

Historical Note:
Formerly National Corrugated Metal Pipe Association. NCSPA's mission is to promote sound public policy relating to the use of corrugated steel drainage structures in private and public construction. Membership: $550-5,500 (Company); $660-1,320 (Affiliate).

Meetings/Conferences: Annual

Publications:
E-News; on-line
Membership Directory; on-line

Membership List Available to Non-members

National Costumers Association *(1923)*
121 N. Bosart Ave.
Indianapolis, IN 46201
Tel: (317) 351-1940 *Fax:* (317) 351-1941
TollFree: (800) 622-1321
E-Mail: office@costumers.org
Website: costumers.org
Members: 525 theatrical costumers and suppliers
Staff: 2
Annual Budget: $100-250,000

Personnel:
Membership Secretary: Jennifer Skarstedt
Manager, Publications: Diane Despopoulos Sheibley
    E-Mail: pub@costumers.org

Historical Note:
NCA encourages and promotes diversified use of costumes in all fields of human activity. Members are theatrical,

masquerade, dance, academic and religious. Membership: $300 (Rental/Retail/Wholesaler/Manufacturer/Costume Professional); $100 (Affiliate); $125 (Secondary Member/Additional Location); $75 (Student).

Publications:
NCA Magazine; adv.

National Cotton Batting Institute *(1954)*
4322 Bloombury St.
Southaven, MS 38672
Tel: (901) 218-2393 *Fax:* (662) 449-0046
E-Mail: info@natbat.com
Website: natbat.com
Members: 25 companies and 40 individuals
Staff: 2
Annual Budget: $10-25,000

Personnel:
Executive Secretary and Treasurer: Fred Middleton

Historical Note:
NCBI represents U.S. companies that manufacture and sell batting for use in mattresses, futons, home furnishings, and upholstered products. NCBI provides a range of services to assist its members in expanding markets, monitoring and contributing to legislative and regulatory decisions that affect the industry, and conducting consumer education and information programs. NCBI's mission is to protect and enhance the growth, profitability and stature of the U.S.cotton batting-manufacturing industry.

Publications:
Membership Directory; on-line
NCBI Magazine; adv.

Membership List Available to Non-members

National Cotton Council of America *(1938)*
P.O. BOX 2995
Cordova, TN 38088-2995
Tel: (901) 274-9030 *Fax:* (901) 725-0510
E-Mail: info@cotton.org
Website: cotton.org
Members: 21974 individuals
Staff: 14
Annual Budget: $10-25,000,000
Tax: 501(c)(6)

Personnel:
President and Chief Executive Officer: Dr. Mark D. Lange
Vice President, Economics and Policy Analysis: Dr. Gary
    Adams
Director, Meeting and Travel Services: Ellen C. Ferrell
Director, Membership Services: John Gibson
Vice President, Technical Services: Dr. Bill M. Norman
Assistant Treasurer: R. E. Shellabarger
Director, Communications, Production and AV Services:
    Marjory L. Walker

Historical Note:
Trade association representing U.S. cotton industry

Meetings/Conferences:
Conference Chair: Ellen C. Ferrell
2013 - San Antonio, TX (San Antonio Marriott
    Rivercenter)/Jan. 7 - 10
2013 - Memphis, TN (Peabody Memphis)/Feb. 7 - 11
2014 - Washington, DC (JW Marriott Washington,
    D.C.)/Feb. 6 - 9

Publications:
Cotton Counts Its Customers; annually
Cotton Economic Review; monthly
Cotton Physiology Today; daily
Cotton's Week; weekly
Daily Cotton eNews; daily
Journal of Cotton Science
Monthly Outlook; monthly
Weekly Cotton Market Report; weekly

National Cotton Ginners' Association *(1937)*
P.O. Box 2995
Cordova, TN 38088-2995
Tel: (901) 274-9030 *Fax:* (901) 725-0510
Website: cotton.org/ncga
Members: 680 individuals
Staff: 2
Annual Budget: $50-100,000
Tax: 501(c)(6)

Personnel:
Executive Vice President: W. Harrison Ashley
    E-Mail: hashley@cotton.org
President: Lee Tiller

Historical Note:

NCGA is the umbrella organization for eight state and regional ginner associations. Members are state and regional associations representing cotton ginners and processors. Administrative support provided by National Cotton Council.

Continuing Education:
Enrollment: 325
Certification Designation/s: CGP

Publications:
Member Directory; on-line

National Cottonseed Products Association *(1897)*
866 Willow Tree Cir.
Cordova, TN 38018-6376
Tel: (901) 682-0800 *Fax:* (901) 682-2856
E-Mail: info@cottonseed.com
Website: cottonseed.com
Members: 300 businesses
Staff: 2
Annual Budget: $250-500,000

Personnel:
Executive Vice President and Secretary: Ben Morgan BS, MBA
Treasurer: Sandi Stine

Historical Note:
Founded as the Interstate Cottonseed Crushers Association, it assumed its present name in 1929. NCPA is the trade association of the cottonseed processing industry in the United States and represents the industry's interests. Members are oil mills, refiners, product dealers and product brokers. Membership: $500/year (Regular/Dealer).

Meetings/Conferences: Annual
2013 - Tucson, AZ (JW Marriott Tucson Starr Pass Resort and Spa)/May 4 - 7
Number of non-conference events/year: 1

Publications:
Newsletter

National Council for Accreditation of Teacher Education *(1954)*
2010 Massachusetts Ave. NW
Suite 500
Washington, DC 20036
Tel: (202) 466-7496 *Fax:* (202) 296-6620
E-Mail: ncate@ncate.org
Website: ncate.org
Members: 33 organizations
Staff: 28
Annual Budget: $2-5,000,000
Tax: 501(c)(3)

Personnel:
President: James G. Cibulka
   E-Mail: jim@ncate.org
Vice President, State Relations: Shari L. Francis
   E-Mail: shari@ncate.org
Director, Finance and Administration: Nancy Groth
Chief Information Officer: Frank Huang
   E-Mail: frank@ncate.org
Vice President, Communications: Jane Leibbrand
   E-Mail: jane@ncate.org
Vice President, Program Review: Monique C. Lynch

Historical Note:
NCATE is the teaching profession's organization to help establish high quality teacher, specialist, and administrator preparation. They believes every student deserves a caring, competent, and highly qualified teacher.

Meetings/Conferences: Semi-Annual
Conference Chair: Monique C. Lynch
Number of non-conference events/year: 14

Publications:
NCATE Newsletter; semi-annually

Membership List Available to Non-members

National Council for Advanced Manufacturing *(1989)*
2025 M St. NW
Suite 800
Washington, DC 20036
Tel: (202) 367-1178 *Fax:* (202) 429-2422
E-Mail: nacfam@nacfam.org
Website: nacfam.org
Members: 3000 organizations
Staff: 12
Annual Budget: $250-500,000
Tax: 501(c)(3)

Personnel:

Chairman and Chief Executive Officer: Robert "Rusty" Patterson
   E-Mail: pattersonr@nacfam.org
Executive Vice President, Industry Relations and Workforce Development: Fred Wentzel
   E-Mail: wentzelf@nacfam.org

Historical Note:
NACFAM encourages the interests of United States manufacturers by improving their product quality, market share and productivity through the deployment of advanced manufacturing processes, related management strategies, and technical training. Members are companies, educational institutions, research entities, government agencies, labor unions, trade and professional associations, workforce development groups, economic development groups, and individuals. Membership: $5,000-50,000 (Company, based on annual sales); $1,000 (Alliance).

Meetings/Conferences: Annual
Conference Chair: Fred Wentzel

Publications:
Manufacturing Metrics; weekly
Policy Insights; quarterly

National Council for Agricultural Education *(1983)*
1410 King St.
Suite 400
Alexandria, VA 22314
Tel: (703) 838-5881 *Fax:* (703) 838-5888
TollFree: (800) 772-0939
E-Mail: council@teamaged.org
Website: ffa.org/thecouncil/Pages/index.html
Staff: 2
Annual Budget: $100-250,000
Tax: 501(c)(3)

Personnel:
National FFA Advisor: Steve Brown
   E-Mail: sbrown@ffa.org
Contact, Media Relations: Tony Small

Historical Note:
The National Council for Agricultural Education (The Council) strives to stimulate positive growth in agricultural education.The Council has provided leadership for stakeholders in agriculture, food, fiber and natural resources systems education.It strives to surface issues important to agricultural education and stimulate actions to support those issues.NCAE's mission is to provide leadership and coordination to shape the future of school-based agricultural education.

Publications:
Monday Morning Monitor; weekly
The Agricultural Education

National Council for Air and Stream Improvement, Inc. *(1943)*
P.O. Box 13318
Research Triangle Park, NC 27709-3318
Tel: (919) 941-6400 *Fax:* (919) 941-6401
Website: ncasi.org
Members: 75 companies
Staff: 90
Annual Budget: $10-25,000,000

Personnel:
President: Dr. Ronald Yeske PhD
   E-Mail: ryeske@ncasi.org

Historical Note:
Formerly (1968) known as the National Council for Stream Improvement. NCASI's mission is to serve the forest products industry as a center of excellence for providing technical information and scientific research needed to achieve the industry's environmental goals and principles. Membership is open to forest products companies in the United States, Canada, and beyond North America. Sustaining Membership is open to suppliers, consulting firms, testing laboratories, and engineering firms allied to the forest products industry. Membership: Dues based on production.

Meetings/Conferences: Annual
Number of non-conference events/year: 3

Publications:
Bulletin Board; bi-weekly
Environmental News for Recyclers; quarterly
Forestry Environmental Program News; bi-weekly
Misc Doc
NCASI-Canada Bulletin
Podcast; weekly
Research Brief; on-line

National Council for Community Behavioral Healthcare *(1970)*
1701 K St. NW
Suite 400
Washington, DC 20006
Tel: (202) 684-7457 *Fax:* (202) 386-9391
E-Mail: communications@thenationalcouncil.org
Website: thenationalcouncil.org
Members: 1,950 companies
Staff: 27
Annual Budget: $5-10,000,000

Personnel:
President and Chief Executive Officer: Linda Rosenberg MSW
   E-Mail: lindar@thenationalcouncil.org
Information Technology Support and System Administrator: Samson Ayele
   E-Mail: SamsonA@thenationalcouncil.org
Executive Vice President: Jeannie Campbell
   E-Mail: jeanniec@thenationalcouncil.org
Vice President, Marketing and Communications: Meena Dayak MA
   E-Mail: meenad@thenationalcouncil.org
Director, Public Education: Bryan Gibb
   E-Mail: bryang@thenationalcouncil.org
Vice President, Public Policy: Charles Ingoglia
   E-Mail: chucki@thenationalcouncil.org
Director, Conferences: Danny Linden
   E-Mail: dannyl@thenationalcouncil.org
Chief Financial Officer and Vice President, Finance and Administration: Bruce Pelleu
   E-Mail: BruceP@thenationalcouncil.org
Associate, Marketing and Communications: Nathan Sprenger
   E-Mail: nathans@thenationalcouncil.org
Vice President, Membership Services and Corporate Development: Kara Sweeney
   E-Mail: karas@thenationalcouncil.org

Historical Note:
Founded as National Council of Community Mental Health Centers; became National Community Mental Healthcare Council in 1993, and assumed its current name in 1997. Absorbed Association of Mental Health Administrators in 1998. Mission is to advance members ability to deliver proactive and holistic healthcare services. Members are healthcare organizations offering critical mental health and addiction treatment services. Membership: $3,100 (Organizations); $3,965 (Association); $5,000 (Affiliate).

Meetings/Conferences: Annual
Conference Chair: Danny Linden
2013 - Las Vegas, NV (Caesars Palace)/April 8 - 10

Publications:
Addictions News Now; monthly
Behavioral Healthcare
Compliance Watch
Drug Abuse Weekly; weekly
Health Weekly; weekly
Journal of Behavioral Health Services and Research; quarterly
National Council Magazine; quarterly; adv.
Public Policy Update; weekly
Technical Assistance Update; semi-monthly

Membership List Available to Non-members

National Council for Geographic Education *(1915)*
1145 17th St. NW
Room 7620
Washington, DC 20036
Tel: (202) 857-7695 *Fax:* (202) 234-2744
E-Mail: ncge@ncge.org
Website: ncge.org
Members: 2561 individuals
Staff: 4
Annual Budget: $500-1,000,000
Tax: 501(c)(3)

Personnel:
Director, Operations: Zachary R. Dulli
   E-Mail: zach@ncge.org
Coordinator, Membership: Ashley Thomas
   E-Mail: athomas@ncge.org
Director, Educational Affairs: Jacqueline Waite
   E-Mail: jwaite@ncge.org

Historical Note:
Formerly the National Council of Geography Teachers. NCGE's mission is to enhance the status, quality, and

effectiveness of geography teaching in North America.
Members include both U.S. and International teachers,
professors, students, businesses, and others who support
geographic education. Membership: $15-1500 /year.

Meetings/Conferences: Annual
Conference Chair: Jacqueline Waite
2013 - Denver, CO (Denver Marriott City Center)/Aug.
  1 - 4
2014 - Memphis, TN (Peabody Memphis)/July 31 -
  Aug. 3
2015 - Washington, DC (JW Marriott Washington,
  D.C.)/Aug. 6 - 9

Publications:
Journal of Geography; bi-monthly
Perspective; bi-monthly
The Geography Teacher; semi-annually

Membership List Available to Non-members

National Council for History Education *(1990)*
7100 Baltimore Ave.
Suite 510
College Park, MD 20740
Tel: (440) 835-1776 *Fax:* (240) 523-0245
E-Mail: NCHE@nche.net
Website: nche.net
Staff: 8
Annual Budget: $1-2,000,000

Personnel:
Interim Executive Director: Jim Cameron
  E-Mail: peter@nche.net
Director, Conference and Events: John Csepegi
  E-Mail: john@nche.net
Director, Membership Services, Communications and Editor:
  Mary Malicki
  E-Mail: mary@nche.net
Coordinator, Membership Services: Kionna Winston
  E-Mail: kionna@nche.net

Historical Note:
The National Council for History Education builds bridges
between K-12 teachers, college and university faculty and
museums/libraries/historical societies who all share a
common passion for teaching history. Membership: $30
(Student/Retired); $50 (Partner); $100 (Patron); $300
(Sustaining); $1000 (Chairman's Club).

Meetings/Conferences:
Conference Chair: John Csepegi
2013 - Columbia, SC (Westwood High School)/Jan. 25
  - 26
2013 - Richmond, VA (Richmond Marriott)/March 21 -
  23/700 attendees/over 100 exhibitors

Publications:
History Matters

National Council for Impacted Schools *(1999)*
4002 Eagle Crest Dr.
Muskogee, OK 74403
Tel: (918) 684-9019 *Fax:* (918) 684-6675
Website: ncisweb.com
Members: 300 Schools
Staff: 13

Personnel:
Executive Director: Ray Henson
Secretary and Treasurer: Tom Crimmins

Historical Note:
NCIS's mission is to establish an equitable proration
formula for impact aid payments when the program is not
full funded, ensure weights properly reflect the loss of taxes
to a district and provide full eligibility of all federal students
in districts meeting the program standards. Membership:
$125-8,000, depending on the federal impact aid that your
school receives.

Publications:
Newsletter; bi-weekly

National Council for Interior Design Qualifications
(1972)
1602 L St. NW
Suite 200
Washington, DC 20036-5681
Tel: (202) 721-0220 *Fax:* (202) 721-0221
E-Mail: inquiries@ncidq.org
Website: ncidq.org
Staff: 6

Personnel:
Executive Director: Jeffrey F. Kenney
Program Manager, Special Projects and Committees: Ken
  Baker

Deputy Director: Kathleen Butler
Manager, Office and Customer Service: Leslie Ford
Accountant: Lola Liao
Director, Operations: Joshua Prentice

Historical Note:
Founded as a basis for issuing credentials to professional
interior design practitioners, the council was formalized
as a nonprofit organization in 1974. NCIDQ's mission
is to develope and administer the examination and also
provides research and expertise that informs state and
provincial licensing laws and regulations for the interior
design profession. Members are state and provincial boards
that regulate the profession of interior design.

Continuing Education:
Certification Designation/s: NCIDQ

Publications:
QLetter Newsletter; monthly

Membership List Available to Non-members

National Council for International Visitors *(1961)*
1420 K St. NW
Suite 800
Washington, DC 20005
Tel: (202) 842-1414 *Fax:* (202) 289-4625
E-Mail: info@nciv.org
Website: nciv.org
Members: 95 nonprofit organizations
Staff: 10
Annual Budget: $5-10,000,000
Tax: 501(c)(3)

Personnel:
President: Jennifer Clinton
Program Associate, Communications: Zachary Carr
Program Officer, Finance and Administration: Leah
  Tomlins
Program Associate, Membership and Training: Haley
  Willis

Historical Note:
Serves the international exchange community. Members
design and implement professional programs, provide
cultural activities, and offer home hospitality for foreign
leaders, specialists, and scholars participating in the U.S.
Department of State International Visitor Leadership
Program (IVLP) and other exchanges. Membership:
$125-500 (Community Organization); $150-250
(Associate Member); $60 (Individual); $25 (Student).

Meetings/Conferences: Annual

Publications:
NCIV Network News; monthly

National Council for Languages and International Studies *(1988)*
4646 40th St. NW
Suite 310
Washington, DC 20016
Tel: (202) 966-8477 *Fax:* (202) 966-8310
E-Mail: info@languagepolicy.org
Website: languagepolicy.org
Members: 59 organizations
Staff: 2
Annual Budget: $100-250,000
Tax: 501(c)(4)

Personnel:
Executive Director: Dr. William P. Rivers
  E-Mail: wrivers@languagepolicy.org
Office Manager: Walter Martinez

Historical Note:
NCLIS works on the mission that all Americans must
have the opportunity to learn and use English and at
least one other language. Supported by 64 language and
international studies organizations.

Publications:
Member Spotlight
Modern Language Journal

National Council for Marketing and Public Relations *(1974)*
P.O. Box 336039
Greeley, CO 80633
Tel: (970) 330-0771 *Fax:* (970) 330-0769
Website: ncmpr.org
Members: 1550 individuals
Staff: 3
Annual Budget: $500-1,000,000
Tax: 501(c)(6)

Personnel:
Executive Director: Becky Olson

  E-Mail: bolson@ncmpr.org
Associate Director Counsel and Editor: Debra Halsey
  E-Mail: dhalsey@ncmpr.org
Coordinator, Membership Services: Shirley Medbery
  E-Mail: smedbery@ncmpr.org

Historical Note:
Formerly (1988) the National Council for Community
Relations. NCMPR aims to provide professional development
opportunities, advocate on behalf of the profession and
the institutions it serves, and recognize professional
excellence. Members are individuals involved in marketing,
communications, public relations and enrollment
management at community, junior and technical colleges.
Membership: $225 (Individual); $450 (College/Educational
Associate); $650 (Corporate Associate); $95 (Student/
Retired).

Meetings/Conferences: Annual
Conference Chair: Becky Olson
2013 - Chicago, IL (Fairmont Chicago Millennium
  Park)/March 10 - 13

Publications:
Counsel Magazine; quarterly; adv.
E-News; on-line
Membership Directory; on-line

National Council for Prescription Drug Programs
(1977)
9240 E. Raintree Dr.
Scottsdale, AZ 85260-7518
Tel: (480) 477-1000 *Fax:* (480) 767-1042
TollFree: (877) 647-0295
E-Mail: ncpdp@ncpdp.org
Website: ncpdp.org
Members: 1582 individuals and 954
organizations
Staff: 42
Annual Budget: $5-10,000,000

Personnel:
President: Lee Ann Stember
  E-Mail: lstember@ncpdp.org
Director, Marketing and Communications: Maggie Bruce
  E-Mail: mbruce@ncpdp.org
Senior Manager, Meeting Planning and Membership
  Services: Beth Fagan
Specialist, Human Resources: Rich Gerry
  E-Mail: rgerry@ncpdp.org
Senior Vice President, Industry Information Technology:
  John Klimek
  E-Mail: jklimek@ncpdp.org
Senior Manager, Finance and Administration: Sandy
  Kovalik
  E-Mail: skovalik@ncpdp.org
Senior Vice President, Operations: Joanne Longie
  E-Mail: jlongie@ncpdp.org
Coordinator, Marketing: Jim McIntyre
  E-Mail: jmcintyre@ncpdp.org
Senior Vice President, Communications and Industry
  Relations: Steve Mullenix
  E-Mail: smullenix@ncpdp.org
Manager, Membership Services: Jenny Powers
  E-Mail: jpowers@ncpdp.org
Specialist, Government Affairs: Nicole Schultz
  E-Mail: nschultz@ncpdp.org

Historical Note:
NCPDP's provides a place wherein members can develop
business solutions, including ANSI-accredited standards,
and guidance for promoting information exchanges related
to medications, supplies, and services within the healthcare
system. Membership: $650/year (Individual).

Meetings/Conferences: Annual
Conference Chair: Beth Fagan
2013 - Phoenix, AZ (Arizona Biltmore Resort & Spa)/
  May 5 - 9/1-10 exhibitors
Number of non-conference events/year: 10

Publications:
Membership Directory; on-line
NCPDP News; weekly

National Council for Research on Women *(1981)*
11 Hanover Sq.
24th Floor
New York, NY 10005
Tel: (212) 785-7335
E-Mail: ncrw@ncrw.org
Website: ncrw.org
Members:
2,000 researchers and specialists

120 leading research, policy and advocacy centers
Staff: 9
Annual Budget: $1-2,000,000

Personnel:
President: Linda Basch PhD
Web Master: Jonathan Bourland
Liaison, Member Center Relations: Kadija Ferryman
Director, Operations: Andrea Greenblatt
Director, Communications: Vivienne Heston-Demirel
Director, Research and Programs: Shyama Venkateswar PhD

Historical Note:
NCRW's mission is dedicated to improving the lives of women and girls and to provide the latest news, analysis and strategies needed to ensure fully informed debates, effective policies and inclusive practices.

Meetings/Conferences:
Number of non-conference events/year: 1

Publications:
IQ

Membership List Available to Non-members

National Council for Science and the Environment (1990)
1101 17th St. NW
Suite 250
Washington, DC 20036
Tel: (202) 530-5810 *Fax:* (202) 628-4311
E-Mail: info@ncseonline.org
Website: ncseonline.org
Staff: 25
Annual Budget: $2-5,000,000
Tax: 501(c)(3)

Personnel:
Executive Director: Peter D Saundry PhD
  E-Mail: peter@ncseonline.org
Officer, Communications and Managing Editor: Lyle Birkey
  E-Mail: lbirkey@NCSEonline.org
Director, Education and Senior Scientist: David E. Blockstein PhD
  E-Mail: david@ncseonline.org
Director, Finance: Andi Glashow
  E-Mail: andi@NCSEonline.org
Director, University Membership and Relations: Shelley Kossak
  E-Mail: shelley@NCSEonline.org
Meetings Contact and Office Manager: Christopher Prince
  E-Mail: cprince@ncseonline.org

Historical Note:
The National Council for Science and the Environment (NCSE) was founded in 1990 as the Committee for the National Institute for the Environment (CNIE).NCSE's mission is to improve the scientific basis for environmental decision making.

Meetings/Conferences: Annual
Conference Chair: Christopher Prince
2013 - Washington, DC (Ronald Reagan Building and International Trade Center)/Jan. 15 - 17
Number of non-conference events/year: 2

Publications:
NCSE Quarterly; quarterly

National Council for the Social Studies (1921)
8555 16th St.
Suite 500
Silver Spring, MD 20910
Tel: (301) 588-1800 *Fax:* (301) 588-2049
TollFree: (800) 296-7840
Website: socialstudies.org
Members: 25,000 educators
Staff: 20
Annual Budget: $2-5,000,000
Tax: 501(c)(3)

Personnel:
Executive Director: Susan Griffin
  E-Mail: sgriffin@ncss.org
Director, Meetings and Exhibits: David Bailor
  E-Mail: dbailor@ncss.org
Director, Administration: Timothy Daly
  E-Mail: tdaly@ncss.org
Director, Finance: Brenda Luper CAE
  E-Mail: brenda@ncss.org

Director, External Relations and Council Communications: Ana M. Chiquillo Post
  E-Mail: apost@ncss.org
Director, Membership Processing: Cassandra Roberts
  E-Mail: croberts@ncss.org
Director, Publications: Michael Simpson
  E-Mail: msimpson@ncss.org

Historical Note:
NCSS seeks to provide leadership, service, and support for all social studies educators. Serves as an umbrella organization for elementary, secondary, and college teachers of history, civics, geography, economics, political science, sociology, psychology, anthropology, and law-related education. Membership is open to any person or institution interested in the social studies. Membership: $37-79 (Individual); $47-79 (Comprehensive); $37-47 (Student/Retired); $115-130 (Institution).

Meetings/Conferences: Annual
Conference Chair: David Bailor
2013 - St. Louis, MO (Cervantes Convention Center at America's Center)/Nov. 22 - 24
2014 - Boston, MA (John P. Hynes Veterans Memorial Convention Center)/Nov. 21 - 23
2015 - New Orleans, LA (Ernest N. Morial Convention Center)/Nov. 13 - 15
2016 - Washington, DC (Walter E. Washington Convention Center)/Dec. 2 - 4
2017 - San Francisco, CA (Moscone West-Moscone Center)/Nov. 17 - 19
2018 - Chicago, IL (Hyatt Regency)/Nov. 30 - Dec. 2
Number of non-conference events/year: 20

Publications:
Membership Directory; on-line
Middle Level Learning; on-line
Social Education
Social Studies and the Young Learner; quarterly; adv.
The Social Studies Professional
Theory and Research in Social Education; quarterly

Membership List Available to Non-members

National Council for Therapeutic Recreation Certification (1981)
Seven Elmwood Dr.
New City, NY 10956
Tel: (845) 639-1439 *Fax:* (845) 639-1471
E-Mail: nctrc@nctrc.org
Website: nctrc.org
Members: 12000 individuals
Staff: 11
Annual Budget: $1-2,000,000

Personnel:
Executive Director: Bob Riley CTRS, PhD
  E-Mail: briley@nctrc.org

Historical Note:
NCTRC's mission is to protect the consumer of therapeutic recreation services by promoting the provision of quality therapeutic recreation services by NCTRC certificants.

Continuing Education:
Certification Designation/s: CTRS, NCTRC

Publications:
NCTRC e-News; on-line

National Council for Workforce Education
1050 Larrabee Ave.
Suite 104-308
Bellingham, WA 98225
Fax: (231) 591-3539
E-Mail: ncwe@ncwe.org
Website: ncwe.org
Members: 650 individuals
Staff: 6
Annual Budget: $250-500,000

Personnel:
Executive Director: Darlene G. Miller
  E-Mail: executivedirector@ncwe.org

Historical Note:
NCWE is committed to promoting excellence and growth in workforce education. Membership: $150 (Individual/Organization/nonprofit one member/Institutional one member); $360 (Nonprofit three member/Institutional, three members); $595 (Nonprofit five member/Institutional, five members); $75 (Student).

Meetings/Conferences: Annual
Conference Chair: Kay Moormann

Publications:
Workplace; quarterly

Membership List Available to Non-members

National Council of Acoustical Consultants (1962)
9100 Purdue Rd.
Suite 200
Indianapolis, IN 46268
Tel: (317) 328-0642 *Fax:* (317) 328-4629
E-Mail: info@ncac.com
Website: ncac.com
Members: 138 companies
Staff: 5
Annual Budget: $100-250,000
Tax: 501(c)(6)

Personnel:
Executive Director: Jackie Williams, CPA
  E-Mail: jwilliams@ncac.com
Vice President, Marketing and Communications: Stephanie Adams
Coordinator, Membership Services and Meetings: Bethany Patton
Vice President, Finance: James Phillips
Vice President, Membership Services: James Phillips

Historical Note:
NCAC is an international organization committed to support the acoustical profession by promoting opportunities for peer interaction. It also seeks to provide a reference tool for the public to learn more about the profession and to find a consultant matched to their needs. Membership: $185/year (Indexed based on firm size).

Meetings/Conferences: Annual
Conference Chair: Bethany Patton
2013 - Denver, CO (Denver Marriott City Center)/Aug. 24 - 25

Publications:
Membership Directory; on-line
The NCAC Newsletter; quarterly; adv.

National Council of Agricultural Employers (1964)
8233 Old Courthouse Rd.
Suite 200
Vienna, VA 22182
Tel: (703) 790-9039 *Fax:* (703) 790-0845
E-Mail: info@ncaeonline.org
Website: ncaeonline.org
Members:
200 organizations
100 individuals
Staff: 2
Annual Budget: $500-1,000,000
Tax: 501(c)(6)

Personnel:
Jr., Executive Vice President for NCAE: Frank A. Gasperini Jr., CAE
  E-Mail: frank@ncaeonline.org
Administration Manager: Matthew A. Coffindaffer
  E-Mail: matt@ncaeonline.org

Historical Note:
NCAE's mission is to advocate, promote, educate and report on legislative and regulatory, policy, and legal issues of importance to agricultural employers, their critical allies and others whose business interests revolve around labor intensive agriculture. Their members are growers, associations, and others whose business interests revolve around labor intensive agriculture. Membership: $15000 (Leader); $7000 (Patron); $3700 (Benefactor); $1700 (Supporter); $500 (Subscriber/Associate).

Meetings/Conferences:
2013 - Washington, DC (Hotel Monaco Washington D.C.)/Feb. 5 - 6

National Council of Architectural Registration Boards (1919)
1801 K St. NW
Suite 700K
Washington, DC 20006-1310
Tel: (202) 783-6500 *Fax:* (202) 783-0290
Website: ncarb.org
Members: 54 state registration boards
Staff: 75
Annual Budget: $10-25,000,000
Tax: 501(c)(6)

Personnel:
Chief Executive Officer: Michael J. Armstrong
Vice President, Operations: Mary S. de Sousa CAE
  E-Mail: mdesousa@ncarb.org
Director, Information Systems: Guillermo Ortiz de Zarate
Director, Communications: Kim Kerker
  E-Mail: kkerker@ncarb.org

Vice President, Programs: Stephen Nutt AIA, CAE
    E-Mail: snutt@ncarb.org
Director, Administration: Zerrin Sayar AIA, CAE

Historical Note:
NCARB's mission is to protect the public health, safety, and welfare by leading the regulation of the practice of architecture through the development and application of standards for licensure and credentialing of architects. Membership: $4,500/year (State Regulatory Boards).

Continuing Education:
Enrollment: 35000
Certification Designation/s: EESA, ARE, IDP, NCARB

Publications:
ARE e-news; quarterly
Direct Connection; semi-annually
e-Connection; semi-annually
IDP e-news; quarterly
IDP Supervisor e-News; quarterly

National Council of Art Administrators *(1972)*
Megram Consulting Services, Ltd.
3-247 Barr St.
Renfrew, ON K7V 1J6
Tel: (613) 432-9491
E-Mail: rshay@uky.edu
Website: ncaaarts.org
Members: 200 individuals
Staff: 4

Personnel:
Association Management Executive: Bonnie James
    E-Mail: bonnie@megram.com

Historical Note:
The purpose of NCAA is to promote communication between institutions, share ideas and facilitate growth in the organization. Members are visual arts administrators in higher education. Membership: $50/year (Individual).

Meetings/Conferences: Annual

National Council of Athletic Training *(1976)*
1900 Association Drive
Reston, VA 20191
Tel: (800) 213-7193 *Fax:* (703) 476-8316
Members: 18000 individuals
Staff: 42
Annual Budget: $5-10,000,000

Personnel:
Staff Liaison: Anita James

Historical Note:
Formerly (1976) NAGWS Athletic Training Committee amd (1986) Athletic Training Council. Members are members of the National Association for Girls and Women in Sport and the National Association for Sport and Physical Education who have an interest in the profession of athletic trainer. Administrative support is provided by the National Association for Sport and Physical Education. Membership: $125/year (individual).

National Council of Chain Restaurants *(1965)*
325 Seventh St. NW
Suite 1100
Washington, DC 20004
Tel: (202) 783-7971 *Fax:* (202) 737-2849
TollFree: (800) 673-4692
E-Mail: info@nrf.com
Website: nccr.net
Members: 40 companies
Staff: 6
Annual Budget: $250-500,000

Personnel:
Executive Director: Robert J. Green
    E-Mail: greenr@nccr.net
Senior Director, Media Relations: Stephen Schatz
Director, Membership Development: Jessica Viator
    E-Mail: viatorj@nrf.com
Vice President: Scott Vinson
    E-Mail: vinsons@nccr.net

Historical Note:
Formerly (1973) American Restaurant Institute and (1990) Foodservice and Lodging Institute, NCCR's mission is to work for sound public policy that best serves the interests of restaurant businesses and the people they employ. It also litigates issues of common interest to the majority of its membership. Membership: $3,000-40,000/year (Fees based on Sales).

Meetings/Conferences: Annual
Conference Chair: Shawna Purvis

Publications:
NCCR Highlights Newsletter; weekly

NRF SmartBrief; daily
Restaurant SmartBrief; daily
STORES; monthly

National Council of Coal Lessors *(1951)*
300 Summers St., Suite 1050
Charleston, WV 25301
Tel: (304) 757-8886
Members: 50 companies
Staff: 1
Annual Budget: $50-100,000

Personnel:
Assistant Secretary: Lynn Lawson

Historical Note:
A trade group of companies who own and lease coal-bearing land.

National Council of Commercial Plant Breeders *(1954)*
225 Reinekers Ln.
Alexandria, VA 22314
Website: nccpb.org
Members: 29 companies and individuals
Staff: 3
Annual Budget: $25-50,000
Tax: 501(c)(6)

Personnel:
Executive Vice President: Andrew LaVigne
    E-Mail: alavigne@amseed.org
Secretary and Treasurer: Ann Jorss
    E-Mail: ajorss@amseed.org

Historical Note:
Founded in 1954 by representatives of thirteen commercial firms as a non- profit organization and NCCPB's mission is to promote plant breeding and genetic research for seed and trait improvement. Membership: $100-5,000 (Active Member, depending on sales volume); $200 (Associate).

National Council of Erectors, Fabricators and Riggers *(1969)*
10382 Main St., Suite 200
P.O. Box 280
Fairfax, VA 22038
Tel: (703) 591-1870 *Fax:* (703) 591-1895
Members: 3 organizations
Staff: 3
Annual Budget: $50-100,000

Personnel:
President: Fred H. Codding

Historical Note:
NCEFR serves as an interface with construction unions. Members are the Specialized Carriers and Rigging Association, the National Association of Reinforcing Steel Contractors, and the National Association of Miscellaneous Ornamental and Architectural Products Contractors.

National Council of Examiners for Engineering and Surveying *(1920)*
280 Seneca Creek Rd.
Seneca, SC 29678
Tel: (864) 654-6824 *Fax:* (864) 654-6824
TollFree: (800) 250-3196
Website: ncees.org
Members: 70 member boards
Staff: 60
Annual Budget: $10-25,000,000
Tax: 501(c)(3)

Personnel:
Executive Director: Jerry Carter
    E-Mail: jcarter@ncees.org
Manager, Corporate Communications: Keri Anderson
Manager, Exam Publications: Ashley Cheney
Director, Information Technology: Steven Matthews
Manager, Meetings and Outreach Logistics: Trish McAlister
Director, Human Resources: Donna Moss PHR
Director, Public Affairs: Nina Norris
Director, Exam Administration Services: Pam Powell
Director, Finance: Jeannie Van der Zalm CPA

Historical Note:
Formerly (1967) National Council of State Boards of Engineering Examiners, and (1989) National Council of Engineering Examiners. NCEES seeks to advance licensure for engineers and surveyors in order to protect the health, safety, and welfare of the public. Develops, scores, and administers the examinations used for engineering and surveying licensure throughout the United States. Membership: $5,000/year (Company).

Continuing Education:
Certification Designation/s: FE, PE, SE, FS, PS
Meetings/Conferences: Annual
Conference Chair: Trish McAlister
2013 - San Antonio, TX/Aug. 21 - 24
2014 - Seattle, WA/Aug. 20 - 23
2015 - Williamsburg, VA/Aug. 19 - 22
2016 - Indianapolis, IN/Aug. 24 - 27
Number of non-conference events/year: 3

National Council of Exchangors *(1975)*
8255 Las Vegas Blvd., South
Suite 1202
Las Vegas, NV 89123
Tel: (702) 475-5331
E-Mail: nce@ncexchangors.com
Website: NCExchangors.com
Members: 400 individuals
Staff: 5
Annual Budget: $50-100,000

Personnel:
President: William Jones
Treasurer: Lance Warner

Historical Note:
NCE is a network of real estate professionals who specialize in marketing real estate equities primarily through the medium of the real estate exchange. Membership: $115/year (Individual).

Continuing Education:
Certification Designation/s: EMS

Meetings/Conferences:
2013 - Las Vegas, NV (Tuscany Suites & Casino)/April 16 - 19
2013 - Las Vegas, NV (Tuscany Suites & Casino)/Oct. 14 - 17

Publications:
NCEmail Newsletter; weekly

National Council of Farmer Cooperatives *(1929)*
50 F St. NW
Suite 900
Washington, DC 20001
Tel: (202) 626-8700 *Fax:* (202) 626-8722
E-Mail: info@ncfc.org
Website: ncfc.org
Members: 3,026 local farmer cooperatives and state and regional councils of cooperatives
Staff: 13
Annual Budget: $5-10,000,000
Tax: 501(c)(6)

Personnel:
President and Chief Executive Officer: Charles F. Conner
Senior Vice President and General Counsel, Legal, Tax and Accounting: Marlis Carson
    E-Mail: mcarson@ncfc.org
Vice President, Communications: Justin Darisse
    E-Mail: jdarisse@ncfc.org
Planner, Meetings: Kate Disbrow
    E-Mail: kdisbrow@ncfc.org
Director, Finance and Administration: Bonita Harrison
    E-Mail: bharrison@ncfc.org
Manager, Membership Relations and Development: Kathleen Heron
    E-Mail: kheron@ncfc.org
Vice President and Chief of Staff, Government Affairs: Lisa Kelley
    E-Mail: lkelley@ncfc.org
Vice President, Legislative and Regulatory Affairs: Kevin Natz
    E-Mail: knatz@ncfc.org
Manager, Legal, Tax and Accounting Committee: Suzanne Spence
    E-Mail: sspence@ncfc.org

Historical Note:
NCFC's mission is to advance the business and policy interests of America's cooperatives and other farmer-owned enterprises. Members include regional and national farmer cooperatives.

Meetings/Conferences: Annual
Conference Chair: Kate Disbrow
2013 - Scottsdale, AZ (Westin Kierland Resort and Spa)/Feb. 6 - 8
2014 - New Orleans, LA (Roosevelt New Orleans)/Feb. 12 - 14
Number of non-conference events/year: 2

Publications:

Membership Directory; on-line
NCFC Update

Membership List Available to Non-members

National Council of Higher Education Loan Programs (1961)
1100 Connecticut Ave. NW
Ste. 1200
Washington, DC 20036-4110
Tel: (202) 822-2106 Fax: (202) 822-2143
E-Mail: info@nchelp.org
Website: nchelp.org
Members: 175 organizations
Staff: 9
Annual Budget: $2-5,000,000

Personnel:
President: Shelly Repp
    E-Mail: shelly_repp@nchelp.org
Vice President, Communications: Kristen Earle
    E-Mail: kearle@nchelp.org
Manager, Meetings: Stefanie Gramm
    E-Mail: sgramm@nchelp.org
Director, Membership Services: Chris Martin
    E-Mail: cmartin@nchelp.org
Chief Technology Officer: Mark Putman
    E-Mail: mputman@nchelp.org

Historical Note:
Formerly (1969) National Conference of Executives of Higher Education Loan Plans. NCHELP's purpose is to inform the public about the availability of the Federal Family Education Loan Program (FFELP) and private education loans as a method to ensure open access to postsecondary education. Members are private and state non-profit corporations that guarantee student loans under the Higher Education Act of 1965, secondary markets, lenders, servicers, collectors, institutions of higher education and other organizations involved in the administration of the Federal Family Education Loan Program.

Meetings/Conferences:
Conference Chair: Stefanie Gramm
2013 - New Orleans, LA (St. James Parish)/July 23 - 28
Number of non-conference events/year: 3

Publications:
Daily Briefing; daily

Membership List Available to Non-members

National Council of Investigative and Security Services Inc. (1975)
7501 Sparrows Point Blvd.
Baltimore, MD 21219-1927
Fax: (410) 388-9746
TollFree: (800) 445-8408
E-Mail: NCISS@comcast.net
Website: nciss.org
Members:
525 state associations and firms
1028 members
Staff: 5
Annual Budget: $50-100,000

Personnel:
Executive Director: Carolyn Ward
    E-Mail: NCISS@comcast.net
Chair, Public Relations and Membership Promotion: Gary Kuty
Chairman, Legislative Services: Jimmie Mesis
    E-Mail: jim@nciss.org

Historical Note:
National Council of Investigative and Security Services works to monitor national legislative and regulatory activities affecting the investigation and security industry. Membership: $140 (Regular Member/Affiliate); $75 (Associate Member); $250 (Service Member); $1-100 (Association Member).

Meetings/Conferences: Annual

Publications:
The NCISS Directory; on-line
The Report; quarterly; adv.

National Council of Juvenile and Family Court Judges (1937)
P.O. Box 8970
Reno, NV 89507
Tel: (775) 784-6012 Fax: (775) 784-6628
E-Mail: staff@ncjfcj.org
Website: ncjfcj.org
Members: 30000 individuals
Staff: 97

Annual Budget: $10-25,000,000
Tax: 501 (c)(3)

Personnel:
Chief Executive Officer: Mari Kay Bickett
Director, Conference Planning and Marketing: Diane Barnette
    E-Mail: dbarnette@ncjfcj.org
Director, Human Resources: Steve Casper
    E-Mail: scasper@ncjfcj.org
Chief Financial Officer: Cheryl Dailey
    E-Mail: cdailey@ncjfcj.org
Executive Assistant: Dorothy Hall
    E-Mail: dhall@ncjfcj.org
Director, Government Affairs and Policy: Nancy Miller
    E-Mail: nmiller@ncjfcj.org
Senior Coordinator, Publications and Communications: Jackie Ruffin
    E-Mail: jruffin@ncjfcj.org
Associate Program Manager: Nancy Tierney
    E-Mail: ntierney@ncjfcj.org
Manager, Information Technology: Robin Whyms
    E-Mail: rwhyms@ncjfcj.org

Historical Note:
NCJFCJ's mission is to provide all judges, courts, and related agencies involved with juvenile, family, and domestic violence cases with the knowledge and skills to improve the lives of the families and children who seek justice. Membership: $195 (Active Judge); $145 (Associate); $175 (NCJFCJ-NJCSA Joint); $35 (Student).

Meetings/Conferences: Annual
Conference Chair: Diane Barnette
Number of non-conference events/year: 3

Publications:
Juvenile and Family Court Journal; quarterly
Juvenile and Family Justice Today; quarterly; adv.
Juvenile and Family Law Digest; monthly
Membership Directory; on-line
Synergy; bi-annually

National Council of Legislators from Gaming States (1995)
385 Jordan Rd.
Troy, NY 12180
Tel: (518) 687-0615 Fax: (518) 687-0401
E-Mail: info@nclgs.org
Website: nclgs.org
Members: 51 member states
Staff: 2
Annual Budget: $50-100,000
Tax: 501 (c)(4)

Personnel:
President: Rep. James Waldman
Treasurer: Rep. James Buskey

Historical Note:
Members of NCLGS are committees responsible for the regulation of gaming in their state legislative houses.

Meetings/Conferences: Annual
2013 - Las Vegas, NV (Rio All Suite Hotel)/Jan. 4 - 6

Publications:
NLC Newsletter

National Council of Minorities in Energy
1725 I St. NW
Suite 300
Washington, DC 20006
Tel: (202) 663-9045 Fax: (866) 663-8007
TollFree: (866) 663-9045
E-Mail: contact@minoritiesinenergy.org
Website: minoritiesinenergy.org
Staff: 3
Annual Budget: $10-25,000

Personnel:
Chairman: Ezekiel Patten Jr.
General Counsel: William "Bill" J. Bethune
Treasurer: Frank L. Torbert
    E-Mail: ftorbert@minoritiesinenergy.org

Historical Note:
The organization promotes the development and utilization of minority-owned and women-owned businesses in the energy sector and energy related industries across the United States and in international markets. Membership in the organization is available to companies involved in, or associated with, the energy industry. Membership: $5000-20,000 (Corporate); $500-7,500 (Minority Business); $500-5,000 (Associate).

Publications:
Membership Directory; on-line

Newsletter; quarterly

National Council of Nonprofits (1989)
1200 New York Ave. NW
Suite 700
Washington, DC 20005
Tel: (202) 962-0322 Fax: (202) 962-0321
E-Mail: ncna@ncna.org
Website: councilofnonprofits.org
Members: 24000 Non-Profits and 36 State Associations of Non-Profits
Staff: 9
Annual Budget: $1-2,000,000

Personnel:
President and Chief Executive Officer: Timothy Delaney
    E-Mail: tdelaney@ncna.org
Vice President and Director, Network Support and Knowledge Transfer: Jennifer Chandler
    E-Mail: jchandler@councilofnonprofits.org
Director, Administration and Operations: Rick Cohen
    E-Mail: rcohen@councilofnonprofits.org
Vice President, Public Policy: David Thompson CAE, CMP
    E-Mail: dthompson@councilofnonprofits.org

Historical Note:
A coalition of state associations of non-profit organizations. Represents over 20,000 non-profits whose purpose is to enhance the quality of life in their respective communities. Merged with the Center for Lobbying in the Public Interest.

Publications:
Non Profit Advocacy Matters; monthly
Non Profit Knowledge Matters; monthly

National Council of Postal Credit Unions (1984)
P.O. Box 160
Del Mar, CA 92014-0160
Tel: (858) 792-3883 Fax: (858) 792-3884
E-Mail: ncpcu@ncpcu.org
Website: ncpcu.org
Members: 160 credit unions
Staff: 2
Annual Budget: $100-250,000
Tax: 501 (c)(6)

Personnel:
Contact, Communications: Bob Spindler
    E-Mail: Bob@ncpcu.org

Historical Note:
NCPCU is a council for credit unions serving postal employees and acts for its membership, and develops programs targeted to the special interests of postal credit unions. Membership: $100-1,000/year (Credit Union-based on assets).

Meetings/Conferences: Annual
2013 - Nashville, TN (Sheraton Nashville Downtown Hotel)/April 14 - 16

Publications:
NCPCU e-Courier Newsletter; on-line
Postal Credit Union Directory; on-line

National Council of Property Taxation (1990)
P.O. Box 763185
Dallas, TX 75376
Tel: (972) 296-0664 Fax: (972) 780-7741
E-Mail: ncpt@ncpt.net
Website: ncpt.net
Staff: 1

Personnel:
Executive Director: Lanette Andrews

Historical Note:
NCPT's mission is to protect and defend the rights of taxpayers and tax professionals. Membership: $1,000 (Regular-Voting); $250 (Associate Regular/Associate/ Subscribing/Affiliate - Non-Voting).

National Council of Real Estate Investment Fiduciaries (1982)
180 N. Stetson Ave.
Two Prudential Plaza, Suite 2515
Chicago, IL 60601
Tel: (312) 819-5890 Fax: (312) 819-5891
E-Mail: info@ncreif.org
Website: ncreif.com
Members: 300 companies
Staff: 9
Annual Budget: $2-5,000,000

Personnel:
Chief Executive Officer: Peter Steil

Chief Information Officer: Dan Dierking
Director, Research: Jeffrey Havsy
Director, Meetings: Tamara Pendley
   E-Mail: tpendley@ncreif.org

Historical Note:
NCREIF aims to serve the institutional real estate investment community as a non-partisan collector, processor, validator and disseminator of real estate performance information. Membership: $7,500-20,000 (NPI- Qualifying Data Contributing Members); $4,500 (Non-NPI Qualifying Data Contributing Members-Affiliate); $3,500 (Professional); $250 (Academic); $200 (Plan Sponsor).

Meetings/Conferences: Semi-Annual
Conference Chair: Tamara Pendley
2013 - Phoenix, AZ (Arizona Biltmore)/Feb. 27 - March 1
2013 - Boston, MA (Fairmont Copley Plaza)/July 9 - 11

Publications:
Membership Directory; on-line
NCREIF News; monthly

Membership List Available to Non-members

National Council of Self-Insurers *(1946)*
1253 Springfield Ave.
P.O. Box 345
New Providence, NJ 07974
Tel: (908) 665-2152 *Fax:* (908) 665-4020
E-Mail: natcouncil@aol.com
Website: natcouncil.com
Members: 3500 employers
Staff: 2
Annual Budget: $500-1,000,000
Tax: 501(c)(6)

Personnel:
Executive Director: Lawrence J. Holt
   E-Mail: natcouncil@aol.com

Historical Note:
Formerly (1973) National Council of State Self-insurers Associations. NCSI aims to preserve workers' compensation system and to protect it as the most effective means of resolving claims for industrial injuries and occupational diseases between employers and employees. Members are organizations and individuals concerned with self-insurance under the workmen's compensation laws. Membership: $300-600 (Individual Company, depending on number of employees); $475 (Group Self-Insurer/State Self- Insurance Guaranty Fund); $500 (Professional Member Serving Self-Insurers).

Meetings/Conferences: Annual
2013 - San Diego, CA (Rancho Bernardo Inn)/May 19 - 22

National Council of Social Security Management Associations *(1970)*
418 C St. NE
Washington, DC 20002
Tel: (202) 547-8530 *Fax:* (202) 547-8532
Website: ncssma.org
Members: 3400 SSA management positions
Staff: 5
Annual Budget: $100-250,000

Personnel:
President: Stephen Clifton
   E-Mail: stephen.clifton@ssa.gov
Treasurer: Anna Gutierrez
   E-Mail: anna.gutierrez@ssa.gov
Membership Committee Chair: Ryan Nelson

Historical Note:
NCSSMA is dedicated to improving management and program administration in the social security administration by assuring that the knowledge and experience of front-line management are included in all phases of agency planning and decision making. Members are managers and supervisors of Social Security field offices and teleservice centers in the U. S. and Puerto Rico. Has no paid officers or full-time staff. Membership in a regional association is required to also be a member of the association.

Meetings/Conferences: Annual

Publications:
FrontLine; quarterly
Membership Directory; on-line

National Council of State Agencies for the Blind
4600 Valley Rd.
Suite 100
Lincoln, NE 68510-4844
Tel: (402) 471-8100 *Fax:* (402) 471-3009

E-Mail: cannonp@michigan.gov
Website: ncsab.org
Members: 54 agencies
Staff: 3
Annual Budget: $100-250,000

Personnel:
President: David De Notaris
   E-Mail: ddenotaris@pa.gov
Secretary: Katy Morris
   E-Mail: katy.morris@arkansas.gov
Treasurer: Pearl Van Zandt
   E-Mail: Pearl.vanzandt@nebraska.gov

Historical Note:
NCSAB strives to promote through advocacy, coordination, and education the delivery of specialized services that enable individuals who are blind and visually impaired to achieve personal and vocational independence.

Meetings/Conferences: Annual

Publications:
NCSAB Directory; on-line

National Council of State Boards for Nursing *(1978)*
111 E. Wacker Dr.
Suite 2900
Chicago, IL 60601-4277
Tel: (312) 525-3600 *Fax:* (312) 279-1032
TollFree: (866) 293-9600
E-Mail: info@ncsbn.org
Website: ncsbn.org
Members: 60 boards
Staff: 99
Annual Budget: $50-100,000,000

Personnel:
Chief Executive Officer: Kathy Apple MS, RN
   E-Mail: dkappel@ncsbn.org
Director, Membership Relations: Alicia Byrd
   E-Mail: abyrd@ncsbn.org
Chief Financial Officer: Robert Clayborne
Chief Officer, Examinations: Philip Dickison
Director, Human Resources: Joseph Dudzik
Manager, Executive Office: Kate Jones
   E-Mail: kjones@ncsbn.org
Director, Marketing and Communications: Dawn Kappel
   E-Mail: dkappel@ncsbn.org
Chief Information Officer: Nur Rajwany
Director, Regulatory Innovations: Nancy Spector

Historical Note:
NCSBN's mission is to provide education, service, and research through collaborative leadership to promote evidence-based regulatory excellence for patient safety and public protection. Membership: $1,500/year.

Continuing Education:
Certification Designation/s: NNAAP, NCLEX, CGFNS, CCNE, NLNAC, MACE

Meetings/Conferences: Annual

Publications:
Council Connector
Directory of Nurse Aide Registries; annually
Journal of Nursing Regulation; quarterly; adv.
Leader to Leader
Membership Directory; on-line
Staff Directory; on-line

National Council of State Directors of Community Colleges *(1969)*
C/O American Association of Community Colleges
One Dupont Cir. NW, Suite 410
Washington, DC 20036-1176
Tel: (202) 728-0200 *Fax:* (202) 833-2467
Website: statedirectors.org
Members: 1500 individuals
Staff: 46
Annual Budget: $10-25,000

Personnel:
Executive Director: Charles N. Earl

Historical Note:
NCSDCC provides a forum for the exchange of information about developments, trends and problems in state systems of community colleges. Membership: $20/year.

Publications:
NCSDCC Newsletter; on-line

National Council of State Housing Agencies *(1974)*

444 N. Capitol St. NW
Suite 438
Washington, DC 20001
Tel: (202) 624-7710 *Fax:* (202) 624-5899
Website: ncsha.org
Members: 300 affiliate members and 350 agencies
Staff: 18
Annual Budget: $5-10,000,000
Tax: 501(c)(4)

Personnel:
Executive Director: Barbara J. Thompson
   E-Mail: bthompson@ncsha.org
Director, Finance and Operations: Kevin B. Burke CPA
   E-Mail: kburke@ncsha.org
Director, Meetings: Maury L. Edwards
   E-Mail: medwards@ncsha.org
Director, Marketing and Communications: Kristine B. Lewis
   E-Mail: klewis@ncsha.org
Director, Housing Advocacy and Strategic Initiatives: Garth B. Rieman
   E-Mail: grieman@ncsha.org
Associate, Operations and Membership Services: Phaedre Stoger
   E-Mail: pstoger@ncsha.org

Historical Note:
Formerly (1987) the Council of State Housing Agencies. NCSHA seeks to advance through advocacy and education the nation's state Housing Finance Agencies' efforts to provide affordable housing to those who need it. Members are the housing finance agencies of Washington, DC, Virgin Islands, Puerto Rico, and New York City. Annual Affiliate dues are determined by category, business size and the extent of professional relationship with HFAs.

Meetings/Conferences:
Conference Chair: Maury L. Edwards
2013 - Washington, DC (Marriott Hotel - Washington)/ Jan. 13 - 18
2013 - San Francisco, CA (San Francisco Marriott Marquis)/June 24 - 27
2013 - New Orleans, LA (New Orleans Marriott)/Oct. 19 - 22
2014 - Washington, DC (JW Marriott Hotel - Washington)/Jan. 12 - 17
2014 - Chicago, IL (Hyatt Regency Chicago)/June 24 - 27
2014 - Boston, MA (Sheraton Boston Hotel)/Oct. 18 - 21
2015 - Washington, DC (JW Marriott Washington, D.C.)/Jan. 11 - 16
2015 - Los Angeles, CA (JW Marriott Los Angeles L.A. LIVE)/June 1 - 4
2015 - Nashville, TN (Omni Nashville Hotel)/Sept. 26 - 29
2016 - Seatle, WA (Sheraton Seattle Hotel)/June 13 - 16
Number of non-conference events/year: 8

Publications:
Membership Directory; on-line

National Council of State Supervisors for Languages *(1960)*
1265 Millington Ct.
Columbus, OH 43235-4062
Tel: (502) 564-2106 *Fax:* (502) 564-9848
Website: ncssfl.org
Members: 50 individuals
Staff: 2
Annual Budget: Under $10,000

Personnel:
President: Gregory Fulkerson
   E-Mail: gfulkerson@doe.k12.de.us
Treasurer: Jon Valentine
   E-Mail: jvalentine@doe.k12.ga.us

Historical Note:
NCSSFL's mission is to provide leadership in facilitating and promoting policies and practices that support language education. Membership: $40 (Regular/Associate); $20 (Retired).

National Council of State Tourism Directors *(1969)*
1100 New York Ave. NW
Suite 450
Washington, DC 20005-3934
Tel: (202) 408-8422 *Fax:* (202) 408-1255

Website: ustravel.org/member-services/national-
council-
Members: 56 individuals
Staff: 2
Annual Budget: Under $10,000

Personnel:
Senior Director, National Councils: Nan Marchand
Beauvois

Historical Note:
*A council of the Travel Industry Association of America,
which provides administrative support. Members are
state and territorial government travel offices. Formerly
(1978) the Council of Regional Travel Executives (CORTE).
Membership: $1,500/year and up, based on size of budget.*

Meetings/Conferences: Annual
2013 - Las Vegas, NV (Las Vegas Convention Center)/
June 8 - 12/1200 attendees/over 100 exhibitors

Publications:
NCSTD Directory; on-line

National Council of Structural Engineers Associations
645 N. Michigan Ave.
Suite 540
Chicago, IL 60611
Tel: (312) 649-4600 *Fax:* (312) 649-5840
E-Mail: execdir@ncsea.com
Website: ncsea.com
Members: 100 companies
Staff: 5
Annual Budget: $1-2,000,000

Personnel:
Executive Director: Jeanne M. Vogelzang
Director, Development and Education: Jan Diepstra
Director, Meetings and Marketing: Melissa Matarrese
E-Mail: melissa@ncsea.com

Historical Note:
*NCSEA's mission is to advance the practice of structural
engineering and, as the national voice for practicing
structural engineers, protect the public's right to safe,
sustainable and cost effective buildings, bridges and other
structures. Members include architects, building code and
enforcement authorities, construction industry, owners,
developers, public building agencies, disaster response
organizations, licensing and registration boards, legislatures
and regulatory agencies. Membership: $1,000 (Commercial
Organization); $500 (Non-Commercial Organization/
Affiliate); $250 (Sustaining).*

Continuing Education:
Enrollment: 1700
Certification Designation/s: SECB

Meetings/Conferences: Annual
Conference Chair: Melissa Matarrese
2013 - Atlanta, GA/Sept. 18 - 21
2014 - New Orleans, LA/Sept. 17 - 20
Number of non-conference events/year: 1

Publications:
Membership Directory; on-line
NCSEA Newsletter; on-line; adv.
Structural Connection; quarterly; adv.
Structure Magazine; monthly; adv.

National Council of Supervisors of Mathematics
(1968)
6000 E. Evans Ave.
Suite 3-205
Denver, CO 80222-5423
Tel: (303) 758-9611 *Fax:* (303) 758-9616
E-Mail: office@ncsmonline.org
Website: mathedleadership.org
Members: 2900 individuals
Staff: 5
Annual Budget: $500-1,000,000
Tax: 501(c)(3)

Personnel:
President: Suzanne Mitchell
Coordinator, Conferences: Cathy Carroll
E-Mail: ccarroll@wested.org
Contact, Technology Liaison: Charlene Chausis
E-Mail: cchausis@mathedleadership.org
Editor: Linda Ruiz Davenport
E-Mail: ldavenport@boston.k12.ma.us
Treasurer: Randy Pippen
E-Mail: ncsmtreasurer@aol.com

Historical Note:
*NCSM's mission is to provide professional learning
opportunities necessary to support and sustain improved*

student achievement. *Membership: $85 (Individual); $55
(Emeritus).*

Meetings/Conferences: Annual
Conference Chair: Cathy Carroll
2013 - Denver, CO (Denver Downtown Hyatt
Regency)/April 15 - 17
2014 - New Orleans, LA/April 7 - 9
2015 - Boston, MA/April 13 - 15
2016 - San Francisco, CA/April 11 - 13
Number of non-conference events/year: 3

Publications:
Membership Directory; on-line
NCSM Journal of Mathematics Education Leadership;
semi-annually
NCSM Newsletter; quarterly; adv.

Membership List Available to Non-members

National Council of Teachers of English *(1911)*
1111 W. Kenyon Rd.
Urbana, IL 61801-1096
Tel: (217) 328-3870 *Fax:* (217) 328-9645
TollFree: (877) 369-6283
Website: ncte.org
Members: 20000 institutions and 80000
individuals
Staff: 90
Annual Budget: $10-25,000,000
Tax: 501(c)(3)

Personnel:
Executive Director: Kent D. Williamson
Contact, Communications: Lori Bianchini
Director, Convention: Jacqui Joseph-Biddle
E-Mail: jbiddle@ncte.org

Historical Note:
*The NCTE Homepage provides the latest information on
upcoming events and opportunities with NCTE, as well as
resources for educators.*

Meetings/Conferences: Annual
Conference Chair: Jacqui Joseph-Biddle
2013 - Boston, MA/Nov. 21 - 24/1-10 exhibitors
2014 - Washington, DC/Nov. 20 - 23/1-10 exhibitors
2015 - Minneapolis, MN/Nov. 19 - 22/1-10 exhibitors
Number of non-conference events/year: 6

Publications:
English Journal
Membership Directory; on-line
NCTE INBOX; weekly; adv.
NCTE Journals; on-line
The Council Chronicle; on-line

National Council of Teachers of Mathematics *(1920)*
1906 Association Dr.
Reston, VA 20191-1502
Tel: (703) 620-9840 *Fax:* (703) 476-2970
TollFree: (800) 235-7566
E-Mail: nctm@nctm.org
Website: nctm.org
Members: 90,000 individuals and 230 affiliated
groups
Staff: 27
Annual Budget: $10-25,000,000
Tax: 501(c)(3)

Personnel:
Executive Director: Kichoon Yang
Director, Information Systems and Services: Richard
Aldridge
*Associate Executive Director, Research, Learning, and
Development:* David Barnes
Director, Publications: Joanne Hodges
*Senior Director, Membership Services, Marketing and
Business Development:* Jennifer J. Johnson
Associate Executive Director, Communications: Ken
Krehbiel
Director, Professional Development Programs and Services:
Monique C. Lynch
Senior Director, Human Resource Development: Melanie S.
Ott
*Associate Chief Operating Officer and Executive Director,
Business Services:* David M. Shayka
E-Mail: dshayka@nctm.org
Manager, Accounting: Jody Wolfe
Director, Conference Services: Mark E. Workman

Historical Note:
*NCTM's mission is to support teachers to ensure better
mathematics education, providing vision, leadership*

and professional development to support teachers in
ensuring mathematics learning of the highest quality for all
students. *Membership: $81-108 (Individual); $69-$94 (E-
Membership); $40-$54 (Student E-Membership/Emeritus);
$104 (Institutional); $135 (PreK-8 School).*

Meetings/Conferences: Annual
Conference Chair: Mark E. Workman
2013 - Denver, CO/April 17 - 19
2013 - Denver, CO (Colorado Convention Center)/April
17 - 20
2014 - New Orleans, LA/April 9 - 12
2015 - Boston, MA/April 15
2015 - Boston, MA/April 15 - 18
2016 - San Francisco, CA/April 13 - 16
Number of non-conference events/year: 9

Publications:
Bright Ideas; adv.
Journal for Research in Mathematics Education;
quarterly; adv.
Mathematics Teacher; monthly; adv.
Mathematics Teaching in the Middle School; adv.
Student Explorations in Mathematics; on-line
Summing Up; semi-monthly; adv.
Teaching Children Mathematics; monthly; adv.

National Council of Textile Organizations
469 Hospital Dr.
Suite C
Gastonia, NC 28054
Tel: (704) 824-3522 *Fax:* (704) 671-2366
Website: ncto.org
Staff: 5
Annual Budget: $1-2,000,000
Tax: 501(c)(6)

Personnel:
Director, Finance & Administration: Robin Haynes
E-Mail: rhaynes@ncto.org
Vice President: Mike Hubbard

Historical Note:
*NCTO's mission is focused on creating powerful alliances
and coalitions to advance the interests of the U.S. textile
industry. Represents entire spectrum of the textile industry.*

Meetings/Conferences:
Conference Chair: Robin Haynes

Publications:
Membership Directory; on-line

Membership List Available to Non-members

National Council of the Multifamily Housing Industry
821 st. North
Lousiana, TX 56007
Staff: 31
Annual Budget: $10-25,000,000

Personnel:
Treasurer: Jones burg

National Council of Travel Attractions
1100 New York
Washington, DC 20005
Website: ustravel.org/member-services/national-
council-of-attractions
Staff: 1

Personnel:
president: john wage

National Council of University Research Administrators *(1959)*
1015 18th St. NW
Suite901
Washington, DC 20036
Tel: (202) 466-3894 *Fax:* (202) 223-5573
E-Mail: info@ncura.edu
Website: ncura.edu
Members: 3100 individuals
Staff: 14
Annual Budget: $5-10,000,000
Tax: 501(c)(3)

Personnel:
Executive Director: Kathleen M. Larmett
E-Mail: larmett@ncura.edu
Senior Coordinator, Membership Services: Neosoty
Abreu-Hernandez
E-Mail: abreu@ncura.edu
Manager, Meetings: Stephanie McJury
E-Mail: mcjury@ncura.edu

Assistant Executive Director and Manager, Education Program Development: Marc Schiffman
  E-Mail: schiffman@ncura.edu
Assistant, Marketing and Meetings: Justin Severini
  E-Mail: wood@ncura.edu
Director, Finance: Ivone Wells
  E-Mail: wells@ncura.edu

Historical Note:
NCURA strives to serve its members and advance the field of research administration through education and professional development programs. Members are individuals with professional interests in problems and policies relating to the administration of sponsored research, education and training activities at colleges and universities. Membership: $175/year (Individual).

Meetings/Conferences: Semi-Annual
Conference Chair: Stephanie McJury
2013 - New Orleans, LA/March 10 - 12
2013 - Washington, DC/Aug. 4 - 7
Number of non-conference events/year: 1

Publications:
Membership Directory; on-line
NCURA Journal
NCURA Magazine

Membership List Available to Non-members

National Council of Urban Education Associations
1201 16th St. NW
Washington, DC 20036-3290
Tel: (202) 833-4000 *Fax*: (202) 822-7974
Website: nea.org/ncuea
Staff: 2
Annual Budget: $250-500,000

Personnel:
President: Katherine Underwood
Secretary and Treasurer: Shannon Rasmussen

Historical Note:
An advocacy organization of local affiliates of the National Education Association

National Council of Writing Program Administrators (1975)
Grand Valley State University
312 Lake Ontario Hall
Allendale, MI 49401
Tel: (773) 508-2794 *Fax*: (773) 508-8696
Website: wpacouncil.org
Members: 700 individuals and institutions
Staff: 10
Annual Budget: $25-50,000
Tax: 501(c)(3)

Personnel:
President: Duane Roen
  E-Mail: president@wpacouncil.org
Journal Editor: Alice Horning
Treasurer and Web Developer: Charles Lowe
Secretary: Keith Rhodes
  E-Mail: rhodekei@gvsu.edu

Historical Note:
WPA's mission is to provide opportunities to focus on matters attendant to the administration of college and university writing programs. Members include directors of freshman composition or undergraduate writing, WAC coordinators, writing center directors, department chairs, and so on. Graduate students and faculty with professional interests in writing program administration. Membership: $20-40 Individual); $60 (Sustaining); $20 (Student); $80 (Libraries).

Meetings/Conferences: Annual
2013 - Savannah, GA/July 14 - 21
2014 - Normal, IL/July 13 - 20
2015 - Boise, ID/July 12 - 19
2016 - Raleigh, NC/July 10 - 17
2017 - Knoxville, TN/July 16 - 23

Publications:
WPA Journal; semi-annually
WPA News; quarterly; adv.

Membership List Available to Non-members

National Council on Aging (1950)
1901 L St. NW
Fourth Floor
Washington, DC 20036
Tel: (202) 479-1200 *Fax*: (202) 479-0735
TollFree: (800) 677-1116
E-Mail: info@ncoa.org
Website: ncoa.org

Members: 14000 Organizations
Staff: 92
Annual Budget: $50-100,000,000
Tax: 501(c)(3)

Personnel:
President and Chief Executive Officer: James P. Firman EdD
  E-Mail: james.firman@ncoa.org
Vice President, Public Policy and Advocacy: Howard Bedlin
  E-Mail: Howard.Bedlin@ncoa.org
Controller: Bradley Gretter
  E-Mail: bradley.gretter@ncoa.org
Vice President, Communications: Scott L. Parkin
  E-Mail: scott.parkin@ncoa.org
Vice President, Human Resources: Rina Pennacchia
Senior Vice President: S. Stuart Spector
  E-Mail: stuart.spector@ncoa.org
Senior Vice President and Chief Financial Officer: Donna Whitt
  E-Mail: donna.whitt@ncoa.org

Historical Note:
NCOA's mission is to improve the lives of older adults, especially those who are vulnerable and disadvantaged. Membership: $145 (Individual); $195 (Business Affiliate); $45 (Student/Retired); $500 (Corporate Affiliate).

Meetings/Conferences: Annual
2013 - Chicago, IL (Hyatt Regency Chicago)/March 19 - 23
Number of non-conference events/year: 3

Publications:
Aging in Stride; quarterly
Innovations
Membership Directory; on-line
Senior Center Voice; monthly

National Council on Compensation Insurance, Inc. (1922)
444 N. Capitol St. NW
Suite 203
Washington, DC 20001
Tel: (202) 661-4724 *Fax*: (561) 893-5614
E-Mail: customer_service@ncci.com
Website: ncci.com
Members: 750 insurance companies and carriers
Staff: 1000
Annual Budget: Over $100,000,000

Personnel:
Washington Affairs Executive and Counsel: Mary Jane Cleary
  E-Mail: maryjane_cleary@ncci.com

Historical Note:
NCCI's mission is to foster a healthy workers compensation system by providing quality information and analytical services that result into adequate loss costs/rates, objective reform evaluation, self-funded residual markets and tangible value for the stakeholders. Members include stock companies, mutual companies, competitive state funds and reciprocals. Membership: based on sliding scale.

Meetings/Conferences: Annual
Number of non-conference events/year: 3

Publications:
NCCI Newsletter; biennially

National Council on Crime and Delinquency (1907)
1970 Broadway
Suite 500
Oakland, CA 94612
Tel: (510) 208-0500 *Fax*: (510) 208-0511
E-Mail: info@sf.nccd-crc.org
Website: nccd-crc.org
Members: 500 individuals
Staff: 28
Annual Budget: $5-10,000,000
Tax: 501(c)(3)

Personnel:
President: Alexander Busansky
Specialist, Human Resources: Rula Adranly
Director, Information Systems: Joel Ehrlich
Communications Coordinator: Michelle Ghafar
Editor: Debra Illingworth Greene
Manager, Communications: Renee Plog
Coordinator, Administration: Keely Stotlar

Historical Note:

Mission is to promote effective, humane, fair and economically sound solutions to family, community and justice problems.

Publications:
Perspectives; semi-annually

Membership List Available to Non-members

National Council on Education for the Ceramic Arts (1966)
77 Erie Village Sq.
Suite 280
Erie, CO 80516-6996
Tel: (303) 828-2811 *Fax*: (303) 828-0911
TollFree: (866) 266-2322
E-Mail: office@nceca.net
Website: nceca.net
Members: 4000 individuals
Staff: 9
Annual Budget: $1-2,000,000
Tax: 501(c)(3)

Personnel:
Executive Director: Josh Green
  E-Mail: josh@nceca.net
Bookkeeper: Helen Anderson
  E-Mail: helen@nceca.net
Director, Publications: Marko Fields
  E-Mail: markofields@msn.com
Manager, Website and Communications: Candice Finn
  E-Mail: candice@nceca.net
Contact, Membership Services and Office Administrator: Jacqueline Hardy
  E-Mail: jacqueline@nceca.net
Administrator, Information Technology, Marketing and Webmaster: Jonathan Hopper
Manager, Conferences: Dori Nielsen
  E-Mail: dori@nceca.net
Manager, Projects: Kate Vorhaus
  E-Mail: kate@nceca.net

Historical Note:
NCECA fosters global education and appreciation for the ceramic arts and its programs, exhibitions, publications, opportunities and resources inspire advancement of the field. Members are faculty, professional studio artists, students and others concerned with the ceramic arts. Membership: $25-500/year.

Meetings/Conferences: Annual
Conference Chair: Dori Nielsen
2013 - Houston, TX (George R. Brown Convention Center)/March 20 - 23
2014 - Milwaukee, WI (Frontier Airlines Center)/March 19 - 22
Number of non-conference events/year: 4

Publications:
Membership Directory; on-line
NCECA E-NEWS; monthly
NCECA Journal; annually; adv.
NCECA Newsletter; adv.

National Council on Family Relations (1938)
1201 W. River Pkwy.
Suite 200
Minneapolis, MN 55454-1115
Tel: (763) 781-9331 *Fax*: (763) 781-9348
TollFree: (888) 781-9331
E-Mail: info@ncfr.org
Website: ncfr.org
Members: 3500 individuals
Staff: 12
Annual Budget: $2-5,000,000
Tax: 501(c)(3)

Personnel:
Executive Director: Diane L. Cushman
  E-Mail: dianecushman@ncfr.org
Manager, Membership Relations and Coordinator, Exhibits: Lynda Bessey
  E-Mail: lyndabessey@ncfr.org
Director, Education: Dawn Cassidy MEd, CFLE
  E-Mail: dawncassidy@ncfr.org
Director, Membership and Marketing: Charles Cheesebrough
  E-Mail: charlescheesebrough@ncfr.org
Director, Public Affairs: Nancy Gonzalez CFLE, MEd
  E-Mail: nancy@ncfr.org
Director, Finance: Tahera Mamdani
Manager, Information Technology: Jason A. Samuels
  E-Mail: jasonsamuels@ncfr.org
Planner, Conferences and Meetings: Judy Schutz

E-Mail: judyschutz@ncfr.org
Manager, Governance and Operations: Jeanne A. Strand
    E-Mail: jeannestrand@ncfr.org

Historical Note:
NCFR's mission is to provide an educational forum for family researchers, educators, and practitioners to share in the development and dissemination of knowledge about families and family relationships, establish professional standards, and work to promote family well-being. Membership: $65-200/year.

Continuing Education:
Enrollment: 1500
Certification Designation/s: CFLE

Meetings/Conferences: Annual
Conference Chair: Judy Schutz
2013 - San Antonio, TX (Grand Hyatt San Antonio)/
    Nov. 5 - 9/1100 attendees
2014 - Baltimore, MD (Hilton Baltimore)/Nov. 18 - 22

Publications:
CFLE Network; quarterly; adv.
Family Relations; adv.
Journal of Family Theory & Review; bi-monthly; adv.
Journal of Marriage and Family; adv.
Journal of Marriage and Family (JMF); bi-monthly; adv.
Membership Directory; on-line
NCFR Report (Magazine); quarterly; adv.
Zippy News; weekly

Membership List Available to Non-members

National Council on International Trade Development *(1967)*
1901 Pennsylvania Ave. NW
Suite 804
Washington, DC 20006
Tel: (202) 872-9280 *Fax:* (202) 293-0495
E-Mail: registrar@ncitd.org
Website: ncitd.org
Members:
60 companies
100 individuals
Staff: 2
Annual Budget: $50-100,000
Tax: 501(c)(6)

Personnel:
Executive Director: Robin Lanier
Legal Counsel: Douglas N. Jacobson

Historical Note:
Formerly (1988) National Council on International Trade Documentation and (1995) NCITD-International Trade Facilitation Council. NCITD provides direct expertise on a wide range of international trade topics. Members are exporters, importers and other professionals serving the international trade industry. Membership: $500-3,000/year (Corporate, dues based on gross sales).

Meetings/Conferences: Semi-Annual
Number of non-conference events/year: 1

Publications:
Membership Directory; on-line

National Council on Measurement in Education
2424 American Ln.
Madison, WI 53704
Tel: (608) 443-2487 *Fax:* (608) 443-2474
Website: ncme.org
Staff: 4
Annual Budget: $250-500,000

Personnel:
Executive Director: Plumer Lovelace III
Contact, Membership Services: Nate Ehresman
    E-Mail: nehresman@ncme.org
Meetings Planner: Drew Nelesen

Historical Note:
NCME is a professional organization for individuals involved in assessment, evaluation, testing, and other aspects of educational measurement.Their mission is to advance the science and practice of measurement in education Members are involved in the construction and use of standardized tests; new forms of assessment, including performance-based assessment; program design; and program evaluation. Membership $70 (Active/Associate); $35 (Student/Emeritus).

Meetings/Conferences: Annual
Conference Chair: Drew Nelesen
2013 - Atlanta, GA/April 10 - 14
2013 - San Francisco, CA/April 26 - 30
2014 - Philadelphia, PA/April 2 - 6

Publications:

ABCs of School Testing
Educational Measurement: Practice and Issues;
    quarterly
ITEMS: The Instructional Topics in Educational
    Measurement Series
JEM: The Journal of Educational Measurement;
    quarterly
NCME Newsletter; quarterly

Membership List Available to Non-members

National Council on Problem Gambling
730 11th St. NW
Suite 601
Washington, DC 20001
Tel: (202) 547-9204 *Fax:* (202) 547-9206
E-Mail: ncpg@ncpgambling.org
Website: ncpgambling.org
Staff: 3
Annual Budget: $500-1,000,000

Personnel:
Executive Director: Keith Whyte
    E-Mail: Keithw@ncpgambling.org
Administrative Assistant: Melissa Eckenrode
    E-Mail: MelissaE@ncpgambling.org
Director, Development and Membership Services: Barbara
    Rollins
    E-Mail: barbarar@ncpgambling.org

Historical Note:
NCPG's mission is to increase public awareness of pathological gambling, ensure the widespread availability of treatment for problem gamblers and their families, and to encourage research and programs for prevention and education.

Continuing Education:
Certification Designation/s: ICGC

Meetings/Conferences: Annual
2013 - Seattle, WA (DoubleTree by Hilton Hotel Seattle
    Airport)/July 19 - 20

Publications:
NCPG Newsletter; quarterly; adv.

Membership List Available to Non-members

National Council on Public History *(1980)*
425 University Blvd.
327 Cavanaugh Hall-IUPUI
Indianapolis, IN 46202-5140
Tel: (317) 274-2716 *Fax:* (317) 278-5230
E-Mail: ncph@iupui.edu
Website: ncph.org
Members: 1700 individuals
Staff: 5
Annual Budget: $250-500,000
Tax: 501(c)(3)

Personnel:
Executive Director: John Dichtl
Editor: Randolph Bergstrom
Director, Program: Carrie Dowdy
    E-Mail: dowdyc@iupui.edu
Secretary and Treasurer: Kristine Navarro-McElhaney
Membership Assistant: Alice Smith

Historical Note:
The NCPH works to promote professionalism among history practitioners and their engagement with the public. Members are museum professionals, historical consultants, historians employed in government, archivists, historical administrators, corporate and business historians, cultural resource managers, curators, film and media producers, oral historians, policy advisers, teachers, professors and students with public history interests. Membership: $70 (Individual); $90 (Individual International); $40 (New Professional); $30 (Student); $125 (Sustaining); $50 (Student International); $60 (New Professional International); $600 (Patron); $400 (Partner).

Meetings/Conferences: Annual
Conference Chair: Carrie Dowdy
2013 - Ottawa, ON (Delta Ottawa City Center)/April 17
    - 20
2014 - Monterey, CA (Monterey Conference Center)/
    March 19 - 22
2015 - Nashville, TN (Sheraton Nashville Downtown
    Hotel)/April 15 - 18

Publications:
Public History News; quarterly; adv.

Membership List Available to Non-members

National Council on Public Polls *(1969)*
1425 Broad St.

Suite Seven
Clifton, NJ 07013
Tel: (973) 857-8500 *Fax:* (973) 857-8578
TollFree: (800) 786-8000
E-Mail: info@ncpp.org
Website: ncpp.org
Members: 40 companies
Staff: 2
Annual Budget: Under $10,000

Personnel:
President: Evans Witt
Secretary and Treasurer: Jay Leve

Historical Note:
Formerly National Committee on Public Polls. NCPP's mission is to set the professional standards for public opinion pollsters, and to advance the understanding, among politicians, the media and general public, of how polls are conducted and how to interpret poll results. Membership: $750 (Large); $500 (Medium); $250 (Small).

Publications:
Membership Directory; annually

Membership List Available to Non-members

National Council on Qualifications for the Lighting Professions *(1991)*
P.O. Box 142729
Austin, TX 78714-2729
Tel: (512) 973-0042 *Fax:* (512) 973-0043
E-Mail: info@ncqlp.org
Website: ncqlp.org
Members: 972 individuals
Staff: 3
Annual Budget: $250-500,000

Personnel:
Executive Director: Mary Jane Kolar CAE

Historical Note:
NCQLP's purpose is to promote effective and efficient lighting practice through a peer-review process, with education, experience and examination requirements for baseline certification across the lighting profession.

Continuing Education:
Certification Designation/s: LC

National Council on Radiation Protection and Measurement *(1964)*
7910 Woodmont Ave.
Suite 400
Bethesda, MD 20814-3095
Tel: (301) 657-2652 *Fax:* (301) 907-8768
TollFree: (800) 229-2652
E-Mail: ncrp@ncrponline.org
Website: ncrponline.org
Members: 100 individuals
Staff: 9
Annual Budget: $2-5,000,000
Tax: 501(c)(3)

Personnel:
Executive Director: James R. Cassata
Office Manager and Coordinator, Meetings: Laura J.
    Atwell
    E-Mail: atwell@ncrponline.org
Managing Editor: Cindy L. O'Brien
    E-Mail: obrien@ncrponline.org
Manager, Publications, Sales and Marketing: Carlotta M.
    Teague
    E-Mail: ncrppubs@ncrponline.org
Manager, Financial Records: Myrna A. Young
    E-Mail: young@ncrponline.org

Historical Note:
Formerly (1929) the Advisory Committee on X-ray and Radium Protection, (1947) National Committee on Radiation Protection and (1957) National Committee on Radiation Protection and Measurements. NCRP seeks to support radiation protection by providing independent scientific analysis, information, and recommendations that represent the consensus of scientists.

Meetings/Conferences: Annual
Conference Chair: Laura J. Atwell
2013 - Bethesda, MD/March 11 - 12

Publications:
Membership Directory; on-line

National Council on Rehabilitation Education *(1955)*
1099 E. Champlain Dr., Suite A
P.O. Box 137
Fresno, CA 93720

Tel: (559) 906-0787 Fax: (559) 412-2550
E-Mail: info@ncre.org
Website: ncre.org
Members: 600 individuals and 90 institutions
Staff: 3
Annual Budget: $100-250,000
Tax: 501(c)(6)

Personnel:
President: Ken Hergenrather
Chief Operating Officer: Charles Arokiasamy
    E-Mail: charlesa@csufresno.edu
Editor: Maureen McGuire-Kueltz
    E-Mail: mkuletz@gwu.edu

Historical Note:
NCRE provides a forum for educators and researchers in
the rehabilitation field to discuss critical issues, develop new
approaches, collaborate on legislative and policy issues, and
test new theories and strategies. Members are professional
educators and researchers with expertise in various facets
of vocational rehabilitation, and educational institutions
offering academic training programs and conducting
research related to rehabilitation education and services.
Membership: $450 (Organization); $75 (Individual); $40
(Student); $75 (Associate Individual); $250 (Associate
Institutional).

Meetings/Conferences:
2013 - San Francisco, CA (SFO Airport Marriott Hotel)/
    April 17 - 19

Publications:
Membership Directory; on-line
NCRE Newsletter; on-line
Rehabilitation Research, Policy, and Education;
    quarterly

National Council on Student Development (1960)
P.O. Box 3948
Parker, CO 80134
Tel: (866) 972-0717 Fax: (303) 755-7363
TollFree: (866) 972-0717
E-Mail: ncsd@ncsdonline.org
Website: ncsdonline.org
Members: 700 individuals
Staff: 4
Annual Budget: $50-100,000
Tax: 501(c)(3)

Personnel:
Executive Director: Nicole Singleton
    E-Mail: ncsd@ncsdonline.org

Historical Note:
NCSD's mission is to provide and promote leadership
in student development by enhancing opportunities for
training, leadership and student advocacy for community
college student development professionals. Membership:
$250 (Institution); $35 (Graduate Student); $50 (Faculty);
$25 (Individual, Member Institution); $95 (Individual,
Non- Member Institution).

Meetings/Conferences: Annual
Number of non-conference events/year: 1

Publications:
Membership Directory; on-line
Monograph of Annual Conference; annually
NCSD Newsletter
NSD E-Newsletter; bi-annually

National Council on Teacher Retirement (1924)
7600 Greenhaven Dr.
Suite 302
Sacramento, CA 95831
Tel: (916) 394-2075 Fax: (916) 392-0295
Website: nctr.org
Members: 284 organizations
Staff: 3
Annual Budget: $1-2,000,000
Tax: 501(c)(6)

Personnel:
Executive Director: Jim Mosman
    E-Mail: jmosman@nctr.org
Office Manager: Robyn Gonzales
    E-Mail: rgonzales@nctr.org
Assistant, Communications: Leslie Kranz
    E-Mail: lkranz@nctr.org

Historical Note:
NCTR is constituted as an independent association to
safeguard the integrity of public retirement systems in the
United States and its territories to which teachers belong
and to promote the rights and benefits of all present and
future members of the systems. Membership: $3,200
(Commercial Associate); $1500-2900 (Active); $800

(Educational Associations/Unions/State Agencies); $250
(Retired Teachers Associations).

Meetings/Conferences: Annual
2013 - Washington, DC (Omni Shoreham Hotel,
    Washington D.C.)/Oct. 5 - 9
2014 - Indianapolis, IN (JW Marriott Indianapolis)/Oct.
    11 - 15
2015 - La Jolla, CA (Hilton La Jolla Torrey Pines)/Oct.
    10 - 14
Number of non-conference events/year: 9

Publications:
Membership Directory; on-line
NCTR Newsletter; quarterly

National Counter Intelligence Corps Association (1947)
125 Riverview Dr.
Washington, DC 27889
E-Mail: cicspook1@aol.com
Website: ncica.org
Members: 700 individuals
Staff: 3
Annual Budget: $10-25,000

Personnel:
President and Convention Contact: Theodore S.
    Hinchman
    E-Mail: phinchman@suddenlink.net

Historical Note:
NCICA is dedicated to persons who served or are serving
in all branches of the United States military. Members are
veteran special agents of the counter intelligence corps of
the U.S. Armed Forces. Purpose is dedicated Intelligence
persons who served or are serving in all branches of the
United States military. Membership: $15 (Individual); $200
(Life).

Meetings/Conferences: Annual
Conference Chair: Theodore S. Hinchman

Publications:
Golden Sphinx

National Court Reporters Association (1899)
8224 Old Courthouse Rd.
Vienna, VA 22182-3808
Tel: (703) 556-6272 Fax: (703) 556-6291
TollFree: (800) 272-6272
E-Mail: msic@ncrahq.org
Website: ncra.org
Members: 23000 individuals
Staff: 6
Annual Budget: $5-10,000,000
Tax: 501(c)(6)

Personnel:
Executive Director and Chief Executive Officer: Jim
    Cudahy
Senior Government Relations Specialist: Adam Finkel
    E-Mail: afinkel@ncrahq.org
Contact, Meetings: Brandon Schall
Editor: Jacqueline Schmidt
    E-Mail: jschmidt@ncrahq.org

Historical Note:
NCRA's mission is to promote excellence among those
who capture and convert the spoken word to text and is
committed to supporting every member in achieving the
highest level of professional expertise. Membership: $135
(Participating); $82.50 (Associate); $32.50 (Student).

Continuing Education:
Certification Designation/s: CRI, MCRI, CCP, RDR, RPR,
RMR, CBC, CLVS, CRR

Meetings/Conferences:
Conference Chair: Brandon Schall
2013 - Dana Point, CA (Ritz-Carlton, Laguna Niguel)/
    Feb. 3 - 5
2013 - Scottsdale, AZ (DoubleTree Resort by Hilton
    Hotel Paradise Valley-Scottsdale)/April 19 - 21
2013 - Nashville, TN (Gaylord Opryland Resort and
    Convention Center)/Aug. 8 - 11
2014 - San Francisco, CA (Hilton San Francisco Union
    Square)/July 31 - Aug. 3
2015 - New York City, NY (Hilton New York)/July 30 -
    Aug. 2
2016 - Chicago, IL (Hilton Chicago)/July 28 - 31
Number of non-conference events/year: 2

Publications:
Journal of Court Reporting; adv.
Membership Directory; on-line
State Leadership Newsletter
Up To Speed; quarterly

National CPA Health Care Advisors Association (1992)
624 Grassmere Park Dr.
Suite 15
Nashville, TN 37211
Tel: (615) 373-9880 Fax: (615) 377-7092
TollFree: (800) 231-2524
E-Mail: info@hcaa.com
Website: hcaa.com
Members: 48 firms
Staff: 6
Annual Budget: $100-250,000

Personnel:
Executive Director: Patrick Pruett
    E-Mail: patrick@hcaa.com

Historical Note:
HCAA, an Affiliate of the Alliance of Professional
Associations, is a nationwide network of CPA firms devoted
to serving the health care industry. Members are selected for
their experience and ability to provide proactive solutions to
the accounting needs of physicians and physician groups.
Membership: $1,700/year, based on territorial structure.

Meetings/Conferences: Annual
Publications:
HCAA Member Directory; on-line

Membership List Available to Non-members

National Credit Reporting Association (1992)
701 E. Irving Park Rd.
Suite 306
Roselle, IL 60172
Website: ncrainc.org
Members: 150 companies
Staff: 4
Annual Budget: $250-500,000

Personnel:
Executive Director: Terry W. Clemans
    E-Mail: Tclemans@ncrainc.org
Conference Chair: Nancy Fedich
    E-Mail: Nancy@cisinfo.net
Office Manager and Membership Services: Jan Gerber
    E-Mail: jgerber@ncrainc.org
Vice President and Treasurer: Daphne Large
    E-Mail: Daphnel@datafacts.com

Historical Note:
Formerly (1997) National Association of Independent
Credit Reporting Agencies. NCRA's mission is to encourage
general welfare of its members, credit reporting agencies,
employment screening services, tenant screening companies
and all issuers of consumer reports. It also encourages the
businesses they serve and the consumers whose information
they report. Membership: $650-3,500 (General); $1,000
(Associate, Vendors/Credit Related); $500 (Associate,
Vendors/Non-Credit Related); $400 (Tenant Screening
Membership).

Continuing Education:
Enrollment: 500
Certification Designation/s: FCRAC

Meetings/Conferences: Annual
Conference Chair: Nancy Fedich
Number of non-conference events/year: 1

Publications:
NCRA's Resident Screening e-Newsletter; on-line
RSC Advocate; bi-monthly
The Advocate
The Credit Reporter; quarterly; adv.

Membership List Available to Non-members

National Criminal Justice Association (1971)
720 Seventh St. NW
Washington, DC 20001-3716
Tel: (202) 628-8550 Fax: (202) 448-1723
E-Mail: info@ncja.org
Website: ncja.org
Members: 900 individuals
Staff: 9
Annual Budget: $2-5,000,000
Tax: 501(c)(3)

Personnel:
Executive Director: Cabell C. Cropper
    E-Mail: ccropper@ncja.org
Director, Communications: Bethany Broida
    E-Mail: bbroida@ncja.org
Director, Government Affairs: Elizabeth Pyke
    E-Mail: epyke@ncja.org

Historical Note:

Incorporated in the District of Columbia (1974). Formerly (until 1979) known as the National Conference of State Criminal Justice Planning Administrators. NCJA's mission is to promote a balanced approach to communities' complex public safety and criminal and juvenile justice system problems. Membership open to all criminal justice system practitioners and others with interest in crime prevention and control, law enforcement, the courts, corrections or other aspects of the administration of justice. Membership: $95 (Individual); $225 (Tribal Government); $2,500 (Corporate); $1,200 (Non Profit Organization); $40 (Student); $200-750 (Public Agency).

Continuing Education:
Certification Designation/s: GMTA

Publications:
Beltway Short Takes; semi-monthly
Justice Bulletin; weekly
Member Directory; on-line

National Crop Insurance Services *(1915)*
8900 Indian Creek Pkwy.
Suite 600
Overland Park, KS 66210-1567
Tel: (913) 685-2767 *Fax:* (913) 685-3080
TollFree: (800) 951-6247
Website: ag-risk.org
Members: 135 companies
Staff: 48
Annual Budget: $10-25,000,000

Personnel:
President: Thomas "Tom" P. Zacharias
Media Contact: Laura A. Langstraat
    E-Mail: lauriel@ag-risk.org
Contact, Meetings: Sherri Scharff
    E-Mail: sherris@ag-risk.org

Historical Note:
Formed in 1989 by the merger of the Crop Hail Insurance Actuarial Association and the National Crop Insurance Association. NCIS is an international not-for-profit organization representing the interests of private crop insurance companies. NCIS members are the direct link to production agriculture in America. Membership: dues based upon crop insurance writings.

Meetings/Conferences:
Conference Chair: Sherri Scharff
2013 - Indian Wells, CA/Feb. 11 - 13
2014 - Scottsdale, AZ (Westin Kierland Resort and Spa)/Feb. 9 - 12/3000 attendees

Publications:
CropTalk Newsletter; monthly
The Crop Insurance Journal; semi-annually
Today magazine; quarterly; adv.

National Customs Brokers and Forwarders Association of America *(1897)*
1200 18th St. NW
Suite 901
Washington, DC 20036
Tel: (202) 466-0222 *Fax:* (202) 466-0226
E-Mail: staff@ncbfaa.org
Website: ncbfaa.org
Members: 870 member companies and 100,000 employees
Staff: 12
Annual Budget: $1-2,000,000
Tax: 501(c)(6)

Personnel:
Executive Vice President: Barbara Reilly CAE
    E-Mail: EVP@ncbfaa.org
Coordinator, Education: Cecilia Ferrara
    E-Mail: nei@ncbfaa.org
Director, Communications: Tom Mathers BS
    E-Mail: comm@ncbfaa.org
Accounting Director: Kimberly Murphy
    E-Mail: acct@ncbfaa.org
Coordinator, Conferences and Meetings: Kim O'Beirne
    E-Mail: meetings@ncbfaa.org
Director, Membership Services: Jeff Short
    E-Mail: ncbfaamembership@gmail.com

Historical Note:
Founded (1897) as the Customs-Clerks Association of the Port of New York, became the New York Customs Brokers Association (1922) and was incorporated under the same name in 1933. The association accepted national membership in 1945, and was incorporated as the Customs Brokers and Forwarders Association of America, Inc., in 1948 and the name was changed to National Customs Brokers and Forwarders Association of America, Inc., in 1962. NCBFAA maintains a close watch over legislative

and regulatory issues that affect its members and keeps them informed of these and other related issues through publications and conferences. Internationally, NCBFAA represents its membership at the International Federation of Customs Brokers Association, which represents many foreign countries and maintains ties with APEC and the World Customs Organization. Membership: $540.80-5,349.40 (Regular); $703.05-1,925.55 (Affiliate); $28.10-29.75 (Affiliate Association Member); $432.65 (Associate).

Continuing Education:
Certification Designation/s: CES, COF, CCS

Meetings/Conferences: Annual
Conference Chair: Kim O'Beirne
2013 - Rancho Mirage, CA (The Western Mission Hills Resort & Spa)/April 7 - 10
Number of non-conference events/year: 1

Publications:
Monday Morning Briefing; weekly
Who's Who (Membership Directory); annually; adv.

National Cutting Horse Association *(1946)*
260 Bailey Ave.
Fort Worth, TX 76107
Tel: (817) 244-6188 *Fax:* (817) 244-2015
Website: nchacutting.com
Members: 21000 individuals and 133 affiliated organizations
Staff: 33
Annual Budget: $25-50,000,000
Tax: 501(c)(5)

Personnel:
Executive Director: Alan Steen
Director, Shows: Dave Brian
    E-Mail: dbrian@nchacutting.com
Director, Marketing and Media: Julie Bryant
    E-Mail: jbryant@nchacutting.com
Director, Information Technology: Kenneth Corzine
    E-Mail: kcorzine@nchacutting.com
Director, Membership Services: Julie Davis
    E-Mail: jdavis@nchacutting.com
Director, Publishing: Alan Gold
    E-Mail: adgold@nchacutting.com
Treasurer: Rick Ivey
    E-Mail: raivey@nchacutting.com
Administrative Assistant: Pam Robison
    E-Mail: probison@nchacutting.com

Historical Note:
NCHA works to improve and promote the cutting horse industry. Members are individuals, firms, organizations and riding clubs interested in the development of superior horses and the refinement of true cutting horse competition. Membership: $60 (Individual); $60-90 (Joint); $750 (Life); $15 (Youth); $100 (Youth Life).

Meetings/Conferences:
Conference Chair: Dave Brian
Number of non-conference events/year: 139

Publications:
Daily Chatter; daily
e-Chatter; bi-weekly
Membership Directory; on-line
The Cutting Horse Chatter; monthly; adv.

National Dairy Council *(1915)*
10255 W. Higgins Rd.
Suite 900
Rosemont, IL 60018-5616
Tel: (312) 240-2880
E-Mail: ndc@dairyinformation.com
Website: nationaldairycouncil.org
Members: 300 individuals and 22 organizations
Staff: 60
Annual Budget: $1-2,000,000
Tax: 501(c)(3)

Personnel:
Executive Vice President, Science and Research: Gregory D. Miller MACN, PhD
Vice President, Technology and Packaging: Gail Barnes MBL, PhD
Senior Vice President, Nutrition Affairs: Ann Marie Krautheim LD, MA, RD

Historical Note:
A wholly-owned subsidiary of Dairy Management Inc., which provides administrative support. NDC's purpose is to provide timely, scientifically sound nutrition information to the media, physicians, dietitians, nurses, educators, consumers and others concerned about fostering a healthier

society. Funds are channelled through the United Dairy Industry Association to the National Dairy Council.

Publications:
The Dairy Download E-Newsletter; monthly

National Dairy Herd Information Association
P.O. Box 930399
Verona, WI 53593-0399
Tel: (608) 848-6455 *Fax:* (608) 848-7675
E-Mail: dhia@dhia.org
Website: dhia.org
Members: 4500 individuals
Staff: 4
Annual Budget: $250-500,000

Personnel:
Chief Executive Officer and Administrator: Jay Mattison
    E-Mail: jmattison@requestltd.com
Contact, Communications and Events: JoDee Sattler
    E-Mail: jdsattler@dhia.org
Contact, Quality Certification Services: Steven Sievert
    E-Mail: sjsievert@dhia.org
Contact, Accounting and Bookkeeping: Leslie Thoman
    E-Mail: lthoman@dhia.org

Historical Note:
Represents the DHIA system on issues involving other National and International organizations. Mission is to serve national DHIA members and the diary industry in advancing diary information services. Also promotes accuracy, credibility, and uniformity of DHI records.

Meetings/Conferences: Annual
Conference Chair: JoDee Sattler

National Dance Association *(1932)*
1900 Association Dr.
Reston, VA 20191-1598
Tel: (703) 476-3400 *Fax:* (703) 476-9527
TollFree: (800) 213-7193
E-Mail: nda@aahperd.org
Website: aahperd.org/nda
Members: 2,000 individual dance educators, institutional and affiliate members
Staff: 3
Annual Budget: $100-250,000

Personnel:
Vice President, Education: Nancy Brooks Schmitz
    E-Mail: nschmitz2002@yahoo.com
Program Manager: Colleen Hearn Dean
    E-Mail: cdean@aahperd.org
Contact, Publications: Terry Sweeting
    E-Mail: terry.sweeting@csun.edu

Historical Note:
NDA was originally established as the section on Dance in 1932 by the American Physical Education Association (APEA). NDA is part of the American Alliance for Health, Physical Education, Recreation and Dance (AAHPERD). Mission is to promote quality dance programs in the areas of health, physical education, recreation and dance by initiating and advocating practices that promote healthy lifestyles through dance curriculum, programs and workshops. Members include dancers, choreographers, dance educators, therapists, dance science and medicine specialists, and arts administrators. Membership: $135 (Professional); $50 (Student).

Meetings/Conferences:
Conference Chair: Colleen Hearn Dean

Publications:
Professional Journal; on-line
Spotlight on Dance; semi-annually; adv.
The Nu Delta Alpha Journal; annually; adv.

National Dance Council of America *(1948)*
P.O. Box 22018
Provo, UT 84602
Tel: (801) 422-8124 *Fax:* (801) 422-0541
Website: ndca.org
Members: 15 organizations
Staff: 4
Annual Budget: $250-500,000

Personnel:
Registrar: Eleanor Wiblin

Historical Note:
An inter-association agency that represents the interests of those in the dance profession and other dance related entities and organizations, and cooperates with similar councils in other countries. Membership: $30-85 (Professionals); $35 (Amateur Adult Competitor); $20 (Amateur Student Competitor); $85 (Other).

Publications:

Membership Directory; on-line

National Dance Education Organization (1998)
8609 Second Ave.
Suite 203-B
Silver Spring, MD 20910
Tel: (301) 585-2880 *Fax:* (301) 585-2888
E-Mail: info@ndeo.org
Website: ndeo.org
Members: 150 federal and state agencies
Staff: 7
Annual Budget: $250-500,000
Tax: 501(c)(3)

Personnel:
Founding Executive Director: Jane Bonbright EdD
Director, Finance: Vilma Braja
Director, Marketing and Membership Services: Melissa Greenblatt
E-Mail: membership@ndeo.org
Conference Planner: Helene Scheff
E-Mail: hscheff@ndeo.org

Historical Note:
An autonomous organization that provides the dance artists, educators and administrators a network of resources and support, a base for advocacy, and access to programs and projects that focus on the importance of dance in the human experience. Serves dance teachers and educators, independent schools of dance, associations for dance, arts and education, community resources and recreation centers, businesses and corporations, state arts agencies and departments of education. Membership: $95 (Professional/Ph.D. / Ed.D. Candidate); $150-200 (Institutional); $300 (Corporate); $55 (Retiree); $35 (High School Student); $65 (Graduate Student); $40 (Undergraduate Student).

Meetings/Conferences: Annual
Conference Chair: Helene Scheff

Publications:
Journal of Dance Education

Membership List Available to Non-members

National Defender Investigator Association
460 Smith St.
Suite K
Middletown, CT 06457
Tel: (860) 635-5533 *Fax:* (866) 668-9858
Website: ndia.net
Members: 1200 individuals
Staff: 4
Annual Budget: $100-250,000

Personnel:
Executive Secretary: Beverly Davidson
E-Mail: ndia@cox.net
Webmaster: James B. Tarter
E-Mail: james.b.tarter@gmail.com

Historical Note:
NDIA strives to include all investigators regardless of race, creed, religion, sex, age, nationality, marital status, sexual orientation or the presence of any sensory, mental or physical handicap. Members are criminal defense investigators, paralegals and others in the criminal justice system dedicated to providing services to indigent persons. Membership: $40/year.

Meetings/Conferences: Annual
2013 - Seatle, WA (Sheraton Seattle Hotel)/April 4 - 5

Publications:
Membership Directory; on-line
The Eagle's Eye; quarterly

National Defense Industrial Association (1919)
2111 Wilson Blvd.
Suite 400
Arlington, VA 22201-3061
Tel: (703) 522-1820 *Fax:* (703) 522-1885
E-Mail: info@ndia.org
Website: ndia.org
Members:
1780 companies
87700 individuals
Staff: 70
Annual Budget: $25-50,000,000
Tax: 501(c)(3)

Personnel:
President and Chief Executive Officer: Lt. Gen. Lawrence P. Farrell Jr. USAF (Ret.)
E-Mail: lfarrell@ndia.org
Manager, Exhibits and Operations: Mary Anna Christiansen
E-Mail: mchristiansen@ndia.org
Contact, Business Operations: Trina Dickey
E-Mail: tdickey@ndia.org
Editor: Sandra Erwin
E-Mail: serwin@ndia.org
Media Contact: Stew Magnuson
E-Mail: magnuson@ndia.org
Vice President, Membership Services: Jim McInerney USAF (Ret.)
E-Mail: jmcinerney@ndia.org
Director, Information Technology: Sasan Oghlidos
E-Mail: soghlidos@ndia.org
Assistant Vice President, Marketing: Scott Rekdal
E-Mail: srekdal@ndia.org
Vice President, Government Policy: Pete Steffes
E-Mail: psteffes@ndia.org

Historical Note:
Formed by a merger of the National Security Industrial Association and the American Defense Preparedness Association in 1997. NDIA's mission is to promote a vigorous, responsive, Government Industry National Security Team. Members are industrial, research, legal and educational organizations of all sizes. Membership: $400 (Individual-Lifetime); $30 (Defense Professionals-Individual); $35 (Individual-Allied); $500 (Corporate).

Continuing Education:
Certification Designation/s: CDM

Meetings/Conferences: Annual
Conference Chair: Mary Anna Christiansen

Publications:
Membership Directory; on-line
State Leadership Newsletter

National Defense Transportation Association (1944)
50 S. Pickett St.
Suite 220
Alexandria, VA 22304-7296
Tel: (703) 751-5011 *Fax:* (703) 823-8761
E-Mail: info@ndtahq.com
Website: ndtahq.com
Members: 9250 corporations and individuals
Staff: 12
Annual Budget: $2-5,000,000
Tax: 501(c)(3)

Personnel:
President and Chief Operating Officer: Lt. Gen. Kenneth R. Wykle USA(Ret)
E-Mail: ken@ndtahq.com
Manager, Database: Leah Ashe
E-Mail: leah@ndtahq.com
Vice President, Finance: Patty Casidy
E-Mail: patty@ndtahq.com
Vice President, Marketing and Corporate Development: COL Dennis Edwards Ret.
E-Mail: denny@ndtahq.com
Director, Public Relations: Karen Schmitt CMP
E-Mail: karen@ndtahq.com
Vice President, Membership: COL Mark Victorson Ret.
E-Mail: mark@ndtahq.com

Historical Note:
NDTA's mission is to nurture a better global transportation and distribution system in support of the economy and national security of the United States by advancing the knowledge and science of transportation/distribution within government and industry. Membership: $10-400/Year.

Meetings/Conferences: Annual
Conference Chair: COL Dennis Edwards Ret.
2013 - San Antonio, TX/Sept. 7 - 11
2014 - Orlando, FL/Sept. 13 - 17
2015 - Washington, DC/Sept. 19 - 23
2015 - Washington, DC/Sept. 26 - 30

Publications:
Defense Transportation Journal (DTJ); bi-monthly

National Defined Contribution Council (1995)
714 Hopmeadow St.
Suite Three
Simsbury, CT 06070
Tel: (860) 658-5161 *Fax:* (860) 658-5068
E-Mail: glenna@sparkinstitute.org
Website: ndcconline.org
Members: 300 individuals
Staff: 2
Annual Budget: Under $10,000

Personnel:
Organization Contact: Glenna Best
E-Mail: glenna@sparkinstitute.org
Director, Technical Consulting: Paul D. Bowman

Historical Note:
NDCC strives to promote and protect the interests of the DC industry and the public it serves. Membership: $3,750-7,500 (Regular, based on number of employees); $1,000-7,500 (Associate, based on number of employees); $2,500 (Affiliate).

Meetings/Conferences:
Conference Chair: Paul D. Bowman

Membership List Available to Non-members

National Demolition Association (1972)
16 N. Franklin St.
Suite 203
Doylestown, PA 18901-3536
Tel: (215) 348-4949 *Fax:* (215) 348-8422
TollFree: (800) 541-2412
E-Mail: info@demolitionassociation.com
Website: demolitionassociation.com
Members: 1000 members
Staff: 3
Annual Budget: $1-2,000,000

Personnel:
Executive Director: Michael R. Taylor CAE
E-Mail: mtaylor@demolotionassociation.com

Historical Note:
Formerly National Association of Demolition Contractors; assumed its current name in 2004. NDA's mission is to provide the tools necessary to its members and to serve towards environmental stewardship, safety, education, professional competency and government advocacy. Members are demolition contractors and equipment manufacturers. Membership: $800-1,100 (Regular, based on gross sales); $800 (Associate/International); $25 (Student).

Meetings/Conferences: Annual
2013 - San Diego, CA (San Diego Convention Center)/March 23 - 26/over 100 exhibitors
Number of non-conference events/year: 1

Publications:
Business Owner; bi-monthly
Convention Highlights; annually
Demolition; bi-monthly; adv.
Demolition Insert; annually
Membership Directory; annually
NDA Newsletter; weekly

National Dental Assistants Association (1964)
37785 Amber Dr.
Farmington Hills, MI 48331
Website: ndaonline.org/index.php?
option = com_content&view = article&id = 90&Itemid = 96
Members: 500 individuals
Staff: 5

Personnel:
President: Christine Wright
E-Mail: grannycml@bellsouth.net
Contact, Membership Services: Gracie Hightower
E-Mail: gracieht@aol.com

Historical Note:
An auxillary of the National Dental Association. NDAA's mission is to serve thousands of minority Dental Assistants in the field. Membership: $55/year.

National Dental Association (1913)
3517 16th St. NW
Washington, DC 20010
Tel: (202) 588-1822 *Fax:* (202) 588-1244
Website: ndaonline.org
Members: 10000 individuals
Staff: 6
Annual Budget: $100-250,000
Tax: 501(c)(3)

Personnel:
Executive Director: Robert S. Johns
E-Mail: rsjohns@ndaonline.org
Contact, Membership Services: LaShawne Bryant
E-Mail: lbryant@ndaonline.org
Coordinator, Corporate Relations: Kitty L. Gaines
E-Mail: kgaines@ndaonline.org
Manager, Meetings and Conferences: Lavette C. Henderson
E-Mail: lhenderson@ndaonline.org

Historical Note:
NDA's mission is to represent the concerns of ethnic minorities in dentistry, to elevate the global oral health

concerns of underserved communities. *Membership: $395 (Active); $270 (Active Military/Affiliate/International/ Associate/Full Time Faculty); $100 (Retired).*

Continuing Education:
Certification Designation/s: CPR

Meetings/Conferences: Annual
Conference Chair: Lavette C. Henderson
2013 - Ft. Washington, MD (Gaylord National Hotel and Convention Center)/July 26 - 30
2014 - New Orleans, LA (Hilton New Orleans Riverside Hotel)/July 25 - 28
Number of non-conference events/year: 1

Publications:
Flossline
NDA Today; quarterly; adv.

Membership List Available to Non-members

National Dental EDI Council
4225 W. Glendale Ave.
Suite E104
Phoenix, AZ 85051-8153
Tel: (602) 266-7740 *Fax:* (602) 277-6798
E-Mail: ndedic@ndedic.org
Website: ndedic.com
Staff: 3
Annual Budget: $100-250,000

Personnel:
Executive Director: Carol Watkins CAE
E-Mail: cwatkins@ndedic.org
Treasurer: Jarvis Shockey

Historical Note:
NDEDIC's mission is to unite all stakeholders in promoting the value and increasing the utilization of electronic commerce within the dental industry. Membership: $1095 (Corporate); $99 (Dentist and Dental office Staff); $180 (Professional/Trade Association Members, Government & Schools); $495 (Small Business companies/Institution); $25 (Dental Student).

Meetings/Conferences: Annual
2013 - Huntington Beach, CA (Hilton Waterfront Resort)/April 30 - May 2
2014 - San Antonio, TX (Hyatt Regency San Antonio)/ April 29 - May 1

Publications:
Council Byte; quarterly; adv.

National Dental Hygienists' Association (1932)
P.O. Box 22463
Tampa, FL 33622
TollFree: (800) 234-1096
E-Mail: forndha@aol.com
Website: ndhaonline.org
Members: 200 individuals
Staff: 4

Personnel:
President: T. Carla Newbern MEd, RDH
Secretary: Phillis Dickerson
Vice President and National Convention Chairperson: Tracye Moore
Treasurer: Barbara Thompson BS, RDH

Historical Note:
NDHA's mission is to cultivate and promote the art and science of dental hygiene. Membership: $35 (Student); $50 (Life); $75 (Retired); $125 (National).

Meetings/Conferences: Annual
Conference Chair: Tracye Moore
2013 - Washington, DC/July 17 - 23
2013 - Ft. Washington, MD (Gaylord National Harbor Resort)/July 26 - 30

Publications:
NDHA In Brief; irregular

National District Attorneys Association (1950)
44 Canal Center Plaza
Suite 110
Alexandria, VA 22314
Tel: (703) 549-9222 *Fax:* (703) 836-3195
Website: ndaa.org
Members: 6800 individuals
Staff: 35
Annual Budget: $5-10,000,000
Tax: 501(c)(3)

Personnel:
Executive Director: Scott Burns
E-Mail: sburns@ndaa.org
Director, Government Affairs: Jason Baker

E-Mail: jbaker@ndaa.org
Manager, Information Technology: Bill Gibbs
E-Mail: bgibbs@ndaa.org
Director, Publications: Jean Hemphill
E-Mail: jhemphill@ndaa.org
Director, Conferences and Membership Services: Cathy Yates
E-Mail: cyates@ndaa.org

Historical Note:
A national membership association for state and local prosecutors.

Meetings/Conferences:
Conference Chair: Cathy Yates
Number of non-conference events/year: 1

Publications:
The Prosecutor Magazine; quarterly

Membership List Available to Non-members

National Dog Groomers Association of America, Inc. (1969)
P.O. Box 101
Clark, PA 16113
Tel: (724) 962-2711 *Fax:* (724) 962-1919
E-Mail: ndga@nationaldoggroomers.com
Website: nationaldoggroomers.com
Members: 500 certified master groomers and 2500 individuals
Staff: 2
Annual Budget: $100-250,000

Personnel:
Executive Director: Jeffrey L. Reynolds
Coordinator, Certification: Wendy Booth

Historical Note:
Established to provide professional indentification and continuing education. Awards the designation NCMG (National Certified Master Groomer) and holds 20 certification workshops every year throughout the U.S. Membership: $90 (USA Resident); $96 (Canadian Resident).

Continuing Education:
Certification Designation/s: SEE, NCMG

Meetings/Conferences: Annual
2013 - Denver, CO (Crowne Plaza Hotel Denver-International Airport)/June 7 - 9

Publications:
Membership Directory; annually

National Drilling Association (1972)
2200 S. 4000, West
C/O Major Drilling America
Salt Lake City, UT 84120
Tel: (801) 974-0645 *Fax:* (801) 973-2994
E-Mail: info@nda4u.com
Website: nda4u.com
Members: 250 companies
Staff: 3
Annual Budget: $100-250,000

Personnel:
President: Dan Dunn
E-Mail: dan.dunn@majordrilling.com

Historical Note:
Formerly National Drilling Contractors Association; merged with Drilling Equipment Manufacturers Association and International Drilling Federation and assumed its current name in 1995. Incorporated in the state of Pennsylvania. NDA's mission is to enhance the use of professional drilling contractors and their methods. Members are contractors, manufacturers and affiliated members from the drilling industry representing the geotechnical, environmental and mineral exploration sectors of this industry. Membership: $590-2,000 (Manufacturer); $325- 640 (Contractor/Non-Contractor/Supplier); $270 (Consultant/Associate); $80 (Retired/Student).

Continuing Education:
Certification Designation/s: GKC, MWCC, DSGC

Meetings/Conferences: Annual

Publications:
Drill Bits Magazine; on-line; adv.
Membership Directory; on-line

National Drug Court Institute
1029 N. Royal St.
Suite 201
Alexandria, VA 22314
Tel: (703) 575-9400 *Fax:* (703) 575-9402
Website: ndci.org
Staff: 10

Personnel:
Executive Director: Carolyn Hardin
E-Mail: chardin@ndci.org
Coordinator, Training: Ingrid Gutierrez
E-Mail: igutierrez@ndci.org

Historical Note:
NDCI is supported by the White House Office of National Drug Control Policy.

National Earth Science Teachers Association (1983)
4041 Hanover, P.O. Box 20854
Suite 100
Boulder, CO 80308-3854
Tel: (303) 497-2591 *Fax:* (303) 497-2598
Website: nestanet.org
Members: 1000 individuals
Staff: 2
Annual Budget: $250-500,000
Tax: 501(c)(3)

Personnel:
Executive Director: Roberta Johnson
E-Mail: rmjohnsn@nestanet.org
Administrator: Marlene DiMarco
E-Mail: marlene.dimarco@nestanet.org

Historical Note:
NESTA's mission is to facilitate and advance excellence in earth and space science education. Members are earth science teachers concerned with teaching in grades K-12. Membership: $20 (E-Membership/International); $35 (Domestic); $45(Mexico and Canada); $70 (Domestic Library).

Publications:
NESTA E-News; monthly; adv.
The Earth Scientist; quarterly; adv.

National Eating Disorders Association (2001)
165 W. 46th St.
New York, NY 10036
Tel: (212) 575-6200 *Fax:* (212) 575-1650
TollFree: (800) 931-2237
E-Mail: info@NationalEatingDisorders.org
Website: nationaleatingdisorders.org
Staff: 11
Annual Budget: $2-5,000,000
Tax: 501(c)(3)

Personnel:
President and Chief Executive Officer: Lynn S. Grefe MA
Manager, Communications: Maggi Flaherty
Manager, Financial Services: Carolina Peguero
Office Manager: Judy Renner

Historical Note:
NEDA was formed when Eating Disorders Awareness & Prevention (EDAP) joined forces with the American Anorexia Bulimia Association (AABA). NEDA is committed to providing help and hope to those affected by eating disorders.

Meetings/Conferences: Annual

Publications:
Membership Directory; on-line
NEDA Newsletters; adv.

National Ecological Observatory Network, Inc
1685 38th St.
Suite 100
Boulder, CO 80301
Tel: (720) 746-4844 *Fax:* (720) 746-4870
Website: neoninc.org
Members: 58 Institutional Members
Staff: 66
Annual Budget: $25-50,000,000
Tax: 501(c)(3)

Personnel:
Chief Executive Officer: Russ Lea
E-Mail: rlea@neoninc.org
Communications Specialist: Sandra Chung
E-Mail: schung@neoninc.org
Chief, Education and Public Engagement: Wendy Gram
E-Mail: wgram@neoninc.org
Senior Database Administrator: Allan Reynolds
E-Mail: areynolds@neoninc.org

Historical Note:
NEON's mission is to enable the understanding and forecasting of the impacts of climate change, land-use change and invasive species on continental-scale ecology, by providing infrastructure and consistent methodologies to

support research and education in these areas. Membership: $1,000 (Individual Institute).

Publications:
E-Newsletter; quarterly

National Economic Association (1969)
Department of Economics, Spelman College
P.O. Box 167, 350 Spelman Ln.
Atlanta, GA 30314
E-Mail: info@neaecon.org
Website: neaecon.org
Members: 150 individuals
Staff: 4
Annual Budget: Under $10,000

Personnel:
Secretary: Dr. Romie Tribble
   E-Mail: rtribble@spelman.edu
Meetings Contact: Warren Whatley
   E-Mail: wwhatley@umich.edu

Historical Note:
Formerly (1975) Caucus of Black Economists. NEA promotes black representation in the economics profession, acts as a job clearing house and gives financial assistance to black students of economics. Membership is open to professionals and students. Membership: $50 (Voting Member); $25 (Student).

Meetings/Conferences: Annual
Conference Chair: Warren Whatley
2013 - San Diego, CA (La Jolla, Marriot Marquis and Marina)/Jan. 3 - 5

Publications:
Membership Directory; on-line
NEA Newsletter; on-line

Membership List Available to Non-members

National Education Association (1857)
1201 16th St. NW
Washington, DC 20036-3290
Tel: (202) 833-4000 *Fax:* (202) 822-7974
Website: nea.org
Members: 320000 individuals
Staff: 13
Annual Budget: $500-1,000,000

Personnel:
Executive Director: John C. Stocks
President: Dennis Van Roekel
General Counsel: Robert H. Chanin
   E-Mail: bobchanin@verizon.net
Senior Press Officer: Miguel A. Gonzalez
   E-Mail: mgonzalez@nea.org
Senior Press Officer: Michelle Hudgins
   E-Mail: mhudgins@nea.org
Senior Writer and Editor: Carrie Lewis
   E-Mail: clewis@nea.org
General Counsel: Alice O'Brien
   E-Mail: aobrien@nea.org
Senior Director, Center for Communications: Ramona C. A. Oliver
Secretary and Treasurer: Rebecca "Becky" Pringle
Project Coordinator: Tomas Saucedo
   E-Mail: tosaucedo@nea.org

Historical Note:
NEA's mission is to advocate for education professionals and to unite our members and the nation. NEA is committed to advance the cause of public education.

Meetings/Conferences: Annual
2013 - Atlanta, GA/July 1 - 6
2014 - Denver, CO/July 1 - 6
2015 - Miami, FL/July 1 - 6
2016 - Washington, DC/July 3 - 8
2017 - Boston, MA/June 30 - July 5
2018 - Minneapolis, MN/June 30 - July 5
2019 - Houston, TX/July 2 - 7
Number of non-conference events/year: 6

Publications:
Advocate; bi-monthly
ESEA/NCLB Newsletter; on-line
First Edition; on-line
NEA Announce E-mail; monthly; adv.
NEA e-newsletter; on-line
NEA Today; adv.
NEA Today Go!; adv.
NEAMB Travel Savers Newsletter; bi-monthly; adv.
This Active Life; adv.
Tomorrow's Teachers; annually
Works4Me E-mail Newsletter; weekly; adv.

National Educational Broadband Services Organization
P O Box 121475
Clermont, FL 34712-1475
Tel: (407) 401-4630 *Fax:* (321) 406-0520
E-Mail: info@nebsa.org
Website: nebsa.org/
Staff: 2

Personnel:
Executive Director: Don MacCullough
Treasurer: David Moore

Historical Note:
NEBSA's mission is to Promote and protect the use of EBS spectrum for education, and to provide EBS license holders with relevant, current and expert information that is needed to serve and protect the interests of EBS Licensees.membership: ($300-$1500)Associate Member; ($400-$2500)Corporate Member.

Meetings/Conferences: Annual
2013 - New Orleans, LA (Astor Crowne Plaza)/April 2 - 5

National Educational Telecommunications Association (1967)
P.O. Box 50008
Columbia, SC 29250
Tel: (803) 799-5517 *Fax:* (803) 771-4831
TollFree: (800) 507-7322
E-Mail: skip@netaonline.org
Website: netaonline.org
Members: 97 public broadcasting licensees and 94 individuals
Staff: 38
Annual Budget: $2-5,000,000
Tax: 501(c)(3)

Personnel:
President: Skip Hinton
   E-Mail: skip@netaonline.org
Contact, Education Center: John Chambers
   E-Mail: john@netaonline.org
Contact, Membership Services: Lisa Lehman
   E-Mail: lisa@netaonline.org
Contact, Programming and Information: Gayle Loeber
   E-Mail: gayle@netaonline.org
Contact, Conference Services: Tinia Milhouse
   E-Mail: tinia@netaonline.org
Contact, Communications: Maryanne Schuessler
   E-Mail: maryanne@netaonline.org
Vice President, Finance: Anita Sims
   E-Mail: anita@netaonline.org
Contact, Operations: Gre Tillou
   E-Mail: greg@netaonline.org

Historical Note:
Founded as Southern Educational Communications Association and assumed its current name in 1997 to reflect its national constituency. Members are public television licensees. The purpose of NETA is to connect people and ideas by providing quality programming, educational resources, professional development, management support and national representation.

Meetings/Conferences: Annual
Conference Chair: Tinia Milhouse

Membership List Available to Non-members

National Elder Law Foundation (1994)
6336 N. Oracle Rd.
Suite 326, Number 136
Tucson, AZ 85704
Tel: (520) 881-1076 *Fax:* (520) 203-0277
Website: nelf.org
Members: 400 attorneys
Staff: 3
Annual Budget: $100-250,000

Personnel:
Executive Director: Lori Barbee CMP
   E-Mail: lori@nelf.org

Historical Note:
NELF's mission is to develop and improve of the professional competence of lawyers in the area of elder law.

Continuing Education:
Certification Designation/s: CELA

Publications:
NELF Newsletter; weekly

National Electrical Contractors Association (1901)

Three Bethesda Metro Center
Suite 1100
Bethesda, MD 20814-5330
Tel: (301) 657-3110 *Fax:* (301) 215-4500
Website: necanet.org
Members: 4500 companies
Staff: 15
Annual Budget: $250-500,000

Personnel:
Chief Executive Officer: John M. Grau
   E-Mail: john.grau@necanet.org
Manager, Membership Database: Vivian Brown
Executive Director, Marketing: Robert Colgan
Manager, Education Services: Ace Crawford
Executive Director, Conventions and Expositions: Beth Ellis
   E-Mail: eie@necanet.org
Director, Human Resources: Bunny Fritter
Executive Director, Government Affairs: Marco Giamberardino
Vice President, Labor Relations: Geary Higgins
Director, Legislative Affairs: Blair E Hood
   E-Mail: blair.hood@necanet.org
Senior Associate Editor: Timothy "Tim" Johnson
   E-Mail: timothy.johnson@necanet.org
Director, Communications: Beth Margulies
   E-Mail: beth.margulies@necanet.org
Director, Database Management: Linda O'Neil
Vice President and Chief Operating Officer: Daniel "Dan" G. Walter

Historical Note:
NECA is a national organization serving the management interests of the entire electrical contracting industry. Members are electrical construction companies. Sponsors and supports the Electrical Construction Political Action Committee (ECPAC). Membership: $500 (International); $200 (Regular).

Meetings/Conferences: Annual
Conference Chair: Beth Ellis
2013 - Naples, FL (Naples Beach Hotel and Golf Club)/ Jan. 31 - Feb. 1
2013 - Washington, DC/Oct. 12 - 15
2013 - Washington, DC (Walter E. Washington Convention Center)/Oct. 12 - 15
2014 - Chicago, IL/Oct. 11 - 14
2014 - Chicago, IL/Oct. 11 - 14
2015 - San Francisco, CA/Oct. 3 - 6
2015 - San Francisco, CA/Oct. 3 - 6
2017 - Seatle, WA/Oct. 7 - 10
2017 - Seattle, WA/Oct. 7 - 10

Publications:
Electrical Contractor Magazine; monthly; adv.
MEInsights; irregular
NECA This Week; weekly

National Electrical Manufacturers Association (1926)
1300 N. 17th St.
Suite 1752
Arlington, VA 22209
Tel: (703) 841-3200 *Fax:* (703) 841-5900
Website: nema.org
Members: 450 companies
Staff: 11
Annual Budget: $25-50,000,000
Tax: 501(c)(6)

Personnel:
President and Chief Executive Officer: Evan R. Gaddis
   E-Mail: evan.gaddis@nema.org
Senior Vice President, Operations and Communications: Ric Erdheim
   E-Mail: ric_erdheim@nema.org
Vice President, Finance and Administration: Tom Hixon
Vice President and Chief Economist: Donald R. Leavens PhD
Manager, Meetings: Francine Meyer
   E-Mail: fran_meyer@nema.org
Vice President, Government Relations: Kyle Pitsor
   E-Mail: kyl_pitsor@nema.org
Vice President, Medical Imaging and Technology Alliance: Gail Rodriguez
Vice President, Technical Services: Alvin Scolnik
Manager, Member Relations: Christine Shattuck
General Counsel: Clark R. Silcox
   E-Mail: cla_silcox@nema.org
Senior Vice President, Operations and Communications: Ric Talley

Historical Note:
NEMA is a trade organization for manufacturers of electrical products in the U.S. Organized in 1926 through the merger of several organizations, the oldest of which, Electrical Manufacturers Club (1905). NEMA's mission is to promote the competitiveness of the U.S. electrical product industry through the development of standards, advocacy in federal and state legislatures and executive agencies, and the collection and analysis of economic data. Membership: $3,000/year.

Meetings/Conferences: Annual
Conference Chair: Francine Meyer
2013 - Palm Beach, FL (Breakers Palm Beach)/Nov. 8 - 9

Publications:
eiXtra e-newsletter; on-line; adv.
Electroindustry; monthly; adv.

National Electrical Manufacturers Representatives Association (1969)
28 Deer St.
Suite 302
Portsmouth, NH 03801
Tel: (914) 524-8650 Fax: (603) 319-1667
TollFree: (800) 446-3672
E-Mail: nemra@nemra.org
Website: nemra.org
Members: 1150 companies
Staff: 9
Annual Budget: $1-2,000,000
Tax: 501(c)(6)

Personnel:
President: Kenneth W. Hooper
    E-Mail: khooper@nemra.org
Director, Information Technologies: James W. Bannon
    E-Mail: jim@nemra.org
Manager, Marketing and Membership Services: Kirsty Stebbins
    E-Mail: kstebbins@nemra.org
Office Manager: Sue Todd
    E-Mail: stodd@nemra.org

Historical Note:
NEMRA's mission is to offer its representative membership and manufacturer affiliates the resources to deal with the dynamics of an ever-changing marketplace. Members are independent electrical sales representatives. Membership: $750-4,750/year.

Meetings/Conferences: Annual
2013 - Chicago, IL (Sheraton Chicago Hotel and Towers)/Jan. 30 - Feb. 2
2014 - Atlanta, GA (Atlanta Marriott Century Center)/Feb. 5 - 8
2015 - San Diego, CA (Hilton San Diego Bayfront)/Jan. 28 - 31
2016 - Dallas, TX (Hilton Anatole)/Feb. 3 - 6

Publications:
Economic Updates
Hot Lines; on-line; adv.
NEMRA Newsletter

National Electronic Service Dealers Association (1963)
3608 Pershing Ave.
Ft. Worth, TX 76107-4527
Tel: (817) 921-9061 Fax: (817) 921-3741
E-Mail: info@nesda.com
Website: nesda.com
Members: 800 individuals
Staff: 5
Annual Budget: $500-1,000,000

Personnel:
Executive Director: Mack Blakely
    E-Mail: mack@nesda.com
Coordinator, Membership Services and Trade Shows: Patricia Bohon
    E-Mail: patricia@nesda.com
Director, Communications and Information Technology: Sheila Fredrickson
    E-Mail: sheila@nesda.com
Associate Editor and Graphic Designer: James Keesler
    E-Mail: james@nesda.com
Bookkeeper and Administrative Assistant: Margaret Vazquez
    E-Mail: margaret@iscet.org

Historical Note:
NESDA works for professionals in the business of repairing consumer electronic equipment, appliances, or computers and help independent services be successful through challenging times. Members are electronics service centers. Sponsors International Society of Certified Electronics Technicians. Membership: $325-2,250/year (Corporate/Associate).

Continuing Education:
Certification Designation/s: CSM, CSC, MST, CET

Meetings/Conferences:
Conference Chair: Patricia Bohon
2013 - Dover, DE (Dover Downs Hotel and Casino)/June 5 - 8
2013 - Tunica, MS (Harrah's Veranda Hotel)/July 29 - Aug. 2

Publications:
Membership Directory; annually
ProService Magazine; bi-monthly; adv.

Membership List Available to Non-members

National Elevator Industry, Inc. (1934)
1677 County Route 64
P.O. Box 838
Salem, NY 12865-0838
Tel: (518) 854-3100 Fax: (518) 854-3257
E-Mail: info@neii.org
Website: neii.org
Members: 35 companies
Staff: 3
Annual Budget: $500-1,000,000
Tax: 501(c)(6)

Personnel:
Managing Director and Secretary: Edward A. Donoghue
    E-Mail: edonoghue@neii.org
Consultant, Government Affairs: Amy J. Blankenbiller
    E-Mail: ajblankenbiller@neii.org
Media Contact: Audra Hession
    E-Mail: ahession@gibbs-soell.com

Historical Note:
Formerly National Elevator Manufacturing Industry, Inc. NEII's mission is to promote safe building transportation for new and existing products and technologies and adoption of current codes by local government agencies. Members are firms that manufacture, install, repair and maintain elevators, escalators, moving walks and related equipment and corporations that as part of their regular business, employ members of the International Union of Elevator Constructors(IUEC) and contribute to the benefit trusts established by agreements between the IUEC and NEII. Membership: $2,500-125,000 (Full-Regular, based on sales); $500 (Associate Regular); $1,000 (Individual); $2,000 (Trust member).

Meetings/Conferences:
Number of non-conference events/year: 1

Publications:
Membership Directory; on-line
NEII Now e-Newsletter; on-line
The Insider; bi-monthly

National Emergency Equipment Dealers Association (1996)
P.O. Box 220
Annandale, VA 22003
Tel: (703) 850-8552
E-Mail: kentonp1@aol.com
Website: needa.org
Members: 60 dealers
Staff: 1
Annual Budget: $10-25,000
Tax: 501(c)(6)

Personnel:
Executive Director: Kenton Pattie
    E-Mail: kentonp1@aol.com

Historical Note:
Purpose is to assist dealers to profitably deliver quality products and support the nation's emergency services. NEEDA represents dealers and distributors who sell fire trucks, ambulances, rescue vehicles and all related equipment, parts, maintenance and repair services. Membership: $600/year (Company).

Meetings/Conferences:
Number of non-conference events/year: 3

Publications:
Membership Directory; on-line
NEEDA Congressional Directory; on-line
NEEDA Newsletter; on-line

National Emergency Management Association (1974)
P.O. Box 11910
Lexington, KY 40578-1910

Tel: (859) 244-8000 Fax: (859) 244-8239
E-Mail: nemaadmin@csg.org
Website: nemaweb.org
Members: 300 individuals
Staff: 4
Annual Budget: $500-1,000,000
Tax: 501(c)(3)

Personnel:
Executive Director: Trina R. Sheets
    E-Mail: tsheets@csg.org
Coordinator, Meetings and Marketing: Karen Cobuluis
    E-Mail: kcobuluis@csg.org
Administrative Assistant: Emily Dierig
Technology Analyst: Jennifer Perkins
    E-Mail: jperkins@csg.org

Historical Note:
NEMA provides national leadership and expertise in comprehensive emergency management; serves as a vital emergency management information and assistance resource; and advances continuous improvement in emergency management through strategic partnerships, innovative programs, and collaborative policy positions. Membership: $3200 (State); $300 (Key State Staff, Organizational, International Associate); $500-1200 (Corporate); $200 (Individual); $50 (Student Associate).

Meetings/Conferences: Annual
Conference Chair: Karen Cobuluis

Publications:
Membership Directory; on-line

National Emergency Number Association (1982)
1700 Diagonal Rd.
Suite 500
Alexandria, VA 22314
Tel: (202) 466-4911 Fax: (202) 618-6370
Website: nena.org
Members: 7000 Members
Staff: 13
Annual Budget: $2-5,000,000

Personnel:
Chief Executive Officer: Brian Fontes
    E-Mail: bfontes@nena.org
Manager, Exhibits and Special Projects: Anna Marie Batt
    E-Mail: abatt@nena.org
Director, Finance: Ron Cranston
    E-Mail: rcranston@nena.org
Director, Technical Issues: Roger Hixson
    E-Mail: rhixson@nena.org
Manager, Education Programs: Chris Nussman
    E-Mail: cnussman@nena.org
Manager, Membership Services: Bri Robinson
    E-Mail: brobinson@nena.org

Historical Note:
NENA's mission is to foster the technological advancement, availability and implementation of a universal emergency telephone number system. NENA promotes research, planning, training and education. Membership: $130 (Public Sector/Government Voting Member); $160 (Private Sector/Commercial Voting Member); $85 (Emergency Dispatcher/Associate).

Continuing Education:
Enrollment: 150
Certification Designation/s: ENP

Meetings/Conferences: Annual
Conference Chair: Anna Marie Batt
2013 - Orlando, FL (Caribe Royale)/Feb. 10 - 13
2013 - Charlotte, NC (Charlotte Convention Center)/June 15 - 20
Number of non-conference events/year: 1

Publications:
Emergency Number Professional; bi-monthly; adv.
The Call Magazine; adv.

National Employment Counseling Association (1964)
940 S. Main St.
Suite E
Lebanon, OR 97355
Tel: (541) 258-8210 Fax: (541) 258-8212
E-Mail: talk@people-solutions.us
Website: employmentcounseling.org
Members: 850 individuals
Staff: 3
Annual Budget: $25-50,000

Personnel:
Executive Director, Contact Financial and E-News: John Hakemian

E-Mail: sailorjohn@mindspring.com
Contact, Professional Development and Strategic
  Leadership: Kay Brawley
  E-Mail: kbrawley@mindspring.com
Webmaster and Trustee: Karen Obringer Campbell

Historical Note:
*Formerly (1992) National Employment Counselors
Association, NECA is committed to offering professional
leadership to people who counsel within employment and/
or career development settings. A division of the American
Counseling Association. Membership: $38 (Regular/
Professional); $25 (Student/Retired).*

Continuing Education:
Certification Designation/s: GCDF
Meetings/Conferences:
Number of non-conference events/year: 1

Publications:
Journal of Employment Counseling; quarterly
NECA eNewsletter

National Employment Lawyers Association (NELA)
(1985)
417 Montgomery St.
Fourth Floor
San Francisco, CA 94104
Tel: (415) 296-7629 *Fax:* (866) 593-7521
E-Mail: nelahq@nelahq.org
Website: nela.org
Members: 3000 individuals
Staff: 11
Annual Budget: $1-2,000,000
Tax: 501(c)(6)

Personnel:
Executive Director: Terisa E. Chaw
Director, Membership Services: Colleen Goodin
  E-Mail: cgoodin@nelahq.org
Technology and Office Administrator: Pedro A. Valverde
  E-Mail: pvalverde@nelahq.org

Historical Note:
*National membership organization of employment plaintiff
lawyers.*

Continuing Education:
Certification Designation/s: CLE

Meetings/Conferences: Annual
Number of non-conference events/year: 5

Publications:
Membership Directory; on-line
The Employee Advocate; quarterly; adv.

Membership List Available to Non-members

National EMS Pilots Association *(1984)*
PO Box 2128
Layton, UT 84041-9128
Tel: (877) 668-0430 *Fax:* (866) 906-6023
E-Mail: contactus@nemspa.org
Website: nemspa.org
Members: 143 individuals and organizations
Staff: 4
Annual Budget: $25-50,000

Personnel:
President: Rex J. Alexander
  E-Mail: RAlexander@omniflight.com

Historical Note:
*NEMSPA's mission is to serve helicopter and fixed-wing
aircraft pilots involved in the air-medical transport industry,
and to improving the quality and safety of those services.
Membership: $45 (Pilot); $38 (Affiliate); $500-5,000
(Sponsor).*

Publications:
AIRNET newsletters; on-line
Membership DIrectory; on-line
Rotorcraft Professional Magazine
The Air Medical Journal

National Energy Assistance Directors' Association
(1983)
1232 31st St. NW
Washington, DC 20007
Tel: (202) 333-5915 *Fax:* (202) 237-7316
TollFree: (866) 674-6327
E-Mail: info@neada.org
Website: neada.org
Staff: 1
Annual Budget: $250-500,000
Tax: 501(c)(3)

Personnel:

Executive Director: Mark Wolfe
  E-Mail: mlwolfe@neada.org

Historical Note:
*NEADA's mission is to support states in the development
of Low-Income Home Energy Assistance (LIHEAP) policies.
The association coordinates and cooperates in the collection
and dissemination of information and proposes energy
policies.*

National Energy Services Association
6430 FM 1960 West
Suite 213
Houston, TX 77069
Tel: (713) 856-6525 *Fax:* (713) 856-6199
Website: nesanet.org
Members: 2200 industries
Staff: 3
Annual Budget: $500-1,000,000
Tax: 501(c)(6)

Personnel:
President: Teresa Rice
  E-Mail: trice@nesanet.org
Contact, Conventions: Tracy Cummins
  E-Mail: tcummins@nesanet.org

Historical Note:
*NESA's mission is to share a common expertise in energy
services and a common goal to improve those services
throughout the United States. Membership: $125/year
(Individual).*

Meetings/Conferences: Annual
Conference Chair: Tracy Cummins
Number of non-conference events/year: 1

Publications:
Member Directory; on-line
NESA Newsletter

National Environmental Balancing Bureau *(1971)*
8575 Grovemont Cir.
Gaithersburg, MD 20877
Tel: (301) 977-3698 *Fax:* (301) 977-9589
TollFree: (866) 497-4447
Website: nebb.org
Members: 600 companies
Staff: 8
Annual Budget: $1-2,000,000

Personnel:
Executive Vice President: John M. Schulte
  E-Mail: john@nebb.org
Director, Marketing and Communications: Mandy Kaur
  E-Mail: mandy@nebb.org
Director, Certification and Publications: Elana Noel
  E-Mail: elana@nebb.org
Executive Assistant, Administration and Finance: Connie
  Vitale
  E-Mail: connie@nebb.org

Historical Note:
*NEBB works to assist architects, engineers, building owners,
and contractors in producing buildings with systems that
perform as they were visualized and designed. Members are
contractors in the heating, ventilating and air conditioning
(HVAC) industry. Membership: $650/year.*

Continuing Education:
Certification Designation/s: NEBBC

Meetings/Conferences: Annual
2013 - Montreal, AB (Hyatt Regency)/May 2 - 4
Number of non-conference events/year: 4

Publications:
NEBB Professional; quarterly; adv.

National Environmental Health Association
(1937)
720 S. Colorado Blvd.
Suite 1000-N
Denver, CO 80246-1926
Tel: (303) 756-9090 *Fax:* (303) 691-9490
TollFree: (866) 956-2258
E-Mail: staff@neha.org
Website: neha.org
Members: 4500 professionals
Staff: 26
Annual Budget: $5-10,000,000
Tax: 501(c)(3)

Personnel:
Executive Director: Nelson E. Fabian
  E-Mail: nfabian@neha.org
Manager, Marketing and Communications: Jill
  Cruickshank

  E-Mail: jcruickshank@neha.org
Receptionist and CSR Specialist: Cindy Dimmitt
  E-Mail: cdimmitt@neha.org
*Customer Service Manager, Office Coordinator and Human
  Resources Liaison:* Dawn Jordan
  E-Mail: djordan@neha.org
*Managing Director, Government Affairs and Research and
  Development:* Larry Marcum
  E-Mail: lmarcum@neha.org
Financial Coordinator: Barry Porter
  E-Mail: bporter@neha.org
Editor: Kristen Ruby
  E-Mail: kruby@neha.org
Coordinator, Credentialing Programs: Shelly Wallingford
  E-Mail: swallingford@neha.org

Historical Note:
*Incorporated in California in 1937 as the National
Association of Sanitarians, became the National
Environmental Health Association in 1970. NEHA's
mission is to advance the environmental health and
protection professional for the purpose of providing a
healthful environment for all. It also conducts continuing
education programs and special seminars. Members
represent virtually all environmental health and protection
professionals. Membership: $95 (Individual); $25 (Student/
New Graduate); $125 (Individual, International); $425
(Sustaining); $175 (Educational-School/University).*

Continuing Education:
Certification Designation/s: CP-FS, RHSP, CIOWTS, HHS,
RET, RHSS, CEHT, REHS/RS

Meetings/Conferences: Annual
Number of non-conference events/year: 72

Publications:
Journal of Environmental Health
Membership Directory; on-line
NEHA E-News; on-line

National Environmental, Safety and Health
Training Association *(1977)*
2700 N. Central Ave.
Suite 900
Phoenix, AZ 85004-1147
Tel: (602) 956-6099 *Fax:* (602) 234-1867
E-Mail: neshta@neshta.org
Website: netforum.avectra.com
Members: 900 individuals
Staff: 3
Annual Budget: $500-1,000,000
Tax: 501(c)(3)

Personnel:
Executive Director: Charles L. Richardson

Historical Note:
*Formerly (2003) National Environmental Training
Association. NESHTA's mission is to promote trainer
competency through trainer skills training, continuing
education, voluntary certification, peer networking and the
adoption of national and international training and trainer
standards. Members are trainers of personnel in the field of
air and noise pollution, solid and hazardous waste control,
water supply and waste-water treatment, and occupational
safety and health. Membership: $105 (Individual); $425
(Organizational (Key Member + 4)); $85 (Organizational
(Additional Member)).*

Continuing Education:
Certification Designation/s: CIT, CET

Meetings/Conferences: Annual
Conference Chair: Charles L. Richardson

Publications:
NESHTA eNews; on-line

National Exchange Carrier Association *(1984)*
80 S. Jefferson Rd.
Whippany, NJ 07981-1009
Tel: (973) 884-8000 *Fax:* (973) 884-8469
TollFree: (800) 228-8597
E-Mail: necainfo@neca.org
Website: neca.org
Members: 1350 local telephone companies
Staff: 250

Personnel:
President and Chief Executive Officer: Bill Hegmann
Vice President and Chief Financial Officer: Peter Dunbar
Contact, Media inquiries: Jeff Dupree
  E-Mail: jdupree@neca.org
Editor: Teresa Evert
  E-Mail: tevert@neca.org
Vice President, Operations: James W. Frame
Contact, Employment Inquiries: Andrea Levine

E-Mail: alevine@neca.org
Vice President and General Counsel: Regina McNeil

Historical Note:
NECA is a membership association of U.S. local telephone companies, is dedicated to keeping customers connected on state-of-the-art communications networks.

Continuing Education:
Certification Designation/s: AMA

Meetings/Conferences: Annual
2013 - Las Vegas, NV (Wynn Las Vegas)/Nov. 10 - 14

Publications:
Access Newsletter
Membership Directory; on-line
REGScan; weekly

National Exchange Club *(1917)*
3050 Central Ave.
Toledo, OH 43606-1700
Tel: (419) 535-3232 *Fax:* (419) 535-1989
TollFree: (800) 924-2643
E-Mail: info@nationalexchangeclub.org
Website: nationalexchangeclub.org
Members:
800 clubs
25000 individuals
Staff: 1
Annual Budget: $2-5,000,000
Tax: 501(c)(4)

Personnel:
President: Sid Mobley

Historical Note:
National Exchange Club strives to help exchange clubs realize their full potential of community service.

Meetings/Conferences: Annual
2013 - Greensboro, NC (Sheraton Greensboro at Four Seasons)/July 10 - 13
2014 - New Orleans, LA (Sheraton Hotel New Orleans)/July 9 - 12
2015 - Columbus, OH (Sheraton Columbus at Capitol Square)/July 29 - Aug. 1
2016 - Houston, TX (Hyatt Regency Houston)/July 13 - 16
2017 - Jacksonville, FL (Hyatt Regency Jacksonville Riverfront)/July 12 - 15

National Exchange Traded Fund Association *(2012)*
1290 Broadway
Suite 1100
Denver, CO 80203
Website: nationaletf.org
Staff: 1

Personnel:
Media Contact: Patricia Lobato
E-Mail: patricia.lobato@alpsinc.com

Historical Note:
An industry group composed of firms that issue, sponsor, or are involved in the Exchanged Traded Funds ("ETFs") industry.

National Exercise Trainers Association *(1977)*
5955 Golden Valley Rd.
Suite 240
Minneapolis, MN 55422
Tel: (763) 545-2505 *Fax:* (763) 545-2524
TollFree: (800) 237-6242
E-Mail: neta@netafit.org
Website: netafit.org
Members: 18000 individuals
Staff: 50
Annual Budget: $1-2,000,000
Tax: 501(c)(3)

Personnel:
Executive Director: Mario Crespo
Director, Communications: Linda Benzinger
E-Mail: lbenz@netafit.org

Historical Note:
Formerly (1977) National Dance-Exercise Instructor's Training Association; assumed current name in 2004. NETA's mission is to offer cost effective certification programs and continuing education that teach concepts and theories of health and fitness. Members are aerobic exercise instructors and personal trainers. Membership: $45- 75/ year (based on expiration).

Continuing Education:
Certification Designation/s: NETA-CPT

National Extension Association of Family and Consumer Sciences *(1933)*
20423 State Rd. 7
Suite F6-491
Boca Raton, FL 33498
Tel: (561) 477-8100 *Fax:* (561) 910-0896
E-Mail: info@neafcs.org
Website: neafcs.org
Members: 3300 individuals
Staff: 6
Annual Budget: $500-1,000,000

Personnel:
Executive Director: Jody Rosen Atkins
E-Mail: jrosen@associationsource.com
Conference Planner: Cindy Rosen
E-Mail: crosen@associationsource.com

Historical Note:
Formerly National Home Demonstration Agents' Association and then National Association of Extension Home Economists, assumed its current name in 1995. NEAFCS educates and recognizes extension professionals who impart the quality of life for individuals, families and communities. Members are family and consumer science educators working in the extension system. Membership: $270 (Life Member); $70 (Active).

Meetings/Conferences:
Conference Chair: Cindy Rosen
2014 - Lexington, KY (Hyatt Regency Lexington)/Sept. 15 - 19
Number of non-conference events/year: 3

Publications:
Communique; annually; adv.
eNEAFCS; monthly; adv.
Journal of the National Extension Association of Family and Consumer Sciences; annually; adv.

Membership List Available to Non-members

National Family Caregivers Association *(1993)*
10400 Connecticut Ave.
Suite 500
Kensington, MD 20895-3944
Tel: (301) 942-6430 *Fax:* (301) 942-2302
TollFree: (800) 896-3650
E-Mail: info@thefamilycaregiver.org
Website: nfcacares.org
Members: 9000 individuals
Staff: 5
Annual Budget: $500-1,000,000
Tax: 501(c)(3)

Personnel:
President and Chief Executive Officer: Suzanne G Mintz
Managing Editor: Sandy Rogers
E-Mail: Sandy.rogers@thefamilycaregiver.org
Director, Finance and Program Administration: Christal Willingham
Chief Operating Officer: Lisa Winstel
E-Mail: Lisa.Winstel@thefamilycaregiver.org

Historical Note:
NFCA seeks to empower family caregivers to remove barriers to health and well being. Members are family caregivers, health professionals and organizations with an interest in the provision of home health care. Membership: Free (Family Caregivers); $10 (Family Caregivers Plus); $20 (Family/Friend/Former Caregiver); $40 (Professional); $60-100 (Organization).

Publications:
TAKE CARE!; quarterly

National Family Planning and Reproductive Health Association *(1971)*
1627 K St. NW
12th Floor
Washington, DC 20006
Tel: (202) 293-3114 *Fax:* (202) 293-1990
E-Mail: info@nfprha.org
Website: nationalfamilyplanning.org
Members: 700 organizations and individuals
Staff: 14
Annual Budget: $2-5,000,000

Personnel:
President and Chief Executive Officer: Clare Coleman
E-Mail: ccoleman@nfprha.org
Director, Membership Services and Special Projects: Lily Davidson
E-Mail: ldavidson@nfprha.org
Manager, Communications: Lauren Levenstein
E-Mail: llevenstein@nfprha.org

Senior Policy Director: Dana Thomas
E-Mail: dthomas@nfprha.org

Historical Note:
Formerly (1979) National Family Planning Forum. NFPRHA is established to assure access to voluntary, comprehensive and culturally sensitive family planning and reproductive health care services and to support reproductive freedom for all. Members are clinicians, administrators, researchers, educators, advocates and consumers. Membership: $250 (Professional); $25 (Student); $500-1,500 (Institution); $3,000 (Sustaining).

Meetings/Conferences: Annual
Conference Chair: Lily Davidson
2013 - Alexandria, VA (Westin Alexandria)/April 28 - May 1/1-10 exhibitors

Publications:
Family Planning Matters; bi-monthly
NFPRHA alerts
Reproductive Health Watch e-newsletter; weekly

National Farmers Organization *(1955)*
P.O. Box 2508
528 Billy Sunday Rd., Suite 100
Ames, IA 50010
Tel: (515) 292-2000 *Fax:* (515) 292-7106
TollFree: (800) 247-2110
E-Mail: nfo@nfo.org
Website: nfo.org
Staff: 250

Personnel:
Director, Communications: Perry Garner

Historical Note:
NFO is an agricultural marketing company that utilizes group marketing concepts to achieve returns for its member producers. Membership: $125/year (Individual).

Meetings/Conferences: Annual
2013 - Kansas City, MO (KC Convention Center & Aladdin Holiday Inn Hotel)/Jan. 28 - 31

Publications:
AgWeb (Farm Journal); on-line; adv.
Membership Directory; on-line
National Farmers Magazine; monthly; adv.

National Farmers Union (Farmers Educational & Co-operative Union of America) *(1902)*
20 F St. NW
Suite 300
Washington, DC 20001
Tel: (202) 554-1600
E-Mail: info@nfu.org
Website: nfu.org
Members:
200000 individuals
32 states
Staff: 19
Annual Budget: $500-1,000,000

Personnel:
President: Roger Johnson
E-Mail: tbuis@nfudc.org
Director, Communications: Melisa Augusto
E-Mail: maugusto@nfudc.org
Vice President ,Operations: Jeff Knudson
Director, Education: Maria Miller
E-Mail: mmiller@nfudc.org
Vice President, Membership: Leigh Slayden
E-Mail: lslayden@nfudc.org
Director, Finance: Martha Van Dale
E-Mail: mvdale@nfudc.org
General Counsel: Dave Velde

Historical Note:
Farmers Educational and Co-operative Union of America also known as National Farmers Union, Farmers Union. Members are farm families throughout the nation united for legislative, cooperative and educational purposes.

Meetings/Conferences: Annual
Conference Chair: Melisa Augusto
2013 - Springfield, MA (Mass Mutual Center)/March 2 - 5

Publications:
National Farmers Union E-Newsletter; on-line

National Fastener Distributors Association *(1968)*
10842 Noel St.
Suite 107
Los Alamitos, CA 90720
Tel: (714) 484-7858 *Fax:* (562) 684-0695

TollFree: (877) 487-6332
E-Mail: nfda@nfda-fastener.org
Website: nfda-fastener.org
Members: 220 companies
Staff: 5
Annual Budget: $250-500,000
Tax: 501(c)(6)

Personnel:
Executive Vice President: Vickie Lester MBA CAE
    E-Mail: vlester@nfda-fastener.org

Historical Note:
Absorbed the Southern Association of Industrial Fastener Distributors in 1972. NFDA is a trade association of qualified fastener related companies which recognizes the worldwide nature of the industry. It also seeks to be the resource to meet or exceed the needs of its members to excel in global markets. Membership: $850-2,730/year (Distributors/Associates, based on annual sales volume).

Meetings/Conferences: Annual

Publications:
Economic Outlook; quarterly
Membership Directory; on-line; adv.
NFDA Newsletter; semi-monthly

National Federal Development Association

13408 Glen Lea Way
Rockville, MD 20850
Staff: 4
Annual Budget: $1-2,000,000

Personnel:
Executive Vice President: Dennis Eisen
    E-Mail: deisen@nfda.us

Historical Note:
Trade association of developers of government-leased facilities.

National Federation Coaches Association (1981)

P.O. Box 690
Indianapolis, IN 46206
Tel: (317) 972-6900 *Fax:* (317) 822-5700
Website: nfhs.org
Members: 30000 individuals
Staff: 2
Annual Budget: $500-1,000,000

Personnel:
Assistant Director: Tim Flannery

Historical Note:
NFCA, an affiliate of National Federation of State High School Associations (same address), seeks to enhance the professional development of all high school sports coaches in order to improve interscholastic athletics in America. Members are secondary school athletic coaches. Membership: $20-35/year.

Meetings/Conferences:
2013 - Orlando, FL/Jan. 1
2013 - Orlando, FL (Rosen Shingle Creek)/Jan. 3 - 6
2013 - Orlando, FL/Jan. 6
2013 - Denver, CO (Hyatt Regency Denver Tech Center)/June 23 - 27
2013 - Anaheim, CA (Hilton Anaheim)/Dec. 13 - 17
2014 - Boston, MA (Boston Marriott Copley Place)/ June 28 - July 2
2014 - Ft. Washington, MD (Gaylord National Resort and Convention Center-National Harbor)/Dec. 12 - 16
2015 - New Orleans, LA (New Orleans Marriott)/June 28 - July 2
2015 - Orlando, FL (Orlando World Center Marriott)/ Dec. 11 - 15
2016 - Reno, NV (Peppermill Resort and Casino)/June 28 - July 2
2016 - Nashville, TN (Gaylord Opryland Hotel and Convention Center Nashville, Tennessee)/Dec. 9 - 13
Number of non-conference events/year: 2

National Federation of Advanced Information Services (1958)

1518 Walnut St.
Suite 1004
Philadelphia, PA 19102-3403
Tel: (215) 893-1561 *Fax:* (215) 893-1564
E-Mail: nfais@nfais.org
Website: nfais.org
Members: 60 organizations
Staff: 3
Annual Budget: $250-500,000

Personnel:
Executive Director: Bonnie Lawlor
    E-Mail: blawlor@nfais.org
Manager, Membership and Customer Services: Margaret Manson
    E-Mail: mmanson@nfais.org
Director, Planning and Communications: Jill O'Neill
    E-Mail: jilloneill@nfais.org

Historical Note:
Formerly (1972) National Federation of Science Abstracting and Indexing Services, (1982) National Federation of Abstracting and Indexing Services and (1977) National Federation of Abstracting and Information Services. Cooperates with the American Society for Information Science, the American Library Association and other national and international organizations concerned with information science. NAFIS's mission is to improve member capabilities and contribute to their ongoing success. Members are private organizations and government offices around the world which abstract and index popular and professional literature in print and machine-readable form, as well as online vendors, CD-ROM vendors and others in related fields. Membership fee varies with revenue.

Meetings/Conferences: Annual
2013 - Philadelphia, PA (Hyatt at The Bellevue)/Feb. 24 - 26

Publications:
NFAIS e-Notes; monthly

Membership List Available to Non-members

National Federation of Community Broadcasters (1975)

1970 Broadway
Suite 1000
Oakland, CA 94612
Tel: (510) 451-8200 *Fax:* (510) 451-8208
E-Mail: comments@nfcb.org
Website: nfcb.org
Members: 250 stations
Staff: 3
Annual Budget: $1-2,000,000
Tax: 501(c)(3)

Personnel:
President and Chief Executive Officer: Maxie C. Jackson III
    E-Mail: maxie@nfcb.org
Vice President and Director, Federation Services: Ginny Z. Berson
Coordinator, Communications: Summer Sewell
    E-Mail: summer@nfcb.org

Historical Note:
NFCB seeks to advance community-oriented non-commercial broadcasting and fosters cooperation among broadcasting organizations. Members are non- commercial public radio stations licensed to community organizations, as well as university and other licensees, independent producers, production groups, individuals, organizations, college stations, and religious broadcasters. Membership: $125-950 (Associate); $125 (Individual).

Meetings/Conferences: Annual
Conference Chair: Ginny Z. Berson
2013 - San Francisco, CA (Parc 55 Hotel)/May 29 - June 1

Publications:
Community Radio News; monthly; adv.

Membership List Available to Non-members

National Federation of Community Development of Credit Unions (1974)

39 Bdwy.
Suite 2140
New York, NY 10006-3063
Tel: (212) 809-1850 *Fax:* (212) 809-3274
TollFree: (800) 437-8711
E-Mail: info@cdcu.coop
Website: natfed.org
Members: 244 CDCUs
Staff: 17
Annual Budget: $2-5,000,000
Tax: 501(c)(3)

Personnel:
Interim President and Chief Executive Officer and Director, Education and Training: Pamela Owens CUDE
    E-Mail: powens@cdcu.coop
Director, Membership Development: Pablo DeFillipi CUDE
    E-Mail: pablo@cdcu.coop
Senior Program Officer and Conference Coordinator: Valerie Harrison CUDE

    E-Mail: vharrison@cdcu.coop
Chief Financial Officer and Chief Operating Officer: Michael Strange
    E-Mail: mstrange@cdcu.coop

Historical Note:
NFCDCU's mission is to help low and moderate income people and communities achieve financial independence through credit unions. Membership: $250-5000/year.

Continuing Education:
Certification Designation/s: CDFI, CUDEs, CDCUs

Meetings/Conferences: Annual
Conference Chair: Valerie Harrison CUDE

Publications:
Membership Directory; on-line

National Federation of Federal Employees (1917)

805 15th St. NW
Suite 500
Washington, DC 20005
Tel: (202) 216-4420 *Fax:* (202) 898-1861
Website: nffe.org
Members: 110000 individuals
Staff: 30
Annual Budget: Under $10,000

Personnel:
President: William R. Dougan
    E-Mail: bdougan@nffe.org
Director, Finance: Omar Arnold
    E-Mail: oarnold@nffe.org
Director, Communications: Cory Bythrow
    E-Mail: cbythrow@nffe.org
Legislative Director: Randy Erwin
    E-Mail: rerwin@nffe.org
National Secretary and Treasurer: William D. Fenaughty
    E-Mail: bfenaughty@nffe.org
General Counsel: Stefan Sutich

Historical Note:
Chartered by the American Federation of Labor, NFFE withdrew from the AFL in 1931 objecting to the AFL's position that civil service classification should not be extended to skilled crafts and is now an independent labor union in competition with the American Federation of Government Employees (AFL-CIO). NFFE's mission is to advance the social and economic welfare and education of federal workers through continued work in organizing units of federal employees, representing their interests through collective bargaining, lobbying for legislative action, fighting for better working conditions, and promoting labor-management partnerships in agency decision-making.

Meetings/Conferences: Annual

Publications:
Legislative Updates; on-line
Membership Directory; on-line
NFFE Legal Updates; on-line

National Federation of Federal Employees, Federal Dist. I, IAMAW, AFL-CIO (1917)

805 15th St. NW
Suite 500
Washington, DC 20005
Tel: (202) 216-4420 *Fax:* (202) 898-1861
Website: nffe.org
Staff: 3

Personnel:
President: William R. Dougan
    E-Mail: bdougan@nffe.org
Secretary and Treasurer: William D. Fenaughty
    E-Mail: bfenaughty@nffe.org

Historical Note:
A labor union representing 100,000 federal workers in federal agencies throughout the country.NFFE's mission is to advance the social and economic welfare and education of federal workers through their continued work in organizing units of federal employees, lobbying for legislative action and fighting for better working conditions.

Publications:
Federal Employee; quarterly
Member Directory; on-line

National Federation of Independent Business (NFIB) (1943)

53 Century Blvd.
Suite 250
Nashville, TN 37214
Tel: (615) 872-5800
TollFree: (800) 634-2669
Website: nfib.com
Members: 600000 businesses

Staff: 1124
Annual Budget: $50-100,000,000

Personnel:
President and Chief Executive Officer: Donald "Dan" Danner
   E-Mail: dan.danner@nfib.org
Senior Manager, Media, Research, Legal Center and Young Entrepreneur Foundation: Cynthia Magnuson
   E-Mail: cynthia.magnuson@nfib.org
Administrative Manager: Chris Pitts
Controller and Treasurer: Jeffery L. Smith
   E-Mail: jeff.smith@nfib.org

Historical Note:
Formerly National Federation of Small Business and assumed its present name in 1950. NFIB's mission is to promote and protect the right of its members to own, operate and grow their businesses. Membership: $365-2,400/year (Dues vary on size of the business).

Publications:
MyBusiness |; adv.
NFIB Insight; bi-weekly; adv.
NFIB SmartBrief; daily; adv.

National Federation of Licensed Practical Nurses (1949)
111 W. Main St.
Suite 100
Garner, NC 27529
Tel: (919) 779-0046 *Fax:* (919) 779-5642
Website: nflpn.org
Members: 6000 individuals
Staff: 4
Annual Budget: $100-250,000

Personnel:
Executive Director: Charlene Barbour
President: Missy Moore LPN
   E-Mail: ottamissiah@yahoo.com
Treasurer: Tina Johnson LPN
   E-Mail: johnson_t62@yahoo.com
Director, Membership Services: Anjeanette Sausedo
   E-Mail: nflpn@mgmt4u.com

Historical Note:
NFLPN's mission is to foster better standards of nursing care and promote continued competence through education certification and lifelong learning, with a focus on public protection. Members are licensed practical nurses, licensed vocational nurses and practical/vocational nursing students in the United States. Membership: $100 (Active-Per capita); $65 (Retired); $25 (Student); $70 (Military); $60 (Affiliate); $70 (International/Individual-at-Large).

Continuing Education:
Certification Designation/s: TGC

Meetings/Conferences: Annual

Publications:
NFLPN Newsletter; quarterly; adv.

National Federation of Modern Language Teachers Associations (1916)
460 Pierce St.
Monterey, CA 93940
Tel: (831) 647-6510 *Fax:* (831) 647-6514
E-Mail: mlj@miis.edu
Website: mlj.miis.edu/nfmlta.htm
Members: 18 associations
Staff: 3
Annual Budget: $100-250,000
Tax: 501(c)(3)

Personnel:
President: Caro Klee
   E-Mail: klee@umn.edu
Treasurer: Gerard Ervin
   E-Mail: ervin7841@earthlink.net
Editor: Leo van Lier
   E-Mail: mlj@miis.edu

Historical Note:
NFMLTA provides a forum for the exchange of information of interest to organizations of modern language teachers. Its purpose is to expand, promote, and improve the teaching of languages, literatures, and cultures throughout the U.S. It publishes The Modern Language Journal, which is devoted to research and discussion about the learning and teaching of foreign and second languages. Revenue from the Journal supports the member associations' goals. Membership includes persons involved in the teaching of modern languages.

Meetings/Conferences:
Number of non-conference events/year: 13

Publications:

The Modern Language Journal; quarterly; adv.

National Federation of Municipal Analysts (1983)
P.O. Box 14893
Pittsburgh, PA 15234
Tel: (412) 341-4898 *Fax:* (412) 341-4894
Website: nfma.org
Members: 1,200 members
Staff: 2
Annual Budget: $500-1,000,000
Tax: 501(c)(6)

Personnel:
Executive Director: Lisa Good
   E-Mail: lgood@nfma.org
Administrative Manager: Betsy Harkins

Historical Note:
Founded by four regional organizations of municipal analysts. NFMA promotes the profession of municipal credit analyst, through educational programs, industry communications, and related programming. Membership: $20-35/year.

Meetings/Conferences: Annual
Conference Chair: Lisa Good
2013 - San Diego, CA (Westin Gaslamp Quarter, San Diego)/April 30 - May 3
2014 - Orlando, FL (Disney's Grand Floridian Resort and Spa)/May 6 - 9
2015 - Las Vegas, NV (Four Seasons Hotel Las Vegas)/ May 12 - 15
Number of non-conference events/year: 1

Publications:
Membership Directory; on-line
NFMA E-Newsletter

National Federation of Music Clubs (1898)
1646 Smith Valley Rd.
Greenwood, IN 46142
Tel: (317) 882-4003 *Fax:* (317) 882-4019
E-Mail: info@nfmc-music.org
Website: nfmc-music.org
Members: 206000 organizations and individuals
Staff: 3
Annual Budget: $1-2,000,000

Personnel:
President: Carolyn Nelson
Treasurer: Suzanne Carpenter
Recording Secretary: Melanie Perez

Historical Note:
NFMC is dedicated to finding and fostering young musical talent. Membership: $50 (Individual Senior); $200 (Life Member); $1000 (Subscriber); $2000 (Donor); $10,000 (Patron); $16 (Individual Student); $13 (Individual Junior); $12 (Junior Special); $15 (Student Special-Individual); $20 (Senior Special-Individual); $25 (Contributing/Cradle Roll); $12.50 (Junior Cradle Roll).

Meetings/Conferences:
Number of non-conference events/year: 1

Publications:
Music Clubs Magazine; quarterly; adv.
NFMC Newsletter; monthly; adv.

The National Federation of Nonpublic School State Accrediting Associations (1984)
C/O ANSAA
48 Norfork Dr.
Maumelle, AR 72113
Tel: (501) 803-3888 *Fax:* (501) 803-3888
Website: nfnssaa.com
Members: 5 state agencies
Staff: 2
Annual Budget: Under $10,000
Tax: 501(c)(3)

Personnel:
President: Beverly Gray
   E-Mail: bevgray@sbcglobal.net

Historical Note:
NFNSSAA's mission is to ensure that state chapters are committed to enhancing the quality of education within their member schools through continuous assessment and evaluation of the state's accreditation process. Membership: $250/year.

Publications:
Membership Directory; on-line

The National Federation of Paralegal Associations, Inc. (1974)
23607 Hwy. 99,

Suite 2-C
Edmonds, WA 98026
Tel: (425) 967-0045 *Fax:* (425) 771-9588
E-Mail: info@paralegals.org
Website: paralegals.org
Members: 11050 Individuals, state and local associations
Staff: 4
Annual Budget: $500-1,000,000

Personnel:
Managing Director: Dana J. Murphy-Love CAE
   E-Mail: dana@paralegals.org
Assistant Director, Conventions, Continuing Legal Education and National Paralegal: Celeste Allen
   E-Mail: celeste@paralegals.org
Assistant Director, Website and Technology: Rodney Dunham
   E-Mail: rodney@paralegals.org
Assistant Director, Convention and Education Programs: Kaylin Rasar
   E-Mail: kaylin@paralegals.org

Historical Note:
NFPA strives for advancement of the paralegal profession. Promotes a global presence for the paralegal profession, and leadership in the legal community. Membership: $85 (Individual); $50 (Student/Associate); $200 (Organization); $45 (Military).

Continuing Education:
Certification Designation/s: PACE

Meetings/Conferences: Annual
Conference Chair: Kaylin Rasar
Number of non-conference events/year: 3

Publications:
Membership Directory; on-line
NFPA E-Newsletter; on-line
The National Paralegal Reporter; bi-monthly; adv.

Membership List Available to Non-members

National Federation of Press Women (1937)
P.O. Box 5556
Arlington, VA 22205
Tel: (703) 237-9804 *Fax:* (703) 237-9808
TollFree: (800) 780-2715
E-Mail: presswomen@aol.com
Website: nfpw.org
Members: 2000 individuals
Staff: 6
Annual Budget: $100-250,000
Tax: 501(c)(6)

Personnel:
Executive Director: Carol Pierce
   E-Mail: presswomen@aol.com
President: Lori Potter
   E-Mail: lori.potter@kearneyhub.com
Treasurer: Ellen Crawford
Director, Publications: Cathy Koon
Director, Membership Services: Mary Jane Skalla
Director, Website Services: Allison Stein

Historical Note:
NFPW's mission is to provide a means of communication between woman writers nationally, make possible the expression of a common voice in matters of national interest to press women, and otherwise advance the professional standards of press women. Members are writers, editors and other communications professionals for newspapers, magazines, radio- TV, corporations, wire services, agencies and freelance. Membership: $74 (Professional); $20 (Student); $25 (Retired).

Meetings/Conferences: Annual

Publications:
Membership Directory; on-line
NFPW Newsletter

National Federation of Priests' Councils (1960)
333 N. Michigan Ave.
Suite 1205
Chicago, IL 60601-4002
Tel: (312) 442-9700 *Fax:* (312) 442-9709
TollFree: (888) 271-6372
E-Mail: nfpc@nfpc.org
Website: nfpc.org
Members: 124 councils
Staff: 6
Annual Budget: $250-500,000
Tax: 501(c)(3)

Personnel:
President: Anthony Cutcher

E-Mail: cutcher@nfpc.org
Coordinator, Programs and Events: Rosario Camacho
E-Mail: camacho@nfpc.org
Administrative Secretary: Yahaira Noriega
E-Mail: noriega@nfpc.org
Business Manager: Terry Oldes
E-Mail: oldes@nfpc.org
Director, Development and Institutional Advancement:
David Philippart
E-Mail: philippart@nfpc.org
Project and Research Assistant: Alan Szafraniec
E-Mail: szafraniec@nfpc.org

Historical Note:
A church membership organization representing 124 councils of diocesan and religious clergy. Members are priests' councils; does not offer individual membership.

Meetings/Conferences: Annual
Conference Chair: Rosario Camacho
2013 - Reno, NV/April 22 - 25

Publications:
ThisWeek; weekly
Touchstone

National Federation of Republican Women
(1938)
124 N. Alfred St.
Alexandria, VA 22314
Tel: (703) 548-9688 *Fax:* (703) 548-9836
E-Mail: mail@nfrw.org
Website: nfrw.org
Members: 10000 individuals
Staff: 4
Annual Budget: $1-2,000,000

Personnel:
President: Rae Lynne Chornenky
Treasurer: Carrie Almond
Political Director: Valerie Dowling
E-Mail: vdowling@nfrw.org
Director, Communications: Lisa Ziriax
E-Mail: lziriax@nfrw.org

Historical Note:
Formerly National Federation of Women's Republican Clubs of America (NFWRC), later name was changed in January 1953 to the National Federation of Republican Women (NFRW). NFRW strives to promote an informed public through political education and activity; increase the effectiveness of women in the cause of good government; facilitate cooperation among the National and state Federations of Republican women's clubs. Membership: $50 (National Associate); $15 (Student Associate).

Meetings/Conferences: Biennial
2013 - Louisville, KY (Galt House Hotel)/Sept. 20 - 23

Publications:
NFRW Newsletter; weekly
Republican Woman; adv.

National Federation of State High School Associations *(1920)*
P.O. Box 690
Indianapolis, IN 46206
Tel: (317) 972-6900 *Fax:* (317) 822-5700
Website: nfhs.org
Members: 18500 high schools
Staff: 48
Annual Budget: $10-25,000,000
Tax: 501(c)(3)

Personnel:
Executive Director: Bob Gardner
Editor: Bruce Howard
E-Mail: bhoward@nfhs.org
Contact, Conferences: Mark Koski
E-Mail: mkoski@nfhs.org

Historical Note:
Established as the National Federation of State High School Athletic Associations, assumed its present name in 1970. NFHS mission is to serve its members, related professional organizations and students by providing leadership for the administration of education-based interscholastic activities, which support academic achievement, good citizenship and equitable opportunities. Membership: $30/year (Coach Group/Officials Group).

Meetings/Conferences:
Conference Chair: Mark Koski
2013 - Orlando, FL (Rosen Shingle Creek)/Jan. 3 - 6
2013 - Denver, CO (Hyatt Regency Denver at Colorado Convention Center)/June 23 - 27
2014 - Boston, MA (Boston Marriott Copley Place)/June 28 - July 2

2015 - New Orleans, LA (New Orleans Marriott)/June 28 - July 2
2016 - Reno, NV (Peppermill Resort Spa Casino)/June 28 - July 2

Publications:
High School Today
NFHS Coaches' Quarterly; quarterly
NFHS News
NFHS Officials' Quarterly; quarterly

National Fellowship of Child Care Executives
(1954)
P.O. Box 1195
Somerset, PA 15501
E-Mail: rmiller@cahprogram.org
Website: nfcce.org
Members: 48 organizations
Staff: 3
Annual Budget: Under $10,000

Personnel:
Executive Secretary: Robert Miller
E-Mail: rmiller@cahprogram.org
Treasurer: Steve Hubbard
Contact, website: Jill W. West
E-Mail: jill@umch.net

Historical Note:
Formerly National Association of Homes for Boys, assumed its present name in 1981. NFCCE's mission is to strengthen child care agencies by promoting fellowship among the leaders and providing opportunities for counsel, education and sharing of experiences. Membership: $250/year.

Meetings/Conferences: Annual

Publications:
Membership Directory; annually

National Fenestration Rating Council *(1989)*
6305 Ivy Ln.
Suite 140
Greenbelt, MD 20770
Tel: (301) 589-1776 *Fax:* (301) 589-3884
E-Mail: info@nfrc.org
Website: nfrc.org
Staff: 20
Annual Budget: $2-5,000,000

Personnel:
Chief Executive Officer: James C. Benney CAE
E-Mail: jbenney@nfrc.org
Chief Operating Officer: Deborah Callahan CAE
E-Mail: dcallahan@nfrc.org
Director, Finance: Robin Y. Clayton
E-Mail: danderson@nfrc.org
Manager, Meetings: Cheryl Gendron
E-Mail: cgendron@nfrc.org
Manager, Communications and Marketing: Tom Herron
E-Mail: therron@nfrc.org
Web Manager: Una Moneypenny
E-Mail: umoneypenny@nfrc.org

Historical Note:
NFRC's mission is to develop and administer energy-related rating and certification programs that serve the public by providing fair, accurate, and credible information on fenestration performance. Membership: $1,000 (Fenestration Industry); $500-19,250 (Labs); $500 (General Interest).

Continuing Education:
Certification Designation/s: NFRC, IGC

Meetings/Conferences: Annual
Conference Chair: Cheryl Gendron

Publications:
NFRC News Now; on-line
NFRC Update; monthly

National FFA Organization *(1928)*
National FFA Center
P.O. Box 68960, 6060 FFA Dr.
Indianapolis, IN 46268-0960
Tel: (317) 802-6060 *Fax:* (317) 802-6051
E-Mail: info@ffa.org
Website: ffa.org
Members: 490017 individuals
Staff: 90
Annual Budget: $10-25,000,000

Personnel:
National Advisor: Dr. Steve A. Brown
E-Mail: sbrown@ffa.org
Interim Executive Secretary: Charles Browne

E-Mail: cbrowne@ffa.org
Director, Information Technology and Chief Technology Officer: Mark Cavell
E-Mail: mcavell@ffa.org
Chief operating officer: Bill Fleet
E-Mail: bfleet@ffa.org
Senior Manager, Exhibits: Bryan Kelley
E-Mail: bkelley@ffa.org
Director, Human Resources: Janet Maloney
E-Mail: jmaloney@ffa.org
Director, Education: Tony Small
E-Mail: tsmall@ffa.org
Director, Strategic Communications: Bill Stagg
E-Mail: bstagg@ffa.org
Manager, Publications: Julie Woodard
E-Mail: jwoodard@ffa.org
Team Leader, Membership Services: Clay Worley
E-Mail: cworley@ffa.org

Historical Note:
Formerly (1989) Future Farmers of America. Absorbed the New Farmers of America in 1965. A vocational student organization organized under the National Vocational Education Act to foster character, leadership and good citizenship. FFA is dedicated to making a positive difference in the lives of students by developing their potential for premier leadership, personal growth and career success through agricultural education. It holds a federal charter. Membership: $7/year.

Meetings/Conferences: Annual
Conference Chair: Bryan Kelley
2013 - Louisville, KY/Oct. 30 - Nov. 2
2014 - Louisville, KY/Oct. 29 - Nov. 1

Publications:
FFA New Horizons; bi-monthly
Making a Difference; monthly
Update; monthly

National Field Selling Association *(1987)*
100 N. 20th St.
Fourth Floor
Philadelphia, PA 19103-1443
Tel: (215) 564-1627 *Fax:* (215) 564-2175
E-Mail: nfsa@fernley.com
Website: nfsa.com
Members: 29 Companies
Staff: 3
Annual Budget: $100-250,000

Personnel:
Management Liaison: G.A. Taylor Fernley
Associate Director: Ellen R. Buckley
E-Mail: ebuckley@fernley.com

Historical Note:
NFSA's mission is to uphold the honor and dignity of the direct selling profession and the free enterprise system. Members are committed to fairness in the treatment of all persons involved in the distribution and sale of their products and services, and to conduct business in conformity with the Association's Code of Ethics. Membership: $2500 (Active); $400 (Associate); $25 (Affiliate); $200 (Supporting).

Publications:
NFSA Newsletter; quarterly

National Finance Adjusters *(1947)*
P.O. Box 3855
Baltimore, MD 21217-0855
Tel: (410) 728-2400 *Fax:* (410) 728-2528
E-Mail: homeoffice@nfa.org
Website: nfa.org
Members: 210 individuals
Staff: 4
Annual Budget: $500-1,000,000

Personnel:
Executive Director: Rob Spangler
E-Mail: nfamanager@nfa.com
Contact, Publicity and Newsletter: Joann Cooper
E-Mail: urs20@comcast.net
Chairman, Convention, Budget and Finance and Legal Liaison: Joan Hudson
E-Mail: joan@arboflou.com
Central Office Manager: Helen M. Mullaney

Historical Note:
A forum of information and exchange for professional recovery specialists and installment loan collectors.

Continuing Education:
Certification Designation/s: CCRS

Meetings/Conferences: Annual
Conference Chair: Joan Hudson

Number of non-conference events/year: 1
Publications:
NFA newsletter

National Finishing Contractors Association (1997)
8120 Woodmont Ave.
Suite 520
Bethesda, MD 20814
Tel: (301) 215-7026 *Fax:* (301) 215-7027
TollFree: (866) 322-3477
E-Mail: fca@finishingcontractors.org
Website: finishingcontractors.org
Members: 1150 companies
Staff: 6
Annual Budget: $1-2,000,000
Personnel:
Chief Executive Officer: Anthony "Tony" Darkangelo
    E-Mail: tdarkangelo@finishingcontractors.org
Director, Communications: Kristin Bromberg
    E-Mail: kbromberg@finishingcontractors.org
Associate, Membership and Meetings: Robin Schmuff
    E-Mail: rschmuff@finishingcontractors.org
Vice President: Robert "Bob" Weaver
    E-Mail: bweaver@finishingcontractors.org
Historical Note:
NFCA's mission is to provide their customers with better quality craftsmanship in the finishing trades.
Meetings/Conferences: Annual
Conference Chair: Robin Schmuff
2013 - Philadelphia, PA/May 29 - June 1
Publications:
Contract Insight; quarterly
Federal Connection; monthly
IUPAT Journal
Membership Directory; on-line
National FCA Update
Trustee Update

National Fire Protection Association (1896)
One Batterymarch Park
Quincy, MA 02169-7471
Tel: (617) 770-3000 *Fax:* (617) 770-0700
TollFree: (800) 344-3555
Website: nfpa.org
Members: 75000 individuals
Staff: 12
Annual Budget: Over $100,000,000
Tax: 501(c)(3)
Personnel:
President and Chief Executive Officer: James M. Shannon
Executive Director, Fire Protection Research Foundation:
    Kathleen H. Almand
    E-Mail: kalmand@nfpa.org
Division Manager, Conferences and Meetings: Linda
    Bailey
Vice President and General Counsel: Maureen B. Brodoff
Vice President, Communications: Lorraine Carli
    E-Mail: lcarli@nfpa.org
Vice President, Marketing and Sales: Paul Crossman
Vice President, Field Operations and Education: Gary S.
    Keith
    E-Mail: gkeith@nfpa.org
Senior Vice President, Finance and Chief Financial Officer:
    Bruce Mullen
Vice President, Technical Projects: Robert J. Vondrasek
    E-Mail: rvondrasek@nfpa.org
Vice President, Human Resources: Lisa A. Yarussi
Historical Note:
NFPA's mission is to reduce the worldwide burden of fire and other hazards on the quality of life by providing and advocating consensus codes and standards, research, training, and education. Membership: $165/year (U.S./Canadian/International).
Continuing Education:
Certification Designation/s: CFPS, CBPE, CFPE, CFI, CFI-II, CBI
Meetings/Conferences:
Conference Chair: Linda Bailey
2013 - Chicago, IL (McCormick Place)/June 10 - 13/
    over 100 exhibitors
Publications:
E-Newsletter; on-line
NFPA Journal; bi-monthly; adv.
NFPA Journal® Update; monthly

National Fire Sprinkler Association (1905)
40 Jon Barrett Rd.
Patterson, NY 12563
Tel: (845) 878-4200 *Fax:* (845) 878-4215
E-Mail: info@nfsa.org
Website: nfsa.org
Members: 2600 individuals
Staff: 45
Annual Budget: $2-5,000,000
Personnel:
President: Russ Fleming
    E-Mail: fleming@nfsa.org
Bookkeeper: Linda Daly
    E-Mail: daly@nfsa.org
SQ Advertising Coordinator: Joanne Genadio
    E-Mail: genadio@nfsa.org
Financial Controller: Jeanne M. Kozlowski
    E-Mail: kozlowski@nfsa.org
Vice President, Training and Communications: Jim Lake
    E-Mail: lake@nfsa.org
Director, Internet Services: Jim Murphy
    E-Mail: murphy@nfsa.org
Coordinator, Membership and Database: Michael "Mike"
    Repko
    E-Mail: mrepko@nfsa.org
Manager, Communications and Events: Deborah Somers
    E-Mail: somers@nfsa.org
Director, Product Standards: Victoria Valentine P E
    E-Mail: valentine@nfsa.org
Director, Membership and Communications: David J.
    Vandeyar
    E-Mail: vandeyar@nfsa.org
Historical Note:
Founded as the National Automatic Sprinkler Contractors Association, (1958) National Automatic Sprinkler and Fire Control Association and assumed its present name in 1983. NFSA's mission is to protect lives and property from fire through the wide-spread acceptance of the fire sprinkler concept. Members are makers and installers of automatic fire sprinklers and related equipment. Membership: $165 (Professional); $500 (Friend of the Industry Member); $750 (Contractor Company); $1,500-25,000 (Supplier Company).
Continuing Education:
Certification Designation/s: NICET, CPFST
Meetings/Conferences: Annual
Conference Chair: Deborah Somers
2013 - Las Vegas, NV (Caesars Palace Las Vegas Hotel
    and Casino)/April 4 - 6
2014 - Paradise Island, Bahamas/May 8 - 10
2015 - Orlando, FL (Hilton Bonnet Creek Resort)/April
    30 - May 2
Number of non-conference events/year: 3
Publications:
NFSA Magazine; quarterly
NFSA Newsletter; bi-monthly
SQ Magazine; bi-monthly; adv.

National Fisheries Institute (1945)
7918 Jones Branch Dr.
Suite 700
McLean, VA 22102
Tel: (703) 752-8880 *Fax:* (703) 752-7583
E-Mail: contact@nfi.org
Website: aboutseafood.com
Members: 230 companies
Staff: 17
Annual Budget: $5-10,000,000
Personnel:
President: John P. Connelly
Senior Vice President: Judy Dashiell
Vice President, Government Affairs & General Counsel:
    Robert DeHaan
Director, Membership Relations and Communications:
    Gerrie Thomas
    E-Mail: gthomas@nfi.org
Historical Note:
NFI is comprised of companies engaged in the commercial fish and seafood business. NFI members work together on issues that affect the seafood industry, including legislative and regulatory policies, technical and scientific issues, seafood promotion, and consumer marketing opportunities.Membership: $2,000 (Associates); $1,000-10,000 (Restaurants); $1,000-5,000 (Trade Association); $1,000-75,000 (Seafood Companies); $1,000-50,000 (Broad-Line Distributors And Seafood Restaurants).
Meetings/Conferences: Annual

Conference Chair: Judy Dashiell
2013 - Santa Monica, CA (Loews Santa Monica Beach
    Hotel)/Jan. 29 - 31
Number of non-conference events/year: 2
Publications:
Membership Directory; on-line
NFI Insider; weekly

Membership List Available to Non-members

National Flea Market Association
7812 McElwen Rd.
Suite 200
Dayton, OH 45459
Tel: (937) 223-0636 *Fax:* (937) 223-0154
TollFree: (866) 417-2884
E-Mail: nfma@fleamarkets.org
Website: fleamarkets.org
Staff: 4
Annual Budget: $100-250,000
Personnel:
Membership Committee Chair: Greg Dove
    E-Mail: gdove@levininc.com?
Administrator: Danielle Salyer
Historical Note:
The objective of the Association is to serve the public interest and benefit the flea market industry by fostering high standards of conduct, personally and professionally. Membership: $395 (Regular); $500 (Associate).
Meetings/Conferences: Annual
2013 - Las Vegas, NV (Tropicana Las Vegas)/Feb. 5 - 6
Publications:
FleaBytes Newsletter; irregular
Membership Directory; on-line
NFMA Newsletter

National Fluid Power Association (1953)
3333 N. Mayfair Rd.
Suite 211
Milwaukee, WI 53222-3219
Tel: (414) 778-3344 *Fax:* (414) 778-3361
E-Mail: nfpa@nfpa.com
Website: nfpa.com
Members: 335 companies
Staff: 12
Annual Budget: $2-5,000,000
Tax: 501(c)(6)
Personnel:
Executive Director: Eric Lanke CAE
    E-Mail: elanke@nfpa.com
Director, Association Services and Technology: Pete Alles
    E-Mail: palles@nfpa.com
Manager, International Standards Development: Karen
    Boehme
    E-Mail: kboehme@nfpa.com
Director, Finance: Sue Chase
    E-Mail: schase@nfpa.com
Web and Publications Manager: Janet Long
    E-Mail: jlong@nfpa.com
Manager, Membership Services: Leslie Miller
    E-Mail: lmiller@nfpa.com
Manager, Communications and Meetings: Denise Rockhill
    E-Mail: drockhill@nfpa.com
Manager, Information Technology: Peter Vanderhoef
    E-Mail: pvanderhoef@nfpa.com
Historical Note:
NFPA serves as a forum for all interested stakeholders in the fluid power industry, including manufacturers, distributors, suppliers, educators and customers. Members are fluid power channel partners, manufacturers, distributors, suppliers, customers and educators. Membership: $1,100-61,050 (Manufacturer); $5,500-61,050 (International); $1,100-4,510 (Distributor/Supplier); $3,190 (Service Supplier Members).
Meetings/Conferences: Annual
Conference Chair: Denise Rockhill
2013 - Scottsdale, AZ (Montelucia Resort and Spa)/
    March 5 - 8
Publications:
Member Directory; on-line

The National Flute Association, Inc. (1972)
26951 Reuther Ave.
Suite H
Santa Clarita, CA 91351
Tel: (661) 299-6680 *Fax:* (661) 299-6681
Website: nfaonline.org
Members: 6000 members

Staff: 5
Annual Budget: $2-5,000,000
Tax: 501(c)(3)

Personnel:
Chief Executive Officer: Phyllis T. Pemberton
   E-Mail: ceo@nfaonline.org
Director, Information Technology: Brian Covington
Director, Conventions: Madeline Neumann
   E-Mail: conventionservices@nfaonline.org
Director, Membership Services: Maria Stibelman
   E-Mail: memberservices@nfaonline.org
Director, Publications: Anne Welsbacher
   E-Mail: awelsbacher@nfaonline.org

Historical Note:
NFA works to encourage better standard of artistic excellence for the flute, its performers, and its literature. Members include soloists, orchestral players, jazz, beatbox, and world music flutists, college and university teachers, adult amateurs, students of all ages and astronauts. Membership: $75-2000/year.

Meetings/Conferences: Annual
Conference Chair: Madeline Neumann
2013 - New Orleans, LA (New Orleans Marriott)/Aug. 8 - 11
2014 - Chicago, IL (Hilton Chicago)/Aug. 7 - 10
2015 - Washington, DC (Washington Marriott)/Aug. 13 - 15

Publications:
Flutist Quarterly; quarterly; adv.
Membership Directory; annually
NFA e-News; monthly

Membership List Available to Non-members

National Food Service Security Council

P.O. Box 1725
Olney, MD 20830
Tel: (240) 252-5542
E-Mail: jim.forlenza@nfssconline.org
Website: nfssc.com
Members: 33 restaurant companies
Staff: 1
Annual Budget: $250-500,000
Tax: 501(c)(6)

Personnel:
Executive Director: James Forlenza
   E-Mail: jim.forlenza@nfssconline.org

Historical Note:
NFSSC's mission is to educate its members on those topics that will benefit the corporations it works for. Membership: $700-3500/year (Company Owned Restaurants).

Meetings/Conferences: Annual
Conference Chair: James Forlenza
2013 - Las Vegas, NV (M Resort Spa and Casino)/Aug. 4 - 7/over 100 exhibitors

Publications:
Membership Directory; on-line
NFSSC Notes; monthly

National Football League *(1970)*

345 Park Ave.
New York, NY 10017
Tel: (212) 450-2000 *Fax:* (212) 681-7595
E-Mail: jeff.miller@nfl.com
Website: nfl.com
Members: 30 teams
Staff: 100
Annual Budget: Over $100,000,000
Tax: 501(c)(6)

Personnel:
Executive Vice President, Government Affairs: Joe Browne
   E-Mail: joe.browne@nfl.com
Vice President, Communications: Brian McCarthy
   E-Mail: mccarthyb@nfl.com
Vice President, Entertainment Marketing and Promotions: Tracy Perlman
Senior Vice President, Events: Frank Supovitz

Historical Note:
Founded as the American Professional Football Association on September 17, 1920 in the showroom of the Huppmobile agency in Canton, Ohio with Jim Thorpe as President, assumed its present name in 1922 and merged with the American Football League on February 1, 1970. NFL is dedicated in bringing its teams at a level that attracts the broadest audience and makes NFL football a better sports entertainment in the world.

Meetings/Conferences: Annual
Conference Chair: Frank Supovitz

2013 - Honolulu, HI/Jan. 27
Number of non-conference events/year: 11

National Football League Players Association
(1970)
1133 20th St. NW
Washington, DC 20036
Tel: (202) 756-9100 *Fax:* (202) 756-9320
TollFree: (800) 372-2000
E-Mail: nflpaexecutivedept@nflplayers.com
Website: nflplayers.com
Members: 1800 individuals
Staff: 100
Annual Budget: Over $100,000,000
Tax: 501(c)(5)

Personnel:
Executive Director: DeMaurice Smith
Public Policy Counsel: Joe Briggs
   E-Mail: joe.briggs@nflplayers.com
General Counsel: Thomas DePaso
Director, Communications: Carl Francis
   E-Mail: carl.francis@nflplayers.com
Vice President, Marketing: Christina Francis
   E-Mail: Christina.Francis@nflplayers.com
Director, Player Services and Development: Dana Hammonds
   E-Mail: dana.hammonds@nflplayers.com
Administrative Assistant: Robyn Harrison
   E-Mail: robyn.harrison@nflplayers.com
Manager, Human Resources: Kimberly Murray
Director, Information Systems: Richard Persons
   E-Mail: richard.persons@nflplayers.com
Director, Finance and Asset Management: Charles Ross

Historical Note:
NFLPA is formed as a result of a merger of the National Football League Players Association (1956) and the American Football League Players Association (1959). NFLPA's mission is to strengthen communities across America by working to provide comfortable and suitable housing opportunities for individuals and families in need through cooperative programs of NFLPA and NAHB-affiliated local groups.

Meetings/Conferences:
Conference Chair: Robyn Harrison

Publications:
NFLPlayers.com Fan Newsletter; on-line

National Foreign Trade Council, Inc. *(1914)*
1625 K St. NW
Suite 200
Washington, DC 20006
Tel: (202) 887-0278 *Fax:* (202) 452-8160
E-Mail: nftcinformation@nftc.org
Website: nftc.org
Members: 300 companies
Staff: 13
Annual Budget: $2-5,000,000
Tax: 501(c)(6)

Personnel:
President: William A. Reinsch
   E-Mail: breinsch@nflc.org
Senior Director, Operations: Marshall Lane
   E-Mail: mlane@nftc.org
Office Manager: Vivian Myers
   E-Mail: vmyers@nftc.org
Vice President, Tax Policy: Catherine G. Schultz
   E-Mail: catherine.schultz@att.net
Vice President, Human Resources: William R. Sheridan
   E-Mail: wsheridan@nftc.org

Historical Note:
Established 1914. Represents the foreign trade and investment interests of the 550-plus U.S. corporations who make up its membership. Favors open international economic system and expansion of international trade and investment. Formed the U.S.-South Africa Business Council in 1993.

Publications:
Council Highlights; bi-monthly
Trade Matters; weekly

National Forensic Association *(1972)*
107 Agency Rd.
Mankato, MN 56001
Tel: (507) 387-3010 *Fax:* (507) 387-3068
Website: nationalforensics.org
Members: 400 colleges and members
Staff: 10

Annual Budget: $10-25,000
Tax: 501(c)(3)

Personnel:
President: Larry Schnoor
   E-Mail: lgene9535@aol.com
Webmaster: Michael Dreher
   E-Mail: mdreher@bethel.edu
Director, Tournaments: Brendan Kelly
   E-Mail: bkelly@uwf.edu
Vice President, Professional Development: Richard Paine
   E-Mail: repaine@noctrl.edu
Secretary and Treasurer: Dan Smith
   E-Mail: dan@bumail.bradley.edu

Historical Note:
NFA's mission is to promote forensics competition at the collegiate level.

Meetings/Conferences:
Conference Chair: Brendan Kelly
Number of non-conference events/year: 1

Publications:
National Forensic Journal; semi-annually
NFA Newsletter; irregular

National Forest Recreation Association *(1948)*
P.O. Box 488
Woodlake, CA 93286
Tel: (559) 564-2365 *Fax:* (559) 564-2048
E-Mail: info@nfra.org
Website: nfra.org
Members: 300 individuals
Staff: 2
Annual Budget: $50-100,000
Tax: 501(c)(6)

Personnel:
Executive Director: Marily Reese
President: Warren Meyer

Historical Note:
NFRA is an association assisting owners and operators of recreational and commercial facilities on National Forest, Bureau of Land Management and National Park Service lands, in their relationship with their respective agencies. Members include resorts, youth camps, campgrounds, pack stations, outfitters, tour and shuttle services, marinas, stores and restaurants. Membership dues are based upon revenue scale of the applicant. Membership: $250-2,500 (General); $100 (Supporting); $500 (Vendor/Supplier).

Publications:
NFRA Newsletters

Membership List Available to Non-members

National Forum for Black Public Administrators
(1983)
777 N. Capitol St. NE
Suite 807
Washington, DC 20002
Tel: (202) 408-9300 *Fax:* (202) 408-8558
Website: nfbpa.org
Members: 2600 memebrs
Staff: 6
Annual Budget: $1-2,000,000
Tax: 501(c)(3)

Personnel:
Executive Director: John E. Saunders III, CAE
   E-Mail: jsaunders@nfbpa.org
Fiscal Director: Malick Diagne
   E-Mail: mdiagne@nfbpa.org
Coordinator, Technology and Operations: Awa Fall
   E-Mail: afall@nfbpa.org
Coordinator, Membership Services and Programs: Yvette Harris
   E-Mail: yharris@nfbpa.org
Program Coordinator, Leadership, Scholarship and Mentor Programs: Valerie Reed
   E-Mail: vreed@nfbpa.org
Executive Secretary: Jacqueline Whitman
   E-Mail: jwhitman@nfbpa.org

Historical Note:
NFBPA's mission is to strengthen the position of Blacks within the field of public administration; to increase the number of Blacks appointed to executive positions in public service organizations; and, to groom and prepare younger, aspiring administrators for senior public management posts in the years ahead. Members are city and county managers, chief administrative officers, agency and department directors, rank-and-file professionals and deans, faculty members and graduate students at schools of public administration. Membership: $25-5000/year.

Meetings/Conferences: Annual
Conference Chair: Valerie Reed
2013 - Atlanta, GA/April 20 - 24/1000 attendees
2013 - Atlanta, GA/April 20 - 23
2014 - San Antonio, TX/April 12 - 16/1000 attendees
2014 - San Antonio, TX/April 12 - 15

Publications:
Forum Issues
The Forum Magazine; quarterly

National Foster Parent Association *(1972)*
2021 E. Hennepin Ave.
Suite 320
Minneapolis, MN 55413-1769
Tel: (800) 557-5238 *Fax:* (888) 925-5634
TollFree: (800) 557-5238
E-Mail: Info@NFPAonline.org
Website: nfpainc.org
Staff: 4
Annual Budget: $100-250,000

Personnel:
President: Irene Clements
     E-Mail: iclements@nfpaonline.org
Treasurer: Aubrey Manuel
     E-Mail: aubreym@pacbell.net
Information Technology and Web Master: Dennis Seger
     E-Mail: dseger@nfpaonline.org
Editor: Carolyn Walker
     E-Mail: cwalker@nfpaonline.org

Historical Note:
Mission is to support foster parents in achieving safety, permanence and well-being for the children and youth in their care. Membership: $ 35 (Regular); $50-100 (Agency/Affiliate); $15-50 (Friends of NFPA).

Meetings/Conferences: Annual
2013 - Long Beach, CA (Renaissance Long Beach Hotel)/June 5 - 8

Publications:
Fostering Families Today magazine
National Advocate; adv.
NFPA Newsletter
NFPA Updates

National Foundation for Credit Counseling *(1951)*
2000 M St. NW
Suite 505
Washington, DC 20036
Tel: (202) 677-4300
E-Mail: info@nfcc.org
Website: nfcc.org
Members: 90 member agencies and 700 offices
Staff: 23
Annual Budget: $10-25,000,000
Tax: 501(c)(3)

Personnel:
Senior Director, Information Technology Management: Steve Grabowski
     E-Mail: sgrabowski@nfcc.org
Vice President, Marketing and Communications: Drew Kessler
     E-Mail: dkessler@nfcc.org
Chief Financial Officer: Denis M. Russell
     E-Mail: drussell@nfcc.org

Historical Note:
Founded as National Foundation for Consumer Credit; assumed its current name in 2000. Members are non-profit community Consumer Credit Counseling Services and creditors. NFCC's promotes the national agenda for financially responsible behavior and builds capacity for its members to deliver the quality financial education and counseling services.

Continuing Education:
Certification Designation/s: CCP

Meetings/Conferences: Annual

Publications:
Membership Directory; on-line

National Foundation for Women Legislators *(1938)*
910 16th St. NW
Suite 100
Washington, DC 20006
Tel: (202) 293-3040 *Fax:* (202) 293-5430
E-Mail: nfwl@womenlegislators.org
Website: womenlegislators.org
Members: 3300 individuals
Staff: 5

Annual Budget: $500-1,000,000
Tax: 501(c)(3)

Personnel:
President and Chief Executive Officer: Robin Read
     E-Mail: Robin_Read@womenlegislators.org
Membership Contact, Development and Policy Coordinator: Samatha Green
     E-Mail: Sami_Green@womenlegislators.org
Director, Policy and Communications: Jennifer Rosen
     E-Mail: Jennifer_Rosen@womenlegislators.org
Director, Public Policy and Operations: Julie Swaney
     E-Mail: julie_swaney@womenlegislators.org

Historical Note:
NFWL's mission is to provide strategic resources to women leaders for leadership development and effective governance through conferences, seminars, education materials, professional and personal relationships, and networking at both the state and federal levels. Membership: $100 (Women State Legislators/Individual); $5,000-50,000 (Corporate).

Meetings/Conferences: Annual

National Frame Building Association *(1970)*
4700 W. Lake Ave.
Glenview, IL 60025
Fax: (847) 375-6495
TollFree: (800) 557-6957
E-Mail: nfba@nfba.org
Website: nfba.org
Members: 1,200 members
Staff: 12
Annual Budget: $1-2,000,000

Personnel:
Chair Elect: Rick Hess
Secretary and Treasurer: Ken Gieseke
Advertising Representative: Randy Graper
     E-Mail: randy.graper@fwpubs.com
Contact, Conventions: Kyler Pope
     E-Mail: kyler.pope@fwpubs.com
Manager, Education: Daniel Weinstock
     E-Mail: dweinstock@nfba.org

Historical Note:
NFBA is a non-profit trade association that promotes the interests of the post-frame construction industry and its member professionals throughout the United States. Members are primarily post-frame builders, suppliers, manufacturers, building material dealers, code and design professionals, and structural engineers. Membership: $55-2,625/year.

Meetings/Conferences: Annual
Conference Chair: Kyler Pope
2013 - Memphis, TN (Memphis Cook Convention Center)/Feb. 20 - 22

Publications:
Frame Building News; adv.
Membership Directory; on-line

National Franchisee Association *(1988)*
1701 Barrett Lakes Blvd. NW
Suite 180
Kennesaw, GA 30144
Tel: (678) 797-5160 *Fax:* (678) 797-5170
Website: nfabk.org
Staff: 7

Personnel:
Contact, Government Relations: Misty Chally
Contact, Information Technology: Jaysen Hortenstine
Contact, Communications and Marketing: Kristi Keith-Hoffman
Contact, General Administration: Amy Kuhn
Contact, Advertising, Sponsorship and Associate Membership: Jeff Reynolds
Contact, Member Services: Hope Sevin
Contact, Education and Training: Christy Williams

Historical Note:
A trade association of Burger King franchisees. The National Franchisee Association (NFA) serves the BURGER KING® franchisee community through advocacy, education and training, networking and member-focused programs, services and benefits. NFA committees focus on specific areas and issues to offer operational and strategic guidance to franchisees and advice to Burger King Corporation management, while supporting the association's objectives and policies.

Meetings/Conferences: Annual
Number of non-conference events/year: 1

Publications:
FLAME; quarterly; adv.

Franchisee Directory
Newsletter; monthly; adv.

National Fraternal Order of Police *(1915)*
701 Marriott Dr.
Nashville, TN 37214
Tel: (615) 399-0900 *Fax:* (615) 399-0400
E-Mail: glfop@grandlodgefop.org
Website: fop.net/contact/index.shtml#Admin
Members: 325000 individuals
Staff: 13
Annual Budget: $500-1,000,000
Tax: 501(c)(3)

Personnel:
National Secretary: Patrick Yoes
     E-Mail: pyoes@fop.net
Administrator, Information Technology and Webmaster: Andrew Bittner
     E-Mail: abittner@fop.net
Associate General Counsel: Mike Coviello
     E-Mail: mecoviello@fop.net
Editor and Coordinator, Seminars: Marquie Hale
     E-Mail: mhale@fop.net
Representative, Membership Services: Tiffany Handley
     E-Mail: thandley@fop.net
General Counsel: Larry H. James
Director, Labor Services: Rick Weisman

Historical Note:
The Fraternal Order of Police (FOP) is an organization of sworn law enforcement officers in the United States. Members are regularly appointed or elected and full-time employed law enforcement officers of the United States, any state or political subdivision thereof, or any agency.

Meetings/Conferences: Annual
Conference Chair: Marquie Hale

Publications:
FOP Journal; quarterly

National Freight Transportation Association *(1905)*
P.O. Box 1321
Exton, PA 19341
Tel: (610) 363-7747 *Fax:* (610) 363-2971
E-Mail: nfta2000@aol.com
Website: nftahq.org
Members: 410 individuals
Staff: 2
Annual Budget: $100-250,000
Tax: 501(c)(6)

Personnel:
Executive Director: George Turner
     E-Mail: nfta2000@aol.com

Historical Note:
NFTA provides a forum for transportation executives of industrial firms and transportation companies to consider and discuss developments affecting the quality of transportation service, methods of enhancing transportation service, and government activity affecting the transportation industry and its customers. Members are senior executives of railroads, motor carriers, water carriers, and rail car leasing companies. Industrial member companies include most manufacturers of agricultural products, chemicals, paper, metals, automobiles, forest products, food, and consumer products. Membership: $475/year (Individual).

Meetings/Conferences: Annual
2013 - Orlando, FL (Omni Orlando Resort at ChampionsGate)/March 20 - 24

National Frozen and Refrigerated Foods Association *(1945)*
P.O. Box 6069
Harrisburg, PA 17112-0069
Tel: (717) 657-8601 *Fax:* (717) 657-9862
E-Mail: info@nfraweb.org
Website: nfraweb.org
Members: 400 companies
Staff: 9
Annual Budget: $2-5,000,000
Tax: 501(c)(6)

Personnel:
President and Chief Executive Officer: H. V. "Skip" Shaw Jr.
     E-Mail: skip@nfraweb.org
Vice President, Communications: Julie W. Henderson
     E-Mail: julie@nfraweb.org
Administrative Assistant, Meetings and Membership Services: Dayna Jackson

Legal Counsel: William Kitchens Esq.
Vice President, Finance: Jessica Kurtz
  E-Mail: jessica@nfraweb.org
Vice President, Membership Services: Leeann
  MacWilliams CHSP
  E-Mail: Leeann@nfraweb.org
Executive Vice president and Chief Operating Officer: Jeff
  Rumachik

Historical Note:
*Formerly (2002) National Frozen Food Association,
NFRA works to promote the sales and consumption of
frozen & refrigerated foods through: education, training,
research and sales planning. Membership; $1,730-13,530
(Manufacturer, based on food sales per millions); $560
(Regional Manufacturer); $1,150-4,430 (Distributor,
based on sales); $775 (Sales Agent); $1,185 (Supplier);
$885-1,430 (Logistics Provider); $560 (Retailer/
Wholesaler/International).*

Meetings/Conferences: Annual
Conference Chair: Dayna Jackson
2013 - San Diego, CA (Hilton San Diego Bayfront)/Oct.
  19 - 22

Publications:
NFRA Update; monthly; adv.

Membership List Available to Non-members

National Frozen Pizza Institute (1975)
2000 Corporate Ridge
Suite 1000
McLean, VA 22102
Tel: (703) 821-0770 *Fax:* (703) 821-1350
Website: frozenpizzafacts.org
Staff: 5
Annual Budget: $100-250,000
Tax: 501(c)(6)

Personnel:
Executive Director: Corey Henry
  E-Mail: chenry@frozenpizzafacts.org
Manager, Conferences: Kristen Holmes
  E-Mail: kholmes@frozenpizzafacts.org
Director, Industry and Public Affairs: Adrienne Richards
  E-Mail: arichards@frozenpizzafacts.org
Vice President, Government Affairs: Kristin Pearson
  Wilcox
  E-Mail: kwilcox@frozenpizzafacts.org

Historical Note:
*Managed by American Frozen Food Institute. NFPI monitors
federal regulatory and legislative activities which impact
the frozen pizza industry and promotes the frozen pizza
category to consumers and the retail trade. Membership:
$634-2,500,000 (Firms, based on revenue); $780
(Associate).*

Meetings/Conferences:
Conference Chair: Kristen Holmes
2013 - Las Vegas, NV (Las Vegas Convention Center)/
  March 19 - 21/700 attendees/over 100 exhibitors

Publications:
Buyer's Guide; on-line
Pizza Piece - Newsletter; monthly

National Funeral Directors and Morticians Association (1924)
6290 Shannon Pkwy.
Union City, GA 30291
Tel: (770) 969-0064 *Fax:* (770) 969-0505
TollFree: (800) 434-0958
E-Mail: nfdma@nfdma.org
Website: nfdma.com
Members: 1500 individuals
Staff: 4
Annual Budget: $1-2,000,000

Personnel:
Executive Director: Carol T. Williams
Executive Assistant: Valeria Clark
Education and Membership Coordinator: Cornell W.
  Robinson-Carroll
Meetings and Conventions Planner: Ella M. Young
  E-Mail: ellamwebb@yahoo.com

Historical Note:
*NFD&MA's mission is to foster research, conduct
workshops and seminars, investigate funeral practices,
develop and maintain standards of conduct designed to
improve the business condition of its members and to
maintain high standards of service for the benefit of the
public. Membership: $350/year.*

Continuing Education:
Certification Designation/s: CEU

Meetings/Conferences: Annual
Conference Chair: Ella M. Young

Publications:
Exhibitor Directory; on-line
NFDMA Newsletter; on-line
The Scope; on-line; adv.

Membership List Available to Non-members

National Funeral Directors Association (1882)
13625 Bishop's Dr.
Brookfield, WI 53005-6607
Tel: (262) 789-1880 *Fax:* (262) 789-6977
TollFree: (800) 228-6332
E-Mail: jfitch@nfda.org
Website: nfda.org
Members:
19000 individuals
10200 funeral homes
Staff: 48
Annual Budget: $5-10,000,000
Tax: 501(c)(6)

Personnel:
Chief Executive Officer: Christine Reichelt-Pepper CAE
  E-Mail: cpepper@nfda.org
Managing Editor: Dawn M. Behr
Vice President, Member Relations Division: Anna Bernfeld
  E-Mail: abernfeld@nfda.org
Director, Information Technology: Thomas Brockman
Accounting Manager: Todd Etheridge
Manager, Human Resource: Patti King
Manager, Public Relations: Jessica A. Koth
  E-Mail: jkoth@nfda.org
Director, Convention, Events and Meetings: David Larsen
Communications Director: Gail Marquardt
Director, Business Development: Kellie Schilling
  E-Mail: kschilling@nfda.org
Senior Vice President, Professional Development: Connie
  Smith
  E-Mail: csmith@nfda.org
Senior Vice President, Operations: Michael Watkins
  E-Mail: mwatkins@nfda.org

Historical Note:
*NFDA's purpose is to promote ethical standards and
help members provide meaningful services to families. It
also sponsors and supports the NFDA Political Action
Committee. Membership: $0-1,250/year.*

Continuing Education:
Enrollment: 1300
Certification Designation/s: CPC

Meetings/Conferences:
Conference Chair: David Larsen
2013 - Austin, TX/Oct. 20 - 23
Number of non-conference events/year: 4

Publications:
Convention Souvenir Program & Expo Buyer's Guide;
  annually; adv.
Directory of Members & Transportation Guide;
  biennially
Memorial Business Journal; weekly
NFDA Bulletin; weekly; adv.
The Director; monthly; adv.

National Futures Association (1982)
300 S. Riverside Plaza
Suite 1800
Chicago, IL 60606-6615
Tel: (312) 781-1300 *Fax:* (312) 781-1467
TollFree: (800) 621-3570
E-Mail: information@nfa.futures.org
Website: nfa.futures.org
Members: 4,200 firms and 55,000 associates
Staff: 250
Annual Budget: $50-100,000,000
Tax: 501(c)(6)

Personnel:
President and Chief Executive Officer: Daniel J. Roth
  E-Mail: droth@nfa.futures.org
Director, Human Resources: Nancy C. Bohanon
  E-Mail: nbohanon@nfa.futures.org
Senior Manager, Membership Services and Registration:
  Yvette Christman
  E-Mail: ychristman@nfa.futures.org
Vice President, Market Regulation: Edward Dasso III
  E-Mail: edasso@nfa.futures.org
Director, Communications and Education: Larry A.
  Dyekman

  E-Mail: ldyekman@nfa.futures.org
Senior Vice President, Information Systems: Kenneth F.
  Haase
  E-Mail: khaase@nfa.futures.org
Vice President, Chief Financial Officer and Treasurer:
  David L. Hawrysz
  E-Mail: dhawrysz@nfa.futures.org
Senior Vice President, General Counsel and Secretary:
  Thomas W. Sexton III
  E-Mail: tsexton@nfa.futures.org

Historical Note:
*NFA seeks to develop rules, programs and services that
safeguard market integrity, protect investors and help its
members meet their regulatory responsibilities. Members
are future commission merchants (FCMs), commodity
trading advisors (CTAs), commodity pool operators (CPOs),
introducing brokers (IBs), exchanges and associated
personnel. Membership: $1,500-1,000,000 (FCM/FDM);
$750 (CPO/CTA/IB); $2,500 (Firms).*

Publications:
Annual Review; annually
Member Newsletter
NFA Investor Newsletter; quarterly
NFA Membership Directory; annually

National Garden Clubs (1929)
4401 Magnolia Ave.
St. Louis, MO 63110
Tel: (314) 776-7574 *Fax:* (314) 776-5108
E-Mail: headquarters@gardenclub.org
Website: gardenclub.org
Members:
5800 clubs
190000 members
Staff: 7
Annual Budget: $1-2,000,000

Personnel:
Contact, Communications: Patricia Binder
Treasurer: Betty Grimes
  E-Mail: ggrimes2@aol.com
Webmaster: Kathy Thomas
  E-Mail: ngcwebsite@aol.com

Historical Note:
*Formerly (2001) National Council of State Garden Clubs.
NGC's mission is to provide education, resources and
national networking opportunities for the members, to
promote the love of gardening, floral design, civic, and
environmental responsibility. Supported by dues of 25 cents
per person from its member clubs. Sponsors the National
Garden Week. Membership: $15 (National Affiliate); $25
(International Affiliate).*

Meetings/Conferences: Annual
2013 - Seattle, WA (Sheraton Seattle Hotel)/May 24 -
  26
Number of non-conference events/year: 2

Publications:
Keeping In Touch; quarterly
The National Gardener; quarterly; adv.

National Genealogical Society (1903)
3108 Columbia Pike
Suite 300
Arlington, VA 22204-4370
Tel: (703) 525-0050 *Fax:* (703) 525-0052
TollFree: (800) 473-0060
E-Mail: ngs@ngsgenealogy.org
Website: ngsgenealogy.org
Members: 11000 individuals
Staff: 6
Annual Budget: $1-2,000,000
Tax: 501(c)(3)

Personnel:
President: Ann Hilke CG
  E-Mail: president@ngsgenealogy.org
Manager, Membership Services: Illyce Mac Donald
  E-Mail: imacdonald@ngsgenealogy.org
Editor: Thomas W. Jones CG, CGL
  E-Mail: ngsq@ngsgenealogy.org
Conference Manager: Erin Shifflett
  E-Mail: eshifflett@ngsgenealogy.org
Manager, Accounting: Karen Soch
  E-Mail: ksoch@ngsgenealogy.org
Manager, Education: Pat Stamm CG, CGL
  E-Mail: education@ngsgenealogy.org

Historical Note:
*NGS's mission is to serve and grow the genealogical
community by providing education and training, fostering
increased quality and standards, and promoting access to*

and preservation of genealogical records.. Membership: $60 (Individual); $15 (Additional Family Member); $50 (Organizational Subscription); $160 (Contributing); $310 (Sustaining); $560 (Patron); $1,060 (Benefactor); $2,500 (Lifetime).

Meetings/Conferences: Annual
Conference Chair: Erin Shifflett
2013 - Las Vegas, NV (Las Vegas Hotel and Casino)/ May 8 - 11

Publications:
Membership Directory; on-line
NGS Magazine; quarterly
NGS Online Store; on-line
Upfront with NGS; monthly

National Gerontological Nursing Association
(1984)
3493 Lansdowne Dr.
Suite Two
Lexington, KY 40517
Tel: (859) 977-7453 *Fax:* (859) 271-0607
TollFree: (800) 723-0560
E-Mail: info@ngna.org
Website: ngna.org
Members:
6 companies
1600 individuals
Staff: 4
Annual Budget: $100-250,000
Tax: 501(c)(3)

Personnel:
Executive Director: Brian Doty
Director, Meetings and Conventions: Sarah Clements CAE
   E-Mail: sclements@ngna.org
Director, Marketing and Communications: Stephanie Czuhajewski CAE
Manager, Member Services: Tonda Preston
   E-Mail: tpreston@ngna.org

Historical Note:
NGNA is dedicated to the clinical care of older adults across diverse care settings. It also seeks to improve the quality of nursing care given to older adults. Members include clinicians, educators, and researchers with vastly different educational preparation, clinical roles, and interest in practice issues. Membership: $65 (Student); $95 (Senior/Nursing Assistant); $110 (Associate/Regular); $130 (International); $1,000(Institution).

Continuing Education:
Certification Designation/s: NGNP, GN, CSG

Meetings/Conferences: Annual
Conference Chair: Sarah Clements CAE
Number of non-conference events/year: 1

Publications:
Geriatric Nursing
Member Directory; on-line
Newsletter
Organization Directory; on-line

National Glass Association *(1948)*
1945 Old Gallows Rd.
Suite 750
Vienna, VA 22182
Tel: (703) 442-4890 *Fax:* (703) 442-0630
TollFree: (866) 342-5642
E-Mail: nga@glass.org
Website: glass.org
Members: 2,200 member companies
Staff: 24
Annual Budget: $5-10,000,000
Tax: 501(c)(6)

Personnel:
President and Chief Executive Officer: Philip J. James CAE
   E-Mail: pjames@glass.org
Director, Information Technology: Marc G. Doggett CCP
   E-Mail: mdoggett@glass.org
Vice President, Association Services: Jim Gandorf CAE
Vice President and Publisher: Nicole Harris CAE
   E-Mail: nharris@glass.org
Director, Administration and Finance: Pamela S. Paroline
   E-Mail: pparoline@glass.org
Vice President, Industry Events: Denise M. Sheehan
   E-Mail: dsheehan@glass.org

Historical Note:
Formerly the National Auto & Flat Glass Dealers Association and the National Glass Dealers Association (until 1984). NGA is the trade association serving the architectural glass, automotive glass, and window and door industries. Members are architectural and automobile

glass manufacturers, wholesalers, fabricators, distributors, installers and companies that do work related to the industry, such as companies that manufacture and/or are otherwise concerned with windows, mirrors, sealants, tools, and material handling equipment. Membership: $45-5190/ year (Based upon annual sales).

Continuing Education:
Certification Designation/s: GIC, AGC, CMAGT, CAGRT, CGI, CAGT

Meetings/Conferences: Semi-Annual
Conference Chair: Denise M. Sheehan
2013 - Atlanta, GA (Georgia World Congress Center)/ Sept. 10 - 12/over 100 exhibitors
2013 - Milan, Italy (Fieramilano)/Oct. 23 - 26
Number of non-conference events/year: 2

Publications:
e-glass weekly; weekly; adv.
Glass Magazine; monthly; adv.
W & D Weekly; weekly; adv.
Window & Door; adv.

National Golf Course Owners Association *(1979)*
291 Seven Farms Dr.
Charleston, SC 29492
Tel: (843) 881-9956 *Fax:* (843) 881-9958
TollFree: (800) 933-4262
E-Mail: info@ngcoa.org
Website: ngcoa.org
Members: 4000 clubs
Staff: 20
Annual Budget: $1-2,000,000
Tax: 501(c)(3)

Personnel:
Chief Executive Officer: Mike Hughes
   E-Mail: mhughes@ngcoa.org
Manager, Marketing: Sarah Gurley
   E-Mail: sgurley@ngcoa.org
Director, Player Development program questions and information, event dates: Anne Lyndrup
   E-Mail: alyndrup@ngcoa.org
Business Development Account Manager: Kelly MacPherson
   E-Mail: kmacpherson@ngcoa.org
Contact, Communications: Sarah Masche
   E-Mail: smasche@ngcoa.org
Contact, Government relations: Joe Rice
   E-Mail: jrice@ngcoa.org
Director, Information Technology: Thomas Smith
   E-Mail: tsmith@ngcoa.org

Historical Note:
Established as the National Association of Public Golf Courses under the aegis of the National Golf Foundation, became fully independent as Golf Course Association in 1982 and assumed its present name in 1991. NGCOA's mission is to enhance the lives of golf course owners by making their business more profitable, more efficient, better managed and more stable. Members are privately-owned golf courses. Membership: $190-1,100 (Individual); $450 (Corporate).

Meetings/Conferences: Annual
Conference Chair: Anne Lyndrup
2013 - San Diego, CA/Feb. 4 - 8
Number of non-conference events/year: 10

Publications:
American Express Business Insights e-newsletter; monthly
Golf Business; monthly
Membership Directory; on-line

Membership List Available to Non-members

National Golf Foundation *(1936)*
1150 S. US Hwy. One
Suite 401
Jupiter, FL 33477
Tel: (561) 744-6006 *Fax:* (561) 744-6107
TollFree: (800) 275-4643
E-Mail: general@ngf.org
Website: ngf.org
Members: 4625 organizations and 4,000 members
Staff: 27
Annual Budget: $2-5,000,000

Personnel:
President and Chief Executive Officer: Joseph Beditz
   E-Mail: jbeditz@ngf.org
Senior Vice President, Membership Services: Greg Nathan
   E-Mail: gnathan@ngf.org

Director, Consulting Services: Richard Singer
   E-Mail: rsinger@ngf.org

Historical Note:
NGF is to support all the people, companies, facilities and associations that earn their living in the golf business. Membership: $199 (Facility); $495 (Business); $5,000 (Business Elite).

Publications:
Inside the Ropes; monthly
NGF Dashboard; monthly

Membership List Available to Non-members

National Government Publishing Association
(1977)
629 N. Main St.
Hattiesburg, MS 39401
Tel: (601) 582-3330 *Fax:* (601) 582-3354
E-Mail: info@govpublishing.org
Website: govpublishing.org
Members: 125 jurisdictions
Staff: 2
Annual Budget: $50-100,000

Personnel:
Executive Director: Lamar Evans
Treasurer: John Wright

Historical Note:
NGPA's mission is to provide a forum for representatives of government print agencies, publishers, document and information management groups, related data service providers, and procurement entities to educate and exchange information among members, vendor partners, and industry experts for the development of more efficient, valued operations, resulting in the improvement of services to the general public and others served by members. Membership: $400 (Full); $750 (Corporate); $225 (International); Free (Honorary/Retired).

Meetings/Conferences: Annual

Publications:
Membership Directory; annually

National Governors Association *(1908)*
444 N. Capitol St.
Suite 267
Washington, DC 20001-1512
Tel: (202) 624-5300 *Fax:* (202) 624-5313
Website: nga.org
Members: 55 governors
Staff: 100

Personnel:
Executive Director: Dan Crippen
   E-Mail: dcrippen@nga.org
Director, Conference Management: Susan Dotchin
   E-Mail: sdotchin@nga.org
Director, Administration and Finance: Bill Gainer
Director, Committees on Health and Human Services: Heather Hogsett
   E-Mail: hhgosett@nga.org
Director, Communications: Jodi Omear
   E-Mail: jomear@nga.org
Director, Federal Relations: David C. Quam
   E-Mail: dquam@nga.org
Director, Corporate Relations: Kevin Sillard
Director, Information Technology: Bob Thomas
Controller: John Thornburg
Director, Education, Early Childhood and Workforce Committee: Joan Wodiska

Historical Note:
Formerly (1977) National Governors Conference. A bipartisan organization of the nation's governors. NGA's mission is to promote visionary state leadership, shares best practices and speaks with a collective voice on national policy. Members are Governors of the 50 states and five territories of the U.S.

Meetings/Conferences: Annual
Conference Chair: Susan Dotchin
2013 - Williamsburg, VA/July 12 - 15

Publications:
Front & Center Newsletters; weekly
NGA Newsletter

National Grain and Feed Association *(1896)*
1250 I St. NW
Suite 1003
Washington, DC 20005
Tel: (202) 289-0873 *Fax:* (202) 289-5388
E-Mail: ngfa@ngfa.org
Website: ngfa.org

Members: 1000 companies
Staff: 13
Annual Budget: $2-5,000,000
Tax: 501(c)(6)

Personnel:
Acting President and Vice President, Communications and Government Relations: Randall C. Gordon
   E-Mail: rgordon@ngfa.org
Vice President, General Counsel and Secretary: Charles M. Delacruz
Manager, Meetings and Event Marketing: Rebecca Grubbs
Vice President, Marketing and Treasurer: Todd E. Kemp
Director, Communications: Heather McElrath
Manager, Database and Membership Services: Faith Silvers

Historical Note:
NGFA's mission is to foster an efficient free-market environment that produces an abundant, safe and high-quality supply of grain, feed and feeding ingredients for domestic and world consumers. Membership: $600-48000 (Active); $600-2500 (NGFA Associate/Trading); $600-1500 (NGFA Regular Associate).

Meetings/Conferences:
Conference Chair: Rebecca Grubbs
2013 - San Francisco, CA (Westin St. Francis)/March 17 - 19
Number of non-conference events/year: 9

Publications:
NGFA Directory; adv.
NGFA Newsletter; bi-monthly

National Grain Trade Council *(1936)*
1300 L St. NW
Suite 1020
Washington, DC 20005-4113
Tel: (202) 842-0400 *Fax:* (202) 789-7223
E-Mail: jkinnaird@ngtc.org
Website: grainnet.com/companies/
   National_Grain_Trade_Co
Members: 40 companies and organizations
Staff: 2
Annual Budget: $250-500,000

Personnel:
President: Jula J. Kinnaird
   E-Mail: jkinnaird@ngtc.org
Treasurer: Victoria Schantz

Historical Note:
NGTC members are commodity exchanges, boards of trade, national grain marketing associations and grain related businesses.

National Grange *(1867)*
1616 H St. NW
Washington, DC 20006
Tel: (202) 628-3507 *Fax:* (202) 347-1091
TollFree: (888) 447-2643
E-Mail: info@nationalgrange.org
Website: nationalgrange.org
Members: 200000 individuals
Staff: 14
Annual Budget: $1-2,000,000

Personnel:
President: Ed Luttrell
   E-Mail: eluttrell@nationalgrange.org
Director, Legislative: Grace Boatright
   E-Mail: gboatright@nationalgrange.org
Director, Communications: Amanda Leigh Brozana
   E-Mail: abrozana@nationalgrange.org
Executive Assistant and Meeting Planner: Jessica Cope
   E-Mail: jcope@nationalgrange.org
Coordinator, Marketing: Beverly Mitchell
   E-Mail: bmitchell@nationalgrange.org
Manager, Information Technology: Stephanie Wilkins
   E-Mail: swilkins@nationalgrange.org

Historical Note:
The National Grange members initiate non-partisan political action, support and participate in community service projects and provide volunteer leadership training and education. Membership: $12 (EMembership); $25 (National Associate).

Meetings/Conferences: Annual
Conference Chair: Jessica Cope
2013 - Manchester, NH (Radisson Hotel Manchester)/ Nov. 12 - 16
2014 - Sandusky, OH (Kalahari Waterpark Resort and Convention Center)/Nov. 11 - 15

2015 - Lincoln, NE (The Cornhusker)/Nov. 3 - 5

Publications:
New Grange Newsletter; on-line

National Grants Management Association *(1978)*
2100 M St. NW
Suite 170
Washington, DC 20037
Tel: (202) 308-9443 *Fax:* (703) 648-9024
E-Mail: info@ngma.org
Website: ngma.org
Members: 950 individuals
Staff: 3
Annual Budget: $250-500,000
Tax: 501(c)(6)

Personnel:
President: Merril Oliver
Director, Business Services: Shelly Slebrch
   E-Mail: slebrch@ngma.org

Historical Note:
NGMA connects professionals in the grants field to improve and unify the grants delivery process. Membership: $125/ year (Individual).

Continuing Education:
Certification Designation/s: CGMS

Meetings/Conferences: Annual
2013 - Arlington, VA (Crystal Gateway Marriott)/May 5 - 9

Publications:
Journal of the National Grants Management Association; bi-annually
Membership Directory; on-line
NGMA Member and Industry News; on-line

The National Greenhouse Manufacturers Association *(1958)*
4305 N. Sixth St.
Suite A
Harrisburg, PA 17110
Tel: (717) 238-4530 *Fax:* (717) 238-9985
TollFree: (800) 792-6462
E-Mail: info@ngma.org
Website: ngma.com
Members: 80 companies
Staff: 5
Annual Budget: $100-250,000

Personnel:
Executive Director: Denise Calabrese
   E-Mail: info@ngma.com
Director, Membership: Angela Burkett
   E-Mail: customerservice@ngma.com
Director, Conferences and Events: Jen Cramer
   E-Mail: events@ngma.com
Manager, Communications: Alison Evans
   E-Mail: communications@ngma.com

Historical Note:
NGMA's mission is to serve the interest of the industry and its members and to gather, develop and disseminate information vital to the greenhouse industry. Membership: $1500 (Structural Manufacture Member/Component Manufacture Member/Service Membership); $25 (University).

Meetings/Conferences: Annual
Conference Chair: Jen Cramer
2013 - Tucson, AZ/April 14 - 16
Number of non-conference events/year: 6

Publications:
E-Newsletter; quarterly
Membership Directory; annually

National Greyhound Association *(1906)*
P.O. Box 543
Abilene, KS 67410
Tel: (785) 263-4660 *Fax:* (785) 263-4689
E-Mail: nga@ngagreyhounds.com
Website: ngagreyhounds.com
Staff: 2
Annual Budget: $2-5,000,000
Tax: 501(c)(6)

Personnel:
President: Kenny Allen
   E-Mail: korjallen@live.com
Executive Editor, Secretary and Treasurer: Gary Guccione
   E-Mail: garyg@ngagreyhounds.com

Historical Note:

NGA, a voluntary nonprofit association that serves the Greyhound racing industry. It is concerned with issues relating to Greyhound racetracks and individual racing jurisdictions, as well as foreign Greyhound registries and governing bodies as the sole registry for racing Greyhounds in North America. Membership: $170 (Individual); $50 (Associate).

Publications:
Buyer's Guide; on-line
Membership Directory; on-line
NGA Newsletter; bi-monthly

National Grocers Association *(1982)*
1005 N. Glebe Rd.
Suite 250
Arlington, VA 22201-5758
Tel: (703) 516-0700 *Fax:* (703) 516-0115
E-Mail: info@nationalgrocers.org
Website: nationalgrocers.org
Members: 2000 retailers and wholesalers
Staff: 21
Annual Budget: $5-10,000,000
Tax: 501(c)(6)

Personnel:
President and Chief Executive Officer: Peter S. Larkin
Manager, Database: Janice Coon
   E-Mail: jcoon@nationalgrocers.org
Director, Marketing: Christine Cunnick
   E-Mail: ccunnick@nationalgrocers.org
Director, Government Affairs: Gregory B. Ferrara
   E-Mail: gferrara@nationalgrocers.org
Controller, Accounting Services: Perry Maison
   E-Mail: pmaison@nationalgrocers.org
Director, Communications: Hayley McConnell
   E-Mail: HMcConnell@NationalGrocers.org
Director, Education and Research: Aileen Dullaghan Munster
   E-Mail: amunster@nationalgrocers.org
Director, Membership Services: Matt Ott MS
   E-Mail: mott@nationalgrocers.org
Director, Expo Management: Karen Voorhies
   E-Mail: kvoorhies@nationalgrocers.org
Executive Vice President and General Counsel: Thomas F. Wenning
   E-Mail: twenning@nationalgrocers.org

Historical Note:
Formed with merger of the National Association of Retail Grocers of the U. S. (1893) and the Cooperative Food distributors of America (1937). NGA's mission is to ensure independent, community-focused retailers and wholesalers the opportunity to succeed and better serve the consumer through its policies, advocacy, programs and services. Represents the retail and wholesale grocers who comprise the independent sector of the food industry which accounts for nearly one- half of all food store sales in the U. S. Retail and wholesale grocers. Membership: $400 (Retailer); $1,000-12,000 (Associate), $1,000 (Wholesaler).

Meetings/Conferences:
Conference Chair: Karen Voorhies
2013 - Las Vegas, NV (Mirage Hotel and Casino)/Feb. 10 - 13
Number of non-conference events/year: 3

Publications:
Express Lanes; weekly
Membership Directory; on-line
Washington Briefs; monthly

National Ground Water Association *(1948)*
601 Dempsey Rd.
Westerville, OH 43081
Tel: (614) 898-7791 *Fax:* (614) 898-7786
TollFree: (800) 551-7379
E-Mail: ngwa@ngwa.org
Website: ngwa.org
Members: 13000 members
Staff: 39
Annual Budget: $5-10,000,000

Personnel:
Chief Executive Officer: Kevin B. McCray CAE
   E-Mail: kmccray@ngwa.org
Manager, Human Resources and Accounts Payable: Denise Bierkortte
   E-Mail: dbierkortte@ngwa.org
Director, Professional Development: Kathy Butcher
   E-Mail: kbutcher@ngwa.org
Director, Marketing: David Evener
   E-Mail: devener@ngwa.org
Director, Membership Services: Trisha Freeman

E-Mail: tfreeman@ngwa.org
Vice President, Operations and Chief Financial Officer:
 Paul Humes
 E-Mail: phumes@ngwa.org
Director, Information Technology: Mark Kibble
 E-Mail: mkibble@ngwa.org
Director, Expositions and Meeting Planning: Greg Phelps
 E-Mail: gphelps@ngwa.org
Director, Publishing and Knowledge Products: Thad
 Plumley
 E-Mail: tplumley@ngwa.org
Director, Government Affairs: Chris Reimer
 E-Mail: creimer@ngwa.org
Director, Public Awareness: Cliff Treyens
 E-Mail: ctreyens@ngwa.org

Historical Note:
*Formerly (1948) National Water Well Association and
changed its name in 1991 as National Groundwater
Association. NGWA's purpose is to provide guidance
to members, government representatives and the public
for sound scientific, economic, beneficial development,
protection, and management of the world's groundwater
resources. Mission is dedicated to advancing groundwater
knowledge. Membership: $25 (Student); $300 (Company,
Contractor); $320 (International Company Contractor);
$115-320 (Scientist/Engineer); $330-1,460 (Manufacturer,
dues based on sales volume); $385-400 (Supplier); $110
(Individual); $125 (International).*

Continuing Education:
Certification Designation/s: CPI, MGWC, CWD, CWD/PI,
CSP, CGWP

Meetings/Conferences: Annual
Conference Chair: Greg Phelps
2013 - San Antonio, TX/April 28 - May 2

Publications:
Ground Water; adv.
Ground Water Monitoring & Remediation; quarterly;
 adv.
Membership Directory; on-line
Water Well Journal; monthly; adv.

National Guard Association of the U.S. *(1878)*
One Massachusetts Ave. NW
Washington, DC 20001
Tel: (202) 789-0031 *Fax:* (202) 682-9358
TollFree: (888) 226-4287
E-Mail: ngaus@ngaus.org
Website: ngaus.org
Members: 45000 current, former Guard officers
Staff: 26
Annual Budget: $5-10,000,000

Personnel:
President: Ret. Maj. Gen. Gus Hargett
 E-Mail: president@ngaus.org
Director, Financial Operations: Pam Buckler-Bowers
 E-Mail: pam.buckler@ngaus.org
Deputy Director, Membership Services: Bonnie Carter
 E-Mail: bonnie.carter@ngaus.org
Director, Communications: John Goheen
 E-Mail: johngoheen@ngaus.org
Director, Legislative Programs: Richard M. Green
 E-Mail: richard.green@ngaus.org
Senior Writer and Editor: Ron Jensen
 E-Mail: ron.jensen@ngaus.org
Director, Contracts, Finance and Human Resources:
 Patricia R. O'Connell
 E-Mail: patricia.oconnell@ngaus.org
Chief-of-Staff and General Conference Coordinator: COL
 Randy Williams Ret.
 E-Mail: cos@ngaus.org

Historical Note:
*NGAUS works to promote the national security of the
United States of America. Membership: $168 (General);
$153 (Lieutenant General); $139 (Major General); $123
(Brigadier General); $108 (Colonel); $85 (Lieutenant
Colonel); $72 (Major); $59 (Captain); $45 (First
Lieutenant); $30 (Second Lieutenant); $73 (Chief Warrant
Officer 5); $59 (Chief Warrant Officer 4); $46 (Chief
Warrant Officer 3); $35 (Chief Warrant Officer 2); $26
(Warrant Officer 1).*

Meetings/Conferences: Annual
Conference Chair: COL Randy Williams Ret.
2013 - Honolulu, HI/Sept. 20 - 23
2014 - Chicago, IL/Aug. 22 - 25
2015 - Nashville, TN/Sept. 10 - 13
2016 - Baltimore, MD/Sept. 9 - 12

Publications:
Membership Directory; on-line

National Guard; monthly; adv.
Staff Directory; on-line
Washington Report; weekly; adv.

National Guard Executive Directors Association
3706 Crawford Ave.
Austin, TX 78731
Tel: (512) 454-7300 *Fax:* (512) 467-6803
Website: ngeda.org
Members:
200 individuals
23 Companies
Staff: 2
Annual Budget: $50-100,000
Tax: 501(c)(3)

Personnel:
Secretary and Treasurer: Ray Lindner CAE
 E-Mail: rlindner@ngat.org

Historical Note:
*NGEDA's mission is to provide a forum for the exchange of
timely information of common interest for the mutual benefit
of members and the organizations they represent. NGEDA
provides the link between the National Guard Association
and the states. Membership: $30/year (Individual).*

Meetings/Conferences: Annual
2013 - Honolulu, HI/Jan. 21 - 25
2013 - Honolulu, HI (Sheraton Waikiki)/Jan. 22 - 25
2014 - Chicago, IL/Jan. 13 - 15
2014 - Chicago, IL/Jan. 14 - 16

National Guardianship Association *(1988)*
174 Crestview Dr.
Bellefonte, PA 16823-8516
Tel: (877) 326-5992 *Fax:* (814) 355-2452
TollFree: (877) 326-5992
E-Mail: info@guardianship.org
Website: guardianship.org
Members: 700 individuals
Staff: 16
Annual Budget: $250-500,000
Tax: 501(c)(3)

Personnel:
Business Manager: Patricia E. Heuser

Historical Note:
*NGA's mission is to advance the nationally recognized
standard of excellence in guardianship. Composed of
individuals and organizations in the United States, Canada
and Australia; includes guardians, conservators, fiduciaries,
representative payees, physicians, hospitals, others
interested in guardianship and surrogacy, attorneys, social
workers, bankers and advocates. Membership: $50 (Family/
Retired); $170 (Individual); $250 (Organization).*

Continuing Education:
Certification Designation/s: CGC

Meetings/Conferences: Semi-Annual
2013 - Chicago, IL (Chicago Marriott O'Hare)/May 16
 - 17
2013 - Tampa, FL (Grand Hyatt Tampa Bay)/Oct. 12 -
 15

Publications:
Membership Directory; annually; adv.
National Guardian; adv.

National Guild for Community Arts Education
(1937)
520 Eighth Ave.
Suite 302
New York, NY 10018
Tel: (212) 268-3337 *Fax:* (212) 268-3995
E-Mail: guildinfo@nationalguild.org
Website: nationalguild.org
Members: 460 member organizations and 16,000
teaching artists
Staff: 10
Annual Budget: $1-2,000,000

Personnel:
Executive Director: Jonathan Herman
 E-Mail: jonathanherman@nationalguild.org
Associate Director: Kenneth T. Cole
 E-Mail: kencole@nationalguild.org
External Affairs Coordinator: Lindsey Cosgrove
 E-Mail: lindseycosgrove@nationalguild.org
Director, Marketing and Communications: Heather
 Ikemire
 E-Mail: heatherstickeler@nationalguild.org
Coordinator, Member Services: Claire Wilmoth
 E-Mail: clairewilmoth@nationalguild.org

Historical Note:
*Formerly known as National Guild of Community Schools
of the Arts. The National Guild for Community Arts
Education supports and advances access to lifelong learning
opportunities in the arts. Members are community schools
of the arts, arts centers, and arts education divisions
of performing arts institutions, universities, museums,
and other organizations. Membership: $200- 2,500
(Full); $175-2,000 (Education Affiliate); $250 (Business
Affiliate); $100 (Individual); $30 (Students).*

Meetings/Conferences: Annual
Conference Chair: Kenneth T. Cole
Number of non-conference events/year: 1

Publications:
GuildNotes Newsletter; quarterly; adv.
Member E-bulletin; semi-monthly
Membership Directory; annually; adv.

Membership List Available to Non-members

National Guild of Piano Teachers *(1929)*
P.O. Box 1807
Austin, TX 78767-1807
Tel: (512) 478-5775 *Fax:* (512) 478-5843
E-Mail: ngpt@pianoguild.com
Website: pianoguild.com
Members: 850 audition centers
Staff: 10
Annual Budget: $1-2,000,000

Personnel:
President: Richard Allison
Editor: Pat McCabe-Leche

Historical Note:
*A division of the American College of Musicians. NGPT's
purpose is to encourage growth and enjoyment through the
study of piano. Membership: $75/year.*

Continuing Education:
Certification Designation/s: ACM

Publications:
Piano Guild Notes; quarterly

National Guild of Professional Paperhangers
(1973)
136 S. Keowee St.
Dayton, OH 45402
Tel: (800) 254-6477 *Fax:* (937) 222-5794
E-Mail: ngpp@ngpp.org
Website: ngpp.org
Members: 1000 individuals
Staff: 1
Annual Budget: $100-250,000

Personnel:
Executive Vice President: Kimberly Fantaci

Historical Note:
*NGPP is an organization of wallcovering installers that
works to provide better craftsmanship in the hanging of
every type of wallpaper. Membership: $200 (Installer
with or with out Chapter Affiliation); $450 (National
Associate); $175 (Local Associate with Chapter affiliation).*

Continuing Education:
Enrollment: 50
Certification Designation/s: CP

Meetings/Conferences: Annual

Publications:
National Membership Directory; annually; adv.
The Wallcovering Installer; bi-monthly; adv.

National Hardwood Lumber Association *(1898)*
P.O. Box 34518
Memphis, TN 38184
Tel: (901) 377-1818
TollFree: (800) 933-0318
E-Mail: info@nhla.com
Website: nhla.com
Members: 1700 companies
Staff: 22
Annual Budget: $5-10,000,000
Tax: 501(c)(6)

Personnel:
Executive Director: Mark Barford CAE
 E-Mail: m.barford@nhla.com
Director, Conventions: Lisa Browne
 E-Mail: l.browne@nhla.com
Director, Education: Chris Churchill
 E-Mail: c.churchill@nhla.com
Director, Marketing: John Hester
 E-Mail: j.hester@nhla.com
Director, Communications: Renee Hornsby

E-Mail: r.hornsby@nhla.com
Administrator, Information Technology Systems: Paula
May
E-Mail: p.may@nhla.com
Director, Finance and Chief Accounting Officer: Denise
Stewart
E-Mail: d.stewart@nhla.com

Historical Note:
NHLA's mission is to serve its members in the North
American Hardwood Lumber Industry by maintaining order,
structure, rules, and ethics in the changing hardwood
marketplace. Membership: $55-8820/year.

Meetings/Conferences: Annual
Conference Chair: Lisa Browne

Publications:
NHLA Directory; on-line

National Hay Association (1895)
151 Treasure Island Cswy.
Suite Two
St. Petersburg, FL 33706
Tel: (727) 367-9702 Fax: (727) 367-9608
TollFree: (800) 707-0014
Website: nationalhay.org
Members: 660 individuals
Staff: 1
Annual Budget: $250-500,000

Personnel:
Executive Director: Donald F. Kieffer

Historical Note:
NHA works daily within the industry, federal agencies and
the Congress itself to create an environment that benefits
hay merchants and the people who depend on hay and
straw in their commerce. Represents hay producers, brokers,
dealers and consumers of forage products, as well as
disciplines and activities of businesses that provide products
and services to the hay industry. Membership: $260/year.

Meetings/Conferences: Annual
Number of non-conference events/year: 1

Publications:
Hay There; monthly; adv.
Membership Directory; annually

National Head Start Association (1973)
1651 Prince St.
Alexandria, VA 22314-2818
Tel: (703) 739-0875 Fax: (703) 739-0878
TollFree: (866) 677-8724
Website: nhsa.org
Members: 200000 individuals
Staff: 20
Annual Budget: $5-10,000,000
Tax: 501(c)(3)

Personnel:
Executive Director: Yasmina S. Vinci
E-Mail: yvinci@nhsa.org
Director, Membership Development and Services: Jane
Adams
E-Mail: jadams@nhsa.org
Professional Development Operations Specialist: Julie
Antoniou
E-Mail: julie@nhsa.org
Director, Technical Services: Lori Christianson
E-Mail: lchristianson@nhsa.org
Senior Director, Membership and Professional Development:
Edward Condon
E-Mail: econdon@nhsa.org
Manager, Meetings and Conferences: Sharon Kirksey-
Walcott
E-Mail: swalcott@nhsa.org
Director, Marketing: Gregg Porter
E-Mail: gporter@nhsa.org
Deputy Director: Carolyn Stennett
E-Mail: cstennett@nhsa.org

Historical Note:
The members of the NHSA's four affiliate associations
merge into one association on June 7,1990. NHSA's
mission is to coalesce and take up the Head Start field as
a leader in early childhood development and education.
Members include staff, parents, directors, agencies and
other organizations concerned with the Head Start program.
Membership: $50 (Head Start Staff/Friend of Head Start);
$80 (Academic); $5 (Parent); $25 (Student); $10 (Head
Start Alumnus); $400-4,500 (Program); $250 (Associate);
$600 (Corporate); $200-600 (Affiliate).

Meetings/Conferences:

2013 - Washington, DC (Omni Shoreham Hotel)/Jan.
28 - Feb. 1

Publications:
Exchange Everyday; on-line
Exchange Magazine
Family Connections Newsletter
NHSA Dialog: A Research-to-Practice Journal for the
Early Intervention Field; quarterly

National Health Association (1948)
P.O. Box 30630
Tampa, FL 33630-3630
Tel: (813) 961-6100 Fax: (813) 961-6114
E-Mail: lgrudnik@healthscience.org
Website: healthscience.org/
Members: 7000 individuals
Staff: 2
Annual Budget: $250-500,000

Personnel:
Executive Director and Editor: Lynn Grudnik
E-Mail: lgrudnik@healthscience.org
Treasurer: Mark Alan Epstein

Historical Note:
Founded as American Natural Hygiene Society assumed its
current name in 1998. NHA's mission is to educate and
empower individuals to understand that health results from
healthful living. Membership: $35 (US and Canada); $55
(Other Countries).

Meetings/Conferences: Annual

Publications:
Health Science Magazine; quarterly
NHA Newsletter; on-line

National Health Care Anti-Fraud Association
(1985)
1201 New York Ave. NW
Suite 1120
Washington, DC 20005
Tel: (202) 659-5955 Fax: (202) 785-6764
E-Mail: NHCAA@nhcaa.org
Website: nhcaa.org
Members: 100 private health insurers
Staff: 9
Annual Budget: $2-5,000,000
Tax: 501(c)(6)

Personnel:
Chief Executive Officer: Louis Saccoccio
Senior Director, Education and Training: Erin Carlson
Deputy Director, Business Development and Marketing:
Deanie Griffin
Director, Government Affairs: Leigh McKenna
Manager, Information Systems and Services: Miriam
Ntsomi
Director, Administration: Tia Theriaque
Director, Communications and Membership: Michael T.
Williams

Historical Note:
NHCAA's mission is to protect and serve the public
interest by increasing awareness and improving the
detection, investigation, civil and criminal prosecution
and prevention of health care fraud. Members are private
health insurers and public-sector law enforcement and
regulatory agencies. Membership: $195 (Individual);
$6,500-22,500 (Supporting Member); $15,000-30,000
(Affiliate); $11,000-27,500 (Organization).

Continuing Education:
Certification Designation/s: AHFI

Meetings/Conferences: Annual

Publications:
NHCAA Legal Brief; on-line
NHCAA News Brief; on-line
The Beacon e-newsletter; monthly

Membership List Available to Non-members

National Health Club Association (1988)
640 Plaza Dr., Suite 300
Highlands Ranch, CO 80129
Tel: (303) 986-9563 Fax: (303) 986-6813
Members: 3000 health clubs
Staff: 6
Annual Budget: $100-250,000

Personnel:
Executive Vice President: Robert Riches

Historical Note:
Absorbed the Fitness Trade Association in 1990. NHCA
members are fitness centers.

National Health Council (1920)
1730 M St. NW
Suite 500
Washington, DC 20026-4561
Tel: (202) 785-3910 Fax: (202) 785-5923
E-Mail: info@nhcouncil.org
Website: nhcouncil.org
Members: 120 national organizations
Staff: 11
Annual Budget: $2-5,000,000
Tax: 501(c)(3)

Personnel:
Executive Vice President and Chief Operating Officer: Marc
M. Boutin JD
E-Mail: mboutin@nhcouncil.org
Director, Government Affairs: Eric Gascho
E-Mail: egascho@nhcouncil.org
Vice President, Communications and Marketing: Nancy
Hughes APR
E-Mail: nhughes@nhcouncil.org
Vice President, Membership Services: Susan Lau
Assistant Vice President, Organizational Affairs and
Meetings: Donna K. O'Leary
E-Mail: oleary@nhcouncil.org
Chief Financial Officer: Carol Sadoff CPA
E-Mail: csadoff@nhcouncil.org
President: Myrl Weinberg CAE
E-Mail: weinberg@nhcouncil.org

Historical Note:
NHC's mission is to provide a united voice for people with
chronic diseases and disabilities, to improve the health of
all people, increase support for health research, strengthen
the community of patient advocacy organizations.
Membership: $1,300-39,900 (Voluntary Health Agencies);
$1,000-8,600 (Professional); $1,300-5,500 (Nonprofit
Organizations); $18,100 (Business/Industry); $10,100
(Associate).

Continuing Education:
Certification Designation/s: NHCSE

Meetings/Conferences: Annual
Conference Chair: Donna K. O'Leary
2013 - Ponte Vedra Beach, FL (Ponte Vedra Inn and
Club)/Feb. 13 - 15

Publications:
Council Currents; quarterly
Membership Directory; on-line
Resource Directory; on-line

Membership List Available to Non-members

National Health Federation (1955)
P.O. Box 688
Monrovia, CA 91017
Tel: (626) 357-2181 Fax: (626) 303-0642
E-Mail: contact-us@thenhf.com
Website: thenhf.com
Staff: 3
Annual Budget: $250-500,000
Tax: 501(c)(4)

Personnel:
President and Legal Counsel: Scott Tips JD
Secretary: Dan Kenner LAc, PhD
Treasurer: Susan J. Negus PhD

Historical Note:
Established in 1955, the National Health Federation is
an international nonprofit, consumer-education, health-
freedom organization working to protect individuals' rights
to choose to consume healthy food, take supplements, and
use alternative therapies without government restrictions.
Membership: $81 (International); $100-$1000 (Gift).

Meetings/Conferences:
Conference Chair: Scott Tips JD

Publications:
Health Freedom News magazine; quarterly; adv.
Membership Directory; on-line

National Hearing Conservation Association
(1976)
3030 W. 81st Ave.
Westminster, CO 80031
Tel: (303) 224-9022 Fax: (303) 458-0002
E-Mail: nhcaoffice@hearingconservation.org
Website: hearingconservation.org
Members: 450 companies and individuals
Staff: 5
Annual Budget: $250-500,000

Personnel:

Executive Director: Erin Erickson
    E-Mail: nhcaoffice@hearingconservation.org
Director, Membership Services: Lynnette Bardolf PhD
    E-Mail: lynnette.bardolf@us.army.mil
Director, Marketing and Public Relations: Renee Bessette
    E-Mail: renee.bessette@gmail.com
Director, Education: Kristen Casto AuD, PhD
    E-Mail: kristen.casto@us.army.mil
Director, Communications: Laura Kauth CCC-A, MA
    E-Mail: lstkauth@gmail.com

Historical Note:
Established and incorporated in Colorado. NHCA's mission is to prevent hearing loss due to noise and other environmental factors in all sectors of society. Membership: $190 (Individual/Associate); $450 (Professional Service Provider Organization); $985 (Commercial).

Meetings/Conferences: Annual
Conference Chair: Erin Erickson
2013 - St. Petersburg, FL (Hilton St. Petersburg Bayfront)/Feb. 21 - 23
2014 - Las Vegas, NV (JW Marriott Las Vegas Spa and Resort)/March 13 - 15
2015 - New Orleans, LA (Astor Crowne Plaza Hotel)/Feb. 19 - 21

Publications:
Membership Directory; on-line; adv.
Spectrum; on-line; adv.

National Hemophilia Foundation *(1948)*
116 W. 32nd St.
11th Floor
New York, NY 10001
Tel: (212) 328-3700 *Fax:* (212) 328-3777
TollFree: (800) 424-2634
E-Mail: handi@hemophilia.org
Website: hemophilia.org
Members: 3000 individuals
Staff: 40
Annual Budget: $10-25,000,000
Tax: 501(c)(3)

Personnel:
Chief Executive Officer: Val Bias
Director, Human Resources and Organization Development: Marie Cramer
    E-Mail: mcramer@hemophilia.org
Vice President, Research and Medical Information: Neil Frick MS
    E-Mail: nfrick@hemophilia.org
Vice President, Marketing and Communications: John Indence
    E-Mail: jindence@hemophilia.org
Vice President, Development: Mary Ann Ludwig
    E-Mail: mludwig@hemophilia.org
Senior Vice President , Finance and Administrative Services: Jordana Zeger

Historical Note:
NHF's mission is to find the cures for inherited bleeding disorders.Membership: $1,000-2,500/year (Student).

Meetings/Conferences: Annual

Publications:
HemAware Jr; bi-monthly
Membership Directory; on-line
NHF eNotes; monthly

National HEP-CAMP Association
Pennsylvania State University
319 Grange Building
University Park, PA 16802
Tel: (814) 863-9440
Website: hepcamp.org
Staff: 3
Annual Budget: $100-250,000

Personnel:
President: Scott Willison
    E-Mail: swillis@boisestate.edu
Treasurer: Susy Sarmiento
    E-Mail: susy@unm.edu

Historical Note:
Represents interests of High School Equivalence Programs (HEP) and College Assistant Migrant Programs (CAMP).HEP-CAMP's mission is to serve, educate, and empower farm workers.

National Hereford Hog Record Association *(1934)*
826 140th St.
Aledo, IL 61231
Tel: (309) 299-5122

Website: nationalherefordhogassociation.com
Members: 150 individuals
Staff: 2
Annual Budget: Under $10,000
Tax: 501(c)(5)

Personnel:
Secretary and Contact, Sales and Show: Becky Hyett

Historical Note:
Organized to promote Hereford Hogs and so Hereford Hog breeders could register and transfer Hereford hogs. Established and incorporated in Iowa. Maintains registry of pedigrees. Membership: $10 (Individual-Lifetime); $100 (Organization/Company- Lifetime).

Meetings/Conferences:
Conference Chair: Becky Hyett
Number of non-conference events/year: 1

Publications:
Breeder's Directory; on-line

Membership List Available to Non-members

National High School Athletic Coaches Association *(1965)*
P.O. Box 3181
Clearwater, FL 33767
Tel: (407) 592-9212 *Fax:* (507) 206-3902
Website: nhsaca.org
Members: 55000 individuals
Staff: 4
Annual Budget: $50-100,000

Personnel:
Executive Director: Donald R. Prokes
Contact, Sponsorship and Advertising: Ron Bowden
    E-Mail: ron@bowdenproductions.com

Historical Note:
NHSACA represents the interests of those in the high school coaching profession and sponsors programs of recognition (High School Coach of the Year Awards for 16 different sports), education and competition and is involved in varied activities in the commercial, educational, governmental and communications fields. Members are high school coaches and athletic directors. Membership: $25/year (Individual).

Meetings/Conferences: Annual

Publications:
NHSACA Newsletter; monthly

National Hispanic Corporate Council *(1985)*
1050 Connecticut Ave. NW
Tenth Floor
Washington, DC 20036
Tel: (202) 772-1100 *Fax:* (202) 772-3101
TollFree: (800) 792-9639
Website: nhcchq.org
Members: 1500 companies
Staff: 4
Annual Budget: $500-1,000,000
Tax: 501(c)(3)

Personnel:
President and Chief Executive Officer: Pat Martinez
    E-Mail: pmartinez@nhcchq.org
Vice President and Director, Operations: Zuleika Cuevas
    E-Mail: zcuevas@nhcchq.org
Senior Manager, Communications: Claudia L. Torres
    E-Mail: ctorres@nhcc-hq.org

Historical Note:
NHCC seeks to maximize the Hispanic market opportunity among Fortune 1000 corporations. Members are Fortune 1000 firms, with interest in the fastest growing market segment within the United States. Membership: $7,500 (Company); $750 (Additional Representatives).

Meetings/Conferences: Annual

Publications:
Membership Directory; on-line
NHCC Newsletter; irregular

National Hispanic Medical Association *(1994)*
1920 L St.
Suite 725
Washington, DC 20036
Tel: (202) 628-5895 *Fax:* (202) 628-5898
E-Mail: nhma@nhmamd.org
Website: nhmamd.org
Members: 45000 licensed Hispanic physicians in U.S.
Staff: 7
Annual Budget: $2-5,000,000
Tax: 501(c)(6)

Personnel:
President and Chief Executive Officer: Elena V. Rios MD, MSPH
    E-Mail: erios@nhmamd.org
Program and Membership Officer: Sara Classen
    E-Mail: sclassen@nhmamd.org
Director, Program: Astrid Jimenez
    E-Mail: ajimenez@nhmamd.org

Historical Note:
Mission is to improve the health of Hispanics and other underserved populations. NHMA provides policymakers and health care providers with expert information and support in strengthening health service delivery to Hispanic communities across the nation. Members are physicians, residents, medical students and associates. Membership: Free (Basic Member); $10 (Medical Student); $50 (Resident); $150 (Associate); $100 (Council of Medical Society Member); $200 (Physician); $20 (Health Professional Student Member).

Meetings/Conferences: Annual
2013 - Washington, DC (Marriott Wardman Park Hotel)/April 25 - 28
Number of non-conference events/year: 2

Publications:
NHMA NET Newsletter; monthly

National Hockey League *(1917)*
1185 Avenue of the Americas
15th Floor
New York, NY 10036
Tel: (212) 789-2000 *Fax:* (212) 789-2020
E-Mail: nhlrbk@reebok.com
Website: nhl.com
Members: 30 teams
Staff: 160
Annual Budget: $50-100,000,000
Tax: 501(c)(6)

Personnel:
Commissioner: Gary B. Bettman
Senior Vice President, Communications: Bernadette Mansur

Historical Note:
NHL is a professional ice hockey league based in Canada and the United States. NHL presents several trophies each year such as Stanley Cup, Presidents' Trophy and many more. National Hockey League games are aired nationally by CBC, TSN etc. Regional games are broadcast by a number of networks including Rogers Sportsnet (RSN). NHL is divided into two fifteen-team conferences, each of which consists of three five-team divisions.

Publications:
Membership Directory; on-line

National Home Furnishings Association *(1920)*
3910 Tinsley Dr.
Suite 101
High Point, NC 27265-3610
Tel: (336) 886-6100 *Fax:* (336) 801-6102
TollFree: (800) 888-9590
E-Mail: info@nhfa.org
Website: nhfa.org
Members: 2,000 corporate entities
Staff: 35
Annual Budget: $1-2,000,000

Personnel:
Executive Vice President: Steve DeHaan
    E-Mail: sdehaan@nhfa.org
Senior Director, Membership and Member Services: Karin Mayfield CMP
    E-Mail: kmayfield@nhfa.org
Senior Director, Accounting and Operations: Trishonda Patrick
    E-Mail: tpatrick@nhfa.org
Editor-in-Chief: Mary Wynn Ryan
    E-Mail: wynnryan@rcn.com
Senior Director, Marketing and Communications: Tim Timmons
    E-Mail: ttimmons@nhfa.org

Historical Note:
Formerly (1970) National Retail Furniture Association. NHFA's mission is to provide its members with the information, education, products and services they need to remain successful. Membership: $495 -1,795 (Retailer); $1,000-20,000 (Industry Partner).

Meetings/Conferences: Annual
Conference Chair: Tim Timmons
2013 - New Orleans, LA/June 2 - 4

Publications:

Currents; monthly
Home Furnishings Retailer; monthly; adv.
Member Directory; on-line

National Home Infusion Association *(1991)*
100 Daingerfield Rd.
Alexandria, VA 22314
Tel: (703) 549-3740 *Fax:* (703) 683-1484
Website: nhia.org
Staff: 10
Annual Budget: $2-5,000,000
Tax: 501(c)(6)

Personnel:
President and Chief Executive Officer: Russell Bodoff
    E-Mail: russell.bodoff@nhia.org
Editor in Chief: Jeannie Counce
    E-Mail: jeanniecounce@earthlink.net
Director, Corporate Marketing: David Gershman
    E-Mail: david.gershman@nhia.org
Vice President, Operations and Chief Operating Officer:
    Steve Jurich
    E-Mail: steve.jurich@nhia.org
Vice President Legislative Affairs: John R. Magnuson
    E-Mail: john.magnuson@nhia.org
Associate Director, Education and Research: Kristen
    Santaromita
    E-Mail: kristen.santaromita@nhia.org
Associate Director, Design, Production and Website
    Activities: Jason Shelton
    E-Mail: jason.shelton@nhia.org
Manager, Office Services: Jennifer Waugh
    E-Mail: jennifer.waugh@nhia.org
Administrative Assistant: Tamiqua Wood
    E-Mail: tamiqua.wood@nhia.org

Historical Note:
*Trade association that represents and advances the interests
of organizations and individuals that provide infusion
and specialized pharmacy products and services to the
entire spectrum of home-based patients. Membership:
$600-40,000 (Provider member, based on Net Sales);
$600 (Individual Consulting Practice Affiliate); $1,000
(Associate); $500 (Individual Affiliate); $2,500-10,000
(Business Firm Affiliate - Gold/Silver); $200 (Academic);
$50 (Student).*

Meetings/Conferences: Annual
2013 - Dallas, TX (Hilton Anatole)/April 8 - 11

Publications:
Exhibitor Newsletter; on-line
Infusion; bi-monthly; adv.

Membership List Available to Non-members

National Home Performance Council, Inc. *(2007)*
1620 Eye St. NW
Suite 501
Washington, DC 20006
Tel: (202) 463-2005
E-Mail: info@nhpci.org
Website: nhpci.org
Staff: 2
Annual Budget: $250-500,000

Personnel:
Executive Director: Kara Saul Rinaldi
    E-Mail: kara.saul-rinaldi@nhpci.org
Managing Director: Robin LeBaron
    E-Mail: robin.lebaron@nhpci.org

Historical Note:
*The mission of the National Home Performance Council
is to encourage improved home energy performance using
a whole-house approach by facilitating coordination and
alignment between public and private sector stakeholders;
developing standardized practices; and conducting research,
analysis and education.*

Publications:
NHPC Newsletter; quarterly

National Honey Packers and Dealers Association
(1952)
3301 Route 66
Suite 205, Building C
Neptune, NJ 07753
Tel: (732) 922-3008 *Fax:* (732) 922-3590
E-Mail: info@nhpda.org
Website: nhpda.org
Members: 35 companies
Staff: 5
Annual Budget: $50-100,000

Personnel:

Executive Vice President: Bob Bauer
Administrative Assistant: Greg Eckhardt

Historical Note:
*NHPDA, a section of the Association of Food Industries
(see separate listing), is a trade association for packers and
dealers of honey. NHPDA is committed to industry quality
and welfare of packers and importers of honey.*

National Horsemen's Benevolent and Protective Association *(1940)*
870 Corporate Dr.
Suite 300
Lexington, KY 40503-5419
Tel: (859) 259-0451 *Fax:* (859) 259-0452
TollFree: (866) 245-1711
E-Mail: racing@hbpa.org
Website: hbpa.org
Members: 35000 individuals
Staff: 4
Annual Budget: $2-5,000,000

Personnel:
Chief Executive Officer: Philip Hanrahan
    E-Mail: phanrahan@hbpa.org
Director, Operations: Laura Plato
    E-Mail: lplato@hbpa.org
Contact, Administration and Bookkeeping: Robert Scott
    E-Mail: rscott@hbpa.org

Historical Note:
*HBPA's mission is to provide insurance services to its
members, disseminate vital information on critical issues
to horsemen and to foster the exchange of ideas and
information, promote the development of threshold levels for
therapeutic medication particularly and generally promote
needed reform in medication rules and research, provide a
national voice for horsemen on matters of national policy
and of national interest.*

Meetings/Conferences:
2013 - Clearwater, FL (Sheraton Sand Key Resort)/Feb.
    20 - 24

Publications:
Horsemen's Journal; adv.

National Horsemen's Association, Inc.
111 W. St.
Gouldbusk, TX 54875
Staff: 1

Personnel:
President: Maria Cardona

Historical Note:
Promote and support various equine affiliated organizations

National Hospice & Palliative Care Organization
(1978)
1731 King St.
Suite 100
Alexandria, VA 22314
Tel: (703) 837-1500 *Fax:* (703) 837-1233
TollFree: (800) 658-8898
E-Mail: nhpco_info@nhpco.org
Website: nhpco.org
Members:
2700 provider members
25000 combinations
Staff: 68
Annual Budget: $10-25,000,000
Tax: 501(c)(3)

Personnel:
President and Chief Executive Officer: Donald J.
    Schumacher PsyD
    E-Mail: pbouchard@nhpco.org
Vice President, Professional Development: Barbara
    Bouton MA
Editor: Sue Canuteson MA
Manager, Corporate Relations and Exhibits: David Cherry
    CEM
Director, Membership Relations and Administration: Andy
    Duncan
Associate Director, Information Technology: Clinton
    Garrison
*Senior Vice President, Office of Administration and Chief
    Financial Officer:* Cathy Gibney CPA
Senior Vice President, Health Policy: Jonathan Keyserling
    JD
    E-Mail: jkeyserling@nhpco.org
Vice President, Communications: Jon Radulovic MA
Manager, Meetings: Sharon Shackelford-Campbell CMP

Associate Director, Human Resources: Jeff Williamson
    PHR

Historical Note:
*Formerly National Hospice Organization. Assumed current
name in 2000. NHPCO's mission is to lead and mobilize
social change for improved care at the end of life. Members
are hospice and palliative care programs and professionals.
Membership: $1000 (Provider); $500 (Palliative Care
Provider).*

Meetings/Conferences: Annual
Conference Chair: Sharon Shackelford-Campbell CMP
2013 - Ft. Washington, MD (Gaylord National Resort
    and Convention Center-National Harbor)/April 25 -
    27
2013 - Kansas City, MO (Sheraton Kansas City Hotel at
    Crown Center)/Sept. 26 - 28
2014 - Ft. Washington, MD (Gaylord National Resort
    and Convention Center-National Harbor)/March 27
    - 29
2014 - Nashville, TN (Gaylord Opryland Resort and
    Convention Center)/Oct. 27 - 29
2015 - Ft. Washington, MD (Gaylord National Resort
    and Convention Center-National Harbor)/April 30 -
    May 2
2016 - Ft. Washington, MD (Gaylord National Resort
    and Convention Center-National Harbor)/April 21 -
    23
2016 - Kissimmee, FL (Gaylord Palms Resort and
    Convention Center-Kissimmee)/Nov. 3 - 5
2017 - Ft. Washington, MD (Gaylord National Resort
    and Convention Center-National Harbor)/April 27 -
    30
Number of non-conference events/year: 1

Publications:
Hospice and Palliative Care Buyer's Guide; annually
Journal of Pain and Symptom Management; monthly
Membership Directory; on-line
NewsBriefs; weekly
NewsLine; monthly; adv.

Membership List Available to Non-members

National Housing and Rehabilitation Association
(1971)
1400 16th St. NW
Suite 420
Washington, DC 20036-2244
Tel: (202) 939-1750 *Fax:* (202) 265-4435
E-Mail: info@housingonline.com
Website: housingonline.com
Members: 350 individuals
Staff: 10
Annual Budget: $1-2,000,000
Tax: 501(c)(6)

Personnel:
Executive Director and Executive Vice President: Thom
    Amdur
    E-Mail: tamdur@dworbell.com
President and Chief Executive Officer: Peter H. Bell
    E-Mail: pbell@dworbell.org
Manager, Financial Operations: Violet Arthur
    E-Mail: varthur@dworbell.com
Vice President, Communications: Marty Bell
    E-Mail: mbell@dworbell.com
Associate, Education, Membership and Research: Anne
    Tyler Feldmann
    E-Mail: afeldmann@dworbell.com
Operations Specialist: Jeri Greaves
    E-Mail: jgreaves@dworbell.com
Manager, Membership Services and Subscriptions: Linda
    Latimore
    E-Mail: llatimore@housingonline.com
General Counsel: Ken Lore
Director, Sales and Marketing: Scott Oser
    E-Mail: soser@dworbell.com
Editor: Glenn Petherick
    E-Mail: gpetherick@dworbell.com

Historical Note:
*Formerly (1985) National Housing Rehabilitation
Association. NH&RA promotes partnerships among
professionals and involved in affordable housing, historic
rehabilitation and new markets tax credit development.
Members include organizations and individuals in
construction, finance, property management and real estate
development. Membership: $6,000-25,000 (Sustaining)
$1,250(NCHMA Practitioner); $1900 (Full); $1400
(Associate); $450 (Public); $2,350 (Board).*

Meetings/Conferences:

2013 - Miami Beach, FL (The Loews Miami Beach Hotel)/March 6 - 9
2013 - Washington, DC (Hyatt Regency Hotel)/April 2 - 3
Number of non-conference events/year: 1

Publications:
Housing Online Weekly; weekly; adv.
Tax Credit Advisor; monthly; adv.

Membership List Available to Non-members

National Housing Conference (1931)
1900 M St. NW
Suite 200
Washington, DC 20036
Tel: (202) 466-2121 *Fax:* (202) 466-2122
E-Mail: nhc@nhc.org
Website: nhc.org
Members: 800 individuals and organizations
Staff: 19
Annual Budget: $2-5,000,000
Tax: 501(c)(3)

Personnel:
President and Chief Executive Officer: Chris Estes
Vice President, Marketing and Communications: Cynthia Dodd Adcock
    E-Mail: cadcock@nhc.org
Director, Operations, Meetings and Events: Thea Beckering
    E-Mail: tbeckering@nhc.org
Director, Administration: Mary Cousins
    E-Mail: mcousins@nhc.org
Vice President, Policy and Advocacy: Ethan Handelman
    E-Mail: ehandelman@nhc.org
Director, Member Services and Resource Development: Leah Logan
    E-Mail: llogan@nhc.org

Historical Note:
NHC's mission is to ensure safe, decent and affordable housing for all in America. Membership: $25-50,000/year.

Meetings/Conferences:
Conference Chair: Thea Beckering

Membership List Available to Non-members

National Human Resources Association (1951)
PO Box 5455
Manchester, NH 03108-5455
Tel: (603) 891-5760 *Fax:* (603) 718-3124
TollFree: (866) 523-4417
E-Mail: info@humanresources.org
Website: humanresources.org
Members: 2000 individuals
Staff: 20
Annual Budget: $100-250,000

Personnel:
Association Manager: Sue Murphy

Historical Note:
Formerly (1992) International Association for Personnel Women. NHRA is a network of local affiliates focused on advancing the development of human resource professionals. Members are HR practitioners. Membership: $50-130 (Members-at-Large); $100-250 (Regular); $50 (Student); $225-350 (Corporate).

Meetings/Conferences:
Number of non-conference events/year: 8

Publications:
Membership Directory; on-line

Membership List Available to Non-members

National Human Services Assembly (2005)
1101 14th St. NW
Suite 600
Washington, DC 20004
Tel: (202) 347-2080 *Fax:* (202) 393-4517
Website: nassembly.org
Members: 70 organizations
Staff: 9
Annual Budget: $1-2,000,000
Tax: 501(c)(3)

Personnel:
President and Chief Executive Officer: Irv Katz
    E-Mail: irv@nassembly.org
Office Manager: Willa Jackson
    E-Mail: wjackson@nassembly.org
Coordinator, Membership and Communications: Bridget McCabe
    E-Mail: bmccabe@nassembly.org

Policy Director: Hayling Price
    E-Mail: hprice@nassembly.org

Historical Note:
Established as the National Social Work Council, it became the National Social Welfare Assembly in 1945, the National Assembly for Social Policy and Development in 1967, National Assembly of Health and Human Services Organizations in 1974, and assumed its present name in 2005. NHSA's mission is to strengthen health and human services in the United States through the active involvement and leadership of its members. Membership: dues are calculated by each member organization, based on revenue for the most recent fiscal year.

Meetings/Conferences: Annual

Publications:
Human Services Newsbytes; semi-monthly

Membership List Available to Non-members

National Humanities Alliance (1981)
21 Dupont Cir. NW
Suite 800
Washington, DC 20036
Tel: (202) 296-4994 *Fax:* (202) 872-0884
Website: nhalliance.org
Members: 90 associations
Staff: 4
Annual Budget: $250-500,000
Tax: 501(c)(4)

Personnel:
Interim Executive Director: Duane Webster
Grassroots Manager: Robert Madrid
Assistant Director, Communications and Membership Services: Erin Smith Mosley
    E-Mail: esmith@nhalliance.org

Historical Note:
NHA is an advocacy coalition dedicated to the advancement of humanities education, research, preservation, and public programs. Membership: $1000 (Active/Associate); $1000-2500 (Institutional).

Meetings/Conferences: Annual
2013 - Washington, DC (The George Washington University campus and Capitol Hill.)/March 18 - 19

Membership List Available to Non-members

National Hydropower Association (1983)
25 Massachussetts Ave. NW
Suite 450
Washington, DC 20001
Tel: (202) 682-1700 *Fax:* (202) 682-9478
E-Mail: help@hydro.org
Website: hydro.org
Members: 180 organizations
Staff: 6
Annual Budget: $2-5,000,000

Personnel:
Executive Director: Linda Church Ciocci
    E-Mail: linda@hydro.org
Director, Government Affairs: Jeffrey A. Leahey
    E-Mail: jeff@hydro.org
Contact, Membership Services: Diane C. Lear
    E-Mail: diane@hydro.org
Assistant Manager, Strategic Communications: Matthew Nocella
Executive Assistant and Contact, Meetings: Kathryn Steele
    E-Mail: kathryn@hydro.org

Historical Note:
NHA dedicated exclusively to advance the interests of the hydropower industry. It seeks to secure hydropower's place as a climate-friendly, renewable and reliable energy source that serves national environmental and energy policy objectives. Membership: $1,725 (Individual); $5,365-14,500 (Service/Industry); $1,775-14,935 (Equipment and Services Providers); $9,270 (Canadian Generators).

Meetings/Conferences: Annual
Conference Chair: Kathryn Steele
2013 - Washington, DC (Capitol Hilton)/April 22 - 24
Number of non-conference events/year: 1

Publications:
NHA Newsletter; bi-weekly

National Ice Cream Mix Association (1945)
2101 Wilson Blvd.
Suite 400
Arlington, VA 22201
Tel: (703) 243-6111 *Fax:* (703) 841-9328

E-Mail: nicma@nmpf.org
Website: icecreammix.org
Members: 115 companies
Staff: 3
Annual Budget: $50-100,000

Personnel:
Executive Director: Tom Balmer
Vice President, Scientific and Regulatory Affairs: Jamie Jonker
Program Administrator and Meeting Manager: Gail Mobley

Historical Note:
Provides technical and business support to ice cream mix manufacturers. Administrative support provided by the National Milk Producers Federation. Members are companies across the United States who share a common interest in the soft serve mix industry.

Meetings/Conferences: Annual
Conference Chair: Gail Mobley
2013 - Ft. Lauderdale, FL (Lago Mar Resort and Club)/ Jan. 20 - 23

National Ice Cream Retailers Association (1933)
1028 W. Devon Ave.
Elk Grove Village, IL 60007
Tel: (847) 301-7500 *Fax:* (847) 301-8402
TollFree: (866) 303-6960
E-Mail: info@nicra.org
Website: nicra.org
Members: 500 companies
Staff: 2
Annual Budget: $250-500,000

Personnel:
Executive Director: Lynda Utterback

Historical Note:
Formerly (1960) the National Association of Retail Ice Cream Manufacturers, (1989) National Ice Cream Retailers Association and (2003) National Ice Cream and Yogurt Retailers Association. NICRA's mission is to help, support, and educate the frozen dessert industry. Membership: $225-450 (Company); $275 (Supplier).

Meetings/Conferences: Annual
Conference Chair: Lynda Utterback
2013 - St. Louis, MO (Hilton St. Louis Frontenac)/Nov. 5 - 7

Publications:
Membership Directory; on-line
NICRA Bulletin; monthly; adv.
NICRA Newsletter; monthly
The National Dipper Magazine; bi-monthly

National Immigration Project of the National Lawyers Guild (1970)
14 Beacon St.,
Suite 602
Boston, MA 02108
Tel: (617) 227-9727 *Fax:* (617) 227-5495
Website: nationalimmigrationproject.org
Staff: 5
Annual Budget: $500-1,000,000

Personnel:
Executive Director: Dan Kesselbrenner
    E-Mail: dan@nationalimmigrationproject.org
Director, Development and Communications: Pamela Goldstein
    E-Mail: pamela@nationalimmigrationproject.org
Director, Legal Advocacy: Ellen Kemp
    E-Mail: ellen@nationalimmigrationproject.org
Assistant, Administration: Ana Manigat
    E-Mail: ana@nationalimmigrationproject.org
Office Manager: Rosa Thomas
    E-Mail: rosa@nationalimmigrationproject.org

Historical Note:
The National Immigration Project is a national non-profit that provides legal and technical support to immigrant communities, legal practitioners, and all advocates seeking to advance the rights of noncitizens. The National Immigration Project's mission is to protect the rights of the most disenfranchised and vulnerable populations, including women who are victims of domestic violence, people with HIV/AIDS, children, and noncitizen criminal offenders.

Publications:
Kurzban's Immigration Law Sourcebook

National Independent Automobile Dealers Association (1946)
2521 Brown Blvd.

Arlington, TX 76006
Tel: (817) 640-3838 *Fax:* (817) 649-5866
TollFree: (800) 682-3837
Website: niada.com
Members: 20000 Professional
Staff: 18
Annual Budget: $1-2,000,000
Tax: 501(c)(6)

Personnel:
President, Chief Executive Officer and Publisher: Michael R. Linn CPP
    E-Mail: mike@niada.com
Director, Events: Ginger Barrientez CMP
    E-Mail: ginger@niada.com
Director, Education: Georgia Brown
    E-Mail: georgia@niada.com
Federal Lobbyist: Sante J. Esposito
Director, Communications and Editor: Andy Friedlander
    E-Mail: andy@niada.com
Manager, Media Sales: Troy Graff
    E-Mail: troy@niada.com
Chief Operations Officer: Steve Jordan
Executive Assistant and Administrative Director: Angela Ledbetter
    E-Mail: angela@niada.com
Vice President, Membership Services: Scott Lilja
    E-Mail: scott@niada.com
Legislative Counsel: Shaun Petersen
Director, Information Technology and Membership Services: Cindy Sirkel
    E-Mail: cindy@niada.com

Historical Note:
NIADA's mission is to Promote, educate and advance the independent motor vehicle dealer. Membership: $199/year.

Continuing Education:
Certification Designation/s: CMD

Meetings/Conferences: Annual
Conference Chair: Ginger Barrientez CMP
2013 - Las Vegas, NV (Caesars Palace Las Vegas Hotel and Casino)/June 23 - 27
2014 - Las Vegas, NV (Caesars Palace Las Vegas Hotel and Casino)/June 22 - 26
Number of non-conference events/year: 7

Publications:
Membership Directory; on-line
State Magazines; adv.
Used Car Dealer Magazine; monthly; adv.

National Independent Concessionaires Association (1993)
1043 E. Brandon Blvd.
Brandon, FL 33511
Tel: (813) 438-8926 *Fax:* (813) 438-8928
E-Mail: nica@nicainc.org
Website: nicainc.org
Members: 1200 members
Staff: 6
Annual Budget: $250-500,000

Personnel:
Executive Director: Barbara Hensinger
    E-Mail: barb@nicainc.org
Director, Graphics and Marketing: Kaitlyn Loos
    E-Mail: graphics@nicainc.org
Coordinator, Membership Services: Jill Omel
    E-Mail: nica@nicainc.org

Historical Note:
NICA's mission is dedicated to strengthening relationships with the Fair, Festival and Special Events Industries through effective communication, benefits, leadership and solutions.Membership: $50-125 (Independent Concessionaire); $40-125 (Associate).

Continuing Education:
Certification Designation/s: CCE

Meetings/Conferences: Annual
2013 - Tampa, FL (USF Embassy Suites)/Feb. 4 - 6

Publications:
Membership Directory; on-line
NICA News; monthly

National Independent Fire Alarm Distributors
1001 Office Park Rd.
Suite 105
Des Moines, IA 50265
Tel: (515) 440-6057 *Fax:* (515) 440-6055
E-Mail: apmsthomas@aol.com
Website: nifad.com

Staff: 2
Annual Budget: $10-25,000

Personnel:
Executive Director: Beverly V. Thomas

Historical Note:
NIFAD provides marketing, safety, promotional and other materials to its members. Membership: $250 (Distributor); $350 (Affiliate/Supplier).

Meetings/Conferences: Annual
Number of non-conference events/year: 1

Publications:
Newsletter

Membership List Available to Non-members

National Independent Flag Dealers Association
2685 Land Park Dr.
Pacific Coast Flag
Sacramento, CA 95818
Fax: (916) 444-8555
TollFree: (800) 453-3524
E-Mail: info@nifda.org
Website: nifda.net
Members: 120 flag dealers and manufacturers
Staff: 2
Annual Budget: $50-100,000

Personnel:
President: James Giraudo
    E-Mail: jgiraudo@msn.com

Historical Note:
NIFDA is an organization of flag and banner retailers and manufacturers located throughout the United States. Membership: $425/year.

Meetings/Conferences: Annual

National Independent Laboratory Association
906 Olive St.
Suite 1200
St. Louis, MO 63101
Tel: (314) 241-1445 *Fax:* (314) 241-1449
Website: aab.org/aab/NILA.asp
Staff: 1

Personnel:
Administrator: Mark S. Birenbaum PhD

Historical Note:
NILA's mission is to focus on business/management issues facing laboratories, such as marketing/sales, contracting with managed care companies, finding and keeping good employees, financial management, expanding test menus, managing growth, competing with big, publicly traded laboratories, and acting on legislative and regulatory issues facing the laboratory industry. Membership: $1,000 (a laboratory to two director/owner members).

Meetings/Conferences: Semi-Annual

National Independent Living Association (1980)
4203 Southpoint Blvd.
Jacksonville, FL 32216
Tel: (904) 296-1038 *Fax:* (904) 296-1953
E-Mail: info@nilausa.org
Website: nilausa.org
Members: 200 individuals
Staff: 4
Annual Budget: Under $10,000

Personnel:
Executive Director: Trevor Quinlan
President and Chief Executive Officer: James Clark
    E-Mail: jclark@danielkids.org
Treasurer: Tricia Phillips
    E-Mail: tricia.l.phillips@dss.mo.gov
Conference Coordinator: Stephanie Waugerman
    E-Mail: swaugerman@danielkids.org

Historical Note:
NILA's mission is to champion youth and young adults ensuring their successful transition into adulthood and self-sufficiency. Members are individuals and organizations providing services to youth and adolescents in child welfare programs. Membership is free.

Meetings/Conferences: Annual
Conference Chair: Stephanie Waugerman
Number of non-conference events/year: 1

Publications:
NILA Newsletter

National Independent Nursery Furniture Retailers Association (1973)
8312 Jefferson Hwy.

Suite Two
Baton Rouge, LA 70809
Tel: (225) 927-0719 *Fax:* (225) 927-8611
E-Mail: info@ninfra.com
Website: ninfra.com
Members: 100 stores
Staff: 2
Annual Budget: $100-250,000

Personnel:
Executive Director: Rafael De Castro
    E-Mail: rafael@ninfra.com

Historical Note:
NINFRA's mission is to provide service to pick the products, handle special orders, and provide with the customer service.

Publications:
Membership Directory; on-line
NINFRA Newsletter; monthly; adv.

National Independent Private Schools Association (1983)
10134 SW, 78th Court
Miami, FL 33156
Tel: (305) 630-2557 *Fax:* (305) 275-8881
Website: nipsa.org
Members: 20 schools
Staff: 1
Annual Budget: $100-250,000
Tax: 501(c)(6)

Personnel:
Executive Director: James F.M. E. Williams
    E-Mail: jaws1139@aol.com

Historical Note:
NIPSA's mission is to advocate for the interests of proprietary academic schools, and the students and communities they serve. Membership: $700 (Regular Academic Schools); $1000 (Online and Virtual Schools/ Candidate and Certified Schools).

Meetings/Conferences:
Number of non-conference events/year: 1

Publications:
NIPSA Newsletter

National Indian Education Association (1969)
110 Maryland Ave. NE
Suite 104
Washington, DC 20002-5626
Tel: (202) 544-7290 *Fax:* (202) 544-7293
E-Mail: niea@niea.org
Website: niea.org
Members: 3000 individuals
Staff: 6
Annual Budget: $2-5,000,000
Tax: 501(c)(3)

Personnel:
Executive Director: Ahniwake Rose
Director, Communications: RiShawn Biddle
    E-Mail: rbiddle@niea.org
Interim Office Manager: Nancy Dewire
    E-Mail: ndewire@niea.org
Manager, Conventions: Wanda Johnson
    E-Mail: wjohnson@niea.org
Administrative Assistant: Ashley Martin
    E-Mail: niea@niea.org

Historical Note:
NIEA seeks to support traditional native cultures and values, to enable native learners to become contributing members of their communities and to improve educational opportunities and resources for American Indians, Alaska Natives, and Native Hawaiians throughout the United States. Membership: $50 (General/Associate/ International); $25 (Student/Elder).

Meetings/Conferences: Annual
Conference Chair: Wanda Johnson
2013 - Rapid City, SD/Oct. 29 - Nov. 3
2014 - Anchorage, AK/Oct. 16 - 19

Publications:
NIEA NEWS Magazine; quarterly; adv.

National Indian Gaming Association (1985)
224 Second St. SE
Washington, DC 20003-1943
Tel: (202) 546-7711 *Fax:* (202) 546-1755
TollFree: (800) 286-6442
E-Mail: info@indiangaming.org
Website: indiangaming.org
Members: 184 Indian Nations

Staff: 14
Annual Budget: $5-10,000,000
Tax: 501(c)(6)

Personnel:
Chairman: Ernest L. Stevens Jr.
   E-Mail: estevens@indiangaming.org
Executive Director: Jason Giles
   E-Mail: jgiles@indiangaming.org
Legislative Director: Danielle Her Many Horses
   E-Mail: dhermanyhorses@indiangaming.org
Director, Trade Shows: Dana Melton
   E-Mail: dmelton@indiangaming.org
Business Manager: Angelica Molina
   E-Mail: amolina@indiangaming.org
Senior Advisor: Mark Van Norman
   E-Mail: mvannorman@indiangaming.org
Director, Media and Communications: Michael
   Woestehoff
   E-Mail: mwoestehoff@indiangaming.org

Historical Note:
NIGA's mission is to advance the lives of Indian peoples economically, socially and politically. It operates as a clearinghouse and educational, legislative and public policy resource for tribes, policymakers and the public on Indian gaming issues and tribal community development. Membership: $800-25,000/year.

Meetings/Conferences: Annual
Conference Chair: Dana Melton
2013 - Phoenix, AZ (Phoenix Convention Center)/
   March 24 - 27/over 100 exhibitors
Number of non-conference events/year: 1

Publications:
NIGA Newsletter; monthly

Membership List Available to Non-members

National Indian Head Start Directors Association
(1965)
919 Hwy. 395.,South
Gardnerville, NV 89410
Tel: (775) 265-1074 *Fax:* (775) 265-5568
Website: nihsda.org
Staff: 2
Annual Budget: $100-250,000
Tax: 501(c)(3)

Personnel:
President: Gil Gonzales
   E-Mail: ggonzales@washoetribe.us

Historical Note:
NIHSDA is a professional organization, promotes and supports high quality comprehensive early childhood development and education services for native Americans in the United States and Canada. Membership: $100/year (Associate); $150-850/year (Director).

Publications:
AIANPB Head Start Directory

National Indian Health Board
926 Pennsylvania Ave. SE
Washington, DC 20003
Tel: (202) 507-4070 *Fax:* (202) 507-4071
Website: nihb.org
Staff: 5
Annual Budget: $2-5,000,000
Tax: 501(c)(3)

Personnel:
Executive Director and Media Contact: Stacy A. Bohlen
   E-Mail: sbohlen@nihb.org
Legislative Director: Jennifer Cooper
   E-Mail: jcooper@nihb.org
Executive Assistant and Office Manager: Jacquelynn
   Engebretson
   E-Mail: jengebretson@nihb.org
Director, Health Information Technology: Jason Heinecke
   E-Mail: jheinecke@nihb.org
Director, Operations: Valerie Walker
   E-Mail: vwalker@nihb.org

Historical Note:
The National Indian Health Board (NIHB) represents Tribal governments—both those that operate their own health care delivery systems through contracting and compacting, and those receiving health care directly from the Indian Health Service.

Meetings/Conferences: Annual

Publications:
Health Reporter; quarterly
Meth and Suicide Prevention E-Newsletter; on-line

Washington Report; on-line

National Industrial Council - Employer Association Group *(1907)*
1331 Pennsylvania Ave. NW
Sixth Floor
Washington, DC 20004-1703
Tel: (202) 637-3052 *Fax:* (202) 637-3182
E-Mail: staff@niba.org
Members: 75 organizations
Staff: 3
Annual Budget: $100-250,000

Personnel:
Executive Director: Amy Foscue
   E-Mail: afoscue@nam.org

Historical Note:
A federation of state and local manufacturers' associations. Affiliated with National Association of Manufacturers. Founded as the National Council for Industrial Defense by the National Association of Manufacturers in 1907; became the National Industrial Council in 1918. Known as the National Industrial Council - Industrial Relations Group until 1990. Composed of two groups of employer associations, each with its own executive director: the Employer Association Group and the State Associations Group (see separate entry). Primarily interested in labor relations and employment law issues. Membership: $600-2, 200/year. (association).

Meetings/Conferences:
Number of non-conference events/year: 3

National Industrial Council - State Associations Group *(1907)*
1331 Pennsylvania Ave. NW
Sixth Floor
Washington, DC 20004-1703
Tel: (202) 637-3054 *Fax:* (202) 637-3182
Members: 140 Companies
Staff: 3
Annual Budget: $100-250,000

Personnel:
Executive Director: Barry Buzby
Membership Services Assistant: Catherine Cataldo
   E-Mail: ccataldo@nam.org

Historical Note:
The NIC is composed of two groups of industrial employer associations: NIC State Associations Group and NIC Employer Association Group (see listing). Forty-eight states plus the Commonwealth of Puerto Rico are represented in the SAG. While associations vary in size, structure and primary activities, their goals are to maintain and strengthen the private enterprise system in the U. S., to encourage individual initiative, progress and freedom. SAG represents a business constituency interested in federal and state legislation. Membership: $400-$2, 000/year (Organization).

National Industrial Sand Association *(1936)*
2011 Pennsylvania Ave. NW
Suite 301
Washington, DC 20006
Tel: (202) 457-0200 *Fax:* (202) 457-0287
E-Mail: info@sand.org
Website: sand.org
Members: 22 businesses
Staff: 4
Annual Budget: $250-500,000
Tax: 501(c)(6)

Personnel:
President: Mark G. Ellis
   E-Mail: markellis@sand.org
Vice President, Government Affairs: Christopher K.
   Greissing
   E-Mail: chrisgreissing@sand.org
Financial Assistant: Paige Huggins
Executive Vice President: Darrell K. Smith CIH, PhD
   E-Mail: darrellsmith@sand.org

Historical Note:
NISA provides industrial sand information and services to the public and its members. It provides member companies with programs including silicosis prevention and other safety and health initiatives, government relations, and technical support. Membership: $1500/year (Minimum, based on sales).

The National Industrial Transportation League
(1907)
1700 N. Moore St.
Suite 1900
Arlington, VA 22209-1904

Tel: (703) 524-5011 *Fax:* (703) 524-5017
E-Mail: info@nitl.org
Website: nitl.org
Members: 1500 individuals
Staff: 4
Annual Budget: $1-2,000,000
Tax: 501(c)(6)

Personnel:
President and Chief Executive Officer: Bruce J. Carlton
   E-Mail: carlton@nitl.org
Executive Vice President: Peter J. Gatti
   E-Mail: gatti@nitl.org
*Vice President, Finance, Administration and Membership
   Services:* Ellie Gilanshah
   E-Mail: gilanshah@nitt.org

Historical Note:
Founded as National Industrial Traffic League, assumed its current name in 1982. NITL's mission is to serve shippers in their dealings with various regulatory bodies. Membership: $1,100-9,765 (Members); $1,100-1,525 (Organizations); $400 (Affiliates).

Meetings/Conferences: Annual
2013 - Houston, TX/Nov. 16 - 20
2014 - Ft. Lauderdale, FL/Nov. 15 - 19
2015 - Anaheim, CA/Nov. 14 - 18
2016 - Houston, TX/Nov. 12 - 16
Number of non-conference events/year: 1

Publications:
Member Directory; on-line
STAFF DIRECTORY; on-line
The Notice; weekly; adv.

National Industries for the Blind *(1938)*
1310 Braddock Pl.
Alexandria, VA 22314-1691
Tel: (703) 310-0500
TollFree: (800) 433-2304
E-Mail: info@nib.org
Website: nib.org
Members: 180 agencies, distribution channels
and outlets
Staff: 100
Annual Budget: $50-100,000,000
Tax: 501(c)(3)

Personnel:
President and Chief Executive Officer: Kevin A. Lynch
Vice President and Chief Financial Officer: Steve T. Brice
   E-Mail: sbrice@nib.org
Executive Vice President: Angela Hartley
   E-Mail: ahartley@nib.org
Administrative Specialist and Event Planner: Michelle
   Hobby
   E-Mail: mhobby@aol.com
Vice President, Human Resources: Lynn Millar
   Konetschni
   E-Mail: lkonetschni@nib.org
Vice President, Communications: Laura Reimers
Vice President, Strategic Business Issues: Arun Shimpi

Historical Note:
In 1971, the Act was amended to include the purchase of products and services from industries employing people who are blind or severely disabled. The Act later became known as the Javits-Wagner-O'Day Act. NIB's mission is to enhance the opportunities for economic and personal independence of persons who are blind, primarily through creating, sustaining and improving employment.

Meetings/Conferences: Annual
Conference Chair: Michelle Hobby

Publications:
NIB Newsletter; weekly
Opportunity Magazine; quarterly

National Information Standards Organization
(1939)
3600 Clipper Mill Rd.
Suite 302
Baltimore, MD 21211
Tel: (301) 654-2512 *Fax:* (410) 685-5278
TollFree: (866) 957-1593
E-Mail: nisohq@niso.org
Website: niso.org
Members: 70 organizations
Staff: 6
Annual Budget: $500-1,000,000

Personnel:
Executive Director: Todd Carpenter
   E-Mail: tcarpenter@niso.org

Editor: Cynthia Hodgson
Manager, Business Development and Operations: Victoria R. Kinnear
   E-Mail: nisohq@niso.org
Associate Director, Programs: Nettie Lagace
   E-Mail: nlagace@niso.org
Coordinator, Membership Services: Anna Martin
   E-Mail: amartin@niso.org
Manager, Standards Program: Karen A. Wetzel
   E-Mail: kwetzel@niso.org

Historical Note:
Incorporated as education association in 1983 and assumed its current name in 1984. NISO, an association accredited by the American National Standards Institute (ANSI), fosters the development and maintenance of standards that facilitate the creation, persistent management, and interchange of information. It is designated by ANSU to represent U.S. interests to the International Organization for Standardization's (ISO) Technical Committee 46 on Information and Documentation. Membership: $1,525-11,500 (Voting); $495-995 (Library Standards Alliance).

Meetings/Conferences: Semi-Annual
Conference Chair: Nettie Lagace

Publications:
Membership Directory; on-line
Information Standards Quarterly; quarterly; adv.
Newsline; monthly

Membership List Available to Non-members

National Installment Lenders Association
P.O. Box 65615
Washington, DC 20035
Website: nilaonline.org
Staff: 1
Annual Budget: $500-1,000,000
Tax: 501(c)(6)

Personnel:
Contact, Communications: Phillip Holt
   E-Mail: phillip.holt@nilaonline.org

Historical Note:
The National Installment Lenders Association is a group of lenders committed to ethical lending and advertising practices.

Publications:
Weekly Update; on-line

National Institute for Animal Agriculture (1916)
13570 Meadowgrass Drive
Suite 201
Colorado Springs, CO 80921
Tel: (719) 538-8843 *Fax:* (719) 538-8847
E-Mail: niaa@animalagriculture.org
Website: animalagriculture.org
Members: 300 organizations
Staff: 7
Annual Budget: $250-500,000

Personnel:
Director, Operations: Scharee Atchison
   E-Mail: slatchison@animalagriculture.org
Director, Membership Services: Katie Ambrose
   E-Mail: katie.ambrose@animalagriculture.org
Director, Communications: Teres Lambert
   E-Mail: tlambert@animalagriculture.org
Coordinator, Events: Anne Mann
   E-Mail: annehmann@gmail.com

Historical Note:
Formerly (1976) Livestock Conservation Inc. and (2000) Livestock Conservation Institute. Formed by a merger of the National Livestock Sanitary Committee and the National Livestock Loss Prevention Board (founded in 1916). NIAA provides a forum for diverse segments of the livestock industry to discuss common issues, build consensus, and offer solutions to the challenges facing meat animal production in North America. The organization specializes in producing educational materials and enhancing the industry's communications efforts. Issues addressed by NIAAI include animal health, livestock care and handling, food safety, and uniform livestock identification. Membership: $1,000 (National Associations and Commercial Organizations); $500 (State-Level Associations and Publicly Supported Institutions/Agencies); $250 (Individuals Self-Employed).

Meetings/Conferences: Annual
Conference Chair: Anne Mann
2013 - Madison, WI/Oct. 1 - 5
2014 - Madison, WI/Sept. 30 - Oct. 4
2015 - Madison, WI/Sept. 29 - Oct. 3
2016 - Madison, WI/Oct. 4 - 8

Publications:
Membership Directory; on-line
News & Information for Animal Agriculture; quarterly

National Institute for Farm Safety, Incorporation (1962)
895 Smith Rd.
Charles Town, WV 25414
Tel: (304) 728-0011
E-Mail: ghetzel@citilink.net
Website: isash.org
Members: 200 individuals
Staff: 2
Annual Budget: $100-250,000

Personnel:
President: Marsha Purcell
   E-Mail: marshap@fb.org
Interim Treasurer: Nancy Hetzel

Historical Note:
Currently known as International Society for Agricultural Safety and Health (ISASH). Mission is to prevent agricultural injuries and illnesses to the agricultural community professionals concerned with agricultural safety. Membership: $115 (Full); $85 (Associate); $50 (Student).

Publications:
Membership Directory; annually
newsletters; quarterly

National Institute for State Credit Union Examination (1982)
1655 N. Fort Myer Dr.
Suite 650
Arlington, VA 22209
Tel: (703) 528-8351 *Fax:* (703) 528-3248
E-Mail: offices@nascus.org
Website: nascus.org
Staff: 4
Annual Budget: $100-250,000
Tax: 501(c)(3)

Personnel:
Vice President, Public Relations and Legislative Affairs: Kate Hartig
   E-Mail: kate@nascus.org

Historical Note:
The National Institute for State Credit Union Examination (NISCUE) advances the quality of state credit union examinations, increases the skill levels of state examiners, and broadens examiners' understanding of state credit union issues and philosophy.

National Institute of American Doll Artists (1962)
109 Ladder Hill North
Weston, CT 06883
Tel: (203) 557-3169
E-Mail: niada@niada.org
Website: niada.org
Members: 200 individuals
Staff: 4
Annual Budget: $25-50,000

Personnel:
President and Conference Chair: Donna May Robinson
   E-Mail: donnamaydolls@optonline.net
Webmaster: Chris Chomick
   E-Mail: webmaster@niada.org

Historical Note:
Represents doll artists, supportive patrons friends whose purpose is to promote the art of the original handmade doll. Membership is by election. Patron membership is open to anyone, but artist membership must be voted on. Membership: $50/year.

Meetings/Conferences: Annual
Conference Chair: Donna May Robinson

Publications:
Membership Directory; on-line
NIADA Newsletter

National Institute of Building Sciences (1974)
1090 Vermont Ave. NW
Suite 700
Washington, DC 20005-4905
Tel: (202) 289-7800 *Fax:* (202) 289-1092
E-Mail: nibs@nibs.org
Website: nibs.org
Members: 800 individuals and organizations
Staff: 22
Annual Budget: $10-25,000,000
Tax: 501(c)(3)

Personnel:
President: Henry L. Green AIA
   E-Mail: hgreen@nibs.org
Vice President, BSC/MMC: Claret M. Heider
   E-Mail: cheider@nibs.org
Editor and Director, Communications: Gretchen Hesbacher
   E-Mail: ghesbacher@nibs.org
Senior Vice President and Chief Operating Officer: Earle W. Kennett
   E-Mail: ekennett@nibs.org
General Counsel: John Keys
   E-Mail: jkeys@nibs.org
Vice President and Chief Financial Officer: John G. Lloyd
   E-Mail: jlloyd@nibs.org
Director, Information Technology: Bob Payn
   E-Mail: bpayn@nibs.org
Director, Marketing and Publication: Pamela R. Towns
   E-Mail: ptowns@nibs.org

Historical Note:
NIBS's mission is to improve regulation of the building process, facilitate the introduction of innovative building technology, and disseminate technical and regulatory information. Membership includes individuals, companies, associations, government bodies and unions. Membership: $75 (Institute Member-Public Interest); $25 (Student); $150 (Institute Member-Industry); $1000 (Sustaining); $5000 (Contributing).

Meetings/Conferences: Annual
Conference Chair: Earle W. Kennett
2013 - Washington, DC (Washington Marriott at Metro Center)/Jan. 7 - 10/1-10 exhibitors
Number of non-conference events/year: 2

Publications:
Building Sciences Newsletter; monthly

National Institute of Business and Industrial Chaplaincy
1900 St. James Pl.
Suite 880
Houston, TX 77056
Tel: (713) 266-2456 *Fax:* (713) 266-0845
E-Mail: info@nibic.com
Website: nibic.com
Staff: 1

Personnel:
Executive Director: Diana C. Dale AAC, Dmin, LMFT
   E-Mail: dcdale@worklifeinstitute.com

Historical Note:
NIBIC promotes and conducts training and other educational programs geared toward developing qualified business and indusrial chaplains. Members are ministers, priests, rabbis, and other religious professionals employed in the private sector. Membership: $65 (Certified Chaplain/Clinical/Professional); $50 (Associate/Lay Affiliate/Retired); $30 (Student); $100 (Organizational).

Publications:
Journal of Pastoral Care & Counseling; adv.
Membership Directory; on-line
NIBIC News

National Institute of Ceramic Engineers (1938)
c/o The American Ceramic Society
600 N. Cleveland Ave., Suite 210
Westerville, OH 43082
Tel: (240) 646-7054 *Fax:* (240) 396-5637
TollFree: (866) 721-3322
E-Mail: customerservice@ceramics.org
Website: ceramics.org/classes/national-institute-of-
Members: 1291 individuals
Staff: 1
Annual Budget: $50-100,000

Personnel:
Senior Manager, Member Services: Marcia Stout
   E-Mail: mstout@ceramics.org

Historical Note:
Professional society of ceramic engineers, dedicated to the development, promotion and advancement of ceramic engineering interests. Founded by the American Ceramic Society, of which it remains a class. Also affiliated with the American Association of Engineering Socs., the Accreditation Board for Engineering and Technology, the National Society of Professional Engineers and the National Council of Engineering Examiners. Membership: $120(Individual); $325-1,000(Corporate); $30 (Student)

Publications:

International Journal of Applied Ceramic Technology;
on-line
The International Journal of Applied Glass Science; on-
line
The Journal of the American Ceramic Society; on-line

National Institute of Electromedical Information
(1984)
P.O. Box 4633
Bay Terrace, NY 11360-4633
Tel: (718) 849-1044 *Fax:* (718) 849-6523
E-Mail: sniei@aol.com
Website: niei.org
Members: 1570 individuals and companies
Staff: 5
Annual Budget: $100-250,000
Tax: 501(c)(3)

Personnel:
President: Stanley H. Kornhauser PhD

Historical Note:
*NIEI provides an educational forum and communication
network for the development and use of Electromedical
devices and therapies in all areas of healthcare.
Membership: $60 (Individual); $250 (Charter); $1000
(Life); $5000 (Sponsoring Patron); $30 (Student); $80
(Institutional/Corporate).*

National Institute of Governmental Purchasing
(1944)
151 Spring St.
Herndon, VA 20170-5223
Tel: (703) 736-8900 *Fax:* (703) 736-2818
TollFree: (800) 367-6447
Website: nigp.org
Members: 2,600 member agencies and 16,000
professionals
Staff: 34
Annual Budget: $5-10,000,000
Tax: 501(c)(3)

Personnel:
Chief Executive Officer: Rick Grimm CPPO, CPPB
  E-Mail: rgrimm@nigp.org
Director, Education and Professional Development: Carol
  Hodes CAE
  E-Mail: chodes@nigp.org
Director, Marketing: Brent Maas
  E-Mail: bmaas@nigp.org
Director, Information Technology: Derek McNeill
  E-Mail: dmcneill@nigp.org
Manager, Human Resources: Julie Ollmann
  E-Mail: jollmann@nigp.org
Manager, Communications: Catherine Patin
  E-Mail: cpatin@nigp.org
Executive Director, Conferences and Meetings: Carrie
  Rawn
  E-Mail: crawn@nigp.org

Historical Note:
*NIGP's mission is to develop, support and promote
the public procurement profession through educational
and research programs, professional support, and
advocacy initiatives that benefit members and constituents.
Organizational members are government purchasing
agencies at local, state and federal levels in the U. S. and
Canada. Membership: $330-5,400 (Agency/Organisation/
Associate); $175 (Individual/Former Public Procurement
Professional); $35 (Retired); Free (Student/Faculty).*

Continuing Education:
Certification Designation/s: CPPB, UPPCC, CPPO

Meetings/Conferences: Annual
Conference Chair: Carrie Rawn
2013 - Orlando, FL (Orlando World Center Marriott)/
  Aug. 24 - 28
2014 - Philadelphia, PA (Philadelphia Convention
  Centre)/Aug. 22 - 27
2015 - Kansas City, MO (Kansas City Convention
  Center)/July 31 - Aug. 5
2016 - Ft. Washington, MD (Gaylord National Hotel
  and Convention Center)/Aug. 19 - 23
2018 - Orlando, FL (Gaylord Palms Resort and
  Convention Center-Orlando)/Aug. 24 - 28

Publications:
Membership Directory; on-line

National Institute of Oilseed Products *(1934)*
529 14th St. NW
750 National Press Building
Washington, DC 20045
Tel: (202) 591-2461 *Fax:* (202) 223-9741

E-Mail: niop@kellencompany.com
Website: niop.org
Members: 120 companies
Staff: 4
Annual Budget: $250-500,000

Personnel:
Executive Director: Lauren LeMunyan Newberry
  E-Mail: lnewberry@kellencompany.com
Executive Vice President: Richard E. Cristol
  E-Mail: rcristol@kellencompany.com
Manager, Meetings: Sean Hewitt

Historical Note:
*NIOP's mission is to promote the general business welfare
of persons, firms and corporations engaged in the buying,
selling, processing, shipping, storage and use of vegetable
oils and raw materials. Members are importers, exporters,
storage tank operators, and brokers in copra, palm,
coconut, soybean and other edible oils and related raw
material. Membership: $1350/year.*

Meetings/Conferences: Annual
Conference Chair: Sean Hewitt
2013 - Scottsdale, AZ (The Camelback Inn)/March 10
  - 12
2014 - San Antonio, TX (J.W. Hill Country)/March 16
  - 18
2015 - Scottsdale, AZ (The Camelback Inn)/March 15
  - 17

Publications:
Trading Rules; on-line

National Institute of Packaging, Handling and Logistics Engineers *(1956)*
1187 W. Spring Valley Pike
Dayton, OH 45458-3109
Tel: (937) 985-9375
E-Mail: admin@niphle.com
Website: niphle.com
Members: 660 individuals
Staff: 3
Annual Budget: $50-100,000

Personnel:
Executive Director: Richard D. Owen
  E-Mail: niphle@dejazzd.com
Director, Marketing: Marcel Bakx
  E-Mail: mbakx@packiq.com
Contact, Education: John Gerrish
  E-Mail: john@airpack.com

Historical Note:
*NIPHLE is an assemblage of professionals whose interests
in the complex and diverse practice of distribution and
logistics is a common bond. Membership: $250 (Regular);
$125 (Government); $50 (Retired/Life/Academia); $1000
(Gold); $345 (Silver); $2500 (Sustaining).*

Meetings/Conferences: Annual

Publications:
Membership Directory; on-line
NIPHLE Newsletter; bi-monthly

National Institute of Pension Administrators *(1983)*
401 N. Michigan Ave.
Suite 2200
Chicago, IL 60611-4267
Tel: (904) 491-0612 *Fax:* (312) 673-6609
TollFree: (800) 999-6472
E-Mail: nipa@nipa.org
Website: nipa.org
Members: 1800 member organizations and
individuals
Staff: 10
Annual Budget: $1-2,000,000
Tax: 501(c)(6)

Personnel:
Executive Director: Laura J. Rudzinski
  E-Mail: lrudzinski@nipa.org
Senior Associate, Membership Services: Mark Hurst
  E-Mail: mhurst@nipa.org
Senior Manager, Marketing: Kim Jones
  E-Mail: kjones@nipa.org
Director, Education: Kimberly B. Martin APA, CPC, QPA
  E-Mail: kmartin@nipa.org
Director, Operations: Bridget McLaughlin
  E-Mail: bmclaughlin@nipa.org
Coordinator, Trade Shows: Catherine Perkins
  E-Mail: cperkins@nipa.org
Manager, Editorial Services: Theresa Wojtalewicz
  E-Mail: twojtalewicz@nipa.org

Historical Note:
*NIPA strives to enhance professionalism in the retirement
plan industry. Members are administrators, owners,
principals or partners of independent administration firms;
pension administration personnel, investment programs or
trusts; actuaries; lawyers; CPAs; or insurance executives
whose work entails the planning, implementation, and/or
administration of pension and employee benefit programs.
Membership: $495 (Business Owner); $385 (Executive);
$310 (Affiliate); $195 (Student); $0 (Guest Membership).*

Continuing Education:
Certification Designation/s: DACP, LACP, APA, APR

Meetings/Conferences:
Conference Chair: Catherine Perkins
2013 - Las Vegas, NV (The Cosmopolitan of Las
  Vegas)/April 28 - May 1

Publications:
Membership Directory; on-line
News from nipa.org; on-line
NIPA News; bi-weekly

National Institute of Senior Centers *(1970)*
1901 L St. NW
Fourth Floor
Washington, DC 20036
Tel: (202) 479-1200 *Fax:* (202) 479-0735
TollFree: (800) 373-4906
Website: ncoa.org/national-institute-of-senior-
  centers
Members: 2500 centers
Staff: 1

Personnel:
Association Coordinator: Maureen Arsenault
  E-Mail: maureen.arsenault@ncoa.org

Historical Note:
*Originally (1962) the National Advisory Committee on
Senior Centers of the National Council on the Aging. NISC
is a network of professionals who represent the senior center
field, which serves over several million older Americans
annually through its community-based senior centers
around throughout the country. Membership: $145/year*

Meetings/Conferences:
Conference Chair: Maureen Arsenault

Publications:
Aging in Stride; quarterly
Senior Center Voice; monthly

National Institute of Senior Housing *(1979)*
1901 L St. NW
Fourth Floor
Washington, DC 20036
Tel: (202) 479-1200 *Fax:* (202) 479-0735
E-Mail: info@ncoa.org
Website: ncoa.org/content.cfm?sectionid = 45
Members: 3500 individuals
Staff: 1

Personnel:
President and Chief Executive Officer: James Firman

Historical Note:
*A special interest group of the National Council on the
Aging, NISH focuses on aging in place-helping older
Americans remain in their homes as long as possible.
Members include senior centers, area agencies on aging,
adult day service centers, faith- based service organizations,
senior housing facilities, employment services, consumer
groups and leaders from academia, business and labor.*

Publications:
Aging in Stride; quarterly
Innovations; quarterly
NCOA Week; weekly
Senior Center Voice; monthly

National Institute of Steel Detailing *(1969)*
1810 Catalina Ct.
Livermore, CA 94550-6416
Tel: (925) 294-9626 *Fax:* (925) 294-9621
E-Mail: nisd@sbcglobal.net
Website: nisd.org
Members: 400 firms and individuals
Staff: 4
Annual Budget: $100-250,000

Personnel:
Administrator: Stephanie Andrew
  E-Mail: nisd@sbcglobal.net
Editor: John Linn
  E-Mail: JLA-JTL@pacbell.net

Historical Note:

NISD is an international association which advocates, promotes and serves the interests of the steel detailing industry. Members are unified company owners and individuals at local, regional and international levels. Membership: $290-450 (Regular); $360 (Associates); $65 (Individual Associate); $100 (Emeritus); $450 (Overseas).

Continuing Education:
Certification Designation/s: IDC

Meetings/Conferences: Annual

Publications:
Connection Newsletter; quarterly; adv.
Membership Directory; on-line

National Institute for Water Resources (1974)
322 E. Front St.
Suite 242
Boise, ID 83702
Tel: (208) 332-4422 Fax: (208) 332-4400
E-Mail: support@niwr.net
Website: niwr.net
Members: 54 individuals
Staff: 2
Annual Budget: $100-250,000
Tax: 501(c)(4)

Personnel:
Secretary and Treasurer: Dr. John C. Tracy
E-Mail: tracy@uidaho.edu

Historical Note:
Formed in 1974 to coordinate the institute program both internally and externally. Formerly (1992) the National Association of Water Institute Directors. NIWR is dedicated to provide representation for the State Water Research Institutes and centers in collective activities to implement the provisions of the Water Resources Research Act of 1984. Membership consists of the directors of 54 institutes. Membership: $2700/year.

Meetings/Conferences: Annual
2013 - Washington, DC/Feb. 11 - 13

National Insulation Association (1953)
12100 Sunset Hills Rd.
Suite 330
Reston, VA 20190
Tel: (703) 464-6422 Fax: (703) 464-5896
E-Mail: niainfo@insulation.org
Website: insulation.org
Members: 450 headquarter company members
Staff: 10
Annual Budget: $2-5,000,000
Tax: 501(c)(6)

Personnel:
Executive Vice President and Chief Executive Officer: Michele M. Jones CMP
E-Mail: mjones@insulation.org
Assistant Manager, Membership Services: Holly Colbert
E-Mail: hcolbert@insulation.org
Director, Meetings and Education: Julie Cupp CMP
E-Mail: jcupp@insulation.org
Contact, Advertising and Sales: Kim Kelemen
E-Mail: ads@insulation.org
Director, Publications and Publisher: Julie A. McLaughlin
E-Mail: JMcLaughlin@insulation.org
Editor, Communications: Katie Photiadis
E-Mail: editor@insulation.org

Historical Note:
Formerly (1970) Insulation Distributor-Contractors National Association, (1989) National Insulation Contractors Association and (1995) National Insulation and Abatement Contractors Association. NIA seeks to provide essential services to all members at acceptable costs. Members are industrial and commercial insulation contractors, manufacturers and distributors. Membership: $735-8,770 (Active); $3,285 (Associate); $735 (Holding Company); $1,375 (International Affiliate); $1,325 (Consultant/Manufacturers/Representative/Associate Supplier); $1,000 (Affiliate).

Meetings/Conferences: Annual
Conference Chair: Julie Cupp CMP
2013 - Bonita Springs, FL (Hyatt Regency Coconut Point Resort and Spa)/April 17 - 20/100 attendees
2014 - Indian Wells, CA (Hyatt Grand Champions Resort, Villas and Spa)/April 2 - 5/100 attendees/51-100 exhibitors
Number of non-conference events/year: 11

Publications:
Insulation Outlook; quarterly; adv.
Membership Directory & Resource Guide; annually; adv.

NIA News

National Insurance Crime Bureau (1992)
1111 E. Touhy Ave.
Suite 400
Des Plaines, IL 60018
Tel: (847) 544-7000 Fax: (847) 544-7100
TollFree: (800) 447-6282
Website: nicb.org
Members: 1100 insurance companies
Staff: 330
Annual Budget: $25-50,000,000
Tax: 501(c)(4)

Personnel:
President and Chief Executive Officer: Joseph H. Wehrle Jr.
Senior Vice President and Chief Information Officer: Dan G. Abbott
E-Mail: dabbott@nicb.org
Director, Marketing: Michelle Curtis
E-Mail: mcurtis@nicb.org
Vice President, Government Affairs: Judith M. Fitzgerald
E-Mail: jfitzgerald@nicb.org
Senior Vice President and Chief Financial Officer: Bob Jachnicki
Vice President, Human Resources: Barbara M. Low
Vice President and Chief Communications Officer: Roger Morris
E-Mail: rmorris@nicb.org
Director, Membership Services: Bill Schroeder
E-Mail: wschroeder@nicb.org
Senior Vice President and General Counsel: Andrew J. Sosnowski
Vice President, Training: Thomas F. Welsh
E-Mail: twelsh@nicb.org

Historical Note:
Formed by the merger of Insurance Crime Prevention Institute (1970) and National Automobile Theft Bureau (1912). NICB's mission is to lead a united effort of insurers, law enforcement agencies and representatives of the public to prevent and combat insurance fraud and crime through data analytics, investigations, training, legislative advocacy and public awareness.

Publications:
Member Directory; on-line

National Intercollegiate Soccer Officials Association (1964)
541 Woodview Dr.
Longwood, FL 32779-2614
Tel: (407) 862-3305 Fax: (407) 862-8545
Website: nisoa.com
Members: 5000 individuals
Staff: 2
Annual Budget: $500-1,000,000

Personnel:
Executive Director: C. Cliff McCrath
Director, Operations: John Van De Vaarst
E-Mail: vandevaj@comcast.net

Historical Note:
NISOA's mission is to provide qualified and certified soccer officials for colleges and high schools. Membership: $100/year.

Meetings/Conferences:
Conference Chair: John Van De Vaarst

Publications:
Intercollegiate Newsletter; semi-annually

National Interscholastic Athletic Administrators Association (1977)
9100 Keystone Crossing
Suite 650
Indianapolis, IN 46240
Tel: (317) 587-1450 Fax: (317) 587-1451
Website: niaaa.org
Members: 8051 individuals and state associations
Staff: 5
Annual Budget: $1-2,000,000
Tax: 501(c)(3)

Personnel:
Executive Director: Bruce Whitehead
E-Mail: bwhitehead@niaaa.org
Contact Membership Services and Communications: Shannon Arvin
E-Mail: sarvin@niaaa.org
Administrator, Organizational Affairs: Patricia Conrad
E-Mail: pconrad@niaaa.org

Manager, Professional Development: Cheryl Van Paris
E-Mail: cvanparis@niaaa.org
Director, Marketing: Walter Sargent
E-Mail: wsargent@niaaa.org

Historical Note:
NIAAA preserves, enhances and promotes the educational values of interscholastic athletics through the professional development of its members in the areas of education, leadership, and service. Members are high school and middle school athletic administrators. Membership: $80 (Regular/Associate); $300-800 (Lifetime); $15 (Student); $30-60 (Retired); $25-500 (Organization).

Continuing Education:
Enrollment: 700
Certification Designation/s: CMAA, RAA, CAA

Meetings/Conferences: Annual
Conference Chair: Patricia Conrad
2013 - Anaheim, CA (Anaheim Marriott)/Dec. 13 - 17
2014 - Ft. Washington, MD (Gaylord National Resort and Convention Center-National Harbor)/Dec. 12 - 16
2015 - Orlando, FL (Orlando World Center Marriott)/Dec. 11 - 15
2016 - Nashville, TN (Gaylord Hotels Resorts and Convention Centers-Nashville)/Dec. 9 - 15

Publications:
Interscholastic Athletic Administration; quarterly
Professional Development Program; annually

National Interscholastic Swimming Coaches Association (1934)
29 Fairview Ave.
Great Neck, NY 11023
Website: niscaonline.org
Members: 1800 individuals
Staff: 2
Annual Budget: $100-250,000

Personnel:
President: Arvel McElroy
E-Mail: president@niscaonline.org
Treasurer: Tom Wojslawowicz
E-Mail: treas-member@nisca.net

Historical Note:
NISCA represents interscholastic swimming, diving and water polo coaches. Membership: $50 (Individual); $150 (Special Team); $40 (Retired); $70-165 (Joint).

Meetings/Conferences: Annual
2013 - Indianapolis, IN/March 28 - 30

Publications:
Membership Directory; on-line
NISCA Journal; bi-monthly
NISCA Newsletters ; monthly
Swimming World Magazine; monthly; adv.

National Interstate Council of State Boards of Cosmetology (1936)
7622 Briarwood Cir.
Little Rock, AR 72205
Tel: (501) 227-8262 Fax: (501) 227-8212
Website: nictesting.org
Members: 500 individuals and boards
Staff: 5
Annual Budget: $2-5,000,000
Tax: 501(c)(6)

Personnel:
Contact, Administrative Services and Coordinator, Conferences and Meetings: Debra Norton
E-Mail: dnorton@nictesting.org
Editor: Jerry Brooks
Coordinator, National Examination Program: Mary Manna
E-Mail: mmanna@nictesting.org
Comptroller: Patrick Ulsh

Historical Note:
NICSBC formed by the merger of National Council of State Boards of Cosmetology and Interstate Council of State Boards of Cosmetology (1956), seeks to provide a forum for the exchange of state regulatory ideas to encourage the standards for consumer safety.

Meetings/Conferences: Annual
Conference Chair: Debra Norton

Publications:
NIC Membership Directory; annually

National Intramural-Recreational Sports Association (1950)
4185 SW Research Way

Corvallis, OR 97333-1067
Tel: (541) 766-8211 *Fax:* (541) 766-8284
E-Mail: nirsa@nirsa.org
Website: nirsa.org
Members: 4000 individuals
Staff: 37
Annual Budget: $2-5,000,000
Tax: 501(c)(3)

Personnel:
Executive Director: Pam Watts
Director, Information Technology: John Bernert MBA
    E-Mail: john@nirsa.org
Assistant Director, Marketing and Communications: Simon Bravo
    E-Mail: simon@nirsa.org
Director, Membership and Publications: Mary Callender
    E-Mail: mary@nirsa.org
Director, Professional Development: Cheri Hawkins
    E-Mail: cheri@nirsa.org
Director, Finance and Human Resources: Marty Kaye
    E-Mail: controller@nirsa.org
Senior Director, Membership and Marketing: Ashley Murphy
    E-Mail: marketingdir@nirsa.org

Historical Note:
Formerly (1973) National Intramural Association, NIRSA seeks to promote the advancement of recreational sports programs and the professional growth of individuals. Members include recreational sports professionals, institutions, and students. Membership: $153-413 (Professional); 123-331 (Professional Member at Member Institution); $1,401 (Professional Life Member); $67-181 (Student); $56-151 (Student Member at Member Institution); $475 (Associate); $430-4220 (Four year Colleges and Universities); $289-2423 (Two year Colleges); $325-1355 (Military, Parks and Recreation).

Meetings/Conferences:
Conference Chair: Mary Callender
2013 - Las Vegas, NV/Feb. 25 - March 7
2013 - Las Vegas, NV/March 4 - 8

Publications:
eFASTNEWS; bi-weekly
NIRSA Know; monthly
Recreational Sports Directory (Membership Directory); annually; adv.
Recreational Sports Journal; semi-annually; adv.

National Investment Banking Association *(1982)*
P.O. Box 6625
Athens, GA 30604
Tel: (706) 208-9620 *Fax:* (706) 993-3342
Website: nibanet.org
Members: 202 Associates and Broker Dealers
Staff: 2
Annual Budget: $500-1,000,000
Tax: 501(c)(3)

Personnel:
Executive Director: Emily Foshee
    E-Mail: emily@nibanet.org
Chief Information and Technology Officer: D. Scott Foshee

Historical Note:
NIBA's mission is to add value to the members, client companies, investors and the securities industry at large by being at service for small capital companies seeking access and exposure to underwriters and broker/dealers. It seeks to be the point of contact for all those looking to enhance the capital formation environment for small companies. Members are regional and independent broker-dealer and investment banking firms, and related capital market service providers.

Meetings/Conferences: Annual

Publications:
Membership Directory; on-line

National Investment Company Service Association *(1962)*
8400 Westpark Dr.
Second Floor
McLean, VA 22102
Tel: (508) 485-1500 *Fax:* (508) 485-1560
E-Mail: info@nicsa.org
Website: nicsa.org
Members: 10400 individuals and firms
Staff: 4
Annual Budget: $1-2,000,000

Personnel:
President: Theresa Hamacher CFA
    E-Mail: thamacher@nicsa.org

Manager, Meetings and Communications: Bethany Alvare
    E-Mail: balvare@nicsa.org
Coordinator, Program and Membership Services: Katie McNealy
    E-Mail: kmcnealy@nicsa.org
Vice President and Marketing Director: Ellen Weinraub
    E-Mail: eweinraub@nicsa.org

Historical Note:
NICSA's mission is to be the provider of independent education and networking forums to professionals in the global investment management community. Membership: $13,700 (Global Leader); $1,750-8,600 (National Corporate); $575 (International Corproate); $325 (Associate).

Continuing Education:
Certification Designation/s: CPE

Meetings/Conferences: Annual
Conference Chair: Bethany Alvare
2013 - Miami, FL (Doral Golf Resort and Spa)/Feb. 10 - 13
Number of non-conference events/year: 3

Publications:
Membership Directory; on-line
NICSA News; quarterly

National Investor Relations Institute *(1969)*
225 Reinekers Ln.
Suite 560
Alexandria, VA 22314
Tel: (703) 562-7700 *Fax:* (703) 562-7701
E-Mail: info@niri.org
Website: niri.org
Members: 4400 individuals
Staff: 15
Annual Budget: $5-10,000,000
Tax: 501(c)(6)

Personnel:
President and Chief Executive Officer: Jeffrey D. Morgan
    E-Mail: jmorgan@niri.org
Vice President, Communications: Matt Brusch
    E-Mail: mbrusch@niri.org
Vice President, Professional Development: Kraig Conrad
    E-Mail: kconrad@niri.org
Director, Research: Ariel Finno
    E-Mail: afinno@niri.org
Director, Technology and Database Management: Anita Joshi
    E-Mail: ajoshi@niri.org
Vice President, Marketing and Membership Development: Michael C. McGough
    E-Mail: mmcgough@niri.org
Editor: Al Rickard
    E-Mail: arickard@associationvision.com
Manager, Meeting Planning and Travel: Sharon Wall
    E-Mail: swall@niri.org
Vice President, Finance and Administration: Carolyn Wheatley
    E-Mail: cwheatley@niri.org

Historical Note:
NIRI's mission is to advance the practice of investor relations and professional competency and stature of its members. Members represent the publicly held corporations in the U.S. and many small and mid-sized companies. Membership: $595 (Corporate/Counselor/Service Provider/Affiliated); $100 (Academic).

Meetings/Conferences: Annual
Conference Chair: Sharon Wall
2013 - Hollywood, FL/June 9 - 12

Publications:
Executive Alert
Investor Relations Update; monthly; adv.
IR Advisor
IR Services Directory; on-line; adv.
IR Weekly; weekly; adv.
Membership Directory; on-line

National Judges Association *(1979)*
222 Gilbert Ave.
P.O. Box 325
Glendale, OR 97442
Fax: (541) 832-2647
TollFree: (888) 366-3652
E-Mail: njaoffice@yahoo.com
Website: nationaljudgesassociation.org/
Members: 400 individuals
Staff: 2
Annual Budget: $10-25,000

Tax: 501(c)(6)

Personnel:
Executive Director and Treasurer: Candace Hissong
Director, Public Relations: Tom B. Webb

Historical Note:
NJA's mission is to preserve the existence of the non-attorney judge and to foster improved performance of traditional duties of the non-attorney judges. Membership: $25 (Regular/Retired); $300 (Retired-lifetime); $50 (Associate); $100 (Contribution Sponsors).

Meetings/Conferences: Annual

Publications:
The Gavel

National Junior College Athletic Association *(1938)*
1631 Mesa Ave.
Suite B
Colorado Springs, CO 80906
Tel: (719) 590-9788 *Fax:* (719) 590-7324
Website: njcaa.org
Members: 520 junior colleges
Staff: 9
Annual Budget: $1-2,000,000
Tax: 501(c)(3)

Personnel:
Executive Director: Mary Ellen Leicht
    E-Mail: meleicht@njcaa.org
Contact, Membership Services and Bookkeeper: Lorna Brizzie
    E-Mail: lbrizzie@njcaa.org
Director, Information Technologies: Rob Bushway
    E-Mail: rbushway@njcaa.org
Administrative Assistant: Dee DuBois
    E-Mail: ddubois@njcaa.org
Director, Championship Events: Stephanie Hazzard
    E-Mail: shazzard@njcaa.org
Assistant Executive Director, Sports Information and Media Relations: Mark Krug
    E-Mail: mkrug@njcaa.org

Historical Note:
NJCAA's mission is to promote and foster junior college athletics on intersectional and national levels. NJCAA members are two year institutions recognized by the American Association of Community and Junior Colleges.

Meetings/Conferences:
Conference Chair: Stephanie Hazzard

Publications:
Eligibility Rules of NJCAA; annually
NJCAA Review Magazine; adv.

National Juvenile Court Services Association *(1970)*
C/O Correctional Management Institute of Texas
George J. Beto Criminal Justice Center, Sam Houston State University
Huntsville, TX 77341-2296
Tel: (936) 294-1227 *Fax:* (936) 294-1671
Website: njcsa.org
Members: 678 individuals
Staff: 2
Annual Budget: Under $10,000
Tax: 501(c)(3)

Personnel:
Executive Director: Amanda Bilnoski
    E-Mail: bilnoski@shsu.edu

Historical Note:
NJCSA works to strengthen the competencies of juvenile justice personnel through training, education, management development, advocacy and standard setting. Membership: $45/year (Individual).

Continuing Education:
Certification Designation/s: PJJM, PJJA

Publications:
Juvenile and Family Court Journal; quarterly
Juvenile and Family Justice TODAY; quarterly
Membership Directory; on-line
RAPPORT; quarterly

National Kitchen and Bath Association *(1963)*
687 Willow Grove St.
Hackettstown, NJ 07840
Tel: (877) 652-2776 *Fax:* (908) 852-1695
TollFree: (800) 843-6522
E-Mail: feedback@nkba.org
Website: nkba.org

Members: 40000 individuals
Staff: 6
Annual Budget: $10-25,000,000
Tax: 501(c)(6)

Personnel:
Chief Executive Officer: Bill Darcy
   E-Mail: bdarcy@nkba.org
Director, Learning: Nancy Barnes
Director, Marketing and Communications: Timothy
   Captain
Senior Director, Finance: Stephen Graziano
Director, Membership Services: Claudette Hoffmann
   E-Mail: choffmann@nkba.org
General Counsel and Director, Legislative Affairs: Edward
   S. Nagorsky Esq.
   E-Mail: enagorsky@nkba.org

Historical Note:
Formerly (1982) the American Institute of Kitchen Dealers. NKBA's mission is to enhance member success and excellence, promote professionalism and ethical business practices, and provide leadership and direction for the kitchen and bath industry worldwide. Members are Kitchen equipment manufacturers, suppliers, wholesalers, retail dealers, distributors and designers. Membership: $100-750 (Company/Self-Employed); $50-150 (Employee); $300 (Educational); $1,475-9,500 (Industry/Corporate).

Meetings/Conferences: Annual

Publications:
NKBA Magazine; quarterly; adv.
QuickClicks Newsletter; monthly

National Labor Relations Board Professional Association (1962)
1099 14th St. NW
Suite 8824
Washington, DC 20570-0001
Fax: (202) 273-4283
Members: 160 individuals
Staff: 1
Annual Budget: $10-25,000

Personnel:
President: John Mantz

Historical Note:
Independent union of lawyers working for the N.L.R.B. in Washington. In additon to representing attorneys, the association also represents law clerks and law students employed by the Board's Division of Administrative Law Judges. Has no headquarters or paid staff. Officers are elected annually. Membership: $78/year.

National Lamb Feeders Association (1950)
1270 Chemeketa St. NE
Salem, OR 97301-4145
Tel: (503) 370-7024 *Fax:* (503) 585-1921
E-Mail: info@nlfa-sheep.org
Website: nlfa-sheep.org
Members: 300 individuals
Staff: 3
Annual Budget: $50-100,000
Tax: 501(c)(5)

Personnel:
President: Don Gnos
Treasurer: Clay Drake
Secretary: Tom Watson

Historical Note:
NLFA's mission is to initiate, sponsor and carry out plans, programs and policies to promote, encourage and improve the production of lambs and sheep. Membership: $25 (Associate/Non-Voting); $100 (Full Voting); $500 (Industry Associate).

Meetings/Conferences: Semi-Annual
2013 - San Antonio, TX (Hyatt Regency Hill Country
   Resort and Spa)/Jan. 25

Publications:
Feeder News Newsletter; irregular; adv.
NLFA Newsletter

National Lawyers Guild (1937)
132 Nassau St.
Room 922
New York, NY 10038
Tel: (212) 679-5100 *Fax:* (212) 679-2811
E-Mail: nlgno@nlg.org
Website: nlg.org
Members: 4000 individuals
Staff: 6
Annual Budget: $250-500,000

Tax: 501(c)(4)

Personnel:
Executive Director: Heidi Boghosian
   E-Mail: director@nlg.org
Executive Vice President: Ian Head
   E-Mail: nlgno@nlg.org
Coordinator, Membership Services: Jamie Munroe
   E-Mail: membership@nlg.org
Coordinator, Communications: Nathan Tempey

Historical Note:
NLG is dedicated to basic and progressive change in the structure of the US political and economic system. Members are lawyers, law students, jailhouse lawyers and legal workers. Membership: $15 (Law Students); $30-50 (New Attorneys/Legal Workers); $45-500 (Others, Based on income).

Publications:
Guild Notes; quarterly
NLG Review; quarterly
Referral Directory; on-line

National League for Nursing (1893)
61 Broadway
33rd Floor
New York, NY 10006
Tel: (212) 363-5555 *Fax:* (212) 812-0391
TollFree: (800) 669-1656
E-Mail: generalinfo@nln.org
Website: nln.org
Members:
1200 organizations
34000 individuals
Staff: 71
Annual Budget: $10-25,000,000
Tax: 501(c)(3)

Personnel:
Chief Executive Officer: Beverly Malone FAAN, PhD, RN
Senior Director, Professional Development: Janice
   Brewington FAAN, PhD, RN
Chief Financial Officer: Stephen Cerame
   E-Mail: scerame@nln.org
Chief Communications Officer: Karen R. Klestzick
   E-Mail: kklestzick@nln.org
Chief Program Officer: M.Elaine Tagliareni EdD, RN
   E-Mail: etaglareni@nln.org

Historical Note:
Formerly (1912) American Society of Superintendents of Training Schools for Nurses, the first organization for nursing. Became National League for Nursing Education (NLNE) and in 1952, NLNE, the National Organization for Public Health Nursing, and the Association for Collegiate Schools of Nursing combined to establish the NLN. Purpose is to promote excellence in nursing education to build a strong and diverse nursing workforce. Membership: $110 (Full Individual); $75 (Graduate Student /Retired); $1,0750-1,575 (Education Agency); $525 (Associate).

Continuing Education:
Certification Designation/s: CNE

Meetings/Conferences: Annual
Conference Chair: M.Elaine Tagliareni EdD, RN
2013 - Washington, DC (Washington Marriott)/Sept.
   18 - 21
2014 - Phoenix, AZ (Hyatt Regency Phoenix)/Sept. 17
   - 20
2015 - Las Vegas, NV (Caesars Palace Las Vegas Hotel
   and Casino)/Sept. 30 - Oct. 4
2016 - Orlando, FL (Orlando World Center Marriott)/
   Sept. 21 - 24

Publications:
Faculty Development Bulletin; monthly
NLN Member Update; bi-weekly
Nursing Education Perspectives; bi-monthly; adv.
Nursing Education Policy Newsletter; bi-monthly
The NLN Report; quarterly

National League of American Pen Women (1897)
1300 17th St. NW
Pen Arts Building
Washington, DC 20036-1973
Tel: (202) 785-1997 *Fax:* (202) 452-6868
E-Mail: nlapw1@verizon.net
Website: nlapw.org
Members: 250 branches
Staff: 6
Annual Budget: $100-250,000
Tax: 501(c)(3)

Personnel:

President: Sharyn Bowman Greberman
Treasurer: Fran Chadwick
Meetings Contact: Mimi Gould
Contact, Public Relations: Sylvia Hoehns Wright
Publications Contact: Marilyn Lewis-Alim
Editor: April Myers
   E-Mail: eggrollcreative@yahoo.com

Historical Note:
Organized in Washington, DC as the League of American Pen Women. Assumed its present name and was incorporated in 1926. NLAPW's mission is to encourage, recognize, and promote the production of creative work of professional standard in Art, Letters, and Music. Members are journalists, painters, choreographers, sculptors, illustrators, songwriters, poets. Membership: $55-65 (Art/Music/Letters).

Meetings/Conferences: Biennial
Conference Chair: Mimi Gould
Number of non-conference events/year: 3

Publications:
The Pen Woman Magazine; quarterly

National League of Cities (1924)
1301 Pennsylvania Ave. NW
Suite 550
Washington, DC 20004-1701
Tel: (202) 626-3100 *Fax:* (202) 626-3043
E-Mail: info@nlc.org
Website: nlc.org
Members: 19,000 cities and towns
Staff: 100
Annual Budget: $25-50,000,000
Tax: 501(c)(4)

Personnel:
Executive Director: Donald J. Borut
   E-Mail: borut@nlc.org
*Principal Associate, Communication and Technology,
   Federal Relations:* Laura Bonavita
   E-Mail: bonavita@nlc.org
Center Director, Federal Relations: Carolyn M. Coleman
   E-Mail: coleman@nlc.org
Center Director, Public Affairs and Member Relations: Amy
   Elsbree
   E-Mail: elsbree@nlc.org
*Program Director, Finance, Economic Development and
   Federal Relations:* Lars Etzkorn
   E-Mail: etzkorn@nlc.org
Chief Finance Officer, Operations: Carlsen Griffith
   E-Mail: griffith@nlc.org
Manager, Editorial Services and Public Affairs: Cyndy
   Hogan
   E-Mail: hogan@nlc.org
Director, Human Resources: Anna Langham
   E-Mail: langham@nlc.org
Manager, Media Relations: Gregory N. Minchak
   E-Mail: minchak@nlc.org
Center Director, Conferences, Education and Training:
   Janice Pauline
   E-Mail: pauline@nlc.org
Director, Membership Programs: Cathy Spain
   E-Mail: spain@nlc.org
Coordinator, Editorial Services: Laura Turner
   E-Mail: lturner@nlc.org

Historical Note:
Known until 1964 as the American Municipal Association, NLC was founded by reform-minded state municipal leagues to represent the interests of its members to the federal and state governments. Membership: $750-1250/year (Associate Members).

Meetings/Conferences: Annual
Conference Chair: Janice Pauline
2014 - Seattle, WA/Nov. 12 - 16

Publications:
Membership Directory; on-line

Membership List Available to Non-members

National League of Postmasters of the United States (1887)
One Beltway Center, 5904 Richmond Hwy.
Suite 500
Alexandria, VA 22303-1864
Tel: (703) 329-4550 *Fax:* (703) 329-0466
E-Mail: information@postmasters.org
Website: postmasters.org
Members: 30000 individuals
Staff: 30
Annual Budget: $2-5,000,000

Tax: 501(c)(5)

Personnel:
President: Mark W. Strong
  E-Mail: mstrong@postmasters.org
Director: Frank J Augustosky
Contact, Media: Martha M. Lostrom
Director, Improved Managers Program: Mary Mueller
  E-Mail: impmueller@hotmail.com
Assistant Director, Meetings and Conventions: Michael J. Perrone
  E-Mail: mjp@surfshop.net
National Secretary and Treasurer: Shelly M. Souders
  E-Mail: rsstigall@wk.net

Historical Note:
NLPM was organized in Washington, DC by about 200 Third and Fourth Class Postmasters to represent the interests of professional postmasters. It also sponsors the Postmasters Benefit Plan, a health insurance program operated under the Federal Employees Health Benefits Program. Membership: $9.26-50.27 (monthly dues based on different levels); $7 (Associates - monthly basis); $6.50 (Retirees - monthly basis).

Meetings/Conferences: Annual
Conference Chair: Barbara H. Veech
2013 - San Diego, CA (Town and Country Resort Hotel)/July 21 - 25
Number of non-conference events/year: 1

Publications:
The Postmasters Advocate; monthly; adv.

National Leased Housing Association *(1972)*
1900 L St. NW
Suite 300
Washington, DC 20036
Tel: (202) 785-8888 *Fax:* (202) 785-2008
E-Mail: info@hudnlha.com
Website: hudnlha.com
Members: 550 organizations
Staff: 5
Annual Budget: $500-1,000,000
Tax: 501(c)(6)

Personnel:
Executive Director: Denise B. Muha
  E-Mail: dmuha@hudnlha.com
Coordinator, Meetings: Cynthia Melton Bitterman
  E-Mail: cbitterman@hudnlha.com
Accountant: Donna Croce
  E-Mail: dacroce@aol.com

Historical Note:
Founded by developers and financers of federally funded housing under the government's Section 8 rent subsidy program for the poor. With the demise of the Section 8 new construction/substantial rehabilitation program, NLHA has broadened its purview to all government-related rental housing programs. Represents all major participants private and public in the affordable multifamily rental housing industry. NLHA is a vital and effective advocate for housing provider organizations and their consultants, specializing in federally assisted rental housing. Mission is committed to the provision and maintenance of quality affordable rental housing for low and moderate income Americans. Membership: $1,000 (Standard Private/Large Agency/ Non-profit Public); $650 (Affiliate Private); $500 (Standard Public); $2,500 (Sustaining Private/Public).

Meetings/Conferences: Annual
Conference Chair: Cynthia Melton Bitterman
2013 - Naples, FL (Naples Beach Hotel and Golf Club)/ Jan. 23 - 25
2013 - Washington, DC (The Washington Marriott Hotel)/June 19 - 21
2014 - Indian Wells, CA (Renaissance Esmeralda Indian Wells Resort and Spa)/Jan. 29 - 31
2014 - Washington, DC (The Washington Marriott Hotel)/June 18 - 20
Number of non-conference events/year: 3

Publications:
Bulletin; monthly
Membership Directory; on-line

National Legal Aid and Defender Association
(1958)
1140 Connecticut Ave. NW
Suite 900
Washington, DC 20036
Tel: (202) 452-0620 *Fax:* (202) 872-1031
E-Mail: info@nlada.org
Website: nlada.org
Members:

3500 organizations and associates
1200 individuals
Staff: 29
Annual Budget: $2-5,000,000
Tax: 501(c)(3)

Personnel:
President and Chief Executive Officer: Jo-Ann Wallace
  E-Mail: j.wallace@nlada.org
Manager, Human Resources: Bettie Biehn
  E-Mail: b.biehn@nlada.org
Vice President, Defender Legal Services: Ed Burnette
  E-Mail: e.burnette@nlada.org
Director, Research and Evaluation: David Carroll
  E-Mail: d.carroll@nlada.org
Manager, Information Technology: Todd Christensen
  E-Mail: t.christensen@nlada.org
Vice President, Strategic Alliances: Julie Clark
  E-Mail: j.clark@nlada.org
Director, Training and Professional Development: Karl Doss
  E-Mail: k.doss@nlada.org
Vice President, Marketing, Communications and Development: Deborah E. Dubois
  E-Mail: d.dubois@nlada.org
Accounting Manager: Yvette Hatcher
  E-Mail: y.hatcher@nlada.org
Manager, Training and Conferences: Melva Jones
  E-Mail: melva.jones@nlada.org
Director, Membership Services: Kevin Mills
  E-Mail: k.mills@nlada.org

Historical Note:
Organized in 1911 by fifteen legal assistance programs as the National Alliance of Legal Aid Societies, it became the National Association of Legal Aid Organizations in 1923. Changed name to National Legal Aid Association in 1949 and assumed its present name in 1958. NLADA serves the equal justice community by providing first-rate products and services and as a voice in public policy and legislative debates on the many issues affecting the equal justice community. Membership: $20-2500/year.

Meetings/Conferences:
Conference Chair: Melva Jones
2013 - Los Angeles, CA (Westin Bonaventure Hotel and Suites, Los Angeles)/Nov. 7 - 10
Number of non-conference events/year: 5

Publications:
CLASP Services memos; on-line
Cornerstone; adv.
NLADA Update; semi-monthly; adv.
The Directory of Legal Aid and Defender Offices and Resources; annually; adv.

National Lesbian and Gay Journalists Association
(1990)
2120 L St. NW
Suite 850
Washington, DC 20037
Tel: (202) 588-9888 *Fax:* (202) 588-1818
E-Mail: info@nlgja.org
Website: nlgja.org
Members: 1100 individuals
Staff: 3
Annual Budget: $250-500,000
Tax: 501(c)(3)

Personnel:
Executive Director: Michael Tune
  E-Mail: mtune@nlgja.org
Communications and Program Coordinator: Bach Polakowski
  E-Mail: bach@nlgja.org
Coordinator, Membership Services: Matthew Rose
  E-Mail: mrose@nlgja.org

Historical Note:
NLGJA's mission is to serve journalists, media professionals, educators and students working from within the news industry to foster fair and accurate coverage of LGBT issues. Membership: $75 (Basic/Associate); $25 (Student/Friends/International/Retiree); $45 (LGBT Media).

Continuing Education:
Certification Designation/s: JEP

Meetings/Conferences: Annual
2013 - Boston, MA (The Boston Park Plaza Hotel and Towers)/Aug. 22 - 25

Publications:
Career Watch (E-mailed to members); monthly
NLGJA News; bi-monthly
NLGJA Outlook; semi-annually

National Lesbian and Gay Law Association *(1988)*
1301 K St. NW
Suite 1100 E. Tower
Washington, DC 20005
Tel: (202) 637-7661 *Fax:* (202) 639-6066
E-Mail: info@LGBTbar.org
Website: lgbtbar.org
Members: 7500 individuals
Staff: 3
Annual Budget: $25-50,000
Tax: 501(c)(6)

Personnel:
Executive Director: D'Arcy Kemnitz
  E-Mail: darcy@nlgla.org
Director, Development and Communications: Kelly Simon
  E-Mail: kelly@lgbtbar.org
Administrator: Liz Youngblood
  E-Mail: liz@lgbtbar.org

Historical Note:
Founded as National Lesbian and Gay Lawyers Association; assumed its current name in 1999. The LGBT Bar promotes justice in and through the legal profession for the LGBT community in all its diversity. It's an association of lawyers, judges and other legal professionals, law students, activists and affiliated lesbian, gay, bisexual and transgender legal organizations. Membership: $60-175/year (Professional, based on annual income); $40/year (Law student); $100/ year (Law student group).

Meetings/Conferences:
Number of non-conference events/year: 5

Publications:
Membership Directory; on-line
Newsletter; on-line

National Lieutenant Governors Association
(1962)
75 Cavalier Blvd.
Suite 226
Florence, KY 41042
Tel: (859) 283-1400 *Fax:* (859) 244-8001
Website: nlga.us
Members: 55 individuals
Staff: 3
Annual Budget: $500-1,000,000

Personnel:
Executive Director: Julia Hurst
  E-Mail: jhurst@csg.org

Historical Note:
Formerly (2002) National Conference of Lieutenant Governors. NLGA promotes the exchange of information, fosters interstate cooperation, and seeks to improve the efficiency and effectiveness of the office of the lieutenant governor. Membership: $5,000-10,000/year.

Meetings/Conferences: Annual
2013 - Oklahoma City, OK (The Skirvin hotel)/July 17 - 19

Publications:
NLGA Focus; quarterly; adv.

Membership List Available to Non-members

National Lighting Bureau *(1976)*
8811 Colesville Rd.
Suite G106
Silver Spring, MD 20910
Tel: (301) 587-9572 *Fax:* (301) 589-2017
E-Mail: info@nlb.com
Website: nlb.com
Staff: 1
Tax: 501(c)(3)

Personnel:
Executive Director: John P. Bachner
  E-Mail: john@nlb.org

Historical Note:
The National Lighting Bureau (NLB) is a not-for-profit organization founded to educate lighting decision-makers about the benefits of High-Benefit Lighting. NLB exists to create demand for High-Benefit Lighting, efficent lighting designed to optimize human performance, health, safety, and commerce by educating those who make and influence decisions about lighting.

National Lime Association *(1902)*
200 N. Glebe Rd.
Suite 800
Arlington, VA 22203
Tel: (703) 243-5463 *Fax:* (703) 243-5489
E-Mail: natlime@lime.org

Website: lime.org
Members: 21 manufacturers
Staff: 4
Annual Budget: $1-2,000,000
Tax: 501(c)(6)

Personnel:
Executive Director and General Counsel: Arline M. Seeger
    E-Mail: aseeger@lime.org
Director, Meetings and Membership Services: Ada Lucero
Director, Government Affairs: Hunter Prillaman
    E-Mail: hprillaman@lime.org

Historical Note:
The trade association for U.S. and Canadian manufacturers of high calcium quicklime, dolomitic quicklime, and hydrated lime. Represents the interests of its members in Washington, provides input on standards and specifications for lime, and funds and manages research on current and new uses for lime. Membership: $7500 (Associate); $750 (Affiliate).

Meetings/Conferences:
Conference Chair: Ada Lucero

Publications:
Membership Directory; on-line

National Limousine Association (1985)
49 S. Maple Ave.
Marlton, NJ 08053
Tel: (856) 596-3344 *Fax:* (856) 596-2145
TollFree: (800) 652-7007
E-Mail: info@limo.org
Website: limo.org
Members: 2000 companies
Staff: 3
Annual Budget: $500-1,000,000

Personnel:
Executive Director: Patricia A. Nelson
    E-Mail: patricia.nelson@limo.org
Manager, Association Programs: Darcie-Jo Benard
    E-Mail: darcie.benard@limo.org
Coordinator, Membership Services: Kim Werbos
    E-Mail: kim.werbos@limo.org

Historical Note:
NLA's mission is to inform, educate and professionalize its members to ensure the continued growth, development and prosperity of their organizations and chauffeured transportation industry. Members are limousine company owners, suppliers and manufacturers. Membership: $102.50-780 (Operator, based on Fleet size); $257.50 (Supplier); $182.50 (Association); $517.50 (Manufacturers/Coachbuilders/Networks).

Meetings/Conferences: Annual
Conference Chair: Darcie-Jo Benard
2013 - Las Vegas, NV (MGM Grand Hotel and Casino)/ Feb. 5
Number of non-conference events/year: 2

Publications:
Limo Scene; bi-monthly; adv.
Membership Directory; annually
NLA E-News; bi-weekly
NLA News & Views; quarterly

Membership List Available to Non-members

National Lincoln Sheep Breeders Association (1891)
8291 S. Cedar Creek Rd.
Dowling, MI 49050
Tel: (314) 308-7491
E-Mail: info@lincolnsheep.com
Website: lincolnsheep.com
Members: 85 individuals
Staff: 2
Annual Budget: Under $10,000

Personnel:
President: Brian Larson
    E-Mail: longwools@mei.net

Historical Note:
Members are breeders and fanciers of Lincoln sheep. Membership: $25 (New Senior Members); Free (Junior Members), plus $10 initiation fee.

Meetings/Conferences: Annual

Publications:
The Lincoln Newsletter

National Lipid Association (2002)
6816 Southpoint Pkwy.
Suite 1000
Jacksonville, FL 32216

Tel: (904) 998-0854 *Fax:* (904) 998-0855
Website: lipid.org
Members: 3500 individuals
Staff: 14
Annual Budget: $2-5,000,000
Tax: 501(c)(6)

Personnel:
Executive Director: Christopher R. Seymour MBA
Director, Education: Chris DeVille
Web Developer: Tad Kellermann
Office Manager: Cindy Moore
Director, Information Technology: Clark Morgan
Director, Business Development and Meeting Management: Shannon O'Leary
Director, Development Programs: Lindsay Otto
Manager, Events: Maggie Schaefer
Manager, Publications: Megan Seery
Coordinator, Communications: Katie Smith
Director, Communications: Judi Spann APR, CPRC
Coordinator, Membership: Deborah Walker

Historical Note:
NLA was created out of the success established by the Southeast Lipid Association (SELA), which was formed in 1997 by a group of pioneering lipid researchers and clinicians from the Southeastern United States. NLA's mission is to enhance the practice of lipid management in clinical medicine and to reduce deaths related to high cholesterol. Members are medical and scientific professionals who manage patients with lipid disorders and increased cardiovascular risk. Membership: $100 (Active/ Industry/International); Free (Fellow/Trainee); $250 (Three Year Member).

Continuing Education:
Certification Designation/s: ML, LMTC, ACCL, ABCL

Meetings/Conferences:
Conference Chair: Maggie Schaefer
Number of non-conference events/year: 29

Publications:
Journal of Clinical Lipidology; bi-monthly; adv.
Member Directory; on-line
The Lipid Spin Newsletter; quarterly

National Livestock Producers Association (1921)
13570 Meadowgrass Dr.
Suite 201
Colorado Springs, CO 80921
Tel: (719) 538-8843 *Fax:* (719) 538-8847
TollFree: (800) 237-7193
E-Mail: nlpa@nlpa.org
Website: nlpa.org
Members: 10 livestock marketing cooperatives
Staff: 3
Annual Budget: $500-1,000,000
Tax: 501(c)(5)

Personnel:
President and Chief Executive Officer: R. Scott Stuart
    E-Mail: scott.stuart@nlpa.org
Director, Operations: Scharee Atchison
    E-Mail: slatchison@nlpa.org
Director, Communications: Melissa Schneider
    E-Mail: maschneider@nlpa.org

Historical Note:
Formerly (1943) National Live Stock Marketing Association. NLPA is a federation of cooperative livestock marketing agencies and regional credit corporations whose services are designed to help member marketing agencies and credit corporations become more effective and efficient for their producer-patrons.

Meetings/Conferences: Annual
Conference Chair: Scharee Atchison
Number of non-conference events/year: 1

Publications:
Membership Directory; on-line
National Producer; bi-monthly
Weekly News Brief; weekly

National Lubricating Grease Institute (1933)
4635 Wyandotte St.
Suite 202
Kansas City, MO 64112-1542
Tel: (816) 931-9480 *Fax:* (816) 753-5026
E-Mail: nlgi@nlgi.com
Website: nlgi.org
Members: 300 companies
Staff: 2
Annual Budget: $500-1,000,000
Tax: 501(c)(6)

Personnel:
Executive Director: Kimberly Bott
    E-Mail: kim@nlgi.org
Assistant, Administration: Marilyn Brohm

Historical Note:
Incorporated as the National Association of Lubricating Grease Manufacturers, assumed its present name in 1937. NLGI's mission is to disseminate information that can lead to the development of better lubricating greases for the consumer and to provide better grease lubrication engineering service to the industry. Membership: $945 (Active Manufacturing/Associate/Supplier); $620-945 (Marketing); $345 (Technical/Consumer).

Continuing Education:
Enrollment: 50
Certification Designation/s: CLGS

Meetings/Conferences: Annual

Publications:
Membership Directory; annually
NLGI Grease Production Survey; annually
NLGI Spokesman; bi-monthly; adv.

National Luggage Dealers Association (1925)
1817 Elmdale Ave.
Glenview, IL 60026
Tel: (847) 998-6869 *Fax:* (847) 998-6884
E-Mail: inquiry@nlda.com
Website: nlda.com
Members: 200 individuals
Staff: 13
Annual Budget: $500-1,000,000

Personnel:
Executive Director: Marrilyn Murray
    E-Mail: Marilyn@nlda.com

Historical Note:
NLDA operates as a volunteer buying organization. NLDA acts as a purchasing office for membership. Members are retailers of luggage, leather goods, gifts and handbags with over 300 stores nationally. Membership fee based on retail volume.

Meetings/Conferences: Annual
2013 - Chicago, IL (Navy Pier Park)/June 20 - 21

Publications:
Membership Directory; on-line

National Lumber and Building Material Dealers Association (1917)
2025 M St. NW
Suite 800
Washington, DC 20036-3309
Tel: (202) 367-1169 *Fax:* (202) 367-2169
TollFree: (800) 634-8645
E-Mail: info@dealer.org
Website: dealer.org
Members: 6000 companies
Staff: 7
Annual Budget: $500-1,000,000
Tax: 501(c)(6)

Personnel:
President and Chief Executive Officer: Michael O'Brien CAE
    E-Mail: mike@dealer.org
Director, Legislative Affairs and Grassroots Activities: Ben Gann
    E-Mail: ben@dealer.org
Contact, Communications and Operations Associate: Stephen Kendrick
    E-Mail: stephen@dealer.org
Government Affairs Counsel: Frank Moore
    E-Mail: frank@dealer.org
Director, Membership Services: Jonathan M. Paine
    E-Mail: jonathan@dealer.org
Manager, Meetings: John Rubsamen
    E-Mail: john@dealer.org

Historical Note:
Formed in Chicago as National Retail Lumber Dealers Association, assumed its current name in 1962. NLBMDA's mission is to advance the national agenda for America's building material suppliers. Member services include government affairs, trend analysis, best practice research, industry- specific education and training, and networking. Membership: $5,000/year.

Meetings/Conferences: Annual
Conference Chair: John Rubsamen
Number of non-conference events/year: 1

Publications:
Membership Directory; on-line

NLBMDA Manufacturers & Services Council Directory;
on-line; adv.

National Mail Order Association (1972)

2807 Polk St. NE
Minneapolis, MN 55418-2954
Tel: (612) 788-1673
E-Mail: info@nmoa.org
Website: nmoa.org
Members: 10000 individuals and companies
Staff: 5
Annual Budget: $100-250,000

Personnel:
President: John D. Schulte
   E-Mail: schulte@nmoa.org
Editor: Brad Lee
   E-Mail: mrBmagic@aol.com
Vice President, Business Development: Cindy Schulte
   E-Mail: cindy@nmoa.org

Historical Note:
NMOA's mission is to provide education, information, and business connections to entrepreneurs and small businesses around the world. NMOA helps small-to-midsize firms in mail order and other direct marketing areas. Membership: $365 (Reseller, within U.S. or International/Service Provider/Product Promotion Package); $400 (Reseller, International); $199 (Individual and New Business Package, within U.S. or International); $234 (Individual and New Business Package, International).

Publications:
Direct Marketing Digest; monthly
Direct Marketing Resource Directory; on-line

National Management Association (1925)

2210 Arbor Blvd.
Dayton, OH 45439
Tel: (937) 294-0421 *Fax:* (937) 294-2374
E-Mail: nma@nma1.org
Website: nma1.org
Members: 18000 individuals
Staff: 6
Annual Budget: $500-1,000,000
Tax: 501(c)(6)

Personnel:
President: Steve Bailey
   E-Mail: steve@nma1.org
Manager, Membership Services: Robin Furlong
   E-Mail: robin@nma1.org
Vice President, Integration and Operations: Sue Kappeler
   E-Mail: sue@nma1.org
Vice President, Professional Development: Karen Tobias

Historical Note:
Formerly (1956) National Association of Foremen. Absorbed International Management Council in 2004. NMA creates leadership development products and opportunities that maximize the potential of its members, sponsoring organizations, and communities. Members are middle level and supervisory management personnel united to professionalize management and promote American competitive enterprise. Membership: $48/year (Individual, with a one time registration fee of $20).

Continuing Education:
Certification Designation/s: CM, CMP

Meetings/Conferences: Annual
Number of non-conference events/year: 2

Publications:
Newsletters

National Marine Bankers Association (1979)

One Melvin Ave.
C/O Sterling Acceptance Corporation
Annapolis, MD 21401
Tel: (800) 525-0554 *Fax:* (410) 268-3755
E-Mail: bmcardle@nmma.org
Website: marinebankers.org
Members: 80 companies
Staff: 3
Annual Budget: $100-250,000

Personnel:
President: Karen Trostle
   E-Mail: karen@sterlingacceptance.com

Historical Note:
NMBA's purpose is to educate current and prospective lenders in marine financing procedures, encourage the extension of credit to consumer and trade borrowers, maintain alliances with industry partners, measure and report on the vitality of the marine lending market, and actively maintain networking and communication benefits

for its members. *Membership: $445/year, plus $100 initiation fee.*

Publications:
Membership Directory; on-line
NMBA Newsletter; on-line
The Business of Pleasure Boats; irregular

National Marine Distributors Association (1965)

37 Pratt St.
Essex, CT 06426-1159
Tel: (860) 767-7898 *Fax:* (860) 767-7932
E-Mail: info@nmdaonline.com
Website: nmdaonline.com
Members: 225 individuals
Staff: 2
Annual Budget: $250-500,000
Tax: 501(c)(6)

Personnel:
Executive Director: Nancy Cueroni
   E-Mail: executivedirector@nmdaonline.com

Historical Note:
NMDA's mission is to promote the common business interests and conditions of wholesale distributors of marine accessories and of the marine industry in general. Members are wholesalers of marine accessories and hardware.

Meetings/Conferences: Annual
Conference Chair: Nancy Cueroni

Publications:
Membership Directory; on-line
NMDA eNewsletter; on-line
The Journal

National Marine Educators Association (1976)

P.O. Box 1470
Ocean Springs, MS 39566-1470
Tel: (228) 896-9182 *Fax:* (228) 701-1771
E-Mail: nmea@usm.edu
Website: marine-ed.org/
Members: 1200 individuals
Staff: 3
Annual Budget: $50-100,000

Personnel:
Editor: Lisa Tooker
   E-Mail: ltooker@sbcglobal.net
Membership Secretary: Sharon Walker
   E-Mail: sharon.walker@usm.edu

Historical Note:
NMEA's purpose is to provide a focus for marine and aquatic studies all over the world. NMEA is affiliated with American Association Foor the Advancement of Science and National Science Teachers Association. Membership: $50 (Active/Institutional); $45 (Affiliate); $65 (Associate); $600 (Life); $25 (Student); $300 (Corporate) ; $75 (Family) .

Meetings/Conferences: Annual
2013 - Mobile, AL (Spring Hill College)/July 22 - 26
2014 - Annapolis, MD (Loews Annapolis Hotel)/July 19 - 24

Publications:
Journal of Marine Education; quarterly
NMEA News; quarterly

National Marine Electronics Association (1957)

Seven Riggs Ave.
Severna Park, MD 21146
Tel: (410) 975-9425 *Fax:* (410) 975-9450
E-Mail: info@nmea.org
Website: nmea.org
Members: 550 members
Staff: 4
Annual Budget: $500-1,000,000

Personnel:
Interim Executive Director: Bruce Angus
   E-Mail: bangus@nmea.org
Office Manager: Cindy Love
   E-Mail: clove@nmea.org
Technical Director: Steve Spitzer
   E-Mail: sspitzer@nmea.org

Historical Note:
NMEA's mission is to promote the technical marine electronics dealer through education, communication, training and certification, to strengthen the industry's reputation in the marketplace through industry standards and recognition of excellence. Membership: $175-1,425/year.

Continuing Education:
Certification Designation/s: CMET, MEI

Meetings/Conferences: Annual

Publications:
Marine Electronics Journal; bi-monthly
Sighs Matter; adv.

National Marine Manufacturers Association (1979)

231 S. LaSalle St.
Suite 2050
Chicago, IL 60604
Tel: (312) 946-6200 *Fax:* (312) 946-0388
Website: nmma.org
Members: 1700 companies
Staff: 33
Annual Budget: $25-50,000,000

Personnel:
President: Thomas J. Dammrich
   E-Mail: tdammrich@nmma.org
Chief Marketing Officer and Senior Vice President, Marketing and Communications: Carl Blackwell
   E-Mail: cblackwell@nmma.org
Senior Vice President, Finance and Chief Financial Officer: Craig Boskey
   E-Mail: cboskey@nmma.org
Show Director, International BoatBuilders' Exhibition and Conference: Anne Dunbar
Director, Trade Events and Meeting Services: Stephen Evans
   E-Mail: sevans@nmma.org
Vive President, Engineering Standards: Thomas Marhevko
   E-Mail: tmarhevko@nmma.org
Director, Information Technology: Robert Marino
   E-Mail: rmarino@nmma.org
Director, Advertising: Cindy Pechous
   E-Mail: cpechous@nmma.org
Director, Human Resources: Kate Plush
   E-Mail: kplush@nmma.org
Director, Membership Services: Bryan Welsh
   E-Mail: bwelsh@nmma.org

Historical Note:
NMMA is dedicated to advocating for and promoting the strength of marine manufacturing, the sales and service networks of its members, and the boating lifestyle. Represents companies that manufacture products or provide services to the recreational boating industry, including boats, engines, trailers and electronic marine accessories. Membership: $1,000-3,00,000 (Manufacturing, dues based on Sales); $650 (Associate).

Continuing Education:
Certification Designation/s: CE

Meetings/Conferences: Annual
Conference Chair: Stephen Evans

Publications:
Boat Show Exhibitor
Boating Industry Statistics Dashboard; monthly
Boating News Net Economic Report; on-line
Currents; on-line
Membership Directory; on-line
MSR/Monthly Shipment Report; monthly
New Powerboat Registrations Report; quarterly
Powerboat Registrations Report; quarterly
US Statistical Abstract; annually
Washington Wave; on-line

National Marine Representatives Association (1960)

8200 Hampson St.
Suite 300
New Orleans, LA 70118
Tel: (847) 662-3167 *Fax:* (847) 336-7126
E-Mail: info@nmraonline.org
Website: nmraonline.org
Members: 530 individuals
Staff: 2
Annual Budget: $25-50,000

Personnel:
President: Chris Kelly

Historical Note:
NMRA serves as a networking tool and information source, promoting the benefits of utilizing independent marine representatives for sales. Members are independent boat and marine accessory sales representatives. Membership: $300 (Full/Affiliate, Initially); $75 (Associate); $150 (Affiliate, Thereafter).

Publications:
Membership Directory; annually

Tidings; quarterly

National Maritime Alliance (1988)
Adm. Ernest Eller House
Greenville, NC 27858-4353
Tel: (252) 328-6097 *Fax:* (252) 328-6754
Website: hnsa.org/nam.htm
Staff: 2
Annual Budget: $100-250,000

Personnel:
Contact: Karen Underwood

Historical Note:
NMA represents individuals and organizations involved in preserving and promoting America's maritime heritage.

National Maritime Safety Association (1956)
919 18th St. NW
Suite 901
Washington, DC 20006
Tel: (202) 587-4830 *Fax:* (202) 587-4888
E-Mail: mto@nmsa.us
Website: nmsa.us
Members: 15 Companies
Staff: 4
Annual Budget: $100-250,000

Personnel:
Executive Director: Charles "Chuck" T. Carroll Jr.
  E-Mail: carroll@nmsa.us
General Counsel: F.E. Win Froelich
Editor: Meg Kane
Meetings Coordinator and Office Manager: Elain Tendler
  E-Mail: elaine@nmsa.us

Historical Note:
NMSA's mission is to aid, promote and support safety in marine cargo handling operations. NMSA represents the marine cargo handling Industry in United States in safety and health matters arising under various statutes.

Meetings/Conferences: Annual
Conference Chair: Elain Tendler
2013 - Napa, CA (Silverado Resort and Spa)/June 26 - 28

National Mastitis Council (1961)
421 S. Nine Mound Rd.
Verona, WI 53593
Tel: (608) 848-4615 *Fax:* (608) 848-4671
E-Mail: nmc@nmconline.org
Website: nmconline.org
Members: 2000 individuals
Staff: 1
Annual Budget: $250-500,000

Personnel:
Executive Director: Anne Saeman
  E-Mail: anne@nmconline.org

Historical Note:
Formerly the National Mastitis Council. NMC provides a forum for education and global exchange of information on milk quality, mastitis and relevant research. Members are dairy industry professionals. Membership: $125 (Individual); $25 (Full Time Student) ; $150-550 (Organization).

Meetings/Conferences: Annual
2013 - San Diego, CA (Omni San Diego Hotel)/Jan. 27 - 29
Number of non-conference events/year: 2

Publications:
Membership Directory; on-line
Udder Topics; bi-monthly

National Medical Association (1895)
8403 Colesville Rd.
Suite 920
Silver Spring, MD 20910
Tel: (202) 347-1895 *Fax:* (202) 347-0722
TollFree: (800) 662-0554
Website: nmanet.org
Members: 30000 individuals
Staff: 35
Annual Budget: $50-100,000
Tax: 501(c)(3)

Personnel:
President: Cedric M. Bright FACP, MD
Associate Executive Director, Community and Mission Services: Ivonne Fuller-Bertrand MPA

Historical Note:

NMA's mission is to enhance the art and science of medicine for people of African descent through education, advocacy, and health policy to encourage health and wellness, eliminate health disparities, and sustain physician viability. Membership: $20-1000/year.

Continuing Education:
Certification Designation/s: CME

Meetings/Conferences: Annual
Number of non-conference events/year: 3

Publications:
NMA E-Newsletter; monthly
NMA Journal; monthly

National Migrant and Seasonal Head Start Association (1969)
1726 M St. NW
Suite 602
Washington, DC 20036
Tel: (202) 223-9889 *Fax:* (202) 828-6005
Website: nmshsaonline.org
Staff: 6
Annual Budget: $250-500,000
Tax: 501(c)(3)

Personnel:
Executive Director: Cleofas "Cleo" Rodriguez Jr.
  E-Mail: crodriguez@nmshsaonline.org

Historical Note:
NMSHSA's purpose is to advocate for resources, create partnerships, and affect public policy for its members. Helps member agencies provide quality comprehensive services to farm worker children and their families.

Meetings/Conferences: Annual
2013 - Washington, DC (Gaylord National Resort and Convention Center)/April 28 - May 3

Publications:
NMSHSA Newsletter

National Military Family Association, Inc. (1969)
2500 N. Van Dorn St.,
Suite 102
Alexandria, VA 22302-1601
Tel: (703) 931-6632 *Fax:* (703) 931-4600
TollFree: (800) 260-0218
E-Mail: Info@MilitaryFamily.org
Website: militaryfamily.org
Staff: 9
Annual Budget: $10-25,000,000
Tax: 501(c)(3)

Personnel:
Executive Director: Joyce Wessel Raezer
  E-Mail: families@nmfa.org
Director, Development and Membership: Kathleen Burke
Chief Financial Officer: Britt Hetherington
Director, Communications: Michelle Joyner
Director, Government Relations: Kathleen Moakler
  E-Mail: Kathleen.moakler@nmfa.org
Director, Administration and Human Resources: Pat Travis

Historical Note:
National Military Family Association mission is to fight for benefits and programs that strengthen and protect uniformed services families and reflect the Nation's respect for their Service. Membership: $20 (Military Family/Parent Member/Civilian Family).

Publications:
E-Newsletter

National Military Intelligence Association (1973)
256 Morris Creek Rd.
Cullen, VA 23934
Tel: (434) 542-5929 *Fax:* (703) 738-7847
E-Mail: admin@nmia.org
Website: nmia.org
Members:
2500 individuals
42 corporate members
Staff: 4
Annual Budget: $100-250,000
Tax: 501(c)(6)

Personnel:
President: Joseph Keefe COl, USAF (Ret.)
Contact, Corporate Liaisons and Meeting Contact: Deb Davis
  E-Mail: admin@nmia.org
Treasurer: Mark Lovingood
Editor: William C. Spracher PhD

Historical Note:

Formerly (1974) Army intelligence professional organization. A professional association focusing on defense intelligence, including strategic, tactical and counter intelligence affecting the security of the United States. NMIA's mission is to support the professional development of military intelligence practitioners and help improve the effectiveness of joint military intelligence operations in support of armed forces and homeland security efforts. Members are current and former U. S. intelligence professionals and U. S. citizens interested in supporting defense intelligence through educational efforts. Membership: $50-75 (Individual); $750-1,500 (Corporate).

Meetings/Conferences: Annual
Conference Chair: Deb Davis

Publications:
NMIA Z-GRAM and CABLE Gram; daily; adv.

Membership List Available to Non-members

National Milk Producers Federation (1916)
2101 Wilson Blvd.
Suite 400
Arlington, VA 22201
Tel: (703) 243-6111 *Fax:* (703) 841-9328
E-Mail: info@nmpf.org
Website: nmpf.org
Members: 30 dairy cooperatives
Staff: 19
Annual Budget: $25-50,000,000

Personnel:
President and Chief Executive Officer: Jerry Kozak
  E-Mail: JKozak@nmpf.org
Executive Vice President: Tom Balmer
  E-Mail: tbalmer@nmpf.org
Senior Vice President, Strategic Initiatives and Trade Policy: Jaime Castaneda
  E-Mail: jcastaneda@nmpf.org
Director, Regulatory Affairs: Betsy Flores
  E-Mail: BFlores@NMPF.org
Senior Vice President, Communications: Christopher Galen
  E-Mail: cgalen@nmpf.org
Senior Director, Executive Office and Member Relations: Anuja Miner
  E-Mail: aminer@nmpf.org
Director, Finance and Administration: Gail Mobley
  E-Mail: GMobley@nmpf.org
Senior Vice President, Marketing and Economic Research: Jim Tillison
  E-Mail: JTillison@nmpf.org

Historical Note:
The National Cooperative Milk Producers Federation assumed its present name in 1966 and absorbed the National Creameries Association in 1966. NMPF provides a forum through which dairy farmers and their cooperatives formulate policy on national issues that affect milk production and marketing.

Meetings/Conferences: Annual
2013 - Phoenix, AZ (Arizona Biltmore Resort and Spa)/ Nov. 11 - 13
2014 - Grapevine, TX (Gaylord Texan Hotel and Convention Center, Dallas Texas)/Oct. 27 - 29

Publications:
Dairy Research Insights; monthly
News for Dairy Coops

National Miniature Donkey Association (1989)
6450 Dewey Rd.
Rome, NY 13440
Tel: (315) 336-0154 *Fax:* (315) 339-4414
E-Mail: nmdaasset@aol.com
Website: nmdaasset.com
Staff: 3
Annual Budget: $50-100,000

Personnel:
General Manager and Asset Editor: Lynn Gattari
  E-Mail: deweymeadowsfarm@aol.com

Historical Note:
NMDA Purpose is to protect and promote the miniature donkey breed. Membership: $35 (Domestic); $60 (International).

Publications:
ASSET Magazine; adv.

National Mining Association (1995)
101 Constitution Ave. NW
Suite 500 East
Washington, DC 20001-2133

Tel: (202) 463-2600 *Fax:* (202) 463-2666
Website: nma.org
Members: 325 corporations
Staff: 40
Annual Budget: $25-50,000,000
Tax: 501(c)(6)

Personnel:
President and Chief Executive Officer: Harold P. Quinn Jr.
  E-Mail: hquinn@nma.org
Federal lobbyist and Associate General Counsel: Tawny
  Bridgeford
  E-Mail: tbridgeford@nma.org
Associate General Counsel: Bradford V. Frisby
  E-Mail: bfrisby@nma.org
M. Richardson "Rich" Nolan
  E-Mail: rnolan@nma.org
Senior Vice President, Membership Services: Moya
  Phelleps
  E-Mail: mphelleps@nma.org
Vice President, External Communications: Luke Popovich
  E-Mail: lpopovich@nma.org
Senior Vice President, Communications: Carol Raulston
  E-Mail: craulston@nma.org
Senior Vice President, Administration and Finance: Roger
  Roberts
Contact, Legal and Regulatory Affairs: Katie Sweeney
  E-Mail: ksweeney@nma.org
Manager, Meetings and Member Services: Ashley West
  E-Mail: awest@nma.org

Historical Note:
*NMA was formed as the result of the 1995 merger of the
National Coal Association (NCA) and the American Mining
Congress (AMC). NMA's mission is to create and maintain
a broad base of political support for the mining industry
and to help the nation realize the economic and national
security benefits of America's domestic mining capability.*

Meetings/Conferences: Annual
Conference Chair: Ashley West
Number of non-conference events/year: 2

Publications:
Coal Industry Employment/Production Reports; bi-
  annually
Facts About Coal and Minerals
Gold Publications
Health & Safety
International Coal Review; monthly
Membership Directory; on-line
Statistical Publications
Weekly Statistical Summary; weekly

Membership List Available to Non-members

National Minority Business Council *(1972)*
120 Broadway
19th Floor
New York, NY 10271
Tel: (212) 693-5050 *Fax:* (212) 693-5048
E-Mail: info@nmbc.org
Website: nmbc.org/home
Members: 550 companies and 350 vendor firms
Staff: 1
Annual Budget: $250-500,000
Tax: 501(c)(3)

Personnel:
President and Chief Executive Officer: John F. Robinson

Historical Note:
*NMBC is dedicated to provide business assistance,
educational opportunities, seminars, purchasing listings and
related services to hundreds of businesses throughout the
tri-state area and across the nation. Membership: $375/
year.*

Publications:
Business Directory
Minority Business Journal; bi-monthly

National Minority Supplier Development Council
(1972)
1359 Broadway
Tenth Floor
New York, NY 10018
Tel: (212) 944-2430 *Fax:* (212) 719-9611
Website: nmsdc.org
Members: 3500 Corporate Members and 37
  regional councils
Staff: 22
Annual Budget: $10-25,000,000
Tax: 501(c)(3)

Personnel:

President: Joset B. Wright
Director, Communications: Kim Brown
  E-Mail: kim.brown@nmsdc.org
Director, Learning Programs: Maggie Chaparro
  E-Mail: maggie.chaparro@nmsdc.org
Manager, Marketing Database: Terri Childress
  E-Mail: theresa.childress@nmsdc.org
Vice President, Finance and Administration: Casilda Del
  Valle
  E-Mail: casilda.delvalle@nmsdc.org
Director, Conferences: Suzette Eaddy
Vice President, Information Technology and Services: Len
  Leach
  E-Mail: len.leach@nnmsdc.org
Director, Development and Membership Services: Maureen
  Vialva
  E-Mail: maureen.vialva@nmsdc.org

Historical Note:
*Formerly (1980) the National Minority Purchasing Council,
NMSDC works to provide increased procurement and
business opportunities for minority businesses of all sizes.
Members are publicly-owned, privately-owned and foreign-
owned companies, as well as universities, hospitals and
other buying institutions. Membership fee based on a sliding
scale.*

Continuing Education:
Certification Designation/s: CMS

Meetings/Conferences: Annual
Conference Chair: Suzette Eaddy
2013 - San Antonio, TX (Henry B. Gonzalez
  Convention Center and the Lila Cockrell Theatre)/
  Oct. 27 - 30
2014 - Orlando, FL (Orange County Convention
  Center)/Nov. 2 - 5

Publications:
Field Operations Report; on-line
MInority Supplier News

National Mitigation Banking Association *(1998)*
1155 15th St. NW
Suite 500
Washington, DC 20005
Tel: (202) 457-8409
E-Mail: info@mitigationbanking.org
Website: mitigationbanking.org
Members: 85 member companies
Staff: 1
Annual Budget: $100-250,000
Tax: 501(c)(6)

Personnel:
Executive Director: Christopher M. Murphy

Historical Note:
*NMBA's mission is to promote federal legislation and
regulatory policy that encourages mitigation banking as a
means of compensating for adverse impacts to the nation's
environment.*

Publications:
NMBA Newsletter; quarterly; adv.

National Mobility Equipment Dealers Association
(1988)
3327 W. Bearss Ave.
Tampa, FL 33618
Tel: (813) 264-2697 *Fax:* (813) 962-8970
TollFree: (866) 948-8341
Website: nmeda.com
Members: 600 Members
Staff: 6
Annual Budget: $2-5,000,000

Personnel:
Chief Executive Officer: Dave Hubbard
Coordinator, Quality Assurance Programs: Kristen
  Clevidence
Coordinator, Membership Services: Doris Santiago
  Cruzado
  E-Mail: doris@nmeda.org
Manager, Creative and Communications: Jenna DeTrapani

Historical Note:
*NMEDA is an association of mobility equipment dealers,
driver rehabilitation specialists, and other professionals
dedicated to broadening the opportunities for people with
disabilities to drive or be transported in vehicles modified
with mobility equipment. Membership: $1,050-2,100
(Dealer/Manufacturer, based on gross sales); $52.50
(Associate).*

Continuing Education:
Certification Designation/s: QAP

Meetings/Conferences: Annual
2013 - Daytona Beach, FL (Hilton Daytona Beach
  Resort/Ocean Walk Village)/Feb. 6 - 8

Publications:
Circuit Breaker; quarterly
NMEDA Newsletter; on-line

Membership List Available to Non-members

The National Money Transmitters Association
(1999)
12 Welwyn Rd.
Suite C
Great Neck, NY 11021
Tel: (516) 829-2742
Website: nmta.us
Staff: 1
Annual Budget: $100-250,000

Personnel:
Executive Director: David Landsman
  E-Mail: david@nmta.us

Historical Note:
*NMTA's mission is to promote a sense of community
and information sharing among members. Membership:
$295-10,000/year.*

National Motor Freight Traffic Association, Inc.
(1956)
1001 N. Fairfax St.
Suite 600
Alexandria, VA 22314
Tel: (703) 838-1810 *Fax:* (703) 683-6296
TollFree: (866) 411-6632
E-Mail: customerservice@nmfta.org
Website: nmfta.org
Members: 800 motor carriers and other
  transportation companies.
Staff: 18
Annual Budget: $5-10,000,000
Tax: 501(c)(6)

Personnel:
General Manager: Paul Levine
  E-Mail: levine@nmfta.org
Coordinator, Meetings: Colleen Airgood
Chief Technology Officer: Urban Jonson
Manager, Marketing: Betty Stenaka
Manager, Finance and Human Resources: Leslie Tate

Historical Note:
*NMFTA's mission is to serve as a research and development
organization providing the transportation industry with
the necessary information to advance and improve their
interests and welfare. Membership: $290-13,314/year.*

Meetings/Conferences:
Conference Chair: Colleen Airgood
2013 - San Diego, CA (Westin San Diego)/Jan. 27
2013 - Alexandria, VA (Hilton Alexandria Old Town)/
  June 2 - 3
2013 - Alexandria, VA (Hilton Alexandria Old Town)/
  Sept. 22 - 23
2014 - Tucson, AZ (Omni Tucson National Golf Resort
  and Spa)/Jan. 26 - 29
2014 - Ft. Lauderdale, FL (Lago Mar Resort and Club)/
  May 18 - 21

Publications:
Continental Directory of Standard Point Location
  Codes; annually
Directory of Standard Carrier Alpha Codes; annually
National Motor Freight Classification; annually
NMFTA Newsletter; on-line

National Motorsports Press Association *(1959)*
P.O. Box 500
Darlington, SC 29540
Tel: (843) 395-8900 *Fax:* (843) 393-3911
Website: nmpaonline.com
Members: 300 individuals
Staff: 2
Annual Budget: $50-100,000
Tax: 501(c)(3)

Personnel:
Executive Secretary: Bridget Holloman
  E-Mail: bholloman@darlingtonraceway.com
Secretary and Treasurer: Dustin long
  E-Mail: Dustin.Long@news-record.com

Historical Note:
*Formerly Southern Motorsports Press Association. The
National Motorsports Press Association consists of qualified*

members of the media who report on the sport of auto racing through his or her affiliation with print, radio, television or the Internet news organizations. *Membership: $35 (Press); $75 (Associate).*

Meetings/Conferences:
Number of non-conference events/year: 12

Publications:
Membership Directory; on-line

National Multi-Housing Council (*1978*)
1850 M St. NW
Suite 540
Washington, DC 20036-5803
Tel: (202) 974-2300 *Fax:* (202) 775-0112
E-Mail: info@nmhc.org
Website: nmhc.org
Members:
950 companies
1600 individuals
Staff: 31
Annual Budget: $10-25,000,000

Personnel:
President: Douglas M. Bibby
    E-Mail: dbibby@nmhc.org
Vice President, Employment Policy and Counsel: Elizabeth Feigin Befus
    E-Mail: ebefus@nmhc.org
Senior Vice President, Public Affairs and Industry Initiatives: Kimberly D. Duty
    E-Mail: kduty@nmhc.org
Director, Technology and Industry Initiatives: Lauren Dwyer
    E-Mail: ldwyer@nmhc.org
Senior Vice President, Finance and Administration: Kenny Emson
    E-Mail: kemson@nmhc.org
Senior Vice President, Government Affairs: Julianne Goodfellow
    E-Mail: jgoodfellow@nmhc.org
Vice President, Property Operations and Technology: Rick Haughey
Chief Economist and Vice President, Research: Mark H. Obrinsky
    E-Mail: mobrinsky@nmhc.org
Vice President, Membership, Marketing and Meetings: Julie Stalknecht
    E-Mail: jstalknecht@nmhc.org

Historical Note:
NMHC advocates on behalf of rental housing, conducts apartment-related research, encourages the exchange of strategic business information, and promotes the desirability of apartment living. Members are the principal officers of firms engaged in all aspects of the apartment industry, including ownership, development, management, and financing. Membership: $20,000 (Executive Committee); $15,000 (Board of Directors); $10,000 (Board of Directors-First Year); $5,000 (Advisory Committee); $2,500 (Associate).

Meetings/Conferences: Annual
Conference Chair: Julie Stalknecht
2013 - Palm Spring, CA (La Quinta Resort and Club, A Waldorf Astoria Resort)/Jan. 22 - 24
2013 - Dallas, TX (Four Seasons Hotel)/April 23 - 24
2013 - Dallas, TX (Dallas Parkway Hilton)/Nov. 11 - 13
2014 - Boca Raton, FL (Boca Raton Resort and Club)/ Jan. 21 - 23
2014 - Orlando, FL (Hilton Orlando Bonnet Creek)/ Nov. 17 - 19
2015 - Palm Spring, CA (La Quinta Resort and Club, A Waldorf Astoria Resort)/Jan. 20 - 22
2015 - San Diego, CA (Hilton San Diego Bayfront)/Nov. 17 - 19
2016 - Boca Raton, FL (Boca Raton Resort and Club)/ Jan. 19 - 21
Number of non-conference events/year: 16

Publications:
Member Directory; on-line
NMHC Newsletter; weekly

National Multiple Sclerosis Society (*1946*)
733 Third Ave.
New York, NY 10017-3288
Tel: (212) 986-3240 *Fax:* (212) 986-7981
TollFree: (800) 344-4867
E-Mail: nat@nmss.org
Website: nationalmssociety.org
Members: 480000 volunteers
Staff: 1350

Annual Budget: Over $100,000,000
Tax: 501(c)(3)

Personnel:
President and Chief Executive Officer: Joyce M. Nelson
Association Vice President, Public Affairs: Arney Rosenblat
    E-Mail: Arney.rosenblat@nmss.org

Historical Note:
Mission of NMSS is to end multiple sclerosis (MS), neurological disease of the central nervous system. NMSS funds MS research, offers services to people with MS, provides professional education programs and advances advocacy efforts. Membership: $25/year.

National Music Council (*1940*)
425 Park St.
Montclair, NJ 07043
Tel: (973) 655-7974 *Fax:* (973) 655-5432
Website: musiccouncil.org
Members: 50 organizations
Staff: 1
Annual Budget: $25-50,000
Tax: 501(c)(3)

Personnel:
Director: Dr. David Sanders PhD
    E-Mail: sandersd@mail.montclair.edu

Historical Note:
NMC's mission is to enhance and support music and music education as an integral part of the curricula in schools and the lives of American citizens.

Publications:
Membership Directory; on-line
NMC Newsletter

National Music Publishers Association (*1917*)
975 F St. NW
Suite 375
Washington, DC 20004
Tel: (202) 393-6672 *Fax:* (202) 393-6673
E-Mail: pr@nmpa.org
Website: nmpa.org
Members: 2500 members
Staff: 6
Annual Budget: $1-2,000,000

Personnel:
President and Chief Executive Officer: David M. Israelite
Vice President, Government Affairs: Allison Halatei
Director, Member Relations: Jamie R. Marotta
    E-Mail: jmarotta@nmpa.org
Senior Vice President and General Counsel: Jay Rosenthal
    E-Mail: jrosenthal@nmpa.org

Historical Note:
Formerly Music Publishers Protective Association. NMPA seeks to protect, promote, and advance the interests of music's creators. Members are publishers of music concentrated principally around New York, Los Angeles and Nashville. Membership: $100/year (Individual).

Meetings/Conferences: Annual

Publications:
The Note; quarterly; adv.

National Narcotics Officers Associations' Coalition (*1960*)
P.O. Box 2456
Covina, CA 91793-2456
Tel: (626) 960-3328 *Fax:* (626) 960-3328
E-Mail: rmsloan626@verizon.net
Website: natlnarc.org
Members:
55000 law enforcement officers
40 state narcotic associations
Staff: 2

Personnel:
Executive Director: Richard M. Sloan
    E-Mail: rmsloan626@verizon.net
Treasurer: Phil Little
    E-Mail: plittle@bladenco.org

Historical Note:
Comprised of individual state associations representing more than 50, 000 narcotic law enforcement officers. NNAOC actively monitors and supports legislative initiatives designed to increase the effectiveness of narcotic enforcement and law enforcement in general. Membership: $200-500/year.

Meetings/Conferences:
Conference Chair: Richard M. Sloan
Number of non-conference events/year: 1

Publications:
Membership Directory; on-line
The Coalition Magazine

National Naval Officers Association (*1972*)
P.O. Box 10871
Alexandria, VA 22310-0871
Tel: (703) 231-8554
E-Mail: nnoa@nnoa.org
Website: nnoa.org
Staff: 3
Annual Budget: $100-250,000

Personnel:
President: Col. Robert Clements
    E-Mail: President@nnoa.org
National Membership Director: Maj. Melissa Ayres
    E-Mail: Membership@nnoa.org
National Treasurer: Lt. Col. Grady Belyeu
    E-Mail: Treasurer@nnoa.org

Historical Note:
NNOA supports the Sea Services in recruiting, retaining, and developing the careers of minority officers. It also provides professional development and mentoring for its members. Membership: $5-750/year.

The National NeedleArts Association (*1975*)
1100-H Brandywine Blvd.
Zanesville, OH 43701-7303
Tel: (740) 455-6773 *Fax:* (740) 452-2552
TollFree: (800) 889-8662
E-Mail: info@tnna.org
Website: tnna.org
Members: 2600 businesses
Staff: 4
Annual Budget: $1-2,000,000
Tax: 501(c)(6)

Personnel:
Executive Director: Patty Parrish
    E-Mail: pparrish@offinger.com
Manager, Events: Rise Fulmer

Historical Note:
Originally National Needwork Association, assumed its current name in 2004. TNNA's mission is to advance its community of professional businesses by encouraging the passion for needlearts through professional and consumer education, industry knowledge exchange and a marketplace. Members are needlework manufacturers, designers, retailers, and distributors. Membership: $225-850 (Wholesale-based on sales volume); $60 (Retail/Affiliate).

Meetings/Conferences:
Conference Chair: Rise Fulmer
2013 - Long Beach, CA (Long Beach Convention Center)/Feb. 2 - 4
2013 - Columbus, OH (Greater Columbus Convention Center)/June 22 - 24
Number of non-conference events/year: 2

Publications:
Membership Directory; annually; adv.
Show Directory; annually
TNNA Today; adv.

The National Network for Social Work Managers (*1985*)
605 W. Olympic Blvd., Suite 600
C/O Special Service for Groups
Los Angeles, CA 90015
Tel: (213) 553-1870 *Fax:* (213) 553-1822
E-Mail: info@socialworkmanager.org
Website: socialworkmanager.org
Members: 801 organizations and individuals
Staff: 4
Annual Budget: $100-250,000
Tax: 501(c)(6)

Personnel:
President: Marilyn Sheldon Flynn PhD
    E-Mail: mflynn@usc.edu
Treasurer: Anthony J Bibbo ACSW, LICSW
    E-Mail: ajbibbo@aol.com
Program Analyst, Special Projects: Wendy Chiu MSW
    E-Mail: wchiu@ssgmain.org
Administrator Coordinator: Jennifer Roecklein

Historical Note:
NNSWM's mission is to enhance and promote effective, values-based social work management. Members are administrators and managers of human services with degrees in social work. Membership: $150 (Individual); $55 (Student/Retired/Unemployed); $100 (International); $500 (Organizational).

Continuing Education:
Certification Designation/s: CSWM

Meetings/Conferences: Annual
2013 - Newark, NJ (Paul Robeson Campus Center)/
May 16 - 17

Publications:
Social Work Manager Newsletter; monthly

National Network of Depression Centers
2929 Plymouth Rd.
Suite 300
Ann Arbor, MI 48105
Tel: (734) 332-3914 *Fax:* (734) 332-3939
Website: nndc.org
Members: 21 Institutions
Staff: 3
Annual Budget: $500-1,000,000
Tax: 501(c)(3)

Personnel:
Executive Director: John R. Hayes MD
Chief Operating Officer: Gail Campanella MBA
Research and Project Coordinator: Lauren Hart

Historical Note:
NNDC's mission is to advance scientific discovery and access to evidence-based care by developing knowledge and translating it into patient care through the collaboration of centers of excellence.

Meetings/Conferences: Annual

National Network of Estate Planning Attorneys
(1989)
3500 DePauw Blvd.
Suite 2090
Indianapolis, IN 46268
Tel: (800) 638-8681
TollFree: (800) 638-8681
E-Mail: info@nnepa.com
Website: nnepa.com
Members: 400 individuals
Staff: 10
Annual Budget: $1-2,000,000

Personnel:
President and Chief Executive Officer: Richard Randall
Counselor, Law: Rock Allen
Counselor, Membership: Deborah L. Murdock

Historical Note:
NNEPA is an interactive alliance of about 400 estate planning attorneys nationwide that provides leadership in innovative estate planning techniques to assist families from various income levels in preserving their assets and perpetuating philanthropy.

Meetings/Conferences: Biennial
2013 - Indianapolis, IN (Crowne Plaza)/April 29 - May
3
2014 - Reno, NV/Oct. 6 - 10

Publications:
e mail Newsletter; bi-weekly
Membership Directory; on-line

National Network of Grantmakers *(1980)*
2801 21st Ave. South, Suite 132
Minneapolis, MN 55407
Tel: (612) 724-0702 *Fax:* (612) 724-0705
E-Mail: nng@nng.org
Members: 450 individuals
Staff: 2
Annual Budget: $500-1,000,000

Personnel:
Executive Director: Ron McKinley

Historical Note:
NNG members are staff or trustees of private, public and corporate philanthropic organizations dedicated to social and economic justice. Membership:$200/year (individual); $1000/year (organization).

National Newspaper Association *(1885)*
P.O. Box 7540
Columbia, MO 65205-7540
Tel: (573) 777-4980 *Fax:* (573) 777-4985
TollFree: (800) 829-4662
E-Mail: info@nna.org
Website: nnaweb.org
Members: 2400 newspapers
Staff: 6
Annual Budget: $1-2,000,000
Tax: 501(c)(6)

Personnel:
Chief Executive Officer: Tonda F. Rush
E-Mail: tonda@nna.org
Planner, Annual Convention and Trade Show, Advertising and Sponsorship Sales: Cindy Joy-Rodgers
E-Mail: cindyjoy-rodgers@nna.org
Director, Communications: Stan Schwartz
E-Mail: stan@nna.org
Manager, Programs and Outreach: Sara Walsh
E-Mail: sarawalsh@nna.org

Historical Note:
Formerly (1960) National Editorial Association. NNA's mission is to protect, promote and enhance America's community newspapers. Members are suppliers to the newspaper industry, students, journalism professors, and retired publishers/owners . Membership: $155-1,288 (Newspaper); $200-300 (College Newspaper); $50-95 (Individual); $225 (Broker); $5,000 (Allied Partner); $500 (Online Newspaper/Allied); $125 (Single-title Newspapers).

Meetings/Conferences: Annual
Conference Chair: Sara Walsh
2013 - Arlington, VA (Crystal City Marriott at Reagan
National Airport)/March 13 - 15

Publications:
Allied Vendor Directory; on-line
Membership Directory; on-line
Publishers' Auxiliary; monthly; adv.
rE-print; weekly; adv.

National Newspaper Publishers Association
(1940)
3200 13th St. NW
Washington, DC 20010-2410
Tel: (202) 588-8764 *Fax:* (202) 588-5029
E-Mail: admin@nnpa.org
Website: nnpa.org
Members: 200 newspaper publishers
Staff: 4
Annual Budget: $5-10,000,000
Tax: 501(c)(3)

Personnel:
President and Chief Executive Officer: William G.
Tompkins Jr.
Treasurer: Yvonne Coleman-Bach
Editor-in-Chief: George E. Curry
E-Mail: George@nnpa.org

Historical Note:
Formerly the National Negro Publishers Association and also known as the Black Press of America. NNPA's mission is harmonizing its energies in a common purpose for the benefit of Negro journalism. It has also launched a print and web advertising-placement and press release distribution service. Membership: $150-660/year (based on circulation).

Meetings/Conferences: Annual
Number of non-conference events/year: 1

National Notary Association *(1957)*
P.O. Box 541032
Los Angeles, CA 90054-1032
Tel: (818) 739-4000 *Fax:* (800) 833-1211
TollFree: (800) 876-6827
E-Mail: nna@nationalnotary.org
Website: nationalnotary.org
Members: 310000 individuals
Staff: 200
Annual Budget: $25-50,000,000
Tax: 501(c)(3)

Personnel:
President and Chief Executive Officer: Thomas A.
Heymann
Executive Vice President and Chief Financial Officer: Jane
Eagle
Vice President, Notary Affairs: Charles N. Faerber
Director, Marketing: Thomas K. Hayden

Historical Note:
Established as the California Notary Association, assumed its present name in 1964. NNA's mission is to educate and serve Notaries throughout the U.S. and enhancing high ethical standards of conduct and sound notarial practices. Membership: $52 (NNA Member); $32 (Section Member).

Continuing Education:
Certification Designation/s: NSA

Meetings/Conferences: Annual
2013 - Austin, TX (Renaissance Austin Hotel)/June 2 -
5

Publications:

The National Notary

National Nurses United *(2009)*
8630 Fenton St.
Suite 1100
Silver Spring, MD 20910
Tel: (240) 235-2000 *Fax:* (240) 235-2019
E-Mail: info@nationalnursesunited.org
Website: nationalnursesunited.org
Members: 160,000 members
Staff: 21
Annual Budget: $5-10,000,000

Personnel:
Executive Director: Rose Ann DeMoro

Historical Note:
NNU is the professional association of registered nurses. Formed in 2009 from a merger of the United American Nurses, the California Nurses Association/National Nurses Organizing Committee and Massachusetts Nurses Association. Membership: $58.13 (Associate); $29.07 (Retired).

Publications:
National Nurse Magazine

National Ocean Industries Association *(1972)*
1120 G St. NW
Suite 900
Washington, DC 20005-3801
Tel: (202) 347-6900 *Fax:* (202) 347-8650
Website: noia.org
Members: 270 member companies
Staff: 10
Annual Budget: $2-5,000,000
Tax: 501(c)(6)

Personnel:
President: Randal Luthi
Director, Conferences: Ann Chapman
E-Mail: ann@noia.org
Vice President, Communications and External Relations:
Nicolette Nye
E-Mail: nicolette@noia.org
*Chief Administrative Officer and Director, Member
Development:* Franki K Stuntz
E-Mail: franki@noia.org

Historical Note:
NOIA is dedicated to the safe development of offshore energy for the continued growth and security of the United States. Membership includes companies involved in or branching out to pursue offshore renewable and alternative energy opportunities. Membership: $1,320-44,400/year (Company, based on gross sales allocated to U.S. offshore operations).

Meetings/Conferences: Semi-Annual
Conference Chair: Ann Chapman
2013 - Washington, DC (The Ritz-Carlton)/April 17 -
19
2013 - Colorado Springs, CO (The Broadmoor)/Oct. 2
- 4
2014 - Washington, DC (Mandarin Oriental
Washington D.C.)/April 9 - 11
2014 - Naples, FL (Ritz Carlton Golf Resort)/Nov. 5 - 7
2015 - Washington, DC (The Ritz-Carlton)/April 15 -
17
2015 - Scottsdale, AZ (The Phoenician)/Oct. 22 - 24

Publications:
Membership Directory; on-line

National Office Managers Association of America
P.O. Box 232
Dallastown, PA 17313
Tel: (877) 782-5141 *Fax:* (866) 359-0561
E-Mail: info@nomaa.net
Website: nomaa.net
Staff: 1

Personnel:
Executive Director and Founder: Desiree R. Baylin
E-Mail: desiree@nomaa.net

Historical Note:
NOMAA is a national professional association for Office Managers from all types of businesses. The National Office Managers Association of America (NOMAA) is a sister association of Physician Office Managers Association of America (POMAA). Membership: $78/year.

Continuing Education:
Certification Designation/s: COM

Publications:
Member Directory; on-line

Newsletter; monthly

National Office Products Alliance (1904)
301 N. Fairfax St.
Suite 200
Alexandria, VA 22314
Tel: (800) 542-6672
TollFree: (800) 542-6672
Website: nopanet.org
Staff: 6

Personnel:
President: Chris Bates
  E-Mail: cbates@nopanet.org
Director, Communications and Marketing: Alicia Ellis
  E-Mail: aellis@nopanet.org
Manager, Accounting: Antonio Payne
  E-Mail: apayne@iopfda.org
Director, Events and Member Services Administration:
  Billie Zidek
  E-Mail: bzidek@iopfda.org

Historical Note:
*NOPA's mission is to foster growth and improved
profitability among independent U.S. and Canadian
office products dealers and their key business
partners. Membership: $ 495 (Dealer); $ 1000
(Manufacturer, depending on the annual sales); $ 350-550
(Manufacturers, depending on the no. of employees); $ 850
(Service Provider); $ 850-4000 (Wholesaler, depending on
the annual sales).*

Meetings/Conferences:
Conference Chair: Billie Zidek

Publications:
E-Newsletter; weekly
eZine; monthly
Membership Directory; on-line

National Oilseed Processors Association (1929)
1300 L St. NW
Suite 1020
Washington, DC 20005-4168
Tel: (202) 842-0463 Fax: (202) 842-9126
E-Mail: nopa@nopa.org
Website: nopa.org
Members: 15 companies
Staff: 4
Annual Budget: $1-2,000,000

Personnel:
President: Thomas A. Hammer
  E-Mail: thammer@nopa.org
Executive Vice President, Government Relations: David J.
  Hovermale
  E-Mail: dhovermale@nopa.org
General Counsel: Elroy H. Wolff Esquire

Historical Note:
*Formerly (1929) National Soybean Processors Association,
assumed its current name in 1989. NOPA's mission is to
assist the industries to be competitive and profitable oilseed
processing industries in the world and is engaged in issues
such as international trade policy, environment and resource
management, domestic farm program and health and
safety issues. It cooperates with the U. S. Departments of
Agriculture, State and Commercial organizations concerned
with oilseed products. Members include firms engaged in
the actual processing of oilseeds, and ten associate member
firms who are consumers of vegetable oil or oilseed meal,
including some refiners and mixed feed manufacturers.
Membership is upon the approval of the Board of Directors.*

Meetings/Conferences: Annual
2013 - Marana, AZ (Ritz-Carlton, Dove Mountain)/Feb.
  10 - 14
2014 - Miami, FL (Ritz-Carlton Coconut Grove)/Feb. 10
  - 14
Number of non-conference events/year: 5

National On-Site Testing Association
2300 Commerce Pl.
McDonough, GA 30253
Fax: (770) 957-6995
Website: nationalonsitetesting.com
Staff: 2

Personnel:
President and Chief Executive Officer: John Hill
  E-Mail: john@nationalonsitetesting.com

Historical Note:
*Providing timely and accurate specimen collection for
substance abuse testing.*

National Onion Association (1913)

822 Seventh St.
Suite 510
Greeley, CO 80631-3277
Tel: (970) 353-5895 Fax: (970) 353-5897
Website: onions-usa.org
Members: 600 individuals and companies
Staff: 3
Annual Budget: $500-1,000,000
Tax: 501(c)(6)

Personnel:
Executive Vice President: Wayne Mininger
Administrative Assistant: Monna Canaday
Director, Public and Industry Relations: Kim Reddin
  E-Mail: kreddin@onions-usa.org

Historical Note:
*NOA is the official organization representing growers,
shippers, brokers, and commercial representatives of
the U.S. onion industry. Voluntary contributions (dues/
assessments) are sole means of support. Membership:
$175-1,500/year.*

Meetings/Conferences: Semi-Annual
2013 - Loveland, CO/July 17 - 20

Publications:
Membership Directory; annually
NOA Newsletter; monthly; adv.

National Onsite Wastewater Recycling Association (1991)
601 Wythe St.
Alexandria, VA 22314
Fax: (703) 535-5263
TollFree: (800) 966-2942
E-Mail: info@nowra.org
Website: nowra.org
Members: 75000 individuals
Staff: 3
Annual Budget: $100-250,000
Tax: 501(c)(6)

Personnel:
President: Dick Otis DEE, P E, PhD
Secretary and Treasurer: Gregory D. Graves

Historical Note:
*NOWRA promotes the advancement and growth of the
onsite and decentralized wastewater industry by promoting
sustainable wastewater management on a watershed
basis through education and outreach. Membership: $95
(Regular); $60 (Regulator); $35 (Student).*

Meetings/Conferences: Annual

Publications:
Membership Directory; on-line
Onsite Journal; quarterly; adv.

National Opera Association (1955)
P.O. Box 60869
Canyon, TX 79016-0869
Tel: (806) 651-2857 Fax: (806) 651-2958
Website: noa.org
Members: 550 individuals
Staff: 5
Annual Budget: $50-100,000

Personnel:
Executive Director: Robert Hansen
  E-Mail: rhansen@noa.org
Editor: Bonnie Cutsforth-Huber
  E-Mail: bbc10@psu.edu
Treasurer: Carol Ann Modesitt
  E-Mail: modesitt@suu.edu
Vice President, Programs: Gordon Ostrowski
  E-Mail: gostrowski@msmnyc.edu

Historical Note:
*NOA seeks to promote opera and music theatre by
enhancing pedagogy. Members are opera companies,
schools of music, opera directors, composers, conductors,
librettists, teachers, and other professionals whose work is
opera-related. Sponsors the nationwide Opera Production
Competition, the New Opera Competition, and the NOA
Voice Competition. Membership: $70 (Individual); $85
(Organization); $50 (Library Subscription - Opera Journal
only); $30 (Student).*

Meetings/Conferences: Annual
Conference Chair: Gordon Ostrowski
2013 - Portland, OR (Hilton Portland Executive
  Towers)/Jan. 3 - 6

Publications:
NOA Notes Newsletter; bi-monthly; adv.
Opera Journal; quarterly; adv.
Sacred in Opera Newsletter; on-line; adv.

National Operating Committee for Standards of Athletic Equipment (1969)
11020 King St.
Suite 215
Overland Park, KS 66210
Tel: (913) 888-1340 Fax: (913) 498-8817
Website: nocsae.org
Staff: 3
Annual Budget: $1-2,000,000

Personnel:
Executive Director and Legal Counsel: Mike Oliver
  E-Mail: Mike.Oliver@nocsae.org
Meetings contact: Melinda Cook
  E-Mail: mlc@orlawyers.net
Treasurer: Terry Schlatter

Historical Note:
*NOCSAE is a leading force in the effort to improve athletic
equipment and as a result, reduce injuries.*

Meetings/Conferences: Semi-Annual
2013 - Phoenix, AZ (Royal Palms Resort and Spa)/Jan.
  25 - 26
2013 - Seatle, WA/June 28 - 29

Publications:
Newsletter; quarterly

National Optometric Association (1969)
5009 Beatties Ford Rd.
Suite 107, Room No. 278
Charlotte, NC 28216
Tel: (219) 398-4483
TollFree: (877) 394-2020
E-Mail:
info@nationaloptometricassociation.com
Website: natoptassoc.org
Members: 600 individuals
Staff: 4
Annual Budget: $100-250,000
Tax: 501(c)(6)

Personnel:
President: Dr. Vicki L. Hughes
Treasurer: Dr. Stella Korieocha
Executive Liaison: Dr. Edwin C. Marshall
  E-Mail: marshall@indiana.edu
Meeting Planner: Dr. Melantha Nephews

Historical Note:
*NOA is Nationally affiliated with ADA, NDEP, AOA,
American Public Health Association, Anhauser-Busch
Community Health Program, ASCO, BCHLE, Congressional
Black Caucus (CBC) Health Brain Trust, IOOL, NEHEP and
NHBPEP. NOA's mission is to advance the visual health of
minority populations. Membership: $225 (Regular); $22
(Corporate/Affiliate); $0 (Newly Graduated).*

Meetings/Conferences: Annual
Conference Chair: Dr. Melantha Nephews

Publications:
Membership Directory; on-line
NOA Newsletter; on-line

National Organization for Associate Degree Nursing (1984)
7794 Grow Dr.
Pensacola, FL 32514
Tel: (850) 484-6948 Fax: (850) 484-8762
TollFree: (877) 966-6236
E-Mail: noadn@noadn.org
Website: noadn.org
Members: 1120 individuals
Staff: 7
Annual Budget: $250-500,000
Tax: 501(c)(6)

Personnel:
President: Donna Meyer
  E-Mail: dmeyer@lc.edu
Account Executive: Harriet McClung CAE, CMA, MBA
Contact, Convention Services: Jenna Vallimont
Contact, Membership Services: Mirta Wallace

Historical Note:
*NOADN is a professional network and forum for ideas
concerning associate degree nursing recruitment, education
and practice.It promotes Associate Degree Nursing through
collaboration, advocacy, and education to ensure excellence
in the future of health care and professional nursing
practice. Membership: $115 (Individual/Retired); $400
(Agency); $90 (Associate).*

Meetings/Conferences: Annual
Conference Chair: Jenna Vallimont

Publications:
N-OADN First Tuesday; monthly; adv.
Teaching and Learning in Nursing; quarterly; adv.

Membership List Available to Non-members

National Organization for Human Service (1975)
3760 Sixes Rd,
Suite126, Room No 262
Canton, GA 30114
Tel: (770) 924-8899 *Fax:* (678) 494-5076
E-Mail: info@nationalhumanservices.org
Website: nationalhumanservices.org
Members: 600 individuals
Staff: 5
Annual Budget: $100-250,000

Personnel:
President: Robert (Rob) Olding
    E-Mail: president@nationalhumanservices.org
Vice President ,Public Relations: Sheri Goik-Kurn
    E-Mail: pr@nationalhumanservices.org
Treasurer: Franklyn Rother
    E-Mail: treasurer@nationalhumanservices.org
Vice President, Professional Development and Education:
    James Stinchcomb
Vice president, Conference: Jennifer Waite
    E-Mail: conference@nationalhumanservices.org

Historical Note:
*NOHS's mission is to strengthen the recognition of
human services professionals by increasing professional
development opportunities and developing a public policy
process. Members are educators, students, direct care
professionals, administrators as well as organizations in
both the United States and Canada. Membership: $95
(Regular); $190 (Organization); $35 (Student); $60
(Retired); $80 (Additional Organization).*

Continuing Education:
Certification Designation/s: CHSP

Meetings/Conferences: Annual
Conference Chair: Jennifer Waite

Publications:
Journal of Human Services; adv.
The Link; quarterly; adv.

National Organization for the Professional Advancement of Black Chemists and Chemical Engineers (1972)
P.O. Box 77040
Washington, DC 20013
Tel: (800) 776-1419 *Fax:* (202) 667-1705
TollFree: (800) 776-1419
E-Mail: president@nobcche.org
Website: nobcche.org
Members: 1000 individuals
Staff: 2
Annual Budget: $250-500,000

Personnel:
President: Victor McCrary PhD
    E-Mail: president@nobcche.org
Treasurer: Dale Mack
    E-Mail: treasurer@nobcche.org

Historical Note:
*NOBCChE was founded as an ad hoc group in 1972, and
incorporated in 1975. Its mission is to increase the number
of minorities in the fields of science and engineering.
Membership: $100 (Regular); $60 (Associate); $20
(Student).*

Meetings/Conferences: Annual
2013 - Indianapolis, IN (JW Marriott Indianapolis)/Oct.
    1 - 4

Publications:
NOBCChE News; on-line

Membership List Available to Non-members

National Organization of Black County Officials (1982)
1090 Vermont Ave. NW
Suite 1290
Washington, DC 20005
Tel: (202) 350-6696 *Fax:* (202) 350-6699
E-Mail: nobco@nobcoinc.org
Website: nobcoinc.org
Members: 3000 county officials in 50 States
Staff: 3
Annual Budget: $250-500,000

Personnel:
Interim Executive Director: Liz Humphrey

Contact, Media, Public Relations and Development: Edith
    Billups
Treasurer: Andrea Harrison

Historical Note:
*NOBCO provides education and training to black county
officials, others in government, representatives from
community based organizations and agencies and
concerned citizens. Membership: $100 (Regular Member);
$40 (Associate Member).*

Meetings/Conferences: Annual

Publications:
Member Directory

National Organization of Black Law Enforcement Executives (1976)
4609-F Pinecrest Office Park Dr.
Alexandria, VA 22312-1442
Tel: (703) 658-1529 *Fax:* (703) 658-9479
E-Mail: noble@noblenatl.org
Website: noblenatl.org
Members: 2300 individuals
Staff: 9
Annual Budget: $50-100,000

Personnel:
Interim Executive Director: Joseph Akers
Coordinator, Conferences: Kelli Bland
Coordinator, Membership Services and Accounting: Aaron
    Brooks
    E-Mail: abrooks@noblenatl.org
Research-Reports, Studies and Statistics: Sarah Johnson
    E-Mail: sjohnson@noblenatl.org
Director, Conferences and Meetings: Valerie Shuford
    E-Mail: vshuford@noblenatl.org

Historical Note:
*NOBLE's mission is to ensure equity in the administration
of justice in the provision of public service to all
communities, and to serve as the conscience of law
enforcement by being committed to justice by action.
Members are minority law enforcement executives
including police chiefs, command-level officers and
others. Membership: $150 (Regular); $100 (Associate);
$55 (Supporting); $525 (Sustaining), $1,525 (Regular
Life Members), $1,095 (Associate and Supporting Life
Members).*

Meetings/Conferences: Annual
Conference Chair: Kelli Bland
2013 - Pittsburgh, PA (David L. Lawrence Convention
    Center)/Aug. 3 - 7
2014 - Grand Rapids, MI (DeVos Performance Hall)/
    July 12 - 14

Publications:
E-Newsletter; weekly
NOBLE Actions; quarterly

National Organization of Industrial Trade Unions (1954)
148-06 Hillside Ave.
Jamaica, NY 11435
Tel: (718) 291-3434 *Fax:* (718) 526-2920
E-Mail: iapquestions@noitu.org
Website: noitu.org
Members: 10000 individuals
Staff: 2
Annual Budget: $2-5,000,000
Tax: 501(c)(5)

Personnel:
National Executive Vice President: Gerald Hustick Jr.
National President: Gerard A. Jones

Historical Note:
*NOITU is the Parent National Union that is comprised of
five (5) affiliated independent autonomous local Unions.
These local Unions represent skilled, semi-skilled and
unskilled industrial workers in a variety of different fields
and classifications. NOITU's mission is to advocate better
wages, hours, and conditions for its members.*

Meetings/Conferences: Annual

National Organization of Legal Services Workers (1972)
256 W. 38th St.
Suite 705
New York, NY 10018
Tel: (212) 228-0992 *Fax:* (212) 228-0097
Website: nolsw.org
Members: 4800 individuals
Staff: 12
Annual Budget: $2-5,000,000

Personnel:
President: Gordon Deane
    E-Mail: gedeane@nolsw.org
National Vice President, Legal Services: Robert Garza
Union Administrator: Diane Lanigan
National Vice President, Human Services: Vicki Roebuck
Administrative Assistant: Ellen Schulman
Financial Secretary and Treasurer: Robert T. (Tim) Yeager
    E-Mail: rtyeager@nolsw.org

Historical Note:
*Labor union affiliated with the AFL-CIO. NOLSW's mission
is to sustain and build the legal services movement by
organizing strong local legal services unions, and to ensure
decent wages and work conditions, workplace democracy
and fairness for those whose life work is to advocate for
others. Represents majority of those who work in federally-
funded legal services programs across USA and workers in
many other advocacy organizations, law offices and human
services programs.*

Publications:
Member Directory; on-line

National Organization of Life and Health Insurance Guaranty Association (1983)
13873 Park Center Rd.
Suite 329
Herndon, VA 20171
Tel: (703) 481-5206 *Fax:* (703) 481-5209
E-Mail: info@nolhga.com
Website: nolhga.com
Members: 52 associations
Staff: 15
Annual Budget: $5-10,000,000

Personnel:
Executive Vice President and Chief Operating Officer:
    Richard W. Klipstein
President: Peter G. Gallanis
Senior Vice President and General Counsel: William P.
    O'Sullivan
Vice President, Accounting and Finance: Paul A. Peterson
Vice President, Administrative Services: Holly L. Wilding

Historical Note:
*NOLHGA assists its member associations in providing quick
and cost-effective coverage to policyholders in the event of
a multi-state life or health insurer insolvency. NOLHGA
members are state life and health insurance guaranty
associations.*

Meetings/Conferences: Annual
2013 - Clearwater, FL/Jan. 8 - 10
2013 - Salt Lake City, UT/April 9 - 10
Number of non-conference events/year: 12

Publications:
GA Update
Membership Directory; on-line
NOLHGA Journal
NOLHGA Wire

National Organization of Nurse Practitioner Faculties (1980)
900 19th St. NW
Suite 200B
Washington, DC 20006
Tel: (202) 289-8044 *Fax:* (202) 384-1444
E-Mail: nonpf@nonpf.org
Website: nonpf.org
Members:
780 organizations
1200 individuals
Staff: 3
Annual Budget: $500-1,000,000
Tax: 501(c)(3)

Personnel:
President: Debra J. Barksdale ANP-BC, CNE, FAANP,
    FNP-BC, PhD
Executive Director: Kitty Werner MPA
Coordinator, Meetings and Membership: Candi Hoffman
    E-Mail: choffman@nonpf.org

Historical Note:
*NONPF promotes continuous quality improvement
and evidence-based approaches to nurse practitioner
education through the development of standards, guidelines,
teaching instruments, resources, and networking exchanges
for faculty. Serves the public interest by assuring the
preparation of highly qualified health care professionals.
Members are Nurse Practitioner (NP) educators.
Membership: $175 (Individual); $145 (Associate); $115
(Student); $60 (Retired); $700 (Program-upto 4 faculty
representatives); $120 (Program-each additional faculty
representative); Free (Honorary).*

Meetings/Conferences: Annual
Conference Chair: Candi Hoffman
2013 - Pittsburgh, PA (Wyndham Grand Pittsburgh
    Downtown)/April 11 - 14
2014 - Denver, CO/April 3 - 6
2015 - Maryland City, MD (Hilton in Baltimore)/April
    23 - 26

Publications:
Newsletter; quarterly

National Organization of Social Security Claimants' Representatives (1979)
560 Sylvan Ave.
Suite 2200
Englewood Cliffs, NJ 07632
Tel: (201) 567-4228 Fax: (201) 567-1542
E-Mail: info@nosscr.org
Website: nosscr.org
Members: 4000 members
Staff: 8
Annual Budget: $10-25,000,000

Personnel:
Executive Director: Nancy G. Shor
    E-Mail: info@nosscr.org

Historical Note:
NOSSCR's purpose is to provide quality representation for claimants, to maintan a system of full and fair adjudication for every claimant and to advocating for beneficial change in the disability determination and adjudication process. Members are attorneys and advocates. Membership: $200 (Regular); $375 (Sustaining).

Meetings/Conferences: Semi-Annual
2013 - Washington, DC (The JW Marriott)/May 15 -
    18
2013 - San Diego, CA (Manchester Grand Hyatt)/Oct.
    9 - 12

Publications:
Social Security Forum; monthly

National Organization of State Associations for Children
320 N. Washington Sq.
Suite 100
Lansing, MI 48933
Website: nosac.org
Staff: 1
Tax: 501(c)(3)

Personnel:
Executive Director: Jenny Crichton

Historical Note:
NOSAC's mission is to facilitate networking and to share information among its member associations. Membership: $250/year.

National Organization of State Offices of Rural Health (1995)
44648 Mound Rd.
Sterling Heights, MI 48314
Tel: (586) 739-9940 Fax: (586) 739-9941
Website: nosorh.org
Staff: 7
Annual Budget: $500-1,000,000

Personnel:
Director: Teryl Eisinger
    E-Mail: teryle@nosorh.org
Coordinator, Special Projects: Jessica Burkard
    E-Mail: jessicab@nosorh.org
Coordinator, Education: Stephanie Hansen
    E-Mail: steph@nosorh.org
Administrative Coordinator: Donna Pfaendtner

Historical Note:
NOSORH's mission is to promote the capacity of state offices of rural health to improve health care in rural America through leadership development, advocacy, education, and partnerships.National Organization of State Offices of Rural Health was established to help State Offices of Rural Health in their efforts to improve access to, and enhance the quality of, health care for America's 61 million rural citizens. Membership: $100 (Associate).

Meetings/Conferences:
Conference Chair: Jessica Burkard

Publications:
Membership Directory; on-line
The Branch Newsletter; monthly

National Orientation Directors Association (1976)

The University of Minnesota
1313 Fifth St. SE, Mail Unit 72
Minneapolis, MN 55414
Tel: (612) 627-0150 Fax: (612) 627-0153
E-Mail: noda@umn.edu
Website: noda.orgsync.com
Members: 1700 individuals
Staff: 4
Annual Budget: $500-1,000,000

Personnel:
Executive Director: Joyce Holl
    E-Mail: holl@umn.edu
Vice President, Internal Relations and Membership:
    Danielle Bristow
    E-Mail: danielle_bristow@wustl.edu
Director, Annual Conferences: April Mann
    E-Mail: asmann@email.unc.edu
Coordinator, Events: Keri Stenemann
    E-Mail: muenc007@umn.edu

Historical Note:
NODA's mission is to provide education, leadership and professional development in the fields of college student orientation, transition and retention. Members are college personnel professionals, graduate and undergraduate students who are responsible for student orientation programs. Membership: $100 (Professional/Faculty); $30 (Student); $500 (Associate).

Meetings/Conferences: Annual
Conference Chair: April Mann
2013 - San Antonio, TX/Nov. 3 - 6
2014 - Orlando, FL/Nov. 2 - 5
2015 - Denver, CO/Oct. 23 - 27
Number of non-conference events/year: 1

Publications:
Orientation Review Newsletter; quarterly
The Journal of College Orientation and Transition;
    semi-annually

Membership List Available to Non-members

National Ornamental and Miscellaneous Metals Association (1958)
805 S. Glynn St.
Suite 127, Apartment 311
Fayetteville, GA 30214
Tel: (888) 516-8585 Fax: (888) 279-7994
E-Mail: nonmainfo@nomma.org
Website: nomma.org
Members: 1,000 members and 1000 companies
Staff: 4
Annual Budget: $500-1,000,000
Tax: 501(c)(6)

Personnel:
Executive Director and Editor: J. Todd Daniel
    E-Mail: todd@nomma.org
Manager, Member Care and Operations: Liz Johnson
    E-Mail: liz@nomma.org
Manager, Meetings and Expositions: Martha Pennington
    E-Mail: martha@nomma.org
Director, Sales: Sherry Theien
    E-Mail: stheien@att.net

Historical Note:
NOMMA founded as National Ornamental Iron Manufacturers Association. Changed its name to National Ornamental Metal Manufacturers Association in 1961 and adopted present name in 1977. NOMMA's mission is to serve its members and advance the industry through education and the encouragement of a positive business environment. Membership: $425 (Fabricator); $375-595 (Supplier); $310 (Affiliate).

Meetings/Conferences: Annual
Conference Chair: Martha Pennington
2013 - Albuquerue, NM (Hyatt Regency Albuquerque)/
    March 20 - 23

Publications:
Fabricator; bi-monthly; adv.

Membership List Available to Non-members

National Ornamental Goldfish Growers Association (1981)
6916 Black's Mill Rd.
Thurmont, MD 21788
Tel: (301) 271-7475 Fax: (301) 271-7059
Members: 6 companies
Staff: 1
Annual Budget: Under $10,000

Personnel:
Executive Secretary: Raymond W. Klinger

Historical Note:
NOGGA was established by professional goldfish growers in the U. S. to fund research on goldfish, principally disease research. Commercial growers and breeders of ornamental goldfish. Conducts and sponsors research on diseases affecting ornamental goldfish.

National Pace Association (1990)
801 N. Fairfax St.
Suite 309
Alexandria, VA 22314
Tel: (703) 535-1565 Fax: (703) 535-1566
E-Mail: info@npaonline.org
Website: npaonline.org
Staff: 13
Annual Budget: $2-5,000,000
Tax: 501(c)(3)

Personnel:
President and Chief Executive Officer: Shawn M. Bloom
    E-Mail: shawnb@npaonline.org
Manager, Association Services: Sharon Cochraham
    E-Mail: SharonC@npaonline.org
Vice President, Education and Learning: Venise Lewis
    E-Mail: venisel@npaonline.org
Director, Data and Technical Operations: Berry McCarthy
    E-Mail: BerryM@npaonline.org
Vice President, Finance and Administration: Rhonda Rose
    E-Mail: RhondaR@npaonline.org
Senior Vice President, Public Policy: Christine van
    Reenen
    E-Mail: chrisvr@npaonline.org

Historical Note:
NPA exists to advance the efforts of programs of all-inclusive care for the elderly (PACE). PACE programs coordinate and provide all needed preventive, primary, acute and long term care services so that older individuals can continue living in the community. Membership: $3,000 (Exploring PACE); $10,800 (Prospective Provider/Capitated Provider); $3,000 (Technical Assistance Center, which is an existing Provider Member); $2,800 (Individuals or organizations that are not owned or operated by a PACE); $4,000 (Associate).

Meetings/Conferences: Annual
2013 - Miami, FL (Loews Miami Beach Hotel)/Oct. 21
    - 24
Number of non-conference events/year: 2

Publications:
Member Directory; on-line
PACE Newsletter; bi-weekly

National Pan-Hellenic Council (1930)
3951 Snapfinger Pkwy.
Suite 218
Decatur, GA 30035
Tel: (404) 592-6145 Fax: (404) 806-9943
E-Mail: info@nphchq.org
Website: nphchq.org
Members: 9 fraternities and sororities
Staff: 2
Annual Budget: $250-500,000

Personnel:
Executive Director: Beverly Burks
    E-Mail: execdirector@nphchq.org
Treasurer: Francine Young
    E-Mail: Treasurer@nphchq.org

Historical Note:
NPHC promotes interaction through forums, meetings and other mediums for the exchange of information and engages in cooperative programming and initiatives through various activities and functions. Membership: $175 (Undergraduate); $275-400 (Alumni Based on no. of Chapters).

Meetings/Conferences:
Conference Chair: Beverly Burks

Publications:
Council Directory; on-line
NPHC newsletter

National Panhellenic Conference (1902)
3901 W. 86th St.
Suite 398
Indianapolis, IN 46268
Tel: (317) 872-3185 Fax: (317) 872-3192
E-Mail: npccentral@npcwomen.org
Website: npcwomen.org
Members: 26 national sororities
Staff: 3
Annual Budget: $50-100,000

Tax: 501(c)(3)

Personnel:
Executive Director: Nicki Meneley
  E-Mail: nicki@npcwomen.org
Coordinator, Business Operations: Emily Ruch
  E-Mail: emily@npcwomen.org
Contact, Communications and Programs: Julia "Jules" Schenk
  E-Mail: julia@npcwomen.org

Historical Note:
NPC's mission is to promote the values of and to serve as an advocate for its member groups in collaboration with those members, campuses and communities.

Meetings/Conferences: Annual

Publications:
NPC Newsletter; on-line

National Paralegal Association *(1982)*
P.O. Box 406
Solebury, PA 18963-0406
Tel: (215) 297-8333 *Fax:* (215) 297-8358
E-Mail: admin@nationalparalegal.org
Website: nationalparalegal.org
Members: 24500 individuals and schools and firms
Staff: 6

Personnel:
Executive Director: H. Jeffrey Valentine

Historical Note:
The NPA is an international organization offering benefits and services to individuals, law firms, corporate legal departments, independent paralegals, paralegal training schools and colleges as well as those offering services or products to those involved in the paralegal profession. Members are paralegals, paralegal educators, independent paralegals, paralegal schools, corporate law departments, law libraries, law firms, paralegal students, and others with an interest in the advancement of the profession. Membership: $70 (First year); $45 (Full Member); $70 (Associate); $30 (Student); $20 (Pre-Student).

Publications:
Membership Directory; on-line

Membership List Available to Non-members

National Parent Teachers Association *(1897)*
1250 N. Pitt St.
Alexandria, VA 22314
Tel: (703) 518-1200 *Fax:* (703) 836-0942
TollFree: (800) 307-4782
E-Mail: info@pta.org
Website: pta.org
Members: 23000 individuals
Staff: 45
Tax: 501(c)(3)

Personnel:
Executive Director: Eric Hargis
Deputy Executive Director, Finance and Operations: Heather Dean
Director, Government Affairs: Mishaela Duran
Manager, Editorial: Marilyn Ferdinand
Manager, Human Resources: Sonia Hicks
Manager, Membership Services: Joy Lindsey
Senior Manager, Media and Public Relations: James Martinez
Director, Information Technology: John Reeb
Director, Meetings and Events: Donna Taylor
Manager, Marketing and Communications: LaWanda Toney

Historical Note:
PTA serves as a powerful voice for all children, a relevant resource for families and communities, and a strong advocate for the education and well-being of every child. Membership: $25/year.

Meetings/Conferences: Annual
Conference Chair: Donna Taylor
2013 - Cincinnati, OH/June 20 - 23

Publications:
PTA Magazine

National Park Hospitality Association *(1919)*
1225 New York Ave. NW
Suite 450
Washington, DC 20005
Tel: (202) 682-9530 *Fax:* (202) 682-9529
E-Mail: info@nphassn.org
Website: parkpartners.org
Members: 125 companies and individuals

Staff: 3
Annual Budget: $250-500,000

Personnel:
Chairman: Joe K. Fassler
  E-Mail: lfassler@viad.com
Counselor: Derrick A. Crandall
  E-Mail: dcrandall@funoutdoors.com
Treasurer: Carol Metzler
  E-Mail: feltyco@mindspring.com

Historical Note:
NPHA's mission is to provide premier services and opportunities for experiences by park visitors appropriate to the units in which the concessioners operate. Membership: $500-35,125 (Regular, based on revenue from park business); $750 (Associate); $2,500 (Vendors).

Publications:
Federal Parks and Recreation Newsletter
NPHA Newsletter; monthly

National Parking Association *(1951)*
1112 16th St. NW
Suite 840
Washington, DC 20036
Tel: (202) 296-4336 *Fax:* (202) 296-3102
TollFree: (800) 647-7275
E-Mail: info@npapark.org
Website: npapark.org
Members: 1200 organizations
Staff: 7
Annual Budget: $1-2,000,000
Tax: 501(c)(6)

Personnel:
President: Christine Banning CAE, MA
  E-Mail: ChristineBanning@npapark.org
Managing Editor, Parking: Denise Gable
  E-Mail: DeniseGable@npapark.org
Director, Marketing and eBusiness: Lawrence D. McFadden MBA
  E-Mail: LawrenceMcFadden@npapark.org
Vice President, Marketing and Communications: Heather Sieber CAE, MA
  E-Mail: HeatherSieber@npapark.org
Director, Business Development and Events: Denise Stone CEM, CPM
  E-Mail: DeniseStone@npapark.org

Historical Note:
NPA's mission is to serve the parking industry and its members by offering quality education, networking opportunities, advocacy, products and services. NPA collects and publishes research, provides networking and educational opportunities and offers cost-cutting business services. Members include private operators, parking consultants, colleges and universities, municipalities, parking authorities, hospitals and medical centers, industry vendors, and full-time university students. Membership: $50-10,500/year.

Continuing Education:
Certification Designation/s: CPP

Meetings/Conferences: Annual
Conference Chair: Denise Stone CEM, CPM
2013 - Chicago, IL (Hyatt Regency Chicago)/Oct. 7 - 11
Number of non-conference events/year: 1

Publications:
Between the Lines (e-Newsletter); weekly; adv.
Membership Directory; on-line
NPA NewsBrief; weekly; adv.
Parking; adv.

Membership List Available to Non-members

National Parks Conservation Association *(1919)*
777 Sixth St. NW
Suite 700
Washington, DC 20001
Tel: (202) 223-6722 *Fax:* (202) 454-3333
E-Mail: npca@npca.org
Website: npca.org
Members: 600000 individuals
Staff: 100
Annual Budget: $50-100,000,000
Tax: 501(c)(3)

Personnel:
President: Thomas C. Kiernan
Vice President, Human Resources: Karen Allen
Regional Director, Texas Field Office: Suzanne Dixon
  E-Mail: sdixon@ncpa.org
General Counsel: Elizabeth Fayad
Program Manager, Northwest Office: David G. Graves

  E-Mail: dgraves@npca.org
Vice President, Regional Operations: Tony Jewett
  E-Mail: tjewett@npca.org
Director, Water Program: Chad Lord
  E-Mail: clord@npca.org
Manager, Publications: Elizabeth Meyers
Executive Vice President: Theresa Pierno
  E-Mail: tpierno@npca.org
Vice President, Communications: Linda M. Rancourt
Vice President, Membership Services: Mina Stanard
Senior Vice President, Policy: Ron Tipton
  E-Mail: rtipton@npca.org

Historical Note:
Formerly (1970) National Parks Association, (1999) National Parks and Conservation Association. NPCA works to protect and enhance America's national parks for present and future generations. Members are individuals interested in conservation, protection of national parks, wildlife and the wilderness. Membership: $25-1,000/year.

Publications:
National Parks Magazine; quarterly; adv.
NPCA e-News; on-line
Park Lines; monthly

National Party Boat Owners Alliance *(1952)*
181 Thames St.
Groton, CT 06340
Tel: (860) 535-2066 *Fax:* (860) 535-8389
Members: 500 individuals
Staff: 1
Annual Budget: Under $10,000

Personnel:
President and Executive Director: Bradley J. Glas

Historical Note:
Established in 1952 in response to increased federal legislation affecting the industry, NPBOA members are Coast Guard licensed Operators or Masters of passenger-for-hire charter/party boats. NPBOA's principal activity is monitoring proposed and new laws or regulations that might be detrimental to its segment of the maritime industry. Membership: $30/year (individual).

National Pasta Association *(1904)*
529 14th St. NW
750 National Press Building
Washington, DC 20045
Tel: (202) 637-5888 *Fax:* (202) 223-9741
E-Mail: info@ilovepasta.org
Website: ilovepasta.org
Members: 30 businesses
Staff: 3
Annual Budget: $500-1,000,000
Tax: 501(c)(6)

Personnel:
Executive Director: Carol Freysinger
  E-Mail: cfreysinger@kellencompany.com
Account Manager: Rick Cristol
  E-Mail: rcristol@kellencompany.com
Legal Counsel: Gary J. Kushner

Historical Note:
Formerly National Macaroni Manufacturers Association. Absorbed the National Macaroni Institute in 1979 and assumed its present name in 1981. NPA's mission is to increase the consumption of pasta, to promote the development of sound public policy and, act as a center of knowledge for the industry. NPA member manufacturers provide a wide variety of pasta products for the retail and foodservice markets.

Publications:
Food Insight

National Pawnbrokers Association *(1988)*
P.O. Box 508
Keller, TX 76244
Tel: (817) 337-8830 *Fax:* (817) 337-8875
TollFree: (888) 808-7296
E-Mail: info@nationalpawnbrokers.org
Website: nationalpawnbrokers.org
Members: 2000 individuals
Staff: 7
Annual Budget: $1-2,000,000
Tax: 501(c)(6)

Personnel:
Executive Director: Dana Meinecke
  E-Mail: dana@nationalpawnbrokers.org
Administrator, Government Relations: Matthew Church
  E-Mail: matthew@nationalpawnbrokers.org
Director, Public Relations: Emmett Murphy

E-Mail: media@nationalpawnbrokers.org
Communication Specialist: Chris Pearcey
E-Mail: chris@nationalpawnbrokers.org
Director, Membership Services: Margie Swoyer
E-Mail: margie@nationalpawnbrokers.org
Director, Meetings and Events: Lindsay Wilson
E-Mail: lindsay@nationalpawnbrokers.org

Historical Note:
NPA's mission is to accurately represent pawnbrokers and their interests through education, mentoring and legislation. Members are pawn companies. Membership: $550-600 (Pawnbroker); $250-300 (International Pawnbroker); $600 (Student/Apprentice); $500-1,000 (Partner).

Meetings/Conferences:
Conference Chair: Lindsay Wilson
Number of non-conference events/year: 2

Publications:
Membership Directory; on-line
National Pawnbroker Magazine; quarterly
NPA NewsBrief; weekly
Pawn Industry Marketplace; daily
Pawn TV; monthly

National Payroll Reporting Consortium
P.O. Box 850
Henrietta, NY 14467-0850
Tel: (610) 827-1591
E-Mail: nprc@nprc-inc.org
Website: nprc-inc.org
Staff: 1
Annual Budget: $50-100,000

Personnel:
Contact, Communications: Pete Isberg

Historical Note:
NPRC is a non-profit trade association of organizations that provide payroll processing and employment tax services directly to employers. Membership: $6,000-10,000/year (Based on number of annual clients).

Publications:
NPRC Newsletter

National Peach Council (1958)
22 Triplett Court
Dillsburg, PA 17019
Tel: (717) 329-8421 *Fax:* (803) 865-8090
E-Mail: PeachCouncil@att.net
Website: nationalpeachcouncil.org
Members: 2000 individuals
Staff: 2
Annual Budget: $50-100,000

Personnel:
Managing Director: Charles Walker
E-Mail: charleswalker@worldnet.att.net

Historical Note:
NPC provides a consistent, meaningful, strong voice on issues impacting the industry. Comprised of growers, packers, shippers, processors, and others affiliated with the U.S. freestone peach industry.

National Peanut Buying Point Association (1973)
115 W. Second St.
P.O. Box 314
Tifton, GA 31793
Tel: (229) 386-1716 *Fax:* (229) 386-8757
E-Mail: spearmanagency@friendlycity.net
Website: npbpa.org
Staff: 3

Personnel:
President: Kenny Brownlee
E-Mail: kennyb@planttel.net
Executive Secretary: Tyron Spearman
E-Mail: spearmanagency@friendlycity.net

Historical Note:
Formerly Southern Peanut Warehouseman's Association. The National Peanut Buying Points Association seeks to represent America's 400+ buying locations that receive, weigh, clean, dry, inspect, grade and prepare peanuts for storage and shelling. The Association's goal is to be an informed liaison between the farmer and the sheller, to strive for fair and friendly government and private regulations. Membership: $400 (Regular); $500 (Elite/Email); $560 (Elite/Fax).

Meetings/Conferences: Annual
2013 - New Orleans, LA/Feb. 14 - 18

Publications:
Membership Directory; annually

National Pecan Shellers Association (1943)
1100 Johnson Ferry Rd.
Suite 300
Atlanta, GA 30342
Tel: (404) 252-3663 *Fax:* (452) 252-0774
E-Mail: npsa@kellencompany.com
Website: ilovepecans.org
Members: 60 companies
Staff: 4
Annual Budget: $50-100,000
Tax: 501(c)(3)

Personnel:
Contact: Vickie Mabry
E-Mail: vmabry@kellencompany.com

Historical Note:
Formerly (1985) the National Pecan Shellers and Processors Association. NPSA strives to educate culinary and health professionals, food technologists and the general public about the nutritional benefits and variety of uses and about the taste of pecans. Members are pecan shellers, processors, brokers, accumulators, growers, packaging equipment and ingredient suppliers to the industry. Membership: $1,000-10,000 (Active); $250-2,500 (Affiliate).

Publications:
In A Nutshell
Membership Directory; annually

National Perinatal Association (1976)
457 State St.
Binghamton, NY 13901
Fax: (607) 772-0468
TollFree: (888) 971-3295
E-Mail: npa@nationalperinatal.org
Website: nationalperinatal.org
Members: 1100 individuals
Staff: 3
Annual Budget: $100-250,000

Personnel:
President: Mary Anne Laffin
E-Mail: mlaffin@nationalperinatal.org
Vice President, Programs: Karen D'Apolito PhD
E-Mail: kdapolito@nationalperinatal.org
Treasurer: Marylouise Martin MSN, RNC
E-Mail: mmartin@nationalperinatal.org

Historical Note:
NPA aims to improve pregnancy and birth outcomes in the United States and promote the expertise of perinatal health providers and to support families. Members are individuals providing health care with particular emphasis on care for the pregnant woman, fetus and newborn. Membership: $75 (Individual); $45 (Student/Retiree/Parent/Family Support Group); $90-15,000 (Corporation/Hospitals/CBP's/Public Health Entities); $200 (State Perinatal Association).

Meetings/Conferences: Annual
Conference Chair: Karen D'Apolito PhD

Publications:
Member Directory; on-line

National Pest Management Association (1933)
10460 N. St.
Fairfax, VA 22030
Tel: (703) 352-6762 *Fax:* (703) 352-3031
TollFree: (800) 678-6722
E-Mail: NPMATeam@vaultcommunications.com
Website: npmapestworld.org
Members: 7,000 companies
Staff: 23
Annual Budget: $5-10,000,000

Personnel:
Executive Vice President: Robert F. Lederer Jr.
E-Mail: lederer@pestworld.org
Director, Technical Services: Dr. Jim Fredericks
E-Mail: jfredericks@pestworld.org
Vice President, Public Affairs: Missy Henriksen
E-Mail: mhenriksen@pestworld.org
Chief Financial Officer and Director, Finance: Gary McKenzie
E-Mail: mckenzie@pestworld.org
Director, Membership Services: Jean Neun
E-Mail: jneun@pestworld.org
Director, Marketing and Communications: Janay Rickwalder
Senior Vice President, Government Affairs: Robert Rosenberg
E-Mail: rosenberg@pestworld.org

Vice President, Conventions and Professional Development: Dominique Stumpf CMP
E-Mail: dstumpf@pestworld.org

Historical Note:
Formerly (1937) the National Association of Exterminators and Fumigators; (2000) National Pest Control Association. NPMA is an organization committed to the protection of public health, food and property. Members are companies engaged in the integrated management of insects, rodents, birds and other pests which inhabit buildings or structures of any kind.

Meetings/Conferences: Annual
Conference Chair: Dominique Stumpf CMP
2013 - Orlando, FL (Florida Hotel and Conference Center)/Jan. 8 - 9
2013 - Scottsdale, AZ (Phoenician Resort)/Oct. 23 - 26
Number of non-conference events/year: 9

Publications:
ePestWorld; weekly; adv.
Membership Directory; on-line
Pest Gazette; semi-annually
PestWorld; bi-monthly; adv.

Membership List Available to Non-members

National Petroleum Council (1946)
1625 K St. NW
Suite 600
Washington, DC 20006
Tel: (202) 393-6100 *Fax:* (202) 331-8539
E-Mail: info@npc.org
Website: npc.org
Members: 200 individuals
Staff: 12
Annual Budget: $2-5,000,000
Tax: 501(c)(6)

Personnel:
Executive Director: Marshall W. Nichols
E-Mail: mnichols@npc.org

Historical Note:
NPC is a self supporting federal advisory body to the Secretary of Energy. NPC represents the views of the oil and natural gas industries in advising, informing, and making recommendations to the Secretary of Energy with respect to any matter relating to oil and natural gas, or to the oil and gas industries submitted to it or approved by the secretary.

Publications:
Membership Directory; on-line

National Petroleum Management Association
10908 Courthouse Rd.
Suite 102-301
Fredericksburg, VA 22408
Tel: (540) 507-4371 *Fax:* (540) 507-4372
Website: npma-fuelnet.org
Members:
125 companies
798 members
Staff: 3
Annual Budget: $250-500,000

Personnel:
President: Jack Lavin
Marketing Officer: Ruth Lavin
Website Administrator: Jeremy Reger

Historical Note:
NPMA's mission is to provide a professional work force through training and career enhancement opportunities designed to reduce personnel turnover, and eliminate the potential for accidents and fuel quality mishaps. Membership: $75 (Middle-tier Associate level); $50 (Basic-tier Associate level); $100 (Senior-tier Associate level).

Continuing Education:
Certification Designation/s: PCP

Meetings/Conferences: Annual

Publications:
Membership Directory; on-line
The Fuel Handler

National Pharmaceutical Council (1953)
1717 Pennsylvania Ave. NW
Suite 800
Washington, DC 20006
Tel: (202) 827-2100 *Fax:* (202) 827-0314
E-Mail: info@npcnow.org
Website: npcnow.org
Members: 16 companies
Staff: 15
Annual Budget: $5-10,000,000

Personnel:
President: Dan Leonard
Chief Science Officer: Robert W. Dubois
Director, Member Relations: Kathryn L. Gleason
Director, Communications: Andrea Hofelich
    E-Mail: ahofelich@npcnow.org

Historical Note:
NPC is a policy research organization dedicated to the advancement of good evidence and science, and to fostering an environment in the United States that supports medical innovation. Members are research-intensive companies producing brand name prescription medicines.

Meetings/Conferences: Semi-Annual
Number of non-conference events/year: 1

Publications:
E.V.I.dently; monthly

National Phlebotomy Association (1978)
1901 Brightseat Rd.
Landover, MD 20785
Tel: (301) 386-4200 *Fax:* (301) 386-4203
E-Mail: naltphle@aol.com
Website: nationalphlebotomy.org
Members: 15000 individuals
Staff: 5
Annual Budget: $500-1,000,000
Tax: 501(c)(3)

Personnel:
Chief Executive Officer and Founder: Diane C. Crawford
Chief Operating Officer: Horace E. J. Crawford
Secretary: Altonese Reese

Historical Note:
NPA's mission is to educate and research in phlebotomy and provide certification to individuals through school programs. Has an accreditation mechanism for phlebotomy training programs. Membership: $100 (Certification); $65 (Renewal Fee).

Continuing Education:
Certification Designation/s: CPT, CPR

Publications:
NPA Newsletter

National Plant Board (1925)
P.O. Box 847
Elk Grove, CA 95759
Tel: (916) 709-3484 *Fax:* (916) 689-2385
E-Mail: npb@agr.wa.gov
Website: nationalplantboard.org
Members: 51 individuals
Staff: 2
Annual Budget: $250-500,000
Tax: 501(c)(5)

Personnel:
President: Mike Cooper
    E-Mail: Mike.Cooper@agri.idaho.gov
Executive Secretary: Aurelio Posadas
    E-Mail: aureliop@elkgrove.net

Historical Note:
NPB strives to provide national representation for the Eastern Plant Board, the Southern Plant Board, the Central Plant Board, and the Western Plant Board, and to receive, consider and implement to the extent possible, all regional plant board recommendations.

Meetings/Conferences: Annual

Publications:
Membership Directory; on-line

National Plasterers Council (1988)
4344 Laura St.
Port Charlotte, FL 33980
Tel: (941) 766-0634 *Fax:* (941) 764-6050
TollFree: (866) 483-4672
E-Mail: npconline@comcast.net
Website: npconline.org
Staff: 5
Annual Budget: $500-1,000,000
Tax: 501(c)(6)

Personnel:
Executive Director: Mitch Brooks
Director, Finance: Karen Hobby
Director, Member Services: Natalya Mabarak
Director, Web Development: Fadi Mabarak
Associate Executive Director: Andy Mallison

Historical Note:
NPC's mission is to promote, advance and advocate the common interests of its members in pool plastering and

related activities. *Membership: $400 (Active); $600 (Associate); $200 (Auxiliary).*

Meetings/Conferences: Annual

Publications:
Membership Directory; on-line
NPC's Newsletter; bi-monthly; adv.

National Police and Security Officers Association of America (1955)
P.O. Box 663
S. Plainfield, NJ 07080-0663
E-Mail: npsoaa@usacops.com
Website: npoaa.tripod.com
Members: 620 individuals
Staff: 2
Annual Budget: $50-100,000

Personnel:
Chief Executive Officer: John R. Moore

Historical Note:
Founded as National Police Officers Association of America; assumed its current name in 2003. NPOA active members are law enforcement, corrections, security, and military officers. Promotes training through scholarships, seminars, and a yearly conference. Membership: $35/year.

National Pork Producers Association
10664 Justin Dr.
Urbandale, IA 50322
Tel: (515) 278-8012 *Fax:* (515) 278-8014
Website: nppc.org
Members: 67000 pork producers
Staff: 8

Personnel:
Chief Executive Officer: Neil Dierks
    E-Mail: dierksn@nppc.org
Director, Trade Show Marketing: Doug Fricke
    E-Mail: fricked@nppc.org
Director, Projects and Events: Alicia Irlbeck
    E-Mail: irlbecka@nppc.org
Accounting Administrator: Meryem Merritt
    E-Mail: merrittm@nppc.org
Administrative Assistant: Bette Murray
    E-Mail: murrayb@nppc.org

Historical Note:
NPPC's mission is to fight for reasonable legislation and regulations, develop revenue and market opportunities and protect the livelihoods of America's 67,000 pork producers. Membership: $2000/year

Publications:
LEADR Letter; bi-monthly
Legislative magazine; monthly

National Pork Producers Council (1954)
10664 Justin Dr.
Urbandale, IA 50332
Tel: (515) 278-8012 *Fax:* (515) 278-8014
Website: nppc.org
Members: 67000 pork producers
Staff: 25
Annual Budget: $10-25,000,000
Tax: 501(c)(5)

Personnel:
Chief Executive Officer: Neil Dierks
    E-Mail: dierksn@nppc.org
Director, Trade Show Marketing: Doug Fricke
    E-Mail: fricked@nppc.org
Director, Projects and Events: Alicia Irlbeck
    E-Mail: irlbecka@nppc.org

Historical Note:
Established as the National Swine Growers Council, assumed its present name in 1967 and is now a federation of 43 state associations. NPPC strives to fight for reasonable legislation and regulations, develop revenue and market opportunities. Membership: $2,000/year (Alliance Member).

Meetings/Conferences:
Conference Chair: Alicia Irlbeck
Number of non-conference events/year: 1

Publications:
Capital Pork Report Magazine; monthly
Capital Update; weekly

National Portable Storage Association
3312 Broadway
Suite 105
Kansas City, MO 64111
Tel: (816) 960-6552 *Fax:* (816) 960-6575

TollFree: (866) 777-0635
E-Mail: info@npsa-us.org
Website: npsa-us.org
Members: 500 individuals and companies
Staff: 2
Annual Budget: $500-1,000,000
Tax: 501(c)(6)

Personnel:
Executive Director: John Finnessy CMP
    E-Mail: john@npsa.org
Operations Manager: Joel Rathbone
    E-Mail: joel@npsa.org

Historical Note:
NPSA's purpose is to advance the portable storage industry. It assists members with industry, regulatory and workforce issues, and offers members networking, marketing and legislative support at national, state and local levels. Membership: $600-2600 (Portable Storage, depending on revenue); 1100-2600 (Associate).

Meetings/Conferences: Semi-Annual
Number of non-conference events/year: 2

Publications:
Membership Directory; on-line
NPSA Newsletter; quarterly

National Postal Mail Handlers Union
1101 Connecticut Ave. NW
Suite 500
Washington, DC 20036
Tel: (202) 833-9095 *Fax:* (202) 833-0008
Website: npmhu.org
Members: 47000 mail handler craft members
Staff: 66
Annual Budget: $25-50,000,000

Personnel:
National President: John F. Hegarty
Manager: William J. Flynn Jr.
National Secretary and Treasurer: Mark A. Gardner
    E-Mail: mgardner@npmhu.org
Assistant Legislative and Political Director: Robert P. Losi

Historical Note:
NPMHU's purpose is to negotiate and enforce a National Agreement with the U.S. Postal Service, a contract that establishes wages, cost-of-living adjustments and other pay increases, working conditions and fringe benefits for all workers within its jurisdiction. The Union also protects workers' rights by representing them in day-to-day problems on the job, like discipline, violations of seniority, discrimination, or other management abuse, and addresses such work-place concerns as safety, health, and the impact of technological change.

Meetings/Conferences: Annual

Publications:
The Mail Handler Magazine; quarterly
The Mail Handler Update

Membership List Available to Non-members

National Postal Policy Council (1981)
529 14th St. NW
750 National Press Bldg.
Washington, DC 20045
Tel: (202) 955-0097 *Fax:* (202) 223-9741
Website: postalcouncil.org
Staff: 2
Annual Budget: $250-500,000

Personnel:
Executive Director: Art Sackler
Treasurer: Ken Metroff

Historical Note:
Organization that works with the United States Postal Service to promote an improved national postal system with quality service at an affordable price.

Publications:
Membership Directory; on-line

National Postsecondary Agriculture Student Organization (1979)
1055 SW Praire Trail
Parkway
Ankeny, IA 50023
Tel: (515) 964-6866 *Fax:* (317) 802-5220
E-Mail: info@nationalpas.org
Website: nationalpas.org
Members: 1400 individuals and institutions
Staff: 4
Annual Budget: $100-250,000

Personnel:

Executive Director: Craig A. McEnany
  E-Mail: rparker@nationalpas.org
Coordinator, Finance: Holly Feldmann
  E-Mail: hfeldmann@nationalpas.org
Coordinator, Marketing: Brian Johnson
  E-Mail: bjohnson@nationalpas.org

Historical Note:
PAS provides opportunities for individual growth, leadership and career preparation. Members are institutions educating agricultural students at the college level. Membership: $20 (Individual); $1500 (Institution Chapter).

Meetings/Conferences: Annual
2013 - Louisville, KY (Galt House Hotel)/March 18 - 21

National Potato Council (1948)
1300 L St. NW
Suite 910
Washington, DC 20005
Tel: (202) 682-9456 Fax: (202) 682-0333
E-Mail: spudinfo@nationalpotatocouncil.org
Website: nationalpotatocouncil.org
Members: 8000 individuals
Staff: 5
Annual Budget: $2-5,000,000
Tax: 501(c)(5)

Personnel:
Chief Executive Officer and Executive Vice President: John Keeling
  E-Mail: johnk@nationalpotatocouncil.org
Director, Meetings and Industry Outreach: Hollee Alexander
  E-Mail: holleea@nationalpotatocouncil.org
Manager, Industry Communications and Outreach: Marie Joanis
  E-Mail: mariejoanismariejoanis@
  nationalpotatocouncil.org
Senior Director, Legislative and Regulatory Affairs: Ryan Krabill
  E-Mail: ryank@nationalpotatocouncil.org
Director, Public Relations: Mark Szymanski
  E-Mail:
  mark.szymanski@nationalpotatocouncil.org

Historical Note:
NPC's aim is to encourage the greater consumption of Irish potatoes and to nationally represent potato farmers on legislative and regulatory matters. Membership: $50 (silver); $100 (Gold); $200 (platinum); $3,000 (Sustaining).

Meetings/Conferences:
Conference Chair: Hollee Alexander
2013 - Las Vegas, NV (Caesars Palace)/Jan. 9 - 11
2013 - Las Vegas, NV (Caesars Palace)/Jan. 11 - 12
2013 - Washington, DC (Madison Hotel)/Feb. 25 - 28
2013 - Walla Walla, WA (Marcus Whitman Hotel and Conference Center)/June 24 - 28
2014 - San Antonio, TX (The Henry B. Gonzalez Convention Center)/Jan. 8 - 10
2014 - San Antonio, TX (The Henry B. Gonzalez Convention Center)/Jan. 10 - 11
2014 - Washington, DC (Madison Hotel)/Feb. 24 - 27
Number of non-conference events/year: 1

Publications:
NPC Insider Report; weekly

National Poultry and Food Distributors Association (1967)
2014 Osborne Rd.
St. Marys, GA 31558
Tel: (770) 535-9901 Fax: (770) 535-7385
TollFree: (877) 845-1545
E-Mail: kkm@npfda.org
Website: npfda.org
Members: 250 companies
Staff: 2
Annual Budget: $100-250,000
Tax: 501(c)(6)

Personnel:
Executive Director and Corporate Secretary: Kristin McWhorter
  E-Mail: kkm@npfda.org

Historical Note:
Formerly (1992) National Independent Poultry and Food Distributors Association. NPFDA's mission is to promote the poultry and food distributors, processors, and allied industries by bringing them together and providing a forum to foster long term business relationships. Members consist of poultry distributors, further processors, processors,

transportation companies, marketing specialist and allied supplier companies. Membership: $500 (Active); $100 (Member Branches).

Continuing Education:
Certification Designation/s: CDP

Meetings/Conferences: Semi-Annual
Conference Chair: Kristin McWhorter
2013 - Atlanta, GA (Hyatt Regency Atlanta)/Jan. 29 - Feb. 1

Publications:
Membership Directory; annually
NPFDA Newsletter; monthly

National Practitioners Network for Fathers and Family
1003 K St. NW
Suite 565
Washington, DC 20001
Tel: (202) 737-6680 Fax: (202) 737-6683
TollFree: (800) 346-7633
E-Mail: info@npnff.org
Website: fcnetwork.org/fatherhood/
  aboutnpnff.html
Staff: 2
Annual Budget: Under $10,000

Personnel:
Executive Director: John Pride

Historical Note:
NPNFF's mission is to build the profession of practitioners working to increase the responsible involvement of fathers in the lives of their children.

National Precast Concrete Association (1965)
1320 City Center Dr.
Suite 200
Carmel, IN 46032
Tel: (317) 571-9500 Fax: (317) 571-0041
TollFree: (800) 366-7731
E-Mail: npca@precast.org
Website: precast.org
Members: 1100 companies
Staff: 27
Annual Budget: $5-10,000,000

Personnel:
President: Ty E. Gable CAE
  E-Mail: tgable@precast.org
Events Coordinator and Executive Assistant: Denise Bradburn
  E-Mail: dbradburn@precast.org
Director, Technical Services: Claude Goguen LEED AP, PE
  E-Mail: cgoguen@precast.org
Director, Education and Safety: Marti Harrell
  E-Mail: mharrell@precast.org
Vice President, Finance and Administration: Claudia Hunter
  E-Mail: chunter@precast.org
Managing Editor: Ron Hyink
  E-Mail: rhyink@precast.org
Manager, Development and Membership Services: Elizabeth Lyndon
  E-Mail: elyndon@precast.org
Finance and Operations Manager: Alice K. Tiemann, CPA
  E-Mail: atiemann@precast.org
Director, Communications: Bob Whitmore
  E-Mail: rwhitmore@precast.org

Historical Note:
NPCA is dedicated to expanding the use of quality precast concrete. It represents manufacturers of plant produced precast concrete products and companies that provide the equipment, supplies and services to make these products. Membership: $1500 (Associate); $1,200-2,700 (Producer, based on annual sales volume); $1200 (Branches/Multiple Locations).

Continuing Education:
Certification Designation/s: NPCA

Meetings/Conferences:
Conference Chair: Denise Bradburn
2013 - Indianapolis, IN (Indiana Convention Center)/Jan. 11 - 13/over 100 exhibitors
2013 - Hot Springs, VA (Homestead)/Oct. 9 - 12
2014 - Houston, TX (George R. Brown Convention Center)/March 6 - 8
2015 - Orlando, FL (Rosen Shingle Creek Hotel)/Feb. 5 - 7

Publications:
Membership Directory; on-line

Precast Inc.; bi-monthly; adv.

National Press Photographers Association (1946)
3200 Croasdaile Dr.
Suite 306
Durham, NC 27705
Tel: (919) 383-7246 Fax: (919) 383-7261
E-Mail: info@nppa.org
Website: nppa.org
Members: 10000 individuals
Staff: 6
Annual Budget: $1-2,000,000
Tax: 501(c)(6)

Personnel:
Executive Director: Mindy Hutchinson
  E-Mail: director@nppa.org
Director, Professional Services: Thomas Kenniff
  E-Mail: tkenniff@nppa.org
Director, Information Technology Services: Stephen Sample
  E-Mail: netgeek@nppa.org
Editor: Donald R. Winslow
  E-Mail: magazine@nppa.org

Historical Note:
Mission is to advance visual journalism, its creation, practice, training, editing and distribution in all news media and works to promote its role as a vital public service. Membership: $110 (Professional); $65 (Student/Retired); $60 (Family); $125-180 (International).

Meetings/Conferences:
Number of non-conference events/year: 4

Publications:
Close Up; weekly
News Photographer; monthly; adv.

Membership List Available to Non-members

National Prison Hospice Association (1991)
11 S. Angell St.
suite 303
Providence, RI 02906
Website: npha.org
Members: 10 hospice care organizations
Staff: 3
Annual Budget: $25-50,000
Tax: 501(c)(3)

Personnel:
Executive Director: Elizabeth Craig
President: Fleet Maull MA, PhD
  E-Mail: fleetmaull@comcast.net
Treasurer: Felice Owens

Historical Note:
NPHA works to promote hospice and similar palliative care programs for seriously ill inmates throughout the United States.

Publications:
NPHA Newsletter

National Private Truck Council (1939)
950 N. Glebe Rd.
Suite 530
Arlington, VA 22203-4183
Tel: (703) 683-1300 Fax: (703) 683-1217
E-Mail: info@nptc.org
Website: nptc.org
Members: 700 companies
Staff: 6
Annual Budget: $2-5,000,000
Tax: 501(c)(6)

Personnel:
President and Chief Executive Officer: Gary F. Petty
  E-Mail: gpetty@nptc.org
Senior Vice President, Education: Tom Moore CTP
  E-Mail: tmoore@nptc.org
Executive Vice President and Chief Operating Officer: George Mundell
  E-Mail: gmundell@nptc.org
Manager, Membership Services: Serena Porter
  E-Mail: sporter@nptc.org
General Counsel and Contact, Government Affairs: Rick Schweitzer
  E-Mail: rpschweitzer@rpslegal.com
Manager, Education: Kristen Todd
  E-Mail: ktodd@nptc.org

Historical Note:
Founded as National Council of Private Motor Truck Operators. Became Private Truck Council of America in

1953. Assumed current name in 1988 after merger with Private Truck Council of America. NPTC's mission is to be recognized and respected as the national trade association representing the private fleet and corporate transportation and distribution field, professional fleet managers, affiliated service and product providers. Membership: $685-950 (Fleet); $695-8,665 (Allied).

Continuing Education:
Enrollment: 50
Certification Designation/s: CTP

Meetings/Conferences: Annual
Conference Chair: George Mundell

Publications:
Annual Membership Directory and Buyer's Guide; on-line; adv.
CTP Insider; on-line; adv.
NPTC FO Newsletter; bi-monthly

The National Procurement Institute, Inc (1968)
P.O. Box 370192
Las Vegas, NV 89137
Tel: (702) 989-8095 Fax: (702) 967-0744
TollFree: (866) 877-7641
E-Mail: info@npiconnection.org
Website: npiconnection.org
Members: 600 individuals
Staff: 2
Annual Budget: $100-250,000

Personnel:
Executive Director: Craig Rowley
    E-Mail: executivedirector@npiconnection.org
Treasurer: Michele Brand

Historical Note:
Formerly (1973) known as Southern Purchasing Institute, (2011) National Purchasing Institute. NPI became an affiliate of the Institute for Supply Management (formerly NAPM) in 1990. NPI's mission is to promote the achievement of excellence in governmental and institutional procurement through education, certification, professional development and networking of its membership. Members are educational, government, and institutional purchasing administrators. Membership: $230 (Regular); $90 (Dual/Associate).

Meetings/Conferences: Annual

Publications:
Membership Directory; on-line
NPInsights
NPInsights; bi-monthly
Public Purchasing Review

Membership List Available to Non-members

National Propane Gas Association (1931)
1899 L St. NW
Suite 350
Washington, DC 20036
Tel: (202) 466-7200 Fax: (202) 466-7205
E-Mail: info@npga.org
Website: npga.org
Members: 3500 marketers, producers and suppliers
Staff: 24
Annual Budget: $5-10,000,000
Tax: 501(c)(6)

Personnel:
President and Chief Executive Officer: Richard R. Roldan
    E-Mail: rroldan@npga.org
Vice President, Regulatory and Technical Services: Mike A. Caldarera
    E-Mail: mcaldarera@npga.org
Manager, Human Resources and Scholarship Foundation: Joanne Casey
    E-Mail: jcasey@npga.org
Vice President, Finance and Administration: Brian E. Dunlap CPA
    E-Mail: bdunlap@npga.org
Coordinator, Communications: Rachel Grant
    E-Mail: rgrant@npga.org
Director, Membership Services: Darlene Hawk
    E-Mail: dhawk@npga.org
Program Manager, Certification and Technical Services: Jacqueline McCracken
    E-Mail: jmccracken@npga.org
Director, Media Relations: Mollie O'Dell
Senior Vice President, Government and Public Affairs: Philip A. Squair
    E-Mail: psquair@npga.org
Director, Conventions and Meetings: Jennifer Tomb CMP
    E-Mail: jtomb@npga.org

Historical Note:
Founded as National Bottled Gas Association. 1937-Liquified Petroleum Gas Association (LPGA). 1964-merger with the National LP-Gas Council (an organization formed in 1949) to form National LP-Gas Association (NLPGA). Present name was adopted in 1988. NPGA's mission is to advance safety and to increase the use of propane through sound public policy. Members are producers and distributors of liquefied petroleum gas and propane and manufacturers of equipment for its use. Membership: $1,008-5,305(Producer/Non-producing Broker/Wholesaler of LP- gas); $96-371(Marketers); $266 (International; $106 (Retired).

Continuing Education:
Certification Designation/s: CETP

Meetings/Conferences: Annual
Conference Chair: Jennifer Tomb CMP
2013 - Atlanta, GA (Georgia World Congress Center)/
    April 13 - 15
2014 - Atlanta, GA (Georgia World Congress Center)/
    April 12 - 14
2015 - Atlanta, GA (Georgia World Congress Center)/
    April 11 - 13
2016 - Atlanta, GA (Georgia World Congress Center)/
    April 9 - 11

Publications:
Membership Directory; on-line
NPGA Newsletter
NPGA Reports; weekly

National Property Management Association (1970)
4025 Tampa Rd.
Suite 1203
Oldsmar, FL 34677
Tel: (813) 475-6998 Fax: (813) 749-0812
E-Mail: hq@npma.org
Website: npma.org
Members: 4200 individuals
Staff: 6
Annual Budget: $1-2,000,000
Tax: 501(c)(6)

Personnel:
Executive Director: Paul Nesbitt CPP
    E-Mail: pnesbitt@npma.org
Administrative Assistant: Ashley DiCicco
    E-Mail: membership@npma.org
Manager, Public Relations and Communications: Felicia Johnson
    E-Mail: fjohnson@npma.org
Manager, Events and Education: Maria Maggio CMP
    E-Mail: mmaggio@npma.org
Manager, Membership Service and Certification: Penny Parker
    E-Mail: pparker@npma.org
Accountant: Denise Wylie
    E-Mail: dwylie@npma.org

Historical Note:
NPMA's mission is to advance the profession of personal property and fixed-asset management. Members benefit from products, programs and services that promote their professional development. Membership: $100-250 (Individual); $20 (Retiree); $20 (Student); $80-225 (Group Membership-Corporate/Employee).

Continuing Education:
Certification Designation/s: NPMAC, CPPA, CPPM

Meetings/Conferences: Annual
Conference Chair: Maria Maggio CMP
2013 - San Antonio, TX (Menger Hotel)/May 2 - 3
Number of non-conference events/year: 2

Publications:
Journal of Property & Asset Management; on-line
NPMA Newsletter; weekly; adv.
Property Professional; bi-monthly; adv.
Vendor Directory; on-line

Membership List Available to Non-members

National Psychological Association for Psychoanalysis (1948)
40 W. 13th St.
New York, NY 10011
Tel: (212) 924-7440 Fax: (212) 989-7543
E-Mail: info@npap.org
Website: npap.org
Members: 365 individuals
Staff: 6
Annual Budget: $100-250,000

Personnel:

President: Carl Weinberg
Administrator and Registrar: Doris Mare

Historical Note:
NPAP's mission is to promote advancement in the science of psychoanalysis as a distinct discipline separate from the practice of medicine and offers low-fee psychoanalysis and psychotherapy to the community at large.

Meetings/Conferences:
Conference Chair: Doris Mare
Number of non-conference events/year: 2

Publications:
NPAP News and Reviews; quarterly; adv.

Membership List Available to Non-members

National Public Employer Labor Relations Association (1971)
1012 S. Coast Hwy.
Suite M
Oceanside, CA 92054
Tel: (760) 433-1686 Fax: (760) 433-1687
TollFree: (877) 673-5721
E-Mail: info@npelra.org
Website: npelra.org
Members: 2000 Members
Staff: 4
Annual Budget: $500-1,000,000
Tax: 501(c)(6)

Personnel:
Executive Director: Michael T. Kolb
    E-Mail: mkolb@npelra.org
Administrative Specialist: Yvonne Gillengerten
    E-Mail: yvonne@npelra.org
Office Manager: Sandy Kostelny
    E-Mail: sandy@npelra.org

Historical Note:
NPELRA works to provide professional development, networking, and advocacy services to labor relations and human resources professionals in public service. Members are federal, state, county and municipal labor and employee relations professionals. Membership: $175 (Active/Affiliate); $150 (Associate); $25 (Student); $100 (Retiree).

Meetings/Conferences: Annual

Publications:
Connections; monthly
Membership Directory; on-line

Membership List Available to Non-members

National Quartz Producers Council (1967)
P.O. Box 1719
Wheat Ridge, CO 80034-1719
Tel: (303) 432-0044 Fax: (303) 467-0107
Members: 10 producers
Staff: 1
Annual Budget: Under $10,000

Personnel:
President: Marc R. Busley

Historical Note:
Members are producers of crushed quartz for use in decorative architectural concrete.

National Railroad Construction and Maintenance Association, Inc. (1967)
500 New Jersey Ave. NW
Suite 400
Washington, DC 20001
Tel: (202) 715-2919 Fax: (202) 318-0867
TollFree: (800) 883-1557
E-Mail: info@nrcma.org
Website: nrcma.org
Members: 150 companies
Staff: 4
Annual Budget: $1-2,000,000
Tax: 501(c)(6)

Personnel:
President: Chuck Baker
    E-Mail: cbaker@nrcma.org
Senior Policy Advisor: Ray B. Chambers
Director, Operations: Matt Ginsberg
    E-Mail: mginsberg@nrcma.org
Contact, Government Affairs: Keith Hartwell

Historical Note:
Formerly (1978) known as Railroad Construction and Maintenance Association. Incorporated, affiliated with Laborers' International Union of North America and the International Union of Operating Engineers.NRC's mission is to promote, develop and protect the railroad

and rail transit construction industry. Membership:
$650-2,900 (Contractors, based on Annual Revenues);
$650 (Associate); $850 (Supplier/Affiliate).

Meetings/Conferences: Annual
2013 - Miami Beach, FL (Loews Miami Beach Hotel)/
   Jan. 9 - 12
2014 - Palm Desert, CA/Jan. 5 - 8
2015 - Hollywood, FL/Jan. 7 - 10
2016 - San Diego, CA/Jan. 6 - 9

Publications:
Membership Directory; on-line; adv.
NRC e-Newsletter; monthly

National Railway Historical Society (1935)
100 N. 20th St.
Suite 400
Philadelphia, PA 19103-1462
Tel: (215) 557-6606 Fax: (215) 963-9785
Website: nrhs.com
Members: 170 chapters
Staff: 2
Annual Budget: $500-1,000,000
Tax: 501(c)(3)

Personnel:
President: Gregory P. Molloy
General Counsel: John Fiorilla

Historical Note:
An association of rail enthusiasts in the U.S. Its mission
to preserve rail heritage and to educate current and future
generations about railroads and their history. Membership:
$37 (Individual); $36 (Chapter); $16 (Student); $5
(Youth).

Meetings/Conferences: Annual
2013 - Williamsburg, VA/Jan. 12 - 13
2013 - Anchorage, AK (Hilton Anchorage)/Sept. 18 -
   22

Publications:
Membership Directory; on-line
NRHS News; bi-monthly

National Railway Labor Conference (1963)
1901 L St. NW
Washington, DC 20036
Tel: (202) 862-7200 Fax: (202) 862-7253
Website: nrlc.ws
Staff: 18
Annual Budget: $5-10,000,000

Personnel:
Chairman: Robert F. Allen
Media Manager: Joanna Moorhead
   E-Mail: jmoorhead@raillaborfacts.org

Historical Note:
NRLC represents member railroads in dealing with
representatives of organized employees on a national level
in matters involving railroad labor relations, health and
welfare benefits, appropriate matters before the courts,
Congressional committees, and other governmental bodies,
and other matters of interest or concern to its members.

National Ready Mixed Concrete Association
(1930)
900 Spring St.
Silver Spring, MD 20910
Tel: (301) 587-1400 Fax: (301) 585-4219
TollFree: (888) 846-7622
E-Mail: info@nrmca.org
Website: nrmca.org
Members: 1200 producers
Staff: 38
Annual Budget: $10-25,000,000
Tax: 501(c)(6)

Personnel:
President: Robert A. Garbini PE
   E-Mail: rgarbini@nrmca.org
Senior Director, Information Technology: Lawrence Afable
   E-Mail: lafable@nrmca.org
Senior Vice President, Membership Services and
   Communications: Kathleen Carr-Smith
   E-Mail: kcarrsmith@nrmca.org
Vice President, Education: Eileen Dickson
   E-Mail: edickson@nrmca.org
Manager, Customer Services: Jacques Jenkins
   E-Mail: jjenkins@nrmca.org
Senior Vice President, Government and Political Affairs:
   Kerri Leininger
   E-Mail: kleininger@nrmca.org

Senior Vice President, Sustainable Development: Lionel
   Lemay PE, SE
   E-Mail: llemay@nrmca.org
Senior Vice President, Marketing: Glenn Ochsenreiter
   E-Mail: gochsenreiter@nrmca.org
Vice President, Finance and Administration: Michael
   Olivarri CPA
   E-Mail: molivarri@nrmca.org
Director, Meetings: Jessica Walgenbach
   E-Mail: jmoore@nrmca.org

Historical Note:
NRMCA's mission is to provide exceptional value for its
members by responsibly representing and serving the
entire ready mixed concrete industry through leadership,
promotion, education and partnering to ensure ready mixed
concrete is the building material of choice. Membership:
$1,000-5,000 (Associate, based upon Company's sales);
$1,000 (Contractors); $350 (Producer, dues based on cubic
yard production).

Continuing Education:
Certification Designation/s: CCSP, CGBSC, CCSP, CDPC,
PMC, GSCP, PCC, PTC, FMC, NRMCA, CSPC, EPC

Meetings/Conferences: Annual
Conference Chair: Jessica Walgenbach
2013 - San Antonio, TX (JW Marriott Hill Country
   Resort & Spa)/March 3 - 15
Number of non-conference events/year: 20

Publications:
Advocacy; weekly
Concrete InFocus Magazine; quarterly
E-News; weekly; adv.
Membership Directory; on-line

National Real Estate Investors Association (1993)
525 W. Fifth St.
Suite 101
Covington, KY 41011
Tel: (859) 261-3335 Fax: (859) 581-5993
TollFree: (888) 762-7342
E-Mail: info@nationalreia.com
Website: nationalreia.com
Members: 230 organizations
Staff: 5
Annual Budget: $250-500,000
Tax: 501(c)(6)

Personnel:
Executive Director: Rebecca McLean
Office Manager: Lori Hudson
Director, Business Development and Events: Troy Miller
Coordinator, Projects: Kathy Rogg

Historical Note:
Formerly (1993) known as Real Estate Leadership
Conference. REIA works to develop, support and promote
local real estate investor organizations while serving the
interests of the real estate investment industry through
networking, education and leadership on legislative issues
and promoting professionalism and standards in the
industry. Membership: $2,500-5,000 (Annual Chapter);
$250-2150 (Affiliate).

Continuing Education:
Certification Designation/s: NPHP, CARI

Meetings/Conferences: Annual
Conference Chair: Troy Miller
2013 - Pittsburgh, PA (Sheraton Station Square Hotel)/
   June 20

Publications:
Personal Real Estate Investor Magazine
ThisWeek@NationalREIA; bi-weekly

National Recreation and Parks Association
(1965)
22377 Belmont Ridge Rd.
Ashburn, VA 20148-4501
Tel: (703) 858-0784 Fax: (703) 858-0794
TollFree: (800) 626-6772
E-Mail: public-policy@nrpa.org
Website: nrpa.org
Members: 21000 professionals, citizen advocates,
   educators, and students
Staff: 77
Annual Budget: $10-25,000,000
Tax: 501(c)(3)

Personnel:
President and Chief Executive Officer: Barbara Tulipane
   CAE
   E-Mail: btulipane@nrpa.org
Managing Editor: Beth Beard

   E-Mail: ebeard@nrpa.org
Vice President, Finance and Chief Financial Officer: Sandy
   Bishop CPA
   E-Mail: sbishop@nrpa.org
Director, Information Technology: Kevin Conley
   E-Mail: kconley@nrpa.org
Generalist, Human Resources: Martin Dease
   E-Mail: mdease@nrpa.org
Vice President, Membership and Professional Development:
   Tara Fitzpatrick-Navarro CPRP, CPSI, CTRS
   E-Mail: tfitzpatrick-navarro@nrpa.org
Editorial Director, Parks & Recreation magazine: Phil
   Hayward
   E-Mail: phayward@nrpa.org
Senior Manager, Public Relations and Communications:
   Lauren Hoffmann
   E-Mail: lhoffmann@nrpa.org
Senior Manager, Marketing: Dave Kelley
   E-Mail: dkelley@nrpa.org
Director, Conferences, Exhibits and Sponsorships: Karla
   Kelly
   E-Mail: kkelly@nrpa.org
Senior Director, Membership and Certification: Jessica
   Lytle
   E-Mail: jlytle@nrpa.org
Director, Education and Accreditation: Beth Wickline
   E-Mail: bwickline@nrpa.org
Vice President, Operations: M. Lauren Yost
   E-Mail: lyost@nrpa.org

Historical Note:
Formed by a merger of the American Association of
Zoological Parks and Aquariums (founded in 1924),
the American Institute of Park Executives (formed in
1898), the American Recreation Society (formed in 1938),
the National of State Parks (founded in 1921) and the
National Recreation Association (founded in 1906). NRPA's
mission is to advance parks, recreation and environmental
conservation efforts that enhance the quality of life for all
people. Membership: $150 (Professional); $99 (Young
Professional); $62 (Retired); $45 (Student); $60 (Citizen);
$600 (Agency); $360 (Group); $850 (Industry Supplier).

Continuing Education:
Certification Designation/s: AFO, CPSI, CPRP, CPRE

Meetings/Conferences: Annual
Conference Chair: Karla Kelly
2013 - Houston, TX/Oct. 8 - 10/7000 attendees/over
   100 exhibitors
2014 - Charlotte, NC/Oct. 14 - 16/7000 attendees/over
   100 exhibitors
2015 - Las Vegas, NV/Oct. 15 - 17/7000 attendees/
   over 100 exhibitors
2016 - St. Louis, MO/Oct. 4 - 6/7000 attendees/over
   100 exhibitors
2017 - New Orleans, LA/Sept. 26 - 28/7000 attendees/
   over 100 exhibitors
2018 - Indianapolis, IN/Sept. 25 - 27/7000 attendees/
   over 100 exhibitors
2019 - Baltimore, MD/Sept. 24 - 26/7000 attendees/
   over 100 exhibitors
2021 - Nashville, TN/Sept. 14 - 16/7000 attendees/
   over 100 exhibitors
Number of non-conference events/year: 6

Publications:
Journal of Leisure Research (JLR); quarterly
NRPA Express; monthly
Parks & Recreation Magazine; monthly; adv.
Parks and Recreation Weekly; weekly
Schole; annually
Therapeutic Recreation Journal (TRJ); quarterly

National Recycling Coalition (1978)
1220 L St. NW
Suite 100-155
Washington, DC 20005
Tel: (202) 618-2107 Fax: (202) 789-1431
E-Mail: info@nrc-recycle.org
Website: nrcrecycles.org
Members: 3,000 members
Staff: 3
Annual Budget: $100-250,000
Tax: 501(c)(3)

Personnel:
President: Mark Lichtenstein
   E-Mail: MarkL@nrcrecycles.org
Vice President, Treasurer: Margretta "Meg" Morris
   E-Mail: Meg@NRCrecycles.org
Contact, Communications and Education: Michele Nestor
   E-Mail: MicheleN@nrcrecycles.org

Historical Note:
NRC's mission is to partner with and facilitate activities between and among non-profit organizations (NGO's), businesses, trade associations, individuals and government to maintain a prosperous and productive American recycling system that is committed to the conservation of natural resources. Membership: $1,000 (Friend); $6,000 (Contributor); $15,000 (Supporter); $25,000 (Sustainer); $50,000 (Partner); $1,00,000 (Leader).

Meetings/Conferences: Annual
Publications:
Newsletter

National Register of Health Service Providers in Psychology (1974)
1200 New York Ave. NW
Suite 800
Washington, DC 20005-3801
Tel: (202) 783-7663 *Fax:* (202) 347-0550
Website: nationalregister.org
Members: 14000 individuals
Staff: 10
Annual Budget: $2-5,000,000
Tax: 501(c)(3)

Personnel:
Executive Officer: Judy E. Hall PhD
E-Mail: judy@nationalregister.org
Manager, Marketing and Communications: Andrew P. Boucher
E-Mail: andrew@nationalregister.org
Director, Finance and Administration: Camille L. Burke
E-Mail: camille@nationalregister.org
Analyst, Legislation and Regulatory Affairs: Alex Krigstein
E-Mail: alex@nationalregister.org
Manager, Professional Practice and Education: Stephanie Jackson Young MS
E-Mail: stephanie@nationalregister.org

Historical Note:
NRHSPP's mission is to promote credentialed psychologists to consumers, provides distinction and value to Registrants, guides psychology students toward credentialing, enhances psychologists' contributions to integrated healthcare, and facilitates identification of qualified psychologists in a global community. Membership: $145-350 (Applicants - Credential Review); $50-150 (Students/Trainees); $25-390 (Registrants); $499 (Healthcare Organizations).

Continuing Education:
Certification Designation/s: CE
Meetings/Conferences:
Number of non-conference events/year: 10

Publications:
Legal Briefs
Membership Directory; on-line
The Register Report

National Registry of Environmental Professionals (1983)
P.O. Box 2099
Glenview, IL 60025-6099
Tel: (847) 724-6631 *Fax:* (847) 724-4223
E-Mail: nrep@nrep.org
Website: nrep.org
Members: 17000 individuals
Staff: 3
Annual Budget: $500-1,000,000
Tax: 501(c)(6)

Personnel:
Executive Director: Richard A. Young PE, PhD, REM
E-Mail: ryoung@nrep.org
Director, Operations: Christopher Young

Historical Note:
NREP is dedicated to professionally and legally enhancing the recognition of those individuals who possess the education, training, and experience as qualified environmental engineers, technologists, managers, technicians and scientists. Membership: $90/year.

Continuing Education:
Certification Designation/s: CEA, REP, CESM, CES, CRCM, CMI, RELT, FMM, SIM, MAS, CIAQM, CIET, RHCMM, REPA, AEP, REM

Meetings/Conferences: Annual
Publications:
Fore Front Magazine; on-line
Journal of Science & Sustainability; on-line
Membership Directory; on-line

National Rehabilitation Association (1925)
633 S. Washington St.

Alexandria, VA 22314
Tel: (703) 836-0850 *Fax:* (703) 836-0848
TollFree: (888) 258-4295
E-Mail: info@nationalrehab.org
Website: nationalrehab.org
Members: 11000 individuals
Staff: 6
Annual Budget: $500-1,000,000

Personnel:
Executive Director: Beverlee Stafford
E-Mail: beverlee@nationalrehab.org
Director, Membership Services: Brian Coupe
E-Mail: Membership@nationalrehab.org
Director, Governmental Affairs: Patricia Leahy
E-Mail: patricia@nationalrehab.org

Historical Note:
NRA seeks to provide advocacy, awareness and career advancement for professionals in the fields of rehabilitation. Members include rehabilitation counselors, physical, speech and occupational therapists, job trainers, consultants, independent living instructors, students in rehabilitation programs, and other professionals involved in the advocacy of programs and services for people with disabilities. Membership: $48 (Student); $700 (Organization); $108 (New Professional/Affiliate); $75 (Individual); $1,500 (Institution);

Meetings/Conferences: Annual
Number of non-conference events/year: 8
Publications:
Contemporary Rehab; bi-monthly; adv.
Journal of Rehabilitation; quarterly; adv.

National Rehabilitation Counseling Association (1958)
P.O. Box 4480
Manassas, VA 20108
Tel: (703) 361-2077 *Fax:* (703) 361-2489
E-Mail: info@nrca-net.org
Website: nrca-net.org
Members: 1800 individuals
Staff: 5
Annual Budget: $50-100,000
Tax: 501(c)(6)

Personnel:
Webmaster: Jennifer Pipinou
Editor: Jamie Satcher
E-Mail: jsatcher@bamaed.ua.edu

Historical Note:
Founded as a professional division of National Rehabilitation Association; became an independent organization in 2005. NRCA represents the unique concerns of practicing rehabilitation counselors. Membership consists of rehabilitation counselors practicing in a variety of work settings: private non-profit agencies, hospital medical settings, educational programs, private-for-profit businesses, state/federal agencies, private practice, unions, and others. Membership: $80 (Professional/Member/Affiliate); $25-35(Student); $700 (Life).

Continuing Education:
Certification Designation/s: CRCC
Publications:
The Journal of Applied Rehabilitation Counseling; quarterly

National Reining Horse Association (1966)
3000 NW Tenth St.
Oklahoma City, OK 73107-5302
Tel: (405) 946-7400 *Fax:* (405) 946-8425
Website: nrha1.com
Members: 15000 individuals
Staff: 32
Annual Budget: $5-10,000,000
Tax: 501(c)(5)

Personnel:
Executive Director: Dan Wall
E-Mail: nrha@nrha.com
Senior Director, Sponsorship and Television Programming: Todd Barden
E-Mail: tbarden@nrha.com
Program Analyst and Database Administrator: Dan Dobbs
E-Mail: ddobbs@nrha.com
Chief Financial Officer: John Foy
E-Mail: jfoy@nrha.com
Senior Director, Marketing: Christa Morris
E-Mail: cmorris@nrha.com
Senior Director, Shows and Affiliate Programs: Chris Potter
E-Mail: cpotter@nrha.com

Senior Director, Publications: Carol Trimmer
E-Mail: ctrimmer@nrha.com
Manager, Member Services and Judges Program Supervisor: Michelle Wrigley
E-Mail: mwrigley@nrha.com
Operations Chief: Dennis York
E-Mail: dyork@nrha.com

Historical Note:
NRHA is an organization dedicated to the promotion of the reining horse. Mission is to promote and encourage development of and public interest in agriculture and ranching through the promotion of public Reining Horse Shows. Membership: $3-2000/year.

Meetings/Conferences: Annual
Conference Chair: Chris Potter

Publications:
Newsletter
Reiner Magazine; monthly

National Religious Broadcasters (1944)
9510 Technology Dr.
Manassas, VA 20110
Tel: (703) 330-7000 *Fax:* (703) 330-7100
E-Mail: info@nrbnetwork.tv
Website: nrb.org
Staff: 10
Annual Budget: $2-5,000,000
Tax: 501(c)(3)

Personnel:
President and Chief Executive Officer: Frank Wright
E-Mail: fwright@nrb.org
Director, Marketing: Steve Cross
Senior Vice President , Strategic Partnerships, Membership: Dr. Ron Harris
Vice President, Conventions and Technology Development: David Keith
E-Mail: dkeith@nrb.org
Vice President, Finance: Mike Kisha
Director, Communications: Laurel MacLeod
Vice President, Government Relations: Aaron Mercer
Senior Vice President, Communications and General Counsel: Craig Parshall
E-Mail: cparshall@nrb.org
Director, Convention Operations: Tammy Singleton
Executive Vice President and Chief Operating Officer: Linda W. Smith

Historical Note:
NRB's mission is to keep the doors of electronic media open for the spread of the Gospel and to promote standards of excellence, integrity, and accountability, networking, educational, ministry, and fellowship opportunities for its members. Membership: $370 (Puerto Rico/Individual); $485 (Educational); $485-15,830 (Organizational); $370-670 (Associate); $50 (Student).

Meetings/Conferences:
Conference Chair: David Keith
2013 - Nashville, TN (Gaylord Hotels Resorts and Convention Centers-Nashville)/March 2
2013 - Nashville, TN (Omni Nashville Hotel)/March 2 - 5
2014 - Nashville, TN (Gaylord Hotels Resorts and Convention Centers-Nashville)/Feb. 22
2014 - Nashville, TN (Gaylord Hotels Resorts and Convention Centers-Nashville)/Feb. 22 - 25
2015 - Nashville, TN (Gaylord Hotels Resorts and Convention Centers-Nashville)/Feb. 21
2015 - Nashville, TN (Gaylord Hotels Resorts and Convention Centers-Nashville)/Feb. 21 - 25

Publications:
NRB Today; weekly; adv.

National Religious Broadcasters, Music License Committee
4880 Santa Rosa Rd.
Camarillo, CA 93012
Tel: (805) 482-8570 *Fax:* (805) 384-4522
Website: nrbmlc.com
Staff: 2

Personnel:
Executive Director: Russell R. Hauth
General Counsel: Bruce Joseph

Historical Note:
NRBMLC works to serve its member stations in negotiating fair and nondiscriminatory music licenses with the performance rights organizations (the "P.R.O.s" – ASCAP, BMI and SESAC and with SoundExchange for Internet streaming).

Publications:
NRBMLC Newsletter; on-line

National Religious Campaign Against Torture
110 Maryland Ave. NE
Suite 502
Washington, DC 20002
Tel: (202) 547-1920 *Fax:* (202) 547-1921
E-Mail: campaign@nrcat.org
Website: nrcat.org
Members: 300 Organizations
Staff: 4
Annual Budget: $500-1,000,000
Tax: 501(c)(3)

Personnel:
Executive Director: Rev. Richard Killmer
   E-Mail: rkillmer@nrcat.org
Director for Policy Coordination: Matthew Hawthorne
   E-Mail: mhawthorne@nrcat.org
Director, Finance And Operations: Tara C. Morrow

Historical Note:
Inter-faith coalition to end U.S. sponsored torture.

Publications:
NRCAT Newsletter; quarterly

National Remotivation Therapy Organization
(1971)
P.O. Box Five
New Tripoli, PA 18066
Tel: (610) 767-5026
Website: remotivation.com
Members: 400 individuals
Staff: 2
Annual Budget: Under $10,000
Tax: 501(c)(3)

Personnel:
Executive Secretary: Beverly Gruber CPO
Contact, Website Services: John Bierma
   E-Mail: biermajr@yahoo.com

Historical Note:
NRTO strives to educate interested persons in remotivation, unite into one organization all persons trained in remotivation, keep remotivators informed of developments that will enhance their delivery and to work cooperatively with other groups interested in remotivation. Members are certified remotivation therapists. Membership: $30/year (Individual).

National Renal Administrators Association
(1977)
100 N. 20th St.
Suite 400
Philadelphia, PA 19103
Tel: (215) 320-4655 *Fax:* (215) 564-2175
E-Mail: nraa@nraa.org
Website: nraa.org
Members:
25 companies
800 individuals
Staff: 3
Annual Budget: $2-5,000,000
Tax: 501(c)(6)

Personnel:
Executive Director: Marc Chow
Contact, Membership and Communication: Lisa Chester
   E-Mail: lchester@fernley.com
Manager, Meeting: Tina Phelan
   E-Mail: tphelan@fernley.com

Historical Note:
NRAA serves as the resource and voice for the independent, regional and community based dialysis providers. Membership: $300 (Active/Affiliate); $150 (Associate).

Meetings/Conferences:
Conference Chair: Tina Phelan
2013 - Seatle, WA (Grand Hyatt Seattle)/Sept. 25 - 27

Publications:
NRAA Membership Directory; on-line
Renal Watch Newsletter; weekly; adv.

National Renderers Association *(1933)*
801 N. Fairfax St.
Suite 205
Alexandria, VA 22314
Tel: (703) 683-0155 *Fax:* (703) 683-2626
E-Mail: renderers@nationalrenderers.com
Website: nationalrenderers.org

Members: 51 members companies, 205 rendering plants, 16 international members and 120 associate members.
Staff: 9
Annual Budget: $2-5,000,000

Personnel:
President: Tom M. Cook
   E-Mail: tcook@nationalrenderers.com
Director, Scientific Education and Communication: Jessica Meisinger
   E-Mail: jmeisinger@nationalrenderers.com

Historical Note:
NRA is an alliance that represents the interests of its members in public, government and regulatory affairs, and provides services, programs and technical support to the North American rendering industry in national and international markets.

Meetings/Conferences: Annual
Conference Chair: Marty Covert

Publications:
NRA Membership Directory
Render Magazine; bi-monthly

National Republican Congressional Committee
(1866)
320 First St. SE
Washington, DC 20003
Tel: (202) 479-7000
Website: nrcc.org
Staff: 2

Personnel:
Executive Director: Guy Harrison
   E-Mail: guy@nrccmail.org
Political Director: Mike Shields

Historical Note:
NRCC supports the election of Republicans to the House through direct financial contributions to candidates and Republican Party organizations; technical and research assistance to Republican candidates and Party organizations; voter registration, education and turnout programs; and other Party-building activities.

National Research Council *(1916)*
500 Fifth St. NW
Washington, DC 20001
Tel: (202) 334-2000
Website: nationalacademies.org/nrc/index.html
Staff: 7

Personnel:
Executive Officer: Bruce B. Darling
Deputy Executive Officer and Chief Operating Officer: James F. Hinchman
Executive Director, Congressional and Government Affairs: James E. Jensen
General Counsel: Audrey Byrd Mosley
Director, Administration: Joseph Papa
Chief Financial Officer: Mary "Didi" Salmon
Director, Human Resources: Shelia B. Wright

Historical Note:
NRF seeks to improve government decision making and public policy, increase public understanding, and promote the acquisition and dissemination of knowledge in matters involving science, engineering, technology, and health.

Publications:
Members Directory; on-line
Report to Congress; annually
Transportation Research E-Newsletter; weekly

National Restaurant Association *(1919)*
2055 L St. NW
Washington, DC 20036
Tel: (202) 331-5900 *Fax:* (202) 331-2429
E-Mail: media@dineout.org
Website: restaurant.org
Members: 380000 individuals
Staff: 225
Annual Budget: $50-100,000,000
Tax: 501(c)(6)

Personnel:
Treasurer: Ken Conrad

Historical Note:
NRA is a business association for the restaurant industry. NRA's goal is to enhance America's restaurant industry and strives to help every member build customer loyalty, find financial success and provide rewarding careers in food service. Membership: $500-7,500 (Allied); $95 (Faculty); $75 (Student); $195 (Not For Profit); $250 (International).

Continuing Education:
Certification Designation/s: FMP
Meetings/Conferences: Annual
2013 - Chicago, IL (McCormick Place)/May 18 - 21/ over 100 exhibitors

Publications:
Washington Weekly; weekly

National Retail Federation *(1981)*
325 Seventh St. NW
Suite 1100
Washington, DC 20004-2802
Tel: (202) 783-7971 *Fax:* (202) 737-2849
TollFree: (800) 673-4692
Website: nrf.com
Members: 16 million associations
Staff: 111
Annual Budget: $25-50,000,000
Tax: 501(c)(3)

Personnel:
President and Chief Executive Officer: Matthew Shay
Senior Director, Membership Administration: Jannise Corry
   E-Mail: corryj@nrf.com
Senior Vice President, General Counsel: Mallory B. Duncan
   E-Mail: duncanm@nrf.com
Senior Vice President, Government Relations: David G. French
   E-Mail: frenchd@nrf.com
Senior Vice President, Member Relations: Mike Gatti
   E-Mail: gattim@nrf.com
Director, Sales: Mike Gribbin
   E-Mail: gribbinm@nrf.com
Senior Vice President, Retail Operations and Chief Information Officer: David Hogan
   E-Mail: hogand@nrf.com
Vice President, Human Resources: Bruce Lampron
   E-Mail: lampronb@nrf.com
Vice President, Retail Technologies: Tom Litchford
Senior Vice President, Conferences: Susan Newman
Vice President, Education Strategies: Eric Olson
   E-Mail: olsene@nrf.com
Executive Assistant: Eileen Pryor
   E-Mail: pryore@nrf.com
Editor, Stores Media: Susan Reda
   E-Mail: redas@nrf.com
Director, Retail Finance and Accounting: Rachel Ryan
   E-Mail: ryanr@nrf.com
Senior Director, Media Relations: Stephen Schatz
   E-Mail: schatzs@nrf.com
Senior Vice President, Communications and Public Affairs: Bill Thorne
Vice President, Communications and Public Affairs: Katie Wilson
   E-Mail: wilsonk@nrf.com

Historical Note:
NRF's mission is to advance the interests of the retail industry through advocacy, communications and education. Divisions include the Association for Retail Technology Standards, the National Council of Chain Restaurants and the Retail Advertising and Marketing Association.

Meetings/Conferences:
Conference Chair: Susan Newman
2013 - New York City, NY (Jacob K. Javits Convention Center)/Jan. 13 - 16/1-10 exhibitors
2013 - San Diego, CA (San Diego Convention Center)/ June 12 - 14
Number of non-conference events/year: 6

Publications:
Membership Directory; on-line
NRF SmartBrief; daily
STORES Magazine; monthly
STORES Weekly; weekly

Membership List Available to Non-members

National Retail Hobby Stores Association *(1992)*
214 N. Hale St.
Wheaton, IL 60187
Tel: (630) 510-4596 *Fax:* (630) 510-4501
E-Mail: info@nrhsa.org
Website: nrhsa.org
Members: 300 Individuals
Staff: 4
Annual Budget: $50-100,000

Personnel:

Executive Director: Janet Svazas
   E-Mail: jsvazas@integrated-solutions.com
Editor: Jeanette L. Helfrich
   E-Mail: jhelfrich@integrated-solutions.com
Administrative Director: Holly Lundgren
   E-Mail: hlundgren@integrated-solutions.com

Historical Note:
NRHSA strives to improve member businesses by providing
marketing and operating information to its members.
Members are hobby store operators and suppliers to
the retail hobby trade. Membership: $120-250/year
(Company-based on gross annual store sales).

Meetings/Conferences: Annual
2013 - Las Vegas, NV (The Orleans Hotel)/April 28 -
   May 1

Publications:
E-Commerce Magazine
Member E-Link; on-line
The Link Newsletter; bi-monthly

National Retail Tenants Association (1997)
60 Shaker Rd.
E. Longmeadow, MA 01028-2760
Tel: (413) 525-4565 Fax: (413) 525-4590
Website: retailtenants.org
Members: 520 individual professionals
Staff: 2
Annual Budget: $250-500,000

Personnel:
Executive Director: Paul Kinney
Manager, Membership Services: Carole Fiola

Historical Note:
NRTA's mission is to enhance the personal and professional
education of its members and the profitability of its member
companies. Membership: $175 (Regular); $375 (Primary
Annual Affiliate).

Meetings/Conferences: Annual
2013 - Orlando, FL (The Renaissance Orlando at Sea
   World)/Sept. 22 - 25
2014 - Reno, NV (Peppermill Resort Spa Casino)/Sept.
   7 - 10

Publications:
Membership Roster; on-line
Tenants In-Common; quarterly; adv.

National Reverse Mortgage Lenders Association
(1997)
1400 16th St. NW
Suite 420
Washington, DC 20036
Tel: (202) 939-1760 Fax: (202) 265-4435
Website: nrmlaonline.org
Members: 125 companies
Staff: 9
Annual Budget: $2-5,000,000
Tax: 501(c)(6)

Personnel:
President and Chief Executive Officer: Peter H. Bell
   E-Mail: pbell@dworbell.org
Executive Vice President, Marketing and Communications:
   Marty Bell
   E-Mail: mbell@dworbell.com
Vice President, Communications: Darryl Hicks
   E-Mail: dhicks@dworbell.com
Executive Vice President: Steve Irwin
   E-Mail: stephenirwin09@comcast.net
Director, Membership Services: Linda Latimore
   E-Mail: llatimore@dworbell.com
Chief Financial Officer: Patty Winter
   E-Mail: pwinter@dworbell.com

Historical Note:
NRMLA's mission is to educate consumers about reverse
mortgages, to train lenders to, to enforce their code
of conduct and best practices, and to promote reverse
mortgages in the news media. Membership: $350 (Public/
Counseling Agency); $1,500 (Associate); $1,000-2,750
(Lender); $10,000 (Government-Sponsored Enterprises/
Investor-for each firm); $50 (Additional Delegates, per
firm/person).

Continuing Education:
Certification Designation/s: CRMP

Meetings/Conferences: Annual
Conference Chair: Darryl Hicks
Number of non-conference events/year: 3

Publications:
Reverse Mortgage Online Update; monthly
The Monday Report; weekly

Vendor Directory; on-line

National Rifle Association of America (1871)
11250 Waples Mill Rd.
Fairfax, VA 22030
Tel: (800) 672-3888 Fax: (703) 267-3918
TollFree: (800) 672-3888
E-Mail: nra-contact@nra.org
Website: nra.org
Members: 1000000 individuals
Staff: 550
Annual Budget: Over $100,000,000
Tax: 501(c)(4)

Personnel:
Executive Vice President: Wayne R. LaPierre Jr.
   E-Mail: nra-contact@nra.org
Chief Lobbyist: Christopher W. Cox
   E-Mail: nra-contact@nra.org
Executive Director, Publications: Joe Graham
Director, Education and Training: Bill Poole
   E-Mail: bpoole@nrahq.org

Historical Note:
NRA's mission is to promote and encourage rifle shooting
on a scientific basis. Membership: $35 (Regular); $1,000
(Life).

Meetings/Conferences: Annual
2013 - Houston, TX (George R. Brown Convention
   Center)/May 3 - 5/51-100 exhibitors

Publications:
America's 1st Freedom
American Hunter
American Rifleman; monthly
Insights; monthly
Regional Report; monthly

National Risk Retention Association (1987)
16133 Ventura Blvd.
Suite 1055
Encino, CA 91436
Tel: (818) 995-3274 Fax: (800) 421-5981
TollFree: (800) 928-5809
E-Mail: info@nrra-usa.org
Website: nrra-usa.org
Members: 105 companies and 44 individuals
Staff: 2
Annual Budget: $250-500,000
Tax: 501(c)(6)

Personnel:
Executive Director: Joseph E. Deems
   E-Mail: joe@riskretention.org

Historical Note:
NRRA represents risk retention and purchasing group
liability insurance programs, organized pursuant to the
Federal Liability Risk Retention Act. Its purpose is to
promote Risk Retention Act-authorized group insurance
programs as practical and financially sound options
for distributing the liability risks of members.NRRA
is the only national association dedicated to the
successful development, education and promotion of U.S.
domiciled alternatives to traditional liability insurance.
NRRA provides a forum where the country's most
knowledgeable individuals in risk retention insurance may
exchange valuable and timely information. Membership:
$350-3,500/year.

Meetings/Conferences: Annual

Publications:
Membership Directory; annually; adv.
Newsletter; monthly; adv.

National Roadside Vegetation Management
Association (1984)
5616 Lynchburg Cir.
Hueytown, AL 35023
Tel: (205) 491-7574 Fax: (205) 491-2725
Website: nrvma.org
Members: 750 individuals
Staff: 1
Annual Budget: $50-100,000
Tax: 501(c)(5)

Personnel:
Executive Director: John R. Reynolds CAE
   E-Mail: jreynoldsnrvma@charter.net

Historical Note:
NRVMA is an educational, non-profit organization
dedicated to providing expertise, solutions and networking
opportunities to personnel involved in integrated roadside
vegetation management. NRVMA's mission is to promote
coordinated, integrated efforts among those interested and

engaged in roadside vegetation management. Members are
individuals concerned with the management, beautification
and maintenance of roadside vegetation. Membership: $25
(General); $250 (Affiliate); $475 (Basic Exhibitor); $1200
(Supporting Member); $3600 (Sustaining Member).

Continuing Education:
Certification Designation/s: CPRM, CPRT

Meetings/Conferences: Annual
Conference Chair: John R. Reynolds CAE

Publications:
Land and Water; bi-monthly; adv.
The Dirt; bi-weekly; adv.

National Roof Deck Contractors Association
(1959)
P.O. Box 1582
Westford, MA 01886-4996
Tel: (800) 217-7944 Fax: (978) 250-9788
E-Mail: nrdca@nrdca.org
Website: nrdca.org
Members: 60 companies
Staff: 2
Annual Budget: $50-100,000
Tax: 501(c)(6)

Personnel:
Executive Director: Hubert T. Dudley

Historical Note:
Formerly (1980) known as the Gypsum Roof Deck
Foundation, NRDCA's mission is to provide, install or
support the application of engineered composite roof deck
substrates in the commercial roof top market. Members
are contractors installing poured gypsum, lightweight
insulating concrete and cementitious wood fiber structural
roof deck systems. Membership: $1,000 (Contractor);
$2,000 (Supplier); $500 (Associate).

Continuing Education:
Certification Designation/s: LWIC

Meetings/Conferences: Annual

National Roofing Contractors Association (1886)
10255 W. Higgins Rd.
Suite 600
Rosemont, IL 60018-5607
Tel: (847) 299-9070 Fax: (847) 299-1183
TollFree: (800) 323-9545
E-Mail: nrca@nrca.net
Website: nrca.net
Members: 4000 companies
Staff: 71
Annual Budget: $10-25,000,000
Tax: 501(c)(6)

Personnel:
Executive Vice President: William Good CAE
Associate Executive Director, Information Technology: Paul
   Apostolos MCSD
Senior Director, Communications and Editor: Ambika
   Puniani Bailey
Director, Education Media and Programs: Michele
   Biesiada
Manager, Human Resources and Payroll: Enrica Burian
Associate Executive Director, Communications and
   Marketing: Carl Good
   E-Mail: cgood@nrca.net
Associate Executive Director, Meeting Services: Bennett
   Judson CMP
   E-Mail: bjudson@nrca.net
Vice President, Operations and Membership Development:
   Alison LaValley CAE
   E-Mail: alavalley@nrca.net
Associate Executive Director, Finance: Harry Ryder CPA
   E-Mail: hryder@nrca.net

Historical Note:
NRCA's mission is to inform and assist the roofing industry,
act as its principal advocate and help members in serving
their customers. Members are roofing professionals.
Membership: $345-14,685/year.

Continuing Education:
Certification Designation/s: CERTA

Meetings/Conferences: Annual
Conference Chair: Bennett Judson CMP
2013 - San Antonio, TX/Feb. 3 - 7
2013 - San Antonio, TX (The Henry B. Gonzalez
   Convention Center)/Feb. 5 - 7
2014 - Las Vegas, NV (Mandalay Bay Convention
   Center)/Feb. 24 - 28
Number of non-conference events/year: 2

Publications:

E-News; weekly; adv.
Membership Directory; on-line
Professional Roofing; monthly; adv.

Membership List Available to Non-members

National Rural Economic Developers Association
(1989)
1255 SW Prairie Trail Pkwy
Ankeny, IA 50023
Tel: (515) 284-1421 *Fax:* (515) 334-1167
Website: nreda.org
Members: 236 members
Staff: 1
Annual Budget: $100-250,000
Tax: 501(c)(6)

Personnel:
Executive Director: Lynn M. Harkin
    E-Mail: director@nreda.org

Historical Note:
NREDA's mission is to provide education, advocacy and networking opportunities to rural and suburban utilities and affiliated organizations. It is an individual-member organization for the advancement of rural development and achievement of social and human service objectives in rural areas. Connects professionals in energy, telecommunications, water and sewer systems, transportation, housing, health care, education and financing. Members are economic development professionals with a special interest in rural utility and telecommunications projects. Membership: $325 (Individual/Associate); $250 (Individual Corporate/Associate Corporate); $50 (Student, Non-Voting); $0 (Honorary)).

Meetings/Conferences: Annual
2013 - Austin, TX (Driskill Hotel)/July 17 - 19
2014 - Cleaveland, OH (Wyndham Cleveland Playhouse Square Hotel)/July 23 - 25

Publications:
Rural Developer; quarterly

National Rural Education Association *(1907)*
C/O Purdue Unversity, Beering Hall of Libarel
Arts and Education
100 N. University St.
West LaFayette, IN 47907-2098
Tel: (765) 494-0086 *Fax:* (765) 496-1228
Website: nrea.net
Members: 2000 individuals and organizations
Staff: 1
Annual Budget: $100-250,000
Tax: 501(c)(3)

Personnel:
Executive Director: Dr. John Hill
    E-Mail: jehill@purdue.edu

Historical Note:
Established as the Department of Rural and Agricultural Education of the National Education Association, it became the Rural Education Association in 1959, the Rural Regional Education Association in 1975, the Rural Education Association in 1986 and assumed its present name in 1987. NREA works to improve and expand public education in rural areas. Membership: $400 (School District); $75 (Institutional/Teacher); $50 (Retired Educator/Library, Domestic Subscription); $100 (Individual/Library, Foreign Subscription).

Meetings/Conferences: Annual
Conference Chair: Dr. John Hill

Publications:
NREA Update; semi-monthly
The Rural Educator

National Rural Electric Cooperative Association
(1942)
4301 Wilson Blvd.
Arlington, VA 22203-1860
Tel: (703) 907-5500 *Fax:* (703) 907-5516
E-Mail: nreca@nreca.org
Website: nreca.org
Members: 900 cooperatives
Staff: 500
Annual Budget: $50-100,000,000
Tax: 501(c)(6)

Personnel:
Chief Executive Officer: Glenn L. English
    E-Mail: glenn.english@nreca.coop
Principal, Legislative Affairs: Cliff Humphrey
    E-Mail: cliff.humphrey@nreca.org

Executive Vice President, Government Relations: Kirk Johnson
    E-Mail: kirk.johnson@nreca.org
Director, Media Relations: Patrick Lavigne
    E-Mail: patrick.lavigne@nreca.coop
Associate Manager, Membership Services: Nancy McMahen
    E-Mail: nancy.mcmahen@nreca.coop
Director, Member Communications: Eleanor Miller
    E-Mail: eleanor.miller@nreca.org
Senior Director and Editor: Perry A. Stambaugh
    E-Mail: perry.stambaugh@nreca.coop
Employee Benefits Legislative Counsel: Chris Stephen
    E-Mail: chris.stephen@nreca.org
General Counsel and Vice President, Energy Policy: Wallace F. Tillman
    E-Mail: wallace.tillman@nreca.org
Senior Principal and Counsel: H. Montee Wynn Jr.
    E-Mail: montee.wynn@nreca.org
Contact, Conferences: Charla Young
    E-Mail: charla.young@nreca.coop

Historical Note:
NRECA is dedicated to representing the national interests of cooperative electric utilities and the consumers they serve. Members include consumer-owned local distribution systems.

Meetings/Conferences: Annual
Conference Chair: Nancy McMahen
Number of non-conference events/year: 6

Publications:
Membership Directory; on-line
NRECA International TieLine; quarterly
RE Magazine; monthly; adv.

National Rural Health Association *(1977)*
521 E. 63rd St.
Kansas City, MO 64110-3329
Tel: (816) 756-3140 *Fax:* (816) 756-3144
E-Mail: npaige@NRHArural.org
Website: ruralhealthweb.org
Members: 20000 members
Staff: 15
Annual Budget: $2-5,000,000
Tax: 501(c)(3)

Personnel:
Director, Communications and Marketing: Lindsey Corey
    E-Mail: lcorey@NRHArural.org
Vice President, Government Affairs and Policy: Maggie Elehwany
    E-Mail: elehwany@nrharural.org
Vice President, Program Services: Amy L. Elizondo
    E-Mail: elizondo@nrharural.org
Chief Financial Officer: Robert G. McVay
    E-Mail: mcvay@NRHArural.org
Accountant: Geno Poarch
    E-Mail: poarch@NRHArural.org
Manager, Meeting Logistics: Kathy Siress
    E-Mail: siress@nrharural.org
Senior Vice President, Membership Services: Brock Slabach
    E-Mail: bslabach@nrharural.org

Historical Note:
NRHA's mission is to provide leadership on rural health issues; through advocacy, communications, education, and research. Membership: $10-3500/year.

Meetings/Conferences: Annual
Conference Chair: Kathy Siress
2013 - Louisville, KY/May 7 - 10
Number of non-conference events/year: 5

Publications:
Rural Health Connect; monthly; adv.
Rural Roads; quarterly; adv.
The Journal of Rural Health; quarterly; adv.

National Rural Letter Carriers' Association
(1903)
1630 Duke St.
Alexandria, VA 22314-3465
Tel: (703) 684-5545 *Fax:* (703) 548-8735
Website: nrlca.org
Members: 112000 individuals
Staff: 25
Annual Budget: $10-25,000,000
Tax: 501(c)(5)

Personnel:
President: Jeanette P. Dwyer

Secretary and Treasurer: Clifford D. Dailing
Director, Labor Relations: Joey C. Johnson
Managing Editor: Melissa Ray
Vice President: Ronnie W. Stutts
Director, Governmental Affairs: Paul Swartz
    E-Mail: pswartz@nrlca.org

Historical Note:
NRLCA's purpose is to improve the methods used by rural letter carriers, to benefit their conditions of labor with the United States Postal Service (USPS), and to promote a fraternal spirit among its members. Membership: $4-624/year.

Publications:
Membership Directory; on-line
The National Rural Letter Carrier; monthly; adv.

Membership List Available to Non-members

National Rural Telecommunications Cooperative
(1986)
2121 Cooperative Way
Herndon, VA 20171-4542
Tel: (703) 787-0874 *Fax:* (703) 464-5300
TollFree: (800) 995-5592
E-Mail: info@nrtc.coop
Website: nrtc.coop
Members: 1400 members
Staff: 5

Personnel:
Chief Executive Officer: Tim Bryan
General Counsel: Bob Fuhrer
Vice President, Finance and Strategic Planning: Terry Gilmore
Director, Training: Tracey Klepic
    E-Mail: training@nrtc.coop
Vice President and Chief Technology Officer: Kurt Schaubach

Historical Note:
Founded by the National Rural Electric Cooperative Association and the National Rural Utilities Cooperative Finance Corporation. NRTC's mission is to lead and support members by delivering telecommunication solutions to strengthen member businesses, promote economic development and improve the quality of life in rural America. Members work to bring advanced telecommunications solutions to rural America. Membership: $1,000 (Class A/Class B); $500 (Class C/Class Group).

Publications:
NRTConnects; monthly
The Provider; monthly

National Rural Water Association *(1976)*
2915 S. 13th St.
Duncan, OK 73533
Tel: (580) 252-0629 *Fax:* (580) 255-4476
Website: nrwa.org
Members: 120 associate members and 900 individuals
Staff: 29
Annual Budget: $50-100,000,000
Tax: 501(c)(6)

Personnel:
Business Manager: Robert K. Johnson
    E-Mail: nrwarj@nrwa.org
Chief Financial Officer: Claudette Atwood
    E-Mail: nrwaca@nrwa.org
Contact, Membership Services: Dena Harms
    E-Mail: nrwadh@nrwa.org
Contact, Membership Services: Dawn Myers
    E-Mail: nrwadm@nrwa.org
Program Manager, Training: Bill O'Connell
Contact, Data Services and Technology: Chris Wilson
    E-Mail: nrwacw@nrwa.org

Historical Note:
NRWA is a water, wastewater and groundwater public utility membership organization representing over 26,000 utilities through state rural water affiliates. NRWA provides training, technical assistance, and legislative representation services, and sponsors and supports the NRWA Political Action Committee (Water PAC). Membership: $25 (Individual); $845 (Corporate).

Publications:
Rural Water Magazine; quarterly; adv.
Rural Water Wire; on-line; adv.

National Safe Skies Alliance *(1997)*
110 McGhee Tyson Blvd.
Suite 201

Alcoa, TN 37701
Tel: (865) 970-0515 *Fax:* (865) 970-0506
TollFree: (888) 609-4957
Website: sskies.org
Members: 24 Companies
Staff: 42
Annual Budget: $2-5,000,000
Tax: 501(c)(3)

Personnel:
President and Chief Executive Officer: Scott Broyles
Senior Vice President and Chief Financial Officer: Jennifer
  Roberts

Historical Note:
*National Safe Skies Alliance's mission is improving
the safety and security of air travel and providing a
public-private forum for the discussion of related issues.
Membership: $3,000-6,000 (Airline/Airport); $3,000
(University); $6,000 (National Laboratory/Association);
$2,000-6,000 (Corporate).*

Publications:
Carpe Diem; monthly

National Safety Council *(1913)*
1121 Spring Lake Dr.
Itasca, IL 60143-3201
Tel: (630) 285-1121 *Fax:* (630) 285-1315
TollFree: (800) 621-7615
E-Mail: info@nsc.org
Website: nsc.org
Members: 20000 companies
Staff: 220
Annual Budget: $25-50,000,000
Tax: 501(c)(3)

Personnel:
President and Chief Executive Officer: Janet P. Froetscher
  E-Mail: janet.froetscher@nsc.org
Contact, Meetings: Sloane Grubb
  E-Mail: sloane.grubb@nsc.org
Contact, Publications: Suzanne Powills
  E-Mail: suzanne.powills@nsc.org
Director, Membership Services: Ingrid Schoen
  E-Mail: ingrid.schoen@nsc.org

Historical Note:
*NSC works to prevent injuries and deaths at work, in
homes, communities and on the roads, through research,
education and advocacy. Membership: $295-395 plus $1
per employee over 100 (Organization, based on the number
of employees); Free (College Students in Safety and Health).*

Meetings/Conferences:
Conference Chair: Sloane Grubb

Publications:
Driver Trainer; monthly
Family Safety and Health magazine; quarterly
Injury Facts; annually
Journal of Safety Research
Membership Advantage; quarterly
News Alert; weekly
OSHA Up To Date; monthly
Safety + Health; monthly; adv.
Today's Supervisor; monthly
Traffic Safety; monthly

Membership List Available to Non-members

The National Safety Management Society *(1966)*
P.O. Box 4460
Walnut Creek, CA 94596-0460
Tel: (925) 944-7094 *Fax:* (573) 441-1765
TollFree: (800) 321-2910
E-Mail: info@nsms.us
Website: nsms.us
Members: 800 individuals
Staff: 3
Annual Budget: $25-50,000
Tax: 501(c)(3)

Personnel:
Executive Director: Jeffrey Y. Chung CSHM, PhD
Office Manager: Joyce Curtis
Director, Programs: Charles W. McGlothlin

Historical Note:
*NSMS's mission is to promote advancement of the
safety/loss control function through the application of
management principles. Membership: $70-102 (Regular-
US/Canada/Foreign); $35-56 (Affiliate/Retired- US/
Canada/Foreign); $35 (Student).*

Continuing Education:
Certification Designation/s: NOCA, CSHM, CST, CSS

Meetings/Conferences:

Conference Chair: Charles W. McGlothlin

Publications:
The NSMS Digest; monthly

National Scholastic Press Association *(1921)*
2221 University Ave. SE
Suite 121
Minneapolis, MN 55414
Tel: (612) 625-8335 *Fax:* (612) 626-0720
E-Mail: info@studentpress.org
Website: studentpress.org/nspa/
Staff: 6
Annual Budget: $1-2,000,000
Tax: 501(c)(3)

Personnel:
Executive director: Logan Aimone
Accountant: Kay Dawson
Administrative Assistant: Jackie Flaum
Director, Membership Services: Emily Griesser
Director, Communications and Technology: Marc Wood

Historical Note:
*NSPA's mission is to provide journalism education services
to students, teachers, media advisers and others throughout
the United States and in other countries. Membership: $109
(Level One); $189 (Level Two); $59 (Junior High/Middle
School); $69 (Broadcast); $35 (Supercritique).*

Meetings/Conferences:
2013 - San Francisco, CA (San Francisco Marriott
  Marquis)/April 25 - 28
2013 - Boston, MA (Sheraton Boston and Hynes
  Convention Center)/Nov. 14 - 17
2014 - San Diego, CA (Hilton Bayfront Hotel)/April 10
  - 13
2014 - Washington, DC (Marriott Wardman Park
  Hotel)/Nov. 6 - 9
2015 - Denver, CO (Sheraton)/April 16 - 20
2015 - Orlando, FL (Walt Disney World Swan And
  Dolphin)/Nov. 12 - 16
Number of non-conference events/year: 7

Publications:
NSPA Newsletter; on-line

National School Boards Association *(1940)*
1680 Duke St.
Alexandria, VA 22314-3493
Tel: (703) 838-6722 *Fax:* (703) 683-7590
E-Mail: info@nsba.org
Website: nsba.org
Members:
53 state level organizations
90,000 local school board members
Staff: 125
Annual Budget: $10-25,000,000
Tax: 501(c)(3)

Personnel:
Executive Director: Dr. Anne L. Bryant
  E-Mail: abryant@nsba.org
Director, Marketing: Holly Abrams
  E-Mail: habrams@nsba.org
Director, Finance and Business: Robert Billups
  E-Mail: rbillups@nsba.org
Manager, Human Resources: Katie Brennan
  E-Mail: kbrennan@nsba.org
Paralegal: Tom Burns
  E-Mail: tburns@nsba.org
*Publisher, American School Board Journal and Executive
  Editor:* Glenn Cook
  E-Mail: gcook@nsba.org
Senior Editor: Naomi Dillon
  E-Mail: ndillon@nsba.org
Deputy General Counsel: Naomi Gittins
  E-Mail: ngittins@nsba.org
*General Counsel and Administrative Assistant, Legal
  Advocacy and Legal Services:* Lenora Johnson
  E-Mail: ljohnson@nsba.org
Associate Executive Director and General Counsel:
  Francisco M. Negron Jr.
  E-Mail: fnegron@nsba.org
Assistant Executive Director: Robin Preston
  E-Mail: rpreston@nsba.org
*Associate Executive Director, Federal Advocacy and Public
  Policy:* Michael A. Resnick
  E-Mail: mresnick@nsba.org
Director, Communications: Alexis Rice
  E-Mail: arice@nsba.org
Director, Information Technology: Carole Stover

  E-Mail: cstover@nsba.org
Senior Staff Attorney: Sonja Trainor
  E-Mail: strainor@nsba.org
Deputy Executive Director and Chief Operating officer:
  Joseph S. Villani
  E-Mail: jvillani@nsba.org
Director, Leadership and Governance Services: Kanisha
  Williams-Jones
  E-Mail: kwilliams-jones@nsba.org

Historical Note:
*Formerly (1940) National Council of State School Boards
Associations. NSBA's mission is to advocate equity and
excellence in public education through School Board
Leadership.*

Meetings/Conferences: Annual
Conference Chair: Robin Preston
2013 - San Diego, CA (San Diego Convention Center)/
  April 13 - 15/26-50 exhibitors
2014 - New Orleans, LA/April 5 - 7
Number of non-conference events/year: 55

Publications:
Action Alerts; weekly
American School Board Journal; monthly; adv.
Health Link
Leadership Insider; bi-monthly; adv.
School Board News Today; on-line; adv.

National School Public Relations Association *(1935)*
15948 Derwood Rd.
Rockville, MD 20855-2123
Tel: (301) 519-0496 *Fax:* (301) 519-0494
E-Mail: info@nspra.org
Website: nspra.org
Members: 1997 individuals
Staff: 7
Annual Budget: $500-1,000,000
Tax: 501(c)(3)

Personnel:
Executive Director: Rich D. Bagin
  E-Mail: rbagin@nspra.org
Assistant, Member Services and Operations: Cynthia
  Frazier
  E-Mail: cfrazier@nspra.org
Manager, Business Services: Tommy Jones
  E-Mail: tjones@nspra.org
*Associate Director, Communication Audits, Public
  Engagement Activities and Seminar Programs:* Karen H.
  Kleinz APR
  E-Mail: kkleinz@nspra.org
Manager, Seminars and Programs: Elaine Willis
  E-Mail: ewillis@nspra.org

Historical Note:
*Formerly (1950) School Public Relations Association,
NSPRA's is dedicated to building support and trust for
education through responsible public relations that leads
to success for all students. Membership: $160-250
(Individual/Subscription School District); $395-485
(Institutional); $90 (Retired); $80 (Student).*

Continuing Education:
Enrollment: 25
Certification Designation/s: APR

Meetings/Conferences:
Conference Chair: Elaine Willis

Publications:
Communication Matters; on-line
NSPRA Alert; bi-monthly
NSPRA Counselor Newsletter; quarterly
NSPRA Network; monthly
NSPRA Opportunities Newsletter; bi-monthly
NSPRA This Week; weekly
NSPRA Website; weekly
Principal Communicator; monthly

National School Supply and Equipment Association *(1916)*
8380 Colesville Rd.
Suite 250
Silver Spring, MD 20910
Tel: (301) 495-0240 *Fax:* (301) 495-3330
TollFree: (800) 395-5550
E-Mail: nssea@nssea.com
Website: nssea.org
Members: 1300 companies
Staff: 10
Annual Budget: $2-5,000,000

Personnel:

President and Chief Executive Officer: Jim McGarry
  E-Mail: jmcgarry@nssea.org
Vice President, Marketing and Communications: Adrienne
  Watts Dayton
  E-Mail: awatts@nssea.org
Vice President, Operations and Meetings: Bill Duffy
  E-Mail: bduffy@nssea.org
Director, Membership Services: Karen Prince
  E-Mail: kprince@nssea.org
Director, Communications: DeShuna Spencer
  E-Mail: dspencer@nssea.org
Director, Exhibits: Tom Tucker

Historical Note:
*Formerly (1958) the National School Service Institute.
NSSEA's mission is to provide quality tradeshows for
the distribution of educational products and services.
Membership: based on gross annual sales.*

Meetings/Conferences: Semi-Annual
Conference Chair: Bill Duffy
2013 - Atlanta, GA/Jan. 16 - 18
2013 - Tampa, FL/March 13 - 15
2013 - San Antonio, TX/Dec. 4 - 6
2014 - Tampa, FL/Jan. 15 - 17
2014 - Tampa, FL/Oct. 29 - 31
Number of non-conference events/year: 19

Publications:
Essentials Magazine; quarterly; adv.
Essentials Weekly; weekly; adv.
Membership Directory; on-line; adv.

National School Transportation Association

(1964)
113 S. West St.
Fourth Floor
Alexandria, VA 22314
Tel: (800) 222-6782 *Fax:* (703) 684-3212
TollFree: (800) 222-6782
E-Mail: info@yellowbuses.org
Website: yellowbuses.org
Members: 1500 companies and individuals
Staff: 7
Annual Budget: $1-2,000,000

Personnel:
Executive Director: Ronna Sable Weber
Meeting Planner: Jennifer Hickey Bruce CMP
  E-Mail: jcarroll@yellowbuses.org
Consultant, Industry Technology: Bob Pudlewski
Lobbyist: Becky B. Weber

Historical Note:
*Formerly (1975) National Association of School Bus
Contract-Operators. NSTA seeks to provide school
transportation professionals with the tools and resources
they need to make school buses safe, affordable, and
efficient nationwide. Membership: $4,000 (Manufacturer);
$2,000 (Multi State Supplier); $1,000 (Single State
Supplier); $150 (Contractor).*

Meetings/Conferences: Semi-Annual
Conference Chair: Jennifer Hickey Bruce CMP
2013 - Bonita Springs, FL/Jan. 12 - 16
2013 - Tulsa, OK/July 19 - 24
Number of non-conference events/year: 1

Publications:
Member Directory; on-line
NSTA Newsletter; bi-monthly

Membership List Available to Non-members

National Science Education Leadership Association *(1959)*

1219 N. 54th St.
Omaha, NE 68132
Tel: (402) 561-0176
Website: nsela.org
Members: 1200 individuals
Staff: 4
Annual Budget: $100-250,000

Personnel:
Executive Director: Susan Koba
  E-Mail: skoba@cox.net

Historical Note:
*Formerly (1994) National Science Supervisors Association.
An affiliate of the National Science Teachers Association
and the American Association for the Advancement of
Science. NSELA's mission is to reflect the changing
nature of science leaders. NSELA members include
department heads, supervisors, consultants, administrators,
coordinators and directors of science programs in public
and private educational institutions. Membership: $45
(Individual/Company); $15 (Retired).*

Meetings/Conferences:
Number of non-conference events/year: 1-10

Publications:
Navigator Newsletter
Science Educator; bi-annually

National Science Teachers Association *(1944)*

1840 Wilson Blvd.
Arlington, VA 22201
Tel: (703) 243-7100 *Fax:* (703) 243-7177
TollFree: (800) 722-6782
Website: nsta.org
Members: 60000 individuals
Staff: 110
Annual Budget: $25-50,000,000
Tax: 501(c)(3)

Personnel:
Executive Director: Francis Q. Eberle
Contact, Operations and Membership Services: Moira
  Fathy Baker
  E-Mail: mfathybaker@nsta.org
Contact, Publications and Product Development: David
  Beacom
Assistant Executive Director, Conferences and Meetings:
  Delores Howard
*Associate Executive Director, Professional Programs and
  Conferences:* Zipporah Miller
Coordinator, Exhibit Services: Marcelo Nunez
  E-Mail: mnunez@nsta.org
Assistant Executive Director, Legislative Affairs: Jodi
  Peterson
  E-Mail: jpeterson@nsta.org
Contact, Marketing and Sales: Ed Rock
*Assistant Executive Director, Membership and Chapter
  Relations:* Howard Walhberg

Historical Note:
*NSTA's mission is to promote excellence and innovation
in science teaching and learning for all. Membership: $75
(Individual); $34 (New Teacher/Student/Retired); $90
(Joint NSTA/SCST Individual); $39 (Joint NSTA/SCST
Student); $95-218 (Institutional).*

Meetings/Conferences:
Conference Chair: Delores Howard
2013 - San Antonio, TX/April 11 - 14
2013 - Portland, OR/Oct. 24 - 26
2013 - Charlotte, NC/Nov. 7 - 9
2013 - Denver, CO/Dec. 12 - 14
2014 - Boston, MA/April 3 - 6
2014 - Richmond, VA/Oct. 16 - 18
2014 - Orlando, FL/Nov. 6 - 8
2014 - Long Beach, CA/Dec. 4 - 6
2015 - Chicago, IL/March 26 - 29

Publications:
Membership Directory; on-line
NSTA E-Newsletter; on-line; adv.
NSTA Express; weekly
NSTA's Book Beat; monthly
Science & Children; adv.
Science Class; monthly
Science Scope; adv.
Scientific Principals; monthly
The Leaders Letter; monthly
The Science Teacher; adv.

Membership List Available to Non-members

National Sculpture Society *(1893)*

C/O ANS
75 Varick St., 11th Floor
New York, NY 10013
Tel: (212) 764-5645 *Fax:* (212) 764-5651
Website: nationalsculpture.org
Members: 4000 individuals
Staff: 5
Annual Budget: $500-1,000,000
Tax: 501(c)(3)

Personnel:
Executive Director: Gwen Pier
  E-Mail: gwen@nationalsculpture.org
Editor: Patricia Delahanty
  E-Mail: patty@nationalsculpture.org
Office Manager and Director, Circulation: Elizabeth Helm
  E-Mail: elizabeth@nationalsculpture.org
Legal Advisor: James F. Kelly
Website Coordinator: Tom Slaughter

Historical Note:

*NSS's mission is to advance excellence in sculpture
throughout the United States. Membership: $75 (US
Residents); $90 (Outside US); $350 (Patrons); $100 (Allied
Professional).*

Meetings/Conferences:
Conference Chair: Patricia Delahanty

Publications:
Membersip directory; on-line
News Bulletin; bi-monthly
Sculpture Review; quarterly

National Seasoning Manufacturers Association

(1972)
2527 Mill Race Rd.
Frederick, MD 21701-6812
Tel: (240) 426-6843 *Fax:* (301) 299-7523
E-Mail: alsmeyerfood@isp.com
Members: 23 companies
Staff: 1
Annual Budget: $10-25,000
Tax: 501(c)(3)

Personnel:
Executive Director: Richard H. Alsmeyer
  E-Mail: alsmeyerfood@isp.com

Historical Note:
*Established as the Industrial Meat Seasoning Manufacturers
Association; later became the National Association of Meat
Seasoning Manufacturers. In 1981, became the National
Association of Meat and Food Seasoning Manufacturers;
assumed its present name in 1984. Promotes scientific
study and research in the seasoning industry. Membership:
$800/year.*

Publications:
Federal Food Regulatory Agency Policy Manual;
  annually

National Senior Corps Association *(2007)*

1316 E. McKinney
C/O RSVP Denton County
Denton, TX 76209
Tel: (940) 383-1508
E-Mail: info@nscatogether.org
Website: nscatogether.org
Staff: 2
Annual Budget: $50-100,000
Tax: 501(c)(3)

Personnel:
President: Fred Lugo
  E-Mail: fred.lugo@co.travis.tx.us
Treasurer: Normalyn Powers
  E-Mail: npowers@berkshire.rr.com

Historical Note:
*NSC's mission is to promote, represent, advocate for and
enhance the power of Senior Corps programs nationwide.
Membership:$100-$250 (Professional), $50 (Associate),
$25 (Volunteer), $100(Business/Organization).*

Publications:
Membersship directory; on-line
NSCA e-Newsletter; on-line

National Shellfisheries Association *(1908)*

Indian River Research and Education Center
2199 S. Rock Rd.
Ft. Pierce, FL 34945
Tel: (772) 468-3922 *Fax:* (772) 468-3973
E-Mail: secretariat@shellfish.org
Website: shellfish.org
Members: 600 members
Staff: 5
Annual Budget: $250-500,000
Tax: 501(c)(3)

Personnel:
President: R. LeRoy Creswell
  E-Mail: creswell@ufl.edu

Historical Note:
*Formerly National Association of Shellfish Commissioners,
assumed its present name in 1930 and was incorporated
in Maryland in 1968. NSA is an organization of scientists,
management officials and members of industry, deeply
concerned with the biology, ecology, production, economics
and management of shellfish resources. Members are
individuals interested in research of mollusks and
crustaceans. Membership: $85 (Regular); $45 (Student);
$200 (Sustaining); $356-375 (Institutional).*

Meetings/Conferences:
2013 - Nashville, TN (Renaissance Nashville Hotel)/
  Feb. 21 - 25
2014 - Jacksonville, FL/March 29 - April 2

2016 - Las Vegas, NV/Feb. 22 - 26
Number of non-conference events/year: 2

Publications:
Membership Directory; on-line
The Journal of Shellfish Research
The Quarterly Newsletter; quarterly

National Sheriffs' Association *(1940)*
1450 Duke St.
Alexandria, VA 22314-3490
Tel: (800) 424-7827 *Fax:* (703) 838-5349
TollFree: (800) 424-7827
E-Mail: nsamail@sheriffs.org
Website: sheriffs.org
Members: 25000 individuals
Staff: 30
Annual Budget: $5-10,000,000
Tax: 501(c)(4)

Personnel:
Executive Director: Aaron D. Kennard
    E-Mail: exec@sheriffs.org
Manager, Membership Services and Training: Hilary
    Burgess
    E-Mail: hburgess@sheriffs.org
Director, Publications and Marketing: Susan H. Crow
    E-Mail: scrow@sheriffs.org
Director, Government Affairs: Stephanie Garlock
    E-Mail: sgarlock@sheriffs.org
Director, Finance: Darlene Hicks
    E-Mail: dhicks@sheriffs.org
Director, Sales, Exhibits and Corporate Relations: Karen
    Killpack
    E-Mail: kkillpack@sheriffs.org
Director, Conferences: Ross F. Mirmelstein CMP, MA
    E-Mail: rossmir@sheriffs.org
General Counsel: Richard Weintraub Esq.
    E-Mail: rmwein@sheriffs.org
*Division Director, Research, Development, Grants and
    Interim Director, Government Affairs:* Tim Woods
    E-Mail: twoods@sheriffs.org

Historical Note:
*NSA is dedicated to assisting sheriffs and other law
enforcement practitioners in performing their duties
professionally. Membership: $50- 500 (Active); $35
(Auxiliary/Student/Deputy Member); $60 (International);
$65 (Chief of Police/Executive/Agency Director); $45
(Other Active Members/Deputy Member).*

Meetings/Conferences: Annual
Conference Chair: Ross F. Mirmelstein CMP, MA
2013 - Washington, DC (JW Marriott Washington,
    D.C.)/Jan. 30 - Feb. 2
2013 - Charlotte, NC/June 22 - 26
2014 - Washington, DC (JW Marriott Washington,
    D.C.)/Jan. 22 - 25
2014 - Ft. Worth, TX/June 20 - 25
2015 - Washington, DC (JW Marriott Washington,
    D.C.)/Jan. 21 - 24
2015 - Baltimore, MD/June 26 - July 1
2016 - Minneapolis, MN/June 25 - 29
2017 - Reno, NV/June 23 - 28
2018 - New Orleans, LA/June 15 - 20
2019 - Louisville, KY/June 14 - 19

Publications:
Deputy and Court Officer Magazine
NSA Bulletin; monthly
Sheriff magazine; bi-monthly; adv.
Sheriffs' Directory; on-line

National Shippers Strategic Transportation Council *(1952)*
9382 Oak Ave.
Waconia, MN 55387
Tel: (952) 442-8850 *Fax:* (952) 442-3941
Website: nasstrac.org
Staff: 6

Personnel:
Executive Director: Brian Everett
    E-Mail: brian2008@NASSTRAC.org
Contact, Administrative Services: Karen Everett
    E-Mail: karen2008@NASSTRAC.org
Manager, Marketing and Communications: Nancy
    LaRoche
    E-Mail: nancy2008@tmcatoday.org

Historical Note:
*NASSTRAC has been providing education and advocacy for
shippers and carriers.Membership: $550-2000 (Regular/
Associate).*

Meetings/Conferences: Annual
Conference Chair: Karen Everett

Publications:
E-Link
Member Directory.; on-line
NewsLink

National Shoe Retailers Association *(1912)*
7386 N. La Cholla Blvd.
Tucson, AZ 85741
Tel: (520) 209-1710 *Fax:* (410) 381-1167
TollFree: (800) 673-8446
E-Mail: info@nsra.org
Website: nsra.org
Members: 1800 companies
Staff: 10
Annual Budget: $500-1,000,000
Tax: 501(c)(6)

Personnel:
President: Chuck Schuyler

Historical Note:
*NSRA's mission is to improve the business performance of
its members through continuing education programs, cost-
saving benefits and services, and networking opportunities.
Members are owners and managers of independent
shoe stores. Membership: $190-1100 (Voting); $220
(International); $35 (Branch Store Members/Additional
Executive).*

Meetings/Conferences: Annual

Publications:
NSRA Online (e-newsletter); bi-weekly
Shoe Retailing Today; bi-monthly

National Shooting Sports Foundation *(1961)*
Flintlock Ridge Office Center, 11 Mile Hill Rd.
Newtown, CT 06470-2359
Tel: (203) 426-1320 *Fax:* (203) 426-1087
E-Mail: info@nssf.org
Website: nssf.org
Members: 7000 individuals
Staff: 47
Annual Budget: $25-50,000,000

Personnel:
President and Chief Executive Officer: Stephen L. Sanetti
    E-Mail: ssanetti@nssf.org
Director, Public Affairs: Michael G. Bazinet
    E-Mail: mbazinet@nssf.org
Director, Communications: Bill Brassard
    E-Mail: bbrassard@nssf.org
Director, Exhibitions and Conferences: Diedra Cauley
    E-Mail: dcauley@nssf.org
Managing Director, Business Development: Randy Clark
    E-Mail: rclark@nssf.org
Vice President and Chief Financial Officer: Nancy Coburn
    E-Mail: ncoburn@nssf.org
Director, Industry Research and Analysis: Jim Curcuruto
    E-Mail: jcurcuruto@nssf.org
Senior Vice President and Chief Marketing Officer: Chris
    Dolnack
    E-Mail: cdolnack@nssf.org
Managing Director, Marketing Communications: Bill Dunn
    E-Mail: bdunn@nssf.org
Senior Vice President and General Counsel: Lawrence G.
    Keane
    E-Mail: lkeane@nssf.org
Managing Director, Human Resources and Administration:
    Deb Kenney SPHR
    E-Mail: dkenney@nssf.org
Director, Government Relations and State Affairs: Jake
    McGuigan
    E-Mail: jmcguigan@nssf.org
Director, Information Technology and Facilities: Dave
    Patterson
    E-Mail: dave.patterson@nssf.org
Director, Editorial Services: Glenn Sapir
    E-Mail: gsapir@nssf.org
Director, Recruitment and Retention: Melissa Schilling
    E-Mail: mschilling@nssf.org
Director, Membership Services: Bettyjane Swann
    E-Mail: bswann@nssf.org

Historical Note:
*NSSF is the trade association for the firearms industry
whose mission is to promote, protect and preserve hunting
and the shooting sports. Membership: $1,000-250,000
(Voting); $450-600 (Supporting); $200 (Non- Profit
Association); $75-15,000 (Shooting Range/Firearms
Retailer); $50 (Individual); $25 (Media); .$1,500-15,000*

*(SHOT Show Special); $50 (Individual); $25 (Media
Individual).*

Meetings/Conferences: Annual
Conference Chair: Diedra Cauley
2013 - Las Vegas, NV (Sands Expo & Convention
    Center)/Jan. 15 - 18

Publications:
Bullet Points; on-line
Government Relations Report; on-line
Shot Business; bi-monthly; adv.

National Show Horse Registry *(1982)*
P.O. Box 862
Lewisburg, OH 45338
Tel: (937) 962-4336 *Fax:* (937) 962-4332
E-Mail: nshowhorse@aol.com
Website: nshregistry.org
Members: 1400 individuals and 14 organizations
Staff: 1
Annual Budget: $100-250,000

Personnel:
Contact, Promotions and Public Relations: Cindy Clinton
    E-Mail: cindi@infinet.com

Historical Note:
*NSHR's mission is to maintain a fiscally sound organization
to promote the breeding and showing of the National
Show Horse and to increase popularity and participation
within the general public through innovative programs.
Membership: $60 (Adult/Farm/Corporate); $25 (Youth);
$30 (Associate/NSHR Non-Member); $1,000 (Life).*

Publications:
National Show Horse (NHS) Magazine; adv.

National Ski and Snowboard Retailers Association *(1987)*
1601 Feehanville Dr.
Suite 300
Mt. Prospect, IL 60056-6035
Tel: (847) 391-9825 *Fax:* (847) 391-9827
TollFree: (888) 527-1168
E-Mail: info@nssra.com
Website: nssra.com
Members: 400 companies
Staff: 2
Annual Budget: $10-25,000
Tax: 501(c)(6)

Personnel:
President: Larry Weindruch CAE
    E-Mail: lweindruch@nssra.com
Treasurer: Greg Dekdebrun

Historical Note:
*Formerly (1996) National Ski Retailers Association.
NSSRA's mission is to provide ski and snowboard
shops with business-related services and representation.
Membership: $135-275 (Annual Retailer, based on Stores);
$350 (Supporting).*

Meetings/Conferences: Annual
2014 - Savannah, GA/April 30 - May 3

Publications:
Membership Directory; on-line
NSSRA Cost of Doing Business Survey; biennially
NSSRA Newsletter

Membership List Available to Non-members

National Ski Area Association *(1962)*
133 S. Van Gordon St.
Suite 300
Lakewood, CO 80228
Tel: (303) 987-1111 *Fax:* (303) 986-2345
E-Mail: nsaa@nsaa.org
Website: nsaa.org
Members: 797 suppliers and ski areas.
Staff: 13
Annual Budget: $2-5,000,000

Personnel:
President: Michael Berry
    E-Mail: nsaa@nsaa.org
Director, Risk Management: David Byrd
    E-Mail: dbyrd@nsaa.org
Managing Editor: Troy Hawks
    E-Mail: thawks@nsaa.org
Director, Education: Wenda Huseman
    E-Mail: whuseman@nsaa.org
Director, Finance: Laura Lewis
    E-Mail: lauram@nsaa.org
Director, Public Policy: Geraldine Link

E-Mail: glink@nsaa.org
Director, Conventions and Meetings: Tom Moore
  E-Mail: tmoore@nsaa.org
Director, Technical Services: Sid Roslund
  E-Mail: sidr@nsaa.org
Director, Sponsorships: Amy Steele
  E-Mail: asteele@nsaa.org
Director, Membership Services: Emily Torres
  E-Mail: etorres@nsaa.org

Historical Note:
Formerly (1989) NSAA merged with SIA (SnowSports Industries America) and moved to McLean, Va. The merger was dissolved in 1992 and NSAA was relocated to Lakewood, Colorado. NSAA's mission is to represent, serve and vigorously promote the mutual interest of its membership. Membership: $25-4000/year.

Meetings/Conferences: Annual
Conference Chair: Tom Moore
2013 - Palm Spring, CA (Westin Mission Hills Resort and Spa)/April 30 - May 3
Number of non-conference events/year: 9

Publications:
Membership Directory; on-line
The NSAA Journal; bi-monthly

National Ski Patrol System *(1938)*
133 S. Van Gordon St.
Suite 100
Lakewood, CO 80228-1706
Tel: (303) 988-1111 *Fax:* (303) 988-3005
E-Mail: nsp@nsp.org
Website: nsp.org
Members: 27000 individuals
Staff: 16
Annual Budget: $50-100,000

Personnel:
Executive Director: Tim White
  E-Mail: twhite@nsp.org
Director, Finance: Wayne Block
  E-Mail: wblock@nsp.org
Director, Education: Darcy Hanley
  E-Mail: dhanley@nsp.org
Director, Marketing and Events: Melanie Hood
  E-Mail: mhood@nsp.org
Director, Communications: Candace Horgan
  E-Mail: chorgan@nsp.org
Director, Membership Registration and National Awards Administrator: Cheri Overton
  E-Mail: coverton@nsp.org
Manager, Information Technology: Mitch Shanley
  E-Mail: mshanley@nsp.org

Historical Note:
NSP's mission is to serve the public and outdoor recreation industry by providing education and credentialing to emergency care and safety services providers. Members are trained in all phases of ski patrolling, including W. E. C. first aid, ski mountaineering, avalanche patrol and lift evacuation. Membership: $27/year.

Continuing Education:
Enrollment: 2000
Certification Designation/s: OEC

Meetings/Conferences: Annual
Conference Chair: Melanie Hood
2013 - Denver, CO (Grand Hyatt Denver)/Jan. 31 - Feb. 3
Number of non-conference events/year: 1

Publications:
Membership Directory; on-line
Ski Patrol Magazine; adv.

National Slag Association *(1918)*
P.O. Box 1197
Pleasant Grove, UT 84062
Tel: (801) 785-4535 *Fax:* (801) 785-4539
E-Mail: info@nationalslag.org
Website: nationalslag.org
Members: 35 processors
Staff: 2
Annual Budget: $250-500,000
Tax: 501(c)(6)

Personnel:
President: Karen Kiggins
  E-Mail: kkiggins@nationalslag.org

Historical Note:
Members are processors of iron and steel slags for use as a mineral aggregate in construction and manufacturing applications.

Publications:
Slag Runner Newsletter; on-line

National Small Business Association *(1937)*
1156 15th St. NW
Suite 1100
Washington, DC 20005
Tel: (800) 345-6728 *Fax:* (202) 847-8453
TollFree: (800) 345-6728
Website: nsba.biz
Members: 150000 individuals
Staff: 24
Tax: 501(c)(6)

Personnel:
President: Todd McCracken
  E-Mail: tmccracken@nsba.biz
Vice President, Public Affairs: Molly Baldwin
  E-Mail: mbrogan@nsba.biz
General Counsel: David R. Burton
Marketing Coordinator: Lauren Hausmann
Vice President, Membership Development: Patrick Post
Vice President, Administration: Rosa Wright

Historical Note:
NSBA is a volunteer directed association. Originally the National Small Business Men's Association, it became the National Small Business Association in 1962, the same year in which the American Association of Small Business was absorbed. Merged with Small Business United in 1986 and changed its name to National Small Business United; reverted to the NSBA name in 2003. Sponsors and supports the NSBU Political Action Committee. Acts as an advocate for the small business community. NSBA's mission is to advocate state and federal policies which are beneficial to small business, the state, and the nation and to promote the growth of free enterprise. Membership: $250-5,500/year (Based on Number of Individuals).

Publications:
NSBA Advocate Magazine; bi-monthly; adv.
The Weekly Advocate; weekly

National Soccer Coaches Association of America *(1941)*
800 Ann Ave.
Kansas City, KS 66101
Tel: (913) 362-1747 *Fax:* (913) 362-3439
TollFree: (800) 458-0678
E-Mail: info@nscaa.com
Website: nscaa.com
Members: 30000 individuals
Staff: 19
Annual Budget: $5-10,000,000
Tax: 501(c)(3)

Personnel:
Chief Executive Officer and Executive Director: Joe Cummings
  E-Mail: jcummings@nscaa.com
Director, Coaching Education: Ian Barker
  E-Mail: ibarker@nscaa.com
Director, Marketing: Chris Burt
  E-Mail: cburt@nscaa.com
Chief Financial Officer: Tammy Reder
  E-Mail: treder@nscaa.com
Director, Events: Geoff VanDeusen
  E-Mail: gvandeusen@nscaa.com
Associate Executive Director: Steve Veal
  E-Mail: sveal@nscaa.com
Manager, Membership Services: Sandy Williamson-Smith
  E-Mail: swilliamson@nscaa.com
Manager, Conventions and Programs: Rudy Zimmermann
  E-Mail: rzimmermann@nscaa.com

Historical Note:
The National Soccer Coaches Association of America (NSCAA) helps its members excel in their coaching careers as well as advances the coaching of soccer, thereby improving players, through a commitment to provide the best coaching education, convention, and member services and benefits to the soccer community. Membership: $85 (Standard); $125 (European); $135 (Non-European Member); $65 (Retired/Inactive Member).

Meetings/Conferences: Annual
Conference Chair: Rudy Zimmermann
2013 - Indianapolis, IN/Jan. 16 - 20/9000 attendees
2014 - Philadelphia, PA/Jan. 15 - 19/9000 attendees
2015 - Philadelphia, PA/Jan. 14 - 18/9000 attendees
2016 - Baltimore, MD/Jan. 13 - 17/9000 attendees
2017 - Los Angeles, CA/Jan. 11 - 15/9000 attendees
2018 - Philadelphia, PA/Jan. 10 - 14/9000 attendees
2020 - Baltimore, MD/Jan. 15 - 19/9000 attendees

Number of non-conference events/year: 19

Publications:
Soccer Journal
Soccer Journal; adv.
The Technical Area; bi-weekly

Membership List Available to Non-members

National Society for Experiential Education *(1971)*
C/O Talley Management Group, Inc.
19 Mantua Rd.
Mt. Royal, NJ 08061
Tel: (856) 423-3427 *Fax:* (856) 423-3420
E-Mail: nsee@talley.com
Website: nsee.org
Members: 1500 individuals
Staff: 2
Annual Budget: $250-500,000
Tax: 501(c)(3)

Personnel:
Executive Director: Haley J. Brust
  E-Mail: hbrust@talley.com

Historical Note:
Formerly (1992) the National Society For Internships and Experiential Education. NSEE's mission is to foster the effective use of experience as an integral part of education, in order to empower learners and promote the common good. Members are college and K-12 faculty, directors of internship, service- learning, school to work, and cooperative education programs; principals, superintendents, and deans, career counselors and employers who sponsor interns. Membership: $40-900/year.

Continuing Education:
Certification Designation/s: EEA

Meetings/Conferences: Annual

Publications:
Experiential Education Review (EER)
Membership Directory; on-line
NSEE Quarterly; semi-monthly

National Society for Graphology *(1972)*
250 W. 57th St.
Suite 1228-A
New York, NY 10107
Tel: (212) 265-1148 *Fax:* (212) 307-5671
E-Mail: rogwrite@aol.com
Members: 300 individuals
Staff: 1
Annual Budget: Under $10,000

Personnel:
Contact, Communications: Janice Klein
  E-Mail: irenicnyc@aol.com

Historical Note:
NSG promotes the study and practice of gestalt graphology. Members are professional graphologists and individuals interested in graphology. Membership: $65/year (Individual).

Meetings/Conferences:
Number of non-conference events/year: 1

National Society for Hebrew Day Schools *(1944)*
1090 Coney Island Ave.
Brooklyn, NY 11230
Tel: (212) 227-1000 *Fax:* (212) 406-6934
E-Mail: umesorah@aol.com
Website: torah-umesorah.com/
Members: 675 organizations
Staff: 25
Annual Budget: $500-1,000,000
Tax: 501(c)(3)

Personnel:
Executive Vice President: Dovid Nojowitz
Program Director: Dennis Me. Eisenberg

Historical Note:
Originally organized as Torah Umesorah by Rabbinical leaders of Eastern Europe who wished to re-establish Jewish centers of learning in the country. NSHDS is the North American organization for Torah Umesorah, supporting the religious and secular learning traditions of the Hebrew Day School. Provides a range of services to member schools.

National Society for Histotechnology *(1973)*
8850 Stanford Blvd
Suite 2900
Columbia, MD 21045
Tel: (443) 535-4060 *Fax:* (443) 535-4055

E-Mail: histo@nsh.org
Website: nsh.org
Members: 4000 individuals
Staff: 6
Annual Budget: $1-2,000,000
Tax: 501(c)(6)

Personnel:
Executive Director: Carrie Diamond
    E-Mail: carrie@nsh.org
Manager, Membership Services: Brenda Royce
    E-Mail: brenda@nsh.org
Manager, Meetings: Aubrey M.J. Wanner
    E-Mail: aubrey@nsh.org
Administrative Assistant: Beth Wise
    E-Mail: beth@nsh.org

Historical Note:
NSH is a non-profit organization. NSH's mission is committed to the advancement of histotechnology, its practitioners and quality standards of practice through leadership, education and advocacy. Members are laboratory personnel who study tissues and prepare slides for diagnosis by a pathologist. Membership: $80 (Professional/International); $40 (Retired/Student); $250 (Sustaining).

Continuing Education:
Certification Designation/s: CMP

Meetings/Conferences: Annual
Conference Chair: Aubrey M.J. Wanner
2013 - Providence, RI/Sept. 20 - 26
2014 - Austin, TX/Aug. 21 - 27
2015 - Washington, DC/Aug. 28 - Sept. 2
2017 - Orlando, FL/Sept. 15 - 20

Publications:
Journal of Histotechnology; quarterly; adv.
Membership Directory; on-line
NSH in Action; quarterly

Membership List Available to Non-members

National Society of Accountants (1945)

1010 N. Fairfax St.
Alexandria, VA 22314
Tel: (703) 549-6400 *Fax:* (703) 549-2984
TollFree: (800) 966-6679
E-Mail: members@nsacct.org
Website: nsacct.org
Members: 30000 individuals
Staff: 13
Annual Budget: $2-5,000,000
Tax: 501(c)(6)

Personnel:
Executive Vice President: John G. Ams
    E-Mail: jams@nsacct.org
Director, Education Programs: Sally Brasse
    E-Mail: sbrasse@nsacct.org
Vice President and Director, Marketing and Membership Services: Jodi Goldberg
    E-Mail: jgoldberg@nsacct.org
Director, Financial Services: Allison Ingram
    E-Mail: aingram@nsacct.org
Manager, Communications: Julene Joy
    E-Mail: jjoy@nsacct.org
Contact, Technology Support: Jay West
    E-Mail: jwest@nsacct.org

Historical Note:
Formerly (1996) National Society of Public Accountants and adopted its present name in 1995. NSA's mission is to provide national leadership and helps its members achieve success in the profession of accountancy and taxation through the advocacy of practice rights and the promotion of high standards in ethics, education, and professional excellence. Membership: $199 (Active/Associate); $54 (Educator Associate); $30 (Student Associate).

Meetings/Conferences: Annual
2013 - Indianapolis, IN (Hyatt Indianapolis)/Aug. 21 - 24

Publications:
Main Street Practitioner; bi-monthly
MemberLink; bi-weekly; adv.
NSA Practice Advisor
NSAlert; bi-weekly

National Society of Accountants for Cooperatives (1936)

136 S. Keowee St.
Dayton, OH 45402
Tel: (937) 222-6707 *Fax:* (937) 222-5794
E-Mail: info@nsacoop.org

Website: nsacoop.org
Members: 2000 individuals
Staff: 10
Annual Budget: $500-1,000,000
Tax: 501(c)(6)

Personnel:
Executive Director: Kim Fantaci
Manager, Event and CPE Specialist: Kelley Alexander
Event Manager and CPE Specialist: Amy Ford
Client Accounting Manager: Krista Saul
Manager, Administration: Tina Schneider

Historical Note:
NSAC provides accounting, tax and business education uniquely tailored to cooperatives. Members are accountants, attorneys, financial officers and other professionals actively involved in the financial planning and management of cooperative businesses. Membership: $175 (Regular); $50 (Retired).

Meetings/Conferences: Annual
Conference Chair: Kelley Alexander
Number of non-conference events/year: 6

Publications:
Membership Directory and Resource Guide; on-line
The Cooperative Accountant; quarterly

National Society of Black Engineers (1975)

205 Dangerfield Rd.
Alexandria, VA 22314
Tel: (703) 549-2207 *Fax:* (703) 683-5312
E-Mail: info@nsbe.org
Website: nsbe.org
Members: 29900 members
Staff: 7
Annual Budget: $10-25,000,000
Tax: 501(c)(3)

Personnel:
Executive Director: Carl B. Mack
    E-Mail: cmack@nsbe.org
Director, Membership Services: Njemile A. Crawley PE
    E-Mail: membership@nsbe.org
Administrator, Information Technology: Sylvester Harriett
Director, Accounting and Finance: Shon McGhee
    E-Mail: smcghee@nsbe.org
Contact, Convention and Meeting Planning: Al Rutherford
Publications, New Media and Communications: Pamela D. Sharif
    E-Mail: psharif@nsbe.org
Coordinator, Publication: Lashonda M. Winston
    E-Mail: lwinston@nsbe.org

Historical Note:
NSBE's mission is to increase the number of culturally responsible Black Engineers who excel academically, succeed professionally and positively impact the community. Membership: $50 (Alumni Extension/Technical Professional); $5 (Pre-College Student); $15 (Collegiate); $1200 (Lifetime).

Meetings/Conferences:
Conference Chair: Al Rutherford

Publications:
NSBE Bridge Magazine; adv.
NSBE Enewsletter; monthly
NSBE Magazine; quarterly; adv.

Membership List Available to Non-members

National Society of Black Physicists (1977)

1100 N. Glebe Rd.
Suite 1010
Arlington, VA 22201
Tel: (703) 536-4207 *Fax:* (703) 536-4203
E-Mail: headquarters@nspb.org
Website: nsbp.org
Members: 300 individuals
Staff: 3
Annual Budget: $50-100,000
Tax: 501(c)(3)

Personnel:
Administrative Executive Officer and Editor: Hakeem Oluseyi
Treasurer: Byron Freelon
President and Technical Executive Officer (acting): Paul Gueye

Historical Note:
NSBP's seeks to develop and support efforts to increase opportunities for African Americans in physics and to increase their numbers and visibility of their scientific work. Membership: $95 (Professional); $35 (Graduate Student); $25 (Undergraduate Student); $45 (Postdocs).

Meetings/Conferences: Annual
Number of non-conference events/year: 5

Publications:
Waves & Packets E-news brief; weekly; adv.

National Society of Certified Healthcare Business Consultants (2006)

12100 Sunset Hills Rd.
Suite 130
Reston, VA 20190
Tel: (703) 234-4099 *Fax:* (703) 435-4390
E-Mail: info@nschbc.org
Website: nschbc.org
Members: 350 individuals
Staff: 2
Annual Budget: $250-500,000

Personnel:
Executive Director: Carol Wynne
    E-Mail: carol.wynne@nschbc.org
Program manager: Rachael Shaw
    E-Mail: rachael.shaw@nschbc.org

Historical Note:
Founded by the membership of the Institute of Certified Healthcare Business Consultants, the National Association of Healthcare Consultants (NAHC) and the Society of Medical Dental Management Consultants. NSCHBC seeks to advance the profession of healthcare business consultants by setting standards for its members through education, certification and professional interaction. Members are consultants in healthcare industry. Membership : $625/ year (Individual).

Continuing Education:
Certification Designation/s: CHBC

Meetings/Conferences: Annual
Number of non-conference events/year: 1

Publications:
E-Newsletter; bi-monthly

Membership List Available to Non-members

National Society of Compliance Professionals (1987)

22 Kent Rd.
Cornwall Bridge, CT 06754
Tel: (860) 672-0843 *Fax:* (860) 672-3005
E-Mail: info@nscp.org
Website: nscp.org
Members: 1750 individuals
Staff: 8
Annual Budget: $1-2,000,000
Tax: 501(c)(6)

Personnel:
Executive Director: Joan Hinchman
    E-Mail: jhinchman@nscp.org
Director, Marketing: Sarah Bowman
    E-Mail: sbowman@nscp.org
Manager, Membership Development: Eric Cieplik
    E-Mail: ecieplik@nscp.org
Contact, Membership, Meetings and Bookkeeper: Wendy Hill
Director, Publications and Information Technology: Frederick Vorck
    E-Mail: vorck@nscp.org
Director, Meetings: Liza Wentworth
    E-Mail: lwentworth@nscp.org

Historical Note:
NSCP provides professional analyses and counsel in regard to securities laws and regulations authorized by the states, federal agencies and the SROs and promotes professionalism among compliance officials within the securities industry. Membership: $450 (Individual); $292.50-360 (Group, depending on the number of members).

Continuing Education:
Certification Designation/s: CSCP

Meetings/Conferences: Annual
Conference Chair: Liza Wentworth

Publications:
Currents; bi-monthly; adv.

National Society of Film Critics (1966)

New York Metro
444 Madison Ave., Fourth Floor
New York, NY 10022
Tel: (800) 624-8301
Website: nationalsocietyoffilmcritics.com
Members: 55 critics
Staff: 1

Annual Budget: Under $10,000

Personnel:
Chairman: David Sterritt

Historical Note:
NFSC members are film critics working in print and broadcast. The Society represents movie criticism in the United States by supplying the official critic delegate to the The National Film Preservation Board (NFPB). It responds to specific issues such as colorization, film preservation, or the ratings system. Has no paid officers or full-time staff.

National Society of Genetic Counselors (1978)
401 N. Michigan Ave.
Chicago, IL 60611
Tel: (312) 321-6834 *Fax:* (312) 673-6972
E-Mail: nsgc@nsgc.org
Website: nsgc.org
Members: 2600 individuals
Staff: 13
Annual Budget: $1-2,000,000

Personnel:
Executive Director: Meghan Carey
    E-Mail: mcarey@nsgc.org
Specialist:, Membership Services: Elizabeth Allen
    E-Mail: eallen@nsgc.org
Senior Associate, Conventions: Dana Almdale
    E-Mail: sstuaffer@nsgc.org
Manager, Marketing: Jennifer Kasowicz
    E-Mail: jkasowicz@nsgc.org
Manager, Accounts: Sarah Lombardi
    E-Mail: slombardi@nsgc.org
Manager, Operations: Meg Orsi
    E-Mail: morsi@nsgc.org
Director, Government Relations: John Richardson
    E-Mail: jrichardson@smithbucklin.com
Education Specialist: Kathryn Schafer
    E-Mail: kschafer@nsgc.org

Historical Note:
NSGC's mission is to advance the various roles of genetic counselors in health care by fostering education, research, and public policy to ensure the availability of genetic services. Members are health professionals with specialized graduate degrees and experience in the areas of medical genetics and counseling. Membership: $265 (Full); $224 (Associate); $100 (Student); $173 (New Genetic Counselor); $95 (Emeritus).

Meetings/Conferences: Annual
Conference Chair: Dana Almdale

Publications:
Journal of Genetic Counseling

Membership List Available to Non-members

National Society of Hispanic MBAs (1988)
450 E. John Carpenter Fwy.
Suite 200
Irving, TX 75062
Tel: (214) 596-9338 *Fax:* (214) 596-9325
TollFree: (877) 467-4622
E-Mail: membership@nshmba.org
Website: nshmba.org
Members: 16,000 members
Staff: 23
Annual Budget: $1-2,000,000
Tax: 501(c)(3)

Personnel:
Chief Executive Officer: Manny Gonzalez
    E-Mail: mgonzalez@nshmba.org
Senior Manager, Education and University Relations: Bibiana Am
    E-Mail: bam@nshmba.org
Chief Financial Officer: Selene Benavides
    E-Mail: sbenavidez@nshmba.org
Specialist, Marketing and Communications: Mandy Brown
    E-Mail: mbrown@nshmba.org
Director, Business Development, Marketing and Membership: Lynn Handley
    E-Mail: lhandley@nshmba.org
Manager, Information Technology: Brandon Jennings
    E-Mail: bjennings@nshmba.org
Internet Services Manager: Jacqueline Rodriguez
    E-Mail: jrodriguez@nshmba.org
Manager, Events and Logistics: Severine Stephenson
    E-Mail: sstephenson@nshmba.org

Historical Note:
NSHMBA's mission is to foster Hispanic leadership through graduate management education and professional development in order to improve the society. Membership: $200 (Premier); $1,000 (Executive); Free (Associate).

Meetings/Conferences: Annual
Conference Chair: Severine Stephenson

Publications:
NSHMBA Magazine; bi-annually; adv.
The Bottom Line; monthly; adv.
The Business Journal of Hispanic Research; adv.

National Society of Insurance Premium Auditors (1975)
P.O. Box 936
Columbus, OH 43216-0936
Fax: (877) 835-5798
TollFree: (888) 846-7472
E-Mail: nsipa@nsipa.org
Website: associationdatabase.com/aws/NSIPA/ pt/sp/Hom
Members: 880 individuals
Staff: 4
Annual Budget: $100-250,000
Tax: 501(c)(6)

Personnel:
Executive Director: Brad L. Feldman CAE, MPA, IOM
Director ,Communications and Managing Editor: Nikkita Cohoon
    E-Mail: nikki@executive-office.org
Administrative Assistant: Christie Engler
    E-Mail: christie@executive-office.org
Director, Membership: Debra Seiple
    E-Mail: deb@executive-office.org

Historical Note:
NSIPA provides a forum for the exchange, development, and dissemination of technical information. Membership: $95 (Individual); $15 (Life).

Continuing Education:
Certification Designation/s: CITPA, CIPA, APA

Meetings/Conferences: Annual
Number of non-conference events/year: 2

Publications:
Newsline; quarterly

National Society of Mural Painters (1895)
450 W. 31st St.
Seventh Floor
New York, NY 10001
Tel: (212) 244-2800
E-Mail:
info@nationalsocietyofmuralpainters.com
Website: nationalsocietyofmuralpainters.com
Members: 120 individuals
Staff: 1
Annual Budget: Under $10,000

Personnel:
President: Jeff Greene

Historical Note:
Formerly, The Mural Painters. Member of the Fine Arts Federation of New York. NSMP,s purpose is concerned with the advancement of techniques and standards for the design and execution of mural art. NSMP presents exhibitions, organizes and conducts competitions. Members are muralists from around the world chosen by a majority vote of the organization after a review of slides and biographical material. Membership: $45 (Individual); $25 (Student).

Publications:
NSMP ListServe; on-line

Membership List Available to Non-members

National Society of Newspaper Columnists (1977)
P.O. Box 411532
San Francisco, CA 94141
Tel: (415) 488-6762 *Fax:* (484) 297-0336
E-Mail: director@columnists.com
Website: columnists.com
Members: 510 individuals
Staff: 4
Annual Budget: $10-25,000

Personnel:
Executive Director: Luenna H. Kim
Treasurer: James Casto
Editor: Robert Haught
Director, Online Media Services: Ben Pollock

Historical Note:
NSNC's mission is to promote professionalism and camaraderie among North American newspaper columnists.

Members are columnists of daily newspapers. Membership: $50 (Regular); $35 (Student); $500 (Lifetime).

Meetings/Conferences: Annual
2013 - Hartford, CT/June 27 - 30

Publications:
Member directory; on-line
Newsletter

The National Society of Painters in Casein and Acrylic (1952)
5513 Jaclyn Ln.
Bethlehem, PA 18017
Tel: (610) 264-7472
Website:
    nationalsocietyofpaintersincaseinandacrylic.or
Staff: 2
Annual Budget: $10-25,000

Personnel:
Honorary Life President: Mark Freeman
Contact, Membership: Nessa Grainger

Historical Note:
NSPCA was founded to give artists the opportunity to exhibit work regardless of style, school or subject matter. Membership is limited to 150 professional artists. Full Membership is by invitation only. Membership: $25/year (Associate/Individual).

Meetings/Conferences: Annual

National Society of Professional Engineers (1934)
1420 King St.
Alexandria, VA 22314-2794
Tel: (703) 684-2800 *Fax:* (703) 836-4875
TollFree: (888) 285-6773
E-Mail: memserv@nspe.org
Website: nspe.org
Members: 55554 individuals, state societies and chapters
Staff: 47
Annual Budget: $10-25,000,000
Tax: 501(c)(6)

Personnel:
Executive Director: Lawrence A. Jacobson
    E-Mail: ljacobson@nspe.org
Director, Membership Development and Services: Felisha Battle
    E-Mail: fbattle@nspe.org
Director, Meetings: Polly Collins
    E-Mail: pcollins@nspe.org
Senior Manager, Marketing: Becky McCarthy
    E-Mail: marketing@nspe.org
Senior Manager, Government Relations: Sarah E. Ogden
    E-Mail: sogden@nspe.org
Senior Manager, Education: Marcia Prichard
    E-Mail: mprichard@nspe.org
Deputy Executive Director and General Counsel: Arthur Edward Schwartz CAE
Director, Communications: David Siegel
    E-Mail: dsiegel@nspe.org
Director, Information Technology and Systems: Alan Thompson

Historical Note:
NSPE, in partnership with the State Societies, is the organization of licensed Professional Engineers (PEs) and Engineer Interns (EIs). Through education, licensure advocacy, leadership training, multi-disciplinary networking, and outreach, NSPE enhances the image of its members and their ability to ethically and professionally practice engineering. Consists of 54 state societies and more than 500 chapters. Membership: $140-220 (Licensed Member); $0-50 (Student); $67.20 (Graduated).

Meetings/Conferences: Annual
Conference Chair: Polly Collins
2013 - Minneapolis, MN/July 17 - 21
Number of non-conference events/year: 25

Publications:
Daily Designs; daily
NSPE Update
PE magazine; adv.
U.S. Engineering Press Review; weekly
Young PE Quarterly; quarterly

National Society of Professional Surveyors (1981)
5119 Pegasus Ct.
Suite Q
Frederick, MD 21704
Tel: (240) 439-4615 *Fax:* (240) 439-4956
Website: nsps.us.com

Members: 4500 individuals
Staff: 4
Annual Budget: $500-1,000,000
Tax: 501(c)(3)

Personnel:
Executive Director: Curtis W. Sumner
    E-Mail: curtis.sumner@acsm.net
Accounting Manager: Bob Jupin
    E-Mail: bob.jupin@acsm.net
Contact, Certifications: Sara Maggi
    E-Mail: sara.maggi@nsps.us.com
Office Manager, Membership Services, and Book Sales:
    Trisha Milburn
    E-Mail: trisha.milburn@nsps.us.com

Historical Note:
Formerly Land Surveys Division of ACSM until 1981, became a self- governing organization named the National Society of Professional Surveyors in 1983. NSPS strives to establish and further common interests, objectives, and political effort that would help bind the surveying profession into a unified body in the U.S. It is also a member organization of the American Congress on Surveying and Mapping. Membership is open to all professional surveyors and to persons trained, registered, or interested in the profession of surveying and mapping. Membership is concurrent. Membership: $240 (Licensed or Regular Member); $155 (Associate Member); $30 (Student).

Continuing Education:
Certification Designation/s: CST, HSCC

Meetings/Conferences: Annual

Publications:
ACSM Bulletin; bi-monthly
Surveying and Land Information Science Journal;
    quarterly

National Society of Real Estate Appraisers, Inc.
(1956)
275 N. Union Blvd.
Suite 1420
St. Louis, MO 63108
Tel: (314) 367-9449 *Fax:* (786) 524-8169
E-Mail: nsrea2001@yahoo.com
Website: nsrea.org
Staff: 2
Annual Budget: Under $10,000
Tax: 501(c)(6)

Personnel:
Executive Vice President: Lawrence Netterville
    E-Mail: lnetter@swbell.net

Historical Note:
NSREA's mission is to provide exceptional services for its members in the core areas of Education, Training/ Mentoring, Communication, Recertification and Business Development. Members are licensed real estate practitioners, with advanced college or university training and are well known appraisers in their communities. Membership: $250 (Designated/Candidate/Associate); $100 (Mentoring); $500 (Allied).

Continuing Education:
Certification Designation/s: MREA, CRA, RA

Meetings/Conferences: Annual

Publications:
Membership Directory; on-line
NSREA Newsletter

National Solid Wastes Management Association
(1962)
4301 Connecticut Ave. NW
Suite 300
Washington, DC 20008-2304
Tel: (202) 244-4700 *Fax:* (202) 966-4824
TollFree: (800) 424-2869
E-Mail: membership@envasns.org
Website: environmentalseveryday.org/about-
    nswma-soli
Members: 2000 companies
Staff: 8
Annual Budget: $250-500,000

Personnel:
President and Chief Executive Officer: Sharon H. Kneiss
    E-Mail: skneiss@envasns.org
General Counsel and Director, Safety: David Biderman
    E-Mail: davidb@nswma.org
Director, Member Services: Christine Hutcherson
    E-Mail: chutcherson@nswma.org
Director, Education: Alice Jacobsohn
    E-Mail: alicej@nswma.org

Contact, Publication sales: Carey Lawrence
    E-Mail: clawrence@nswma.org
Director, Finance: Pat Lyddane
    E-Mail: plyddane@nswma.org
Manager, Meetings: Catherine Maimon
    E-Mail: cmaimon@nswma.org
Director, Communications and Public Affairs: Thom
    Metzger
    E-Mail: tmetzger@nswma.org

Historical Note:
A constituent group of the Environmental Industries Associations. NSWMA strives to promote the management of waste in a manner that is environmentally responsible, efficient, profitable and ethical. Members are small haulers and recyclers and facility owners and operators. Membership: $600-32,450/year.

Meetings/Conferences: Annual
Conference Chair: Catherine Maimon
Number of non-conference events/year: 4

Publications:
NSWMA E-News; weekly
Safety Monday; weekly
Waste Industry News; quarterly

National Sorghum Producers *(1985)*
4201 N. Interstate-27
Lubbock, TX 79403
Tel: (806) 749-3478 *Fax:* (806) 749-9002
TollFree: (800) 749-3478
E-Mail: ngsp@sorghumgrowers.com
Website: sorghumgrowers.com
Members: 4000 individuals
Staff: 6
Annual Budget: $500-1,000,000

Personnel:
Chief Executive Officer: Tim Lust
    E-Mail: tim@sorghumgrowers.com
Coordinator, Communications: Jennifer Blackburn
    E-Mail: jennifer@sorghumgrowers.com
Director, Strategic Business: Chris Cogburn
    E-Mail: chris@sorghumgrowers.com
Manager, Operations: Shari Connel
    E-Mail: shari@sorghumgrowers.com
Director, External Affairs and Editor: Lindsay Kennedy
    E-Mail: lindsay@sorghumgrowers.com

Historical Note:
Formerly (1985) known as the Grain Sorghum Producers Association, NSP is affiliated with the Texas Grain Sorghum Producers Board that works to serve producers and acts as the voice of the sorghum industry for farmers through legislative and regulatory representation. Membership: $60/ year.

Meetings/Conferences:
Number of non-conference events/year: 2

Publications:
e-Newsletters; monthly
Sorghum Grower Magazine; quarterly; adv.
Sorghum Notes; weekly

National Speakers Association *(1973)*
1500 S. Priest Dr.
Tempe, AZ 85281
Tel: (480) 968-2552 *Fax:* (480) 968-0911
E-Mail: information@nsaspeaker.org
Website: nsaspeaker.org
Members: 3200 individuals
Staff: 14
Annual Budget: $2-5,000,000
Tax: 501(c)(6)

Personnel:
Chief Executive Officer: Stacy Tetschner CAE
Technology Manager: Patrick Berens
Executive Assistant: Kim Cook
Manager, Marketing: Andrea DiMickele
    E-Mail: andrea@nsaspeaker.org
Manager, Meetings: Nikki Harris
    E-Mail: nikki@nsaspeaker.org
Director, Membership and Foundation Executive Director:
    Dustin McKissen
Director, Publications: Barbara Parus
    E-Mail: barbara@nsaspeaker.org
Director, Finance and Administration: William Peterson
Director, Professional Development: Cara Tracy CMP,
    CMM
    E-Mail: cara@nsaspeaker.org

Historical Note:

NSA is the organization for professional speakers and provides resources and education designed to advance the skills, integrity and value of its members and the speaking profession. Membership: $75-600/year.

Continuing Education:
Enrollment: 350
Certification Designation/s: CSP

Meetings/Conferences:
Conference Chair: Nikki Harris
2013 - Philadelphia, PA (Philadelphia Marriott
    Downtown)/July 27 - 30
2014 - San Diego, CA (San Diego Marriott Marquis and
    Marina)/June 29 - July 2
2015 - Washington, DC (Marriott Wardman Park
    Hotel)/July 18 - 21
Number of non-conference events/year: 2

Publications:
Member Handbook; annually
NSA Now; quarterly
Speaker Magazine; adv.
Voices of Experience; on-line

Membership List Available to Non-members

National Speleological Society *(1941)*
2813 Cave Ave.
Huntsville, AL 35810-4431
Tel: (256) 852-1300 *Fax:* (256) 851-9241
E-Mail: nss@caves.org
Website: caves.org
Members: 10000 individuals and 250 grottos
Staff: 4
Annual Budget: $1-2,000,000
Tax: 501(c)(3)

Personnel:
President: Wm Shrewsbury
    E-Mail: president@caves.org
Contact, Media Relations: Jay Jorden
    E-Mail: media@caves.org
Vice-President,Operations: David Lukins
    E-Mail: ovp@caves.org
Vice-President, Administration: Geary Schindel
    E-Mail: avp@caves.org

Historical Note:
NSS's purpose is to promote interest in and to advance in any and all ways the study and science of speleology, the protection of caves and their natural contents, and to promote fellowship among those interested therein. Membership: $24 (Basic- Individual); $40 (Regular- Individual); $30 (Associate-Individual); $99 (Institutional); $120 (Sustaining-Individual); $800 (Life-Individual); $125 (Regular Conservation-Individual); $8-50 (Family); $400 (Family, Life).

Meetings/Conferences: Annual
2013 - Shippensburg, PA/Aug. 5 - 9
2014 - Huntsville, AL (NSS Headquarters)/July 14 - 18
Number of non-conference events/year: 3

Publications:
American Caving Accidents; biennially; adv.
Caving Magazine; monthly
Journal of Cave and Karst Studies; quarterly; adv.
NSS News; monthly; adv.

National Spinal Cord Injury Association *(1948)*
75-20 Astoria Blvd.
Jackson Heights, NY 11370
Tel: (718) 803-3782 *Fax:* (866) 387-2196
E-Mail: info@spinalcord.org
Website: spinalcord.org
Members:
60 support group and chapters
50 hospital, buisiness and organizational
members
Staff: 4
Annual Budget: $500-1,000,000
Tax: 501(c)(3)

Personnel:
President and Chief Executive Officer: Paul J. Tobin
Treasurer: Janeen Earwood
Manager, Resource Center: Bill Fertig
    E-Mail: bfresource@spinalcord.org

Historical Note:
Founded in response to the medical and social problems arising from spinal cord injury within the civilian population. NSCIA is the membership division of United Spinal Association. NSCIA's mission is to enable people with spinal cord injury and disease (SCI/D) to achieve their level of independence, health, and personal fulfillment by providing resources, services, and peer support. Members

are individuals with spinal cord injuries, their families, health professionals, and others. Individual membership is free.

Publications:
SCI e-News; monthly; adv.
SCI Life; bi-monthly; adv.

Membership List Available to Non-members

National Sporting Goods Association *(1929)*
1601 Feehanville Dr.
Suite 300
Mt. Prospect, IL 60056
Tel: (800) 815-5422 *Fax:* (847) 391-9827
TollFree: (800) 815-5422
E-Mail: info@nsga.org
Website: nsga.org
Members: 22500 retail outlets and suppliers
Staff: 14
Annual Budget: $10-25,000,000
Tax: 501(c)(6)

Personnel:
President and Chief Executive Officer: Matt Carlson
    E-Mail: mcarlson@nsga.org
Director, Marketing and Communication: Bruce
    Hammond
    E-Mail: bhammond@nsga.org
Director, Research and Information: Dan Kasen
    E-Mail: dkasen@nsga.org
Director, Membership and Sales: Darlene Plunkett
    E-Mail: dplunkett@nsga.org
Chief Financial Officer: Richard Schascheck
    E-Mail: rschascheck@nsga.org
Director, Education and Strategic Planning: Chuck Suritz
    E-Mail: csuritz@nsga.org

Historical Note:
Formerly Sporting Goods Distributors Association, changed its name to the National Sporting Goods Distributors Association in 1930 and assumed its present name in 1936. NSGA provides information, education and cost-saving services to the sporting goods industry. Membership consists of manufacturers, retailers, dealers, wholesalers, sales agents and media in the sporting goods industry. Membership: $111-285 (Retailer/Dealer/Wholesaler); $279-484 (Industry Associate); $566-966 (Manufacturer).

Meetings/Conferences: Annual
2013 - Palm Beach Gardens, FL (PGA National Resort and Spa)/May 5 - 8

Publications:
NSGA Athletic Footwear newsletter; monthly; adv.
NSGA Huddle; monthly
NSGA Research newsletter; monthly
NSGA Retail Focus magazine; bi-monthly; adv.
SNEWS; on-line
Sporting Goods Dealer; bi-monthly
Sporting Goods Market; monthly
Sports Executive Weekly; weekly

Membership List Available to Non-members

National Sportscasters and Sportswriters Association and Hall of Fame *(1959)*
P.O. Box 1545
Salisbury, NC 28145-1545
Tel: (704) 633-4275 *Fax:* (704) 633-2027
E-Mail: nssa@nssahalloffame.com
Website: nssafame.com
Members: 700 individuals
Staff: 2
Annual Budget: $10-25,000

Personnel:
Executive Director: Dave Goren
    E-Mail: dgoren@nssafame.com
Administrative Assistant: Irene Beyer
    E-Mail: admin@nssafame.com

Historical Note:
NSSA is dedicated to honoring, preserving and celebrating the legacy of sportscasters and sportswriters in the United States. It also seeks to develop educational opportunities for those who are interested in pursuing a career in sports media, through networking, mentoring and scholarship programs. Membership: $30 (Full); $20 (Associate); $15 (Student); $110 (AIPS).

Publications:
Member Directory; on-line
Staff Directory; on-line

National Spotted Saddle Horse Association *(1979)*

P.O. Box 898
Murfreesboro, TN 37133-0898
Tel: (615) 890-2864 *Fax:* (615) 896-8738
E-Mail: nssha898@aol.com
Website: nssha.com
Members: 4000 individuals
Staff: 2
Annual Budget: Under $10,000

Personnel:
Recording Secretary: Shirley Hayes

Historical Note:
NSSHA is dedicated to establishing a uniform breed saddle horse that is naturally gaited and performs without the use of punishing training aids or substances. Membership: $50/year.

Meetings/Conferences: Quarterly
Number of non-conference events/year: 4

Publications:
NSSHA Journal; quarterly; adv.
NSSHA Newsletter; monthly

National Spotted Swine Records *(1914)*
P.O. Box 9758
Peoria, IL 61612-9758
Tel: (309) 693-1804 *Fax:* (309) 691-0168
E-Mail: cpspeoria@mindspring.com
Website: cpsswine.com/spots/spotted.htm
Members: 565 individuals
Staff: 3
Annual Budget: $100-250,000

Personnel:
Executive Secretary: Jack Wall

Historical Note:
Formerly the National Spotted Poland China Record. At the 1960 Annual Meeting, the breed's Board of Directors and members voted to change the name of the association from the National Spotted Poland China Record to the National Spotted Swine Record, Inc. Further, it was voted to refer to the breed as Spotted Swine or SPOTS, rather than the longer previously used name for the breed. Membership: $30 (Life-Sr); $10 (Junior- 9-18 yrs); $50 (Senior Members).

Continuing Education:
Certification Designation/s: CPS

Publications:
Breeders Digest; on-line; adv.

National Staff Development and Training Association *(1930)*
1133 Nineteenth St.NW
Suite 400
Washington, DC 20036
Tel: (202) 682-0100 *Fax:* (202) 204-0071
E-Mail: memberservice@aphsa.org
Website: nsdta.aphsa.org
Members: 500 individuals
Staff: 34
Annual Budget: $5-10,000,000

Personnel:
Contact, Membership Services and Conference Coordinator: Dee Gross
    E-Mail: dee.gross@aphsa.org

Historical Note:
Affiliate unit of the American Public Welfare Association, which provides administrative support. NSDTA's mission is to build professional and organizational capacity in the human services through a national network of membership sharing ideas and resources on organizational development, staff development, and training. Membership: $150 (Individual); $35 (Student).

Meetings/Conferences: Annual
Conference Chair: Dee Gross

Publications:
NSDTA Newsletter
NSDTA's Journal

National Star Route Mail Contractors Association *(1933)*
324 E. Capitol St.
Washington, DC 20003-3897
Tel: (202) 543-1661 *Fax:* (202) 543-8863
E-Mail: info@starroutecontractors.org
Website: starroutecontractors.org
Members: 17000 small businessmen and women
Staff: 4
Annual Budget: $500-1,000,000
Tax: 501(c)(5)

Personnel:
Executive Director: John V. "Skip" Maraney
    E-Mail: jmaraney@starroutecontractors.org

Historical Note:
Formerly (1982) National Star Route Mail Carriers Association, NSRMCA is a non-profit association whose major goal is to provide legislative and regulatory protection to its members. It represents Contractors in all 50 States and U.S. Territories. Membership: $20 (Associate, Non Contractors); $100 (Affiliate, Non Contractors); Contractor dues are based on a formula.

Publications:
The Star Carrier; monthly

National Steel Bridge Alliance
One E. Wacker Dr.
Suite 700
Chicago, IL 60601-1802
Tel: (312) 670-5401
Website: aisc.org/contentnsba.aspx?id = 20844
Staff: 2

Personnel:
Executive Director: Roger Ferch
    E-Mail: ferch@aisc.org
Director, Marketing: Brian Raff
    E-Mail: raff@steelbridges.org

Historical Note:
NSBA's mission is to establish steel as the material of choice for bridges and the NSBA's goal is to increase steel's share of the bridge market.

Meetings/Conferences: Annual
Number of non-conference events/year: 1

Publications:
NSBA Newsletter; monthly

National Stone, Sand, and Gravel Association *(1903)*
1605 King St.
Alexandria, VA 22314
Tel: (703) 525-8788 *Fax:* (703) 525-7782
TollFree: (800) 342-1415
E-Mail: info@nssga.org
Website: nssga.org
Members: 500 producers and manufacturers and services
Staff: 30
Annual Budget: $5-10,000,000
Tax: 501(c)(6)

Personnel:
President and Chief Executive Officer: Jennifer Joy
    Pinniger
    E-Mail: jwilson@nssga.org
Associate Vice President, Communications: Peggy Disney
    E-Mail: pdisney@nssga.org
President and Chief Executive Officer: R. A. "Gus"
    Edwards III
    E-Mail: gedwards@nssga.org
Director, Meetings and Conventions: Cynthia McDowell
    CSEP
    E-Mail: cmcdowell@nssga.org
Senior Vice President, Marketing and Membership Services:
    Tim Reagan
    E-Mail: treagan@nssga.org
Associate Vice President , Administration and Finance:
    Tina M. Richards
    E-Mail: trichards@nssga.org
Director, Information Technology: Chris Richards
    E-Mail: crichards@nssga.org
Director, Finance: Cesar Silva
    E-Mail: csilva@nssga.org
Manager, Education: Catherine Whalen
    E-Mail: cwhalen@nssga.org

Historical Note:
Founded as National Sand and Gravel Association; became National Aggregates Association in 1987. Merged with National Stone Association and assumed its current name in 2001. NSSGA's purpose is to represent the crushed stone, sand and gravel-or aggregates- industries.

Meetings/Conferences: Annual
Conference Chair: Cynthia McDowell CSEP
2013 - San Antonio, TX/March 17 - 20
2014 - Las Vegas, NV/March 17 - 20
2015 - Baltimore, MD/March 16 - 18
2015 - Baltimore, MD/March 16 - 18
Number of non-conference events/year: 1

Publications:

e-Digest and Washington Watch Electronic Newsletter; weekly
Stone, Sand & Gravel Review; bi-monthly

National Strength and Conditioning Association
(1978)
1885 Bob Johnson Dr.
Colorado Springs, CO 80906
Tel: (719) 632-6722 *Fax:* (719) 632-6367
TollFree: (800) 815-6826
E-Mail: nsca@nsca.com
Website: nsca.com
Members: 33000 individuals
Staff: 76
Annual Budget: $10-25,000,000
Tax: 501(c)(3)

Personnel:
Chief Financial Officer: Lee Madden
    E-Mail: Lee.Madden@nsca.com
Chief Technology Director: David Ashley
    E-Mail: David.Ashley@nsca.com
Director, Publications: Keith E. Cinea CSCS, MA
    E-Mail: Keith.Cinea@nsca.com
Director, Marketing: Scott Douglas
    E-Mail: Scott.Douglas@nsca.com
Senior Director, Human Resources: Kim Ginter
    E-Mail: Kim.Ginter@nsca.com
Director, Membership Services: Curtis Lords
    E-Mail: Curtis.Lords@nsca.com
Director, Conferences and Events: Virginia Meier
    E-Mail: Virginia.Meier@nsca.com
Manager, Education: Peter Melanson
    E-Mail: pmelanson@nsca-lift.org
Director, Certification: Torrey Smith CSCS, MA
    E-Mail: Torrey.Smith@nsca.com

Historical Note:
Supports and disseminates research-based knowledge and its practical application to improve athletic performance and fitness. Membership: $120 (Professional); $65 (Student); $47 (Associate).

Continuing Education:
Certification Designation/s: NSCA-CPT, CSCS, CSPS

Meetings/Conferences:
Conference Chair: Virginia Meier
2013 - Nashville, TN (Renaissance Nashville Hotel)/ Jan. 4 - 5/600 attendees
2013 - Norfolk, VA (Marriott Norfolk Waterside)/April 16 - 18
2013 - Las Vegas, NV (Paris Hotel)/July 10 - 13/2000 attendees/over 100 exhibitors
Number of non-conference events/year: 3

Publications:
Journal of Strength and Conditioning Research; monthly
NSCA Bulletin; monthly
NSCA's Performance Training Journal; bi-monthly
Strength and Conditioning Journal; bi-monthly
Tactical Strength and Conditioning Report; bi-monthly

Membership List Available to Non-members

National Stripper Well Association (1934)
P.O. Box 18336
Oklahoma City, OK 73154
Tel: (405) 228-4112 *Fax:* (580) 332-4714
Website: nswa.us
Members: 300 owners
Staff: 3
Annual Budget: $250-500,000
Tax: 501(c)(6)

Personnel:
Executive Director: Somerlyn Cothran
Contact, Governmental Affairs: Bill Brewster
Treasurer: John Pilkington

Historical Note:
NSWA states that producers and operators of marginally producing wells have a unique set of needs and concerns regarding federal legislation and regulation. Membership: $10,000 (Executive); $5,000 (Governing); $2,500 (Supervisory); $1,000 (Guardian); $500 (Benefactor); $250 (Individual or Company Single).

Publications:
NSWA Newsletter; monthly

National Stroke Association (1984)
9707 E. Easter Ln.
Suite B
Centennial, CO 80112

Tel: (800) 787-6537 *Fax:* (303) 649-1328
TollFree: (800) 787-6537
E-Mail: info@stroke.org
Website: stroke.org
Members: 10000 individuals
Staff: 16
Annual Budget: $2-5,000,000
Tax: 501(c)(3)

Personnel:
Chief Executive Officer: James "Jim" Baranski
    E-Mail: JBaranski@stroke.org
Manager, Special Events: Crystal Blaylock
    E-Mail: CBlaylock@stroke.org
Director, Marketing and Communications: Taryn Fort
    E-Mail: tfort@stroke.org
Manager, Database and Accounting: Jill Hare
    E-Mail: Jhare@stroke.org
Director, Education: Amy Jensen
    E-Mail: ajenson@stroke.org
Manager, Professional Membership Programs: Linda Kuhrt
    E-Mail: Lkuhrt@stroke.org
Editor: Amy McCraken
    E-Mail: amccraken@stroke.org

Historical Note:
NSA's mission is to reduce the incidence and impact of stroke by developing compelling education and programs focused on prevention, treatment, rehabilitation and support for all impacted by stroke. Membership: $80-175 (Professional); $2100 (Organization).

Meetings/Conferences:
Conference Chair: Amy Jensen
Number of non-conference events/year: 1

Publications:
Brain Alert; quarterly
Membership Directory; on-line
Professional Education e-Newsletter; bi-annually
StrokeSmart; quarterly

Membership List Available to Non-members

National Structured Settlements Trade Association (1985)
1100 New York Ave. NW
Suite 750W
Washington, DC 20005
Tel: (202) 289-4004
E-Mail: info@nssta.com
Website: nssta.com
Members: 1200 licensed consultants, attorneys, insurance companies and professionals
Staff: 10
Annual Budget: $1-2,000,000
Tax: 501(c)(6)

Personnel:
Executive Director: Eric Vaughn
Deputy Director: Peter Arnold
Manager, Membership Relations: Courtney Hill
Director, Communications and Social Media: Raushanna Salhi
Administrator, Continuing Education: Debbie Sink
General Counsel: John Stanton

Historical Note:
NSSTA advances the use of structured settlements as a means of using periodic payments to resolve personal injury claims, workers compensation, and other types of claims. It works towards through public advocacy, legislative action, and educational programs. Producer membership is on a company basis, and is scaled on the number of principals, partners and producers in the firm. Membership: $2,175 minimum (Producer); $10,000-55,000 (Provider Company-based on annual premium volume); $965 (User Company); $735 (Associate-Individual).

Continuing Education:
Enrollment: 40
Certification Designation/s: CSSC

Meetings/Conferences:
Number of non-conference events/year: 1

Publications:
Membership Directory; on-line

Membership List Available to Non-members

National Student Employment Association (1976)
715 Northill Dr.
C/O June Hagler
Richardson, TX 75080
Tel: (972) 690-8772 *Fax:* (972) 767-5131
E-Mail: nsea@nsea.info
Website: nsea.info

Members: 500 individuals
Staff: 6
Annual Budget: $100-250,000

Personnel:
Office Manager: June M. Hagler
    E-Mail: nsea@nsea.info

Historical Note:
Formerly (1975) National Association on Work and the College Student and (1997) National Association of Student Employment Administrators. NSEA's mission is to support and promote student employment through research, publications, professional development opportunities and open exchange of information. Membership: $125 (Individual); $375 (Institutional); $750 (Corporate); $50 (Retired).

Meetings/Conferences: Annual
2013 - New Orleans, LA (LePavillon Hotel)/Oct. 16 - 18

Publications:
Membership Directory; annually
NSEA Newsletter; on-line; adv.
The Journal of Student Employment; on-line; adv.

National Student Nurses Association (1952)
45 Main St.
Suite 606
Brooklyn, NY 11201
Tel: (718) 210-0705 *Fax:* (718) 797-1186
E-Mail: nsna@nsna.org
Website: nsna.org
Members: 60000 members
Staff: 12
Annual Budget: $2-5,000,000
Tax: 501(c)(6)

Personnel:
Executive Director: Diane J. Mancino CAE, EdD, RN
    E-Mail: nsna@nsna.org
Managing Editor: Jonathan Buttrick MPW
    E-Mail: jonathan@nsna.org
Consultant, Conference and Program Planning: Judith Tyler MA, RN
    E-Mail: nsna@nsna.org
Director, Membership Development: Susan Wong BS, CAE
    E-Mail: nsna@nsna.org

Historical Note:
NSNA's mission is to mentor students preparing for initial licensure as registered nurses, and to convey the standards, ethics, and skills that students will need as responsible and accountable leaders and members of the profession. Membership: $50 (Individual); $35 (New Graduate); $250 (Local or State Agency/Organization/School of Nursing); $500 (National Organization).

Meetings/Conferences: Annual
Conference Chair: Judith Tyler MA, RN
2013 - Charlotte, NC/April 3 - 7/11-25 exhibitors

Publications:
Imprint; quarterly; adv.
NSNA News; on-line; adv.
NSNA Weekly Update; on-line; adv.

National Student Osteopathic Medical Association
(1970)
142 E. Ontario St.
Chicago, IL 60611-2864
Tel: (312) 202-8193 *Fax:* (312) 202-8200
TollFree: (800) 621-1773
E-Mail: somanat@studentdo.com
Website: studentdo.com
Members: 7000 individuals
Staff: 7
Annual Budget: $100-250,000

Personnel:
Administrator: Elizabeth Hodor
    E-Mail: somanat@studentdo.com
Director, Public Relations: Tim Beals
Coordinator, Convention: Kaitlin Dewhirst
    E-Mail: convention@studentdo.com
Director, Political Affairs: Whitney Fix-Lanes
    E-Mail: politicalaffairs@studentdo.com
Coordinator, Membership: Brittany Grady
    E-Mail: membership@studentdo.com
Director, Research and Development: Kelsey Neufeld
National President: Sam Rabor
    E-Mail: president@studentdo.com

Historical Note:
SOMA's mission is to promote osteopathic ideals and unity within the profession and to educate future osteopathic physicians to establish and maintain lines of communication

among healthcare professionals to improve the quality of healthcare.

Meetings/Conferences: Annual

Publications:
SOMA Newsletter - The Student DOctor; irregular

Membership List Available to Non-members

National Student Speech Language Hearing Association (1972)
2200 Research Blvd.
Suite 322
Rockville, MD 20850
Tel: (301) 296-5700 *Fax:* (301) 571-0481
TollFree: (800) 498-2071
E-Mail: nsslha@asha.org
Website: nsslha.org
Members: 13000 individuals
Staff: 2
Annual Budget: $500-1,000,000

Personnel:
Director, Operations: Dawn D. Dickerson
    E-Mail: ddickerson@asha.org
Membership Administrator and Web Liaison: Lisa Marie Fields
    E-Mail: lfields@asha.org

Historical Note:
Formed as National Student Speech and Hearing Association through a merger of Sigma Alpha Eta and the Student Journal Group of American Speech and Hearing Association and assumed its present name in 1980, NSSLHA is the national organization for graduate and undergraduate students interested in the study of normal and disordered human communication. Members are undergraduates and master's degree candidates working in the field of speech-language pathology and audiology.Membership: $60/year.

Publications:
CICSD; on-line; adv.
In the Loop; on-line; adv.
NSSLHA Now; adv.

Membership List Available to Non-members

National Subcontractors Alliance (2003)
76 E. North St.
Akron, OH 44304
Tel: (330) 762-9951 *Fax:* (330) 762-9960
TollFree: (866) 889-9701
E-Mail: info@nationalsubcontractors.com
Website: nationalsubcontractors.com
Members:
11 associations
3500 member companies
Staff: 2

Personnel:
Executive Director: Lynne Black
    E-Mail: director@nationalsubcontractors.com

Historical Note:
NSA's mission is to promote the exchange of information between its member organizations, and to foster opportunities for representation at the national level on industry issues. Membership in NSA is open to any local, regional or state association that is dedicated to promoting the interests and protecting the rights of construction industry subcontractors. Membership: $1,500-2,500/year (Organization).

Meetings/Conferences: Annual

Publications:
Member Chapter Newsletter

National Sunflower Association (1975)
2401 46th Ave. SE
Suite 206
Mandan, ND 58554-4829
Tel: (701) 328-5100 *Fax:* (701) 663-8652
TollFree: (888) 718-7033
E-Mail: info@sunflowernsa.com
Website: sunflowernsa.com
Members: 28315 individuals
Staff: 5
Annual Budget: $2-5,000,000
Tax: 501(c)(5)

Personnel:
Executive Director: John SandBakken
    E-Mail: johns@sunflowernsa.com
Meeting Planner and Advertising Sales: Lerrene Kroh
    E-Mail: lkroh@sunflowernsa.com
Manager, Business and Office: Tina Mittelstaedt

E-Mail: tinam@sunflowernsa.com
Director, Communications: Sonia Mullally
    E-Mail: soniam@sunflowernsa.com

Historical Note:
Formerly the Sunflower Association of America. NSA's mission is to insure the profitability and long term growth of the sunflower crop through industry wide leadership. Membership includes growers and the support industry. Membership: $500 (Regular/Foreign); $325 (Associate); $250 (Checkoff Elevator-only North and South Dakota elevators); $40 (Farmer).

Meetings/Conferences: Annual
Conference Chair: Lerrene Kroh
Number of non-conference events/year: 3

Publications:
Sunflower Week in Review; bi-weekly
The Sunflower Magazine; bi-monthly; adv.
Universities and Government Agencies; on-line

National Sunroom Association (1997)
1300 Sumner Ave.
Cleveland, OH 44115-2851
Tel: (216) 241-7333 *Fax:* (216) 241-0105
E-Mail: info@nationalsunroom.org
Website: nationalsunroom.org
Members: 45 manufacturers and producers
Staff: 4
Annual Budget: $100-250,000
Tax: 501(c)(6)

Personnel:
President: John H. Addington
    E-Mail: jaddington@thomasamc.com
Account Executive: Craig Addington
    E-Mail: caddington@thomasamc.com
Director, Technical Services: Daniel J. Walker
    E-Mail: dwalker@thomasamc.com

Historical Note:
NSA is a member-directed trade association dedicated to the advancement of the manufacture and construction of safe, energy efficient and environmentally conscious sunrooms, patio rooms and solariums. Members are manufacturers and producers of sunrooms, patio rooms, solariums and related structures. Membership: $2,000-6,000 (Manufacturers); $3,000 (Affiliate); $500 (Affiliate Organization); $75-200 (Dealer-Sponsor).

Meetings/Conferences: Annual

Publications:
NSA Newsletter; on-line

National Surgical Assistant Association (1983)
2615 Amesbury Rd.
Winston-Salem, NC 27103
Tel: (336) 768-4443 *Fax:* (336) 464-2974
TollFree: (888) 633-0479
E-Mail: nsaa@namgmt.com
Website: nsaa.net
Members: 800 individuals
Staff: 2
Annual Budget: $250-500,000
Tax: 501(c)(6)

Personnel:
Executive Director: Ruth Helein
    E-Mail: ruth@namgmt.com
Contact, Educational Liaison: Walter Lampeter
    E-Mail: walterlampeter@aol.com

Historical Note:
Originally established as the Virginia Association of Surgical Assistants and later became NSAA. NSAA's mission is to set standards of professionalism, proficiency and continued education for non physician surgical assistants throughout the country. Membership: $25 (Student); $150 (Associate-Non-Certified); $300 (Certified Member).

Continuing Education:
Certification Designation/s: CSA

Meetings/Conferences: Annual
2013 - Norfolk, VA (Marriott Norfolk Waterside)/May 3 - 5

National Sweetener and Ingredient Marketing Association (1903)
3000 Chestnut Ave.
Suite 100A
Baltimore, MD 21211
Tel: (410) 467-6965 *Fax:* (410) 467-9552
Website: nsima.org
Members: 47 sugar brokers
Staff: 2

Annual Budget: $10-25,000

Personnel:
President: Raymond A. Washmera
Secretary and Treasurer: Bruce W. Penner

Historical Note:
NSIMA's mission is to provide reliable guidance to the buyer and professional service to a principal.Members are brokers of food ingredients.

Publications:
NSIMA Newsletter

Membership List Available to Non-members

National Swine Improvement Federation (1975)
University of Tennessee, Department of Animal Science
2640 Morgan Cir. Dr.
Knoxville, TN 37996-4588
Tel: (865) 974-7238 *Fax:* (865) 974-9043
Website: nsif.com
Members: 60 individuals
Staff: 1
Annual Budget: Under $10,000

Personnel:
Professor and Extension Swine Specialist: Glenn Conatser
    E-Mail: gconatser@utk.edu

Historical Note:
Established in Missouri and incorporated in Nebraska. NSIF's mission is to advance and stimulate individual and collaborative efforts of swine breeding stock suppliers, academic personnel, and pork industry affiliates in the research, development, and utilization of scientific genetic improvement programs and associated practices for the economically efficient production of quality, nutritious pork. Members are central testing stations, field performance testing programs, purebred breed associations and the National Pork Producers Council. Membership: $100/year.

Continuing Education:
Certification Designation/s: UC

National Swine Registry (1994)
2639 Yeager Rd.
West LaFayette, IN 47906
Tel: (765) 463-3594 *Fax:* (765) 497-2959
E-Mail: nsr@nationalswine.com
Website: nationalswine.com
Members: 2500 individuals
Staff: 29
Annual Budget: $5-10,000,000
Tax: 501(c)(5)

Personnel:
Chief Executive Officer: Mike Paul
    E-Mail: mike@nationalswine.com
Vice President, Member Outreach and Youth Development: Brian Arnold
    E-Mail: arnold@nationalswine.com
Vice President, Global Technical Services: Dr. Justin Fix
    E-Mail: justin@nationalswine.com
Director, Marketing and Communications: Jen Gillespie
    E-Mail: jen@nationalswine.com
Administrative Secretary: Lisa Kennedy
    E-Mail: lisa@nationalswine.com
Assistant Editor: Katie Maupin
    E-Mail: katie@nationalswine.com

Historical Note:
NSR's mission is to develop and implement programs and services to enhance the value and influence of U.S. Duroc, Hampshire, Landrace, and Yorkshire swine within all segments of the global purebred industry through avenues of technology, genetic service and youth development. Services include litter registrations, performance pedigrees, breed promotion and marketing assistance. It creates various educational materials, including a swine-judging video. Also provides free swine-related genetic consultation, across-herd genetic evaluations, and a National Four-Breed Sire Summary. Membership: $85/year (Individual).

Publications:
Breeder Directory; on-line
Pinnacle; quarterly
Seedstock EDGE; adv.

National Systems Contractors Association (1980)
3950 River Ridge Dr. NE
Cedar Rapids, IA 52402
Tel: (319) 366-6722 *Fax:* (319) 366-4164
TollFree: (800) 446-6722
E-Mail: nsca@nsca.org
Website: nsca.org
Members: 2500 individuals and companies

|

Staff: 9
Annual Budget: $1-2,000,000
Tax: 501(c)(6)

Personnel:
Executive Director: Chuck Wilson
  E-Mail: cwilson@nsca.org
General Manager and Vice President, Operations: Katie Chism
  E-Mail: kchism@nsca.org
Director, Marketing and Communications: Kendra Fish
  E-Mail: kfish@nsca.org
Specialist, Member Relations: Debra Gaskill
  E-Mail: dgaskill@nsca.org
Senior Director, Professional Development: Norah Hammond
  E-Mail: nhammond@nsca.org
Senior Director, Government Affairs and Industry Outreach: Cathy Mrosko
  E-Mail: cmrosko@nsca.org
Events Specialist: Bonnie Taylor
  E-Mail: btaylor@nsca.org

Historical Note:
Formerly (1994) National Sound and Communications Association. NSCA works to provide its members and the commercial electronic systems contracting industry with formal educational opportunities, professional development, information exchange and member services. Members are installers and servicers of electronic communications equipment. Membership: $150-300 (Affiliate/Architect/ Specifying Engineer/Business Consultant/Independent Design Consultant/Independent Programmer/Press); $150-595 (Contractor/ Integrator); $150-1800 (Distributor/Manufacturer); $150-480 (Independent Sales Representative); $30 (Student).

Continuing Education:
Certification Designation/s: CWD, MGWC, CWD/PI, CGWP, CPI, CSP

Meetings/Conferences: Annual
Conference Chair: Norah Hammond
2013 - Phoenix, AZ (Arizona Grand Resort)/Feb. 21 - 23
Number of non-conference events/year: 1

Publications:
Building Connections; bi-monthly
Member Directory; on-line
The Business Owner; bi-monthly

Membership List Available to Non-members

National Tactical Officers Association of America *(1983)*
P.O. Box 797
Doylestown, PA 18901
Tel: (215) 230-7616 *Fax:* (215) 230-7552
TollFree: (800) 279-9127
E-Mail: membership@ntoa.org
Website: ntoa.org
Members: 35,000 member Organizations
Staff: 12
Annual Budget: $2-5,000,000

Personnel:
Executive Director: Mark Lomax
Bookkeeper: Joan Detweiler
  E-Mail: jdetweiler@ntoa.org
Coordinator, Conference: Laura Gerhart
  E-Mail: lauragerhart@ntoa.org
Editor: Mary Heins
  E-Mail: maryheins@ntoa.org
Assistant, Administration: Sarah Johnson
  E-Mail: sarah.johnson@ntoa.org
Marketing Director: Corey Luby
  E-Mail: corey.luby@ntoa.org
Coordinator, Membership: Marsha Martello
  E-Mail: marshamartello@ntoa.org

Historical Note:
NTOA's is to enhance the performance and professional status of law enforcement personnel by providing a credible and proven training resource as well as a forum for the development of tactics and information exchange. Membership: $40-45 (Individual); $150-200 (Team).

Meetings/Conferences: Annual
Conference Chair: Laura Gerhart

Publications:
The Tactical Edge; quarterly; adv.

National Tank Truck Carriers *(1945)*
950 N.Glebe Rd.
Suite 520

Arlington, VA 22203-4183
Tel: (703) 838-1960 *Fax:* (703) 838-8860
E-Mail: nttcstaff@tanktruck.org
Website: tanktruck.org
Members: 200 trucking companies and 250 associate members
Staff: 9
Annual Budget: $2-5,000,000

Personnel:
President: Daniel Furth
  E-Mail: dfurth@tanktruck.org
Director, Membership Services and Regulatory Affairs: George (Fritz) Mead
  E-Mail: fmead@tanktruck.org
Vice-President, Finance and Administration: Laura Niel
  E-Mail: lniel@tanktruck.org

Historical Note:
NTTC strives to enhance the safety and profitability of the industry by providing relevant and useful information to carrier management on a timely basis. Membership: $275-30,000 (Carrier, based on annual tank truck revenues); $700 (Associate).

Meetings/Conferences:
2013 - Austin, TX (Hilton Austin)/April 28 - 30
Number of non-conference events/year: 2

Publications:
Membership Directory; on-line
NTTC Newsletter

National Tax Association *(1907)*
725 15th St. NW
Suite 600
Washington, DC 20005-2109
Tel: (202) 737-3325 *Fax:* (202) 737-7308
E-Mail: natltax@aol.com
Website: ntanet.org
Members: 1400 individuals and institutions
Staff: 4
Annual Budget: $250-500,000
Tax: 501(c)(3)

Personnel:
Executive Director: J. Fred Giertz
  E-Mail: jgiertz@ad.uiuc.edu

Historical Note:
Merged in 1973 with the Tax Institute of America (formed 1932), NTA provides the taxpayer, tax administrator, practitioner, educator, and student with a vehicle for national research, discussion, and dissemination of information. It also fosters the study and discussion of complex and controversial issues in tax theory, practice and policy, and other aspects of public finance. Membership: $500 (Sustaining); $350 (Corporation); $370 (Government Agency); $140 (Corporate Individual/ Professional); $100 (Government/Academic Individual); $40 (Full-time Student); $45 (Retiree).

Meetings/Conferences:
Number of non-conference events/year: 3

Publications:
National Tax Journal; quarterly
NTA Network Newsletter; quarterly

Membership List Available to Non-members

National Tax Lien Association *(1997)*
P.O. Box 1491
Jupiter, FL 33468
Tel: (561) 644-1109 *Fax:* (561) 449-2483
E-Mail: info@ntalinfo.org
Website: thentla.com
Members: 100 individuals
Staff: 3
Annual Budget: $250-500,000
Tax: 501(c)(6)

Personnel:
Executive Director: Bradley P. Westover
Legal Counsel: Donald R. Dinan Esq.
Treasurer: Jim Meeks

Historical Note:
NTLA aims to establish a centralized voice for the tax lien industry and engaged in legislative monitoring and lobbying activities.NTLA's mission is to be the primary organization advancing the legislative, regulatory, business, public relations and educational interests of the tax lien industry in the United States Membership: $2000-28,000/year.

Meetings/Conferences: Annual
Number of non-conference events/year: 5

Publications:
Membership Directory; on-line

National Taxidermists Association *(1972)*
108 Branch Dr.
Slidell, LA 70461
Tel: (985) 641-4682 *Fax:* (985) 641-9463
TollFree: (866) 662-9054
E-Mail: ntahq@aol.com
Website: nationaltaxidermists.com
Members: 2500 individuals
Staff: 5
Annual Budget: $100-250,000
Tax: 501(c)(6)

Personnel:
Executive Director: Greg Crain
Contact, Conventions: Cindy Crain

Historical Note:
NTA endorses education, solidarity, and standards for the entire taxidermy industry. Membership: $65 (Individual); $88 (Family/Canada/Mexico); $625 (Life); $750 (Family Lifetime); $113(Foreign); $138 (Business); $50 (Lifetime judges).

Continuing Education:
Certification Designation/s: CT

Meetings/Conferences: Annual
Conference Chair: Cindy Crain
2013 - Baton Rouge, LA (Crowne Plaza Baton Rouge)/ July 15 - 23
2014 - Rogers, AR (Embassy Suites NorthWest Arkansas-Hotel, Spa and Convention Center)/July 15 - 20
Number of non-conference events/year: 1

Publications:
Outlook Magazine; on-line; adv.

Membership List Available to Non-members

National Technical Association *(1925)*
2705 Bladensburg Rd. NE
Washington, DC 20018
Tel: (202) 575-4682
E-Mail: info@ntaonline.org
Website: ntaonline.org
Members: 2000 individuals
Staff: 2
Annual Budget: $25-50,000
Tax: 501(c)(3)

Personnel:
President: Allan Harris
  E-Mail: President@ntaonline.org
National Treasurer: Dr. Cecilia Wright Brown
  E-Mail: Treasurer@ntaonline.org

Historical Note:
NTA's purpose is to nurture scientists, engineers, technologists & educators. Membership: $1,350 (Life Fellow); $100 (Full Membership); $60 (Associate); $45 (Trail Blazer); $25 (Student).

Meetings/Conferences: Annual

Publications:
NTA newsletter; quarterly

National Telecommunications Cooperative Association *(1954)*
4121 Wilson Blvd.
Tenth Floor
Arlington, VA 22203
Tel: (703) 351-2000 *Fax:* (703) 351-2001
E-Mail: communications@ntca.org
Website: ntca.org
Members: 1135 communications providers, vendors and state telecom associations
Staff: 120
Annual Budget: $10-25,000,000
Tax: 501(c)(6)

Personnel:
Chief Executive Officer: Shirley A. Bloomfield
  E-Mail: sbloomfield@ntca.org
Manager, Design and Marketing: Sharolyn R. Auckerman
  E-Mail: sauckerman@ntca.org
Esq. General Counsel: James K. Bass
Director, Legal and Industry: Jill M. Canfield
  E-Mail: jcanfield@ntca.org
Manager, Publications: Christian A. Hamaker
  E-Mail: chamaker@ntca.org
Director, Membership: April-Marie Irwin
  E-Mail: airwin@ntca.org
Director, Communications: Wendy Mann
  E-Mail: wmann@ntca.org

Director, Training and Development: Dennis McGarry
   E-Mail: dmcgarry@ntca.org
Director, Meetings: Noni Nicolaou
   E-Mail: nnicolaou@ntca.org
Vice President, Human Resources: Barbara W. Ritter
   E-Mail: britter@ntca.org
Senior Vice President, Policy: Michael R. Romano
   E-Mail: mromano@ntca.org
Director, Information Technology: Denise M. Skotek
   E-Mail: dskotek@ntca.org
Director, Finance: Michael Smith
   E-Mail: msmith@ntca.org

Historical Note:
NTCA represents both cooperative and commercial, independent rural communications providers throughout America. Dedicated to improving the quality of life in rural communities through advanced telecommunications. Services Management Corporation (SMC) is a wholly owned subsidiary of NTCA. NTCA's membership is divided into 10 geographic regions. Membership: $300-700 (Subsidiary); $500 (International); $25 (Association).

Meetings/Conferences: Semi-Annual
Conference Chair: Noni Nicolaou
2013 - San Antonio, TX (Loews Grand Hyatt San Antonio)/Jan. 16 - 18
2013 - Lake Buena Vista, FL (Disney's Yacht and Beach Club)/Feb. 3 - 6
2013 - Austin, TX (Hyatt Regency Lost Pines Resort and Spa)/March 24 - 26
2013 - Minneapolis, MN (Hyatt Regency Minneapolis)/April 16 - 18
2013 - Atlanta, GA (InterContinental Buckhead Atlanta)/May 19 - 21
2013 - Memphis, TN (Peabody Memphis)/Aug. 26 - 29
2013 - Chicago, IL (Sheraton Chicago Hotel and Towers)/Sept. 15 - 18
2014 - San Antonio, TX (San Antonio Marriott Riverwalk)/Feb. 2 - 5
2014 - Orlando, FL (Walt Disney World Swan & Dolphin Resort)/June 15 - 17
2014 - San Francisco, CA (Hilton San Francisco Union Square)/Sept. 21 - 24
2015 - Scottsdale, AZ (Phoenician Resort)/Feb. 1 - 4
2015 - Phoenix, AZ (Phoenix Convention Center and Hyatt Regency)/March 8 - 11
2015 - Boston, MA (Sheraton Boston Hotel)/Sept. 19 - 23
2016 - Lake Buena Vista, FL (Disney's Yacht and Beach Club)/Jan. 31 - Feb. 3
2017 - San Diego, CA (Manchester Grand)/Feb. 5 - 8
Number of non-conference events/year: 25

Publications:
Membership Directory; on-line
Rural Telecom; bi-monthly; adv.
The New Edge; bi-weekly; adv.

Membership List Available to Non-members

National Terrazzo and Mosaic Association *(1924)*
138 W. Lower Crabapple
P.O. Box 2605
Fredericksburg, TX 78624
Tel: (800) 323-9736 *Fax*: (888) 362-2770
E-Mail: info@ntma.com
Website: ntma.com
Members: 200 individuals
Staff: 2
Annual Budget: $1-2,000,000

Personnel:
Chief Executive Officer: Richard Burns

Historical Note:
Mission is to provide complete specifications, color plates and general information to architects and designers free of cost. Membership is limited to competent Terrazzo Contractors. Associate membership is available to material suppliers who meets the NTMA standards. Membership: $1,932/year.

Publications:
Membership Directory; on-line

National Textile Association *(1854)*
Six Beacon St.
Suite 1125
Boston, MA 02108-3812
Tel: (617) 542-8220 *Fax*: (617) 542-2199
E-Mail: info@nationaltextile.org
Website: nationaltextile.org
Members: 200 companies
Staff: 8

Annual Budget: $500-1,000,000

Personnel:
President: Karl H. Spilhaus
   E-Mail: kspilhaus@nationaltextile.org
Office Administrator: Jane Lomas
Vice President, Regulatory and Technical Affairs: Hardy Poole
Director, Finance: Barry Ripley
Finance Director: Barry Ripley
Vice President, International Trade: David Trumbull
Treasurer: Henry Truslow III

Historical Note:
Established as the Nation Council of Cotton Manufacturing, later became the Northern Textile Association and then (2002) merged with the Knitted Textile Association to form the present organization, NTA's members are companies that work in a number of sectors of the textile industry and in supplier industries.

Continuing Education:
Certification Designation/s: CPSC

Publications:
NTA Newsletter; monthly

Membership List Available to Non-members

National Therapeutic Recreation Society
22377 Belmont Ridge Rd.
Ashburn, VA 20148-4501
Tel: (800) 626-6772
E-Mail: membership@nrpa.org
Website: recreationtherapy.com/history/ntrs/ntrs2005arc
Staff: 1

Personnel:
President: Jerry Jordan CTRS, PhD

Historical Note:
A branch of the National Recreation and Park Association, it specializes in the provision of therapeutic recreation services for persons with disabilities in clinical facilities and in the community. Members include practitioners, administrators, educators, volunteers, students, and consumers.

National Thoroughbred Racing Association *(1998)*
2525 Harrodsburg Rd.
Suite 400
Lexington, KY 40504
Tel: (859) 245-6872 *Fax*: (859) 223-3945
TollFree: (800) 792-6872
E-Mail: ntra@ntra.com
Website: ntra.com
Members: 30000 members
Staff: 12
Annual Budget: $5-10,000,000

Personnel:
President and Chief Executive Officer: Alex Waldrop
   E-Mail: alexwaldrop@ntra.com
Contact, Marketing: Keith Chamblin
   E-Mail: keithchamblin@ntra.com
Contact, Legislative Affairs: Peggy Hendershot
   E-Mail: phendershot@ntra.com
Contact, Media and Communications: Eric Wing
   E-Mail: ericwing@ntra.com

Historical Note:
NTRA's mission is to improve the popularity of Thoroughbred horse racing and to improve economic conditions in the industry for NTRA stakeholders.

National Tile Contractors Association *(1947)*
P.O. Box 13629
Jackson, MS 39236
Tel: (601) 939-2071 *Fax*: (601) 932-6117
Website: tile-assn.com
Members: 800 companies
Staff: 5
Annual Budget: $1-2,000,000
Tax: 501(c)(6)

Personnel:
Executive Director and Publisher: Bart A. Bettiga
   E-Mail: bart@tile-assn.com
Editor, TileLetter: Lesley A. Goddin
   E-Mail: lesley@tile-assn.com
Accountant: Lisa Murphy
   E-Mail: lisa@tile-assn.com
Contact, TileLetter and TADA Advertising Sales: Mary Shaw-Olson
   E-Mail: mary@tile-assn.com

Director, Training: Gerald Sloan
   E-Mail: gerald@tile-assn.com

Historical Note:
Formerly (1988) the Association of Tile Terrazzo, Marble Contractors and Affiliates and the Southern Tile, Terrazzo, Marble Contractors Association. NTCA serves every segment of the tile and stone industry, spearheading education for the professional installation of ceramic tile and allied products. Members are manufacturers, distributors, contractors, architects, designers and builders. Membership: $500 (Contractor/Manufacturer); $350 (Distributor); $250 (Consultant).

Meetings/Conferences: Annual
Number of non-conference events/year: 28

Publications:
E-Mail Newsletter; weekly
Membership Directory; annually; adv.
Tileletter Canada; quarterly; adv.
Tileletter US; monthly; adv.

Membership List Available to Non-members

National Tooling and Machining Association *(1943)*
1357 Rockside Rd.
Cleveland, OH 44134
Fax: (216) 264-2840
TollFree: (800) 248-6862
E-Mail: info@ntma.org
Website: ntma.org
Members: 2000 members
Staff: 21
Annual Budget: $25-50,000

Personnel:
President: David Tilstone
   E-Mail: dtilstone@ntma.org
Chief Operating Officer: Robert Akers
   E-Mail: rakers@ntma.org
Membership Officer: Rich Basalla
   E-Mail: rbasalla@ntma.org
Chief Financial Officer: John Capka
   E-Mail: jcapka@ntma.org
Director, Marketing: James R. Grosmann
   E-Mail: jgrosmann@ntma.org
Director, Events: Lynda Khoury
   E-Mail: lkhoury@ntma.org
Director, Information Systems: Bill Koppes
   E-Mail: bkoppes@ntma.org
Event Planner: Amanda Namenek
   E-Mail: anamenek@ntma.org

Historical Note:
Established as the National Tool and Die Manufacturers Association, it became the National Tool, Die and Precision Machining Association in 1960, and assumed its present name in 1980. NTMA's mission is to help members of the U.S. precision custom manufacturing industry achieve business success in a global economy through advocacy, advice, networking, information, programs, and services.

Meetings/Conferences:
Conference Chair: Lynda Khoury
2013 - Waikoloa, HI (Hilton Waikoloa Village)/March 5 - 8

Publications:
Membership Directory; on-line

National Tour Association *(1951)*
101 Prosperous Pl.
Suite 350
Lexington, KY 40509
Tel: (859) 264-6540 *Fax*: (859) 264-6570
TollFree: (800) 682-8886
E-Mail: questions@nta.travel
Website: ntaonline.com
Members: 3600 tour operators, destinations and suppliers
Staff: 30
Annual Budget: $5-10,000,000

Personnel:
President: Lisa Simon CTP
   E-Mail: lisa.simon@NTAstaff.com
Controller and Director, Human Resources: Cathy Boyd
   E-Mail: cathy.boyd@NTAstaff.com
Accounting Clerk: Claudia Duncan
   E-Mail: Claudia.Duncan@ntastaff.com
Director, Industry and Government Relations: Matt Grayson
   E-Mail: grayson@NTAstaff.com
Director, Marketing: Susan McDaniel

E-Mail: Susan.McDaniel@ntastaff.com
Director, Membership Relations: Katey Pease
E-Mail: katey.pease@ntastaff.com
Manager, Events: Lauren-Ashley Pope
E-Mail: Lauren-Ashley.Pope@ntastaff.com
Senior Vice President, Strategic Development: Catherine Prather
E-Mail: catherine.prather@NTAstaff.com
Public Affairs Advocate: Steve Richer
Manager, Public Relations: Bob Rouse
E-Mail: bob.rouse@NTAstaff.com
Manager, Education and Research: Jason Terwilliger
E-Mail: jason.terwilliger@ntastaff.com
Public Relations Specialist: Madeline Vied
E-Mail: madeline.vied@ntastaff.com
Editor in Chief: Penny Whitman
E-Mail: Penny.Whitman@NTAservicesinc.com

Historical Note:
Founded as National Tour Brokers Association; became (1983) National Tour Association. NTA is committed to providing business opportunities and professional education in an environment where its members can foster relationships with one another. Membership: $400 (Operator); $550-1,500 (Supplier); $550 (DMO); $135 (Educator); $335 (Associate).

Meetings/Conferences: Annual
Conference Chair: Lauren-Ashley Pope
2013 - Orlando, FL/Jan. 19 - 23
2013 - Orlando, FL (Orange County Convention Center)/Jan. 20 - 24
2014 - Los Angeles, CA/Feb. 16 - 20
2015 - New Orleans, LA/Jan. 17 - 21

Publications:
Courier magazine; monthly; adv.
Membership Directory; annually
Tuesday; weekly; adv.

National Tractor Parts Dealer Association *(1986)*
P.O. Box 1181
Gainesville, TX 76241
Tel: (940) 668-0900 *Fax*: (940) 668-1627
TollFree: (877) 668-0900
E-Mail: ntpda@ntpda.com
Website: ntpda.com
Members: 200 companies
Staff: 2
Annual Budget: $100-250,000

Personnel:
Manager, Operations: Kim Carroll
E-Mail: kim@ntpda.com
Coordinator, Events, Meeting Planner and Editor: Phyllis Cox

Historical Note:
NTPDA's purpose is to develop and maintain a quality of service oriented attitude that will improve the industry and create a sustainable competitive advantage for all members of the Association. Membership: $400/year (Regular/Associate).

Meetings/Conferences: Annual
Conference Chair: Phyllis Cox
2013 - Little Rock, AR (The Peabody Little Rock)/Jan. 30 - Feb. 2

Publications:
NTPDA Bulletin; quarterly; adv.

National Tractor Pullers Association *(1969)*
6155-B Huntley Rd.
Columbus, OH 43229
Tel: (614) 436-1761 *Fax*: (614) 436-0964
Website: ntpapull.com
Members: 5600 individuals
Staff: 9
Annual Budget: $25-50,000

Personnel:
Executive Director: David P. Schreier
Contact, Sales and Marketing: Kara Baker
Event Producer: Jim Miller
Office General Manager: Gregg Randall
E-Mail: gregg@ntpapull.com
Director, Technical Services and Event Operations: Larry Richwine
Contact, Accounting: Bev Ross
E-Mail: bev@ntpapull.com
Contact, Communications Technology and Scoreboard Operations: Joshua Steinmetz
Contact, Membership Operations: Helen Swartz
E-Mail: helen@ntpapull.com

Editor, Publications, Subscriptions and Web Mall: Sarah Toland
E-Mail: sarah@ntpapull.com

Historical Note:
NTPA's mission is to produce the quality performance forced induction systems, components and accessories, resulting in customer satisfaction and leading edge technology, based on a proven history of engineering and racing experience.

Meetings/Conferences:
Conference Chair: Jim Miller

Publications:
Membership Directory; on-line
Puller magazine; monthly

National Trailer Dealers Association *(1990)*
9864 E. Grand River Ave., Suite 110
P.O. Box 290
Brighton, MI 48116
Tel: (810) 229-5960 *Fax*: (810) 229-5961
TollFree: (800) 800-4552
E-Mail: info@ntda.org
Website: ntda.org
Members: 500 companies
Staff: 4
Annual Budget: $250-500,000
Tax: 501(c)(6)

Personnel:
Executive Director: Gwendolyn Brown
E-Mail: gwen@ntda.org

Historical Note:
NTDA's purpose is to promote the general good will and public relations of the independent trailer dealers. Members are companies with interests in all aspects of the semi-trailer industry. Membership: $399 (Dealer); $599 (Allied); $200 (Branch).

Meetings/Conferences: Annual

Publications:
Membership Directory; on-line; adv.
NTDA News Alert; monthly; adv.
TrailerTalk; bi-monthly; adv.

National Training and Simulation Association *(1988)*
2111 Wilson Blvd.
Suite 400
Arlington, VA 22201-3061
Tel: (703) 247-9471 *Fax*: (703) 243-1659
Website: trainingsystems.org
Members: 925 companies and individuals
Staff: 5
Annual Budget: $1-2,000,000

Personnel:
President: RADM James A. Robb
Director, Exhibits: Debbie L. Dyson
E-Mail: ddyson@ndia.org
Director, Conferences and Programs: Barbara McDaniel
E-Mail: bmcdaniel@ndia.org
Director, Membership Services: Patrick Rowe
E-Mail: prowe@ndia.org

Historical Note:
Changed its name from National Training Systems Association and merged with NDIA in 1992. NTSA fosters communication between the training agencies regarding requirements, procurement issues and policies and also provides industry forums, market surveys, business development information and other services to members. Represents companies in the simulation and training industry and training support services. Membership: $5,000 (Sustaining Corporate); $1,250-3,750 (Regular Corporate); $500 (Associate Corporate); $125 (Individual).

Continuing Education:
Enrollment: 250
Certification Designation/s: CMSP

Meetings/Conferences:
Conference Chair: Barbara McDaniel
Number of non-conference events/year: 3

Publications:
NTSA Newsletter; bi-monthly

Membership List Available to Non-members

National Transit Benefits Association
P.O. Box 25
Clifton, VA 20124
Tel: (703) 222-9373 *Fax*: (703) 222-9374
E-Mail: inquiries@ntba.info
Website: ntba.info

Staff: 2

Personnel:
Executive Director: Cynthia Fondriest Capelli
President: Larry Filler

Historical Note:
NTBA's purpose is to promote transit and vanpooling through the use of federal, state and local tax programs in order to reduce traffic congestion and improve air quality.

Publications:
Membership Directory; on-line
NTBA Newsletter; monthly

National Translator Association *(1962)*
6868 Vivian St.
Arvada, CO 80004
Tel: (303) 378-8209 *Fax*: (303) 465-4067
Website: tvfmtranslators.com
Members: 250 translator stations
Staff: 2
Annual Budget: $50-100,000
Tax: 501(c)(6)

Personnel:
Business Manager: Susan Hansen
E-Mail: shansen885@aol.com

Historical Note:
NTPA is dedicated to the preservation of free over-the-air TV and FM in all geographical areas. Membership: $200/year (Individual/Organization/Company).

Meetings/Conferences: Annual

Publications:
Membership Directory; on-line

National Trappers Association *(1959)*
2815 Washington Ave.
Bedford, IN 47421-2247
Tel: (812) 277-9670 *Fax*: (812) 277-9672
TollFree: (866) 680-8727
E-Mail: ntaheadquarters@nationaltrappers.com
Website: nationaltrappers.com
Members: 9000 individuals
Staff: 6
Annual Budget: $500-1,000,000
Tax: 501(c)(6)

Personnel:
President: Kraig Kaatz
E-Mail: kaatz@nationaltrappers.com
Manager, Finance: Aimee Carlisle
E-Mail: carlisle@nationaltroopers.com
Editor: Buddy Marsyada
E-Mail: marsyada@nationaltrappers.com
Secretary, Membership Services: Beth Roberts
E-Mail: broberts@nationaltrappers.com
Coordinator, Conventions: Daniel Skurski
E-Mail: skurski@nationaltrappers.com

Historical Note:
Formerly (1969) National Trappers Association of America. NTA is committed to defending and promoting the safe and ethical harvest of furbearing mammals and to the preservation and enhancement of their habitats. Membership: $30 (Individual); $35 (Canadian/Foreign U.S. Funds); $15 (Junior Members/Family Members); $350-750 (US Lifetime Members); $200 (US Senior Lifetime Members).

Meetings/Conferences: Annual
Conference Chair: Daniel Skurski
Number of non-conference events/year: 7

Publications:
American Trapper; quarterly; adv.

National Treasury Employees Union *(1938)*
1750 H St. NW
Suite 700
Washington, DC 20006
Tel: (202) 572-5500 *Fax*: (202) 572-5642
E-Mail: nteu-pr@nteu.org
Website: nteu.org
Members: 150000 Individuals and 31 Federal Agencies
Staff: 9
Annual Budget: $10-25,000,000
Tax: 501(c)(5)

Personnel:
National President: Colleen M. Kelley
E-Mail: nteu-pr@nteu.org
National Executive Vice President: Frank D. Ferris
E-Mail: fferr@nteu.org

Legislative and Political Director: Maureen Gilman
  E-Mail: maureen.gilman@nteu.org

Historical Note:
Founded as National Association of Collectors of Internal Revenue, became National Association of Internal Revenue Employees in 1970 and assumed its current name in 1973. NTEU's mission is to organize federal employees to work together to ensure that every federal employee is treated with dignity and respect.

Publications:
Membership Directory; on-line
NTEU DHS Update; monthly
NTEU Political Insider

Membership List Available to Non-members

National Trooper's Coalition (1977)
1875 I (Eye) St. NW
Suite 500
Washington, DC 20006
Tel: (202) 857-5200 *Fax:* (202) 429-9574
E-Mail: info@ntctroopers.com
Website: ntctroopers.com
Members: 42 Member Associations
Staff: 6
Tax: 501(c)(5)

Personnel:
Executive Director: Dennis Hallion
Contact, Government Relations: Bradford A. Card
Legal Counsel: Richard E. Mulvaney
Director, Communications: Michael Muth
Treasurer: William R. Staviski

Historical Note:
An advocacy group for state troopers. The NTC offers a vehicle for continuing efforts to better police services to the public. NTC is the national organization that solely represents the interests of State Trooper and Highway Patrol Associations.

Meetings/Conferences:
Conference Chair: David M. Latimer III

Publications:
NTC Magazine

National Truck and Heavy Equipment Claims Council (1961)
P.O. Box 5928
Fresno, CA 93755-5928
Tel: (559) 431-3774 *Fax:* (559) 436-4755
E-Mail: contact pr@nthecc.org
Website: nthecc.org
Members:
18 companies
55 individuals
Staff: 3
Annual Budget: $100-250,000

Personnel:
Administrator: Richard Bruce
  E-Mail: pr@nthecc.org

Historical Note:
Formerly, Truck and Heavy Equipment Claims Council, assumed it's current name in 1992. NTHECC's purpose is to promote and develop a standard of ethics in the handling of insurance claims and to promote activities designed to enable members to expedite and to make more efficient the servicing of insurance claims for the public. Membership: $150/year.

Meetings/Conferences:
2013 - Dallas, TX/May 3 - 4
2013 - Portland, OR/Oct. 10 - 12

Publications:
Member Listing; on-line; adv.

National Truck Equipment Association (1964)
37400 Hills Tech Dr.
Farmington Hills, MI 48331-3414
Tel: (248) 489-7090 *Fax:* (248) 489-8590
TollFree: (800) 441-6832
E-Mail: info@ntea.com
Website: ntea.com
Members: 1600 companies
Staff: 28
Annual Budget: $5-10,000,000
Tax: 501(c)(6)

Personnel:
Executive Director: Steve Carey CAE
  E-Mail: steve@ntea.com
Manager, Information Technology: Derek Eng
  E-Mail: derek@ntea.com

Director, Trade Shows and Events: Rob Gutierrez
  E-Mail: rob@ntea.com
Manager, Membership Services: Jim Hamilton
Manager, News and Information Services: Summer Marrs
  E-Mail: summer@ntea.com
Director, Communications: Terrie Skully
  E-Mail: terrie@ntea.com
Director, Sales and Services: Kathy Swartzentrover
  E-Mail: kathy@ntea.com

Historical Note:
NTEA's mission is to further the growth, profitability and professionalism of its members and function as the hub for the work truck industry. NTEA membership is composed of companies concerned with all aspects of the commercial truck and transportation equipment industry. Membership: $650- 1,700 (Distributor, based on annual sales volume); $950-2,700 (Manufacturer, based on annual sales volume); $325 (Distributor Branch).

Continuing Education:
Enrollment: 350
Certification Designation/s: MVP

Meetings/Conferences: Annual
Conference Chair: Rob Gutierrez
2013 - Indianapolis, IN (Indiana Convention Center)/
  March 6 - 8/10000 attendees/over 100 exhibitors

Publications:
Membership Roster and Product Directory; annually; adv.
NTEA Industry News Brief; weekly; adv.
NTEA Insider; bi-monthly; adv.
NTEA News; monthly; adv.
Work Truck Show News; on-line

Membership List Available to Non-members

National Truck Leasing System (1944)
1S450 Summit Ave.
Suite 300
Oakbrook Terrace, IL 60181-3990
Tel: (630) 953-8878 *Fax:* (630) 953-0040
TollFree: (800) 729-6857
E-Mail: Info@NationaLease.com
Website: nationalease.com
Members: 175 independent businesses and 22,000 people
Staff: 29
Annual Budget: $1-2,000,000

Personnel:
Chief Executive Officer: Doug Clark
Contact, Annual Meetings: Kate Barnes
  E-Mail: kbarnes@nationalease.com
Vice President, Member Services: Jane Clark

Historical Note:
Truck leasing organization in North America, with more than 700 facilities throughout the U. S and Canada, merged with AmeriQuest leasing members (2006). NTLS's mission is to provide customers with a flexible, quick response to their transportation needs. Members are independent truck leasing companies. Membership: based on size of company.

Meetings/Conferences: Annual
Conference Chair: Kate Barnes

National Tuberculosis Controllers Association
2452 Spring Rd. SE
Smyrna, GA 30080-3828
Tel: (678) 503-0503 *Fax:* (678) 503-0805
TollFree: (877) 503-0806
E-Mail: info@tbcontrollers.org
Website: tbcontrollers.org
Staff: 3
Annual Budget: $250-500,000

Personnel:
Executive Director: Carol Pozsik
  E-Mail: cpozsik@tbcontrollers.org

Historical Note:
NTCA seeks to advance the elimination of tuberculosis (TB) in the U.S. through the collective, concerted action of the officials of state, local, and territorial government who are empowered by their jurisdiction with the responsibility for carrying out programs to prevent and control TB. Membership: $100 (Active); $55 (Associate).

Meetings/Conferences: Tri-annual

Publications:
Member Directory; annually

National Tunis Sheep Registry (1929)
222 Main St.
P.O. Box 51

Milo, IA 50166
Tel: (641) 942-6402 *Fax:* (641) 942-6502
Website: tunissheep.org
Members: 187 individuals
Staff: 2
Annual Budget: $25-50,000

Personnel:
President and Interim Treasurer: Bill Kerns
  E-Mail: billkerns@charter.net
Editor: Louise Dunham
  E-Mail: tunis@bright.net

Historical Note:
NTSRI's mission is to provide information about the Tunis sheep breed, encourages its breeding, maintains a register of the pure-breds and issues certificates of registration and transfers. Membership: $20 (Senior); $10 (Junior).

Meetings/Conferences:
Number of non-conference events/year: 5

Publications:
Breeder Directory; on-line
Newsletter; quarterly

National Turf Writers and Broadcasters (1960)
3920 Grassy Creek Dr.
Lexington, KY 40514
Tel: (859) 219-9437 *Fax:* (859) 223-8338
E-Mail: info@turfwriters.org
Website: ntwab.org
Members: 225 individuals
Staff: 7
Annual Budget: $10-25,000

Personnel:
Contact, Membership: Ed DeRosa II

Historical Note:
The National Turf Writers and Broadcasters, formerly known as the National Turf Writers Association, changed its bylaws in 2010 to include members of the broadcasting profession. The NTWAB is organized to build a closer relationship among its members, improved working conditions, and better understanding of Thoroughbred racing and breeding.

Publications:
NTWA Member Roster; on-line
NTWAB Newsletter; on-line

National Turfgrass Federation (1991)
P.O. Box 106
Beltsville, MD 20704
Tel: (301) 504-5125 *Fax:* (301) 504-5167
E-Mail: info@turfresearch.org
Website: turfresearch.org
Staff: 1
Annual Budget: $25-50,000
Tax: 501(c)(6)

Personnel:
Executive Director: Kevin Morris

Historical Note:
NTF, was formed as the parent organization of the National Turfgrass Evaluation Program (NTEP). Now it is a new organization which coordinates the activities of the National Turfgrass Research Initiative (NTRI). The mission of NTF is to promote the need for turfgrass research and its associated value to society.

National Turkey Federation (1939)
1225 New York Ave. NW
Suite 400
Washington, DC 20005
Tel: (202) 898-0100 *Fax:* (202) 898-0203
E-Mail: info@turkeyfed.org
Website: eatturkey.com
Members: 4000 individuals
Staff: 12
Annual Budget: $1-2,000,000

Personnel:
President: Joel Brandenberger
  E-Mail: jbrandenberger@turkeyfed.org
Director, Membership Services: Jennifer Zukowski Dansereau
Vice President, Marketing and Communications: Sherrie L. Rosenblatt
  E-Mail: srosenblatt@turkeyfed.org
Vice President, Government Affairs: Damon Wells
  E-Mail: dwells@turkeyfed.org

Historical Note:
NTF is a national advocate for all segments of the turkey industry. Provides support to the U.S turkey industry in

marketing and government relations. Members of NTF include growers, processors, hatchers, breeders, distributors, allied services and state associations. Membership: $165-10,350/year.

Meetings/Conferences: Annual
Conference Chair: Jennifer Zukowski Dansereau

Publications:
Membership Directory; on-line
NTF Newsletter

Membership List Available to Non-members

National Tutoring Association (1992)
P.O. Box 6840
Lakeland, FL 33807-6840
Tel: (863) 529-5206 Fax: (863) 937-3390
E-Mail: ntatutor@aol.com
Website: ntatutor.com
Members: 16000 tutors
Staff: 2
Annual Budget: $50-100,000
Tax: 501(c)(3)

Personnel:
Executive Director and Interim Treasurer: Dr. Sandi Ayaz
   E-Mail: sayaz@ntatutor.com
Editor: Ray Blum

Historical Note:
NTA founded as National Organization of Tutoring and Mentoring Centers in 1992, became National Association of Tutoring in 1993. Purpose is to promote education, specialization, and scientific research. Members are individuals who are actively engaged in tutoring or tutoring program administration, and others with an interest in the field. Membership: $55 (Professional); $125 (Program); $455 (Institutional); $650-2,500 (Corporate); $10 (Student); $5-10 (International).

Continuing Education:
Certification Designation/s: NTACA

Meetings/Conferences: Annual

Publications:
NTA Newsletter; on-line

National U.S.-Arab Chamber of Commerce (1987)
1023 15th St. NW, Suite 400
Washington, DC 20005
Tel: (202) 289-5920 Fax: (202) 289-5938
E-Mail: info@nusacc.org
Website: nusacc.org
Members: 25,000 companies
Staff: 11
Annual Budget: $1-2,000,000
Tax: 501(c)(6)

Personnel:
President and Chief Executive Officer: David Hamod
Associate Director, Certifications: Nazha Benchaln CAE
   E-Mail: nbenchaln@nusacc.org
Associate Director, Communications: Dylan Davis
Director, Business Development: Amin Salam
Executive Vice President: Curt Silvers
   E-Mail: csilvers@nusacc.org

Historical Note:
NUSACC promotes business between the United States and the Arab world. Membership: $2500 (Gold); $5000 (Platinum); $15000 (Platinum Plus).

Publications:
Trade Data; annually
U.S.-Arab Trade Monitor
U.S.-Arab Tradeline; quarterly

National United Merchants Beverage Association (1979)
609 Ann St.
Homestead, PA 15120
Tel: (412) 678-9583 Fax: (412) 678-9584
Website: numba.biz/the_organization.html
Members: 5000 individuals
Staff: 3
Annual Budget: $100-250,000
Tax: 501(c)(6)

Personnel:
President: Melvin Cornelious
Administrative Secretary: Rosemary Allen
Financial Secretary: Gloria Bell

Historical Note:
NUMBA's goal is to strengthen the image of African Americans in the beverage industry by assisting in developing culturally sensitive, age appropriate marketing programs.

Meetings/Conferences: Annual

National Utility Contractors Association (NUCA) (1964)
3925 Chain Bridge Rd.
Suite 300
Fairfax, VA 22030
Tel: (703) 358-9300 Fax: (703) 358-9307
Website: nuca.com
Members: 2000 companies
Staff: 12
Annual Budget: $1-2,000,000

Personnel:
Vice President, Marketing and Communications: Bonnie Williams
   E-Mail: Bonnie@nuca.com

Historical Note:
NUCA represents companies that build, repair, and maintain water, wastewater, gas, telecommunications, and electric systems. Members are contractors, suppliers, and manufacturers involved in water, sewer, gas, electric, telecommunications, site work, and other segments of the industry.

Meetings/Conferences: Annual
2013 - Phoenix, AZ (Sheraton Phoenix Downtown Hotel)/Feb. 11 - 15
Number of non-conference events/year: 4

Publications:
Membership Directory; on-line
Safety Newsletters; on-line
Utility Contractor Magazine; monthly

Membership List Available to Non-members

National Vehicle Leasing Association (1968)
7250 Parkway Dr.
Suite 510
Hanover, MD 21076
Tel: (410) 782-2342 Fax: (410) 712-4038
TollFree: (800) 225-6852
E-Mail: info@nvla.org
Website: nvla.org
Members: 300 companies
Staff: 2
Annual Budget: $100-250,000
Tax: 501(c)(6)

Personnel:
Executive Director: Jack Tracey CAE

Historical Note:
Founded as an amalgamation of two separate groups of pioneer lessors (1968) in San Francisco, as the Automotive Leasing Association. Merged with the Southern California Leasing Association to become the California Vehicle Leasing Association. Expanded membership in 1981 to become the Western Vehicle Leasing Association and in 1984 voted to act as a national body under the name National Vehicle Leasing Association. NVLA's mission is to provide educational opportunities, promote responsible legislation and communicate with members regarding developments and trends in vehicle leasing. Membership: $695-2,495 (Regular); $695-1,295 (Associate).

Continuing Education:
Certification Designation/s: CVLE, CVLA

Meetings/Conferences: Annual

National Venture Capital Association (1973)
1655 N. Fort Myer Dr.
Suite 850
Arlington, VA 22209
Tel: (703) 524-2549 Fax: (703) 524-3940
Website: nvca.org
Members: 400 members
Staff: 13
Annual Budget: $5-10,000,000
Tax: 501(c)(6)

Personnel:
President: Mark G. Heesen
   E-Mail: mheesen@nvca.org
Accounting Manager: Beverley Badley
   E-Mail: bbadley@nvca.org
Manager, Administration and Meetings: Allyson Chappell
   E-Mail: achappell@aeeg.org
Senior Vice President, Federal Policy and Political Advocacy: Jennifer Connell Dowling
   E-Mail: jcdowling@nvca.org
Vice President, Membership and Member Firm Liaison: Janice Mawson
   E-Mail: jmawson@nvca.org

Vice President, Communications: Emily Mendell
   E-Mail: emendell@nvca.org
Chief Marketing Officer: Jeanne Lazarus Metzger
   E-Mail: jmetzger@nvca.org
Senior Vice President: Molly M. Myers
   E-Mail: mmyers@nvca.org
Manager, Membership and Database: Terry Samm
   E-Mail: tsamm@nvca.org
Head, Research: John S Taylor
   E-Mail: jstaylor@nvca.org

Historical Note:
NVCA ia an economic development group and serves as the definitive resource for venture capital data and unites members through a full range of professional services. Membership: $6,400-39,000/year.

Meetings/Conferences: Annual
Conference Chair: Allyson Chappell

Publications:
Membership Directory; on-line; adv.
NVCA Today; monthly
The Venture Capital Review; annually

National Verbatim Reporters Association (1967)
721 Cypress Point Dr.
Chappells, SC 29037
Tel: (601) 582-4345 Fax: (601) 582-3354
E-Mail: nvra@nvra.org
Website: nvra.org
Staff: 3
Annual Budget: $100-250,000

Personnel:
President: Becky Bazzle CVR

Historical Note:
NVRA advances the understanding, practice, education and professional standards of verbatim reporters and related reporting professionals by promoting ethical behavior, professional development, educational opportunities and support of individual reporters. Membership: $200 (General); $150 (Military); $185 (Associate); $100 (Student).

Publications:
NVRA's eVoice; monthly
SpeedMaster
Voice Writing Method

National Volunteer Fire Council (1976)
7852 Walker Dr.
Suite 450
Greenbelt, MD 20770
Tel: (202) 887-5700 Fax: (202) 887-5291
TollFree: (888) 275-6832
E-Mail: nvfcoffice@nvfc.org
Website: nvfc.org
Members: 13,097 individuals and associations
Staff: 13
Annual Budget: $2-5,000,000
Tax: 501(c)(3)

Personnel:
Executive Director: Heather Schafer CAE
   E-Mail: hschaefer@nvfc.org
Director, Finance: Melaku Alito
   E-Mail: malito@nvfc.org
Contact, Graphic Design Services: Susan Dyer
   E-Mail: advertising@nvfc.org
Director, Government Relations: David Finger
   E-Mail: dfinger@nvfc.org
Program Manager: Lori Moon
   E-Mail: lmoon@firecorps.org
Director, Communications: Kimberly Quiros
   E-Mail: kettinger@nvfc.org

Historical Note:
NVFC is a non-profit membership association representing the interests of the volunteer fire, EMS and rescue services. Members include state level organizations that represent volunteer firefighters and EMS personnel, volunteer fire departments, individual firefighters, corporate members, and a number of allied organizations. Membership: $15-10,000/year.

Meetings/Conferences:
Conference Chair: Lori Moon
Number of non-conference events/year: 4

Publications:
Dispatch; monthly; adv.
EMS Update; monthly; adv.
National Junior Firefighter Program E-news; bi-monthly; adv.
The Fire Corps E-Update; monthly; adv.

The Heart-Healthy Firefighter E-News; monthly; adv.

National Water Resources Association *(1932)*
3800 N. Fairfax Dr.
Suite Four
Arlington, VA 22203
Tel: (703) 524-1544 *Fax:* (703) 524-1548
E-Mail: nwra@nwra.org
Website: nwra.org
Members: 5000 individuals
Staff: 3
Annual Budget: $500-1,000,000

Personnel:
Executive Vice President: Thomas F. Donnelly
    E-Mail: tdonnelly@nwra.org
Vice President, Government Relations: Kris D. Polly
    E-Mail: kpolly@nwra.org

Historical Note:
Formerly (1970) National Reclamation Association. Operates in 16 western states. Members are directors of water resource development projects such as irrigation districts, canal companies, conservancy districts and water users in general. NWRA advocates federal policies, legislation and regulations promoting protection, management, development and beneficial use of water resources. Memberships available through state associations and the Professional Services Council.

Meetings/Conferences: Annual
2014 - Coronado, CA (Hotel del Coronado)/Nov. 12 - 14
2016 - Coronado, CA (Hotel del Coronado)/Nov. 30 - Dec. 2
Number of non-conference events/year: 2

Publications:
Water News Daily; daily

National Watercolor Society *(1920)*
915 S. Pacific Ave.
San Pedro, CA 90731
Tel: (310) 831-1099
E-Mail: nws-art@hotmail.com
Website: nationalwatercolorsociety.org
Members: 1700 individuals
Staff: 15
Annual Budget: $100-250,000
Tax: 501(c)(3)

Personnel:
President: Linda A. Doll
    E-Mail: NWSPresident@gmail.com
Director, Annual Exhibition: Penny Hill
    E-Mail: NWSAnnualExhib@gmail.com
Director, Membership and Communications: Kathleen Mooney
    E-Mail: kmooney@iserv.net
Treasurer: Vickie Myers
    E-Mail: NWSTreasurer@gmail.com

Historical Note:
Formerly, California National Watercolor Society (1967) and assumed its current name in 1975. NWS is committed to the exhibition and promotion of water media painting. Membership: $40/year (Associate).

Meetings/Conferences: Annual
Conference Chair: Penny Hill

Publications:
Membership Direcotry; annually
NWS News - Newsletter; quarterly

National Watermelon Association *(1914)*
5129 S. Lakeland Dr.
Suite One
Lakeland, FL 33813
Tel: (863) 619-7575 *Fax:* (863) 619-7577
E-Mail: nwa@tampabay.rr.com
Website: nationalwatermelonassociation.com
Members: 700 individuals
Staff: 2
Annual Budget: $1-2,000,000
Tax: 501(c)(6)

Personnel:
Executive Director: Bob Morrissey
    E-Mail: bmorrissey@tampabay.rr.com
Secretary and Bookkeeper: Monica McCook
    E-Mail: nwa@tampabay.rr.com

Historical Note:
Formerly (1945) known as National Watermelon Growers and Distributors Association, assumed its current name in 1979. NWA's purpose is to promote the interests of the Watermelon Industry from production to consumption. Members are producers, distributors and sellers of watermelons and related support industries. Membership: $150/year (Individual).

Meetings/Conferences: Annual
2013 - San Antonio, TX (Westin La Cantera Hill Country Resort)/Feb. 20 - 24
2014 - Savannah, GA (Savannah Marriott Riverfront)/ Feb. 19 - 23
2015 - La Quinta, CA (La Quinta Resort and Club, A Waldorf Astoria Resort)/Feb. 18 - 22
2016 - New Orleans, LA (Hyatt Regency)/Feb. 24 - 28
Number of non-conference events/year: 11

Publications:
Off The Vine; quarterly
The Vineline magazine; quarterly; adv.

National Waterways Conference *(1960)*
1100 N. Glebe Rd.
Suite 1010
Arlington, VA 22201
Tel: (703) 224-8007 *Fax:* (866) 371-1390
E-Mail: info@waterways.org
Website: waterways.org
Members: 350 businesses
Staff: 2
Annual Budget: $250-500,000
Tax: 501(c)(6)

Personnel:
President: Amy W Larson Esq.
    E-Mail: amy@waterways.org
Director, Internal Operations: Carole Wright

Historical Note:
NWC's mission is to effect policies and programs, recognizing the public value of the Nation's water resources and their contribution to public safety, a competitive economy, national security, environmental quality and energy conservation. Membership includes waterway associations, carriers, public agencies, shippers, and waterway services. Membership: $1050 (Associations); $1,500 (Corporate); $1305 (Public Members).

Meetings/Conferences: Annual
2013 - Washington, DC (The Madison)/March 11 - 13

Publications:
Membership Directory; on-line; adv.
NWC Newsletter; quarterly
The Waterways Journal

National Weather Association *(1975)*
228 W. Millbrook Rd.
Raleigh, NC 27609-4304
Tel: (919) 845-7121 *Fax:* (919) 845-2956
E-Mail: exdir@nwas.org
Website: nwas.org
Members: 54 corporations and 3000 individuals
Staff: 2
Annual Budget: $250-500,000
Tax: 501(c)(6)

Personnel:
Executive Director: Stephen W Harned CCM
    E-Mail: exdir@nwas.org
Newsletter Technical Editor: Winnie Crawford
    E-Mail: nwanewsletter@nwas.org

Historical Note:
NWA is a professional association supporting and promoting excellence in operational meteorology and related activities. Awards Radio-Television Weather-caster Seal of Approval through testing and a continuing education requirement. Sponsors an annual awards program; provides grants to teachers to help improve teaching of meteorology in grades K-12; and has recently started a college scholarship program. Membership: $45 (Regular); $18 (Student/Retired/Military Member/Spouse of Regular Member); $200 (Corporate).

Meetings/Conferences: Annual
2013 - North Charleston, SC (Charleston Convention Center)/Oct. 12 - 17
Number of non-conference events/year: 7

Publications:
Electronic Journal of Operational Meteorology; on-line
National Weather Digest; semi-annually; adv.
NWA Newsletter; monthly; adv.

National Weather Service Employees Organization *(1976)*
601 Pennsylvania Ave. NW
Suite 900
Washington, DC 20004-2612
Tel: (202) 907-3036 *Fax:* (703) 293-9651
Website: nwseo.org
Members: 4000 Individuals
Staff: 4
Annual Budget: $500-1,000,000
Tax: 501(c)(5)

Personnel:
National President: Daniel "Dan" Sobien
    E-Mail: president@nwseo.org
General Counsel and Director, Legislative: Richard J. Hirn
Director, Communications: Lisa Luciani
    E-Mail: mediarelations@nwseo.org
Director, Membership Services: Peter J. Nuhn
    E-Mail: Peter@nwseo.org

Historical Note:
NWSEO is the labor organization and professional association that represents 4,000 employees of the National Oceanic and Atmospheric Administration in the U.S. Department of Commerce. Membership: $555.67 (Annual Membership); $65 (Associate); $45 (Retiree).

Meetings/Conferences: Annual

Publications:
Four Winds -Newsletter
Membership Directory; on-line

National Wellness Institute, Inc. *(1977)*
1300 College Ct.
P.O. Box 827
Stevens Point, WI 54481-0827
Tel: (715) 342-2969 *Fax:* (715) 342-2979
E-Mail: nwi@nationalwellness.org
Website: nationalwellness.org
Members: 1215 individuals
Staff: 5
Annual Budget: $500-1,000,000
Tax: 501(c)(3)

Personnel:
Executive Director and Director, Membership and Operations: Brandan DuChateau
    E-Mail: brandan@nationalwellness.org
Coordinator, Conference and Manager, Business and Records: Mandy Koch
    E-Mail: mandy@nationalwellness.org
Director, Education and Outreach: Trina Laube
    E-Mail: trina@nationalwellness.org
Marketing and Outreach Associate: Jennifer Mitchell
    E-Mail: jennifer@nationalwellness.org
Programmer Systems Analyst Consultant: Walter Wright
    E-Mail: walter@nationalwellness.org

Historical Note:
NWI's mission is to serve the professionals and organizations that promote optimal health and wellness in individuals and communities. Membership: $275-375 (Organization); $125-225 (Individual); $15 (Student).

Continuing Education:
Certification Designation/s: CWPD, CWPC, CWPM, CWP

Meetings/Conferences: Annual
Conference Chair: Mandy Koch
2013 - Stevens Point, WI (University of Wisconsin, Stevens Point)/July 15 - 18

Publications:
Member Directory; on-line
The American Journal of Health Promotion; bi-monthly; adv.

Membership List Available to Non-members

National Wheelchair Basketball Association *(2010)*
1130 Elkton St.
Suite C
Colorado Springs, CO 80907
Tel: (719) 266-4082 *Fax:* (719) 266-4876
Website: nwba.org
Staff: 2
Annual Budget: $500-1,000,000

Personnel:
Executive Director: Randy Schubert
    E-Mail: randyschubert@nwba.org
Contact, Web Administration: Cesar Hernandez
    E-Mail: cesar@nwba.org

Historical Note:
NWBA provides qualified individuals with physical disabilities the opportunity to play, learn and compete in the sport of wheelchair basketball.

Publications:
Down to Earth Newsletter

Men Matters; on-line
NWBA Newsletter; on-line

National WIC Association (1983)
2001 S St. NW
Suite 580
Washington, DC 20009-1165
Tel: (202) 232-5492 *Fax:* (202) 387-5281
Website: nwica.org
Members: 2800 individuals and agencies
Staff: 8
Annual Budget: $2-5,000,000
Tax: 501(c)(3)

Personnel:
President & Chief Executive Officer: Rev. Douglas A.
  Greenaway MArch
  E-Mail: douglasg@nwica.org
Events Coordinator and Executive Assistant: DuWvaughn
  Pierre Francois
  E-Mail: dfrancois@nwica.org
Coordinator, Communications, Media and Marketing:
  Samantha Lee
  E-Mail: slee@nwica.org
Coordinator, Membership Services: Robert A. Lee
  E-Mail: rlee@nwica.org
Director, Nutrition Programs and Staff: Cecilia
  Richardson MS RD LD
  E-Mail: crichardson@nwica.org

Historical Note:
*NWA provides service for supporting, inspiring and
empowering the WIC Community through creativity,
teamwork and leadership to serve America's low-income,
high-risk women, infants and children. Members are state
and local agency directors and nutrition coordinators of the
Special Supplemental Nutrition Program for Women, Infants
and Children Membership: $25,000 (Sustaining-Business
Council Partner, minimum); $50- 400 (State/Local agency);
$2,500-20,000 (Sustaining- Founder/Benefactor/Patron/
Donor); $10-50 (Individual/Student/Retired).*

Meetings/Conferences:
Conference Chair: DuWvaughn Pierre Francois
Number of non-conference events/year: 2

Publications:
Association Update
Food Price Brief; monthly
Legislative Alert; weekly
Membership Directory; on-line
Monday Morning Report; weekly

National Wildlife Federation (1936)
P.O. Box 1583
Merrifield, VA 22116-1583
Tel: (703) 438-6000
TollFree: (800) 822-9919
Website: nwf.org
Staff: 13
Annual Budget: Over $100,000,000
Tax: 501(c)(3)

Personnel:
President and Chief Executive Officer: Larry J. Schweiger
Chief Financial Officer: Dulce Gomez-Zormelo
Executive Vice President and Chief Operating Officer:
  Jaime Berman Matyas

Historical Note:
*NWF's mission is to inspire Americans to protect wildlife for
the future and it provides resources on wildlife conservation
and at-risk species to the public and media. Membership:
$30/year.*

Continuing Education:
Certification Designation/s: WHC

Meetings/Conferences: Annual

Publications:
Eco-Schools USA E-Newsletters; monthly
National Wildlife magazine; adv.
Wildlife Online: Habitats; quarterly

National Wildlife Rehabilitators Association
(1982)
2625 Clearwater Rd.
Suite 110
St. Cloud, MN 56301
Tel: (320) 230-9920 *Fax:* (320) 230-3077
E-Mail: nwra@nwrawildlife.org
Website: nwrawildlife.org
Members: 250 organizations and 1500
individuals
Staff: 4

Annual Budget: $250-500,000
Tax: 501(c)(3)

Personnel:
Manager, Central Office: Deb Dohrmann
Editor: Lessie Davis
  E-Mail: editor@nwrawildlife.org
Webmaster: Michele Goodman
Book keeper and Accounting Clerk: Deb Mortenson

Historical Note:
*NWRA's mission is to improve and promote the profession
of wildlife rehabilitation and its contributions to preserving
natural ecosystems. Members are professional wildlife
rehabilitators and others with an interest in wild animal
care. Membership: $25-2,500/year.*

Meetings/Conferences: Annual
2013 - Portland, OR (DoubleTree by Hilton)/March 5 -
  9/400 attendees

Publications:
Newsletter
NWRA Membership Directory; annually

National Woman's Party (1916)
144 Constitution Ave. NE
C/O Sewall-Belmont House and Museum
Washington, DC 20002-5608
Tel: (202) 546-1210
E-Mail: info@sewallbelmont.org
Website: sewallbelmont.org/learn/national-
  womans-party
Staff: 28
Annual Budget: $500-1,000,000

Personnel:
Executive Director: Page Harrington
Manager, Public Programs and Outreach: Elisabeth Crum
Manager, Membership and Development: Chitra Panjabi

Historical Note:
*In 1917, the two organizations formally merged to form the
National Woman's Party (NWP). NWP seeks to educate the
public about the women's rights movement and to use and
preserve the Sewall-Belmont House, with its outstanding
historic library and suffragist and ERA archives, to tell
the inspiring story of a century of courageous activism by
American women.*

Meetings/Conferences:
Conference Chair: Elisabeth Crum

National Women's Studies Association (1977)
11 E. Mount Royal Ave.
Suite 100
Baltimore, MD 21202
Tel: (410) 528-0355 *Fax:* (410) 528-0357
E-Mail: nwsaoffice@nwsa.org
Website: nwsa.org
Members: 3000 individuals
Staff: 8
Annual Budget: $500-1,000,000
Tax: 501(c)(3)

Personnel:
Executive Director: Allison Kimmich
  E-Mail: allison.kimmich@nwsa.org
Contact, Membership, Educational Outreach and Programs:
  Nupur Chaudhuri
Operations Manager: Kira Wisniewski

Historical Note:
*NWSA members are teachers, students, independent
scholars, program administrators, and community activists.
NWSA promotes the field of women's studies in educational
and social transformation. Membership: $150-235
(Individual, based on income); $90 (Student/Unemployed/
Retired); $225-600 (Institution/Affiliate Institution).*

Meetings/Conferences: Annual
Conference Chair: Nupur Chaudhuri
2013 - Cincinnati, OH (Hilton Cincinnati Netherland
  Plaza)/Nov. 7 - 10
2015 - Milwaukee, WI (Hilton Milwaukee Downtown)/
  Nov. 12 - 15

Publications:
Member Directory

Membership List Available to Non-members

National Wood Flooring Association (1986)
111 Chesterfield Industrial Blvd.
Chesterfield, MO 63005
Tel: (636) 519-9663 *Fax:* (636) 519-9664
TollFree: (800) 422-4556
E-Mail: info@nwfa.org
Website: nwfa.org

Members: 3500 Individuals
Staff: 17
Annual Budget: $2-5,000,000
Tax: 501(c)(6)

Personnel:
President and Chief Executive Officer: Michael Martin
  E-Mail: michaelm@nwfa.org
Director, Technical Support: Don Conner
  E-Mail: donc@nwfa.org
Contact, Membership Services: Penny Erb
  E-Mail: pennye@nwfa.org
Director, Communications and Contact, Conventions:
  Anita Howard
  E-Mail: anitah@nwfa.org

Historical Note:
*Merged (2009) with NOFMA, the Wood Flooring
Manufacturers Association. An international trade
association for the wood flooring industry, providing
technical training, publications, educational videos,
management education programs, and membership services
that assist members in operating their businesses more
successfully. NWFA's worldwide membership includes wood
flooring manufacturers, dealers, contractors and wholesale
distributors. Membership: $425/year.*

Continuing Education:
Certification Designation/s: NWFA CP, WFI, S&F,
WFI,S&C, WFSC

Meetings/Conferences: Annual
Conference Chair: Anita Howard
2013 - Dallas, TX (Gaylord Texan Hotel and
  Convention Center-Dallas)/April 2 - 5

Publications:
Hardwood Floors E-News; on-line; adv.

National Wood Tank Institute (1854)
5500 N. Water St.
P.O. Box 2755
Philadelphia, PA 19120
Tel: (215) 329-9022 *Fax:* (215) 329-1177
E-Mail: woodtanks@aol.com
Website: woodtank.com
Members: 8 companies
Staff: 1
Annual Budget: Under $10,000

Personnel:
General Manager: Jack Hillman
  E-Mail: jackhillman@woodtank.com

Historical Note:
*NWTI members are companies and individuals in the
U.S. and Canada involved in the manufacture of wood
tanks, vats and pipes. Goal is to continue manufacturing,
servicing, installing and inspecting wooden tanks the
way it has always been meant; with care, quality and
craftsmanship.*

Publications:
S-82-Specifications for Wood Tanks and Pipes

National Wooden Pallet and Container
Association (1947)
1421 Prince St.
Suite 340
Alexandria, VA 22314-2805
Tel: (703) 519-6104 *Fax:* (703) 519-4720
Website: palletcentral.com
Members: 700 companies
Staff: 12
Annual Budget: $2-5,000,000
Tax: 501(c)(6)

Personnel:
President: Sam McAdow
Director, Administration: Edna Coppage
  E-Mail: ecoppage@palletcentral.com
Technical Director: Edgar Deomano PhD
  E-Mail: palletinfo@palletcentral.com
Director, Sales and Membership Services: Darryl Gale
  E-Mail: dgale@palletcentral.com
General Counsel: Jan Holt
Publisher: Pamela Krewson
  E-Mail: pkrewson@palletcentral.com
Manager, Membership Services: Karen Saucier
  E-Mail: ksaucier@palletcentral.com
Director, Meetings and Education: Isabel "Mimi" Sullivan
  E-Mail: msullivan@palletcentral.com
Vice President, Industry and Government Affairs: Karen
  Wanamaker
  E-Mail: kwanamaker@palletcentral.com

Historical Note:

Founded National Wooden Pallet Manufacturers Association. Merged with National Wooden Pallet Manufacturers Association and assumed the current name in 1966. NWPCA is dedicated to serve its members by helping them create cost-effective, environmentally responsible solutions to meet their customers' changing unit load handling needs. Members are manufacturers, recyclers and distributors of pallets, containers and reels, and companies that supply products, equipment, and services to the industry. Membership: $500-5,000 (Industry); $800-1,500 (International); $1,325-2,350 (Associate); $825 (End User).

Meetings/Conferences: Annual
Conference Chair: Isabel "Mimi" Sullivan
2013 - Orlando, FL (Loews Portofino Bay Hotel)/Feb. 16 - 19
2013 - Dallas, TX (Dallas Marriott City Center)/Oct. 11 - 13
2014 - Ft. Lauderdale, FL (Marriott Harbor Beach Fort Lauderdale Resort and Spa)/March 1 - 4
Number of non-conference events/year: 2

Publications:
Membership Directory; on-line
PalletCentral; adv.
PalletCentral newsletter; monthly; adv.

National Woodland Owners Association (1983)
374 Maple Ave., East
Suite 310
Vienna, VA 22180
Tel: (703) 255-2700 Fax: (703) 281-9200
TollFree: (800) 476-8733
E-Mail: info@woodlandowners.org
Website: woodlandowners.org
Members: 25000 individuals
Staff: 4
Annual Budget: $100-250,000

Personnel:
President and Chief Executive Officer: Keith A Argow
E-Mail: argow@nwoa.net
Treasurer: Dale Zaug
E-Mail: northcentral@nwoa.net

Historical Note:
NWOA's purpose is to develop policy, legislation and representation at the national level as one unified voice as well as provide educational and networking opportunities to landowners throughout the country. Membership: $35 (Individual); $45 (Sustaining).

Continuing Education:
Certification Designation/s: GTFC

Publications:
Family Lands & Conservation magazine
National Woodlands magazine; quarterly

National Wrestling Coaches Association (1928)
P.O. Box 254
Manheim, PA 17545
Tel: (717) 653-8009 Fax: (717) 653-8270
Website: nwcaonline.com
Staff: 11
Annual Budget: $1-2,000,000

Personnel:
Executive Director: Mike Moyer
E-Mail: mmoyer@nwca.cc
Office Manager: Amy Dicato
E-Mail: adicato@nwca.cc
Coordinator, Coaching Development: John Licata
E-Mail: jlicata@nwca.cc
Manager, Finance: Don Shelly
E-Mail: dshelly@nwca.cc
Chief Operating Officer: Pat Tocci
E-Mail: ptocci@nwca.cc

Historical Note:
NWCA's mission is dedicated to serve and provide leadership for the advancement of all levels of the sport of wrestling with primary emphasis on scholastic and collegiate wrestling programs. The membership embraces all people who are interested in amateur wrestling.Membership: $30-225/year

Meetings/Conferences: Annual
2013 - Los Cabos, MX (Westin Resort and Spa)/Aug. 2 - 4

Publications:
Amateur Wrestling News; monthly
WIN Magazine

National Writers Association (1937)
10940 S. Parker Rd.

Suite 508
Parker, CO 80134-7440
Tel: (303) 841-0246 Fax: (303) 841-2607
E-Mail: natlwritersassn@hotmail.com
Website: nationalwriters.com
Members: 3000 individuals
Staff: 1
Annual Budget: $50-100,000
Tax: 501(c)(3)

Personnel:
Executive Director: Sandy Whelchel

Historical Note:
NWA's mission is to to enhance the future of writers by fostering continuing education through awarding scholarships and providing no or low cost workshops and seminars. A non-profit organization that provides education and an ethical resource for writers at all levels of experience. Membership: $65 (Professional); $85 (Professional); $35 (Student).

Publications:
PROFESSIONAL FREELANCE WRITER'S DIRECTORY; on-line
AUTHORSHIP MAGAZINE; quarterly
NWA MARKET UPDATE; quarterly
NWA NEWSLETTER; monthly

National Writers Union (1983)
256 W. 38th St.
Suite 703
New York, NY 10018
Tel: (212) 254-0279 Fax: (212) 254-0673
E-Mail: nwu@nwu.org
Website: nwu.org
Members: 1600 members
Staff: 17
Annual Budget: $1-2,000,000

Personnel:
President: Larry Goldbetter
Contact, Membership Services: Leanna Millan
E-Mail: lmillan@nwu.org
Financial Secretary and Treasurer: Mitzi Runyard

Historical Note:
Originated in New York City in October, 1981 in connection with the American Writers Congress, it's an independent union established to improve the working conditions of freelance writers through the collective strength of its members. NWU members include journalists, novelists, biographers, historians, poets, children's book authors, textbook authors, commercial writers, technical writers and cartoonists. Membership: $120-340/year (based on Income).

National Yogurt Association (1987)
2000 Corporate Ridge
Suite 1000
McLean, VA 22102
Tel: (703) 821-0770 Fax: (703) 821-1350
Website: aboutyogurt.com
Members: 5 companies
Staff: 5
Annual Budget: $250-500,000
Tax: 501(c)(6)

Personnel:
Executive Director: Elise Cortina
E-Mail: ecortina@affi.com
President: Kraig R. Naasz
E-Mail: knaasz@affi.com
Vice President, Communications: Corey Corey Henry
E-Mail: chenry@aboutyogurt.com
Senior Vice President, Public Policy and International Affairs: Robert L. Garfield
E-Mail: rgarfield@affi.com

Historical Note:
NYA strives to advance the interests of the live and active culture yogurt industry. Members are manufacturers and marketers of live and active culture yogurt products and the suppliers to the industry.

National Young Farmers Education Association
P.O. Box 20326
Montgomery, AL 36120
Tel: (334) 213-3276 Fax: (334) 213-0421
E-Mail: natloffice@nyfea.org
Website: nyfeaweb.org
Staff: 2
Annual Budget: $100-250,000
Tax: 501(c)(3)

Personnel:

President: C. J. Fleenor
secretary: Allen Tyler

Historical Note:
National Young Farmer Educational Association, is the official adult student organization for agricultural education as recognized by the USA. Membership: $250 (Affiliate).

Meetings/Conferences: Annual

Publications:
NYFEA E-Update; quarterly

Native American Contractors Association (2003)
1514 P St. NW
Suite Two
Washington, DC 20005
Tel: (202) 758-2676 Fax: (202) 355-1399
E-Mail: membership@nativecontractors.org
Website: nativecontractors.org
Members: 49 member companies
Staff: 7
Annual Budget: $1-2,000,000

Personnel:
Executive Director: Kevin J. Allis
Director, Legislative: Lael Echo-Hawk
Director, External Affairs: Jennine J. Elias
Executive Assistant: Denise Pollock

Historical Note:
The Native American Contractors Association's (NACA's) mission is to enhance self-determination through preservation and enhancement of government contracting participation based on the unique relationship between Native Americans and the federal government. Membership: $530-25,032.50/year.

Meetings/Conferences: Annual

Publications:
Member Legislative and Media Alerts; bi-weekly

Native American Journalists Association (1983)
University of Oklahoma, Gaylord College
395 W. Lindsey St.
Norman, OK 73019-4201
Tel: (405) 325-9008 Fax: (405) 325-6945
Website: naja.com
Members: 600 individuals
Staff: 3
Annual Budget: $250-500,000
Tax: 501(c)(3)

Personnel:
President: Rhonda LeValdo
E-Mail: rhondalevaldo@gmail.com
Treasurer: Tristan Ahtone
E-Mail: tahtone@gmail.com
Director, Marketing: Heather Dutcher
E-Mail: has@ou.edu

Historical Note:
Formerly Native American Press Association (NAPA), the name was changed in 1990, to the Native American Journalists Association. NAJA serves and empowers Native journalists through programs and actions designed to enrich journalism and promote Native cultures. Membership: $1,000 (Lifetime Individual/Lifetime Associate); $55 (Individual/Associate); $20 (Student); $10 (High School Student); $250-500 (Institutional).

Publications:
Annual Conference Program; annually; adv.
NAJA Student Projects; annually; adv.

Natural Areas Association
P.O. Box 1504
Bend, OR 97709
Tel: (541) 317-0199 Fax: (541) 317-0140
Website: naturalarea.org
Staff: 3
Annual Budget: $100-250,000

Personnel:
Director: Deb Kraus
Editor: Dr. Ronald Hiebert
Administrative Assistant and Membership Coordinator: Karen Lorberau

Historical Note:
The mission of the Natural Areas Association is to advance the preservation of natural diversity. The Association works to inform, unite, and support persons engaged in identifying, protecting, managing, and studying natural areas and biological diversity across landscapes and ecosystems. Membership: $60 (Individual); $35(Student/ Retired); $175 (Library); $240 (Agency/Organization/ Business); $90 (Family); $1,000 (Individual Life).

Publications:
Newsletter
Natural Areas Journal; quarterly

Natural Colored Wool Growers Association
(1977)
19477 Indian Rd.
Kellyville, OK 74039
Tel: (918) 247-4082 *Fax:* (918) 688-3365
Website: ncwga.org
Members: 850 individuals
Staff: 4
Annual Budget: $10-25,000

Personnel:
Secretary: Kate Lowder
  E-Mail: kmlowder@aol.com

Historical Note:
NCWGA's purpose is to assist members in the development and promotion of naturally-colored sheep and their wool, providing educational information on wool growth, quality, and color genetics. Membership: $20 (Regular); $15 (Associate); $5 (Junior).

Publications:
Membership Directory; on-line
The Marker; quarterly; adv.

Natural Gas Supply Association *(1965)*
1620 Eye St. NW
Suite 700
Washington, DC 20006
Tel: (202) 326-9300 *Fax:* (202) 326-9330
Website: ngsa.org
Members: 12 companies
Staff: 8
Annual Budget: $2-5,000,000
Tax: 501(c)(6)

Personnel:
President: R. Skip Horvath
  E-Mail: skip.horvath@ngsa.org
Vice President, Markets and Government Relations:
  Jennifer "Jenny" Fordham
  E-Mail: jfordham@ngsa.org
President And Chief Executive Officer: Ralph E. Horvath
Senior Vice President: Patricia Jagtiani
  E-Mail: pjagtiani@ngsa.org
Director, Political Communications: Jeff Schrade
  E-Mail: jeff.schrade@ngsa.org

Historical Note:
Formerly (1979) Natural Gas Supply Committee. NGSA encourages the use of natural gas within a balanced national energy policy, and promotes the benefits of competitive markets for transportation, delivery, and increasing the supply of natural gas to U.S. customers. Members are domestic natural gas producers and marketers.

Natural Products Association *(1936)*
1773 T St. NW
Washington, DC 20009
Tel: (202) 223-0101 *Fax:* (202) 223-0250
TollFree: (800) 966-6632
E-Mail: natural@npainfo.org
Website: npainfo.org
Members: 1,900 members and 10000 retailers,
manufacturers and distributors, etc
Staff: 17
Annual Budget: $2-5,000,000
Tax: 501(c)(3)

Personnel:
Executive Director and Chief Executive Officer: John Shaw
  E-Mail: jshaw@NPAinfo.org
Vice President, Membership Services: Gabrielle
  Alahouzos
Director, Government Relations: Elizabeth Hurst
  E-Mail: ehurst@NPAinfo.org
Manager, Communications: Sandra Y. Jackson
  E-Mail: sjackson@naturalproductsassoc.org
Director, Communications: Michael Keaton
  E-Mail: mkeaton@NPAInfo.org
Director, Marketing: Meg Mader
  E-Mail: mmader@NPAInfo.org
Senior Vice President and Chief Financial Officer: Brent
  Weickert
  E-Mail: bweickert@npainfo.org

Historical Note:
Absorbed the American Dietary Retailers Association in 1969, became the National Nutritional Foods Association in 1970 and assumed its present name in 2007. NPA's mission is to advocate for the rights of consumers to

have access to products that will maintain and improve their health, and for the rights of retailers and suppliers to sell these products. Members are natural, nutritional, and dietary food retailers, distributors and producers. *Membership:* $49 (Retailer); $670-1,910 (Associate Non-voting); $515-40,400 (Supplier-Voting) /year.

Continuing Education:
Certification Designation/s: NPA GMPC

Meetings/Conferences: Annual

Publications:
Federal Focus; monthly; adv.
Natural Products Association Natural News Update;
  weekly; adv.
Natural Products Association Now; bi-monthly
Science Matters; monthly; adv.

Natural Science Collections Alliance *(1972)*
Florida Museum of Natural History
P.O. Box 112710
Gainesville, FL 32611
Tel: (352) 337-6649
E-Mail: nsca@burkinc.com
Website: nscalliance.org
Members: 108 institutions and societies
Staff: 3
Annual Budget: $50-100,000
Tax: 501(c)(3)

Personnel:
President: Lawrence Page

Historical Note:
Formerly (2001) Association of Systematics Collections. NSC's mission is to support natural science collections, their human resources, the institutions that house them, and their activities. Members are museums, zoos, botanic gardens and other systematic collections housed at universities, non-profit research institutions, state-funded institutions, governmental agencies, and professional societies of individuals interested in the systematics of organisms. Membership: $750-6,000 (Institution).

Publications:
Membership Directory; on-line
Washington Report; semi-monthly

Natural Stone Council
P.O. Box 539
Hollis, NH 03049
Tel: (978) 391-4130 *Fax:* (978) 391-4130
E-Mail: info@genuinestone.org
Website: naturalstonecouncil.org
Staff: 1
Annual Budget: $100-250,000
Tax: 501(c)(6)

Personnel:
Executive Director: Duke Pointer

Historical Note:
The Natural Stone Council formed in 2003 to advocate "Genuine Stone" in all building applications

Naval Enlisted Reserve Association *(1957)*
6703 Farragut Ave.
Falls Church, VA 22042-2189
Tel: (800) 776-9020 *Fax:* (301) 219-2647
TollFree: (800) 776-9020
E-Mail: members@nera.org
Website: nera.org
Members: 15000 individuals
Staff: 4
Annual Budget: $250-500,000
Tax: 501(c)(19)

Personnel:
Executive Director: Stephen R. Sandy DCCM, USNR
  E-Mail: neraexec@nera.org
Administrative Manager: Jennifer Abbott
  E-Mail: jabbott@nera.org
Managing Editor: Joanne Elliott
  E-Mail: marineeditor@nera.org

Historical Note:
NERA represents the interests of Enlisted Sea Service Reservists in the U.S. Navy, the Marine Corps and the Coast Guard. Members are the enlisted personnel in the Navy, Marine Corps and Coast Guard Reserve. Membership: $30 (Active/Associate); $300 (Life).

Meetings/Conferences: Annual

Publications:
Newsletter
The Mariner

Naval Submarine League *(1982)*
P. O. Box 1146
Annandale, VA 22003-9146
Tel: (703) 256-0891 *Fax:* (703) 642-5815
E-Mail: nslmem@navalsubleague.com
Website: navalsubleague.com
Members: 3500 Members
Staff: 3
Annual Budget: $500-1,000,000

Personnel:
Executive Director: CAPT Michael C. Garverick USN
  (Ret.)
Contact, Counsel: CAPT Earl N. Griggs USN (Ret.)
Treasurer: CAPT Robert C. Wagoner USN (Ret.)

Historical Note:
The Naval Submarine League (NSL) is a professional organization for submariners and submarine advocates. Membership: $35 (Regular); $50-1,000 (Contribution Levels).

Meetings/Conferences: Annual

Publications:
Membership Directory; on-line
NSL Updates; daily
The Submarine Review; quarterly

Navy League of the United States *(1902)*
2300 Wilson Blvd.
Suite 200
Arlington, VA 22201-5424
Tel: (703) 528-1775 *Fax:* (703) 528-2333
TollFree: (800) 356-5760
Website: navyleague.org
Members: 65000 active members
Staff: 9
Annual Budget: $1-2,000,000
Tax: 501(c)(3)

Personnel:
National Executive Director: Dale Lumme
  E-Mail: dlumme@navyleague.org
Director, Publications, Seapower: Kerri Carpenter
  E-Mail: kcarpenter@navyleague.org
Senior Director, Membership: Salvador Chairez
  E-Mail: schairez@navyleague.org
Senior Director, Communications and Marketing: John
  Daniels
  E-Mail: jdaniels@navyleague.org
*Senior Director, Government Operations and
  Administration:* Sara Fuentes
  E-Mail: sfuentes@navyleague.org
Senior Director, Finance: Howard Siegel
  E-Mail: hsiegel@navyleague.org
Senior Director, Corporate Development and Marketing:
  Kevin Traver
  E-Mail: ktraver@navyleague.org
Senior Director, Regional Activities, Training: Bill Waylett
  E-Mail: wwaylett@navyleague.org

Historical Note:
Founded in 1902. A patriotic, educational civilian non-profit association that supports a strong defense establishment, especially the sea services, and a foreign policy consistent with maintaining America's security. Membership: $50 (Regular individual); $85 (Husband/wife joint); $500 (Life); $750 (Husband/wife joint life); $30 (Active duty spouse); $4,400 (Corporate); $14,000 (Corporate Gold); $1,600 (Business Associate).

Meetings/Conferences: Semi-Annual
Conference Chair: Bill Waylett
2013 - Ft. Washington, MD (Gaylord National Resort
  and Convention Center-National Harbor)/April 8 -
  10
2013 - Long Beach, CA (Hilton Long Beach and
  Executive Meeting Center)/June 19 - 23
2014 - Ft. Washington, MD (Gaylord National Resort
  and Convention Center-National Harbor)/April 7 - 9
2014 - San Diego, CA (Sheraton San Diego Hotel and
  Marina)/June 18 - 22
2015 - Ft. Washington, MD (Gaylord National Resort
  and Convention Center-National Harbor)/April 13 -
  15
2016 - Ft. Washington, MD (Gaylord National Resort
  and Convention Center-National Harbor)/April 4 - 6
2017 - Ft. Washington, MD (Gaylord National Resort
  and Convention Center-National Harbor)/April 3 - 5
2018 - Ft. Washington, MD (Gaylord National Resort
  and Convention Center-National Harbor)/April 9 -
  11

Publications:

Corporate Newsletter
Membership Directory; on-line
SEAPOWER; monthly; adv.
The Navy League's newsletter; quarterly

NCSL International (1961)
2995 Wilderness Pl.
Suite 107
Boulder, CO 80301-5404
Tel: (303) 440-3339 *Fax:* (303) 440-3384
E-Mail: info@ncsli.org
Website: ncsli.org
Members: 1500 laboratories
Staff: 3
Annual Budget: $500-1,000,000
Tax: 501(c)(3)
Personnel:
Executive Director: Craig Gulka
    E-Mail: cgulka@ncsli.org
Vice President, Marketing: Jesse Morse
Historical Note:
*Founded as National Conference of Standards Laboratories,
assumed its current name in 2001. NCSL's mission is
to invest in the advancement of measurement science.
It provides measurement science (metrology) resources,
education and training, scholarships and metrology
outreach to improve the quality of products and
services supporting excellence in calibration and testing.
Membership: $150 (Individual Professional); $550
(Organization); $250 (Associate); 50 (Student).*
Meetings/Conferences:
2013 - Nashville, TN (Gaylord Hotels Resorts and
    Convention Centers-Nashville)/July 14 - 18/51-100
    exhibitors
2014 - Lake Buena Vista, FL (Walt Disney World Swan
    and Dolphin)/Aug. 3 - 4/51-100 exhibitors
2015 - Grapevine, TX (Gaylord Texan Hotel and
    Convention Center-Grapevine)/July 19 - 23/51-100
    exhibitors
Publications:
Membership Directory; on-line
Metrologist Magazine ; on-line; adv.
NCSLI Measure Journal; on-line; adv.
NCSLI Newsletter

Network Advertising Initiative (1999)
62 Portland Rd.
Suite 44
Kennebunk, ME 04043
Tel: (207) 467-3500 *Fax:* (207) 985-2523
E-Mail: help@networkadvertising.org
Website: networkadvertising.org
Members: 90 online advertising companies
Staff: 3
Annual Budget: $1-2,000,000
Personnel:
Counsel and Senior Director, Technology: David Wainberg
Historical Note:
*NAI's mission is to oversee the self-regulation of the online
advertising industry through enforceable standards and
ongoing compliance efforts and strive to infuse their self-
regulatory program with accountability, serious compliance,
and enforcement.*
Publications:
Membership Directory; on-line

Network Branded Prepaid Card Association
(2005)
110 Chestnut Ridge Rd.
Suite 111
Montvale, NJ 07645-1706
Tel: (201) 746-0725
Website: nbpca.com
Members: 52 Principal Members, 27 Affiliate
Members
Staff: 2
Annual Budget: $1-2,000,000
Tax: 501(c)(6)
Personnel:
President and Executive Director: Kirsten Trusko
Treasurer: William E. Saunders
Historical Note:
*NBPCA is a trade association open to all companies
involved in providing prepaid cards that carry a brand
network logo (American Express, Discover, MasterCard or
Visa) to consumers, businesses and government, which can
be used at numerous retailers nationwide.*

Network of Executive Women in Hospitality
(1984)
P.O. Box 322
Shawano, WI 54166
Tel: (800) 593-6394 *Fax:* (800) 693-6394
E-Mail: office@newh.org
Website: newh.org
Members: 1500 individuals
Staff: 7
Annual Budget: $1-2,000,000
Tax: 501(c)(3)
Personnel:
Executive Director: Sheila Lohmiller
Manager, Financial: Julie Buntrock
Coordinator, Administrative and Membership: Kathy
    Coughlin
Coordinator, Education and Sustainable: Nicole Crawford
Manager, Membership and Events: Diane Federwitz
Manager, Marketing and Tradeshow: Jena Seibel
Historical Note:
*NEWH is the premier networking resource for the
hospitality industry, providing scholarships, education,
leadership development, recognition of excellence, and
business development opportunities. Membership: $80-182
(General); $50 (Associate); Free (Student/Professional).*
Meetings/Conferences:
Conference Chair: Diane Federwitz
2013 - San Francisco, CA (Grand Hyatt Union Square)/
    Jan. 25 - 26
Number of non-conference events/year: 1
Publications:
Membership Directory; on-line
NEWH Magazine

Network of Ingredient Marketing Specialists
(1981)
P.O. Box 681864
Marietta, GA 30068-0032
Tel: (770) 971-8116 *Fax:* (770) 971-1094
E-Mail: kreynolds@nimsgroup.com
Website: nimsgroup.com
Members: 13 companies
Staff: 1
Annual Budget: $10-25,000
Personnel:
Executive Director: Kenneth W. Reynolds
    E-Mail: kreynolds@nimsgroup.com
Historical Note:
*Formerly (1998) known as North American Ingredient
Marketing Specialists, NIMS members strive to offer a
better means of reaching national, regional and local
markets with a variety of important marketing, sales,
and administrative services. Members are food ingredient
brokers and ingredient manufacturers.*
Publications:
Membership Directory; on-line
Membership List Available to Non-members

Network of Nonprofit Search Consultants (2002)
29 N. Wacker Dr.
Suite 200
Chicago, IL 60606
Tel: (708) 837-9937
Website: nnsc.org
Staff: 1
Personnel:
Administrator: Megan Lewis
Historical Note:
*NNSC's purpose is to provide a forum for the development
of better practices through the participation of executive
search consultants who conduct retained services
exclusively or predominantly for nonprofit organizations,
institutions and non-governmental organizations.
Membership is by invitation only. Individual members are
nonprofit executive search consultants.*
Publications:
Membership Directory
Membership List Available to Non-members

Network Professional Association (1991)
1401 Hermes Ln.
San Diego, CA 92154
Tel: (614) 221-1900 *Fax:* (614) 221-1989
E-Mail: npa@npa.org
Website: npa.org
Staff: 1

Tax: 501(c)(6)
Personnel:
Executive Director: Lori Landry
    E-Mail: executivedirector@npa.org
Historical Note:
*NPA's mission is to advance the computer networking
industry. Members are network administrators and
other professionals involved in computer network
deployment, maintenance and administration. Membership:
$125 (Professional Member); $1,000 (Executive); $0
(Community).*
Continuing Education:
Certification Designation/s: CNP
Publications:
Membership Directory; on-line
The NPA Journal; quarterly; adv.

Neuro-Developmental Treatment Association
(1967)
1540 S. Coast Hwy.
Suite 203
Laguna Beach, CA 92651
Tel: (800) 869-9295 *Fax:* (949) 376-3456
E-Mail: info@ndta.org
Website: ndta.org
Members: 1600 individuals
Staff: 6
Annual Budget: $250-500,000
Personnel:
Executive Director: Bradley J. Lund
    E-Mail: brad@ndta.org
Coordinator, Education: Julie Pitz
    E-Mail: julie@ndta.org
Coordinator, Exhibits: Stacy Spalding
    E-Mail: stacy@ndta.org
Director, Conferences: Gail Sunshine CMP
    E-Mail: gail@ndta.org
Associate Director: Mark Toof
    E-Mail: mark@ndta.org
Historical Note:
*NDTA's mission is to provide specialized clinical training to
health care professionals, supporting clinical research, and
supporting clients and families with education, resources
and information. Membership: $25-250/year.*
Continuing Education:
Certification Designation/s: NDT/BC
Meetings/Conferences: Annual
Conference Chair: Gail Sunshine CMP
Number of non-conference events/year: 10
Publications:
e-news; monthly
Member Directory; on-line
Network on the Net; bi-monthly; adv.

Neurofibromatosis, Inc., Northeast
Nine Bedford St.
Burlington, MA 01803
Tel: (781) 272-9936 *Fax:* (781) 272-9937
Website: nfincne.org
Staff: 4
Annual Budget: $500-1,000,000
Tax: 501(c)(3)
Personnel:
Executive Director: Karen Peluso
    E-Mail: kpeluso@nfincne.org
Executive Associate, Marketing: Jennifer Brickley
    E-Mail: msmith@nfincne.org
Director, Special Event: Sonja Nathan
    E-Mail: snathan@nfincne.org
Executive Associate and Outreach Coordinator: Linda Yew
    E-Mail: lyew@nfincne.org
Historical Note:
*A non profit organization, provided research grants to
scientists at leading institutions around the country.*
Meetings/Conferences:
Conference Chair: Sonja Nathan
Number of non-conference events/year: 1
Publications:
NF News

The Neuropathy Association (1995)
60 E. 42nd St.
Suite 942
New York, NY 10165
Tel: (212) 692-0662 *Fax:* (212) 692-0668
E-Mail: info@neuropathy.org

Website: neuropathy.org
Members: 50,000 members
Staff: 6
Annual Budget: $1-2,000,000

Personnel:
President and Chief Executive Officer: Tina M.
Tockarshewsky

Historical Note:
*The Association focuses on helping and healing people with
peripheral neuropathy by providing neuropathy awareness,
education, support, advocacy and research. Membership:
$45-99 (Contributing Supporter); $100-999 (Sponsor);
$1,000 (Benefactor).*

Publications:
Neuropathy E-News; monthly
Neuropathy News
Support Group Network Directory; annually

Neurosurgical Society of America (1948)
Department of Neurological Surgery
Northwestern University Feinberg School of
Medicine
676 North St. Clair, Suite 2210
Chicago, IL 60611-5934
Tel: (312) 695-6200 *Fax:* (312) 695-0225
E-Mail: help@neurosurgicalsociety.com
Website: neurosurgicalsociety.com
Members: 210 individuals
Staff: 3
Annual Budget: $250-500,000
Tax: 501(c)(3)

Personnel:
President: H. Hunt Batjer MD
E-Mail: hbatjer@nmff.org

Historical Note:
*NSA works to enhance the advancement of the specialty of
neurological surgery in America.*

Meetings/Conferences:
2013 - Sea Island, GA (Cloisters)/April 7 - 10
2013 - Minneapolis, MN/Sept. 20 - 22

Neurotechnology Industry Organization (2006)
315 30th St.
San Francisco, CA 94131
Tel: (415) 341-0193 *Fax:* (415) 358-5888
Website: neurotechindustry.org
Members: 200 organizations
Staff: 2
Annual Budget: $100-250,000
Tax: 501(c)(6)

Personnel:
Founder and Executive Director: Zack Lynch
E-Mail: zack@neurotechindustry.org
Director, Public Policy: John Reppas

Historical Note:
*NIO is spearheading new Federal legislation aimed to
accelerate translational neurotech innovation and improving
the timeliness of the FDA review process. Membership is
open to organizations that research, develop, manufacture
or market pharmaceuticals, biologics, medical devices,
as well as diagnostic and surgical equipment for the
treatment of neurological diseases, nervous systems ailments
and psychiatric illnesses. Membership is also open to
university neuroscience research centers, non-profit brain-
state charities, and non-profit brain research centers.
Membership: $1,000-30,000/year.*

Meetings/Conferences: Annual
2013 - San Francisco, CA/May 23 - 24/250 attendees

Publications:
Memberhp Directory; on-line
Neurotech Insights; monthly; adv.

New America Alliance (1999)
1050 Connecticut Ave. NW, Tenth Floor
Washington, DC 20036
Tel: (202) 772-1044 *Fax:* (214) 466-6415
E-Mail: info@naaonline.org
Website: naaonline.org
Members: 104 members
Staff: 3
Annual Budget: $100-250,000

Personnel:
Chief Executive Officer: Maria de Pilar Avila
E-Mail: pavila@naaonline.org
Director, Finance and Operations: Jessica Cardoza
E-Mail: jcardoza@naaonline.org

Director, Membership Services and Marketing: Lisa
Rodriguez
E-Mail: lrodriguez@naaonline.org

Historical Note:
*Organization of American Latino business leaders
united to promote the well being of the American Latino
community with a focus on education, economic and
political empowerment and strategic philanthropy. It is a
501(c)6 and a 501(c)3 organization. Membership: $10,000
(General); $7,500 (Associate); $2,500 (Young Leader/
Non-profit).*

Meetings/Conferences: Annual

Publications:
Membership Directory; on-line

New Dramatists (1949)
424 W. 44th St.
New York, NY 10036
Tel: (212) 757-6960 *Fax:* (212) 265-4738
E-Mail: newdramatists@newdramatists.org
Website: newdramatists.org
Staff: 12
Annual Budget: $1-2,000,000

Personnel:
Executive Director: Joel K. Ruark
Director, Finance and New Media: Morgan Allen
Director, Development: Christie Brown
Director, Operations: Ron Riley

Historical Note:
*Mission is to find gifted playwrights and give them the time,
space, and tools to develop their craft, so that they may
fulfill their potential and make lasting contributions to the
theatre.*

Membership List Available to Non-members

New England Club Managers Association (1914)
William F. Connell Golf House & Museum
300 Arnold Palmer Blvd., Suite 227
Norton, MA 02766-1365
Tel: (774) 430-9050 *Fax:* (774) 430-9051
E-Mail: necma@necma.org
Website: necma.org
Members: 212 individuals
Staff: 2
Annual Budget: $100-250,000
Tax: 501(c)(6)

Personnel:
Manager Director: Lee Norton Kelly
E-Mail: managing.director@necma.org
Secretary: William J. Roman
E-Mail: conference@necma.org

Historical Note:
*NECMA seeks to provide education to persons connected
with the management of clubs and other associations of
similar character, to promote and encourage efficient and
successful club management, and to advance friendly
relations among its members. Maine, Massachusetts, New
Hampshire, Rhode Island, Vermont are affiliated states.
Membership: $125-350 (Regular); $175 (Alumnus);
$350 (Assiciate); $50 (Faculty); $55 Retired, active). Free
(Student/Inactive Retired).*

Continuing Education:
Certification Designation/s: CCM, CCE

Meetings/Conferences:
Conference Chair: William J. Roman
Number of non-conference events/year: 2

Publications:
Chapter News; on-line
Member Directory; on-line

The New Media Consortium (1993)
6101 W. Courtyard
Building One, Suite 100
Austin, TX 78730
Tel: (512) 445-4200 *Fax:* (512) 445-4205
E-Mail: info@nmc.org
Website: nmc.org
Members: 429 NMC Member Organizations
Staff: 11
Annual Budget: $2-5,000,000
Tax: 501(c)(3)

Personnel:
Chief Executive Officer: Laurence F. Johnson PhD
E-Mail: johnson@nmc.org
Editorial Associate: Victoria Estrada
E-Mail: victoria@nmc.org
Senior Director, Communications Group: Paul Hicks

E-Mail: paul@nmc.org
Director, Internet Services: Arp Laszlo
Senior Director, Member Services and Meeting Planner:
Nancy Reeves CMP
E-Mail: nancy@nmc.org
Controller and Senior Director, Financial Services: Anne
Treadway CPA
E-Mail: anne@nmc.org

Historical Note:
*Founded on October 17, 1993 by a group of hardware
manufacturers, software developers, and publishers and
moved its national headquarters from San Francisco to
Austin, Texas in 2002. NMC is a community of hundreds
of leading universities, colleges, museums, and research
centers. The organization stimulates and furthers the
exploration and use of new media and technologies for
learning and creative expression. All content Creative
Commons. Membership: $2,500 (Regular); $5,000
(Corporate Partner Sustaining); $10,000 (Corporate Partner
Distinguished); $25,000 (Corporate Partner Platinum).*

Meetings/Conferences: Annual
Conference Chair: Nancy Reeves CMP
2013 - Hilton Head Island, SC (Hilton Head)/June 4 - 7

Publications:
The Pulse; monthly

The New York Academy of Sciences (1817)
Seven World Trade Center
250 Greenwich St., 40th Floor
New York, NY 10007-2157
Tel: (212) 298-8600 *Fax:* (212) 888-2894
E-Mail: nyas@nyas.org
Website: nyas.org
Members: 24000 individuals
Staff: 15
Annual Budget: $10-25,000,000
Tax: 501(c)(3)

Personnel:
President and Chief Executive Officer: Ellis Rubinstein
E-Mail: erubinstein@nyas.org
Director, Scientific Publications: Douglas Braaten PhD
E-Mail: dbraaten@nyas.org
Director, Meeting and Event Operations: Erica Johnson
Cullman
E-Mail: ecullmann@nyas.org
Executive Vice President and Chief Operating Officer: Mike
Goldrich
E-Mail: mgoldrich@nyas.org
Director, Membership and Marketing: John Grifferty
E-Mail: jgrifferty@nyas.org
Director, K12 Education and Science and the City:
Meghan Groome PhD
E-Mail: mgroome@nyas.org
Vice President, Administration and Human Resources:
Wendy Caruso Schneider
E-Mail: wschneider@nyas.org

Historical Note:
*NYAS's mission is to advance scientific knowledge, to help
resolve the major global challenges facing society with
science-based solutions, and to increase the number of
scientifically informed individuals. Membership: $108-129
(Individual-U.S) $135-155 (Professional); $36-52
(Student and Postdoc- U.S./International); $258 (Patron).*

Meetings/Conferences: Annual
Conference Chair: Erica Johnson Cullman
Number of non-conference events/year: 2

Publications:
Academy eBriefings; on-line; adv.
Annals of the New York Academy of Sciences; on-line;
adv.
Membership Directory; on-line
NYAS eNews; monthly; adv.
Science & the City; weekly; adv.
The New York Academy of Sciences Magazine;
quarterly

New York E-Health Collaborative (2006)
40 Worth St.
Fifth Floor
New York, NY 10013
Tel: (646) 619-6400
E-Mail: info@nyehealth.org
Website: nyehealth.org
Staff: 6

Personnel:
Executive Director: Dave Whitlinger
Director, Business Development: Anuj Desai
Director, Policy: Sara Kay

Director, Marketing and Communications: Erin Lippincott
Chief Operating Officer: Inez Sieben
Chief Technology Officer: Nick VanDuyne

Historical Note:
NYeC is a not-for-profit organization, working to improve healthcare for all New Yorkers through health information technology (health IT).

Newspaper Association Managers (1923)
P.O. Box 458
Essex, MA 091929
Tel: (978) 338-2555
Website: nammanagers.com
Members: 70 individuals
Staff: 1
Annual Budget: $50-100,000

Personnel:
Clerk: Morley L. Piper
  E-Mail: mlpiper52@comcast.net

Historical Note:
NAM is an association of managers of state, regional, national and international press associations.

Meetings/Conferences: Annual

Newspaper Association of America (1992)
4401 Wilson Blvd.
Suite 900
Arlington, VA 22203-1867
Tel: (571) 366-1000 *Fax:* (571) 366-1195
E-Mail: irc@naa.org
Website: naa.org
Members: 2000 newspapers
Staff: 140
Annual Budget: $10-25,000,000
Tax: 501(c)(6)

Personnel:
President and Chief Executive Officer: Caroline H. Little
  E-Mail: caroline.little@naa.org
Coordinator, Member Services and Events: Jeanne Boone
  E-Mail: jeanne.boone@naa.org
Senior Vice President, Public Policy: Paul J. Boyle
  E-Mail: paul.boyle@naa.org
Director, Human Resources: Sarah Burkman
  E-Mail: sarah.burkman@naa.org
Vice President, Research and Industry Analysis: Jim Conaghan
  E-Mail: jim.conaghan@naa.org
Vice President, Advertising: Mort Goldstrom
  E-Mail: mort.goldstrom@naa.org
Senior Manager, Communications: Marina Hendricks
  E-Mail: marina.hendricks@naa.org
Vice President, Legal Affairs and General Counsel: Rene Milam
  E-Mail: Rene.Milam@naa.org
Manager, Marketing Communications: Joanie Mills
  E-Mail: joanie.mills@naa.org
Vice President, Information Technology: Gary Peifer
  E-Mail: Gary.Peifer@naa.org
Senior Vice President and Chief Financial Officer, Finance and Operations: Margaret Vassilikos
  E-Mail: margaret.vassilikos@naa.org

Historical Note:
NAA was formed by the merger of seven associations serving the newspaper industry. The associations included the American Newspaper Publishers Association (founded in 1887), the Newspaper Advertising Bureau, the Association of Newspaper Classified Advertising Managers, the International Circulation Managers Association, the International Newspapers Advertising and Marketing Executives, the Newspaper Advertising Co-op Network, and the Newspaper Research Council. NAA is a nonprofit organization representing newspapers and their multiplatform businesses in the United States and Canada. NAA serves the newspaper industry by Communicating the vitality of newspaper media to external constituencies, including the advertising community, news media and Wall Street. Members include daily newspapers, as well as non-dailies, other print publications and online products. Membership: $2000/year (Associate).

Meetings/Conferences: Annual
Conference Chair: Jeanne Boone
2013 - Orlando, FL (Hilton Bonnet Creek Resort)/April 14 - 17

Publications:
NAA on Your Side; quarterly
PRESSTIME Update; weekly; adv.

The Newspaper Guild (1995)
501 Third St. NW
Sixth floor
Washington, DC 20001-2797
Tel: (202) 434-7177 *Fax:* (202) 434-1472
E-Mail: guild@cwa-union.org
Website: newsguild.org
Members: 34000 individuals
Staff: 32
Annual Budget: $2-5,000,000

Personnel:
President and Vice President: Bernard J. Lunzer
  E-Mail: blunzer@cwa-union.org
Editor: Janelle Hartman
Secretary and Treasurer: Carol D. Rothman
  E-Mail: crothman@cwa-union.org
Administrative Director to the Vice President: Timothy Schick

Historical Note:
Formerly the Wire Service Guild, assumed the current name in 1970 and merged with the Communications Workers of America in 1995. TNG is a labor union representing editorial and commercial department employees of two wire services, Associated Press and United Press International whose mission is to advance the economic interests and to improve the working conditions of its members. Members are journalists, sales and media workers of all kinds.

Meetings/Conferences:
Number of non-conference events/year: 5

Publications:
Guild Reporter; monthly; adv.

Newspaper Purchasing Management Association (1958)
14237 Bookcliff Ct.
Suite 200
Purcellville, VA 20132
Tel: (703) 421-4060 *Fax:* (703) 421-4068
Website: infe.org/npma/newsite/extranet/ npma.asp
Members: 100 individuals
Staff: 2
Annual Budget: $25-50,000

Personnel:
President: Wade Walker
  E-Mail: wwalker@bhamnews.com
Treasurer: Steve Bower
  E-Mail: stephen.bower@scripps.com

Historical Note:
Purpose is to promote the study, development and application of improved purchasing methods, practices and techniques in the newspaper publishing industry. Membership: $150 (Regular); $100 (Associate).

NFHS Music Association (1983)
P.O. Box 690
Indianapolis, IN 46206
Tel: (317) 972-6900 *Fax:* (317) 822-5700
TollFree: (800) 776-3462
E-Mail: webmaster@nfhs.org
Website: nfhs.org
Members: 850 individuals
Staff: 2
Annual Budget: Under $10,000

Personnel:
Editor: Bob Gardner
Contact, Meetings: Angela Hays

Historical Note:
NFHSMA's mission is to identify and meet the common needs of music educators who participate in or sponsor high school interscholastic activities, an educational extension of the school music curriculum. Membership: $20/year (Individual).

Meetings/Conferences: Annual
Conference Chair: Angela Hays

Publications:
NFHS Music Association Journal; bi-annually

NFHS Speech Debate and Theatre Association (1986)
P.O. Box 690
Indianapolis, IN 46206
Tel: (317) 972-6900 *Fax:* (317) 822-5700
Website: nfhs.org
Members: 1250 individuals
Staff: 2
Annual Budget: Under $10,000

Personnel:

Executive Director: Robert Gardner
Contact, Meetings and Conventions: Angela Hays
  E-Mail: ahays@nfhs.org

Historical Note:
Founded as the NFHS Speech, Debate and Theatre Association, assumed its current name in 2003 and affiliated with the National Federation of State High School Associations. NFHS SDTA works for the development of education-based interscholastic sports and activities that help students succeed in their lives. Members are secondary and post-secondary speech, drama and debate coaches. Membership: $20 (NFHS Speech, Debate and Theatre Association Membership); $4 (NFHS Speech, Debate and Theater Association).

Meetings/Conferences:
Conference Chair: Angela Hays

Publications:
Directory of Summer Institutes in Speech, Debate and Theatre for Secondary Students and Teachers; on-line
Forensic Quarterly; quarterly
The Forensic Educator

NGNP Industry Alliance
P.O. Box 837
Ridgeland, MS 39158-0837
Tel: (601) 368-5933
Website: ngnpalliance.org
Members: 11 Companies
Staff: 2

Personnel:
Executive Director: Don Halter
  E-Mail: executivedirector@ngnpalliance.org
Secretary and Treasurer: John Mahoney
  E-Mail: secretary@ngnpalliance.org

Historical Note:
NGNPIA's mission is to work with Government to commercialize High Temperature Gas-cooled Reactor (HTGR) technology expanding the use of clean nuclear energy and significantly reducing the dependence on premium fossil fuels. NGNP Industry Alliance is a member of: United States Nuclear Infrastructure Council and Nuclear Energy Institute.

Publications:
Membership Directory; on-line

NGVAmerica (1988)
400 N. Capitol St. NW
Washington, DC 20001
Tel: (202) 824-7366 *Fax:* (202) 824-7087
E-Mail: rkolodziej@ngvc.org
Website: ngvc.org
Members: 180 companies
Staff: 6
Annual Budget: $1-2,000,000

Personnel:
President: Richard R. Kolodziej
  E-Mail: rkolodziej@ngvamerica.org
General Counsel and Director, Regulatory Affairs: Jeffrey Clarke
  E-Mail: jclarke@ngvamerica.org
Director, Government Relations: Paul Kerkhoven
  E-Mail: pkerkhoven@ngvamerica.org
Director, Marketing: Stephe Yborra
  E-Mail: syborra@ngvamerica.org

Historical Note:
Formerly the Natural Gas Vehicle Coalition, and most recently the Natural Gas Vehicle for America, NGVA strives to develop a growing, sustainable and profitable market for vehicles powered by natural gas or hydrogen. Members are organizations with an interest in encouraging the development of natural gas powered vehicles. Membership: $500-25,200/year (based on type of company and business volume).

Meetings/Conferences: Annual
Number of non-conference events/year: 6

Publications:
Business Directory; on-line
NGVAmerica Newsletter; weekly

NIBA - The Belting Association (1927)
6737 W. Washington St.
Suite 1300
Milwaukee, WI 53214
Tel: (414) 389-8606 *Fax:* (414) 276-7704
E-Mail: staff@niba.org
Website: niba.org
Members: 250 companies

Staff: 3
Annual Budget: $500-1,000,000
Tax: 501(c)(6)

Personnel:
Executive Director: Jennifer Rzepka
    E-Mail: jennifer@niba.org
Accounts Coordinator: Tiffany Taticek
    E-Mail: tiffany@niba.org

Historical Note:
Formerly (1926) American Leather Belting Association, (1977) National Industrial Leather Association and (2001) National Industrial Belting Association. NIBA's mission is to promote the common business interests of all distributor or fabricators and manufacturers of conveyor and flat power transmission belting and material that enhances or changes belt. Membership: $600-1,190/year.

Meetings/Conferences: Annual
2013 - San Antonio, TX (JW Marriott San Antonio Hill
    Country Resort and Spa)/Sept. 12 - 15
2014 - Seattle, WA (Seattle Sheraton)/Sept. 24 - 27

Publications:
Belt Line; quarterly
NIBA Member Directory; annually

Nickel Institute *(1984)*
Brookfield Place
161 Bay St., Suite 2700
Toronto, ON M5J 2S1
Tel: (416) 591-7999
E-Mail: ni_toronto@nickelinstitute.org
Website: nickelinstitute.org
Members: 25 Companies
Staff: 4

Personnel:
Executive Director: Dr. Hudson Bates
Director, Promotion: Dr. Peter Cutler
Director, Global Government Affairs and Advocacy: Dr.
    Veronique Steukers

Historical Note:
Founded as Nickel Development Institute (NiDI), merged with Nickel Producers Environmental Research Association (NiPERA), originally formed in 1980 to form Nickel Institute. A non-profit organization funded by metal producers promotes promote on behalf of its members the production, use and re-use (through recycling) of nickel in a socially and environmentally responsible manner.

Publications:
Nickel Advantage
Nickel Magazine; semi-annually; adv.

Nine to Five, National Association of Working Women *(1973)*
207 E. Buffalo St.
Suite 211
Milwaukee, WI 53202
Tel: (414) 274-0925 *Fax:* (414) 272-2870
TollFree: (800) 522-0925
E-Mail: 9to5@9to5.org
Website: 9to5.org
Members: 15000 individuals
Staff: 13
Annual Budget: $1-2,000,000
Tax: 501(c)(3)

Personnel:
Executive Director: Linda Meric
    E-Mail: lindam@9to5.org
Director, Operations: Linda Garcia Barnard
    E-Mail: lindagb@9to5.org
Director, Development: Nasreen Jilani
    E-Mail: nasreen@9to5.org

Historical Note:
9to5's mission is to build a movement to achieve economic justice by engaging directly affected women to improve working conditions. Members are low-wage women, women in traditionally female jobs, and those who have experienced any form of discrimination. Membership is open to all. Membership: $25 (Individuals); $40 (Institutions).

Meetings/Conferences:
Number of non-conference events/year: 4

Publications:
National Newsline; quarterly
Working Women's Voter Guide; annually

Nisei Farmers League *(1971)*
1775 N. Fine
Fresno, CA 93727-1616
Tel: (559) 251-8468 *Fax:* (559) 251-8430

Website: niseifarmersleague.com
Staff: 5
Annual Budget: $500-1,000,000
Tax: 501(c)(6)

Personnel:
President: Manuel Cunha Jr.
Executive Vice President: Don Patrick

Historical Note:
Agricultural Association. NFL represent flower and Christmas tree producers and farm labor contractors.

Non Commissioned Officers Association (NCOA)
(1970)
9330 Corporate Dr.
Suite 701
Selma, TX 78154
Tel: (800) 662-2620 *Fax:* (703) 549-0245
E-Mail: membersuc@ncoausa.org
Website: ncoausa.org
Members: 65000 individuals
Staff: 25
Annual Budget: $10-25,000,000
Tax: 501(c)(19)

Personnel:
Executive Director: Scoop Davis
    E-Mail: execdir@ncoausa.org
Manager, Sales and Marketing: Shelley Conklin
    E-Mail: sconklin@ncoausa.org
Director, Operations: Jeri Glowacki
    E-Mail: jglow@ncoausa.org
Executive Director, Government Affairs: Richard C.
    Schneider
    E-Mail: rschneider@ncoadc.org

Historical Note:
NCOA works to enhance and maintain the quality of life for noncommissioned and petty officers in all branches of the Armed Forces, National Guard and Reserves. Membership: $30 (Regular/Veterans/Associate); $20 (International Auxiliary/Apprentice).

Meetings/Conferences: Annual
Conference Chair: Tina Kish

Publications:
NCOA Journal; bi-monthly; adv.
NCOA Magazine

Membership List Available to Non-members

Non-Ferrous Founders' Society *(1943)*
1480 Renaissance Dr.
Suite 310
Park Ridge, IL 60068
Tel: (847) 299-0950 *Fax:* (847) 299-3598
E-Mail: nffstaff@nffs.org
Website: nffs.org
Members: 120 companies
Staff: 5
Annual Budget: $500-1,000,000
Tax: 501(c)(6)

Personnel:
Executive Director: James L. Mallory CAE
    E-Mail: jlm@nffs.org
Manager, Membership Services: Ryan J. Moore CAE
    E-Mail: ryanm@nffs.org
Director, Education: Jerrod A. Weaver CAE
    E-Mail: jerrod@nffs.org

Historical Note:
NFFS's mission is to provide members and industry with information and services relevant to their current and future business needs, to effectively represent the concerns and the interests of the non-ferrous metal casting industry. Members are manufacturers of bronze, brass and aluminum castings. Membership: $900-4,250 (Company, based on number of employees).

Continuing Education:
Certification Designation/s: NSF

Meetings/Conferences: Annual
2013 - Scottsdale, AZ (Talking Stick Resort)/Oct. 11 -
    14

Publications:
Member Directory
NFFS e-Newsletter; semi-monthly; adv.
NFFScene; quarterly; adv.
The Crucible magazine; bi-monthly; adv.

Nonprofit Technology Network *(2000)*
1020 SW Taylor St.
Suite 800

Portland, OR 97205
Tel: (415) 397-9000 *Fax:* (415) 814-4056
Website: nten.org
Staff: 7
Annual Budget: $1-2,000,000
Tax: 501(c)(3)

Personnel:
Executive Director: Holly Ross
    E-Mail: holly@nten.org
Chief Financial Officer and Chief Operating Officer: Jill
    Farrow
    E-Mail: jill@nten.org
Manager, Information Technology: Karl Hedstrom
    E-Mail: karl@nten.org
Director, Publications: Annaliese Hoehling
    E-Mail: annaliese@nten.org
Manager, Educational Programs: John Kenyon
    E-Mail: john@nten.org
Director, Communications: Brett Mayer
    E-Mail: brett@nten.org
Director, Membership Services: Amy Sample Ward
    E-Mail: amy@nten.org

Historical Note:
NTEN's mission is to facilitate the exchange of knowledge and information within the community; connect members to each other, by providing professional development opportunities, educate constituency on issues of technology use in nonprofits, and spearhead groundbreaking research, advocacy, and education on technology issues affecting entire community. A membership organization of nonprofit technology professionals. Membership: $85 (Individual); $1,000 (Organization).

Meetings/Conferences: Annual
2013 - Minneapolis, MN/April 11 - 13/11-25 exhibitors
2014 - Washington, DC/March 13 - 15/11-25
    exhibitors
2016 - San Francisco, CA/March 22 - 24/11-25
    exhibitors

Publications:
NTEN: Change Journal; quarterly; adv.
NTEN Connect; monthly; adv.

NORA: Association of Responsible Recyclers
(1985)
5965 Amber Ridge Rd.
Haymarket, VA 20169
Tel: (703) 753-4277 *Fax:* (703) 753-2445
E-Mail: sparker@noranews.org
Website: noranews.org
Members: 250 companies
Staff: 4
Annual Budget: $500-1,000,000

Personnel:
Executive Director: Scott D. Parker
    E-Mail: sparker@noranews.org
Coordinator, Communications and Marketing: Justin
    Hancher
    E-Mail: justin@noranews.org
Associate Director: Casey Parker
    E-Mail: casey@noranews.org
Office Manager: Peggy Schochet
    E-Mail: peggy@noranews.org

Historical Note:
Formerly known as the National Oil Recyclers Association, absorbed National Association of Chemical Recyclers in 2000, and assumed its current name in 2001. NORA's mission is to fight the hazardous waste designation of used oil and aid in the development of the EPA's used oil management standards. Membership: $825-6,600 (Recyler); $1100 (Associate); $550 (International).

Meetings/Conferences: Annual
Conference Chair: Casey Parker
2013 - Las Vegas, NV/Feb. 27 - March 1
2013 - Nashville, TN/June 19 - 21
Number of non-conference events/year: 1

Publications:
Liquid Recycling; bi-monthly; adv.
Membership Directory; on-line; adv.

**North American Association of Floor Covering
Distributors** *(1971)*
401 N. Michigan Ave.
Suite 2400
Chicago, IL 60611-4267
Tel: (312) 321-6836 *Fax:* (312) 673-6962
E-Mail: info@nafcd.org
Website: nafcd.org

Members:
400 companies
300 individuals
Staff: 7
Annual Budget: $500-1,000,000

Personnel:
Executive Director: Michelle Parrilli Miller
    E-Mail: mmiller@smithbucklin.com
Manager, Conferences: Sarah Haukap
    E-Mail: shaukap@smithbucklin.com
Manager, Sales: Scott Narug
    E-Mail: snarug@smithbucklin.com
Senior Coordinator, Marketing: Andy Younger
    E-Mail: ayounger@smithbucklin.com
Associate, Membership Services: Kyle Zapalik
    E-Mail: KZapalik@smithbucklin.com

Historical Note:
NAFCD's mission is to promote the wholesale distribution in the floor covering industry and to provide members with resources for enhancing their performance as industry suppliers. It also offers member development programs and conferences. Membership: $595-1,745 (Distributor); $2,145 (Manufacturer/Allied).

Meetings/Conferences: Annual
Conference Chair: Sarah Haukap

Publications:
e-Newsletters; weekly
Membership Directory; on-line

North - American Interfraternity Conference
(1909)
3901 W. 86th St.
Suite 390
Indianapolis, IN 46268-1791
Tel: (317) 872-1112 *Fax:* (317) 872-1134
E-Mail: nic@nicindy.org
Website: nicindy.org
Members: 75 fraternities
Staff: 7
Annual Budget: $1-2,000,000
Tax: 501(c)(3)

Personnel:
President and Chief Executive Officer: Peter Smithhisler
    E-Mail: pete@nicindy.org
Vice President, Education: Will Foran
    E-Mail: foran@nicindy.org
Director, Member Services: Andy Huston
    E-Mail: andy@nicindy.org
Director, University Relations and Public Policy: Wade Lowhorn
    E-Mail: wade@nicindy.org
Office Manager: Shelley Meltzer
    E-Mail: nic@nicindy.org
Director, Student Affairs: Jameson Root
    E-Mail: root@nicindy.org

Historical Note:
Formerly (1999) National Interfraternity Conference. NIC's mission is to advocate the needs of its member fraternities through enrichment of the fraternity experience and enhancement of the educational mission of host institution. Membership: $400/year.

Meetings/Conferences: Annual
2013 - St. Louis, MO (Ritz Carlton)/April 14 - 15

Publications:
Greek News; monthly
Membership Directory; on-line

Membership List Available to Non-members

North American Academy of Ecumenists *(1957)*
3838 W. Cypress St
Tampa, FL 33647
Tel: (813) 435-5335 *Fax:* (928) 268-8765
Website: naae.net
Members: 300 individuals
Staff: 1
Annual Budget: Under $10,000

Personnel:
Acting Treasurer and Past-President: Russell L. Meyer
    E-Mail: treasurer@naae.net

Historical Note:
Formerly Association of Professors of Ecumenics, NAAE works to inform, relate, and encourage men and women whose profession or ministry in the church involves them in ecumenical activities and studies. Members are ecumenically active clergy and laity as well as professors and students. Membership: $30 (Special); $60 (Regular).

Meetings/Conferences: Annual

Publications:
Membership Directory; annually
NAAE Links - Newsletter; semi-annually

Membership List Available to Non-members

North American Academy of Liturgy *(1975)*
Columbia Theological Seminary
505 S. Columbia Dr.
Decatur, GA 30030
Tel: (404) 687-4652
E-Mail: naaltreasurer@aol.com
Website: naal-liturgy.org
Staff: 4
Annual Budget: $100-250,000

Personnel:
Delegate, Membership Services: Martha Moore-Keish
    E-Mail: membership@naal-liturgy.org
Meeting Manager: Courtney Murtaugh
    E-Mail: meetings@naal-liturgy.org

Historical Note:
NAAL is an ecumenical and inter-religious association of liturgical scholars who collaborate in research. Members are scholars, religious leaders, artists, and others who contribute to liturgical understanding and practice across a broad spectrum of Christian and Jewish traditions. Membership: $75 (Regular); $35 (Retired/Student).

Meetings/Conferences: Annual
Conference Chair: Courtney Murtaugh
2013 - Albuquerue, NM (Hyatt Regency Albuquerque)/ Jan. 3 - 6
2014 - Orlando, FL/Jan. 2 - 5
2015 - Minneapolis, MN/Jan. 2 - 5
2016 - Houston, TX/Jan. 7 - 10
2018 - Vancouver, BC/Jan. 4 - 7

Publications:
NAAL Newsletter

North American Agricultural Marketing Officials
(1920)
C/O Debra May, Florida Department of Agriculture and Consumer Services, Division of Marketing
407 S. Calhoun St., Suite 421
Tallahassee, FL 32399-0800
Tel: (850) 921-1727 *Fax:* (850) 488-7127
Website: naamo.org
Members: 45 individuals
Staff: 2
Annual Budget: $25-50,000

Personnel:
President: Debra Cox May
    E-Mail: mayd2@doacs.state.fl.us

Historical Note:
Formerly (1977) National Association of Marketing Officials, assumed current name in 1992. NAAMO is a subsidiary of the National Association of State Department of Agriculture. NAAMO's mission is to promote education, communication and cooperation among its membership, and thereby enhance worldwide market opportunities for North American agricultural products. Members are state and provincial officials responsible for agricultural products marketing programs in the United States, Canada and ultimately Mexico. Membership: $300 (Executive); $25 (Associate).

Meetings/Conferences: Annual

Publications:
Membership Directory; on-line
Newsletter

North American Association for Environmental Education *(1971)*
2000 P St. NW
Suite 540
Washington, DC 20036
Tel: (202) 419-0412 *Fax:* (202) 419-0415
E-Mail: email@naaee.org
Website: naaee.org
Members: 2000 individuals
Staff: 4
Annual Budget: $1-2,000,000
Tax: 501(c)(3)

Personnel:
Executive Director: Judy Braus
    E-Mail: jbraus@naaee.org
Manager, Conferences: Bridget Chisholm
    E-Mail: bchisholm@naaee.org
Office Manager: Darlene D. Dorsey

Editor and Member Services: Mary Ocwieja
    E-Mail: maryo@naaee.org

Historical Note:
Formerly (1985) the National Association for Environmental Education. Merged with the Conservation Education Association in 1990. NAAEE's purpose is to assist and support the work of individuals and groups engaged in environmental education, research and service in order for present and future generations to benefit from a safe and healthy environment and a better quality of life. Membership: $55 (Retired); $1800 (Lifetime); $35 (Student); $300 (Partner Government); $150-200 (Affiliate/supporter); $80 (Professional); $17 (Mexico Professional/Mexico Student/Mexico Retired); $250 (Partner Nonprofit); $400 (Corporate Small); $500 (Corporate Large).

Continuing Education:
Certification Designation/s: EE, CAC

Meetings/Conferences: Annual
Conference Chair: Bridget Chisholm
Number of non-conference events/year: 4

Publications:
EE- News; irregular

North American Association for the Study of Religion *(1985)*
St. Thomas Aquinas College
125 Route 340
Sparkill, NY 10976
E-Mail: cmartin@stac.edu
Website: naasr.com
Members: 75 individuals
Staff: 3

Personnel:
President: William Arnal
    E-Mail: william.arnal@uregina.ca
Contact, Meetings: Christopher Lehrich
    E-Mail: clehrich@bu.edu
Executive Secretary and Treasurer: Craig Martin
    E-Mail: cmartin@stac.edu

Historical Note:
NAASR encourages the historical, comparative and structural study of religion in North America. Membership: $35 (Faculty Member); $15 (Student/Retired Member); $180 (Six Year Member); $350 (Life Member).

Meetings/Conferences: Semi-Annual
Conference Chair: Christopher Lehrich

Publications:
Method & Theory in the Study of Religion; quarterly
Newsletter

North American Association of Central Cancer Registries *(1987)*
2121 W. White Oaks Dr.
Suite B
Springfield, IL 62704-7412
Tel: (217) 698-0800 *Fax:* (217) 698-0188
Website: naaccr.org
Staff: 9
Annual Budget: $1-2,000,000

Personnel:
Executive Director: Betsy Kohler CTR, MPH
    E-Mail: bkohler@naaccr.org
Chief Operating Officer: Charlie Blackburn
    E-Mail: cblackburn@naaccr.org
Program Manager, Education and Training: Shannon Vann
    E-Mail: svann@naaccr.org
Administrator, Information Technology: Joshua Whitley
    E-Mail: jwhitley@naaccr.org

Historical Note:
NAACCR's mission is to promote uniform data standards for cancer registration. It provides education and training; certifies population-based registries; aggregates and publishes data from central cancer registries; and promotes the use of cancer surveillance data and systems for cancer control and epidemiologic research, public health programs, and patient care. Membership: $125 (Individual); $375 (Full); $500-1000 (Sustaining); $2,000 (Sponsoring).

Meetings/Conferences: Annual
2013 - Austin, TX/June 8 - 14
2014 - Ottawa, ON/June 21 - 27
2015 - Charlotte, NC/June 13 - 19

Publications:
NAACCR Membership Directory
NAACCR Narrative Newsletter; quarterly

North American Association of Christians in Social Work (1954)

P.O. Box 121
Botsford, CT 06404-0121
Tel: (203) 270-8780
TollFree: (888) 426-4712
E-Mail: info@nacsw.org
Website: nacsw.org
Members: 1950 individuals
Staff: 9
Annual Budget: $100-250,000
Tax: 501(c)(3)

Personnel:
Executive Director: Rick Chamiec-Case MAR, MSW, PhD

Historical Note:
NACSW equips its members to integrate Christian faith and professional social work practice. Membership: $90 (Individual); $28(Student); $250- 495 (Organization, based on Budget).

Meetings/Conferences: Annual
2013 - Atlanta, GA (Sheraton Atlanta Hotel)/Oct. 17 - 20
2014 - Annapolis, MD (Anne Arundel Medical Center)/ Nov. 6 - 9

Publications:
Catalyst; bi-monthly; adv.
Membership Directory; on-line
Social Work & Christianity; quarterly; adv.

Membership List Available to Non-members

North American Association of Commencement Officers (2001)

191 Clarksville Rd.
Princeton Junction, NJ 08550
Fax: (609) 799-7032
TollFree: (877) 622-2606
E-Mail: info@naaco.org
Website: naaco.co/
Members: 118 universities
Staff: 5
Annual Budget: $250-500,000

Personnel:
Executive Director: Gabrielle Copperwheat
Contact, Meetings: Lisa Arakaki
    E-Mail: lisa.arakaki@american.edu
Membership Coordinator: Josephine Crutchley
    E-Mail: jcrutchley@naaco.org
Media Relations: Meghan Higgins
    E-Mail: mhiggins@cmasolutions.com

Historical Note:
NAACO's mission is to help the individual commencement and convocation officers at member colleges and universities sharpen their skills, broaden their knowledge of how other institutions deal with these major events, and exchange ideas and information. Membership: $300/year (Institution).

Meetings/Conferences: Annual
Conference Chair: Lisa Arakaki
2013 - Washington, DC (Mayflower Renaissance Hotel)/Feb. 17 - 19

Publications:
Membership Directory; on-line
NAAco Newsletter

North American Association of Educational Negotiators (1970)

P.O. Box 1068
Salem, OR 97308
Tel: (503) 588-2800 *Fax:* (503) 588-2813
Website: naen.org
Members: 480 individuals
Staff: 2
Annual Budget: $50-100,000
Tax: 501(c)(6)

Personnel:
Executive Director: Ron Wilson
    E-Mail: execdir@naen.org
Meeting Planner: Josie Hummert
    E-Mail: jhummert@osba.org

Historical Note:
Established as the Association of Educational Negotiators; later became the National Association of Educational Negotiators and assumed its present name in 1991. NAEN's mission is to improve the knowledge and performance of K-12 school district, community college,
and university, management negotiators by advancing their professional status, providing a forum for effective communication, and encourage information exchanges among educational negotiators. Membership: $125 (Individual); $346-554 (Institution); $50 (Student).

Meetings/Conferences: Annual
Conference Chair: Josie Hummert
2013 - San Antonio, TX (Hyatt Regency San Antonio)/ March 10 - 13

Publications:
NAEN Bulletin; bi-monthly
NAEN's Membership Directory; on-line

North American Association of Food Equipment Manufacturers (1948)

161 N. Clark St.
Suite 2020
Chicago, IL 60601
Tel: (312) 821-0201 *Fax:* (312) 821-0202
E-Mail: info@nafem.org
Website: nafem.org
Members: 550 foodservice equipment and supplies manufacturers
Staff: 8
Annual Budget: $2-5,000,000
Tax: 501(c)(6)

Personnel:
Executive Vice President: Deirdre Flynn CFSP
    E-Mail: dflynn@nafem.org
Manager, Marketing: Marianne Byrne
    E-Mail: mbyrne@nafem.org
Membership Manager: Celeste Fuchs
    E-Mail: cfuchs@nafem.org
Manager, Communications: Alice Konopasek
    E-Mail: akonopasek@nafem.org
Director, Shows: Buffy Levy
Program Coordinator, Member Services: Vonceil Roberts
    E-Mail: robertsv@nafem.org
Director, Membership Services: Charlie Souhrada
    E-Mail: csouhrada@nafem.org

Historical Note:
NAFEM represents the food industry in Washington and supports programs and organizations that move the industry forward. Membership: $2,500/year (Associate).

Continuing Education:
Certification Designation/s: CFSP

Meetings/Conferences: Biennial
Conference Chair: Buffy Levy
2013 - Orange, FL (Orange County Convention Center)/Feb. 7 - 9/over 100 exhibitors
2015 - Anaheim, CA (Anaheim Convention Center)/ Feb. 19 - 21
2017 - Orange, FL (Orange County Convention Center)/Feb. 9 - 11
2019 - Orange, FL (Orange County Convention Center)/Feb. 7 - 9
Number of non-conference events/year: 70

Publications:
Associate Member Directory; on-line
NAFEM for operators; quarterly; adv.
NAFEM Membership Directory; on-line
NAFEM online; on-line

North American Association of Professors of Christian Education (1947)

Biola University
13800 Biola Ave.
La Mirada, CA 90639
Tel: (562) 903-6000 *Fax:* (714) 352-6680
E-Mail: mail@napce.org
Website: napce.org
Members: 275 individuals
Staff: 2
Annual Budget: $50-100,000

Personnel:
Executive Administrator: Freddy Cardoza
    E-Mail: freddy.cardoza@biola.edu

Historical Note:
NAPCE was formerly (1992) known as National Association of Professors of Christian Education. NAPCE serves to enhance the international teaching mission of the church through the cultivation of personal and professional growth of professors within the broad field of educational ministries. Membership: $75 (Regular); $45 (Student).

Continuing Education:
Enrollment: 275

Meetings/Conferences: Annual

Publications:
Christian Education Journal; semi-annually; adv.
Membership Directory; on-line
NAPCE Newsletter

North American Association of State and Provincial Lotteries (1971)

One S. Broadway
Geneva, OH 44041
Tel: (440) 466-5630 *Fax:* (440) 466-5649
E-Mail: info@nasplhq.org
Website: naspl.org
Staff: 3

Personnel:
President: Buddy Roogow
Treasurer: Terry Rich
Contact, Membership: Andy White
    E-Mail: awhite@nasplhq.org

Historical Note:
Became the North American Association of State and Provincial Lotteries in 1987. The mission of NASPL is to assemble and disseminate information and benefits of state and provincial lottery organizations through education and communications and where appropriate publicly advocate the positions of the Association on matters of general policy. Membership: $5,000-80,000/year (Associate).

Meetings/Conferences: Annual
2013 - Providence, RI (The Westin Providence Hotel)/ Oct. 1 - 4
2014 - Atlantic City, NJ/Sept. 30 - Oct. 3

Publications:
Lottery Insights; monthly; adv.
NASPL Online Office ; on-line

North American Association of State and Provincial Lotteries (1971)

One S. Broadway
Geneva, OH 44041
Tel: (440) 466-5630 *Fax:* (440) 466-5649
E-Mail: info@nasplhq.org
Website: naspl.org
Members: 52 organizations
Staff: 6
Annual Budget: $1-2,000,000

Personnel:
Executive Director: David B. Gale
    E-Mail: dgale@nasplhq.org
Contact, Vendor Relations: Jean Pierre Bayard
Contact, Legal: Kurt Freedlund
Coordinator, Conferences: Tamika R. Ligon MPA
    E-Mail: tligon@nasplhq.org
Chair, Conferences: Terry Rich
Director, Administration: Thomas C. Tulloch
    E-Mail: ttulloch@nasplhq.org

Historical Note:
Founded as the National Association of State Lotteries (NASL), later changed as NASPL (1984). NASPL works to assemble and disseminate information and benefits of state and provincial lottery organizations through education and communications and, when appropriate, publicly advocates its positions on matters of general policy. Membership $5000-80,000 (Association)/year.

Meetings/Conferences: Annual
Conference Chair: Tamika R. Ligon MPA
2013 - Providence, RI (The Westin Providence Hotel)/ Oct. 1 - 4
2014 - Atlantic City, NJ/Sept. 30 - Oct. 3
Number of non-conference events/year: 1

Publications:
Lottery Insights; monthly

North American Association of Summer Sessions (1964)

1501 W. Bradley Ave.
Peoria, IL 61625
Fax: (309) 677-3321
TollFree: (866) 880-9607
Website: naass.org
Members: 450 summer session administrators
Staff: 2
Annual Budget: $100-250,000
Tax: 501(c)(3)

Personnel:
Executive Director: Janet Lange
    E-Mail: lange@bradley.edu
Contact, Events and Membership: Candy Hall
    E-Mail: cld@bradley.edu4

Historical Note:
Established as the National Association of College and University Summer Sessions, it became the National Association of Summer Sessions in 1968 and assumed its present name in 1975. NAASS's purpose is to develop quality summer programming, academic standards and present the opportunity for stimulation and professional growth. Members are deans and directors of college and university summer programs located throughout the United States, Canada and Mexico. Membership: $50 (Affiliated/ Retired); $200 (Professional); $250 (University-College).

Meetings/Conferences: Annual
Conference Chair: Candy Hall

Publications:
Membership Directory; on-line

Membership List Available to Non-members

North American Association of Wardens and Superintendents *(1970)*

P.O. Box 11037
Albany, NY 12211-0037
Tel: (607) 738-3374
E-Mail: NAAWSinfo@aol.com
Website: corrections.com/naaws
Members: 1150 active and retired wardens
Staff: 4
Annual Budget: $100-250,000

Personnel:
Executive director: Gloria Hultz
    E-Mail: ghultz@stny.rr.com
Editor and Publisher: Arthur A. Leonardo
    E-Mail: elart26@aol.com
Treasurer: Cherry Lindamood
President: Darrel Vannoy

Historical Note:
Formerly (1971) Wardens' Association of America and (1980) American Association of Wardens and Superintendents. NAAWS is committed to setting goals and achieving results that make a difference when it comes to jail and prison operations. Activities include communication, networking, training and recognition. Membership is open to all CEO's of Adult and Youth facilities in both the public and private sector. Membership: $25/year.

Meetings/Conferences: Annual
2013 - Houston, TX (George R. Brown Convention Center)/Jan. 25 - 30
2013 - Columbus, OH (Hilton Columbus Downtown)/ May 29 - June 1
Number of non-conference events/year: 1

Publications:
Grapevine; monthly

Membership List Available to Non-members

North American Bar-Related Title Insurers *(1965)*

1430 Lee St.
Des Plaines, IL 60018
Tel: (847) 298-8300 *Fax:* (847) 298-8388
Website: nabrti.com
Members: 10 companies
Staff: 2
Annual Budget: $25-50,000

Personnel:
Executive Vice President: Joanne P. Elliot
    E-Mail: joanne@elliottlaw.com
Webmaster: Catherine Loveland
    E-Mail: catherineloveland@catic-e.com

Historical Note:
Formerly (1979) the National Conference of Bar-Related Title Insurers, assumed its current name in 2005. NABRTI's mission is to play an active part in maintaining the role of the real estate lawyer by closely monitoring, lobbying, and introducing (where necessary) legislation that would have an impact on the real estate practitioner.

Publications:
NABRTI Newsletter; bi-monthly

North American Blueberry Council *(1965)*

80 Iron Point Cir.
Suite 114
Folsom, CA 95630-8593
Tel: (916) 983-2279 *Fax:* (916) 983-9370
Website: nabcblues.org
Members: 85 grower organizations
Staff: 3
Annual Budget: $500-1,000,000
Tax: 501(c)(5)

Personnel:

Executive Director: Mark Villata
    E-Mail: mvillata@nabcblues.org
Administrative Assistant: Jo Dee Gowan
    E-Mail: jgowan@nabcblues.org
Compliance Coordinator: Mary Nezbeth
    E-Mail: mnezbeth@blueberry.org

Historical Note:
NABC is a non-profit agricultural association representing cultivated blueberry growers and marketers in the United State and Canada. Members are blueberry growers and marketers from the U.S. and Canada. Membership: $100-1,000 (Grower, based on annual production); $700 (Associate).

Meetings/Conferences: Annual

Publications:
Membership Directory; on-line

North American Building Material Distribution Association *(1952)*

401 N. Michigan Ave.
Chicago, IL 60611
Tel: (312) 321-6845 *Fax:* (312) 644-0310
TollFree: (888) 747-7862
E-Mail: info@nbmda.org
Website: nbmda.org
Members: 250 Companies
Staff: 5
Annual Budget: $500-1,000,000
Tax: 501(c)(6)

Personnel:
Executive Vice President: Kevin Gammonley
    E-Mail: kgammonley@nbmda.org
Senior Associate, Member Services: Kari Aylward
    E-Mail: kaylward@nbmda.org
Manager, Convention: Sarah Haukap
    E-Mail: shaukap@smithbucklin.com
Membership and Operations Manager: Mark Swets
    E-Mail: mswets@nbmda.org
Senior Coordinator, Marketing and Communications: Andy Younger
    E-Mail: ayounger@smithbucklin.com

Historical Note:
Absorbed (1964) National Plywood Distributors Association and formerly (1994) National Building Material Distributors Association, merged (1994) with the Canadian National Building Materials Distributors Association. Mission is to develop and promote the effectiveness of distribution processes to improve member profitability and growth. NBMDA represents a network of distributors and manufacturers . Membership: $795- 4,595 (Distributor); $995-3,595 (Associate); $495 (Allied).

Continuing Education:
Certification Designation/s: UID, PCID, MID

Meetings/Conferences: Annual
Conference Chair: Kari Aylward

Publications:
Membership Directory; on-line
NAW publications; on-line

Membership List Available to Non-members

North American Calorimetry Conference *(1945)*

Department of Chemistry and Chemical Biology, Rutgers University
610 Taylor Rd.
Piscataway, NJ 08854
Tel: (732) 445-3958 *Fax:* (732) 445-5312
E-Mail: calcon@rci.rutgers.edu
Website: calorimetry-conference.org
Members: 250 individuals
Staff: 2
Annual Budget: $10-25,000
Tax: 501(c)(3)

Personnel:
Secretary and Treasurer: Conceicao A.S.A Minetti
    E-Mail: cminetti@rci.rutgers.edu

Historical Note:
Formerly (1950) the Low Temperature Calorimetry Conference. CALCON serves as the collegial forum for the dissemination of current research and state-of-the-art technological developments in calorimetry and thermodynamics. Members are scientists in academia, government, and industry whose research interests primarily focus on the development and application of calorimetric methods and/or thermochemical techniques. Membership: $20/year.

Meetings/Conferences: Annual

North American Carbon Capture & Storage Association

C/O Blue Source LLC
12012 Wickchester, Suite 660
Houston, TX 77079
Tel: (281) 668-8488
E-Mail: michael.moore@naccsa.org
Website: naccsa.org
Members: 14 Organisations
Staff: 2
Annual Budget: $250-500,000

Personnel:
Executive Director: Michael Moore
    E-Mail: michael.moore@naccsa.org

Historical Note:
NACCSA is a non-profit organization that supports the development of the carbon capture and storage industry. Its primary purpose is to educate policymakers and the public about the CCUS industry. Members of the association include companies involved in developing commercial processes that seek to mitigate atmospheric emissions through carbon capture and storage, and specialists engaged in the technical, commercial, financial and developmental aspects of CCUS activities in both the U.S. and Canada.

Meetings/Conferences:
Number of non-conference events/year: 1

Publications:
Membership Directory

North American Cartographic Information Society *(1980)*

The Florida State University, Florida Resources and Environmental Analysis Center
UCC2200
Tallahassee, FL 32306-2641
Tel: (850) 644-7362 *Fax:* (850) 644-7360
E-Mail: nacis@nacis.org
Website: nacis.org
Members: 540 individuals and members
Staff: 6
Annual Budget: $50-100,000

Personnel:
Executive Director, Annual Meeting Operations: Lou Cross
    E-Mail: nacis@nacis.org

Historical Note:
NACIS's mission is to improve communication, coordination and cooperation among the producers, disseminators, curators, and users of cartographic information. Members are cartographers and others interested in the creation and use of accurate maps. Membership: $42 (Regular); $20 (Student); $72 (Affiliate).

Meetings/Conferences: Annual
Conference Chair: Lou Cross

Publications:
Cartographic Perspectives

North American Case Research Association *(1958)*

Department of Economics, Scobey 504
South Dakota State University
Brookings, SD 57007
Tel: (605) 688-4849
Website: nacra.net
Members: 500 individuals
Staff: 5
Annual Budget: $50-100,000

Personnel:
President: Jeffrey P. Shay
    E-Mail: shayj@wlu.edu
Vice President, Communications and Editor: Carol Cumber
    E-Mail: carol.cumber@sdstate.edu
Editor: Deborah Ettington
    E-Mail: dxe12@psu.edu
Secretary and Treasurer: Kay Guess
    E-Mail: aguess@samford.edu
Vice President, Case Marketing: Susan Peters
    E-Mail: speters@fmarion.edu

Historical Note:
Founded as the Southern Case Writers, became the Southern Case Research Association in 1971, and assumed its current name in 1981. NACRA works to enhance the legitimacy and status of case research and pedagogy within academic institutions and professional associations. Members are persons interested in case research, writing and teaching in business and other academic disciplines. Membership: $50/year.

Meetings/Conferences: Annual
2013 - Victoria, BC (The Fairmont Empress Hotel)/Oct.
   17 - 19

Publications:
Membership Directory; on-line
NACRA Newsletter; semi-annually

North American Catalysis Society (1956)
3801 W. Chester Pike
LyondellBasell Industries
Newtown Square, PA 19073
Tel: (610) 359-2500
Website: nacatsoc.org
Members: 2000 individuals
Staff: 3
Annual Budget: $100-250,000
Tax: 501(c)(3)

Personnel:
Director, Communications: Edrick Morales
   E-Mail: edrick.morales@lyondell.com

Historical Note:
*Formerly The Catalysis Society (North America). Fosters
an interest in heterogeneous and homogeneous catalysis in
the U.S., Mexico, and Canada. Organizes national meetings
for the purpose of discussing the latest developments in
the field. Members are chemists and chemical engineers
engaged in the study and use of reactions involving
catalysts, substances used to accelerate reactions and which
may be recovered virtually unchanged. Membership: $20
(Non-Student); $5 (Student).*

Meetings/Conferences: Semi-Annual
2013 - New Orleans, LA/March 7 - 11
2013 - Indianapolis, IN/Sept. 8 - 12
2014 - Washington, DC/March 16 - 20
2014 - San Francisco, CA/Sept. 7 - 11
Number of non-conference events/year: 21

Publications:
NACS Newsletter

North American Clinical Dermatologic Society
(1959)
C/O Dr. Judith Koperski
9850 Genesee Ave., Suite 530
La Jolla, CA 92037
Tel: (858) 558-0677 *Fax:* (858) 558-3077
Website: nacds.com
Members: 180 individuals
Staff: 4
Annual Budget: $100-250,000
Tax: 501(c)(3)

Personnel:
President: James Stewart MD
Director, Professional Relations: Robert Berger MD
   E-Mail: rsbcsb@aol.com
Vice President and Chairman, Membership Services: Judith
   A. Koperski MD
   E-Mail: jakoperski@yahoo.com
General Secretary: Richard L. Spielvogel MD

Historical Note:
*NACDS is nationally affiliated with American Academy
of Dermatology. NACDS's mission is to provide clinical
education to its members through its program of organized
visits to dermatology clinics and related institutions around
the world. NACDS regularly provides donations to local
medical facilities such as the National Leprosarium in
Istanbul and the Skin and Cancer Foundation of Australia.
Has no paid officers or full-time staff. Membership: $175/
year.*

Meetings/Conferences: Annual
2013 - Barcelona, Spain (University of Barcelona)/
   April 23 - May 5
Number of non-conference events/year: 1

North American Clun Forest Association (1925)
21727 Randall Dr.
Houston, MN 55943-9801
Tel: (507) 864-7585
Website: clunforestsheep.org
Members:
8 farms
60 individuals
Staff: 3
Annual Budget: Under $10,000

Personnel:
Secretary and Treasurer: Bets Reedy
   E-Mail: bramble@acegroup.cc

Historical Note:

*NACFA's mission is to provide for the recording of
pedigrees, the issuance of registration certificates to animals
whose pedigrees have been deemed to be pure and which
meet such other qualifications. Membership: $25 (Voting);
$10 (Associate).*

Meetings/Conferences: Annual

Publications:
Member Directory; on-line

North American Coalition for Christian
Admissions Professionals (1970)
P.O. Box 5211
Huntington, IN 46750
Tel: (260) 356-5211 *Fax:* (260) 359-0101
TollFree: (888) 423-2477
Website: naccap.org
Members: 300 schools
Staff: 19
Annual Budget: $1-2,000,000
Tax: 501(c)(3)

Personnel:
Executive Director: Chant Thompson
Treasurer: Julie Featherston

Historical Note:
*NACCAP is an organization recognized for serving
and engaging its members by providing professional
development and initiatives that champion the cause for
Christian Education. Members are admissions and guidance
personnel from over 300 Christian high schools, liberal arts
colleges and universities, Bible colleges, graduate schools
and seminaries throughout North America. Membership:
$50-300/year.*

Meetings/Conferences: Annual
2013 - Grantham, PA (Messiah College)/May 28 - June
   1

North American Colleges and Teachers of
Agriculture (1955)
151 W. 100 South
Rupert, ID 83350
Tel: (208) 436-0692 *Fax:* (208) 436-1384
E-Mail: nactasec@pmt.org
Website: nactateachers.org
Members: 1000 individuals
Staff: 5
Annual Budget: $50-100,000

Personnel:
Editor: Rick Parker
   E-Mail: ricpar@pmt.org
Secretary and Treasurer: Marilyn B. Parker
   E-Mail: nactasec@pmt.org

Historical Note:
*Formerly (2002) National Association of Colleges and
Teachers of Agriculture. NACTA's purpose is to promote
teaching of agriculture and related disciplines at the postsecondary level. Members of NACTA are from two-year
and four-year colleges, public and private. Membership:
$75 (Institutional Active); $100 (Active); $25 (Emeritus/
Graduate Student); $750 (Lifetime).*

Meetings/Conferences: Annual
2013 - Blacksburg, VA (Virginia Tech)/June 25 - 29

Publications:
NACTA Journal; quarterly
NACTA Newsletter; monthly

North American Conference on British Studies
(1950)
Department of History, University of Colorado
Denver
CB 182, P.O. Box 173364
Denver, CO 80217
Tel: (303) 556-2896 *Fax:* (303) 556-6037
E-Mail: axa24@psu.edu
Website: nacbs.org
Members: 673 individuals
Staff: 3
Annual Budget: $50-100,000

Personnel:
Executive Secretary: Marjorie Levine-Clark
   E-Mail: marjorie.levine-clark@ucdenver.edu

Historical Note:
*Formerly known as the Conference on British Studies (CBS),
adopted its current name in 1980. NACBS, an affiliate
of the American Historical Association, is committed to
all aspects of the study of British civilization. Members
are teachers at universities in countries outside North
America, secondary school teachers, and independent*

*scholars. Membership: $71 (Individual); $38 (Student);
$119 (Sustaining).*

Meetings/Conferences:
Conference Chair: Marjorie Levine-Clark
2013 - Portland, OR/Nov. 8 - 10
Number of non-conference events/year: 3

Publications:
Journal of British Studies; quarterly
NACBS Directory (Membership Directory)

North American Corriente Association (1982)
P.O. Box 2698
Monument, CO 80132
Tel: (816) 421-1992 *Fax:* (816) 421-1991
Website: corriente.us
Members: 675 individuals
Staff: 2
Annual Budget: $50-100,000
Tax: 501(c)(5)

Personnel:
Executive Director: Ellen Hamilton
   E-Mail: ellen@corriente.us
Executive Editor: James A. Spawn

Historical Note:
*NACA's mission is to promote the use of Corriente cattle
and institute and monitor a registered breeding program to
preserve the true breed and make it available for the fast-
growing rodeo circuit. Membership: $600 (Lifetime); $35
(Active Member); $20 (Associate); $10 (Junior).*

Meetings/Conferences: Annual
Number of non-conference events/year: 3

Publications:
Corriente Corresponder; adv.
Membership Directory; on-line

North American Council of Automotive Teachers
(1974)
P.O. Box 80010
Charleston, SC 29416
Tel: (843) 556-7068 *Fax:* (843) 556-7068
E-Mail: office@nacat.com
Website: nacat.com
Members:
50 companies
750 individuals
Staff: 4
Annual Budget: $50-100,000
Tax: 501(c)(6)

Personnel:
Treasurer: Charles Ginther
Executive Manager and Vice President, Conferences: Dan
   Perrin

Historical Note:
*Formerly (1991) the National Association of College
Automotive Teachers. NACAT's purpose is to advance all
levels of automotive education and operates the NACAT
Foundation to provide funding for scholarships and
other worthy causes. Members are automotive teachers
and supporting companies in the automotive industry.
Membership: $50 (Individual); $45 (Per Member-Group
Membership).*

Meetings/Conferences: Annual
Conference Chair: Dan Perrin
2013 - Québec, QC/July 22 - 26
2014 - Greenville, SC/July 21 - 25

Publications:
Membership Directory
NACAT News; adv.

North American Deer Farmers Association (1983)
1428 Market Ave., North
Canton, OH 44714
Tel: (330) 454-3944 *Fax:* (330) 454-3950
E-Mail: info@nadefa.org
Website: nadefa.org
Members: 650 individuals
Staff: 9
Annual Budget: $250-500,000

Personnel:
Executive Director: Shawn Schafer
   E-Mail: schafer@nadefa.org

Historical Note:
*NADeFA is dedicated to the encouragement of deer farming
and ranching as an agricultural pursuit and serves its
members through educational programs and publications.
NADeFA's mission is to foster a greater association*

among people who raise deer for commercial purposes.
Membership: $35-1,500/year.

Meetings/Conferences: Annual
2013 - Cincinnati, OH/March 14 - 16

North American Die Casting Association (1989)
241 Holbrook Dr.
Wheeling, IL 60090-5809
Tel: (847) 279-0001 Fax: (847) 279-0002
E-Mail: nadca@diecasting.org
Website: diecasting.org
Members: 3400 individuals
Staff: 15
Annual Budget: $2-5,000,000
Tax: 501(c)(6)

Personnel:
President: Daniel L. Twarog
    E-Mail: twarog@diecasting.org
Manager, Advertising and Promotions: Athena Catlett
    E-Mail: catlett@diecasting.org
Contact, Membership Services: Donna Hutchins
    E-Mail: hutchins@diecasting.org
Manager, Education and Meetings: Melisa Ryzner
    E-Mail: mryzner@diecasting.org
Director, Research, Education and Technology: Steve
    Udvardy
    E-Mail: udvardy@diecasting.org

Historical Note:
NADCA aims at promoting industry awareness, domestic
growth in the global marketplace and member exposure.
Members are individual members and corporate members
located throughout United States, Canada and Mexico.
Membership: $25-11,300/year.

Continuing Education:
Certification Designation/s: MDCM, CDCT, MDCT, MDCP

Meetings/Conferences: Annual
2013 - Schaumburg, IL (Renaissance Schaumburg
    Convention Center Hotel)/April 8 - 11
2013 - Louisville, KY (Kentucky International
    Convention Center)/Sept. 16 - 18/5000 attendees/
    over 100 exhibitors
2015 - Indianapolis, IN (Indianapolis Convention
    Center)/Oct. 5 - 7/5000 attendees/over 100
    exhibitors
Number of non-conference events/year: 3

Publications:
Die Casting Engineer; bi-monthly
Insight; monthly
Leadership Directory; on-line
LINKS; bi-monthly; adv.
Membership Directory; on-line
NADCA Update; weekly; adv.

North American Electric Reliability Corporation (1968)
3353 Peachtree Rd. NE
Suite 600, North Tower
Atlanta, GA 30326
Tel: (404) 446-2560 Fax: (404) 446-2595
E-Mail: info@nerc.com
Website: nerc.com
Members: 500 regional councils
Staff: 151
Annual Budget: $25-50,000,000
Tax: 501(c)(6)

Personnel:
President and Chief Executive Officer: Gerry W. Cauley
Meeting Planning Specialist: Stacia-Ann Chambers
Director, Human Resources: Damon Epperson
Director, Training, Education and Personnel Certification:
    Peter Knoetgen
Manager, Communications: Kimberly Mielcarek
    E-Mail: Kimberly.Mielcarek@nerc.net
Senior Legal Assistant: Sara Minges
    E-Mail: sara.minges@nerc.net
Director, Information Technology and Services: Marvin
    Santerfeit

Historical Note:
Formerly (2007) National Electric Reliability Council,
NERC's help maintain and improve the reliability of North
America's bulk power system and provides a number of
additional programs and services designed to support
owners, operators and users of the bulk power system in
their efforts to attain operational excellence.

Continuing Education:
Certification Designation/s: SOC

Meetings/Conferences: Annual

Conference Chair: Stacia-Ann Chambers
Number of non-conference events/year: 4

Publications:
Membership Directory; on-line
NERC News; monthly

Membership List Available to Non-members

North American Elk Breeders Association (1990)
3160 Rd. 435 South
Havre, MT 59501
Tel: (406) 395-4556
E-Mail: info@naelk.org
Website: naelk.org
Members: 1800 individuals
Staff: 10
Annual Budget: $50-100,000

Personnel:
President: Kim Kafka
    E-Mail: kdiamondK@mtintouch.net

Historical Note:
An affiliate of the U.S. Animal Health Association, and
is nationally afiliated with North American Deer Farmers
Association. NAEBA educates its members and the
general public about the rewards and opportunities that
are available through participation in the industry as a
legitimate diversified agricultural pursuit. Also maintains
a registry of pure bred Wapiti (North American Elk),
and provides education and support to member breeders.
Membership: $25-2,500/year.

Meetings/Conferences: Annual
2013 - Sioux Falls, SD (Best Western Plus Ramkota
    Hotel)/Aug. 1 - 3
Number of non-conference events/year: 1

Publications:
Membership Directory; on-line
NAEBA Newsletter

North American Equipment Dealers Association (1900)
1195 Smizer Mill Rd.
Fenton, MO 63026-3480
Tel: (636) 349-5000 Fax: (636) 349-5443
E-Mail: naeda@naeda.com
Website: naeda.com
Members: 5000 retail dealers
Staff: 10
Annual Budget: $2-5,000,000
Tax: 501(c)(6)

Personnel:
Director, Communications: Kathy Bernard
    E-Mail: bernardk@naeda.com
Director, Member Services: Joseph (Joe) R. Dykes
    E-Mail: dykesj@naeda.com
Corporate Counsel: Lance Formwalt
    E-Mail: lancef@sblsg.com
Publisher and Editor-in-Chief: Jack Odle
    E-Mail: jodle@progressivefarmer.com
Vice President, Government Relations: Michael Williams
    E-Mail: williamsm@naeda.com

Historical Note:
Founded as the National Retail Farm Equipment
Association, became the National Farm and Power
Equipment Dealers Association in 1962 and assumed its
present name in 1988. NAEDA strives to build a better
business environment for North American equipment
dealers. Members are retail dealers of agricultural,
industrial and outdoor power equipment in the United
States and Canada. Membership: $500/year (Associate).

Meetings/Conferences: Annual
Conference Chair: Joseph (Joe) R. Dykes
2013 - Louisville, KY (Kentucky Exposition Center)/
    Oct. 23 - 25
2014 - Louisville, KY (Kentucky Exposition Center)/
    Oct. 22 - 24
2015 - Louisville, KY (Kentucky Exposition Center)/
    Oct. 21 - 23
Number of non-conference events/year: 1

Publications:
NAEDA Update; bi-weekly; adv.

North American Export Grain Association, Inc. (1912)
1250 I St. NW
Suite 1003
Washington, DC 20005
Tel: (202) 682-4030 Fax: (202) 682-4033
E-Mail: info@naega.org

Website: naega.org
Members: 35 companies
Staff: 3
Annual Budget: $500-1,000,000
Tax: 501(c)(6)

Personnel:
President and Chief Executive Officer: Gary C. Martin
    E-Mail: gcmartin@naega.org
Director, Operations: Patrick Hayden
    E-Mail: phayden@naega.org

Historical Note:
NAEGA's purpose is to promote the commercial export of
grain and oilseed trade from the United States. Membership
includes private and public companies and farmer
cooperatives involved in North American grain and seed
trade.

Meetings/Conferences:
Conference Chair: Patrick Hayden

Publications:
Membership Directory; annually
NAEGA OUTREACH; weekly

North American Farm Show Council (1972)
590 Woody Hayes Dr.
Columbus, OH 43210
Tel: (614) 292-4278 Fax: (614) 292-9448
E-Mail: gamble.19@osu.edu
Website: farmshows.org
Members:
24 member shows
12 associates
Staff: 2
Annual Budget: $25-50,000
Tax: 501(c)(6)

Personnel:
President: Doug Wagner
Secretary and Treasurer: Chuck Gamble
    E-Mail: gamble.19@osu.edu

Historical Note:
NAFSC strives to improve the value of its member shows
through education, communication and evaluation.
Membership: $700 (Regular); $100 (Associate).

Meetings/Conferences:
Number of non-conference events/year: 23

Publications:
Membership Directory; on-line

North American Fiberboard Association (1991)
2118 Plum Grove Rd.
Suite 283
Rolling Meadows, IL 60008
Tel: (847) 934-8394 Fax: (847) 934-8394
E-Mail: afa@fiberboard.org
Website: fiberboard.org
Members: 6 companies
Staff: 2
Annual Budget: $100-250,000

Personnel:
Executive Director: Louis E. Wagner
    E-Mail: lwagner@voyager.net
Legal Counsel: William C. Ives

Historical Note:
Formerly American Fiberboard Association. AFA serves
as the central clearinghouse for industry and technical
information for architects, builders, contractors, distributors,
dealers, government agencies, and the general public.
Members are manufacturers of cellulosic fiberboard
products.

Publications:
Member Roster; on-line

North American Flowerbulb Wholesalers Association (1983)
Marlboro Bulb Company
2424 Hwy. 72/221 East
Greenwood, SC 29649
Tel: (864) 229-1618 Fax: (864) 229-5719
TollFree: (800) 999-0567
E-Mail: nafwa1@aol.com
Website: nafwa.com
Members: 50 companies
Staff: 4
Annual Budget: $25-50,000

Personnel:
President: Thijs Leenders
    E-Mail: tleenders@dutchbulbs.com

Director, Research: Ron Beck
   E-Mail: rbeck@fredgloeckner.com
Contact, Membership: Patricia de Vroomen
Secretary and Treasurer: Jack De Vroomen
   E-Mail: nafwa1@aol.com

Historical Note:
NAFWA's purpose is to promote the interest of companies whose trade is wholesaling flowerbulbs by developing programs, services and networking opportunities that contribute to the overall business success of the industry.

Meetings/Conferences: Annual

Publications:
Bill Miller's Research Newsletter

North American Fuzzy Information Processing Society *(1981)*
C/O Dr. Bill Tastle
School of Business, 424 Smiddy Hall, Ithaca College
Ithaca, NY 14850
Tel: (607) 274-3669 *Fax:* (607) 274-1152
Website: nafips.ece.ualberta.ca
Members: 120 individuals
Staff: 4
Annual Budget: Under $10,000

Personnel:
President: Vladik Kreinovich
   E-Mail: president@nafips.org
Editor-in-Chief: Piero P. Bonissone
Treasurer: Atsushi Inoue
   E-Mail: treasurer@nafips.org
Board Director: Bill Tastle
   E-Mail: tastle@ieee.org

Historical Note:
NAFIPS's mission is to promote and disseminate studies related to theories of fuzzy sets and related topics and to study of their application in such fields as artificial intelligence, medicine, image processing, speech, linguistics, control theory, operations research, economics, and decision theory. Membership: $19/year (Individual).

Meetings/Conferences: Annual

Publications:
International Journal of Approximate Reasoning; adv.
NAFIPS Newsletter; quarterly

Membership List Available to Non-members

North American Gamebird Association *(1931)*
P.O. Box 338
Cambridge, MD 21613
Tel: (410) 228-3755 *Fax:* (410) 228-3238
TollFree: (800) 624-2967
E-Mail: info@mynaga.org
Website: mynaga.org
Members: 1500 individuals
Staff: 3
Annual Budget: $50-100,000

Personnel:
Executive Director: Ladd Johnson
   E-Mail: laddjohnson@verizon.net
Treasurer: Vern Beavers
   E-Mail: vernbeavers@live.com
News Editor: Sue Bookhout

Historical Note:
Formerly (1981) known as North American Game Breeders and Shooting Preserve Operators Association, NAGA tries to improve the methods of game bird production and hunting preserve management. Membership: $65 (Individual); $75 (Canada and Foreign); $125 (Business); $300 (Sponsor); $2,500 (Diamond Sponsor).

Meetings/Conferences: Annual
2013 - Kansas City, MO (InterContinental Hotel)/Feb. 4 - 6

Publications:
NAGA Membership Directory; on-line
NAGA News Magazine; bi-monthly

North American Gaming Regulators Association *(1984)*
1000 Westgate Dr.
Suite 252
St. Paul, MN 55114
Tel: (651) 203-7244 *Fax:* (651) 290-2266
E-Mail: info@nagra.org
Website: nagra.org
Members: 120 regular member agencies and trade affiliates

Staff: 4
Annual Budget: $100-250,000
Tax: 501(c)(6)

Personnel:
President: Simone Syrenne
   E-Mail: ssyrenne@mgcc.mb.ca
Secretary: Rachel Farr
   E-Mail: rachel.farr@mgc.dps.mo.gov
Treasurer: Joseph Koss
   E-Mail: joe.koss@alaska.gov
Contact, Publications: Anna Wrisky
   E-Mail: annaw@ewald.com

Historical Note:
NAGRA brings together agencies that regulate gaming activities and provides them a forum for the mutual exchange of regulatory information and techniques. Its activities include collecting and disseminating regulatory and enforcement information, procedures, and experiences from all jurisdictions. It also provides on-going gaming education and training for all members and a forum to speak on legislative matters. Membership: $475 (Regular-Organization); $725 (Trade Affiliate-Organization).

Meetings/Conferences: Annual
2013 - Virginia Beach, VA (Hilton Virginia Beach Oceanfront)/June 3 - 7

Publications:
NAGRA News; quarterly

Membership List Available to Non-members

North American Horticultural Supply Association *(1988)*
100 N. 20th St.
Suite 400
Philadelphia, PA 19103-1443
Tel: (215) 320-3877 *Fax:* (215) 564-2175
E-Mail: nahsa@fernley.com
Website: nahsa.org
Members: 54 manufacturers and distributors
Staff: 3
Annual Budget: $100-250,000

Personnel:
Account Manager: Jason Harbonic
   E-Mail: jharbonia@fernley.com
Meeting Manager: Stephanie Ritter
   E-Mail: sritter@fernley.com

Historical Note:
NAHSA's mission is to strengthen and support the distribution and manufacturing of horticultural products and services. Membership: $745 (Associate); $450-1,050 (Distributor), $875 (Manufacturer).

Meetings/Conferences: Annual
Conference Chair: Stephanie Ritter

Publications:
Membership Directory; annually; adv.
The Landscape; quarterly; adv.

North American Insulation Manufacturers Association *(1933)*
44 Canal Center Plaza
Suite 310
Alexandria, VA 22314
Tel: (703) 684-0084 *Fax:* (703) 684-0427
E-Mail: insulation@naima.org
Website: naima.org
Members: 14 companies
Staff: 9
Annual Budget: $5-10,000,000

Personnel:
President, Chief Executive Officer and Treasurer: Kate Offringa
Vice President, Finance and Administration: Michelle Bunch
   E-Mail: mbunch@naima.org
Vice President, Technical Services: Charles Cottrell
Executive Vice President and General Counsel: Angus Crane
Director, Government Affairs and Communications: Kevin Koonce

Historical Note:
Formerly the National Rock and Slag Wool Association, the National Mineral Wool Association, (1980) the National Mineral Wool Insulation Association, and (1992) the Mineral Insulation Manufacturers Association. NAIMA's mission is to promote energy efficiency and environmental preservation through the use of fiber glass, rock wool, and slag wool insulation products and to encourage safe production and use of these insulation products. Members

are manufacturers of fiber glass, rock wool, and slag wool insulation products.

Publications:
Membership Directory; on-line

North American Lake Management Society *(1980)*
P.O. Box 5443
Madison, WI 53705-0443
Tel: (608) 233-2836 *Fax:* (608) 233-3186
E-Mail: info@nalms.org
Website: nalms.org
Members: 2500 individuals
Staff: 3
Annual Budget: $500-1,000,000
Tax: 501(c)(3)

Personnel:
Coordinator, Membership Services: Greg Arenz
   E-Mail: garenz@nalms.org
Manager, Programs: Philip Forsberg
   E-Mail: forsberg@nalms.org

Historical Note:
The purpose of the Society is to forge partnerships among citizens, scientists, and professionals to foster the management and protection of lakes and reservoirs. Members are academics, lake managers and others having an interest in furthering the understanding of lake ecology. Membership: $35-500/year.

Continuing Education:
Certification Designation/s: CLM, CLP

Meetings/Conferences: Annual
Conference Chair: Philip Forsberg
Number of non-conference events/year: 1

Publications:
Lake and Reservoir Management; quarterly; adv.
LakeLine Magazine; quarterly; adv.

North American Limousin Foundation *(1968)*
Six Inverness Ct. East
Suite 260
Englewood, CO 80112-5595
Tel: (303) 220-1693 *Fax:* (303) 220-1884
E-Mail: limousin@nalf.org
Website: nalf.org
Members: 4000 individuals
Staff: 7
Annual Budget: $1-2,000,000
Tax: 501(c)(5)

Personnel:
Executive Director: Mark Anderson
   E-Mail: mark@nalf.org
Director, Communications: Brooke Bennett
   E-Mail: brooke@nalf.org
Director, Commercial Marketing: Joe Epperly
   E-Mail: joe@nalf.org
Director, Activities: Bobbi Hartwig
   E-Mail: bobbi@nalf.org
Director, Program Administration: Carol Johnson
   E-Mail: carol@nalf.org
Specialist, Registry and Membership Services: Stephanie Kramer-Beddo
   E-Mail: steph@nalf.org
Director, Membership Services: Alison Pagel
   E-Mail: Lalison@nalf.org

Historical Note:
NALF is organized to promote, improve, and develop the Limousin breed of cattle. Seeks to maintain the Limousin Herdbook, which includes information on ownership, bloodlines, and performance of Limousin cattle. Members are breeders or owners of cattle. Membership: $100 (Annual); $50 (Junior/Associate); $50 (Partner, Life Time).

Meetings/Conferences:
Conference Chair: Carol Johnson
Number of non-conference events/year: 30

Publications:
Bottom Line Newsletter; adv.
Limousin World; monthly; adv.
Member Directory; on-line
Members Memo
NALF Line; monthly
NALF News; monthly
NALF Partners e-Newsletter; bi-weekly
NALF Report; monthly

North American Manufacturing Research Institution of SME *(1981)*
One SME Dr.

P.O. Box 930
Dearborn, MI 48128
Tel: (313) 425-3000 *Fax:* (313) 425-3000
TollFree: (800) 733-4763
Website: sme.org/namri
Members: 200 individuals
Staff: 2
Annual Budget: $25-50,000

Personnel:
President: Jian Cao FSME, PhD
  E-Mail: jcao@northwestern.edu
Secretary: Robert W. Ivester PhD
  E-Mail: ivester@nist.gov

Historical Note:
*Founded and supported by the Society of Manufacturing
Engineers. NAMRI/SME brings together researchers from
companies, government laboratories, academic institutions
and industrial think tanks located around the world for the
purpose of advancing the scientific foundation of discrete-
parts manufacturing. Members are individuals engaged
in manufacturing research and technology development.
Membership: $125/year.*

Continuing Education:
Certification Designation/s: CMfgT, CMfgE, CEM

Meetings/Conferences: Annual

Publications:
The Transactions of NAMRI/SME; annually

North American Maple Syrup Council *(1959)*
P.O. Box 581
Simsbury, CT 06070
Website: northamericanmaple.org
Members: 16 commercial maple producing states
and Canadian provinces
Staff: 4
Annual Budget: $50-100,000

Personnel:
Executive Director: Michael A. Girard
  E-Mail: mgirard@simscroft.com
Editor: Roy S. Hutchinson
  E-Mail: mapledigest@tds.net
Coordinator, Conferences: Bill Robinson
  E-Mail: robinmap@hurontel.on.ca

Historical Note:
*NAMSC works to promote the interests of all maple syrup
producers. Members are state and provincial maple syrup
associates.*

Meetings/Conferences: Annual
Conference Chair: Bill Robinson
Number of non-conference events/year: 1

Publications:
Maple Syrup Digest; adv.

North American Meat Association *(2012)*
1910 Association Dr.
Reston, VA 20191-1547
Tel: (703) 758-1900 *Fax:* (703) 758-8001
TollFree: (800) 368-3043
Website: meatassociation.com
Members: 400 meat processing members, 230
associate members (suppliers) and 70 allied
members.
Staff: 16
Annual Budget: $500-1,000,000
Tax: 501(c)(6)

Personnel:
Chief Executive Officer: Barry Carpenter
  E-Mail: barry@meatassociation.com
Executive Director: Philip H. Kimball CAE
  E-Mail: phil@meatassociation.com
Director, Membership Services Association Development:
  Jim Goldberg
  E-Mail: jim@meatassociation.com
Operations Manager: Jen Kempis-Persons
  E-Mail: jen@meatassociation.com
Director, Meetings: Sabrina Moore
  E-Mail: sabrina@meatassociation.com
Associate Director, Administration: Etta Reyes
  E-Mail: etta@meatassociation.com
Director, Science, Technical Outreach and Education: Ann
  Wells
  E-Mail: ann@meatassociation.com

Historical Note:
*Formed in 2012 from the merger of the North American
Meat Processors Association and the National Meat
Association. It is an organization of global meat trade.*

Meetings/Conferences: Annual
Conference Chair: Sabrina Moore
2013 - Las Vegas, NV (MGM Resorts International)/
  Feb. 10 - 13
Number of non-conference events/year: 5

Publications:
Membership Direcctory; on-line
NAMP e-Newsletter; on-line

North American Membrane Society *(1985)*
University of Arkansas, Dept. of Chemical
Engineering
3202 Bell Engineering Center
Fayetteville, AR 72701-1201
Tel: (479) 575-3419 *Fax:* (479) 575-7926
E-Mail: nams@uark.edu
Website: membranes.org
Members: 600 individuals
Staff: 3
Annual Budget: $100-250,000

Personnel:
Secretary: Jamie Hestekin
  E-Mail: jhesteki@uark.edu

Historical Note:
*NAMS's purpose is to promote all aspects of membrane
science and technology. Membership: $20 (Student); $60
(Individual); $25 (Retiree).*

Meetings/Conferences: Annual
2013 - Boise, ID (Grove Hotel)/June 8 - 12

Publications:
Membrane Quarterly; quarterly

North American Menopause Society *(1989)*
5900 Landerbrook Dr.
Suite 390
Mayfield Heights, OH 44124
Tel: (440) 442-7550 *Fax:* (440) 442-2660
TollFree: (800) 774-5342
E-Mail: info@menopause.org
Website: menopause.org
Members: 2000 health professionals
Staff: 10
Annual Budget: $2-5,000,000
Tax: 501(c)(3)

Personnel:
Executive Director: Margery L.S. Gass MD
  E-Mail: mgass@menopause.org
Director, Administration: Carolyn Develen
  E-Mail: carolyn@menopause.com
Director, Outreach: Mary A. Nance
  E-Mail: mary@menopause.org
Coordinator, Membership Services: Lynne Povhe
  E-Mail: members@menopause.org
Manager, Operations: Elizabeth K. Slogar
  E-Mail: beth@menopause.org
Managing Editor: Kathryn J. Wisch
  E-Mail: kathy@menopause.org

Historical Note:
*NAMS's mission is to promote the health and quality of
life of women through an understanding of menopause and
healthy aging. Membership: $180-235 (Active); $155-160
(Associate).*

Continuing Education:
Enrollment: 700
Certification Designation/s: NCMP

Meetings/Conferences: Annual
2013 - Dallas, TX (Gaylord Texan Hotel and
  Convention Center-Dallas)/Oct. 9 - 12
2014 - Washington, DC (Gaylord National-
  Washington)/Oct. 15 - 18
2015 - Las Vegas, NV (Caesars Palace Las Vegas Hotel
  and Casino)/Sept. 30 - Oct. 3
2016 - Orlando, FL/Oct. 5 - 8

Publications:
NAMS Daily News; daily
First to Know; monthly
Menopause; monthly; adv.
Menopause e-consult (e-newsletter for members);
  quarterly
Menopause Flashes; on-line
The Female Patient; bi-monthly

Membership List Available to Non-members

North American Metal Packaging Alliance, Inc. (NAMPA) *(1993)*
2200 Pennsylvania Ave. NW

Suite 100
Washington, DC 20037
Tel: (866) 522-0950
Website: metal-pack.org
Members: 16 companies
Staff: 1
Annual Budget: $250-500,000

Personnel:
Executive Director: Kathleen Robertson

Historical Note:
*A trade association for the North American light metal
packaging industry.*

Publications:
Ethical Corporation Magazine
Journal of Pediatrics Study
Wall Street Journal; adv.

North American Millers' Association *(1998)*
600 Maryland Ave. SW
Suite 305 West
Washington, DC 20024
Tel: (202) 484-2200 *Fax:* (202) 488-7416
E-Mail: generalinfo@namamillers.org
Website: namamillers.org
Members: 48 companies
Staff: 6
Annual Budget: $1-2,000,000
Tax: 501(c)(6)

Personnel:
President: Mary K. Waters
  E-Mail: mwaters@namamillers.org
Vice President: James A. Bair
  E-Mail: jbair@namamillers.org
Director, Government Relations: Sherri Lehman
  E-Mail: slehman@namamillers.org
Director, Communications and Meetings: Terri Long
  E-Mail: tlong@namamillers.org

Historical Note:
*Formerly (1998) Millers' National Federation. Absorbed
the National Soft Wheat Association in 1976, the Durum
Wheat Institute in 1982, the American Corn Millers
Federation and Protein Grain Products International
in 1998, and the American Oat Association in 1999.
Represents the dry milling of wheat, corn, oats and rye.
NAMA's mission is to enable its members to grow and
prosper by providing leadership through education,
information and advocacy to members, policy makers,
customers and suppliers in the areas of regulation and
legislation, trade, supply and consumption. Membership is
based on hundred weights of production.*

Meetings/Conferences: Annual
Conference Chair: Terri Long
2013 - Washington, DC (Hotel Sofitel Washington D.C.
  Lafayette Square)/Oct. 28 - 30

Publications:
Membership Directory; on-line
NAMA Newsletter; monthly

Membership List Available to Non-members

North American Mycological Association *(1959)*
P.O. Box 64
Christiansburg, VA 24068
Tel: (540) 230-7603
Website: namyco.org
Members: 2000 individuals and 75 affiliated
mycological societies
Staff: 8
Annual Budget: $25-50,000
Tax: 501(c)(3)

Personnel:
President: Bob Fulgency
  E-Mail: robjoful@comcast.net
Contact, Finance: Angelica Miller
  E-Mail: miller1121@sbcglobal.net
Executive Secretary: Rebecca H. Rader
  E-Mail: rebeccahrader@hotmail.com
Webmaster: David Rust
  E-Mail: webmaster@namyco.org
Contact, Education: Sandy Sheine
  E-Mail: ssheine@aol.com
Editor: Dianna Smith
  E-Mail: diannasmith@optonline.net

Historical Note:
*Originated at Ohio State University in November 1959 as
the Committee on Fungi and incorporated in Ohio as the
North American Mycological Association in 1967. NAMA
is committed to the promotion of scientific and educational*

activities related to fungi. Also supports the protection of natural areas and their biological integrity. Membership: $15–5,000 and up/year; $500 (Lifetime).

Meetings/Conferences: Annual
Number of non-conference events/year: 2

Publications:
McIlvainea: Journal of American Amateur Mycology; annually
NAMA Directory; annually
The Mycophile; bi-monthly

North American Natural Casing Association
(1990)
494 Eighth Ave.
Suite 805
New York, NY 10001
Tel: (212) 695-4980 *Fax:* (212) 695-7153
E-Mail: nanca18hq@yahoo.com
Website: nanca.org
Members:
17 companies
2000 individuals
Staff: 4
Annual Budget: $50-100,000

Personnel:
President: Barbara Negron
    E-Mail: nanca18hq@yahoo.com
Treasurer: Eric Svendsen

Historical Note:
NANCA's mission is to protect its industry from unfair trade practices by foreign countries and to work with member governments to ease trade among its member countries and throughout the world. It also strives to obtain legislation favorable to the industry's interests and prevent or change unfavorable legislation at local, state and federal levels.

Publications:
Member Directory; on-line

North American Nature Photography Association
(1994)
6382 Charleston Rd.
Alma, IL 62807
Tel: (618) 547-7616 *Fax:* (618) 547-7438
E-Mail: info@nanpa.org
Website: nanpa.org
Members: 3000 individuals
Staff: 5
Annual Budget: $250-500,000
Tax: 501(c)(6)

Personnel:
Executive Director: Susan Day
    E-Mail: susanday@nanpa.org

Historical Note:
NANPA promotes the art and science of nature photography as a medium of communication, nature appreciation, and environmental protection. Membership: $100 (General/International); $150 (Joint); $25 (Student); $250-$999 (Friends of NANPA); $250-5000 + (Corporate).

Meetings/Conferences: Annual
2013 - Jacksonville, FL/Feb. 27 - March 2
2013 - Jacksonville, FL (Hyatt Regency Jacksonville Riverfront)/Feb. 28 - March 3
Number of non-conference events/year: 1

Publications:
Currents; quarterly; adv.
Expressions Magazine; annually
Membership Directory; annually
Ripples Newsletter; bi-monthly; adv.

North American Neuro-Ophthalmology Society
(1975)
5841 Cedar Lake Rd.
Suite 204
Minneapolis, MN 55416
Tel: (952) 646-2037 *Fax:* (952) 545-6073
E-Mail: info@nanosweb.org
Website: nanosweb.org
Members: 400 members
Staff: 3
Annual Budget: $500-1,000,000
Tax: 501(c)(3)

Personnel:
Executive Director: Janel Fick
Editor: Lanning B. Kline MD
Exhibits Coordinator: Tami Page

Historical Note:

NANOS is committed to the achievement of excellence in patient care through the support and promotion of education, communication, research, and the practice of neuro-ophthalmology. Membership: $400/year.

Meetings/Conferences: Annual
Conference Chair: Tami Page
2013 - Snowbird, UT (Snowbird Ski and Summer Resort)/Feb. 9 - 14
2014 - Rio Grande, PR (Rio Mar Beach Resort and Spa)/March 1 - 6

Publications:
Journal of Neuro-Ophthalmology; quarterly; adv.
Membership Directory; on-line

Membership List Available to Non-members

North American Neuromodulation Society *(1994)*
4700 W. Lake Ave.
Glenview, IL 60025
Tel: (847) 375-4714 *Fax:* (847) 375-6424
E-Mail: info@neuromodulation.org
Website: neuromodulation.org
Members: 600 members
Staff: 3
Annual Budget: $1-2,000,000
Tax: 501(c)(3)

Personnel:
Executive Director: Chris Welber
    E-Mail: cwelber@neuromodulation.org
Editor-in-Chief, Neuromodulation: Robert Levy
    E-Mail: rml199@northwestern.edu
Treasurer: B. Todd Sitzman MD, MPH
    E-Mail: toddsitzman@msn.com

Historical Note:
Formerly (2004) American Neuromodulation Society. NANS is dedicated to being the premier organization representing neuromodulation. NANS promotes multidisciplinary collaboration among clinicians, scientists, engineers, and others to advance neuromodulation through education, research, innovation and advocacy. Through these efforts NANS seeks to promote and advance the highest quality patient care. Membership: $285 (New); $260 (Renewal); $25 (Student).

Meetings/Conferences: Annual

Publications:
Member Directory; on-line
NANS Newsletter; semi-annually
Neuromodulation: Technology at the Neural Interface; quarterly

North American Olive Oil Association *(1982)*
3301 Route 66
Suite 205, Building C
Neptune, NJ 07753
Tel: (732) 922-3008 *Fax:* (732) 922-3590
E-Mail: info@naooa.org
Website: naooa.org
Members: 110 importers, distributors, and suppliers
Staff: 5

Personnel:
President: Bob Bauer

Historical Note:
NAOOA is a trade association for importers and distributors of olive oil, and for their suppliers abroad. Mission is to support scientific and other forms of research that will benefit the olive oil industry. Memebrship: $2,400-9,660 (Regular); $1,500 (Brokers/Agents); $899 (Introductory/Associate); $995 (Foreign Trade Association).

Meetings/Conferences: Annual

Publications:
Member Directory; on-line

North American Performing Arts Managers and Agents *(1979)*
459 Columbus Ave.
Suite 133
New York, NY 10024
Tel: (510) 643-3786 *Fax:* (510) 643-6707
TollFree: (800) 867-3281
E-Mail: info@napama.org
Website: napama.org
Members: 125 companies
Staff: 5
Annual Budget: $25-50,000

Personnel:
President: Robert Baird
    E-Mail: robert@napama.org

Webmaster: Andrew Gilpin
    E-Mail: mail@gilpin.ca
Treasurer: Robin Pomerance
    E-Mail: r_pomerance@hotmail.com
Vice President, Communications: Jerry Ross
    E-Mail: jross@harmonyartists.com
Vice President, Membership Services: David Wannen
    E-Mail: david@nygasp.org

Historical Note:
Formerly (2000) National Association of Performing Arts Managers and Agents. NAPAMA aims to enhance the professionalism of its members. Membership: $100-300 (Presenting Organization); $150-350 (Agent/Manager); $350 (Business Associate); $100 (Individual/Member Artist/Staff); $150 (Individual Professional); $50 (Student/Emeritus).

Continuing Education:
Certification Designation/s: CPAE

Meetings/Conferences: Annual
Number of non-conference events/year: 1

Publications:
Membership Directory; on-line
NAPAMA email blasts; on-line
NAPAMA Newsletter; quarterly

Membership List Available to Non-members

North American Perishable Agricultural Receivers
1301 Pennsylvania Ave. NW
Suite 501
Washington, DC 20004
Tel: (202) 360-4949 *Fax:* (866) 900-6099
E-Mail: pdavis@fmi.org
Website: naparassoc.org
Staff: 1

Personnel:
President: John J. Motley III

Historical Note:
Represents independent produce wholesale receivers. Membership: $500 (Supporter); $1200 (Contributor); $1000 (Associate).

Publications:
E-Newsletter; on-line

North American Peruvian Horse Association
(1970)
P.O. Box 2187
Santa Rosa, CA 95405
Tel: (707) 544-5807 *Fax:* (707) 544-5857
E-Mail: mhwmd@aol.com
Website: napha.net
Members:
500 individuals
700 Members
Staff: 2
Annual Budget: $250-500,000
Tax: 501(c)(5)

Personnel:
Executive Director: Donna Bearer
    E-Mail: donna@napha.net
Registrar: Arlynda Castro
    E-Mail: arlynda@napha.net

Historical Note:
Founded as Peruvian Paso Horse Registry of North America. In 2006, the merger of the American Association of Owners & Breeders of Peruvian Paso Horses and the Peruvian Paso Horse Registry of North America was finalized to form the North American Peruvian Horse Association. NAPHA's mission is to serve as a member-represented equine association and to protect the integrity and accuracy of breed records and registration process. Membership: $70 (Owner Member); $50 (Aficionado); $25 (Junior) $80 (International)

Meetings/Conferences: Annual
Conference Chair: Arlynda Castro
Number of non-conference events/year: 11

Publications:
Membership Directory; annually
NAPHA e-Newsletter; quarterly

Membership List Available to Non-members

North American Polyelectrolyte Producers Association *(1996)*
1250 Connecticut Ave. NW
Suite 700
Washington, DC 20036
Tel: (202) 419-1500
E-Mail: info@regnet.com

Members: 5 companies
Staff: 2
Tax: 501(c)(6)

Personnel:
Executive Director: Robert J. Fensterheim CAE

Historical Note:
Founded as Acrylamide Monomer Producers Association; assumed its current name in 2003. NAPPA represents the major manufacturers and importers of synthetically produced coagulants and flocculants, which are generically referred to as polyelectrolytes. Monitors regulatory issues affecting manufacturers in the chemical industry.

North American Punch Manufacturers Association
(1963)
21 Turquoise Ave.
Naples, FL 34114-8239
Tel: (239) 775-7245 *Fax:* (239) 775-7245
Website: napmaa.org
Members: 10 companies
Staff: 1
Annual Budget: $10-25,000

Personnel:
Contact, Communications: Robert May
  E-Mail: bobjanmay@aol.com

Historical Note:
Formerly (1996) known as the National Association of Punch Manufacturers. Mission of NAPMA is to establish and promote standardization of punches, dyes and accessories for the benefit of the end user in the Stamping and Forming Industry. Membership: $1,000 (Full); $350 (Associate).

Publications:
Membership Directory; on-line

The North American Rail Shippers Association
(1927)
2115 Portsmouth Dr.
Richardson, TX 75082-4839
Tel: (972) 690-4740 *Fax:* (972) 644-8208
E-Mail: nars@railshippers.com
Website: railshippers.com
Members: 1506 individuals and regional associations
Staff: 2
Annual Budget: $50-100,000

Personnel:
Executive Director: E. Leo Mountjoy

Historical Note:
Formerly (1984) National Association of Shippers Advisory Boards, National Association of Rail Shippers Advisory Board (1985), and (2003) National Association of Rail Shippers. NARS's mission is to provide a common meeting ground between rail owners, vendors and users to establish transportation requirements and ensure a smooth transition from the present era to the future in the rail industry. Members are industrial traffic executives using rail transportation. NARS has no dues. Administrative support provided by Association of American Railroads.

Meetings/Conferences: Annual
Conference Chair: E. Leo Mountjoy
2013 - Baltimore, MD (Hilton Inner Harbor Hotel)/May 29 - 31

North American Raspberry & Blackberry Association *(1987)*
1138 Rock Rest Rd.
Pittsboro, NC 27312
Tel: (919) 542-4037 *Fax:* (866) 511-6660
TollFree: (866) 511-6660
E-Mail: info@raspberryblackberry.com
Website: raspberryblackberry.com
Staff: 1
Annual Budget: $50-100,000
Tax: 501(c)(5)

Personnel:
Executive Secretary: Debby Wechsler

Historical Note:
Formerly known as North American Bramble Growers Association. NARBA's mission is to promote the production and marketing of raspberries and blackberries in North America through communication, education, and research. Membership: $85 (Grower); $40 (Researchers/Extension/Students); $150 (Industry).

Meetings/Conferences: Annual
2013 - Portland, OR/Jan. 27 - 30

Publications:
Membership Directory; annually

The Bramble; quarterly; adv.

North American Retail Dealers Association
(1943)
222 S. Riverside Plaza
Suite 2100
Chicago, IL 60606
Tel: (312) 648-0649 *Fax:* (312) 648-1212
TollFree: (800) 621-0298
E-Mail: nardasvc@narda.com
Website: narda.com
Members: 1000 dealers
Staff: 2
Annual Budget: $2-5,000,000
Tax: 501(c)(6)

Personnel:
Executive Director: Otto Papasadero
  E-Mail: canmarto@aol.com
General Counsel: Bob Goldberg

Historical Note:
Formerly the National Electrical Retailers Association, (1948) the National Appliance and Radio TV Dealers Association and (1974) the National Association of Retail Dealers of America. NARDA's mission is to provide the power of knowledge to independent retailers and services through progressive education, information, and services, with friendly and prompt service. Members are independent retailers, selling and servicing kitchen and laundry appliances, consumer home and mobile electronics, computers and other home and small office products, furniture, sewing machines, vacuum cleaners, room air conditioners, and other consumer home products. Membership: $295 (Retail/Service Owners-per Company); $8,000 (Associate); $4,500 (Affiliate); $2,000 (Allied). Year Founded 1943

Continuing Education:
Certification Designation/s: CFC

Publications:
NARDA E-Newsletter; bi-monthly

North American Retail Hardware Association
(1900)
6325 Digital Way
Suite 300
Indianapolis, IN 46278-1787
Tel: (317) 290-0338 *Fax:* (317) 328-4354
TollFree: (800) 772-4424
E-Mail: contact@nrha.org
Website: nrha.org
Members: 15000 individuals
Staff: 47
Annual Budget: $50-100,000

Personnel:
President and Chief Executive Officer: Bill Lee
Coordinator, Membership Services and Events: Allison Dewitt
  E-Mail: adewitt@nrha.org
Director, Publications: Dan Tratensek
  E-Mail: dant@nrha.org
Vice President, Member Services: Scott Wright
  E-Mail: swright@nrha.org

Historical Note:
Formerly known as National Retail Hardware Association and later assumed its current name in 2005. NRHA strives to help independent home improvement retailers to become better and more profitable merchants. Members are hardware retailers. Membership: $195 (U.S. Retailers); $295 (Canadian Retailers).

Meetings/Conferences: Annual
Conference Chair: Allison Dewitt
2013 - Las Vegas, NV (Las Vegas Convention Center)/May 7 - 9
Number of non-conference events/year: 24

Publications:
Hardware Retailing; on-line; adv.

North American Saxophone Alliance *(1976)*
Department of Music, Harmon Fine Arts Center, Drake University
2507 University Ave.
Des Moines, IA 50311-4505
Tel: (515) 271-3104
Website: saxalliance.org
Members: 1600 individuals
Staff: 4
Annual Budget: $50-100,000
Tax: 501(c)(3)

Personnel:

President: John Nichol
Treasurer: Frank Bongiorno
Director, Publications: Thomas Liley
Director, Membership Services: James Romain
  E-Mail: james.romain@drake.edu

Historical Note:
NASA's purpose is to provide resources for saxophonists at all levels of skill, of all ages and backgrounds, and of varied musical styles by disseminating information about saxophone performance. Members are professional saxophonists, university faculty and students, high school students, and interested amateurs. Membership: $25 (Student); $35 (Professional); $50 (Overseas/Institutional); $10 (Youth).

Meetings/Conferences: Biennial

Publications:
The Saxophone Symposium; adv.
Update; bi-monthly; adv.

North American Securities Administrators Association (NASAA) *(1919)*
750 First St. NE
Suite 1140
Washington, DC 20002
Tel: (202) 737-0900 *Fax:* (202) 783-3571
E-Mail: info@nasaa.org
Website: nasaa.org
Members: 67 state, provincial, and territorial securities administrators
Staff: 17
Annual Budget: $2-5,000,000

Personnel:
Executive Director: Russel Iuculano
  E-Mail: ri@nasaa.org
General Counsel: Joseph Brady
  E-Mail: jb@nasaa.org
Director, Policy: Michael Canning
Manager, Membership Services and Finance: Gina Haidle
  E-Mail: gh@nasaa.org
Executive Assistant, Office Manager and Benefits Coordinator: Jennifer Marsoni
  E-Mail: jm@nasaa.org
Manager, Membership and Meetings: Lonnie Martin
  E-Mail: jm@nasaa.org
Director, Communications: Bob Webster
  E-Mail: bw@nasaa.org
Manager, Training and Technology: Jason Wolf
  E-Mail: jw@nasaa.org

Historical Note:
NASAA works to advocate and act for the protection of investors, especially those who lack the expertise, experience and resources to protect their own interests.

Meetings/Conferences: Annual
Number of non-conference events/year: 1

Publications:
Membership Directory; on-line
NASAA Insight; quarterly

North American Serials Interest Group *(1985)*
1902 Ridge Rd.
P.O. Box 305
West Seneca, NY 14224-3312
E-Mail: info@nasig.org
Website: nasig.org
Members: 1200 individuals
Staff: 3
Annual Budget: $100-250,000

Personnel:
President: Bob Boissy
Editor-in-Chief: Angela Dresselhaus

Historical Note:
NASIG's mission is to promote communication, understanding, and sharing of ideas among all members of the serials information community. Membership: $75 (Regular); $25 (Student/Retired); $1,500 (Organizational).

Meetings/Conferences: Annual
2013 - Buffalo, NY/June 6 - 9
2014 - Ft. Worth, TX (Hilton Fort Worth)/May 1 - 4

Publications:
Human Resources Directory; on-line
Membership Directory; on-line
NASIG Newsletter; quarterly

North American Skull Base Society *(1989)*
11300 W. Olympic Blvd.
Suite 600
Los Angeles, CA 90064

Tel: (310) 424-3326 *Fax:* (310) 437-0585
E-Mail: info@nasbs.org
Website: nasbs.org
Members: 500 individuals
Staff: 5
Annual Budget: $100-250,000
Tax: 501(c)(3)

Personnel:
Executive Director: Jaclyn Weinstein
    E-Mail: jackie@nasbs.org
Senior Meetings Planner: Maribeth Balon
    E-Mail: maribeth@nasbs.org
Manager, Membership Services: Tressa MacKelvie
    E-Mail: membership@nasbs.org

Historical Note:
The North American Skull Base Society works to promote dissemination of information about the anatomy, physiology, pathology, and clinical management of diseases involving the skull base. Members include neurosurgeons, otolaryngologists, plastic surgeons, ophthalmologists, pathologists, anesthesiologists and radiologists. Membership: $275/year (Active/Candidate/ Affiliate/International).

Meetings/Conferences: Annual
Conference Chair: Maribeth Balon
2013 - Miami, FL (Sugarloaf Elementary School)/Feb. 15 - 17

Publications:
NASBS Online Membership Directory; annually
Skull Base Surgery Journal; bi-monthly
The NASBS Newsletter; adv.

North American Small Business International Trade Educators *(1988)*
1860 E. 18th St.
BU327
Cleveland, OH 44115
Tel: (216) 802-3381
E-Mail: info@nasbite.org
Website: nasbite.org
Members: 300 individuals and organizations
Staff: 2
Annual Budget: $50-100,000

Personnel:
Executive Director: Donna Davisson
    E-Mail: d.davisson@csuohio.edu

Historical Note:
Founded as National Association of Small Business International Trade Educators; assumed its current name in 1999. NASBITE works to promote and enhance the involvement and competitiveness of small businesses in international trade. Mission is to improve global competitiveness through effective education and training. NASBITE members include U.S. Dept. of Education, Commerce, State and U.S. Small Business Administration officials. Membership: $95 (Individual); $285 (Institutional, first 4 members, plus additional fee depending on the number of members); $25 (Student).

Continuing Education:
Certification Designation/s: CGBP

Meetings/Conferences: Annual
2013 - Albuquerue, NM (Embassy Suites)/April 8 - 12
Number of non-conference events/year: 2

Publications:
Membership Directory

Membership List Available to Non-members

North American Snowsports Journalists Association *(1963)*
11728 SE Madison
Portland, OR 97216-3946
Tel: (503) 255-3771 *Fax:* (503) 255-3771
E-Mail: execsec@nasja.org
Website: nasja.org
Members:
250 individuals
120 firms
Staff: 1
Annual Budget: $25-50,000

Personnel:
Executive Secretary and Treasurer: Vicki Andersen
    E-Mail: execsec@nasja.org

Historical Note:
Founded as the United States Ski Writers Association, became North American Ski Journalists Association in 1991, and assumed its current name in 1998. NASJA provides a forum for ski and snowboard journalists to exchange ideas and opinions, and aids in their professional

advancement. Members are writers, photographers, filmmakers and broadcasters who report ski and snowboard-related news and information. Membership: $25 (Press/Media); $175 (Corporate).

Meetings/Conferences: Annual
2013 - Mammoth Mountain, CA/March 7 - 12
2013 - Mammoth Mountain, CA/April 7 - 11

Publications:
Annual Membership Directory and Industry Source Book; annually

North American Society for Cardiovascular Imaging *(1972)*
1891 Preston White Dr.
Reston, VA 20191
Tel: (703) 476-1350 *Fax:* (703) 264-2093
E-Mail: info@nasci.org
Website: nasci.org
Members: 515 individuals
Staff: 7
Annual Budget: $250-500,000

Personnel:
President: Geoffrey D Rubin MD
Executive Director: Michele Wittling
    E-Mail: mwittling@acr.org
Treasurer: Jill E. Jacobs
Contact, Website, Abstracts and General Questions: Ronni Levine
    E-Mail: rlevine@acr.org
Program Manager: Melissa Randolph
    E-Mail: mrandolph@acr-arrs.org
Contact, CME Certificates and Reprints: Kia Reid
    E-Mail: kreid@acr.org
Contact, Meetings and Programs: Sarah Tate
    E-Mail: state@acr.org

Historical Note:
NASCI is a scientific, educational and professional organization dedicated to the advancement of cardiovascular imaging. Mission of NASCI is to develop and disseminate the knowledge regarding Cardiovascular Imaging Membership: $250 (Active); $0 (In-Training Member).

Meetings/Conferences: Annual
Conference Chair: Sarah Tate
2013 - Atlanta, GA (Atlanta Marriott Marquis)/Sept. 28 - Oct. 1

Publications:
International Journal for Cardiovascular Imaging; bi-monthly
Membership Directory; on-line
NASCI Beat e-Newsletter; quarterly

Membership List Available to Non-members

North American Society for Dialysis and Transplantation *(1981)*
4010 Bentley Dr.
Pearland, TX 77584
Tel: (281) 997-1944
E-Mail: phelderman@comcast.net
Website: nasdat.org
Members: 200 individuals
Staff: 2
Annual Budget: $50-100,000
Tax: 501(c)(3)

Personnel:
Executive Director: Laura Brazil-Nichols
    E-Mail: lbrazil@nasdat.org

Historical Note:
NASDAT works to share the most recent advances in the science and practice of nephrology and transplantation with interested practitioners in the community and at the university. Members are health professionals concerned with kidney dialysis and transplantation procedures.

Meetings/Conferences: Annual
2013 - Maui, HI (Ritz Carlton Kapalua)/July 14 - 18

North American Society for Oceanic History *(1973)*
Deptartment of History, Texas Christian University
P.O. Box 297260
Fort Worth, TX 76129
Tel: (202) 707-1409
Website: nasoh.org
Members: 220 individuals
Staff: 2
Annual Budget: $50-100,000

Tax: 501(c)(3)

Personnel:
President: Warren Riess
Secretary: Michael W. Kegerreis

Historical Note:
NASOH promotes the exchange of information among its members and others interested in the history of the seas, lakes and inland waterways. Members are academics and others with an interest in the study of seafaring and inland waterways. Membership: $65 (Individual/Institutional); $18 (Student); $25 (Gift/CNRS/NASOH-Dual).

Meetings/Conferences: Annual
2013 - Alpena, MI (Holiday Inn Alpena)/May 15 - 19

Publications:
The Northern Mariner; quarterly

North American Society for Pediatric Gastroenterology, Hepatology and Nutrition *(1972)*
P.O. Box Six
Flourtown, PA 19031
Tel: (215) 233-0808 *Fax:* (215) 233-3918
E-Mail: naspghan@naspghan.org
Website: naspghan.org
Members: 1400 individuals
Staff: 4
Annual Budget: $2-5,000,000
Tax: 501(c)(3)

Personnel:
Executive Director: Margaret K. Stallings
    E-Mail: mstallings@naspghan.org
Coordinator, Membership Services: Kim Rose
    E-Mail: krose@naspghan.org

Historical Note:
The mission of the NASPGHAN is to advance understanding of normal development, physiology and pathophysiology of diseases of the gastrointestinal tract and liver in children, improve quality of care by fostering the dissemination of this knowledge through scientific meetings, professional and public education, and policy development, and serve as an effective voice for members and the profession.

Meetings/Conferences: Annual
2013 - Chicago, IL (Hilton Chicago)/Oct. 10 - 13

Publications:
Journal of Pediatric Gastroenterology and Nutrition; monthly; adv.
Membership Directory; on-line
NASPGHAN Newsletter; quarterly

North American Society for Social Philosophy *(1984)*
P.O. Box 7147
Charlottesville, VA 22906-7147
Tel: (434) 220-3300 *Fax:* (434) 220-3301
TollFree: (800) 444-2419
E-Mail: order@pdcnet.org
Website: pitt.edu/~nassp/nassp.html
Members: 200 individuals
Staff: 3

Personnel:
President: Margaret Crouch
Treasurer: Jim Boettcher
Archivist: Nancy Snow

Historical Note:
NASSP's purpose is to facilitate discussion between social philosophers on all topics of interest, primarily by sponsoring conferences and publications. Members are academics drawn from a wide range of disciplines with an interest in social philosophy. Membership: $40-65 (Individual); $25-50 (Student/Unemployed).

Meetings/Conferences: Annual
2013 - Hamden, CT (Quinnipiac University)/July 11 - 13

Publications:
NASSP Newsletter; on-line
The Journal of Social Philosophy

North American Society for Sport History *(1972)*
P.O. Box 1026
Lemont, PA 16851-1026
Tel: (814) 238-1288 *Fax:* (814) 238-1288
Website: nassh.org
Members: 950 individuals and institutions
Staff: 2
Annual Budget: $25-50,000

Personnel:

Secretary and Treasurer: Ronald A. Smith
    E-Mail: secretary-treasurer@nassh.org
Manager, Conventions: Rita Liberti

Historical Note:
NASSH is committed for the research and teaching of the history of sport, exercise and physical activity through annual conferences.NASSH's mission is to enhance, stimulate, and encourage study and research and writing of the history of sport. It also supports and cooperate with local, national, and international organizations having the same purposes. Membership: $60 (Regular); $70 (Foreign Regular); $30 (Student/Retired); $95 (Sustaining); $95 (Institution); $105 (Foreign Institution);$700(Lifetime).

Meetings/Conferences: Annual
Conference Chair: Rita Liberti
2013 - Halifax, NS (Saint Mary's University)/May 24 - 27

Publications:
Journal of Sport History; adv.
NASSH Newsletter; on-line

North American Society for Sport Management
(1985)
135 Winterwood Dr.
Butler, PA 16001
Tel: (724) 482-6277 *Fax:* (724) 738-4858
E-Mail: businessoffice@nassm.com
Website: nassm.com
Members: 475 individuals
Staff: 6

Personnel:
Office Manager: Dr. Robin Ammon Jr.
    E-Mail: robert.ammon@sru.edu

Historical Note:
NASSM is involved in supporting and assisting professionals working in the fields of sport, leisure and recreation. Purpose is to stimulate and encourage study, research, scholarly writing and professional development in the area of sport management - both theoretical and applied aspects. Membership: $125 (Professional); $55 (Student/Emeritus Member with JSM); $20 (Emeritus Member without JSM).

Meetings/Conferences: Annual
2013 - Austin, TX (Hilton Austin)/May 28 - June 1

Publications:
Journal of Sport Management; bi-monthly
Membership Directory; on-line
NASSM Newsletter
Sport Management Education Journal; annually

North American Society for the Psychology of Sport and Physical Activity *(1966)*
University of Tennessee
1914 Andy Holt Ave.
Knoxville, TN 37996-2700
Tel: (865) 974-3616
E-Mail: naspspa@hotmail.com
Website: naspspa.org
Members: 600 individuals
Staff: 4
Annual Budget: $100-250,000

Personnel:
Director, Communications: Jeffrey T. Fairbrother
    E-Mail: jfairbr1@utk.edu
Contact, Membership: Jackie Moore
    E-Mail: jackiem@hkusa.com

Historical Note:
NASPSPA multidisciplinary association of scholars from the behavioral sciences and related professions. Members are kinesiologists, physical education and physical therapy professionals and others with an interest in motor skills development, motor/learning control, and sport and exercise psychology. Membership: $60 (Professional); $30 (Retired); $25 (Student).

Meetings/Conferences: Annual
2013 - New Orleans, LA (Hilton Riverside Hotel)/June 13 - 15

Publications:
e-news; on-line
Membership Directory; on-line
NASPSPA Newsletter

North American Society for the Sociology of Sport
(1978)
264F Gym Annex
School of Foundations, Leadership and Administration, 350 Midway Dr., Kent State University

Kent, OH 44242
E-Mail: treasurer@nasss.org
Website: nasss.org
Members: 400 individuals
Staff: 6
Annual Budget: $50-100,000

Personnel:
President: Faye Wachs
    E-Mail: fayewachs@hotmail.com
Member Liaison: Robert Pitter
    E-Mail: Robert.pitter@acadiau.ca
Treasurer: Brenda Riemer
    E-Mail: briemer@emich.edu
Conference, Site Director: Maureen Smith
    E-Mail: smithmm@csus.edu
Newsletter Editor: Sean Smith
    E-Mail: sean.smith@rogers.com
Member Liaison: Theresa Walton
    E-Mail: members@nasss.org

Historical Note:
NASSS's purpose is to promote, stimulate and encourage the sociological study of play, games and sport and to support and cooperate with local, national and international organizations having the same purposes. Members are academics concerned with the sociology of sport. Membership: $95-145 (Professional); $15-50 (Student); $35-70 (Retired/Unemployed).

Meetings/Conferences: Annual
Conference Chair: Maureen Smith

Publications:
Sociology of Sport Journal; quarterly

North American Society for Trenchless Technology
(1990)
C\O Losi & Ranger, PLLC
7445 Morgan Rd.
Liverpool, NY 13090
Tel: (703) 351-5252 *Fax:* (613) 424-3037
E-Mail: nastt@nastt.org
Website: nastt.org
Members: 1200 members
Staff: 3
Annual Budget: $500-1,000,000

Personnel:
Communications And Training Manager: Michelle Hill
    E-Mail: mhill@nastt.org

Historical Note:
An affiliate of the International Society for Trenchless Technology, NASTT's mission is to advance trenchless technology and to promote its benefits for the public and the environment by increasing awareness and knowledge through information dissemination, research and development, education and training and partnerships with organizations and agencies interested in trenchless technology and its benefits. Members are individuals and organizations interested in the construction, maintenance and rehabilitation of utility service lines without the use of trenches. Membership: $200 (Individual); $1,000 (Corporate/Organizational); $300 (Governmental/ Educational Institutions).

Meetings/Conferences: Annual
2013 - Sacramento, CA (Hyatt Regency Sacramento)/ March 3 - 7
2014 - Kissimmee, FL (Gaylord Palms Hotel and Convention Center, Orlando Florida)/April 13 - 17
2016 - Dallas, TX (Gaylord Texan Hotel and Convention Center-Dallas)/March 20 - 24
2017 - Washington, DC (Gaylord National Hotel and Convention Center)/April 9 - 13

Publications:
Membership Directory; on-line
NASTT Newsletter; bi-monthly
Trenchless Today Magazine; adv.

North American Society of Adlerian Psychology
(1952)
429 E. Dupont Rd.
Suite 276
Ft. Wayne, IN 46825
Tel: (717) 579-8795 *Fax:* (717) 533-8616
E-Mail: info@alfredadler.org
Website: alfredadler.org
Members: 1000 individuals
Staff: 3
Annual Budget: $100-250,000
Tax: 501(c)(3)

Personnel:
Executive Director: John F. Newbauer EdD

Treasurer: Susan (Zsuzsanna) Burak
Conference Coordinator: Becky LaFountain
    E-Mail: rmlafo@comcast.net

Historical Note:
Formerly (1976) American Society of Adlerian Psychology. The purpose of NASAP is to foster and promote the research, knowledge, training, and application of Adlerian Psychology, maintaining its principles and encouraging its growth. Members are individuals interested in the teachings of the Austrian psychiatrist, Alfred Adler (1870-1937). Membership: $135 (Individual/Affiliate Organization); $45 (Retired); $35 (Associate); $55 (Family Member); $25 (Student).

Meetings/Conferences: Annual
Conference Chair: Becky LaFountain
2013 - San Diego, CA (Hyatt Regency)/June 20 - 23

Publications:
Journal of Individual Psychology; quarterly; adv.
Membership Directory; annually
Newsletter; bi-monthly

North American South Devon Association *(1974)*
19590 E. Main St.
Suite 104
Parker, CO 80138
Tel: (303) 770-3130 *Fax:* (303) 770-9302
E-Mail: nasouthdevon@aol.com
Website: southdevon.com
Members: 220 individuals
Staff: 4
Annual Budget: $50-100,000
Tax: 501(c)(5)

Personnel:
Contact, Registry Services: Sherry Doubet

Historical Note:
NASDA promotes the superior quality characteristics of the South Devon breed with integrity, forethought and leadership for a prospering livestock industry satisfying consumer demand. Membership: $25 (Active/Associate); $15 (Junior).

Meetings/Conferences:
Number of non-conference events/year: 1

Publications:
Animal Directory; on-line
Membership Directory; on-line
NASDA Newsletter; on-line

North American Spine Society *(1985)*
7075 Veterans Blvd.
Burr Ridge, IL 60527
Tel: (630) 230-3600 *Fax:* (630) 230-3700
TollFree: (866) 960-6277
E-Mail: info@spine.org
Website: spine.org
Members: 7,000 members
Staff: 20
Annual Budget: $10-25,000,000
Tax: 501(c)(3)

Personnel:
Executive Director: Eric J. Muehlbauer CAE
    E-Mail: muehlbauer@spine.org

Historical Note:
Formed by the merger of the American College of Spine Surgeons and the North American Lumbar Spine Association. NASS's mission is to foster the quality, evidence-based and ethical spine care by promoting education, research, and advocacy. Members are physicians, orthopedists, osteopaths and other health professionals with an interest in the treatment of the spine. Membership: $595 (Active/Associate); $250-300 (Affiliate); $250 (Corresponding).

Meetings/Conferences: Annual
2013 - New Orleans, LA/Oct. 9 - 12
2014 - San Francisco, CA/Nov. 12 - 15
2015 - Chicago, IL/Oct. 14 - 17
2016 - Boston, MA/Oct. 26 - 29

Publications:
NASS Newsletter; on-line; adv.
SpineLine; bi-monthly; adv.
The Spine Journal; adv.

North American Students of Cooperation *(1968)*
P. O. Box 180048
Chicago, IL 60618
Tel: (773) 404-2667
Website: nasco.coop
Staff: 1
Annual Budget: $250-500,000

Personnel:
Director of Education: Emma Rubin
  E-Mail: emma@nasco.coop

Historical Note:
NASCO's mission is to educate affordable group equity co-ops and their members for the purpose of promoting a community oriented cooperative movement. Membership: $10/person and $36 for new member; $150 to $1,000 (Associate depending on gross revenue); $35-$50/year (Individual -Low income/Regular); $151-$1000/year (Supporting/Sustaining).

Meetings/Conferences: Annual

Membership List Available to Non-members

North American Technician Excellence (1997)
2111 Wilson Blvd.
Suite 510
Arlington, VA 22201
Tel: (703) 276-7247 *Fax*: (703) 527-2316
TollFree: (877) 420-6283
E-Mail: mail@natex.org
Website: natex.org
Members: 30000 certificants
Staff: 7
Annual Budget: $2-5,000,000
Tax: 501(c)(6)

Personnel:
President and Chief Executive Officer: Peter W. Schwartz
  E-Mail: pschwartz@natex.org
Manager, Marketing and Communications: Dana Anaman
  E-Mail: danaman@natex.org

Historical Note:
NATE is the non-profit certification organization for heating, ventilation, air conditioning and refrigeration technicians. It is governed, owned, operated, developed and supported by the HVACR industry.

Continuing Education:
Enrollment: 5000
Certification Designation/s: HVAC/R

Meetings/Conferences: Annual

Publications:
NATE Advantage; quarterly
NATE Magazine; annually; adv.
NATE Newsletter
Trade News; quarterly; adv.

North American Thermal Analysis Society (1968)
2413 Nashville Rd., C2
Bowling Green, KY 42101
Tel: (270) 745-2530 *Fax*: (270) 745-2221
E-Mail: natas@wku.edu
Website: natasinfo.org
Staff: 6
Annual Budget: $100-250,000

Personnel:
Education Councilor: Quentin Lineberry
  E-Mail: quentin.lineberry@wku.edu
Contact, Membership Services: Terrill D. Martin
  E-Mail: natas@wku.edu

Historical Note:
NATAS is an affiliate of the International Confederation for Thermal Analysis and Calorimetry (ICTAC). NATAS's mission is to promote the understanding and advancement of thermal analysis and provide members with pertinent information and knowledge. Membership: $60 (Full); $10 (Student).

Meetings/Conferences: Annual
Conference Chair: Bob Howell
2013 - Bowling Green, KY (Holiday Inn University
  Plaza-Bowling Green)/Aug. 4 - 7
2014 - Santa Fe, NM/Sept. 15 - 17
2015 - Ottawa, ON/Aug. 10 - 12
2016 - Orlando, FL/Aug. 8 - 11

Publications:
Membership Directory; on-line
NATAS Notes
THERMAL Listserver

North American Transportation Employee Relations Association (1987)
1300 19th St. NW
Suite 700
Washington, DC 20036
Tel: (202) 719-2041 *Fax*: (202) 719-2077
E-Mail: haitken@fordharrison.com
Website: natera.org
Members: 128 individuals

Staff: 4
Annual Budget: $50-100,000

Personnel:
Executive Director and Secretary: Herve H. Aitken Esq.
  E-Mail: haitken@fordharrison.com
Contact, Meetings: Marsha Alexandrovic
Executive Vice President, Government Affairs: R. Bruce Josten

Historical Note:
Founded as National Trucking Industrial Relations Association, became North American Trucking Industrial Relations Association in 1997 and assumed its current name in 2001. NATERA's mission is to provide a forum for creation, exchange and dissemination of ideas and information concerning human resources and labor relations matters, issues, regulations, legislation and current laws. Members are trucking executives and lawyers concerned with personnel and labor relations issues. Membership: $175/year.

Meetings/Conferences: Annual
Conference Chair: Marsha Alexandrovic

Publications:
Member Directory; on-line

Membership List Available to Non-members

North American Transportation Management Institute (1944)
2460 W. 26th Ave.
Suite 245-C
Denver, CO 80211
Tel: (303) 952-4013 *Fax*: (775) 370-4055
E-Mail: info@natmi.org
Website: natmi.org
Members: 1050 individuals and organizations
Staff: 3
Annual Budget: $500-1,000,000

Personnel:
Executive Director: Jeffrey Arnold MAM
  E-Mail: jeff@natmi.org
Administrator: Kelly Long Crow
  E-Mail: kelly@natmi.org
Seminar Coordinator: Vicki Schrock
  E-Mail: seminars@natmi.org

Historical Note:
Founded as National Committee for Motor Fleet Supervisor Training; assumed its current name in 1997. NATMI is dedicated to providing internationally recognized university affiliated professional certification and training seminars for truck, bus, and transit fleet professionals. Membership: $250 (Fleet/Associate); $150 (Fleet Additional/Associate Additional); $100 (Government/Truck Driving School).

Continuing Education:
Enrollment: 500
Certification Designation/s: CSM/E, CDM/E, CCSP, CDS, CSS, CDT

Meetings/Conferences:
Conference Chair: Vicki Schrock

Publications:
Accident Investigation; adv.
Guardrail Magazine; semi-annually; adv.
Member Directory; on-line
Motor Fleet Monthly; monthly; adv.

North American Wensleydale Sheep Association (1999)
4589 Fruitland Rd.
Loma Rica, CA 95901
Tel: (530) 743-5262
E-Mail: info@wensleydalesheep.org
Website: wensleydalesheep.org
Members: 34 herds
Staff: 2
Tax: 501(c)(3)

Personnel:
President: Barbara Burrows
Treasurer: Lois Olund

Historical Note:
NAWSA's mission is to develop and promote Wensleydale Longwool Sheep in North America. Maintains a pedigree registry on behalf of its member breeders. Has no paid officers or full-time staff. Membership: $25 (Active); $15 (Associate).

Publications:
Membership Directory; on-line

North American Wholesale Lumber Association (1893)
3601 Algonquin Rd.

Suite 400
Rolling Meadows, IL 60008
Tel: (847) 870-7470 *Fax*: (847) 870-0201
TollFree: (800) 527-8258
E-Mail: info@nawla.org
Website: nawla.org
Members: 650 forest products and building material industry wholesalers, manufacturers and industry affiliated companies
Staff: 5
Annual Budget: $1-2,000,000

Personnel:
Executive Director and Interim Chief Executive Officer: Mark Palmer
  E-Mail: mpalmer@nawla.org
Accountant: Jennifer Chan
  E-Mail: jchan@nawla.org
Director, Marketing and Communications: Kevin Ketchum
  E-Mail: kketchum@nawla.org
President: Gary Vitale
  E-Mail: gvitale@nawla.org
Manager, Meetings and Education: Stacey M. Woldt CMP
  E-Mail: swoldt@nawla.org

Historical Note:
Formerly (1972) National American Wholesale Lumber Association. NAWLA is dedicated to efficient distribution of lumber products and the responsible stewardship of forest resources. Represents wholesalers, manufacturers, and service provider companies throughout the distribution supply chain. Membership: $25-2,285/year.

Meetings/Conferences: Annual
Conference Chair: Stacey M. Woldt CMP

Publications:
Membership Directory; on-line
NAWLA Bulletin; monthly

North American-Bulgarian Chamber of Commerce (1998)
851 Irwin St.
Suite 200
San Rafael, CA 94901
Tel: (415) 251-2322 *Fax*: (415) 454-2046
E-Mail: usa@nabcc.org
Website: nabcc.org
Staff: 3

Personnel:
Chief Executive Officer: Emil A. Dimitroff
Manager, Marketing and Public Relation: Reneta Denkova

Historical Note:
Promotes business ties between the United States and Bulgaria. Membership: $1500 (Corporate); $1050 (Medium); $850 (Small Business); $650 (Individual); $100 (Student).

North American-Chilean Chamber of Commerce (1918)
866 United Nations Plaza
Suite 4019
New York, NY 10017
Tel: (212) 317-1959 *Fax*: (212) 758-8598
E-Mail: info@nacchamber.com
Website: nacchamber.com
Members: 120 businesses
Staff: 5
Annual Budget: $50-100,000

Personnel:
President: Mario J. Paredes
Treasurer: Carlos Bianchi
Marketing and Communications: Alejandro Cerda
Vice president: David Spencer
Legal Advisor: Roger W. Thomas

Historical Note:
Founded as the Chile-American Association, Inc. (CAA), changed its name to North American-Chilean Chamber of Commerce, Inc. (NACCC) and merged with Chile-American Association in 1918. NACCC's mission is to promote knowledge and understanding of political, economic, regulatory matters affecting the business/commercial environment between Chile and United States. Members are interested in fostering improved trade and commerce between their respective countries. Membership: $150 (Individual); $50 (Student and Senior); $500 (Bronze Corporate); $1,000 (Silver Corporate); $5,000 (Gold Corporate).

Meetings/Conferences:
Number of non-conference events/year: 1

Publications:
NACCC Newsletter; on-line

Northeast Organic Farming Association

P.O. Box 164
Stevenson, CT 06491
Tel: (203) 888-5146
E-Mail: bduesing@mac.com
Website: nofa.org
Members: 5000 farmers, gardeners, landscape
professionals and consumers
Staff: 7
Annual Budget: $250-500,000

Personnel:
President: Bill Duesing
E-Mail: bduesing@mac.com

Historical Note:
NOFA's purpose is to advocate for and educate about
organic and sustainable agriculture, family-scale farming
and homesteading both rural and urban, agricultural
justice, and related issues. The NOFA Interstate Council
serves essentially as the Board of the overall NOFA
organization.

Meetings/Conferences: Annual
Conference Chair: Bob Minnocci

Publications:
The Natural Farmer; quarterly; adv.

Northern Nut Growers Association (1910)

P.O. Box 6216
Hamden, CT 06517-0216
Website: northernnutgrowers.org
Members: 825 individuals
Staff: 2
Annual Budget: $25-50,000
Tax: 501(c)(3)

Personnel:
President: Dennis Fulbright
Treasurer: William Sachs
E-Mail: wsachs@alumni.princeton.edu

Historical Note:
NNGA's mission is to advance interest in nut-bearing
trees, promote scientific research in their breeding
and culture and nut-tree products. Members are nut
culturists, farmers, amateur and commercial nut growers,
experiment station workers, horticultural teachers and
scientists, nut tree breeders, nursery people, and foresters.
Membership: $40 (Individual, U.S.); $45 (Individual,
Canada); $50 (Overseas and Mexican/Family- U.S); $55
(Family-Canada); $60 (Contributing); $80 (Sustaining);
$1000-1600 (Life).

Meetings/Conferences: Annual

Publications:
Membership Directory; on-line
The Nutshell; quarterly; adv.

Northwest Fruit Exporters (1980)

105 S. 18th St., Suite 227
Yakima, WA 98901
Tel: (509) 576-8004 Fax: (509) 576-3616
Members: 17 companies
Staff: 3
Annual Budget: $500-1,000,000
Tax: 501(c)(5)

Personnel:
Manager: Jim Archer
E-Mail: nfe@goodfruit.com

Historical Note:
A Webb-Pomerene Act association.

Northwest Natural Resource Group

1917 Firsst Ave., Level A
Suite 200
Seattle, WA 98101
Tel: (206) 971-3709
E-Mail: info@nnrg.org
Website: nnrg.org
Staff: 6
Annual Budget: $250-500,000
Tax: 501(c)(3)

Personnel:
Executive Director: Dan Stonington
Director, Operations and Finance: Eric Ruthford
Director, Member Services: Hannah Yourd

Historical Note:
NNRG's mission is to promote innovative forest
management strategies that improve the health of forest
and freshwater ecosystems while increasing economic
development in rural communities.

Publications:

Member Listing; on-line
NNRG Newsletter

Norwegian-American Chamber of Commerce (1915)

655 Third Ave.
Suite 1810
New York, NY 10017
Tel: (212) 885-9737 Fax: (281) 587-9284
E-Mail: nacc@ntcny.org
Website: naccusa.org
Members: 800 members
Staff: 4
Annual Budget: $250-500,000

Personnel:
President: Blaine Collins
Executive Vice President: Craig Dykers
Treasurer: Cameron Beard
General Manager: Inger M. Tallaksen
E-Mail: itallaksen@naccusa.org

Historical Note:
NACC is dedicated to the service of the Norwegian-
American Business Community. Membership: $475/year.

Meetings/Conferences: Annual
Number of non-conference events/year: 3

Publications:
NACCNews; quarterly

Not-For-Profit Services Association (1995)

624 Grassmere Park Dr.
Suite 15
Nashville, TN 37211
Tel: (615) 377-3392 Fax: (615) 377-7092
TollFree: (800) 231-2524
E-Mail: info@nonprofitcpas.com
Website: nonprofitcpas.com
Members: 17 firms
Staff: 6

Personnel:
Executive Director: Patrick Pruett
E-Mail: patrick@the-apa.com

Historical Note:
NPAC is a independently owned accounting firms committed
to delivering exceptional financial and consulting services
to nonprofit organizations.NPAC's mission is to provide its
members with resources in education and marketing as well
as foster networking among members in order to provide
high-quality comprehensive business advisory services to
the nonprofit industry.Membership Dues:$2,400(Annual);
$1,500(one time).

Continuing Education:
Certification Designation/s: CNAP

Publications:
Member Directory; on-line

NPES, The Association for Suppliers of Printing, Publishing, and Converting Technologies (1933)

1899 Preston White Dr.
Reston, VA 20191-4367
Tel: (703) 264-7200 Fax: (703) 620-0994
E-Mail: npes@npes.org
Website: npes.org
Members: 400 companies
Staff: 32
Annual Budget: $2-5,000,000

Personnel:
Director, Finance and Administration: Judy B. Durham
E-Mail: jdurham@npes.org
President, Programs and Meetings: Ralph J. Nappi
E-Mail: rnappi@npes.org
Director, Government Affairs: Mark J. Nuzzaco
E-Mail: mnuzzaco@npes.org
Managing Editor: Jane Pratt
E-Mail: jpratt@npes.org
Manager, Administration Technical Services: Jesus A.
Romero
E-Mail: jromero@npes.org
Vice President, Global Programs: William K. Smythe Jr.
E-Mail: ksmythe@npes.org
Director, Communications and Marketing: Deborah B.
Vieder
E-Mail: dvieder@npes.org

Historical Note:
Established as the National Printing Equipment
Association; became the National Printing Equipment
and Supply Association in 1979 and assumed its present
name in 1998. NPES's purpose is to strengthen the

entire industry and aid member firms in the areas of
statistics and marketing, safety and industry standards,
international trade, and government relations. Members
are manufacturers and distributors of equipment, systems,
software, and supplies. Membership: $1,000 (Associate);
$295-5,500 (Full Member; based on annual sales volume).

Meetings/Conferences:
Conference Chair: Ralph J. Nappi
2013 - Tucson, AZ/March 10 - 13
2013 - Chicago, IL (McCormick Place)/Sept. 8 - 12
2014 - Chicago, IL (McCormick Place)/Sept. 28 - Oct. 1

Publications:
NPES Member Directory and Digital Product Locator;
on-line
NPES News; monthly; adv.

NPTA Alliance (1903)

401 N. Michigan Ave.
Suite 2200
Chicago, IL 60611
Tel: (312) 321-4092 Fax: (312) 673-6736
TollFree: (800) 355-6782
E-Mail: npta@gonpta.com
Website: gonpta.com
Members: 2850 individuals and wholesalers
Staff: 6
Annual Budget: $2-5,000,000

Personnel:
Chief Executive Officer: Kevin Gammonley
E-Mail: kgammonley@gonpta.com
Manager, Marketing and Communications: Victoria
Crews-Anderson
E-Mail: vcrewsanderson@smithbucklin.com
Associate, Membership Services: Ronnie Hwang
E-Mail: rhwang@gonpta.com
Contact, Event Services: Jen Manfredo
E-Mail: jmanfredo@gonpta.com
Manager, Operations: Sean Samet
E-Mail: ssamet@gonpta.com

Historical Note:
Formerly National Paper Trade Association; assumed
current name in 2001. NPTA's mission is to actively
support the success of members through the delivery of
networking, advocacy, education, and research that focuses
on the health of the distribution channel. It serves the paper,
packaging and supplies distribution channel. Membership:
$420-74,000 (Distributor); $1,800-25,000 (Supplier);
$695 (Service Providers).

Continuing Education:
Enrollment: 500
Certification Designation/s: MDP

Meetings/Conferences:
Conference Chair: Jen Manfredo
2013 - Naples, FL (The Ritz-Carlton Golf Resort)/Jan.
15 - 17
2013 - Chicago, IL/March 17 - 19

Publications:
NPTA Member Directory; on-line
Paper & Packaging; quarterly; adv.
Paper & Packaging Update; monthly; adv.

Nuclear Energy Institute (1981)

P.O. Box 27768
Suite 400
Washington, DC 20038
Tel: (202) 739-8000 Fax: (202) 785-4019
Website: nei.org
Members: 350 organizations
Staff: 138
Annual Budget: $50-100,000,000
Tax: 501(c)(6)

Personnel:
President and Chief Executive Officer: Marvin S. Fertel
E-Mail: msf@nei.org
Senior Manager, Human Resources: Lori Brady
E-Mail: resumes@nei.org
Contact, Publications: Tonya Cameron
E-Mail: tjc@nei.org
Senior Vice President, Governmental Affairs: Alex Flint
Vice President, General Counsel and Secretary: Ellen C.
Ginsberg
E-Mail: ecg@nei.org
Vice President, Communications: J. Scott Peterson
Senior Vice President and Chief Nuclear Officer: Anthony
"Tony" R. Pietrangelo
E-Mail: arp@nei.org
Senior Vice President and Chief Financial Officer: Phyllis
M. Rich

E-Mail: pmr@nei.org
Senior Director and Assistant Corporate Secretary: Lisa
   Steward
   E-Mail: membership@nei.org

Historical Note:
*Established as the Committee for Energy Awareness, it
became the U.S. Council for Energy Awareness in 1987.
Absorbed the American Nuclear Energy Council and the
Nuclear Management and Resources Council and assumed
its present name in 1994. In July 1987, the Atomic
Industrial Forum was merged with the Council. NEI's
mission is to ensure the formation of policies that promote
the beneficial uses of nuclear energy and technologies in the
United States and around the world. Members consist of
utilities, manufacturers of electrical generating equipment,
researchers, architects, engineers, labor unions, milling and
mining companies, constructors, laboratories, educational
institutions and government agencies with interest in the
generation of electricity by nuclear power. Membership dues
vary, based on type of company.*

Meetings/Conferences: Annual
2013 - Washington, DC (Grand Hyatt Washington)/
   May 20 - 22
Number of non-conference events/year: 7

Publications:
Nuclear Energy Insight; monthly
Nuclear Performance; monthly

Nuclear Information and Records Management Association *(1977)*
Ten Almas Rd.
Windham, NH 03087
Tel: (603) 432-6476 *Fax:* (603) 432-3024
E-Mail: nirma@nirma.org
Website: nirma.org
Members: 275 individuals
Staff: 3
Annual Budget: $100-250,000

Personnel:
Executive Director: Jane Hannum
   E-Mail: jnirma@nirma.mv.com

Historical Note:
*Formerly (1985) the Nuclear Records Management
Association. NIRMA supports regulated nuclear and
selected energy-related industries. Purpose is to improve
the management of corporate information and records
relating to nuclear facilities. Membership includes utility
company employees, architectural engineers and industrial
consultants. Membership: $200 (Individual); $3,000
(Corporate-Silver); $6,000 (Corporate-Gold).*

Continuing Education:
Certification Designation/s: ICRM, CRM, NS

Meetings/Conferences: Annual

Publications:
Nirma Newsletter

Nuclear Suppliers Association *(1984)*
P.O. Box 1354
Westerly, RI 02891
Tel: (401) 637-4224 *Fax:* (401) 637-4822
E-Mail: nsanews@charter.net
Website: nuclearsuppliers.org
Members: 60 companies
Staff: 1
Annual Budget: $100-250,000
Tax: 501(c)(6)

Personnel:
Executive Administrator: DeeDee McNeill

Historical Note:
*NSA's mission is to provide a more organized approach to
maximize business promotion and professional relationship
building among nuclear industry suppliers. Members
are companies which specialize in the manufacture and
distribution of products and services for the nuclear
industry. Membership: $200/year (Organization).*

Meetings/Conferences: Annual
Number of non-conference events/year: 5

Publications:
Membership Directory; on-line

Membership List Available to Non-members

Nursery and Landscape Association Executives of North America *(1947)*
2130 Stella Ct.
Columbus, OH 43215
Tel: (614) 487-1117 *Fax:* (614) 487-1216
E-Mail: nlae@ofa.org
Website: nlae.org

Members: 100 association executives
Staff: 4
Annual Budget: $25-50,000
Tax: 501(c)(6)

Personnel:
Executive Director: Michael V. Geary CAE
Contact, Membership Services: Laura A. Kunkle
   E-Mail: lkunkle@ofa.org
Contact, Event Information: Margaret McGuire
   E-Mail: mmcguire@ofa.org
Contact, E-newsletters and Website: Alicia Wells
   E-Mail: awells@ofa.org

Historical Note:
*Formerly (1972) Nursery Association Secretaries, (1987)
Nursery Association Executives, and (2000) Nursery
Association Executives of North America. NLAE's mission
is to develop its members, providing information and
opportunities for growth on important topics. Members are
chief executives of nursery associations of the U.S. and
Canada. Membership: $150-450 (Member, based on the
total operational budget of the association); $50 (Additional
Member).*

Meetings/Conferences: Annual
Conference Chair: Margaret McGuire

Publications:
Membership Directory; on-line

Nurses Organization of Veterans Affairs *(1980)*
47595 Watkins Island Sq.
Sterling, VA 20165
Tel: (703) 444-5587 *Fax:* (703) 444-5597
E-Mail: nova@vanurse.org
Website: vanurse.org
Members: 2600 individuals
Staff: 2
Annual Budget: $250-500,000
Tax: 501(c)(6)

Personnel:
Executive Director: Susan Dove
   E-Mail: sdove@vanurse.org
Director, Administration and Membership Services: Luba
   Litvinova
   E-Mail: luba@vanurse.org

Historical Note:
*Formerly (1989) Nurses Organization of the Veterans
Administration. NOVA works to shape and influence
healthcare in the Department of Veterans Affairs. Members
are registered nurses employed by the Department of
Veterans Affairs. Membership: $105 (Active); $50
(Emeritus); $200 (Legacy).*

Obesity Society
8757 Georgia Ave.
Suite 1320
Silver Spring, MD 20910
Tel: (301) 563-6526 *Fax:* (301) 563-6595
Website: obesity.org
Members: 2000 basic and clinical researchers
Staff: 17
Annual Budget: $2-5,000,000

Personnel:
Executive Director: Francesca M. Dea CAE
   E-Mail: fdea@obesity.org
Senior Director, Finance and Administration: Kathie
   Cleary
   E-Mail: kcleary@obesity.org
Assistant, Membership Services: Kelly Evans
   E-Mail: kevans@obesity.org
Director, Education and Scientific Meetings: Lauren Maza
   E-Mail: lmaza@obesity.org
Director, Marketing and Communications: Jane Pratt
   E-Mail: jpratt@obesity.org
Editorial Assistant: Deborah Rice
   E-Mail: drice@obesity.org
*Senior Director, Publications, Marketing, and
   Communications:* Hedy Ross
   E-Mail: hross@obesity.org

Historical Note:
*The Obesity Society is committed to improving the lives of
those with obesity, nurturing careers of obesity scientists
and practitioners and promoting the interdisciplinary
nature of obesity research, management and education.
Membership: $225-250 (Regular/Fellow); $235-260
(Overseas Member); $30-125 (Student); $85-135
(Overseas Student); Free (New Student).*

Continuing Education:
Certification Designation/s: COMP, CME

Meetings/Conferences: Annual

Conference Chair: Lauren Maza
2013 - Atlanta, GA/Nov. 12 - 16

Publications:
Membership Directory; on-line
Obesity Journal; adv.
The Obesity Society Newsletter; monthly; adv.

Object Management Group *(1989)*
109 Highland Ave.
Needham, MA 02494
Tel: (781) 444-0404 *Fax:* (781) 444-0320
E-Mail: info@omg.org
Website: omg.org
Members: 450 companies
Staff: 12
Annual Budget: $2-5,000,000

Personnel:
President and Chief Operating Officer: Bill Hoffman
   E-Mail: hoffman@omg.org
Chairman and Chief Executive Officer: Richard Soley
   E-Mail: soley@omg.org
Vice President, Business Development: Kenneth Berk
   E-Mail: ken.berk@omg.org
Director, Membership Services: Juergen Boldt
   E-Mail: juergen@omg.org
Manager, Marketing Communications: Stephanie L.
   Covert
   E-Mail: scovert@omg.org
System Administrator: Joe Harth
   E-Mail: joe@omg.org
Senior Technical Editor: Linda Heaton
   E-Mail: linda@omg.org
Marketing Specialist and Manager, Certification Program:
   Becky Higgins
   E-Mail: becky@omg.org
Senior Vice President, Finance: Suzanne Leon
   E-Mail: suzanne@omg.org
Manager, Marketing Programs and Events: Mike Narducci
   E-Mail: mike@omg.org
Webmaster: Svetlana Orlova
   E-Mail: svetlana@omg.org
Vice President and Technical Director: Andrew Watson
   E-Mail: andrew@omg.org

Historical Note:
*OMG's mission is to create software standards that improve
the process of developing complex applications while
increasing ROI. Membership includes many large and
smaller companies in the computer industry. Membership:
$11,000-75,000 (Contributing Member, based on
Annual Gross Revenue); $5,500-37,500 (Domain/
Platform Members, based on Annual Gross Revenue);
$3,000-21,500 (Influencing Members, based on Annual
Gross Revenue); $12,850 (Government Members); $2,150
(Trial); $550 (University).*

Continuing Education:
Certification Designation/s: OCSMP, OCRES, OCUP,
OCEB

Meetings/Conferences:
Conference Chair: Mike Narducci
2013 - Reston, VA (Hyatt Regency Reston)/March 18 -
   22
2013 - Berlin, Germany (Radisson Blu Hotel)/June 17
   - 21
Number of non-conference events/year: 1

Publications:
THE OMG STANDARD

Ocean Carrier Equipment Management Association (OCEMA)
1627 I St. NW
Suite 1100
Washington, DC 20006
E-Mail: info@ocema.org
Website: ocema.com
Members: 20 major ocean common carriers
Staff: 1
Annual Budget: $250-500,000

Personnel:
Executive Director: Jeff Lawrence
   E-Mail: jlawrence@ocema.org

Historical Note:
*OCEMA's focus is on operational and safety matters
pertaining to the intermodal transportation of ocean freight
within the US.*

Publications:
Membership Directory; on-line

Ocean Research & Conservation Association
(2005)
1420 Seaway Dr.
C/O Duerr Laboratory for Marine Conservation
Ft. Pierce, FL 34949
Tel: (772) 467-1600 *Fax:* (772) 467-1602
E-Mail: inquiries@teamorca.org
Website: teamorca.org
Staff: 13
Annual Budget: $1-2,000,000
Tax: 501(c)(3)

Personnel:
President, Chief Executive Officer and Senior Scientist: Dr.
Edith "Edie" Widder
E-Mail: ewidder@teamorca.org
Senior Education Associate: Sue Cook PhD
E-Mail: scook@teamorca.org
Managing Director: Warren Falls
E-Mail: wfalls@teamorca.org
Graphics and Communications Consultant: Christopher
Hayden
E-Mail: chayden@teamorca.org
Bookkeeper and Administrative Assistant: Halley Rohm
E-Mail: hrohm@teamorca.org
Marketing Coordinator and Executive Assistant: Lauren
Tracy
E-Mail: ltracy@teamorca.org

Historical Note:
*ORCA's mission to protect and restore aquatic ecosystems
while providing citizens with the guidance and support they
need to make measurable environmental improvements and
promote others to do the same. A donation of $50 or more
will qualify an individual to become a member of Team
ORCA. Membership: $50 (Individual); $100 (Couple); $150
(Family).*

Publications:
eNewsletter

Ocean Stewards Institute
750 Nineth St. NW
Suite 750
Washington, DC 20001-4524
Website: oceanstewards.org
Staff: 2
Annual Budget: $50-100,000

Personnel:
Contact, Communications: Kelly Coleman
E-Mail: kcoleman@hawaii.rr.com
Contact, Administrative Services: Carolyn Cuppernull
E-Mail: admin@oceanstewards.org

Historical Note:
*A trade organization that advocates for open ocean
aquaculture.*

Oceanic Engineering Society
114 S. Fork Ct.
Hertford, NC 27944
Tel: (252) 426-1226 *Fax:* (252) 426-5135
E-Mail: kferer@ieee.org
Website: oceanicengineering.org
Members: 2200 individuals
Staff: 6

Personnel:
Contact, Membership Services: Kenneth Ferer
E-Mail: kferer@ieee.org
Vice President, Conference Operations: Rene Garello
E-Mail: rene.garello@telecom-bretagne.eu

Historical Note:
*OES's mission is to work for scientific, literary, and
educational character and to strive for the advancement of
the theory and practice of electrotechnology applied to the
ocean environment, allied branches of engineering and of
the related arts and sciences, and the maintenance of a high
professional standards among its members and affiliates.
Membership: $19/year.*

Meetings/Conferences: Annual
Conference Chair: Rene Garello
2013 - San Diego, CA/Sept. 22 - 28

Publications:
IEEE Journal of Oceanic Engineering; quarterly
Membership Directory; on-line
OES Newsletter; quarterly

Membership List Available to Non-members

The Oceanography Society *(1988)*
P.O. Box 1931
Rockville, MD 20849-1931

Tel: (301) 251-7708 *Fax:* (301) 251-7709
E-Mail: info@tos.org
Website: tos.org
Members: 1500 individuals
Staff: 3
Annual Budget: $500-1,000,000
Tax: 501(c)(3)

Personnel:
Executive Director: Jennifer Ramarui
Editor: Ellen S. Kappel
E-Mail: ekappel@geo-prose.com

Historical Note:
*Mission of TOS is to promote communication among
oceanographers, and to provide a constituency for
consensus-building across all the disciplines of the field.
TOS members are oceanographers, scientists and engineers
with a professional interest in oceanography and related
fields. Membership: $60 (Regular); $30 (Student); $110
(Sponsoring); $500 (Corporate/Institution).*

Meetings/Conferences:
2014 - Honolulu, HI/Feb. 23 - 28

Publications:
Member Directory; on-line
Oceanography Magazine; quarterly; adv.

OESP - National Association of Oil and Energy Service Professionals *(1954)*
P.O. Box 67
E. Petersburg, PA 17520-0067
Tel: (717) 625-3076 *Fax:* (717) 625-3077
TollFree: (888) 552-0900
Website: naohsm.org
Members: 1400 individuals
Staff: 1
Annual Budget: $250-500,000

Personnel:
Executive Director: Judy Garber
E-Mail: jgarber@thinkoesp.org

Historical Note:
*Formerly National Association of Oil Heating Service
Managers. OESP's mission is education. Works for the
advancement of oilheating service professionals and
provides members with technical tapes, books and speakers
to train their employee technicians. Members are oil heat
service managers and small business owners. Membership:
$100 (National Direct); $545 (Corporate).*

Meetings/Conferences: Annual
Conference Chair: Judy Garber
2013 - Hershey, PA/May 19 - 23
Number of non-conference events/year: 3

Publications:
Advantage E-Newsletter; on-line

Off-Road Business Association
1701 Westwind Dr.
Suite 216
Bakersfield, CA 93301
Tel: (661) 323-1464 *Fax:* (661) 323-1487
Website: orba.biz
Members: 353 Members
Staff: 3
Annual Budget: $100-250,000

Personnel:
President and Chief Executive Officer: Fred Wiley
E-Mail: FWiley@ORBA.biz
Office Manager: Deborah Burgess
E-Mail: DBurgess@ORBA.biz
Chief Financial Officer: Randy Weisser

Historical Note:
*A professional trade association of off-road related business
owners, formed to preserve the sport of off-road recreation
in an environmentally responsible manner. Makes decisions
and takes actions that maintain and expand off-highway
vehicle recreation opportunities. Works closely with its
partner organizations on local, state and federal issues
that have potential impacts to the off-road industry.
Membership: $1,000 (Regular); $3,000 (Silver); $1,250/
quarter (Gold); $2,500/quarter (Platinum).*

Meetings/Conferences:
Number of non-conference events/year: 2

Publications:
Freedom Trails
Member Directory
Off-Road Business Magazine

Membership List Available to Non-members

Office and Professional Employees International Union (OPEIU) *(1945)*
80 Eighth Ave. 265 W. 14th St.
20th Floor
New York, NY 10011
Tel: (212) 675-3210 *Fax:* (212) 727-3466
TollFree: (800) 346-7348
E-Mail: opeiu@opeiu.org
Website: opeiu.org
Members: 125000 members
Staff: 63
Annual Budget: $1-2,000,000

Personnel:
General Counsel: Melvin Schwarzwald

Historical Note:
*Organized in Cincinnati, Ohio January 8, 1945 as the
Office Employees International Union and chartered by the
American Federation of Labor at the same time, absorbed
the Associated Unions of America in 1972, absorbed
the Leather Workers International Union (previously in
Peabody, MA) in 1992. OPEIU sponsors and supports the
voice of the Electorate Political Action Committee. Members
are employees and independent contractors in banking
and credit unions, insurance, higher education, shipping,
hospitals, medical clinics, utilities, transportation, hotels,
administrative offices. Professional organizations and Guilds
affiliated with OPEIU are a group that includes physicians,
pharmacists, chiropractors, appraisers, podiatrists, clinical
social workers, hypnotists, teachers and helicopter pilots.
Membership: fee varies by local union.*

Publications:
Member Directory; on-line
union's Research News

Office Business Center Association International
(1986)
2030 Main St.
Suite 1300
Irvine, CA 92614
Tel: (949) 260-9023 *Fax:* (949) 260-9021
TollFree: (800) 237-4741
E-Mail: rmeyers@obcai.org
Website: globalworkspace.org
Members: 600 companies
Staff: 12
Annual Budget: $250-500,000
Tax: 501(c)(6)

Personnel:
Executive Director: Richard Meyers
E-Mail: rmeyers@obcai.com
Bookkeeping: Julie Jacinto
Annual Meeting Planner: Cathy Palmateer
Manager, Communications: Ruth Sarreal
Database Management and Deputy Executive Director:
Valerie Tomlin
Tax Preparation: Rick Whittaker

Historical Note:
*Formerly (1993) Executive Suite Network and (2001)
Executive Suite Association and Office Business Center
Association International. Global Workspace Association
seeks to advance and promote the office business center
industry. Members are business center owners, managers
and support staff as well as vendors who service business
centers. Membership: $495-2,500 (Regular); $595
(Associate).*

Continuing Education:
Certification Designation/s: CCM

Meetings/Conferences: Annual
Conference Chair: Cathy Palmateer

Office Furniture Dealers Alliance
301 N. Fairfax St.
Suite 200
Alexandria, VA 22314
Tel: (800) 542-6672
Website: ofdanet.org/
Members: 400 Members
Staff: 4

Personnel:
President: Chris Bates
E-Mail: cbates@iopfda.org
Director, Marketing and Communications: Alicia Ellis
E-Mail: aellis@iopfda.org
Manager, Accounting: Antonio Payne
E-Mail: apayne@iopfda.org
Director, Events and Administration, Membership Services:
Billie Zidek
E-Mail: bzidek@iopfda.org

Historical Note:
OFDA's mission is to advance growth and improve profitability among independent U.S. and Canadian office furniture and interior products dealers and their key business partners through delivery of leading edge business performance benchmarking services, management education and online resources and implementation tools.

Meetings/Conferences: Annual
Conference Chair: Billie Zidek

Publications:
eNewsletter; weekly
Membership Directory; monthly

Office Furniture Distribution Association *(1923)*
282 N. Ridge Rd.
Brooklyn, MI 49230
Tel: (517) 467-9355 *Fax:* (517) 467-9056
Website: theofda.org
Members: 51 companies
Staff: 3

Personnel:
Managing Director: Russ Matthews
    E-Mail: russ111@comcast.net

Historical Note:
Formerly Metal Office Furniture Traffic League, adopted by Steel Office Furniture Institute in 1931, (1934) Steel Office Furniture Traffic Association, (1976) Office Furniture Distribution Management Association, (1986) Office Furniture Distribution Association. OFDA's mission is to hold down freight costs for the office furniture industry and the education of its members. Membership: $300/year (Company).

Meetings/Conferences: Annual

Publications:
Membership Directory; on-line
OFDA Newsletter; monthly

Offshore Marine Service Association *(1957)*
990 N. Corporate Dr.
Suite 210
Harahan, LA 70123-3324
Tel: (504) 734-7622 *Fax:* (504) 734-7134
Website: offshoremarine.org
Members: 270 corporations
Staff: 6
Annual Budget: $1-2,000,000

Personnel:
President And Chief Executive Officer : Jim Adams
    E-Mail: jim@offshoremarine.org
Director, Government Relations: Sarah Branch
    E-Mail: sarah@offshoremarine.org
Manager, Membership Services: Kelly L. Pettigrew
    E-Mail: kelly@offshoremarine.org

Historical Note:
OMSA's mission is to provide regulatory input on issues of concern to the offshore business community. Members are owners and operators of offshore installations or of vessels servicing such installations, and suppliers to the industry. Membership $90-$2,950 (Regular members); $1,500-$3,500 (Associate members).

Meetings/Conferences: Quarterly

Publications:
e-News Updates; monthly
Membership Directory; on-line
OMSA Newsletter

Omega Delta *(1917)*
Southern College of Optometry
2575 Yorba Linda Blvd.
Fullerton, CA 92831
Tel: (901) 722-3200
Website: omegadelta.org/entities
Members: 90 individuals
Staff: 3
Annual Budget: $100-250,000

Personnel:
Co-President: Jeff Binstock
Treasurer: Teresa Lam
Contact, Public Relations: Ryan Zamanigan

Historical Note:
Omega Delta is a professional fraternity serving optometry that promotes cultural awareness and provides an environment for academic and social success.

Omega Tau Sigma *(1906)*
P.O. Box 876
Ithaca, NY 14851-0876
Tel: (217) 868-5095 *Fax:* (217) 868-5080

E-Mail: alumnirecords@omegatausigma.org
Website: omegatausigma.org
Members: 8054 individuals
Staff: 8
Annual Budget: Under $10,000

Personnel:
President and Treasurer: Anne Gemensky Metzler
    DACVO, DVM, MS
    E-Mail: metzler.134@osu.edu
Secretary and Historian: Ann Walther DVM, G'94
    E-Mail: paws4ann@aol.com

Historical Note:
Professional veterinary medical fraternity, established at the University of Pennsylvania School of Veterinary Medicine. Member of the Professional Fraternity Association. OTS encourages and fosters the development of well-rounded, ethical veterinarians and through them create a better profession on the basis of friendship, cooperation, and respect for their fellow professional.

Meetings/Conferences: Annual
Number of non-conference events/year: 1

Omicron Kappa Upsilon *(1914)*
University of Medicine and Dentistry of New Jersey
110 Bergen St., Suite D-860
Newark, NJ 07103
Tel: (973) 972-4635 *Fax:* (973) 972-3164
Website: oku.org
Members: 17000 individuals
Staff: 4
Annual Budget: $25-50,000

Personnel:
Editor: James L. Delahanty
    E-Mail: j.delahanty@umdnj.edu

Historical Note:
Organized by the faculty of Northwestern University Dental School. OKU's mission is to promote and recognize scholarship and character among students of dentistry. Membership includes dental students who have distinguished themselves by excellence in scholarship.

Publications:
Membership Directory; on-line
OKU Bulletin; annually

Oncology Nursing Society *(1975)*
125 Enterprise Dr.
Pittsburgh, PA 15275-1214
Tel: (412) 859-6100 *Fax:* (412) 859-6162
TollFree: (877) 369-5497
E-Mail: customer.service@ons.org
Website: ons.org
Members: 37000 individuals
Staff: 130
Annual Budget: $25-50,000,000
Tax: 501(c)(6)

Personnel:
Chief Executive Officer: Paula Trahan Rieger
    E-Mail: prieger@ons.org
*Executive Director, External Relations and Business
    Development:* Michele R Dietz
    E-Mail: mdietz@ons.org
Manager, Public Relations: Jeanette Kent
    E-Mail: jkent@ons.org
Executive Director, Business Development: Michele R.
    McCorkle MSN, RN
    E-Mail: mmccorkle@ons.org
Director, Publications: Barbara A. Sigler MNEd, RN
    E-Mail: bsigler@ons.org
Health Policy Director: Alec Stone
    E-Mail: astone@ons.org
Director, Membership Services and Component Relations:
    Brian Theil
    E-Mail: btheil@ons.org

Historical Note:
ONS's mission is to promote excellence in oncology nursing and quality cancer care. Members are nurses and other health care professionals involved in the treatment and care of cancer patients and dedicated to education, research, and administration in oncology nursing. Membership: $102 (Active/Associate); $51 (Student/Physically Challenged); $21-41 (International Tiered); $62 (Senior Registered Nurse).

Meetings/Conferences: Annual
2013 - Washington, DC/April 25 - 28
Number of non-conference events/year: 3

Publications:

Clinical Journal of Oncology Nursing
Membership Directory; on-line
ONS Connect; adv.

Online Audiovisual Catalogers *(1980)*
20 Cooper Sq.
Third Floor
New York, NY 10003
Fax: (212) 995-4366
Website: olacinc.org
Members: 700 individuals
Staff: 5
Annual Budget: Under $10,000
Tax: 501(c)(3)

Personnel:
President: Heidi Frank
    E-Mail: hf36@nyu.edu
Organizer, Conferences: Julia Huskey
    E-Mail: huskey_je@mercer.edu

Historical Note:
OLAC's mission is to provide a means of exchange of information, opportunities for continuing education, and works towards a common understanding of practices and standards. OLAC represents catalogers of audiovisual materials and computer files. Membership: $20-55 (Individual, based on years); $25-70 (Institution/Other Countries); $50 (Contributing).

Meetings/Conferences: Annual
Conference Chair: Julia Huskey

Publications:
Membership Directory; on-line
OLAC Newsletter; quarterly

Membership List Available to Non-members

Online Lenders Alliance
P.O. Box 320130
Alexandria, VA 22320
Tel: (202) 567-6418
E-Mail: contact@onlinelendersalliance.org
Website: onlinelendersalliance.org
Staff: 1
Annual Budget: $2-5,000,000

Personnel:
Manager, Conference Sponsorship: Liz Jones
    E-Mail: ljones@onlinelendersalliance.org

Historical Note:
The Online Lenders Alliance is a professional trade organization representing the growing industry of companies offering online consumer small, short-term loans.

Meetings/Conferences:
Conference Chair: Liz Jones

Publications:
OLA Newsletter

Online News Association *(1999)*
P.O. Box 65741
Washington, DC 20035
Tel: (646) 290-7900
Website: journalists.org
Members: 1600 Professional Members
Staff: 5
Annual Budget: $1-2,000,000
Tax: 501(c)(3)

Personnel:
Executive Director: Jane McDonnell
    E-Mail: director@journalists.org
Director, Community Engagement: Jeanne Brooks
    E-Mail: jbrooks@journalists.org
Manager, Communications and Social Media: Jennifer
    Mizgata
    E-Mail: jennifer@journalists.org
Digital Manager: Jeremiah Patterson
    E-Mail: jeremiah@journalists.org
Senior Manager, Business Development and Sales:
    Branden Smith
    E-Mail: branden.smith@journalists.org

Historical Note:
ONA's mission is to inspire innovation and excellence among digital journalists to better serve the public.Members include news writers, producers, designers, editors, photographers, technologists and others who produce news for the Internet or other digital delivery systems, as well as academic members and others interested in the development of online journalism. Membership: $75 (Academic/Associate/Professional); $25 (Student).

Meetings/Conferences:

Conference Chair: Jeanne Brooks
Publications:
Nieman Reports; quarterly

Online Publishers Association, Inc. *(2001)*
249 W. 17th St.
New York, NY 10011
Tel: (212) 204-1495 *Fax:* (212) 204-1514
E-Mail: info@online-publishers.org
Website: online-publishers.org
Members:
52 publisher organizations
31 publisher organizations
Staff: 8
Annual Budget: $2-5,000,000
Tax: 501(c)(6)

Personnel:
President: Pam Horan
Contact, Membership Services: Emily Peck
Vice President, Government Affairs: Christopher Pedigo

Historical Note:
OPA's mission is to advance the business interests of online content providers before the advertising community, the press, the government and the public and to help its members fairly compete in the marketplace. Membership: $26,250-63,000 (Organizations); $26,250 (Affiliate); $5,250 (Supporter).

Publications:
Industry Intelligence; bi-weekly

Open Applications Group *(1994)*
P.O. Box 4897
Marietta, GA 30061-4897
Tel: (404) 402-1962 *Fax:* (801) 740-0100
E-Mail: oagis@openapplications.org
Website: oagi.org
Members: 48 Companies
Staff: 3
Annual Budget: $500-1,000,000
Tax: 501(c)(6)

Personnel:
Chief Executive Officer: David M. Connelly
Vice President, Operations: Ralph Hertlein
Business Manager: Michelle Rascoe

Historical Note:
OAGi is a process driven standards organization. OAGi's mission is to promote business process interoperability for both inter and intra enterprise business processes. Members are enterprise application software developers. Membership: $20,000-30,000 (Policy Board); $10,000-15,000 (Industry Council/Architecture Council); $325-8,000 (General).

Publications:
OAGi News; monthly

Open Geospatial Consortium *(1994)*
35 Main St.
Suite 5
Wayland, MA 01778
Tel: (508) 655-5858 *Fax:* (508) 655-2237
E-Mail: info@opengeospatial.org
Website: opengeospatial.org
Members: 473 companies, government agencies and universities
Staff: 18
Annual Budget: $2-5,000,000

Personnel:
President and Chief Executive Officer: Mark Reichardt
Research and Academic Advocate: David Arctur
   E-Mail: darctur@opengeospatial.org
Web Developer: Joe Brumley
   E-Mail: jbrumley@opengeospatial.org
Director, Outreach and Communication Services: Greg Buehler
   E-Mail: gbuehler@opengeospatial.org
Vice President, Operations and Finance: Jeff Burnett

Historical Note:
OGC's mission is to serve as a global forum for the collaboration of developers and users of spatial data products and services, and to advance the development of international standards for geospatial interoperability. Membership: $500-4400 (Associate); $11000 (Technical); $55000 (Principal); $250,000 (Strategic).

Meetings/Conferences:
Number of non-conference events/year: 3

Publications:
eNewsletter; monthly

The Open Group *(1983)*
44 Montgomery St.
Suite 960
San Francisco, CA 94104-4704
Tel: (415) 374-8280 *Fax:* (415) 374-8293
Website: opengroup.org
Members: 350 member organizations
Staff: 50
Annual Budget: $2-5,000,000

Personnel:
President and Chief Executive Officer: Allen Brown
   E-Mail: a.brown@opengroup.org
Contact, Marketing and Sales: Mitch Dalition
Vice President, Membership Services and Events: Patricia Donovan
   E-Mail: p.donovan@opengroup.org
Chief Technical Officer and Vice President, Services: Dave Lounsbury
   E-Mail: d.lounsbury@opengroup.org
Vice President and Chief Operating Officer: Steve Nunn
Director, Marketing: Steve Philp
   E-Mail: s.philp@opengroup.org
Vice President, Certification: James de Raeve
   E-Mail: j.deraeve@opengroup.org
Chief Financial Officer: James Scott

Historical Note:
Founded as the Electronic Messaging Association, became EMA -The E- Business Forum in 1999, and assumed its present name in 2002. The Open Group works towards enabling access to integrated information within and between enterprises based on open standards and global interoperability. Members are corporate users plus telecommunications carriers, computer equipment and software manufacturers, and consultants. Membership: $1,000- 2,500 (Academic); $6,250-31,250 (Gold); $2,500-20,000 (Silver).

Continuing Education:
Certification Designation/s: WAP, COE, UNIX, NASPL, TOGAF, LDAP, CORBA, POSIX, SIF, SSM, OAC, OCITS, ArchiMate

Meetings/Conferences: Quarterly
Conference Chair: Patricia Donovan
2013 - Newport Beach, CA/Jan. 28 - 31
2013 - Sydney, Australia/April 15 - 18
2013 - Washington, DC/July 15 - 18
2013 - London, United Kingdom/Oct. 21 - 24

Publications:
Membership Directory; on-line

Open Mobile Alliance *(2002)*
4330 La Jolla Village Dr.
Suite 110
San Diego, CA 92122
Fax: (858) 623-0743
Website: openmobilealliance.org
Members: 400 members
Staff: 7
Annual Budget: $2-5,000,000

Personnel:
General Manager: Seth Newberry
   E-Mail: snewberry@omaorg.org
Contact, Membership: Michelle Janata
   E-Mail: mjanata@omaorg.org
Contact, Events: Megan Leonard
Director, Market Development: Eshwar Pittampalli
Accounting Staff: Lisa Robotti
Director of Communications: Elizabeth Rose

Historical Note:
OMA seeks to provide interoperable service enablers working across countries, operators and mobile terminals. Members are wireless vendors, information technology companies, mobile operators application and content providers. Membership: $85,000 (Sponsor Members); $39,000 (Full Members); $9,000 (Associate Members); $600 (Supporter Members); $650 (Explorer Members).

Meetings/Conferences: Annual
Conference Chair: Megan Leonard

Publications:
Current OMA Members (Membership Directory); on-line
OMA Quarterly; quarterly

OpenTravel Alliance *(1999)*
1740 Massachusetts Ave.
Boxborough, MA 01719
Tel: (978) 263-7606 *Fax:* (978) 263-0696
E-Mail: opentravel@opentravel.org
Website: opentravel.org
Members: 125 companies
Staff: 2
Annual Budget: $500-1,000,000

Personnel:
President and Chief Executive Officer: Valyn Perini
   E-Mail: valyn.perini@opentravel.org
Office Manager: Caliene Isaacs
   E-Mail: caliene.isaacs@opentravel.org

Historical Note:
A trade group developing a common standard for the exchange of information within the travel industry. OpenTravel's mission is to engineer specifications to ensure traveler and supplier information flow smoothly throughout travel, tourism and hospitality. It creates, expands and drives adoption of open specifications, including but not limited to the use of XML, for the electronic exchange of business information among all sectors of the travel industry. Membership: $950-11,250 (Based on a company's annual revenue).

Publications:
Newsletter

OPERA America *(1970)*
330 Seventh Ave.
16th Floor
New York, NY 10001
Tel: (212) 796-8620 *Fax:* (212) 796-8631
E-Mail: info@operaamerica.org
Website: operaamerica.org
Members: 18450 individuals
Staff: 22
Annual Budget: $5-10,000,000

Personnel:
President and Chief Executive Officer: Marc A. Scorca
   E-Mail: mscorca@operaamerica.org
Director, Finance and Operations: Larry Bomback
   E-Mail: LBomback@operaamerica.org
Manager, Marketing and Communications: Patricia Kiernan Johnson
   E-Mail: pkjohnson@operaamerica.org
Editor: Kelley Rourke
   E-Mail: krourke@operaamerica.org
Manager, Membership Services: Sam Snook
   E-Mail: SSnook@operaamerica.org
Director, Research and Chief Information Officer: Kevin M. Sobczyk
   E-Mail: ksobczyk@operaamerica.org

Historical Note:
OPERA America is dedicated to support the creation, presentation and enjoyment of opera. Membership: $125 (Career Service Center); $75 (Individual); $250 (Associate); $300 (Business Member); $350 (Educational Producing Associate).

Meetings/Conferences: Annual
Conference Chair: Patricia Kiernan Johnson
2013 - Vancouver, BC/May 7 - 11

Publications:
North American Opera Journal; semi-annually
Opera America; quarterly; adv.

Operations Security Professionals Society *(1990)*
P. O. Box 150515
Alexandria, VA 22315-0515
Tel: (540) 338-3048 *Fax:* (703) 738-7145
E-Mail: opssociety@comcast.net
Website: opsecsociety.org
Members: 780 individuals
Staff: 2
Annual Budget: $100-250,000
Tax: 501(c)(6)

Personnel:
President: Dan Philips
Treasurer: Tim Rockwell

Historical Note:
Also known as OPSEC Professionals Society. OPSEC's mission is to advance the interests of the United States and its allies by serving as a means of educating and informing the American people with regard to the role of operations security in maintaining a strong national defense. Membership: $55 (Regular); $35 (Student); $500 (Life Time); $500- 7,500 (Corporate).

Continuing Education:
Certification Designation/s: OAP, OCP

Publications:
Membership Directory; on-line
Newsletter
OPSEC Journal

Operative Plasterers and Cement Masons International Association of the United States and Canada (1864)

11720 Beltsville Dr.
Suite 700
Beltsville, MD 20705
Tel: (301) 623-1000 Fax: (301) 623-1032
E-Mail: opcimiaintl@opcmia.org
Website: opcmia.org
Members:
56000 members
55000 individuals
Staff: 43
Annual Budget: $10-25,000,000

Personnel:
Executive Vice President: Daniel E. Stepano
General President: Patrick Finley
General Secretary and Treasurer: Earl F. Hurd

Historical Note:
Formerly (1864) the National Plasterers Organization of the United States, (1889) the Operative Plasterers International the United States and Canada. OPCMIA's mission is to protect and promote the quality of the industry and the livelihood of members. It is a labor union that represents plasterers and cement masons in the construction industry in North America.

Continuing Education:
Certification Designation/s: CPR

Publications:
E-Journal News
Membership Directory; on-line
The Plasterer and Cement Mason; irregular

Ophthalmic Photographers' Society (1969)

1887 W. Ranch Rd.
Nixa, MO 65714-8262
Tel: (417) 725-0181 Fax: (417) 724-8450
TollFree: (800) 403-1677
E-Mail: ops@opsweb.org
Website: opsweb.org
Members: 1200 individuals
Staff: 2
Annual Budget: $250-500,000

Personnel:
Executive Director: Barbara S. McCalley

Historical Note:
OPS's mission is to provide continuing education in the field of ophthalmic photography, to set and maintain standards for the profession through a multi-level certification program and to promote scientific advancement in the technology. Members are health professionals actively engaged in ophthalmic photography including ophthalmic photographers, ophthalmologists, ophthalmic technicians and basic scientific researchers. Membership: $90/year.

Continuing Education:
Certification Designation/s: CRA, OCT

Meetings/Conferences: Annual

Publications:
Journal of Ophthalmic Photography; semi-annually; adv.
OPS Directory; annually
OPS Newsletter; quarterly; adv.

Membership List Available to Non-members

Opportunity Finance Network (1986)

620 Chestnut St., Suite 572
Public Ledger Building
Philadelphia, PA 19106
Tel: (215) 923-4754 Fax: (215) 923-4755
E-Mail: info@opportunityfinance.net
Website: opportunityfinance.net
Members: 180 funds
Staff: 34
Annual Budget: $25-50,000,000
Tax: 501(c)(3)

Personnel:
President and Chief Executive Officer: Mark Pinsky
    E-Mail: mpinsky@opportunityfinance.net
Vice President, Accounting: Laurie Curran
    E-Mail: lcurran@opportunityfinance.net
Senior Associate, Human Resources: Tamara Frye
    E-Mail: tfrye@opportunityfinance.net
Vice President, Membership Services: Seth Julyan
    E-Mail: sjulyan@opportunityfinance.net
Chief Financial Officer: Beth Lipson
    E-Mail: blipson@opportunityfinance.net

Senior Vice President, Policy Development: Cheryl Neas
    E-Mail: cneas@opportunityfinance.net
Executive Vice President, Strategic Communications: Lina Page
    E-Mail: lpage@opportunityfinance.net

Historical Note:
Founded as National Association of Community Development Loan Funds, Formerly known as National Community Capital Association, assumed its current name in 2006. OFN's mission is to lead CDFIs and their partners to ensure that low-income, low-wealth, and other disadvantaged people and communities have access to affordable, responsible financial products and services. Membership depends on assets. Membership: $250-3,000/year.

Meetings/Conferences: Annual

Publications:
e-Newsletter; monthly

Membership List Available to Non-members

Optical Imaging Association (1918)

P.O. Box 428
Fairfax, VA 22038
Tel: (703) 836-1360 Fax: (703) 836-6644
Website: lpanet.org
Members: 14 companies
Staff: 2
Annual Budget: $50-100,000

Personnel:
Executive Director: Clark Mulligan CAE
    E-Mail: cmulligan@lpanet.org
Director of Membership Services, Marketing and Communications: Lauren Hefner

Historical Note:
The Optical Imaging Association is a part of the Laboratory Products Association which was founded in 1918. The OPIA represents companies that manufacture or distribute microscopes and/or products, components and peripherals for microscopy and the microscopy imaging market. Membership: $3,200-7,950 (Active); $500-3200 (Associate).

Meetings/Conferences: Annual
Conference Chair: Clark Mulligan CAE

Publications:
Membership Directory; on-line

Membership List Available to Non-members

The Optical Lab Division (1894)

225 Reinekers Ln.
Suite 700
Alexandria, VA 22314
Tel: (703) 548-6619 Fax: (703) 548-4580
TollFree: (800) 477-5652
E-Mail: ola@ola-labs.org
Website: ola-labs.org
Members: 200 companies
Staff: 8
Annual Budget: $500-1,000,000
Tax: 501(c)(6)

Personnel:
Manager, Convention and Member Services: Carmen Sevilla
    E-Mail: csevilla@thevisioncouncil.org

Historical Note:
Formerly (1977) the Optical Wholesalers Association and Optical Laboratories Association. OLA provides forums for optical laboratories and develops information and services for members for business improvement. Membership: $960 (Individual); $1200 (Associate).

Meetings/Conferences: Annual
Conference Chair: Carmen Sevilla
Number of non-conference events/year: 9

Publications:
Membership Directory; on-line
OLA Newsletter; monthly

Membership List Available to Non-members

Optical Society of America (1916)

2010 Massachusetts Ave. NW
Washington, DC 20036-1023
Tel: (202) 223-8130 Fax: (202) 223-1096
E-Mail: info@osa.org
Website: osa.org
Members: 15000 individuals
Staff: 164
Annual Budget: $25-50,000,000
Tax: 501(c)(3)

Personnel:
Chief Executive Officer: Elizabeth A. Rogan
    E-Mail: oed@osa.org
Chief Financial Officer: Kathy Bosak
Senior Director, Human Resources and Administration: Genaro Esposito-Montanez
Senior Director, Science Policy: Tom G. Giallorenzi
    E-Mail: tgiall@osa.org
Chief Marketing Officer: Beth T. Hampton
    E-Mail: omsc@osa.org
Senior Advisor, Engineering and Applications: Tom Hausken
Senior Director, Information Technology: Deborah C. Herrin
    E-Mail: dherri@osa.org
Chief Strategy Officer: Grace Klonoski
    E-Mail: gklono@osa.org
Chief Meetings Officer: Chad Stark
    E-Mail: cstark@osa.org

Historical Note:
OSA's mission is to promote the generation, application and archiving of knowledge in optics and photonics and to disseminate this knowledge worldwide. Membership: $120 (Individual/Fellow); $35 (Student/Teacher); $45 (Recent Graduate); $55 (Emeritus), $2,360 (Lifetime).

Meetings/Conferences: Annual
Conference Chair: Chad Stark
2013 - San Jose, CA (San Jose Convention Center)/June 9 - 14/1-10 exhibitors
Number of non-conference events/year: 1

Publications:
Applied Optics
Journal of the Optical Society of America
Journal of the Optical Society of America B; monthly
Membership Directory
Optical Materials Express; monthly
Optics and Photonics News (OPN); monthly
Optics Express; bi-weekly
Optics Letters (OL); semi-monthly
The Journal of Optical Networking (JON); monthly
The Journal of the Optical Society of America (JOSA)
The Journal of the Optical Society of America A (JOSA A); monthly
Virtual Journal for Biomedical Optics

Optical Storage Technology Association (1992)

19925 Stevens Creek Blvd.
Cupertinoc, CA 95014
Tel: (408) 253-3695 Fax: (408) 253-9938
E-Mail: questions@osta.org
Website: osta.org
Staff: 3
Annual Budget: Under $10,000

Personnel:
President: David Bunzel
    E-Mail: dbunzel@osta.org
Administrator: Debbie Maguire
    E-Mail: debbie@osta.org

Historical Note:
OSTA was incorporated as an international trade association in 1992 to promote the use of recordable optical technologies and products. OSTA's mission is to promote market demand for optical recording products.

Meetings/Conferences:
Conference Chair: Debbie Maguire

Publications:
OSTA Newsletter

Opticians Association of America (1926)

4064 E. Fir Hill Dr.
Lakeland, TN 38002
Tel: (901) 388-2423 Fax: (901) 388-2348
E-Mail: oaa@oaa.org
Website: oaa.org
Members: 3500 individuals 500 retail optical companies
Staff: 1
Annual Budget: $250-500,000

Personnel:
Executive Director: Christopher "Chriss" M. Allen

Historical Note:
Formerly (1972) Guild of Prescription Opticians of America. OAA seeks to promote and expand opticianry by improving its professional stature through leadership, education, legislative representation and communication. Members are dispensing opticians or students enrolled in 2 year opticianry program. Membership: $25-500/year.

Meetings/Conferences: Annual
2013 - Orlando, FL (Buena Vista Palace)/Jan. 17 - 19

Publications:
Member Directory
Newsletter

Membership List Available to Non-members

Optoelectronics Industry Development Association (1991)
2010 Massachusetts Ave. NW
Washington, DC 20036
Tel: (202) 416-1449 *Fax:* (202) 416-6130
E-Mail: OIDAInfo@osa.org
Website: oida.org
Staff: 4
Annual Budget: $500-1,000,000

Personnel:
Executive Technical Director: Ganesh Gopalakrishnan
    E-Mail: ganesh@oida.org
Manager, Program: Brooke Hirsh
    E-Mail: bhirsc@oida.org

Historical Note:
OIDA's mission is to advance the competitiveness of its members by focusing on the business of technology and to provide a network for the exchange of ideas and information within the optoelectronics community. Membership: $1,500-16,500 (Associate, based on revenue); $3,500 (Affiliate).

Meetings/Conferences:
Conference Chair: Brooke Hirsh
2013 - Munich, Germany/June 17 - 20
Number of non-conference events/year: 1

Publications:
Membership Directory; on-line
OIDA Newsletter

Optometric Extension Program Foundation (1928)
1921 E. Carnegie Ave.
Suite 3-L
Santa Ana, CA 92705-5510
Tel: (949) 250-8070 *Fax:* (949) 250-8157
Website: oepf.org
Staff: 8
Annual Budget: $1-2,000,000
Tax: 501(c)(3)

Personnel:
Executive Director: Robert A. Williams
    E-Mail: RWilliams@oep.org
Director, Publications: Sally Marshall Corngold
    E-Mail: SMCorngold@oep.org
President: Gregory Kitchene
    E-Mail: GregoryKitchener@oep.org
Administrative Assistant: Karen Ruder
    E-Mail: Karen.Ruder@verizon.net

Historical Note:
OEP's mission is to advance human progress through research and education on vision, the visual process, and clinical care.

Meetings/Conferences:
2013 - St. Pete Beach, FL/May 2 - 4

Publications:
Clinical Curriculum
The Journal of Behavioral Optometry

Oral History Association (1966)
P.O. Box 1773
Dickinson College
Carlisle, PA 17013-2896
Tel: (717) 245-1036 *Fax:* (717) 245-1046
Website: oralhistory.org
Members: 1200 individuals
Staff: 2
Annual Budget: $250-500,000
Tax: 501(c)(3)

Personnel:
President: Mary Larson
    E-Mail: mary.larson@okstate.edu
Executive Secretary: Madelyn Campbell
    E-Mail: oha@dickinson.edu

Historical Note:
OHA's mission is to promote better standards in the collection, preservation, dissemination and uses of oral testimony. Members are historians and others involved in recording, transcribing, and preserving conversations with persons who have participated in seminal developments of

history. *Membership: $1,000 (Lifetime); $65 (Regular); $142-170 (Institutional); $35 (Student).*

Meetings/Conferences: Annual
2013 - Oklahoma City, OK (Skirvin Hilton Oklahoma City)/Oct. 29 - Nov. 3

Publications:
Membership Directory; on-line
OHA Newsletter; adv.
The Oral History Review; semi-annually; adv.

Order Fulfillment Solutions (1986)
8720 Red Oak Blvd., Suite 201
C/O Material Handling Industry of America
Charlotte, NC 28217-3992
Tel: (704) 676-1190 *Fax:* (704) 676-1199
Website: mhia.org/industrygroups/ofs
Members: 60 associations
Staff: 2
Annual Budget: $50-100,000

Personnel:
Managing Executive: Mike Ogle

Historical Note:
Members are storage industry manufacturers. OSSSC is a Council of the Material Handling Industry Association. OFS is dedicated to developing properly applied order fulfillment solutions. OFS's members achieve this mission through Education and Membership Development.

Oregon Farm Bureau Federation (1932)
3415 Commercial St.
Salem, OR 97302-5169
Tel: (503) 399-1701 *Fax:* (503) 399-8082
TollFree: (800) 334-6323
E-Mail: luann@oregonfb.org
Website: oregonfb.org
Members: 60,000 Oregon families
Staff: 6
Annual Budget: $2-5,000,000
Tax: 501(c)(5)

Personnel:
President: Barry Bushue
    E-Mail: barry@oregonfb.org
Executive Vice President: David B. Dillon
Contact, Membership Records And Services: Melissa Armour
    E-Mail: melissa@oregonfb.org
National Affairs, Grassroots Specialist: Gail Greenman
    E-Mail: gail@oregonfb.org
Director, Communication: Anne Marie Moss
    E-Mail: annemarie@oregonfb.org
Accounting Director, Treasurer: Candace Seal
    E-Mail: candace@oregonfb.org

Historical Note:
The Oregon Farm Bureau (OFB) is a voluntary, grassroots, nonprofit organization representing the interests of the state's farmers and ranchers in the public and policymaking arenas.

Publications:
Multnomah County Farm Bureau Newsletter; monthly

Organic Crop Improvement Association International (1985)
1340 N. Cotner Blvd.
Lincoln, NE 68505-1838
Tel: (402) 477-2323 *Fax:* (402) 477-4325
E-Mail: info@ocia.org
Website: ocia.org
Members: 50000 growers/processors/ manufacturers
Staff: 27
Annual Budget: $2-5,000,000

Personnel:
Executive Director: Amanda Brewster
    E-Mail: abrewster@ocia.org
Manager, Human Resources: Lisa Schroedl
    E-Mail: lschroedl@ocia.org

Historical Note:
OCIA is dedicated to providing the quality organic certification services and access to global organic markets. Members are farmers, processors, manufacturers and traders of organic crops from different parts of the world. Membership: $50 (Supporting Member); $95 (Direct Member/General Member).

Continuing Education:
Certification Designation/s: RFCO, MAFF, IFOAM, MAG, CAAQ, NOP

Publications:

OCIA Communicator; quarterly; adv.
OCIA Outlook; semi-annually
Organic Updates; on-line

Membership List Available to Non-members

Organic Reactions Catalysis Society (1975)
PO Box 999
C/O Pacific Northwest National Laboratory
Richland, WA 99352
Tel: (978) 784-5403 *Fax:* (978) 784-5200
E-Mail: treasurer@orcs.org
Website: orcs.org
Members: 250 individuals
Staff: 1
Annual Budget: $25-50,000

Personnel:
Secretary and Treasurer: Karl Albrecht
    E-Mail: treasurer@orcs.org

Historical Note:
Members are chemists and researchers interested in reagents that increase or provoke chemical reactions. Has no paid officers or full-time staff. The Organic Reactions Catalysis Society seeks to advance practical applications of catalysis for making organic compounds by fostering discussions, providing opportunities for members to present their work, and facilitating dissemination of scientific knowledge.

Meetings/Conferences: Biennial

Publications:
ORCS Newsletter

Organic Trade Association (1985)
28 Vernon St.
Suite 413
Brattleboro, VT 53011
Tel: (802) 275-3800 *Fax:* (802) 275-3801
E-Mail: info@ota.com
Website: ota.com
Members: 1600 businesses
Staff: 27
Annual Budget: $2-5,000,000

Personnel:
Executive Vice President: Laura Batcha
    E-Mail: lbatcha@ota.com
Chief Operating Officer: David Gagnon
    E-Mail: dgagnon@ota.com
Senior Writer and Editor: Barbara Haumann
    E-Mail: bhaumann@ota.com
Manager, Membership: Linda Lutz
    E-Mail: llutz@ota.com
Manager, Internet Marketing and Webmaster: Jen Mavris
    E-Mail: jmavris@ota.com

Historical Note:
Formerly (1994) Organic Foods Production Association of America, absorbed (1991) Organic Food Alliance. OTA seeks to promote and protect the growth of organic trade to benefit the environment, farmers, the public and the economy. Members are businesses involved in the organic products industry. Membership: $300-32,025 (Trade Member); $330-3,150 (Business Associate); $330 (Provisional Member/Government Associate/Non Profit Associate).

Meetings/Conferences: Annual
Conference Chair: David Gagnon

Publications:
The Organic Pages (The member directory); on-line; adv.
The Organic Report; quarterly; adv.
What's News in Organic

Organization Development Institute (1968)
11234 Walnut Ridge Rd.
Chesterland, OH 44026-1299
Tel: (440) 729-7419 *Fax:* (440) 729-9319
E-Mail: donwcole@aol.com
Website: odinstitute.org
Members: 455 individuals
Staff: 1
Annual Budget: $25-50,000

Personnel:
President: Donald W. Cole
    E-Mail: donwcole@aol.com

Historical Note:
ODI strives to promote an understanding of the field of organization development. Membership: $110 (Regular); $150 (Professional Consultant); $80 (Full time Student/ Senior, not employed full-time).

Meetings/Conferences:
Number of non-conference events/year: 1

Membership List Available to Non-members

Organization Development Network (1964)
401 N. Michigan Ave.
Suite 2200
Chicago, IL 60611
Tel: (312) 321-5136 *Fax:* (312) 673-6836
E-Mail: odnetwork@odnetwork.org
Website: odnetwork.org
Members: 4000 individuals
Staff: 11
Annual Budget: $500-1,000,000
Tax: 501(c)(3)

Personnel:
Executive Director: Laura J. Rudzinski
    E-Mail: odnetwork@odnetwork.org
Education Manager: Lauren Brosio
    E-Mail: LBrosio@smithbucklin.com
Manager, Conferences: Jennifer Dotson
    E-Mail: jdotson@odnetwork.org
Coordinator, Membership Services: Danielle Driscoll
Director , Operations: Sara Giacalone
    E-Mail: SGiacalone@odnetwork.org
Contact, Membership Services and Event Registration: Tim Meadows
    E-Mail: tmeadows@odnetwork.org
Financial Management Manager: Chris Migala
    E-Mail: odnetwork@odnetwork.org
Managing Editor: John Vogelsang
    E-Mail: jvogelsang@earthlink.net
Director, Events: Katie Walsh
    E-Mail: kawalsh@smithbucklin.com
Manager, Sales: Andrew Werfelmann
    E-Mail: awerfelmann@odnetwork.org
Director, Marketing and Communications: Andrew Younger
    E-Mail: ayounger@odnetwork.org

Historical Note:
OD Network strives to provide resources, professional development and networking opportunities for organization development professionals. It works to advance the theory and practice of organization development by promoting more visibility, credibility, and influence for its members. Members are scholars, practitioners and others with an interest in human, organizational, and systems development. Membership: $200 (Individual); $100 (Student/Senior); $159 (Organizational).

Meetings/Conferences: Annual
Conference Chair: Jennifer Dotson

Publications:
Member Directory
OD Practitioner; quarterly

Membership List Available to Non-members

Organization for International Investment (1991)
1225 19th St. NW
Suite 501
Washington, DC 20036
Tel: (202) 659-1903 *Fax:* (202) 659-2293
Website: ofii.org
Members: 136 companies
Staff: 14
Annual Budget: $2-5,000,000

Personnel:
President and Chief Executive Officer: Nancy L. McLernon
    E-Mail: nmclernon@ofii.org
Senior Director, Operations and Events: Monica L. Coates
    E-Mail: mcoates@ofii.org
Vice President, Public Policy and Governmental Affairs: John Lettieri
    E-Mail: jlettieri@ofii.org
Manager, Marketing and Communications: Brennan Marshall
    E-Mail: bmarshall@ofii.org
Vice President, External Affairs: Abigail Martin
    E-Mail: amartin@ofii.org
Contact, Communications: Amanda Reid
    E-Mail: Amanda.Reid@ErvinHillStrategy.com

Historical Note:
OFII is involved in issues of U.S. subsidiaries of companies headquartered abroad or "Insourcing" companies. It is a clearinghouse for statistical information (both government and private data) on the role of international investment in the United States. Membership is exclusive to the U.S. operations of companies headquartered abroad.

Meetings/Conferences:
Conference Chair: Monica L. Coates

Organization for Safety and Asepsis Procedures (1984)
1997 Annapolis Exchange Pkwy., Suite 300
P.O. Box 6297
Annapolis, MD 21401
Tel: (410) 571-0003 *Fax:* (410) 571-0028
TollFree: (800) 298-6727
E-Mail: office@osap.org
Website: osap.org
Staff: 5
Annual Budget: $250-500,000
Tax: 501(c)(6)

Personnel:
Executive Director: Therese Long MBA CAE
    E-Mail: tlong@osap.org
Executive Assistant and Office Manager: Suzanne Bauman
Editor and Director, Website: Patricia Podolak

Historical Note:
OSAP's mission is to strive for safe oral healthcare for people everywhere. Membership: $115 (Individual, US); $25 (Student); $2,500 (Corporate); $100 (Web); $250 (Associate); $150-250 (Academic) $150 (Professional Practice).

Meetings/Conferences:
2013 - San Diego, CA (Hyatt Regency Mission Bay Spa and Marina-San Diego)/June 13 - 15
Number of non-conference events/year: 1

Publications:
Infection Control in Practice (ICIP); bi-monthly
Membership Directory
The OSAP Report Online (TORO); monthly

Organization for the Advancement of Structured Information Standards
25 Corporate Dr.
Suite 103
Burlington, MA 01803-4238
Tel: (781) 425-5073 *Fax:* (781) 425-5072
E-Mail: info@oasis-open.org
Website: oasis-open.org
Members: 5,600 participants, organizations and individual members
Staff: 13
Annual Budget: $2-5,000,000

Personnel:
Executive Director: Laurent Liscia
    E-Mail: laurent.liscia@oasis-open.org
Director, Technology: Greg Carpenter
    E-Mail: greg.carpenter@oasis-open.org),
General Counsel: James Bryce Clark
    E-Mail: jamie.clark@oasis-open.org
Coordinator, Member Service: Barbara Erbes
    E-Mail: barbara.erbes@oasis-open.org
Senior Director, Communications and Development: Carol Geyer
    E-Mail: carol.geyer@oasis-open.org
Manager, Events: Jane Harnad
    E-Mail: jane.harnad@oasis-open.org
Chief Operating Officer: Scott McGrath
    E-Mail: scott.mcgrath@oasis-open.org
Senior Manager, Development and Advocacy: Dee Schur
    E-Mail: dee.schur@oasis-open.org

Historical Note:
OASIS is a not-for-profit consortium that drives the development, convergence and adoption of open standards for the global information society. Membership: $300-50,000/year.

Meetings/Conferences: Annual
Conference Chair: Jane Harnad

Publications:
OASIS News; bi-weekly
XML Daily Newslink; daily

Organization for the Promotion and Advancement of Small Telecommunications Companies (1963)
2020 K St. NW
Seventh Floor
Washington, DC 20006
Tel: (202) 659-5990 *Fax:* (202) 659-4619
Website: opastco.org
Members: 560 companies and 175 associate members
Staff: 19

Annual Budget: $2-5,000,000
Tax: 501(c)(3)

Personnel:
Director, Finance and Administration: Michael Viands
    E-Mail: mlv@opastco.org
Regulatory Counsel: Brian Ford
    E-Mail: bjf@opastco.org
Technical Director: John McHugh
    E-Mail: jtm@opastco.org
Coordinator, Public Relations: Caroline O'Reilly
    E-Mail: cao@opastco.org
Vice President, Regulatory Policy and Business Development: Stuart Polikoff
    E-Mail: sep@opastco.org
Director, Education and Events: Kathleen Kelley Riesett
    E-Mail: kkr@opastco.org
Director, Public Relations: Martha Silver
    E-Mail: mks@opastco.org

Historical Note:
Formerly (1996) the Organization for the Protection and Advancement of Small Telephone Companies. OPASTCO protects the interests of small, rural, independent commercial telephone companies and cooperatives that have less than 50,000 access lines. It also provides educational programs, conventions and publications that create forums for sharing rural telecom knowledge. Membership: $12,240 (Local Exchange Carrier); $425-1,450 (Associate); Associate Dues + $1,500 (Medallion); $5,970 (International ILEC); $500 (Individual).

Meetings/Conferences:
Conference Chair: Kathleen Kelley Riesett
2013 - Kauai, HI (Grand Hyatt Kauai)/Jan. 5 - 9
2013 - Lake Buena Vista, FL (Walt Disney World Dolphin Resort)/Feb. 3 - 6
2013 - Orlando, FL (Disney Yacht and Beach Resort)/July 13 - 17

Publications:
Advocate Newsletter; weekly
Associate Member Newsletter; quarterly
Convention Wrap-up; semi-annually
Membership Directory; on-line
OPASTCO 411 Newsletter; semi-monthly
Roundtable Magazine; quarterly; adv.

Organization for the Study of Sex Differences (2006)
1025 Connecticut Ave. NW
Suite 701
Washington, DC 20036
Tel: (202) 496-5009 *Fax:* (202) 833-3472
Website: ossdweb.org
Staff: 3

Personnel:
Executive Director: Christine L. Carter

Historical Note:
From 2006-2012, OSSD operated as a program of the Society for Women's Health Research (SWHR), and in 2012 became an independent non-profit educational organization. OSSD's mission is to promote research in, and knowledge of, sex and gender differences in biology and medicine. Members are basic and clinical scientists from various disciplines who share an interest in exploring sex/gender differences in all areas of biological, medical, and behavioral science. Membership: $150 (Regular); $50 (Students/Postdoctoral Fellows/Residents/Trainees).

Meetings/Conferences: Annual
2013 - Weehawken, NJ (Sheraton Lincoln Harbor Hotel)/April 25 - 29

Publications:
Biology of Sex Differences; monthly; adv.
Membership Directory; on-line; adv.
OSSD e-newsletter; bi-monthly; adv.

Organization for Tropical Studies (1963)
Duke University
P.O. Box 90630
Durham, NC 27708-0630
Tel: (919) 684-5774 *Fax:* (919) 684-5661
E-Mail: ots@duke.edu
Website: ots.ac.cr
Members: 64 institutions
Staff: 19
Annual Budget: $10-25,000,000

Personnel:
President and Chief Executive Officer: Elizabeth Losos
    E-Mail: elosos@duke.edu
Development Staff Specialist: Sarah Clem
    E-Mail: sarah.clem@duke.edu

Business Manager: Susan Gillispie
   E-Mail: susan.gillispie@duke.edu
Vice President, Finances: Bethany Hawkins
   E-Mail: beth.hawkins@duke.edu
Vice President, Global Programs and Partnerships: Ed
   Stashko
   E-Mail: estashko@duke.edu

Historical Note:
*OTS is an organization of universities and research
institutions with graduate and undergraduate programs
in tropical ecology studies. OTS's mission is to provide
leadership in education, research and the responsible
use of natural resources in the tropics. Membership: $35
(Individual); $8,800 (Organization).*

Meetings/Conferences: Annual
2013 - San Jose, Costa Rica (Ramada Herradura
   Convention Center)/June 23 - 27

Publications:
e-Canopy; on-line
View From the Canopy

Membership List Available to Non-members

Organization of American Historians *(1907)*
112 N. Bryan Ave.
P.O. Box 5457
Bloomington, IN 47408-4141
Tel: (812) 855-7311 *Fax:* (812) 855-0696
E-Mail: oah@oah.org
Website: oah.org
Members:
11000 institutions
7800 historians
Staff: 19
Annual Budget: $2-5,000,000
Tax: 501(c)(3)

Personnel:
Executive Director: Katherine M. Finley
   E-Mail: kmfinley@oah.org
Accounting and Financial Support Specialist: Jonathan
   Apgar
   E-Mail: jmapgar@oah.org
Director, Membership Services: Ginger Foutz
   E-Mail: glfoutz@oah.org
Executive Editor: Edward T. Linenthal
   E-Mail: etl@oah.org
Coordinator, Sponsorship, Exhibit and Advertising: Teresa
   Ransdell
   E-Mail: transdell@oah.org
Marketing and Communications Specialist: Michael Regoli
   E-Mail: mregoli@oah.org
Director, Meetings: Amy Stark
   E-Mail: astark@oah.org

Historical Note:
*Formerly (1964) Mississippi Valley Historical Association.
OAH promotes excellence in the scholarship, teaching,
and presentation of American history, and encourages
wide discussion of historical questions and equitable
treatment of all practitioners of history. Members are
professors, teachers, students, archivists, public historians,
and institutional subscribers. Membership: $60-200
(Individual); $45 (Student); $60 (Other).*

Meetings/Conferences: Annual
Conference Chair: Amy Stark
2013 - San Francisco, CA (Hilton San Francisco Union
   Square)/April 11 - 14
2014 - Atlanta, GA/April 10 - 13
2015 - St. Louis, MO/April 16 - 19

Publications:
Journal of American History; quarterly
OAH Magazine of History; quarterly; adv.
OAH Outlook; quarterly

Organization of American Kodaly Educators
(1975)
10951 Pico Blvd
Suite 405
Los Angeles, CA 90064
Tel: (310) 441-3555 *Fax:* (310) 441-3577
E-Mail: info@oake.org
Website: oake.org
Members: 1700 individuals
Staff: 4
Annual Budget: $250-500,000

Personnel:
President: Kelly Foster Griffin
   E-Mail: president@oake.org

Historical Note:

*OAKE's mission is to advocate Kodaly's concept of
"Music for Everyone" through the improvement of
music education in schools. Members are music teachers
and others interested in the Kodaly approach to music
education. Membership: $75 (Active/Institutional); $70
(Corresponding/Library); $20 (Full-Time Student); $1,000
(Lifetime); $40 (Retired); $125 (Sustaining).*

Meetings/Conferences: Annual
Conference Chair: Nancy Johnson
2013 - Hartford, CT/March 21 - 23

Publications:
Member Directory; on-line
The Kodály Envoy; adv.

Organization of Black Designers *(1990)*
300 M St. SW
Suite N-110
Washington, DC 20024
Tel: (202) 659-3918 *Fax:* (202) 488-3838
E-Mail: info@obd.org
Website: obd.org
Members: 10,000 individuals
Staff: 6
Annual Budget: $10-25,000

Personnel:
Executive Director: Shauna D. Stallworth
Membership Contact: Bill Browne
   E-Mail: bill@obd.org
Secretary and Treasurer: Barbara G. Laurie AIA

Historical Note:
*OBD members are African-Americans working as fashion,
graphic, product, interior or industrial designers. OBD's
mission is to enhance and improve the totality of the
American design professions by energizing them with
creative diversity. Membership: $175 (Professional/
Affiliate/Intern Professional/Educator Associate); $75
(Student); $500 (Corporate).*

Organization of Flying Adjusters *(1958)*
1380 W. Hume Rd.
Lima, OH 45806
Tel: (567) 712-2097 *Fax:* (800) 207-9324
Website: ofainc.com
Members: 50 companies
Staff: 4
Annual Budget: $10-25,000

Personnel:
Meeting Chairman: Donald H. Hendricks
   E-Mail: dh2729@sbcglobal.net

Historical Note:
*OFA's mission is to promote and develop a standard
of ethics in the handling of aviation insurance claims.
Membership: $175/year (Regular).*

Meetings/Conferences: Annual

Publications:
Directory
OFA Newsletter; semi-annually

Organization of Professional Employees of the U.S. Department of Agriculture (OPEDA) *(1929)*
P.O. Box 23762
Washington, DC 20026-3762
Tel: (202) 720-4898 *Fax:* (202) 720-6692
E-Mail: opeda@usda.gov
Website: opeda.net
Members: 4000 individuals
Staff: 5
Annual Budget: $25-50,000

Personnel:
Executive Vice President: Edward Dickerhoof
Executive Director: Dr. Dora (Holly) Hambley
Vice President, Member Services: Mark Benedict
Vice President, Membership: Teresa Pickett
Vice President, Professionalism: Caroline Thorpe

Historical Note:
*OPEDA's mission is to enhance the effectiveness of
members in the performance of their duties and to promote
the efficient and effective operation of agencies of the
U.S. Department of Agriculture. Membership is open
to all USDA employees and retirees regardless of race,
color, national origin, sex, religion, age, disability, sexual
orientation, marital or familial status, political beliefs,
parental status, receipt of public assistance, or protected
genetic information. Membership: $52 (Active Employees);
$25 (Retired).*

Publications:
OPEDA Newsletter

Organization of Wildlife Planners *(1978)*
C/O Nebraska Game and Parks Commission
2200 N. 33rd St.
Lincoln, NE 68503
Website: owpweb.org
Members: 100 individuals
Staff: 3
Annual Budget: $10-25,000
Tax: 501(c)(4)

Personnel:
President: Dave Chadwick
   E-Mail: dave.chadwick@state.co.us
Treasurer: Loren Chase
   E-Mail: lchase@azgfd.gov
Editor: Juliette Wilson
   E-Mail: juliette_wilson@comcast.net

Historical Note:
*OWP's mission is to help improve the management
of fish and wildlife agencies and to help support the
professional lives of the people that participate in the
profession. Membership is comprised of fish and wildlife
professionals from all parts of the country. Membership:
$250 (Governmental/University); $50 (Associate
Organization), $25 (Associate Individual).*

Meetings/Conferences: Annual

Publications:
Management Tracks; semi-annually
Membership Directory; on-line

Organization of Women in International Trade *(1989)*
1707 L St. NW
Suite 570
Washington, DC 20036
E-Mail: info@owit.org
Website: owit.org
Members: 3000 individuals
Staff: 8
Annual Budget: $25-50,000

Personnel:
President: Angela Marshall Hofmann
   E-Mail: president@owit.org
Vice President, Partnerships: Susan Baka
   E-Mail: coVPpartnerships@owit.org
Vice President, Communications: Allison Campbell
   E-Mail: Communications@owit.org
Assistant Treasurer: Tamuna Gabilaia
   E-Mail: Treasurer@owit.org
Vice President, Conferences: Margaret Heine
   E-Mail: conference@owit.org
Vice President, Marketing: Kim Holizna
   E-Mail: marketing@owit.org
General Counsel: Camelia Mazard
   E-Mail: General-Counsel@owit.org
Vice President, Information Technology: Grace
   Montealegre
   E-Mail: it@owit.org

Historical Note:
*A member of the International Alliance for Women (TIAW),
OWIT is designed to promote women doing business in
international trade by providing networking and educational
opportunities. OWIT shares national affiliation with The
Association of Women in International Trade. Membership
consists of women and men around the world sharing
knowledge, mentoring youth and peers, connecting with
counterparts in other countries and exchanging business
contacts and referrals. Membership: $50/year (Virtual
Member).*

Meetings/Conferences: Annual
Conference Chair: Margaret Heine

Publications:
Membership Directory; on-line

Organizational Behavior Teaching Society *(1973)*
Marist College: School of Management
3399 North Rd.
Poughkeepsie, NY 12601-1387
Tel: (845) 569-1800 *Fax:* (845) 569-3885
Website: obts.org
Members: 450 individuals
Staff: 3
Annual Budget: $100-250,000
Tax: 501(c)(3)

Personnel:
President: Rae Andre
   E-Mail: president@obts.org
Contact, Communications: Gary Coombs

E-Mail: communications@obts.org

Historical Note:
OBTS is dedicated to enhance the quality and promote the importance of teaching and learning across the management disciplines. Members are academics, consultants and other teaching professionals with an interest in management education training. Membership: $55 (Regular); $35 (Student).

Meetings/Conferences: Annual

Publications:
Journal of Management Education

Membership List Available to Non-members

Organizational Systems Research Association
(1982)
Dept. of Information Systems, Morehead State Univ.
P. O. Box 2478
Morehead, KY 40351-1689
Tel: (606) 783-2718 *Fax:* (606) 783-5025
Website: osra.org
Members: 150 individuals
Staff: 6
Annual Budget: $10-25,000
Tax: 501(c)(3)

Personnel:
Executive Director and Editor: Donna R. Everett
    E-Mail: d.everett@moreheadstate.edu
President: L. Roger Yin
    E-Mail: yinl@mail.uww.edu
Vice President, Publications: Susan Feather-Gannon
    E-Mail: sfeathergannon@pace.edu
Treasurer: Melinda "Mindy" McCannon
    E-Mail: mmccannon@northwesterntech.edu
Vice President, Professional Studies: Daniel Norris
    E-Mail: dnorris@sc.edu
Vice President, Membership Services: Elizabeth A. Regan
    E-Mail: e.regan@moreheadstate.edu

Historical Note:
Organized as Office Systems Research Association in 1980, officially chartered in the State of Ohio in June 1981, absorbed (1995) Office Automation Society International and assumed its current name in 2000. OSRA's mission is to Promote research and the implementation and application of information technologies to enhance individual, group, and organizational performance. OSRA promotes research and application of information technology in the end-user environment to support work processes, improve employee performance, and enhance overall organizational effectiveness in direct support of goals and strategies. Members are individuals from business, government or education interested in a professional approach to the planning of office systems. Membership: $55 (Individual/Student Chapter); $35 (Retired/Student); $300 (Corporate).

Meetings/Conferences: Annual

Publications:
Information Technology, Learning, and Performance Journal; bi-annually; adv.
OSRA Newsletter; quarterly; adv.

Oriental Rug Importers Association of America
(1958)
100 Park Plaza Dr.
Secaucus, NJ 07094-3606
Tel: (201) 866-5054 *Fax:* (201) 866-6169
E-Mail: oria@oria.org
Website: oria.org
Members: 90 companies
Staff: 2
Annual Budget: $10-25,000

Personnel:
Executive Director: Lucille J. Laufer
Treasurer: Behrooz Hakimian

Historical Note:
ORIA's purpose is to foster ethical business practices and to promote the interests of Oriental Rug Trade in the United States and in countries that produce Oriental rugs. ORIA financially committed in improving the lives of children in rug weaving counties for over a decade. Members are importers/wholesalers of handmade carpets. Membership: $750 (Regular); $350 (Associate).

Meetings/Conferences: Annual
Number of non-conference events/year: 1

Publications:
Membership Directory; on-line
The Area Magazine; quarterly; adv.

Oriental Rug Retailers of America, Inc. *(1969)*

P.O. Box 71831
Richmond, VA 23255
Tel: (804) 270-3195 *Fax:* (804) 270-3196
E-Mail: orra@orrainc.com
Website: orrainc.com
Members: 245 individuals
Staff: 4
Annual Budget: $25-50,000
Tax: 501(c)(4)

Personnel:
Executive Director: Elizabeth Arnold
    E-Mail: orraarnold@verizon.net
Senior Advisor: Allan Furman

Historical Note:
ORRA is a non-profit membership organization supporting Oriental Rug retailers, wholesalers, importers and service-related companies. Mission is to promote ethical practices in the Oriental rug business. Membership: $275/year (Normal).

Continuing Education:
Certification Designation/s: CRA

Meetings/Conferences: Annual

Publications:
ORRA Newsletter; semi-annually

Original Equipment Suppliers Association *(1998)*
1301 W. Long Lake Rd.
Suite 225
Troy, MI 48098-5724
Tel: (248) 952-6401 *Fax:* (248) 952-6404
E-Mail: info@oesa.org
Website: oesa.org
Members: 400 companies
Staff: 15
Annual Budget: $2-5,000,000
Tax: 501(c)(6)

Personnel:
President and Chief Executive Officer: Neil De Koker
    E-Mail: ndekoker@oesa.org
Senior Vice President, Operations and International Affairs: Margaret Baxter
    E-Mail: mbaxter@oesa.org
Executive Director, Marketing and Communications: Greg Janicki
    E-Mail: gjanicki@oesa.org
Manager, Information Systems and Membership Services: Michelle Maki
    E-Mail: mmaki@oesa.org
Manager, Events and Membership Services: Pamela Minard
    E-Mail: pminard@oesa.org
Vice President, Sales and Membership Services: Glenn Stevens
    E-Mail: gstevens@oesa.org
Senior Vice President, Government Affairs: Ann Wilson
    E-Mail: awilson@mema.org

Historical Note:
An affiliate of Motor and Equipment Manufacturers Association. OESA's mission is to provide a strategic forum for the automotive industry's original equipment suppliers. Membership encompasses suppliers of components, modules, systems, materials and equipment used by the original equipment automotive industry. Membership: $2,000-22,000 (Regular); $4,000 (Affiliate/International); $1,200 (Divisional); $1,500 (Extra MSA).

Meetings/Conferences: Annual
Conference Chair: Pamela Minard
Number of non-conference events/year: 6

Publications:
APRC Tidbits; on-line
OESA Membership Directory; annually; adv.
OESA News; monthly; adv.
OESA Weekly; weekly; adv.

Membership List Available to Non-members

Ornamental Concrete Producers Association
(1991)
759 Phelps Johnson Rd.
Leitchfield, KY 42754
Tel: (270) 879-6319 *Fax:* (270) 879-0399
E-Mail: ocpa@windstream.net
Website: ocpainfo.com
Members: 500 companies
Staff: 2
Annual Budget: $50-100,000

Personnel:

Executive Director: Dona Dunkelberger
Editor: Scott Dunkelberger
    E-Mail: sdunk@windstream.net

Historical Note:
Primarily concerned with education in ornamental concrete production. OCPA aims at providing an educational environment for its members and sharing information, product knowledge, methods and techniques. Membership: $50/year (Producers/Apprentice/Allied).

Meetings/Conferences: Annual
Conference Chair: Dona Dunkelberger

Publications:
Membership Directory; annually
Ornamental Observer; bi-monthly; adv.

Orthodox Theological Society in America *(1966)*
50 Goddard Ave.
Brookline, MA 02445
E-Mail: dkatos@hchc.edu
Website: otsamerica.org
Members: 150 individuals
Staff: 3
Annual Budget: Under $10,000

Personnel:
President: Fr. Radu Bordeianu PhD
Secretary: Fr. Gabriel C R.
Treasurer: Gayle E. Wo

Historical Note:
OTSA is an academic society of Orthodox Christian scholars that meets to advocate Orthodox theology. Members are Orthodox Christian theologians. The members of OTSA belong to jurisdictions of SCOBA. A candidate for membership typically will have at least a Master's degree in theology (or its equivalent) or a Master's degree in Arts, as well as significant additional graduate studies in theology or related disciplines. Membership: $25/year.

Meetings/Conferences: Annual

Publications:
Member Directory; on-line

Orthopaedic Research Society *(1954)*
6300 N. River Rd.
Suite 602
Rosemont, IL 60018-4237
Tel: (847) 823-5770 *Fax:* (847) 823-5772
E-Mail: ors@ors.org
Website: ors.org
Members: 2200 individuals
Staff: 7
Annual Budget: $2-5,000,000
Tax: 501(c)(3)

Personnel:
Executive Director: Brenda Frederick
    E-Mail: Frederick@ors.org
Coordinator, Meetings: Mary Jo Harrold
    E-Mail: Harrold@ors.org
Manager, Development and Communications: Annie Carpenter Hayashi
    E-Mail: Hayashi@ors.org
Manager, Education: Mary Jo Heflin
    E-Mail: heflin@ors.org
Coordinator, Membership Services: Matt Zuleg
    E-Mail: Zuleg@ors.org

Historical Note:
ORS's mission is to advance the global orthopaedic research agenda through excellence in research, education, collaboration, communication and advocacy. Membership: $220 (Active/Affiliate); $50 (Associate/Student); $0 (Emeritus).

Continuing Education:
Certification Designation/s: CME

Meetings/Conferences: Annual
Conference Chair: Mary Jo Harrold
2013 - San Antonio, TX (The Henry B. Gonzalez Convention Center)/Jan. 26 - 30
2014 - New Orleans, LA (Hyatt Regency)/March 15 - 18
2015 - Las Vegas, NV (MGM Grand Hotel and Casino)/ March 24 - 28

Publications:
Journal of Orthopaedic Research; on-line
Membership Directory; on-line
ORS Newsletter; on-line

Orthopaedic Section - American Physical Therapy Association *(1974)*
2920 E. Ave., South

Suite 200
La Crosse, WI 54601-7202
Tel: (608) 788-3982 *Fax:* (608) 788-3965
TollFree: (800) 444-3982
Website: orthopt.org
Members: 15000 individuals
Staff: 249
Annual Budget: $25-50,000,000

Personnel:
Executive Director: Terri A. DeFlorian
    E-Mail: tdeflorian@orthopt.org
Managing Editor: Sharon Klinski
    E-Mail: sklinski@orthopt.org

Historical Note:
Orthopaedic Section - American Physical Therapy Association's mission is to serve as an advocate and resource for the practice of Orthopaedic Physical Therapy by fostering quality patient and client care and encouraging professional growth. Members are orthopaedic physical therapists. Membership: $15 (Student Physical Therapist/ Student Physical Therapist Assistant); $30 (Physical Therapist Assistant/Retired Physical Therapist/Retired Physical Therapist Assistant); $50 (Physical Therapist/ Physical Therapist - Post-Professional Student).

Meetings/Conferences: Annual
2013 - Orlando, FL (Marriott World Center)/May 2 - 4
2013 - Dubai, United Arab Emirates (The Intercontinental Hotel)/Oct. 27 - 31

Publications:
JOSPT; monthly; adv.
Membership Directory; on-line

Orthopaedic Trauma Association

6300 N. River Rd.
Suite 727
Rosemont, IL 60018-4226
Tel: (847) 698-1631 *Fax:* (847) 823-0536
E-Mail: ota@aaos.org
Website: ota.org
Members: 1067 individuals
Staff: 5
Annual Budget: $2-5,000,000
Tax: 501(c)(3)

Personnel:
Executive Director: Kathleen A. Caswell
    E-Mail: caswell@aaos.org
Coordinator, Abstracts, Marketing and Social Media, Annual Meeting Program and Pre-Meeting Courses,:
    Paul M. Hiller
    E-Mail: hiller@aaos.org
Coordinator, Web, Membership, Annual Meeting Registrar:
    Darlene Meyer
    E-Mail: meyer@aaos.org
Manager, Exhibits, Annual Meeting Programs, Abstracts, and Courses: Sharon Moore
    E-Mail: smoore@aaos.org
Manager, Education and Research: Diane Vetrovec
    E-Mail: vetrovec@aaos.org

Historical Note:
OTA's mission is to promote care for the injured patient, through provision of scientific forums and support of musculoskeletal research and education of orthopaedic surgeons and the public. Membership: $50-600/year.

Continuing Education:
Enrollment: 1800
Certification Designation/s: AMA PRA

Meetings/Conferences: Annual
Conference Chair: Sharon Moore
2013 - Phoenix, AZ (JW Marriott Phoenix Desert Ridge Resort and Spa)/Oct. 10 - 12/1100 attendees
2014 - Tampa, FL/Oct. 15 - 18
2015 - San Diego, CA/Oct. 7 - 10
2016 - Ft. Washington, MD/Oct. 5 - 8
2018 - Orlando, FL/Oct. 3 - 6

Publications:
Journal of Orthopaedic Trauma; adv.
OTA Newsletter; quarterly

Orthopedic Surgical Manufacturers Association
(1954)
P.O. Box 38805
Germantown, TN 38183-0805
Tel: (901) 758-0806 *Fax:* (201) 760-8350
E-Mail: secretary@osma.net
Website: osma.net
Members: 21 companies
Staff: 3

Annual Budget: $100-250,000

Personnel:
President: Sharon Starowicz
Treasurer: Ed Chin

Historical Note:
OSMA's mission is to facilitate the timely availability of quality orthopedic technologies by advocating clear, consistent and efficient implementation of government regulations and industry standards. Member companies are manufacturers and distributors of orthopedic devices, instrumentation and biological materials used to treat orthopedic conditions. Membership: $1,000-9,500 (Corporate, varies on gross sales); $750 (Associate).

Meetings/Conferences:
Number of non-conference events/year: 1

Publications:
Membership Directory; on-line
Orthopedics This Week; on-line

Osborne Association *(1931)*
175 Remsen St.
Suite 800
Brooklyn, NY 11201
Tel: (718) 637-6560 *Fax:* (718) 237-0686
E-Mail: info@osborneny.org
Website: osborneny.org
Members: 5500 Individuals
Staff: 271
Annual Budget: $10-25,000,000

Personnel:
Executive Director: Elizabeth Gaynes
    E-Mail: egaynes@osborneny.org
Associate Executive Director and Chief Financial Officer:
    Carolina Cordero Dyer
Contact, Communications: Melissa Grigg
    E-Mail: mgrigg@osborneny.org

Historical Note:
Formed by merger of the National Society of Penal Information and the Welfare League Association of New York. The Osborne Association offers opportunities for individuals who have been in conflict with the law to transform their lives through innovative, effective, and replicable programs that serve the community by reducing crime and its human and economic costs.

Publications:
Daily News; daily
Membership Directory; on-line

Membership List Available to Non-members

Osteoarthritis Research Society International
(1990)
15000 Commerce Pkwy.
Suite C
Mount Laurel, NJ 08054
Tel: (856) 439-1385 *Fax:* (856) 439-0525
E-Mail: oarsi@ahint.com
Website: oarsi.org
Members: 630 individuals
Staff: 4
Annual Budget: $1-2,000,000

Personnel:
Executive Director: Diann Stern MS
    E-Mail: dstern@ahint.com
Manager, Meetings: Anthony Celenza CMP
    E-Mail: acelenza@ahint.com
Editor-in-Chief: Stefan Lohmander MD, PhD
    E-Mail: stefan.lohmander@med.lu.se
Administrative Assistant: Priscilla Rodriguez
    E-Mail: prodriguez@ahint.com

Historical Note:
OARSI's mission is to promote and encourage fundamental and applied research, and to disseminate the results of that research in order to permit better knowledge of osteoarthritis and of its treatment. Members are physicians, researchers, and other health industry personnel. Membership: $195 (Regular Member); $125 (Associate Member); $7,000 (Industry Partner); $50 (Student Membership); $125 (Allied Health Professional).

Meetings/Conferences: Annual
Conference Chair: Anthony Celenza CMP
2013 - Philadelphia, PA (Philadelphia Marriott Downtown)/April 25
Number of non-conference events/year: 1

Publications:
Osteoarthritis and Cartilage Journal

Osteopathic Cranial Academy *(1947)*
3535 E. 96th St.

Suite 101
Indianapolis, IN 46240
Tel: (317) 594-0411 *Fax:* (317) 594-9299
E-Mail: info@cranialacademy.org
Website: cranialacademy.org
Members: 1200 individuals
Staff: 2
Annual Budget: $250-500,000

Personnel:
Executive Director: Sidney N. Dunn
Coordinator, Administration: Jennifer Southworth

Historical Note:
Formerly (1960) Osteopathic Cranial Association. CA's mission is to teach, advocate, and advance Osteopathy. Membership: $195 (Regular); $170 (Associate/Affiliate); $55 (Intern/Resident); $35 (Student); $2,925 (LifeTime).

Publications:
Membership Information Directory; on-line
The Cranial Letter; quarterly

Outdoor Advertising Association of America
(1891)
1850 M St. NW
Suite 1040
Washington, DC 20036-5803
Tel: (202) 833-5566 *Fax:* (202) 833-1522
E-Mail: info@oaaa.org
Website: oaaa.org
Members: 800 companies
Staff: 14
Annual Budget: $2-5,000,000

Personnel:
President and Chief Executive Officer: Nancy J. Fletcher
    E-Mail: nfletcher@oaaa.org
Marketing Research Manager and Website Administrator:
    Monisha Blair
    E-Mail: mblair@oaaa.org
Chief Marketing Officer: Stephen Freitas
    E-Mail: sfreitas@oaaa.org
Director, Communications: Nicole Hayes
    E-Mail: nhayes@oaaa.org
Executive Vice President: Ken Klein
    E-Mail: kklein@oaaa.org
Vice President, State, Local and Regulatory Affairs: Myron Laible
    E-Mail: mlaible@oaaa.org
Vice President, Membership Services and Administration:
    Marci Werlinich
    E-Mail: mwerlinich@oaaa.org

Historical Note:
The OAAA is the trade association representing the outdoor advertising industry. Mission is to provide leadership, services, and standards to promote, protect and advance the outdoor advertising industry. Membership: $2,500 (Attorney/Financial/Supplier); $500 (Advertisers Council/ Affiliate); $1,800 (International).

Publications:
Electronic Newsletter; weekly
Membership Directory; on-line
Outdoor Outlook; weekly

Outdoor Amusement Business Association *(1964)*
1035 S. Semoran Blvd.
Suite 1045A
Winter Park, FL 32792
Tel: (407) 681-9444 *Fax:* (407) 681-9445
TollFree: (800) 517-6222
E-Mail: oaba@oaba.org
Website: oaba.org
Members: 4000 companies
Staff: 5
Annual Budget: $1-2,000,000

Personnel:
President: Robert Johnson
    E-Mail: bobj@oaba.org
Senior Vice President: Al DeRusha

Historical Note:
OABA's mission is to encourage the growth and preservation of the outdoor amusement industry through leadership, legislation, education and membership services. Represents circuses, carnivals and concessionaires in the mobile amusement industry. Membership consists of road shows, food and beverage and games suppliers, carnivals and equipment suppliers. Membership: $40-500 (Circus); $40-2000 (Carnival).

Meetings/Conferences: Annual
2013 - Tampa, FL (Embassy Suites Hotel)/Feb. 7 - 8

Publications:
Midway Marquee - Membership Directory; annually; adv.
ShowTime Magazine; monthly; adv.
Xtra Top 3 News Stories; weekly; adv.

Outdoor Industry Association (1989)
4909 Pearl E. Cir.
Suite 200
Boulder, CO 80301
Tel: (303) 444-3353 *Fax:* (303) 444-3284
E-Mail: info@outdoorindustry.org
Website: outdoorindustry.org
Members: 4000 members
Staff: 11
Annual Budget: $2-5,000,000
Tax: 501(c)(6)

Personnel:
President and Chief Executive Officer: Frank Hugelmeyer
    E-Mail: fhugelmeyer@outdoorindustry.org
Vice President, Government Affairs: Kirk A. Bailey
    E-Mail: kbailey@outdoorindustry.org
Manager, Education Services: Loraine Gruber
    E-Mail: lgruber@outdoorindustry.org
Controller: Cindy Haddox
    E-Mail: chaddox@outdoorindustry.org
Executive Vice President and Chief Operating Officer: Lori Herrera
    E-Mail: lherrera@outdoorindustry.org
Director, Website and Information Systems: Bryan Mahler
    E-Mail: bmahler@outdoorindustry.org
Director, Membership Services: Ingrid Malmberg
    E-Mail: imalmberg@outdoorindustry.org
Manager, Marketing: Donna Martino
    E-Mail: dmartino@outdoorindustry.org
Vice President, Communications: I Ling Thompson
    E-Mail: ithompson@outdoorindustry.org

Historical Note:
Comprised of companies in the active outdoor recreation business. OIA works to raise the standards of the industry, increase participation in outdoor recreation to strengthen business markets, provide support services to improve member profitability, represent member interests in the legislative/regulatory process, promote professional training and education, support innovation, and offer cost-saving member benefits. Membership: $350-10,000 (Manufacturer/Supplier); $250-10,000 (Speciality Retailer/ Sales Representative); $500 (Associate).

Meetings/Conferences:
Number of non-conference events/year: 4

Publications:
CEO Brief; monthly; adv.
Membership Directory; on-line
WebNews; weekly; adv.

Outdoor Power Equipment Aftermarket Association (1986)
341 S. Patrick St.
Alexandria, VA 22314
Tel: (703) 549-7608 *Fax:* (703) 549-7609
E-Mail: opeaa@opeaa.org
Website: opeaa.org
Members: 75 companies
Staff: 4
Annual Budget: $100-250,000
Tax: 501(c)(6)

Personnel:
President and Chief Executive Officer: Kris Kiser
    E-Mail: kkiser@opei.org
Vice President, Industry Affairs: Gerry Coons
    E-Mail: gcoons@opei.org
Senior Vice President, Finance and Administration: Jean Haws
Manager, Member Services: Kristen Reamy
    E-Mail: kreamy@opei.org

Historical Note:
OPEAA's mission is to promote the quality of replacement parts as an equivalent and economical means for the maintenance and repair of outdoor power equipment. Membership is composed of small to medium-sized businessmen dedicated to promoting the use of aftermarket (spare) parts in outdoor power equipment (lawnmowers, chain saws, etc.). Membership: $540-5,525 (Corporate); $770 (Regional Distributor); $710 (International/Affiliate).

Meetings/Conferences: Annual
Conference Chair: Kristen Reamy
2013 - Palm Beach Gardens, FL (PGA National Resort and Spa)/Feb. 16 - 19

Publications:
Membership Directory; annually
The Cutting Edge; quarterly

Outdoor Power Equipment and Engine Service Association (1980)
37 Pratt St.
Essex, CT 06426-1159
Tel: (860) 767-1770 *Fax:* (860) 767-7932
E-Mail: info@opeesa.com
Website: opeesa.com
Members: 200 companies
Staff: 3
Annual Budget: $250-500,000

Personnel:
Executive Director: Nancy Cueroni
    E-Mail: executivedirector@opeesa.com
Webmaster: Leslie Bonk
    E-Mail: Leslie.l.Bonk@bmpr.com

Historical Note:
Formerly (2002) the Outdoor Power Equipment Distributors Association, absorbed the Engine Service Association in 2002. OPEESA's mission is to assist distributors in achieving better channel performance. Membership: $550-1,560 (Distributor); $1245-1,560 (Manufacturer/ Affiliate).

Continuing Education:
Certification Designation/s: EETC

Meetings/Conferences: Annual
2013 - St. Pete Beach, FL (Loews Don CeSar Hotel)/ March 3 - 6

Publications:
Membership Directory; on-line
Monthly In-the-Know; monthly
OPE News
OPEESA eNewsletter; monthly
Weekly eNewsletter; weekly

Outdoor Power Equipment Institute (1952)
341 S. Patrick St.
Alexandria, VA 22314
Tel: (703) 549-7600 *Fax:* (703) 549-7604
E-Mail: kreamy@opei.org
Website: opei.org
Members: 73 companies
Staff: 8
Annual Budget: $2-5,000,000
Tax: 501(c)(6)

Personnel:
President and Chief Executive Officer: Kris Kiser
    E-Mail: kkiser@opei.org
Senior Vice President, Finance and Administration: Jean Hawes
Director, Meetings: Marla Popkin
    E-Mail: mpopkin@opei.org
Manager, Member Services: Kristen Reamy
    E-Mail: kreamy@opei.org

Historical Note:
Established as the Lawn Mower Institute, OPEI assumed its present name in 1960. OPEI assists, advances, and fosters the economic interest of its membership by providing accurate and timely worldwide information, sponsoring the industry's international tradeshow, promoting the effective and safe use of outdoor power equipment, and representing the members' interests in legislative and regulatory affairs. Members are manufacturers of all types of mechanized lawn and garden equipment and industry suppliers of major components. Membership: $250 (Regular); $5,000-7,000 (Associate, based on ope-related sales); $3,000 (Affiliate).

Meetings/Conferences: Annual
Conference Chair: Marla Popkin
2013 - Williamsburg, VA (Williamsburg Lodge)/June 19 - 21

Publications:
Outdoor Power Report - Quarterly Update; quarterly

Outdoor Writers Association of America (1927)
615 Oak St.
Suite 201
Missoula, MT 59801
Tel: (406) 728-7434 *Fax:* (406) 728-7445
TollFree: (877) 730-4863
E-Mail: info@owaa.org
Website: owaa.org
Members:
300 corporations, nonprofits and government agencies
1400 individuals

Staff: 4
Annual Budget: $250-500,000
Tax: 501(c)(3)

Personnel:
Executive Director: Robin Giner
    E-Mail: rginer@owaa.org
Marketing Intern: Drew Easton
    E-Mail: deaston@owaa.org
Contact, Membership and Conference Services: Jessica Pollett
Director, Publications and Communications: Ashley Schroeder
    E-Mail: aschroeder@owaa.org

Historical Note:
OWAA's mission is to improve the professional skills of its members, encourage public enjoyment and conservation of natural resources, and be mentors for the next generation of professional outdoor communicators. Membership: $150 (Active/Associate); $10 (Student); $375 (Supporter).

Meetings/Conferences: Annual
Conference Chair: Robin Giner
2013 - Lake Placid, NY (Lake Lure Inn and Spa)/Sept. 14 - 16

Number of non-conference events/year: 1

Publications:
Membership Directory; on-line
Outdoor Market Listings; monthly
Outdoors Unlimited; monthly; adv.
OWAA Newsletter; monthly

Membership List Available to Non-members

Outfitters Association of America (1999)
P.O. Box 3255
Ray City, GA 31645
Tel: (229) 686-7621 *Fax:* (229) 686-5273
E-Mail: info@oaoa.net
Website: oaoa.net
Staff: 1

Personnel:
Executive Director: Wayne Pearson

Historical Note:
Provides services, benefits, and accrediation to hunting outfitters, fishing guides and recreational businesses of all types. Membership: Associate member $ 250 yearly; Gold member $500 yealy; Premium membership $1,000 yealy.

Outpatient Ophthalmic Surgery Society (1981)
6564 Umber Cir.
Arvada, CO 80007
Tel: (866) 892-1101 *Fax:* (303) 940-7780
TollFree: (866) 892-1001
E-Mail: info@ooss.org
Website: ooss.org
Members: 1000 individuals
Staff: 3
Annual Budget: $500-1,000,000

Personnel:
Executive Director: Claudia A. McDougal
    E-Mail: claudiamcdougal@ooss.org

Historical Note:
OOSS represents the surgeon owners and surgeon utilizers of ophthalmic ambulatory surgery centers. Members are ophthalmic surgeon/owners of ambulatory surgery centers. Membership: $1,500-2,500/year (dues based on procedures performed in the facility); $500 (International Facility).

Meetings/Conferences:
Number of non-conference events/year: 1

Publications:
OOSS Washington Update Online
Outlook Magazine Online

Overseas Press Club of America (1939)
40 W. 45th St.
New York, NY 10036
Tel: (212) 626-9220 *Fax:* (212) 626-9210
E-Mail: info@opcofamerica.org
Website: opcofamerica.org
Members: 600 individuals
Staff: 3
Annual Budget: $250-500,000

Personnel:
Executive Director: Sonya K. Fry
Treasurer: Dorinda Elliott
Editor: Aimee Vitrak

Historical Note:

OPC's mission is to help and educate upcoming journalists, contribute to the freedom and independence of journalists and the press throughout the world, and work toward better communication and understanding among people. Members are professional journalists. Membership: $25-500/year.

Publications:
Membership Directory; on-line
The Bulletin; monthly

Owner-Operator Independent Drivers Association, Inc. (1973)
One NW Ooida Dr.
P.O. BOX 1000
Grain Vally, MO 64029
Tel: (816) 229-5791
TollFree: (800) 444-5791
E-Mail: ooida@ooida.com
Website: ooida.com/
Members: 150000 individuals
Staff: 18
Annual Budget: $2-5,000,000
Tax: 501(c)(6)

Personnel:
President: James J. Johnston
  E-Mail: jim_johnston@ooida.com
Executive Vice President: Todd Spencer
  E-Mail: Todd_Spencer@ooida.com
Accounting: Sherri Aronson
  E-Mail: Sherri_Aronson@ooida.com
Executive Assistant: Angel Burnell
  E-Mail: angel_burnell@ooida.com
Contact, Membership Services: Sylvia Dodson
  E-Mail: Sylvia_Dodson@ooida.com
Contact, Information Technology: Debbie Hines
  E-Mail: Debbie_Hines@ooida.com
Director, Human Resources: Suzanne Johnson
  E-Mail: Suzanne_Johnson@ooida.com
Contact, Marketing: Mike Schermoly
  E-Mail: mike_schermoly@ooida.com
Contact, Land Line Magazine: Sandi Soendker
  E-Mail: Sandi_Soendker@landlinemag.com
Contact, Public Affairs: Norita Taylor
  E-Mail: norita_taylor@ooida.com

Historical Note:
OOIDA strives to serve owner-operators, small fleets and professional drivers, to work for a business climate where truckers are treated equally and fairly, to boost highway safety and responsibility among all highway users, and to enhance a better business environment for all truck operators. Members are professional truckers from company drivers and owner-operators to retired truckers and spouse members. Membership: $45/year.

Publications:
Land Line Magazine
Land Line Magazine; adv.
Membership Directory; on-line

Pacific Coast Marine Firemen, Oilers, Watertenders and Wipers Association (1883)
Marine Firemen's Union
240 Second St.
San Francisco, CA 94105
Tel: (415) 362-4592 *Fax:* (415) 348-8864
E-Mail: mfow@pacbell.net
Website: mfoww.org
Staff: 1

Personnel:
President, Secretary and Treasurer: Anthony Poplawski
  E-Mail: mfow_president@yahoo.com

Historical Note:
Founded in 1883, Pacific Coast Marine Firemen, Oilers, Watertenders and Wipers Association is affiliated with the Seafarers International Union of North America, AFL-CIO.

Publications:
Marine Firemann; monthly

Pacific Maritime Association
555 Market St.
San Francisco, CA 94105-2800
Tel: (415) 576-3200 *Fax:* (415) 348-8392
TollFree: (888) 762-1234
Website: pmanet.org
Staff: 205
Annual Budget: $50-100,000,000

Personnel:
President and Chief Executive Officer: James C. McKenna
Consultant, Public Relations: Cheryl Heinonen

E-Mail: cheryl.heinonen@bm.com

Historical Note:
The principal business of the Pacific Maritime Association is to negotiate and administer maritime labor agreements with the International Longshore and Warehouse Union. Member companies are cargo carriers, terminal operators and stevedores that operate at West Coast ports.

Publications:
PMA Newsletter

Pacific Telecommunications Council (1978)
914 Coolidge St.
Honolulu, HI 96826-3085
Tel: (808) 941-3789 *Fax:* (808) 944-4874
E-Mail: info@ptc.org
Website: ptc.org
Members: 3000 members
Staff: 29
Annual Budget: $2-5,000,000

Personnel:
Chief Executive Officer: Sharon Nakama
Clerk, Accounting Services: Janice Kuniyuki
Communications Officer: Anamarcia Lacayo
Membership Coordinator: Emily Lee
Administrator, Information Technology Systems and Network: Alisa Lum
Executive Assistant: Colleen Shishido
  E-Mail: colleen@ptc.org
Coordinator, Lead Conference and Human Resources: Lori Takeuchi
  E-Mail: lori@ptc.org
Conference Coordinator: Jamie Wan-Lopaz

Historical Note:
PTC promotes the development and use of telecommunications and information and communication technologies to enhance the lives of people living in the Pacific Hemisphere. Membership: $250-4500 (For-Profit based on number of Employees); $250-750 (Non-Profit based on number of employees); $150 (Individual); $250 (Affiliate); $25 (Student developing countries); $65 (All other Students).

Meetings/Conferences: Annual
Conference Chair: Jamie Wan-Lopaz
2013 - Honolulu, HI/Jan. 20 - 23/1500 attendees

Publications:
Member Directory; on-line

Packaging Machinery Manufacturers Institute (1933)
11911 Freedom Dr.
Suite 600
Reston, VA 20190
Tel: (703) 243-8555 *Fax:* (703) 243-8556
TollFree: (888) 275-7664
Website: pmmi.org
Members: 600 companies
Staff: 39
Annual Budget: $25-50,000,000

Personnel:
President and Chief Executive Officer: Charles (Chuck) D. Yuska
  E-Mail: cyuska@pmmi.org
Director, Member Communications: Kate Achelpohl
  E-Mail: kachelpohl@pmmi.org
Senior Director, Communications and Public Relations: Julie Ackerman
  E-Mail: jackerman@pmmi.org
Vice President, Administration: Katie Bergmann
  E-Mail: kbergmann@pmmi.org
Vice President, Industry Services: Tom Egan
  E-Mail: tegan@pmmi.org
Vice President, Meetings and Events: Patti Fee
  E-Mail: pfee@pmmi.org
Senior Director, Education and Workforce Development: Maria Ferrante
  E-Mail: maria@pmmi.org
Manager, Workforce Solutions: Stephan Girard
  E-Mail: sgirard@pmmi.org
Director, Technical Services: Fred Hayes
  E-Mail: fhayes@pmmi.org
Vice President, Market Development: Jorge Izquierdo
  E-Mail: jorge@pmmi.org
Education Coordinator: Danny Martinez
  E-Mail: dmartinez@pmmi.org
Manager, Communications: Matt Sedlak
  E-Mail: msedlak@pmmi.org
Vice President, Finance: Craig Silverio

E-Mail: csilverio@pmmi.org
Director, International Tradeshows: Laura Thompson
  E-Mail: laura@pmmi.org

Historical Note:
PMMI's mission is to improve and promote members abilities to succeed in a global marketplace. Members are manufacturers of packaging and packaging- related converting equipment. Membership: $1,500 (General); $2,000 (Supplier/Materials/Processing).

Continuing Education:
Certification Designation/s: PMMICT

Meetings/Conferences:
Conference Chair: Patti Fee
2013 - Guadalajara, JL (Expo Guadalajara)/Feb. 27 - March 1/4000 attendees/51-100 exhibitors
2013 - Las Vegas, NV (Las Vegas Convention Center)/ Sept. 23 - 25
Number of non-conference events/year: 5

Publications:
Membership Directory; on-line
Packaging Machinery Technology Magazine; bi-monthly; adv.
PMMI Reports Newsletter; monthly

The Paddlesports Industry Association (1977)
2700 Flat Creek Valley Rd.
Lake Toxaway, NC 28747
Tel: (828) 577-2484 *Fax:* (828) 966-4716
E-Mail: cometocanoe@citcom.net
Website: propaddle.com
Members: 1300 companies
Staff: 4
Annual Budget: $250-500,000
Tax: 501(c)(6)

Personnel:
Interim Chief Executive Officer: Debi Whitmire
  E-Mail: dwhitmire@propaddle.com

Historical Note:
Established as National Association of Canoe Liveries and Outfitters (NACLO); assumed its current name in 1995. Incorporated in the state of Michigan. Formerly known as the Professional Paddlesports Association (PPA) it has assumed the current name in 2006. Promotes canoeing and related sports, works to preserve waterways for human-powered recreation, and protects the interests of professional outfitters and outfitting firms. Membership: $240-325 (Renters, Retailers, Instruction Schools, Sales Reps); $325-3500 (Paddlesports Manufacturers); $240 (Independent Paddlesports Sales Representatives); $500 (Other Vendors); $750 (Insurance); $125 (Supporters).

Continuing Education:
Certification Designation/s: CPP

Meetings/Conferences: Annual

Publications:
Membership Directory; on-line

Paint and Decorating Retailers Association (1947)
1401 Triad Center Dr.
St. Peters, MO 63376
Tel: (636) 326-2636 *Fax:* (636) 229-4750
E-Mail: info@pdra.org
Website: pdra.org
Members: 6500 companies and 3500 individuals
Staff: 11
Annual Budget: $1-2,000,000

Personnel:
Executive Vice President and Publisher: Dan Simon
  E-Mail: dan@pdra.org
Managing Editor: Michael Austin
  E-Mail: mike@pdra.org
Director, Marketing and Senior Art: Larry DeWitt
  E-Mail: larry@pdra.org
Director, Finance and Human Resources: Renee Nolte
  E-Mail: renee@pdra.org

Historical Note:
Formerly Retail Paint & Wallpaper Distributors of America, (1972) Paint and Wallpaper Association of America, and (1996) National Decorating Products Association. PDRA's mission is to educate and support the independent paint and decorating retailers. Members are independent dealers and interior designers selling decorating products. Membership: $149 (Company).

Meetings/Conferences:
2013 - Las Vegas, NV (Las Vegas Convention Center)/ May 7 - 9/over 100 exhibitors

Publications:

Paint & Decorating Retailer magazine; monthly; adv.

Painting and Decorating Contractors of America
(1937)
2316 Millpark Dr.
St. Louis, MO 63043
Tel: (314) 514-7322 *Fax:* (314) 514-9417
TollFree: (800) 332-7322
E-Mail: ihoren@pdca.org
Website: pdca.org
Members: 3000 firms and 10000 individuals
Staff: 8
Annual Budget: $1-2,000,000
Tax: 501(c)(6)

Personnel:
Chief Executive Officer: Richard Greene CAE, MBA
   E-Mail: rgreene@pdca.org
Coordinator, Membership Services: Marsha Bass
   E-Mail: mbass@pdca.org
Manager, Communications and Marketing: Jessi Goodhart
   E-Mail: jgoodhart@pdca.org
Manager, Education: Libby Loomis
   E-Mail: lloomis@pdca.org
Chief Financial Officer: Beth McDaniel
   E-Mail: bmcdaniel@pdca.org

Historical Note:
Formerly Master House Painters Association of the United States and Canada, assumed the name the Master House Painters and Decorators Association of the United States of America in 1890, in 1903 "and Canada" was restored to the name and in 1904 the title was amplified to International Association of Master House Painters and Decorators. Incorporated in 1928, assumed the name Master Painters and Decorators and in 1937 assumed the present name. PDCA's mission is to provide quality products, programs, services and opportunities essential to the success of its members. Members are professional painting and decorating contractors. Membership: $24-400/year.

Meetings/Conferences: Annual
Conference Chair: Marsha Bass
2013 - St. Louis, MO (Hyatt Regency)/March 3 - 6

Publications:
Colors Newsletter
DECO Magazine; quarterly
Membership Directory; on-line
The Briefer; bi-monthly

Pakistan American Business Association *(1986)*
9302 Old Keene Mill Rd.
Suite B
Burke, VA 22015-4278
Tel: (703) 440-1111 *Fax:* (703) 451-7777
E-Mail: info@pabausa.org
Website: pabausa.com
Staff: 3
Annual Budget: $50-100,000

Personnel:
Executive Director: Harry Wiggins
Director, Technology: Shakeel Tufail
Treasurer and Director: Steve Webster

Historical Note:
PABA's mission is to bring together business men and women of diverse occupations, providing opportunities for them to help themselves and other grow personally and professionally through leadership, education, networking support and national recognition.

Publications:
Membership Directory; on-line

Paleontological Research Institution *(1932)*
1259 Trumansburg Rd.
Ithaca, NY 14850
Tel: (607) 273-6623 *Fax:* (607) 273-6620
Website: museumoftheearth.org
Members: 1100 combinations
Staff: 32
Annual Budget: $2-5,000,000
Tax: 501(c)(3)

Personnel:
Director: Warren D. Allmon
   E-Mail: allmon@museumoftheearth.org
Director, Exhibits: Cathy Blackburn
   E-Mail: blackburn@museumoftheearth.org
Associate, Education: Carlyn Buckler
   E-Mail: csb36@cornell.edu
Director, Collections: Greg Dietl
   E-Mail: dietl@museumoftheearth.org

Associate Director, Administration: Michael Lucas
   E-Mail: lucas@museumoftheearth.org
Associate Director, Science and Director, Publications:
   Paula Mikkelsen
   E-Mail: mikkelsen@museumoftheearth.org
Manager, Marketing: Cassie Mundt
   E-Mail: mundt@museumoftheearth.org
Manager, Database and Membership Services: Abigail
   Scaduto
   E-Mail: scaduto@museumoftheearth.org
Manager, Exhibitions: Beth Stricker
   E-Mail: stricker@museumoftheearth.org

Historical Note:
PRI's mission is to serve society by increasing and disseminating knowledge about the history of life on Earth. Membership: $40 (Individual); $30 (Student/Senior/ Subscriber); $50 (International Subscriber); $65-75 (Household); $100 (Explorer Circle); $250 (Excavator Circle); $500 (Curator Circle); $1,000-10,000 (Society).

Meetings/Conferences:
Conference Chair: Cathy Blackburn

Publications:
American Paleontologist; quarterly
Bulletins of American Paleontology; semi-annually
Journal of Paleontology
Membership Directory; on-line
Palaeontographica Americana
PRI Newsletter; monthly

Paleontological Society *(1908)*
P.O. Box 9044
Boulder, CO 80301
Tel: (855) 357-1032 *Fax:* (303) 357-1070
E-Mail: paleosoc@geosociety.org
Website: paleosoc.org
Members: 1700 individuals
Staff: 3
Annual Budget: $500-1,000,000

Personnel:
President: Philip D. Gingerich
   E-Mail: gingeric@umich.edu
Secretary: Mark A. Wilson
   E-Mail: mwilson@wooster.edu
Coordinator, Education: Margaret (Peg) Yacobucci
   E-Mail: mmyacob@bgsu.edu

Historical Note:
PS is devoted to the advancement of the science of paleontology through the dissemination of research by publication and meetings. Membership: $55 (Regular); $30 (Student); $25 (Spouse); $50 (Retired); $0 (Emeritus).
Meetings/Conferences:
Number of non-conference events/year: 1

Publications:
Journal of Paleontology; bi-monthly; adv.
Palaeontologica Electronica; on-line
Paleobiology; quarterly; adv.
Priscum; quarterly

Palomino Horse Association *(1936)*
P.O. Box 125, Route One
10171 Nectar Ave.
Nelson, MO 65347
Tel: (660) 859-2064 *Fax:* (660) 859-2058
Website: palominohorseassoc.com
Members: 500 individuals
Staff: 2
Annual Budget: $10-25,000

Personnel:
Contact, Communications: Patricia Rebuck
   E-Mail: palominorebuck@yahoo.com

Historical Note:
The original registry for the Palomino horse. Members are owners and breeders of Palomino horses. Membership: $30 (Individual, US); $35 (Individual, foreign); $250 (Lifetime).

Publications:
PHA Newsletter; quarterly

Palomino Horse Breeders of America *(1941)*
15253 E. Skelly Dr.
Tulsa, OK 74116-2637
Tel: (918) 438-1234 *Fax:* (918) 438-1232
E-Mail: yellahrses@palominohba.com
Website: palominohba.com
Members: 12011 individuals
Staff: 8
Annual Budget: $500-1,000,000

Personnel:

President: Melonie Furnish
Contact, Membership and Accounting: Tina Beel
   E-Mail: membership@palominohba.com
General Manager: Terri Green
   E-Mail: tgreen@palominohba.com

Historical Note:
PHBA's mission is to record and preserve the pedigree of the palomino horse while maintaining the integrity of the breeds and to provide member services which enhance and encourage palomino ownership and participation. Membership: $40-400 (Lifetime, age dependent); $200 (Youth).

Meetings/Conferences:
2013 - Tulsa, OK (Hyatt Regency Tulsa)/March 13 - 16

Publications:
Palomino Horses Magazine
PHBA newsletter; monthly

Pan American Allergy Society *(1956)*
1317 Wooded Knoll
San Antonio, TX 78258
Tel: (210) 495-9853 *Fax:* (210) 495-9852
Website: paas.org
Members: 400 groups
Staff: 2
Annual Budget: $100-250,000

Personnel:
Executive Director: Ann Brey
   E-Mail: panamallergy@sbcglobal.net

Historical Note:
In 1956, the Gulf Coast Allergy Study Group was organized by a group of students of Dr. Herbert J. Rinkel of Kansas City, Missouri. In 1968, the name of the organization was changed to The Pan American Allergy Society. The PAAS's mission is to provide quality continuing medical education in quantitative skin testing and other scientifically validated methods for the diagnosis and treatment of allergy and sensitivity disorders.Membership $350 (Physicians); $175 (Affiliate)

Meetings/Conferences: Annual
2013 - Dallas, TX (Dallas Marriott City Center)/March
   21 - 24
2014 - Dallas, TX (Dallas Marriott City Center)/March
   20 - 23

Publications:
Membership Directory; on-line

Pan American Association of Ophthalmology
(1940)
1301 S. Bowen Rd.
Suite 450
Arlington, TX 76013
Tel: (817) 275-7553 *Fax:* (817) 275-3961
E-Mail: info@paao.org
Website: paao.org
Staff: 3
Annual Budget: $500-1,000,000

Personnel:
Executive Director: Teresa J. Bradshaw
   E-Mail: teresa.bradshaw@paao.org
Administrator and Contact, Membership Services: Terri L.
   Grassi
   E-Mail: terri.grassi@paao.org
Contact, Public Relations: Mapy Padilla
   E-Mail: mapy.padilla@paao.org

Historical Note:
PAAO's mission is the prevention of blindness through lifelong education and cultural exchange among ophthalmologists in the Western Hemisphere. Membership: $150 (Active); $100 (Corresponding); $50 (Member-in-Training); $75 (Affiliate).

Publications:
Membership Directory; on-line
PAAO Newsletter; monthly
Vision Pan-America; quarterly

Panelized Home Building Council *(1942)*
1201 15th St. NW
Washington, DC 20005
Tel: (202) 266-8200 *Fax:* (202) 266-8400
TollFree: (800) 368-5242
Website: nahb.org/page.aspx/category/
   sectionID = 814
Staff: 1

Personnel:
Chief Executive Officer: Gerald "Jerry" M. Howard
Historical Note:

PHBC advocates building with systems. Panelized home construction techniques utilize advanced technology and a controlled work environment to construct an energy-efficient, durable home in less time.

Publications:
Sales + Marketing Ideas magazine; bi-monthly; adv.
Systems-Built Advantage Newsletter; bi-monthly; adv.

Membership List Available to Non-members

Paper and Plastic Representatives Management Council (1995)
P.O. Box 150229
Arlington, TX 76015
Tel: (682) 518-6008 *Fax:* (682) 518-6476
E-Mail: assnhqtrs@aol.com
Website: pprmc.com
Members: 20 companies
Staff: 2
Annual Budget: $25-50,000

Personnel:
Executive Director: Pamela L. Bess

Historical Note:
PPRMC seeks to provide members a forum to improve sales, marketing skills, and other business practices. Member companies provide professional sales representation that is shown by their commitment towards business acumen, technical competence, ethical standards, and continuing education. Membership: dues are billed monthly and are minimal.

Publications:
Membership Directory; on-line

Membership List Available to Non-members

Paper Shipping Sack Manufacturers' Association, Inc. (1933)
5050 Blue Church Rd.
Coopersburg, PA 18036
Tel: (610) 282-6845 *Fax:* (610) 282-1577
E-Mail: admin@pssma.org
Website: pssma.com
Members: 50 companies
Staff: 3
Annual Budget: $250-500,000
Tax: 501(c)(6)

Personnel:
President: Richard E. Storat
  E-Mail: dick.storat@pssma.org
Contact, Administration and Meetings: Wendy Storat
Contact, Operations: Gregory Storat

Historical Note:
PSSMA seeks to provide its member companies with programs and services which further the industry's objectives. Members are producers of multiwall shipping sacks. Membership: $3,000 (Regular); $2,500 (Associate/International).

Meetings/Conferences: Annual
Conference Chair: Wendy Storat
Number of non-conference events/year: 1

Publications:
Member Roster; on-line
The Outlook For Paper Shipping Sacks; semi-annually

Paperboard Packaging Council (1964)
1350 Main St.
Suite 1508
Springfield, MA 01103-1670
Tel: (413) 686-9191 *Fax:* (413) 747-7777
E-Mail: info@ppcnet.org
Website: ppcnet.org
Members: 120 principal and associate members
Staff: 8
Annual Budget: $1-2,000,000
Tax: 501(c)(6)

Personnel:
President: Ben Markens
  E-Mail: ben@ppcnet.org
Director, Marketing and Communications: Kim Guarnaccia
  E-Mail: kim@ppcnet.org
Director, Industry Information and Research: Cindy Healy
  E-Mail: cindy@ppcnet.org
Vice President and Chief-of-Staff: Lou Kornet
  E-Mail: lou@ppcnet.org
Controller: Susan Martins
  E-Mail: susan@ppcnet.org
Manager, Marketing Communications and Director, Membership Services: Emily Rae

  E-Mail: emily@ppcnet.org

Historical Note:
Originally, known as the Paraffin Carton Association, and later the Protective.Package Association and then the Institute of Better Packaging.PPC seeks to grow, promote and protect the paperboard packaging industry, and provide tools for members to compete in the marketplace. It also provides various programs and services for package manufacturers, structural and graphic designers, financial experts, marketing professionals, human resource managers, top-level executives and others within the paperboard packaging industry. Membership fee varies, based on annual sales.

Meetings/Conferences: Annual
2013 - Nashville, TN/April 3 - 5
Number of non-conference events/year: 2

Publications:
Directory of Members; annually; adv.
Marketflash; monthly
PPC Weekly Update; weekly
Safety Boxscore; monthly
Trends; annually

Parachute Industry Association
3833 W. Oakton St.
Skokie, IL 60076
Tel: (847) 674-9742 *Fax:* (847) 674-9743
Website: pia.com
Staff: 3
Annual Budget: $250-500,000

Personnel:
President: Cliff Schmucker
  E-Mail: president@pia.com
Treasurer: Dori Bachman
  E-Mail: treasurer@pia.com
Secretary: Elizabeth Johnson
  E-Mail: secretary@pia.com

Historical Note:
PIA is actively pursuing many technical, safety, and promotional projects that benefit its members and the industry it serves. Membership: $500 (Sustaining); $300 (Full); $150 (Affiliate)

Continuing Education:
Enrollment: 1

Meetings/Conferences: Annual
2013 - Philadelphia, PA (DoubleTree by Hilton Hotel Philadelphia Center City)/Aug. 23 - 24

Publications:
Member Directory; on-line
PIA Newsletter; bi-monthly

Paramount Citrus Association (1950)
1901 S. Lexington St.
Delano, CA 93215
Tel: (661) 720-2400 *Fax:* (661) 720-2403
E-Mail: contact_us@paramountcitrus.com
Website: paramountcitrus.com
Staff: 2

Personnel:
General Manager, Operations: Redd Owens
Vice President, Sales and Marketing: Scott Owens
  E-Mail: sowens@paramountcitrus.com

Historical Note:
A citrus grower, packer, shipper and marketer. Aim is to satisfy customers with high quality, good value fresh citrus products year round.

Parapsychological Association (1957)
P.O. Box 24173
Columbus, OH 43224
Tel: (202) 318-2364 *Fax:* (202) 318-2364
E-Mail: business@parapsych.org
Website: parapsych.org
Members: 300 individuals
Staff: 1
Annual Budget: $50-100,000
Tax: 501(c)(3)

Personnel:
Executive Director: Annalisa Ventola
  E-Mail: annalisa@publicparapsychology.org

Historical Note:
PA is the international professional organization of scientists and scholars engaged in the study of psi (or psychic). Membership open to persons doing research or scholarly work of publishable quality in the field, also professionals and students in other academic disciplines with a serious interest in this field. Membership: $95 (Full/

Affiliate/Associate/Supporting/Professional); $40 (Student Affiliate); Free (Honorary Member).

Meetings/Conferences: Annual
2013 - Viterbo, Italy (Ora Domus La Quercia)/Aug. 8 - 11

Publications:
Journal of Parapsychology
The Mindfield Bulletin; on-line

Parcel Shippers Association (1953)
1420 King St.
Suite 620
Alexandria, VA 22314
Tel: (571) 257-7617 *Fax:* (571) 257-7613
E-Mail: psa@parcelshippers.org
Website: parcelshippers.org
Members: 200 companies
Staff: 2
Annual Budget: $250-500,000
Tax: 501(c)(6)

Personnel:
Executive Vice President: Pierce Myers

Historical Note:
Formerly (1977) the Parcel Post Association. PSA's mission is to foster competition in the parcel delivery market, creating value for its members by promoting quality service at the lowest possible costs. Members are firms that ship parcels for themselves or others and firms that supply merchandise, materials or services to shippers. Membership: $2,000-15,000 (Member, Based on annual parcel shipping expense); $3,000 (Associate).

Parenteral Drug Association (1946)
4350 E.W. Hwy.
Suite 150
Bethesda, MD 20814-6133
Tel: (301) 656-5900 *Fax:* (301) 986-0296
Website: pda.org
Members: 9,500 members
Staff: 34
Annual Budget: $10-25,000,000

Personnel:
President: Richard M. Johnson
  E-Mail: johnson@pda.org
Senior Vice President, Programs and Registration Services: Wanda Neal Ballard CMP
  E-Mail: neal@pda.org
Senior Manager, Information Systems: Feng Chen
  E-Mail: chen@pda.org
Senior Vice President Quality and Regulatory Affairs and PDA Training and Research Institute: Robert Dana
  E-Mail: dana@pda.org
Senior Vice President and Chief Financial Officer: Craig Elliott
  E-Mail: elliott@pda.org
Vice President, Marketing Services: Adrienne Fierro
  E-Mail: fierro@pda.org
Director, Membership Services and Chapters: Hassana Howe
  E-Mail: howe@pda.org
Senior Vice President, Scientific and Regulatory Affairs: Richard Levy PhD
  E-Mail: levy@pda.org
Director, Publishing: Walter L. Morris III
  E-Mail: morris@pda.org

Historical Note:
PDA's mission is to develop technical information and resources to advance science and regulation for the pharmaceutical and bio pharmaceutical industry through the expertise of global membership. Members are makers of parenteral (injectable) drugs and other pharmaceuticals, as well as suppliers, academia, regulatory and compendial bodies, and other interested parties. Membership: $249 (Standard/Individual Membership); $30 (Student); $100 (Academic/Government/Health Authority/Developing Economy Membership); $25 (Retired).

Meetings/Conferences: Annual
Conference Chair: Wanda Neal Ballard CMP
2013 - Orlando, FL (Peabody Orlando)/April 15 - 17
Number of non-conference events/year: 4

Publications:
Membership Directory; on-line; adv.
PDA Journal of Pharmaceutical Science and Technology; adv.
PDA Letter; adv.

Parenting Media Association (1988)
1970 E. Grand Ave.

Suite 330
El Segundo, CA 90245
Tel: (310) 364-0193 *Fax:* (310) 364-0196
E-Mail: info@parentmedia.org
Website: parentingpublications.org
Members: 120 publications
Staff: 4
Annual Budget: $100-250,000

Personnel:
Executive Director: James C. Dowden
    E-Mail: admin@parentmedia.org
Chair, Associate Membership: Sharon Bay
Staff Associate: Tracey Dowden
    E-Mail: tracey@parentmedia.org
Editor: Barton Ortberg
    E-Mail: bart.ortberg@dowdenmanagement.com

Historical Note:
Formerly known as the Parenting Publications of America, PMA's mission is to promote the growth, success and development of the regional parenting publication companies which constitute its membership. Membership: $835-8,620 (Total Circulation); $1,600 (Associate).

Meetings/Conferences: Annual
Conference Chair: Tracey Dowden

Publications:
Membership Directory
PPA Email Newsletter; on-line

Membership List Available to Non-members

Parliamentary Associates *(1990)*
P.O. Box 1102
Independence, MO 64051-0602
Tel: (800) 572-8328
TollFree: (800) 572-8328
E-Mail: info@parliassoc.com
Website: parliassoc.com
Members: 40 individuals
Staff: 2
Annual Budget: $10-25,000

Personnel:
Administrative Assistant: Helene Goldsmith

Historical Note:
Members are credentialed professional parliamentarians.

Partnership for Air-Conditioning, Heating Refrigeration Accreditation *(2000)*
2111 Wilson Blvd.
Suite 500
Arlington, VA 22201-3001
Tel: (703) 524-8800 *Fax:* (703) 528-3816
E-Mail: pahra@pahrahvacr.org
Website: pahrahvacr.org
Staff: 2
Annual Budget: $25-50,000

Personnel:
Contact, Communications: Warren Lupson
    E-Mail: wlupson@pahrahvacr.org

Historical Note:
PAHRA's purpose is to improve the quality of training offered at all levels of education by meeting or exceeding established industry standards in the heating, ventilation, air conditioning and refrigeration (HVACR) industry.

Partnership for Philanthropic Planning *(1988)*
233 McCrea St.
Suite 400
Indianapolis, IN 46225-1030
Tel: (317) 269-6274 *Fax:* (317) 269-6276
E-Mail: info@pppnet.org
Website: pppnet.org
Members: 11500 individuals
Staff: 8
Annual Budget: $25-50,000
Tax: 501(c)(3)

Personnel:
President and Chief Executive Officer: Tanya Howe Johnson CAE
    E-Mail: thjohnson@ncpg.org
Manager, Membership Operations: Belinda Gillett
    E-Mail: bgillett@pppnet.org
Manager, Communications Services: Ron Tellmann
    E-Mail: rtellmann@ncpg.org
Manager, Finance: Staci Tingley
    E-Mail: stingley@ncpg.org
Director, Operations and Editor: Barbara Yeager
    E-Mail: byeager@ncpg.org

Historical Note:
Formerly National Committee on Planned Giving (NCPG). Assumed its current name in 2006. PPP's mission is to help people and organizations create charitable giving experiences that are the most meaningful in achieving both charitable mission and the philanthropic, financial, family and personal goals of the donor. Members are professionals involved in the process of planning and cultivating charitable gifts. Membership: $150-190/year (Individual).

Meetings/Conferences: Annual

Publications:
Membership Directory; on-line
The Journal of Gift Planning; quarterly; adv.

Paso Fino Horse Association, Inc. *(1972)*
4047 Iron Works Pkwy.
Suite One
Lexington, KY 40511
Tel: (859) 825-6000 *Fax:* (859) 258-2125
Website: pfha.org
Members: 8500 individuals
Staff: 8
Annual Budget: $1-2,000,000
Tax: 501(c)(5)

Personnel:
Executive Director: Don Vizi
    E-Mail: dvizi@pfha.org
Contact, Membership Services and Administrative Assistant: Shanon Hawkins
    E-Mail: shawkins@pfha.org
Editor and Consultant, Media Sales and Marketing Paso Fino Horse World: Catherine King
    E-Mail: cking@pfha.org
Events Manager and Operations Assistant: Andy Smith
    E-Mail: asmith@pfha.org

Historical Note:
Formerly (1986) Paso Fino Owners and Breeders Association and was incorporated in Tennessee. PFHA was formed to promote the Paso Fino horse and to maintain the integrity of the Registry of the PFHA. Mission is to maintain and preserve the Registry of the PFHA. Members are owners and breeders of Paso Fino horses. Membership: $55 (Junior Active); $2,500 (life).

Meetings/Conferences: Annual
Conference Chair: Andy Smith
2013 - New Orleans, LA/Jan. 11 - 12
Number of non-conference events/year: 16

Publications:
Paso Fino Horse World Magazine; adv.
PFHA E-News; weekly

Passenger Vessel Association *(1971)*
103 Oronoco St.
Suite 200
Alexandria, VA 22314
Tel: (703) 518-5005 *Fax:* (703) 518-5151
TollFree: (800) 807-8360
E-Mail: pvainfo@passengervessel.com
Website: passengervessel.com
Members: 600 companies
Staff: 9
Annual Budget: $2-5,000,000
Tax: 501(c)(6)

Personnel:
Executive Director: John Groundwater
    E-Mail: jgroundwater@passengervessel.com
General Counsel: Steven Bers
    E-Mail: sbers@wtplaw.com
Chief Financial Officer: Lee Hill
    E-Mail: lhill@passengervessel.com
Director, Finance: Leslie Kagarise
    E-Mail: lkagarise@passengervessel.com
Managing Editor: Karen Rainbolt
    E-Mail: pvafoghorn@aol.com
Legislative Director: Edmund B. Welch
    E-Mail: ewelch@passengervessel.com
Manager, Membership and Public Affairs: Jennifer Wilk
    E-Mail: jwilk@passengervessel.com

Historical Note:
Formerly National Association of Passenger Vessel Owners. PVA represents operators of tours, excursions, ferries, charter vessels, dinner boats, and other small passenger vessels. It also focuses on the issues and concerns relevant to owners and operators of passenger vessels, manufacturers of maritime-related products and services and other service companies dedicated to develop a conducive business environment. Membership: $125 (Individual/Retired Member); $434-7,725 (Vessel

Members, based on passenger capacity); $1,258 (National Associate); $953 (Regional Associate); $5,174-9,265 (Packaging).

Meetings/Conferences: Annual
2013 - Jacksonville, FL (Hyatt Regency Jacksonville Riverfront)/Feb. 16 - 19
Number of non-conference events/year: 7

Publications:
FOGHORN

Patent and Trademark Office Society *(1917)*
P.O. Box 2089
Arlington, VA 22202
Tel: (703) 557-6511
Website: ptos.org
Members: 230 individuals
Staff: 5
Annual Budget: $100-250,000
Tax: 501(c)(4)

Personnel:
President: Matthew Bradley
Treasurer: Philip Bonzell
Vice President: Aimee Li
Administrator: Jared Rutz
    E-Mail: Jared.Rutz@uspto.gov
Editor-in-Chief: Joshua Schwartz
    E-Mail: editor@jptos.org

Historical Note:
Labor union of Patent Office Trademark examiners. The Society promotes the systems' growth and well-being and the social and intellectual welfare of members. Affiliated with the National Treasury Employees Union, Chapter 245. All members are attorneys. Membership: $60-90 (Associate); $240-360 (Corporate); $8 (Employee); $52-82 (Student/Retired).

Meetings/Conferences:
Number of non-conference events/year: 1

Publications:
Journal of the Patent & Trademark Office Society; quarterly; adv.
Unofficial Gazette/E-Gazette; on-line

Patent Office Professional Association *(1964)*
P.O. Box 25287
Arlington, VA 22313
Website: popa.org
Members: 4000 examiners, classifiers, computer scientists
Staff: 7
Annual Budget: $250-500,000

Personnel:
President: Robert D. Budens
Secretary: Kathleen Duda
Treasurer: Randy Myers

Historical Note:
An independent labor union representing all non-managerial professionals (other than trademark professionals) in the U.S. Patent and Trademark Office. Membership: $5/Bi-Weekly Pay Period.

Publications:
POPA News

Membership List Available to Non-members

Path to Purchase Institute *(1994)*
7400 Skokie Blvd.
Skokie, IL 60077
Tel: (847) 675-7400 *Fax:* (847) 675-7494
Website: p2pi.org
Members: 7,000 Professionals
Staff: 8

Personnel:
Executive Director and Chief Executive Officer: Peter W. Hoyt
Manager, Human Resources: Jeanine Caughlin
Director, Information Technology: Jack Dare
Director, Education and Faculty Administration: Ronit Lawlor
Manager, Events: Peggy Milbrandt
Director, Marketing and Communications: Michele Weston Rowe
Chief Operating and Financial Officer: Chris Stark
Director, New Business Development: Scott Taylor
    E-Mail: staylor@p2pi.org

Historical Note:
A global association serving the needs of retailers, brands and the entire ecosystem of solution providers along the path to purchase. It's mission is to advance best practices

and a deeper understanding of all marketing efforts and touch-points that influence and culminate in purchase decisions at retail. Membership: $11,088 (Universal); $5,544 (Universal Subsidiary); $5,082 (Corporate); $2,541 (Corporate Subsidiary).

Publications:
Digital; daily; adv.
Newsletters; weekly; adv.
Shopper Marketing Magazine; biennially; adv.
The Path to Purchase Marketer; monthly; adv.
This Week in P-O-P Design; weekly; adv.

Patient Centered Primary Care Collaborative
601 13th St. NW.
Suite 430 North
Washington, DC 20005
Tel: (202) 417-2081 Fax: (202) 393-6148
Website: pcpcc.net
Members: 1500 companies
Staff: 4
Annual Budget: $1-2,000,000
Tax: 501(c)(6)

Personnel:
Executive Director: Marci Nielsen MPH, PhD
Chief Operating Officer: Amy Gibson MS, RN
   E-Mail: agibson@pcpcc.net
Manager, Membership Relations and Communications:
   Ana Lojanica
   E-Mail: ana@pcpcc.net
Director, Information Technology: Loren Vandegrift
   E-Mail: loren@songlinedesign.com

Historical Note:
The mission of the Patient-Centered Primary Care Collaborative is to advance an effective and efficient health system built on a strong foundation of primary care and the patient-centered medical home (PCMH).

PCIA - The Wireless Infrastructure Association
(1949)
901 N. Washington St.
Suite 600
Alexandria, VA 22314-1561
Tel: (800) 759-0300 Fax: (703) 836-1608
TollFree: (800) 759-0300
Website: pcia.com
Members: 3000 companies
Staff: 12
Annual Budget: $2-5,000,000

Personnel:
President and Chief Executive Officer: Jonathan S. Adelstein
Director, Operations: Don Andrew
   E-Mail: andrewd@pcia.com
Manager, Information Technology: Renu Batheja
   E-Mail: renu.batheja@pcia.com
Government Affairs Counsel: D. Zachary Champ
   E-Mail: zac.champ@pcia.com
Manager, Communications and Public Affairs: Caitlin Colligan
   E-Mail: caitlin.colligan@pcia.com
Vice President, Marketing and External Relation: Tim House
   E-Mail: houset@pcia.com
Director, Finance and Administration: Praneet Mathur
   E-Mail: praneet.mathur@pcia.com
Manager, Marketing and Sales: Nancy Touhill
   E-Mail: touhilln@pcia.com

Historical Note:
PCIA supports the infrastructure necessary to make wireless communications and information available at all times and places. Represents carriers, infrastructure providers and professional services firms. Membership: $2,500-50,000 (Carrier); $1,250-50,000 (Tower); $1,750-25,000 (Vendor).

Meetings/Conferences:
Conference Chair: Nancy Touhill

Publications:
Member Directory; on-line
Membership Directory; on-line
PCIA NewsWeekly; weekly

Peanut and Tree Nut Processors Association
(1969)
P.O. Box 2660
Alexandria, VA 22301
Tel: (301) 365-2521 Fax: (301) 365-7705
Website: ptnpa.org
Members: 156 companies

Staff: 3
Annual Budget: $500-1,000,000
Tax: 501(c)(6)

Personnel:
Executive Director: Jeannie Shaughnessy Hodges
   E-Mail: jhodges@ptnpa.org

Historical Note:
Formerly (1978) Peanut Butter Manufacturers and Nut Salters Association, and (1995) Peanut Butter and Nut Processors Association. PTNPA's mission is to proactively advance America's nut industry through professional networks, advocacy and education. Membership: $3,000-5,000 (Active); $2,000 (Associate).

Meetings/Conferences: Annual
2013 - Rancho Mirage, CA (The Westin Mission Hills)/ Jan. 19 - 21/26-50 exhibitors
2014 - Marco Island, FL (Marco Island Marriott Beach Resort, Golf Club and Spa)/Jan. 18 - 21/26-50 exhibitors

Publications:
Membership Directory; annually
Newsletter

Peanut Growers Cooperative Marketing Association
1001 Campbell Ave.
P.O. Box 59
Franklin, VA 23851
Tel: (757) 562-4103 Fax: (757) 562-0744
Website: pgcma.org
Staff: 1

Personnel:
Manager: Dell Cotton

Historical Note:
PGCMA's mission is to produce good quality peanuts.

Pediatric Endocrine Society (1971)
6728 Old McLean Village Dr.
McLean, VA 22101
Tel: (703) 556-9222 Fax: (703) 556-8729
E-Mail: info@pedsendo.org
Website: lwpes.org
Members: 1200 individuals
Staff: 3
Annual Budget: $1-2,000,000
Tax: 501(c)(3)

Personnel:
Executive Director: George K. Degnon CAE

Historical Note:
Formerly the Lawson Wilkins Pediatric Endocrine Society (2009). Mission of PES is to advance the care of children and adolescents with endocrine disorders. The Society influences policy-making that advances research, clinical care, reimbursement, and education in pediatric endocrinology. Members are pediatric endocrinologists.

Meetings/Conferences: Annual
2013 - Washington, DC/May 4 - 7
2014 - Vancouver, BC/May 3 - 6
2015 - San Diego, CA/April 25 - 28
2016 - Baltimore, MD/April 30 - May 3
2017 - San Francisco, CA/May 6 - 9
2018 - Toronto, ON/May 5 - 8
2019 - Baltimore, MD/April 27 - 30
2020 - Philadelphia, PA/May 2 - 5

Publications:
Member Directory; on-line
PES Newsletter; on-line

Pediatric Nursing Certification Board (1975)
800 S. Frederick Ave.
Suite 204
Gaithersburg, MD 20877-4152
Tel: (301) 330-2921 Fax: (301) 330-1504
TollFree: (888) 641-2767
E-Mail: pncb@pncb.org
Website: pncb.org
Staff: 14
Annual Budget: $2-5,000,000

Personnel:
Chief Executive Officer: Peg Harrison MS, RN
Director, Marketing: Lori Boocks
   E-Mail: lboocks@pncb.org
Chief Financial Officer and Chief Operating Officer: Andrea Burns CPA, MBA, CPE
   E-Mail: aburns@pncb.org

Historical Note:

PNCB's mission is to advocate better healthcare for children through the better quality credentialing services.

Continuing Education:
Enrollment: 23000
Certification Designation/s: CPEN, CPNP-AC, CPN, CPNP-PC

Publications:
Proctor Newsletter; on-line

Membership List Available to Non-members

Pediatric Orthopedic Society of North America
(1982)
6300 N. River Rd.
Suite 727
Rosemont, IL 60018-4226
Tel: (847) 698-1692 Fax: (847) 823-0536
E-Mail: posna@aaos.org
Website: posna.org
Members: 769 individuals
Staff: 3
Annual Budget: $1-2,000,000

Personnel:
Executive Director: Teri Stech
Society Coordinator: Cristina Cabral

Historical Note:
Formerly (1985) the Society of Pediatric Orthopedics. The Pediatric Orthopedic Society of North America (POSNA) strives to develop and implement quality education of pediatric orthopedists and thereby assure better possible care of musculoskeletal pediatric patients. Membership: $300/year.

Meetings/Conferences: Annual
2013 - Toronto, ON (Sheraton Centre Toronto Hotel)/ May 1 - 4
2014 - Los Angeles, CA (Renaissance Hollywood Hotel and Spa)/April 30 - May 3
2015 - Atlanta, GA (Atlanta Marriott Century Center)/ April 29 - May 2
2016 - Indianapolis, IN (JW Marriott Indianapolis)/ April 27 - 30

Publications:
Membership Directory

Pedorthic Footwear Association (1958)
8400 Westpark Dr.
2nd Floor
McLean, VA 22102
Tel: (703) 610-9035 Fax: (703) 995-4456
E-Mail: info@pedorthics.org
Website: pedorthics.org
Members: 2100 Companies and Individuals
Staff: 13
Annual Budget: $1-2,000,000

Personnel:
Manager, Convention and Meeting: Annette Suriani CMP

Historical Note:
PFA's mission is to enhance the effectiveness and efficiency of the credentialed pedorthist through education.

Meetings/Conferences: Annual
Conference Chair: Annette Suriani CMP
Number of non-conference events/year: 6

Publications:
Current Pedorthics magazine; bi-monthly; adv.

PeerSpan (1978)
216 W. Jackson Blvd.
Suite 625
Chicago, IL 60606
Tel: (312) 263-1755 Fax: (312) 750-1203
E-Mail: info@peerspan.org
Website: peerspan.org
Members: 205 individuals
Staff: 4
Annual Budget: $100-250,000

Personnel:
President: Patrick Connors
Senior Vice President and Chief Financial Officer: Paul Hawkins
Contact, Communications: Kim Klein
Treasurer: Todd Pearson
   E-Mail: tpearson@peerspan.org

Historical Note:
Formerly, National Association of Real Estate Companies (NAREC). PeerSpan's mission is to provide real world solutions to real estate financial and tax challenges through collaborative relationships, education and knowledge sharing.Membership: $550/year.

Continuing Education:
Certification Designation/s: NASBA

Meetings/Conferences: Annual
2013 - Laguna Beach, CA (Montage Laguna Beach)/
June 18 - 21
Number of non-conference events/year: 2

Publications:
NAREC Newsletter; quarterly

Pellet Fuels Institute (1982)
1901 N. Moore St.
Suite 600
Arlington, VA 22209
Tel: (703) 522-6778 *Fax:* (703) 522-0548
E-Mail: pfimail@pelletheat.org
Website: pelletheat.org
Members: 145 companies
Staff: 4
Annual Budget: $500-1,000,000
Tax: 501(c)(6)

Personnel:
Executive Director and Media Contact: Jennifer Hedrick
   E-Mail: hedrick@pelletheat.org
Associate, Membership and Government Affairs: Jason
   Berthiaume
   E-Mail: berthiaume@pelletheat.org
Director, Public Affairs: John Crouch
   E-Mail: Crouch@pelletheat.org

Historical Note:
Formerly Fiber Fuels Institute. The Fiber Fuels Institute later merged with the Association of Pellet Fuel Industries and formed the Pellet Fuels Institute. PFI is a North American trade association promoting energy independence through the efficient use of clean, renewable densified biomass fuel. Members are manufacturers of pellet and briquette fuel, suppliers and others. Membership: $2,000-12,000 (Pellet fuel manufacturer); $1,500 (Supplier); $5,000 (Supplier Gold); $3,000 (Supplier Silver); $500 (Associate).

Meetings/Conferences: Annual

Publications:
Member Directory
PFI Newsletter; quarterly

Pension Real Estate Association (1979)
100 Pearl St.
13th Floor
Hartford, CT 06103
Tel: (860) 692-6341 *Fax:* (860) 692-6351
E-Mail: membership@prea.org
Website: prea.org
Members: 400 corporate members, 1400
individuals
Staff: 8
Annual Budget: $2-5,000,000
Tax: 501(c)(6)

Personnel:
President: Gail C. Haynes

Historical Note:
Mission is to serve its members engaged in institutional real estate investment through the sponsorship of objective forums for education, research and intiatives. Membership: $5,990 (Full Corporate); $3,570 (Standard Corporate); $2,845 (Basic Corporate); $330 (Academic Institution/ Institutional Investor, Non-Profit); $1,950 (Institutional Investor, Profit).

Meetings/Conferences:
2013 - Washington, DC/March 13
2013 - Washington, DC/March 14 - 15
2013 - Chicago, IL/Oct. 28 - 30

Publications:
Journal of Real Estate Portfolio Management
PREA Quarterly Magazine; quarterly

Percheron Horse Association of America (1876)
10330 Quaker Rd.
P. O. Box 141
Fredericktown, OH 43019-0141
Tel: (740) 694-3602 *Fax:* (740) 694-3604
E-Mail: percheron@percheronhorse.org
Website: percheronhorse.org
Members: 3400 individuals
Staff: 3
Annual Budget: $100-250,000
Tax: 501(c)(5)

Personnel:
Secretary and Treasurer: Elaine Beardsley

Historical Note:

Formerly known as Norman-Percheron Association and then Percheron Society of America. Later changed its name to Percheron Horse Association of America. Its purpose is the preservation and promotion of the purebred Percheron Horse. Members are owners and breeders of Percheron horses. Membership: $40 (Regular); $500 (Lifetime).

Publications:
Percheron News Magazine; quarterly; adv.
The Percheron Postscript; monthly

Percussion Marketing Council (1995)
P.O. Box 33252
Cleveland, OH 44133
Tel: (440) 582-7006 *Fax:* (440) 230-1346
Website: playdrums.com
Members: 35 individuals
Staff: 3
Annual Budget: $25-50,000

Personnel:
Co-Executive Director: Karl Dustman
   E-Mail: kbdustman@aol.com
Co-Executive Director and Editor: Brad Smith
   E-Mail: bsmith@halleonard.com
Contact, Membership Services: Phil Hood
   E-Mail: philhood@pacbell.net

Historical Note:
PMC's mission is to provide professional marketing and advertising campaigns, programs and activities that bring increased public awareness to drumming, thus increasing the number of people playing all types of drums. Members are drum and percussion manufacturers, suppliers and dealers.

Publications:
PMC Newsletter; semi-annually

Percussive Arts Society (1961)
110 W. Washington St.
Suite A
Indianapolis, IN 46204
Tel: (317) 974-4488 *Fax:* (317) 974-4499
E-Mail: percarts@pas.org
Website: pas.org
Members:
50 chapters in the United States, and 28 chapters
outside the United States
8500 individuals
Staff: 21
Annual Budget: $1-2,000,000

Personnel:
Executive Director: Michael Kenyon
   E-Mail: mkenyon@pas.org
Director, Marketing and Communications: Matthew
   Altizer
Director, Event Production and Marketing: Jeff Hartsough
Publications Editor: Rick Mattingly
Director, Information Technology and Interactive Media:
   Marianella Moreno
Manager , Membership Services: Justin Ramirez
Coordinator, Programs and Operations: Heath Towson

Historical Note:
PAS is a music service organization that promotes percussion music education, research, performance and appreciation throughout the world. Members are teachers and performers on drums and other percussion instruments. Membership: $35-60 (Student); $60-100 (Professional); $175 (Friend); $60 (Senior Citizen); $475-2,300 (Sustaining).

Meetings/Conferences: Annual
Conference Chair: Jeff Hartsough
2013 - Indianapolis, IN/Nov. 13 - 16

Publications:
Percussion News; bi-monthly; adv.
Percussive Notes; bi-monthly; adv.
The PAS Online Research Journal; bi-monthly

Perennial Plant Association (1983)
3383 Schirtzinger Rd.
Hilliard, OH 43026
Tel: (614) 771-8431 *Fax:* (614) 876-5238
E-Mail: ppa@perennialplant.org
Website: perennialplant.org
Members: 1400 firms and individuals
Staff: 4
Annual Budget: $250-500,000
Tax: 501(c)(5)

Personnel:
Executive Director: Steven M. Still PhD
   E-Mail: sstill@perennialplant.org

Contact, Web and Information Resources: Sara Crawford
Contact, Membership Services: Rayma King
   E-Mail: rking@perennialplant.org
Associate Director: Carolyn Still
   E-Mail: cstill@perennialplant.org

Historical Note:
The purpose of the PPA is to increase awareness and knowledge of the many fine perennial plants that can enhance its gardens. Voting membership in PPA is open to firms or individuals who are actively engaged in the growing, landscape planting, landscape designing or merchandising of perennials. Membership: $95-500 (Voting Members); $20-125 (Non-voting Members).

Meetings/Conferences: Annual
2013 - Vancouver, BC/June 21 - 27

Publications:
Membership Directory; on-line
Perennial Plants Journal; quarterly; adv.
PPA News; bi-monthly

Performance Track Participants Association
1155 15th St. NW
Suite 500
Washington, DC 20005
Website: ptpaonline.org
Staff: 2
Annual Budget: $100-250,000
Tax: 501(c)(6)

Personnel:
Executive Director: John Flatley
Director: Anne Vogel-Marr
   E-Mail: steplightly@verizon.net

Historical Note:
PTPA strives to provide a forum for corporations, trade associations and public entities dedicated to improving their environmental performance through the vehicle of the Environmental Protection Agency's (EPA) Performance Track program. Membership: $200-5,0000 (Company); $10,000 (Corporate).

Performance Warehouse Association (1971)
41-701 Corporate Way
Suite One
Palm Desert, CA 92260
Tel: (760) 346-5647 *Fax:* (760) 346-5847
E-Mail: info@pwa-par.org
Website: pwa-par.com
Members: 600 individuals
Staff: 4
Annual Budget: $500-1,000,000

Personnel:
President: John Towle
   E-Mail: john@pwa-par.org
Contact, Advertising: Roxanne Ries
   E-Mail: ROXANNE@PWA-PAR.ORG

Historical Note:
PWA's mission is to assist the specialty automotive warehouse distributors in their efforts to expand, maintain and promote the profitable distribution of specialty automotive products through the manufacturer/warehouse distributor/retailer/consumer channel. Members are distributors of specialty automotive parts and suppliers. Membership: $350-400 (Warehouse Distributor, based on annual sales); $150-400 (Manufacturer, based on annual sales); $100 (Manufacturer Affiliate); $100-200 (Manufacturer's Representative); $100-300 (Supporting Distributor/Media/Advertising/Trade Associations/Service Providers, based on annual sales).

Meetings/Conferences: Annual
2013 - Phoenix, AZ/Sept. 21 - 25
2014 - Phoenix, AZ/Sept. 13 - 17
2015 - Phoenix, AZ/Sept. 26 - 30
Number of non-conference events/year: 8

Publications:
Membership Directory; on-line
PAR Newsletter; quarterly
PWA & PAR Newsletter; bi-monthly
PWA Newsline; adv.

Performing Arts Alliance (1977)
1211 Connecticut Ave. NW
Suite 200
Washington, DC 20036
Tel: (202) 207-3850 *Fax:* (202) 833-1543
E-Mail: info@theperformingartsalliance.org
Website: theperformingartsalliance.org
Members: 18000 organizational and individuals
Staff: 1

Annual Budget: $250-500,000
Tax: 501(c)(3)

Personnel:
Manager: Townley Clardy
 E-Mail: tclardy@artspresenters.org

Historical Note:
Formerly the American Arts Alliance. PAA advocates for America's professional nonprofit art organizations, artists and public before the Congress and key policy makers. Through legislative and grassroots action, the American Arts Alliance advocates for national policies which recognize, enhance, and foster the contributions the arts make to America. Members include the professionals belonging to nonprofit performing arts and presenting fields. Member art organizations include the Association of Performing Arts Presenters, Dance/USA, Opera America and Theatre Communications Group.

Publications:
Membership Directory; on-line
PAA Newsletter; on-line

Periodical and Book Association of America
(1965)
481 Eighth Ave.
Suite 826
New York, NY 10001
Tel: (212) 563-6502 *Fax:* (212) 563-4098
E-Mail: info@pbaa.net
Website: pbaa.net
Members: 120 companies
Staff: 2
Annual Budget: $250-500,000
Tax: 501(c)(4)

Personnel:
Executive Director: Lisa W. Scott
 E-Mail: lisawscott@hotmail.com
Associate Director: Jose L. Concio
 E-Mail: JCancio@pbaa.net

Historical Note:
PBAA's mission is to build awareness, identify trends, educate, and bring positive reinforcement to the issues at hand while bringing the publishing community closer together. Members are organizations which publish and distribute magazines and books in the United States and abroad.

Meetings/Conferences: Annual
Number of non-conference events/year: 4

Publications:
Membership Directory; on-line

Perlite Institute *(1949)*
4305 N. Sixth St.
Suite A
Harrisburg, PA 17110
Tel: (717) 238-9723 *Fax:* (717) 238-9985
E-Mail: info@perlite.org
Website: perlite.org
Members: 40 companies
Staff: 7
Annual Budget: $100-250,000

Personnel:
Executive Director: Denise Calabrese
 E-Mail: info@perlite.org
Director, Membership Services: Angela Burkett
 E-Mail: customerservice@perlite.org
Director, Conferences and Events: Jen Cramer
 E-Mail: events@perlite.org
Manager, Communications: Alison Evans
 E-Mail: communications@perlite.org
Administrative Assistant: Leona Wagner
 E-Mail: admin@perlite.org

Historical Note:
PI's purpose is to increase the public's awareness and knowledge of perlite through publicity and advertising programs. Membership: $2,000 (Regular/Furnace); $500 (Associate); $2,000-10,000 (Ore Producer).

Meetings/Conferences: Annual
Conference Chair: Jen Cramer

Publications:
Membership Directory; on-line

Personal Care Products Council *(1894)*
1101 17th St. NW
Suite 300
Washington, DC 20036-4702
Tel: (202) 331-1770 *Fax:* (202) 331-1969
Website: personalcarecouncil.org

Members: 600 companies
Staff: 8
Annual Budget: $10-25,000,000
Tax: 501(c)(6)

Personnel:
Executive Director: Louanne Roark
 E-Mail: roarkl@personalcarecouncil.org
Executive Vice President, Legal and General Counsel: Elizabeth H. Anderson
 E-Mail: andersone@personalcarecoucil.org
Executive Vice President, Public Affairs and Communications: Kathleen Dezio
 E-Mail: deziok@personalcarecouncil.org
Executive Vice President, Government Affairs: John A. Hurson
 E-Mail: hursonj@personalcarecouncil.org
Senior Vice President, Public Affairs and Communications: Lisa Powers
Vice President, Meetings: Jeanie Tulipane CMP
 E-Mail: tulipanej@personalcarecouncil.org
President and Chief Executive Officer: Lezlee Westine

Historical Note:
Formerly the Cosmetic, Toiletry and Fragrance Association. PCPC advocates for consumer safety and continued access to new, innovative products. Membership: $2,700/year(International Active/International Associate).

Continuing Education:
Certification Designation/s: CFS

Meetings/Conferences: Annual
2013 - Florida City, FL (The Breakers in Palm Beach)/ Feb. 25 - 27
Number of non-conference events/year: 3

Publications:
Membership Directory; on-line

Membership List Available to Non-members

Personal Watercraft Industry Association (PWIA)
(1987)
444 N. Capitol St. NW
Suite 645
Washington, DC 20001
Tel: (202) 737-9768 *Fax:* (202) 628-4716
E-Mail: info@pwia.org
Website: pwia.org
Members: 4 companies
Staff: 3
Annual Budget: $1-2,000,000
Tax: 501(c)(6)

Personnel:
Director, State Government Relations: David Dickerson
 E-Mail: ddickerson@nmma.org
Manager, State Government Relations and Legislative Counsel: Nicole Vasilaros
 E-Mail: nvasilaros@nmma.org

Historical Note:
PWIA supports and actively advocates for reasonable regulations, strong enforcement of boating and navigation laws, and mandatory boating safety education for all PWC operators.

Pet Food Institute *(1958)*
2025 M St. NW
Suite 800
Washington, DC 20036
Tel: (202) 367-1120 *Fax:* (202) 367-2120
E-Mail: info@petfoodinstitute.org
Website: petfoodinstitute.org
Members: 100 companies
Staff: 5
Annual Budget: $2-5,000,000
Tax: 501(c)(6)

Personnel:
President: Duane Ekedahl
Director, Communications and Export Development: Kurt Gallagher
 E-Mail: kurt@petfoodinstitute.org
Manager, Technical and Regulatory Affairs: Pat Tovey

Historical Note:
PFI is dedicated to promote the overall care and well-being of pets. Members are dog and cat food manufacturers.

Meetings/Conferences: Annual

Publications:
PFI Monitor; semi-annually; adv.

Pet Industry Distributors Association *(1968)*
2105 Laurel Bush Rd.

Suite 200
Bel Air, MD 21015
Tel: (443) 640-1060 *Fax:* (443) 640-1031
E-Mail: pida@ksgroup.org
Website: pida.org
Members: 300 companies
Staff: 4
Annual Budget: $1-2,000,000
Tax: 501(c)(6)

Personnel:
President: Steven T. King, CAE
 E-Mail: steve@ksgroup.org
Director, Finance: Debbie Dacre
 E-Mail: debbie@kingmgmt.com
Director, Meetings and Membership Services: Marci Hickey CMP
 E-Mail: marci@ksgroup.org
Director, Online Education: Stephanie Kaplan
 E-Mail: Stephanie@kingmgmt.com

Historical Note:
PIDA's mission is to enhance the well-being of the wholesaler-distributor, to promote partnerships with their suppliers and customers, and to work cooperatively in fostering the human-companion animal bond. Membership: $500-4,300 (Active/Pet Food Wholesaler/Affiliate); $250-3,000 (Manufacturer Representative); $250 (Associate); $425 (Pet Wholesaler).

Continuing Education:
Certification Designation/s: PSP

Meetings/Conferences:
Conference Chair: Marci Hickey CMP
2013 - Carlsbad, CA (Park Hyatt Aviara Resort)/Jan. 21 - 24
2013 - Orlando, FL (Orange County Convention Center)/Feb. 20 - 22/11-25 exhibitors

Publications:
Membership Directory; on-line
PIDA Bulletin; on-line

Pet Industry Joint Advisory Council *(1971)*
1146 19th St. NW
Suite 350
Washington, DC 20036
Tel: (202) 452-1525 *Fax:* (202) 452-1516
TollFree: (800) 553-7387
E-Mail: info@pijac.org
Website: pijac.org
Members: 2000 firms and associations
Staff: 7
Annual Budget: $1-2,000,000
Tax: 501(c)(6)

Personnel:
President and Chief Executive Officer: Michael F. Canning CAE, Esq.
 E-Mail: mcanning@pijac.org
Vice President, Marketing and Communications: Cathy Calliotte
 E-Mail: cathy@pijac.org
Director, Administration and Member Services: Nancy Knutson
 E-Mail: nancy@pijac.org
Vice President, Governmental Affairs and General Counsel: Michael Maddox
 E-Mail: michael@pijac.org

Historical Note:
PIJAC's mission is to promote responsible pet ownership and animal welfare, fosters environmental stewardship, and ensures the availability of pets. Members are pet shop retailers, companion animal breeders and importers, product manufacturers, pet hobbyist groups, and distributors. Membership: $25-50,000/year.

Continuing Education:
Certification Designation/s: CAS, CCS, CFS, CRS, CSAS

Meetings/Conferences: Annual
2013 - Napa, CA (Meritage Resort and Spa)/April 23 - 25/26-50 exhibitors

Publications:
Membership Directory; on-line
PetLetter; quarterly
PIJAC eNews; bi-weekly

Membership List Available to Non-members

Pet Partners *(1977)*
875 124th Ave. NE
Suite 101
Bellevue, WA 98005
Tel: (425) 679-5500 *Fax:* (425) 679-5539

E-Mail: info@deltasociety.org
Website: deltasociety.org
Members: 10300 individuals, member companies
and organizations
Staff: 9
Annual Budget: $250-500,000
Tax: 501(c)(3)

Personnel:
President and Chief Executive Officer: Stephen R.
Browning
E-Mail: stephenb@petpartners.org
Development Coordinator: Lisa Erwin
E-Mail: LisaE@DeltaSociety.org
Vice President, Marketing: Bill Kueser
E-Mail: BillK@DeltaSociety.org
Director, Finance: Michelle Matheson
E-Mail: michellem@petpartners.org
Director, Operations: Frances Pak
E-Mail: francesp@petpartners.org
Director, Programs: Rachel Wright
E-Mail: rachelw@petpartners.org

Historical Note:
Formerly Delta Society. Mission of Pet Partners is to
advance human health and well-being through positive
interactions with animals. Serves as an international,
educational, research and service resource on the
relationships between people, animals and nature. Members
include veterinarians, psychiatrists, health workers,
volunteers, administrators, teachers, and pet owners.
Membership: $50/year (Individual).

Meetings/Conferences:
Conference Chair: Rachel Wright

Publications:
Interactions Magazine; semi-annually
Pet Partners; adv.

Membership List Available to Non-members

PET Resin Association
355 Lexington Ave.
Suite 1500
New York, NY 10017-6603
Tel: (212) 297-2108 Fax: (212) 370-9047
E-Mail: info@PETresin.org
Website: petresin.org
Members: 6 Organizations
Staff: 1

Personnel:
Executive Director: Ralph Vasami
E-Mail: RVasami@PETresin.org

Historical Note:
PETRA's mission is to promote the growth of PET products
and to represent the North American PET resin producers.
PET Resin Association is an affiliate member of the
Association of Postconsumer Plastic Recyclers.

Pet Sitters International (1994)
201 E. King St.
King, NC 27021
Tel: (336) 983-9222 Fax: (336) 983-5266
E-Mail: info@petsit.com
Website: petsit.com
Members: 8000 companies
Staff: 16
Annual Budget: $1-2,000,000

Personnel:
Founder, President and Editor: Patti J. Moran
Senior Communication Director: Terry Chance
E-Mail: terrychance@petsit.com
Manager, Academics: Ellen Price
E-Mail: ellen@petsit.com
Marketing Manager: Beth Stultz
E-Mail: bethstultz@petsit.com

Historical Note:
Mission is to foster continuous learning in the pet-sitting
profession by providing education and tools of the trade.
Membership: $140 (U.S. Members); $125 (Canadian); $75
(International).

Continuing Education:
Enrollment: 400
Certification Designation/s: APS, CPPS, POA

Meetings/Conferences: Annual

Publications:
Pet Owner's WORLD; annually; adv.
Pet Sitter's WORLD; bi-monthly; adv.
The Scoop; monthly; adv.

Petroleum Convenience Alliance for Technology Standards (2003)
1600 Duke St.
Alexandria, VA 22314
Tel: (703) 518-7960
Website: pcats.org
Members: 70 retailer and supplier members,
20,000 convenience stores
Staff: 3
Annual Budget: $500-1,000,000

Personnel:
Executive Director: Gray Taylor
E-Mail: gtaylor@pcats.org
Office Manager: Ann Zecca
E-Mail: azecca@pcats.org

Historical Note:
PCATS is devoted to the development, maintenance and
implementation of standards, education and best practices
for the convenience store and petroleum retail segments.
Members of PCATS collaborate and focus on key industry
challenges and initiatives.

Publications:
Membership Directory; on-line

Petroleum Equipment Institute (1951)
P.O. Box 2380
Tulsa, OK 74101-2380
Tel: (918) 494-9696 Fax: (918) 491-9895
E-Mail: info@pei.org
Website: pei.org
Members: 1600 companies
Staff: 11
Annual Budget: $2-5,000,000
Tax: 501(c)(6)

Personnel:
Executive Vice President and General Counsel: Robert N.
Renkes
E-Mail: rrenkes@pei.org
Director, Information Services: J. Rex Brown
E-Mail: jrbrown@pei.org
Coordinator, Membership Services: Carletta Denison
E-Mail: cdenison@pei.org
Contact, Convention Planning: Connie Dooley
E-Mail: cdooley@pei.org
Accounting and Office Manager: Sondra Sutton
E-Mail: ssutton@pei.org
Director, Publications and Marketing: Sarah West
E-Mail: swest@pei.org
Contact, Shipping, Receiving and Publication Orders: Keith
Wilson
E-Mail: kwilson@pei.org

Historical Note:
Established as the National Association of Oil Equipment
Jobbers; assumed its present name in 1966. PEI's mission
is to be the source of information for the petroleum and
energy handling equipment industry. Members are makers
and distributors of equipment used in service stations,
bulk plants and other petroleum marketing facilities.
Membership: $350-900 (Operations & Engineering).

Meetings/Conferences:
Conference Chair: Connie Dooley
2013 - Clearwater, FL (Sheraton Sand Key Resort)/Feb.
6 - 8

Publications:
PEI Directory; annually
The PEI Journal; quarterly
Tulsa Letter

Petroleum Equipment Suppliers Association (1933)
1240 Blalock Rd.
Suite 110
Houston, TX 77055
Tel: (713) 932-0168 Fax: (713) 932-0497
E-Mail: info@pesa.org
Website: pesa.org
Members: 200 companies and 175 individuals
Staff: 6
Annual Budget: $2-5,000,000
Tax: 501(c)(6)

Personnel:
President: Sherry A. Stephens
Director, Communications: Chris Evans
Meeting Administrator: Geri Perini
Financial Administrator: Juanita Ybarra

Historical Note:

Formerly (1938) American Petroleum Equipment Suppliers.
PESA seeks to assist the federal government in preparing
a fair practice code for the oilfield equipment industry.
Members are makers of oil field production and drilling
equipment, well site services and suppliers, equipment
manufacturers, well site service companies and supply
companies serving the drilling and production segments of
the petroleum industry.

Meetings/Conferences: Annual
Conference Chair: Geri Perini
2013 - San Diego, CA (The Grand Del Mar)/April 3 - 6
2014 - Tucson, AZ (Loews Ventana Canyon Resort)/
April 2 - 5
Number of non-conference events/year: 2

Publications:
Member Service Point Directory; on-line
PESA News; monthly

Petroleum Marketers Association of America (1941)
1901 N. Fort Myer Dr.
Suite 500
Arlington, VA 22209-1604
Tel: (703) 351-8000 Fax: (703) 351-9160
TollFree: (800) 300-7622
E-Mail: info@pmaa.org
Website: pmaa.org
Members: 51 associations
Staff: 7
Annual Budget: $1-2,000,000
Tax: 501(c)(6)

Personnel:
President: Daniel Gilligan
E-Mail: dgilligan@pmaa.org
Director, Programs and Administration: Susan Isard
E-Mail: sisard@pmaa.org
Vice President: Sherri Stone
E-Mail: sstone@pmaa.org
Manager, Regulatory Affairs and Communications:
Brandon Wright
E-Mail: bwright@pmaa.org

Historical Note:
PMAA was origininated in 1909, when the Independent
Petroleum Marketers Association of the United States
was formed. This association became defunct, but in
1940, the President's Council of Petroleum Marketers
Association was formed. In 1948, that group became the
National Oil Jobbers Council; assumed its current name in
1984. PMAA is a national organization representing the
nation's independent petroleum marketers. Mission is to
nationally unify petroleum marketers through their state
and regional associations in order to effectively further
the common business interests of the petroleum marketing
industry. Provides legislative and regulatory representation,
and organizes events where members can learn about
and develop consensus on important issues. PMAA is
a federation of state and regional petroleum marketing
trade associations which represent approximately 8,000
independent petroleum marketers.

Meetings/Conferences:
Conference Chair: Susan Isard
2013 - Washington, DC (Washington Court Hotel)/May
15 - 17

Publications:
PMAA Journal; quarterly; adv.

Petroleum Packaging Council (1989)
C/O ATD Management, Inc.
1519 Via Tulipan
San Clemente, CA 92673
Tel: (949) 369-7102 Fax: (949) 366-1057
E-Mail: PPC@ATDmanagement.com
Website: ppcouncil.org
Members: 400 individuals
Staff: 4
Annual Budget: $250-500,000

Personnel:
Executive Director: Brenda Baker
E-Mail: bbaker@atdmanagement.com
Chair, Communications and Membership Services:
Matthew Miller
Secretary and Treasurer: John Ressler
E-Mail: jressler@designlabel.com

Historical Note:
PPC's mission is to provide technical education to the
Petroleum Packaging Industry. Various forums are used
to disseminate information and technical knowledge to
members. Membership: $525 (Regular); $575 (Associate);
$2,000 (Corporate); $2300 (Associate Corporate).

Meetings/Conferences: Semi-Annual
2013 - St. Augustine, FL (Renaissance Resort at World
Golf Village)/March 17 - 19
2013 - Nashville, TN (Nashville Marriott, Vanderbilt
University)/Aug. 18 - 20

Publications:
NewsFlash; monthly

Petroleum Technology Transfer Council (1994)
P.O. Box 710942
Oak Hill, VA 20171
Tel: (703) 928-5020 *Fax:* (571) 485-8255
E-Mail: hq@pttc.org
Website: pttc.org
Staff: 7
Annual Budget: $1-2,000,000
Tax: 501(c)(3)

Personnel:
Contact, Financial Affairs and Business Affairs: Kathy
Chapman
E-Mail: kchapman@pttc.org
Director, Advertising Sales: Russell Lindsay
E-Mail: Russell.lindsay7@gmail.com
Editor: Kristi Lovendahl
E-Mail: klovendahl@pttc.org
Operations Manager: Viola Rawn-Schatzinger
E-Mail: vschatzinger@pttc.org

Historical Note:
*PTTC aims to encourage the effective transfer of exploration
and production technology to US petroleum producers. The
technical information that the PTTC transfers to producers
comes from the research and development community and
intermediary providers of technology including: government,
universities, professional and trade societies, national
labs, major companies, the service industry, etc. Although
the PTTC is not involved directly with any research and
development efforts, PTTC identifies the best mechanisms
for improving near-term and long-term technology transfer
to domestic operators.*
Meetings/Conferences:
Number of non-conference events/year: 2

Publications:
PTTC Network News; quarterly

Petroleum Transportation and Storage Association
4200 Wisconsin Ave. NW
Suite 106
Washington, DC 20016
Tel: (202) 364-6767
Staff: 1

Personnel:
Executive Director: Mark S. Morgan

Historical Note:
*The Petroleum Transportation and Storage Association
(PTSA) is a national trade association representing small
business petroleum marketers engaged in the shipment,
storage and sale of petroleum products throughout the
country.*

The PGA Tour, Inc. (1969)
112 PGA TOUR Blvd.
Suite 36
Ponte Vedra Beach, FL 32082-5023
Tel: (904) 285-3700
Website: pgatour.com
Members: 50 individuals
Staff: 7
Annual Budget: Over $100,000,000
Tax: 501(c)(6)

Personnel:
General Manager: Lee Bushkell
Sales Manager: Michele Bryan
Editorial Coordinator: Lauren Deason
Senior Vice President, New Media: Paul Johnson
Managing Editor: Mike McAllister
Senior Manager, Website Operations: Patrick Regan

Historical Note:
*PGATTA provides structured ShotLink data sets to
credentialed higher education institutions for research and
other approved academic purposes.*

Publications:
LINKS Magazine; weekly
Newsletter; monthly
Players Directory; adv.

Pharmaceutical Care Management Association
(1975)

601 Pennsylvania Ave. NW
Suite 740 South
Washington, DC 20004
Tel: (202) 207-3610 *Fax:* (202) 207-3623
Website: pcmanet.org
Members: 75 companies
Staff: 17
Annual Budget: $25-50,000,000
Tax: 501(c)(6)

Personnel:
President and Chief Executive Officer: Mark Merritt
*Senior Vice President, Policy and Federal Government
Affairs:* Kristin Bass
Assistant Vice President, Strategic Communications:
Charles Cote
Director, Accounting and Operations: Ryan Hickey
Vice President State Affairs and General Counsel: Barbara
A. Levy
E-Mail: blevy@pcmanet.org
Vice President, Industry Relations and Operations: Brian
McCarthy
E-Mail: bmccarthy@pcmanet.org
Chief Financial Officer: Brenda W. Palmer
Senior Director, Industry Relations and Conferences:
Kristen Pumphrey

Historical Note:
*Formerly (1989) National Association of Mail Service
Pharmacies, (1996) American Managed Care Pharmacy
Association. PCMA's mission is to enhance the proven
tools and techniques pioneered by PBMs that generate
savings and access for consumers and payors. Affiliate
members include partners in pharmaceutical care such
as pharmaceutical manufacturers, retail pharmacies,
disease management firms, drug wholesalers, and
others. Membership: $12,000 (Affiliate Industry/Service
Company); $250 (Academic/Governmental Institution).*

Meetings/Conferences: Annual
Conference Chair: Kristen Pumphrey
2013 - Rancho Palos Verdes, CA (Terranea Resort in
Rancho Palos Verdes)/Oct. 28 - 30
Number of non-conference events/year: 2

Publications:
PCMA Today's News; daily
Reality Check e-newsletter; bi-monthly

Pharmaceutical Education and Research Institute
(1989)
1616 N. Ft. Myer Dr.
Suite 1430
Arlington, VA 22209
Tel: (703) 276-0178 *Fax:* (703) 276-0069
Website: peri.org
Staff: 1
Annual Budget: $1-2,000,000

Personnel:
President: Judith K. Jones MD, PhD
E-Mail: julio.rodriguez@peri.org

Historical Note:
*PERI's mission is to enhance the professional effectiveness
of constituencies by providing training and accredited
continuing education for physicians, nurses, pharmaceutical
professionals and others, that meets or exceeds established
standards.*

Continuing Education:
Certification Designation/s: PERICP

Pharmaceutical Industry Labor Management Association (PILMA)
101 N. Union St.
Alexandria, VA 22314
Tel: (703) 548-4721
Website: pilma.org
Staff: 1
Annual Budget: $1-2,000,000
Tax: 501(c)(6)

Personnel:
Chairman: Walter Wise

Historical Note:
PILMA promotes medical innovation to cure disease.

Pharmaceutical Marketing Research Group
(1961)
P.O. Box 1449
Minneola, FL 34755
Tel: (352) 243-8585
E-Mail: info@pmrg.org
Website: pmrg.org

Staff: 5
Annual Budget: $1-2,000,000
Tax: 501(c)(6)

Personnel:
Executive Director: Stephanie Reynders
E-Mail: stephanie@pmrg.org
Director, Events: Heidi Boyle
E-Mail: heidi@pmrg.org
Treasurer: Jeff Kozloff
E-Mail: jkozloff@verilogue.com
Director, Membership Services and Marketing: Rochelle
Cinque Scott
E-Mail: rochelle@pmrg.org
Legal Counsel: Mike Slotznick
E-Mail: mslotznick@comcast.net

Historical Note:
*PMRG advances the principles, practice and power of
healthcare marketing research by creating a community that
both supports individual professional development and acts
as an advocate for the profession as a whole. Membership:
$150 (Individual); $500-1875 (Client-Manufacturer).*

Meetings/Conferences:
2013 - Maryland, WA (Gaylord National Resort)/
March 10 - 12
2013 - Jersey City, NJ (Hyatt Regency Jersey City on the
Hudson)/Oct. 20 - 22
2014 - Orlando, FL (Gaylord Palms Resort and
Convention Center-Orlando)/March 9 - 11
2014 - New Brunswick, NJ (Hyatt Regency New
Brunswick)/Oct. 19 - 21
2015 - Ft. Washington, MD (Gaylord National Hotel
and Convention Center)/March 15 - 17

Publications:
Membership Directory; on-line
PMGR e-Newsletter; monthly
PMRG Meetings & More; semi-annually

Pharmaceutical Printed Literature Association
(2001)
P.O. Box 722
Batavia, IL 60510
Tel: (630) 777-5709
E-Mail: info@pplaonline.org
Website: pplaonline.org
Members: 25 corporate members
Staff: 4
Annual Budget: $100-250,000
Tax: 501(c)(6)

Personnel:
Executive Director: Robert Brooks
E-Mail: rbrooks@evergreendc.com

Historical Note:
*PPLA provides a forum for members to improve delivery
of information for patient protection, and supports health
care professionals through the advancement of printed
literature to legislative, regulatory and other decision-
making bodies. Represents companies involved in the
production of printed instructional matter for pharmacists,
other health professionals, and consumers.*

Publications:
Membership Directory; on-line

Pharmaceutical Research and Manufacturers of America (PhRMA) (1958)
950 F St. NW
Suite 300
Washington, DC 20004
Tel: (202) 835-3400 *Fax:* (202) 835-3414
Website: phrma.org
Members: 110 companies
Staff: 218
Annual Budget: Over $100,000,000

Personnel:
President and Chief Executive Officer: John J. Castellani
Director, Membership: Mary Beth Aring
E-Mail: MBAring@phrma.org
Senior Vice President, Communications and Public Affairs:
Matt Bennett
E-Mail: mbennett@phrma.org
Executive Vice President, Advocacy: Chip Davis
Deputy Compliance Officer And Assistant General Counsel:
Paul J. Larsen
E-Mail: plarsen@phrma.org

Historical Note:
*Formerly (1994) Pharmaceutical Manufacturers
Association. PhRMA's mission is to conduct effective
advocacy for public policies that encourage discovery of*

important new medicines for patients by pharmaceutical and biotechnology research companies. Members are engaged in the manufacture and marketing of finished dosage form ethical pharmaceutical or biological products or in R&D activities of the same.

Meetings/Conferences: Annual

Publications:
Innovation Insights; on-line
Rx Minute Newsletter; on-line

Membership List Available to Non-members

Phi Alpha Delta (1902)
345 N. Charles St.
Third Floor
Baltimore, MD 21201-4300
Tel: (410) 347-3118 *Fax:* (410) 347-3119
E-Mail: info@pad.org
Website: pad.org
Members: 265000 individuals
Staff: 9
Annual Budget: $1-2,000,000

Personnel:
Executive Director: Andrew D. Sagan
 E-Mail: andrew@pad.org
Director, Technical Development and Editor: Leslie
 Plummer
 E-Mail: leslie@pad.org
Director, Pre-Law Operations: Byron Rupp
 E-Mail: dco@pad.org
Accountant: Kelly Williams
 E-Mail: kelly@pad.org
Coordinator, Membership Services: Rachel Zillig
 E-Mail: rachel@pad.org

Historical Note:
Phi Alpha Delta seeks to advance integrity, compassion and courage through service to the student, the school, the profession and the community. Absorbed Phi Delta Delta, a women's professional law sorority, in 1972. Membership: $25-110/year (Individual).

Publications:
P.A.D. Spotlight; on-line

Phi Alpha Theta (1921)
University of South Florida
4202 E. Fowler Ave. SOC 107
Tampa, FL 33620-8100
Tel: (813) 974-8212 *Fax:* (813) 974-8215
TollFree: (800) 394-8195
E-Mail: info@phialphatheta.org
Website: phialphatheta.org
Members: 350000 individuals
Staff: 3
Annual Budget: $500-1,000,000
Tax: 501(c)(3)

Personnel:
Executive Director: Graydon (Jack) A. Tunstall Jr.
 E-Mail: tunstall@usf.edu
Editor: Kees Boterbloem
 E-Mail: historian@cas.usf.edu

Historical Note:
PAT's mission is to promote the study of history through the encouragement of research, good teaching, publication and the exchange of learning and ideas among historians. PAT seeks to bring students and teachers together for intellectual and social exchanges, which promote and assist historical research and publication by members in a variety of ways. One-time initiation fee: $40.00 (student).

Continuing Education:
Enrollment: 9500

Meetings/Conferences: Biennial

Publications:
PAT Newsletter; quarterly
The Historian; quarterly

Phi Beta Fraternity (1912)
3119 E. Wallings Rd.
Broadview Heights, OH 44147
E-Mail: president@phibeta.com
Website: phibeta.com
Members:
3 collegiate and 10 alumni chapters
400 individuals
Staff: 6
Annual Budget: $10-25,000

Personnel:
National Director, Fraternity Education: Jamie Auberg
 E-Mail: education@phibeta.com

National President: Carrie Frederick
 E-Mail: president@phibeta.com
National Director, Awards: Ann Marie Hardulak
 E-Mail: awardsdirector@phibeta.com
Treasurer: Sam Jones
 E-Mail: treasurer@phibeta.com
National Director, Public Relations: Charlotte Murray
 E-Mail: publicrelations@phibeta.com
National Editor: Cora Willett
 E-Mail: editor@phibeta.com

Historical Note:
Phi Beta Fraternity's mission is to enhance the best in the creative and performing arts, to live a life of service and to seek and develop the highest type of humanity. Membership: $45/year (Individual).

Meetings/Conferences: Annual
Conference Chair: Ann Marie Hardulak

Phi Chi Theta (1924)
1508 E. Belt Line Rd.
Suite 104
Carrollton, TX 75006
Tel: (972) 245-7202
Website: phichitheta.org
Members: 47000 individuals
Staff: 2
Annual Budget: $100-250,000

Personnel:
Executive Director: Saundra Finley
 E-Mail: executivedirector@phichitheta.org
Editor in Chief: David Casey
 E-Mail: iriseditor@phichitheta.or

Historical Note:
Phi Chi Theta is a national professional fraternity. PCT's mission is to provide an opportunity to develop and practice those professional leadership skills and abilities necessary to succeed in the business community and to Provide a local and national network to share resources, ideas and concepts. Membership: $60/year (Individual).

Meetings/Conferences: Annual
Number of non-conference events/year: 1

Publications:
eEdNews; adv.

Phi Delta Chi (1883)
116 N. Lafayette
Suite B
South Lyon, MI 48178
Tel: (800) 732-1883 *Fax:* (248) 486-1906
E-Mail: execdir@phideltachi.org
Website: phideltachi.org
Members: 50000 individuals
Staff: 2
Annual Budget: $100-250,000

Personnel:
Executive Director: Kenny Walkup
 E-Mail: execdir@phideltachi.org
Administrative Assistant: Becky Griffith
 E-Mail: office@phideltachi.org

Historical Note:
PDC's mission is to develop leaders to advance the profession of pharmacy. Membership: $60/year.

Publications:
The e-Communicator; monthly
e-Communicator; adv.
Membership directory; on-line
The Communicator

Phi Delta Epsilon International Medical Fraternity (1904)
1005 N. Northlake Dr.
Hollywood, FL 33019
Tel: (786) 302-1120 *Fax:* (786) 472-7133
E-Mail: phide@phide.org
Website: phide.org
Members: 35000 individuals
Staff: 1

Personnel:
Chief Executive Officer: Karen Katz MD

Historical Note:
PhiDE strives to create physicians with a commitment to its guiding principles of philanthropy, deity and education through fellowship, service, mentoring and formal training in leadership, science and ethics. Membership: $110 (Graduate); $100 (New Student); $50 (Returning Student).

Meetings/Conferences: Annual

Phi Delta Kappa International (1906)
P.O. Box 7888
Bloomington, IN 47407-7888
Tel: (812) 339-1156 *Fax:* (812) 339-0018
TollFree: (800) 766-1156
E-Mail: memberservices@pdkintl.org
Website: pdkintl.org
Members: 36000 individuals
Staff: 31
Annual Budget: $5-10,000,000
Tax: 501(c)(3)

Personnel:
Executive Director: Bill Bushaw
 E-Mail: bbushaw@pdkintl.org
Contact, Accounts Payable: Shirley Carter
 E-Mail: scarter@pdkintl.org
Chief Financial Officer: Gihis de Leede
Assistant Director, Marketing and Communications:
 Carolyn Dew
 E-Mail: cdew@pdkintl.org
Director, Membership and Communications: Ashley
 McDonald Kincaid
 E-Mail: akincaid@pdkintl.org
Assistant Director, Membership Development: Robyn
 Mintier
 E-Mail: rmintier@pdkintl.org
*Executive Admin Assistant and Manager, Admin and
 Technology:* Debbie Webb
 E-Mail: dwebb@pdkintl.org
Managing Editor, Web and Publications: Erin Young
 E-Mail: eyoung@pdkintl.org

Historical Note:
PDK is the professional association for educators. Promotes and enhances teaching through the tenets of leadership, research, and service. Membership: $75 (Professional); $40 (Undergraduate Student/International).

Meetings/Conferences: Annual
2013 - Orlando, FL/April 26 - 28

Publications:
Classroom Tips; on-line
Member Directory; on-line
PDK Connection; quarterly
PDK Edge; bi-monthly
Phi Delta Kappan
The Core; bi-annually

Membership List Available to Non-members

Phi Epsilon Kappa (1913)
901 W. New York St.
Indianapolis, IN 46202
Tel: (317) 627-8745 *Fax:* (317) 278-2041
Website: phiepsilonkappa.org
Members: 3000 individuals
Staff: 2
Annual Budget: $50-100,000

Personnel:
Executive Director: Jeff Vessely
 E-Mail: jvessel@iupui.edu
Journal Editor: Thomas H. Sawyer
 E-Mail: thomas.sawyer@indstate.edu

Historical Note:
PhiEK fosters scientific research and facilitates the exchange of information and experience gained in the various countries of the world. Members are persons engaged in or pursuing careers in physical education, health, recreation, dance, human performance, exercise science, sports medicine and sports management. Membership: $100/year.

Publications:
Black and Gold Bulletin
The Physical Educator; quarterly

Phi Gamma Nu Fraternity (1924)
6745 Cheryl Ann Dr.
Seven Hills, OH 44131
Tel: (216) 524-0019
E-Mail: exedir2@yahoo.com
Website: phigammanu.com
Members: 30000 individuals
Staff: 3

Personnel:
Executive Director: Lorraine A. Scott
 E-Mail: exedir2@yahoo.com
Webmaster: Rahim Ghelani
 E-Mail: webmaster@phigammanu.com
President: Shachar Golan

E-Mail: shachar.golan@gmail.com

Historical Note:
PGN's purpose is to foster the study of business in colleges and universities and to provide a standard of commercial ethics and culture in civic and professional enterprises. Membership: $200/group (Chapter fee); $70 (Individual).

Phi Mu Alpha Sinfonia *(1898)*
10600 Old State Rd.
Evansville, IN 47711
Tel: (812) 867-2433 *Fax:* (812) 867-0633
TollFree: (800) 473-2649
E-Mail: lyrecrest@sinfonia.org
Website: sinfonia.org
Members: 100000 individuals
Staff: 10
Annual Budget: $1-2,000,000

Personnel:
Administrative Coordinator: Kimberly J. Daily
   E-Mail: daily@sinfonia.org
Chief Operating Officer: Jeremy M. Evans
   E-Mail: evans@sinfonia.org
Director, Programs and Education: William C. Lambert
   E-Mail: lambert@sinfonia.org
Retreat Coordinator and Programs Associate: Cameron Miller
   E-Mail: miller@sinfonia.org
Director, Communications: Mark A. Wilson
   E-Mail: wilson@sinfonia.org

Historical Note:
The objective of the fraternity is for the development of the mutual welfare and brotherhood of musical students and to serve music students and to promote the advancement of music in America. Membership: $50 (Lifetime/Sustaining).

Meetings/Conferences: Annual
Conference Chair: Mark A. Wilson
Number of non-conference events/year: 1

Publications:
Membership Directory; on-line
Sinfonia Resonance; bi-monthly
The Red & Black; quarterly
The Sinfonian; semi-annually

Phi Rho Sigma Medical Society *(1890)*
P.O. Box 90264
Indianapolis, IN 46290-0264
Website: phirhosigma.org
Members: 31000 individuals
Staff: 4
Annual Budget: $25-50,000
Tax: 501(c)(7)

Personnel:
President: Elisabeth Righter
Secretary and Treasurer: Julie Best
Editor: Gabriel Cuka
Editor: Sheryl Mascarenhas

Historical Note:
Phi Rho Sigma Medical Society is dedicated to the enhancement of medical education, service to humanity, and fellowship among its members. Membership: $35/year.

Publications:
Membership Directory; on-line
The Journal of Phi Rho Sigma

The Philanthropy Roundtable *(1991)*
1730 M St. NW
Suite 601
Washington, DC 20036
Tel: (202) 822-8333 *Fax:* (202) 822-8325
E-Mail: main@philanthropyroundtable.org
Website: philanthropyroundtable.org
Members: 650 individuals
Staff: 22
Annual Budget: $5-10,000,000
Tax: 501(c)(3)

Personnel:
President: Adam Meyerson
   E-Mail: ameyerson@philanthropyroundtable.org
Director, Technology: Brian Anderson
   E-Mail: banderson@philanthropyroundtable.org
Director, K-12 Education Programs: Dan Fishman
   E-Mail: dfishman@philanthropyroundtable.org
Director, External Affairs: Alison Hawkins
   E-Mail: ahawkins@philanthropyroundtable.org
Manager, Membership Services: Michael Horn
   E-Mail: mhorn@philanthropyroundtable.org
Editor-in-Chief: Christopher Levenick

E-Mail: clevenick@philanthropyroundtable.org
Director, Finance and Human Resources: Suzi Marchena
   E-Mail: smarchena@philanthropyroundtable.org
Director, Regional Events: Dorothy Martinez
   E-Mail: dmartinez@philanthropyroundtable.org
Director, Annual Meetings: Lindsay Miller
   E-Mail: lmiller@philanthropyroundtable.org
Senior Vice President, Public Policy: Sue Santa
   E-Mail: ssanta@philanthropyroundtable.org
Chief Operating Officer: Shannon Toronto
   E-Mail: storonto@philanthropyroundtable.org

Historical Note:
Mission is to foster excellence in philanthropy, to protect philanthropic freedom, to assist donors in achieving their philanthropic intent, and to help donors advance liberty, opportunity, and personal responsibility in America and abroad. Members gain access to a donor community interested in philanthropic strategies and programs that actually work. Members include corporate giving representatives, foundation staff, estate officers and individual donors. Membership: $500-25,000/year.

Meetings/Conferences: Annual
Conference Chair: Lindsay Miller
2013 - Rancho Palos Verdes, CA (Terranea Resort)/Oct. 17 - 19
2014 - Salt Lake City, UT (Grand America Hotel)/Oct. 9 - 11
Number of non-conference events/year: 2

Publications:
Philanthropy

Philosophy of Education Society *(1941)*
1015 W. Main St.
Richmond, VA 23284-2020
Tel: (804) 827-8415
Website: philosophyofeducation.org
Members: 500 individuals
Staff: 1
Annual Budget: $25-50,000

Personnel:
Executive Director: Kurt Stemhagen
   E-Mail: krstemhagen@vcu.edu

Historical Note:
PES's mission is to promote the fundamental philosophic treatment of the problems of education. Membership: $35-85 (Individual, based on income); $25 (Emeriti).

Meetings/Conferences: Annual
2013 - Portland, OR (Benson Hotel)/March 14 - 18

Publications:
Educational Theory; bi-monthly; adv.
Membership Directory; annually
PES Yearbook; annually

Philosophy of Science Association *(1934)*
Bloomsburg University
Department of Philosophy
Bloomsburg, PA 17815
Tel: (570) 389-4174 *Fax:* (949) 824-8388
Website: philsci.org
Members: 950 individuals
Staff: 3
Annual Budget: $50-100,000
Tax: 501(c)(3)

Personnel:
President: James Woodward
Executive Secretary and Treasurer: Gary Hardcastle
   E-Mail: ghardcas@bloomu.edu

Historical Note:
PSA is a member of the International Union of History and Philosophy of Science. PSA's mission is to promote research, teaching, and free discussion of issues in the philosophy of science from diverse standpoints. Membership: $72-209 (Individual-Income); $28 (Student/Retired); $46 (Members-British Society for the Philosophy of Science).

Meetings/Conferences: Biennial

Publications:
Philosophy of Science; adv.
PSA Newsletter; irregular

Membership List Available to Non-members

Photo Chemical Machining Institute *(1967)*
11 Robert Toner Blvd.
Suite 234
N. Attleboro, MA 02763
Tel: (508) 385-0085 *Fax:* (508) 232-6005
E-Mail: info@pcmi.org

Website: pcmi.org
Members: 210 companies
Staff: 2
Annual Budget: $100-250,000
Tax: 501(c)(6)

Personnel:
Executive Director and Meeting Contact: Catherine Flaherty CAE
   E-Mail: cflaherty@pcmi.org
Treasurer: Philip Greiner

Historical Note:
PCMI's mission is to monitor developments in photo chemical machining and to address problems that may affect the process or the industry worldwide. PCMI members are manufacturers and users of photo chemically machined parts, companies that supply raw materials, equipment and services used to produce its products. Membership: $1,300 (Regular/Allied/Associate); $950 (Associate Membership-Artwork only); Free (Senior).

Meetings/Conferences: Annual
Conference Chair: Catherine Flaherty CAE

Publications:
Membership Directory; annually; adv.
PCMI Journal; semi-annually; adv.

Photoimaging Manufacturers and Distributors Association *(1939)*
7600 Jericho Tnpk.
Suite 301
Woodbury, NY 11797
Tel: (516) 802-0895 *Fax:* (516) 364-0140
Website: pmda.com
Members: 78 companies
Staff: 3
Annual Budget: $250-500,000

Personnel:
Executive Director: Jerry Grossman
   E-Mail: jerry@pmda.com
Editor: Jackie Augustine
   E-Mail: jackie@pmda.com
Administrator: Michelle Tramantano
   E-Mail: michellepmda@hotmail.com

Historical Note:
Formerly (1999) Photographic Manufacturers and Distributors Association. PMDA seeks to advocate imaging, to involve member companies in charting the industry's future and to gain perspective on technologies and business methods that will enhance its members' standing in the marketplace. Members are photo imaging product manufacturers and distributors. Membership: $750 (Associate); $1,500 (Voting).

Publications:
ENewsletter; on-line

Membership List Available to Non-members

Photoluminescent Safety Association *(2006)*
2001 Jefferson Davis Hwy.
Suite 1004
Arlington, VA 22202-3617
Tel: (703) 416-0060 *Fax:* (703) 416-0014
E-Mail: info@plsafety.org
Website: plsafety.org
Staff: 2
Annual Budget: $25-50,000

Personnel:
President: Phil Befumo
Treasurer: Al Carlson

Historical Note:
PSA's mission is to generate broad-based acceptance of safety-grade photoluminescent products. Photoluminescent products improve safety through such products as exit signs, low-level egress pathway marking systems, and general safety signage. Membership is open to photoluminescent manufacturers and distributors, as well as organizations in allied fields. Membership: $2000 (Regular); $250 (Service Organization); $100 (Associate).

Meetings/Conferences: Annual
Number of non-conference events/year: 1

Publications:
Membership Directory; on-line

Phycological Society of America *(1946)*
C/O John Wiley and Sons Inc.
350 Main St.
Malden, MA 02148
Tel: (781) 388-8599 *Fax:* (781) 388-8270
TollFree: (800) 835-6770

E-Mail: cs-membership@wiley.com
Website: psaalgae.org
Members: 1200 individuals
Staff: 5
Annual Budget: $250-500,000

Personnel:
President: Juan M. Lopez-Bautista
  E-Mail: jlopez@bama.ua.edu
Director, Programs: Dale Casmatta
  E-Mail: dcasamat@unf.edu
Managing Editor: Michael H. Graham
  E-Mail: jphycol@mlml.calstate.edu
Director, Communications: Louise A. Lewis
  E-Mail: louise.lewis@uconn.edu
Director, Membership: Deborah L. Robertson
  E-Mail: DebRobertson@clarku.edu

Historical Note:
PSA aims to promote research and teaching in all fields
of Phycology and in particular, basic and applied research
of algae. Members are individuals interested in phycology.
Membership: $25-100 (USA); $25-105 (Canada/Mexico);
$25-125 (Rest of World); $2,200 (Life); $65 (Individual);
$195 (Institution); $45 (Student).

Meetings/Conferences: Annual
Conference Chair: Dale Casmatta
2014 - Portland, OR/May 18 - 23

Publications:
Journal of Phycology; bi-monthly; adv.
Membership Directory; on-line
Phycological Newsletter; on-line

Physician Assistant Education Association (1972)
300 N. Washington St.
Suite 710
Alexandria, VA 22314
Tel: (703) 548-5538 Fax: (703) 548-5539
E-Mail: info@PAEAonline.org
Website: paeaonline.org
Members:
142 PA Programs, 1500 individuals
131 programs
Staff: 15
Annual Budget: $2-5,000,000
Tax: 501(c)(3)

Personnel:
Executive Director: Timi Agar Barwick
  E-Mail: tbarwick@paeaonline.org
Assistant Director, Communications and Information
  Technology: Geraldene Darden
  E-Mail: gdarden@paeaonline.org
Research Assistant: Rachel Hamann
  E-Mail: rhamann@paeaonline.org
Assistant Director, Finance & Administration: Lynn
  Heitzman
  E-Mail: lheitzman@paeaonline.org
Associate Executive Director, Director, Meeting Services and
  Education: Jennifer Jarmin
  E-Mail: jjarmin@paeaonline.org
Director, Communication: Jeanette Smith
  E-Mail: jsmith@PAEAonline.org
Manager, Communications and Marketing: Todd Usher
  E-Mail: tusher@paeaonline.org

Historical Note:
PAEA was founded under the name of APAP in 1972.
PAEA's mission is to pursue excellence, foster faculty
development, advance the body of knowledge that defines
quality education and patient- centered care, and promote
diversity in all aspects of physician assistant education.
Membership: $3,065 (Program Member); $2,220
(Institutional Colleague); $75 (Individual).

Meetings/Conferences: Annual
Conference Chair: Jennifer Jarmin
2013 - Memphis, TN (Peabody Memphis)/Oct. 14 - 19
2014 - Philadelphia, PA (Marriott Philadelphia
  DownTown)/Oct. 15 - 19

Publications:
Journal of Physician Assistant Education; quarterly
PAEA Networker; monthly

Physician Insurers Association of America (1977)
2275 Research Blvd.
Suite 250
Rockville, MD 20850-6213
Tel: (301) 947-9000 Fax: (301) 947-9090
Website: piaa.us
Members: 69 companies
Staff: 18

Annual Budget: $2-5,000,000

Personnel:
President and Chief Executive Officer: Brian Atchinson
  E-Mail: batchinson@piaa.us
Director, Public Relations and Marketing: Eric R.
  Anderson
  E-Mail: eanderson@piaa.us
Manager, Information Technology and Database: Wen-Lu
  Chao
  E-Mail: wchao@piaa.us
Director, Business Development and Membership Services:
  Ginny Echeverria
  E-Mail: ginnye@piaa.us
Director, Finance and Accounting: Betty Hong
  E-Mail: bhong@piaa.us
Director, Human Resources and Administration: Jill K. Kerr
  E-Mail: jknerr@piaa.us
Director, Loss Prevention and Research: P. Divya Parikh
  E-Mail: dparikh@piaa.us
Director, Meetings and Education: Jan Ross
  E-Mail: jross@piaa.us
Director, Government Relations: Mike Stinson
  E-Mail: mstinson@piaa.us

Historical Note:
PIAA's mission is to assist its members through education,
patient safety initiatives, research, and government
relations. Membership: $8,300-53,750 (Domestic Regular/
Domestic Associate); $7,225-45,150 (International
Regular/International Associate).

Meetings/Conferences: Annual
Conference Chair: Jan Ross
2013 - Palm Desert, CA (JW Marriott Desert Springs
  Resort and Spa)/May 15 - 17
2014 - Toronto, ON (Fairmont Royal York)/May 14 - 16
2015 - Las Vegas, NV (Caesars Palace Las Vegas Hotel
  and Casino)/May 13 - 15
Number of non-conference events/year: 10

Publications:
Cryptogram; bi-annually
Newsbriefs; weekly
Physician Insurer Magazine; quarterly
Research Notes; bi-annually

Physician Office Managers Association of America (2008)
P.O. Box 232
Dallastown, PA 17313
Tel: (717) 825-0094 Fax: (866) 359-0561
TollFree: (877) 782-5141
E-Mail: national@pomaa.net
Website: pomaa.net
Staff: 3

Personnel:
Executive Director and Founder: Desiree R. Baylin
  E-Mail: desiree@pomaa.net
Director, Membership and Certification Services: Denys
  Meade
  E-Mail: Denys@pomaa.net
Director, Corporate Sponsorship and Exhibitors: Jeanine
  Villabon
  E-Mail: Jeanine@pomaa.net

Historical Note:
POMAA is a national professional organization for medical
office and practice managers to help with the needs of
physician office management. POMAA has a board of
several practice and administrative managers along with a
physician and national healthcare speaker working in the
healthcare environment. Membership: $155.00 (Student/
Billing Manager/Specialist/Practice/Administrative
Managers); $500.00 (Sponsorship for Corporations);
$40.00 (International).

Continuing Education:
Certification Designation/s: CPM, CHRS, CMPCS, CMOS,
CMBM, CHITS

Meetings/Conferences:
Conference Chair: Jeanine Villabon
2013 - Orlando, FL (Walt Disney World Swan)/Sept. 18
  - 21

Publications:
E-News; weekly
Membership Directory; on-line
Practice Made Perfect - News from POMAA

Pi Gamma Mu (1924)
1001 Millington
Suite B
Winfield, KS 67156

Tel: (620) 221-3128 Fax: (620) 221-7124
E-Mail: pgm@sckans.edu
Website: pigammamu.org
Members: 150 active chapters
Staff: 2
Annual Budget: $100-250,000

Personnel:
Executive Director: Sue Watters
  E-Mail: pgm@sckans.edu
Legal Counsel: Michelle Price

Historical Note:
Formerly The National Social Science Honor Society, Pi
Gamma Mu, Inc.,Pi Gamma Mu's mission is to encourage
and promote excellence in the social sciences and to uphold
the ideals of scholarship and service. Membership: $40
(international).

Meetings/Conferences: Triennial
2014 - North Charleston, SC (Crowne Plaza Charleston
  Airport - Convention Center)/Oct. 16 - 18

Publications:
International Social Science Review; semi-annually
PI GAMMA MU NEWSLETTER

Pi Lambda Theta (1910)
P.O. Box 7888
Bloomington, IN 47407-7888
Tel: (812) 339-1156 Fax: (812) 339-0018
TollFree: (800) 766-1156
E-Mail: plt@pdkintl.org
Website: pilambda.org
Members: 13000 individuals
Staff: 9
Annual Budget: $500-1,000,000
Tax: 501(c)(3)

Personnel:
Executive Director: Bill Bushaw
  E-Mail: bbushaw@pdkintl.org
Assistant Director, Marketing and Communications:
  Carolyn Dew
Assistant Director, Office Operations: Jacquie Groves
  E-Mail: jgroves@pdkintl.org
Director, Marketing and Communications: Ashley
  McDonald Kincaid
  E-Mail: akincaid@pdkintl.org
Assistant Director, Membership Development: Robyn
  Mintier
  E-Mail: rmintier@pdkintl.org
Chief Financial Officer: Cathy Ruf
  E-Mail: cruf@pdkintl.org
Assistant Director, Resource Development: Holly Thrasher
  E-Mail: hthrasher@pdkintl.org
Graphic Designer: Victoria Voelker
  E-Mail: vvoelker@pdkintl.org
Managing Editor, Web and Publications: Erin Young
  E-Mail: eyoung@pdkintl.org

Historical Note:
PLT's mission is to honor the accomplishments of exemplary
educators and support the continuing development of
knowledge and skills aimed at providing leadership for
colleagues and enhanced learning for students. In 2010,
Pi Lambda Theta joined the PDK International family
of associations, which includes PDK International and
the Future Educators Association. Membership: $29-40
(Student/Professional).

Publications:
Educational Horizons; quarterly
The Core; bi-monthly

Pi Sigma Epsilon (1952)
3747 S. Howell Ave.
Milwaukee, WI 53207
Tel: (414) 328-1952 Fax: (414) 328-1953
E-Mail: pse@pse.org
Website: pse.org
Staff: 7
Annual Budget: $250-500,000

Personnel:
Executive Director: Ann Devine
  E-Mail: ann.devine@pse.org
Director, Membership: Lynnette Hahn
Manager, Communications: Tracy Krueger
Media Manager and Website Administrator: Tracy
  McCarthy
  E-Mail: tracy.mccarthy@pse.org
Manager, Finance: Eric Rosandich

Historical Note:

PSE, a professional fraternity affiliated with Sales and Marketing Executives, International, works to develop the sales and marketing skills of its members through lifelong opportunities. Membership: $125-350/year.

Meetings/Conferences: Annual
2013 - San Diego, CA (Town and Country Resort Hotel)/April 1 - 7

Publications:
Dotted Lines
Journal of Personal Selling & Sales Management; quarterly
Slice of Pi

Piano Manufacturers Association International (1891)
14070 Proton Rd.
Suite 100, LB 9
Dallas, TX 75244
Tel: (972) 233-9107 *Fax:* (972) 490-4219
Members: 20 companies
Staff: 1
Annual Budget: $250-500,000
Tax: 501(c)(6)

Personnel:
President: Brian Chung

Historical Note:
Formerly (1986) the National Piano Manufacturers Association. Supports the National Piano Foundation (same address) as its educational arm.

Publications:
NPF Piano Notes; quarterly

Piano Technicians Guild (1957)
4444 Forest Ave.
Kansas City, KS 66106
Tel: (913) 432-9975 *Fax:* (913) 432-9986
E-Mail: ptg@ptg.org
Website: ptg.org
Members: 4100 individuals
Staff: 8
Annual Budget: $1-2,000,000

Personnel:
Executive Director: Barbara Cassaday
  E-Mail: barbara@ptg.org
Manager, Marketing: Shawn Bruce
  E-Mail: shawn@ptg.org
Internet Developer: Alec Foster
  E-Mail: alec@ptg.org
Manager, Finance and Administration: Jason Hensley
  E-Mail: jason@ptg.org
Manager, Development and Merchandise: Kathy Maxwell
  E-Mail: kathy@ptg.org
Manager, Member Services and Conventions: Sandy Roady
  E-Mail: sandy@ptg.org
Art and Design Manager: Jason Wheeler
  E-Mail: jasonw@ptg.org

Historical Note:
Formed in 1957 by a consolidation of the American Society of Piano Technicians and the National Association of Piano Tuners. PTG's mission is to promote service and technical standards among its members, piano tuners and technicians. Membership dues are decided on annual basis.

Meetings/Conferences: Annual
Conference Chair: Sandy Roady
2013 - Chicago, IL (Hyatt Regency O'Hare)/July 10 - 14
Number of non-conference events/year: 6

Publications:
Membership Directory; annually
Piano Technicians Journal; monthly; adv.

Pickle Packers International (1893)
1620 I St. NW
Suite 925
Washington, DC 20006
Tel: (202) 331-2465 *Fax:* (202) 463-8998
Website: ilovepickles.org
Members: 250 companies
Staff: 3
Annual Budget: $500-1,000,000

Personnel:
Executive Vice President: Brian Bursiek
  E-Mail: bbursiek@therobertsgroup.net

Historical Note:
Formerly (1963) National Pickle Packers Association. PPI is a voluntary not for profit trade association representing pickled vegetables worldwide. Members are manufacturers

of pickles and other fermented or acidified vegetables, suppliers of salt, salt stock brokers, and other suppliers to the industry. Membership: 1530/year(Manufacturer/Associate/Broker).

Meetings/Conferences: Annual

Publications:
Membership Directory; on-line

Picture Archive Council of America (1951)
23046 Avenida de la Carlota
Suite 600
Laguna Hills, CA 92653-1537
Tel: (714) 815-8427 *Fax:* (949) 282-5066
Website: pacaoffice.org
Members: 170 firms
Staff: 3
Annual Budget: $250-500,000

Personnel:
Executive Director: Cathy Aron
  E-Mail: execdirector@pacaoffice.org
Assistant Director: Morgan Dawirs
  E-Mail: assistdirector@pacaoffice.org

Historical Note:
PACA's mission is to support and protect the interests of the picture archive community through advocacy, education and communication. Membership: $565 (International); $875-27,500 (General); $425 (Friend of PACA); $795-5,670 (Corporate Sponsor).

Meetings/Conferences: Annual
Conference Chair: Cathy Aron

Publications:
Membership Directory; on-line
PACA Update; bi-weekly
What's New; semi-monthly; adv.

Piedmontese Association of the United States (1984)
57975 703 Rd.
Diller, NE 68342-4001
E-Mail: paus343@yahoo.com
Website: pauscattle.org
Members: 400 individuals
Staff: 3
Annual Budget: $50-100,000

Personnel:
President: Dennis Hennerberg

Historical Note:
PAUS's mission is to promote, stimulate, encourage, develop and regulate the breeding of the Piedmontese cattle in the United States. Membership: $100 (Annual); $50 (Associate); $25 (Junior); $1,000 (Lifetime, New); $150 (International Annual); $75 (International Associate).

Meetings/Conferences:
Conference Chair: Dennis Hennerberg

Publications:
Membership Directory; annually; adv.
PAUS On The MOO-VE; quarterly; adv.
Piedmontese Profile; semi-annually; adv.

Membership List Available to Non-members

Pierre Fauchard Academy (1936)
P.O. Box 3718
Mesquite, NV 89024-3718
Tel: (702) 345-2950 *Fax:* (702) 345-5031
TollFree: (800) 232-0099
Website: fauchard.org
Members:
50 state organizations
6000 individuals
Staff: 2
Annual Budget: $500-1,000,000
Tax: 501(c)(6)

Personnel:
Executive Director: Judith D. Kozal
  E-Mail: pfajdk@aol.com

Historical Note:
An international honorary dental organization that recognizes achievements by dentists. PFA's mission is to advance the field of dental health through scholarships, provision of needed services to the public, continuing education, faculty development, and support of other charitable projects in dentistry. Funds are provided through bequests, donations, planned giving memorial donations, investments and grants. Academy members are dentists. Membership: $100/year.

Meetings/Conferences: Annual
2013 - New Orleans, LA/Oct. 31 - Nov. 5

Publications:
Dental Abstracts; bi-monthly
Dental World; bi-monthly
Membership Directory; on-line
PFA Newsletter

Membership List Available to Non-members

Pile Driving Contractors Association (1996)
1857 Wells Rd., Suite 6
P.O. Box 66208
Orange Park, FL 32065
Tel: (904) 215-4771 *Fax:* (904) 215-2977
TollFree: (888) 311-7322
E-Mail: steve@piledrivers.org
Website: piledrivers.org
Members: 300 companies
Staff: 3
Annual Budget: $250-500,000
Tax: 501(c)(6)

Personnel:
Executive Director: Stevan A. Hall
  E-Mail: steve@piledrivers.org
Director, Education and Events: Lori L. Schneider
  E-Mail: lori@piledrivers.org

Historical Note:
PDCA is an organization of pile driving contractors that seeks to increase the use of driven piles for deep foundations and earth retention systems. PDCA's mission is to advocate driven piles and provide exceptional support and services to their members. Membership: $100-850 (Contractor/National Associate); $100 (Technical Affiliate/Retired Industry/Affiliate Labor Organization); $20 (Student); $50 (Individual/Retired).

Meetings/Conferences: Annual
Conference Chair: Lori L. Schneider
Number of non-conference events/year: 1

Publications:
E-Letters; monthly
Pile Driver Magazine

Pine Chemicals Association (1947)
1098 Ashbury Dr.
Decatur, GA 30030
Tel: (404) 994-6267 *Fax:* (404) 994-6267
Website: pinechemicals.org
Members: 60 companies
Staff: 2
Annual Budget: $500-1,000,000

Personnel:
President and Chief Operating Officer: Charlie Morris
  E-Mail: cwmorris@pinechemicals.org

Historical Note:
Formerly known as the Tall Oil Association. PCA is an association of producers, processors and consumers of pine chemicals that promotes innovative, safe and environmentally responsible practices to assure a reliable supply of products. Membership: $2,500 (Producer); $5,000-20,000 (Fractionator); $2,000-4,000 (User Pine Chemicals); $1,000-2,000 (Associate).

Meetings/Conferences:
Conference Chair: Cheryl Morgan
2013 - Barcelona, Spain (Hotel Rey Juan Carlos I)/Sept. 15 - 17

Publications:
Member Directory; on-line
PCA Newsletter; quarterly

Pinto Horse Association of America (1956)
7330 NW 23rd St.
Bethany, OK 73008
Tel: (405) 491-0111 *Fax:* (405) 787-0773
E-Mail: membership@pinto.org
Website: pinto.org
Members: 12000 membership units
Staff: 13
Annual Budget: $1-2,000,000
Tax: 501(c)(5)

Personnel:
Executive Vice President and Chief Operating Officer: Darrell L. Bilke
  E-Mail: membership@pinto.org
Director, Communications, Marketing and Editor: Meriruth Cohenour
  E-Mail: mcohenour@pinto.org
Contact, Human Resources: Dorothy Fread
  E-Mail: dfread@pinto.org

Contact, Conventions, World Show and Congress Stalling: Kim Hall

    E-Mail: khall@pinto.org

Contact, Information Technology: Fred Kinder

    E-Mail: fkinder@pinto.org

Historical Note:

PtHA maintains the registry for the Pinto breed and sets standards for conformation, color, performance and encourages the showing of the Pinto breed. Members are breeders and owners of Pinto horses. Membership: $40 (Individual/Corporate/Partnership); $15 (Youth); $10 (Amateur/Novice).

Meetings/Conferences:

Conference Chair: Kim Hall

Publications:

Pinto Horse Online; quarterly

The Pinto Horse Quarterly; quarterly

Pipe Fabrication Institute (1913)

511 Avenue of the Americas

Suite 601

New York, NY 10011

Tel: (514) 634-3434 Fax: (514) 634-9736

E-Mail: pfi@pfi-institute.org

Website: pfi-institute.org

Members: 54 companies

Staff: 2

Annual Budget: $250-500,000

Tax: 501(c)(6)

Personnel:

Executive Director: Guy Fortin

    E-Mail: guy.fortin@pfi-institute.org

Legal Counsel: Scott Zimmerman Esq.

    E-Mail: szimmerman@reedsmith.com

Historical Note:

PFI's primary purpose is to promote standards of excellence in the pipe fabrication industry. Membership: $1,800 (Charter); $600 (Contractor/Affiliate); $1,200 (Associate).

Meetings/Conferences: Semi-Annual

2013 - Pittsburgh, PA (Fairmont Pittsburgh)/May 29 - June 4

2014 - Tuscaloosa, AL (Hotel Capstone)/March 29 - April 1

Number of non-conference events/year: 1

Membership List Available to Non-members

Pipe Line Contractors Association (1948)

1700 Pacific Ave.

Suite 4100

Dallas, TX 75201-4675

Tel: (214) 969-2700 Fax: (214) 969-2705

E-Mail: plca@plca.org

Website: plca.org

Members: 130 companies

Staff: 4

Annual Budget: $1-2,000,000

Tax: 501(c)(6)

Personnel:

Executive Director: Kevin N. Barrett

    E-Mail: kbarrett@plca.org

Administrative Manager: Kerrie Horn

    E-Mail: plca@plca.org

Managing Director and General Counsel: J. Patrick Tielborg

    E-Mail: jptielborg@plca.org

Historical Note:

PLCA negotiates labor agreements, encourage safe practices in pipeline construction and seek the resolution of problems common to all those in the industry. Members are builders of cross-country pipelines and their suppliers. Membership: $4,000 (Associate); $4,000-25,000 (Regular).

Meetings/Conferences: Annual

2013 - Scottsdale, AZ (Hyatt Regency Scottsdale Resort and Spa)/Feb. 12 - 16

2014 - Bonita Springs, FL (Hyatt Regency Coconut Point Resort and Spa)/Feb. 18 - 22

2015 - Carlsbad, CA (Park Hyatt Aviara)/Feb. 24 - 28

Publications:

Labor Newsletter; weekly

Members Directory; on-line

PLCA Weekly Newsletter; weekly

Membership List Available to Non-members

Pipe Tobacco Council, Inc. (1988)

818 Connecticut Ave. NW

Suite 200

Washington, DC 20006

Tel: (202) 223-8204 Fax: (202) 833-0379

Website: cigarassociation.org

Members: 10 companies

Staff: 1

Annual Budget: $50-100,000

Tax: 501(c)(6)

Personnel:

President: Craig P. Williamson

Historical Note:

A division of Cigar Association of America. PTA advances and fosters the economic interests of its members who represent the pipe and smoking tobacco industry.

Pipeline Research Council International, Inc. (1952)

3141 Fairview Park Dr.

Suite 525

Falls Church, VA 22042

Tel: (703) 205-1600 Fax: (703) 205-1607

E-Mail: info@prci.org

Website: prci.org

Members: 53 corporations

Staff: 10

Annual Budget: $10-25,000,000

Tax: 501(c)(6)

Personnel:

President: Cliff Johnson

Senior Program Manager: Gary Choquette

Research Manager: Carrie Greaney

Administrative Assistant: Holly Sauer

Manager, Membership and Communications: Natalie M. Tessel

    E-Mail: ntessel@prci.org

Historical Note:

Founded as Pipeline Research Committee, an autonomous program of the American Gas Association. PRCI's mission is to conduct a collaboratively funded research program that enables energy pipeline companies around the world to provide safe, reliable, environmentally compatible, and cost effective service to meet customer energy requirements. Members are companies operating natural gas transmission and crude oil and petroleum products pipelines, companies that have a commitment to the energy pipeline industry and capabilities in technology transfer, particularly commercialization.

Meetings/Conferences: Annual

Conference Chair: Gary Choquette

Publications:

Throughput; quarterly

PKF North American Network (1969)

1745 N. Brown Rd.

Suite 350

Lawrenceville, GA 30043

Tel: (770) 279-4560 Fax: (770) 279-4566

Website: pkfna.com

Members: 244 member firms

Staff: 21

Annual Budget: $5-10,000,000

Personnel:

President and Chief Executive Officer: Terry L. Snyder CPA

    E-Mail: tsnyder@pkfnan.org

Chief Operating Officer: Jack Charlesworth CITP, CPA

Media Contact: Melissa Gracey

    E-Mail: mgracey@bdpb.com

Contact, Member Development: Carolyn Morgan

    E-Mail: cmorgan@pkfna.org

Historical Note:

Formerly (1998) Associated Regional Accounting Firms. PKF North American Network is an association of independently owned and operated accounting and consulting firms with offices throughout North America. The association helps members to improve, become more profitable and remain independent.

Continuing Education:

Certification Designation/s: CRM

Meetings/Conferences: Semi-Annual

Conference Chair: Jack Charlesworth CITP, CPA

Number of non-conference events/year: 2

Plains Cotton Growers, Inc. (1956)

4517 W. Loop 289

Lubbock, TX 79414-1235

Tel: (806) 792-4904 Fax: (806) 792-4906

E-Mail: pcg@plainscotton.org

Website: plainscotton.org

Members: 25000 growers

Staff: 5

Annual Budget: $5-10,000,000

Tax: 501(c)(5)

Personnel:

Executive Vice President: Steve Verett

    E-Mail: steve@plainscotton.org

Director, Communications and Public Affairs: Mary Jane Buerkle

    E-Mail: maryjane@plainscotton.org

Director, Policy Analysis and Research: Shawn Wade

    E-Mail: shawn@plainscotton.org

Office Manager: Julie Wheeler

    E-Mail: julie@plainscotton.org

Historical Note:

PCG works to encourage and protect the interests of plains cotton producers, provide an additional medium of information for plains cotton producers and to foster improvement of the conditions under which plains cotton is produced and sold. Membership: $25/year.

Meetings/Conferences: Annual

Publications:

Cotton News; weekly

Membership List Available to Non-members

Plan Sponsor Council of America (1947)

20 N. Wacker Dr.

Suite 3700

Chicago, IL 60606

Tel: (312) 419-1863 Fax: (312) 419-1864

E-Mail: psca@psca.org

Website: psca.org

Members: 1200 companies

Staff: 15

Annual Budget: $1-2,000,000

Personnel:

Interim President and Executive Director: Robert A. Benish

    E-Mail: bob.benish@psca.org

Vice President, Membership Development: Tom Brace

    E-Mail: tom.brace@psca.org

Consultant, Communications and Editor: Kara Clark

    E-Mail: kara@psca.org

Manager, Research: Hattie Greenan

    E-Mail: hattie@psca.org

Associate, Marketing: Meredith Kopelman

    E-Mail: meredith.kopelman@psca.org

Director, Marketing and Events: Jen Rogers

    E-Mail: jennifer.rogers@psca.org

Historical Note:

PSCA promotes the idea that profit sharing, 401(k) and related savings and incentive programs strengthen the free-enterprise system, empower and motivate the workforce, improve domestic and international competitiveness and provide a vital source of retirement income. PSCA's mission is to encourage the use of profit sharing, 401(k) and related savings and incentive programs by increasing business, employee, government, media, academia and public awareness of their benefits. Membership: $315-4,095/year (Associate, Based Number of People Employed).

Meetings/Conferences: Annual

Conference Chair: Jen Rogers

2013 - Scottsdale, AZ (Fairmont Scottsdale Princess)/ Sept. 9 - 12

Number of non-conference events/year: 2

Publications:

Defined Contribution Insights Magazine; bi-monthly

Membership Roster; on-line

PSCA's Executive Report; monthly

PlanetSpace, Inc. (2005)

39 S. LaSalle

Suite 600

Chicago, IL 60603

Tel: (877) 872-7928 Fax: (312) 726-1812

E-Mail: info@planetspace.org

Website: planetspace.org

Staff: 1

Personnel:

President and Chief Executive Officer: Geoff Sheerin

Historical Note:

PlanetSpace, Inc. is a leader in commercializing space and developer of space related technologies. Its mission is to make space travel accessible to the general public.

Plant Growth Regulation Society of America (1973)

1018 Duke St.
Alexandria, VA 22314
Tel: (703) 836-4606 *Fax:* (706) 883-8215
E-Mail: pgrsa@ashs.org
Website: pgrsa.org
Members: 25 companies and 300 individuals
Staff: 3
Annual Budget: $25-50,000

Personnel:
Executive Director: Dr. Sonja L. Maki PhD
  E-Mail: smaki@carleton.edu
Executive Secretary: Dawn Mancini
  E-Mail: dmancini@ashs.org
Business Manager: Sally Mayeux

Historical Note:
*PGRSA's primary purpose is to disseminate information
concerning regulation of plant growth that results in safe,
environmentally sound, and efficient production of food,
fiber, and ornamentals. Membership: $40 (Individual, North
America, U.S., Canada and Mexico); $55 (International);
$15 (Student); $500-2500 (Sustaining).*

Continuing Education:
Certification Designation/s: CCA, PCA

Meetings/Conferences: Annual
Number of non-conference events/year: 2

Publications:
PGRSA Quarterly - Newsletter; quarterly

Plasma Protein Therapeutics Association *(1992)*
147 Old Solomons Island Rd.
Suite 100
Annapolis, MD 21401
Tel: (202) 789-3100 *Fax:* (410) 263-2298
E-Mail: ppta@pptaglobal.org
Website: pptaglobal.org
Members: 51 Companies
Staff: 25
Annual Budget: $10-25,000,000
Tax: 501(c)(6)

Personnel:
President and Chief Executive Officer: Jan M. Bult
  E-Mail: jbult@pptaglobal.org
Senior Vice President: Julie A. Birkofer
  E-Mail: jbirkofer@pptaglobal.org
Senior Director, Legal Affairs: John Delacourt
  E-Mail: jdelacourt@pptaglobal.org
Director, Finance: Laurella Ganey
  E-Mail: lganey@pptaglobal.org
Vice President, Global Regulatory Policy: Mary Gustafson
  E-Mail: mgustafson@pptaglobal.org
Director, Membership Services: Cathy Izzi
  E-Mail: cizzi@pptaglobal.org
Director, Federal Affairs: Kym Kilbourne
  E-Mail: kkilbourne@pptaglobal.org
Senior Manager, Communications: Lisa LoVullo
  E-Mail: llovullo@pptaglobal.org
Director, Information Technology and Facilities: Mike
  McCormick
  E-Mail: mmccormick@pptaglobal.org
Manager, Office and Events: Sophie Van Puyvelde
  E-Mail: sophie@pptaglobal.eu
Manager, Certification Programs: Mary Straub
  E-Mail: mstraub@pptaglobal.org

Historical Note:
*PPTA's mission is to promote the availability of and access
to safe and effective plasma protein therapeutics for all
patients in the world. It also acts an advocate for producers
of plasma-based and recombinant biological therapeutics.*

Continuing Education:
Certification Designation/s: QSEAL, IQPP

Meetings/Conferences:
Conference Chair: Sophie Van Puyvelde
Number of non-conference events/year: 1

Publications:
Health Policy Update
Leadership Briefing; weekly
Source Essentials; quarterly
The Source Magazine; quarterly; adv.

Plastic Pipe and Fittings Association *(1978)*
800 Roosevelt Rd.
Building C, Suite 312
Glen Ellyn, IL 60137
Tel: (630) 858-6540 *Fax:* (630) 790-3095
Website: ppfahome.org
Members: 77 companies

Staff: 5
Annual Budget: $1-2,000,000
Tax: 501(c)(6)

Personnel:
Association Coordinator: Briana Gunn
  E-Mail: brianag@cmservices.com

Historical Note:
*PPFA is the national trade association of manufacturers
of plastic piping products used for plumbing applications.
Members include pipe and fitting processors, prime
resin suppliers, equipment suppliers, solvent cement
manufacturers and suppliers of compounding ingredients.*

Meetings/Conferences: Semi-Annual
2013 - Indian Wells, CA (Hyatt Grand Champions
  Resort, Villas and Spa)/March 2 - 5
2013 - Napa, CA (Silverado Resort and Spa)/Oct. 5 - 8

Plastic Shipping Container Institute *(1976)*
1701 Pennsylvania Ave. NW
Suite 300
Washington, DC 20006
Tel: (202) 253-4347 *Fax:* (202) 330-5092
E-Mail: info@pscionline.org
Website: pscionline.org
Members: 45 companies
Staff: 1
Annual Budget: $100-250,000
Tax: 501(c)(6)

Personnel:
General Counsel: David H. Baker
  E-Mail: dhbakerlaw@aol.com

Historical Note:
*PSCI seeks to advocate the common interests of and
the general well being of the plastic shipping container
industry, including consideration of local, state and federal
regulatory and legislative issues and international trade
issues impacting customers, suppliers and consumers.
Members are manufacturers of open head plastic shipping
containers or companies producing virgin high density
polyethylene, component parts for shipping containers and
companies, manufacturing machines and service companies.
Membership: $5,000 (Regular); $2,000 (Associate).*

Meetings/Conferences: Annual
2013 - Yountville, CA (Hotel Yountville)/April 21 - 22

Publications:
Membership Directory; on-line

Membership List Available to Non-members

Plastic Surgery Administrative Association
(1974)
C/O Edina Plastic Surgery, Ltd
6525 France Ave., Suite 300
Edina, MN 55435
Tel: (952) 767-3170 *Fax:* (952) 925-1579
TollFree: (800) 373-0302
Website: plasticadmin.org
Members: 200 individuals
Staff: 4
Annual Budget: $10-25,000
Tax: 501(c)(6)

Personnel:
Executive Director: Orla McClure
  E-Mail: orla@edinaplasticsurgery.com

Historical Note:
*PSAA works to further the efficiency of the professional
offices where the members are employed. Membership:
$150/year (Individual).*

Meetings/Conferences: Annual
Conference Chair: R. Andrew Guth

Publications:
Member Directory; on-line; adv.
The Administrator Review; semi-annually; adv.

Plastic Surgery Research Council *(1955)*
45 Lyme Rd.
Suite 304
Hanover, NH 03755
Tel: (603) 643-2325 *Fax:* (603) 643-1444
E-Mail: psrc@conmx.net
Website: ps-rc.org
Members: 598 individuals
Staff: 5
Annual Budget: $250-500,000
Tax: 501(c)(3)

Personnel:
Executive Director: Catherine Foss
  E-Mail: catherine@conmx.net

Manager, Marketing: Jodie Ambrose
  E-Mail: jodie@conmx.net
Manager, Membership Services: Jordan Carney
  E-Mail: jordan@conmx.net
Meeting Registrar: Gael DeBeaumont
  E-Mail: gael@conmx.net
Accounting Manager: Ed Tracey
  E-Mail: ed@conmx.net

Historical Note:
*PSRC's purpose is to promote basic research in plastic and
reconstructive surgery. Membership: $225 (Active); $175
(Associate); $25 (Resident).*

Meetings/Conferences: Annual
Conference Chair: Gael DeBeaumont
2013 - Santa Monica, CA (Loews Santa Monica Beach
  Hotel)/May 2 - 4

Publications:
Lab Directory; on-line
PRS Supplement; annually; adv.

Plastics Foodservice Packaging Group *(1988)*
1300 Wilson Blvd.
Eighth Floor
Arlington, VA 22209
Fax: (703) 741-6050
E-Mail: pspc@plastics.org
Website: plastics.americanchemistry.com/pfpg
Members: 13 companies
Staff: 2
Annual Budget: $500-1,000,000

Personnel:
Contact, Media Relations: Allyson Wilson
  E-Mail: Allyson_Wilson@americanchemistry.com

Historical Note:
*PFPG serves to create and implement programs to educate
the public about the importance and benefits of polystyrene
and plastics food packaging. Members are resin suppliers
as well as manufacturers of polystyrene and plastics
foodservice products. Membership: $350 (Polystyrene
Resin Supplier and Non Polystyrene Resin Supplier/Foam
Polystyrene Fabricator Existing/Solid Oriented Polystyrene
Existing/Non-Polystyrene Fabricator/Converter Existing);
$2,500 (Foam Polystyrene Fabricator New Member/
Solid Oriented Polystyrene New Member/Non-Polystyrene
Fabricator/Converter New Member); $5,000 (International/
International Association).*

Plastics Pipe Institute *(1950)*
105 Decker Ct.
Suite 825
Irving, TX 75062
Tel: (469) 499-1044 *Fax:* (469) 499-1063
E-Mail: info@plasticpipe.org
Website: plasticpipe.org
Members: 125 corporate members
Staff: 9
Annual Budget: $2-5,000,000

Personnel:
Executive Director: Tony Radoszewski
  E-Mail: tonyr@plasticpipe.org
Coordinator, Administrative Division: Debora Bechtloff
  E-Mail: dbechtloff@plasticpipe.org
Technical Director: Stephen Boros
  E-Mail: sboros@plasticpipe.org
Manager, Marketing Communications: Dana Gecker
  E-Mail: dgecker@plasticpipe.org
Director, Engineering: Camille Rubeiz PE
  E-Mail: crubeiz@plasticpipe.org

Historical Note:
*Mission is to make plastics the material of choice for
all piping applications. Membership is comprised of
manufacturers of plastics pipe, fittings and valves.
Membership varies by sales level (Corporate).*

Meetings/Conferences:
Conference Chair: Tony Radoszewski
2013 - St. Pete Beach, FL/May 5 - 8
2013 - Charlotte, NC/Sept. 29 - Oct. 2

Membership List Available to Non-members

Plumbing and Drainage Institute *(1928)*
800 Turnpike St.
Suite 300
N. Andover, MA 01845
Tel: (978) 557-0720 *Fax:* (978) 557-0721
TollFree: (800) 589-8956
E-Mail: pdi@PDIonline.org
Website: pdionline.org
Members: 14 companies and 13 licensees

Staff: 1
Annual Budget: $100-250,000
Tax: 501(c)(6)

Personnel:
Executive Director: Rand Ackroyd

Historical Note:
Formerly (1949) Plumbing and Drainage Manufacturers Association. Incorporated in 1954 in the state of Illinois. Mission is to promote the advancement of engineered plumbing products through publicity, public relations, research, and standardization of product requirements. Members are manufacturers of engineered plumbing products, including drains, cleanouts, backwater valves, and other drainage specialties. PDI works for the development and implementation of engineering standards for the industry.

Publications:
Membership Directory; on-line

Membership List Available to Non-members

Plumbing Contractors of America *(1989)*
1385 Piccard Dr.
Rockville, MD 20850
Tel: (301) 869-5800 *Fax:* (301) 990-9690
TollFree: (800) 556-3653
Website: mcaa.org/pca
Members: 1300 firms and 2300 contractors
Staff: 1
Annual Budget: $2-5,000,000

Personnel:
Director, Industry Programs: Sean McGuire
    E-Mail: smcguire@mcaa.org

Historical Note:
Founded as the National Plumbing Bureau; assumed its present name in 1999. Represents the interests of union plumbing contractors on a national level. In addition to lobbying, the PCA works with other industry groups and associations. Members of the PCA sit on the Board of Directors for IAPMO, work directly with the UA, ASSE, ASPE and the World Plumbing Council.

Meetings/Conferences: Annual
Conference Chair: Sean McGuire

Publications:
MCAA Membership Directory; on-line

Plumbing Manufacturers Institute *(1975)*
1921 Rohlwing Rd.
Unit G
Rolling Meadows, IL 60008
Tel: (847) 481-5500 *Fax:* (847) 481-5501
E-Mail: pmiadmin@pmihome.org
Website: pmihome.org
Members: 40 companies
Staff: 5
Annual Budget: $1-2,000,000

Personnel:
Executive Director: Barbara C. Higgens
    E-Mail: bhiggens@pmihome.org
Contact, Membership Services: Amy Berg-Ferguson
    E-Mail: abergferguson@pmihome.org
Legal Counsel: Michael Sennett
    E-Mail: msennett@jonesday.com
Technical Director: Len Swatkowski
    E-Mail: lswatkowski@pmihome.org

Historical Note:
Formerly Plumbing Brass Institute and then changed its name to the Plumbing Manufacturers Institute. In 2011 changed its name to Plumbing Manufacturers International. PMI functions as a sounding board for its members, a source for industry and market information, and as a coordinating and decision- making body for dealing with industry issues. Membership in PMI is open to manufacturers of plumbing industry products. PMI's Mission is to provide a forum for the exchange of information and industry education. Membership: $10,300-78,280 (Based on Sales).

Meetings/Conferences: Annual
2013 - Austin, TX/April 7 - 10

Publications:
Member Directory; on-line
PMI News
PMI This Week; weekly
Tech Talk

Plumbing-Heating-Cooling Contractors - National Association *(1883)*
180 S. Washington St.
P.O. Box 6808

Falls Church, VA 22046
Tel: (703) 237-8100 *Fax:* (703) 237-7442
TollFree: (800) 533-7694
E-Mail: naphcc@naphcc.org
Website: phccweb.org
Members: 4000 individuals
Staff: 22
Annual Budget: $2-5,000,000

Personnel:
Manager, QSC Membership and Marketing: Elina Gross
    E-Mail: gross@naphcc.org
Executive Vice President: Gerard J. Kennedy Jr.
    E-Mail: kennedy@naphcc.org
Vice President, Member Services: Elicia Magruder
    E-Mail: magruder@naphcc.org
Senior Director, Communications: Charlotte R. Perham
    E-Mail: perham@naphcc.org
Director, Government Relations: Mark Riso
    E-Mail: riso@naphcc.org
Vice President, Technical Services and Code Services: Chuck White
    E-Mail: mailto:white@naphcc.org
Vice President, Finance and Administration and Chief Financial Officer: Penny Young
    E-Mail: young@naphcc.org
Vice President, Education and Programs: John Zink
    E-Mail: zink@naphcc.org

Historical Note:
Established as the National Association of Master Plumbers, became (1953) the National Association of Plumbing Contractors and (1962) National Association of Plumbing-Heating-Cooling Contractors before assuming its present name in 1997. PHCC is dedicated to the promotion, advancement, education and training of the industry, for the protection of environment and the health, safety, and comfort of society. Members are plumbing and HVACR businesses and technicians. Membership: $436/year.

Meetings/Conferences: Annual
2013 - Las Vegas, NV (Rio Las Vegas Hotel and Casino)/Oct. 16 - 19

Publications:
Contractor Magazine; monthly; adv.
PHCC Connection; monthly
PHCC Online; weekly
PHCC Online Buyers' Guide; on-line; adv.
Who's Who in PHCC Membership Directory; annually; adv.

PMA - The Worldwide Community of Imaging Associations *(1924)*
2282 Springport Rd.
Suite F
Jackson, MI 49202
Tel: (517) 788-8100 *Fax:* (517) 788-8371
TollFree: (800) 762-9287
Website: pmai.org
Members: 20000 individuals
Staff: 95
Annual Budget: $5-10,000,000

Personnel:
Executive Director and Secretary: Jim Esp
Executive, Corporate Communications: Tom Crawford
    E-Mail: tcrawford@pmai.org
Contact, Chapters Relations and Competitions: Heather Kelso
    E-Mail: hkelso@pmai.org

Historical Note:
Formed by a merger of National Photo Dealers Association and Master Photo Finishers of America, (1974) Master Photo Dealers, (2006) Finishers' Association, Photo Marketing Association International. PMA's mission is to disseminate timely information, products and services and provide forums contributing to increased profitability, business growth. Membership is open to any firm in the photographic industry. Membership: $75/year.

Continuing Education:
Certification Designation/s: SPFE, MCPF, CPC, CPF, QDPC

Meetings/Conferences: Annual
Conference Chair: Tom Crawford
2013 - Las Vegas, NV (LVH-Las Vegas Hotel and Casino)/Jan. 6 - 11/26-50 exhibitors

Publications:
In Compliance; monthly
Membership Directory; on-line; adv.
Mini Lab Focus; monthly
PMA Magazine; monthly; adv.
PMA Newsline; weekly

PMA Washington Report; monthly
The 6Sight Report; bi-monthly
Weekly Business Focus Newsletter; weekly

PMCA: An International Association of Confectioners *(1907)*
2980 Linden St.
Suite E3
Bethlehem, PA 18017
Tel: (610) 625-4655 *Fax:* (610) 625-4657
E-Mail: info@pmca.com
Website: pmca.com
Members: 405 Companies in 30 different countries.
Staff: 4
Annual Budget: $250-500,000

Personnel:
Administrative Director: Yvette Thomas
    E-Mail: Yvette.Thomas@pmca.com
Membership Contact: Brandy Kresge
    E-Mail: Brandy.Kresge@pmca.com
Treasurer: Paul Myler
President: Marlene Stauffer

Historical Note:
PMCA's mission is to provide an open forum for the free exchange of information, promote and direct basic and applied scientific research and educate and train confectionery technical personnel worldwide. Membership: $400 to $2,000 (depending on locations in/outside U.S).

Meetings/Conferences: Annual
2013 - Lancaster, PA (Lancaster Convention Center)/ April 15 - 17

Publications:
Member Directory; on-line
Newsletters; semi-annually

Poetry Society of America *(1910)*
15 Gramercy Park
New York, NY 10003
Tel: (212) 254-9628 *Fax:* (212) 673-2352
TollFree: (888) 872-7636
Website: poetrysociety.org
Members: 3000 individuals
Staff: 4
Annual Budget: $250-500,000
Tax: 501(c)(3)

Personnel:
Executive Director: Alice Quinn
Director, Programs: Darrel Alejandro Holnes
    E-Mail: darrel@poetrysociety.org
Coordinator, Membership Services and Development: Elsbeth Pancrazi
    E-Mail: elsbeth@poetrysociety.org

Historical Note:
PSA's mission is to create a public forum for the advancement, enjoyment, and understanding of poetry. It also works to build a larger audience for poetry, to encourage a deeper appreciation of the art, and to place poetry at the crossroads of American life. Membership: $45 (Individual); $25 (Student); $65 (Supporter); $100 (Sustainer); $250 (Patron); $500 (Centennial Friend); $1,000 (Centennial Angel); $2,000 (Centennial Sponsor); $5,000 (Centennial Muse).

Meetings/Conferences:
Conference Chair: Darrel Alejandro Holnes
Number of non-conference events/year: 20

Publications:
E-News; on-line

Membership List Available to Non-members

Point of Purchase Advertising Institute *(1936)*
1660 L St. NW
10th Floor
Washington, DC 20036
E-Mail: kcurtis@popai.com
Website: popai.com
Members: 1700 Member Companies.
Staff: 5

Personnel:
President: Richard Winter
    E-Mail: rwinter@popai.com
Executive, Member Services and Accounts: Michael Cure
    E-Mail: mcure@popai.com
Office Administrator: Elise Grosso
    E-Mail: tmulcahy@popai.com
Manager, Events: Tammy Mulcahy
    E-Mail: tmulcahy@popai.com

Director, Communications: Gregory Smith
  E-Mail: gsmith@popai.com

Historical Note:
POPAI is an international trade association for the marketing at retail industry. POPAI is focused on strengthening global partnerships, enriching research and educational programs, and utilizing technology to better serve the members.

Meetings/Conferences:
Conference Chair: Tammy Mulcahy

Publications:
Connections; quarterly
Cosmo magazine; adv.
E-Newsletter; monthly
Impulse; quarterly
Interactive Briefings; quarterly
Journal of Marketing at Retail (JMAR); quarterly

Poland China Record Association (1876)
P.O. Box 9758
Peoria, IL 61612-9758
Tel: (309) 691-6301 *Fax:* (309) 691-0168
E-Mail: cpspeoria@mindspring.com
Website: cpsswine.com/poland/polands.htm
Members: 275 individuals
Staff: 1
Annual Budget: $100-250,000

Personnel:
Chief Executive Officer: Jack Wall

Historical Note:
Breeders and fanciers of Poland China swine. Member of the National Society of Livestock Record Associations. Membership: $10 (first year); $75/year (thereafter - includes magazine subscription, listing in breeders directory, and maintenance fee).

Continuing Education:
Certification Designation/s: CPS

Publications:
Breeders Digest Magazine; bi-monthly; adv.

Police Executive Research Forum (1976)
1120 Connecticut Ave. NW
Suite 930
Washington, DC 20036
Tel: (202) 466-7820 *Fax:* (202) 466-7826
E-Mail: perf@policeforum.org
Website: policeforum.org
Members: 1100 individuals
Staff: 36
Annual Budget: $5-10,000,000
Tax: 501(c)(3)

Personnel:
Executive Director: Chuck Wexler
  E-Mail: cwexler@policeforum.org
Director, Communications: Craig Fischer
  E-Mail: cfischer@policeforum.org
Director, Finance: Ken F Hartwick
  E-Mail: khartwick@policeforum.org
Chief-of-Staff: Andrea Luna
  E-Mail: aluna@policeforum.org
Director, Management Education: Tony Narr
  E-Mail: tnarr@policeforum.org
Administrator, Membership Services and Operations:
  Rebecca Neuburger
  E-Mail: rneuburger@policeforum.org

Historical Note:
PERF is a police research organization and a provider of management services, technical assistance, and executive-level education to support law enforcement agenciesAn organization of police executives from large city, county and state law enforcement agencies and it's mission is to improve policing and advancing professionalism through research and involvement in public policy debate. Membership is limited to nominated leaders of large police departments. Membership: $300 (General); $160 (Subscribing).

Meetings/Conferences:
Number of non-conference events/year: 3

Publications:
Subject to Debate; monthly

Membership List Available to Non-members

Polyisocyanurate Insulation Manufacturers Association (1986)
7315 Wisconsin Ave.
Suite 400E
Bethesda, MD 20814

Tel: (301) 654-0000 *Fax:* (301) 951-8401
E-Mail: pima@pima.org
Website: pima.org
Members: 27 companies
Staff: 2
Annual Budget: $1-2,000,000

Personnel:
President: Jared O. Blum
  E-Mail: joblum@pima.org
Director, Membership Services: Renee LaMura
  E-Mail: rlamura@pima.org

Historical Note:
PIMA strives to be a voice for the polyiso industry and a proactive advocate for safe, cost-effective, sustainable and energy efficient construction. PIMA membership promotes the polyiso industry through leadership, advocacy and education.

Meetings/Conferences: Annual

Publications:
Membership Directory; on-line
Technical Bulletin; irregular; adv.

Polyurethane Foam Association (1980)
334 Lakeside Plaza
Loudon, TN 37774
Tel: (865) 657-9840 *Fax:* (865) 381-1292
Website: pfa.org
Members: 53 companies
Staff: 1
Annual Budget: $250-500,000
Tax: 501(c)(6)

Personnel:
Executive Director: Robert J. Luedeka
  E-Mail: rluedeka@pfa.org

Historical Note:
Formerly (1981) the Flexible Polyurethane Foam Manufacturers Association. PFA strives to educate customers and other groups about flexible polyurethane foam and to promote its use in manufactured and industrial products. Members are companies that manufacture flexible polyurethane foam in U.S. facilities from chemical raw materials and companies that supply raw materials, equipment and technology services to U.S. flexible polyurethane foam manufacturers.

Meetings/Conferences: Semi-Annual
2013 - St. Petersburg, FL (Renaissance Vinoy Resort and Golf Club)/May 22 - 23
2013 - New Orleans, LA (New Orleans Downtown Marriott at the Convention Center)/Nov. 6 - 7
Number of non-conference events/year: 3

Publications:
InTOUCH; on-line

Polyurethane Manufacturers Association (1971)
6737 W. Washington Ave.
Suite 1300
Milwaukee, WI 53214
Tel: (414) 431-3094 *Fax:* (414) 276-7704
E-Mail: info@pmahome.org
Website: pmahome.org
Members: 90 companies
Staff: 4
Annual Budget: $250-500,000
Tax: 501(c)(6)

Personnel:
President: Payam Towfigh
  E-Mail: payam.state@mts.net
Manager, Technology: R. Scott Archibald
  E-Mail: scott.archibald@chemtura.com
Manager, Marketing: Joe Bell
Treasurer: Mike Kocak
  E-Mail: mikek@cue-inc.com

Historical Note:
PMA's mission is to advocate the polyurethane elastomer industry and drive the growth of its member companies. Membership includes processors of solid cast, microcellular, RIM and thermoplastic urethane elastomers, manufacturers, suppliers, distributors and sales agents of raw materials, additives or processing equipment, and individuals or companies providing publishing, education, research, or consulting services to the industry. Membership: $750 (Processors); $1,000-5,000 (Suppliers, based on annual sales); $150 (Academic/Research Laboratory/Consultant); $50 (Associate).

Continuing Education:
Certification Designation/s: RCSC

Meetings/Conferences: Annual
2013 - Las Vegas, NV (Caesars Palace)/May 5 - 7

Publications:
Member Directory; on-line
Polytopics Newsletter; quarterly

Membership List Available to Non-members

Pony of the Americas Club (1954)
3828 S. Emerson Ave.
Indianapolis, IN 46203
Tel: (317) 788-0107 *Fax:* (317) 788-8974
E-Mail: officemanager@poac.org
Website: poac.org
Members: 1800 individuals
Staff: 5
Annual Budget: $500-1,000,000

Personnel:
President: Jackie Guthrie
  E-Mail: jguthrie0234@yahoo.com
Interim Executive Secretary: Joyse L. Banister
  E-Mail: officemanager@poac.org
Assistant, Show Department and Administration: Kelly Gideon
  E-Mail: showdept@poac.org
Editor: Tammy Virzi
  E-Mail: tkr.mkr@gmail.com

Historical Note:
POAC is devoted to the furtherment of youth riders. Members are breeders and fanciers of the Pony of the Americas breed, an Appaloosa-type pony used in pleasure, performance, and halter competitions. Membership: $70 (Active); $25 (Junior); $35 (Associate); $82 (International).

Meetings/Conferences: Annual
Conference Chair: Joyse L. Banister

Publications:
Membership Directory; annually
POA Magazine; monthly

POPAI The Global Association for Marketing at Retail (1936)
440 N. Wells St.
Suite 740
Chicago, IL 60654
Tel: (312) 863-2900 *Fax:* (312) 229-1152
E-Mail: info@popai.com
Website: popai.com
Members: 1700 companies
Staff: 6
Annual Budget: $5-10,000,000

Personnel:
President: Richard Winter
  E-Mail: rwinter@popai.com
Manager, Education: Savia A. Coutinho PhD
  E-Mail: scoutinho@popai.com
Vice President, Membership Services: Kevin Murphy
  E-Mail: kmurphy@popai.com
Director, Events: Alicia Rutherford
  E-Mail: arutherford@popai.com
Director, Communications: Gregory Smith CAE
  E-Mail: gsmith@popai.com
Manager, Finance and Accounting: Sihin Tsegaye
  E-Mail: tsegaye@popai.com

Historical Note:
Formerly the Point-of-Purchase Advertising International, assumed current name in 2005. POPAI is dedicated to serving its members internationally by promoting, protecting, and advancing the broader interests of marketing at retail through research, education, trade forums, networking, and legislative efforts. Membership: $2,400-13,600 (Advertising Agency/Brand Marketer/ Producer/Supplier/Vendor); $150 (Educator); $900 (Retailer).

Continuing Education:
Certification Designation/s: MaRC

Meetings/Conferences:
Conference Chair: Alicia Rutherford
Number of non-conference events/year: 6

Publications:
Connections; bi-monthly
imPULSE; bi-weekly
Interactive Briefings
Journal of Marketing at Retail (JMAR)

Population Action International (1965)
1300 19th St. NW
Suite 200
Washington, DC 20036-1624
Tel: (202) 557-3400 *Fax:* (202) 728-4177
E-Mail: pai@popact.org

Website: populationaction.org
Staff: 33
Annual Budget: $5-10,000,000
Tax: 501(c)(3)

Personnel:
President and Chief Executive Officer: Suzanne Ehlers
　E-Mail: sehlers@popact.org
Vice President, Development: Michele Duryea
　E-Mail: mduryea@popact.org
Vice President, Communications: Michael Khoo
　E-Mail: mkhoo@popact.org
Director, United States Government Relations: Craig
　Lasher
　E-Mail: clasher@popact.org
Vice President, Finance and Administration: Rachael
　Murray Rakestraw
　E-Mail: rmr@popact.org
Director, Information Technology: Sarah Reidy
　E-Mail: sreidy@popact.org
Chief Operating Officer: Carolyn Gibb Vogel
　E-Mail: cvogel@popact.org

Historical Note:
*PAI works to ensure that every person has the right and
access to sexual and reproductive health. It uses research
and advocacy to improve access to family planning and
reproductive health care across the world.*

Publications:
The Washington Memo; quarterly
TIP Sheet

Population Association of America *(1931)*
8630 Fenton St.
Suite 722
Silver Spring, MD 20910-3812
Tel: (301) 565-6710 Fax: (301) 565-7850
E-Mail: membersvc@popassoc.org
Website: populationassociation.org
Members: 3000 individuals
Staff: 3
Annual Budget: $1-2,000,000
Tax: 501(c)(3)

Personnel:
Executive Director: Stephanie D. Dudley
　E-Mail: stephanie@popassoc.org
Coordinator, Membership Services: Lois Brown
　E-Mail: lmbrown@popassoc.org
Director, Government and Public Affairs: Mary Jo
　Hoeksema
　E-Mail: paaapc@crosslink.net

Historical Note:
*Incorporated in New York in 1937. PAA's mission is to
advance research in human population. PAA members
include demographers, sociologists, economists, public
health professionals, and other individuals interested in
research and education in the population field. Membership:
$118 (Regular); $55 (Joint Member); $47 (Student); $77
(Emeritus); $39 (Citizen/Resident of Low-income Country);
$321 (Corporate Member).*

Meetings/Conferences: Annual
2013 - New Orleans, LA (Sheraton New Orleans
　Hotel)/April 11 - 13
2014 - Boston, MA (Boston Marriott Copley Place)/
　May 1 - 3
2015 - San Diego, CA (Hilton San Diego Bayfront)/
　April 30 - May 2
2016 - Washington, DC (Marriott Wardman Park
　Hotel)/March 31 - April 2

Publications:
Applied Demography; semi-annually
Demography; quarterly; adv.
Government and Public Affairs Update; semi-annually
Membership Directory; on-line
PAA Affairs; quarterly

Membership List Available to Non-members

Porcelain Enamel Institute *(1930)*
P.O. Box 920220
Norcross, GA 30010
Tel: (770) 676-9366 Fax: (770) 409-7280
Website: porcelainenamel.com
Members: 90 companies
Staff: 2
Annual Budget: $250-500,000

Personnel:
Executive Vice President: Cullen L. Hackler

Historical Note:

*PEI's misssion is to advance the common interests of
porcelain enameling plants and suppliers of porcelain
enameling materials and equipment. Membership:
$2,625-6,850 (Steel Companies); $2,100-3,360
(Enamellers-Appliances); $2,100-5,250 (Other
Enamellers); $1,575-36,000 (Suppliers); $1,050
(Companies).*

Meetings/Conferences: Semi-Annual
Number of non-conference events/year: 2

Publications:
First Firing

Portable and Stationary Crushing Bureau
6737 W. Washington St.
Suite 2400
Milwaukee, WI 53214-5647
Tel: (414) 272-0943 Fax: (414) 272-1170
E-Mail: aem@aem.org
Website: aem.org/Groups/Groups/Group.asp?
　G = 62
Staff: 1

Personnel:
Manager, Technical and Safety Services: Mark Benishek
　E-Mail: mbenishek@aem.org

Historical Note:
*PSCB is one of the association of AEM groups. PSCB serves
the needs of manufacturers of portable and stationary
crushing equipment. Members engage in lawful activities,
calculated to provide information relating to and to promote
the business of the portable and stationary crushing
equipment as a segment of the construction industry.*

Portable Computer and Communications Association *(1992)*
P.O. Box 680
Hood River, OR 97031
Tel: (541) 490-5140 Fax: (413) 410-8447
E-Mail: pcca@pcca.org
Website: pcca.org
Members: 65 firms and organizations
Staff: 1
Annual Budget: $50-100,000
Tax: 501(c)(6)

Personnel:
Executive Director: Peter Rysavy
　E-Mail: rysavy@rysavy.com

Historical Note:
*PCCA publishes and disseminates information, standards,
software, and other materials to facilitate the synthesis of
computing and communications technologies. Membership:
$100 (Individual); $750 (Affiliate); $2,500 (Associate);
$5,000 (Executive).*

Meetings/Conferences:
Number of non-conference events/year: 4

Publications:
Newsletter

Portable Sanitation Association International *(1971)*
7760 France Ave. South
11th Floor
Minneapolis, MN 55435
Tel: (952) 854-8300 Fax: (952) 854-7560
TollFree: (800) 822-3020
E-Mail: info@psai.org
Website: psai.org
Members: 700 companies
Staff: 4
Annual Budget: $250-500,000

Personnel:
Director, Membership Services: Sean Melon
　E-Mail: seanm@psai.org

Historical Note:
*PSAI's mission is to expand and improve portable sanitation
services and facilities worldwide. Membership: $195-1,150
(Regular-US); $185-550 (Regular-International); $395
(Associate).*

Continuing Education:
Certification Designation/s: CHSWCP

Meetings/Conferences: Annual
2013 - Myrtle Beach, SC (Sheraton Myrtle Beach
　Convention Center Hotel)/Oct. 29 - Nov. 2/over 100
　exhibitors
Number of non-conference events/year: 3

Publications:
PSAI In Action; bi-monthly

Portfolio Management Institute
301 Tresser Blvd.
12th Floor
Stamford, CT 06901
Tel: (203) 356-0807 Fax: (203) 967-7006
E-Mail: admin@pminstitute.org
Website: pminstitute.org
Members: 100 investment managers
Staff: 4
Annual Budget: $250-500,000

Personnel:
President: Gary Klingner CPM
　E-Mail: gary.w.klingner@smithbarney.com
Treasurer: Paul McCauley CPM
　E-Mail: paul.d.mccauley@smithbarney.com

Historical Note:
*PMI's mission is to improve the skills of participants in the
Smith Barney Portfolio Management Program. PMI provides
educational opportunities and professional development
opportunities. PMI members are investment managers.
Membership: $295/year (Individual Voting/Associate/
Branch Manager/Regional Manager).*

Meetings/Conferences: Annual
2013 - Houston, TX (Omni Houston Hotel)/April 17 -
　19

Publications:
The Exchange; quarterly

Portland Cement Association *(1916)*
5420 Old Orchard Rd.
Skokie, IL 60077
Tel: (847) 966-6200 Fax: (847) 966-8389
E-Mail: info@cement.org
Website: cement.org
Members: 30 cement companies
Staff: 103
Annual Budget: $50-100,000,000
Tax: 501(c)(6)

Personnel:
Director, Communications: Patti Flesher
　E-Mail: pflesher@cement.org
Managing Director, Research and Technical Services:
　Steven H. Kosmatka
　E-Mail: skosmatka@cement.org

Historical Note:
*Absorbed American Portland Cement Alliance in 2002.
PCA's mission is to improve and expand the uses of
Portland cement and concrete.*

Continuing Education:
Certification Designation/s: LEED, ACI

Publications:
Membership Directory; on-line
PCA e-newsletter; weekly

Membership List Available to Non-members

Portugal-US Chamber of Commerce *(1979)*
590 Fifth Ave.
Fourth Floor
New York, NY 10036
Tel: (212) 354-4627 Fax: (212) 575-4737
E-Mail: chamber@portugal-us.com
Website: portugal-us.com
Members: 50 businesses
Staff: 2
Annual Budget: $10-25,000

Personnel:
President: Donzelina A. Barroso
Treasurer: Cesaltine Gregorio

Historical Note:
*PUSCC is a bilateral chamber of commerce that stimulates
economic development, trade and investment, and cultural
exchange between the United States and Portugal.
Membership: $1,100 (Sustaining); $550 (Corporate); $220
(Individual).*

Meetings/Conferences: Annual

Publications:
Membership Directory; on-line

Post-Tensioning Institute *(1976)*
38800 Country Club Dr.
Farmington Hills, MI 48331
Tel: (248) 848-3180 Fax: (248) 848-3181
E-Mail: info@post-tensioning.org
Website: post-tensioning.org
Members: 90 Companies and 700 Individuals
Staff: 8

Annual Budget: $1-2,000,000
Tax: 501(c)(6)

Personnel:
Executive Director: Theodore L. Neff PE
　E-Mail: ted.neff@post-tensioning.org
Coordinator, Certification Programs: Tracey M. Bales
　E-Mail: tracey.bales@post-tensioning.org
Lead Accountant: Stacey A. Clement
　E-Mail: stacey.clement@post-tensioning.org
Event Planner: Jeffrey D. Ponder
　E-Mail: jeff.ponder@post-tensioning.org
Editor and Graphic Designer: Kelli R. Slayden
　E-Mail: kelli.slayden@post-tensioning.org
Coordinator, Membership Services: Michelle J. Stern
　E-Mail: michelle.stern@post-tensioning.org
Director, Technical and Certification: Miroslav F. Vejvoda MBA, PE
　E-Mail: miroslav.vejvoda@post-tensioning.org

Historical Note:
PTI's mission is to expand post-tensioning applications through marketing, education, research, teamwork, and code development while advancing the quality, safety, efficiency, profitability, and use of post- tensioning systems. Membership: $2,500-30,640 (PT Companies); $2500-12,000 (PC Strand Manufacturer); $1,900-2,900 (Associate); $840 (Consulting/Installing/Affiliate); $125 (Professional); $150 (International Professional); $40 (student); $300-900 (International); $1,200 (Association); $600 (International);

Continuing Education:
Certification Designation/s: PCP, FCP

Meetings/Conferences: Annual
Conference Chair: Jeffrey D. Ponder
2013 - Scottsdale, AZ (Hilton Scottsdale Resort and Villas)/May 5 - 7

Publications:
Membership Directory; on-line
Newsletter; irregular
PTI Journal; adv.

Membership List Available to Non-members

Potato Association of America *(1913)*
University of Maine
5719 Crossland Hall, Room 220
Orono, ME 04469-5719
Tel: (207) 581-3042 *Fax:* (207) 581-3015
E-Mail: umpotato@maine.edu
Website: potatoassociation.org
Members: 1000 individuals
Staff: 3
Annual Budget: $100-250,000
Tax: 501(c)(3)

Personnel:
President: Leigh Morrow
Treasurer: Larry Hiller
Administrator: Lori Wing

Historical Note:
Founded in New York as the National Potato Association of America, became the Potato Association of America, Inc. in 1917. PAA is a professional society for potato research, extension, utilization and technical workers in all aspects of the American potato industry. Membership: $0-500/year.

Continuing Education:
Certification Designation/s: AGC

Meetings/Conferences: Annual
2013 - Québec, QC/July 28 - Aug. 2

Publications:
American Journal of Potato Research; bi-monthly
Membership Directory; on-line
The PAA Insider Newsletter; quarterly; adv.

Membership List Available to Non-members

Poultry Breeders of America *(1959)*
U.S. Poultry and Egg Association, 1530 Cooledge Rd.
Tucker, GA 30084-7303
Tel: (770) 493-9401 *Fax:* (770) 493-9257
E-Mail: info@poultryegg.org
Website: poultryegg.org
Members: 27 companies
Staff: 6
Annual Budget: Under $10,000

Personnel:
President: John Starkey
　E-Mail: jstarkey@poultryegg.org

Executive Assistant and Expo Hotel Coordinator: Caroline E. Hanson
　E-Mail: chanson@poultryegg.org
Vice President, Education Programs: Barbara Jenkins
　E-Mail: bjenkins@uspoultry.org
Executive Vice President: Charles Olentine PhD
　E-Mail: colentine@poultryegg.org
Vice President, Information Technology: Jason Rivera
　E-Mail: jrivera@poultryegg.org
Director, Communications: Gwen Venable
　E-Mail: gvenable@poultryegg.org

Historical Note:
An affiliate of US Poultry and Egg Association. PBA serves the mutual interests of poultry breeders by exchanging information, conducting the National Breeders Roundtable, and representing the industry before government agencies. Membership: $400/year (Regular/Associate/Allied/International).

Meetings/Conferences: Annual
Conference Chair: Charles Olentine PhD

Publications:
Membership Directory; annually
The Communicator; quarterly
USPOULTRY Wire; on-line

Poultry Science Association *(1908)*
1800 S. Oak St.,
Suite 100
Champaign, IL 61820
Tel: (217) 356-5285 *Fax:* (217) 398-4119
E-Mail: psa@assochq.org
Website: poultryscience.org
Members: 1500 individuals
Staff: 3
Annual Budget: $1-2,000,000

Personnel:
Executive Director: Stephen E. Koenig
　E-Mail: steve.koenig@poultryscience.org
Director, Business Operations: Jon A. Cole
　E-Mail: jonc@assochq.org
Managing Editor: Susan M. Pollock
　E-Mail: susanp@assochq.org

Historical Note:
Originated in 1908 as the International Association of Instructors and Investigators in Poultry Husbandry. Became the American Association of Instructors and Investigators in Poultry Husbandry in 1912 and the Poultry Science Association, Inc. in 1926. PSA is dedicated to discover and disseminate knowledge generated by poultry research, that enhances human and animal health and well-being and provides for the ethical, sustainable production of food. Members are university and industry researchers involved in poultry, avian science, and related disciplines. Membership: $120 (Professional); $30 (Student); $25-100 (Individual Sustaining); Free (Emeritus).

Meetings/Conferences: Annual
Conference Chair: Jon A. Cole
2013 - San Diego, CA (Town and Country Resort Hotel)/July 21 - 25
2014 - Corpus Christi, TX (Omni Corpus Christi Hotel Bayfront Tower)/July 14 - 17

Publications:
Journal of Applied Poultry Research
Membership Directory
Poultry Science® journal
PSA Newsletter

Powder Actuated Tool Manufacturers Institute *(1952)*
136 S. Main St.
Suite 2E
St. Charles, MO 63301
Tel: (636) 578-5510 *Fax:* (314) 725-6592
E-Mail: info@patmi.org
Website: patmi.org
Members: 7 companies
Staff: 2
Annual Budget: $50-100,000

Personnel:
Executive Director: James A. Borchers
　E-Mail: jborchers@patmi.org

Historical Note:
PATMI, a member of the National Safety Council and the American National Standards Institute, provides a common industry voice for manufacturers of powder actuated fastening systems. Membership: $5,500/year.

Publications:
Membership Directory; on-line

Membership List Available to Non-members

Powder Coating Institute *(1981)*
2170 Buckthorne Pl.
Suite 250
The Woodlands, TX 77380
Tel: (832) 585-0770 *Fax:* (832) 585-0220
TollFree: (800) 988-2628
E-Mail: pci-info@powdercoating.org
Website: powdercoating.org
Members: 320 companies
Staff: 5
Annual Budget: $1-2,000,000

Personnel:
Director, Programs: Jennifer Egan
　E-Mail: jegan@powdercoating.org
Contact, Marketing and Communications: Ginny Robinson
　E-Mail: grobinson@powdercoating.org
Director, Publications: Brett Ryden
　E-Mail: bryden@powdercoating.org
Technical Manager: Mike Wittenhagen
　E-Mail: mwitten@powdercoating.org

Historical Note:
PCI is committed to serving its members by promoting the benefits of powder coating technology. Members are companies producing powder coatings, application equipment, related materials and services for finishing a wide range of products. Membership: $3,300-10,100 (Diamond); $1,500-8,300 (Star); $300-7,400 (Gold); $195 (Company Affiliate); $95 (Individual).

Continuing Education:
Certification Designation/s: PCI 3000, PCI 4000

Meetings/Conferences: Annual
Conference Chair: Jennifer Egan

Publications:
Membership Directory; on-line
PCI News Brief; on-line
PCI Newsletter; irregular
Powder Coated Tough Magazine; quarterly; adv.

Powder Metallurgy Equipment Association *(1958)*
105 College Rd., East
C/O Metal Powder Industries Federation
Princeton, NJ 08540
Tel: (609) 452-7700 *Fax:* (609) 987-8523
E-Mail: info@mpif.org
Website: mpif.org/AboutMPIF/pmea.asp?
　linkid = 32
Staff: 15

Personnel:
Executive Director and Chief Executive Officer: C. James Trombino CAE
　E-Mail: jtrombino@mpif.org
Director, Technical Services: James P. Adams
　E-Mail: jadams@mpif.org
Vice President, Member and Industry Relations: James R. Dale
　E-Mail: jdale@mpif.org
Manager, Meetings and Conferences: Sandra E. Leatherman
　E-Mail: sleatherman@mpif.org
Director, Communications: Donni Magid
　E-Mail: dmagid@mpif.org
Vice President, Finance and Administration.: Jillaine K. Regan
　E-Mail: jregan@mpif.org
Manager, Advertising and Exhibit: Jessica S. Tamasi
　E-Mail: jtamasi@mpif.org

Historical Note:
A constituent of the Metal Powder Industries Federation. PMEA's mission is to improve and promote the products of powder metallurgy processing equipment and its supply industries. It promotes education, practice, and application of powder metallurgy processing equipment, and provides services for the collection and dissemination of information pertaining to the industry.

Meetings/Conferences: Annual
Conference Chair: Sandra E. Leatherman

Powder Metallurgy Parts Association *(1957)*
105 College Rd., East
Princeton, NJ 08540
Tel: (609) 452-7700 *Fax:* (609) 987-8523
E-Mail: info@mpif.org
Website: mpif.org/aboutmpif/pmpa.asp?
　linkid = 30

Staff: 8

Personnel:

Executive Director and Chief Executive Officer: C. James
   Trombino CAE
   E-Mail: jtrombino@mpif.org
Manager, Office Services: Turner T. Abbott
   E-Mail: tabbott@mpif.org
Director, Technical Services: James P. Adams
   E-Mail: jadams@mpif.org
Vice President, Member and Industry Relations: James R.
   Dale
   E-Mail: jdale@mpif.org
Manager, Meetings and Conferences: Sandra E.
   Leatherman
   E-Mail: sleatherman@mpif.org
Publication Coordinator: Peggy LeBedz
   E-Mail: plebedz@mpif.org
Director, Communications: Donni Magid
   E-Mail: dmagid@mpif.org
Vice President, Finance and Administration: Jillaine K.
   Regan
   E-Mail: jregan@mpif.org

Historical Note:
*PMPA is one of the six trade associations of the Metal
Powder Industries Federation that advocates wider usage
and improved quality of powder metallurgy parts.*

Meetings/Conferences: Semi-Annual
Conference Chair: Sandra E. Leatherman
2013 - Orlando, FL (Hilton Orlando Lake Buena Vista)/
   March 4 - 6
2013 - Chicago, IL (Sheraton Chicago Hotel and
   Towers)/June 24 - 27
2015 - San Diego, CA/May 17 - 20

Publications:
FOCUS: PM e-newsletter; bi-weekly; adv.
PM Industry NewsLine; monthly; adv.
PM Newsbytes e-newsletter; weekly; adv.

Membership List Available to Non-members

Power and Communications Contractors Association *(1945)*
1908 Mt. Vernon Ave.
Second Floor
Alexandria, VA 22301
Tel: (703) 212-7734 *Fax:* (703) 548-3733
TollFree: (800) 542-7222
E-Mail: info@pccaweb.org
Website: pccaweb.org
Members: 350 member companies
Staff: 6
Annual Budget: $500-1,000,000

Personnel:
President-Elect: Steve Sellenriek
Executive Vice President: Timothy Wagner
   E-Mail: twagner@pccaweb.org
Vice President, Communication: Michael Ancell
   E-Mail: mancell@pccaweb.org
Membership Associate: Stacy Bowdring
   E-Mail: sbowdring@pccaweb.org
Marketing Associate: Vitoria Elie
   E-Mail: velie@pccaweb.org
Meeting Associate: Mackenzie Fluharty
   E-Mail: mfluharty@pccaweb.org

Historical Note:
*Formerly (1950) Rural Electrical Contractors Association,
the Power and Communication Contractors Association is
the national trade association for companies constructing
electric power facilities, including transmission and
distribution lines and substations and telephone, fiber optic,
and cable television systems. Membership: $1000/year
(Contractor/Associate).*

Meetings/Conferences: Annual
2013 - Naples, FL (Naples Beach Hotel and Golf Club)/
   March 1 - 6
2013 - Colorado Springs, CO (The Broadmoor)/July 10
   - 13
2014 - St. Thomas, VI (Frenchman's Reef Marriott
   Beach Resort)/March 14 - 19

Publications:
PCCA Journal; quarterly; adv.
The Annual PCCA Directory & Buyer's Guide; annually

Power Crane and Shovel Association *(1945)*
6737 W. Washington St., Suite 2400
C/O Association of Equipment Manufacturers
Milwaukee, WI 53214-5647
Tel: (414) 272-0943 *Fax:* (414) 272-1170

Website: aem.org/Groups/Groups/Group.asp?
   G = 65
Staff: 1

Personnel:
Manager, Technical and Safety Services: John Wagner

Historical Note:
*The Power Crane & Shovel Association (PCSA) provides
services tailored to meet the needs of the lattice boom
and truck crane industry. PCSA explores business
issues, technological questions and legislative and
regulatory concerns (domestic and worldwide) that effect
manufacturers of cranes.*

Power Sources Manufacturers Association *(1985)*
P.O. Box 418
Mendham, NJ 07945-0418
Tel: (973) 543-9660 *Fax:* (973) 543-6207
E-Mail: power@psma.com
Website: psma.com
Members: 153 companies
Staff: 2
Annual Budget: $50-100,000
Tax: 501(c)(4)

Personnel:
Executive Director: Joseph "Joe" Horzepa
   E-Mail: ipstrategy@worldnet.att.net
Associate Director and Managing Editor: Judy Horzepa
   E-Mail: judy@psma.com

Historical Note:
*PSMA's mission is to integrate the resources of the power
sources industry to more effectively and profitably serve
the needs of the power sources users, providers and PSMA
members. Members are manufacturers and users of AC
and DC power source systems and related components.
Membership: $650-2,250 (Regular, based on revenue);
$600 (Associate); $125 (Affiliate).*

Meetings/Conferences: Annual
Number of non-conference events/year: 2

Publications:
Electronic Transformers and Circuits; irregular
Soft Ferrites; irregular
Update Newsletter; quarterly; adv.

Power Tool Institute, Inc. *(1937)*
1300 Sumner Ave.
Cleveland, OH 44115-2851
Tel: (216) 241-7333 *Fax:* (216) 241-0105
E-Mail: pti@powertoolinstitute.com
Website: powertoolinstitute.com
Members: 17 companies
Staff: 3
Annual Budget: $500-1,000,000
Tax: 501(c)(6)

Personnel:
Executive Manager: Charles (Chuck) M. Stockinger
   E-Mail: cstockinger@thomasamc.com
Director, Technology: Robert Stoll

Historical Note:
*Formerly (1969) Electric Tool Institute. PTI works to
harmonize global product listing standards and develops
educational programs on the safe use of power tools.*
Meetings/Conferences:
Number of non-conference events/year: 1

Publications:
Directory; annually

Membership List Available to Non-members

Power Transmission Distributors Association *(1960)*
230 W. Monroe St.
Suite 1410
Chicago, IL 60606-4703
Tel: (312) 516-2100 *Fax:* (312) 516-2101
E-Mail: ptda@ptda.org
Website: ptda.org
Members: 390 companies
Staff: 11
Annual Budget: $1-2,000,000
Tax: 501(c)(6)

Personnel:
Executive Vice President and Chief Executive Officer: Ann
   Arnott
   E-Mail: aarnott@ptda.org
Manager, Meetings and Education: Kelly Butler
   E-Mail: kbutler@ptda.org
Director, Communications and Research: Mary Neil
   Crosby

   E-Mail: mncrosby@ptda.org
Operations, Coordinator: Andrea Lebron
   E-Mail: alebron@ptda.org
Manager, Marketing and Communications: Ginger
   Wheeler
   E-Mail: gwheeler@ptda.org

Historical Note:
*Established as Mechanical Power Transmission Equipment
Distributors Association, assumed its present name
in 1966. PTDA is dedicated to advancing distribution
and strengthening members to be successful, profitable
and competitive in a changing marketing environment.
Members are industrial power transmission/motion control
distributor firms. Membership: $740-7,760 (Distributor/
Manufacturer, based on sales volume); $975 (Associate);
$150 (Educational Institution).*

Meetings/Conferences: Annual
Conference Chair: Kelly Butler
2013 - San Antonio, TX (Hotel Contessa)/March 21 -
   23
2013 - Palm Desert, CA (JW Marriott Desert Springs
   Resort and Spa)/Oct. 3 - 5

Publications:
Membership Directory; on-line
PTDA Spotlight; monthly; adv.

Membership List Available to Non-members

Power Washers of North America *(1992)*
P.O. Box 270634
St. Paul, IL 55127
Tel: (651) 207-9544 *Fax:* (651) 213-0369
TollFree: (800) 393-7962
E-Mail: info@pwna.org
Website: thepwna.org
Members: 450 companies
Staff: 2
Annual Budget: $100-250,000

Personnel:
Executive Director: Jackie Tacheny
Treasurer: John Nearon

Historical Note:
*PWNA strives to develop and communicate better
standards in ethical business practices, environmental
awareness, and safety through continuing education and
active representation of the membership. Members are
power washing contractors, suppliers, distributors and
manufacturers. Membership: $350 (Contractor/Associate/
Retired); $500 (Supplier).*

Continuing Education:
Certification Designation/s: FWC, WRC, KEC, HWC

Meetings/Conferences: Annual

Publications:
Membership Directory; on-line
Waterworks; quarterly

Power-Motion Technology Representatives Association *(1972)*
C/O MANA, 16A Journey
Suite 200
Aliso Viejo, CA 92656
Tel: (949) 859-2885 *Fax:* (949) 855-2973
TollFree: (888) 817-7872
E-Mail: info@ptra.org
Website: ptra.org
Members: 195 companies and 75 allied members
Staff: 3
Annual Budget: $250-500,000
Tax: 501(c)(6)

Personnel:
Executive Director: Doug Bower
   E-Mail: dbower@ptra.org
Treasurer: Kurt Fisher
Legal Counsel: Mitchell Kramer
   E-Mail: mkramer@kramerandkramer.com

Historical Note:
undefined

Continuing Education:
Certification Designation/s: CPMR, CSP

Meetings/Conferences: Annual
2013 - Rio Grande, PR (Rio Mar Beach Resort and
   Spa)/April 17 - 20

Publications:
Membership Directory; on-line
The Focus Newsletter; quarterly

Practising Law Institute *(1933)*

810 Seventh Ave.
21st Floor
New York, NY 10019-5818
Tel: (212) 824-5700 *Fax:* (800) 321-0093
TollFree: (800) 260-4754
E-Mail: info@pli.edu
Website: pli.edu
Members: 60000 individuals
Staff: 100
Annual Budget: $50-100,000,000
Tax: 501(c)(3)

Personnel:
President: Victor J. Rubino
    E-Mail: vrubino@pli.edu
Vice President, Publishing: William C. Cubberley
    E-Mail: wcubberley@pli.edu
Chief Financial Officer and Treasurer: Frank DeVivo
    E-Mail: fdevivo@pli.edu
Chief Information Officer: Kenneth Moskowitz
    E-Mail: kmoskowitz@pli.edu
Director, Patent Professional Development: John M. White

Historical Note:
PLI's mission is to enhance the professionalism of attorneys and other qualified persons by providing, in a cost effective manner, the quality and most innovative programs, publications and other services to enable them to practice law competently and ethically and to fulfill pro bono responsibilities. Membership: $100-975 (Based on the number of practicing attorneys in the firm); $3,495 (Individual Privileged).

Continuing Education:
Certification Designation/s: MPRE
Meetings/Conferences:
Number of non-conference events/year: 150

Publications:
Membership Directory; on-line

PRBA - The Rechargeable Battery Association
(1991)
1776 K St.
Fourth Floor
Washington, DC 20006
Tel: (202) 719-4978
E-Mail: PRBAtt@gmail.com
Website: prba.org
Members: 130 companies
Staff: 2
Annual Budget: $1-2,000,000
Personnel:
Executive Director: George A. Kerchner
    E-Mail: prbatt@gmail.com
Contact, Membership Services: Donna Lehman

Historical Note:
PRBA's mission is to provide service in obtaining consistent domestic and international solutions to transportation, environmental and other selected issues affecting the transport, use, recycling and disposal of small sealed rechargeable batteries. Members are manufacturers, distributors, users, and sellers of small rechargeable batteries and battery-powered products. Membership: $5,500-35,750 (Active); $5,500 (Associate).

Meetings/Conferences: Semi-Annual
Number of non-conference events/year: 1

Publications:
Membership Directory; on-line
Recharger; quarterly; adv.
Regulatory and Legislative Updates; monthly
Weekly News Updates; weekly

Precast/Prestressed Concrete Institute *(1954)*
200 W. Adams St.
Suite 2100
Chicago, IL 60606
Tel: (312) 786-0300 *Fax:* (312) 621-1114
E-Mail: info@pci.org
Website: pci.org
Members: 2550 firms, engineers and architects
Staff: 33
Annual Budget: $5-10,000,000
Personnel:
President: James G. Toscas PE
    E-Mail: jtoscas@pci.org
Director, Publishing and Art Direction: Paul Grigonis
Managing Director, Technical Activities: Jason J. Krohn PE
    E-Mail: jkrohn@pci.org
Manager, Events: Megan Lanning CMP

Managing Director, Business Development: Brian Miller
    AP, LEED, PE
    E-Mail: bmiller@pci.org
Director, Educational Activities: Alex Morales MEd
Manager, Sales and Member Development: Kirstin
    Osgood
Manager, Communications: Whitney Stephens
Coordinator, Member Services: Cynthia A. Ward
    E-Mail: cward@pci.org

Historical Note:
Formerly (1989) the Prestressed Concrete Institute. PCI, an organization dedicated to fostering greater understanding and use of precast and prestressed concrete, maintains a full staff of technical and marketing specialists. Membership: $900 (Foreign Producer); $2,000-10,000 (Service Associate/Supplier Associate); $110 (Professional US/ Affiliate US); $140 (Professional Non-US/Affiliate Non-US); $50 (Professional Associate US); $75 (Professional Associate Non-US); $0 (Student US/Non-US); $1600-6,500 (Erector Associate).

Continuing Education:
Certification Designation/s: PQPC

Meetings/Conferences:
Conference Chair: Megan Lanning CMP
2013 - Chicago, IL (Hyatt Magnificant Mile)/April 25 -
    28
2013 - Grapevine, TX (Gaylord Texan Hotel and
    Convention Center-Grapevine)/Sept. 21 - 25
2014 - Washington, DC (Gaylord National-
    Washington)/Sept. 6 - 10
2015 - Nashville, TN (Gaylord Hotels Resorts and
    Convention Centers-Nashville)/Sept. 19 - 23
Number of non-conference events/year: 1

Publications:
Ascent Magazine
Aspire; quarterly
E-trends E-Newsletter; irregular
inFORM E-Newsletter; bi-monthly
PCI Journal; bi-monthly
PCI Newsletter; monthly

Precision Machined Products Association *(1933)*
6700 W. Snowville Rd.
Brecksville, OH 44141
Tel: (440) 526-0300 *Fax:* (440) 526-5803
Website: pmpa.org
Members: 500 companies
Staff: 9
Annual Budget: $1-2,000,000
Tax: 501(c)(6)

Personnel:
Executive Director: Michael B. Duffin
    E-Mail: mduffin@pmpa.org
Director, Industry Research and Technology: Miles K. Free
    E-Mail: mfree@pmpa.org
Director, Technical Programs: Monte C. Guitar
    E-Mail: mguitar@pmpa.org
Accounting Assistant: Andrea J. Jeric
    E-Mail: ajeric@pmpa.org
Director, Government Affairs and Communications: Robert
    C. Kiener
    E-Mail: rkiener@pmpa.org
Director, Membership Services: Jeffrey Remaley
    E-Mail: jremaley@pmpa.org

Historical Note:
Formerly the National Screw Machine Products Association. PMPA is an international trade association representing the interests of the precision machined products industry. It seeks to provide programs and services for the industry through dissemination of the latest technological advancements, government regulations, benchmarking, business intelligence and management information. Membership: $700-5,500 (Active, minimum-varies with previous years sales); $1,200 (Associate, minimum-varies with no. of machines); $250 (Affiliate, per location); $1,000-3,000 (Technical).

Meetings/Conferences: Annual
Conference Chair: Robert C. Kiener
2013 - Glendale, AZ (Renaissance Glendale Hotel and
    Spa)/Feb. 15 - 17
Number of non-conference events/year: 2

Publications:
Membership Directory; annually
Production Machining; monthly; adv.
Reports Weekly; weekly

Precision Metalforming Association *(1913)*
6363 Oak Tree Blvd.

Independence, OH 44131-2500
Tel: (216) 901-8800 *Fax:* (216) 901-9190
E-Mail: info@pma.org
Website: pma.org
Members: 10000 companies
Staff: 41
Annual Budget: $2-5,000,000
Tax: 501(c)(6)

Personnel:
Executive Director, PMAEF: David C. Sansone CAE
    E-Mail: dsansone@pma.org
Accounting Assistant: Lori Bailey
    E-Mail: lbailey@pma.org
Director, Programs: Bruce Broman
    E-Mail: bbroman@pma.org
Manager, Government Affairs: Christie Carmigiano
    E-Mail: ccarmigiano@pma.org
President: William E. Gaskin CAE
    E-Mail: wgaskin@pma.org
Director, Membership Services: Allison Grealis
    E-Mail: agrealis@pma.org
Manager, Exhibition Sales: Roger Judson
    E-Mail: rjudson@pma.org
Director, Information Technology: William Koppes
    E-Mail: wkoppes@pma.org
Editor: Brad Kuvin
    E-Mail: bkuvin@pma.org
Senior, Event Planner: Erin Peterman
    E-Mail: epeterman@pma.org

Historical Note:
Established as the Pressed Metal Institute, it became the American Metal Stamping Association in 1961, and assumed its present name in 1987. Custom Roll Forming Institute was merged with PMA in August, 1992. PMA's mission is to represent the metalforming industry and to lead innovative member companies toward competitiveness and profitability. Membership: $900-1,130 (Manufacturer, based on metalforming sales); $190-4,290 (Associate, based on company sales).

Meetings/Conferences: Semi-Annual
Conference Chair: Erin Peterman
2013 - Monterrey, NL (Cintermex)/May 7 - 9/7000
    attendees/over 100 exhibitors
2013 - Chicago, IL/Nov. 18 - 21
Number of non-conference events/year: 9

Publications:
Action Alert; on-line
Membership Directory; on-line
MetalForming magazine; monthly; adv.
PMA e-newsletter; weekly
PMA Update; monthly

Pressure Sensitive Tape Council *(1953)*
1833 Center Point Cir.
Suite123
Naperville, IL 60563
Tel: (630) 544-5048 *Fax:* (630) 544-5055
TollFree: (877) 523-7782
E-Mail: info@pstc.org
Website: pstc.org
Members: 35 affiliate supplier companies and
tape companies
Staff: 6
Annual Budget: $500-1,000,000
Tax: 501(c)(6)

Personnel:
Executive Vice President: Glen R. Anderson
    E-Mail: ganderson@pstc.org
Executive Director: Patrick M. Farrey
    E-Mail: pfarrey@pstc.org
Manager, Meetings: Kriston Ewoldt
    E-Mail: kewoldt@pstc.org
Legal Counsel: Terrence Hutton
    E-Mail: th@howehutton.com

Historical Note:
PSTC's mission is to help the industry produce quality pressure sensitive adhesive tape products in the global marketplace. Members are manufacturers of pressure sensitive tape located in North America. Membership: $4,500-17,600 (Manufacturer); $16,500 (Affiliate Supplier).

Continuing Education:
Certification Designation/s: RTM

Meetings/Conferences: Annual
Conference Chair: Kriston Ewoldt
2013 - New Orleans, LA (Sheraton New Orleans
    Hotel)/May 13 - 17

Publications:
Tape Products Directory; on-line

Pressure Vessel Manufacturers Association
(1975)
800 Roosevelt Rd., Building C
Suite 312
Glen Ellyn, IL 60137
Tel: (630) 942-6590 *Fax:* (630) 790-3095
E-Mail: info@pvma.org
Website: pvma.org
Members: 29 companies
Staff: 3
Annual Budget: $50-100,000

Personnel:
Executive Director: Jeff Church
Association Coordinator: Briana Gunn
    E-Mail: brianag@cmservices.com

Historical Note:
PVMA's mission is with matters pertaining to regulations, standards and codes to which the industry is subject. Members are manufacturers and suppliers for the pressure vessel fabricating industry. Membership: $1,500-4,500 (Company, based on sales volume); $1,500 (Associate).

Meetings/Conferences: Semi-Annual
2013 - Bonita Springs, FL (Hyatt Regency Coconut
    Point Resort and Spa)/March 24 - 25
2013 - Columbus, OH (Crowne Plaza Columbus
    North)/Sept. 9 - 10

Publications:
Member Directory; annually

Membership List Available to Non-members

Pressure Washer Manufacturers Association
(1997)
1300 Sumner Ave.
Cleveland, OH 44115-2851
Tel: (216) 241-7333 *Fax:* (216) 241-0105
E-Mail: pwma@pwma.org
Website: pwma.org
Members: 4 companies
Staff: 4
Annual Budget: $10-25,000

Personnel:
Executive Director: John H. Addington

Historical Note:
The Pressure Washer Manufacturers Association (PWMA) is a nonprofit trade association of manufacturers of pressure washers. The association was formed in 1997 to develop standards pertinent to pressure washers, to increase understanding of pressure washers, and to promote the interests of the pressure washer industry.

Preventive Cardiovascular Nurses Association
(1992)
613 Williamson St.
Suite 200
Madison, WI 53703
Tel: (608) 250-2440 *Fax:* (608) 250-2410
E-Mail: info@pcna.net
Website: pcna.net
Members: 2500 individuals
Staff: 7
Annual Budget: $2-5,000,000
Tax: 501(c)(3)

Personnel:
Chief Executive Officer: Sue Koob MPA
    E-Mail: skoob@pcna.net
Meeting Planner: Tracey Bockhop CMP
Contact, Public Relations and Marketing: Abby Despins
Contact, Membership and Component Relations: Megan
    Halverson
Director, Clinical Education Project: Suzanne Hughes
    MSN, RN

Historical Note:
Formerly (2000) Lipid Nurse Task Force. PCNA is the leading nursing organization dedicated to preventing cardiovascular disease (CVD) through assessing risk, facilitating lifestyle changes, and guiding individuals to achieve treatment goals. Membership: $75 (Regular); $50 (Student).

Continuing Education:
Certification Designation/s: ANCC, ACCL

Meetings/Conferences: Annual
Conference Chair: Tracey Bockhop CMP
2013 - Las Vegas, NV (Paris Las Vegas)/May 2 - 4

Publications:

E-Newsletter; monthly; adv.
Journal of Cardiovascular Nursing; bi-monthly; adv.
Membership Directory; on-line

Membership List Available to Non-members

Print Council of America *(1956)*
Spencer Museum of Art
University of Kansas
Lawrence, KS 66045
Tel: (785) 864-4710 *Fax:* (785) 864-3112
Website: printcouncil.org
Members: 200 individuals
Staff: 1
Annual Budget: $25-50,000

Personnel:
President and Project Coordinator: Stephen Goddard
    E-Mail: goddard@ku.edu

Historical Note:
Professional organization of museum curators of prints, drawings, and photographs. PCA fosters the creation, dissemination, and appreciation of fine prints, old and new. Membership: $40/year.

Print Services & Distribution Association *(1946)*
401 N. Michigan Ave.
Suite 2200
Chicago, IL 60611
Tel: (800) 230-0175 *Fax:* (312) 673-6880
E-Mail: psda@psda.org
Website: psda.org
Members: 25000 companies
Staff: 32
Annual Budget: $2-5,000,000

Personnel:
Executive Vice President: Matt Sanderson
    E-Mail: msanderson@psda.org
Manager, Advertising, Sales and Sponsorship: Ryan Abell
    E-Mail: rabell@psda.org
Editor: John Delavan
    E-Mail: jdelavan@psda.org
Manager, Marketing: Carli Franks
    E-Mail: cfranks@psda.org
Manager, Events: Lydia Goessel
    E-Mail: lgoessel@psda.org
Senior Manager, Event Services: Eric Johnson
    E-Mail: ejohnson@psda.org
Manager, Operations: Barbara O'Connor
    E-Mail: boconnor@psda.org
Director, Finance: Jason Roe
    E-Mail: jroe@psda.org
Manager, Marketing and Communications Services:
    Marcie Valerio
    E-Mail: mvalerio@psda.org

Historical Note:
Formerly (2007) Document Management Industries Association and (1996) National Business Forms Association. PSDA seeks to enhance the success of the independent distribution channel for print, marketing and related services. Members are print distributors, trade printers, suppliers and technology partners. Membership: $250-18,000 (Print Distributors/Trade Printers/Suppliers); $500 (International Companies).

Continuing Education:
Certification Designation/s: CDC

Meetings/Conferences: Annual
Conference Chair: Eric Johnson
2013 - Chicago, IL (Navy Pier Park)/May 7 - 9/1-10
    exhibitors

Publications:
Membership Directory; on-line
Print Solutions Magazine; monthly; adv.
Print Solutions Weekly; weekly

Printing Brokerage/Buyers Association International *(1985)*
1530 Locust St.
Mezanine 124
Philadelphia, PA 19102
Tel: (215) 821-6581 *Fax:* (561) 845-7130
E-Mail: contactus@pbba.org
Website: pbba.org
Members: 1800 companies, international
companies and individuals
Staff: 3
Annual Budget: $1-2,000,000

Personnel:
Director: Vincent Mallardi CMC, MBA

E-Mail: vince@pbba.org

Historical Note:
Formerly (1993) the Printing Brokerage Association. PBBA promotes business relationships between brokers, buying groups, manufacturers and related companies in the printing industry, sets standards and codes of ethical conduct and acts as a source of information and referral. Members are printing intermediaries: group buying/outsourcing services, Independent manufacturers' representatives, and value-added resellers. Membership: $399 (Associate); $599 (Corporate); $999 (Print Vendor).

Publications:
The Broker Age; quarterly

Printing Industries of America *(1887)*
601 13th St. NW
Suite 360S
Washington, DC 20005-3807
Tel: (202) 730-7970 *Fax:* (202) 730-7987
TollFree: (800) 910-4283
E-Mail: printing@printing.org
Website: printing.org
Members: 12000 companies
Staff: 33
Annual Budget: $5-10,000,000

Personnel:
Assistant Vice President, Human Resources: Jim Kyger
    E-Mail: jkyger@printing.org
Vice President, Government Affairs: Lisbeth Lyons
    E-Mail: llyons@printing.org

Historical Note:
PIA is a federation of national, regional, state, and city associations incorporated under the laws of the District of Columbia. Established as United Typothetae of America; became Printing Industry of America in 1945 and assumed its present name in 1965. The 1999 consolidation of PIA and GATF brought together two powerful partners—the world's largest graphic arts trade association, and a technical, scientific, and educational organization dedicated to the advancement of the graphic communications industries worldwide. Sections include Binding Industries of America, Graphic Arts Marketing Information Service, International Thermographers Association, Label Printing Industries of America, Magazine Printers Section, Non-Heatset Web Section, Printing Industry Financial Executives, Print Information Center, and Web Offset Association. PIA along with its affiliates, delivers products and services that enhance the growth and profitability of its members and the industry through advocacy, education, research, and technical information. Membership: $49-105 (Educator/Teacher); $25-85 (Student); $199 (International).

Meetings/Conferences: Annual
Conference Chair: Elise Cohen

Publications:
FOCUS:Membership Newsletter; quarterly
imPRINT Health; quarterly
imPRINT Newsletter; on-line
Print Points Newsletter; bi-weekly
The Magazine; bi-monthly

Printing Industry Credit Executives *(1977)*
1100 Main St.
Buffalo, NY 14209
Tel: (212) 964-8600 *Fax:* (716) 878-0479
TollFree: (800) 226-0722
E-Mail: info@pice.com
Website: pice.com
Members: 125 individuals
Staff: 5
Annual Budget: $50-100,000
Tax: 501(c)(3)

Personnel:
President: Pat Rydzik
Legal Counsel: James E. Anderson
Treasurer: Steve Langager
Administrator: Michael Meyers
Programs Chairman: Judy Telep

Historical Note:
PICE member companies include printers, paper houses, and related graphic arts firms located throughout the United States and Canada. Members are primarily printers of books, catalogues, magazines, and direct mail, and they serve a customer base that includes advertising agencies, publishers, brokers, and end-users. Membership: $900/year (Organization) plus a one-time setup fee of $225.

Meetings/Conferences: Annual
Conference Chair: Judy Telep

Publications:
Member Directory; on-line

Printing Industry Financial Executives
200 Deer Run Rd.
Sewickley, PA 15143
Tel: (412) 741-6860 *Fax:* (412) 741-2311
TollFree: (800) 910-4283
Website: printing.org/pife
Staff: 1

Personnel:
Contact, Media: Justin Goldstein
  E-Mail: jgoldstein@printing.org

Historical Note:
PIFE is a network of professionals who hold positions in finance and administration at Printing Industries of America-member printing companies.PIFE's mission is to deliver products and services that enhance the growth and profitability of its members and the industry through advocacy, education, research, and technical information.

Private Art Dealers Association *(1990)*
P.O. Box 872
Lenox Hill Station
New York, NY 10021
Tel: (212) 572-0772 *Fax:* (212) 572-8398
E-Mail: pada99@msn.com
Website: pada.net
Members: 60 individuals
Staff: 3
Annual Budget: $25-50,000

Personnel:
President: Robert Simon
Contact, Counsel: Christopher Robinson
Administrator: Christine Rath Selhi
  E-Mail: pada99@msn.com

Historical Note:
PADA represents professional art dealers in the private market. Services include appraisals for estate purposes and donations. PADA offers a fine art appraisal service that provides tax valuations for estate purposes and donations to charitable institutions at competitive rates. Membership: $650/year (Individual).

Publications:
Member Listing; on-line

Private Equity Growth Capital Council
950 F St. NW
Suite 550
Washington, DC 20004
Tel: (202) 465-7700 *Fax:* (202) 347-7154
E-Mail: info@pegcc.org
Website: pegcc.org
Members: 36 Firms
Staff: 4
Annual Budget: $5-10,000,000
Tax: 501(c)(6)

Personnel:
Vice President, Finance, Operations and Membership:
  Jennifer Colfelt
General Counsel: Jason Mulvihill
Vice President, Public Affairs and Communications: Ken
  Spain

Historical Note:
PEGCC is committed to developing long-term value by investing in and building enduring companies through the alignment of interests between investors and management and providing financial, operational and strategic resources and direction.

Publications:
PEGCC Quarterly Newsletter; quarterly

Private Label Manufacturers Association *(1979)*
630 Third Ave.
New York, NY 10017
Tel: (212) 972-3131 *Fax:* (212) 983-1382
E-Mail: info@plma.com
Website: plma.com
Members: 3300 member companies
Staff: 45
Annual Budget: $5-10,000,000
Tax: 501(c)(6)

Personnel:
President: Brian Sharoff
Director, Programs and Conferences: Linda Morales
Director, Public Relations: Dane Twining
  E-Mail: dtwining@plma.com

Historical Note:

PLMA's purpose is to promote the purchase of private label or store brand products by consumers. Members are registered retailers and wholesalers.

Continuing Education:
Enrollment: 55
Certification Designation/s: PLMA

Meetings/Conferences:
Conference Chair: Linda Morales
2013 - Prague, Czech Republic/Feb. 27 - 28/over 100
  exhibitors
2013 - Amsterdam, Netherlands (Amsterdam RAI
  Exhibition and Convention Centre)/May 28 - 29/
  over 100 exhibitors
Number of non-conference events/year: 1

Publications:
Market Update; annually
PLMA e-Scanner; monthly

Process Equipment Manufacturers' Association
(1960)
201 Park Washington Ct.
Falls Church, VA 22046-4527
Tel: (703) 538-1796 *Fax:* (703) 241-5603
E-Mail: info@pemanet.org
Website: pemanet.org
Members: 50 companies
Staff: 4
Annual Budget: $250-500,000
Tax: 501(c)(6)

Personnel:
Executive Director: Susan A. Denston
  E-Mail: sdenston@pemanet.org
Management Counsel: Harry W. Buzzerd Jr., CAE, Jr.
  CAE
  E-Mail: hbuzzerd@pemanet.org
Manager, Meetings: Michelle Savoie
Manager, Marketing and Communications: Dawn M.
  Shiley-Danzeisen

Historical Note:
PEMA purpose is to maintain an organization of capital equipment manufacturers. Member companies are engaged in the manufacture and supply of equipment for food, chemical, pulp and paper, water and wastewater processing, air pollution control, liquids-solids separation, etc. Membership: $1,915-5,215/year.

Meetings/Conferences: Semi-Annual
2013 - St. Petersburg, FL/April 10 - 14
2013 - Alexandria, VA (Westin Alexandria)/Sept. 9 - 10
Number of non-conference events/year: 2

Publications:
Newsletter

Produce Marketing Association *(1949)*
1500 Casho Mill Rd.
P.O. Box 6036
Newark, DE 19714-6036
Tel: (302) 737-7100 *Fax:* (302) 731-2409
Website: pma.com
Members: 3000 companies and individuals
Staff: 100
Annual Budget: $10-25,000,000
Tax: 501(c)(6)

Personnel:
President and Chief Executive Officer: Bryan E.
  Silbermann CAE
Vice President, Meetings and Trade Shows: Kent Allaway
  CAE, CMP, IOM
  E-Mail: kallaway@pma.com
Chief Financial Officer: Yvonne Bull
Executive Vice President and Chief Operating Officer:
  Lorna Christie
  E-Mail: lchristie@pma.com
Director, Business Development: Daniel "Dan"
  Henderson
Vice President, Membership Programs: Julie Koch CAE
  E-Mail: jkoch@pma.com
Vice President, Marketing and Communications: Kelly
  Koczak
  E-Mail: kkoczak@pma.com
Vice-President, Government Relations and Public Affairs:
  Katherine "Kathy" A. Means
  E-Mail: kmeans@pma.com
Director, Information Technology: Shawn Merrifield
Director, Public Relations: Meg Miller
Director, Human Resources: Donna Moss
Senior Vice President, Membership Value Creation:
  Anthony "Tony" Parassio

  E-Mail: tparassio@pma.com
Senior Director, Events: Eboni Wall
  E-Mail: ewall@pma.com
Manager, Education and Training: Richard "Lisl"
  Wilkinson

Historical Note:
Formerly (1956) Produce Prepackaging Association, Produce Packaging Association (1967), Produce Packaging and Marketing Association (1971). PMA seeks to serve the entire produce and floral supply chains by enhancing the marketing of produce, floral, and related products and services worldwide. Members are companies, corporations, organizations, or individuals engaged in any facet of marketing fresh produce and floral products, or providing equipment, supplies, transportation, or other services to the fresh produce and floral industry. Membership: $865-2,435/year.

Meetings/Conferences: Annual
Conference Chair: Kent Allaway CAE, CMP, IOM
2013 - New Orleans, LA/Oct. 18 - 21
2013 - New Orleans, LA/Oct. 18 - 20/18500
  attendees/over 100 exhibitors
2014 - Anaheim, CA/Oct. 17 - 20
2014 - Anaheim, CA/Oct. 17 - 19/18500 attendees/
  over 100 exhibitors
2015 - Atlanta, GA/Oct. 23 - 26
2015 - Atlanta, GA/Oct. 23 - 25/18500 attendees/over
  100 exhibitors
Number of non-conference events/year: 3

Publications:
Fresh Magazine; quarterly; adv.
Membership Directory; on-line

Producers Guild of America *(1950)*
8530 Wilshire Blvd.
Suite 450
Beverly Hills, CA 90211
Tel: (310) 358-9020 *Fax:* (310) 358-9520
E-Mail: info@producersguild.org
Website: producersguild.org
Members: 5,000 members
Staff: 12
Annual Budget: $2-5,000,000

Personnel:
Executive Director: Vance Van Petten
Director, Membership: Bryce Averitt
Administrative Assistant: Scott Bengston
Supervisor, Communications: Chris Green
Director, Arbitration and Legal Affairs:: Nikki Livolsi
Sponsorship Specialist: Diane Salerno
Director, Operations: Jo-Ann West

Historical Note:
Formerly (1967) Screen Producers Guild. PGA is the non-profit trade group that represents, protects and promotes the interests of all members of the producing team in film, television and new media. Members vary from producers to production coordinators of motion pictures, television and new media. Membership: $395 (Producers Council); $195 (AP Council/New Media Council).

Meetings/Conferences:
Conference Chair: Diane Salerno

Publications:
Produced By magazine; adv.
The Networker; quarterly; adv.
The Networker newsletter; quarterly

Product Development and Management Association *(1976)*
401 N. Michigan Ave.
Suite 2200
Chicago, IL 60611
Tel: (312) 321-5145 *Fax:* (312) 673-6885
TollFree: (800) 232-5241
E-Mail: pdma@pdma.org
Website: pdma.org
Members: 3500 individuals
Staff: 17
Annual Budget: $1-2,000,000

Personnel:
Executive Director: Brad Barbera
  E-Mail: bbarbera@pdma.org
Editor: John Delavan
  E-Mail: jdelavan@pdma.org
Senior Director, Education and Certification: Susan Farrel
  E-Mail: sfarrell@pdma.org
Senior Coordinator, Education and Certification: Amada
  Fiesler
  E-Mail: pdma@pdma.org

Senior Manager, Event Services: Eric Johnson
    E-Mail: ejohnson@pdma.org
Senior Director, Marketing and Communications: Linda
    Schwartz
    E-Mail: lschwartz@pdma.org
Manager, Operations: Amy Westercamp
    E-Mail: awestercamp@pdma.org
Director, Marketing and Communications: Amanda Wood
    E-Mail: pdma@pdma.org

Historical Note:
PDMA's mission is to improve the effectiveness of
individuals and organizations in product development and
management. Members are practitioners, service providers,
academics and students. Membership: $235 (Professional);
$145 (Academic); $35 (Student); $700 (Team Leader);
$100 (Basic).

Continuing Education:
Certification Designation/s: NPDP

Meetings/Conferences: Annual
Conference Chair: Eric Johnson
Number of non-conference events/year: 12

Publications:
Journal of Product Innovation Management (JPIM); bi-
    monthly
Membership Directory; on-line
Visions Magazine; quarterly; adv.

Product Liability Advisory Council (1983)
1850 Centennial Park Dr.
Suite 510
Reston, VA 20191-1517
Tel: (703) 264-5300 Fax: (703) 264-5301
E-Mail: plac@plac.net
Website: plac.com
Members: 100 corporate members
Staff: 3
Annual Budget: $1-2,000,000

Personnel:
President: Hugh F. Young Jr.
    E-Mail: hyoung@plac.net
Director, Membership Services: Kimberly J. Condon
    E-Mail: kcondon@plac.net
Vice President, Legal Services: Jonathan M. Harrison
    E-Mail: jharrison@plac.net

Historical Note:
PLAC seeks to contribute to the reform of laws governing
the liability of manufacturers in the U.S. and elsewhere.

Meetings/Conferences: Annual

Publications:
Membership Directory; on-line

Production and Operations Management Society
(1989)
C/O Florida International University
11200 SW Eighth St., University Park, RB 250
Miami, FL 33199
Tel: (305) 348-1413 Fax: (305) 348-4126
E-Mail: poms@fiu.edu
Website: poms.org
Members: 1200 individuals
Staff: 3
Annual Budget: $250-500,000

Personnel:
Executive Director: Sushil K. Gupta PhD

Historical Note:
POMS aims to extend and integrate knowledge that
contributes to the understanding and practice of production
and operations management. Members are professionals
and academics with an interest in production and
operations management. Membership: $125 (Regular);
$155 (Joint); $25 (Student); $30 (Retired); $25 (Colleges/
Management); $10 (Latin Chapter); $5 (Other Chapters).

Meetings/Conferences: Annual
Conference Chair: Manoj K. Malhotra
2013 - New Orleans, LA/April 26 - 29
2013 - Denver, CO (Denver Marriott City Center)/May
    3 - 6
Number of non-conference events/year: 1

Publications:
POMS Chronicle
POMS Journal

Production Engine Remanufacturers Association
(1946)
28203 Woodhaven Rd.
Edwards, MO 65326
Tel: (417) 998-5057 Fax: (417) 998-5056

Website: pera.org
Members: 150 companies
Staff: 2
Annual Budget: $100-250,000
Tax: 501(c)(6)

Personnel:
Executive Vice President: Nancie Boland
    E-Mail: nancieboland@pera.org

Historical Note:
Formerly (1970) Western Engine Rebuilders Association
and (1973) Production Engine Rebuilders Association,
PERA's goal is to provide its members with the opportunity
to exchange the ideas, methods and procedures necessary
to produce remanufactured products. Members are
manufacturers, remanufacturers and parts suppliers to the
production line combustion engine industry. Membership:
$750-1500 (Remanufacturer); $1,050-1,500 (Core
Suppliers); $400-1,250 (Supplier).

Meetings/Conferences: Annual
Number of non-conference events/year: 1

Publications:
Enginews Newsletter; semi-annually; adv.

Membership List Available to Non-members

Production Equipment Rental Association (1992)
P.O. Box 77327
San Francisco, CA 94107-7327
E-Mail: info@peraonline.org
Website: peraonline.org
Members: 200 companies
Staff: 2
Annual Budget: $25-50,000

Personnel:
Secretary and Treasurer: Lee Utterbach
    E-Mail: lee@lucamera.com
President: Kay Baker
    E-Mail: kbaker@fvesco.com

Historical Note:
An industry association and user community for the film
and video professional production and entertainment
industry. Dedicated to promoting the professional
advancement of new technologies available from member
companies to meet the requirements of clients' artistic
challenges. Members are rental companies who supply
production equipment to the entertainment industry.
Membership is international, with roughly half concentrated
in southern California. Membership: $265-1,600/year
(company).

Professional and Organizational Development
Network in Higher Education (1975)
P.O. Box 3318
Nederland, CO 80466
Tel: (303) 258-9521 Fax: (970) 377-9282
E-Mail: podoffice@podnetwork.org
Website: podnetwork.org
Members: 1800 individuals
Staff: 2
Annual Budget: $100-250,000

Personnel:
Executive Director: Hoag Holmgren
    E-Mail: hoag.holmgren@gmail.com

Historical Note:
POD's purpose is to provide support and services for its
members through publications, conferences, consulting,
and networking, to offer services and resources to
others interested in faculty development and to fulfill an
advocacy role, nationally, seeking to inform and persuade
educational leaders the value of faculty, instructional,
and organizational development in institutions of higher
education. Membership: $110 (Individual International);
$95 (Individual); $225 (Institutional international, for 3
persons and $75 for Additional persons); $45 (Student/
Retired, Canada, the United States, and Mexico); $50
(Student/Retired International).

Meetings/Conferences: Semi-Annual

Publications:
POD Network News
The Annual Membership Directory; annually

Membership List Available to Non-members

Professional and Technical Consultants
Association (1975)
P.O. Box 2261
Santa Clara, CA 95055
Tel: (408) 971-5902 Fax: (866) 746-1053
TollFree: (800) 747-2822
E-Mail: info@patca.org

Website: patca.org
Members: 400 individuals
Staff: 2
Annual Budget: $25-50,000

Personnel:
Executive Director: Tonia Forbus

Historical Note:
PATCA provides clients with an unparalleled network of
outstanding professional and technical consultants, at no
cost to client businesses. Members are independent technical
consultants and small consulting firms. Membership: $345
(Associate/Full); $690 (Company); $125 (Affiliate).

Meetings/Conferences: Annual
Number of non-conference events/year: 6

Publications:
Membership Directory; on-line

Professional Association of Christian Educators
(1970)
Biola University
13800 Biola Ave.
La Mirada, CA 90639
E-Mail: mail@napce.org
Members: 341 individuals
Staff: 1
Annual Budget: $50-100,000

Personnel:
Executive Administrator: Freddy Cardoza
    E-Mail: freddy.cardoza@biola.edu

Historical Note:
NAPCE is a community of Christian educators committed to
the teaching and equipping ministry of the church. NAPCE
encourages collaboration, networking and fellowship for
current and future professors in Christian educational
ministries. Annual dues are only $75.00 (Graduate
students, $45.00)

Publications:
Christian Education Journal; semi-annually
The Journal of Family Ministry

Membership List Available to Non-members

Professional Association of Diving Instructors
(1966)
30151 Tomas St.
Rancho Santa Margarita, CA 92688-2125
Tel: (949) 858-7234 Fax: (949) 267-1267
TollFree: (800) 729-7234
Website: padi.com
Members: 135000 individuals and 6000 dive
stores
Staff: 220
Annual Budget: $25-50,000,000

Personnel:
Chairman and Chief Executive Officer: Brian P. Cronin
Media Contact: Theresa Gulledge
    E-Mail: theresa.gulledge@padi.com
Vice President, Training and Customer Services: James
    Morgan
Chief Financial Officer: Gary Prenovost

Historical Note:
PADI exists to develop programs that encourage and
fulfill the public interest in recreational scuba diving and
snorkeling worldwide.

Continuing Education:
Certification Designation/s: PADISD

Publications:
PADI Newsletter; on-line

Professional Association of Health Care Office
Management (1988)
1576 Bella Cruz Dr.
Suite 360
Lady Lake, FL 32159
Tel: (847) 375-4717 Fax: (407) 386-7006
TollFree: (800) 451-9311
E-Mail: info@pahcom.com
Website: pahcom.com
Members: 3300 individuals and 100 companies
Staff: 8
Annual Budget: $500-1,000,000

Personnel:
Founder and Executive Director: Richard Blanchette
    E-Mail: richardb@pahcom.com
Contact, Membership Services: Darlene Born CMM
Chief Technology Officer: Daniel Labelle
    E-Mail: dan@pahcom.com

Editor: Mary Miller
Administrative Assistant: Heather Schumacher

Historical Note:
PAHCOM was founded as the Professional Association of Health Care Office Managers, with the purpose of providing a networking system to managers of medical practices. Assumed its current name in 2002. Membership: $195 (Individual); $125 (Student); $1,000 (Corporate).

Continuing Education:
Certification Designation/s: CMM

Meetings/Conferences: Annual

Publications:
Member Directory; on-line
The PAHCOM Journal; bi-monthly

Professional Association of Innkeepers International *(1988)*
295 Seven Farms Dr.
Suite 236-C
Charleston, SC 29492
Tel: (856) 310-1102 *Fax:* (856) 895-0432
TollFree: (800) 468-7244
E-Mail: membership@paii.org
Website: paii.org
Members: 3000 members
Staff: 6
Annual Budget: $500-1,000,000

Personnel:
President and Chief Executive Officer: Jay Karen
    E-Mail: jay@paii.org
Sales Coordinator, Membership Services: Isabel Abreu
    E-Mail: isabel@paii.org
Director, Education and Events: Jessie Robinson
    E-Mail: jessie@paii.org
Manager, Communications and Marketing: Ingrid Thorson
    E-Mail: ingrid@paii.org

Historical Note:
PAII is committed to fostering a knowledgeable, caring and conscientious community of professional innkeepers, networking with each other throughout the world. Membership: $89-399/year.

Meetings/Conferences: Annual
Conference Chair: Jessie Robinson
2013 - Las Vegas, NV (Tropicana Las Vegas)/Jan. 28 - 31
Number of non-conference events/year: 6

Publications:
INNfo; weekly
Innkeeping; monthly
Innkeeping Quarterly; quarterly

Professional Association of Resume Writers and Career Coaches *(1990)*
1388 Brightwaters Blvd. NE
St. Petersburg, FL 33704
Tel: (727) 821-2274 *Fax:* (727) 894-1277
TollFree: (800) 822-7279
E-Mail: PARWhq@aol.com
Website: parw.com
Members: 950 companies
Staff: 2
Annual Budget: $250-500,000

Personnel:
Executive Director: Frank Fox
    E-Mail: parwhq@aol.com

Historical Note:
PARW/CC's mission is to strive to exchange information, enhance skills or demonstrate commitment to provide professional services to the general public. Members include independent business owners, as well as non-profit career centers such as colleges and universities, military bases, workforce development offices, and state Departments of Labor. Membership: $150/year (Individual).

Continuing Education:
Certification Designation/s: CPRW, CEIP, CPCC

Publications:
Membership Directory; on-line
Spotlight; monthly

Professional Association of Volleyball Officials *(1992)*
P.O. Box 780
Oxford, KS 67119
Tel: (316) 721-2860 *Fax:* (620) 455-3800
TollFree: (888) 791-2074
E-Mail: pavo@pavo.org

Website: pavo.org
Members: 97 boards and 1900 individuals
Staff: 2
Annual Budget: $250-500,000
Tax: 501(c)(3)

Personnel:
Executive Director: Marcia Alterman
    E-Mail: executive.director@pavo.org
Contact, Membership Services: Miki Kennedy
    E-Mail: pavo@pavo.org

Historical Note:
Founded as the Affiliated Boards of Officials and formerly (1992) a division of National Association for Girls and Women in Sport, assumed its present name in 1994. PAVO strives to increase the number of competent officials through education and mentoring and promotes involvement in the governing bodies of other volleyball officiating groups. Membership: $35/year.

Continuing Education:
Certification Designation/s: SC, NNRC, NRC, LJC

Meetings/Conferences: Annual
Number of non-conference events/year: 4

Publications:
Membership Directory; on-line
Official Word; bi-monthly
PAVO Officials' Guidebook; annually
Rules Interpretation - Newsletter; irregular

Professional Aviation Maintenance Association *(1972)*
972 E Tuttle Rd.
Building 204
Ionia, MI 48846
Tel: (800) 356-1671
E-Mail: hq@pama.org
Website: pama.org
Members:
250 Companies
4500 Individuals
Staff: 5
Annual Budget: $25-50,000
Tax: 501(c)(6)

Personnel:
President: Dale Forton

Historical Note:
PAMA's mission is to promote continuous improvement in aviation safety by enhancing the professionalism and recognition of the Aviation Maintenance Technician through communication, education, representation and support. Membership: $20 (Student); $49 (Standard/Associate); $25 (Active); $99 (Educational members); $650 (Corporate).

Continuing Education:
Certification Designation/s: CC, RMC, TLS, AME, AMS, TLE

Meetings/Conferences: Annual

Publications:
JetBlast! Newsletter

Professional Aviation Safety Specialists (AFL-CIO) *(1977)*
1150 17th St. NW
Suite 702
Washington, DC 20036
Tel: (202) 293-7277 *Fax:* (202) 293-7727
Website: passnational.org
Members: 11000 Federal Aviation Administration (FAA) and Department of Defense (DoD) employees
Staff: 15
Annual Budget: $2-5,000,000

Personnel:
National President: Tom Brantley
    E-Mail: president@passnational.org
Legislative and Administrative Director: Abby H. Bernstein
    E-Mail: abernstein@passnational.org
Representative, Legislative and Public Relations: Kori Blalock Keller
    E-Mail: kbkeller@passnational.org
Editor: Jessica Cigich
    E-Mail: jhoffman@passnational.org
Counsel: Mike Derby
    E-Mail: mderby@passnational.org
Manager, Member Services and Special Projects: Emily Edwards
    E-Mail: eedwards@passnational.org

Labor Relations Specialist and Paralegal: Allyn Van Vechten
    E-Mail: avanvechten@passnational.org

Historical Note:
Formerly the Professional Airways Systems Specialists (AFL-CIO), PASS, an aviation labor union, was formed to provide exclusive representation for the FAA's technician bargaining unit. Members include Technical Operations and DoD employees (systems specialists, electronics technicians and computer specialists). Membership: $75 (Retired); $120 (Associate).

Meetings/Conferences: Annual

Publications:
Pass Times; bi-monthly

Professional Bail Agents of the United States *(1981)*
1718 M St NW
Suite 136
Washington, DC 20036
Tel: (202) 783-4120 *Fax:* (202) 783-4125
TollFree: (800) 883-7287
E-Mail: info@pbus.com
Website: pbus.com
Members: 15500 bail agents
Staff: 3
Annual Budget: $250-500,000
Tax: 501(c)(6)

Personnel:
Chief Executive Officer and Executive Director: Melanie Ledgerwood
    E-Mail: mledgerwood@pbus.com
Vice President: Dennis H. Sew
    E-Mail: dennis@pbus.com

Historical Note:
PBUS's mission is to provide information, education and representation for the 14,500 bail agents nationwide and support of bail agent certification, enhanced liability insurance and development of a code of ethics. Membership: $300 (Individual-Voting); $675 (Agency); $1,500 (Insurance Company); $120 (Individual).

Continuing Education:
Enrollment: 250
Certification Designation/s: CBA

Meetings/Conferences:
Number of non-conference events/year: 2

Publications:
Membership Directory; on-line
PBUS Newsletter; quarterly

Membership List Available to Non-members

Professional Baseball Athletic Trainers Society *(1983)*
400 Colony Sq., Suite 1750
1201 Peachtree St.
Atlanta, GA 30361
Tel: (404) 892-8919 *Fax:* (404) 892-8560
Website: pbats.com
Members: 60 individuals
Staff: 3
Annual Budget: $500-1,000,000
Tax: 501(c)(6)

Personnel:
President: Richie Bancells
General Counsel: Rollin E. Mallernee II
Director, Public Relations: Neil Romano

Historical Note:
PBATS serves as an educational resource for the major league and minor league baseball athletic trainers.

Professional Basketball Writers' Association *(1972)*
P.O. Box 4744
Baltimore, MD 21211
Tel: (410) 523-0635
E-Mail: richdubroff@aol.com
Website: sportswriters.net
Members: 150 individuals
Staff: 1
Annual Budget: Under $10,000
Tax: 501(c)(6)

Personnel:
Treasurer: Rich Dubroff
    E-Mail: richdubroff@aol.com

Historical Note:
Members are sports editors and reporters who cover professional basketball. Membership: $20/year.

Professional Beauty Association | National Cosmetology Association (2004)

15825 N. 71st St.
Suite 100
Scottsdale, AZ 85254
Tel: (480) 281-0424 *Fax:* (480) 905-0708
TollFree: (800) 468-2274
E-Mail: info@probeauty.org
Website: probeauty.org
Members:
1400 firms and 12000 industry professionals
12000 industry professionals
Staff: 25
Annual Budget: $2-5,000,000

Personnel:
Executive Director: Steve Sleeper CAE, CPA
   E-Mail: steve@probeauty.org
Director, Membership Services: Elizabeth Fantetti
   E-Mail: elizabeth@probeauty.org
Director, Event Operations: Susie Howard
   E-Mail: susan@probeauty.org
Director, Government Affairs: Myra Y. Irizarry
   E-Mail: myra@probeauty.org
Director, Industry Programs and Education: Jessi Marshall
   E-Mail: jessi@probeauty.org
Manager, Education and Training: Kelley McCarthy
   E-Mail: kelley@probeauty.org
Director, Marketing and Communications: Marissa
   Porcaro
   E-Mail: marissa@probeauty.org
Chief Financial Officer: Steve Wilkerson
   E-Mail: swilkerson@probeauty.org

Historical Note:
Formerly (1904) the Barber Supply Dealers of America and then the Beauty and Barber Supply Institute; assumed current name in 2004. PBA's mission is to provide resources, education, ideas and advocacy to enhance the power and performance of the professional beauty community. Offers business tools, education, advocacy, networking and more to improve individual businesses and the industry as a whole. Membership: $175-7,500 (Manufacturers/Distributors/Salon Owners); $115 (Beauty Professionals).

Continuing Education:
Certification Designation/s: CBE

Meetings/Conferences:
Conference Chair: Susie Howard
2013 - Long Beach, CA (Long Beach Convention and
   Entertainment Center)/Jan. 26 - 28
Number of non-conference events/year: 1

Publications:
Membership Directory; on-line

Membership List Available to Non-members

Professional Bowlers Association (1958)

719 Second Ave.
Suite 701
Seattle, WA 98104
Tel: (206) 332-9688 *Fax:* (206) 332-9722
E-Mail: info@pba.com
Website: pba.com
Members: 4300 individuals
Staff: 23
Annual Budget: $5-10,000,000

Personnel:
Chief Executive Officer and Commissioner: Fred Schreyer
Accountant: Allyson Beaver
Manager, Information Technology: Brian Foraker
Vice President and Director, Business and Legal Affairs:
   Cara Frey
Director, Community Relations and Events: Janay Leddy
Sales Manager: Sam Mulligan
Contact, Media Relations: Jerry Schneider

Historical Note:
PBA hosts regional, national, and senior tournaments throughout the year. Members must have a minimum average of 200 established for 66 or more games per season for the 2 most recent seasons prior to applying for membership. Membership: $144 (Standard Member); $300/year.

Meetings/Conferences:
Conference Chair: Janay Leddy
Number of non-conference events/year: 7

Publications:
PBA Newsletter; weekly

Professional Communications Society (1957)

445 Hoes Ln.
Piscataway, NJ 08854-4141
Tel: (732) 981-0060
Website: ewh.ieee.org/soc/pcs
Members: 2500 individuals
Staff: 1

Personnel:
President: Julia Williams

Historical Note:
A technical society of the Institute of Electrical and Electronics Engineers (IEEE). Membership in the Society, open only to IEEE members, includes a subscription to a technical periodical in the field published by IEEE. All administrative support is provied by IEEE.

Meetings/Conferences: Annual
2013 - Vancouver, BC (Walter Gage conference hotel)/
   July 15 - 17

Publications:
PCS Newsletter

Professional Construction Estimators Association of America (1956)

P.O. Box 680336
Charlotte, NC 28216
Tel: (704) 489-1494 *Fax:* (704) 489-1495
TollFree: (877) 521-7232
E-Mail: pcea@pcea.org
Website: pcea.org
Members: 1000 individuals
Staff: 3
Annual Budget: $50-100,000
Tax: 501(c)(3)

Personnel:
President: Lance Pollock
Treasurer: Wesley Ferree

Historical Note:
PCEA's mission is to further the recognition of construction estimating as a professional field within the construction industry. Membership: $295/year.

Continuing Education:
Certification Designation/s: ASPE

Publications:
Estimator; quarterly; adv.
PCEA National Membership and Resource Directory;
   annually; adv.

Professional Convention Management Association (1958)

35 E. Wacker Dr.
Suite 500
Chicago, IL 60601
Tel: (312) 423-7262 *Fax:* (312) 423-7222
TollFree: (877) 827-7262
Website: pcma.org
Members: 6000 individuals
Staff: 42
Annual Budget: $5-10,000,000
Tax: 501(c)(6)

Personnel:
President and Chief Executive Officer: Deborah Sexton
   CAE
   E-Mail: deborah.sexton@pcma.org
Vice President, Marketing and Communications: Carolyn
   Clark
Director, Education: Kristin Crane
   E-Mail: kcrane@pcma.org
Systems Administrator: Scott Evtuch
   E-Mail: sevtuch@pcma.org
Director, Online Marketing: Mary Reynolds Kane
   E-Mail: mkane@pcma.org
Chief Operating Officer: Sherrif Karamat
   E-Mail: skaramat@pcma.org
Associate Director, Membership Development: Dorothy
   Kolpak
   E-Mail: dkolpak@pcma.org
Executive Director, PCMA Education Foundation and Head,
   PCMA Education: Brad Lewis
   E-Mail: blewis@pcma.org
Director, Human Resources: Gina Meier
   E-Mail: gmeier@pcma.org
Senior Vice President, Meetings and Events: Kelly Peacy
   CAE CMP
   E-Mail: kpeacy@pcma.org
Vice President, Finance: Paulette Phillips
   E-Mail: pphillips@pcma.org
Editor in Chief, Convene: Michelle Russell

E-Mail: mrussell@pcma.org

Historical Note:
Incorporated in Illinois, February 28, 1958. PCMA's mission is to deliver superior and innovative education and promote the value of professional convention management. Membership consists of convention managers, CEOs, meeting planners, and suppliers. Membership: $40-485/ year.

Meetings/Conferences:
Conference Chair: Kelly Peacy CAE CMP
2013 - Orlando, FL (Orange County Convention
   Center)/Jan. 13 - 16/3000 attendees
2013 - Ottawa, ON/July 28 - 30

Publications:
Convene Magazine; monthly; adv.
Membership Directory; on-line
PCMA E-Newsletter; weekly

Professional Currency Dealers Association (1985)

P. O. Box 7157
Westchester, IL 60154
Tel: (414) 421-3484 *Fax:* (414) 423-0343
E-Mail: nge3@comcast.net
Website: pcdaonline.com
Members: 75 individuals
Staff: 5
Annual Budget: $50-100,000

Personnel:
Secretary: James A. Simek
   E-Mail: nge3@comcast.net
Webmaster: Bruce Perdue
   E-Mail: bdperdue1@netscape.net
Treasurer: Austin M. Sheheen Jr.

Historical Note:
PCDA seeks to encourage, stimulate and progress the profession of dealing in all forms of currency and related items and to boost the study of paper money, knowledgeable and ethical dealing between members and the public. Members are specialists in currency, stocks and bonds, fiscal documents, and related paper items. Membership: $250/year.

Meetings/Conferences: Annual
Conference Chair: Kevin Foley
2013 - Rosemont, IL (Crowne Plaza Chicago O'Hare,
   Rosemont)/Nov. 20 - 23

Publications:
Membership Directory; on-line

Professional Engineers in Private Practice (1956)

1420 King St.
Alexandria, VA 22314-2794
Tel: (703) 684-2800 *Fax:* (703) 836-4875
E-Mail: pepp@nspe.org
Website: nspe.org/InterestGroups/PEPP/
   index.html
Members: 24000 individuals
Staff: 2
Annual Budget: $1-2,000,000

Personnel:
Chair: Dawn Edgell
   E-Mail: dawn_edgell@hotmail.com
Staff Director: Kim "Kimberly" Shoop Granados CAE

Historical Note:
Formed in 1955 as an autonomous division of the National Society of Professional Engineers to address concerns of individual consulting professional engineers; reorganized in 1965 with independent dues structure. Mission is to provide information and lobbying efforts on practice management, professional liability, and career development interests of members.

Publications:
PEPP Talk; monthly; adv.

Professional Football Athletic Trainers Society (1982)

400 Colony Sq.
Suite 1750
Atlanta, GA 30361
Tel: (404) 875-4000 *Fax:* (404) 892-8560
Website: pfats.com
Members: 120 individuals
Staff: 1
Annual Budget: $100-250,000

Personnel:
President: John Norwig

Historical Note:

PFATS is composed of all the athletic trainers in the NFL. Promotes the professional interests of NFL athletic trainers. It holds national affiliation with National Athletic Trainers Association.

Publications:
Pro Football Athletic Trainer; annually

Professional Football Writers of America (1962)
12030 Cedar Lake Ct.
Maryland Heights, MO 63043
Tel: (314) 453-0755
Website: pfwa.org
Members: 400 individuals
Staff: 1
Annual Budget: $10-25,000

Personnel:
Secretary: Howard Balzer
E-Mail: howardbalzer@pfwa.org

Historical Note:
PFWA's mission is to include improving access to practices and locker rooms, developing working relationships with all teams and ensuring that football writers are treated in a professional manner. Members are sportswriters and columnists who cover professional football regularly. Promotes good working relationships between writers and leagues, and clubs and players' associations. Membership: $50/year.

Publications:
PFWA Newsletter; irregular; adv.

Professional Fraternity Association (1978)
3649 Shinn St.
New York, NY 10004
Tel: (512) 789-9530 Fax: (512) 472-4820
E-Mail: info@profraternity.org
Website: profraternity.org
Members: 37 fraternities and sororities
Staff: 1
Annual Budget: $50-100,000

Personnel:
Executive Director: Michael Abraham
E-Mail: mike.abraham@thetatau.org

Historical Note:
Established through a merger of the Professional Panhellenic Association (1925) and the Professional Interfraternity Conference (1928). PFA's mission is to be the trusted resource for educating and serving its members. Membership: $200 (Associate); $250 (Fraternal).

Meetings/Conferences:
Conference Chair: Michael Abraham

Publications:
Membership Directory; on-line

Professional Golfers Association of America (1916)
100 Ave. of the Champions
Palm Beach Gardens, FL 33410
Tel: (561) 624-8400 Fax: (561) 624-8448
Website: pga.com
Members: 27000 individuals
Staff: 115
Annual Budget: Over $100,000,000
Tax: 501(c)(6)

Personnel:
Chief Executive Officer: Joe Steranka
Director, PGM Recruiting and Internships: Bill Cioffoletti
E-Mail: recruiting@pgahq.com
Director, Communications and Publications: Kelly Elbin

Historical Note:
Founded in New York City in 1916, PGA is a sports organization comprised of men and women promoting the game of golf to everyone, everywhere. Members are golf professionals managing golf courses.

Meetings/Conferences: Annual
2013 - Orlando, FL (Hilton Orlando)/Jan. 22 - 24
2014 - Las Vegas, NV (Venetian Resort Hotel Casino)/ Aug. 21 - 22
Number of non-conference events/year: 1

Publications:
PGA Magazine; monthly; adv.

Professional Grounds Management Society (1911)
720 Light St.
Baltimore, MD 21230-3816
Tel: (410) 223-2861 Fax: (410) 752-8295
E-Mail: pgms@assnhqtrs.com
Website: pgms.org

Members: 1500 individuals
Staff: 5
Annual Budget: $250-500,000
Tax: 501(c)(4)

Personnel:
Executive Director: Thomas C. Shaner APR, CAE
E-Mail: pgms@assnhqtrs.com
Director, Communications and Marketing: Molly Baldwin
E-Mail: mollybaldwin@assnhqtrs.com
Assistant Director ,Communications and Marketing: Meghan Brady
E-Mail: meghanbrady@assnhqtrs.com
Associate Director and Membership Coordinator: Kelly Mesaris
E-Mail: kellymesaris@assnhqtrs.com
Manager, Finance: Monica Shaner
E-Mail: monicashaner@assnhqtrs.com

Historical Note:
Formerly (1971) National Association of Professional Gardeners. PGMS is a professional society for the individual whose purpose is education and professional advancement. Members are professionals involved in the care and maintenance of schools, universities, parks, office parks, shopping malls, municipalities, sports grounds, etc. Membership: $175 (Active); $125 (Affiliate); $400 (Supplier); $35 (Student/Educator/Researcher); $450 (Institutional).

Continuing Education:
Certification Designation/s: CGM, CGK, CGT, SGM

Meetings/Conferences: Annual
Number of non-conference events/year: 1

Publications:
Forum- Newsletter; bi-monthly
Membership Directory

Professional Handlers Association (1926)
17017 Norbrook Dr.
Olney, MD 20832
Tel: (301) 924-0089
E-Mail: manager@phadoghandlers.com
Website: phadoghandlers.com
Members: 250 individuals
Staff: 3
Annual Budget: $25-50,000

Personnel:
Executive Vice President: Kathleen Bowser
E-Mail: kathy@phadoghandlers.com

Historical Note:
PHA represents the interests of professional dog handlers and furthering the sport of showing dogs throughout the United States. PHA is organized into six geographical zones across the United States. PHA seeks to advocate a beneficial working relationship among members, clients, other handler organizations, and the American Kennel Club. Members are individuals who show purebred dogs professionally as well as others interested in improving the stature of professional dog handling.

Publications:
PHA Handlers Directory; on-line

Professional Hockey Writers' Association (1967)
1480 Pleasant Valley Way, Suite 44
W. Orange, NJ 07052
Tel: (973) 669-8607
E-Mail: sherrydarlingnj@aol.com
Members: 350 individuals
Staff: 2
Annual Budget: Under $10,000

Personnel:
President: Helene Elliott CAE
E-Mail: helene.elliott@latimes.com
Secretary-Treasurer: Sherry J. Ross
E-Mail: sherrydarlingnj@aol.com

Historical Note:
Formerly (1971) National Hockey League Writers' Association. PHWA members are journalists covering the teams of the National Hockey League. Has no paid officers or full-time staff. Membership: $25/year (individual).

Professional Housing Management Association (1973)
154 Ft. Evans Rd. NE
Leesburg, VA 20176
Tel: (703) 771-1888 Fax: (703) 771-0299
E-Mail: phmainfo@earthlink.net
Website: phma.com
Members: 120 organizations and 3000 individuals

Staff: 6
Annual Budget: $1-2,000,000
Tax: 501(c)(6)

Personnel:
Executive Director: Jon R. Moore DHD
E-Mail: jonrmoore@earthlink.net
Manager, Publication and Advertising Project: Melissa Cooper
E-Mail: mkcooper@earthlink.net
Contact, Membership Services: Dana Fikes
E-Mail: phmamembership@earthlink.net
Contact, Trade Expo and Corporate Memberships: Monique Jenkins Esq.
E-Mail: phmaadmin@earthlink.net
Manager, Membership Project and Administration Project: Breanna Smith
E-Mail: breannamsmith@earthlink.net
Manager, Events Management Project: Kati Trump
E-Mail: katitrump@earthlink.net

Historical Note:
PHMA's mission is to contribute towards better quality housing for military members and their families through improved communications and networking; education and training; certification; and professional recognition. Members are federal government employees, civilian or military, who are directly involved in the profession of housing management or whose responsibility provides direct support to the field of housing management. Membership: $30 (Regular); $20 (GS-5/below- Regular); $350 (Corporate-Silver); $1,000 (Corporate-Gold); $3,500 (Corporate-Platinum).

Continuing Education:
Certification Designation/s: CDAM, CDRS, CHCSR, CDUHM, DHP, DHD, CDPM, DFS, DHM

Meetings/Conferences: Annual
Conference Chair: Monique Jenkins Esq.

Publications:
Defense Communities: The Magazine of Military Housing, Lodging and Lifestyles; bi-monthly; adv.

Membership List Available to Non-members

Professional Insurance Communicators of America (1954)
3601 Vincennes Rd.
P.O. Box 68700
Indianapolis, IN 46268-0700
Tel: (317) 875-5250 Fax: (317) 879-8408
Website: pro-ins-coa.org
Members: 30 individuals
Staff: 1
Annual Budget: Under $10,000
Tax: 501(c)(3)

Personnel:
Assistant Secretary and Treasurer: Janet E. H. Wright ABC, APR, Jr.
E-Mail: jwright@namic.org

Historical Note:
Formerly (1969) Mutual Insurance Council of Editors, (1981) the Mutual Insurance Communicators. An affiliate of the National Association of Mutual Insurance Companies. Committed to the continuing education and professional development of its members and the positive promotion of the insurance industry to its many audiences. Members produce communication media for insurance companies and organizations, to include written and online communication. Membership: $275 (Full, Single); $325 (Full, Corporate); $300 (Affiliate).

Meetings/Conferences: Annual
Number of non-conference events/year: 1

Publications:
Membership Directory; on-line

Professional Insurance Marketing Association (1975)
35 E. Wacker Dr.
Suite 850
Chicago, IL 60601-2106
Tel: (817) 569-7462 Fax: (312) 644-8557
E-Mail: pima@pima-assn.org
Website: pima-assn.org
Members: 140 companies
Staff: 4
Annual Budget: $500-1,000,000

Personnel:
Chief Executive Officer: Mona Buckley
E-Mail: mona@pima-assn.org
Contact, Meetings: Meaghan Corkrey
Director, Membership Services: Ramona Hopkins

E-Mail: ramona@pima-assn.org
Director, Communications and Operations: Jeanne Sheehy
   E-Mail: jeanne@pima-assn.org

Historical Note:
Formerly (1982) the Professional Independent Mass-Marketing Administrators and (1999) the Professional Insurance Mass-Marketing Administrators; assumed its present name in 1999. PIMA's mission is to craft strategic relationships, develop business opportunities and perfect their expertise. Membership dues for companies and agencies are based upon annual mass- marketed premium volume. Membership: $800-4,200 (Agency); $5,600-9,700 (Company); $1,500 (Business Partner).

Meetings/Conferences:
Conference Chair: Meaghan Corkrey
2013 - San Diego, CA (Hotel del Coronado)/Feb. 7 - 10
2013 - Southampton, Bermuda (The Fairmont Southampton)/July 25 - 28
2014 - Miami Beach, FL (Eden Roc Renaissance Miami Beach)/Jan. 23 - 26
Number of non-conference events/year: 1

Publications:
e-ConnXions; monthly
Membership Directory & Buyers Guide; on-line; adv.
PIMA ConnXions; adv.

Professional Landcare Network (2005)
950 Herndon Pkwy.
Suite 450
Herndon, VA 20170
Tel: (703) 736-9666 *Fax:* (703) 736-9668
TollFree: (800) 395-2522
E-Mail: info@landcarenetwork.org
Website: landcarenetwork.org
Members: 3500 Firms
Staff: 29
Annual Budget: $2-5,000,000

Personnel:
Chief Executive Officer: Sabeena Hickman CAE, CMP
   E-Mail: sabeenahickman@landcarenetwork.org
Vice President, Membership and Services: Shaine Anderson CAE
   E-Mail: shaineanderson@landcarenetwork.org
Publications and Communications Assistant: Scott Carter
   E-Mail: scottcarter@landcarenetwork.org
Director, Education and Events: Joan Haller
   E-Mail: joanhaller@landcarenetwork.org
Director, Marketing and Communications: Jessica Howard
   E-Mail: jessicahoward@landcarenetwork.org
Vice President, Finance and Administration: Carol Keeling
   E-Mail: carolkeeling@landcarenetwork.org
Director, Public Relations: Lisa Schaumann
   E-Mail: lisaschaumann@landcarenetwork.org

Historical Note:
Formed by the merger of the Associated Landscape Contractors of America (ALCA) and the Professional Lawn Care Association of America (PLCAA) in 2005. PLANET's mission is to advance and communicate the interests of its members in the conduct of effective and environmentally responsible landscape services. Membership: $325-8,400 (Green Industry Service Provider); $545-1,915 (Green Industry Supplier); $140 (Student Chapter); $100 (Affiliate); $25 (Student); 125 (State/Allied Regional Association); $175 (Dealer); $325-6,615 (New Franchisee); $475 (International); $80 (Branch).

Continuing Education:
Certification Designation/s: CTP-CSL, CTP, COLP, CLP, CLT-I, CLT-E

Meetings/Conferences: Annual
Conference Chair: Joan Haller
2013 - Las Vegas, NV (Cosmopoliton)/Feb. 21 - 24/1-10 exhibitors
2013 - Auburn, AL/March 7 - 10/1-10 exhibitors
Number of non-conference events/year: 3

Publications:
Front Page News; monthly; adv.
Personnel Notebook; monthly
PLANET advantage; quarterly; adv.
PLANET Multibrief; weekly; adv.
PLANET News; bi-monthly; adv.
PLANET News Interior; monthly; adv.
Safety $ense; monthly

Professional Liability Agents Network (1984)
P.O. Box 1632
Monterey, CA 93942
Tel: (831) 372-3706 *Fax:* (831) 372-6647

TollFree: (877) 960-7526
E-Mail: info@plan.org
Website: plan.org
Members: 48 insurance agencies
Staff: 1
Annual Budget: $250-500,000

Personnel:
Executive Director: Tom Owens

Historical Note:
PLAN is a select group of insurance agencies specializing in risk management and loss prevention programs for architects, engineers and environmental consultants.

Publications:
Member Directory; on-line
PLAN Newsletter

Professional Liability Underwriting Society (1986)
5353 Wayzata Blvd.
Suite 600
Minneapolis, MN 55416
Tel: (952) 746-2580 *Fax:* (952) 746-2599
TollFree: (800) 845-0778
E-Mail: info@plusweb.org
Website: plusweb.org
Members: 6100 individuals
Staff: 12
Annual Budget: $10-25,000,000
Tax: 501(c)(6)

Personnel:
Executive Director: Derek B. Hazeltine CAE
   E-Mail: dhazeltine@plusweb.org
Director, Operations: Scott A. Billey
   E-Mail: sbilley@plusweb.org
Director, Meetings and Events: Diane Dukes CMP
   E-Mail: ddukes@plusweb.org
Director, Strategic Marketing: Lance Helgerson
   E-Mail: lhelgerson@plusweb.org
Director, Communications: Kimberly T. Holland
   E-Mail: kholland@plusweb.org
Director, Education: Deborah Ropelewski ARM, AU, CPCU, CPIW
   E-Mail: dropelewski@plusweb.org
Director, Chapter Relations: Glenda Swan
   E-Mail: gswan@plusweb.org

Historical Note:
PLUS's mission is to enhance the professionalism of its members through education and other activities and to responsibly address issues related to professional liability. Membership: $150 (Individual); $1,000 (Corporate Sponsor); $100 (Corporate Affiliate); $25 (Academic); $50 (Future PLUS).

Continuing Education:
Certification Designation/s: RPLU

Meetings/Conferences:
Conference Chair: Diane Dukes CMP
2013 - New York City, NY (Marriott Marquis Hotel)/ Feb. 6 - 7
2013 - Chicago, IL (Hyatt Regency Chicago)/April 10 - 11
2013 - Orlando, FL/Nov. 4 - 6
2014 - Las Vegas, NV/Nov. 5 - 7
2015 - Dallas, TX/Nov. 11 - 13
2016 - Chicago, IL/Nov. 9 - 11
2017 - Atlanta, GA/Nov. 1 - 3

Publications:
PLUS Journal; monthly
PLUS Member Directory; annually

Professional Lighting and Sound Association (1987)
630 nineth Ave.
Suite 609
New York, NY 10036
Tel: (212) 244-1505 *Fax:* (212) 244-1502
E-Mail: info.na@plasa.org
Website: plasa.org
Members: 641 members
Staff: 7
Annual Budget: $1-2,000,000

Personnel:
Chief Executive Officer and Director, Events: Matthew Griffiths
   E-Mail: matthew.griffiths@plasa.org
Editor: Beverly Inglesby
   E-Mail: binglesby@esta.org

Chief Operating Officer and Director, Finance: Shane McGreevy
   E-Mail: shane.mcgreevy@plasa.org
Manager, Certification: Meredith Moseley-Bennett
   E-Mail: mmbennett@esta.org
Director, Membership, Skills, Standards and Technical : Lori Rubinstein
   E-Mail: lori.rubinstein@plasa.org
Manager, Technical Standards: Karl G. Ruling
   E-Mail: kruling@esta.org
Director, Media, Sales and Marketing: Jackie Tien
   E-Mail: jackie.tien@plasa.org

Historical Note:
Formerly (1994) Theatrical Dealers Association. and (2012) Entertainment Services and Technology Association. PLASA promotes and enhances the interests of its members and the industry. Members are manufacturers, dealers, distributors, production companies, service companies, consultants, designers and others providing goods and services to the live entertainment industry in North America and around the world. Membership: $165-1100/year.

Continuing Education:
Certification Designation/s: ETCP

Meetings/Conferences:
Conference Chair: Matthew Griffiths
2013 - London, United Kingdom (Hotel Earls Court)/ Sept. 8 - 11/12000 attendees/over 100 exhibitors
2014 - London, United Kingdom (Hotel Earls Court)/ Sept. 14 - 17/12000 attendees/over 100 exhibitors
Number of non-conference events/year: 3

Publications:
ESTA Essentials; on-line
Job Board; on-line
Membership Directory; annually; adv.
Standards Watch; bi-monthly

Professional Managers Association (1981)
P.O. Box 77235
Washington, DC 20013-0235
Tel: (202) 874-0126 *Fax:* (202) 874-1739
E-Mail: info@promanager.org
Website: promanager.org
Members: 2000 individuals
Staff: 3
Annual Budget: $100-250,000

Personnel:
Executive Director: Thomas R. Burger
   E-Mail: burger@promanager.org
National Treasurer: Katheleen Kruchten
   E-Mail: Kruchten@promanager.org
Contact, Membership Services: Brenda Lind
   E-Mail: Lind@promanager.org

Historical Note:
PMA's mission is to promote leadership and management excellence within the federal service. Represents more than 200,000 federal managers and management officials in the U.S. government.

Publications:
IRS Updates; irregular
Management Matters; weekly
The Public Manager; quarterly

Professional Photographers of America (1880)
229 Peachtree St. NE
Suite 2200
Atlanta, GA 30303
Tel: (404) 522-8600 *Fax:* (404) 614-6400
TollFree: (800) 786-6277
E-Mail: csc@ppa.com
Website: ppa.com
Members: 20000 individuals
Staff: 50
Annual Budget: $5-10,000,000

Personnel:
Chief Executive Officer: David Trust CAE
   E-Mail: trustd@ppa.com
Director, Marketing and Communications: Therese Aleman
   E-Mail: taleman@ppa.com
Director, Member Value and Experience: Christel Aprigliano
Chief Financial Officer and Chief Operating Officer: Scott Kurkian CAE, CPA
   E-Mail: skurkian@ppa.com
Executive Assistant: Sandra Lang
   E-Mail: slang@ppa.com

Manager, Copyright and Government Affairs: Maria D. Matthews
  E-Mail: mmatthews@ppa.com
Director, Information Technology: Scott Morgan
Director, Administration: Wilda Oken
  E-Mail: woken@ppa.com
Director, Education: Dawn Robb
Director, Events and Education: Lenore Taffel
  E-Mail: ltaffel@ppa.com

Historical Note:
Formerly (1958) the Photographers' Association of America. PPA's mission is to creating a vibrant community of successful professional photographers by providing education, resources and industry standards of excellence. Membership: $323 (Professional Active); $273 (Without Malpractice Protection); $246 (Additional Associate Member); $500-5,000 (Corporate Membership); $220 (Only Canadian); $170 (Non US States); $194 (Aspiring Photographer).

Continuing Education:
Certification Designation/s: CPP, CEP

Meetings/Conferences: Annual
Conference Chair: Lenore Taffel
2013 - Atlanta, GA (Georgia World Congress Center)/ Jan. 20 - 22
2014 - Phoenix, AZ/Jan. 12 - 14
2015 - San Antonio, CA/Jan. 18 - 20
2015 - Nashville, TN (Gaylord OprylandResort and Convention Center)/Feb. 1 - 3
2016 - Nashville, TN (Gaylord OprylandResort and Convention Center)/Jan. 31 - Feb. 2
Number of non-conference events/year: 44

Publications:
Action News; adv.
Membership Directory; on-line
Professional Photographer Magazine; monthly; adv.

Professional Picture Framers Association (1971)
2282 Springport Rd.
Suite F
Jackson, MI 49202
Tel: (517) 788-8100 *Fax:* (517) 788-8371
TollFree: (800) 762-9287
E-Mail: ppfa@ppfa.com
Website: pmai.org/ppfa
Members: 3500 shops and suppliers
Staff: 7

Personnel:
Secretary and Executive Director: Jim Esp
  E-Mail: jesp@pmai.org
Director, Marketing Research: Dimitrios Delis
  E-Mail: ddelis@pmai.org
Contact, Trade Exhibits Sales: Jeff Frazine
  E-Mail: jfrazine@pmai.org
FMO: Sheila Pursglove
  E-Mail: spursglove@pmai.org
Contact, Member Relations, Certification and Business Resources: Nick Shaver
  E-Mail: nshaver@pmai.org
Contact, Publications: Elaine Truman
  E-Mail: etruman@pmai.org

Historical Note:
PPFA's is a trade association of manufacturers, wholesalers, print publishers, importers and retailers selling art, framing, and related supplies. Sponsors an educational program and professional certification. Membership: $175-2,495 (Voting); $325-3,995 (Supplier).

Continuing Education:
Certification Designation/s: MCPF, CPF

Meetings/Conferences: Annual
Conference Chair: Jeff Frazine
2013 - Las Vegas, NV (Mirage Hotel and Casino)/Jan. 26 - 30

Publications:
Membership Directory; annually
PPFA Newsletter; monthly

Professional Putters Association (1959)
8105 Timberlake Rd.
Lynchburg, VA 24502
Tel: (434) 237-7888
E-Mail: ppainfo@proputters.com
Website: proputters.com
Members: 1117 individuals
Staff: 25
Annual Budget: $100-250,000

Personnel:

Executive Director: Joe Aboid
  E-Mail: joe@proputters.com

Historical Note:
PPA offers enhanced programs and benefits to its members. Members are individuals over the age of 18 who compete in national putting tournaments as well as golf course owners, managers and suppliers. Membership: $75 (PPA Pro); $25 (Amateur Putters Association Members).

Publications:
Membership Directory; annually
Putt-Putt World

Membership List Available to Non-members

Professional Reactor Operator Society (1981)
P.O. Box 484
Byron, IL 61010-0484
Tel: (815) 234-8140 *Fax:* (815) 234-8140
Website: nucpros.com
Members: 500 individuals
Staff: 1
Annual Budget: $10-25,000
Tax: 501(c)(6)

Personnel:
Manager: Mark Rasmussen

Historical Note:
PROS exists to serve individuals involved with safe nuclear reactor operations and also works to communicate and promote the knowledge and professional values of members, and to offer constructive input to the regulatory process on issues related to Operators. Membership is open to any individual or company that shares the goal of promoting safe reactor operation. Membership: $35/year (Individual).

Publications:
The Communicator; quarterly; adv.

Professional Records and Information Services Management International (1980)
4700 W. Lake Ave.
Glenview, IL 60025
Tel: (847) 375-6344 *Fax:* (847) 375-6343
E-Mail: info@prismintl.org
Website: prismintl.org
Members: 500 individuals
Staff: 9
Annual Budget: $1-2,000,000
Tax: 501(c)(6)

Personnel:
Executive Director: Dave Bergeson CAE, PhD
  E-Mail: dbergeson@prismintl.org
National Sales Manager: Patrick Filippelli
  E-Mail: pfilippelli@prismintl.org
Senior Manager, Professional Relations: Brian Fitzgerald
  E-Mail: bfitzgerald@prismintl.org
Managing Editor: Rachel Frank
  E-Mail: rfrank@prismintl.org
Administrator: Connie French
  E-Mail: cfrench@prismintl.org
Director, Meetings: Kay Granath CAE, CMP
  E-Mail: kgranath@prismintl.org
Member Services Representative: Justin Smith
  E-Mail: jsmith@prismintl.org
Education Manager: Jennifer M. Velazquez
  E-Mail: jvelazquez@prismintl.org
Manager, Senior Operations: Nicole Wallace
  E-Mail: nwallace@prismintl.org

Historical Note:
PRISM's mission is to increase professionalism through the enforcement of ethical, business and personal standards of conduct and operation. Provides educational and advocacy resources to promote smart records and information management solutions for its members and the business public. Membership: $300 (Affiliate/Associate); $786 (Corporate); $862-13,464 (Company).

Meetings/Conferences: Semi-Annual
Conference Chair: Kay Granath CAE, CMP
2013 - Bonita Springs, FL (Hyatt Regency Coconut Point)/May 13 - 17

Publications:
InFo Newsletter; weekly
inFocus Journal; quarterly; adv.

Professional Retail Store Maintenance Association
14850 Quorum Dr.
Suite 120
Dallas, TX 75254
Tel: (972) 231-9810 *Fax:* (972) 231-4081
TollFree: (866) 963-1895

E-Mail: info@prsm.com
Website: prsm.com
Members:
790 companies
2300 individuals
Staff: 11
Annual Budget: $5-10,000,000
Tax: 501(c)(6)

Personnel:
Executive Director: Patricia Dameron
  E-Mail: pdameron@prsm.com
Office Manager: Nelda Alston
  E-Mail: nalston@prsm.com
Director, Member Relations: Kay Altom
  E-Mail: kaltom@prsm.com
Director, Vendor Relations: Jeff Bond
  E-Mail: jbond@prsm.com
Director, Communications and Public Relations: Brian Bourque
  E-Mail: bbourque@prsm.com
Director, Learning Experiences and Certifications: Kip Eads CAE
  E-Mail: keads@prsm.com

Historical Note:
PRSM commits to serve facilities management professionals and to develop the industry by providing resources, solutions networking and knowledge sharing. Membership: $150-475 (Professional Corporate Member-Retail); $250-975 (Allied Corporate, based on Annual Sales).

Continuing Education:
Certification Designation/s: RFMP

Meetings/Conferences:
Conference Chair: Jeff Bond
2013 - Dallas, TX (Dallas Convention Center)/April 3 - 5
2014 - Orlando, FL (Rosen Shingle Creek)/April 6 - 8
Number of non-conference events/year: 1

Publications:
Member Directory; on-line
Professional Retail Store Maintenance Magazine; bi-monthly
PRSM Weekly (e-newsletter); weekly
ShopTalk (e-Newsletter); monthly

Professional Rodeo Cowboys Association (1936)
101 Pro Rodeo Dr.
Colorado Springs, CO 80919
Tel: (719) 593-8840 *Fax:* (719) 548-4876
TollFree: (800) 234-7722
E-Mail: prca@prorodeo.com
Website: prorodeo.org
Members: 11375 individuals
Staff: 94
Annual Budget: $10-25,000,000

Personnel:
Commissioner: Karl Stressman
  E-Mail: kstressman@prorodeo.com
Director, Member Relations: John Davis
  E-Mail: jdavis@prorodeo.com
Director, Rodeo Administration: Aaron Enget
  E-Mail: aenget@prorodeo.com
Manager, Industry Outreach: Julie Jutten
  E-Mail: jjutten@prorodeo.com
Vice President, Technology: Dan Martinez
  E-Mail: dmartinez@prorodeo.com
Director, Marketing: Sara Muirheid
  E-Mail: smuirheid@prorodeo.com
Managing Editor: Neal Reid
Director, Communications: Kendra Santos
  E-Mail: ksantos@prorodeo.com
Managing Editor: Eric Schmoldt
  E-Mail: eschmoldt@prorodeo.com
Chief Financial Officer: Joe Shafer
  E-Mail: jshafer@prorodeo.com
Coordinator, Marketing and Special Events: Sara Tadken
  E-Mail: stadken@prorodeo.com
Director, Human Resources: Shelley Warner
  E-Mail: swarner@prorodeo.com

Historical Note:
Formerly (1945) Cowboys Turtle Association. Became Rodeo Cowboys Association, (1975) Professional Rodeo Cowboys Association. PRCA's mission is to provide vital services like central entry system, rodeo administration, professional judging, media relations assistance, sponsor information and membership services. Membership: $500/year (Individual).

Meetings/Conferences: Annual

Conference Chair: Sara Tadken

Publications:
Membership Directory; on-line

Professional School Photographers Association International *(1951)*
2282 Springport Rd.
Suite F
Jackson, MS 49202
Tel: (517) 788-8100 *Fax:* (517) 788-8371
TollFree: (800) 762-9287
Website: pmai.org/pspa/
Staff: 2

Personnel:
Secretary and Executive Director: Jim Esp
   E-Mail: jesp@pmai.org
Technical Advisor: James W Pool

Historical Note:
Formerly, (1924) the Photo Finishers Association of America, (1940) Master Photo Dealers and Finishers' Association and (1974) the Photo Marketing Association International and assumed its current name in 2006. PSPAI's mission is to advocate the growth of the imaging industry. Membership: $95/year.

Meetings/Conferences: Annual
2013 - Las Vegas, NV (Bally's Las Vegas)/Jan. 6 - 7

Publications:
Buisness Focus Newsletter; weekly
PMA Magazine; bi-monthly
PMA Newsline; daily

Professional Service Association *(1989)*
71 Columbia St.
Cohoes, NY 12047
Tel: (518) 237-7777 *Fax:* (518) 237-0418
TollFree: (888) 777-8851
E-Mail: psaworld@aol.com
Website: psaworld.com
Members: 712 companies
Staff: 1
Annual Budget: $50-100,000

Personnel:
Executive Director: Ron Sawyer
   E-Mail: psaworld@aol.com

Historical Note:
PSA's mission is to be the voice of the independent service provider and to assess and identify industry related problems and provide solutions. PSA is dedicated to providing educational training, certification, business management training, support and fairness to the independent service industry. PSA encourages professionalism and honesty and publicly identifies those technicians who provide a level of service professionalism that meets the criteria established by the service industry, with industry approved certification credentials. Membership: $200/year.

Continuing Education:
Certification Designation/s: CAP-MT, CCS, CSM, CGT, CST, CT, CMT

Publications:
PSA Update; monthly; adv.

Professional Services Council *(1972)*
4401 Wilson Blvd.
Suite 1110
Arlington, VA 22203
Tel: (703) 875-8059 *Fax:* (703) 875-8922
Website: pscouncil.org
Members: 330 companies and 4 associations
Staff: 14
Annual Budget: $5-10,000,000
Tax: 501(c)(6)

Personnel:
President and Chief Executive Officer: Stan Z. Soloway
   E-Mail: soloway@pscouncil.org
Manager, Marketing: Bryan Bowman
Manager, Membership Services: Matthew Busby
   E-Mail: busby@pscouncil.org
Vice President, Marketing and Membership Services: Joe Carden
   E-Mail carden@pscouncil.org
Executive Vice President and Counsel: Alan Chvotkin
   E-Mail: chvotkin@pscouncil.org
Executive Vice President and Counsel: Alan L. Chvotkin
   E-Mail: chvotkin@pscouncil.org
Office Manager and Receptionist: Karen Holmes
   E-Mail: holmes@pscouncil.org

Director, Government Affairs: Roger Jordan CAE, CPSM, FSMPS
   E-Mail: jordan@pscouncil.org
Director, Communications: Carrie S. Lake
   E-Mail: lake@pscouncil.org
Director, Meetings and Events: Melissa Phillips
   E-Mail: phillips@pscouncil.org
Director, Finance: Robert Piening
   E-Mail: piening@pscouncil.org

Historical Note:
Formerly (1972) the National Council of Professional Services Firms, assumed its current name in 1982 and merged with Contract Services Association of America (CSA) in 2008. PSC works to be an advocate and resource for the federal professional and technical services industry. Members are companies that provide professional and technical services to the government and private industry. Membership: $100 (Trade/Professional Association); $750-35,000 (Regular); $2,650-5,600 (Associate).

Meetings/Conferences: Annual
Conference Chair: Melissa Phillips

Publications:
PSC Insider; monthly
Public Policy Action Update; monthly

Professional Show Managers Association *(1987)*
One Regency Dr.
P.O. Box 30
Bloomfield, CT 06002-0030
Tel: (860) 243-3977 *Fax:* (860) 286-0787
Website: psmashows.org
Members: 180 individuals
Staff: 1
Annual Budget: $25-50,000

Personnel:
Executive Director: C. Mitchell Sorensen CAE
   E-Mail: msorensen@ssmgt.com

Historical Note:
PSMA is aimed at advancing the professional standards of the show business and represents show managers of all types of consumer and trade shows. Members are professional show managers, event promoters, event producers, exhibition organizers of shows, fairs, festivals and street shows. Membership: $200 (Regular); $150 (Associate).

Membership List Available to Non-members

Professional Skaters Association *(1938)*
3006 Allegro Park. SW
Rochester, MN 55902
Tel: (507) 281-5122 *Fax:* (507) 281-5491
E-Mail: office@skatepsa.com
Website: skatepsa.com
Members: 6000 individuals
Staff: 11
Annual Budget: $1-2,000,000
Tax: 501(c)(6)

Personnel:
Executive Director: Jimmie Santee
   E-Mail: jsantee@skatepsa.com
Art Director: Lee Green
   E-Mail: lgreen@skatepsa.com
Office Administrator: Ann Miksch
   E-Mail: amiksch@skatepsa.com
Contact, Membership Services: Elizabeth Peschges
   E-Mail: epeschges@skatepsa.com
Contact, Membership Services: Pat Phillips
   E-Mail: pphillips@skatepsa.com
Contact, Education and Accreditation: Carol Rossignol
   E-Mail: crossignol@skatepsa.com
Staff Accountant: Donna Wells
   E-Mail: dwells@skatepsa.com
Contact, Marketing and Events: Barb Yackel
   E-Mail: byackel@skatepsa.com

Historical Note:
PSA's mission is to provide continuing education and accreditation to ice skating professionals in a safe and ethical environment. Members are ice skaters, coaches, judges and others interested in the sport. Membership: $125 (Full/State Technical/Program Director); $75 (Associate); $180 (Family); $80 (Intern); $30 (Patron); $45 (Patron Family).

Continuing Education:
Certification Designation/s: PACE

Meetings/Conferences: Annual
Conference Chair: Barb Yackel
2013 - Chicago, IL (Hyatt Regency O'Hare)/May 23 - 25

Number of non-conference events/year: 5

Publications:
PS Magazine; bi-monthly; adv.

Professional Society for Sales and Marketing Training *(1940)*
2885 Sanford Ave. SW
Suite 17425
Grandville, MI 49418
TollFree: (877) 763-2948
E-Mail: info@smt.org
Website: smt.org
Members: 170 individuals
Staff: 1
Annual Budget: $100-250,000

Personnel:
President: Laurie Weed

Historical Note:
Formerly (1993) National Society of Sales Training Executives. SMT is the network for sales and marketing training professionals, and is dedicated to improving sales performance through training. Membership: $150 (Individual); $350 (Corporate).

Continuing Education:
Certification Designation/s: SMT

Publications:
SMT Connections; on-line
SMT News; weekly

Membership List Available to Non-members

Professional Tennis Registry *(1976)*
P.O. Box 4739
Hilton Head Island, SC 29938
Tel: (843) 785-7244 *Fax:* (843) 686-2033
TollFree: (800) 421-6289
E-Mail: ptr@ptrtennis.org
Website: ptrtennis.org
Members: 14000 individuals
Staff: 10
Annual Budget: $2-5,000,000

Personnel:
Chief Executive Officer: Dan Santorum
   E-Mail: dan@ptrtennis.org
Contact, Membership Services: Paige Cooper
Director, Communications and Editor: Peggy Edwards
Vice President, Marketing and Special Events: Julie Jilly
   E-Mail: julie@ptrtennis.org
Director, Information Technology: Amanda Mitchell-Grooms
Accountant: Vicki Neitzel
   E-Mail: vicki@ptrtennis.org
Director, Operations and Training: Dave Ritter

Historical Note:
Formerly United States Professional Tennis Registry, assumed its current name in 2002. An international association of officially recognized, certified and registered tennis teaching professionals in 122 countries, PTR's mission is to educate, certify and service tennis teachers and coaches around the world in order to grow the game. Membership: $195 (Certified, based on month); $150 (Campus Certified , based on month); $95 (Affiliate/Recreational Coach/Scholastic Coach/Touring, based on month).

Continuing Education:
Certification Designation/s: JDC, ADC, PC

Meetings/Conferences: Annual
Conference Chair: Julie Jilly
Number of non-conference events/year: 6

Publications:
Membership Directory; on-line
Tennis Pro; bi-monthly; adv.

Professional Women Controllers *(1978)*
P.O. Box 950085
Oklahoma City, OK 73195-0085
Tel: (310) 322-4403
E-Mail: info@pwcinc.org
Website: pwcinc.org
Members: 1000 individuals
Staff: 4
Annual Budget: $100-250,000

Personnel:
President: Robin Rush
   E-Mail: president@pwcinc.org
Director, Membership Service: Dianna Eldridge
   E-Mail: membership@pwcinc.org
Treasurer: Tina Santiago

Editor: Patty Swenor

Historical Note:
PWC was recognized by the Federal Aviation Administration (FAA) in 1980. PWC's mission is to provide support, training, encouragement, and camaraderie for all air traffic professionals. Members are professional air traffic controllers. Membership: $156 (Active); $78 (Associate); $400 (Corporate); $30 (Student).

Meetings/Conferences: Annual
Conference Chair: Dianna Eldridge
2013 - Philadelphia, PA (Sheraton Society Hill Hotel)/
    April 8 - 11

Publications:
Membership Directory; on-line
WATCH; quarterly

Membership List Available to Non-members

Professional Women in Construction *(1980)*
315 E. 56th St.
New York, NY 10022
Tel: (212) 486-4712 *Fax:* (212) 486-0228
E-Mail: pwc@pwcusa.org
Website: pwcusa.org/v2/
Members: 1000 individuals
Staff: 3
Annual Budget: $250-500,000
Tax: 501(c)(3)

Personnel:
President: Lenore Janis
    E-Mail: pwc@pwcusa.org
Secretary and Special Advisory Counsel: Priscilla J. Triolo Esq.

Historical Note:
Formerly (1982) the Association of Business and Professional Women in Construction. PWC is a nonprofit organization committed to advancing professional, entrepreneurial and managerial opportunities for women and other "non-traditional" populations in construction and related industries. Membership is open to individual women and men, companies and government agencies engaged in construction and related fields and industries. Membership: $65-750/year.

Publications:
New York Real Estate Journal
Real Estate; weekly

Membership List Available to Non-members

Professional Women Photographers *(1975)*
119 W. 72nd St.
Suite 223
New York, NY 10023
Tel: (212) 330-8225
E-Mail: info@pwponline .org
Website: pwponline.org
Members: 200 individuals
Staff: 5
Annual Budget: $50-100,000
Tax: 501(c)(3)

Personnel:
Director, Publications: Kelly Ann Barbieri
Director, Development: Terry Berenson
Director, Membership Services: Karen Corrigan
Director, Exhibitions: Fabienne Cuter
President: Beth Portnoi Shaw

Historical Note:
PWP strives to support and promote the work of women photographers through the sharing of ideas, resources and experiences. Members are full time working photographers, photo editors, photo researchers and curators. Membership: $125 (General); $1,850 (Lifetime); $75 (Young Member); $100 (Non-metro Area Resident).

Meetings/Conferences: Annual
Conference Chair: Fabienne Cuter
Number of non-conference events/year: 1

Publications:
ENews; on-line
Imprints Magazine; on-line; adv.
Membership Directory; on-line
PWP Magazine; adv.

Professional Women Singers Association *(1982)*
Ansonia Stn.
P.O. Box 231162
New York, NY 10023
E-Mail: info@womensingers.org
Website: womensingers.org
Members: 50 individuals

Staff: 2
Annual Budget: Under $10,000
Tax: 501(c)(3)

Personnel:
President: Christina Rosas
Treasurer: Mary Lou Zobel

Historical Note:
PWSA promotes talents of its singers to the greater musical community. PWSA serves as an information resource and referral network for professional women in opera, oratorio, musical theater, and related genres. Membership: $50 (Affiliate); $115 (Individual); $25 (Friend).

Professional Women's Appraisal Association *(1986)*
1224 N. Nokomis Ave. NE
Alexandria, MN 56308
Tel: (320) 763-7626 *Fax:* (320) 763-9290
Members: 1250 individuals
Staff: 6
Annual Budget: $100-250,000

Personnel:
Executive Director: Deborah S. Johnson
Contact: Keith Starkey

Historical Note:
PWAA provides professional recognition to women involved in real estate valuation. Membership: $75/year (individual).

Progressive Gardening Trade Association *(1997)*
7809 FM 179
Shallowater, TX 79363
Tel: (806) 832-5306 *Fax:* (806) 832-5244
E-Mail: info@pgta.org
Website: pgta.org
Members: 191 companies
Staff: 5
Annual Budget: $100-250,000
Tax: 501(c)(6)

Personnel:
Executive Director: Robert C. LaGasse CAE
    E-Mail: execdir@pgta.org
Secretary and Treasurer: Christine Hubbard

Historical Note:
Formerly Hydroponic Merchants Association. PGTA is an international organization of retailers and related businesses bringing earth-friendly, water-wise and organic products and practices to the gardening community. It focuses on the implementation of progressive gardening techniques into the mainstream gardening community via trade representation and education. Membership: $300 (Retail Members/ Allied organization); $350 (Consultant Members); $1,000 (Distributor/Wholesaler/Manufacturer).

Meetings/Conferences: Annual

Publications:
Membership Directory; on-line

Project Management Institute *(1969)*
14 Campus Blvd.
Newtown Square, PA 19073-3299
Tel: (610) 356-4600 *Fax:* (610) 482-9971
E-Mail: customercare@pmi.org
Website: pmi.org
Members: 600,185 Members and Institutions
Staff: 175
Annual Budget: Over $100,000,000
Tax: 501(c)(6)

Personnel:
President and Chief Executive Officer: Mark Langley CPA
    E-Mail: mark.langley@pmi.org
Vice President, Brand Management: Lesley Bakker
    E-Mail: lesley.bakker@pmi.org
Vice President, Finance and Administration: John J. Doyle MBA
Vice President, Human Resources: Dorothy McKelvy MA, SPHR
Secretary and Treasurer: Peter Monkhouse PMP
    E-Mail: peter.monkhouse@bod.pmi.org
Vice President and General Counsel: William Scarborough J D
    E-Mail: wscarborough@pmi.org
Vice President, Information Technology: Frank Schettini MBA

Historical Note:
PMI's mission is to encourage career and professional development and organizational maturity in the field. It also offers certification, networking and community involvement opportunities. Membership: $129 (Individual); $40 (Student); $60 (Retiree).

Continuing Education:
Certification Designation/s: CAPM, PgMP, PMI-RMPSM, PMI-SPSM, PMP

Meetings/Conferences: Annual
Conference Chair: Peter Monkhouse PMP

Publications:
Community Post; semi-monthly
Manage India; on-line
PM KnowledgeWire; quarterly
PM Network; monthly; adv.
PMI Community Post; bi-monthly
PMI Today; monthly; adv.
Project Management Journal

Membership List Available to Non-members

PROMAX/BDA *(1997)*
1522-E Cloverfield Blvd.
Santa Monica, CA 90404
Tel: (310) 788-7600 *Fax:* (310) 788-7616
Website: prod.promaxbda.org/index.aspx
Members: 4300 companies
Staff: 10
Annual Budget: $1-2,000,000

Personnel:
President and Chief Executive Director: Jonathan Block-Verk
    E-Mail: jbv@promaxbda.org
Director, Marketing and Communications: Shawn Anderson
    E-Mail: shawn@promaxbda.org
Chief Information Officer: Lucian Cojescu
    E-Mail: lucian@promaxbda.org
Editorial Director: Shanna Green
    E-Mail: shanna@promaxbda.org
Director, Events and Production: Tripp Mahan
    E-Mail: tripp@promaxbda.org
Contact, Sales and Partnership Development: Jay Milla
    E-Mail: jay@promaxbda.org
Manager, Member Services: Anush Payaslyan
    E-Mail: anush@promaxbda.org
Chief Financial Officer: Randy Smith
    E-Mail: randy@promaxbda.org

Historical Note:
Formed by the merger of the Broadcast Design Association (BDA) and PROMAX in 1997. PromaxBDA's mission is to provide education and interaction for creative and strategic professionals in the business of entertainment and information content marketing, promotion and design. Membership: $1,995 (Elite); $49 (Academic); $199 (Individual).

Meetings/Conferences: Annual
Conference Chair: Anush Payaslyan
2013 - Paris, France/March 11 - 12
Number of non-conference events/year: 3

Promotion Marketing Association *(1911)*
650 First Ave.
Suite Two-SW
New York, NY 10016
Tel: (212) 420-1100 *Fax:* (212) 533-7622
Website: pmalink.org
Members: 500 companies
Staff: 10
Annual Budget: $1-2,000,000

Personnel:
President: Bonnie J. Carlson
    E-Mail: bcarlson@pmalink.org
Executive Assistant: Noelle Boddewyn
    E-Mail: nboddewyn@pmalink.org
Chief Legal Officer: Edward M. Kabak
    E-Mail: ekabak@pmalink.org
Manager, Events: Michelle Lynch
    E-Mail: mlynch@pmalink.org
Director, Web and Information Technology: Debbie Martin
    E-Mail: lmavresh@pmalink.org
Chief Financial Officer: Lana Mavreshko
    E-Mail: lmavresh@pmalink.org
Contact, Marketing and Sales: Jane McDermott
    E-Mail: jmcdermott@pmalink.org
Vice President, Member Development: Dave Wallace
    E-Mail: dwallace@pmalink.org

Historical Note:
Formerly (1998) Promotion Marketing Association of America. PMA's mission is to deliver member value by providing resources and best practices through education, research, networking and community. Membership:

$825 (Corporate Small Company); $1,100 (Corporate International); $1,925 (Primary Corporate); $1,100 (Non-Profit Organizations); $500 (Academic/Associate); $50 (Student).

Meetings/Conferences:
Conference Chair: Michelle Lynch
2013 - Chicago, IL (Westin Chicago River North)/April 3 - 4
Number of non-conference events/year: 5

Publications:
e-Newsletter
Membership Directory

Promotional Products Association International (1903)
3125 Skyway Cir. North
Irving, TX 75038-3526
Tel: (888) 426-7724 *Fax:* (972) 258-3004
TollFree: (888) 426-7724
Website: ppa.org
Members: 8000 companies
Staff: 79
Annual Budget: $10-25,000,000
Tax: 501(c)(6)

Personnel:
President and Chief Executive Officer: Paul Bellantone CAE
    E-Mail: paulb@ppa.org
Senior Manager, Membership Services: Marcia Bohannan
Director, Expositions and Meetings: Darel Cook
    E-Mail: darelc@ppa.org
Director, Finance: Dennis Cormany
    E-Mail: dennisc@ppa.org
Director, Information Technology: Paul Elfstrom
    E-Mail: paule@ppa.org
Editor: Tina Berres Filipski
Director, Human Resources: Kathy Goodin-Mitchell
    E-Mail: kathygm@ppa.org
Manager, Regional Programs: Melissa Hendrick
    E-Mail: melissajh@ppai.org
Director, Public Affairs: Anne Lardner-Stone
    E-Mail: annel@ppa.org
Executive Vice President: Bob McLean
    E-Mail: bobm@ppai.org
Director, Marketing: Keith Vincent
    E-Mail: keithv@ppa.org

Historical Note:
Formerly Advertising Manufacturers Association. PPAI serves its members best by serving its industry first. Its an international trade association for supplier and distributors in the promotional products industry.

Continuing Education:
Enrollment: 200
Certification Designation/s: CAS, MAS

Meetings/Conferences: Annual
Conference Chair: Darel Cook
2013 - Las Vegas, NV (Mandalay Bay Convention Center)/Jan. 14 - 18/11000 attendees/over 100 exhibitors
Number of non-conference events/year: 2

Publications:
PC Today; daily
PPAI Navigator; on-line
PPB Magazine
PPB Newslink; weekly
Promotional Consultant; on-line

Propane Engine Fuel Committee/Propane Education and Research Council
1140 Connecticut Ave. NW
Suite 1075
Washington, DC 20036
Tel: (202) 452-8975 *Fax:* (202) 452-9054
Website: propanecouncil.org
Staff: 7

Personnel:
President and Chief Executive officer: Roy W. Willis
Chief Financial Officer and Vice President, Administration: James Harris
Chief Information Officer: Kay Howell
Manager, Meetings: Anna W. Lombardo
Chief Marketing Officer: Jesse Marcus
Editorial and Publications Manager: Burney Simpson
    E-Mail: burney.simpson@propane.com
Director, Communications: Gregg Walker
    E-Mail: gregg.walker@propane.com

Historical Note:

PERC's mission is to promote the safe and efficient use of odorized propane gas. It accomplishes this through wide-ranging programs that support safety, training, and the development and commercialization of promising propane technologies.

Meetings/Conferences: Annual
Conference Chair: Anna W. Lombardo
2013 - New York City, NY/July 10 - 11
2013 - Portland, OR/Oct. 9 - 10
2013 - Amelia Island, FL/Dec. 10 - 11
2014 - Louisville, KY/Oct. 22 - 24
2015 - Louisville, KY/Oct. 21 - 23

Publications:
PERC Update; on-line

The Propeller Club of the United States (1927)
3927 Old Lee Hwy.
Suite 101A
Fairfax, VA 22030
Tel: (703) 691-2777 *Fax:* (703) 691-4173
E-Mail: propclubhq@aol.com
Website: propellerclubhq.com
Members: 68 club ports and student port clubs
Staff: 4
Annual Budget: $250-500,000
Tax: 501(c)(6)

Personnel:
International Executive Vice President: Andrew Riester
    E-Mail: andrew@propellerclubhq.com
International President: R. Wade Wetherington
    E-Mail: rww@whhlaw.com
International Vice President, Student Ports: Bill Van Voorhis
    E-Mail: bvanvoorhis@gmail.com

Historical Note:
Founded in 1923 as The Propeller Club of New York, it became a multi-club national organization and assumed its present name in 1927. PCUS advocates and supports American water-borne commerce and the development of river, great lakes and harbor improvements, the enhancement and well-being of all interests of the maritime community on a national and international basis.

Meetings/Conferences: Annual
2014 - Louisville, KY/Oct. 15 - 17

Publications:
The quarterly magazine; quarterly

Property Casualty Insurers Association of America (2004)
2600 S. River Rd.
Des Plaines, IL 60018-3203
Tel: (847) 297-7800 *Fax:* (847) 297-5064
E-Mail: pci@pciaa.net
Website: pciaa.net
Members: 1000 companies
Staff: 240
Annual Budget: $25-50,000,000
Tax: 501(c)(6)

Personnel:
President and Chief Executive Officer: David A. Sampson
Senior Vice President, Membership and Marketing Communications: Joanne Orfanos
    E-Mail: joanne.orfanos@pciaa.net
Director, Meetings: Courtney Thomas
    E-Mail: courtney.thomas@pciaa.net
Senior Vice President, Finance and Administration: Deborah Wensel
    E-Mail: deborah.wensel@pciaa.net

Historical Note:
Formerly National Association of Independent Insurers, merged with Alliance of American Insurers and assumed its current name in 2004. PCI's mission is to foster a competitive insurance marketplace to benefit both insurers and consumers. Membership comprises of property-liability companies.

Meetings/Conferences: Annual
Conference Chair: Courtney Thomas
Number of non-conference events/year: 8

Publications:
Daily Digest; daily
Membership Directory; on-line

Property Loss Research Bureau (1947)
3025 Highland Pkwy.
Suite 800
Downers Grove, IL 60515-1291
Tel: (630) 724-2200 *Fax:* (630) 724-2260

TollFree: (888) 711-7572
E-Mail: plrb-main@plrb.org
Website: plrb.org
Members: 800 insurance companies
Staff: 35
Annual Budget: $5-10,000,000
Tax: 501(c)(6)

Personnel:
President and Chief Executive Officer: Thomas W. Mallin CPCU, JD
    E-Mail: tmallin@plrb.org
Vice President, Liability Services and Membership: Paul C. Dispensa
    E-Mail: pdispensa@plrb.org
Manager, Marketing and Exhibits: Tom O'Dowd
    E-Mail: todowd@plrb.org
Vice President, Educational and Technical Services: Scott Powell
    E-Mail: spowell@plrb.org

Historical Note:
Founded as the Mutual Loss Research Bureau, assumed its present name in 1972. The purpose of PLRB is to disseminate information on property and liability issues among members and within the insurance industry. Members are mutual and stock property and casualty insurance companies. Membership: $1,190-86,324 (Subscriber). $850-45,000 (Affiliate).

Meetings/Conferences: Annual
Conference Chair: Tom O'Dowd
2013 - Boston, MA (Boston Marriott Copley Place)/March 17 - 20
2014 - Indianapolis, IN/March 16 - 19
Number of non-conference events/year: 7

Publications:
PLRB Front Lines; weekly
PLRB Service Provider Directory; on-line

Property Owners Association (1949)
1072 Madison Ave.
Lakewood, NJ 08701
Tel: (732) 780-1966 *Fax:* (732) 780-1611
E-Mail: info@poanj.org
Website: poanj.org
Members: 550 individuals
Staff: 1
Annual Budget: $100-250,000

Personnel:
Executive Director: Kelly Voicheck
    E-Mail: poanj@worldnet.att.net

Historical Note:
POA exists to bring together owners and operators of residential real estate, interested persons, and related industry personnel for educational and information sharing purposes. The organization is comprised of owners and managers of apartment units and other individuals who work in fields related to the housing industry. Membership: $249 (Individual); $349 (Super Star).
Meetings/Conferences:
Number of non-conference events/year: 1

Publications:
Membership Directory; annually
News and Views; adv.

Property Records Industry Association (2002)
2501 Aerial Center Pkwy.
Suite 103
Morrisville, NC 27560
Tel: (919) 459-2081 *Fax:* (919) 459-2075
E-Mail: coordinator@pria.us
Website: pria.us
Staff: 3
Annual Budget: $250-500,000
Tax: 501(c)(6)

Personnel:
Chief Staff Officer: Stevie Hughes Kernick
    E-Mail: stevie@pria.us
Chief Technology Officer: Charlie Epperson
    E-Mail: cepperson@signiadocs.com
Coordinator, Membership Services: Erin Huber
    E-Mail: erinh@imiae.com

Historical Note:
PRIA's mission is to foster dialog among property record industry participants and to promote mutual understanding of different perspectives on issues of common interest and to develop consensus leading to shared standards and practices. Membership: $55-385 (Regular- depending on population); $2,200 (Association/Organization- National/

International); $550 (Association/Organization-State); $50 (Associate Member/Non Voting).

Meetings/Conferences:
2013 - Washington, DC (The Washington Marriott Hotel)/Feb. 27 - March 1

Publications:
For The Record; quarterly; adv.
In Touch; bi-weekly; adv.

Membership List Available to Non-members

The Protein Society (1986)
9650 Rockville Pike
Bethesda, MD 20814-3998
Tel: (301) 634-7411 *Fax:* (301) 634-7271
TollFree: (800) 992-6466
E-Mail: staff@proteinsociety.org
Website: proteinsociety.org
Members: 3200 individuals
Staff: 3
Annual Budget: $1-2,000,000
Tax: 501(c)(3)

Personnel:
Managing Director: Jody L. McGinness
    E-Mail: jmcginness@proteinsociety.org
Secretary and Treasurer: Jaqueline Fetrow

Historical Note:
Mission is to provide national and international forums to facilitate communication, cooperation and collaboration with respect to all aspects of the study of proteins. Membership: $245 (Full); $100 (Post Doctoral); $220 (Virtual Plenary); $50 (Graduate); $25 (Undergraduate/ Emeritus).

Meetings/Conferences: Annual
2013 - Boston, MA/July 20 - 24
2014 - San Diego, CA/July 26 - 30
2015 - Boston, MA/July 25 - 29
2016 - San Diego, CA/July 9 - 13

Publications:
Membership Directory; on-line
Protein Science Journal; monthly; adv.
The Protein Society News; semi-annually; adv.

Membership List Available to Non-members

Protestant Church-Owned Publishers Association (1951)
6631 Westbury Oaks Ct.
Springfield, VA 22152
Tel: (703) 220-5989
E-Mail: mulder@pcpaonline.org
Website: pcpaonline.org
Members:
33 publishing houses
8 adjunct members
Staff: 2
Annual Budget: $25-50,000
Tax: 501(c)(3)

Personnel:
Association Director: Gary Mulder
    E-Mail: mulder@pcpaonline.org
Webmaster: David Schrader
    E-Mail: david.schrader@lifeway.com

Historical Note:
PCPA's mission is to enable its members to serve their denominations by providing visionary leadership through the ministry of Christian publishing. Membership: $750/ year (Adjunct Member).

Meetings/Conferences: Annual
Conference Chair: Gary Mulder

Publications:
Heads of House Newsletter; bi-monthly
Member Directory; on-line

Membership List Available to Non-members

Psi Omega Fraternity (1892)
1040 Savannah Hwy.
Charleston, SC 29407
Tel: (843) 556-0573 *Fax:* (843) 556-6311
E-Mail: psiomega@bellsouth.net
Website: psiomegafraternity.org
Members: 24500 individuals
Staff: 3
Annual Budget: $50-100,000

Personnel:
Co-Executive Director: B. Thomas Kays
    E-Mail: kayst@psiomegafraternity.org

Co-Executive Director: Dr. James A. Rivers
    E-Mail: riversj@psiomegafraternity.org
Editor: Emily W. Lemacks
    E-Mail: emily@psiomegafraternity.org

Historical Note:
Psi Omega Fraternity seeks to maintain and advance the standards of dentistry by instilling in its members the spirit of fraternal cooperation, and to exert its influence for the advancement of the dental profession in its methods of teaching, practice, research, ethics and jurisprudence. Membership: $60 (Student, depending upon the year of graduation); $600 (Alumni Life Member).

PSIA-AASI (1961)
133 S. Van Gordon St.
Suite 200
Lakewood, CO 80228
Tel: (303) 987-9390 *Fax:* (303) 987-9489
E-Mail: mist@thesnowpros.org
Website: thesnowpros.org
Members:
31000 individuals
335 schools
Staff: 15

Personnel:
Executive Director and Chief Executive Officer: Mark Dorsey
Director, Information Services: Patrick Bragg
Director, Marketing: Andy Hawk
Director, Membership Services: Sara Nakon
Manager, Professional Development: Earl Saline
Manager, Information Technology: John Sarazen
Communications Director and Editor: Wendy Schrupp
Director, Finance and Chief Financial Officer: Tom Spiess

Historical Note:
The Professional Ski Instructors of America (PSIA) and American Association of Snowboard Instructors (AASI) are nonprofit associations dedicated to promoting the sports of skiing and snowboarding through instruction. PSIA-AASI's mission is to support the members, as a part of the snowsports industry, to develop personally and professionally, create positive learning experiences and have more fun.

Publications:
32 Degrees: The Journal of Professional Snowsports Instruction; adv.
Education E-News; on-line
Membership Directory; on-line

Psychology Society (1960)
100 Beekman St., #25D
New York, NY 10038-1810
Members: 3500 individuals
Staff: 5
Annual Budget: $250-500,000

Personnel:
Director: Pierre C. Haber PhD

Historical Note:
The Society represents practitioners of clinical psychology. It seeks to promote the use of psychology in the treatment of human ills, social and political discord and other problems involving humanity. In 2004, the society added financial advisory service for members who seek help in selecting investments and retirement planning. Membership: $200/ year (individual).

Psychometric Society (1935)
University of North Carolina-Greensboro
210 Curry Building, P.O. Box 26170
Greensboro, NC 27402-6170
Tel: (336) 334-3474 *Fax:* (336) 256-0405
Website: psychometricsociety.org
Members: 600 individuals
Staff: 4
Annual Budget: $100-250,000

Personnel:
Managing Editor and Webmaster: Gwen Exner
    E-Mail: pmetrika@uncg.edu

Historical Note:
Psychometric Society's mission is to promote the use of quantitative models for psychological phenomena and quantitative methodology in the social and behavioral sciences. Membership: $90 (Regular); $110 (Family); $25 (Emeritus/Student).

Meetings/Conferences: Annual
2013 - Arnhem, Netherlands/July 22 - 26
Number of non-conference events/year: 1

Publications:

Member Directory; on-line
Psychometrika; quarterly

The Psychonomic Society (1959)
2424 American Ln.
Madison, WI 53704-3102
Tel: (608) 441-1070 *Fax:* (608) 443-2474
E-Mail: info@psychonomic.org
Website: psychonomic.org
Members: 2000 individuals and 650 associate members
Staff: 25
Annual Budget: $1-2,000,000

Personnel:
Executive Director: Kathy Kuehn
    E-Mail: kkuehn@reesgroupinc.com
Coordinator, Membership Services: Linda Potchoiba

Historical Note:
PS advocates the communication of scientific research in psychology and allied sciences. Members are qualified to conduct and supervise scientific research. Membership: $70- $40 (Outside US); $53.65 (Members U.S.); $20 (Associate).

Meetings/Conferences: Annual
Conference Chair: Andrew Conway
2013 - Toronto, ON/Nov. 14 - 17
2014 - Long Beach, CA/Nov. 20 - 22
2014 - Long Beach, CA/Nov. 20 - 23
2015 - Chicago, IL/Nov. 19 - 22
2016 - Boston, MA/Nov. 17 - 20

Publications:
Attention, Perception and Psychophysics; on-line; adv.
Behavior Research Methods; on-line; adv.
Cognitive, Affective and Behavioral Neuroscience; quarterly; adv.
Learning and Behavior; quarterly; adv.
Membership Directory; on-line
Memory and Cognition; quarterly; adv.

Public Affairs Council (1954)
2121 K St. NW
Suite 900
Washington, DC 20006
Tel: (202) 787-5950 *Fax:* (202) 787-5942
E-Mail: pac@pac.org
Website: pac.org
Members: 550 corporations and organizations
Staff: 20
Annual Budget: $2-5,000,000
Tax: 501(c)(4)

Personnel:
Associate Director, Political Involvement Programs: Rikki D. Amos
    E-Mail: ramos@pac.org
Contact, Publications Assistant: Mary Beaver
    E-Mail: mbeaver@pac.org
Director, Communications and Editorial: Erika Pontarelli Compart
    E-Mail: ecompart@pac.org
Manager, Membership Services: Shelly Deavy
    E-Mail: sdeavy@pac.org
Manager, Conference Logistics: Kristin Hanley
    E-Mail: khanley@pac.org
Manager, Technology, Office Operations and Graphic Design: Bonnie Moore
    E-Mail: bmoore@pac.org
Director, Finance and Administration: Reggie Nance
    E-Mail: rnance@pac.org
President: Doug G. Pinkham
    E-Mail: dpinkham@pac.org

Historical Note:
Formed as the Effective Citizens Organization, it assumed its present name in 1965. PAC's mission is to advance the field of public affairs and to provide members with the training and information resources they need to achieve success while maintaining the ethical standards. Membership: $2,200-11,000 (Corporations); $2,000 -2,400 (Associations); $2,000-2,800 (Consulting/Law Firms); $2,400 (Non-Corporate Entities).

Continuing Education:
Enrollment: 30
Certification Designation/s: PAJ

Meetings/Conferences:
Conference Chair: Kristin Hanley
2013 - Miami Beach, FL (Eden Roc Renaissance Miami Beach)/March 4 - 7
Number of non-conference events/year: 6

Publications:
Impact Newsletter; monthly
Membership Directory; on-line

Public Agency Risk Managers Association *(1974)*
P.O. Box 6810
San Jose, CA 95150
Tel: (888) 907-2762 *Fax:* (888) 907-2762
TollFree: (888) 907-2762
E-Mail: info@parma.com
Website: parma.com
Members: 600 public entity members and
associate members
Staff: 3
Annual Budget: $500-1,000,000
Tax: 501(c)(6)

Personnel:
Contact, Conferences: Brenda Reisinger
    E-Mail: brenda.reisinger@parma.com

Historical Note:
*PARMA's mission is to provide an environment that
advocates better practices, professional education, and
strategies to manage a broad spectrum of risk. Membership:
$100 (Regular/Public Agency); $275 (Associate); $50
(Retired Public Agency Representative).*

Meetings/Conferences: Annual
Conference Chair: Brenda Reisinger
2013 - Rancho Mirage, CA (The Westin Mission Hills)/
    Feb. 3 - 6

Publications:
Membership Directory; on-line
PARMA Facts; on-line

Public Education Network
P.O. Box 166
Washington, DC 20004
Tel: (202) 628-7460
E-Mail: pen@publiceducation.org
Website: publiceducation.org
Staff: 16
Annual Budget: $1-2,000,000

Personnel:
President: Wendy D. Puriefoy
    E-Mail: WPuriefoy@PublicEducation.org
Senior Associate, Data Collection and Analysis: Adam
Brown
    E-Mail: Abrown@publiceducation.org
Director, Membership Practice: Cindy Cisneros
    E-Mail: CCisneros@publiceducation.org
Director, Public Engagement and Advocacy: Arnold Fege
    E-Mail: AFege@PublicEducation.org
Associate, Communications and Advocacy: Kathleen
Mercier
    E-Mail: KMercier@publiceducation.org
Director, Operations: Jeanette Vaughn
    E-Mail: JVaughn@PublicEducation.org

Historical Note:
*PEN's mission is to build public demand and mobilize
resources for quality public education for all children
through a national constituency of local education funds
and individuals. Membership: $1,000-3,000 (Based on
Organization Budget).*

Publications:
Membership Directory; on-line
PEN Weekly NewsBlast; weekly

Public Employees Roundtable *(1982)*
P.O. Box 75248
Washington, DC 20013-5248
Tel: (202) 927-4926 *Fax:* (202) 927-4920
E-Mail: per@excelgov.org
Website: keyinsurancequotes.com/pssp.html
Members: 50 organizations and institutions
Staff: 5
Annual Budget: $250-500,000

Personnel:
Chief Financial Officer: Bridgette Bell
    E-Mail: bbell@theroundtable.org
Chief Operating Officer: Adam Bratton
    E-Mail: abratton@theroundtable.org

Historical Note:
*PER strives to inform about the quality of people in
government and the services they provide. It also seeks to
develop a stronger spirit de corps among public service
employees and encourage interest in public service careers.
Membership: $50 (Individual); $1,000 (Government
Agencies); $2,000 (Corporate).*

Publications:
PER newsletter

Membership List Available to Non-members

Public Housing Authorities Directors Association
(1979)
511 Capitol Ct. NE
Washington, DC 20002-4937
Tel: (202) 546-5445 *Fax:* (202) 546-2280
Website: phada.org
Members: 1900 housing authorities
Staff: 8
Annual Budget: $2-5,000,000
Tax: 501(c)(6)

Personnel:
Executive Director: Timothy G. Kaiser
    E-Mail: tkaiser@phada.org
Director, Membership Services: Norma Bellew
    E-Mail: nbellew@phada.org
Director, Government Affairs: Ted Van Dyke
    E-Mail: tvandyke@phada.org
Director, Communications: Yaniv Goury
    E-Mail: ygoury@phada.org
Administrative Assistant: Gwen Lyda
    E-Mail: glyda@phada.org
Director, Meetings: Malena Malone
    E-Mail: mmalone@phada.org
Financial Assistant and Production Manager: Godfrey
Swindall
    E-Mail: gswindall@phada.org

Historical Note:
*PHADA works closely with members of Congress in efforts
to develop public housing statutes and obtain funding for
low-income housing programs. Members receive discounts
on guidebooks and manuals. Membership: $120-5,150/
year (Agency, based on size).*

Meetings/Conferences: Semi-Annual
Conference Chair: Malena Malone
2013 - San Diego, CA (Hilton San Diego Bayfront)/Jan.
    13 - 16
2013 - San Antonio, TX (Grand Hyatt San Antonio)/
    May 19 - 22
2014 - Orlando, FL (Hyatt Regency Grand Cypress)/
    Jan. 12 - 15
Number of non-conference events/year: 1

Publications:
Advocate-Newsletter; bi-weekly

Public Investors Arbitration Bar Association
(1990)
2415 A Wilcox Dr.
Norman, OK 73069
Tel: (405) 360-8776 *Fax:* (405) 360-2063
TollFree: (888) 621-7484
Website: piaba.org
Staff: 8
Annual Budget: $500-1,000,000

Personnel:
Executive Director: Robin S. Ringo
Administrative Assistant: April Bowers
Administrator, Information Technology: Tiffany Zachary

Historical Note:
*PIABA's mission is to advocate the interests of the public
investor in securities and commodities arbitration by
protecting public investors from abuses in the arbitration
process, such as those associated with document production
and discovery.*

Meetings/Conferences: Annual
2013 - Orlando, FL (JW Marriott Orlando Grande
    Lakes)/Oct. 16 - 19

Publications:
PIABA Bar Journal; quarterly

Public Lands Council *(1968)*
1301 Pennsylvania Ave. NW
Suite 300
Washington, DC 20004
Tel: (202) 347-0228 *Fax:* (202) 638-0607
Website: publiclandscouncil.org
Staff: 2
Annual Budget: $100-250,000

Personnel:
Executive Director, Public Lands Council: Dustin Van Liew
    E-Mail: vanliew@beef.org
Manager, Legislative Affairs: Theodora Dowling
    E-Mail: tdowling@beef.org

Historical Note:
*A non-profit group that represents livestock operators who
hold permits to graze livestock on public lands.*

Meetings/Conferences:
2013 - Washington, DC/April 15 - 16

Publications:
Newsletter

Public Library Association *(1944)*
50 E. Huron
Chicago, IL 60611
Tel: (312) 280-5752 *Fax:* (312) 280-5029
TollFree: (800) 545-2433
E-Mail: pla@ala.org
Website: pla.org
Members: 11000 members
Staff: 11
Annual Budget: $500-1,000,000

Personnel:
Executive Director: Barb Macikas
    E-Mail: bmacikas@ala.org
Manager, Professional Development: Linda Bostrom
    E-Mail: lbostrom@ala.org
Manager, Web Communications: Steven Hofmann
    E-Mail: shofmann@ala.org
Manager, Publications: Kathleen Marie Hughes
    E-Mail: khughes@ala.org
Planner, Meetings and Special Events: Melissa Faubel
Johnson CMP
    E-Mail: mfaubel@ala.org
Coordinator, Programs: Julianna Kloeppel
    E-Mail: jkloeppel@ala.org
Manager, Marketing and Communications: Amy Sargent
    E-Mail: asargent@ala.org

Historical Note:
*PLA's mission is to focus its efforts on serving the needs of
its members, address issues which affect public libraries,
commit to quality public library services that benefit the
general public. Membership: $50 (Regular/International/
Associate/Trustee); $15 (Student); $50 (Inactive/Retired/
Unemployed/Full/Part-Time).*

Continuing Education:
Certification Designation/s: CPLA

Meetings/Conferences: Biennial
Conference Chair: Melissa Faubel Johnson CMP
2014 - Indianapolis, IN/March 11 - 15
2016 - Denver, CO/April 5 - 9
2018 - Philadelphia, PA/March 20 - 24

Publications:
PLA E-News; on-line; adv.
PLDS Statistical Report; annually
Public Libraries Magazine; bi-monthly; adv.

Membership List Available to Non-members

Public Media Business Association *(1982)*
1760 Old Meadow Rd.
Suite 500
McLean, VA 22102
Tel: (703) 506-3292 *Fax:* (703) 506-3266
E-Mail: info@pbma.org
Website: pbma.org
Members: 300 stations
Staff: 4
Annual Budget: $100-250,000
Tax: 501(c)(3)

Personnel:
Executive Director: Andy Schwarz
    E-Mail: aschwarz@pmbaonline.org
Senior Manager, Member Services: Michelle DelaRosa
    E-Mail: mdelarosa@pmbaonline.org
Treasurer: Jocelyn V Enriquez
Events Manager: Mary Katherine Saladino CMP
    E-Mail: msaladino@pmbaonline.org

Historical Note:
*Formerly Public Telecommunications Financial Management
Association. PMBA's mission is to enhance and sustain
public broadcasting and public service media through
management excellence. Membership: $660 (Associate);
$220-825 (Public Broadcasting).*

Meetings/Conferences: Annual

Publications:
PMBA Newsletter; bi-monthly

Public Notice Resource Center *(2003)*
P.O. Box 5337
Arlington, VA 22205

Tel: (703) 237-9806 Fax: (703) 237-9808
E-Mail: info@pnrc.net
Website: pnrc.net
Staff: 1
Annual Budget: $100-250,000

Personnel:
Executive Director: David Placher

Historical Note:
Established in 2003 by the American Court and Commercial Newspapers, Inc. (ACCN). Mission of PNRC is to collect, analyze, and disseminate information on public and private notifications to the public through local newspapers, and to educate the public on the value and use of its right to know.

Public Radio News Directors Incorporated (1985)
P.O. Box 838
Sturgis, SD 57785-0838
Tel: (605) 490-3033 Fax: (605) 720-0632
Website: prndi.org
Members: 125 individuals
Staff: 2
Annual Budget: $25-50,000

Personnel:
President: George Bodarky
    E-Mail: gbodarky@wfuv.org
Business Manager: Christine Paige Diers
    E-Mail: cpaigediers@gmail.com

Historical Note:
Formerly (1994) Public Radio News Directors Association. PRNDI's purpose is to improve local news and information programming by serving public radio journalists and organize to promote standards, ethical principles and significant public service.

Meetings/Conferences: Annual
2013 - Cleaveland, OH (Cleveland Playhouse Square Hotel)/June 18 - 22

Public Radio Program Directors Association
(1987)
38 Milford St.
Hamilton, NY 13346
Tel: (315) 824-8226 Fax: (315) 824-8227
E-Mail: info@prpd.org
Website: prpd.org
Members: 200 stations and networks and producers
Staff: 2
Annual Budget: $500-1,000,000

Personnel:
President and Chief Executive Officer: Arthur Cohen
Office Manager: David Hollis

Historical Note:
PRPD sponsors an annual conference and provides other networking opportunities for programmers and program directors at public radio stations in the U.S. Membership: $370 (Individual); $800-4000 (Institutional); $425-4000 (Stations).

Meetings/Conferences: Annual

The Public Relations Society of America (1947)
33 Maiden Ln.
11th Floor
New York, NY 10038-5150
Tel: (212) 460-1400 Fax: (212) 995-0757
E-Mail: pr@prsa.org
Website: prsa.org
Members:
31000 professionals and students
100 chapters and districts
Staff: 66
Annual Budget: $10-25,000,000

Personnel:
President and Chief Operating Officer: William Murray DDS
    E-Mail: william.murray@prsa.org
Chief Financial Officer: Philip Bonaventura
    E-Mail: philip.bonaventura@prsa.org
Director, Publications: John Elsasser
    E-Mail: john.elsasser@prsa.org
Vice President, Education: Jeneen Garcia
    E-Mail: jeneen.garcia@prsa.org
Vice President, Membership Services: Rachel O'Leary
    E-Mail: rachel.oleary@prsa.org
Vice President, Corporate Development and Industry Partnerships: John D. Robinson DDS
    E-Mail: john.robinson@prsa.org
Vice President, Special Events and Programs: Karla Voth

    E-Mail: karla.voth@prsa.org
Vice President, Public Relations: Arthur Yann
    E-Mail: arthur.yann@prsa.org

Historical Note:
PRSA provides professional development, sets standards of excellence. Purpose is to build value, demand and global understanding for public relations. Membership: $60-225/year.

Continuing Education:
Certification Designation/s: APR

Meetings/Conferences: Annual
Conference Chair: Karla Voth
2013 - Philadelphia, PA/Oct. 26 - 29
Number of non-conference events/year: 2

Publications:
Public Relations Journal; on-line; adv.
Public Relations Strategist; quarterly; adv.
Public Relations Tactics; monthly; adv.
The Strategist Online; on-line

Public Relations Student Society of America
(1968)
33 Maiden Ln.
11th Floor
New York, NY 10038-5150
Tel: (212) 460-1474 Fax: (212) 995-0757
E-Mail: prssa@prsa.org
Website: prssa.org
Members: 10000 individuals
Staff: 8
Annual Budget: $100-250,000

Personnel:
President: Lauren Gray
    E-Mail: laurenkgray2@gmail.com
Vice President, Education: Jeneen Garcia CAE
    E-Mail: jeneen.garcia@prsa.org
Editor in Chief: Ashley Mauder
    E-Mail: a-mauder@onu.edu
Administrative Assistant: Kevin Monahan
    E-Mail: kevin.monahan@prsa.org
Vice President, Advocacy: Zane Riley
    E-Mail: zaneriley@gmail.com
Vice President, Public Relations: Lauren Rosenbaum
    E-Mail: Lauren.G.Rosenbaum@gmail.com
Vice President, Member Services: Kate Ryan
    E-Mail: kryan2013@gmail.com
Vice President, Professional Development: Danielle Stewart
    E-Mail: ds.lynne@gmail.com

Historical Note:
PRSSA's mission is to serve its members by enhancing their knowledge of public relations and providing access to professional development opportunities and to serve the public relations profession by helping to develop highly qualified, well-prepared professionals. Membership: $60 (Associate/Student); $255 (Regular).

Continuing Education:
Certification Designation/s: CEPR

Meetings/Conferences: Annual

Publications:
Biweekly Update; bi-weekly; adv.
Public Relations Journal; quarterly; adv.

Public Risk Management Association (1978)
700 S. Washington St.
Suite 218
Alexandria, VA 22314
Tel: (703) 528-7701 Fax: (703) 739-0200
E-Mail: info@primacentral.org
Website: primacentral.org
Members: 3800 entities and jurisdictions.
Staff: 14
Annual Budget: $1-2,000,000
Tax: 501(c)(3)

Personnel:
Executive Director: Marshall Davies PhD
    E-Mail: mdavies@primacentral.org
Deputy Executive Director: Jennifer Ackerman CAE
    E-Mail: jackerman@primacentral.org
Manager, Membership Services: Bles Dones
    E-Mail: bdones@primacentral.org
Manager, Education and Training: Jessica Konrath
    E-Mail: jkonrath@primacentral.org
Manager, Meetings and Conferences: Jennifer W. Morris
    E-Mail: jmorris@primacentral.org

Historical Note:

Formerly (1989) Public Risk and Insurance Management Association. PRIMA promotes and encourages effective public risk management and risk management professionalism in the public sector. Members are local and state government entities, including intergovernmental risk pools. Member representatives include risk managers and other public servants who fulfill the risk management function including loss control, litigation and claims management, contract management, employee benefits, occupational safety and health insurance and risk financing. Membership: $25-770/year.

Meetings/Conferences: Annual
Conference Chair: Jennifer W. Morris
2013 - Tampa, FL (Tampa Bay Convention Center)/ June 2 - 5
2014 - Long Beach, CA (Long Beach Convention and Entertainment Center)/June 8 - 11
2015 - Houston, TX (George R. Brown Convention Center)/June 6 - 10

Publications:
Public Risk magazine

Public Utilities Risk Management Association
(1996)
1900 W. Park Dr.
Suite 150
Westborough, MA 01581
Tel: (508) 599-3422 Fax: (508) 599-3427
Website: purma.org
Members: 38 Organizations
Staff: 3
Annual Budget: $250-500,000
Tax: 501(c)(6)

Personnel:
Executive Director: Diane Belanger
    E-Mail: DBelanger@purma.org
Director, Administration: Andrea Friberg
    E-Mail: AFriberg@purma.org

Historical Note:
PURMA mission is to provide members superior solutions to all their risk management needs. Members are publicly owned, nonprofit electric, gas, water, telecommunications, cable TV, and sewer utilities. Membership: $1150 (Utility); $1,200 (Non-Voting Contributing); $650 (Non-Voting Associate).

Public Works Historical Society (1975)
2345 Grand Blvd.
Suite 700
Kansas City, MO 64108-2625
Tel: (816) 472-6100 Fax: (816) 472-1610
TollFree: (800) 848-2792
Website: apwa.net/PWHS
Members: 850 individuals
Staff: 2
Annual Budget: $25-50,000

Personnel:
Manager, Technical Services Program: Teresa Hon
    E-Mail: thon@apwa.net

Historical Note:
The mission of the PWHS is to enhance the planning and management of public works programs, document public works history and to promote public understanding and appreciation of the role of public works in the growth and development of civilization. Membership: $35 (US); #37 (Canada).

Meetings/Conferences: Annual

Publications:
Public Works History Journal
SHOT Newsletter; quarterly

Publishers' Publicity Association (1963)
Random House Children's
1745 Broadway
New York, NY 10019
Tel: (212) 782-8626 Fax: (212) 782-9004
E-Mail: jhaut@randomhouse.com
Members: 250 individuals
Staff: 2
Annual Budget: $10-25,000

Personnel:
President: Judith Haut
    E-Mail: jhaut@randomhouse.com
Vice President: Margaret McAllister
    E-Mail: meg@mcallrow.com

Historical Note:
The PPA was originally a part of the Publishers' Ad Club, which was founded in 1921. In 1963, the Publishers'

Publicity Association was founded. PPA's purpose is to raise the professional level of book publishers publicity by conducting research into all media and by providing a meeting place for the discussion and exchange of ideas and techniques. Membership: $75-110/year.

Meetings/Conferences:
Number of non-conference events/year: 1

Pulp and Paper Safety Association *(1944)*

P.O. Box 531
Perry, FL 32348
Tel: (850) 584-3639 *Fax:* (850) 584-3636
E-Mail: ppsasecy@fairpoint.net
Website: ppsa.org
Members: 380 individuals
Staff: 2
Annual Budget: $100-250,000
Tax: 501(c)(6)

Personnel:
Secretary and Treasurer: John Sunderland
    E-Mail: john_sunderland@bkitech.com
Website Service: Ed Corlew
    E-Mail: Ed.Corlew@mohawkpaper.com

Historical Note:
Formerly Southern Pulp and Paper Safety Association. PPSA's purpose is to promote safety, to set reasonable and attainable goals, to educate its members, and to give the members a forum for discussion. PPSA members are safety and health professionals in the industry. Membership: $275 (Vendor); $100-300 (Organization, based on number of employees).

Meetings/Conferences: Annual
2013 - Williamsburg, VA (Williamsburg Lodge)/June 9 - 12

Publications:
Newsletter
Quarter Review; quarterly; adv.

Purebred Dairy Cattle Association *(1940)*

3310 Latham Dr.
Madison, WI 53713
Tel: (608) 224-0400 *Fax:* (608) 224-0300
E-Mail: wde@wdexpo.com
Website: purebreddairycattle.com
Members: 7 cattle breeders associations
Staff: 3
Annual Budget: $10-25,000

Personnel:
General Manager: Mark Clarke
Contact: Lisa Behnke

Historical Note:
Members are breeders of Ayrshire, Brown-Swiss, Guernsey, Holstein, Milking Shorthorn, Red and White and Jersey breed registry associations.

Meetings/Conferences: Annual
2013 - Madison, WI (Alliant Energy Center)/Oct. 1 - 5

Purebred Morab Horse Association *(1984)*

P.O. Box 203
Hodgenville, KY 42748
Fax: (270) 358-8727
E-Mail: pmha@puremorab.com
Website: puremorab.com
Members: 150 individuals
Staff: 2
Annual Budget: $10-25,000
Tax: 501(c)(3)

Personnel:
President: Donna J. Lassanske

Historical Note:
Founded as North American Horse Association; assumed its current name in 1998. Absorbed the Hearst Memorial Morab Horse Registry in 1985. PMHA's mission is to develop quality horses of Morgan and Arabian lineage through a representative government of breeders and owners. Membership: $30 (Individual); $50 (Club); $45 (Family); $100 (Corporate); $30 (Individual Award); $15 (Youth Member).

Meetings/Conferences: Annual

Publications:
Breeders Roster; on-line

Membership List Available to Non-members

Pyramid Society *(1969)*

4067 Iron Works Pkwy.
Suite Two
Lexington, KY 40511

Tel: (859) 231-0771 *Fax:* (859) 255-4810
E-Mail: info@pyramidsociety.org
Website: pyramidsociety.org
Staff: 8
Annual Budget: $500-1,000,000

Personnel:
Executive Director: Anna Bishop
    E-Mail: anna@pyramidsociety.org
Membership Coordinator: Carol Aldridge
    E-Mail: carol@pyramidsociety.org
Financial Manager: Melissa Virgin
    E-Mail: melissa@pyramidsociety.org
Coordinator, Marketing and Public Relations: Kory Wilcox
    E-Mail: kory@pyramidsociety.org

Historical Note:
The Pyramid Society is an international breeders' organization dedicated to the preservation, perpetuation, and promotion of the Straight Egyptian Arabian horse as the premiere source of classic Arabian type in the world. Membership: $175 (Supporting); $350 (Premium); $5,000 (Lifetime).

Publications:
Chariot E-Newsletter; monthly
Member Directory

Pyrotechnics Guild International *(1969)*

813 Appleton St.
Menasha, WI 54952
Tel: (920) 558-4681 *Fax:* (920) 725-6194
Website: pgi.org
Members: 3500 individuals
Staff: 3
Annual Budget: $500-1,000,000
Tax: 501(c)(6)

Personnel:
Manager, Membership Services: Robin Cleveland
    E-Mail: membership@pgi.org

Historical Note:
PGI promotes the safe and sane display and use of pyrotechnics and encourages the display of pyrotechnics in conjunction with local and national events. Provides education to members, the media, politicians and public. Members are amateur and professional fireworks enthusiasts. Membership: $100(Full); $60 (Junior); $1750 (Life).

Continuing Education:
Certification Designation/s: PGI-DOC

Meetings/Conferences: Annual
2013 - Butler, PA/Aug. 10 - 16
2014 - Mason, IA/Aug. 9 - 15
2015 - Fargo, ND/Aug. 8 - 14
2016 - La Porte, IN/Aug. 6 - 12

Publications:
Bulletin; bi-monthly

Quail Unlimited *(1981)*

308 Third Ave.
P.O. Box 70518
Albany, GA 31708
Tel: (229) 883-3209 *Fax:* (229) 883-3979
Website: qu.org
Staff: 4

Personnel:
President: Bill Bowles
    E-Mail: bbowles@qu.org
Editor: Diana J. Kogon
    E-Mail: dkogon@qu.org
Administrative Assistant and Contact, Membership Services: Debbie Powell
    E-Mail: dneuman@qu.org
Director, Art and Technical Services: Donald Tilton
    E-Mail: djtilton@qu.org

Historical Note:
QU's mission is to restore America's quail populations for future generations. Membership: $35 (Annual); $50 (Mentor); $150 (Foundation); $250 (Sponsor); $1,500 (Life); $15 (Youth); $350 (Hunting Property); $10,000-20,000 (Life Sponsor).

Meetings/Conferences: Annual
2013 - Albany, GA (Albany Civic Center)/Jan. 24 - 26

Publications:
QU Newsletter; quarterly
Quail Unlimited; adv.

Qualitative Research Consultants Association *(1983)*

1000 Westgate Dr.

Suite 252
St. Paul, MN 55114
Tel: (651) 290-7491 *Fax:* (651) 290-2266
TollFree: (888) 674-7722
E-Mail: admin@qrca.org
Website: qrca.org
Members: 1000 individuals
Staff: 7
Annual Budget: $500-1,000,000
Tax: 501(c)(6)

Personnel:
Executive Director: Shannon Pfarr Thompson
    E-Mail: exdir@qrca.org
Director, Membership Services: Darrin Hubbard
    E-Mail: membership@qrca.org

Historical Note:
QRCA's mission is to promote excellence in the field of qualitative research by pooling experience and expertise to create a base of shared knowledge. Members are owners and employees of independent marketing and social research firms conducting qualitative research. Membership: $290/year (Individual).

Meetings/Conferences: Annual

Publications:
Membership Directory; on-line
QRCA Connections Newsletter; monthly
QRCA VIEWS magazine; quarterly; adv.

Membership List Available to Non-members

Quality Bakers of America Cooperative *(1922)*

1275 Glenlivet Dr.
Suite 100
Allentown, PA 18106-3107
Tel: (973) 263-6970 *Fax:* (973) 263-0937
E-Mail: info@qba.com
Website: qba.com
Members: 35 companies
Staff: 25
Annual Budget: $1-2,000,000

Personnel:
Contact, Membership Services: Norm Trapp
    E-Mail: ntrapp@qba.com

Historical Note:
QBA is owned by a group of US wholesale bakers. Its member bakers own the Sunbeam brand name and trademark. Mission is to enhance the growth of SUNBEAM® branded breads, rolls and related products. Members also manufacture and market bakery products under their own brand names. Membership is available to bakers and bakery suppliers.

Quality Chekd Daries *(1944)*

901 Warrenville Rd.
Suite 405
Lisle, IL 60532
Tel: (800) 222-6455 *Fax:* (630) 717-1126
E-Mail: qchekd@qchekd.com
Website: qchekd.com
Members: 27 independent dairy processors with 59 manufacturing facilities
Staff: 6

Personnel:
President: Peter Horvath
    E-Mail: phorvath@qchekd.com
Manager, Accounting and Administration: Mary DeMarco
    E-Mail: mdemarco@qchekd.com
Director, Human Resource and Training: Steve Drabek
    E-Mail: sdrabek@qchekd.com
Director, Member Relations: Molly Iovino
    E-Mail: miovino@qchekd.com

Historical Note:
Member-owned organization of 27 independent dairy processors with 59 manufacturing facilities located throughout the United States, Guatemala and Colombia.

Publications:
Dairy Field Article
QC Member Directory

Quality Service Contractors *(1994)*

180 S. Washington St.
P.O. Box 6808
Falls Church, VA 22046
Tel: (703) 237-8100 *Fax:* (703) 237-7442
TollFree: (800) 533-7694
E-Mail: quality@qsc-phcc.org
Website: qsc-phcc.org
Staff: 4

Personnel:
Vice President, Executive Director, Chief Operating Officer:
  Charlie Wallace
    E-Mail: cwallace@qsc-phcc.org
Administrative Coordinator: Dawn Dalton
    E-Mail: ddalton@qsc-phcc.org
Coordinator, Membership: Patrice Jackson
    E-Mail: pjackson@qsc-phcc.org

Historical Note:
QSC's mission is to provide service contractors with training, technology, and professional development, resulting in better client service and satisfaction. Membership: Full, Active PHCC-National Association membership is a prerequisite for QSC membership.
Meetings/Conferences:
Number of non-conference events/year: 4

Quarter Century Wireless Association (1947)
P.O. Box 2088
Malakoff, TX 75148-2088
Tel: (903) 375-7507 *Fax:* (800) 219-8048
TollFree: (800) 219-8048
E-Mail: N1CC@qcwa-hq.com
Website: qcwa.org
Staff: 5
Annual Budget: $250-500,000

Personnel:
General Manager: Jim LaPorta
Webmaster: Bob Roske
    E-Mail: broske@hutchtel.net

Historical Note:
QCWA Promotes friendship and cooperation among Amateur Radio operators who were licensed at least a quarter century ago, and are licensed today.

Publications:
Member Directory
Newsletter; monthly
QCWA Bulletin; quarterly
QCWA E Journal; quarterly

Quarters Furniture Manufacturers Association
(1995)
8425 Progress Dr.
Suite BB
Frederick, MD 21701
Tel: (240) 215-9700 *Fax:* (240) 215-9721
Website: qfma.net
Members: 20 companies
Staff: 3
Annual Budget: $50-100,000

Personnel:
President: Michael Gittinger
Treasurer: Allyn Richert
    E-Mail: arichert@tradeproductscorp.com
Membership Contact: Matt Yanson

Historical Note:
QFMA's mission is to facilitate positive changes that support and reconcile the often-differing viewpoints on issues that exist between GSA contractors and federal government customers. Membership: $850 (Class A); $425 (Class B); $250 (Class C); $100 (Class D).

Publications:
Membership Directory; on-line

Membership List Available to Non-members

QVM/CMC Vehicle Manufacturers Association
(1989)
P.O. Box 3070
Warrenton, VA 20188
Tel: (540) 347-0743 *Fax:* (540) 347-0742
Members: 7 companies
Staff: 1
Annual Budget: $25-50,000

Personnel:
General Counsel: Jerome C. Loftus

Historical Note:
Formerly (2003) Limousine Industry Manufacturers Organization. QVM/CMC/VMA is the trade association of the limousine manufacturing industry. Non-voting Supplier-Service Firm and Associate Member memberships are available for companies or individuals involved in the industry in a non-manufacturing capacity. Membership: $1,500/year (organization/company).

R & E Council of the NAPL (1947)
One Meadowlands Plaza
Suite 1511
East Rutherford, NJ 07073

Tel: (201) 634-9600 *Fax:* (201) 634-0324
TollFree: (800) 642-6275
E-Mail: naplmemberservice@napl.org
Website: napl.org
Members: 250 companies
Staff: 4
Annual Budget: $500-1,000,000

Personnel:
Vice President, Member Relations: Dean D'Ambrosi
    E-Mail: ddambrosi@napl.org
Senior Vice President, Accounting: Timothy Fischer
    E-Mail: tfischer@napl.org
Senior Director, Communications: Dawn Lospaluto
    E-Mail: dlospaluto@napl.org
Coordinator, Marketing: Carol Rocke
    E-Mail: crocke@napl.org

Historical Note:
Formerly (1950) Research and Engineering Council of the Graphics Arts; became the Research and Engineering Council of the NAPL in 2002 when it became a member of the National Association for Printing Leadership. R&E Council's mission is to enhance the competitiveness of the graphic communications community by facilitating the practical and profitable integration of technologies. Membership: $795-1,200 (Corporate, based on employees); $1,200-3,500 (Associate, based on employees); $250 (Education); $750 (International Internet).
Meetings/Conferences:
Number of non-conference events/year: 1

Publications:
Twenty:10 Newsletter; on-line

R-Calf (1998)
P.O. Box 30715
Billings, MT 59107
Tel: (406) 252-2516 *Fax:* (406) 252-3176
E-Mail: r-calfusa@r-calfusa.com
Website: r-calfusa.com
Staff: 2

Personnel:
Chief Executive Officer: Bill Bullard
Coordinator, Membership Services and Contact, Website Services: Laurel Masterson

Historical Note:
The R-Calf mission is to ensure the continued profitability and viability of independent U.S. cattle producers. Membership: $50/year

Meetings/Conferences: Annual
2013 - Pierre, SD (Best Western Ramkota Pierre Hotel)/
  Aug. 2 - 3

Publications:
The Cattlemen's Newsletter; on-line

Rabbinical Assembly (1901)
3080 Broadway
New York, NY 10027
Tel: (212) 280-6000 *Fax:* (212) 749-9166
E-Mail: info@rabbinicalassembly.org
Website: rabbinicalassembly.org
Members: 1600 individuals
Staff: 10
Annual Budget: $1-2,000,000

Personnel:
Executive Vice President: Rabbi Julie Schonfeld
    E-Mail: jschonfeld@rabbinicalassembly.org
Administrator, Web and Digital Media: Yossi Hoffman
    E-Mail: yhoffman@rabbinicalassembly.org
Director, Special Projects: Rabbi Jan Caryl Kaufman
    E-Mail: jkaufman@rabbinicalassembly.org
Accountant: Ursula Morillo
    E-Mail: accounting@rabbinicalassembly.org

Historical Note:
RA's goal is to serve the Jewish religion and strengthen the conservative and Masorti movement among rabbis. Members are rabbis serving conservative Jewish congregations and educational institutions.

Meetings/Conferences: Annual
Conference Chair: Rabbi Jan Caryl Kaufman

Publications:
Conservative Judaism (CJ); quarterly

Rack Manufacturers Institute (1958)
8720 Red Oak Blvd.
Suite 201
Charlotte, NC 28217-3992
Tel: (704) 676-1190 *Fax:* (704) 676-1199

Website: mhia.org/industrygroups/rmi
Members: 27 companies
Staff: 3
Annual Budget: $100-250,000
Tax: 501(c)(6)

Personnel:
Managing Director: John Nofsinger
    E-Mail: jnofsinger@mhia.org
Executive Assistant: Victoria Wheeler
    E-Mail: vwheeler@mhia.org

Historical Note:
RMI's mission is to strive for continuous improvement in both product design and application and also for the Professional and Ethical Standards of Performance.

Continuing Education:
Certification Designation/s: R-Mark

Racking Horse Breeders Association of America
(1971)
67 Horse Center Rd.
Suite B
Decatur, AL 35603
Tel: (256) 353-7225 *Fax:* (256) 353-7266
E-Mail: info@rackinghorse.com
Website: rackinghorse.com
Members: 3000 individuals
Staff: 10
Annual Budget: $500-1,000,000

Personnel:
Secretary, Manager and Director, Marketing: Melisa L.
  Taylor
    E-Mail: MelisaRhbaa@aol.com

Historical Note:
RHBAA aims to advocate and preserve the Racking Horse breed through the Official Breed Registry and other activities. Members are persons directly connected with Racking horses and the Racking horse industry. Membership: $35 (Individual); $45 (Family).

Meetings/Conferences: Annual

Membership List Available to Non-members

Radiant Panel Association (1993)
18927 Hickory Creek Dr.
Suite 140
Mokena, IL 60448
Tel: (315) 303-4735 *Fax:* (315) 303-5559
TollFree: (800) 427-6601
E-Mail: RPA@radiantprofessionalsalliallance.org
Website: radiantpanelassociation.org
Members: 1000 companies
Staff: 7
Annual Budget: $250-500,000
Tax: 501(c)(3)

Personnel:
Executive Director: Ted Lowe
    E-Mail: tlowe@rpa-info.com
Manager, Publications: Rich St. Angelo
    E-Mail: Rich.StAngelo@iapmo.org
Director, RPA Technical Services: Michael Geagan
    E-Mail: Michael.Geagan@
    radiantprofessionalsalliance.org
Director, Government Relations: Dain Hansen
    E-Mail: Dain.Hansen@iapmo.org
Director, Marketing and Communications: Duane Huisken
    E-Mail: Duane.Huisken@iapmo.org
Manager, Education Programs: Sherard Jones
    E-Mail: Education@radiantprofessionalsalliance.org
Director, Membership Services: Alan Wald
    E-Mail:
    Membership@radiantprofessionalsalliance.org

Historical Note:
RPA's mission is to partner with members to provide superior leadership to the radiant industry through comprehensive education while providing a clearinghouse of experience, ideas, and information on radiant heating and cooling. Membership: $100 (Student/Retired); $1,200 (Educational/Non-Profit Organizations); $300-500 (Trade Associate/Dealer/Contractor); $1,200-$10,000 (Manuafacturer).

Continuing Education:
Certification Designation/s: AIA, NATE

Meetings/Conferences: Annual
Number of non-conference events/year: 1

Publications:
Membership Directory; on-line
Radiant Living Magazine
Radiant Panel Report; monthly

Radiation Research Society (1952)

P.O. Box 7050
Lawrence, KS 66044-8897
Fax: (785) 843-6153
TollFree: (800) 627-0326
E-Mail: info@radres.org
Website: radres.org
Members: 2025 individuals
Staff: 4
Annual Budget: $2-5,000,000
Tax: 501(c)(3)

Personnel:
Executive Director: Kathy Votaw
   E-Mail: kvotaw@allenpress.com
Treasurer: Eleanor A. Blakely PhD
Editor-in-Chief: Marc S. Mendonca
Association Manager: Scott Starr
   E-Mail: sstarr@allenpress.com

Historical Note:
RRS is a professional society of individuals the effects of radiation. It is affiliated with the International Association for Radiation Research. It's mission is to advocate dissemination of knowledge in these and related fields through publications, meetings and educational symposia. Membership: $180 (Active Members); $145 (Associate Members); $25-75 (SIT Members); $1,250 (Corporate Members); $1,000-2,000 (Institutional Members).

Meetings/Conferences: Annual

Publications:
Membership Directory; annually
Radiation Research; monthly; adv.
rrsNews; quarterly

Radiation Therapy Oncology Group (1968)

1818 Market St.
Suite 1600
Philadelphia, PA 19103
Fax: (215) 928-0153
Website: rtog.org
Members: 250 research institutions
Staff: 5

Personnel:
Director, Data Management: Wendy Bergantz RN
   E-Mail: wbergantz@acr.org
Associate, Membership Services: Yvette Brantley
   E-Mail: RTOG-Membership@acr.org
Coordinator, Meetings and Administrative Assistant:
Michelle Buado
   E-Mail: mbuado@acr.org
Associate, Publications: Lisa Morabito
   E-Mail: RTOG-Publications@acr.org
Group Administrator: Sharon Hartson Stine BA
   E-Mail: shartson@acr.com

Historical Note:
An affiliate of the American College of Radiology. RTOG's mission is to improve the survival outcome and quality of life of adults with cancer through the conduct of high-quality clinical trials. Members are medical and research institutions.

Meetings/Conferences: Semi-Annual
Conference Chair: Michelle Buado
2013 - San Diego, CA (Manchester Grand Hyatt)/Jan. 24 - 27
2013 - Philadelphia, PA (Loews Philadelphia Hotel)/ June 13 - 16

Publications:
Member Listing; on-line
RTOG Newsletter

Radical Philosophy Association (1982)

Butler University, Philosophy and Religion Department
4600 Sunset Ave.
Indianapolis, IN 46208
Tel: (317) 940-9974
E-Mail: hvanderl@butler.edu
Website: radicalphilosophyassociation.org
Staff: 3

Personnel:
Interim, Executive Editor: Richard A. Jones
   E-Mail: rajones19@cox.net
Managing Editor: Peter Gratton
   E-Mail: pgratton@sandiego.edu
Treasurer: Harry van der Linden
   E-Mail: hvanderl@butler.edu

Historical Note:
RPA is an international nonsectarian forum for philosophical discussion of fundamental change. RPA states its enterprise to be inherently interdisciplinary and welcome persons not trained in philosophy. Membership: $69 (Institutions), $42 (Individuals) and $25 (Students).

Meetings/Conferences: Annual

Publications:
Radical Philosophy Review (RPR); bi-annually
RPA Newsletter; quarterly

Radio Advertising Bureau (1951)

125 W. 55th St.
21st Floor
New York, NY 10019
Tel: (800) 252-7234 Fax: (212) 681-7223
Website: rab.com
Members: 6000 stations and 8000 members and associates
Staff: 26
Annual Budget: $5-10,000,000

Personnel:
President and Chief Executive Officer: Erica Farber
   E-Mail: efarber@rab.com
Executive Vice President and Chief Financial Officer: Van Allen
   E-Mail: vallen@rab.com
Senior Vice President, Technical Services: Thomas Barnhardt
   E-Mail: tbarnhardt@rab.com
Senior Vice President, Marketing and Communications: Leah Kamon
   E-Mail: lkamon@rab.com
Senior Vice President, Professional Development: John Potter
   E-Mail: rramirez@rab.com
Senior Vice President, Membership Services: Dick Rakovan
   E-Mail: drakovan@rab.com

Historical Note:
Established originally as the Department of Radio Advertising of the National Association of Broadcasters, became independent in 1951 as the Broadcast Advertising Bureau and assumed its present name in 1955. RAB's mission is to lead industry initiatives and provide organizational, educational, research and advocacy programs and services that benefit the RAB membership and the Radio industry as a whole.

Continuing Education:
Certification Designation/s: CDMC, CRMC, CPCC

Publications:
Radio Sales Today; daily
Sales Meetings on Demand; semi-monthly

Radio and Television Correspondents Association (1939)

U.S. Capitol, Room S-325
Washington, DC 20510
Tel: (202) 224-6421
Members: 2400 individuals
Staff: 1
Annual Budget: $10-25,000

Personnel:
President: Joe Johns

Historical Note:
Formerly (1949) Radio Correspondents Association. Members are correspondents covering Congress. Its sole purpose is to oversee the work of the Senate and House press galleries. Has no paid staff; officers change annually. Membership: $15/year (individual).

Radio Technical Commission for Maritime Services (1947)

1800 N. Kent St.
Suite 1060
Arlington, VA 22209
Tel: (703) 527-2000 Fax: (703) 351-9932
E-Mail: information@rtcm.org
Website: rtcm.org
Members: 120 member organizations
Staff: 1
Annual Budget: $250-500,000
Tax: 501(c)(3)

Personnel:
President: R. L. Markle

Historical Note:
RTCM is an international non-profit scientific, professional and educational organization. RTCM members are organizations (not individuals) that are both non-
government and government. Founded in 1947 as a U.S. State Department advisory committee, it is now an independent non-profit membership organization.

Meetings/Conferences: Annual
2013 - San Diego, CA (Sheraton San Diego Hotel and Marina)/Sept. 22 - 27

Radio Television Digital News Association (1946)

529 14th St. NW
Suite 425
Washington, DC 20045
Tel: (202) 659-6510 Fax: (202) 223-4007
TollFree: (800) 807-8632
E-Mail: rtdna@rtnda.org
Website: rtnda.org
Members: 3000 individuals
Staff: 8
Annual Budget: $2-5,000,000

Personnel:
Executive Director: Mike Cavender
   E-Mail: mikec@rtdna.org
Director, Education Projects: Carol Knopes
   E-Mail: carolk@rtdna.org
Manager, Communications, Marketing and Digital Media: Ryan Murphy
   E-Mail: ryanm@rtdna.org
Manager, Meetings and Events: Noukla Ruble
   E-Mail: nouklar@rtdna.org
Manager, Programs, Awards and Membership: Katie Switchenko
   E-Mail: katies@rtdna.org

Historical Note:
Formerly Radio-Television Digital News Association. RTNDA is dedicated to setting standards for newsgathering and reporting and committed to encouraging excellence in the electronic journalism industry. Members are broadcast journalists, suppliers and educators. Membership: $85-199 (TV/Radio News Professional); $140 (Educator); $65 (Student); $199 (Associate); $185 (Government Associate); $70 (Retired); $535 (Supplier).

Meetings/Conferences: Semi-Annual
Conference Chair: Noukla Ruble
Number of non-conference events/year: 2

Publications:
Membership Directory; on-line

Membership List Available to Non-members

Radiological Society of North America (1915)

820 Jorie Blvd.
Oak Brook, IL 60523-2251
Tel: (630) 571-2670 Fax: (630) 571-7837
TollFree: (800) 381-6660
Website: rsna.org
Members: 46000 individuals
Staff: 203
Annual Budget: $50-100,000,000

Personnel:
Executive Director: Mark G. Watson
   E-Mail: mwatson@rsna.org
Assistant Executive Director, Publications and Communications: Roberta E. Arnold MA, MHPE
   E-Mail: rarnold@rsna.org
Controller: Olimpia Ballmaier
   E-Mail: oballmaier@rsna.org
Assistant Executive Director, Science and Education: Linda B. Bresolin CAE
   E-Mail: lbresolin@rsna.org
Director, Convention Operations: Janet Cooper
   E-Mail: jcooper@rsna.org
Director, Marketing: Jennifer Divelbiss
   E-Mail: jdivelbiss@rsna.org
Director, Advertising: James Drew
   E-Mail: jdrew@rsna.org
Director, Membership Services: Kolleen Klein
   E-Mail: kklein@rsna.org
Director, Administration and Human Resources: Mark Lichtenberger
   E-Mail: mlichtenb@rsna.org
Director, Public Information and Communications: Marijo Millette
   E-Mail: mmillette@rsna.org
Assistant Executive Director, Finance and Administration: Sally Nikkel
   E-Mail: snikkel@rsna.org
Director, Information Systems: David Pede
   E-Mail: dpede@rsna.org

Historical Note:

The mission of RSNA is to promote and develop the standards of radiology and related sciences through education and research. Members are individuals interested in the application of radiology to medicine. Membership: $430 (Active/Associate/Corresponding Member); $215 (Member).

Continuing Education:
Certification Designation/s: PQI

Meetings/Conferences: Annual
Conference Chair: Janet Cooper
2013 - Chicago, IL (McCormick Place)/Dec. 1 - 6
2014 - Chicago, IL (McCormick Place)/Nov. 30 - Dec. 5

Publications:
Directory of Members; annually
RadioGraphics; bi-monthly; adv.
Radiology; monthly; adv.
RSNA News; monthly; adv.
Scientific Assembly Program; annually; adv.

Membership List Available to Non-members

Radiology Business Management Association
(1968)
10300 Eaton Pl.
Suite 460
Fairfax, VA 22030
Tel: (703) 621-3355 *Fax:* (703) 621-3356
TollFree: (888) 224-7262
E-Mail: info@rbma.org
Website: rbma.org
Members:
2400 radiology practice managers and radiology business professionals
200 corporate
Staff: 15
Annual Budget: $2-5,000,000

Personnel:
Executive Director: Michael R. Mabry
    E-Mail: mike.mabry@rbma.org
Director, Communications and Development: Daphne Gawronski
    E-Mail: daphne.gawronski@rbma.org
Director, Education: Kimberly Mydland
    E-Mail: kimberly.mydland@rbma.org

Historical Note:
RBMA is a professional organization for radiology business management, offering education, resources and solutions for its members and the healthcare community. Membership: $410 (Active); $1050 (Corporate); $310 (Additional Member from a Practice/Additional Corporate Representative).

Continuing Education:
Certification Designation/s: RCCB

Meetings/Conferences:
2013 - Colorado Springs, CO (Broadmoor)/May 19 - 22
2013 - Boston, MA (Seaport Boston Hotel)/Sept. 8 - 11

Publications:
Conference Guide; annually; adv.
Corporate Partner Directory; on-line
eFlash; on-line
RadCast; semi-monthly
RBMA Bulletin; bi-monthly

RadTech (1986)
7720 Wisconsin Ave.
Suite 208
Bethesda, MD 20814
Tel: (240) 497-1242 *Fax:* (240) 209-2340
E-Mail: uveb@radtech.org
Website: radtech.org
Staff: 2
Annual Budget: $250-500,000

Personnel:
Senior Director: Mickey Fortune
    E-Mail: mickey@radtech.org

Historical Note:
RadTech's mission is to promote the use and development of UV & EB processing as an industrial technique offering energy savings, elimination of pollution, greater productivity, higher yields and the opportunity for improved, new or unique products. Membership: $85 (Affiliate); $1,000 (Corporate End User); $75 (Individual Corporate); $200 (Individual End User); $950 (Developing Corporate); $3,950 (Expanding Corporate); $1,950 (Growing Corporate); $7,450 (Major Corporate).

Meetings/Conferences: Biennial
Conference Chair: Mickey Fortune

Publications:
Buyer's Guide; on-line
RadTech Report; quarterly; adv.

Railway Engineering-Maintenance Suppliers Association (1965)
500 New Jersey Ave. NW
Suite 400
Washington, DC 20001
Tel: (202) 715-2921 *Fax:* (202) 204-5753
TollFree: (888) 337-3672
E-Mail: contact@remsa.org
Website: remsa.org
Members:
200 companies
216 individuals
Staff: 3
Annual Budget: $100-250,000
Tax: 501(c)(6)

Personnel:
Executive Director: David Soule
Manager, Operations: Urszula Soucie

Historical Note:
Formed by merger (1965) of National Railway Appliance Association (1894) and Association of Track and Structures Suppliers (1914). REMSA's mission is to provide global business development opportunities to members. Members are distributors and manufacturers of railway maintenance-of-way equipment, products and services. Membership: $705/year (Organization).

Meetings/Conferences: Semi-Annual
2013 - Miami, FL/Jan. 9 - 12/800 attendees
2013 - Indianapolis, IN/Sept. 29 - Oct. 2

Publications:
Mainline; quarterly
REMSA Buyer's Guide; annually

Membership List Available to Non-members

Railway Industrial Clearance Association (1969)
10330-S Lake Rd.
Building K
Houston, TX 77070
Tel: (281) 826-0009
Website: rica.org
Members: 400 members
Staff: 2
Annual Budget: $250-500,000

Personnel:
President: Steven Evans
    E-Mail: president@rica.org
Secretary and Treasurer: Michael R. Scott
    E-Mail: secretarytreasurer@rica.org

Historical Note:
RICA's mission is to serve the heavy and dimensional transportation industry and to explore opportunities to solve problems arising from transporting large dimension, excess weight, excess center of gravity or unusual shipments and to improve professional and social cooperation between members. Membership: $100/year (Active).

Publications:
Membership Directory; on-line
RICA News and Views Newsletter; quarterly
RICA Newsletter; on-line

Railway Supply Institute (1962)
425 Third St. SW
Suite 920
Washington, DC 20001
Tel: (202) 347-4664 *Fax:* (202) 347-0047
E-Mail: rsi@railwaysupply.org
Website: rsiweb.org
Members: 500 Companies
Staff: 5
Annual Budget: $1-2,000,000

Personnel:
President: Thomas D. Simpson
    E-Mail: simpson@rsiweb.org
Assistant Vice President, Government Affairs: Nicole Brewin
    E-Mail: gamache@rpi.org
Coordinator, Membership Services and Grassroots: Brian M. Kellman
    E-Mail: kellman@rsiweb.org
Office Manager: Robyn M. Leach
    E-Mail: leach@rsiweb.org
Contact, Trade Shows and Marketing: Amanda T. Patrick
    E-Mail: patrick@rsiweb.org

Historical Note:
RSI was formalized in January, 2003, with a consolidation of the Railway Supply Association and the Railway Progress Institute. The Railway Progress Institute was organized as the Railway Business Association in 1908, and changed its name in 1955. The Railway Supply Association was organized in 1938 under the name Allied Mechanical Association, and later morphed into the Railway Supply Association. RSI's mission is to support, connect and advocate for railway suppliers. Membership: $1,000 (Railroads/Banks/Law Firms/Industry Publications); $1,000-25,000 (Company, based on gross global rail related sales).

Meetings/Conferences: Annual
Conference Chair: Robyn M. Leach
2013 - Indianapolis, IN (Indiana Convention Center)/ Sept. 29 - Oct. 2

Publications:
Membership Directory; on-line
RSI newsletter; on-line

Railway Systems Suppliers, Inc (1966)
9306 New LaGrange Rd.
Suite 100
Louisville, KY 40242
Tel: (502) 327-7774 *Fax:* (502) 327-0541
E-Mail: rssi@rssi.org
Website: rssi.org
Members: 260 member companies
Staff: 2
Annual Budget: $1-2,000,000
Tax: 501(c)(6)

Personnel:
Executive Director: Michael A. Drudy
Executive Assistant: Sharon R. Morris

Historical Note:
Founded as the Railway Signal and Communication Suppliers Association Inc. In 1972 the corporate name was changed to Railway Systems Suppliers, Inc. RSSI's mission is to serve the communication and signal segment of the rail transportation industry. Its primary activity is organizing and managing a trade show for its members to exhibit their products and services. Membership: $350/year (Active/ Associate).

Meetings/Conferences: Annual
Conference Chair: Sharon R. Morris
2013 - Indianapolis, IN (Indiana Wesleyan University)/ Sept. 29 - Oct. 1/2000 attendees/over 100 exhibitors

Publications:
RSSI Newsletter; annually

The Railway Tie Association (1919)
115 Commerce Dr.
Suite C
Fayetteville, GA 30214
Tel: (770) 460-5553 *Fax:* (770) 460-5573
E-Mail: ties@rta.org
Website: rta.org
Members: 3200 companies
Staff: 3
Annual Budget: $500-1,000,000
Tax: 501(c)(6)

Personnel:
Executive Director: Jim Gauntt
    E-Mail: jgauntt@rta.org
Administrator: Debbie Corallo
    E-Mail: dcorallo@rta.org
Coordinator, Committee and Website: Barbara Stacey
    E-Mail: bstacey@rta.org

Historical Note:
RTA's purpose is to enhance the economical and environmentally sound use of wood crossties. Membership is comprised of crosstie producers, sawmill owners, chemical manufacturers, wood preservation companies, railroad maintenance engineers, purchasing officials and others interested in the manufacture and procurement of wood railroad ties. Membership: $425 (Producer); $595 (Supplier); $75 (Associate); $195 (Contractor/Recycling Management/Timberland Owner/Global Associate); $195-525 (Railroad Corporate).

Meetings/Conferences: Annual
Conference Chair: Barbara Stacey
Number of non-conference events/year: 2

Publications:
Crossties Magazine; bi-monthly

Ranchers-Cattlemen Action Legal Fund, United Stockgrower of America (1998)
P.O. Box 30715

Billings, MT 59107
Tel: (406) 252-2516 *Fax:* (406) 252-3176
E-Mail: r-calfusa@r-calfusa.com
Website: r-calfusa.com
Members: 15000 individuals
Staff: 4
Annual Budget: $250-500,000
Tax: 501(c)(3)

Personnel:
Chief Executive Officer: Bill Bullard
    E-Mail: billbullard@r-calfusa.com
Coordinator, Communications: Shae Dodson-Chambers
    E-Mail: sdodson@r-calfusa.com
Coordinator, Membership Services: Laurel Masterson
    E-Mail: laurelmasterson@r-calfusa.com

Historical Note:
Mission is to represent the U.S. cattle industry in national and international trade and marketing issues to ensure the continued profitability and viability of U.S. cattle producers. It consists primarily of cow-calf operators, cattle backgrounders, and feedlot owners. Membership: $50/year.
Meetings/Conferences:
Number of non-conference events/year: 1

Rapid Technologies & Additive Manufacturing Community of SME

One SME Dr.
Dearborn, MI 48128
Tel: (313) 425-3000 *Fax:* (313) 425-3404
TollFree: (800) 733-4763
E-Mail: techcommunities@sme.org
Website: sme.org/rtam
Members: 2000 individuals
Staff: 1

Personnel:
Manager, Community Relations: Jane Wellington
    E-Mail: techcommunities@sme.org

Historical Note:
Part of Technical Community Network of SME, a program of the Society of Manufacturing Engineers, which provides administrative support. RTAM/SME's mission is to showcase the innovative technologies represented by its technical groups to promote and accelerate adoption within the global manufacturing community.

Raptor Breeders of America

111 W. St.
El Paso, TX 54865
Website: raptorbreedersofamerica.org
Staff: 1

Personnel:
Treasurer: Jon Mathew

Historical Note:
A raptor breeders association.

RCI, Inc. *(1983)*

1500 Sunday Dr.
Suite 204
Raleigh, NC 27607-5041
Tel: (919) 859-0742 *Fax:* (919) 859-1328
TollFree: (800) 828-1902
E-Mail: rci@rci-online.org
Website: rci-online.org
Members: 2600 individuals
Staff: 12
Annual Budget: $2-5,000,000

Personnel:
Executive Vice President and Chief Executive Officer: James R. Birdsong
    E-Mail: jbirdsong@rci-online.org
Director, Publications: Kristen Ammerman
    E-Mail: kammerman@rci-online.org
Director, Educational Services: Rebecca Cunningham
    E-Mail: rcunningham@rci-online.org
Associate Director and Director, Membership Services and Registrations: Micki Kamszik
    E-Mail: mkamszik@rci-online.org
Director, Conventions and Meetings: Karen McElroy
    E-Mail: kmcelroy@rci-online.org
Director, Marketing Communications: William Myers
    E-Mail: wmyers@rci-online.org
Manager, Finance: Tammy M. Patterson
    E-Mail: tpatterson@rci-online.org
Director, Technical Services: Walter J. Rossiter
    E-Mail: wrossiter@rci-online.org

Historical Note:

Formerly Roof Consultants Institute, assumed its current name in 2006. RCI's mission is to ensure the credibility of the roofing, waterproofing, and exterior wall consulting professions. Members are professional building analysis consultants (those who derive their income from building analysis consulting) and industry members (individuals involved in contracting, sales or manufacturing). Membership: $420 (Professional); $474 (Industry); $149 (Quality Assurance Observer); $115 (Facility Manager); $69 (Student); $266 (Professional Affiliate/Industry Affiliate/Associate).
Continuing Education:
Certification Designation/s: RWC, RRC, RRO, REBC
Meetings/Conferences:
Conference Chair: Karen McElroy
2013 - Orlando, FL (Rosen Shingle Creek Hotel)/March 14 - 19

Publications:
Interface Journal; monthly; adv.
Membership Directory; on-line
RCI E-News; on-line; adv.
RCItems Newletter; monthly

Membership List Available to Non-members

React International *(1962)*

P.O. Box 21064
Glendale, CA 91221
E-Mail: RI.HQ@REACTIntl.org
Website: reactintl.org
Staff: 1
Annual Budget: $25-50,000

Personnel:
NIMS Coordinator: John Mahon
    E-Mail: J.Mahon@REACTIntl.org

Historical Note:
Mission is to provide public service communications to individuals, organizations, and government agencies to save lives, prevent injuries, and give assistance wherever and whenever needed.

Publications:
REACT'er magazine; adv.

Real Estate Buyers Agent Council *(1988)*

430 N. Michigan Ave.
Chicago, IL 60611
Tel: (312) 329-8656 *Fax:* (312) 329-8632
TollFree: (800) 648-6224
E-Mail: rebac@realtors.org
Website: rebac.net
Members: 50000 individuals
Staff: 21
Annual Budget: $5-10,000,000

Personnel:
Executive Director: Marc Gould
Manager, Business Development: Dawn Headtke
    E-Mail: dheadtke@realtors.org
Manager, Marketing: Jessica White
    E-Mail: jwhite@realtors.org

Historical Note:
REBAC's mission is to provide training and support that helps buyer's representatives be successful in their business and to educate consumers about the benefits of buyer representation and the ABR designation, in order to improve their home buying experience. Became an affiliate of National Association of Realtors in 1996. Membership: $110/year.
Meetings/Conferences:
Number of non-conference events/year: 7

Publications:
Membership Directory; on-line
RISMedia's Real Estate Magazine; monthly
TBR Hotsheet; weekly
Today's Buyer's Rep; monthly

Real Estate Educators Association *(1979)*

2000 Interstate Park Dr.
Suite 306
Montgomery, AL 36109
Tel: (334) 625-8650 *Fax:* (334) 260-2903
E-Mail: MemberCare@REEA.org
Website: reea.org
Members: 1000 individuals
Staff: 3
Annual Budget: $100-250,000
Tax: 501(c)(6)

Personnel:
Executive Director: Joe McClary
    E-Mail: Joe.McClary@reea.org

Coordinator, Membership Services: Meloney Gwin
    E-Mail: Meloney.Gwin@reea.org
Historical Note:
REEA's mission is to provide resources and opportunities for professional development to individuals and organizations involved in Real Estate education. Members are individuals involved in all types of real estate training and education. Membership: $349 (Institutional); $1,099 (Patron); $549 (Sustaining); $149 (Individual).

Continuing Education:
Certification Designation/s: DREI, NAR

Meetings/Conferences: Annual

Publications:
Membership Directory; on-line
REEAline; quarterly
REEANews; quarterly

Membership List Available to Non-members

Real Estate Information Professionals Association *(1995)*

2501 Aerial Center Pkwy.
Suite 103
Morrisville, NC 27560
Tel: (919) 459-2070 *Fax:* (919) 459-2075
Members: 110 individuals
Staff: 5
Annual Budget: $1-2,000,000
Tax: 501(c)(6)

Personnel:
Executive Director: Sarah Gillian Carlton
    E-Mail: sarah@imiae.com
Shalonda Maggitt

Historical Note:
REIPA supports professional information providers in the real estate industry. Membership: $1,595/year (Corporate).

Real Estate Investment Securities Association *(2002)*

Two Meridian Plaza, 10401 N. Meridian St.
Suite 202
Indianapolis, IN 46290
Tel: (317) 663-4180 *Fax:* (317) 815-0871
TollFree: (866) 353-8422
E-Mail: reisa@reisa.org
Website: reisa.org
Staff: 5
Annual Budget: $1-2,000,000

Personnel:
Executive Director and Chief Executive Officer: John P. Harrison CAE, CMP, MBA
    E-Mail: jharrison@reisa.org
Coordinator, Education and Meetings: Tanisha Bibbs
    E-Mail: tbibbs@reisa.org
Director, Marketing: Jennifer Fitzgerald
    E-Mail: jfitzgerald@reisa.org
Director, Business Development: Tony Grego
    E-Mail: tgrego@reisa.org
Director, Membership Services and Accounting: Deborah Lowe
    E-Mail: dlowe@reisa.org

Historical Note:
Formerly Tenant-in-Common Association. Organization of industry related companies focused exclusively on the success of the fractional ownership industry. Purpose is to provide members with quality education, information resources and networking opportunities. Membership: $1,000 (Associate/Affiliate); $199 (Individual); $2,500 (Affiliate Company).
Meetings/Conferences: Semi-Annual
Conference Chair: Tanisha Bibbs
2013 - Scottsdale, AZ (DoubleTree Resort by Hilton Hotel Paradise Valley-Scottsdale)/April 10 - 13
2014 - Chicago, IL (Hilton Chicago)/May 12 - 17

Publications:
E-Blasts; on-line
FYI; bi-monthly
Member Directory; on-line

Real Estate Management Brokers Institute

8543 S. Stony Island Ave.
Chicago, IL 60617
Tel: (773) 375-1600 *Fax:* (773) 375-1631
E-Mail: info@rembi.org
Website: rembi.org
Staff: 4

Personnel:
President: E. Jean Webber

E-Mail: jdawnwebb1@yahoo.com
Editor: Calvin Berry
Secretary: Lydia Kirkland
   E-Mail: lydiakirkland@aol.com
Treasurer: Evelyn Reeves
   E-Mail: fsico@sbcglobal.net

Historical Note:
REMBI's mission is to unite realtists specializing in the management of income producing properties in order to enhance and better the professional real estate manager. Membership: $50 (Broker/Salesperson); $75 (Local Chapter); $150 (Government Accredited Real Estate Organizations); $200 (Accredited Real Estate Organizations, Non- Government).

Continuing Education:
Certification Designation/s: CREM, CRM, AREMO

Publications:
REMBI Newsletter; on-line

Real Estate Roundtable *(1969)*
Market Sq., West, 801 Pennsylvania Ave. NW
Suite 720
Washington, DC 20004
Tel: (202) 639-8400 *Fax:* (202) 639-8442
E-Mail: info@rer.org
Website: rer.org
Members: 200 firms
Staff: 11
Annual Budget: $2-5,000,000

Personnel:
President and Chief Executive Officer: Jeffrey D. DeBoer
   E-Mail: jdeboer@rer.org
Director, Public Affairs: Xenia ("Ksen'ya") Jowyk
   E-Mail: xjowyk@rer.org
Systems Administrator: Elizabeth H. Karch
Director, Administration: Nancy G. Pitcher
   E-Mail: npitcher@rer.org
Director, Meetings and Executive Assistant: Michelle M. Reid
   E-Mail: mreid@rer.org
Director, Public Affairs: Scott Sherwood
   E-Mail: sherwood@rer.org

Historical Note:
Founded as the National Realty Committee, assumed its present name in 1999. The Roundtable's business and trade association leaders seek to ensure a cohesive industry voice is heard by government officials and the public about real estate and its important role in the global economy. Membership is by invitation only.

Meetings/Conferences: Annual
Conference Chair: Michelle M. Reid
Number of non-conference events/year: 6

Publications:
Membership Directory; on-line
Roundtable Weekly; weekly

Real Estate Valuation Advocacy Association
734 15th St. NW
Suite 900
Washington, DC 20005
TollFree: (888) 498-1114
Website: revaa.org
Staff: 2

Personnel:
Executive Director: Donald E. Kelly
   E-Mail: Don.Kelly@revaa.org
Manager, Communications: Elizabeth Kelley
   E-Mail: Libbi.Kelley@revaa.org

Historical Note:
The Real Estate Valuation Advocacy Association (REVAA) is a nonprofit trade association dedicated to the maintenance and further development of high quality.

REALTORS Land Institute *(1944)*
430 N. Michigan Ave.
Chicago, IL 60611
Tel: (312) 329-8446 *Fax:* (312) 329-8633
TollFree: (800) 441-5263
E-Mail: rli@realtors.org
Website: rliland.com
Members: 1600 individuals
Staff: 3
Annual Budget: $500-1,000,000
Tax: 501(c)(6)

Personnel:
Managing Director: Michele Cohen
   E-Mail: mcohen@realtors.org

Manager, Operations and Member Records: Karen Calaro
   E-Mail: kcalarco@realtors.org
Manager, Member Services and Accreditation: Lindsey Urban
   E-Mail: lpurban@realtors.org

Historical Note:
Formerly the Farm & Land Institute, the REALTORS Land Institute, an affiliate of the National Association of REALTORS, represents real estate professionals who specialize in the sale, brokerage, leasing, management, and development of land assets. RLI's mission is to build knowledge, relationships, and business for its members. The organization confers the Accredited Land Consultant (ALC) designation to those land professionals who achieve the highest levels of education and success in the marketplace. Members specialize in land brokerage related to farms, ranches, recreational, and other specialty land properties, undeveloped tracts of land, transitional and development land, subdivision and lot wholesaling, site selection and assemblage of land parcels. Membership: $395 (ALC Candidate/Accredited/Government and Non-Profit Employee); $145 (Non-Practitioner); $50 (Life); $75 (Student).

Continuing Education:
Certification Designation/s: ALC

Meetings/Conferences: Semi-Annual
Number of non-conference events/year: 2

Publications:
Membership Roster; on-line
Terra Firma Newsletter; adv.

Receptive Services Association of America *(1991)*
2365 Harrodsburg Rd.
Suite A325
Lexington, KY 40504
Tel: (859) 219-3545 *Fax:* (859) 226-4404
TollFree: (866) 939-0934
E-Mail: headquarters@rsana.com
Website: rsana.com
Members: 400 companies
Staff: 6
Annual Budget: $250-500,000

Personnel:
Executive Director: Matt Grayson
   E-Mail: matt.grayson@rsana.com
Member Services Administrator: Kate Hendle
Financial Analyst: Michelle Meade
Sales Manager: Jason Wallin
   E-Mail: sales@rsana.com

Historical Note:
Founded as Receptive Services Association of New York and New Jersey in 1990, RSA became a national organization in 1995 that strives to bring together all of the major receptive tour operators and suppliers in the New York and New Jersey region. RSAA's mission is to connect, educate and promote professionalism, defining the worldwide standard of the U.S. inbound travel industry. Members are companies who provide tour and travel related services to groups visiting the U. S. from overseas. Membership: $500 (Regular); $600 (Associate); $300 (International).

Meetings/Conferences: Annual
2013 - Atlantic City, NJ/Feb. 20 - 21
Number of non-conference events/year: 3

Publications:
Membership Directory; on-line
RSAA RTO Directory; on-line

Recognition Professionals International *(1998)*
1000 Westgate Dr.
Suite 252
St. Paul, MN 55114
Tel: (651) 290-7490 *Fax:* (651) 290-2266
E-Mail: rpi@recognition.org
Website: recognition.org
Members: 265 organizations
Staff: 3
Annual Budget: $250-500,000

Personnel:
Treasurer: Sean Schooling
   E-Mail: sean.schooling@telus.com

Historical Note:
RPI's mission is to enhance organizational performance through workforce recognition by providing access to best practice standards, education, research and the exchange of ideas. Membership: $250 (Practitioner); $400 (Resource Provider); $1,000-1,850 (Corporate Practitioner); $2,500-10,000 (Corporate Resource Provider); $75 (Student).

Continuing Education:

Certification Designation/s: CRP

Meetings/Conferences: Annual
2013 - New Orleans, LA (Hilton New Orleans Riverside)/April 27 - May 1
Number of non-conference events/year: 2

Publications:
Membership Directory; on-line
RPI Newsletter

Recording Industry Association of America (RIAA) *(1952)*
1025 F St. NW
Tenth Floor
Washington, DC 20004
Tel: (202) 775-0101 *Fax:* (202) 775-7253
E-Mail: webmaster@riaa.com
Website: riaa.com
Members: 350 companies
Staff: 72
Annual Budget: $25-50,000,000

Personnel:
Chairman and Chief Executive Officer: Cary Sherman
Senior Vice President, Public Policy and Industry Relations: Michele Ballantyne
Senior Executive Vice President: Mitch Glazier
   E-Mail: mglazier@riaa.com
Executive Vice President, Communications: Jonathan Lamy
   E-Mail: JLamy@riaa.com
Executive Vice President and General Counsel: Steven M. Marks

Historical Note:
Formerly (1970) Record Industry Association of America. RIAA seeks to foster a business and legal climate that supports and promotes its members creative and financial vitality. Member companies create, manufacture and market approximately 90% of all legitimate recordings produced and sold in the U.S.

Publications:
Fast Tracks Newsletter; on-line

Recreation Vehicle Dealers Association of North America *(1968)*
3930 University Dr.
Fairfax, VA 22030-2515
Tel: (703) 591-7130 *Fax:* (703) 359-0152
E-Mail: info@rvda.org
Website: rvda.org
Members: 1500 companies
Staff: 10
Annual Budget: $2-5,000,000
Tax: 501(c)(6)

Personnel:
Director, Finance: Hank Fortune
   E-Mail: hfortune@rvda.org
Vice President, Administration: Ronnie Hepp CAE
   E-Mail: rhepp@rvda.org
President: Phil Ingrassia CAE
   E-Mail: pingrassia@rvda.org
Director, Industry Relations: Jeff Kurowski
   E-Mail: jkurowski@rvda.org
Registrar, Technician Certification: Isabel McGrath
   E-Mail: imcgrath@rvda.org
Associate General Counsel and Director, Legal and Regulatory Affairs: Brett Richarson CAE, Esq.
   E-Mail: brichardson@rvda.org
Editor: Mary Anne Shreve
   E-Mail: mashreve@rvda.org

Historical Note:
Formerly (1976) Recreation Vehicle Dealers Institute. Absorbed Recreation Vehicle Rental Association in 1982 and Recreation Vehicle After Market Association in 1986. RVDA is dedicated to advance the RV retailer's interests through education, member services, industry leadership, and market expansion programs that promote the increased sale and use of RVs and that enhance the positive image of the RV experience. Members are RV dealers, RV rental fleet operators, RV service centers, and AfterMarket stores. Membership: $499 (RV Dealer); $230 (Rental Association).

Continuing Education:
Certification Designation/s: SW/A, WA, ST, SM

Meetings/Conferences: Annual
Number of non-conference events/year: 12

Publications:
RV Executive Today; monthly
RVDA Online Membership Directory & Resource Guide; on-line

Recreational Park Trailer Industry Association
(1993)
30 Greenville St.
Second Floor
Newnan, GA 30263-2602
Tel: (770) 251-2672 *Fax:* (770) 251-0025
E-Mail: info@rptia.com
Website: rptia.com
Members: 150 firms and organizations
Staff: 2
Annual Budget: $250-500,000

Personnel:
Executive Director: Bill Garpow
    E-Mail: bill.garpow@rptia.com
Assistant Director: Laraine H. Ayers
    E-Mail: layers@rptia.com

Historical Note:
*RPTIA is a nonprofit trade association that represents
and provides information and assistance to all segments
of the Park Trailer industry, agencies of government,
members of the media and product owners or potential
owners. Keeping the Standard up to date and insuring that
the inspections and enforcement procedures are uniform
in their application are two of the primary missions of
the Association. Membership: $75 (Individual); $600
(Supplier); $1,500-9,000 (Manufacturer).*

Meetings/Conferences:
Number of non-conference events/year: 3

Publications:
Member Directory; on-line

Membership List Available to Non-members

The Recreational Vehicle Aftermarket Association
(1969)
1833 Centre Point Cir.
Suite 123
Naperville, IL 60563
Tel: (630) 596-9004
E-Mail: info@rvaahq.org
Website: rvaahq.com
Members: 150 companies
Staff: 7
Annual Budget: $100-250,000

Personnel:
Executive Director: Patrick Farrey
    E-Mail: pfarrey@rvaahq.org
Director,Communications: Chris Barry
    E-Mail: cbarry@rvaahq.org
Finance and Operations: Barbara Ciulla
    E-Mail: bciulla@rvaahq.org
Business Development: Michael Greskiewicz
    E-Mail: michaelg@rvaahq.org
Member Services: Laura Hallen
Contact, Events and Awards: Meg Pawelski
    E-Mail: mpawelski@rvaahq.org
Manager, Operations: Sarah Washburn
    E-Mail: swashburn@rvaahq.org

Historical Note:
*Formerly (2001) known as Warehouse Distributors
Association. RVAA's mission is to improve the efficiency
of the RV aftermarket by establishing and promoting
programs and industry partnerships to enhance the RV
lifestyle. Members are wholesale distributors of parts
for manufactured housing and recreational vehicles.
Membership: $875/year (Manufacturer/Distributor/
Supplier).*

Meetings/Conferences: Annual
2013 - Boston, MA (Omni Parker House)/Aug. 13 - 16

Publications:
Aftermarket Update; on-line
Executive Magazine; monthly; adv.
Membership Directory; on-line
RVAAHQ Bulletin; on-line

Recreation Vehicle Industry Association (1963)
1896 Preston White Dr.
Reston, VA 20191
Tel: (703) 620-6003 *Fax:* (703) 620-5071
TollFree: (800) 336-0154
Website: rvia.org
Members: 520 companies
Staff: 53
Annual Budget: $10-25,000,000
Tax: 501(c)(6)

Personnel:
Vice President and General Counsel: Craig A. Kirby
    E-Mail: ckirby@rvia.org

Vice President, Public Relations and Advertising: James
    Ashurst
    E-Mail: jashurst@rvia.org
Senior Director, Publications and Communications: Bill
    Baker
    E-Mail: bbaker@rvia.org
Vice President, Administration: Mac Bryan
    E-Mail: mbryan@rvia.org
Vice President, Government Affairs: Dianne Farrell
    E-Mail: dfarrell@rvia.org
Vice President, Meetings and Shows: Mary Hutya
    E-Mail: mhutya@rvia.org
Research Analyst: Tatiana Samoylin
    E-Mail: tsamoylin@rvia.org
Coordinator, Membership Services: Diane Stuebing
    E-Mail: dstuebing@rvia.org
Manager, Information Technology and Market Information:
    Menges Tecle
    E-Mail: mtecle@rvia.org
Manager, Human Resources: Alice Wang
    E-Mail: awang@rvia.org
Director, Accounting: Carolyn Wood
    E-Mail: cwood@rvia.org

Historical Note:
*Established in 1963 as the Recreational Vehicle Institute,
Inc. Merged in 1968 with Camping Trailer Manufacturers
Association and American Institute of Travel Trailer and
Camper Manufacturers, Inc. The name was changed in
1975 to Recreation Vehicle Industry Association. RVIA
serves as a unifying force for safety and professionalism
within the RV industry and works with both federal and
state government agencies to protect the interests of its
members. Represents recreation vehicle (RV) manufacturers
and their component parts suppliers. Provides free materials
to consumers and other publics about RV travel and
camping and actively works with the media nationwide to
educate the public about the benefits of RVing.*

Continuing Education:
Certification Designation/s: CRVST

Meetings/Conferences: Annual
Conference Chair: Mary Hutya
2013 - Tampa, FL (Tampa Marriott Waterside Hotel
    and Marina)/Jan. 17 - 20
Number of non-conference events/year: 2

Publications:
Campgrounds Directory; on-line
Dealers Directory; on-line
Manufacturers Directory; on-line
Media Buzz; on-line
Membership Directory; on-line
Owner Clubs Directory; on-line
RV Shows Directory; on-line
RVIA Newsletter; quarterly; adv.
RVIA Today; quarterly

Membership List Available to Non-members

Recreation Vehicle Rental Association (1982)
3930 University Dr.
Fairfax, VA 22030
Tel: (703) 591-7130 *Fax:* (703) 359-0152
E-Mail: info@rvda.org
Website: rvda.org
Members: 2000 companies
Staff: 15
Annual Budget: $1-2,000,000

Personnel:
President: Phil Ingrassia CAE
    E-Mail: pingrassia@rvda.org
Contact, Membership Services: Chuck Boyd
    E-Mail: cboyd@rvda.org
Director, Finance: Hank Fortune
    E-Mail: hfortune@rvda.org
Director, Legal and Regulatory Affairs: Brett Richardson
    CAE, Esq.
    E-Mail: brichardson@rvda.org
Coordinator, Education: Liz Shoemaker
    E-Mail: lshoemaker@rvda.org
Editor: Mary Anne Shreve
    E-Mail: mashreve@rvda.org

Historical Note:
*A division of National RV Dealers Association (RVDA).
See RVDA's listing. Membership: $499 (RV Dealer); $230
(RV Rental); $224 (AfterMarket); $134 (Branch); $200
(California Dealers); $129 (Arizona Dealers).*

Meetings/Conferences: Annual

Publications:
Digital RVTechnician Magazine; on-line; adv.

Membership Directory; on-line
RV Executive Today; monthly; adv.

Recycled Paperboard Technical Association
(1953)
P.O. Box 5774
Suite 306
Elgin, IL 60121-5774
Tel: (847) 622-2544 *Fax:* (847) 622-2546
E-Mail: rpta@rpta.org
Website: rpta.org
Members: 100 companies
Staff: 4
Annual Budget: $500-1,000,000
Tax: 501(c)(6)

Personnel:
Executive Director: Amy Schaffer
    E-Mail: aschaffer@rpta.org
Media Contact: Joanne Arnold
    E-Mail: jarnold@rpta.org

Historical Note:
*Formerly Boxboard Research and Development Association
(BRDA) and renamed RPTA in 1991 . RPTA is a non-
profit association organized and operated as a business
league dedicated to the improvement of recycled paperboard
and related products. Membership dues are based on the
common denominator of annual total tons produced/sold of
relevant material.*

Meetings/Conferences:
Number of non-conference events/year: 27

Publications:
Membership Directory; on-line

Red and White Dairy Cattle Association (1964)
308B Ogden Ave.
Clinton, WI 53525
Tel: (608) 676-4900 *Fax:* (608) 299-0800
E-Mail: rwdcanicole@gmail.com
Website: redandwhitecattle.com
Members: 1400 individuals
Staff: 6
Annual Budget: $250-500,000

Personnel:
President: Jake Skinner
Manager & Executive Secretary: Stephanie Stout
    E-Mail: rwdcastephanie@gmail.com
Operation Manager: Elmo Wendorf
    E-Mail: rwdcaelmo@gmail.com

Historical Note:
*Founded as American Red and White Dairy Cattle Society,
assumed its current name in 1966. RWDCA strives to
encourage and promote the progressive breeding and
development of Red & White dairy cattle by providing
breeders with information, programs and services to help
track, evaluate and improve the breed from one generation
to the next. Members are owners and breeders of Red
and White dairy cattle, a hybrid of Red Holstein and
Milking Shorthorn. Membership: $20 (Junior); $50 (U.S.
Membership); $55 (Canada Membership); $75 (Foreign
Membership).*

Meetings/Conferences: Annual

Publications:
Bull Briefs; monthly
Red & White Breeder Directory; annually
The Red Bloodlines; adv.

Red Angus Association of America (1954)
4201 N. Interstate 35
Denton, TX 76207-3415
Tel: (940) 387-3502 *Fax:* (888) 829-5573
E-Mail: info@redangus.org
Website: redangus.org
Members: 2200 individuals
Staff: 18
Annual Budget: $2-5,000,000

Personnel:
Chief Executive Officer: Greg Comstock
    E-Mail: greg@redangus.org
Junior Programs Coordinator: Dawn Bernhard
    E-Mail: dawn@redangus.org
Director, Commercial Marketing: Clint Berry
    E-Mail: clint@redangus.org
Managing Editor: Ann Holsinger
    E-Mail: ann@redangus.org
Director, Accounting: Jeanene McCuistion
    E-Mail: jeanene@redangus.org
Director, Information Technology: Kip McEntire
    E-Mail: kip@redangus.org

Director, Communications: Jennifer Noble
  E-Mail: jennifer@redangus.org
Director, Member Services: Kenda Ponder
  E-Mail: kenda@redangus.org

Historical Note:
Member of National Pedigree Livestock Council, National Cattlemen's Association, U.S. Beef Breeds Council and Beef Improvement Federation. RAAA's mission is to provide its members and their customers with innovative programs and services, to continue advancing the quality, reliability and value of Red Angus and Red Angus influenced seedstock used in the commercial beef industry. Members are breeders and improvers of Red Angus Beef Cattle. Membership: $100 (Regular); $20 (Junior); $30 (Associate).

Meetings/Conferences: Annual
Conference Chair: Kenda Ponder
2013 - Denver, CO/Jan. 10 - 14

Publications:
ARA Magazine; monthly; adv.

Red Tag News Publications Association *(1971)*
1415 N. Dayton
Chicago, IL 60622
Tel: (312) 274-2215 *Fax:* (312) 266-3363
TollFree: (800) 460-4434
Website: redtag.org
Members: 57 publications
Staff: 4
Annual Budget: $50-100,000

Personnel:
Executive Director: Jim Franklin
  E-Mail: jim@redtag.org
Staff Consultant: Ed Mayhew
  E-Mail: ed@redtag.org
Monitor Administrator: Joanna Zygmont
  E-Mail: joanna@redtag.org

Historical Note:
RTNPA is a not-for-profit association of consumer and business magazines who have a common interest in improving the delivery of their publications in the mail. Members are publications classified by the U. S. Postal Service as newspapers. Membership: Fee varies based on circulation.

Meetings/Conferences:
Conference Chair: Ed Mayhew

Publications:
RTNPA Newsletter; on-line

Membership List Available to Non-members

The Refractories Institute *(1951)*
325 Maple Ave.
P.O. Box 8439
Pittsburgh, PA 15218
Tel: (412) 244-1880 *Fax:* (412) 281-1881
E-Mail: info@refractoriesinstitute.org
Website: refractoriesinstitute.org
Members: 60 companies
Staff: 1
Annual Budget: $500-1,000,000
Tax: 501(c)(6)

Personnel:
President: Robert W. Crolius
  E-Mail: rob@refractoriesinstitute.org

Historical Note:
Incorporated as a national trade association for refractory manufacturers, suppliers of equipment, raw material, and contractors/installers. TRI's mission is to advocate the interests of the refractories industry. Membership: $3,380-40,004 (Active); $400-3,500 (Affiliate); $2,816-6,756 (Associate); $848 (Contractors/Installers).

Publications:
Product Directory of the Refractories Industry; on-line; adv.
Refractory News; irregular; adv.
TRI newsletter; irregular; adv.

Refractory Ceramic Fibers Coalition *(1992)*
2300 N. St. NW
Room 6178
Washington, DC 20037
Tel: (202) 663-9188 *Fax:* (202) 354-5230
E-Mail: rcfc@buffnet.net
Website: rcfc.net
Members: 3 companies
Staff: 1
Annual Budget: $500-1,000,000
Tax: 501(c)(6)

Personnel:
President: Dean E. Venturin
  E-Mail: rcfc@buffnet.net

Historical Note:
Formed by refractory ceramic fiber manufacturers after the dissolution of TIMA (Thermal Insulation Manufacturers Association) in 1992. RCFC promotes proper work practices and standards for the RCF industry.

Publications:
Member Listing; on-line

Membership List Available to Non-members

Refractory Metals Association *(1971)*
105 College Rd. East
C/O Metal Powder Industries Federation
Princeton, NJ 08540
Tel: (609) 452-7700 *Fax:* (609) 987-8523
E-Mail: info@mpif.org
Website: mpif.org/aboutmpif/rma.asp?linkid = 33
Staff: 14

Personnel:
Executive Director and Chief Executive Officer: C. James Trombino CAE
  E-Mail: jtrombino@mpif.org
Manager, Office Services: Turner T. Abbott
Director, Technical Services: James P. Adams
  E-Mail: jadams@mpif.org
Vice President, Membership Services and Industry Relations: James R. Dale
  E-Mail: jdale@mpif.org
Manager, Meetings and Conferences: Sandra E. Leatherman
  E-Mail: sleatherman@mpif.org
Coordinator, Publications: Peggy LeBedz
  E-Mail: plebedz@mpif.org
Director, Communications: Donni Magid
  E-Mail: dmagid@mpif.org
Vice President, Finance and Administration: Jillaine K. Regan
  E-Mail: jregan@mpif.org

Historical Note:
Formerly (1975) Refractory and Reactive Metals Association. RMA is composed of producers of powders and products made from tungsten, molybdenum, tatalum and niobium that strive to serve for the refractory metals industries in dealing with agencies of the government on stockpiling, import and export regulations, defense programs, general communications, and any other such matters of concern.

Meetings/Conferences: Annual
Conference Chair: Sandra E. Leatherman

Publications:
Membership Directory; on-line

Refrigerated Foods Association *(1980)*
1640 Powers Ferry Rd.
Building Two, Suite 200A
Marietta, GA 30067
Tel: (770) 303-9905 *Fax:* (770) 303-9906
E-Mail: info@refrigeratedfoods.org
Website: refrigeratedfoods.org
Members: 150 companies
Staff: 5
Annual Budget: $500-1,000,000

Personnel:
Executive Director: Erik Lawser CAE
Director, Communications: Katy Fisher
Coordinator, Membership Services: Megan Levin

Historical Note:
Formerly (1991) Salad Manufacturers Association. RFA's mission is to educate its members on technical aspects of manufacturing and distributing prepared refrigerated foods. Members are manufacturers and suppliers of refrigerated prepared foods, who are committed to advance and safeguard the industry. Membership: $400-4,150 (Manufacturer, based on sales volume); $700 (Associate); $2,000 (Affiliate); $50 (Academic); $300-3112 (International).

Meetings/Conferences: Annual
2013 - Miami, FL (Doral Golf Resort and Spa)/Feb. 24 - 27

Publications:
Commodity Enews; quarterly
Membership Directory; annually; adv.
RFA Newsletter; quarterly
Technical E-News; weekly

Membership List Available to Non-members

Refrigerating Engineers and Technicians Association *(1910)*
P.O. Box 1819
Salinas, CA 93902
Tel: (831) 455-8783 *Fax:* (831) 455-7856
E-Mail: info@reta.com
Website: reta.com
Members: 2300 individuals
Staff: 4
Annual Budget: $1-2,000,000
Tax: 501(c)(6)

Personnel:
Executive Director: Don Tragethon
  E-Mail: don@reta.com
Contact, Education and Certifications: Scott Henderson MS
  E-Mail: scott@reta.com
Editor-in-Chief and Conference Manager: Julie Mower-Payne
  E-Mail: julie@reta.com
Contact, Membership Services and Accounting: Jan Tragethon
  E-Mail: jan@reta.com

Historical Note:
Formerly National Association of Practical Refrigerating Engineers. RETA's mission is to enhance the professional development of industrial refrigeration operating and technical engineers. Members are designers, installers, operators and maintainers of central refrigeration and air conditioning equipment. Membership: $125 (Individual/Student Member); $155 (International Individual/Student Member); $655 (Corporate); $680 (International Corporate).

Meetings/Conferences: Annual
Conference Chair: Julie Mower-Payne
2013 - Bellevue, WA/Oct. 30 - Nov. 2
2014 - Atlanta, GA/Nov. 4
2014 - Atlanta, GA/Nov. 4 - 7

Publications:
Conference Chronicle; daily; adv.
RETA Breeze; bi-monthly; adv.
Technical Report; monthly; adv.

Refrigeration Service Engineers Society *(1933)*
1911 Rohlwing Rd.
Suite A
Rolling Meadows, IL 60016-1397
Tel: (847) 297-6464 *Fax:* (847) 297-5038
TollFree: (800) 297-5660
E-Mail: general@rses.org
Website: rses.org
Members: 11000 members
Staff: 23
Annual Budget: $2-5,000,000
Tax: 501(c)(6)

Personnel:
Executive Vice President: Mark Lowry
  E-Mail: mlowry@rses.org
Manager, Conferences and Seminars: Jean Birch
  E-Mail: jbirch@rses.org
Manager, Educational Publications: Tim Gioe
  E-Mail: tgioe@rses.org
Manager, Marketing: Kim Heselbarth
  E-Mail: kheselbarth@rses.org
Manager, Member and Chapter Relations: Anna Szmajchel
  E-Mail: aszmajchel@rses.org
Director, Finance and Administration: Kelly Womack
  E-Mail: kwomack@rses.org

Historical Note:
RSES's mission is to provide opportunities for enhanced technical competence for its members, by offering education and certification. It works to advance the professionalism and proficiency of the industry through alliances with other HVACR associations. Members work in HVACR-related jobs, such as air conditioning, refrigeration, warm-air heating and ventilation. Membership: $128 (Individual); $150-1,000 (Corporate); $51.50 (Student); $2,000 (Lifetime).

Continuing Education:
Certification Designation/s: CM, CMS

Meetings/Conferences: Annual
Conference Chair: Jean Birch

Publications:
Refrigeration Service Engineer (RSE); monthly; adv.

Regional Airline Association *(1975)*

2025 M St. NW
Suite 800
Washington, DC 20036-3309
Tel: (202) 367-1170 *Fax:* (202) 367-2170
E-Mail: raa@raa.org
Website: raa.org
Members: 280 associate members and 32 airlines
Staff: 6
Annual Budget: $1-2,000,000
Tax: 501(c)(6)

Personnel:
President: Roger Cohen
  E-Mail: cohen@raa.org
Senior Vice President, Legislative Affairs: Faye Malarkey
  Black
  E-Mail: malarkey@raa.org
Senior Vice President, Operations and Safety: Scott W.
  Foose
Director, Advertising: Cheryl Goldsby
  E-Mail: cheryl@emeraldmediaus.com
Operations Manager and Contact, Membership Services:
  Staci Morgan
  E-Mail: morgan@raa.org
Editor: Kelly Murphy
  E-Mail: kelly@emeraldmediaus.com

Historical Note:
*In 1968 the Association of Commuter Airlines merged with
the National Air Taxi Conference to form what became
the National Air Transportation Conferences and later,
the National Air Transportation Associations. In 1975,
this group again became independent under the name
Commuter Airline Association of America and assumed
its present name in 1981. RAA's purpose is to provide
technical, government relations and public relations services
for regional airlines. Membership: $650/year.*

Meetings/Conferences: Annual
Conference Chair: Staci Morgan
2013 - Montreal, QC/May 6 - 9
Number of non-conference events/year: 1

Publications:
Airline Member Directory; on-line
Associate Member Directory; on-line
Regional Horizons; quarterly; adv.

Membership List Available to Non-members

Regional Plan Association (1922)
Four Irving Pl.
Seventh Floor
New York, NY 10003
Tel: (212) 253-2727 *Fax:* (212) 253-5666
Website: rpa.org
Staff: 33
Annual Budget: $2-5,000,000

Personnel:
Executive Director: Thomas K. Wright
  E-Mail: twright@rpa.org
Director, Creative and Technology: Jeff Ferzoco
  E-Mail: jferzoco@rpa.org
Director, Finance and Management: Jim Finch
  E-Mail: jfinch@rpa.org
Vice President, Development: Rossana Ivanova
  E-Mail: rivanova@rpa.org
Director, Strategic Initiatives: Juliette Michaelson
  E-Mail: jmichaelson@rpa.org
Director, Communications: Wendy Pollack
  E-Mail: wendy.pollack@rpa.org
Senior Accountant: Roma Tejada
  E-Mail: roma@rpa.org

Historical Note:
*A not-for-profit organization focused on improving the
quality of life for the New York, New Jersey and Connecticut
metropolitan regions. RPA is the distinguished independent
urban research and advocacy group.*

Publications:
RPA Blueprint
Spotlight; bi-weekly

Register of Professional Archeologists (1998)
5024-R Campbell Blvd.
Baltimore, MD 21236
Tel: (410) 933-3486 *Fax:* (410) 931-8111
E-Mail: info@rpanet.org
Website: rpanet.org
Members: 1800 individuals
Staff: 2
Annual Budget: $100-250,000

Personnel:

Associate Director: Donna Liberto
  E-Mail: donnal@clemonsmgmt.com
Association Coordinator: Ally Lancaster
  E-Mail: ally@clemonsmgmt.com

Historical Note:
*Formerly (1976) Society of Professional Archeologists,
assumed current name in 1998. RPA is a listing of
archaeologists who have agreed to abide by a code of
conduct and standards of research performance, who hold a
graduate degree in archaeology, anthropology, art history,
classics, history, or another germane discipline and who
have substantial practical experience. Membership: fee
varies, based on income.*

Publications:
Directory of Registered Professional Archaeologists;
  annually
RPA Notes; semi-annually

Registry of Interpreters for the Deaf (1964)
333 Commerce St.
Alexandria, VA 22314
Tel: (703) 838-0030 *Fax:* (703) 838-0454
Website: rid.org
Members: 57 affiliate chapters and 15000
individuals
Staff: 17
Annual Budget: $2-5,000,000
Tax: 501(c)(3)

Personnel:
Acting Executive Director: Matthew O'Hara MS
  E-Mail: MOHara@rid.org
Government Affairs Representative: Janet L. Bailey
  E-Mail: govtaffairs@rid.org
Director, Membership Services: Ryan Butts
  E-Mail: RButts@rid.org
Accountant: Sarah Luo
  E-Mail: SLuo@rid.org
Director, Certification and Education: Phara Georges
  Rodrigue MA
  E-Mail: PRodrigue@rid.org
Meetings Manager: Laura Romaine
  E-Mail: LRomaine@rid.org
Senior Director, Member Programs and Services: Tina
  Maggio Schultz
  E-Mail: TSchultz@rid.org
Acting Director, Operations: Elijah Sow
  E-Mail: ESow@rid.org
Communications Manager: Lindsey Walter
  E-Mail: LWalter@rid.org

Historical Note:
*RID is a national membership organization representing the
professionals who facilitate communication between people
who are deaf or hard of hearing and people who hear.
Interpreters serve as professional communicators in a vast
array of settings such as: churches, schools, courtrooms,
hospitals and theaters, as well as on political grandstands
and television. Membership: $15-165/year.*

Continuing Education:
Certification Designation/s: CI, CT, CDI-P, CDI, OTC,
NAD, CLIP-R, SC:L, NIC, CSC, MCSC, RSC, OIC:C,
OIC:S/V, OIC:V/S, IC/TC , Ed: K-12

Meetings/Conferences: Annual
Conference Chair: Laura Romaine
2013 - Indianapolis, IN (JW Marriott Indianapolis)/
  Aug. 9 - 14
2015 - New Orleans, LA (Hyatt Regency New Orleans)/
  Aug. 11 - 18

Publications:
Journal of Interpretation
RID's newsletter
VIEWS; quarterly

Membership List Available to Non-members

Regulatory Affairs Professionals Society (1976)
5635 Fishers Ln.
Suite 550
Rockville, MD 20852
Tel: (301) 770-2920 *Fax:* (301) 770-2924
E-Mail: raps@raps.org
Website: raps.org
Members: 12000 Individuals
Staff: 24
Annual Budget: $5-10,000,000
Tax: 501(c)(3)

Personnel:
Executive Director: Sherry Keramidas PhD, CAE
  E-Mail: skeramidas@raps.org

Senior Manager, Communications: Zachary Brousseau
  E-Mail: zbrousseau@raps.org

Historical Note:
*RAPS is an international membership organization
of regulatory professionals in the medical device,
pharmaceutical and biotechnology sectors.RAPS's mission
is to create and promote a clear identity for the regulatory
profession, establish standards for the profession, assure
access to resources to meet the standards, and recognize
achievement. Members are regulatory affairs professionals,
lawyers and consultants from drug, medical device, biologic
and health care related industries who work with the Food
and Drug Administration and other regulatory agencies
worldwide. Membership: $185 (Active/Associate); $65
(Student); $60-99 (Emerging Markets).*

Continuing Education:
Certification Designation/s: RAC

Meetings/Conferences: Annual
2013 - Boston, MA/Sept. 28 - Oct. 2
2014 - Austin, TX/Sept. 27 - Oct. 1
2015 - Baltimore, MD/Oct. 24 - 28
Number of non-conference events/year: 4

Publications:
Member Directory; on-line
Newsletter
Regulatory Focus; monthly

Membership List Available to Non-members

Rehabilitation Engineering and Assistive Technology Society of North America (1979)
1700 N. Moore St.
Suite 1540
Arlington, VA 22209-1903
Tel: (703) 524-6686 *Fax:* (703) 524-6630
E-Mail: info@resna.org
Website: resna.org
Members: 1300 individuals
Staff: 10
Annual Budget: $1-2,000,000

Personnel:
Executive Director: M. Nell Bailey
  E-Mail: nbailey@resna.org
Government Affairs Committee Chair: Paul M.A. Baker
  E-Mail: paul.baker@cacp.gatech.edu
Treasurer: Paul J. Schwartz ATP
  E-Mail: schwartzpa@uwstout.edu
Director, Certification: Anjali Weber
  E-Mail: aweber@resna.org

Historical Note:
*Formerly (1995) RESNA, the Association for the
Advancement of Rehabilitation Technology then became
(1986) Rehabilitation Engineering Society of North
America. RESNA's mission is to improve the potential
of people with disabilities to achieve their goals through
the use of technology. A member society of the American
Institute for Medical and Biological Engineering.
Membership: $150 (Regular/Certified ATP holders); $75
(Student/Consumer); $100 (New).*

Continuing Education:
Certification Designation/s: ATP, RET, ATS

Meetings/Conferences: Annual
2013 - Bellevue, WA (Hyatt Regency Beleluve)/June 20
  - 24

Publications:
Assistive Technology Journal; on-line
Membership Directory; on-line
RESNA E-News; on-line

Membership List Available to Non-members

Reinsurance Association of America (1968)
1445 New York Ave.
Seventh Floor
Washington, DC 20005
Tel: (202) 638-3690
E-Mail: infobox@reinsurance.org
Website: reinsurance.org
Members: 28 companies
Staff: 25
Annual Budget: $5-10,000,000
Tax: 501(c)(6)

Personnel:
President: Franklin W. Nutter
  E-Mail: nutter@reinsurance.org
Contact, General Media: Barbara Carroll
  E-Mail: carroll@reinsurance.org
Senior Vice President and Director, Education: Marsha A.
  Cohen

E-Mail: cohen@reinsurance.org
Senior Vice President and General Counsel: Tracey W. Laws
    E-Mail: laws@reinsurance.org
Senior Vice President, Membership Services and Business Operations: Robyn L. Morriss
    E-Mail: morriss@reinsurance.org
Vice President and Director, Federal Affairs: Mary Z. Seidel
    E-Mail: seidel@reinsurance.org
Vice President and Director, Information Services: J. Christopher Shue
    E-Mail: shue@reinsurance.org
Senior Vice President and Director, Financial Services: Joseph B. Sieverling
    E-Mail: sieverling@reinsurance.org
Vice President, Financial Analysis: W. Scott Williamson
    E-Mail: williamson@reinsurance.org
Vice President, State Relations and Assistant General Counsel: Matthew T. Wulf
    E-Mail: wulf@reinsurance.org

Historical Note:
Incorporated in the District of Columbia as the National Association of Property and Casualty Reinsurers. Became the Reinsurance Association of America in 1970. RAA is committed to promote a regulatory environment that ensures the industry remains globally competitive and financially robust, unhindered by conflicting state and federal regulation.

Publications:
Membership Directory; on-line
Reinsurance Underwriting Report; quarterly

Reliability Society
2866 Blue Jay Way
Lafayette, CO 80026
Website: rs.ieee.org
Members: 4000 individuals
Staff: 6
Annual Budget: $50-100,000

Personnel:
President: Dennis Hoffman
    E-Mail: d.hoffman@ieee.org
Vice President, Meetings: Marsha Abramo
    E-Mail: m.t.abramo@ieee.org
Vice President, Membership: Lon Chase
    E-Mail: l.chase@ieee.org
Vice President, Publications: Bob Loomis
    E-Mail: rloomis@ieee.org
Managing Editor: Jason Rupe
    E-Mail: Jrupe@ieee.org
Vice President, Technical Operations: W. Eric Wong
    E-Mail: ewong@utdallas.edu

Historical Note:
A technical society of the Institute of Electrical and Electronics Engineers (IEEE). Membership in the Society, open only to IEEE members, includes a subscription to a technical periodical in the field published by IEEE. All administrative support is provided by IEEE.

Meetings/Conferences:
Conference Chair: Marsha Abramo

Publications:
Reliability Society Newsletter; quarterly
Transactions on Reliability

Religion Communicators Council *(1929)*
475 Riverside Dr.
Room 1355
New York, NY 10115
Tel: (212) 870-2985 *Fax:* (212) 870-2171
E-Mail: rccrprc@rcn.com
Website: religioncommunicators.org
Members: 500 individuals
Staff: 1
Annual Budget: $50-100,000
Tax: 501(c)(3)

Personnel:
Executive Director: Shirley Whipple-Struchen
    E-Mail: sstruchen@rcn.com

Historical Note:
Founded as Religious Publicity Council; later became Religious Public Relations Council, and assumed its current name in 1999. Members are individuals working in advertising, public relations or communications for any religious communion, organization or related agency. Membership: $100 (Professional); $85 (Associate); $30 (Student).

Meetings/Conferences: Annual

2013 - Indianapolis, IN (Sheraton Indianapolis City Centre Hotel)/April 3 - 6

Publications:
eCounselor; quarterly; adv.
Membership Directory; on-line

Religion Newswriters Association *(1949)*
P.O. Box 2037
Westerville, OH 43086-2037
Tel: (573) 355-5201 *Fax:* (888) 707-3755
Website: rna.org
Members: 600 individuals
Staff: 6
Annual Budget: $100-250,000
Tax: 501(c)(6)

Personnel:
Executive Director: Debra L. Mason
    E-Mail: masondl@rna.org
Marketing Director: Wendy Gustufson
    E-Mail: Wendy@ReligionNews.com
Web Administrator: David Herrera
    E-Mail: Herrera@RNA.org
Administrative Assistant: Amy Schiska
    E-Mail: Schiska@RNA.org
Development Director: Yonat Shimron
    E-Mail: Yonat.Shimron@gmail dot com
Manager, Business and Human Resources: Michelle Stacho
    E-Mail: stacho@rna.org

Historical Note:
RNA is a professional association of journalists covering religion for the general circulation news media. Membership: $50 (Active); $100 (Associate); $25 (Students/Retiree).

Meetings/Conferences: Annual
Conference Chair: Wendy Gustufson
2013 - Austin, TX/Sept. 26 - 28

Publications:
e-Extra newsletter; on-line
Membership Directory; on-line

Membership List Available to Non-members

Religious Communication Association *(1973)*
Department of Communication, University of Texas
3900 University Blvd.
Tyler, TX 75799
Tel: (903) 566-7093 *Fax:* (903) 566-7287
Website: americanrhetoric.com/rca
Members: 212 individuals and institutions
Staff: 4
Annual Budget: Under $10,000
Tax: 501(c)(3)

Personnel:
Coordinator, Electronic Communications: Michael E. Eidenmuller
    E-Mail: eiden@uttyler.edu

Historical Note:
Formerly (1998) Religious Speech Communication Association. Until 1973 Religious Speech Division of the Speech Communication Association. RCA's mission is to promote honest, respectful and profound dialogue which reflects the diversity of religious beliefs, subject matter concerns, methodologies, and professions of its members. Members include teachers, students, clergy, broadcasters and other scholars and professionals. Membership: $25 (Regular); $50 (Institution); $12.50 (Student); $45 (Sustaining); $250 (Life); Add $10 per category of international membership.

Meetings/Conferences: Annual

Publications:
Journal of the Religious Communication Association; semi-annually
Membership Directory; on-line
The RCA News; irregular

Membership List Available to Non-members

Religious Conference Management Association *(1972)*
7702 Woodland Dr.
Suite 120
Indianapolis, IN 46278
Tel: (317) 632-1888 *Fax:* (317) 632-7909
E-Mail: rcma@rcmaweb.org
Website: rcmaweb.org
Members: 3314 individuals
Staff: 5

Annual Budget: $500-1,000,000
Tax: 501(c)(3)

Personnel:
Executive Director: Harry Schmidt
Special Projects Coordinator: Debbie Hochstetler
Director, Conferences and Events: Dean Jones
Director, Administration: Judy Valenta
Director, Finance: Donna Woodring

Historical Note:
A nonprofit international organization of professionals responsible for planning and/or managing meetings, seminars, conferences, conventions, assemblies, or other gatherings for religious organizations. Formerly (1982) the Religious Convention Managers Association. Membership: $50 (Religious); $100 (Associate).

Continuing Education:
Certification Designation/s: CMP

Meetings/Conferences:
2013 - Minneapolis, MN/Jan. 29 - Feb. 1
2014 - Sacramento, CA/Feb. 4 - 7

Publications:
RCMA Highlights; daily; adv.
Religious Conference Manager; bi-monthly; adv.
Religious Conference Manager Extra; monthly; adv.
Who's Who in Religious Conference Management; annually; adv.

Religious Education Association *(1903)*
409 Prospect St.
New Haven, CT 06511
Tel: (765) 225-8836 *Fax:* (203) 432-5356
E-Mail: reaappre@msn.com
Website: religiouseducation.net
Members: 2600 individuals and libraries
Staff: 3
Annual Budget: $50-100,000
Tax: 501(c)(3)

Personnel:
President: Dean Blevins
    E-Mail: dgblevins@nts.edu
Coordinator, Networking: Sybrina Atwaters
    E-Mail: webmaster@religiouseducation.net
Executive Secretary: Lucinda Huffaker
    E-Mail: secretary@religiouseducation.net

Historical Note:
Merged with Association of Professors and Researchers in Religious Education in 2005. REA's mission is to create opportunities for exploring and advancing the interconnected practices of scholarship, research, teaching, and leadership in faith communities, academic institutions, and the wider world community. Membership: $35-95/year (Individual, based on annual income).

Meetings/Conferences: Annual
2013 - Boston, MA/Nov. 1 - 3
2014 - Chicago, IL/Nov. 7 - 9
2015 - Denver, CO/Nov. 6 - 8

Publications:
Membership Directory; on-line
REACH Newsletter; quarterly
Religious Education

Membership List Available to Non-members

Religious Research Association *(1959)*
618 SW Second Ave.
Galva, IL 61434-1912
Tel: (309) 932-2727 *Fax:* (309) 932-2282
Website: rra.hartsem.edu
Members: 600 individuals,college and universities
Staff: 4
Annual Budget: $50-100,000
Tax: 501(c)(3)

Personnel:
President: John P Bartkowski
Executive Officer: William H. Swatos Jr., PhD
    E-Mail: williamswatos@augustana.edu
Editor: Adair Lummis
    E-Mail: alummis@hartsem.edu
Treasurer: David Roozen

Historical Note:
RRA is a professional society of individuals engaged in religious behavior research including social scientists, church researchers and planners, theologians, teachers, administrators, members of the clergy, editors and religious educators. Formally organized as the Religious Research Fellowship on June 21, 1951. RRA's mission is to increase understanding of the function of religion in persons and society through application of social scientific and other

scholarly methods. Was originally under the auspices of the Institute of Social and Religious Research in association with the Federal Council of Churches. *Membership*: $35 (Sustaining); $20 (Student); $90 (Library Subscription).

Meetings/Conferences: Annual

Publications:
Context of Religious Research; semi-annually
Review of Religious Research; quarterly; adv.

Remanufacturing Institute (1995)
4460 Brookfield Corporate Dr.
Suite H
Chantilly, VA 20151-1671
Tel: (703) 968-2772 *Fax:* (703) 968-2878
E-Mail: gager@buyreman.com
Website: reman.org
Staff: 2
Annual Budget: $50-100,000

Personnel:
Chairman: William C. Gager

Historical Note:
TRI's mission is to help and develop the next generation of remanufacturing technology, to disseminate information throughout the industry and to make remanufacturing more competitive throughout the world. *Membership:* $500 (Associates); $200-1,000 (Remanufacturers); $25 (Others).

Meetings/Conferences:
2013 - Amsterdam, Netherlands (Amsterdam RAI Exhibition and Convention Centre)/June 16 - 18

Publications:
Remanufacturing Today; weekly; adv.
The ORG Quarterly; quarterly

The Renaissance Society of America (1954)
C/O Graduate School and University Center, City University of New York
365 Fifth Ave., Room 5400
New York, NY 10016-4309
Tel: (212) 817-2130 *Fax:* (212) 817-1544
E-Mail: rsa@rsa.org
Website: rsa.org
Members: 3400 individuals
Staff: 4
Annual Budget: $500-1,000,000

Personnel:
Executive Director: Ann E. Moyer
    E-Mail: amoyer@rsa.org
Editorial and Website Assistant: Maura Kenny
Program Manager: Erika Suffern
    E-Mail: rsa@rsa.org
Editor: Nicholas Terpstra
    E-Mail: nicholas.terpstra@utoronto.ca

Historical Note:
A professional society of scholars of the Renaissance. RSA brings together members from many backgrounds who are interested in a wide variety of disciplines related to this period. *Membership:* $70 (Regular); $110 (Patron); $53 (Retiree); $35(Student); $3000 (Life).

Meetings/Conferences: Annual
Conference Chair: Erika Suffern
2013 - San Diego, CA (San Diego Sheraton Hotel and Marina)/April 4 - 6/1500 attendees/over 100 exhibitors
2014 - New York City, NY/March 27 - 29/1500 attendees/over 100 exhibitors
2015 - Berlin, Germany/March 26 - 28/1500 attendees/over 100 exhibitors
2016 - Boston, MA/March 31 - April 2/1500 attendees/over 100 exhibitors
2017 - Chicago, IL/March 30 - April 1/1500 attendees/ over 100 exhibitors

Publications:
Membership Directory; on-line
Renaissance News & Notes; semi-annually
Renaissance Quarterly; quarterly; adv.

Renal Physicians Association (1973)
1700 Rockville Pike
Suite 220
Rockville, MD 20852
Tel: (301) 468-3515 *Fax:* (301) 468-3511
TollFree: (800) 772-7525
E-Mail: rpa@renalmd.org
Website: renalmd.org
Members: 3500 individuals
Staff: 10
Annual Budget: $2-5,000,000

Personnel:
Executive Director: Dale Singer MHA
    E-Mail: dsinger@renalmd.org
Director, Public Policy: Robert Blaser
    E-Mail: rblaser@renalmd.org
Director, Meetings: Desiree Bryant CMP
    E-Mail: dbryant@renalmd.org
Director, Membership Services and Marketing: Rose Butts
    E-Mail: rbutts@renalmd.org
Director, Finance and Administration: Rona Eisenberger
    E-Mail: reisenberger@renalmd.org

Historical Note:
RPA's purpose is to represent nephrologists and other members in their pursuit and to deliver quality renal health care. Members are physicians, practice managers, advanced practice nurses and physician assistants specializing in treatment of renal disease. *Membership:* $0-375/year.

Meetings/Conferences:
Conference Chair: Desiree Bryant CMP
2013 - New Orleans, LA/March 14 - 17
Number of non-conference events/year: 1

Publications:
RPA eNews; monthly; adv.
RPA News; adv.

Membership List Available to Non-members

Renewable Fuels Association (1981)
425 Third St. SW
Suite 1150
Washington, DC 20024
Tel: (202) 289-3835 *Fax:* (202) 289-7519
E-Mail: info@ethanolrfa.org
Website: ethanolrfa.org
Members: 75 companies
Staff: 10
Annual Budget: $5-10,000,000
Tax: 501(c)(6)

Personnel:
President and Chief Executive Officer: Bob Dinneen
Vice President, Research and Analysis: Geoff Cooper
    E-Mail: gcooper@ethanolrfa.org
General Counsel: Edward S. Hubbard Esq., Jr.
    E-Mail: ehubbard@ethanolrfa.org
Director, Membership Services: Randy Klein
    E-Mail: rklein@ethanolrfa.org
Vice President, Technical Services: Kristy Moore
    E-Mail: kmoore@ethanolrfa.org
Communications Specialist: Taryn Morgan
    E-Mail: tmorgan@ethanolrfa.org
Chief Financial Officer: Alex Obuchowski
    E-Mail: alex@ethanolrfa.org
Vice President, Government Affairs: Samantha Slater
    E-Mail: sslater@ethanolrfa.org
President and Chief Executive Officer: Robert White
    E-Mail: rwhite@ethanolrfa.org

Historical Note:
RFA represents the domestic ethanol industry, and promotes the increased production and use of fuel ethanol before Congress and federal agencies.

Meetings/Conferences: Annual
2013 - Las Vegas, NV (Wynn Las Vegas)/Feb. 18 - 20

Publications:
Ethanol Report; bi-weekly
Membership Directory; on-line

Renewable Natural Resources Foundation (1972)
5430 Grosvenor Ln.
Bethesda, MD 20814-2142
Tel: (301) 493-9101 *Fax:* (301) 493-6148
E-Mail: info@rnrf.org
Website: rnrf.org
Members: 10 societies
Staff: 5
Annual Budget: $250-500,000
Tax: 501(c)(3)

Personnel:
Executive Director: Robert D. Day
    E-Mail: day@rnrf.org

Historical Note:
RNRF is a consortium of professional, scientific and educational organizations that advances sciences and public education in renewable natural resources and fosters cooperation among professionals. *Membership:* $50-99 (Associate); $100-499 (Sustaining Associate); $500-999 (Sponsor Associate); $1,000 or more (Patron Associate).

Publications:
Renewable Resources Journal; quarterly

Reprographic Services Association (1988)
8778 Wolff Ct.
Suite 102
Westminster, CO 80031
Tel: (303) 428-0479 *Fax:* (303) 428-0481
TollFree: (800) 445-8629
E-Mail: info@rsacorporation.com
Website: rsacorporation.com
Members: 80 companies
Staff: 1

Personnel:
Executive Director: Mark Beilman
    E-Mail: markb@rsacorporation.com

Historical Note:
RSA is a network of independent businesses operated by stockholders of the Reprographic Services Association.

Republican Governors Association (1963)
1747 Pennsylvania Ave. NW
Suite 250
Washington, DC 20006
Tel: (202) 662-4140 *Fax:* (202) 662-4924
E-Mail: info@rga.org
Website: rga.org
Staff: 18

Personnel:
Executive Director: Phil Cox
    E-Mail: pcox@rga.org
Counsel and Deputy Executive Director: Mike Adams
    E-Mail: madams@rga.org
Director, Events: Jane Batson
    E-Mail: jbatson@rga.org
National Recruitment Coordinator: Amy Burggraf
    E-Mail: aburggraf@rga.org
Membership Director: Cara Edmundowicz
    E-Mail: carae@rga.org
Finance Director: Paige Hahn
    E-Mail: phahn@rga.org
Political Director: Josh Robinson
    E-Mail: jrobinson@rga.org
Director, Communications: Mike Schrimpf
    E-Mail: mschrimpf@rga.org
Press Secretary: Jon Thompson
    E-Mail: jthompson@rga.org
Executive Assistant: Larissa Ziemann
    E-Mail: lziemann@rga.org

Historical Note:
RGA's mission is to help elect Republicans to governorships throughout the nation and to provide the governors with the resources to help them govern effectively. Members can join the association through freedom fund. *Membership:* $25-5,000/year.

Meetings/Conferences:
Conference Chair: Jane Batson

Republican National Lawyers Association
P.O. Box 18965
Washington, DC 20036
Tel: (703) 719-6335 *Fax:* (202) 747-2873
E-Mail: info@republicanlawyer.net
Website: rnla.org
Staff: 2

Personnel:
Executive Director: Michael B. Thielen
    E-Mail: thielen@republicanlawyer.net

Historical Note:
A national organization of Republican lawyers that strives to advance professionalism; open, fair and honest elections; career opportunity; and Republican ideals. $100 (Regular); $190 (regular 2 years); $150 (Contributing); $300 (Sustaining); $1000 (Advisory Council); $10 (Law Student).

Meetings/Conferences: Annual
Number of non-conference events/year: 5

Publications:
Membership Directory; adv.
Newsletter; monthly

Research and Development Associates for Military Food and Packaging Systems (1946)
16607 Blanco Rd.
Suite 501
San Antonio, TX 78232
Tel: (210) 493-8024 *Fax:* (210) 493-8036
E-Mail: hqs@militaryfood.org
Website: militaryfood.org
Members: 1100 individuals

Staff: 3
Annual Budget: $500-1,000,000

Personnel:
Executive Director: James F. Fagan
  E-Mail: jfagan@militaryfood.org
Meeting Planner: Marygene Fagan
  E-Mail: mfagan@militaryfood.org

Historical Note:
R&DA's mission is to provide safe and quality food and food service to the U.S. Armed Forces. R&DA coordinates research and development activities in food, food service, foodservice equipment and packaging systems among agencies, academic institutions and private industry. Membership: $125 (Consultant); $100 (Associate); $50 (Individual/Institutional); $10 (Student); $400 (Industrial).

Continuing Education:
Certification Designation/s: CCN, CHP, CBP, CSP, CPFM, MCFP

Meetings/Conferences:
Conference Chair: Marygene Fagan
2013 - Amelia Island, FL (Villas of Amelia Island Plantation)/May 20 - 22/26-50 exhibitors

Publications:
The Link; bi-annually

Research Association of Minority Professors (1975)
Texas A&M University
College Station, TX 77843
Tel: (979) 845-3211
Members: 985 individuals
Staff: 1
Annual Budget: $10-25,000
Tax: 501(c)(3)

Personnel:
Executive Director: Jeffrey J. Guidry PhD

Historical Note:
RAMP's purpose is to provide an opportunity for minority professors to engage in culturally relevant research projects and encourage students to become involved in systematic research activities. Membership: $65 (Regular); $45 (Student).

Meetings/Conferences: Annual

Publications:
Journal of the Research Association of Minority Professors (JRAMP); annually

Research Chefs Association (1996)
1100 Johnson Ferry Rd.
Suite 300
Atlanta, GA 30342
Tel: (404) 252-3663 Fax: (404) 252-0774
E-Mail: rca@kellencompany.com
Website: culinology.com
Members: 2500 individuals
Staff: 8
Annual Budget: $1-2,000,000
Tax: 501(c)(6)

Personnel:
Executive Vice President: Jim Fowler CAE
  E-Mail: jfowler@kellencompany.com
Director, Membership Services: Kristi Johnson
  E-Mail: kjohnson@kellencompany.com
Director, Education and Certifications: Tim Kline
  E-Mail: tkline@kellencompany.com
Manager, Meetings: Darrel McCook
  E-Mail: dmccook@kellencompany.com
Specialist, Communications: Laura Wilkins
  E-Mail: lwilkins@kellencompany.com

Historical Note:
RCA's mission is to promote the value of culinology and empower its community. Membership is comprised of chefs and food scientists working in food manufacturing, chain restaurants, hotels, ingredient supply houses, consulting and academia, and other food professionals in R&D, sales, marketing, manufacturing, distribution, and the media. Membership: $135 (Affiliate/Chef/Food Science and Technology/Culinology); $400 (Associate); $30 (Student).

Continuing Education:
Enrollment: 100
Certification Designation/s: CCS, CRC

Meetings/Conferences: Annual
Conference Chair: Darrel McCook
2013 - Charlotte, NC/March 6 - 9

Publications:
Culinology; quarterly; adv.
Culinology Currents; semi-annually; adv.

Member Directory; on-line
RCA Insider; monthly; adv.

Research Council on Structural Connections (1947)
C/O AISC, One E. Wacker Dr.
Suite 700
Chicago, IL 60601
Tel: (312) 670-5414
Website: boltcouncil.org
Members: 70 companies, associations and individuals
Staff: 4
Annual Budget: $25-50,000

Personnel:
Chair, Executive Committee: Charles Carter
  E-Mail: carter@aisc.org
Secretary and Treasurer: Chad Larson

Historical Note:
Formerly Research Council on Riveted and Bolted Structural Joint. In 1979, the name of the Council was changed to the Research Council on Structural Connections whose mission is to stimulate and support such investigation as may be deemed necessary and valuable to determine the suitability, strength and behavior of various types of structural connections. Membership: $50-$1000 (Annual Individual and Company Research Contributions); $1000-$10000 (Annual Association and Institute Research Contributions).

Meetings/Conferences: Annual

Publications:
Membership Directory; on-line

Research Institute for Fragrance Materials (1966)
50 Tice Blvd.
Suite 325
Woodcliff Lake, NJ 07677
Tel: (201) 689-8089 Fax: (201) 689-8090
E-Mail: rifm@rifm.org
Website: rifm.org
Members: 78 companies
Staff: 25
Annual Budget: $5-10,000,000

Personnel:
President: David K. Wilcox PhD
Contact, Membership: Christen Sachse-Vasquez
  E-Mail: csachse-vasquez@rifm.org
Technical Manager: Saloni Sharma
  E-Mail: ssharma@rifm.org

Historical Note:
RIFM purpose is to gather and analyze scientific data, engage in testing and evaluation, distribute information, cooperate with official agencies and to encourage uniform safety standards related to the use of fragrance ingredients. Membership: $2,510-400,000/year.

Meetings/Conferences: Annual

Research Society on Alcoholism (1976)
7801 N. Lamar Blvd.
Suite D-89
Austin, TX 78752
Tel: (512) 454-0022 Fax: (512) 454-0812
E-Mail: RSAstaff@sbcglobal.net
Website: rsoa.org
Members: 1600 individuals
Staff: 4
Annual Budget: $1-2,000,000
Tax: 501(c)(3)

Personnel:
Director: Debra Sharp
  E-Mail: DebbyRSA@sbcglobal.net
Administrative Assistant: Rae Peurifoy

Historical Note:
RSA provides a forum for communication among scientists conducting research that may contribute to the prevention and treatment of alcoholism. Members are qualified scientists interested in alcohol research, including all biomedical sciences, clinical fields and psychosocial sciences. Membership: $150/year (Individual).

Meetings/Conferences: Annual
2013 - Orlando, FL (Grand Cypress)/June 22 - 26
2014 - Seatle, WA (Bellevue)/June 21 - 25
2015 - San Antonio, TX/June 20 - 24

Publications:
Alcoholism: Clinical & Experimental Research (ACER)
Membership Directory; on-line

Research!America (1989)
1101 King St.
Suite 520
Alexandria, VA 22314-2960
Tel: (703) 739-2577 Fax: (703) 739-2372
TollFree: (800) 366-2873
E-Mail: info@researchamerica.org
Website: researchamerica.org
Staff: 4
Annual Budget: $2-5,000,000
Tax: 501(c)(3)

Personnel:
President: Mary Woolley
  E-Mail: mwoolley@researchamerica.org
Chief Operating Officer: Michael Coburn
  E-Mail: mcoburn@researchamerica.org
Vice President, Communications: Suzanne Ffolkes
  E-Mail: sffolkes@researchamerica.org
Senior Director, Development and Membership: Carol Kennedy
  E-Mail: ckennedy@researchamerica.org

Historical Note:
Association of research organizations.

Publications:
The Research Advocate; bi-monthly

Reserve Officers Association of the U.S. (1922)
One Constitution Ave. NE
Washington, DC 20002-5618
Tel: (202) 479-2200 Fax: (202) 547-1641
TollFree: (800) 809-9448
E-Mail: membership@roa.org
Website: roa.org
Members: 60000 individuals
Staff: 25
Annual Budget: $2-5,000,000
Tax: 501(c)(19)

Personnel:
Executive Director: MAJ Drew Davis USMC (Ret.)
  E-Mail: adavis@roa.org
Director, Industry Affairs and Business Operations: Lani Burnett
  E-Mail: lburnett@roa.org
Manager, Meetings and Events: Kim Echols CMP
  E-Mail: kechols@roa.org
Director, Strategic Education: Lt. Col. Robert E. Feidler USAR (Ret.)
  E-Mail: rfeidler@roa.org
Legislative Director: Capt. Marshall A. Hanson USNR (Ret.)
  E-Mail: mhanson@roa.org
Director, Member Services: Diane Markham
  E-Mail: dmarkham@roa.org
Director, Web Development and Graphics: Kelly Matthews
  E-Mail: kmatthews@roa.org
Director, Resource Development: Richard Thralls
  E-Mail: rthralls@roa.org
Director, Communications: Keith Weller
  E-Mail: kweller@roa.org
Director, Service Members Law Center: CAPT Samuel F. Wright JAGC, USN Ret.
  E-Mail: swright@roa.org

Historical Note:
Chartered by Congress and in existence since 1922, ROA strives to support and promote the development and execution of a military policy for the United States that will provide adequate national security. Membership: $70-225 (Regular); $35-113 (Spouse); $265-600 (Life); $150-300 (Spouse Life); $200 (Virtual); $55-210 (Regular Term Membership with Co-Membership Discount); $20 (Cadet/ROTC).

Continuing Education:
Enrollment: 200
Certification Designation/s: JOPDS

Meetings/Conferences: Annual
Conference Chair: Kim Echols CMP
Number of non-conference events/year: 1

Publications:
112th Congress Directory; on-line
Defense Education Forum (DEF) Newsletter; on-line
Legislative Updates; daily
Membership Directory; on-line
ROA SmartBrief; daily
The Intersect; weekly
The Officer Journal; bi-monthly; adv.

The ReserveVoice; weekly; adv.
Weekly e-Newsletter; weekly

Residential Space Planners International (1963)
P.O. Box 14393
Scottsdale, AZ 85267-4393
Tel: (480) 473-0986 Fax: (480) 473-0757
TollFree: (800) 548-0945
E-Mail: maryfisherdesigns1@cox.net
Website: maryfisherdesigns.com
Members: 30 architects and designers
Staff: 2

Personnel:
Executive Director: Mary Knott
    E-Mail: maryfisherdesigns1@cox.net

Historical Note:
RSPI members are architects and interior designers
specializing in planning residential interiors and kitchen
design. Membership: $85/year.

Resilient Floor Covering Institute (1929)
115 Broad St.
Suite 201
La Grange, GA 30240
E-Mail: info@rfci.com
Website: rfci.com
Members: 19 companies
Staff: 2
Annual Budget: $1-2,000,000

Personnel:
Contact, Communications: Janice Hofmann
    E-Mail: Janice@creativestrategiespr.com

Historical Note:
Formerly (1973) Asphalt and Vinyl Asbestos Tile Institute
and (1976) the Resilient Tile Institute. Purpose is to support
the interests of the total resilient floor covering industry and
the people who use its products.

Resistance Welding Manufacturing Alliance
(1935)
550 NW LeJeune Rd.
Miami, FL 33126
Tel: (305) 443-9353 Fax: (305) 443-5647
TollFree: (800) 443-9353
E-Mail: rwma@aws.org
Website: aws.org/rwma
Members: 100 companies
Staff: 3
Annual Budget: $100-250,000

Personnel:
Manager, Programs: Susan Hopkins
    E-Mail: susan@aws.org
Contact, Membership: Keila DeMoraes
Vice Chair: Ed Langhenry Jr.
    E-Mail: ed.langhenry@watteredge.com

Historical Note:
A committee of the American Welding Society, representing
an alliance of organizations interested in the advancement
of the resistance welding process. RWMA's mission is to
advance the resistance welding technology, broaden its use,
and promote its economic benefits. Membership: $525/year
(Regular; Company-requires AWS Sustaining or Supporting
Membership).

Meetings/Conferences: Annual
Conference Chair: Susan Hopkins
Number of non-conference events/year: 1

Publications:
Membership Directory; on-line; adv.
RWMA News

Resolve, The National Infertility Association
(1974)
1760 Old Meadow Rd.
Suite 500
McLean, VA 22102
Tel: (703) 556-7172 Fax: (703) 506-3266
E-Mail: info@resolve.org
Website: resolve.org
Members: 7000 members
Staff: 9
Annual Budget: $1-2,000,000
Tax: 501(c)(3)

Personnel:
President and Chief Executive Officer: Barbara Collura
    E-Mail: bcollura@resolve.org
Director, Strategic Partnerships and Projects: Rebecca
    Flick

E-Mail: rflick@resolve.org
Manager, Professional Outreach: Dawn Gannon
    E-Mail: dgannon@resolve.org
Specialist, Resource Development: Heather Gasser
    E-Mail: hgasser@resolve.org
Manager, Development: Tracy Kaylie
Administrative Assistant: Aretha Lee
Director, Public Relations: Andy Schwarz
    E-Mail: aschwarz@resolve.org

Historical Note:
RESOLVE seeks to provide timely, compassionate support
and information to people who are experiencing infertility
and to increase awareness of infertility issues through public
education and advocacy. Membership: $55 (Consumer);
$150 (Professional).

Publications:
Professional Services Directory; on-line
Resolve, for the journey and beyond; quarterly; adv.

Resort and Commercial Recreation Association
(1981)
P.O. Box 1564
Dubuque, IA 52004-1564
Tel: (563) 690-3233 Fax: (563) 690-3296
E-Mail: info@rcra.org
Website: rcra.org
Members: 300 companies and 1500 individuals
Staff: 2
Annual Budget: $50-100,000

Personnel:
President: Lisa Linden
    E-Mail: lisa.linden@rcra.org
Treasurer: Steve Geisz
    E-Mail: steve.geisz@rcra.org

Historical Note:
RCRA works to serve as a vehicle to communicate, educate
and promote standards of professionalism within the
industry and to provide opportunities for continuing
education, networking and awareness of industry trends.
Membership: $115 (Professional); $130 (Vendor); $50
(Student); $230 (Agency/Educational Institution); $40
(Affiliated Student).

Meetings/Conferences: Annual

Publications:
Membership Directory; on-line
Update; adv.

Resort Hotel Association (1987)
2100 E. Cary St.
Suite Three
Richmond, VA 23223
Tel: (804) 525-2020 Fax: (804) 525-2021
E-Mail: info@rhainsure.com
Website: rhainsure.com
Staff: 11

Personnel:
President and Chief Executive Officer: Brooks W. Chase
    E-Mail: brooks@rhainsure.com
Administrative Manager: Sara Amman
    E-Mail: sara@rhainsure.com
Vice President, Marketing and Member Relations: Bree
    Brostko
    E-Mail: bree@rhainsure.com
Program Manager: Tamara B. Glaser
    E-Mail: tammy@rhainsure.com
Senior Vice President, Business Development: David A.
    Kean
    E-Mail: david@rhainsure.com
Chief Financial Officer: Christine Longfield
    E-Mail: christine@rhainsure.com

Historical Note:
A not-for-profit insurance association, specializing in
insurance programs that address the risks unique to
independent resorts, hotels, city clubs and spas.

Meetings/Conferences: Annual
Conference Chair: Tamara B. Glaser
2013 - Seattle, WA (The Edgewater Hotel)/July 14 - 17
Number of non-conference events/year: 2

Publications:
Newsletter; quarterly

Resource Center for Religious Institutes (1981)
8824 Cameron St.
Silver Spring, MD 20910
Tel: (301) 589-8143 Fax: (301) 589-2897
E-Mail: trcri@trcri.org
Website: trcri.org

Members: 600 individuals
Staff: 5
Annual Budget: $500-1,000,000
Tax: 501(c)(3)

Personnel:
Executive Director: Daniel J. Ward J D, OSB
    E-Mail: dward@trcri.org
Business Manager: Bobbi Besley
    E-Mail: bbesley@trcri.org
Associate Director: Helen Burke
    E-Mail: hburke@trcri.org
Executive Assistant, Meetings: Kenita Hidalgo
    E-Mail: shidalgo@trcri.org
Administrative Assistant: Rita Waters RSM
    E-Mail: rwaters@trcri.org

Historical Note:
Formerly National Association for Treasurers of Religious
Institutes. RCRI's mission is to address the fiscal, legal
and administrative responsibilities specific to religious
institutes in the U.S. Membership: $410 (Individual); $600
(Organization).

Meetings/Conferences: Annual
Conference Chair: Kenita Hidalgo
2013 - Anaheim, CA/Oct. 20 - 25
2014 - St. Louis, MO/Nov. 3 - 7
2015 - Orlando, FL/Oct. 26 - 30
2016 - Anaheim, CA/Oct. 9 - 14
Number of non-conference events/year: 3

Publications:
News In Brief; quarterly
RCRI Bulletin; bi-annually

Respiratory Nursing Society (1990)
3816 Hawthorne Ave.
Richmond, VA 23222
E-Mail: dcbond@carilion.com
Website: respiratorynursingsociety.org
Members: 200 Registered Nurses
Staff: 6
Annual Budget: $25-50,000

Personnel:
President: Tracy Estes FNP BC, PhD, RN
    E-Mail: tsestes@vcu.edu

Historical Note:
RNS's mission is to advocate the practice of respiratory
nursing through professional development of its members
and to promote safe and effective respiratory health care
for society. Membership: $75 (Voting/Associate); $50
(Student/Retired); $1,500 (Corporate).

Meetings/Conferences: Annual
Conference Chair: Casey Norris RN

Publications:
Perspectives in Respiratory Nursing; irregular
Respiratory Nursing; adv.

RESPRO (Real Estate Services Providers Council)
(1993)
2000 L St. NW
Suite 522
Washington, DC 20036
Tel: (202) 862-2051 Fax: (202) 862-2052
E-Mail: info@respro.org
Website: respro.org
Staff: 3
Annual Budget: $500-1,000,000

Personnel:
Executive Director: Susan E. Johnson
    E-Mail: sjohnson@respro.org
Director, Meetings and Marketing: Rae Brevard
    E-Mail: rbrevard@respro.org

Historical Note:
RESPRO seeks to cultivate a business and regulatory
environment that better enables all its members to efficiently
offer affiliated services through subsidiaries, joint ventures,
and strategic partnerships. Members are real estate broker-
owners, franchisers, mortgage lenders/brokers, title
insurers/agents, home builders, home warranty companies
and other settlement service providers. Membership:
$1,100-2,200 (General); $5,500- 33,000 (Board); $1,100
(Associate).

Meetings/Conferences: Annual
Conference Chair: Rae Brevard
2013 - Washington, DC/March 25 - 27
Number of non-conference events/year: 1

Publications:
RESPRO® E-News; on-line
RESPRO® Quarterly Magazine; quarterly; adv.

Restaurant Facility Management Association

5600 Tennyson Pkwy.
Suite 180
Plano, TX 75024
Tel: (972) 805-0905 *Fax:* (972) 805-0906
Website: rfmaonline.com
Members: 350 individual
Staff: 4
Annual Budget: $1-2,000,000

Personnel:
Executive Director: Tracy Tomson
    E-Mail: tracy@rfmaonline.com
Manager, Education and Membership: Debi Kensell
    E-Mail: debi@rfmaonline.com
Coordinator, Membership Services: Jennifer Moore
    E-Mail: debi@rfmaonline.com
Coordinator, Marketing and Communications: Heather
    Webb
    E-Mail: heather@rfmaonline.com

Historical Note:
*RFMA's mission is to advance industry awareness
of restaurant facility management, while promoting
professional and ethical standards to serve the customer
with added value. Membership: $250 (Primary/Restaurant
Professional Independent Contractor); $75 (Restaurant
Professional Brand/Restaurant Professional Independent/
Retired Professional/Retired Allied); $50 (Student);
$500-1,250 (Vendor-Allied Corporate).*

Continuing Education:
Certification Designation/s: CRFP

Meetings/Conferences: Annual
2013 - Orlando, CO (Gaylord Palms Resort and
    Convention Center-Orlando)/March 10 - 12

Publications:
Facilitator Magazine; bi-monthly; adv.
Membership Directory; on-line
The Dish E-Newsletter; on-line

Restoration Industry Association (1946)

12339 Carroll Ave.
Rockville, MD 20852
Tel: (301) 231-6505 *Fax:* (301) 231-6569
E-Mail: info@restorationindustry.org
Website: restorationindustry.org
Members: 1350 companies
Staff: 11
Annual Budget: $1-2,000,000
Tax: 501(c)(6)

Personnel:
Executive Director: Timothy Shaw
    E-Mail: tshaw@restorationindustry.org
Director, Communications and Editor-in-Chief: Patricia L.
    Harman
    E-Mail: communications@restorationindustry.org
Director, Training and Certification: Cynthia A. Mullaly
    E-Mail: education@restorationindustry.org
Accountant: Valorie D. Seely
    E-Mail: accounting@restorationindustry.org
Director, Membership Services: Gina M. Valerio
    E-Mail: membership@restorationindustry.org

Historical Note:
*Formerly Association of Specialists in Cleaning and
Restoration International, (1984) the Association of Interior
Decor Specialists Divisions, (1971) Carpet and Upholstery
Cleaning Institute, (1971) Drapery Specialists Institute,
(1993) Mechanical Systems Hygiene Institute, (1968)
National Institute of Disaster Restoration, (1946) National
Institute of Rug and Drapery Cleaning, (1994) Water Loss
Institute. RIA's mission is to provide industry leadership and
promotes practices in the cleaning and restoration industry.
Membership: $1,000 (Contractors); $1,725 (Franchisors/
Suppliers); $420-1,725 (International).*

Continuing Education:
Certification Designation/s: CEC, CFS, CMH, CR, CRS,
CMP, WLS

Meetings/Conferences: Annual
2013 - Las Vegas, NV/April 23 - 25/1-10 exhibitors
Number of non-conference events/year: 11

Publications:
Cleaning and Restoration; monthly; adv.
Conference Directories; semi-annually; adv.
Directory of Cleaning and Restoration Firms; annually;
    adv.
Media Kit; monthly
NewsBreak; weekly
Organization Directory; on-line; adv.

Retail Advertising and Marketing Association International (1952)

325 Seventh St. NW
Suite 1100
Washington, DC 20004-2802
Tel: (202) 661-3052 *Fax:* (202) 737-2849
Website: rama-nrf.com
Members: 2000 individuals
Staff: 6
Annual Budget: $500-1,000,000

Personnel:
Executive Director: Mike Gatti
    E-Mail: gattim@nrf.com
Senior Vice President: Kelly Gilmore
    E-Mail: gilmorek@rama-nrf.com
Manager, Media Relations: Kathy Grannis
    E-Mail: grannisk@nrf.com
Vice President, Strategic Marketing: Libby Landen
    E-Mail: landenl@nrf.com
Director, Membership Development: Jessica Viator
    E-Mail: viatorj@nrf.com
Director, Speaker and Conference Management: Rachel
    Weintraub
    E-Mail: WeintraubR@nrf.com

Historical Note:
*Formerly (1991) the Retail Advertising Conference. RAMA
provides leadership that promotes creativity, innovation and
excellence within all marketing disciplines that strategically
elevates members and the industry.*

Meetings/Conferences: Annual
Conference Chair: Rachel Weintraub
2013 - New York City, NY (Jacob K. Javits Convention
    Center)/Jan. 13 - 16/51-100 exhibitors

Publications:
Retail Industry Indicators; annually
Retail Sales Outlook; quarterly
Stores Magazine; monthly
Washington Retail Insight; weekly

Retail Bakers of America (1918)

202 Village Cir.
Suite one
Slidell, LA 70458
Tel: (985) 643-6504 *Fax:* (985) 643-6929
E-Mail: Info@RBAnet.com
Website: retailbakersofamerica.org
Members: 2000 companies
Staff: 6
Annual Budget: $500-1,000,000
Tax: 501(c)(6)

Personnel:
Executive Director: Susan Nicolais CAE
    E-Mail: snicolais@retailbakersofamerica.org
Director, Marketing and Communications: Jim Fulton
    E-Mail: jfulton@retailbakersofamerica.org
Program Administrator: Kelley Mcclendon
    E-Mail: kmcclendon@retailbakersofamerica.org
Director, Marketing and Communications: Dawn Rivera
    E-Mail: drivera@retailbakersofamerica.org
Director, Finance: Paul Sapienza
    E-Mail: psapienza@retailbakersofamerica.org
Director, Education: Lynn Schurman
    E-Mail: lschurman@retailbakersofamerica.org

Historical Note:
*Formerly (2004) Retailers' Bakery of America, (1994)
Retail Bakers of America and (1996) Retailer's Bakery-
Deli Association. RBA's mission is to improve the operation
and profitability of retail bakeries. Membership: $200-400
(Retail); $350 (International Retail); $150 (School); $50
(Individual).*

Continuing Education:
Enrollment: 20
Certification Designation/s: CD, CMB, CB, CJB, CBB

Meetings/Conferences:
Conference Chair: Kelley Mcclendon
2013 - Las Vegas, NV (Las Vegas Convention Center)/
    Oct. 6 - 9

Publications:
Baker's Rack; quarterly; adv.
Flour Facts; weekly
Membership Directory; on-line
RBA NewsBrief; weekly
RBA Update; monthly; adv.
The Business Owner newsletter; on-line

Membership List Available to Non-members

Retail Confectioners International (1917)

2053 S. Waverly
Suite C
Springfield, MO 65804
Tel: (417) 883-2775 *Fax:* (417) 883-1108
TollFree: (800) 545-5381
E-Mail: info@retailconfectioners.org
Website: retailconfectioners.org
Members: 520 companies
Staff: 7
Annual Budget: $250-500,000

Personnel:
Executive Director: Kelly Brinkmann
    E-Mail: kelly@retailconfectioners.org
Manager, Marketing: Denise Alvarez
Manager, Office and Membership Services: Jordan Reppell
Manager, Event Planning: Lisa Wainwright

Historical Note:
*Formerly (1960) Associated Retail Confectioners of the
United States; (1969) Associated Retail Confectioners of
North America. RCI provides a forum for confectioners to
meet, network, share ideas, solve mutual problems, and
develop their candy making and entrepreneurial skills.
Members are confectioners and industry suppliers, from
small, independently owned businesses to large, multi-
million-dollar corporations. Membership: $100-1,200
(Active Candy Makers); $100-1,500 (Associate/Suppliers);
$100 (Retired).*

Meetings/Conferences: Annual
Conference Chair: Lisa Wainwright
2013 - Cincinnati, OH/June 24 - 28
Number of non-conference events/year: 3

Publications:
Annual Convention Magazine; annually; adv.
Candy Scoop; monthly
Kettle Talk; quarterly; adv.
Membership Directory and Buyer's Guide; annually;
    adv.

Retail Florist Association (2001)

197 Woodland Pkwy.
Suite 104-280
San Marcos, CA 92069
Fax: (323) 657-5379
E-Mail: info@retailflorist.com
Website: etfa.org
Members: 13000 individuals
Staff: 50
Annual Budget: $2-5,000,000

Personnel:
President: Marilee Just

Historical Note:
*Founded as Florists Telegraph Delivery Association;
became FTD Association in 1998, Extra Touch Flourists
Association in 2001 and assumed current name in 2011. A
partner of InterFlora, Inc., the international florists delivery
organization. Provides collaborative marketing, educational
programs, and networking opportunities to member florists.
Membership: $800/year.*

Retail Industry Leaders Association (1969)

1700 N. Moore St.
Suite 2250
Arlington, VA 22209
Tel: (703) 841-2300 *Fax:* (703) 841-1184
Website: rila.org
Members: 600 member companies
Staff: 46
Annual Budget: $10-25,000,000

Personnel:
President: Sandra L. Kennedy
    E-Mail: sandy.kennedy@retail-leaders.org
Vice President, Government Affairs: Sarah C. Arbes
    E-Mail: sarah.arbes@rila.org
Vice President, Communications and Advocacy: Jason
    Brewer
    E-Mail: jason.brewer@rila.org
Senior Vice President, Communications and State Affairs:
    Brian A. Dodge
    E-Mail: brian.dodge@rila.org
Manager, Communications: Liz Jennings
    E-Mail: liz.jennings@rila.org
Executive Vice President, Membership Services: Jenny
    Keehan
    E-Mail: jenny.keehan@rila.org
Executive Vice President, Public Affairs: Katherine Lugar
    E-Mail: katherine.lugar@retail-leaders.org

Vice President, Sustainability and Retail Operations: Adam
Siegel
E-Mail: adam.siegel@rila.org
Senior Vice President, Membership Services and Marketing:
Suzie Squier
E-Mail: suzie.squier@rila.org
Director, Membership Services: Giorgia Sumilas
E-Mail: giorgia.sumilas@rila.org
Executive Vice President and General Counsel: Deborah R.
White

Historical Note:
Announced plans to merge with National Retail Federation
(2009). Formerly (1969) Mass Merchandising Research
Foundation, (1976) National Mass Retailing Institute,
(1986) Merged with Association of General Merchandise
Chains (AGMC), (1988) International Mass Retailing
Association (IMRA). Adopted the present name in 2004.
RILA promotes consumer choice and economic freedom
through public policy and industry operational excellence.
Membership: $2,500-25,000 (Product Manufacturer);
$5,000-50,000 (Retailer); $2,500-15,000 (Associate).

Continuing Education:
Certification Designation/s: LPC

Meetings/Conferences:
2013 - Orlando, FL (Gaylord Palms Resort and
Convention Center-Orlando)/Feb. 17 - 20/1-10
exhibitors

Publications:
Human Resources; quarterly
Membership Directory; on-line
RILA Report; quarterly
RILA Report: Asset Protection; bi-monthly
RILA Report: Privacy; quarterly
RILA Report: Supply Chain; bi-monthly
RILA Report: Sustainability; bi-monthly
Tax Newsletter; adv.

Retail Packaging Manufacturers Association
(1990)
P.O. Box 17656
Covington, KY 41017-0656
Tel: (859) 341-9623 Fax: (859) 341-9624
E-Mail: info@retailpackaging.org
Website: rpma.org
Members:
100 associates
150 individuals
Staff: 2
Annual Budget: $100-250,000

Personnel:
Executive Director: Nancy Coons

Historical Note:
RPMA provides comprehensive educational and
networking services and organizes an annual trade
show for its members. Members of the association
include manufacturers, manufacturer representatives and
distributors of retail packaging.

Retail Print Music Dealers Association *(1976)*
14070 Proton Rd.
Suite 100, LB9
Dallas, TX 75244
Tel: (972) 233-9107 Fax: (972) 490-4219
E-Mail: office@printmusic.org
Website: printmusic.org
Members: 295 businesses
Staff: 2
Annual Budget: $100-250,000
Tax: 501(c)(6)

Personnel:
Executive Director: Madeleine Crouch

Historical Note:
RPMDA's mission is to provide a common meeting ground
for the congenial interchange of ideas among print music
dealers, to promote ethical standards and policies in dealing
with music publishers and to enhance better and more
meaningful dealer-publisher relations. Members are dealers,
publishers, or suppliers, large or small, full-line or print
only. Membership: $225/year (Associate/Dealer).

Meetings/Conferences: Annual
2013 - Columbus, OH/May 1 - 4/230 attendees/26-50
exhibitors

Publications:
Membership Directory; on-line
The Measure Newsletter; quarterly

Membership List Available to Non-members

Retail Solutions Providers Association *(1948)*
10130 Perimeter Pkwy.
Suite 420
Charlotte, NC 28216
Tel: (704) 357-3124 Fax: (704) 357-3127
TollFree: (800) 782-2693
E-Mail: info@gorspa.org
Website: gorspa.org
Members: 650 companies
Staff: 16
Annual Budget: $2-5,000,000

Personnel:
President and Chief Executive Officer: J. Joseph Finizio
E-Mail: jfinizio@gorspa.org
Supervisor, Member Services: Stephen Gift
E-Mail: sgift@gorspa.org
Manager, Meetings and Events: Amy Hanzel
E-Mail: ahanzel@gorspa.org
Manager, Education and Certification: Amber Murdock
E-Mail: AMurdock@GoRSPA.org
Manager, Marketing and Communications: Kristen Oleson
E-Mail: KOleson@GoRSPA.org
Manager, Member Services: Sara Petrus
E-Mail: SPetrus@GoRSPA.org
Manager, Education: Lauren Stark
E-Mail: lstark@gorspa.org
Controller: Elena Turner
E-Mail: ETurner@GoRSPA.org

Historical Note:
Established in 1948 in Dayton, OH in protest to a ceiling
on prices of used cash registers and formerly (2004)
the Independent Cash Register Dealers Association and
later merged with the SDA (Systems Dealer Association).
RSPA's purpose is to improve the retail technology
industry. Members are resellers, distributors, hardware
manufacturers, software developers, consultants and service
providers. Membership: $100-4,000/year.

Continuing Education:
Certification Designation/s: RSPA, SS, PCIwise, RC, VC

Meetings/Conferences: Annual
Conference Chair: Amy Hanzel
2013 - Curacao, Netherlands (Hyatt Regency Curacao
Golf Resort and Spa)/Jan. 20 - 23
Number of non-conference events/year: 1

Publications:
Connect Magazine; monthly; adv.
Juice e-news; monthly; adv.
RSPA Member Directory; annually

Retail, Wholesale and Department Store Union
(1937)
30 E. 29th St.
Fourth Floor
New York, NY 10016
Tel: (212) 684-5300 Fax: (212) 779-2809
E-Mail: info@rwdsu.org
Website: rwdsu.info
Members: 100000 individuals
Staff: 40
Annual Budget: $25-50,000,000
Tax: 501(c)(5)

Personnel:
President: Stuart Appelbaum
Director, Communications: Dan Morris
E-Mail: dmorris@rwdsu.org
Secretary and Treasurer: Jack Wurm

Historical Note:
Established in 1937 by dissidents from the Retail Clerks
International Union and chartered by the Congress of
Industrial Organizations as the United Retail Employees
of America. Became the United Retail, Wholesale and
Department Store Employees of America in 1940, a title
that was later shortened to its present form. Absorbed
the Distributive, Processing and Office Workers of
America as well as the Playthings, Jewelry and Novelty
Workers International Union in 1954 and the Cigar
Makers International Union of America in 1974. RWDSU
represents workers throughout much of the United States
and Canada. Mission is to better advance the interests and
protect the rights as working people.

Publications:
New Motts Newsletter

Membership List Available to Non-members

The Retired Enlisted Association *(1963)*
1111 S. Abilene Ct.
Aurora, CO 80012
Tel: (303) 752-0660 Fax: (303) 752-0835

TollFree: (800) 338-9337
E-Mail: treahq@trea.org
Website: trea.org
Staff: 7
Annual Budget: $2-5,000,000
Tax: 501(c)(19)

Personnel:
Coordinator, Publications and Interim Director, Operations:
Tammy Clowers
E-Mail: editor@trea.org
Contact, Membership Services: Charles Perry
E-Mail: cperry@trea.org

Historical Note:
Premier source of grassroots lobbying, legislative and
health care information for active duty military and retired
enlisted personnel. TREA's to enhance the quality of life
for uniformed services enlisted personnel, their families
and survivors-including active components, Reserves, and
National Guard, and all retirees. Membership: $30 (1
Year); $55 (3 Years); $400 (Lifetime).

Meetings/Conferences: Annual
2013 - Colorado Springs, CO (DoubleTree by Hilton
Hotel Colorado Springs)/Sept. 23

Publications:
The VOICE; bi-monthly; adv.

Retirement Industry Trust Association *(1987)*
4251 Pasadena Cir.
Sarasota, FL 34233
Tel: (941) 724-0900 Fax: (941) 866-7321
Website: ritaus.org
Members: 13 companies
Staff: 1
Annual Budget: $100-250,000

Personnel:
Executive Director: Mary L. Mohr JD, MBA
E-Mail: mlmohr.e.d.RITA@comcast.net

Historical Note:
RITA serves the self-directed retirement plan industry
and the general public by promoting ethical, efficient
and compliant practices among its regulated, financial
institutions. It aims at helping Americans reach their
retirement goals. Members are trust and custodian
companies providing professional guidance for self-directed
retirement savings plans and related instruments. Has no
paid officers or full-time staff. Membership: $600/year
(Individual).

Meetings/Conferences: Annual

Publications:
RITA Member Directory

Reusable Industrial Packaging Association *(1942)*
51 Monroe St.
Suite 812
Rockville, MD 20850
Tel: (301) 577-3786 Fax: (301) 577-6476
E-Mail: ripa@ripaus.com
Website: reusablepackaging.org
Members: 160 individuals
Staff: 4
Annual Budget: $500-1,000,000
Tax: 501(c)(3)

Personnel:
President: Paul W. Rankin
E-Mail: prankin@ripaus.com
General Counsel: Larry "Lawrence" W. Bierlein Esq.
Office Administrator and Conference Planner: Aisyah
Maskiell
E-Mail: amaskiell@ripaus.com
Vice President, Regulatory and Technical Affairs: C. L.
Pettit
E-Mail: cpettit@igc.org

Historical Note:
Formerly (1987) National Barrel and Drum Association
and (1999) Association of Container Reconditioners.
RIPA's mission is to promote safe, efficient and
environmentally responsible design, manufacturing,
collection, reconditioning, remanufacturing and reuse
of reusable industrial packaging, including preparation
for recycling at the end of its useful life. Members are
reconditioners and dealers of steel and plastic drums,
as well as intermediate bulk containers. Membership:
$2,790- 39,300 (U.S. Reconditioner/International,
Voting); $1,210-19,580 (Canadian Reconditioner);
$1,000 (International, Non-Voting); $5,500-16,500
(Manufacturer); $425 (Packager); $2,500 (Supplier/
Associate).

Meetings/Conferences:
Conference Chair: Aisyah Maskiell

2013 - Amsterdam, Netherlands (NH Grand Hotel Krasnapolsky)/June 5 - 7

Publications:
Membership Directory; on-line
Reusable Packaging; monthly
RIPA Newsletter; on-line

Rhetoric Society of America (1968)
1 Campus Dr.
Allendale, MI 49401-9403
Tel: (616) 331-5000
E-Mail: info@rhetoricsociety.org
Website: associationdatabase.com
Members: 1500 individuals
Staff: 3
Annual Budget: $100-250,000
Tax: 501(c)(3)

Personnel:
Executive Director: Frederick J. Antczak
    E-Mail: antczakf@gvsu.edu

Historical Note:
The purpose of RSA is to gather information of all relevant fields of study and to disseminate among its members, current knowledge of rhetoric and to encourage experimentation in the teaching of rhetoric. Membership: $50 (Student); $100 (International); $90 (Regular); $200 (Institutional); $2,000 (Lifetime); $3,000 (Enhanced Lifetime); $120 (Sustaining).

Meetings/Conferences: Biennial
2014 - San Antonio, TX (San Antonio Marriott Rivercenter)/May 22 - 26
Number of non-conference events/year: 2

Publications:
Rhetoric Society Quarterly; quarterly; adv.

Rheumatology Nurses Society (2007)
1810-J York Rd.
Suite 178
Lutherville, MD 21093
Tel: (800) 380-7081 *Fax:* (410) 384-4222
E-Mail: rns@dancyamc.com
Website: rns-network.org
Staff: 3
Annual Budget: $500-1,000,000

Personnel:
Director, Conference: Brent Carver

Historical Note:
RNS aims to empowering nurses through development and education to benefit its members, patients, family, and community. Members are rheumatology nurses and other healthcare professionals. Membership: $75 (Active); $35 (Student); $50 (Associate); $85 (Sustaining).

Meetings/Conferences: Annual
Conference Chair: Brent Carver
2013 - Nashville, TN (Gaylord Opryland Resort and Convention Center)/Aug. 1 - 3

Publications:
Membership Directory; on-line
Rheumatology Nurse; on-line
RNS Journal

Membership List Available to Non-members

Rice Millers' Association (1899)
2101 Wilson Blvd.
Suite 610
Arlington, VA 22201
Tel: (703) 236-2300 *Fax:* (703) 236-2301
TollFree: (800) 888-7423
E-Mail: riceinfo@usarice.com
Website: usarice.com
Members: 29 mills and cooperatives
Staff: 9
Annual Budget: $1-2,000,000
Tax: 501(c)(6)

Personnel:
President and Chief Executive Officer: Betsy Ward
Vice President, Meetings and Membership Services: Patricia Alderson
Manager, Membership Services and Meetings: Kim Broome
    E-Mail: kbroome@usarice.com
Director, Legislative Affairs and Communications: Johnny Broussard
    E-Mail: jbroussard@usarice.com
Director, Meetings: Jeanette Davis
Senior Director, Communications: Stacy Fitzgerald-Redd

Senior Director, Human Resources and Administration: Lisa L. Gargano
Vice President, Government Affairs: Reece Langley
    E-Mail: rlangley@usarice.com
Vice President, Finance and Administration: Linda Sieh

Historical Note:
RMA is national trade association of the United States' rice milling industry. Membership includes both independent rice milling companies and farmer-owned cooperative rice milling firms which together mill virtually all rice produced in the United States. RMA is a charter member of the USA Rice Federation which provides administrative support. Membership: $9000 (Trader); $5000 (Broker/ Merchandiser/User); $1500 (Allied Sliver).

Meetings/Conferences: Annual
Conference Chair: Jeanette Davis
Number of non-conference events/year: 2

Publications:
RMA Online; on-line

The Ripon Society (1962)
1300 L St. NW
Suite 900
Washington, DC 20005
Tel: (202) 216-1008
E-Mail: info@riponsoc.org
Website: riponsoc.org
Staff: 7
Annual Budget: $1-2,000,000

Personnel:
President and Chief Executive Officer: James K. Conzelman
Director, Membership Services: Robin Kessler
Editor and Communications Director: Lou Zickar
    E-Mail: editor@riponsociety.org

Historical Note:
A moderate Republican public policy organization founded in 1962, the Ripon Society works to strengthen the American family and protect the safety and future of its children.

Publications:
The Ripon Forum; quarterly

RISE (Responsible Industry for a Sound Environment) (1991)
1156 15th St. NW
Suite 400
Washington, DC 20005
Tel: (202) 872-3860 *Fax:* (202) 463-0474
E-Mail: info@pestfacts.org
Website: pestfacts.org
Staff: 2

Personnel:
President: Aaron Hobbs
    E-Mail: ahobbs@pestfacts.org
Director, Communications: Karen Reardon
    E-Mail: kreardon@pestfacts.org

Historical Note:
An association affiliated with the CropLife America representing manufacturers, suppliers, and distributors of non-agricultural urban use pesticides.

Risk and Insurance Management Society, Inc. (RIMS) (1950)
1065 Avenue of the Americas
13th Floor
New York, NY 10018
Tel: (212) 286-9292 *Fax:* (212) 986-9716
E-Mail: info@rims.org
Website: rims.org
Members:
3700 businesses and organizations
10000 individuals
Staff: 13
Annual Budget: $10-25,000,000
Tax: 501(c)(6)

Personnel:
Executive Director: Mary Roth
    E-Mail: mroth@rims.org
Accountant: Martha Agostini
Manager, Communications: Amy Benson
    E-Mail: abenson@rims.org
Director, Meetings and Events: Salvatore Chiarelli
Director of Government Affairs: Kathy Doddridge
    E-Mail: kdoddridge@rims.org
Manager, Human Resources: Deborah Flam
Chief Financial Officer: Jack Harrington

Director, Membership and Chapter Services: Jill Levy
Director, Publications and Editor-in- Chief: Morgan O'Rourke
Director, Information Technology: Michael Peters
Director, Professional Development: Kate Powers
General Counsel: Mark Prysock
Director, Marketing and Communications: Nikole TenBrink

Historical Note:
Founded as the National Insurance Buyers Association, became the American Society of Insurance Management in 1954 and assumed its present name in 1975. RIMS provides timely and innovative information, education, networking and advocacy. Membership consists of corporations, municipalities, universities and other entities that plan and purchase insurance or insurance services. Membership: $490 (Company); $500 (Associate); $100 (Educational); $50 (Student); $75 (Affiliate); $100 (Retired); $160 (Additional Deputy).

Continuing Education:
Certification Designation/s: RIMS

Meetings/Conferences:
Conference Chair: Salvatore Chiarelli
2013 - Los Angeles, CA (Los Angeles Convention Center)/April 21 - 25
2013 - Victoria, Australia/Oct. 6 - 9
Number of non-conference events/year: 33

The Risk Management Association (1914)
1801 Market St.
Suite 300
Philadelphia, PA 19103-1628
Tel: (215) 446-4000 *Fax:* (215) 446-4101
TollFree: (800) 677-7621
Website: rmahq.org
Members: 2,500 institutional members
Staff: 80
Annual Budget: $25-50,000,000
Tax: 501(c)(6)

Personnel:
President and Chief Executive Officer: William F. Githens
    E-Mail: bgithens@rmahq.org
Editor: Kathleen M. Beans
    E-Mail: kbeans@rmahq.org
General Counsel: Edward J. DeMarco
    E-Mail: edemarco@rmahq.org
Director, Chapters and Community Banks: Lisa McBride
    E-Mail: lmcbride@rmahq.org
Director, Information Technology: Frank McShay
    E-Mail: fmcshay@rmahq.org
Director, Strategic Planning and Organizational Development: Linda O'Loughlin
    E-Mail: loloughlin@rmahq.org
Chief Financial Officer: Dwight Overturf
    E-Mail: doverturf@rmahq.org
Director, Marketing: Mark Shafer
    E-Mail: mshafer@rmahq.org

Historical Note:
Formerly (1994) Robert Morris Associates, the National Association of Bank Loan and Credit Officers, and (2000) Robert Morris Associates the Association of Lending and Risk Professionals. RMA's purpose is to advance sound risk principles to improve institutional performance and financial stability, and enhance the risk competency of individuals through information, education, peer sharing, and networking. Membership: $595-76,500 (Institutional); $65-70 (Associate); $250-270 (Professional); $150-162 (Academic); $20 (student).

Continuing Education:
Certification Designation/s: CRC

Meetings/Conferences: Annual
2013 - Hong Kong, China/March 5 - 7
2013 - Cambridge, MA/April 17 - 18

Publications:
Membership Directory; on-line
The RMA Journal; adv.

Membership List Available to Non-members

River Management Society (1988)
P.O. Box 5750
Takoma Park, MD 20913-5750
Tel: (301) 585-4677 *Fax:* (301) 585-4677
E-Mail: rms@river-management.org
Website: river-management.org
Members:
40 companies and organizations
500 individuals
Staff: 1

Annual Budget: $250-500,000
Tax: 501(c)(3)

Personnel:
Executive Director: Risa Shimoda
  E-Mail: executivedirector@river-management.org

Historical Note:
Formed by the merger of the American River Management Society and the River Federation in 1996. RMS's mission is to support professionals who study, protect and manage North America's rivers. Members are government agency employees, companies and organizations and other private and public-sector individuals concerned with holistic and ecosystem approaches to water quality, riparian health and watershed management. Membership: $50 (Professional); $25 (Student); $120 (Organization-Government/Corporate); $60 (Organization- Nonprofit/NGO); $30 (Associate); $500 (Lifetime).

Meetings/Conferences: Annual
2013 - Grand Junction, CO (Colorado Mesa University)/March 11 - 15
Number of non-conference events/year: 2

Publications:
Membership Directory; on-line
RMS Journal; quarterly
RMS News; quarterly

Membership List Available to Non-members

RNA Society (1993)
9650 Rockville Pike
Bethesda, MD 20814-3998
Tel: (301) 634-7120 *Fax:* (301) 634-7420
E-Mail: rna@faseb.org
Website: rnasociety.org
Members: 1000 individuals
Staff: 4
Annual Budget: $1-2,000,000
Tax: 501(c)(3)

Personnel:
Chief Executive Officer: James McSwiggen
Chief Financial Officer: James P. Bruzik

Historical Note:
RNA members are scientists engaged in research on ribonucleic acid. Formed to facilitate sharing and dissemination of experimental results and emerging concepts in ribonucleic acid research. RNA Society's mission is to facilitate sharing and dissemination of experimental results and emerging concepts in RNA search. Membership: $183 (Full/Editorial Board member, Journal-Print and Electronic Access); $89 (Student/Post Doc, with Journal-Print and Electronic access); $154 (Full/Editorial Board, Journal-Electronic Access Only); $36 (Student/Post Doc, Journal-Electronic Access Only).

Meetings/Conferences: Annual
2013 - Davos, Switzerland (Congress Center Davos)/June 11 - 16
2014 - Québec, QC (Centre des Congrès de Québec)/June 3 - 8
Number of non-conference events/year: 4

Publications:
RNA Society newsletter; bi-annually
Society Directory; on-line
The RNA Journal; monthly; adv.

Robotic Industries Association (1974)
900 Victors Way
Suite 140
Ann Arbor, MI 48108
Tel: (734) 994-6088 *Fax:* (734) 994-3338
E-Mail: ria@robotics.org
Website: robotics.org
Members: 270 companies
Staff: 13
Annual Budget: $1-2,000,000

Personnel:
President: Jeffrey Burnstein
  E-Mail: jburnstein@robotics.org
Director, Marketing and Public Relations: Brian Huse

Historical Note:
Formerly (1983) Robot Institute of America. RIA represents the robotics automation industry in North America. Concerned with developing industry guidelines and collecting and dispensing accurate information on research and applications. Member companies include leading robot manufacturers, users, system integrators, component suppliers, research groups, and consulting firms. Membership: $1,000-10,000 (Supplier); $350 (Educator/Researcher); $1,500-3,000 (System Integrator); $400-800 (Consultant); $150-1,000 (User).

Meetings/Conferences: Annual
2013 - Orlando, FL (Orlando World Center Marriott)/Feb. 20 - 22

Publications:
Robotics Online; on-line; adv.

Robotics and Automation Society (1989)
2001 L St. NW
Suite 700
Washington, DC 20036-4910
Tel: (202) 785-0017 *Fax:* (202) 785-0835
E-Mail: ieeeusa@ieee.org
Website: ieee-ras.org
Members: 7000 individuals
Staff: 8
Annual Budget: $100-250,000

Personnel:
President: David Orin
  E-Mail: d.orin@ieee.org
Administrator: Kathy Colabaugh
  E-Mail: k-colabaugh@ieee.org
Vice President, Publications: Alessandro De Luca
  E-Mail: deluca@dis.uniroma1.it
Treasurer: Ronald Lumia
  E-Mail: lumia@unm.edu
Vice President, Financial Services: Anthony Maciejewski
  E-Mail: aam@colostate.edu
Vice President, Conferences: Nikos Papanikolopoulos
  E-Mail: npapas@cs.umn.edu
Vice President, Member Services: Stefano Stramigioli
  E-Mail: s.stramigioli@ieee.org
Vice President, Technical Services: Satoshi Tadokoro

Historical Note:
A technical society of the Institute of Electrical and Electronics Engineers (IEEE). Membership in the Council is open only to IEEE members. All administrative support is provided by IEEE. RAS's mission is to support exchange of information and knowledge among researchers and practitioners, standards development, career development, education, public outreach including pre-college students, and to support IEEE. Membership: $78.50 (Society Affiliate).

Meetings/Conferences: Annual
Conference Chair: Nikos Papanikolopoulos
2013 - Karlsruhe, Germany (Kongresszentrum Karlsruhe)/May 6 - 10
2014 - Hong Kong, China (Hong Kong International Convention Centre)/May 5 - 10
Number of non-conference events/year: 16

Publications:
IEEE Transactions on Automation Science and Engineering (T-ASE); quarterly
IEEE TRANSACTIONS ON ROBOTICS; bi-monthly
Robotics and Automation Magazine; quarterly

Robotics & Flexible Machinery Tech Group (1980)
One SME Dr.
C/O Society of Manufacturing Engineers
Dearborn, MI 48128
Tel: (313) 425-3000 *Fax:* (313) 425-3400
TollFree: (800) 733-4763
Website: i.sme.org/roboticsandflexiblemachinery/Home
Members: 3500 individuals
Staff: 3

Personnel:
Executive Director and Chief Executive Officer: Mark C. Tomlinson CMfgE, EMCP
  E-Mail: leadership@sme.org

Historical Note:
A member association of the Society of Manufacturing Engineers. Members are scientists, engineers and managers involved in all phases of robotics research, design, application, installation, human factors, and education and training related to robots. Certification as CMfgE (Certified Manufacturing Engineer) or CMfgT (Certified Manufacturing Technologist) is offered through the Manufacturing Engineering Certification Institute of SME. Membership: $60/year (initiation fee $15).

Publications:
Directory

Rocky Mountain Llama & Alpaca Association (1982)
P.O. Box 385403
Waikoloa, HI 80302
Tel: (808) 883-1887
Website: rmla.com

Members: 176 members
Staff: 3
Annual Budget: $50-100,000

Personnel:
President: Lougene Baird
  E-Mail: lougenebaird@hawaiiantel.net

Historical Note:
Incorporated in 1983. RMLA's mission is to share the information about llamas and alpacas with fellow owners and the general public. Membership: $40 (Regular Adult); $500 (Life); $10 (Youth/Young Adult).

Meetings/Conferences: Annual

Publications:
Membership Directory; annually; adv.
RMLA Newsletter
The RMLA Journal; quarterly; adv.

Rolf Institute of Structural Integration (1971)
5055 Chaparral Ct.
Suite 103
Boulder, CO 80301
Tel: (303) 449-5903 *Fax:* (303) 449-5978
TollFree: (800) 530-8875
E-Mail: info@rolf.org
Website: rolf.org
Members: 1700 individuals
Staff: 46
Annual Budget: $1-2,000,000

Personnel:
Executive Director: Diana Yourell
  E-Mail: dyourell@rolf.org
Manager, Membership Services: Heidi Hauge
  E-Mail: membership@rolf.org
Director, Education: James "Jim" Jones
  E-Mail: jjones@rolf.org
Accountant: Gena Rauschke
  E-Mail: grauschke@rolf.org
Manager, Marketing and Public Relations: Susan Winter
  E-Mail: swinter@rolf.org

Historical Note:
RISI brings Rolfing Structural Integration to the world through its training program for certified rolfers.

Continuing Education:
Certification Designation/s: ACR, CR, RMP

Publications:
Structural Integration

Roller Skating Association International (1937)
6905 Corporate Dr.
Indianapolis, IN 46278
Tel: (317) 347-2626 *Fax:* (317) 347-2636
E-Mail: rsa@rollerskating.com
Website: rollerskating.org
Members: 1100 skating centers and manufacturers and 2500 individuals
Staff: 10
Annual Budget: $1-2,000,000
Tax: 501(c)(3)

Personnel:
Executive Director: Susan Melenchuk
  E-Mail: smelenchuk@rollerskating.com
Accountant: Tonya Crenshaw
  E-Mail: accounting@rollerskating.com
Coordinator, Marketing and Promotions: Shelley Grogg
  E-Mail: sgrogg@rollerskating.com
Coordinator, Membership and Pepsi Account: Matt Nimrick
  E-Mail: membership@rollerskating.com
Accounting Assistant, Honors, and Public Information: Alice Sloat
  E-Mail: orders@rollerskating.com
Coordinator, Conventions, Education and Chapter Affairs: Breanne Talbott
  E-Mail: btalbott@rollerskating.com

Historical Note:
Formerly (1991) Roller Skating Rink Operators Association of America. RSA strives to serve commercial (for-profit) skating center owner and operators. It also serves those involved in various facets of the roller related industry such as teachers, coaches, manufacturers, distributors and other elements of the family entertainment industry. Membership: $360 (Supplier/Manufacturer); $460 (Future Operators); $30-60 (Coaches/Judges); $225-360 (Skating Center).

Meetings/Conferences: Annual
Conference Chair: Breanne Talbott
2013 - Reno, NV (Silver Legacy Resort Casino)/May 5 - 8

Publications:
Roller Skating Business Magazine; bi-monthly; adv.
RSA Membership Directory; annually
RSA Today; adv.

Romance Writers of America (1980)
14615 Benfer Rd.
Houston, TX 77069
Tel: (832) 717-5200 *Fax:* (832) 717-5201
E-Mail: info@rwa.org
Website: rwa.org
Members: 10000 individuals and 145 chapters
Staff: 11
Annual Budget: $2-5,000,000

Personnel:
Executive Director: Allison Kelley CAE
    E-Mail: allison.kelley@rwa.org
Editor: Erin Fry
    E-Mail: erin.fry@rwa.org
Manager, Education, Bookseller and Librarian Liaison:
    Stephani Fry
    E-Mail: steph.fry@rwa.org
Event Planner: Tiffany René
    E-Mail: tiffany.rene@rwa.org
Manager, Professional Relations: Carol Ritter
    E-Mail: carol.ritter@rwa.org
Coordinator, Membership and Chapter Services: Leslie
    Scantlebury
    E-Mail: leslie.scantlebury@rwa.org
Contact, Data Services: Judy Scott
    E-Mail: judy.scott@rwa.org

Historical Note:
RWA works to advance the professional interests of career-focused romance writers through networking and advocacy. Membership: $85 (General /Associate); $10 (Affiliate).

Meetings/Conferences: Annual
Conference Chair: Tiffany René
2013 - Atlanta, GA (Atlanta Marriott Marquis)/July 17
    - 21/2100 attendees
2014 - San Antonio, TX (San Antonio Marriott
    Rivercenter)/July 23 - 26/2100 attendees
2015 - New York City, NY (New York Marriott
    Downtown)/July 22 - 25/2100 attendees
2016 - San Diego, CA (San Diego Marriott Marquis and
    Marina)/July 13 - 16/2100 attendees
2017 - Lake Buena Vista, FL (Walt Disney World Swan
    and Dolphin)/July 26 - 29

Publications:
eNotes; bi-monthly
Romance Writers Report; monthly; adv.

Romanian Studies Association of America (1973)
Guilford College, English Department, Bauman
B-4
Greensboro, NC 27410
Tel: (512) 245-3073 *Fax:* (512) 245-8298
Website: thersaa.org
Members: 55 individuals
Staff: 1
Annual Budget: Under $10,000

Personnel:
President: Letitia Guran
    E-Mail: letitia_guran@yahoo.com

Historical Note:
RSAA's purpose is to foster Romanian Studies on the American continent, particularly in the United States and Canada. By advancing the scholarship and the intellectual exchanges between East-Central Europe and the West. Membership:$12/year.

Publications:
RSAA Newsletter; semi-annually; adv.

Romanian-American Chamber of Commerce (1990)
Two Wisconsin Cir.
Suite 700
Chevy Chase, MD 20815-7003
Tel: (240) 235-6060 *Fax:* (240) 235-6061
E-Mail: racc@racc.ro
Website: racc.ro
Members: 150 businesses
Staff: 1
Annual Budget: $50-100,000

Personnel:
Executive Director: Jay McCrensky PhD

Historical Note:

RACC is a bilateral trade association dedicated to the development of prosperous business relationships between Romania and the United States. Members are businesses, organizations, and individuals currently involved in or seeking business relationships in the Romanian-American marketplace. Membership: $300 (Small Business/Non Profit Organization); $600 (Corporate); $2,500 (Corporate Council/Infrastructure Council); Free (Individual).

Meetings/Conferences: Annual

Publications:
Membership Directory; on-line

Romanian-U.S. Business Council (1974)
15303 N. Dallas Pkwy.
Suite 1030
Addison, TX 75001
Tel: (855) 692-3226
E-Mail: info@usrobc.org
Website: usrobc.com
Staff: 1

Personnel:
President: Luana Gagu

Historical Note:
Founded as the Romanian-United States Economic Council, assumed its current name in 2000. USROBC is a private business development organization that bridges United States and Romania by identifying market, investment and technology opportunities and facilitates networking and cooperation between both countries. Members are U.S. Companies interested in business opportunities in Romania.

Meetings/Conferences: Annual

Roof Coatings Manufacturers Association (1983)
750 National Press Building
529 14th St. NW
Washington, DC 20045
Tel: (202) 591-2452 *Fax:* (202) 223-9741
E-Mail: questions@roofcoatings.org
Website: roofcoatings.org
Members: 70 companies
Staff: 8
Annual Budget: $250-500,000
Tax: 501(c)(6)

Personnel:
Executive Director: Reed B. Hitchcock
    E-Mail: Rhitchcock@kellencompany.com
Coordinator, Member Services: Penny Alston
    E-Mail: Palston@kellencompany.com
Coordinator, Industry Affairs: Shawn Richardson
    E-Mail: Srichardson@kellencompany.com

Historical Note:
RCMA provides a unified voice to advance, promote, and expand the international market for roof coatings through education, technical advancement, and advocacy of industry issues. Membership: $1,622.25-5,995.65/year.

Publications:
Suppliers Directory; on-line

RTCA, Inc. (1935)
1150 18th St. NW
Suite 910
Washington, DC 20036
Tel: (202) 833-9339 *Fax:* (202) 833-9434
E-Mail: info@rtca.org
Website: rtca.org
Members: 400 government, industry and
academic organizations
Staff: 11
Annual Budget: $2-5,000,000

Personnel:
President: Margaret Jenny
Senior Manager, Business Operations: Mary Beth
    Guaspari
Office Administrator and Receptionist: Stephanie Lamay

Historical Note:
RTCA, Inc. develops consensus-based recommendations regarding communications, navigation, surveillance, and air traffic management (CNS/ATM) system issues. Member $600-12500 (based on gross revenue); $1,200 (Academic Institutions); $ 2,200 (International Government Associate).

Meetings/Conferences: Annual
2013 - Washington, DC (Washington Convention
    Center)/June 5 - 6

Publications:
Membership Directory; on-line

Rubber and Plastics Industry Conference of the United Steelworkers of America (1935)
Five Gateway Center
Pittsburgh, PA 15222
Tel: (412) 562-2400
Members: 90000 individuals
Staff: 3
Annual Budget: $10-25,000,000

Personnel:
President: Leo W. Gerard
International Secretary-Treasurer: James D. English

Historical Note:
Organized in Akron, Ohio September 12, 1935 as the United Rubber Workers of America and chartered as an industrial union the following year by the Congress of Industrial Organization. Became United Rubber, Cork, Linoleum and Plastic Workers of America in 1945; Merged with United Steelworkers of America and assumed its current name in 1995. Has an annual budget of approximately $12. 5 million.

Rubber Manufacturers Association (1900)
1400 K St. NW
Suite 900
Washington, DC 20005
Tel: (202) 682-4800 *Fax:* (202) 682-4854
E-Mail: info@rma.org
Website: rma.org
Members: 100 companies
Staff: 18
Annual Budget: $5-10,000,000

Personnel:
President and Chief Executive Officer: Charlie Cannon
Senior Vice President, Policy, Technical and Legal Issues:
    Tracey Norberg
    E-Mail: tracey@rma.org
Senior Vice President, Public Affairs: Daniel Zielinski
    E-Mail: dzielinski@rma.org

Historical Note:
Founded as the New England Rubber Club, incorporated in 1915 as the Rubber Club of America and became the Rubber Association of America in 1917, assumed its current name in 1919. RMA is the national trade association for the elastomer products industry. Members are manufacturers of rubber products of all types. Membership: $3,000-45,000 (Manufacturer, Depending on Sales); $3,450-11,500 (Supplier).

Meetings/Conferences: Annual

Publications:
Membership Directory

Rubber Pavements Association (1985)
1801 S. Jentilly Ln.
Suite A-Two
Tempe, AZ 85281-5738
Tel: (480) 517-9944 *Fax:* (480) 517-9959
TollFree: (877) 517-9944
Website: rubberpavements.org
Members: 34 companies
Staff: 3
Annual Budget: $250-500,000
Tax: 501(c)(6)

Personnel:
Executive Director: Mark Belshe
    E-Mail: MBelshe@rpamail.org
Office Manager: Guadalupe Dickerson
    E-Mail: gdickerson@rpamail.org

Historical Note:
Formerly (1993) the Asphalt Rubber Producers Group. RPA is to dedicated to encouraging greater usage of high quality, cost effective asphalt pavements containing recycled tire rubber. Membership: $35-2,000/year.

Meetings/Conferences:
Number of non-conference events/year: 1

Publications:
RPA Newsletter

Membership List Available to Non-members

Rubber Trade Association of North America (1914)
220 Maple Ave., Suite 205
P.O. Box 196
Rockville Centre, NY 11571
Tel: (516) 536-7228 *Fax:* (516) 536-3771
Members: 43 companies
Staff: 2

Personnel:

Secretary: Fred B. Finley CML, CMST

Historical Note:
The purpose of the organization is to foster and promote the common business interests of the rubber trade as a whole for the benefit of all concerned; importers, brokers, dealers, agents, consumers and those servicing the natural rubber trade.

Rural Electricity Resource Council *(1952)*
P.O. Box 309
Wilmington, OH 45177-0309
Tel: (937) 383-0001 *Fax:* (937) 383-0003
E-Mail: info@rerc.org
Website: rerc.org
Members: 150 companies
Staff: 3
Annual Budget: $100-250,000
Tax: 501(c)(6)

Personnel:
President and Executive Manager: Richard S. Hiatt PE
    E-Mail: rhiatt@rerc.org
Vice President, Business Development: Jim Bausell
Administrative Assistant: Dorthy (Dot) Campbell
    E-Mail: dcampbell@rerc.org

Historical Note:
Formerly National Food and Energy Council. RERC delivers information and technical assistance on the efficient use of energy, with an emphasis on rural applications. Membership: $550-2100 (Based on total number of meters served); $600 (REC Statewide Assn.); $900 (G&T); $375 (Equip. Suppliers/Allies/Other); $3,100 (Group); $4,000 (Holding Company).

Publications:
Current Marketing; annually

The Rural Sociological Society *(1937)*
Brigham Young University
2019 JFSB
Provo, UT 80234
Tel: (801) 422-7386 *Fax:* (801) 422-0625
E-Mail: rural_sociology@byu.edu
Website: ruralsociology.org
Members: 820 individuals
Staff: 3
Annual Budget: $250-500,000
Tax: 501(c)(3)

Personnel:
Executive Director and Treasurer: Ralph B. Brown
    E-Mail: ralph_brown@byu.edu
Web Manager: Elizabeth Arteaga
Manager, Business Office and Financial: Nathan Barton

Historical Note:
Originally a section of the American Sociological Society, the Rural Sociological Society became independent in 1937. RSS is a social science association that promotes the generation, application and dissemination of sociological knowledge. The Society seeks to enhance the quality of rural life, communities and the environment. Membership: $55-125 (Regular Professional, dues varies based on salary); $110-250 (Sustaining Professional); $63 (Emeritus); $41 (Regular Student); $1,500 (Life); $63 (Emeritus); $82 (Sustaining Student); $126 (Sustaining Emeritus).

Meetings/Conferences: Annual
2013 - New York City, NY (Sheraton New York Hotel)/
    Aug. 6 - 9
2014 - New Orleans, LA (Roosevelt New Orleans, A
    Waldorf Astoria Hotel)/July 30 - Aug. 3
2016 - Seatle, WA (Hyatt Regency Bellevue on Seattle's
    Eastside)/Aug. 16 - 21

Publications:
Membership Directory; monthly
Rural Sociology; quarterly; adv.
The Rural Sociologist; quarterly; adv.

Rural Telecommunications Group
Ten G St. NE
Suite 710
Washington, DC 20002-4288
Tel: (202) 551-0025 *Fax:* (202) 371-1558
E-Mail: rtg@bennetlaw.com
Website: ruraltelecomgroup.org
Members: 100000 subscribers
Staff: 6
Annual Budget: $100-250,000

Personnel:
Executive Director: Tanya Sullivan
    E-Mail: tanya.sullivan@ruraltelecomgroup.org

General Counsel: Caressa D. Bennet
    E-Mail: cbennet@bennetlaw.com
Director, Industry Affairs: James Mardis
    E-Mail: james.mardis@ruraltelecomgroup.org
Technology Advisor: Art Prest
    E-Mail: prest@prest.biz

Historical Note:
RTG's mission is to promote wireless opportunities for rural telecommunications companies through advocacy and education in a manner that best represents the interests of its membership. Membership: $3,000-$10,000 (Voting based on carriers), $4,000 (Supporting), $2,500 (Associate).

Meetings/Conferences:
2013 - San Antonio, TX (Grand Hyatt San Antonio)/
    Jan. 16 - 18

Publications:
Membership Directory; on-line

Ruth Jackson Orthopaedic Society *(1983)*
6300 N. River Rd.
Suite 727
Rosemont, IL 60018-4226
Tel: (847) 698-1626 *Fax:* (847) 823-0536
E-Mail: rjos@aaos.org
Website: rjos.org
Members: 525 individuals
Staff: 2
Annual Budget: $100-250,000

Personnel:
Society Manager: Susan Koshy
    E-Mail: koshy@aaos.org
Society Coordinator: Stella Gauthier
    E-Mail: gauthier@aaos.org

Historical Note:
Formerly (1990) the Ruth Jackson Society. RJOS's mission is to advocate and support women in orthopaedic surgery. Members are women engaged in the practice of orthopaedic surgery. All active members are certified by the American Board of Orthopaedic Surgery, belong to the American Academy of Orthopaedic Surgeons, or are in training programs leading to these two qualifications. Membership: $250 (Active/Associate/Affiliate); $50 (Fellows/Residents); $35 (Students); $75 (Allied Health Member); $25 Corresponding (International).

Meetings/Conferences: Annual
Number of non-conference events/year: 1

Publications:
RJOS Newsletter; on-line

Ryan White Medical Providers Coalition *(2006)*
1300 Wilson Blvd.
Arlington, VA 20910
E-Mail: rwmpc@hivma.org
Website: hivma.org/RWMPC.aspx
Staff: 1

Personnel:
Co-Chair: J. Kevin Carmichael MD

Historical Note:
Uniting medical providers facing the challenges involved in offering HIV services and treatments.

S-Corporation Association *(1996)*
805 15th St. NW
Suite 650
Washington, DC 20005
Tel: (202) 466-8700 *Fax:* (202) 466-9666
Website: s-corp.org
Staff: 2
Annual Budget: $100-250,000
Tax: 501(c)(6)

Personnel:
Executive Director: Brian Reardon
    E-Mail: breardon@s-corp.org
President: Stephanie E. Silverman
    E-Mail: ssilverman@vennstrategies.com

Historical Note:
S-Corp is a not-for-profit, tax-exempt trade and educational organization formed from an association of companies organized under the subchapters of the internal revenue code. Mission is to protect America's family and closely-held businesses from excessive taxes and government mandates. Membership: $95 (New); $895-20,000 (Business); $2,000 (Trade Association/ Professional Services).

Publications:
Washington Wire

SACNAS (Society for Advancement of Chicanos and Native Americans in Science) *(1973)*
P.O. Box 8526
Santa Cruz, CA 95061-8526
Tel: (831) 459-0170 *Fax:* (831) 459-0194
TollFree: (877) 722-6271
E-Mail: juditcamacho@sacnas.org
Website: sacnas.org
Staff: 19
Annual Budget: $250-500,000
Tax: 501(c)(3)

Personnel:
Executive Director: Dr. Kristine (Tina) Garza PhD
Vice President, Science Policy and Strategic Initiatives:
    Robert E. Barnhill PhD
Director, Communications: Sara Clarenbach JD
Coordinator, Information Technology: Eric Estrada
Publications Manager and Senior Editor: Jenny Kurzweil
    E-Mail: jenny@sacnas.org
Manager, Marketing: Megan Longcor
Director, Development and Events: Jennifer Macotto
Director, Operations: Beth Roszman

Historical Note:
SACNAS is a society of scientists dedicated to advancing Hispanics/Chicanos and Native Americans in science. Membership: $15-1,000/year.

Meetings/Conferences: Annual
Conference Chair: Jennifer Macotto
2013 - San Antonio, TX/Oct. 3 - 6

Publications:
Membership Directory; on-line
SACNAS News; bi-annually

SAE International *(1905)*
400 Commonwealth Dr.
Warrendale, PA 15096-0001
Tel: (724) 776-4841 *Fax:* (724) 776-0790
E-Mail: customerservice@sae.org
Website: sae.org
Members: 132000 individuals
Staff: 254
Annual Budget: $50-100,000,000
Tax: 501(c)(3)

Personnel:
Chief Executive Officer: David L. Schutt PhD
    E-Mail: david.schutt@sae.org
Manager, Corporate Communications: Shawn Andreassi
    E-Mail: shawna@sae.org
Contact, Human Resources: Donna Anglemyer
Contact, Information Technology: Joe Astorino
    E-Mail: joe@sae.org
General Counsel: Gregory L. Bradley
Director, Human Resources: Sandra L. Dillner
Contact, Publications: Dawn Frenchak
    E-Mail: dawn@sae.org
Chief Information Officer: Brian Kaleida
Chief Financial officer: Dana M. Pless CAE, CPA
Contact, Membership Benefits: Sandra Sutermaster
*Director, Global Business Development, Sales and
    Marketing:* Scott Sward

Historical Note:
Originated in 1905 as the Society of Automobile Engineers, became the Society of Automotive Engineers in 1916, and assumed its current name in 2001. SAE is a network of engineers, business executives, educators and students from more than 80 countries who come together to share information and exchange ideas for advancing the engineering of mobility systems. Advances all aspects of the design, construction and use of self- propelled mechanisms, prime movers, their components and related equipment. Service Technicians Society is a division of SAE. Membership: $79-249 (Professional); $25 (Retired); $20 (Student).

Continuing Education:
Certification Designation/s: DTC, FDSC, GMLC, PLIC, VDC

Meetings/Conferences:
Number of non-conference events/year: 21

Publications:
Aerospace Engineering; adv.
Automotive Engineering International; adv.
Momentum; bi-monthly; adv.
SAE Off-Highway Engineering; adv.
SAE Update; monthly; adv.
SAE Vehicle Electrification; adv.
SAE Vehicle Engineering; on-line; adv.
Truck & Bus Engineering; on-line; adv.

Safe and Vault Technicians Association (1986)
3500 Easy St.
Dallas, TX 75247
Tel: (214) 819-9733 *Fax:* (214) 819-9736
TollFree: (800) 532-2562
E-Mail: savta@savta.org
Website: savta.org
Members: 2000 individuals
Staff: 3

Personnel:
Executive Director: David M. Lowell CML, CAE
Director, Marketing and Public Relations: Ellen McEwen
   E-Mail: media@aloa.org

Historical Note:
SAVTA is devoted entirely to serving professional safe and vault technicians worldwide. Members are retail locksmiths. Associate membership is available for manufacturers, distributors and others with an interest in the industry. Membership: $180 (Individual); $240 (Overseas); $195 (Canada).

Meetings/Conferences: Annual
2013 - Lexington, KY (Hilton Lexington)/May 6 - 11

Publications:
Safe & Vault Technology magazine; monthly

SAFE Association (1956)
300 N. Mill St., Unit B
P.O. Box 130
Creswell, OR 97426-0130
Tel: (541) 895-3012 *Fax:* (541) 895-3014
E-Mail: safe@peak.org
Website: safeassociation.com
Members: 950 individuals
Staff: 1
Annual Budget: $250-500,000
Tax: 501(c)(6)

Personnel:
Association Administrator: Jeani E. Benton

Historical Note:
Established as the Space and Flight Equipment Association at Edwards Air Force Base. Incorporated in California in 1964; name changed to Survival and Flight Equipment Association in 1969; adopted the present name in 1976. SAFE promotes the science of survival and the development of safety in all forms of transportation. Members belong to all fields and include equipment manufacturers, college professors, students, airline flight attendants, government officials, pilots and military life support specialists. Membership: $60 (Individual); $10 (Student); $500 (Corporate).

Meetings/Conferences: Annual
Conference Chair: Jeani E. Benton

Publications:
SAFE Newsletter; quarterly

Safety Glazing Certification Council (1971)
100 W. Main St.
P.O. Box 730
Sackets Harbor, NY 13685
Tel: (315) 646-2234 *Fax:* (315) 646-2297
E-Mail: staff@amscert.com
Website: sgcc.org
Members: 250 companies
Staff: 3
Annual Budget: $1-2,000,000

Personnel:
Administrator: Brandy Redder
Administrator, Programs: John G. Kent

Historical Note:
SGCC maintains a certification program under which manufacturers of safety glazing products voluntarily submit their products for testing to an SGCC- approved independent testing laboratory. Members are manufacturers of safety glazing products, building code officials, and others concerned with public safety.

Continuing Education:
Certification Designation/s: SGCC

Meetings/Conferences: Annual
Number of non-conference events/year: 1

Publications:
SGCC Certified Products Directory; semi-annually

Membership List Available to Non-members

Safety Pharmacology Society (2000)
1821 Michael Faraday Dr.
Suite 300
Reston, VA 20190

Tel: (703) 547-0874 *Fax:* (703) 438-3113
E-Mail: spshq@safetypharmacology.org
Website: safetypharmacology.org
Staff: 1
Annual Budget: $500-1,000,000
Tax: 501(c)(3)

Personnel:
Executive Director: Clarissa Russell Wilson
   E-Mail: cwilson@safetypharmacology.org

Historical Note:
SPS's mission is to further the discovery, development and safe use of biologically active chemical entities by identification, monitoring and characterization of potentially undesirable pharmacodynamic activities in nonclinical studies. Members belong to the pharmaceutical industry, academia, government, contract research organizations, service industries, consulting agencies, and private organizations world-wide. Membership: $100 (Full); $50 (Student).

Meetings/Conferences: Annual
2013 - Rotterdam, Netherlands/Sept. 16 - 19

Publications:
Journal of Pharmacological and Toxicological Methods; on-line
Membership Directory; on-line

Membership List Available to Non-members

Sail America (1990)
50 Water St.
Warren, RI 02885
Fax: (401) 247-0074
E-Mail: info@sailamerica.com
Website: sailamerica.com
Staff: 5
Annual Budget: $500-1,000,000

Personnel:
Executive Director: Jonathan Banks
   E-Mail: jbanks@sailamerica.com
Manager, Finance: Kayce Florio
   E-Mail: kflorio@sailamerica.com
Manager, Administration and Membership: Stephanie Grove
   E-Mail: sgrove@sailamerica.com
Coordinator, Events: Rachel LaMarre
   E-Mail: rlamarre@sailamerica.com
Editor: Wanda Kenton Smith
   E-Mail: wanda@kentonsmithmarketing.com

Historical Note:
Sail America's mission is to Produce and support sailboat shows,Promote the sailing lifestyle,Provide ongoing business education and market data,Communicate industry news and trends and Represent the interests of the sailing industry.Membership: $375-3650 (Corporate); $50-150 (Associate).

Publications:
Membership Directory; on-line
Sail America Newsletter

Sailors' Union of the Pacific (1885)
450 Harrison St.
San Francisco, CA 94105
Tel: (415) 777-3400 *Fax:* (415) 777-5088
Website:
sailors.org/
sailors.org
Staff: 16
Annual Budget: $1-2,000,000

Personnel:
Director, Workforce Development: Berit Eriksson
Administrator: Michelle Chang
   E-Mail: mcsupsiupd@sbcglobal.net

Historical Note:
Formerly named Steamship Sailors' Union merged with the Coast Seamen's Union to form the Sailors' Union of the Pacific.

Publications:
West Coast Sailor; monthly

Sales and Marketing Executives International, Inc. (1935)
P.O. Box 1390
Sumas, WA 98295-1390
Tel: (312) 893-0751 *Fax:* (312) 893-0751
E-Mail: admin@smei.org
Website: smei.org
Members: 10000 individuals
Staff: 5

Annual Budget: $250-500,000
Tax: 501(c)(6)

Personnel:
President and Chief Executive Officer: Willis H. Turner CAE, CSE

Historical Note:
Established as National Federation of Sales Executives, it became National Sales Executives International in 1949 and assumed its present name in 1961. SMEI's mission is to work for ethical standards, continuing professional development, knowledge sharing, mentoring students and advancing free enterprise. Membership: $200/year (Individual).

Continuing Education:
Certification Designation/s: CSE, CME, SCPS

Meetings/Conferences: Annual
Number of non-conference events/year: 2

Publications:
Marketing Times; quarterly; adv.
Sales & Marketing Directory; on-line
SMEI Exchange; on-line
SMEI Newsletter; on-line

Sales Association of the Chemical Industry (1921)
25 Charles St.
Westwood, NJ 07675
Tel: (201) 358-9399 *Fax:* (201) 358-9398
E-Mail: info@sacionline.com
Website: sacionline.com
Members: 300 individuals
Staff: 1
Annual Budget: $10-25,000

Personnel:
President: James Stowe

Historical Note:
Formerly Salesmen's Association of the American Chemical Industry. SACI's mission is to be its members' primary resource for business and professional networking opportunities. To be recognized as a leading source of opportunities for networking in the chemical industries. Membership is concentrated in New York, New Jersey and Connecticut. Membership: $130 (Regular); $65 (Associate); $30 (Student).

Meetings/Conferences:
Number of non-conference events/year: 2

Publications:
SACI Newsletter; semi-annually

Sales Association of the Paper Industry (1919)
225 N. Franklin Tnpk.
Ramsey, NJ 07446
Tel: (866) 307-7274 *Fax:* (201) 818-8720
Website: sapionline.com
Members: 500 individuals and companies
Staff: 2
Annual Budget: $25-50,000

Personnel:
Executive Director: Sheila Borgese

Historical Note:
Formerly (1972) Salesmen's Association of the Paper Industry. SAPI provides service to individuals engaged in sales, marketing, advertising, sales promotion and related activities for primary producers and distributors of paper, pulp and paperboard. Membership: $125/year.

Sales Lead Management Association
19783 Santiago Blvd.
Suite 107-339
Villa Park, CA 92861
Tel: (714) 637-6989
E-Mail: info@salesleadmgmtassn.com
Website: salesleadmgmtassn.com
Members: 4301 members
Staff: 11

Personnel:
Chief Executive Officer and Executive Director: James W. Obermayer
   E-Mail: jobermayer@salesleadmgmtassn.com
Vice President, Marketing and Membership Services: Sue Campanale
   E-Mail: scampanale@salesleadmgmtassn.com
Executive Vice President: Mark Friedman
   E-Mail: mark@velosgroup.com
Vice President, Business Development: Ronald P. Goodman
   E-Mail: rgoodman@salesleadmgmtassn.com
Director, Public Relations: Christel Hall

E-Mail: christel@prowrite-pr.com
Contributing Editor: Stu Heinecke
E-Mail: stu.heinecke@stuheinecke.com

Historical Note:
SLMA's mission is to promote helping companies become more successful in the critical business process of managing sales leads. Provides practices for marketing and sales management so that the marketing dollars put at risk have a predictable rate of return.

Publications:
SLMA Newsletter; monthly

Salt Institute (1914)
700 N. Fairfax St.
Suite 600
Alexandria, VA 22314-2040
Tel: (703) 549-4648 *Fax:* (703) 548-2194
E-Mail: info@saltinstitute.org
Website: saltinstitute.org
Members: 50 companies
Staff: 6
Annual Budget: $2-5,000,000
Tax: 501(c)(6)

Personnel:
President: Lori Roman
E-Mail: lori@saltinstitute.org
Director, Communications: Jorge Amselle
Director, Administration: Tammy Goodwin
E-Mail: tammy@saltinstitute.org
Vice President, Science and Research: Mort Satin
E-Mail: mort@saltinstitute.org

Historical Note:
Founded as the Salt Producers Association, assumed its current name in 1963. SI's mission is to increase understanding regarding the contributions of responsible salt use, enabling improved quality of life, better health and safer and more reliable transportation. Membership in the Salt Institute is restricted to companies that produce and sell sodium chloride (salt producers). Membership: $12,000 (Regular); $5000-13000 (Associate); $1000 (Affiliate); $2000 (Consulting Company).

Meetings/Conferences: Annual
2013 - West Palm Beach, FL (Ritz Carlton)/March 6 - 8

Publications:
Salt and Health Newsletter; quarterly
Salt and Highway Deicing Newsletter; quarterly
Salt and Trace Minerals Newsletter; quarterly
SI Report Newsletter; monthly

Sanitary Supply Wholesaling Association (1980)
P.O. Box 98
Swanton, OH 43558
Tel: (419) 825-3055 *Fax:* (419) 825-1815
E-Mail: info@sswa.com
Website: sswa.com
Members: 75 companies
Staff: 3
Annual Budget: $50-100,000

Personnel:
Executive Director: Donna Frendt
E-Mail: dfrendt@sswa.com
President: Lane Crosser
Treasurer: Tom Zatkulak

Historical Note:
SSWA is a professional trade association whose global members work together to advance wholesaling through partnerships and common goals. Membership: $845 (Wholesaler/Manufacturer); $745 (Associate).

Meetings/Conferences: Annual
Number of non-conference events/year: 2

Publications:
Membership Directory; on-line
The Wholesaler - Newsletter

Santa Gertrudis Breeders International (1951)
P.O. Box 1257
Kingsville, TX 78364
Tel: (361) 592-9357 *Fax:* (361) 592-8572
E-Mail: info@santagertrudis.com
Website: santagertrudis.com
Members: 1300 individuals
Staff: 3
Annual Budget: $500-1,000,000
Tax: 501(c)(5)

Personnel:
Executive Director: John E. Ford
E-Mail: jford@santagertrudis.com

Vice President, Marketing and Promotion: Allen Grainger
E-Mail: allen.grainger@santagertrudis.com
Specialist, Registration and Membership Services: Diana L. Ruiz
E-Mail: druiz.sgbi@sbcglobal.net

Historical Note:
SGBI is dedicated to the improvement of Santa Gertrudis cattle throughout the world. Membership: $125 (Active); $75 (Junior); $55 (Commercial/Non-Voting/Non-Registering).

Meetings/Conferences: Annual

Publications:
Magazine; monthly; adv.
SGBI Membership Directory; annually

Satellite Broadcasting and Communications Association (1986)
1100 17th St. NW
Suite 1150
Washington, DC 20036
Tel: (202) 349-3620 *Fax:* (202) 349-3621
TollFree: (800) 541-5981
E-Mail: info@sbca.org
Website: sbca.com
Members: 1400 companies
Staff: 10
Annual Budget: $2-5,000,000

Personnel:
Executive Director: Joseph Widoff
Manager, Membership Services and Data Management: Martin Esteves
E-Mail: mesteves@sbca.org
Manager, Communications and Online Member Services: Amy Hager
E-Mail: ahager@sbca.org
Senior Director, Information Systems: Shahzad Haider
Deputy Executive Director, Education and Training: Steven Hill
Director, Public Policy and Outreach: Lisa Volpe McCabe
E-Mail: lmccabe@sbca.org
Senior Director, Finance and Human Resources: Abdul Salam

Historical Note:
Formerly (1985) the Society for Private and Commercial Earth Stations and (1986) Satellite Television Industry Association. SBCA's mission is to improve the customer experience through professional development and training opportunities to industry installation professionals and to protect the rights of consumers to receive satellite delivered video audio and data services through education, training and public outreach. Represents all segments of the satellite television industry, including manufacturers, distributors, dealers, programmers, and satellite service providers. Membership: $25-100,000/year.

Continuing Education:
Certification Designation/s: SBCA, NSTP

Meetings/Conferences:
Conference Chair: Martin Esteves

Publications:
SBCA SmartBrief Newsletter; weekly

Satellite Industry Association (1995)
1200 18th St. NW
Suite 1001
Washington, DC 20036
Tel: (202) 503-1560 *Fax:* (202) 503-1590
E-Mail: info@sia.org
Website: sia.org
Members: 40 Companies
Staff: 5
Annual Budget: $1-2,000,000
Tax: 501(c)(6)

Personnel:
President: Patricia Cooper
Director, Policy: Sam Black
Administrative Assistant: Kathleen Orem
Director, Communications: Marie-Pierre Pluvinage

Historical Note:
Represents major commercial satellite companies in the United States. Formed in 1995 as an out-growth of the Satellite Super Skyway Coalition. Purpose is to promote the benefits and uses of commercial satellite technology and its role in national security, homeland security, disaster relief and recovery, and the global information infrastructure and economy. Membership: $18,000-45,000 (Executive); $7,500-18,000 (Associate); $5,000 (Trial Associate Membership).

Meetings/Conferences: Annual

SAVE International (1959)
136 S. Keowee St.
Dayton, OH 45402
Tel: (937) 224-7283 *Fax:* (937) 222-5794
E-Mail: info@value-eng.org
Website: value-eng.org
Members: 1100 individuals
Staff: 7
Annual Budget: $500-1,000,000

Personnel:
Executive Director: Kimberly Fantaci
E-Mail: info@value-eng.org

Historical Note:
Formerly Society of American Value Engineers (1998). SAVE's mission is to promote, support, and advance the practice of value enhancing methods through global exchange, networking, certification, member services, professional growth, and recognition. Membership: $150 (Individual); $415 (Regular-Corporate); $1065 (Sustaining Corporate); $90 (Additional Corporate).

Continuing Education:
Enrollment: 200
Certification Designation/s: AVS, VMP, CVS

Meetings/Conferences: Annual
Conference Chair: Richard L. Johnson CVS, DEE, PE
2013 - Arlington, VA (Crystal Gateway Marriott)/June 24 - 27
Number of non-conference events/year: 10

Publications:
Consultants directory; on-line; adv.
Interactions; monthly; adv.
Membership Directory; on-line
Value World; adv.

Membership List Available to Non-members

SB Latex Council (1988)
1250 Connecticut Ave. NW
Suite 700
Washington, DC 20036
Tel: (202) 419-1500 *Fax:* (202) 637-9178
E-Mail: info@regnet.com
Website: regnet.com/sblc
Members: 4 manufacturers
Staff: 9
Annual Budget: $250-500,000
Tax: 501(c)(6)

Personnel:
Executive Director: Robert J. Fensterheim CAE

Historical Note:
SBLC's mission is to promote the safe manufacture, use, handling and disposal of SB latex. SBLC is managed by RegNet Environmental Services.

Scaffold Industry Association (1972)
400 Admiral Blvd.
Kansas City, MO 64106
Tel: (816) 595-4860 *Fax:* (816) 472-7765
E-Mail: info@scaffold.org
Website: scaffold.org
Members: 925 companies
Staff: 6
Annual Budget: $1-2,000,000
Tax: 501(c)(6)

Personnel:
Executive Director: Laurie Weber
E-Mail: laurie@scaffold.org
Director, Sales and Marketing: Bryon Bowman
E-Mail: bryon@scaffold.org
Director, Training and Education: Granville Loar
E-Mail: granville@scaffold.org
Director, Operations: DeAnna Martin
E-Mail: deanna@saiaonline.org
Webmaster: Greg Plough
E-Mail: greg@robstan.com
Director, Membership Services and Marketing: Sara Schorr
E-Mail: sara@saiaonline.org

Historical Note:
SIA's mission is to protect and promote the interests of manufacturers, dealers and distributors of access and scaffold equipment. Membership: $825-3250 (Regular); $100-300 (Regular Branch); $400-1500 (Affiliate); $700-900 (Allied).

Meetings/Conferences:
2013 - New Orleans, LA (Loews New Orleans Hotel)/ Feb. 24 - 26

2013 - Nashville, TN/July 21 - 24
Number of non-conference events/year: 2

Publications:
Membership Directory; annually; adv.
Scaffold Industry; monthly; adv.
SI Connect e-Newsletter; on-line; adv.

Membership List Available to Non-members

Scaffolding, Shoring and Forming Institute
(1960)
1300 Sumner Ave.
Cleveland, OH 44115
Tel: (216) 241-7333 *Fax:* (216) 241-0105
E-Mail: ssfi@ssfi.org
Website: ssfi.org
Members: 20 companies
Staff: 2
Annual Budget: $50-100,000
Tax: 501(c)(6)

Personnel:
Managing Director: R. Christopher Johnson
Administrative Assistant: Louise M. Skellhammer

Historical Note:
Formerly (1969) Steel Scaffolding and Shoring Institute and (1980) Scaffolding and Shoring Institute. SSFI is a trade association of manufacturers of scaffolding, suspended scaffolding, shoring, forming, planks, platforms and related components.

Scale Manufacturers Association *(1945)*
P.O. Box 26972
Columbus, OH 43226-0972
Tel: (866) 372-4627 *Fax:* (239) 514-3470
TollFree: (866) 372-4627
E-Mail: info@scalemanufacturers.org
Website: scalemanufacturers.org
Members: 12 companies
Staff: 3
Annual Budget: $100-250,000

Personnel:
Executive Director: Robert A. Reinfried
    E-Mail: bob@scalemanufacturers.org

Historical Note:
SMA's purpose is to advance the science of weighing and force measuring, and the engineering and manufacturing of instruments, apparatus, equipment and facilities. Members are manufacturers, integrators, and assemblers of weighing equipment. Membership: $2,500/year.

Meetings/Conferences: Annual

Publications:
Membership Directory; annually
Weighlog; semi-annually

Schiffli Lace and Embroidery Manufacturers Association *(1937)*
Seven Commercial Ave.
Fairview, NJ 07022-1614
Tel: (201) 943-7730 *Fax:* (201) 941-5447
Website: schiffli.org
Members: 150 companies
Staff: 2
Annual Budget: $10-25,000

Personnel:
President: Larry Squiccimari
Contact, Communications: Vincent Mesiano
    E-Mail: vincent@schiffli.org

Historical Note:
SLEMA was formerly Embroidery Manufacturers Bureau. Members are manufacturers of machine-made embroideries and laces, or firms in allied trades (concentrated principally in northern New Jersey and New York City). Membership: $125/year (Machine/Allied trade).

School Nutrition Association *(1946)*
120 Waterfront St.
Suite 300
Ft. Washington, MD 20745
Tel: (301) 686-3100 *Fax:* (301) 686-3115
E-Mail: servicecenter@schoolnutrition.org
Website: schoolnutrition.org
Members: 55000 individuals
Staff: 57
Annual Budget: $5-10,000,000
Tax: 501(c)(4)

Personnel:
Chief Executive Officer: Frank DiPasquale

Washington Counsel: Marshall L. Matz
Staff Vice President, Communications: Maria Robertson
Vice President, Child Nutrition and Policy: Cathy Schuchart
Vice President, Meetings: Cheryl Thompson

Historical Note:
Formerly American School Food Service Association; assumed its current name in 2004. SNA is dedicated solely to the support and well being of school nutrition professionals in advancing good nutrition for all children. Members are individuals working in food services in elementary and secondary non-profit schools, state programs, CNP, and other non-profit community child nutrition programs. Membership: $125/year (International).

Continuing Education:
Certification Designation/s: CNU, NC

Meetings/Conferences:
Conference Chair: Cheryl Thompson
2013 - Kansas City, MO/July 13 - 17
2013 - Kansas City, MO (Kansas City Convention Center)/July 14 - 17
2014 - Boston, MA/July 12 - 16
2015 - Salt Lake City, UT/July 11 - 15
2016 - San Antonio, TX/July 10 - 13
2017 - Atlanta, GA/July 9 - 12
2018 - Las Vegas, NV/July 8 - 11
2019 - St. Louis, MO/July 14 - 17
Number of non-conference events/year: 5

Publications:
CN Direct; bi-weekly; adv.
Industry Insider
Regional Director
School Nutrition Magazine
The Daily Mix; on-line; adv.
The Journal of Child Nutrition & Management
Tuesday Morning

School Science and Mathematics Association
(1901)
Oklahoma State University
College of Education, 245 Willard
Stillwater, OK 74078
Tel: (405) 744-8018 *Fax:* (405) 744-6290
E-Mail: office@ssma.org
Website: ssma.org
Members: 500 individuals
Staff: 4
Annual Budget: $100-250,000

Personnel:
Co-Executive Director: Julie Thomas
Editor: Carla Johnson
    E-Mail: johnsonssmj@gmail.com
Contact, Membership Services: Michael Maroney
    E-Mail: mmaroney@wiley.com
Contact, Conventions: Melanie Shores
    E-Mail: mshores@uab.edu

Historical Note:
Incorporated in Illinois as the Central Association of Science and Mathematics Teachers, Inc. SSMA strives to be an inclusive professional community bringing together researchers and teachers to enhance research, scholarship, and practice to improve school science and mathematics. Membership: $25-60/year.

Meetings/Conferences: Annual
Conference Chair: Melanie Shores
2013 - San Antonio, TX/Nov. 14 - 16

Publications:
School Science and Mathematics Journal; monthly
The Math-Science Connector Newsletter

School Social Work Association of America
(1994)
P.O. Box 1086
Sumner, WA 98390
Tel: (253) 266-7464
E-Mail: contact@sswaa.org
Website: sswaa.org
Members: 64 Participants
Staff: 4
Annual Budget: $250-500,000
Tax: 501(c)(6)

Personnel:
Executive Director: Frederick Streeck
    E-Mail: fstreeck@comcast.net
Director, Conference Planning: Dot Kontak
    E-Mail: dkontak1@aol.com
Director, Government Relations: Myrna Mandlawitz

    E-Mail: mmandlawitz@sswaa.org
Director, Policy and Advocacy: Libby Kuffner Nealis
    E-Mail: Libby@sswaa.org

Historical Note:
SSWAA works to advance the profession of school social work and advocates the profession of school social work to enhance the social and emotional growth and academic outcomes of all students. Membership: $75 (Regular/Full/Associate); $60 (Affiliate/Retired/Student).

Meetings/Conferences: Annual
Conference Chair: Dot Kontak
2013 - San Diego, CA (Sheraton San Diego Hotel and Marina)/March 20 - 23
Number of non-conference events/year: 1

Publications:
E-bell; weekly
Membership Directory; on-line

Membership List Available to Non-members

Schools Interoperability Framework Association
1090 Vermont Ave. NW
Sixth Floor
Washington, DC 20005
Tel: (202) 789-4460 *Fax:* (202) 289-7097
E-Mail: staff@sifassociation.org
Website: sifinfo.org
Members: 3200 software vendors
Staff: 6
Annual Budget: $1-2,000,000
Tax: 501(c)(3)

Personnel:
Executive Director and Chief Executive Officer: Larry Fruth
    E-Mail: lfruth@sifassociation.org
Chief Technology Officer: Ron Kleinman
    E-Mail: rkleinman@sifassociation.org
Manager, Community Development: Penny Murray
    E-Mail: pmurray@sifassociation.org

Historical Note:
The goal of the SIF Association is to make it possible for school administrators, teachers and other school personnel to have access to the most current and accurate data available. Membership: $2000-$26000 (Based on Vendors Gross Revenue).

Continuing Education:
Certification Designation/s: SIF

Meetings/Conferences: Annual
Conference Chair: Penny Murray
2013 - Washington, DC (Sheraton Crystal City Hotel)/Jan. 15 - 17

Publications:
SIF Newsletters

Membership List Available to Non-members

Science Fiction and Fantasy Writers of America
(1965)
P.O. Box 3238
Enfield, CT 06083-3238
Tel: (410) 778-2211 *Fax:* (410) 778-3052
Website: sfwa.org
Members: 1800 individuals
Staff: 3
Annual Budget: $250-500,000
Tax: 501(c)(6)

Personnel:
President: John Scalzi
Office Manager, Membership: Kate Baker
Treasurer: Bud Sparhawk

Historical Note:
Formerly (1992) Science Fiction Writers of America. An organization of professional writers in the science fiction and fantasy field, SFWA informs, supports, promotes, defends and advocates for its members. Membership is open to authors, artists and other industry professionals, including graphic novelists. Membership: $80 (Active); $70 (Associate/Estate); $100 (Institutional); $60 (Affiliate).

Meetings/Conferences: Annual

Publications:
Bulletin - Magazine; bi-monthly; adv.
Membership Directory; on-line

Membership List Available to Non-members

Scientific Equipment and Furniture Association
(1988)
1205 Franklin Ave.
Suite 320
Garden City, NY 11530

Tel: (516) 294-5424 *Fax:* (516) 294-4765
TollFree: (877) 294-5424
E-Mail: info@sefalabs.com
Website: sefalabs.com
Members: 83 companies
Staff: 3
Annual Budget: $250-500,000
Tax: 501(c)(6)

Personnel:
Executive Director and General Counsel: David J. Sutton
CAE, JD
E-Mail: david@sefalabs.com

Historical Note:
*SEFA works to enable and support all involved parties
in creating humane, safe and effective laboratory
environments. It represents designers and manufacturers of
equipment and furniture for laboratories and other scientific
installations. Membership: $880 (Associate); $2513-4774
(Executive based on company's revenues); $1,885-3,770
(Sustaining).*

Continuing Education:
Certification Designation/s: SEFA8CTL

Meetings/Conferences: Annual

Publications:
Member Directory; on-line
SEFAMember Update; on-line

Scoliosis Research Society (1966)
555 E. Wells St.
Suite 1100
Milwaukee, WI 53202-3823
Tel: (414) 289-9107 *Fax:* (414) 276-3349
E-Mail: info@srs.org
Website: srs.org
Members: 1000 individuals
Staff: 5
Annual Budget: $2-5,000,000
Tax: 501(c)(3)

Personnel:
Executive Director: Tressa Goulding CAE, CMP
E-Mail: tgoulding@srs.org
Director, Meetings: Megan Kelley
E-Mail: mkelley@execinc.com
Executive Assistant: Courtney Kissinger
E-Mail: ckissinger@srs.org
Manager, Programs: Brian Lueth
E-Mail: blueth@srs.org
Manager, Membership Services: Nilda Toro
E-Mail: ntoro@srs.org

Historical Note:
*SRS's purpose is to foster the optimal care of all patients
with spinal deformities. Members are physicians with an
interest in spinal deformities. Membership: $125-500
(Active/Associate); $90-350 (Associate).*

Meetings/Conferences: Annual
Conference Chair: Megan Kelley
2013 - Lyon, France/Sept. 18 - 21
2014 - Anchorage, AK/Sept. 10 - 14
2014 - Anchorage, AK/Sept. 10 - 13
2015 - Minneapolis, MN/Sept. 30 - Oct. 4
Number of non-conference events/year: 2

Publications:
SRS newsletter; quarterly

SCORE Association (1964)
1175 Herndon Pkwy.
Suite 900
Herndon, VA 20170
Tel: (703) 487-3612 *Fax:* (703) 487-3066
TollFree: (800) 634-0245
Website: score.org
Members: 13000 volunteers
Staff: 23
Annual Budget: $10-25,000,000

Personnel:
Chief Executive Officer: W. Kenneth Yancey Jr.
Director, Finance: John Fuqua
Vice President, Technology: Jim Gephart
Vice President, Education and Partnership Services: K. Jai
Hokimi
Communications Manager: Shalini 'Shelly' Karnani
Bonjour
E-Mail: media@score.org
*Director, Business Development and Contact, Conventions
and Meetings:* Resa Kierstein
E-Mail: resa.kierstein@scorefoundation.org

Marketing Director: Bridget Weston Pollack
Director, Human Resource and Recruiting: Keith Scott

Historical Note:
*SCORE is a nonprofit association dedicated to educating
entrepreneurs and helping small businesses start, grow, and
succeed nationwide.*

Meetings/Conferences:
Conference Chair: Resa Kierstein

Publications:
SCORE eNews; on-line

Scottish Blackface Breeders Association (1982)
1699 H H Hwy.
Willow Springs, MO 65793
Tel: (417) 962-5466
E-Mail: sbsba@fidnet.com
Website: ramshornstudio.com/
scottish_blackface.htm
Members: 65 companies and 90 individuals
Staff: 1
Annual Budget: Under $10,000

Personnel:
Secretary: Richard "Dick" J. Haward

Historical Note:
*SBSBA aids breeders in finding and perpetuating new blood
lines. Members are breeders of Scottish Blackface sheep and
others interested in the breed. Promotes the breed and works
to establish its pedigree. Membership: $10/year.*

Scrap Tire Management Council (1990)
1400 K St. NW
Suite 900
Washington, DC 20005
Tel: (202) 682-4800
E-Mail: info@rma.org
Website: scraptire.org
Staff: 2

Personnel:
President and Chief Executive Officer: Charlie Cannon
Senior Vice President, Public Affairs: Daniel Zielinski

Historical Note:
*The Rubber Manufacturers Association (RMA) is the
national trade association for tire manufacturers that make
tires in the U.S.*

Meetings/Conferences: Annual

Publications:
Member Directory; on-line

Screen Actors Guild - American Federation of Television and Radio Artists (1930)
5757 Wilshire Blvd.
Seventh Floor
Los Angeles, CA 90036-3600
Tel: (323) 954-1600 *Fax:* (323) 549-6648
TollFree: (800) 724-0767
E-Mail: saginfo@sag.org
Website: sagaftra.org
Members: 160000 individuals
Staff: 15
Annual Budget: $25-50,000,000

Personnel:
National Executive Director: David White
Chief Administrative Officer and General Counsel: Duncan
Crabtree-Ireland
E-Mail: direland@sag.org
Assistant National Executive Director, Communications:
Pamela Greenwalt
E-Mail: pgreenwalt@sag.org
Chief Information Officer: Erin Griffin
E-Mail: erin.griffin@sag.org
Chief Financial Officer: Arianna Ozzanto

Historical Note:
*Screen Actors Guild underwent merger with American
Federation of Television and Radio Artists to form Screen
Actors Guild - American Federation of Television and Radio
Artists in 2012. SAG is an autonomous branch union of
Associated Actors and Artistes America. SAG-AFTRA's
mission is to educate and engage members so that they
may be full participants in the workings of their union.
Membership: $116/year (Individual).*

Publications:
Membership Directory; on-line
Nevada
SAG Newsletters
Screen Actor

Screen Manufacturers Association (1955)

10526 S. Ave.
Chicago, IL 60617
Tel: (717) 365-3400 *Fax:* (888) 432-8036
Website: smainfo.org
Members: 35 companies
Staff: 3
Annual Budget: Under $10,000

Personnel:
President: Robert D. Williams
Contact, Membership Services: Kathryn R. Fitzgerald
E-Mail: kathryn@smainfo.org

Historical Note:
*Formerly (1957) Frame Screen Manufacturers Association.
SMA's mission is to inform and educate the public about
the primary intent of screens, which is a device to provide
ventilation and protection from insects, not a product
designed as protection from falls.Members are manufacturer
of window screens, swinging or sliding screen doors and
people associated with the fabrication of window screen and
doors. Membership: $1,000-3,000/year.*

Meetings/Conferences: Annual
2013 - Chicago, IL/May 2 - 3
2013 - Chicago, IL/May 6 - 7
2014 - Chicago, IL/May 2 - 3
2014 - Chicago, IL/May 5 - 6

Publications:
Membership Directory; on-line

Scribes-The American Society of Legal Writers (1953)
C/O Thomas Cooley Law School, 300 S. Capitol
Ave.
P.O. Box 13038
Lansing, MI 48901
Tel: (517) 371-5140 *Fax:* (517) 334-5781
E-Mail: platen@cooley.edu
Website: scribes.org
Members:
45 institutions
2600 individuals
Staff: 3
Annual Budget: $10-25,000

Personnel:
Executive Director: Norman E. Plate
E-Mail: platen@cooley.edu
Journal Editor: Joseph Kimble
E-Mail: Scribes-journal-editor@scribes.org

Historical Note:
*ASLW works to foster a feeling of fraternity among those
who write about the law and especially among its members.
Members are judges, editors of legal publications, writers on
legal topics, law professors and others with an interest in
legal writing. Membership: $65 (Regular/Associate); $100
(Sustaining); $35 (Scrivener only); $15 (Student-Editor);
$1000 (Life); $650 (Institutional).*

Meetings/Conferences: Annual

Publications:
The Scribes Journal of Legal Writing; annually
The Scrivener; quarterly

SCSI Trade Association (1996)
572-B Ruger St.
P.O. Box 29920
San Francisco, CA 94129-0920
Tel: (415) 561-6273 *Fax:* (415) 561-6120
E-Mail: info@scsita.org
Website: scsita.org
Members: 20 individuals
Staff: 3
Annual Budget: $250-500,000
Tax: 501(c)(6)

Personnel:
Executive Director: Chris Lyon
E-Mail: clyon@scsita.org
Contact, Communications: Linda Capcara
E-Mail: Linda@SCSITA.org
Contact, Communications: Lea Schwartz
E-Mail: pointpr@msn.com

Historical Note:
*STA develops and disseminates information about the
SCSI (Small Computer System Interface) technology for
member OEMs, resellers and IT professionals. Membership:
$25,000 (Sponsorship Member); $10,000 (Principal
Member); $4,500 (Promotional Member).*

Meetings/Conferences:
Number of non-conference events/year: 5

Sculptors Guild (1937)
55 Washington St.
Suite 256
Brooklyn, NY 11201
Tel: (718) 422-0555 Fax: (212) 431-5669
E-Mail: sculptorsguild@gmail.com
Website: sculptorsguild.org
Members: 123 individuals
Staff: 5
Annual Budget: $10-25,000
Tax: 501(c)(3)

Personnel:
President: Robert Michael Smith
Contact, Public Relations: Lucy Hodgson
    E-Mail: pr@sculptorsguild.org
Treasurer: Stephen Keltner
Contact, Administration: Sherrie Lynne
    E-Mail: admin@sculptorsguild.org
Vice President, Exhibitions: David Morris

Historical Note:
SC's mission is to is to promote, encourage, and serve as an advocate for sculpture and to make contemporary sculpture a relevant part of the cultural experience. Membership: $250/year.

Meetings/Conferences:
Conference Chair: David Morris

Sea Grant Association
University of New Hampshire, 102 Chase Ocean Engineering Laboratory
24 Colovos Rd.
Durham, NH 03824
Tel: (603) 862-2921 Fax: (603) 862-0241
Website: sga.seagrant.org
Staff: 2
Annual Budget: $100-250,000

Personnel:
President: Jonathan Pennock
    E-Mail: jonathan.pennock@unh.edu
Treasurer and Communications Representative: Linda Duguay
    E-Mail: duguay@usc.edu

Historical Note:
The Sea Grant Association represents our nation's most advanced capabilities in marine, coastal, and Great Lakes research, education

Meetings/Conferences: Semi-Annual

Seafarers International Union of North America (1938)
5201 Auth Way
Camp Springs, MD 20746
Tel: (301) 899-0675 Fax: (301) 899-7355
Website: seafarers.org
Members: 80000 individuals
Staff: 125
Annual Budget: $1-2,000,000
Tax: 501(c)(5)

Personnel:
Executive Vice President: Augustin "Augie" Tellez
Administrative Assistant and Associate Editor: Misty Dobry
    E-Mail: mdobry@seafarers.org
Vice President, Government Services: Kermett Mangram

Historical Note:
Chartered by the American Federation of Labor as an outgrowth of the Sailor's Union of the Pacific, SIU is a politically active organization that aims to protect its membership's job security. It is composed of 18 autonomous affiliated unions of seamen, fishermen, fish cannery workers, inland boatmen, transportation workers and industrial workers in the U.S., Canada, U.S. Virgin Islands and Puerto Rico.

Publications:
Seafarers LOG; monthly

Sealant, Waterproofing and Restoration Institute (1976)
400 Admiral Blvd.
Kansas City, MO 64106
Tel: (816) 472-7974 Fax: (816) 472-7765
E-Mail: info@swrionline.org
Website: swrionline.org
Members: 250 companies
Staff: 4
Annual Budget: $500-1,000,000

Personnel:
Executive Vice President: Kenneth "Ken" R. Bowman
    E-Mail: kenb@robstan.com
Director, Membership Services: Nicole Cervantes
    E-Mail: nicole@robstan.com
Vice President: Jennifer Crane
    E-Mail: jenniferc@robstan.com
Legal Counsel: Jon W. Gilchrist
    E-Mail: jwg@paynejones.com

Historical Note:
Formerly the Sealant and Waterproofers Institute; adopted its present name in 1989. SWRI's mission is to promote the exchange of ideas for the development of operating efficiency within the sealant, waterproofing and restoration industry; to create lasting good will between the members and those who manufacture, specify and purchase sealant, waterproofing and restoration materials and services. Membership: $600-1,200 (Contractor); $600 (Associate); $1,200-1,500 (Manufacturer); $250 (Senior); $25 (Student).

Meetings/Conferences: Semi-Annual
2013 - Scottsdale, AZ (Montelucia Resort and Spa)/ March 3 - 6

Publications:
Member Briefs
Membership Directory; on-line
The Applicator Magazine; quarterly; adv.

Membership List Available to Non-members

SEAMS Association (1967)
4921-C Broad River Rd.
Columbia, SC 29212
Tel: (803) 772-5861 Fax: (803) 731-7709
TollFree: (800) 476-5289
E-Mail: sarah@seams.org
Website: seams.org
Members: 150 companies
Staff: 2
Annual Budget: $100-250,000
Tax: 501(c)(6)

Personnel:
Executive Director: Sara Y. Friedman
    E-Mail: sarah@seams.org

Historical Note:
Founded as the South Carolina Needle Trades Association, assumed its present name in 1999 and became a national organization. SEAMS Association's mission is to support the resurging US sewn products industry through educational programs that will improve the quality and productivity of the sewn products industry collectively. Membership: $200-$1005/year.

Meetings/Conferences: Semi-Annual

Publications:
Membership Directory; on-line; adv.
SEAMS Association Newsletter
SEAMS Important; irregular; adv.

Membership List Available to Non-members

Seaplane Pilots Association (1972)
3859 Laird Blvd.
Lakeland, FL 33811
Tel: (863) 701-7979 Fax: (863) 701-7588
TollFree: (888) 772-8923
E-Mail: spa@seaplanes.org
Website: seaplanes.org
Members: 8000 individuals
Staff: 4
Annual Budget: $500-1,000,000

Personnel:
Executive Director: Steve McCaughey
    E-Mail: steve@seaplanes.org
Contact, Advertising and Sales: Chester Baumgartner
    E-Mail: cbaum111@mindspring.com
Administrative Assistant: Ann Gaines
    E-Mail: anng@seaplanes.org
Editor: Mark Twombly
    E-Mail: editor@seaplanes.org

Historical Note:
SPA's mission is to represent the interests of the seaplane enthusiast community on the federal, state, and local levels. Membership: $45 (Domestic); $55 (International).

Meetings/Conferences:
Number of non-conference events/year: 10

Publications:
Water Flying Update; bi-monthly
Water Landing Directory
WaterFlying Magazine; bi-monthly; adv.

Search - The National Consortium for Justice Information and Statistics (1969)
7311 Greenhaven Dr., Suite 145
Sacramento, CA 95831
Tel: (916) 392-2550 Fax: (916) 392-8440
Website: search.org
Staff: 33
Annual Budget: $2-5,000,000

Personnel:
Executive Director: Ronald P. Hawley
    E-Mail: ron@search.org
Director, Finance and Administration: Rose Marie Florita
    E-Mail: rosemarie@search.org
Director, Law and Policy: Owen M. Greenspan
    E-Mail: owen@search.org
Director, High-Tech Crime Training Services: Timothy Lott
    E-Mail: tlott@search.org
Director, Systems and Technology: Mark Perbix
    E-Mail: mark@search.org
Manager, Corporate Communications: Twyla R. Putt
    E-Mail: twyla@search.org
Assistant, Human Resources and Bookkeeper: Anne E. Stites
    E-Mail: anne@search.org

Historical Note:
Search's mission is to to improve the quality of justice and public safety through the use, management and exchange of information, application of new technologies and responsible law and policy, while safeguarding security and privacy. Members are primarily state-level justice officials responsible for operational decisions and policymaking concerning the management of criminal justice information, particularly criminal history information.

Meetings/Conferences: Annual
Number of non-conference events/year: 4

Secondary Materials and Recycled Textiles Association (1932)
2105 Laurel Bush Rd.
Suite 200
Bel Air, MD 21015
Tel: (443) 640-1050 Fax: (433) 640-1086
E-Mail: smartinfo@kingmgmt.org
Website: smartasn.org
Members: 225 companies
Staff: 5
Annual Budget: $250-500,000

Personnel:
Executive Director: Jackie King
    E-Mail: jackie@KINGmgmt.org
Media Contact: Paul Bailey
    E-Mail: paul.bailey@fallstongroup.com
Director, Finance: Debbie Dacre
    E-Mail: Debbie@KINGmgmt.org
Director, Meetings and Member Services: Heather Zucker
    E-Mail: heather@KINGmgmt.org

Historical Note:
Founded as the Sanitary Institute of America, became the National Association of Wiping Cloth Manufacturers, (1977) the International Association of Wiping Cloth Manufacturers, and (1993) Secondary Materials and Recycled Textiles Association. SMART's mission is to promote the interdependence of all its industry segments by providing a common forum for networking, education, and trade. Members are manufacturers and distributors of industrial wiping cloths, used clothing, mill ends, remnants, and recycled textiles. Membership: $2,995 (International/ Associate/Industry); $1,395 (Regular).

Meetings/Conferences: Annual
Conference Chair: Heather Zucker
2013 - Ponte Vedra Beach, FL (Ponte Vedra Inn and Club)/March 17 - 20

Publications:
Membership Directory; annually

Section for Women in Public Administration
1301 Pennsylvania Ave. NW, Suite 840
C/O American Society for Public Administration (ASPA)
Washington, DC 20004
Tel: (202) 393-7878
Website: aspaonline.org/swpa/
Staff: 2

Personnel:
Contact, Website: Roslyn Alic-Batson

Historical Note:

Section on Women in Public Administration (SWPA) is the section of American Society for Public Administration (ASPA). The SWPA mission can be summed up as a Section where women and men work together on projects and programs promoting participation and recognition of women at all levels and areas of the public sector. Membership: $17/Year.

Meetings/Conferences: Annual

Publications:
Bridging the Gap
Membership Directory; on-line

Securities Industry and Financial Markets Association (SIFMA) (2006)
120 Broadway
35th Floor
New York, NY 10271-0080
Tel: (212) 313-1200 Fax: (212) 313-1301
E-Mail: inquiries@sifma.org
Website: sifma.org
Members:
800,000 individuals
650 firms
Staff: 199
Annual Budget: $50-100,000,000
Tax: 501(c)(3)

Personnel:
President and Chief Executive Officer: T. Timothy Ryan Jr.
  E-Mail: tryan@sifma.org
Executive Vice President, Communications: Cheryl Crispen
  E-Mail: ccrispen@sifma.org
Senior Managing Director and General Counsel: Ira D. Hammerman
  E-Mail: ihammerman@sifma.org
Chief Financial and Chief Administrative Officer: David Krasner
Executive Vice President, Member Engagement: Ileane F. Rosenthal
Executive Vice President: Randy Snook

Historical Note:
Formed in 2006 from the merger of the Securities Industry Association and the Bond Market Association. SIFMA's mission is to develop policies and practices which strengthen financial markets and which encourage capital availability, job creation and economic growth while building trust and confidence in the financial industry.

Meetings/Conferences: Semi-Annual

Publications:
Asset Management Update; quarterly
Communications; weekly
Energy/Carbon Update; weekly
Global Weekly Update; weekly
Infrastructure Update; weekly
Private Client Today; on-line
Rates Update; weekly
Regulatory Update; weekly
Retirement & Savings Review; monthly
SIFMA Dashboard; weekly
SIFMA Research Reports; on-line
SmartBrief; daily
SSG Update; weekly
STATE-news; monthly
Washington Weekly Update; weekly

The Securities Transfer Association (1911)
P.O. Box 5220
Hazlet, NJ 07730-5220
Tel: (732) 888-6040 Fax: (732) 888-2121
E-Mail: cgaffney@stai.org
Website: stai.org
Members: 150 registered transfer agents
Staff: 2
Annual Budget: $500-1,000,000

Personnel:
Executive Director and Program Chairperson: Cynthia Jones
  E-Mail: cjones@stai.org
Administrator: Carol A. Gaffney
  E-Mail: cgaffney@stai.org

Historical Note:
STA's mission is to encourage and promote an interchange of information, experience, and ideas, among the association membership. It also provides educational, consultative, and advocacy services to its members. Membership: $500-1,500 plus $0.0025/account (Commercial Transfer Agent); $1,000-1,500 (Mutual Fund

Transfer Agent/Fixed Asset Transfer Agent); $1,000 (In-House Transfer Agent/Corporate); $2,000 (Non-Agent).

Meetings/Conferences:
Conference Chair: Cynthia Jones
Number of non-conference events/year: 3

Publications:
STA Newsletter; on-line
STA Vendor Directory; on-line

Security Hardware Distributors Association (1940)
105 Eastern Ave.
Suite 104
Annapolis, MD 21403
Tel: (410) 940-6346 Fax: (410) 263-1659
E-Mail: info@shda.org
Website: associationdatabase.com/aws/SHDA/pt/sp/
Members: 150 manufacturers and distributors
Staff: 7
Annual Budget: $250-500,000

Personnel:
Executive Director: Patricia A Lilly
  E-Mail: plilly@shda.org
President: Karen Hoffman-Kahl
Director, Membership Services: Amy Luckado
  E-Mail: aluckado@shda.org
Treasurer: Jennie Berg Pagano
Office Manager: Janice Sunderland
Associate Executive Director: Kristin B. Thompson
  E-Mail: kthompson@shda.org
Manager, Conferences: Molly Thompson

Historical Note:
Formerly (1997) National Locksmith Suppliers Association. SHDA's mission is to continually improve, through education and services, the proficiency of Security Distributors in order that they are the most effective and efficient conduit to the marketplace. Membership: $600-$1,500 (Distributor, based on Annual Sales Volume); $1,500 (Associate/Manufacturers).

Meetings/Conferences: Annual
Conference Chair: Molly Thompson
2013 - Phoenix, AZ (Pointe Hilton Squaw Peak Resort)/April 30 - May 3

Publications:
Membership Directory; on-line
SHDA Newsletter; quarterly
Unlocked Newsletter; semi-annually

Security Industry Association (1969)
8405 Colesville Rd.
Suite 500
Silver Spring, MD 20910-6343
Tel: (301) 804-4700 Fax: (703) 683-2469
E-Mail: info@siaonline.org
Website: siaonline.org
Members: 650 firms
Staff: 16
Annual Budget: $5-10,000,000
Tax: 501(c)(6)

Personnel:
Chief Executive Officer: Donald R. Erickson
  E-Mail: derickson@siaonline.org
Director, Government Relations: Marcus Dunn
  E-Mail: mdunn@siaonline.org
Director, Technical Standards: Joe Gittens
  E-Mail: jgittens@siaonline.org
Manager, Technical Writing and Special Projects: Ronald Hawkins
  E-Mail: rhawkins@siaonline.org
Director, Membership Services: Kevin Murphy
  E-Mail: kmurphy@siaonline.org
Manager, Events and Operations: Shawn Pearson
  E-Mail: spearson@siaonline.org
Chief Operating Officer: Rand C. Price CAE
  E-Mail: rprice@siaonline.org
Director, Marketing: Patricia Sherwood
  E-Mail: psherwood@siaonline.org
Manager, Communications: Rob Traister
  E-Mail: rtraister@siaonline.org
Director, Education and Training: Arminda Valles-Hall
  E-Mail: avalleshall@siaonline.org
Director, Research and Technology: Mark A. Visbal
  E-Mail: mvisbal@siaonline.org

Historical Note:
Product of a merger of the Security Equipment Manufacturers Association and the Security Equipment

Distributors Association. SIA protects and advances its members' interests by producing leading-edge global market research and by creating open industry standards that enable integration. Membership: $250-5000/year.

Continuing Education:
Certification Designation/s: CSOI, CSPM

Meetings/Conferences:
Conference Chair: Shawn Pearson
Number of non-conference events/year: 3

Publications:
Market Research Reports; quarterly
Membership Directory; on-line
Quarterly Research Update; quarterly
Quarterly Technical Update; quarterly
SIA News; monthly

Security Traders Association (1934)
80 Broad St.
Fifth Floor
New York, NY 10004
Tel: (212) 837-7765
Website: securitytraders.org
Members: 26 affiliate organizations and 4,200 professional trade industry members
Staff: 17
Annual Budget: $1-2,000,000
Tax: 501(c)(6)

Personnel:
President and Chief Executive Officer: James Toes
  E-Mail: jtoes@securitytraders.org

Historical Note:
Formerly (1988) National Security Traders Association. STA's mission is to promote the interests of its members throughout the global financial markets and providing representation of these interests in the legislative, regulatory and technological processes. Members are security traders and others involved in the securities industry. Membership: $50/year (Individual, excluding local affiliate membership).

Meetings/Conferences: Annual

Publications:
STA Newsletter; monthly
Traders Annual; annually; adv.

Seismological Society of America (1906)
400 Evelyn Ave.
Suite 201
Albany, CA 94706-1375
Tel: (510) 525-5474 Fax: (510) 525-7204
E-Mail: info@seismosoc.org
Website: seismosoc.org
Members: 1900 individuals
Staff: 8
Annual Budget: $1-2,000,000
Tax: 501(c)(3)

Personnel:
Executive Director: Susan Newman
  E-Mail: snewman@seismosoc.org
Contact, Press Relations: Nan Broadbent
  E-Mail: press@seismosoc.org
Coordinator, Membership Services: Katie Kadas
  E-Mail: membership@seismosoc.org
Managing Editor, BSSA: Carol Mark
  E-Mail: bssa@seismosoc.org
Administrative Assistant: Sissy Stone
  E-Mail: registration@seismosoc.org
Director, Operations: Joy Troyer
  E-Mail: joy@seismosoc.org

Historical Note:
Established in San Francisco, CA, and incorporated in California the same year. SSA works for the advancement of seismology and its applications in understanding and mitigating earthquake hazards and in imaging the structure of the earth. A member society of the American Geological Institute. Promotes scientific research in seismology and related phenomena, and informs the public on how to insure itself against damage by proper studies of earthquakes' geographic distribution, historical sequence, activities and effects on buildings. Membership: $100 (Regular); $25 (Student); $130 (Foreign); $60 (Affiliate); $45 (Developing Country); $1,000 (Corporate).

Meetings/Conferences:
Conference Chair: Sissy Stone
2013 - Salt Lake City, UT (Salt Palace Convention Center)/April 17 - 19
2014 - Anchorage, AK/April 30 - May 2

Publications:
Bulletin of the Seismological Society of America; quarterly

Membership Directory; on-line
Seismological Research Letters; bi-monthly; adv.

Membership List Available to Non-members

Select Registry/Distinguished Inns of North America *(2000)*

501 E. Michigan Ave.
P.O. Box 150
Marshall, MI 49068
Tel: (269) 789-0393 *Fax:* (269) 789-0970
TollFree: (800) 344-5244
E-Mail: maincontact@selectregistry.com
Website: selectregistry.com
Members: 400 inns and establishments
Staff: 6
Annual Budget: $1-2,000,000
Tax: 501(c)(3)

Personnel:
Executive Director: Will Carlson
    E-Mail: will@selectregistry.com
Office Coordinator and Contact, Communications: Bev
    Hiscock
    E-Mail: bev@selectregistry.com
Coordinator, Member Services: Lois Huver
    E-Mail: lois@selectregistry.com
Director, Membership Services and Quality Assurance:
    Carol Riggs
    E-Mail: criggs@selectregistry.com

Historical Note:
*Founded as the Independent Innkeepers Association.
DINA's mission is to promote and elevate niche, specialty
accommodations into a universal, recurring pursuit.
Members are independent, full-service Inns and Bed &
Breakfasts in the U.S. and Canada.*
Meetings/Conferences:
Number of non-conference events/year: 258

Membership List Available to Non-members

Selected Independent Funeral Homes *(1917)*

500 Lake Cook Rd.
Suite 205
Deerfield, IL 60015
Tel: (847) 236-9401 *Fax:* (847) 236-9968
TollFree: (800) 323-4219
E-Mail: info@selectedfuneralhomes.org
Website: selectedfuneralhomes.org
Members: 1300 firms
Staff: 10
Annual Budget: $2-5,000,000
Tax: 501(c)(6)

Personnel:
Executive Director: Robert Paterkiewicz CAE
    E-Mail: robp@selectedfuneralhomes.org
Director, Communications: Lauren Ehle
    E-Mail: lauren.ehle@selectedfuneralhomes.org
Director, Meetings and Education: Amy Hunt
    E-Mail: ahunt@selectedfuneralhomes.org
General Counsel: Sarah Pojanowski
    E-Mail: sarahp@selectedfuneralhomes.org
Executive Assistant and Office Manager: Angie Stark
    E-Mail: angies@selectedfuneralhomes.org
Director, Member Programs: Denise Zoephel
    E-Mail: denisez@selectedfuneralhomes.org

Historical Note:
*Formerly National Selected Morticians (NSM). SIFH's
purpose is to provide a continuing forum for the exchange,
development and dissemination of knowledge and
information beneficial to members and the public. Members
are independent, locally owned funeral homes. Membership:
$2,200-5,200/year.*
Meetings/Conferences:
Conference Chair: Amy Hunt
2013 - Austin, TX (Omni Austin Hotel Downtown)/Oct.
    16 - 19

Publications:
H.O.P.E; adv.
Membership Directory; on-line
The Bulletin; monthly; adv.

Self Storage Association *(1975)*

1901 N. Beauregard St.
Suite 450
Alexandria, VA 22311
Tel: (703) 575-8000 *Fax:* (703) 575-8901
TollFree: (888) 735-3784
E-Mail: info@selfstorage.org
Website: selfstorage.org

Members: 58,500 facilities
Staff: 12
Annual Budget: $2-5,000,000
Tax: 501(c)(6)

Personnel:
President and Chief Executive Officer: Mike T. Scanlon Jr.
    E-Mail: mscanlon@selfstorage.org
Director, Advertising Sales: Tom Comi
    E-Mail: tcomi@selfstorage.org
Vice President, Government Relations: Timothy J. Dietz
    E-Mail: tdietz@selfstorage.org
Editor: John Dunlap
    E-Mail: jdunlap@selfstorage.org
General Counsel: D. Carlos Kaslow
Vice President, Finance and Administration: Derek E.
    Knights
    E-Mail: dknights@selfstorage.org
Director, Membership Services and Marketing: Stacey
    Loflin
    E-Mail: sloflin@selfstorage.org
Director, Registrations, Vendor and Sponsorship Relations:
    Jennifer Pettigrew
    E-Mail: jpettigrew@selfstorage.org

Historical Note:
*Formerly (1989) Self-Service Storage Association. SSA's
mission is to advance the public awareness and to enhance
the image of the industry in the eyes of the general public,
government, the news media and its residential and
commercial customers. Membership: $100-775/year.*

Continuing Education:
Certification Designation/s: CSSM
Meetings/Conferences:
Conference Chair: Jennifer Pettigrew
2013 - Beaver Creek, CO (The Westin Riverfront Resort
    & Spa)/Feb. 4 - 7
2013 - Philadelphia, PA (Mariott Downtown)/April 23
    - 25
2013 - Las Vegas, NV (Caesars Palace)/Sept. 4 - 6

Publications:
Membership Directory; on-line
Self Storage Legal Review; bi-monthly
SSA Facility Managers' Memo; monthly
SSA Globe Magazine; monthly; adv.
SSA Globe Yearbook; annually
SSA Monday Morning Memo; weekly

Self-Insurance Institute of America, Inc. *(1981)*

P.O. Box 1237
Simpsonville, SC 29681
Tel: (864) 962-2208 *Fax:* (864) 962-2483
TollFree: (800) 851-7789
E-Mail: legislative@siia.org
Website: siia.org
Members: 1000 companies
Staff: 8
Annual Budget: $2-5,000,000
Tax: 501(c)(6)

Personnel:
Executive Vice President: Erica Massey
    E-Mail: emassey@siia.org
Director, Membership: Jennifer Ivy
    E-Mail: jivy@siia.org
Manager, Database: Michiale Machado
    E-Mail: mmachado@siia.org
Director, Marketing: Justin Miller
    E-Mail: jmiller@siia.org
Coordinator, Conference: Amy L. Troiano
    E-Mail: atroiano@siia.org

Historical Note:
*SIIA's mission is to identify opportunities to create and
increase membership value for companies involved with
self-insured group health plans and to assist the association
in communicating its membership services to this market
niche. Membership: $500-25000/year.*

Meetings/Conferences: Annual
Conference Chair: Amy L. Troiano
Number of non-conference events/year: 1

Publications:
Membership Directory; on-line
The Self-Insurer; monthly; adv.
Washington Report; weekly

SEMATECH *(1987)*

257 Fuller Rd.
Albany, NY 12203
Tel: (518) 649-1000
Website: sematech.org

Staff: 3

Personnel:
President and Chief Executive Officer: Dan Armbrust
Contact, Media Relations: Erica McGill
    E-Mail: media.relations@sematech.org
Senior Vice President and Chief Administrative Officer:
    David Saathoff

Historical Note:
*SEMATECH is the catalyst for accelerating the
commercialization of technology innovations into
manufacturing solutions.*
Meetings/Conferences:
Number of non-conference events/year: 2

Publications:
TECHreport Newsletter

Semiconductor Environmental Safety and Health Association *(1978)*

1313 Dolley Madison Blvd.
Suite 402
McLean, VA 22101-3926
Tel: (703) 790-1745 *Fax:* (703) 790-2672
E-Mail: sesha@burkinc.com
Website: seshaonline.org
Members:
35 companies
500 members
Staff: 12
Annual Budget: $100-250,000

Personnel:
Executive Director: Brett Burk CAE
    E-Mail: BBurk@BurkInc.com
Contact, Accounting: Tiffany Becker
    E-Mail: tbecker@burkinc.com
Editor: Mary Majors
    E-Mail: majorsma@airproducts.com
Director, Membership Services: Heide Rohland
    E-Mail: hrohland@burkinc.com
Manager, Meetings and Exhibits: Lori Strong
    E-Mail: lstrong@burkinc.com

Historical Note:
*Formerly (2002) the Semiconductor Safety Association.
SESHA is the environmental, safety and health association
serving the global semiconductor and associated technology
industries. Membership: $125 (Associate); $25 (Student).*
Meetings/Conferences: Annual
Conference Chair: Lori Strong
2013 - Long Beach, CA (Queen Mary)/March 18 - 22

Publications:
Membership Directory; on-line
SESHA E-Journal; on-line; adv.

Membership List Available to Non-members

Semiconductor Equipment and Materials International *(1970)*

3081 Zanker Rd.
San Jose, CA 95134
Tel: (408) 943-6900 *Fax:* (408) 428-9600
E-Mail: semihq@semi.org
Website: semi.org
Members: 2000 companies
Staff: 13
Annual Budget: $25-50,000,000
Tax: 501(c)(6)

Personnel:
President and Chief Executive Officer: Dennis P. McGuirk
Senior Director, Global Human Resources: Maureen
    McDonough
*Executive Vice President, Emerging Markets Group and
    Chief Marketing Officer:* Tom Morrow
*Chief Financial Officer and Executive Vice President, Global
    Member Alliances:* Richard Salsman

Historical Note:
*Formerly (1988) Semiconductor Equipment and Materials
Institute. SEMI is an international trade association
representing firms supplying equipment, materials and
also serving the manufacturing supply chains for the
microelectronic, display and photovoltaic industries. Mission
is to help members grow their profit, create new markets
and meet common industry challenges. Maintains regional
offices in Brussels, Tokyo, Seoul, Moscow, Washington,
D.C. and Singapore. Membership: $100 (Individual);
$1,200-5,200 (Corporate); $250 (Business Affiliate).*

Publications:
SEMI Global Update; monthly
SEMI Quarterly; quarterly
SEMI Tsushin; monthly

Semiconductor Manufacturing Newsletter; bi-weekly
Membership List Available to Non-members

Semiconductor Industry Association (1977)
1101 K St. NW
Suite 450
Washington, DC 20005
Tel: (202) 446-1700 *Fax:* (202) 216-9745
TollFree: (866) 756-0715
E-Mail: mailbox@sia-online.org
Website: sia-online.org
Members: 125 companies
Staff: 14
Annual Budget: $5-10,000,000
Tax: 501(c)(6)

Personnel:
President and Chief Executive Officer: Brian Toohey
Director, Communications: John Greenagel
    E-Mail: mailbox@sia-online.org
Vice President, Government Policy: David Isaacs

Historical Note:
Represents U.S. producers of all semiconductor products, such as discrete components, integrated circuits and microprocessors. SIA's mission is to provide domestic semiconductor companies to advance the global competitiveness of the $115 billion U.S. microchip industry and also provides a spectrum of services to aid members in growing their own businesses.

Semiotic Society of America (1976)
University of West Florida
11000 University Pkwy., P.O. Box 32009
Pensacola, FL 32514
Tel: (850) 474-2186 *Fax:* (713) 942-3452
Website: semioticsocietyofamerica.org
Members: 600 individuals and institutions
Staff: 3
Tax: 501(c)(3)

Personnel:
Executive Director: Terry J. Prewitt
    E-Mail: tprewitt@uwf.edu
Editor: Joseph Brent
    E-Mail: amgjlb@worldnet.att.net
Managing Editor: John Deely
    E-Mail: jndeely@stthom.edu

Historical Note:
SSA is an interdisciplinary professional organization serving a diverse community of scholars with common interests in the study of signs and sign-systems. SSA members are academics and institutions with an interest in the function of signs and symbols. Membership: $50 (Individual Print); $85 (Individual, Print and Online); $30 (Student Print); $65 (Student, Print and Online).

Meetings/Conferences: Annual

Publications:
Semiotics
The American Journal of Semiotics

Senior Army Reserve Commanders Association (1949)
P.O. Box 5050
Springfield, VA 22150
Tel: (703) 342-4099
E-Mail: execdirector@sarca.us
Website: sarca.us
Members: 600 individuals
Staff: 3
Annual Budget: $10-25,000
Tax: 501(c)(3)

Personnel:
Executive Director: COL Joseph Moravec
    E-Mail: jmoravec@sarca.us
Treasurer: COL Douglas J. Lamude
    E-Mail: treasurer@sarca.us

Historical Note:
SARCA's mission is to support the army reserve in its role, develop and mentor senior leaders of the USAR and provide a forum for dialogue among senior USAR leaders. Membership: $175 (General Officer, Pay Status); $125 (Colonel/Lt.Colonel, Pay Status); $55 (General Officer, Non-Pay Status/Retired/Colonel, Pay Status); $500-1000 (Life).

Meetings/Conferences: Annual

Senior Executives Association (1980)
77 K St. NE
Suite 2600
Washington, DC 20002

Tel: (202) 927-7000 *Fax:* (202) 927-5192
E-Mail: action@seniorexecs.org
Website: seniorexecs.org
Members: 3000 individuals
Staff: 9
Annual Budget: $500-1,000,000
Tax: 501(c)(5)

Personnel:
President: Carol A. Bonosaro
    E-Mail: seniorexec@aol.com
General Counsel: William L. Bransford
Director, Membership Services: Marc Owen
Administrative Assistant: Ryan Pearce
Director, Communications: Jeff Spinella
    E-Mail: action@seniorexecs.com
Office Manager: Vicky Zorrilla

Historical Note:
Founded as a tax-exempt, non-profit professional association representing career Federal executives, Advocate the interests of career federal executives, especially members of SEA. Membership includes senior level (SL) and senior technical and professional (ST) executives and Boards of Contract Appeals judges. Membership: $293 (Active); $100 (Retiree); $1,500 (Lifetime-Active); $750 (Lifetime-Retired); $140 (Organization, minimum).

Publications:
Action; monthly; adv.
Member Alert; bi-weekly
Member Directory; on-line

SEPM - Society for Sedimentary Geology (1926)
4111 S. Darlington
Suite 100
Tulsa, OK 74135-6373
Tel: (918) 610-3361 *Fax:* (918) 621-1685
TollFree: (800) 865-9765
Website: sepm.org
Members: 5000 individuals
Staff: 7
Annual Budget: $1-2,000,000
Tax: 501(c)(3)

Personnel:
Executive Director: Dr. Howard Harper
    E-Mail: hharper@sepm.org
Associate, Membership Services: Janice Curtis
    E-Mail: jcurtis@sepm.org
Administrative Associate: Edythe Ellis
    E-Mail: eellis@sepm.org
Associate Director and Business Manager: Theresa L. Scott
    E-Mail: tscott@sepm.org
Coordinator, Publications and Technology: Michele Tomlinson
    E-Mail: mtomlinson@sepm.org

Historical Note:
Formerly Society of Economic Paleontologists and Mineralogists, assumed its present name in 1989. SEPM is committed to the dissemination of scientific information on sedimentology, stratigraphy, paleontology, environmental sciences, marine geology, hydrogeology, and many additional related specialties. Membership: $300 (Sustaining); $40 (Spouse); $10-35 (Student).

Meetings/Conferences: Annual

Publications:
PALAIOS; monthly
The Journal of Sedimentary Research; monthly
The Sedimentary Record

Serbian-American Chamber of Commerce (1987)
448 W. Barry Ave.
Chicago, IL 60657
TollFree: (877) 686-7222
E-Mail: info@serbianamericanchamber.org
Website: serbianamericanchamber.org
Staff: 2

Personnel:
President and Chief Executive Officer: Milos Dedovic
    E-Mail:
    milos.dedovic@serbianamericanchamber.org
Treasurer: Vladimir Rokvic

Historical Note:
SACC's mission is to promote bilateral business relations between the United States and Serbia. Membership: $80 (Individual); $300 (Corporate); $750 (Corporate Gold).

Service Dealers Association (1986)
P.O. Box 151389

Austin, TX 78715
Fax: (512) 292-1221
Website: psd.info
Members: 2400 individuals
Staff: 1
Annual Budget: $25-50,000

Personnel:
President: Oscar Cavazos

Historical Note:
SDA represents dealers and distributors of power equipment. Membership: $95/year (individual); $250/year (company).

Service Employees International Union (1921)
1800 Massachusettes Ave. NW
Washington, DC 20036
Tel: (202) 730-7000
TollFree: (800) 424-8592
E-Mail: media@seiu.org
Website: seiu.org
Members: 225000 individuals
Staff: 750
Annual Budget: Over $100,000,000
Tax: 501(c)(5)

Personnel:
President: Mary Kay Henry
Associate General Counsel: Alma C. Henderson
    E-Mail: alma.henderson@seiu.org
Director, Legislative Department: Alison Reardon
    E-Mail: alison.reardon@seiu.org

Historical Note:
SEIU, a union of more than 2 million service sector employees, works to improve the lives of workers and their families.

Publications:
Uniting Our Strength e-News; weekly

Service Industry Association (1985)
2164 Historic Decatur Rd.
Villa 19
San Diego, CA 92106
Tel: (619) 221-9200 *Fax:* (619) 221-8201
E-Mail: cbetzner@servicenetwork.org
Website: servicenetwork.org
Members: 250 companies
Staff: 1
Annual Budget: $100-250,000
Tax: 501(c)(6)

Personnel:
Executive Director: Claudia Betzner
    E-Mail: cbetzner@aol.com

Historical Note:
SIA's mission is to enhance the high-tech industry by promoting an open environment of interdependence and co-operation between manufacturers, independent servicers and users by providing value-adding solutions for customers.SIA members are high tech service companies. Membership: $425-1,300 (Regular/Associate); $20,000 (Platinum); $10,000 (GoldPlus); $6,000 (Gold); $3,000 (Silver); $2,250 (Bronze).

Meetings/Conferences: Annual
2013 - Las Vegas, NV (Mirage Hotel and Casino)/ March 17 - 19

Publications:
Membership Directory
SIA Newsletter; quarterly; adv.

Service Specialists Association (1981)
160 Symphony Way
Suite Two
Elgin, IL 60120
Tel: (847) 760-0067
E-Mail: kholliday@wade-partners.com
Website: truckservice.org
Members: 163 companies
Staff: 2
Annual Budget: $100-250,000
Tax: 501(c)(6)

Personnel:
Executive Director: Bill Wade CIC, CPCU
Manager: Randy Brothers
    E-Mail: rbrothers@wade-partners.com

Historical Note:
Formerly (1990) the Spring Service Association and The Suspension Specialists Association (1996). SSA's mission is to provide a forum for the exchange of technical and business information in order that members may understand them better. Members are persons, firms, or corporations

who have operated a full line heavy duty repair service shop for at least one year with sufficient inventory to service market area, have rebuilding department capable of making all necessary repairs. *Membership: $750/year.*

Meetings/Conferences: Annual
Number of non-conference events/year: 1

Publications:
The Leaf; quarterly; adv.

Membership List Available to Non-members

Service Station Dealers of America and Allied Trades (1947)
1532 Pointer Ridge Pl.
Suite E
Bowie, MD 20716
Tel: (301) 390-4405 *Fax:* (301) 390-3161
E-Mail: mgates@wmda.net
Website: ssda-at.org
Members: 20000 individuals
Staff: 5
Annual Budget: $100-250,000

Personnel:
Vice President: Billy Hillmuth
President: Peter S. Kischak
Executive Vice President: Roy E. Littlefield
Treasurer: Hugh Campbell
Director, Federal Government Affairs: Amy Littlefield
    E-Mail: ssda-at@mindspring.com

Historical Note:
Formerly (1980) National Congress of Petroleum Retailers, Inc. SSDA-AT serves as a voice for its members on the Capitol Hill, and before federal regulators, media, courts, and suppliers. Members are independent gasoline dealers who sell gasoline under the brand name of their supplier. Membership includes individual and state affiliate associations representing service repair facilities, car washes and convenience stores. Membership: $99 (Regular); $300 (Associate).

Meetings/Conferences: Annual

Sewing and Craft Alliance (1928)
P.O. Box 369
Monroeville, PA 15146
Tel: (412) 372-5950
Website: gotsewing.com
Members: 900 companies
Staff: 4
Annual Budget: $1-2,000,000

Personnel:
Executive Director: Joyce Perhac
    E-Mail: jperhac@sewing.org

Historical Note:
Formerly (1976) the National Notion Association; Assumed its current name in 1997. SCA provides education and creative resources to the sewing and craft enthusiast. It offers opportunities for retailers and businesses in the sewing, quilting, crafting or textile industries to showcase their products and services to the creative community through advertising, sponsorships and promotions. Membership: varies according to sales volume or number of stores.

Publications:
SEW-lutions Newsletter; monthly

Sewn Products Equipment and Suppliers of the Americas (1990)
9650 Strickland Rd.
Suite 103-324
Raleigh, NC 27615
Tel: (919) 872-8909 *Fax:* (919) 872-1915
TollFree: (888) 447-7372
E-Mail: info@spesa.org
Website: spesa.org
Members: 110 companies
Staff: 5
Annual Budget: $500-1,000,000
Tax: 501(c)(3)

Personnel:
President: Benton W. Gardner
    E-Mail: benton@spesa.org
Managing Director: Dave Gardner
    E-Mail: dave@spesa.org
Administration and Website: Laura Kelly
    E-Mail: laura@spesa.org

Historical Note:
Founded as Sewn Products Equipment Suppliers Association; assumed its current name in 2002. Mission is to provide its members with quality networking,

educational, and marketing opportunities for advancing their businesses within the sewn products industries. Members are companies engaged in or connected with supplying equipment, including replacement parts and computer software, to the sewn products industry. *Membership: $850-5,000 (Supplier, based on annual sales); $750 (Associate).*

Meetings/Conferences: Annual
Number of non-conference events/year: 1

Publications:
Behind The Seams; bi-weekly; adv.
Membership Directory; on-line
SPESA Speaks; on-line

Shareholder Services Association (1946)
1100 SW Sixth Ave. P11D
c/o StanCorp Financial Group
Portland, OR 97204
Tel: (706) 596-3385 *Fax:* (706) 596-3488
Website: shareholderservices.org
Members: 240 individuals
Staff: 3
Annual Budget: $250-500,000

Personnel:
President: Karen V. Danielson
    E-Mail: kdanielson@na.ko.com
Treasurer: Christopher G. Dowd
    E-Mail: cdowd@georgeson.com
Membership Chair: Jane Keister
    E-Mail: jane.keister@standard.com

Historical Note:
Formerly (1946) Corporate Transfer Agents Association (CTA). SSA's mission is to support corporate issuers in effectively meeting their responsibilities for shareholder recordkeeping and service. Members are corporate employees responsible for the transfer of stock, shareholder services and related functions. Membership: $495/year (Individual/Company/Association).

Meetings/Conferences: Annual
2013 - Stowe, VT (Stowe Mountain Lodge)/July 16 - 19

Publications:
Corporate Secretary Magazine
The Shareholder Service Optimizer; quarterly

Sheet Metal and Air Conditioning Contractors' National Association (1943)
4201 Lafayette Center Dr.
Chantilly, VA 20151-1219
Tel: (703) 803-2980 *Fax:* (703) 803-3732
E-Mail: info@smacna.org
Website: smacna.org
Members: 103 chapters and 1834 members
Staff: 34
Annual Budget: $500-1,000,000
Tax: 501(c)(6)

Personnel:
Chief Executive Officer: Vincent R. Sandusky
    E-Mail: vsandusky@smacna.org
Director, Business Management and Membership Services: Bridgette Bienacker CAE
    E-Mail: bbienacker@smacna.org
Executive Director, Technical Services: Eli P. Howard III
    E-Mail: ehoward@smacna.org
Controller: Jerrold Marans
    E-Mail: jmarans@smacna.org
Director, Communications and Public Relations: Rosalind P. Raymond
    E-Mail: rraymond@smacna.org
Director, Accounting Services: Leila Sader
    E-Mail: lsader@smacna.org
Executive Director, Market Sectors: Thomas J. Soles Jr.
    E-Mail: tsoles@smacna.org
Administrative Assistant, Publications: Carolyn M. Williams
    E-Mail: cwilliams@smacna.org
Executive Director, Labor Relations: Deborah A. Wyandt Esq.
    E-Mail: dwyandt@smacna.org

Historical Note:
Formerly (1956) Sheet Metal Contractors National Association. SMACNA's mission is to provide products, services, and representation to enhance businesses, markets and profitability. Membership: $100-1500 (Regular/International); $1500-20000 (Associate).

Meetings/Conferences: Annual
Conference Chair: Deborah A. Wyandt Esq.
2013 - Maui, HI (Wailea Beach Marriott Resort and Spa)/Oct. 20 - 24

Number of non-conference events/year: 6

Publications:
Architectural Metal (E-Mail); semi-annually
HVAC Systems Expertise; biennially
Industrial Insights (E-Mail); semi-annually
Membership Directory; on-line
Products & Services Update; monthly; adv.
Residential Report (E-Mail); semi-annually
Safety Focus; quarterly
SMACNews (E-Mail); monthly

Sheet Metal Workers' International Association (1888)
1750 New York Ave. NW
Sixth Floor
Washington, DC 20006
Tel: (202) 783-5880 *Fax:* (202) 662-0866
E-Mail: info@smwia.org
Website: smwia.org
Members: 150000 individuals
Staff: 125
Annual Budget: $50-100,000,000
Tax: 501(c)(5)

Personnel:
General President: Joseph J. Nigro
    E-Mail: jnigro@smwia.org
Director, Communications: Bill Butler
    E-Mail: bbutler@smwia.org
Director, Education: Chris E. Carlough
Chief International Representative: Charles F. Mulcahy
Director, Governmental Affairs: Vincent A. Panvini
Legal Counsel: Patrick Riley

Historical Note:
SMWIA's mission is to establish and maintain desirable working conditions and thus provide comfort, happiness, and security to its members. Serves to protect and raise the living standards of skilled men and women employed throughout the United States, Canada and Puerto Rico.

Publications:
Members' Voices; bi-monthly
Partners in Progress; semi-annually
The Journal; bi-monthly

Shelf-Stable Food Processors Association (1923)
1150 Connecticut Ave. NW
12th Floor
Washington, DC 20036
Tel: (202) 587-4273 *Fax:* (202) 587-4303
E-Mail: sfpa@meatami.com
Website: meatami.com/ht/d/sp/i/8423/pid/8423
Members: 35 companies
Staff: 8
Annual Budget: $100-250,000
Tax: 501(c)(6)

Personnel:
President and Chief Executive Officer: Patrick J. Boyle
Executive Vice President: James H. Hodges
    E-Mail: jhodges@meatami.com
Director, Administration: Susan Backus
    E-Mail: sbackus@meatami.com
Senior Vice President, Regulatory Affairs/General Counsel: Mark Dopp
Senior Vice President, Legislative Affairs: Dale Nellor
Chief Financial Officer: Ron Nunnery
Senior Vice President, Public Affairs and Professional Development: Janet Riley
Vice President, Education and Professional Development: Marie D. Ternieden
    E-Mail: mternieden@meatami.com

Historical Note:
Formerly (1923) the National Meat Canners Association and assumed its present name in 2007. SFPA advocates the interests of packers of commercially sterile canned meats, can equipment suppliers, and encourages scientific and practical research. Managed by the American Meat Institute. Membership: $2,000/year.

Meetings/Conferences: Annual
2013 - Palm Beach Gardens, FL (PGA National Resort and Spa)/March 10 - 12
2014 - Phoenix, AZ (Arizona Biltmore)/March 9 - 11

Publications:
Membership Directory; on-line

Shipbuilders Council of America (1920)
655 Fifteenth St. NW
Suite 225
Washington, DC 20005

Tel: (202) 347-5762 *Fax:* (202) 347-5464
Website: shipbuilders.org
Staff: 5
Annual Budget: $500-1,000,000

Personnel:
President: Matthew Paxton
E-Mail: mpaxton@dc.bjllp.com
Manager, Government Affairs: Ian H. Bennitt
E-Mail: ibennitt@dc.bjllp.com
Senior Defense Advisor: Joe Carnevale
E-Mail: jcarnevale@balljanik.com

Historical Note:
SCA is a trade association representing the U.S. shipyard industry. SCA members build, repair and service America's fleet of commercial vessels. Membership: $5,000-55,000(Shipyard);$1,550-5,150 (Affiliate).

Meetings/Conferences: Biennial
Membership List Available to Non-members

Shipowners Claims Bureau, Inc. *(1917)*
One Battery Park Plaza
31st Floor
New York, NY 10004
Tel: (212) 847-4500 *Fax:* (212) 847-4599
E-Mail: info@american-club.com
Website: american-club.com
Members: 31 companies
Staff: 30

Personnel:
Chairman and Chief Executive Officer: Joseph E.M. Hughes
E-Mail: joe.hughes@american-club.com
President and Chief Operating Officer: Vincent J. Solarino
E-Mail: vince.solarino@american-club.com
Senior Vice President, Information Technology: Manny Beri
E-Mail: manny.beri@american-club.com
Senior Vice President, Corporate Compliance: Charles J. Cuccia
E-Mail: charles.cuccia@american-club.com
Senior Vice President and Treasurer: Arpad A. Kadi
E-Mail: arpad.kadi@american-club.com
Senior Vice President, Loss Prevention: William H. Moore
E-Mail: william.moore@american-club.com
Vice President, Human Resources: Vicki A. Paradise
E-Mail: vicki.paradise@american-club.com
Senior Vice President, Underwriting: Stuart Todd
E-Mail: stuart.todd@american-club.com
Senior Vice President, Claims and General Counsel: George J. Tsimis
E-Mail: george.tsimis@american-club.com

Historical Note:
SCB members are claim managers and adjusters for shipping lines and protection and indemnity clubs. The American Club, a mutual P&I association for the shipping industry is managed by SCB.

Publications:
Currents; irregular
Member Alerts; on-line

Shippers of Recycled Textiles *(1989)*
2105 Laurel Bush Rd.
Suite 200
Bel Air, MD 21015
Tel: (443) 640-1050 *Fax:* (443) 640-1086
Website: sorti.com
Members: 50 companies
Staff: 3
Annual Budget: $25-50,000
Tax: 501(c)(6)

Personnel:
Association Coordinator: Casey Joseph
E-Mail: casey@ksgroup.org

Historical Note:
SORT is an association for members of SMART created to benefit members and provide reduced ocean freights and additional services for the transportation of used clothing, wipers, textiles and textile waste products for shipment by sea and land. Membership: $200 (Plan A, based on no. of containers); $65 (Plan B, for each container).

Publications:
Membership Directory; on-line

Shock Society *(1978)*
160 Convent Ave.
Harris Hall 207
New York, NY 10031

Tel: (212) 650-6880 *Fax:* (212) 650-7797
Website: shocksociety.org
Members: 800 individuals
Staff: 2
Annual Budget: $250-500,000

Personnel:
Secretary: Sonna Goyert PhD
E-Mail: sgoyert@med.cuny.edu

Historical Note:
SS's mission is to improve the care of victims of trauma, shock, and sepsis through promoting clinically relevant research into the basic biology of trauma, shock, and sepsis. Membership composed of individuals interested in extending basic and clinical knowledge of the nature and treatment of shock and trauma. Membership: $220 (Full); $50-170 (Student); $265 (International Full); $210 (International Student).

Meetings/Conferences: Annual
Conference Chair: Mary Schuerman
2013 - San Diego, CA (Sheraton San Diego Hotel and Marina)/June 1 - 4
2014 - Charlotte, NC (Westin Charlotte)/June 7 - 10

Publications:
Membership Directory; on-line
Shock Journal; monthly
Shock Society Newsletter

Showmen's League of America *(1913)*
P.O. Box 64980
Chicago, IL 60664-0980
Tel: (312) 332-6236 *Fax:* (312) 332-6237
Website: showmensleague.org
Members: 1500 individuals
Staff: 3
Annual Budget: $100-250,000
Tax: 501(c)(10)

Personnel:
President: Sam Johnston
Executive Secretary: Joe Burum
E-Mail: joeb@showmensleague.org
Treasurer: John Hanschen

Historical Note:
SLA promotes friendship and fellowship between its members and the outdoor amusement industry and pledges to assist those in need through its many programs. Membership: $25 (Individual); $625 (Life).

Meetings/Conferences: Annual

Sigma Epsilon Delta Dental Fraternity *(1859)*
211 E. Chicago Ave.
Chicago, IL 60611-2678
Tel: (312) 440-2500
Website: ada.org/ada/organizations/ orgdetail.asp?OrganizationID = 938
Staff: 1
Annual Budget: $25-50,000

Personnel:
Executive Director: Nathan Massoff

Historical Note:
ADA is the source for oral health related information for dentists and their patients. ADA's mission is to foster the success of a diverse membership and advance the oral health of the public.

Publications:
Member Directory; on-line
The Journal of the American Dental Association; on-line

Sigma Phi Delta *(1924)*
P.O. Box 2234
Mansfield, TX 76063
Tel: (773) 564-9728 *Fax:* (214) 686-2240
TollFree: (877) 744-7447
E-Mail: webissues@sigmaphidelta.org
Website: sigmaphidelta.org
Members: 7500 individuals
Staff: 6

Personnel:
Director, Professional Development: Shane Bartus PhD
E-Mail: professionaldevelopment@sigmaphidelta.org
Manager, Information Systems: Edward A. Hurst
E-Mail: ism@sigmaphidelta.org
Communications Director: Naoki Tokuhashi
E-Mail: cd@sigmaphidelta.org

Historical Note:

A professional and social fraternity of engineering students and alumni. It promotes the advancement of the engineering profession, and a greater spirit of cooperation among engineering students and organizations.

Meetings/Conferences: Annual
2013 - Bethesda, MD (Bethesda North Marriott Hotel and Conference Center)/Aug. 8 - 11
Number of non-conference events/year: 1

Publications:
Membership Directory

Sigma Theta Tau International *(1922)*
550 W. North St.
Indianapolis, IN 46202
Tel: (317) 634-8171 *Fax:* (317) 634-8188
TollFree: (888) 634-7575
E-Mail: stti@stti.iupui.edu
Website: nursingsociety.org
Members: 450000 individuals
Staff: 78
Annual Budget: $10-25,000,000
Tax: 501(c)(3)

Personnel:
Chief Executive Officer: Patricia E. Thompson EdD, FAAN, RN
E-Mail: ceo@stti.iupui.edu
Director, Marketing and Communications: Rachael McLaughlin
E-Mail: Rachael@stti.iupui.edu
Treasurer: Nancy Sharts-Hopko

Historical Note:
STTI was founded at the Indiana University School of Nursing. It provides leadership and scholarship in practice, education and research to enhance public health, and supports the learning and professional development of its members to improve nursing care worldwide. International Annual Membership Dues: $43.90-99.50/year. (Based on Income).

Meetings/Conferences:
2013 - Indianapolis, IN (JW Marriott Indianapolis)/ Nov. 16 - 20
Number of non-conference events/year: 4

Publications:
Always a Nurse
Chapter Leader Emphasis; bi-annually
Journal of Nursing Scholarship; quarterly; adv.
Membership Directory
Newsletter for Developing Chapters; quarterly
Nursing Focal Points; monthly
Reflections on Nursing Leadership; quarterly; adv.
RNL Magazine; adv.
STTIconnect; monthly; adv.
Worldviews on Evidence-Based Nursing; quarterly; adv.

Sigma Xi, The Scientific Research Society *(1886)*
P.O. Box 13975
3106 E. NC Hwy. 54
Research Triangle Park, NC 27709
Tel: (919) 549-4691 *Fax:* (919) 549-0090
TollFree: (800) 243-6534
E-Mail: info@sigmaxi.org
Website: sigmaxi.org
Members: 60000 individuals
Staff: 36
Annual Budget: $5-10,000,000

Personnel:
Executive Director: Jerome F. Baker CAE
E-Mail: jerry.baker@sigmaxi.org
Manager, Communications: Charles Blackburn
E-Mail: cblackburn@sigmaxi.org
Chief Operating Officer: Barry C. Collin
E-Mail: barry.collin@sigmaxi.org

Historical Note:
Sigma Xi promotes the health of the scientific enterprise and honors scientific achievement. Membership is by invitation. Membership: $90 (Regular/Full/Associate); $63 (Emeritus/ Transitional); $25 (Student).

Meetings/Conferences: Annual

Publications:
Member Newletter; monthly
Sigma Xi Today; bi-monthly
Year in Review; annually

Silica Fume Association *(1998)*
38860 Sierra Ln.
Lovettsville, VA 20180

Tel: (540) 822-9455 *Fax:* (540) 822-9456
Website: silicafume.org
Staff: 1
Annual Budget: $50-100,000

Personnel:
President: Mark B. Benedict
    E-Mail: markb@silicafume.org

Historical Note:
Assists the producers of silica fume by promoting its usage in concrete. The SFA advances the use of silica fume in the nation's concrete infrastructure and works to increase the awareness and understanding of silica-fume concrete in the private civil engineering sector among state transportation officials and in the academic community.

Publications:
HPC Bridge Views; bi-monthly

Silicones Environmental, Health and Safety Council of North America *(1971)*
2325 Dulles Corner Blvd.
Suite 500
Herndon, VA 20171
Tel: (703) 788-6570
E-Mail: sehsc@sehsc.com
Website: sehsc.com
Members: 7 companies
Staff: 3
Annual Budget: $2-5,000,000

Personnel:
Executive Director: Karluss Thomas
    E-Mail: Kthomas@sehsc.com

Historical Note:
SEHSC's primary focus is to coordinate scientific research on health, safety and environmental issues involving silicones. It is also involved in legislative and regulatory issues relating to silicone materials. Members are North American silicone chemical producers and importers.

Silver Council
The Silver Council C/O I3A 701 Westchester Ave.
Suite 317W
White Plains, NY 10604
Tel: (914) 285-4933 *Fax:* (914) 285-4937
E-Mail: i3ainfo@i3a.org
Website: pmairegs.com/silvercouncil/index.htm
Staff: 1

Personnel:
President: Lyndon B. Johnson

Historical Note:
Silver Council is an organization developing and promoting the most equitable and environmentally-sound methods of handling silver resulting from photographic processes.

The Silver Institute *(1971)*
888 16th St. NW
Suite 303
Washington, DC 20006
Tel: (202) 835-0185 *Fax:* (202) 835-0155
E-Mail: info@silverinstitute.org
Website: silverinstitute.org
Members: 35 companies
Staff: 5
Annual Budget: $1-2,000,000

Personnel:
Executive Director and Secretary: Michael DiRienzo

Historical Note:
SI's purpose is to enhance the development and uses of silver and silver products and foster research and development related to the present and prospective uses of silver.

Publications:
Membership Directory; on-line
Silver News - Newsletter; quarterly

Silver Users Association *(1947)*
11240 Waples Mill Rd.
Suite 200
Fairfax, VA 22030
Tel: (703) 934-0219 *Fax:* (703) 359-7562
E-Mail: pmiller@mwcapitol.com
Website: silverusersassociation.org
Members: 28 companies
Staff: 1
Annual Budget: $50-100,000

Personnel:
Executive Director: Paul A. Miller
    E-Mail: pmiller@mwcapitol.com

Historical Note:
SUA serves as industry spokesperson for accurate silver market information and also monitors domestic and international silver activity. SUA's mission is to inform members, government and the public on all facets of the silver market in a timely manner. Membership: $2,500/year

Publications:
Washington Report Newsletter; monthly

Single Ply Roofing Institute *(1981)*
411 Waverley Oaks Rd.
Suite 331B
Waltham, MA 02452
Tel: (781) 647-7026 *Fax:* (781) 647-7222
E-Mail: info@spri.org
Website: spri.org
Members: 59 companies
Staff: 1
Annual Budget: $500-1,000,000
Tax: 501(c)(6)

Personnel:
Managing Director: Linda King

Historical Note:
SPRI provides a forum for its members to collectively focus their industry expertise and efforts on critical industry issues. SPRI represents sheet membrane and related component suppliers in the commercial roofing industry. Membership: $1,500-7,500/year (Depending on company product).

Meetings/Conferences:
2013 - Indian Wells, CA (Miramonte Resort and Spa)/
    Jan. 11 - 13

Publications:
Member Directory; on-line

Slag Cement Association
38800 Country Club
Farmington Hills, MI 48331
Tel: (847) 977-6920
E-Mail: info@slagcement.org
Website: slagcement.org
Members: 7 Companies
Staff: 1
Annual Budget: $100-250,000
Tax: 501(c)(6)

Personnel:
Executive Director: Tony Fiorato
    E-Mail: tony@slagcement.org

Historical Note:
SCA's mission is to serve as the source of knowledge for slag cement and slag blended cements through continuous research, promotion and education.

Sleep Research Society *(1961)*
2510 N. Frontage Rd.
Darien, IL 60561
Tel: (630) 737-9763 *Fax:* (630) 737-9790
E-Mail: srsmembership@srsnet.org
Website: sleepresearchsociety.org
Members: 1500 individuals
Staff: 3
Annual Budget: $500-1,000,000
Tax: 501(c)(3)

Personnel:
Executive Director: Jerome A. Barrett
Administrative Coordinator: Nick Cekosh
    E-Mail: ncekosh@srsnet.org
Secretary and Treasurer: Sean P.A. Drummond PhD

Historical Note:
Founded as Association for the Psycho Physiological Study of Sleep.Membership: $180 (Full Member);$90 (Associate/ Postdoctorial Fellow);$45(Predoctorial/Undergraduate); $40 (Emeritus);$100(Corresponding member).

Meetings/Conferences: Annual
Number of non-conference events/year: 1

Publications:
Journal SLeep
Member Directory; on-line
Sleep and Biological Rhythms; on-line
Sleep and Breathing
Sleep Medicine; on-line
Sleep Medicine Clinics; on-line
Sleep Medicine Reviews; on-line
the International Journal of Sleep and Wakefulness
the Journal of Clinical Sleep Medicine; on-line
The Open Sleep Journal; on-line

Membership List Available to Non-members

Slovak Studies Association *(1977)*
Wayne State University, Department of Political Science
2040 F/AB
Detroit, MI 48220
Tel: (313) 577-2630 *Fax:* (313) 993-3435
E-Mail: slovakstudies@gmail.com
Website: slovakstudies.org
Members: 80 individuals
Staff: 3
Annual Budget: Under $10,000

Personnel:
President: Kevin Deegan-Krause
    E-Mail: slovakstudies@gmail.com
Treasurer: Bradley Abrams
    E-Mail: bradleyabrams4@gmail.com

Historical Note:
SSA is an international society of scholars. SSA's mission is to promote inter-disciplinary research, publication and teaching related to the Slovak experience. Affiliated with American Society for the Advancement of Slavic Studies. Membership: $5/year.

Publications:
SSA Newsletter; bi-annually

Small Business Council of America *(1979)*
1523 Concord Pike, Suite 300
Brandywine East
Wilmington, DE 19803
Tel: (302) 691-7222 *Fax:* (302) 691-6833
Website: sbca.net
Members: 700 businesses
Staff: 6
Annual Budget: $100-250,000
Tax: 501(c)(6)

Personnel:
Secretary: Leanne H. Redstone
    E-Mail: lredstone@shanlaw.com

Historical Note:
SBCA is a national organization representing the federal tax and employee benefit interests of small business. Mission is to prevent federal tax laws from becoming more burdensome on small businesses and their owners. Membership: $500 (Institutional); $225 (Professional); $315 (Individual); $1,000-50,000 (Others).
Meetings/Conferences:
Number of non-conference events/year: 6

Publications:
Membership Directory; annually

Small Business Exporters Association of the United States *(1937)*
1156 15th St. NW
Suite 1100
Washington, DC 20005-1755
Tel: (202) 659-9320 *Fax:* (202) 872-8543
TollFree: (800) 345-6728
E-Mail: info@sbea.org
Website: sbea.org
Members: 150000 members
Staff: 2
Tax: 501(c)(6)

Personnel:
Office Contact: Jody Milanese
Contact, Communications and Public Affairs: Molly
    Baldwin

Historical Note:
SBEA is a nonprofit association dedicated to small and mid-size business exporters in the United States. SBEA's mission is to provide governmental advocacy on behalf of all small exporters and individual member companies that encounter government difficulties as they export. Membership: $200-5500/year (varies on the number of employees).

Publications:
SBEA Newsletter

National Association of Small Business Investment Companies *(1958)*
1100 H St. NW
Suite 610
Washington, DC 20005
Tel: (202) 628-5055 *Fax:* (202) 628-5080
E-Mail: info@sbia.org
Website: sbia.org
Members: 400 companies
Staff: 5
Annual Budget: $1-2,000,000

Personnel:
President: Brett Palmer
   E-Mail: bpalmer@nasbic.org
Office Manager: Vanessa Fountain-Allen
Director, Meeting Planning and Operations: Jeanette
   Diana Paschal
   E-Mail: jpaschal@nasbic.org
Senior Director, Marketing and Events: Lisa G. Slaydon
   E-Mail: lslaydon@nasbic.org
Senior Director, Governmental and Regulatory Affairs:
   Chris Walters

Historical Note:
*NASBIC is the professional association for the Small
Business Investment Company (SBIC) industry. SBIA's
mission is to provide advocacy power with federal regulators
and on Capitol Hill, and access to exceptional networking
opportunities. Membership: $1,000 (Limited Partner);
$2,000 (Affiliate); $5,000 (Associate); 1,000-8,500
(Fund).*

Meetings/Conferences:
Conference Chair: Lisa G. Slaydon
Number of non-conference events/year: 2

Publications:
Membership Directory; annually
Report & Outlook

Small Business Legislative Council *(1976)*
1100 H St. NW
Suite 610
Washington, DC 20005
Tel: (202) 639-8500 *Fax:* (202) 296-5333
E-Mail: email@sblc.org
Website: sblc.org
Members: 106 small business associations
Staff: 2
Annual Budget: $100-250,000

Personnel:
President and General Counsel: John S. Satagaj

Historical Note:
*SBLC is a coalition of trade and professional association
who share a common concern with advancing the interests
of small business. Members represent the interests of
small businesses in diverse economic sectors such as
manufacturing, retailing, distribution, professional and
technical services, construction, transportation, and
agriculture. Membership: $650-3500/year (Organization,
based on member association's budget).*
Meetings/Conferences:
Number of non-conference events/year: 6

Publications:
Membership Directory; on-line
SBLC Weekly; weekly

Small Business Technology Coalition (SBTC)
1156 15th St. NW, Suite 1100
Washington, DC 20005-1704
Tel: (202) 785-4300
Website: sbtc.org
Staff: 1

Personnel:
Treasurer: Kenneth J. Thurber

Historical Note:
*The Small Business Technology Council is a non-partisan,
non-profit industry association of companies dedicated to
promoting the creation and growth of research-intensive,
technology-based U.S. small business.*

Publications:
Membership Directory; on-line
SBCT Newsletter; monthly

Small Luxury Hotels of the World *(1985)*
370 Lexington Ave.
Suite 1506
New York, NY 10017
Tel: (212) 953-2064 *Fax:* (212) 953-0576
Website: slh.com
Members: 350 hotels
Staff: 60

Personnel:
Public Relations and Marketing Executive: Mallory Miller
   E-Mail: pr@slh.com

Historical Note:
*Founded as Small Luxury Hotels and Resorts in 1985,
the organization became Small Luxury Hotels following a
merger with Prestige Hotels, and assumed its current name
in 1991. Members are independently owned and managed
deluxe hotels with less than 200 rooms.*

Publications:

Membership Directory; on-line

Small Publishers Association of North America
(1996)
P.O. Box 9725
Colorado Springs, CO 80932-0725
Tel: (719) 924-5534 *Fax:* (719) 213-2602
E-Mail: info@spannet.org
Website: spannet.org
Members: 800 individuals
Staff: 5
Annual Budget: $50-100,000
Tax: 501(c)(6)

Personnel:
Executive Director: Brad Poulson
Business Manager: Debi Flora
Online Community Manager: Brad Flora
Director, Membership: Kaye Krassner

Historical Note:
*SPAN is committed to supporting authors and independent
publishers as a nonprofit trade association and to build
successful writing and publishing businesses. Members are
small presses, self-publishers, authors and vendors offering
products or services to the industry. Membership: $89 (Pro
Member); $60 (Pro Member - Partner); $150 (Associate).*

Publications:
Membership Directory; on-line
SPAN Connection; monthly

Membership List Available to Non-members

Smart Card Alliance *(2001)*
191 Clarksville Rd.
Princeton, NJ 08550
Tel: (609) 799-6000 *Fax:* (609) 799-7032
TollFree: (800) 556-6828
E-Mail: info@smartcardalliance.org
Website: smartcardalliance.org
Members: 170 companies
Staff: 6
Annual Budget: $1-2,000,000

Personnel:
Executive Director: Randy Vanderhoof
   E-Mail: rvanderhoof@smartcardalliance.org
Contact, Administrative and Membership Services: Nicole
   Lauzon
   E-Mail: nlauzon@cmasolutions.com
Manager, Communications and Operations: Debbie
   Marshall
   E-Mail: dmarshall@smartcardalliance.org
*Senior Programs Director, Technology and Industry
   Councils:* Cathy Medich
   E-Mail: cmedich@smartcardalliance.org

Historical Note:
*Formerly known as Smart Card Industry Association;
absorbed Smart Card Forum. SCA's mission is to influence
standards that are relevant to smart card adoption and
implementation and maintain a voice in public policy that
affects smart card adoption and implementation. It also
serve as an educational resource to its members and the
industry. Membership: $12,000 (Leadership Council);
$5,000 (General); $1,750 (Government/University);
$1,200 (Associate).*

Continuing Education:
Certification Designation/s: CSCIP, LEAP
Meetings/Conferences: Annual
Conference Chair: William Rutledge

Publications:
Membership Directory; on-line
Smart Card Industry Daily News; daily
Smart Card Products and Services Directory; on-line
Smart Card Talk; monthly; adv.

Membership List Available to Non-members

SMMA - The Motor and Motion Association
(1975)
P.O. Box P182
S. Dartmouth, MA 02748
Tel: (508) 979-5935 *Fax:* (508) 979-5845
E-Mail: info@smma.org
Website: smma.org
Members: 140 companies
Staff: 2
Annual Budget: $100-250,000

Personnel:
Executive Director: Elizabeth B. Chambers
   E-Mail: betsy.chambers@smma.org%20
Director, Operations: William H. Chambers

   E-Mail: bill.chambers@smma.org

Historical Note:
*Founded as Small Motor Manufacturers Association;
became Small Motors and Motion Association in 1993,
and assumed its current name in 2001. SMMA's mission is
to provide a structure, through management and technical
knowledge, skills and resources of the member companies.
Members are users, suppliers, and manufacturers of
fractional and sub-fractional horsepower motors and
controls; membership also includes consulting firms in the
industry. Membership: $1095 (Regular); $595 (Affiliate).*

Meetings/Conferences:
Conference Chair: William H. Chambers
2013 - Orlando, FL (Villas of Grand Cypress Orlando
   Hotel)/May 7 - 9
2013 - Tampa, FL (Marriott Tampa Airport Hotel)/Nov.
   5 - 7

Publications:
Member Company Product Index; on-line
Membership Directory; on-line

Smocking Arts Guild of America *(1979)*
Ten Marsh Hawk
Amelia Island, FL 32034
Tel: (817) 350-4883 *Fax:* (817) 886-0393
E-Mail: director@smocking.org
Website: smocking.org
Members: 3000 individuals
Staff: 3
Annual Budget: $100-250,000
Tax: 501(c)(3)

Personnel:
President: Liz Perch
   E-Mail: president@smoking.org
President Elect, Education: Susanne Brisach
   E-Mail: Presidentelect@smoking.org

Historical Note:
*SAGA's purpose is to preserve and foster the art of
smocking and related needlework for future generations
through education, communication and quality
workmanship. Membership: $65-70 (Sustaining); $35-40
(Standard); $17.50 (Junior Student); $20 (College Student);
$1,000 (Lifetime).*

Meetings/Conferences: Annual
2013 - Frisco, TX (Embassy Suites Hotel and
   Conference Center)/Oct. 23 - 27

Publications:
SAGANews; quarterly

Snack Food Association *(1937)*
1600 Wilson Blvd.
Suite 650
Arlington, VA 22209
Tel: (703) 836-4500 *Fax:* (703) 836-8262
TollFree: (800) 628-1334
E-Mail: sfa@sfa.org
Website: sfa.org
Members: 400 companies
Staff: 6
Annual Budget: $2-5,000,000
Tax: 501(c)(6)

Personnel:
President and Chief Executive Officer: James A. McCarthy
   E-Mail: jmccarthy@sfa.org
Vice President, Operations and Membership Services:
   Chris Clark
   E-Mail: cclark@sfa.org
Contact, Communications: Allie Mamone
   E-Mail: amamone@sfa.org
Director, Meetings: Elizabeth Wells
   E-Mail: lwells@sfa.org

Historical Note:
*SFA's mission is to offer services and relationships that
strengthen the performance of member companies and
support industry growth.*

Meetings/Conferences:
Conference Chair: Elizabeth Wells
2013 - Tampa, FL (Tampa Marriott Waterside Hotel
   and Marina)/March 16 - 19
2014 - Dallas, TX (Dallas Convention Center)/March 1
   - 4
Number of non-conference events/year: 6

Publications:
Membership Directory; on-line
Snack World Magazine

Snow & Ice Management Association *(1996)*

7670 N. Port Washington Rd.
Suite 105
Milwaukee, WI 53217
Tel: (414) 375-1940 *Fax:* (414) 375-1945
E-Mail: info@sima.org
Website: sima.org
Staff: 7
Annual Budget: $1-2,000,000

Personnel:
Executive Director: Martin B. Tirado CAE
 E-Mail: Martin@sima.org
Coordinator, Membership and Meetings: Heather Carew
 E-Mail: Heather@sima.org
Director , Education and Outreach: Phill Sexton
 E-Mail: Phill@sima.org

Historical Note:
SIMA's mission is to ensure professionalism and safer communities by helping those who manage snow and ice master essential skills and practices. Membership: $180-450 (General Member); $320-450 (Associate); $265 (Affiliate).

Continuing Education:
Certification Designation/s: CSP

Meetings/Conferences: Annual
Conference Chair: Heather Carew
2013 - Minneapolis, MN (Hyatt Regency Minneapolis)/
 June 19 - 22
Number of non-conference events/year: 3

Publications:
Membership Directory; on-line
SIMA e-newsletter; monthly
Snow Business

Membership List Available to Non-members

Snow Control Equipment Manufacturers Committee (*1979*)
37400 Hills Tech Dr.
Farmington Hills, MI 48331-3414
E-Mail: scemcinfo@ntea.com
Website: ntea.com/vango/core/committees.aspx?
 committee =
Staff: 1

Personnel:
Director, Communications: Terrie Skully

Historical Note:
SCEMC is an Affiliate division of NTEA. SCEMC's mission is to promote the manufacture and use of safe and efficient snow control equipment.

SnowSports Industries America (*1954*)
8377-B Greensboro Dr.
McLean, VA 22102-3587
Tel: (703) 556-9020 *Fax:* (703) 821-8276
E-Mail: siamail@snowsports.org
Website: snowsports.org
Members: 650 companies
Staff: 20
Annual Budget: $5-10,000,000

Personnel:
President: David J. Ingemie
 E-Mail: dingemie@snowsports.org
Associate Director, Meetings, Events and Education:
 Maggie Bittner
 E-Mail: mbittner@snowsports.org
Manager, Communications and Public Relations: Anovia
 Daniels
 E-Mail: adaniels@snowsports.org
Director, Research: Kelly Davis
 E-Mail: kdavis@snowsports.org
Manager, Print Production: Sherry Gilbert
 E-Mail: sgilbert@snowsports.org
Manager, Information Technology: Bryan Ginn
 E-Mail: bginn@snowsports.org
Associate Director, Marketing and Communications: Mary
 Cecile Neville
 E-Mail: mcneville@snowsports.org
Director, Finance and Operations: Bob Orbacz
 E-Mail: rorbacz@snowsports.org
Director, Sales and Membership Services: Chris Semon
 E-Mail: chris@snowsports.org

Historical Note:
Formerly (1997) Ski Industries of America. Merged with the National Ski Areas Association in 1989 to form the United Ski Industries Association. In 1992 SIA again became an independent trade association upon the dissolution of USIA. Purpose is to promote awareness and participation in snow sports, which will result in increased sales of member's

products. Membership: $1200 (Exhibiting Supporting Member/Standard Member); $500 (Non- Exhibiting Supporting Member); $75 (Sales Representative); $199 (Supporting Retail Member).

Meetings/Conferences: Annual
Conference Chair: Maggie Bittner
2013 - Denver, CO (Colorado Convention Center)/Jan.
 31 - Feb. 3

Publications:
SIA Directory; on-line
SIA Retailer Newsletter; monthly; adv.

Soaring Society of America (*1932*)
P.O. Box 2100
Hobbs, NM 88241-2100
Tel: (575) 392-1177 *Fax:* (575) 392-8154
Website: ssa.org
Members: 16000 individuals
Staff: 8
Annual Budget: $1-2,000,000
Tax: 501(c)(3)

Personnel:
Chief Financial and Administrative Officer: Alan Gleason
Chief Administrative Officer: Denise Layton
 E-Mail: dlayton@ssa.org

Historical Note:
SSA promotes all phases of soaring and gliding for its members. Membership: $64 (Full); $36 (Family/Youth); $1,600 (Life); $200 (Business); $52 (Subscriber).

Publications:
E-Newsletter; on-line
Sailplane Directory; on-line
SOARING Magazine; monthly; adv.

Membership List Available to Non-members

SOCAP International (*1973*)
675 N. Washington St.
Suite 304
Alexandria, VA 22314-1939
Tel: (703) 519-3700 *Fax:* (703) 549-4886
E-Mail: socap@socap.org
Website: socap.org
Members: 3000 individuals
Staff: 7
Annual Budget: $2-5,000,000

Personnel:
President and Chief Executive Officer: Matthew R. D'Uva
 CAE
 E-Mail: matthew@socap.org
Vice President, Education and Communications: Marjorie
 Bynum
 E-Mail: marjorie@socap.org
Director, Membership and Chapter Relations: Ike Casey
 E-Mail: ike@socap.org
Manager, Marketing and Communications: Brian Cheung
 E-Mail: brian@socap.org
Manager, Exhibits, Sponsorship and Advertising: Ken
 Silverstein
 E-Mail: ken@socap.org

Historical Note:
Formerly (2002) known as Society of Consumer Affairs Professionals in Business. SCAP's mission is to develop experts who add business value through customer engagement. Members are vice presidents, directors, managers and supervisors of customer care and consumer affairs. Membership: $395 (Regular); $175 (Associate); $1,495-2,995 (Corporate); $50(Student).

Meetings/Conferences: Annual
Conference Chair: Ken Silverstein
Number of non-conference events/year: 2

Publications:
Customer Relationship Management Magazine (CRM);
 on-line; adv.
e-Newsletter; on-line
Membership Directory; on-line
SOCAP journal; on-line

Soccer Industry Council of America (*1985*)
1150 17th St. NW
Suite 850
Washington, DC 20036
Tel: (301) 495-6321 *Fax:* (301) 495-6322
E-Mail: info@sgma.com
Website: sgma.org
Members: 110 companies and 120 individuals
Staff: 8
Annual Budget: $100-250,000

Personnel:
President and Chief Executive Officer: Tom Cove
 E-Mail: tcove@sgma.com
Chief Financial Officer: Chip Baldwin
 E-Mail: cbaldwin@sgma.com
Director, Communications: Mike May
 E-Mail: mmay@sgma.com
Business Operations Manager: Vincent Mayor
 E-Mail: vmayor@sgma.com
Manager, Membership Services: Jonathan Michaels
 E-Mail: jmichaels@sgma.com
Research Director: Neil Schwartz
 E-Mail:
 neil.schwartz@sportsmarketingsurveysusa.com
Vice President, Government Relations: Bill Sells
 E-Mail: bsells@sgma.com
Marketing Manager: Lauren Wallace
 E-Mail: lwallace@sgma.com

Historical Note:
SICA members are soccer goods manufacturers, distributors, representatives, sales agents, retailers and other soccer related businesses. SICA is a committee of the Sporting Goods Manufacturers Association, which provides administrative support. Membership: $550- 5, 000/year (full member); $100/year (contributing); $700-$35, 000 (Corporate Members, based on Annual Sales Volume); $700 (Associate Members).

Meetings/Conferences:
Conference Chair: Lauren Wallace
2013 - Washington, DC (Capitol Hill)/March 12 - 13

Social Science History Association (*1976*)
Journals Department, Duke University Press
P.O. Box 90660
Durham, NC 27708-0660
Tel: (919) 687-3600 *Fax:* (919) 688-4574
TollFree: (888) 651-0122
E-Mail: erik@icpsr.umich.edu
Website: ssha.org
Members:
450 libraries
1100 individuals
Staff: 4
Annual Budget: $50-100,000

Personnel:
Executive Director: William C. Block
 E-Mail: block@cornell.edu
President: William H. Sewell Jr.
 E-Mail: wsewell@uchicago.edu
Treasurer: Philip Vandermeer
 E-Mail: p.vander.meer@asu.edu
Coordinator, Conferences: Judy Warner
 E-Mail: juewarne@indiana.edu

Historical Note:
SSHA strives to improve the quality of historical explanation in every manner possible, but particularly by encouraging the selective use and adaptation in historical teaching and research of relevant theories and methods from related disciplines, particularly the social sciences. Members are historians and social scientists with an interest in interdisciplinary applications. Membership: $70 (Individual); $25 (Student).

Meetings/Conferences:
Conference Chair: Judy Warner
2013 - Chicago, IL (Palmer House a Hilton Hotel)/Nov.
 21 - 24
2014 - Toronto, ON (Fairmont Royal York)/Nov. 6 - 9
2015 - Baltimore, MD (Hyatt Regency Baltimore)/Nov.
 12 - 15
2016 - Chicago, IL (Palmer House a Hilton Hotel)/Nov.
 17 - 20
2019 - Chicago, IL (Palmer House a Hilton Hotel)/Nov.
 21 - 24

Publications:
Social Science History Journal; quarterly; adv.
SSHA Newsletter

Social Venture Network
P.O. Box 29221
San Francisco, CA 94129-0221
Tel: (415) 561-6501 *Fax:* (415) 561-6435
E-Mail: svn@svn.org
Website: svn.org
Members: 500 CEOs, founders, nonprofit leaders,
investors, and senior executives
Staff: 9
Annual Budget: Under $10,000

Personnel:

Executive Director: Deb Nelson
    E-Mail: debn@svn.org
Senior Manager, Events: Tina Beck
    E-Mail: tinab@svn.org
Director, Finance and Administration: Nathan Joblin
    E-Mail: nathanj@svn.org
Associate, Administrative Services and Systems: Casey
    Lauderdale
    E-Mail: caseyl@svn.org
Director, Recruitment and Marketing: Erin Roach
    E-Mail: erinr@svn.org

Historical Note:
*Social Venture Network connects, supports and
inspires business leaders and social entrepreneurs in
expanding practices that build a just and sustainable
economy.Membership $1,100 (individual); $2,750
(supporting); $5,500 (impact); $11,000 (mission); $27,500
(leadership); $100,000 and Up (lifetime).*

Meetings/Conferences:
Conference Chair: Tina Beck

Publications:
Membership Directory; annually
Networker; monthly

Society for a Science of Clinical Psychology
(1966)
P. O. Box 1082
Niwot, CO 80544
Website: sites.google.com/site/sscpwebsite/
Staff: 3

Personnel:
President: Richard Heimberg
    E-Mail: heimberg@temple.edu
Webmaster: Frank Farach
    E-Mail: sscp.webmaster@gmail.com
Secretary and Treasurer: David A. Smith
    E-Mail: dsmith11@nd.edu

Historical Note:
*SSCP's purpose is to affirm and continue to promote
the integration of the scientist and the practitioner in
training, research, and applied endeavors. Membership:
$40 (Divisional/Member at Large); $10 (Student); $7.50
(Doctoral Program); $12 (Retirees over the age of 60)*

Society for Academic Emergency Medicine *(1970)*
2340 S. River Rd.
Suite 208
Des Plaines, IL 60018
Tel: (847) 813-9823 *Fax:* (847) 813-5450
E-Mail: saem@saem.org
Website: saem.org
Members: 6000 individuals
Staff: 11
Annual Budget: $2-5,000,000
Tax: 501(c)(3)

Personnel:
Executive Director: Ron Moen
    E-Mail: rmoen@saem.org
Manager, Marketing and Membership Services: Holly
    Gouin MBA
    E-Mail: hgouin@saem.org
Coordinator, Meetings: Maryanne Greketis CMP
    E-Mail: mgreketis@saem.org
Help Desk Specialist: Neal Hardin
    E-Mail: nhardin@saem.org
Accountant: Mai Luu
    E-Mail: mluu@saem.org
Manager, Education: Kirsten Nadler
    E-Mail: knadler@saem.org

Historical Note:
*Formerly (1977) the University Association for Emergency
Medicine, merged with the Society of Teachers of Emergency
Medicine in 1988. SAEM's mission is advancement of
emergency care through education and research, advocacy
and professional development in academic emergency
medicine. Membership is open to physicians, nurses, allied
health professionals and those interested in academic
emergency medicine. Membership: $560 (Active); $250
(Associate); $335 (Young Physician); $165 (Resident/
Fellow); $140 (Medical Student/Resident Groups); $495
(Faculty Group); $120 (Emeritus); $100 (Academy).*

Meetings/Conferences: Annual
Conference Chair: Maryanne Greketis CMP
2013 - Atlanta, GA/May 15 - 18
2014 - Dallas, TX/May 14 - 17
2015 - San Diego, CA/May 13 - 16

Publications:
Academic Emergency Medicine journal; monthly; adv.

Membership Directory; on-line
Resident eNews; bi-monthly
The SAEM eNewsletter; bi-monthly
Membership List Available to Non-members

The Society for Adolescent Medicine *(1968)*
111 Deer Lake Rd.
Suite 100
Deerfield, IL 60015
Tel: (847) 753-5226 *Fax:* (847) 480-9282
E-Mail: sahm@adolescenthealth.org
Website: adolescenthealth.org
Members: 1300 individuals
Staff: 7
Annual Budget: $1-2,000,000

Personnel:
Executive Director: Susan L. Tibbitts
Manager, Marketing and Communications: Kasia Chalko
Accountant: William Chandler
Meeting Manager: Lyn Maddox
Administrative Director: Ryan Norton
Education Manager: Kismet Saglam

Historical Note:
*SAHM is the international organization dedicated to
advancing the health and well-being of adolescents.
Members are health professionals throughout the world
who are involved in service, teaching, or research concerned
with the health and well-being of adolescents including
physicians, nurses, social workers, and psychologists.
Membership: $320 (Doctorate Level); $255 (Non-
Doctorate Level); $190 (International); $155 (Students
with Post-Advanced Degrees and Fellows-in-Training); $95
(Graduate Students); $75 (Pre-baccalaureate students).*

Meetings/Conferences: Annual
Conference Chair: Lyn Maddox
2013 - Atlanta, GA (Omni Hotel at CNN Center)/March
    13 - 16
2014 - Austin, TX/March 23 - 26

Publications:
Journal of Adolescent Health; monthly
SAHM Newsletter; quarterly

Membership List Available to Non-members

Society for Advancement of Consulting *(2004)*
P.O. Box 746
E. Greenwich, RI 02818
Tel: (401) 886-4097 *Fax:* (401) 884-5068
TollFree: (800) 825-6153
E-Mail: info@consultingsociety.com
Website: consultingsociety.com
Members: 300 individuals
Staff: 1

Personnel:
Chief Executive Officer: Alan Weiss
    E-Mail: alan@consultingsociety.com

Historical Note:
*SAC's mission is to improve the business of solo
practitioners and small firms in the consulting and related
professional services fields and to accomplish this through
branding of organization, publicity for the profession,
in-service training for practitioners, leading-edge and
innovative practices, an active community of colleagues,
and similar methods recommended by membership.
Membership: $400 (Affiliate); $300 (Full Membership).*

Publications:
Membership Directory; on-line
Weiss Advice; monthly

Society for Advancement of Management *(1912)*
6300 Ocean Dr.
OCNR 330, Unit 5807
Corpus Christi, TX 78412-5807
Tel: (361) 825-6045 *Fax:* (361) 825-2725
TollFree: (888) 827-6077
E-Mail: sam@samnational.org
Website: samnational.org
Members: 5000 individuals
Staff: 2
Annual Budget: $100-250,000
Tax: 501(c)(3)

Personnel:
President and Chief Executive Officer: Moustafa H.
    Abdelsamad
    E-Mail: moustafa.abdelsamad@tamucc.edu
Treasurer: Kent Byus

Historical Note:

---

*SAM's mission is to provide an opportunity for the members
to increase management skills and expertise through
participation in programs and services designed to improve
the professional quality of their knowledge, performance,
and leadership ability. Membership: $80 (Individual); $45
(Retired); $55 (Academic, International); $65 (Academic,
US); $30 (Student, US); $40 (Associate/Graduate Student,
US); $50 (Associate/Graduate Student, International).*

Meetings/Conferences: Annual
2013 - Arlington, VA (Key Bridge Marriott)/March 21 -
24

Publications:
Management In Practice (MIP); quarterly
SAM Advanced Management Journal (AMJ); quarterly
SAM International News; on-line

Membership List Available to Non-members

Society for American Archaeology *(1934)*
1111 14th St. NW
Suite 800
Washington, DC 20005-5622
Tel: (202) 789-8200 *Fax:* (202) 789-0284
E-Mail: headquarters@saa.org
Website: saa.org
Members: 7000 members
Staff: 8
Annual Budget: $1-2,000,000
Tax: 501(c)(3)

Personnel:
Executive Director: Tobi Brimsek
    E-Mail: tobi_brimsek@saa.org
Coordinator, Administrative and Financial Services:
    Shelley Adams
    E-Mail: shelley_adams@saa.org
Manager, Government Affairs: David Lindsay
    E-Mail: david_lindsay@saa.org
Manager, Public Education: Maureen Malloy
    E-Mail: maureen_malloy@saa.org
Manager, Publications: John Neikirk
    E-Mail: john_neikirk@saa.org
Manager, Membership Services and Marketing: Meghan
    Tyler
    E-Mail: meghan_tyler@saa.org
Manager, Information Services: Cheng Zhang
    E-Mail: cheng_zhang@saa.org

Historical Note:
*SAA is an international organization dedicated to the
research, interpretation and protection of the archaeological
heritage of the Americas. Members include student,
avocational and professional archaeologists working
in a variety of settings including government agencies,
colleges and universities, museums and the private sector.
Membership: $135 (Regular); $70 (Student); $82 (Retired);
$59 (Associate); $48 (Joint); $26,000 (Life).*

Meetings/Conferences: Annual
2013 - Honolulu, HI/April 3 - 7
2014 - Austin, TX/April 23 - 27
2015 - San Francisco, CA/April 15 - 19
2016 - Orlando, FL/April 6 - 10

Publications:
American Antiquity; quarterly; adv.
Latin American Antiquity; quarterly; adv.
The Saa Archaeological Record; adv.

Membership List Available to Non-members

Society for American Baseball Research *(1971)*
4455 E. Camelback Rd.
Suite D-140
Phoenix, AZ 85018
Tel: (602) 343-6455 *Fax:* (602) 595-5690
TollFree: (800) 969-7227
E-Mail: info@sabr.org
Website: sabr.org
Members: 6700 individuals
Staff: 9
Annual Budget: $500-1,000,000
Tax: 501(c)(3)

Personnel:
Executive Director: Marc Appleman
    E-Mail: mappleman@sabr.org
Director, Publications: Nicholas Frankovich
    E-Mail: frankovich@sabr.org
Contractor, System Administration and Web Development:
    Peter Garver
    E-Mail: pgarver@sabr.org
Director, Membership Services and Events: Deborah Jayne
    E-Mail: djayne@sabr.org

Web Content Editor and Producer: Jacob Pomrenke
    E-Mail: jpomrenke@sabr.org
Director, Operations: Jeff Schatzki
    E-Mail: jschatzki@sabr.org
Contact, Publications: Cecilia Tan
    E-Mail: ctan@sabr.org

Historical Note:
SABR strives to encourage research and literary efforts to establish and maintain the accurate historical record of baseball. Membership: $45-75/year.

Meetings/Conferences:
Conference Chair: Deborah Jayne
2013 - Phoenix, AZ (Hilton Phoenix East/Mesa)/March 7 - 9
Number of non-conference events/year: 2

Publications:
Baseball Research Journal
The National Pastime
The Sporting News

Membership List Available to Non-members

Society for Ancient Greek Philosophy *(1953)*
C/O Binghamton University
Binghamton, NY 13902-6000
Tel: (607) 777-2886 *Fax:* (607) 777-6255
E-Mail: apreus@binghamton.edu
Website: societyforancientgreekphilosophy.com
Members: 500 individuals
Staff: 3
Annual Budget: Under $10,000

Personnel:
President: Deborah Modrak
Secretary, Membership and Meetings Contact: Anthony Preus
    E-Mail: apreus@binghamton.edu
Webmaster: Chris Tennberg
    E-Mail:
    webmaster@societyofchristianphilosophers.com

Historical Note:
SAGP exists primarily to give those who are working in ancient philosophy an opportunity to exchange their views in a variety of venues. Members are academics and others with an interest in classical philosophy. Membership: $10 (Individual, for electronic receipt of the papers); $20 (Individual, for hard copy receipt of papers).

Meetings/Conferences: Annual
Conference Chair: Anthony Preus

Publications:
Membership Directory; on-line
SAGP Newsletter; on-line

Society for Anthropology in Community Colleges *(1978)*
Department of Anthropology, Miramar College
10440 Black Mountain Rd.
San Diego, CA 92126
Tel: (619) 388-7534
Website: aaanet.org/sections/sacc
Staff: 3

Personnel:
President: Laura Gonzalez
    E-Mail: Lagonzal@sdccd.edu
Vice President, Membership and Development: Tad McIlwaith
    E-Mail: mcilwraitht@douglascollege.ca

Historical Note:
SACC's purpose is to encourage dialogue and collaboration among teachers of anthropology across sub-disciplines and institutional settings, and to promote excellence in the teaching of anthropology. Members are people who teach anthropology in community colleges, two-year and four-year colleges, universities and pre-collegiate institutions. SACC is a section of the American Anthropological Association (AAA).

Meetings/Conferences: Annual
2013 - Austin, TX/April 10 - 13

Publications:
SACC Notes; semi-annually

Membership List Available to Non-members

Society for Applied Anthropology *(1941)*
P.O. Box 2436
Oklahoma City, OK 73101-2436
Tel: (405) 843-5113 *Fax:* (405) 843-8553
E-Mail: info@sfaa.net
Website: sfaa.net

Members: 2500 individuals
Staff: 3
Annual Budget: $250-500,000
Tax: 501(c)(3)

Personnel:
Executive Director: J. Thomas May
    E-Mail: tom@sfaa.net
Editor: James (Tim) Wallace
    E-Mail: tmwallace237@gmail.com

Historical Note:
SfAA advocates the interdisciplinary scientific study of the principles controlling the relations of human beings to one another, and the wide application of those principles to practical problems. Membership: $110 (Sustaining Fellow); $90 (Fellow); $70 (Regular); $40 (Student/Joint Member); $45 (Emeritus Fellow); $40 (Emeritus Member); $100 (Joint Sustaining Fellow); $60 (Joint Fellow); $40 (Joint Member).

Meetings/Conferences: Annual
2013 - Denver, CO (Denver Marriott City Center Hotel)/March 19 - 23

Publications:
Human Organization; quarterly; adv.
Human Rights: The Scholar as Activist
Practicing Anthropology; quarterly; adv.
SfAA Newsletter; quarterly; adv.

Membership List Available to Non-members

Society for Applied Learning Technology *(1972)*
50 Culpeper St.
Warrenton, VA 20186
Tel: (540) 347-0055 *Fax:* (540) 349-3169
Website: salt.org
Members: 300 individuals
Staff: 5
Annual Budget: $5-10,000,000
Tax: 501(c)(3)

Personnel:
Executive Director and Editor: John G. Fox

Historical Note:
The Society works to enhance the knowledge and job performance of an individual by participating in society sponsored meetings and through receiving society sponsored publications. Members include industrial, military and academic managers involved in the design production or use of technology-based educational systems. Membership: $100/year.

Meetings/Conferences:
2013 - Orlando, FL (Caribe Royale Hotel)/March 6 - 8

Publications:
Membership Directory; on-line
SALT Newsletter; weekly
The Journal of Educational Technology Systems; quarterly
The Journal of Instruction Delivery Systems; quarterly
The Journal of Interactive Instruction Development; quarterly

Membership List Available to Non-members

Society for Applied Spectroscopy *(1958)*
5320 Spectrum Dr.
Suite C
Frederick, MD 21703
Tel: (301) 694-8122 *Fax:* (301) 694-6860
E-Mail: office@s-a-s.org
Website: s-a-s.org
Members: 3000 individuals
Staff: 5
Annual Budget: $500-1,000,000
Tax: 501(c)(3)

Personnel:
Executive Director: Bonnie Saylor
    E-Mail: exdir@s-a-s.org
Managing Editor: Rebecca Airmet
Administrative Affairs Associate: Victor Hutcherson
Office Manager: Stephanie Iocco
Membership Coordinator: Gloria M. Story
    E-Mail: story.gm@pg.com

Historical Note:
The Federation of Spectroscopic Societies was founded in Pittsburgh in March 1956. From this grew the Society for Applied Spectroscopy, incorporated in Pennsylvania in 1960. SAS is a nonprofit organization formed to advance and disseminate knowledge and information concerning the art and science of spectroscopy and other allied sciences. Membership: $15-75/year.

Meetings/Conferences: Annual
2013 - Milwaukee, WI/Sept. 29 - Oct. 4

Publications:
Applied Spectroscopy; monthly; adv.
Membership Directory; on-line
SAS Spectrum - Newsletter; monthly

Membership List Available to Non-members

Society for Archaeological Sciences *(1977)*
Department of Earth and Environment
Franklin & Marshall College
Lancaster, PA 17604-3003
Tel: (717) 291-4134 *Fax:* (717) 291-4186
Website: socarchsci.org
Members: 600 individuals
Staff: 10
Annual Budget: $10-25,000

Personnel:
President: Patrick Degryse
    E-Mail: Patrick.Degryse@ees.kuleuven.be
Vice President, Membership Services: Michael Gregg
    E-Mail: greggmic@sas.upenn.edu
General Secretary: Rob Sternberg
    E-Mail: rob.sternberg@fandm.edu

Historical Note:
SAS aims to provide communication between scholars applying methods from the physical sciences to archaeological questions. Members are archaeological scientists working in business, academic, and government settings. Membership: $20 (Regular); $15 (Students/Retired); $35 (Institutional); $300 (Lifetime).

Meetings/Conferences:
Number of non-conference events/year: 1

Publications:
Archaeological and Anthropological Sciences
Archaeometry
Journal of Archaeological Science; bi-monthly
Membership Directory; on-line
The Society for Archaeological Sciences Bulletin; quarterly

Society for Asian and Comparative Philosophy *(1967)*
Dept. of History, Kingsborough/CUNY
2001 Oriental Blvd.
Brooklyn, NY 11235
E-Mail: Michael.Barnhart@kbcc.cuny.edu
Website: sacpweb.org
Members: 200 individuals
Staff: 3
Annual Budget: Under $10,000
Tax: 501(c)(3)

Personnel:
President: Roger Ames
    E-Mail: rtames@hawaii.edu.edu
Treasurer: Michael Barnhart
    E-Mail: Michael.Barnhart@kbcc.cuny.edu

Historical Note:
SACP is aimed at advancing the development of the disciplines of Asian and comparative philosophy in the international academic arena, and bringing together Asian and Western philosophers. SACP members are academics and others with an interest in Asian philosophic systems. Membership: $20 (Student/Emeritus); $35 (Regular).

Meetings/Conferences: Annual

Publications:
Forum Newsletter; semi-annually
Membership Directory; on-line
Philosophy East and West; quarterly

Society for Asian Music *(1959)*
P.O. Box 7819
University of Texas, Journal Division
Austin, TX 78713-7819
Tel: (512) 232-7621 *Fax:* (512) 232-7178
Website: asianmusic.skidmore.edu
Members: 500 individuals
Staff: 3
Annual Budget: Under $10,000

Personnel:
President: Frederick Lau
    E-Mail: fredlau@hawaii.edu
Managing Editor: Ricardo Trimillos
    E-Mail: rtrimil@hawaii.edu
Treasurer: Andrew Weintraub
    E-Mail: anwein@pitt.edu

Historical Note:
SAM members are academics and others with an interest in the music of the middle and far east. Has no paid officers

or full-time staff. *Membership:* $35 (Individual); $25 (Student); $65 (Institutional); $650 (Life time).

Publications:
Journal of the Society for Asian Music; semi-annually

Society for Assisted Reproductive Technology (1985)
1209 Montgomery Hwy.
Birmingham, AL 35216-2809
Tel: (205) 978-5000 *Fax:* (205) 978-5018
Website: sart.org
Members: 375 individuals and member practices
Staff: 2
Annual Budget: $1-2,000,000

Personnel:
Administrator and Coordinator, Member Services: Kelley Jefferson
    E-Mail: kjefferson@asrm.org

Historical Note:
SART's mission is to promote and advance the standards for the practice of assisted reproductive technology to the benefit of their patients, members, and society at large. Members are practice facilities offering assisted reproductive procedures and all members of the ART team. Administrative support provided by the American Society of Reproductive Medicine. Membership: $25 (Individual); $800 (Organization).

Publications:
Fertility and Sterility; irregular; adv.
Menopausal Medicine; on-line
Sexuality, Reproduction, and Menopause (SRM); on-line
The Journal of Assisted Reproduction and Genetics; on-line

Society for Biomaterials (1974)
15000 Commerce Pkwy.
Suite C
Mt. Laurel, NJ 08054
Tel: (856) 439-0826 *Fax:* (856) 439-0525
E-Mail: info@biomaterials.org
Website: biomaterials.org
Members: 1000 individuals
Staff: 8
Annual Budget: $1-2,000,000
Tax: 501(c)(3)

Personnel:
Executive Director: Daniel "Dan" Lemyre
    E-Mail: dlemyre@ahint.com
Senior Manager, Meeting: Anthony Celenza CMP
    E-Mail: acelenza@ahint.com
Director, Membership Services: Rebecca "Becky" Riedesel
    E-Mail: rriedesel@ahint.com

Historical Note:
SFB serves to promote research, development, and education in the biomaterial sciences. Seeks to cooperate with scientific organizations, private industry, government agencies and other interested parties, to establish the standards and terms for biomaterials. Membership: $195-433 (Active/Associate); $100-335 (Associate Post Graduate); $60-318 (Student Associate).

Meetings/Conferences: Annual
Conference Chair: Anthony Celenza CMP
2013 - Boston, MA (John B. Hynes Veterans Memorial Convention Center)/April 10 - 13
Number of non-conference events/year: 2

Publications:
Applied Biomaterials; adv.
Biomaterials Forum; quarterly; adv.
Journal of Biomedical Materials Research; adv.

Society for Buddhist-Christian Studies
1720 S. Michigan Ave.
Suite 3303
Chicago, IL 60616-4865
Website: society-buddhist-christian-studies.org
Members: 450 individuals
Staff: 3

Personnel:
Contact, Membership Services: Guy McCloskey

Historical Note:
SBCS's mission is to serve as a coordinating body supporting activities related to the comparative study of, and the practical interaction between, Buddhism and Christianity, whether by groups or individuals. SBCS members of the society provide an ongoing format and organization for those committed to study and practice

of Buddhism and Christianity. A program of Council of Societies for the Study of Religion, which provides administrative support. *Membership:* $45 (Regular); $25 (Senior); $10 (Student).

Publications:
News of the Society; semi-annually

Society for Business Ethics (1980)
C/O University of New Brunswick
P.O. Box 4400
Fredericton, NB E3B 5A3
Website: societyforbusinessethics.org
Members: 600 individuals
Staff: 2
Annual Budget: $50-100,000

Personnel:
Executive Director: Jeff Frooman
    E-Mail: frooman@unb.ca
Website Administrator: Brent Brewer
    E-Mail: brentbrewer@essentialstudios.ca

Historical Note:
SBE's mission is to promote the study of business ethics and provide a forum in which moral, legal, empirical, and philosophical issues of business ethics may be openly discussed and analyzed. Members are academics and practitioners (such as ethics and compliance officers) and other interested in the field. Membership: $75-100 (Individual, depending on Income); $40 (Students/Retirees).

Meetings/Conferences: Annual

Publications:
Business Ethics Quarterly; quarterly
Membership Directory

Membership List Available to Non-members

Society for Cardiovascular Angiography and Interventions (1976)
2400 N St. NW
Suite 604
Washington, DC 20037-1153
Tel: (202) 741-9854 *Fax:* (800) 863-5202
TollFree: (800) 992-7224
E-Mail: info@scai.org
Website: scai.org
Members: 4,000 adult and congenital interventional cardiologists
Staff: 20
Annual Budget: $5-10,000,000

Personnel:
Executive Director: Norm Linsky
    E-Mail: nlinsky@scai.org
Senior Director, Education, Meetings and Communications: Kerry Curtis
    E-Mail: kcurtis@scai.org
Director, Public Relations: Kathy Boyd David
    E-Mail: kbdavid@scai.org

Historical Note:
SCAI's mission is to promote excellence in invasive and interventional cardiovascular medicine through physician education and representation, and the advancement of quality standards to enhance patient care. Membership: $525 (Fellows-in-Training, Fellow); $335 (International Fellow); $100 (International Associate Member).

Continuing Education:
Enrollment: 2000
Certification Designation/s: CME

Meetings/Conferences: Annual
2013 - Orlando, FL (Convention Center/The Peabody Orlando)/May 8 - 11
2014 - Las Vegas, NV (Caesar's Palace)/May 7 - 10
2015 - San Diego, CA (Hilton Bayfront Hotel)/May 6 - 9
2016 - Orlando, FL (Convention Center/The Peabody Orlando)/May 4 - 7
Number of non-conference events/year: 1

Publications:
Catheterization and Cardiovascular Interventions Journal; monthly; adv.
SCAI Newsletter; bi-monthly
SCAI This Week E-brief; weekly

Membership List Available to Non-members

Society for Cardiovascular Magnetic Resonance (1994)
19 Mantua Rd.
Mt. Royal, NJ 08061
Tel: (856) 423-8955 *Fax:* (856) 423-3420
E-Mail: hq@scmr.org

Website: scmr.org
Members: 1300 individuals
Staff: 4
Annual Budget: $500-1,000,000

Personnel:
President: Andrew Arai
    E-Mail: a.arai@scmr.org
Executive Director: Deborah Berkowitz
    E-Mail: d.berkowitz@scmr.org
Senior Meeting Manager: Kathy Baumer
    E-Mail: kbaumer@scmr.org
Treasurer: Lon Simonetti

Historical Note:
SCMR is an organization for medical practitioners who are interested in applications of magnetic resonance in diagnosis of heart and circulatory conditions. Membership: $225 (Regular); $60 (Trainee); $60 (Technologist/Allied Health Member/Emeritus).

Meetings/Conferences: Annual
Conference Chair: Andrew Arai
2013 - San Francisco, CA (Hilton San Francisco Union Square)/Jan. 31 - Feb. 3

Publications:
Newsletter; quarterly

Society for Chaos Theory in Psychology and Life Sciences (1991)
P.O. Box 484
Pewaukee, WI 53072
Tel: (414) 288-6900 *Fax:* (414) 288-5333
E-Mail: register@societyforchaostheory.org
Website: societyforchaostheory.org
Members:
3 organizations
300 individuals
Staff: 12
Annual Budget: $25-50,000
Tax: 501(c)(3)

Personnel:
President: Dick Thompson
    E-Mail: dick@hpsys.com
Treasurer: Stephen J. Guastello
    E-Mail: stephen.guastello@marquette.edu
Secretary and Editor: Sara Nora Ross PhD
    E-Mail: saraross2@roarunner.com

Historical Note:
The Society is an international forum that brings together researchers, theoreticians, and practitioners interested in applying dynamical systems theory, self-organization, neural nets, fractals, cellular automata, agent-based modeling, and related forms of chaos, catastrophes, bifurcations, nonlinear dynamics, and complexity theories to psychology and the life sciences. Membership: $85 (Regular); $70 (Students).

Meetings/Conferences: Annual

Publications:
Nonlinear Dynamics, Psychology and Life Sciences; quarterly
SCTPLS Newsletter; quarterly; adv.

Society for Cinema and Media Studies (1959)
640 Parrington Oval
Wallace Old Science Hall, Room 300
Norman, OK 73019-3060
Tel: (405) 325-8075 *Fax:* (405) 325-7135
E-Mail: office@cmstudies.org
Website: cmstudies.org
Members: 2500 individuals
Staff: 4
Annual Budget: $500-1,000,000
Tax: 501(c)(3)

Personnel:
Administrative Coordinator: Jane Dye
    E-Mail: njdye@ou.edu
Editor: Heather Hendershot
Manager, Conferences: Leslie LeMond
    E-Mail: leslielemond@mac.com
Account and Budget Representative III: Debbie Rush

Historical Note:
Formerly (2003) know as Society for Cinema Studies. SCMS's mission is to promote a understanding of film, television, and related media through research and teaching grounded in the contemporary humanities tradition. Membership: $55-204 (Individuals); $300 (Institutional).

Meetings/Conferences: Annual
Conference Chair: Leslie LeMond
2013 - Chicago, IL (The Drake Hotel)/March 6 - 10

Publications:
Cinema Journal; quarterly; adv.
Membership Directory; on-line
SCMS eNewsletter; quarterly

Membership List Available to Non-members

Society for Clinical and Experimental Hypnosis
(1949)
P.O. Box 252
Southborough, MA 01772
Tel: (508) 598-5553 *Fax:* (866) 397-1839
E-Mail: info@sceh.us
Website: sceh.us
Members: 400 individuals
Staff: 2
Annual Budget: $100-250,000
Tax: 501(c)(3)

Personnel:
Executive Director: Michele Spilberg Hart
    E-Mail: michele@sceh.us

Historical Note:
SCEH's mission is to promote excellence and progress in hypnosis research, education, and clinical practice. Members are psychologists, psychiatrists, social workers, nurses, dentists and physicians who are in the field of scientific inquiry and the conscientious application of hypnosis in the clinical setting. Membership: $139 (Clinical/Experimental); $45 (Student).

Continuing Education:
Certification Designation/s: SCEH-ACE

Meetings/Conferences: Annual
2013 - Berkeley, CA/Oct. 2 - 6

Publications:
FOCUS-SCEH's Newsletter; quarterly
International Journal of Clinical and Experimental Hypnosis; quarterly; adv.

Society for Clinical Data Management *(1994)*
1444 St.NW.
Suite 700
Washington, DC 20005
Tel: (202) 712-9023 *Fax:* (202) 216-9646
E-Mail: info@scdm.org
Website: scdm.org
Members: 2600 Members
Staff: 7
Annual Budget: $1-2,000,000
Tax: 501(c)(6)

Personnel:
Executive Director: Pol Van de Perre
    E-Mail: PVandeperre@scdm.org
Manager, Operations: Lysan Drabon
    E-Mail: LDrabon@scdm.org
Manager, Education: Dorothy Henry
    E-Mail: DHenry@scdm.org
Contact, Publications: Kimberly Jahnke
    E-Mail: kjahnke@scdm.org
Manager, Marketing and Communications: Michel Marques
    E-Mail: MMarques@scdm.org
Manager, Meetings: Margaret Trotter
    E-Mail: mtrotter@scdm.org
Director, Marketing: Jean Wenzel
    E-Mail: jwenzel@scdm.org

Historical Note:
SCDM is committed to advocating excellence in clinical data management through professional development education and certification. Key products and programs include Good Clinical Data Management practices, CCDM certification, online learning, and annual conference. Membership: $90/ year.

Continuing Education:
Certification Designation/s: CCDM

Meetings/Conferences: Annual
Conference Chair: Margaret Trotter

Publications:
Data Basics; quarterly; adv.
Data Connections; monthly; adv.
Membership Directory; on-line

Society for Clinical Trials *(1978)*
100 N. 20th St.
Fourth Floor
Philadelphia, PA 19103
Tel: (215) 320-3878 *Fax:* (215) 564-2175
E-Mail: sct@fernley.com
Website: sctweb.org

Members: 800 individuals
Staff: 2
Annual Budget: $250-500,000

Personnel:
Executive Director: Elizabeth Franks
    E-Mail: efranks@fernley.com
Editor: Joanne Lombardi
    E-Mail: jlombardi@fernley.com

Historical Note:
SCT is an international professional organization dedicated to the development and dissemination of knowledge about the design, conduct and analysis of government and industry- sponsored clinical trials and related health care research methodologies. Membership: $170 (Full); $50 (Student).

Meetings/Conferences: Annual
2013 - Boston, MA (Sheraton Boston Hotel)/May 19 - 22
2014 - Las Vegas, NV (Caesars Palace Las Vegas Hotel and Casino)/May 18 - 21

Publications:
Clinical Trials: Journal of the Society for Clinical Trials; bi-monthly; adv.
Membership Directory; on-line
SCT Newsletter; semi-annually; adv.

Society for Clinical Vascular Surgery *(1970)*
500 Cummings Center
Suite 4550
Beverly, MA 01915
Tel: (978) 927-8330 *Fax:* (978) 524-8890
E-Mail: scvs@prri.com
Website: scvs.org
Members: 1034 individuals
Staff: 2
Annual Budget: $500-1,000,000
Tax: 501(c)(3)

Personnel:
Executive Director: Stan Alger III
    E-Mail: salger@prri.com
Coordinator, Exhibits: Jennifer Gecawicz
    E-Mail: jgecawicz@prri.com

Historical Note:
SCVS's mission is to advance the art and science of vascular surgery, to provide a forum for vascular surgeons and to improve the delivery of health care in vascular disease. Members are surgeons who are involved in the clinical practice of vascular surgery. Membership: $175/ year (Active).

Meetings/Conferences: Annual
Conference Chair: Jennifer Gecawicz
2013 - Miami Beach, FL (Fontainebleau Miami Beach)/ March 13 - 16
2014 - Carlsbad, CA (La Costa Resort and Spa)/March 17 - 22

Publications:
Journal of Vascular Surgery; monthly; adv.
Membership Directory; on-line
SCVS Newsletter; semi-annually

Society for College and University Planning
(1965)
1330 Eisenhower Pl.
Ann Arbor, MI 48108
Tel: (734) 764-2000 *Fax:* (734) 661-0157
E-Mail: info@scup.org
Website: scup.org
Members: 5000 individuals
Staff: 23
Annual Budget: $2-5,000,000
Tax: 501(c)(3)

Personnel:
Executive Director: Jolene L Knapp CAE
    E-Mail: jolene.knapp@scup.org
Director, Media Relations and Publications: Terry Calhoun JD, MA
    E-Mail: terry.calhoun@scup.org
Director, Planning and Education: Phyllis Grummon PhD
    E-Mail: phyllis.grummon@scup.org
Associate Director, Information Services and Systems Architecture: Marc Johns
    E-Mail: marc.johns@scup.org
Assistant, Regional Programs: Michelle Pierson
    E-Mail: michelle.pierson@scup.org
Financial Specialist: Anne Przykucki
    E-Mail: anne.przykucki@scup.org

Director, Member Relations and Marketing: Susan K. Rogers ABC, APR
    E-Mail: susan.rogers@scup.org
Director, Administrative Services: Karen Verhey CMP
    E-Mail: karen.verhey@scup.org

Historical Note:
SCUP is a community that provides its members with the knowledge and resources to establish and achieve institutional planning goals within the context of best practices and emerging trends. Membership: $780-1,890 (Institutional); $780-870 (Small Non-Institutional Group); $1,560-1740 (Large Non- Institutional Group); $345-375 (Individual); $75-150 (Retired); $50 (Student).

Meetings/Conferences: Annual
2013 - San Diego, CA (Hilton San Diego Bayfront)/July 27 - 31
2014 - Pittsburgh, PA/July 12 - 16
2015 - Chicago, IL/July 11 - 15
2016 - Vancouver, BC/July 9 - 13
2017 - Washington, DC/July 8 - 12
Number of non-conference events/year: 3

Publications:
Membership Directory; annually; adv.
Planning for Higher Education; quarterly
SCUP Email News; weekly

Society for Community Research and Action
(1982)
4440 PGA Blvd.
Suite 600
Palm Beach Gardens, FL 33410
Tel: (561) 623-5323
Website: scra27.org
Staff: 3
Annual Budget: $250-500,000

Personnel:
President: Jean Hill
Treasurer: Jim Emshoff
Editor: Jacob Kraemer Tebes

Historical Note:
A division of the American Psychological Association, SCRA's mission is to advance theory, research, and social action. SCRA serves many different disciplines that focus on community research and action. Membership: $75 (Individual); $30 (Student); $60 (International); $15 (Senior).

Meetings/Conferences: Biennial
2013 - Coral Gables, FL (University of Miami)/June 26 - 29

Publications:
Membership Directory; on-line
The Community Psychologist (TCP)

Membership List Available to Non-members

Society for Computers in Psychology *(1971)*
Department of Psychological and Brain Sciences, Indiana University
1101 E. Tenth St.
Bloomington, IN 47405
Tel: (812) 856-1490 *Fax:* (812) 855-4691
Website: scip.ws
Members: 70 psychologists
Staff: 2

Personnel:
Secretary and Treasurer: Rick Dale
    E-Mail: rdale@ucmerced.edu

Historical Note:
Formerly (1982) the Society for the Use of On-Line Computers in Psychology. SCIP's purpose is to "increase and diffuse knowledge of the use of computers in psychological research." Over the past several years the organization has set a special goal of aiding psychologists in using microcomputers in their teaching and research. SCiP members are psychologists and others with an interest in the application of computers in psychological research. Membership: $50/year.

Meetings/Conferences: Annual

Publications:
International Journal of Internet Science; annually

Society for Conservation Biology *(1985)*
1017 O St. NW
Washington, DC 20001-4229
Tel: (202) 234-4133 *Fax:* (703) 995-4633
E-Mail: info@conbio.org
Website: conbio.org
Members: 12000 individuals

Staff: 12
Annual Budget: $2-5,000,000
Tax: 501(c)(3)

Personnel:
Executive Director: Anne Hummer
    E-Mail: ahummer@conbio.org
Administrative Assistant: Lauren Krizel
    E-Mail: lkrizel@conbio.org
Senior Editor: Ellen Main
    E-Mail: emain@conbio.org
Coordinator, Communications and Marketing: Nathan
Spillman
    E-Mail: nspillman@conbio.org

Historical Note:
SCB's mission is to advance the science and practice of conserving the earth's biological diversity. The Society's membership comprises a wide range of people interested in the conservation and study of biological diversity: resource managers, educators, government and private conservation workers, and students. Membership: $80 (Professional); $20 (Student/Retired/All Types of membership, Developing Countries).

Meetings/Conferences: Biennial
2013 - Baltimore, MD/July 21 - 25/1600 attendees
Number of non-conference events/year: 7

Publications:
Conservation; quarterly; adv.
Conservation Biology Journal; bi-monthly; adv.
Conservation Letters; on-line
Journal Watch Online; on-line
Neotropical Conservation; bi-monthly; adv.
SCB Newsletter; quarterly; adv.

Society for Consumer Psychology
Clarkson University School of Business
P.O. Box 5795, Eight Clarkson Ave.
Potsdam, NY 13699
Fax: (315) 268-3810
E-Mail: scp@clarkson.edu
Website: myscp.org
Staff: 4
Annual Budget: $250-500,000
Tax: 501(c)(3)

Personnel:
President: Michel Tuan Pham
    E-Mail: tdp4@columbia.edu
Executive Officer: Larry D. Compeau
    E-Mail: compeau@clarkson.edu
Editor: Cornelia (Connie) Pechmann
    E-Mail: cpechman@uci.edu
Secretary and Treasurer: Tiffany Barnett White
    E-Mail: tbwhite@illinois.edu

Historical Note:
A division of the American Psychological Association. SCP aims at advancing consumer psychology as a scientific discipline through the support of intellectual contributions to consumer psychology, promotion of research in consumer psychology and the improvement of research methods and conditions. Membership: $50 (Academic/Practitioner); $25 (Retired); $30 (Student).

Meetings/Conferences:
2013 - San Antonio, TX (Omni La Mansion del Rio)/
Feb. 28 - March 2

Publications:
Journal of Consumer Psychology
The Communicator

Society for Cross-Cultural Research (1971)
Univ. of Nevada
Dept. of Anthropology
Las Vegas, NV 89154
Tel: (702) 895-3610 *Fax:* (702) 895-4823
Website: sccr.org
Members: 200 individuals
Staff: 5
Annual Budget: Under $10,000

Personnel:
President: William R. Jankowiak
    E-Mail: jankowiak@spamarrest.com
Editor: Hemalatha Ganapathy-Coleman
Webmaster: David Shwalb
    E-Mail: shwalb@suu.edu

Historical Note:
An interdisciplinary organization whose primary goal is to support and encourage comparative research which will aid in the establishment of scientifically derived generalizations about human behavior. Members come from a wide variety

of social, behavioral and scientific professions. Membership: $55-65 (Regular); $40-50 (Retired); $35-45 (Student).

Meetings/Conferences: Annual
2013 - Mobile, AL (The Battle House Renaissance
Mobile Hotel and Spa)/Feb. 20 - 23

Publications:
Cross-Cultural Research; quarterly
Culture & Psychology; quarterly
Journal of Material Culture; quarterly
Membership Directory; on-line
Newsletter; bi-annually

Membership List Available to Non-members

Society for Cryobiology (1964)
C/O Department of Molecular and Cellular
Biology
University of California
Davis, CA 95616
Tel: (530) 756-7247
Website: societyforcryobiology.org
Members: 300 individuals
Staff: 2
Annual Budget: $100-250,000

Personnel:
President: John H. Crowe
    E-Mail: jhcrowe@ucdavis.edu

Historical Note:
Founded on March 20, 1964 and incorporated in the same year in Maryland. SC strives to advocate scientific research in low temperature biology to improve scientific understanding in this field and to disseminate and apply this knowledge to the benefit of mankind. Membership: $800 (Corporate); $275 (Institution); $165 (Sustaining); $60-130 (Individual); $45 (Retired); $40 (Student).

Meetings/Conferences: Annual
2013 - Bethesda, MD (Marriott Bethesda North Hotel
and Conference Center)/July 28 - 31

Publications:
Cryobiology; bi-monthly
E-Bulletin; irregular

Society for Cultural Anthropology (1983)
College of William and Mary
Department of Anthropology
Williamsburg, VA 23187
Website: sca.culanth.org
Staff: 3

Personnel:
President: Brad Weiss
    E-Mail: blweis@wm.edu

Historical Note:
A section of the American Anthropological Association that provides administrative support. Its mission is holding small biannual meetings in untraditional locations, encouraging broad participation by keeping fees low, and spotlighting student members. Membership: $42 (Postdoctoral Members); $21 (Students).

Meetings/Conferences: Biennial

Publications:
Cultural Anthropology; quarterly; adv.

Society for Developmental and Behavioral Pediatrics (1982)
6728 Old McLean Village Dr.
McLean, VA 22101
Tel: (703) 556-9222 *Fax:* (703) 556-8729
E-Mail: info@sdbp.org
Website: sdbp.org
Members: 750 individuals
Staff: 3
Annual Budget: $500-1,000,000
Tax: 501(c)(3)

Personnel:
Executive Director: Laura E. Degnon CAE
    E-Mail: laura@sdbp.org
Editor: Suzanne D. Dixon MD, MPH
    E-Mail: jdbp@earthlink.net
Association Manager: Amy Schull
    E-Mail: amy@sdbp.org

Historical Note:
Formerly (1995) Society for Behavioral Pediatrics. SDBP's mission is to improve the health care of infants, children, and adolescents by promoting research and teaching in developmental and behavioral pediatrics. Members are pediatricians, child psychologists and other professionals with an interest in developmental and behavioral pediatrics by advancing research, education, evidence-based clinical

practice and advocacy. Membership: $210 (Regular); $110 (Associate/Non Doctorate/Developing World Professional).

Meetings/Conferences: Annual
2013 - Baltimore, MD (Renaissance Baltimore
Harborplace Hotel)/Sept. 27 - 30

Publications:
Behavioral Developments; semi-annually; adv.
Journal of Developmental & Behavioral Pediatrics
(JDBP); adv.
Member Directory; on-line

Membership List Available to Non-members

Society for Developmental Biology (1939)
9650 Rockville Pike
Bethesda, MD 20814-3998
Tel: (301) 634-7815 *Fax:* (301) 634-7825
E-Mail: sdb@sdbonline.org
Website: sdbonline.org
Members: 2000 individuals
Staff: 4
Annual Budget: $1-2,000,000
Tax: 501(c)(3)

Personnel:
Executive Officer: Ida Chow PhD
    E-Mail: ichow@sdbonline.org
Contact, Publications: Marsha Lucas
    E-Mail: mlucas@sdbonline.org
Treasurer: Sally Moody

Historical Note:
Formerly (1965) the Society for the Study of Development and Growth, SDB's purpose is to further the study of development in all organisms and at all levels, to represent and promote communication among students of development, and to promote the field of developmental biology. Membership includes developmental biologists at all stages of their careers from around the world - students, postdocs, professors, and Nobel laureates and those who care about developmental biology and who seek contacts in the field. Membership: $80 (Full); $35 (Postdoctoral); $15 (Student).

Meetings/Conferences: Annual
2013 - Cancun, QR (Cancun Center Conventions and
Exhibitions)/June 16 - 20
Number of non-conference events/year: 5

Publications:
Developmental Biology
SDB e-news; quarterly

Society for Disability Studies (1982)
107 Commerce Centre Dr.
Suite 204
Huntersville, NC 28078
Tel: (704) 274-9240 *Fax:* (704) 948-7779
E-Mail: info@disstudies.org
Website: disstudies.org
Members: 350 individuals
Staff: 3
Annual Budget: $100-250,000

Personnel:
Executive Officer: Stephan J. Hamlin-Smith
Treasurer: Mariette Bates
Editor: Brenda Brueggeman

Historical Note:
Formerly (1986) known as the Section for the Study of Chronic Illness, Impairment, and Disability. SDS's purpose is to advocate the study of disability in social, cultural and political contexts. Membership is composed of scholars in the social sciences and humanities. Membership: $40 (Student/Low Income); $135 (Professional); $350 (Organizational); $1,450 (Life).

Meetings/Conferences: Annual

Publications:
Disability Studies Quarterly; quarterly; adv.
Member Directory; on-line
SDS Newsletter

Society for Ear, Nose and Throat Advances in Children (1973)
3901 Rainbow Blvd.
Mail Stop 3010
Kansas City, KS 66160
Tel: (913) 588-6683 *Fax:* (913) 588-6708
Website: sentac.org
Members: 300 health care professionals
Staff: 3
Annual Budget: $50-100,000

Personnel:

President: Udayan Shah MD
Treasurer: Ravindhra Elluru MD
Webmaster: Marc Steele

Historical Note:
SENTAC's primary purpose is to continually update the science and practice of medicine, surgery and habilitation as it relates to diseases and disorders of the ear, nose and throat areas of the body in infants and children.

Meetings/Conferences: Annual

Publications:
International Journal of Pediatric Otorhinolaryngology;
   annually; adv.
SENTAC Newsletter
SENTAC Newsletter; annually; adv.

Society for Ecological Restoration International (1987)
1017 O St. NW
Washington, DC 20001
Tel: (202) 299-9518 *Fax*: (270) 626-5485
E-Mail: info@ser.org
Website: ser.org
Members: 2500 individuals
Staff: 5
Annual Budget: $100-250,000
Tax: 501(c)(3)

Personnel:
Executive Director: Steve Bosak
   E-Mail: steve@ser.org
Coordinator, Communications: Leah Bregman
   E-Mail: leah@ser.org
Manager, Membership: Caroline Bronaugh
   E-Mail: caroline@ser.org

Historical Note:
Formerly Society for Ecological Restoration and Management. SER's mission is to promote ecological restoration as a means of sustaining the diversity of life on earth and reestablishing an ecologically healthy relationship between nature and culture. SER members are academics, scientists, ecological consultants, government agencies and others with an interest in ecological restoration. Membership: $5 (Associate); $250 (Student); $20-45 (Full); $75-125 (Professional); $175-250 (Organizational); $10-50 (Individual); $20-200 (Group).

Meetings/Conferences: Biennial
2013 - Madison, WI (Monona Terrace Community and
   Convention Center)/Oct. 6 - 11/1500 attendees
Number of non-conference events/year: 8

Publications:
Restoration Ecology; bi-monthly
SERNews; quarterly

Membership List Available to Non-members

Society for Economic Anthropology
Western Washington University
Department of Anthropology
Bellingham, WA 98225
Tel: (360) 650-4785
E-Mail: sea.webmaster@gmail.com
Website: econanthro.org
Members: 500 individuals
Staff: 5

Personnel:
President: Katherine E. Browne
General Editor: Lisa Cliggett
Treasurer: Robert Marshall

Historical Note:
SEA is a group of anthropologists, economists and other scholars who are interested in the connections between economics and social life. Members are scientists and academics interested in economic systems and their relevance to human and cultural development. Membership: $35 (Basic Professional); $10 (Basic Student); $50 (Standard Professional); $30 (Standard Student).

Meetings/Conferences: Annual
Conference Chair: Carolyn K. Lesorogol
2013 - St. Louis, MO (Campus of Washington
   University)/April 11 - 13

Publications:
SEA Newsletters; semi-annually

Membership List Available to Non-members

Society for Economic Botany (1959)
P.O. Box 299
St. Louis, MO 63166-0299
Tel: (314) 577-9566 *Fax*: (314) 577-9515
E-Mail: seb@botany.org

Website: econbot.org
Members: 1500 members
Staff: 4
Annual Budget: $100-250,000
Tax: 501(c)(3)

Personnel:
President: Gail Wagner
   E-Mail: president@econbot.org
Secretary: Heather McMillen
Treasurer: Sy Sohmer
   E-Mail: treasurer@econbot.org
Editor-in-Chief: Bob Voeks PhD
   E-Mail: editor@econbot.org

Historical Note:
SEB's mission is to foster scientific research, education, and related activities on the past, present and future uses of plants and the relationship between plants and people. It works to make the results of such research available to the scientific community and the general public through meetings and publications. Membership: $35 (Emeritus/Retired); $30 (Student); $60 (Regular); $150-249 (Sustaining); $250- 499 (Patron); $500 (Benefactor); $1,000 (Life); $150 (Corporate); $1000 (Life); $10 (Associate).

Meetings/Conferences: Annual
2013 - Plymouth, United Kingdom (Plymouth
   University)/June 28 - July 3

Publications:
Economic Botany; quarterly
Membership Directory; on-line
Plants and People; bi-annually

Society for Education in Anesthesia (1984)
520 N. Northwest Hwy.
Park Ridge, IL 60068-2573
Tel: (847) 825-5586 *Fax*: (847) 825-5658
E-Mail: sea@asahq.org
Website: seahq.org
Members: 600 individuals
Staff: 3
Annual Budget: $250-500,000
Tax: 501(c)(3)

Personnel:
Executive Director: Nicole C. Bradle CAE, CMP, MA
   E-Mail: n.bradle@asahq.org
Contact, Membership Services: Angelica Castillo
   E-Mail: a.castillo@asahq.org
Administrative Assistant: Tish Neff
   E-Mail: t.neff@asahq.org

Historical Note:
Formerly (1994) Society of Education in Anesthesia. SEA is an educational organization for anesthesiologists who strive to enhance their abilities and scholarly endeavors in the field of education. Members are individuals within anesthesia departments responsible for direct involvement in teaching, administration and planning educational programs for residents and medical students. Membership: $225 (Active); $30 (International); $15 (Resident/Medical Student).

Meetings/Conferences: Semi-Annual
Conference Chair: Nicole C. Bradle CAE, CMP, MA
2013 - Salt Lake City, UT (Hilton Salt Lake City
   Center)/May 31 - June 2
2013 - San Francisco, CA/Oct. 11

Publications:
Journal of Clinical Anesthesia (JCA)
Membership Directory; on-line
SEA Newsletter; quarterly

Society for Environmental Geochemistry and Health (1971)
4698 S. Forest Ave.
Springfield, MO 65810
Tel: (417) 885-1166 *Fax*: (417) 881-6920
Website: segh.net
Members: 400 individuals
Staff: 2
Annual Budget: Under $10,000
Tax: 501(c)(3)

Personnel:
President: Xiangdong Li
   E-Mail: cexdi@polyu.edu.hk
Secretary: Suzette Morman
   E-Mail: smorman@usgs.gov

Historical Note:
SEGH was formed to promote a multi-disciplinary approach to research in fields of geochemistry and health, to facilitate and expand communication among scientists within

these disciplines and to advance knowledge in the area. Membership: $85 (Individual); $48 (Student); $250 (Life Member), Life Members pay a $48 annual Journal fee.

Society for Environmental Graphic Design (1973)
1000 Vermont Ave. NW
Suite 400
Washington, DC 20005
Tel: (202) 638-5555 *Fax*: (202) 478-2286
E-Mail: segd@segd.org
Website: segd.org
Members: 1720 individuals and companies
Staff: 7
Annual Budget: $25-50,000

Personnel:
Chief Executive Officer: Jessica W. London
   E-Mail: jessica@segd.org
Associate, Membership Services: Nadia Adona
   E-Mail: nadia@segd.org
Manager, Programs: Jennette Keiser
   E-Mail: jennette@segd.org
Director, Communications: Pat Matson Knapp
   E-Mail: pat@segd.org
Chief Operating Officer: Ann Makowski
   E-Mail: ann@segd.org
Director, Education and Professional Development: Justin
   Molloy
   E-Mail: justin@segd.org
Director, Sponsorship: Sara Naegelin
   E-Mail: sara@segd.org

Historical Note:
Formerly (1992) Society of Environmental Graphic Designers. SEGD's mission is to serve as a source of education and inspiration for community. Members are individuals and corporations engaged in or affiliated with environmental graphic design including individuals from the fields of graphic design, architecture, interior and industrial design, education, research and sign manufacturing. Membership: $55-1,700/year.

Meetings/Conferences:
Conference Chair: Jennette Keiser
2013 - San Francisco, CA/June 6 - 8

Publications:
Membership Directory; on-line
SEGD e-newsletter; monthly
segdDESIGN Magazine; quarterly; adv.

Society for Epidemiologic Research (1968)
P.O. Box 990
Clearfield, UT 84089
Tel: (801) 525-0231 *Fax*: (801) 525-6549
E-Mail: membership@epiresearch.org
Website: epiresearch.org
Members: 2500 individuals
Staff: 5
Annual Budget: $250-500,000

Personnel:
Manager, Membership Services: Jacqueline C. Brakey
   E-Mail: membership@epiresearch.org

Historical Note:
SER is committed to keep epidemiologists at the vanguard of scientific developments. Membership: $190 (Regular); $25-100 (Student); $120 (Emeritus/Retired).

Meetings/Conferences: Annual
Conference Chair: Peggy Christensen
2013 - Boston, MA (The Boston Park Plaza Hotel)/June
   18 - 21
2014 - Seatle, WA/June 24 - 27
2015 - Denver, CO/June 15 - 18
Number of non-conference events/year: 2

Publications:
American Journal of Epidemiology; monthly
Epidemiologic Reviews; annually; adv.
SER Newsletter; on-line

Society for Ethnomusicology (1955)
1165 E. Third St.
Morrison Hall 005
Bloomington, IN 47405-3700
Tel: (812) 855-6672 *Fax*: (812) 855-6673
E-Mail: sem@indiana.edu
Website: ethnomusicology.org
Members: 1800 individuals
Staff: 2
Annual Budget: $250-500,000

Personnel:
Executive Director: Steve Stuempfle

Program Assistant: Heather McFadden
    E-Mail: semprog@indiana.edu

Historical Note:
*SEM's mission is to promote the research, study, and
performance of music in all historical periods and cultural
contexts. SEM is a Member of American Council of
Learned Societies. Has an international membership.
Membership: $60-105 (Individual, based on income); $40
(Student); $1400 (Life); $1600 (Spouse/Partner Life); $120
(Institutional).*

Meetings/Conferences: Annual
2013 - Indianapolis, IN (Indiana University
    Bloomington)/Nov. 14 - 17
2014 - Pittsburgh, PA (University of Pittsburgh)/Nov.
    13 - 16
Number of non-conference events/year: 1

Publications:
Ethnomusicology; adv.
Membership Directory; on-line
SEM Newsletter; quarterly
SEM Student News; bi-annually

Society for Excellence in Eyecare *(1989)*
P.O. Box 2153
Goodlettsville, TN 37070-2153
Tel: (615) 892-0863 *Fax:* (615) 859-3941
E-Mail: info@excellenteyesurgery.com
Website: excellenteyesurgery.com
Members: 100 individuals
Staff: 3
Annual Budget: $250-500,000

Personnel:
Executive Director: Trent Roark

Historical Note:
*SEE seeks to develop and implement standards of practice
for the provision of ophthalmologic services to the general
public, and to act as a patient's advocate to promote
quality, cost-effective eye care services. Membership is
open to ophthalmologists and optometrists who meet the
standards of SEE. Membership: $1,000/year (Individual).*

Meetings/Conferences: Annual
2013 - San Juan, PR (The Ritz-Carlton San Juan)/Feb.
    8 - 12
Number of non-conference events/year: 1

Publications:
Membership directory; on-line

Membership List Available to Non-members

Society for Experimental Biology and Medicine *(1903)*
130 W. Pleasant Ave.
Suite 334
Maywood, NJ 07607-1727
Tel: (201) 962-3519 *Fax:* (201) 962-3522
E-Mail: sebm@inch.com
Website: sebm.org
Members: 1500 individuals
Staff: 3
Annual Budget: $500-1,000,000
Tax: 501(c)(3)

Personnel:
Executive Director: Felice O'Grady
Administrative and Editorial Assistant: Nancy E. Blake
Editor-in-Chief: Steven R. Goodman PhD
    E-Mail: goodmans@upstate.edu

Historical Note:
*SEBM advocates investigation in the biomedical sciences
by encouraging and facilitating interchange of scientific
information among disciplines. The Society also advances
the career development of students and new investigators.
Membership: $90 (Regular); $50 (Associate); $20
(Student).*

Publications:
Experimental Biology and Medicine; monthly; adv.
Membership Directory; on-line

Society for Experimental Mechanics, Inc. *(1943)*
Seven School St.
Bethel, CT 06801-1405
Tel: (203) 790-6373 *Fax:* (203) 790-4472
E-Mail: sem@sem1.com
Website: sem.org
Members: 1800 individuals
Staff: 6
Annual Budget: $500-1,000,000
Tax: 501(c)(3)

Personnel:

Executive Director: Thomas "Tom" Proulx
    E-Mail: director@sem1.com
Contact, Membership Services: Alessandra de la Vega
    E-Mail: alessandra@sem1.com
Contact, Publication Sales: Shari Matthews
    E-Mail: pubsales@sem1.com
Contact, Exhibits: Joni Normandin CAE, MPA
    E-Mail: joni@sem1.com
Contact, Conferences: Jennifer Tingets
    E-Mail: meetings@sem1.com

Historical Note:
*Incorporated in Delaware in 1961. Formerly (1984) the
Society for Experimental Stress Analysis. SEM's mission
is to increase the knowledge of physical phenomena
and to further the understanding of the behavior of
materials, structures and systems. Members belong to
academia, government, and industry who are committed
to interdisciplinary application, research and development,
education, and active promotion of experimental methods.
Membership: $72 (Individual); $325-1,000 (Corporate);
$13-24 (Student); $1,100 (Life).*

Meetings/Conferences:
Conference Chair: Jennifer Tingets
2013 - Orlando, FL (Rosen Plaza Hotel)/Feb. 3 - 6
2013 - Garden Grove, CA (Hyatt Regency Orange
    County)/Feb. 11 - 14
2013 - Lombard, IL (The Westin Lombard Yorktown
    Center)/June 3 - 6
2014 - Greenville, SC (Hyatt Regency Greenville)/June
    2 - 4
Number of non-conference events/year: 1

Publications:
Experimental Mechanics; bi-monthly
Experimental Techniques; bi-monthly; adv.

Membership List Available to Non-members

Society for Features Journalism *(1947)*
University of Maryland
1100 Knight Hall
College Park, MD 20742-7111
Tel: (301) 314-2631
E-Mail: aasfe@jmail.umd.edu
Website: featuresjournalism.org
Members: 200 individuals
Staff: 2
Annual Budget: $50-100,000
Tax: 501(c)(6)

Personnel:
Executive Director: Merrilee Cox
    E-Mail: merrileesfj@gmail.com
Secretary and Treasurer: Kathy Blackwell
    E-Mail: kblackwell@statesman.com

Historical Note:
*Formerly the American Association of Sunday and Feature
Editors, the Society for Features Journalism promotes
the craft of writing and innovation in lifestyle, arts and
entertainment journalism. Membership: $25-150/year
(dues are based on daily circulation).*

Meetings/Conferences: Annual

Publications:
Membership Directory; on-line
SFJ's Newsletter; monthly

Society for Foodservice Management *(1979)*
455 S. Fourth St.
Suite 650
Louisville, KY 40202
Tel: (502) 574-9931 *Fax:* (502) 589-3602
E-Mail: sfm@ahint.com
Website: sfm-online.org
Members: 1971 individuals
Staff: 7
Annual Budget: $500-1,000,000

Personnel:
Executive Director: Tony Butler
    E-Mail: tbutler@hqtrs.com
Contact, Marketing and Communications: Michael
    Alderson
    E-Mail: malderson@hqtrs.com
Contact, Finance and Operations: John Bunker
    E-Mail: jbunker@hqtrs.com
Contact, Sponsorship and Advertising Sales: Lorraine
    Houghton
    E-Mail: lhoughton@hqtrs.com
Contact, Public Relations and Digital Media: Andrea Parr
    E-Mail: aparr@hqtrs.com
Contact, Event Services: Peg Plaut

    E-Mail: pplaut@hqtrs.com
Coordinator, Membership Services: Candice Zavatsky
    E-Mail: czavatsky@hqtrs.com

Historical Note:
*Formed as the result of a merger of the Association for
Food Service Management (established 1970) and the
National Industrial Cafeteria Managers' Association
(established 1949) on July 1, 1979. Represents the interest
of executives in the onsite foodservice industry. SFM's
mission is to enhance the ability of its members to achieve
career and business objectives in an ethical, responsible
and professional climate. Members are executives who
are responsible for non-commercial food service, such as
employee cafeterias, colleges and universities and healthcare
facilities. Membership: $395 (Active); $595 (Associate);
$75 (Emeritus); $25 (Student); $99 (Young Professional).*

Meetings/Conferences: Annual
Conference Chair: Peg Plaut

Publications:
FastFacts; monthly; adv.
Membership Directory; on-line

Membership List Available to Non-members

Society for Free Radical Biology and Medicine *(1987)*
8365 Keystone Crossing
Suite 107
Indianapolis, IN 46240
Tel: (317) 205-9482 *Fax:* (317) 205-9481
E-Mail: info@sfrbm.org
Website: sfrbm.org
Members: 1400 individuals
Staff: 7
Annual Budget: $500-1,000,000
Tax: 501(c)(6)

Personnel:
President: Harry Ischiropoulos PhD
    E-Mail: ischirop@mail.med.upenn.edu
Executive Director: Kent Lindeman CMP
    E-Mail: info@sfrbm.org
Vice President, Finance: Margaret Briehl PhD
    E-Mail: mmbriehl@email.arizona.edu
Vice President Research and Scientific Excellence: Henry
    Forman PhD
    E-Mail: hjforman@gmail.com
Vice President, Communications: Chris Kevil PhD
    E-Mail: ckevil@lsuhsc.edu
Vice President, Membership: Sally Nelson PhD
    E-Mail: snelson@somalogic.com
Manager, Meetings: Lori Pearson
    E-Mail: lpearson@hp-assoc.com

Historical Note:
*SFRBM fosters a balanced approach to understanding both
the advantageous and deleterious properties of free radicals
and reactive oxygen and nitrogen species. Membership:
$125-$160 (Regular/Active); $95-$130 (Associate); $55-
$90 (Post Doctoral); $20-$90 (Student).*

Meetings/Conferences: Annual
2013 - San Antonio, TX (Grand Hyatt San Antonio)/
    Nov. 20 - 24
2014 - Seatle, WA (Sheraton Seattle Hotel)/Nov. 19 -
    23
2015 - Boston, MA (Westin Waterfront Hotel)/Nov. 19
    - 22
2016 - San Francisco, CA (Hyatt Regency Embarcadero
    Hotel)/Nov. 17 - 20

Publications:
Free Radical Biology and Medicine; bi-weekly
Membership Directory; on-line
The DOT; quarterly

Society for French Historical Studies *(1955)*
551-101 Milton Ct.
Long Beach, CA 90803
Tel: (562) 494-6764
Website: societyforfrenchhistoricalstudies.net
Members: 1450 individuals
Staff: 3
Annual Budget: $10-25,000
Tax: 501(c)(3)

Personnel:
Executive Director: Linda L. Clark
    E-Mail: lclark2@csulb.edu
Financial Officer: Barry Bergen
Editor: Rachel Fuchs

Historical Note:

SFHS ia a professional society concerned with scholarly research and teaching on French History. Membership: $45 (Individual); $25 (Students).

Meetings/Conferences: Annual
2013 - Cambridge, MA (Cambridge Marriott Hotel)/ April 4 - 6

Publications:
French Historical Studies; quarterly

The Society for Freshwater Science (1953)
3206 Maple Leaf Dr.
Glenview, IL 60026
Tel: (847) 564-9905 Fax: (254) 776-3767
E-Mail: sfs@sgmeet.com
Website: freshwater-science.org
Members: 1800 individuals
Staff: 4
Annual Budget: $250-500,000

Personnel:
President: Dave Penrose
Secretary: Sue Norton
Business Manager: Irwin Polls
 E-Mail: ipolls@comcast.net

Historical Note:
Founded as Midwest Benthological Society, Society for Freshwater Science (SFS), formerly North American Benthological Society (NABS), changed name to SFS in May 2011 SFS now serves as an international membership association. Purpose is to promote better understanding of the biotic communities of lake and stream bottoms and their role in aquatic ecosystems, by providing media and disseminating new investigation results, new interpretations, and other benthological information to aquatic biologists and to the scientific community at large. Members are scientists concerned with freshwater-habitat ecology. Membership: $40-75/year.

Meetings/Conferences: Annual
2013 - Jacksonville, FL (Hyatt Regency Jacksonville Riverfront)/May 19 - 23

Publications:
Freshwater Science
In the Drift - Newsletter
Membership Directory; annually

Membership List Available to Non-members

Society for General Music (1982)
111 St.
New York, NY 54786
Staff: 1

Personnel:
Treasurer: Jon Rag

Society for German-American Studies (1968)
Scott Community College
500 Belmont Rd.
Bettendorf, IA 52722-5649
Tel: (319) 441-4319
E-Mail: communications@soci.org
Website: sgas.org/
Members: 600 Individuals
Staff: 5

Personnel:
President: Randall P. Donaldson
 E-Mail: rdonaldson@loyola.edu
Editor: William D. Keel
 E-Mail: wkeel@ku.edu
Coordinator, Membership Services: J. Gregory Redding
 E-Mail: reddingg@wabash.edu
Vice President: William Roba

Historical Note:
SGAS members are academics and others with an interest in German-American studies. SGAS promotes research in the history, culture, folklore, genealogy, language, literature and the creative arts of the German element in North America. Membership: $30 (Regular); $35 (Outside North America), $15 (Student); $40 (Joint); $35 (Institutional); $50 (Outside North America); $500 (Life).

Publications:
SGAS Newsletter

Society for Gynecologic Investigation (1952)
888 Bestgate Rd.
Suite 420
Annapolis, MD 21401
Tel: (202) 863-2544 Fax: (202) 863-0739
Website: sgionline.org
Members: 1200 individuals

Staff: 5
Annual Budget: $1-2,000,000

Personnel:
Executive Director: Ava Ann Tayman
 E-Mail: sgiava@aol.com
Program Specialist and Webmaster: Linda Gildersleeve
 E-Mail: lgildersleeve@sgionline.org
Director, Advancement and Liaison: Leslie Myatt
 E-Mail: myattl@uthscsa.edu
Administrative Assistant and Membership Services: Stephanie Ponta
Director, Development: John Tyson FRCS, MD
 E-Mail: jtcare@aol.com

Historical Note:
SGI's mission is to establish the scientific basis and clinical translation of reproductive science and women's health by providing and promoting leadership and excellence in research, international forums for scientific exchange, mentoring, career development and education. Membership: $50/year.

Meetings/Conferences: Annual
Conference Chair: Linda Gildersleeve
2013 - Orlando, FL (Hilton Orlando Bonnet Creek)/ March 20 - 23
2014 - Florence, Italy/March 26 - 29
2015 - San Francisco, CA/March 25 - 28
2016 - Montreal, QC/March 16 - 19
Number of non-conference events/year: 2

Publications:
Reproductive Sciences; monthly

Society for Healthcare Consumer Advocacy (1972)
155 N. Wacker Dr.
Suite 400
Chicago, IL 60606
Tel: (312) 422-3700 Fax: (312) 278-0881
E-Mail: shca@aha.org
Website: shca-aha.org
Members: 1000 individuals
Staff: 2
Annual Budget: $250-500,000

Personnel:
Program Specialist, Marketing: Diana Hammer
 E-Mail: dhammer@aha.org
Program Manager, Meetings and Membership Services: Kourtney Sproat
 E-Mail: ksproat@aha.org

Historical Note:
SHCA seeks to lead the advancement of healthcare consumer advocacy by supporting the role of professionals who represent and advocate for consumers across the healthcare continuum.Membership: $150 (Individuals); $200 (Associate); $75 (Students); $500 (Corporate); $80 (Retired).

Meetings/Conferences: Annual
Conference Chair: Kourtney Sproat
2013 - St. Louis, MO/April 3 - 5

Publications:
Membership Directory; on-line; adv.
Newsletter; quarterly; adv.

Membership List Available to Non-members

Society for Healthcare Epidemiology of America (1980)
1300 Wilson Blvd.
Suite 300
Arlington, VA 22209
Tel: (703) 684-1006 Fax: (703) 684-1009
E-Mail: info@shea-online.org
Website: shea-online.org
Members: 1200 individuals
Staff: 7
Annual Budget: $2-5,000,000

Personnel:
Executive Director: Jennifer Bright MPA
 E-Mail: jbright@shea-online.org
Senior Manager, Education Programs: Kimberly Belaunde
Manager, Member Services: Wanda M. Brown
Director, Member Services and Communications: Kristy Weinshel
 E-Mail: kweinshel@shea-online.org
Director, Policy and Strategic Initiatives: Melanie Young
 E-Mail: myoung@shea-online.org

Historical Note:
Formerly (1994) Society for Hospital Epidemiology of America. SHEA strives to advance expertise and education

in hospital epidemiology and quality assurance. Members work in all branches of medicine, public health, and healthcare epidemiology. Membership: $225 (Domestic Member/Fellow); $250 (International Member/Fellow); $70 (Developing Nation Member/Fellow); $100-160 (Emeritus Member/Member- in-Training); $185-200 (Associate); $275-375 (Corporate).

Meetings/Conferences: Annual

Publications:
Infection Control & Hospital Epidemiology
Membership Directory; on-line
SHEA News

Society for Healthcare Strategy and Market Development (1996)
155 N. Wacker Dr.
Suite 400
Chicago, IL 60606
Tel: (312) 422-3888 Fax: (312) 278-0883
E-Mail: shsmd@aha.org
Website: shsmd.org
Members: 4500 individuals
Staff: 6
Annual Budget: $25-50,000

Personnel:
Executive Director: Lauren A. Barnett
 E-Mail: lbarnett@aha.org
Interim Conference Planners: Jayne Ayers
 E-Mail: jayne@jayneayersassociates.com
Senior Specialist, Membership Services and Marketing Communications: Emily McCracken Lee
 E-Mail: elee@aha.org
Project Coordinator, Membership Services: Juana Sanchez
 E-Mail: jsanchez@aha.org
Project Director, Conferences: Paula Szyper
 E-Mail: pszyper@aha.org
Project Coordinator, Education: Sharon L. Warren
 E-Mail: swarren@aha.org

Historical Note:
Founded in 1996 as the result of a merger between Society for Healthcare Planning and Marketing (founded 1977) and American Society for Health Care Marketing and Public Relations (founded 1964). SHSMD's mission is to provide healthcare planning, marketing, and communications professionals with several resources for professional development. Membership: $235 (Individual); $85 (Student); $105 (Faculty).

Meetings/Conferences:
Conference Chair: Paula Szyper

Publications:
Calendar of Health Observances & Recognition Days; on-line
CareerLink; weekly; adv.
Futurescan; annually
Membership Directory; on-line
Spectrum; bi-monthly

Membership List Available to Non-members

Society for Hematopathology (1981)
3643 Walton Way Extension
Augusta, GA 30909
Tel: (706) 733-7550 Fax: (706) 733-8033
E-Mail: sh@uscap.org
Website: socforheme.org
Members: 500 individuals
Staff: 3
Annual Budget: $25-50,000
Tax: 501(c)(3)

Personnel:
Coordinator: Carolyn Lane
 E-Mail: sh@uscap.org

Historical Note:
The society was created for the promotion and exchange of knowledge and the stimulation of clinical, morphologic, and functional investigation of the hematopoietic and lymphoreticular systems as its primary objective.

Meetings/Conferences: Annual
Number of non-conference events/year: 1

Publications:
Journal of Hematopathology; on-line
Membership Directory; on-line
newsletter; annually

Society for Historians of American Foreign Relations (1967)
Department of History, Ohio State University
230 W. 17th Ave., 106 Dulles Hall

Columbus, OH 43210
Tel: (614) 292-1951 *Fax:* (614) 292-2282
E-Mail: shafr@osu.edu
Website: shafr.org
Members: 1700 individuals
Staff: 2
Annual Budget: $500-1,000,000
Tax: 501(c)(3)

Personnel:
Executive Director: Peter L. Hahn
   E-Mail: shafr@osu.edu
Program Committee Co-Chair: David Engerman
   E-Mail: program-chair@shafr.org

Historical Note:
SHAFR's mission is to maintain society of historians for the study, advance and disseminate the knowledge of American foreign relations and the doing of all acts incidental to the accomplishment thereof. Membership: $50 (Regular); $20 (Student/Unwaged Member).

Meetings/Conferences: Annual
Conference Chair: David Engerman
2013 - Arlington, VA (Renaissance Arlington Capital
   View Hotel)/June 20 - 22
Number of non-conference events/year: 1

Publications:
Diplomatic History
Diplomatic History; adv.
Membership Directory; on-line
Passport; adv.

Society for Historians of the Early American Republic *(1977)*
3355 Woodland Walk
Philadelphia, PA 19104-4531
Tel: (215) 746-5393 *Fax:* (215) 573-3391
E-Mail: info@shear.org
Website: shear.org
Members: 1500 individuals and organizations
Staff: 4
Annual Budget: $100-250,000
Tax: 501(c)(3)

Personnel:
President: Andrew Cayton
Executive Coordinator: Amy L. Baxter-Bellamy
Advisory Council: Daniel K. Richter
Program Committee Chair: Stacey Robertson
   E-Mail: smr@bumail.bradley.edu

Historical Note:
SHEAR's mission is to foster the study of the early republican period among professional historians, students, and the general public. Membership: $30-137/year.

Meetings/Conferences: Annual
Conference Chair: Stacey Robertson
2013 - St. Louis, MO/July 18 - 21
Number of non-conference events/year: 1

Publications:
Journal of the Early Republic; quarterly

Society for Historians of the Gilded Age and Progressive Era *(1988)*
406 Natural Science
Michigan State University
East Lansing, MI 48824-1115
Tel: (517) 432-5134 *Fax:* (517) 355-8363
E-Mail: wgamber@indiana.edu
Website: h-net.org/~shgape
Members: 300 individuals
Staff: 3
Annual Budget: $10-25,000

Personnel:
President: Maureen Flanagan
   E-Mail: maureen.flanagan@iit.edu
Executive Secretary: Wendy Gamber
   E-Mail: wgamber@indiana.edu
Treasurer: Philip Vandermeer
   E-Mail: p.vander.meer@asu.edu

Historical Note:
H-SHGAPE is the online forum of the Society for Historians of the Gilded Age and Progressive Era and one of the founding lists on H-NET. Mission is to encourage lively and professional discussion and collaboration of important information about the Gilded Age and Progressive Era.

Publications:
The Journal of the Gilded Age and Progressive Era
   (JGAPE); quarterly

Society for Historical Archaeology *(1967)*
13017 Wisteria Dr.
Suite 395
Germantown, MD 20874
Tel: (301) 972-9684 *Fax:* (866) 285-3512
E-Mail: hq@sha.org
Website: sha.org
Members: 2350 organizations and individuals
Staff: 3
Annual Budget: $500-1,000,000
Tax: 501(c)(3)

Personnel:
Executive Director: Karen Hutchison CAE
   E-Mail: karen@sha.org

Historical Note:
SHA works to enhance scholarly research and the dissemination of knowledge concerning historical archaeology. Membership: $135 (Regular); $80 (Student/Retired); $175 (Friend); $250 (Developer); $400 (Benefactor); $3600 (Life); $45 (Adjunct); $215 (Institution).

Meetings/Conferences: Annual
Conference Chair: Kate Fitzgerald CMP
2013 - Leicester, United Kingdom/Jan. 9 - 12
Number of non-conference events/year: 1

Publications:
Historical Archaeology; quarterly; adv.
Membership Directory; on-line
SHA Newsletter; quarterly; adv.

Society for History Education *(1972)*
1250 Bellflower Blvd.
Long Beach, CA 90840-1601
Tel: (562) 985-2573 *Fax:* (562) 985-5431
E-Mail: info@societyforhistoryeducation.org
Website: societyforhistoryeducation.org
Members: 2000 individuals
Staff: 12
Annual Budget: $50-100,000

Personnel:
President: Troy Johnson
Editor and Secretary: Jane Dabel
Treasurer: Nancy Quam-Wickham

Historical Note:
Formerly (1967) the History Teachers Association. SHE was founded for the purpose of supporting and improving history education in the university, community college and K-12 classroom. Society for History Education holds National affiliate with American Historical Association. Membership: $32 (Individual); $22 (Student/Retired); $63 (Institution); $300 (Lifetime).

Publications:
The History Teacher Journal; quarterly; adv.

Society for History in the Federal Government *(1979)*
Ben Franklin Station
P.O. Box 14139
Washington, DC 20044-4139
Tel: (202) 354-2009
Website: shfg.org
Members: 500 individuals
Staff: 9
Annual Budget: Under $10,000
Tax: 501(c)(3)

Personnel:
President: Marc Rothenberg
   E-Mail: mrothenb@nsf.gov
Membership Coordinator: Eric Boyle
   E-Mail: SHFGmembership@gmail.com
Secretary: Sejal Patel
   E-Mail: sejal.patel@nih.gov
Treasurer: Karen Kruse Thomas
   E-Mail: Kthoma48@jhmi.edu

Historical Note:
SHFG's mission is to enhance study and broad understanding of the history of the U.S. government. SHFG is a professional society of historians, archivists, curators and others with an interest in the historical and archival activities of the U.S. government. Membership: $40 (Regular); $30 (Retired); $20 (Student); $100 (Patron/ Institutions).

Meetings/Conferences: Annual

Publications:
Federal History; annually
The Federalist; quarterly

Society for Human Ecology *(1981)*
105 Eden St.
College of the Atlantic
Bar Harbor, ME 04609
Tel: (801) 694-0001 *Fax:* (207) 288-3780
Website: societyforhumanecology.org
Members: 250 individuals
Staff: 3
Annual Budget: $10-25,000
Tax: 501(c)(3)

Personnel:
Executive Director: Ken Hill
   E-Mail: khill@coa.edu
Secretary: Barbara Carter
   E-Mail: carter@coa.edu

Historical Note:
SHE promotes the use of an ecological perspective in both research and application. Members are academics, scientists, health professionals and others with an interest in studying the interrelationship of man's actions and his environment. Membership: $60 (Regular); $30 (Student); $1000 (Sustaining); $150 (Contributing).

Meetings/Conferences: Annual
2013 - Canberra, Australia (The Australian National
   University)/Feb. 5 - 8

Publications:
Human Ecology Review; semi-annually

Society for Human Resource Management *(1948)*
1800 Duke St.
Alexandria, VA 22314
Tel: (703) 548-3440 *Fax:* (703) 535-6490
TollFree: (800) 283-7476
E-Mail: shrm@shrm.org
Website: shrm.org
Members: 250000 individual members
Staff: 350
Annual Budget: Over $100,000,000
Tax: 501(c)(6)

Personnel:
President and Chief Executive Officer: Henry G. Jackson
  CPA
   E-Mail: ceo@shrm.org
Vice President: Michael P. Aitken
   E-Mail: maitken@shrm.org
Senior Vice President, Membership, Marketing and External Affairs: J. Robert Carr J.D., SPHR
   E-Mail: rcarr@shrm.org
Senior Vice President, Knowledge Development: Deb
  Cohen PhD
   E-Mail: Deb.Cohen@shrm.org
General Counsel: Henry A. Hart J.D.
   E-Mail: hhart@shrm.org
Chief Financial Officer: Mary Mohney
   E-Mail: Mary.Mohney@shrm.org
Chief Human Resources and Strategy Officer: Jeff Pon
   E-Mail: Jeff.Pon@shrm.org
Senior Vice President, Publishing and E-Media: Gary K.
  Rubin
   E-Mail: Gary.Rubin@shrm.org

Historical Note:
Formerly American Society for Personnel Administration (ASPA). An organization dedicated to excellence in human resource management. Includes more than 93,000 individuals working for a cross-section of employers, from smaller family operations to large, multi-national corporations. Membership: $180 (Full membership); $90 (Internet-only membership).

Continuing Education:
Certification Designation/s: PHR, SPHR, GPHR

Meetings/Conferences:
2013 - Chicago, IL/June 16 - 19
Number of non-conference events/year: 1

Publications:
California Employment Law; monthly; adv.
Compensation & Benefits Update; adv.
Global HR; bi-weekly; adv.
HR Job Seekers; adv.
HR Magazine; monthly; adv.
HR News
HR Technology Briefing; adv.
HR Week; weekly; adv.
Legal Report; quarterly
Organizational and Employee Development Update;
   monthly; adv.
Safety & Security; bi-monthly; adv.

SHRM Vendor Directory; on-line; adv.
Staffing Management; monthly; adv.
Staffing Management magazine
Supervisory Newsletter
The Diversity newsletter; monthly; adv.

Society for Humanistic Judaism (1969)
28611 W. 12 Mile Rd.
Farmington Hills, MI 48334
Tel: (248) 478-7610 *Fax:* (248) 478-3159
E-Mail: info@shj.org
Website: shj.org
Members: 2500 individuals
Staff: 4
Annual Budget: $500-1,000,000
Tax: 501(c)(3)
Personnel:
Executive Director: M. Bonnie Cousens
Editor: Harriet Maza
Historical Note:
SHJ's mission is to mobilize people to celebrate Jewish identity and culture consistent with a humanistic philosophy of life. Membership: $95 (National); $25 (Young Adult); $1800 (Lifetime).
Meetings/Conferences:
Number of non-conference events/year: 2
Publications:
Humanorah; semi-annually; adv.

Society for Imaging Informatics in Medicine (1980)
19440 Golf Vista Plaza
Suite 330
Leesburg, VA 20176-8264
Tel: (703) 723-0432 *Fax:* (703) 723-0415
E-Mail: info@siimweb.org
Website: siimweb.org
Members: 2200 individuals, 35 corporations and 90 institutions
Staff: 5
Annual Budget: $1-2,000,000
Tax: 501(c)(3)
Personnel:
Executive Director: Anna Marie Mason
    E-Mail: amason@siimweb.org
Manager, Education: Nikki Smith Medina
    E-Mail: nsmith@siimweb.org
Director, Meetings: Andrea Saris
    E-Mail: asaris@siimweb.org
Director, Membership and Database Management Systems: Steven "Steve" M. Smith
    E-Mail: ssmith@siimweb.org
Historical Note:
Formerly (2006) known as the Society of Computer Applications in Radiology. SIIM's mission is to advance computer applications and information technology in medical imaging through education and research. Members are physicians and other health care professionals with an interest in the application of computers in medical imaging and designers/manufacturers of image management equipment. Membership: $65-1500 (Individuals/Institutional); $2,000 (Corporate, minimum,-includes 10 sponsored individuals, Additional blocks of 10 sponsored members for $1,000).
Meetings/Conferences: Annual
Conference Chair: Andrea Saris
2013 - Grapevine, TX (Gaylord Texan Hotel and Convention Center, Dallas Texas)/June 6 - 9
2014 - Long Beach, CA (Long Beach Convention and Entertainment Center)/May 15 - 17
2015 - Washington, DC (Gaylord National Resort and Convention Center)/May 28 - 31
2017 - Grapevine, TX (Gaylord Texan Hotel and Convention Center-Grapevine)/June 1 - 4
2019 - Washington, DC (Gaylord National Resort and Convention Center)/May 30 - June 2
Number of non-conference events/year: 1
Publications:
Directory; on-line
Journal of Digital Imaging; bi-monthly; adv.
SIIM Expert Hotline; on-line

Membership List Available to Non-members

Society for Imaging Science and Technology (1947)
7003 Kilworth Ln.
Springfield, VA 22151

Tel: (703) 642-9090 *Fax:* (703) 642-9094
E-Mail: info@imaging.org
Website: imaging.org
Members: 2000 individuals
Staff: 10
Annual Budget: $1-2,000,000
Personnel:
Executive Director: Suzanne E. Grinnan
    E-Mail: sgrinnan@imaging.org
Manager, Conference Programs: Diana Gonzalez
    E-Mail: dgonzalez@imaging.org
Manager, Special Projects: Jennifer O'Brien
Contact, Membership Services, Conference Registration, Procurement and Facilities Manager: Mark Reynolds
    E-Mail: mreynolds@imaging.org
Contact, Financial Management: Marion Zoretich
Historical Note:
Originated as the Society of Photographic Engineers, merged in 1957 with the Technical Division of the Photographic Society of America to form the Society of Photographic Scientists and Engineers. Became (1986) Society for Imaging Science and Technology. Mission is to keep members and others aware of the latest scientific and technological developments in the field of imaging, and is achieved through conferences, educational programs and publications. Members are persons who engage in imaging science or engineering or teachers of photography or imaging science. Membership: $95 (Regular-Domestic); $100 (Regular- Foreign); $25 (Student); $0 (Emeritus); $1,250 (Donor Corporate); $2,500 (Supporting Corporate); $5,000 (Sustaining Corporate).
Meetings/Conferences: Annual
Conference Chair: Diana Gonzalez
2013 - San Francisco, CA/Feb. 3 - 7
2013 - Washington, DC/April 2 - 5
2013 - Albuquerque, NM/Nov. 4 - 8
Number of non-conference events/year: 7
Publications:
IS&T Reporter; bi-monthly
Journal of Electronic Imaging; quarterly
Journal of Imaging Science and Technology (JIST); bi-monthly; adv.
Membership Directory; on-line

Society for In Vitro Biology (1946)
514 Daniels St.
Suite 411
Raleigh, NC 27605
Tel: (919) 562-0600 *Fax:* (919) 562-0608
E-Mail: sivb@sivb.org
Website: sivb.org
Members: 1000 individuals
Staff: 3
Annual Budget: $250-500,000
Personnel:
President: William J. Smith
    E-Mail: william.j.smith3@us.army.mil
Manager, Publications: Michele Schultz
    E-Mail: michele@sivb.org
Historical Note:
Formerly, the Tissue Culture Commission. Became the Tissue Culture Association in 1950 and assumed its current name in 1994. SIVB's mission is to advance exchange, publication and teaching of knowledge related to in vitro biology of cells, tissues and organs and also focuses on biological problems of significance to science and society. Membership: $160 (Regular); $105 (Post Doctoral); $55 (Student).
Meetings/Conferences: Annual
Publications:
In Vitro Cellular & Developmental Biology-Animal; monthly; adv.
In Vitro Cellular & Developmental Biology-Plant; bi-monthly; adv.
In Vitro Report Newsletter; quarterly; adv.

Membership List Available to Non-members

Society for Industrial & Applied Mathematics (1952)
3600 Market St.
Sixth Floor
Philadelphia, PA 19104-2688
Tel: (215) 382-9800 *Fax:* (215) 386-7999
TollFree: (800) 447-7426
E-Mail: service@siam.org
Website: siam.org
Members: 500 academic, manufacturing, research and development, service and

consulting organizations, government, and military organizations and 13,000 individual members.
Staff: 40
Annual Budget: $10-25,000,000
Tax: 501(c)(3)
Personnel:
Executive Director: James M. Crowley
    E-Mail: jcrowley@siam.org
Associate, Marketing Communications: Dan Cleary
    E-Mail: cleary@siam.org
Technical Director: William Kolata
    E-Mail: kolata@siam.org
Publisher: David K. Marshall
    E-Mail: marshall@siam.org
Director, Marketing and Sales: Michelle Montgomery
    E-Mail: montgomery@siam.org
Director, Finance and Administration: Susan A. Palantino
    E-Mail: palantino@siam.org
Manager, Membership Services: Susan Whitehouse CAE
    E-Mail: whitehouse@siam.org
Director, Conferences: Connie Young
    E-Mail: cyoung@siam.org
Historical Note:
Organized in Philadelphia in November 1951 and incorporated in Delaware in April 1952. SIAM's mission is to advance the application of mathematics and computational science to engineering, industry, science, and society. Membership: $10-680/year.
Meetings/Conferences: Annual
Conference Chair: Connie Young
2013 - San Diego, CA (Town and Country Resort Hotel)/July 8 - 12
2014 - Chicago, IL (Palmer House a Hilton Hotel)/July 7 - 11
Publications:
Membership Directory; on-line
Multiscale Modeling and Simulation
SIAM Journal on Applied Dynamical Systems
SIAM Journal on Applied Mathematics; bi-monthly; adv.
SIAM Journal on Computing
SIAM Journal on Control and Optimization
SIAM Journal on Discrete Mathematics; quarterly; adv.
SIAM Journal on Financial Mathematics
SIAM Journal on Imaging Sciences
SIAM Journal on Mathematical Analysis
SIAM Journal on Matrix Analysis and Applications; quarterly; adv.
SIAM Journal on Numerical Analysis
SIAM Journal on Optimization
SIAM Journal on Scientific Computing
SIAM Review
Theory of Probability and Its Applications

Society for Industrial and Organizational Psychology Inc. (1946)
440 E. Poe Rd.
Suite 101
Bowling Green, OH 43402-0087
Tel: (419) 353-0032 *Fax:* (419) 352-2645
E-Mail: siop@siop.org
Website: siop.org
Members: 6600 individuals
Staff: 6
Annual Budget: $2-5,000,000
Tax: 501(c)(6)
Personnel:
Executive Director: David Nershi
    E-Mail: dnershi@siop.org
Manager, Publications: Jenny Baker
    E-Mail: jbaker@siop.org
Manager, Communications: Stephany Below
    E-Mail: sbelow@siop.org
Director, Administrative Services: Linda Lentz
    E-Mail: llentz@siop.org
Manager, Information Technology: Larry Nader
    E-Mail: lnader@siop.org
Manager, Membership Services: Tracy Vanneman
    E-Mail: tvanneman@siop.org
Historical Note:
SIOP's mission is to enhance human well-being and performance in organizational and work settings by promoting the science, practice, and teaching of industrial-organizational psychology. Membership: $69 (Professional); $34.50 (Student/Retired).
Meetings/Conferences: Annual

2013 - Houston, TX (Sugar Land Marriott Town
Square)/April 11 - 13
2014 - Honolulu, HI (Hilton Hawaiian Village Waikiki
Beach Resort)/May 15 - 17
2015 - Philadelphia, PA (Philadelphia Marriott
Downtown)/April 23 - 25
2016 - Anaheim, CA (Disney's Grand Californian Hotel
and Spa)/April 14 - 16

Publications:
Industrial and Organizational Psychology: Perspectives
on Science and Practice (IOP); quarterly
Member Directory; on-line
Newsbrief e-newsletter; monthly
SIOP International Directory; on-line
TIP: The Industrial-Organizational Psychologist;
quarterly; adv.

Membership List Available to Non-members

Society for Industrial Archeology (1971)
Department of Social Sciences, Michigan
Technological University
1400 Townsend Dr.
Houghton, MI 49931-1295
Tel: (906) 487-1889 Fax: (906) 487-2468
E-Mail: sia@mtu.edu
Website: sia-web.org
Members: 1700 individuals
Staff: 6
Annual Budget: $50-100,000

Personnel:
President: Duncan Hay
E-Mail: duncan_hay@nps.gov
Treasurer: Nanci K. Batchelor
E-Mail: nkbatch@msn.com
Office Manager: Don Durfee
E-Mail: sia@mtu.edu
Executive Secretary and Editor: Patrick Martin
E-Mail: pemartin@mtu.edu

Historical Note:
SIA strives to encourage the study, interpretation and
preservation of historically significant industrial sites,
structures, artifacts and technology. Membership: $50
(Individual/Institutional); $55 (Household/Joint); $20
(Student); $100 (Contributing); $150 (Sustaining); $500
(Corporate).

Meetings/Conferences: Annual
Conference Chair: Ronald Petrie
2013 - Minneapolis, MN (The Twin Cities)/May 30 -
June 2
Number of non-conference events/year: 1

Publications:
E-News; on-line
Membership Directory
SIA Newsletter; quarterly; adv.
The Journal of the Society for Industrial Archeology;
semi-annually; adv.

Society for Industrial Microbiology (1949)
3929 Old Lee Hwy.
Suite 92A
Fairfax, VA 22030-2421
Tel: (703) 691-3357 Fax: (703) 691-7991
E-Mail: info@simhq.org
Website: simhq.org
Members: 1300 individuals
Staff: 5
Annual Budget: $1-2,000,000

Personnel:
Executive Director: Christine Lowe
Manager, Visual Communications: Suzannah Eller
E-Mail: suzi.eller@simhq.org
Coordinator, Meetings: Nancy Gorell
E-Mail: nancy.gorell@simhq.org
Director, Membership Services: Jennifer Johnson
E-Mail: jennifer.johnson@simhq.org
Accountant: Esperanza Montesa

Historical Note:
SIM's mission is to advance microbiological sciences,
especially as they apply to industrial products,
biotechnology, materials and processes. Membership: $40
(Student for SIM News only); $70 (Student SIM News and
Journal); $110 (US Regular); $130 (Non-US Regular);
$700-2,000 (Corporate).

Meetings/Conferences:
Conference Chair: Nancy Gorell
2013 - San Diego, CA (Sheraton San Diego)/Aug. 11 -
15

Publications:
Journal of Industrial Microbiology & Biotechnology;
monthly; adv.
Membership Directory; on-line
SIM News; bi-monthly; adv.

Membership List Available to Non-members

Society for Information Display (1962)
1475 S. Bascom Ave.
Suite 114
Campbell, CA 95008-4006
Tel: (408) 879-3901 Fax: (408) 879-3833
E-Mail: office@sid.org
Website: sid.org
Members: 6000 individuals
Staff: 4
Annual Budget: $2-5,000,000

Personnel:
President: Brian Berkeley
E-Mail: SID1@theberkeleys.net
Business Manager: Doug Bragdon
E-Mail: doug@sid.org
Treasurer: Yong-Seog Kim
E-Mail: yskim@wow.hongik.ac.kr

Historical Note:
SID's mission is to advance the display of technology,
manufacturing, and applications. Membership: $100
(Individual/Associate); $5 (Student); $950 (Sustaining
Corporate Member); $25 (Unemployed); Free (Life
Member).

Meetings/Conferences: Annual
2013 - Vancouver, BC (Vancouver Convention Center)/
May 19 - 24
2014 - San Diego, CA/June 1 - 6
Number of non-conference events/year: 2

Publications:
Digest of Technical Papers; annually
Information Display; monthly
Journal of the SID; monthly
Membership Directory; on-line

Membership List Available to Non-members

Society for Information Management (1969)
15000 Commerce Pkwy.
Suite C
Mount Laurel, NJ 08054
Tel: (800) 387-9746 Fax: (856) 439-0525
E-Mail: sim@simnet.org
Website: simnet.org
Members: 3500 individuals
Staff: 10
Annual Budget: $2-5,000,000
Tax: 501(c)(6)

Personnel:
Chief Executive Officer: Steve Hufford
E-Mail: steve.hufford@simnet.org
Vice President, Conferences and Seminars: Andrew
Jackson
Program Manager: Vincenzo Nelli
E-Mail: vnelli@ahint.com
Chief Staff Executive: Amy Williams
E-Mail: awilliams@ahint.com
Contact, Membership Services and Chapter Relations:
Karen Zader
E-Mail: kzader@simnet.org

Historical Note:
SIM's mission is to enhance international recognition of
information as a basic organizational resource and to
enhance the utilization and management of this resource
towards the improvement of management performance.
Membership: $80-7,850 (Individual); $420-25,500
(Corporate); $1,750-3,000 (Academic).

Meetings/Conferences: Annual
Conference Chair: Andrew Jackson
Number of non-conference events/year: 2

Publications:
MIS Quarterly Executive (MISQE); quarterly
SIM Connect; weekly
SIM News Extra; monthly

Society for Integrative and Comparative Biology
(1890)
1313 Dolley Madison Blvd.
Suite 402
McLean, VA 22101
Tel: (703) 790-1745 Fax: (703) 790-2672

TollFree: (800) 955-1236
E-Mail: sicb@burkinc.com
Website: sicb.org
Members: 2400 individuals
Staff: 6
Annual Budget: $500-1,000,000
Tax: 501(c)(3)

Personnel:
Executive Director: Brett Burk CAE
E-Mail: BBurk@BurkInc.com
Director, Membership Services: Heide Rohland
E-Mail: hrohland@burkinc.com
Director, Meetings: Lori Strong
E-Mail: LStrong@BurkInc.com
Executive Project Assistant: Sandra White
E-Mail: swhite@burkinc.com

Historical Note:
Formed as the American Society of Zoologists through a
1902 merger of two societies, the Central Naturalists and
the American Morphological Society, changed its name
to the Society for Integrative and Comparative Biology in
1996. SICB's mission is to advocate the pursuit and public
dissemination of important information relating to biology.
Membership is open to individuals who are actively engaged
in the field of zoology. Membership: $105 (Full Member);
$41 (Student); $65-145 (Family); $50 (Postdoctoral);
$1,500 (20 Year Single); $2,000 (20 Year Family); $3,000
(Life Single); $4,000 (Life Family).

Meetings/Conferences: Annual
Conference Chair: Lori Strong
2013 - San Francisco, CA (Hilton San Francisco Union
Square)/Jan. 3 - 7
2014 - Austin, TX/Jan. 3 - 7

Publications:
Integrative and Comparative Biology
Member Directory
SICB Newsletter; bi-annually

Society for Invertebrate Pathology (1967)
P.O. Box 11
Marceline, MO 64658
Tel: (660) 376-3586 Fax: (660) 376-3586
TollFree: (888) 486-1505
E-Mail: sip@sipweb.org
Website: sipweb.org
Members: 1100 individuals
Staff: 4
Annual Budget: $25-50,000
Tax: 501(c)(3)

Personnel:
General Editor: Eric Haas-Stapleton
E-Mail: ehaas@csulb.edu
Contact, Meetings: Nina Jenkins
E-Mail: nej2@psu.edu

Historical Note:
SIP promotes research and scientific inquiry into
invertebrate pathology. Membership: $45 (Regular); $20
(Student); Free (Emeritus).

Meetings/Conferences: Annual
Conference Chair: Nina Jenkins
2013 - Pittsburgh, PA (Sheraton Hotel at Station
Square)/Aug. 11 - 15

Publications:
Journal of Invertebrate Pathology
Membership Directory; annually
SIP Newsletter

Membership List Available to Non-members

The Society for Investigative Dermatology (1937)
526 Superior Ave., East
Suite 540
Cleveland, OH 44114
Tel: (216) 579-9300 Fax: (216) 579-9333
E-Mail: sid@sidnet.org
Website: sidnet.org
Members: 1700 individuals
Staff: 7
Annual Budget: $2-5,000,000

Personnel:
Executive Director, Chief Program and Development Officer:
Becky "Rebecca" Minnillo MPA
E-Mail: minnillo@sidnet.org
President Elect: Paul Bergstresser MD
JID Managing Editor: Elizabeth Blalock
E-Mail: blalock@sidnet.org
Manager, Membership and Association Services: Tracy
Martin

E-Mail: martin@sidnet.org
Director, Meetings and Events: Carolyn Slade
E-Mail: slade@sidnet.org

Historical Note:
SID's mission is to advance and promote the sciences relevant to skin health and disease through education, advocacy, and scholarly exchange of scientific information. Membership: $75-1,500/year.

Meetings/Conferences: Annual
Conference Chair: Carolyn Slade
2013 - Edinburgh, United Kingdom (Edinburgh International Conference Centre)/May 8 - 11
2014 - Albuquerue, NM (Albuquerque Convention Center)/May 7 - 10
2015 - Atlanta, GA (Hilton Atlanta)/May 6 - 9
2016 - Scottsdale, AZ (Westin Kierland Resort and Spa)/May 11 - 14

Publications:
Journal of Investigative Dermatology (JID); monthly; adv.

Society for Italian Historical Studies *(1956)*
Department of History, Boston College
140 Commonwealth Ave.
Chestnut Hill, MA 02467-3806
Tel: (617) 552-3814
Website: italianhistoricalstudies.org
Members: 350 individuals
Staff: 2
Annual Budget: Under $10,000

Personnel:
President: Carol Lansing
Editor, Executive Secretary and Treasurer: Alan J. Reinerman
E-Mail: alan.reinerman@bc.edu

Historical Note:
SIHS encourages the study and teaching of Italian history, promotes research, and awards prizes. Members are professors and students of Italian history. Membership: $12 (Regular); $5 (Graduate Students/Part-Time Instructors/ Retirees/Unemployed).

Meetings/Conferences: Annual
2013 - New Orleans, LA (New Orleans Marriott)/Jan. 3 - 6
2014 - Washington, DC (Washington Marriott Wardman Park)/Jan. 2 - 5
2015 - New York City, NY (Hilton New York)/Jan. 2 - 5
2016 - Atlanta, GA (Hilton Atlanta/Marietta Hotel and Conference Center)/Jan. 7 - 10
2017 - Denver, CO (Hyatt Regency Denver Tech Center)/Jan. 5 - 8
2018 - Washington, DC (Marriott Wardman Park and Omni Shoreham)/Jan. 4 - 7
2019 - Chicago, IL (Hilton Chicago)/Jan. 3 - 6
2020 - New York City, NY (Hilton New York)/Jan. 3 - 5

Society for Laboratory Automation and Screening *(2010)*
100 Illinois St.
Suite 242
St. Charles, IL 60174
Tel: (630) 256-7527 *Fax:* (630) 741-7527
TollFree: (877) 990-7527
E-Mail: slas@slas.org
Website: slas.org
Staff: 13
Annual Budget: $5-10,000,000

Personnel:
Chief Executive Officer: Greg Dummer CAE
E-Mail: gdummer@slas.org
Director, Global Events: Brenda Dreier CMP
E-Mail: bdreier@slas.org
Contact, Legal Services: Peter Gaido Esq.
E-Mail: peter@gaido-fintzen.com
Manager, Administrative and Member Services: Mary Geismann
E-Mail: mgeismann@slas.org
Director, Publishing: Nan Hallock
E-Mail: nhallock@slas.org
Director, Education: Steven Hamilton PhD
E-Mail: shamilton@slas.org
Director, Marketing Communications: Tom Manning
E-Mail: tmanning@slas.org
Financial Director: Dave Wasielewski
E-Mail: davew@krdcpas.com
Web Service Manager: Ellen Zidar
E-Mail: ellen@podi.com

Historical Note:
Formed by merger of Society for Biomolecular Sciences (SBS) and the Association for Laboratory Automation (ALA). SLAS is a global organization that exists to provide forums for education and information exchange to encourage the study of, and improve the science and practice of, laboratory automation and screening. Membership: $120-200 (Regular); $60-100 (Emerging Economy/Early Career Professional/Retired); $25-50 (Student).

Meetings/Conferences: Annual
Conference Chair: Brenda Dreier CMP
2013 - Orlando, FL (Gaylord Palms Resort and Convention Center)/Jan. 12 - 16
2014 - San Diego, CA/Jan. 18 - 22
2015 - Washington, DC/Feb. 7 - 11
2016 - San Diego, CA/Jan. 23 - 27
2017 - Washington, DC/Feb. 4 - 8
2018 - San Diego, CA/Feb. 3 - 7
2019 - Washington, DC/Feb. 2 - 6

Publications:
Journal of Biomolecular Screening; adv.
Journal of Laboratory Automation; bi-monthly; adv.
Member Directory
Point to Point; adv.

Society for Leukocyte Biology *(1954)*
9650 Rockville Pike
Bethesda, MD 20814
Tel: (301) 634-7814 *Fax:* (301) 634-7455
E-Mail: slb@faseb.org
Website: leukocytebiology.org
Members: 1300 individuals
Staff: 3
Annual Budget: $1-2,000,000
Tax: 501(c)(3)

Personnel:
President: Jill Suttles
E-Mail: jill.suttles@louisville.edu
Treasurer: Lee-Ann H. Allen
Director, Publications: Jennifer Pesanelli
E-Mail: jpesanelli@faseb.org

Historical Note:
The goals of the Society are to promote the discipline of leukocyte biology. Membership consists of those interested in phagocytic cells of the body, especially as relating to host defense, immunity and cancer. Membership: $20 (Students); $75 (Regular Full); $25 (Post-Doc); $1000 (Corporate).

Meetings/Conferences: Annual

Publications:
iSLB newsletter; on-line; adv.
Journal of Leukocyte Biology; monthly; adv.

Membership List Available to Non-members

Society for Light Treatment and Biological Rhythms *(1988)*
2601 de la Canardiere F4500
Quebec City, QC G1J 2G3
Tel: (418) 663-5000 *Fax:* (418) 654-2131
E-Mail: sltbrinfo@gmail.com
Website: sltbr.org
Members:
200 individuals
7 companies
Staff: 1
Annual Budget: $25-50,000

Personnel:
President: Marc Hebert
E-Mail: marc.hebert@crulrg.ulaval.ca

Historical Note:
SLTBR's purpose is to foster research, professional development and clinical applications in the fields of light therapy and biological rhythms. Membership: $85 (Regular/Associate); $15 (Student); $600 (Corporate); $45 (Retired).

Meetings/Conferences: Annual

Publications:
Chronobiology International
Membership Directory; on-line

Society for Linguistic Anthropology *(1983)*
1009 E. South Campus Dr.
PO Box 210030
Tucson, AZ 85721
Website: linguisticanthropology.org
Staff: 5

Personnel:
President: Norma Mendoza-Denton
E-Mail: nmd@u.arizona.edu

Historical Note:
SLA helps to explore ways in which practices of language use shape patterns of communication, formulate categories of social identity and group membership, organize large-scale cultural beliefs and ideologies, and, in conjunction with other semiotic practices, equip people with common cultural representations of their natural and social worlds.

Meetings/Conferences:
Conference Chair: Jocelyn Ahlers

Publications:
Anthropology Newsletter
Journal of Linguistic Anthropology

Membership List Available to Non-members

Society for Maintenance & Reliability Professionals *(1992)*
1100 Johnson Ferry Rd.
Suite 300
Atlanta, GA 30342
Fax: (404) 252-0774
TollFree: (800) 250-7354
E-Mail: info@smrp.org
Website: smrp.org
Members: 3800 individuals
Staff: 7
Annual Budget: $1-2,000,000
Tax: 501(c)(3)

Personnel:
Executive Director: Jon Krueger
E-Mail: JKrueger@kellencompany.com
Coordinator, Membership and Staff Associate: Marella Bivins
E-Mail: mbivins@kellencompany.com
Manager, Business Development: Laura B. Keane
E-Mail: lkeane@smrp.org
Director, Certification and Education: Tim Kline
E-Mail: TKline@kellencompany.com
Executive Vice President: Russ Lemieux
Manager, Meetings: Sandy M. Stevens CMP
E-Mail: sstevens@kellencompany.com
Coordinator, Marketing and Communications: Christine Wang
E-Mail: cwang@kellencompany.com

Historical Note:
SMRP's mission is to develop and promote leaders in reliability and physical asset management. Membership: $25 (Emerging Professional); $125 (Individual/ Industry Partner Individual); $250-2,500 (Academic); $1,250-17,500 (Executive).

Continuing Education:
Enrollment: 2800
Certification Designation/s: CMRT, CMRP

Meetings/Conferences: Annual
Number of non-conference events/year: 7

Publications:
Buyers Guide; semi-annually; adv.
Member Directory; on-line
SMRP SmartBrief; on-line
SMRP Solutions; bi-monthly; adv.

Society for Marketing Professional Services *(1973)*
123 N. Pitt St.
Suite 400
Alexandria, VA 22314
Tel: (703) 549-6117 *Fax:* (703) 549-2498
TollFree: (800) 292-7677
E-Mail: info@smps.org
Website: smps.org
Members: 6,000 marketing and business development professionals
Staff: 13
Annual Budget: $2-5,000,000
Tax: 501(c)(6)

Personnel:
Chief Executive Officer: Ronald D. Worth
E-Mail: ron@smps.org
Senior Vice President, Communications and Marketing: Lisa Bowman
E-Mail: lisa@smps.org
Director, Education, Certification, and Information Technology: Mark DellaPietra
E-Mail: mark@smps.org
Manager, Certification and Information Technology: Kevin Doyle

E-Mail: kevin@smps.org
Senior Vice President, Membership and Chapter Services:
Tina M. Myers CAE
E-Mail: tina@smps.org
Manager, Education and Events: Daniel Reilly
E-Mail: dan@smps.org
Director, Marketing: Michele Santiago
E-Mail: michele@smps.org
Manager, Membership: Denise Schjenken
E-Mail: denise@smps.org

Historical Note:
SMPS' mission is to advocate for, educate, and connect leaders in the building industry. Members are marketing and business development professionals from architectural, engineering, planning, interior design, construction, and specialty consulting firms located throughout the United States and Canada. Membership: $405 (New); $30 (Emeritus); $25 (Student).

Continuing Education:
Certification Designation/s: CPSM

Meetings/Conferences: Annual
Conference Chair: Daniel Reilly
Number of non-conference events/year: 3

Publications:
Connections; bi-weekly
Marketer; bi-monthly
Membership Directory; on-line
SMPS Connections; weekly; adv.

Society for Maternal-Fetal Medicine *(1977)*
409 12th St. SW
Washington, DC 20024
Tel: (202) 863-2476 *Fax:* (202) 554-1132
E-Mail: smfm@smfm.org
Website: smfm.org
Members: 2000 individuals
Staff: 6
Annual Budget: $2-5,000,000
Tax: 501(c)(3)

Personnel:
Executive Director: Patricia D. Stahr
E-Mail: pstahr@smfm.org
Contact, Communications: Vicki Bendure
E-Mail: vicki@bendurepr.com
Administrative Assistant: Debbie Gardner
E-Mail: dgardner@smfm.org
Membership Coordinator and Project Specialist: Sarah Kyger
E-Mail: skyger@smfm.org
Director, Industry Relations: Julie Miller
E-Mail: jmiller@smfm.org
Director, Finance and Meetings, Services Manager: Terri Mobley
E-Mail: tmobley@smfm.org

Historical Note:
Formerly (1998) Society of Perinatal Obstetricians, SMFM's purpose is to raise the standards of prevention, diagnosis, and treatment of maternal and fetal disease by focusing on the advancement and dissemination of knowledge. Membership: $450 (Regular); $400 (Associate/Affiliate); $50 (Fellow in Training/Resident); $100 (Coding).

Meetings/Conferences: Annual
Conference Chair: Terri Mobley
2013 - San Francisco, CA (Hilton San Francisco Union Square)/Feb. 11 - 16
2014 - New Orleans, LA (Hilton New Orleans Riverside)/Feb. 3 - 8
2015 - San Diego, CA (Hilton San Diego Bayfront)/Feb. 2 - 7
Number of non-conference events/year: 3

Publications:
Special Delivery

Membership List Available to Non-members

Society for Mathematical Biology
P.O. Box 11283
Boulder, CO 80301
Tel: (303) 661-9942 *Fax:* (303) 665-8264
E-Mail: smbnet@smb.org
Website: smb.org
Members: 500 individuals
Staff: 5
Annual Budget: $50-100,000
Tax: 501(c)(6)

Personnel:
President: Gerda de Vries
E-Mail: devries@math.ualberta.ca

Treasurer: Torcom Chorbajian
E-Mail: tchorbaj@concentric.net
Contact, Membership Services: Avner Friedman
E-Mail: afriedman@mbi.osu.edu
Webmaster: Will Heuett
E-Mail: wheuett@marymount.edu
Director, Publications: Sharon Lubkin
E-Mail: lubkin@smb.org

Historical Note:
SMB's mission is to promote and foster interactions between the mathematical and biological sciences communities through membership, journal publications, travel support and conferences. Members are academics and others with an interest in the application of mathematics in biological research. Membership: $50/year.

Meetings/Conferences: Annual
2013 - Tempe, AZ (Tempe Mission Palms Hotel and Conference Center)/June 10 - 13

Publications:
Bulletin of Mathematical Biology
SMB Digest; on-line
SMB Newsletter

Society for Medical Anthropology *(1968)*
C/O The College at Brockport
350 New Campus Dr.
Brockport, NY 14420-2914
Website: medanthro.net/
Staff: 4

Personnel:
President: Douglas A. Feldman
E-Mail: dfeldman@brockport.edu

Historical Note:
SMA, a section of the American Anthropological Association, works to promote the study of anthropological aspects of health, illness, disease, health care, and related topics. Membership: $10-75/year.

Meetings/Conferences: Annual

Publications:
SMA Newsletter

Society for Medical Decision Making *(1978)*
390 Amwell Rd.
Suite 402
Hillsborough, NJ 08844
Tel: (908) 359-1184 *Fax:* (908) 450-1119
E-Mail: info@smdm.org
Website: smdm.org
Members: 1000 individuals
Staff: 2
Annual Budget: $500-1,000,000

Personnel:
Executive Director: Jill Metcalf MBA
E-Mail: jill.metcalf@smdm.org
Association Manager: Marie Cortsen
E-Mail: arie@smdm.org

Historical Note:
SMDM's mission is to improve health outcomes through the advancement of proactive systematic approaches to clinical decision making and policy-formation in health care by providing a scholarly forum that connects and educates researchers, providers, policy-makers, and the public. Membership: $255 (Regular); $75 (Trainee); $140 (Emeritus).

Meetings/Conferences: Annual
2013 - Baltimore, MD (Hilton Baltimore)/Oct. 20 - 23/600 attendees
2014 - Miami, FL (Doral Golf Resort and Spa Miami)/Oct. 19 - 22/600 attendees
2015 - St. Louis, MO (Hyatt Regency St Louis at the Arch)/Oct. 17 - 21
Number of non-conference events/year: 1

Publications:
Medical Decision Making; bi-monthly; adv.
SMDM Newsletter; quarterly

Membership List Available to Non-members

Society for Medieval and Renaissance Philosophy *(1978)*
University of Missouri, Department of Philosophy (MC 73)
599 Lucas Hall, One University Blvd.
St. Louis, MO 63121-4499
Tel: (314) 516-5439
E-Mail: mcginnis@umsl.edu
Website: smrphil.org
Members: 325 individuals

Staff: 3
Annual Budget: Under $10,000
Tax: 501(c)(3)

Personnel:
Secretary, Membership Contact and Treasurer: Jon McGinnis
E-Mail: mcginnis@umsl.edu

Historical Note:
SMRP members are academics with an interest in medieval or renaissance philosophy. Membership: $10 (Regular); $15 (Contributing); $5 (Student); $150 (Life).

Meetings/Conferences: Annual

Publications:
Journal of the History of Philosophy
Newsletter; bi-annually

Society for Menstrual Cycle Research *(1979)*
333 E. 45th St.
Suite 21D
New York, NY 10017
E-Mail: info@menstruation.org
Website: menstruationresearch.org
Members: 150 individuals
Staff: 5
Annual Budget: Under $10,000
Tax: 501(c)(3)

Personnel:
President: Margaret L. (Peggy) Stubbs PhD
E-Mail: mstubbs@chatham.edu
Treasurer and Membership Contact: Alexandra Jacoby
E-Mail: info@menstruationresearch.org
Conference Coordinator: Ingrid Johnston-Robledo
E-Mail: Ingrid.Johnston-Robledo@fredonia.edu

Historical Note:
SMCR's mission is to be the source of guidance, expertise, and ethical considerations for researchers, practitioners, policy makers and funding resources interested in the menstrual cycle. Membership is open to individuals who have demonstrated an interest in research on the menstrual cycle or related issues, and who support the purposes of the Society. Membership: $50 (Individual); $20 (Student).

Meetings/Conferences: Biennial
Conference Chair: Margaret L. (Peggy) Stubbs PhD
2013 - New York City, NY (Marymount Manhattan College)/June 6 - 8

Publications:
SMRC Newsletter; quarterly

Society for Military History *(1933)*
The George C. Marshall Library
Virginia Military Institute
Lexington, VA 24450
Website: smh-hq.org
Members: 2400 individuals
Staff: 11
Annual Budget: $500-1,000,000
Tax: 501(c)(3)

Personnel:
Executive Director: Robert H. Berlin
E-Mail: rhberlin@aol.com

Historical Note:
Formerly American Military History Foundation, American Military Institute. SMH is devoted to stimulate and advance the study of military history. Members are scholars and others with an interest in the study of military history. Membership: $50 (Individual); $25 (Student); $100 (Sustaining); $75 (Institution).

Meetings/Conferences: Annual
2013 - New Orleans, LA (Sheraton Hotel New Orleans)/March 14 - 17
2014 - Kansas City, MO (Sheraton Kansas City Hotel at Crown Center)/April 3 - 7
2015 - Montgomery, AL (Renaissance Montgomery Hotel and Spa at the Convention Center)/April 9 - 12
2016 - Ottawa, ON (Ottawa Marriott Hotel)/April 14 - 17

Publications:
Headquarters Gazette; quarterly
Journal of Military History; quarterly
Member Directory; on-line

Membership List Available to Non-members

Society for Mining, Metallurgy and Exploration, Inc. *(1957)*
12999 E. Adam Aircraft Cir.

Englewood, CO 80112
Tel: (303) 948-4200 *Fax:* (303) 973-3845
TollFree: (800) 763-3132
E-Mail: cs@smenet.org
Website: smenet.org
Members: 12500 individuals
Staff: 37
Annual Budget: $5-10,000,000

Personnel:
Executive Director: David L. Kanagy
   E-Mail: kanagy@smenet.org
Manager, Meetings: Carol Cudworth
   E-Mail: cudworth@smenet.org
Manager, Membership Services: Tara Davis
   E-Mail: davis@smenet.org
Director, Public Affairs and Government Relations: John
   Hayden
   E-Mail: hayden@smenet.org
Director, Finance and Administration: Mike Hedges
   E-Mail: hedges@smenet.org
Manager, Information Systems: Paul Hoiberg
   E-Mail: hoiberg@smenet.org
Publications Editor: Steve Kral
   E-Mail: kral@smenet.org
Coordinator, Education: Mona Vandervoort
   E-Mail: vandervoort@smenet.org

Historical Note:
*A member society of the American Institute of Mining,
Metallurgical and Petroleum Engineers (AIME), SME's
roots date back to 1871. Founded as the Society of Mining
Engineers, the Society adopted its present name in 1989.
SME is an international society of professionals in the
minerals industry. Membership: $31-1500/year.*

Meetings/Conferences:
Conference Chair: Carol Cudworth
2013 - Denver, CO (Colorado Convention Center)/Feb.
   24 - 27
2014 - Salt Lake City, UT (Salt Palace Convention
   Center)/Feb. 23 - 26
2015 - Denver, CO (Colorado Convention Center)/Feb.
   22 - 25
Number of non-conference events/year: 6

Publications:
Membership Directory; on-line
Minerals and Metallurgical Processing Journal;
   quarterly
Mining Engineering; monthly; adv.
SME eNews; weekly

Membership List Available to Non-members

The Society for Modeling and Simulation International *(1952)*
2598 Fortune Way
Suite 1
Vista, CA 92081
Tel: (858) 277-3888 *Fax:* (858) 277-3930
E-Mail: scs@scs.org
Website: scs.org
Members: 1900 individuals
Staff: 3
Annual Budget: $1-2,000,000
Tax: 501(c)(3)

Personnel:
Executive Director: Oletha Darensburg
   E-Mail: oletha.darensburg@sbcglobal.net
Director, Membership: Aleah Hockridge
   E-Mail: aleah@scs.org
Manager, Publications and Editor: Vicki M. Pate
   E-Mail: vmpate@earthlink.net

Historical Note:
*Founded in Oxnard, CA as the Simulation Council and
incorporated in California in 1957 as Simulation Councils,
Inc. Became Society for Computer Simulation in 1973.
SCS's mission is to facilitate communication among
professionals in the field of simulation. Membership: $85
(Regular); $140 (Professional); $240 (Premier); $30
(Student); $500-5,000 (Organization).*

Meetings/Conferences:
2013 - Tampa, FL (Renaissance Tampa International
   Plaza Hotel)/Jan. 28 - Feb. 1
2013 - San Diego, CA (Bahia Resort Hotel)/April 7 - 10

Publications:
JDMS; quarterly; adv.
SCS M&S Magazine; quarterly; adv.
SCS M&S Newsletter; monthly
Simulation; monthly; adv.

Membership List Available to Non-members

Society for Mucosal Immunology *(1987)*
11950 W. Lake Park Dr.
Suite 320
Milwaukee, WI 53224-3049
Tel: (414) 359-1650 *Fax:* (414) 359-1671
E-Mail: info@socmucimm.org
Website: socmucimm.org
Members: 700 scientists and clinicians
Staff: 4
Annual Budget: $100-250,000
Tax: 501(c)(3)

Personnel:
Executive Director: Gail L. Bast CAE, MBA
   E-Mail: gbast@socmucimm.org
Association Manager: Lori Rathje
   E-Mail: lrathje@socmucimmo.org
Manager, Meetings: Andrea E. Rowe

Historical Note:
*SMI's purpose is to advance research, literary and
educational aspects of the scientific field of mucosal
immunology and fosters communication among
immunologists studying both human and animal tissues.
Membership $150 (Regular); $50 (Trainee/Student);
$7,500 (Corporate).*

Meetings/Conferences: Biennial
Conference Chair: Andrea E. Rowe

Publications:
Membership Directory; on-line
Mucosal Immunology; bi-monthly; adv.
SMI Newsletter; quarterly

Society for Natural Philosophy *(1963)*
University of Houston, Department of
Mechanical Engineering
N207 Engineering Building One
Houston, TX 77204-4006
Website: ms.uky.edu/~snp
Members: 300 individuals
Staff: 1
Annual Budget: Under $10,000

Personnel:
Treasurer: Yi-chao Chen
   E-Mail: chen@uh.edu

Historical Note:
*SNP advances specific research aimed at the unity of
mathematical and physical science, and seeks to recognize
and promote work of quality. Members are mathematicians,
chemists, engineers, physicists, and other scientists
interested in the foundations of mathematical sciences in
nature. Membership: $30 (Individual). Free (Students).*

Meetings/Conferences: Annual

Society for Neuro-Oncology *(1994)*
PO Box 273296
Houston, TX 77277-3296
Website: soc-neuro-onc.org
Staff: 3
Annual Budget: $1-2,000,000
Tax: 501(c)(3)

Personnel:
Executive Director: J. Charles Haynes JD
Chief Administrative Officer: Jan Esenwein
Manager, Membership Services: Linda Greer
   E-Mail: linda@soc-neuro-onc.org

Historical Note:
*SNO is dedicated to promoting advances in neuro-oncology
through research and education. Membership: $200
(Associate); $75 (Trainee).*

Meetings/Conferences: Annual

Publications:
Neuro-Oncology Journal; monthly
SNO Newsletter; on-line

Society for Neuroscience *(1969)*
1121 14th St. NW
Suite 1010
Washington, DC 20005
Tel: (202) 962-4000 *Fax:* (202) 962-4941
E-Mail: info@sfn.org
Website: sfn.org
Members: 42000 individuals
Staff: 90
Annual Budget: $25-50,000,000
Tax: 501(c)(3)

Personnel:
Executive Director: Marty Saggese
   E-Mail: marty@sfn.org
Director, Public Information and Outreach: Todd Bentsen
   E-Mail: tbentsen@sfn.org
Director, Membership Services and Marketing: Barry Black
   E-Mail: bblack@sfn.org
*Senior Director, Membership Services and Professional
   Development:* Eun-Joo Chang
   E-Mail: eun-joo@sfn.org
Senior Director, Meeting Services: Paula Kara
   E-Mail: paula@sfn.org
Senior Director, Communications and Public Affairs: Mona
   Miller
   E-Mail: mmiller@sfn.org
*Senior Director, Finance and Administration and Chief
   Financial Officer:* Lara Moninghoff
   E-Mail: lara@sfn.org
Director, Technology Services: Scott Moore
   E-Mail: scott@sfn.org
Director, Policy and Advocacy: Allen Segal
   E-Mail: asegal@sfn.org
Director, Professional and Global Programs: Mark Storey
   E-Mail: mstorey@sfn.org
Director, Human Resources and Administration: Adrianne
   Troilo
   E-Mail: atroilo@sfn.org

Historical Note:
*SFN's mission is to advance the understanding of the brain
and the nervous system, provide professional development
activities, information, and educational resources for
neuroscientists, promote public information and general
education, inform legislators and other policymakers.
Members are scientists and physicians who study the brain
and nervous system. Membership: $140-185 (Regular);
$27-65 (Student); $185 (Affiliate); $110-285 (Institutional
Program).*

Meetings/Conferences: Annual
Conference Chair: Paula Kara
2013 - San Diego, CA/Nov. 9 - 13
Number of non-conference events/year: 6

Publications:
Brain Briefings
Membership Directory; on-line
Neuroscience Nexus; bi-weekly
Neuroscience Quarterly; quarterly
Scholars Newsletter
The Journal of Neuroscience

Society for Neuroscience in Anesthesiology and Critical Care *(1973)*
2209 Dickens Rd.
Richmond, VA 60068-2573
Tel: (847) 825-5586 *Fax:* (847) 825-5658
TollFree: (800) 245-3001
E-Mail: snacc@snacc.org
Website: snacc.org
Members: 500 individuals
Staff: 3
Annual Budget: $250-500,000
Tax: 501(c)(3)

Personnel:
Executive Director: Stewart A. Hinckley
   E-Mail: stewart@societyhq.com

Historical Note:
*Formerly (1987) known as the Society of Neurosurgical
Anesthesia and Neurological Supportive Care and later the
Society of Neurosurgical Anesthesia and Critical Care, the
mission of SNACC is to advance the art and science of the
care of the neurologically impaired patients. Membership:
$125-295 (Active); $125-305 (International); $25-195
(Medical Student/Resident/Fellow/Emeritus (Retired)).*

Meetings/Conferences: Annual
2013 - San Francisco, CA/Oct. 10 - 11

Publications:
Journal of Neurosurgical Anesthesiology; quarterly
Membership Directory; on-line
SNACC Fall, 2011 Newsletter; annually; adv.

Society for News Design *(1979)*
424 E. Central Blvd.
Suite 406
Orlando, FL 32801
Tel: (407) 420-7748 *Fax:* (407) 420-7697
E-Mail: snd@snd.org
Website: snd.org
Members: 2500 individuals
Staff: 3

Annual Budget: $250-500,000
Tax: 501(c)(6)

Personnel:
Executive Director: Stephen Komives
    E-Mail: skomives@snd.org
Director, Education: Julie Elman
    E-Mail: elman@ohio.edu
Manager, Membership Services: Susan Santoro
    E-Mail: susans@snd.org

Historical Note:
Formerly (1981) Society of Newspaper Designers, (1998) Society of Newspaper Design in 1981. SND strives to enhance communication around the world through excellence in visual journalism. Members include designers, publishers, graphics artists, editors, illustrators, photographers, art directors, paginators, advertising artists, students and faculty who design newspapers, magazines and web pages. Membership: $90-135 (Professional); $60 (Full-time Students); $130-135 (Corporate).

Meetings/Conferences: Annual

Publications:
Design; semi-annually
The Best of Newspaper Design™; annually
Update; on-line

Society for Nonprofit Organizations (1983)
P.O. Box 510354
Livonia, MI 48151
Tel: (734) 451-3582 Fax: (734) 451-5935
E-Mail: info@snpo.org
Website: snpo.org
Members: 6000 members
Staff: 3
Annual Budget: $100-250,000
Tax: 501(c)(3)

Personnel:
President: Katie Burnham Laverty
    E-Mail: kburnham@snpo.org
Director, Membership Services: Jason Chmura
Editor: Jill Muehrcke

Historical Note:
SNPO's mission is to provide nonprofit staff members, volunteers, and board members with affordable resources and information to work effectively and efficiently. Membership: $150 (Organization/Group); $69 (Individual); $49 (Electronic); $25 (Affiliate).

Meetings/Conferences:
Number of non-conference events/year: 2

Publications:
Funding Alert e-newsletter; monthly; adv.
GrantStation Insider; weekly
Membership Directory; on-line
Nonprofit World Magazine; bi-monthly; adv.

Membership List Available to Non-members

Society for Nutrition Education and Behavior (1967)
9100 Purdue Rd.
Suite 200
Indianapolis, IN 46268
Tel: (317) 328-4627 Fax: (317) 280-8527
TollFree: (800) 235-6690
E-Mail: info@sneb.org
Website: sne.org
Members: 1000 individuals
Staff: 4
Annual Budget: $500-1,000,000
Tax: 501(c)(6)

Personnel:
Executive Director: Jackie Williams, CPA
    E-Mail: jwilliams@sneb.org
Director, Membership and Marketing: Rachel Daeger
    E-Mail: rdaeger@sne.org
Managing Editor: Kristin Faust
    E-Mail: managingeditor@jneb.org
Coordinator, Membership and Meetings: Sarah Gould
    E-Mail: sgould@sneb.org

Historical Note:
SNEB promotes effective nutrition education and communication to support and improve healthful behaviors. Membership: $60-5,000/year.

Continuing Education:
Certification Designation/s: ADA, SNA, CPE, AAFCS

Meetings/Conferences: Annual
Conference Chair: Sarah Gould
2013 - Portland, OR (Hilton Portland and Executive Tower)/Aug. 9 - 12

2014 - Milwaukee, WI/June 28 - July 1
2015 - Pittsburgh, PA/July 25 - 28

Publications:
Abstracts; annually; adv.
Journal of Nutrition Education and Behavior; bi-monthly; adv.
Member Directory; on-line; adv.
SNE eCommunicator; monthly; adv.
SNE Supplement; annually

Membership List Available to Non-members

Society for Obstetric Anesthesia and Perinatology (1968)
520 N. Northwest Hwy.
Park Ridge, IL 60068-2573
Tel: (847) 825-6472 Fax: (847) 825-5658
E-Mail: soap@soap.org
Website: soap.org
Members: 1200 individuals
Staff: 2
Annual Budget: $500-1,000,000
Tax: 501(c)(3)

Personnel:
Executive Director: Karen A. Hurley MA
Administrative Assistant: Michelle Rarick

Historical Note:
SOAP's mission is to improve pregnancy-related outcomes for women and neonates through the support of obstetric anesthesiology research, the provision of education to its members, other providers, and pregnant women, and the promotion of clinical anesthetic care. Membership: $200 (Active/Associate); $65 (Retired/Resident/Fellow/Medical Student); $320 (Joint IARS and SOAP).

Meetings/Conferences: Annual
2013 - San Juan, PR (Caribe Hilton San Juan)/April 24 - 28/11-25 exhibitors
2014 - Toronto, ON (Sheraton Centre Toronto Hotel)/May 14 - 18/11-25 exhibitors
2015 - Colorado Springs, CO (Broadmoor)/May 13 - 17
Number of non-conference events/year: 1

Publications:
Membership Directory; on-line
SOAP Newsletter; annually; adv.

Society for Occupational and Environmental Health (1972)
1010 Vermont Ave. NW
Suite 513
Washington, DC 20005
Tel: (202) 347-4976 Fax: (202) 347-4950
TollFree: (888) 347-2632
E-Mail: soeh@degnon.org
Website: soeh.org
Members: 300 individuals
Staff: 3
Annual Budget: $50-100,000
Tax: 501(c)(3)

Personnel:
Executive Director: Katherine H. Kirkland DrPH, MPH
    E-Mail: kkirkland@aoec.org

Historical Note:
SOEH's mission is to reduce occupational and environmental health hazards through the presentation of scientific data and the dynamic exchange of information across institutions and disciplines. Membership: $90 (Regular); $30 (Student/Emeritus).

Publications:
American Journal of Industrial Medicine
SOEH Bulletin

Society for Organic Petrology (1984)
C/O U.S. Geological Survey
956 National Center
Reston, VA 20192
Tel: (703) 648-6458 Fax: (703) 648-6419
E-Mail: info@tsop.org
Website: tsop.org
Members: 250 individuals
Staff: 4
Annual Budget: $10-25,000
Tax: 501(c)(3)

Personnel:
President: Isabel Suárez-Ruiz
    E-Mail: isruiz@incar.csic.es
Treasurer: Mike Avery

E-Mail: tsop.mavery@gmail.com
Chair, Membership: Paul Hackley
    E-Mail: phackley@usgs.gov
Editor: Rachel Walker
    E-Mail: rwalker@coalpetrography.com

Historical Note:
TSOP are scientists and engineers with an interest in coal petrology, kerogen petrology, organic geochemistry and related fields. TSOP's mission is to provide a forum, disseminate information and provide educational opportunities in organic petrology. Membership: $25 (Individual); $15 (Student).

Meetings/Conferences: Annual

Publications:
International Journal of Coal Geology
Membership Directory; on-line
TSOP Newsletter

Membership List Available to Non-members

Society for Pediatric Anesthesia (1956)
2209 Dickens Rd.
Richmond, VA 23230-2005
Tel: (804) 282-9780 Fax: (804) 282-0090
E-Mail: spa@societyhq.com
Website: pedsanesthesia.org
Members: 4000 individuals
Staff: 10
Annual Budget: $1-2,000,000
Tax: 501(c)(3)

Personnel:
President: Lynn D. Martin FAAP, FCCM, MBA, MD

Historical Note:
SPA's mission is to continually advance the safety and quality of anesthetic care, perioperative management, and alleviation of pain in children. Membership: $175 (Active/Affiliate); $50 (International); $40 (Resident/Fellow); $200 (Active Joint SPA/CCAS/Affiliate Joint SPA/CCAS).

Continuing Education:
Certification Designation/s: CME

Meetings/Conferences: Semi-Annual
2013 - Las Vegas, NV (Red Rock Casino Resort and Spa)/March 14 - 17
2013 - San Francisco, CA/Oct. 11
2014 - Ft. Lauderdale, FL (Marriott Harbor Beach Resort & Spa)/March 6 - 9

Publications:
SPA Newsletter; on-line

Society for Pediatric Dermatology (1976)
8365 Keystone Crossing
Suite 107
Indianapolis, IN 46240
Tel: (317) 202-0224 Fax: (317) 205-9481
E-Mail: spd@hp-assoc.com
Website: pedsderm.net
Members: 550 individuals
Staff: 3
Annual Budget: $500-1,000,000

Personnel:
Executive Director: Kent Lindeman CMP
    E-Mail: spd@hp-assoc.com

Historical Note:
SPD's purpose is to promote, develop and advance education, research and care of skin disease in all pediatric age groups. Members are physicians with an interest in pediatric dermatology. Membership:$100-300 (Practicing Physicians); $85-100 (Residents in Training); $300 (Associate).

Continuing Education:
Enrollment: 400

Meetings/Conferences: Annual
2013 - Miami, FL/Feb. 28
2013 - Milwaukee, WI (Pfister Hotel)/July 11 - 14
2014 - Denver, CO/March 20
2014 - Coeur d#Alene, ID (Coeur d' Alene Resort)/July 9 - 12
2015 - San Francisco, CA/March 19
2015 - Boston, MA (InterContinental Hotel)/July 9 - 12
2016 - Washington, DC/March 3
2017 - Orlando, FL/March 2
2018 - San Diego, CA/Feb. 15
2019 - Washington, DC/Feb. 28
Number of non-conference events/year: 3

Publications:
Pediatric Dermatology; bi-monthly

Membership List Available to Non-members

Society for Pediatric Pathology (1965)

C/O U.S. and Canadian Academy of Pathology
3643 Walton Way Extension
Augusta, GA 30909
Tel: (706) 364-3375 *Fax:* (706) 733-8033
E-Mail: spp@uscap.org
Website: spponline.org
Members: 500 individuals
Staff: 3
Annual Budget: $250-500,000
Tax: 501(c)(3)

Personnel:
President: Kathy Patterson
Contact, Membership Services: Carolyn Lane
    E-Mail: carolyn@uscap.org
Secretary and Treasurer: Sara Vargas

Historical Note:
SPP's mission is to promote expertise, effective teaching and productive research in the practice of pediatric pathology and promote the development and recognition of resident/ fellow training programs in pediatric pathology and, through the American Board of Pathology, establish and maintain a means by which pathologists may be certified as having special competency in pediatric pathology. Members are pathologists and other physicians substantially involved in pathology as it relates to pediatric medicine. Membership: $300 (Regular); $100 (Junior); $120 (Affiliate).

Meetings/Conferences: Semi-Annual

Publications:
Membership Directory; on-line
SPP newsletter

Membership List Available to Non-members

Society for Pediatric Psychology (1969)

P.O. Box 3968
Lawrence, KS 66046
Tel: (785) 856-0713 *Fax:* (785) 856-0759
E-Mail: apadiv54@gmail.com
Website: societyofpediatricpsychology.org
Members: 1400 individuals
Staff: 1
Annual Budget: $100-250,000

Personnel:
Administrative Officer and Database Manager: Karen Roberts
    E-Mail: APADiv54@gmail.com

Historical Note:
SPP's mission is to promote the health and development of children, adolescents, and their families through use of evidence-based methods. Membership: $50 (Member of American Psychological Association/ Psychologist/ Physician/Allied professional); $20 (Student).

Publications:
Journal of Pediatric Psychology
Membership Directory; on-line
Progress Notes

Membership List Available to Non-members

Society for Pediatric Radiology (1958)

1891 Preston White Dr.
Reston, VA 20191
Tel: (703) 648-0680 *Fax:* (703) 648-1863
E-Mail: spr@acr.org
Website: pedrad.org
Members: 1400 individuals
Staff: 4
Annual Budget: $1-2,000,000
Tax: 501(c)(3)

Personnel:
Executive Director: Jennifer K. Boylan CMP
Secretary: Jim Donaldson MD
Contact, Membership Services: Barbara Quattrone
    E-Mail: bquattrone@acr.org
Director, Meetings and Education: Karen Schmitt CMP
    E-Mail: kschmitt@acr-arrs.org

Historical Note:
SPR's mission is to foster excellence in pediatric health care through imaging and image-guided care. Membership: $400 (Active/Associate); $25 (Corresponding).

Meetings/Conferences:
Conference Chair: Karen Schmitt CMP
2013 - San Antonio, TX (Hyatt Regency Hill Country Resort and Spa)/May 14 - 18
2014 - Washington, DC (JW Marriott Washington, D.C.)/May 13 - 17

2015 - Seatle, WA (Hyatt Regency Bellevue on Seattle's Eastside)/April 27 - May 1

Publications:
Membership Directory; on-line
Pediatric Radiology; monthly; adv.
SPR Newsletter; on-line

Society for Pediatric Research (1929)

3400 Research Forest Dr.
Suite B-7
The Woodlands, TX 77381-4259
Tel: (281) 419-0052 *Fax:* (281) 419-0082
E-Mail: info@aps.spr.org
Website: aps-spr.org
Members: 3000 individuals
Staff: 7
Annual Budget: $2-5,000,000
Tax: 501(c)(3)

Personnel:
Executive Director: Debbie Anagnostelis
    E-Mail: debbie@aps-spr.org
Associate Executive Director: Kathy Cannon JD
    E-Mail: kathyc@aps-spr.org
Manager, Accounts: Kate Culliton
    E-Mail: katec@aps-spr.org
Managing Editor: Stephanie Dean
    E-Mail: stephanie.dean@pedres.org
Director, Information Technology: Antonio Moreno
    E-Mail: antonio.moreno@aps-spr.org
Executive Secretary: Jana Wells
    E-Mail: jwells@aps-spr.org
Manager, Web and Marketing: Deb Zirkle
    E-Mail: deb.zirkle@aps-spr.org

Historical Note:
SPR's purpose is to provide a forum for pediatric researchers to present and receive information currently available in all fields of pediatric research. Membership: $210 (Active); $120 (Senior); $35 (Affiliate); $0 (Emeritus).

Meetings/Conferences: Annual
Conference Chair: Kathy Cannon JD
2013 - Washington, DC (Walter E Washington Convention Center)/May 4 - 7
2014 - Vancouver, BC/May 3 - 6
2015 - San Diego, CA/April 25 - 28
2016 - Baltimore, MD/April 30 - May 3
2017 - San Francisco, CA/May 6 - 9
2018 - Toronto, ON/May 5 - 8
2019 - Baltimore, MD/April 27 - 30
2020 - Philadelphia, PA/April 25 - 28
2020 - Philadelphia, PA/May 2 - 5

Publications:
Membership Directory; on-line
SPR Newsletter; on-line; adv.

Society for Pediatric Urology

900 Cummings Center
Suite 4550
Beverly, MA 01915
Tel: (978) 927-8330 *Fax:* (978) 524-8890
E-Mail: spu@prri.com
Website: spuonline.org
Members: 350 individuals
Staff: 1
Annual Budget: $100-250,000
Tax: 501(c)(3)

Personnel:
Executive Director: Lorraine O'Grady

Historical Note:
SPC's mission is to promote pediatric urology, appropriate practice, education as well as exchanges between practitioners involved in the treatment of genito urinary disorders in children. Membership: $100/year (Individual).

Continuing Education:
Certification Designation/s: PSC

Meetings/Conferences: Annual
2013 - San Diego, CA/May 3 - 5

Publications:
Membership Directory; on-line
SPU Journal; monthly

Society for Personality and Social Psychology (1974)

Department of Psychology, Cornell University
239 Uris Hall
Ithaca, NY 14853
Tel: (607) 254-5416

Website: spsp.org
Members: 7000 Individuals
Staff: 4
Annual Budget: $1-2,000,000

Personnel:
Manager, Member Services: Christie Marvin
    E-Mail: cc286@cornell.edu

Historical Note:
A division of the American Psychological Association. SPSP's mission is to promote peace, social justice, and sustainable living through public education, research and the advancement of psychology. Membership: $50 (Doctorate); $25 (Undergraduate/Graduate Student/ Retired).

Meetings/Conferences: Annual
2013 - New Orleans, LA (Ernest N. Morial Convention Center)/Jan. 17 - 19

Publications:
Dialogue; semi-annually
Personality and Social Psychology Bulletin; monthly; adv.
Personality and Social Psychology Review; quarterly
Social Psychological and Personality Science

Society for Personality Assessment (1938)

6109H Arlington Blvd.
Falls Church, VA 22044
Tel: (703) 534-4772 *Fax:* (703) 534-6905
E-Mail: manager@spaonline.org
Website: personality.org
Members: 1500 individuals
Staff: 2
Annual Budget: $500-1,000,000
Tax: 501(c)(3)

Personnel:
Administrative Director: Paula J. Garber
    E-Mail: manager@spaonline.org

Historical Note:
Founded as the Rorschach Research Exchange. Name changed to the Society for Projective Techniques and then the Society for Projective Techniques and Personality Assessment; assumed its current name in 1971. SPA is dedicated to the development of methods of personality assessment, the advancement of research on their effectiveness, the exchange of ideas about the theory and practice of assessment and the promotion of the applied practice of personality assessment. Membership: $120 (Fellow/Member/Associate); $32 (Student); $60 (New Doctoral Graduates); $85 (Second-Year Doctoral Graduate).

Continuing Education:
Enrollment: 400
Certification Designation/s: CE

Meetings/Conferences: Annual
Conference Chair: Paula J. Garber
2013 - San Diego, CA (Westin Gaslamp Quarter, San Diego)/March 20 - 24/500 attendees
2014 - Arlington, VA (Westin Arlington Gateway)/ March 19 - 23/500 attendees

Publications:
Journal of Personality Assessment; bi-monthly
Membership Directory; annually
The Exchange; semi-annually; adv.

Membership List Available to Non-members

Society for Phenomenology and Existential Philosophy (1962)

Department of Philosophy
Southern Illinois University
Carbondale, IL 62901
E-Mail: shannnonspep@gmail.com
Website: spep.org
Members: 2000 individuals
Staff: 3
Annual Budget: $50-100,000

Personnel:
Executive Co-Director: Anthony Steinbock
    E-Mail: steinboc@siu.edu

Historical Note:
SPEP is the Society for Phenomenology and Existential Philosophy, a professional organization committed to supporting philosophy inspired by continental European traditions. SPEP sponsors an annual conference and other activities promoting philosophical inquiry inspired by the traditions of continental Europe. Membership: $100 (Individual); $40 (Student/Retired/Underemployed).

Meetings/Conferences: Annual
2013 - Eugene, OR/Oct. 24 - 26

Publications:
Phenomenology and Existential Philosophy

Society for Philosophy and Technology (1976)
Philosophy Department, Sonoma Sate University,
1801 E Cotati Ave.
Rhonert Park, CA 94928-3613
Tel: (707) 664-2277
TollFree: (800) 444-2419
Website: spt.org
Members: 300 individuals
Staff: 1
Tax: 501(c)(3)

Personnel:
Secretary and Treasurer: John Sullins
    E-Mail: john.sullins@sonoma.edu

Historical Note:
*SPT is an independent international organization that
encourages, supports and facilitates philosophically
significant considerations of technology. Members are
academics and other researchers studying the philosophical
ramifications of technological innovation. Membership: $65
(Individual); $45 (Student).*

Meetings/Conferences: Annual
2013 - Lisbon, Portugal/July 4 - 6

Publications:
SPT Newsletters; semi-annually
Techné: Research in Philosophy and Technology;
    quarterly

Society for Photographic Education (1963)
2530 Superior Ave.
Suite 403
Cleveland, OH 44114
Tel: (216) 622-2733 *Fax:* (216) 622-2712
E-Mail: membership@spenational.org
Website: spenational.org
Members: 1900 individuals
Staff: 7
Annual Budget: $500-1,000,000
Tax: 501(c)(3)

Personnel:
Executive Director: Virginia Morrison
    E-Mail: vmorrison@spenational.org
Coordinator, Advertising, Publications and Exhibitions:
    Nina Barcellona
    E-Mail: advertising@spenational.org
Registrar: Meghan Borato
    E-Mail: membership@spenational.org
Editor: Stacey McCarroll Cutshaw
    E-Mail: exposure@spenational.org
Legal Counsel: Allan M. Harris Esq.
Coordinator, Events and Publications: Ginenne Lanese
    CMP
    E-Mail: events@spenational.org
Office and Accounts Manager: Carla Pasquale
    E-Mail: admin@spenational.org

Historical Note:
*SPE's mission is to advocate the understanding of
photography in all of its forms and to foster the
development of its practice, teaching, scholarship and
critical analysis. Members are college and university
teachers of photography, photographers, museum curators
and students of photography. Membership: $125 (Regular);
$55 (Student); $75 (Senior/Retired); $170 (Adjunct/Part-
time); $225 (Sustaining); $600 (Corporate); $90 (Part
Time); $400 (Institutional).*

Meetings/Conferences: Annual
Conference Chair: Ginenne Lanese CMP
2013 - Chicago, IL (Palmer House Hilton Hotel)/March
7 - 10

Publications:
Exposure; bi-annually; adv.
Membership Directory and Resource Guide; annually;
    adv.
National Conference Program Guide; annually; adv.
SPE Newsletter; adv.

Membership List Available to Non-members

Society for Physical Regulation in Biology and Medicine (1980)
1210 Amsterdam Ave.
Mail Code: 8904
New York, NY 10027
Tel: (212) 854-6196 *Fax:* (212) 854-8725
E-Mail: crj2111@columbia.edu
Website: sprbm.org

Members: 100 individuals
Staff: 2
Annual Budget: $50-100,000
Tax: 501(c)(3)

Personnel:
President: X. Edward Guo
    E-Mail: exg1@columbia.edu
Secretary and Treasurer: Christopher Jacobs
    E-Mail: crj2111@columbia.edu

Historical Note:
*Founded as Bioelectrical Repair and Growth Society,
assumed its current name in 1994. SPRBM members
are persons conducting research relevant to electric or
magnetic field effects on repair, growth, regeneration or
other activity of living tissue and related fields including
biologists, physical scientists, physicians, surgeons,
engineers and members of industry. Membership: $200
(Individual/Affiliate); $80 (Early Career); $30 (Student);
$25 (Corresponding).*

Meetings/Conferences: Annual
2013 - Weimea, HI (Hapuna Beach Prince Hotel)/Jan.
    2 - 5

Society for Physician Assistants in Pediatrics (1994)
P.O. Box 121
Schertz, TX 78154
Tel: (210) 722-7622 *Fax:* (210) 568-6375
TollFree: (800) 481-0384
E-Mail: info@planitsat.com
Website: spaponline.org
Members: 250 individuals
Staff: 4
Annual Budget: $50-100,000

Personnel:
President: Erin Hoffman
    E-Mail: erin.hoffman@unmc.edu
Treasurer: Lauren Davey
    E-Mail: gibsol18@gmail.com
Conference Planner and Manager: Monique Mohr
    E-Mail: monique@planitsat.com
Secretary: Brian Wingrove
    E-Mail: bwingrove@gppa.net

Historical Note:
*SPAP seeks to improve the health care of children by
supporting Physician/PA teams who provide cost effective,
quality care to pediatric patients and by advocating
a network for communication and education between
providers committed to the well being of children.
Members are physician assistants interested in pediatrics.
Membership: $75 (Fellow); $20 (Student); $90 (Associate/
Affiliate); $750 (Corporate); $67.50 (AAP/SPAP).*

Meetings/Conferences: Annual
Conference Chair: Monique Mohr
2013 - Atlanta, GA (Sheraton Atlanta Hotel)/March 8 -
10

Society for Psychological Anthropology (1977)
Dept. of Anthropology, Pitzer College
1050 N. Mills Ave.
Claremont, CA 91711
Tel: (909) 607-3063
Website: aaanet.org/sections/spa
Staff: 3

Personnel:
President: Claudia Strauss
    E-Mail: claudia_strauss@pitzer.edu

Historical Note:
*SPA works for cultural, psychological, and social
interrelations of people at all levels. An affiliate of American
Anthropological Association (AAA). Membership: $290
(Professional); $70 (Student).*

Meetings/Conferences: Biennial
2013 - San Diego, CA (Hyatt Regency Mission Bay Spa
    and Marina-San Diego)/April 4 - 7

Publications:
Culture, Mind, and Society
Ethos; quarterly

Membership List Available to Non-members

Society for Psychophysiological Research (1960)
2424 American Ln.
Madison, WI 53704
Tel: (608) 443-2472 *Fax:* (608) 443-2474
E-Mail: spr@reesgroupinc.com
Website: sprweb.org
Members: 2000 individuals

Staff: 6
Annual Budget: $250-500,000

Personnel:
Executive Director: Susan M. Rees
    E-Mail: srees@reesgroupinc.com
Manager, Membership Services: Amy Bayer
    E-Mail: abayer@reesgroupinc.com
Treasurer: Diane Filion
    E-Mail: filiond@umkc.edu
Webmaster: John Hofmann
    E-Mail: jhofmann@reesgroupinc.com
Meeting Planner: Brooke Miller
    E-Mail: bmiller@reesgroupinc.com
Editor: Robert F. Simons
    E-Mail: rsimons@psych.udel.edu

Historical Note:
*SPR's purpose is to foster research on the interrelationships
between the physiological and psychological aspects of
behavior. Membership: $75 (Full); $25 (Student); $50
(Full, with early career discount).*

Meetings/Conferences: Annual
Conference Chair: Brooke Miller
2013 - Florence, Italy (Firenze Fiera Congress and
    Exhibition Center)/Oct. 2 - 6

Publications:
Membership Directory; annually
Psychophysiology; adv.

Society for Public Health Education (1950)
10 G St. NE
Suite 605
Washington, DC 20002-4242
Tel: (202) 408-9804 *Fax:* (202) 408-9815
E-Mail: info@sophe.org
Website: sophe.org
Members: 4000 individuals and 20 chapters
Staff: 15
Annual Budget: $2-5,000,000
Tax: 501(c)(3)

Personnel:
Chief Executive Officer: M. Elaine Auld CHES, MPH
    E-Mail: eauld@sophe.org
Project Director, Media: Laura Boyle
    E-Mail: lboyle@sophe.org
Administrative Assistant: Saundra Flegler
    E-Mail: sflegler@sophe.org
Director, Public Health Policy: Jerrica Mathis
    E-Mail: jmathis@sophe.org
Director, Professional Development: Allison T. McElvaine
    PhD
    E-Mail: amcelvaine@sophe.org
Director, Membership Services and Marketing: Celena T.
    NuQuay
    E-Mail: cnuquay@sophe.org
Assistant Chief Executive Officer: Melanie Sellers
Editorial and Project Coordinator: Katherine Will
    E-Mail: kwill@sophe.org

Historical Note:
*Formerly (1950) Society of Public Health Educators, Inc.
SOPHE's mission is to provide global leadership to the
profession of health education and health promotion and
to promote the health of society. Membership: $120 (New
Member); $165 (Active); $75 (Full-time Student); $105
(Emeritus); $100 (Student Member International); $145
(New Member International).*

Continuing Education:
Enrollment: 500
Certification Designation/s: CHES

Meetings/Conferences: Annual
Conference Chair: M. Elaine Auld CHES, MPH
2013 - Orlando, FL/April 17 - 19

Publications:
Health Education & Behavior; bi-monthly; adv.
Health Promotion Practice; bi-monthly; adv.
Membership Directory; on-line
News and Views; bi-monthly
News U Can Use; weekly

Membership List Available to Non-members

Society for Radiation Oncology Administration (1984)
5272 River Rd.
Suite 630
Bethesda, MD 20816
Tel: (301) 718-6510 *Fax:* (301) 656-0989
TollFree: (866) 458-7762
E-Mail: sroa@paimgmt.com

Website: sroa.org
Members: 500 individuals
Staff: 4
Annual Budget: $500-1,000,000
Tax: 501(c)(3)

Personnel:
Executive Director: Mark H. Epstein ScD
    E-Mail: mepstein@paimgmt.com
Meeting Registrar: Robert Coneys
    E-Mail: rconeys@paimgmt.com
Account Manager: Kristen Flemming
    E-Mail: kflemming@paimgmt.com
Coordinator, Membership and Meetings Registrar:
    Melynda Maurelus

Historical Note:
SROA's mission is to improve the administration of the business and nonmedical management aspects of radiation oncology and the practice of radiation oncology as a cost-effective form of health care delivery. Provides a forum for dialogue between the members on matters of professional interest. Membership: $200 (Active); $275 (Contributing Member).

Meetings/Conferences: Annual
Conference Chair: Melynda Maurelus
2013 - Atlanta, GA/Sept. 21 - 25
2014 - San Francisco, CA/Sept. 14 - 18
2015 - San Antonio, TX/Oct. 17 - 21

Publications:
Member Directory
Newsletter

Society for Range Management *(1948)*
10030 W. 27th Ave.
Wheat Ridge, CO 80215-6601
Tel: (303) 986-3309 *Fax:* (303) 986-3892
E-Mail: info@rangelands.org
Website: rangelands.org
Members: 4200 individuals
Staff: 9
Annual Budget: $1-2,000,000
Tax: 501(c)(3)

Personnel:
Executive Vice President: Jess Peterson
    E-Mail: evp@rangelands.org
Annual and ESD Meeting and Registration Manager: Kate
    Counter
    E-Mail: SRMmeeting@allenpress.com
Director, Finance: Denisha Marino
    E-Mail: dmarino@rangelands.org
Director, Outreach and Leadership Development: Aleta
    Rudeen
    E-Mail: arudeen@rangelands.org
Deputy Director, Event Operations: Bo Wagner
    E-Mail: bwagner@vintage5.us
Information and Technology Specialist: Ryan Wingerter
    E-Mail: ryan@techout.net

Historical Note:
Formerly (1971) American Society of Range Management. SRM aims to promote the professional development and continuing education of members and the public and the stewardship of rangeland resources. Members are land managers, scientists, educators, students, producers and conservationists. Membership: $85 (Regular); $80 (Regular Unsectioned); $25 (Regular International); $35 (Student); $30 (Student Unsectioned); $205 (Institutional); $525 (Commercial); $1,500-1,750 (Life).

Continuing Education:
Certification Designation/s: CPRM

Meetings/Conferences: Annual
Conference Chair: Kate Counter
2013 - Oklahoma City, OK (Renaissance Oklahoma
    City Convention Center Hotel)/Feb. 3 - 7
2014 - Orlando, FL (Caribe Royal Resort)/Feb. 7 - 15
2015 - Sacramento, CA/Jan. 30 - Feb. 7
2016 - Corpus Christi, TX/Jan. 29 - Feb. 6

Publications:
Rangeland Ecology & Management; bi-monthly; adv.
Rangelands; bi-monthly; adv.

Society for Reproductive Endocrinology and Infertility *(1983)*
1209 Montgomery Hwy.
Birmingham, AL 35216-2809
Tel: (205) 978-5000 *Fax:* (205) 978-5005
E-Mail: asrm@asrm.org
Website: socrei.org
Members: 936 individuals

Staff: 3
Annual Budget: $250-500,000

Personnel:
Executive Director: Robert W. Rebar
Editor: Bill Catherino MD
Treasurer: Stuart, S. Howards

Historical Note:
Formerly Society of Reproductive Endocrinologists (1998). SREI's mission is to foster the training and career development of students, residents, associates, members, and affiliates. Members are physicians, both in private practice and academia, who are certified by the American Board of Obstetrics and Gynecology as reproductive endocrinologists. SREI gets administrative support from the American Society for Reproductive Medicine.

Publications:
Membership Directory; on-line

Society for Research in Child Development *(1933)*
2950 S. State St.
Suite 401
Ann Arbor, MI 48104
Tel: (734) 926-0600 *Fax:* (734) 926-0601
E-Mail: info@srcd.org
Website: srcd.org
Members: 5500 researchers, practitioners, and
human development professionals
Staff: 16
Annual Budget: $5-10,000,000
Tax: 501(c)(3)

Personnel:
Executive Director: Lonnie Sherrod PhD
    E-Mail: sherrod@srcd.org
Manager, Membership Services and Marketing: Amy D.
    Glaspie
    E-Mail: aglaspie@srcd.org
Deputy Executive Director: Susan Lennon
    E-Mail: slennon@srcd.org
Managing Editor: Adam Martin
    E-Mail: amartin@srcd.org
Manager, Program Operations: Thelma Tucker
    E-Mail: tetucker@srcd.org

Historical Note:
Founded in 1933 in the District of Columbia as an outgrowth of the Committee on Child Development of the National Research Council. The Committee, formed in 1925, was the successor to a subcommittee on Child Development under the Division of Anthropology and Psychology of the National Research Council, which began in 1922. Affiliated with the American Association for the Advancement of Science. SRCD's purpose is to promote multidisciplinary research in the field of human development, to advance the exchange of information among scientists and other professionals of various disciplines, and to encourage applications of research findings. Membership: $160 (Regular); $305 (2-Year Regular) $65 (Spouse); $75 (Graduate Student); $55 (Undergraduate); $95 (Early Career); $150 (Developed Country); $75-142 (Tier 2 Country).

Continuing Education:
Certification Designation/s: EBPF, CFCD

Meetings/Conferences:
Conference Chair: Thelma Tucker
2013 - Seatle, WA/April 18 - 20
2015 - Philadelphia, PA/March 19 - 21
2015 - Philadelphia, PA/March 26 - 28

Publications:
Child Development; bi-monthly; adv.
Child Development Perspectives
Developments; quarterly; adv.
Membership Directory; on-line
Monographs of the Society for Research in Child
    Development; bi-monthly

Society for Research on Adolescence *(1984)*
2950 S. State St.
Suite 401
Ann Arbor, MI 48104
Tel: (734) 926-0700 *Fax:* (734) 926-0701
E-Mail: info@s-r-a.org
Website: s-r-a.org
Members: 1200 individuals
Staff: 12
Annual Budget: $250-500,000
Tax: 501(c)(6)

Personnel:
Executive Officer: Susan Lennon

    E-Mail: slennon@s-r-a.org
Controller: Rick Burdick
    E-Mail: rburd@s-r-a.org
Coordinator, Membership and Marketing: Amy D. Glaspie
    E-Mail: aglaspie@s-r-a.org
Managing Editor: Adam Martin
    E-Mail: amartin@s-r-a.org
Meeting Planner: Anne Perdu
    E-Mail: aperdue@s-r-a.org

Historical Note:
SRA's mission is to foster high quality scholarship on adolescence; encourage and foster global exchange and collaboration among adolescent researchers from diverse disciplines. Membership: $120 (Full); $53 (Student); $85 (New Professional/Emeritus); $35 (Student, Non-Journal).

Meetings/Conferences: Biennial
Conference Chair: Anne Perdu
2014 - Austin, TX/March 20 - 22

Publications:
Journal of Research on Adolescence; quarterly
Membership Directory; on-line

Society for Research on Nicotine and Tobacco *(1994)*
2424 American Ln.
Madison, WI 53704
Tel: (608) 443-2462 *Fax:* (608) 443-2474
E-Mail: info@srnt.org
Website: srnt.org
Members: 900 individuals
Staff: 6
Annual Budget: $500-1,000,000
Tax: 501(c)(3)

Personnel:
Executive Director: Bruce Wheeler
    E-Mail: bwheeler@reesgroupinc.com
Dianne Benson: Dianne Benson
Editor: Karen Cropsey PhD
    E-Mail: klcropsey@vcu.edu
Contact, Electronic Communications and Web: John
    Hofmann
    E-Mail: jhofmann@reesgroupinc.com
Coordinator, Membership Services: Linda Potchoiba
Meeting Planner: Jane Shepard

Historical Note:
SRNT's mission is to stimulate the generation of new knowledge concerning nicotine in all its manifestations from molecular to societal. Members are international scientists and other researchers interested in societal, biobehavioral, and political aspects of tobacco and tobacco use. Membership: $30-150 (Full/Affiliate); $85 (Retired); $48 (Student/Trainee).

Meetings/Conferences: Annual
Conference Chair: Jane Shepard
2013 - Boston, MA (Westin Boston Waterfront Hotel)/
    March 13 - 16
2014 - Seatle, WA (Sheraton Seattle Hotel)/Feb. 5 - 8
2015 - Philadelphia, PA (Philadelphia Marriott Hotel)/
    Feb. 23 - 28
Number of non-conference events/year: 2

Publications:
Member Directory; on-line
Nicotine & Tobacco Research
SRNT Newsletter

Society for Risk Analysis *(1982)*
1313 Dolley Madison Blvd.
Suite 402
McLean, VA 22101-3926
Tel: (703) 790-1745 *Fax:* (703) 790-2672
E-Mail: sraburkmgt@aol.com
Website: sra.org
Members: 2090 individuals
Staff: 15
Annual Budget: $500-1,000,000
Tax: 501(c)(6)

Personnel:
President: Ann Bostrom
    E-Mail: abostrom@u.washington.edu
Executive Secretary: David A. Drupa
    E-Mail: ddrupa@burkinc.com
Media Contact: Steve Gibb
Managing Editor: Mary Walchuk
    E-Mail: mwalchuk@hickorytech.net

Historical Note:
SRA is an international society that provides an open forum for all those who are interested in risk analysis.

SRA encourages applications of risk analysis methods and promotes advancement of the state-of-the-art in research and education on risk analysis. Membership: $105 (Full); $155 (Supporting); $55 (Student/Reduced Fee); $0-40 (Regional Organization); $0-15 (Specialty Group).

Meetings/Conferences: Annual
2013 - Baltimore, MD/Dec. 8 - 11
Number of non-conference events/year: 3

Publications:
Risk Analysis
RISK Newsletter; quarterly; adv.

Society for Romanian Studies (1973)
Department of Political Science
P.O. Box 261790
Greensboro, NC 17412
Tel: (480) 965-4658
Website: society4romanianstudies.org
Members: 200 individuals
Staff: 3
Annual Budget: Under $10,000

Personnel:
Editor: Roland Clark
    E-Mail: roloclark80@gmail.com
Treasurer: William Crowther
    E-Mail: wecrowth@uncg.edu

Historical Note:
SRS promotes professional study, criticism, and research on all aspects of Romanian culture and civilization, particularly concerning the countries of Romania and Moldova. Annual meetings held in conjunction with the AAASS. Membership: $0-500/year.

Meetings/Conferences:
Number of non-conference events/year: 1

Publications:
SRS Newsletter

Society for Scholarly Publishing (1978)
10200 W. 44th Ave.
Suite 304
Wheat Ridge, CO 80033-2840
Tel: (303) 422-3914 Fax: (303) 422-8894
E-Mail: info@sspnet.org
Website: sspnet.org
Members: 885 individuals and organizations
Staff: 4
Annual Budget: $500-1,000,000
Tax: 501(c)(3)

Personnel:
Executive Director: Ann Mehan Crosse CMP, CAE
    E-Mail: amehan@resourcecenter.com
Secretary and Treasurer: Todd A. Carpenter
    E-Mail: tcarpenter@niso.org

Historical Note:
SSP's mission is to promote and advance communication among all sectors of the scholarly publication community through networking, information dissemination and facilitation of new developments in the field. Members are individuals, publishing companies and professional societies involved in the production of scholarly books and periodicals. Membership: $135 (Regular); $75 (Librarian/Early Career); $30 (Student); $1,390 (Supporting Organization); $3,275 (Sustaining Organization).

Meetings/Conferences:
2013 - San Francisco, CA (San Francisco Marriott Marquis)/June 5 - 7
2013 - San Francisco, CA (San Francisco Marriott Marquis)/July 5 - 7
Number of non-conference events/year: 2

Publications:
Learned Published; on-line
Membership Directory; annually
Services Directory; on-line; adv.
SSP News; on-line
SSP President's e-Letter

Society for Sex Therapy and Research (1975)
6311 W. Gross Point Rd.
Niles, IL 60714
Tel: (847) 647-8832 Fax: (847) 647-8940
E-Mail: info@sstarnet.org
Website: sstarnet.org
Members: 200 individuals
Staff: 7
Annual Budget: $100-250,000

Personnel:
Manager: Linda Getty

E-Mail: lindag@celticchicago.com

Historical Note:
Formerly the Eastern Association of Sex Therapy, SSTAR aims to facilitate communication among clinicians who treat problems of sexual function, sexual identity, and reproductive life. Membership includes professionals in varying disciplines including psychology, medicine (including psychiatry, Ob/Gyn, urology, internal medicine, family medicine), social work, marriage and family therapy, nursing, sexology and the sciences. Membership: $30 (Student); $180 (Full/Associate).

Meetings/Conferences:
Conference Chair: Chris Kraft PhD
2013 - Baltimore, MD/April 4 - 7
Number of non-conference events/year: 1

Publications:
Directory of Clinical Professionals; on-line
SSTAR Newsletter; on-line

Society for Simulation in Healthcare (2004)
214 N. Hale St.
Wheaton, IL 60187
Tel: (630) 510-4586 Fax: (952) 252-8096
E-Mail: admin@ssih.org
Website: ssih.org
Members: 2000 individuals
Staff: 7
Annual Budget: $2-5,000,000
Tax: 501(c)(3)

Personnel:
Executive Director: Kathryn B. Aberle CAE, MBA
    E-Mail: kaberle.ssh@gmail.com
Director, Continuing Education: Kathy Adams
    E-Mail: kadams@ssih.org
Managing Editor: Karl W. Durst
Director, Meetings and Exhibits: Judy Larson
    E-Mail: jlarson@ssih.org
Manager, Membership: Valerie Lippert
Manager, Communications: Holly Simonton
    E-Mail: communications.ssh@gmail.com
Director, Finance: Alan Togliatti
    E-Mail: atogliatti@integrated-solutions.com

Historical Note:
Represents a group of educators and researchers who utilize a variety of simulation techniques for education, testing, and research in health care. SSH strives to facilitate excellence in multi-specialty health care education, practice, and research through simulation modalities. Membership: $165 (Full); $75 (Retired/Student/Resident).

Meetings/Conferences: Annual
Conference Chair: Judy Larson
2013 - Orlando, FL (Peabody Orlando)/Jan. 26 - 30

Publications:
Simulation in Healthcare - Journal; bi-monthly
SSH Newsletter; monthly

Society for Slovene Studies (1973)
University of Washington, Suzzallo Library
P.O. Box 352900
Seattle, WA 98195
Tel: (206) 937-1250
Website: slovenestudies.com
Members: 350 individuals
Staff: 3
Annual Budget: Under $10,000

Personnel:
Secretary: Michael Biggins
    E-Mail: mbiggins@u.washington.edu

Historical Note:
An affiliate of American Association for the Advancement of Slavic Studies and American Association of Teachers of Slavic and East European Languages. SSS is a non-profit association of scholars dedicated to the research of Slovene culture. SSS's purpose is to promote the dissemination of scholarly information on Slovene studies through meetings, conferences, and the preparation of scholarly works for publication. Membership: $20 (Regular/Sustaining); $10 (Students);$300 (Lifetime).

Publications:
Slovene Studies
SSS Letter - Newsletter

Society for Social Studies of Science (1975)
Louisiana State University, Department of Sociology
126 Stubbs Hall
Baton Rouge, LA 70803
Tel: (225) 578-5311 Fax: (225) 578-5102

Website: 4sonline.org
Members: 550 individuals
Staff: 2
Annual Budget: $250-500,000
Tax: 501(c)(3)

Personnel:
President: Trevor Pinch
    E-Mail: tjp2@cornell.edu
Secretary: Wesley Shrum
    E-Mail: shrum@lsu.edu

Historical Note:
Affiliated with American Association for the Advancement of Science. Also known as 4S. 4S's mission is to facilitate communication across conventional boundaries that separate the disciplines and across national boundaries that separate scholars. Members include scholars in sociology, anthropology, history, philosophy, political science, economics, and psychology. Membership: $45 (Professional); $22 (Students, Retirees, and Scholars from non-OECD countries).

Meetings/Conferences: Annual
2013 - San Diego, CA (Town and Country Resort Hotel)/Oct. 9 - 12

Publications:
Science, Technology, and Human Values; bi-monthly; adv.
Technoscience Updates; monthly; adv.

Society for Social Work Leadership in Health Care (1965)
100 N. 20th St.
Fourth Floor
Philadelphia, PA 19103
Tel: (215) 599-6134 Fax: (215) 564-2175
TollFree: (866) 237-9542
E-Mail: lgroff@fernley.com
Website: sswlhc.org
Members: 700 individuals
Staff: 5
Annual Budget: $25-50,000
Tax: 501(c)(6)

Personnel:
Management Liaison: Lindsay Groff
    E-Mail: lgroff@fernley.com
Account Manager: Kyle Fernley
    E-Mail: kfernley@fernley.com
Senior Meeting Planner: Trish Keppler CMP

Historical Note:
Formerly (1993) the Society for Hospital Social Work Directors, (1994) Social Work Administrators in Health Care and (1998) Society for Social Work Administrators in Health Care. The SSWLHC works to support emerging leaders in all roles, provide leadership knowledge and skills and be the force for advocacy through its collective leadership in all health care arenas. Membership: $140 (Management); $90 (Direct Patient Care); $85 (Transitional/Faculty); $165 (Associate); $55 (Student/EMERITUS).

Meetings/Conferences: Annual
Conference Chair: Trish Keppler CMP

Publications:
Membership Directory
Social Work in Health Care
Social Work Leader

Society for Software Quality (1984)
P.O. Box 27634
San Diego, CA 92198
E-Mail: info@ssq.org
Website: ssq.org
Members: 250 individuals
Staff: 2
Annual Budget: Under $10,000
Tax: 501(c)(3)

Personnel:
President: Theodore Hahn
Treasurer: Leo Shchupak

Historical Note:
SSQ's mission is to improve the quality of software and to provide a means of communication between academia, industry and software professionals. Membership: $45/year.

Society for Surgery of the Alimentary Tract (1960)
900 Cummings Center
Suite 4550
Beverly, MA 01915

Tel: (978) 927-8330 Fax: (978) 524-8890
E-Mail: ssat@prri.com
Website: ssat.com
Members: 2700 individuals
Staff: 6
Annual Budget: $1-2,000,000
Tax: 501(c)(6)

Personnel:
President: John G. Hunter MD
Treasurer: Selwyn M. Vickers MD

Historical Note:
Formerly Association of Colon Surgery. SSAT's mission is to stimulate, foster, and provide surgical leadership in the art and science of patient care; to teach and research the diseases and functions of the alimentary tract; to provide a forum for the presentation of such knowledge; and to encourage training opportunities, funding, and scientific publications supporting the foregoing activities. Membership: $155 (Active Member); $80 (Candidate Member); $20 (Candidate/Resident Member).

Continuing Education:
Certification Designation/s: MIS

Meetings/Conferences: Annual
2013 - Orlando, FL (Orange County Convention Center)/May 17 - 21

Publications:
Journal of Gastrointestinal Surgery (JOGS); monthly
Membership Directory; on-line
SSAT Newsletter

Society for Technical Communication (1953)
9401 Lee Hwy.
Suite 300
Fairfax, VA 22031
Tel: (703) 522-4114 Fax: (703) 522-2075
Website: stc.org
Members: 12000 individuals and 120 chapters
Staff: 8
Annual Budget: $2-5,000,000
Tax: 501(c)(3)

Personnel:
Manager, Web Content and Information Technology: Chip Boyd
E-Mail: chip.boyd@stc.org
Manager, Media: Kevin Cuddihy
E-Mail: kevin.cuddihy@stc.org
Manager, Meetings: Elaine Gilliam
E-Mail: elaine.gilliam@stc.org
Manager, Business Development: Stacey O'Donnell
E-Mail: stacey.odonnell@stc.org
Director, Publications and Editor: Liz Pohland
E-Mail: liz.pohland@stc.org
Manager, Membership Services: Barbra Sanders
E-Mail: barbra.sanders@stc.org
Senior Accountant: Marta Sokol
E-Mail: marta.sokol@stc.org
Deputy Executive Director: Lloyd Tucker
E-Mail: lloyd.tucker@stc.org

Historical Note:
STC's mission is to advance the practice and theory of technical communications and promotes the value of technical communicators globally. Members include technical writers and editors, content developers, documentation specialists, technical illustrators, instructional designers, academics, information architects, usability and human factors professionals, visual designers, Web designers and developers, and translators. Membership: $215 (Basic); $395 (Gold); $75 (Student); $145 (Retired), $160 (New TC Professional).

Continuing Education:
Certification Designation/s: CPTC

Meetings/Conferences: Annual
Conference Chair: Elaine Gilliam
2013 - Atlanta, GA (Hyatt Regency Atlanta)/May 5 - 8/11-25 exhibitors
Number of non-conference events/year: 3

Publications:
Intercom; monthly; adv.
News & Notes; monthly
Technical Communication; quarterly

Membership List Available to Non-members

Society for Technological Advancement of Reporting
222 S. Westmonte Dr.
Suite 101
Altamonte Springs, FL 32714

Tel: (407) 774-7880 Fax: (407) 774-6440
TollFree: (800) 565-6054
E-Mail: star@staronline.org
Website: staronline.org
Members: 700 companies
Staff: 3
Annual Budget: $100-250,000

Personnel:
Executive Director: Tina Kautter CAE

Historical Note:
STAR's purpose is to help its members to exchange information, evaluate products, and present their ideas to the manufacturer with a united voice. Membership: $150 (Reporting/Agency); $75 (Associate); $40 (Student).

Meetings/Conferences: Annual
2013 - Ft. Lauderdale, FL (Marriott Harbor Beach Resort & Spa)/March 7 - 9
2013 - Washington, DC (Liaison Capitol Hill)/Oct. 3 - 5
2014 - Las Vegas, NV (Caesars Palace)/March 13 - 15

Publications:
Membership Directory; on-line
STAR-Dot-STAR; quarterly; adv.

Society for Textual Scholarship (1979)
Indiana University Press
601 N. Morton St.
Bloomington, IN 47404
Website: textual.org
Members: 50 institutions and 600 individuals
Staff: 2
Annual Budget: $10-25,000

Personnel:
Executive Director: John K. Young
E-Mail: youngj@marshall.edu
Treasurer: Gabrielle Dean
E-Mail: gnodean@jhu.edu

Historical Note:
STS is dedicated to explore how the various cultures of textual production shape the creation, reception, dissemination, and understanding of texts. Membership: $80 (Basic); $250 (Sustaining); $40 (Student); $41.50 (Retiree).

Meetings/Conferences:
2013 - Chicago, IL (Loyola University)/March 6 - 8

Publications:
Membership Directory; on-line
Textual Cultures; adv.

Society for the Advancement of American Philosophy (1972)
9001 Stockdale Hwy.
Bakersfield, CA 93311-1099
Tel: (618) 536-6641
Website: american-philosophy.org
Members: 900 individuals
Staff: 4

Personnel:
President: Jacquelyn Kegley
E-Mail: jkegley@csub.edu

Historical Note:
SAAP's mission is to promote interest and research in the history of American Philosophy. Members are academics and others with an interest in the field of American Philosophy. Membership: $150 (Benefactor); $100 (Sustaining); $20-65(Regular).

Meetings/Conferences: Annual
2013 - Galloway, NJ (The Richard Stockton College)/March 7 - 9

Publications:
Contemporary Pragmatism
The Pluralist

Society for the Advancement of Behavior Analysis (1980)
550 W. Center Ave.
Suite One
Portage, MI 49024-5364
Tel: (269) 492-9310 Fax: (269) 492-9316
E-Mail: mail@abainternational.org
Website: abainternational.org/saba
Members: 400 donors
Staff: 3
Annual Budget: $25-50,000
Tax: 501(c)(3)

Personnel:
President: Richard W. Malott

E-Mail: dickmalott@dickmalott.com
Secretary and Treasurer: Maria E. Malott PhD
E-Mail: mmalott@abainternational.org

Historical Note:
SABA is the fundraising arm of Association for Behavior Analysis, which provides administrative support. SABA's purpose is to provide instruction and training in behavior analysis and to disseminate information concerning it.

Society for the Advancement of Economic Theory (1990)
University of Illinois, Deapartment of Economics
410 David Kinley Hall, 1407 W. Gregory
Urbana, IL 61801
Tel: (217) 333-0120 Fax: (217) 244-6678
Website: saet.illinois.edu
Members: 170 individuals
Staff: 1

Personnel:
Founder, Treasurer and Editor: Nicholas C. Yannelis
E-Mail: nyanneli@uiuc.edu

Historical Note:
Purpose of SEAT is to advance knowledge in theoretical economics and to facilitate communication among researchers in economics, mathematics, game theory or any other field which is potentially useful to economic theory. Members are individuals with an interest in theoretical economics. Membership: $69 (Individual); $39 (Student).

Meetings/Conferences: Annual
2013 - Paris, France (Mines ParisTech)/July 22 - 27

Publications:
SAET Bulletin

Society for the Advancement of Education (1939)
22-11 Valley Rd.
Apt 11
Drexel Hill, PA 19026
Tel: (484) 461-9000
E-Mail: info@educationsaveschildren.org
Website: educationsaveschildren.org
Members: 1900 individuals
Staff: 3
Annual Budget: $100-250,000

Personnel:
President: Faraz Sheikh
E-Mail: fmasoodsheikh@gmail.com

Historical Note:
SAVE's mission is to serve the poorest and the most needy children in poor regions of the world. Initially, they are focusing on poor areas in Pakistan.Membership: $29/year.

Society for the Advancement of Material and Process Engineering (1944)
1161 Park View Dr.
Suite 200
Covina, CA 91724-3759
Tel: (626) 331-0616 Fax: (626) 332-8929
TollFree: (800) 562-7360
E-Mail: sampe@sampe.org
Website: sampe.org
Members: 4500 individuals
Staff: 14
Annual Budget: $2-5,000,000
Tax: 501(c)(6)

Personnel:
Executive Director: Gregg Balko
E-Mail: gregg@sampe.org
Webmaster: Janie Drake
E-Mail: janie@sampe.org
Manager, Information Technology: Jack Hsiung
E-Mail: jack@sampe.org
Controller, Accounting and Finance: Mike Keilty
E-Mail: mike@sampe.org
Manager, Conference and Exhibits: Rosemary Loggia
E-Mail: rosemary@sampe.org
Coordinator, Membership Services: Patricia Padelford
E-Mail: patricia@sampe.org
Manager, Business Development: Efren Pavon
E-Mail: efren@sampe.org
Journal Production Manager: Jennifer Stephens
E-Mail: jennifer@sampe.org
Manager, Marketing and Education: Michelle Tubb
E-Mail: michelle@sampe.org

Historical Note:
Founded as the Society of Aircraft Material and Process Engineers and incorporated in California in 1960 as the Society of Aerospace Material and Process Engineers and

assumed its present name in 1973. SAMPE's mission is to provide a global forum for information, education and professional fellowship for those who define the leading edge and application of materials and processes advancement. Membership: $122 (Professional/Associate-US); $20 (Student); $39 (Retiree); $99-113 (Professional/Associate-International); $26 (Student-International).

Meetings/Conferences: Annual
Conference Chair: Rosemary Loggia
2013 - Long Beach, CA (Long Beach Convention Center)/May 6 - 9
2013 - Wichita, KS (Century II Convention Center)/Oct. 21 - 24/over 100 exhibitors
2014 - Seattle, WA/June 2 - 5
Number of non-conference events/year: 2

Publications:
The SAMPE Journal; bi-monthly; adv.

Society for the Advancement of Scandinavian Study (1911)
Brigham Young University, Scandinavian Studies
P.O. Box 26118
Provo, UT 84602-6118
Tel: (801) 422-5598 *Fax:* (801) 422-0307
E-Mail: sass@byu.edu
Website: scandinavianstudy.org
Members: 800 individuals
Staff: 3
Annual Budget: $100-250,000
Tax: 501(c)(3)

Personnel:
President: Mark Sandberg
  E-Mail: sandberg@berkeley.edu
Secretary and Treasurer: Richard L. Jensen
  E-Mail: richard_l_jensen@byu.edu
Managing Editor: Steven P. Sondrup
  E-Mail: steven_sondrup@byu.edu

Historical Note:
SASS advocates Scandinavian study and instruction in America. Members are scholars, teachers and researchers of Scandinavian language, literature and culture. Membership: $55-70 (Regular); $30-45 (Student/Retired); $70- 85 (Patron); $750-900 (Life).

Meetings/Conferences: Annual
2013 - San Francisco, CA/May 2 - 4
2014 - New Haven, CT/March 13 - 15

Publications:
Membership Directory; on-line
SASS Newsletter

Society for the Anthropology of Food and Nutrition (1974)
Emory University
1557 Dickey Dr.
Atlanta, GA 30322
Tel: (404) 727-5248
E-Mail: info@nutritionalanthro.org
Website: foodanthro.com
Staff: 5

Personnel:
President: Craig Hadley
  E-Mail: chadley@emory.edu

Historical Note:
Formerly the Council on Nutritional Anthropology; a section of the American Anthropological Association, became SAFN in 2004. SAFN's mission is to promote interest and research in the anthropological study of food and nutrition. Membership: $20 (Student); $30 (Professional).

Meetings/Conferences:
Conference Chair: Sera Young

Publications:
Anthropology Newsletter

Society for the Anthropology of North America
2200 Wilson Blvd.
Suite 600
Arlington, VA 22201
Tel: (703) 528-1902 *Fax:* (703) 528-3546
Website: sananet.org
Staff: 4

Personnel:
President: Julian Brash
  E-Mail: brashj@mail.montclair.edu
Editor: Susan Falls
  E-Mail: sfalls@scad.edu
Webmaster: Martin Hoyem
  E-Mail: mh@americanethnography.com

Treasurer: Marina Peterson
  E-Mail: petersom@ohio.edu

Historical Note:
The goal of the Society for the Anthropology of North America is to address the need for a focused voice and institutional presence for the Anthropology of the United States, Canada and Mexico. Membership: $25 (Professor and Professional); $10 (Student).

Publications:
North American Dialogue; semi-annually; adv.

Society for the Anthropology of Work (1980)
2200 Wilson Blvd., Suite 600
C/O American Anthropological Association
Arlington, VA 22201
Tel: (703) 528-1902 *Fax:* (703) 528-3546
Website: aaanet.org/sections/saw
Staff: 6

Personnel:
President: Samuel Collins
  E-Mail: scollins@towson.edu
Webmaster: Angela Jancius
  E-Mail: jancius3022@comcast.net
Meetings Contact: Carrie Lane
  E-Mail: clane@fullerton.edu
Editor: Sarah Lyon
  E-Mail: sarah.lyon@uky.edu
Treasurer: Charles Menzies
  E-Mail: cmenzies@interchange.ubc.ca
Student Representative: Theodore Rose
  E-Mail: theorose81@yahoo.com

Historical Note:
SAW's mission is to advance the study of work in all aspects, by anthropologists from all areas of the discipline and to encourage the communication of such study.

Meetings/Conferences:
Conference Chair: Carrie Lane

Publications:
Anthropology of Work Review Journal

Society for the Exploration of Psychotherapy Integration (1984)
1550 Wilson Blvd.
Suite 600
Arlington, VA 22209
Tel: (301) 598-0969
Website: sepiweb.com
Members: 750 individuals
Staff: 3
Annual Budget: $25-50,000
Tax: 501(c)(3)

Personnel:
Contact, Publications: Jerry Gold
  E-Mail: jrgold99@gmail.com
Webmaster: Sven Schneider
  E-Mail: sven.schneider@uni-ulm.de
Treasurer: George Stricker PhD
  E-Mail: geostricker@gmail.com

Historical Note:
SEPI's mission is to advocate the development and evaluation of approaches to psychotherapy that are not limited by a single orientation. Members are mental health professionals with an interest in integrating theories and techniques in psychotherapy. Membership: $59 (Regular); $29 (Full time Student).

Continuing Education:
Certification Designation/s: CEU

Meetings/Conferences: Annual
2013 - Barcelona, Spain/June 6 - 9

Publications:
Journal of Psychotherapy Integration; on-line
Membership Directory; on-line

Membership List Available to Non-members

Society for the History of Authorship, Reading and Publishing (1991)
2006 Columbia Rd. NW
Apartment 42
Washington, DC 20009
Tel: (202) 462-3105 *Fax:* (410) 516-3866
E-Mail: members@sharpweb.org
Website: sharpweb.org
Members: 1000 individuals
Staff: 4
Annual Budget: $50-100,000

Personnel:

Editor: Sydney Shep
  E-Mail: editor@sharpweb.org
Secretary, Membership Services: Eleanor F. Shevlin
  E-Mail: members@sharpweb.org

Historical Note:
SHARP promotes research and education in the historical sociology of literature, i. e., the creation, diffusion, and reception of the written and printed word. Membership: $55-60 (Full Individual); $20-25 (Student); $25-30 (Library/Institution) $100 (Sustaining).

Meetings/Conferences: Annual
2013 - Antwerp, Belgium/May 23 - 24
2013 - Philadelphia, PA (University of Pennsylvania)/ July 18 - 21

Publications:
Book History; annually
Membership & Periodicals Directory; annually
Sharp News; quarterly

Society for the History of Discoveries (1960)
5904 Mt. Eagle Dr.
Apt. 118
Alexandria, VA 22303-2535
Website: sochistdisc.org
Members: 300 individuals
Staff: 4
Annual Budget: $10-25,000
Tax: 501(c)(3)

Personnel:
Treasurer: Donald Perkins
  E-Mail: Perkwyn53@cox.net
Editor: Marguerite Ragnow
  E-Mail: editor@sochistdisc.org

Historical Note:
SHD's purpose is to stimulate interest in teaching, research, and publishing the history of geographical exploration. Membership: $30 (Regular); $50 (Contributing); $15 (Student/Retiree).

Meetings/Conferences: Annual
2013 - Tampa, FL (Tampa Marriott Waterside Hotel and Marina)/Oct. 31 - Nov. 2

Publications:
Membership list; annually
Terra Cognita; annually
Terrae Incognitae; semi-annually

Society for the History of Technology (1958)
C/O Department of Science, Technology & Society, University of Virginia
P.O. Box 400744
Charlottesville, VA 22904-4744
Tel: (434) 987-6230 *Fax:* (434) 975-2190
E-Mail: shot@virginia.edu
Website: historyoftechnology.org
Members: 2000 individuals
Staff: 4
Annual Budget: $100-250,000

Personnel:
President: Ron Kline
  E-Mail: rrk1@cornell.edu
Secretary: W. Bernard Carlson
  E-Mail: shotsecy@virginia.edu
Treasurer: Hugh Gorman
  E-Mail: hsgorman@mtu.edu
Editor: Suzanne Moon
  E-Mail: suzannemoon@techculture.org

Historical Note:
Formed in Cleveland (1958) and incorporated Ohio (1959). SHOT is dedicated to the historical study of technology and its relations with politics, economics, labor, business, the environment, public policy, science, and the arts. Membership: $64 (Individual); $34 (Student); $44 (Emeritus).

Meetings/Conferences: Annual
2013 - Portland, ME/Oct. 10 - 13
2014 - Dearborn, MI/Nov. 6 - 9

Publications:
SHOT Newsletter; quarterly
Technology and Culture Journal; quarterly

Membership List Available to Non-members

Society for the Philosophy of Sex and Love (1977)
University of Illinois at Urbana-Champaign,
Department of Philosophy
105 Gregory Hal, 810 S. Wright St., M/C 468

Urbana, IL 61801
Tel: (217) 333-2889 Fax: (217) 244-8355
E-Mail: caraway@grove.iup.edu
Website: philosophyofsexandlove.org
Members: 60 individuals
Staff: 1
Annual Budget: Under $10,000

Personnel:
Co-President: Helga Varden
    E-Mail: hvarden@illinois.edu

Historical Note:
SPSL encourages and facilitates the philosophical study of
sexuality, gender, love, friendship, marriage, and related
topics. Members are academics and others. Membership:
Free.

Meetings/Conferences: Annual
2013 - San Francisco, CA/March 27 - 31

Society for the Preservation of Oral Health
(1960)
P.O. Box 2945
La Grange, GA 30241
Tel: (706) 845-9085 Fax: (706) 883-8215
Website: spoh.org
Members: 75 individuals
Staff: 1
Annual Budget: $25-50,000

Personnel:
Contact: Rebecca Smith
    E-Mail: rsmith@asginfo.net

Historical Note:
Members are those who have practiced dentistry for at least
five years and who concentrate on or have a strong interest
in preventive dentistry. Membership: $500/year.

Meetings/Conferences:
Conference Chair: Rebecca Smith

Society for the Psychological Study of Ethnic Minority Issues
750 First St. NE
Washington, DC 20002-4242
Tel: (202) 336-6121 Fax: (202) 218-3599
Website: division45.org/about/
Staff: 3

Personnel:
Contact, Administration: Chad Rummel MEd

Historical Note:
Society for the Psychological Study of Ethnic Minority
Issues works to advance psychology as a science and to
promote public welfare through research, to apply research
findings towards addressing ethnic minority issues, and to
encourage professional relationships among psychologists
with these interests. A division of American Psychological
Association Council. Members are psychologists who
conduct research on ethnic minority concerns. Membership:
$57 (Regular/Professional Affiliate); $27 (Student).

Meetings/Conferences: Annual
2013 - Houston, TX (Royal Sonesta Houston)/Jan. 17
    - 18

Publications:
Cultural Diversity and Ethnic Minority Psychology;
    quarterly
Focus Newsletter; semi-annually

Society for the Psychological Study of Lesbian and Gay Issues (1892)
2B Carl A. Kroch Library
Cornell University
Ithaca, NY 14853-5302
Tel: (607) 255-3530 Fax: (607) 255-9524
Website: apadivision44.org/
Staff: 4

Personnel:
President: Arlene Noriega
    E-Mail: dranor@bellsouth.net
Secretary and Treasurer: Chris Downs
    E-Mail: chris.downs215@gmail.com
Editor: Doug Kimmel
    E-Mail: dougkimmel@tamarackplace.com
Website Editor: Deborah Miller
    E-Mail: Deborah Miller, djmiller2@bsu.edu

Historical Note:
The Society for the Psychological Study of Lesbian, Gay,
Bisexual and Transgender Issues (SPSLGBTI) welcomes all
those interested in psychological research, education and
training, practice, and advocacy on lesbian, gay, bisexual
and transgendered issues and all lesbian women, gay men,

bisexual women, bisexual men, transgendered people, and
their allies.

Meetings/Conferences: Annual

Publications:
Newsletter

Society for the Psychological Study of Men and Masculinity (1995)
C/O American Psychological Association
750 First St. NE
Washington, DC 20002-4242
Tel: (202) 336-6013 Fax: (202) 218-3599
TollFree: (800) 374-2721
Website: apa.org/divisions/div51
Members: 774 members
Staff: 3

Personnel:
President: Jay Wade PhD
    E-Mail: jwade@fordham.edu
Treasurer: Sam Buser PhD
    E-Mail: sbuser@comcast.net
Contact, Membership Services: Jim O'Neil
    E-Mail: jimoneil1@aol.com

Historical Note:
A division of the American Psychological Association.
SPSMM is committed to the enhancement of men's capacity
to experience their full human potential. Membership:
$5-57 (Associate); $15-50 (Professional Affiliates);
$0-25(Student Affiliates).

Meetings/Conferences: Annual
2013 - Houston, TX (Royal Sonest Hotel)/Jan. 18 - 20

Publications:
Psychology of Men & Masculinity; quarterly

Membership List Available to Non-members

Society for the Psychological Study of Science Issues (1936)
208 I St. NE
Washington, DC 20002-4340
Tel: (202) 675-6956 Fax: (202) 675-6902
TollFree: (877) 310-7778
E-Mail: spssi@spssi.org
Website: spssi.org
Members: 3000 scientists
Staff: 6
Annual Budget: $500-1,000,000

Personnel:
Executive Director: Susan Dudley
    E-Mail: sdudley@spssi.org
Administrative and Awards Coordinator: Anila Balkissoon
    E-Mail: abalkissoon@spssi.org
Policy Coordinator: Alex Ingrams
    E-Mail: aingrams@spssi.org

Historical Note:
SPSSI is an association of psychologists, allied scientists,
and others, who are interested in the application of research
on the psychological aspects of important social issues
to public policy solutions. Membership: $25 (Graduate
Student/Undergraduate); $1500 (Sustaining); $50
(Affiliate).

Meetings/Conferences: Annual

Publications:
Analyses of Social Issues and Public Policy
Forward
Journal of Social Issues; quarterly
Social Issues and Policy Review; annually
The Rookie

Society for the Psychological Study of Social Issues (1936)
208 I St. NE
Washington, DC 20002-4340
Tel: (202) 675-6956 Fax: (202) 675-6902
TollFree: (877) 310-7778
E-Mail: spssi@spssi.org
Website: spssi.org
Members: 3000 psychologists, allied scientists
and students
Staff: 3
Annual Budget: $1-2,000,000
Tax: 501(c)(3)

Personnel:
Executive Director: Susan Dudley
    E-Mail: sdudley@spssi.org
Coordinator, Administration and Awards: Anila
    Balkissoon

    E-Mail: abalkissoon@spssi.org

Historical Note:
SPSSI seeks to bring behavioral and social science theory,
empirical evidence and practice into focus on human
problems. A division of the American Psychological
Association. Members are college students or professionals.
Membership: $25 (Student); $1,500 (Sustaining Member);
$50 (Affiliate); $40-100 (Individual) Free (Lifetime).

Meetings/Conferences: Biennial

Publications:
Analyses of Social Issues and Public Policy (ASAP);
    annually
Journal of Social Issues (JSI); quarterly
Social Issues and Policy Review (SIPR); annually
The Forward
The Rookie; quarterly

Membership List Available to Non-members

Society for the Science & the Public (1921)
1719 N. St. NW
Washington, DC 20036
Tel: (202) 785-2255
Website: societyforscience.org
Staff: 8
Annual Budget: $10-25,000,000

Personnel:
Manager, Information Technology Projects: Vikram Surya
    Chiruvolu
Contact, Web Specialist and Editorial Secretary:
    Gwendolyn K. Gillespie
Director, Science Education Programs: Michele Glidden
Director, Events: Cait Goldberg
President and Publisher: Elizabeth Marincola
Chief Financial Officer: Gregory L. Mitchell
Manager, Accounting and Contact, Human Resources: Lisa
    Proctor
Senior Manager, Communications: Sarah Wood

Historical Note:
SSP promotes the understanding and appreciation of science
and the vital role it plays in human advancement: to inform,
educate, and inspire.

Meetings/Conferences:
Conference Chair: Cait Goldberg

Publications:
Science News Bulletin; weekly
Science News for Kids; on-line
Science News magazine; bi-weekly
SSP E-Newsletter; monthly

Society for the Scientific Study of Religion (1949)
IUPUI Cavanaugh Hall 417
425 University Blvd.
Indianapolis, IN 46202-5140
Tel: (371) 278-6491
E-Mail: sssr@iupui.edu
Website: sssrweb.org
Members: 2500 libraries and individuals
Staff: 3
Annual Budget: $100-250,000
Tax: 501(c)(3)

Personnel:
Executive Officer: Arthur E. Farnsley II
Treasurer: James Cavendish
Business Manager: Joy Sherrill

Historical Note:
SSSR's mission is to foster interdisciplinary dialogue
and collaboration among scholars from sociology,
religious studies, psychology, political science, economics,
international studies, gender studies, and many other fields.
Membership: $35 (Regular); $45 (Contributing); $60
(Supporting); $100 (Patron); $15 (Student); $20 (Emeritus/
International Associate).

Meetings/Conferences: Annual
2013 - Boston, MA (Boston Waterfront Hotel)/Nov. 8 -
    10
2014 - Indianapolis, IN (JW Marriott Indianapolis)/Oct.
    31 - Nov. 2

Publications:
Journal for the Scientific Study of Religion; quarterly;
    adv.
Membership Directory; on-line

Membership List Available to Non-members

Society for the Scientific Study of Sexuality
(1957)
881 Third St.

Suite B-5
Whitehall, PA 18052
E-Mail: thesociety@sexscience.org
Website: sexscience.org
Members: 800 individuals
Staff: 3
Annual Budget: $250-500,000
Tax: 501(c)(3)

Personnel:
Executive Director: Joseph Fay MA
President: Bean Robinson PhD

Historical Note:
SSSS is committed to advancing knowledge of sexuality. The Society also support a world-wide, interdisciplinary community for professionals who, regardless of their specialization, are committed to a serious, scholarly, and scientific approach to acquiring and disseminating knowledge of sexuality. Membership: $245 (Member/ Associate); $355 (Couple); $155 (Retired Member); $85 (Student, without journal); $125 (Student, with journal); $145 (Developing Professional).

Meetings/Conferences: Annual
Conference Chair: Mandy L. Peters
2013 - San Diego, CA (Paradise Point Resort and Spa)/ Nov. 14 - 17

Publications:
Annual Review of Sex Research; annually; adv.
Journal of Sex Research; quarterly; adv.
Membership Directory; on-line; adv.
Sexual Science; quarterly; adv.

Membership List Available to Non-members

Society for the Study of Amphibians and Reptiles (1958)

C/O Central Michigan University, Deptartment of Biology
217 Brooks Hall
Mt. Pleasant, MI 48859
Tel: (989) 774-3758 *Fax:* (989) 774-3462
Website: ssarherps.org
Members: 2500 individuals and institutions
Staff: 4
Annual Budget: $250-500,000
Tax: 501(c)(3)

Personnel:
Treasurer: Kirsten Nicholson
    E-Mail: kirsten.nicholson@cmich.edu

Historical Note:
SSAR's mission is to advance research, conservation, and education concerning amphibians and reptiles. Membership: $70 (Regular); $35 (Student/Zoo Keeper Member); $85 (Family); $100 (Sustaining); $200 (Contributing); $500 (Patron); $1,400 (Life); $95-475 (Plenary).

Meetings/Conferences: Annual
Number of non-conference events/year: 1

Publications:
Herpetological Review; quarterly; adv.
Journal of Herpetology; quarterly

Society for the Study of Evolution (1946)

P.O. Box 299
St. Louis, MO 63166-0299
Tel: (510) 643-7711 *Fax:* (314) 577-9515
Website: evolutionsociety.org
Members: 3100 individuals
Staff: 8
Annual Budget: $1-2,000,000
Tax: 501(c)(3)

Personnel:
Executive Vice-President and Contact, Finance Committee: Edmund D. ("Butch") Brodie III
    E-Mail: bbrodie@virginia.edu
Director, Membership and Subscriptions: Heather Cacanindin
Contact, Business Office: William M. Dahl
    E-Mail: wdahl@botany.org
Managing Editor: Jennifer Mahar
    E-Mail: jmahar@wiley.com

Historical Note:
Founded as an outgrowth of the Committee on Common Problems of Genetics, Paleontology and Systematics, which was established in 1943 by the National Research Council. SSE absorbed the Society for the Study of Speciation. SSE promotes the study of organic evolution and the integration of the various fields of science concerned with evolution. Membership: $40 (Regular); $20 (Regular Developoing Nation/Emeritus/Student/K-12 Education); $700 (Lifetime).

Meetings/Conferences: Annual
2013 - Snowbird, UT/June 21 - 25
Number of non-conference events/year: 2

Publications:
Evolution

Society for the Study of Indigenous Languages of the Americas (1981)

P.O. Box 1295
Denton, TX 76202
Website: ssila.org
Members: 900 individuals
Staff: 4
Annual Budget: $10-25,000

Personnel:
President: Patricia Shaw
    E-Mail: patricia.a.shaw@ubc.ca
Executive Secretary: Ivy Doak
    E-Mail: ssila2@gmail.com
Editor: Karen Sue Rolph
    E-Mail: ssila_editor@hotmail.com

Historical Note:
Founded as the international scholarly organization representing American Indian linguistics and incorporated in 1997. Membership in SSILA is open to all those who are interested in the scientific study of the languages of the native peoples of North, Central and South America. Membership: $20/year.

Meetings/Conferences: Annual
2013 - Boston, MA (Boston Marriott Copley Place)/Jan. 3 - 6
Number of non-conference events/year: 1

Publications:
Membership Directory; annually
SSILA Newsletter; quarterly
The SSILA Bulletin; monthly

Society for the Study of Male Psychology and Physiology (1975)

321 Iuka Rd.
Montpelier, OH 43543
Tel: (419) 485-3602
Members: 180 individuals
Staff: 1
Annual Budget: Under $10,000

Personnel:
Executive Officer: Jerry Bergman PhD

Historical Note:
SSMPP members are psychiatrists, psychologists, sociologists and other professionals with an interest in the field.

Society for the Study of Reproduction (1967)

1619 Monroe St.
Suite Three
Madison, WI 53711-2063
Tel: (608) 256-2777 *Fax:* (608) 256-4610
E-Mail: ssr@ssr.org
Website: ssr.org
Members: 2450 individuals
Staff: 1
Annual Budget: $2-5,000,000
Tax: 501(c)(3)

Personnel:
Executive Director: Judith Jansen

Historical Note:
Founded in 1967 at the University of Illinois, with roots that go back to the 1953 Biennial Symposia of Reproduction. SSR's mission is to promote the study of reproduction by fostering interdisciplinary communication among scientists, holding conferences, and publishing meritorious studies. Members are researchers and clinicians representing many fields including physiology, immunology, molecular biology, genetic engineering, animal science, endocrinology and embryology. Membership: $225 (Regular/Associate); $50 (Trainee Pre-Doctorate); 65 (Post-Doctorate); $0 (Emeritus).

Meetings/Conferences: Annual
2013 - Montreal, QC/July 22 - 26
2014 - Grand Rapids, MI/July 19 - 23
Number of non-conference events/year: 9

Publications:
Biology of Reproduction; monthly
SSR Membership Directory; annually
SSR Newsletter
SSR Newsletter; adv.

Membership List Available to Non-members

Society for the Study of Social Biology (1926)

Syracuse University, Center for Policy Research
426 Eggers Hall
Syracuse, NY 13244-1020
Tel: (213) 740-1707 *Fax:* (213) 740-0792
E-Mail: clhimes@maxwell.syr.edu
Website: usc.edu/dept/gero/sssb
Members: 400 individuals
Staff: 2
Annual Budget: $10-25,000

Personnel:
Secretary and Treasurer: Christine Himes
    E-Mail: clhimes@maxwell.syr.edu
Editor: Tim Heaton
    E-Mail: biodemography@byu.edu

Historical Note:
Founded, organized and incorporated in New York in January 1926 as the American Eugenics Society, Inc.; assumed its present name in 1973. SSSB's mission is to promote the study of the biological and sociocultural forces affecting the structure and composition of human populations. The society is in the process of renaming itself to the Society of Biodemography and Social Biology (SBSB). Membership: $60 (Individual); $30 (Student/Emeritus).

Publications:
Biodemography and Social Biology; semi-annually

Society for the Study of Social Problems (1951)

901 McClung Tower
University of Tennessee
Knoxville, TN 37996-0490
Tel: (865) 689-1531 *Fax:* (865) 689-1534
E-Mail: sssp@utk.edu
Website: sssp1.org
Members: 2000 individuals
Staff: 4
Annual Budget: $500-1,000,000
Tax: 501(c)(3)

Personnel:
Executive Officer: Hector L. Delgado
    E-Mail: hector.delgado49@gmail.com
Associate, Graduate Research and Webmaster: Lisa East
    E-Mail: eeast2@utk.edu
Administrative Officer and Manager, Meetings: Michele Smith Koontz
    E-Mail: mkoontz3@utk.edu

Historical Note:
SSSP's objective is to promote social science research and teaching in order to bring scholarly and practical attention to the social world and its problems. Membership is open to anyone who supports its goals. Membership: $70-1700/ year; Free (Life Members/Emeriti).

Meetings/Conferences: Annual
Conference Chair: Michele Smith Koontz
2013 - New York City, NY (Westin New York at Times Square)/Aug. 9 - 11
2014 - San Francisco, CA (Hilton San Francisco Union Square)/Aug. 15 - 17
2015 - Chicago, IL (Radisson Blu Aqua Hotel)/Aug. 21 - 23

Publications:
Membership Directory; on-line; adv.
Social Problems Forum-Newsletter; adv.
Social Problems Journal; on-line; adv.
The SSSP Newsletter; monthly; adv.

Membership List Available to Non-members

Society for the Study of Symbolic Interaction (1975)

University of Illinois, Institute of Communications Research
229 Gregory Hall, 810 S. Wright St.
Urbana, IL 89154-5033
Tel: (217) 333-0795 *Fax:* (217) 244-9580
E-Mail: symbolic@unlv.nevada.edu
Website: symbolicinteraction.org/
Members: 650 individuals
Staff: 4
Annual Budget: $50-100,000

Personnel:
President: Simon Gottschalk
Editor: Robert Dingwall
Vice President: Melinda Milligan
    E-Mail: melinda.milligan@sonoma.edu
Treasurer: Linda Morrison

Historical Note:

SSSI is an international professional organization of scholars interested in the study of symbolic interactionism as it relates to a range of social issues. Has no paid officers or full-time staff. Membership: Dues based on level of income.

Meetings/Conferences: Annual
Conference Chair: Melinda Milligan

Publications:
SSSI Notes
Symbolic Interaction; quarterly

Membership List Available to Non-members

Society for the Teaching of Psychology
P.O. Box 5609
Wakefield, RI 02880
Tel: (401) 374-5042
E-Mail: stp@teachpsych.org
Website: teachpsych.org
Staff: 5

Personnel:
Executive Director: Theodore Bosack
   E-Mail: mailto:stp@teachpsych.org
Editor: Andrew N. Christopher
   E-Mail: top@albion.edu
Vice President for Recruiting, Retention and Public Relations: Diane Finley
   E-Mail: dfinley@pgcc.edu
Treasurer: David Kreiner
   E-Mail: kreiner@ucmo.edu
Director, Professional Development Program: Laura G. Lunsford
   E-Mail: mentoring@teachpsych.org

Historical Note:
A division of the American Psychological Association, STP advances understanding of the discipline by promoting excellence in the teaching and learning of psychology. Membership: $15 (Student); $25 (Non Student); $15 (Retirees).

Meetings/Conferences: Annual

Publications:
Membership Directory
Teaching of Psychology Journal; quarterly
TOPNEWS; monthly

Society for Theriogenology (1973)
P.O. Box 3007
Montgomery, AL 36109-3007
Tel: (334) 395-4666 *Fax:* (334) 270-3399
E-Mail: info@therio.org
Website: therio.org
Members: 2446 individuals
Staff: 4
Annual Budget: $250-500,000
Tax: 501(c)(5)

Personnel:
Executive Director: Charles F. Franz DVM
   E-Mail: charles@franzmgt.com
Coordinator, Membership Services: Linda Cargile
   E-Mail: Linda@Franzmgt.com
Director, Meetings and Membership Services: Roberta Norris
   E-Mail: roberta@franzmgt.com
Director, Public Relations and Communications: Melissa Williford
   E-Mail: melissa@franzmgt.com

Historical Note:
Formerly (1975) American Veterinary Society for the Study of Breeding Soundness. SFT's mission is to establish and advocate standards of excellence, provide forums to disseminate emerging information to veterinarians and students. Serves as a resource for scientific exchange, foster client education and awareness and encourage a network for collegial exchange. Members are veterinarians interested in animal reproduction. American College of Theriogenologists is the examination and certifying arm of SFT. Membership: $110 (Active/Associate); $10 (Student).

Meetings/Conferences:
Conference Chair: Roberta Norris

Publications:
Membership Directory; on-line
SFT newsletter; quarterly
Theriogenology; adv.

Society for Thermal Medicine (1986)
Duke University Medical Center, Radiation
Oncology Department
P.O. Box 3295 DUMC

Durham, NC 27710
Tel: (919) 681-1675
TollFree: (800) 627-0326
E-Mail: stm@allenpress.com
Website: psfebus.allenpress.com/eBusSFTM/
  HOME.aspx
Members: 200 individuals
Staff: 25
Annual Budget: $100-250,000
Tax: 501(c)(3)

Personnel:
Secretary and Treasurer: Dr. Oana I. Craciunescu PhD
Editor: Mark W. Dewhirst DVM, PhD

Historical Note:
Founded as North American Hyperthermia Society; assumed its current name in 2004. STM's mission is to facilitate interaction and communication between theoreticians, experimentalists, and clinical practitioners from the disciplines of physical and engineering sciences, biological and chemical sciences, and clinical and medical sciences that contribute to the understanding and use of hyperthermia. STM members are professionals from the physical, engineering, biological, chemical, and clinical and medical sciences with an interest in the field of hyperthermia. Membership: $75-299 (Active Member); $50-160 (Emeritus/New Investigator).

Meetings/Conferences: Annual
2013 - Aruba, Aruba (The Westin Resort & Casino)/
  April 17 - 21

Publications:
The International Journal of Hyperthermia

Society for Uroradiology (1966)
4550 Post Oak Pl.
Suite 342
Houston, TX 77027
Tel: (713) 965-0566 *Fax:* (713) 960-0488
E-Mail: info@uroradiology.org
Website: uroradiology.org
Members: 300 individuals
Staff: 1
Annual Budget: $100-250,000
Tax: 501(c)(3)

Personnel:
Executive Director: Lynne K. Tiras CMP

Historical Note:
SUR's mission is to promote interest and investigation in the advancement of urinary and genital tract imaging and to stimulate the study of both normal and abnormal processes with emphasis upon the integration of current imaging and interventional practice. Membership is offered to physicians and other scientists who have an interest in the practice, teaching, or research of genitourinary imaging.

Publications:
Membership Directory; on-line

Society for Values in Higher Education (1923)
C/O Portland State University
P.O. Box 751 - SVHE
Portland, OR 97207-0751
Tel: (503) 725-2575 *Fax:* (503) 725-2577
E-Mail: society@pdx.edu
Website: svhe.org
Members: 1200 individuals
Staff: 15
Annual Budget: $100-250,000
Tax: 501(c)(3)

Personnel:
Executive Director: Eric Bain-Selbo
Business Manager: Pamela "Pam" Montgomery

Historical Note:
Formerly (1962) National Council on Religion in Higher Education and (1976) Society for Religion in Higher Education. SVHE is a fellowship of teachers and others who care deeply about ethical issues such as integrity, diversity, social justice and civic responsibility facing higher education and the wider society. Membership: $80-135 (Regular); $35 (Introductory); $250 (Institution); $1000 (Life); $50 (Unemployed).

Meetings/Conferences: Annual
Number of non-conference events/year: 1

Publications:
Directory; on-line
Soundings: An Interdisciplinary Journal; quarterly
SVHE News: Views and Values; quarterly

Society for Vascular Medicine (1989)
111 Deer Lake Rd.

Suite 100
Deerfield, IL 60015
Tel: (847) 480-2961 *Fax:* (847) 480-9282
E-Mail: info@vascularmed.org
Website: vascularmed.org
Members: 413 individuals
Staff: 1
Annual Budget: $500-1,000,000
Tax: 501(c)(3)

Personnel:
Executive Director: Lee Ann Clark

Historical Note:
Formerly the Society for Vascular Medicine and Biology, assumed its current name in 2008. SVM's mission is to stimulate the formation of vascular medicine training programs and to foster formal vascular research and educational activities for medical students, residents and fellows. Membership: $125 (Advanced Practitioner Member); $350 (SVM Doctorate or Fellow Member); $90 (SVM Vascular Care Team Member); $25 (SVM Associate).

Meetings/Conferences:
2013 - Cleaveland, OH (InterContinental Hotel Suites
  Cleveland)/June 12 - 15
Number of non-conference events/year: 7

Publications:
Member Directory; on-line
SVM Newsletter; quarterly
Vascular Medicine; on-line

Society for Vascular Nursing (1982)
100 Cummings Center
Suite 124 A
Beverly, MA 01915
Tel: (978) 927-7800 *Fax:* (978) 927-7872
TollFree: (888) 536-4786
E-Mail: svn@administrare.com
Website: svnnet.org
Members: 800 individuals
Staff: 5
Annual Budget: $100-250,000

Personnel:
President: Marge Lovell CVN, MEd, RN
   E-Mail: Marg.Lovell@LHSC.ON.CA
Editor: Cindy Lewis MSN, RN
Contact, Conventions: Angela Wetherbee
   E-Mail: angela@administrare.com

Historical Note:
Formerly (1992) the Society for Peripheral Vascular Nursing. SVN strives to provide a professional community for vascular nursing. It provides national educational programs, helps development of local programs, and supports research in this specialized field. Membership: $110 (Active/Associate); $125 (International); $55 (Student/Graduate Nurse); $90 (Military).

Continuing Education:
Certification Designation/s: CVN

Meetings/Conferences: Annual
Conference Chair: Angela Wetherbee
2013 - Boston, MA (Sheraton Boston Hotel)/May 8 - 11

Publications:
Journal of Vascular Nursing; quarterly; adv.
SVN...prn - Newsletter; quarterly; adv.

Membership List Available to Non-members

Society for Vascular Surgery (1947)
633 North St., Clair St.
24th Floor
Chicago, IL 60611
Tel: (312) 334-2300 *Fax:* (312) 334-2320
TollFree: (800) 258-7188
E-Mail: vascular@vascularsociety.org
Website: vascularweb.org
Members: 3000 individuals
Staff: 23
Annual Budget: $10-25,000,000
Tax: 501(c)(6)

Personnel:
Executive Director: Rebecca Maron CAE
   E-Mail: rmaron@vascularsociety.org
Managing Editor: Jessica Brabant
   E-Mail: jbrabant@vascularsociety.org
Director, Education: Julie Chan
   E-Mail: jchan@vascularsociety.org
Director, Marketing Communications: Jill Goodwin CAE
   E-Mail: jgoodwin@vascularsociety.org
Constituencies Manager: Emily Kalata
   E-Mail: ekalata@vascularsoceity.org

Administrative Assistant and Accounting Specialist: Ronna
  Kalinga
  E-Mail: rkalinga@vascularsociety.org
Coordinator, Membership Services: Tracy Levy
  E-Mail: tlevy@vascularsociety.org
Technology Director: Sonia Soto
  E-Mail: ssoto@vascularsociety.org
Director, Meetings: Debbie Wallentin CMP
  E-Mail: dwallentin@sbcglobal.net

Historical Note:
Organized in Virginia in 1945 at a meeting of the Southern
Surgical Association. Mission is to promote, encourage
and improve the dissemination of knowledge concerning all
aspects of vascular disease and health; provide education
for vascular surgeons in new science, surgical techniques
and practice; serve as a strong advocate for members in all
areas of vascular surgery and endovascular surgery and
address social, economic, ethical and legal issues that relate
to vascular surgery. Membership: $500 (Active/Associate);
$50 (Affiliate); $65 (Candidate); $150-500 (International);
Complimentary (Honorary/Senior).

Meetings/Conferences: Annual
Conference Chair: Debbie Wallentin CMP
2013 - San Francisco, CA (Doubletree Hotel San
  Francisco)/May 30 - June 1
2014 - Boston, MA (Hynes Convention Center)/June 5
  - 7
2015 - Ft. Washington, MD (Gaylord National Resort
  and Convention Center-National Harbor)/June 4 - 6
Number of non-conference events/year: 2

Publications:
Journal of Vascular Surgery®
On the Cutting Edge

Membership List Available to Non-members

Society for Vascular Ultrasound (1977)
4601 Presidents Dr.
Suite 260
Lanham, MD 20706-4831
Tel: (301) 459-7550 Fax: (301) 459-5651
TollFree: (800) 788-8346
E-Mail: info@svunet.org
Website: svunet.org
Members: 4600 individuals
Staff: 4
Annual Budget: $1-2,000,000
Tax: 501(c)(3)

Personnel:
Executive Director: Thomas L. Stefaniak CAE
Director, Marketing and Communications: Frankie
  Hamme
  E-Mail: fhamme@svunet.org
Director, Membership Services and Meetings: Missi
  McLean
  E-Mail: mmclean@svunet.org

Historical Note:
Formerly (1988) Society of Noninvasive Vascular
Technology and (2002) Society for Vascular Technology,
SVU works for the advancement of noninvasive vascular
technology used in the diagnosis of vascular disease
through education programs, publications, and certification.
Members are vascular technologists, vascular physicians,
vascular lab managers, nurses, and other allied medical
ultrasound professionals. Membership: $125 (Regular);
$150 (International); $25 (Student); $60 (Student
Transitional); $45 (Retired/Disabled).

Continuing Education:
Certification Designation/s: RPVI

Meetings/Conferences: Annual
Conference Chair: Missi McLean
2013 - San Francisco, CA (Moscone Center West)/May
  30 - June 1

Publications:
e-Spectrum Newsletter; monthly; adv.
Journal for Vascular Ultrasound; quarterly; adv.
Membership Directory; on-line
Student Directory; on-line

Membership List Available to Non-members

Society for Vector Ecology (1968)
1966 Compton Ave.
Corona, CA 92881-3318
Tel: (951) 340-9792 Fax: (951) 340-2515
E-Mail: sove@sove.org
Website: sove.org
Members: 850 individuals
Staff: 4
Annual Budget: $100-250,000

Personnel:
President: Kenneth Linthicum
  E-Mail: kenneth.linthicum@ars.usda.gov
Secretary and Treasurer: Major S. Dhillon PhD
  E-Mail: mdhillon@northwestmvcd.org
Webmaster: Ryan Reneau
  E-Mail: webmaster@sove.org

Historical Note:
Formerly (1971) California Association of Vector Ecologists;
(1988) Society of Vector Ecologists. SOVE's mission is
to solve many complex problems encountered in the field
of vector biology and control like suppression of nuisance
organisms and disease vectors through environmental
management, biological control, public education, and
appropriate chemical control technology. Members are
group of individuals involved in vector biology and control
programs in California. Membership: $70 (Regular); $35
(Student/Retired); $100 (Institutional); $200 (Sustaining).

Meetings/Conferences: Annual

Publications:
Journal of Vector Ecology; bi-annually; adv.
SOVE Newsletter; on-line

Society for Wetland Scientists
22 N. Carroll St.
Suite 300
Madison, WI 53703
Tel: (608) 310-7855 Fax: (608) 251-5941
E-Mail: bolson@sws.org
Website: sws.org
Members: 3500 individuals
Staff: 3
Annual Budget: $500-1,000,000

Personnel:
President: George Lukacs
  E-Mail: George.Lukacs@jcu.edu.au
Treasurer: Julia Cherry
  E-Mail: julia.cherry@ua.edu
Editor: Marinus L. Otte
  E-Mail: marinus.otte@ndsu.edu

Historical Note:
The mission of the Society of Wetland Scientists is to
promote understanding, scientifically based management,
and sustainable use of wetlands. Membership: $75-95
(Active); $25 (Student); $110 (Family); $1500 (Lifetime);
$50 (Emeritus).

Meetings/Conferences: Annual
2013 - Duluth, MN (Duluth Entertainment Convention
  Center)/June 2 - 6

Publications:
Member Directory; on-line
The SWS Research Brief
Wetland Science & Practice
Wetlands; on-line; adv.

Society of Abdominal Radiology (1971)
C/O International Meeting Managers
4550 Post Oak Pl., Suite 342
Houston, TX 77027
Tel: (713) 965-0566 Fax: (713) 960-0488
E-Mail: admin@abdominalradiology.org
Website: sgr.org
Members: 319 individuals
Staff: 9
Annual Budget: $100-250,000
Tax: 501(c)(3)

Personnel:
Executive Director: Lynne K. Tiras CMP
Secretary and Treasurer: Deborah A. Baumgarten
First Director-in-Succession: Judy Yee MD

Historical Note:
Formally known as Society of Gastrointestinal
Radiologists .The merger of SGR and SUR became Society
of Abdominal Radiology (SAR).SAR's mission is to
furnish leadership and to foster advances in diagnosis
and intervention within the areas of gastrointestinal and
genitourinary radiology, to enhance the study and practice
of abdominal radiology by establishing lectureships,
scholarships, and foundations in abdominal radiology.
Members are radiologists with an interest in diseases of the
gastrointestinal tract.Membership Dues: $300 / Year

Meetings/Conferences: Annual
2013 - Maui, HI (Grand Waila Resort)/Feb. 24 - March
  1
2014 - Boca Raton, FL (Boca Raton Resort and Club)/
  March 23 - 28

Publications:
Membership Directory

Society of Accredited Marine Surveyors (1986)
7855 Argyle Forest Blvd.
Suite 203
Jacksonville, FL 32244
Tel: (904) 384-1494 Fax: (904) 388-3958
E-Mail: samshq@marinesurvey.org
Website: marinesurvey.org
Members: 1000 individuals
Staff: 8
Annual Budget: $500-1,000,000

Personnel:
President: Joseph B. Lobley
  E-Mail: jblmarine@roadrunner.com
Vice President, Public Relations: Thomas C. Benton
  E-Mail: tom.benton@marinesurveyor.com
Treasurer: Lloyd E. Kittredge
  E-Mail: kitt@netnitco.net
Vice president, Meetings and Conventions: Paul Logue
  E-Mail: marinesurvey@comcast.net
Vice President, Testing: Alison Mazon
Vice-President, Membership Services: George J. Sepel
  E-Mail: marinesurvey@gci.net
Office Manager: Rhea Shea
  E-Mail: samshq@marinesurvey.org
Vice President, Education: Kenneth Weinbrecht
  E-Mail: oceanbaymarine@yahoo.com

Historical Note:
Incorporated in the state of Florida. SAMS strives to assist
other marine organizations in technical matters, provide
information and training for persons interested in the
profession, and suggest standards for technical procedures
to members. Membership: $500/year (Accredited Marine
Surveyor).

Continuing Education:
Certification Designation/s: AMS

Meetings/Conferences: Quadrennial
Conference Chair: Paul Logue

Publications:
Sams Newsletter; bi-annually

Society of Actuaries (1949)
475 N. Martingale Rd.
Suite 600
Schaumburg, IL 60173-2226
Tel: (847) 706-3500 Fax: (847) 706-3599
E-Mail: customerservice@soa.org
Website: soa.org
Members: 22,000 individuals
Staff: 90
Annual Budget: $25-50,000,000
Tax: 501(c)(3)

Personnel:
Executive Director: Greg Heidrich
  E-Mail: gheidrich@soa.org
Senior Director, Events: Colleen Bagnasco
  E-Mail: cBagnasco@soa.org
Director, Governance: Sheree Baker
  E-Mail: sbaker@soa.org
Managing Director, Marketing and Communications:
  Patrick Gould
  E-Mail: pgould@soa.org
Managing Director, Education: Ken Guthrie
  E-Mail: kguthrie@soa.org
Managing Director, Strategy and Technology: Margaret
  Ann Jordan
  E-Mail: mjordan@soa.org
Director, Human Resources: Carol Kozlowski
  E-Mail: ckozlowski@soa.org
Deputy Executive Director and Chief Financial Officer:
  Stacy Lin
  E-Mail: slin@soa.org
Director, Communications: Lisamarie Lukas
  E-Mail: llukas@soa.org
Membership Representative, Customer Service: Dorothy
  Pedroza
  E-Mail: dpedroza@soa.org
Manager, Publications: Karen Perry
  E-Mail: kperry@soa.org
General Counsel: Richard Veys
  E-Mail: rveys@soa.org

Historical Note:
Formed by a merger of the American Institute of Actuaries
and the Actuarial Society of America. SOA's mission
is to advance actuarial knowledge and to enhance the
ability of actuaries to provide expert advice and relevant
solutions for financial, business, and societal problems
involving uncertain future events. Membership: $575-630

(Fellows/Associates who became Associates prior to 2009); $290-345 (Associates who became Associates after 2008).

Continuing Education:
Certification Designation/s: APC, FAP, VEE, FAC

Meetings/Conferences: Annual
Conference Chair: Colleen Bagnasco
2013 - San Diego, CA (San Diego Convention and Visitors Bureau)/Oct. 20 - 23
2014 - Orlando, FL/Oct. 26 - 29
Number of non-conference events/year: 19

Publications:
Actuarial Research Clearing House (ARCH)
ImageWatch; monthly
Membership Directory; on-line
Professional Development Opportunities (e-Newsletter); semi-monthly
Section Newsletters
SOA News Today
The Actuarial Practice Forum (APF)
The Actuary Magazine; bi-monthly
The Future Actuary; annually
The North American Actuarial Journal (NAAJ)

Society of Air Force Clinical Surgeons *(1951)*
1511 Paddington Way
Plumas Lake, CA 95961-9129
Tel: (530) 741-0682 *Fax:* (530) 741-0680
Website: safcs.org
Members: 645 individuals
Staff: 1
Annual Budget: $50-100,000
Tax: 501(c)(6)

Personnel:
Executive Director: Rose A. Thomas
E-Mail: rose@safcs.org

Historical Note:
SAFCS's mission is to promote surgery within the Air Force, and serves as a forum for presentation of scientific papers, fosters esprit de corps and promulgates military surgical objectives. Members are doctors of medicine and osteopathy who practice surgery, anesthesiology, emergency medicine, podiatric medicine, doctors of dentistry who limit their practice to oral surgery and certified registered nurse anesthetists. Membership: $25 (Resident); $75 (Active); $100 (Senior/Associate); Life membership is free and honorary members are elected by unanimous agreement of the Board of Governors.

Meetings/Conferences: Annual
Number of non-conference events/year: 4

Publications:
Journal of Surgical Education; bi-monthly
Membership Directory; on-line

Membership List Available to Non-members

Society of Air Force Physician Assistants
2833 Gramercy Pl.
Beavercreek, OH 45431
E-Mail: info@safpa.org
Website: safpa.org
Staff: 2

Personnel:
President: Maj Randy Stevens
Secretary and Treasurer: Brandi Ritter

Historical Note:
SAFPA's mission is to promote quality, cost- effective, and accessible health care and to promote the professional and personal development of Air Force physician assistants. Membership: $35/year.

Continuing Education:
Certification Designation/s: CME

Meetings/Conferences: Annual

Publications:
Towner-Schafer Report Newsletter

Society of Allied Weight Engineers *(1939)*
P.O. Box 60024
Terminal Annex
Los Angeles, CA 90060
Tel: (562) 596-2873 *Fax:* (562) 596-2874
E-Mail: saweron@charton.net
Website: sawe.org
Members: 828 individuals, companies and libraries
Staff: 4
Annual Budget: $100-250,000

Personnel:

Vice President, Internet Operations: Andrew Brooks
E-Mail: andy...@sawe.org
Vice President, Training: Errol Oguzhan
E-Mail: trai...@sawe.org
Vice President, Publications: Robert Ridenour

Historical Note:
Formerly Society of Aeronautical Weight Engineers, SAWE's mission is to promote recognition of mass properties engineering as a specialized discipline in the entire spectrum of professional engineering. Members are engaged in mass properties engineering or in work, which contributes to the advancement of this specialized branch of engineering. Membership: $60 (Individual); $30 (Retired); $20 (Student); $900 (Life).

Meetings/Conferences: Semi-Annual
2013 - St. Louis, MO (Marriot St. Louis Union Station)/ May 18 - 20
Number of non-conference events/year: 1

Publications:
SAWE Newsletter; quarterly; adv.
Weight Engineering; adv.

Membership List Available to Non-members

Society of American Business Editors and Writers *(1964)*
Walter Cronkite School of Journalism and Mass Communication, Arizona State University
555 N. Central Ave., Suite 302
Phoenix, AZ 85004-1248
Tel: (602) 496-7862 *Fax:* (602) 496-7041
E-Mail: sabew@sabew.org
Website: sabew.org
Members: 3200 members
Staff: 5
Annual Budget: $250-500,000
Tax: 501(c)(3)

Personnel:
Executive Director: Warren Watson
E-Mail: watson@sabew.org
Coordinator, Marketing: Sue Davis
E-Mail: davis@sabew.org
Coordinator, Membership Services: Mark J. Scarp
E-Mail: scarp@sabew.org

Historical Note:
Formerly (1986) the Society of American Business Writers, SABW's mission is to advance business journalism and to encourage comprehensive reporting of economic events without fear or favoritism and to upgrade skills and knowledge through continuous educational efforts. Members are financial, business and economic news writers and editors for print and broadcast outlets. Membership: $55 (Individual); $75 (Associate); $10 (Student); $105-345 (Institutions).

Meetings/Conferences:
2013 - Washington, DC (The George Washington University)/April 4 - 6
Number of non-conference events/year: 1

Publications:
The Business Journalist; quarterly

Society of American Fight Directors *(1977)*
1350 E. Flamingo Rd.
Suite 25
Las Vegas, NV 89119
Website: safd.org
Members: 1000 individuals
Staff: 3
Annual Budget: $100-250,000
Tax: 501(c)(3)

Personnel:
Manager, Business Operations: Angela Bonacasa
E-Mail: goodhouse@hotmail.com
Editor-In-Chief: Michael Mueller
E-Mail: mjmueller3@gmail.com
Web Administrator: John Teague
E-Mail: jteague@safd.org

Historical Note:
SAF's mission is to advocate safety and fostering excellence in the art of directing staged combat/theatrical violence. Members are stage fight choreographers, actors and other interested individuals including professional actors, directors, producers, educators, dancers, singers, stunt performers, historians, and armorers working in theatre, film, television, all levels of academia, stunt shows, opera, and the video gaming industry. Membership: $45 (Domestic-USA); $55 (Outside USA).

Continuing Education:
Certification Designation/s: CSCI

Meetings/Conferences:
Number of non-conference events/year: 3

Publications:
Member Directory; on-line
The Cutting Edge; bi-monthly

Membership List Available to Non-members

Society of American Florists *(1884)*
1601 Duke St.
Alexandria, VA 22314-3406
Tel: (703) 836-8700 *Fax:* (703) 836-8705
TollFree: (800) 336-4743
E-Mail: info@safnow.org
Website: safnow.org
Members: 15000 members
Staff: 24
Annual Budget: $2-5,000,000

Personnel:
Executive Vice President and Chief Executive Officer: Peter J. Moran
E-Mail: pmoran@safnow.org
Manager, Membership and Data Services: Krissy Doyle
E-Mail: krissydoyle@safnow.org
Director, Communications: Shelley Estersohn
E-Mail: sestersohn@safnow.org
Manager, Member Services: Brian Gamberini
E-Mail: bgamberini@safnow.org
Chief Operating Officer: Drew N. Gruenburg
E-Mail: dgruenburg@safnow.org
Vice President, Publishing and Communications: Kate Penn
E-Mail: kpenn@safnow.org
Senior Director, Government Relations: Lin Schmale
E-Mail: lschmale@safnow.org
Director, Research and Information: Ira T. Silvergleit
E-Mail: isilverg@safnow.org
Chief Information Officer: Renato Cruz Sogueco
E-Mail: rsogueco@safnow.org
Vice President, Marketing: Jennifer Sparks
E-Mail: jsparks@safnow.org
Director, Meetings and Conventions: Laura Weaver CMP
E-Mail: lweaver@safnow.org

Historical Note:
SAF is the association that provides marketing, government advocacy, industry intelligence and practices information for all participants in the U.S. floral industry. Represents all segments of the U.S. floral industry. Members include retailers, growers, wholesalers, importers, manufacturers, suppliers, educators, students and allied organizations. Membership: $384-1614 (Retailer); $654-1614 (Grower/ Wholesaler/Importer/Manufacturer/Supplier).

Meetings/Conferences: Annual
Conference Chair: Laura Weaver CMP
Number of non-conference events/year: 1

Publications:
E-Brief; weekly; adv.
Floral Management; monthly; adv.
Floral Trend Tracker; quarterly; adv.
MagnetMail; on-line
Membership Directory; on-line
Sales Wake-Up!; weekly
Washington Week in Review; weekly

Society of American Foresters *(1900)*
5400 Grosvenor Ln.
Bethesda, MD 20814-2198
Tel: (301) 897-8720 *Fax:* (301) 897-3690
TollFree: (866) 897-8720
E-Mail: safweb@safnet.org
Website: safnet.org
Members: 15000 individuals
Staff: 18
Annual Budget: $5-10,000,000
Tax: 501(c)(3)

Personnel:
Executive Vice President and Chief Executive Officer: Michael T. Goergen Jr.
E-Mail: goergenm@safnet.org
Manager, Education: Pat Cillay
E-Mail: cillayp@safnet.org
Chief Financial Officer: Jorge Esguerra
E-Mail: esguerraj@safnet.org
Director, Conferences and Meetings: Carlton Gleed
E-Mail: gleedc@safnet.org
Manager, Accounting and Data Processing: Carol McKernon
E-Mail: mckernoc@safnet.org

Director, Publications and Managing Editor: Matthew Walls
  E-Mail: wallsm@safnet.org
Senior Director, Marketing and Membership: Christopher Whited
  E-Mail: whitedc@safnet.org

Historical Note:
Founded by Gifford Pinchot and six other pioneer foresters. SAF's mission is to advance the science, education, technology, and practice of forestry; to enhance the competency of its members; to establish professional excellence; and, to use the knowledge, skills, and conservation ethic of the profession to ensure the continued health and use of forest ecosystems and the present and future availability of forest resources to benefit society. Membership: $40-240/year.

Continuing Education:
Certification Designation/s: CFE, CFP

Meetings/Conferences: Annual
Conference Chair: Carlton Gleed
Number of non-conference events/year: 3

Publications:
Forest Science; bi-monthly; adv.
Journal of Applied Forestry; quarterly; adv.
Journal of Forestry; adv.

Society of American Gastrointestinal and Endoscopic Surgeons *(1980)*
11300 W. Olympic Blvd.
Suite 600
Los Angeles, CA 90064
Tel: (310) 437-0544 *Fax*: (310) 437-0585
E-Mail: sagesweb@sages.org
Website: sages.org
Members: 5,000 surgeons and allied health professionals.
Staff: 15
Annual Budget: $5-10,000,000
Tax: 501(c)(6)

Personnel:
Executive Director: Sallie Matthews
  E-Mail: sallie@sages.org
Treasurer: L. Michael Brunt MD

Historical Note:
SAGES's mission is to provide education and training for gastrointestinal and/or abdominal surgeons and surgeons-in- training. Members are surgeons performing gastrointestinal endoscopy and related minimal-access surgeries. Membership: $285 (Active/International/ Associate Active); $150 (Allied Health); $60 (Candidate).

Meetings/Conferences: Annual
2013 - Baltimore, MD (Hilton Baltimore)/April 17 - 20
2014 - Salt Lake City, UT (Salt Palace Convention Center)/April 2 - 5
2015 - Nashville, TN (Gaylord Hotels Resorts and Convention Centers-Nashville)/April 15 - 18

Publications:
Annals of Surgical Oncology
Journal of Gastrointestinal Surgery
Mini-SCOPE; quarterly; adv.
Scope; bi-annually; adv.
Surgical Endoscopy; adv.
World Journal of Surgery

Membership List Available to Non-members

Society of American Graphic Artists *(1915)*
32 Union Sq.
Room 1214
New York, NY 10003
Tel: (212) 260-5706
E-Mail: sagaprints@verizon.net
Website: sagaprints.org
Members: 250 individuals
Staff: 5
Annual Budget: $10-25,000

Personnel:
President: Shelley Thorstensen
Treasurer: Joseph Essig
Counsel: Lawrence Fox
Corresponding Secretary: Marion Lerner-Levine
  E-Mail: mlerlev@aol.com
Secretary: Barbara Minton

Historical Note:
Founded as the Brooklyn Society of Etchers, adopted its present name in 1952. SAGA's mission is to promote the making of art through printmaking. Membership includes printmakers of America. Membership: $45/year.

Meetings/Conferences: Annual

Publications:
SAGA Notes; on-line
SAGAzine; semi-annually

Society of American Historians *(1939)*
603 Fayerweather MC 2538
Columbia University
New York, NY 10027
Tel: (212) 854-6495
E-Mail: amhistsociety@columbia.edu
Website: sah.columbia.edu
Members: 350 individuals
Staff: 3
Annual Budget: $10-25,000
Tax: 501(c)(3)

Personnel:
President: Walter Isaacson
Administrative Secretary: Ene Sirvet
Executive Secretary: Andie Tucher

Historical Note:
SAH's goal is to encourage literary distinction in the writing of history and biography by awarding of prizes, promoting historical studies and interests, and cooperating with publishers and other institutions.

Publications:
American Heritage

Society of American Law Teachers *(1972)*
P.O. Box 451098, 4505 S. Maryland Pkwy.
C/O Boyd School of Law, UNLV
Las Vegas, NV 89154-1098
Tel: (702) 895-2476
E-Mail: info@saltlaw.org
Website: saltlaw.org
Members: 750 individuals
Staff: 2
Annual Budget: $100-250,000

Personnel:
Treasurer: Patricia A. Cain
Editor: Raleigh Levine

Historical Note:
SALT strives to make the legal profession more inclusive.SALT's mission is to make the legal profession more inclusive and reflective of the great diversity of this nation. Membership: $55 (Fellows/visiting assistant professors); $75 (Adjunct faculty/retired teachers); $100 (Non-tenure track faculty/librarians/academic support/ staff); $125 (Tenure track faculty); $150 (Tenured faculty/ senior administrative personnel); $1200 (Lifetime).

Meetings/Conferences: Annual

Publications:
Member Directory; on-line
SALT Electronic Newsletter; weekly

Society of American Magicians *(1902)*
P.O. Box 505
Parker, CO 80134
E-Mail: samadministrator@magicsam.com
Website: magicsam.com
Members: 8500 individuals
Staff: 5
Annual Budget: $250-500,000
Tax: 501(c)(10)

Personnel:
National President: Christopher Bontjes
  E-Mail: christopher@magicalentertainer.net
Editor: Michael Close
  E-Mail: mumeditor@gmail.com
National Treasurer: Eric Lampert
  E-Mail: ebl00@aol.com
National Administrator: Manon Rodriguez
  E-Mail: samadministrator@magicsam.com
Contact, Public Relations: George Schindler

Historical Note:
SAM's mission is to enhance an environment for the worldwide magic community that fosters fellowship, preservation of the magical arts, ethical standards, education, and personal growth. Membership is open to professional and amateur magicians, manufacturers of magical apparatus, collectors, writers, and hobbyists. Membership: $65 (Individual); $25 (Household).

Meetings/Conferences: Annual
2013 - Arlington, VA (Mariott Hotel Crystal Gateway)/ July 3 - 6

Publications:
M-U-M Magazine; monthly; adv.

Membership List Available to Non-members

Society of American Military Engineers *(1920)*
607 Prince St.
Alexandria, VA 22314-3117
Tel: (703) 549-3800 *Fax*: (703) 684-0231
E-Mail: info@same.org
Website: same.org
Members: 26100 individuals and 3100 corporations
Staff: 35
Annual Budget: $5-10,000,000

Personnel:
Executive Director: Robert D. Wolff PE, PhD
  E-Mail: rwolff@same.org
Director, Member and Post Support: Diana Dawkins
  E-Mail: ddawkins@same.org
Director, Communications and Marketing and Associate Publisher: L. Eileen Erickson
  E-Mail: erickson@same.org
Office Manager: Desyreé Jones
  E-Mail: djones@same.org
Director, Meetings and Expositions: Ann McLeod CAE, CEM
  E-Mail: amcleod@same.org
Database Manager: Natasha Rocheleau
  E-Mail: nroch@same.org
Director, Finance and Accounting: Kathleen Wilson CPA
  E-Mail: kwilson@same.org

Historical Note:
SAME's mission is to promote and facilitate engineering support for national security by developing and enhancing relationships and competencies among uniformed services, public- and private-sector engineers and related professionals, and by developing future engineers through outreach and mentoring. Members are professional engineers, architects, planners, designers, other related professionals, and contractors, suppliers, and manufacturers of engineering and engineering-related products. Membership: $55-82 (Public Sector); $85-127 (Private Sector); $35-52 (Young Member); $60 (Uniform Service Member); $400 (Non Profit Organization); $250 (Public Agency).

Meetings/Conferences:
Conference Chair: Ann McLeod CAE, CEM
2013 - San Diego, CA (San Diego Convention Center)/ May 21 - 24/1-10 exhibitors
2014 - Orlando, FL (Jacksonville Post)/May 20 - 23
2015 - Houston, TX (Houston-Galveston Post)/May 19 - 22/over 100 exhibitors
Number of non-conference events/year: 14

Publications:
Directory of Member Companies and Public Agencies; annually
The Military Engineer; bi-monthly; adv.

Society of American Registered Architects *(1956)*
P.O. Box 280
Newport, TN 37822
Tel: (423) 721-0129
TollFree: (888) 385-7272
Website: sara-national.org
Members: 800 individuals
Staff: 3
Annual Budget: $50-100,000

Personnel:
Executive Director: Cathie Moscato
  E-Mail: cmoscato@sara-national.org

Historical Note:
Established in Kansas City by Wilfred Gregson of Atlanta. Founded as a professional society that includes the participation of all architects regardless of their roles in the architectural community. SARA's purpose is to provide a professional society for all who carry an architectural license regardless of their role in the building and designing industry and to allow those individuals opportunities to unite as a common voice to work together for the betterment of the profession. Membership: $270 (Professional-Registered Architects/Affiliate-Industry/ Professional); $78 (Associate-Non-Registered Architects); $295 (International-Registered Architects); $18 (Student).

Meetings/Conferences: Annual
Conference Chair: Cathie Moscato
Number of non-conference events/year: 1

Publications:
Directory; on-line
SARAScope; bi-monthly; adv.

Society of American Silversmiths *(1989)*

P.O. Box 786
Warwick, RI 02893
Tel: (401) 461-6840 *Fax:* (401) 461-6841
E-Mail: sas@silversmithing.com
Website: silversmithing.com
Members: 220 individuals
Staff: 1
Annual Budget: Under $10,000

Personnel:
Executive Director: Jeffrey "Jeff" Herman

Historical Note:
SAS is dedicated to the preservation and promotion of silversmithing. It also educates the public in silversmithing techniques, silver care, restoration & conservation, and the aesthetic value of this art form. Membership: $45 (Artisan); $40 (Supporting); $20 (Associate); $30 (Supporting).

Publications:
Membership Directory; on-line
SAS Newsletter

Membership List Available to Non-members

Society of American Travel Writers *(1956)*
11950 W. Lake Park Dr.
Suite 320
Milwaukee, WI 53224-3049
Tel: (414) 359-1625 *Fax:* (414) 359-1671
E-Mail: info@satw.org
Website: satw.org
Members: 1300 individuals
Staff: 6
Annual Budget: $1-2,000,000
Tax: 501(c)(3)

Personnel:
Executive Director: Cindy Lemek MA
Manager, Finance and Administration: Laura Beddingfield CPA
Contact, Technical Support: Sarah Martis CAE
Coordinator, Membership and Administration Services: Kelsey Weaver MBA

Historical Note:
Organized as the American Association of Travel Writers in Ellinor Village, Florida, assumed its present name in 1957 and incorporated in the District of Columbia in 1958. SATW's mission is to promote responsible journalism, provide professional support and development for its members and encourage the conservation and preservation of travel resources worldwide. Members include writers, photographers, editors, electronic media and journalists, film lecturers, broadcast/video/film producers and public relations representatives. Membership: $50 (Active); $100 (Associate).

Meetings/Conferences: Annual

Publications:
Membership Directory; on-line
SATW E-Mail Newsletter; weekly; adv.
Traveler; quarterly; adv.

Membership List Available to Non-members

Society of Animal Artists *(1960)*
5451 Sedona Hills Dr.
Berthoud, CO 80513
Tel: (970) 532-3127 *Fax:* (970) 532-2537
E-Mail: admin@societyofanimalartists.com
Website: societyofanimalartists.com
Members: 360 individuals
Staff: 6
Annual Budget: $100-250,000
Tax: 501(c)(3)

Personnel:
President: Diane Mason
Treasurer: Renee Headings-Bemis
Contact, Social Media Communications: Jan Martin McGuire
Administrative Assistant: Teresa Rives
Webmaster: Wes Siegrist
Editor: Lynn Understiller
    E-Mail: SAAEditor@live.com

Historical Note:
SAA strives to advocate portrayal of the creatures sharing the planet, and educates the public through its informative art seminars, lectures and teaching demonstrations. Members are artists in the portrayal of animals. Membership: $160 (Artist/Signature Member); $100 (Associate); $100-249 (Patron Member); $250-499 (Sponsoring Member); $500-999 (Supporting Member); $1000-4,999 (Sustaining Member); $5,000+ (Partner Member).

Publications:

Member Listing; on-line
SAA Newsletter; semi-annually
Wildlife Art; on-line; adv.

Society of Architectural Historians *(1940)*
1365 N. Astor St.
Chicago, IL 60610-2144
Tel: (312) 573-1365 *Fax:* (312) 573-1141
E-Mail: info@sah.org
Website: sah.org
Members: 3500 individuals
Staff: 5
Annual Budget: $2-5,000,000
Tax: 501(c)(3)

Personnel:
Executive Director: Pauline Saliga
    E-Mail: psaliga@sah.org
Director, Membership Services: Anne Bird
    E-Mail: membership@sah.org
Director, Operations and Comptroller: Bob Drum
    E-Mail: bdrum@sah.org
Media and Communications Editor: Kara Elliott-Ortega
    E-Mail: kelliott-ortega@sah.org
Director, Programs: Kathy Sturm
    E-Mail: ksturm@sah.org

Historical Note:
SAH's mission is to preserve important structures, landscapes and other aspects of the built environment. Membership: $125-135 (Individual); $175-195 (Joint); $225 (Supporting); $55-65 (Student); $400 (Patron); $550 (Donor); $2,700 (Life); $7,500 (Benefactor); $350-380 (Active); $450-480 (Sustaining); $1,000 (Corporate).

Continuing Education:
Enrollment: 20
Certification Designation/s: AIA, CES

Meetings/Conferences: Annual
Conference Chair: Kathy Sturm
2013 - Buffalo, NY/April 10 - 16
2013 - Buffalo, NY (Hyatt Regency Buffalo Hotel And Conference Center)/April 10 - 14
Number of non-conference events/year: 2

Publications:
Journal of the Society of Architectural Historians (JSAH); quarterly; adv.
SAH News; quarterly; adv.

Society of Armenian Studies *(1974)*
California State University, 5245 N. Backer Ave.
P.O. Box Four
Fresno, CA 93740-8001
Tel: (559) 278-2669 *Fax:* (559) 278-2129
E-Mail: barlowd@csufresno.edu
Website: armenianstudies.csufresno.edu/sas
Members: 300 individuals
Staff: 3
Annual Budget: Under $10,000

Personnel:
President: Kevork B. Bardakjian
    E-Mail: kbar@umich.edu
Editor: Joseph Kechichian
    E-Mail: joegcc@aol.com
Treasurer: Hovann Simonian
    E-Mail: hovanns@aol.com

Historical Note:
SAS's mission is to promote the study of Armenian culture and society, including history, language, literature, and social, political, and economic questions. Membership: $50 (Regular); $20 (Student); $25 (Retired); $100 (Patrons); $10 (Scholars, living in Republic of Armenia); $40 (Supporting).

Meetings/Conferences: Annual

Publications:
JSAS
Membership Directory; annually
SAS Newsletter

Society of Army Physician Assistants *(1977)*
P.O. Box 4068
Waynesville, MO 65583-4068
Tel: (573) 528-2307 *Fax:* (888) 711-8543
Website: sapa.org
Members: 1050 individuals
Staff: 33
Annual Budget: $100-250,000

Personnel:
Executive Director: Paul W. Lowe

    E-Mail: lowepw@earthlink.net

Historical Note:
SAPA's mission is to provide a forum for discussion, representation with the AAPA (American Academy of Physician Assistance) and to provide high quality, low cost CME (continuing medical education) to the Society's members and the PA profession. Membership: $25 (Fellow/Associate/Affiliate); $5 (Student).

Continuing Education:
Certification Designation/s: CME

Meetings/Conferences:
Conference Chair: Orie R. Potter
Number of non-conference events/year: 1

Publications:
SAPA Journal
SAPA Newsletter; bi-monthly

Society of Atherosclerosis Imaging and Prevention *(1999)*
8601 Aqueduct Rd.
Potomac, MD 20854
Tel: (301) 251-8864 *Fax:* (301) 251-1125
E-Mail: info@sai-p.org
Website: sai-p.org
Staff: 1
Annual Budget: $25-50,000
Tax: 501(c)(3)

Personnel:
Executive Director: Lawrence H. Leong

Historical Note:
SAI strives to disseminate information regarding plaque imaging by various modalities, development of guidelines on use and interpretation of imaging data. Membership: $200 (Physician/Ph.D.); $100 (Student/Post-doc/Fellow/ Government Employee/Technologist).

Meetings/Conferences: Annual

Publications:
Newsletter

Society of Automotive Analysts *(1987)*
P.O. Box 362
Lake Orion, MI 48361
Tel: (248) 804-6433
E-Mail: info@saaautoleaders.org
Website: saaautoleaders.org
Members: 500 individuals
Staff: 3
Annual Budget: $100-250,000

Personnel:
President: Anthony Pratt
Treasurer: Lauren Eisbrenner
Contact, Media Relations: Neal Zipser
    E-Mail: nzipser@SAAautoleaders.org

Historical Note:
SAA's mission is to provide information on the latest trends, technologies and developments affecting the automotive industry. Members are analysts involved in the automotive industry through various fields such as marketing, finance, advertising, production and public relations. Membership: $150-350 (Individual); $99 (Young Professionals).

Meetings/Conferences: Annual
2013 - Detroit, MI (Cobo Hall)/Jan. 13
Number of non-conference events/year: 2

Publications:
Membership Directory; on-line

Society of Behavioral Medicine *(1978)*
555 E. Wells St.
Suite 1100
Milwaukee, WI 53202-3823
Tel: (414) 918-3156 *Fax:* (414) 276-3349
E-Mail: info@sbm.org
Website: sbm.org
Members: 3000 individuals
Staff: 6
Annual Budget: $1-2,000,000

Personnel:
Executive Director: Amy Stone
    E-Mail: astone@sbm.org
Director, Administration: Robert Kopchinski
    E-Mail: rkopchinski@sbm.org
Manager, Education and Meetings: Holland LaFave
    E-Mail: hlafave@sbm.org
Manager, Programs: Benjamin Stumpf
    E-Mail: bstumpf@sbm.org

Senior Manager, Communications and Membership
  Services: Alicia Sukup
    E-Mail: asukup@sbm.org

Historical Note:
SBM is a multidisciplinary organization of clinicians, educators and scientists committed to advocate the study of the interactions of behavior with biology and the environment to improve the health and well being of individuals, families, communities and populations. Members are primarily physicians, psychologists, nurses and health educators concerned with the interactions of health, illness and behavior. Membership: $287 (Full/ Associate); $97 (Trainee/Student); $210 (Transition); $0 (Emeritus).

Meetings/Conferences: Annual
Conference Chair: Holland LaFave
2013 - San Francisco, CA (Hilton San Francisco Union Square)/March 20 - 23
2014 - Philadelphia, PA (Philadelphia Marriott Downtown)/April 23 - 26
2015 - San Antonio, TX (San Antonio Marriott Rivercenter)/April 22 - 25
2016 - Washington, DC (Washington Hilton)/March 30 - April 2
2017 - San Diego, CA (Hilton San Diego Bayfront)/ March 29 - April 1
Number of non-conference events/year: 1

Publications:
Annals of Behavioral Medicine
Membership Directory; on-line
Translational Behavioral Medicine; quarterly

Society of Biblical Literature *(1880)*
825 Houston Mill Rd.
Atlanta, GA 30329
Tel: (404) 727-3100 *Fax:* (404) 727-3101
TollFree: (866) 727-9955
E-Mail: sblexec@sbl-site.org
Website: sbl-site.org
Members: 8500 individuals
Staff: 23
Annual Budget: $2-5,000,000
Tax: 501(c)(3)

Personnel:
Executive Director: John Kutsko
    E-Mail: john.kutsko@sbl-site.org
Director, Publications: Bob Buller
    E-Mail: bob.buller@sbl-site.org
Director, Technology Services: Missy Colee
    E-Mail: missy.colee@sbl-site.org
Manager, Marketing: Kathie Klein
    E-Mail: kathie.klein@sbl-site.org
Director, Global Conferences: Trista Krock
    E-Mail: trista.krock@sbl-site.org
Director, Finance and Administration: Susan Madara
    E-Mail: susan.madara@sbl-site.org
Manager, Membership and Subscriptions: Navar Steed
    E-Mail: navar.steed@sbl-site.org

Historical Note:
SBL is devoted to the critical investigation of the Bible from a variety of academic disciplines. Mission is to advance the academic study of biblical texts and their contexts as well as the traditions and contexts of biblical interpretation. Membership: $85 (Full); $40 (Student); $60 (Associate).

Meetings/Conferences:
Conference Chair: Trista Krock
2013 - Scotland, United Kingdom (St. Andrews)/July 7 - 11
2013 - Baltimore, MD/Nov. 23 - 26/3000 attendees
2014 - Vienna, Austria/June 6 - 10
2014 - San Diego, CA/Nov. 22 - 25
2015 - Buenos Aires, Argentina/July 20 - 24
2015 - Atlanta, GA/Nov. 21 - 24
2016 - San Antonio, TX/Nov. 19 - 22
2017 - Boston, MA/Nov. 18 - 21
2018 - Denver, CO/Nov. 17 - 20
2019 - San Diego, CA/Nov. 23 - 26
2020 - Boston, MA/Nov. 21 - 24
2021 - San Antonio, TX/Nov. 20 - 23
Number of non-conference events/year: 3

Publications:
Journal of Biblical Literature; quarterly; adv.
Member Directory; on-line

Membership List Available to Non-members

Society of Biological Psychiatry *(1945)*
C/O Mayo Clinic

4500 San Pablo Rd., Birdsall 310
Jacksonville, FL 32224
Tel: (904) 953-2842 *Fax:* (904) 953-7117
E-Mail: sobp@sobp.org
Website: sobp.org
Members: 965 individuals
Staff: 4
Annual Budget: $2-5,000,000
Tax: 501(c)(3)

Personnel:
Executive Director: Maggie Peterson MBA
    E-Mail: maggie@mayo.edu
Director, Programs: Mimi Macke
    E-Mail: sobp@sobp.org
Editor: Elliott Richelson MD
    E-Mail: sobp@sobp.org

Historical Note:
Founded in San Francisco and incorporated in California in 1949. SOBP's mission is to advocate excellence in scientific research and education in fields that investigate the nature, causes, mechanisms, and treatments of disorders of thought, emotion, or behavior. Membership: $250 (Regular/Associate); $125 (Student).

Meetings/Conferences: Annual
Conference Chair: Mimi Macke
2013 - San Francisco, CA (Hilton San Francisco Union Square)/May 18 - 22
2014 - New York City, NY/May 3 - 7
2014 - New York City, NY (The New York Helmsley Hotel)/May 8 - 10
2015 - Toronto, ON/May 14 - 16
2015 - Toronto, ON/May 16 - 20
2016 - Atlanta, GA/May 12 - 14
2016 - Atlanta, GA/May 14 - 18
2017 - San Diego, CA/May 18 - 20
2018 - New York City, NY/May 3 - 5
2019 - San Francisco, CA/May 16 - 19
2019 - San Francisco, CA/May 16 - 18

Publications:
Society of Biological Psychiatry Newsletter; quarterly; adv.

Membership List Available to Non-members

Society of Broadcast Engineers *(1964)*
9102 N. Meridian St.
Suite 150
Indianapolis, IN 46260
Tel: (317) 846-9000 *Fax:* (317) 846-9120
Website: sbe.org
Members:
112 local chapters
5500 individuals
Staff: 10
Annual Budget: $500-1,000,000
Tax: 501(c)(6)

Personnel:
Executive Director: John L. Poray CAE
    E-Mail: jporay@sbe.org
Executive Assistant and Manager, Advertising Sales: Debbie Hennessey
    E-Mail: dhennessey@sbe.org
Manager, Database: Scott Jones
    E-Mail: kjones@sbe.org
Director, Education: Kimberly Kissel
    E-Mail: kkissel@sbe.org
Manager, Communications: Hannah Trowbridge
    E-Mail: htrowbridge@sbe.org

Historical Note:
Founded as the Institute of Broadcast Engineers, SBE strives for the advancement of all levels and types of broadcast engineering. Membership includes studio and transmitter operators, announcer technicians, chief and staff engineers of large and small television and radio stations and others involved in broadcast engineering. Membership: $10 (Youth); $20 (Student); $68 (Regular/ Associate/Reinstatement/Change in grade to Member); $600 (Sustaining).

Continuing Education:
Enrollment: 5100
Certification Designation/s: 8-VSB, CTO, AMD, CBTE, CBRE, CSRE, CEA, CBT, CRO, CEV, CPBE, DRB, CSTE, CBNT

Meetings/Conferences: Annual
Conference Chair: John L. Poray CAE
Number of non-conference events/year: 4

Publications:
Career Advancement Newsletter; monthly

Membership Directory and Buyers' Guide; annually; adv.
SBE-news; semi-monthly; adv.
The Connector
The Signal; bi-monthly; adv.

Society of Cable Telecommunications Engineers *(1969)*
140 Philips Rd.
Exton, PA 19341-1318
Tel: (800) 542-5040 *Fax:* (610) 363-5898
TollFree: (800) 542-5040
E-Mail: scte@scte.org
Website: scte.org
Members:
250 companies
14000 individuals
Staff: 30
Annual Budget: $2-5,000,000

Personnel:
President and Chief Executive Officer: Mark Dzuban
    E-Mail: mdzuban@scte.org
Vice President, National Conferences: Lori Bower
    E-Mail: lbower@scte.org
Director, Information Systems: Derek DiGiacomo
    E-Mail: ddigiacomo@scte.org
Director, Event Marketing and Business Development: Heather Gosciniak
    E-Mail: hgosciniak@scte.org
Senior Vice President, Operations: Cathy Oakes
    E-Mail: coakes@scte.org
Vice President, Standards: Steve Oksala
    E-Mail: soksala@scte.org
Director, Member Marketing, Planning and Publications: Bill Schankel
    E-Mail: bschankel@scte.org
Vice President, Marketing and Business Development: Debra Swann
    E-Mail: dswann@scte.org
Vice President, Marketing and Membership: Bernadette Vernon
    E-Mail: bvernon@scte.org

Historical Note:
SCTE provides technical leadership for the telecommunications industry and serves its members through professional development, standards, certification and information. Membership is open to person employed full or part time in the engineering or technical operations, cable television, broadband communications or broadcasting systems or companies who have an interest in the purposes of the Society. Membership: $68 (Individual); $34 (Retired/Disabled/Student/In Transition); $750 (Expo Partner); $950 (Lifetime); Free (New Emeritus).

Continuing Education:
Certification Designation/s: BPI, BPE, BPT, IPEP, BTS, BCE, BTCS, BCT, DVEP, BDS, BPS

Meetings/Conferences:
Conference Chair: Lori Bower
Number of non-conference events/year: 1

Publications:
SCTE Interval; monthly

Society of Cardiovascular Anesthesiologists *(1978)*
2209 Dickens Rd.
Richmond, VA 23230-2005
Tel: (804) 282-0084 *Fax:* (804) 282-0090
E-Mail: sca@societyhq.com
Website: www2.scahq.org
Members: 5000 individuals
Staff: 16
Annual Budget: $2-5,000,000

Personnel:
Association Manager: Dana Gibson
    E-Mail: dana@societyhq.com
President: Solomon Aronson MD, FACC, FACCP
    E-Mail: solomon.aronson@duke.edu

Historical Note:
SCA's mission is to promote excellence in patient care through education and research in preoperative care for patients undergoing cardiothoracic and vascular procedures. Membership: $40-210/year.

Meetings/Conferences:
Conference Chair: Dana Gibson
2013 - Miami Beach, FL (Fontainebleau Miami Beach)/ April 6 - 10
2013 - Atlanta, GA (JW Marriott Atlanta Buckhead)/ May 6 - 11

Number of non-conference events/year: 66
Publications:
SCA Bulletin; bi-monthly; adv.
Membership List Available to Non-members

Society of Certified Insurance Counselors (1969)
P.O. Box 27027
Austin, TX 78755-2027
Tel: (800) 633-2165 *Fax:* (512) 349-6194
E-Mail: alliance@scic.com
Website: scic.com
Members: 27000 individuals
Staff: 104
Annual Budget: $10-25,000,000
Tax: 501(c)(6)
Personnel:
President and Chief Executive Officer: William T. Hold
CIC, CLU, CPU, PhD
Senior Vice president, Program Administration: Paula
Cook
E-Mail: pcook@scic.com
Director, Human resources: Amy Schott PHR
Historical Note:
*The association aims at creating, developing, and delivering
practical continuing education programs for everyone
involved in the insurance and risk management industries.
Membership: $85/year.*
Continuing Education:
Certification Designation/s: CSRM, CIC, CRM, CISR

Society of Chairmen of Academic Radiology Oncology Programs (1966)
8280 Willow Oaks Corporate Drive
Suite 500
Fairfax, VA 22031
Website: astro.org/SCAROP/Index.aspx
Members: 3300 individuals
Staff: 20
Personnel:
President: Theodore S. Lawrence MD, PhD
Secretary and Treasurer: Stephen M. Hahn MD
Contact, Communications: Kathy Thomas
Historical Note:
*Formerly Society of Chairmen of Academic Radiology
Departments, then Society of Chairmen of Academic
Radiology Oncology Programs; assumed current name in
2000.*

Society of Chemical Industry, American Section (1894)
315 Chestnut St.
Philadelphia, PA 19106
Tel: (215) 873-8232 *Fax:* (215) 629-5232
E-Mail: communications@soci.org
Website: soci.org
Members: 800 individuals
Staff: 1
Annual Budget: $100-250,000
Tax: 501(c)(6)
Personnel:
Director, Finance and Information and Technology,:
Hamza Ali
E-Mail: accounts@soci.org
Historical Note:
*SCIAS provides technical information and support to
practitioners throughout the sciences and to advance
applied chemistry in all its branches. Membership: $30
(Student); $150 (Member).*
Publications:
Biofuels, Bioproducts and Biorefining
C&I Magazine; adv.
Greenhouse Gases: Science and Technology
Membership Directory; on-line
Pest Management Science
Polymer International
The Journal of Chemical Technology and
Biotechnology
The Journal of the Science of Food and Agriculture

Society of Chemical Manufacturers and Affiliates Inc. (1921)
1850 M St. NW
Suite 700
Washington, DC 20036-5810
Tel: (202) 721-4100 *Fax:* (202) 296-8120
E-Mail: info@socma.org
Website: socma.com

Members: 300 companies
Staff: 6
Annual Budget: $10-25,000,000
Tax: 501(c)(6)
Personnel:
President and Chief Executive Officer: Larry Sloan
President and Chief Executive Officer: Lawrence D. Sloan
E-Mail: website@socma.com
Senior Director, Membership Services: Dolores Alonso
E-Mail: membership@socma.com
Director, Marketing and Public Relations: Liesa Brown
E-Mail: info@socma.com
Director, Recruitment and Retention: Todd Brown
E-Mail: brownt@socma.com
Assistant Manager, Publications and Public Relations:
Jenny Gaines
E-Mail: public.relations@socma.com
Senior Director, Human Resources and Administration:
Charlena Patterson
E-Mail: info@socma.com
Senior Manager, Site Administration: Ana C. Penaranda
E-Mail: website@socma.com
Senior Manager, Personal Relations and Media: Christine
Sanchez
E-Mail: public.relations@socma.com
Director, Finance and Administration and Department Lead:
Francis Shafer
Historical Note:
*Formerly (2009) the Synthetic Organic Chemical
Manufacturers Association. SOCMA promotes innovative,
safe and environmentally responsible operations that are
internationally competitive and contribute to a healthy,
productive economy. Membership: $6,500-71,000 (Active/
International); $5,000-25,000 (Associate); $5,900
(Affiliate).*
Meetings/Conferences: Annual
Conference Chair: Alicia Massey
Publications:
Capitol Connect Newsletter; quarterly
Chemical Bond Express Newsletter; weekly
ChemStewards® e-Newsletter; bi-weekly
Commercial Guide; annually; adv.
Executive Briefing; monthly
Executive Briefing Newsletter; biennially
Member Spotlight Newsletter; quarterly
Membership Directory; annually
SOCMA e-Newsletter; weekly; adv.
SOCMA Newsletter; irregular; adv.

Society of Children's Book Writers and Illustrators (1971)
8271 Beverly Blvd.
Los Angeles, CA 90048-4515
Tel: (323) 782-1010 *Fax:* (323) 782-1892
E-Mail: scbwi@scbwi.org
Website: scbwi.org
Members: 22000 individuals
Staff: 14
Annual Budget: $2-5,000,000
Personnel:
Executive Director: Lin Oliver
Director, Operations and Membership Services: Gee Cee
Addison
E-Mail: geeceeaddison@scbwi.org
Administrator: Kayla Heinen
Chief Operating Officer: Sara Rutenberg
Director, Special Projects: Kim Turrisi
E-Mail: kimturrisi@scbwi.org
Historical Note:
*SCBWI's mission is to act as a network for the exchange
of knowledge between children's writers, illustrators,
editors, publishers and agents. Members include writers
and illustrators of children's books, magazine stories and
articles, writers and producers of children's television,
children's book and magazine editors and publishers,
agents, children's librarians, teachers and educators,
bookstore owners and personnel. Membership: $85/year.*
Meetings/Conferences:
2013 - New York City, NY (Hyatt Regency Grand
Central)/Feb. 1 - 3
Number of non-conference events/year: 2
Publications:
Membership Directory; on-line
SCBWI Bulletin; bi-monthly

Society of Christian Ethics (1959)
P.O. Box 5126

St. Cloud, MN 56302-5126
Tel: (320) 253-5407 *Fax:* (320) 252-6984
E-Mail: sce@scethics.org
Website: scethics.org
Members: 900 individuals
Staff: 2
Annual Budget: $100-250,000
Tax: 501(c)(3)
Personnel:
Executive Director: Stacey M. Floyd-Thomas
Associate Executive Director: Linda Schreiber
Historical Note:
*Formerly (1980) American Society of Christian Ethics,
SCE's mission is to advocate research in the history of
ethics and moral theology, theoretical issues relating to the
interplay of theology and ethics, methodology in ethical
reflection and investigation and comparative religious
ethics. Society of Christian Ethics holds National affiliation
with American Council of Learned Societies. Membership:
$30 (Unemployed/Student/Retired); $0 (life); $35-245
(Full,based on current salary).*
Meetings/Conferences: Annual
2013 - Chicago, IL (Hilton Chicago)/Jan. 3 - 6/550
attendees/11-25 exhibitors
2014 - Seatle, WA (Westin Seattle)/Jan. 9 - 12
Publications:
Journal of the Society of Christian Ethics; semi-
annually; adv.
Membership List Available to Non-members

Society of Christian Philosophers (1978)
Department of Philosophy, Calvin College
1845 Knollcrest Cir. SE
Grand Rapids, MI 49546-4402
Tel: (616) 526-6419 *Fax:* (616) 526-8551
Website: societyofchristianphilosophers.com
Members: 1100 individuals
Staff: 3
Annual Budget: $250-500,000
Tax: 501(c)(3)
Personnel:
Executive Director: Christina Van Dyke
E-Mail: cvdyke@calvin.edu
Editor: Thomas Flint
Treasurer: Lee Hardy
Historical Note:
*SCP's purpose is to boost fellowship among christian
philosophers and to stimulate study and discussion of
issues which arise from their Christian and philosophical
commitments. Membership: $45 (Regular); $25
(Unemployed/Retiree); $10 (Student, plus $7 for Canadian
or $9 for other non-US postage).*
Publications:
Faith and Philosophy journal; quarterly; adv.
SCP Newsletter
Membership List Available to Non-members

Society of Cleaning and Restoration Technicians (1972)
4402 S. Danville Dr.
Abilene, TX 79605
Tel: (325) 692-1892 *Fax:* (325) 692-1823
TollFree: (800) 949-4728
E-Mail: info@scrt.org
Website: scrt.org
Members: 500 companies
Staff: 5
Annual Budget: $50-100,000
Personnel:
President: Gary Glenn
E-Mail: garyg@a-town.net
Administrator: Debbie Glenn
E-Mail: administrator@scrt.org
Historical Note:
*Formerly (1993) Society of Cleaning Technicians and
(2004) International Society of Cleaning Technicians.
SCRT seeks to provide members with up-to- date technical,
management, and marketing information. SCRT's mission is
to be the leading worldwide resource that provides members
with up-to-date technical, management, and marketing
information. Members are professional on-site carpet and
upholstery cleaners, restorers and suppliers to the industry.
A shareholder of the Institute of Inspection, Cleaning and
Restoration Certification. Membership: $275 (Regular);
$395 (Associate).*
Meetings/Conferences: Annual
Publications:

SCRT Directory; on-line
The Monitor; bi-monthly; adv.

Society of Clinical and Medical Hair Removal (1985)
2424 American Ln.
Madison, WI 53704-3102
Tel: (608) 443-2470 *Fax:* (608) 443-2474
E-Mail: homeoffice@scmhr.org
Website: scmhr.org
Members: 500 individuals
Staff: 2
Annual Budget: $100-250,000
Tax: 501(c)(6)

Personnel:
Executive Secretary: Lisa M. Nelson
   E-Mail: lisan@scmhr.org

Historical Note:
Founded as Society of Clinical and Medical Electrologists by the merger of the National Electrolysis Organization and the Electrolysis Society of America. SCMHR sponsors and supports the International Commissioner for Hair Removal Certificate. Membership: $195 (Individual U.S. Member); $140 (Individual Foreign Member).

Continuing Education:
Certification Designation/s: ICHRC, CCE, CME, CLHRP, CPLHRP

Meetings/Conferences: Annual
2013 - Dallas, TX/May 4 - 6

Publications:
Dermascope Magazine; monthly; adv.
Member Directory; on-line
Perspectives Newsletter; quarterly

Society of Collision Repair Specialists (1982)
P.O. Box 346
Smyrna, DE 19977
Tel: (302) 423-3537 *Fax:* (877) 435-6028
TollFree: (877) 841-0660
E-Mail: info@scrs.com
Website: scrs.com
Members: 31 state affiliates 750 companies
Staff: 2
Annual Budget: $250-500,000

Personnel:
Executive Director: Aaron Schulenburg
   E-Mail: aaron@scrs.com
Administrative Assistant: Linda Atkins

Historical Note:
SCRS is committed to the future of the collision repair industry: to provide the leadership needed; raise the professional image of the individual and the industry; and develop new leaders to carry forward. Members are owners and managers of auto collision repair shops, suppliers, insurance and educational associates and suppliers in the U.S., Canada, Australia, and New Zealand. Membership: $300 (General); $1,000 (Platinum); $1,250 (Company); $5,000 (Corporate); $350 (Affiliate).

Meetings/Conferences: Annual

Publications:
Newsletter; quarterly

Society of Commercial Seed Technologists (1922)
101 E. State St.
Suite 214
Ithaca, NY 14850
Tel: (607) 256-3313 *Fax:* (607) 273-1638
E-Mail: scst@twcny.rr.com
Website: seedtechnology.net
Members: 250 individuals
Staff: 2
Annual Budget: $100-250,000

Personnel:
Executive Director: Anita Hall
   E-Mail: scst@twcny.rr.com
Editor-in-Chief: Dennis Tekrony
   E-Mail: dtekrony@uky.edu

Historical Note:
Formerly (1946) functioned as a liaison between the Association of Official Seed Analysts (AOSA) and the American Seed Trade Association (ASTA). SCST's mission is to advocate professionalism, advance uniformity and ensure proficiency. Members are professionals involved in the testing and analysis of seeds, research on seed physiology, and seed production and handling based on the modern botanical and agricultural sciences. Membership: $250 (Registered Seed Technologist); $100 (Associate/ Research).

Continuing Education:
Certification Designation/s: CGT, CPT, RGT, RST, CVT

Meetings/Conferences: Biennial
Number of non-conference events/year: 3

Publications:
Membership Directory; on-line
Seed Technologist Newsletter; adv.

Society of Competitive Intelligence Professionals (1986)
P.O. Box 277
Falls Church, VA 22040
Tel: (703) 739-0696 *Fax:* (703) 739-2524
E-Mail: info@scip.org
Website: scip.org
Members: 3000 individuals
Staff: 6
Annual Budget: $2-5,000,000
Tax: 501(c)(6)

Personnel:
Chief Executive Officer: Ken Garrison
   E-Mail: kgarrison@scip.org
Vice President, Membership Services: Patrice Davenport
   E-Mail: pdavenport@scip.org
Manager, Programs: Joanna Molina
   E-Mail: jmolina@scip.org
Vice President, Education and Training: Sandy Skipper
   E-Mail: sskipper@scip.org

Historical Note:
Formerly the Society of Competitive Intelligence Professionals. SCIP provides education and networking opportunities for business professionals working in the field of competitive intelligence (CI). Mission is to enhance the success of members through leadership, education, advocacy, and networking. SCIP members have backgrounds in market research, government intelligence, or science and technology. Membership: $75-345/year; $5000 (Lifetime).

Continuing Education:
Certification Designation/s: CIP

Meetings/Conferences: Annual
Conference Chair: Joanna Molina
2013 - Orlando, FL (Caribe Royal Resort)/May 6 - 9/500 attendees/51-100 exhibitors
Number of non-conference events/year: 2

Publications:
Competitive Intelligence; quarterly
Journal of Competitive Intelligence and Management
Membership Directory; on-line
SCIP.Insight - Newsletter; monthly

The Society of Composers and Lyricists (1945)
8447 Wilshire Blvd.
Suite 401
Beverly Hills, CA 90211
Tel: (310) 281-2812 *Fax:* (310) 284-4861
Website: thescl.com
Members: 1000 individuals
Staff: 2
Annual Budget: $100-250,000
Tax: 501(c)(6)

Personnel:
Executive Director: Laura Dunn
   E-Mail: ExecDir@TheSCL.com
Chief Financial Officer and Treasurer: Christopher Farrell

Historical Note:
SCL is committed to advancing the interests of the film and television music community. Members are professional composers and songwriters active in production and composition of music for films, television and/or multimedia. Membership: $85-1,000/year.

Meetings/Conferences: Annual
Number of non-conference events/year: 4

Publications:
Membership Directory; on-line
The Score; quarterly

Society of Composers, Inc. (1966)
P.O. Box 687
Mineral Wells, TX 76068-0687
E-Mail: secretary@societyofcomposers.org
Website: societyofcomposers.org
Members: 1500 individuals
Staff: 2
Annual Budget: $50-100,000

Personnel:
President: Thomas Wells

General Manager: Gerald Warfield

Historical Note:
Formerly known as the American Society of University Composers (ASUC). SCI is dedicated to promote the composition, performance, understanding and dissemination of new and contemporary music. Members include composers and performers. Membership: $30-1100/year.

Meetings/Conferences: Annual
2013 - Columbus, OH (Ohio State University)/Feb. 13 - 16

Publications:
iSCI; on-line
Member Directory
SCION; on-line; adv.
The SCI Journal of Music Scores
The SCI Newsletter; bi-monthly

Society of Computed Body Tomography and Magnetic Resonance (1977)
1891 Preston White Dr.
Reston, VA 20191
Tel: (703) 476-1117 *Fax:* (703) 264-2093
E-Mail: info@scbtmr.org
Website: scbtmr.org
Members: 675 individuals
Staff: 6
Annual Budget: $500-1,000,000

Personnel:
Executive Director: Michele Wittling
   E-Mail: mwittling@acr.org
Chief Membership Officer: Erik K. Paulson MD
Manager, Meetings: Pamela Plater
   E-Mail: pplater@acr.org
Contact, CME Certificates and Reprints: Kia Reid
   E-Mail: kreid@acr.org
Director, Membership Services: Heidi Saikeld
   E-Mail: hsalkeld@acr.org
Contact, Meetings and Programs: Sarah Tate
   E-Mail: state@acr.org

Historical Note:
SCBT-MR's mission is to improve patient care through the appropriate use of CT and MR by fostering innovative research and educating radiologists. Membership in the society is competitive, selecting only those physicians actively involved in academic practice and research dealing with body computed tomography and magnetic resonance imaging. Membership: $250 (Regular); Free (In-Training).

Meetings/Conferences:
Conference Chair: Pamela Plater
2013 - Tucson, AZ (Hilton El Conquistador Resort)/ Oct. 12 - 16/350 attendees

Publications:
Membership Directory; on-line
President's Newsletter; semi-annually
SCBT-MR Newsletter; on-line

Membership List Available to Non-members

Society of Corporate Secretaries and Governance Professionals (1946)
240 W. 35th St.
Suite 400
New York, NY 10001
Tel: (212) 681-2000 *Fax:* (212) 681-2005
Website: governanceprofessionals.org
Members: 3100 individuals
Staff: 13
Annual Budget: $2-5,000,000

Personnel:
President and Chief Executive Officer: Kenneth A. Bertsch
   E-Mail: kbertsch@governanceprofessionals.org
Director, Information Technology: Russell M. Benasaraf
   E-Mail: rbenasaraf@governanceprofessionals.org
Director, Meeting Administration: Ophelia King
   E-Mail: oking@governanceprofessionals.org
Senior Vice President: Suzanne Walker
   E-Mail: swalker@governanceprofessionals.org
Director, Membership and Marketing: Teresa Webb
   E-Mail: twebb@governanceprofessionals.org

Historical Note:
Formerly American Society of Corporate Secretaries; assumed its current name on January 1, 2005. Mission is to promote and assist in the voluntary exchange of information and experience relating to the duties, problems, and practices of corporate secretaries and their companies through the Society's committees, chapters, publications and research, and its seminars and conferences. Membership: $645 (First Member/Service Provider); $325-495 (Additional Members).

Meetings/Conferences:
Conference Chair: Suzanne Walker
2013 - Seatle, WA (Seattle Sheraton Hotel)/July 10 - 13
2014 - Boston, MA (Sheraton Boston Hotel)/June 25 - 28
Number of non-conference events/year: 11

Publications:
Membership Directory; on-line
Newsletter; quarterly

Membership List Available to Non-members

Society of Cosmetic Chemists *(1945)*
120 Wall St.
Suite 2400
New York, NY 10005-4088
Tel: (212) 668-1500 *Fax:* (212) 668-1504
E-Mail: scc@scconline.org
Website: scconline.org
Members: 4000 individuals
Staff: 4
Annual Budget: $1-2,000,000
Tax: 501(c)(3)

Personnel:
Executive Director: Bill Cowen
    E-Mail: bcowen@scconline.org
Coordinator, Meetings: Annmarie Lynch
    E-Mail: alynch@scconline.org
Contact, Membership Services: Helen McCarren
    E-Mail: hmccarren@scconline.org

Historical Note:
Member of the International Federation of Societies of Cosmetic Chemists. SCC's mission is to further the interests and recognition of cosmetic scientists while maintaining the confidence of the public in the cosmetic and toiletries industry. Membership: $140 (Individual/National Affiliate); $35 (Student); $70 (Junior).

Meetings/Conferences: Annual
Conference Chair: Annmarie Lynch
2013 - St. Louis, MO (St. Louis Union Station Marriott)/June 6 - 7
Number of non-conference events/year: 2

Publications:
Journal of Cosmetic Science; bi-monthly
SCC Newsletter; monthly

Society for Critical Care Medicine *(1970)*
500 Midway Dr.
Mt. Prospect, IL 60056
Tel: (847) 827-6869 *Fax:* (847) 827-6886
E-Mail: info@sccm.org
Website: sccm.org
Members: 14000 individuals
Staff: 62
Annual Budget: $10-25,000,000
Tax: 501(c)(3)

Personnel:
Executive Vice President and Chief Executive Officer: David Julian Martin CAE
    E-Mail: dmartin@sccm.org
Manager, Accounting: Jim Brown
Director, Meetings and Conventions: Pamela S. Dallstream CMP, CMM
    E-Mail: pdallstream@sccm.org
Director, Marketing: James Flanigan
    E-Mail: jflanigan@sccm.org
Manager, Marketing and Communications: Julie Oswald
Director, Publications: Lynn Retford
    E-Mail: lretford@sccm.org
Director, Technology: Jeff Schaefer
Manager, Membership Services and Marketing: Ewa Stankiewicz
Director, Program Development and Professional Affairs: Nancy Stonis BSN, RN
Manager, Human Resources: Ellen Turney PHR, SPHR
    E-Mail: eturney@sccm.org

Historical Note:
Formerly (1988) the American College of Critical Care Medicine. SCCM's mission is to secure the quality care for all critically ill and injured patients. Membership: $130 (Healthcare Professional); $355 (Physician); $250 (International Physician); $195 (Young Physician); $85 (In-training); $55 (International Associate).

Meetings/Conferences:
Conference Chair: Pamela S. Dallstream CMP, CMM
2013 - Ft. Washington, MD (Gaylord National Hotel and Convention Center)/May 16 - 19/11-25 exhibitors

2013 - Johannesburg, South Africa (Sandton Sun Hotel)/Aug. 25 - Sept. 2
2014 - Los Angeles, CA (Los Angeles Convention Center)/Feb. 8 - 12

Publications:
Critical Care eNewsletter; bi-monthly
Critical Care Medicine
Critical Connections; bi-monthly
Membership Directory; on-line
Pediatric Critical Care Medicine; bi-monthly

Membership List Available to Non-members

Society of Dance History Scholars *(1982)*
3416 Primm Ln.
Birmingham, AL 35216
Tel: (205) 978-1404 *Fax:* (205) 823-2760
E-Mail: info@sdhs.org
Website: sdhs.org
Members: 450 individuals
Staff: 2
Annual Budget: $25-50,000
Tax: 501(c)(3)

Personnel:
Website Content Editor: Ken Pierce
    E-Mail: kpierce@mit.edu
Contact, Communication: Robert Ranieri

Historical Note:
Formerly (1983) Dance History Scholars, SDHS strives to advance the field of dance studies through research, publication, performance and outreach to audiences across the arts, humanities and social sciences. Members are academics and teachers in the field of dance. Membership: $85 (Regular); $45 (Student); $65 (Retired/Senior); $160 (Institutional); $500 (Benefactor).

Meetings/Conferences: Annual
2013 - Trondheim, Norway (NTNU Campus Dragvoll)/June 8 - 11
2013 - Riverside, CA (Mission Inn Hotel and Spa)/Nov. 14 - 17

Publications:
Ballet Alert!; on-line
Conversations Across the Field of Dance Studies; annually
Dance Online; weekly
Irish Dancing Magazine; monthly

Society of Depreciation Professionals *(1987)*
P.O. Box 67100
Harrisburg, PA 17106
Tel: (717) 763-7212
E-Mail: admin@depr.org
Website: depr.org
Staff: 2
Annual Budget: $100-250,000
Tax: 501(c)(3)

Personnel:
President: John Spanos
    E-Mail: jspanos@gfnet.com

Historical Note:
SDP's mission is to recognize the professional field of depreciation and those individuals contributing to this field. Membership: $750 (Sustaining); $300 (Business Patron); $200 (Individual Patron); $100 (Friend); $75 (Senior/Associate/Student); $85 (Individual).

Continuing Education:
Enrollment: 220
Certification Designation/s: CDP

Publications:
Membership Directory; on-line
SDP Journal; annually; adv.
SDP Newsletter; irregular

Society of Diagnostic Medical Sonographers *(1970)*
2745 Dallas Pkwy.
Suite 350
Plano, TX 75093-8730
Tel: (214) 473-8057 *Fax:* (214) 473-8563
TollFree: (800) 229-9506
Website: sdms.org
Members: 21000 combinations
Staff: 15
Annual Budget: $2-5,000,000
Tax: 501(c)(3)

Personnel:

Chief Executive Officer and Executive Director: Donald F. Haydon CAE
    E-Mail: dhaydon@sdms.org
Manager, Creative Services: Chris Alcott
    E-Mail: calcott@sdms.org
Manager, Information Technology: Scott Farmer BS, MCP
    E-Mail: sfarmer@sdms.org
Membership Marketing and Services Coordinator: Keith Gentry
    E-Mail: kgentry@sdms.org
Chief Operating Officer and Deputy Executive Director: Donald E. Kerns CAE
    E-Mail: dkerns@sdms.org
Director, Accounting and Human Resources and Director, Membership Marketing and Services: Mary Rodriguez CAE
    E-Mail: mrodriguez@sdms.org
Director, Education and Meetings: Amy Westerman CAE, CMP
    E-Mail: awesterman@sdms.org

Historical Note:
Formerly (1981) the American Society of Ultrasound Technical Specialists, SDMS's aim is to promote, advance and educate its members and the medical community in the science of diagnostic medical sonography. Membership: $145 (Active/Associate/Supporting); $495 (Corporate/Business/Institutional); $40 (Student); $179 (Advanced Practice Sonographer).

Meetings/Conferences: Annual
Conference Chair: Amy Westerman CAE, CMP
2013 - Las Vegas, NV (Sugar Loaf Ct)/Oct. 10 - 13/1100 attendees/over 100 exhibitors
2014 - Louisville, KY (Kentucky Exposition Center)/Sept. 26 - 29/1100 attendees/over 100 exhibitors

Publications:
Membership Directory; on-line
News Wave; bi-monthly
The Journal of Diagnostic Medical Sonography (JDMS); bi-monthly; adv.
The SDMS Sound News; monthly

Membership List Available to Non-members

Society of Economic Geologists *(1920)*
7811 Shaffer Pkwy.
Littleton, CO 80127-3732
Tel: (720) 981-7882 *Fax:* (720) 981-7874
E-Mail: seg@segweb.org
Website: segweb.org
Members: 6000 individuals
Staff: 9
Annual Budget: $5-10,000,000
Tax: 501(c)(3)

Personnel:
Executive Director: Brian Hoal
    E-Mail: director@segweb.org
Contact, Publications: Alice Bouley
    E-Mail: editing@segweb.org
Contact, Membership Services: Sydney Crawford
    E-Mail: sydneycrawford@segweb.org
Website Coordinator: Jeff Doyle
    E-Mail: jeffdoyle@segweb.org
Contact, Events and Publication Sales: Frances Kotzé
    E-Mail: franceskotze@segweb.org
Contact, Student Programs: Vicky Sternicki
    E-Mail: studentprograms@segweb.org
Contact, Accounting: Anna Thoms
    E-Mail: accounting@segweb.org

Historical Note:
SEG advances the science of geology in relation to minerals exploration, mining and related industries. Membership includes geoscientists from 68 countries. Membership: $95-115 (Fellow/Regular); $20-75 (Student); $35 (Couple);

Meetings/Conferences:
Conference Chair: Frances Kotzé
2013 - Leicester, United Kingdom (University of Leicester)/Jan. 3 - 4
2013 - Townsville, Australia/June 2 - 5
Number of non-conference events/year: 2

Publications:
Economic Geology; quarterly
Membership Directory; annually
Newsletter; quarterly; adv.

Society of Emergency Medicine Physician Assistants *(1990)*
1125 Executive Cir.

Irving, TX 75038-2522
TollFree: (877) 297-7594
E-Mail: sempa@sempa.org
Website: sempa.org
Members: 750 individuals
Staff: 1
Annual Budget: $250-500,000
Tax: 501(c)(6)

Personnel:
Executive Director: Michelle Parker
   E-Mail: mparker@sempa.org

Historical Note:
SEMPA's mission is to advocate and support the professional, clinical and personal development of physician assistants involved with emergency medicine and to advance the practice of emergency medicine. It was created to enhance the Emergency Medicine Physician Assistant's ability to provide the best quality patient care. Affiliated with the American Academy of Physician Assistants. Membership: $125 (Fellow); $150 (Associate); $25 (Student); $75 (Resident); $82.50(Life Member).

Continuing Education:
Certification Designation/s: CME

Meetings/Conferences: Annual
2013 - Las Vegas, NV (Mirage Resort and Casino)/
   March 17 - 21

Publications:
Annals of Emergency Medicine
e-newsletter
SEMPA News; daily

Society of Engineering Science *(1963)*
University of Illinois at Urbana-Champaign,
Beckman Institute for Advanced Science and
Technology
405 N. Mathews Ave., Room 3361
Urbana, IL 61801
E-Mail: ses@sesinc.org
Website: sesinc.org
Members: 300 individuals
Staff: 3
Annual Budget: Under $10,000

Personnel:
President: Horacio Espinosa
   E-Mail: espinosa@northwestern.edu
Treasurer: Yi-Chao Chen
   E-Mail: chen@uh.edu
Meeting Contact: David McDowell

Historical Note:
Multidisciplinary society of scientists and engineers concerned with research and communication between the fields of engineering and science. SES's mission is to promote the development and strengthening of the interfaces between various disciplines in engineering, sciences, and mathematics. Membership: $50/year (Individual).

Meetings/Conferences: Annual
Conference Chair: David McDowell

Society of Environmental Journalists *(1990)*
P.O. Box 2492
Jenkintown, PA 19046
Tel: (215) 884-8174 *Fax:* (215) 884-8175
E-Mail: sej@sej.org
Website: sej.org
Members: 1500 individuals
Staff: 4
Annual Budget: $500-1,000,000
Tax: 501(c)(3)

Personnel:
Executive Director: Beth Parke
   E-Mail: bparke@sej.org
Editor: Joseph A. Davis
   E-Mail: jdavis2@starpower.net
Director, Annual Conferences: Jay Letto
   E-Mail: jletto@sej.org
*Director, Awards, Senior Programs Manager and Systems
   Analyst:* Christine Rigel
   E-Mail: crigel@sej.org

Historical Note:
SEJ's mission is to strengthen the quality, reach and viability of journalism across all media to advance public understanding of environmental issues. Members are journalists and educators. Membership: $20 (U.S.); $15 (Canada/Mexico/Student/Outside North America).

Meetings/Conferences: Annual
Conference Chair: Jay Letto

Publications:

EJToday news service; daily
Member Directory; on-line
SEJournal; quarterly; adv.
The Daily Glob; daily
TipSheet; bi-weekly
WatchDog TipSheet; bi-weekly

Membership List Available to Non-members

Society of Environmental Toxicology and Chemistry *(1979)*
229 S. Baylen St.
Second Floor
Pensacola, FL 32502
Tel: (850) 469-1500 *Fax:* (850) 469-9778
E-Mail: setac@setac.org
Website: setac.org
Members: 5000 individuals
Staff: 10
Annual Budget: $1-2,000,000
Tax: 501(c)(6)

Personnel:
Executive Director: Greg Schiefer
   E-Mail: greg.schiefer@setac.org
Manager, Information Technology: Jason F. Andersen
   E-Mail: jason@setac.org
Communications Specialist: Sabine Barrett
   E-Mail: sabine.barrett@setac.org
Contact, Finance and Membership: Terresa Daugherty
   E-Mail: terresa.daugherty@setac.org
Manager, Finance: Linda Fenner
   E-Mail: linda.fenner@setac.org
Manager, Publications: Mimi Meredith
   E-Mail: mmeredith@setac.org
Coordinator, Events: Nikki Turman
   E-Mail: nikki.turman@setac.org

Historical Note:
SETAC's mission is to support the development of principles and practices for protection, enhancement and management of sustainable environmental quality and ecosystem integrity. Members are professionals in the fields of chemistry, toxicology, biology, ecology, atmospheric sciences, health sciences, earth sciences, and environmental engineering. Membership: $25-10,000/year.

Meetings/Conferences: Annual
Conference Chair: Nikki Turman
2013 - Nashville, TN (Gaylord Opryland Hotel and
   Convention Center Nashville, Tennessee)/Nov. 17 -
   21
2014 - Vancouver, BC/Nov. 9 - 13
Number of non-conference events/year: 8

Publications:
Environmental Toxicology and Chemistry (ET&C);
   monthly; adv.
Integrated Environmental Assessment and
   Management; quarterly; adv.
Membership Directory; on-line
SETAC Globe; bi-weekly
SETAC News; bi-weekly

Society of Ethnobiology *(1977)*
Department of Geography, University of North
Texas
1155 Union Cir. Suite 305279
Denton, TX 76203-5017
Tel: (940) 565-4987 *Fax:* (940) 369-7550
E-Mail: treasurer@ethnobiology.org
Website:
ethnobiology.org
ethnobiology.org/
Members: 530 individuals and institutions
Staff: 5
Annual Budget: $100-250,000

Personnel:
President: Justin M. Nolan
   E-Mail: president@ethnobiology.org
Coordinator, Conferences: Denise Glover
   E-Mail: conference@ethnobiology.org
Editor: Virginia Popper
   E-Mail: editor@ethnobiology.org
Webmaster: Cheryl Takahashi
   E-Mail: webmaster@ethnobiology.org
Treasurer: Steve Wolverton
   E-Mail: treasurer@ethnobiology.org

Historical Note:
SoE's mission is to promote the understanding of the past and present relationships between humans and their biological worlds. Also promotes and perpetuates the

interdisciplinary study of the relationships of plants and animals with human cultures worldwide, including past and present relationships between peoples and the environment. Members include academic and non-academic individuals who share a binding interest in exploring human-biological relationships. Membership: $50 (Regular); $75 (Family); $92 (Institution-US); $35 (Student); $85 (Sustaining); $1,000 (Life); $102 (Institution-Non US).

Meetings/Conferences: Annual
Conference Chair: Denise Glover
2013 - Denton, TX (Univ of North Texas)/May 15 - 18

Publications:
Contributions in Ethnobiology; on-line
Ethnobiology Letters; on-line
Journal of Ethnobiology; bi-annually
Membership directory; annually

Society of Experimental Test Pilots *(1955)*
P.O. Box 986
Lancaster, CA 93584-0986
Tel: (661) 942-9574 *Fax:* (661) 940-0398
E-Mail: setp@setp.org
Website: setp.org
Members: 2000 individuals
Staff: 4
Annual Budget: $500-1,000,000
Tax: 501(c)(6)

Personnel:
Executive Director: Paula S. Smith
   E-Mail: setp@setp.org
Contact, Membership Office: Becki Hoffman
   E-Mail: Becki@setp.org
Contact, Publications: Shawna Mullen
   E-Mail: shawna@setp.org
Office Manager: Laurie Simmons
   E-Mail: laurie@setp.org

Historical Note:
Incorporated in California (1956). SETP seeks to promote air safety and contributes to aeronautical advancement by promoting sound aeronautical design and development. Membership: $110 (Members/Associate Fellows/Fellows); $100 (Associate).

Meetings/Conferences: Annual

Publications:
COCKPIT Magazine; quarterly; adv.
SETP Newsletter; on-line; adv.

Society of Exploration Geophysicists *(1930)*
P.O. Box 702740
Tulsa, OK 74170-2740
Tel: (918) 497-5500 *Fax:* (918) 497-5557
E-Mail: web@seg.org
Website: seg.org
Members: 33000 individuals
Staff: 82
Annual Budget: $10-25,000,000

Personnel:
Executive Director: Steven H. Davis
   E-Mail: sdavis@seg.org
Director, Professional Development: Tom Agnew
   E-Mail: tagnew@seg.org
Director, Publications: Ted Bakamjian
   E-Mail: tbakamjian@seg.org
Advertising Sales Representative: Mel R. Buckner
   E-Mail: mbuckner@seg.org
Director, Finance and Operations: Nancy Carter
   E-Mail: ncarter@seg.org
Director, Communications: Dan DeMellier
   E-Mail: ddemellier@seg.org
Specialist, Professional Development: Cecilia Martin
   E-Mail: cmartin@seg.org
Manager, Human Resources and Membership Services:
   Judy Paull
   E-Mail: jpaull@seg.org
Manager, Programs and Events: Kristi Smith CMP
   E-Mail: ksmith@seg.org
Director, Global Relations and Meetings: Terry Todd
   E-Mail: ttodd@seg.org

Historical Note:
Founded in Houston in 1930 and incorporated in Oklahoma. SEG advocates the science of geophysics and the education of applied geophysicists. Membership: $12-90 (Active/Associate); $6-45 (Emeritus); $21 (Student).

Meetings/Conferences: Annual
Conference Chair: Kristi Smith CMP
2013 - Houston, TX (George R. Brown Convention
   Center)/Sept. 22 - 27

2014 - Denver, CO/Oct. 26 - 31
Number of non-conference events/year: 4

Publications:
Carrying the Torch; monthly
Geophysics; bi-monthly; adv.
The Leading Edge (TLE); monthly; adv.

Society of Eye Surgeons *(1968)*
10801 Connecticut Ave.
Kensington, MD 20895
Tel: (240) 290-0263 *Fax:* (240) 290-0269
E-Mail: info@iefusa.org
Website: iefusa.org
Members: 100 individuals
Staff: 10
Annual Budget: $2-5,000,000

Personnel:
President and Chief Executive Officer: Victoria M.
    Sheffield
    E-Mail: vsheffield@iefusa.org
Public Affairs Officer: Calvin Baerveldt
    E-Mail: cbaerveldt@iefusa.org
Vice President, Finance and Administration: Edwin M.
    Henderson
    E-Mail: ehenderson@iefusa.org

Historical Note:
*An auxiliary of the International Eye Foundation (same
address), SES's purpose is to assist programs dedicated
to the restoration of sight/prevention of blindness. It
also promotes understanding of blindness. Membership:
$50-100/year.*

Publications:
ENewsletter; on-line
SightReach Surgical
SRS News; on-line

Society of Federal Labor and Employee Relations Professionals *(1973)*
P.O. Box 25112
Arlington, VA 22202
Tel: (703) 403-3039 *Fax:* (703) 852-4461
E-Mail: info@sflerp.org
Website: sflerp.org
Members: 500 individuals
Staff: 1
Annual Budget: $50-100,000

Personnel:
Treasurer and Executive Director: Paco Martinez-Alvarez
    E-Mail: sflerp@sflerp.org

Historical Note:
*Formerly (2002) Society of Federal Labor Relations
Professionals. SFLERP's mission is to enhance the value
and stature of the federal labor- employee management
relations program and to increase the understanding and
visibility of federal labor-employee management relations.
Membership: $50 (Individual); $10 (Student); $100
(Organizational); $15 (Sponsored).*

Meetings/Conferences: Annual

Publications:
SFLERP Reporter; quarterly

Society of Financial Examiners *(1973)*
12100 Sunset Hills Rd.
Suite 130
Reston, VA 20190
Tel: (703) 234-4140 *Fax:* (703) 435-4390
TollFree: (800) 787-7633
E-Mail: sofe@sofe.org
Website: sofe.org
Members: 1700 individuals
Staff: 4
Annual Budget: $500-1,000,000
Tax: 501(c)(6)

Personnel:
Executive Director: L. Brackett
    E-Mail: lbrackett@sofe.org
Administrator: Judy Judy Estus
    E-Mail: sofe@sofe.org
Director: Jeanne Lachapelle
    E-Mail: jeanne@sofe.org
General Counsel: William D. Latza Esq.
    E-Mail: wlatza@stroock.com

Historical Note:
*SOFE's mission is to promote uniform ethical standards
that enable employers and public to identify professionally
qualified practitioners, and enforcing of requirements of
conduct, training, and expertise for members engaged*

*in financial examination. Membership: $65 (General/
Regulatory); $250 (Associate); $1,000 (Institution); $90
(Retired); $100 (Reinstatement Fees for Inactive Status);
Free (Student).*

Continuing Education:
Certification Designation/s: CFE, AFE, AES, CRE

Meetings/Conferences: Annual

Publications:
Insight; monthly
Membership Directory; on-line
The Examiner; quarterly

Society of Financial Service Professionals *(1928)*
19 Campus Blvd.
Suite 100
Newtown Square, PA 19073-3239
Tel: (610) 526-2500 *Fax:* (610) 527-1499
TollFree: (800) 392-6900
E-Mail: info@financialpro.org
Website: financialpro.org
Members: 18000 individuals
Staff: 43
Annual Budget: $5-10,000,000
Tax: 501(c)(6)

Personnel:
Chief Executive Officer: Joseph E. Frack CPA
    E-Mail: jfrack@financialpro.org
Chief Financial Officer: Donna Conrad ChFC
    E-Mail: dconrad@financialpro.org
Director, Human Resources: Bev Meyers Fox
    E-Mail: bfox@financialpro.org
Chief Operations and Technology Officer: Brian Horn
    E-Mail: bhorn@financialpro.org
Director, Meetings: Amy Johnson
    E-Mail: ajohnson@financialpro.org
Managing Director, Professional Development: Marshall
    Lipson CLU
    E-Mail: mlipson@financialpro.org
Director, Publications: Mary Anne Mennite
    E-Mail: mmennite@financialpro.org
General Counsel: Anne M. Rigney
    E-Mail: arigney@financialpro.org
Managing Director, Marketing and Corporate Development:
    Anthony Smith ChFC, CLU
    E-Mail: tsmith@financialpro.org
Director, Membership Services: Amy Whicker
    E-Mail: awhicker@financialpro.org

Historical Note:
*FSP's mission is to empower networks that create a
professional home identified by a set of core values, beliefs
and the opportunity for learning and growth. Membership:
$280 (Regular); $210 (Young Professional); $35 (Student),
140 (Retired/Disabled/Associate/Full-time Professor).*

Meetings/Conferences: Annual
Conference Chair: Amy Johnson
2013 - Tucson, AZ (Westward Look Wyndham Grand
    Resort and Spa)/Jan. 27 - 31

Publications:
FSP NewsBrief; weekly
FSP Newsletter
Journal of Financial Service Professionals

Society of Fire Protection Engineers *(1950)*
7315 Wisconsin Ave.
Suite 620 East
Bethesda, MD 20814
Tel: (301) 718-2910 *Fax:* (301) 718-2242
E-Mail: sfpehqtrs@sfpe.org
Website: sfpe.org
Members: 5000 individuals
Staff: 8
Annual Budget: $1-2,000,000
Tax: 501(c)(6)

Personnel:
Executive Director: Allan Freedman
    E-Mail: afreedman@sfpe.org
Program Manager, Education: Julie A. Gordon CMP
    E-Mail: jgordon@sfpe.org
Technical Director: Morgan J. Hurley PE
    E-Mail: mhurley@sfpe.org
Manager, Membership Services: Sean Kelleher
    E-Mail: skelleher@sfpe.org
Office Manager: Diane A. Sylvester
    E-Mail: dsylvester@sfpe.org

Historical Note:
*Established in 1950 and incorporated as an independent
organization in 1971. Mission is to advance the science and*

*practice of fire protection engineering and its allied fields, to
maintain ethical standards among its members and to foster
fire protection engineering education. Membership: $107.50
(Allied Professional); $215 (Affiliate).*

Continuing Education:
Enrollment: 200
Certification Designation/s: NICET, AIA, NCEES

Meetings/Conferences: Annual
2013 - Austin, TX (Omni Hotel & Resorts Downtown
    Austin)/Oct. 27 - Nov. 1

Publications:
Career Connections Magazine; biennially; adv.
Emerging Trends eNewsletter; on-line
Fire Protection Engineering Magazine; quarterly; adv.
Membership Directory; on-line
SFPE Update; monthly
SPE Today; bi-monthly; adv.

Society of Flavor Chemists *(1959)*
3301 Route 66
Suite 205, Building C
Neptune, NJ 07753
Tel: (732) 922-3393 *Fax:* (732) 922-3590
E-Mail: administrator@flavorchemist.org
Website: flavorchemist.org
Members: 500 individuals
Staff: 5
Annual Budget: $50-100,000

Personnel:
Chairman: Aaron Graham
    E-Mail: chairman@flavorchemist.org

Historical Note:
*SFC's mission is to advance the field of flavor technology
and related sciences by encouraging the exchange of ideas
and personal contacts. Society members are primarily
chemists and food scientists. Membership: $75 (USD); $90
(Foreign Currency).*

Meetings/Conferences: Annual
Number of non-conference events/year: 3

Publications:
Membership Directory; on-line
Society News

Society of Flight Test Engineers *(1968)*
44814 N. Elm Ave.
Lancaster, CA 93534
Tel: (661) 949-2095 *Fax:* (661) 949-2096
E-Mail: sfte@sfte.org
Website: sfte.org
Members: 1013 individuals and companies
Staff: 4
Annual Budget: $100-250,000

Personnel:
Executive Director: Margaret Drury
    E-Mail: sfte@sfte.org
Webmaster: Steve Lewis
    E-Mail: webmaster@sfte.org
Treasurer: Steve Martin
    E-Mail: treasurer@sfte.org
Editor, Newsletter: Carmen Prater
    E-Mail: editor@sfte.org

Historical Note:
*SFTE's mission is to improve communications in the fields
of flight test operations, analysis, instrumentation and
data systems. Members are engineers whose principal
professional interest is flight and ground testing of
aerospace vehicles. Membership: $55 (Individual/ Affiliate/
Associate); $15 (Student); $30 (Senior); $400-1,400
(Lifetime, based on age); $900-2,500 (Corporate, based on
annual revenue).*

Meetings/Conferences: Annual
Number of non-conference events/year: 1

Publications:
SFTE Newsletter; on-line

Society of Forensic Toxicologists *(1970)*
One MacDonald Center
One N. MacDonald St., Suite 15
Mesa, AZ 85201
TollFree: (888) 866-7638
E-Mail: office@soft-tox.org
Website: soft-tox.org
Members: 621 individuals
Staff: 4
Annual Budget: $500-1,000,000

Personnel:
President: Marc LeBeau PhD

Vice President: Dan Anderson MS
  E-Mail: danderson@coroner.lacounty.gov
Coordinator, Meetings and Webmaster: Bruce Goldberger PhD
Treasurer: Peter Stout PhD

Historical Note:
SOFT is an organization composed of practicing forensic toxicologists and those interested in the discipline for the purpose of promoting and developing forensic toxicology. Membership: $60 (Full/Associate); $15 (Student Affiliate).

Meetings/Conferences: Annual
Conference Chair: Bruce Goldberger PhD
2013 - Orlando, FL/Oct. 26 - Nov. 3
2013 - Orlando, FL/Oct. 27 - Nov. 1
2014 - Grand Rapids, MI/Oct. 18 - 25
2015 - Atlanta, GA/Oct. 17 - 25
2016 - Dallas, TX/Oct. 15 - 23

Publications:
Journal of Analytical Toxicology
The Journal of Analytical Toxicology
ToxTalk; quarterly

Society of Former Special Agents of the Federal Bureau of Investigation *(1937)*
3717 Fettler Park Dr.
Dumfries, VA 22025
Tel: (703) 445-0026 *Fax:* (703) 445-0039
TollFree: (800) 527-7372
E-Mail: socxfbi@socxfbi.org
Website: socxfbi.org
Members: 8000 individuals
Staff: 8
Annual Budget: $500-1,000,000

Personnel:
Executive Director: Roger Trott
  E-Mail: roger.trott@socxfbi.org
Financial and Administrative Assistant: Sandy Allyson
  E-Mail: sandy.allyson@socxfbi.org
Planner, Meetings and Conventions: Susan Anderson
  E-Mail: susan.anderson@socxfbi.org
Manager, Communications: Mary Coffman-Burke
Contact, Membership Services: Hilary B. Shampine
  E-Mail: hilary.shampine@socxfbi.org

Historical Note:
SFSAFBI's mission is to promote the welfare of its members, preserve friendships and loyalties among former Special Agents of the FBI, and support the FBI and law enforcement as positive forces in American society. Provides assistance to needy members, deceased members' families, rehabilitation of the ill and education. Membership: $67.50 (Associate); $135 (Retired/Resigned Agent).

Meetings/Conferences: Annual
Conference Chair: Susan Anderson

Publications:
Grapevine; monthly
Membership Directory; on-line

Society of Gastroenterology Nurses and Associates *(1973)*
401 N. Michigan Ave.
Chicago, IL 60611-4267
Tel: (312) 321-5165 *Fax:* (312) 673-6694
TollFree: (800) 245-7462
E-Mail: sgna@smithbucklin.com
Website: sgna.org
Members: 8000 individuals
Staff: 22
Annual Budget: $2-5,000,000
Tax: 501(c)(6)

Personnel:
Executive Director: Dale West CAE
  E-Mail: dwest@smithbucklin.com
Senior Associate, Operations and Education: Mollie Corbett
  E-Mail: mcorbett@smithbucklin.com
Manager, Operations: Kristin Dee
  E-Mail: kdee@smithbucklin.com
Senior Director, Education and Programming Services: Susan Farrell
  E-Mail: sfarrell@smithbucklin.com
Coordinator, Conventions: Mia Friel
  E-Mail: mfriel@smithbucklin.com
Senior Manager, Marketing and Communications: Jennifer Kasowicz
  E-Mail: jkasowicz@smithbucklin.com
Managing Editor: Lynn Valastyan
  E-Mail: valastyan@att.net

Historical Note:
Formerly (1989) the Society of Gastrointestinal Assistants. SGNA's mission is to advance the science and practice of gastroenterology and endoscopy nursing through education, research, advocacy, and collaboration, and by advocating the professional development of its members in an atmosphere of mutual support. Members are nurses and other allied health care individuals working in the fields of gastroenterology and endoscopy. Membership: $125-235 (Voting Licensed Nurse/Associate); $110-220 (Non-voting Affiliate); $60-120 (Non-voting/ Non-practicing).

Continuing Education:
Enrollment: 1800
Certification Designation/s: CGRN

Meetings/Conferences: Annual
Conference Chair: Mia Friel

Publications:
Membership Directory; on-line
SGNA News; on-line
SGNA's Journal; annually

Membership List Available to Non-members

Society of General Internal Medicine *(1978)*
1500 King St.
Suite 303
Alexandria, VA 22314
Tel: (202) 887-5150 *Fax:* (202) 887-5405
TollFree: (800) 822-3060
E-Mail: info@sgim.org
Website: sgim.org
Members: 3000 individuals
Staff: 11
Annual Budget: $2-5,000,000
Tax: 501(c)(3)

Personnel:
Executive Director: David Karlson PhD
  E-Mail: karlsond@sgim.org
Director, Information Technology: Smith Bullington
  E-Mail: bullingtons@sgim.org
Director, Finance and Project Management: Leslie Dunne
  E-Mail: dunnel@sgim.org
Director, Meetings: Sarajane Garten
  E-Mail: gartens@sgim.org
Director, Communications and Publications: Francine Jetton
  E-Mail: jettonf@sgim.org
Chief Operating Officer: Kay Ovington
  E-Mail: ovingtonk@sgim.org
Coordinator, Meetings: Quione Rice
  E-Mail: riceq@sgim.org
Director, Membership Services: Chris Wojcik
  E-Mail: wojcikc@sgim.org

Historical Note:
SGIM's mission is to promote improved patient care, research and education in primary care and general internal medicine. Members are health professionals interested in teaching and research related to general and primary care internal medicine. Membership: $345 (Full Member); $100 (Associate Member); $110 (International Member).

Meetings/Conferences: Annual
Conference Chair: Sarajane Garten
2013 - Denver, CO (Sheraton Denver Downtown Hotel)/April 24 - 27
2014 - San Diego, CA (Manchester Grand)/April 23 - 26
2015 - Toronto, ON (Sheraton Centre Toronto Hotel)/April 22 - 25
2016 - Hollywood, FL (Westin Diplomat Resort and Spa)/May 11 - 15

Publications:
Journal of General Internal Medicine and Supplement; monthly; adv.
Membership Directory; on-line
SGIM E-News; on-line
SGIM Forum Newsletter; monthly; adv.

Membership List Available to Non-members

Society of General Physiologists *(1946)*
P.O. Box 257
Woods Hole, MA 02543-0257
Tel: (508) 540-6719 *Fax:* (508) 540-0155
E-Mail: sgp@mbl.edu
Website: sgpweb.org
Members: 1000 individuals
Staff: 2
Annual Budget: $1-2,000,000
Tax: 501(c)(3)

Personnel:
Executive Secretary: Susan Shephard
  E-Mail: sgp@mbl.edu

Historical Note:
Founded in 1946 at the Marine Biological Laboratory, Woods Hole, and incorporated in Massachusetts in 1966. SGP's mission is to advocate interdisciplinary research and education about how living organisms function. Membership: $75 (Regular); $30 (Young Investigator). Emeritus membership is available free of cost to retired physiologists.

Meetings/Conferences: Annual
2013 - Woods Hole, MA (Marine Biological Laboratory)/Sept. 4 - 8
2014 - Woods Hole, MA (Marine Biological Laboratory)/Sept. 3 - 7
Number of non-conference events/year: 2

Publications:
Journal of General Physiology; monthly
Membership Directory; annually
Synapses; semi-monthly

Society of Geriatric Cardiology *(1986)*
7910 Woodmont Ave.
Suite 1050
Bethesda, MD 20814
Tel: (301) 656-1802 *Fax:* (301) 654-4137
E-Mail: info@sgcard.org
Website: sgcard.org
Members: 500 individuals
Staff: 1
Annual Budget: $100-250,000

Personnel:
Executive Director: Deborah Williams-Martinez
  E-Mail: dmartinez@sgcard.org

Historical Note:
SGC was formed to meet the problems resulting from cardiovascular diseases in aging men and women in the U.S. and around the world. Membership is open to all health care professionals who have demonstrated a commitment to geriatric cardiology and are certified in their area of professional expertise by an appropriate agency. Membership: $95/year (physician); $50/year (associate); $50/year (trainee); $150/year (fellowship).

Society of Glass and Ceramic Decorated Products *(1871)*
P.O. Box 2489
Zanesville, OH 43702
Tel: (740) 588-9882 *Fax:* (740) 588-0245
E-Mail: info@sgcd.org
Website: sgcd.org
Members:
48 Companies
750 individuals
Staff: 3
Annual Budget: $100-250,000
Tax: 501(c)(6)

Personnel:
Executive Director: Myra Warne

Historical Note:
SGCDpro provides designers, decorators and marketers of glass, ceramic and related products with resources for maximizing profitability, technical applications and regulatory compliance. Membership: $1400 (Corporate); $395 (Individual); $140 (Independent); $75 (Student).

Meetings/Conferences: Annual

Publications:
Membership Directory; on-line
Newsletter

Membership List Available to Non-members

Society of Government Economists *(1970)*
P.O. Box 77082
Washington, DC 20013
Tel: (202) 643-1743
E-Mail: sge@paintedcup.net
Website: sge-econ.org
Members: 300 individuals
Staff: 3
Tax: 501(c)(6)

Personnel:
Executive Director: Farhad Niami
  E-Mail: farhad.niami@sge-econ.org
Director, Membership Services: Mark Ledbetter
Conference Committee Chair: Brian W. Sloboda
  E-Mail: brian.w.sloboda@usps.gov

Historical Note:
SGE's mission is to support the professional development of government economists, and those who are interested in public policy economics, by providing them with research, publication, and professional communication opportunities. Membership: $25 (Regular); $150 (Institutional).

Meetings/Conferences: Annual
Conference Chair: Brian W. Sloboda
2013 - San Diego, CA/Jan. 4 - 6

Publications:
SGE newsletter; monthly

Society of Government Meeting Professionals
(1980)
908 King St.
Lower Level
Alexandria, VA 22314
Tel: (703) 549-0892 *Fax:* (703) 549-0708
Website: sgmp.org
Members: 3800 individuals
Staff: 9
Annual Budget: $1-2,000,000
Tax: 501(c)(6)

Personnel:
Interim Chief Executive Officer: Rob Bergeron CAE, CGMP
 E-Mail: rob.bergeron@sgmp.org
Manager, Conference and Meetings: Krystal Bushell CGMP
 E-Mail: krystal.bushell@sgmp.org
Director, Membership Services and Information Technology: Michael Downard CGMP
 E-Mail: michael.downard@sgmp.org
Manager, Membership Communications: Kimberly Kowal CGMP
 E-Mail: kimberly.kowal@sgmp.org
Manager, Accounting: Anna Marie Stewart
 E-Mail: anna.marie.stewart@sgmp.org

Historical Note:
Formerly (1996) the Society of Government Meeting Planners. SGMP's mission is to improve the quality and promote the cost effectiveness of government meetings. It aims to achieve this by improving the knowledge and expertise of individuals in the planning and management of government meetings through education, training, and industry relationships. Members are persons involved in planning government meetings and individuals who supply services to government planners. Membership: $25-350/ year.

Continuing Education:
Enrollment: 425
Certification Designation/s: CGMP

Meetings/Conferences: Annual
Conference Chair: Krystal Bushell CGMP
2013 - Orlando, FL/May 22 - 24
Number of non-conference events/year: 14

Publications:
Government Connections; quarterly; adv.
Membership Directory; on-line
Newsletters

Society of Government Service Urologists *(1972)*
1100 E. Woodfield Rd.
Suite 520
Schaumburg, IL 60173
Tel: (847) 517-7225 *Fax:* (847) 517-7229
E-Mail: info@sgsu.org
Website: sgsu.org
Members: 731 individuals
Staff: 3
Annual Budget: $100-250,000

Personnel:
President: Richard Steven Stack MD
Executive Director: Wendy J. Weiser
Treasurer: Joseph Y. Clark MD

Historical Note:
SGSU provides a comprehensive update on the full spectrum of urologic diseases, in addition to addressing specific needs of government service urologists, including care of combat-related injuries and practice management in federal health facilities. Membership: $100 (Active Duty Military); $1000 (Lifetime); $150 (All others); $100 (VA/USPHS/Indian Health Service (currently employed)).

Meetings/Conferences: Annual
2013 - Honolulu, HI (Waikiki Beach Marriott Resort and Spa)/Jan. 20 - 25

Publications:
SGSU news; quarterly

Society of Government Travel Professionals
(1983)
P.O. Box 158
Glyndon, MD 21071
Tel: (202) 241-7487 *Fax:* (202) 379-1775
E-Mail: info@sgtp.org
Website: sgtp.org
Members: 530 organizations
Staff: 3
Annual Budget: $250-500,000

Personnel:
Executive Director: Rick Singer
 E-Mail: rsinger@sgtp.org
Treasurer: Scott Lamb
 E-Mail: scott.lamb@hilton.com

Historical Note:
Formerly Society of Travel Agents in Government, SGTP is dedicated to collaboration between Government Travel Managers and Travel Industry Suppliers to facilitate the combined needs of both groups as the travel environment evolves. Members are ARC-appointed travel agents holding government travel contracts or servicing government contractors, suppliers and government or contractor travel managers. Membership: $495 (TMC Regular/ Supplier Regular); $215 (TMC Small Business/Government Employee Federal/Employee State or Municipal/Supplier Supporting).

Continuing Education:
Certification Designation/s: CGTP

Publications:
Accessibility of Federal Government Travel Rates; annually
Membership Directory; on-line; adv.
SGTP 101: Principles of Government Travel Management; semi-annually; adv.
SGTP eNews; biennially
State & Provincial Travel Procurement Practices & Procedures; annually; adv.

Membership List Available to Non-members

Society of Gynecologic Oncologists *(1969)*
230 W. Monroe St.
Suite 710
Chicago, IL 60606
Tel: (312) 235-4060 *Fax:* (312) 235-4059
E-Mail: sgo@sgo.org
Website: sgo.org
Members: 1500 individuals
Staff: 12
Annual Budget: $2-5,000,000

Personnel:
Executive Director: Mary Eiken MS
 E-Mail: mary.eiken@sgo.org
Director, Meetings: Jenna Cummins CMP
 E-Mail: jenna.cummins@sgo.org
Manager, Education: Rachel Newman
 E-Mail: rachel.newman@sgo.org
Director, Corporate Communications and Advocacy: Ellen Sullivan
 E-Mail: ellen.sullivan@sgo.org
Director, Finance and Administration: Michael Vogl
 E-Mail: michael.vogl@sgo.org
Director, Membership Services and Marketing: Chrissy Ward CAE, MS
 E-Mail: chrissy.ward@sgo.org

Historical Note:
Formerly (1994) Society of Gynecological Oncologists. Founded by a small group of doctors, SGO is interested in advancing knowledge and raising standards of practice in gynecologic oncology within the disciplines of obstetrics and gynecology. SGO's mission is to promote the good quality of comprehensive clinical care through education and research in the prevention and treatment of gynecologic cancers. Membership: $25-500/year.

Meetings/Conferences:
Conference Chair: Jenna Cummins CMP
2013 - Avon, CO (Westin Riverfront)/Feb. 7 - 9
2013 - Los Angeles, CA (Los Angeles Convention Center)/March 9 - 13
2014 - Tampa, FL (Tampa Bay Convention Center)/ March 23 - 26
2015 - Chicago, IL (Hilton Chicago)/March 29 - April 1
2016 - San Diego, CA (San Diego Convention and Visitors Bureau)/March 20 - 23
Number of non-conference events/year: 2

Publications:
Membership Directory; on-line

Society of Hispanic Professional Engineers *(1974)*
13181 Crossroads Pkwy., North
Suite 450
Industry, CA 91746-3497
Tel: (323) 725-3970 *Fax:* (323) 725-0316
E-Mail: shpenational@shpe.org
Website: shpe.org
Members: 10000 individuals
Staff: 15
Annual Budget: $2-5,000,000
Tax: 501(c)(4)

Personnel:
Chief Executive Officer: Pilar Montoya
 E-Mail: Pilar.Montoya@shpe.org
Manager, Information Technology: Frank Barragan
 E-Mail: frank.barragan@shpe.org
Manager, National Meetings and Events: Beatriz Garcia
 E-Mail: beatriz.garcia@shpe.org
Director, Finance and Administration: Carlyn Hemminger
 E-Mail: Carlyn.Hemminger@shpe.org
Manager, Corporate Affairs: Carmen Peralta
 E-Mail: carmen.peralta@shpe.org
Manager, Membership Services: Valerie Valenzuela
 E-Mail: valerie.valenzuela@shpe.org

Historical Note:
SHPE's mission is to improve the equality of all people through the use of science and technology. It changes lives by empowering the Hispanic community to realize their fullest potential and impacts the world through STEM awareness, access, support and development. Membership: $45 (Professional); $500 (Lifetime Regular/Professional); $400 (Lifetime-Associate); $35 (Associate); $5 (Student); $15 (Graduate Student); $5 (Undergraduate).

Meetings/Conferences: Annual
Conference Chair: Beatriz Garcia
2013 - Indianapolis, IN/Oct. 30 - Nov. 3/5000 attendees
Number of non-conference events/year: 1

Publications:
Membership Directory; on-line
SHPE Magazine; quarterly; adv.

Society of Hospital Medicine *(1997)*
1500 Spring Garden St.
Suite 501
Philadelphia, PA 19130
Fax: (267) 702-2690
TollFree: (800) 843-3360
E-Mail: membership@hospitalmedicine.org
Website: hospitalmedicine.org
Members: 10000 individuals
Staff: 53
Annual Budget: $10-25,000,000
Tax: 501(c)(3)

Personnel:
Chief Executive Officer: Laurence Wellikson MD
 E-Mail: lwellikson@hospitalmedicine.org
Office Manager: Marikay Brown
 E-Mail: mbrown@hospitalmedicine.org
Director, Marketing: Irisa Gold
 E-Mail: igold@hospitalmedicine.org
Senior Manager, Membership Services: Ethan Gray
 E-Mail: egray@hospitalmedicine.org
Director, Information Technology: Michael Porreca
 E-Mail: mporreca@hospitalmedicine.org
Editor, The Hospitalist: Danielle Scheurer
 E-Mail: scheured@musc.edu
Manager, Business Development: Kristin Scott
 E-Mail: kscott@hospitalmedicine.org
Human Resource Generalist: Joi Seabrooks
 E-Mail: jseabrooks@hospitalmedicine.org
Associate Vice President, Communications: Brendon Shank
 E-Mail: bshank@hospitalmedicine.org
Senior Director, Education and Meetings: Catharine Smith
 E-Mail: csmith@hospitalmedicine.org
Senior Vice President, Operations: Todd Von Deak CAE, MBA
 E-Mail: tvondeak@hospitalmedicine.org
Vice President, Finance: Robert A. Zipperlen
 E-Mail: bzipperlen@hospitalmedicine.org

Historical Note:
SHM's purpose is to promote quality care for all hospitalized patients. SHM is committed to promoting excellence in the practice of hospital medicine through education, advocacy and research. Membership: $300

(Physician/Affiliates/Allied Health Professionals); $155 (Resident/Fellow).

Meetings/Conferences: Annual
2013 - Ft. Washington, MD (Gaylord National Resort & Convention Center)/May 16 - 19
2014 - Las Vegas, NV (Mandalay Bay)/March 24 - 27
Number of non-conference events/year: 2

Publications:
eWire; monthly
Journal of Hospital Medicine; adv.
The Hospitalist; monthly

Society of Illustrators (1901)
128 E. 63rd St.
New York, NY 10065
Tel: (212) 838-2560 *Fax:* (212) 838-2561
E-Mail: info@societyillustrators.org
Website: societyillustrators.org
Members: 1055 individuals
Staff: 14
Annual Budget: $1-2,000,000
Tax: 501(c)(3)

Personnel:
Executive Director: Anelle Miller
   E-Mail: anelle@societyillustrators.org
Director, Operations: John Capobianco
   E-Mail: john@societyillustrators.org
Director, Exhibitions: Kate Feirtag
   E-Mail: kate@societyillustrators.org
Bookkeeper: Mary Molloy
   E-Mail: mary@societyillustrators.org

Historical Note:
SI's mission is to promote the art and appreciation of illustration, its history and evolving nature. It achieves this through exhibitions, lectures, education, and fostering open discussion. Membership: $150-500 (Illustrator) $300-500 (Associate); $580 (Educator); $1,500 (Corporate); $250 (Friend); $35 (Student).

Meetings/Conferences:
Conference Chair: Kate Feirtag

Publications:
Society News; on-line

Society of Incentive & Travel Executives (1973)
401 N. Michigan Ave.
Chicago, IL 60611
Tel: (312) 321-5148 *Fax:* (312) 527-6783
E-Mail: site@siteglobal.com
Website: siteglobal.com
Members: 2100 individuals
Staff: 10
Annual Budget: $2-5,000,000
Tax: 501(c)(6)

Personnel:
Managing Director: Allison Summers
   E-Mail: asummers@siteglobal.com
Manager, Accounting: Jennifer Buzalski
   E-Mail: jbuzalski@siteglobal.com
Manager, International Conference: Kelly Geegan
   E-Mail: kgeegan@siteglobal.com
Manager, Education and Certification: Lydia Goessel
   E-Mail: lgoessel@siteglobal.com
Director, International Conference: Eric Johnson CMM, CMP
   E-Mail: ejohnson@siteglobal.com
Senior Coordinator, Education: Carrie Johnson
Director, Operations: Christie Pruyn
   E-Mail: cpruyn@siteglobal.com
Senior Coordinator, Marketing: Jennie Snider
   E-Mail: jsnider@siteglobal.com
Contact, Membership Services, North America: Leslie Teague
   E-Mail: lteague@siteglobal.com

Historical Note:
Formerly (1996) the Society of Incentive Travel Executives. SITE provides educational seminars and information services to those who design, develop, promote, sell, administer, and operate motivational programs as an incentive to increase productivity in business. Members are corporate users, airlines, tourism boards, cruise lines, destination management companies, consultants, hotels/resorts, travel agents, incentive travel houses and publications. Membership: $115-445/year (Individual).

Continuing Education:
Certification Designation/s: CITE

Meetings/Conferences: Annual
Conference Chair: Eric Johnson CMM, CMP

2013 - Antwerp, Belgium/March 11 - 13
2013 - Orlando, FL (Loews Portofino Bay Hotel at Universal Orlando)/Dec. 7 - 10

Society of Independent Gasoline Marketers of America (SIGMA) (1958)
3930 Pender Dr.
Suite 340
Fairfax, VA 22030
Tel: (703) 709-7000 *Fax:* (703) 709-7007
E-Mail: sigma@sigma.org
Website: sigma.org
Members: 250 corporate members
Staff: 11
Annual Budget: $2-5,000,000
Tax: 501(c)(6)

Personnel:
Executive Vice President: Kenneth A. Doyle CAE
   E-Mail: kdoyle@sigma.org
Director, Communications and Education: Susan Crosby
   E-Mail: scrosby@sigma.org
Assistant Director, Membership Services: Brian Inglis
   E-Mail: binglis@sigma.org
Director, Meetings: Mary Alice Kutyn
   E-Mail: makutyn@sigma.org
Director, Advertising and Sponsorship Sales: Nancy Muskett
   E-Mail: nmuskett@sigma.org
Director, Business Development: Marilyn Selvitelle
   E-Mail: mselvitelle@sigma.org

Historical Note:
Absorbed the Southeast Independent Oil Marketers Association in 1988, SIGMA's mission is to benefit its members by ensuring a free and unencumbered economic environment for the fully competitive marketing of motor fuels. Members are independent gasoline marketers. Dues for Regular Membership vary, based on number of outlets and on sales volume of motor fuel. Membership: $3,000-6,180/year (Associate).

Meetings/Conferences: Semi-Annual
Conference Chair: Mary Alice Kutyn
2013 - Telluride, CO (Peaks Resort and Spa)/Jan. 27 - 30
2013 - Scottsdale, AZ (Hyatt Regency Scottsdale Resort and Spa at Gainey Ranch)/May 2 - 5
2014 - Rancho Mirage, CA (Westin Mission Hills Resort and Spa)/April 10 - 13
Number of non-conference events/year: 3

Publications:
Independent Gasoline Marketing Magazine; bi-monthly; adv.
Membership Directory; on-line

Society of Independent Professional Earth Scientists (1963)
4925 Greenville Ave.
Suite 1106
Dallas, TX 75206-4008
Tel: (214) 363-1780 *Fax:* (214) 363-8195
E-Mail: sipes@sipes.org
Website: sipes.org
Members: 1400 individuals
Staff: 2
Annual Budget: $250-500,000
Tax: 501(c)(6)

Personnel:
Executive Director: Diane M. Finstrom

Historical Note:
Founded in Houston, TX and chartered as a professional and scientific society in 1963, SIPES is a member society of the American Geological Institute and a cooperative association with the Independent Petroleum Association of America. SIPES's mission is to further the professional and business interests of independent practitioners of earth sciences. Members are geologists, geophysicists, engineers and other earth scientists with at least twelve years professional experience who are independent or self-employed. Membership: $75/year.

Meetings/Conferences: Annual
Conference Chair: Diane M. Finstrom
2013 - Santa Fe, NM (El Dorado Hotel and Spa)/June 17 - 20

Publications:
Membership Directory; biennially
SIPES Newsletter; quarterly; adv.

Society of Independent Show Organizers (1990)
2601 Ocean Park Blvd.

Suite 200
Santa Monica, CA 90405
Tel: (310) 450-8831 *Fax:* (310) 450-9305
TollFree: (877) 937-7476
E-Mail: info@siso.org
Website: siso.org
Members: 120 companies
Staff: 3
Annual Budget: $250-500,000
Tax: 501(c)(6)

Personnel:
Executive Director: Lew R. Shomer
   E-Mail: lshomer@shomex.com
Contact, Membership Services: Gillian Campbell
   E-Mail: gcampbell@shomex.com
Contact, Operations: Anna Osnower
   E-Mail: aosnower@shomex.com

Historical Note:
SISO's mission is to meet the common needs of its members, by providing peer networking opportunities, education, industry information, streamlined business processes and best practices in the industry. Membership: $295-1,825/year (Organization/Company, based on gross annual revenue).

Meetings/Conferences: Annual
2013 - Kiawah Island, SC (Sacntuary Kiawah Island Golf Resort)/April 8 - 11

Publications:
Membership Directory; on-line

Society of Industrial and Office Realtors (1941)
1201 New York Ave. NW
Suite 350
Washington, DC 20005-6126
Tel: (202) 449-8200 *Fax:* (202) 216-9325
E-Mail: admin@sior.com
Website: sior.com
Members: 3000 members
Staff: 20
Annual Budget: $2-5,000,000

Personnel:
Executive Vice President: Richard E. Hollander
   E-Mail: rhollander@sior.com
Director, Communications: Alexis Fermanis
   E-Mail: afermanis@sior.com
Vice President, Marketing and Programs: Pamela "Pam" Fitzgerald
   E-Mail: pfitzgerald@sior.com
Manager, Meetings and Events: Kourtney Frawley
   E-Mail: kfrawley@sior.com
Senior Vice President, Operations: Robert Hammond
   E-Mail: rhammond@sior.com
Director, Programs: Lizzy Koenst
   E-Mail: lkoenst@sior.com
Director, Information Technology: Michael Roberts
   E-Mail: mroberts@sior.com
Director, Membership Services: Michael T. Topp
   E-Mail: mtopp@sior.com

Historical Note:
Formerly (1986) Society of Industrial Realtors. A professional affiliate of the National Association of Realtors, SIR was founded in Washington just prior to World War II at the instigation of the War Department to help locate specialized facilities suitable for the production of military equipment. Incorporated in the state of Illinois, SIOR strives to establish, maintain, and sustain a designation of the highest level for commercial real estate providers. Active members are brokers, consultants and appraisers. Associate membership includes corporate executives, developers, educators, and other involved in the commercial real estate industry. Membership: $1280 (Active); $200-1,500 (Associate); $100-200 (Retired).

Continuing Education:
Certification Designation/s: SIOR

Meetings/Conferences: Semi-Annual
Conference Chair: Pamela "Pam" Fitzgerald
2013 - Palm Spring, CA/May 2 - 4
Number of non-conference events/year: 1

Publications:
Membership Directory; annually; adv.

Membership List Available to Non-members

Society of Infectious Diseases Pharmacists (1990)
14061 Hartman Ave.
Omaha, NE 68164
E-Mail: sidp@eami.com

Website: sidp.org
Members: 400 members
Staff: 2
Annual Budget: $250-500,000
Tax: 501(c)(6)

Personnel:
President: Elizabeth Hermsen
  E-Mail: edhermsen@hotmail.com

Historical Note:
SIDP promotes the appropriate use of antimicrobials. Provides education, advocacy, and leadership in all aspects of the treatment of infectious diseases. SIDP is comprised of pharmacists and other health care professionals involved in patient care, research, teaching, drug development, and governmental regulation that are concerned with all facets of antimicrobial use and committed to infectious diseases pharmacotherapy. Membership: $100 (Active/Associate); $25 (Trainee Associate).

Meetings/Conferences: Annual
2013 - Denver, CO/Sept. 10 - 13
2014 - Washington, DC/Sept. 5 - 8

Publications:
Newsletter; quarterly

Society of Insurance Financial Management
(1959)
P.O. Box 9001
Mt. Vernon, NY 10552
Tel: (914) 966-3180 *Fax:* (914) 966-3264
E-Mail: sifm@cinn.com
Website: sifm.org
Members: 800 individuals and 250 companies
Staff: 1
Annual Budget: $100-250,000

Personnel:
President: Edward J. Majkowski

Historical Note:
Formerly known as the Society of Insurance Accountants until 1994. SIFM's mission is to provide forum for discussing current insurance industry issues relating to financial accounting and reporting, reinsurance, taxation, regulatory developments and other relevant topics. Membership: $125/year (Individual).

Meetings/Conferences: Quarterly

Publications:
Membership Directory; on-line

Society of Insurance Research *(1970)*
631 Eastpointe Dr.
Shelbyville, IN 46176-2291
Tel: (317) 398-3684 *Fax:* (317) 642-0535
E-Mail: sir.mail@comcast.net
Website: sirnet.org
Members: 450 individuals
Staff: 7
Annual Budget: $100-250,000
Tax: 501(c)(6)

Personnel:
Executive Director: Ed Budd CPCU
Vice President, Controller: Tom Forristell
Vice President, Education and Educational Outreach: Terrie Lemon
Vice President, Annual Conference: Sharon Markovsky
Vice President, Events: Richard Skyba
Vice President, Public Relations and Communications: Todd Walker MAAA
Vice President, Marketing: Michael Warner

Historical Note:
Founded under the sponsorship of the Griffith Foundation for Insurance Education and Ohio State University, SIR provides a forum for the free exchange of ideas in all areas of insurance research. Members are individuals actively engaged in some form of insurance research. Membership: $195 (Individual); $2,000 (Corporate Value); $3,000 (Associate Corporate).

Meetings/Conferences: Annual
Conference Chair: Richard Skyba

Publications:
SIR Member Directory; on-line
SIR Newsletter; adv.

Society of Insurance Trainers and Educators
(1953)
1821 University Ave. W
Suite S256
St. Paul, MN 55104
Tel: (651) 999-5354 *Fax:* (651) 917-1835

E-Mail: ed@insurancetrainers.org
Website: insurancetrainers.org
Members: 1000 individuals
Staff: 5
Annual Budget: $100-250,000
Tax: 501(c)(6)

Personnel:
Executive Director: Melissa Palank
  E-Mail: ed@insurancetrainers.org
Treasurer: Tammy Alsene
  E-Mail: tammy.alsene.bcz2@statefarm.com
Vice President, Member Services: Paul Balbresky
  E-Mail: pbalbresky@verizon.net
Vice President, Annual Conferences: Brenda Davis
  E-Mail: bdavis@alliantinsurance.com
Vice President, Marketing: Angela Siegfried AIP
  E-Mail: siegfra1@nationwide.com

Historical Note:
Formerly (1985) Insurance Company Education Directors Society. SITE's mission is to provide professional development to Society members through programs, networking opportunities and services. Membership is composed of education and training professionals, organizational/performance development and HR directors, curriculum designers, classroom and online instructors, and solution providers for training and education in the insurance/financial services industry. Membership: $125 (Designee); $95 (Associate); $45 (Retiree); $60 (Student); $1,000-8,000 (Corporate).

Continuing Education:
Enrollment: 10
Certification Designation/s: ITP

Meetings/Conferences: Annual
Conference Chair: Brenda Davis
2013 - Portland, OR (Hilton Portland and Executive Tower)/June 22 - 26
2014 - Bonita Springs, FL (Hyatt Regency Coconut Point Resort and Spa)/June 21 - 24
2015 - Colorado Springs, CO/June 20 - 23
Number of non-conference events/year: 1

Publications:
In-Site Newsletter; bi-monthly
Member Directory; on-line

Society of International Business Fellows *(1981)*
191 Peachtree St. NE
Suite 3950
Atlanta, GA 30303
Tel: (404) 525-7423 *Fax:* (404) 525-5331
E-Mail: info@sibf.org
Website: sibf.org
Members: 400 members
Staff: 7
Annual Budget: $2-5,000,000

Personnel:
Executive Director: Nancy Haselden
  E-Mail: nancy.haselden@sibf.org
Coordinator, Communications: Marco Coelho
Treasurer: Ryan Losi
Vice President, Program Development: Randy Nuckolls
Vice President, Membership: Rick Walker

Historical Note:
SIBF educates and connects leaders throughout the world to further their professional and personal success. Members are a diverse and experienced base of 450 CEOs and other high- level executives who share a keen interest in global commerce. Membership: $1,500/year.

Meetings/Conferences: Annual
Conference Chair: Randy Nuckolls
2013 - Toronto, ON (Four Seasons)/Oct. 3 - 6
Number of non-conference events/year: 4

Publications:
Member Directory.; on-line

Society of Interventional Radiology *(1973)*
3975 Fair Ridge Dr.
Suite 400 North
Fairfax, VA 22033
Tel: (703) 691-1805 *Fax:* (703) 691-1855
TollFree: (800) 488-7284
E-Mail: info@sirweb.org
Website: sirweb.org
Members: 4500 members and 29 companies and organizations
Staff: 34
Annual Budget: $10-25,000,000
Tax: 501(c)(6)

Personnel:
Executive Director: Susan E. Sedory Holzer CAE, MA
Director, Publications and Managing Editor: Noemi C. Arthur
  E-Mail: narthur@sirweb.org
Director, Membership Services, Marketing and Graduate Medical Affairs: Joy Gornal
  E-Mail: gornal@sirweb.org
Assistant Executive Director, Meetings and Education: Erica Holland
  E-Mail: holland@sirweb.org
Senior Director, Finance: Jeff Nielsen
Director, Communications and Public Relations: Maryann Verrillo
Director, Information Technology and Web Development: Phil White MCP

Historical Note:
Founded as Society of Cardiovascular and Interventional Radiology. Assumed its current name in 2003. SIR's mission is to improve the health of the public through pioneering advances in image-guided therapy. Membership: $300-520 (Associate); $650 (Active); $25-300 (Student); $280 (Corresponding); $440 (Public Health/Military).

Continuing Education:
Certification Designation/s: MOC, CME

Meetings/Conferences:
Conference Chair: Erica Holland
2013 - New Orleans, LA/April 13 - 18/11-25 exhibitors
2014 - San Diego, CA/March 23 - 28
Number of non-conference events/year: 1

Publications:
IR News; bi-monthly
JVIR; monthly
Membership Directory; on-line
STAT and E-News; on-line

Membership List Available to Non-members

Society of Invasive Cardiovascular Professionals
(1993)
1500 Sunday Dr.
Suite 102
Raleigh, NC 27607
Tel: (919) 861-4546 *Fax:* (919) 787-4916
E-Mail: director@sicp.com
Website: sicp.com
Members: 1200 members
Staff: 4
Annual Budget: $50-100,000
Tax: 501(c)(6)

Personnel:
Executive Director: Nicole Shore
  E-Mail: director@sicp.com
Coordinator, Advocacy: Penney De Pas
  E-Mail: pdepas@sicp.com
Coordinator, Membership: Verena Rojas
  E-Mail: membership@sicp.com
Review Course Coordinator: Tracy Steadman
  E-Mail: meetings@sicp.com

Historical Note:
SICP aims to promote and encourage participation of the invasive cardiovascular professional in organization. Members are cardiac catheter laboratory professionals. Membership: $50 (Professional/Student); $170 (Group).

Meetings/Conferences: Annual
Conference Chair: Tracy Steadman
Number of non-conference events/year: 2

Publications:
SICP News

Society of Laparoendoscopic Surgeons *(1990)*
7330 SW 62nd Pl.
Suite 410
Miami, FL 33143-4825
Tel: (305) 665-9959 *Fax:* (305) 667-4123
TollFree: (800) 446-2659
E-Mail: info@sls.org
Website: sls.org
Members: 6000 individuals
Staff: 8
Annual Budget: $1-2,000,000

Personnel:
Operations Officer: Janis Chinnock Wetter
  E-Mail: janis@sls.org
Contact, Conferences: Lynne Davidson
  E-Mail: Lynne@SLS.org
Director, Membership Services: Lauren Frede

E-Mail: lauren@sls.org
Administrator, Publications: J. Gisele Muller
E-Mail: gisele@sls.org
Administrative Assistant: Flor Tilden
E-Mail: flor@sls.org

Historical Note:
SLS established to provide an open forum for surgeons and other health professionals interested in laparoscopic, endoscopic and minimally invasive surgery. Members are surgeons from various specialties and other health professions who are interested in advancing their expertise in the diagnostic and therapeutic uses of laparoendoscopic techniques. Membership: $250 (Physician); $75 (Resident-In-Training/Fellow-In-Training/Nurse/Technician/Retired Physicians).

Meetings/Conferences: Annual
Conference Chair: Lynne Davidson
2013 - Reston, VA (Hyatt Regency Reston)/Aug. 28 - 31
2014 - Las Vegas, NV (Caesar's Palace)/Sept. 10 - 13
2015 - New York City, NY (Sheraton New York Hotel and Towers)/Sept. 2 - 5

Publications:
Journal of the Society of Laparoendoscopic Surgeons; quarterly
Laparoscopy Today; semi-annually
Membership Directory; on-line

Society of Manufacturing Engineers (1932)
One SME Dr.
Dearborn, MI 48128
Tel: (313) 425-3000 Fax: (313) 425-3400
TollFree: (800) 733-4763
Website: sme.org
Members: 24000 individuals, Student Chapters and Senior Chapters
Staff: 150
Annual Budget: $25-50,000,000
Tax: 501(c)(3)

Personnel:
Executive Director and Chief Executive Officer: Mark C. Tomlinson
E-Mail: leadership@sme.org
Director, Membership Services: Joe LaRussa PE
E-Mail: membership@sme.org
Manager, Business: Gary Mikola
E-Mail: mikogar@sme.org
Manager, Manufacturing Education and Research Community: Mark Stratton
E-Mail: membership@sme.org

Historical Note:
Formerly (1932) the Society of Tool Engineers, a year later renamed as American Society of Tool Engineers, assumed its current name in 1969. SME's mission is to encourage an increased awareness of manufacturing engineering and keep manufacturing professionals up to date on leading trends and technologies. Membership: $138-152 (Regular); $20 (Student); $259-665 (Reciprocal).

Continuing Education:
Certification Designation/s: CMfgE, CMfgT

Meetings/Conferences:
Conference Chair: Gary Mikola
Number of non-conference events/year: 15

Publications:
Daily Executive Briefing; daily
Journal of Manufacturing Processes
Journal of Manufacturing Systems
Lean Directions; monthly
Manufacturing Engineering; monthly
Showcase; bi-monthly
SME e-Newsletters; monthly
The SME Member Newsletter; quarterly

Society of Marine Port Engineers (1946)
P.O. Box 369
Eatontown, NJ 07724
Tel: (732) 389-2009 Fax: (732) 389-2264
E-Mail: dmoore@smpe.org
Website: smpe.org
Members: 550 individuals
Staff: 1
Annual Budget: $25-50,000

Personnel:
Contact, Communications: Diane Moore
E-Mail: dmoore@smpe.org

Historical Note:
SMPE seeks to develop a cooperative spirit and friendship among members, to be of mutual assistance to each other, and to encourage and protect the interests and welfare of

the American Merchant Marine. Members are students in engineering and related fields interested in pursuing a maritime career at sea or ashore. Membership: $100/year (Full/Associate); Free (Students).

Meetings/Conferences:
Number of non-conference events/year: 2

Publications:
Dinner Dance Journal; annually; adv.

Society of Maritime Arbitrators (1963)
30 Broad St.
Seventh Floor
New York, NY 10004-2304
Tel: (212) 344-2400 Fax: (212) 344-2402
E-Mail: info@smany.org
Website: smany.org
Members: 100 individuals
Staff: 3
Annual Budget: $50-100,000

Personnel:
President: Austin L. Dooley
E-Mail: president@smany.org
Administrative Secretary: Patricia E Leahy
Governor: Klaus C.J. Mordhorst

Historical Note:
SMA's purpose is to help settle disputes arising from contracts involving movements by water, or those involving shipbuilding and repair. It helps maintain uniformity in U. S. maritime arbitration proceedings. Members are drawn from such fields as surveying, engineering, finance, brokerage, stevedoring, construction, repairs, sales, insurance, and terminal and vessel operations.

Publications:
Membership Roster; on-line
The Arbitrator; quarterly; adv.

Membership List Available to Non-members

Society of Medical Consultants to the Armed Forces (1946)
Five Southern Way
Fredericksburg, VA 22406
Tel: (540) 361-2587 Fax: (540) 361-2589
Website: smcaf.org
Members: 700 individuals
Staff: 3
Annual Budget: $10-25,000
Tax: 501(c)(19)

Personnel:
Assistant to the President: Margo Cabrero
E-Mail: margo@smcaf.org

Historical Note:
Formerly Society of U.S. Medical Consultants in W. W. II. Organized by specialists who were consultants to the Armed Forces during World War II. SMCAF's mission is to preserve and encourage the beneficial association of authorities in various fields of medical endeavor and assist in development and maintenance of standard medical practice in the armed forces. Membership: $100 (Active Member); $40 (Associate Member).

Meetings/Conferences: Annual

Publications:
SMCAF Newsletter

Society of Mexican American Engineers and Scientists (1974)
2437 Bay Area Blvd.
Suite 100
Houston, TX 77058
Tel: (281) 557-3677 Fax: (281) 715-5100
E-Mail: questions@maes-natl.org
Website: mymaes.org
Members: 6000 individuals
Staff: 9
Annual Budget: $500-1,000,000
Tax: 501(c)(3)

Personnel:
National President: Will Davis
E-Mail: wcdavis@maes-natl.org
Executive Director: Raul Munoz
E-Mail: raul@mymaes.org
Editor: Lynne Andrews
E-Mail: magazine@maes-natl.org
National Vice President, Administration: John Florez
E-Mail: john@mymaes.org
Assistant Vice President, Finance: Esther Moreno Gonzales
E-Mail: treasurer@maes-natl.org

National Vice President, Finance: Nancy Lowery
E-Mail: nancy@mymaes.org
National Vice President, Operations: Connie Medina
E-Mail: connie@mymaes.org
National Vice President, Programs and Events: Gil Saenz
E-Mail: gsaenzj@gmail.com
National Vice President, Membership Services and Chapters: Mark Venzor
E-Mail: mark@mymaes.org

Historical Note:
MAES's mission is to advocate, cultivate, and honor excellence in education and leadership among Latino engineers and scientists. Membership: $35 (Professional); $1,000 (Lifetime); $10 (Student); $0 (Associate).

Meetings/Conferences: Annual
Conference Chair: Will Davis
Number of non-conference events/year: 1

Publications:
Membership Directory; on-line
The Society of Mexican American Engineers and Scientists Magazine; quarterly

Society of Military Orthopaedic Surgeons (1958)
110 West Rd.
Suite 227
Towson, MD 21204
Tel: (866) 494-1778 Fax: (410) 494-0515
E-Mail: info@somos.org
Website: somos.org
Members: 785 individuals
Staff: 2
Annual Budget: $500-1,000,000
Tax: 501(c)(3)

Personnel:
President: Tad Gerlinger MD
Treasurer: Travis Burns

Historical Note:
SOMOS's mission is to provide a forum for the interchange of medical knowledge as it relates to the practice of orthopaedic surgery in the military. Members are orthopedic surgeons who are on active duty or who have served in the armed forces. Membership: $150 (Active/Allied); $125 (Associate); $75 (Affiliate); Free (Resident/Emeritus).

Meetings/Conferences: Annual

Publications:
Member Directory; on-line
SOMOS Newsletter

Society of Military Otolaryngologists - Head and Neck Surgeons (1952)
P.O. Box 923
Converse, TX 78109-0923
Tel: (210) 945-9006 Fax: (210) 945-2010
Website: miloto.org
Members: 309 individuals
Staff: 1
Annual Budget: Under $10,000

Personnel:
Administrator: Sue M. Pearce
E-Mail: spearce@att.net

Historical Note:
SMO works to bring into one organization the otolaryngologists of the Army, Air Force, and Navy, to further the social and professional contacts of military otolaryngologists and for the advancement of the science and art of otolaryngology in the military services. Members are residents in training and otolaryngologists on active duty or who have served in the armed forces. Membership: $30/year (Associate Fellow).

Publications:
Laryngology
Otology

Society of Military Widows (1968)
5535 Hempstead Way
Springfield, VA 22151-4094
Tel: (703) 750-1342 Fax: (703) 354-4380
TollFree: (800) 842-3451
E-Mail: naus@naus.org
Website: naus.org
Members: 160000 individuals
Staff: 10
Annual Budget: $2-5,000,000
Tax: 501(c)(19)

Personnel:
President: Jack W. Klimp
E-Mail: jklimp@naus.org

Treasurer and Director, Membership: Tamea A. Boone
E-Mail: taboone@naus.org
Chief Financial Officer and Director, Membership Services:
Windora Bradburn
E-Mail: wbradburn@naus.org
Marketing Director: Steve Hein
E-Mail: shein@naus.org
Legislative Director/PAC: Rick Jones
E-Mail: rjones@naus.org

Historical Note:
Promotes development and support of legislation to sustain the morale of the Armed Forces and provide fair and equitable consideration for all members of the uniformed services. NAUS affiliated with the Society of Military Widows in 1984. Sponsors the National Association for Uniformed Services Political Action Committee (NAUS-PAC). Membership: $25/year (Single), $19/year (widows); $45/year (couple).

Publications:
Military Times; weekly
Uniformed Services Journal; bi-monthly

Society of Mineral Analysts *(1987)*
P.O. Box 404
Lewiston, ID 83501
Tel: (208) 799-3286 *Fax:* (775) 786-3613
E-Mail: services@sma-online.org
Website: sma-online.org
Members: 250 individuals
Staff: 2
Annual Budget: $10-25,000

Personnel:
Managing Secretary and Contact, Membership and Events:
Patrick Braun
E-Mail: secretary@sma-online.org
Editor: Mark F. Lewis APR, CAE
E-Mail: mlewis@lmine.com

Historical Note:
SMA's purpose is to promote mutual cooperation in the mineral industry through the discussion and free exchange of information relating to the analysis of both chemical and physical, of minerals and mineral products. Membership: $30/year.

Meetings/Conferences: Annual
Conference Chair: Patrick Braun

Publications:
Membership Directory
SMA News; on-line
The Alchemist Digest; quarterly

Society of Mortgage, Appraisal, Real Estate and Title Professionals *(2005)*
1410 Grant St.
Suite C209
Denver, CO 80203
Tel: (303) 437-9160 *Fax:* (720) 875-0594
E-Mail: cstreiff@qwest.net
Website: smartprofessionals.org
Members: 100 companies
Staff: 1
Annual Budget: $25-50,000

Personnel:
Director: Chris Streiff
E-Mail: cstreiff@qwest.net

Historical Note:
SMART's mission is to promote integrity, professionalism and goodwill to the community. Membership: $500 (Mortgage Broker/Owners and Realtor Professional); $1,200 (Affiliate); $100 (Associate).

Publications:
Membership Directory; on-line

Society of Motion Picture and Television Engineers *(1916)*
Three Barker Ave.
Fifth Floor
White Plains, NY 10601
Tel: (914) 761-1100 *Fax:* (914) 761-3115
Website: smpte.org
Members: 200 Sustaining institutional members
Staff: 10
Annual Budget: $2-5,000,000

Personnel:
Executive Director: Barbara Lange
Director, Operations: Sally-Ann D'Amato
Manager, Member Relations: Roberta Gorman
Managing Editor: Dianne Purrier

Executive Assistant: June Marie Sobrito
E-Mail: jsobrito@smpte.org
Director, Professional Development: Joel E. Welch

Historical Note:
Founded in 1916 as the Society of Motion Picture Engineers, assumed its current name in 1950. SMPTE's purpose is to advocate networking interaction and communicating the latest developments in technology. Membership: $135-390 (Professional); $245 (Executive Professional); $35 (Student/Associate).

Meetings/Conferences: Annual
Number of non-conference events/year: 2

Publications:
Engineering Standards; irregular
Membership Directory; on-line
Newsletters; monthly
SMPTE Motion Imaging Journal; monthly

Society of Multivariate Experimental Psychology *(1960)*
Department of Psychology, University of Victoria,
P. O. Box 3050
Victoria, BC V8W3P5
Tel: (212) 998-7895 *Fax:* (212) 995-4866
E-Mail: pat.shrout@nyu.edu
Website: smep.org
Members: 65 individuals
Staff: 5
Annual Budget: $100-250,000

Personnel:
Coordinating Officer: Scott Michael Hofer
E-Mail: smhofer@uvic.ca
Editor: Joseph L. Rodgers
E-Mail: jrodgers@ou.edu

Historical Note:
SMEP members are researchers in behavioral psychology. Has no paid officers or full-time staff. Membership is limited to 65 members, and is by invitation only.

Meetings/Conferences: Annual

Publications:
Multivariate Behavioral Research; bi-monthly; adv.

Society of Municipal Arborists *(1964)*
P.O. Box 641
Watkinsville, GA 30677
Tel: (706) 769-7412 *Fax:* (706) 769-7307
E-Mail: urbanforestry@prodigy.net
Website: urban-forestry.com
Members: 1324 individuals
Staff: 1
Annual Budget: $250-500,000
Tax: 501(c)(6)

Personnel:
Executive Director: Jerri J. LaHaie CAE

Historical Note:
SMA is an organization of municipal arborists and urban foresters. Mission is to promote and improve the practice of professional municipal arboriculture. Membership: $75 (Professional); $140 (Corporate); $25-$140 (Municipal); $40 (Student/Senior/Affiliate).

Continuing Education:
Certification Designation/s: CAMS

Meetings/Conferences: Annual
Number of non-conference events/year: 1

Publications:
City Trees; bi-monthly; adv.

The Society of Naval Architects and Marine Engineers *(1893)*
601 Pavonia Ave.
Suite 400
Jersey City, NJ 07306-3881
Tel: (201) 798-4800 *Fax:* (201) 798-4975
TollFree: (800) 798-2188
Website: sname.org
Members: 9000 individuals
Staff: 16
Annual Budget: $2-5,000,000
Tax: 501(c)(3)

Personnel:
Executive Director: Erik Seither
E-Mail: eseither@sname.org
Director, Events: Alana Alissa Yoshiko Anderson
E-Mail: alana@sname.org
Senior Web and Communications Strategist: Mark Eichler
E-Mail: meichler@sname.org

Coordinator, Scholarships and Education and Administrative Assistant: Erlinda Faustino
E-Mail: efaustino@sname.org
Director, Publications: Susan Evans Grove
E-Mail: sevans@sname.org
Director, Membership Services: Mike Hall
E-Mail: mhall@sname.org
Coordinator, Technical and Research Programs: Alex Landsburg
E-Mail: alandsburg@sname.org
Executive Administrator: Barbara Trentham
E-Mail: btrentham@sname.org

Historical Note:
SNAME's mission is to advance the art, science and practice of naval architecture, marine engineering, ocean engineering and other marine- related professions. Membership: $55-175/year (Affiliate/Associate).

Meetings/Conferences: Annual
Conference Chair: Alana Alissa Yoshiko Anderson

Publications:
Journal of Ship Production and Design (JSPD); quarterly
Member Directory; on-line
SNAME e-Newsletter; bi-weekly; adv.

Membership List Available to Non-members

Society of Nematologists *(1961)*
c/o Rosewood Business Solutions
108 W. Burwell Ave.
Loudonville, OH 44842
Tel: (419) 994-3419 *Fax:* (419) 994-2419
E-Mail: societyofnematologists@gmail.com
Website: nematologists.org
Members: 600 individuals
Staff: 2
Annual Budget: $100-250,000

Personnel:
Business Manager: Lisa Miller
Editor-in-Chief: Nancy Kokalis-Burelle

Historical Note:
SON's mission is to advance the science of nematology in its fundamental and economic aspects. Member of the American Institute of Biological Sciences. Membership: $30 (Student); $60 (Individual Regular); $500 (Sustaining Associate); Free (Emeritus).

Meetings/Conferences: Annual

Publications:
Journal of Nematology; quarterly
Membership Directory; annually
Nematology Newsletter; quarterly

Society of Neurointerventional Surgery *(1992)*
3975 Fair Ridge Dr.
Suite 460 North
Fairfax, VA 22033
Tel: (703) 691-2272 *Fax:* (703) 537-0650
E-Mail: info@snisonline.org
Website: snisonline.org
Members: 600 members
Staff: 7
Annual Budget: $2-5,000,000
Tax: 501(c)(6)

Personnel:
Executive Director: Marie Williams CAE
Meeting Planner: Eden Capuano
Consultant, Information Technology: Michael Drobnis
Accountant: Amy Fox CPA
Specialist, Public Relations: Becca Hall
Coordinator, Administration: Anthony Portillo
Director, Member Services: Eddie Woods

Historical Note:
Formerly the American Society of Interventional and Therapeutic Neuroradiology. SNIS's mission is to foster the growth of the discipline of neurointervention and support its multi-disciplinary physician members to provide the highest quality of neurointerventional patient care through research, education, standard-setting, and advocacy. Membership: $350 (Active); $150 (Corresponding); $100 (Associate/Senior); $50 (Junior/Clinical Associate); $25 (Medical Student).

Meetings/Conferences:
2013 - Honolulu, HI (Sheraton Waikiki)/Feb. 4 - 5
2013 - Miami, FL (Loews Miami Beach Hotel)/July 29 - Aug. 1

Publications:
Journal of NeuroInterventional Surgery
Membership Directory; on-line

The Embolus

Society of Neurological Surgeons (1920)
660 S Euclid Ave. #8057
St Louis, MT 63110-1010
Tel: (314) 362-5039 *Fax:* (314) 362-2107
E-Mail: burchiek@ohsu.edu
Website: societyns.org
Members: 200 individuals
Staff: 3
Annual Budget: $250-500,000

Personnel:
President: Ralph G. Dacey
   E-Mail: daceyr@wustl.edu

Historical Note:
SNS is the honorary society of neurological surgery in the United States. Purpose is to enhance the role and stature of neurosurgical units in academic medical centers.

Meetings/Conferences: Annual
2013 - Boston, MA (Brandeis University)/June 7 - 11
2014 - Rochester, MN (Mayo Civic Center)/May 18 -
   20

Publications:
Membership Directory; on-line

Society of North American Goldsmiths (1969)
540 Oak St.
Suite A
Eugene, OR 97401
Tel: (541) 345-5689 *Fax:* (541) 345-1123
E-Mail: info@snagmetalsmith.org
Website: snagmetalsmith.org
Members: 3300 individuals
Staff: 4
Annual Budget: $500-1,000,000
Tax: 501(c)(3)

Personnel:
Executive Director: Dana Singer
   E-Mail: dsinger@snagmetalsmith.org
Manager, Programs: Ellen Laing
   E-Mail: elaing@snagmetalsmith.org
Editor: Suzanne Ramljak
   E-Mail: editor@snagmetalsmith.org
Advertising Director: Jean Savarese
   E-Mail: jsavarese@snagmetalsmith.org

Historical Note:
SNAG's mission is to support and advance the professional practice of artists, designers, jewelers and metalsmiths. Membership is open to anyone passionate about jewelry, design and metalsmithing. Membership: $49-95 (Gold); $25-49 (Silver).

Meetings/Conferences: Annual
Conference Chair: Ellen Laing
2013 - Toronto, ON/May 15 - 18
2014 - Minneapolis, MN (Hilton Minneapolis)/April 23
   - 26

Publications:
Digital Metalsmith; on-line
Membership Directory; annually
Metalsmith; annually; adv.
SNAG News Newsletter; on-line
SNAG's Weekly Announcements; weekly

Membership List Available to Non-members

Society of Nuclear Medicine (1954)
1850 Samuel Morse Dr.
Reston, VA 20190
Tel: (703) 708-9000 *Fax:* (703) 708-9015
Website: snm.org
Members: 16000 Individuals
Staff: 45
Annual Budget: $10-25,000,000
Tax: 501(c)(3)

Personnel:
Chief Executive Officer: Virginia M. Pappas CAE
   E-Mail: vpappas@snm.org
Director, Meetings: Judy Brazel CMP
   E-Mail: jbrazel@snm.org
Senior Manager, Membership Services: Christine
   Cachuela
   E-Mail: ccachuela@snmmi.org
Director, Health Policy and Regulatory Affairs: Hugh
   Cannon
   E-Mail: hcannon@snm.org
Director, Education: Pam Colman Colman
   E-Mail: pcolman@snmmi.org

Systems Manager: Leonard Getzin
   E-Mail: lgetzin@snm.org
Director, Communications: Rebecca Maxey
   E-Mail: rmaxey@snm.org
Director, Membership Services: Cecilia Noblett
   E-Mail: cnoblett@snm.org
Chief Financial Officer: Vincent Pistilli
   E-Mail: vpistilli@snm.org
Director, Marketing: Joanna Spahr CAE
   E-Mail: jspahr@snm.org
Coordinator, Publications: Mark Sumimoto
   E-Mail: msumimoto@snm.org

Historical Note:
SNM's mission is to promote the science, technology and practical application of nuclear medicine. Members are physicians, technologists and scientists specializing in the research and practice of nuclear medicine. $375 (Full Membership); $119-250 (Associate); $104 (Technologist/ Scientific Laboratory Professionals); $275 (Affiliate).

Meetings/Conferences: Annual
Conference Chair: Judy Brazel CMP
2013 - New Orleans, LA (Sheraton New Orleans
   Hotel)/Jan. 24 - 27
2013 - Vancouver, BC/June 8 - 12
2014 - Palm Spring, CA (Palm Springs Renaissance at
   the Convention Center)/Feb. 6 - 9
2014 - St. Louis, MO/June 7 - 11
2015 - Baltimore, MD/June 6 - 10
2016 - San Diego, CA/June 11 - 15
2017 - Denver, CO/June 10 - 14
2018 - Philadelphia, PA/June 23 - 27
Number of non-conference events/year: 6

Publications:
CTN Newsletter
Journal of Nuclear Medicine; adv.
Journal of Nuclear Medicine Technology; quarterly;
   adv.
Leadership Update
Membership Directory; on-line
Molecular Imaging; bi-monthly
SNM SmartBrief; daily
Uptake

Membership List Available to Non-members

Society of Otorhinolaryngology and Head-Neck Nurses (1976)
207 Downing St.
New Smyrna Beach, FL 32168
Tel: (386) 428-1695 *Fax:* (386) 423-7566
E-Mail: info@sohnnurse.com
Website: sohnnurse.com
Members: 1200 individuals
Staff: 3
Annual Budget: $250-500,000
Tax: 501(c)(3)

Personnel:
Executive Director: Sandra Schwartz MS, RN
   E-Mail: sohnnet@aol.com
Treasurer: Sharon Jamison RN

Historical Note:
SOHN strives to foster the professional growth of the ORL nurse through education and research. It also strives to develop an organization that is responsive to the needs of the membership. Members are nurses for the care of patients with ear, nose and throat disorders and head and neck cancer. Membership: $100 (Voting Full Member/Non-Voting Associate Member); $50 (Retired Full Member/ Retired Associate Member).

Continuing Education:
Certification Designation/s: NCBOHN

Publications:
ORL-Head and Neck Nursing; quarterly; adv.
Update Newsletter; adv.

Membership List Available to Non-members

Society of Outdoor Recreation Professionals (1983)
P.O. Box 221
Marienville, PA 16239
Tel: (814) 927-8212 *Fax:* (814) 927-6659
E-Mail: info@narrp.org
Website: narrp.org
Members: 230 individuals
Staff: 5
Annual Budget: $100-250,000
Tax: 501(c)(3)

Personnel:

Association Manager: Brenda Adams-Weyant
   E-Mail: brenda@narrp.org

Historical Note:
Formerly known as the National Association of Recreation Resource Planners and previous to that known as National Association of State Recreation Planners (1994). SORP's mission is to provide the public opportunities for the enjoyment and benefits of quality outdoor recreation, in balance with natural, cultural, historic, and scenic resource protection. Membership: $80 (Regular); $80 (Institutional, for the first member); $70 (Institutional, for each additional member); $35 (Student/Retiree).

Meetings/Conferences: Annual
2013 - Traverse City, MI (Park Place Hotel)/May 19 -
   23

Publications:
Membership Directory; on-line
NARRP Newsletter; on-line; adv.
News from NARRP; weekly

Society of Pediatric Nurses (1990)
7044 S. 13th St.
Oak Creek, WI 53154
Tel: (414) 908-4950
E-Mail: spn@puetzamc.com
Website: pedsnurses.org
Members: 3000 individuals
Staff: 3
Annual Budget: $500-1,000,000
Tax: 501(c)(3)

Personnel:
Association Manager: Nancy Short
   E-Mail: n.short@pedsnurses.org

Historical Note:
SPN's mission is to promote nursing care of children and their families through support of its members clinical practice, education, research and advocacy. Membership: $125-345 (Regular); $70 (Retired); $80 (Associate/ Student); $1000 (Corporate).

Continuing Education:
Certification Designation/s: CE

Meetings/Conferences: Annual
2013 - Nashville, TN (Gaylord Opryland Resort and
   Convention Center)/April 11 - 14

Publications:
The Journal of Pediatric Nursing

Society of Pediatric Psychology
P.O. Box 3968
Lawrence, KS 66046
Tel: (785) 856-0713 *Fax:* (785) 856-0759
Website: societyofpediatricpsychology.org
Staff: 3

Personnel:
President: Tonya Palermo PhD
Treasurer: T. David Elkin PhD
Editor: Grayson Holmbeck

Historical Note:
The society aims to promote the health and psychological well-being of children, youth and their families through science and an evidence-based approach to practice, education, training, advocacy and consultation. Membership: $50 (Psychologists/Allied professionals); $20 (Undergraduate students/ Graduate students/Students in post-doctoral training).

Meetings/Conferences: Annual
2013 - New Orleans, LA/April 11 - 13

Publications:
Clinical Practice in Pediatric Psychology
Journal of Pediatric Psychology; adv.
Member Directory; on-line
SPP newsletter

Society of Pelvic Reconstructive Surgeons (1987)
75 Claremont St.
Kalispell, MT 59901
Tel: (406) 863-9133 *Fax:* (713) 799-9028
E-Mail: info@sprs.org
Website: sprs.org
Staff: 1
Annual Budget: $100-250,000

Personnel:
Executive Director: Sarah Daniels MD
   E-Mail: pelvicsurgeonsinc@gmail.com

Historical Note:

SPRS seeks to promote the standards of care in pelvic reconstructive and vaginal surgery. Membership: $200(Individual).

Publications:
email newsletter; monthly; adv.

Society of Pelvic Surgeons (1952)
9500 Euclid Ave., Q10
Cleveland, FL 44195
Tel: (216) 444-6320 *Fax:* (216) 636-4492
E-Mail: info@societyofpelvicsurgeons.org
Website: societyofpelvicsurgeons.org
Members: 125 individuals
Staff: 2
Annual Budget: $50-100,000
Tax: 501(c)(3)

Personnel:
President: Neville Hacker

Historical Note:
SPS' mission is to achieve excellence in the surgical management of diseases and disorders of the pelvic organs and also to explore the frontiers affecting the surgical treatment of patients through translational research and the development of new surgical techniques.

Meetings/Conferences: Annual
2013 - Duesseldorf and Leiden, Germany/July 7 - 13

Publications:
SPS Newsletter; monthly

Society of Petroleum Engineers (1913)
222 Palisades Creek Dr.
Richardson, TX 75080-2040
Tel: (972) 952-9393 *Fax:* (972) 952-9435
TollFree: (800) 456-6863
E-Mail: service@spe.org
Website: spe.org
Members: 97000 individuals
Staff: 222
Annual Budget: $25-50,000,000

Personnel:
Executive Director: Mark A. Rubin
   E-Mail: mrubin@spe.org
Vice President, Finance: Kenneth E. Arnold
Director, Communications: Georgeann Bilich
Director, Member Programs and Services: Jane Boyce
Director, Business Services and Chief Financial Officer: Steve Byrne
Director, Information Technology: Robert Wyatt
   E-Mail: rwyatt@spe.org

Historical Note:
SPE's mission is to collect, disseminate, and exchange technical knowledge concerning the exploration, development and production of oil and gas resources, and related technologies for the public benefit; and to provide opportunities for professionals to enhance their technical and professional competence. Membership: $10-$90 (Professional); $10-14 (Student).

Continuing Education:
Certification Designation/s: SPE

Meetings/Conferences: Annual
2013 - New Orleans, LA (Ernest N. Morial Convention Center)/Sept. 30 - Oct. 2
2014 - Amsterdam, Netherlands (Amsterdam RAI Exhibition and Convention Centre)/Oct. 27 - 29
2015 - Houston, TX (George R. Brown Convention Center)/Oct. 12 - 14
Number of non-conference events/year: 68

Publications:
Journal of Petroleum Technology; monthly; adv.
Membership Directory; on-line

Society of Petroleum Evaluation Engineers (1962)
5535 Memorial Dr.
Suite F654
Houston, TX 77007
Tel: (713) 651-1639 *Fax:* (713) 951-9659
E-Mail: info@spee.org
Website: spee.org
Members: 495 individuals
Staff: 2
Annual Budget: $250-500,000
Tax: 501(c)(6)

Personnel:
Executive Secretary: B.K. Buongiorno
   E-Mail: bkspee@aol.com
Editor: Diane Pollard

E-Mail: dpollard@austin.rr.com

Historical Note:
SPEE attempts to provide educational and other services to its members and to the oil and gas industry. Members are engineers specializing in the evaluation of petroleum and natural gas properties.

Meetings/Conferences: Annual
2013 - Sun Valley, ID (Sun Valley Resort)/June 8 - 11

Publications:
Journal of SPEE
Membership Directory
SPEE Newsletter; quarterly; adv.

Society of Petrophysicists and Well Log Analysts (1959)
8866 Gulf Fwy.
Suite 320
Houston, TX 77017-6531
Tel: (713) 947-8727 *Fax:* (713) 947-7181
E-Mail: spwla@spwla.org
Website: spwla.org
Members: 3300 individuals
Staff: 4
Annual Budget: $1-2,000,000

Personnel:
Executive Director: Sharon Johnson
   E-Mail: sharon@spwla.org
Contact, Membership Services and Administration: Lydia Wacasey
   E-Mail: membership@spwla.org
Manager, Publications: Jorja Zywczuk
   E-Mail: jorja@spwla.org

Historical Note:
Formerly (2003) Society of Professional Well Log Analysts. SPWLA's mission is to advance the science of petrophysics and formation evaluation, through well logging and other formation evaluation techniques and to the application of these techniques to the exploitation of gas, oil and other minerals. Members are actively engaged in formation evaluation through analysis of well logs and/or related data. Membership: $75/year.

Meetings/Conferences:
2013 - New Orleans, LA (Hyatt Regency Hotel)/June 22 - 26
Number of non-conference events/year: 1

Publications:
Membership Directory; on-line
Transactions; annually

Society of Pharmaceutical and Biotech Trainers (1971)
4423 Pheasant Ridge Rd.
Suite 100
Roanoke, VA 24014-5274
Tel: (540) 725-3859 *Fax:* (540) 989-7482
E-Mail: info@spbt.org
Website: spbt.org
Members: 1000 trainers
Staff: 8
Annual Budget: $2-5,000,000
Tax: 501(c)(3)

Personnel:
Executive Director: Kevin Kruse
   E-Mail: kkruse@spbt.org
Director, Communications: Kristen Brill
   E-Mail: kbrill@spbt.org
Manager, Business Services: Miki Saint Clair
   E-Mail: mstclair@spbt.org
Director, Events: Christine Gaudet
   E-Mail: cgaudet@spbt.org
Director, Advertising and Publisher: Gregg Haunroth
   E-Mail: ghaunroth@spbt.org
Director, Membership Services: Scott Sauve RPh
   E-Mail: ssauve@spbt.org

Historical Note:
Formerly (2000) National Society of Pharmaceutical Sales Trainers. SPBT's mission is to advance professional training in the pharmaceutical, biotech, medical device industries and medical diagnostic companies. Members are training personnel employed by pharmaceutical and biotechnology companies. Membership: $175 (Full); $49 (Associate).

Meetings/Conferences: Annual
Conference Chair: Christine Gaudet
2013 - Orlando, FL (Peabody Orlando)/June 10 - 13/ over 100 exhibitors

Publications:
Focus Magazine; quarterly; adv.

Membership Directory; on-line

Society of Philosophers in America (1985)
The University of Mississippi, Department of Public Policy Leadership
105 Odom Hall
University, MS 38677
Tel: (662) 915-1336 *Fax:* (662) 915-1954
Website: philosophersinamerica.com
Members: 120 individuals
Staff: 1
Annual Budget: Under $10,000

Personnel:
Executive Director and Treasurer: Dr. Eric Thomas Weber
   E-Mail: etweber@olemiss.edu

Historical Note:
Dedicated to revitalizing the professional life of professors and teachers of philosophy in the U.S. Has no paid officers or full-time staff. Aim is to promote education in the philosophical ideas, practices and traditions of America and of other world cultures. Membership: $25 (Regular); $10 (Student); $200 (Sustaining).

Society of Photo-Technologists (1958)
11112 S. Spotted Rd.
Cheney, WA 99004-9038
Tel: (509) 624-9621 *Fax:* (509) 634-5320
E-Mail: cc5@earthlink.net
Website: spt.info
Staff: 1
Annual Budget: $50-100,000
Tax: 501(c)(6)

Personnel:
Executive Director: Chuck Bertone

Historical Note:
SPT is an international association of camera technicians and businesses and has served the camera repair industry for over 50 years. Membership: $195 (Class A); $225 (Class B); $245 (Class C); $355 (Sustaining); $125 (Associate/Technician/Student).

Society of Piping Engineers and Designers (1980)
9211 West Rd.
Suite 143-219
Houston, TX 77064
Tel: (832) 286-3404 *Fax:* (713) 221-2712
E-Mail: spedexec@spedweb.com
Website: spedweb.com
Members: 800 individuals and companies
Staff: 2
Annual Budget: $250-500,000
Tax: 501(c)(6)

Personnel:
Executive Director: William G. Beazley
   E-Mail: spedexec@spedweb.com
Contact, Membership Services, Training, Certification and Sales: Sarah Evans
   E-Mail: spedsrvs@spedweb.com

Historical Note:
SPED strives to promote excellence and quality in the practice of piping engineering and design. Members are piping professionals and technical experts interested in staying abreast of the technological advances in the field of piping and plant design. Membership: $0-1,000/year.

Continuing Education:
Certification Designation/s: PPD

Meetings/Conferences: Annual

Publications:
Membership Directory; on-line
SPED Update; monthly; adv.

Society of Plastics Engineers (1942)
13 Church Hill Rd.
Newtown, CT 06470
Tel: (203) 775-0471 *Fax:* (203) 775-8490
E-Mail: info@4spe.org
Website: 4spe.org
Members: 20,000 plastics professionals
Staff: 21
Annual Budget: $2-5,000,000

Personnel:
Chief Executive Officer: Willem De Vos
   E-Mail: wdevos@4spe.org
Senior Manager, Events: Lesley Kyle
   E-Mail: lskyle@4spe.org

Historical Note:

Founded December 2, 1941 in Detroit as the Society of Plastics Sales Engineers and incorporated in Michigan in 1942. SPE's mission is to promote the scientific and engineering knowledge relating to plastics. Membership: $144 (Individual); $31 (Student).

Meetings/Conferences:
Conference Chair: Lesley Kyle
2013 - Houston, TX (Hilton Houston North)/Feb. 24 - 27/51-100 exhibitors

Publications:
Plastics Engineering
Plastics Engineering Directory; on-line
Polymer Composites; bi-monthly
Polymer Engineering & Science; quarterly

Society of Professional Asset-Managers and Record Keepers
Nine Phelps Ln.
Simsbury, CT 06070
E-Mail: info@sparkinstitute.org
Website: sparkusa.org
Members: 250 companies
Staff: 6

Personnel:
Executive Director: Robert G. Wuelfing
 E-Mail: bob@rgwstaff.com
Director, Advertising and Public Relations: Jeffrey S. Close
 E-Mail: jeff@sparkinstitute.org
General Counsel: Larry H. Goldbrum
 E-Mail: larry@sparkinstitute.org
Chief Financial Officer: Marlene D. Jung CPA, MST
 E-Mail: marlene@sparkinstitute.org
Events Coordinator: Betty Kolding
 E-Mail: betty@sparkinstitute.org

Historical Note:
The Society of Professional Asset-Managers and Record Keepers (SPARK) is an inter-industry professional association servicing mutual fund companies, banks, insurance companies, investment advisors, third party administration, record keepers and benefit consulting firms in the retirement plan industry. Membership: $895 (Full/Vendor); $100 (Adjunct).

Meetings/Conferences: Annual
Conference Chair: Betty Kolding
2013 - Washington, DC (The Mandarin Oriental)/June 16 - 18

Publications:
The SPARK Journal; quarterly

Society of Professional Audio Recording Services
(1979)
P.O. Box 606
Palacios, TX 77465
Fax: (214) 722-1442
TollFree: (800) 771-7727
E-Mail: info@spars.com
Website: spars.com
Members: 250 companies/individuals
Staff: 2
Annual Budget: $10-25,000
Tax: 501(c)(6)

Personnel:
Executive Director: Paul A. Christensen
 E-Mail: paul@spars.com
Treasurer: Jessica Dally
 E-Mail: Jessica.am.dally@gmail.com

Historical Note:
SPARS's mission is to provide excellence through innovation, education and communication. Membership consists of commercial recording facilities, manufacturers, suppliers, educators, and individual professionals. Membership: $150 (Active Member); $99 (Individual); $25 (Student); $350(Manufacturer/Support Service Provider); $250 (Educational), $1,000 (Platinum Sponsorship).

Publications:
Membership Directory
Sound Bytes; on-line

Society of Professional Benefit Administrators
(1975)
Two Wisconsin Cir.
Suite 670
Chevy Chase, MD 20815-7003
Tel: (301) 718-7722 *Fax:* (301) 718-9440
E-Mail: info@spbatpa.org
Website: spbatpa.org
Members: 400 TPA firms
Staff: 6

Annual Budget: $1-2,000,000
Tax: 501(c)(6)

Personnel:
President: Anne C. Lennan
 E-Mail: anne@spbatpa.com
Director, Government Relations and Legal Affairs: Elizabeth Ysla Leight
 E-Mail: elizabeth@spbatpa.com

Historical Note:
SPBA works for government policy- shapers. It also serves to share insights from and for SPBA members and entities with whom they deal. Members are third- party contract administration firms (TPAs), which administer employee benefit plans for client employers and unions. Membership: $1,050- 7,000 (TPA Firm, based on category); $4,500 (Stop-Loss Service Partners).

Publications:
List of State TPA Statutes; annually
Membership Directory; annually
SPBA UPDATE

Membership List Available to Non-members

Society of Professional Investigators *(1956)*
P.O. Box 1087
Bellmore, NY 11710
Tel: (646) 584-9081 *Fax:* (212) 349-0338
E-Mail: info@spionline.org
Website: spionline.info
Members: 375 individuals
Staff: 4
Annual Budget: $10-25,000

Personnel:
President: Bruce Sackman
 E-Mail: BruceS@spionline.info
Contact, Membership Services: Donna N. Karp
 E-Mail: DonnaK@spionline.info
Treasurer: David Roberts
 E-Mail: DavidR@spionline.info
General Counsel: Marvin E. Schecter
 E-Mail: MarvinS@spionline.info

Historical Note:
SPI is dedicated to ethical principals in the field of private investigation. The mission of SPI is to provide the very best forum possible for the education, training and networking of members. Membership consists of individuals with at least five years of experience in investigation, along with attorneys, accountants, CFE's and law enforcement officers. Membership: $65/year (Individual).

Continuing Education:
Certification Designation/s: BCIP
Meetings/Conferences:
Number of non-conference events/year: 9

Publications:
SPI Online; adv.

Society of Professional Journalists *(1909)*
Eugene S. Pulliam Nat'l Journalism Center, 3909 N. Meridian St.
Indianapolis, IN 46208-4045
Tel: (317) 927-8000 *Fax:* (317) 920-4789
E-Mail: spj@spj.org
Website: spj.org
Members: 9000 individuals
Staff: 16
Annual Budget: $1-2,000,000
Tax: 501(c)(6)

Personnel:
Executive Director: Joe Skeel
 E-Mail: jskeel@spj.org
Communications Coordinator: Christine DiGangi
 E-Mail: cdigangi@spj.org
Director, Events: Heather Dunn
 E-Mail: hdunn@spj.org
Director, Membership Services: Linda A. Hall
 E-Mail: lhall@spj.org
Director, Education: Scott Leadingham
 E-Mail: sleadingham@spj.org
Web Administrator: Billy O'Keefe
 E-Mail: billyok@mac.com
Associate Executive Director: Chris Vachon
 E-Mail: cvachon@spj.org

Historical Note:
Founded at DePauw University in Greencastle, Indiana in 1909 as Sigma Delta Chi; became the Society of Professional Journalists, Sigma Delta Chi in 1972; assumed its present name in 1988. SPJ is dedicated to the perpetuation of a free press as the cornerstone of the

nation and liberty. Membership is comprised of men and women in every field of journalism. Maintains over 300 local professional and campus chapters. Membership: $37.50-1,000/year.

Meetings/Conferences: Annual
Conference Chair: Heather Dunn

Publications:
Membership Directory; on-line
Quill Online; bi-monthly; adv.
SPJ Leads; weekly; adv.

Society of Professional Rope Access Technicians
P.O. Box 1678
Tempe, AZ 85280-1678
E-Mail: info@sprat.org
Website: sprat.org
Members: 90 individuals
Staff: 2
Annual Budget: $100-250,000
Tax: 501(c)(6)

Personnel:
Treasurer: Matt Hudson
 E-Mail: matt@sprat.org

Historical Note:
SPRAT is dedicated to promote the safe development of industrial rope access standards in the US, Canada, Mexico and beyond. Membership in the organization is open to any company or individual that uses rope access. Membership: $350-950 (Organization); $100 (Individual).

Continuing Education:
Certification Designation/s: SPRAT

Meetings/Conferences: Annual
2013 - Anaheim, CA (Disney's Paradise Pier Hotel)/ Feb. 6 - 9

Publications:
Newsletter; quarterly

Membership List Available to Non-members

Society of Professors of Child and Adolescent Psychiatry *(1969)*
3615 Wisconsin Ave. NW
Washington, DC 20016
Tel: (202) 966-7300 *Fax:* (202) 966-2037
E-Mail: societyofprofessors@gmail.com
Website: spcap.org
Members: 175 individuals
Staff: 2
Annual Budget: $10-25,000
Tax: 501(c)(3)

Personnel:
Executive Director: Earl Magee
 E-Mail: societyofprofessors@gmail.com
Membership Chair: A. Jack Naftel MD

Historical Note:
Formerly (1987) Society of Professors of Child Psychiatry. SPCAP is a division of American Academy of Child and Adolescent Psychiatry, which provides administrative support. Purpose is to provide a forum for discussion and exchange of ideas among the child and adolescent psychiatry program directors in medical schools in the United States and elsewhere. Membership: $175/year (Individual).

Meetings/Conferences: Annual
Conference Chair: Earl Magee
2013 - Washington, DC (Hyatt Regency Washington on Capitol Hill/May 9 - 11
Number of non-conference events/year: 1

Publications:
Membership Directory; annually

Society of Professors of Education *(1902)*
Department of ELPS, UWG, College of Education
1600 Maple St.
Carrollton, GA 30118-5160
Tel: (678) 839-6132
Website: unm.edu/~spe
Members: 400 individuals
Staff: 3
Annual Budget: Under $10,000

Personnel:
President: William G. Wraga
Secretary and Treasurer: Robert C. Morris
 E-Mail: rmorris@westga.edu
Editor, Professing Education: John M. Novak
 E-Mail: profed@ed.brocku.ca

Historical Note:

Formerly (1969) National Society of College Teachers of Education. SPE's mission is to provide a forum for consideration of major issues, tasks, problems and challenges confronting professional educators. Members include both theoreticians and practitioners in education. Membership: $50 (Patron/Library); $40 (Regular); $15 (Student); $25 (Retired).

Publications:
Professing Education; semi-annually
The DeGarmo Lecture; annually
The Sophist's Bane

Society of Publication Designers (1965)
27 Union Sq., West
Suite 207
New York, NY 10003
Tel: (212) 223-3332 Fax: (212) 223-5880
E-Mail: mail@spd.org
Website: spd.org
Members: 1300 individuals
Staff: 2
Annual Budget: $500-1,000,000

Personnel:
Interim Executive Director: Keisha Dean
Treasurer: Gail Bichler

Historical Note:
SPD's mission is to promote and encourage excellence in editorial design. Members are art directors, designers, photo editors, editors and graphics professionals. Membership: $195 (Professional); $25 (Student).

Publications:
SPD Newsletter; weekly; adv.

Society of Quality Assurance (1984)
154 Hansen Rd.
Suite 201
Charlottesville, VA 22911
Tel: (434) 297-4772 Fax: (434) 977-1856
E-Mail: sqa@sqa.org
Website: sqa.org
Members: 2500 individuals
Staff: 3
Annual Budget: $1-2,000,000

Personnel:
President: Nancy J. Gongliewski
Treasurer: Tammy White Barkalow
    E-Mail: treasurer@sqa.org
Contact, Advertising: Erin Irtenkauf
    E-Mail: erin.irtenkauf@sqa.org

Historical Note:
Formerly Quality Assurance Roundtable, became SQA in 1984. SQA's mission is to promote and advance the principles and knowledge of quality assurance essential to human, animal and environmental health. Members are professionals in the toxicological, pharmaceutical, biological, and chemical sciences responsible for quality assurance and standards maintenance in the laboratory and workplace. Membership: $150 (Active/Affiliate).

Meetings/Conferences: Annual
2013 - Indianapolis, IN (JW Marriott Indianapolis)/ April 28 - May 3
2014 - Las Vegas, NV (The Cosmopolitan of Las Vegas)/April 6 - 11
Number of non-conference events/year: 1

Publications:
Annual Meeting Program; annually; adv.
Membership Directory; on-line
Quality Matters; quarterly; adv.

Society of Quantitative Analysts (1989)
P.O. Box 6
Rutledge, MO 63563
Tel: (585) 545-6925
TollFree: (800) 918-7930
E-Mail: sqa@sqa-us.org
Website: sqa-us.org
Members: 350 individuals
Staff: 3
Annual Budget: $50-100,000

Personnel:
President: Irina Bogacheva
    E-Mail: irina.bogacheva@qsinvestors.com
Treasurer: Peg DiOrio
    E-Mail: peg.diorio@gmail.com
Associate Editor: Getmansky Sherman

Historical Note:
Formerly (1972) the Computer Applications Symposium of the New York Society of Security Analysts and (1980) the

Investment Technology Association. Absorbed the Society of Quantitative Analysts upon incorporation in 1989. SQA's mission is to encourage the dissemination and discussion of leading-edge ideas and innovations related to the work of the quantitatively-oriented investment professional, including analytical techniques and technologies for investment research and management. Membership: $200 (Regular); $100 (Academic); $50 (Transitional); $25 (Student).

Meetings/Conferences:
Number of non-conference events/year: 6

Publications:
Journal of Alternative Investments; annually; adv.
Journal of Derivatives; annually; adv.
Journal of Fixed Income; annually; adv.
Journal of Investing; annually; adv.
Journal of Investment Management; on-line
Journal of Private Equity; annually; adv.
Journal of Trading; annually; adv.
Member Directory; on-line
The Journal of Structured Finance; annually; adv.
The Journal of Wealth Management; on-line; adv.

Society of Radiologists in Ultrasound (1976)
1891 Preston White Dr.
Reston, VA 20191
Tel: (703) 858-9210 Fax: (703) 880-0295
E-Mail: info@sru.org
Website: sru.org
Members: 1100 individuals
Staff: 3
Annual Budget: $500-1,000,000
Tax: 501(c)(6)

Personnel:
Executive Director and Managing Editor: Susan Roberts
Treasurer: John J. Cronan
    E-Mail: jcronan@lifespan.org
Contact, Meetings and Events: Pamela Plater
    E-Mail: pplater@acr.org

Historical Note:
SRU advocates the use of diagnostic ultrasound in the field of academic radiology. Membership is open to all board-certified or board-eligible radiologists with an interest in ultrasound. Membership: $300 (General); $150 (Transitional Member).

Continuing Education:
Certification Designation/s: CME

Meetings/Conferences: Annual
Conference Chair: Pamela Plater
2013 - Chicago, IL (The Westin Michigan Avenue Hotel)/Oct. 18 - 20
2014 - Denver, CO (The Denver Marriott City Center)/ Oct. 24 - 26
2015 - Chicago, IL (The Westin Michigan Avenue Hotel)/Oct. 23 - 25

Publications:
Radiology and Ultrasound Quarterly; quarterly
SRU Newsletter; quarterly
Ultrasound Quarterly Journal; quarterly; adv.

Membership List Available to Non-members

Society of Reliability Engineers (1966)
250 Durham Hall
C/O Virginia Tech
Blacksburg, VA 24061-0118
Website: sre.org
Members: 1000 individuals
Staff: 1
Annual Budget: $10-25,000

Personnel:
Contact, Scholarship: Dr. J. A. Nachlas

Historical Note:
SRE's mission is to contribute and attain distinction in reliability- related disciplines. Membership: $10-50/year.

Publications:
Lambda Notes

Society of Reproductive Surgeons (1984)
1209 Montgomery Hwy.
Birmingham, AL 35216-2809
Tel: (205) 978-5000 Fax: (205) 978-5005
E-Mail: asrm@asrm.org
Website: reprodsurgery.org
Members: 500 individuals
Staff: 5
Annual Budget: $25-50,000

Personnel:

President: Mark Sigman MD
Editor: Bala Bhagavath MD
Secretary and Treasurer: Jeffrey Goldberg MD

Historical Note:
SRS strives to promote excellence in gynecologic and urologic reproductive surgery by providing and encouraging professional education, lay education, and by fostering research. Members are doctors specializing in reproductive surgery. Membership: $75/year

Meetings/Conferences: Annual

Publications:
Fertility and Sterility (F&S) medical journal; adv.
Journal of Assisted Reproduction and Genetics (JARG) journal
Sexuality, Reproduction, and Menopause (SRM)
SRS Newsletter

Society of Research Administrators International (1967)
500 N. Washington St.
Suite 300
Falls Church, VA 22046
Tel: (703) 741-0140 Fax: (703) 741-0142
E-Mail: info@srainternational.org
Website: srainternational.org
Members: 4000 individuals
Staff: 12
Annual Budget: $2-5,000,000

Personnel:
Chief Executive Officer: Elliott Kulakowski
    E-Mail: exedir@srainternational.org
Director, Administration and Human Resources: Valerie Ducker
    E-Mail: vducker@srainternational.org
Director, Meetings and Education: Ellen Lupinski
    E-Mail: elupinski@srainternational.org
Accountant: Yvette Rector
    E-Mail: yrector@srainternational.org
Director, New Program Development and Strategic Partnerships: Rebecca Vandall
    E-Mail: rvandall@srainternational.org
Director, Membership Services and Benefits: Brian J. Walrath
    E-Mail: membership@srainternational.org

Historical Note:
SRA is committed to the education and professional development of research administrators working in varied organizational settings as well as the advancement of research administration as a profession around the world. Membership: $205 (Individual/Institutional); $40 (Affiliate); $70 (Student/Retired).

Meetings/Conferences: Annual
Conference Chair: Ellen Lupinski
2013 - New Orleans, LA (Sheraton Hotel New Orleans)/Oct. 26 - 30

Publications:
Membership Directory; on-line
SRA Catalyst; on-line; adv.
SRA eConnections; monthly; adv.
The Journal of Research Administration; adv.

Society of Rheology (1929)
C/O American Institute of Physics, Two Huntington Quadrangle
Suite 1N01
Melville, NY 11747-4502
Tel: (516) 576-2397 Fax: (516) 576-2223
E-Mail: rheology@aip.org
Website: rheology.org/sor
Members: 1700 individuals
Staff: 5
Annual Budget: $500-1,000,000

Personnel:
President: A. Jeffrey Giacomin
    E-Mail: giacomin@wisc.edu
Secretary, Webmaster: Albert Co
    E-Mail: albertco@maine.edu
Editor: Ralph H. Colby
    E-Mail: colby@matse.psu.edu
Contact, Membership Services: Doreen Hall
Treasurer: Montgomery T. Shaw
    E-Mail: montgomery.shaw@uconn.edu

Historical Note:
SoR comprises of chemists, physicists, biologists, chemical engineers, and others concerned with the theory and precise measurement of the flow of matter, and the response of

materials to mechanical force. Membership: $40 (Regular); $25 (Student/Retired).

Meetings/Conferences: Annual
2013 - Pasadena, CA (CBD)/Feb. 10 - 14
2013 - Montreal, QC (CBD)/Oct. 13 - 17
2014 - Philadelphia, PA (CBD)/Oct. 5 - 9
2015 - Baltimore, MD (CBD)/Oct. 11 - 15

Publications:
Journal of Rheology; bi-monthly; adv.
Membership Directory; on-line
Rheology Bulletin; semi-annually; adv.

Membership List Available to Non-members

Society of Risk Management Consultants (1984)
330 S. Executive Dr.
Suite 301
Brookfield, WI 53005-4275
Tel: (262) 754-1160 *Fax:* (262) 754-1161
TollFree: (800) 765-7762
Website: srmcsociety.org
Members: 100 individuals
Staff: 1
Annual Budget: $25-50,000

Personnel:
Contact, Communications: Jill Sherman ARM, CPCU
   E-Mail: sherman@tebrennan.com

Historical Note:
SRMC's mission is to advance professions to benefit the consultants, their clients and the public through research, education, exchange of information through conferences, networking. SRMC is an organization of professionals engaged in risk management, insurance and employee benefits consulting. Membership: $300/year.

Meetings/Conferences: Semi-Annual

Publications:
Consultants Roster; on-line

Society of Satellite Professionals International (1983)
New York Information and Technology Center
250 Park Ave., Seventh Floor
New York, NY 10177
Tel: (212) 809-5199 *Fax:* (212) 825-0075
Website: sspi.org
Members: 1700 individuals
Staff: 5
Annual Budget: $500-1,000,000

Personnel:
Executive Director: Robert Bell
   E-Mail: rbell@sspi.org
Director, Membership Services: Tamara Bond
   E-Mail: tbond@sspi.org
Manager, Communications and Editor: Orly Konig Lopez
   E-Mail: orly@sspi.org
Editor: Linda Thornburg
   E-Mail: lthornburg@sspi.org
Director, Development: Louis Zacharilla
   E-Mail: lzacharilla@sspi.org

Historical Note:
Formerly (1988) Society of Satellite Professionals, SSPI's mission is to attract, retain and support the incredible talents that make this industry such an integral part of daily life. Members are individuals in the fields of business, education, entertainment, media, science and industry who share common interests in satellite technology. Membership: $100 (Professional); Free (Students).

Continuing Education:
Certification Designation/s: SPCE

Meetings/Conferences:
Conference Chair: Louis Zacharilla

Publications:
Journal of Space Communication; quarterly; adv.
The Orbiter; monthly; adv.

Society of School Librarians International (1985)
19 Savage St.
Charleston, SC 29401
Tel: (843) 577-5351
E-Mail: sbssteve@aol.com
Website: societyofschoollibrarians.webs.com
Members: 1200 individuals
Staff: 2
Annual Budget: $100-250,000
Tax: 501(c)(3)

Personnel:
Executive Director: Jeanne Schwartz

Historical Note:
SSLI's mission is to speak singularly and forcefully for the unique needs of school librarians in the educational community. Members are librarians involved with selection and utilization of technology and children's books in education. Membership: $75 (Corporate/Vendor); $25 (Professional/Retired/Student); $400 (Life).

Society of Scribes (1974)
P.O. Box 933
New York, NY 10150
Tel: (212) 452-0139
E-Mail: info@societyofscribes.org
Website:
societyofscribes.org
societyofscribes.org
Members: 500 individuals
Staff: 6
Annual Budget: $25-50,000
Tax: 501(c)(3)

Personnel:
President: Chi Nguyen
Vice President and Contact, Programs and Special Events: Cynthia Dantzic
Contact, Website: Rebecca Farber
Contact, Newsletter: Anna Pinto
President and Contact, Advertising and Publicity: Susan Steele

Historical Note:
SOS strives to promote the study, teaching and practice of calligraphy and related disciplines. It also seeks to foster the appreciation, understanding and acceptance of calligraphy as a fine art. Membership: $40 (Basic); $75 (Supporting); $100 (Patron); $45 (Canada/Mexico/Overseas).

Meetings/Conferences: Annual
Conference Chair: Cynthia Dantzic

Publications:
Letters from New York; on-line; adv.
SOS Newsletter; on-line; adv.

Society of State Leaders of Health and Physical Education (1926)
P.O. Box 40186
Arlington, VA 22204
Tel: (202) 286-9138 *Fax:* (703) 995-4639
E-Mail: info@thesociety.org
Website: thesociety.org
Members: 180 individuals
Staff: 5
Annual Budget: $500-1,000,000
Tax: 501(c)(3)

Personnel:
Executive Director: Patricia K. Anderson MPA
   E-Mail: panderson@thesociety.org

Historical Note:
Formerly the Society of State Directors of Health, Physical Education and Recreation. SSLHPE is a professional association whose members supervise and coordinate programs in health, physical education, and related fields within state departments of education. Membership: $0-135 /year.

Meetings/Conferences: Annual

Publications:
Membership Directory; annually
Society Newsletter; weekly

Society of Surgical Oncology (1940)
85 W. Algonquin Rd.
Suite 550
Arlington Heights, IL 60005-4425
Tel: (847) 427-1400 *Fax:* (847) 427-9656
Website: surgonc.org
Members: 2300 members
Staff: 4
Annual Budget: $2-5,000,000

Personnel:
President: Michael Morrow
Executive Director: M. Eileen Widmer CAE
Secretary: Jeffrey A. Drebin MD, PhD
Director, Meetings and Conventions: Gina Seegers
   E-Mail: ginaseegers@surgonc.org

Historical Note:
Founded as the James Ewing Society. Became the Society of Surgical Oncology in 1975. Mission is to promote the quality of surgical oncology care by advancing the education and training of its members and fostering oncology research needed to improve multidisciplinary

cancer patient care. Membership: $395 (Active, US); $245 (Associate); $50 (Candidate).

Meetings/Conferences: Annual
Conference Chair: Gina Seegers
2013 - Ft. Washington, MD (Gaylord National Hotel and Convention Center)/March 6 - 9
2013 - Washington, DC/March 7 - 10/1500 attendees/ over 100 exhibitors
2014 - Phoenix, AZ/March 12 - 15/1500 attendees/ over 100 exhibitors
2014 - Phoenix, AZ/March 13
2015 - Houston, TX/March 25 - 28/over 100 exhibitors

Publications:
Annals of Surgical Oncology; monthly; adv.
Membership Directory; on-line
SSO NEWS- Newsletter; quarterly
Surgical Oncology Research- Reports; weekly

Society of Systematic Biologists (1948)
Department of Biological Sciences
University of Idaho
Moscow, ID 83844-3051
Website: systbio.org
Members: 1700 individuals
Staff: 3
Annual Budget: $100-250,000

Personnel:
President: Jack Sullivan
Editor-in-Chief: Ronald W. DeBry
   E-Mail: ronald.debry@uc.edu

Historical Note:
Formerly (1991) known as Society of Systematic Zoology. SSB is dedicated to the advancement of the science of systematic biology in all its aspects of theory, principles, methodology, and practice, for both living and fossil organisms, with emphasis on areas of common interest to all systematic biologists regardless of individual specialization. Membership: $16-1129/year.

Meetings/Conferences: Annual

Publications:
Membership Directory; on-line
Systematic Biology; bi-monthly; adv.

Society of Teachers of Family Medicine (1967)
11400 Tomahawk Creek Pkwy.
Suite 540
Leawood, KS 66211
Tel: (913) 906-6000 *Fax:* (913) 906-6096
TollFree: (800) 274-7928
E-Mail: stfmoffice@stfm.org
Website: stfm.org
Members: 5000 individuals
Staff: 16
Annual Budget: $2-5,000,000
Tax: 501(c)(6)

Personnel:
Executive Director: Stacy Brungardt CAE
   E-Mail: sbrungardt@stfm.org
Assistant, Publications: Jan Cartwright
Chief Financial Officer: Dana Greco CAE
   E-Mail: dgreco@stfm.org
Senior Meeting Planner: Priscilla Noland
   E-Mail: pnoland@stfm.org
Director, Publications and Community: Traci Nolte CAE
   E-Mail: tnolte@stfm.org
Director, Information Technology: Larry Peery
   E-Mail: lpeery@stfm.org
Director, Conferences and Member Relations: Ray Rosetta CMP
   E-Mail: rrosetta@stfm.org
Director, Government Relations: Hope R. Wittenberg MA
   E-Mail: oafmdc@stfm.org

Historical Note:
Affiliated with the American Board of Family Practice, the American Academy of Family Physicians, and the American Academy of Family Physicians Foundation, STFM's purpose is to advance family medicine to improve health through a community of teachers and scholars. Membership: $275 (Active Physician Member); $200 (Active Nonphysician Member); $130 (Associate Member/International Member); $90 (Fellow-in-Training); $70 (Resident); $25 (Student). Emeritus membership is free.

Meetings/Conferences:
Conference Chair: Ray Rosetta CMP
2013 - San Antonio, TX (Grand Hyatt San Antonio)/ Jan. 24 - 27
2013 - Baltimore, MD (Baltimore Marriott Waterfront)/ May 1 - 5/1500 attendees

2014 - Nashville, TN (Opryland Resort)/Jan. 30 - Feb. 2
Number of non-conference events/year: 2
Publications:
Annals of Family Medicine
Family Medicine; monthly; adv.
Membership Directory; on-line
STFM Messenger; semi-monthly; adv.
The Teaching Physician E-Newsletter; quarterly; adv.
Membership List Available to Non-members

Society of Telecommunications Consultants
(1976)
13275 State Hwy. 89
P.O. Box 70
Old Station, CA 96071
Tel: (530) 335-7313 *Fax:* (530) 335-7360
E-Mail: stchdq@stcconsultants.org
Website: stcconsultants.org
Members: 190 Individual Consultant Members
And Vendor Advisory Council Members
Staff: 1
Annual Budget: $100-250,000
Tax: 501(c)(6)
Personnel:
President: James O'Gorman
    E-Mail: jogorman@ce-inc.com
Historical Note:
Established to meet the need for a self-regulating body in the profession. STC's Mission is to serve its constituencies - information and communication technology consultants and their clients and represents its members in regulatory, legislative and commercial affairs and maintains a vendor advisory council, comprised of companies offering telecommunications products and services, which supports consultant members with technical information and provides assistance in solving problems in the field. STC members are telecommunications professionals who serve clients in business, industry and government.Membership: $275-$475 (Consultant/Associate); $850 (Vendor); $350 (Affiliate); $50 (Student).
Meetings/Conferences: Annual
Publications:
Membership Directory; on-line
The STC Newsletter

Society of the Plastics Industry *(1937)*
1667 K St. NW
Suite 1000
Washington, DC 20006
Tel: (202) 974-5200 *Fax:* (202) 296-7005
Website: plasticsindustry.org
Members: 1000 companies
Staff: 38
Annual Budget: $5-10,000,000
Personnel:
President and Chief Executive Officer: William R. Carteaux
    E-Mail: wcarteaux@plasticsindustry.org
Senior Vice President, Communications and Marketing: Tracy H. Cullen CAE
    E-Mail: tcullen@plasticsindustry.org
Manager, Government Affairs: John Grant
Senior Vice President, Government & Industry Affairs: Jonathan Kurrle
Senior Vice President, Trade Shows and Conferences: Gene Sanders
Historical Note:
SPI works to preserve the plastics industry by providing government advocacy based on current member needs and facilitates networking. Member companies represent the entire plastics industry supply chain, including processors, machinery and equipment manufacturers and raw materials suppliers. Membership: $1,200-50,000 (Materials Supplier/Equipment/Moldmakers); $1,200-27,600 (Recycler/Processor/Purchasers/Distributors/Manufacturers Representatives/Industrial Services/Associate); $1,200 (Service Provider).
Continuing Education:
Certification Designation/s: NCP
Meetings/Conferences: Semi-Annual
Conference Chair: Gene Sanders
Number of non-conference events/year: 24
Publications:
Membership Directory; on-line
Membership List Available to Non-members

Society of Thoracic Radiology *(1982)*

1202 1/2 Seventh St. NW
Suite 209
Rochester, MN 55901
Tel: (507) 288-5620 *Fax:* (507) 288-0014
E-Mail: str@thoracicrad.org
Website: thoracicrad.org
Members: 700 individuals
Staff: 4
Annual Budget: $500-1,000,000
Tax: 501(c)(3)
Personnel:
Administrator: Barbara McLeod CMP
    E-Mail: barbara@matrixmeetings.com
Contact, Membership Services: Jhoesel Newman
    E-Mail: jhoesel@matrixmeetings.com
Meeting Planner: Tracy Parks CMP
    E-Mail: tracy@matrixmeetings.com
Historical Note:
STR's mission is to promote excellence in cardiothoracic imaging and improve patient care through research and education. Membership: $390 (Senior/Associate); $235 (Members-in-training).
Meetings/Conferences: Annual
2013 - Seoul, Republic of Korea (South Korea)/June 8 - 11
2014 - Antonio, TX (Grand Hyatt San Antonio)/March 16 - 19
Publications:
Journal of Thoracic Imagery; quarterly; adv.
STR Newsletter; quarterly

Society of Thoracic Surgeons *(1964)*
633 N. St. Clair St.
Floor 23
Chicago, IL 60611-3658
Tel: (312) 202-5800 *Fax:* (312) 202-5801
Website: sts.org
Members: 6600 individuals
Staff: 20
Annual Budget: $25-50,000,000
Tax: 501(c)(6)
Personnel:
Executive Director and General Counsel: Robert A. Wynbrandt
Director, Marketing and Communications: Natalie Boden
    E-Mail: nboden@sts.org
Director, Government Relations: Phillip A. Bongiorno
    E-Mail: pbongiorno@sts.org
Director, Meetings and Conventions: Joyce A. Gambino
Director, Education and Membership Services: Damon K. Marquis
    E-Mail: dmarquis@sts.org
Director, Finance and Administration: Sylvia Novick
    E-Mail: snovick@sts.org
Director, Research and Scientific Affairs: Cynthia M. Shewan
    E-Mail: cshewan@sts.org
Administrator, Information Technology: Michael Skallas
    E-Mail: mskallas@sts.org
Historical Note:
STS's mission is to enhance the ability of cardiothoracic surgeons to provide quality patient care through education, research, and advocacy. Membership: $750 (Active/International-US); $650 (Active/International-Canada); $300 (Active/International, Outside US and Canada); $100 (Candidate); $25 (Pre-Candidate); $250 (Associate).
Meetings/Conferences: Annual
Conference Chair: Joyce A. Gambino
2013 - Los Angeles, CA/Jan. 26 - 30
Publications:
Annals of Thoracic Surgery; quarterly
Beltway Briefings; on-line
Coding Newsletter
Membership Directory; on-line
STS News; quarterly
STS Newsletter
Membership List Available to Non-members

Society of Toxicologic Pathologists *(1971)*
1821 Michael Faraday Dr.
Suite 300
Reston, VA 20190-5332
Tel: (703) 438-7508 *Fax:* (703) 438-3113
TollFree: (800) 826-6762
E-Mail: stp@toxpath.org
Website: toxpath.org

Members: 1150 individuals
Staff: 4
Annual Budget: $1-2,000,000
Tax: 501(c)(3)
Personnel:
Executive Director: Sue Pitsch
    E-Mail: spitsch@toxpath.org
Manager, Meetings and Exhibits: Maureen Kettering
    E-Mail: mkettering@toxpath.org
Director, Membership Services: Tierre Miller
    E-Mail: tmiller@aim-hq.com
Historical Note:
Originated as Society of Pharmacological and Environmental Pathologists and incorporated in New Jersey in 1971, assumed its present name in 1980. STP's mission is to advance pathology as it pertains to changes elicited by pharmacological, chemical and environmental agents, and factors that modify these responses. Membership: $225 (Full/Associate); $65 (Student with Journal); $30 (Student without Journal); $0 (Emeritus/Honorary).
Meetings/Conferences: Annual
Conference Chair: Maureen Kettering
2013 - Portland, OR (Oregon Convention Center)/June 16 - 20
2014 - Washington, DC (Marriott Wardman Park Hotel)/June 22 - 26
Number of non-conference events/year: 1
Publications:
Membership Directory; on-line
The Scope; quarterly
ToxPath Journal
Membership List Available to Non-members

Society of Toxicologic Pathology *(1971)*
1821 Michael Faraday Dr.
Suite 300
Reston, VA 20190
Tel: (703) 438-7508 *Fax:* (703) 438-3113
E-Mail: stp@toxpath.org
Website: toxpath.org
Members: 1150 individuals
Staff: 4
Annual Budget: $1-2,000,000
Tax: 501(c)(3)
Personnel:
Executive Director: Sue Pitsch
    E-Mail: spitsch@toxpath.org
Contact, Continuing Education: Krystle Correll
    E-Mail: kcorrell@toxpath.org
Manager, Meetings and Exhibits: Maureen Kettering
    E-Mail: mkettering@toxpath.org
Director, Membership Services: Tierre Miller
    E-Mail: tmiller@aim-hq.com
Historical Note:
Originally Society of Pharmacological and Environmental Pathologists and incorporated in New Jersey in 1971, assumed its present name in 1980. STP aims at the advancement of pathology as it pertains to changes elicited by pharmacological, chemical and environmental agents, and factors that modify these responses. Membership: $225 (Full/Associate); $30-65 (Student).
Meetings/Conferences: Annual
Conference Chair: Maureen Kettering
2013 - Portland, OR (Oregon Convention Center)/June 16 - 20
2014 - Washington, DC (Washington Marriott Wardman Park)/June 22 - 26
Number of non-conference events/year: 2
Publications:
Member Directory; on-line
Scope Newsletter; on-line
ToxPath Journal; on-line
Membership List Available to Non-members

Society of Toxicology *(1961)*
1821 Michael Faraday Dr.
Suite 300
Reston, VA 20190-5332
Tel: (703) 438-3115 *Fax:* (703) 438-3113
E-Mail: sothq@toxicology.org
Website: toxicology.org
Members: 6000 individuals
Staff: 30
Annual Budget: $25-50,000,000
Tax: 501(c)(3)
Personnel:
Executive Director: Shawn Douglas Lamb

E-Mail: shawnl@toxicology.org
Contact, Membership Services: Rosibel Alvarenga
    E-Mail: rosibel@toxicology.org
Director, Education: Betty Eidemiller PhD
    E-Mail: bettye@toxicology.org
Legal Counsel: William E. Hays
Manager, Communications and Media Relations: Martha Lindauer
    E-Mail: martha@toxicology.org
Director, Meetings: Heidi Prange
    E-Mail: heidi@toxicology.org

Historical Note:
SOT works to create a safer and healthier world by advancing the science of toxicology. Members are scientists concerned with the effects of chemicals on humankind and the environment. Membership: $135 (Full/Associate); $35 (Postdoctoral); $20 (Graduate Student); $51-85 (Retired).

Meetings/Conferences: Annual
Conference Chair: Heidi Prange
2013 - San Antonio, TX (Henry B. Gonzalez Convention Center and the Lila Cockrell Theatre)/ March 10 - 14
2014 - Scottsdale, AZ (Phoenician Resort)/March 23 - 27
2015 - San Diego, CA (San Diego Convention and Visitors Bureau)/March 22 - 26
2016 - New Orleans, LA (Ernest N. Morial Convention Center)/March 13 - 17
2017 - Baltimore, MD (Baltimore Convention Center)/ March 12 - 16

Publications:
Membership Directory; on-line; adv.
The Communique; quarterly
The Toxicologist; annually
Toxicological Sciences; monthly; adv.

Membership List Available to Non-members

Society of Trauma Nurses *(1986)*
3493 Lansdowne Dr.
Suite two
Lexington, KY 40517
Tel: (859) 977-7456 *Fax:* (859) 271-0607
E-Mail: info@traumanurses.org
Website: traumanurses.org
Members: 1200 individuals
Staff: 5
Annual Budget: $500-1,000,000
Tax: 501(c)(3)

Personnel:
Executive Director: Stephanie Czuhajewski
    E-Mail: sczuhajewski@traumanurses.org
Project Coordinator: Sarah Clements
    E-Mail: sclements@traumanurses.org
Coordinator, Meetings and Education: Brian Doty
    E-Mail: bdoty@traumanurses.org
Contact, Memberships Services and Enrollment: Tonda Preston
    E-Mail: tpreston@traumanurses.org
Webmaster: Chris Walls
    E-Mail: cwalls@traumanurses.org

Historical Note:
STN is a membership-based, non-profit organization whose members represent trauma nurses from around the world. Mission is to ensure optimal trauma care to all people locally, regionally, nationally and globally through initiatives focused on trauma nurses related to prevention, education and collaboration with other healthcare disciplines. Membership: $100 (Domestic); $115 (International).

Continuing Education:
Certification Designation/s: TOPIC, ATCN

Meetings/Conferences: Annual
Conference Chair: Brian Doty
2013 - Las Vegas, NV (Caesars Palace)/April 3 - 5

Publications:
Journal of Trauma Nursing; quarterly; adv.
Membership Directory; on-line
STN News; on-line

Membership List Available to Non-members

Society of Tribologists and Lubrication Engineers *(1944)*
840 Busse Hwy.
Park Ridge, IL 60068-2302
Tel: (847) 825-5536 *Fax:* (847) 825-1456
E-Mail: information@stle.org
Website: stle.org

Members:
150 companies and organizations
10000 individuals
Staff: 12
Annual Budget: $2-5,000,000
Tax: 501(c)(3)

Personnel:
Executive Director: Edward P. Salek
    E-Mail: esalek@stle.org
Director, Professional Development: Dr. Robert Gresham
    E-Mail: rgresham@stle.org
Contact, Meetings Management: Merle Hedland
    E-Mail: mhedland@bacon-hedland.com
Manager, Digital Marketing: Bruce Murgueitio
    E-Mail: BMurgueitio@stle.org
Associate Manager, Publishing and Communications: Karl Phipps
    E-Mail: kphipps@stle.org
Manager, Information Systems: Myrna Scott-Perez
    E-Mail: mscott@stle.org
Manager, Education: Kara Sniegowski
    E-Mail: klemar@stle.org

Historical Note:
Formerly (1987) the American Society of Lubrication Engineers. STLE's mission is to advance the science of tribology and the practice of lubrication engineering in order to foster innovation, improve the performance of equipment and products, conserve resources and protect the environment. Members are technical experts who research, develop and market the methods and products that make industry successful. Membership: $135-9270/year.

Continuing Education:
Certification Designation/s: CMFS, OMA, CLS

Meetings/Conferences: Annual
Conference Chair: Merle Hedland
2013 - Detroit, MI (Marroitt Renaissance)/May 5 - 9
2013 - Torino, Italy/Sept. 8 - 13
2014 - Lake Buena Vista, FL (Disneys Contemporary Resorts)/May 18 - 22
2015 - Dallas, TX (Omni Hotel)/May 17 - 21
2016 - Las Vegas, NV (Bally's Las Vegas)/May 15 - 19
Number of non-conference events/year: 4

Publications:
Tribology & Lubrication Engineering (TLT); monthly
Tribology Letters
Tribology Transactions Journal; quarterly

Society of United States Air Force Flight Surgeons *(1960)*
P.O. Box 1776
Fairborn, OH 45324
Tel: (210) 536-2845 *Fax:* (210) 536-1779
Website: sousaffs.org
Members: 900 individuals
Staff: 4
Annual Budget: Under $10,000

Personnel:
Executive Officer: David Miller
    E-Mail: executive@sousaffs.org
Technical Editor: Sandy Kawano
    E-Mail: elaine.kawano@wpafb.af.mil
Treasurer: Sparky Matthews
    E-Mail: treasurer@sousaffs.org
Executive Editor: Patricia Pankey
    E-Mail: patricia.pankey@wpafb.af.mil

Historical Note:
SoUSAFFS provides a forum for education, cross-talk, mentoring and networking. Members are Air Force Flight Surgeons - active, guard, reserve, and retired. Membership: $20 (Individuals/Associate/Subscribers); $200 (Lifetime); Free (Members Emeritus /Honorary).

Publications:
Membership Directory; on-line
Sousaffs Newsletter; adv.

Society of University Otolaryngologists-Head and Neck Surgeons *(1964)*
2709 San Marcos Dr.
Pasadena, CA 91107
Tel: (626) 683-7313 *Fax:* (626) 683-7313
Website: suo-aado.org
Members: 525 individuals
Staff: 2
Annual Budget: $50-100,000

Personnel:
Executive Director: Donna Hoffman MA
    E-Mail: donna.hoffman05@gmail.com

Historical Note:
SUO-HNS's mission to give exchange of ideas and relevant information germane to practice of medicine in an academic setting. Members are otolaryngologist-head and neck surgeon, teacher, or investigator, or pursuing a successful career in Otolaryngology Head and Neck Surgery. Membership: $80/year (Active).

Meetings/Conferences: Annual

Publications:
SUO Newsletter; on-line

Society of University Surgeons *(1938)*
341 N. Maitland Ave.,
Suite 130
Maitland, FL 32751
Tel: (407) 647-7714 *Fax:* (407) 629-2502
E-Mail: info@susweb.org
Website: susweb.org
Members: 1400 individuals
Staff: 5
Annual Budget: $100-250,000

Personnel:
Executive Vice President: Phil Pyster CAE
    E-Mail: phil@crow-segal.com

Historical Note:
SUS's mission is to advance the art and science of surgery by the encouragement of its members to pursue original investigations both in the clinic and in the laboratory. Free and informal interchange of ideas pertaining to the above subjects as a limited membership and common aims. Membership: $225 (Active); $160 (Senior Member).

Meetings/Conferences: Annual
2013 - New Orleans, LA (Roosevelt New Orleans Hotel)/Feb. 5 - 7
2014 - San Diego, CA (Hyatt Regency La Jolla)/Feb. 4 - 6

Publications:
Membership Directory; on-line

Society of University Urologists *(1967)*
1100 E. Woodfield Rd.
Suite 520
Schaumburg, IL 60173
Tel: (847) 517-7225 *Fax:* (847) 517-7229
E-Mail: info@suunet.org
Website: suunet.org
Members: 465 individuals
Staff: 2
Annual Budget: $25-50,000

Personnel:
Executive Director: Wendy J. Weiser
Secretary and Treasurer: Michael Coburn

Historical Note:
SUU's mission is to promote standards of urologic education and research. Members are urologists at United States and Canadian academic urologic training institutions who have demonstrated interest and achievement in urologic education. Membership: $70/year.

Meetings/Conferences: Annual
2013 - San Diego, CA/May 3

Publications:
Membership Directory; on-line

Society of Urologic Nurses and Associates *(1972)*
E. Holly Ave.
P.O. Box 56
Pitman, NJ 08071-0056
Tel: (856) 256-2335 *Fax:* (856) 589-7463
TollFree: (888) 827-7862
E-Mail: suna@ajj.com
Website: suna.org
Members: 3000 individuals
Staff: 4
Annual Budget: $1-2,000,000
Tax: 501(c)(3)

Personnel:
President: Valre W. Welch MSN

Historical Note:
Formed as American Urological Association Allied, adopted its current name in 1995. SUNA is a professional organization committed to excellence in clinical practice and research through education of its members, patients, family and community. Membership: $75 (Active); $115 (Sustaining); $37.50 (Student); $95 (International).

Continuing Education:
Certification Designation/s: CBUNA

Meetings/Conferences: Annual

2013 - Savannah, GA (Hyatt Regency Savannah)/
March 7 - 9
2013 - Chicago, IL (Hyatt Regency)/Oct. 11 - 14
2014 - Lake Buena Vista, FL (Disney's Board Walk
Inn)/Oct. 31 - Nov. 3
2015 - Nashville, TN (Omni Hotel)/Feb. 26 - 28
Number of non-conference events/year: 1

Publications:
E-Newsletter; bi-monthly
Membership Directory; on-line
SUNA's Urogram
Urologic Nursing; adv.

Society of Vacuum Coaters *(1957)*
71 Pinon Hill Pl. NE
Albuquerque, NM 87122-1914
Tel: (505) 856-7188 *Fax:* (505) 856-6716
E-Mail: svcinfo@svc.org
Website: svc.org
Members: 1000 individuals
Staff: 3
Annual Budget: $1-2,000,000
Tax: 501(c)(6)

Personnel:
Executive Director: Vivienne Harwood Mattox
Administrative Assistant: Jacque Matanis
E-Mail: svcinfo@svc.org
Manager, Marketing and Communications: Beth Strong
E-Mail: publications@svc.org

Historical Note:
*SVC's mission is to advocate technical excellence by
providing a global forum to inform, educate and engage the
members, the technical community, and the public on all
aspects of vacuum coating, surface engineering and related
technologies. Members are individuals concerned with the
use and development of vacuum coatings for large and
small scale applications. Membership: $110 (Individual);
$40 (Student/Young Member/Group Member); $550
(Corporate).*

Meetings/Conferences: Annual
2013 - Providence, RI (Rhode Island College)/April 20
- 25
2014 - Chicago, IL (Hyatt Regency Chicago)/May 3 - 8
2015 - Santa Clara, CA (Santa Clara Convention
Center)/April 25 - 30

Publications:
SVC Bulletin; adv.
SVConnections; monthly; adv.

Membership List Available to Non-members

Society of Vertebrate Paleontology *(1940)*
111 Deer Lake Rd.
Suite 100
Deerfield, IL 60015
Tel: (847) 480-9095 *Fax:* (847) 480-9282
E-Mail: svp@vertpaleo.org
Website: vertpaleo.org
Members: 2400 individuals
Staff: 4
Annual Budget: $1-2,000,000
Tax: 501(c)(3)

Personnel:
Executive Director: Debbie Trueblood
Communications Liaison: Meagan Comerford
E-Mail: mcomerford@vertpaleo.org
Director, Conference: Liz Freyn
Administrator: Diane Rutherford

Historical Note:
*SVP's mission is to advance the science of vertebrate
paleontology, and to serve the common interests and
facilitate the cooperation of all persons concerned with the
history, evolution, comparative anatomy and taxonomy of
vertebrate animals, as well as the field occurrence, collection
and study of fossil vertebrates and the stratigraphy of the
beds in which they are found. Membership: $115-130
(Regular); $50-60 (Student); $25 (Emeritus/Junior); $50
(Spousal/Second Member).*

Meetings/Conferences: Annual
Conference Chair: Liz Freyn
2013 - Los Angeles, CA (Westin Bonaventure Hotel and
Suites, Los Angeles)/Oct. 30 - Nov. 2
Number of non-conference events/year: 3

Publications:
Journal of Vertebrate Paleontology; bi-monthly; adv.
Membership Directory; on-line
SVP News Bulletin; semi-annually

Membership List Available to Non-members

The Society of Wine Educators *(1974)*
1319 F St. NW
Suite 303
Washington, DC 20004
Tel: (202) 408-8777 *Fax:* (202) 408-8677
E-Mail: info@societyofwineeducators.org
Website: societyofwineeducators.org
Members: 1800 individuals and members
Staff: 8
Annual Budget: $1-2,000,000
Tax: 501(c)(3)

Personnel:
Executive Director: Carla J. Williams CSS
E-Mail: cwilliams@societyofwineeducators.org
Manager, Membership Services and Outreach: Ben Coffelt
E-Mail: bcoffelt@societyofwineeducators.org
General Manager: Shields Hood CWE
E-Mail: shood@societyofwineeducators.org
Events Manager: Andrew Knerr
E-Mail: AKnerr@societyofwineeducators.org

Historical Note:
*SWE's mission is to advance wine education through
professional development and certification. Members include
those who teach wine education classes, those who write
about wine, and those associated with its production,
restaurant, retail and wholesale areas. Membership: $2,500
(Corporate); $500 (Industry); $250 (Non-Profit); $135
(Professional); $85 (Associate); $40 (Student).*

Continuing Education:
Certification Designation/s: CSS, CWE, CSW

Meetings/Conferences: Annual
Conference Chair: Shields Hood CWE

Publications:
Membership Directory; on-line; adv.
Smart Sip Newsletter; quarterly

Society of Woman Geographers *(1925)*
415 E. Captiol St. SE
Washington, DC 20003-3810
Tel: (202) 546-9228 *Fax:* (202) 546-5232
E-Mail: swghq@verizon.net
Website: iswg.org
Members: 500 individuals
Staff: 1
Annual Budget: $500-1,000,000
Tax: 501(c)(3)

Personnel:
President: Kimberly Crews

Historical Note:
*The Society of Woman Geographers is an organization of
accomplished women whose common link is the intellectual
and scientific exploration of some area or aspect of
the earth's phenomena, including human adaptations.
Membership by invitation only and officers change
every three years in May. Membership: $75 (Active/
Associate Group); $50 (Active/Associate-At Large); $50
(Corresponding); $15 (Student).*

Meetings/Conferences: Triennial
Number of non-conference events/year: 16

Publications:
Membership Directory; annually
SWG Newsletter; quarterly

Society of Women Engineers *(1950)*
203 N La Salle St.
Suite 1675
Chicago, IL 60601
Tel: (312) 596-5223 *Fax:* (312) 596-5252
TollFree: (877) 793-4636
E-Mail: hq@swe.org
Website: societyofwomenengineers.swe.org
Members: 17100 individuals and institutions
Staff: 15
Annual Budget: $5-10,000,000
Tax: 501(c)(3)

Personnel:
Chief Executive Officer and Executive Director: Betty A.
Shanahan CAE
E-Mail: executive-director@swe.org
Director, Membership Relations: Mary Carravallah
E-Mail: membership@swe.org
Manager, Conferences: Jeanne Elipani
E-Mail: jeanne.elipani@swe.org
Director, Editorial and Publications: Anne Perusek
E-Mail: swemag@swe.org
Director, Education: Kelly Griswold Schable

E-Mail: director-education@swe.org

Historical Note:
*SWE's mission is to encourage women to achieve full
potential in careers as engineers and leaders, expand the
image of the engineering profession as a positive force in
improving the quality of life, and demonstrate the value
of diversity. Membership: $100 (Individual); $3,000
(Corporate); $20 (Collegiate); $50 (Retired); $2,000
(Lifetime); $120 (Professional).*

Meetings/Conferences: Annual
Conference Chair: Jeanne Elipani
2013 - Baltimore, MD/Oct. 24 - 26

Publications:
All Together E-Newsletter; on-line
SWE Magazine; adv.
SWE News; monthly

Society of Wood Science and Technology *(1958)*
P.O. Box 6155
Monona, WI 53716-6155
Tel: (608) 577-1342 *Fax:* (608) 467-8979
Website: swst.org
Members: 450 individuals
Staff: 2
Annual Budget: $100-250,000
Tax: 501(c)(6)

Personnel:
Executive Director: Victoria L. Herian
E-Mail: vicki@swst.org
Newsletter Editor: P. David Jones
E-Mail: pdjones@cfr.msstate.edu

Historical Note:
*Formerly (1961) American Society of Wood Engineering.
SWST seeks to provide member services that develop,
maintain, and advance the educational, scientific, and
ethical standards defining the wood technology profession,
and to advocate socially responsible production and use
of wood and other lignocellulosic products. Membership:
$75 (Individual); $25 (Student); $40 (Retiree); $5-130
(Emerging Country).*

Meetings/Conferences: Annual
Conference Chair: Victoria L. Herian

Publications:
Membership Directory; annually
SWST Newsletter; bi-monthly; adv.
Wood and Fiber Science; quarterly

Sociological Practice Association *(1978)*
c/o SMSU, Sociology and Anthropology Dept.
901 National Ave.
Springfield, MO 65804
Tel: (614) 292-3114 *Fax:* (614) 292-9750
Members: 200 individuals
Staff: 1
Annual Budget: Under $10,000

Personnel:
President: Melodye G. Lehnerer

Historical Note:
*Members include organizational developers, program
planners, community organizers, sociotherapists,
counselors, gerontologists, conflict interventionists,
applied social science researchers, policy planners on all
levels including international practice, and many others
who practice, study, teach or do research by applying
sociological knowledge for positive social change. Has
no paid officers or full-time staff. Membership: $80/year
(individual); $150/year (organization/company).*

Software & Information Industry Association
(SIIA) *(1984)*
1090 Vermont Ave. NW
Sixth Floor
Washington, DC 20005-4095
Tel: (202) 289-7442 *Fax:* (202) 289-7097
Website: siia.net
Members: 800 companies
Staff: 41
Annual Budget: $5-10,000,000

Personnel:
President: Kenneth Wasch
E-Mail: kwasch@siia.net
Chief Litigation Counsel and Director, Internet Anti-piracy:
Scott Bain
E-Mail: sbain@siia.net
Vice President, Education Division: Karen Billings
E-Mail: kbillings@siia.net
Managing Director, Financial and Information Services:
Tom Davin

E-Mail: tdavin@siia.net
Vice President, Membership Services: Eric Fredell
E-Mail: efredell@siia.net
Director, Communications: Laura Greenback
E-Mail: lgreenback@siia.net
Director, Events and Sponsor: Anika King
E-Mail: aking@siia.net
General Counsel and Senior Vice President,Intellectual
Property: Keith Kupferschmid
E-Mail: kkupfer@siia.net
Vice President, Public Policy: Mark MacCarthy PhD
E-Mail: mmaccarthy@siia.net
Vice President, Administration and Finance: Tom
Meldrum
Senior Vice President, Sales and Marketing: Brian
Rosenberg
E-Mail: brosenberg@siia.net
Vice President and General Manager, Content Division:
Kathy Greenler Sexton
E-Mail: kgsexton@siia.net

Historical Note:
SIIA's mission is to promote the common interests of the
software and digital content industries, to protect the
intellectual property of member companies, and advocates
a legal and regulatory environment that benefits the
industries. Members are full time employees of software
and information publishers and online software and
information-based service providers and their subsidiaries,
professional service firms with software and information
industry interests, venture capital firms. Membership:
$850-1,25,000 (Full and Entity Corporate Member);
$1,995-10,895 (Associate); $1,000-4,000 (VC Associate),
$5,000-25,000 (Market Data User Associate Member).

Meetings/Conferences:
Conference Chair: Anika King

Publications:
Membership Directory; on-line
SIIA All About the Cloud Weekly; weekly
SIIA Content Weekly; weekly
SIIA Digital Policy Roundup; weekly
SIIA Ed Tech Daily; daily
SIIA Intellectual Property Roundup; weekly
SIIA Software Industry Daily; daily

Membership List Available to Non-members

Softwood Export Council (1998)
P.O. Box 80517
Portland, OR 97280
Tel: (503) 620-5946 Fax: (503) 684-8928
Website: softwood.org
Members: 20 organizations
Staff: 2
Annual Budget: $2-5,000,000
Tax: 501(c)(6)

Personnel:
President: Craig L. Larsen CFP
E-Mail: clarsen@softwood.org
Manager, International Marketing: Natalie Macias
E-Mail: Natalie@softwood.org

Historical Note:
SEC's mission is to coordinate overseas market development
activities for the U.S. softwood industry with the Foreign
Agricultural Service, and aids American exports of softwood
products by providing information and assistance to agents,
importers, designers, and users of these products in other
countries. Membership: $125 (Individual); $250 (Small
Company); $375 (Large Company).

Meetings/Conferences:
Number of non-conference events/year: 12

Publications:
SEC Newsletter

Soil and Plant Analysis Council (1970)
347 N. Shores Cir.
Windsor, CO 80550
Tel: (970) 686-5702 Fax: (402) 476-0302
Website: spcouncil.com
Members: 350 individuals
Staff: 2
Annual Budget: $10-25,000
Tax: 501(c)(3)

Personnel:
President: Rigas Karamanos
E-Mail: r.karamanos@westcoag.com
Secretary and Treasurer: Robert Miller
E-Mail: rmiller@lamar.colostate.edu

Historical Note:

Formerly Council on Soil Testing and Plant Analysis
(1994). SPAC is an international organization of educators,
scientists and industrialists who are committed to advancing
nutrient analysis of soil, plant, water, and manure. SPAC
is dedicated to nutrient analysis for better crops and
environment. Membership: $100 (Individual); $300
(Laboratory); $450 (Company/Corporate/Sustaining).

Meetings/Conferences: Annual

Publications:
Lab Directory; on-line
SPAC Newsletter; quarterly

Soil and Water Conservation Society (1945)
945 SW Ankeny Rd.
Ankeny, IA 50021
Tel: (515) 289-2331 Fax: (515) 289-1227
TollFree: (800) 843-7645
E-Mail: swcs@swcs.org
Website: swcs.org
Members: 5000 individuals
Staff: 8
Annual Budget: $1-2,000,000
Tax: 501(c)(3)

Personnel:
Executive Director: Jim Gulliford
E-Mail: jim.gulliford@swcs.org
Specialist, Membership Services: Cammie Callen
E-Mail: memberservices@swcs.org
Director, Publications and Journal Editor: Oksana
Gieseman
E-Mail: oksana.gieseman@swcs.org
Specialist, Membership Services: Robin Hockaday
E-Mail: memberservices@swcs.org
Comptroller: Jody Ogg
E-Mail: jody.ogg@swcs.org

Historical Note:
Formerly (1987) the Soil Conservation Society of America.
SWCS's mission is to foster the science and art of
natural resource conservation. Members are researchers,
consultants and practitioners of soil and water conservation,
both in the public and private sectors. Membership: $200
(President's Club); $130 (Leader); $80 (Conservationist);
$25 (Student).

Meetings/Conferences: Annual
2013 - Reno, NV (Peppermill Reno)/July 21 - 24
Number of non-conference events/year: 11

Publications:
Journal of Soil and Water Conservation; bi-monthly;
adv.
SWCS Newsletter
The Conservogram; monthly; adv.

Soil Science Society of America (1936)
5585 Guilford Rd.
Madison, WI 53711-5801
Tel: (608) 273-8080 Fax: (608) 273-2021
E-Mail: headquarters@soils.org
Website: soils.org
Members: 6000 individuals
Staff: 41
Annual Budget: $2-5,000,000

Personnel:
Chief Executive Officer: Ellen G.M. Bergfeld
E-Mail: ebergfeld@sciencesocieties.org
Director, Government Relations: Karl Anderson
E-Mail: kanderson@sciencesocieties.org
Director, Business Development, Advertising, Exhibits and
Sponsorships: Alexander Barton
E-Mail: abarton@sciencesocieties.org
Director, Membership Services: Susan Chapman
E-Mail: schapman@sciencesocieties.org
Director, Publications: Mark Mandelbaum
E-Mail: mmandelbaum@sciencesocieties.org
Chief Financial Officer: Wes Meixelsperger
E-Mail: wm@sciencesocieties.org
Director, Information Technology and Operations: Ian
Popkewitz
E-Mail: ipopkewitz@sciencesocieties.org
Director, Meetings and Conventions: Keith Schlesinger
E-Mail: kschlesinger@sciencesocieties.org
Director, Certification Programs: Luther Smith
E-Mail: lsmith@sciencesocieties.org
Member Communications Manager, Awards and
Communities: Sara Uttech
E-Mail: suttech@sciencesocieties.org

Historical Note:

SSSA fosters the transfer of knowledge and practices to
sustain global soils. Members are individuals or companies
who are interested in the objectives of ASA, CSSA, and/or
SSSA. Membership: $15-125/year.

Continuing Education:
Certification Designation/s: CPA, CPSC, CCA, CPSS

Meetings/Conferences: Annual
Conference Chair: Keith Schlesinger
2013 - Tampa, FL/Nov. 3 - 7/3200 attendees/over 100
exhibitors
2014 - Long Beach, CA/Nov. 2 - 6/3200 attendees/
over 100 exhibitors
2015 - Minneapolis, MN/Nov. 15 - 18/3200 attendees/
over 100 exhibitors
2016 - Phoenix, AZ/Nov. 6 - 9
2017 - Tampa, FL/Oct. 22 - 25
2020 - Phoenix, AZ/Nov. 8 - 11

Publications:
CSA News Magazine; monthly; adv.
Journal of Environmental Quality; bi-monthly; adv.
Journal of Plant Registrations; adv.
Member Directory; on-line
Soil Science Society of America Journal; bi-monthly;
adv.
Vadose Zone Journal; on-line

Membership List Available to Non-members

Solar Alliance
P.O. Box 534
N. Scituate, MA 02060
Tel: (202) 879-4400
E-Mail: info@solaralliance.org
Website: solaralliance.org
Staff: 3
Annual Budget: $1-2,000,000

Personnel:
President: Carrie Cullen Hitt
Contact, Membership: Holly Gordon

Historical Note:
Solar Alliance works with state administrators, legislators
and utilities to establish cost-effective solar policies and
programs.

Solar Electric Power Association (1992)
1220 19th St. NW
Suite 800
Washington, DC 20036-2405
Tel: (202) 857-0898 Fax: (202) 559-2035
E-Mail: info@solarelectricpower.org
Website: solarelectricpower.org
Members: 1000 members
Staff: 24
Annual Budget: $5-10,000,000
Tax: 501(c)(3)

Personnel:
President and Chief Executive Officer: Julia Hamm
E-Mail: jhamm@solarelectricpower.org
Director, Policy: Darren Deffner
Director, Membership: Emily Easley
E-Mail: eeasley@solarelectricpower.org
Senior Manager, Marketing Communications: Laurie
Ehrlich
E-Mail: lreese@solarelectricpower.org
Vice President, Finance and Operations: Mark C. Kimble
E-Mail: mkimble@solarelectricpower.org
Vice President, Outreach: Don Lintvet
E-Mail: dlintvet@solarelectricpower.org
Director, Research: Mike Taylor
E-Mail: mtaylor@solarelectricpower.org

Historical Note:
SEPA's mission is to facilitate solutions for the use and
integration of solar electric power by utilities, electric service
providers, and their customers. Members include utility and
electric service providers, manufacturers, installers as well
as government and research organizations. Membership:
$500-7,500/year.

Meetings/Conferences: Annual
2013 - Portland, OR/April 16 - 17
2013 - Chicago, IL (Hyatt Regency McCormick Place)/
Oct. 21 - 24
2014 - Las Vegas, NV (Las Vegas Convention Center)/
Oct. 7 - 9
2015 - Chicago, IL (Hyatt Regency McCormick Place)/
Oct. 26 - 29
Number of non-conference events/year: 6

Publications:
Member Directory; on-line

SEPA Newsletter; bi-weekly

Solar Energy Industries Association (SEIA) *(1974)*
575 Seventh St. NW
Suite 400
Washington, DC 20004
Tel: (202) 682-0556 *Fax:* (202) 682-0559
E-Mail: info@seia.org
Website: seia.org
Members: 14 state chapters,1000 companies and
900 members
Staff: 30
Annual Budget: $5-10,000,000
Tax: 501(c)(6)

Personnel:
President and Chief Executive Officer: Rhone Resch
  E-Mail: rresch@seia.org
Vice President, Regulatory Affairs and Counsel: Daniel M.
  Adamson
  E-Mail: dadamson@seia.org
Director, Research: Scott Fenn
  E-Mail: sfenn@seia.org
Director, Communications: Monique Hanis
  E-Mail: mhanis@seia.org
Director, Legislative Affairs and General Counsel: Scott
  Hennessey
  E-Mail: shennessey@seia.org
Director, Membership Services: Karen Nedbal
  E-Mail: knedbal@seia.org
Vice President, Trade and Competitiveness: John Smirnow
  E-Mail: jsmirnow@seia.org
Executive Vice President, Government Affairs: John M.
  Stanton
  E-Mail: jstanton@seia.org
Director, Meetings and Conventions: Shannon M. Watson
  CMP, CAE
  E-Mail: swatson@seia.org

Historical Note:
*As the national trade association in the U.S., the Solar
Energy Industries Association (SEIA) is the power behind
solar energy. In January 2012, SEIA merged with the Solar
Alliance, an advocacy organization working to establishing
solar policies at the state level. The two organizations now
operate under the SEIA brand in order to present a unified
solar industry voice in all state and federal advocacy efforts.
SEIA's mission is to build a strong solar industry to power
America. Membership: $500-100,000 based on business
type and the combined total of revenue from U.S. solar
energy related products/services and government-sponsored
R&D from the last fiscal year.*

Meetings/Conferences: Semi-Annual
Conference Chair: Shannon M. Watson CMP, CAE
Number of non-conference events/year: 1

Publications:
Member Directory; on-line
National Journal; adv.
SEIA Newsletter

Solar Rating and Certification Corporation
(1980)
400 High Point Dr.
Suite 400
Cocoa, FL 32926
Tel: (321) 213-6037 *Fax:* (321) 821-0910
E-Mail: srcc@solar-rating.org
Website: solar-rating.org
Members: 19 companies
Staff: 3
Annual Budget: $1-2,000,000
Tax: 501(c)(6)

Personnel:
Executive Director: Eileen Prado
  E-Mail: EPrado@Solar-Rating.org
Technical Director: Jim Huggins
  E-Mail: JHuggins@Solar-Rating.org
Administration Support Specialist: Teresa Johnson
  E-Mail: Teresa@Solar-Rating.org

Historical Note:
*SRCC's purpose is development and implementation
of certification programs for solar energy equipment
including solar collectors and solar water heating systems.
In addition to its certification programs, the corporation
also administers a laboratory accreditation program for
independent test facilities evaluating solar components,
subsystems and systems. Membership: $30-3,500/year.*

Continuing Education:
Certification Designation/s: SCCP, SSCP
Publications:

SOLE - The International Society of Logistics
(1966)
14625 Baltimore Ave.
Suite 303
Laurel, MD 20707-4902
Tel: (310) 459-8446 *Fax:* (301) 459-1522
E-Mail: solehq@erols.com
Website: sole.org
Members: 6000 individuals
Staff: 6
Annual Budget: $250-500,000
Tax: 501(c)(3)

Personnel:
President: Timothy H. Overstreet
Editor: Benjamin S. Blanchard
  E-Mail: bsblanch@vt.edu
Vice President, Communications: Catherine A. Elder
Vice President, Education: Dianne S. Kurec
Vice President, Finance: Jeffrey L. Schafer
Vice President, Administration: Joanne Stone Wyman

Historical Note:
*SOLE, formerly known as the Society of Logistics Engineers,
is an international professional society composed of
individuals organized to enhance the art and science
of logistics technology, education and management.
Membership: $140 (Regular); $85 (Retired); $75 (Young
Logistician); $40 (Student); $1,000-3,000 (Corporate).*

Continuing Education:
Certification Designation/s: CML, CPL, DML
Meetings/Conferences: Annual
Publications:
SOLEtech Newsletter; monthly

Solid-State Circuits Society
445 Hoes Ln.
Piscataway, NJ 08854
Tel: (732) 981-3400 *Fax:* (732) 981-3410
E-Mail: sscs@ieee.org
Website: ewh.ieee.org/soc/sscs
Members: 10000 members
Staff: 6

Personnel:
Executive Director: Mike Kelly
  E-Mail: m.p.kelly@ieee.org
Membership Contact: Tzi-Dar Chiueh
President: Rakesh Kumar
Treasurer: H.S. Lee
Meetings Chair: Ken O
*Senior Administrator, Staff Magazine Managing and News
  Editor:* Katherine Olstein
  E-Mail: k.olstein@ieee.org

Historical Note:
*A technical society of the Institute of Electrical and
Electronics Engineers (IEEE). Membership, open only
to IEEE members, includes subscription to a technical
periodical in the field published by IEEE. All administrative
support is provided by IEEE.*

Meetings/Conferences: Annual
Conference Chair: Ken O
2013 - San Francisco, CA/Feb. 17 - 21/4000 attendees
2014 - San Francisco, CA/Feb. 9 - 13/3000 attendees
2015 - San Francisco, CA/Feb. 22 - 26/4000 attendees
2016 - San Francisco, CA/Feb. 21 - 25/3500 attendees
2017 - San Francisco, CA/Feb. 5 - 9/3000 attendees

Publications:
JSSC; monthly; adv.
Solid-State Circuits Magazine; adv.

Solution Mining Research Institute *(1958)*
105 Apple Valley Cir.
Clarks Summit, PA 18411
Tel: (570) 585-8092 *Fax:* (570) 585-8091
E-Mail: smri@solutionmining.org
Website: solutionmining.org
Members: 150 organizations
Staff: 2
Annual Budget: $500-1,000,000

Personnel:
Executive Director: John Voigt
  E-Mail: jvoigt@solutionmining.org

Historical Note:
*SMRI's purpose is to sponsor and engage in research
related to solution mining, cavern storage or utilization. It
also serve as a technology center and representative for the*

Solar Watch; quarterly; adv.

*industry. Membership: $4,000 (Regular); $1,000-2,000
(Associate).*

Meetings/Conferences:
2013 - Lafayette, LA/April 21 - 24
2013 - Avignon, France/May 13

Publications:
Membership Directory; on-line
Membership List Available to Non-members

Sommelier Society of America *(1954)*
P.O. Box 20080
W. Village Station
New York, NY 10014-0708
Tel: (212) 679-4190 *Fax:* (212) 255-8959
E-Mail: info@sommeliersocietyofamerica.org
Website: sommeliersocietyofamerica.org
Members: 500 individuals
Staff: 5
Annual Budget: $50-100,000

Personnel:
Chairman: Robert S. Moody

Historical Note:
*A wine teaching organization devoted to create a vital
wine society for the passionate consumer, the oenophile, as
well as for the industry professionals. Members are wine
importers and merchants, restaurant owners, caterers and
others. Membership: $150 (Students); $600 (Businesses/
Trade Associate).*

Songwriters Guild of America *(1931)*
5120 Virginia Way
Suite C22
Brentwood, TN 37027
Tel: (615) 742-9945 *Fax:* (615) 630-7501
TollFree: (800) 524-6742
E-Mail: nash@songwritersguild.com
Website: songwritersguild.com
Members: 4500 individuals
Staff: 20
Annual Budget: $250-500,000

Personnel:
President: Rick Carnes
Central Regional Project Manager: Kimberly Maiers Shaw
  E-Mail: kshaw@songwritersguild.com

Historical Note:
*Formerly called as Songwriters Protective Association
and American Guild of Authors and Composers, SGA's
mission is to promote, advance and benefit the profession
of songwriters. Membership: $60 (Gold); $84 (Platinum);
$225 (Diamond).*

Publications:
e-newsletter; monthly
SGA newsletter; bi-annually

Sorptive Minerals Institute *(1970)*
1155 15th St. NW
Suite 500
Washington, DC 20005
Tel: (202) 289-2760 *Fax:* (202) 530-0659
E-Mail: lcoogan@navista.net
Website: sorptive.org
Members: 11 companies
Staff: 4
Annual Budget: $100-250,000
Tax: 501(c)(6)

Personnel:
Executive Director: Lee Coogan
  E-Mail: lcoogan@navista.net

Historical Note:
*SMI is a not-for-profit industry trade association that would
serve as the marketing, promotion and research arm of the
absorbent clay industry with the goal of enhancing long-
range growth and profitability. Membership is based on
tonnage.*

South Asian Journalists Association *(1994)*
Columbia University, School of Journalism Lerner
Hall, 2950 Broadwy.
Room 705
New York, NY 10027
Tel: (212) 854-5979 *Fax:* (212) 854-7837
E-Mail: saja@columbia.edu
Website: saja.org
Members: 350 individuals
Staff: 3
Annual Budget: Under $10,000
Tax: 501(c)(3)

Personnel:
President: Anusha Shrivastava
    E-Mail: president@saja.org
Treasurer: John Laxmi
    E-Mail: treasurer@saja.org
Co-Founder: Sreenath Sreenivasan
    E-Mail: sree@sree.net

Historical Note:
The South Asian Journalists Association (SAJA) is a non-profit organization that provides a networking and resource forum for journalists of South Asian origin and journalists interested in South Asia or the South Asian Diaspora. Members are journalists of South Asian origin. Membership: $40 (Full Member/Associate); $20 (Student); $300 (Full Life/Associate Life).

Publications:
Public Member Directory

Membership List Available to Non-members

Southeastern Livestock Network (2009)
176 Pasadena Dr.
Lexington, KY 40503
Tel: (859) 278-0899 *Fax:* (859) 260-2060
E-Mail: info@slnllc.com
Website: slnllc.com
Staff: 3
Annual Budget: $500-1,000,000

Personnel:
Director, Industry Relations: Jim Collins
    E-Mail: jcollins@slnllc.com

Historical Note:
The primary purpose of the Southeastern Livestock Network, LLC is to represent the interests of regional livestock producers in the regulatory and legislative arenas that impact their ability to manage and market their animals and to provide data management services for cattlemen, auction markets, order buyers, and the beef industry.

Southeastern Theatre Conference (1949)
1175 Revolution Mill Dr.
Suite 14
Greensboro, NC 27405
Tel: (336) 272-3645 *Fax:* (336) 272-8810
Website: setc.org
Staff: 10
Annual Budget: $1-2,000,000

Personnel:
Executive Director: Betsey Baun
    E-Mail: Betsey@setc.org
Program Associate: Quiana Clark-Roland
    E-Mail: Quiana@setc.org
Administrative Assistant: Riley Driver
    E-Mail: riley@setc.org
Manager, Communications and Marketing: Judi Rossabi
    E-Mail: Judi@setc.org
Accounts Receivable & Professional Services Associate:
    Mark Snyder
    E-Mail: Mark@setc.org
Coordinator, Educational Theatre Services: Claire
    Wisniewski
    E-Mail: Claire@setc.org

Historical Note:
SETC is the strongest and broadest network of theatre practitioners in the United States. Provide extensive resources and year-round opportunities for their constituents. SETC connects individuals to opportunities in Theatre. Membership: $70 (Individual/Organization); $40 (Student); $50 (Senior Discount); $1200 (Life).

Meetings/Conferences: Annual
Conference Chair: Quiana Clark-Roland
2013 - Louisville, KY (Galt House Hotel)/March 6 - 10

Publications:
Membership Directory; on-line
SETC News; bi-monthly
Southern Theatre Magazine; quarterly; adv.
Theatre Symposium; annually

Southern Cypress Manufacturers Association
(1905)
665 Rodi Rd.
Suite 305
Pittsburgh, PA 15235
Tel: (412) 323-9320
Website: cypressinfo.org
Members: 15 companies
Staff: 2
Annual Budget: $25-50,000

Personnel:
President: Chuck Harris
Media Contact: Ian Faight

Historical Note:
SCMA acts as a national clearinghouse for information on construction applications of cypress products.

Publications:
e-Newsletter; on-line

Southern Shrimp Alliance (2002)
P.O. Box 1577
Tarpon Springs, FL 34688
Tel: (727) 934-5090
E-Mail: info@shrimpalliance.com
Website: shrimpalliance.com
Staff: 3
Annual Budget: $250-500,000

Personnel:
Executive Director: John Williams
Contact, Media Relations: Deborah Long
    E-Mail: Deborah@CohesiveCommunications.com

Historical Note:
SSA's mission is to ensure the continued vitality and existence of the U.S. shrimp industry. Members are shrimp fishermen and shrimp processors. Membership: $25 (Supporting); $100 (Small Vessel); $200 (Large Vessel); $300 (Associate).

Publications:
SSA Newsletter

Southwest Airlines Pilots Association (1978)
Brookview Plaza, 1450 Empire Central
Suite 737
Dallas, TX 75247
Tel: (214) 722-4200 *Fax:* (214) 350-0647
TollFree: (800) 969-7972
Website: swapa.org
Members: 6,100 pilots
Staff: 26
Annual Budget: $10-25,000,000
Tax: 501(c)(5)

Personnel:
Second Vice President: Jason L. Pettit
Director, Communications: Neal Hanks
    E-Mail: nhanks@swapa.org

Historical Note:
Trade union representing the pilots of Southwest Airlines. Provides a members only login and union press releases.

Souvenir Wholesale Distributors Association
(1973)
2105 Laurel Bush Rd.
Suite 200
Bel Air, MD 21015
Tel: (443) 640-1055 *Fax:* (443) 640-1031
E-Mail: swda@ksgroup.org
Website: souvenircentral.org
Members: 110 companies
Staff: 3
Annual Budget: $50-100,000
Tax: 501(c)(6)

Personnel:
Executive Vice President: Marci L. Hickey CMP
    E-Mail: marci@ksgroup.org
Financial Director: Debbie Dacre
    E-Mail: debbie@kingmgmt.org

Historical Note:
Formerly Post Card Distributors Association of North America and changed its name to Post Card and Souvenir Distributors Association (PCSDA) in 2000. Assumed its present name in 2008. Mission of SWDA is to promote the distribution of souvenirs by providing education, networking opportunities and access to vendors. Membership $375 (Distributor); $275 (Supplier).

Meetings/Conferences: Annual
2013 - Las Vegas, NV (SpringHill Suites Las Vegas
    Convention Center)/Sept. 14 - 16

Publications:
Membership Directory; on-line
SWDA Today newsletter; quarterly

Souvenirs, Gifts and Novelties Trade Association
(1962)
10 E. Athens Ave.
Suite 208
Ardmore, PA 19003
Tel: (610) 645-6940 *Fax:* (610) 645-6943

E-Mail: info@sgnmag.com
Website: sgnmag.com
Members: 1900 individuals
Staff: 10
Annual Budget: $500-1,000,000

Personnel:
President and Executive Editor: Scott C. Borowsky
    E-Mail: editorsgnmag@kanec.com
Accounts Executive: Mitchell Pfeffer

Historical Note:
Association covers the gift, souvenir and sporty merchandise industry.

Meetings/Conferences: Annual
2013 - Houston, TX (George R. Brown Convention
    Center)/Jan. 19 - 22

Publications:
Career Center Bulletin; monthly; adv.
EMail Reports; weekly; adv.
SGN Newsletter
Souvenirs, Gifts & Novelties Magazine; bi-monthly;
    adv.
Souvenirs, Gifts and Novelties Magazine; adv.

Soyfoods Association of North America (1978)
1050 17th St. NW
Suite 600
Washington, DC 20036
Tel: (202) 659-3520 *Fax:* (202) 659-3522
E-Mail: info@soyfoods.org
Website: soyfoods.org
Members: 48 companies
Staff: 2
Annual Budget: $500-1,000,000

Personnel:
Executive Director: Nancy Chapman

Historical Note:
Assumed its current name in 1997, SANA is an advocate for information about the health benefits and nutritional advantages of soy consumption. Members are large and small soyfoods companies, growers and suppliers of soybeans, nutritionists, equipment representatives, food scientists, and retailers.SANA's mission is to provide information about the health benefits and nutritional advantages of soy consumption Membership: $250-35,000/year.

Meetings/Conferences: Annual
Number of non-conference events/year: 1

Publications:
Membership Directory
Update; monthly

Space Transportation Association (1989)
4305 Underwood St.
University Park, MD 20782
Tel: (703) 855-3917
Website: spacetransportation.us
Members: 20 organizations
Staff: 1
Annual Budget: $250-500,000

Personnel:
President: Richard Coleman
    E-Mail: rich@spacetransportation.us

Historical Note:
STA supports policies that advance robust, affordable space transportation for NASA, DOD, and commercial markets. The association's corporate members are launch manufacturers and launch service providers.

The Spain-United States Chamber of Commerce
(1959)
Empire State Building
350 Fifth Ave., Suite 2600
New York, NY 10118
Tel: (212) 967-2170 *Fax:* (212) 564-1415
E-Mail: info@spainuscc.org
Website: spainuscc.org
Members: 400 companies
Staff: 5
Annual Budget: $500-1,000,000

Personnel:
Executive Director: Gemma Cortijo
    E-Mail: gcortijo@spainuscc.org
*Manager, Professional Exchange Program and Events
    Department:* Sandra Martin
Professional Exchange Program and Office Manager:
    Maria Padilla

Historical Note:
The Spain-United States Chamber of Commerce is a forum for fostering business and commerce between Spain and the U.S. Members are some of the most influential companies in the world of business, commerce, and investment. Membership: $100-1,500/year.

Meetings/Conferences: Annual
Conference Chair: Sandra Martin

Publications:
Newsletter; monthly; adv.
The Business Link; semi-annually; adv.

Spanish Barb Horse Association *(1972)*
P.O. Box 1628
Silver City, NM 88062
E-Mail: info@spanishbarb.com
Website: spanishbarb.com
Members: 125 individuals
Staff: 3
Annual Budget: Under $10,000

Personnel:
President: Steve Dobrott
Treasurer: Maggie Engler

Historical Note:
Formerly known as the Spanish Barb Breeders Association (SBBA). SBHA's mission is the preservation, perpetuation and promotion of the Spanish Barb Horse. Members are owners and breeders of Spanish-Barb horses. Membership: $15 (Individual); $20 (Family); $25 (Owner/Breeder).

Publications:
SBHA Newsletter; semi-annually

SPARC *(1997)*
21 Dupont Cir. NW
Suite 800
Washington, DC 20036
Tel: (202) 296-2296 *Fax:* (202) 872-0884
Website: arl.org/sparc
Staff: 5
Annual Budget: $500-1,000,000

Personnel:
Executive Director: Heather Joseph
    E-Mail: heather@arl.org
Manager, Communications: Andrea Brusca
    Higginbotham
    E-Mail: andrea@arl.org
Programs and Operations Associate: Stacie Lemick
    E-Mail: stacie@arl.org

Historical Note:
SPARC, the Scholarly Publishing and Academic Resources Coalition, is an international alliance of academic and research libraries working to correct imbalances in the scholarly publishing system. Its pragmatic focus is to stimulate the emergence of new scholarly communication models that expand the dissemination of scholarly research and reduce financial pressures on libraries.

Publications:
SPARC Open Access Newsletter; monthly

Special Care Dentistry *(1998)*
401 N. Michigan Ave.
Suite 2200
Chicago, IL 60611
Tel: (312) 527-6764 *Fax:* (312) 673-6663
E-Mail: scda@scdaonline.org
Website: scdonline.org
Members: 550 individuals
Staff: 3
Annual Budget: $500-1,000,000

Personnel:
Executive Director: Meghan Carey
    E-Mail: mcarey@smithbucklin.com
Associate, Membership Services: Elizabeth Allen
    E-Mail: eallen@smithbucklin.com
Operations Manager: Kate Martinez
    E-Mail: kmartinez@smithbucklin.com

Historical Note:
SCDA's mission is to act as a central focus for diverse individuals and groups with a common interest in oral health for people with special needs and direct its resources accordingly. Membership: $285 (Regular); $60-70 (Resident/Student); $85 (Retired); $20 (Student Network Membership); $165 (Supporting Associate).

Meetings/Conferences: Annual
2013 - New Orleans, LA (Astor Crowne Plaza New Orleans)/April 18 - 21
Number of non-conference events/year: 1

Publications:
SCDA Journal; adv.

Special Care Dentistry Association
401 N. Michigan Ave.
Suite 2200
Chicago, IL 60611
Tel: (312) 527-6764 *Fax:* (312) 673-6663
E-Mail: scda@scdaonline.org
Website: scdonline.org
Members: 1500 individuals
Staff: 3
Annual Budget: $500-1,000,000

Personnel:
Executive Director: Meghan Carey
    E-Mail: mcarey@scdaonline.org
Associate, Membership Services: Elizabeth Allen
    E-Mail: eallen@smithbucklin.com
Manager, Operations: Kate Martinez
    E-Mail: kmartinez@smithbucklin.com

Historical Note:
SCDA bring together professionals from the American Association of Hospital Dentists (AAHD), the Academy of Dentistry for Persons with Disabilities (ADPD) and the American Society for Geriatric Dentistry (ASGD).Because many of the goals and activities of these three practice areas overlap, the component groups joined forces and formed SCDA.It acts as a central focus for diverse individuals and groups with a common interest in oral health for people with special needs and direct its resources accordingly.Membership: $60-255/year.

Continuing Education:
Certification Designation/s: CDE

Meetings/Conferences: Annual
2013 - New Orleans, LA (Astor Crowne Plaza Hotel)/
April 18 - 21

Publications:
Interface newsletter; quarterly; adv.
Special Care in Dentistry Journal; bi-monthly; adv.

Special Event Sites Marketing Alliance *(2002)*
P.O. Box 332
Bel Air, MD 21014
Tel: (443) 617-2191 *Fax:* (410) 420-8679
E-Mail: info@sesma.org
Website: sesma.org
Members: 100 properties and companies
Staff: 3
Annual Budget: $50-100,000
Tax: 501 (c)(6)

Personnel:
Executive Director: Gina Kazimir
    E-Mail: gina@sesma.org
Events and Meetings Manager: Peggy Martz
Managing Director, Conferences and Events: Andrew Osborne
    E-Mail: andrew.osborne@houseofsweden.com

Historical Note:
SESMA's mission is to develop cooperative marketing programs that bring its members' special event sites to the attention of the meeting/event professionals and wedding planners throughout the country who seek unique venues for their functions. Membership: $500 (Primary Member-Event Site); $600 (Associate) $150 (Affiliate).

Meetings/Conferences:
Conference Chair: Andrew Osborne

Publications:
SESMA Newsletter; quarterly

Special Interest Group for Algorithm and Computation Theory
251 Mercer St.
New York, NY 10012-1185
Tel: (212) 998-3119 *Fax:* (212) 995-4124
Website: sigact.acm.org
Members: 2220 individuals
Staff: 2
Annual Budget: $250-500,000

Personnel:
Editor: Brendan Mumey
    E-Mail: editor.sigact@sigact.acm.org
Secretary and Treasurer: Tal Rabin
    E-Mail: secretary.sigact@sigact.acm.org

Historical Note:
Formerly (1992) Special Interest Group for Automata and Computability Theory. SIGACT's mission is to foster and promote the discovery and dissemination of high quality research in theoretical computer science (TCS), the

formal analysis of efficient computation and computational processes. Membership: $9-213/year.

Publications:
SIGACT News; quarterly; adv.

Special Interest Group for Architecture of Computer Systems
1210 W. Dayton St.
Madison, WI 53726
Tel: (608) 263-7463
E-Mail: infodir_sigarch@acm.org
Website: sigarch.org
Members: 3600 individuals
Staff: 4

Personnel:
Chair: David A. Wood
    E-Mail: chair_SIGARCH@acm.org
Editor: Doug DeGroot
    E-Mail: editors_SIGARCH@acm.org
Director, Information Services: Kevin Lim
    E-Mail: infodir_SIGARCH@acm.org

Historical Note:
SIGARCH's mission is to promote the interest of its members by affording opportunity for discussion of problems of common interest. A semi-autonomous subsidiary of the Association for Computing Machinery, SIGARCH members' specialty is the architecture of computer systems. Membership: $99-198 (Professional); $19-62 (Student).

Publications:
SIGARCH Newsletter; quarterly

Special Interest Group for Computer Science Education *(1970)*
C/O College of Charleston
66 George St.
Charleston, SC 29424
Tel: (843) 805-5507
Website: sigcse.org
Members: 2000 individuals
Staff: 3
Annual Budget: $25-50,000

Personnel:
Chair: Renee McCauley
    E-Mail: chair@sigcse.org

Historical Note:
SIGCSE, a semi-autonomous subsidiary of the Association for Computing Machinery, provides a forum for the problems common among college educators involved in computer science programs. Membership: $25 (Professional Member); $8 (Student).

Meetings/Conferences: Annual
Conference Chair: Dorothea Heck
2013 - Denver, CO (The Sheraton Downtown)/March
6 - 9

Publications:
SIGCSE Bulletin; quarterly

Special Interest Group for Computer-Human Interaction *(1972)*
P.O. Box 30777
New York, NY 10087-0777
Website: sigchi.org
Members: 5700 individuals
Staff: 6
Annual Budget: $2-5,000,000

Personnel:
President: Gerrit van der Veer
    E-Mail: sigchi-president@acm.org
Vice President, Conferences: John "Scooter" Morris
    E-Mail: sigchi-VP-Conferences@acm.org
Vice President, Publications: Dan Olsen
    E-Mail: sigchi-VP-Publications@acm.org
Vice President, Finance: Gary Olson
    E-Mail: sigchi-VP-Finances@acm.org
Vice President, Operations: Fred Sampson
    E-Mail: sigchi-VP-Operations@acm.org

Historical Note:
SIGCHI is a semi-autonomous subsidiary of the Association for Computing Machinery. Formerly (1982) the Special Interest Group for Social and Behavioral Science Computing. SIGCHI is concerned with the study of the human-computer interaction process and with research and development efforts leading to the design and evaluation of user interfaces. Membership: $30 (ACM Member); $57 (Non-ACM).

Meetings/Conferences: Annual
Conference Chair: John "Scooter" Morris

2013 - Paris, France/April 27 - May 2
2014 - Toronto, ON/April 26 - May 1

Publications:
interactions; bi-monthly; adv.
Membership Directory; on-line
SIGCHI Bulletin; on-line

Membership List Available to Non-members

Special Interest Group for Computers and Society
(1972)
C/O Association for Computing Machinery
P.O. Box 30777
New York, NY 10087-0777
Tel: (212) 626-0500 *Fax:* (212) 944-1318
TollFree: (800) 342-6626
Website: sigcas.org
Members: 800 individuals
Staff: 1
Annual Budget: $10-25,000

Personnel:
Chair: Andrew A. Adams
    E-Mail: chair_sigcas@acm.org

Historical Note:
SIGCAS was created by the Association for Computing Machinery in 1969 and given permanent status in 1972. SIGCAS's mission is to raise the awareness about the impact that technology has on society, and to support the efforts of those who are involved in this important work. Membership: $20 (ACM member); $56 (Non-ACM).

Publications:
Computers and Society Magazine; quarterly
SIGCAS Newsletter; irregular

Special Interest Group for Data Communication
(1970)
1414 Massachusetts Ave.
Boxborough, MA 01719
Website: sigcomm.org
Members: 5000 individuals
Staff: 4
Annual Budget: $100-250,000

Personnel:
Chair: Bruce S. Davie
    E-Mail: bdavie@mit.edu

Historical Note:
SIGCOMM provides a forum for research and development in computer communications with a special focus on networks and network applications. A semi-autonomous subsidiary of the Association for Computing Machinery. Membership: $19-62/year (Student).

Meetings/Conferences: Annual
Conference Chair: Jaudelice Cavalcante de Oliveira
2013 - Hong Kong, China (Chinese University of Hong Kong)/Aug. 12 - 16

Publications:
Computer Communication Review
SIGCOMM Newsletter; quarterly

Special Interest Group for Design of Communication *(1975)*
Two Penn Plaza
Suite 701
New York, NY 10121-0701
E-Mail: frawley@hq.acm.org
Website: sigdoc.org
Members: 1050 individuals
Staff: 4
Annual Budget: $500-1,000,000

Personnel:
Chair: Rob Pierce
Secretary and Treasurer: Kathie Gossett
Newsletter Editor, Vice Chair: Liza Potts
Director, Information: Ashley Williams
    E-Mail: ashleyw@acm.org

Historical Note:
Formerly (2003) Special Interest Group on Documentation, SIGDOC is a semi-autonomous subsidiary of the Association for Computing Machinery. SIGDOC's mission is to promote the professional development of its members and encourage interdisciplinary problem solving related to online and print documentation and to communication technologies. Membership: $35 (ACM Member); $45 (Non-ACM Member) $19 (Student Membership) $99 (ACM Proffesional Membership)

Meetings/Conferences: Annual
2013 - Greenville, NC (East Carolina University Heart Institute)/Feb. 25 - 26

Publications:
Membership Directory; quarterly
Newsletter; quarterly; adv.

Special Interest Group for Information Retrieval
(1966)
100 Bureau Dr.
Mail Stop 8940
Gaithersburg, MD 20899-8940
E-Mail: infodir_sigir@acm.org
Website: sigir.org
Members: 1250 individuals
Staff: 1
Annual Budget: $100-250,000

Personnel:
Treasurer: Ian Soboroff

Historical Note:
SIGIR members work in all aspects of information storage, retrieval and dissemination including research strategies, output schemes and system evaluation. Of special note is SIGIR's involvement with the National Science Foundation's initiative to form a National Electronic Science, Engineering, and Technology Library. A semi-autonomous subsidiary of the Association for Computing Machinery. Membership: $30/year (ACM member), $65/year (non-ACM); $15/year (student).

Meetings/Conferences:
2013 - Rome, Italy (Auditorium Antonianum)/Feb. 4 - 8
2013 - Moscow, Russia (Higher School of Economics)/ March 24 - 27
2013 - Dublin, Ireland (The Mansion House)/July 28 - Aug. 1

Publications:
D-Lib Magazine; on-line
International Journal of Cooperative Information Systems (IJCIS)
International Journal of Intelligent Systems
International Journal of Uncertainty, Fuzziness and Knowledge-Based Systems (IJUFKS)
International Journal on Digital Libraries
International Journal on Document Analysis and Recognition
Journal of Documentation (JDoc)
Journal of Intelligent Information Systems (JIIS)
Journal of the American Society for Information Science and Technology (JASIST)
Membership Directory; on-line
SIGIR Forum Newsletter; on-line

Special Interest Group for Measurement and Evaluation *(1971)*
2 Penn Plaza
Suite 701
New York, NY 10121-0701
Website: sigmetrics.org
Members: 1900 individuals
Staff: 1
Annual Budget: $25-50,000

Personnel:
President: Alain Chesnais

Historical Note:
SIGMETRICS provides a forum for those interested in the measurement and evaluation of computer system performance. A semi-autonomous subsidiary of the Association for Computing Machinery (ACM). Membership: $20/year (ACM member), $25/year (non-ACM).

Special Interest Group for Teacher Educators
1151 S. Forest Ave.
Tempe, AZ 85281
Website: iste.org/connect/special-interest-groups/sig-d
Staff: 3

Personnel:
President: Teresa Foulger
    E-Mail: teresa.foulger@asu.edu

Historical Note:
SIGTE serves professors and other professionals focused on teacher education with a peer-reviewed journal and other venues that address inservice training, research in computer education, and appropriate training materials. Members include higher education faculty teaching in graduate and undergraduate programs, graduate students, K–12 teachers, administrators, information technology specialists, and curriculum specialists teaching and conducting research in teacher preparation and instructional technology.

Special Interest Group for Technology Coordinators
1710 Rhode Island Ave. NW
Suite 900
Washington, DC 20036
Tel: (202) 861-7777 *Fax:* (202) 861-0888
Website: iste.org/connect/special-interest-groups/sig-d
Staff: 3

Personnel:
President: Bret Gensburg
Communications Officer: Jeffery Thomas
Contact, Newsletter: Tammy Vaugh
    E-Mail: tvaught64@clemson.edu

Historical Note:
SIGTC is a professional organization that helps technology coordinators meet the challenges of their rapidly changing field. It also addresses current legislation and advancements in technology leadership.

Publications:
Newsletter

Special Interest Group for University and College Computing Services *(1962)*
Two Penn Plaza
Suite 701
New York, NY 10121-0701
Tel: (212) 626-0500 *Fax:* (212) 944-1318
E-Mail: infodir_siguccs@acm.org
Website: siguccs.org
Members: 550 individuals
Staff: 4
Annual Budget: $100-250,000

Personnel:
Program Coordinator: Irene Frawley

Historical Note:
Formerly (1984) the Special Interest Group for University Computing Centers, SIGUCCS is a semi-autonomous subsidiary of the Association for Computing Machinery. SIGUCCS's mission is to support the professional development of those involved in the support, delivery, management, and leadership of information technology services in higher education. Membership: $25 (Professional Member).

Meetings/Conferences: Annual
Conference Chair: Irene Frawley
2013 - Chicago, IL (Holiday Inn Mart Plaza)/Nov. 3 - 8

Publications:
SIGUCCS Newsletter

Special Interest Group on Accessible Computing
(1970)
C/O Association for Computing Machinery
Two Penn Plaza, Suite 701
New York, NY 10121-0701
Tel: (212) 626-0500 *Fax:* (212) 944-1318
TollFree: (800) 342-6626
E-Mail: acmhelp@acm.org
Website: sigaccess.org
Members: 250 individuals
Staff: 4
Annual Budget: $10-25,000
Tax: 501(c)(3)

Personnel:
Secretary and Treasurer: Shari Trewin
    E-Mail: treasurer_sigaccess@acm.org
Information Director: Jeffrey P. Bigham
    E-Mail: infodir_sigaccess@acm.org
Editor: Jinjuan Heidi Feng
    E-Mail: editors_sigaccess@acm.org
Director, Programs: Irene Frawley
    E-Mail: frawley@hq.acm.org

Historical Note:
Formerly (1978) the Special Interest Committee for Computers and the Physically Handicapped, and (2004) the Special Interest Group for Accessible Computing. SIGACCESS promotes the professional interests of computing personnel with disabilities and the application of computing and information technology in solving relevant disability problems. Membership: $20/year (ACM Member).

Meetings/Conferences: Annual

Publications:
Accessibility & Computing; quarterly
SIGACCESS Newsletter

Special Interest Group on Ada Programming Language *(1981)*

1155 Academy Park Loop
Colorado Springs, CO 80910
Tel: (703) 845-6666 *Fax:* (703) 845-6848
E-Mail: clyderoby@acm.org
Website: sigada.org
Members: 1000 individuals
Staff: 5
Annual Budget: $100-250,000

Personnel:
Chairman: Ricky E. Sward
　E-Mail: RSward@MITRE.Org

Historical Note:
SIGAda is a semi-autonomous subsidiary of the Association for Computing Machinery. Operates exclusively for educational, scientific, and technical purposes like collecting and disseminating information in the specialty, through a newsletter and other publications approved by the publications board of the ACM. Membership: $25 (Professional); $10 (Student).

Meetings/Conferences:
Conference Chair: Irene Frawley
2013 - Berlin, Germany/June 10 - 14

Publications:
ADA Letter; annually

Membership List Available to Non-members

Special Interest Group on Applied Computing
801 Leroy Pl.
Socorro, NM 87801
Website: sigapp.org
Members: 400 individuals
Staff: 2

Personnel:
Treasurer: Lorie M. Liebrock
　E-Mail: liebrock@cs.nmt.edu

Historical Note:
SIGAPP is a forum for the exchange of information on advanced and unique computing applications which involve the integration of such traditional computing disciplines as graphics, database, communication, software engineering, artificial intelligence, and office automation with emerging technologies like neural networks, logic and symbolic programming, expert systems, image information systems, parallel processing and object oriented programming. SIGAPP is a semi-autonomous subsidiary of the Association for Computing Machinery. Membership: $15/year (ACM member).

Special Interest Group on Artificial Intelligence
(1966)
Two Penn Plaza
Suite 701
New York, NY 10121-0701
Tel: (212) 626-0605 *Fax:* (212) 302-5826
E-Mail: frawley@acm.org
Website: sigart.org
Members: 2700 individuals
Staff: 3
Annual Budget: $50-100,000

Personnel:
Treasurer: Gautam Biswas
　E-Mail: treasurer_sigart@acm.org
Contact, Communications: Irene Frawley
　E-Mail: frawley@acm.org
Information Officer: Weike Pan
　E-Mail: infodir_sigart@acm.org

Historical Note:
SIGART's mission is to understand and apply the principles and mechanisms underlying intelligent behavior. Promotes meetings and discussions on artificial intelligence. SIGART is a subsidiary of the Association for Computing Machinery. Membership: $25 (ACM/Non-ACM Member); $11 (ACM/Non-ACM Student).

Publications:
SIGART Bulletin and Intelligence Magazine

Special Interest Group on Hypertext/Hypermedia
Two Penn Plaza
Suite 701
New York, NY 10121-0701
Tel: (212) 626-0605
E-Mail: infodir_sigweb@acm.org
Website: sigweb.org
Members: 700 individuals
Staff: 1
Annual Budget: $100-250,000

Personnel:
Coordinator, Programs: Irene Frawley

Historical Note:
An affiliate of Association for Computing Machinery that provides administrative support, SIGWEB addresses the concerns of the multi-disciplinary fields of hypertext and hypermedia. Membership: $30 (ACM /Non-ACM Member); $19 (Student).

Meetings/Conferences:
Number of non-conference events/year: 2

Publications:
Bibliometrics

Special Interest Group on Management Information Systems *(1960)*
College of Business and Economics
University of Wisconsin Whitewater
Whitewater, WI 53190
Tel: (262) 472-7034
E-Mail: ignatoff@hq.acm.org
Website: sigmis.org
Members: 1250 individuals
Staff: 2
Annual Budget: $100-250,000

Personnel:
Secretary and Treasurer: Christina Outlay
　E-Mail: outlayc@uww.edu

Historical Note:
Formerly (1993) the Special Interest Group on Business Data Processing and Management and (1995) Special Interest Group on Business Information Technology. SIGMIS merge with the Special Interest Group on Computer Personnel Research(SIGCPR). SIGMIS is a semi-autonomous subsidiary of the Association for Computing Machinery. SIGMIS's mission is to promote best practice, research, education in information systems and technologies for management and the management of information systems and technologies to increase the value of these resources to management. Members are primarily interested in information systems and technologies for management and the management of these systems and technologies. Membership: $29 (ACM Member); $49 (Non-ACM Member); $19 (Student).

Meetings/Conferences: Annual
2013 - Cincinnati, OH/May 30 - June 1

Publications:
DATA BASE; quarterly; adv.

Special Interest Group on Management of Data *(1976)*
University of Pittsburgh
Pittsburgh, PA 15260-9161
Tel: (412) 624-8843
Website: sigmod.org
Members: 2500 individuals
Staff: 4

Personnel:
Treasurer: Alexandros Labrinidis
　E-Mail: labrinid@cs.pitt.edu
Coordinator, Conferences: K. Selçuk Candan
Director, Information Services: Curtis Dyreson
Editor: Ioana Manolescu

Historical Note:
SIGMOD is concerned with the development, management and evaluation of database technology. Formerly (1973) Special Interest Group for File Description and Translation. A semi-autonomous subsidiary of the Association for Computing Machinery. Membership: $20/year (ACM member); $15/year (Professional non-ACM member); $10 (Student non-ACM member).

Meetings/Conferences: Annual
Conference Chair: K. Selçuk Candan

Special Interest Group on Mobility of Systems, Users, Data and Computing *(1995)*
C/O Intel Labs Santa Clara, 2200 Mission College Blvd.
Mail-Stop:RN6-61
Santa Clara, CA 95052-8819
Tel: (408) 765-9204 *Fax:* (408) 653-9861
Website: sigmobile.org
Staff: 3

Personnel:
Director, Information Technology: Dr. Robert Steele
　E-Mail: robert.steele@sydney.edu.au

Historical Note:
SIGMOBILE, a semi-autonomous subsidiary of the Association for Computing Machinery, is concerned with issues involving the mobility of systems, users, data and computing. Membership: $30 (Non-ACM Members); $20 (Student).

Meetings/Conferences: Annual
Conference Chair: Fran Spinola
2013 - Taipei, Taiwan/June 25 - 28

Publications:
Mobile Computing and Communications Review (MC2R); quarterly; adv.
SIGMOBILE E-News

Special Interest Group on Operating Systems *(1965)*
Two Penn Plaza
Suite 701
New York, NY 10121-0701
Tel: (212) 626-0603
Website: sigops.org
Members: 3000 individuals
Staff: 4
Annual Budget: $50-100,000

Personnel:
Director, Information: Muli Ben-Yehuda
　E-Mail: muli@cs.technion.ac.il
Treasurer: Dilma Da Silva
　E-Mail: dilmasilva@us.ibm.com
Program Coordinator: Fran Spinola
　E-Mail: spinola@hq.acm.org

Historical Note:
SIGOPS is a semi-autonomous subsidiary of the Association for Computing Machinery. Concerned with computer operating systems and architecture for multiprogramming, multiprocessing, time-sharing, and networking; distributed computing systems resource management; evaluation and stimulation; reliability, integrity, and security of data; and communications among computing processes. Membership: $15 (Professional); $5 (Student).

Publications:
Operating Systems Review; quarterly

Special Interest Group on Security, Audit, and Control *(1981)*
890 Oval Dr.
3320 Engineering Building II
Raleigh, NC 27695-8206
Tel: (919) 513-4457 *Fax:* (919) 515-7896
Website: sigsac.org
Members: 789 individuals
Staff: 1
Annual Budget: $100-250,000

Personnel:
Secretary and Treasurer: Peng Ning
　E-Mail: pning@ncsu.edu

Historical Note:
SIGSAC's mission is to develop the information security profession by sponsoring quality research conferences and workshops. Membership: $9-225/year.

Meetings/Conferences: Annual

Publications:
SIGSAC Annual Report; annually

Special Interest Group on Software Engineering
2 Penn Plaza
Suite 701
New York, NY 10121-0701
Tel: (212) 626-0603 *Fax:* (212) 302-5826
Website: sigsoft.org/
Members: 6000 individuals
Staff: 2
Annual Budget: $250-500,000

Personnel:
Chair, Editor: Will Tracz
Information Director: Greg Cooper
　E-Mail: infodir_sigsoft@acm.org

Historical Note:
SIGSOFT is a semi-autonomous subsidiary of the Association for Computing Machinery. SIGSOFT is concerned with techniques and principles involved in the production of high quality software for practical application including solutions to problems inherent in program development, system design methodology, debugging, documentation, portability of programs, program validation and quality assurance. Membership: $12-$25/year

Publications:
ACM Journals
ACM Magazines
ACM SIGSOFT newsletter.; bi-monthly

Special Libraries Association *(1909)*

331 S. Patrick St.
Alexandria, VA 22314-3501
Tel: (703) 647-4900 *Fax:* (703) 647-4901
E-Mail: sla@sla.org
Website: sla.org
Members: 15000 individuals
Staff: 21
Annual Budget: $5-10,000,000
Tax: 501(c)(3)

Personnel:
Chief Executive Officer: Janice R. Lachance
    E-Mail: janice@sla.org
Chief Financial Officer: Linda Broussard
    E-Mail: lbroussard@sla.org
Director, Membership Services: Paula Diaz
    E-Mail: pdiaz@sla.org
Senior Writer and Editor: Stuart C. Hales
    E-Mail: shales@sla.org
Director, Marketing and Exhibits: Jeff Leach
    E-Mail: jleach@sla.org
Chief Technology Officer: Quan O. Logan
    E-Mail: qlogan@sla.org
Manager, Events: Caroline Rives
    E-Mail: crives@sla.org
Director, Education and Information Services: Carolyn
    Sosnowski
    E-Mail: csosnowski@sla.org
Manager, Communications and Marketing: John Walsh
    E-Mail: jwalsh@sla.org

Historical Note:
*A member of the Council of National Library and
Information Associations and the International Federation
of Library Associations and Institutions. Incorporated in
Rhode Island in 1928 and later in New York in 1959.
SLA's mission is to promote and strengthen its members
through learning, advocacy and networking initiatives.
Membership: $40-200 (Full, based on annual salary);
$750 (Organizational); $40 (Student).*

Meetings/Conferences: Annual
Conference Chair: Caroline Rives
2013 - San Diego, CA/June 9 - 12
2013 - San Diego, CA/June 9 - 11
2014 - Vancouver, BC/June 8 - 11
2014 - Vancouver, BC/June 8 - 10
2015 - Boston, MA/June 14 - 17
2015 - Boston, MA/June 14 - 16

Publications:
Connections; on-line
Membership Directory; on-line
SLA Newsletter; on-line

Membership List Available to Non-members

Specialized Carriers and Rigging Association
(1948)
2750 Prosperity Ave.
Suite 620
Fairfax, VA 22031-4312
Tel: (703) 698-0291 *Fax:* (703) 698-0297
E-Mail: info@scranet.org
Website: scranet.org
Members: 1300 members
Staff: 12
Annual Budget: $2-5,000,000
Tax: 501(c)(6)

Personnel:
Executive Vice President: Joel M. Dandrea
    E-Mail: jdandrea@scranet.org
Manager, Membership Services: Patrick Corr
    E-Mail: pcorr@scranet.org
Director, Web and Information Technology: Kurt Hoffman
    E-Mail: khoffman@scranet.org
Director, Finance and Administration: Lisa Lieu
    E-Mail: llieu@scranet.org
Meetings Manager: Christine Montgomery
    E-Mail: cmontgomery@scranet.org
Director, Marketing and Foundation Manager: Jackie
    Roskos
    E-Mail: jroskos@scranet.org
Contact, Publications: Pat Sharkey
    E-Mail: pat.sharkey@khl.com
Manager, Communications: Terry White
    E-Mail: twhite@scranet.org

Historical Note:
*Established as the Heavy Specialized Carriers Section-
Local Cartage National Conference, SC&RA became
the Heavy Specialized Carriers Conference in 1959 and
assumed its present name in 1981. SC&RA's purpose*

*is to help members run businesses by monitoring and
affecting pending legislation and regulatory policies at the
state and national levels. Members are carriers, crane and
rigging operators and millwrights engaged in the lifting and
transport of heavy goods. Membership: $595/year (Full).*

Meetings/Conferences:
Conference Chair: Christine Montgomery
2013 - Scottsdale, AZ (Westin Kierland Resort and
    Spa)/April 2 - 6
Number of non-conference events/year: 4

Publications:
American Cranes & Transport; monthly; adv.
International Cranes & Specialized Transport; monthly;
    adv.
SC&RA Directory of Members and Equipment;
    annually
SC&RA Weekly Newsletter; weekly

Membership List Available to Non-members

Specialized Information Publishers Association
(1977)
8229 Boone Blvd.
Suite 260
Vienna, VA 22182
Tel: (703) 992-9339 *Fax:* (703) 992-7512
E-Mail: sipa@sipaonline.com
Website: sipaonline.com
Members: 600 corporate members
Staff: 5
Annual Budget: $500-1,000,000
Tax: 501(c)(6)

Personnel:
Executive Director: Matt Salt
    E-Mail: msalt@sipaonline.com
Manager, Membership: Julie Anthony
    E-Mail: janthony@sipaonline.com
Managing Editor: Ronn Levine
    E-Mail: rlevine@sipaonline.com
Meetings Coordinator: Anne Moore
    E-Mail: amoore@sipaonline.com
Associate Director, Operations: Julie Utano
    E-Mail: jutano@sipaonline.com

Historical Note:
*Merged with and became a division of the Software &
Information Industry Association in 2012. SIPA's purpose
is to serve its member newsletter and other specialized-
information publishers worldwide through education,
training, networking and advocacy to foster growth,
profitability and professional excellence. Membership:
$495-14,995/year (fee is based on annual company gross
revenue).*

Publications:
Membership Directory & Buyer's Guide; on-line; adv.
SIPA Hotline newsletter; monthly; adv.
SIPAlert; daily; adv.

Specialty Coffee Association of America *(1982)*
330 Golden Shore
Suite 50
Long Beach, CA 90802
Tel: (562) 624-4100 *Fax:* (562) 624-4101
E-Mail: info@scaa.org
Website: scaa.org
Members: 3000 companies
Staff: 22
Annual Budget: $2-5,000,000
Tax: 501(c)(6)

Personnel:
Executive Director: Ric Rhinehart
    E-Mail: rhinehart@scaa.org
Director, Community Development: Marcus Boni
Manager, Membership Development: Mansi Chokshi
    E-Mail: mchokshi@scaa.org
Director, Events: Cindy Cohn
Director, Professional Development: Ellie Hudson-
    Matuszak
Specialist, Communications: Lily Kubota
Senior Advisor: Ted Lingle
    E-Mail: tlingle@scaa.org
Director, Accounting: David Roberson
    E-Mail: droberson@scaa.org
Director, Marketing and Communications: Tara Shenson

Historical Note:
*SCAA's aim is to improve the quality of specialty coffee
from seed to cup and ensure its availability in the
future. Members belong to all segments of the specialty
coffee industry from growers to roasters and retailers.
Membership: $195-1175/year.*

Continuing Education:
Certification Designation/s: CBT, BGA, CBC, CJLC
Meetings/Conferences:
Conference Chair: Marcus Boni
2013 - Boston, MA (Renaissance Boston Waterfront
    Hotel)/April 10 - 14
2013 - Boston, MA/April 10 - 11
2013 - Boston, MA (Boston Convention and Exhibition
    Center)/April 11 - 14
Number of non-conference events/year: 10

Publications:
Membership Directory; annually; adv.
The Specialty Coffee Chronicle

Specialty Equipment Market Association *(1963)*
1575 S. Valley Vista Dr.
P.O. Box 4910
Diamond Bar, CA 91765-0910
Tel: (909) 396-0289 *Fax:* (909) 860-0184
E-Mail: info@sema.org
Website: sema.org
Members:
2000 companies
7094 members
Staff: 9
Annual Budget: $50-100,000,000
Tax: 501(c)(6)

Personnel:
President and Chief Executive Officer: Christopher J.
    Kersting CAE
Vice President and Chief Financial Officer: George
    Afremow
Director: Jamie Eriksen
    E-Mail: jamiee@sema.org
Vice President, Events and Communications: Peter
    MacGillivray
    E-Mail: peterm@sema.org
Vice President, Government Affairs: Stephen B.
    McDonald
    E-Mail: stevemac@sema.org
Vice President, Internal Systems and Project Teams: Alise
    Miner
Vice President, Marketing and Market Research: Tom
    Myroniak
    E-Mail: member@sema.org
Vice President, Councils and Membership: Nathan
    Ridnouer

Historical Note:
*Formerly (1966) Speed Equipment Manufacturers
Association, and (1979) Specialty Equipment
Manufacturers Association, SEMA works to help its
members' businesses succeed and prosper. Members are the
producers and marketers of specialty equipment products
and services for the automotive aftermarket. Membership:
$350-2,000 (Category 1); $100- 1,000 (Category 2);
$200-300 (Category 3); $150 (Category 4).*

Meetings/Conferences: Annual
Conference Chair: Peter MacGillivray
Number of non-conference events/year: 3

Publications:
SEMA e-News; weekly
SEMA News; monthly; adv.

Membership List Available to Non-members

Specialty Graphic Imaging Association *(1948)*
10015 Main St.
Fairfax, VA 22031-3489
Tel: (703) 385-1335 *Fax:* (703) 273-0456
TollFree: (888) 385-3588
E-Mail: sgia@sgia.org
Website: sgia.org
Members: 4500 companies
Staff: 31
Annual Budget: $10-25,000,000
Tax: 501(c)(6)

Personnel:
President and Chief Executive Officer: Michael Robertson
    E-Mail: miker@sgia.org
Vice President, Marketing and Membership: Sondra Fry
    Benoudiz
    E-Mail: sondra@sgia.org
Vice President, Government and Business Information:
    Marcia Kinter
    E-Mail: marcik@sgia.org
Manager, Exhibit Logistics: Jean Lambert
    E-Mail: jean@sgia.org
Vice President, Technical Services: Johnny Shell

E-Mail: jshell@sgia.com

Historical Note:
Formerly (1968) the Screen Process Printing Association, (1994) the Screen Printing Association International and (2003) the Screenprinting and Graphic Imaging Association International. SGIA's mission is to provide imaging professionals with the tools and information needed to make better business decisions. Membership: $475-800 (Corporate); $1000 (Global Membership); $40 (Membership Plaque).

Meetings/Conferences: Annual
2013 - Orlando, FL (Orange County Convention Center)/Oct. 23 - 25
2014 - Las Vegas, NV (Las Vegas Convention Center)/Oct. 22 - 24
2015 - Atlanta, GA (Georgia World Congress Center)/Nov. 4 - 6
2016 - Las Vegas, NV (Las Vegas Convention Center)/Sept. 13 - 16
2017 - New Orleans, LA (Ernest N. Morial Convention Center)/Oct. 10 - 12
2018 - Las Vegas, NV (Las Vegas Convention Center)/Sept. 26 - 28
Number of non-conference events/year: 2

Publications:
Membership Directory; on-line
SGIA Industry Ink; on-line
SGIA Journal; bi-monthly

Specialty Sleep Association (1995)
46639 Jones Ranch Rd.
Friant, CA 93626
Tel: (559) 868-4187 Fax: (559) 868-4185
E-Mail: info@sleepinformation.org
Website: sleepinformation.org
Members: 80 companies
Staff: 1
Annual Budget: $250-500,000
Tax: 501(c)(6)

Personnel:
Executive Director: Tambra Jones
E-Mail: tambra@sleepinformation.org

Historical Note:
Formed from a merger of the National Waterbed Retailers Association and the Waterbed Manufacturers Association in 1994 as the Waterbed Council; assumed its current name in 1996. SSA's purpose is to facilitate the growth and positive awareness of the specialty sleep category through consumers, retailers and manufacturers. SSA develop, manufacture, market and sell innovative, new-technology mattress and bedding products. Membership: $150-1,000 (Retailers); $350-1,000 (Manufacturers); $125-200 (Associate).

Publications:
Bedroom Magazine; quarterly; adv.
Industry News; on-line
Membership Directory; on-line

Specialty Steel Industry of North America (1962)
3050 K St. NW
Suite 400
Washington, DC 20007
Tel: (202) 342-8630 Fax: (202) 342-8451
TollFree: (800) 982-0355
Website: ssina.com
Members: 21 companies
Staff: 1
Annual Budget: $2-5,000,000

Personnel:
Secretary and Counsel: David A. Hartquist

Historical Note:
Formerly (1983) Tool and Stainless Steel Industry Committee and (1994) Specialty Steel Industry of the U.S. SSINA's purpose is to promote the expanded use and a recognition of stainless steel. Members of SSINA produce a variety of products including bar, rod, wire, angles, plate, sheet and strip, in stainless steel and other specialty steels.

Continuing Education:
Certification Designation/s: SSSC

Meetings/Conferences: Annual

Specialty Tobacco Council (1984)
102 W. Third St.
Suite 200B, Lobby Level
Winston-Salem, NC 27101
Tel: (336) 723-4311 Fax: (336) 759-0965
Website: specialtytobacco.org
Staff: 1

Annual Budget: $100-250,000

Personnel:
Executive Director: Henry C Roemer III
E-Mail: hroemer@specialtytobacco.org

Historical Note:
The STC provides information about specialty tobacco products, especially clove cigarettes and cigars, to the public, the media and legislators. STC's mission is to advocate the business interests that are common to its members in the eyes of legislators and the general public in the United States.

Specialty Tools and Fasteners Distributors Association (1976)
500 Elm Grove Rd., Suite 210
P.O. Box 44
Elm Grove, WI 53122
Tel: (262) 784-4774 Fax: (262) 784-5059
TollFree: (800) 352-2981
E-Mail: info@stafda.org
Website: stafda.org
Members: 2,500 + leading Distributors, Manufacturers, and Rep Agents
Staff: 4
Annual Budget: $2-5,000,000

Personnel:
Executive Director: Georgia H. Foley
E-Mail: ghfoley@stafda.org
Director, Membership Services: Catherine P. Usher
E-Mail: cusher@stafda.org
Senior Accountant: Anne Venturelli
E-Mail: anne@stafda.org

Historical Note:
STAFDA's mission is to promote a better understanding of the economic value of the functions performed by distributors of power tools, construction fasteners, and related accessories among customers and suppliers. Membership: $350/year (Distributor/Manufacturer/Associate/Independent Rep/Agent).

Meetings/Conferences: Annual
2013 - Las Vegas, NV (Mandalay Bay Convention Center)/Nov. 10 - 12
2014 - Charlotte, NC (Charlotte Convention Center)/Nov. 9 - 11
2015 - Phoenix, AZ (Phoenix Convention Center)/Nov. 8 - 10
2016 - Atlanta, GA (Georgia World Congress Center)/Nov. 6 - 8

Publications:
Membership Directory; annually
Trade News; quarterly

Specialty Vehicle Institute of America (1983)
Two Jenner St.
Suite 150
Irvine, CA 92618-3806
Tel: (949) 727-3727 Fax: (949) 727-4216
E-Mail: info@intix.org
Website: atvsafety.org
Members: 10 companies
Staff: 40
Annual Budget: $5-10,000,000
Tax: 501(c)(6)

Personnel:
President: Tim Buche
E-Mail: tbuche@mic.org
Vice President, Administration: Joe Di Corpo
E-Mail: jdicorpo@mic.org
Executive Business Assistant: Wendy Larkin
E-Mail: wlarkin@svia.org
Executive Vice President and General Counsel: Paul Vitrano
E-Mail: pvitrano@mic.org

Historical Note:
SVIA is a national, non-profit trade association representing manufacturers and distributors of all-terrain vehicles whose purpose is to foster and promote the safe and responsible use of specialty vehicles manufactured and/or distributed in the U.S.

SPIE - The International Society for Optical Engineering (1955)
P.O. Box Ten
Bellingham, WA 98227-0010
Tel: (360) 676-3290 Fax: (360) 647-1445
E-Mail: customerservice@spie.org
Website: spie.org
Members:

320 companies
17500 individuals
Staff: 152
Annual Budget: $10-25,000,000

Personnel:
Chief Executive Director: Eugene G. Arthurs
Secretary and Treasurer: Brain Lula
Director, Digital Library Sales: Marybeth Manning
E-Mail: marybeth@spie.org
Manager, Public Relations: Amy Nelson
E-Mail: amy@spie.org
Director, Publications: Eric Pepper
E-Mail: eric@spie.org
Director, Education and Community Services: Krisinda Plenkovich
E-Mail: krisindap@spie.org

Historical Note:
Formerly Society of Photographic Instrumentation Engineers; (1983) Society of Photo-Optical Instrumentation Engineers. SPIE's mission is to advance an interdisciplinary approach to the science and application of light. Members are scientists, engineers and companies interested in technology and applications of optical, electro-optical, fiber-optic, laser and photonic systems. Membership: $105 (Individual): $55 (Early Career Professionals); $20 (Student); $449-2,299 (Corporate); $699 (Non-Profit).

Meetings/Conferences:
2013 - San Jose, CA (San Jose Convention Center)/Feb. 24 - 28
2013 - San Diego, CA (Town & Country Resort and Convention center)/March 10 - 14
2013 - Baltimore, MD (Baltimore Convention Center)/April 29 - May 3
2013 - Rochester, NY (Rochester Riverside Convention Center)/Oct. 14 - 17
2014 - Montreal, QC (Palais des congrès)/June 22 - 27
Number of non-conference events/year: 10

Publications:
Journal of Applied Remote Sensing; annually
Journal of Biomedical Optics
Journal of Micro/Nanolithography, MEMS, and MOEMS; quarterly
Journal of Nanophotonics; on-line
Journal of Photonics for Energy
Membership Directory; on-line
Optical Engineering; monthly
SPIE Letters Virtual Journal
SPIE Reviews

Spill Control Association of America (1973)
103 Oronoco St.
Suite 200
Alexandria, VA 22314
Tel: (571) 451-0433
E-Mail: info@scaa-spill.org
Website: scaa-spill.org
Members: 50 companies and organizations
Staff: 5
Annual Budget: $100-250,000
Tax: 501(c)(6)

Personnel:
Executive Director: John Allen
E-Mail: JAllen@ses.ckor.com
Contact, Public Relations: Anne Burns
Contact, Meetings and Events: Marilyn Clark
Association Manager: Lee Hill
Contact, Information Technology Development and Marketing: Katie Hill

Historical Note:
Established as the Oil Spill Control Association of America, assumed its present name in 1978. SCAA's mission is to promote the interests of all groups within the spill response community. Membership includes spill response contractors, manufacturers, distributors, consultants, instructors, government & training institutions and corporations working in the industry. Membership: $1,750 (Full); $750 (Associate); $250 (Government/Educational).

Meetings/Conferences: Annual
Conference Chair: Marilyn Clark

Publications:
Membership Directory; on-line
Small Business Legislative Council (SBLC) Report; weekly
Spill Briefs; on-line

Sponge and Chamois Institute (1933)
10024 Office Center Ave.
Suite 203

St. Louis, MO 10583-6721
Tel: (314) 842-2230 *Fax:* (314) 842-3999
E-Mail: scwaters@swbell.net
Website: chamoisinstitute.org
Members: 4 companies
Staff: 2
Annual Budget: $10-25,000

Personnel:
Contact, Communications: Susan Waters
   E-Mail: scwaters@swbell.net

Historical Note:
SCI's mission is to educate the public about the benefits of genuine chamois and natural sponges. Members are dealers and suppliers of natural sponges and chamois leather.

Sporting Arms and Ammunition Manufacturers' Institute Inc. *(1926)*
11 Mile Hill Rd.
Newtown, CT 06470-2359
Tel: (203) 426-4358 *Fax:* (203) 426-3592
E-Mail: webmaster@nssf.org
Website: saami.org
Members: 27 companies
Staff: 1
Annual Budget: $1-2,000,000
Tax: 501(c)(6)

Personnel:
Managing Director: Richard Patterson
   E-Mail: rpatterson@saami.org

Historical Note:
SAAMI is active primarily in technical matters relating to voluntary industry standards and product safety. Membership is open to any domestic primary manufacturer producing and selling within the United States, or domestic designing firm or corporation causing to be manufactured to its basic design and selling within the United States under its own name, sporting firearms or ammunition subject to the United States manufacturer's excise tax or propellants for sporting ammunition. SAAMI's mission is to Create and Promulgate Technical, Performance, and Safety Standards for Commerce in Firearms, Ammunition, and Components.

Publications:
Membership Directory; on-line

Sports and Entertainment Alliance in Technology
5795 S. Sandhill Rd.
Suite F
Las Vegas, NV 89120-2558
Tel: (602) 639-1807 *Fax:* (623) 243-4160
Website: seatconsortium.com
Members: 68 Organisations
Staff: 2

Personnel:
Founder and Chief Executive Officer: Christine Stoffel
   E-Mail: Christine.Stoffel@seatconsortium.com
Executive Vice President, Business Development: Chris Dill
   E-Mail: Chris.Dill@seatconsortium.com

Historical Note:
Sports & Entertainment Alliance in Technology (SEAT) joins forces with the ALSD to present a one-of-a kind conference dedicated to the technology executives.

Meetings/Conferences: Annual
2013 - Indianapolis, IN/June 9 - 11
2013 - Kansas City, MO/Aug. 4 - 7

Sports and Fitness Industry Association *(1906)*
8505 Fenton St.
Suite 211
Silver Spring, MD 20910
Tel: (301) 495-6321 *Fax:* (301) 495-6322
E-Mail: info@sgma.com
Website: sgma.com
Members: 1000 goods manufacturers, retailers and marketers
Staff: 9
Annual Budget: $2-5,000,000

Personnel:
Chief Executive Officer: Tom Cove
   E-Mail: tcove@sgma.com
Chief Financial Officer: Chip Baldwin
   E-Mail: cbaldwin@sgma.com
Director, Communications: Mike May
   E-Mail: mmay@sgma.com
Business, Operation Manager: VJ Mayor
   E-Mail: vmayor@sfia.org
Manager, Membership Services: Jonathan Michaels
   E-Mail: jmichaels@sgma.com

Senior Vice President, Marketing and Business Development: Ron Rosenbaum
   E-Mail: rrosenbaum@sgma.com
Vice President, Government Relations: Bill Sells
   E-Mail: bsells@sgma.com
Manager, Marketing: Lauren Wallace
   E-Mail: lwallace@sgma.com

Historical Note:
Established as the Athletic Goods Manufacturers Association, became Sporting Goods Manufacturers Association in 1906. SGMA's mission is to support its member companies and promote a healthy environment for the sporting goods industry by providing access to research, advancing policies that increase participation and industry connections. Membership: $700- 35,000 (Corporate, based on annual sales volume); $1,000-5,000 (Associate, based on annual sales volume); $700 (Non-Profit).

Meetings/Conferences: Annual

Publications:
e-newsletter In Brief; on-line; adv.

Sports Lawyers Association *(1976)*
12100 Sunset Hills Rd.
Suite 130
Reston, VA 20190
Tel: (703) 437-4377 *Fax:* (703) 435-4390
E-Mail: sla@sportslaw.org
Website: sportslaw.org
Members: 1200 individuals
Staff: 3
Annual Budget: $250-500,000
Tax: 501(c)(6)

Personnel:
Executive Director: Rick A Guggolz
Deputy Executive Director: William M Drohan CAE
Director, Publications: Gabe Feldman

Historical Note:
SLA's mission is to provide educational opportunities and disseminate data and information regarding specific areas of sports law. Provides a forum for lawyers representing athletes, teams, leagues, conferences, civic recreational programs, educational institutions and other organizations. Members are attorneys specializing in sports law. Membership: $100 (New Lawyer); $245 (Regular); $440 (Associate); $115 (Law Educator); $75 (Law Student).

Meetings/Conferences: Annual
2013 - Braselton, GA (Chateau Elan Winery and Resort)/May 16 - 18
2014 - Chicago, IL (Fairmont Chicago Millenium Park)/May 15 - 17
2015 - Baltimore, MD (Marriott Waterfront)/May 14 - 16

Publications:
Annual Membership Directory; annually
SportsBusiness Journal; annually; adv.
The Sports Law Weekly; weekly; adv.
The Sports Lawyer; on-line; adv.
The Sports Lawyers Journal; annually

Sports Turf Managers Association *(1981)*
805 New Hampshire St.
Suite E
Lawrence, KS 66044-2774
Tel: (785) 843-2549 *Fax:* (785) 843-2977
TollFree: (800) 323-3875
E-Mail: stmainfo@stma.org
Website: STMA.org
Members:
350 commercial companies
2400 individuals
Staff: 5
Annual Budget: $1-2,000,000
Tax: 501(c)(6)

Personnel:
Chief Executive Officer: Kimberly "Kim" Heck
   E-Mail: kheck@stma.org
Manager, Sales and Marketing: Patrick Allen
   E-Mail: pallen@stma.org
Manager, Education: Kristen Althouse
   E-Mail: kalthouse@stma.org
Manager, Member Programs: Leah Craig
   E-Mail: lcraig@stma.org
Manager, Finance and Operations: Nora Dunnaway-McIntire
   E-Mail: ndmcintire@stma.org

Historical Note:
STMA's mission is to be the recognized leader in strengthening the sports turf industry and enhancing

members' competence and acknowledgement of their professionalism. Membership: $25-295/year.

Continuing Education:
Enrollment: 20
Certification Designation/s: CSFM

Meetings/Conferences: Annual
2013 - Daytona Beach, FL (Hilton Daytona Beach Resort/Ocean Walk Village)/Jan. 14 - 19
2014 - San Antonio, TX/Jan. 21 - 25
2015 - Denver, CO/Jan. 13 - 16
2016 - San Diego, CA/Jan. 19 - 22

Publications:
Membership Directory; annually
News Online; on-line
Sports Turf Insider; weekly
SportsTurf Magazine; monthly; adv.

Sportsplex Operators and Developers Association *(1981)*
P.O. Box 24263 - Westgate Stn.
Rochester, NY 14624-0263
Tel: (585) 426-2215 *Fax:* (585) 247-3112
TollFree: (800) 878-4308
E-Mail: info@sportsplexoperators.com
Website: sportsplexoperators.com
Members: 1125 sports facilities
Staff: 2
Annual Budget: $25-50,000
Tax: 501(c)(6)

Personnel:
Executive Director: Don Aselin
   E-Mail: don@sportsplexoperators.com
Treasurer: Norm Rice

Historical Note:
Founded as Sportsplex Owners and Directors of America. Assumed its current name in 1994. SODA's mission is to provide its members with opportunities for exchange of experiences, ideas and opinions through discussion, study and publications. Membership: $995 (Sustained); $350 (Professional/Associate); $225 (Social); $100 (Affiliate).

Publications:
SODAsite Magazine; bi-monthly; adv.
SODAsite Newsletter

Spotted Saddle Horse Breeders' and Exhibitors' Association *(1985)*
P.O. Box 1046
Shelbyville, TN 37162
Tel: (931) 684-7496 *Fax:* (931) 684-7215
E-Mail: info@sshbea.org
Website: sshbea.org
Members: 4000 members
Staff: 3
Annual Budget: $250-500,000

Personnel:
Manager, Operations: Janice Prince Pope
   E-Mail: jprince@sshbea.org

Historical Note:
SSHBEA is a non-profit, member-owned corporation formed to preserve the pedigree of and to promote the Spotted Saddle Horse. SHBEA affiliates horse shows, licenses judges, approves designated qualified persons, and establishes official rules for registering and showing of the Spotted Saddle Horse. Membership: $50 (Adult); $80 (Family); $40 (Associate); $600 (Life).

Publications:
SSH News
SSHBEA Newsletter

Spray Polyurethane Foam Alliance *(1987)*
4400 Fair Lakes Ct.
Suite 105
Fairfax, VA 22033
Tel: (800) 523-6154 *Fax:* (703) 222-5816
Website: sprayfoam.org
Members: 320 companies
Staff: 4
Annual Budget: $1-2,000,000
Tax: 501(c)(6)

Personnel:
Executive Director: Kurt Riesenberg
   E-Mail: kurtriesenberg@sprayfoam.org
Director, Technical Services: Rick Duncan PE, PhD
Manager, Training: Kelly Marcavage
Contact, Membership Services: Lisa Smith
   E-Mail: lisasmith@sprayfoam.org

Historical Note:

SPFA develops tools designed to educate and influence the construction industry with the positive benefits of spray polyurethane foam roofing, insulation, and climate control systems.

Meetings/Conferences: Annual
2013 - Jacksonville, FL (Jacksonville Hyatt)/Feb. 12

Publications:
Membership Directory; on-line
SPF Industry Report; monthly
SprayFoam Magazine; quarterly; adv.

Membership List Available to Non-members

Spring Manufacturers Institute *(1933)*
2001 Midwest Rd.
Suite 106
Oak Brook, IL 60523-1335
Tel: (630) 495-8588 *Fax:* (630) 495-8595
E-Mail: info@smihq.org
Website: smihq.org
Members: 335 companies
Staff: 5
Annual Budget: $500-1,000,000

Personnel:
President: Scott Rankin
Executive Vice President: Russ Bryer
General Manager: Lynne Carr
    E-Mail: lynne@smihq.org
Director, Technology: Jim Kobrinetz
    E-Mail: jim@smihq.org
Managing Editor: Gary McCoy
    E-Mail: gmccoy@fairwaycommunications.com

Historical Note:
SMI's purpose is to serve as a clearinghouse and source of information on the precision spring manufacturing industry and to inspire professional business standards among members. Members are companies that manufacture springs and their associate suppliers. Membership: $847-4,373 (Regular); $2860 (Internal Producer); $1,485-3,685 (Associate).

Continuing Education:
Certification Designation/s: ISO, QS, TS

Meetings/Conferences: Annual
2013 - Marana, AZ (Ritz-Carlton Dove Mountain)/
    April 4 - 9

Publications:
Springs; quarterly; adv.

Spring Research Institute *(1933)*
422 Kings Way
Naples, FL 34104
Tel: (317) 439-4811 *Fax:* (239) 643-7769
Website: springresearch.org
Members:
12 manufacturers
6 associates
Staff: 3
Annual Budget: $100-250,000
Tax: 501(c)(6)

Personnel:
President: John D. Thomson
    E-Mail: johndthomson@comcast.net
Secretary: Elizabeth Thomson
    E-Mail: elisabeththomson@comcast.net

Historical Note:
SRI's mission is to enhance the manufacture and distribution of high quality leaf springs and related products for use in replacement markets, through the dissemination of technical information.

Publications:
Member Listing; on-line

SSPC: the Society for Protective Coatings *(1950)*
40 24th St.
Sixth Floor
Pittsburgh, PA 15222-4656
Tel: (412) 281-2331 *Fax:* (412) 281-9992
TollFree: (877) 281-7772
E-Mail: info@sspc.org
Website: sspc.org
Members: 8240 individuals and organizations
Staff: 31
Annual Budget: $5-10,000,000

Personnel:
Executive Director: William L. Shoup
    E-Mail: shoup@sspc.org
Coordinator, Publications Fulfillment: Jeannine Bodack

    E-Mail: bodack@sspc.org
Coordinator, Conference Administration: Dee Boyle
    E-Mail: boyle@sspc.org
Director, Marketing: Michael E. Kline
    E-Mail: kline@sspc.org
Specialist, Accounting and Administration: Monica Pierce
    E-Mail: pierce@sspc.org
Director, Membership Services: Terry Sowers
    E-Mail: sowers@sspc.org
Manager, Network and Information Technology: Brian Spahr
    E-Mail: spahr@sspc.org
Manager, Certifications: Norm Suzich
    E-Mail: suzich@sspc.org

Historical Note:
Founded as Steel Structures Painting Council, assumed its current name in 1997. SSPC's mission is to advance the technology and promote the use of protective coatings to preserve industrial, marine and commercial structures, components and substrates. Members include paint manufacturers, raw material suppliers, specifiers, applicators, government agencies, and a wide variety of end-users. Membership: $95 (Individual-Domestic); $120 (Individual-Foreign); $700-5,500 (Organizational).

Continuing Education:
Certification Designation/s: PCS, PCI, CCI, BCI, MCI, CAS, PCCP

Meetings/Conferences: Annual
Conference Chair: Dee Boyle
2013 - San Antonio, TX (The Henry B. Gonzalez Convention Center)/Jan. 14 - 17/1-10 exhibitors

Publications:
Journal of Protective Coatings and Linings; monthly
SSPC eNews; monthly

Membership List Available to Non-members

Stable Value Investment Association *(1990)*
1025 Connecticut Ave. NW
Suite 1000
Washington, DC 20036
Tel: (202) 580-7620 *Fax:* (202) 580-7621
E-Mail: info@stablevalue.org
Website: stablevalue.org
Staff: 2
Annual Budget: $500-1,000,000
Tax: 501(c)(4)

Personnel:
President: Gina Mitchell

Historical Note:
SVIA is committed to educating retirement plan sponsors and the public about the importance of saving for retirement and the contribution stable value can make toward a financially secure retirement. Membership: $195 (Corporate-Plan Sponsors/Associate); $7,500 (Corporate-Service Providers) $5000-$15000(Value Program).

Meetings/Conferences: Annual
2013 - Palm Beach, FL (Four Seasons Resort Palm Beach)/April 14 - 16

Publications:
Stable Times; semi-annually

Stadium Managers Association *(1974)*
525 SW Fifth St.
Suite A
Des Moines, IA 50309-4501
Tel: (515) 282-8192 *Fax:* (515) 282-9117
E-Mail: sma@assoc-mgmt.com
Website: stadiummanagers.org
Members: 500 individuals
Staff: 3
Annual Budget: $500-1,000,000
Tax: 501(c)(6)

Personnel:
Executive Director: Mary Mycka
    E-Mail: mmycka@assoc-mgmt.com
Director, Membership Services: Kate Banasiak
Legal Counsel: George McCormick

Historical Note:
MA's mission is to advocate the professional, efficient and state-of-the- art management of stadiums around the world. Members are administrators, operators, and marketing personnel from teams, government entities, colleges and universities, and suppliers to the industry. Membership: $200 (Stadium Manager/Affiliate); $750 (Corporate Member); $50 (Student); $150 (Faculty Member); $3000 -3,500 (Corporate Sponsor).

Meetings/Conferences: Annual

2013 - Miami Beach, FL (Eden Roc Renaissance Miami Beach)/Feb. 3 - 7
Number of non-conference events/year: 1

Publications:
Membership Directory
SMA Newsletter; monthly

Stage Directors and Choreographers Society *(1959)*
1501 Broadway
Suite 1701
New York, NY 10036-5653
Tel: (212) 391-1070 *Fax:* (212) 302-6195
TollFree: (800) 541-5204
E-Mail: info@sdcweb.org
Website: sdcweb.org
Members: 2300 individuals and associates
Staff: 15
Annual Budget: $1-2,000,000
Tax: 501(c)(3)

Personnel:
Executive Director: Laura Penn
    E-Mail: lpenn@sdcweb.com
Administrative Assistant: Lena Abrams
    E-Mail: LAbrams@SDCweb.org
Senior Business Associate: Michele Holmes
    E-Mail: MHolmes@SDCweb.org
Director, Finance and Administration: Cole Jordan
    E-Mail: cjordan@sdvweb.org
Publications and Online Media Manager: Elizabeth Miller
    E-Mail: EMiller@SDCweb.org
Director, Membership Services: Barbara Wolkoff
    E-Mail: bwolkoff@sdcweb.org

Historical Note:
SDC's mission is to foster a national community of professional stage Directors and Choreographers by protecting the rights, health and livelihoods of all its members. To facilitate the exchange of ideas, information and opportunities, while educating the current and future generations about the role of Directors and Choreographers and providing effective administration, negotiations and contractual support. Membership: $200 (Full); $60 (Associate).

Publications:
Membership Directory; on-line
SDC E-Newsletter; bi-monthly

Stage Managers Association *(1982)*
P.O. Box 275
Times Square Station
New York, NY 10108-0275
E-Mail: info@stagemanagers.org
Website: stagemanagers.org
Staff: 3

Personnel:
Secretary: Katrina Renee Herrmann
Treasurer: Marci Skolnick

Historical Note:
A professional organization for stage managers. Seeks to create a network inorder to share problems and ideas. Provides contracts, benefits, and tax information, computer light boards, stage combat and weaponry, theatre architecture and design, emergency medical services in NYC, mental and physical health care to performing arts professionals, managing large events and education of stage managers in undergraduate and graduate programs. Membership: $40 (Full); $30 (Associate); $20 (Student).

Publications:
Membership Directory; on-line

Stained Glass Association of America *(1903)*
9313 E. 63rd St.
Raytown, MO 64133
Tel: (800) 737-2090 *Fax:* (816) 737-2801
TollFree: (800) 438-9581
E-Mail: headquarters@sgaaonline.com
Website: stainedglass.org
Members: 590 individuals
Staff: 3
Annual Budget: $100-250,000
Tax: 501(c)(6)

Personnel:
Executive Administrator: Katherine "Katei" E. Gross
    E-Mail: sgaa@kcnet.com
Editor and Director, Media: Richard Gross
    E-Mail: richard@richardgross.net

Historical Note:

SGAA works to advance the awareness of stained glass, offers programs to assure the survival of the craft by offering guidelines, instruction and training to craftspersons, and defends the industry against unwarranted regulations. Membership: $100 (Affiliate/Related Profession Affiliate); $50 (Student Affiliate); $200 (Associate); $500 (Fully Accredited); $300 (Active Accredited).

Meetings/Conferences: Annual
Conference Chair: Katherine "Katei" E. Gross

Publications:
Kaleidoscope - Newsletter
Sourcebook - Membership Directory; annually
The Stained Glass Quarterly; quarterly; adv.

Standards Engineering Society (1947)
1950 Lafayette Rd.
P. O. Box One
Portsmouth, NH 03801
Tel: (603) 926-0750 Fax: (603) 610-7101
E-Mail: admin@ses-standards.org
Website: ses-standards.org
Members: 503 individuals and organizations
Staff: 6
Annual Budget: $100-250,000
Tax: 501(c)(6)

Personnel:
Executive Director: Mike Morrell
Director, Marketing: Patti Ensor
Director, Publications: Joy Fitzpatrick
Director, Education: Ashley Griggs
Director, Membership Services: Matt Williams
Director, Technical Services: Trudie Williams

Historical Note:
Formally Standards Engineering Society.SES strives to create and maintain a professional website for the society's products and services. SES's mission is to provide opportunities for professional development through quality programs and services for standards users and professionals, and to promote the awareness, use, and value of standards and standardization to the private and public sectors. SES holds National Affiliation with ASTM International. Members are standards developers, users, managers, and information specialists from industry, government, standards developing organizations, trade associations, and academia. Membership: $100 (Regular, U.S. and Canada); $150 (Regular, International); $750 (Organization, U.S. and Canada); $850 (Organization, International); $50 (Student, U.S. and Canada), 75 (Student, International); $55 (Subscriber, U.S. and Canada); $90 (Subscriber, International).

Continuing Education:
Enrollment: 10
Certification Designation/s: CStd, AStd

Meetings/Conferences: Annual

Publications:
Membership Directory; biennially
Standards Engineering; bi-monthly

State Capital Group (1989)
1717 Pennsylvania Ave. NW
Suite 1200
Washington, DC 20006
Tel: (202) 659-6601 Fax: (202) 659-6641
E-Mail: info@statecapitalgroup.org
Website: statecapitalgroup.org
Members: 145 Independent Law Firms
Staff: 2

Personnel:
Chief Executive Officer: David E. Poisson Esq.
    E-Mail: dpoisson@statecapitalgroup.org
Executive Assistant: Diane B. Case
    E-Mail: dcase@statecapitalgroup.org

Historical Note:
A group of independent law firms. Formed in 1989 by 17 former state governors and their law firms.State Capital Group provides an effective and trusted resource for identifying local counsel worldwide. Membership is strictly by invitation.

Meetings/Conferences: Annual

Publications:
Member Directory; on-line
SCG News from the NETWORK; monthly

State Debt Management Network (1991)
P.O. Box 11910
Lexington, KY 40578-1910
Tel: (859) 244-8175 Fax: (859) 244-8053
E-Mail: nast@csg.org
Website: sdmn.org

Members: 50 individuals
Staff: 1

Personnel:
Coordinator, Membership: Michele West
    E-Mail: mwest@csg.org

Historical Note:
SDMN members are state officials concerned with the issuance or management of state debt. Affiliated with the National Association of State Treasurers, serves as a professional organization for individuals responsible for the management of oversight of public debt at the state level. The purpose is to enhance debt management practices through training, development of educational materials, and data collection and dissemination. Membership: $500/year (voting/Corporate); $100/year (associate).

Meetings/Conferences:
Number of non-conference events/year: 2

Publications:
Membership Directory; on-line

State Education Technology Directors Association (2001)
P.O. Box 10
Glen Burnie, MD 21060
Tel: (202) 715-6636 Fax: (202) 715-6636
E-Mail: setda@setda.org
Website: setda.org
Staff: 4
Annual Budget: $500-1,000,000
Tax: 501(c)(3)

Personnel:
Executive Director: Douglas A. Levin
    E-Mail: dlevin@setda.org
Director, Administration and Membership: Tera Daniels
    E-Mail: tdaniels@setda.org
Manager, Technology: Lia Dossin
Director, Educational Leadership and Research: Christine Fox
    E-Mail: cfox@setda.org

Historical Note:
The State Educational Technology Directors Association (SETDA) is the national member association that serves, supports and represents the interests of the educational technology leadership of state education agencies in all 50 states, the District of Columbia, the Bureau of Indian Affairs, American Samoa, and the U.S. Virgin Islands.

Meetings/Conferences: Annual
2013 - Washington, DC/April 10 - 13

Publications:
SETDA Newsletter; monthly

State Government Affairs Council (1975)
515 King St.
Suite 325
Alexandria, VA 22314
Tel: (703) 684-0967 Fax: (703) 684-0968
E-Mail: stategov@sgac.org
Website: sgac.org
Members: 150 companies
Staff: 3
Annual Budget: $500-1,000,000
Tax: 501(c)(6)

Personnel:
Executive Director: Elizabeth A. Loudy
    E-Mail: eloudy@sgac.org
Manager, Programs and Events: Crislyn Lumia
    E-Mail: clumia@sgac.org
Manager, Member Services: Tina Phillips
    E-Mail: tphillips@sgac.org

Historical Note:
SGAC seeks to conduct educational activities that benefit members of the Council, legislative and public policy organizations and their members. Members are representatives of major U.S. companies and associations that participate in the state-level public policy process. Membership: $5,000/year.

Meetings/Conferences: Annual
Conference Chair: Crislyn Lumia

Publications:
Member Directory; on-line

State Guard Association of the United States (1985)
P.O. Box 1416
Fayetteville, GA 30214-1416
Tel: (770) 460-1215
E-Mail: director@sgaus.org

Website: sgaus.org
Members: 2600 individuals, 33 states and territories
Staff: 2
Annual Budget: $50-100,000
Tax: 501(c)(6)

Personnel:
Executive Director: Byers W. Coleman
    E-Mail: director@sgaus.org
Treasurer: Roland Candee

Historical Note:
Formed as the State Defense Force Association of the United States (SDF AUS) and assumed its current name in 1993. SGAUS's mission is to advocate for the advancement and support of regulated state military forces established by state governments under the authority of Title 32, Section 109, of the United States Code. It also seeks to sponsor and promote federal and state legislation in support of state military forces. Members are active and retired members of state defense forces. Membership: $16 (Enlisted/NCO); $25 (Officer/Civilian); $30 (General Officer); $300 (Lifetime).

Meetings/Conferences: Annual

Publications:
Journal Newsletter

State Higher Education Executive Officers (1954)
3035 Center Green Dr.
Suite 100
Boulder, CO 80301-2205
Tel: (303) 541-1600 Fax: (303) 541-1639
E-Mail: sheeo@sheeo.org
Website: sheeo.org
Members: 29 coordinating boards of higher education and 28 statewide governing boards
Staff: 17
Annual Budget: $2-5,000,000

Personnel:
President: Paul E. Lingenfelter
    E-Mail: plingenfelter@sheeo.org
Administrative and Editorial Assistant: Gloria Auer
    E-Mail: gauer@sheeo.org
Director, Administrative Operations: Gladys Kerns
    E-Mail: gkerns@sheeo.org
Vice President, Research and Information Resources: Hans P. L'Orange
    E-Mail: hlorange@sheeo.org
Vice President, Policy Analysis and Academic Affairs: Charles S. Lenth
    E-Mail: clenth@sheeo.org
Administrator, Information Technology: Chris Ott
    E-Mail: cott@sheeo.org

Historical Note:
SHEEO's mission is to assist its members and the states in developing and sustaining systems of higher education. Members are chief executive officers serving statewide coordinating boards and governing boards of postsecondary education. Members include 49 states, the District of Columbia, and the Commonwealth of Puerto Rico.

Meetings/Conferences: Annual
Conference Chair: Gladys Kerns
Number of non-conference events/year: 2

Publications:
Consultant Directory; on-line
Membership Directory; on-line
Newsletter on Current Technical and Policy Issues; quarterly

State Risk and Insurance Management Association (1974)
1712 E. Riverside Dr.
Suite 265
Austin, TX 78741
Tel: (512) 936-1502
Website: strima.org
Members: 50 individuals
Staff: 2
Annual Budget: $100-250,000
Tax: 501(c)(3)

Personnel:
President Elect and Conference Host: Jonathan Bow
    E-Mail: txstrimaconf@gmail.com

Historical Note:
STRIMA's mission is to advance the development and application of effective risk management principles and practices in state governments. STRIMA is an association of 38 State and 3 Canadian Provincial members who meet annually at a 5 day conference hosted by one of its State members. Members are state government risk and

insurance managers. *Membership:* $200(Organization); $300 (Associate).

Meetings/Conferences: Annual
Conference Chair: Jonathan Bow

Publications:
STRIMA Newsletter; on-line

StateNets Radio (1973)
17911 Harwood Ave.
Homewood, IL 60430
Tel: (708) 799-6676 *Fax:* (708) 799-6698
E-Mail: tdobrez@statenets.com
Website: statenets.com
Members: 30 companies
Staff: 13
Annual Budget: $250-500,000

Personnel:
Executive Director: Tom Dobrez
   E-Mail: tdobrez@statenets.com
Contact, Communications: Sharon Kitchell

Historical Note:
Formerly National Association of State Radio Networks (NASRN). StateNets works with various marketers in creating client specific programming opportunities. Members are companies that broadcast news and other informational programming to affiliated radio stations, over 1700 radio stations a day via satelite transmission.

States Organization for Boating Access (1986)
P.O. Box 7921
Madison, WI 53707-7921
E-Mail: info@sobaus.org
Website: sobaus.org
Members: 50 states and provinces
Staff: 2
Annual Budget: $100-250,000
Tax: 501(c)(3)

Personnel:
President: Steven W. Miller

Historical Note:
SOBA's mission is to encourage, promote and support federal and state programs that provide safe, high-quality and environmentally sound public recreational boat access to the waterways of the United States and its territories. Membership: $600 (Voting); $500 (Associate); $300 (Advisory); $125 (Individual); $50 (Affiliated Professional).

Meetings/Conferences:
2013 - Portland, OR (Hilton DoubleTree Hotel and
   Conference Center)/Sept. 30 - Oct. 3

Publications:
SOBA Newsletters; quarterly

Membership List Available to Non-members

Station Representatives Association (1948)
16 W. 77th St., Suite 9-E
New York, NY 10024-5126
Tel: (212) 362-8868
Members: 9 organizations
Staff: 1
Annual Budget: $10-25,000

Personnel:
Managing Director: Jerome R. Feniger Jr.

Historical Note:
Founded (1948) as the National Association of Radio Station Representatives, Inc. Became Station Representatives Association Inc. in 1952. Broadcast sales organizations, not affiliated with a national network, who sell non-network broadcast advertising.

Steamfitters Local Union 449 (1913)
1517 Woodruff St.
Pittsburgh, PA 15220
Tel: (412) 381-1133 *Fax:* (412) 381-7875
TollFree: (800) 253-6960
Website: ua449.com
Members: 1,500 union-trained steamfitters
Staff: 19
Annual Budget: $2-5,000,000

Personnel:
President: Michael M. Leaf
Business Manager: Kenneth J. Broadbent
   E-Mail: kjb@ua449.com
Secretary and Treasurer: Joseph M. Little
   E-Mail: jml@ua449.com

Historical Note:
Steamfitters Local 449 represent union-trained steamfitters, and are affiliated with the United Association of Journeymen

and Apprentices of the Plumbing and Pipefitting Industry of the United States and Canada.

Steel Deck Institute (1939)
P.O. Box 25
Fox River Grove, IL 60021-0025
Tel: (847) 458-4647 *Fax:* (847) 458-4648
Website: sdi.org
Members: 29 companies
Staff: 3
Annual Budget: $250-500,000
Tax: 501(c)(6)

Personnel:
Managing Director: Steven A. Roehrig
   E-Mail: Steve@sdi.org

Historical Note:
Formerly the Metal Roof Deck Technical Institute. A non-profit association of steel deck producers and associate members furnishing products allied to steel deck use in construction. SDI provides uniform industry guidelines for the engineering, design, manufacture and field usage of steel decks.

Meetings/Conferences: Annual

Publications:
Membership Directory; annually
SDI E-News; on-line

Membership List Available to Non-members

Steel Door Institute (1954)
30200 Detroit Rd.
Westlake, OH 44145-1967
Tel: (440) 899-0010 *Fax:* (440) 892-1404
E-Mail: info@steeldoor.org
Website: steeldoor.org
Members: 11 companies
Staff: 5
Annual Budget: $250-500,000
Tax: 501(c)(6)

Personnel:
Managing Director: Jeffrey J. Wherry
   E-Mail: jjw@wherryassoc.com

Historical Note:
SDI tests steel doors and frames for strength, quality, consistency, security, weather and fire resistance, wear and tear, and longevity. Represents producers of standard steel doors and frames for commercial and industrial construction.

Publications:
Membership Directory; on-line
SDI Newsletter; on-line

Steel Founders' Society of America (1902)
780 McArdle Dr.
Unit G
Crystal Lake, IL 60014
Tel: (815) 455-8240 *Fax:* (815) 455-8241
Website: sfsa.org
Members: 80 corporations
Staff: 5
Annual Budget: $2-5,000,000
Tax: 501(c)(6)

Personnel:
Executive Vice President: Raymond W. Monroe
   E-Mail: monroe@sfsa.org
Manager, Information Services: Rob Blair
   E-Mail: blairr@sfsa.org
Vice President, Technology: Malcolm Blair
   E-Mail: blairm@sfsa.org
Director, Finance and Administration: Kelly DiGiacomo
   CPA
   E-Mail: kdigiacomo@sfsa.org

Historical Note:
SFSA seeks to serve the steel casting industry in North America. Members are companies that produce steel castings, but is not limited to U.S. companies. Membership: $300-5,000/quarter.

Meetings/Conferences: Annual
2013 - Half Moon Bay, CA/Sept. 7 - 10
Number of non-conference events/year: 9

Publications:
Casteel Reporter newsletter; monthly
Directory of Steel Foundries; on-line

Steel Joist Institute (1928)
234 W. Cheves St.
Florence, SC 29501

Tel: (843) 407-4091 *Fax:* (843) 407-4091
Website: steeljoist.org
Members: 18 Companies
Staff: 3
Annual Budget: $500-1,000,000

Personnel:
Managing Director: J. Kenneth Charles III
   E-Mail: kcharles@steeljoist.org

Historical Note:
SJI seeks to address the lack of uniform joist standards within the industry. The Institute also holds continuing education seminars, provides technical information and promotes the use of steel joists through a national communications program. Members are active joist manufacturers and other individuals and entities connected to the industry.

Publications:
Newsletter

Steel Manufacturers Association (1988)
1150 Connecticut Ave. NW
Suite 715
Washington, DC 20036
Tel: (202) 296-1515 *Fax:* (202) 296-2506
Website: steelnet.org
Members: 157 Associate member and steel companies
Staff: 4
Annual Budget: $1-2,000,000
Tax: 501(c)(6)

Personnel:
President: Thomas A. Danjczek
   E-Mail: danjczek@steelnet.org
Manager, Membership Services and Administration: Aimee
   Cipicchio
   E-Mail: cipicchio@steelnet.org
Vice President, Policy and Communications: Adam Parr
   E-Mail: parr@steelnet.org
Vice President, Environment and Energy: Eric J. Stuart
   E-Mail: danjczek@steelnet.org

Historical Note:
SMA is the trade association for scrap-based electric arc furnace (EAF) steelmakers and rerollers.

Meetings/Conferences: Annual
Number of non-conference events/year: 7

Publications:
Membership Directory; annually

Steel Plate Fabricators Association Division of STI/SPFA (2004)
944 Donata Ct.
Lake Zurich, IL 60047
Tel: (847) 438-8265 *Fax:* (847) 438-8766
E-Mail: info@steeltank.com
Website: steeltank.com
Members: 100 companies
Staff: 13

Personnel:
Executive Vice President: Wayne B. Geyer
   E-Mail: wgeyer@steeltank.com
Director, Technical Services: Lorri Grainawi
   E-Mail: Lgrainawi@steeltank.com
Contact, Administrative Services: Lucy Hales
   E-Mail: lhales@steeltank.com
Controller: Kevin Kroll
   E-Mail: kkroll@steeltank.com
Coordinator, Meetings and Education: Marie Scimeca
   E-Mail: mscimeca@steeltank.com
*Coordinator, Administration, Membership Services and
   Meetings:* Elizabeth Whitney
   E-Mail: ewhitney@steeltank.com
Contact, Membership Services and Communications: Noel
   Zak
   E-Mail: nzak@steeltank.com

Historical Note:
Formed when the Steel Tank Institute (1916) and the Steel Plate Fabricators Association (1933) combined their operations. STI/SPFA's mission is to protect the environment and preservation of air and water quality which are key concerns for the owners and operators of tanks, pressure vessels, specialty fabrications and piping systems. It shares its staff with the Steel Plate Institute Division of STI/SPFA. Members are fabricators of steel construction products. Membership: $1,535 (Active: Shop Fabricated Atmospheric Tank Section); $1,120 (Active: Field Erected Tanks); $1,980-825 (Affiliate); $170 (Individual); $175 (Industry).

Meetings/Conferences: Annual
Conference Chair: Elizabeth Whitney
2013 - Bonita Springs, FL (Hyatt Regency Coconut
    Point)/March 23 - 26

Publications:
Membership Directory; annually
Tank Talk; on-line

Steel Recycling Institute (1988)
680 Andersen Dr.
Pittsburgh, PA 15220-2700
Tel: (412) 922-2772 *Fax:* (412) 922-3213
TollFree: (800) 876-7274
E-Mail: sri@recycle-steel.org
Website: recycle-steel.org
Members: 60 companies
Staff: 10
Annual Budget: $500-1,000,000

Personnel:
Executive Director: Gregory L. Crawford
    E-Mail: gcrawford@steel.org
President: William M. Heenan Jr.
    E-Mail: bheenansri@aol.com
Director, Public and Education Relations: James Woods
    E-Mail: jimw@recycle-steel.org

Historical Note:
*Formerly (1993) Steel Can Recycling Institute. Merged
with the American Iron and Steel Institute (1999) as a
department, and continues to operate under the SRI name.
Promotes and sustains the recycling of all steel products.
SRI educates the solid waste industry, government, business
and ultimately the consumer about the benefits of steel's
continuous recycling cycle.*

Continuing Education:
Certification Designation/s: LEED

Steel Shipping Container Institute (1944)
P.O. Box 100907
Arlington, VA 22210
Tel: (610) 286-3918 *Fax:* (610) 646-3267
E-Mail: ssci@steelcontainers.com
Website: steelcontainers.com
Members: 57 companies
Staff: 2
Annual Budget: $10-25,000

Personnel:
Executive Director: John A. McQuaid
    E-Mail: mcquaid@steelcontainers.com
Counsel: Jerry W. Cox
    E-Mail: jerry.w.cox@cox.net

Historical Note:
*SSCI's purpose is to promote the interests of the steel
shipping container industry, collect information on matters
of interest to the industry, and develop research to discover
better methods of operating the industry. SSCI is an
independent affiliate of IPANA. Members are makers of steel
drums, barrels and pails.*

Publications:
SSCI Newsletter; bi-monthly

Steel Tank Institute Division of STI/SPFA (1916)
944 Donata Ct.
Lake Zurich, IL 60047
Tel: (847) 438-8265 *Fax:* (847) 438-8766
Website: steeltank.com
Members: 100 companies
Staff: 12
Annual Budget: $1-2,000,000

Personnel:
Executive Vice President: Wayne B. Geyer
    E-Mail: wgeyer@steeltank.com
Director, Technical Services and Operations: Lorri
    Grainawi
    E-Mail: Lgrainawi@steeltank.com
Controller: Kevin Kroll
    E-Mail: kkroll@steeltank.com
Manager, Meetings and Education: Marie Scimeca
    E-Mail: mscimeca@steeltank.com
Coordinator, Administration, Membership and Meetings:
    Elizabeth Whitney
    E-Mail: Ewhitney@steeltank.com
Contact, Membership and Communications: Noel Zak
    E-Mail: nzak@steeltank.com

Historical Note:
*Formerly the Steel Tank Institute; became a division of STI/
SPFA and assumed its current name in 2004. Absorbed
(1990) Association for Composite Tanks. Conducts research
and develops underground and above ground storage tank*

*technologies and standards for the steel industry, and
provides educational training and certificates. Represents
its members to regulatory agencies. Shares staff with
another division of STI/SPFA, the Steel Plate Fabricators
Association of STI/SPFA.*

Continuing Education:
Certification Designation/s: ATSI, CPT

Meetings/Conferences: Annual
Conference Chair: Marie Scimeca
2013 - Bonita Springs, FL/March 23 - 26
Number of non-conference events/year: 7

Publications:
Tank Talk; quarterly

Membership List Available to Non-members

Steel Tube Institute of North America (1930)
2516 Waukegan Rd.
Suite 172
Glenview, FL 60025
Tel: (847) 461-1701 *Fax:* (847) 660-7981
E-Mail: stina@steeltubeinstitute.org
Website: steeltubeinstitute.org
Members: 66 companies
Staff: 1
Annual Budget: $500-1,000,000

Personnel:
Executive Director: William A. Wolfe

Historical Note:
*Formerly (1960) the Formed Steel Tube Institute and
(1988) Welded Steel Tube Institute. STI seeks to promote
the growth and competitiveness of North America's steel
tubular products industry. Members make steel tubes and
pipes produced from carbon, stainless or alloy steel, for
applications ranging from large structural tubing to small
redrawn tubing. Membership: $3,005-6,445 (Active);
$3,850 (Associate).*

Meetings/Conferences: Annual

Publications:
Membership directory; annually

Membership List Available to Non-members

Steel Window Institute (1920)
1300 Sumner Ave.
Cleveland, OH 44115-2851
Tel: (216) 241-7333 *Fax:* (216) 241-0105
E-Mail: swi@steelwindows.com
Website: steelwindows.com
Members: 6 companies
Staff: 3
Annual Budget: $50-100,000
Tax: 501(c)(6)

Personnel:
Executive Secretary: John H. Addington

Historical Note:
*Formerly the Metal Window Institute, SWI members are
United States manufacturers of windows made from hot-
rolled, solid steel sections and such related products as
castings, trim, mechanical operators, screens and moldings.*

Publications:
The Specifiers Guide to Steel Windows

Membership List Available to Non-members

Storage Equipment Manufacturer's Association (1972)
8720 Red Oak Blvd.
Suite 201
Charlotte, NC 28217-3992
Tel: (704) 676-1190 *Fax:* (704) 676-1199
Website: mhia.org/sma
Members: 18 individuals and 10 companies
Staff: 2
Annual Budget: $25-50,000

Personnel:
Managing Director: John Nofsinger
    E-Mail: jnofsinger@mhia.org

Historical Note:
*Formerly (1998) Shelving Manufacturers Association.
Members are the Industry's leading suppliers of industrial
storage equipment. SMA, formed as an outgrowth of the
Rack Manufacturers Institute, focuses specifically on the
shelving industry. SMA is a product section of the Material
Handling Industry Association.*

Strategic Account Management Association (1999)
33 N. LaSalle St.
Suite 3700

Chicago, IL 60602
Tel: (312) 251-3131 *Fax:* (312) 251-3132
Website: strategicaccounts.org
Members: 3900 individuals
Staff: 14
Annual Budget: $2-5,000,000

Personnel:
President and Chief Executive Officer: Bernard Quancard
    E-Mail: quancard@strategicaccounts.org
Editor: Greg Bartlett
    E-Mail: bartlett@strategicaccounts.org
Director, Knowledge and Programming: Elisabeth Cornell
    E-Mail: cornell@strategicaccounts.org
Manager, Membership and Operations: Frankie Cusimano
    E-Mail: cusimano@strategicaccounts.org
Manager, Meetings and Registration: Rhodonna Espinosa
    E-Mail: espinosa@strategicaccounts.org
Director, Corporate Business: Matt Fegley
    E-Mail: fegley@strategicaccounts.org
Administrator, Web and Database: Scot Goodhart
    E-Mail: goodhart@strategicaccounts.org
Director, Operations: Katherine Gotsick
    E-Mail: gotsick@strategicaccounts.org
Manager, Marketing: Matt Micou
    E-Mail: micou@strategicaccounts.org
Art Director: Aimee Waddell
    E-Mail: waddell@strategicaccounts.org

Historical Note:
*Founded as National Account Marketing Association,
became National Account Management Association and
assumed its current name in 1999. SAMA is a knowledge-
sharing organization devoted to developing, promoting and
advancing the concept of customer supplier collaboration
through communities of practice. Members are company
executives concerned with sales or marketing to major
national and global accounts and the special management
they require. Membership: $550/year (Practitioner/
Consultant/Academic).*

Continuing Education:
Certification Designation/s: CSAM

Meetings/Conferences: Annual
Conference Chair: Rhodonna Espinosa
2013 - Berlin, Germany/March 10 - 12
2013 - Hollywood, FL (Westin Diplomat Resort and
    Spa)/May 20 - 23

Publications:
SAMA newsletter
Velocity magazine; quarterly

Strategic Marketplace Initiative
22 Colonel Mansfield Dr.
Scituate, MA 02066
Tel: (781) 378-1107
E-Mail: info@smisupplychain.com
Website: smisupplychain.com
Staff: 4
Annual Budget: $500-1,000,000
Tax: 501(c)(6)

Personnel:
Executive Director: Thomas Hughes
    E-Mail: thughescih@aol.com
Communications Coordinator: Christine Dean
    E-Mail: cdean@smisupplychain.com
Administrative Director: Teri Gallagher
    E-Mail: tgallagher@smisupplychain.com
Senior Director: Dennis Orthman
    E-Mail: dorthman@smisupplychain.com

Historical Note:
*SMI is a consortium of healthcare supply chain executives
united to reengineer and advance the future of the
healthcare supply chain.*

Meetings/Conferences: Annual

Publications:
Newsletter

Strategic Rail Finance (1994)
1700 Sansom St.
Suite 500
Philadelphia, PA 19103
Tel: (215) 564-3122 *Fax:* (215) 564-3288
E-Mail: msussman@strategicrail.com
Website: strategicrail.com
Staff: 1

Personnel:
President: Michael Sussman
    E-Mail: msussman@strategicrail.com

Historical Note:
SRF purpose is to enhance programs for Railroad Rehabilitation and Improvement through promoting a comprehensive understanding of rail assets, railroad finance, and the capital marketplace.

Structural Building Components Association
(1983)
6300 Enterprise Ln.
Madison, WI 53719
Tel: (608) 274-4849 *Fax:* (608) 274-3329
E-Mail: sbca@sbcindustry.com
Website: sbcindustry.com
Members: 1100 companies
Staff: 35
Annual Budget: $2-5,000,000
Tax: 501(c)(6)

Personnel:
Executive Director: Kirk Grundahl PE
Director, Communications: Melinda Caldwell
    E-Mail: mcaldwell@qualtim.com
Managing Director: Suzanne Grundahl
    E-Mail: sgrundahl@qualtim.com
Coordinator, Educational and Technical Project: Trish Kutz
    E-Mail: tkutz@qualtim.com
Director, Sales and Marketing: Peggy Meskan
    E-Mail: pmeskan@qualtim.com
Coordinator, Publications: Eric Monson
    E-Mail: emonson@qualtim.com
Director, Membership and Chapter Development: Anna L. Stamm
    E-Mail: astamm@qualtim.com

Historical Note:
SBCA is an international not-for-profit trade association formerly known as Wood Truss Council of America. SBCA's mission is to promote the safe, economic and structurally sound use of structural building components thereby increasing their market penetration. Membership: varies based on sales volume, $432-18,888 (Regular); $684 (Supplier); $132-14,724 (Builder/Framer); $132 (Professional).

Continuing Education:
Certification Designation/s: TATO, TTT, QC, OS, CTW, SCORE

Meetings/Conferences: Annual
Conference Chair: Anna L. Stamm
Number of non-conference events/year: 5

Publications:
SBC Magazine; monthly; adv.

Membership List Available to Non-members

Structural Insulated Panel Association *(1990)*
P.O. Box 1699
Gig Harbor, WA 98335
Tel: (253) 858-7472 *Fax:* (253) 858-0272
E-Mail: info@sips.org
Website: sips.org
Members: 200 companies and organizations
Staff: 3
Annual Budget: $500-1,000,000
Tax: 501(c)(6)

Personnel:
Executive Director: William "Bill" Wachtler
    E-Mail: bill@sips.org

Historical Note:
SIPA's mission is to increase the use and acceptance of SIPs in green, high performance building by providing an industry forum for promotion, communication, education, quality assurance, and technical and marketing research. Membership: $125 (Builder/Design and Architect/Associate); $250 (Dealer/Distributor).

Meetings/Conferences: Annual
Number of non-conference events/year: 2

Publications:
Membership Directory; on-line

Structural Stability Research Council *(1944)*
C/O Missouri University of Science and Technology
1401 N. Pine St., 301 Butler Carlton Hall
Rolla, MO 65409-0030
Tel: (573) 341-6610 *Fax:* (573) 341-4476
E-Mail: ssrc@mst.edu
Website: stabilitycouncil.org
Members:
100 companies and organizations
400 individuals
Staff: 2

Annual Budget: $50-100,000
Tax: 501(c)(3)

Personnel:
Faculty Liaison and Treasurer: Roger LaBoube
    E-Mail: laboube@mst.edu
Administrative Secretary: Christina Stratman

Historical Note:
An outgrowth of the American Society of Civil Engineers Committee on Design of Structural Members and formerly known as the Column Research Council. SSRC works to review and resolve the conflicting opinions and practices that existed at the time with respect to solutions to stability problems, and to facilitate and promote economical and safe design. Members are representatives from Government Agencies, International Organizations, Private Corporations and Educational Institutions concerned with specifications and design procedures for metal structures, representatives of consulting firms engaged in engineering practice, members-at-large selected from universities and design offices, and corresponding members from various countries who are in touch with stability research for their region. Membership: $60-2399/year.

Meetings/Conferences: Annual
2013 - St. Louis, MO/April 16 - 20

Publications:
Member Directory; on-line
SSRC Newsletter; quarterly

Stucco Manufacturers Association *(1957)*
500 E. Yale Loop
Irvine, CA 92614
Tel: (949) 387-7611 *Fax:* (949) 701-4476
E-Mail: info@stuccomfgassoc.com
Website: stuccomfgassoc.com
Members: 30 companies and 30 individuals
Staff: 2
Annual Budget: $25-50,000
Tax: 501(c)(6)

Personnel:
Executive Director: Norma S. Fox
    E-Mail: info@stuccomfgassoc.com
Treasurer: Ted Jones

Historical Note:
SMA is a non-profit trade association that works to advance the knowledge and encourage the use of three-coat colored cementitious stucco. Members are manufacturers of stucco in North America and their related suppliers. Membership: $1,000-2,000/year (Stucco Member).

Publications:
E-Newsletter; on-line
Membership Directory; on-line

Student National Medical Association *(1964)*
5113 Georgia Ave. NW
Washington, DC 20011
Tel: (202) 882-2881 *Fax:* (202) 882-2886
Website: snma.org
Members: 6,000 medical students, pre-medical students, residents and physicians
Staff: 5
Annual Budget: $1-2,000,000

Personnel:
Associate Director, Membership Services: Marlene Sherrill
    E-Mail: memberinfo@snma.org
Associate Director, Programs and Conference Services:
    Annette McLane
    E-Mail: conferences@snma.org
Administrative Assistant: Marcus McNeil
Manager, Marketing, Publications and Media Resources:
    DeJuana Thompson
    E-Mail: marketing@snma.org

Historical Note:
Student National Medical Association (SNMA) is committed to supporting current and future underrepresented minority medical students, addressing the needs of underserved communities, and increasing the number of clinically excellent, culturally competent and socially conscious physicians. Membership: $30 (Active); $25 (Associate); $50 (Physician/Patron); $250 (Institution); $500 (Corporate); $300 (Life Member/Active/Associate); $600 (Life Member/Physician/Patron).

Meetings/Conferences: Annual
Conference Chair: Annette McLane
2013 - Louisville, KY (Galt House Hotel)/March 27 - 31/1000 attendees

Publications:
Journal of the Student National Medical Association (JSNMA); quarterly; adv.

Student Youth and Travel Association
8400 Westpark Dr.
Second Floor
McLean, VA 22102-5116
Tel: (703) 610-1264 *Fax:* (703) 610-0270
E-Mail: info@syta.org
Website: syta.org
Staff: 6
Annual Budget: $1-2,000,000

Personnel:
Executive Director: Carylann Assante CAE
    E-Mail: cassante@syta.org
Manager, Membership and Database: Jenny Burke
    E-Mail: jburke@syta.org
Senior Meetings Manager: Barbara Hutchison
    E-Mail: bhutchison@mmgevents.com

Historical Note:
A nonprofit, professional trade association that promotes student and youth travel. Members are student travel professionals. Active membership is available to tour operators, travel agencies, and wholly-owned subsidiaries of active members. Associate membership is available to hotels, restaurants, tourist attractions, airlines and destination marketing organizations. Membership dues: $500/year.

Continuing Education:
Certification Designation/s: CSTP

Meetings/Conferences: Annual
Conference Chair: Barbara Hutchison
2013 - Los Angeles, CA/Aug. 23 - 27
2014 - Toronto, ON/Aug. 21 - 26

Publications:
SYTA Conference Newsletter; adv.
SYTA Magazine
Teach&Travel

Stuntmen's Association of Motion Pictures *(1961)*
5200 Lankershim Blvd.
Suite 190
Hollywood, CA 91601
Tel: (818) 766-4334 *Fax:* (818) 766-5943
E-Mail: hq@stuntmen.com
Website: stuntmen.com
Members: 137 individuals
Staff: 2
Annual Budget: $50-100,000

Personnel:
President: J. Mark Donaldson
Treasurer: Hugh Aodh O'Brien

Historical Note:
The Stuntmen's Association of Motion Pictures is an honorary society of motion picture stunt coordinators, stuntmen, and second unit directors committed to achieving and enhancing the filmmaker's ceative vision with a better degree of safety. Members of Screen Actor's Guild are only eligible for applying membership in SAMP.

Publications:
Membership Directory; on-line

Membership List Available to Non-members

Stuntwomen's Association of Motion Pictures *(1967)*
12457 Ventura Blvd., Suite 208
Studio City, CA 91604-2411
Tel: (818) 762-0907 *Fax:* (818) 762-9534
E-Mail: stuntwomen@stuntwomen.com
Website: stuntwomen.com
Members: 34 individuals
Staff: 1
Annual Budget: $25-50,000

Personnel:
President: Jane Austen
    E-Mail: stuntwomen@stuntwomen.com

Historical Note:
SWAMP is an organization representing professional stuntwomen who are also full members of the Screen Actors Guild and the American Federation of Television and Radio Artists. Applicants for membership must have been earning a living exclusively as a stuntperson for a minimum of five years.

Subcontractors Trade Association *(1966)*
1430 Broadway
Suite 1600
New York, NY 10018
Tel: (212) 398-6220 *Fax:* (212) 398-6224
E-Mail: subcontractorstrade@verizon.net

Website: stanyc.com
Members: 370 Members
Staff: 3
Annual Budget: $500-1,000,000
Tax: 501(c)(6)

Personnel:
Executive Director: Ronald S. Berger
 E-Mail: stanyc.berger@verizon.net
Administrative Assistant: Jenny Lee
 E-Mail: jennylee@stanyc.com

Historical Note:
STA advocates to improve and enhance subcontractors' economic position in the construction industry. STA represents its members in dealing with the public agencies, authorities and private developers. Membership: $1,475 (Larger Sized Company); $995 (Medium Sized Company); $845 (Smaller Sized Company).

Meetings/Conferences:
Number of non-conference events/year: 1

Publications:
Membership Directory; on-line
STA Newsletter; monthly

Submersible Wastewater Pump Association
(1976)
1866 Sheridan Rd.
Suite 212
Highland Park, IL 60035
Tel: (847) 681-1868 *Fax:* (847) 681-1869
E-Mail: swpaexdir@sbcglobal.net
Website: swpa.org
Members: 50 companies
Staff: 2
Annual Budget: $100-250,000
Tax: 501(c)(6)

Personnel:
Executive Director: Adam Stolberg
 E-Mail: swpaexdir@sbcglobal.net
Administrator Director: Carol Stolberg
 E-Mail: cfs66@sbcglobal.net

Historical Note:
SWPA is a national trade association representing and serving the manufacturers of submersible pumps for municipal and industrial applications.

Meetings/Conferences: Annual
Number of non-conference events/year: 4

Publications:
Membership Roster; annually

Substance Abuse Librarians and Information Specialists *(1978)*
P.O. Box 9513
Berkeley, CA 94709-0513
Tel: (510) 769-1831 *Fax:* (510) 865-2467
E-Mail: salis@salis.org
Website: salis.org
Members: 150 individuals
Staff: 3
Annual Budget: $25-50,000
Tax: 501(c)(3)

Personnel:
Executive Director and Editor: Andrea Mitchell
 E-Mail: amitchell@salis.org
Webmaster and Listserv manager: Nancy Sutherland
 E-Mail: webmaster@salis.org

Historical Note:
SALIS serves as an international network for librarians and information professionals working with material on alcohol and drugs. Members are librarians, information professionals, technology professionals, and others employed in or interested in ATOD information dissemination and services who support the mission, goals, and activities of SALIS. Membership: $50 (Associate/ Retired/unemployed/Students); $60 (Elisad Member); $100 (Full).

Meetings/Conferences: Annual
2013 - Reno, NV (University of Nevada Reno)/April 30 - May 3

Publications:
Membership Directory; on-line
SALIS News; quarterly

Membership List Available to Non-members

Substance Abuse Program Administrators Association *(1992)*
1014 Whispering Oak Dr.
Bardstown, KY 40004

Fax: (281) 664-3152
TollFree: (800) 672-7229
E-Mail: exdir2@sapaa.com
Website: sapaa.com
Staff: 1
Annual Budget: $250-500,000

Personnel:
Executive Director: Jeff M. Morrison
 E-Mail: exdir2@sapaa.com

Historical Note:
SAPAA strives to establish, promote, and communicate better standards of quality, integrity, and professionalism in the administration of workplace substance abuse prevention programs through education, training and the exchange of ideas. Membership: $550 (Regular- Classification A); $175 (Regular-Classification B-Government).

Continuing Education:
Certification Designation/s: C-SAPA

Meetings/Conferences: Annual

Publications:
Membership Directory; on-line
SAPAA Online Certified Collector's Directory; on-line

Sugar Association *(1947)*
1300 L St. NW
Suite 1001
Washington, DC 20005
Tel: (202) 785-1122 *Fax:* (202) 785-5019
E-Mail: sugar@sugar.org
Website: sugar.org
Members: 16 companies
Staff: 7
Annual Budget: $2-5,000,000
Tax: 501(c)(6)

Personnel:
President and Chief Executive Officer: Andrew C. Briscoe III
 E-Mail: briscoe@sugar.org
Vice President, Public Policy and Education: Cheryl Digges
 E-Mail: digges@sugar.org
General Counsel: James Meers Esq.
 E-Mail: jcmeers@aol.com
Media Contact: Megan Mitchell
 E-Mail: mitchell@sugar.org
Administrative Assistant: Lisa Swanson
 E-Mail: lisa@sugar.org

Historical Note:
Founded (1943) as Sugar Research Foundation, assumed its present name in 1947. SA's mission is to promote the consumption of sugar as part of a healthy diet and lifestyle through the use of sound science and research. Members are processors and refiners of beet and cane sugar. Supplies science-based information on the role of sugar and carbohydrates in a healthful diet. Membership: $500 (Associate); $1000 (International).

Publications:
Membership Directory; on-line
The Sugar Packet

Sugar Industry Technologists *(1941)*
201 Cypress Ave.
Clewiston, FL 33440
Tel: (863) 983-3637 *Fax:* (863) 983-7855
E-Mail: sitcontact@sucrose.com
Website: sucrose.com/sit
Members: 550 individuals and companies
Staff: 2
Annual Budget: $100-250,000

Personnel:
Executive Director: Edgar L. Aguirre PhD

Historical Note:
SIT's purpose is to serve the professional interests of its members by dissemination of scientific and other technical aspects of sugar refining at an annual technical meeting. It encourages original research and cooperates with other engineering, technical and scientific societies. Members are technical and administrative personnel in the cane sugar refining industry. Membership: $40 (Associate); $450 (Corporate); $60 (Affiliate).

Meetings/Conferences: Annual
2013 - Guangzhou, China/May 12 - 15
2014 - Toronto, ON/May 18 - 21

Publications:
Membership Directory; on-line

The Sulphur Institute *(1960)*

1020 19th St. NW
Suite 520
Washington, DC 20036
Tel: (202) 331-9660 *Fax:* (202) 293-2940
E-Mail: sulphur@sulphurinstitute.org
Website: sulphurinstitute.org
Members: 36 companies
Staff: 5
Annual Budget: $1-2,000,000
Tax: 501(c)(6)

Personnel:
President and Chief Executive Officer: Catherine A. Randazzo
 E-Mail: crandazzo@sulphurinstitute.org
Manager, Communications: Joshua C. Maak
 E-Mail: TDunn@sulphurinstitute.org
Vice President, Agricultural Programs: Donald L. Messick
 E-Mail: dmessick@sulphurinstitute.org
Manager, Meetings, Membership Relations and Office Services: Stephanie A. Santini
 E-Mail: SSantini@sulphurinstitute.org

Historical Note:
TSI's mission is to promote and expand the use of sulphur in all forms throughout the world and monitors, shares, evaluates, addresses, and expands knowledge about environmental, health, and safety issues impacting sulphur operations. Membership: $17,500 (Producers, plus surcharge of $0.055 per long ton); $17,500 (Traders/ Brokers, plus a surcharge of $0.02 per long ton transacted); $17,500 (Consumers, plus a surcharge of $0.02 per long ton consumed); $17,500 (Companies with sales above $15 million); $6000 (Companies under $15 million in sales).

Meetings/Conferences: Annual
Conference Chair: Stephanie A. Santini
2013 - Beijing, China (The Kerry Hotel)/April 24

Publications:
TSI Newsletter; weekly

Sump and Sewage Pump Manufacturers Association *(1956)*
P.O. Box 647
Northbrook, IL 60065-0647
Tel: (847) 559-9233 *Fax:* (847) 559-9235
E-Mail: hdqtrs@sspma.org
Website: sspma.org
Members: 16 companies
Staff: 3
Annual Budget: $50-100,000
Tax: 501(c)(6)

Personnel:
Managing Director: Pamela W. Franzen
President: Susan O'Grady
Secretary and Treasurer: Jeff Hawks

Historical Note:
Formerly (1981) Sump Pump Manufacturers Association. SSPMA's mission is to represent the industry in a manner consistent with the highest standards of business practice and its obligations under law and regulation, by educating the industry, general public, legislative and regulatory groups, in the proper application, use, installation, and maintenance of the products and services offered by its members.

Continuing Education:
Certification Designation/s: CEU

Sunglass Association of America
225 Reinekers Ln.
Suite 700
Alexandria, VA 33935
Tel: (863) 612-0085 *Fax:* (863) 612-0250
Website: thevisioncouncil.org/members/ content_24
Members: 70 companies
Staff: 2
Annual Budget: Under $10,000
Tax: 501(c)(6)

Personnel:
Contact, Communications: Kenneth "Ken" Frederick
 E-Mail: kfred@gvtc.com

Historical Note:
Sunglass Association of America- has joined The Vision Council and become the Sunglass and Reader Division. Members of the Association consist of firms actively engaged in the manufacture and/or importation and distribution of sunglasses, sunglass parts, components or materials, or reading glasses. Promotes both function and fashion benefits of sunwear and readers to media, trade, and consumers by Providing member guidance regarding regulatory and standards compliance.

Meetings/Conferences:
Conference Chair: Kenneth "Ken" Frederick

Publications:
Newsletter; quarterly

Suntanning Association for Education (1984)
P.O. Box 1181
Gulf Breeze, FL 32562-1181
Tel: (850) 939-3388 Fax: (801) 348-9571
TollFree: (800) 536-8255
E-Mail: suntanningedu@gmail.com
Website: suntanningedu.com
Members: 500 companies
Staff: 1
Annual Budget: $250-500,000

Personnel:
Executive Vice President: Paul Germek
    E-Mail: suntanningedu@gmail.com

Historical Note:
SAE is a non-profit trade association established to provide educational resources and legislative assistance to the indoor tanning industry. Membership: $115 (Salon); $350 (Distributor); $750 (Manufacturer).

Continuing Education:
Certification Designation/s: TOC

Supima (1954)
4141 E. Broadway Rd.
Phoenix, AZ 85040-8831
Tel: (602) 792-6002 Fax: (602) 792-6004
E-Mail: info@supima.com
Website: supima.com
Members: 2400 individuals
Staff: 4
Annual Budget: $2-5,000,000
Tax: 501(c)(6)

Personnel:
President: Jesse W. Curlee
    E-Mail: jesse@supima.com
Executive Vice President: Marc A. Lewkowitz
    E-Mail: marc@supima.com
Vice President, Marketing and Promotions: Buxton S. Midyette
    E-Mail: buxton@supima.com

Historical Note:
Founded in 1954, Supima is the promotional organization of the American Pima cotton growers whose primary objective is to promote the increased consumption of American Pima cotton around the world.

Meetings/Conferences: Annual

Publications:
Supima News Newsletter; monthly; adv.

Supply Chain Council (1996)
12320 Barker Cypress Rd., Suite 600
P.O. Box 321
Cypress, TX 77429-8329
Tel: (202) 962-0440 Fax: (202) 540-9027
E-Mail: info@supply-chain.org
Website: supply-chain.org
Members: 1000 corporations
Staff: 6
Annual Budget: $2-5,000,000

Personnel:
Executive Director: Joseph Francis
    E-Mail: jfrancis@supply-chain.org
Director, Operations and Research: Caspar Hunsche
    E-Mail: chunsche@supply-chain.org
Global Director, Membership Services: Carolyn Lawrence
    E-Mail: clawrence@supply-chain.org
Director, Member Programs: Melinda Spring
    E-Mail: mspring@supply-chain.org

Historical Note:
SCC is a global non-profit association whose methodology, diagnostic and benchmarking tools help its member organizations improve their supply chain processes. Membership: $5,000 (Global); $3,000 (Standard); $1,500 (SME); $300 (NP).

Continuing Education:
Certification Designation/s: SCOR-P, SCOR-S

Meetings/Conferences: Annual
Conference Chair: Carolyn Lawrence
Number of non-conference events/year: 11

Publications:
Supply-Chain Council Newsletter; quarterly

The Surety and Fidelity Association of America (1908)
1101 Connecticut Ave. NW
Suite 800
Washington, DC 20036
Tel: (202) 463-0600 Fax: (202) 463-0606
E-Mail: information@surety.org
Website: surety.org
Members: 650 companies
Staff: 12
Annual Budget: $2-5,000,000
Tax: 501(c)(6)

Personnel:
President: Lynn M. Schubert
    E-Mail: lschubert@surety.org
General Counsel: Edward G. Gallagher
    E-Mail: egallagher@surety.org
Vice President, Government Affairs: Lenore Marema
    E-Mail: lmarema@surety.org
Director, Information Technology: Joseph Orgovan
    E-Mail: jorgovan@surety.org
Director, Regulatory Affairs, Membership and Publications: Barbara Finnegan Reiff
    E-Mail: breiff@surety.org
Associate, Communications: Stephanie Robichaux
    E-Mail: srobichaux@surety.org

Historical Note:
Absorbed the Towner Rating Bureau in 1947 and formerly known as the Surety Association of America, assumed its current name in 2007. SFAA's purpose is to perform a leadership role in promoting and preserving the use of fidelity and surety bonds to protect public and private interests. Members are insurance companies underwriting fidelity, surety and forgery bonds. All members pay an annual assessment fee based upon their latest three-year surety, fidelity, forgery and financial guaranty direct premium writings in addition to a minimum assessment. Foreign affiliates are assessed at a lower rate. Assessments for new members are pro-rated to reflect the actual effective date of membership. There are no additional charges for state filing authorizations.

Meetings/Conferences: Annual
Number of non-conference events/year: 8

Publications:
Newsletter; bi-monthly

Surface Design Association (1976)
P.O. Box 360
Sebastopol, CA 95473-0360
Tel: (707) 829-3110 Fax: (707) 829-3285
E-Mail: info@surfacedesign.org
Website: surfacedesign.org
Members: 300 businesses, schools, libraries and 3700 individuals
Staff: 6
Annual Budget: $250-500,000
Tax: 501(c)(3)

Personnel:
Executive Director: Diane Sandlin
    E-Mail: executivedirector@surfacedesign.org
Administrator, Group Communications: Geraldine Congdon
    E-Mail: groupcommunications@surfacedesign.org
Editor, Surface Design Journal: Marci McDade
    E-Mail: journaleditor@surfacedesign.org
Manager, Conferences: Dorothy Moye
Director, Finance and Membership Services: Joy Stocksdale
    E-Mail: administration@surfacedesign.org
Director, Membership Services: Saaraliisa Ylitalo

Historical Note:
SDA's mission is to increase awareness, understanding, and appreciation of textiles in the art and design communities as well as the general public. Membership consists of individuals involved in printing, designing and dyeing art fabrics, fibers and other materials. Membership: $60 (Individual-US); $72 (Individual- Canada/Mexico); $80 (Individual-International); $500 (Business/Benefactor); $50 (Supporting); $200 (Sponsor/Professional); $1,000 (Fellow); $35 (Student); $100 (Institution, Basic); $180 (Institution, Advanced).

Meetings/Conferences: Annual
Conference Chair: Dorothy Moye
2013 - San Antonio, TX (Crowne Plaza Riverwalk)/June 6 - 9

Publications:
eNews; monthly
Surface Design Journal; quarterly; adv.

Membership List Available to Non-members

Surface Engineering Coating Association (1999)
University at Buffalo Technology Center
1576 Sweet Home Rd., Suite 102
Amherst, NY 14228
Tel: (716) 791-8100 Fax: (716) 278-8768
E-Mail: info@surfaceengineering.org
Website: surfaceengineering.org
Members: 10 companies
Staff: 4
Annual Budget: $10-25,000
Tax: 501(c)(3)

Personnel:
Managing Director: Frederick J. Teeter JD
    E-Mail: fred@surfaceengineering.org
Contact, Accounting and Statistics Services: Catherine Golonka CPA
Legal Counsel: Robert Patterson JD
Contact, Administrative Services: Shirley Teeter
    E-Mail: shirley@surfaceengineering.org

Historical Note:
SECA's mission is to serve and promote the interests of the surface engineering industry, particularly the PVD and CVD thin film vacuum coating service industry. It also promotes communication and dissemination of knowledge in the technology and use of thin films for the members and their end users. Full Members provide PVD and or CVD coating services within North America. Associate Members are companies or individuals providing services to the PVD/CVD coating industry. Membership dues are based on total CVD and PVD sales of the previous year.

Publications:
Associate Member Directory; on-line
Full Member Directory; on-line

Membership List Available to Non-members

Surface Mount Technology Association (1984)
5200 Willson Rd.
Suite 215
Edina, MN 55424-1316
Tel: (952) 920-7682 Fax: (952) 926-1819
E-Mail: smta@smta.org
Website: smta.org
Members: 550 companies and 4100 individuals
Staff: 9
Annual Budget: $1-2,000,000

Personnel:
Executive Administrator: JoAnn Stromberg
    E-Mail: joann@smta.org
Administrative Assistant: Karen Bergseth
    E-Mail: karen@smta.org
Director, Communications and Information Technology: Ryan Flaherty
    E-Mail: ryan@smta.org
Director, Education: Patti Hvidhyld
    E-Mail: patti@smta.org
SMTAI Director, Sales: Gayle Jackson
    E-Mail: gayle@smta.org
Director, Membership Services: Krissy Ohnstad
    E-Mail: krissy@smta.org
Director, Exhibitions: Seana Wall
    E-Mail: seana@smta.org

Historical Note:
The SMTA membership is an international network of professionals who build skills, share practical experience and develop solutions in electronic assembly technologies, including microsystems, emerging technologies, and related business operations. Membership: $5-1495/year.

Continuing Education:
Certification Designation/s: SMAT-CE

Meetings/Conferences: Annual
Conference Chair: Seana Wall
Number of non-conference events/year: 1

Publications:
Membership Directory; on-line; adv.

Surfaces in Biomaterials Foundation (1993)
1000 Westgate Dr.
Suite 252
St. Paul, MN 55114
Tel: (651) 290-6267 Fax: (651) 290-2266
E-Mail: surfacesinbiomaterials@ewald.com
Website: surfaces.org
Members: 30 institutions and 250 individuals
Staff: 3
Annual Budget: $100-250,000

Tax: 501(c)(3)

Personnel:
Executive Director: Andy Shelp
  E-Mail: andys@ewald.com
Planner, Events and Meetings: Ashley Crunstedt
  E-Mail: ashleyc@ewald.com
Web Coordinator and Newsletter Managing Editor: Cody Zwiefelhofer
  E-Mail: codyz@ewald.com

Historical Note:
An international society of research professionals interested in the manufacture and development of new biomaterials. SIBF is dedicated to exploring creative solutions to technical challenges in the biointerface by fostering education and multidisciplinary cooperation among industrial, academic, clinical and regulatory communities. Membership: $50 (Individual/Student); $625 (Academic); $2,000-2,500 (Supporting).

Meetings/Conferences: Annual
Conference Chair: Ashley Crunstedt

Publications:
Membership Directory; on-line
SurFACTS in Biomaterials - Newsletter; bi-monthly; adv.

Surgical Infection Society (1981)
P.O. Box 1278
East Northport, NY 11731
Tel: (631) 368-1880 *Fax:* (631) 368-4466
Website: sisna.org
Staff: 2
Annual Budget: $250-500,000
Tax: 501(c)(3)

Personnel:
Executive Director: Lynn Hydo
Administrative Assistant: Diane Catalano
  E-Mail: dbac66@aol.com

Historical Note:
SIS's mission is to educate health care providers and the public about infection in surgical patients and to promote research in the understanding, prevention and management of surgical infections. Members are surgeons and other medical specialists with an interest in surgical infection. Membership: $200/year.

Meetings/Conferences: Annual
2013 - Las Vegas, NV (Four Seasons Hotel Las Vegas)/ April 12 - 15
2013 - Las Vegas, NV/April 14 - 16
2014 - Baltimore, MD/April 29 - May 3

Publications:
SIS Newsletter
Surgical Infections

Sustainable Buildings Industry Council (1980)
1090 Vermont Ave.
Suite 700
Washington, DC 20005
Tel: (202) 289-7800 *Fax:* (202) 289-1092
E-Mail: sbic@sbiccouncil.org
Website: sbicouncil.org
Members: 70 companies
Staff: 4
Annual Budget: $250-500,000
Tax: 501(c)(6)

Personnel:
Contact: Ryan Colker
  E-Mail: rcolker@nibs.org
Technical Editor: Stephanie Vierra
  E-Mail: svierra@sbicouncil.org

Historical Note:
Formerly (1999) known as the Passive Solar Industries Council. SBIC's mission is to unite and inspire the building industry towards better performance through education, outreach, advocacy and the mutual exchange of ideas. Membership is comprised mainly of trade associations, manufacturers and suppliers interested in the construction of buildings. Membership: $100 (Individual); $500 (Small Business); $1,500-7,000 (Regular, based on revenue).

Publications:
Membership Directory; on-line
SBIC Newsletter; monthly

SWANA - Solid Waste Association of North America (1961)
1100 Wayne Ave.
Suite 700
Silver Spring, MD 20910
Fax: (301) 589-7068

TollFree: (800) 467-9262
E-Mail: info@swana.org
Website: swana.org
Members: 8000 solid waste professionals
Staff: 25
Annual Budget: $100-250,000

Personnel:
Deputy Executive Director: Lori Scozzafava
Executive Director and Chief Executive Officer: John H. Skinner
  E-Mail: jskinner@swana.org
Manager, Marketing and Communications: Kellie Bove
  E-Mail: kbove@swana.org
Manager, Division and Conference Programs: Sue Bumpous
Associate Director: Kathy Callaghan
Manager, Membership and Chapter Services Department: Estela Martinez
Director, Information Technology: Guy Riso
Director, Administration: Cathy Wilde
Coordinator, Marketing: Naddia Williams
Director, Education and Marketing: Meri Beth Wojtaszek
  E-Mail: mwojtaszek@swana.org

Historical Note:
Formerly the Governmental Refuse Collection and Disposal Association (1990). SWANA's mission is to promote and advance the practice of environmentally and economically sound management of municipal solid waste in North America. Members are professionals in the private and public sectors. Membership: $183 (Public Sector Individual); $343 (Private Sector Individual); $243 (Small Business Individual); $62 (Student); $72 (Retired).

Continuing Education:
Certification Designation/s: CM, CTA, CI

Meetings/Conferences:
Conference Chair: Kathy Callaghan
2013 - Long Beach, CA/Sept. 17
2014 - Dallas, TX/Aug. 26
Number of non-conference events/year: 7

Publications:
E-Newsletter; monthly
Member Directory; on-line
Professional Services Directory; on-line
Tech News; quarterly

Swedish-American Chambers of Commerce of the USA, Inc. (1906)
2900 K St. NW
Suite 403
Washington, DC 20007
Tel: (202) 536-1520 *Fax:* (703) 836-6561
E-Mail: info@sacc-usa.org
Website: sacc-usa.org
Members:
20 regional chambers
2300 members
Staff: 6
Annual Budget: $500-1,000,000
Tax: 501(c)(6)

Personnel:
President: Therese Linde
  E-Mail: therese.linde@sacc-usa.org
Communications and Member Services Trainee Scholar: Jimmy Gustafsson
  E-Mail: jimmy@sacc-usa.org
Director, Trainee Program: Cecilia Kullman
  E-Mail: ck@sacc-usa.org
Marketing Intern: Marcus Nygren
  E-Mail: marketing@sacc-usa.org
Financial Officer: Therese Gustavsson Schardt
  E-Mail: therese@sacc-usa.org
Editor: Jordan Zaner

Historical Note:
The purpose of SACC-USA is to advance, foster and expand harmonious commerce and trade between Sweden and the US. Provides leadership and guidance to its regional chamber network and to Swedish and American companies. Membership: $250 (Individual); $800-15,000 (Corporation).

Publications:
Currents Magazine; quarterly; adv.
Membership Directory; annually; adv.
Newsletter eCurrents; quarterly; adv.
Subsidiary Listing; annually; adv.

Synthetic Turf Council (2003)
400 Galleria Pkwy.

Suite 1500
Atlanta, GA 30339
Tel: (678) 385-6720 *Fax:* (678) 385-6501
Website: syntheticturfcouncil.org
Staff: 3
Annual Budget: $500-1,000,000

Personnel:
President: Rick Doyle
  E-Mail: rick@syntheticturfcouncil.org
Director, Member Services: Melanie Taylor
  E-Mail: office@syntheticturfcouncil.org
Marketing And Education Director: Terrie Ward
  E-Mail: terrie@syntheticturfcouncil.org

Historical Note:
The Synthetic Turf Council serves as a neutral unbiased source to encourage, promote, facilitate and communicate a better understanding between all parties of the essential elements required in the selection, delivery and use of synthetic turf systems that will result in greater end user satisfaction. Membership: $1500-$15000 (Full member); $500-$1500 (Special Full); $25-$75 (Affiliate).

Meetings/Conferences: Annual
2013 - Orlando, FL (Renaissance Orlando at SeaWorld)/March 20 - 22

Publications:
STC Newsletter; quarterly

Synthetic Yarn and Fiber Association (1971)
737 Park Trail Ln.
Clover, NC 29710
Tel: (704) 589-5895 *Fax:* (803) 746-5566
Website: thesyfa.org
Members:
350 companies
300 individuals
Staff: 2
Annual Budget: $50-100,000

Personnel:
Managing Director: Kim Petit
  E-Mail: kpettit@thesyfa.org
Executive Secretary: Jerry N. King
  E-Mail: jerry_king@milliken.com

Historical Note:
Formerly Textured Yarn Association of America. SYFA seeks to promote the production, improvement, and use of synthetic yarns and fibers and to facilitate various end uses. The association also provides members a forum for discussion and presentations related to the improvement of synthetic yarns and fibers and their downstream applications and review of current trade issues. Membership: $140 (Individual); $500 (Company).

Meetings/Conferences: Annual
2013 - Charlotte, NC (Sheraton Airport Hotel)/April 18 - 19

System Safety Society (1962)
P.O. Box 70
Unionville, VA 22567-0070
Tel: (540) 854-8630 *Fax:* (540) 854-4561
E-Mail: systemsafety@system-safety.org
Website: system-safety.org
Members: 20 companies and 900 individuals
Staff: 9
Annual Budget: $250-500,000
Tax: 501(c)(6)

Personnel:
President: Gary Braman
Administrative Secretary: Cathy Carter
Director, Member Services: Saralyn Dwyer
  E-Mail: sdwyer@apt-research.com
Director, Publicity and Media and Editor: Clifton A. Ericson II
  E-Mail: cliftonericson@cs.com
Executive Secretary: Jean Jean Sauerman
Director, Education and Professional Development: Chuck Muniak
  E-Mail: cmuniak@stevens.edu
Executive Vice President: Robert Schmedake
  E-Mail: robert.a.schmedake@boeing.com
Director, Conferences: Dave Shampine
  E-Mail: dave.shampine@urs.com
Treasurer: Rod Simmons

Historical Note:
Formerly known as Aerospace System Safety Society and assumed its current name in 1967, SSS works to improve communications in the fields of flight test operations, analysis, instrumentation and data systems. Membership:

$100 (Affiliate); $35 (Senior); $110 (International); $45 (Fellow); $500 (Corporate).

Meetings/Conferences: Annual
Conference Chair: Dave Shampine
2013 - Boston, MA (Boston Marriott Copley Place)/
    Aug. 11 - 16
2014 - St. Louis, MO (St. Louis Union Station
    Marriott)/Aug. 1 - 10
2015 - San Diego, CA (Manchester Grand Hyatt San
    Diego)/Aug. 21 - 29
2016 - Orlando, FL (Renaissance Orlando at
    SeaWorld)/Aug. 6 - 14

Publications:
Journal of System Safety; bi-monthly; adv.

Tag and Label Manufacturers Institute *(1933)*
One Blackburn Center
Gloucester, MA 01930
Tel: (978) 282-1400 *Fax:* (978) 282-3238
E-Mail: office@tlmi.com
Website: tlmi.com
Members: 320 companies
Staff: 5
Annual Budget: $1-2,000,000

Personnel:
President: Frank A. Sablone
    E-Mail: fas@timi.com
Director, Communications: Jennifer Dochstader
    E-Mail: editor@tlmi.com
Office Administrator: Elizabeth Morris
    E-Mail: beth@tlmi.com
Meeting Planner: Vicki Runyeon
    E-Mail: vicki@tlmi.comm

Historical Note:
Formerly (1962) known as the Tag Manufacturers Institute. TLMI is a member-driven association committed to providing business solutions that enhance the prosperity of its members and the narrow web tag, label, and packaging industries. Membership: $800-4,000 (Converter); $2,500 (Supplier); $300 (International).

Continuing Education:
Enrollment: 25
Certification Designation/s: LIFE

Meetings/Conferences:
Conference Chair: Vicki Runyeon
2013 - Palm Beach, FL (Four Seasons Resort Palm
    Beach)/March 3 - 6
2013 - Chicago, IL (Hyatt Regency Chicago)/Sept. 3 - 5
2013 - San Antonio, TX (JW Marriott San Antonio Hill
    Country Resort and Spa)/Oct. 20 - 23
2014 - Newport Beach, CA (The Resort at Pelican Hill)/
    March 9 - 12
2014 - Dana Point, CA (St. Regis Monarch Beach
    Resort)/Oct. 12 - 15
Number of non-conference events/year: 2

Publications:
Hot Off the Press; quarterly
Membership Directory; on-line
TLMI Illuminator; bi-monthly

Tall Ships America *(1973)*
29 Touro St.
P.O. Box 1459
Newport, RI 02840
Tel: (401) 846-1775 *Fax:* (401) 849-5400
E-Mail: asta@tallshipsamerica.org
Website: sailtraining.org
Staff: 6
Tax: 501(c)(3)

Personnel:
Executive Director: Bert Rogers
    E-Mail: bert@tallshipsamerica.org
Director, Operations: Lori A. Aguiar
    E-Mail: lori@tallshipsamerica.org
Office Manager and Bookkeeper: Darlene Godin
    E-Mail: darlene@tallshipsamerica.org

Historical Note:
Formerly American Sail Training Association (ASTA). The mission of the American Sail Training Association is to encourage character building through sail training, promote sail training to the North American public, and support education under sail. Membership: $25-1,000 (Associate); $375-1,075 (Organizational).

Meetings/Conferences: Annual
2013 - Erie, PA (Sheraton Erie Bayfront Hotel)/Feb. 4 -
    6

Publications:

e-Running Free; monthly
Sail Tall Ships! Directory; adv.

Tamworth Swine Association *(1923)*
621 N. 850 West
Greencastle, IN 46135-7771
Tel: (765) 653-4913
E-Mail: tamassoc@webtv.net
Website: tamworthswine.org
Members: 150 individuals
Staff: 2
Annual Budget: Under $10,000

Personnel:
Secretary, Treasurer and Contact, Conferences: Shirley R.
    Brattain
    E-Mail: SBrattain@TamworthSwine.org

Historical Note:
Members are breeders and fanciers of Tamworth swine. Membership: $20-35 (Members); $25-40 (Non Members).

Meetings/Conferences:
Conference Chair: Shirley R. Brattain

Publications:
Membership Directory; on-line

TASH *(1975)*
1001 Connecticut Ave. NW
Suite 235
Washington, DC 20036
Tel: (202) 540-9020 *Fax:* (202) 540-9019
E-Mail: info@TASH.org
Website: tash.org
Members: 2000 individuals
Staff: 7
Annual Budget: $250-500,000
Tax: 501(c)(3)

Personnel:
Executive Director: Barbara Trader
    E-Mail: btrader@tash.org
Editor: Martin Agran PhD
    E-Mail: magran@uwyo.edu
Manager, Programs: Haley Kimmet
    E-Mail: hkimmet@tash.org
Manager, Advocacy Communications: Jonathan
    Riethmaier
    E-Mail: jriethmaier@tash.org
Coordinator, Conferences: Mary Staley
    E-Mail: mstaley@tash.org

Historical Note:
Mission of TASH is to promote the full inclusion and participation of children and adults with significant disabilities in every aspect of their community, and to eliminate the social injustices that diminish human rights. Membership: $30-350/year.

Meetings/Conferences: Annual
Conference Chair: Mary Staley

Publications:
Research and Practice for Persons with Severe
    Disabilities (RPSD); quarterly
TASH Connections; quarterly; adv.
TASH in Action; bi-weekly; adv.

Tau Beta Pi Association *(1885)*
P.O. Box 2697
Knoxville, TN 37901-2697
Tel: (865) 546-4578 *Fax:* (865) 546-4579
E-Mail: tbp@tbp.org
Website: tbp.org
Members:
238 US colleges and universities and a total
membership of 535,617
238 US colleges and universities and a total
membership of 535,617
Staff: 12
Annual Budget: $5-10,000,000
Tax: 501(c)(3)

Personnel:
Executive Director, Secretary, Treasurer and Editor: Curtis
    D. Gomulinski
    E-Mail: curt@tbp.org
Administrative Assistant: Angela B. Boles
    E-Mail: angie@tbp.org
Member Records Specialist: Debbie A. Dewine
    E-Mail: debbie@tbp.org
Communications Specialist: Dylan Lane
    E-Mail: dylan@tbp.org
Director, Development: Patricia B. McDaniel

E-Mail: pat@tbp.org

Historical Note:
Mission is to mark in a fitting manner those who have conferred honor upon their Alma Mater by distinguished scholarship and exemplary character as students in engineering.

Meetings/Conferences: Annual
2013 - Ames, IA/Oct. 31 - Nov. 2

Publications:
Membership Directory; on-line
THE BENT; quarterly; adv.
The Engineering Honor Society; quarterly

Tau Epsilon Rho Law Society *(1921)*
133 Paisley Place
Hainesport, NJ 08036
Tel: (609) 864-1838
Website: ter-law.org
Members: 7500 individuals
Staff: 2
Tax: 501(c)(10)

Personnel:
National Treasurer and Executive Director: Alan M.
    Tepper Esq.
    E-Mail: tepesq@verizon.net
Editor: Barry L. Lippitt
    E-Mail: barry@lippittlaw.com

Historical Note:
TER's mission is to provide opportunities to its members to network, associate, and socialize, both nationally and locally, with other members of the bench and bar who share common values and interests. Membership is open to all attorneys and judges and students attending law school. Membership: $95/year (New Member).

Meetings/Conferences: Annual

Publications:
The Summons; semi-annually

TAUC - The Association of Union Constructors *(1969)*
1501 Lee Hwy.
Suite 202
Arlington, VA 22209-1109
Tel: (703) 524-3336 *Fax:* (703) 524-3364
Website: tauc.org
Members: 2500 companies
Staff: 11
Annual Budget: $1-2,000,000
Tax: 501(c)(6)

Personnel:
Chief Executive Officer: Stephen R. Lindauer
    E-Mail: slindauer@tauc.org
Manager, Communications: David Acord
    E-Mail: dacord@tauc.org
Manager, Meetings and Events: Gwen Jackson
    E-Mail: gjackson@tauc.org
Senior Manager, Database and Information Systems:
    Pamela Livinski
    E-Mail: plivinski@tauc.org
Director, Administration: Mike Marrone
*Senior Director, Government Affairs and Membership
    Services:* Todd R. Mustard
    E-Mail: tmustard@tauc.org

Historical Note:
Formerly National Steel Erectors Association and then NEA - The Association of Union Constructors became TAUC - The Association of Union Constructors in 2007. TAUC's mission is to serve as an advocate for the union construction industry, advancing the cause through an educated and action-driven membership. Members are steel erectors, general contractors and industrial maintenance firms. Membership: $750 (Regular); $5000 (Governing); $4000 (Affiliate/Local Employer Organization).

Meetings/Conferences:
Conference Chair: Gwen Jackson
Number of non-conference events/year: 6

Publications:
Membership Directory; on-line
TAUC About Construction; monthly; adv.
TAUC E-Newsletter; monthly; adv.
The Construction User Magazine; quarterly

Membership List Available to Non-members

Tax Executives Institute, Inc. *(1944)*
1200 G St. NW
Suite 300
Washington, DC 20005-3814

Tel: (202) 638-5601 *Fax:* (202) 638-5607
E-Mail: asktei@tei.org
Website: tei.org
Members: 7000 individuals
Staff: 19
Annual Budget: $5-10,000,000
Tax: 501(c)(6)

Personnel:
Executive Director: Timothy J. McNormally
  E-Mail: tmccormally@tei.org
Tax Counsel: Daniel B. De Jong
  E-Mail: ddejong@tei.org
Director, Information Technology and Web Services: Lars
  M. DeSalvio
  E-Mail: ldesalvio@tei.org
Chief Tax Counsel: Eli J. Dicker
  E-Mail: edicker@tei.org
Director, Conference Planning: Deborah K. Gaffney
  E-Mail: dgaffney@tei.org
Director, Administration: Deborah C. Giesey
  E-Mail: dgiesey@tei.org
Manager, Publications: Christine Hayes
  E-Mail: chayes@tei.org
Director, Membership Services and Chapter Relations:
  Coleman J. Kane
  E-Mail: ckane@tei.org
Senior Tax Counsel: Jeffery P. Rasmussen
  E-Mail: jrasmussen@tei.org
Tax Counsel: Ben R. Shreck
  E-Mail: bshreck@tei.org
Bookkeeper: Joy D. Wolfe
  E-Mail: jwolfe@tei.org

Historical Note:
*TEI's mission is to enhance and improve the tax system and
facilitates interaction among, and the training of, members
and their staffs, by effectively advocating its members views,
and by promoting competence and professionalism in both
the private and government sectors. Membership is open to
corporate officers and employees charged with administering
their company's tax affairs. Membership: $225/year.*

Meetings/Conferences: Annual
Conference Chair: Deborah K. Gaffney
2013 - Washington, DC (Grand Hyatt Washington)/
  March 17 - 20
Number of non-conference events/year: 2

Publications:
Membership Directory; on-line
TEI Membership Roster; annually
The Tax Executive Magazine; bi-monthly

Taxicab, Limousine & Paratransit Association
(1917)
3200 Tower Oaks Blvd.
Suite 220
Rockville, MD 20852
Tel: (301) 984-5700 *Fax:* (301) 984-5703
E-Mail: info@tlpa.org
Website: tlpa.org
Members: 1,100 taxicab companies, executive
sedan and limousine services
Staff: 5
Annual Budget: $1-2,000,000
Tax: 501(c)(6)

Personnel:
Chief Executive Officer: Alfred B. LaGasse
  E-Mail: alagasse@tlpa.org
Manager, Meetings: Michelle A. Hariston CMP
  E-Mail: mhariston@tlpa.org
Executive Vice President: Harold Morgan
  E-Mail: hmorgan@tlpa.org
Manager, Communications: Leah New
  E-Mail: lnew@tlpa.org

Historical Note:
*TLPA is a non-profit trade association of and for the private
passenger transportation industry. Mission is to provide
its membership with a network of programs, services
and support that will enhance their ability to effectively
and profitably serve local public transportation needs.
Membership: $144 (U.S./ International Fleet Operator);
$500-788 (Associate); $250-538 (Public Sector/Trade
Association).*

Meetings/Conferences: Annual
Conference Chair: Michelle A. Hariston CMP
Number of non-conference events/year: 2

Publications:
Member Directory; annually
Newsbriefs; bi-monthly; adv.

Transportation Leader; quarterly; adv.
Membership List Available to Non-members

Tea Association of the United States of America
(1899)
362 Fifth Ave.
Suite 801
New York, NY 10001
Tel: (212) 986-9415 *Fax:* (212) 697-8658
E-Mail: info@teausa.com
Website: teausa.com
Members: 100 companies
Staff: 4
Annual Budget: $500-1,000,000
Tax: 501(c)(6)

Personnel:
President: Joseph P. Simrany

Historical Note:
*The Association is committed to a proactive stance in
formulating and articulating positions on regulatory
and legislative issues. Membership: $2,375-198,000
(Trade Category A); $2,000-40,000 (Trade Category B);
$1,250-10,000 (Associate).*

Continuing Education:
Enrollment: 500
Certification Designation/s: TCP

Publications:
Membership Directory; on-line
TeaBits Newsletter; quarterly

Membership List Available to Non-members

Tea Council of the U.S.A. *(1950)*
362 Fifth Ave.
Suite 801
New York, NY 10001
Tel: (212) 986-9415 *Fax:* (212) 697-8658
E-Mail: info@teausa.com
Website: teausa.com
Members: 84 companies and governments
Staff: 3
Annual Budget: $1-2,000,000

Personnel:
President: Joseph P. Simrany
  E-Mail: simrany@teausa.org

Historical Note:
*TC seeks to increase the consumption of hot and iced tea.
Represents importer, wholesaler, domestic retail, food service
and specialty tea companies. TC Promotes tea consumption
by leveraging positive attributes of tea helping the annual
dollar growth of tea sales.*

Meetings/Conferences: Annual
Number of non-conference events/year: 1

Publications:
TeaBits Newsletter; quarterly

Teaching-Family Association *(1975)*
P.O. Box 2007
Midlothian, VA 23113
Tel: (804) 632-0155 *Fax:* (804) 639-9212
E-Mail: info@teaching-family.org
Website: teaching-family.org
Members:
30 agencies
400 individuals
Staff: 1
Annual Budget: $100-250,000
Tax: 501(c)(3)

Personnel:
Executive Director: Peggy McElgunn
  E-Mail: peggymcelgunn@comcast.net

Historical Note:
*Formerly (1992) the National Teaching-Family Association.
The mission of TFA is to support its members effectively
and to promote the Teaching- Family Model. Membership:
$30 (Individual); $40 (Couple); $60 (Supportive); $4,000
(Agency).*

Continuing Education:
Certification Designation/s: TFA

Meetings/Conferences: Annual

Publications:
TFA Newsletter; adv.

Teamsters Brewery and Soft Drink Workers Conference *(1886)*
25 Louisiana Ave. NW
Washington, DC 20001

Tel: (202) 624-6800 *Fax:* (202) 624-8137
E-Mail: brewery@teamster.org
Website: teamster.org
Members: 75 individuals
Staff: 2

Personnel:
Director: Dave Laughton
Secretary and Treasurer: Ken Hall

Historical Note:
*Founded in 1886 as the National Union of United Brewery
Workmen. In 1903, the union changed its name to the
International Union of United Brewery Workmen of
America. Became International Union of United Brewery,
Flour, Cereal and Soft Drink Workers of America in 1920.
Assumed the present name after merger with United
Brewery Workers in 1973. BSWC is the beverage trade
division of the International Brotherhood of Teamsters.
It brings together all the Teamster locals in the U.S. and
Canada employed in the brewing and soft drink industries,
and allied industries such as fruit juices, wine coolers,
bottled water and can manufacturing.*

Publications:
Teamster Magazine; monthly

TechAmerica (fka Technology Association of America) *(2008)*
601 Pennsylvania Ave. NW, N. Building
Suite 600
Washington, DC 20004
Tel: (202) 682-9110 *Fax:* (202) 682-9111
E-Mail: csc@techamerica.org
Website: techamerica.org
Members: 1,200 Companies
Staff: 84
Annual Budget: $10-25,000,000

Personnel:
Chief of Staff,General Counsel and Secretary: Benjamin
  "Ben" Aderson
Chief Financial Officer: Jeff Bates
Senior Director, Member Relations: Meryl Hickman
Vice President, Business Development: Pete Kaminskas
*Vice President and Counsel, Communications, Privacy, and
  Internet Policy:* Christopher "Chris" E. Wilson
  E-Mail: chris.wilson@techamerica.org

Historical Note:
*Formed in 2008 by the merger of the Information
Technology Association of America, the American
Electronics Association, the Cyber Security Industry
Alliance and the Government Electronics & Information
Technology Association. The largest technology association
in the United States. Consists of four divisions: American
Software Association, Information Technology Services,
Processing and Network Services, and Systems Integration.
Absorbed the Association of Independent Software
Companies in 1972. ITAA provides leadership in business
development, public policy advocacy, market forecasting
and standards development to its corporate members.
Membership fee based on size of company.*

Continuing Education:
Certification Designation/s: ISC

Publications:
Membership Directory; on-line
TechAmerica Newsletter

TechLaw Group *(1986)*
c/o Ackerman Public Relations
1111 Northshore Dr., Suite N-400
Knoxville, TN 37919
Tel: (865) 588-7456 *Fax:* (865) 588-3009
Website: techlaw.org
Members: 17 firms
Staff: 2
Annual Budget: $100-250,000

Personnel:
Executive Director: Lisa Skinner
  E-Mail: lskinner@techlaw.org

Historical Note:
*TechLaw is an international network of law firms which
serve the interests of businesses, institutions, and
individuals involved with technology industries. Member
firms comprise over 7, 000 lawyers.*

Publications:
Membership Directory

Technical Association of the Graphic Arts *(1948)*
200 Deer Run Rd.
Sewickley, PA 15143-2600
Tel: (412) 259-1706 *Fax:* (412) 741-2311
TollFree: (800) 910-4283

E-Mail: taga@printing.org
Website: printing.org/taga
Members: 300 individuals
Staff: 4
Annual Budget: $50-100,000
Tax: 501(c)(6)

Personnel:
Administrator: John Bodnar
  E-Mail: jbodnar@printing.org
Managing Director: Mark Bohan
  E-Mail: mbohan@printing.org
Conference Assistant: Elise Cohen
  E-Mail: ecohen@printing.org

Historical Note:
TAGA's mission is to provide a worldwide forum for sharing and disseminating theoretical, functional and practical information on current and emerging technologies for Graphic Arts print production and related processes. Membership: $125 (Professional); $50 (Retired/ Undergraduate/Graduate Student); $1,500 (Corporate Sponsor).

Meetings/Conferences: Annual
Conference Chair: Elise Cohen
2013 - Portland, OR (Portland Marriott Downtown Waterfront)/Feb. 3 - 6

Publications:
Journal of Graphic Technology; semi-annually
Membership Directory; on-line
TAGA Newsletter; on-line

Technical Association of the Pulp and Paper Industry (1915)
15 Technology Pkwy., South
Norcross, GA 30092
Tel: (770) 446-1400 Fax: (770) 446-6947
TollFree: (800) 332-8686
E-Mail: memberconnection@tappi.org
Website: tappi.org
Members: 8000 individuals
Staff: 29
Annual Budget: $5-10,000,000

Personnel:
President and Chief Executive Officer: Larry N. Montague
  E-Mail: lmontague@tappi.org
Vice President, Corporate Relations and Marketing: David Bell
  E-Mail: dbell@tappi.org
Marketing Specialist: Deborah Chafin
  E-Mail: dchafin@tappi.org
Director, Membership Services, Global Development and Training: Mary Beth Cornell
  E-Mail: mcornell@tappi.org
Content Development Specialist: Chelsie Durie
  E-Mail: cdurie@tappi.org
Administrative Assistant: Sarah Ellsworth
  E-Mail: sellsworth@tappi.org
Chief Financial Officer: Chuck Fiveash
  E-Mail: chuck@ffcpa.net
Director, Marketing: Simona Marcellus
  E-Mail: smarcellus@tappi.org
Manager, Accounting Services: Craig McKinney
  E-Mail: cmckinney@tappi.org
Technical Lead, Publications: Ken Patrick
  E-Mail: kpatrick@tappi.org
Senior Manager, Events: Ed Robie
  E-Mail: erobie@tappi.org
Webmaster: Karen Roman
  E-Mail: kroman@tappi.org
Manager, Membership Services: Lori Madeline Smith
  E-Mail: lmadeline@tappi.org
Manager, Press Operations: Lisa Stephens
  E-Mail: lstephens@tappi.org

Historical Note:
Organized as a section of the American Paper and Pulp Association. The articles of organization were revised at the first annual meeting in 1916 and the name was changed to the Technical Association of the Pulp and Paper Industry. TAPPI's mission is to engage the people and resources of the association in providing solutions to the workplace problems and opportunities that challenge the current and future members. Membership: $174 (Professional); $119 (Young Professional); $500-1,500 (Patron); $355 (Affiliate); $35 (Student); $92 (Retired).

Meetings/Conferences:
Conference Chair: Ed Robie
2013 - Green Bay, WI (Hyatt on Main, Green Bay)/ Sept. 15 - 18
Number of non-conference events/year: 10

Publications:
Ahead of the Curve; weekly; adv.
Bioenergy Technologies Quarterly; quarterly
BioPro News Wire; monthly; adv.
Caught in the Net; weekly; adv.
Eucalyptus Newsletter; irregular; adv.
Frontline Focus; monthly; adv.
Journal of Engineered Fibers and Fabrics; quarterly; adv.
Membership Directory; adv.
Paper 360; monthly; adv.
PLACE Weekly Wrap-Up; weekly; adv.
Progress in Paper Recycling; quarterly; adv.
TAPPI Journal; on-line; adv.
TAPPI Star; on-line; adv.
Tissue Edition; monthly; adv.

Technology and Maintenance Council of American Trucking Associations (1954)
950 N. Glebe Rd.
Suite 210
Arlington, VA 22203-4181
Tel: (703) 838-1763 Fax: (703) 838-1701
E-Mail: tmc@trucking.org
Website: truckline.com/Federation/Councils/ TMC/Pages/default.aspx
Members: 45000 companies
Staff: 9
Annual Budget: $2-5,000,000

Personnel:
Executive Director: Carl Kirk
Technical Director: Robert Braswell
Director, Council Development: Janet Howells-Tierney

Historical Note:
TMC seeks to improve transport equipment, its maintenance and maintenance management. It also conducts industry surveys and promotes the voluntary cooperation among designers and manufacturers of transport equipment and those who specify, purchase, and manage such equipment. Members are trucking executives, maintenance specialists, manufacturers, and suppliers interested in the improvement of trucking equipment, its maintenance, and maintenance management. Membership: $75-460 (ATA Member/Non-ATA Member).

Meetings/Conferences: Annual
Conference Chair: Janet Howells-Tierney
2013 - Nashville, TN (Opryland Hotel)/March 11 - 14
2013 - Pittsburgh, PA (David L. Lawrence Convention Center)/Sept. 10 - 13
Number of non-conference events/year: 1

Publications:
Fleet Advisor; monthly
Fleet Maintenance and Technology; quarterly
The Trailblazer; on-line
TMC's Membership Directory; annually
Transport Topics; weekly

The Technology Institute for Music Educators (1995)
7503 Kingwood Ct.
Suite 220
Fairview, TN 37062
Tel: (615) 285-9750
E-Mail: timemused@ti-me.org
Website: ti-me.org
Staff: 1
Annual Budget: $50-100,000
Tax: 501(c)(3)

Personnel:
Executive Director: Z. Kay Fitzpatrick CAE, JD
  E-Mail: execdirector@ti-me.org

Historical Note:
TI:ME's mission is to assist music educators in applying technology to improve teaching and learning in music. Membership: $40 (Regular); $20-40 (Group); $20 (Student); $30 (Library); $495(Institutional/Commercial).

Continuing Education:
Certification Designation/s: TI:ME 1A, TI:ME 2A

Meetings/Conferences: Annual

Publications:
Electronic Musician Magazine; on-line
Music Educators Journal; adv.
TI:ME Newsletter; monthly

Technology Services Industry Association (1975)
17065 Camino San Bernardo
Suite 200

San Diego, CA 92127
Tel: (858) 674-5491
E-Mail: info@tsia.com
Website: tsia.com
Members: 2000 companies
Staff: 16
Annual Budget: $2-5,000,000

Personnel:
Executive Director: Thomas Lah
President and Chief Executive Officer: J. B. Wood
Senior Vice President, Membership Development: Diane Brundage
Senior Research Director, Education Services: Maria Manning Chapman
Vice President, Technology Research: John Ragsdale
Senior Vice President, Programs: Tom Rich
Senior Vice President, Operations and Chief Financial Officer: Stephen Smith

Historical Note:
Formerly (1985) Association of Field Service Managers and (1989) Association of Field Service Managers International and Association for Services Management. TSIA strives to help service professionals and service organizations deliver more value for their customers. Members are executives and managers in the high technology services/support industry. Membership: $4,000 (Companies); $299 (Individual).

Continuing Education:
Certification Designation/s: CSP-S, CSP-I, CSQ, CSP-II

Meetings/Conferences: Semi-Annual
Conference Chair: Tom Rich

Publications:
ConferenceNews; monthly
Inside Technology Services; quarterly
Technology Services Community Insight; quarterly
Technology Services Research Quarterly

Technology Student Association (1978)
1914 Association Dr.
Reston, VA 20191-1540
Tel: (703) 860-9000 Fax: (703) 758-4852
TollFree: (888) 860-9010
E-Mail: general@tsaweb.org
Website: tsaweb.org
Members: 175000 individuals
Staff: 9
Annual Budget: $1-2,000,000
Tax: 501(c)(3)

Personnel:
Executive Director: Rosanne T. White
  E-Mail: rwhite@tsaweb.org
Systems Manager: Leanne Guido
  E-Mail: lguido@tsaweb.org
Program Manager: Lynda Haitz
Manager, Programs: Sandy Honour
Project Manager: Catherine Wetherby
Business Manager: Virginia Williams

Historical Note:
TSA fosters personal growth, leadership, and opportunities in technology, innovation, design, and engineering. Members apply and integrate science, technology, engineering and mathematics concepts through co-curricular activities, competitive events and related programs.

Meetings/Conferences: Annual
Conference Chair: Sandy Honour
2013 - Orlando, FL (Rosen Shingle Creek Hotel)/June 28 - July 2

Technology Transfer Society (1975)
2005 Arthur Ln.
Austin, TX 78704
Tel: (512) 447-4409 Fax: (512) 447-1814
E-Mail: t2s@t2society.org
Website: t2society.org
Members: 200 individuals
Staff: 2
Annual Budget: $10-25,000

Personnel:
President: Donald Siegel
  E-Mail: sieged@rpi.edu
Contact, Advertising: Jiten Ruparel
  E-Mail: ruparelj@franklin.edu

Historical Note:
T2S's mission is to share methods, opportunities and schools of thought with the technology transfer community. Membership: $125 (Individual, U.S.); $600 (For-profit Organization); $300 (Not-for-profit Organization); $65

(Student/Retiree); $150 (Individual, International); $320 (Others).

Publications:
T'Squared; monthly
The Journal of Technology Transfer; quarterly
Membership List Available to Non-members

TechServe Alliance (1987)
1420 King St.
Suite 610
Alexandria, VA 22314
Tel: (703) 838-2050 *Fax:* (703) 838-3610
E-Mail: staff@techservealliance.org
Website: techservealliance.org
Members: 350 IT solutions and IT consulting firms
Staff: 12
Annual Budget: $2-5,000,000
Tax: 501(c)(6)

Personnel:
Chief Executive Officer: Mark Roberts
    E-Mail: roberts@techservealliance.org
Director, Programs and Public Policy: Susan K. Donohoe
    E-Mail: donohoe@techservealliance.org
Communications Assistant: Tom Haskard
    E-Mail: haskard@techservealliance.org
Director, Member Relations: Julie Price-Shehan
Manager, Business Development: Nikki Ramlogan
    E-Mail: ramlogan@techservealliance.org

Historical Note:
Formerly National Association of Computer Consultant Businesses (NACCB). A computer consultancy firm. TechServe Alliance is a collaboration of IT services firms, clients, consultants and suppliers dedicated to advancing excellence and ethics within the IT services industry. Mission is to help member companies achieve their business goals and fostering IT services industry growth and advancement. Membership: $1,350 -13,400/year (Based on Firm Size).

Meetings/Conferences:
Conference Chair: Susan K. Donohoe

Publications:
camera-ready Client and Consultant; quarterly
Client and Contractor Newsletters; quarterly
IT Contractor Update
IT Services Update
Membership Directory; on-line
NACCB Monitor; quarterly
News You Can Use; weekly; adv.
Wednesday Weekly; weekly; adv.

Telecommunications Benchmarking International Group (1992)
4606 FM 1960 West
Suite 250
Houston, TX 77069
Tel: (281) 440-5044 *Fax:* (281) 440-6677
E-Mail: tbig@benchmarkingnetwork.com
Members: 3500 individuals
Staff: 21
Annual Budget: $1-2,000,000

Personnel:
President: Mark T. Czarnecki

Historical Note:
Members are professionals in telecommunications firms. TBIG collects data from its members on best practices in the industry.

Telecommunications Industry Association (1988)
2500 Wilson Blvd.
Suite 300
Arlington, VA 22201-3834
Tel: (703) 907-7700 *Fax:* (703) 907-7727
E-Mail: tia@tiaonline.org
Website: tiaonline.org
Members: 600 companies
Staff: 51
Annual Budget: $10-25,000,000

Personnel:
President: Grant E. Seiffert
    E-Mail: gseiffert@tiaonline.org
Vice President, Marketing and Communications: Eileen Bramlet
    E-Mail: ebramlet@tiaonline.org
Director, Technical Programs: John Derr
    E-Mail: jderr@tiaonline.org

Senior Vice President, Membership Services, Marketing and Business Development: John Jacobs
    E-Mail: jjacobs@tiaonline.org
Vice President and Corporate Counsel: Andrew Kurtzman
    E-Mail: akurtzman@tiaonline.org
Director, Human Resources: Lisa Maghraoui
    E-Mail: lmaghraoui@tiaonline.org
Manager, Events: Michelle Melsop
    E-Mail: mmelsop@tiaonline.org
Director, Public Relations: Mike Snyder
    E-Mail: msnyder@tiaonline.org
Vice President, Networking and Intelligence: Taly Walsh
    E-Mail: twalsh@tiaonline.org
Senior Director, Operations: Mary Piper Waters
    E-Mail: mwaters@tiaonline.org
Senior Manager, Information and Technology Services: Tony Zarafshar
    E-Mail: tzarafshar@tiaonline.org

Historical Note:
Formerly (1988) the United States Telecommunications Suppliers Association. Originally a part of the United States Independent Telephone Association with which it was affiliated, TIA is a trade group of manufacturers, suppliers and support service organizations of the telecommunications industry. Membership: $1,200-72,000 (General Manufacturer/Supplier/General Service Provider/ Enterprise); $1,200-6000 (Associate).

Continuing Education:
Certification Designation/s: CTP, CCNT

Meetings/Conferences: Annual
Conference Chair: Michelle Melsop
2013 - Washington, DC (Gaylord National-Washington)/Oct. 8 - 10

Publications:
ICT2020; on-line
Industry Beat
PULSE online; monthly
TIA Network; weekly

Television Bureau of Advertising (1955)
Three E. 54th St.
Tenth Floor
New York, NY 10022-3108
Tel: (212) 486-1111 *Fax:* (212) 935-5631
E-Mail: info@tvb.org
Website: tvb.org
Members: 600 television stations
Staff: 27
Annual Budget: $5-10,000,000

Personnel:
President and Chief Executive Officer: Steve Lanzano
    E-Mail: steve@tvb.org
Executive Vice President and Chief Marketing Officer: Abby Auerbach
    E-Mail: aauerbach@tvb.org
Vice President, Finance and Administration: Susan Converse
    E-Mail: susanc@tvb.org
Web Administrator: Anne Conway
    E-Mail: anne@tvb.org
Accountant: Arleen Fong
    E-Mail: arleen@tvb.org
Senior Vice President, Business Development and Marketing: Scott Roskowski
    E-Mail: scott@tvb.org
Manager, Marketing and Communications: Don Seaman
    E-Mail: don@tvb.org

Historical Note:
TVB actively promotes local media marketing solutions to the advertising community, and in so doing works to develop advertising dollars for the medium's multiple platforms, including on-air, website and mobile. Members are television broadcast groups, advertising sales reps, syndicators, international broadcasters, associate members and individual television stations.

Meetings/Conferences: Annual

Publications:
Membership Directory; on-line

Telework Advisory Group for World at Work (1955)
1100 13th St. NW.
Suite 800
Washington, DC 20005
Tel: (202) 315-5500 *Fax:* (202) 315-5550
Website: workingfromanywhere.org/
Staff: 1

Personnel:
Government Training and Education: Glynnis Gillespie
    E-Mail: glynnis.gillespie@worldatwork.org

Historical Note:
ITAC's mission is to advance Telework.

Tennis Industry Association (1981)
P.O. Box 7845
Hilton Head Island, SC 29938
Tel: (843) 686-3036 *Fax:* (843) 686-3078
TollFree: (866) 686-3036
E-Mail: info@tennisindustry.org
Website: tennisindustry.org
Members: 150 Organizations
Staff: 4
Annual Budget: $1-2,000,000
Tax: 501(c)(6)

Personnel:
Executive Director: Jolyn de Boer
    E-Mail: jolyn@tennisindustry.org
Director, Information Technology: Matt Allen
    E-Mail: matt@tennisindustry.org
Contact, Media Relations: Peter Francesconi
    E-Mail: Peter@TennisIndustry.org
Marketing Manager: Brian O'Donnell
    E-Mail: brian@tennisindustry.org

Historical Note:
TIA was established in 1974 as the American Tennis Industry. In 1993 the name was changed to the Tennis Industry Association to better reflect the global interests of the membership. The TIA's mission is to increase tennis participation through the support of grow the game activities and image campaigns by working closely with the USTA and industry partners. Membership: $100 (Individual); $295 (Associate); $1,000 (Supporting Members); $3,000 (Affiliate); $500 (Lifetime Individual).

Meetings/Conferences: Annual

Publications:
Tennis Industry Association Newsletter; monthly; adv.

Teratology Society (1960)
1821 Michael Faraday Dr.
Suite 300
Reston, VA 20190-5332
Tel: (703) 438-3104 *Fax:* (703) 438-3113
E-Mail: tshq@teratology.org
Website: teratology.org
Members: 750 individuals
Staff: 2
Annual Budget: $500-1,000,000
Tax: 501(c)(3)

Personnel:
Executive Director: Tonia M. Masson
Treasurer: Wafa A. Harrouk PhD

Historical Note:
TS's mission is to promote research and the exchange of ideas and research results that reveal the causes, improve the diagnosis and treatment, and prevent the occurrence of abnormal development and birth defects. Membership: $126 (Regular/Associate); $10 (Student); $4,000 (Platinum Sustaining); $2,000-4,000 (Gold Sustaining); $750-2,000 (Silver Sustaining).

Meetings/Conferences: Annual
2013 - Tucson, AZ (Loews Ventana Canyon Resort)/June 22 - 26
2014 - Bellevue, WA (Hyatt Regency Bellevue)/June 28 - July 2
2015 - Montreal, QC (Hilton Montreal Bonaventure)/June 27 - July 2
2016 - San Antonio, TX (Grand Hyatt San Antonio)/June 25 - 29

Publications:
Birth Defects Research
Membership Directory; on-line
TS Newsletters; quarterly

TESOL International Association (1966)
1925 Ballenger Ave.
Suite 550
Alexandria, VA 22314-6820
Tel: (703) 836-0774 *Fax:* (703) 836-7864
TollFree: (888) 547-3369
E-Mail: info@tesol.org
Website: tesol.org
Members: 12000 individuals and 40000 educators
Staff: 20

Annual Budget: $2-5,000,000
Tax: 501(c)(3)

Personnel:
Executive Director: Rosa Aronson PhD
   E-Mail: raronson@tesol.org
Director, Education Programs: John Donaldson
   E-Mail: jdonaldson@tesol.org
Director, Conference Services: Lisa Dyson CMP
   E-Mail: ldyson@tesol.org
Manager, Publications: Carol Edwards CAE
   E-Mail: cedwards@tesol.org
Manager, Information Technology: Jaime Mattos
   E-Mail: jmattos@tesol.org
Director, Marketing and Membership Services: Barry
   Pilson CAE
   E-Mail: bpilson@tesol.org
Associate Executive Director, Advocacy and Professional
   Relations: John Segota
   E-Mail: jsegota@tesol.org
Director, Finance: Jim Trope
   E-Mail: jtrope@tesol.org

Historical Note:
TESOL International Association was formerly
known as Teachers of English to Speakers of Other
Languages. TESOL's mission is to develop and maintain
professional expertise in English language teaching and
learning for speakers of other languages worldwide.
Membership: $95 (Individual); $35 (Global Professional/
Global Electronic); $33 (Student); $55 (Retired/New
Professional).

Meetings/Conferences: Annual
Conference Chair: Lisa Dyson CMP
2013 - Dallas, TX (Dallas Convention Center)/March
   20 - 23
2014 - Portland, OR (Oregon Convention Center)/
   March 26 - 29
2015 - Toronto, ON (Metro Toronto Convention
   Centre)/March 25 - 28
2016 - Baltimore, MD/April 5 - 8
2017 - Seatle, WA/March 21 - 24
Number of non-conference events/year: 2

Publications:
Community Newsletters; on-line
Member Directory; on-line
TESOL Connections; on-line; adv.
TESOL Journal; on-line; adv.
TESOL Quarterly; quarterly; adv.

Membership List Available to Non-members

Tetrahydrofuran Task Force (1921)
2200 Pennsylvania Ave. NW
Suite 100W
Washington, DC 20037
Tel: (202) 833-6580
Staff: 26
Annual Budget: $25-50,000
Tax: 501(c)(6)

Personnel:
Treasurer: Glyn jones

Historical Note:
The Tetrahydrofuran Task Force represents U.S.
manufacturers and users of tetrahydrofuran (THF). Its
mission is to address scientific, regulatory, and product
stewardship issues concerning the health, safety, or
environmental aspects of THF or products using THF. All
administration is provided by B&C Consortia Management.

Texas Alliance of Energy Producers (2000)
719 Scott Ave.
Suite 930
Wichita Falls, TX 76301
Tel: (940) 723-4131 Fax: (940) 723-4132
E-Mail: taep@texasalliance.org
Website: texasalliance.org
Members: 3350 members
Staff: 6
Annual Budget: $1-2,000,000
Tax: 501(c)(6)

Personnel:
President: Alex Mills
   E-Mail: alexm@texasalliance.org
Director, Meetings: Donna Brown
   E-Mail: donnab@texasalliance.org
Director, Membership Services: Sharon Davis
   E-Mail: sharond@texasalliance.org
Public Relations Specialist: A. D. Koen
Legal Advisor: Gloria Leal

E-Mail: gleallaw@sbcglobal.net
Vice President, Development: Sandi Simon
   E-Mail: sandis@texasalliance.org

Historical Note:
Formed by the merger of the North Texas Oil and Gas
Association and the West Central Texas Oil and Gas
Association. The Alliance brings together members in
300 cities and 29 states for the common purpose of
protecting the oil and gas industry and developing programs
- insurance, public education - that make them more
profitable. Membership: $240 (Basic); $325 (Corporate).

Meetings/Conferences: Annual
Conference Chair: Donna Brown
2013 - Wichita Falls, TX/April 23 - 24/4000
   attendees/over 100 exhibitors

Publications:
Membership Directory; on-line; adv.
NewsLine; monthly; adv.

Texas Longhorn Breeders Association of America (1964)
2315 N. Main, Suite 402
P.O. Box 4430
Fort Worth, TX 76164
Tel: (817) 625-6241 Fax: (817) 625-1388
E-Mail: tlbaa@tlbaa.org
Website: tlbaa.org
Members: 4600 individuals
Staff: 10
Annual Budget: $500-1,000,000
Tax: 501(c)(5)

Personnel:
Contact, Events: Pam Galloway
   E-Mail: pam.galloway@tlbaa.org
Contact, Registrations and Membership and Office
   Manager: Rick Fritsche
   E-Mail: rick@tlbaa.org
Contact, Financial Services: Donna Shimanek
   E-Mail: donna@tlbaa.org
Editor in Chief: Laura Standley
   E-Mail: laura@tlbaa.org

Historical Note:
TLBAA's aim is to recognize Texas Longhorn cattle as a
distinct breed in order to protect the unique heritage of the
Texas Longhorn and its link with the history of America, to
encourage breeding practices, to preserve its purity. Member
of the National Pedigree Livestock Council, National
Cattlemen's Association, and U.S. Beef Breeds Council.
Membership: $100 (Active); $25 (Junior); $75 (Associate).

Meetings/Conferences:
Conference Chair: Pam Galloway
Number of non-conference events/year: 2

Publications:
Breeders Directory; on-line
E-Trails; weekly
Texas Longhorn Trails Magazine; monthly

Text and Academic Authors Association (1987)
P.O. Box 56359
St. Petersburg, FL 33732-6359
Tel: (727) 563-0020 Fax: (727) 563-0050
E-Mail: textandacademicauthors@taaonline.net
Website: taaonline.net
Members: 1950 individuals
Staff: 11
Annual Budget: $1-2,000,000
Tax: 501(c)(6)

Personnel:
Executive Director: Richard T. Hull
   E-Mail: richard.hull@taaonline.net
Contact, Information Technology: Robin Casey
   E-Mail: rcasey4@gmail.com
Manager, Marketing and Membership Services: Maureen
   Foerster
   E-Mail: Maureen.Foerster@taaonline.net
Production Editor: Paula Heimbecker
   E-Mail: pheimbecker@winona.msus.edu
Database Manager: Jodi Matson
   E-Mail: jodi.matson@taaonline.net
Assistant, Programs: Susanna Patrick
   E-Mail: susanna.patrick@taaonline.net
Associate Executive Director: Kim Pawlak
   E-Mail: kim.pawlak@taaonline.net

Historical Note:
Formerly (1993) Textbook Authors Association. TAA's
mission is to enhance the quality of textbooks and other
academic materials, such as journal articles, monographs
and scholarly books, in all fields and disciplines, by

providing its textbook and academic author members
with educational and networking opportunities. Members
are creators of academic intellectual property at all
levels. Membership: $15 (Graduate students/Instructors/
Postdoctoral Fellows); $30 (Assistant Professor); $55
(Associate Professors); $75 (Professor); $200(Sustaining).

Meetings/Conferences: Annual
Conference Chair: Kim Pawlak
2013 - Reno, NV (Silver Legacy Hotel)/June 21 - 22
Number of non-conference events/year: 2

Publications:
Membership Directory; on-line
TAA News Alerts; bi-monthly; adv.
The Academic Author; monthly; adv.

Textile Bag and Packaging Association (1934)
3000 Royal Marco Way PH-N
Marco Island, FL 34145
Tel: (616) 481-4730
E-Mail: sccashapir@aol.com
Website: textilepackaging.org
Members: 140 firms
Staff: 3
Annual Budget: $50-100,000
Tax: 501(c)(6)

Personnel:
Executive Director: Maxine Shapiro
   E-Mail: sccashapir@aol.com
President: Jeff Chalabi
   E-Mail: jeffchalabi@centralbagcompany.com
Contact, Website Issues: Karen Wasserman

Historical Note:
Formerly (1968) National Burlap Bag Dealers Association
and (1984) Textile Bag Processors Association; assumed
its present name in 1985. TBPA's mission is to promote
the trade and build membership through meetings,
newsletters and roster listing. Members are manufacturers
and distributors of textile bags and packaging supplies.
Membership: $475/year.

Meetings/Conferences: Annual
Conference Chair: Maxine Shapiro
2013 - Tucson, AZ (Loews Ventana Canyon Resort)/
   March 17 - 19
2013 - Las Vegas, NV (Caesars Palace)/Sept. 23 - 25

Publications:
Association Newsletter; quarterly; adv.
Membership Directory; on-line

Textile Care Allied Trades Association (1920)
271 Route 46 West
Suite D203
Fairfield, NJ 07004
Tel: (973) 244-1790 Fax: (973) 244-4455
E-Mail: info@tcata.org
Website: tcata.org
Members: 250 companies
Staff: 2
Annual Budget: $250-500,000

Personnel:
Chief Executive Officer: David Cotter
   E-Mail: david@tcata.org

Historical Note:
Formerly (1982) the Laundry and Cleaners Allied Trades
Association. TCATA seeks to increase professionalism
through business operations and sales improvement
education, provide forums where business challenges
are discussed and solved, generate and apply business
intelligence, and create a favorable business climate by
seeking fair regulation and legislation. Members are
manufacturers and distributors of commercial laundry
and dry cleaning machinery, equipment and supplies.
Membership: $760-2,940 (North American Supply/
Machinery Manufacturer); $625-2,675 (North American
Distributor); $625 (International Company/Trade
Journal/General/Manufacturers Representative/Niche
Manufacturers).

Meetings/Conferences: Annual
Conference Chair: David Cotter
2013 - San Diego, CA (Rancho Bernardo Inn)/July 31 -
   Aug. 3

Publications:
American Trade Magazines; on-line; adv.
TIDINGS Newsletter; monthly; adv.

Textile Fibers and By-Products Association (1931)
1531 Industrial Dr.
Griffin, GA 30224
Tel: (770) 412-2325 Fax: (770) 227-6321
E-Mail: info@tfbpa.org

Website: tfbpa.org
Members:
52 companies
166 individuals
Staff: 2
Annual Budget: $10-25,000

Personnel:
Executive Secretary: C.E. "Chubby" Williams Jr.

Historical Note:
Formerly (1966) Textile Waste Exchange, TFBPA promotes the interests of dealers and processors in the textile by-products business. Upon receipt of an inquiry for information concerning membership, the Executive Secretary shall transmit to the inquirer form letter outlining the general procedure for application for membership as well as a copy of the general information brochure. If the inquirer then indicates a desire to become a member, he/she will be sent a copy of a standard application form.

Meetings/Conferences:
Conference Chair: C.E. "Chubby" Williams Jr.
Number of non-conference events/year: 1

Publications:
Membership Directory

Membership List Available to Non-members

Textile Producers and Suppliers Association

437 Madison Ave., 35th Floor
New York, NY 10022-7302
Tel: (212) 907-7300 *Fax:* (212) 754-0330
Members: 25 individuals
Staff: 1
Annual Budget: $100-250,000

Personnel:
Counsel: Richard S. Taffet

Historical Note:
TPSA was formed to address the problem of unauthorized copying of textile and decorative home furnishing designs in international markets.

Textile Rental Services Association of America
(1913)
1800 Diagonal Rd.
Suite 200
Alexandria, VA 22314
Tel: (703) 519-0029 *Fax:* (703) 519-0026
TollFree: (877) 770-9274
E-Mail: info@trsa.org
Website: trsa.org
Members: 600 companies
Staff: 20
Annual Budget: $2-5,000,000

Personnel:
President: Joseph Ricci
    E-Mail: jricci@trsa.org
Director, Membership Services: Charles Brigham
    E-Mail: cbrigham@trsa.org
Manager, Industry Affairs and Programs: Salita Jones
    E-Mail: sjones@trsa.org
Multimedia Designer and Developer: Dennis Mangual
    E-Mail: dmangual@trsa.org
Director, Government Relations: Kevin Schwalb
    E-Mail: KSchwalb@trsa.org
Manager, Advertising Production: Mittie Spruill
    E-Mail: mspruill@trsa.org

Historical Note:
Formerly (1979) Linen Supply Association of America, TRSA seeks to advance the professionalism of its members and promote their success through government advocacy, education, marketing and business enhancing services. Members are textile rental service companies which provide uniform, linen and towel rental services to business and industry. Associate members are manufacturers, distributors and suppliers. It also sponsors and supports the Textile Rental Services Association Political Action Committee. Membership: $1500-75000 (Operator); $2500-23000 (Associate).

Meetings/Conferences: Annual
Conference Chair: Salita Jones
2013 - Sonoma, CA (Fairmont Sonoma Mission Inn and Spa)/Sept. 22 - 25
Number of non-conference events/year: 5

Publications:
Textile Rental; monthly
TR Weekly; weekly
TRSA's Membership Directory

Theatre Communications Group *(1961)*
520 Eighth Ave.

24th Floor
New York, NY 10018-4156
Tel: (212) 609-5900 *Fax:* (212) 609-5901
E-Mail: tcg@tcg.org
Website: tcg.org
Members: 12000 individuals, 700 member theatres and affiliate organizations
Staff: 70
Annual Budget: $5-10,000,000
Tax: 501(c)(3)

Personnel:
Executive Director: Teresa Eyring
Director, Government and Education Programs: Laurie Baskin
Director, Membership Services: Jennifer Cleary
Director, Technology: Joe Cucchiara
Director, Advertising: Carol Van Keuren
Director, Communications and Conferences: Dafina McMillan
Editor: Jim O'Quinn
Chief Financial Officer: Robin Schlinger
Operations Manager: Mark Thornton
Director, Marketing: Leigh A. Zona

Historical Note:
TCG works to strengthen, nurture and advocate the professional not-for-profit American theatre. Membership: $35-200 (Individual); $20-35 (Student); $100- 550 (Affiliate).

Meetings/Conferences: Annual
Conference Chair: Dafina McMillan
2013 - Dallas, TX/June 6 - 8

Publications:
American Theatre Magazine; monthly; adv.
ARTSEARCH; semi-monthly; adv.
Field Letter; monthly
Individual Member Wire; bi-monthly
TCG Bulletin; monthly
TCG Membership Directory; on-line

Membership List Available to Non-members

Theatre Library Association *(1937)*
C/O New York Public Library for the Performing Arts
40 Lincoln Center Plaza
New York, NY 10023
Tel: (212) 000-0000
E-Mail: info@tla-online.org
Website: tla-online.org
Members:
125 institutions
175 individuals
Staff: 5
Annual Budget: $10-25,000
Tax: 501(c)(3)

Personnel:
President: Kenneth Schlesinger
    E-Mail: kenneth.schlesinger@lehman.cuny.edu
Legal Counsel: Georgia Harper
    E-Mail: gharper@austin.utexas.edu
Executive Secretary and Webmaster: David Nochimson
    E-Mail: davidnoc@softhome.net
Treasurer: Colleen Reilly
Editor: Angela Weaver
    E-Mail: aw6@u.washington.edu

Historical Note:
Founded in 1937. An affiliate of the American Library Association and the International Federation for Theatre Research. TLA's purpose is to promote professional practices in acquisition, organization, access and preservation of performing arts resources in libraries, archives, museums, private collections, and the digital environment. Membership: $30 (Personal Members/ Students/Non-Salaried Members (non-U.S.)); $40 (Institutional Members/Personal Members (non-U.S.)); $50 (Institutional Members (non-U.S.)); $20 (Students/Non-Salaried Members (U.S.)).

Meetings/Conferences: Annual
Number of non-conference events/year: 1

Publications:
Broadside; adv.
Broadside, Newsletter of the Theatre Library Association
Membership Directory; on-line
Performing Arts Resources; irregular; adv.

Membership List Available to Non-members

Therapeutic Touch International Association
(1978)
P.O. Box 419
Craryville, NY 12521
Tel: (518) 325-1185 *Fax:* (509) 693-3537
E-Mail: nhpai@therapeutic-touch.org
Website: therapeutic-touch.org
Members: 700 individuals
Staff: 7
Annual Budget: $25-50,000

Personnel:
President: Sue Conlin
    E-Mail: president@therapeutic-touch.org
Contact, Education: Chery Brady
    E-Mail: education@therapeutic-touch.org
Contact, Membership Services: Judy Custer
Contact, Communications: Lin Reilly
    E-Mail: communications@therapeutic-touch.org
Contact, Membership: David Shields
    E-Mail: membership@therapeutic-touch.org
Treasurer: Kathleen Archibald Simon
    E-Mail: treasurer@therapeutic-touch.org
Treasurer: Glenn Wood
    E-Mail: ttwood52@gmail.com

Historical Note:
Formerly Professional Associates International, Inc. (NH-PAI). TTIA's mission is to guide, inspire and advance excellence in Therapeutic Touch SM as a healing practice and lifeway. Has no paid officers or full-time staff. Membership: $50(Individual/International); $50(Senior/ Student); $15(Associate).

Continuing Education:
Certification Designation/s: QTTP, QTTT

Meetings/Conferences: Annual

Publications:
CfH Newsletter; on-line
Cooperative Connection; on-line
Membership Directory; on-line

Thermoforming Institute
2151 Michelson Dr.
Suite 240
Irvine, CA 92612
Tel: (949) 261-6979 *Fax:* (949) 261-6959
Website: spithermoformers.org
Members: 45 manufacturers
Staff: 1

Personnel:
Director, Business Unit: Jill Brandts
    E-Mail: jbrandts@plasticsindustry.org

Historical Note:
Ti's mission is to promote the growth and prestige of the thermoforming industry by encouraging the use of good manufacturing practices in compliance with recognized standards of practice.

Theta Tau *(1904)*
1011 San Jacinto
Suite 205
Austin, TX 78701
Tel: (512) 472-1904 *Fax:* (512) 472-4820
TollFree: (800) 264-1904
E-Mail: central.office@thetatau.org
Website: thetatau.org
Members: 30000 individuals
Staff: 2
Annual Budget: $250-500,000

Personnel:
Executive Director: Michael T. Abraham

Historical Note:
A professional fraternity in engineering. Founded at the University of Minnesota. Purpose is to develop and maintain a standard of professional interest among its members, and to unite them in a strong bond of fraternal fellowship.

Publications:
Gear of Theta Tau; biennially; adv.
Member Directory; on-line
Velocitas
Velocitas (Officers Newsletter); adv.

Thoroughbred Club of America *(1932)*
P.O. Box 8098
Lexington, KY 40533-8098
Tel: (859) 254-4282 *Fax:* (859) 231-6131
E-Mail: contact@thethoroughbredclub.com

Website: thethoroughbredclub.com
Members: 1500 individuals
Staff: 30
Annual Budget: $1-2,000,000

Personnel:
Executive Director: Betty Stone Flynn
    E-Mail: BettyFlynn@thethoroughbredclub.com

Historical Note:
Founded as the Thoroughbred Club; name was changed to its present form the following year. TCA's mission is to provide a forum for the discussion and interchange of ideas, methods and information relating to the breeding, racing and marketing of Thoroughbred horses and to encourage public interest.

Publications:
Monthly News; monthly

Thoroughbred Owners and Breeders Association (1961)

P.O. Box 910668
Lexington, KY 40591-0668
Tel: (859) 276-2291 *Fax:* (859) 276-2462
TollFree: (888) 606-8622
E-Mail: toba@toba.org
Website: toba.org
Members: 2500 individuals
Staff: 7
Annual Budget: $500-1,000,000
Tax: 501(c)(6)

Personnel:
President: Daniel J. Metzger
    E-Mail: metzger@toba.org
Coordinator, Membership and Education: Amy Bunt
Director, Marketing and Communications: Erin Crady
    E-Mail: ecrady@toba.org
Manager, Membership Development: Terry Leffel
Executive and Financial Assistant: Helen Proffitt
Director, Industry Relations and Development: Andrew Schweigardt

Historical Note:
TOBA's mission is to improve the economics, integrity and pleasure of the sport on behalf of owners and breeders. Members include individual owners, breeders, trainers, jockeys, veterinarians, as well as twenty eight state breeders' organizations. Membership: $275 (Individual); $375 (Family); $550 (Corporate); $1,000 (Sponsor); $75 (Student).

Meetings/Conferences: Annual

Publications:
Membership Directory; annually; adv.
The Blood-Horse Magazine; adv.
TOBA Times; quarterly

Thoroughbred Racing Associations of North America (1942)

420 Fair Hill Dr.
Suite One
Elkton, MD 21921-2573
Tel: (410) 392-9200 *Fax:* (410) 398-1366
E-Mail: info@tra-online.com
Website: tra-online.com
Members: 48 racing associations
Staff: 4
Annual Budget: $500-1,000,000

Personnel:
Executive Vice President: Christopher N. Scherf
    E-Mail: cscherf@tra-online.com
Director, Services: Jane Murray
    E-Mail: jmurray@tra-online.com

Historical Note:
Formerly (1977) the Thoroughbred Racing Associations of the U. S., TRA strives to create various programs, activities, ventures, and enterprises related to thoroughbred racing. The Thoroughbred Racing Protective Bureau is a wholly owned subsidiary of the TRA.

Meetings/Conferences: Annual

Publications:
Membership Directory; on-line
Weekly Leaders; weekly

Membership List Available to Non-members

Tile Contractors' Association of America (1903)

10434 Indiana Ave.
Kansas City, MO 64137
Tel: (816) 868-9300 *Fax:* (816) 767-0194
TollFree: (800) 655-8453
E-Mail: info@tcaainc.org

Website: tcaainc.org
Members: 150 companies
Staff: 2
Annual Budget: $100-250,000
Tax: 501(c)(6)

Personnel:
Executive Director: Carole Damon
    E-Mail: caroled@tcaainc.org
Associate Director: Chris Pattavina
    E-Mail: chrisp@tcaainc.org

Historical Note:
Formerly (1936) the Tile and Mantle Contractors Association of America. TCAA's mission is to promote the tile industry and to ensure that its members have the information, skills and tools needed to ensure better levels of professionalism, reliability, skilled craftsmanship and technical performance in the industry. Membership: $950/year.

Continuing Education:
Enrollment: 20
Certification Designation/s: TOE

Meetings/Conferences: Annual

Publications:
9300 Contractor; quarterly; adv.
Membership Directory; on-line
TCAA Tuesday; weekly

Tile Council of North America, Inc. (1945)

100 Clemson Research Blvd.
Anderson, SC 29625
Tel: (864) 646-8453 *Fax:* (864) 646-2821
E-Mail: info@tileusa.com
Website: tcnatile.com
Members: 160 companies
Staff: 13
Annual Budget: $1-2,000,000

Personnel:
Executive Director: Eric Astrachan
    E-Mail: eastrachan@tileusa.com
Contact, Accounting: Leisa Grasty
    E-Mail: lgrasty@tileusa.com
Marketing and Communications Specialist: D.J. Liefer
    E-Mail: djliefer@tileusa.com

Historical Note:
Formerly (2003) Tile Council of America (TCA). TCNA is dedicated to expanding the market for ceramic tile manufactured in North America. Represents manufacturers of ceramic tile, tile installation materials, tile equipment, raw materials, and other tile-related products. Members are manufacturers and suppliers of ceramic wall and floor tiles. Membership: $1,200 (Regular); $1,000-7,500 (Associate); $1,000- 2,000 (Affiliated); $250-750 (Associate Art/Studio).

Continuing Education:
Certification Designation/s: PTCA

Meetings/Conferences: Annual
2013 - Atlanta, GA (Georgia World Congress Center)/
    April 29 - May 2/over 100 exhibitors

Publications:
Membership Directory; on-line

Membership List Available to Non-members

Tile Roofing Institute (1971)

35 E. Wacker Dr.
Suite 850
Chicago, IL 60601-2106
Tel: (312) 670-4177 *Fax:* (312) 644-8557
TollFree: (888) 321-9236
E-Mail: info@tileroofing.org
Website: tileroofing.org
Members: 192 companies
Staff: 2
Annual Budget: $500-1,000,000
Tax: 501(c)(6)

Personnel:
Managing Director: Jeanne Sheehy
    E-Mail: jsheehy@tileroofing.org
Technical Director: Rick Olson
    E-Mail: Rolson@tileroofing.org

Historical Note:
Formerly National Tile Roofing Manufacturers Association, assumed its current name in 2004. TRI's mission is to promote greater awareness of concrete and clay tile as the preferred roofing material used worldwide and its suitability for all roofing installations. Membership: $6,000 (Importer); $1,000-4,000 (Associate Supplier); $1,500 (Associate Distributor); $249-500 (Associate Contractor/Associate Professional/Associate General).

Continuing Education:
Certification Designation/s: IC, SC
Meetings/Conferences:
Number of non-conference events/year: 1

Publications:
Marketing Materials
Membership Directory; on-line
Technical Briefs
TRI eNewsletter; irregular; adv.

Tillage & Ground Engaging Equipment Product Council

1000 Executive Pkwy.
Suite 100
St. Louis, MO 63141
Tel: (314) 878-2304
Website: farmequip.org/product_councils/tillage
Staff: 1

Personnel:
Chairman: Doug Bruce
    E-Mail: dgb@osmundson.com

Historical Note:
The Tillage & Ground Engaging Equipment Product Council provide service to issues specifically impacting tillage equipment and/or tillage equipment accessories.

Tilt-up Concrete Association (1986)

113 First St., West
P.O. Box 204
Mt. Vernon, IA 52314-0204
Tel: (319) 895-6911 *Fax:* (320) 213-5555
E-Mail: info@tilt-up.org
Website: tilt-up.org
Members: 480 companies
Staff: 4
Annual Budget: $250-500,000
Tax: 501(c)(6)

Personnel:
Executive Director: J. Edward Sauter
    E-Mail: esauter@tilt-up.com
Technical Director: James Baty II
    E-Mail: jbaty@tilt-up.org
Manager, Project: Mitch Bloomquist
    E-Mail: mbloomquist@tilt-up.org

Historical Note:
Incorporated in Illinois. TCA strives to improve the quality and acceptance of site-cast Tilt-Up construction combining the advantages of reasonable cost with low maintenance, durability, speed of construction and minimal capital investment. TCA represents builders, engineers and suppliers involved with tilt-up concrete construction. Membership: $1,100 (Global Associate); $750 (Contractors); $600 (Local Associate); $500 (Professional Firm/Developer/Owner/Speciality Trade); $75 (Educator/Student); $2,000 (Sustaining).

Meetings/Conferences: Annual
Number of non-conference events/year: 1

Publications:
Tilt-Up Today; quarterly
Membership Directory; on-line

Timber Frame Business Council (1995)

46 Chambersburg St.
Gettysburg, PA 17325
Tel: (717) 334-5234 *Fax:* (717) 334-5571
TollFree: (888) 560-9251
E-Mail: info@timberframe.org
Website: timberframe.org
Staff: 1
Annual Budget: $100-250,000
Tax: 501(c)(6)

Personnel:
Executive Director: Pam Hinton
    E-Mail: pam@timberframe.org

Historical Note:
TFBC's mission is to strengthen the timber framing industry through professional and public outreach, professional development, education, and major industry initiatives Membership: $0-1810/year.

Meetings/Conferences: Semi-Annual
Number of non-conference events/year: 1

Publications:
In Touch; monthly
Member Directory; on-line

Timber Framers Guild (1985)

P.O. Box 295

9 Mechanic St.
Alstead, NH 03602-0295
Tel: (559) 834-8453 *Fax:* (888) 453-0879
TollFree: (888) 453-0879
E-Mail: info@tfguild.org
Website: tfguild.org
Members: 1700 individuals and companies
Staff: 4
Annual Budget: $500-1,000,000
Tax: 501(c)(3)

Personnel:
Executive Director: Joel McCarty
    E-Mail: joel@tfguild.org
Administrative Assistant: Susan Norlander
    E-Mail: susan@tfguild.org
Director, Publications: Ken Rower
    E-Mail: kenrower@myfairpoint.net
Editor: Susan Witter
    E-Mail: witter@mysoundideas.us

Historical Note:
*Formerly (2000) Timber Framers Guild of North America.
TFG advocates the centuries-old craft of timber framing.
Members are architects, designers and other building
professionals; suppliers of tools and materials to the timber
frame trade; owner-builders; timber frame owners and
others with an interest in the craft. Membership: $100
(Individual/International Student); $65 (Student); $125
(Family); $135 (International); $160 (International Family).*

Meetings/Conferences: Annual
Number of non-conference events/year: 5

Publications:
Member Directory; annually; adv.
Scantlings; monthly; adv.
Timber Framing; quarterly; adv.

Timber Products Manufacturers Association
(1916)
951 E. Third Ave.
Spokane, WA 99202
Tel: (509) 535-4646 *Fax:* (509) 534-6106
E-Mail: tpm@tpmrs.com
Website: tpmrs.com
Members: 225 companies
Staff: 17
Annual Budget: $1-2,000,000
Tax: 501(c)(6)

Personnel:
President: Adam Molenda
    E-Mail: amolenda@tpmrs.com
Administrative Assistant and Publications Coordinator:
    Shelley Jeffers
    E-Mail: sjeffers@tpmrs.com

Historical Note:
*Established as the Loggers Club in 1916 and assumed its
present name in 1969. TPM's mission is to advance the
wood products industry by providing profitable and valuable
business solutions.*

Publications:
Frontline; monthly
Legal Briefing; monthly
TPM Bulletin; monthly

Tin Stabilizers Association *(2001)*
100 N. 20th St., Fourth Floor
Philadelphia, PA 19103
Tel: (215) 564-3484 *Fax:* (215) 564-2175
E-Mail: tsa@fernley.com
Website: tinstabilizers.org
Members: 5 companies
Staff: 2
Annual Budget: Under $10,000

Personnel:
Executive Director: John D. McGreevey

Historical Note:
*TSA was formed to promote the safe use of tin stabilizers,
an additive used in vinyl and other plastics to improve
processing characteristics.*

Tire and Rim Association *(1903)*
175 Montrose W. Ave.
Suite 150
Copley, OH 44321
Tel: (330) 666-8121 *Fax:* (330) 666-8340
E-Mail: tra@us-tra.org
Website: us-tra.org
Members: 85 companies
Staff: 3

Annual Budget: $250-500,000
Tax: 501(c)(6)

Personnel:
Executive Vice President: J.F. Pacuit

Historical Note:
*On April 11, 1933, the Association was incorporated in
Ohio and its name changed to Tire and Rim Association,
Inc. TRA is the technical standardizing body for tire, rim
and valve manufacturers.*

Publications:
Membership Directory; on-line

Tire Industry Association *(2002)*
1532 Pointer Ridge Pl.
Suite G
Bowie, MD 20716-1883
Tel: (301) 430-7280 *Fax:* (301) 430-7283
TollFree: (800) 876-8372
E-Mail: info@tireindustry.org
Website: tireindustry.org
Members: 6000 companies
Staff: 17
Annual Budget: $2-5,000,000

Personnel:
Executive Vice President: Roy E. Littlefield
    E-Mail: rlittlefield@tireindustry.org
Director, Communications: Mark Cook
    E-Mail: media@tireindustry.org
Director, Government and Business Relations: Paul Fiore
Director, Meeting Planning and Advertising: Lakisha
    Pindell
    E-Mail: lpindell@tireindustry.org
Manager, Public Relations and Promotions: Richard Porter
    E-Mail: cwood@tireindustry.org
Senior Vice President, Training: Kevin Rohlwing
Director, Membership Services: Megan L. Walsh
    E-Mail: mwalsh@tireindustry.org

Historical Note:
*Formed by the merger of the International Tire & Rubber
Association (ITRA) and the Tire Association of North
America (TANA). Membership represents segments of the
tire industry, including those that manufacture, repair,
recycle, sell, service or use new or retreaded tires, and
also suppliers or individuals who furnish equipment,
material or services to the industry. Associate Members
are suppliers, marketers, consultants, wholesalers and
others. Membership: $250-3,000 (US Member); $200
(International Member).*

Continuing Education:
Certification Designation/s: ETS, ATS, CTS

Meetings/Conferences:
Conference Chair: Lakisha Pindell
2013 - Rio Grande, PR (Gran Melia Golf Resort)/Feb.
    20 - 23
Number of non-conference events/year: 1

Publications:
Membership Directory; on-line; adv.
Retreader's Journal; adv.
TIA Member eNews; monthly; adv.
Today's Tire Industry; quarterly; adv.

Tire Retread and Repair Information Bureau
(1974)
1013 Birch St.
Falls Church, VA 22046
Tel: (703) 533-7677 *Fax:* (703) 533-7678
TollFree: (877) 394-6811
E-Mail: info@retread.org
Website: retread.org
Members: 500 companies
Staff: 2
Annual Budget: $250-500,000
Tax: 501(c)(6)

Personnel:
Managing Director: David Stevens

Historical Note:
*TRIB is a member supported association formerly known
as Tire Retread Information Bureau. It is dedicated to
promote the safe recycling of tires through tire retreading
and time repairing. Membership: $150 (Individual); $350
(Associations); $200 (Trucking Companies); $1,000
(Manufacturers); $350 (Retreaders/Tire Dealers/Suppliers/
Casing Dealers, minimum first two locations, plus $175 for
each additional retread plant).*

Publications:
Flat Tire! Now What? A Consumers Guide to Proper
    Tire Repair; on-line
The Voice of Retreading Fast Read Newsletter; monthly

Understanding Retreading: The facts, the industry, the
    process and the benefits; on-line

Membership List Available to Non-members

Tissue Banks International *(2009)*
815 Park Ave.
Baltimore, MD 21201
Tel: (410) 752-3800 *Fax:* (410) 783-0183
Website: tbionline.org
Staff: 296
Annual Budget: $25-50,000,000

Personnel:
President and Chief Executive Officer: Timothy E. Askew
*Chief Quality Officer and Vice President, Regulatory and
    Quality:* James SaFranko
Chief Operating Officer: Jeffery A. Sandler
Vice President, Marketing and Communications: Nancy
    Thrush

Historical Note:
*TBI is a non-profit network of medical eye and tissue
banks dedicated to the relief of human suffering through
transplantation.*

Tobacco Associates, Inc. *(1947)*
1306 Annapolis Dr.
Suite 102
Raleigh, NC 27608-2136
Tel: (919) 821-7670 *Fax:* (919) 821-7674
E-Mail: taw@tobaccoassociatesinc.org
Website: tobaccoassociatesinc.org
Members: 3000 individuals
Staff: 4
Annual Budget: $500-1,000,000
Tax: 501(c)(5)

Personnel:
President: Kirk Wayne
Office Manager and Bookkeeper: Veronica Martins
    E-Mail: tar@tobaccoassociatesinc.org

Historical Note:
*TA's mission is to enhance understanding of US flue-cured
tobacco and assist manufacturers interested in adding
quality US leaf to their products.*

Meetings/Conferences:
Conference Chair: Kirk Wayne

Tobacco Merchants Association of the United
States *(1915)*
P.O. Box 8019
Princeton, NJ 08543-8019
Tel: (609) 275-4900 *Fax:* (609) 275-8379
E-Mail: tma@tma.org
Website: tma.org
Members: 167 companies
Staff: 1
Annual Budget: $1-2,000,000

Personnel:
President: Farrell Delman

Historical Note:
*TMA's mission is to be the provider of accurate,
comprehensive, and objective information on the global
tobacco industry for its members, contributors and other
interested parties, delivered in a timely, innovative and
cost-effective manner as well as a provider of forums for
education and dialogue on issues of interest and concern
to the industry. Membership: $2,250-15,000 (Non-
Manufacturers); $5000 (US Cigarette Manufacturers);
$2250 (Non US cigarette manufacturers).*

Meetings/Conferences: Annual

Publications:
Membership Directory; on-line
US Tobacco Weekly; weekly

Membership List Available to Non-members

Tobacco Vapor Electronic Cigarette Association
1920 N. St. NW
Suite 800
Washington, DC 20035
Tel: (202) 331-8800 *Fax:* (202) 331-8330
E-Mail: info@tveca.com
Website: tveca.com
Members: 16 Companies
Staff: 3
Tax: 501(c)(6)

Personnel:
Chief Executive Officer: Ray Story
    E-Mail: ray@tveca.com

Contact, Legal: Thompson Hine
Chief Financial Officer: Thomas R. Kiklas

Historical Note:
The Tobacco Vapor Electronic Cigarette Association is the voice for all media and legislative requests for information on the electronic cigarette (e-cig). The TVECA's mission is to provide the tools and information necessary for policy-makers, opinion leaders, media and private sector companies worldwide to make informed decisions about the management and use of electronic cigarette technologies, particularly the most recent advances and applications. Membership: $250 (Member); $500 (Manufacturer).

Publications:
TVECA Newsletter

Tobacconists' Association of America *(1968)*
P.O. Box 81152
Conyers, GA 30013
Tel: (770) 597-6264 *Fax:* (812) 479-5939
E-Mail: t-a-a@t-a-a.us
Website: t-a-a.com
Members: 100 companies
Staff: 2
Annual Budget: $250-500,000

Personnel:
Executive Director: Ted Clark

Historical Note:
TAA's mission is to provide an open forum of ideas, strategies, and problem solving between retail tobacconist and vendors to the trade. Members are retail tobacco dealers representing outlets throughout the U. S.

Meetings/Conferences: Annual
2013 - Casa de Campo, Dominican Republic (Casa de Campo in the Domincan Republic)/April 7 - 11

Publications:
Membership Directory; on-line

Tooling, Manufacturing and Technologies Association *(1933)*
28237 Orchard Lake Rd.
Suite 101
Farmington Hills, MI 48334
Tel: (248) 488-0300 *Fax:* (248) 488-0500
TollFree: (800) 969-9682
Website: thetmta.com
Members: 600 individuals
Staff: 6
Annual Budget: $500-1,000,000

Personnel:
President and Chief Executive Officer: Robert J. Dumont
    E-Mail: rob@thetmta.com
Controller: Charles Barnes
    E-Mail: charlie@thetmta.com
Manager, Membership Services: Elaine F. Burrger-Laskosky
    E-Mail: elaine@thetmta.com
Administrative Assistant: Stella Krupansky
    E-Mail: stella@thetmta.com
Technical Coordinator: Ron Mariutto
    E-Mail: ron@thetmta.com

Historical Note:
TMTA is a non- profit organization. TMTA's mission is to serve, enhance and promote the success of its member companies for the mutual benefit of all concerned through the increased power of group strength and leadership. Membership: $ 75-690/year (Quarterly Dues, based on number of employees).

Meetings/Conferences: Annual

Publications:
Membership Directory; on-line
TMTA TALK; monthly; adv.

Tortilla Industry Association *(1989)*
1600 Wilson Blvd.
Suite 650
Arlington, VA 22209
Tel: (800) 944-6099 *Fax:* (800) 944-6177
TollFree: (800) 944-6099
E-Mail: info@tortilla-info.com
Website: tortilla-info.com
Members: 180 companies
Staff: 2
Annual Budget: $500-1,000,000
Tax: 501(c)(6)

Personnel:
Chief Executive Officer: Jim Kabbani
    E-Mail: jkabbani@tortilla-info.com

Historical Note:
TIA serves the emerging tortilla industry, now the fastest growing segment of the baking industry. Members include tortilla manufacturers, industry suppliers and distributors. Affiliate members are industry suppliers. Membership: $250-2,000 (Regular, depending on annual sales); $2,000 (Affiliate); $250 (International Affiliate Membership); $500 (Associate); $300 (In Store).

Meetings/Conferences: Annual
Number of non-conference events/year: 1

Publications:
Membership Directory; on-line
TIA News - Newsletter; quarterly

Membership List Available to Non-members

Touchstone Energy Cooperatives *(1998)*
4301 Wilson Blvd.
Arlington, VA 22203-1860
Tel: (703) 907-5500 *Fax:* (703) 907-5554
Website: touchstoneenergy.com
Members: 700 local, consumer-owned electric cooperatives
Staff: 2
Annual Budget: $5-10,000,000

Personnel:
Contact, Communications and Media Relations: Ann Maggard
    E-Mail: ann.maggard@nreca.coop
Contact, Meetings: Kristine Jackson
    E-Mail: kristine.jackson@nreca.coop

Historical Note:
Alliance of consumer-owned electric cooperatives. Touchstone Energy co-operatives collectively deliver power and energy solutions to about 30 million members in rural America.

Meetings/Conferences: Annual
Conference Chair: Kristine Jackson

Tourist Railway Association Inc. *(1972)*
P.O. Box 1189
Covington, GA 30015
Tel: (770) 278-0088 *Fax:* (575) 756-1238
TollFree: (800) 678-7246
E-Mail: train@valornet.com
Website: traininc.org
Members: 200 companies
Staff: 4
Annual Budget: $50-100,000

Personnel:
Executive Director: Suzanne Grace

Historical Note:
TRAIN's mission is to foster the development and operation of tourist railways and museums and the free exchange amongst members of research data. TRAIN members are railway museums, tourist railroads, product suppliers, railroad publishers, private car owners, excursion operators, and other interested persons and organizations. Membership: $250 (Vendor); $115 (Associate); $175-575 (Full, based on gross operating income).

Meetings/Conferences: Annual

Publications:
Membership Directory; on-line
Railway Museum Quarterly / Trainline; quarterly; adv.
Trainline Newsletter; bi-monthly; adv.

Towing and Recovery Association of America *(1979)*
2121 Eisenhower Ave.
Suite 200
Alexandria, VA 22314-4686
Tel: (703) 684-7713 *Fax:* (703) 684-6720
TollFree: (800) 728-0136
E-Mail: towserver@aol.com
Website: towserver.net
Members: 1500 companies
Staff: 3
Annual Budget: $250-500,000
Tax: 501(c)(6)

Personnel:
Executive Director: Harriet Cooley
Contact, Marketing, Advertising, Web Design and Branding: Sherri Arnaiz
Director, Certification Operations: Natasha Patterson
    E-Mail: natasha@towserver.net

Historical Note:
TRAA's mission is to foster and promote the interest and welfare of all towing and recovery operators in North America and to towing professionalism and quality customer service throughout the world. Members are companies operating tow-trucks and automotive recovery equipment. Membership: $30-500/year.

Continuing Education:
Certification Designation/s: NDC
Meetings/Conferences:
Number of non-conference events/year: 1

Publications:
National Directory; annually; adv.
National Towing News; quarterly; adv.

Towing Equipment Manufacturers Association
37400 Hills Tech Dr.
C/O NTEA
Farmington Hills, MI 48331-3414
Tel: (248) 489-7090 *Fax:* (248) 489-8590
TollFree: (800) 441-6832
E-Mail: info@ntea.com
Website: ntea.com/vango/core/committees.aspx?
    committee = COMMITTEE/TEMA-R
Staff: 1

Personnel:
Executive Director: Steve Carey CAE

Historical Note:
Towing Equipment Manufacturers Association is an NTEA affiliate organization. The group works to expand and improve the wrecker body and towing equipment market through advertising and industry education programs while improving communications and working relationships with truck chassis manufacturers.

Toxicology Forum *(1975)*
1300 Eye St. NW
Suite 1010 East
Washington, DC 20005-3314
Tel: (202) 659-0030 *Fax:* (202) 789-0905
Website: toxforum.org
Members: 127 individuals
Staff: 2
Annual Budget: $500-1,000,000
Tax: 501(c)(3)

Personnel:
President and Chief Operating Officer: Dr. David G. Longfellow
    E-Mail: dlongfellow@toxforum.org
Executive Coordinator: Catherine Rytkonen
    E-Mail: crytkonen@toxforum.org

Historical Note:
Mission is to encourage open dialogue on human health and environmental issues that drive public concerns, academic involvement, industry action and regulatory decision making. Membership: $100 (Individual); $2,000 (Associate); $8,000-15,000 (Corporate).

Meetings/Conferences: Annual
2013 - Washington, DC/Jan. 29 - 31

Publications:
Membership Directory; on-line

Membership List Available to Non-members

Toy Industry Association *(1916)*
1115 Broadway
Suite 400
New York, NY 10010
Tel: (212) 675-1141 *Fax:* (212) 633-1429
E-Mail: info@toyassociation.org
Website: toyassociation.org
Members: 550 toy manufacturers and importers
Staff: 48
Annual Budget: $10-25,000,000
Tax: 501(c)(6)

Personnel:
President: Carter E. Keithley
    E-Mail: ckeithley@toyassociation.org
Senior Manager, Public Relations: Adrienne Citrin Appell
    E-Mail: aappell@toyassociation.org
Vice President, Meetings and Events: Marian Bossard
    E-Mail: mbossard@toyassociation.org
Vice President, Membership Services: Jean Butler
    E-Mail: jbutler@toyassociation.org
Senior Director, Trade Show and Event Marketing: Kimberly Carcone
    E-Mail: kcarcone@toyassociation.org
Events Operations Coordinator: Richard Chow
    E-Mail: rchow@toyassociation.org
Senior Vice President, Technical Affairs: Alan P. Kaufman
    E-Mail: akaufman@toyassociation.org

Vice President, Strategic Communications: Stacy Leistner
  E-Mail: sleistner@toyassociation.org
Accountant and Manager, Human Resources: Angela Oliveri
  E-Mail: aoliveri@toyassociation.org
Vice President, Finance and Administration: Paul Vitale
  E-Mail: pvitale@toyassociation.org

Historical Note:
Formerly (1996) the Toy Manufacturers of the U.S. Toy Manufacturers of America (2001), absorbed the American Toy Export Association in 1992. TIA is committed to addressing the needs of the diverse membership, building on the history of leadership in safety standards, advocacy on legislative and trade issues, visibility in the media, and philanthropy to children. Members are American toy manufacturers and importers. Membership: $0-250,000/ year.

Continuing Education:
Certification Designation/s: TSCP

Meetings/Conferences: Annual
Conference Chair: Marian Bossard
2013 - New York City, NY (Jacob K. Javits Convention Center)/Feb. 10 - 13/over 100 exhibitors
2013 - Scottsdale, AZ (Hyatt Regency Scottsdale Resort and Spa)/May 15 - 17

Publications:
Membership Directory
Toy News Tuesday; weekly

Trade Exchange of America *(1978)*
23200 Coolidge Hwy.
Oak Park, MI 48237
Tel: (248) 544-1350 *Fax:* (248) 544-1546
Website: tradefirst.com
Members: 16 Companies
Staff: 2

Personnel:
Media: Nan Keilman
  E-Mail: media@tradefirst.com
Marketing: Justin Stenson
  E-Mail: marketing@tradefirst.com

Historical Note:
TradeFirst is a nationwide e-commerce network of businesses that work together, trading goods and services in order to generate new business, offset cash expenses, and increase profits by utilizing excess capacity and inventory.

Publications:
D Business Magazine
Membership Directory; on-line
Newsletter; adv.
The Wall Street Journal

Trade Promotion Management Associates *(1989)*
51 Cragwood Rd.
Suite 200
S. Plainfield, NJ 07080
Tel: (646) 442-3473 *Fax:* (908) 755-7451
E-Mail: headquarters@tpmaww.com
Website: tpmaww.com
Members: 100 individuals
Staff: 4
Annual Budget: $250-500,000

Personnel:
Chairman: Kim Zablocky
  E-Mail: kzablocky@vcfww.com
Director, Operations: Susan Haupt
  E-Mail: shaupt@tpmaww.com
Director: Bob Houk
  E-Mail: bhouk@tpmaww.com
Director, Sales and Marketing: Sheri Kurdakul
  E-Mail: skurdakul@tpmaww.com

Historical Note:
Formerly the National Association for Advertising and Promotional Allowances (NAPAA). TPMA's mission is to explore best practices and address forecasting and inventory concerns while working collaboratively with suppliers to assure that product flow is sufficient to meet demand of seasonal sales and promotion. Members are companies and organizations that rely on cooperative advertising and promotions. Membership: $2,750-4,750 (VCF Membership); $2,750 (Service Provider).

Publications:
TPMA Outlook; bi-weekly; adv.
VCF Report; monthly

Traffic Audit Bureau for Media Measurement, Inc. *(1933)*
271 Madison Ave.

Suite 1504
New York, NY 10016
Tel: (212) 972-8075 *Fax:* (212) 972-8928
E-Mail: inquiry@tabonline.com
Website: tabonline.com
Members: 425 companies
Staff: 12
Annual Budget: $2-5,000,000

Personnel:
President and Chief Executive Officer: Joseph C. Philport
Chief Financial Officer: Shawn Ballard
  E-Mail: sballard@tabonline.com
Vice President and Director, Audit Operations and Research: Jeff Casper
  E-Mail: jcasper@tabonline.com
Vice President, Audit Policy and Membership Services: Larry Hennessy
  E-Mail: larryhennessy@tabonline.com
Vice President, Information Technology: Sean McCarthy
  E-Mail: smccarthy@tabonline.com
Office Administrator: Velvet A. Ross

Historical Note:
Formerly Traffic Audit Bureau, assumed its present name in 1990. TAB acts as an independent third party provider of standardized and valid circulation measures for out of home media. Mission is to prepare and disseminate standardized factual statements setting forth the circulation value and/or proof of out-of-home media advertising. Membership: $418-1,276 (Advertisers); $3,500-50,000 (Advertising Agencies and Media Buying Services); $2,000-450,000 (Plant Operators); $418 (Associates).

Publications:
The Foundation; weekly; adv.

Training Directors' Forum *(1985)*
60 Industrial Pkwy.
PMB Suite 650
Cheektowaga, NY 14227
E-Mail: training@showcare.com
Website: trainingdirectorsforum.com
Members: 500 individuals
Staff: 5

Personnel:
Director, Sales, Training Magazine and Events: Sean Nodland
  E-Mail: sean.nodland@nielsen.com
Director, Group Marketing: Shereen Abuzobaa
  E-Mail: shereen.abuzobaa@nielsen.com

Historical Note:
Focuses on job-related, employer-sponsored training and education in the working world, including business, industry, government, and service organizations.

Continuing Education:
Certification Designation/s: PCC, RIMC, OLMC, SPC
Meetings/Conferences:
Number of non-conference events/year: 1

Membership List Available to Non-members

Training Officers Consortium *(1938)*
2025 M St. NW
Suite 800
Washington, DC 20036
Tel: (202) 973-8683 *Fax:* (202) 331-0111
E-Mail: info@trainingofficers.org
Website: trainingofficers.org
Members: 200 individuals
Staff: 1
Annual Budget: $250-500,000
Tax: 501(c)(3)

Personnel:
Chair: Karen Hoffman
  E-Mail: khoffman@ftc.gov

Historical Note:
Formerly (Training Officers Conference). TOC members are federal trainers and other professionals from industry and academe who are interested in contributing to the knowledge and practice of human resources and training. Has no paid officers or full-time staff. Membership: $850/ year.

Meetings/Conferences: Annual
2013 - Virginia Beach, VA (Founders Inn and Spa)/ April 28 - May 1

Publications:
MEMBER DIRECTORY; on-line
TOC NEWSLETTER; monthly; adv.

Trans-Atlantic American Flag Liner Operators and Trans-Pacific American Flag Berth Operators *(1985)*
80 Wall St.
Suite 1117
New York, NY 10005
Tel: (212) 269-2415 *Fax:* (212) 269-2418
E-Mail: halevy1@nyct.net
Website: taaflo-tpafbo.com
Members: 4 companies
Staff: 1
Annual Budget: $100-250,000

Personnel:
Administrator: Howard A. Levy
  E-Mail: halevy1@attglobal.net

Historical Note:
Formerly (1985) Atlantic and Gulf American Flag Berth Operators. TAAFLO/TPAFBO's purpose is to provide publication of ocean freight rates on movements of military goods. TAAFLO Members operate U.S. flag vessels in ocean common service between ports in the U.S. and ports in Europe and elsewhere. Members provide transportation by sea for general commercial cargo as well as cargo reserved by law for such transport to vessels of U.S. flag registry including household goods and personal effects of U.S. military personnel and other U.S. governmental employees (Military HHGs).

Transaction Processing Performance Council *(1988)*
572B Ruger St.
P.O. Box 29920
San Francisco, CA 94129-0920
Tel: (415) 561-6272 *Fax:* (415) 561-6120
E-Mail: info@tpc.org
Website: tpc.org
Members: 31 manufacturers
Staff: 1
Annual Budget: $100-250,000
Tax: 501(c)(6)

Personnel:
Contact, Public Relations: Michael Majdalany
  E-Mail: majdalany@tpc.org

Historical Note:
The TPC is a corporation whose mission is to define transaction processing and database benchmarks and to disseminate objective, verifiable TPC performance data to the industry. Members are computer and database manufacturers and individuals with an interest in transaction processing. Membership: $15,000 (Full); $1,500 (Associate).

Publications:
Newsletter

Membership List Available to Non-members

The Transformer Association *(1974)*
1300 Sumner Ave.
Cleveland, OH 44115
Tel: (216) 241-7333 *Fax:* (216) 241-0105
E-Mail: info@transformer-assn.org
Website: transformer-assn.org
Members: 58 companies
Staff: 4
Annual Budget: $100-250,000
Tax: 501(c)(6)

Personnel:
Senior Account Executive: Craig Addington
  E-Mail: caddington@thomasamc.com
Administrative Assistant: Christine Devor
  E-Mail: cdevor@thomasamc.com

Historical Note:
Formerly (1994) Power Conversion Products Council, International and later (2000) PCPCI, TTA is a manufacturing trade association whose mission is to gather, monitor, and disseminate industry data and trends including economic and industry issues. Corporate members include transformer and power supply manufacturers, their suppliers, safety agencies and consultants. Membership: $895 (Manufacturer/Safety Agency); $995 (Industry); 1,395 (IMA Group); $400 (Educator).

Meetings/Conferences: Annual

Publications:
Membership Directory; on-line; adv.
newsletter; quarterly
Product Index; on-line; adv.

Membership List Available to Non-members

Transpacific Stabilization Agreement *(1989)*

1901 Harrison St., Suite 1620
Oakland, CA 94612
Tel: (510) 208-0440 Fax: (510) 208-0452
E-Mail: info@tsacarriers.org
Website: tsacarriers.org
Staff: 1
Annual Budget: $1-2,000,000
Tax: 501(c)(6)

Personnel:
President: Ken Glenn

Historical Note:
The Transpacific Stabilization Agreement is a research and discussion forum of major ocean container shipping lines that carry cargo from Asia to ports and inland points in the U.S.

Transport Workers Union of America, AFL-CIO (1934)
501 Third St. NW
Ninth Floor
Washington, DC 20001
Tel: (202) 719-3900 Fax: (202) 347-0454
Website: twu.org
Members: 130114 individuals and autonomous locals
Staff: 60
Annual Budget: $5-10,000,000

Personnel:
International Vice President: Roger Tauss
    E-Mail: dcguy@twu.org

Historical Note:
Formerly the Transport Workers Union and chartered by the Congress of Industrial Organizations, assumed its present name in 1937. TWU holds national affiliation with AFL-CIO. TWU's mission is to protect and improve working conditions and living standards of all workers and demand respect, dignity and equality for all.

Publications:
ATD Insider; quarterly
TWU Express

Transportation and Logistics Council (1974)
120 Main St.
Huntington, NY 11743-0630
Tel: (631) 549-8988 Fax: (631) 549-8962
E-Mail: tlc@transportlaw.com
Website: tlcouncil.org
Members: 300 companies
Staff: 4
Annual Budget: $100-250,000

Personnel:
Executive Director: George Carl Pezold
    E-Mail: george.pezold@transportlaw.com
Editor: Stephen W. Beyer
    E-Mail: sbeyer@transportlaw.com
General Counsel: Raymond A. Selvaggio
    E-Mail: rselvaggio@transportlaw.com
Executive Secretary: Diane Smid
    E-Mail: diane@transportlaw.com

Historical Note:
Formerly (1990) Shippers National Freight Claim Council, Inc, (1996) Transportation Claims and Prevention Council, Inc. TLC's mission is to serve the interests of the shipping community through education and representation in issues relating to the transportation of goods. Membership: $395 (Regular); $345 (Associate); $200 (Multiple Subscriber).

Meetings/Conferences: Annual
2013 - San Diego, CA/April 22 - 24

Publications:
Trans Digest; monthly; adv.

Transportation Clubs International (1920)
P.O. Box 2223
Ocean Shores, WA 98569
Fax: (360) 289-3188
TollFree: (877) 858-8627
E-Mail:
info@transportationclubsinternational.com
Website: transportationclubsinternational.com
Members:
70 traffic and transportation clubs
6000 members
Staff: 12
Annual Budget: $50-100,000
Tax: 501(c)(6)

Personnel:
Executive Director: Katie Dejonge

President: Caci Case
    E-Mail:
    cacicase@transportationclubsinternational.com

Historical Note:
TCI's purpose is to create, stimulate and perpetuate discussion of topics relating to local and national transportation issues. Membership: $250 (Company/Corporate); $50 (Individual); $1000 (Club); $4-50 (Based on members).

Meetings/Conferences: Annual
Conference Chair: Caci Case

Publications:
Membership Directory; on-line
TCI Newsletter; weekly

Transportation Communications International Union/IAM (1899)
Three Research Pl.
Rockville, MD 20850
Tel: (301) 948-4910 Fax: (301) 948-1872
E-Mail: websteward@tcunion.org
Website: goiam.org/index.php/tcunion/about-tcu
Members: 46000 individuals
Staff: 60

Personnel:
National President: Robert A. Scardelletti
Carmen Division General President and International Vice President: Richard A. Johnson
National Secretary and Treasurer: Russell C. Oathout

Historical Note:
Founded as the Order of Railroad Clerks of America in 1899. Became the Brotherhood of Railway and Steamship Clerks, Freight Handlers, Express and Station Employees in 1919 and then the Brotherhood of Railway, Airline, and Steamship Clerks, Freight Handlers, Express and Station Employees (BRAC) in 1967. Merged with Brotherhood Railway Carmen of the United States in 1986 and assumed the current name in 1987.

Membership List Available to Non-members

Transportation Development Association (1971)
Ten E. Doty St.
Suite 201
Madison, WI 53703
Tel: (608) 256-7044 Fax: (608) 256-7079
E-Mail: general@tdawisconsin.org
Website: tdawisconsin.org
Members: 400 transportation stakeholders
Staff: 2
Annual Budget: $250-500,000

Personnel:
Executive Director: Craig Thompson
    E-Mail: craig.thompson@tdawisconsin.org
Business Manager: Debby Jackson
    E-Mail: debby.jackson@tdawisconsin.org

Historical Note:
TDA is committed to advance the best in transportation. Members include businesses, labor unions, citizen groups, units of government and individuals.

Meetings/Conferences: Annual
2013 - Washington, DC (Grand Hyatt Washington)/April 10 - 11

Publications:
Membership Directory; on-line
TDA Newsletter; on-line

Transportation Elevator and Grain Merchants Association (1918)
P.O. Box 26426
Kansas City, MO 64196
Tel: (816) 569-4020 Fax: (816) 221-8189
Website: tegma.org
Members: 45 companies
Staff: 3
Annual Budget: $100-250,000
Tax: 501(c)(6)

Personnel:
President: Robert R. Petersen
    E-Mail: bob.petersen@tegma.org
Director, Communications: Abigail Hiles
    E-Mail: abigail.hiles@tegma.org
Secretary and Treasurer: Erica Venancio
    E-Mail: erica.venancio@tegma.org

Historical Note:
TEGMA seeks to provide a forum where the grain-based agribusiness industry can debate, discuss and facilitate resolution of operational and business issues bringing

insight to its membership and stakeholders. Membership: $700-3250/year.

Meetings/Conferences:
2013 - Scottsdale, AZ (Montelucia Resort and Spa)/Jan. 24 - 25

Publications:
Industry News; on-line
Membership Directory; on-line

Transportation Intermediaries Association (1978)
1625 Prince St.
Suite 200
Alexandria, VA 22314-2883
Tel: (703) 299-5700 Fax: (703) 836-0123
E-Mail: info@tianet.org
Website: tianet.org
Members: 1200 companies
Staff: 7
Annual Budget: $2-5,000,000

Personnel:
President and Chief Executive Officer: Robert A. Voltmann
    E-Mail: voltmann@tianet.org
Director, Education and Meetings: Cindy Amos
    E-Mail: amos@tianet.org
Director, Sales and Marketing: Jessica Mizell
    E-Mail: mizell@tianet.org
Director, TIA Services: Nancy O'Liddy
    E-Mail: oliddy@tianet.org
Vice President, Policy and Government Affairs: John T. Stirrup
    E-Mail: stirrup@tianet.org
Manager, Communications: Walter Weart
    E-Mail: wweart@transportwriter.com

Historical Note:
Working with truckers, carriers and shippers to arrange the transport of general freight. The Logistics Conference, the Intermodal Conference, the North American Conference of Freight Forwarders, the Perishable Agricultural and Foodstuff Conference, and the Transportation Brokers Conference of America are subsidiaries of TIA. TIA provides resources, education, information, advocacy and connections to establish, maintain and expand ethical, profitable and growing businesses in service to their customers. Membership: $200-18000 (Regular/Associate, Based on Gross Annual Revenue); $40-150 (Branch).

Continuing Education:
Certification Designation/s: CTB, TIAPC

Meetings/Conferences: Annual
Conference Chair: Cindy Amos
2013 - Las Vegas, NV (Red Rock Casino Resort and Spa)/April 10 - 13
2014 - Tucson, AZ/April 2 - 5
2015 - Orlando, FL/April 15 - 18
2016 - San Antonio, TX/April 4 - 9
2017 - Las Vegas, NV/April 5 - 8
2018 - Tucson, AZ/March 21 - 24

Publications:
The Logistics Journal; monthly; adv.
TIA Logistics Weekly; weekly; adv.
TIA Online Directory; on-line; adv.

Transportation Lawyers Association (1983)
P.O. Box 15122
Lenexa, KS 66285-5122
Tel: (913) 895-4615 Fax: (913) 895-4652
E-Mail: tla-info@goamp.com
Website: translaw.org
Members: 900 lawyers
Staff: 3
Annual Budget: $500-1,000,000
Tax: 501(c)(6)

Personnel:
President: Gordon Hearn
    E-Mail: gord@fernandeshearn.com
Secretary and Treasurer: Steven B. Novy
    E-Mail: snovy@cyp-law.com

Historical Note:
Founded in Louisville, KY as the Motor Carrier Lawyers Association (MCLA); assumed its present name in 1983. TLA is dedicated to keeping its members ahead of the constant changes in all aspects of the specialized legal environment affecting the transportation community, regardless of the particular legal discipline involved. Membership: $185 (Active Members); $75 (Law Professor Members); $125 (Government Attorney Members); $25 (Student Members).

Meetings/Conferences: Annual

2013 - Napa, CA (The Meritage Resort and Spa)/April 30 - May 4
2014 - St. Petersburg, FL (Marriott Vinoy Renaissance Resort and Golf Club)/April 29 - May 3
Publications:
Membership Directory; on-line

Transportation Research Forum (1958)
C/O NDSU Department 2880
P.O. Box 6050
Fargo, ND 58108-6050
Tel: (701) 231-7766 *Fax:* (701) 231-1945
E-Mail: info@trforum.org
Website: trforum.org
Members: 250 individuals
Staff: 6
Annual Budget: $50-100,000
Tax: 501(c)(6)

Personnel:
Executive Director: Denver Tolliver
    E-Mail: denver.tolliver@ndsu.edu
Vice President: Jack Ventura
    E-Mail: ProgramVP@trforum.org
Vice President, Academic Affairs: Eric Jessup
    E-Mail: eric_jessup@wsu.edu
Vice President, Public Relations: Joshua Schank
Treasurer: Carl A. Scheraga
    E-Mail: cscheraga@fairfield.edu
Vice President, Membership Services: Bob Walton

Historical Note:
TRF is an independent organization of transportation professionals that works to provide an impartial meeting ground for carriers, shippers, government officials, consultants, university researchers, suppliers, and others seeking an exchange of information and ideas related to both passenger and freight transportation. Membership: $120 (Regular); $30 (Student); $45 (Retired); $175 (Supporting); $325 (Sustaining); $1000 (Sponsor); $25 (Local/Young).

Meetings/Conferences: Annual
Conference Chair: Jack Ventura
2013 - Annapolis, MD (Doubletree Hotel Annapolis)/ March 21 - 23

Publications:
Journal of the Transportation Research Forum (JTRF); quarterly
Membership Directory; on-line
The Journal of the Transportation Research Forum (JTRF); adv.
TRF Newsletter; on-line; adv.

Transportation Safety Equipment Institute (1962)
2741 SE 32nd St.
Topeka, KS 66605
Tel: (916) 406-8841 *Fax:* (866) 286-3641
E-Mail: tsei@mema.org
Website: tsei.org
Members: 25 companies
Staff: 2
Annual Budget: $100-250,000
Tax: 501(c)(6)

Personnel:
Executive Director: Michelle Brown
    E-Mail: Michelle_Brown@tsei.org
Legal Counsel: Christopher H. Grigorian
    E-Mail: chris@arentfox.com

Historical Note:
Formerly (1986) the Truck Safety Equipment Institute. TSEI provides government representation and market research services, monitors proposed and enacted legislation and regulations, and serves as a technical forum to resolve industry problems.

Publications:
Member Directory; on-line

Transportation Trades Department, AFL-CIO (1990)
815 16th St. NW
Fourth Floor
Washington, DC 20006
Tel: (202) 628-9262 *Fax:* (202) 628-0391
Website: ttd.org
Members: 32 unions
Staff: 13
Annual Budget: $2-5,000,000

Personnel:

President: Edward Wytkind
    E-Mail: edw@ttd.org
Director, Communications: Jennifer McCormick
    E-Mail: jeniferm@ttd.org
Secretary-Treasurer: Larry I. Willis
    E-Mail: larryw@ttd.org

Historical Note:
TTD represents 32 unions whose members work in the aviation, rail, transit, highway, trucking, longshore.

Publications:
Membership Directory; on-line

Transworld Advertising Agency Network (1936)
814 Watertown St.
Newton, MN 02465
Tel: (617) 795-1706 *Fax:* (419) 730-1706
E-Mail: info@taan.org
Website: taan.org
Members: 47 agencies
Staff: 2
Annual Budget: $100-250,000

Personnel:
President: Peter Gerritsen
    E-Mail: peterg@taan.org
Legal Counsel: John Feldman Esq.

Historical Note:
Established as the Transamerica Advertising Agency Network, assumed its present name in 1975. TAAN's mission is to enhance the intelligence, expertise, reach and personal effectiveness of the owners of its member agencies. Members are established and independently operated agencies.

Meetings/Conferences: Semi-Annual
Publications:
TAAN Newsletter; semi-annually

Membership List Available to Non-members

Trauma Care International (1988)
P.O. Box 4826
Baltimore, MD 21211
Tel: (410) 235-7697 *Fax:* (410) 235-8084
E-Mail: info@itaccs.com
Website: itaccs.com
Members: 1000 individuals
Staff: 2

Personnel:
Executive Director and President: Christopher M. Grande MD, MPH
Managing Editor: Ann Donaldson
    E-Mail: morann@aol.com

Historical Note:
Originally (1988) known as International Trauma Anesthesia and Critical Care Society before assuming its current name. ITACCS's mission is to coordinate the development of policies pertaining to trauma care and disseminates related information as needed. Membership: $200 (Full Member); $1,000 (Corporate); $40 (Member in Training).

Publications:
TraumaCare; semi-annually; adv.

The Travel and Tourism Research Association (1970)
5300 Lakewood Rd.
Whitehall, MI 49461
Tel: (248) 708-8872 *Fax:* (248) 814-7150
E-Mail: info@ttra.com
Website: ttra.com
Members: 800 firms, universities and agencies
Staff: 4
Annual Budget: $250-500,000
Tax: 501(c)(6)

Personnel:
Chief Executive Officer: Michael Palmer
    E-Mail: mpalmer@ttra.com
Accounting Assistant: Bailey Boyer
Associate Executive Director: Rita Brummett
    E-Mail: rbrummett@ttra.com
Executive Director and Director, Events: Kathy Palmer
    E-Mail: kpalmer@ttra.com

Historical Note:
Established as the Travel Research Association as a result of the merger of the Eastern and Western Councils for Travel Research. The present name was adopted in 1980. TTRA's mission is to advocate standards and promotes the application of quality travel and tourism research and marketing information. TTRA fosters development of travel

and tourism research and related curricula in institutes of higher education. Membership: $200 (Standard/Additional Organization); $345 (Premier); $575 (Organization-2 members); $50 (Student); $25 (Student Organization).

Meetings/Conferences:
Conference Chair: Kathy Palmer
2013 - Dublin, Ireland/April 17 - 19

Publications:
Supplier Directory; on-line; adv.
TTRA Connects; quarterly; adv.

Travel Goods Association (1938)
301 N. Harrison St.
Suite 412
Princeton, NJ 08540-3512
Tel: (877) 842-1938 *Fax:* (877) 842-1938
E-Mail: info@travel-goods.org
Website: travel-goods.org
Members: 250 companies and 300individuals
Staff: 7
Annual Budget: $2-5,000,000
Tax: 501(c)(6)

Personnel:
President and Chief Executive Officer: Michele Marini Pittenger
Vide President, Trade Shows: Cathy Hays
Director, Government Relations: Nate Herman
    E-Mail: nate@travel-goods.org
Vice President and Chief Financial Officer: Rob Holmes
Contact, Media Relations: Kate Ryan
Director, Membership Services: Cathy Trecartin
Creative Director: Kim Wong

Historical Note:
Formerly called as Luggage and Leather Goods Manufacturers of America till 2000. TGA's mission is to promote the growth, profitability and image of the travel goods industry. Members include manufacturers, retailers and distributors of luggage, personal leather goods, business and computer cases, business and travel accessories, and handbags. Membership: $250-6,200 (Manufacturer/Affiliate); $100-1,000 (Retailer); $50 (Independent Sales Representative).

Meetings/Conferences: Annual
Conference Chair: Cathy Hays
2013 - Las Vegas, NV (Mandalay Bay)/Feb. 27 - March 1/51-100 exhibitors

Publications:
Membership Directory; on-line
TGA Industry News Briefs; weekly
Travel Goods Showcase; quarterly; adv.
Washington Report - Newsletter; monthly

Membership List Available to Non-members

The Travel Institute (1964)
945 Concord St.
Framingham, MA 01701
Tel: (781) 237-0280 *Fax:* (781) 237-3860
TollFree: (800) 542-4282
E-Mail: info@thetravelinstitute.com
Website: thetravelinstitute.com
Members: 7000 individuals
Staff: 6
Annual Budget: $1-2,000,000

Personnel:
Chief Operating Officer: Diane Petras CMP, CTIE
    E-Mail: dpetras@thetravelinstitute.com
Manager, Testing and Certification: Ulmer "Steven" Coy
    E-Mail: scoy@thetravelinstitute.com
Director, Program Development: Patricia J. Gagnon
    E-Mail: pgagnon@thetravelinstitute.com
Director, Sales: Patty Noonan
    E-Mail: pnoonan@thetravelinstitute.com
Manager, Marketing, Communications and Membership Services: Carla Smith
    E-Mail: csmith@thetravelinstitute.com
Director, Marketing and Technology: Chelle Honiker Yarbrough
    E-Mail: cyarbrough@thetravelinstitute.com

Historical Note:
Formerly the Institute of Certified Travel Agents; assumed its current name in 2007. The Travel Institute serves as a community of knowledge and insight for all travel professionals. Provides innovative education programs, professional certifications and customized learning solutions. Membership: $2500 (Lifetime): $1000 (Corporate); $95 (Student).

Continuing Education:
Certification Designation/s: CTIE, LS, CTC, DS, CTA

Meetings/Conferences:
Conference Chair: Diane Petras CMP, CTIE
Number of non-conference events/year: 1

Publications:
Conde Nast Traveller Magazine
Membership Directory
Membership List Available to Non-members

Travel Journalists Guild (1980)
4701 S. Lakeshore Dr.
Suite One
Tempe, AZ 85282
Tel: (480) 897-3331 *Fax:* (480) 897-3332
Website: tjgonline.com
Members: 75 individuals
Staff: 2
Annual Budget: $10-25,000

Personnel:
Executive Director: Mike Finney
    E-Mail: director@tjgonline.com
President: Kerrick James
    E-Mail: kjames5@cox.net

Historical Note:
TJG is a group of professional travel writers and photographers. Members are freelance authors, photographers, artists, lecturers and file makers. Membership: $150/year plus $250 initial fee (Individual).

Publications:
Member Directory; on-line
Membership List Available to Non-members

Treated Wood Council (2003)
1111 19th St. NW
Suite 800
Washington, DC 20036
Tel: (202) 463-2045 *Fax:* (202) 463-2059
Website: treated-wood.org
Members: 470 organizations
Staff: 1
Annual Budget: $500-1,000,000

Personnel:
Executive Director: Jeffrey T. Miller
    E-Mail: jeff_miller@treated-wood.org

Historical Note:
TWC's mission is to serve all segments of the treated wood industry in the field of government affairs. Members are firms msanufacturing pressure-treated wood products, that use EPA-registered wood preservatives, chemical companies whose wood preservative products are EPA registered or accepted by the building codes, and associations and companies related to the preserved wood market.

Treatment Communities of America (1975)
1601 Connecticut Ave. NW
Suite 803
Washington, DC 20009
Tel: (202) 296-3503 *Fax:* (202) 518-5475
E-Mail: tca.office@verizon.net
Website: therapeuticcommunitiesofamerica.org
Members: 600 programs sites
Staff: 3
Annual Budget: $250-500,000
Tax: 501(c)(3)

Personnel:
Executive Director: Patricia Beauchemin
    E-Mail: Pat.tca@verizon.net
Editor: Sushma D. Taylor PhD

Historical Note:
Formerly known as Therapeutic Communities of America, TCA's mission is to increase the efficacy and efficiency of substance abuse and mental health treatment programs by promoting cooperation among TCA members. Membership: $125 (Associate TCA Membership).

Publications:
TCA News
The TCA Membership Directory; on-line

Tree Care Industry Association (1938)
136 Harvey Rd.
Suite 101
Londonderry, NH 03053
Tel: (603) 314-5380 *Fax:* (603) 314-5386
TollFree: (800) 733-2622
E-Mail: tcia@treecareindustry.org
Website: tcia.org
Members: 2000 commercial tree care firms and affiliated companies

Staff: 29
Annual Budget: $2-5,000,000
Tax: 501(c)(6)

Personnel:
President: Mark Garvin
    E-Mail: garvin@tcia.org
Director, Marketing: Jennifer Isham
    E-Mail: isham@tcia.org
Director, Membership Services: David Lee
    E-Mail: lee@tcia.org
Vice President, Corporate Relations and Marketing: Sachin Mohan
    E-Mail: mohan@tcia.org
Meeting Planner: Diane Morgan
    E-Mail: morgan@tcia.org
Chief Program Officer: Bob Rouse
Director, Information Technology: Bruce White
    E-Mail: white@tcia.org

Historical Note:
Formerly (2003) known as National Arborist Association. TCIA's mission is to advance tree care companies and their interests. Membership: $299 (Regular); $326 (Affiliate).

Continuing Education:
Enrollment: 240
Certification Designation/s: CTSP
Meetings/Conferences: Annual
Conference Chair: Diane Morgan

Publications:
TCIA Reporter; monthly
Tree Care Industry Equipment Locator; semi-annually; adv.
Tree Care Industry Magazine; monthly; adv.
Tree Care Manager e-newsletter; on-line
Treeworker; monthly; adv.

Tree-Ring Society (1935)
University of Arizona
Building 58
Tucson, AZ 85721
Tel: (520) 621-1608 *Fax:* (520) 621-8229
E-Mail: pgress@hrr.arizona.edu
Website: treeringsociety.org
Members: 350 individuals and institutions
Staff: 3
Annual Budget: Under $10,000

Personnel:
President: Elaine Kennedy-Sutherland
    E-Mail: sutherland.elaine@gmail.com
Editor: Steven W. Leavitt
    E-Mail: sleavitt@ltrr.arizona.edu
Treasurer: Thomas W. Swetnam
    E-Mail: tswetnam@ltrr.arizona.edu

Historical Note:
TRS's purpose is to advocate tree-ring research to the global scientific community, and to encourage research in dendrochronology throughout the world. Membership consists of those interested in dendrochronology, the science of determining dates by matching tree-rings for archaeological, hydrological or climatological purposes. Membership: $48.95 (Individual); $26.95 (Student); $59.95 (Institution).

Meetings/Conferences: Annual
2013 - Tucson, AZ/May 13 - 18

Publications:
Tree-Ring Research

Trencher Equipment Committee (1974)
6737 W. Washington St., Suite 2400
C/O Association of Equipment Manufacturers
Milwaukee, WI 53214-5647
Tel: (414) 272-0943 *Fax:* (414) 272-1170
Website: aem.org/Groups/Groups/Group.asp?
    G = 82
Staff: 1

Personnel:
Manager, Technical and Safety Services: John Wagner

Historical Note:
Formerly Underground Equipment Council. Mission is to promote and further the interests of the Trencher Equipment Committee on issues related to safety, standards and regulations, statistics and market data, education, public policy and enhancement of the industry's stature.

Trenchless Equipment Committee (1987)
6737 W. Washington St.
Suite 2400
Milwaukee, WI 53214-5647

Tel: (414) 272-0943 *Fax:* (414) 272-1170
Website: aem.org/Groups/Groups/Group.asp?
    G = 83#.T1eDn8DCnIY
Staff: 1

Personnel:
Manager, Technical and Safety Services: John Wagner
    E-Mail: jwagner@aem.org

Historical Note:
Established in 1987 as the Manufacturers of Horizontal Earth Boring Equipment. Gained its current name in 1990. TEC's mission is to encourage and further its interests on issues related to safety, standards and regulations, statistics and marketing data, education, public policy and the enhancement of the industry's stature.

Tributyl Phosphate Task Force (1987)
1850 M St. NW, Suite 700
C/O Society of Chemical Manufacturers and Affiliates
Washington, DC 20036
Tel: (202) 721-4100 *Fax:* (202) 296-8120
Website: socma.com/AssociationManagement/?
    subSec = 9&articleID = 47#TPTF
Staff: 1

Personnel:
Executive Director: C. Tucker Helmes PhD

Historical Note:
The Tributyl Phosphate (TBP) Task Force was created to respond to EPA's proposed TSCA Section 4 test rule for tributyl phosphate. Member companies import, manufacture, or process tributyl phosphate in the United States. The Task Force sponsors health and environmental effects testing and coordinates industry discussions with government agencies.

Triological Society
13930 Gold Circle
Suite 103
Omaha, NE 68144
Tel: (402) 346-5500 *Fax:* (402) 346-5300
E-Mail: info@triological.org
Website: triological.org
Staff: 3

Personnel:
President: Jesus E. Medina FACS, MD
Treasurer: Myles L. Pensak
Editor: Michael G. Stewart FACS, MD, MPH

Historical Note:
Triological Society's mission is to encourage and assist otolaryngologist-head and neck surgeons and other health care professionals to develop, maintain, and enhance their knowledge and skills in their pursuit of improved patient care through education, research, and fellowship.

Meetings/Conferences:
2013 - Scottsdale, AZ (Westin Kierland Resort and Spa)/Jan. 24 - 26
2013 - Orlando, FL (JW Marriott Grande Lakes)/April 10 - 14

Publications:
Membership Directory; on-line
The Laryngoscope; monthly; adv.

Triumvirate Environmental
200 Inner Belt Rd.
Somerville, MA 02143
Tel: (617) 628-8098
TollFree: (800) 966-9282
Website: triumvirate.com
Staff: 4

Personnel:
Chairman, President and Chief Executive Officer: John McQuillan
Chief Operating Officer: Doug Youngen

Historical Note:
A hazardous waste management firm. Mission is to build the most productive, long-term, customer-intimate, environmental services firm.

Publications:
Industrial Insights Newsletter

Truck and Engine Manufacturers Association (1968)
333 W. Wacker Dr.
Suite 810
Chicago, IL 60606
Tel: (312) 929-1970 *Fax:* (312) 929-1975
E-Mail: ema@emamail.org

Website: enginemanufacturers.org
Members: 28 companies
Staff: 14
Annual Budget: $5-10,000,000

Personnel:
President: Jed R. Mandel
    E-Mail: jmandel@emamail.org
Director, Public Affairs: Joseph L. Suchecki
    E-Mail: jsuchecki@emamail.org

Historical Note:
Formerly (1968) Internal Combustion Engine Institute.
Became Engine Manufacturers Association. Assumed the
present name to represent the integration with the Truck
Manufacturers Association in 2011. EMA's mission is to
advance its member companies' interests on emissions
and air quality issues before legislative and regulatory
bodies, both in the United States and abroad. Members are
manufacturers of internal combustion engines used for any
purpose except aircraft or passenger car use.

Publications:
Membership Directory; on-line

Truck Mixer Manufacturers Bureau (1945)
900 Spring St.
Silver Spring, MD 20910
Tel: (301) 587-1400 Fax: (301) 587-1605
Website: tmmb.org
Members: 8 companies
Staff: 4
Annual Budget: $25-50,000
Tax: 501(c)(6)

Personnel:
Executive Secretary: Robert A. Garbini PE
    E-Mail: bgarbini@tmmb.org
Executive Administrator: Deana Angelastro
    E-Mail: dangelastro@nrmca.org
Administrator: Nicole R. Maher
    E-Mail: nmaher@nrmca.org

Historical Note:
TMMB's mission is to develop standards and guidelines for
equipment production.

Truck Renting and Leasing Association (1978)
675 N. Washington St.
Suite 410
Alexandria, VA 22314
Tel: (703) 299-9120 Fax: (703) 299-9115
Website: trala.org
Members: 400 Companies
Staff: 6
Annual Budget: $1-2,000,000
Tax: 501(c)(6)

Personnel:
President and Chief Executive Officer: Thomas M. James
    E-Mail: tjames@trala.org
Director, Communications and Events: Shannon Davison
    E-Mail: sdavison@trala.org
Director, Finance and Business Operations: Tonya Gibbs
    E-Mail: tgibbs@trala.org
Director, Membership Services: Brian Hefner
    E-Mail: bhefner@trala.org
Vice President, Government Relations: Jake Jacoby
    E-Mail: jjacoby@trala.org

Historical Note:
TRALA's mission is to foster a positive legislative and
regulatory climate within which companies engaged in
leasing and renting vehicles and trailers, as well as related
businesses, can compete without discrimination in the North
American marketplace. Members are firms active in full-
service truck and trailer leasing, dedicated contract carriage,
commercial daily truck rental, and consumer truck rental.
Membership: $1,495-5,980 (Associate); $2,500-10,000
(Industry Council); $399-195,000 (Regular).

Meetings/Conferences:
Conference Chair: Shannon Davison
2013 - Naples, FL (The Naples Grande Beach Resort)/
    March 11 - 15

Publications:
En Route; bi-weekly
Inside TRALA; quarterly
TRALA Industry Wire; monthly
TRALA Membership Directory and Buyers Guide;
    annually; adv.
Weekly Wire; weekly

Truck Trailer Manufacturers Association (1941)
8506 Wellington Rd.
Suite 101

Manassas, VA 20109
Tel: (703) 549-3010 Fax: (703) 549-3014
Website: ttmanet.org
Members: 137 companies
Staff: 5
Annual Budget: $500-1,000,000

Personnel:
President: Jeff N. Sims
    E-Mail: Jeff@ttmanet.org
Contact, Administrative Services: Nancy Livingston

Historical Note:
TTMA's mission is to establish confidence between
manufacturers of truck trailers, cargo tanks, intermodal
containers and their suppliers to bring about a
mutual understanding of the problems confronting all
manufacturers.

Publications:
Membership Directory; on-line

Membership List Available to Non-members

Truck Writers of North America (1988)
4429 Back Creek Church Rd.
Charlotte, NC 28213
Tel: (704) 779-9515 Fax: (704) 509-4932
E-Mail: admin@twna.org
Website: twna.org
Members: 150 individuals
Staff: 3
Annual Budget: $10-25,000

Personnel:
Executive Director: Tom Kelley
Contact, Membership Services: Regina Mitchell
    E-Mail: Admin@TWNA.org

Historical Note:
TWNA works to improve the quality of trucking journalism.
Membership is composed of writers, editors, freelance
journalists, public relations and communications specialists,
sales and marketing personnel and others involved in the
business of producing information related to the world
of trucking. Membership: $50 (Individual-Press); $65
(Associate-Nonprofit); $100 (Associate-Business); $500
(Associate-Corporate).

Publications:
Dispatch
TWNA's Membership Directory; adv.

Truck-frame and Axle Repair Association (1966)
364 W. 12th St.
Erie, PA 16501
Fax: (877) 735-1688
TollFree: (877) 735-1687
E-Mail: leafspg@aol.com
Website: taraassociation.com
Members: 102 associations and companies
Staff: 2
Annual Budget: $25-50,000

Personnel:
President: Paul Jones
    E-Mail: pjonesafa@aol.com
Secretary and Treasurer: Bill Hinchcliffe
    E-Mail: bill@hawkframe.com

Historical Note:
TARA's mission is to advocate and protect the interests
of the owners, firms and employees engaged in the heavy
truck and frame repair industry. Membership is open to all
companies which have been in business for two years.

Meetings/Conferences: Annual

Publications:
TARA News; quarterly

Trucking Management, Inc. (1963)
P.O. Box 860725
Shawnee, KS 66286-0725
Tel: (913) 568-5873
E-Mail: info@tmiweb.org
Website: tmiweb.org
Members: 5 companies
Staff: 2
Annual Budget: $1-2,000,000
Tax: 501(c)(6)

Personnel:
President and Chief Executive Officer: David Smith
    E-Mail: david.smith@tmiweb.org
Director, Labor Services: Steve Miller
    E-Mail: steve.miller@tmiweb.org

Historical Note:

Founded as Trucking Employers (TEI), became Trucking
Management in 1978 and in 1997 TMI became a division
of MFCA. On October 1, 2005, MFCA was changed to
Trucking Management, Inc. (TMI). TMI is the primary
multi-employer bargaining arm of the unionized general
freight trucking industry. It negotiates and administers
the National Master Freight Agreement on behalf of its
membership.

Truckload Carriers Association (1938)
555 E. Braddock Rd.
Alexandria, VA 22314
Tel: (703) 838-1950 Fax: (703) 836-6610
E-Mail: tca@truckload.org
Website: truckload.org
Members: 650 carriers and 300 affiliates
Staff: 15
Annual Budget: $2-5,000,000
Tax: 501(c)(6)

Personnel:
President: Christopher Burruss
    E-Mail: cburruss@truckload.org
Manager, Systems Integration: Joy Douglas
    E-Mail: jdouglas@truckload.org
Executive Vice President, Conventions and Marketing:
    William Giroux CMP
    E-Mail: wgiroux@truckload.org
Director, Education: Ron Goode
    E-Mail: rongoode@truckload.org
Director, Safety and Policy: Dave Heller
    E-Mail: dheller@truckload.org
Director, Communications: Michael Nellenbach
    E-Mail: mnellenbach@truckload.org
Vice President, Development: Deborah Sparks
    E-Mail: dsparks@truckload.org

Historical Note:
Formed by the merger in 1983 of the Common Carrier
Conference- Irregular Route (founded in 1941) and the
Contract Carrier Conference (founded in 1939). Formerly
(1997) Interstate Truckload Carriers Conference and (1988)
Interstate Carriers Conference. TCA's mission is to create
success for the truckload industry and the communities
it serves and serves as the national coordinating point,
lobbying organization, and promotional arm for irregular-
route common and contract truckload motor carriers.
Membership: 1,375 (Associate); $350 (School).

Meetings/Conferences: Annual
Conference Chair: William Giroux CMP
2013 - Las Vegas, NV (Wynn Las Vegas and Encore
    Resort)/March 3 - 6
2014 - Grapevine, TX (Gaylord Texan Hotel and
    Convention Center-Grapevine)/March 23 - 26
2015 - Kissimmee, FL (Gaylord Palms Resort and
    Convention Center-Kissimmee)/March 8 - 11
Number of non-conference events/year: 3

Publications:
Membership Directory; on-line; adv.
TCA Newsletter; weekly; adv.

Membership List Available to Non-members

Truss Plate Institute (1961)
218 N. Lee St.
Suite 312
Alexandria, VA 22314
Tel: (703) 683-1010 Fax: (866) 501-4012
E-Mail: info@tpinst.org
Website: tpinst.org
Members: 400 licensee members
Staff: 3
Annual Budget: $500-1,000,000

Personnel:
Executive Director: Michael "Mike" A. Cassidy
    E-Mail: mcassidy@tpinst.org

Historical Note:
TPI's mission is to maintain the truss industry on a sound
engineering basis. Members are truss plate manufacturers,
allied suppliers and truss manufacturers. Membership:
$300/year (Associate).

Tube and Pipe Association, International (1983)
833 Featherstone Rd.
C/O Fabricators and Manufacturers Association,
Intl.
Rockford, IL 61107-6302
Tel: (815) 399-8700 Fax: (815) 484-7700
TollFree: (888) 394-4362
E-Mail: info@fmanet.org

Website: fmanet.org/members/tpa-
membership.cfm
Members: 1800 individuals and companies
Staff: 68
Personnel:
President and Chief Executive Officer: Ed Youdell
Vice President, Expositions and Media Relations: Mark
  Hoper
Director, Marketing: Pat Lee
Membership, Education, Training and Certification: Jim
  Warren
Director, Information Technology: Vicki Webb

Historical Note:
Formed as Tube and Pipe Fabricators Association by the
merger of the Tube Fabricating Division of the Fabricators
and Manufacturers Association, International and the
International Pipe Association in 1990, merged with
American Tube Association and assumed its current name
in 1996. TPA is an educational technology association
serving the metal tube and pipe producing and fabricating
industries. TPA is the technology affiliate of the Fabricators
& Manufacturers Association, Intl. (FMA). TPA members
are eligible for FMA member benefits. Membership: $25
(Student); $150 (Basic); $49 (Young Professional);
$450-1950 (Advantage -Multisite).

Meetings/Conferences: Annual
Conference Chair: Mark Hoper

Publications:
Canadian Industrial Machinery; adv.
Fabricating Update; monthly
Fabricator
Fabrinomics Economic e-Newsletter; on-line; adv.
Green Manufacturer; adv.
Member Directory
Practical Welding Today
Practical Welding Today; adv.
Stamping Journal; bi-monthly; adv.
Stamping News Brief; on-line
The Fabricator; adv.
TPJ, The Tube & Pipe Journal; bi-monthly; adv.
Tube Talk; monthly
Welding Wire; monthly

Tube Council of North America (1938)
187 Cane Creek Blvd.
Danville, VA 24540
Tel: (434) 822-8007 Fax: (434) 822-8043
Website: tube.org
Members: 11 companies
Staff: 2
Annual Budget: $50-100,000
Personnel:
Vice President: Ted Sojourner
  E-Mail: ted.sojourner@ep.esselgroup.com
Contact, Membership Services: Paul Goodman
  E-Mail: paul.goodman@plastube.com

Historical Note:
Established as the Collapsible Metal Tube Association;
became the Metal Tube Packaging Council of North America
in 1966 and assumed its present name in 1983. TCNA is
dedicated to promoting the tube as the package of choice for
dentifrice, cosmetic, pharmaceutical, household/industrial
and food products. Membership fee varies, based on volume
of production. Membership: $3,000 (Companies); $3,500
(Corporate Associate Members); $0 (Individual).

Publications:
TCNA Tube News; on-line
Tube Council E-Newsletter; on-line

Tubular Exchanger Manufacturers Association
(1939)
25 N. Broadway
Tarrytown, NY 10591
Tel: (914) 332-0040 Fax: (914) 332-1541
E-Mail: tema@tema.org
Website: tema.org
Members: 23 companies
Staff: 5
Annual Budget: $100-250,000
Personnel:
Secretary: Richard C. Byrne
  E-Mail: rbyrne@taminc.com

Historical Note:
Sets standards for the industry, known as TEMA Standards,
which are sold to the chemical processing and petroleum
refining industries.

Tuna Council (1976)

7918 Jones Branch Dr.
Suite 700
McLean, VA 22102
Tel: (703) 752-8880 Fax: (703) 752-7583
Website: healthytuna.com
Staff: 3
Personnel:
Media Contact: Gavin Gibbons
  E-Mail: ggibbons@nfi.org

Historical Note:
Forerunner to the current Tuna Council, the U.S. Tuna
Foundation (USTF), the trade association of the U.S. tuna
fishing industry. Headquartered in Washington, DC. The
organization announced that it will be merging with the
National Fisheries Institute in the spring of 2007. In 2007,
the U. S. Tuna Foundation was dissolved and a new council
created within the National Fisheries Institute (NFI) called
the Tuna Council. The combined office will be based out of
McLean, VA.

Turf and Ornamental Communicators Association
(1990)
120 W. Main St.
P.O. Box 156
New Prague, MN 56071
Tel: (952) 758-6340 Fax: (952) 758-5813
E-Mail:
toca@gardnerandgardnercommunications.com
Website: toca.org
Members: 200 individuals
Staff: 3
Annual Budget: $100-250,000
Tax: 501(c)(6)
Personnel:
Executive Director: Den Gardner
Director, Membership Services: Kathy Heyda

Historical Note:
TOCA serves communicators in the Green Industry by
fostering an open exchange of information regarding
issues that affect how people communicate to their various
audiences. TOCA members are individuals and companies
involved in communications in the turf and ornamentals
industry. Membership: $125/year (Individual). For Group
membership, add $75 for each additional member from the
same company or association; $25 (Student).

Meetings/Conferences: Annual
2013 - Portland, OR (Embassy Suites Portland Hotel)/
  May 7 - 10

Publications:
TOCA Talk; quarterly

Membership List Available to Non-members

Turf Equipment Technicians Association (1985)
2225 Willow Lakes Dr.
Plainfield, IL 60586-6260
Tel: (815) 254-8240 Fax: (815) 254-8241
E-Mail: info@teta-online.org
Website: teta-online.org
Staff: 2
Annual Budget: $10-25,000
Personnel:
President: Don Briggs
  E-Mail: donbriggs@teta-online.org
Executive Director: Wes Danielewicz
  E-Mail: wes@teta-online.org

Historical Note:
Formerly, the Chicagoland Golf Course Mechanics
Association. TETA promotes the image, stature, reputation
and skills of professional turf equipment industry
technicians. Membership: $130/year.

Continuing Education:
Enrollment: 7

Publications:
TETA Newsletter; adv.

Turfgrass Producers International (1967)
Two E. Main St.
Dundee, IL 60118
Tel: (847) 649-5555 Fax: (847) 649-5678
TollFree: (800) 405-8873
E-Mail: info@turfgrasssod.org
Website: turfgrasssod.org
Members: 1200 companies
Staff: 8
Annual Budget: $1-2,000,000
Personnel:
Executive Director: Kirk Hunter

E-Mail: khunter@turfgrasssod.org
Managing Editor: Lynn Grooms
Manager, Membership Services and Marketing: Veronica
  Iwanski
  E-Mail: VIwanski@TurfGrassSod.org
Manager, Public Relations: Jim Novak
  E-Mail: jnovak@turfgrasssod.org
Manager, Meetings: Sandy Reynolds
  E-Mail: meetings@turfgrasssod.org

Historical Note:
Formerly (1994) American Sod Producers Association.
TPI's mission is to represent and advance the turfgrass
sod industry worldwide through the promotion of improved
practices and the professional development of members
and the enhancement of the environment. Membership:
$495-1,175 (Turfgrass Sod Producer, based on number
of acres); $800 (Supplier/Manufacturer); $50 (Formal
Educator); $265 (Industry Associate); $50 (Student); $140
(Retired).

Meetings/Conferences: Semi-Annual
Conference Chair: Sandy Reynolds
2013 - San Antonio, TX (San Antonio Marriott
  Rivercenter)/Feb. 11 - 15
2013 - Chicago, IL (The Drake)/July 22 - 25

Publications:
Business Management Newsletter; bi-monthly
Membership Directory; on-line
TPI E-Newsletter; monthly; adv.
Turf News; bi-monthly; adv.

Turkish Studies Association (1971)
University of S. Carolina, Dept. of Geography
Callcott Bldg., Rm. 127, 709 Bull St.
Columbia, SC 29208
Tel: (803) 777-5688 Fax: (803) 777-4972
Website: h-net.org/~thetsa
Members: 500 individuals
Staff: 2
Annual Budget: Under $10,000
Personnel:
Secretary and Treasurer: Amy Mills
  E-Mail: amills@sc.edu

Historical Note:
TSA membership consists of academics, institutions and
professional organizations with an interest in Turkish
culture, history and language. Sponsors several awards in
recognition of achievement in Turkish/Ottoman scholarship,
language, and education. Membership: $30 (Regular);
$40 (Joint); $15 (Student/Retired); $15 (In Turkey, Pay to
ARIT).

Publications:
Insight Turkey
Turkish Studies Association Journal; semi-annually

Turnaround Management Association (1988)
150 S. Wacker Dr.
Suite 900
Chicago, IL 60606
Tel: (312) 578-6900 Fax: (312) 578-8336
E-Mail: info@turnaround.org
Website: turnaround.org
Members: 9000 individuals
Staff: 18
Annual Budget: $2-5,000,000
Tax: 501(c)(6)
Personnel:
Executive Director: Gregory J. Fine CAE
  E-Mail: gfine@turnaround.org
Director, Education: Jennifer Bethke
  E-Mail: jbethke@turnaround.org
Manager, Education and Meeting: Stephanie Bodanyi
  E-Mail: sbodanyi@turnaround.org
Chief Financial Officer: Jim Gavin
  E-Mail: jgavin@turnaround.org
Director, Marketing and Communications: Dan Goldberg
  E-Mail: dgoldberg@turnaround.org
Senior Manager, Communications and Editor: Eddy
  McNeil
  E-Mail: emcneil@turnaround.org
Manager, Membership Services: Allison Pietrzak
  E-Mail: apietrzak@turnaround.org
Manager, Operations and Executive Assistant: Julie
  Schwenk
  E-Mail: jschwenk@turnaround.org
Director, Chapters and Infrastructure: John Warnik
  E-Mail: jwarnik@turnaround.org

Historical Note:

TMA's mission is to provide opportunities for professional development, networking, certification and reference/ research services for its members. Members are in the corporate renewal industry, comprised of turnaround practitioners, attorneys, accountants, investors, lenders, venture capitalists, appraisers, liquidators, executive recruiters and consultants. Membership is also available for individuals in academia or government. *Membership: $300 (Regular); $150 (Next Generation); $125 (Academic/ Government); $75 (Full-Time Student).*

Continuing Education:
Enrollment: 400
Certification Designation/s: CTP

Meetings/Conferences:
Conference Chair: Stephanie Bodanyi
2013 - Las Vegas, NV (Mirage/ Bellagio)/Feb. 6 - 8
2013 - Chicago, IL (JW Marriott Chicago)/May 14 - 16
2013 - Washington, DC (Marriott Wardman Park Hotel)/Oct. 3 - 5
2014 - Las Vegas, NV (Mirage/ Bellagio)/Feb. 5 - 7
2014 - Toronto, ON (Westin Harbour Castle)/Sept. 29 - Oct. 1
Number of non-conference events/year: 10

Publications:
Membership Directory; on-line
The Journal of Corporate Renewal; monthly
The Journal of Private Equity; quarterly
TMA Newsletter; on-line

Twentieth-Century Spanish Association of America *(1976)*
Temple University, Anderson Hall
1114 W. Berks St.
Philadelphia, PA 19122
Tel: (215) 204-2877 *Fax:* (215) 204-2652
E-Mail: sssas@temple.edu
Members: 1000 individuals
Staff: 3

Personnel:
Executive Secretary: Luis T. Gonzalez del Valle
    E-Mail: gonzalez@temple.edu
Senior Publication Assistant: Annete Vega
    E-Mail: annette.vega@temple.edu

Historical Note:
Formerly (2000) Society of Spanish and Spanish-American Studies. Members are academics and others with an interest in contemporary Spanish and Spanish-American art, literature and culture.

Type Directors Club *(1946)*
347 W. 36th St.
Suite 603
New York, NY 10018
Tel: (212) 633-8943 *Fax:* (212) 633-8944
E-Mail: director@tdc.org
Website: tdc.org
Members: 750 individuals and 8 corporations
Staff: 2
Annual Budget: $250-500,000

Personnel:
Executive Director: Carol Wahler
    E-Mail: director@tdc.org
Treasurer: Brian Miller

Historical Note:
TDC's purpose is to support typography, both in print and on screen. Members are professionals involved in typography. Membership: $175-195 (Regular); $1,000 (Corporate); $175 (Associate); $75 (Student).

Meetings/Conferences:
Conference Chair: Brian Miller

Publications:
Typography Annual; annually

U. S. Airline Pilots Association
200 E. Woodlawn Rd.
Suite 250
Charlotte, NC 28217
Tel: (877) 332-3342 *Fax:* (704) 936-4592
Website: usairlinepilots.org
Members: 5,200 mainline pilots
Staff: 5
Annual Budget: $10-25,000,000

Personnel:
President: Captain Gary Hummel

Historical Note:
USAPA's mission is to ensure safe flights for their passengers by guaranteeing that their lives are in the hands

of only the most qualified, competent and well-equipped pilots.

U.S. Hereditary Angioedema Association *(1999)*
Seven Waterfront Plaza
500 Ala Moana Blvd., Suite 400
Honolulu, HI 96813
Fax: (508) 437-0303
TollFree: (866) 798-5598
Website: haea.org
Staff: 12
Annual Budget: $2-5,000,000

Personnel:
President: Anthony Castaldo
Assistant Vice President, Patient Services and Clinical Programs: Donna Davis
Contact, Operations: Miranda Harreys
Financial Director: Larry Salus
Administrator: Michelle Williamson
Manager, Information Technology: Joyce Wilmot

Historical Note:
US Hereditary Angioedema Association, Inc. (US HAEA). Founded and staffed by HAE patients and HAE patient caregivers. HAEA's mission is to help HAE patients and their families to achieve lifelong health.

Publications:
Fall 2010; bi-annually
Spring 2011; bi-annually
Winter 2011; bi-annually

U.S. Metric Association *(1916)*
2032 Mendon Dr.
Rancho Palos Verdes, CA 90275-1620
Tel: (310) 832-3763
Website: lamar.colostate.edu/~hillger
Members: 1500 individuals
Staff: 5
Annual Budget: $10-25,000
Tax: 501(c)(3)

Personnel:
Executive Director: Valerie Antoine
    E-Mail: valerie.antoine@verizon.net

Historical Note:
USMA works to advocate increased usage of the modernized metric system (SI) in the United States with the ultimate objective of complete conversion to it. Members are companies, government agencies, libraries, educators, industry personnel and other individuals with an interest in the metric system. Membership: $30 (Individual); $150 (Corporate); $500 (Lifetime); $15 (Full Time Student); $35 (Individual, Foreign); $150 (Business Member).

Continuing Education:
Certification Designation/s: CAMS, CMS

Publications:
Metric Today; bi-monthly; adv.

U.S. Rice Producers Group
2101 Wilson Blvd.
Suite 610
Arlington, VA 22201
Tel: (703) 236-2300 *Fax:* (703) 236-2301
Website: usarice.com/index.php?
    option = com_content&view = article&id = 130&Itemid = 325
Staff: 1

Personnel:
Chairperson: Linda Raun

Historical Note:
USA Rice Federation is made up of the USA Rice Producers' Group, which is composed entirely of rice farmers. This representative body assures a forum for policy development on the issues that affect rice farmers, and a voice for rice farmers to advance and implement activities to address those issues.

Publications:
Magazine

US Travel Association *(2009)*
1100 New York Ave. NW
Suite 450
Washington, DC 20005-3934
Tel: (202) 408-8422 *Fax:* (202) 408-1255
E-Mail: feedback@ustravel.org
Website: ustravel.org
Members: 2200 organizations
Staff: 57
Annual Budget: $10-25,000,000
Tax: 501(c)(6)

Personnel:
President and Chief Executive Officer: Roger J. Dow
    E-Mail: rdow@ustravel.org
Senior Director, Membership Services: Judith L. Harris
Senior Vice President, Research: David Huether
Vice President, Meetings and Events Services: Barbara Logan
Vice President, Finance: David Mimm
    E-Mail: dmimm@tia.org
Senior Vice President, Business Development: Gary A. Oster
    E-Mail: goster@tia.org
Senior Vice President, Communications: Dennis Petroskey
    E-Mail: dpetroskey@tia.org
Director, Human Resources: Karen Reinhard
Senior Vice President, Public Affairs and Government Relations: Blain Rethmeier
General Counsel: Michelle Tuffin
Senior Vice President, Marketing Product Development: Adam Vance
Vice President, Technology: Eric Weber
    E-Mail: eweber@tia.org

Historical Note:
Formed by a merger of Discover America (1965) and the National Association of Travel Organizations (1941). In (1980) known as Discover America Travel Organizations and the Travel Industry Association of America (2007). Assumed its current name after merger with the Travel Business Roundtable (2009). It leverages the collective strength of everyone who benefits from travel to grow their business beyond what they can do individually, advocates industry-wide initiatives to grow and sustain travel and ensure the freedom to travel. Membership: $350-15,000 (Regular); $195 (Trial); $495 (Affiliate).

Meetings/Conferences: Annual
Conference Chair: Barbara Logan
2013 - Las Vegas, NV/June 8 - 12
Number of non-conference events/year: 3

Publications:
Membership Directory; on-line
Research Alert; irregular

Membership List Available to Non-members

U.S.A. Toy Library Association *(1984)*
2719 Broadway Ave.
Evanston, IL 60201
Tel: (847) 612-6966 *Fax:* (847) 864-8473
E-Mail: director@usatla.org
Website: usatla.org
Members: 230 individuals and companies
Staff: 2
Annual Budget: $10-25,000

Personnel:
Executive Director: Judith Q. Iacuzzi
    E-Mail: jqi@comcast.net

Historical Note:
USATLA is actively involved in the International Association of Toy Libraries. European leaders in the field of early childhood tie in closely to the toy library and play movement there. Membership: $20 (Student); $60 (Basic); $75 (Basic, Outside US and Canada); $175 (Comprehensive); $195 (Comprehensive, Outside US and Canada).

Meetings/Conferences: Annual

Publications:
Child's Play Newsletter; quarterly; adv.
Toy Library Operators Manual

Ultrasonic Industry Association *(1956)*
P.O. Box 2307
Dayton, OH 45401-2307
Tel: (937) 586-3725 *Fax:* (937) 586-3699
E-Mail: uia@ultrasonics.org
Website: ultrasonics.org
Members: 106 companies
Staff: 4
Annual Budget: $50-100,000

Personnel:
Executive Director: Francine "Fran" W. Rickenbach CAE, IOM
Contact, Web Publications: Robert Muratore
Chair, Membership Services: Jay Sheehan

Historical Note:
UIA strives to change the world of medicine and industry through ultrasonics by providing access to educators, researchers, engineers, users, products and applications leading to the advancement of ultrasonic technology. Members are users, manufacturers, and researchers of

ultrasonics. Membership: $75 (Student); $150 (Individual); $575 (Corporate); $995 (Sustaining); Free (Honorary/Affinity).

Meetings/Conferences: Annual
2013 - Lake Buena Vista, FL (Hilton Orlando Lake Buena Vista)/April 22 - 24

Publications:
Membership Directory; on-line
Vibrations Newsletter; quarterly; adv.

Underground Equipment Manufacturers Council (2005)
6737 W. Washington St.
Suite 2400
Milwaukee, WI 53214-5647
Tel: (414) 298-4164
Website: aem.org/Groups/Groups/Group.asp?
  G = 86
Staff: 1

Personnel:
Contact, Communications: Kira Henschel

Historical Note:
Established in 2005 as a consolidation of four existing AEM product groups: the Trencher Equipment Council, Trenchless Equipment Council, Underground Electronics Committee, and Vacuum Excavation Equipment Manufacturers Council. UEMC's mission is to promote and further the interests of the members of the Underground Equipment Manufacturers Council on issues related to safety, standards and regulations, education, public policy and enhancement of the industry's stature.

Undersea and Hyperbaric Medical Society (1967)
21 W. Colony Pl.
Suite 280
Durham, NC 27705
Tel: (919) 490-5140 Fax: (919) 490-5149
TollFree: (877) 533-8467
E-Mail: uhms@uhms.org
Website: membership.uhms.org
Members: 2000 individuals
Staff: 11
Annual Budget: $1-2,000,000
Tax: 501(c)(3)

Personnel:
Executive Director: Peter Bennet DSc, PhD
    E-Mail: peterbennett@uhms.org
Managing Editor: Renee Duncan
    E-Mail: renee@uhms.org
Coordinator, Education: Cindi Easterling
    E-Mail: cindi@uhms.org
Coordinator, Membership Services and CME: Stacy Rupert
    E-Mail: stacy@uhms.org
Office Manager and Meeting Planner: Lisa Tidd
    E-Mail: lisa@uhms.org

Historical Note:
Formerly (1986) Undersea Medical Society. UHMS's mission is to foster the advancement of medical science in the fields of undersea medicine and hyperbaric medicine. Serves as a source of scientific information for diving and hyperbaric medicine physiology worldwide. Membership: $120-2,000/year.

Continuing Education:
Certification Designation/s: CHT, CHRN

Meetings/Conferences: Annual
Conference Chair: Lisa Tidd
2013 - Orlando, FL (DoubleTree by Hilton at the Entrance to Universal Orlando)/June 13 - 15
2014 - St. Louis, MO (Hyatt Regency St. Louis at The Arch)/June 18 - 21
Number of non-conference events/year: 1

Publications:
UH MS E-blast; monthly
UHM Journal; bi-monthly

Underwater Construction Corporation
110 Plains Rd.
Essex, CT 06426
Tel: (860) 767-8256 Fax: (860) 767-0612
Website: uccdive.com
Staff: 2

Personnel:
Director, Global Nuclear Services: Phil Mcdermott
    E-Mail: pmcdermott@uccdive.com
Contact, Employment and Human Resources: Cathy Alexander
    E-Mail: cathya@uccdive.com

Historical Note:
UCC is a global service provider specializing in underwater services to a diverse customer base. UCC's goal is to bring the highest degree of professionalism to every job. UCC provides basic and speciality services under the general categories of inspection, Maintenance, Construction and Technical Support.

Underwater Society of America (1959)
P.O. Box 628
Daly City, CA 94017
Tel: (650) 583-8492 Fax: (650) 583-6184
Website: underwater-society.org
Staff: 3

Personnel:
President and Editor: Carol Rose
    E-Mail: croseusoa@aol.com
Contact, Legislation: Anne Giesecke
    E-Mail: info@a-dpolicyanalysis.com
Contact, Membership: Elizabeth Hughes

Historical Note:
Functions of the Society is in education and information keeping divers, councils and clubs aware of the issues affecting them. Membership: $15/year.

Publications:
Newsletter; quarterly

Unfinished Furniture Association (1990)
P.O. Box 520
Spofford, NH 03462
Tel: (518) 832-7939 Fax: (518) 824-5719
TollFree: (800) 487-8321
E-Mail: ufa@realwoodfurniture.org
Website: unfinishedfurniture.org
Members: 700 companies
Staff: 7
Annual Budget: $50-100,000
Tax: 501(c)(6)

Personnel:
Executive Director: Fred Moriarty
    E-Mail: ufa.exdir@gmail.com

Historical Note:
UFA is a not-for-profit trade organization that supports the growth of the unfinished furniture industry and association membership through education and awareness. Membership: $99 (Premium/Independent Sales Representative); $350-15,000 (Manufacturer); $200 (Associate); $120 (Premium PLUS).

Continuing Education:
Certification Designation/s: RWFCP

Publications:
UBOnline; monthly; adv.

Membership List Available to Non-members

Uni-Bell PVC Pipe Association (1971)
2711 LBJ Fwy.
Suite 1000
Dallas, TX 75234
Tel: (972) 243-3902 Fax: (972) 243-3907
E-Mail: info@uni-bell.org
Website: uni-bell.org
Members: 56 companies
Staff: 3
Annual Budget: $1-2,000,000
Tax: 501(c)(6)

Personnel:
Executive Director: Bruce Hollands
    E-Mail: bhollands@uni-bell.org

Historical Note:
Uni-Bell's mission is to advocate use of longer-life, lower-maintenance, corrosion-proof PVC piping in water and wastewater systems-for real sustainability, strength and long-term asset management. Association members are producers of gasketed PVC pipe used in buried water, sewer and irrigation lines.

Meetings/Conferences: Annual

Publications:
Membership Directory; on-line

Membership List Available to Non-members

Unified Abrasives Manufacturers Association (1999)
30200 Detroit Rd.
Cleveland, OH 44145-1967
Tel: (440) 899-0010 Fax: (440) 892-1404
E-Mail: contact@uama.org
Website: uama.org

Members: 37 companies
Staff: 5
Annual Budget: $250-500,000
Tax: 501(c)(6)

Personnel:
Managing Director: Jeffrey J. Wherry
    E-Mail: jjw@wherryassoc.com

Historical Note:
UAMA was formed from the merging of four predecessor organizations: the Abrasive Grain Association, Coated Abrasives Manufacturers' Institute, Diamond Wheel Manufacturers' Institute and the Grinding Wheel Institute. The mission of the UAMA is to undertake those activities that can be pursued more effectively by an Association than individual companies in order to enable the industry to freely create and market safe, productive abrasive products throughout the world.

Meetings/Conferences: Semi-Annual

Publications:
Member Directory; on-line

Uniform Retailers Association (2007)
1100-H Brandywine Blvd.
Zanesville, OH 43701-7303
Tel: (740) 452-4541 Fax: (740) 452-2552
E-Mail: ura@uniformretailers.org
Website: uniformretailers.org
Staff: 2
Annual Budget: $250-500,000

Personnel:
President: Steve Land
    E-Mail: sland1313@gmail.com
Secretary and Treasurer: Jason Paulsgrove

Historical Note:
The Uniform Retailers Association is managed by Offinger Management Company. URA is a non-profit trade association dedicated to the growth and prosperity of the independent uniform retailer. Assists its members throughout the year by providing education, communication, valuable member benefits and promotion of the independent uniform retailer. Membership is for retailers only. Membership: $150/year.

Meetings/Conferences: Annual

Publications:
Member Directory; on-line
Resource Guide; on-line
Retailer to Retailer eNews; monthly

Uniformed Services Academy of Family Physicians (1972)
1503 Santa Rosa Rd.
Suite 207
Richmond, VA 23229
Tel: (804) 968-4436 Fax: (804) 968-4418
Website: usafp.org
Members: 2000 individuals
Staff: 6
Annual Budget: $500-1,000,000

Personnel:
Executive Director: Terrence Schulte CAE
    E-Mail: tschulte@vafp.org
Associate Executive Director: Mary Lindsay White
    E-Mail: mlwhite@vafp.org

Historical Note:
USAFP is a services chapter of the American Academy of Family Physicians. USAFP's mission is to be the primary professional organization to support, represent, and advance the Uniformed Family Physician in scholarship, readiness, patient care, and leadership. Membership: $395 (Active); $30 (Resident); $35 (International Student); $270 (Supporting).

Meetings/Conferences: Annual
Conference Chair: Mary Lindsay White
2013 - Lake Buena Vista, FL (Swan and Dolphin Resorts)/March 21 - 26

Publications:
Uniformed Family Physician; quarterly; adv.

Membership List Available to Non-members

UniForum Association (1981)
P.O. Box 3177
Annapolis, MD 21403
Tel: (410) 715-9500 Fax: (240) 465-0207
TollFree: (800) 333-8649
Website: uniforum.org
Members: 5000 individuals
Staff: 2

Personnel:
President: Alan Fedder
  E-Mail: afedder@uniforum.org
Vice President, Professional Training and Development:
Deb Murray
  E-Mail: dmurray@uniforum.org

Historical Note:
Founded as International Association of Open Systems, assumed its current name in 1997. UniForum's mission is the delivery of high quality educational programs, conferences, publications, on-line services and peer group interaction. Membership: $95/year (General).

Publications:
Membership Directory; on-line
The Journal of Open Computing
UniNews; bi-weekly; adv.

Union for Radical Political Economics *(1968)*
418 N. Pleasant St.
Amherst, MA 01002
Tel: (413) 577-0806 *Fax:* (413) 577-0261
E-Mail: urpe@labornet.org
Website: urpe.org
Members: 1100 individuals
Staff: 2
Annual Budget: $100-250,000

Personnel:
Editor: Frances Boyes
  E-Mail: franceskboyes@gmail.com

Historical Note:
An interdisciplinary association devoted to the study, development, and application of political economic analysis to social problems. A member of the Allied Social Science Associations. Membership: $30 (Low-Income/Student); $55 (Individuals); $20 (Limited Member).

Meetings/Conferences: Annual
2013 - San Diego, CA/Jan. 4 - 6

Publications:
Review of Radical Political Economics (RRPE); quarterly
URPE Newsletter; quarterly; adv.

Membership List Available to Non-members

Union Label and Service Trades Department *(1909)*
815 16th St. NW
Washington, DC 20006
Tel: (202) 508-3700
Website: unionlabel.org
Staff: 2
Annual Budget: $250-500,000

Personnel:
President: Richard Kline
  E-Mail: rkline@aflcio.org
Secretary and Treasurer: James Dunn

Historical Note:
UL&STD mission is to promote the products and services produced in America by trade union members, especially those products and services identified by a union label, shop card, store card or service button. The department is a constitutionally mandated department of the AFL-CIO and has affiliates. It is supported by per capita payments from AFL-CIO National and International Unions.

Publications:
The Label Letter; bi-monthly

Union of American Physicians and Dentists *(1972)*
180 Grand Ave.
Suite 1380
Oakland, CA 94612
Tel: (510) 839-0193 *Fax:* (510) 763-8756
TollFree: (800) 622-0909
E-Mail: uapd@uapd.com
Website: uapd.com
Members: 10000 individuals
Staff: 19
Annual Budget: $2-5,000,000

Personnel:
Executive Director: Al W. Groh
Bookkeeper: Cheryl A. Clark
  E-Mail: cheryl@uapd.com
Office Manager: Gloria A. Duarte
Representative and Communications Specialist: Sue Wilson
  E-Mail: swilson@uapd.com

Historical Note:

UAPD is affiliated with AFSCME, AFL-CIO. UAPD's mission is to help physicians maintain control of their practices and fulfill a role in American healthcare. Membership: $440/year.

Meetings/Conferences: Triennial

Publications:
Membership Directory; on-line
The UAPD Report; quarterly

Membership List Available to Non-members

UNITE-HERE *(1891)*
275 Seventh Ave.
Tenth Floor
New York, NY 10001
Website: unitehere.org
Members: 450000 individuals
Staff: 1000
Annual Budget: Over $100,000,000
Tax: 501(c)(5)

Personnel:
President: John W. Wilhelm
Specialist, Communications: Annemarie Strassel
  E-Mail: astrassel@unitehere.org

Historical Note:
Formerly International Ladies Garment Workers Union and chartered by the American Federation of Labor in 1900; merged (1995) with Amalgamated Clothing and Textile Workers Union to become Union of Needletrades, Industrial and Textile Employees; (2003) UNITE. Merged with Hotel Employees and Restaurant Employees International Union and assumed its current name in 2004. UNITE represents workers throughout the U.S. and Canada who work in the hospitality, gaming, food service, manufacturing, textile, laundry, and airport industries.

Publications:
Membership Directory; on-line

United Abrasives Manufacturers Association, Coated Division *(1933)*
30200 Detroit Rd.
Cleveland, OH 44145-1967
Tel: (440) 899-0010 *Fax:* (440) 892-1404
E-Mail: contact@uama.org
Website: uama.org
Members: 4 companies
Staff: 2

Personnel:
Director: Paul Freedenberg

Historical Note:
Founded as the Coated Abrasives Manufacturers Institute, assumed its present name in 1999. Members are individuals, partnerships or corporations that manufacture coated abrasives and coated abrasive products. Mission of the UAMA is to undertake those activities that can be pursued more effectively by an Association than individual companies in order to enable the industry to freely create and market safe, productive abrasive products throughout the world.

Publications:
Membership Directory; on-line

United Applications Standards Group *(1999)*
8265 E. Serene Ridge Ln.
Anaheim, CA 92808-2531
Tel: (800) 840-6368 *Fax:* (714) 281-2206
TollFree: (800) 840-6368
Website: uasg.org
Members: 43 companies
Staff: 2
Annual Budget: $50-100,000

Personnel:
Contact, Administration: Sharon Paxton

Historical Note:
UASG is an organization made up of companies that employ full time installers. Members are graphics installation contractors, screen printers, designers and others involved in the commercial graphics industry. The organization's focus, activities, services, and dues are determined by the members themselves.UASG's mission is to provide a forum for professional development and growth of graphic installation companies.

Publications:
Member Directory; on-line

United Association for Labor Education *(1959)*
14951 SW 157 Terrace
Miami, FL 33187
Tel: (305) 348-2371 *Fax:* (617) 287-7404

E-Mail: info@uale.org
Website: uale.org
Members: 540 institutions and individuals
Staff: 3
Annual Budget: $50-100,000
Tax: 501(c)(6)

Personnel:
Treasurer: Dawn Addy
  E-Mail: addyd@fiu.edu

Historical Note:
Formed as a result of the merger between the Workers' Education Local 189 and the University and College Labor Education Association, assumed its current name in 2000. UALE's mission is to promote and encourage the development of labor and worker education, to make labor education accessible to all working people, and to promote collective bargaining and the right to organize. Members are institutions with labor education programs and individuals with an interest in labor education. Membership: $35-200/year.

Meetings/Conferences: Annual
Conference Chair: Dawn Addy
2013 - Toronto, ON (Metropolitan Hotel)/April 17 - 20
Number of non-conference events/year: 3

Publications:
Individual Membership Directory; on-line
The Labor Studies Journal; quarterly

Membership List Available to Non-members

United Association of Equipment Leasing *(1974)*
78120 Calle Estado
Suite 201
La Quinta, CA 92253
Tel: (760) 564-2227 *Fax:* (760) 564-2206
E-Mail: jwoodley@uael.org
Members: 400 companies
Staff: 6
Annual Budget: $500-1,000,000

Personnel:
Executive Director: Joe Woodley
  E-Mail: jwoodley@uael.org
Contact: Andy Alper
  E-Mail: aalper@frandzel.com
Contact: Brian Bjella
  E-Mail: brian@gvfin.com
Contact: Adolph Chang
  E-Mail: achang@bankofthewest.com
Director, Membership and Marketing: Bill Grohe
  E-Mail: bill@uael.org
Manager, Operations: Kim King
  E-Mail: kim@uael.org

Historical Note:
Founded as Western Association of Equipment Lessors; became UAEL: a National Equipment Leasing Association in 1993, and assumed its current name in 1995. UAEL works towards providing a forum for the personal and professional growth and mutual success of its members by uniting them through networking, education and involvement. Membership: $595-$1295/year (Broker/ Lessor); $1995/year (Funding Source); $795/year (Service Provider); $1495/year (Service Provider).

Continuing Education:
Certification Designation/s: CLP

Meetings/Conferences:
Conference Chair: Adolph Chang
Number of non-conference events/year: 1

United Association of Journeymen and Apprentices of the Plumbing and Pipe Fitting Industry of the U.S. and Canada *(1889)*
Three Park Pl.
Annapolis, MD 21401
Tel: (410) 269-2000 *Fax:* (410) 267-0262
Website: ua.org
Members: 340000 individuals
Staff: 150
Annual Budget: $5-10,000,000

Personnel:
General President: William P. Hite
  E-Mail: billh@uanet.org
Senior Executive Vice President: Rick Terven
  E-Mail: rickt@uanet.org

Historical Note:
Formerly the United Association of Journeymen, Plumbers, Gas Fitters, Steam Fitters and Steam Fitters Helpers of the United States and Canada. Affiliated with the American Federation of Labor in 1897, assumed its current name in 1947. UA's mission is to improve member's skills through

training programs and assists qualified members to obtain information and identify opportunities regarding training and employment in the union pipe trades industry.

Meetings/Conferences:
Conference Chair: Rick Terven

Publications:
Membership Directory; on-line

United Auto Workers (UAW) (1935)
8000 E. Jefferson Ave.
Detroit, MI 48214
Website: uaw.org
Members: 390000 active members and 600000 retired members
Staff: 5

Personnel:
President: Bob King
Director, Public Relations and Publications: Michele Martin

Historical Note:
UAW represents workers in the auto industry as well as aircraft manufacture and other industries in the U.S. Members pay monthly dues equal to two hours pay or, for salaried workers, 1.15% of their monthly salary.

Meetings/Conferences: Annual

Publications:
Solidarity; bi-monthly

United Braford Breeders (1969)
422 E. Main
Suite 218
Nacogdoches, TX 75961
Tel: (936) 569-8200
E-Mail: info@brafords.org
Website: brafords.org
Members: 500 individuals
Staff: 2
Annual Budget: $100-250,000

Personnel:
Executive Director: Rodney L. Roberson PhD
    E-Mail: roberson@brafords.org

Historical Note:
Formerly (1994) International Braford Association. International Braford Association and American Braford Association joined forces on June 1, 1994, to form UBB. UBB represents the interests of all braford breeders throughout the U. S. and its programs are focused on assisting members in their efforts to breed functional braford cattle. Members are breeders of braford cattle. Membership: $85 (Active/Full); $40 (Junior)

Publications:
Membership Directory; annually
The Braford News; quarterly; adv.

United Brotherhood of Carpenters and Joiners of America (1881)
101 Constitution Ave. NW
Washington, DC 20001
Tel: (202) 546-6206 *Fax:* (301) 420-3023
Website: carpenters.org
Members: 520000 individuals
Staff: 150
Annual Budget: $100-250,000
Tax: 501(c)(5)

Personnel:
General President: Douglas J. McCarron
General Vice President: Douglas Banes
Legislative Director: Thomas Flyee
General Secretary and Treasurer: Andris J. Silins

Historical Note:
Established August 8, 1881 in Chicago as the Brotherhood of Carpenters and Joiners. Merged in 1888 with the United Order of Carpenters to form the present organization. Absorbed the Wood, Wire and Metal Lathers International Union in 1979. Absorbed the Tile, Marble, Terrazzo, Finishers, Shopworkers & Granite Cutters International Union in 1988. UBC's mission is to stand for signatory contractors and help them succeed in today's marketplace by supplying them with motivated, knowledgable crews that demonstrate skills, productivity, and a strong work ethic every day.

Publications:
Carpenter
Membership Directory; on-line

Membership List Available to Non-members

United Cerebral Palsy (1949)
1825 K St.NW

Suite 600
Washington, DC 20006
Tel: (202) 776-0406 *Fax:* (202) 776-0414
TollFree: (800) 872-5827
E-Mail: ucpnatl@ucp.org
Website: ucp.org
Staff: 7
Annual Budget: $500-1,000,000
Tax: 501(c)(3)

Personnel:
President and Chief Executive Officer: Stephen Bennett
    E-Mail: sbennett@ucp.org
Director, Marketing and Communications: Lauren Cozzi
    E-Mail: lcozzi@ucp.org
Staff Accountant and Manager of Human Resources:
    Chiquitta Hewitt
    E-Mail: chewitt@ucp.org
Senior Vice President, External Affairs: Michael Hill
    E-Mail: mhill@ucp.org
Director, Finance: Tanneka Jones
    E-Mail: tjones@ucp.org
Senior Director, Public Policy, Communications and Advocacy: Kaelan Richards
    E-Mail: krichards@ucp.org
Vice President, Corporate Affairs and General Counsel:
    Chris Thomson
    E-Mail: christopher@ucp.org

Historical Note:
UCP strives to advance the independence, productivity and full citizenship of people with disabilities through an affiliate network.

Meetings/Conferences: Annual
2013 - San Diego, CA/April 24 - 27/11-25 exhibitors
Number of non-conference events/year: 1

Publications:
Capitol Insider; weekly
United Cerebral Palsy Newsletter; monthly

Membership List Available to Non-members

United Dairy Industry Association
10255 W. Higgins Rd.
Suite 900
Rosemont, IL 60018-5616
TollFree: (800) 853-2479
Website: dairycheckoff.com
Staff: 1
Annual Budget: $25-50,000,000

Personnel:
Director, Producer Relations: Joe Bavido

Historical Note:
A federation of state and regional dairy producer-funded promotion organizations that provides marketing programs that are developed and implemented in coordination with its members. UDIA is overseen by a board comprised of dairy producers elected by their respective boards of their member organizations.

United Development Council
4018 Chartres
Houston, TX 77004
Tel: (713) 987-7000 *Fax:* (713) 987-7004
Website: developmentedu.com
Staff: 1

Personnel:
Chief Executive Officer: John Conners MBA

Historical Note:
UDC is dedicated to promoting the inclusion and representation of minorities within the planning and development of community development projects located in high density urban areas where its members are actively engaged in development and the brokerage of real estate.

Continuing Education:
Certification Designation/s: UDCC

United Egg Producers (1968)
1720 Windward Concourse
Suite 230
Alpharetta, GA 30005
Tel: (770) 360-9220 *Fax:* (770) 360-7058
Website: unitedegg.com
Members: 220 manufacturers
Staff: 10

Personnel:
President and Chief Executive Officer: Gene Gregory
    E-Mail: gene@unitedegg.com
Administrative Assistant: Vicki Brandenburg
    E-Mail: Vicki@unitedegg.com

Senior Vice President: Chad Gregory
    E-Mail: chaduep@unitedegg.com
Vice President, Finance: Sherry Shedd
    E-Mail: sherryshedd@unitedegg.com

Historical Note:
Created as a federated Capper-Volstead Agriculture Cooperative of five regional marketing cooperatives. UEP engages professional consultants for government relations, animal welfare, food safety, and the environment in order to provide the best service possible to its members.

Continuing Education:
Certification Designation/s: UEP

Publications:
United Voices Newsletter; bi-weekly

United Electrical Radio & Machine Workers of America (1936)
One Gateway Center
Suite 1400
Pittsburgh, PA 15222-1416
Tel: (412) 471-8919 *Fax:* (412) 471-8999
E-Mail: ue@ranknfile-ue.org
Website: ranknfile-ue.org
Members: 35000 individuals
Staff: 90
Annual Budget: $2-5,000,000
Tax: 501(c)(5)

Personnel:
President: John H. Hovis Jr.
    E-Mail: jhovis@ranknfile-ue.org
Editor: Alan Hart
Director, Organization: Robert B. Kingsley
Secretary and Treasurer: Bruce J. Klipple
    E-Mail: bklipple@ranknfile-ue.org

Historical Note:
UE is an independent union representing workers in a variety of manufacturing, public sector and private non-profit sector jobs and has a democratic structure and progressive policies. Members include teachers, speech pathologists and nurses clerical workers, graduate instructors, graduate researchers, scientists, librarians, and day care workers.

Meetings/Conferences: Biennial

Publications:
UE News; on-line

Membership List Available to Non-members

United Engineering Foundation (1904)
P.O. Box 70
Mount Vernon, VA 22121-0070
Tel: (973) 244-2328 *Fax:* (973) 882-5155
E-Mail: engfnd@aol.com
Website: uefoundation.org
Members: 5 engineering organizations
Staff: 2
Annual Budget: $500-1,000,000

Personnel:
Executive Director: David L. Belden PE, PhD
    E-Mail: engfnd@aol.com

Historical Note:
Founded as the United Engineering Society, became Engineering Foundation in 1930, then became the United Engineering Trustees in 1931 and assumed its current name in 1999. UET's mission is to support engineering and education by, among other means, making grants. Members are the American Institute of Chemical Engineers (AIChE), American Institute of Mining Engineers (AIME), American Society of Civil Engineers (ASCE), American Society of Mechanical Engineers, and Institute of Electrical and Electronics Engineers (IEEE).

United Farm Workers of America (1962)
29700 Woodford-Tehachapi Rd.
P.O. Box 62
Keene, CA 93531
Tel: (661) 823-6151 *Fax:* (661) 823-6177
E-Mail: execoffice@ufw.org
Website: ufw.org
Members: 27000 Individuals
Staff: 102
Annual Budget: $5-10,000,000

Personnel:
President: Arturo S. Rodriguez
Secretary and Treasurer: Sergio Guzman
Contact, Events: Teresa Romero
    E-Mail: execoffice@ufw.org

Historical Note:

Organized in 1962 by Cesar E. Chavez as the National Farm Workers Association, in 1966 the National Farm Workers Association and the Agricultural Workers Organizing Committee merged to become the United Farm Workers of America affiliated with the AFL-CIO. UFW works to provide farm workers and other working people with the inspiration and tools to share in society's bounty. It also sponsors and supports the National United Farm Workers Volunteer Political Action Committee. Membership: 2% of what each member earns while they earn while they work.

Meetings/Conferences:
Conference Chair: Teresa Romero

United Federation of Police & Security Officers (1980)
540 N. State Rd.
P.O. Box 76
Briarcliff Manor, NY 10510-0076
Tel: (914) 941-4103 *Fax:* (914) 941-4472
TollFree: (800) 227-4291
E-Mail: mailroom@securityfederation.com
Website: securityfederation.com
Members: 200 individuals
Staff: 7
Annual Budget: $250-500,000
Tax: 501(c)(5)

Personnel:
President: Ralph M. Purdy
    E-Mail: rpurdy@securityfederation.com
Secretary and Treasurer: Vance Sullivan
    E-Mail: damittt@aol.com

Historical Note:
UFSPSO's mission is to advocate the welfare of its members, including greater acknowledgement of their professionalism, betterment of working conditions and financial security for the individual members and their dependents; to endorse, support and propose legislation beneficial to its members and oppose any legislation contrary to the members' mutual well-being and financial security. Membership: $7.50/week.

Publications:
UFPSO Newsletter; on-line

United Federation of Teachers
52 Broadway
New York, NY 10004
Tel: (212) 777-7500
Website: uft.org
Members: 200,000 members
Staff: 1034
Annual Budget: Over $100,000,000

Personnel:
President: Michael Mulgrew
    E-Mail: mmulgrew@uft.org
Treasurer: Mel Aaronson
    E-Mail: maaronson@uft.org

Historical Note:
The UFT is the sole bargaining agent for most of the non-supervisory educators who work in New York City public schools.

United Food and Commercial Workers International Union (1979)
1775 K St. NW
Washington, DC 20006-1598
Tel: (202) 223-3111 *Fax:* (202) 466-1562
E-Mail: press@ufcw.org
Website: ufcw.org
Members: 130000 individuals
Staff: 5
Annual Budget: Over $100,000,000
Tax: 501(c)(5)

Personnel:
Executive Vice President: William T. McDonough
Director, Communications: Jill Cashen
Chief Lobbyist: Mia Dell
International President: Joseph T. Hansen
International Secretary and Treasurer: Anthony M.
    Perrone

Historical Note:
Formed (1979) by a merger of the Retail Clerks International Union (founded in 1888) and Amalgamated Meat Cutters and Butcher Workmen of North America (founded in 1897). Absorbed Affiliated Barbers, Beauticians, and Allied Industries International Association in 1980; United Retail Workers in 1981; Insurance Workers International Union in 1983; Canadian Brewery and Distillery Workers in 1986; International Union of Life

Insurance Agents in 1992; United Garment Workers of America in 1994; Distillery, Wine and Allied Workers' International Union in 1996 and International Chemical Workers Union in 1997. UFCW's mission is to change the communities where members work and live so that all workers have the better opportunity. Members are workers in the retail, meat packing, food processing, hair care, insurance, health care, footwear and fur industry.

Publications:
Membership Directory; on-line
UFCW Newsletter

United Fresh Produce Association (1904)
1901 Pennsylvania Ave. NW
Suite 1100
Washington, DC 20006
Tel: (202) 303-3400 *Fax:* (202) 303-3433
E-Mail: united@unitedfresh.org
Website: unitedfresh.org
Members: 1000 companies
Staff: 27
Annual Budget: $5-10,000,000
Tax: 501(c)(6)

Personnel:
President and Chief Executive Officer: Thomas E. Stenzel
    E-Mail: tstenzel@unitedfresh.org
Vice President, Communications: Ray Gilmer
    E-Mail: rgilmer@unitedfresh.org
Senior Vice President, Public Policy: Robert L. Guenther
    E-Mail: rguenther@unitedfresh.org
Chief Financial Officer: Dan Hilleary
    E-Mail: dhilleary@unitedfresh.org
Director, Meetings and Events: Leslie N. Howard CMP
    E-Mail: lhoward@unitedfresh.org
Manager, Marketing: Marinell Saville
    E-Mail: msaville@unitedfresh.org
Vice President, Business Development: Claudia Wenzing
    E-Mail: cwenzing@unitedfresh.org
Senior Director, Membership Services: Miriam Miller
    Wolk CAE
    E-Mail: mmiller@unitedfresh.org
Manager, Education: Shannon Young
    E-Mail: syoung@unitedfresh.org

Historical Note:
Formed as a merger of the United Fresh Fruit and Vegetable Association and the International Fresh-Cut Produce Association. UFPA is a trade association committed to driving the growth and success of produce companies and their partners. Members are companies involved in the processing of fresh fruits and vegetables for commercial distribution. Membership: $890-25,745 (Regular); $815-1,615 (Customer); $1,025-4,495 (Associate); $595-7,295 (Allied Organization); $250 (University).

Meetings/Conferences:
Conference Chair: Leslie N. Howard CMP
2013 - San Diego, CA (San Diego Convention Center)/
    May 14 - 16
Number of non-conference events/year: 8

Publications:
Fresh Impact Magazine; annually
Inside United Fresh; weekly
Membership Directory; on-line

United Gamefowl Breeders Association, Inc. (1976)
P.O. Box 457
Daleville, AL 36322
Tel: (334) 503-4336
E-Mail: united069@troycable.net
Website: ugba.info
Staff: 2
Annual Budget: $25-50,000

Personnel:
Director Emeritus and Editor: Verna Dowd
Contact, Membership: D'Renda Lewis

Historical Note:
UGBA members include gamefowl breeders and others who recognize the importance of preserving the gamefowl industry and this unique breed of fowl. Membership: $1000/year.

Publications:
The Feathered Warrior

United Inventors Association of the U.S.A. (1990)
1025 Connecticut Ave.
Suite 1000
Washington, DC 20036
E-Mail: admin@uiausa.org

Website: uiausa.org
Staff: 2
Annual Budget: $100-250,000
Tax: 501(c)(3)

Personnel:
Executive Director: Mark T. Reyland
    E-Mail: mark@uiausa.org
Contact, Tradeshow: Jen Lawlor
    E-Mail: JenLawlor@uiausa.org

Historical Note:
UIA is dedicated to inventor education and support. Mission is to provide reliable information to inventors, as well as Certification to groups and inventor-friendly firms who agree to comply with rigorous professional and ethical standards.

Meetings/Conferences: Annual
Conference Chair: Jen Lawlor
2013 - Chicago, IL/March 2 - 5/65000 attendees/over
    100 exhibitors

Publications:
UIA Newsletter; monthly

United Lightning Protection Association (1936)
426 North Ave.
Libertyville, IL 60048
Tel: (800) 668-8572 *Fax:* (847) 362-6443
E-Mail: info@ulpa.org
Website: ulpa.org
Members: 95 individuals
Staff: 2
Annual Budget: $50-100,000

Personnel:
President: Mark Hicks
Treasurer: Jeffrey Harger

Historical Note:
ULPA's mission is to render services to the lightning protection industry and to promote its welfare and development, provide opportunities for dialogue, education, advancement and improvement of all aspects of the lightning protection industry through meetings, seminars, publications and other programs and activities. Members are comprised of lightning protection manufacturers, engineers, contractors and technicians. Membership: $200 (Full); $50 (Associate).

Meetings/Conferences: Annual

Publications:
Membership Directory; on-line
More Static Newsletter; irregular; adv.

United Methodist Association of Health and Welfare Ministries (1940)
2800 W. Main St.
Tupelo, MS 38801-3027
Tel: (662) 269-2955 *Fax:* (662) 269-2956
TollFree: (800) 441-4901
E-Mail: uma@umassociation.org
Website: umassociation.org
Members:
400 organizations
354000 individuals
Staff: 4
Annual Budget: $500-1,000,000
Tax: 501(c)(3)

Personnel:
President and Chief Executive Officer: Stephen L. Vinson
    E-Mail: svinson@mss.org
Coordinator, Membership Services: Kristen P. Cress
    E-Mail: kcress@umassociation.org
Treasurer: Jill C. Hreben

Historical Note:
Organized in 1940 as the National Association of Methodist Hospitals and Homes, UMA became the National Association of Health and Welfare Ministries, United Methodist Church in 1969 and assumed its present name in 1983. It is now independent of the United Methodist Church and provides services such as long-term care, retirement, family and children's service and community organizations related to the UMC. UMA promotes, inspires, empowers and recognizes excellence in healing and caring ministries. Membership: $80 (Individual); $40 (Retired/Emeritus); $730-4,910 (Organization, based on budget); $95 (Community Service Ministries); $180 (Conference Related Units/Local Congregation Ministries).

Meetings/Conferences: Annual
2013 - Orlando, FL (Hilton in the Walt Disney World(R) Resort)/March 4 - 6

Publications:
UMA Newsletter; weekly; adv.

United Mine Workers of America (1890)
18354 Quantico Gateway Dr.
Suite 200
Triangle, VA 22172-1179
Tel: (703) 291-2400
E-Mail: general@umwa.org
Website: umwa.org
Members: 120000 individuals
Staff: 5
Annual Budget: Over $100,000,000
Tax: 501(c)(5)

Personnel:
President: Cecil E. Roberts
Secretary and Treasurer: Daniel J. Kane
Director, Communications and Editor: Phil Smith

Historical Note:
The United Mine Workers of America is a growing
union with membership that includes coal miners, clean
coal technicians, health care workers, truck drivers,
manufacturing workers and public employees throughout
the United States and Canada.

Publications:
UMW Journal; bi-monthly
UMWA Activist Alert; on-line

Membership List Available to Non-members

United Motorcoach Association (1971)
113 S. W. St.
Fourth Floor
Alexandria, VA 22314-2824
Tel: (703) 838-2929 Fax: (703) 838-2950
TollFree: (800) 424-8262
E-Mail: info@uma.org
Website: uma.org
Members: 1000 companies
Staff: 7
Annual Budget: $5-10,000,000
Tax: 501(c)(6)

Personnel:
President and Chief Executive Officer: Victor S. Parra
    E-Mail: vparra@uma.org
Coordinator, Membership Services: Greg Lange
    E-Mail: glange@uma.org
Manager, Meetings and Operations: Maggie Masterson
    E-Mail: mmasterson@uma.org
Director, Marketing and Membership Services: Michele
    Nosko
    E-Mail: mnosko@uma.org

Historical Note:
Formerly (1995) United Bus Owners of America. UMA's
mission is to protect and promote the interests and welfare
of privately owned common carriers of passengers and
UMA serves the intercity bus industry, with particular
emphasis on charter and tour transportation companies.
Membership: $250-1,550 (Active); $395-1,700
(Associate); $395 (Travel Partners).

Meetings/Conferences: Annual
Conference Chair: Maggie Masterson
2013 - Orlando, FL (Orange County Convention
    Center)/Jan. 20 - 24

Publications:
Membership Directory; on-line; adv.
The Docket; bi-monthly; adv.

Membership List Available to Non-members

United Nations Staff Union (1946)
866 United Nations Plaza, 48th St.
Room A-0248, Second Floor
New York, NY 10017
Tel: (212) 963-7075 Fax: (212) 963-3367
E-Mail: SUnion-User1@un.org
Website: u-seek.org
Members: 17000 individuals
Staff: 3
Annual Budget: $1-2,000,000

Personnel:
President: Barbara Tavora-Jainchill
Treasurer: Meriam Gueziel

Historical Note:
Open to all staff of the United Nations Secretariat.
Membership: $198/year (Member).

Publications:
UNSU Newsletter; on-line

United Natural Products Alliance (1991)
1075 Hollywood Ave.

Salt Lake City, UT 84105
Tel: (801) 474-2572 Fax: (801) 474-2571
Website: unpa.com
Members: 37 Companies
Staff: 4

Personnel:
Executive Director: Loren D. Israelsen
Director, Member Services: Kira Olsen
    E-Mail: kira@unpa.com
Senior Political Advisor: Peter Reinecke
Director, Programs and Seminars: Lindsay Wright

Historical Note:
Formerly (2005) Utah Natural Products Alliance. An
association of dietary supplement and functional food
companies that share a commitment to provide consumers
with natural health products of superior quality, benefit, and
reliability.

Meetings/Conferences:
Conference Chair: Lindsay Wright

United Ostomy Associations of America (1962)
P.O. Box 512
Northfield, MN 55057-0512
TollFree: (800) 826-0826
E-Mail: info@ostomy.org
Website: ostomy.org
Members: 34000 individuals
Staff: 8
Annual Budget: $250-500,000

Personnel:
President: Dave Rudzin
    E-Mail: rudyman22@uoaa.org
Advocacy Chair: Linda Aukett
Director, Administrative Services: Joan McGorry
Publisher: Ian Settlemire

Historical Note:
Mission to provide provision of information, advocacy
and service to, and for, its affiliated support groups, their
members and the intestinal/urinary diversion community at
large. Membership: $25 (Association); $50 (Professional);
$30 (Affiliation).

Meetings/Conferences: Annual
2013 - Jacksonville, FL (Hyatt Regency Jacksonville
    Riverfront)/Aug. 7 - 10
Number of non-conference events/year: 4

Publications:
Phoenix; quarterly; adv.
UOAA Update; monthly

United Potato Growers of America (2005)
5320 S. 900 East
Suite 120
Salt Lake City, UT 84117-7250
Tel: (801) 517-9000 Fax: (801) 981-4470
E-Mail: info@unitedpotatousa.com
Website: unitedpotatousa.com
Staff: 4

Personnel:
President and Chief Executive Officer: Jerry P. Wright
    E-Mail: jerry@unitedpotatousa.com
Chief Operating Officer: Buzz Shahan
Chief Communications Officer: Barb Shelley
    E-Mail: barb@unitedpotatousa.com

Historical Note:
UPGA's mission is to bring order and stability to the North
American potato growing industry and increase its member
potato growers economic potential by the effective use of
cooperative principles.

Meetings/Conferences: Annual

Publications:
UPGA Newsletter

United Producers Formulators and Distributors
Association (1968)
2034 Beaver Ruin Rd.
Norcross, GA 30071
Tel: (770) 417-1418 Fax: (770) 417-1419
Website: upfda.com
Members: 100 companies
Staff: 2
Annual Budget: $50-100,000

Personnel:
Executive Director: Valera B. Jessee
    E-Mail: Valera@gpca.org

Historical Note:

Formerly (1988) United Pesticide Formulators and
Distributors Association. UPFDA's mission is to recognize
the requirements and needs of its customers and to promote
better cooperation and communication with government
authorities. Members are firms which are directly involved
in formulating and distributing products or equipment to the
pest control industry. Membership: $725 (Active); $72.50
(Affiliate).

Meetings/Conferences: Annual
2013 - Orlando, FL/April 23 - 25

Publications:
Membership Directory; on-line
Updated; quarterly

United Producers, Inc. (1999)
8351 N. High St.
Suite 250
Columbus, OH 43235
Tel: (614) 890-6666 Fax: (614) 890-4776
TollFree: (800) 456-3276
Website: uproducers.com
Members: 45000 individuals
Staff: 1
Annual Budget: $50-100,000

Personnel:
President and Chief Executive Officer: Dennis Bolling

Historical Note:
Formed in 1999 through the consolidation in operations
of Producers Livestock Association (Ohio/Indiana) and
MFA Livestock (Missouri). UPI is a cooperative marketing
organization owned by farmers and ranchers in the United
States' corn belt, Midwest and Southeast whose mission
is to provide necessary livestock services on a cooperative
basis to its members in a business-like manner that will
improve their income and be competitive in the industry.

United Professional Horsemen's Association
(1968)
1345 Scotts Ferry Rd., East
Versailles, KY 40383-7011
Tel: (859) 879-8322 Fax: (859) 873-2951
E-Mail: uphakgr@aol.com
Website: uphaonline.com
Members: 1300 individuals
Staff: 3
Annual Budget: $50-100,000
Tax: 501(c)(5)

Personnel:
President: Bret C. Day
    E-Mail: daygreyridge@aol.com

Historical Note:
UPHA seeks to advance the horse show industry, define and
clarify their professionalism within the industry and works
to improve the conditions of those engaged in the pursuit
of various equine related activities. Membership is open to
anyone who has been a bonafide professional horse trainer
for a period of one year prior to application and people who
are involved and interested in the horse industry but do not
make their primary living from horses. Membership: $65
(Individual); $35 (Junior).

Meetings/Conferences: Annual
2013 - Las Vegas, NV (Caesars Palace)/Jan. 3 - 5
Number of non-conference events/year: 1

Publications:
Membership Directory; on-line
UPHA Newsletter

United Shoe Retailers Association (1977)
P.O. Box 4931
W. Hills, CA 91308
Tel: (818) 703-6062 Fax: (818) 703-6063
Website: usraonline.org
Members: 1000 store locations
Staff: 2
Annual Budget: $250-500,000
Tax: 501(c)(6)

Personnel:
Executive Director: Linda Hauss
    E-Mail: linda@usraonline.org

Historical Note:
USRA serves the independent shoe retailer and provides
the independent retailer with special benefits to enable
them to run their businesses in a more profitable manner.
Membership: $95/year.

Meetings/Conferences: Annual
2013 - Phoenix, AZ (Wigwam Resort)/May 5 - 7
Number of non-conference events/year: 1

Publications:

Newsletter

United Soybean Board (1990)
16305 Swingley Ridge Rd.
Suite 150
Chesterfield, MO 63017
Fax: (636) 530-1560
TollFree: (800) 989-8721
E-Mail: info@unitedsoybean.org
Website: unitedsoybean.org
Staff: 5
Annual Budget: $25-50,000,000

Personnel:
Chief Executive Officer: John Becherer
    E-Mail: jbecherer@unitedsoybean.com
Manager, Internal Communications: Maria Bingaman
    E-Mail: mbingaman@unitedsoybean.org
Director, Finance: Brenda Malottke
    E-Mail: bmalottke@unitedsoybean.org
Executive Director: Lisa O'Brien
    E-Mail: lobrien@unitedsoybean.org
Manager, Programs: Shelly Reinagel
    E-Mail: sreinagel@unitedsoybean.org

Historical Note:
USB administers soybean checkoff activities focusing on research and market development and expansion. Provides promotion, marketing, and research activities to create increased profitability for U.S. soybean farmers.

Meetings/Conferences: Annual
Conference Chair: Shelly Reinagel
Number of non-conference events/year: 3

Publications:
Beyond the Bean - BTB Magazine; monthly
Beyond the Bean Update Soybean farmers and the greater USB family; monthly
Checkoff Chronicle
Global Opportnties Briefings; irregular
GO Beyond the Bean; quarterly
Soybean Link; irregular

United Spinal Association (1946)
75-20 ASTORIA BLVD.
Jackson Heights, NY 11370
Tel: (718) 803-3782 *Fax:* (718) 803-0414
E-Mail: info@unitedspinal.org
Website: unitedspinal.org
Members: 35000 Members
Staff: 86
Annual Budget: $10-25,000,000
Tax: 501(c)(3)

Personnel:
President and Chief Executive Officer: Paul J. Tobin
Treasurer: Janeen Earwood
Secretary: Michael B. Kinne

Historical Note:
United Spinal Association's mission is to advance the quality of life of all people living with spinal cord injuries and disorders . Membership is free and open to all individuals with spinal cord injuries and diseases.

Publications:
Life in Action Online Magazine; on-line
No Nusiance; on-line
United Spinal Newsletter

United States-Taiwan Business Council (1976)
1700 N. Moore St.
Suite 1703
Arlington, VA 22209
Tel: (703) 465-2930 *Fax:* (703) 465-2937
E-Mail: council@us-taiwan.org
Website: us-taiwan.org
Members: 300 organizations
Staff: 4
Annual Budget: $500-1,000,000

Personnel:
President: Rupert J. Hammond-Chambers
    E-Mail: Council@us-taiwan.org
Vice President,Corporate Affairs: Lotta Danielsson
    E-Mail: Council@us-taiwan.org
Director, Finance and Administration: Christine Kupfer Messick

Historical Note:
Formed as USA-ROC Economic Council (1976). Formerly US-ROC (Taiwan) Business Council in 1996 and US-Taiwan Business Council in 2001. USA-TBC's purpose is to develop the trade and business relationship between the United States and Taiwan, serves its members as a portal to Taiwan, and aspires to be an effective representative in dealing with business, trade, and investment matters. Members consist of public and private companies with business interests in Taiwanis and is dedicated towards giving members access to the people and the information that they need to succeed.. Membership: $7,500 (Corporate); $15,000 (Chairman's Circle Level).

Meetings/Conferences: Annual

Publications:
Annual Review; annually
Defense & Security Report; quarterly
Semiconductor Report; quarterly
Taiwan Banking & Finance Bulletin; weekly
Taiwan Business Bulletin; weekly
Taiwan Defense & Security Bulletin; weekly
Taiwan Semiconductor Bulletin; weekly
Taiwan Technology Bulletin; weekly

United States Advanced Ceramics Association (1985)
1020 19th St. NW
Suite 375
Washington, DC 20036
Tel: (202) 467-5459 *Fax:* (202) 467-5469
E-Mail: usaca@strategicmi.com
Website: advancedceramics.org
Members: 21 companies
Staff: 3
Annual Budget: $250-500,000
Tax: 501(c)(6)

Personnel:
Executive Director: Theodore D. Lynch
    E-Mail: ted@startegicmi.com
Contact, Conventions: Glenton Mandigo
    E-Mail: glen@strategicmi.com

Historical Note:
USACA's mission is to develop and maintain close working relationships between its members and industry and to provide liaison between members and Congress, government agencies, and other targeted industries. Membership: $5,000 (Regular); $2,000 (Associate).

Meetings/Conferences: Semi-Annual
Conference Chair: Glenton Mandigo

Publications:
Membership Directory; on-line
USACA Newsletter

Membership List Available to Non-members

United States Air Force Medical Service Corps Association (1992)
4008 Plantation House Rd.
Summerville, SC 29485-6239
Tel: (866) 818-2110
E-Mail: info@mscassociation.org
Website: mscassociation.org
Members: 700 individuals
Staff: 5

Personnel:
Treasurer: Col. Al Obuchowski
    E-Mail: Treasurer@mscassociation.org

Historical Note:
The USAF MSC Association is a professional organization for health care administrators. It provide a way for to stay in touch with other MSCs, support survivors upon the death of a member and maintain a focus on documenting the history of the Medical Service Corps. Membership: $15 (majors and below); $20 (others).

Publications:
USAF MSC Newsletter; quarterly

United States Air Tour Association
111 St.
Las Vegas, NV 54786
Staff: 1
Annual Budget: $50-100,000

Personnel:
President: John A. Catsimatidis

Historical Note:
Federal Aviation Administration.

United States and Canadian Academy of Pathology (1906)
3643 Walton Way Extension
Building Six
Augusta, GA 30909-4507
Tel: (706) 733-7550 *Fax:* (706) 733-8033
E-Mail: help@uscap.org
Website: uscap.org
Members: 9300 individuals
Staff: 13
Annual Budget: $5-10,000,000

Personnel:
Executive Director: Kerry Crockett
    E-Mail: kerry@uscap.org
Director, Education: Kia Gray
    E-Mail: kia@uscap.org
Director, Marketing and Development: Victoria Hann
    E-Mail: victoria@uscap.org
Director, Membership Services: Carolyn Lane
    E-Mail: carolyn@uscap.org
Accountant: Richard Matthews CPA
    E-Mail: richard@uscap.org
Assistant Meeting Planner: Nancy West
    E-Mail: nancy@uscap.org

Historical Note:
Formerly International Association of Medical Museums and (1987) International Academy of Pathology. USCAP seeks to advance Pathology teaching, practice and research and also provides its members with new information both at the investigative and applied practice levels so as to reinforce and update their knowledge in their area of interest and expertise. Membership: $200 (Regular/Individual); $35 (Junior); $240 (Sustaining).

Continuing Education:
Certification Designation/s: CME

Meetings/Conferences: Annual
Conference Chair: Nancy West
2013 - Baltimore, MD (Baltimore Convention Center)/ March 2 - 8/4880 attendees/51-100 exhibitors
2014 - San Diego, CA (Convention Center)/March 1 - 7/4880 attendees/51-100 exhibitors
2015 - Boston, MA (John B. Hynes Veterans Memorial Convention Center)/March 21 - 27/4880 attendees/51-100 exhibitors

Publications:
Academy Newsletter; bi-monthly
Membership Directory; on-line
USCAP Journal; on-line; adv.

United States Animal Health Association (1897)
421 Mitchell Ave.
St. Joseph, MO 64507
Tel: (816) 671-1144 *Fax:* (816) 671-1201
E-Mail: usaha@usaha.org
Website: usaha.org
Members: 18 organizations and 1400 individuals
Staff: 3
Annual Budget: $250-500,000

Personnel:
Executive Director: Benjamin Richey
    E-Mail: brichey@usaha.org
Coordinator, Meetings: Linda B. Ragland

Historical Note:
Formed as the National Association of State Livestock Sanitary Boards to combat one disease affecting cattle, it became the United States Livestock Sanitary Association in 1911 and assumed its present name in 1968. Absorbed the National Assembly of Chief Livestock Health Officials in 1973. USAHA's prime objective is to prevent, control and eliminate livestock diseases that cost ranchers, farmers and consumers approximately $1 billion per year. Members are state and federal animal health officials, national allied organizations, regional representatives, and individual members. Membership: $150 (Individual); $600 (Official Agency/Allied Organization).

Meetings/Conferences: Annual
Conference Chair: Linda B. Ragland
2013 - San Diego, CA (Town and Country Resort Hotel)/Oct. 17 - 23
2014 - Kansas City, MO (Sheraton Kansas City at Crown Center)/Oct. 16 - 22

Publications:
Membership Directory; on-line
News Alerts; daily
USAHA Newsletter; semi-annually

United States Apple Association (1996)
8233 Old Courthouse Rd.
Suite 200
Vienna, VA 22182
Tel: (703) 442-8850 *Fax:* (703) 790-0845
TollFree: (800) 781-4443
E-Mail: info@usapple.org
Website: usapple.org
Members: 450 companies

Staff: 8
Annual Budget: $2-5,000,000

Personnel:
President and Chief Executive Officer: Nancy E. Foster
    E-Mail: nfoster@usapple.org
Director, Membership and Communications: Mark Gedris
    E-Mail: mgedris@usapple.org
Vice President, Public Affairs: Diane Kurrle
    E-Mail: dkurrle@usapple.org
Director, Consumer Health and Education: Allison Parker
MS, RD
    E-Mail: aparker@usapple.org

Historical Note:
Formed by the merger of the International Apple Association (1895) and the National Apple Institute (1935) as International Apple Institute; assumed its current name in 1996. USApple's mission is to provide information on matters pertaining to the apple industry. Members are U.S. and foreign firms, other than retailers, which handle apples. Membership: $100-200 (Grower); $500-2500 (Apple Industry Business); $250-2500 (Associate); $500 (Special); $100 (Academic/Government).

Meetings/Conferences: Annual

Publications:
An Apple a Day; quarterly
Apple News; monthly
Market News; monthly
Membership Directory; on-line

United States Aquaculture Suppliers Association
(1989)
c/o AREA, P.O. Box 901303
Homestead, FL 33090
Tel: (305) 248-4205 *Fax:* (305) 248-1756
E-Mail: psaworld@aol.com
Website: aquaculturesuppliers.org
Members: 60 businesses
Staff: 1

Personnel:
Secretary: Jason Mulvihill
    E-Mail: jason@areainc.com

Historical Note:
USASA members are companies producing feed, equipment, and other materials for use in aquaculture. Has no paid officers or full-time staff. Membership: $125/year.

United States Army Warrant Officers Association
(1972)
462 Herndon Pkwy.
Suite 207
Herndon, VA 20170-5235
Tel: (703) 742-7727 *Fax:* (703) 742-7728
TollFree: (800) 587-2962
E-Mail: usawoamdb@verizon.net
Website: usawoa.org
Members:
5 Corporations
6000 individuals
Staff: 3
Annual Budget: $100-250,000
Tax: 501(c)(4)

Personnel:
Executive Director and Editor: Jack John Du Teil
Bookkeeper and Payroll Clerk: Terri Theresa Casteel
Membership and Chapter Information: Herb Rundgren
CPO, USN

Historical Note:
USAWOA helps to the improvement of the Warrant Officer Corps through the dissemination of professional information. Membership is open to Army warrant officers regardless of component or status (Active, Reserve or Retired). Membership: $30-100I.

Meetings/Conferences: Annual
2013 - Sacramento, CA (Radisson Hotel Colonia del
    Sacramento)/Oct. 14 - 18
Number of non-conference events/year: 100

Publications:
Newsliner; monthly; adv.
USAWOA Online; on-line

United States-ASEAN Business Council Inc.
(1983)
1101 17th St. NW
Suite 411
Washington, DC 20036
Tel: (202) 289-1911 *Fax:* (202) 289-0519
E-Mail: mail@usasean.org

Website: us-asean.org
Members: 600 million people
Staff: 16
Annual Budget: $2-5,000,000
Tax: 501(c)(3)

Personnel:
President: Alexander Feldman
    E-Mail: afeldman@usasean.org
Director, Information Services and ICT Working Group:
    Putri Alam
    E-Mail: palam@usasean.org
Director, Programs: Cheryle Davis
    E-Mail: cdavis@usasean.org
Manager, Programs and Events: Elease Dennis
    E-Mail: edennis@usasean.org
Vice President, Policy: Marc Mealy
    E-Mail: mmealy@usasean.org
Chief Financial Officer: Michael Shue
    E-Mail: mshue@usasean.org
Senior Manager, Membership and Food and Agriculture
    Working Group: Mads Stockwell

Historical Note:
Formerly (1997) US-ASEAN Council for Business and Technology, the council strives to expand trade and investment ties between the U.S. and ASEAN (Association of Southeast Asian Nations, including Brunei Darussalam, Indonesia, Malaysia, Philippines, Singapore Thailand and Vietnam) by implementing programs which assist companies to identify and compete for opportunities. Its mission is to strengthen bilateral and US- ASEAN relations through strong economic and commercial ties.

Meetings/Conferences:
Conference Chair: Cheryle Davis
Number of non-conference events/year: 2

Publications:
Membership Directory; on-line

United States Association for Computational Mechanics *(1988)*
C/O Department of Mechanical Engineering
6141 Etcheverry Hall, University of California
Berkeley, CA 94720-1740
Tel: (510) 642-1338 *Fax:* (510) 642-6163
E-Mail: info@usacm.org
Website: usacm.org
Members: 500 individuals and institutions
Staff: 3
Annual Budget: $25-50,000

Personnel:
President: Tarek Zohdi
    E-Mail: zohdi@me.berkeley.edu
Secretary and Treasurer: Leszek Demkowicz
    E-Mail: leszek@ices.utexas.edu

Historical Note:
USACM's mission is to promote, foster, organize and coordinate various activities concerning computational mechanics in the United States. Members are individuals and institutions concerned with computational mechanics. Membership: $25/year.

Meetings/Conferences:
Conference Chair: Ruth Hengst
2013 - Raleigh, NC (Raleigh Convention Center)/July
    22 - 25
2015 - San Diego, CA/July 27 - 30
Number of non-conference events/year: 1

Publications:
USACM Digest; weekly
USACM News

United States Association for Energy Economics
(1994)
28790 Chagrin Blvd.
Suite 350
Cleveland, OH 44122
Tel: (216) 464-2785 *Fax:* (216) 464-2768
E-Mail: usaee@usaee.org
Website: usaee.org
Members: 1010 individuals and companies
Staff: 1
Annual Budget: $250-500,000
Tax: 501(c)(6)

Personnel:
Executive Director: David L. Williams

Historical Note:
USAEE's mission is to provide a forum for exchange of ideas, experience and issues among professionals interested in energy economics. Members include economists,

corporate planners, engineers, geologists, environmentalists, consultants, journalists, researchers from private industry and government and faculty from colleges and universities. Membership: $100 (Individual); $40 (Student); $1,500 (Sustaining); $1,000 (Academic Institutions).

Meetings/Conferences: Annual
2013 - Anchorage, AK/July 28 - 31

Publications:
IAEE Energy Forum; quarterly; adv.
IAEE/USAEE Membership Directory; annually; adv.
Online Membership Directory; on-line
The Energy Journal; quarterly; adv.
USAEE Dialogue; quarterly; adv.

Membership List Available to Non-members

United States Association of Former Members of Congress *(1970)*
1401 K St. NW
Suite 503
Washington, DC 20005
Tel: (202) 222-0972 *Fax:* (202) 222-0977
E-Mail: admin@usafmc.org
Website: usafmc.org
Staff: 6
Annual Budget: $500-1,000,000

Personnel:
Chief Executive Officer: Peter M. Weichlein
    E-Mail: pweichlein@usafmc.org
Office Manager: Andrew Loeb Shoenig
Treasurer: Jim Walsh
Manager, Member Services: Sharon Witiw

Historical Note:
A nonpartisan, non-profit, educational, research, and social organization with under 600 members. The organization has been chartered by Congress. Promotes improved public understanding of the role of Congress as a unique institution as well as the importance of representative democracy as a system of government, both domestically and internationally.FMC's mission is to promote public service and strengthen representative democracy domestically and abroad.

Publications:
FMC Newsletter; annually

United States Association of Importers of Textiles and Apparel *(1988)*
1140 Connecticut Ave.
Suite 950
Washington, DC 20036
Tel: (202) 419-0444 *Fax:* (202) 783-0727
E-Mail: info@usaita.com
Website: usaita.com
Members: 200 companies
Staff: 4
Annual Budget: $500-1,000,000
Tax: 501(c)(6)

Personnel:
President: Julia K. Hughes
    E-Mail: jhughes@usaita.com
Coordinator, Membership: Jana Kalish
    E-Mail: jkalish@usaita.com
Director, Communications: Samantha Sault
    E-Mail: ssault@usaita.com
Counsel: David M. Spooner

Historical Note:
USA-ITA, formed by nine founding company members in January 1989, represents members' interests to the government and within the industry. The mission for USA-ITA is to offer members access to the information that they need to do business and understand and comply with complex regulations in the United States and overseas. Membership: $1,100-16,500 (Retailers/Brands/Importers); $1500(Associate); $5000 (International Affiliate).

Meetings/Conferences: Annual

Publications:
e-Newsletter; monthly

United States Association of Independent Gymnastic Clubs *(1972)*
450 North End Ave.
Suite 20F
New York, NY 10282
Tel: (212) 227-9792 *Fax:* (212) 227-9793
TollFree: (800) 480-0201
E-Mail: info@usaigc.com
Website: usaigc.com
Members: 300 clubs
Staff: 3

Annual Budget: $100-250,000
Tax: 501(c)(6)

Personnel:
Vice President: Paul Spadaro
    E-Mail: usaigcpsny2@aol.com
Director, Technical Services: Mary Bakke Spadaro
    E-Mail: M143BNY@aol.com

Historical Note:
USAIGC's mission is to provide a competitive program that is educationally sound, progressively challenging and fun. Members are not- for-profit clubs. Membership: $100/year.

Meetings/Conferences: Annual
Number of non-conference events/year: 3

Publications:
Member Directory; on-line

United States Basketball Writers Association (1956)

1818 Chouteau Ave.
St. Louis, MO 63103
Fax: (314) 421-3505
Website: sportswriters.net/usbwa
Members: 1000 individuals
Staff: 3
Annual Budget: $100-250,000
Tax: 501(c)(6)

Personnel:
Executive Director: Joe Mitch
    E-Mail: mitch@mvc.org
Editor: John Akers
Webmaster: Ted Gangi
    E-Mail: ted.gangi@sportswriters.net

Historical Note:
USBWA has served the interests of writers who follow college and high school basketball in the United States, fighting for access to and professional relations. Membership: $50 (Individuals); $25 (Students/Retired).

Publications:
Tipoff; quarterly
USBWA Directory; on-line

United States Beef Breeds Council (1952)

19590 E. Main St.
Suite 202
Parker, CO 80138
Tel: (303) 770-9292 *Fax:* (303) 770-9302
Members: 22 associations
Staff: 1
Annual Budget: $10-25,000

Personnel:
Executive Vice President: Sherry Doubet

Historical Note:
Members are the chief executive officers of national purebred cattle organizations.

United States Beet Sugar Association (1911)

1156 15th St. NW
Suite 1019
Washington, DC 20005
Tel: (202) 296-4820 *Fax:* (202) 331-2065
TollFree: (800) 872-0127
E-Mail: beetsugar@aol.com
Website: beetsugar.org
Members: 21 processing factories and 8 companies
Staff: 4
Annual Budget: $2-5,000,000
Tax: 501(c)(6)

Personnel:
President: James W. Johnson Jr.
Vice President, Public Affairs: Elin Peltz
    E-Mail: epeltz@beetsugar.org
Director, Administration: Claudia Tidwell

Historical Note:
Formerly, the United States Beet Sugar Industry and in 1926, the Association adopted its present name. USBSA's purpose is to encourage the interchange of ideas and to promote the honorable, economical, efficient and useful conduct of the beet sugar industry in the United States.

Publications:
Member Directory; on-line

United States Bowling Congress (2005)

621 Six Flags Dr.
Arlington, TX 76011
Tel: (414) 423-3332 *Fax:* (817) 385-8269

TollFree: (800) 514-2695
E-Mail: bowlinfo@bowl.com
Website: bowl.com
Members: 32 organizations
Staff: 372
Annual Budget: $25-50,000,000

Personnel:
Executive Director: Stu Upson
Managing Director, Information Technology: Jon-Paul Estes
Managing Director and Chief Financial Officer: Susan Merrill
    E-Mail: susan.merrill@bowl.com
Managing Director, Communications: Jason Overstreet
    E-Mail: jason.overstreet@bowl.com
Managing Director, Marketing and Membership Services: Kevin Terry
    E-Mail: kevin.terry@bowl.com
Managing Director, Media and Events: Pete Tredwell
    E-Mail: pete.tredwell@bowl.com

Historical Note:
Formed by a merger of the American Bowling Congress (founded in 1895), Women's International Bowling Congress (founded in 1916), Young American Bowling Alliance (founded in 1982) and USA Bowling, combined its operations with the Bowling Proprietors' Association of America (BPAA). USBC's mission is to provide benefits, resources and programs that enhance the bowling experience. Membership: $10-30/year.

Meetings/Conferences: Annual
Conference Chair: Pete Tredwell
2013 - Reno, NV (Silver Legacy Resort Casino)/April 30 - May 4
Number of non-conference events/year: 13

Publications:
US Bowler E-Magazine; on-line

United States Business and Industry Council (1933)

512 C St. NE
Washington, DC 20002
Tel: (202) 266-3980 *Fax:* (202) 266-3981
TollFree: (800) 767-2267
E-Mail: usbicef@aol.com
Website: americaneconomicalert.org
Members: 1500 companies
Staff: 2
Annual Budget: $500-1,000,000
Tax: 501(c)(6)

Personnel:
President: Kevin L. Kearns
    E-Mail: kearns@usbusiness.org

Historical Note:
Formerly United States Business and Industrial Council (1998). Established as the Southern States Industrial Council; became (1973) the United States Industrial Council and assumed its current name in 1998. USBIC members come from family-owned and closely held domestic companies; USBIC represents their interests in trade, taxation, regulation and other matters relevant to domestic businesses. Membership: $125-$1,500 (Non-Profit Organization -based on budget): $500-$999 (Contributing Member) $1,000 -$2,499 (Supporting Member); $2,500- $4,999 (Sustaining Member); $5,000 or more (Patron).

United States Canola Association (1989)

600 Pennsylvania Ave. SE
Suite 320
Washington, DC 20003-4316
Tel: (202) 969-8113 *Fax:* (202) 969-7036
E-Mail: info@uscanola.com
Website: uscanola.com
Members: 50 producers and processors
Staff: 4
Annual Budget: $500-1,000,000

Personnel:
Executive Director: John D. Gordley
    E-Mail: john@uscanola.com
Director, Communications: Angela Dansby
    E-Mail: angela@uscanola.com
Representative, Advertising Sales: Mary O'Donohue
    E-Mail: mary@uscanola.com

Historical Note:
USCA's purpose is to increase U.S. canola production to meet the growing public demand for healthy products. Members are producers and processors of canola and rapeseed. Membership: $25 (Producer Members); $5,000 (Industry Members); $500 (Associate Members).

Meetings/Conferences: Annual

Publications:
Canola Quick Bytes; adv.
U.S. Canola Digest; quarterly; adv.

United States Cattlemen's Association

P.O. Box 339
San Lucas, CA 93954
Tel: (831) 385-5316
E-Mail: usca@uscattlemen.org
Website: uscattlemen.org
Staff: 1
Annual Budget: $100-250,000
Tax: 501(c)(12)

Personnel:
President: Jon Wooster

Historical Note:
USCA's mission is to present an effective voice for the United States cattle industry. Represents the interests of US cattle producers on legislation, regulation and trade. Membership: $1-1,000/year.

Publications:
USCA newsletter

United States Chamber of Commerce (1912)

1615 H St. NW
Washington, DC 20062-2000
Tel: (202) 659-6000 *Fax:* (202) 463-5836
TollFree: (800) 638-6582
Website: uschamber.com
Members: 18392 businesses and organizations
Staff: 1100
Annual Budget: $50-100,000,000

Personnel:
Executive Director, Business Development: Kelley Cox
    E-Mail: kcox@uschamber.com
Senior Manager, Let's Rebuild America: Murphie Barrett
    E-Mail: mbarrett@uschamber.com
Executive Director, Brazil-U.S. Business Council: Steven Bipes
    E-Mail: sbipes@uschamber.com
Executive Vice President and Chief Operating Officer: David C. Chavern
Senior Vice President, Communications and Strategy: Thomas J. Collamore
    E-Mail: Collamore@uschamber.com
Vice President, Small Business Policy: Giovanni Coratolo
    E-Mail: gcoratolo@uschamber.com
Senior Vice President, Administration: Shannon DiBari
President and Chief Executive Officer: Thomas J. Donohue
Senior Vice President, Political Affairs and Federation Relations and National Political Director: Rob Engstrom
Senior Vice President, Chief Financial Officer and Chief Information Officer: Stan Harrell
Chief Tax Counsel and Executive Director, Tax Policy: Caroline Harris
    E-Mail: charris@uschamber.com
Executive Director, Transportation and Infrastructure: Janet F. Kavinoky
    E-Mail: jkavinoky@uschamber.com
Senior Director, Communications: Blair Latoff
Senior Vice President, Congressional and Public Affairs: Rolf Lundberg Jr.
Vice President, Asia: Tami Overby
    E-Mail: toverby@uschamber.com
Vice President, Senior Associate General Counsel: Judith K. Richmond
    E-Mail: jrichmon@uschamber.com
Executive Director, Digital Strategic Communications: Nick Schaper
Coordinator, Research: David Tulley
Vice President, Communications and Strategy: Mia Kelly Walton
Executive Director: Ashley Wilson

Historical Note:
USCC's purpose is to fight for free enterprise before Congress, the White House, regulatory agencies, the courts, the court of public opinion, and governments around the world. Membership: $500 (Signature Members); $2500 (Advantage Members); $5000 (Elite Members).

Meetings/Conferences: Annual
2013 - Washington, DC (Capitol Hill)/April 29 - May 1
Number of non-conference events/year: 6

United States Clay Producers Traffic Association

101 Wood Ave.

Iselin, NJ 08830-2703
Website: usclayproducers.org
Staff: 1
Annual Budget: $50-100,000

Personnel:
Senior Vice President and Chief Commercial Officer: Paul McClintock

United States Clean Heat & Power Association
(1999)
105 N. Virginia Ave.
Suite 204
Falls Church, VA 22046
Tel: (703) 436-2257 *Fax:* (703) 647-6259
E-Mail: info@uschpa.org
Website: uschpa.org
Staff: 1

Personnel:
Executive Director: Jessica Bridges
   E-Mail: jbridges@uschpa.org

Historical Note:
USCHPA brings together diverse market interests to promote the growth of clean, efficient energy in the United States. USCHPA's mission is to increase deployment of combined heat and power and waste energy recovery systems to benefit the environment and the economy. Membership dues levels are determined by the member's gross annual revenues.

Publications:
Membership Directory; on-line

United States Club Soccer *(2000)*
192 E. Bay St.
Suite 301
Charleston, SC 29401
Tel: (843) 614-4140
Website: usclubsoccer.org
Staff: 10

Personnel:
Executive Director: Bill Sage
   E-Mail: bsage@usclubsoccer.org
Director, Membership Services and Adult League Development: John Borozzi
   E-Mail: jborozzi@usclubsoccer.org
Director, Event Marketing and Operations: Leo Garcia
Director, Projects and Communications: Greg Hutton
   E-Mail: ghutton@usclubsoccer.org

Historical Note:
Formerly known as the National Association of Competitive Soccer Clubs (NACSC), US Club Soccer is a non-profit organization whose mission is to develop competitive club soccer in the United States.

Meetings/Conferences:
Conference Chair: Leo Garcia

Publications:
Membership Directory; on-line

United States Coast Guard Chief Petty Officers Association *(1969)*
5520-G Hempstead Way
Springfield, VA 22151-4009
Tel: (703) 941-0395 *Fax:* (703) 941-0397
E-Mail: cgcpoa@aol.com
Website: uscgcpoa.org
Staff: 5
Annual Budget: $100-250,000
Tax: 501(c)(19)

Personnel:
Executive Director: Randy Reid
Webmanager: Joe D'Elia
   E-Mail: webmanager@uscgcpoa.org
Public Relations and Outreach Coordinator: Sarah B. Foster
   E-Mail: sarah.foster@uscg.mil
Contact, Meetings: Bill Segelken
   E-Mail: cpoaconvention@gmail.com
Treasurer: Mark Tahtinen
   E-Mail: mark.t.tahtinen@uscg.mil

Historical Note:
CPOA works to take care of members and their dependents who may be in urgent need of assistance financial or otherwise. Membership: $24 (Regular/Associate); $400-500 (Lifetime).

Meetings/Conferences: Annual
Conference Chair: Bill Segelken
2013 - Houston, TX/Aug. 12 - 15

Publications:
The Chief

United States Committee on Irrigation and Drainage *(1952)*
1616 17th St.
Suite 483
Denver, CO 80202
Tel: (303) 628-5430 *Fax:* (303) 628-5431
E-Mail: stephens@uscid.org
Website: uscid.org
Members: 520 individuals and Compaanies
Staff: 2
Annual Budget: $100-250,000

Personnel:
President: Jerrold D. Gregg
   E-Mail: jgregg@pn.usbr.gov
Executive Vice President: Larry D. Stephens
   E-Mail: stephens@uscid.org

Historical Note:
Formerly (1967) United States National Committee, International Commission on Irrigation and Drainage and (1984) United States Committee on Irrigation, Drainage and Flood Control. USCID, a not- for-profit professional organization, is the U. S. national committee of the International Commission on Irrigation and Drainage.USCID's mission is to foster sustainable, socially acceptable and environmentally responsible irrigation, drainage and flood control systems and practices for providing food, clothing and shelter to the people of the United States and the World. It also provides a forum for multidisciplinary discussion on issues related to irrigation, drainage and flood control. Membership: $90 (Regular); $1700 (Life); $50 (Young Professional); $20 (student); $0 (Designated Individual); $675 (Organizational); $2900 (Sustaining); $75 (Associate); $50 (Senior).

Meetings/Conferences: Annual
2013 - Phoenix, AZ/April 16 - 19

Publications:
USCID Membership Directory; on-line; adv.
USCID Newsletter; adv.

United States Composting Council *(1991)*
5400 Grosvenor Ln.
Bethesda, MD 20814
Tel: (301) 897-2715 *Fax:* (301) 530-5072
E-Mail: uscc@compostingcouncil.org
Website: compostingcouncil.org
Members: 520 businesses and individuals
Staff: 7
Annual Budget: $1-2,000,000
Tax: 501(c)(6)

Personnel:
Executive Director: Michael Virga
   E-Mail: michaelvirga@compostingcouncil.org
Office Manager: Rosa Bottoni
   E-Mail: uscc@compostingcouncil.org
Accounts Manager: Michele Doyle
   E-Mail: accounting@compostingcouncil.org
Director, Education and Outreach: Cary Oshins
   E-Mail: cary.oshins@compostingcouncil.org
Director, Market Development and STA: Alfred Rattie
   E-Mail: al.rattie@compostingcouncil.org
Manager, Membership Services and Communications: Leanne Spaulding
   E-Mail: leannespaulding@compostingcouncil.org
Event Planner and Program Coordinator: Cherrie Yang
   E-Mail: cherrieyang@compostingcouncil.org

Historical Note:
Established in 1990, USCC works to develop, expand, and promote the composting industry through encouraging, supporting, and performing research, improving management practices, establishing standards, educating professionals. USCC's mission is to advance composting and promotes compost use to enhance soils and provide economic and environmental benefits for members and society.. USCC members include compost producers, marketers, equipment manufacturers, product suppliers, academic institutions, public agencies, nonprofit groups and consulting/engineering firms. Membership: $10,000 (Benefactor); $5,000 (Corporate Sustaining); $2,500 (Corporate); $1,000 (Large Business); $500 (Large Government/Medium Business); $250 (University/Government/Small Business); $150 (Non-Profits/Farm Composter); $100 (Individual); $25 (Students/Friend of Composting);

Meetings/Conferences: Annual
Conference Chair: Cherrie Yang
2013 - Lake Buena Vista, FL (Buena Vista Palace Hotel and Spa)/Jan. 28 - 31/26-50 exhibitors

Number of non-conference events/year: 2

Publications:
Compost Communicator 2011 Conference Edition; quarterly

Membership List Available to Non-members

United States Conference of Catholic Bishops *(1966)*
3211 Fourth St. NE
Washington, DC 20017-1194
Tel: (202) 541-3000 *Fax:* (202) 541-3054
Website: usccb.org
Members: 400 individuals
Staff: 350
Annual Budget: $25-50,000,000
Tax: 501(c)(3)

Personnel:
Executive Director: Patrick Markey
   E-Mail: pmarkey@usccb.org
Associate Director, Public Policy: Sr. Suzanne Bellenoit SSJ
   E-Mail: ssjsbellenoit@usccb.org
Assistant Director, Promotions: Mary Mencarini Campbell
   E-Mail: mcampbell@usccb.org
Assistant Director, Technology: Gina Laurent
   E-Mail: glaurent@usccb.org
Assistant Director, Higher Education: Barbara Humphrey McCrabb
   E-Mail: bmccrabb@usccb.org
Assistant Director, Information Services: Katherine Nuss
   E-Mail: knuss@usccb.org
Associate Director, Government Relations: Terry Boykin Thames
   E-Mail: tthames@usccb.org
Director, Media Relations: Sr. Mary Ann Walsh
   E-Mail: mwalsh@usccb.org

Historical Note:
Founded in 1966 as the joint National Conference of Catholic Bishops (NCCB) and United States Catholic Conference, adopted its current name in July 2001. The purpose of the Conference is to promote the greater good which the Church offers humankind, especially through forms and programs of the apostolate fittingly adapted to the circumstances of time and place.

Publications:
Membership Directory; on-line
USCCB Newsletter; on-line

United States Conference of Mayors *(1932)*
1620 Eye St. NW
Washington, DC 20006
Tel: (202) 293-7330 *Fax:* (202) 293-2352
E-Mail: info@usmayors.org
Website: usmayors.org
Members: 30000 individuals
Staff: 45
Annual Budget: $5-10,000,000
Tax: 501(c)(3)

Personnel:
Executive Director: Tom Cochran
Director, Meetings: Carol Edwards
   E-Mail: cedwards@usmayors.org
Contact, Membership Services: Katie Pirolt
   E-Mail: kpirolt@usmayors.org
Contact, Communications: Elena Temple
   E-Mail: etemple@usmayors.org

Historical Note:
USCM's mission is to create a forum in which mayors can share ideas and information. Membership: $1,992-102,721/year (varies with the population of the city).

Meetings/Conferences: Semi-Annual
Conference Chair: Carol Edwards
2013 - Washington, DC/Jan. 17 - 19
2013 - Las Vegas, NV/June 21 - 24

Publications:
Membership Directory; on-line
U.S. MAYOR Newspaper; bi-monthly
USCM Newsletter; on-line

United States Contract Tower Association *(1995)*
601 Madison St.
Fourth Floor
Alexandria, VA 22314
Tel: (703) 825-0500 *Fax:* (703) 820-1395
Website: contracttower.org

Members: 209 Individuals
Staff: 1
Annual Budget: $250-500,000

Personnel:
Executive Director: Spencer Dickerson
    E-Mail: spencer.dickerson@airportnet.org

Historical Note:
The mission of USCTA is to advance aviation safety and enhance the future viability. A division of American Association of Airport Executives, which provides administrative support.

Publications:
USCTA newsletter; irregular

United States Court Reporters Association
(1946)
8430 Gross Point Rd.
Suite 115
Skokie, IL 60077-2036
Tel: (847) 470-9500 *Fax:* (847) 470-9505
E-Mail: info.uscra@gmail.com
Website: uscra.org
Members: 400 individuals
Staff: 3
Annual Budget: $50-100,000

Personnel:
Editor-in-Chief: Regina McBride
    E-Mail: editor.uscra@gmail.com

Historical Note:
USCRA is committed to promoting and maintaining the standards of verbatim reporting, quality services, professional ethics, fidelity to the ideals of the judicial system and to advocating continuing education as well as the utilization of state-of-the-art technologies. Members are official reporters in the United States District Courts. Membership: $150 (Regular, Full Time); $75 (Regular, Job Share); $35 (Student); $50 (Associate/Supporting Member).

Continuing Education:
Certification Designation/s: FCRR

Meetings/Conferences: Annual
Number of non-conference events/year: 1

Publications:
Member Directory; on-line
The Circuit Rider; quarterly; adv.

United States Cross Country Coaches Association
5327 Newport Dr.
Lisle, IL 60532
Tel: (630) 960-3049 *Fax:* (630) 960-3218
E-Mail: xcpoll@aol.com
Members: 300 individuals
Staff: 1
Annual Budget: Under $10,000

Personnel:
Director, Public Relations: Dan Kopriva

Historical Note:
Formerly National Collegiate Cross Country Coaches Association. Membership is drawn from NCAA-accredited men's track programs. USCCCA strives to gather the most relevant information for its members. Has no paid officers or full-time staff. Membership: $225/year (Individual).

United States Custom Harvesters, Inc. *(1983)*
119 W. Sherman
Hutchinson, KS 67501
Tel: (620) 664-6297 *Fax:* (620) 664-6265
E-Mail: office@uschi.com
Website: uschi.com
Members: 600 individuals/companies
Staff: 1
Annual Budget: $500-1,000,000

Personnel:
Manager, Operations and Coordinator, Trade Shows: Pam Shmidl
    E-Mail: manager@uschi.com

Historical Note:
The mission of the US Custom Harvesters, Inc. is to advance the cause of the members of the Corporation by representing and promoting the harvesting industry. Membership: $200 (Harvester); $150 (Associate); $250 (Non-U.S. Harvester); $1750 (Lifetime).

Meetings/Conferences: Annual
Conference Chair: Pam Shmidl
2013 - Kansas City, MO (Kansas City Convention Center)/Jan. 29 - 31

Publications:

Harvest News; monthly; adv.
Membership Directory; annually

United States Cutting Tool Institute *(1988)*
1300 Sumner Ave.
Cleveland, OH 44115-2851
Tel: (216) 241-7333 *Fax:* (216) 241-0105
E-Mail: uscti@uscti.com
Website: uscti.com
Members: 100 companies
Staff: 3
Annual Budget: $250-500,000
Tax: 501(c)(6)

Personnel:
President: David J. Povich
Senior Vice President: Thomas Haag
Director, Meetings: Anya Hodgson
    E-Mail: ahodgson@thomasamc.com

Historical Note:
USCTI was formed by the merger of the Metal Cutting Tool Institute and the Cutting Tool Manufacturers of America. USCTI works to represent, advocate, and expand the U.S. cutting tool industry and to promote the benefits of buying American-made cutting tools manufactured by its members. Members belong to seven product divisions-Carbide Tooling, Drill & Reamer, Milling Cutter, PCD & PCBN, Tap & Die, Tool Holder and All Other Tooling. Members are North American manufacturers/remanufacturers of cutting tools, and post-fabrication tool surface treatment providers. Membership: based on company size.

Meetings/Conferences: Semi-Annual
Conference Chair: Anya Hodgson
2013 - Kyoto, Japan/May 13 - 16
2013 - Austin, TX (The Driskill)/Oct. 12 - 14
2014 - Amelia Island, FL (Omni Amelia Island Plantation Resort)/May 3 - 5
Number of non-conference events/year: 1

Publications:
Informer; quarterly
Member Directory; on-line

Membership List Available to Non-members

United States Dairy Export Council *(1995)*
2101 Wilson Blvd.
Suite 400
Arlington, VA 22201-3061
Tel: (703) 528-3049 *Fax:* (703) 528-3705
E-Mail: dingram@usdec.org
Website: usdec.org
Staff: 29
Annual Budget: $10-25,000,000

Personnel:
President: Tom Suber
    E-Mail: tsuber@usdec.org
Executive Vice President, Strategy and Insights: Marc Beck
    E-Mail: mbeck@usdec.org
Director, Market Access and Regulatory Affairs: Sandra Benson
Director, Information Resources: Daniel Ingram
    E-Mail: dingram@usdec.org
Coordinator, Global Marketing: Diana King
Vice President, Communications: Alan Levitt
Manager, Communications and Membership: Clemente Santiago
    E-Mail: csantiago@usdec.org
Senior Vice President, Strategy and Industry Communications: Margaret Speich
    E-Mail: mspeich@usdec.org
Senior Vice President, Operations and Evaluation: Chuck Timpko
Administrative Assistant: Rebecca Vidal

Historical Note:
USDEC's mission is to enhance international demand for U.S. dairy products and assist the industry to increase the volume and value of their exports.

Meetings/Conferences: Annual

Publications:
Dairy Market Outlook; monthly
Dairy Research Insights; monthly
Export Profile; quarterly
Global Dairy eBrief; weekly
Management Report; bi-monthly
Membership Directory; on-line
Trade Data; monthly

United States Durum Growers Association *(1957)*

1605 E. Capitol Ave.
Bismarck, ND 58501
Tel: (701) 214-3203 *Fax:* (701) 223-4645
E-Mail: dawn@durumgrowers.com
Website: durumgrowers.com
Members: 1000 individuals
Staff: 1
Annual Budget: $100-250,000

Personnel:
Executive Director: Deana Wiese
    E-Mail: clearone@btinet.net

Historical Note:
USDGA provides a voice for durum producers on agricultural policy and the durum industry, while striving to keep producers informed about the latest technology in durum production. It also seeks to advocate the production and marketing of durum and semolina. Membership: $75 (Grower); $100 (Associate); $1,000 (Lifetime).

Publications:
Durum Kernel

United States Energy Association *(1930)*
1300 NW. Pennsylvania Ave.
Suite 550
Washington, DC 20004-3022
Tel: (202) 312-1230 *Fax:* (202) 682-1682
E-Mail: reply@usea.org
Website: usea.org
Members: 156 businesses and individuals
Staff: 21
Annual Budget: $5-10,000,000

Personnel:
Executive Director: Barry K. Worthington
    E-Mail: bworthington@usea.org
Coordinator, Membership Services: Kim Grover
    E-Mail: kgrover@usea.org
Manager, Program: John Hammond
Chief Financial Officer: Brian Kearns

Historical Note:
The United States Energy Association (USEA) is the U.S. Member Committee of the World Energy Council (WEC). It is an association of public and private energy-related organizations, corporations, and government agencies. USEA's mission is to develop the sustainable supply and use of energy. Membership: $2,000-5,000 (Companies/Trade Associations/Manufacturers); $1,000 (Professional Societies/Federal Government Agencies/Professional Service Firms/Universities/Educational Organizations/State Government Agencies).

Meetings/Conferences: Annual
Conference Chair: John Hammond
Number of non-conference events/year: 3

Publications:
USEA Now; on-line

United States Equestrian Federation *(1917)*
4047 Iron Works Pkwy.
Lexington, KY 40511
Tel: (859) 258-2472 *Fax:* (859) 231-6662
Website: usef.org
Members: 143 organizations and 80000 individuals
Staff: 157
Annual Budget: $25-50,000,000

Personnel:
Chief Executive Officer: John Long
    E-Mail: jlong@usef.org
President: David O'Connor
    E-Mail: doconnor@usef.org
Director, Travel and Events: Ilse Dehner
    E-Mail: idehner@usef.org
Controller: David Harris
    E-Mail: dharris@usef.org
Coordinator, Membership Care: Mary Henson
    E-Mail: mhenson@usef.org
Senior Vice President and General Counsel: Sonja Keating
    E-Mail: skeating@usef.org
Manager, Human Resource and Payroll: Becki McGee
    E-Mail: bmcgee@usef.org
Senior Vice President, Marketing and Communications: Kathy Meyer
    E-Mail: kmeyer@usef.org
Director, Information Technology: Justin Provost
    E-Mail: jprovost@usef.org
Executive Director, Administration and Finance: Lori Rawls
Editor: Brian Sosby

E-Mail: bsosby@usef.org
Director, Education: Charles Walker
    E-Mail: cwalker@usef.org

Historical Note:
Founded as American Horse Shows Association became Equestrian USA in 2002, before merging (2004) with the United States Equestrian team to form the present organization. USEF is dedicated to uniting the equestrian community, honoring achievement, and serving as guardians of equestrian sport. Membership: $15-150/year; $2500 (Life-Time).

Meetings/Conferences: Annual
Conference Chair: Ilse Dehner
2013 - Louisville, KY (Louisville Marriott Downtown)/
Jan. 16 - 19

Publications:
Equestrian Magazine; quarterly; adv.
PHR Newsletter; monthly; adv.

United States Federation for Culture Collections
(1970)
1519 Little Farms Rd.
Oxnard, CA 93030-4738
Tel: (805) 984-6947
Website: usfcc.us
Members: 150 organizations and individuals
Staff: 1
Annual Budget: Under $10,000
Tax: 501(c)(3)

Personnel:
Treasurer: Mary Meeker

Historical Note:
USFCC's purpose is to further the science and practice of culture maintenance and systematic microbiology. Members are individuals and organizations concerned with maintaining culture collections and running taxonomic studies on micro-organisms. Membership: $25 (Individual); $45 (Affiliate); $200 (Sustaining); $12 (Student/Emeritus).

Meetings/Conferences: Annual

Publications:
USFCC Newsletter; on-line; adv.

United States Federation of Scholars and Scientists *(1937)*
Department of Physics, California State
University
P.O. Box 6866
Fullerton, CA 92834-6866
Tel: (714) 278-3366 *Fax:* (714) 278-5810
E-Mail: aejmchq@aol.com
Members: 50 individuals
Staff: 2
Annual Budget: Under $10,000
Tax: 501(c)(3)

Personnel:
President: Roger Dittmann
    E-Mail: rdittman@fullerton.edu
Director: Jarrett Lovell
    E-Mail: jlovell@fullerton.edu

Historical Note:
Formerly (1988) American Association of Scientific Workers, the U.S. affiliate of the World Federation of Scientific Workers, primarily concerned with the impact of science upon society, especially on a global/international scale. It is also affiliated with the American Association for the Advancement of Science. Its other affiliates are Concerned Philosophers for Peace, Southern California Federation of Scientists, and the California Peace Academy. Membership: $25 (Individual); $2.50 per capita/year (Organization).

United States Fencing Coaches Association
(1941)
514 NW 164th St.
Edmond, OK 73013-2001
Tel: (215) 862-5741
Website: usfca.org
Members: 400 individuals
Staff: 11
Annual Budget: Under $10,000
Tax: 501(c)(3)

Personnel:
President: Abdel Salem
    E-Mail: president@usfca.org
Treasurer: Carolyn Gresham-Fiegel
    E-Mail: treasurer@usfca.org
Webmaster: Ray Parker
    E-Mail: Support@usfca.org

Historical Note:
Formerly, National Fencing Coaches Association of America and assumed its present name in 1982. USFCA is committed to developing and maintaining the quality of fencing instruction, and to serve the many needs of fencing coaches in the United States. Membership: $50-120 (Full); $1,000 (Life).

Continuing Education:
Certification Designation/s: USFCA

Meetings/Conferences: Annual

Publications:
Membership Directory; on-line

United States Golf Association *(1894)*
P.O. Box 708
Far Hills, NJ 07931-0708
Tel: (908) 234-2300 *Fax:* (908) 234-9687
E-Mail: usga@usga.org
Website: usga.org
Members:
9700 golf clubs, golf courses and qualified
training facilities
750000 individuals
Staff: 5
Annual Budget: Over $100,000,000
Tax: 501(c)(3)

Personnel:
Executive Director: Mike Davis
Director, Construction Education: James F. Moore
    E-Mail: jmoore@usga.org
General Counsel: Mark E. Newell

Historical Note:
Mission is to serve members and individuals interested in golf. USGA conducts the U.S. Open, U.S. Women's Open and U.S. Senior Open, and national amateur championships. Membership: $110/year.

Publications:
USGA Newsletter

United States Grains Council *(1960)*
1400 K St. NW
Suite 1200
Washington, DC 20005
Tel: (202) 789-0789 *Fax:* (202) 898-0522
E-Mail: grains@grains.org
Website: grains.org
Members: 140 Organizations
Staff: 41
Annual Budget: $10-25,000,000

Personnel:
President and Chief Executive Officer: Thomas N. Sleight
    E-Mail: tsleight@grains.org
Manager, Communications: Marri Carrow
    E-Mail: mcarrow@grains.org
Manager of International, Operations and Marketing:
    Kevin Roepke
    E-Mail: kroepke@grains.org
Manager, Membership Services: Valerie Smiley
    E-Mail: vsmiley@grains.org

Historical Note:
Formerly (1998) U.S. Feed Grains Council. USGC is a private, non-profit organization dedicated to building export markets for barley, corn, sorghum and their products, enable trade and improve live.
Meetings/Conferences:
Number of non-conference events/year: 1

Publications:
Grain News; bi-monthly
Membership Directory; on-line

Membership List Available to Non-members

United States Green Building Council
2101 L St. NW
Suite 500
Washington, DC 20037
Tel: (202) 828-7422 *Fax:* (202) 828-5110
TollFree: (800) 795-1747
E-Mail: info@usgbc.org
Website: usgbc.org
Members: 16,000 member companies and
organizations
Staff: 9
Annual Budget: $100-250,000
Tax: 501(c)(3)

Personnel:
President and Chief Executive Officer: S. Richard Fedrizzi
Chief Financial Officer: Jim Craig

General Counsel: Susan E. Dorn
Vice President, National Policy: Jason Hartke
    E-Mail: jhartke@usgbc.org
Vice President, Conferences and Events: Kimberly Lewis
Chief Operating Officer: Mahesh Ramanujam
Vice President, Education and Research: Peter Templeton
Senior Vice President, Marketing and Communications:
    Judith Webb
Vice President, Finance and Administration: David Witek
    E-Mail: dwitek@usgbc.org

Historical Note:
USGBC's mission is to transform the way buildings and communities are designed, built and operated, enabling an environmentally and socially responsible, healthy, and prosperous environment that improves the quality of life. Membership: $300-5,000 (Contractors/Builders/ Professional Societies/Trade Association); $1,000- 5,000 (Corporate/Retail); $300-2,000 (Educational Institutions); $1,000 (Federal Government); $2,500-3,500 (Insurance Companies/Financial Institutions); $300-750 (Nonprofit/Environmental Organizations); $500- 12,500 (Product Manufacturers/Building Controls/Service Contractors/Distributors); $300-3,500 (Professional Firms); $750-4,000 (Real Estate/Real Estate Service Providers); $500-1,000 (State/Local Governments); $750-3,500 (Utility/Energy Service Companies).

Meetings/Conferences:
Conference Chair: Kimberly Lewis
Number of non-conference events/year: 1

Publications:
Member Directory
Newsletter

The United States Harness Writers' Association
(1947)
P.O. Box 1314
Mechanicsburg, PA 17055
Tel: (717) 651-5889
E-Mail: ushwa@paonline.com
Website: ushwa.org
Members: 300 individuals
Staff: 2
Annual Budget: $25-50,000

Personnel:
President: Steve Wolf
    E-Mail: stevejw@bellsouth.net
Secretary: Jerry Connors

Historical Note:
USHWA's mission is to bring a closer relationship among the media, racetracks and horsemen to promote the sport. Members are journalists who cover harness racing. Membership: $40 (Regular); $25 (Associate); Free (Retired/ Life).

Meetings/Conferences: Annual

Publications:
Awards Journal; adv.
Membership Directory; on-line
Newsletter; quarterly

United States Hide, Skin and Leather Association
(1980)
1150 Connecticut Ave. NW
12th Floor
Washington, DC 20036
Tel: (202) 587-4250 *Fax:* (202) 587-4303
Website: ushsla.org
Members: 80 companies
Staff: 2
Annual Budget: $100-250,000

Personnel:
President: John Reddington
    E-Mail: jreddington@meatami.com

Historical Note:
Formed by a merger of the American Association of Hides, Skins and Leather Merchants (established 1918) and the National Hide Association (established 1945). Represents the hide and skin industry in the United States. Membership: $1,450-5650 (Regular, based on the volume of hides per week, averaged over one year); $1,250 (Associate).

Meetings/Conferences: Annual

Publications:
Membership Directory; annually

United States High Speed Rail Association
10 G St. NE, Suite 710
Washington, DC 20002-4288
Tel: (202) 248-5001

E-Mail: email@ushsr.com
Website: ushsr.com
Staff: 5
Annual Budget: $500-1,000,000
Tax: 501(c)(6)

Personnel:
President and Chief Executive Officer: Andy Kunz
Vice President, Government Affairs and General Counsel: Thomas Hart Esq.
Manager, Operations: Anthony Le
Director, Public Outreach: Emy Louie
Vice President, Member Services: Joseph Shelhorse

Historical Note:
USHSR's mission is to build widespread public, business, and political support for a major investment in a national high speed rail network. Membership: $75 (Individual Advocate); $35 (Student Advocate);

Publications:
Member Directory; on-line
USHSR Newsletter; monthly

United States Hispanic Chamber of Commerce
(1979)
1424 K St. NW
Suite 401
Washington, DC 20005
Tel: (202) 842-1212 *Fax:* (202) 842-3221
TollFree: (800) 874-2286
E-Mail: ushcc@ushcc.com
Website: ushcc.com
Members: 200 chamber members and 160 corporate partners
Staff: 20
Annual Budget: $5-10,000,000
Tax: 501(c)(6)

Personnel:
President and Chief Executive Officer: Javier Palomarez
    E-Mail: palomarez@ushcc.com
Director, Events: Yesmin Asmar
    E-Mail: yesmin.asmar@eliteglobalevents.com
Vice President, Finance and Administration: Manuel Cosme
    E-Mail: mcosme@ushcc.com
Chief of staff and Vice President, Strategy Affairs: DeVere Kutscher
    E-Mail: dkutscher@ushcc.com
Vice President, Business Development and Procurement Services: Eduardo Pereira
    E-Mail: epereira@ushcc.com
Director, Government Relations: Jesse Salazar
    E-Mail: jsalazar@ushcc.com
Contact, Membership Services: Jennifer Tarazon
Communications Associate: Chadwick Vale
    E-Mail: cvale@ushcc.com

Historical Note:
USHCC is a national trade association of local Hispanic chambers of commerce, business associations and individuals advocating Hispanic domestic and international economic interests. Mission is to foster Hispanic economic development and to create sustainable prosperity for the benefit of American society. Membership: $25-100/year.

Meetings/Conferences: Annual
Conference Chair: Yesmin Asmar
Number of non-conference events/year: 2

Publications:
Chamber News; on-line

United States Industrial Fabrics Institute
1801 County Rd. B, West
Roseville, MN 55113-4061
Tel: (651) 222-2508 *Fax:* (651) 631-9334
TollFree: (800) 225-4324
Website: usifi.com
Staff: 1
Annual Budget: $1-2,000,000

Personnel:
Managing Director: Ruth Stephens
    E-Mail: rastephens@ifai.com

Historical Note:
A division of Industrial Fabrics Association International. USIFI's mission is to build a strong coalition of U.S. fiber, fabric, and end product manufacturers and to serve member company interests both domestically and internationally. Membership: $2,135 (Supplier); $1,535 (Sponsoring); $1,435 (Affiliate); $1,460-2,135 (Manufacturing Company).

Meetings/Conferences: Annual

Publications:
e-Newsletter; weekly

United States Institute for Theatre Technology
(1960)
315 S. Crouse Ave.
Suite 200
Syracuse, NY 13210-1844
Tel: (315) 463-6463 *Fax:* (315) 463-6525
TollFree: (800) 938-7488
E-Mail: info@office.usitt.org
Website: usitt.org
Members: 3800 individuals
Staff: 8
Annual Budget: $2-5,000,000
Tax: 501(c)(3)

Personnel:
Executive Director: David Grindle
    E-Mail: david@office.usitt.org
Director, Finance and Human Resources: Carol B. Carrigan
    E-Mail: carol@office.usitt.org
Director, Communications: Barbara E.R. Lucas
    E-Mail: barbara@office.usitt.org
Marketing Sales and Services Associate: Jim Lucas
    E-Mail: jim@office.usitt.org
Director, Membership Services: Monica L. Merritt
    E-Mail: monica@office.usitt.org
Editor: David Rodger

Historical Note:
USITT's mission is to connect performing arts design and technology communities to ensure a vibrant dialogue among practitioners, educators, and students. Membership: $108 (Individual); $1,135 (Contributing); $715 (Sustaining); $270 (Supporting); $162 (Professional); $65 (Student); $75 (Early Career); $87 (Senior, must be 65 years of age or older).

Meetings/Conferences: Annual
Conference Chair: Monica L. Merritt
2013 - Milwaukee, WI (Frontier Airlines Center)/March 20 - 23/over 100 exhibitors
2014 - Ft. Worth, TX (Fort Worth Convention Center)/March 26 - 29
2015 - Cincinnati, OH (Duke Energy Convention Center)/March 18 - 21

Publications:
Membership Directory; annually; adv.
Sightlines; monthly; adv.
Theatre Design & Technology; quarterly; adv.

United States Internet Industry Association
(1994)
P.O. Box 302
Luray, VA 22835
Tel: (540) 742-1928
Website: usiia-net.org
Members: 400 companies
Staff: 4
Annual Budget: $50-100,000
Tax: 501(c)(6)

Personnel:
President and Chief Executive Officer: David P. McClure
    E-Mail: dmcclure@usiia.org
Association Legal Counsel: James Anderson
Association Financial Counsel: Michael A. Freedman
Chief Technology Officer: Stephen B. May

Historical Note:
Founded as Association of Online Professionals; assumed its present name in 1999. USIIA's goal is to foster the growth of the Internet industry through the development and support of its members. Membership: $500 (Institutional/ Individual Professionals); $500-40,000 (Corporate); 99 (Student).

Publications:
The USIIA Bulletin; weekly

United States Internet Service Provider Association *(1991)*
700 12th St. NW
Suite 700E
Washington, DC 20005
Tel: (202) 904-2351 *Fax:* (202) 261-0604
Website: usispa.org
Members: 8 corporations
Staff: 5
Annual Budget: $100-250,000
Tax: 501(c)(6)

Personnel:
Executive Director: Kate Dean
    E-Mail: kdean@usispa.org

Historical Note:
Founded as Commercial Internet Exchange Association, assumed its current name in 2002. USISPA's mission is to serve as the ISP community's representative during policy debates and serves its members to share information and develop practices for handling specific legal matters. Members are companies that offer TCP/IP or OSI data internetworking to the general public. Members shall pay dues as established by the board of directors from time to time, and the payment of such dues shall be a condition precedent to effective membership in the association.

Publications:
Membership Directory; on-line

United States-Israel Science & Technology Foundation (USISTF) *(1995)*
1300 Pennsylvania Ave. NW
Suite 700
Washington, DC 20004
Tel: (202) 204-3102 *Fax:* (202) 289-7322
E-Mail: ann@usistf.org
Website: usistf.org
Staff: 3
Annual Budget: Under $10,000
Tax: 501(c)(3)

Personnel:
Executive Director: Ann Liebschutz
    E-Mail: ann@usistf.org
Program Manager: Eve Copeland
    E-Mail: eve@usistf.org
Project Consultant: Na'ama Termechi
    E-Mail: naama@usistf.org

Historical Note:
The U.S.-Israel Science and Technology Foundation "USISTF" seeks to foster the broadest possible range of collaborative opportunities in high technology for American and Israeli entities for the mutual benefit of the people and economies of both nations.

United States Junior Chamber (Jaycees) *(1920)*
100 Chesterfield Business Pkwy.
Suite 200
Chesterfield, MO 63005
Tel: (636) 681-1857 *Fax:* (636) 681-1401
E-Mail: customerservice@usjaycees.org
Website: jci.cc/local/info/usa
Members:
2600 chapters
107000 individuals
Staff: 5
Annual Budget: Under $10,000
Tax: 501(c)(4)

Personnel:
Executive Director: Joel Harper
    E-Mail: execdirector@usjaycees.org
Contact, Customer Service and Data Processing: Karen Fitzgerald
    E-Mail: Customerservice@usjaycees.org
Communications Specialist: Sharon Gutowski
    E-Mail: customerservice@usjaycees.org

Historical Note:
Also known as the U.S. Jaycees. USJC promotes personal growth and leadership development for individuals of ages 18-40 through service to the community and social interaction in order to achieve personal success and to have a positive impact on the community.

Meetings/Conferences: Semi-Annual
2013 - St. Louis, MO/Jan. 10 - 13
2013 - Seatle, WA/June 5 - 8
Number of non-conference events/year: 1

Publications:
Connections; monthly
USJC Postmark; monthly; adv.

United States Lacrosse *(1998)*
113 W. University Pkwy.
Baltimore, MD 21210
Tel: (410) 235-6882 *Fax:* (410) 366-6735
E-Mail: info@uslacrosse.org
Website: uslacrosse.org
Members: 200000 individuals
Staff: 79
Annual Budget: $10-25,000,000
Tax: 501(c)(3)

Personnel:

President and Chief Executive Officer: Steve Stenersen
  E-Mail: sstenersen@uslacrosse.org
Associate Director, Public Relations and Marketing: Paul
  Krome
  E-Mail: pkrome@uslacrosse.org
Director, Communications: Brian Logue
  E-Mail: blogue@uslacrosse.org
Chief Financial Officer: Cara Morris
  E-Mail: cmorris@uslacrosse.org
Managing Director, Membership and Chapters: Sara Noon
  E-Mail: snoon@uslacrosse.org
Art Director: Gabriella Ferraro O'Brien
  E-Mail: gobrien@uslacrosse.org
Director, Special Events: Beth Porreca
  E-Mail: bporreca@uslacrosse.org
Managing Director, Marketing: Bill Rubacky
  E-Mail: brubacky@uslacrosse.org
Director, Education and Training: Erin Smith
  E-Mail: esmith@uslacrosse.org
Director, Information Technology: James Wilson
  E-Mail: jwilson@uslacrosse.org

Historical Note:
Mission is to increase playing opportunities for post-collegiate athletes and facilitate women's continued involvement to grow and share the sport. Membership: $25 (Youth); $35 (High School); $50 (Adult).

Continuing Education:
Certification Designation/s: CEP

Meetings/Conferences: Annual
Conference Chair: Beth Porreca
2013 - Philadelphia, PA (Philadelphia Courtyard
  Marriott)/Jan. 11 - 13
2014 - Philadelphia, PA (Philadelphia Courtyard
  Marriott)/Jan. 10 - 12

Publications:
e-mail Newsletter; on-line
Lacrosse Magazine; monthly; adv.
Membership Directory; on-line

United States Lactation Consultant Association

2501 Aerial Center Pkwy.
Suite 103
Morrisville, NC 27560
Tel: (919) 861-4543 *Fax:* (919) 459-2075
E-Mail: info@uslca.org
Website: ilca.org/i4a/pages/index.cfm?
  pageid = 3509
Staff: 7
Annual Budget: $250-500,000
Tax: 501(c)(3)

Personnel:
President: Alisa Sanders
  E-Mail: AlisaSanders@uslcaonline.org
Executive Director: Scott Sherwood
  E-Mail: ScottSherwood@uslcaonline.org
Secretary and Treasurer: Michele Bunker-Alberts
  E-Mail: secretary@uslca.org
Director, Membership Services: Regina Camillieri IBCLC
  E-Mail: reginacamillieri@uslcaonline.org
Director, External Affairs: Sylvia Edwards
  E-Mail: externalaffairs@uslca.org
Director, Marketing: Debi Page Ferrarello
  E-Mail: marketing@uslca.org
Director, Professional Development: Barbara Robertson
  MA, IBCLC
  E-Mail: barbararobertson@uslcaonline.org

Historical Note:
USLCA's mission is to build and sustain a national association that advocates for lactation professionals. Membership: $182 (Contributing Professional); $150 (Standard).

Meetings/Conferences: Annual
2013 - St. Louis, MO (St. Louis Science Center)/May 3
  - 5

Publications:
Clinical Lactation; quarterly; adv.
USLCA Newsletter; monthly

United States Lifesaving Association *(1964)*

P.O. Box 322
Avon-By-the-Sea, NJ 07717
TollFree: (866) 367-8752
Website: usla.org
Members: 6000 individuals
Staff: 5
Annual Budget: $100-250,000
Tax: 501(c)(3)

Personnel:
President: Chris B. Brewster
  E-Mail: president@usla.org
Contact, Public Information and Media Relations: Tom Gill
  E-Mail: mediarep@usla.org
Executive Delegate and Contact, Membership Services:
  Charles Hartl
  E-Mail: membershipliaison@usla.org
Legal Advisor: John "Chip" More
  E-Mail: legaladvisor@usla.org
Treasurer: Rob Williams
  E-Mail: treasurer@usla.org

Historical Note:
Formerly (1979) the National Surf Life Saving Association of America. USLA works to reduce the incidence of death and injury in the aquatic environment through public education, national aquatic rescue standards, training programs, promotion of high levels of readiness, and other means. Members are open water lifeguards and rescue personnel. Membership: $30 (Professional/Alumnus/Associate); $10 (Associate Junior); $1,000 (Perpetual); $500 (Corporate).

Continuing Education:
Certification Designation/s: LACP, ARRTCP, CCLA

Meetings/Conferences: Tri-annual

Publications:
American Lifeguard Magazine

United States Maglev Coalition (USMC)

607 14th St. NW
Washington, DC 20005
Tel: (202) 508-5872 *Fax:* (202) 508-5858
Website: usmaglevcoalition.com
Staff: 1
Annual Budget: $10-25,000

Personnel:
Treasurer: Kenneth Waugh

Historical Note:
Magnetic levitation transportation technology. USMC's mission is to support the development of superspeed magnetic levitation (Maglev) transportation technology in the United States. $2500-$5000(Board Member); $50-$2500(Regular member).

United States Marine Safety Association *(1987)*

5050 Industrial Rd.
Suite Two
Wall Township, NJ 07727
Tel: (732) 751-0102 *Fax:* (732) 751-0508
Website: usmsa.org
Members: 145 companies
Staff: 2
Annual Budget: $100-250,000

Personnel:
Executive Director : Tom Thompson

Historical Note:
Formerly U. S. Lifesaving Manufacturing Association. USMSA's purpose is to advocate safety and survival for all who earn a living at sea. It serves as a forum for the effective use of marine safety equipment. Members are manufacturers and service organizations, including trainers, for all types of marine safety equipment. Membership: $1,435 (Manufacturer); $750 (Secondary Manufacturer/Service Organization); $495 (Associate); $195 (Subscriber).

Publications:
Marine Safety Newsletter; monthly; adv.
Membership Directory; annually

United States Maritime Alliance (USMX) *(1997)*

485-C Route One South
Suite 100
Iselin, NJ 08830
Tel: (732) 404-2960 *Fax:* (732) 750-0587
Website: usmx.com
Staff: 8
Annual Budget: $5-10,000,000

Personnel:
Chairman and Chief Executive Officer: Capo James A.
  E-Mail: jcapo@usmx.com
Senior Vice President, Chief Operating Officer: David F.
  Adam
  E-Mail: dadam@usmx.com
Senior Vice President, Chief Financial Officer: Anthony J.
  Dalonges
  E-Mail: adalonges@usmx.com
Administrative Assistant: Kim Perez
  E-Mail: kperez@usmx.com

Historical Note:
USMX's mission is to preserve and protect the interests of its members in matters associated with the maritime industry, including all labor relations issues affecting longshore and related activities. USMX is an alliance of container and port associations serving the East and Gulf Coasts of the United States

United States Meat Export Federation *(1976)*

1855 Blake St.
Suite 200
Denver, CO 80202
Tel: (303) 623-6328 *Fax:* (303) 623-0297
E-Mail: migoe@usmef.org
Website: usmef.org
Members: 214 organizations
Staff: 33
Annual Budget: $25-50,000,000
Tax: 501(c)(6)

Personnel:
President and Chief Executive Officer: Philip M. Seng
  E-Mail: pseng@usmef.org
Director, Meeting Services: Jackie Boubin
  E-Mail: jboubin@usmef.org
Director, Executive Services: Jody Falletta Carman
  E-Mail: jcarman@usmef.org
Senior Vice President, Export Services: Paul Clayton
  E-Mail: pclayton@usmef.org
Chief Financial Officer: Ron Goss
  E-Mail: rgoss@usmef.org
Assistant Vice President, International Marketing and
  Programs: Greg Hanes
  E-Mail: ghanes@usmef.org
Vice President, Communications: Jim Herlihy
  E-Mail: jherlihy@usmef.org
Assistant and Vice President, Industry Relations: John
  Hinners
  E-Mail: jhinners@usmef.org

Historical Note:
USMEF's mission is to increase the value and profitability of the U.S. meat industry by enhancing demand for their products in export markets through the partnership of all stakeholders. USMEF is funded by USDA, exporting companies, and the beef, pork, corn and soybean checkoff programs. Membership: $2,500-6,000/year (Organization).

Meetings/Conferences: Annual
Conference Chair: Jackie Boubin

Publications:
Daily news; daily
Membership Directory; on-line
The Export Newsline; weekly

United States National Committee of the International Dairy Federation *(1980)*

421 S. Nine Mound Rd.
P.O. Box 930398
Verona, WI 53593
Tel: (608) 219-4115 *Fax:* (608) 262-1278
E-Mail: usidfsec@usidf.org
Website: usnac.org
Members: 57 companies
Staff: 1
Annual Budget: $100-250,000

Personnel:
National Secretary: Debra Wendorf Boyke
  E-Mail: usnacsec@usnac.org

Historical Note:
US-IDF's mission is to provide scientific expertise and knowledge in support of development and promotion of quality milk and dairy products to deliver consumers with nutrition, health and well-being. Members are milk producers, dairy product manufacturers and suppliers, dairy scientists and educators, associations and other representatives of the U.S. dairy industry. US-IDF is a member of the International Dairy Federation, which is headquartered in Brussels, Belgium. Membership: $100 (Individual); $1,250 (Institutional); 6,000 (Sustaining); $3,000 (Corporate).

Meetings/Conferences: Annual
2013 - Yokohama, Japan/Oct. 28 - Nov. 1

Publications:
Membership Directory; on-line

United States of America Dry Pea and Lentil Council, Inc. *(1965)*

2780 W. Pullman Rd.
Moscow, ID 83843-4024
Tel: (208) 882-3023 *Fax:* (208) 882-6406

E-Mail: pulse@pea-lentil.com
Website: pea-lentil.com
Members: 5000 individuals
Staff: 8
Annual Budget: $500-1,000,000
Tax: 501(c)(3)

Personnel:
Chief Executive Officer: Tim D. McGreevy
  E-Mail: mcgreevy@pea-lentil.com
Manager, Communications: Erica Beck
  E-Mail: ebeck@pea-lentil.com
Director, Marketing: Pete Klaiber
  E-Mail: klaiber@pea-lentil.com
Office Manager, Meetings and Fundraising: Kim Monk
  E-Mail: kmonk@pea-lentil.com
Director, Information and Research: Todd Scholz
  E-Mail: scholz@pea-lentil.com
Compliance Manager: Brenda Udy
  E-Mail: udy@pea-lentil.com

Historical Note:
Formerly known as "Idaho Dry Pea and Lentil
Commission." Gained its name in 1970 as the USA Dry
Pea & Lentil Council, Inc. (USADPLC) by bringing together
the WA and ID pea and lentil growers and the processors
and exporters association. USADPLC's mission is to
provide research support, development of new markets and
increased awareness of US grown dry peas, lentils, and
chickpeas worldwide. Membership: $325 (Warehousemen);
$650 (Exporter); $325 (Broker/Commission Agent); $150
(Associate Member); $650 (Associate International Firm);
$25 (Retired Member).

Meetings/Conferences:
Conference Chair: Kim Monk

Publications:
Foodservice Newsletter; quarterly; adv.
Take Your Pulse; on-line; adv.

United States of America Gymnastics (1963)
132 E. Washington St., Suite 700
Indianapolis, IN 46204
Tel: (317) 237-5050 Fax: (317) 237-5069
TollFree: (800) 345-4719
Website: usagym.org
Members: 110,000 athletes and professionals
Staff: 59
Annual Budget: $10-25,000,000
Tax: 501(c)(3)

Personnel:
President and Chief Executive Officer: Steve Penny
  E-Mail: spenny@usagym.org
Manager, Computer Systems: Mike Bowman
  E-Mail: mbowm@usagym.org
Chief Operating Officer: Ron Galimore
  E-Mail: rgali@usagym.org
Chief Financial Officer: John Hewett
  E-Mail: jhewett@usagym.org
Vice President, Member Services: Cheryl Jarrett
  E-Mail: cjarrett@usagym.org
Vice President, Marketing: Lee Johnson
  E-Mail: ljohnson@usagym.org
Vice President, Communications: Leslie King
  E-Mail: lking@usagym.org
Graphic Designer: Jeannie Shaw
  E-Mail: jshaw@usagym.org
Director, Events: Jeff Smith
  E-Mail: jsmith@usagym.org

Historical Note:
Mission of USA Gymnastics is to encourage participation
and the pursuit of excellence in all aspects of gymnastics.
Membership: $15-350/year.

Meetings/Conferences: Annual
Conference Chair: Jeff Smith

Publications:
Acrobatic Gymnastics Program Newsletters; monthly
Member News; monthly
Technique Magazine
USA Gymnastics Magazine

United States of Ayrshire Breeders' Association (1875)
1224 Alton Darby Creek Rd.
Suite B
Columbus, OH 43228
Tel: (614) 335-0020 Fax: (614) 335-0023
E-Mail: info@usayrshire.com
Website: usayrshire.com
Members: 1100 individuals

Staff: 2
Annual Budget: $100-250,000

Personnel:
Executive Secretary: Becky Payne
  E-Mail: bpayne@usayrshire.com

Historical Note:
Breeders and fanciers of Ayrshire dairy cattle. Member
of the National Society of Livestock Record Associations.
Membership is available to individuals, partnerships and
corporations who own registered Ayrshires. Membership:
$25 (Adult); $10 (Junior).

Meetings/Conferences: Annual

Publications:
Ayrshire Breeders Directory; on-line
Membership Directory; on-line

U.S. Oil and Gas Association (1917)
1101 K St. NW
Suite 425
Washington, DC 20005
Tel: (202) 638-4400 Fax: (202) 638-5967
E-Mail: usoil@usoga.com
Website: usoga.org
Members: 150 member companies
Staff: 2
Annual Budget: $1-2,000,000

Personnel:
President: Albert L. Modiano
  E-Mail: amodiano@usoga.org

Historical Note:
Formerly the Mid-Continent Oil & Gas Association. The
Mission of the Association is to establish and maintain
reasonable statewide public policy regarding legislative and
regulatory issues and to work on regional and federal issues
which could have a significant impact on the industry.

Publications:
The Washington Flash

United States Organizations for Bankruptcy Alternatives (USOBA)
P. O. Box 91323
Houston, TX 77291
Tel: (877) 768-7622 Fax: (713) 456-2837
E-Mail: info@usoba.org
Website: usoba.org
Staff: 1

Personnel:
Executive Director: Jenna Keehnen

Historical Note:
Represent the debt negotiation industry to advocate for fair
regulation and protect consumers. Membership: $4,800/
year (Vendor); $1,565 to $4,800 (Gold/Silver/Platinum/
Regular Non-vendor).

Publications:
USOBA Newsletter, "The Bottom Line"

United States Pan Asian American Chamber of Commerce (1984)
1329 18th St. NW
Washington, DC 20036
Tel: (202) 296-5221 Fax: (202) 296-5225
E-Mail: administrator@uspaacc.org
Website: uspaacc.com
Members: 8000 individuals and companies
Staff: 13
Annual Budget: Under $10,000
Tax: 501(c)(3)

Personnel:
National President and Chief Executive Officer: Susan Au
  Allen Esq.
  E-Mail: susanallen@uspaacc.com
Marketing Specialist: Janice Tu
  E-Mail: janice@uspaacc.com
Director, National Programs: Anna Zawacki
  E-Mail: anna@uspaacc.com

Historical Note:
A national non-profit organization representing Asian
American and other businesses and professionals. Provides
members with a wide variety of educational, information
and advocacy programs. Membership: $15,000 (National
Corporate Platinum); $10,000 (National Corporate Gold);
$5,000 (National Corporate); $2,500 (National Non-
Profit).

Continuing Education:
Enrollment: 1800
Certification Designation/s: USPAACC, AABC

Meetings/Conferences: Quarterly

Publications:
E-News; bi-weekly; adv.
National Directory of Asian American Businesses and
  Resource Guide; annually; adv.
Receive East West Report; quarterly; adv.

Membership List Available to Non-members

United States Parachute Association (1946)
5401 Southpoint Center Blvd.
Fredericksburg, VA 22407
Tel: (540) 604-9740 Fax: (540) 604-9741
E-Mail: uspa@uspa.org
Website: uspa.org
Members: 33000 members
Staff: 16
Annual Budget: $2-5,000,000

Personnel:
Executive Director: Edward "Ed" Scott
  E-Mail: escott@uspa.org
Director, Safety and Training: Jim Crouch
  E-Mail: Safety@uspa.org
Director, Communications: Elijah Florio
  E-Mail: Communications@uspa.org
Director, Government Relations: Randy Ottinger
  E-Mail: govrelations@uspa.org
Managing Editor: Laura Sharp
  E-Mail: Communications@uspa.org
Director, Membership Services: Clint Vincent
  E-Mail: membership@uspa.org
Director, Accounting and Human Resources: Stephanie
  Whittaker
  E-Mail: USPA@uspa.org

Historical Note:
Formerly (1957) Parachute Club of America. USPA's
mission is to encourage unity among all persons interested
in skydiving. Membership: $65-74 (New Member); $55-64
(Renewal); $1000-2500 (Lifetime, U.S.).

Meetings/Conferences: Annual
2013 - Ottawa, IL (Skydive Chicago)/Sept. 12 - 24

Publications:
Membership Directory; on-line
Parachutist magazine; monthly
USPA Professional; monthly
USPA Update; monthly

Membership List Available to Non-members

United States Pharmacopeia (1820)
12601 Twinbrook Pkwy.
Rockville, MD 20852-1790
Tel: (301) 881-0666 Fax: (301) 816-8236
TollFree: (800) 227-8772
E-Mail: info@usp.org
Website: usp.org
Members: 400 organizations, institutions and
  agencies
Staff: 25

Personnel:
Chief Executive Officer: Roger L. Williams MD
  E-Mail: rlw@usp.org
Vice President, Human Resources: Susan A. Bach
Executive Vice President and Chief Legal Officer: Susan S.
  de Mars J D
  E-Mail: sdm@usp.org
Director, Government Affairs: Ben Firschein
  E-Mail: baf@usp.org
Vice President, Publishing: Linda Guard
Senior Vice President, Information and Services: Scott
  Henderson MS
Chief Operating Officer: Brian L. Hendrix MS
Vice President, Administrative Services: Drew Lutz
Vice President, Finance and Accounting: James P.
  Thompson CPA
Vice President, Sales and Marketing: Richard Wailes
  MBA

Historical Note:
USP's mission is to improve the public health of people
around the world through public standards and related
programs that help ensure the quality, safety, and benefit of
medicines and foods.

Publications:
The Standard; quarterly

United States Potato Board (1971)
7555 E. Hampden Ave.
Suite 412
Denver, CO 80231-4835

Tel: (303) 369-7783 *Fax:* (303) 369-7718
E-Mail: info@uspotatoes.com
Website: uspotatoes.com
Members: 2,500 potato growers and handlers
Staff: 17
Annual Budget: $10-25,000,000

Personnel:
President and Chief Executive Officer: Timothy O'Connor
   E-Mail: toconnor@uspotatoes.com
Executive Administrator: Robin Vest Angelo
   E-Mail: rvest@uspotatoes.com
Vice President, Industry Communications and Policy:
   David Fraser
   E-Mail: david.fraser@uspotatoes.com
Vice President, Finance and Information Technology:
   Diana LeDoux
   E-Mail: Diana@uspotatoes.com
Manager, Public Relations: Meredith Myers
   E-Mail: meredithm@uspotatoes.com
Vice President, International Marketing: John Toaspern
   E-Mail: johnt@uspotatoes.com

Historical Note:
*Also known as The National Potato Promotion Board.
USPB is the nation's potato marketing and research
organization. Mission is to increase demand for potatoes
and potato products through an integrated promotion
program, thereby providing US producers with expanding
markets for their production.*

Meetings/Conferences:
Conference Chair: Robin Vest Angelo
2013 - Las Vegas, NV (Caesar's Palace)/Jan. 9 - 12
2013 - Colorado Springs, CO (The Broadmoor)/March
   12 - 15

Publications:
USPB Newsletter

U.S Poultry and Egg Association *(1947)*
1530 Cooledge Rd.
Tucker, GA 30084-7303
Tel: (770) 493-9401 *Fax:* (770) 493-9257
E-Mail: info@poultryegg.org
Website: poultryegg.org
Members: 600 companies
Staff: 24
Annual Budget: $2-5,000,000

Personnel:
President: John Starkey
   E-Mail: jstarkey@uspoultry.org
Controller: Seals Burdell
   E-Mail: sburdell@uspoultry.org
Vice President, Education Programs: Barbara Jenkins
   E-Mail: bjenkins@uspoultry.org
*Executive Vice President and Contact, International Poultry
Expo:* Charles Olentine PhD
   E-Mail: colentine@uspoultry.org
Vice President, Information Technology: Jason Rivera
   E-Mail: jrivera@uspoultry.org
Director, Communications: Gwen Venable
   E-Mail: gvenable@uspoultry.org
Administrative Assistant to Executive Vice President: Sarah
   Williams
   E-Mail: swilliams@poultryegg.org

Historical Note:
*Founded as the Southeastern Poultry and Egg Association
to promote the poultry and egg industries. USPOULTRY is
committed to the advancement of research and education
in poultry science and technology. Members are producers
of broiler, eggs, or turkeys, and firms that provide products
and services to the poultry industry. Membership: $400/
year (Regular/Associate/Allied/International).*

Meetings/Conferences: Annual
Conference Chair: Charles Olentine PhD
2013 - Atlanta, GA (Georgia World Congress Center)/
   Jan. 29 - 31
Number of non-conference events/year: 9

Publications:
Expo Flash; monthly
Membership Directory; on-line
News & Views; quarterly
People Matters (e-newsletter); weekly
Poultry Wire (e-newsletter); daily

United States Professional Tennis Association
(1927)
3535 Briarpark Dr.
Suite One
Houston, TX 77042

Tel: (713) 978-7782 *Fax:* (713) 978-7780
TollFree: (800) 877-8248
E-Mail: USPTA@uspta.org
Website: uspta.org
Members: 15000 individuals
Staff: 27
Annual Budget: $5-10,000,000
Tax: 501(c)(6)

Personnel:
Chief Executive Officer: Tim Heckler
   E-Mail: tim.heckler@uspta.org
Director, Marketing: John Dettor
   E-Mail: john.dettor@uspta.org
Director, Operations: Rich Fanning
   E-Mail: rich.fanning@uspta.org
Manager, Publications and Managing Editor: Kimberly
   Forrester
   E-Mail: kim.forrester@uspta.org
Director, Finance: Kathy Ladner
   E-Mail: kathy.ladner@uspta.org
Director, Communications: Shawna Riley
   E-Mail: shawna.riley@uspta.org
Director, Public Relations: Poornima Rimm
   E-Mail: poornima.rimm@uspta.org
Director, Membership Services and Certifications: Vicky
   Tristan
   E-Mail: vicky.tristan@uspta.org
Director, Professional Development: Fred Viancos
   E-Mail: fred.viancos@uspta.org
Director, Information Technology: Dan Wilson
   E-Mail: dan.wilson@uspta.org

Historical Note:
*USPTA's mission is to improve the standards of tennis-
teaching professionals and coaches. Membership:
$61.25-285.83 (United States-Its territories and Canada);
$57.50-268.33 (International Members).*

Continuing Education:
Certification Designation/s: APC

Meetings/Conferences: Annual
Conference Chair: Rich Fanning

Publications:
ADDvantage Magazine; monthly
Convention Commemorative Program; annually; adv.
Membership Directory; annually
Tennis Magazine
USPTA e-news; monthly

United States Psychiatric Rehabilitation
Association *(1975)*
1760 Old Meadow Rd,
Suite 500
McLean, VA 22102
Tel: (410) 789-7054 *Fax:* (410) 789-7675
E-Mail: info@uspra.org
Website: uspra.org
Members:
348 agencies
1400 individuals
Staff: 12
Annual Budget: $500-1,000,000
Tax: 501(c)(3)

Personnel:
Chief Executive Officer: Dawn M. Bauman
Contact, Accounts Payable and Publications: Karla
   Bingman
   E-Mail: kbingman@uspra.org
Senior Manager, Education and Training: Janet Bradley
   E-Mail: jbradley@uspra.org
Senior Manager, Membership and Chapters: Sara B.
   Duginske
   E-Mail: sduginske@uspra.org
Chief Staff Officer, Certification Program: Casey Ward
   Goldberg
   E-Mail: cgoldberg@uspra.org
Chief Financial Officer: David Manke
   E-Mail: dmank@uspra.org
Director, Communications: Nancy Seiss
   E-Mail: nseiss@uspra.org

Historical Note:
*Formerly (2004) known as International Association of
Psychosocial Rehabilitation Services. USPRA's goal is
to help advance the role, scope and quality of services
designed to facilitate the community readjustment of
people with psychiatric disabilities. Membership: $110
(Individual Member); $30 (Associate Individual Member);
$620 (Associate Organizational Membership); $190-4,400*

---

*(Organization, varies according to budget); $275-5,000
(VA Membership,Based on # of Full-Time Employees).*

Continuing Education:
Enrollment: 2600
Certification Designation/s: CPRP

Meetings/Conferences: Annual
2013 - Atlanta, GA (Hyatt Regency Atlanta)/June 9 - 12

Publications:
Psychiatric Rehabilitation Journal; quarterly
PsyR Connections Newsletter; quarterly

United States Racquet Stringers Association
(1975)
P.O. Box 3392
Duluth, GA 30096
Tel: (760) 536-1177 *Fax:* (760) 536-1171
E-Mail: usrsa@racquettech.com
Website: racquettech.com
Members: 7000 individuals
Staff: 7
Annual Budget: $500-1,000,000

Personnel:
Executive Director: David Bone
   E-Mail: dave@racquettech.com
Contact, Advertising sales: John Hanna
   E-Mail: hanna@knowatlanta.com
Director, Membership Services and Office Manager:
   Dianne Pray
   E-Mail: dianne@racquettech.com
Contact, Technical Support and Webmaster: Greg Raven
   E-Mail: greg@usrsa.com
Contact, Certification Testing: Jonathan Wolfe
   E-Mail: jonathan@racquettech.com

Historical Note:
*USRSA's mission is to educate all its constituencies
to better understand, service, perform with, and enjoy
racquets, strings, balls, courts, shoes, and stringing
machines. Members are racquet technicians, teaching
professionals, racquet sports retailers, manufacturers and
sales organizations, and tennis, racquetball, squash, and
badminton enthusiasts. Membership: $119 (U.S); $149
(Canadian); $154 (Mexican); $165 (International).*

Continuing Education:
Certification Designation/s: MRT

Publications:
Membership Directory; on-line
Racquet Sports Industry magazine; monthly
The Stringer's Digest; bi-annually

Membership List Available to Non-members

United States Rowing Association
Two Wall St.
Princeton, NJ 08540
Tel: (609) 751-0700 *Fax:* (609) 924-1578
TollFree: (800) 314-4769
E-Mail: members@usrowing.org
Website: usrowing.org
Members: 17,100 individuals and organizations
Staff: 39
Annual Budget: $5-10,000,000
Tax: 501(c)(3)

Personnel:
Chief Executive Director: Glenn Merry
   E-Mail: glenn@usrowing.org
Manager, Education: Willie Black
   E-Mail: willieb@usrowing.org
Manager, Events: A. J. Dominique
   E-Mail: alvin@usrowing.org
Manager, Communications: Allison Frederick
   E-Mail: allison@usrowing.org
Director, Operations: Brett Johnson
   E-Mail: brett@usrowing.org
Chief Financial Officer: Brian Klausner
   E-Mail: brian@usrowing.org
Coordinator, Member Services: Hillary Levitz
   E-Mail: hillary@usrowing.org
Manager, Membership Services, Marketing and Database:
   Alison Pollini
   E-Mail: Pollini@usrowing.org
Coordinator, Membership Services: Wendy Rahn
   E-Mail: wendy@usrowing.org

Historical Note:
*Formed (1982) by the merger of the National Association of
Amateur Oarsmen (est. 1872) and the National Women's
Rowing Association (est. in the early 1960s). USRowing
selects, trains and manages the teams that represent the
U. S. in international competition including the world*

---

championships, Pan American Games and Olympics. USRowing serves and promotes the sport on all levels of competition. Membership includes American rowers – juniors, collegians, masters and those who row for recreation, competition or fitness. Membership: $45 (Individual-Age 26 and under); $65 (Individual-Age 27 and older); $75 (International).

Continuing Education:
Certification Designation/s: CPR, CEL

Meetings/Conferences: Annual
Conference Chair: A. J. Dominique
Number of non-conference events/year: 12

Publications:
USRowing E-Magazine; bi-monthly; adv.
USRowing This Month e-newsletter; monthly; adv.

U.S.-Russia Business Council *(1993)*
1110 Vermont Ave. NW
Suite 350
Washington, DC 20005
Tel: (202) 739-9180 *Fax:* (202) 659-5920
E-Mail: info@usrbc.org
Website: usrbc.org
Members: 300 companies
Staff: 12
Annual Budget: $2-5,000,000
Tax: 501(c)(6)

Personnel:
President and Chief Executive Officer: Edward S. Verona
    E-Mail: verona@usrbc.org
Manager, Membership Affairs and Programs: Julia Bacon
    E-Mail: bacon@usrbc.org
Senior Director, Policy and Programs: Jeffrey Barnett
    E-Mail: jbarnett@usrbc.org
Vice President, Administration and Finance: Jo Bottalico
    E-Mail: bottalico@usrbc.org
Director, Research: Keith Bush
    E-Mail: bush@usrbc.org
Executive Vice President: Randi B. Levinas
    E-Mail: Levinas@usrbc.org
Director, Communications and External Affairs: Svetlana Minjack
    E-Mail: sminjack@usrbc.org

Historical Note:
A non-profit, Washington-based trade organization that represents the interests of 300 member companies operating in the Russian market. Its mission is to expand and enhance the U.S.-Russia commercial relationship.

Meetings/Conferences: Annual
Number of non-conference events/year: 4

United States Ski and Snowboard Association *(1905)*
One Victory Ln.
P.O. Box 100
Park City, UT 84060
Tel: (435) 649-9090 *Fax:* (435) 649-3613
E-Mail: info@ussa.org
Website: ussa.org
Members: 30000 individuals
Staff: 123
Annual Budget: $250-500,000
Tax: 501(c)(3)

Personnel:
President and Chief Executive Officer: Bill Marolt
    E-Mail: bmarolt@ussa.org
Director, Membership Services: Sheryl Barnes
    E-Mail: sbarnes@ussa.org
Vice President, Events: Calum Clark
Vice President and Chief Marketing Officer: Michael Jaquet
Vice President, Communications: Tom Kelly
Executive Vice President and Chief Financial Officer: Mark Lampe
    E-Mail: mlampe@ussa.org
Director, Human Resources: Shauna Vanderlinden
    E-Mail: svanderlinden@ussa.org

Historical Note:
Formerly National Ski Association of America and became (1990) United States Ski Association. USSA's mission is to provide strong leadership that establishes and supports athletic excellence in accordance with USSA core values. Membership: $60-165/year.

Meetings/Conferences: Annual
Conference Chair: Calum Clark
2013 - Park City, UT/May 14 - 18

Publications:

Membership Directory; on-line
Ski Racing Magazine
USSA Club eNewsletter; monthly
USSA Coach eNewsletter; irregular
USSA Judges and Officials Newsletter; irregular
USSA Medical Newsletter; bi-annually

Membership List Available to Non-members

United States Soccer Federation *(1913)*
1801 S. Prairie Ave.
Chicago, IL 60616
Tel: (312) 808-1300 *Fax:* (312) 808-1301
Website: ussoccer.com
Members: 106 affiliated associations
Staff: 598
Annual Budget: $50-100,000,000
Tax: 501(c)(3)

Personnel:
Executive Vice president: Mike Edwards
Chief Executive Officer and Secretary General: Daniel "Dan" T. Flynn
President: Sunil K. Gulati
Manager, Development Academy Programs: Melissa Biniewicz
    E-Mail: mbiniewicz@ussoccer.org
Staff Attorney: Greg Fike
    E-Mail: gfike@ussoccer.org
Manager, Coaching Programs: Scott Flood
    E-Mail: sflood@ussoccer.org
Manager, Marketing: Steve Hoffman
    E-Mail: shoffman@ussoccer.org
Coordinator, Communications: Elizabeth Sanchez
    E-Mail: esanchez@ussoccer.org

Historical Note:
Formerly United States Football Association, assumed its current name in 1974. Mission is to make soccer, in all its forms, a preeminent sport in the United States and to continue the development of soccer at all recreational and competitive levels. Membership includes associate, disabled service organization, indoor professional league, affiliate, professional league, state association, life member and individual sustaining member.

Meetings/Conferences: Annual
Conference Chair: Melissa Biniewicz
Number of non-conference events/year: 5

Publications:
U.S. Soccer Wire; weekly

United States Society on Dams *(1932)*
1616 17th St.
Suite 483
Denver, CO 80202
Tel: (303) 628-5430 *Fax:* (303) 628-5431
Website: ussdams.org
Members: 1150 individuals and companies
Staff: 2
Annual Budget: $250-500,000
Tax: 501(c)(3)

Personnel:
Executive Director: Larry D. Stephens
    E-Mail: stephens@ussdams.org
Public Affairs Officer: Ronald A. Corso
    E-Mail: ron.corso@meadhunt.com

Historical Note:
Founded as United States Committee on Large Dams, assumed its current name in 2000. USSD is dedicated to fostering dam technology for socially, environmentally and financially sustainable water resources systems. Membership: $25-2,900/year; $1,080 (Life).

Meetings/Conferences: Annual
2013 - Phoenix, AZ/Feb. 11 - 15

Publications:
Membership Directory; annually; adv.
USSD Newsletter; adv.

United States-Sudan Business Council
United States-Sudan Business Council
Bowie, MD 78735
Staff: 1

Personnel:
Executive Director: Andrew Mangan

United States Superyacht Association *(2006)*
757 SE 17th St.
Suite 662
Ft. Lauderdale, FL 33316
Tel: (954) 792-8666 *Fax:* (954) 523-0607

TollFree: (800) 208-5801
E-Mail: info@ussuperyacht.com
Website: ussuperyacht.com
Staff: 3
Annual Budget: $100-250,000

Personnel:
Advocacy Manager: Kitty McGowan
Treasurer: Mark Cline
General Counsel: Michael Karcher

Historical Note:
USSA's mission is to promote the Superyacht industry of the United States and to serve as its voice. Members are businesses with a presence in the Superyacht industry. Membership: $500/year (Business/Affiliate).

Meetings/Conferences: Annual

Publications:
Membership Directory; on-line

United States Swim School Association *(1988)*
P.O. Box 17208
Fountain Hills, AZ 85269
Tel: (480) 837-5525 *Fax:* (480) 836-8277
E-Mail: Admin@usswimschools.org
Website: usswimschools.org
Members: 400 swim schools (domestic & international)
Staff: 2
Annual Budget: $250-500,000

Personnel:
Executive Director: Sue Mackie
    E-Mail: suemackie@usswimschools.org

Historical Note:
Mission is to provide resources to assist members in achieving their goals in the learn to swim business. Members are companies who provide products and services to the U.S. Swim School Association and/or its members. Membership: $349 (U.S); $225 (International); $50 (Retired).

Meetings/Conferences: Annual
Number of non-conference events/year: 2

Publications:
Membership Directory; on-line
Swimformation; quarterly; adv.

United States Synchronized Swimming *(1977)*
132 E. Washington St.
Suite 820
Indianapolis, IN 46204
Tel: (317) 237-5700 *Fax:* (317) 237-5705
Website: usasynchro.org
Staff: 8
Annual Budget: $1-2,000,000

Personnel:
Executive Director: Terry Harper
    E-Mail: terry.harper@usasynchro.org
Manager, Finance: Jennifer Hawkins
    E-Mail: jennifer@usasynchro.org
Contact, Media: Dax Lowery
    E-Mail: media@usasynchro.org
Administrative Assistant: Janice Sherman
Manager, Membership: Elizabeth Simonson
    E-Mail: mbrservices@usasynchro.org
Director, Education: Kevin Warner
    E-Mail: kevin@usasynchro.org

Historical Note:
The inaugural synchronized swimming U.S. National Championships were held in 1946, just one year after the Amateur Athletic Union (AAU) first recognized the sport. A few years later, the 1955 Pan American Games included synchronized swimming events, and the World Aquatic Championships soon followed.USSS's mission is to provide leadership and resources for the promotion and growth of synchronized swimming, to achieve competitive excellence at all levels and to develop broad based participation.Membership $15-100((Individual); $50 (Club); $2,500 (Life).

Publications:
USA Synchro Magazine; quarterly

United States Targhee Sheep Association *(1951)*
7009 Via Campanile Ave.
Las Vegas, NV 89131
Tel: (702) 292-5715
E-Mail: ustargheesheep@gmail.com
Website: ustargheesheep.org
Members: 270 individuals
Staff: 2

Annual Budget: $25-50,000

Personnel:
Contact, Communications: Mardy Rutledge

Historical Note:
A member of the National Pedigreed Livestock Council, USTSA seeks to develop profitable range raised sheep requiring minimal human intervention. Membership: $26/ year (Lifetime).

Publications:
Targhee Talk - Newsletter; irregular

United States Telecom Association *(1897)*
607 14th St. NW
Suite 400
Washington, DC 20005-2136
Tel: (202) 326-7300 *Fax:* (202) 315-3603
Website: ustelecom.org
Members: 1200 telephone companies
Staff: 73
Annual Budget: $10-25,000,000
Tax: 501(c)(6)

Personnel:
President and Chief Executive Officer: Walter B. McCormick Jr.
  E-Mail: wmccormick@usta.org
Vice President, Government Affairs: William R. Deere
Senior Vice President, Administration and Chief Financial Officer: Mark Kulish
Vice President, Media Affairs: Anne Veigle
  E-Mail: media@ustelecom.org

Historical Note:
Formerly Independent Telephone Association of America, (1983) National Independent Telephone, (2000) United States Telephone Association. Originally formed to represent domestic non-Bell System companies in the telephone industry, USTA works to advance policies that spur investment and help make broadband's promise real for every American. Members are companies previously affiliated with AT&T. Membership: $2,000 (Associate); Active and International membership dues are based on total gross domestic telecom revenues.

Meetings/Conferences: Annual

Publications:
Broadband Connection; bi-weekly
Broadband Connection In-Depth; weekly
Membership Directory; on-line
USTelecom dailyLead; daily

Membership List Available to Non-members

United States Tennis Association *(1881)*
70 W. Red Oak Ln.
White Plains, NY 10604-3602
Tel: (914) 696-7000 *Fax:* (914) 696-7167
TollFree: (800) 990-8782
E-Mail: officiating@usta.com
Website: usta.com
Members: 707000 individual and organizational members
Staff: 606
Annual Budget: Over $100,000,000

Personnel:
Executive Director and Chief Operating Officer: Gordon Smith
Chief Financial Officer: Harry Beeth
Chief Information Officer: Lawrence Bonfante
Managing Director, Tournament Operations: Jim Curley
General Counsel and Chief Legal Officer: Andrea S. Hirsch
Managing Director, Membership Services: Barrie Markowitz
  E-Mail: markowitz@usta.com
Director, Marketing: Daran Miner
  E-Mail: miner@usta.com
Director, Human Resources: Dario R. Otero
Editorial Director: Mark Preston
Senior Director, Public Relations and Communications: Chris Widmaier
  E-Mail: widmaier@usta.com

Historical Note:
Formerly (1975) United States Lawn Tennis Association. USTA's mission is to promote and develop the growth of tennis. Membership: $42 (Adult); $19 (Junior); $68 (Family-2 or more members of same family); $35-110 (Organization); $750 (Life Member Individual).

Publications:
SMASH Magazine; on-line
TENNIS

USTA & US Open Newsletter; on-line
USTA Magazine

United States Tobacco Cooperative Inc *(1946)*
1304 Annapolis Dr.
Raleigh, NC 27608
Tel: (919) 821-4560 *Fax:* (919) 821-4564
Website: ustobaccofarmer.com
Members: 3500 individuals
Staff: 8
Annual Budget: $1-2,000,000

Personnel:
President: Tommy Bunn
  E-Mail: tbunn@ipass.net
Manager, Information Technology: Robert Booker
  E-Mail: rbooker@ipass.net
Treasurer: Ken Bopp
  E-Mail: kbopp@ipass.net
Senior Vice President, Sales and Marketing: Mike Lynch
  E-Mail: mlynch@ipass.net
Chief Financial Officer: Stuart Thompson
  E-Mail: sthompson@usleaf.com
Manager, Human Resources: Sam Tie
  E-Mail: stie@ipass.net

Historical Note:
Formerly (1967) Tobacco Growers Services Inc. (2004) Flue-Cured Tobacco Cooperative Stabilization Corporation, USTC's mission is to enhance the livelihood of its member farmers by educating potential customers about the superior taste and aroma of U.S. flue-cured tobacco and promoting its use in increasing percentages to companies that produce tobacco products.

Publications:
Scoop; quarterly; adv.

United States Tour Operators Association *(1972)*
345 Seventh Ave.
Suite 1801
New York, NY 10001
Tel: (212) 599-6599 *Fax:* (212) 599-6744
E-Mail: information@ustoa.com
Website: ustoa.com
Members: 740 Members, 35 companies
Staff: 4
Annual Budget: $2-5,000,000
Tax: 501(c)(6)

Personnel:
President: Terry L. Dale

Historical Note:
USTOA seeks to foster a level of professionalism within the tour operator industry and protect consumers and travel agents from financial loss in the event of a member's bankruptcy or insolvency. Membership: $2,000- 9,500 (Active); $750 (Associate); $350 (Allied).

Meetings/Conferences: Annual
2013 - Scottsdale, AZ (Fairmont Scottsdale Princess)/ Dec. 5 - 7
2014 - Boca Raton, FL (Boca Raton Resort and Club)/ Dec. 5 - 7

Publications:
USTOA Annual Directory; annually

Membership List Available to Non-members

United States Trotting Association *(1939)*
750 Michigan Ave.
Columbus, OH 43215-1191
Tel: (614) 224-2291 *Fax:* (614) 224-4575
TollFree: (877) 800-8782
Website: ustrotting.com
Members: 25000 members and 256 tracks
Staff: 61
Annual Budget: $5-10,000,000
Tax: 501(c)(6)

Personnel:
Executive Vice President: Mike Tanner
  E-Mail: mike.tanner@ustrotting.com
Director, Information Technology: Sherry Antion-Mohr
  E-Mail: itmanager@ustrotting.com
Executive Editor: T. J. Burkett
  E-Mail: tj.burkett@ustrotting.com
Controller: Dennis Fisher
  E-Mail: dennis.fisher@ustrotting.com
Director, Registry and Membership Services: T. C. Lane
  E-Mail: tc.lane@ustrotting.com
Director, Communications: Dan Leary
  E-Mail: dan.leary@ustrotting.com
Manager, Human Resources: Rini Moskos

  E-Mail: moskos@ustrotting.com

Historical Note:
USTA's mission is to license owners, trainers, drivers, and officials, formulate the rules of racing and maintain and disseminate racing information and records. Members include officials, breeders, owners, trainers and drivers of standard bred trotting horses. USTA licenses drivers/ officials and maintains a registry of horses. Membership: $70 (New Members); $55 (Renewal); $105 (Driver/ Trainer); $20-50 (Officers).

Continuing Education:
Enrollment: 22500

Publications:
Membership Directory; on-line
Youth Beats Magazine; semi-annually

Membership List Available to Non-members

United States Trout Farmers Association *(1954)*
P.O. Box 1647
Pine Bluff, AR 71613
Tel: (870) 850-7900 *Fax:* (870) 850-7902
E-Mail: ustfa@thenaa.net
Website: ustfa.org
Staff: 3
Annual Budget: $25-50,000

Personnel:
President: Charlie Conklin
Treasurer: Marvin Emerson
Office Administrator: Kelly Goodwin

Historical Note:
USTFA's mission is to protect and ensure the interests of trout farmers in the United States on legislative and marketing fronts. Membership: $30-1,500/year.

Meetings/Conferences:
Number of non-conference events/year: 3

Publications:
Membership Directory; on-line
Trout Talk; quarterly; adv.

United States Wheat Associates, Inc. *(1980)*
3103 Tenth St., North
Suite 300
Arlington, VA 22201
Tel: (202) 463-0999 *Fax:* (703) 524-4399
E-Mail: info@uswheat.org
Website: uswheat.org
Members: 19 state organizations
Staff: 85
Annual Budget: $10-25,000,000

Personnel:
President: Alan T. Tracy
  E-Mail: alan_tracy@uswheat.org
Vice President, Marketing Programs: Rick Callies
  E-Mail: callies@uswheat.org
Convention Planner and Coordinator, State Outreach: Nancy Fisher
  E-Mail: nancy_fisher@uswheat.org
Director, Information Services: Terry Herman
  E-Mail: herman@uswheat.org
Vice President, Finance: Kevin McGarry
  E-Mail: mcgarry@uswheat.org
Director, Communications: Steve Mercer
  E-Mail: smercer@uswheat.org
Director, Policy: Shannon Schlecht
  E-Mail: sschlecht@uswheat.org
Program Manager: Alain Sellier
  E-Mail: sellier@uswheat.org

Historical Note:
USW's mission is to export market development organization representing the U.S. wheat industry. Market development activities include trade servicing, technical assistance, market analysis, and consumer promotion.

Meetings/Conferences:
Conference Chair: Nancy Fisher
2013 - Washington, DC (Hyatt Regency Washington on Capitol Hill)/Jan. 27 - 30
2013 - Rapid City, SD (Holiday Inn Rapid City-Rushmore Plaza)/June 29 - July 1
2013 - Portland, OR (Nines Hotel)/Nov. 3 - 6
2014 - Washington, DC (Hyatt Regency Washington on Capitol Hill)/Jan. 29 - Feb. 1
2014 - Omaha, NE (DoubleTree Omaha)/June 8 - 11
Number of non-conference events/year: 6

Publications:
Membership Directory; on-line
USW Wheat Letter; bi-monthly

United States-Austrian Chamber of Commerce (1949)

165 W. 46th St.
Suite 1112
New York, NY 10036
Tel: (212) 819-0117 *Fax:* (212) 819-0345
E-Mail: info@usatchamber.com
Website: usaustrianchamber.org
Members: 120 companies
Staff: 3
Annual Budget: $50-100,000

Personnel:
President: Johannes P. Hofer
Counsel: Stephen M. Harnik Esq.
Board Secretary: Elizabeth Shuman

Historical Note:
Mission is to promote the development of trade and personal relationships between the United States and Austria by merging traditional values with the exciting opportunities provided by information technology. Membership: $500 (Corporate); $200 (Small Business); $75 (Individual) $1500 (Flagship).

United States-China Business Council (1973)

1818 N St. NW
Suite 200
Washington, DC 20036-2470
Tel: (202) 429-0340 *Fax:* (202) 775-2476
E-Mail: info@uschina.org
Website: uschina.org
Members: 225 companies
Staff: 29
Annual Budget: $2-5,000,000

Personnel:
President: John Frisbie
   E-Mail: jfrisbie@uschina.org
Vice President: Erin Ennis
   E-Mail: eennis@uschina.org
Director, Membership Services: E. Palmer Golson
   E-Mail: pgolson@uschina.org
Director, Programs: Gloria Gonzalez-Micklin
   E-Mail: ggonzalezmicklin@uschina.org
Director, Finance and Administration: Shonda Hightower
   E-Mail: shightower@uschina.org
Director, Business Advisory Services: Ryan Ong
   E-Mail: ryanong@uschina.org
Director, Communications and Publications: Marc A. Ross
   E-Mail: mross@uschina.org

Historical Note:
USCBC's mission to expand the US-China commercial relationship to the benefit of its membership and, more broadly, the US economy. Membership is limited to companies incorporated in the United States. Individuals, non- profit organization, and government and academic institutions are not eligible for membership. Membership: $2,750-19,500 (Parent Company); $2,750-11,000 (Professional Services Firms); $11,000-16,500 (Venture Capital Firms/Private Equity Firms).

Meetings/Conferences: Annual
Conference Chair: Gloria Gonzalez-Micklin
Number of non-conference events/year: 2

Publications:
China Business Review; bi-monthly; adv.
China Market Intelligence; bi-weekly
USBC China News Headlines; weekly
Washington Update; on-line

United States-China Chamber of Commerce (1993)

55 W. Monroe St., Suite 630
Chicago, IL 60603
Tel: (312) 368-9911 *Fax:* (312) 368-9922
E-Mail: Info@usccc.org
Website: usccc.org
Members: 350 corporations and professionals
Staff: 2
Annual Budget: Under $10,000
Tax: 501(c)(6)

Personnel:
Executive Director: Mai Hoang
   E-Mail: maihoang@usccc.org
Legal Counsel and Co-Editor: Philip Wong

Historical Note:
USCCC is a not-for-profit, bi-national membership organization dedicated to developing U.S.-China trade and investment activities. Membership: $10,000 (Chairman's

Circle Member); $2,000 (Corporate Sponsor); $350 (General Member).

Meetings/Conferences: Annual

Publications:
China Alert
USCCC Newsletter

United Steelworkers of America (1942)

Five Gateway Center
Pittsburgh, PA 15222
Tel: (412) 562-2400
Website: usw.org
Members: 660000 individuals
Staff: 900
Annual Budget: $50-100,000

Personnel:
International President: Leo W. Gerard
   E-Mail: lgerard@uswa.org

Historical Note:
Established as the Steel Workers Organizing Committee (SWOC) in 1936 to coordinate the massive drive to organize the North American steel industry, the organization became the United Steelworkers in 1942. It underwent a 2005 merger with Paper, Allied-Industrial, Chemical and Energy Workers International Union (PACE). It works to improve jobs, build a better future for steelworkers' families and to promote fairness, justice and equality both on the job and in society.

Publications:
FrontLines
Membership Directory; on-line
Pulp Truth
SOAR
The Oil Worker
USW@Work Magazine; quarterly

United Suffolk Sheep Association (1935)

P.O. Box 995
Ottumwa, IA 52501-0995
Tel: (641) 684-5291 *Fax:* (641) 682-9449
E-Mail: info@u-s-s-a.org
Website: u-s-s-a.org
Members: 2500 individuals
Staff: 12
Annual Budget: $100-250,000
Tax: 501(c)(5)

Personnel:
Executive Secretary: Amanda Evarts

Historical Note:
Merged with American Suffolk Sheep Association in 1998 and a member of the National Pedigree Livestock Council, USSA encourages and supports Suffolk breeders of all ages in their efforts to maintain pedigree registry and promote the Suffolk breed. It also oversees the National Junior Suffolk Sheep Association. Membership: $35/year (Individual).

Meetings/Conferences: Annual
2013 - Choteau, MT (Weatherbeater Barn)/Sept. 7

United Synagogue of Conservative Judaism (1913)

820 Second Ave.
Tenth Floor
New York, NY 10017-4504
Tel: (212) 533-7800 *Fax:* (212) 353-9439
E-Mail: info@uscj.org
Website: uscj.org
Members: 760 congregations
Staff: 47
Annual Budget: $10-25,000,000
Tax: 501(c)(3)

Personnel:
Chief Executive Officer: Rabbi Steven Wernick
   E-Mail: wernick@uscj.org
Director, Book and Media Center: Dorrie Berkowitz
   E-Mail: berkowitz@uscj.org
Assistant to the Director, Book Service: Elaine Bieber
   E-Mail: bieber@uscj.org
Director, Solomon Schechter Day School Network: Dr. Elaine Cohen
   E-Mail: cohen@uscj.org
Director, Online Communications, Media and Marketing: Andrea Glick
   E-Mail: aglick@uscj.org
Chief Operating Officer: Jerry Herman
   E-Mail: herman@uscj.org
Director, Facilities and Meetings: Adam Kofinas
   E-Mail: kofinas@uscj.org

Director, Information Technology: Martin S. Kunoff MBA
   E-Mail: kunoff@uscj.org
Director, Human Resources: Vivian Lewis
   E-Mail: vlewis@uscj.org
Chief Resource Development and Marketing Officer: Barry Mael
   E-Mail: mael@uscj.org

Historical Note:
-Associated with the Federation of Jewish Men's Clubs, the Women's League for Conservative Judaism, the Jewish Theological Seminary of America and the Rabbinical Assembly. Mission of USCJ is to strengthen and serve congregations and their members. Also works in concert with other institutions and organizations of the conservative movement to promote, nurture and foster a vibrant movement. Member congregations are conservative U.S. and Canadian congregations.

Meetings/Conferences: Biennial
Conference Chair: Adam Kofinas
Number of non-conference events/year: 1

Publications:
CJ: Voices of Conservative/Masorti Judaism; quarterly; adv.
eNews; monthly
Leadership News/Next Step Newsletter
Membership Directory; annually

United Transportation Union (1969)

24950 Country Club Blvd.
Suite 340
North Olmsted, OH 44070-5333
Tel: (216) 228-9400 *Fax:* (216) 228-5755
Website: utu.org
Members: 125,000 active and retired railroad, bus and mass transit workers
Staff: 100
Annual Budget: $25-50,000,000
Tax: 501(c)(5)

Personnel:
International President: Malcolm B. Futhey Jr.
   E-Mail: president@utu.org
Assistant director, Marketing and Sales: Laurie Baker
   E-Mail: l_baker@utu.org
Executive Director, Finance and Human Resources: Stu Collins
   E-Mail: s_collin@utu.org
Assistant General Counsel: Erika A. Diehl
   E-Mail: e_diehl@utu.org
Director, Information Systems: Matt Dolin
   E-Mail: m_dolin@utu.org
Director, Accounting and Financial Reporting: Rick Kusnic
   E-Mail: r_kusnic@utu.org
Director, Marketing Management: Dan Lough
   E-Mail: d_lough@utu.org
General Secretary and Treasurer: Kim Thompson
   E-Mail: gst@utu.org
Director, Membership Services: Jeff Weisbarth
   E-Mail: j_weisba@utu.org

Historical Note:
UTU's purpose is to set the pace in national and state legislative activity, collective bargaining, and in efforts to improve safety and working conditions on the railroads and in the bus, transit and airline industries. Members are conductors, brakemen, switchmen, ground service personnel, locomotive engineers, hostlers and workers in associated crafts.

Publications:
Directory of UTU Designated Legal Counsel; on-line
UTU International Directory; on-line
UTU News; monthly

United Union of Roofers, Waterproofers and Allied Workers (1919)

1660 L St. NW
Suite 800
Washington, DC 20036-5646
Tel: (202) 463-7663 *Fax:* (202) 463-6906
E-Mail: roofers@unionroofers.com
Website: unionroofers.com
Members: 22000 individuals
Staff: 7
Annual Budget: $10-25,000,000
Tax: 501(c)(5)

Personnel:
International President: Kinsey M. Robinson
   E-Mail: roofers@unionroofers.com
Director, Research and Education: John Barnhard
   E-Mail: johnb@unionroofers.com

International Secretary and Treasurer: Robert J. Danley
Vice President: James Hadel
    E-Mail: jimh@unionroofers.com
Director, Financial Services: Frank Massey
Media Director: Erin C. McDermott
    E-Mail: erinm@unionroofers.com
Director, Market Development: Jordan Ritenour

Historical Note:
UURWAW works to promote and maintain the unionized roofing industry by providing welfare, vacation, pension and annuity benefits to it's members.

Meetings/Conferences: Annual

Publications:
The Journeyman Roofer & Waterproofer Magazine; quarterly

Universities Council on Water Resources *(1962)*
C/O Southern Illinois University Carbondale
1000 Faner Dr., Room 4543
Carbondale, IL 62901
Tel: (618) 453-6020
E-Mail: ucowr@siu.edu
Website: ucowr.org
Members: 93 institutions and foreign affiliations
Staff: 2
Annual Budget: $100-250,000

Personnel:
Executive Director and Editor: Christopher L. Lant PhD
    E-Mail: clant@siu.edu
Office Administrator: Laura Germann
    E-Mail: felix@siu.edu

Historical Note:
Formerly (1964) known as the Universities Council on Hydrology. UCOWR is a voluntary organization of universities engaged in education, research, public service, international activities and legislative pursuits relevant to all aspects of water resources. Membership: $20 (Student); $70 (Regular); $450 (Academic); $450-4000 (Non- Academic Organizations, based on total number of employees).

Meetings/Conferences: Annual
2013 - Lake Tahoe, CA/June 11 - 13

Publications:
Delegate Directory; on-line
Journal of Contemporary Water Research and Education; quarterly; adv.

Universities Research Association *(1965)*
1111 19th St. NW
Suite 400
Washington, DC 20036
Tel: (202) 293-1382 *Fax:* (202) 293-5012
E-Mail: info@ura-hq.org
Website: ura-hq.org
Members: 85 universities
Staff: 8
Annual Budget: $1-2,000,000
Tax: 501(c)(3)

Personnel:
Executive Director: Dr. Marta Cehelsky

Historical Note:
URA is a consortium of universities whose purpose is to educate and train technical, research and student personnel in said sciences. Initial membership cost: $10,000; no annual dues.

Universities Space Research Association *(1969)*
10211 Wincopin Cir.
Suite 500
Columbia, MD 21044-3432
Tel: (410) 730-2656 *Fax:* (410) 730-3496
E-Mail: info@usra.edu
Website: usra.edu
Members: 104 institutions
Staff: 18
Annual Budget: $50-100,000,000
Tax: 501(c)(3)

Personnel:
President and Chief Executive Officer: Dr. Frederick A. Tarantino
    E-Mail: ftarantino@usra.edu
Chief Financial Officer: Karin Hilser
Director, University Relations: Hussein D. Jirdeh
    E-Mail: hjirdeh@usra.edu
Chief Information Officer: Alan Marchant
Vice President, Program Development and General Counsel: Dr. Scot Williamson

Historical Note:
USRA seeks to advance the space-related sciences and exploration through innovative research, technology, and educational programs. Only Ph.D.-granting universities having graduate programs in space sciences or technology are eligible for membership. Membership: $1,200 (University, one-time assessment fee).

Meetings/Conferences:
Number of non-conference events/year: 1

Publications:
Astronomy and Astrophysics; on-line
Biomedicine and Biotechnology; on-line
Member Directory; on-line
Planetary Science; on-line

Membership List Available to Non-members

University and College Designers Association *(1970)*
199 W. Enon Springs Rd.
Suite 300
Smyrna, TN 37167
Tel: (615) 459-4559 *Fax:* (615) 459-5229
E-Mail: info@ucda.com
Website: ucda.com
Members: 1200 individuals
Staff: 2
Annual Budget: $250-500,000

Personnel:
Executive Director: Tadson Bussey
    E-Mail: tadson@ucda.com
Director, Membership Services: Walter T. Bowen Sr.
    E-Mail: bowenw@ucda.com

Historical Note:
UCDA's mission is to promote excellence in visual communications for educational institutions. Members are designers, design educators, art directors, creative directors, managers, directors of print shops, editors, writers, directors of media services, photographers, and businesses associated with visual communication. Membership: $195 (Professional/Associate); $150 (Educator); $250 (Corporate); $50 (Student/Subscriber); $75 (Retired).

Meetings/Conferences: Annual
Number of non-conference events/year: 1

Publications:
Designer Magazine; quarterly
Home Page Newsletter; monthly
Membership Directory; on-line

University Aviation Association *(1947)*
3410 Skyway Dr.
Auburn, AL 36830-6444
Tel: (334) 844-2434 *Fax:* (334) 844-2432
E-Mail: uaamail@uaa.aero
Website: uaa.aero
Members:
105 colleges
525 members
Staff: 3
Annual Budget: $250-500,000
Tax: 501(c)(3)

Personnel:
Executive Director: Carolyn Williamson CAE
    E-Mail: uaamail@uaa.aero
Coordinator, Office Administration: Mary Chandler
Coordinator, Member Services: David McAlister

Historical Note:
UAA's mission is to promote and foster excellence in collegiate aviation education by providing a forum for students, faculty, staff and practitioners to share ideas, to enhance the quality of education, and to develop stronger programs and curricula. Members are individuals, institutions, and corporations concerned with aviation education at the university level. Membership: $80 (Individual); $550 (Corporate/Institutional); $250 (High School); $30 (Student).

Meetings/Conferences: Annual

Publications:
Collegiate Aviation News; quarterly
Collegiate Aviation Review; semi-annually
Institutional Membership List; semi-annually

Membership List Available to Non-members

University Council for Educational Administration *(1957)*
Curry School of Education, The University of Virginia, 405 Emmet St. South
P. O. Box 400287
Charlottesville, VA 22904

Tel: (434) 243-1041 *Fax:* (434) 924-1384
E-Mail: ucea@virginia.edu
Website: ucea.org
Members: 74 universities
Staff: 10
Annual Budget: $500-1,000,000

Personnel:
Executive Director: Michelle D. Young
    E-Mail: mdy8n@virginia.edu
Executive Assistant: Rhonda Douthit
    E-Mail: rmdouthit@virginia.edu
Manager, Events and Special Projects: Kirstine Sigloh
    E-Mail: ksiglohva@gmail.com
Director, Finance: Lisa C. Wright
    E-Mail: lcw@lisacwrightcpa.com

Historical Note:
UCEA's mission is to improve the professional preparation of educational administrators to promote the development of professional knowledge in school improvement and administration. Membership: $2,000/year.

Meetings/Conferences: Annual
Conference Chair: Kirstine Sigloh
2013 - Indianapolis, IN (Hyatt Regency Indianapolis)/ Nov. 7 - 10/1-10 exhibitors
2014 - Washington, DC (Washington Hilton)/Nov. 20 - 24/1-10 exhibitors

Publications:
Journal of Research on Leadership Education; annually
Membership Directory; on-line
UCEA Connections; monthly

Membership List Available to Non-members

University Film and Video Association *(1947)*
960 War Eagle Dr. South
Colorado Springs, CO 80919
E-Mail: ufvahome@aol.com
Website: ufva.org
Members: 1000 professionals and institutions
Staff: 3
Annual Budget: $500-1,000,000
Tax: 501(c)(3)

Personnel:
President: Rob Sabal
    E-Mail: robert_sabal@emerson.edu
Editorial Vice President: Steve Lipkin
    E-Mail: steven.lipkin@wmich.edu
Treasurer: Tom Sanny
    E-Mail: tsanny@me.com

Historical Note:
Originally the University Film Producers Association, it became the University Film Association in 1968 and assumed its present name in 1982. UFVA is an international organization where media production and writing meets the history, theory and criticism of the media. Members are image-makers and artists, teachers and students, archivists and distributors, college departments, libraries and manufacturers. Membership: $95 (Active); $175 (Institutional); $30 (Student); $325 (Sustaining).

Meetings/Conferences: Annual

Publications:
Member Directory; on-line
The Journal of Film and Video

University Photographers Association of America *(1961)*
Moraine Valley Community College
9000 W. College Pkwy.
Palos Hills, IL 60465
Tel: (708) 974-5495 *Fax:* (585) 395-2723
Website: upaa.org
Members: 300 individuals
Staff: 2
Annual Budget: $10-25,000

Personnel:
President: Glenn Carpenter
    E-Mail: carpenter@morainevalley.edu
Treasurer: Nick Romanenko
    E-Mail: nroman@rci.rutgers.edu

Historical Note:
UPAA is an international organization of college and university photographers concerned with the application and practice of photography and is committed to photographic excellence through continuing education and networking with professional colleagues. Members are college and university photographers who are concerned with the application and practice of photography. Membership: $50 (Full); $35 (Associate); $25 (Student).

University Professional & Continuing Education Association (1915)

One Dupont Cir.
Suite 615
Washington, DC 20036
Tel: (434) 243-1041 *Fax:* (434) 924-1384
E-Mail: ucea@virginia.edu
Website: ucea.edu
Members:
425 institutions
2000 individuals
Staff: 10
Annual Budget: $1-2,000,000
Tax: 501(c)(3)

Personnel:
Chief Executive Officer: Bob Hansen
    E-Mail: rhansen@upcea.edu
Contact, Finance: Lori Derkay CAE
    E-Mail: lderkay@upcea.edu
Director, Communications: Kandace Gilligan MA
    E-Mail: kgilligan@ucea.edu
Financial Manager: Ron Hart
    E-Mail: rhart@ucea.edu
Chief Learning Officer: Amy Heitzman MA, MD
    E-Mail: aheitzman@upcea.edu
Interim Executive Director and Director, Membership and International Affairs: Cyrus K. Homayounpour
    E-Mail: cyrus@ucea.edu
Director, Conferences: Natalia Kats
    E-Mail: nkats@ucea.edu
Manager, Member Services: Megan Mills
    E-Mail: mmills@upcea.edu
Coordinator, Administrative and Meetings: Shelby Scango
    E-Mail: sscango@upcea.edu
Director, Corporate Relations and Associate Director: Cheri Simpson MBA, PhD
    E-Mail: csimpson@upcea.edu

Historical Note:
Formerly (1980) known as the National University Extension Association and then (1996) National University Continuing Education Association and University Continuing Education Association. UPCEA's mission is to assist institutions of higher learning and affiliated non-profit organizations and to provide national leadership in support of policies that advance workforce and professional development. Members are accredited colleges and universities with continuing higher education programs and professional staff. Membership: $1,100-3,000(Institution); $4,800-6,400 (Proprietary); $980-2,800 (Others).

Meetings/Conferences: Annual
Conference Chair: Natalia Kats
2013 - Boston, MA (Boston Marriott Copley)/April 4 - 6
Number of non-conference events/year: 6

Publications:
Continuing Higher Education Review; annually
InFocus; quarterly

University Professional & Continuing Education Association (1915)

One Dupont Cir.
Suite 615
Washington, DC 20036
Tel: (202) 659-3130 *Fax:* (202) 785-0374
Website: upcea.edu
Members:
350 institutional and affiliates
2200 professional
Staff: 6
Annual Budget: $1-2,000,000
Tax: 501(c)(3)

Personnel:
Chief Executive Officer: Dr. Robert J. Hansen
    E-Mail: rhansen@upcea.edu
Director, Center for Research and Consulting: Jim Fong
    E-Mail: jfong@upcea.edu
Director, Communications: Kandace Gilligan MA
    E-Mail: kgilligan@upcea.edu
Chief Learning Officer: Amy Heitzman MA, MEd
    E-Mail: aheitzman@upcea.edu
Manager, Member Services: Megan Mills
    E-Mail: mmills@upcea.edu
Coordinator, Administrative and Meetings: Shelby Scango
    E-Mail: sscango@upcea.edu

Historical Note:
Formerly known as National University Continuing Education Association. UPCEA's seeks to advance

university professional and continuing education. Members include both public and private accredited colleges and universities, as well as nonprofit organizations. Membership: $650-6570 (Institutional/Professional); $980 (Affiliate); $50 (Additional Professional Individual).

Meetings/Conferences: Annual
Conference Chair: Amy Heitzman MA, MEd
2013 - Boston, MA/April 3 - 6
2013 - Boston, MA (Copley Place Marriott)/April 3 - 5
Number of non-conference events/year: 2

Publications:
Continuing Higher Education Review; annually
e-News; on-line
InFocus Newsletter; monthly; adv.

University Risk Management and Insurance Association (1966)

P.O. Box 1027
Bloomington, IN 47402-1027
Tel: (812) 855-6683 *Fax:* (812) 856-3149
E-Mail: urmia@urmia.org
Website: urmia.org
Members:
500 colleges and universities
100 companies
Staff: 6
Annual Budget: $1-2,000,000

Personnel:
Executive Director: Jenny Whittington
    E-Mail: jenny@urmia.org
Administrator, Office and Membership Services: Keely Davenport
Administrator, Database and Website: Leslie Ems
    E-Mail: leslie@urmia.org
Associate, Communications and Marketing: Christie Wahlert
    E-Mail: christie@urmia.org

Historical Note:
URMIA's mission is to promote the advancement and application of effective risk management principles and practices in institutions of higher education. Members are colleges and universities with insurance or risk management offices. Membership: $400-550 (Institutional); $100-200 (Additional Deputy); $850 (Affiliate); $100 (Individual); $200 (International).

Meetings/Conferences: Annual
2013 - Phoenix, AZ (Arizona Biltmore Resort and Spa)/ Oct. 12 - 16
2014 - Louisville, KY (Louisville Marriott Downtown)/ Sept. 20 - 24
Number of non-conference events/year: 8

Publications:
Membership Directory
URMIA Insights; monthly
URMIA Journal; annually

University/Resident Theatre Association (1969)

1560 Broadway
Suite 1103
New York, NY 10036-1518
Tel: (212) 221-1130 *Fax:* (212) 869-2752
E-Mail: info@urta.com
Website: urta.com
Members: 41 graduate schools and theaters
Staff: 162
Annual Budget: $1-2,000,000
Tax: 501(c)(3)

Personnel:
Executive Director: Scott L. Steele
    E-Mail: slsteele@urta.com

Historical Note:
Our member institutions have training programs which involve a comprehensive approach to theatre training; include one or more degree offerings leading to an MFA in theatre; and contain a graduate student body of a significant size and scope as to allow students to artistically collaborate with and intellectually stimulate one another.Membership: $2698/year (Organization).

Continuing Education:
Enrollment: 41
Certification Designation/s: CMP

Meetings/Conferences:
Number of non-conference events/year: 3

Publications:
Directory of U/RTA; annually; adv.
U/RTA Update Newsletter; semi-monthly; adv.

Membership List Available to Non-members

Urban Affairs Association (1969)

C/O University of Wisconsin-Milwaukee
P.O. Box 413
Milwaukee, WI 53201-0413
Tel: (414) 229-3025 *Fax:* (302) 831-4225
E-Mail: info@uaamail.org
Website: urbanaffairsassociation.org
Members: 638 institutional, individual and student members
Staff: 3
Annual Budget: $250-500,000
Tax: 501(c)(3)

Personnel:
Executive Director: Margaret Wilder
    E-Mail: mwilder@udel.edu
Webmaster and Manager, Communications: Sue Peacock
Event Planner: Shelvia (Shelly) Tillinghast
    E-Mail: shelviat@udel.edu

Historical Note:
Formerly (1981) the Council of University Institutes for Urban Affairs. UAA's mission is to promote more effective policies and procedures relating to the study of urban affairs and urbanization. Members are urban specialists from private or public universities who are involved in teaching, research or public service. Membership: $345 (Institutional); $60 (Individual); $30 (Student).

Meetings/Conferences: Annual
Conference Chair: Shelvia (Shelly) Tillinghast
2013 - San Francisco, CA (The Fairmont Hotel)/April 3 - 6
2014 - San Antonio, TX (Westin Riverwalk)/March 19 - 22

Publications:
Membership Directory; on-line
The Journal of Urban Affairs; adv.
Urban Affairs; semi-annually

Membership List Available to Non-members

Urban and Regional Information Systems Association (1963)

701 Lee St.
Suite 680
Des Plaines, IL 60016
Tel: (847) 824-6300 *Fax:* (847) 824-6363
E-Mail: info@urisa.org
Website: urisa.org
Members: 2000 individuals
Staff: 6
Annual Budget: $1-2,000,000
Tax: 501(c)(3)

Personnel:
Executive Director: Wendy Nelson
    E-Mail: wnelson@urisa.org
Accountant and Finance Administrator: Ann Bishopp
    E-Mail: abishopp@urisa.org
Coordinator, Conferences and Meetings: Patricia Francis
    E-Mail: pfrancis@urisa.org
Manager, Education: Jennifer Griffith
    E-Mail: jgriffith@urisa.org
Registrar, Database Manager and Contact, Publications: Verlanda McBride
    E-Mail: vmcbride@urisa.org

Historical Note:
URISA's mission is to encourage a multi-disciplinary approach to the design and use of urban and regional information systems and provide quality professional education. Membership: $87.50-218.75 (Professional, Based on Submittal Date); $10-25 (Student, Submittal Date).

Continuing Education:
Certification Designation/s: GISPC

Meetings/Conferences: Annual
Conference Chair: Patricia Francis
2013 - Albuquerue, NM/March 4 - 7
2013 - Miami, FL (Hyatt Regency Miami)/June 17 - 20
Number of non-conference events/year: 11

Publications:
The GIS Professional; bi-monthly; adv.
URISA Digest; semi-monthly
URISA Journal; bi-annually; adv.
URISA Membership Directory; on-line

Membership List Available to Non-members

Urban Financial Services Coalition (1974)

1200 G St. NW
Suite 800

Washington, DC 20005
Tel: (202) 289-8335 Fax: (202) 434-8707
TollFree: (800) 996-8335
E-Mail: usfc@ufscnet.org
Website: ufscnet.org
Members: 2000 affiliates and 35 corporate
members
Staff: 7
Annual Budget: Under $10,000

Personnel:
President: Ditu Kasuyi
    E-Mail: kasuyiditu@gmail.com
Vice-President, Technology: Marlene Braithwaite
    E-Mail: mbraithwaite@msn.com
Secretary: Renee Coffiel
    E-Mail: secretary@ufscnet.org
Vice-President, Membership Services: Roderick Hayes
    E-Mail: Membership@ufscnet.org
Treasurer: Akili M. Johnson
    E-Mail: treasurer@ufscnet.org
Vice President, Legal Affairs: Melanie Lee
    E-Mail: MelanieLee@mleelaw.com

Historical Note:
Formerly (2000) National Association of Urban Bankers.
UFSC provides professional development programs,
supports educational advancement and promotes economic
empowerment for its members and minority communities
at large. Members, primarily from large institutions in
major metropolitan areas, are minority professionals in the
banking industry and related fields. Membership: $125/
year (National).

Meetings/Conferences: Annual
2013 - St. Louis, MO/June 13 - 15

Publications:
Membership Directory; on-line
Newsletter

Urban History Association (1988)
Department of History, University of Dayton
300 College Park
Dayton, OH 45469-1540
Tel: (312) 281-3145 Fax: (312) 281-3132
Website: uha.udayton.edu
Members: 425 individuals
Staff: 4
Annual Budget: $10-25,000
Tax: 501(c)(3)

Personnel:
President: Jon Teaford
Executive Secretary and Treasurer: Janet R. Bednarek
    E-Mail: janet.bednarek@notes.udayton.edu
Editor: David Goldfield

Historical Note:
UHA is affiliated with the International Planning History
Society. UHA's mission is to stimulate interest and
forwarding research and study in the history of the city
in all periods and geographical areas. Membership: $27
(Individual); $12 (Graduate Students/Libraries); $7
(Undergraduate); $135 (Six-year); $400 (Lifetime).

Meetings/Conferences: Biennial

Publications:
Journal of Urban History; bi-monthly
Urban History
Urban History Newsletter; bi-annually

Urban Libraries Council (1971)
125 S. Wacker Dr.
Suite 1050
Chicago, IL 60606
Tel: (312) 676-0999 Fax: (312) 676-0950
E-Mail: info@urbanlibraries.org
Website: urbanlibraries.org
Members: 25 Associates and 125 Libraries and 19
Corporate members
Staff: 6
Annual Budget: $1-2,000,000
Tax: 501(c)(3)

Personnel:
President and Chief Executive Officer: Susan B. Benton
    E-Mail: susanbenton@urbanlibraries.org
Contact, Media and Marketing: Mary Colleen Bragiel
    E-Mail: mcbragiel@urbanlibraries.org
Program Leader, Education: Amy Eshleman
    E-Mail: aeshleman@urbanlibraries.org
Contact, Administration and Finance: Angela B. Goodrich
    E-Mail: agoodrich@urbanlibraries.org

Contact, Membership Services and Communications: Jodi
Lazar
    E-Mail: jlazar@urbanlibraries.org

Historical Note:
A member organization of North America's public library
systems, ULC serves as a forum for research widely
recognized and used by public and private sector leaders.
Its members are thought leaders dedicated to leadership,
innovation and the continuous transformation of libraries to
meet community needs. Membership: $650-16,875/year.

Meetings/Conferences: Annual

Publications:
Member Directory; on-line
ULC e-Brief; weekly

Urgent Care Association of America (2004)
387 Shuman Blvd.
Suite 235W
Naperville, IL 60563
Tel: (877) 698-2262 Fax: (331) 457-5439
E-Mail: info@ucaoa.org
Website: ucaoa.org
Staff: 8
Annual Budget: $1-2,000,000
Tax: 501(c)(6)

Personnel:
Chief Executive Officer: Joanne Ray
Manager, Administration: Laura Carta
    E-Mail: lcarta@ucaoa.org
Director, Marketing: Laura Gaskill
    E-Mail: lgaskill@ucaoa.org
Director, Education: Carla Jamison
    E-Mail: cjamison@ucaoa.org
Manager, Membership: Jami Kral
    E-Mail: jkral@ucaoa.org
Director, Events: Colleen Richter
    E-Mail: crichter@ucaoa.org

Historical Note:
Represents professionals working in urgent care. Provides
leadership, education and resources for the practice
of urgent care. Membership open to physicians, non-
physicians, urgent care practices and other health related
organizations.

US Navy Veterans Association
1718 M St. NW
Washington, DC 20036
Tel: (202) 736-1725
Website: navyvets.tripod.com
Staff: 1
Annual Budget: $2-5,000,000

Personnel:
Chief Executive Officer: Jack L. Nimitz

US Rice Producers Association (1997)
2825 Wilcrest Dr.
Suite 505
Houston, TX 77042
Tel: (713) 974-7423 Fax: (713) 974-7696
Website: usriceproducers.com
Staff: 6
Annual Budget: $2-5,000,000
Tax: 501(c)(6)

Personnel:
President and Chief Executive Officer: Dwight Roberts
    E-Mail: dwight@usriceproducers.com
Vice president and General counsel: Fred Clark
Marketing Director: Marcela Garcia
    E-Mail: marcela@usriceproducers.com
Financial Director: Karen Miles
    E-Mail: karen@usriceproducers.com
Associate, Public Relations and Marketing: Kristen
O'Brien
Coordinator, Member Services: Veronica Vargas

Historical Note:
The US Rice Producers Association, representing rice
producers in Arkansas, California, Louisiana, Mississippi,
Missouri and Texas, is the only national rice producers'
organization comprised by producers, elected by producers
and representing producers in all six rice-producing states.

Publications:
RiceCAP Newsletter

USA Archery (1879)
711 N. Tejon St.
Colorado Springs, CO 80903
Tel: (719) 866-4576 Fax: (719) 632-4733

E-Mail: info@usarchery.org
Website: teamusa.org/USA-Archery.aspx
Staff: 15

Personnel:
Chief Executive Officer: Denise Parker
    E-Mail: dparker@usarchery.org
Specialist, Accounting and Finance: Cindy Clark
    E-Mail: cclark@usarchery.org
Contact, Public Relations and Marketing: Teresa Laconi
    E-Mail: tiaconi@usarchery.org
Manager, National Events: Katrina Weiss
    E-Mail: kweiss@usarchery.org

Historical Note:
USA Archery's mission is to provide the necessary resources
to foster strong athlete participation, competition and
training in the sport of archery. Membership: $50-1,500/
year.

Meetings/Conferences:
Conference Chair: Katrina Weiss
Number of non-conference events/year: 13

USA Maritime
1700 K St. NW
Washington, DC 20006
Tel: (202) 282-5000 Fax: (202) 282-5100
Website: usamaritime.org
Members: 19 Companies
Staff: 1
Annual Budget: $250-500,000

Personnel:
Chairman: James L. Henry

Historical Note:
Cargo preference laws, sustainment Food for Peace
program, food aid programs generally. USA Maritime is
a coalition of carriers and maritime unions committed to
promoting and protecting the U.S. Maritime Industry.

USA Rice Council
4301 N. Fairfax Dr.
Suite 425
Arlington, VA 22203
Tel: (703) 236-2300 Fax: (703) 236-2301
E-Mail: riceinfo@usarice.com
Website: usarice.com
Staff: 29
Annual Budget: $5-10,000,000
Tax: 501(c)(6)

Personnel:
President and Chief Executive Officer: Betsy Ward
Vice President, Meetings and Membership Services:
    Patricia Alderson
Director, Legislative Affairs and Communications: Johnny
Broussard
    E-Mail: jbroussard@usarice.com
Director, Meetings: Jeanette Davis
Senior Director, Communications: Stacy Fitzgerald-Redd
Senior Director, Human Resources and Administration:
    Lisa L. Gargano
Vice President, International Promotion: Jim Guinn
Vice President, Government Affairs: Reece Langley
    E-Mail: rlangley@usarice.com
Vice President, Finance and Administration: Linda Sieh

Historical Note:
Mission to promote and protect the interests of producers,
millers, merchants and allied businesses. International
promotion activities are directed at increasing awareness
and consumption of U.S. rice around the world.

Meetings/Conferences:
Conference Chair: Patricia Alderson

Publications:
USA Rice Daily; daily

USA Rice Federation (1994)
2101 Wilson Blvd.
Suite 610
Arlington, VA 22201
Tel: (703) 236-2300 Fax: (703) 236-2301
TollFree: (800) 888-7423
E-Mail: riceinfo@usarice.com
Website: usarice.com
Members: 150 organizations
Staff: 21
Annual Budget: $10-25,000,000
Tax: 501(c)(6)

Personnel:
President and Chief Executive Officer: Betsy Ward

Vice President, Meeting and Membership Services: Patricia Alderson
   E-Mail: talderson@usarice.com
Director, Legislative Affairs and Communications: John E. Broussard
   E-Mail: jbroussard@usarice.com
Chief Operating Officer: Robert "Bob" E. Cummings
   E-Mail: rcummings@usarice.com
Director, Meetings: Jeanette Davis
   E-Mail: jdavis@usarice.com
Senior Director, Communications: Stacy Fitzgerald-Redd
   E-Mail: sfitzgerald-redd@usarice.com
Senior Director, Human Resources and Administration: Lisa L. Gargano
Vice President, Government Affairs: Reece Langley
   E-Mail: rlangley@usarice.com
Director, National Consumer Education and Foodservice Marketing: Judy Rusignuolo
   E-Mail: jrusignuolo@usarice.com
Vice President, Finance and Administration: Linda Sieh

Historical Note:
Founded as The Rice Industry. Became the Rice Council for Market Development in 1960, and assumed its present name in 1990. Mission is to promote and protect the interests of producers, millers, merchants and allied businesses. The USA Rice Federation is an umbrella organization representing three associations: U.S. Rice Producers Group, Rice Millers Association, and U.S.A. Rice Council. USARF supports the U.S. rice producers, millers, marketers and others allied industries. Membership: $1500-9,000/year.

Meetings/Conferences: Annual
Conference Chair: Jeanette Davis

Publications:
Membership Directory; on-line
USA Rice Daily; daily

Membership List Available to Non-members

USA Sprinkler Fitter Business Managers Association *(1996)*
115 W Walnut St.
Suite 2
Lodi, CA 95240
Tel: (209) 368-5229 *Fax:* (209) 367-1722
E-Mail: randy@usasprinklerfitters.org
Website: usasprinklerfitters.org
Staff: 1

Personnel:
Executive Director: Randy D. Roxson
   E-Mail: randy@usasprinklerfitters.org

Historical Note:
Sprinkler Fitters & Apprentice in Seattle, WA is a private company categorized under Trade Union. Current estimates show this company has an annual revenue of unknown and employs a staff of approximately 1 to 4. Companies like Sprinkler Fitters & Apprentice usually offer: Labour Unions, Central Labor Union, Afl Cio Labor Unions, Trade Labor Unions and Organizing Labor Unions.

USA Taekwondo *(1945)*
One Olympic Plaza
Suite 104 C
Colorado Springs, CO 80909
Tel: (719) 866-4632 *Fax:* (719) 866-4642
Website: usa-taekwondo.us
Members: 15000 individuals
Staff: 18
Annual Budget: $2-5,000,000

Personnel:
Chief Executive Officer: Eric Parthen
   E-Mail: Eric.Parthen@usa-taekwondo.us
Director, Communications: Bill Kellick
   E-Mail: bill.kellick@usa-taekwondo.us
Director, Events: Travis Oosthoek
   E-Mail: Travis.Oosthoek@usa-taekwondo.us
Manager, Membership Services: Amanda Rubin
   E-Mail: amanda.rubin@usa-taekwondo.us
Manager, Certification: Penny Warren
   E-Mail: Penny.Warren@usa-taekwondo.us

Historical Note:
USAT's mission is to enable United States athletes to achieve sustained competitive excellence and promote and grow the sport of taekwonda in the United States. Membership: $90-115 (Family); $35 (Individual); $20 (Support); $500 (Life).

Meetings/Conferences: Annual
Conference Chair: Travis Oosthoek

2013 - Colorado Springs, CO (Cheyenne Mountain Resort)/Jan. 12 - 13

Publications:
Magazine; quarterly; adv.
USAT e-Newsletter; monthly

USA Volleyball *(1928)*
4065 Sinton Rd.
Suite 200
Colorado Springs, CO 80907
Tel: (719) 228-6800 *Fax:* (719) 228-6899
Website: teamusa.org/USA-Volleyball.aspx
Members:
250000 individuals
35 organizations
Staff: 7
Annual Budget: $250-500,000

Personnel:
Chief Executive Officer: Doug Beal
   E-Mail: doug.beal@usav.org
Director, Communications and Technology: Brent Buzbee
   E-Mail: brent.buzbee@usav.org
Director, Coaching Education (CAP): Diana Cole
   E-Mail: diana.cole@usav.org
Manager, Media Relations and Publications: B.J. Evans
   E-Mail: bj.evans@usav.org
Senior Director, Financial Services: Stacie Kearns
   E-Mail: stacie.kearns@usav.org
Chief Operating Officer: Chris Vadala
   E-Mail: chris.vadala@usav.org
Manager, National Team Events and Marketing: Melissa Weymouth
   E-Mail: melissa.weymouth@usav.org

Historical Note:
USA Volleyball (USAV) is the National Governing Body (NGB) for the sport of volleyball in the United States and is recognized as such by the Federation International de Volleyball (FIVB) and the United States Olympic Committee (USOC). USAV's mission is to work towards opportunity for all to participate.

Meetings/Conferences:
Conference Chair: Melissa Weymouth

Publications:
International Journal of Volleyball Research
Membership Directory; on-line
Rotations; bi-monthly; adv.
Volleyball USA; quarterly; adv.

Used Textbook Association *(2006)*
7375 Day Creek Blvd.
Suite 103-211
Rancho Cucamonga, CA 91739
Tel: (888) 724-3338
E-Mail: membership@usedtextbookassociation.org
Website: usedtextbookassociation.org
Members: 350 bookstores
Staff: 2
Annual Budget: $50-100,000

Personnel:
Executive Director: Stacey L. Douglas
   E-Mail: stacey.douglas@usedtextbookassociation.org

Historical Note:
UTA's mission is to advocate the role and value of used textbooks in the marketplace and is working toward a marketplace solution to the problem of textbook affordability while still providing students with high-quality educational materials. Only bookstores engaged in the retail sale of textbooks for colleges or universities and maintain a physical location in proximity to a college or university campus can become a member. Membership: $100-600/year (Bookstore, based on annual sales volume).

Publications:
Membership Directory; on-line
UTA Newsletter

Used Truck Association *(1988)*
National Truck Protection
Six Commerce Dr., Suite 200
Canford, NJ 07016
E-Mail: contact@uta.org
Website: uta.org
Members: 286 individuals
Staff: 13
Annual Budget: $50-100,000

Personnel:

President: Rick Clark
   E-Mail: rick@uta.org

Historical Note:
UTA is comprised of used truck professionals and associated businesses committed to strengthening the used truck industry. Membership: $350 (Corporate); $100 (Professional).

Meetings/Conferences: Annual
Conference Chair: Tim Ormsby

Publications:
Industry Watch online; monthly; adv.
Membership Directory; annually

Membership List Available to Non-members

USENIX: The Advanced Computing Systems Association *(1975)*
2560 Ninth St.
Suite 215
Berkeley, CA 94710
Tel: (510) 528-8649 *Fax:* (510) 548-5738
E-Mail: office@usenix.org
Website: usenix.org
Staff: 13
Annual Budget: $2-5,000,000
Tax: 501(c)(3)

Personnel:
Co-Executive Director and Contact, Event Sales and Marketing: Anne Dickison
   E-Mail: anne@usenix.org
Managing Editor: Rikki Endsley
   E-Mail: rikki@usenix.org
Editor: Rik Farrow
   E-Mail: rik@usenix.org
Production Editor, Information Systems and Production: Arnold Gatilao
   E-Mail: arnold@usenix.org
Conference Administrative Assistant: Andrew Gustafson
   E-Mail: andrew@usenix.org
Office and Member Services Administrative Assistant: Sara Hernandez
   E-Mail: sara@usenix.org
Education Director: Dan Klein
   E-Mail: dvk@usenix.org
Manager, Marketing Communications: Julie Miller
   E-Mail: julie@usenix.org
Manager, Human Resource and Finance: Toni Veglia
   E-Mail: toni@usenix.org

Historical Note:
USENIX's mission is to foster technical excellence and innovation, support and disseminate research with a practical bias, provide a neutral forum for discussion of technical issues, encourage computing outreach into the community at large. Membership consists of engineers, system administrators, scientists, and technicians. Membership: $20-495/year.

Meetings/Conferences:
Conference Chair: Andrew Gustafson
2013 - San Jose, CA (Fairmont San Jose)/Feb. 12 - 15
2013 - San Jose, CA/June 25 - 28
2013 - San Jose, CA (Fairmont San Jose)/June 26 - 28
2013 - Washington, DC/Nov. 3 - 8
2014 - Seattle, WA/Nov. 9 - 14
2015 - Washington, DC/Dec. 6 - 11
2016 - Boston, MA/Dec. 4 - 9
Number of non-conference events/year: 11

Publications:
Computing Systems; quarterly
The USENIX Magazine; bi-monthly; adv.

User Experience Professionals Association *(1991)*
140 N. Bloomingdale Rd.
Bloomingdale, IL 60108-1017
Tel: (630) 980-4997 *Fax:* (630) 351-8490
E-Mail: office@usabilityprofessionals.org
Website: usabilityprofessionals.org
Members: 2400 individuals
Staff: 4
Annual Budget: $1-2,000,000
Tax: 501(c)(6)

Personnel:
Executive Director: John E. Kasper CAE, PhD
   E-Mail: executive-director@uxpa.org
Director , Membership Services: Elizabeth Kasper Goins
   E-Mail: member_services@uxpa.org
Manager, Meetings: Emma J. Leighton
Director, Membership Services, Conferences and Manager, Publications: Nicole A. Tafoya

E-Mail: publications@uxpa.org

Historical Note:
Formerly, Usability Professionals' Association, assumed its present name in 2012. UXPA's goal is to work on the practice of usability, user-centered design (UCD), and user experience (UX) and facilitate professional development and education within the UX field. Members are usability specialists, interface/interaction designers, information architects, ethnographers, web design and communicators. Membership: $100 (Professional); $35 (Student).

Meetings/Conferences: Annual
Conference Chair: Nicole A. Tafoya
Number of non-conference events/year: 1

Publications:
Journal of Usability Studies; quarterly
Membership Directory; on-line
UPA Monthly; monthly
UPA Voice; bi-monthly
User Experience Magazine; quarterly; adv.

USFN-America's Mortgage Banking Attorneys
625 The City Dr.
Suite 310
Orange, CA 92868
Tel: (714) 838-7167 *Fax:* (714) 573-2650
TollFree: (800) 635-6128
E-Mail: info@usfn.org
Website: usfn.org
Staff: 7

Personnel:
Executive Director and Chief Executive Officer: Alberta E. Hultman CAE
  E-Mail: ahultman@usfn.org
Accounting and Database Coordinator: Valji Bagada
  E-Mail: vbagada@usfn.org
Director, Education and Marketing: Alexis A. Haughton CMP
  E-Mail: ahaughton@usfn.org
Office Administrator: Kelly J. Mauras
Associate Editor: Celinda Sandoval
  E-Mail: csandoval@usfn.org
Director, Publications and Services: R. Hillary Willett Esq.
  E-Mail: hwillett@usfn.org

Historical Note:
The Mission of USFN is to promote competent, professional and ethical representation among the members and the real estate finance industry. It supports the advancement of the real estate finance industry through education, legislation, political and governmental reform.

Publications:
The USFN e-Update; monthly; adv.
USFN Member Directory; on-line
USFN Report; quarterly; adv.

Utah Association of Public Charter Schools
(2002)
PO Box 2583
Salt Lake City, UT 84110
Tel: (801) 960-2583 *Fax:* (801) 657-4712
E-Mail: info@utahcharters.org
Website: utahcharters.org
Members: 40,000 students
Staff: 1
Annual Budget: $100-250,000
Tax: 501(c)(3)

Personnel:
President: Chris Bleak
  E-Mail: chrisrbleak@utahcharters.org

Historical Note:
UAPCS mission is to promote and support quality charter schools in Utah.

Publications:
Magazine; semi-annually
Newsletter; weekly

Utilimetrics/Alliance for Advanced Metering & Data Management Solutions *(1987)*
401 N. Michigan Ave.
Chicago, IL 60611-4267
Tel: (312) 321-6882 *Fax:* (312) 673-6995
E-Mail: info@utilimetrics.org
Website: utilimetrics.org
Members: 2000 companies
Staff: 11
Annual Budget: $1-2,000,000
Tax: 501(c)(6)

Personnel:

Interim Executive Director: Brad Barbera
  E-Mail: bbarbera@utilimetrics.org
Manager, Operations: Janice Greenberg MPA
  E-Mail: jgreenberg@utilimetrics.org
Senior Manager, Information Technology: Denis Janis
  E-Mail: djanis@utilimetrics.org
Director, Event Services: Perry Juliano
  E-Mail: pjuliano@utilimetrics.org
Senior Vice President, Education and Learning Services: Carol McGury
  E-Mail: cmcgury@smithbucklin.com
Contact, Meetings and Conventions: Matt McLaughlin
  E-Mail: matt_mclaughlin@corcexpo.com
Director, Marketing: Joel Mendes MA
  E-Mail: jmendes@utilimetrics.org
Director, Meeting Services: Louise Pochelski CMP
  E-Mail: lpochelski@utilimetrics.org
Director, Education: Debby Scheck MA
  E-Mail: dscheck@utilimetrics.org
Senior Manager, Financial Services: Jay Schommer CPA
  E-Mail: jschommer@utilimetrics.org
Coordinator, Membership Services: Donna Stevens
  E-Mail: dstevens@utilimetrics.org

Historical Note:
AMRA's mission is to provide education and advocacy for utilities and information about technologies that lead to improved operations, customer service and resource utilization. Members develop and implement automated resource- management technologies and participate in standardization and regulatory activities. Membership: $500-3,500 (Company, based on annual revenue); $500 (Associate); $125 (Student).

Meetings/Conferences: Annual
Conference Chair: Louise Pochelski CMP
2013 - New Orleans, LA/Sept. 8 - 11
2014 - Orlando, FL/Sept. 28 - Oct. 1
Number of non-conference events/year: 1

Publications:
News Link; weekly; adv.
This Week at Utilimetrics; weekly; adv.
Utilimetrics Quarterly; quarterly; adv.

Utilities Telecom Council *(1948)*
1129 20th St. NW
Suite 350
Washington, DC 20036
Tel: (202) 872-0030 *Fax:* (202) 872-1331
TollFree: (800) 900-4882
E-Mail: marketing@utc.org
Website: utc.org
Members: 900 companies
Staff: 22
Annual Budget: $5-10,000,000
Tax: 501(c)(6)

Personnel:
President and Chief Executive Officer: Connie Durcsak
  E-Mail: connie.durcsak@utc.org
Finance Director and Controller: Natasha Bailey
  E-Mail: natasha.bailey@utc.org
Manager, Technology Partner Relations: Andy Browne
  E-Mail: andy.browne@utc.org
Vice President, Government and Industry Affairs and Deputy General Counsel: Brett Kilbourne
  E-Mail: brett.kilbourne@utc.org
Manager, Communications: Shari Nauflett
  E-Mail: shari.nauflett@utc.org
Vice President, Strategic Initiatives and General Counsel: Mike Oldak
  E-Mail: mike.oldak@utc.org
Director, Government Affairs and Legislative Counsel: Prudence Parks
  E-Mail: prudence.parks@utc.org
Specialist, Meetings and Events: Ashley Preece
  E-Mail: ashley.preece@utc.org
Industry Affairs Specialist: Neha Shah
  E-Mail: neha.shah@utc.org
Vice President, Member and Industry Services: Karnel Thomas
  E-Mail: karnel.thomas@utc.org

Historical Note:
UTC is dedicated to creating a favorable business, regulatory, and technological environment for companies that own, manage, or provide critical telecommunications systems in support of their core business. It represents electric, gas, water utilities, natural gas pipelines other critical infrastructure entities and industry stakeholders. Membership: $30,000 (Core Members); $15,000 -24,400 (Associate).

Meetings/Conferences: Annual
Conference Chair: Andy Browne
Number of non-conference events/year: 4

Publications:
Membership Directory; on-line
UTC Alert; monthly
UTC Industry Intelligence; weekly
UTC Journal; quarterly; adv.

Membership List Available to Non-members

Utility Arborist Association *(1974)*
4935 103rd Ln. NE
Blaine, MN 55014
Tel: (513) 623-1737
Website: utilityarborist.org
Members: 2400 individuals
Staff: 2
Annual Budget: $250-500,000

Personnel:
Executive Director: Philip Charlton
  E-Mail: philipcharlton@gmail.com

Historical Note:
An affiliate of International Society of Arboriculture, which provides administrative support. Established with the aim of providing an association where utility arborists, employed by electric utilities, could network and share information, improve their skills and knowledge, and enhance public awareness. UAA members are utility line clearance arborists and others involved in line clearance operations. Membership: $40/year (Individual).

Meetings/Conferences: Annual

Publications:
Utility Arborist Membership Directory; on-line; adv.
Utility Arborist Newsline; bi-monthly; adv.

Utility Communicators International *(1922)*
735 Delaware Rd.
Suite 380
Buffalo, NY 14223-1231
Tel: (716) 957-4505
E-Mail: eboardman@att.net
Website: utilitycommunicators.com
Members: 400 individuals
Staff: 1
Annual Budget: $50-100,000
Tax: 501(c)(6)

Personnel:
Executive Director: M.J. Caliendo
  E-Mail: mjcaliendo.uci@gmail.com

Historical Note:
Formerly (1977) Public Utilities Advertising Association, then became the Public Utilities Communicators Association before adopting its present name in 1989. UCI's mission is to support the needs of communications professionals in utilities and their affiliated organizations. Membership: $275 (Individual); $700 (Corporate).

Meetings/Conferences: Annual
2013 - Chicago, IL/June 11 - 13
Number of non-conference events/year: 1

Publications:
e-newsletter; bi-monthly; adv.

Utility Management & Conservation Association *(1998)*
16526 W. 78th St., Suite 318
P.O. Box 318
Eden Prairie, MN 55346
Website: utilitymca.org
Members: 75 companies
Staff: 5
Annual Budget: $100-250,000

Personnel:
Executive Director: Thanya Gonzalez
  E-Mail: execdirector@utilitymca.org
Treasurer : Jim Nehl
  E-Mail: jnehl@meterlogixllc.com

Historical Note:
Formerly known as National Submetering and Utility Allocation Association. UMCA's mission is to promote increased conservation and cost management of utilities within the multifamily housing industry. This will be accomplished by educating the industry on best practices, latest technology, and regulations relative to utility cost recovery. Membership: $2,500-10,000 (Billing Service Provider/Supplier); $750-2,500 (Technician and Installer).

Meetings/Conferences: Annual

Publications:

Membership Directory; on-line

Utility Smart Network Access Port
17431 Lakeview Dr.
Morgan Hill, CA 95037
Fax: (408) 852-3496
E-Mail: info@usnap.org
Website: usnap.org
Members: 39 Organisations
Staff: 2
Annual Budget: $50-100,000

Personnel:
Secretary and Treasurer: Barry Haaser
   E-Mail: barry @ usnap.org

Historical Note:
The mission of the Utility Smart Network Access Port (USNAP) Alliance is to create a protocol independent serial interface standard that enables any HAN (Home Area Network) standard, present and future, to use any vendor's Smart Meter as a gateway into the home, without adding additional hardware in the Smart Meter. Membership: $1000 to $5000(Contributor depending on Annual sales); $1000 to $5000 (Influencer depending on number of customers).

Utility Workers Union of America *(1945)*
815 16th St. NW
Washington, DC 20006
Tel: (202) 974-8200 *Fax:* (202) 974-8201
TollFree: (888) 843-8982
Website: uwua.net
Members: 50000 individuals
Staff: 23
Annual Budget: $10-25,000,000
Tax: 501(c)(5)

Personnel:
Senior National Researcher: Mark Brooks
   E-Mail: markbrooks@uwua.net
National Organizing Director: Robert Houser
   E-Mail: bobhouser@uwua.net
National Secretary and Treasurer: Gary M. Ruffner
   E-Mail: gruffner@aflcio.org
Director, Regulatory Affairs: Carl Wood
   E-Mail: carlwwood@verizon.net

Historical Note:
Formed through the merger of the Utility Workers Organizing Committee and the Brotherhood of Consolidated Edison Employees and chartered by the Congress of Industrial Organizations the same year, the purpose of UWUA is to improve job security, standard of living, working conditions and society in general. It is also affiliated with AFL-CIO.

Publications:
Utility Worker Magazine; quarterly
UWUA alerts; on-line
UWUA E-News; weekly

UWC - Strategic Services on Unemployment and Workers' Compensation *(1933)*
910 17th St. NW
Suite 315
Washington, DC 20006
Tel: (202) 223-8902 *Fax:* (202) 783-1616
E-Mail: info@uwcstrategy.org
Website: uwcstrategy.org
Staff: 3

Personnel:
Treasurer: Darin R. Hoffner
Office Manager and Executive Assistant: Cheryl Robinson
   E-Mail: robinsonc@uwcstrategy.org

Historical Note:
Formerly (1997) UBA, the association works on behalf of business to control the costs of unemployment and workers' compensation programs and seeks to limit federal government involvement in such programs, preferring state systems as a means of ensuring reasonable benefits at less cost. Members are employers, businesses organizations, or business associations concerned with public policy on unemployment insurance and/or workers' compensation. Government agencies are eligible for associate membership.

Meetings/Conferences: Annual
Conference Chair: Cheryl Robinson

Vacation Rental Managers Association *(1985)*
9100 Purdue Rd.
Suite 200
Indianapolis, IN 46268
Tel: (317) 454-8315 *Fax:* (317) 454-8316
E-Mail: vrma@vrma.com

Website: vrma.com
Members: 600 companies
Staff: 4
Annual Budget: $1-2,000,000
Tax: 501(c)(6)

Personnel:
Executive Director: Steve Ingram
   E-Mail: director@vrma.com
Director, Membership Services: Jill Curtis
   E-Mail: membership@vrma.com
Director, Conferences, Meetings and Education: Sheila King
   E-Mail: education@vrma.com
Director, Communications and Publications: Shelly Pfenninger
   E-Mail: communication@vrma.com

Historical Note:
VRMA's mission is to serve the Vacation Rental Industry by providing invaluable educational and networking opportunities, advocating the value of the Vacation Rental experience and speaking as the authoritative voice to foster professionalism and growth in the industry. Membership: $895 (Supplier/Associate); $495 (Vacation Rental Manager).

Meetings/Conferences: Annual
Conference Chair: Sheila King
2013 - Nashville, TN (Gaylord Opryland Resort and Convention Center)/Oct. 19 - 23
Number of non-conference events/year: 2

Publications:
Newsletter; quarterly

Membership List Available to Non-members

Vacuum Dealers Trade Association/Sewing Dealers Trade Association *(1981)*
2724 Second Ave.
Des Moines, IA 50313-4933
Tel: (515) 282-9101 *Fax:* (515) 282-4483
TollFree: (800) 367-5651
E-Mail: mail@vdta.com
Website: vdta.com
Members: 2200 individuals
Staff: 9
Annual Budget: $250-500,000
Tax: 501(c)(3)

Personnel:
President: Judy Patterson
   E-Mail: jptrson@aol.com
Administrative Assistant: Mary Kay Beall
   E-Mail: marykay@cdmshows.com
Director, Membership Services: Tim Devick
   E-Mail: tim.devick@vdta.com
Contact, Accounting: Sherry Graham
   E-Mail: sherry2@vdta.com
Director, Sales and Marketing and Associate Editor: Rob Heater
   E-Mail: rob@vdta.com
Managing Editor: Beth Vitiritto
   E-Mail: beth@vdta.com

Historical Note:
VDTA/SDTA's mission to support independent vacuum cleaner and sewing machine retailers around the world. Membership includes independent vacuum and sewing retail stores. Membership: $625 (Associate); $121 (Independent Dealer); $150 (International).

Continuing Education:
Certification Designation/s: CFCD, CSD, CCVD, CVI, CSE, CRT

Meetings/Conferences: Annual
2013 - Las Vegas, NV (Las Vegas Convention Center)/ Feb. 10 - 12

Publications:
Floor Care & Central Vac Professional; monthly; adv.
SQE Professional; monthly; adv.

Valve Manufacturers Association of America *(1938)*
1050 17th St. NW
Suite 280
Washington, DC 20036-5521
Tel: (202) 331-8105 *Fax:* (202) 296-0378
E-Mail: vma@vma.org
Website: vma.org
Members: 100 companies
Staff: 4
Annual Budget: $2-5,000,000
Tax: 501(c)(6)

Personnel:
President: William "Bill" S. Sandler CAE
   E-Mail: wsandler@vma.org
Manager, Meetings and Exhibit: Angela Hingston-Oliver
   E-Mail: ahingstonoliver@vma.org
Director, Advertising: Sue Partyke
   E-Mail: spartyke@vma.org
Associate Publisher and Editor-in-Chief and Director, Education: Judith Tibbs
   E-Mail: jtibbs@vma.org

Historical Note:
Formerly (1985) known as the Valve Manufacturers Association. VMA's mission is to promote and facilitate the global interest of members companies with customers,suppliers and governments. Membership: $3,180 (Associate Member); $3,180- 50,000 (Company).

Meetings/Conferences: Annual
Conference Chair: William "Bill" S. Sandler CAE
Number of non-conference events/year: 3

Publications:
Monthly Economic Report; monthly
Quarterly Economic Report; quarterly
Quarterly Shipment and Order Activity; quarterly
Valve Magazine; quarterly; adv.
VMA Quick Read; weekly; adv.

Valve Repair Council *(1989)*
1050 17th St. NW
Suite 280
Washington, DC 20036
Tel: (202) 331-8105 *Fax:* (202) 296-0378
E-Mail: mpasternak@vma.org
Website: vma.org
Members: 100 manufacturers of valves and actuators
Staff: 3
Annual Budget: $50-100,000

Personnel:
Executive Director: Marc Pasternak
   E-Mail: mpasternak@vma.org
Meetings and Exhibit Manager: Angela Hingston-Oliver
   E-Mail: ahingstonoliver@vma.org
Managing Editor: Genilee Parente
   E-Mail: gparente@vma.org

Historical Note:
Formerly (1994) Valve Remanufacturers Council, affiliated with the Valve Manufacturers Association of America, VRC promotes the OEM approach in valve and actuator repair. Membership is open to all VMA members who have either in-house service operations or out-of-plant service facilities as well as their authorized independent facilities. Membership: $3,180-22,550 (Full); $3,180 (Associate).

Meetings/Conferences: Annual
Conference Chair: Angela Hingston-Oliver
Number of non-conference events/year: 1

Publications:
E-Newsletter; weekly
Valve Magazine; quarterly; adv.

Van Alen Institute *(1894)*
30 W. 22nd St.
Sixth Floor
New York, NY 10010
Tel: (212) 924-7000 *Fax:* (212) 366-5836
E-Mail: vai@vanalen.org
Website: vanalen.org
Members: 600 individuals
Staff: 16
Annual Budget: $500-1,000,000

Personnel:
Executive Director: Olympia Kazi
   E-Mail: okazi@vanalen.org
Director, Operations: Susannah Bohlke
   E-Mail: sbohlke@vanalen.org
Development Manager: Marissa Feddema
   E-Mail: mfeddema@vanalen.org
Coordinator, Communications: Zach Postone
   E-Mail: zpostone@vanalen.org

Historical Note:
Established as the Society of Beaux-Arts Architects, became (1916) the Beaux-Arts Institute of Design and then (1956) National Institute for Architectural Education before assuming its current name in 1996. VAI is an independent non-profit architectural organization whose mission is to promote inquiry into the processes that shape the design of the public realm . Membership: $30 (Students); $50 (Friend); $100 (Supporter); $1000 (Benefactors); $1000

(Sustaining Benefactors); $2500 (Patrons); $10000 (New York Prize Fellowship Sponsor); $500 (Donor).

Meetings/Conferences:
Number of non-conference events/year: 1

Publications:
VAI Newsletter; monthly

Membership List Available to Non-members

Van Body Manufacturers Division

37400 Hills Tech Dr.
Farmington Hills, MI 48331-3414
Website: ntea.com/vango/core/committees.aspx?
  committee = COMMITTEE/VBMD-R
Staff: 1

Personnel:
President: VT Hackney

Vanadium Producers and Reclaimers Association (2003)

900 Second St. NE
Suite 201
Washington, DC 20002
Tel: (202) 842-3203 *Fax:* (202) 842-0439
E-Mail: gmiller@khaconsultants.com
Website: vpra.org
Staff: 1
Annual Budget: $250-500,000

Personnel:
President: John W. Hilbert III
  E-Mail: jhilbert@khaconsultants.com

Historical Note:
VPRA's mission is to promote the general welfare of the United States producers and recyclers of vanadium and to engage in all lawful activities to that end.

Variable Electronic Components Institute (1960)

P.O. Box 1070
Vista, CA 92085-1070
Tel: (760) 631-0178 *Fax:* (760) 631-7827
E-Mail: veci2@cox.net
Website: veci-vrci.com
Members: 35 companies
Staff: 2
Annual Budget: $25-50,000
Tax: 501(c)(3)

Personnel:
Executive Director: Stan Kukawka

Historical Note:
Formerly (1964) Precision Potentiometer Manufacturers Association and then (1997) became Variable Resistive Components Institute before assuming its current name. VECI, an association of manufacturers, suppliers and users of a broad line of electro-mechanical devices and specialized components, works to improve the health and image of the industry by encouraging excellence in product quality, performance and reliability. It also maintains and publishes potentiometer and encoder standards, as well as market statistics for potentiometers and encoders. Membership: $2,650 (Regular); $250-1,250 (Associate); $500 (Additional Facility).

Vehicular Technology Society

Three Park Ave., 17th Floor
C/O IEEE
New York, NY 10016-5997
Tel: (212) 419-7900 *Fax:* (212) 752-4929
Website: vtsociety.org
Members: 5000 individuals
Staff: 6

Personnel:
President: Tracy Fulghum
Vice President, Conferences: J.R. Cruz
Vice President, Publications: James Irvine
Treasurer: Thomas N. Rubinstein
Website Editor in Chief: Robert C. Shapiro
Vice President, Membership: William Sommerville

Historical Note:
A technical society of the Institute of Electrical and Electronics Engineers (IEEE). Membership in the Society, open only to IEEE members, includes a subscription to a technical periodical in the field published by IEEE. All administrative support is provided by IEEE. Membership: $9-87.50/Year.

Meetings/Conferences:
Conference Chair: J.R. Cruz

Publications:
IEEE Transactions on Vehicular Technology
IEEE Vehicular Technology Magazine; quarterly

VTS Mobile World

Venezuelan American Association of the U.S. (1936)

641 Lexington Ave.
Suite 1430
New York, NY 10022
Tel: (212) 233-7776 *Fax:* (212) 233-7779
E-Mail: info@andean-us.com
Website: venezuelanamerican.org
Members:
90 companies
50 individuals
Staff: 3
Annual Budget: $100-250,000

Personnel:
Executive President and Chief Executive Officer: Maria
  Rosa Baquerizo
Coordinator, Marketing: Arelis Quiroz

Historical Note:
VAAUS promotes the expansion of trade relations between the U.S and Venezuela. It encourages and facilitates the interchange of investment and trade between the two nations. Membership consists of international business executives, financiers, and professionals. Membership: $200-10,000/year.

Membership List Available to Non-members

Veterinary Botanical Medical Association (2001)

6410 Hwy. 92
Acworth, GA 30102
E-Mail: office@vbma.org
Website: vbma.org
Members: 130 individuals
Staff: 1
Tax: 501(c)(6)

Personnel:
Executive Director and Treasurer: Jasmine C. Lyon CAE
  E-Mail: office@vbma.org

Historical Note:
VBMA is dedicated to developing responsible herbal practice by encouraging research and education, strengthening industry relations, keeping herbal tradition alive as a valid information source, and increasing professional acceptance of herbal medicine for animals. Members are veterinarians and herbalists. Membership: $80 (Regular/Associate/Affiliate); $15 (Student); $45-80 (Multiple); $30 (Developing Countries).

Continuing Education:
Certification Designation/s: VBMA

Meetings/Conferences: Annual
2013 - Norton, MA (Wheaton College)/June 28 - 30
Number of non-conference events/year: 1

Publications:
VBMA Journal; on-line

Membership List Available to Non-members

Veterinary Cancer Society (1976)

P.O. Box 30855
Columbia, MO 65205
Tel: (573) 823-8497 *Fax:* (573) 445-0353
E-Mail: vetcancersociety@yahoo.com
Website: vetcancersociety.org
Members: 1000 individuals
Staff: 3
Annual Budget: $250-500,000
Tax: 501(c)(3)

Personnel:
Executive Director: Sandy Strother
Treasurer: Barbara Biller DVM, PhD
Newsletter Editor: Laura Garrett

Historical Note:
VCS was formed by an interested group of veterinary oncologists. VCS's mission is to help maintain the standards of diagnosis, treatment and prevention of cancer in animals. Membership includes specialists in medical, surgical, and radiation oncology, internists, pathologists, pharmacologists, and general practitioners from all over the United States and the world. Membership: $150 (Professional); $50 (Resident\Intern\Student); $40 (Technician).

Meetings/Conferences:
2013 - Minneapolis, MN (Hilton Minneapolis)/Oct. 17
  - 20
2014 - Asheville, NC (Grove Park Inn)/March 16 - 19
2014 - St. Louis, MO (Hyatt Regency St. Louis at The
  Arch)/Oct. 9 - 12

2015 - Vienna, VA/Oct. 15 - 18
Number of non-conference events/year: 1

Publications:
Membership Directory; on-line
VCS Newsletter; quarterly

Veterinary Hospital Managers Association (1981)

P.O. Box 2280
Alachua, FL 32616-2280
Tel: (518) 433-8911 *Fax:* (888) 795-4520
E-Mail: admin@vhma.org
Website: vhma.org
Members: 1000 individuals
Staff: 4
Annual Budget: $250-500,000
Tax: 501(c)(6)

Personnel:
Executive Director: Christine Quinn Shupe CAE
  E-Mail: christine@vhma.org

Historical Note:
VHMA's mission is to enhance and serve professionals in veterinary management through education, certification, and networking. Members include veterinarians, hospital administrators, practice managers and office managers. Membership: $195 (Individual/Consultant/Team); $125 (Student).

Continuing Education:
Certification Designation/s: CVPM

Meetings/Conferences: Annual
2013 - San Diego, CA/Feb. 8 - 10

Publications:
Membership Directory; on-line
VHMA Newsletter; on-line

Membership List Available to Non-members

Veterinary Orthopedic Society (1972)

P.O. Box 705
Okemos, MI 48805-0705
Tel: (517) 381-2468 *Fax:* (517) 381-2468
Website: vosdvm.org
Members: 650 individuals
Staff: 5
Annual Budget: $250-500,000
Tax: 501(c)(3)

Personnel:
President: Trevor Bebchuk
  E-Mail: gpvs@mts.net
Contact, Research: Derek Fox
  E-Mail: foxdb@missouri.edu
Contact, Communications: W. Michael Karlin
  E-Mail: mkarlindvm@gmail.com
Co-Chair, Advertising and Publicity, Sponsors and Exhibits:
  Ross B. Palmer
Executive Secretary: Maralyn R. Probst
  E-Mail: secretary@vosdvm.org

Historical Note:
VOS's mission is to provide for the association of persons engaged in the practice, teaching, or research in the area of orthopedics for the presentation and discussion of items of common interest, to further scientific investigation, and to upgrade the specialty of orthopedics in order to provide better patient care. Membership: $100 (Individual); $25 (Interns/Residents).

Meetings/Conferences: Annual
2013 - Park City, UT (The Canyons)/March 9 - 16

Publications:
Veterinary and Comparative Orthopaedics and
  Traumatology; bi-monthly
VOS Newsletter

Vibration Institute (1972)

6262 S. Kingery Hwy.
Suite 212
Willowbrook, IL 60527
Tel: (630) 654-2254 *Fax:* (630) 654-2271
E-Mail: vibinst@att.net
Website: vi-institute.org
Members: 3000 individuals
Staff: 4
Annual Budget: $1-2,000,000
Tax: 501(c)(3)

Personnel:
Executive Director: Karen E. Bresson CAE
  E-Mail: kbresson@vi-institute.org
Technical Director, Certification: Ronald L. Eshleman
  E-Mail: reshleman@vi-institute.org

Operations Associate: Ellie Murphy
   E-Mail: emurphy@vi-institute.org
Associate, Membership Services: Bhupinder Puri
   E-Mail: bpuri@vi-institute.org

Historical Note:
Founded as the Vibration Foundation and reorganized in 1973 under its present name. VI's mission is to disseminate practical information on evaluating machinery behavior and condition without commercial interest. Members are companies and individuals concerned with measuring and analyzing machinery vibration. Membership: $75 (Individual U.S.); $120 (Individual Foreign); $500 (Corporate).

Continuing Education:
Enrollment: 1500
Certification Designation/s: CVA, CBT, CVC

Meetings/Conferences: Annual
2013 - Jacksonville, FL (Wyndham Jacksonville Riverwalk)/June 19 - 21/11-25 exhibitors

Publications:
Membership Directory; on-line
Vibrations Magazine; quarterly; adv.

Vibration Isolation and Seismic Control Manufacturers Association *(1999)*
994 Old Eagle School Rd.
Suite 1019
Wayne, PA 19087
Tel: (610) 971-4850 *Fax*: (610) 971-4859
E-Mail: info@viscma.com
Website: viscma.com
Members: 10 member organizations
Staff: 2
Annual Budget: $25-50,000
Tax: 501(c)(6)

Personnel:
Executive Director: Robert H. Ecker
   E-Mail: info@viscma.com

Historical Note:
VISCMA is a professional organization of partnerships, companies and corporations who engage in the seismic restraint, vibration isolation or noise isolation industry.

Meetings/Conferences: Semi-Annual
Number of non-conference events/year: 2

Publications:
Membership Directory; on-line

Membership List Available to Non-members

Victorian Society in America *(1966)*
1636 Sansom St.
Philadelphia, PA 19103
Tel: (215) 636-9872 *Fax*: (215) 636-9873
E-Mail: info@victoriansociety.org
Website: victoriansociety.org
Members: 3000 individuals
Staff: 2
Annual Budget: $250-500,000
Tax: 501(c)(3)

Personnel:
Business Manager: Sue Verzella
   E-Mail: info@victoriansociety.org

Historical Note:
Members are historians, preservationists and others with an interest in the study of nineteenth century America. VSA is committed to historic preservation, protection, understanding, education, and enjoyment of its heritage. Membership: $35-275/year; ($1,650 (Life).

Meetings/Conferences: Annual

Publications:
The Victorian; adv.
The Victorian Quarterly; quarterly; adv.

Video Electronics Standards Association *(1989)*
39899 Balentine Dr.
Suite 125
Newark, CA 94560
Tel: (510) 651-5122 *Fax*: (510) 651-5127
E-Mail: info@vesa.org
Website: vesa.org
Members: 180 companies
Staff: 5
Annual Budget: $1-2,000,000
Tax: 501(c)(6)

Personnel:
Executive Director: Bill Lempesis
   E-Mail: bill@vesa.org

Contact, Public Relations and Marketing: Brian Eble
   E-Mail: beble@brandanimal.net
Secretary and Treasurer: Brian Fetz
Contact, Public Relations: Derek James
   E-Mail: derekjames@mcgrathpower.com
Manager, Membership Services: Joan White
   E-Mail: moderator@vesa.org

Historical Note:
VESA's mission is to to develop, advocate and support open standards for the display industry. Membership: $3,500-8,000/year (Company, based on annual corporate sales revenue).

Meetings/Conferences: Annual
2013 - Las Vegas, NV (South Hall Lower Level)/Jan. 8 - 11

Publications:
VESA Non-Member Newsletter; monthly; adv.

The Vinegar Institute *(1945)*
1100 Johnson Ferry Rd. NE
Suite 300
Atlanta, GA 30342-1733
Tel: (404) 252-3663 *Fax*: (404) 252-0774
E-Mail: vi@kellencompany.com
Website: versatilevinegar.org
Members: 31 companies
Staff: 3
Annual Budget: $100-250,000
Tax: 501(c)(6)

Personnel:
Executive Director: Jeannie Milewski
   E-Mail: jmilewski@kellencompany.com
President: Pamela A. Chumley
Staff Associate: Donna Smith
   E-Mail: dsmith@kellencompany.com

Historical Note:
Formerly known as the Apple Cider Vinegar Association when founded, assumed its current name after reorganization in 1955 and 1967. Membership composed of makers and bottlers of vinegar, as well as suppliers to the industry. VI represents the vast majority of vinegar manufacturers and bottlers. Membership: $1,828-24,800 (Active, based on annual dollar sales); $1,241 (International Member); $1,218-3,048 (Associate, based on sales to vinegar manufacturers & bottlers).

Meetings/Conferences: Annual
Conference Chair: Donna Smith
2013 - Delray Beach, FL (Seagate Hotel & Spa)/March 9 - 12

Publications:
Membership Directory; on-line
VI News; on-line

Membership List Available to Non-members

Vinyl Acetate Council *(1994)*
1250 Connecticut Ave. NW
Suite 700
Washington, DC 20036
Tel: (202) 419-1500 *Fax*: (202) 659-8037
E-Mail: info@vinylacetate.org
Website: vinylacetate.org
Members: 6 companies
Staff: 1
Annual Budget: $500-1,000,000
Tax: 501(c)(6)

Personnel:
Executive Director: Robert J. Fensterheim CAE

Historical Note:
Formerly (1994) Vinyl Acetate Toxicology Group. VAC is dedicated to promoting the safe and continued use of vinyl acetate and vinyl acetate- based products. Represents North American manufactures and major processors of vinyl acetate monomer.

Publications:
Member Listing; on-line

Vinyl Institute *(1982)*
1737 King St.
Suite 390
Arlington, VA 22314
Tel: (571) 970-3400 *Fax*: (571) 970-3271
Website: vinylinfo.org
Members: 17 companies
Staff: 7
Annual Budget: $2-5,000,000
Tax: 501(c)(6)

Personnel:

Technical Director: Rich Krock
   E-Mail: rkrock@vinylinfo.org
Vice President Marketing and Communications: Kevin Mulvaney
   E-Mail: kmulvaney@vinylinfo.org
Director, Marketing and Communications: Jeffrey B. Palmer
   E-Mail: jpalmer@vinylinfo.org

Historical Note:
VI's mission is to seek to advocate the responsible manufacture of vinyl resins, life cycle management of vinyl products, promotion of the value of vinyl to society. Members are manufacturers of vinyl, vinyl chloride monomer, vinyl additives and modifiers, and vinyl packaging materials.

Publications:
VI Executive Update; monthly
Vinyl News Service; on-line
Vinyl Recycling Directory; on-line

Membership List Available to Non-members

Vinyl Siding Institute, Inc. *(1960)*
1201 15th St. NW
Suite 220
Washington, DC 20005
Tel: (202) 587-5100 *Fax*: (202) 587-5127
TollFree: (888) 367-8741
E-Mail: jhuntley@vinylsiding.org
Website: vinylsiding.org
Members:
50 companies
250 individuals
Staff: 6
Annual Budget: $2-5,000,000
Tax: 501(c)(6)

Personnel:
President and Chief Executive Officer: Jery Y. Huntley
   E-Mail: jhuntley@vinylsiding.org
Director, Business and Finance: Mark Baxter
Senior Technical Director: Dave Johnston
Senior Manager , Certification Programs: Elizabeth Nelson
Senior Manager, Communications and Marketing: Suzanne Kay Pittman

Historical Note:
VSI strivers to further the development and growth of the vinyl siding industry by maintaining and expanding markets for vinyl and polymeric siding. Membership: $5,000/year (Associate).

Meetings/Conferences: Biennial

Publications:
SideLines e-newsletter; on-line

Viola da Gamba Society of America *(1962)*
4440 Trieste Dr.
Carlsbad, CA 92010
Tel: (760) 729-6679
E-Mail: phillip@phillipwserna.com
Website: vdgsa.org
Members:
90 organizations and institutions
1100 individuals
Staff: 5
Annual Budget: $250-500,000
Tax: 501(c)(3)

Personnel:
President: Phillip Serna
Education Contact: Jane Hershey
music publications coordinator: Alice Brin Renken
   E-Mail: arenken@sandwich.net
Newsletter Editor: Janet Scott
Treasurer: Russell Wagner

Historical Note:
VdGSA is a not-for-profit national organization dedicated to the support of activities relating to the viola da gamba in the United States and abroad. VdGSA members are professional musicians, music teachers and amateur players of the viola da gamba, a bass instrument related to the cello. Membership: $20 (New Member); $30 (Residents of the U.S. and Canada); $25 (Student in the U.S. and Canada); $35 (Other Countries/Institutions).

Meetings/Conferences: Annual
Number of non-conference events/year: 7

Publications:
Journal of the VdGSA; annually
VdGSA News; quarterly; adv.

Violin Society of America *(1973)*
341 N. Maitland Ave.
Suite 130
Maitland, FL 32751
Tel: (407) 647-8839 *Fax:* (407) 629-2502
E-Mail: info@vsaweb.org
Website: vsa.to
Members: 1800 individuals
Staff: 6
Annual Budget: $500-1,000,000
Tax: 501(c)(3)

Personnel:
President: Rodney Mohr
Executive Vice President: Phil Pyster CAE
    E-Mail: phil@crowsegal.com
Bookkeeper: Debbie Batchelor
    E-Mail: batchelord@bellsouth.net
Editor: Bobby Davis
    E-Mail: bobby@crowsegal.com
Contact, Tradeshow Management: Mark Mitchell
    E-Mail: phil@crowsegal.com
Contact, Membership Services, Registration and Database Management: Andrea Ribera
    E-Mail: andrea@crowsegal.com

Historical Note:
VSA's purpose is to promote the art and science of making, repairing and preserving stringed musical instruments and their bows. Membership is open to all who share an interest in the violin, viola, cello, bass and their bows. It reflects a range of interests and concerns, including craftsmanship, acoustics, innovation, the history of instruments and performers, technique, performance practice, repertory and other matters pertaining to instruments of the violin family. Membership: $100-120 (Individual); 45-60 (Student); $95 (Library/Institution).

Meetings/Conferences: Annual
Conference Chair: Mark Mitchell

Publications:
Journal
VSA Newsletter; bi-annually

The Vision Council *(1985)*
225 Reinekers Ln.
Suite 700
Alexandria, VA 22314
Tel: (703) 548-4560 *Fax:* (703) 548-4580
TollFree: (866) 826-0290
E-Mail: info@thevisioncouncil.org
Website: thevisioncouncil.org
Members: 700 companies
Staff: 27
Annual Budget: $5-10,000,000

Personnel:
Chief Executive Officer: Ed Greene
    E-Mail: egreene@thevisioncouncil.org
General Counsel: Jim Anderson
    E-Mail: janderson@haspc.org
Vice President, Marketing and Communications: Maureen Beddis
    E-Mail: mbeddis@thevisioncouncil.org
Chief Financial Officer and Chief Operating Officer: Brian Carroll
    E-Mail: bcarroll@thevisioncouncil.org
Vice President, Membership Services: Greg Chavez
    E-Mail: gchavez@thevisioncouncil.org
Vice President, Shows and Meetings: Deborah Malakoff
    E-Mail: dmdcastor@thevisioncouncil.org
Senior Manager, Finance and Human Resource: Katrina Schatz
    E-Mail: kschatz@thevisioncouncil.org
Senior Director, Meetings and Education: Rene Soltis
    E-Mail: rsoltis@thevisioncouncil.org
Database Manager: Lisa Wright
    E-Mail: lwright@thevisioncouncil.org
Director, Public Affairs and Advocacy: Eve Zartman-Ball
    E-Mail: ezb@thevisioncouncil.org

Historical Note:
Formerly (2010) Vision Council of America and (1989) Vision Industry Council of America. Absorbed OMA (Optical Industry Association) in 2000. The Vision Council promotes eye care and eye wear in the United States through public relations programs, trade shows and practice building programs for eye care professionals. Represents the manufacturers and suppliers of the optical industry. Membership: $2,000-25,000 (Full/Associate); $3,000 (Trade Media); $1,000 (Laboratory).

Meetings/Conferences:
Conference Chair: Deborah Malakoff

2013 - New York City, NY (Javits Center)/March 14 - 17/15000 attendees/11-25 exhibitors
2013 - Las Vegas, NV/Oct. 2 - 5
2014 - New York City, NY/April 3 - 6
2014 - Las Vegas, NV/Sept. 17 - 20
2015 - New York City, NY/March 19 - 22
2015 - Las Vegas, NV/Oct. 1 - 3
2016 - New York City, NY/April 14 - 17
2016 - Las Vegas, NV/Sept. 21 - 24
Number of non-conference events/year: 2

Publications:
Membership Directory; on-line

Visiting Nurse Associations of America *(1983)*
900 19th St. NW
Suite 200
Washington, DC 20006
Tel: (202) 384-1420 *Fax:* (202) 384-1444
TollFree: (888) 866-8773
E-Mail: vnaa@vnaa.org
Website: vnaa.org
Members: 415 organizations and 12000 employees
Staff: 14
Annual Budget: $2-5,000,000
Tax: 501(c)(3)

Personnel:
Director, Membership Services and Events: Shane Boyle
    E-Mail: sboyle@vnaa.org
Manager, Education: Eileen Grande
    E-Mail: egrande@vnaa.org
Manager, Advocacy: Isabel Jones
    E-Mail: ijones@vnaa.org
Vice President, Administration and Operations: Kristine Metter
    E-Mail: kmetter@vnaa.org
Vice President, Public Policy: Kathleen Sheehan
    E-Mail: ksheehan@vnaa.org
Senior Director, Marketing and Operations: Emily Swanson
    E-Mail: eswanson@vnaa.org
Coordinator, Member Services and Education Programs: Agnes Terry
    E-Mail: aterry@vnaa.org
Chief Financial Officer: Tim Wiltse
    E-Mail: twiltse@vnaa.org

Historical Note:
Associations of America (VNAA) is a national association that supports, promotes and advocates for community based, nonprofit home health.Membership: $5,000 (Associate); $2,100-18,000 (Affiliate); $250 (Individual).

Meetings/Conferences: Annual
Conference Chair: Shane Boyle

Publications:
Membership Directory; on-line
Weekly Member Updates (e-newsletter); weekly

Visiting Physicians Association *(1993)*
500 Kirts Blvd.
Troy, MI 48084
Tel: (248) 824-6000 *Fax:* (248) 824-6001
TollFree: (888) 742-4695
Website: visitingphysicians.com
Staff: 1

Personnel:
Senior Executive: Debbie Elert

Historical Note:
Visiting Physicians Association is an association for house call medicine industry with expertise in geriatric care.

Publications:
VPA® Company Newsletter

Visitor Studies Association *(1988)*
2885 Sanford Ave. SW
Suite 18100
Grandville, MI 49418
Tel: (740) 872-0566 *Fax:* (301) 637-3312
E-Mail: info@visitorstudies.org
Website: visitorstudies.org
Members:
22 organizations
365 individuals
Staff: 1
Annual Budget: $100-250,000

Personnel:
Association Manager: Sarah Cohn

Historical Note:
VSA is an international network of professionals committed to understanding and enhancing visitor experience in informal learning settings through research, evaluation, and dialogue. Membership: $60 (Basic); $100 (Full); $250 (Supporting); $500 (Sustaining); $1,000 (Patron); $300 (Institution); $30 (Student/Retired).

Meetings/Conferences: Annual

Publications:
Membership Directory; on-line
Visitor Studies; semi-annually
VSA e-Newsletter; bi-monthly

Visual Artists Rights Coalition
1025 W. Johnson St., Suite 1152
Madison, WI 53706
Website: protectvisualartists.org
Staff: 1

Personnel:
Treasurer: Sankalp Jon

Historical Note:
United States law protecting artist rights.

Visual Communications Industry Group *(2002)*
4248 Park Glen Rd.
Minneapolis, MN 55416
Tel: (952) 928-4665 *Fax:* (952) 929-1318
TollFree: (800) 784-4636
E-Mail: info@vci-group.org
Website: vci-group.org
Members: 1000 members
Staff: 2
Annual Budget: $250-500,000

Personnel:
Executive Director: Karen Wesloh
    E-Mail: kwesloh@vci-group.org
Manager, Conference: Amy Sellheim
    E-Mail: asellheim@vci-group.org

Historical Note:
Formerly Polycom User Group (2010). VCI-Group is an independent organization dedicated to working to influence the development of Industry-based standards for multimedia collaboration technologies and applications, to improve industry products and services, and to facilitate the exchange of information among its members. Membership: $99-2,250 (Individual); $1000-15000 (Alliance).

Meetings/Conferences: Annual
Conference Chair: Amy Sellheim

Publications:
Alliance Directory; on-line
Membership Directory; on-line
VCI-Group News; on-line

Membership List Available to Non-members

Visual Resources Association *(1982)*
P.O. Box 418232
Boston, MA 02241-8232
E-Mail: info@vraweb.org
Website: vraweb.org
Members: 600 individuals
Staff: 6
Annual Budget: $100-250,000
Tax: 501(c)(6)

Personnel:
Coordinator, Membership Services: Lise Hawkos
    E-Mail: join@vraweb.org
Web Editor: Jackie Spafford
    E-Mail: webeditor@vraweb.org

Historical Note:
VRA is a multi-disciplinary organization dedicated to furthering research and education in the field of image management within the educational, cultural heritage, and commercial environments. Members include slide and photograph curators, electronic media professionals, film and video librarians, photo archivists, slide/microfilm/ digital image producers, rights and reproduction officials, photographers, art historians, and others concerned with visual materials. VRA shares National Affiliation with Society of Architectural Historians, College Art Association. Membership: $40 (Student/Retired/Unemployed); $110 (Individual); $300 (Institutional).

Meetings/Conferences: Annual
Conference Chair: Steven Kowalik
2013 - Providence, RI (Providence Biltmore)/April 3 - 6

Publications:
Images Newsletter; on-line
VRA Bulletin; quarterly
VRA Bulletin-Journal; adv.

VRA Special Bulletin
Membership List Available to Non-members

Visually Impaired Data Processors International
(1970)
1155 15th St. NW, Suite 1004
Washington, DC 20005
Tel: (202) 467-5081
E-Mail: info@acb.org
Website: acb.org/vidpi
Members: 69 individuals
Staff: 11
Annual Budget: Under $10,000

Personnel:
President: Robert Rodgers

Historical Note:
An affiliate of the American Council of the Blind.

VITA *(1982)*
P.O. Box 19658
Fountain Hills, AZ 85269
Tel: (480) 837-7486
E-Mail: info@vita.com
Website: vita.com/
Staff: 4
Annual Budget: $500-1,000,000

Personnel:
Executive Director: Ray Alderman
    E-Mail: exec@vita.com
Director, Editorial and Marketing: Jerry Gipper
Technical Director: John Rynearson
Office Administrator and Product Directory Editor: Lollie
    Wheeler
    E-Mail: lollie@vita.com

Historical Note:
*Founded as the VMEbus Manufacturers Group, became
the VMEbus International Trade Association (VITA) in
1984, and shortened to VITA in 2005, VITA works to
unite manufacturers and users through the acceptance and
implementation of open technology standards. Membership:
$25,000 (Sponsor); $3,000 (Regular).*

Meetings/Conferences: Annual
2013 - Long Beach, CA/Jan. 23 - 24

Publications:
VITA Member Roster; on-line

Vocational Evaluation and Career Assessment Professionals *(1967)*
5500 University Pkwy.
Room CE-120
San Bernardino, CA 92407
Tel: (909) 537-3696 *Fax:* (909) 227-7580
E-Mail: office@vecap.org
Website: vecap.org
Members: 300 individuals
Staff: 2
Annual Budget: $25-50,000
Tax: 501(c)(6)

Personnel:
Coordinator, Home Office: Connie McReynolds
Editor: Steven R. Sligar
    E-Mail: sligars@ecu.edu

Historical Note:
*Formerly Vocational Evaluation and Work Adjustment
Association in 1967, assumed its current name in 2003.
VECAP's mission is to improve and advance the fields
of vocational evaluation and career assessment services.
Membership: $70 (Professional/Associate); $20 (Student).*

Meetings/Conferences: Annual

Publications:
VECAP Journal; semi-annually; adv.
VECAP Newsletter; quarterly; adv.

Voice and Speech Trainers Association *(1986)*
P.O. Box 297510
Fort Worth, TX 76129
Tel: (773) 888-2782
E-Mail: treasurer@vasta.org
Website: vasta.org
Members: 500 members
Staff: 6
Annual Budget: $50-100,000

Personnel:
President: Mandy Rees
    E-Mail: president@vasta.org
Newsletter Editor: Joe Alberti

Director, Technology and Internet Services: Michael J.
    Barnes
    E-Mail: techdirector@vasta.org
Director, Annual Conferences: Vivian Majkowski
Treasurer: Antonio Ocampo-Guzman
    E-Mail: treasurer@vasta.org
Director, Membership: Shannon Vickers

Historical Note:
*A focus group of the Association for Theatre in Higher
Education. VASTA's mission is to practice and encourage
the standards of voice and speech use and artistry in all
professional arenas, serve the needs of voice and speech
teachers and students in training and practice, promote
the concept that the art of the voice and speech specialist
is integral to the successful teaching of acting and to
the development of all professional voice users and to
encourage and facilitate opportunities for ongoing education
and the exchanging of knowledge and information among
professionals in the field. Membership: $80 (Professional/
Institutional); $48 (Student/Retired Professional).*

Meetings/Conferences:
Conference Chair: Vivian Majkowski

Publications:
Membership Directory; on-line
VASTA Voice
Voice and Speech Review; bi-annually

Voices for America's Children *(1984)*
1000 Vermont Ave. NW
Seventh Floor
Washington, DC 20005
Tel: (202) 289-0777 *Fax:* (202) 289-0776
TollFree: (866) 435-2970
E-Mail: voices@voices.org
Website: voices.org
Members: 60 organizations
Staff: 17
Annual Budget: $1-2,000,000
Tax: 501(c)(3)

Personnel:
President and Chief Executive Officer: William Bentley
    MSW
    E-Mail: bentley@voices.org
Senior Research and Evaluation Specialist: Rennie Dutton
    PhD
    E-Mail: dutton@voices.org
Vice President, Communications and Marketing: Roberta
    Heine
    E-Mail: heine@voices.org
Vice President, Membership Services: Marlo Nash
    E-Mail: nash@voices.org
*Senior Vice President, Operations and Chief Financial
    Officer:* Jill Seibert
    E-Mail: seibert@ voices.org
Senior Vice President, Programs: Joe Theissen
    E-Mail: theissen@voices.org

Historical Note:
*Formerly (1984) National Association of Child Advocates;
assumed its current name in 2003. Voices for America's
Children's mission is to improve the lives of children in the
United States by advocating for effective public policies.
Membership: $500/year.*

Publications:
Voices Update; monthly

Voluntary Protection Programs Participants' Association, Inc. *(1985)*
7600-E Leesburg Pike
Suite 100
Falls Church, VA 22043-2004
Tel: (703) 761-1146 *Fax:* (703) 761-1148
E-Mail: administration@vpppa.org
Website: vpppa.org
Members: 2100 companies
Staff: 19
Annual Budget: $2-5,000,000
Tax: 501(c)(3)

Personnel:
Specialist, Conference and Education: Ciarra Cox
    E-Mail: ccox@vpppa.org
Manager, Database and Processing: Richelle Kelly
    E-Mail: rkelly@vpppa.org
Senior Advisor: R. Davis Layne
    E-Mail: rdlayne@vpppa.org
Director, Communications and Outreach: Sanna Raza
    E-Mail: sraza@vpppa.org
Administrative Assistant: Lisa Ridgley
    E-Mail: lridgley@vpppa.org

Director, Membership Services and Development: Cynthia
    Taborda
    E-Mail: ctaborda@vpppa.org

Historical Note:
*VPPPA is dedicated to cooperative occupational safety,
health and environmental management systems. Members
are companies and sites which participate in voluntary
protection programs coordinated by OSHA State Plans or
the Dept. of Energy. Membership: $90-2,500 (Full); $45-
1,250 (Associate); $250 (Corporate); $500 (Affiliate);
$360-4,500 (Agency); $100 (Union); $360 (Non-profit).*

Meetings/Conferences: Annual
2013 - Nashville, TN (Gaylord Hotels Resorts and
    Convention Centers-Nashville)/Aug. 26 - 29
2014 - Ft. Washington, MD (Gaylord National Resort
    and Convention Center-National Harbor)/Aug. 25 -
    28
2015 - Grapevine, TX (Gaylord Texan Hotel and
    Convention Center-Grapevine)/Aug. 24 - 27
2016 - Kissimmee, FL (Gaylord Palms Resort and
    Convention Center-Kissimmee)/Aug. 29 - Sept. 1
Number of non-conference events/year: 10

Publications:
C-Newsletter; bi-weekly; adv.
Membership Directory; on-line
On the Wire; bi-monthly; adv.
Safety News Network; bi-weekly; adv.
The Leader; quarterly; adv.
Washington Update; on-line; adv.

WACRA - World Association for Case Method Research and Application *(1984)*
23 Mackintosh Ave.
Needham, MA 02492-1218
Tel: (781) 444-8982 *Fax:* (781) 444-1548
E-Mail: wacra@rcn.com
Website: wacra.org
Members:
100 organizations
2000 individuals
Staff: 3
Annual Budget: $25-50,000

Personnel:
President and Executive Director: Dr. Hans E. Klein CMA
    E-Mail: hans.klein@wacra.org

Historical Note:
*WACRA's mission is to advance the use of the case method
in teaching, training, and planning, and encourage research
using the case method. Members are professionals and
academicians with an interest in the use of the case method
and other interactive methods in teaching, training and
planning. Membership: $35-950/year.*

Meetings/Conferences: Annual
Conference Chair: Denise M. Smith

Publications:
International Journal of Case Method Research and
    Application (IJCRA); on-line
WACRA Newsletter; quarterly

Walking Horse Owners Association of America *(1976)*
P.O. Box 4007
Murfreesboro, TN 37129
Tel: (615) 494-8822 *Fax:* (615) 494-8825
E-Mail: joinwhoa@aol.com
Website: walkinghorseowners.com
Members: 8000 individuals
Staff: 5
Annual Budget: $100-250,000

Personnel:
Executive Director: Tommy Hall
    E-Mail: tommy.hall@walkinghorseowners.com
Coordinator, Pleasure and Versatility Events: Sis Osborne
    E-Mail: sis.osborne@walkinghorseowners.com
Director, Sales and Marketing: Mark Taylor
    E-Mail: mark.taylor@walkinghorseowners.com

Historical Note:
*WHOA's mission is to advocate the well-being of the
Tennessee Walking Horse so as to ensure the humane
treatment of all Tennessee Walking Horses and to aid in the
development of standards and rules which will eliminate
unfair or unlawful practices affecting the Tennessee
Walking Horse. Membership: $40 (New Membership);
$60 (Regular/Associate); $20 (Youth); $100(Family);
$200-1,000 (Lifetime).*

Continuing Education:
Certification Designation/s: ROM

Meetings/Conferences: Annual

Conference Chair: Sis Osborne
Publications:
WHOA Newsletter; on-line

Walking Horse Trainers Association (1968)
1101 N. Main St.
P.O. Box 61
Shelbyville, TN 37162
Tel: (931) 684-5866 *Fax:* (931) 684-5895
E-Mail: whtrainers@gmail.com
Website: walkinghorsetrainers.com
Members: 850 individuals
Staff: 1
Annual Budget: $250-500,000
Tax: 501(c)(5)

Personnel:
President: Bill Cantrell
   E-Mail: birddogs@bellsouth.net

Historical Note:
WHTA's mission is to actively protect and promote the welfare of the Tennessee Walking Horse. Membership: $250/year.

Meetings/Conferences: Semi-Annual
Number of non-conference events/year: 2

Publications:
WHTA News - Newsletter

Wallcovering Association (1992)
401 N. Michigan Ave.
Suite 2200
Chicago, IL 60611-4267
Tel: (312) 321-5166 *Fax:* (312) 673-6928
Website: wallcoverings.org
Members: 100 companies
Staff: 3
Annual Budget: $250-500,000

Personnel:
Executive Director: Chris Mundschenk
   E-Mail: cmundschenk@wallcoverings.org

Historical Note:
The product of a merger in 1992 of the Wallcovering Manufacturers Association and the Wallcovering Distributors Association. WA provides an excellent vehicle for communication between various segments of the wallcoverings industry while promoting the use of wallcoverings in the marketplace. Mission is to advance the welfare of members engaged in the manufacturing, distribution and sales of wallcoverings. Membership: $4,950 (Wallcoverings Manufacturer/ Wallcoverings Distributor/Associate/Converter/Supplier); $500 (Designer/Sales Representative / Showroom/ Retailer); $500-1,000 (Specialty Manufacturer, Based on Employees).

Meetings/Conferences:
2013 - Clearwater, FL (Sandpearl Resort)/Jan. 27 - 29
Number of non-conference events/year: 3

Publications:
Membership Directory
WA Newsletter; quarterly

Walnut Council (1970)
1007 N. 725 W
West Lafayette, IN 47906-9431
Tel: (765) 583-3501 *Fax:* (765) 583-3512
E-Mail: walnutcouncil@walnutcouncil.org
Website: walnutcouncil.org
Members: 1000 individuals
Staff: 2
Annual Budget: $25-50,000
Tax: 501(c)(3)

Personnel:
Executive Director and Editor: Liz Jackson
   E-Mail: jackson@purdue.edu
Treasurer: Bill Hoover
   E-Mail: whoover@purdue.edu

Historical Note:
WC's purpose is to assist in the technical transfer of forest research to field applications, help build and maintain better markets for wood products and nut crops. Membership: $500 (Life); $25 (National); $30 (Canadian); $40 (International); $60 (Industry/Supporting); $10 (Youth/ Student).

Meetings/Conferences: Annual
2013 - Morgantown, WV/July 28 - 31

Publications:
The Juglans; quarterly
WC Bulletin; adv.

Warehousing Education and Research Council (1977)
1100 Jorie Blvd.
Suite 170
Oak Brook, IL 60523-4413
Tel: (630) 990-0001 *Fax:* (630) 990-0256
E-Mail: wercoffice@werc.org
Website: werc.org
Members: 2000 individuals
Staff: 8
Annual Budget: $2-5,000,000
Tax: 501(c)(6)

Personnel:
Chief Executive Officer: Michael J. Mikitka CAE, CMP
   E-Mail: mmikitka@werc.org
Administrative Support: John Case
   E-Mail: jcase@werc.org
Executive Vice President: Rita M. Coleman
   E-Mail: rcoleman@werc.org
Manager, Member and Chapter Relations: Patrick M. Dockins
   E-Mail: pdockins@werc.org
Office Manager: Roseanna Nania
   E-Mail: rnania@werc.org
Manager, Meetings: Ellen M. Pendola
   E-Mail: ependola@werc.org
Manager, Business Development: Chad Pilbeam
   E-Mail: cpilbeam@werc.org

Historical Note:
WERC works to improve warehousing through education and research. Focuses on practical operations within the context of strategic global matters like technology, globalization, infrastructure, workforce management and legislation. Members are professionals who lead, direct and manage the efficient flow of information, materials and finished goods throughout the supply chain. Membership: $275 (Professional/Mentor); $80 (Educator); $40 (Student); $150 (Protege).

Meetings/Conferences: Annual
Conference Chair: Ellen M. Pendola
2013 - Dallas, TX/April 28 - May 1
2014 - Chicago, IL (Hyatt Regency Chicago)/April 27 - 30
Number of non-conference events/year: 1

Publications:
Member Directory; on-line
WERCSheet; semi-annually
WERCwatch (weekly ezine); weekly; adv.

Warrior Protection & Readiness Coalition
500 New Jersey Ave. NW
Washington, DC 20001
Tel: (202) 805-8480
Website: warriorprotection.net
Members: 32 companies
Staff: 1

Personnel:
Executive Director: Craig W. Heilman

Historical Note:
WPRC's mission is to ensure that warfighters are provided with good quality gear and equipment.

Waste Equipment Technology Association (1972)
4301 Connecticut Ave. NW
Suite 300
Washington, DC 20008-2304
Tel: (202) 244-4700 *Fax:* (202) 966-4824
TollFree: (800) 424-2869
E-Mail: wastecinfo@wastec.org
Website: environmentalisteveryday.org
Members: 225 companies
Staff: 9
Annual Budget: $500-1,000,000

Personnel:
Executive Vice President: Janice Comer Bradley
   E-Mail: jbradley@wastec.org
President and Chief Executive Officer: Sharon H. Kneiss
   E-Mail: skneiss@wastec.org
General Counsel and Director, Safety: David Biderman
   E-Mail: davidb@wastec.org
Director, Member Services: Christine Hutcherson
   E-Mail: chutcherson@wastec.org
Contact, Publication Sales: Carey Lawrence
   E-Mail: clawrence@wastec.org
Manager, Meetings: Catherine Maimon
   E-Mail: cmaimon@wastec.org

Director, Communications and Public Affairs: Thom Metzger
   E-Mail: tmetzger@wastec.org

Historical Note:
Formerly Waste Equipment Manufacturers Institute (WEMI). A constituent group of Environmental Industry Associations, WASTEC is committed to promoting the use of technology and innovation in meeting the needs of the waste services industry in a safe and responsible manner. Members are designers, manufacturers, distributors and consultants of technology and systems for the management of solid wastes and recyclable materials. Membership: $300-1,660/Year (Based on Company Type); $1,100-5,520 (OEM Component/Material Supplier); $1,660-16,100 (Original Equipment Manufacturer); $1,400 (Affiliate).

Meetings/Conferences:
Conference Chair: Catherine Maimon
2013 - New Orleans, LA (Ernest N. Morial Convention Center)/May 20 - 23/11000 attendees/over 100 exhibitors
Number of non-conference events/year: 4

Publications:
Member Directory
WASTEC E-News; monthly

Water and Sewer Distributors of America (1979)
100 N. 20th St.
Suite 400
Philadelphia, PA 19103-1462
Tel: (215) 320-3882 *Fax:* (215) 564-2175
E-Mail: wasda@fernley.com
Website: wasda.com
Members: 134 companies
Staff: 5
Annual Budget: $250-500,000
Tax: 501(c)(6)

Personnel:
Executive Director: Sarah Hagy CAE
   E-Mail: shagy@fernley.com
Management Liaison: Trudie Bruner CAE, MBA
   E-Mail: tbruner@fernley.com
Legal Counsel: Mark Grueskin
   E-Mail: mgrueskin@hpgfirm.com
Senior Manager, Meetings: Trish Keppler CMP
   E-Mail: tkeppler@fernley.com
Associate Director: Patrick Vulgamore
   E-Mail: pvulgamore@fernley.com

Historical Note:
WASDA mission is to strengthen and promote the distribution of water and wastewater products and services. Members are distributors and manufacturers of products to the contractor, municipal water and sewer markets. Membership: $600-6,600 (Distributor); $1,000 (Associate).

Meetings/Conferences:
Conference Chair: Trish Keppler CMP
2013 - Ft. Lauderdale, FL (Hyatt Regency)/Feb. 24 - 27
2013 - Denver, CO (Grand Hyatt Denver)/Oct. 21 - 23
2014 - Scottsdale, AZ (Westin Kierland Resort and Spa)/Feb. 23 - 26

Publications:
Connections Newsletter; quarterly
Membership Directory; on-line

Water and Wastewater Equipment Manufacturers Association (1908)
P.O. Box 17402
Washington, DC 20041
Tel: (703) 444-1777 *Fax:* (703) 444-1779
E-Mail: info@wwema.org
Website: wwema.org
Members: 80 companies
Staff: 3
Annual Budget: $500-1,000,000
Tax: 501(c)(6)

Personnel:
Secretary/President: Dawn Kristof Champney
   E-Mail: dawn@wwema.org
Legal Counsel: Karen McGee Esq.

Historical Note:
Formerly Water and Sewage Works Manufacturers Association, WWEMA's mission is to inform, educate and provide leadership on issues which affect the worldwide water and wastewater equipment industry. Membership: $2,450- 18,000 (Regular); $1,000 (Associate).

Meetings/Conferences: Annual
Publications:

E-Alerts; irregular
Membership Directory; on-line
Washington Analysis newsletter

Membership List Available to Non-members

Water Environment Federation (1928)
601 Wythe St.
Alexandria, VA 22314-1994
Tel: (703) 684-2400 *Fax:* (703) 684-2492
TollFree: (800) 666-0206
E-Mail: csc@wef.org
Website: wef.org
Members: 36000 individuals
Staff: 32
Annual Budget: $10-25,000,000
Tax: 501(c)(3)

Personnel:
Executive Director: Jeff Eger
    E-Mail: jeger@wef.org
Director, Human Resources: Julia Eller
    E-Mail: jeller@wef.org
Exhibition Sales Coordinator: Sarah Evans
    E-Mail: sevans@wef.org
Director, Media Relations: Lori Harrison
    E-Mail: lharrison@wef.org
Editor: Melissa Jackson
    E-Mail: wetmag@wef.org
Director, Membership Services: Lori Jordan
    E-Mail: csc@wef.org
Director, Communications: Linda Kelly
    E-Mail: lkelly@wef.org
Chief Technical Officer: Eileen O'Neill
    E-Mail: eoneill@wef.org
Chief Operating Officer: Timothy Ricker
    E-Mail: tricker@wef.org
Managing Director, Technical and Education Services:
    Matt Ries
    E-Mail: mries@wef.org
Director, Governance and MA Programs: Phyllis Ross
    E-Mail: pross@wef.org
Director, Government Affairs: Timothy S. Williams
    E-Mail: twilliams@wef.org

Historical Note:
*WEF is a not-for-profit technical and educational
organization representing water quality professionals
around the world. Members are water quality specialists
from around the world, including environmental, civil
and chemical engineers, biologists, chemists, government
officials, treatment plant managers and operators,
laboratory technicians, college professors, researchers,
students and equipment manufacturers and distributors.
Membership: $20-350/year.*

Meetings/Conferences:
Conference Chair: Sarah Evans
2013 - Al-Khobar, Saudi Arabia (Le Meridien)/Feb. 4 -
    6
2013 - Indianapolis, IN (Hyatt Regency Indianapolis)/
    Feb. 23 - 26
2013 - Phoenix, AZ (Renaissance Phoenix Glendale
    Hotel and Spa)/March 10 - 13
2013 - Nashville, TN (Renaissance Hotel)/May 6 - 9
2013 - Sacramento, CA (Sacramento Convention
    Center)/June 9 - 12
2013 - Chicago, IL (McCormick Place)/Oct. 5 -
    9/18000 attendees/over 100 exhibitors
Number of non-conference events/year: 4

Publications:
Biosolids Technical Bulletin; bi-weekly; adv.
Industrial Wastewater; bi-monthly
Utility Executive; bi-monthly; adv.
Water Environment & Technology Magazine (WE&T);
    monthly; adv.
Water Environment Laboratory Solutions; semi-
    monthly; adv.
Water Environment Regulation Watch; monthly; adv.
Water Environment Research; monthly
WEF Water Log; bi-weekly; adv.
World Water; adv.
World Water: Water Reuse & Desalination; quarterly;
    adv.

Membership List Available to Non-members

Water Quality Association (1974)
4151 Naperville Rd.
Lisle, IL 60532-3696
Tel: (630) 505-0160 *Fax:* (630) 505-9637
E-Mail: info@wqa.org

Website: wqa.org
Members: 2500 companies
Staff: 31
Annual Budget: $5-10,000,000
Tax: 501(c)(6)

Personnel:
Executive Director: Dave Haataja
Manager, Member Relations and Editor: Peggy Blazek
Director, Membership Services and Marketing: Margit
    Fotre
    E-Mail mfotre@wqa.org
Director, Government Affairs and Communications: David
    Loveday
    E-Mail: dloveday@wqa.org
Director, Education: Tanya Lubner PhD
    E-Mail: tlubner@wqa.org
Manager, Technical Services: Mark T. Unger CWS-VI
    E-Mail: munger@wqa.org
Marketing and Events Manager: Lori Watkins

Historical Note:
*Formed by the Merger of the Water Conditioning
Association International (1945) and the Water
Conditioning Foundation (1948). WQA is a resource
and information source, an educator for professionals,
a laboratory for product testing, and a communicator
to the public. Membership: Based on sales minimum
dues are started; $430 (Dealer); $2,000 (Manufacturer/
Supplier); $900 (International Manufacturer/Supplier);
$915 (Manufacturers Representative); $430 (Consultant).*

Continuing Education:
Certification Designation/s: CI, CSR, CCO, CCWS, CWS

Meetings/Conferences: Annual
Conference Chair: Lori Watkins
2013 - Indianapolis, IN (Indianapolis Convention
    Center)/April 2 - 5
2013 - Incline Village, CA (Hyatt Regency Lake Tahoe
    Resort, Spa and Casino)/Sept. 4 - 6

Publications:
Membership Directory; on-line
WQA Newsletter

Water Sports Industry Association (1977)
P. O. Box 568512
Orlando, FL 32856-8512
Tel: (407) 251-9039 *Fax:* (407) 251-9039
E-Mail: info@wsia.net
Website: wsia.net
Members: 200 companies
Staff: 2
Annual Budget: $100-250,000

Personnel:
Executive Director: Larry Meddock

Historical Note:
*Founded as Water Ski Industry Association. WSIA
works to encourage the sport through national public
relations programs, print media, radio and television,
publications, awards, market research and Census of Sales
Reports. Membership: $300-1,200 (Regular); $180-600
(Associate); $100 (Dealers/SalesRep/Friends/Schools/
Cable Operators); $250 (Parasail Operators).*

Meetings/Conferences:
Number of non-conference events/year: 2

Publications:
Membership Directory; on-line

Membership List Available to Non-members

Water Systems Council (1932)
1101 30th St. NW
Suite 500
Washington, DC 20007
Tel: (202) 625-4387 *Fax:* (202) 625-4363
TollFree: (888) 395-1033
E-Mail: wsc@watersystemscouncil.org
Website: watersystemscouncil.org
Members: 61 companies
Staff: 7
Annual Budget: $1-2,000,000
Tax: 501(c)(6)

Personnel:
Executive Director: Kathleen Stanley
    E-Mail: kstanley@watersystemscouncil.org
Director, Member Services: Kathryn Auth
    E-Mail: kauth@watersystemscouncil.org
Hotline Supervisor: Charlene Greenstreet
    E-Mail: cgreenstreet@watersystemscouncil.org
Coordinator, Public Education: Margaret Martens
    E-Mail: mmartens@watersystemscouncil.org

Policy and Research Advisor: Jesse Richardson Jr.
    E-Mail: jrichardson@watersystemscouncil.org
Communications Specialist and Writer: Angela Stanley
    E-Mail: astanley@watersystemscouncil.org

Historical Note:
*Formerly the National Association of Domestic and Farm
Pump Manufacturers, WSC is a nonprofit organization
focused on household wells and small water well systems.
It is also committed to ensuring that Americans who
get their water from household, private wells have safe,
reliable drinking water and to protecting the nation's
groundwater resources. Membership: $814 (Distributor);
$547 (Allied Interest - Associations/Manufacturers Reps);
$110 (Contractor/Other Individuals); $3,675-46,344
(Manufacturers-depending on annual sales volume).*

Meetings/Conferences:
Number of non-conference events/year: 1

Publications:
Member Directory

WaterJet Technology Association - Industrial and Municipal Cleaning Association (1983)
906 Olive St.
Suite 1200
St. Louis, MO 63101-1448
Tel: (314) 241-1445 *Fax:* (314) 241-1449
E-Mail: wjta-imca@wjta.org
Website: wjta.org
Members: 850 individuals and corporate
Staff: 2
Annual Budget: $100-250,000

Personnel:
Association Manager: Mark S. Birenbaum PhD
    E-Mail: wjta-imca@wjta.org

Historical Note:
*WJTA-IMCA seeks to foster domestic and international
trade of products and services relating to waterjet cutting,
waterjet cleaning, and industrial vacuuming. Members
include high pressure waterjet and industrial vacuum
equipment users, manufacturers, distributors, researchers,
regulators, and consultants. Membership: $60-80
(Individual); $400-460 (Corporate); $45-65 (Corporate
Individual); $20-40 (Student).*

Meetings/Conferences: Annual

Publications:
Directory of Waterjetting Products, Systems and
    Services; annually
Jet News; bi-monthly; adv.
Proceedings of the American Water Jet Conference;
    biennially
WJTA-IMCA Membership Directory; annually; adv.

Membership List Available to Non-members

Waterproofing Contractors Association (1970)
8608 Timberwind Dr.
Raleigh, NC 27615
Tel: (919) 870-0315 *Fax:* (919) 844-4833
E-Mail: info@thewaterproofers.org
Website: thewaterproofers.org
Members: 60 firms
Staff: 4
Annual Budget: $50-100,000

Personnel:
Executive Director and Contact, Website and Newsletter:
    Kelly Andrews
    E-Mail: kellybob@earthlink.net
General Counsel and Contact, Legislation: Andy
    Anderson
Treasurer: John McDougall
    E-Mail: john@blairduron.com
*Contact, Membership Services, Education and Fall
    Convention Planning:* Brian Spencer

Historical Note:
*WCA's aim is to elevate and sustain the professional
character of the members, publish and provide relevant
industry knowledge to educate members on proper
industry practices and new technologies, to represent and
safeguard the common interests of its members and the
public by practicing moral and ethical standards and to
promote goodwill between various phases of construction.
Membership: $290/year (Company).*

Meetings/Conferences: Annual
Conference Chair: Brian Spencer
Number of non-conference events/year: 1

Publications:
Membership Directory; on-line; adv.
The waterproofer; quarterly

Waterways Council, Inc. (2003)
801 N. Quincy St.
Suite 200
Arlington, VA 22203
Tel: (703) 373-2261 Fax: (703) 373-2037
Website: waterwayscouncil.org
Members: 300 Organizations
Staff: 5
Annual Budget: $2-5,000,000
Tax: 501(c)(6)

Personnel:
President and Chief Executive Officer: Michael J. Toohey
    E-Mail: mtoohey@vesselalliance.com
Senior Vice President: Debra Colbert
    E-Mail: dcolbert@vesselalliance.com
Vice President, Government Affairs: John S. Doyle Jr.
Senior Executive Assistant: Medina Moran

Historical Note:
WCI is the national public policy organization that advocates for a properly funded and well-maintained system of inland waterways and ports. Seeks to educate decision-makers in the states and federal government, the news media and the general public about the critical importance of nation's inland waterways and the need to sustain and increase their reliability. Membership: $1,000-50,000/year.

Meetings/Conferences: Annual

Publications:
Capitol Currents
e-brief

Weather Modification Association (1950)
P.O. Box 845
Riverton, UT 84065
Tel: (801) 598-4392
Website: weathermodification.org
Members: 30 corporations 200 individuals
Staff: 4
Annual Budget: $50-100,000

Personnel:
President: Joseph Golden
    E-Mail: joegolden@q.com
Webmaster: Stephanie Beall
    E-Mail: wxbliss21@yahoo.com
Executive Secretary and Treasurer: Laurie Capece
    E-Mail: wmaexecsec@gmail.com
Editor: David Delene
    E-Mail: ddelene@aim.com

Historical Note:
Formerly (1967) Weather Control Research Association. Assumed its current name in 2003. Mission is to enable persons, political entities, and other organizations to make informed decisions about the application of weather modification technologies, to provide adequate water supplies, and to reduce natural weather hazards. Members of weather modification association are individuals, organizations and students. Membership: $75 (Individual); $20 (Student); $2,000 (Associate); $300 (Corporate); $30 (Retired).

Continuing Education:
Certification Designation/s: WMO, WMM

Meetings/Conferences: Annual
2013 - San Antonio, TX (Marriott Plaza San Antonio)/
    April 9 - 13

Publications:
Journal of Weather Modification
Membership Directory; annually

Weather Risk Management Association (1999)
529 14th St. NW
Suite 750
Washington, DC 20045
Tel: (202) 289-3800 Fax: (202) 223-9741
E-Mail: info@wrma.org
Website: wrma.org
Members: 40 companies
Staff: 4
Annual Budget: $250-500,000
Tax: 501(c)(6)

Personnel:
Executive Director: Lauren Newberry
    E-Mail: lnewberry@kellencompany.com
Associate Director: Christina Donnelly
    E-Mail: cdonnelly@kellencompany.com
Communication Strategist: Shirley Savage

Historical Note:
WRMA was created to be the industry association for weather risk management professionals to enhance public awareness of the weather risk industry and promote the growth and general welfare of the weather risk market. Membership: $3,000 (Regular); $500 (University).

Meetings/Conferences: Semi-Annual
Number of non-conference events/year: 1

Publications:
Membership Directory

Web Sling and Tie down Association (1973)
2105 Laurel Bush Rd.
Suite 200
Bel Air, MD 21015
Tel: (443) 640-1070 Fax: (443) 640-1031
E-Mail: wstda@ksgroup.org
Website: wstda.com
Members: 90 companies
Staff: 5
Annual Budget: $250-500,000
Tax: 501(c)(6)

Personnel:
Executive Director: Fred Stringfellow CAE
    E-Mail: fred@ksgroup.org
Director, Finance: Amy Chetelat, CAE
    E-Mail: amy@ksgroup.org
Associate Director: Kathy Demarco
    E-Mail: kathy@stringfellowgroup.net
Director, Meetings: Cynthia Jordan
    E-Mail: cynthia@ksgroup.org

Historical Note:
Formerly (1988) the Web Sling Association. WSTDA's mission is to advance and further, in every lawful manner, the common interests of its members and industry. Members are manufacturers of web slings which are used as hoists in various industrial lifting operations and web tie downs used in cargo control trucking operations. Membership: $1,000-2,200 (Regular/Associate); $1,000 (Affiliate).

Meetings/Conferences:
Conference Chair: Cynthia Jordan
2013 - Napa, CA (The Meritage Resort and Spa)/May
    6 - 9
2013 - Chicago, IL (Sax Chicago – A Thompson Hotel)/
    Oct. 15 - 17
2014 - Charleston, SC (DoubleTree by Hilton Hotel and
    Suites Charleston-Historic District)/May 5 - 8

Publications:
Membership Directory; annually
Uplifting News; semi-annually; adv.

WEB: Worldwide Employee Benefits Network (1982)
2701 W. 15th St.
Suite 323
Plano, TX 75075
E-Mail: info@webnetwork.org
Website: webnetwork.org
Members: 1600 individuals
Staff: 3
Annual Budget: $250-500,000

Personnel:
Executive Director: Sherlynn Hendershot
    E-Mail: sherlynn.hendershot@webnetwork.org

Historical Note:
Incorporated in 1983 as WEB, became WEB, Inc. in 1988, the WEB Network of Benefits Professionals (1997) and assumed its current name in 2000. WEB's mission is to further the development and education of benefits of professionals. Members are administrators, consultants, attorneys, accountants, investment managers, communications experts and benefits managers. Membership: $175-185 (Individual); $144 (Corporate per member); $720 (Corporate, for 5 members); $105-115 (Government); $75-85 (Associate).

Publications:
Membership Directory; on-line
The Network; quarterly; adv.
WEB Newsletter; monthly; adv.

Membership List Available to Non-members

Wedding and Event Videographers Association International (1994)
8499 S. Tamiami Trail
P.O. Box 208
Sarasota, FL 34238
Tel: (941) 923-5334 Fax: (941) 921-3836
E-Mail: admin@weva.com
Website: weva.com
Staff: 1
Annual Budget: $250-500,000

Tax: 501(c)(6)

Personnel:
Director, Communications: Dan Argenas
    E-Mail: da@weva.com

Historical Note:
WEVA International works for advancing the professional interests of wedding and event videographers worldwide through continuing education, technical support, group benefits, advocacy committees and professional development training. Members are professional wedding and event videogaphers. Membership: $249/year.

Publications:
Member Directory
Wedding & Event Videography Resource Guide;
    quarterly
WEVA Magazine
WEVA Newsletter; monthly

Wedding and Portrait Photographers International (1995)
6255 Sunset Blvd.
19th floor
Los Angeles, CA 90028
Tel: (323) 817-3500
Website: wppionline.com
Members: 3500 individuals
Staff: 17
Annual Budget: $250-500,000

Personnel:
Executive Vice President and Group Publisher: George
    Varanakis
    E-Mail: gvaranakis@rfpublishing.com
Director, Education and Membership: Arlene C. Evans
    E-Mail: aevans@rfpublishing.com
Account Executive: Mike Gangel
    E-Mail: Mike.Gangel@nielsen.com
Director, Operations: Cathy Griffith
    E-Mail: Cathy.Griffith@nielsen.com
Editor-in-Chief: Bill Hurter
    E-Mail: bhurter@rfpublishing.com
Manager, Conference: Neeta Lakhani
    E-Mail: Neeta.Lakhani@nielsen.com
Marketing Manager: Sheryl Navarro
    E-Mail: snavarro@rfpublishing.com

Historical Note:
Formerly Wedding Photographers of America and Wedding Photographers International, WPPI assumed its present name in 1995. Mission is to promote artistic and technical standards and to serve as a forum for the exchange of knowledge and experience. Membership: $125 (Basic); $299 (Elite Portfolio); $860 (Premium Portfolio).

Meetings/Conferences: Annual
Conference Chair: Neeta Lakhani
2013 - Las Vegas, NV (MGM Grand Hotel and
    Conference Center)/March 7 - 14/1600 attendees
Number of non-conference events/year: 2

Publications:
Rangefinder; monthly; adv.

Weed Science Society of America (1956)
810 E. Ten St.
P.O. Box 1897
Lawrence, KS 66044-8897
Tel: (785) 843-1235 Fax: (785) 843-1274
TollFree: (800) 627-0629
E-Mail: wssa@allenpress.com
Website: wssa.net
Members: 2000 individuals
Staff: 3
Annual Budget: $500-1,000,000
Tax: 501(c)(3)

Personnel:
Executive Secretary: Joyce Lancaster
    E-Mail: jlancaster@allenpress.com
Managing Editor: Tracy Candelaria
    E-Mail: wssa@allentrack.net
Manager, Meetings: Kate Counter
    E-Mail: kcounter@allenpress.com

Historical Note:
Founded as the Weed Society of America, it absorbed the Association of Regional Weed Control Conferences in 1956 and assumed its present name in 1963. WSSA's mission is to encourage and promote the development of knowledge concerning weeds and their impact on the environment. Membership: $170-190 (Regular); $50-70 (Student).

Meetings/Conferences: Annual
Conference Chair: Kate Counter

2013 - Baltimore, MD/Feb. 4 - 7
Number of non-conference events/year: 13

Publications:
Invasive Plant Science and Management; quarterly
Weed Science; quarterly; adv.
Weed Technology; quarterly
WSSA Directory
WSSA Newsletter; quarterly

Welding Research Council *(1935)*
P.O. Box 1942
New York, NY 10156
Tel: (216) 658-3847 *Fax:* (216) 658-3854
E-Mail: wrc@forengineers.org
Website: forengineers.org/wrc
Members: 300 organizations
Staff: 4
Annual Budget: $250-500,000

Personnel:
Executive Director: Dr. Martin Prager PhD
    E-Mail: mprager@forengineers.org

Historical Note:
Established by the Engineering Foundation to conduct and coordinate welding research. WRC provides a forum for the exchange, evaluation, and dissemination of the pertinent technical information. Time, talent, and funds are focused and committed - ruled solely by the technical significance of the problem at hand. Membership: $1,250 (Domestic); $1,320 (International).

Meetings/Conferences: Annual

Publications:
Bulletin

Wellness Councils of America *(1985)*
17002 Marcy St.
Suite 140
Omaha, NE 68118
Tel: (402) 827-3590 *Fax:* (402) 827-3594
E-Mail: wellworkplace@welcoa.org
Website: welcoa.org
Members: 3028 wellness councils and individuals
Staff: 9
Annual Budget: $1-2,000,000
Tax: 501(c)(3)

Personnel:
President: David M. Hunnicutt PhD
    E-Mail: dhunnicutt@welcoa.org
Associate, Communications: Madeline Jahn
    E-Mail: mjahn@welcoa.org
Director, Marketing: William Kizer Jr., MBA
    E-Mail: bkizer@welcoa.org
Vice President, Operations: Brittanie Leffelman MS
    E-Mail: bleffelman@welcoa.org

Historical Note:
WELCOA's mission is to serve business leaders, workplace wellness practitioners, public health professionals and consultants of all kinds by promoting corporate membership and producing leading-edge worksite wellness publications and health information. Membership: $365/year.

Continuing Education:
Certification Designation/s: WWU

Publications:
Absolute Advantage; on-line
E-Newsletter; weekly
Membership Directory; on-line

Membership List Available to Non-members

The Wellness Plan *(1973)*
7700 Second Ave.
Detroit, MI 48202
Tel: (313) 202-8500 *Fax:* (313) 202-6822
Website: wellplan.com
Staff: 3
Annual Budget: $10-25,000,000

Personnel:
Chief Executive Officer and Executive Director: Anthony V.
    King FACHE, MHSA
    E-Mail: aking@wellplan.com
Director, Financial Services: Gloria Reid
    E-Mail: greid@wellplan.com
Manager, Human Resources: Betty Shelton
    E-Mail: bshelton@wellplan.com

Historical Note:
TWP's mission is to deliver primary healthcare services by means of medical doctors and quality of life information to its thousands of users.

Publications:
Membership Directory

Welsh Pony and Cob Society of America *(1906)*
720 Green St.
Stephens City, VA 22655
Tel: (540) 868-7699
E-Mail: info@welshpony.org
Website: welshpony.org
Members: 1800 individuals
Staff: 5
Annual Budget: $250-500,000
Tax: 501(c)(5)

Personnel:
President: Ruth Wilburn
Executive Secretary and Treasurer and Editor: Lisa L.
    Landis
Contact, Membership Services: Cindy Snyder
    E-Mail: accounts1@welshpony.org

Historical Note:
Formerly known as the Welsh Pony and Cob Society of America in Illinois in 1906; reinstituted after a period of inactivity in Indiana in 1946 as Welsh Pony Society of America. Membership: $45 (Individual); $55 (Organization/Family); $30 (Associate); $25 (Junior, age 18 & under); 1,000 (Life).

Meetings/Conferences: Annual
Number of non-conference events/year: 14

Publications:
Driving Digest; adv.
Equine Journal; adv.
Stallion Directory; on-line
Welsh Review; quarterly; adv.

Membership List Available to Non-members

Western Association for Art Conservation *(1975)*
1156 15th St. NW
Suite 320
Washington, DC 20005
Tel: (202) 452-9545 *Fax:* (202) 452-9328
E-Mail: treasurer@waac-us.org
Website:
cool.conservation-us.org/waac
cool.conservation-us.org
Members: 500 individuals
Staff: 5
Annual Budget: $25-50,000

Personnel:
President: Daniel Cull
    E-Mail: president@waac-us.org

Historical Note:
Formerly (1977) Western Association of Art Conservators. WAAC is a nonprofit membership organization for professional conservators. Membership: $40 (Individual-Domestic); $45 (Individual- Canada and Mexico); $50 (Individual-Overseas); $45 (Institution-Domestic); $50 (Institution-Canada and Mexico); $55 (Institution-Overseas).

Meetings/Conferences: Annual

Publications:
Membership Directory; annually
WAAC Newsletter; adv.

Western Association of Industrial Distributors *(1955)*
2604-B El Camino Real
Box 348
Carlsbad, CA 92008
Tel: (916) 850-5658 *Fax:* (916) 543-1612
E-Mail: connie@waidonline.org
Website: waidonline.org
Members: 42 companies
Staff: 1
Annual Budget: $50-100,000
Tax: 501(c)(6)

Personnel:
Executive Director: Connie Seitz
    E-Mail: connie@waidonline.org

Historical Note:
Formerly (2000) Associated Bearing & Power Transmission Distributors. WAID's mission is to bring value to its members by providing education, networking opportunities and promotion of the industry. Membership: $295/year.

Meetings/Conferences: Annual

Publications:
The Distributor

Western Dredging Association *(1979)*
P.O. Box 5797
Vancouver, WA 98668-5797
Tel: (360) 750-0209 *Fax:* (360) 750-1445
E-Mail: weda@comcast.net
Website: westerndredging.org
Members: 35 companies and 3000 individuals
Staff: 1
Annual Budget: $250-500,000

Personnel:
Executive Director, Secretary and Treasurer: Lawrence M.
    Patella
    E-Mail: weda@comcast.net

Historical Note:
WEDA's mission is to promote the exchange of knowledge in fields related to dredging, navigation, marine engineering and construction by sponsoring or co-sponsoring national and international technical conferences and provide a forum for improvement of communications. Membership: $150 (Standard); $75 (Student); $500 (Sustaining).

Publications:
Membership Directory; on-line
WEDA Newsletter

Western Economic Association International *(1922)*
18837 Brookhurst St.
Suite 304
Fountain Valley, CA 92708-7302
Tel: (714) 965-8800 *Fax:* (714) 965-8829
Website: weai.org
Members: 40 organizations and 1800 individuals
Staff: 3
Annual Budget: $500-1,000,000
Tax: 501(c)(3)

Personnel:
Executive Director: Darwin Hall

Historical Note:
WEAI is a non-profit educational organization which seeks to promote mutually beneficial exchange of ideas between economists in academia and those working in government and business. It also strives to communicate economic knowledge outside the profession. Members are individuals, corporations, universities, and other organizations. Membership: $450- 2,500 (Institutional); $65 (Regular); $30 (Student); $100 (Family); $30-85 (Green Membership).

Meetings/Conferences: Annual
2013 - Tokyo, Japan/March 14 - 17
2013 - Seatle, WA (Grand Hyatt Seattle)/June 28 - July
    2
2014 - Denver, CO/June 27 - July 1

Publications:
Economic Inquiry; quarterly
WEAI Newsletter

Western History Association *(1961)*
University of Alaska Fairbanks
605 Gruening
Fairbanks, AR 99775-6460
Tel: (907) 474-6509 *Fax:* (314) 516-7272
E-Mail: wha@umsl.edu
Website: westernhistoryassociation.org
Members: 1900 individuals and 65 organizations
Staff: 4
Annual Budget: $500-1,000,000
Tax: 501(c)(3)

Personnel:
Executive Director: John Heaton
Administrative Assistant: Betty Jo Ditmeyer
    E-Mail: wha@umsl.edu
Coordinator, Membership Services: Amy Horstman

Historical Note:
WHA seeks to promote the study of the North American West in its varied aspects and broadest sense. Members are academic historians and others with an interest in the history of the American West. Membership: $90 (Regular); $150 (Institution/Sustaning); $30 (Student); $45 (Emeritus/Retired); $95 (Joint); $300 (Patron); $500 (Donor).

Meetings/Conferences: Annual
2013 - Tucson, AZ (Westin La Paloma Resort and Spa)/
    Oct. 9 - 12
2014 - Newport Beach, CA (Newport Beach Marriott
    Hotel and Spa)/Oct. 15 - 18

Publications:
Montana The Magazine of Western History; quarterly

Western Historical Quarterly; quarterly
WHA Newsletter; semi-annually; adv.

Western Literature Association (1965)
C/O Department of English, Texas Tech
University, P.O. Box 43091
Lubbock, TX 79409-3091
Tel: (806) 742-2501 *Fax:* (806) 742-0989
E-Mail: wal@usu.edu
Website: usu.edu/westlit/
Members: 500 individuals
Staff: 5
Annual Budget: $25-50,000
Tax: 501(c)(3)

Personnel:
President: Sara Spurgeon
  E-Mail: sara.spurgeon@ttu.edu

Historical Note:
*WLA unites and recognizes scholars, artists,
environmentalists, and community leaders who value the
West's literary and cultural contributions to American
and world cultures. Fosters student learning and career
advancement in education. Members are scholars and
others with an interest in western regional literary genre.
Membership: $35-60 (Professional); $30-55 (Student/
Retiree); $40-65 (Couple); $75 (Sponsor); $100 (Patron).*

Meetings/Conferences: Annual
Conference Chair: Sara Spurgeon
2013 - Berkeley, CA (DoubleTree by Hilton Berkeley
  Marina)/Oct. 9 - 12
2014 - Victoria, BC (Fairmont Empress)/Nov. 4 - 8

Publications:
Member Directory; on-line
Western American Literature (WAL); adv.

Membership List Available to Non-members

Western Music Association (1988)
P.O. Box 648
Coppell, TX 75019
Tel: (505) 563-0673 *Fax:* (520) 322-0582
E-Mail: westerngroupie@aol.com
Website: westernmusic.com
Members: 1000 individuals
Staff: 3
Annual Budget: $100-250,000

Personnel:
Executive Director: Marsha Short

Historical Note:
*WMA is dedicated to preserving and advancing the history,
literature and performance of western music. Members are
western music aficionados and performers. Membership:
$1,000 (Sponsoring); $600 (Individual Life); $100
(Business/Patron); $65 (Family); $45 (Individual).*

Meetings/Conferences: Annual

Publications:
Membership Directory; on-line
Western Way; quarterly

The Western Red Cedar Pole Association (2000)
14455 N. Hayden Rd.
Suite 226
Scottsdale, AZ 85260
E-Mail: info@wrcpa.org
Website: wrcpa.org
Members: 6 companies
Staff: 2
Annual Budget: $50-100,000
Tax: 501(c)(6)

Personnel:
Executive Chairman and Founder: Bob Parsons

Historical Note:
*WRCPA represents the manufacturers of cedar utility
poles in Western North America and provides educational
material addressing the manufacture and use of cedar utility
poles. Members are electrical utility companies using only
these cedar utility poles.*

Publications:
Cedar Pole News; quarterly

Membership List Available to Non-members

Western Writers of America (1953)
271 CR 219
Encampment, WY 82325
Tel: (307) 329-8942
Website: westernwriters.org
Members: 630 individuals
Staff: 2

Annual Budget: $250-500,000

Personnel:
Executive Director, Secretary and Treasurer: Candy
  Moulton
  E-Mail: wwa.moulton@gmail.com
Contact, Membership Services: Rod Miller
  E-Mail: rod@holmesco.com

Historical Note:
*WWA promotes the literature of the American West
and bestow Spur Awards for distinguished writing in the
Western field. Membership: $75 (Active/Associate); $150
(Sustaining); $250 (Patron).*

Meetings/Conferences: Annual
2013 - Las Vegas, NV (Riviera Hotel and Casino)/June
  24 - 28

Publications:
Roundup Magazine; on-line

Membership List Available to Non-members

Wheat Quality Council (1938)
P.O. Box 966
Pierre, SD 57501-0966
Tel: (605) 224-5187 *Fax:* (605) 224-0517
Website: wheatqualitycouncil.org
Members: 125 organizations
Staff: 2
Annual Budget: $100-250,000
Tax: 501(c)(3)

Personnel:
Executive Vice President: Ben Handcock
  E-Mail: bhwqc@aol.com

Historical Note:
*Formerly (1980) the Kansas Wheat Improvement
Association. WQC's mission is to advocate the development
of new wheat varieties that improve the value of wheat
to all parties in the U.S. supply chain. Membership:
$1,250-12,750 (Millers, based on daily CWT capacity);
$500-7,500 (Wheat Food users, based on annual sales
dollars); $250-1,000 (Grain companies, based on general
size); $100-1,000 (Seed Breeders/Distributors); $250
(Allied); $2,000-6,000 (Professional Organizations).*

Meetings/Conferences: Annual

Publications:
Membership Directory; on-line
WQC Newsletter

White House Correspondents Association (1914)
600 New Hampshire Ave.
Suite 800
Washington, DC 20037
Tel: (202) 266-7453 *Fax:* (202) 266-7454
E-Mail: whca@starpower.net
Website: whca.net
Members: 600 individuals
Staff: 1
Annual Budget: $500-1,000,000
Tax: 501(c)(3)

Personnel:
Executive Director: Julia Whiston

Historical Note:
*Members are media reporters assigned to coverage of
Presidential political news. WHCA represents the White
House press corps in its dealings with the administration on
coverage-related issues. Membership: $50/year (Regular/
Associate).*

Meetings/Conferences: Annual

White House News Photographers Association (1921)
P.O. Box 7119
7119 Ben Franklin Stn.
Washington, DC 20044-7119
Tel: (202) 785-5230 *Fax:* (202) 333-7898
E-Mail: info@whnpa.org
Website: whnpa.org
Members: 525 individuals
Staff: 11
Annual Budget: $250-500,000
Tax: 501(c)(6)

Personnel:
Executive Director: Heidi Elswick
Secretary: Elisa Miller
Legal Counsel: James Lorin Silverberg Esq.

Historical Note:
*Founded with 24 charter members, WHNPA works to
protect and promote photographers' interests in pursuing
their mission. Membership is limited to photojournalists*

*who regularly cover the White House and Washington
Metropolitan area for local and network TV and local and
national newspapers and magazines. Membership: $95
(Active); $75 (Associate); $25 (Student).*

Publications:
Ace Photo Newsletter
Membership Directory; on-line

Wholesale Beer Association Executives of America (1946)
1101 Livingston Ave.
Charleston, WV 25302-1030
E-Mail: info@usacm.org
Members: 43 individuals
Staff: 1

Personnel:
Treasurer: Armilda Perry

Historical Note:
*Formerly (1946) National Association of State Beer
Association Secretaries, (1977) State Beer Association of
Executives of America. Members are executives of state beer
distributor associations. Has no paid officers or full-time
staff; officers change annually. Membership: $125/year
(individual).*

Wholesale Florist and Florist Supplier Association (1926)
Horn Point Harbor Marina
105 Eastern Ave., Suite 104
Annapolis, MD 21403
Tel: (410) 940-6580 *Fax:* (410) 263-1659
TollFree: (888) 289-3372
E-Mail: info@wffsa.org
Website: wffsa.org
Members: 700 companies
Staff: 5
Annual Budget: $500-1,000,000

Personnel:
Executive Vice President: Patricia "Trish" A. Lily
  E-Mail: plilly@wffsa.org
Manager, Accounts: Dorothy Cusack
  E-Mail: dcusack@wffsa.org
Director, Membership: Amy Luckado
  E-Mail: aluckado@wffsa.org
Office Manager: Janice Sunderland
  E-Mail: jsunderland@wffsa.org
Director, Communications and Conference: Kristin
  Thompson
  E-Mail: kthompson@wffsa.org

Historical Note:
*Formerly (1961) the Wholesale Commission Florists of
America. WF&FSA's mission is to provide networking and
business opportunities to wholesale distributors and floral
suppliers. Membership: $570-1,730 (Wholesale/Supplier/
Associate Member, based on annual sales volume); $295
(Sales Representative).*

Meetings/Conferences: Annual
Conference Chair: Kristin Thompson
2013 - Miami, FL (Doral)/Oct. 23 - 25
2014 - Miami, FL (Doral)/Oct. 22 - 24
2015 - Miami, FL (Doral)/Oct. 21 - 23

Publications:
Membership Directory; on-line
WF&FSA netWORK; on-line

Wi-Fi Alliance (1999)
10900-B Stonelake Blvd.
Suite 126
Austin, TX 78759
Tel: (512) 498-9434 *Fax:* (512) 498-9435
Website: wi-fi.org
Members: 400 individuals
Staff: 5
Annual Budget: $5-10,000,000
Tax: 501(c)(6)

Personnel:
Chief Executive Officer: Edgar Figueroa
Director, Marketing: Kelly Davis-Felner
Director, Technical: Greg Ennis
Controller, Finance: Tracy Howard
Media Contact: Karl F. Stetson
  E-Mail: karl.stetson@edelman.com

Historical Note:
*Wi-Fi Alliance provides wireless access locations for people
and seeks to establish a global standard for wireless local
area networking. Membership: $3,750-15,000 (Regular);
$2,500-5,000 (Adopter).*

Continuing Education:

Certification Designation/s: Wi-Fi

Publications:
Wi-Fi Alliance Newsletter

Membership List Available to Non-members

WIFS - Women in Insurance and Financial Services *(1936)*
136 Everett Rd.
Albany, NY 12205
Tel: (518) 694-5506 *Fax:* (518) 935-9232
TollFree: (866) 264-9437
E-Mail: office@w-wifs.org
Website: wifsnational.com
Members: 1000 individuals
Staff: 6
Annual Budget: $500-1,000,000
Tax: 501(c)(6)

Personnel:
Executive Director: Deb Duffy
President: Karen Roberts ChFC, CLU
   E-Mail: karen.roberts@lfg.com
Contact, Communications and Marketing: Megan Geroux
Contact, Programs and Events: Cheryl Gerstler
Contact, Member Services: Tory Owens
Treasurer: Sara M. Samuels

Historical Note:
Formerly (1987) Women Life Underwriters Conference and (2000) WLUC - Women in Insurance and Financial Services. WIFS is dedicated to attracting capable women to the financial services sector, helping them develop their talents and advancing them toward their fullest potential. Membership: $200 (Individual); $100 (Partner Affiliated).

Meetings/Conferences: Annual
Conference Chair: Cheryl Gerstler

Publications:
Member Directory; on-line
Member Newsletter; bi-monthly

Wild Bird Feeding Industry *(1984)*
P. O. Box 502
West End, NC 27376
Tel: (888) 839-1237 *Fax:* (605) 275-6697
TollFree: (855) 233-6362
E-Mail: info@wbfi.org
Website: wbfi.org
Members: 157 companies
Staff: 3
Annual Budget: $100-250,000

Personnel:
Executive Director and Contact, Membership and Events: Susan Hays
   E-Mail: shays@wbfi.org

Historical Note:
WBFI's mission is the progressive expansion of the wild bird and backyard wildlife feeding industry. Members are bird feeder manufacturing, seed packing and processing companies and related brokers, distributors, retailers and suppliers. Membership: $645-7,450 (Packer); $325-1,240 (Distributor/Processor/Retailer); $325-2,500 (Feeder/Accessories).

Meetings/Conferences: Annual
Conference Chair: Susan Hays

Publications:
Membership Directory; on-line

Membership List Available to Non-members

Wild Bird Feeding Institute *(1984)*
P.O. Box 502
West End, NC 27376
Tel: (855) 233-6362
TollFree: (888) 839-1237
Website: wbfi.org
Staff: 1
Annual Budget: $100-250,000

Personnel:
Executive Director: Susan M. Hays
   E-Mail: shays@wbfi.org

Historical Note:
WBFI is dedicated to the progressive expansion of the wild bird and backyard wildlife feeding industry. Serves the interests of its members through promoting responsible feeding, creating alliances, removing barriers, safeguarding gains and enhancing the experience of the consumer.

Publications:
Member Directory; on-line

Wild Blueberry Association of North America *(1981)*
P.O. Box 100
Old Town, ME 04468
Tel: (207) 570-3535 *Fax:* (207) 581-3499
E-Mail: wildblueberries@gwi.net
Website: wildblueberries.com
Members:
15 companies
75 individuals
Staff: 2
Annual Budget: $1-2,000,000
Tax: 501(c)(5)

Personnel:
President: J. Kim Higgins

Historical Note:
WBANA is an international trade association of producers and processors of wild blueberries from Maine and eastern Canada. Membership fee varies, based on production.

Wilderness Education Association *(1978)*
Eigenmann Hall 029, 1900 E. Tenth St.
Bloomington, IN 47406
Tel: (812) 855-4095 *Fax:* (812) 855-8697
E-Mail: wea@indiana.edu
Website: weainfo.org
Members: 500 individuals
Staff: 4
Annual Budget: $100-250,000
Tax: 501(c)(3)

Personnel:
Executive Director: Mary Williams
Committee Chair, Conventions: Kim Collins
Executive Administrative Assistant: Margaret Estock

Historical Note:
WEA's mission is to promote the professionalism of outdoor leadership through establishment of national standards, curriculum design, implementation, advocacy, and research driven initiatives. Membership: $15-1,500/year.

Continuing Education:
Certification Designation/s: SA, OLA, SIA, OLIA

Meetings/Conferences: Annual
Conference Chair: Kim Collins

Publications:
Membership Directory
Outside Magazine
WEA Member Access; monthly

Membership List Available to Non-members

Wilderness Medical Society *(1983)*
2150 S. 1300 East
Suite 500
Salt Lake City, UT 84106
Tel: (801) 990-2988 *Fax:* (801) 990-2987
E-Mail: info@wms.org
Website: wms.org
Members: 2976 individuals
Staff: 4
Annual Budget: $500-1,000,000
Tax: 501(c)(3)

Personnel:
Chief Executive Officer: Loren Greenway FAWM, FCCP, PhD
   E-Mail: loren@wms.org
Managing Editor: Jonna Barry
   E-Mail: jonna@wms.org
Administrative Director: Teri Howell
   E-Mail: teri@wms.org
Director, Information Technology: Jim Ingwersen
   E-Mail: jim@wms.org

Historical Note:
WMS seeks to advance healthcare, research, and education related to wilderness medicine. Membership: $50-225/year; $1,600-2,500 (Life Membership).

Meetings/Conferences: Semi-Annual
2013 - Park City, UT (The Canyons)/Feb. 15 - 20
2013 - Breckenridge, CO (Beaver Run Resort and Conference Center)/July 11 - 17
Number of non-conference events/year: 38

Publications:
Members Directory; on-line; adv.
Practice Guidelines for Emergency Care
Wilderness and Environmental Medicine Journal; quarterly; adv.
Wilderness Medicine Magazine; quarterly; adv.

Wildlife Disease Association *(1951)*
P.O. Box 7065
Lawrence, KS 66044-7065
Tel: (785) 843-1234 *Fax:* (785) 843-1274
TollFree: (800) 627-0326
E-Mail: wda@allenpress.com
Website: wildlifedisease.org
Members: 1000 individuals
Staff: 3
Annual Budget: $250-500,000

Personnel:
President: Dolores Gavier-Widen
Business Manager: Kay Rose
   E-Mail: krose@allenpress.com

Historical Note:
Formed in Milwaukee, WI at the North American Wildlife Conference. Originally the Committee on Wildlife Diseases, the name was changed to the Wildlife Disease Association in 1952 and the association was incorporated in Illinois in 1964. WDA's mission is to acquire, disseminate and apply knowledge of the health and diseases of wild animals in relation to their biology, conservation and interactions with human and domestic animals. Membership: $100-110 (Regular); $30 (Associate); $40-50 (Student).

Meetings/Conferences: Annual
Number of non-conference events/year: 2

Publications:
Journal of Wildlife Diseases; on-line
Wildlife Disease Association Newsletter; quarterly

Wildlife Management Institute *(1911)*
1440 Upper Bermudian Rd.
Gardners, PA 17324
Tel: (717) 677-4480
E-Mail: info@wildlifemgt.org
Website: wildlifemanagementinstitute.org
Members: 700 individuals
Staff: 4
Annual Budget: $2-5,000,000
Tax: 501(c)(3)

Personnel:
President: Steven A. Williams
   E-Mail: swilliams@wildlifemgt.org

Historical Note:
WMI strives for the conservation, enhancement and professional management of North America's wildlife and other natural resources. Membership: $15-1500/year.

Meetings/Conferences: Annual
2013 - Arlington, VA (Crystal Gateway Marriott)/March 25 - 30
2014 - Denver, CO (Sheraton Downtown Denver Hotel)/March 9 - 14
2015 - Omaha, NE (Hilton Omaha)/March 8 - 13

Publications:
Outdoor News Bulletin; monthly

The Wildlife Society *(1937)*
5410 Grosvenor Ln.
Suite 200
Bethesda, MD 20814-2144
Tel: (301) 897-9770 *Fax:* (301) 530-2471
E-Mail: membership@wildlife.org
Website: wildlife.org
Members: 8800 individuals
Staff: 28
Annual Budget: $250-500,000
Tax: 501(c)(3)

Personnel:
Executive Director and Chief Executive Officer: Michael Hutchins
   E-Mail: michael@wildlife.org
Director, Government Affairs: Laura Bies
   E-Mail: laura@wildlife.org
Database and Information Technology Administrator: Aniket Gajare
   E-Mail: agajare@wildlife.org
Manager, Office and Finance: Jane Jorgenson
   E-Mail: jane@wildlife.org
Director, Communications and Editor-in-Chief: Lisa Moore LaRoe
   E-Mail: lmoore@wildlife.org
Program Manager, Subunits and Certification: Shannon Pederson
   E-Mail: shannon@wildlife.org
Operations Manager: Yanin Walker
   E-Mail: yanin@wildlife.org

Director, Membership, Marketing and Conferences: Darryl Walter
E-Mail: dwalter@wildlife.org

Historical Note:
TWS's mission is to represent and serve the professional community of scientists, managers, educators, technicians, planners, and others who work actively to study, manage, and conserve wildlife and habitats worldwide. Membership: $71 (Regular); $46 (New Professional); $36 (Student).

Continuing Education:
Certification Designation/s: PDC, WTC, AWB, CWB

Meetings/Conferences: Annual
Conference Chair: Darryl Walter
2013 - Milwaukee, WI/Oct. 5 - 9
2014 - Pittsburgh, PA/Oct. 25 - 30
2015 - Winnipeg, MB/Oct. 17 - 21

Publications:
Journal of Wildlife Management; quarterly; adv.
The Annual Conference News Update; weekly
The Wildlife Certification Newsletter
The Wildlife Monographs
The Wildlife Professional
The Wildlife Society News Brief; weekly
The Wildlifer; monthly; adv.
Wildlife Policy News; bi-monthly
Wildlife Policy News; on-line
Wildlife Society Bulletin

Membership List Available to Non-members

Wilson Ornithological Society (1888)
P.O. Box 737
Sandusky, OH 44871
Website: wilsonsociety.org
Members: 2500 members
Staff: 3
Annual Budget: $100-250,000

Personnel:
President: Robert Beason
E-Mail: Robert.C.Beason@gmail.com

Historical Note:
The Wilson Ornithological Society is a world-wide organization who share a curiosity about birds. Membership: $40 (Active); $20 (Student); $50 (Family); $100 (Sustaining); $1000 (Life).

Meetings/Conferences: Annual
2013 - Williamsburg, VA (College of William and Mary)/March 7 - 9
2014 - Newport, RI (Salve Regina University)/May 29 - June 1

Publications:
Membership Directory; on-line
Ornithological Newsletter; bi-monthly; adv.
The Wilson Journal of Ornithology; quarterly; adv.
Wilson Bulletin

Window and Door Manufacturers Association (1927)
401 N. Michigan Ave.
Suite 2200
Chicago, IL 60611
Tel: (312) 321-6802 Fax: (312) 673-6922
TollFree: (800) 223-2301
E-Mail: wdma@wdma.com
Website: wdma.com
Members: 150 companies
Staff: 8
Annual Budget: $1-2,000,000

Personnel:
President and Chief Executive Officer: Michael O'Brien CAE
E-Mail: mobrien@wdma.com
Communications and Operations Associate: Stephen Kendrick
E-Mail: skendrick@wdma.com
Vice President, Technical Services: Jeff Lowinski
E-Mail: jlowinski@wdma.com
Vice President, Certification Programs: John McFee
E-Mail: jmcfee@wdma.com
Manager, Membership Services and Operations: Jonathan Paine
E-Mail: jpaine@wdma.com

Historical Note:
Founded as the National Door Manufacturers Association, became the National Woodwork Manufacturers Association Inc. in 1949. In 1985 WDMA became the National Wood Window and Door Association, assumed its current name in 1998. Absorbed the Ponderosa Pine Woodwork

Association in 1975. WDMA defines the standards of excellence in the residential and commercial window, door and skylight industry and advances these standards among industry members. Provides resources, education and professional programs designed to advance industry businesses and provides greater value for their customers. Members are makers of standard building products such as doors, windows, and frames.

Continuing Education:
Certification Designation/s: HC

Meetings/Conferences: Annual

Publications:
WDMA Newsletter

Window Council (1958)
2850 S. Ocean Blvd., Suite 114
Palm Beach, FL 33480-6205
Tel: (561) 533-0991 Fax: (561) 533-7466
Members: 5 companies
Staff: 1
Annual Budget: Under $10,000

Personnel:
President: Frank S. Fitzgerald CAE, DABFE, FACFE

Historical Note:
Organized to develop window safety programs for children.

Window Covering Manufacturers Association (1950)
355 Lexington Ave.
15th Floor
New York, NY 10017-6603
Tel: (212) 297-2122 Fax: (212) 370-9047
Website: wcmanet.org
Members: 11 companies
Staff: 4
Annual Budget: $250-500,000

Personnel:
Executive Director: Ralph Vasami
E-Mail: rvasami@kellencompany.com

Historical Note:
Formerly Venetian Blind Institute; later became the (1977) Venetian Blind Association; (1985) United States Venetian Blind Association ; (1995) American Window Coverings Manufacturers Association . WCMA represents the interests of the window covering industry manufacturers, fabricators and assemblers. Industry products include blinds, shades, shutters, curtains, curtain rods, drapes, drapery hardware, and other window treatments. Membership: $3,000 (Associate); $1,000-15,000 (Manufacturer).

Publications:
Newsletter

Window Covering Safety Council (1994)
355 Lexington Ave.
Suite 1500
New York, NY 10017
Tel: (212) 297-2100 Fax: (212) 370-9047
TollFree: (800) 506-4636
E-Mail: info@windowcoverings.org
Website: windowcoverings.org
Staff: 1
Annual Budget: $500-1,000,000

Personnel:
Executive Director: Peter S Rush

Historical Note:
WCSC is a coalition of major U.S. manufacturers, importers and retailers of window coverings dedicated to educating consumers about window cord safety. WCSC's mission is to educate Americans about potential window-cord hazards facing young children and provide consumers with free retrofit kits and information.

Publications:
Home & Child Safety

Window Coverings Association of America (1987)
9707 Key West Ave.
Suite 100
Rockville, MD 20850
Tel: (240) 404-6490 Fax: (888) 496-0272
TollFree: (888) 298-9222
Website: wcaa.org
Members: 1300 Individuals
Staff: 4
Annual Budget: $250-500,000

Personnel:
Executive Director: Bill Scott CAE
E-Mail: bill@wcaa.org
Meeting Planner: Julie Burgess

E-Mail: meetings@wcaa.org
Manager, Marketing: Julie Hill
E-Mail: marketing@wcaa.org
Manager, Member Services: Shannon Sperati
E-Mail: membership@wcaa.org

Historical Note:
WCAA is dedicated to the retail window coverings industry and its dealers, decorators, designers, and workrooms who are its members. Membership: $150 (Individual); $50 (Student).

Continuing Education:
Certification Designation/s: CWTC, CWP

Meetings/Conferences:
Conference Chair: Julie Burgess

Publications:
Cover Story; bi-monthly
WCAA Membership Directory; on-line; adv.

Wine and Spirits Shippers Association (1976)
11800 Sunrise Valley Dr.
Suite 425
Reston, VA 20191-5396
Tel: (703) 860-2300 Fax: (703) 860-2422
TollFree: (800) 368-3167
E-Mail: info@wssa.com
Website: wssa.com
Members: 600 companies
Staff: 6
Annual Budget: $1-2,000,000

Personnel:
Managing Director: Geoffrey N. Giovanetti
E-Mail: ggiovanetti@wssa.com
Coordinator, Programs: Catherine Jennings
E-Mail: cjennings@wssa.com
Contract and Rate Manager: Geraldine Zilleruelo
E-Mail: gzilleruelo@wssa.com

Historical Note:
WSSA was founded by the Wine and Spirits Wholesalers of America (WSWA) and the National Association of Beverage Importers (NABI) in 1976 as a shipping cooperative. WSSA is dedicated to providing efficient and economical transportation by land, sea, or air, enables its members to tap into a marketplace efficiently and affordably. Members are composed of importers and exporters of beverages and allied products. Membership: $100/year (Company).

Meetings/Conferences:
Conference Chair: Catherine Jennings

Publications:
Member Directory; on-line

Wine and Spirits Wholesalers of America (1943)
805 15th St. NW
Suite 430
Washington, DC 20005-2203
Tel: (202) 371-9792 Fax: (202) 789-2405
E-Mail: Info@wswa.org
Website: wswa.org
Members: 340 companies
Staff: 20
Annual Budget: $5-10,000,000
Tax: 501(c)(6)

Personnel:
President and Chief Executive Officer: Craig Wolf
E-Mail: craig.wolf@wswa.org
Vice President, Finance and Administration: Sam Block
Director, Communications: Ashley Durkin
Director, Interactive Communications and Marketing: Jasmine Henderson
Manager, Meetings and Conventions: Kari Langerman
Vice President and Co-General Counsel, Litigation and Regulatory: Karin Moore
E-Mail: karin.moore@wswa.org
Senior Vice President, Government Affairs: James A. Rowland
E-Mail: jim.rowland@wswa.org
Vice President, Communications: Jeff L. Solsby
Director, Membership Services: Bob Wiggans
E-Mail: bob.wiggans@wswa.org

Historical Note:
WSWA is the national trade organization representing the wholesale tier of the wine and spirits industry. It is dedicated to advancing the interests and independence of wholesale distributors and/or brokers of wine and/or spirits. Membership: $1,000-10,000/year (Associate).

Meetings/Conferences: Annual
Conference Chair: Kari Langerman
2013 - Orlando, FL (Grande Lakes)/April 28 - 30

Number of non-conference events/year: 1

Publications:
Membership Roster & Industry Directory; on-line

Membership List Available to Non-members

WineAmerica (1978)
1015 18th St. NW
Suite 500
Washington, DC 20036
Tel: (202) 783-2756 *Fax:* (202) 347-6341
TollFree: (800) 879-4537
E-Mail: info@wineamerica.org
Website: wineamerica.org
Members: 824 wineries
Staff: 4
Annual Budget: $500-1,000,000
Tax: 501(c)(6)

Personnel:
President: Bill Nelson
Chief Operating Officer: Cary Greene
　　E-Mail: cgreene@wineamerica.org
Director, Communications and Regulatory Affairs: Michael Kaiser
　　E-Mail: mkaiser@wineamerica.org
Director, Grassroots and Political Affairs: Jennifer Montgomery
　　E-Mail: jmontgomery@wineamerica.org

Historical Note:
Formerly the American Vintners Association. WineAmerica's mission is to encourage the growth and development of American wineries and winegrowing through the advancement and advocacy of sound public policy. Membership: $250-1,000 (Supplier); $250 (Wineries).

Publications:
Ezines; quarterly
WineAmerica Newsletter; monthly; adv.

Winegrape Growers of America (1978)
1325 J St.
Suite 1560
Sacramento, CA 95814
Tel: (800) 241-1800 *Fax:* (916) 379-8999
E-Mail: info@cawg.org
Website: winegrapegrowersofamerica.org
Staff: 2
Annual Budget: $25-50,000

Personnel:
Executive Director: John Aguirre
Treasurer: Kim Ledbetter Bronson

Historical Note:
WGA's mission is to represent the national winegrape growing industry. The Winegrape Growers of America (WGA) is based on the power of unity, cooperation and efficiency.

Meetings/Conferences: Annual
2013 - Washington, DC (Holiday Inn Capitol)/March 17 - 20

Publications:
WGA Newsletter

Wire and Cable Industry Suppliers Association (1918)
1867 W. Market St.
Akron, OH 44313
Tel: (330) 864-2122 *Fax:* (330) 864-5298
E-Mail: info@wcisaonline.org
Website: wcisaonline.org
Members: 100 companies
Staff: 1
Annual Budget: $25-50,000

Personnel:
Executive Director: Michael J. McNulty

Historical Note:
Founded as Wire Machinery Builders Association; became Wire Industry Suppliers Association in 1987, and assumed its current name in 2002. WCISA's mission is to promote its members' products and services by providing representation, networking/social opportunities and services at wire and cable trade events and conferences. Membership: $310/year (Company).

Publications:
Membership Directory; on-line
Overview
Wire & Cable Technology International; bi-monthly

Membership List Available to Non-members

The Wire Association International, Inc. (1930)
1570 Boston Post Rd.
P.O. Box 578
Guilford, CT 06437-0578
Tel: (203) 453-2777 *Fax:* (203) 453-8384
Website: wirenet.org
Members: 2400 individuals
Staff: 10
Annual Budget: $500-1,000,000

Personnel:
Executive Director: Steven J. Fetteroll
Manager, Conventions and Events: Livia A. Jacobs
Treasurer: David LaValley
Editor-in-Chief: Mark A. Marselli
Director, Education and Membership Services: Marc L. Murray
Director, Marketing and Corporate Communications: Janice E. Swindells
Administrator, Information Technology: Charles (Chuck) Szymaszek

Historical Note:
Formerly (1977) the Wire Association Inc., WAI's mission is to serve the technical, manufacturing and general business segments of the global wire and cable industry. Members are individuals involved in wire manufacturing, wire forming and fabricating and supplying the wire and cable industry. Membership: $110/year (Individual).

Meetings/Conferences: Annual
Conference Chair: Livia A. Jacobs
2013 - Atlanta, GA (Georgia World Congress Center)/ April 23 - 25
2014 - Indianapolis, IN (Indianapolis Convention Center)/May 6 - 7

Publications:
The WAI Connection; semi-monthly

Wire Fabricators Association (1976)
P.O. Box 304
Montgomery, IL 60538-0304
Tel: (630) 896-1469 *Fax:* (209) 633-6265
Website: wirefabricators.org
Members: 40 companies and 10 associates
Staff: 2
Annual Budget: $50-100,000
Tax: 501(c)(6)

Personnel:
Executive Director and Membership Contact: Roseanne M. Hoban
　　E-Mail: rhoban@wirefabricators.org
Treasurer: Steve Diebold

Historical Note:
WFA's mission is considering and resolving common problems of operation for the industry, addressing health and safety issues, fostering sound and equitable employment relation policies and producing quality products efficiently and economically. Members are manufacturers of items composed principally of low carbon steel wire. Membership: $400-500 (Fabricator, based on number of employees); $1,500 (Associate).

Meetings/Conferences: Annual
2013 - Marco Island, FL/Jan. 24 - 26

Publications:
Labor Review Report; annually

Membership List Available to Non-members

Wire Reinforcement Institute (1930)
942 Main St.
Suite 300
Hartford, CT 06103
Tel: (860) 240-9545 *Fax:* (860) 808-3009
Website: wirereinforcementinstitute.org
Members: 22 companies
Staff: 1
Annual Budget: $100-250,000

Personnel:
Marketing Consultant: Terri Albert
　　E-Mail: wwrinfo@wirereinforcementinstitute.org

Historical Note:
WRI's mission is to be the concrete construction industry's source for timely, objective, credible information on the uses and benefits of Welded Wire Reinforcement and related products. Members produce welded wire reinforcement for reinformed concrete and construction precast components according to the standards and specification of the American Society for Testing and Materials, and the American Concrete Institute. Membership: Based on annual shipments, $7,596-10,131/year (Regular, within US);

$4,558-6,079/year (Regular, outside US); $1,595-6,714/year (Associate, based on business volume).

Publications:
WRI UPDATE newsletter

Membership List Available to Non-members

Wire Rope Technical Board (1959)
801 N. Fairfax St.
Suite 211
Alexandria, VA 22314-1757
Tel: (703) 299-8550 *Fax:* (703) 299-9253
TollFree: (888) 289-9782
E-Mail: wrtb@usa.net
Website: wireropetechnicalboard.org
Members: 5 companies
Staff: 2
Annual Budget: $50-100,000

Personnel:
Executive Director: Kimberly A. Korbel

Historical Note:
An association of engineers from companies who are wire rope manufacturers with a common goal to share technical knowledge, improve the production and quality standards of wire rope industry, extend the uses of wire rope by sharing technical and engineering information to equipment manufacturers.

Wireless Communications Association International (1988)
1333 H St. NW
Suite 700-W
Washington, DC 20005
Tel: (202) 452-7823 *Fax:* (202) 452-0041
Website: wcai.com
Members: 250 companies
Staff: 4
Annual Budget: $500-1,000,000

Personnel:
Director, Operations: Joe Supervielle
　　E-Mail: joe@wcai.com
Director, Membership and Services: Thomas Wilde
　　E-Mail: thomas@wcai.com

Historical Note:
WCA's mission is to foster the growth of such services, including voice, data, Internet, e-commerce and video applications. Membership is comprised of service providers, equipment manufacturers, application developers and other contributors to the wireless broadband industry. Membership: $2,500-10,000 (Operators and Vendors); $1,000(Consultants); Free (Non profits).

Meetings/Conferences:
Conference Chair: Joe Supervielle

Publications:
WCAI's Transmitter; weekly

Wireless Industry Association (1986)
9746 Tappenbeck Dr.
Houston, TX 77055-4102
Tel: (713) 467-0077
TollFree: (800) 624-6918
E-Mail: contact@wirelessindustry.com
Website: wirelessindustry.com
Members: 2500 members
Staff: 36
Annual Budget: $500-1,000,000

Personnel:
President: Robert Hutchinson
　　E-Mail: bob@wirelessindustry.com

Historical Note:
Founded as National Association of Cellular Agents and assumed its current name in 1995. WIA is a clearing house of information and wireless business operations in the industry. Members are cellular and wireless communications agents, dealers, resellers, carriers, manufacturers, distributors and importers. Membership: $1,095 (Wholesaler); $1,295 (Distributor).

Publications:
Wireless Magazine

Wireless Innovation Forum (1996)
12100 Sunset Hills Rd.,
Suite 130
Reston, VA 20190
Website: wirelessinnovation.org
Staff: 4
Annual Budget: $500-1,000,000

Personnel:

Chief Executive Officer: Lee Pucker
    E-Mail: lee.pucker@wirelessinnovation.org
Webmaster: Joel Gluck
    E-Mail: webmaster@wirelessinnovation.org
Contact, Marketing and Communications: Stephanie
    Hamill
    E-Mail: stephaniehamill@wirelessinnovation.org
Account Manager: Don Kaiser
    E-Mail: Don.Kaiser@wirelessinnovation.org

Historical Note:
The Wireless Innovation Forum, working in collaboration
with the Institute of Electrical and Electronic Engineers
(IEEE) P1900.1 group, has worked to establish a definition
of SDR that provides consistency and a clear overview of
the technology and its associated benefits. Membership:
$8500 (Large commercial); $5500 (Medium); $2600
(Small commercial); $2550 (Government and non-profit
organizations); $1500 (Academic Institutions).

Publications:
SDR e-Newsletter

Wiring Harness Manufacturers Association
(1993)
7500 Flying Cloud Dr.
Suite 900
Eden Prairie, MN 55344
Tel: (952) 253-6225 Fax: (952) 835-4774
E-Mail: whma@associationsolutionsinc.com
Website: whma.org
Members: 200 companies
Staff: 3
Annual Budget: $250-500,000

Personnel:
Treasurer and Secretary: Randy Olson
    E-Mail: randy@squires.com

Historical Note:
WHMA represents the interests and concerns of
manufacturers of electronic cable assemblies, cord sets and
wiring harnesses. Membership: $350-650 (Regular, based
on sales volume); $1,000-1,600 (Suppliers).

Continuing Education:
Certification Designation/s: A-620

Meetings/Conferences: Annual
2013 - Las Vegas, NV (Renaissance Las Vegas Hotel)/
    Feb. 20 - 22

Publications:
Hot Wire; monthly
Member Directory; on-line
Wiring Harness News

Women Band Directors International (1969)
2711 Grant Lakes Blvd.
Suite 61
Sugar Land, TX 77479
Tel: (403) 314-9094
Website: womenbanddirectors.org
Members: 355 individuals
Staff: 4
Annual Budget: Under $10,000
Tax: 501(c)(3)

Personnel:
President: Linda Thompson
    E-Mail: lkaythomp@gmail.com
Editor: Kathy Cox
    E-Mail: kathyhcox@aol.com
Treasurer: Carol Nendza
    E-Mail: carolnen@aol.com
Executive Secretary: Gladys Stone Wright
    E-Mail: agwright@verizon.net

Historical Note:
Chartered as Women Band Directors National Association,
assumed current name in 1997. WBDI serves as an
association which supports, promotes, and mentors women
in the band field. Active members are women engaged in
directing bands and women who have been directors but are
not presently so engaged. Membership: $10 (Tenured); $20
(Student); $35 (Active/Affiliate); $40 (International).

Meetings/Conferences: Semi-Annual
2013 - New Orleans, LA/June 19 - 23
Number of non-conference events/year: 1

Publications:
Bandworld; monthly
The Woman Conductor

Women Chefs and Restaurateurs (1993)
P.O. Box 1875
Madison, AL 35758

Tel: (256) 975-1346
TollFree: (877) 927-7787
E-Mail: admin@womenchefs.org
Website: womenchefs.org
Members: 2000 individuals
Staff: 3
Annual Budget: $100-250,000
Tax: 501(c)(6)

Personnel:
Executive Director: Lieann O'Brien
    E-Mail: admin@womenchefs.org
Director, Membership Programs: Joey Belden
    E-Mail: joey@womenchefs.org
Editor: Leila Corcoran
    E-Mail: l.corcoran2@verizon.net

Historical Note:
WCR founded as International Association of Women Chefs
and Restaurateurs in 1993. WCR's mission is to promote
and enhance the education, advancement and connection
of women in the culinary industry. Membership: $195
(Executive); $45 (Student); $55 (Beginning Restaurant
Professional); $95 (Chef/Restaurant/Culinary Professional);
$140 (Friend of WCR); $280 (Small Business); $1,650
(Corporate).

Meetings/Conferences: Annual
2013 - San Francisco, CA (Sir Francis Drake)/Jan. 16 -
18

Publications:
Entrez; quarterly
Membership Directory; on-line

Membership List Available to Non-members

Women Construction Owners and Executives, USA (1983)
1004 Duke St.
Alexandria, VA 22314
Tel: (916) 484-1339 Fax: (202) 330-5151
TollFree: (800) 788-3548
E-Mail: info@wcoeusa.org
Website: wcoeusa.org
Members: 250 individuals
Staff: 2
Annual Budget: $100-250,000
Tax: 501(c)(6)

Personnel:
National Executive Director: Penny Pompei
Treasurer: Deborah Bradley

Historical Note:
WCOE's mission is to promote the growth of women
owners and policy executives in the construction industry.
Provides educational seminars, business connections and
advocacy for issues impacting the industry. Helps members
to build their business through networking and information.
Membership: $25-25,000/year.

Meetings/Conferences: Annual

Publications:
Turning Point; weekly

Women in Aerospace (1984)
204 E St. NE
Washington, DC 20002
Tel: (202) 547-0229 Fax: (202) 547-6348
E-Mail: info@womeninaerospace.org
Website: womeninaerospace.org
Members: 300 individuals
Staff: 8
Annual Budget: $250-500,000

Personnel:
President: Stephanie Schierholz
Executive Director: Annette Summers
    E-Mail: asummers@womeninaerospace.org
Treasurer: Emma Hinds
Vice President, Communications: Jennifer Hoil
Vice President, Membership: Karen Yasumura

Historical Note:
WIA is dedicated to expanding women's opportunities
for leadership and increasing their visibility in the
aerospace community. Members include journalists,
industry executives, government officials and congressional
staff. Membership: $500 (Corporate Nonprofit); $1,000
(Corporate Bronze); $2,500 (Corporate Silver); $5,000
(Corporate Gold); $10,000 (Corporate Platinum); $20-75
(Individual).

Meetings/Conferences: Annual
2013 - Arlington, VA (Key Bridge Marriott)/June 14

Publications:
Connections Newsletter; quarterly

Membership Directory; on-line

Women in Agribusiness
300 Rosewood Dr.
Suite 30
Danvers, MA 01923
Tel: (978) 887-8800
E-Mail: icevinlandusa@sbcglobal.net
Website: womeninag.com
Members: 150 individuals
Staff: 5
Annual Budget: Under $10,000

Personnel:
President: Mark Dineen
    E-Mail: mdineen@soyatech.com
Contact, Sponsorship Sales: Lissa Blake
    E-Mail: lblake@highquestpartners.com
Content Manager, Meetings Contact and Research Analyst:
    Sarah E. Clark
    E-Mail: sclark@highquestpartners.com
Contact, Media Partners: Michelle Marshall
    E-Mail: mmarshall@highquestpartners.com
Contact, Student Scholarships: Frances Pratt
    E-Mail: fpratt@highquestpartners.com

Historical Note:
WIA was established to organize women in agribusiness
and to provide a forum on subjects concerning the industry.
Has no paid officers or full-time staff. Membership: $1,495
(Regular Delegate) ; $795 (Small Farmer/Producer Rate);
$195 (Student).

Meetings/Conferences: Annual
Conference Chair: Sarah E. Clark
2013 - Minneapolis, MN/Oct. 23 - 24

Women in Aviation International (1990)
C/O Morningstar Airport
3647 State Route 503 South
W. Alexandria, OH 45381-9354
Tel: (937) 839-4647 Fax: (937) 839-4645
E-Mail: wai@wai.org
Website: wai.org
Members: 7000 Members
Staff: 13
Annual Budget: $1-2,000,000
Tax: 501(c)(3)

Personnel:
President: Dr. Peggy Baty-Chabrian PhD
    E-Mail: pchabrian@wai.org
Manager, Membership Services and Merchandise: Sue
    Coon
    E-Mail: scoon@wai.org
Manager, Computer Services: Doug Henderson
Manager, Publications: Amy Laboda
    E-Mail: alaboda@wai.org
Manager, Operations and Executive Assistant: Connie
    Lawrence
Coordinator, Conferences: Verne Wiese
    E-Mail: vwiese@wai.org

Historical Note:
WAI works towards the encouragement and advancement
of women in all aviation career fields and interests.
Members include pilots, air traffic controllers, airport
managers, engineers, flight attendants, and others with
an interest in encouraging women to seek professional
opportunites in aviation. Membership: $39 (Individual/
International - Digital Only/International Student); $29
(Student/International Student - Digital); $20 (Family);
$49 (International); $400 (Corporate); $500 (Supersonic
Corporate).

Meetings/Conferences: Annual
Conference Chair: Sue Coon
2013 - Nashville, TN (Gaylord Opryland Resort and
    Convention Center)/March 14 - 16

Publications:
Aviation for Women Magazine; bi-monthly; adv.
Membership Directory; on-line
WAI Connect Newsletter; on-line; adv.

Women in Cable Telecommunications, Inc.
(1979)
14555 Avion Pkwy.
Suite 250
Chantilly, VA 20151
Tel: (703) 234-9810 Fax: (703) 817-1595
E-Mail: membership@wict.org
Website: wict.org
Members: 7880 individuals
Staff: 22

Annual Budget: $2-5,000,000
Tax: 501(c)(3)

Personnel:
President and Chief Executive Officer: Maria Brennan
  E-Mail: mbrennan@wict.org
Director, Events and Programs: Kristie Chang
  E-Mail: kchang@wict.org
Senior Vice President and Chief of Staff: Parthavi Das
  E-Mail: pdas@wict.org
Vice President, Business Development: Lesa Faris
  E-Mail: lfaris@wict.org
Vice President, Communications: Talton Gibson
  E-Mail: tgibson@wict.org
Director, Finance and Administration: Donna McDonald
  E-Mail: dmcdonald@wict.org
Vice President of Education and Program Development:
  Christina Vergara
  E-Mail: cvergara@wict.org
Senior Director, Member Services: Robin Burke Zahory
  E-Mail: rzahory@wict.org

Historical Note:
*Formerly (1994) Women in Cable. WICT's mission
is to develop women leaders. It also seeks to provide
opportunities for leadership, networking, and advocacy
in the industry. Membership: $275 (Executive); $175
(Regular); $75 (Entry); $35 (Student).*

Meetings/Conferences: Annual
Conference Chair: Kristie Chang
Number of non-conference events/year: 1

Publications:
Membership Directory
WICT Newsletters

Women in Cell Biology *(1972)*
8120 Woodmont Ave.
Suite 750
Bethesda, MD 20814-2762
Tel: (301) 347-9300 *Fax:* (301) 347-9310
E-Mail: wicb@ascb.org
Website: ascb.org/index.php?
  option = com_content&view = art
Staff: 1

Personnel:
Contact Associate, WICB: Cheryl Lehr
  E-Mail: clehr@ascb.org

Historical Note:
*WICB serves as a resource for women and men at all stages
in their scientific trajectories. Members are women cell
biologists.*

Women in Endocrinology *(1975)*
5323 Harry Hines Blvd.
Dallas, TX 75390-9032
Tel: (214) 648-9593 *Fax:* (214) 648-8066
Website: women-in-endo.org
Members: 400 individuals
Staff: 2
Annual Budget: $10-25,000
Tax: 501(c)(3)

Personnel:
President: Lisa M. Halvorson MD
  E-Mail: lisa.halvorson@utsouthwestern.edu

Historical Note:
*WE's purpose is to advocate educational opportunities
for women in the science and discipline of Endocrinology.
Membership: $50 (Faculty/Medical/Industry); Free
(Student); $15 (Resident/Post- Doctoral/Fellow).*

Meetings/Conferences: Annual

Publications:
WE Member Directory
WE newsletter

Women in Energy *(1978)*
P.O. Box 105252
Jefferson City, MO 65110-5252
Tel: (573) 635-6448
Members: 50 individuals
Staff: 1
Annual Budget: Under $10,000

Personnel:
President: Judy Gustafson

Historical Note:
*Members are persons employed in energy and related energy
businesses working in areas such as science, engineering,
finance, consumer education, communications, home
economics, etc. Membership: $50/year.*

Women in Film *(1973)*
6100 Wilshire Blvd.
Suite 710
Los Angeles, CA 90048
Tel: (323) 935-2211 *Fax:* (323) 935-2212
E-Mail: info@wif.org
Website: wif.org
Members: 2300 individuals
Staff: 5
Annual Budget: $1-2,000,000
Tax: 501(c)(3)

Personnel:
Executive Director: Gayle Nachlis
  E-Mail: gnachlis@wif.org
Controller: David Kay
  E-Mail: controller@wif.org

Historical Note:
*WIF is a non-profit organization. WIF is dedicated to
help women to achieve their potential within the global
entertainment, communications and media industries and
to preserve the legacy of women within those industries.
General members of WIF must have a minimum of three
years of professional experience in the executive, guild or
craft areas of the industry. Membership: $10,000 (Lifetime);
$150 (General); $85 (Associate); $35 (Student); $440
(Executive); $925 (Friends of Women in Film).*

Publications:
WIF Weekly News; weekly; adv.

Women In Film and Television International *(1997)*
59 E Via Plaza Nueva
Santa Fe, NM 87507
Tel: (212) 679-0870 *Fax:* (212) 679-0899
E-Mail: info@nywift.org
Website: wifti.org
Members:
10000 members
37 chapters
Staff: 1

Personnel:
Vice Chair: Janet Davidson

Historical Note:
*WIFTI's mission is to enhance the international visibility
of women in the entertainment industry, facilitate and
encourage communication and cooperation internationally,
Develop bold international projects and initiatives,
Stimulate professional development and global networking
opportunities for women. It seeks to encourage diverse and
positive representation of women in screen-based media
worldwide.*

Publications:
Member Directory; on-line

Women in Government *(1988)*
1319 F St. NW
Suite 710
Washington, DC 20004
Tel: (202) 333-0825 *Fax:* (202) 333-0875
TollFree: (888) 333-0164
E-Mail: wig@womeningovernment.org
Website: womeningovernment.org
Members: 136 individuals
Staff: 20
Annual Budget: $1-2,000,000
Tax: 501(c)(3)

Personnel:
President and Executive Director: Marjorie Maginn
  E-Mail: mmaginn@womeningovernment.org
Director, Policy and Programs: Libby Derting
  E-Mail: lderting@womeningovernment.org
Director, Meetings and Membership Services: Heather
  Kearns
  E-Mail: hkearns@womeningovernment.org

Historical Note:
*WIG's mission is to provide leadership opportunities,
networking, expert forums, and educational resources to
address and resolve complex public policy issues. WIG
members are women holding elected offices at the state
levels. Friends Membership is open to individuals and
students. Membership: $125 (Legislative); $50 (Individual);
$20 (Student).*

Meetings/Conferences: Annual
Conference Chair: Heather Kearns

Publications:
AccessEd; quarterly
Family Finance; quarterly
Health Matters; quarterly

Prevention Connection; quarterly
Rheumatoid Arthritis Today; quarterly
The Legislative Voice; quarterly

Women in Government Relations, Inc. *(1975)*
8400 Westpark Dr.
Second Floor
McLean, VA 22102
Tel: (703) 610-9030 *Fax:* (703) 995-0528
E-Mail: info@wgr.org
Website: wgr.org
Members: 650 members
Staff: 6
Annual Budget: $250-500,000
Tax: 501(c)(6)

Personnel:
Executive Director: Patricia Gaitan
  E-Mail: pgaitan@wgr.org
Operations Manager: Tracy Cacho
  E-Mail: tcacho@wgr.org
Senior Advisor: Kimberly A. Korbel
  E-Mail: kkorbel@wgr.org
Coordinator, Membership and Events: Heather Outhuse
  E-Mail: houthuse@wgr.org
Specialist, Database: Toya Vigne
  E-Mail: tvigne@wgr.org

Historical Note:
*WGR works for the advancement and empowerment
of women at all career levels of government relations.
Membership: $195 (Private Sector/Vendor/Supplier); $45
(Public Sector); $25 (Fulltime Student); $100 (Associate).*

Meetings/Conferences:
Conference Chair: Heather Outhuse
Number of non-conference events/year: 3

Publications:
Membership Directory; on-line
Newsletter; bi-monthly
WGR Around Town; bi-monthly; adv.

Women in International Security *(1987)*
Center for Strategic and International Studies
1800 K St. NW
Washington, DC 20006
Tel: (202) 887-0200 *Fax:* (202) 775-3199
Website: csis.org/program/wiis
Members: 7000 members
Staff: 4
Annual Budget: $500-1,000,000

Personnel:
Director: Jolynn Shoemaker
  E-Mail: jshoemaker@csis.org
Coordinator, Development: Denise Bertholin
Program Manager: Marie-Laure Poire
Senior Vice President, External Relations: H. Andrew
  Schwartz
  E-Mail: aschwartz@csis.org

Historical Note:
*WIIS is dedicated to increasing the influence of women in
the field of foreign and defense affairs and enhancing the
dialogue on international security. WIIS is an affiliated
program of CSIS. Offers comprehensive programs designed
to foster and promote women in government, business, think
tanks, academia and the media. Membership: $400 (Patron
Level); $125 (Sustaining); $65 (Basic); $45 (Overseas);
$30 (Student); $50 (US - Outside DC area); $275 (Non-
profit Institution); $5,000 (Corporate).*

Meetings/Conferences:
Conference Chair: Marie-Laure Poire
Number of non-conference events/year: 2

Publications:
WIIS JobsHotline

Membership List Available to Non-members

Women in Management *(1978)*
P.O. Box 1032
Dundee, IL 60118-7032
Website: wimonline.org
Members: 200 individuals
Staff: 3
Annual Budget: $25-50,000

Personnel:
President: Cary Sue Lavan
Vice President, Membership Services: Deb Domagalski
Vice President, Communications: Katrina Laflin

Historical Note:

WIM's mission is to promote the professionalism of its members through education, development, encouragement and mentoring. Membership: $100/year.

Publications:
Membership Directory; on-line
WIM Newsletter

Women in Mining National (1981)
P.O. Box 260246
Lakewood, CO 80226-0246
Tel: (303) 298-1535
TollFree: (866) 537-9694
E-Mail: wimnational@womeninmining.org
Website: womeninmining.org
Members: 600 individuals
Staff: 4
Annual Budget: $10-25,000
Tax: 501(c)(6)

Personnel:
President: Stephen Tibbals
Editor: Jackie Dorr
    E-Mail: jdorr@mii.org
Treasurer: Jann Higdem
Secretary: Hannah McNally

Historical Note:
WIM National's purpose is to enhance communication and coordination among chapters, assist formation of new chapters and support chapter educational programs. Membership: $30 (Individual); $300-5,000 (Sustaining Membership Corporate).

Meetings/Conferences: Annual
2013 - Roanoke, VA/April 25 - 27

Publications:
Membership Directory; annually
National Quarterly; quarterly

Women in Municipal Government (1974)
101 paul St.
Chicago, IL 56898
Website: nlc.org/build-skills-networks/networks/
    constituency-groups/wimg
Members: 300 individuals
Staff: 2
Annual Budget: Under $10,000

Personnel:
President: Mitchel Hone

Historical Note:
Members are women holding elected or appointed municipal office. The organization serves as a leadership network for women and colleagues interested in women's issues and policy development. Membership: $35/year (individual); $55/year (organization).

Women in Packaging (1993)
4290 Bells Ferry Rd.
Suite 106-17
Kennesaw, GA 30144-1300
Tel: (678) 594-6872 Fax: (770) 928-2338
E-Mail: wpstaff@womeninpackaging.org
Website: womeninpackaging.org
Members: 800 individuals
Staff: 2
Tax: 501(c)(6)

Personnel:
Executive Director: JoAnn R. Hines
    E-Mail: jrhines@womeninpackaging.org
Director, Publications and Contact, Advertising Sales:
    Michelle Nordlinger
    E-Mail: shellyn@womeninpackaging.org

Historical Note:
WP is dedicated to the growth and success of packaging professionals. Members are professionals employed at all levels in the packaging industry. Membership: $200-600 (Corporate); $150 (Professional); $35 (Student).

Publications:
New e-zine; weekly
Packaging Horizons Magazine; weekly

Women in Technology International (1989)
11500 Olympic Blvd.
Suite 400
Los Angeles, CA 90064
Tel: (818) 788-9484 Fax: (818) 788-9410
TollFree: (800) 334-9484
E-Mail: members-info@corp.witi.com
Website: witi.org
Members:

200 companies
4000 individuals
Staff: 15
Annual Budget: $250-500,000

Personnel:
President: David Leighton
Director, Online: Henry Fan
Chief Technology Officer: Daniel Leighton
Director, Strategic Partnership: Cynthia Roe
    E-Mail: cynthia@corp.witi.com

Historical Note:
Formerly (1989) known as The International Network of Women in Technology and in 2001 evolved as WITI. WITI's purpose is to empower women worldwide to achieve better possibilities and transformations through technology, leadership and economic prosperity. Membership: $250 (Individual); $50 (Student); $1,000 (Lifetime); $95 (Academic/Government); $25,000-50,000 (Corporate).

Meetings/Conferences:
Number of non-conference events/year: 3

Publications:
Member Directory; on-line
WITI Strategist; semi-monthly

Women Networking in Electronic Transactions (2005)
1760 Old Meadow Rd.
Suite 500
McLean, VA 22102
Tel: (877) 772-9638 Fax: (703) 506-3266
TollFree: (877) 772-9638
E-Mail: info@wnetonline.org
Website: w-net.biz/
Staff: 2
Annual Budget: $100-250,000
Tax: 501(c)(3)

Personnel:
Executive Director: Shawn Taylor Zelman
Treasurer: Lisa Shipley

Historical Note:
W.net inspires and empowers women in the electronic transactions industry to maximize their individual potential and position themselves for better personal success. Membership: $200/year.

Meetings/Conferences: Annual

Publications:
W2W Newsletter; quarterly

Women of the Motion Picture Industry, International (1952)
Twentieth Century Fox
P.O. Box 900
Beverly Hills, CA 90213
Tel: (310) 432-2352 Fax: (310) 369-8903
Website: wompi.org
Members: 600 individuals
Staff: 3
Annual Budget: $10-25,000

Personnel:
Contact: Elaine Webb
International Treasurer: Doris McGehee

Historical Note:
WOMPI exists to promote professionalism in the motion picture industry and to contribute to the community through service projects. Membership: $35/year.

Meetings/Conferences: Annual

Women's Basketball Coaches Association (1981)
4646 Lawrenceville Hwy.
Lilburn, GA 30047-3620
Tel: (770) 279-8027 Fax: (770) 279-8473
E-Mail: membership@wbca.org
Website: wbca.org
Members: 4200 individuals
Staff: 12
Annual Budget: $2-5,000,000
Tax: 501(c)(3)

Personnel:
Chief Executive Officer: Beth Bass
    E-Mail: beth_bass@wbca.org
Manager, Legislation and Research: Joanna Britz
    E-Mail: jbritz@wbca.org
Director, Events: Stephanie S. Baron Dollar
    E-Mail: sbaron@wbca.org
Manager, Membership and Convention Services: Felicia
    Folds

    E-Mail: ffolds@wbca.org
Director, Membership, Exhibition and Convention Services:
    Tip Tucker Kendall
    E-Mail: tkendall@wbca.org
Chief Operating Officer: Shannon Reynolds
    E-Mail: shannonr@wbca.org
Controller, Finance and Benefits: Melissa Stevens
    E-Mail: mstevens@wbca.org
Director, Communications: Jack Watford
    E-Mail: jwatford@wbca.org

Historical Note:
WBCA promotes women's basketball by unifying coaches and it also seeks to foster and promote the development of the game of basketball as a sport for women and girls. Membership: $50-220/year.

Meetings/Conferences: Annual
Conference Chair: Stephanie S. Baron Dollar
2013 - New Orleans, LA/April 5 - 9/51-100 exhibitors

Publications:
Coaching Women's Basketball; adv.
Compliance Corner; quarterly
Compliance Now
Fast Break; monthly; adv.
Membership Directory; on-line; adv.

Women's Business Enterprise National Council (1997)
1120 Connecticut Ave. NW
Suite 1000
Washington, DC 20036
Tel: (202) 872-5515 Fax: (202) 872-5505
Website: wbenc.org
Members: 700 companies
Staff: 18
Annual Budget: $5-10,000,000
Tax: 501(c)(3)

Personnel:
President and Chief Executive Officer: Pamela Prince-
    Eason
Senior Director, Development and Corporate Relations:
    Paige Adams
    E-Mail: padams@wbenc.org
Vice President, Marketing: Patricia Birmingham
    E-Mail: pbirmingham@wbenc.org
Director, Finance and Operations: Valerie Bunns
Senior Director, Programs: Betty Cole
    E-Mail: bcole@wbenc.org
Assistant Vice President, Marketing and Communications:
    Cristy McCullough
    E-Mail: cmccullough@wbenc.org
Director, Information Technology: Jason Moore
    E-Mail: jmoore@wbenc.org
Chief Operating Officer: Lynn Grossman Quinn
Office Manager: Alice Spears
    E-Mail: aspears@wbenc.org
Senior Compliance Manager: LaKesha White
    E-Mail: lwhite@wbenc.org

Historical Note:
WBENC's mission is to advance the success of Corporate Members, certified women's business enterprises (WBEs), and government entities in partnership with its Regional Partner Organizations (RPOs). Members include corporations, women's business organizations and certified WBE's. Membership: $6,000-30,000 (Corporate, based on annual revenues); $2,500 (Non-Profit/Government Agency).

Continuing Education:
Certification Designation/s: WBE, WOSB

Meetings/Conferences: Annual
Conference Chair: Betty Cole
2013 - Baltimore, MD (Hilton Baltimore)/March 13 -
    15
Number of non-conference events/year: 2

Publications:
President's Report; monthly
What's New at WBENC; quarterly

Women's Caucus for Art (1972)
P.O. Box 1498
Canal St. Stn.
New York, NY 10013-1498
Tel: (212) 634-0007
E-Mail: info@nationalwca.org
Website: nationalwca.org
Members: 1500 individuals
Staff: 2
Annual Budget: $100-250,000

Tax: 501(c)(3)

Personnel:
Director, Operations: Karin Luner
  E-Mail: karin@nationalwca.org
Editor: Marcia Santore

Historical Note:
WCA's mission is to create community through art, education and social activism. Members are women artists and educators, art historians and critics, gallery and museum professionals and collectors. Membership: $40- 50 (Regular); $25-$35 (Student/Subsidized); $75 (Institutional); $500 (Life Time).

Meetings/Conferences: Annual

Publications:
Artlines; adv.
Email Digest; monthly
Member Directory; on-line

Women's Caucus for Political Science (1969)
Department of Political Science, University of North Texas
1155 Union Cir. P.O. Box 305340
Denton, TX 76203-5340
Website: apsanet.org/~wcps
Members: 900 individuals
Staff: 3

Personnel:
Treasurer: Valerie Martinez-Ebers
  E-Mail: valmartinez@unt.edu

Historical Note:
WCPS seeks to improve the status of women in the profession of political science by promoting equal opportunity for women political scientists in employment, promotion & tenure decisions, as well as graduate school admissions & financial aid decisions. Membership: $10-30 (Faculty members and other professionals); $30 (Institutions); $500 (Life).

Meetings/Conferences: Annual

Publications:
Membership Directory
Newsletter WCPS; quarterly

Women's Classical Caucus (1972)
University of Illinois at Urbana-Champaign, Department of the Classics
4080 Foreign Languages Building, 707 S. Mathews Ave.
Urbana, IL 61801-3676
Tel: (217) 333-7327
Website: wccaucus.org
Members: 600 individuals
Staff: 3
Tax: 501(c)(3)

Personnel:
Secretary and Treasurer: Antony Augoustakis
  E-Mail: aaugoust@illinois.edu
Editor: Alison Jeppesen-Wigelsworth
  E-Mail: Cloelia.WCC@gmail.com
Web Editor: Lisl Walsh
  E-Mail: walshl@beloit.edu

Historical Note:
WCC's mission is to foster feminist and gender-informed perspectives in the study and teaching of all aspects of ancient Mediterranean cultures and classical antiquity.WCC is an affiliate of The American Philological Association Membership: $20 (Regular); $5 (Retiree); $200 (Life); Free (First year Students); $10 (Student, after first year).

Meetings/Conferences: Annual
2013 - Seatle, WA/Jan. 3 - 6

Publications:
WCC Newsletter; annually

Women's Council of REALTORS (1938)
430 N. Michigan Ave.
Chicago, IL 60611-4093
Tel: (312) 329-5967 *Fax:* (312) 329-3290
TollFree: (800) 245-8512
E-Mail: wcr@wcr.org
Website: wcr.org
Members: 16000 individuals
Staff: 5
Annual Budget: $2-5,000,000
Tax: 501(c)(6)

Personnel:
Executive Vice President: Gary Krysler CAE
  E-Mail: gkrysler@wcr.org
President: Bobbie Nelson

  E-Mail: bjnelson@earthlink.net
Recording Secretary: Jo Kenney
  E-Mail: jo@jokenney.com
Financial Secretary: Sindy Ready
  E-Mail: Sindy@AzGreatHomes.com

Historical Note:
A professional development group for women in real estate. WCR provides a referral network and referral, relocation training, leadership training, and chapter programs on the local, state, and national levels. Membership: $110/year (National).

Continuing Education:
Certification Designation/s: PMN, RSPS

Meetings/Conferences: Semi-Annual
Number of non-conference events/year: 4

Publications:
eConnect; monthly; adv.
Membership Directory; on-line

Women's Foodservice Forum (1989)
6750 LBJ Fwy.
Dallas, TX 75240
Tel: (972) 770-9100 *Fax:* (972) 770-9150
E-Mail: info@womensfoodserviceforum.com
Website: womensfoodserviceforum.com
Members: 3000 Individuals
Staff: 10
Annual Budget: $5-10,000,000
Tax: 501(c)(3)

Personnel:
President and Chief Executive Officer: Fritzi Woods
  E-Mail: fwoods@womensfoodserviceforum.com
Executive Administrator: Linda Downey
  E-Mail: ldowney@wff.org
Manager, Administration: Natasha Mandigo Harris
  E-Mail: nharris@womensfoodserviceforum.com
Director, Sponsor and Industry Relations: Karen Lazowski
  E-Mail: klazowski@womensfoodserviceforum.com
Vice President, Operations and General Manager: Anna Mason
  E-Mail: amason@wff.org
Director, Learning: Kathy Murphy
  E-Mail: kmurphy@wff.org
Vice President, Marketing and Communications: Kelly Primus
  E-Mail: kprimus@wff.org
Executive Administrative Assistant: Michelle Russell
  E-Mail: mrussell@womensfoodserviceforum.com
Vice President, Business Development and Industry Relations: Gretchen Sussman
  E-Mail: gsussman@womensfoodserviceforum.com
Coordinator, Operations and Human Resources: Caroline Wolters
  E-Mail: cwolters@wff.org

Historical Note:
WFF is a leadership development community for collective insights and connections that empower women in the food service industry. Members are men and women executives in the food service and hospitality industries. Membership: $295 (Individual/Professional); $150 (Educator).

Meetings/Conferences: Annual
Conference Chair: Anna Mason

Publications:
Elevate Newsletter; on-line

Membership List Available to Non-members

Women's International Network of Utility Professionals (1923)
P.O. Box 64
Grove City, OH 43123-0064
Tel: (614) 738-0603
E-Mail: winup@att.net
Website: winup.org/
Members: 350 individuals
Staff: 2
Annual Budget: $50-100,000

Personnel:
Executive Director: Claudia Powell
Treasurer: Susan Toombs

Historical Note:
Founded as Electrical Women's Round Table; incorporated in New York in 1927. Assumed its current name in 1988. Purpose is to provide a link for developing and recognizing professionals involved with utility business trends, issues, products and services. Membership: $66/year, plus local chapter dues.

Meetings/Conferences: Annual

Publications:
Connection; quarterly

Women's Jewelry Association (1983)
52 Vanderbilt Ave.
19th Floor
New York, NY 10017-3827
Tel: (212) 687-2722 *Fax:* (646) 355-0219
E-Mail: info@womensjewelry.org
Website: wjamarion.memberlodge.com
Members: 1000 individuals
Staff: 5
Annual Budget: $500-1,000,000
Tax: 501(c)(3)

Personnel:
President: Kendra Bridel Weinman
Co-Vice President, Events: Lisa Cochin
Administrative Director and Membership Services: Nicole Lichwick
  E-Mail: Nicole@womensjewelry.org
Vice President, Public Relations: Michelle Orman
Vice President, Education: Anne Valentzas

Historical Note:
WJA's mission is to empower women to achieve their goals in the international jewelry, watch and related businesses. Members are professional women in the jewelry industry. Membership: $160 (New Member); $135 (Renewing Member); $105 (Student); $80 (Renewing Student).

Meetings/Conferences:
Conference Chair: Lisa Cochin
Number of non-conference events/year: 5

Publications:
WJA Newsletter; on-line

Membership List Available to Non-members

Women's National Book Association (1917)
P.O. Box 237
FDR Stn.
New York, NY 10150-0231
Tel: (212) 208-4629 *Fax:* (212) 208-4629
E-Mail: publicity@bookbuzz.com
Website: wnba-books.org
Members: 800 individuals
Staff: 3
Annual Budget: $10-25,000
Tax: 501(c)(3)

Personnel:
Contact, Public Relations: Susannah Greenberg

Historical Note:
WNBA's mission is to enhance reading and to support the role of women in the community. Members include publishers, authors, librarians, literary agents, editors, illustrators and booksellers. Membership: $48 (Regular); $35 (Student/Retiree); $100 (Sponsoror); $500-2,500 (Sustaining, based on annual sales).

Meetings/Conferences:
Number of non-conference events/year: 1

Publications:
National Membership Directory; on-line; adv.
The Bookwoman; adv.

Women's Professional Rodeo Association (1948)
431 S. Cascade
Colorado Springs, CO 80903
Tel: (719) 447-4627 *Fax:* (719) 447-4631
E-Mail: contact@wpra.com
Website: wpra.com
Members: 2300 individuals
Staff: 4
Annual Budget: $1-2,000,000
Tax: 501(c)(6)

Personnel:
Operating Officer and Executive Secretary: Janet Cropper
  E-Mail: jcropper@mlh-services.com
Contact, Finance and Accounting: Mindy Anderson
  E-Mail: mindy@wpra.com
Editor: Mary Anna Clemmons
  E-Mail: mclemons@elpasotel.net
Contact, Membership Services and Approvals: Kelsey Larsen
  E-Mail: kelsey@wpra.com

Historical Note:
Formerly (1980) the Girls' Rodeo Association and (1981) the Professional Women's Rodeo Association, WPRA, originally organized to replace trick riding in the rodeos, works to provide professional-level competitions and prize money for women athletes in the rodeo arena. Members are

competitors in professional girl rodeos and in barrel races in rodeos sanctioned by the Rodeo Cowboys Association. Membership: $300 (WPRA Permit); $375 (WPRA Card); $125 (Active Gold Card); $190 (WPRA Roping Division); $175 (WPRA Futurity/Derby); Free (Inactive Gold Card); $150 (WPRA Junior Division).

Publications:
The Women's Pro Rodeo News (WPRN); monthly; adv.

Women's Regional Publications of America
(1986)
P.O. Box 12955
Albuquerque, NM 87195
Tel: (505) 247-9195
Website: womensregionalpublications.org
Members: 20 publishers
Staff: 3
Annual Budget: $10-25,000

Personnel:
President: Karen Green
    E-Mail: kgreen@womensdigest.net
Vice President and Membership: Jill Duval
    E-Mail: heygals@nmwoman.com
Director, Advertising Information: Ellen Fisher

Historical Note:
Formerly (2002) National Association of Women's Yellow Pages. Purpose is to inform, serve, spotlight women and the organizations, businesses and communities that serve them. Women focused media represented by WRPA includes regional women's magazines, websites, electronic media, directories, newsletters, and calendars. Membership: $150/year.

Publications:
WRPA Directory
WRPA Magazine

Membership List Available to Non-members

Women's Transportation Seminar (WTS International) *(1977)*
1701 K St. NW
Suite 800
Washington, DC 20006
Tel: (202) 955-5085 *Fax:* (202) 955-5088
E-Mail: membership@wtsinternational.org
Website: wtsinternational.org
Members: 4500 individuals
Staff: 5
Annual Budget: $1-2,000,000
Tax: 501(c)(6)

Personnel:
President and Chief Executive Officer: Marcia Ferranto
    E-Mail: mferranto@wtsinternational.org
Executive Assistant and Coordinator, Membership Services: Emily Kinney
    E-Mail: ekinney@wtsinternational.org
Vice President, Development: Pam Mullender
    E-Mail: pmullender@wtsinternational.org
Managing Director: Margaret Mullins
    E-Mail: mmullins@wtsinternational.org
Director, Communications and Social Media: Mary Petto
    E-Mail: mpetto@wtsinternational.org

Historical Note:
WTS's mission is to transform the transportation industry through the advancement of women. Members are male and female transportation professionals, and public and private suppliers of transportation services. Membership: $95-225 (Individual); $100 (Retired Member); $50 (Student Member); $155 (International Member); $225 (Flat Rate Member).

Meetings/Conferences: Annual
2013 - Philadelphia, PA/May 15 - 17

Publications:
Transcript; bi-monthly
W/M DBE Directory; on-line
WTS Membership Directory; on-line

Wood Component Manufacturers Association
(1929)
741 Butlers Gate
Suite 100
Marietta, GA 30068
Tel: (770) 565-6660 *Fax:* (770) 565-6663
E-Mail: wcma@woodcomponents.org
Website: woodcomponents.org
Members: 150 companies
Staff: 3
Annual Budget: $100-250,000
Tax: 501(c)(6)

Personnel:
Executive Director: Steven V. Lawser CAE

Historical Note:
Formerly (1984) Hardwood Dimension Manufacturers Association and (1996) National Dimension Manufacturers Association. WCMA's mission is to promote a friendly exchange of ideas among those engaged in the dimension & component manufacturing business; develop and promote a general demand for the industry's products and services. Members are manufacturers of wood component products for the furniture and kitchen cabinet industries as well as other wood parts users. Membership: $1,000-3,000/year.

Publications:
Membership Directory; annually; adv.
WCMA Newsletter; monthly; adv.

Wood Flooring Manufacturers Association *(2008)*
111 St.
New York, NY 58745
Website: nofma.org
Staff: 1
Annual Budget: $100-250,000

Personnel:
Treasurer: Jon Rack

Wood Machinery Manufacturers of America
(1899)
2105 Laurel Bush Rd.
Suite 201
Bel Air, MD 21015
Tel: (443) 640-1052 *Fax:* (443) 640-1031
E-Mail: info@wmma.org
Website: wmma.org
Members: 205 companies
Staff: 7
Annual Budget: $250-500,000
Tax: 501(c)(3)

Personnel:
Executive Director: Fred Stringfellow CAE
    E-Mail: fred@wmma.org
Director, Finance: Amy Chetelat, CAE
    E-Mail: amy@wmma.org
Coordinator, Membership Services: Laura Izzo
    E-Mail: laura@wmma.org
Director, Meetings: Diane Schafer CMP
    E-Mail: diane@wmma.org
Director, Marketing and Communications: Mary Helen Sprecher
    E-Mail: maryhelen@wmma.org
Chief Staff Executive: Harold R. Zassenhaus
    E-Mail: hzassenhaus@wmma.org

Historical Note:
WMMA's mission is to enhance the competitive position, improve the performance and advocate for domestic manufacturers of machinery, cutting tools and supplies used in the processing of wood and related products. Membership: $650 (Active/Associate); $100 (Affiliate).

Meetings/Conferences: Annual
Conference Chair: Diane Schafer CMP
Number of non-conference events/year: 2

Publications:
Product Guide and Directory; on-line
The Cutting Edge; quarterly

Wood Moulding and Millwork Producers Association *(1963)*
507 First St.
Woodland, CA 95695-4025
Tel: (530) 661-9591 *Fax:* (530) 661-9586
TollFree: (800) 550-7889
E-Mail: info@wmmpa.com
Website: wmmpa.com
Members: 156 companies
Staff: 5
Annual Budget: $100-250,000

Personnel:
Chief Executive Officer and Executive Vice President: Kellie A. Schroeder
    E-Mail: kelli@wmmpa.com
Director, Programs and Finance: Melissa Leal
Legal Counsel: Clark Malak
Contact, Membership Services: Reena Melancon
Technical Advisor: Ric Morrison

Historical Note:
Established as the Western Wood Moulding Producers; became the Western Wood Moulding and Millwork Producers in 1968, named as Wood Moulding and Millwork Producers Association in 1978. MMPA's mission

is to promote quality products produced by its members, develop sources of supply and to promote optimum use of raw materials. Membership: $30-1,100/year (Based on board footage production).

Meetings/Conferences:
2013 - Scottsdale, AZ (Talking Stick Resort)/March 5 - 9
Number of non-conference events/year: 1

Wood Products Manufacturers Association
(1929)
P.O. Box 761
Westminster, MA 01473-0761
Tel: (978) 874-5445 *Fax:* (978) 874-9946
E-Mail: woodprod@wpma.org
Website: wpma.org
Members: 702 companies
Staff: 5
Annual Budget: $250-500,000
Tax: 501(c)(6)

Personnel:
Executive Director: Phillip A. Bibeau
    E-Mail: woodprod@wpma.org

Historical Note:
Formerly Wood Turners Service Bureau and Wood Turners and Shapers Association (1978). Incorporated in Massachusetts in 1967, WPMA members represent all facets of the wood industry. Mission is to provide members with the tools to help their business succeed with the finest information resources and services available. Membership: $495-1,125 (Manufacturing Member, Based on Company Size); $650 (Associate).

Continuing Education:
Certification Designation/s: FSC

Meetings/Conferences: Annual

Publications:
Membership Directory; adv.
WPMA Newsletter; monthly; adv.

Woodworking Machinery Industry Association
(1978)
27 Main St.
Suite One
New Milford, CT 06776
Tel: (860) 350-9642 *Fax:* (860) 354-0677
E-Mail: info@wmia.org
Website: wmia.org
Members: 170 members
Staff: 2
Annual Budget: $500-1,000,000

Personnel:
Executive Vice President: Riccardo Azzoni
    E-Mail: razzoni@wmia.org
Manager, Meetings and Member Services: Linda Nicklos
    E-Mail: lnicklos@wmia.org

Historical Note:
Formerly (1997) the Woodworking Machinery Importers Association of America. WMIA provides the North American wood products industry with technologically advanced woodworking systems available in the global market. It also offers special programs, provides industry awards, scholarships etc to support industry initiatives and address industry issues. Members are chief executives of woodworking machinery importing and distributing companies. Membership: $600 (Importer/Distributor/Associate Member); $100 (Educational Institutions).

Meetings/Conferences: Annual
Conference Chair: Linda Nicklos
2013 - Phoenix, AZ (Phoenix Marriott Tempe at The Buttes)/April 23 - 26

Publications:
WMIA Update; quarterly
WoodworkingTechnology.com; on-line

Work Colleges Consortium
CPO 2163
Berea, KY 40404
Tel: (859) 985-3154
Website: workcolleges.org
Members: 7 distinctive liberal arts colleges
Staff: 1

Personnel:
Executive Director: Robin Taffler
    E-Mail: robin@workcolleges.org

Historical Note:
A work college is a type of institution of higher learning where student work is an integral and mandatory part of

the educational process, as opposed to being an appended requirement.

Meetings/Conferences: Annual

Publications:
Membership Directory; annually
WCC Newsletter; quarterly

Workers United
10 W. 37th St
New York, NY 10018
Website: workersunitedunion.org
Staff: 1
Annual Budget: $10-25,000,000
Tax: 501(c)(5)

Personnel:
Executive Director: P. Catlin Fullwood

Historical Note:
A labor organization.

Workers' Injury Law and Advocacy Group *(1995)*
131 Daniel Webster Hwy.
Suite 614
Nashua, NH 03060
E-Mail: wilg@wilg.org
Website: wilg.org
Members: 675 individuals/law firms
Staff: 4
Tax: 501(c)(6)

Personnel:
Executive Director: Jennifer L. Comer
Research Director: Roselyn Bonanti

Historical Note:
WILG is dedicated to represent the interests of millions of workers and their families who, each year, suffer the consequences of workplace injuries and illnesses. Membership: $295 (Regular/Associate); $1,000 (Advocate/Board); $100 (Paralegal); $2,000 (Benefactor).

Meetings/Conferences: Annual

Publications:
E-newsletter
Workers' First Watch

Membership List Available to Non-members

Workgroup for Electronic Data Interchange *(1991)*
1984 Isaac Newton Sq.
Suite 304
Reston, VA 20190
Tel: (202) 688-2488 *Fax:* (202) 688-2488
Website: wedi.org
Members:
300 companies
100 individuals
Staff: 6
Annual Budget: $1-2,000,000
Tax: 501(c)(6)

Personnel:
President and Chief Executive Officer: Devin A. Jopp EdD
   E-Mail: djopp@wedi.org
Vice President, Administrative and Membership Services: Lisa Berretta
   E-Mail: lberretta@wedi.org
Director, Marketing and Partner Development: Mario Marzette
   E-Mail: mmarzette@wedi.org
Vice President, External Relations and Strategic Initiatives: Ann Marie Railing
   E-Mail: AMRailing@wedi.org
Assistant Director, Programs and Services: Patti Sanderson
   E-Mail: psanderson@wedi.org
Director, Industry Education and Events: Amy Verd
   E-Mail: averd@wedi.org

Historical Note:
WEDI's mission is to provide multi-stakeholder leadership and guidance to the healthcare industry on how to use and leverage the industry's collective technology, knowledge, expertise and information resources to improve the administrative efficiency, quality and cost effectiveness of healthcare information. Membership: $150 (eMember); $300 (Individual); $500 (Affiliate/Regional Entity/ Medicaid); $1,000-5000 (Organizations).

Meetings/Conferences: Semi-Annual
Conference Chair: Amy Verd

Publications:
Membership Directory; on-line

WEDI Newsletter; on-line

Working Group for Investment in Reliable and Economic Electric Systems
1300 I St.
Suite 300 W
Washington, DC 20005
Tel: (202) 898-0368
E-Mail: contact@wiresgroup.com
Website: wiresgroup.com
Staff: 3

Personnel:
President: J. Jolly Hayden
Treasurer: Gary Hickey

Historical Note:
WIRES mission is to reduce or eliminate uneconomic barriers to transmission development and is accomplished through the development and dissemination of information, strategic advocacy, and innovation in regulatory, policy making, industry, and educational forums.

Publications:
WIRES Newsletters

WorkPlace Furnishings *(1963)*
3574 E. Kemper Rd.
Cincinnati, OH 45241
Tel: (513) 563-0048 *Fax:* (513) 563-1822
Website: workplacefurn.com
Members: 90 independent dealers
Staff: 5
Annual Budget: $1-2,000,000

Personnel:
Director, Administration: Janet Vaughn
   E-Mail: jvaughn@workplacefurn.com

Historical Note:
Incorporated in Ohio as MIV (More in Value) Inc., later became National Association of Office Furniture Dealers, and assumed its current name in 1999. WPF is a marketing group providing advertising, catalogues and related services to its member dealers. Membership: $1,200-2,400/year.

Publications:
Membership Directory; on-line

World Affairs Councils of America *(1918)*
1200 18th St. NW
Suite 902
Washington, DC 20036
Tel: (202) 833-4557 *Fax:* (202) 833-4555
E-Mail: waca@worldaffairscouncils.org
Website: worldaffairscouncils.org
Members: 94 organizations
Staff: 7
Annual Budget: $500-1,000,000
Tax: 501(c)(3)

Personnel:
President and Chief Executive Officer: S. Todd Culpepper
Accountant: Jacquiline Black
Officer, Communications and Development: Ian J. Byrne
Program Officer: Althea Georgantas
Associate, Professional Affairs: Sarah Maurizi

Historical Note:
Formerly (1982) the National Council of World Affairs Organizations. WACA's mission is to represent and support the national non-partisan network of local councils that are dedicated to educating, and engaging Americans in international affairs. Membership: $200-3750/year (Organization).

Meetings/Conferences: Annual
Conference Chair: Althea Georgantas

Publications:
WACA Newsletter; monthly

World Airline Entertainment Association *(1979)*
355 Lexington Ave.
15th Floor
New York, NY 10017-6603
Tel: (212) 297-2177 *Fax:* (212) 370-9047
E-Mail: info@apex.aero
Website: apex.aero
Members: 400 companies
Staff: 9
Annual Budget: $2-5,000,000

Personnel:
Executive Director: Russ Lemieux
   E-Mail: rlemieux@kellencompany.com
Manager, Meetings and Expositions: Kirsten Arthur CMP
   E-Mail: kcurnyn@kellencompany.com

General Manager: Katie Goshgarian
   E-Mail: kgoshgarian@kellencompany.com
Director, Communications: Bonnie Sonnenschein
   E-Mail: bsonnenschein@kellencompany.com
Coordinator, Membership Services: Heather Wetzel
   E-Mail: hwetzel@kellencompany.com

Historical Note:
Formerly, World Airline Entertainment Association. APEX serves as a resource to the businesses and professionals that create, deliver, and manage the airline passenger experience, and the association provides the industry with a forum for knowledge sharing, collaboration and networking. Membership: $450 (New Airline); $700 (New Vendor).

Continuing Education:
Enrollment: 1

Meetings/Conferences:
Conference Chair: Kirsten Arthur CMP
2013 - /April 29 - May 1
2013 - Anaheim, CA/Sept. 9 - 12
2014 - Anaheim, CA/Sept. 15 - 18

Publications:
APEXnews SmartBrief; daily; adv.

Membership List Available to Non-members

World Allergy Organization *(1951)*
555 E. Wells St.
Suite 1100
Milwaukee, WI 53202-3823
Tel: (414) 276-1791 *Fax:* (414) 276-3349
E-Mail: info@worldallergy.org
Website: worldallergy.org
Members: 74 regional and national societies
Staff: 10
Annual Budget: $2-5,000,000

Personnel:
Executive Director: Jennie Smazik
Director, Publications, Education, Communications and Managing Editor: Sofia Dorsano
Associate Director, Meetings: Katie Vande Zande

Historical Note:
Founded (1951) as International Association of Allergology and Clinical Immunology at the First International Congress of Allergology in Zurich, Switzerland, assumed current name in 2000. WAO's mission is to be a global resource and advocate in the field of allergy, asthma and clinical immunology advancing excellence in clinical care through education, research and training as a worldwide alliance of allergy, asthma and clinical immunology societies.

Meetings/Conferences: Biennial
Conference Chair: Katie Vande Zande

Publications:
WAO e-News and Notes; monthly
World Allergy Organization Journal

World Aquaculture Society *(1969)*
Louisiana State University
143 J.M. Parker Coliseum
Baton Rouge, LA 70803
Tel: (225) 578-3137 *Fax:* (225) 578-3493
Website: was.org
Members: 3000 individuals
Staff: 3
Annual Budget: $250-500,000
Tax: 501(c)(3)

Personnel:
Director, Home Office: Carol M. Mendoza
   E-Mail: carolm@was.org
Contact, Conferences: John Cooksey
   E-Mail: worldaqua@aol.com
Editor-in-Chief: Dr. Carl Webster
   E-Mail: cwebster@dcr.net

Historical Note:
Formerly (1986) the World Mariculture Society. WAS's purpose is to strengthen and facilitate communication and information exchange on high priority topics and emerging issues within the diverse global aquaculture community. Membership: $10-1100/year.

Meetings/Conferences:
Conference Chair: John Cooksey
2013 - Nashville, TN/Feb. 21 - 25/11-25 exhibitors

Publications:
Journal of the World Aquaculture Society; bi-monthly
Membership Directory; annually
World Aquaculture Magazine; quarterly; adv.

World Association of Veterinary Anatomists *(1957)*

University of Tennessee, College of Veterinary
Medicine
2407 River Dr.
Knoxville, TN 37996-4543
Tel: (865) 974-5822 *Fax:* (865) 974-5640
Website: wava-amav.org
Staff: 2

Personnel:
President: Robert Henry
    E-Mail: rhenry@utk.edu

Historical Note:
*An American Chapter of the international organization,
headquartered in Bern Switzerland, WAVA encourages the
study of anatomy in the field of taxonomy. Membership: $5
(Individual); $50-150 (Lifetime).*

Meetings/Conferences:
Number of non-conference events/year: 1

Publications:
Newsletter; annually

World Council of Credit Unions, Inc.
P.O. Box 2982
Madison, WI 53701-2982
Tel: (608) 395-2000 *Fax:* (608) 395-2001
E-Mail: mail@woccu.org
Website: woccu.org
Staff: 11
Annual Budget: $25-50,000,000
Tax: 501(c)(6)

Personnel:
President and Chief Executive Officer: Brian Branch
Chief Financial Officer: Julie Allen
    E-Mail: jallen@woccu.org
Manager, Marketing and Communications: Jennifer
    Bernhardt
    E-Mail: jbernhardt@woccu.org
Business Manager and Contact, Technical Services: Nicole
    Bice
    E-Mail: nbice@woccu.org
Contact, International Partnerships and Training: Victor
    Miguel Corro
    E-Mail: vcorro@woccu.org
Contact, Certification: Kimberly Hinrichs
    E-Mail: khinrichs@woccu.org
Director, Marketing and Communications: Mike Muckian
    E-Mail: mmuckian@woccu.org
Credit Union Analyst: Liliana Tangwall
    E-Mail: ltangwall@woccu.org
Director, Human Resources: JoAnna Vanderpoel PHR

Historical Note:
*WOCCU's mission is to advocate, platform, development
agency and good governance model for credit unions. The
board of directors review and vote upon new membership
applications three times per year.*

Continuing Education:
Certification Designation/s: MCP

Meetings/Conferences: Annual
Number of non-conference events/year: 5

Publications:
Credit Union World; annually
eCommuniqué; on-line
Focus

World Federation for Mental Health (1948)
P.O. Box 807
Occoquan, VA 22125
Fax: (703) 490-6926
E-Mail: info@wfmh.com
Website: wfmh.org
Staff: 3
Annual Budget: $100-250,000

Personnel:
President: Hong kong
Director, Administration: Deborah Maguire
Treasurer: Helen Millar

Historical Note:
*WFMH's mission is to advocate the advancement of mental
health awareness, prevention of mental disorders, advocacy,
and best practice recovery focused interventions worldwide.
Its organizational and individual membership includes
mental health workers of all disciplines, consumers of
mental health services, family members, and concerned
citizens. Membership: $50-300 (Voting Member
Organization); $50-150 (Affiliate Member Organization);
$15-100 (Individuals); $500 (Life Membership) based on
annual budget.*

Meetings/Conferences: Annual

2013 - Athens, Greece (Royal Olympic Hotel)/March 6
    - 9
Number of non-conference events/year: 5

Publications:
Center News; quarterly
WFMH's Newsletter; quarterly; adv.

World Federation of Public Health Associations
(1967)
800 I St. NW
Washington, DC 20001-3710
Tel: (202) 777-2490 *Fax:* (202) 777-2530
E-Mail: mtaylor@wfpha.org
Website: wfpha.org
Members: 73 organizations
Staff: 2

Personnel:
Executive Manager: Laetitia Bourquin
    E-Mail: laetitia.bourquin@unige.ch
Programme Manager: Marta Lomazzi
    E-Mail: marta.lomazzi@unige.ch

Historical Note:
*WFPHA's mission is to advocate the public's health
through professional exchange, collaboration, and action.
Members include multidisciplinary national and regional
public health societies whose own memberships include
nurses, sanitarians, administrators, physicians, health
educators, pharmacists, anthropologists, researchers,
and many other persons interested in public health.
Membership: $500 (Individual); Free (Regional); $100
(Sustaining/ Full Member/ Associate).*

Meetings/Conferences: Annual
Conference Chair: Marta Lomazzi

Publications:
Journal of Public Health Policy; on-line
WFPHA Newsletter; monthly

World Floor Covering Association (1960)
2211 E. Howell Ave.
Anaheim, CA 92806-6009
Tel: (714) 978-6440 *Fax:* (714) 978-6066
TollFree: (800) 624-6880
E-Mail: wfca@wfca.org
Website: wfca-pro.org
Members: 3,000 flooring and carpet store retailer
Staff: 7
Annual Budget: $5-10,000,000

Personnel:
Chairman of the Board: Harold Chapman CFE
Contact, Communications: Leah Gross-Harmon
    E-Mail: leah@storydept.net

Historical Note:
*Formed as result of merger of the Western Floor Covering
Association and the American Floor covering Association
in 1994. WFCA's mission is to enhance the industy's
professionalism and profitability. Membership: $275
(Regular); $1300 (Manufacturer); $575 (Supplier/
Distributor).*

Continuing Education:
Certification Designation/s: CFP, CFE, CFSC

World Future Society (1966)
7910 Woodmont Ave.
Suite 450
Bethesda, MD 20814-3032
Tel: (301) 656-8274 *Fax:* (301) 951-0394
TollFree: (800) 989-8274
E-Mail: info@wfs.org
Website: wfs.org
Members: 25000 individuals
Staff: 11
Annual Budget: $1-2,000,000
Tax: 501(c)(3)

Personnel:
Business Manager: Jeff Cornish
    E-Mail: jcornish@wfs.org
Executive Editor: Timothy C. Mack
    E-Mail: tmack@wfs.org
Director, Communications: Patrick Tucker
    E-Mail: ptucker@wfs.org
Speaker Coordinator: Sarah Warner
    E-Mail: swarner@wfs.org

Historical Note:
*WFS's mission is to enable thinkers, political personalities,
scientists and lay-people to share an informed, serious
dialogue on what the future will be like. Membership: $79
(Regular); $20 (Student); $295 (Professional); $950-2,950*

*(Life); $450-850 (Institutional); $185 (Nonprofit/
Academic).*

Meetings/Conferences: Annual
Conference Chair: Sarah Warner
2013 - Chicago, IL (Hilton Chicago)/July 26 - 28

Publications:
Futurist Update; monthly; adv.
The Futurist; bi-monthly; adv.
World Future Review: A Journal of Strategic Foresight;
    bi-monthly; adv.

World Gold Trust Services (1987)
424 Madison Ave.
Third Floor
New York, NY 10017
Tel: (212) 317-3800 *Fax:* (212) 688-0410
E-Mail: info@gold.org
Website: gold.org
Members: 23 Individuals
Staff: 11
Annual Budget: $5-10,000,000

Personnel:
Chief Executive Officer: Aram Shishmanian
Director, Corporate Communications: Brenda Bates
Chief Financial Officer: Robin Lee
Managing Director and Principal Executive Officer: Jason
    Toussaint

Historical Note:
*A subsidiary of World Gold Council, World Gold Trust
Services is an organization formed and funded by the gold
mining companies and it's mission is to stimulate desire
for gold by articulating core truths and discovering new
opportunities.*

Meetings/Conferences:
Number of non-conference events/year: 2

Publications:
Gold Bulletin; quarterly; adv.
WGC Newsletter; on-line; adv.

Membership List Available to Non-members

World History Association (1982)
University of Hawaii at Manoa, Department of
History
2530 Dole St.
Honolulu, HI 96822-2383
Tel: (808) 956-7688 *Fax:* (808) 956-9600
E-Mail: thewha@hawaii.edu
Website: thewha.org
Members: 1400 individuals
Staff: 2
Annual Budget: $100-250,000
Tax: 501(c)(3)

Personnel:
Executive Director: Winston Welch ChFC, CLU
    E-Mail: thewha@hawaii.edu
Treasurer: Carolyn Neel
    E-Mail: cneel@hotmail.com

Historical Note:
*WHA's mission is to support teaching and scholarship
within a trans-national, trans-regional, and trans- cultural
perspective. Membership: $75/year (Individual); $60
(Adjunct / Part-Time/New Professional); $40 (Full-Time
Student/Retired/Non-Employed); $125 (Contributing
Member); $200 (Sustaining Member); $2,000 (Life).*

Meetings/Conferences: Annual
2013 - Brooklyn Park, MN (North Hennepin
    Community College)/June 26 - 29
Number of non-conference events/year: 1

Publications:
Journal of World History; quarterly; adv.
World History Bulletin; semi-annually; adv.
World History connected, E-Journal of Teaching and
    Learning; on-line

World International Nail and Beauty Association
(1981)
1221 N. Lake View Ave.
Anaheim, CA 92807
Tel: (714) 779-9892 *Fax:* (714) 779-9971
E-Mail: dkellenberger@inmnails.com
Members: 13000 buyers
Staff: 4
Annual Budget: $250-500,000

Personnel:
Contact Person: David Kellenberger
    E-Mail: dkellenberger@inmnails.com

Historical Note:
Formerly (1984) the National Association of Nail Artists and (1987) the National Aesthetician and Nail Artist Association. Manufactures fingernail files (over 2,000,000 files/month). Members are manicurists, pedicurists and aestheticians as well as manufacturers and suppliers of beauty products. Primarily functions as a buyer's club for its members. Membership: $40/year (individual).

World Jurist Association *(1963)*
7910 Woodmont Ave.
Suite 1440
Bethesda, MD 20814
Tel: (202) 466-5428 *Fax:* (202) 452-8540
E-Mail: wja@worldjurist.org
Website: worldjurist.org
Staff: 2
Annual Budget: $100-250,000
Tax: 501(c)(3)

Personnel:
National President: Peter J. Marcus
General Counsel: Garry E. Hunter

Historical Note:
WJA is a non-profit, non-political organization established under the auspices of the American Bar Association that seeks peaceful international relations under a rule of law. Membership: 25,000 (Benefactor, includes Lifetime Membership); $15,000 (President's Circle, includes Lifetime Membership); $5,000 (Patron, includes Lifetime Membership); $1,000 (Lifetime Member); $250 (Lawyers & Judges); $100 (Law Professors/Legal Professionals from Developing Countries/Young Lawyers/Law Students); $200 (Business Associates).

Publications:
Law/Technology; quarterly
The World Jurist; quarterly

World Media Association
3600 New York Ave. NE, Third Floor
Washington, DC 20002
Tel: (202) 636-3124 *Fax:* (202) 635-9227
E-Mail: media@wmassociation.com
Website: wmassociation.com
Members: 6000 individuals
Staff: 3
Annual Budget: $100-250,000

Personnel:
Executive Director: Larry Moffitt
General Manager: Tomiko Duggan
Editor: Diane M. Falk

Historical Note:
WMA promotes freedom of the press in places and encourages the responsible use of that freedom.

World Pet Association *(1951)*
135 W. Lemon Ave.
Monrovia, CA 91016
Tel: (626) 447-2222 *Fax:* (626) 447-8350
TollFree: (800) 999-7295
E-Mail: info@wpamail.org
Website: worldpetassociation.org
Members: 520 companies
Staff: 12
Annual Budget: $2-5,000,000
Tax: 501(c)(6)

Personnel:
President: Douglas L. Poindexter CAE
 E-Mail: doug.poindexter@wpamail.org
Office Manager: Nancy Bertagna
 E-Mail: nancy@wpamail.org
Director, Shows and Events: Kathy Branson
 E-Mail: kathy@wpamail.org
Director, Communications: Jessica Guzman
 E-Mail: jessica@wpamail.org
Vice President, Sales: Dave Williams
 E-Mail: dave@wpamail.org

Historical Note:
Formerly (1994) Western World Pet Supply Association. Mission is to promote responsible pet care worldwide. WWPIA represents and promotes the interests of pet industry manufacturers, importers, product distributors, breeder/livestock distributors and manufacturers' representatives and retailers. Membership: $750 ((Distributor/Manufacturer/Animal Distributor/Affiliate/E-commerce.); $50-750 (Retail).

Meetings/Conferences:
Conference Chair: Kathy Branson
2013 - Atlantic City, NJ/April 10 - 12
2013 - Las Vegas, NV (Mandalay Bay)/July 23 - 25

2013 - Chicago, IL (Donald Stephens Convention
 Center Chicago)/Sept. 20 - 22
2014 - Las Vegas, NV (Mandalay Bay)/July 22 - 24
2014 - Chicago, IL (Donald Stephens Convention
 Center Chicago)/Sept. 19 - 21
2015 - Las Vegas, NV (Mandalay Bay)/July 21 - 23
2015 - Chicago, IL (Donald Stephens Convention
 Center Chicago)/Sept. 18 - 20

Publications:
Member Directory; on-line
Pet Industry Briefs; weekly

World Research Foundation *(1984)*
41 Bell Rock Plaza
Sedona, AZ 86351
Tel: (928) 284-3300 *Fax:* (928) 284-3530
E-Mail: info@wrf.org
Website: wrf.org
Members: 41000 individuals
Staff: 2
Annual Budget: $100-250,000
Tax: 501(c)(3)

Personnel:
Founder: LaVerne Boeckman
 E-Mail: laverne@wrf.org
Co-founder: Steven A. Ross

Historical Note:
WRF's purpose is to locate, gather, codify, evaluate, classify, and disseminate information dealing with health and the environment. Membership: $40/year (Active Donor).

Publications:
WRF News

World Shipping Council *(2000)*
1156 15th St. NW
Suite 300
Washington, DC 20005
Tel: (202) 589-1230 *Fax:* (202) 589-1231
E-Mail: info@worldshipping.org
Website: worldshipping.org
Members: 28 Members Companies
Staff: 5
Annual Budget: $2-5,000,000
Tax: 501(c)(6)

Personnel:
President and Chief Executive Officer: Christopher L.
 Koch
 E-Mail: ckoch@worldshipping.org
Senior Vice President: Lars Kjaer
 E-Mail: lkjaer@worldshipping.org
Vice President: Don O'Hare
 E-Mail: dohare@worldshipping.org
Vice President: Douglas Schneider
 E-Mail: dschneider@worldshipping.org
Bryan Wood-Thomas
 E-Mail: bwoodthomas@worldshipping.org

Historical Note:
The World Shipping Council's goal is to provide a coordinated voice for the liner shipping industry in its work with policymakers and other industry groups with an interest in international transportation.

World Sign Associates *(1947)*
8774 Yates Dr.
Suite120
Westminster, CO 80030
Tel: (303) 427-7252 *Fax:* (303) 427-7090
Website: wsanetwork.org
Members: 185 companies
Staff: 3
Annual Budget: $250-500,000

Personnel:
Executive Vice President: Jerry L. Righthouse

Historical Note:
WSA members are companies involved in the design, manufacture, installation and maintenance of electrical signs, and suppliers to the industry. Membership: $780/year (company).

World Teleport Association *(1985)*
250 Park Ave.
Seventh Floor
New York, NY 10177
Tel: (212) 825-0218 *Fax:* (212) 825-0075
E-Mail: wta@worldteleport.org
Website: worldteleport.org

Members: 650 individuals, 106 companies and
 130 companies
Staff: 4
Annual Budget: $250-500,000

Personnel:
Executive Director: Robert Bell FACHE
 E-Mail: rbell@worldteleport.org
Director, Membership Services: Randall Barney
 E-Mail: rbarney@worldteleport.org
Manager, Communications: Orly Konig Lopez
 E-Mail: orly@worldteleport.org
Director, Development: Louis Zacharilla
 E-Mail: lzacharilla@worldteleport.org

Historical Note:
WTA's mission is to promote the understanding, development and use of teleports as a means to achieve economic, political and social progress locally, regionally and worldwide. Members are operators of teleports, from independents to multinationals, niche service providers to global hybrid carriers. Membership: $995-3,250 (Companies based on turnover); $8,000 (Industry Patrons); $17,000 (Industry Leaders); $700 (Government and Nonprofit Organization).

Meetings/Conferences:
Number of non-conference events/year: 13

Publications:
Membership Database; on-line
Membership Directory; on-line
The Marketplace; on-line
Uplink news brief; monthly

World Trade Centers Association *(1970)*
420 Lexington Ave.
Suite 518
New York, NY 10170
Tel: (212) 432-2626 *Fax:* (212) 488-0064
TollFree: (800) 937-8886
E-Mail: wtca@wtca.org
Website: wtcaonline.com
Members: 326 members
Staff: 27
Annual Budget: $5-10,000,000
Tax: 501(c)(6)

Personnel:
Chief Executive Officer: Eric R. Dahl
Administrative Assistant: Betel Abebe
 E-Mail: babebe@wtca.org
Manager, Accounting: Yverose Charles
 E-Mail: ycharles@wtca.org
Director, Member Services: Robert Frueh
 E-Mail: rfrueh@wtca.org
Coordinator, Human Resource: Cynthia Gallegos
 E-Mail: cgallegos@wtca.org
Manager, Member Relations and Events: Julia Gonzalez
 E-Mail: jgonzalez@wtca.org
Coordinator, Member Relations and Communications:
 Maryann Kopfer
 E-Mail: mkopfer@wtca.org
Legal Council: Scott Richie
 E-Mail: srichie@wtca.org
Manager, Certification and Programs: Natalie Rideau
 E-Mail: nrideau@wtca.org
Support Coordinator, Information Technology: Felix
 Vargas
 E-Mail: fvargas@wtca.org
Business Development Executive: Scott Wang
 E-Mail: swang@wtca.org

Historical Note:
WTCA strives to encourage the expansion of global trade. Its mission is to foster a global world trade network that promotes prosperity through trade and investment. Membership: $10,000/Year.

Continuing Education:
Certification Designation/s: WTCA

Meetings/Conferences:
Conference Chair: Julia Gonzalez
Number of non-conference events/year: 90

Publications:
WTCA Newsletter; on-line

The World Umpires Association *(2000)*
P.O. Box 394
Neenah, WI 54957
Website: worldumpires.com
Members: 96 umpires
Staff: 2
Annual Budget: $50-100,000

Personnel:
President: John Hirschbeck
Secretary and Treasurer: Jerry Layne

Historical Note:
Supersedes Major League Umpires Association. Acts as bargaining agent in negotiations with Major League Baseball. The WUA is a union managed from within with legal counsel taking an advisory role.

Publications:
Membership Directory; on-line

World War Two Studies Association (1967)
Kansas State University
Department of History, Eisenhower Hall
Manhattan, KS 66506-1002
Tel: (913) 532-0374　*Fax:* (913) 532-7004
Website: h-net.msu.edu/~war/wwtsa
Members: 350 individuals
Staff: 1

Personnel:
*Contact, Communications, Secretary, Editor and
　Membership:* Mark Parillo
　E-Mail: parillo@ksu.edu

Historical Note:
WWTSA was originally called as American Committee on the History of the Second World War. WWTSA strives to promote historical research in the period of World War II in all its aspects. WWTSA is affiliated with the American Historical Association, with the International Committee for the History of the Second World War, and with corresponding national committees in other countries. Members are academics and others with an interest in the study of the World War II period. Membership: $15 (Individual).

Publications:
WWTSA Newsletter; semi-annually

World Waterpark Association (1980)
8826 Santa Fe Dr.
Suite 310
Overland Park, KS 66212
Tel: (913) 599-0300　*Fax:* (913) 599-0520
E-Mail: memberservices@waterparks.org
Website: waterparks.org
Members: 1000 parks and 450 suppliers
Staff: 5
Annual Budget: $500-1,000,000

Personnel:
President: Rick Root
　E-Mail: rroot@waterparks.org
Director, Operations and Membership Services: Kelly
　Harris
　E-Mail: kelly@waterparks.org
Coordinator, Trade Show and Advertising: Andy Miller
　E-Mail: andy@waterparks.org
Director, Trade Shows and Supplier Relations: Patty Miller
　E-Mail: patty@waterparks.org

Historical Note:
WWA provides a forum for the discussion of information related to the water amusement park industry. Furthers safety and profitability in the water leisure industry through educational conferences and publications. Members are owners and operators of water leisure facilities. Membership: $365 (Prospective park developers/Park Member, facilities with an annual attendance of below 250,000); $580 (Park Member, facilities with an annual attendance of 250,000 or more); $585 (Supplier Member).

Meetings/Conferences: Annual
Conference Chair: Patty Miller

Publications:
Buyers Guide; annually; adv.
World Waterpark Magazine; monthly; adv.

World Watusi Association (1984)
J Heart Farm
5625 State Hwy. 94 West
Water Valley, KY 42085
Tel: (270) 832-0515
E-Mail: info@watusicattle.com
Website: watusicattle.com
Members: 300 individuals
Staff: 2
Annual Budget: $10-25,000

Personnel:
President: Vernon Base
　E-Mail: buffalo2@mtelco.net

Historical Note:

WWA is dedicated to the preservation and advancement of African Ankole- Watusi cattle. Maintains breed standards, stud books and the registry. Membership: $25/year.

Meetings/Conferences: Annual

Publications:
Newsletter

World's Poultry Science Association, U.S.A. Branch (1965)
P.O. Box 1705
Clemson, SC 29633-1705
Tel: (864) 633-8633
E-Mail: psa@assochq.org
Website: wpsa.com
Members: 450 individuals
Staff: 2
Annual Budget: $10-25,000

Personnel:
Secretary: Dr. Robert E. Buresh
　E-Mail: bob.buresh@novusint.com

Historical Note:
WPSA strives to advance knowledge and understanding of all aspects of poultry science and the poultry industry. Membership: $50 (Affiliate/Patron); $5-10 (Student); $10-20 (Individual) $500 (Life).

Meetings/Conferences: Annual
Number of non-conference events/year: 2

Publications:
World's Poultry Science Journal
WPSA Newsletter; quarterly

WorldatWork (1955)
14040 N. Northsight Blvd.
Scottsdale, AZ 85260-3627
Tel: (480) 951-9191
TollFree: (877) 951-9191
E-Mail: customerrelations@worldatwork.org
Website: worldatwork.org
Members: 30000 individuals
Staff: 135
Annual Budget: $10-25,000,000
Tax: 501(c)(3)

Personnel:
President and Chief Executive Officer: Anne C Ruddy CCP,
　CPCU
Vice President, Publishing and Community: Ryan M
　Johnson
　E-Mail: rjohnson@worldatwork.org
Vice President, Professional Development: Bonnie Kabin
　CCP
　E-Mail: bkabin@worldatwork.org
Director, Human Resources: Richard "Kip" Kipley
　E-Mail: kip.kipley@worldatwork.org
Manager, Public Relations: Marcia Rhodes APR
　E-Mail: marcia.rhodes@worldatwork.org

Historical Note:
Formerly American Compensation Association and assumed its current name in 2000. WAW's mission is to enable organizations to reward employees in ways that satisfy and engage them and produce desired business results. Membership: $195 (Practitioner); $100 (Academic/ University Professor); $50 (Student).

Continuing Education:
Enrollment: 30000
Certification Designation/s: CECP, CCP, CBP, GRP, WLCP,
CSCP

Meetings/Conferences: Annual
Conference Chair: Bonnie Kabin CCP
2013 - Philadelphia, PA (Pennsylvania Convention
　Center)/April 29 - May 1

Publications:
Membership Directory; on-line
Workspan e-Newsletter; weekly; adv.
WorldatWork Journal; quarterly

Worldwide ERC (1964)
4401 Wilson Blvd.
Suite 510
Arlington, VA 22203
Tel: (703) 842-3400　*Fax:* (703) 527-1552
E-Mail: info@erc.org
Website: worldwideerc.org
Members: 13000 individuals and Corporations
Staff: 45
Annual Budget: $10-25,000,000

Personnel:

President and Chief Executive Officer: Peggy Smith
　E-Mail: psmith@WorldwideERC.org
Senior Vice President, Communications and Marketing:
　Anita Brienza
　E-Mail: abrienza@worldwideerc.org
Vice President, Finance and Operations: Kirk Fabel PhD
　E-Mail: kfabel@WorldwideERC.org
Vice President, Research and Education: Jan Hatfield-
　Goldman
　E-Mail: jhatfield-goldman@WorldwideERC.org
Director, Membership Services and Operations: Terri
　LaGoe
　E-Mail: tlagoe@WorldwideERC.org
General Counsel: Richard H. Mansfield
　E-Mail: rmansfield@WorldwideERC.org
Director, Human Resource Services: Bobbye Mathews
　E-Mail: bmathews@WorldwideERC.org
Vice President, Meetings and Membership Alliances: Cici
　Thompson CAE
　E-Mail: cthompson@WorldwideERC.org
Vice President, Research and Professional Development:
　Christine Wilson
　E-Mail: cwilson@WorldwideERC.org

Historical Note:
Formerly (1973) Employee Relocation Real Estate Advisory Council. Mission is to provide leadership, advocacy, education and networking to professionals and stakeholders in the mobile global workforce through specialized training, credentialing, meetings and exchange of information. Membership: $235-335 (Corporate HR Professionals); $235-865 (Mobility Service Professionals).

Continuing Education:
Certification Designation/s: GMS

Meetings/Conferences: Annual
Conference Chair: Cici Thompson CAE
2013 - San Diego, CA (Manchester Grand)/May 15 -
　17
2014 - Orlando, FL/May 7 - 9
2015 - Las Vegas, NV/May 6 - 8

Publications:
Labour Relations Law Newsletter; on-line
Mobility; monthly; adv.
Worldwide ERC® Roster; on-line; adv.

Worldwide Printing Thermographers Association
305 Plus Park Blvd.
Nashville, TN 37217
Tel: (800) 821-3138　*Fax:* (615) 366-4192
E-Mail: thermographers@earthlink.net
Website: thermographers.org
Staff: 1

Personnel:
Treasurer: Palm Jones

Historical Note:
WPTA works to promote and and advance the art of thermography, and helps raise product quality standards for the thermographic industry. It is organized within the International Engraved Graphics Association.

The Wound, Ostomy and Continence Nurses Society (1968)
15000 Commerce Pkwy.
Suite C
Mt. Laurel, NJ 08054
Tel: (888) 224-9626　*Fax:* (856) 439-0525
TollFree: (888) 224-9626
E-Mail: wocn_info@wocn.org
Website: wocn.org
Members: 105 industry members and 4200
individuals
Staff: 15
Annual Budget: $5-10,000,000
Tax: 501(c)(6)

Personnel:
Executive Director: Pete Pomilio
　E-Mail: ppomilio@ahint.com
Executive Vice President: Nicolette Zuecca
　E-Mail: nzuecca@ahint.com
Senior Manager, Meetings and Exhibits: Chris Brown
　CEM, CMP
　E-Mail: cbrown@wocn.org
Director, Membership Services: Gail Haas
　E-Mail: ghaas@ahint.com
Managing Editor: Gary Mawyer
　E-Mail: gdm@virginia.edu

Historical Note:

Wound Ostomy and Continence Nurses Society is a professional society of healthcare professionals who are experts in wound ostomy and incontinence care. Membership: $60-1,500/year.

Continuing Education:
Certification Designation/s: WOCNCB

Meetings/Conferences: Annual
Conference Chair: Chris Brown CEM, CMP
2013 - Seattle, WA/June 22 - 26
2014 - Nashville, TN/June 21 - 25

Publications:
Journal of Wound, Ostomy, and Continence Nursing;
  bi-monthly; adv.
Membership Directory; on-line
Wound, Ostomy and Continence Nurses Society™, the
  WOCNews; adv.

Membership List Available to Non-members

Woven Wire Products Association *(1942)*
P.O. Box 610280
Birmingham, AL 35261-0280
Tel: (800) 529-6691 *Fax:* (517) 542-2501
TollFree: (800) 529-6691
Website: wovenwire.org
Members: 18 companies
Staff: 1
Annual Budget: $25-50,000
Tax: 501(c)(3)

Personnel:
Vice President, Membership Services: Bonny Des Jardin
  E-Mail: bonnyd@jescoonline.com

Historical Note:
WWPA's purpose is to promote its active member firms and their products. It also offers a forum for the exchange of management and technical information at semi-annual and annual conventions and meetings. Membership: $1,600 (Active); $800 (Associate); Initiation Fee is $125.

Publications:
Member Directory; on-line

Writers Guild of America East *(1954)*
250 Hudson St.
New York, NY 10013
Tel: (212) 767-7800 *Fax:* (212) 582-1909
E-Mail: info@wgaeast.org
Website: wgaeast.org
Members: 4100 individuals
Staff: 27
Annual Budget: $2-5,000,000

Personnel:
Executive Director: Lowell Peterson
  E-Mail: lpeterson@wgaeast.org
Senior Legal Counsel: Ann Burdick
  E-Mail: aburdick@wgaeast.org
Coordinator, Events: Nancy Hathorne
  E-Mail: nhathorne@wgaeast.org
Administrator, Membership Services: Kelly O'Brien
  E-Mail: kobrien@wgaeast.org
Contact, Media Relations: Jay Strell
  E-Mail: strell@sunshinesachs.com
Director, Programs: Dana Weissman
  E-Mail: dweissman@wgaeast.org

Historical Note:
Founded in New York City as an independent labor union. WGAE's mission is to serve professional writers in motion pictures, television, cable, digital media, and broadcast news. Members write for animation, entertainment, network and local news operations, independent stations in major cities, and for any other media production companies which are signatory to Guild agreements. Affiliated states include Maine, New Hampshire, Vermont, Massachusetts, Rhode Island, Connecticut, New York, Pennsylvania, New Jersey, Delaware, Maryland, District of Columbia, West Virginia, Virginia, North Carolina, South Carolina, Georgia, Florida, Puerto Rico, and Virgin Islands.

Meetings/Conferences:
Conference Chair: Nancy Hathorne
Number of non-conference events/year: 1

Publications:
On Writing Magazine; annually
OnWritingONLINE; on-line
Writers Guild Awards Journal; annually

Membership List Available to Non-members

Writers Guild of America West *(1933)*
7000 W. Third St.
Los Angeles, CA 90048-4329

Tel: (323) 951-4000 *Fax:* (323) 782-4800
TollFree: (800) 548-4532
Website: wga.org
Members: 9000 individuals
Staff: 169
Annual Budget: $10-25,000,000

Personnel:
President: Christopher Keyser
Contact, Communications: Greg Mitchell
  E-Mail: gmitchell@wga.org
Director, Public Policy: John Vezina
  E-Mail: jvezina@wga.org

Historical Note:
The Writers Guild of America, West (WGAW) is a labor union representing writers of motion pictures, television, radio, and Internet programming, including news and documentaries.

Publications:
Now Playing (e-Newsletter); on-line
Written By Magazine

Membership List Available to Non-members

Writing Instrument Manufacturers Association *(1943)*
1701 Pennsylvania Ave. NW
Suite 300
Washington, DC 20006
Tel: (202) 253-4347 *Fax:* (202) 330-5092
E-Mail: info@wima.org
Website: wima.org
Members: 40 companies
Staff: 2
Annual Budget: $100-250,000

Personnel:
Executive Director and General Counsel: David Baker
  E-Mail: dhbakerlaw@aol.com

Historical Note:
Formerly (1963) known as the Fountain Pen and Mechanical Pencil Manufacturers Association. Merged with Pencil Makers Association in 1994. WIMA's mission is to promote the overall interest of the writing instrument industry in the United States, Canada and Mexico and strives to keep its members well-informed on issues which affect the industry and individual companies. Member categories are Writing and Marking Instrument Manufacturers, Component Suppliers, Exclusive Distributors, Advertising Specialty Companies and Raw Material Suppliers. Membership: $500-15,000 (Manufacturers and Suppliers, Based on writing instrument sales); $2,500 (Testing).

Continuing Education:
Certification Designation/s: ECP, ICP, PCP

Meetings/Conferences: Annual
2013 - Lake Buena Vista, FL (Hyatt Regency Grand
  Cypress)/May 21 - 23
Number of non-conference events/year: 1

Publications:
Writing Instrument Industry Directory; on-line; adv.

WTA Tour, Inc. *(1973)*
100 Second Ave. S.
Suite 1100-S
St. Petersburg, FL 33701
Tel: (727) 895-5000 *Fax:* (727) 894-1982
Website: sonyericssonwtatour.com
Members: 2400 individuals
Staff: 32
Annual Budget: $50-100,000,000
Tax: 501(c)(6)

Personnel:
Chief Executive Officer and Chairman: Stacey Allaster
Chief Administrative Officer: Matthew Cenedella
Managing Director: Peter Johnston
Senior Vice President, Tour Operations: Peachy Kellmeyer
General Counsel: Diana Myers
Senior Vice President, Operations: Joan Pennello
Vice President, Human Resources: Linda Ryley
Senior Vice President, Information Technology: Murray
  Swartzberg
Vice President, Global Marketing and Communications:
  Andrew Walker
  E-Mail: awalker@wtatour.com

Historical Note:
Originally Women's Tennis Association; became (1986) Women's International Tennis Association; reverted to its original name in 1990. Absorbed WTA Tour Players Association in 1995 and assumed the name WTA Tour. WTA Tour is now also known as Sony Ericsson WTA Tour.

Members are professional women tennis players. Sponsors tournaments in 34 countries worldwide. Membership: $1,000/year (Full).

Publications:
Hero News; weekly

XBRL US, Inc. *(1998)*
100 Walnut Ave.
Suite 103
Clark, DC 20036-5339
Tel: (618) 263-4383 *Fax:* (866) 516-6923
TollFree: (888) 810-6907
E-Mail: info@xbrl.org
Website: xbrl.us
Members: 500 companies and agencies
worldwide
Staff: 11
Annual Budget: $1-2,000,000
Tax: 501(c)(6)

Personnel:
Chief Executive Officer: Campbell Pryde
  E-Mail: campbell.pryde@xbrl.us
Vice President, Communications: Michelle Savage
  E-Mail: michelle.savage@xbrl.us
Vice President, Membership Services: David Tauriello
  E-Mail: david.tauriello@xbrl.us

Historical Note:
XBRL's mission is to support the implementation of XBRL in the United States through the development of taxonomies relevant for use by US public and private sectors. Membership: $2 to $2000-$20000 (for Profit Organisations depending on gross revenue); $2000 to $5000 (Government/Regulatory Entities); $1000 to $10000 (NOn-profit Organizations).

Meetings/Conferences: Annual

Publications:
Interactive Business Reporting (iBR)

Xi Psi Phi Dental Fraternity *(1889)*
160 S. Bellwood Dr.
Suite Z
Alton, IL 62024
Tel: (618) 307-5433 *Fax:* (618) 307-5430
Website: xipsiphi.org
Members: 20000 individuals
Staff: 2

Personnel:
Supreme Secretary and Treasurer: Dr. Keith W. Dickey
  E-Mail: kdickey@siue.edu

Historical Note:
An international professional dental fraternity. Xi Psi Phi promotes intellectual, moral and fellowship virtues among dental students and professionals. Fraternity. Membership varies from campus to campus and from group to group.

Meetings/Conferences: Annual
2013 - Alton, IL/April 6
Number of non-conference events/year: 2

Publications:
Xi Psi Phi Magazine; quarterly

Xplor International *(1981)*
24156 State Rd. 54
Suite Four
Lutz, FL 33559
Tel: (813) 949-6170 *Fax:* (813) 949-9977
TollFree: (800) 669-7567
E-Mail: info@xplor.org
Website: xplor.org
Members: 1400 organizations and 3500
individuals
Staff: 6
Annual Budget: $500-1,000,000
Tax: 501(c)(6)

Personnel:
President and Chief Executive Officer: Skip Henk
  E-Mail: skip@xplor.org
Contact, Sales and Sponsorship Program: Deborah Green
  E-Mail: deborahgreen1@earthlink.net
Coordinator, Programs: Chad Henk
  E-Mail: chad@xplor.org
Director, Information Technology: Quang Nguyen
  E-Mail: xqn@xplor.org
Director, Operations: Lynn Robbins
  E-Mail: lynn@xplor.org

Historical Note:
Formerly known as Electronic Document Systems Association and also known as Xplor International/

Electronics Documents Systems Association. XI strives to provide programs, forums, and related services which enhance the use of electronic document systems to achieve organizational goals. *Membership: $199 (Individual); $795 (Corporate, includes benefits for up to five); $3,750 (Corporate plus, includes member benefits for up to 25); $85 (Student/Unemployed/Retired).*

Continuing Education:
Certification Designation/s: EDP

Meetings/Conferences: Annual
2013 - St. Petersburg, FL (The TradeWinds Island Grand Hotel)/April 17 - 19

Publications:
E-Document News; bi-weekly

Yacht Brokers Association of America (1920)
105 Eastern Ave.
Suite 104
Annapolis, MD 21403-3300
Tel: (410) 940-6345 *Fax:* (410) 263-1659
E-Mail: info@ybaa.com
Website: ybaa.com
Members: 320 companies and 1900 individuals
Staff: 9
Annual Budget: $250-500,000
Tax: 501(c)(6)

Personnel:
Executive Director: Vincent J. Petrella
Manager, Accounting: Dorothy Cusack
  E-Mail: dcusack@thompsonmanagement.com
Assistant, CPYB Program: Amy Luckado
  E-Mail: aluckado@thompsonmanagement.com
Manager, CPYB Program: Colleen McDonough
  E-Mail: cmcdonough@thompsonmanagement.com
Director, Communications and Conferences: Kristin B. Thompson
  E-Mail: kthompson@thompsonmanagement.com
General Manager: Joseph M. Thompson Jr.
  E-Mail: jthompson@thompsonmanagement.com
Editor and Manager, Communications: Nicole Tierney Weber
  E-Mail: nweber@thompsonmanagement.com

Historical Note:
Formerly (1999) known as Yacht Architects and Brokers Association. YBAA promotes the interests of professional yacht brokers through its code of ethics, legislative and regulatory involvement and certification program, as well as conducting education and dissemination of pertinent information. Membership: $330-815 (Corporate/Provisional Corporate); $475 (Affiliate).

Continuing Education:
Enrollment: 400
Certification Designation/s: CPYB

Meetings/Conferences: Annual
Conference Chair: Kristin B. Thompson

Publications:
Membership Directory; annually
Yacht Broker News; monthly; adv.

YMA Fashion Scholarship Fund (1937)
36 W. 20th St.
Third Floor
New York, NY 10011
Tel: (212) 594-6422 *Fax:* (212) 594-9349
Website: fashionscholarshipfund.org
Members: 350 individuals
Staff: 2
Annual Budget: $1-2,000,000
Tax: 501(c)(3)

Personnel:
Executive Director and Secretary: Robert Harry Harrison Jr.
  E-Mail: hharrison@ymafashionscholarshipfund.org
Contact, Marketing, Events and Press Inquiries: Brenner Thomas
  E-Mail: bthomas@laforce-stevens.com

Historical Note:
Formerly (1971) Young Men's Apparel Association of the Men's Apparel Industry (YMAMAI) and (2006) Young Menswear Association, or YMA. YMAFSF reflect its focus beyond men's wear and is committed to advancing the fashion industry by encouraging talented and enterprising young people to pursue careers in design, merchandising, retailing and business disciplines.

Meetings/Conferences:
Conference Chair: Brenner Thomas

Publications:
Member Directory; on-line

Young Adult Library Services Association (1957)
50 E. Huron St.
Chicago, IL 60611
Tel: (312) 280-4390 *Fax:* (312) 280-5276
TollFree: (800) 545-2433
E-Mail: yalsa@ala.org
Website: ala.org/yalsa
Members: 5400 members
Staff: 5
Tax: 501(c)(3)

Personnel:
Executive Director: Beth Yoke
  E-Mail: byoke@ala.org
Program Officer, Continuing Education: Eve Gaus
  E-Mail: egaus@ala.org
Program Officer, Conferences and Events: Nichole Gilbert
  E-Mail: ngilbert@ala.org
Program Coordinator, Membership Services: Letitia Smith
  E-Mail: lsmith@ala.org

Historical Note:
YALSA's purpose is to advocate, promote and strengthen service to young adults as part of the continuum of total library service. Membership: $53-180/year.

Meetings/Conferences: Annual
Conference Chair: Nichole Gilbert
Number of non-conference events/year: 2

Publications:
American Libraries magazine; adv.
Journal of Research on Libraries and Young Adults; quarterly; adv.
Member Directory; on-line
YAttitudes; monthly; adv.
Young Adult Library Services; quarterly; adv.

Membership List Available to Non-members

Young Presidents' Organization (1950)
600 E. Las Colinas Blvd.
Suite 1000
Irving, TX 75039
Tel: (972) 587-1500 *Fax:* (972) 587-1611
TollFree: (800) 773-7976
E-Mail: askypo@ypo.org
Website: ypo.org
Members: 20,000 business leaders
Staff: 3
Annual Budget: $2-5,000,000

Personnel:
Director, Brand Management: Michelle Foster
  E-Mail: mfoster@ypowpo.org
Contact, Meetings: Chris Thomas
  E-Mail: cthomas@ypowpo.org.

Historical Note:
Merged with the World Presidents' Organization in year 2007 to create the premier lifelong leadership network. YPO's mission is to develop better leaders through education and idea exchange. Members are company presidents under age 50 whose companies employ at least 50 individuals and have either $7 million in annual sales or $140 million in total assets. Membership: $2,880/year (International).

Meetings/Conferences: Annual
Conference Chair: Chris Thomas
2013 - Istanbul, Turkey/Feb. 28 - March 2

Publications:
YPO Newsletter; on-line

YPO-WPO (1970)
600 E. Las Colinas Blvd.
Suite 1000
Irving, TX 75039
Tel: (972) 587-1500 *Fax:* (972) 587-1600
TollFree: (800) 773-7976
E-Mail: askypo@ypowpo.org
Website:
wpo.org
ypo.org
Members: 17000 executives
Staff: 3

Personnel:
Chief Executive Officer: Scott Mordell
Chief Marketing Officer: Steve Dobbins
Chief Financial Officer: Terry Wilson

Historical Note:
Founded in 2007 as a result of a merger between the World Presidents Organization (WPO) and the Young Professionals Organization (YPO) and both organizations

have retained their individual identities and serve as a global leadership network providing educational and networking opportunities for executives. WPO provides YPO graduates with opportunities for continued learning and lifelong peer networking at the chapter, regional and international levels.

Meetings/Conferences: Annual
2013 - Istanbul, Turkey/Feb. 28 - March 2

Zero Balancing Health Association (1970)
8640 Guilford Rd.
Suite 241
Columbia, MD 21046
Tel: (410) 381-8956 *Fax:* (410) 381-9634
Website: zerobalancing.com
Staff: 3

Personnel:
Executive Director: Cindi Pridgen
Office Manager: Kara Skeberdis
Administrative Assistant: Charlotte Urgolites

Historical Note:
ZBHA's mission is to help people experience health, well-being and wholeness by facilitating the study, practice and development of Zero Balancing.Membership: $50 (Associate/Retired); $150 (Certified).

Continuing Education:
Certification Designation/s: ZB CP

Meetings/Conferences: Annual
2013 - Buckeystown, MD (The Claggett Center in Buckeystown)/May 3 - 5

Publications:
e-news
Interface; monthly

Zonta International (1919)
1211 W. 22nd St.
Suite 900
Oak Brook, IL 60523
Tel: (630) 928-1400 *Fax:* (630) 928-1559
E-Mail: zontaintl@zonta.org
Website: zonta.org
Members: 30000 individuals and clubs
Staff: 12
Annual Budget: $2-5,000,000
Tax: 501(c)(4)

Personnel:
Executive Director: Jason Friske
Manager, Membership Services: Jill Gehring
Manager, Accounting and Human Resources: Margaret Ingram
Manager, Communications: Megan Radavich
Assistant, Contributions and Membership Database: Brett Simon

Historical Note:
ZI works to advance the status of women worldwide through service and advocacy. Membership in a Zonta Club is by invitation.

Meetings/Conferences: Annual

Publications:
Membership Directory; on-line
The Zontian; bi-annually
Zonta International E-Newsletter; monthly

Zoological Association of America (2005)
P.O. Box 511275
Punta Gorda, FL 33951-1275
Tel: (941) 621-2021
E-Mail: info@zaa.org
Website: zaa.org
Members: 109 Individuals and 5 Companies
Staff: 2
Annual Budget: $100-250,000

Personnel:
Chairman, Conference: Matt Fouts
  E-Mail: conference@zaa.org
Treasurer: John Wortman

Historical Note:
ZAA was formed to advocate responsible ownership, management, conservation, and propagation of animals in both the private and public domains through professional standards in husbandry, animal care, safety and ethics. Membership: $40 (Associate); $60 (Professional); $250 (Private Facility); $350 (Public Facility); $150 (Educational Facility); $500 (Commercial).

Meetings/Conferences: Annual
Conference Chair: Matt Fouts

Publications:

ZAA Newsletter & Journal; quarterly; adv.

Subject Index

Every active association listed in NTPA has been indexed in one or more subject headings, which reflect the products, professions, or industries the association represents. Organizations that make their membership lists available to non-members are marked with an asterisk (*).

ABRASIVES
Abrasive Engineering Society (2)
International Grooving & Grinding Association (549)
Unified Abrasives Manufacturers Association (984)
United Abrasives Manufacturers Association, Coated Division (985)
WaterJet Technology Association - Industrial and Municipal Cleaning Association (1013)*

ACOUSTICS
The Acoustical Society of America (11)
ALMA - The International Loudspeaker Association (26)*
Audio Engineering Society (320)*
National Association of Noise Control Officials (682)
National Council of Acoustical Consultants (733)
National Horsemen's Association, Inc. (760)

ADHESIVES
Adhesion Society (12)
Adhesive and Sealant Council (12)*
Pressure Sensitive Tape Council (856)
Sealant, Waterproofing and Restoration Institute (894)*

ADVERTISING AND MARKETING
Academy of Marketing Science (6)*
Advertising and Marketing International Network (13)
Advertising Council (13)
Advertising Media Credit Executives Association (13)
The Advertising Research Foundation (13)
AIM North America (17)
Alliance for Gray Market and Counterfeit Abatement (23)
American Academy of Advertising (30)*
American Advertising Federation (43)
American Agricultural Marketing Association (44)
American Association for Public Opinion Research (51)*
American Association of Advertising Agencies (53)*
American Catalog Mailers Association (88)
American Floorcovering Alliance (122)
American Insurance Marketing and Sales Society (141)
American Luggage Dealers Association (146)
American Marketing Association (147)
American Photographic Artists (164)
American Railway Development Association (173)
American Teleservices Association (215)
American Wholesale Marketers Association (221)*
Association for Accounting Marketing (238)*
Association for Postal Commerce (253)
Association of Free Community Papers (284)
Association of Hispanic Advertising Agencies (287)
Association of Independent Commercial Producers (287)
Association of Independent Information Professionals (288)
Association of Investment Management Sales Executives (289)
Association of Marketing Service Providers (293)*
Association of National Advertisers (295)
Association of Travel Marketing Executives (315)
Audit Bureau of Circulations (320)*
Automotive Communication Council (322)*
Bluegrass Tourism Marketing Association (332)

BP and AMOCO Marketers Association (334)
BPA Worldwide (334)
Business Marketing Association (339)*
Cabletelevision Advertising Bureau (340)*
Chain Drug Marketing Association (350)*
Cherry Marketing Institute (352)
Chevron and Texaco Petroleum Marketers Association (352)
Color Marketing Group (365)
Communications Marketing Association (369)
Construction Marketing Research Council (380)
Copper Development Association (384)
Copywriters Council of America (385)
Council of American Survey Research Organizations (392)*
Diagnostic Marketing Association (411)
Digital Imaging Marketing Association (412)
Direct Marketing Association (412)
Direct Marketing Association Nonprofit Federation (412)
Direct Marketing Insurance and Financial Services Council (413)
Direct Selling Association (413)
Distributive Education Clubs of America (DECA) (415)
Eight Sheet Outdoor Advertising Association (421)
Electrical Generating Systems Association (422)
Electronic Retailing Association (423)*
Family and Consumer Sciences Education Association (437)
Food Marketing Institute (449)
Fulfillment Management Association (454)
Glass Association of North America (461)
Global Market Development Center (462)
Graphic Arts Sales Foundation (465)
Herb Growing and Marketing Network (474)
Hospitality Sales and Marketing Association International (479)*
ICOM, International Communications Agency Network (482)
Incentive Federation, Inc. (487)
Incentive Manufacturers & Representatives Alliance (487)
Incentive Marketing Association (487)*
Independent Film and Television Alliance (489)*
Independent Professional Representatives Organization (491)
Inflatable Advertising Dealers Association (494)
Institute of Store Planners (503)*
Insurance Marketing Communications Association (505)
Inter-Company Marketing Group (506)
Interactive Advertising Bureau (506)*
Intermarket Agency Network (508)*
International Advertising Association (509)
International Association of Medical Equipment Remarketers and Servicers (IAMERS) (524)
International Housewares Association (550)
International Licensing Industry Merchandisers' Association (554)*
International Newspaper Marketing Association (558)
International Sign Association (564)*
International Society for Quality-of-Life Studies (569)
Internet Marketing Association (582)*
Legal Marketing Association (596)*
Livestock Marketing Association (599)

Local Search Association (fka Yellow Pages Association) (600)
Manufacturers' Agents National Association (603)
Marketing Agencies Association Worldwide (606)
Marketing and Advertising Global Network (606)*
Marketing Association of Credit Unions (606)
Marketing Education Association (606)
Marketing Research Association (606)
Marketing Science Institute (606)
Mass Marketing Insurance Institute (607)
Materials Marketing Associates (608)
Media Credit Association (610)
Medical Marketing Association (611)
Mobile Marketing Association (618)
Multi-Level Marketing International Association (621)*
National Agri-Marketing Association (629)
National Aircraft Resale Association (630)*
National Association for Campus Activities (637)
National Association for Retail Marketing Services (642)
National Association of Collegiate Marketing Administrators (656)
National Association of Export Companies (666)*
National Association of Publishers' Representatives (689)
National Association of Sales Professionals (692)
National Association of Video Distributors (708)
National Automatic Merchandising Association (711)
National Council of Exchangors (734)
National Retail Federation (786)*
Network Advertising Initiative (808)
Network of Ingredient Marketing Specialists (808)*
North American Agricultural Marketing Officials (812)
Outdoor Advertising Association of America (834)
Petroleum Marketers Association of America (843)
Pharmaceutical Marketing Research Group (844)
Photoimaging Manufacturers and Distributors Association (846)*
PMA - The Worldwide Community of Imaging Associations (851)
Point of Purchase Advertising Institute (851)
POPAI The Global Association for Marketing at Retail (852)
Private Label Manufacturers Association (858)
Produce Marketing Association (858)
Product Development and Management Association (858)
Professional Insurance Marketing Association (862)
Professional Society for Sales and Marketing Training (865)*
PROMAX/BDA (866)
Promotion Marketing Association (866)
Promotional Products Association International (867)
Publishers' Publicity Association (870)
Qualitative Research Consultants Association (871)*
Radio Advertising Bureau (873)
Real Estate Buyers Agent Council (875)
Retail Advertising and Marketing Association International (884)
Retail Industry Leaders Association (884)
Sales and Marketing Executives International, Inc. (890)
Sales Lead Management Association (890)
Society for Marketing Professional Services (914)

Society of Independent Gasoline Marketers of America (SIGMA) **(939)**
Special Event Sites Marketing Alliance **(954)**
Specialty Equipment Market Association **(957)***
Station Representatives Association **(962)**
Strategic Marketplace Initiative **(963)**
Television Bureau of Advertising **(971)**
Tobacco Merchants Association of the United States **(975)***
Trade Promotion Management Associates **(977)**
Traffic Audit Bureau for Media Measurement, Inc. **(977)**
Transworld Advertising Agency Network **(979)***
United Producers, Inc. **(988)**
United States Potato Board **(997)**
Utility Communicators International **(1006)**
Wine and Spirits Wholesalers of America **(1018)***

AESTHETICS
Aestheticians International Association **(14)**
American Academy of Esthetic Dentistry **(33)***
American Society for Aesthetic Plastic Surgery **(180)***
American Society for Aesthetics **(180)**
American Society for Dental Aesthetics **(183)***
Indoor Tanning Association **(492)**

AGING
Alliance for Aging Research **(22)**
American Academy of Anti-Aging Medicine **(30)**
American Aging Association **(43)***
American Association for Geriatric Psychiatry **(49)**
American Association of Retired Persons **(72)**
American Association of Retirement Communities **(72)**
American College of Health Care Administrators **(96)***
American Federation for Aging Research **(119)**
American Geriatrics Society **(126)**
American Health Care Association **(129)**
American Seniors Housing Association **(178)**
American Society on Aging **(211)***
Assisted Living Federation of America **(234)**
Association for Adult Development and Aging **(238)***
Association of Jewish Aging Services **(290)**
Coalition for Independent Seniors **(360)**
Gerontological Society of America **(460)***
Hospice Association of America **(479)**
Insured Retirement Institute **(505)**
International Association of Homes and Services for the Ageing **(522)**
International Society for Quality of Life Research **(569)**
LeadingAge (American Association of Homes and Services for the Aging) **(595)**
Meals on Wheels Association of America **(609)**
National Academy of Elder Law Attorneys, Inc. **(627)**
National Active and Retired Federal Employees Association **(629)**
National Adult Day Service Association **(629)**
National Association for the Support of Long Term Care **(644)**
National Association of Activity Professionals **(645)**
National Association of Area Agencies on Aging **(647)**
National Association of County Aging Programs **(659)**
National Association of Foster Grandparent Program Directors **(669)**
National Association of Nutrition and Aging Services Programs **(682)**
National Association of Older Worker Employment Services **(683)**
National Association of Professional Geriatric Care Managers **(687)***
National Association of Retired and Senior Volunteer Program Directors **(692)**
National Association of States United For Aging and Disabilities **(703)**
National Conference on Public Employee Retirement Systems **(729)**
National Council of Social Security Management Associations **(736)**
National Council on Aging **(738)**
National Council on Teacher Retirement **(740)**
National Hospice & Palliative Care Organization **(760)***
National Institute of Senior Centers **(765)**
National Organization of Social Security Claimants' Representatives **(778)**
National Pace Association **(778)**
National Senior Corps Association **(790)**
Pharmaceutical Care Management Association **(844)**
Retirement Industry Trust Association **(885)**

AGRICULTURE/AGRONOMY
Agribusiness Council **(16)**
Agricultural & Applied Economics Association **(16)**
Agricultural and Food Transporters Conference **(16)**
Agricultural History Society **(16)**
Agricultural Retailers Association **(16)**

Agricultural Stewardship Association **(16)**
Agriculture Council of America **(16)***
Alpha Gamma Rho **(26)**
American Agricultural Editors Association **(43)***
American Agricultural Law Association **(44)***
American Agricultural Marketing Association **(44)**
American Agriculture Movement, Inc. **(44)**
American Association for Agricultural Education **(47)***
American Association of Candy Technologists **(55)**
American Association of Cereal Chemists International **(55)**
American Association of Crop Insurers **(59)***
American Association of Grain Inspection and Weighing Agencies **(61)**
American Beekeeping Federation **(80)**
American Corn Growers Association **(108)**
American Cotton Shippers Association **(108)**
American Farm Bureau Federation **(118)**
American Farmland Trust **(118)***
American Feed Industry Association **(120)**
American Forage and Grassland Council **(122)**
American Herbalists Guild **(131)***
American Institute of Biological Sciences **(137)**
American Malting Barley Association **(146)**
American Meat Institute **(148)***
American Mosquito Control Association **(153)**
American Nursery and Landscape Association **(156)***
American Oil Chemists' Society **(157)***
American Oilseed Coalition **(157)**
American Peanut Council **(162)**
American Peanut Product Manufacturers, Inc. **(162)**
American Peanut Research and Education Society, Inc. **(162)**
American Peanut Shellers Association **(162)**
American Phytopathological Society **(165)**
American Polypay Sheep Association **(167)**
American Pomological Society **(167)**
American Seed Trade Association **(178)**
American Sesame Growers Association **(178)**
American Sheep Industry Association **(178)**
American Society of Agricultural and Biological Engineers **(191)***
American Society of Agricultural Appraisers **(191)**
American Society of Agricultural Consultants **(191)**
American Society of Agronomy (ASA, CSSA, SSSA) **(191)***
American Society of Animal Science **(192)**
American Society of Farm Managers and Rural Appraisers **(197)**
American Society of Irrigation Consultants **(201)**
American Society of Plant Biologists **(207)**
American Society of Sugar Beet Technologists **(209)**
American Soybean Association **(211)**
American Sugar Alliance **(214)**
American Sugarbeet Growers Association **(214)***
Animal Health Institute **(223)**
Animal Transportation Association **(223)***
Apple Processors Association **(225)**
Apple Products Research and Education Council **(226)**
Aquacultural Engineering Society **(227)**
Aquatic Plant Management Society, Inc. **(227)**
Association for Communication Excellence **(242)***
Association for International Agricultural and Extension Education **(250)**
The Association for International Agriculture and Rural Development **(250)**
Association for Living History, Farm and Agricultural Museums **(251)**
Association of American Feed Control Officials **(265)***
Association of American Pesticide Control Officials **(265)**
Association of American Plant Food Control Officials **(266)**
The Association of American Seed Control Officials **(266)***
Association of Analytical Communities International **(267)**
Association of Applied IPM Ecologists **(267)**
Association of Farmworker Opportunity Programs **(282)**
Association of Natural Bio-Control Producers **(295)***
Association of Official Seed Analysts, Inc. **(296)**
Association of Official Seed Certifying Agencies **(296)**
Association of Women Soil Scientists **(317)**
Beet Sugar Development Foundation **(327)**
Biotechnology Industry Organization (BIO) **(330)**
Black Farmers and Agriculturists Association **(331)**
Braunvieh Association of America **(334)**
Canola Council of Canada **(341)**
Cattlemen's Beef Promotion and Research Board **(346)**
Cherry Marketing Institute **(352)**
Chilean Avocado Importers Association (CAIA) **(353)**
Commodity Markets Council **(368)**
Concord Grape Association **(373)**
Corn Refiners Association, Inc. **(385)**

Cotton Council International **(387)**
Cotton Growers Warehouse Association **(387)**
Cotton Incorporated **(387)**
Cotton Warehouse Association of America **(387)**
Council for Agricultural Science and Technology **(388)**
Council of Producers & Distributors of Agrotechnology **(396)**
Cranberry Institute **(403)**
Crop Insurance Research Bureau **(404)**
Crop Science Society of America **(404)**
CropLife America **(404)**
Dairy Management, Inc. **(406)**
Distilled Spirits Council of the United States, Inc. **(414)**
Distillers Grains Technology Council **(414)***
Epsilon Sigma Phi **(432)**
Equipment Marketing and Distribution Association **(432)**
Farm Credit Council **(437)**
Farm Equipment Council **(437)**
Farm Labor Organizing Committee **(437)**
The Fertilizer Institute **(443)**
Fluid Fertilizer Foundation **(448)**
Food Processing Suppliers Association **(449)**
Fresh Produce and Floral Council **(453)**
Fresh Produce Association of the Americas **(453)**
Futures Industry Association **(455)**
Grain Elevator and Processing Society **(464)**
Grocery Manufacturers Association (GMA) **(466)**
Growth Energy **(466)**
Herb Growing and Marketing Network **(474)**
Herb Society of America **(474)**
Home Baking Association **(477)**
Hop Growers of America **(478)**
ICE Futures U.S. **(482)**
Industrial Fabrics Association International **(493)**
Industrial/Agricultural Mower Manufacturers Council **(494)**
International Association of Operative Millers **(525)**
International Banana Association **(529)**
International Dairy Foods Association **(539)***
International Fruit Tree Association **(547)**
International Herb Association **(550)***
International Maple Syrup Institute **(555)**
International Plant Nutrition Institute **(560)**
International Silo Association **(564)**
International Weed Science Society **(581)**
International Wild Rice Association **(581)***
Irrigation Association **(585)**
Juice Products Association **(589)**
Kamut Association of North America **(590)**
Land Improvement Contractors of America **(593)**
The Lawn Institute **(594)**
Livestock Marketing Association **(599)**
Methanol Institute **(614)**
National Agri-Marketing Association **(629)**
National Agricultural Alumni and Development Association **(630)**
National Agricultural Aviation Association **(630)**
National Alfalfa Alliance **(631)**
National Alfalfa and Forage Alliance **(631)**
National Alliance of Independent Crop Consultants **(632)***
National Animal Control Association **(634)**
National Animal Supplement Council **(634)**
National Aquaculture Council **(635)**
National Association of Agricultural Educators **(646)***
National Association of Agricultural Fair Agencies **(646)**
National Association of Agriculture Employees **(646)**
National Association of County Agricultural Agents **(659)***
National Association of Crop Insurance Agents **(662)**
National Association of Extension 4-H Agents **(667)**
National Association of Farm Broadcasting **(667)**
National Association of Farm Service Agency County Office Employees **(667)**
National Association of Farmer Elected Committees (NAFEC) **(667)**
National Association of Farmers Market Nutrition Programs **(667)**
National Association of State Departments of Agriculture **(699)**
National Association of Wheat Growers **(709)***
National Barley Growers Association **(712)**
National Black Caucus of State Legislators **(714)**
National Black Farmers Association **(714)**
National Block and Bridle Club **(715)**
National Cannabis Industry Association **(717)**
National Cattlemen's Beef Association **(718)**
National Cherry Growers and Industries Foundation **(720)**
National Chicken Council **(720)**
National Confectioners Association **(725)**
National Cooperative Business Association **(729)**
National Corn Growers Association **(730)**
National Cotton Batting Institute **(730)***
National Cotton Council of America **(730)**

ANIMALS

Mohair Council of America (618)
Montadale Sheep Breeders Association (619)
National Association for Biomedical Research (636)
National Association of Animal Breeders (647)
The National Association of Dog Obedience
    Instructors (663)
National Association of Federal Veterinarians (668)
National Association of Professional Pet Sitters
    (687)*
National Association of Swine Records (704)
National Barrel Horse Association (712)
National Bison Association (713)*
National Block and Bridle Club (715)
National Cattlemen's Beef Association (718)
National Cutting Horse Association (741)
National Dog Groomers Association of America, Inc.
    (743)
National Greyhound Association (756)
National Hereford Hog Record Association (759)*
National Horsemen's Benevolent and Protective
    Association (760)
National Horsemen's Association, Inc. (760)
National Institute for Animal Agriculture (764)
National Lamb Feeders Association (768)
National Lincoln Sheep Breeders Association (770)
National Livestock Producers Association (770)
National Mastitis Council (772)
National Miniature Donkey Association (772)
National Pork Producers Council (781)
National Reining Horse Association (785)
National Renderers Association (786)
National Show Horse Registry (791)
National Spotted Saddle Horse Association (796)
National Spotted Swine Records (796)
National Swine Improvement Federation (798)
National Swine Registry (798)
National Taxidermists Association (799)*
National Thoroughbred Racing Association (800)
National Tunis Sheep Registry (802)
National Turf Writers and Broadcasters (802)
National Wildlife Federation (805)
Natural Colored Wool Growers Association (807)
North American Clun Forest Association (815)
North American Corriente Association (815)
North American Deer Farmers Association (815)
North American Elk Breeders Association (816)
North American Gamebird Association (817)
North American Limousin Foundation (817)
North American Peruvian Horse Association (819)*
North American South Devon Association (822)
North American Wensleydale Sheep Association
    (823)
Palomino Horse Association (837)
Palomino Horse Breeders of America (837)
Paso Fino Horse Association, Inc. (839)
Percheron Horse Association of America (841)
Pet Food Institute (842)
Pet Industry Distributors Association (842)
Pet Industry Joint Advisory Council (842)*
Pet Sitters International (843)
Piedmontese Association of the United States (848)*
Pinto Horse Association of America (848)
Poland China Record Association (852)
Pony of the Americas Club (852)
Professional Handlers Association (862)
Purebred Dairy Cattle Association (871)
Purebred Morab Horse Association (871)*
Pyramid Society (871)
R-Calf (872)
Racking Horse Breeders Association of America
    (872)*
Ranchers-Cattlemen Action Legal Fund, United
    Stockgrower of America (874)
Raptor Breeders of America (875)
Red and White Dairy Cattle Association (877)
Red Angus Association of America (877)
Rocky Mountain Llama & Alpaca Association (887)
Santa Gertrudis Breeders International (891)
Scottish Blackface Breeders Association (893)
Society for Range Management (920)
Spanish Barb Horse Association (954)
Spotted Saddle Horse Breeders' and Exhibitors'
    Association (959)
Tamworth Swine Association (968)
Texas Longhorn Breeders Association of America
    (972)
Thoroughbred Club of America (973)
Thoroughbred Owners and Breeders Association
    (974)
Thoroughbred Racing Associations of North America
    (974)*
United Braford Breeders (986)
United Gamefowl Breeders Association, Inc. (987)
United Producers, Inc. (988)
United Professional Horsemen's Association (988)
United States Beef Breeds Council (991)
United States Cattlemen's Association (991)
United States Equestrian Federation (993)
The United States Harness Writers' Association
    (994)

United States of Ayrshire Breeders' Association (997)
United States Targhee Sheep Association (999)
United Suffolk Sheep Association (1001)
Walking Horse Owners Association of America
    (1011)
Walking Horse Trainers Association (1012)
Welsh Pony and Cob Society of America (1015)*
Wild Bird Feeding Industry (1017)*
Wild Bird Feeding Institute (1017)
Wildlife Management Institute (1017)
The Wildlife Society (1017)*
Wilson Ornithological Society (1018)
Women's Professional Rodeo Association (1023)
World Pet Association (1027)
World Watusi Association (1028)
Zoological Association of America (1030)

APPAREL/TEXTILES INDUSTRY

American Apparel & Footwear Association (46)
American Apparel Producer's Network (46)
American Association of Textile Chemists and
    Colorists (75)
American Border Leicester Association (85)
American Cleaning Institute (91)
American Cotton Shippers Association (108)
American Fiber Manufacturers Association (121)
American Flock Association (122)*
American Floorcovering Alliance (122)
American Home Furnishings Alliance (132)
American Karakul Sheep Registry (143)
American Leather Chemists Association (145)*
American Legend Cooperative (145)
American Naturopathic Association (155)
American Reusable Textile Association (175)
American Sheep Industry Association (178)
American Society for Eighteenth-Century Studies
    (183)*
American Textile Machinery Association (216)*
American Watchmakers-Clockmakers Institute (219)
American Wool Council (222)
Apparel Graphics Institute (225)
Association for Linen Management (251)
Association of Bridal Consultants (270)*
Association of Sewing and Design Professionals
    (308)
Belt Association (328)
Building Service Contractors Association
    International (337)
The Carpet and Rug Institute (343)
Carpet Cushion Council (343)*
Cashmere and Camel Hair Manufacturers Institute
    (344)
Cleaning Equipment Trade Association (357)
Cleaning Management Institute (357)
Coin Laundry Association (361)*
The Color Association of the United States (365)
The Cordage Institute (385)
Costume Society of America (387)*
Cotton Council International (387)
Cotton Growers Warehouse Association (387)
Cotton Warehouse Association of America (387)
Council of Fashion Designers of America (393)
Custom Tailors and Designers Association of
    America (406)
Decorative Furnishings Association (408)
Drycleaning & Laundry Institute (417)
Embroidery Trade Association (425)
Fashion Accessories Shippers Association (438)
Fashion Accessories Shippers Association/Gemini
    Shippers Association (438)
Fashion Group International (438)
Flag Manufacturers Association of America (446)
Fluid Sealing Association (448)*
Footwear Distributors and Retailers of America (450)
Fur Commission USA (454)
Fur Information Council of America (454)
Greater Blouse, Skirt and Undergarment Association
    (466)
Handweavers Guild of America, Inc. (468)*
Home Fashion Products Association (478)
The Hosiery Association (478)
INDA, Association of the Nonwoven Fabrics Industry
    (488)*
Industrial Fabrics Association International (493)
Industrial Fasteners Institute (493)
The Institute of Inspection, Cleaning and Restoration
    Certification (500)
International Association of Clothing Designers and
    Executives (518)
International Federation of Leather Guilds (544)
International Formalwear Association (546)
International Glove Association (548)
International Kitchen Exhaust Cleaning Association
    (553)
International Maintenance Institute (555)
International Sleep Products Association (565)
International Textile and Apparel Association (577)
International Window Cleaning Association (581)*
The Knitting Guild Association (591)
Korean Drycleaners-Laundry Association (591)

Leather Apparel Association (596)
Leather Industries of America (596)
Metal Findings Manufacturers Association (613)
Mohair Council of America (618)
Multi-Housing Laundry Association (621)
NADCA: The HVAC Inspection, Maintenance and
    Restoration Association (623)
National Association of Decorative Fabric
    Distributors (662)
National Association of Resale & Thrift Shops (691)
National Association of Uniform Manufacturers and
    Distributors (707)
National Chimney Sweep Guild (721)
National Cleaners Association (722)
National Costumers Association (730)
National Cotton Council of America (730)
National Council of Textile Organizations (737)*
National Fastener Distributors Association (747)
National Home Furnishings Association (759)
National Luggage Dealers Association (770)
The National NeedleArts Association (774)
National Shoe Retailers Association (791)
National Textile Association (800)*
National Trappers Association (801)
Natural Colored Wool Growers Association (807)
NIBA - The Belting Association (810)
Oriental Rug Importers Association of America (833)
Oriental Rug Retailers of America, Inc. (833)
Pedorthic Footwear Association (840)
Pine Chemicals Association (855)
Power Washers of North America (855)
Restoration Industry Association (884)
Schiffli Lace and Embroidery Manufacturers
    Association (892)
Scottish Blackface Breeders Association (893)
SEAMS Association (894)*
Secondary Materials and Recycled Textiles
    Association (894)
Sewing and Craft Alliance (898)
Sewn Products Equipment and Suppliers of the
    Americas (898)
Shippers of Recycled Textiles (899)
Society of Cleaning and Restoration Technicians
    (932)
Sponge and Chamois Institute (958)
Sports and Fitness Industry Association (959)
Sunglass Association of America (965)
Surface Design Association (966)*
Synthetic Yarn and Fiber Association (967)
Textile Bag and Packaging Association (972)
Textile Care Allied Trades Association (972)
Textile Fibers and By-Products Association (972)*
Textile Producers and Suppliers Association (973)
Textile Rental Services Association of America (973)
Travel Goods Association (979)*
UNITE-HERE (985)
United Food and Commercial Workers International
    Union (987)
United Shoe Retailers Association (988)
United States Association of Importers of Textiles
    and Apparel (990)
United States Hide, Skin and Leather Association
    (994)
Wallcovering Association (1012)
YMA Fashion Scholarship Fund (1030)

ARCHITECTURE AND DESIGN

Airport Consultants Council (21)
American Architectural Foundation (46)
American College of Healthcare Architects (96)
American Council of Engineering Companies (109)*
American Craft Council (111)
American Cultural Resources Association (ACRA)
    (112)
American Design Drafting Association International
    and American Digital Design Association (114)
The American Institute of Architects (137)*
American Institute of Architecture Students (137)
American Institute of Building Design (137)
American Institute of Certified Planners (137)
American Institute of Floral Designers (138)
American Planning Association (166)*
American Society of Architectural Illustrators (192)*
American Society of Furniture Designers (198)
American Society of Golf Course Architects (198)
American Society of Interior Designers (200)*
American Society of Landscape Architects (201)
Architectural Engineering Institute (227)
Architectural Precast Association (228)
Architectural Woodwork Institute (228)*
Association for Bridge Construction and Design
    (240)
Association for Dressings and Sauces (245)
Association of AE Business Leaders (263)
Association of Collegiate Schools of Architecture
    (275)*
Association of Professional Design Firms (301)
Association of University Interior Designers (315)
Bridge Grid Flooring Manufacturers Association
    (335)

League of American Orchestras *(595)*
League of Historic American Theatres *(595)**
League of Resident Theatres *(595)*
Literary Managers and Dramaturgs of the Americas *(599)*
Motion Picture Association of America (MPAA) *(619)*
Mu Phi Epsilon *(621)*
Music and Entertainment Industry Educators Association *(622)*
Music Critics Association of North America *(622)*
Music Distributors Association *(622)*
Music Industry Conference *(622)*
Music Library Association *(622)*
Music Publishers Association of the United States *(622)*
Music Teachers National Association *(622)**
NABIM - the International Band and Orchestral Products Association *(623)*
NAMM - The International Music Products Association *(625)*
Nashville Songwriters Association, International *(625)*
National Academy of Recording Arts and Sciences *(628)*
National Alliance for Musical Theatre *(632)*
National Antique and Art Dealers Association of America *(634)*
National Art Education Association *(635)*
NAMTA - National Art Materials Trade Association *(635)**
National Assembly of State Arts Agencies *(635)*
National Association for Drama Therapy *(638)*
The National Association for Music Education (Formerly MENC) *(641)**
National Association for Printing Leadership *(641)*
National Association of College Wind and Percussion Instructors *(655)*
National Association of Pastoral Musicians *(683)**
National Association of Photo Equipment Technicians *(684)*
National Association of Professional Band Instrument Repair Technicians *(686)*
National Association of Recording Merchandisers (NARM) *(690)*
National Association of School Music Dealers *(692)*
National Association of Schools of Art and Design *(693)**
National Association of Schools of Dance *(693)**
National Association of Schools of Music *(694)**
National Association of Schools of Theatre *(694)**
National Association of Teachers of Singing *(705)*
National Association of Theatre Owners *(706)*
National Association of Women Artists *(709)*
National Ballroom and Entertainment Association *(712)*
National Band Association *(712)*
National Cartoonists Society *(718)*
National Catholic Band Association *(718)*
National Costumers Association *(730)*
National Council of Art Administrators *(734)*
National Council on Education for the Ceramic Arts *(738)*
National Dance Association *(741)*
National Dance Council of America *(741)*
National Dance Education Organization *(742)**
National Federation of Music Clubs *(749)*
The National Flute Association, Inc. *(751)**
National Guild for Community Arts Education *(757)**
National Guild of Piano Teachers *(757)*
National Humanities Alliance *(761)**
National Institute of American Doll Artists *(764)*
National Music Council *(774)*
National Music Publishers Association *(774)*
National Opera Association *(776)*
National Press Photographers Association *(782)**
National Sculpture Society *(790)*
National Society of Mural Painters *(794)**
The National Society of Painters in Casein and Acrylic *(794)*
National Watercolor Society *(804)*
New Dramatists *(809)**
NFHS Music Association *(810)*
NFHS Speech Debate and Theatre Association *(810)*
North American Nature Photography Association *(819)*
North American Performing Arts Managers and Agents *(819)**
North American Saxophone Alliance *(820)*
NPES, The Association for Suppliers of Printing, Publishing, and Converting Technologies *(824)*
OPERA America *(828)*
Ophthalmic Photographers' Society *(829)**
Organization of American Kodaly Educators *(832)*
Percussion Marketing Council *(841)*
Percussive Arts Society *(841)*
Performing Arts Alliance *(841)*
Phi Beta Fraternity *(845)*
Phi Mu Alpha Sinfonia *(846)*
Photo Chemical Machining Institute *(846)*

Photoimaging Manufacturers and Distributors Association *(846)**
Piano Manufacturers Association International *(848)*
Piano Technicians Guild *(848)*
Picture Archive Council of America *(848)*
PMA - The Worldwide Community of Imaging Associations *(851)*
Print Council of America *(857)*
Printing Brokerage/Buyers Association International *(857)*
Private Art Dealers Association *(858)*
Professional Photographers of America *(863)*
Professional School Photographers Association International *(865)*
Professional Women Photographers *(866)*
Professional Women Singers Association *(866)*
R & E Council of the NAPL *(872)*
Recording Industry Association of America (RIAA) *(876)*
Refractory Ceramic Fibers Coalition *(878)**
The Renaissance Society of America *(881)*
Retail Print Music Dealers Association *(885)**
Screen Actors Guild - American Federation of Television and Radio Artists *(893)*
Sculptors Guild *(894)*
Silver Users Association *(900)*
Smocking Arts Guild of America *(901)*
Society for Asian Music *(904)*
Society for Ethnomusicology *(908)*
Society for General Music *(910)*
Society for Imaging Science and Technology *(912)*
Society for Photographic Education *(919)**
Society for Technical Communication *(922)**
Society of American Fight Directors *(928)**
Society of American Graphic Artists *(929)*
Society of Animal Artists *(930)*
The Society of Composers and Lyricists *(933)*
Society of Composers, Inc. *(933)*
Society of Dance History Scholars *(934)*
Society of Illustrators *(939)*
Society of Photo-Technologists *(944)*
Society of Professional Audio Recording Services *(945)*
Society of Publication Designers *(946)*
Society of Scribes *(947)*
Songwriters Guild of America *(952)*
Southeastern Theatre Conference *(953)*
Specialty Graphic Imaging Association *(957)*
SPIE - The International Society for Optical Engineering *(958)*
Stage Directors and Choreographers Society *(960)*
Stage Managers Association *(960)*
Stuntwomen's Association of Motion Pictures *(964)*
Surface Design Association *(966)**
Technical Association of the Graphic Arts *(969)*
The Technology Institute for Music Educators *(970)*
Theatre Communications Group *(973)**
Theatre Library Association *(973)**
Type Directors Club *(983)*
United States Institute for Theatre Technology *(995)*
University Photographers Association of America *(1002)*
University/Resident Theatre Association *(1003)**
Van Alen Institute *(1007)**
Viola da Gamba Society of America *(1009)*
Violin Society of America *(1010)*
Visual Artists Rights Coalition *(1010)*
Visual Resources Association *(1010)**
Wedding and Portrait Photographers International *(1014)*
Western Association for Art Conservation *(1015)*
Western Music Association *(1016)*
White House News Photographers Association *(1016)*
Women Band Directors International *(1020)*
Women's Caucus for Art *(1022)*
Women's Classical Caucus *(1023)*

AUCTIONS

Manuscript Society *(604)*
National Auctioneers Association *(711)*
National Auto Auction Association *(711)*

AUDIO-VISUAL

American Association for Vocational Instructional Materials *(53)*
ASPRS- The Imaging and Geospatial Information Society *(233)*
Association for Educational Communications and Technology *(245)**
Association for Recorded Sound Collections *(255)**
Association of Biomedical Communications Directors *(269)*
Association of Cinema and Video Laboratories *(273)*
Association of Moving Image Archivists *(295)*
Audio Engineering Society *(320)**
Builders Association *(338)*
CALLERLAB - International Association of Square Dance Callers *(341)*

Communications Media Management Association *(369)*
Content Delivery and Security Association *(382)*
Entertainment Merchants Association *(429)*
InfoComm International *(495)*
Interactive Audio Special Interest Group *(507)*
International Association of Audio Visual Communicators *(516)**
International Documentary Association *(541)*
International Society for Performance Improvement *(567)**
International Society of Communication Specialists *(572)*
MIDI Manufacturers Association *(615)**
National Academy of Recording Arts and Sciences *(628)*
National Association of Media and Technology Centers *(680)**
National Association of Recording Merchandisers (NARM) *(690)*
National Association of Self-Instructional Language Programs *(695)*
Online Audiovisual Catalogers *(827)**
Recording Industry Association of America (RIAA) *(876)*
Society for Cinema and Media Studies *(905)**
Society of Professional Audio Recording Services *(945)*
United States Institute for Theatre Technology *(995)*

BANKING/FINANCE/INVESTMENTS

AACE International *(1)*
Abacus International *(2)*
ACA International, The Association of Credit and Collection Professionals *(2)*
Academy of Accounting Historians *(3)*
Accreditation Council for Accountancy and Taxation *(9)*
Actors' Equity Association *(11)*
Advertising Media Credit Executives Association *(13)*
AGN International North America, Inc *(15)*
Allied Finance Adjusters *(26)*
American Accounting Association *(43)*
American Agents Alliance *(43)*
American Alliance of Home Modification Professionals (AAHMP) *(44)*
American Association for Budget and Program Analysis *(48)*
American Association of Attorney-Certified Public Accountants *(54)**
American Association of Bank Directors *(54)*
American Association of Credit Union Leagues *(59)*
American Association of Healthcare Administrative Management *(61)**
American Association of Individual Investors *(63)*
American Association of Private Lenders *(71)*
American Association of Residential Mortgage Regulators *(72)*
American Bail Coalition *(78)*
American Bankers Association *(79)*
American Bankers Association Securities Association (ABASA) *(79)*
American Bankers Insurance Association *(79)*
American Bankruptcy Institute *(79)*
American Cash Flow Association *(88)*
American Council of Life Insurers (ACLI) *(110)**
American Council of State Savings Supervisors *(110)*
American Credit and Collections Association *(111)*
American Education Finance Association *(116)**
American Factoring Association *(118)*
The American Fair Credit Council *(118)*
The American Finance Association *(121)*
American Financial Services Association *(121)*
American Fraternal Alliance *(124)*
American Institute of Certified Public Accountants *(137)*
American Institute of Professional Bookkeepers *(140)**
American Land Title Association *(144)*
American League for Exports and Security Assistance *(145)*
American National Chamber of Commerce *(154)*
American Payroll Association *(162)*
American Recovery Association *(174)*
American Risk and Insurance Association *(175)**
The American Safe Deposit Association *(176)*
American Society of Military Comptrollers *(203)*
American Society of Tax Professionals *(209)*
American Society of Women Accountants (ACC) *(211)*
American Woman's Society of Certified Public Accountants *(221)*
Armed Forces Financial Network *(229)*
Association for Accounting Administration *(237)*
Association for Accounting Marketing *(238)**
Association for Enterprise Opportunity *(245)**
Association for Financial Counseling and Planning Education *(246)*
Association for Financial Professionals, Inc. *(247)*
Association for Financial Technology *(247)*

Association for Governmental Leasing and Finance *(247)*
Association for Management Information in Financial Services *(251)*
The Association of Asian American Investment Managers *(268)*
Association of Chartered Accountants in the United States *(272)*
Association of College and University Auditors *(274)**
Association of Commercial Finance Attorneys *(275)*
Association of Corporate Credit Unions *(277)*
Association of Credit Union Internal Auditors *(278)*
Association of Finance and Insurance Professionals *(283)*
Association of Financial Guaranty Insurers *(283)*
Association of Foreign Investors in U.S. Real Estate *(284)*
Association of Fundraising Professionals *(285)*
Association of Government Accountants *(286)*
Association of Independent Trust Companies *(288)*
Association of Information Technology Professionals *(289)*
Association of Insolvency and Restructuring Advisors *(289)**
Association of Institutional Investors *(289)**
Association of Investment Management Sales Executives *(289)*
Association of Latino Professionals in Finance and Accounting *(291)*
Association of Military Banks of America *(294)*
The Association of Mortgage Investors *(295)*
Association of Public Treasurers of the United States and Canada *(304)*
ATM Industry Association *(320)*
BAFT-IFSA *(325)*
Bank Administration Institute *(326)**
Bank Insurance and Securities Association *(326)*
Benchmarking Network Association *(328)*
Beta Alpha Psi *(328)*
BKR International *(331)*
Broadcast Cable Credit Association *(335)*
Capital Markets Credit Analysts Society *(342)*
CEO Council for Growth *(349)*
CFA Institute *(350)*
Checks Payment Systems Association *(351)*
Coalition of Higher Education Assistance Organizations *(360)*
College Savings Foundation *(364)**
College Savings Plans Network *(364)*
Colombian American Association *(365)**
Commercial Finance Association *(366)**
Committee of Annuity Insurers *(368)*
Community Banking Advisors Network *(370)*
Community Development Venture Capital Alliance *(370)**
Community Financial Services Association of America CFSA *(370)**
Conference of State Bank Supervisors *(376)*
Conference on Consumer Finance Law *(376)*
Consolidated Tape Association *(378)*
Construction Financial Management Association *(379)*
Construction Industry CPAs/Consultants Association *(379)**
Consumer Bankers Association *(380)*
Consumer Credit Industry Association *(381)*
Consumer Data Industry Association *(381)*
Consumer Mortgage Coalition *(381)*
Corporate Facility Advisors, Inc. *(386)*
Council for International Tax Education *(390)**
Council of Development Finance Agencies *(393)*
Council of Federal Home Loan Banks *(393)*
Council of Infrastructure Financing Authorities *(394)*
Council of Institutional Investors *(394)*
The Council of Insurance Agents and Brokers *(394)*
Council of Petroleum Accountants Societies *(396)*
CPA Associates International *(402)*
CPA Auto Dealer Consultants Association *(402)*
CPA USA Network *(402)*
CPAmerica International *(402)*
CPCU Society *(402)**
CRE Finance Council *(403)*
Credit Professionals International *(403)*
Credit Research Foundation *(403)*
Credit Union Executives Society *(403)*
Credit Union National Association, Inc. *(404)*
DBA International *(407)*
DBA International *(407)*
Defense Credit Union Council *(408)*
Ecuadorean American Association *(419)*
Education Credit Union Council *(419)*
Education Finance Council *(419)*
Electronic Funds Transfer Association *(423)*
Electronic Transactions Association *(424)*
Employee Stock Ownership Plan Association *(426)*
EMTA - Trade Association for the Emerging Markets *(427)*
Environmental Bankers Association *(430)*
The ERISA Industry Committee (ERIC) *(433)*

Evangelical Council for Financial Accountability *(434)*
Farm Credit Council *(437)*
FCIB-NACM Corporation *(438)*
The Fiduciary and Investment Risk Management Association *(443)*
Financial and Security Products Association *(444)*
Financial Executives International *(444)*
Financial Industry Regulatory Authority (FINRA) *(444)*
Financial Management Association International *(444)*
Financial Managers Society *(445)**
Financial Markets Association *(445)*
Financial Planning Association *(445)*
Financial Planning Standards Board *(445)*
Financial Services Forum *(445)*
The Financial Services Roundtable *(445)*
Fixed Income Analysts Society *(446)*
Futures Industry Association *(455)*
Global Association of Risk Professionals *(461)*
Government Finance Officers Association of the United States and Canada *(464)*
Government Finance Officers Association, Federal Liaison Center *(464)*
Healthcare Billing and Management Association *(470)*
Healthcare Financial Management Association *(471)*
Hedge Fund Association *(473)*
Hospitality Financial and Technology Professionals *(479)*
IGAF Polaris *(486)**
Independent Community Bankers of America *(488)**
Independent Insurance Agents & Brokers of America, Inc. *(490)*
Information Systems Audit and Control Association *(495)*
Institute for Responsible Housing Preservation *(497)*
Institute for Supply Management *(497)*
Institute Management Accountants *(498)**
The Institute of Financial Operations *(499)*
The Institute of Internal Auditors *(500)*
Institute of International Bankers *(501)*
Institute of International Finance *(501)*
Insurance Accounting and Systems Association *(504)*
Insured Retirement Institute *(505)*
Intermediaries and Reinsurance Underwriters Association *(508)*
International Association of Commercial Collectors *(518)*
International Association of Credit Portfolio Managers *(519)*
International Association of Financial Crimes Investigators *(521)*
International Association of Microfinance Investors *(524)*
International Cost Estimating and Analysis Association effective *(537)*
International Energy Credit Association *(542)*
International Federation of Accountants *(544)*
International Insurance Society *(552)*
International Swaps and Derivatives Association *(576)**
Intertribal Monitoring Association on Indian Trust Funds *(583)*
Investment Adviser Association *(583)*
Investment Company Institute *(584)*
Investment Management Consultants Association *(584)*
Investment Program Association *(584)*
Investment Recovery Association *(584)**
IT Financial Management Association *(586)*
Jewelers Board of Trade *(587)**
Loan Syndication & Trading Association *(599)*
Managed Funds Association *(602)**
Market Technicians Association *(606)*
Marketing Association of Credit Unions *(606)*
Media Credit Association *(610)*
Media Financial Management Association *(610)*
Money Management Institute *(618)*
Mortgage Bankers Association of America *(619)*
Mortgage Insurance Companies of America *(619)*
Mutual Fund Education Alliance *(623)*
NACHA - The Electronic Payments Association *(623)*
National Accounting and Finance Council *(628)*
National Aircraft Finance Association *(630)*
National Association for Fixed Annuities *(639)*
National Association of Active Investment Managers *(645)*
National Association of Affordable Housing Lenders *(646)*
National Association of Bankruptcy Trustees *(647)**
National Association of Black Accountants, Inc. *(648)*
National Association of Bond Lawyers *(650)*
National Association of Catastrophe Adjusters *(651)*
National Association of Certified Valuation Analysts *(652)*
National Association of Chapter Thirteen Trustees (NACTT) *(652)*

National Association of Consumer Advocates *(657)*
National Association of Consumer Bankruptcy Attorneys *(657)*
National Association of Consumer Credit Administrators *(657)*
National Association of Corporate Treasurers *(658)*
National Association of Credit Management *(661)*
National Association of Credit Specialists *(661)*
National Association of Credit Union Chairmen *(661)*
National Association of Credit Union Service Organizations *(661)*
National Association of Credit Union Supervisory and Auditing Committees *(661)*
National Association of Development Companies *(662)*
National Association of Division Order Analysts *(663)*
National Association of Energy Service Companies *(665)*
National Association of Enrolled Agents *(666)*
National Association of Equipment Leasing Brokers *(666)*
National Association of Federal Credit Unions *(667)*
National Association of Government Guaranteed Lenders (NAGGL) *(670)*
National Association of Independent Public Finance Advisors *(675)*
National Association of Industrial Bankers *(675)*
National Association Of Insurance and Financial Advisors(NAIFA) *(676)*
National Association of Investment Companies *(676)*
National Association of Investment Professionals *(676)*
National Association of Investors Corporation *(677)*
National Association of Local Government Auditors *(678)*
National Association of Local Housing Finance Agencies *(678)*
National Association of Mortgage Bankers *(681)*
National Association of Mortgage Brokers *(681)*
National Association of Nonprofit Accountants & Consultants *(682)*
National Association of Personal Financial Advisors *(684)*
National Association of Professional Mortgage Women *(687)*
National Association of Publicly Traded Partnerships *(689)*
National Association of Real Estate Investment Managers *(690)**
National Association of Real Estate Investment Trusts (NAREIT) *(690)*
National Association of Retail Collection Attorneys *(692)**
National Association of Sales Professionals *(692)*
National Association of Securities Professionals *(695)*
National Association of Shareholder and Consumer Attorneys *(696)*
National Association of State & Local Equity Funds *(697)**
National Association of State Auditors, Comptrollers and Treasurers *(698)*
National Association of State Boards of Accountancy *(698)*
National Association of State Budget Officers *(698)*
National Association of State Credit Union Supervisors *(699)*
National Association of State Treasurers *(702)*
National Association of Stock Plan Professionals *(703)*
National Association of Student Financial Aid Administrators *(703)**
National Association of Trade Exchanges *(706)*
National Automotive Finance Association *(711)*
National Bankers Association *(712)*
National Black MBA Association *(714)*
National Center for Employee Ownership *(719)*
National Chemical Credit Association *(720)*
National Committee for Quality Assurance *(724)**
National Conference of Bankruptcy Judges *(726)*
National Conference of CPA Practitioners *(727)*
National Council of Higher Education Loan Programs *(735)**
National Council of Postal Credit Unions *(735)*
National Council of Real Estate Investment Fiduciaries *(735)**
National CPA Health Care Advisors Association *(740)**
National Credit Reporting Association *(740)**
National Customs Brokers and Forwarders Association of America *(741)*
National Defined Contribution Council *(742)**
National Exchange Traded Fund Association *(747)*
National Federation of Community Development of Credit Unions *(748)*
National Federation of Municipal Analysts *(749)*
National Finance Adjusters *(750)*
National Foreign Trade Council, Inc. *(752)*
National Foundation for Credit Counseling *(753)*

National Installment Lenders Association *(764)*
National Institute for State Credit Union
Examination *(764)*
National Institute of Pension Administrators *(765)*
National Investment Banking Association *(767)*
National Investment Company Service Association
(767)
National Investor Relations Institute *(767)*
National Marine Bankers Association *(771)*
National Mitigation Banking Association *(773)*
The National Money Transmitters Association *(773)*
National Pawnbrokers Association *(779)*
National Payroll Reporting Consortium *(780)*
National Real Estate Investors Association *(784)*
National Reverse Mortgage Lenders Association
(787)
National Risk Retention Association *(787)*
National Society of Accountants *(793)*
National Society of Accountants for Cooperatives
(793)
National Society of Insurance Premium Auditors
(794)
National Treasury Employees Union *(801)**
National Vehicle Leasing Association *(803)*
National Venture Capital Association *(803)*
North American Association of State and Provincial
Lotteries *(813)*
North American Securities Administrators
Association (NASAA) *(820)*
Not-For-Profit Services Association *(824)*
Online Lenders Alliance *(827)*
Operations Security Professionals Society *(828)*
Opportunity Finance Network *(829)**
Organization for International Investment *(831)*
Partnership for Philanthropic Planning *(839)*
PeerSpan *(840)*
Pension Real Estate Association *(841)*
Physician Insurers Association of America *(847)*
PKF North American Network *(849)*
Plan Sponsor Council of America *(849)*
Portfolio Management Institute *(853)*
Printing Industry Credit Executives *(857)*
Printing Industry Financial Executives *(858)*
Private Equity Growth Capital Council *(858)*
Professional Liability Agents Network *(863)*
Professional Liability Underwriting Society *(863)*
Public Investors Arbitration Bar Association *(869)*
Reinsurance Association of America *(879)*
Resource Center for Religious Institutes *(883)*
Retirement Industry Trust Association *(885)*
The Risk Management Association *(886)**
S-Corporation Association *(889)*
Securities Industry and Financial Markets
Association (SIFMA) *(895)*
The Securities Transfer Association *(895)*
Security Traders Association *(895)*
Shareholder Services Association *(898)*
Small Business Council of America *(900)*
National Association of Small Business Investment
Companies *(900)*
Smart Card Alliance *(901)**
Society for Information Management *(913)*
Society for Risk Analysis *(920)*
Society of Financial Examiners *(936)*
Society of Financial Service Professionals *(936)*
Society of Insurance Financial Management *(940)*
Society of Insurance Research *(940)*
Society of Mortgage, Appraisal, Real Estate and Title
Professionals *(942)*
Society of Professional Asset-Managers and Record
Keepers *(945)*
Society of Quantitative Analysts *(946)*
The Spain-United States Chamber of Commerce
(953)
Stable Value Investment Association *(960)*
State Debt Management Network *(961)*
State Risk and Insurance Management Association
(961)
Strategic Account Management Association *(963)*
Strategic Rail Finance *(963)*
Tax Executives Institute, Inc. *(968)*
United States Organizations for Bankruptcy
Alternatives (USOBA) *(997)*
University Risk Management and Insurance
Association *(1003)*
Urban Financial Services Coalition *(1003)*
USFN-America's Mortgage Banking Attorneys *(1006)*
Venezuelan American Association of the U.S.
*(1008)**
WACRA - World Association for Case Method
Research and Application *(1011)*
WIFS - Women in Insurance and Financial Services
(1017)
World Council of Credit Unions, Inc. *(1026)*
XBRL US, Inc. *(1029)*

BROOMS & BRUSHES
American Brush Manufacturers Association *(86)*

BUSINESS

Academy of International Business *(5)**
Academy of Legal Studies in Business *(6)*
ACORD - Association for Cooperative Operations
Research and Development *(11)*
Advertising Council *(13)*
Agribusiness Council *(16)*
Alliance of Area Business Publications *(24)*
Alpha Kappa Psi *(26)*
America's Small Business Development Center
Network *(29)*
American Association of Business Valuation
Specialists *(55)*
American Association of Franchisees and Dealers
(61)
American Association of Individual Investors *(63)*
American Association of Medical Assistants *(65)*
American Association of Minority Businesses *(65)*
American Benefits Council *(80)*
American Business Media *(87)*
American Business Women's Association *(87)*
American Chamber of Commerce Executives *(89)*
The American Consultants League *(108)*
American Cultural Resources Association (ACRA)
(112)
American Franchisee Association *(123)*
American Independent Business Alliance *(135)*
American Marketing Association *(147)*
American Senior Benefits Association *(178)*
American Small Manufacturers' Coalition *(180)*
American Society of Business Publication Editors
(194)
American Staffing Association *(213)**
Angel Capital Association *(223)*
APICS The Association for Operations Management
*(224)**
Art Dealers Association of America *(229)*
Asian Women in Business *(232)*
Associated Business Writers of America *(235)*
Association for Accounting Administration *(237)*
Association for Business Communication *(240)*
Association for Business Simulation and Experiential
Learning *(241)*
Association for Corporate Growth *(244)**
Association for Enterprise Information *(245)*
The Association for Research in Business Education
- Delta Pi Epsilon *(255)**
Association for University Business and Economic
Research *(260)*
Association of Business Owners of America *(270)*
Association of Corporate Contributions
Professionals *(277)*
Association of Corporate Counsel *(277)**
Association of Executive and Administrative
Professionals *(281)*
Association of Management/International
Association of Management *(292)*
Association of Private Sector Colleges and
Universities (Career College Association) *(300)*
Association of School Business Officials
International *(306)*
Association of Small Business Development Centers
(308)
Association of Strategic Alliance Professionals, Inc.
(311)
Association of Women's Business Centers *(318)*
The Association to Advance Collegiate Schools of
Business *(319)*
BPA Worldwide *(334)*
BritishAmerican Business Inc. *(335)*
BSA | The Software Alliance *(337)*
Business Council for International Understanding
(338)
Business Executives for National Security *(338)**
Business for Social Responsibility *(339)**
Business Forms Management Association *(339)**
Business Higher Education Forum *(339)*
Business History Conference *(339)*
Business Professionals of America *(339)*
Business Technology Association *(340)**
Canadian-American Business Council *(341)*
CIES - The Food Business Forum *(356)*
Coalition of Service Industries *(361)**
College Athletic Business Management Association
*(362)**
Colombian American Association *(365)**
The Commercial Vehicle Solutions Network *(367)**
Committee of 200 *(368)*
Community Managers International Association
(371)
The Conference Board *(374)*
Consortium for Graduate Study in Management
(378)
Council of Better Business Bureaus *(392)**
Data Interchange Standards Association *(407)*
Delta Sigma Pi *(409)*
Ecuadorean American Association *(419)*
Embroidery Trade Association *(425)*
Emerging Markets Private Equity Association *(425)*
Employer Associations of America *(426)*
Employers Association *(426)*

Employers of America *(427)*
Enactus *(427)*
Entrepreneurs' Organization *(430)*
The Entrepreneurship Institute *(430)*
Ethics and Compliance Officer Association *(433)*
Executive Women International *(435)*
Export Institute of the United States *(436)*
Extruded Polystyrene Foam Association *(436)**
Family Firm Institute, Inc. *(437)**
Financial Management Association International
(444)
Foundation for Russian-American Economic
Cooperation *(453)*
Future Business Leaders of America - Phi Beta
Lambda *(455)*
Futures Industry Association *(455)*
Global Semiconductor Alliance *(463)*
Grand Strand Business Association *(465)*
Health Industry Business Communications Council
(469)
HUBZone Contractors National Council *(480)*
Independent Equipment Dealers Association *(489)*
Independent Hardee's Franchisee Association *(490)*
Industrial Asset Management Council *(492)*
Industrial Foundation of America *(493)*
Information Technology Industry Council *(495)*
Institute of Business Appraisers *(498)*
Institute of Certified Business Counselors *(498)**
Inter-National Association of Business Industry &
Rehabilitation *(506)*
The International Alliance for Women *(510)*
International Association for Business and Society
(511)
International Association of Administrative
Professionals *(515)**
International Association of Airport Duty Free Stores
(515)
International Association of Business
Communicators *(517)*
International Association of Plumbing and
Mechanical Officials *(526)*
International Association of Used Equipment
Dealers *(528)**
International Business Brokers Association *(532)*
International Business Music Association *(532)*
International Contact Center Benchmarking
Consortium *(537)*
International Council for Small Business *(538)*
International Executive Association *(543)*
International Franchise Association *(547)*
International Function Point Users Group *(548)*
International Network of Merger and Acquisition
Partners *(557)*
International Reciprocal Trade Association *(562)*
International Swaps and Derivatives Association
*(576)**
The Knitting Guild Association *(591)*
Latin Business Association *(594)*
NALS *(625)**
National AMBUCS *(633)*
National AMBUCS, Inc *(633)*
National Association for Business Economics *(636)*
National Association for Business Teacher Education
(636)
National Association for the Self-Employed *(644)*
National Association of Black Women Entrepreneurs
(649)
National Association of Blacks in Criminal Justice
(649)
National Association of Business Owners and
Entrepreneurs *(651)*
National Association of Business Political Action
Committees *(651)*
National Association of Church Business
Administration *(653)**
National Association of College and University
Business Officers *(654)**
National Association of Corporate Directors *(658)*
National Association of Development Companies
(662)
National Association of Independent Brokers
Dealers *(674)*
National Association of Investment Companies *(676)*
National Association of Manufacturers *(679)*
National Association of Negro Business and
Professional Women's Clubs *(681)**
National Association of Publicly Traded Partnerships
(689)
National Association of Small Business Contractors
(696)
National Association of Supervisors for Business
Education *(704)**
National Association of Women Business Owners
(709)
National Black Caucus of State Legislators *(714)*
National Black Chamber of Commerce *(714)*
National Black MBA Association *(714)*
National Business Association *(716)*
National Business Education Association *(716)*
National Business Incubation Association *(717)*

National Community Pharmacists Association (725)
National Consumers League (729)
National Cooperative Business Association (729)
National Court Reporters Association (740)
National Federation of Independent Business (NFIB) (748)
National Franchisee Association (753)
National Hispanic Corporate Council (759)
National Mail Order Association (771)
National Minority Business Council (773)
National Minority Supplier Development Council (773)
National Office Managers Association of America (775)
National Organization of Industrial Trade Unions (777)
National Small Business Association (792)
National Society of Hispanic MBAs (794)
Natural Products Association (807)
Nine to Five, National Association of Working Women (811)
North American Case Research Association (814)
North American Small Business International Trade Educators (821)*
Off-Road Business Association (826)*
Operations Security Professionals Society (828)
Organization Development Institute (830)*
Organization Development Network (831)*
Organization for the Promotion and Advancement of Small Telecommunications Companies (831)
Organizational Systems Research Association (833)
Outdoor Amusement Business Association (834)
Outdoor Industry Association (835)
Phi Chi Theta (845)
Phi Gamma Nu Fraternity (845)
Physician Office Managers Association of America (847)
Product Development and Management Association (858)
Professional Retail Store Maintenance Association (864)
Romanian-U.S. Business Council (888)
S-Corporation Association (889)
SCORE Association (893)
Small Business Council of America (900)
Small Business Exporters Association of the United States (900)
National Association of Small Business Investment Companies (900)
Small Business Legislative Council (901)
Small Business Technology Coalition (SBTC) (901)
Small Publishers Association of North America (901)*
SOCAP International (902)
Social Venture Network (902)
Society for Advancement of Consulting (903)
Society for Business Ethics (905)*
Society of American Business Editors and Writers (928)
Society of Competitive Intelligence Professionals (933)
Society of Corporate Secretaries and Governance Professionals (933)*
Society of International Business Fellows (940)
Solar Electric Power Association (951)
Souvenirs, Gifts and Novelties Trade Association (953)
Special Interest Group on Management Information Systems (956)
State Government Affairs Council (961)
Supply Chain Council (966)
Telecommunications Benchmarking International Group (971)
Timber Frame Business Council (974)
Transworld Advertising Agency Network (979)*
United Applications Standards Group (985)
United Development Council (986)
United States-Taiwan Business Council (989)
United States Business and Industry Council (991)
United States Chamber of Commerce (991)
United States Junior Chamber (Jaycees) (995)
United States Pan Asian American Chamber of Commerce (997)*
Venezuelan American Association of the U.S. (1008)*
WACRA - World Association for Case Method Research and Application (1011)
Women's Business Enterprise National Council (1022)
World Trade Centers Association (1027)
Young Presidents' Organization (1030)
YPO-WPO (1030)
Zonta International (1030)

CEMETERIES/FUNERALS

Accredited Pet Cemetery Society (10)
American Institute of Commemorative Art (138)
Associated Funeral Directors International (236)
Casket and Funeral Supply Association of America (344)
Catholic Cemetery Conference (345)
Celebrant Foundation and Institute (347)
Cremation Association of North America (404)
Funeral Consumers Alliance (454)
International Association Of Pet Cemeteries and Crematories (526)
International Cemetery, Cremation and Funeral Association (533)*
International Conference of Funeral Service Examining Boards (536)
International Memorialization Supply Association (556)
International Order of the Golden Rule (559)
Jewish Funeral Directors of America (588)
Monument Builders of North America (619)
National Concrete Burial Vault Association (725)
National Funeral Directors and Morticians Association (754)*
National Funeral Directors Association (754)
Selected Independent Funeral Homes (896)

CHEMICALS & CHEMICAL INDUSTRY

Acrylonitrile Group, Inc. (11)
Adhesion Society (12)
Adhesive and Sealant Council (12)*
Agricultural Retailers Association (16)
Alkylphenols and Ethoxylates Research Council (22)
Alliance for Responsible Atmospheric Policy (23)*
Alpha Chi Sigma Fraternity, Inc. (26)
American Association for Clinical Chemistry, Inc. (48)
American Association of Cereal Chemists International (55)
American Association of Textile Chemists and Colorists (75)
American Chemical Society (89)
American Chemical Society - Rubber Division (90)*
American Chemistry Council (90)
American Cleaning Institute (91)
American Coke and Coal Chemicals Institute (92)
American College of Toxicology (103)
American Fiber Manufacturers Association (121)
American Fire Safety Council (121)
American Fuel & Petrochemical Manufacturers (124)
American Institute of Chemical Engineers (138)*
American Institute of Chemists (138)
American Leather Chemists Association (145)*
American Microchemical Society (151)
American Mosquito Control Association (153)
American Oil Chemists' Society (157)*
American Society for Biochemistry and Molecular Biology (181)
American Society for Mass Spectrometry (186)
American Society for Neurochemistry (187)
American Society of Brewing Chemists (193)
Association for Chemoreception Sciences (241)
Association of Analytical Communities International (267)
Association of Consulting Chemists and Chemical Engineers (276)
Association of Defensive Spray Manufacturers (278)
Association of Official Racing Chemists (296)
Association of Water Technologies (317)*
Basic Acrylic Monomer Manufacturers (326)
Biotechnology Industry Organization (BIO) (330)
Chemical Coaters Association International (351)
Chemical Fabrics and Film Association (351)*
Chemical Heritage Foundation (351)*
Chemical Sources Association (352)*
Chlorinated Paraffins Industry Association (354)
Chlorine Chemistry Council (354)
Chlorine Institute (354)
Chlorobenzene Producers Association (354)
Color Pigments Manufacturers Association, Inc. (365)
The Combustion Institute (366)
Compressed Gas Association (372)
Consumer Aerosol Products Council (380)
Consumer Specialty Products Association (381)
Council for Chemical Research, Inc. (389)
Council of Producers & Distributors of Agrotechnology (396)
CropLife America (404)
Dangerous Goods Advisory Council (407)
Dibasic Esters Group (412)
Drug, Chemical and Associated Technologies Association (417)
The Electrochemical Society (423)
Emulsion Polymers Council (427)
ETAD North America (433)
Ethylene Oxide Sterilization Association, Inc. (433)
Extruded Polystyrene Foam Association (436)*
Federation of Analytical Chemistry and Spectroscopy Societies (440)
The Fertilizer Institute (443)
Formaldehyde Council, Inc. (452)
Geochemical Society (458)
Halogenated Solvents Industry Alliance (468)
Halon Alternatives Research Corporation (468)
The Histochemical Society (476)

Institute of Makers of Explosives (501)
International Association of Color Manufacturers (518)
International Chemical Workers Union Council/UFCW (534)
International Institute of Ammonia Refrigeration (551)
International Isotope Society (552)
International Liquid Terminals Association (554)
International Oxygen Manufacturers Association (559)
International Ozone Association-Pan American Group Branch (559)
International Sanitary Supply Association (563)
International Society of Chemical Ecology (572)
Materials Marketing Associates (608)
Materials Technology Institute (609)
Methacrylate Producers Association (614)
Methanol Institute (614)
National Aerosol Association (629)
National Association for Surface Finishing (643)
National Association of Chemical Distributors (652)
National Chemical Credit Association (720)
National Lime Association (769)
National Organization for the Professional Advancement of Black Chemists and Chemical Engineers (777)*
National Pest Management Association (780)*
North American Catalysis Society (815)
North American Polyelectrolyte Producers Association (819)
Organic Reactions Catalysis Society (830)
Performance Track Participants Association (841)
Photo Chemical Machining Institute (846)
Pine Chemicals Association (848)
Polyisocyanurate Insulation Manufacturers Association (852)
Polyurethane Foam Association (852)
Powder Coating Institute (854)
Process Equipment Manufacturers' Association (858)
Professional Landcare Network (863)
RadTech (874)
RISE (Responsible Industry for a Sound Environment) (886)
Sales Association of the Chemical Industry (890)
SB Latex Council (891)
Silicones Environmental, Health and Safety Council of North America (900)
Society for Environmental Geochemistry and Health (908)
Society of Chemical Industry, American Section (932)
Society of Chemical Manufacturers and Affiliates Inc. (932)
Society of Cosmetic Chemists (934)
Society of Environmental Toxicology and Chemistry (935)
Society of Flavor Chemists (936)
Society of Mineral Analysts (942)
Society of Toxicology (948)*
Soil and Plant Analysis Council (951)
Solution Mining Research Institute (952)*
Spill Control Association of America (958)
Spray Polyurethane Foam Alliance (959)*
Tetrahydrofuran Task Force (972)
Tributyl Phosphate Task Force (980)
Tubular Exchanger Manufacturers Association (982)
Vanadium Producers and Reclaimers Association (1008)
Vinyl Acetate Council (1009)

CHILDREN AND YOUTH

Academic Pediatric Association (3)
Alliance for Children and Families (22)
American Academy of Adoption Attorneys (30)
American Academy of Child and Adolescent Psychiatry (31)
American Academy of Pediatric Dentistry (39)
American Academy of Pediatrics (39)
American Association for Marriage and Family Therapy (50)*
American Association of Children's Residential Centers (56)*
American Association of Early Childhood Educators (60)
American Counseling Association (111)
American Professional Society on the Abuse of Children (168)
American Society of Pediatric Nephrology (206)
American Specialty Toy Retailing Association (212)*
Association for Child Psychoanalysis (241)
Association for Childhood Education International (241)
The Association for Library Service to Children (251)*
The Association for the Study of Play (260)
Association of Administrators of the Interstate Compact on the Placement of Children (263)
Association of Children's Museums (272)

Association of Jewish Family & Children's Agencies (290)
Association of Maternal and Child Health Programs (AMCHP) (293)*
Association of Pediatric Program Directors (298)
Association of Reproductive Health Professionals (305)
Child Care Aware of America (353)
Child Life Council (353)
Child Neurology Society (353)
Child Welfare League of America (353)*
Children's Book Council (353)
Children's Literature Association (353)*
Choristers Guild (355)
The Corps Network (formerly the National Association of Service and Conservation Corps) (386)
Cottage Industry Miniaturists Trade Association (387)
Council for Children with Behavioral Disorders (389)
Council for Exceptional Children (390)*
Council for Professional Recognition (391)
Cristo Rey Network (404)
Family, Career and Community Leaders of America (437)
Foster Family-Based Treatment Association (452)
Future Business Leaders of America - Phi Beta Lambda (455)
Hobby Manufacturers Association (477)
International Academy for Child Brain Development (509)
International Balloon Association (529)
International Formula Council (547)
International Lactation Consultant Association (553)
International Nanny Association (557)
International Society of Psychiatric-Mental Health Nurses (574)
Juvenile Products Manufacturers Association (590)
The Kite Trade Association International (591)
Lamaze International (592)*
National After School Association (629)
National Association for Children's Behavioral Health (NACBH) (637)
National Association for Family Child Care (638)
National Association for Gifted Children (639)*
National Association for the Education of Young Children (644)*
National Association of Child Care Professionals (653)*
National Association of Children's Hospitals and Related Institutions (653)
National Association of Counsel for Children (658)
National Association of Foster Grandparent Program Directors (669)
National Association of Police Athletics/Activities Leagues, Inc. (685)
National Association of Private Special Education Centers (686)
National Association of Public Child Welfare Administrators (688)
National Association of School Psychologists (693)*
National Association of Street Schools (703)
National Child Care Association (721)
National Child Support Enforcement Association (721)
National Collaboration for Youth (723)
National Council of Juvenile and Family Court Judges (735)
National Family Planning and Reproductive Health Association (747)
National Fellowship of Child Care Executives (750)
National FFA Organization (750)
National Foster Parent Association (753)
National Guardianship Association (757)
National Head Start Association (758)
National Independent Living Association (762)
National Juvenile Court Services Association (767)
National Migrant and Seasonal Head Start Association (772)
National Organization of State Associations for Children (778)
National Parent Teachers Association (779)
National Perinatal Association (780)
National Recreation and Parks Association (784)
National WIC Association (805)
Parenting Media Association (838)*
Pediatric Endocrine Society (840)
School Social Work Association of America (892)*
The Society for Adolescent Medicine (903)*
Society for Developmental and Behavioral Pediatrics (907)*
Society for Maternal-Fetal Medicine (915)*
Society for Research in Child Development (920)
Society for Research on Adolescence (920)
Society of Children's Book Writers and Illustrators (932)
Society of Professors of Child and Adolescent Psychiatry (945)
Teaching-Family Association (969)
Toy Industry Association (976)

U.S.A. Toy Library Association (983)
Voices for America's Children (1011)

CIVIL RIGHTS AND LIBERTIES
American Association of Jewish Lawyers and Jurists (64)
American Association of University Women (76)
American Land Rights Association (144)
Asian Pacific American Labor Alliance, AFL-CIO (232)
National Association for Equal Opportunity in Higher Education (638)
National Association for State Community Services Programs (643)
National Association of Jewish Legislators (677)
National Legal Aid and Defender Association (769)
National Religious Campaign Against Torture (786)
Workers' Injury Law and Advocacy Group (1025)*

CLUBS SEE ALSO FRATERNAL ORGANIZATIONS
Alpha Chi Sigma Fraternity, Inc. (26)
Alpha Kappa Psi (26)
Alpha Omega International Dental Fraternity (26)
Alpha Zeta Omega (27)
American Association of State Troopers (73)
American Dental Interfraternity Council (114)
The Association for Research in Business Education - Delta Pi Epsilon (255)*
Association of College and University Clubs (274)
Association of College Honor Societies (274)
Association of Fraternity Advisors (284)*
Association of Private Club Directors (300)
Beta Alpha Psi (328)
Beta Phi Mu (328)
Club Managers Association of America (359)
Continental Dorset Club (382)
Delta Omicron (409)
Delta Sigma Delta (409)
Delta Sigma Pi (409)
Delta Theta Phi (409)
Distributive Education Clubs of America (DECA) (415)
Fraternity Executives Association (453)
Future Business Leaders of America - Phi Beta Lambda (455)
Gamma Iota Sigma (456)
General Federation of Women's Clubs (458)*
International Health, Racquet and Sportsclub Association (549)
International League of Professional Baseball Clubs (554)
International Legal Fraternity of Phi Delta Phi (554)*
International Military Community Executives Association (556)
Kappa Delta Epsilon (590)
Kappa Kappa Iota-National (590)
Kappa Psi Pharmaceutical Fraternity, Inc. (590)
Men of Reform Judaism (612)
Mu Phi Epsilon (621)
National AMBUCS (633)
The National Association of Colored Women's Club, Inc. (656)
National Association of Litho Clubs (678)
National Association of Negro Business and Professional Women's Clubs (681)*
National Block and Bridle Club (715)
National Club Association (722)
National Exchange Club (747)
National Federation of Music Clubs (749)
National Garden Clubs (754)
National Pan-Hellenic Council (778)
National Panhellenic Conference (778)
National Writers Association (806)
North - American Interfraternity Conference (812)*
Omega Delta (827)
Omega Tau Sigma (827)
Omicron Kappa Upsilon (827)
Overseas Press Club of America (835)
Phi Alpha Delta (845)
Phi Beta Fraternity (845)
Phi Delta Epsilon International Medical Fraternity (845)
Phi Epsilon Kappa (845)
Phi Rho Sigma Medical Society (846)
Pi Lambda Theta (847)
Professional Fraternity Association (862)
Psi Omega Fraternity (868)
Sigma Theta Tau International (899)
Theta Tau (973)
Type Directors Club (983)
United States Association of Independent Gymnastic Clubs (990)
Xi Psi Phi Dental Fraternity (1029)

COALITIONS
Abortion Care Network (2)
Alliance for Energy and Economic Growth (23)
Alliance for Responsible Atmospheric Policy (23)*
Alliance of Nonprofit Mailers (25)
American College of Physicians Services, Inc. (101)

American Fraternal Alliance (124)
American Small Manufacturers' Coalition (180)
Association of University Programs in Occupational Health and Safety (316)
Cement Kiln Recycling Coalition (347)*
The Coalition for America's Gateways and Trade Corridors (360)
The Coalition for Government Procurement (360)
Coalition for Independent Seniors (360)
The Coalition for Transportation Productivity (360)
The Coalition of Airline Pilots Associations (360)
Coalition of Black Trade Unionists (360)
Coalition of Higher Education Assistance Organizations (360)
Coalition of Service Industries (361)*
Commercial Vehicle Safety Alliance (367)
Consumer Mortgage Coalition (381)
Continua Health Alliance (382)
Council for Employment Law Equity (CELE) (389)
Demand Response and Smart Grid Coalition (410)
Department for Professional Employees - AFL-CIO (410)
Electric Drive Transportation Association (421)
Federal Forest Resource Coalition (439)
Free Speech Coalition (453)
Global Alcohol Producers Group (461)
Hispanic Association on Corporate Responsibility (475)
Independent Film and Television Alliance (489)*
Industrial Fabrics Association International (493)
International Anti-Counterfeiting Coalition (511)
International SalonSpa Business Network (ISBN) (563)
International Warehouse Logistics Association (580)*
Lighter Association (598)*
Management Association for Private Photogrammetric Surveyors (602)
Midwest Dairy Coalition (615)
NanoBusiness Alliance (625)
Napa Valley Vintners Association (625)
National Agricultural Alumni and Development Association (630)
National Alliance for Hispanic Health (631)
National Alliance for Hospice Access (631)
National Association for Information Destruction, Inc. (640)
National Association for Olmsted Parks (641)
National Association for Proton Therapy (642)
National Association of Publicly Traded Partnerships (689)
National Association of Retired and Senior Volunteer Program Directors (692)
National Association of Shareholder and Consumer Attorneys (696)
National Association of State & Local Equity Funds (697)
National Black MBA Association (714)
National Border Patrol Council (716)
National Coalition for Assistive and Rehab Technology (723)
National Coalition of Black Meeting Planners (723)
National Collaboration for Youth (723)
National Comprehensive Cancer Network (725)
National Council for Advanced Manufacturing (731)
National Narcotics Officers Associations' Coalition (774)
National Recycling Coalition (784)
National Trooper's Coalition (802)
Network Advertising Initiative (808)
New England Club Managers Association (809)
NGVAmerica (810)
Ocean Carrier Equipment Management Association (OCEMA) (825)
Ryan White Medical Providers Coalition (889)
Small Business Technology Coalition (SBTC) (901)
Urban Financial Services Coalition (1003)
Warrior Protection & Readiness Coalition (1012)
XBRL US, Inc. (1029)

COLOR
The Color Association of the United States (365)
Color Marketing Group (365)
Color Pigments Manufacturers Association, Inc. (365)
ETAD North America (433)
Inter-Society Color Council (506)
International Association of Color Manufacturers (518)
National Watercolor Society (804)

COMMODITIES
Agribusiness Council (16)
American Commodity Distribution Association (105)
American Soybean Association (211)
American Sugar Alliance (214)
American Sugarbeet Growers Association (214)*
Environmental Markets Association (431)
Futures Industry Association (455)
Hop Growers of America (478)

ICE Futures U.S. *(482)*
International Franchise Association *(547)*
International Precious Metals Institute *(561)*
Lighter Association *(598)**
Manufacturing Jewelers and Suppliers of America *(604)**
National Association of Wheat Growers *(709)**
National Futures Association *(754)*
National Grain Trade Council *(756)*
National Sorghum Producers *(795)*
Silver Council *(900)*
The Silver Institute *(900)*
Silver Users Association *(900)*
Society of American Silversmiths *(929)**
Society of Mineral Analysts *(942)*
Society of North American Goldsmiths *(943)**
Sugar Association *(965)*
Supima *(966)*
United States Beet Sugar Association *(991)*
US Rice Producers Association *(1004)*
Women in Agribusiness *(1020)*
World Gold Trust Services *(1026)**

COMMUNICATIONS

ABC Children's Group *(2)**
The Academy of American Poets *(3)*
Academy of Aphasia *(4)*
Accrediting Council on Education in Journalism and Mass Communications *(11)**
ACUTA - The Association for Information Communications Technology Professionals in Higher Education *(11)**
Aerospace & Flight Test Radio Coordinating Council *(14)*
Alliance for Telecommunications Industry Solutions *(23)*
Alliance for Women in Media *(24)*
Alliance of Area Business Publications *(24)*
Alliance of Associations of Teachers of Japanese *(24)**
Alliance of Black Telecommunications Employees *(24)*
Alliance of Motion Picture & Television Producers *(25)*
American Academy of Advertising *(30)**
American Academy on Communication in Healthcare *(43)*
American Agricultural Editors Association *(43)**
American Association for Applied Linguistics *(47)*
American Association for Chinese Studies *(48)*
American Association for Vocational Instructional Materials *(53)*
American Association of Dental Editors *(60)*
American Association of Intensive English Programs *(63)*
The American Association of Language Specialists *(64)*
The American Association of Phonetic Sciences *(69)*
American Association of Teachers of Arabic *(74)**
American Association of Teachers of French *(74)**
American Association of Teachers of German *(74)**
American Association of Teachers of Italian *(74)**
American Association of Teachers of Slavic and East European Languages *(75)*
American Association of Teachers of Spanish and Portuguese *(75)*
American Association of Teachers of Turkic Languages *(75)*
American Auto Racing Writers and Broadcasters Association *(78)*
American Book Producers Association *(85)**
American Booksellers Association *(85)**
American Business Media *(87)*
American Cable Association *(87)**
American Classical League *(91)**
American Cleft Palate-Craniofacial Association *(91)**
American Comparative Literature Association *(105)*
American Composers Alliance *(105)*
American Conference for Irish Studies *(106)*
American Council on the Teaching of Foreign Languages *(111)**
American Councils for International Education *(111)**
American Court and Commercial Newspapers *(111)*
American Dialect Society *(115)**
American Disc Jockey Association *(115)*
American Federation of Musicians *(119)*
American Folklore Society *(122)*
American Forensic Association *(123)*
American Horse Publications *(133)*
American Humor Studies Association *(134)*
American Hungarian Educators Association *(134)*
American Independent Writers *(135)*
American Jewish Press Association *(143)**
American Journalism Historians Association *(143)**
American Literary Translators Association *(146)*
American Medical Writers Association *(150)*
American Mideast Business Associates *(151)*
American Mobile Telecommunications Association *(152)*

American Name Society *(154)*
American Neurotology Society *(156)*
American Philological Association *(163)**
American Photographic Artists *(164)*
American Podiatric Medical Writers Association *(166)*
American Press Institute *(167)**
American Public Communications Council *(170)*
American Radio Relay League *(172)*
American Registry for Internet Numbers *(174)**
American Society for Indexing *(186)**
American Society of Access Professionals *(190)*
American Society of Business Publication Editors *(194)*
American Society of Composers, Authors and Publishers (ASCAP) *(195)*
American Society of Geolinguistics *(198)*
American Society of Journalists and Authors *(201)**
American Society of Magazine Editors *(202)*
American Society of Media Photographers *(203)*
American Society of News Editors *(204)*
American Society of Papyrologists *(205)*
American Society of Plant Taxonomists *(207)**
American Speech-Language-Hearing Association *(212)**
American Sportscasters Association *(213)*
American Telemarketing Association *(215)*
American Telemedicine Association *(215)**
American Teleservices Association *(215)*
American Translators Association *(217)*
Antenna Measurement Techniques Association *(224)*
Antiquarian Booksellers Association of America *(224)*
Armed Forces Broadcasters Association *(228)*
Armed Forces Communications and Electronics Association *(228)*
Art Directors Guild/Scenic, Title and Graphic Artists *(230)*
Arthur W. Page Society *(230)*
AscdiNatd *(231)**
Asian American Journalists Association *(231)*
Associated Business Writers of America *(235)*
Associated Church Press *(235)**
Associated Collegiate Press *(235)*
Associated Construction Publications *(235)*
Associated Press Managing Editors *(237)*
Association for Business Communication *(240)*
Association for Communication Administration *(241)*
Association for Communication Excellence *(242)**
Association for Computational Linguistics *(242)*
Association for Conservation Information *(243)*
Association for Documentary Editing *(245)*
Association for Education in Journalism and Mass Communication *(245)**
Association for Educational Communications and Technology *(245)**
Association for Informal Logic and Critical Thinking *(249)*
Association for Information Systems *(250)*
Association for Slavic, East European, and Eurasian Studies *(256)*
Association for Spanish and Portuguese Studies *(256)*
Association for the Calligraphic Arts *(259)*
Association for Women in Communications *(261)*
Association for Women in Sports Media *(262)*
Association Media and Publishing *(262)*
Association of Alternative Newsweeklies *(264)**
Association of American Editorial Cartoonists *(264)*
Association of American Publishers *(266)*
Association of American University Presses *(267)**
Association of Art Editors *(267)*
Association of Authors' Representatives *(268)*
Association of Cable Communicators *(270)*
Association of Catholic Publishers *(271)*
Association of Departments of English *(278)*
Association of Departments of Foreign Languages *(278)**
Association of Directory Publishers *(279)*
Association of Earth Science Editors *(279)*
Association of Educational Publishers *(280)*
Association of Federal Communications Consulting Engineers *(282)*
Association of Food Journalists *(283)*
Association of Free Community Papers *(284)*
Association of Independent Commercial Producers *(287)*
Association of Independents in Radio *(288)*
The Association of Language Companies *(290)*
The Association of Literary Scholars, Critics, and Writers *(291)*
Association of Opinion Journalists *(297)*
Association of Professional Communication Consultants *(301)*
Association of Public Television Stations *(304)*
APCO (Association of Public-Safety Communications Officials) International *(304)*
Association of Schools of Journalism and Mass Communication *(307)*
Association of Teachers of Technical Writing *(313)*

Association of Telehealth Service Providers *(313)*
Association of TeleServices International, Inc. *(313)*
Association of Test Publishers *(313)*
Association of Theatrical Press Agents and Managers *(314)*
Association of Writers and Writing Programs *(318)*
Audio Publishers Association *(320)**
Audit Bureau of Circulations *(320)**
Authors Guild *(320)*
Automotive Communication Council *(322)**
Baptist Communicators Association *(326)*
BICSI *(329)*
Binding Industries Association *(329)**
The Bluetooth Special Interest Group *(332)*
Boating Writers International *(333)*
Book Industry Study Group, Inc. *(333)*
Book Manufacturers' Institute *(333)*
Bowling Writers Association of America *(334)*
BPA Worldwide *(334)*
Broadcast Cable Credit Association *(335)*
Broadcast Education Association *(335)**
Broadcast Technology Society *(336)*
Cable & Telecommunications Association for Marketing *(340)*
Cable and Telecommunications Human Resources Association *(340)*
Cabletelevision Advertising Bureau *(340)**
Calendar Marketing Association *(340)*
Caribbean Cable Communications *(343)*
Catholic Academy for Communication Arts Professionals *(345)*
Catholic Press Association *(346)*
Catholic Radio Association *(346)*
Caucus for Producers, Writers & Directors *(346)*
CBA *(346)*
Children's Book Council *(353)*
Children's Literature Association *(353)**
Chinese American Librarians Association *(354)**
Chinese Language Teachers Association *(354)*
Church Music Publishers Association *(356)**
City and Regional Magazine Association *(357)*
College English Association *(363)*
College Media Association *(363)**
Columbia Scholastic Press Association *(365)*
Communications Fraud Control Association *(369)*
Communications Marketing Association *(369)*
Communications Supply Service Association *(369)*
Communications Workers of America *(369)*
Community College Journalism Association *(370)*
Competitive Carriers Association *(371)*
Competitive Telecommunications Association *(371)**
Computer and Communications Industry Association *(372)*
Computer Assisted Language Instruction Consortium *(372)**
Conference on College Composition and Communication *(376)*
Conference on English Education *(376)*
Conference on English Leadership *(376)*
Consolidated Tape Association *(378)*
Consortium of School Networking *(378)*
Construction Writers Association *(380)*
Copyright Society of the U.S.A. *(385)**
Council of Communication Management *(393)**
Council of Literary Magazines and Presses *(395)**
Council of Science Editors *(397)*
Council of Writing Program Administrators *(398)*
Country Music Association *(401)*
Country Radio Broadcasters, Inc. *(401)*
CTIA - The Wireless Association *(405)*
Dance Critics Association *(406)*
Digital Media Association *(412)**
Digital Screenmedia Association *(412)*
Directors Guild of America *(413)*
Dog Writers' Association of America *(415)**
Dramatists Guild of America *(416)*
Drug Information Association *(417)*
Editorial Freelancers Association *(419)*
Education Writers Association *(420)**
Educational Book and Media Association *(420)*
Educause *(420)**
Electronic Retailing Association *(423)**
Energy Telecommunications and Electrical Association *(428)*
Engineering College Magazines Associated *(429)*
Enterprise Wireless Alliance *(429)*
Entertainment Merchants Association *(429)*
Esperanto-USA *(433)**
Evangelical Christian Publishers Association *(434)*
Evangelical Press Association *(434)*
Federal Communications Bar Association *(439)**
Flexographic Prepress Platemakers Association *(447)*
Flexographic Technical Association *(447)*
Football Writers Association of America *(450)*
Forest Industries Telecommunications *(451)*
Forestry Conservation Communications Association *(452)*
Garden Writers Association *(456)**
German American Business Association *(460)*
German American Chamber of Commerce *(460)*

COMPUTER/TECHNOLOGY

CONSTRUCTION/CONSTRUCTION MATERIALS

EPDM Roofing Association (432)
Expanded Shale, Clay and Slate Institute (435)
Expansion Joint Manufacturers Association, Inc. (436)*
Exterior Insulation and Finish Systems Industry Members Association (EIMA) (436)*
Fastener Industry Coalition (438)
Federal Facilities Council (439)
Federation of Modern Painters and Sculptors (442)
Fiberglass Tank and Pipe Institute (443)
Flight Safety Foundation (448)
Floor Covering Installation Contractors Association (448)*
Foundation for International Meetings (453)
The Fragrance Foundation (453)
Gasket Fabricators Association (457)
Geosynthetic Materials Association (459)*
Golf Course Builders Association of America (463)
Graphic Arts Technical Foundation (465)
Hand Tools Institute (468)
Hardwood Plywood and Veneer Association (468)*
Housing Education and Research Association (479)
Independent Distributors Association (489)
Independent Electrical Contractors (489)
Independent Professional Painting Contractors Association of America (491)
Industrial Fasteners Institute (493)
Industrial Foundation of America (493)
Institute of Makers of Explosives (501)
Insulating Concrete Form Association (504)
Insulation Contractors Association of America (504)*
Interlocking Concrete Pavement Institute (508)*
International Association for Cold Storage Construction (511)
International Association of Bridge, Structural, Ornamental and Reinforcing Iron Workers (517)
International Association of Drilling Contractors (519)
International Association of Heat and Frost Insulators and Asbestos Workers (522)
International Association of Plumbing and Mechanical Officials (526)
International Brotherhood of Boilermakers, Iron Shipbuilders, Blacksmiths, Forgers and Helpers (531)
International Builders Exchange Executives/Builders Exchange Network (532)
International Cadmium Association (532)
International Cast Polymer Alliance (533)
International Concrete Repair Institute (536)
International Council of Employers of Bricklayers and Allied Craftworkers (538)
International Decorative Artisans League (540)*
International District Energy Association (540)*
International Door Association (541)
International Foundation of Employee Benefit Plans (547)
International Furnishings and Design Association (548)
International Grooving & Grinding Association (549)
International Institute for Lath and Plaster (551)
International Masonry Institute (556)
International Municipal Signal Association (557)*
International Slurry Surfacing Association (565)*
International Society for Pharmaceutical Engineering (567)
International Staple, Nail and Tool Association (575)
International Surface Fabricators Association (576)
International Union of Bricklayers and Allied Craftworkers (579)*
International Union of Elevator Constructors (579)
International Union of Painters and Allied Trades (579)
International Window Film Association (581)
The International Wood Products Association (581)
Laborers International Union of North America (592)
Log Home Builders Association of North America (600)
Log Homes Council (600)
Manufactured Housing Association for Regulatory Reform (602)
Manufactured Housing Institute (602)
Manufacturers Standardization Society of the Valve and Fittings Industry (603)
Maple Flooring Manufacturers Association (604)
Marble Institute of America (604)
Mason Contractors Association of America (607)
The Masonry Heater Association of North America (607)*
The Masonry Society (607)
Masonry Veneer Manufacturers Association (607)*
Master Pools Guild, Inc. (608)*
Materials and Methods Standards Association (608)
Mechanical Service Contractors of America (610)*
Metal Building Contractors and Erectors Association (613)
Metal Building Manufacturers Association (613)*
Metal Construction Association (613)
Modular Building Institute (618)
Modular Building Systems Council (618)*

Motorcycle Safety Foundation (620)
National Academy of Building Inspection Engineers (627)
National Asphalt Pavement Association (635)
National Association of Architectural Metal Manufacturers (647)
National Association of Elevator Contractors (665)
National Association of Heavy Equipment Training Schools (672)
National Association of Home Builders (673)*
National Association of Home Builders Research Center (673)
National Association of Home Inspectors (673)
National Association of Minority Contractors (680)
National Association of Miscellaneous, Ornamental and Architectural Products Contractors (681)
National Association of Pipe Coating Applicators (684)
National Association of Pipe Fabricators (684)
National Association of Reinforcing Steel Contractors (691)
National Association of Steel Pipe Distributors (703)
National Association of the Remodeling Industry (705)
National Association of Tower Erectors (706)
National Association of Women in Construction (710)
The National Building Granite Quarries Association (716)
National Certified Pipe Welding Bureau (720)
National Clay Pipe Institute (722)*
National Concrete Burial Vault Association (725)
National Concrete Masonry Association (725)*
National Conference of Bar Foundations (726)*
National Corrugated Steel Pipe Association (730)*
National Council of Erectors, Fabricators and Riggers (734)
National Demolition Association (742)
National Electrical Contractors Association (744)
National Environmental Balancing Bureau (746)
National Fastener Distributors Association (747)
National Fenestration Rating Council (750)
National Finishing Contractors Association (751)
National Foundation for Credit Counseling (753)
National Frame Building Association (753)
National Guild of Professional Paperhangers (757)
National Hemophilia Foundation (759)
National Housing and Rehabilitation Association (760)*
National Housing Conference (761)*
National Institute of Building Sciences (764)
National Institute of Pension Administrators (765)
National Institute of Senior Housing (765)
National Institute of Steel Detailing (765)
National Insulation Association (766)
National Lime Association (769)
National Lumber and Building Material Dealers Association (770)
National Marine Distributors Association (771)
National Multi-Housing Council (774)
National Plasterers Council (781)
National Precast Concrete Association (782)
National Quartz Producers Council (783)
National Railroad Construction and Maintenance Association, Inc. (783)
National Ready Mixed Concrete Association (784)
National Roof Deck Contractors Association (787)
National Roofing Contractors Association (787)*
National Shooting Sports Foundation (791)
National Slag Association (792)
National Society of Mural Painters (794)*
National Star Route Mail Contractors Association (796)
National Stone, Sand, and Gravel Association (796)
National Terrazzo and Mosaic Association (800)
National Tile Contractors Association (800)*
National Utility Contractors Association (NUCA) (803)*
National Watercolor Society (804)
National Wood Flooring Association (805)
Native American Contractors Association (806)
Natural Stone Council (807)
New England Club Managers Association (809)
North American Association of Floor Covering Distributors (811)
North American Building Material Distribution Association (814)*
North American Insulation Manufacturers Association (817)
North American Limousin Foundation (817)
North American Retail Hardware Association (820)
North American Society for Trenchless Technology (822)
Operative Plasterers and Cement Masons International Association of the United States and Canada (829)
Ornamental Concrete Producers Association (833)
Outdoor Power Equipment and Engine Service Association (835)
Paint and Decorating Retailers Association (836)

Painting and Decorating Contractors of America (837)
Panelized Home Building Council (837)*
Perlite Institute (842)
Pile Driving Contractors Association (848)
Pipe Fabrication Institute (849)*
Pipe Line Contractors Association (849)*
Plastic Pipe and Fittings Association (850)
Plastics Pipe Institute (850)*
Plumbing and Drainage Institute (850)*
Plumbing Contractors of America (851)
Plumbing Manufacturers Institute (851)
Plumbing-Heating-Cooling Contractors - National Association (851)
Polyisocyanurate Insulation Manufacturers Association (852)
Porcelain Enamel Institute (853)
Portable Sanitation Association International (853)
Portland Cement Association (853)*
Post-Tensioning Institute (853)*
Powder Coating Institute (854)
Power and Communications Contractors Association (855)
Precast/Prestressed Concrete Institute (856)
Professional Construction Estimators Association of America (861)
Professional Women in Construction (866)*
Quality Service Contractors (871)
RCI, Inc. (875)*
Renewable Natural Resources Foundation (881)
Resilient Floor Covering Institute (883)
Restoration Industry Association (884)
Roof Coatings Manufacturers Association (888)
Rubber Pavements Association (888)*
Safety Glazing Certification Council (890)*
Scaffold Industry Association (891)*
Scaffolding, Shoring and Forming Institute (892)
Screen Manufacturers Association (893)
Sealant, Waterproofing and Restoration Institute (894)*
Service Specialists Association (897)*
Sheet Metal and Air Conditioning Contractors' National Association (898)
Sheet Metal Workers' International Association (898)
Silica Fume Association (899)
Single Ply Roofing Institute (900)
Slag Cement Association (900)
Society of Piping Engineers and Designers (944)
Society of Professional Rope Access Technicians (945)*
Specialty Tools and Fasteners Distributors Association (958)
Spray Polyurethane Foam Alliance (959)*
SSPC: the Society for Protective Coatings (960)*
Steel Deck Institute (962)*
Steel Door Institute (962)
Steel Joist Institute (962)
Steel Window Institute (963)*
Structural Building Components Association (964)*
Structural Insulated Panel Association (964)
Structural Stability Research Council (964)
Stucco Manufacturers Association (964)
Subcontractors Trade Association (964)
Sustainable Buildings Industry Council (967)
TAUC - The Association of Union Constructors (968)*
Tile Contractors' Association of America (974)
Tile Council of North America, Inc. (974)*
Tile Roofing Institute (974)
Tilt-up Concrete Association (974)
Timber Frame Business Council (974)
Timber Framers Guild (974)
Truck Mixer Manufacturers Bureau (981)
Truss Plate Institute (981)
Tube and Pipe Association, International (981)
Underwater Construction Corporation (984)
Uni-Bell PVC Pipe Association (984)*
United Association of Journeymen and Apprentices of the Plumbing and Pipe Fitting Industry of the U.S. and Canada (985)
United Brotherhood of Carpenters and Joiners of America (986)*
United States Advanced Ceramics Association (989)*
United States Contract Tower Association (992)
United States Green Building Council (994)
United Steelworkers of America (1001)
United Union of Roofers, Waterproofers and Allied Workers (1001)
Valve Manufacturers Association of America (1007)
Vinyl Institute (1009)*
Vinyl Siding Institute, Inc. (1009)
Window and Door Manufacturers Association (1018)
Window Council (1018)
Window Covering Manufacturers Association (1018)
Window Covering Safety Council (1018)
Window Coverings Association of America (1018)
Wire and Cable Industry Suppliers Association (1019)*
The Wire Association International, Inc. (1019)
Wire Fabricators Association (1019)*

Wire Reinforcement Institute (1019)*
Wire Rope Technical Board (1019)
Women Construction Owners and Executives, USA (1020)
World Floor Covering Association (1026)
World Research Foundation (1027)
Woven Wire Products Association (1029)

CONSULTANTS

Airport Consultants Council (21)
American Association of Dental Consultants (59)
American Association of Healthcare Consultants (62)
American Association of Legal Nurse Consultants (64)
American Association of Political Consultants (70)
The American Consultants League (108)
American Council of Engineering Companies (109)*
American Society of Agricultural Consultants (191)
American Society of Consultant Pharmacists (195)*
American Society of Consulting Arborists (196)
American Society of Trial Consultants (210)
American Society of Wedding Professionals (211)
Association for Wedding Professionals International (261)
Association of Bridal Consultants (270)*
The Association of Career Firms North America (271)
Association of Consulting Chemists and Chemical Engineers (276)
Association of Consulting Foresters of America (276)
Association of Executive Search Consultants (282)
Association of Federal Communications Consulting Engineers (282)
Association of Image Consultants International (287)
Association of Internal Management Consultants (289)
Association of Management Consulting Firms (292)
Association of Productivity Specialists (300)
Association of Professional Communication Consultants (301)
Association of Professional Investment Consultants (301)
Association of Professional Material Handling Consultants (301)
CPA Auto Dealer Consultants Association (402)
ECRI (418)
Institute of Management Consultants USA (501)
Institute of Tax Consultants (503)
International Association of Career Consulting Firms (517)
International Association of Professional Security Consultants (527)*
International Lactation Consultant Association (553)
International Network of Merger and Acquisition Partners (557)
Investment Management Consultants Association (584)
IT Financial Management Association (586)
National Alliance of Independent Crop Consultants (632)*
National Association of Export Companies (666)*
National Association of Independent Public Finance Advisors (675)
National Association of Personal Financial Advisors (684)
National Association of Vision Professionals (708)
National Council of Acoustical Consultants (733)
North American Association of Educational Negotiators (813)
Parliamentary Associates (839)
Professional and Technical Consultants Association (859)
Professional Services Council (865)
Project Management Institute (866)*
The Public Relations Society of America (870)
Society for Advancement of Consulting (903)
Society of Medical Consultants to the Armed Forces (941)
Society of Risk Management Consultants (947)
Society of Telecommunications Consultants (948)

CONSUMERS

American Council on Consumer Interests (110)
The American Fair Credit Council (118)
American Financial Services Association (121)
American Society for Quality (189)
Association for Consumer Research (243)*
Cabletelevision Advertising Bureau (340)*
Consumer Credit Industry Association (381)
Council of Better Business Bureaus (392)*
DBA International (407)
Electricity Consumers Resource Council (ELCON) (422)
Family and Consumer Sciences Education Association (437)
Healthcare Compliance Packaging Council (470)
IEEE Consumer Electronics Society (483)
Insurance Consumer Affairs Exchange (505)
International Ombudsman Association (558)
NAGMR Consumer Product Brokers (624)

National Association for Information Destruction, Inc. (640)
National Association of Consumer Advocates (657)
National Association of Consumer Agency Administrators (657)*
National Association of Railroad Passengers (689)
National Association of State Utility Consumer Advocates (NASUCA) (702)
National Association of Teacher Educators for Family Consumer Sciences (704)
National Consumers League (729)
National Flea Market Association (751)
National Insurance Crime Bureau (766)
SOCAP International (902)
Society for Consumer Psychology (907)

CONTRACTORS

ADSC: The International Association of Foundation Drilling (12)*
African American Contractors Association (15)
Air Conditioning Contractors of America (18)
American Subcontractors Association (214)
Associated Builders and Contractors (235)
Associated General Contractors of America (AGC) (236)
Associated Specialty Contractors (237)
Association of Bituminous Contractors (269)
Association of the Wall and Ceiling Industry (314)*
Building Service Contractors Association International (337)
Ceilings and Interior Systems Construction Association (347)
Certified Contractors Network (349)
Concrete Foundations Association (373)*
Exhibition Services and Contractors Association (435)
Floor Covering Installation Contractors Association (448)*
Independent Electrical Contractors (489)
Independent Professional Painting Contractors Association of America (491)
Insulation Contractors Association of America (504)*
International Association for Cold Storage Construction (511)
International Association of Drilling Contractors (519)
International Association of Geophysical Contractors (522)
International Association of Lighting Management Companies (524)
International Concrete Repair Institute (536)
International Council of Employers of Bricklayers and Allied Craftworkers (538)
International Institute for Lath and Plaster (551)
The International Stability Operations Association (575)*
Land Improvement Contractors of America (593)
Mason Contractors Association of America (607)
Masonry Institute of America (607)
Mechanical Service Contractors of America (610)*
National Association of Minority Contractors (680)
National Association of Miscellaneous, Ornamental and Architectural Products Contractors (681)
National Association of Reinforcing Steel Contractors (691)
National Association of Small Business Contractors (696)
National Association of Waterproofing and Structural Repair Contractors (709)
National Certified Pipe Welding Bureau (720)
National Contract Management Association (729)*
National Council of Erectors, Fabricators and Riggers (734)
National Demolition Association (742)
National Drilling Association (743)
National Electrical Contractors Association (744)
National Environmental Balancing Bureau (746)
National Insulation Association (766)
National Property Management Association (783)*
National Roof Deck Contractors Association (787)
National Roofing Contractors Association (787)*
National School Transportation Association (790)*
National Subcontractors Alliance (798)
National Tile Contractors Association (800)*
Native American Contractors Association (806)
Painting and Decorating Contractors of America (837)
Pile Driving Contractors Association (848)
Pipe Line Contractors Association (849)*
Plumbing-Heating-Cooling Contractors - National Association (851)
Quality Service Contractors (871)
Scaffold Industry Association (891)*
Sealant, Waterproofing and Restoration Institute (894)*
Sheet Metal and Air Conditioning Contractors' National Association (898)
Subcontractors Trade Association (964)
Tile Contractors' Association of America (974)
United Association of Equipment Leasing (985)

United States Contract Tower Association (992)
Waterproofing Contractors Association (1013)

CONVENTIONS/TRADE SHOWS/EXHIBITS

American Academy of Equine Art (33)
American Federation of Astrologers, Inc. (119)
Association for Convention Marketing Executives (244)
The Association of Collegiate Conference and Events Directors International (275)
Association of Destination Management Executives (278)
Association of Meeting Professionals (294)*
Business History Conference (339)
Center for Exhibition Industry Research (348)
Christian Meetings & Conventions Association (356)
Conference on College Composition and Communication (376)
Connected International Meeting Professionals Association (377)
Convention Industry Council (383)
Council of Protocol Executives (396)
Destination Marketing Association International (411)
Disaster Recovery Contractors Association (DRCA) (413)
Electric Utility Fleet Managers Conference (422)
Electronic Distribution Show Corporation (423)*
Event Planners Association (434)
Event Service Professionals Association (434)
Exhibit Designers and Producers Association (435)*
Exhibition Services and Contractors Association (435)
Exhibitor Appointed Contractors Association (435)
Financial & Insurance Conference Planners (444)
Foundation for International Meetings (453)
Healthcare Convention and Exhibitors Association (471)
International Association for Modular Exhibitry (513)
International Association of Conference Center Administrators (518)
International Association of Conference Centers (518)
International Association of Exhibitions and Events (520)
International Association of Fairs and Expositions (521)
International Association of Venue Managers (528)*
International Festivals and Events Association (545)*
International Laser Display Association (553)
International Society of Meeting Planners (573)
International Special Events Society (575)*
Meeting Professionals International (612)
National Association of Agricultural Fair Agencies (646)
National Association of Consumer Shows (658)
National Association of Reunion Managers (692)
National Catholic Educational Exhibitors (718)
National Coalition of Black Meeting Planners (723)
North American Farm Show Council (816)
Professional Convention Management Association (861)
Professional Show Managers Association (865)*
Religious Conference Management Association (880)
Society of Independent Show Organizers (939)
Visitor Studies Association (1010)

COOPERATIVES

The Association for Consortium Leadership (243)
Association of Cooperative Educators (277)
Association of Large Distribution Cooperatives (291)
Burley Tobacco Growers Cooperative Association (338)
Cooperative Education and Internship Association (384)
Credit Union National Association, Inc. (404)
Farm Credit Council (437)
Funeral Consumers Alliance (454)
International Association for the Study of Cooperation in Education (514)
National Association of Federal Credit Unions (667)
National Association of Housing Cooperatives (673)
National Center for Asia-Pacific Economic Cooperation (719)
National Cooperative Business Association (729)
National Council of Farmer Cooperatives (734)*
National Farmers Organization (747)
National Farmers Union (Farmers Educational & Co-operative Union of America) (747)
National Milk Producers Federation (772)
National Rural Electric Cooperative Association (788)
National Society of Accountants for Cooperatives (793)
National Telecommunications Cooperative Association (799)*
Plan Sponsor Council of America (849)
Quality Bakers of America Cooperative (871)
United Egg Producers (986)

United Producers, Inc. *(988)*
United States Tobacco Cooperative Inc *(1000)*

COPYRIGHTS, PATENTS AND TRADEMARKS

American Intellectual Property Law Association *(141)*
Association for Information Protection *(249)*
Association of American Publishers *(266)*
Association of University Technology Managers *(316)*
Intellectual Property Owners Association *(505)*
International Licensing Industry Merchandisers' Association *(554)**
International Trademark Association *(577)**
Licensing Executives Society *(597)*
National Association of Plant Patent Owners *(685)*
National Humanities Alliance *(761)**
Patent and Trademark Office Society *(839)*
Patent Office Professional Association *(839)**
Special Libraries Association *(956)**

COUNSELING SEE ALSO VOCATIONAL GUIDANCE

The Accrediting Commission of Career Schools and Colleges *(10)*
American Association for Career Education *(48)*
American Association for Employment in Education *(49)*
American Association for Marriage and Family Therapy *(50)**
American Association of Pastoral Counselors *(68)*
American Association of Sexuality Educators, Counselors and Therapists *(73)*
American Board of Vocational Experts *(84)**
American College Counseling Association *(92)*
American College of Counselors *(95)*
American Counseling Association *(111)*
American Family Therapy Academy *(118)**
American Medical Rehabilitation Providers Association *(149)*
American Mental Health Counselors Association *(151)*
American Rehabilitation Counseling Association *(174)*
American School Counselor Association *(177)**
American Technical Education Association *(215)*
Association for Adult Development and Aging *(238)**
Association for Assessment in Counseling and Education *(240)*
Association for Career and Technical Education Research *(241)*
Association for Counselor Education and Supervision *(244)*
Association for Gay, Lesbian, Bisexual, and Transgender Issues in Counseling *(247)*
Association for Multicultural Counseling and Development *(252)*
Association for Skilled and Technical Sciences *(256)*
Association for Specialists in Group Work *(257)*
Association for Spiritual, Ethical and Religious Values in Counseling *(257)*
Association for University and College Counseling Center Directors *(260)*
Association of Career and Technical Education *(271)*
Business Professionals of America *(339)*
Career Planning and Adult Development Network *(343)*
Child Life Council *(353)*
Council of State Administrators of Vocational Rehabilitators *(397)*
Distributive Education Clubs of America (DECA) *(415)*
Family, Career and Community Leaders of America *(437)*
Future Business Leaders of America - Phi Beta Lambda *(455)*
Independent Educational Consultants Association *(489)**
International Association of Addictions and Offender Counselors *(514)**
International Association of Counseling Services *(518)*
International Association of Counselors and Therapists *(519)*
International Association of Jewish Vocational Services *(523)*
National Academic Advising Association *(626)**
National Association for College Admission Counseling *(637)**
National Association of Advisors for the Health Professions *(645)*
National Association of Agricultural Educators *(646)**
National Association of Industrial and Technical Teacher Educators *(675)*
National Association of Pupil Services Administrators *(689)*
National Career Development Association *(717)**
National Conference of Diocesan Vocation Directors *(727)*
National Council on Public History *(739)**

National Employment Counseling Association *(745)*
National FFA Organization *(750)*
National Postsecondary Agriculture Student Organization *(781)*
National Rehabilitation Counseling Association *(785)*
Technology Student Association *(970)*
Vocational Evaluation and Career Assessment Professionals *(1011)*

DISABILITIES

ADARA *(12)*
American Academy of Audiology *(31)**
American Academy of Physical Medicine and Rehabilitation *(40)**
The American Association of Eye and Ear Centers of Excellence *(61)*
American Auditory Society *(78)**
American Congress of Community Supports and Employment Services *(107)*
American Counseling Association *(111)*
American Medical Rehabilitation Providers Association *(149)*
American Neurotology Society *(156)*
American Occupational Therapy Association, Inc. *(157)**
American Orthotic and Prosthetic Association *(159)**
American Speech-Language-Hearing Association *(212)**
Association for Education and Rehabilitation of the Blind & Visually Impaired *(245)*
Association of Academic Physiatrists *(263)*
Association of Technology Act Projects *(313)*
Association of University Centers on Disabilities (AUCD) *(315)*
Association on Higher Education and Disability *(319)**
Blinded Veterans Association *(332)*
Brain Injury Association of America *(334)**
Conference of Educational Administrators of Schools and Programs for the Deaf *(375)*
Council for Children with Behavioral Disorders *(389)*
Council on Education of the Deaf *(399)*
Hearing Industries Association *(472)*
Hearing Loss Association of America *(472)**
Inter-National Association of Business Industry & Rehabilitation *(506)*
International Association of Audio Information Services *(516)**
International Hearing Society *(549)*
International Visual Literacy Association *(580)*
The Learning Disabilities Association *(596)*
National AMBUCS *(633)*
National Association for the Advancement of Orthotics and Prosthetics *(643)*
National Association of Blind Merchants *(650)*
National Association of Blind Teachers *(650)*
National Association of Councils on Developmental Disabilities *(658)*
National Association of Disability Representatives *(663)*
National Association of Rehabilitation Providers and Agencies *(691)*
National Association of State Directors of Developmental Disabilities Services, Inc. *(700)*
National Association of State Directors of Special Education *(700)**
National Council of State Agencies for the Blind *(736)*
National Council on Rehabilitation Education *(739)*
National Hearing Conservation Association *(758)*
National Independent Living Association *(762)*
National Industries for the Blind *(763)*
National Rehabilitation Association *(785)*
National Student Speech Language Hearing Association *(798)**
Pan American Association of Ophthalmology *(837)*
Registry of Interpreters for the Deaf *(879)**
School Social Work Association of America *(892)**
Society for Disability Studies *(907)*
United Cerebral Palsy *(986)**
Visually Impaired Data Processors International *(1011)*

DISASTER

American Fire Safety Council *(121)*
American Fire Sprinkler Association *(121)*
American Pyrotechnics Association *(172)*
Automatic Fire Alarm Association *(321)*
Defense Fire Protection Association *(408)*
Disaster Preparedness and Emergency Response Association *(413)*
Electronic Security Association *(424)*
Fire and Emergency Manufacturers and Services Association *(446)*
Fire Apparatus Manufacturers' Association *(446)*
Fire Department Safety Officers Association *(446)*
Fire Equipment Manufacturer's Association *(446)**
Fire Suppression Systems Association *(446)*
International Association of Arson Investigators *(515)*

International Association of Black Professional Fire Fighters *(517)*
International Association of Emergency Managers *(520)**
International Association of Fire Chiefs *(521)*
International Association of Fire Fighters *(521)*
International Association of Wildland Fire *(528)**
International Association of Women in Fire and Emergency Services *(528)*
International Fire Marshals Association *(545)*
International Fire Photographers Association *(545)*
International Firestop Council *(545)*
International Society of Fire Service Instructors *(572)*
Lighter Association *(598)**
Maritime Fire and Safety Association *(605)*
National Association of Chiefs of Police *(653)*
National Association of Fire Equipment Distributors *(668)*
National Association of Fire Investigators *(668)*
National Association of Flood and Stormwater Management Agencies *(668)*
National Association of Hispanic Firefighters *(672)*
National Association of State Fire Marshals *(701)*
National Emergency Management Association *(745)*
National Fire Protection Association *(751)*
National Fire Sprinkler Association *(751)*
National Independent Fire Alarm Distributors *(762)**
National Volunteer Fire Council *(803)*
Society of Fire Protection Engineers *(936)*
USA Sprinkler Fitter Business Managers Association *(1005)*

DRUG AND ALCOHOL ABUSE

Alliance for Children and Families *(22)*
American Academy of Addiction Psychiatry *(29)**
American Counseling Association *(111)*
Association of Medical Education and Research in Substance Abuse *(293)**
Drug & Alcohol Testing Industry Association *(416)*
Employee Assistance Professionals Association *(426)*
National Association for Alcoholism and Drug Abuse Counselors *(646)*
National Association of Blacks in Criminal Justice *(649)*
National Association of Drug Court Professionals *(663)**
National Association of Psychiatric Health Systems *(688)**
National Association of State Alcohol and Drug Abuse Directors (NASADAD) *(697)*
National Narcotics Officers Associations' Coalition *(774)*
National On-Site Testing Association *(776)*
Research Society on Alcoholism *(882)*
School Social Work Association of America *(892)**
Substance Abuse Program Administrators Association *(965)*
Treatment Communities of America *(980)*

ECONOMICS AND ECONOMIC DEVELOPMENT

AACE International *(1)*
Agricultural & Applied Economics Association *(16)*
American Association of Family and Consumer Sciences *(61)*
American Chamber of Commerce Executives *(89)*
American Economic Association *(115)**
American Enterprise Institute for Public Policy Research *(117)*
American Indonesian Chamber of Commerce *(135)*
American Mideast Business Associates *(151)*
American National Chamber of Commerce *(154)*
American Real Estate and Urban Economics Association *(173)**
American-Israel Chamber of Commerce and Industry *(222)*
American-Uzbekistan Chamber of Commerce *(222)*
Argentine-American Chamber of Commerce *(228)*
Association for Community Affiliated Plans *(242)*
Association for Comparative Economic Studies *(242)*
Association for Enterprise Opportunity *(245)**
Association for Evolutionary Economics *(246)*
Association for Management Information in Financial Services *(251)*
Association for University Business and Economic Research *(260)*
Association of American Chambers of Commerce in Latin America *(264)*
Association of Environmental and Resource Economists *(281)*
Association of Foreign Investors in U.S. Real Estate *(284)*
Association of Private Enterprise Education *(300)*
Association of Small Business Development Centers *(308)*
Association of Third World Studies *(314)*
Automation Alley *(321)*
Belgian-American Chamber of Commerce *(327)*
Brazilian American Chamber of Commerce *(334)**
BritishAmerican Business Inc. *(335)*
Business Roundtable *(339)*

Checks Payment Systems Association (351)
Coalition of Service Industries (361)*
Colombian American Association (365)*
The Commercial Vehicle Solutions Network (367)*
Community Development Venture Capital Alliance (370)*
Conference of Business Economists (374)
Corporate Council on Africa (385)
Council for Community and Economic Research (388)
The Council for Trade and Economic Cooperation (391)
Council of Better Business Bureaus (392)*
Council of Development Finance Agencies (393)
Council of the Americas (398)
The Danish-American Chamber of Commerce (USA) (407)
DBA International (407)
Econometric Society (418)*
Economic History Association (418)*
Ecuadorean American Association (419)
Educational Association of University Centers (420)
European-American Business Council (434)
Financial Management Association International (444)
Finnish American Chamber of Commerce (445)
German American Chamber of Commerce (460)
Hellenic-American Chamber of Commerce (474)
History of Economics Society (476)*
Human Capital Institute (480)
Icelandic American Chamber of Commerce (482)
Institute Management Accountants (498)*
International Association for Energy Economics (512)
International Downtown Association (541)*
International Economic Development Council (541)*
International Electronic Commerce Association (542)
International Society for Ecological Economics (566)
International Society for Pharmacoeconomics and Outcomes Research (568)*
Ireland Chamber of Commerce in the United States (585)
Italy-America Chamber of Commerce (586)
Mexico-U.S. Business Committee, U.S. Council (614)
Mineral Economics and Management Society (617)
National Alliance of Community Economic Development Associations (632)
National Association for Business Economics (636)
National Association of County Community and Economic Development (637)
National Association of Development Organizations (662)
National Association of Foreign Trade Zones (669)
National Association of Forensic Economics (669)
National Association of Regional Councils (690)
National Association of Workforce Boards (NAWB) (710)
National Black Chamber of Commerce (714)
National Black MBA Association (714)
National Center for Asia-Pacific Economic Cooperation (719)
National Community Development Association (725)
National Economic Association (744)*
National Extension Association of Family and Consumer Sciences (747)*
National Foreign Trade Council, Inc. (752)
National U.S.-Arab Chamber of Commerce (803)
North American-Bulgarian Chamber of Commerce (823)
North American-Chilean Chamber of Commerce (823)
Norwegian-American Chamber of Commerce (824)
Opportunity Finance Network (829)*
Pakistan American Business Association (837)
Portugal-US Chamber of Commerce (853)
Regional Plan Association (879)
Romanian-American Chamber of Commerce (888)
Serbian-American Chamber of Commerce (897)
National Association of Small Business Investment Companies (900)
Social Science History Association (902)
Society for Economic Anthropology (908)*
Society for Economic Botany (908)
Society for the Advancement of Economic Theory (922)
Society of American Business Editors and Writers (928)
Society of Automotive Analysts (930)
Society of Government Economists (937)
The Spain-United States Chamber of Commerce (953)
Swedish-American Chambers of Commerce of the USA, Inc. (967)
Union for Radical Political Economics (985)*
United States-Taiwan Business Council (989)
United States Association for Energy Economics (990)*
United States Business and Industry Council (991)
United States Chamber of Commerce (991)
United States Hispanic Chamber of Commerce (995)

United States Junior Chamber (Jaycees) (995)
U.S.-Russia Business Council (999)
United States-Austrian Chamber of Commerce (1001)
Venezuelan American Association of the U.S. (1008)*
Western Economic Association International (1015)

EDUCATION

Academic Language Therapy Association (3)
Academy of Aphasia (4)
Academy of Breastfeeding Medicine (4)
Academy of Criminal Justice Sciences (4)*
Academy of Homiletics (5)
Academy of International Business (5)*
Academy of Management (6)*
Academy of Marketing Science (6)*
Academy of Political Science (8)
Academy of Psychosomatic Medicine (8)
Academy of Radiology Research (8)*
Academy of Security Educators and Trainers (9)
Accreditation Council for Pharmacy Education (10)
Accrediting Bureau of Health Education Schools (10)
The Accrediting Commission of Career Schools and Colleges (10)
Accrediting Council for Continuing Education & Training (10)
Accrediting Council for Independent Colleges and Schools (10)
Accrediting Council on Education in Journalism and Mass Communications (11)*
ACPA College Student Educators International (11)
ACUTA - The Association for Information Communications Technology Professionals in Higher Education (11)*
ADED - The Association for Driver Rehabilitation Specialists (12)
Aerospace Department Chairs Association (14)
AFT - Public Employees (15)
Alliance for Continuing Medical Education (22)
Alliance of Associations of Teachers of Japanese (24)*
Alliance of Professional Tattooists (25)
Alliance of Work/Life Progress (25)
America's Small Business Development Center Network (29)
American Academy for Cerebral Palsy and Developmental Medicine (29)*
American Academy of Advertising (30)*
American Academy of Ambulatory Care Nursing (30)
American Academy of Anesthesiologist Assistants (30)*
American Academy of Child and Adolescent Psychiatry (31)
American Academy of Clinical Psychiatrists (31)
American Academy of Dental Group Practice (32)
American Academy of Dental Practice Administration (32)
American Academy of Environmental Engineers (33)*
American Academy of Estate Planning Attorneys (33)
American Academy of Esthetic Dentistry (33)*
American Academy of Family Physicians (34)*
American Academy of Gold Foil Operators (34)
American Academy of Health Care Providers-Addictive Disorders (34)
American Academy of Health Physics (35)*
American Academy of Matrimonial Lawyers (35)
American Academy of Medical Hypnoanalysts (36)
American Academy of Nurse Practitioners (37)
American Academy of Ophthalmology (37)*
American Academy of Oral Medicine (38)
American Academy of Otolaryngic Allergy (38)
American Academy of Pain Management (39)
American Academy of Pain Medicine (39)
American Academy of Pediatric Dentistry (39)
American Academy of Periodontology (39)*
American Academy of Physician Assistants (40)
American Academy of Professional Coders (40)
American Academy of Psychiatry and the Law (41)
American Academy of Psychotherapists (41)*
American Academy of Religion (41)*
American Academy of Somnology (42)
American Academy of State Certified Appraisers (42)
American Academy of Teachers of Singing (42)
American Academy of Wound Management (42)
American Academy on Communication in Healthcare (43)
American Accounting Association (43)
American Alliance for Health, Physical Education, Recreation and Dance (44)*
American Alliance for Theatre and Education (44)*
American Architectural Foundation (46)
American Association for Adult and Continuing Education (47)
American Association for Agricultural Education (47)*
American Association for Cancer Education (48)
American Association for Career Education (48)
American Association for Chinese Studies (48)

American Association for Employment in Education (49)
American Association for Health Education (49)
American Association for Paralegal Education (50)
American Association for Physical Activity and Recreation (51)
American Association for the Advancement of Slavic Studies (52)
American Association for Vocational Instructional Materials (53)
American Association for Women in Community Colleges (53)
American Association of Attorney-Certified Public Accountants (54)*
American Association of Chairs of Departments of Psychiatry (56)*
American Association of Christian Schools (56)
American Association of Classified School Employees (56)
American Association of Colleges for Teacher Education (57)
American Association of Colleges of Nursing (57)*
American Association of Colleges of Osteopathic Medicine (57)
American Association of Colleges of Pharmacy (57)*
American Association of Colleges of Podiatric Medicine (58)
American Association of Collegiate Registrars and Admissions Officers (58)
American Association of Community Colleges (58)
American Association of Cosmetology Schools (59)
American Association of Diabetes Educators (60)
American Association of Early Childhood Educators (60)
American Association of Family and Consumer Sciences (61)
American Association of Intensive English Programs (63)
American Association of Philosophy Teachers (69)
American Association of Physics Teachers (69)
American Association of Presidents of Independent Colleges and Universities (71)
American Association of School Librarians (72)*
American Association of School Personnel Administrators (73)
American Association of Sexuality Educators, Counselors and Therapists (73)
American Association of State Colleges and Universities (73)
American Association of Teachers of Arabic (74)
American Association of Teachers of French (74)*
American Association of Teachers of German (74)*
American Association of Teachers of Italian (74)*
American Association of Teachers of Spanish and Portuguese (75)
American Association of Teachers of Turkic Languages (75)
American Association of University Administrators (75)
American Association of University Professors (75)*
American Association of University Women (76)
American Bladesmith Society (81)
American Board of Internal Medicine (82)
American Board of Medical Specialties (82)
American Board of Perianesthesia Nursing Certification Inc. (83)
American Bridge Teachers' Association (86)
American Classical League (91)*
American College Counseling Association (92)
American College for Advancement in Medicine (93)*
American College Health Association (93)*
American College of Bankruptcy (93)
American College of Chest Physicians (94)*
American College of Chiropractic Orthopedists (94)
American College of Clinical Pharmacy (94)
American College of Counselors (95)
American College of Dentists (95)
American College of Health Plan Management (96)
American College of Medical Genetics (97)*
American College of Medical Quality (97)*
American College of Mental Health Administration (98)
American College of Musicians (98)
American College of Nutrition (99)
American College of Phlebology (100)
American College of Physicians (101)
American College of Sports Medicine (102)*
American College of Theriogenologists (103)
American College of Veterinary Nutrition (104)
American College Personnel Association (105)
American Collegiate Retailing Association (105)
American Comparative Literature Association (105)
American Conference of Academic Deans (107)
American Congress of Community Supports and Employment Services (107)
American Council for Construction Education (109)
American Council of Learned Societies (109)
American Council on Education (110)*

Business Higher Education Forum *(339)*
Business Professionals of America *(339)*
Campus Safety, Health and Environmental
 Management Association *(341)**
Career Planning and Adult Development Network
 (343)
Catalogue Raisonne Scholars Association *(344)*
CCIM Institute *(347)*
Center for Spiritual and Ethical Education *(348)*
Central Conference of American Rabbis *(348)*
Certified Claims Professional Accreditation Council
 (349)
Chief Administrators of Catholic Education *(352)*
Chinese Language Teachers Association *(354)*
Christian Association for Psychological Studies *(355)*
Christian College Consortium *(355)*
Christian Educators Association International *(355)*
Christian Schools International *(356)*
Coalition of Essential Schools *(360)**
Coalition of Higher Education Assistance
 Organizations *(360)*
College and University Professional Association for
 Human Resources *(362)**
College Art Association *(362)**
College Band Directors National Association *(363)*
The College Board *(363)*
College English Association *(363)*
College Language Association *(363)*
College Media Association *(363)**
College Music Society *(363)**
College of Diplomates of the American Board of
 Orthodontics *(364)*
College Reading and Learning Association *(364)*
College Savings Foundation *(364)**
College Savings Plans Network *(364)*
College Theology Society *(365)*
Commission on Accreditation of Allied Health
 Education Programs *(368)*
Committee on History in the Classroom *(368)*
Community College Business Officers *(370)*
Community College Journalism Association *(370)*
Community Colleges Humanities Association *(370)*
Comparative and International Education Society
 (371)
Computer Assisted Language Instruction
 Consortium *(372)**
Conference Board of the Mathematical Sciences
 (374)
Conference of Educational Administrators of Schools
 and Programs for the Deaf *(375)*
Conference on College Composition and
 Communication *(376)*
Conference on English Education *(376)*
Conference on English Leadership *(376)*
Conference on Faith and History *(376)*
Conference on Jewish Social Studies *(376)*
Conference on Latin American History *(377)*
Consortium for Graduate Study in Management
 (378)
Consortium for North American Higher Education
 Collaboration *(378)*
Consortium of College and University Media Centers
 (378)
Consortium of School Networking *(378)*
Consortium of Social Science Associations *(379)*
Consortium on Financing Higher Education *(379)*
Cooperative Education and Internship Association
 (384)
Correctional Education Association *(386)*
Council for Adult and Experiential Learning *(388)**
Council for Advancement and Support of Education
 *(388)**
Council for American Private Education *(389)**
Council for Art Education *(389)*
Council for Christian Colleges and Universities
 *(389)**
Council for Educational Diagnosticians *(389)*
Council for Elementary Science International *(389)**
Council for European Studies *(390)**
Council for Exceptional Children *(390)**
Council for Higher Education Accreditation *(390)*
Council for Learning Disabilities *(390)**
Council for Opportunity in Education *(390)*
Council for Professional Recognition *(391)*
Council for Resource Development *(391)**
Council for the Advancement of Standards in Higher
 Education *(391)**
Council of Administrators of Special Education *(391)*
Council of American Overseas Research Centers
 (392)
Council of Chief State School Officers *(392)*
Council of Colleges of Acupuncture and Oriental
 Medicine *(392)*
Council of Colleges of Arts and Sciences *(393)*
Council of Educational Facility Planners
 International *(393)*
Council of Graduate Schools *(394)*
Council of Independent Colleges *(394)*
Council of Societies for the Study of Religion *(397)**

Council of State Administrators of Vocational
 Rehabilitators *(397)*
Council of Teaching Hospitals *(398)*
Council of the Great City Schools *(398)**
Council on Anthropology and Education *(398)**
Council on Chiropractic Education *(399)*
Council on Education of the Deaf *(399)*
Council on Governmental Relations *(400)*
Council on Library-Media Technicians *(400)*
Council on Occupational Education *(400)**
Council on Social Work Education *(400)*
Council on Technology Teacher Education *(401)**
Crane Certification Association of America *(403)*
Creative Education Foundation *(403)*
Cristo Rey Network *(404)*
Dance Educators of America *(406)*
Dance Masters of America, Inc. *(406)*
Decision Sciences Institute *(407)**
Direct Marketing Association Nonprofit Federation
 (412)
Distance Education and Training Council *(414)*
Distributive Education Clubs of America (DECA)
 (415)
Early Care and Education Consortium *(417)*
Ecological Farming Association *(418)*
Education Finance Council *(419)*
Education Industry Association *(420)*
Education Law Association *(420)*
Education Writers Association *(420)**
Educational Book and Media Association *(420)*
Educational Theatre Association *(420)**
Educause *(420)**
Electrical and Computer Engineering Department
 Heads Association *(422)*
Engineering College Magazines Associated *(429)*
Esperanto-USA *(433)**
Family and Consumer Sciences Education
 Association *(437)*
Family Firm Institute, Inc. *(437)**
Family, Career and Community Leaders of America
 (437)
Federal Education Association *(439)**
Federation of State Humanities Councils *(442)*
Fire Equipment Manufacturer's Association *(446)**
Future Business Leaders of America - Phi Beta
 Lambda *(455)*
Georgia Charter Schools Association *(459)*
Health Care Education Association *(469)*
Higher Education Consortium for Special Education
 (474)
Higher Education Consortium for Urban Affairs *(475)*
Hispanic Association of Colleges and Universities
 *(475)**
History of Economics Society *(476)**
The History of Education Society *(477)*
Hosa *(478)*
Hospitality Institute of Technology and Management
 (479)
Housing Education and Research Association *(479)*
Humanities Education and Research Association
 (481)
IDEA, The Health and Fitness Association *(482)*
IEEE Education Society *(484)*
Incorporated Research Institutions for Seismology
 *(487)**
Independent Educational Consultants Association
 *(489)**
Independent Research Libraries Association *(491)*
Indian Educators Federation *(492)*
Industrial Research Institute *(494)**
InSight *(496)*
Institute for Certification of Computing Professionals
 (497)
Institute Management Accountants *(498)**
Institute of Behavioral and Applied Management
 (498)
Institute of Certified Business Counselors *(498)**
Institute of Certified Records Managers *(499)*
The Institute of Inspection, Cleaning and Restoration
 Certification *(500)*
Institute of International Finance *(501)*
Instructional Technology Council *(504)*
Intercollegiate Broadcasting System *(507)*
Interior Design Educators Council *(508)**
International Academy of Oral Medicine and
 Toxicology *(509)*
International Academy of Trial Lawyers *(509)*
International Association for Computer Information
 Systems *(511)*
International Association for Continuing Education
 and Training *(511)*
International Association for Language Learning
 Technology *(513)*
International Association for the Study of
 Cooperation in Education *(514)*
International Association for Truancy and Dropout
 Prevention *(514)*
International Association of Baptist Colleges and
 Universities *(516)*

International Association of Campus Law
 Enforcement Administrators *(517)*
International Association of Certified
 Thermographers *(517)**
International Association of Protocol Consultants
 (527)
International Association of School Librarianship
 (527)
The International Childbirth Education Association
 (534)
International Council of Fine Arts Deans *(538)*
International Council on Education for Teaching
 *(539)**
International Council on Hotel, Restaurant and
 Institutional Education *(539)*
International Double Reed Society *(541)**
International Dyslexia Association *(541)**
International Engineering Consortium *(543)*
International Graphic Arts Education Association
 (548)
International Lead Zinc Research Organization *(553)*
International Listening Association *(554)*
International Physical Fitness Association *(560)*
International Reading Association *(562)**
International Society for Educational Planning *(566)*
International Society for Performance Improvement
 *(567)**
International Society for Technology in Education
 *(569)**
International Society for Traumatic Stress Studies
 (570)
International Society of Certified Employee Benefit
 Specialists *(572)*
International Society of Fire Service Instructors *(572)*
International Society of Travel and Tourism
 Educators *(574)*
International Technology and Engineering Educators
 Association *(576)**
International Veterinary Academy of Pain
 Management *(580)*
International Visual Literacy Association *(580)*
International Writing Centers Association *(581)*
Jean Piaget Society *(586)**
Jesuit Association of Student Personnel
 Administrators *(587)*
Jesuit Secondary Education Association *(587)*
Jewish Education Service of North America *(588)*
Jewish Educators Assembly *(588)*
Joint National Committee for Languages *(589)*
Journalism Education Association *(589)*
Kappa Delta Epsilon *(590)*
Kappa Delta Pi *(590)*
Kappa Kappa Iota-National *(590)*
Keyboard Teachers Association International *(590)*
Knowledge Alliance *(591)*
Laborers-Employers Cooperation & Education Trust
 (592)
Latin American Studies Association *(594)**
League for Innovation in the Community College
 (595)
The Learning Disabilities Association *(596)*
Learning Forward *(596)*
Learning Resources Network *(596)*
Literacy Research Association *(599)*
Lutheran Education Association *(600)*
Lutheran Educational Conference of North America
 (600)
Magnet Schools of America *(601)**
Marketing Education Association *(606)*
Mathematical Association of America *(609)**
Middle East Studies Association of North America
 *(615)**
Military Impacted Schools Association *(616)*
Modern Language Association *(618)*
Music and Entertainment Industry Educators
 Association *(622)*
Music Teachers National Association *(622)**
NACE International *(623)*
NAFSA: Association of International Educators *(624)*
National Association of Student Personnel
 Administrators *(626)*
National Abstinence Education Association *(626)*
National Academic Advising Association *(626)**
National Academy of Arbitrators *(627)*
National Academy of Building Inspection Engineers
 (627)
National Academy of Education *(627)**
National Academy of Opticianry *(628)*
National Academy of Sciences *(628)**
National Adult Education Professional Development
 Consortium *(629)*
National After School Association *(629)*
National Alliance of Black School Educators *(632)*
National Art Education Association *(635)*
National Association for Bilingual Education *(636)*
National Association for Black Geologists and
 Geophysicists *(636)*
National Association for Business Teacher Education
 (636)
National Association for Campus Activities *(637)*

National Association for Chicana and Chicano Studies (637)*
National Association for College Admission Counseling (637)*
National Association for Developmental Education (638)
National Association for Equal Opportunity in Higher Education (638)
National Association for Family and Community Education (638)
National Association for Gifted Children (639)*
National Association for Girls and Women in Sport (639)
National Association for Kinesiology in Higher Education (640)
National Association for Multicultural Education (640)
The National Association for Music Education (Formerly MENC) (641)*
National Association for Practical Nurse Education and Service (641)
National Association for Pupil Transportation (642)
National Association for Relationship and Marriage Education (642)
National Association for Research in Science Teaching (642)*
National Association for Sport and Physical Education (643)*
National Association for the Education of Young Children (644)*
National Association for Year-Round Education (645)
National Association of Academic Advisors for Athletes (645)*
National Association of Academies of Science (645)
National Association of African American Studies and Affiliates (646)*
National Association of Agricultural Educators (646)*
National Association of Agricultural Fair Agencies (646)
National Association of Biology Teachers (648)*
National Association of Black Professors (649)
National Association of Blind Teachers (650)
National Association of Catholic School Teachers (651)
National Association of Charter School Authorizers (652)
National Association of College and University Attorneys (654)*
National Association of College and University Business Officers (654)*
National Association of College and University Food Services (655)*
National Association of College Auxiliary Services (655)*
National Association of College Wind and Percussion Instructors (655)
National Association of Colleges and Employers (655)
National Association of Collegiate Directors of Athletics (656)
National Association of Community Health Centers (656)
National Association of Concessionaires (657)*
National Association of Credential Evaluation Services, Inc. (661)
The National Association of Dog Obedience Instructors (663)
National Association of Educational Office Professionals (664)*
National Association of Educational Procurement, Inc. (664)*
National Association of Elementary School Principals (664)
National Association of Episcopal Schools (666)
National Association of Federal Education Program Administrators (667)
National Association of Federally Impacted Schools (668)
National Association of Flight Instructors (668)
National Association of Forensic Economics (669)
National Association of Geoscience Teachers (669)
National Association of Graduate Admissions Professionals (670)*
National Association of Graduate-Professional Students (670)
National Association of Health and Educational Facilities Finance Authorities (671)
National Association of Healthcare Education Centers (671)
National Association of Heavy Equipment Training Schools (672)
National Association of Hispanic and Latino Studies (672)
National Association of Independent Colleges and Universities (674)
National Association of Independent Schools (675)*
National Association of Industrial and Technical Teacher Educators (675)

National Association of Junior Auxiliaries (677)
National Association of Media and Technology Centers (680)*
National Association of Medical Minority Educators, Inc. (680)
National Association of Native American Studies (681)*
National Association of Parliamentarians (683)
National Association of Partners in Education (683)
National Association of Principals of Schools for Girls (686)
National Association of Private Special Education Centers (686)
National Association of Private, Nontraditional Schools and Colleges (686)
National Association of Professional Asian American Women (686)
The National Association of Professional Receptionists (688)
National Association of Professors of Hebrew (688)*
National Association of Pupil Services Administrators (689)
National Association of Rehabilitation Providers and Agencies (691)
National Association of Rehabilitation Research and Training Centers (691)
National Association of School Music Dealers (692)
National Association of School Nurses (693)*
National Association of School Psychologists (693)*
National Association of Schools of Art and Design (693)*
National Association of Schools of Dance (693)*
National Association of Schools of Music (694)*
National Association of Schools of Public Affairs and Administration (694)
National Association of Schools of Theatre (694)*
National Association of Secondary School Principals (694)*
National Association of Self-Instructional Language Programs (695)
National Association of Sports Public Address Announcers (697)
National Association of State Administrators and Supervisors of Private Schools (697)
National Association of State Boards of Education (698)
National Association of State Directors of Career Technical Education Consortium (699)
National Association of State Directors of Migrant Education (700)
National Association of State Directors of Special Education (700)*
National Association of State Directors of Teacher Education and Certification (700)
National Association of State Student Grant and Aid Programs (702)
National Association of Street Schools (703)
National Association of Student Affairs Professionals (703)
National Association of Student Councils (703)
National Association of Student Financial Aid Administrators (703)*
National Association of Supervisors for Business Education (704)*
National Association of Supervisors of Agricultural Education (704)
National Association of Teacher Educators for Family Consumer Sciences (704)
National Association of Teachers' Agencies (705)
National Association of Temple Educators (705)
National Association of Test Directors (705)
National Association of Therapeutic Schools and Programs (NATSAP) (706)
National Association of Underwater Instructors (707)
National Association of University Forest Resources Programs (707)
National Association of University Women (708)
National Association of Veterans Program Administrators (708)*
National Association of Veterans Research and Education Foundations (708)*
National Association of Workforce Boards (NAWB) (710)
National Association of Workforce Development Professionals (710)*
National Associations of State Directors of Pupil Transportation Services (710)
National Black Caucus of State Legislators (714)
National Board for Certification in Occupational Therapy, Inc. (715)
National Board for Professional Teaching Standards (NBPTS) (715)
National Braille Association (716)
National Business Education Association (716)
National Catholic College Admission Association (718)
National Catholic Educational Association (718)
National Catholic Educational Exhibitors (718)

National Certification Commission for Acupuncture and Oriental Medicine (720)*
National Christian School Association (721)
National Coalition of Alternative Community Schools (723)
National Coalition of Girls' Schools (723)
National College of Probate Judges (724)
National Collegiate Athletic Association (724)
National Collegiate Honors Council (724)*
National Collegiate Wrestling Association (724)
National Conference of Yeshiva Principals (729)
National Council for Accreditation of Teacher Education (731)*
National Council for Agricultural Education (731)
National Council for Geographic Education (731)*
National Council for History Education (732)
National Council for Impacted Schools (732)
National Council for Languages and International Studies (732)
National Council for Marketing and Public Relations (732)
National Council for the Social Studies (733)*
National Council for Workforce Education (733)*
National Council of Art Administrators (734)
National Council of Exchangors (734)
National Council of Higher Education Loan Programs (735)*
National Council of State Directors of Community Colleges (736)
National Council of State Supervisors for Languages (736)
National Council of Supervisors of Mathematics (737)*
National Council of Teachers of English (737)
National Council of Teachers of Mathematics (737)
National Council of Urban Education Associations (738)
National Council of Writing Program Administrators (738)*
National Council on Education for the Ceramic Arts (738)
National Council on Family Relations (738)*
National Council on Measurement in Education (739)*
National Council on Rehabilitation Education (739)
National Council on Student Development (740)
National Council on Teacher Retirement (740)
National Dance Association (741)
National Dance Education Organization (742)*
National Drug Court Institute (743)
National Earth Science Teachers Association (743)
National Education Association (744)
National Educational Broadband Services Organization (744)
National Educational Telecommunications Association (744)*
National Extension Association of Family and Consumer Sciences (747)*
National Farmers Union (Farmers Educational & Co-operative Union of America) (747)
National Federation Coaches Association (748)
National Federation of Modern Language Teachers Associations (749)
The National Federation of Nonpublic School State Accrediting Associations (749)
National Federation of State High School Associations (750)
National FFA Organization (750)
National Guild for Community Arts Education (757)*
National Guild of Piano Teachers (757)
National Head Start Association (758)
National HEP-CAMP Association (759)
National High School Athletic Coaches Association (759)
National Humanities Alliance (761)*
National Independent Living Association (762)
National Independent Private Schools Association (762)
National Indian Education Association (762)
National Indian Head Start Directors Association (763)
National Institute for State Credit Union Examination (764)
National Marine Educators Association (771)
National Maritime Alliance (772)
National Migrant and Seasonal Head Start Association (772)
National Music Council (774)
National Organization for Human Service (777)
National Organization of Nurse Practitioner Faculties (777)
National Orientation Directors Association (778)*
National Parent Teachers Association (779)
National Postsecondary Agriculture Student Organization (781)
National Rural Education Association (788)
National School Boards Association (789)
National School Public Relations Association (789)
National School Supply and Equipment Association (789)

National School Transportation Association *(790)**
National Science Education Leadership Association *(790)*
National Science Teachers Association *(790)**
National Society for Experiential Education *(792)*
National Society for Hebrew Day Schools *(792)*
National Student Employment Association *(797)*
National Student Speech Language Hearing Association *(798)**
National Training and Simulation Association *(801)**
National Tutoring Association *(803)*
National Woman's Party *(805)*
National Women's Studies Association *(805)**
National Young Farmers Education Association *(806)*
Naval Submarine League *(807)*
Neurofibromatosis, Inc., Northeast *(808)*
New America Alliance *(809)*
The New York Academy of Sciences *(809)*
NFHS Music Association *(810)*
North American Academy of Ecumenists *(812)**
North American Academy of Liturgy *(812)*
North American Association for Environmental Education *(812)*
North American Association of Commencement Officers *(813)*
North American Association of Educational Negotiators *(813)*
North American Association of Professors of Christian Education *(813)*
North American Association of Summer Sessions *(813)**
North American Coalition for Christian Admissions Professionals *(815)*
North American Colleges and Teachers of Agriculture *(815)*
North American Council of Automotive Teachers *(815)*
North American Flowerbulb Wholesalers Association *(816)*
North American Small Business International Trade Educators *(821)**
North American Technician Excellence *(823)*
Organization for Tropical Studies *(831)**
Organization of American Kodaly Educators *(832)*
Organizational Behavior Teaching Society *(832)**
Organizational Systems Research Association *(833)*
PCIA - The Wireless Infrastructure Association *(840)*
Pediatric Nursing Certification Board *(840)**
Pet Partners *(842)**
Pharmaceutical Education and Research Institute *(844)*
Phi Delta Kappa International *(845)**
Phi Epsilon Kappa *(845)*
Philosophy of Education Society *(846)*
Physician Assistant Education Association *(847)*
Pi Lambda Theta *(847)*
Pi Sigma Epsilon *(847)*
Practising Law Institute *(855)*
Professional and Organizational Development Network in Higher Education *(859)**
Professional Association of Diving Instructors *(859)*
Public Education Network *(869)*
Public Relations Student Society of America *(870)*
Quality Service Contractors *(871)*
Real Estate Educators Association *(875)**
Religious Education Association *(880)**
Research Association of Minority Professors *(882)*
Rhetoric Society of America *(886)*
SAVE International *(891)**
School Nutrition Association *(892)*
School Science and Mathematics Association *(892)*
School Social Work Association of America *(892)**
Schools Interoperability Framework Association *(892)**
Sigma Theta Tau International *(899)*
Society for Academic Emergency Medicine *(903)**
Society for Applied Learning Technology *(904)**
Society for Buddhist-Christian Studies *(905)*
Society for Cinema and Media Studies *(905)**
Society for College and University Planning *(906)*
Society for Education in Anesthesia *(908)*
Society for French Historical Studies *(909)*
Society for Historians of American Foreign Relations *(910)*
Society for History Education *(911)*
Society for Laboratory Automation and Screening *(914)*
Society for Nutrition Education and Behavior *(917)**
Society for Photographic Education *(919)**
Society for Public Health Education *(919)**
Society for Scholarly Publishing *(921)*
Society for Slovene Studies *(921)*
Society for Textual Scholarship *(922)*
Society for the Advancement of Education *(922)*
Society for the Advancement of Scandinavian Study *(923)*
Society for the Teaching of Psychology *(926)*
Society for Values in Higher Education *(926)*
Society of Armenian Studies *(930)*
Society of Certified Insurance Counselors *(932)*

Society of Insurance Trainers and Educators *(940)*
Society of Philosophers in America *(944)*
Society of Professors of Child and Adolescent Psychiatry *(945)*
Society of Professors of Education *(945)*
Society of Scribes *(947)*
Society of State Leaders of Health and Physical Education *(947)*
Society of Teachers of Family Medicine *(947)**
The Society of Wine Educators *(950)*
Solar Rating and Certification Corporation *(952)*
Special Interest Group for Computer Science Education *(954)*
Special Interest Group for Teacher Educators *(955)*
Special Interest Group for Technology Coordinators *(955)*
Special Interest Group for University and College Computing Services *(955)*
State Debt Management Network *(961)*
State Education Technology Directors Association *(961)*
State Higher Education Executive Officers *(961)*
Suntanning Association for Education *(966)*
TASH *(968)*
Teaching-Family Association *(969)*
Technology Student Association *(970)*
TESOL International Association *(971)**
Text and Academic Authors Association *(972)*
Training Directors' Forum *(977)**
The Travel Institute *(979)**
Turkish Studies Association *(982)*
Underwater Society of America *(984)*
United Association for Labor Education *(985)**
United Federation of Teachers *(987)*
United Inventors Association of the U.S.A. *(987)*
United States Federation of Scholars and Scientists *(994)*
United States Swim School Association *(999)*
Universities Council on Water Resources *(1002)*
Universities Research Association *(1002)*
University and College Designers Association *(1002)*
University Aviation Association *(1002)**
University Council for Educational Administration *(1002)**
University Film and Video Association *(1002)*
University Photographers Association of America *(1002)*
University Professional & Continuing Education Association *(1003)*
University Professional & Continuing Education Association *(1003)*
University/Resident Theatre Association *(1003)**
Urban Affairs Association *(1003)**
Used Textbook Association *(1005)*
Utah Association of Public Charter Schools *(1006)*
Van Alen Institute *(1007)**
WACRA - World Association for Case Method Research and Application *(1011)*
Warehousing Education and Research Council *(1012)*
Western History Association *(1015)*
Wilderness Education Association *(1017)**
Work Colleges Consortium *(1024)*
World Future Society *(1026)*
World History Association *(1026)*

EMPLOYEES & EMPLOYMENT

Accrediting Council for Continuing Education & Training *(10)*
ACPA College Student Educators International *(11)*
AFT - Public Employees *(15)*
Alliance of National Staffing and Employment Resources *(25)*
American Association for Employment in Education *(49)*
American Association of Classified School Employees *(56)*
American Association of International Healthcare Recruitment *(63)*
American Association of Occupational Health Nurses *(67)**
American Association of School Personnel Administrators *(73)*
American College of Occupational and Environmental Medicine *(99)*
American College Personnel Association *(105)*
American Congress of Community Supports and Employment Services *(107)*
American Council on International Personnel *(110)*
American Counseling Association *(111)*
American Federation of Government Employees *(119)*
American Federation of Musicians and Employers Pension Fund *(119)*
American Federation of State, County and Municipal Employees *(120)*
American Payroll Association *(162)*
American Society for Healthcare Human Resources Administration *(185)*

American Society for Training and Development *(190)*
American Society of Association Executives-The Center for Association Leadership *(193)*
American Society of Picture Professionals *(207)**
American Staffing Association *(213)**
APSE: The Network on Employment *(226)*
Asian Pacific American Labor Alliance, AFL-CIO *(232)*
Association for Multicultural Counseling and Development *(252)*
Association for Specialists in Group Work *(257)*
Association of Career and Technical Education *(271)*
The Association of Career Firms North America *(271)*
Association of Career Professionals International *(271)*
Association of Executive and Administrative Professionals *(281)*
Association of Executive Search Consultants *(282)*
Association of Farmworker Opportunity Programs *(282)*
Association of Professional Office Managers *(302)*
Association of Talent Agents *(312)**
Association of Test Publishers *(313)*
Board of Certified Safety Professionals *(332)**
Brotherhood of Maintenance of Way Employees Division *(336)*
Cable and Telecommunications Human Resources Association *(340)*
Career Planning and Adult Development Network *(343)*
Cement Employers Association *(347)*
College and University Professional Association for Human Resources *(362)**
Combat Contractor's Association *(366)*
Community Health Charities of America *(371)*
Correctional Vendors Association *(386)*
Council for Employment Law Equity (CELE) *(389)*
Council of State Administrators of Vocational Rehabilitators *(397)*
Council on Employee Benefits *(399)*
Customer Relations Institute Global, LLC *(406)*
Department for Professional Employees - AFL-CIO *(410)*
Direct Care Alliance *(412)*
Drug & Alcohol Testing Industry Association *(416)*
Employee Assistance Professionals Association *(426)*
Employee Assistance Society of North America *(426)*
Employee Benefit Research Institute *(426)*
Employee Services Management Association *(426)*
Employee Stock Ownership Plan Association *(426)*
Employer Associations of America *(426)*
Employers Association *(426)*
Employers Council on Flexible Compensation *(427)*
Employers of America *(433)*
The ERISA Industry Committee (ERIC) *(433)*
Federation of Employers and Workers of America *(441)*
Freelancers Union *(453)*
Heavy Duty Manufacturers Association *(473)*
Hosa *(478)*
HR Policy Association *(480)*
Human Resource People and Strategy *(481)*
Ideas America *(482)*
Independent Staffing Alliance *(492)*
Inter-National Association of Business Industry & Rehabilitation *(506)*
International Alliance of Theatrical Stage Employees, Moving Picture Technicians, Artists and Allied Crafts of the U.S., Its Territories and Canada *(510)*
International Association for Corporate and Professional Recruitment *(511)*
International Association for Human Resource Information Management *(512)**
International Association for Truancy and Dropout Prevention *(514)*
International Association of Correctional Training Personnel *(518)**
International Association of Counseling Services *(518)*
International Association of Jewish Vocational Services *(523)*
International Association of Outsourcing Professionals *(525)*
International Association of Personnel in Employment Security *(526)*
International Association of Rehabilitation Professionals *(527)*
International Association of Workforce Professionals (IAWP) *(529)*
International Brotherhood of Electrical Workers #98 *(531)*
International Brotherhood of Teamsters - Airline Division *(532)*
International Foundation of Employee Benefit Plans *(547)*
International Public Management Association for Human Resources *(562)*

ENERGY/ELECTRICITY

ENGINEERING/MATHEMATICS

Engineering College Magazines Associated *(429)*
Environmental and Engineering Geophysical Society *(430)**
Environmental Technology Council *(431)*
Federal Facilities Council *(439)*
Federation of Materials Societies *(441)*
Friction Material Standards Institute *(454)*
Geoscience and Remote Sensing Society *(459)*
Geosynthetic Materials Association *(459)**
Human Factors and Ergonomics Society *(480)**
IEEE Computer Society *(483)*
IEEE Engineering in Medicine and Biology Society *(484)*
IEEE Instrumentation and Measurement Society *(484)*
IEEE Photonics Society *(485)*
IEEE Power and Energy Society *(485)*
IEEE Signal Processing Society *(485)*
IEEE Society on Social Implications of Technology *(485)*
IEEE Technology Management Council *(486)*
IEEE Ultrasonics, Ferroelectrics and Frequency Control Society *(486)*
Illuminating Engineering Society of North America *(486)**
iNARTE, Inc. *(487)*
Industrial Designers Society of America *(493)*
Industrial Electronics Society *(493)*
Information Theory Society *(495)*
Institute of Electrical and Electronics Engineers (IEEE) *(499)*
Institute of Environmental Sciences and Technology *(499)*
Institute of Hazardous Materials Management *(500)*
Institute of Industrial Engineers *(500)*
Institute of Mathematical Statistics *(501)**
Institute of Noise Control Engineering *(502)*
Institute of Transportation Engineers *(503)**
Insulated Cable Engineers Association *(504)*
Insurance Accounting and Systems Association *(504)*
Insurance Loss Control Association *(505)**
International Association for Mathematical Geosciences *(513)*
International Biometric Society *(530)*
International Council on Systems Engineering *(539)*
International Engineering Consortium *(543)*
International Federation of Professional and Technical Engineers *(544)*
The International Fluid Power Society *(545)*
International Function Point Users Group *(548)*
International Institute of Ammonia Refrigeration *(551)*
International Reprographic Association *(563)*
International Society for Ecological Modelling-North American Chapter *(566)*
International Society for Pharmaceutical Engineering *(567)*
International Society of Automation *(571)*
International Society of Exposure Science *(572)*
International Society of Offshore and Polar Engineers *(573)*
International Society of Weighing and Measurement *(574)*
International Technology and Engineering Educators Association *(576)**
International Test and Evaluation Association *(577)*
International Union of Operating Engineers *(579)*
Joint Electron Device Engineering Council *(589)*
Justice Research and Statistics Association *(589)*
Man and Cybernetics Systems Society *(602)*
Manufactured Housing Institute *(602)*
Manufacturers Standardization Society of the Valve and Fittings Industry *(603)*
Marine Engineers Beneficial Association *(605)*
Marine Technology Society *(605)*
MASINT Association *(607)**
Materials and Methods Standards Association *(608)*
Materials Properties Council *(609)*
Materials Research Society *(609)*
Mathematical Association of America *(609)**
Measurement, Control and Automation Association *(609)*
Media Rating Council *(610)*
Metal Injection Molding Association *(613)*
Metal Powder Producers Association *(614)*
MTM Association for Standards and Research *(620)*
NACE International *(623)*
National Academy of Engineering of the United States of America *(627)*
National Academy of Sciences *(628)**
National Action Council for Minorities in Engineering (NACME) *(628)*
National Alliance of State Science and Mathematics Coalitions *(633)*
National Association for Business Economics *(636)*
National Association of Public Health Statistics and Information Systems *(642)*
National Association of County Engineers *(660)*
National Association of County Information Technology Administrators *(660)*

National Association of Multicultural Engineering Program Advocates *(681)*
National Association of Power Engineers *(685)*
National Board of Boiler and Pressure Vessel Inspectors *(715)*
National Cancer Registrars Association *(717)**
National Certification Commission *(720)*
National Conference on Weights and Measures *(729)*
National Council for Accreditation of Teacher Education *(731)**
National Council for Therapeutic Recreation Certification *(733)*
National Council of Examiners for Engineering and Surveying *(734)*
National Council of Structural Engineers Associations *(737)*
National Council of Supervisors of Mathematics *(737)**
National Council of Teachers of Mathematics *(737)*
National Council on Compensation Insurance, Inc. *(738)*
National Crop Insurance Services *(741)*
National Environmental Balancing Bureau *(746)*
National Fenestration Rating Council *(750)*
National Fire Protection Association *(751)*
National Information Standards Organization *(763)**
National Institute of Building Sciences *(764)*
National Institute of Ceramic Engineers *(764)*
National Institute of Packaging, Handling and Logistics Engineers *(765)*
National Institute of Steel Detailing *(765)*
National Organization for the Professional Advancement of Black Chemists and Chemical Engineers *(777)**
National Society of Black Engineers *(793)**
National Society of Professional Engineers *(794)*
NCSL International *(808)*
North American Die Casting Association *(816)*
North American Fuzzy Information Processing Society *(817)**
North American Manufacturing Research Institution of SME *(817)*
North American Membrane Society *(818)*
North American Technician Excellence *(823)*
Oceanic Engineering Society *(826)**
Phi Alpha Theta *(845)*
Population Association of America *(853)**
Professional Aviation Safety Specialists (AFL-CIO) *(860)*
Professional Engineers in Private Practice *(861)*
Professional Services Council *(865)*
Psychometric Society *(868)*
R & E Council of the NAPL *(872)*
Railway Engineering-Maintenance Suppliers Association *(874)**
Rapid Technologies & Additive Manufacturing Community of SME *(875)*
Refrigerating Engineers and Technicians Association *(878)*
Refrigeration Service Engineers Society *(878)*
Rehabilitation Engineering and Assistive Technology Society of North America *(879)**
Reliability Society *(880)*
Research Council on Structural Connections *(882)*
Robotic Industries Association *(887)*
Robotics and Automation Society *(887)*
Robotics & Flexible Machinery Tech Group *(887)*
SAE International *(889)*
SAVE International *(891)**
Scale Manufacturers Association *(892)*
School Science and Mathematics Association *(892)*
Search - The National Consortium for Justice Information and Statistics *(894)*
Sigma Phi Delta *(899)*
Society for Experimental Mechanics, Inc. *(909)**
Society for Imaging Science and Technology *(912)*
Society for Industrial & Applied Mathematics *(912)*
Society for Maintenance & Reliability Professionals *(914)*
Society for Mathematical Biology *(915)*
Society for Mining, Metallurgy and Exploration, Inc. *(915)**
Society for Natural Philosophy *(916)*
Society for the Advancement of Material and Process Engineering *(922)*
Society for the History of Technology *(923)**
Society of Actuaries *(927)*
Society of Allied Weight Engineers *(928)**
Society of American Military Engineers *(929)*
Society of Automotive Analysts *(930)*
Society of Broadcast Engineers *(931)*
Society of Cable Telecommunications Engineers *(931)*
Society of Engineering Science *(935)*
Society of Fire Protection Engineers *(936)*
Society of Flight Test Engineers *(936)*
Society of Hispanic Professional Engineers *(938)*
Society of Independent Professional Earth Scientists *(939)*
Society of Manufacturing Engineers *(941)*

Society of Marine Port Engineers *(941)*
Society of Mexican American Engineers and Scientists *(941)*
Society of Motion Picture and Television Engineers *(942)*
Society of Multivariate Experimental Psychology *(942)*
The Society of Naval Architects and Marine Engineers *(942)**
Society of Petroleum Engineers *(944)*
Society of Petroleum Evaluation Engineers *(944)*
Society of Piping Engineers and Designers *(944)*
Society of Plastics Engineers *(944)*
Society of Reliability Engineers *(946)*
Society of Rheology *(946)**
Society of Tribologists and Lubrication Engineers *(949)*
Society of Women Engineers *(950)*
Solar Rating and Certification Corporation *(952)*
SOLE - The International Society of Logistics *(952)*
Solid-State Circuits Society *(952)*
Special Interest Group on Mobility of Systems, Users, Data and Computing *(956)*
SPIE - The International Society for Optical Engineering *(958)*
Standards Engineering Society *(961)*
Structural Stability Research Council *(964)*
Surface Engineering Coating Association *(966)**
Surface Mount Technology Association *(966)*
System Safety Society *(967)*
Tau Beta Pi Association *(968)*
Theta Tau *(973)*
Tire and Rim Association *(975)*
The Transformer Association *(977)**
Tubular Exchanger Manufacturers Association *(982)*
U.S. Metric Association *(983)*
United Engineering Foundation *(986)*
United States Advanced Ceramics Association *(989)**
United States Contract Tower Association *(992)*
Utilimetrics/Alliance for Advanced Metering & Data Management Solutions *(1006)*
Vehicular Technology Society *(1008)*
Water Environment Federation *(1013)**
Western Dredging Association *(1015)*

ENVIRONMENT AND CONSERVATION

Acrylonitrile Group, Inc. *(11)*
Air and Waste Management Association *(17)*
Air Conditioning Contractors of America *(18)*
Alliance for Responsible Atmospheric Policy *(23)**
America Outdoors Association *(28)**
American Academy of Environmental Engineers *(33)**
American Academy of Sanitarians *(41)*
American Association for Aerosol Research *(47)*
American Board of Health Physics *(82)*
American Coal Ash Association *(92)*
American College of Occupational and Environmental Medicine *(99)*
American College of Toxicology *(103)*
American Council on Science and Health *(110)*
American Exploration & Production Council *(118)*
American Farmland Trust *(118)**
American Fisheries Society *(121)**
American Geophysical Union *(126)*
American Ground Water Trust *(127)*
American Hiking Society *(131)*
American Industrial Hygiene Association *(135)*
American Institute for Conservation of Historic and Artistic Works *(136)**
American Institute of Biological Sciences *(137)*
American Institute of Hydrology *(139)*
American Land Rights Association *(144)*
American Lands Access Association *(144)*
American Littoral Society *(146)**
American Mountain Guides Association *(153)*
American Nature Study Society *(155)*
American Ornithologists' Union *(158)*
American Public Gardens Association *(170)**
American Public Works Association *(172)*
American Salvage Pool Association *(177)*
American Society for Environmental History *(184)*
American Society of Mining and Reclamation *(203)**
American Society of Sanitary Engineering *(209)*
American Water Resources Association *(220)**
Asbestos Cement Product Producers Association *(231)*
Asphalt Recycling and Reclaiming Association *(233)**
Associated Air Balance Council *(234)*
Association for Conservation Information *(243)*
The Association for Environmental Health and Sciences *(246)*
Association for Facilities Engineering *(246)*
Association for Preservation Technology International *(253)*
Association of American Pesticide Control Officials *(265)*
Association of Boards of Certification *(270)*
Association of Clean Water Administrators *(273)*
Association of Conservation Engineers *(276)*

Association of Consulting Foresters of America *(276)*
Association of Diving Contractors International *(279)*
Association of Ecosystem Research Centers *(279)*
Association of Energy Engineers *(280)**
Association of Environmental and Resource Economists *(281)*
Association of Environmental Engineering and Science Professors *(281)*
Association of Fish and Wildlife Agencies *(283)*
Association of HazMat Shippers *(286)*
Association of Moving Image Archivists *(295)*
Association of Occupational and Environmental Clinics *(296)**
Association of Partners for Public Lands *(298)*
Association of State and Territorial Solid Waste Management Officials *(310)*
Association of State Floodplain Managers *(311)*
Association of State Wetland Managers *(311)*
Association of University Research Parks *(316)*
Association of Zoos and Aquariums *(318)*
Automotive Recyclers Association *(323)*
Baking Industry Sanitation Standards Committee *(325)*
Biotechnology Industry Organization (BIO) *(330)*
Center for Waste Reduction Technologies *(348)*
Clean Technology & Sustainable Industries Organization (CTSI) *(357)*
Coastal Conservation Association *(361)*
Conservation and Preservation Charities of America *(377)**
Conservation Technology Information Center *(378)*
Consumer Specialty Products Association *(381)*
Corporate Environmental Enforcement Council *(386)*
The Corps Network (formerly the National Association of Service and Conservation Corps) *(386)*
Dangerous Goods Advisory Council *(407)*
Delta Waterfowl Foundation *(409)*
Distributed Wind Energy Association *(414)*
Dredging Contractors of America, Inc. *(416)*
Ductile Iron Pipe Research Association *(417)*
Ecological Society of America *(418)*
Emissions Control Technology Association (ECTA) *(426)*
Energy and Environmental Building Association *(427)**
Energy Recovery Council *(428)*
Environmental and Engineering Geophysical Society *(430)**
Environmental and Water Resources Institute of the American Society of Civil Engineers *(430)*
Environmental Assessment Association *(430)*
Environmental Bankers Association *(430)*
Environmental Council of the States *(431)*
Environmental Design Research Association *(431)*
Environmental Industry Associations *(431)*
The Environmental Information Association *(431)*
Environmental Markets Association *(431)*
Environmental Mutagen Society *(431)*
Environmental Technology Council *(431)*
ETAD North America *(433)*
Federal Water Quality Association *(440)*
Federation of Environmental Technologists, Inc. *(441)**
Fluid Sealing Association *(448)**
Forest History Society *(451)*
Forestry Conservation Communications Association *(452)*
Ground Water Protection Council *(466)*
Groundwater Management Districts Association *(466)*
Health Physics Society *(470)*
ICLEI - Local Governments for Sustainability *(482)*
Independent Sealing Distributors *(491)*
Institute of Clean Air Companies *(499)*
Institute of Environmental Sciences and Technology *(499)*
Institute of Noise Control Engineering *(502)*
Institute of Scrap Recycling Industries, Inc. *(503)*
International Association for Food Protection *(512)*
International Association of Amusement Parks and Attractions(IAAPA) *(515)**
International Association of Heat and Frost Insulators and Asbestos Workers *(522)*
International Association of Wildland Fire *(528)**
International Desalination Association *(540)*
The International Ecotourism Society *(542)*
International Emissions Trading Association *(542)*
International Erosion Control Association *(543)**
International Institute for Energy Conservation *(551)*
International Lead Zinc Research Organization *(553)*
International Sanitary Supply Association *(563)*
International Society for Ecological Economics *(566)*
International Society for Ecological Modelling-North American Chapter *(566)*
Interstate Council on Water Policy *(582)*
Investment Recovery Association *(584)**
Irrigation Association *(585)*
Land Improvement Contractors of America *(593)*
Land Trust Alliance *(593)**

Manufacturers of Emission Controls Association *(603)*
Methanol Institute *(614)*
Mining and Metallurgical Society of America *(617)*
Municipal Waste Management Association *(621)*
NADCA: The HVAC Inspection, Maintenance and Restoration Association *(623)*
National Air Filtration Association *(630)*
National Alliance of Forest Owners *(632)*
National Association for Environmental Management *(638)*
National Association for Interpretation *(640)*
National Association for PET Container Resources *(641)**
National Association of Clean Air Agencies *(654)**
National Association of Clean Water Agencies *(654)*
National Association of Conservation Districts *(657)*
National Association of County Park and Recreation Officials *(660)*
National Association of Environmental Professionals *(666)*
National Association of Flood and Stormwater Management Agencies *(668)*
National Association of Local Government Environmental Professionals *(678)*
National Association of Noise Control Officials *(682)*
National Association of Resource Conservation and Development Councils *(691)*
National Association of Sewer Service Companies *(695)*
National Association of State Archaeologists *(697)*
National Association of State Land Reclamationists *(701)*
National Association of State Park Directors *(702)*
National Association of University Fisheries and Wildlife Programs *(707)*
National Association of University Forest Resources Programs *(707)*
National Association of Wastewater Transporters *(708)*
National Conference of Local Environmental Health Administrators *(727)*
National Conference of State Historic Preservation Officers *(728)*
National Council for Air and Stream Improvement, Inc. *(731)*
National Council for Science and the Environment *(733)*
National Council on Radiation Protection and Measurement *(739)*
National Ecological Observatory Network, Inc *(743)*
National Environmental Balancing Bureau *(746)*
National Environmental Health Association *(746)*
National Environmental, Safety and Health Training Association *(746)*
National Forest Recreation Association *(752)**
National Grange *(756)*
National Institute for Animal Agriculture *(764)*
National Institute of Building Sciences *(764)*
National Institute for Water Resources *(766)*
National Onsite Wastewater Recycling Association *(776)*
National Park Hospitality Association *(779)*
National Parks Conservation Association *(779)*
National Pest Management Association *(780)**
National Recreation and Parks Association *(784)*
National Recycling Coalition *(784)*
National Registry of Environmental Professionals *(785)*
National Safety Council *(789)**
National Shellfisheries Association *(790)*
National Solid Wastes Management Association *(795)*
National Speleological Society *(795)*
National Systems Contractors Association *(798)**
National Water Resources Association *(804)*
National Wildlife Rehabilitators Association *(805)*
NORA: Association of Responsible Recyclers *(811)*
North American Association for Environmental Education *(812)*
North American Carbon Capture & Storage Association *(814)*
North American Gamebird Association *(817)*
North American Society for Trenchless Technology *(822)*
Ocean Research & Conservation Association *(826)*
Organization of Wildlife Planners *(832)*
Outdoor Writers Association of America *(835)**
Outfitters Association of America *(835)*
Pellet Fuels Institute *(841)*
Performance Track Participants Association *(841)*
Pet Industry Joint Advisory Council *(842)**
Plant Growth Regulation Society of America *(849)*
Plumbing and Drainage Institute *(850)**
Population Action International *(851)*
Portable Sanitation Association International *(853)*
Process Equipment Manufacturers' Association *(858)*
Recreational Park Trailer Industry Association *(877)**
Regional Plan Association *(879)*
Renewable Fuels Association *(881)*

Renewable Natural Resources Foundation *(881)*
Resilient Floor Covering Institute *(883)*
Reusable Industrial Packaging Association *(885)*
RISE (Responsible Industry for a Sound Environment) *(886)*
Sea Grant Association *(894)*
Seismological Society of America *(895)**
Silicones Environmental, Health and Safety Council of North America *(900)*
Society for Conservation Biology *(906)*
Society for Ecological Restoration International *(908)**
Society for Environmental Geochemistry and Health *(908)*
Society for Human Ecology *(911)*
Society for Occupational and Environmental Health *(917)*
Society for Range Management *(920)*
Society for Wetland Scientists *(927)*
Society of Chemical Manufacturers and Affiliates Inc. *(932)*
Society of Environmental Journalists *(935)**
Society of Environmental Toxicology and Chemistry *(935)*
Society of Municipal Arborists *(942)*
Society of Outdoor Recreation Professionals *(943)*
Soil and Water Conservation Society *(951)*
Steel Recycling Institute *(963)*
Submersible Wastewater Pump Association *(965)*
The Sulphur Institute *(965)*
Surfaces in Biomaterials Foundation *(966)*
SWANA - Solid Waste Association of North America *(967)*
Synthetic Turf Council *(967)*
Toxicology Forum *(976)**
Tree Care Industry Association *(980)*
Triumvirate Environmental *(980)*
Turfgrass Producers International *(982)*
U. S. Airline Pilots Association *(983)*
Underwater Construction Corporation *(984)*
United States Composting Council *(992)**
United States Green Building Council *(994)*
Visitor Studies Association *(1010)*
Waste Equipment Technology Association *(1012)*
Water and Sewer Distributors of America *(1012)*
Water and Wastewater Equipment Manufacturers Association *(1012)**
Water Environment Federation *(1013)**
Water Quality Association *(1013)*
Waterways Council, Inc. *(1014)*
Wildlife Disease Association *(1017)*
Wildlife Management Institute *(1017)*
The Wildlife Society *(1017)**
World Research Foundation *(1027)*
World Waterpark Association *(1028)*

EXECUTIVES

Advertising Media Credit Executives Association *(13)*
American Association of Airport Executives *(53)**
American Association of Bank Directors *(54)*
American Association of Credit Union Leagues *(59)*
American Association of Medical Society Executives *(65)*
American Chamber of Commerce Executives *(89)*
American College of Cardiovascular Administrators *(93)**
American College of Healthcare Executives *(96)*
American College of Physician Executives *(101)**
American College Personnel Association *(105)*
American Conference of Academic Deans *(107)*
American Society of Association Executives-The Center for Association Leadership *(193)*
Analytical Laboratory Managers Association *(223)**
Association for the Accreditation of Human Research Protection Programs *(257)*
Association of Corporate Travel Executives (ACTE) *(277)*
Association of Executive and Administrative Professionals *(281)*
Association of Executive Search Consultants *(282)*
Association of Fundraising Professionals *(285)*
Association of Girl Scout Executive Staff *(285)*
Association of Professional Office Managers *(302)*
Association of State Chamber Professionals *(310)*
Association of Strategic Alliance Professionals, Inc. *(311)*
Association of Travel Marketing Executives *(315)*
Automotive Trade Association Executives *(324)*
Business Executives for National Security *(338)**
Chief Executives Organization *(352)*
Community Action Partnership *(369)*
Congress of Chiropractic State Associations *(377)*
Cosmetic Executive Women *(387)*
Council of Engineering and Scientific Society Executives *(393)*
Council of Protocol Executives *(396)*
Council of State Restaurant Associations *(397)*
Council of State Speech-Language-Hearing Association Presidents *(398)*
County Executives of America *(402)*

Credit Union Executives Society *(403)*
Executive Women in Government *(435)*
Executive Women International *(435)*
Executive Women's Golf Association *(435)*
Financial Executives International *(444)*
Food Industry Association Executives *(449)*
Fraternity Executives Association *(453)*
HR Policy Association *(480)*
Human Resource People and Strategy *(481)*
Incentive Marketing Association *(487)**
International Association of Golf Administrators *(522)*
International Association of Outsourcing Professionals *(525)*
International Association of Protocol Consultants *(527)*
International Association of Railway Operating Officers *(527)*
International Builders Exchange Executives/Builders Exchange Network *(532)*
International Council of Library Association Executives *(538)*
International Downtown Association *(541)**
International Food Service Executives' Association *(546)*
International Military Community Executives Association *(556)*
International Society of Hotel Association Executives *(573)*
Licensing Executives Society *(597)*
Literary Managers and Dramaturgs of the Americas *(599)*
Military Officers Association of America (MOAA) *(616)**
National Alliance of State Pharmacy Associations *(633)*
National Association of Bar Executives *(648)*
National Association of Black County Officials *(649)*
National Association of Catering and Events *(651)*
National Association of Corporate Treasurers *(658)*
National Association of Credit Union Chairmen *(661)*
National Association of Multicultural Media Executives *(681)*
The National Association of Professional Receptionists *(688)*
National Association of State Personnel Executives *(702)**
National Association of Television Program Executives *(705)*
National Association of Ticket Brokers *(706)*
National Fellowship of Child Care Executives *(750)*
National Funeral Directors Association *(754)*
National Naval Officers Association *(774)*
National Organization of Black County Officials *(777)*
Newspaper Association Managers *(810)*
Nursery and Landscape Association Executives of North America *(825)*
Police Executive Research Forum *(852)**
Professional Show Managers Association *(865)**
Professional Society for Sales and Marketing Training *(865)**
Reserve Officers Association of the U.S. *(882)*
Sales and Marketing Executives International, Inc. *(890)*
Senior Executives Association *(897)*
Society of Corporate Secretaries and Governance Professionals *(933)**
Society of Depreciation Professionals *(934)*
Society of Incentive & Travel Executives *(939)*
Stadium Managers Association *(960)*
State Higher Education Executive Officers *(961)*
Tax Executives Institute, Inc. *(968)*
Training Officers Consortium *(977)*
Women Construction Owners and Executives, USA *(1020)*
Young Presidents' Organization *(1030)*
Zonta International *(1030)*

EXPLOSIVES
American Pyrotechnics Association *(172)*
Institute of Makers of Explosives *(501)*
International Society of Explosives Engineers *(572)**

FAMILY & HOME ISSUES/ABORTION/ADOPTION
Abortion Care Network *(2)*
Alliance for Children and Families *(22)*
American Academy of Adoption Attorneys *(30)*
American Academy of Family Physicians *(34)**
American Association for Marriage and Family Therapy *(50)**
American Association of Family and Consumer Sciences *(61)*
American Counseling Association *(111)*
Billings Ovulation Method Association of the United States *(329)*
Family, Career and Community Leaders of America *(437)*
Foster Family-Based Treatment Association *(452)*
Lamaze International *(592)**

National Abortion Federation *(626)*
National Association for Relationship and Marriage Education *(642)*
National Association of Foster Grandparent Program Directors *(669)*
National Child Support Enforcement Association *(721)*
National Council on Family Relations *(738)**
National Family Planning and Reproductive Health Association *(747)*
National Military Family Association, Inc. *(772)*
National Parent Teachers Association *(779)*
National Practitioners Network for Fathers and Family *(782)*
Population Action International *(852)*
Resolve, The National Infertility Association *(883)*
United States Conference of Catholic Bishops *(992)*

FIREARMS/GUN CONTROL
American Custom Gunmakers Guild *(112)*
Association of Firearm and Toolmark Examiners *(283)*
International Association of Law Enforcement Firearms Instructors, Inc. *(523)*
International Hunter Education Association *(550)*
National Association of Arms Shows *(647)*
National Association of Federally Licensed Firearms Dealers *(668)*
National Association of Sporting Goods Wholesalers *(696)**
National Rifle Association of America *(787)*
National Shooting Sports Foundation *(791)*
North American Gamebird Association *(817)*
Sporting Arms and Ammunition Manufacturers' Institute Inc. *(959)*

FISH AND FISHING
American Bluefin Tuna Association *(81)*
American Fisheries Society *(121)**
American Fly Fishing Trade Association *(122)*
American Institute of Fishery Research Biologists *(138)*
American Littoral Society *(146)**
American Shrimp Processors Association *(179)*
American Sportfishing Association *(212)*
Aquarium and Zoo Facilities Association *(227)*
Association of Fish and Wildlife Agencies *(283)*
Association of Zoos and Aquariums *(318)*
At-Sea Processors Association *(319)*
Blue Water Fishermen's Association *(332)*
Catfish Farmers of America *(344)*
The Catfish Institute *(345)*
Central Bering Sea Fisherman's Association *(348)*
Coastal Conservation Association *(361)*
Deep Sea Fishermen's Union *(408)*
Fishing Vessel Owners' Association *(446)*
International Institute of Fisheries Economics and Trade *(551)*
Meat Industry Suppliers Alliance *(610)*
National Fisheries Institute *(751)**
National Ocean Industries Association *(775)*
National Ornamental Goldfish Growers Association *(778)*
National Party Boat Owners Alliance *(779)*
National Shellfisheries Association *(790)*
Outfitters Association of America *(835)*
Southern Shrimp Alliance *(953)*
Tuna Council *(982)*
United States Aquaculture Suppliers Association *(990)*
United States Trout Farmers Association *(1000)*
Waterways Council, Inc. *(1014)*
World Aquaculture Society *(1025)*

FOOD AND BEVERAGE INDUSTRY
Academy of Hospitality Industry Attorneys *(5)*
Academy of Nutrition and Dietetics *(7)*
Agribusiness Council *(16)*
AIB International *(17)*
Alberta Beef Producers *(21)*
Allied Trades of the Baking Industry *(26)*
American Association of Avian Pathologists *(54)*
American Association of Cereal Chemists International *(55)*
American Association of Food Hygiene Veterinarians *(61)*
American Association of Meat Processors *(64)*
American Association of Medical Milk Commissions *(65)*
American Bakers Association *(78)*
American Beekeeping Federation *(80)*
American Beverage Association *(80)*
American Beverage Institute *(81)*
American Beverage Licensees *(81)*
American Butter Institute *(87)*
American Cheese Society *(89)*
American Culinary Federation *(112)*
American Dairy Products Institute *(112)*
American Dairy Science Association *(113)*

American Dehydrated Onion and Garlic Association *(113)*
American Egg Board *(116)*
American Emu Association *(117)*
American Feed Industry Association *(120)*
American Frozen Food Institute *(124)*
American Genetic Association *(126)*
American Herbal Products Association *(130)*
American Homebrewers Association *(133)**
American Honey Producers Association *(133)*
American Importers and Exporters/Meat Products Group *(135)*
American Jersey Cattle Association/National All-Jersey Inc. *(142)*
American Malting Barley Association *(146)*
American Meat Institute *(148)**
American Meat Science Association *(148)*
American Mushroom Institute *(153)*
American National CattleWomen *(154)*
American Oil Chemists' Society *(157)**
American Ostrich Association *(161)*
American Peanut Council *(162)*
American Peanut Product Manufacturers, Inc. *(162)*
American Peanut Research and Education Society, Inc. *(162)*
American Peanut Shellers Association *(162)*
American Poultry Association *(167)*
American Sesame Growers Association *(178)*
American Shrimp Processors Association *(179)*
American Society for Enology and Viticulture *(184)*
American Society for Healthcare Food Service Administrators *(185)*
American Society of Baking *(193)*
American Society of Brewing Chemists *(193)*
American Soybean Association *(211)*
American Spice Trade Association *(212)*
American Sugar Alliance *(214)*
American Veal Association *(218)*
American Wholesale Marketers Association *(221)**
American Wine Society *(221)*
Apiary Inspectors of America *(224)*
Apple Processors Association *(226)*
Apple Products Research and Education Council *(226)*
Association for Dressings and Sauces *(245)*
Association for Healthcare Foodservice *(248)*
Association for the Study of Food and Society *(259)*
Association of Correctional Food Service Affiliates *(277)*
Association of Coupon Professionals *(277)*
Association of Farmworker Opportunity Programs *(282)*
Association of Food and Drug Officials *(283)*
Association of Food Industries *(283)*
Association of Kentucky Fried Chicken Franchisees, Inc. *(290)*
Association of Nutrition & Foodservice Professionals *(296)*
Atlantic Seaboard Wine Association *(319)*
Bakery, Confectionery, Tobacco Workers and Grain Millers International Union *(325)*
Baking Industry Sanitation Standards Committee *(325)*
BCA *(326)*
Beef Improvement Federation *(327)*
Beer Institute *(327)*
Beet Sugar Development Foundation *(327)*
BEMA - The Baking Industry Suppliers Association *(328)*
Beverage Media Group, Inc *(328)*
Biscuit and Cracker Manufacturers' Association *(330)**
BMC - A Foodservice Sales and Marketing Council *(332)*
The Brewers Association *(335)**
Calorie Control Council *(341)*
Can Manufacturers Institute *(341)**
Catfish Farmers of America *(344)*
The Catfish Institute *(345)*
Cattlemen's Beef Promotion and Research Board *(346)*
Certified Milk Producers Association of America *(350)*
Cheese Importers Association of America, Inc. *(351)*
Chemical Sources Association *(352)**
Cherry Marketing Institute *(352)*
Chinese American Food Society *(354)*
CIES - The Food Business Forum *(356)*
The Coca-Cola Bottlers' Association *(361)*
Cocoa Merchants' Association of America *(361)*
Commercial Food Equipment Service Association *(366)*
Concord Grape Association *(373)*
Convenience Caterers & Food Manufacturers Association *(383)*
Cookie and Snack Bakers Association *(383)*
Corn Refiners Association, Inc. *(385)*
Council of Hotel and Restaurant Trainers *(394)*
Council of State Restaurant Associations *(397)*
CROPP Cooperative / Organic Valley *(405)*

Dairy Management, Inc. **(406)**
Distilled Spirits Council of the United States, Inc. **(414)**
Distillers Grains Technology Council **(414)***
Distinguished Restaurants of North America **(414)**
Drug, Chemical and Associated Technologies Association **(417)**
Fermenters International Trade Association **(443)**
Flavor and Extract Manufacturers Association **(446)**
Food and Drug Law Institute **(449)***
Food Distribution Research Society **(449)**
Food Industry Association Executives **(449)**
Food Industry Suppliers Association **(449)**
The Food Institute **(449)**
Food Marketing Institute **(449)**
Food Processing Suppliers Association **(449)**
Food Sanitation Institute **(450)**
Food Shippers of America **(450)**
Foodservice & Packaging Institute, Inc. **(450)***
Foodservice Equipment Distributors Association **(450)**
The Foodservice Group, Inc. **(450)***
Foodservice Sales & Marketing Association **(450)**
Fresh Produce and Floral Council **(453)**
Fresh Produce Association of the Americas **(453)**
Frozen Potato Products Institute **(454)**
Gelatin Manufacturers Institute of America **(457)**
Global Alcohol Producers Group **(461)**
Glutamate Association (United States) **(463)**
Grocery Manufacturers Association (GMA) **(466)**
Herb Growing and Marketing Network **(474)**
Herb Society of America **(474)**
Home Baking Association **(477)**
Hop Growers of America **(478)**
Hospitality Institute of Technology and Management **(479)**
Human Milk Banking Association of North America **(481)**
Independent Bakers Association **(488)**
Institute of Food Technologists **(499)**
Institute of Shortening and Edible Oils **(503)**
International Association for Food Protection **(512)**
International Association of Color Manufacturers **(518)**
International Association of Culinary Professionals **(519)**
International Association of Eating Disorders Professionals **(520)***
International Association of Ice Cream Vendors **(523)**
International Association of Milk Control Agencies **(524)**
International Association of Operative Millers **(525)**
International Association of Refrigerated Warehouses **(527)**
International Banana Association **(529)**
International Beverage Dispensing Equipment Association **(529)**
International Bottled Water Association **(530)**
International Castor Oil Association **(533)**
International Council on Hotel, Restaurant and Institutional Education **(539)**
International Dairy Foods Association **(539)***
International Dairy-Deli-Bakery Association **(540)**
International Food Additives Council **(546)**
International Food & Beverage Association (IFBA) **(546)**
The International Food & Beverage Forum **(546)**
International Food Service Executives' Association **(546)**
International Food, Wine and Travel Writers Association **(546)**
International Foodservice Distributors Association **(546)**
International Foodservice Editorial Council **(546)**
International Foodservice Manufacturers Association **(546)**
International Formula Council **(547)**
International Frozen Food Association **(547)**
International Hydrolized Protein Council **(551)**
International Ice Cream Association **(551)**
International Institute of Ammonia Refrigeration **(551)**
International Jelly and Preserve Association **(553)**
International Liquid Terminals Association **(554)**
International Maple Syrup Institute **(555)**
International Natural Sausage Casing Association **(557)**
International Oil Mill Superintendents Association **(558)**
International Packaged Ice Association **(559)**
International Society of Beverage Technologists **(571)**
International Wild Rice Association **(581)***
Juice Products Association **(589)**
Leafy Greens Council **(595)**
Manufacturers' Agents Association for the Foodservice Industry **(603)**
Master Brewers Association of the Americas **(607)**
Meals on Wheels Association of America **(609)**
Meat Importers Council of America **(609)**
Meat Industry Suppliers Alliance **(610)**

Mexican-American Grocers Association **(614)**
Midwest Dairy Coalition **(615)**
Milking Machine Manufacturers Council **(616)**
Napa Valley Vintners Association **(625)**
National Alcohol Beverage Control Association **(631)**
National Association for the Specialty Food Trade **(644)**
National Association for Alcoholism and Drug Abuse Counselors **(646)**
National Association of Beverage Importers Inc. **(648)**
National Association of Catering and Events **(651)**
National Association of Church Food Service **(653)**
National Association of College and University Food Services **(655)***
National Association of Concessionaires **(657)***
National Association of Convenience Stores **(658)**
National Association of Farmers Market Nutrition Programs **(667)**
National Association of Flavors and Food-Ingredient Systems **(668)**
National Association of Flour Distributors **(668)**
National Association of Margarine Manufacturers **(679)**
National Association of Pizzeria Operators **(685)**
National Association of Produce Market Managers **(686)**
National Association of Truck Stop Operators(NATSO) **(707)**
National Automatic Merchandising Association **(711)**
National Barbecue Association **(712)**
National Beer Wholesalers Association **(713)***
National Candle Association **(717)**
National Cheese Institute **(720)***
National Chicken Council **(720)**
National Coffee Association of the U.S.A. **(723)***
National Commodity Supplemental Food Program Association **(724)**
National Confectioners Association **(725)**
National Confectionery Sales Association **(726)**
National Conference of State Liquor Administrators **(728)**
National Corn Growers Association **(730)**
National Cottonseed Products Association **(731)**
National Council of Chain Restaurants **(734)**
National Dairy Council **(741)**
National Dairy Herd Information Association **(741)**
National Food Service Security Council **(752)**
National Frozen and Refrigerated Foods Association **(753)***
National Frozen Pizza Institute **(754)**
National Grocers Association **(756)**
National Honey Packers and Dealers Association **(760)**
National Ice Cream Mix Association **(761)**
National Ice Cream Retailers Association **(761)**
National Institute of Oilseed Products **(765)**
National Mastitis Council **(772)**
National Milk Producers Federation **(772)**
National Oilseed Processors Association **(776)**
National Onion Association **(776)**
National Park Hospitality Association **(779)**
National Pasta Association **(779)**
National Peach Council **(780)**
National Pecan Shellers Association **(780)**
National Pork Producers Association **(781)**
National Pork Producers Council **(781)**
National Potato Council **(782)**
National Poultry and Food Distributors Association **(782)**
National Renderers Association **(786)**
National Restaurant Association **(786)**
National Seasoning Manufacturers Association **(790)**
National Sunflower Association **(798)**
National Sweetener and Ingredient Marketing Association **(798)***
National Turkey Federation **(802)***
National United Merchants Beverage Association **(803)**
National Watermelon Association **(804)**
National Yogurt Association **(806)**
Natural Products Association **(807)**
Network of Ingredient Marketing Specialists **(808)***
North American Association of Food Equipment Manufacturers **(813)**
North American Export Grain Association, Inc. **(816)**
North American Meat Association **(818)**
North American Metal Packaging Alliance, Inc. (NAMPA) **(818)**
North American Millers' Association **(818)***
North American Mycological Association **(818)**
North American Natural Casing Association **(819)**
Northeast Organic Farming Association **(824)**
Northern Nut Growers Association **(824)**
Organic Trade Association **(830)**
Paramount Citrus Association **(838)**
Peanut and Tree Nut Processors Association **(840)**
Pet Food Institute **(842)**
Pickle Packers International **(848)**

PMCA: An International Association of Confectioners **(851)**
Potato Association of America **(854)***
Poultry Breeders of America **(854)**
Poultry Science Association **(854)**
Process Equipment Manufacturers' Association **(858)**
Produce Marketing Association **(858)**
Quality Bakers of America Cooperative **(871)**
Quality Chekd Daries **(871)**
Red and White Dairy Cattle Association **(877)**
Refrigerated Foods Association **(878)***
Research and Development Associates for Military Food and Packaging Systems **(881)**
Research Chefs Association **(882)**
Research Society on Alcoholism **(882)**
Restaurant Facility Management Association **(884)**
Retail Bakers of America **(884)***
Retail Confectioners International **(884)**
Rice Millers' Association **(886)**
Rural Electricity Resource Council **(889)**
Salt Institute **(891)**
School Nutrition Association **(892)**
Shelf-Stable Food Processors Association **(898)**
Snack Food Association **(901)**
Society for Foodservice Management **(909)***
Society for the Anthropology of Food and Nutrition **(923)**
Society of Flavor Chemists **(936)**
The Society of Wine Educators **(950)**
Sommelier Society of America **(952)**
Southern Shrimp Alliance **(953)**
Soyfoods Association of North America **(953)**
Specialty Coffee Association of America **(957)**
Sugar Association **(965)**
Tea Association of the United States of America **(969)***
Tea Council of the U.S.A. **(969)**
Teamsters Brewery and Soft Drink Workers Conference **(969)**
Tortilla Industry Association **(976)***
Tuna Council **(982)**
United Dairy Industry Association **(986)**
United Egg Producers **(986)**
United Food and Commercial Workers International Union **(987)**
United Fresh Produce Association **(987)**
United Natural Products Alliance **(988)**
United States Apple Association **(989)**
United States Beet Sugar Association **(991)**
United States Canola Association **(991)**
United States Dairy Export Council **(993)**
United States Durum Growers Association **(993)**
United States Lactation Consultant Association **(996)**
United States Meat Export Federation **(996)**
United States National Committee of the International Dairy Federation **(996)**
United States of America Dry Pea and Lentil Council, Inc. **(996)**
United States Potato Board **(997)**
U.S Poultry and Egg Association **(998)**
US Rice Producers Association **(1004)**
USA Rice Federation **(1004)***
The Vinegar Institute **(1009)***
Walnut Council **(1012)**
Wholesale Beer Association Executives of America **(1016)**
Wild Blueberry Association of North America **(1017)**
Wine and Spirits Shippers Association **(1018)**
Wine and Spirits Wholesalers of America **(1018)***
WineAmerica **(1019)**
Women Chefs and Restaurateurs **(1020)***
Women's Foodservice Forum **(1023)***
World's Poultry Science Association, U.S.A. Branch **(1028)**

FOREIGN RELATIONS

The American Bar Association Rule of Law Initiative **(80)**
American Enterprise Institute for Public Policy Research **(117)**
American Foreign Service Association **(122)**
American Friends of Turkey **(124)**
American Hellenic Educational Progressive Association (AHEPA) **(130)**
American Translators Association **(217)**
American–Uzbekistan Chamber of Commerce **(222)**
Arms Control Association **(229)**
Association of Foreign Investors in U.S. Real Estate **(284)**
Association of Former Intelligence Officers **(284)**
Business Executives for National Security **(338)***
Coalition of Service Industries **(361)***
Council of the Americas **(398)**
Diplomatic and Consular Officers, Retired (Dacor) **(412)**
The International Stability Operations Association **(575)***
Iranian American Community of Northern California **(585)**
Joint National Committee for Languages **(589)**

Mexico-U.S. Business Committee, U.S. Council *(614)*
NAFSA: Association of International Educators *(624)*
National Association of Passports and Visa Services *(683)*
National Council for Languages and International Studies *(732)*
Pakistan American Business Association *(837)*
United States Business and Industry Council *(991)*
United States-Sudan Business Council *(999)*
World Jurist Association *(1027)*

FOREIGN SERVICE

American Foreign Service Association *(122)*
American Foreign Service Protective Association *(123)*
Diplomatic and Consular Officers, Retired (Dacor) *(412)*
National Association of Passports and Visa Services *(683)*
Professional Currency Dealers Association *(861)*

FORESTRY

American Forest & Paper Association *(123)*
American Forest Resource Council *(123)**
Aquarium and Zoo Facilities Association *(227)*
Association of Consulting Foresters of America *(276)*
Council On Forest Engineering *(399)*
Forest History Society *(451)*
Forest Industries Telecommunications *(451)*
Forest Landowners Association *(451)*
Forest Landowners Tax Council *(451)*
Forest Products Industry National Labor-Management Committee *(451)*
Forest Products Society *(451)*
Forest Stewardship Council - United States Chapter *(451)*
Forestry Conservation Communications Association *(452)*
Forestry Equipment Council *(452)*
International Concatenated Order of Hoo-Hoo *(536)*
International Fruit Tree Association *(547)*
International Society of Arboriculture *(571)*
National Alliance of Forest Owners *(632)*
National Association of Environmental Professionals *(666)*
National Association of State Foresters *(701)*
National Association of University Forest Resources Programs *(707)*
National Christmas Tree Association *(721)**
National Council of Commercial Plant Breeders *(734)*
National Forest Recreation Association *(752)**
National Plant Board *(781)*
National Woodland Owners Association *(806)*
Renewable Natural Resources Foundation *(881)*
Society of American Foresters *(928)*
Tree Care Industry Association *(980)*
Tree-Ring Society *(980)*
The Wildlife Society *(1017)**

FUNDRAISING

American National Chamber of Commerce *(154)*
Association for Healthcare Philanthropy *(248)*
Association Foundation Group *(262)*
Association of Direct Response Fundraising Counsel *(279)*
Association of Donor Recruitment Professionals *(279)*
Association of Fund-Raising Distributors and Suppliers *(285)*
Association of Fundraising Professionals *(285)*
Association of Professional Researchers for Advancement *(302)*
Council for Advancement and Support of Education *(388)**
Direct Marketing Association Nonprofit Federation *(412)*
Donors Forum *(415)*
Giving Institute *(461)**
Independent Sector *(491)*
National Association of Athletic Development Directors *(647)*
National Association of Independent Colleges and Universities *(674)*
National Catholic Development Conference *(718)**
North American Association of State and Provincial Lotteries *(813)*

FURNITURE/HOME FURNISHINGS

American Craft Council *(111)*
American Edged Products Manufacturers Association *(115)*
American Home Furnishings Alliance *(132)*
American Lighting Association *(145)**
American Society of Furniture Designers *(198)*
American Society of Interior Designers *(200)**
Antiquarian Booksellers Association of America *(224)*
Appliance Parts Distributors Association *(226)*
Art and Antique Dealers League of America *(229)*

Associated Glass and Pottery Manufacturers *(236)*
Association for Retail Environments *(256)*
Association of Home Appliance Manufacturers *(287)*
Association of Progressive Rental Organizations *(303)*
Association of Woodworking and Furnishings Suppliers *(318)*
Business and Institutional Furniture Manufacturers Association International *(338)*
The Carpet and Rug Institute *(343)*
Center for the Polyurethanes Industry *(348)**
Chemical Fabrics and Film Association *(351)**
Cookware Manufacturers Association *(384)*
Furniture Manufacturers Alliance *(454)*
Furniture Retailers of America *(454)*
Futon Association International *(455)*
High Point Market *(474)*
Home Fashion Products Association *(478)*
Home Furnishings Independents Association *(478)**
Independent Office Products and Furniture Dealers Association *(490)*
Industry Council on Tangible Assets *(494)*
The Institute of Inspection, Cleaning and Restoration Certification *(500)*
Interior Design Society *(508)*
International Association of Bedding and Furniture Law Officials *(516)*
International Association of Home Staging Professionals *(522)**
International Association of Movers *(525)*
International Casual Furnishings Association *(533)*
International Furnishings and Design Association *(548)*
International Furniture Rental Association *(548)*
International Furniture Transportation and Logistics Council *(548)*
International Guild of Candle Artisans *(549)*
International Home Furnishings Representatives Association *(550)*
International Housewares Association *(550)*
International Housewares Representatives Association *(550)**
International Interior Design Association *(552)*
International Sleep Products Association *(565)*
International Union of Electronic, Electrical, Salaried, Machine, and Furniture Workers-CWA *(579)*
Juvenile Products Manufacturers Association *(590)*
Kitchen Cabinet Manufacturers Association *(591)*
National Antique and Art Dealers Association of America *(634)*
National Appliance Parts Suppliers Association *(634)*
National Appliance Service Association *(635)*
National Association of Decorative Fabric Distributors *(662)*
National Association of Resale & Thrift Shops *(691)*
National Candle Association *(717)*
National Cotton Batting Institute *(730)**
National Home Furnishings Association *(759)*
National Independent Nursery Furniture Retailers Association *(762)*
National Kitchen and Bath Association *(767)*
National Office Products Alliance *(776)*
North American Association of Floor Covering Distributors *(811)*
North American Retail Dealers Association *(820)*
Office Furniture Dealers Alliance *(826)*
Paint and Decorating Retailers Association *(836)*
Quarters Furniture Manufacturers Association *(872)**
Restoration Industry Association *(884)*
Scientific Equipment and Furniture Association *(892)*
Society of Glass and Ceramic Decorated Products *(937)**
Specialty Sleep Association *(958)*
Sponge and Chamois Institute *(958)*
Unfinished Furniture Association *(984)**
Window Covering Manufacturers Association *(1018)*
Window Covering Safety Council *(1018)*
Wood Component Manufacturers Association *(1024)*
WorkPlace Furnishings *(1025)*
World Floor Covering Association *(1026)*
Writing Instrument Manufacturers Association *(1029)*

GENEALOGY

Association of Professional Genealogists *(301)*
National Genealogical Society *(754)*

GLASS

American Ceramics Society *(89)*
American Scientific Glassblowers Society *(178)**
Associated Glass and Pottery Manufacturers *(236)*
Enhanced Protective Glass Automotive Association *(429)*
Gift Associates Interchange Network *(460)*
Glass Art Society *(461)*
Glass Association of North America *(461)*
Glass Manufacturing Industry Council *(461)*
Glass Packaging Institute *(461)**

Glass, Molders, Pottery, Plastics and Allied Workers International Union *(461)*
International Crystal Federation *(539)*
International Window Cleaning Association *(581)**
National Glass Association *(755)*
National Sunroom Association *(798)*
The Optical Lab Division *(829)**
Society of Glass and Ceramic Decorated Products *(937)**
Stained Glass Association of America *(960)*

GOVERNMENT-RELATED

AASHTO: Transportation Center of Excellence *(2)*
Adjutants General Association of the United States *(12)*
Aerospace Industries Association of America *(14)*
AFT - Public Employees *(15)*
Air Force Association *(18)*
Air Force Sergeants Association *(19)*
Air Traffic Control Association *(19)*
American Academy of Diplomacy *(32)*
American Association for Budget and Program Analysis *(48)*
American Association of Motor Vehicle Administrators *(65)*
American Association of Police Polygraphists *(70)*
American Association of Port Authorities *(70)*
American Association of Public Health Dentistry *(71)*
American Association of Public Welfare Attorneys *(72)*
American Association of State Climatologists *(73)*
American Conference of Governmental Industrial Hygienists *(107)**
American Correctional Association *(108)**
American Correctional Chaplains Association *(108)*
American Council of State Savings Supervisors *(110)*
American Enterprise Institute for Public Policy Research *(117)*
American Federation of Government Employees *(119)*
American Federation of School Administrators *(120)*
American Federation of State, County and Municipal Employees *(120)*
American Foreign Service Association *(122)*
American Institute of Certified Planners *(137)*
American Judges Association *(143)*
American League of Lobbyists *(145)*
American Logistics Association *(146)*
American Maritime Officers *(147)*
American Military Retirees Association *(152)*
American Military Society *(152)*
American National Standards Institute *(154)*
American Public Works Association *(172)*
The American Society for Public Administration *(189)**
American Society of Access Professionals *(190)*
American Society of Military Comptrollers *(203)*
American Society of Naval Engineers *(204)*
APHSA - Information Systems Management *(224)*
Apiary Inspectors of America *(224)*
Armed Forces Broadcasters Association *(228)*
Armed Forces Communications and Electronics Association *(228)*
Armed Forces Special Agents Association *(229)*
Arms Control Association *(229)*
Assisted Living Federation of America *(234)*
Association for Federal Information Resources Management *(246)**
Association for Governmental Leasing and Finance *(247)*
Association for Unmanned Vehicle Systems International *(261)*
Association of Administrative Law Judges *(263)*
Association of Administrators of the Interstate Compact on the Placement of Children *(263)*
Association of American Feed Control Officials *(265)**
Association of American Pesticide Control Officials *(265)*
Association of American Plant Food Control Officials *(266)*
The Association of American Seed Control Officials *(266)**
Association of American State Geologists *(266)**
Association of Boards of Certification *(270)*
Association of Clean Water Administrators *(273)*
Association of Conservation Engineers *(276)*
Association of Correctional Food Service Affiliates *(277)*
Association of Defense Communities *(278)*
Association of Eminent Domain Professionals *(280)*
Association of Film Commissioners International *(283)*
Association of Fish and Wildlife Agencies *(283)*
Association of Food and Drug Officials *(283)*
Association of Former Agents of the U.S. Secret Service *(284)*
Association of Former Intelligence Officers *(284)*
Association of Former OSI Special Agents *(284)*
Association of Government Accountants *(286)*

Association of Labor Relations Agencies *(290)*
Association of Major City and County Building Officials *(292)*
Association of Maternal and Child Health Programs (AMCHP) *(293)**
Association of Metropolitan Water Agencies *(294)*
Association of Military Banks of America *(294)*
Association of Military Colleges and Schools of the United States *(294)*
Association of Military Surgeons of the United States *(294)*
Association of Naval Aviation *(295)**
Association of Official Seed Analysts, Inc. *(296)*
Association of Official Seed Certifying Agencies *(296)*
Association of Old Crows *(297)*
Association of Paroling Authorities International *(297)*
Association of Procurement Technical Assistance Centers *(300)*
Association of Public Health Nurses *(304)*
Association of Public Treasurers of the United States and Canada *(304)*
APCO (Association of Public-Safety Communications Officials) International *(304)*
Association of Racing Commissioners International *(304)*
Association of Real Estate License Law Officials *(305)*
Association of State and Territorial Dental Directors *(310)*
Association of State and Territorial Health Officials *(310)*
Association of State and Territorial Public Health Nutrition Directors *(310)*
Association of State and Territorial Solid Waste Management Officials *(310)*
Association of State Correctional Administrators *(310)*
Association of the United States Army *(313)*
Association of the United States Navy, Inc. *(314)*
Association of University Technology Managers *(316)*
Blinded Veterans Association *(332)*
Business Executives for National Security *(338)**
Chief Officers of State Libraries Agencies *(352)*
Chief Petty Officers Association *(352)*
Chief Warrant and Warrant Officers Association, United States Coast Guard *(352)*
The Coalition for Government Procurement *(360)*
Coalition for Juvenile Justice *(360)**
College Savings Plans Network *(364)*
Combat Helicopter Pilots Association *(366)*
Commercial Vehicle Safety Alliance *(367)*
Commissioned Officers Association of the United States Public Health Service *(368)*
Community Action Partnership *(369)*
Conference of Minority Public Administrators *(375)*
Conference of State Bank Supervisors *(376)*
Conference of State Court Administrators *(376)**
Congressional Legislative Staff Association *(377)*
Council of Chief State School Officers *(392)*
Council of Large Public Housing Authorities *(395)*
Council of Professional Associations on Federal Statistics *(396)*
Council of State Administrators of Vocational Rehabilitators *(397)*
Council of State and Territorial Epidemiologists *(397)*
Council of State Community Development Agencies *(397)*
Council of State Governments *(397)**
Council on Governmental Ethics Laws *(399)*
Council on Governmental Relations *(400)*
Council on Licensure, Enforcement and Regulation *(400)*
Council On State Taxation *(400)*
County Executives of America *(402)*
Defense Credit Union Council *(408)*
Defense Orientation Conference Association *(408)*
Delta Phi Epsilon *(409)*
Democratic Governors Association *(410)*
Democratic Lieutenant Governors' Association (DLGA) *(410)*
Diplomatic and Consular Officers, Retired (Dacor) *(412)*
Directors of Health Promotion and Education (DHPE) *(413)*
DRI International *(416)**
Election Technology Association *(421)*
Energy Bar Association *(428)**
Enlisted Association of the National Guard of the United States *(429)*
Epsilon Sigma Phi *(432)*
Executive Women in Government *(435)*
FAA Managers Association, Inc. *(436)*
Federal Administrative Law Judges Conference *(438)*
Federal Bar Association *(438)*
Federal Criminal Investigators Association *(439)*
Federal Education Association *(439)**
Federal Facilities Council *(439)*
Federal Judges Association *(439)*

Federal Law Enforcement Officers Association *(439)*
Federal Managers Association *(439)*
Federal Network for Sustainability *(439)*
Federal Physicians Association *(439)**
Federal Probation and Pre-trial Officers Association *(440)*
Federal Water Quality Association *(440)*
Federally Employed Women (FEW) *(440)*
Federation of American Scientists *(440)**
Federation of Associations of Regulatory Boards *(441)**
Federation of Environmental Technologists, Inc. *(441)**
Federation of State Medical Boards of the United States *(442)*
Federation of Tax Administrators *(442)*
Fleet Reserve Association *(447)*
Government Finance Officers Association of the United States and Canada *(464)*
Government Finance Officers Association, Federal Liaison Center *(464)*
Government Management Information Sciences *(464)*
Governmental Research Association *(464)*
Governors' Highway Safety Association *(464)*
Groundwater Management Districts Association *(466)*
Hispanic Elected Local Officials *(475)*
Hispanic Lobbyists Association *(475)*
IFIA Americas Committee Inc. *(486)*
International Association of Assessing Officers *(516)**
International Association of Bedding and Furniture Law Officials *(516)*
International Association of Chiefs of Police *(517)*
International Association of Clerks, Recorders, Election Officials and Treasurers *(518)*
International Association of Electrical Inspectors *(520)*
International Association of Emergency Managers *(520)**
International Association of Fire Chiefs *(521)*
International Association of Industrial Accident Boards and Commissions *(523)*
International Association of Milk Control Agencies *(524)*
International Association of Official Human Rights Agencies *(525)**
International Association of Plumbing and Mechanical Officials *(526)*
International Bridge, Tunnel and Turnpike Association *(531)*
International City/County Management Association *(535)*
International Cost Estimating and Analysis Association effective *(537)*
International Fire Marshals Association *(545)*
International Institute of Municipal Clerks *(552)*
International Military Community Executives Association *(556)*
International Municipal Lawyers Association *(557)*
International Municipal Signal Association *(557)**
The International Stability Operations Association *(575)**
Interstate Council on Water Policy *(582)*
Interstate Oil and Gas Compact Commission *(583)**
Justice Research and Statistics Association *(589)*
Marine Corps Association *(604)*
Marine Corps League *(605)*
Marine Corps Reserve Association *(605)**
Military Chaplains Association of the U.S. *(616)*
Military Chaplains Association of the United States *(616)*
Military Impacted Schools Association *(616)*
Military Officers Association of America (MOAA) *(616)**
Military Operations Research Society *(616)**
Mine Safety Institute of America *(616)*
NASTD - Technology Professionals Serving State Government *(626)*
National Academy of Public Administration *(628)*
National Active and Retired Federal Employees Association *(629)*
National Affordable Housing Management Association *(629)*
National Alcohol Beverage Control Association *(631)*
National Alliance of Postal and Federal Employees *(633)*
National Alliance of Preservation Commissions *(633)*
National Alliance of State and Territorial AIDS Directors *(633)*
National American Indian Housing Council *(634)*
National Assembly of State Arts Agencies *(635)*
National Association of County Community and Economic Development *(637)*
National Association for Government Training and Development *(639)*
National Association for Health and Fitness *(639)**
National Association for Program Information and Performance Measurement *(641)*

National Association for Search and Rescue *(642)**
National Association for State Community Services Programs *(643)*
National Association for Uniformed Services *(644)*
National Association of Agricultural Fair Agencies *(646)*
National Association of Agriculture Employees *(646)*
National Association of Assistant United States Attorneys *(647)*
National Association of Attorneys General *(647)*
National Association of Barber Boards of America *(648)*
National Association of Blacks In Government *(649)*
National Association of Chiefs of Police *(653)*
National Association of Clean Water Agencies *(654)*
National Association of Conservation Districts *(657)*
National Association of Consumer Credit Administrators *(657)*
National Association of Counties *(659)*
National Association of County Administrators *(659)*
National Association of County Aging Programs *(659)*
National Association of County Agricultural Agents *(659)**
National Association of County and City Health Officials *(659)*
National Association of County Civil Attorneys *(659)*
National Association of County Engineers *(660)*
National Association of County Health Facility Administrators *(660)*
National Association of County Human Services Administrators *(660)*
National Association of County Information Officers *(660)**
National Association of County Information Technology Administrators *(660)*
National Association of County Intergovernmental Relations Officials *(660)*
National Association of County Park and Recreation Officials *(660)*
National Association of County Recorders, Election Officials and Clerks *(660)**
National Association of County Surveyors *(660)*
The National Association of Crime Victim Compensation Boards *(661)*
National Association of Development Companies *(662)*
National Association of Development Organizations *(662)*
National Association of Farm Service Agency County Office Employees *(667)*
National Association of Farmers Market Nutrition Programs *(667)*
National Association of Federal Credit Unions *(667)*
National Association of Federal Education Program Administrators *(667)*
National Association of Federal Veterinarians *(668)*
National Association of Federally Impacted Schools *(668)*
National Association of Flood and Stormwater Management Agencies *(668)*
National Association of Government Archives and Records Administrators *(669)**
National Association of Government Communicators *(670)*
National Association of Government Defined Contribution Administrators *(670)*
National Association of Government Employees *(670)*
National Association of Government Guaranteed Lenders (NAGGL) *(670)*
National Association of Government Labor Officials *(670)*
National Association of Hispanic Federal Executives *(672)*
National Association of Housing and Redevelopment Officials *(673)*
National Association of Housing Information Managers *(673)*
National Association of Insurance Commissioners *(676)*
National Association of Jewish Legislators *(677)*
National Association of Local Boards of Health *(678)*
National Association of Local Government Auditors *(678)*
National Association of Local Housing Finance Agencies *(678)*
National Association of Manufacturers *(679)*
National Association of Media and Technology Centers *(680)**
National Association of Medicaid Directors *(680)*
National Association of Noise Control Officials *(682)*
National Association of Ordnance and Explosive Waste Contractors *(682)*
National Association of Passports and Visa Services *(683)*
National Association of Postal Supervisors *(685)*
National Association of Postmasters of the United States *(685)*

National Association of Public Child Welfare Administrators **(688)**
National Association of Pupil Services Administrators **(689)**
National Association of Regional Councils **(690)**
National Association of Regulatory Utility Commissioners **(691)***
National Association of Resource Conservation and Development Councils **(691)**
National Association of Secretaries of State **(695)**
National Association of State Administrators and Supervisors of Private Schools **(697)**
National Association of State Agencies for Surplus Property **(697)**
National Association of State Alcohol and Drug Abuse Directors (NASADAD) **(697)**
National Association of State Archaeologists **(697)**
National Association of State Auditors, Comptrollers and Treasurers **(698)**
National Association of State Aviation Officials **(698)**
National Association of State Boards of Accountancy **(698)**
National Association of State Boards of Education **(698)**
National Association of State Boating Law Administrators **(698)**
National Association of State Budget Officers **(698)**
National Association of State Charity Officials **(699)**
National Association of State Chief Administrators **(699)**
National Association of State Chief Information Officers **(699)***
National Association of State Controlled Substances Authorities **(699)**
National Association of State Credit Union Supervisors **(699)**
National Association of State Departments of Agriculture **(699)**
National Association of State Directors of Career Technical Education Consortium **(699)**
National Association of State Directors of Developmental Disabilities Services, Inc. **(700)**
National Association of State Directors of Special Education **(700)***
National Association of State Directors of Teacher Education and Certification **(700)**
National Association of State Directors of Veterans Affairs **(700)**
National Association of State Election Directors **(700)**
National Association of State Energy Officials **(700)**
National Association of State Facilities Administrators **(701)**
National Association of State Fire Marshals **(701)**
National Association of State Foresters **(701)**
National Association of State Head Injury Administrators **(701)**
National Association of State Land Reclamationists **(701)**
National Association of State Mental Health Program Directors **(701)**
National Association of State Outdoor Recreation Liaison Officers **(701)**
National Association of State Park Directors **(702)**
National Association of State Personnel Executives **(702)***
National Association of State Procurement Officials **(702)***
National Association of State Retirement Administrators **(702)**
National Association of State Treasurers **(702)**
National Association of State Utility Consumer Advocates (NASUCA) **(702)**
National Association of State Workforce Agencies **(703)**
National Association of States United For Aging and Disabilities **(703)**
National Association of Towns and Townships (NATAT) **(706)**
National Association of Unclaimed Property Administrators **(707)**
National Association of Veterans Affairs Physicians and Dentists **(708)**
National Association of Veterans Research and Education Foundations **(708)***
National Black Caucus of Local Elected Officials **(714)**
National Black Caucus of State Legislators **(714)**
National Board of Boiler and Pressure Vessel Inspectors **(715)**
National Border Patrol Council **(716)**
National Center for Simulation **(719)**
National Center for State Courts **(720)**
National Chief Petty Officers' Association **(721)**
National Child Support Enforcement Association **(721)**
National Civic League **(722)**
National Classification Management Society **(722)**
National Community Development Association **(725)**
National Conference of Bankruptcy Judges **(726)**

National Conference of Black Mayors **(726)**
National Conference of Commissioners on Uniform State Laws **(727)**
National Conference of Federal Trial Judges **(727)**
National Conference of Insurance Legislators **(727)**
National Conference of Local Environmental Health Administrators **(727)**
National Conference of State Fleet Administrators **(728)**
National Conference of State Historic Preservation Officers **(728)**
National Conference of State Legislatures **(728)***
National Conference of State Liquor Administrators **(728)**
National Conference of State Social Security Administrators **(728)**
National Conference on Public Employee Retirement Systems **(729)**
National Conference on Weights and Measures **(729)**
National Constables Association **(729)**
National Council of Legislators from Gaming States **(735)**
National Council of Social Security Management Associations **(736)**
National Council of State Agencies for the Blind **(736)**
National Council of State Directors of Community Colleges **(736)**
National Council of State Housing Agencies **(736)**
National Council of State Supervisors for Languages **(736)**
National Council of State Tourism Directors **(736)**
National Counter Intelligence Corps Association **(740)**
National Criminal Justice Association **(740)**
National Defense Industrial Association **(742)**
National Defense Transportation Association **(742)**
National District Attorneys Association **(743)***
National Emergency Management Association **(745)**
National Federation of Community Development of Credit Unions **(748)**
National Federation of Federal Employees **(748)**
National Federation of Federal Employees, Federal Dist. 1, IAMAW, AFL-CIO **(748)**
National Federation of Municipal Analysts **(749)**
National Federation of Republican Women **(750)**
National Forum for Black Public Administrators **(752)**
National Foundation for Women Legislators **(753)**
National Government Publishing Association **(755)**
National Governors Association **(755)**
National Grants Management Association **(756)**
National Guard Association of the U.S. **(757)**
National Guard Executive Directors Association **(757)**
National Institute of Governmental Purchasing **(765)**
National League of Cities **(768)***
National League of Postmasters of the United States **(768)**
National Lieutenant Governors Association **(769)***
National Military Family Association, Inc. **(772)**
National Military Intelligence Association **(772)***
National Naval Officers Association **(774)**
National Organization of State Offices of Rural Health **(778)**
National Plant Board **(781)**
National Public Employer Labor Relations Association **(783)***
National School Boards Association **(789)**
National Society of Compliance Professionals **(793)**
National Training and Simulation Association **(801)***
National Treasury Employees Union **(801)***
National Weather Service Employees Organization **(804)**
National WIC Association **(805)**
Naval Enlisted Reserve Association **(807)**
Navy League of the United States **(807)**
Non Commissioned Officers Association (NCOA) **(811)***
North American Agricultural Marketing Officials **(812)**
North American Association of State and Provincial Lotteries **(813)**
North American Gaming Regulators Association **(817)***
North American Insulation Manufacturers Association **(817)**
North American Securities Administrators Association (NASAA) **(820)**
Nurses Organization of Veterans Affairs **(825)**
Organization of Professional Employees of the U.S. Department of Agriculture (OPEDA) **(832)**
Organization of Wildlife Planners **(832)**
Pakistan American Business Association **(837)**
Professional Managers Association **(863)**
Professional Services Council **(865)**
Public Agency Risk Managers Association **(869)**
Public Employees Roundtable **(869)***
Public Housing Authorities Directors Association **(869)**
Public Lands Council **(869)**

Public Risk Management Association **(870)**
Quarters Furniture Manufacturers Association **(872)***
Republican Governors Association **(881)**
Reserve Officers Association of the U.S. **(882)**
The Retired Enlisted Association **(885)**
Senior Army Reserve Commanders Association **(897)**
Senior Executives Association **(897)**
Serbian-American Chamber of Commerce **(897)**
Society for History in the Federal Government **(911)**
Society for Military History **(915)***
Society of Air Force Clinical Surgeons **(928)***
Society of Air Force Physician Assistants **(928)**
Society of American Military Engineers **(929)**
Society of Army Physician Assistants **(930)**
Society of Federal Labor and Employee Relations Professionals **(936)**
Society of Former Special Agents of the Federal Bureau of Investigation **(937)**
Society of Government Economists **(937)**
Society of Government Meeting Professionals **(938)**
Society of Government Service Urologists **(938)**
Society of Government Travel Professionals **(938)***
Society of Medical Consultants to the Armed Forces **(941)**
Society of Military Orthopaedic Surgeons **(941)**
Society of Military Otolaryngologists - Head and Neck Surgeons **(941)**
Society of Military Widows **(941)**
Society of United States Air Force Flight Surgeons **(949)**
State Debt Management Network **(961)**
State Government Affairs Council **(961)**
State Guard Association of the United States **(961)**
State Higher Education Executive Officers **(961)**
State Risk and Insurance Management Association **(961)**
States Organization for Boating Access **(962)***
SWANA - Solid Waste Association of North America **(967)**
Uniformed Services Academy of Family Physicians **(984)***
United States Air Force Medical Service Corps Association **(989)**
United States Animal Health Association **(989)**
United States Army Warrant Officers Association **(990)**
United States Association of Former Members of Congress **(990)**
United States Coast Guard Chief Petty Officers Association **(992)**
United States Conference of Mayors **(992)**
Urban and Regional Information Systems Association **(1003)***
US Navy Veterans Association **(1004)**
UWC - Strategic Services on Unemployment and Workers' Compensation **(1007)**
Voluntary Protection Programs Participants' Association, Inc. **(1011)**
Women in Government **(1021)**
Women in Government Relations, Inc. **(1021)**
Women in Municipal Government **(1022)**
World Affairs Councils of America **(1025)**

GOVERNMENTS (LOCAL/STATE/FEDERAL/FOREIGN)

AASHTO: Transportation Center of Excellence **(2)**
American Federation of State, County and Municipal Employees **(120)**
County Counsels' Association of California **(401)**
County Executives of America **(402)**
Enlisted Association of the National Guard of the United States **(429)**
Federal Physicians Association **(439)***
International Association of Clerks, Recorders, Election Officials and Treasurers **(518)**
Intertribal Monitoring Association on Indian Trust Funds **(583)**
National Association of Black County Officials **(649)**
National Association of Counties **(659)**
National Association of County Administrators **(659)**
National Association of County Aging Programs **(659)**
National Association of County Agricultural Agents **(659)***
National Association of County and City Health Officials **(659)**
National Association of County Civil Attorneys **(659)**
National Association of County Engineers **(660)**
National Association of County Information Officers **(660)***
National Association of County Intergovernmental Relations Officials **(660)**
National Association of County Park and Recreation Officials **(660)**
National Association of County Recorders, Election Officials and Clerks **(660)***
National Association of Passports and Visa Services **(683)**
National Association of State Technology Directors **(702)**
National Council of State Housing Agencies **(736)**

National Organization of State Offices of Rural Health *(778)*

HANDWRITING

American College of Forensic Examiners Institute *(96)*
American Handwriting Analysis Foundation *(128)*
Association for the Calligraphic Arts *(259)*
Council of Graphological Societies *(394)*
National Association of Document Examiners *(663)*
National Society for Graphology *(792)*

HEATING AND AIR CONDITIONING

Air Conditioning Contractors of America *(18)*
Air Conditioning, Heating and Refrigeration Institute (AHRI) *(18)*
Air Diffusion Council *(18)*
Air Distribution Institute *(18)*
Air Movement and Control Association International *(19)*
American Boiler Manufacturers Association *(84)*
American Society of Heating, Refrigerating and Air Conditioning Engineers (ASHRAE) *(199)**
American Solar Energy Society *(211)*
American Supply Association *(214)**
Associated Air Balance Council *(234)*
Associated Specialty Contractors *(237)*
Association of Home Appliance Manufacturers *(287)*
Association of Independent Manufacturers'/ Representatives, Inc. *(288)*
Cooling Technology Institute *(384)*
Council of Industrial Boiler Owners (CIBO) *(394)*
Cryogenic Society of America *(405)*
The Evaporative Cooling Institute *(434)*
Frozen Potato Products Institute *(454)*
Hearth, Patio and Barbecue Association *(472)*
Heat Exchange Institute *(472)*
Heating, Airconditioning and Refrigeration Distributors International *(473)*
Industrial Heating Equipment Association *(493)*
International Association for Cold Storage Construction *(511)*
International Association of Heat and Frost Insulators and Asbestos Workers *(522)*
International Association of Refrigerated Warehouses *(527)*
International District Energy Association *(540)**
International Ground Source Heat Pump Association *(549)*
International Institute of Ammonia Refrigeration *(551)*
International Kitchen Exhaust Cleaning Association *(553)*
The Masonry Heater Association of North America *(607)**
Mechanical Service Contractors of America *(610)**
Mobile Air Conditioning Society Worldwide *(617)**
NADCA: The HVAC Inspection, Maintenance and Restoration Association *(623)*
National Air Filtration Association *(630)*
National Association of Power Engineers *(685)*
National Electrical Contractors Association *(744)*
National Electrical Manufacturers Association *(744)*
National Frozen Pizza Institute *(754)*
OESP - National Association of Oil and Energy Service Professionals *(826)*
Partnership for Air-Conditioning, Heating Refrigeration Accreditation *(839)*
Plumbing-Heating-Cooling Contractors - National Association *(851)*
Pressure Vessel Manufacturers Association *(857)**
Radiant Panel Association *(872)*
Refrigerating Engineers and Technicians Association *(878)*
Refrigeration Service Engineers Society *(878)*
Sheet Metal and Air Conditioning Contractors' National Association *(898)*
Solar Energy Industries Association (SEIA) *(952)*
Sustainable Buildings Industry Council *(967)*

HISTORY/HISTORIC PRESERVATION

Academy of Accounting Historians *(3)*
Academy of Certified Archivists *(4)*
Agricultural History Society *(16)*
American Academy of Research Historians of Medieval Spain *(41)*
American Academy of the History of Dentistry *(42)*
American Antiquarian Society *(45)**
American Association for State and Local History *(51)**
American Association for the History of Medicine *(52)*
American Association for the History of Nursing *(52)*
American Association for the Study of Hungarian History *(52)*
American Association of Museums *(65)**
American Catholic Historical Association *(88)*
American College of Health Care Administrators *(96)**
American Conference for Irish Studies *(106)*

American Council on Education *(110)**
American Cultural Resources Association (ACRA) *(112)*
American Folklore Society *(122)*
American Historical Association *(131)**
American Hungarian Educators Association *(134)*
American Institute for Conservation of Historic and Artistic Works *(136)**
American Institute for Patristic and Byzantine Studies *(136)*
American Institute of Bangladesh Studies *(137)*
American Institute of the History of Pharmacy *(141)*
The American Jewish Historical Society *(143)*
American Journalism Historians Association *(143)**
American Men's Studies Association *(150)*
American Musicological Society *(154)*
American Numismatic Society *(156)*
American Oriental Society *(158)**
American Printing History Association *(167)*
American Society for Environmental History *(184)*
American Society for Ethnohistory *(184)**
American Society for Legal History *(186)**
American Society of Papyrologists *(205)*
American Studies Association *(214)**
Archaeological Institute of America *(227)*
Archivists and Librarians in the History of the Health Sciences *(228)*
Association for Asian Studies *(239)**
Association for Documentary Editing *(245)*
Association for Living History, Farm and Agricultural Museums *(251)*
Association for Spanish and Portuguese Studies *(256)*
Association for Textual Scholarship in Art History *(257)*
Association for the Bibliography of History *(259)*
Association for the Study of African American Life and History *(259)*
Association for the Study of Nationalities *(259)*
Association of Academic Museums & Galleries *(263)**
Association of African American Museums *(263)*
Association of Ancient Historians *(267)*
Association of Art Museum Directors *(267)*
Association of Catholic Diocesan Archivists *(271)*
Association of Children's Museums *(272)*
Association of Moving Image Archivists *(295)*
Association of Personal Historians *(299)**
Association of Railway Museums *(305)*
Association of Science Museum Directors *(307)**
Association of Science-Technology Centers *(307)*
Business History Conference *(339)*
Caribbean Studies Association *(343)*
Charles Homer Haskins Society *(351)*
Cheiron: The International Society for the History of Behavioral and Social Sciences *(351)*
Committee on History in the Classroom *(368)*
Committee on Lesbian and Gay History *(368)*
Conference for the Study of Political Thought *(374)*
Conference of Historical Journals *(375)*
Conference on Asian History *(376)**
Conference on Faith and History *(376)*
Conference on Latin American History *(377)*
Conservation and Preservation Charities of America *(377)**
Coordinating Council for Women in History *(384)*
Costume Society of America *(387)**
Council for European Studies *(390)**
Council for Museum Anthropology *(390)*
Council of American Jewish Museums *(391)*
Council of American Maritime Museums *(391)**
Council of Archives and Research Libraries in Jewish Studies *(392)*
Czechoslovak Studies Association *(406)**
Economic History Association *(418)**
Federation of State Humanities Councils *(442)*
Forest History Society *(451)*
Group for the Use of Psychology in History *(466)*
Historians Film Committee/Film & History *(476)*
Historians of American Communism *(476)**
Historians of Netherlandish Art *(476)*
History of Earth Sciences Society *(476)*
History of Economics Society *(476)**
The History of Education Society *(477)*
History of Science Society *(477)*
Immigration and Ethnic History Society *(487)*
International Association of Art Critics *(516)*
International Museum Theatre Alliance *(557)*
International Psychohistorical Association *(562)*
International Sports Heritage Association *(575)**
Italian American Studies Association *(586)*
Latin American Studies Association *(594)**
Medieval Academy of America *(612)*
Middle East Studies Association of North America *(615)**
Modern Greek Studies Association *(618)**
Museum Education Roundtable *(621)*
Museum Store Association *(621)*
Museum Trustee Association *(621)**
National Alliance of Preservation Commissions *(633)*

National Association for Armenian Studies and Research *(636)*
National Association for Ethnic Studies *(638)*
National Association for Interpretation *(640)*
National Association of Government Archives and Records Administrators *(669)**
National Association of Tribal Historic Preservation Officers *(707)*
National Conference of State Historic Preservation Officers *(728)*
National Council for History Education *(732)*
National Council on Public History *(739)**
National Genealogical Society *(754)*
National Parks Conservation Association *(779)*
Natural Science Collections Alliance *(807)*
North American Conference on British Studies *(815)*
North American Society for Sport History *(821)*
Oral History Association *(830)*
Organization of American Historians *(832)*
Paleontological Research Institution *(837)*
Phi Alpha Theta *(845)*
Public Works Historical Society *(870)*
The Renaissance Society of America *(881)*
Romanian Studies Association of America *(888)*
Social Science History Association *(902)*
Society for Ancient Greek Philosophy *(904)*
Society for French Historical Studies *(909)*
Society for German-American Studies *(910)*
Society for Historians of American Foreign Relations *(910)*
Society for Historians of the Early American Republic *(911)*
Society for Historians of the Gilded Age and Progressive Era *(911)*
Society for Historical Archaeology *(911)*
Society for History Education *(911)*
Society for History in the Federal Government *(911)*
Society for Industrial Archeology *(913)*
Society for Italian Historical Studies *(914)*
Society for Military History *(915)**
Society for Romanian Studies *(921)*
Society for the History of Authorship, Reading and Publishing *(923)*
Society for the History of Discoveries *(923)*
Society for the History of Technology *(923)**
Society of American Historians *(929)*
Society of Architectural Historians *(930)*
Society of Armenian Studies *(930)*
Society of Dance History Scholars *(934)*
Tourist Railway Association Inc. *(976)*
Turkish Studies Association *(982)*
Urban History Association *(1004)*
Victorian Society in America *(1009)*
Visitor Studies Association *(1010)*
Western History Association *(1015)*
Western Music Association *(1016)*
World History Association *(1026)*
World War Two Studies Association *(1028)*

HORTICULTURE AND LANDSCAPING

All-America Rose Selections *(22)**
American Cultural Resources Association (ACRA) *(112)*
American Herbalists Guild *(131)**
American Horticultural Society *(133)*
American Horticultural Therapy Association *(133)*
American Institute of Floral Designers *(138)*
American Mushroom Institute *(153)*
American Nursery and Landscape Association *(156)**
American Pomological Society *(167)*
American Public Gardens Association *(170)**
American Seed Trade Association *(178)*
American Society for Horticultural Science *(185)*
American Society of Consulting Arborists *(196)*
American Society of Landscape Architects *(201)*
American Society of Plant Biologists *(207)*
American Society of Plant Taxonomists *(207)**
Association for Hose and Accessories Distribution *(248)*
Association of Professional Landscape Designers *(301)**
Association of Specialty Cut Flower Growers *(309)*
The Botanical Society of America *(333)*
The Council of Landscape Architectural Registration Boards *(395)*
Council on Botanical and Horticultural Libraries *(399)**
Forest Landowners Association *(451)*
Garden Centers of America *(456)*
Garden Writers Association *(456)**
Holiday and Decorative Association *(477)*
Independent Turf and Ornamental Distributors Association *(492)*
International Cut Flower Growers Association *(539)*
International Erosion Control Association *(543)**
International Fruit Tree Association *(547)*
International Plant Propagators Society *(560)*
International Society of Arboriculture *(571)*
International Turfgrass Society *(579)*

International Waterlily and Water Gardening Society *(580)**

Lawn and Garden Dealers' Association *(594)*

The Lawn Institute *(594)*

Master Pools Guild, Inc. *(608)**

Mulch and Soil Council *(621)*

National Association of Plant Patent Owners *(685)*

National Cannabis Industry Association *(717)*

National Council of Commercial Plant Breeders *(734)*

National Garden Clubs *(754)*

The National Greenhouse Manufacturers Association *(756)*

National Peach Council *(780)*

National Plant Board *(781)*

National Roadside Vegetation Management Association *(787)*

National Turfgrass Federation *(802)*

North American Flowerbulb Wholesalers Association *(816)*

North American Horticultural Supply Association *(817)*

Nursery and Landscape Association Executives of North America *(825)*

Perennial Plant Association *(841)*

Plant Growth Regulation Society of America *(849)*

Professional Grounds Management Society *(862)*

Professional Landcare Network *(863)*

Progressive Gardening Trade Association *(866)*

Retail Florist Association *(884)*

Society of American Florists *(928)*

Society of Municipal Arborists *(942)*

Soil and Plant Analysis Council *(951)*

Tree Care Industry Association *(980)*

Turf Equipment Technicians Association *(982)*

Turfgrass Producers International *(982)*

Utility Arborist Association *(1006)*

Wholesale Florist and Florist Supplier Association *(1016)*

HOUSING

AFL-CIO Housing Investment Trust *(15)*

American Alliance of Home Modification Professionals (AAHMP) *(44)*

American Association of Home Inspectors *(62)*

American Association of Residential Mortgage Regulators *(72)*

American Seniors Housing Association *(178)*

American Society of Home Inspectors *(200)*

Assisted Living Federation of America *(234)*

Consumer Mortgage Coalition *(381)*

Corporate Housing Providers Association *(386)**

Council for Affordable and Rural Housing *(388)*

Council of Large Public Housing Authorities *(395)*

Home Builders Association *(478)*

Housing Partnership Network *(479)*

Institute for Responsible Housing Preservation *(497)*

Manufactured Housing Association for Regulatory Reform *(602)*

Manufactured Housing Institute *(602)*

Manuscript Society *(604)*

National Affordable Housing Management Association *(629)*

National American Indian Housing Council *(634)*

National Apartment Association *(634)*

National Association of County Community and Economic Development *(637)*

National Association of Affordable Housing Lenders *(646)*

National Association of Home Builders Research Center *(673)*

National Association of Housing and Redevelopment Officials *(673)*

National Association of Housing Cooperatives *(673)*

National Association of Independent Housing Professionals *(674)*

National Association of Local Housing Finance Agencies *(678)*

National Black Caucus of State Legislators *(714)*

National Council of State Housing Agencies *(736)*

National Council of the Multifamily Housing Industry *(737)*

National Housing and Rehabilitation Association *(760)**

National Housing Conference *(761)**

National Leased Housing Association *(769)*

National Multi-Housing Council *(774)*

North American Students of Cooperation *(822)**

Public Housing Authorities Directors Association *(869)*

Regional Plan Association *(879)*

HYPNOSIS

American Academy of Medical Hypnoanalysts *(36)*

American Association of Professional Hypnotherapists *(71)*

American Council of Hypnotist Examiners *(109)*

American Guild of Hypnotherapists *(127)*

American Hypnosis Association *(134)*

American Society of Clinical Hypnosis *(194)*

Coalition of Visionary Resources *(361)*

National Board for Certified Clinical Hypnotherapists *(715)*

Society for Clinical and Experimental Hypnosis *(906)*

IMMIGRATION

American Council on International Personnel *(110)*

American Hellenic Educational Progressive Association (AHEPA) *(130)*

American Immigration Lawyers Association *(134)**

National Border Patrol Council *(716)*

National Council of Agricultural Employers *(733)*

National Immigration Project of the National Lawyers Guild *(761)*

INDUSTRIAL RELATIONS

Academy of Rail Labor Attorneys *(8)*

Actors' Equity Association *(11)*

AFL-CIO (American Federation of Labor and Congress of Industrial Organizations) *(14)*

AFL-CIO - Building and Construction Trades Department *(15)*

AFL-CIO - Maritime Trades Department *(15)*

AFL-CIO Housing Investment Trust *(15)*

AFL-CIO Working for America Institute *(15)*

AFT - Public Employees *(15)*

AFT Healthcare *(15)*

Air Line Pilots Association International *(19)*

Aircraft Mechanics Fraternal Association *(20)*

Airline Industrial Relations Conference *(20)*

Allied Pilots Association *(26)*

Amalgamated Transit Union *(28)*

American Association of Classified School Employees *(56)*

American Association of Independent Claims Professionals *(63)*

American Association of University Professors *(75)**

American Congress of Community Supports and Employment Services *(107)*

American Federation of Government Employees *(119)*

American Federation of Labor & Congress of Industrial Organizations *(119)*

American Federation of Musicians *(119)*

American Federation of Musicians and Employers Pension Fund *(119)*

American Federation of School Administrators *(120)*

American Federation of State, County and Municipal Employees *(120)*

American Federation of Teachers (AFL-CIO) *(120)*

American Foreign Service Association *(122)*

American Guild of Musical Artists *(127)*

American Guild of Variety Artists *(128)*

American Maritime Congress *(147)*

American Maritime Officers *(147)*

American Maritime Officers Plans *(147)*

American Military Retirees Association *(152)*

American Military Society *(152)*

American Musicians Union *(154)*

American Postal Workers Union *(167)**

American Rights at Work *(175)**

American Train Dispatchers Association *(217)*

Art Directors Guild/Scenic, Title and Graphic Artists *(230)*

Asian Pacific American Labor Alliance, AFL-CIO *(232)*

Associated Actors and Artistes of America *(234)*

Associated Builders and Contractors *(235)*

Associated Locksmiths of America *(236)*

Association of American Railroads *(266)**

Association of Civilian Technicians *(273)**

Association of Farmworker Opportunity Programs *(282)*

Association of Flight Attendants - CWA *(283)*

Association of Labor Relations Agencies *(290)*

Association of Professional Flight Attendants *(301)*

Association of Theatrical Press Agents and Managers *(314)*

Atlantic Independent Union *(319)*

Bakery, Confectionery, Tobacco Workers and Grain Millers International Union *(325)*

Brotherhood of Locomotive Engineers and Trainmen *(336)*

Brotherhood of Maintenance of Way Employees Division *(336)*

Brotherhood of Railroad Signalmen *(336)**

Brotherhood Railway Carmen/TCU *(336)*

Building Trades Association *(338)*

Christian Labor Association of the United States of America *(355)*

Coalition of Black Trade Unionists *(360)*

Coalition of Labor Union Women *(361)*

Committee of Interns and Residents/ SEIU *(368)*

Communications Workers of America *(369)*

Congress of Independent Unions *(377)*

Council for Employment Law Equity (CELE) *(389)*

Deep Sea Fishermen's Union *(408)*

Democratic Attorneys General Association *(410)*

Department for Professional Employees - AFL-CIO *(410)*

Direct Care Alliance *(412)*

Directors Guild of America *(413)*

Dramatists Guild of America *(416)*

Driver Employer Council of America *(416)*

Employee Benefit Research Institute *(426)*

The ERISA Industry Committee (ERIC) *(433)*

Farm Labor Organizing Committee *(437)*

Federal Education Association *(439)**

Federation of Modern Painters and Sculptors *(442)*

Forest Products Industry National Labor-Management Committee *(451)*

Freelancers Union *(453)*

Glass, Molders, Pottery, Plastics and Allied Workers International Union *(461)*

Graphic Artists Guild *(465)*

Graphic Communications Conference of the International Brotherhood of Teamsters *(465)*

Guild of Italian American Actors *(467)*

Hollywood Radio & Television Society *(477)*

HR Policy Association *(480)*

Independent Pilots Association *(491)*

Indian Educators Federation *(492)*

Industrial Foundation of America *(493)*

Inter-National Association of Business Industry & Rehabilitation *(506)*

International Alliance of Theatrical Stage Employees, Moving Picture Technicians, Artists and Allied Crafts of the U.S., Its Territories and Canada *(510)*

International Allied Printing Trades Association *(510)*

International Association of Bridge, Structural, Ornamental and Reinforcing Iron Workers *(517)*

International Association of Fire Fighters *(521)*

International Association of Heat and Frost Insulators and Asbestos Workers *(522)*

International Association of Machinists and Aerospace Workers *(524)*

International Association of Tool Craftsmen *(528)*

International Brotherhood of Boilermakers, Iron Shipbuilders, Blacksmiths, Forgers and Helpers *(531)*

International Brotherhood of Electrical Workers *(531)*

International Brotherhood of Electrical Workers #98 *(531)*

International Brotherhood of Police Officers *(532)*

International Brotherhood of Teamsters *(532)*

International Brotherhood of Teamsters - Airline Division *(532)*

International Chemical Workers Union Council/ UFCW *(534)*

International Council of Employers of Bricklayers and Allied Craftworkers *(538)*

International Federation of Professional and Technical Engineers *(544)*

International Guards Union of America *(549)*

International Guild of Symphony, Opera and Ballet Musicians *(549)*

International Labor Communications Association *(553)*

International Labor Rights Forum *(553)*

International Longshore and Warehouse Union *(555)*

International Longshoremen's Association, AFL-CIO *(555)*

International Masonry Institute *(556)*

International Plate Printers, Die Stampers and Engravers Union of North America *(560)*

International Union of Bricklayers and Allied Craftworkers *(579)**

International Union of Electronic, Electrical, Salaried, Machine, and Furniture Workers-CWA *(579)*

International Union of Elevator Constructors *(579)*

International Union of Journeymen and Allied Trades *(579)*

International Union of Operating Engineers *(579)*

International Union of Painters and Allied Trades *(579)*

International Union of Police Associations, AFL-CIO *(579)*

Labor and Employment Relations Association *(592)**

Labor Council for Latin American Advancement (LCLAA) *(592)*

Laborers International Union of North America *(592)*

Major League Baseball Players Association *(601)*

Marine Engineers Beneficial Association *(605)*

Mason Contractors Association of America *(607)*

National Active and Retired Federal Employees Association *(629)*

National Air Traffic Controllers Association *(630)*

National Alliance of Postal and Federal Employees *(633)*

National Association for Uniformed Services *(644)*

National Association of Agriculture Employees *(646)*

National Association of Broadcast Employees and Technicians-Communications Workers of America, AFL-CIO (NABET-CWA) *(650)*

National Association of Farm Service Agency County Office Employees *(667)*

National Association of Government Employees *(670)*

National Association of Government Labor Officials **(670)**
National Association of Letter Carriers **(678)**
National Association of Postal Supervisors **(685)**
National Association of Postmasters of the United States **(685)**
National Association of Workforce Boards (NAWB) **(710)**
National Basketball Players Association **(713)**
National Border Patrol Council **(716)**
National Coordinating Committee for Multiemployer Plans **(730)**
National Council of Agricultural Employers **(733)**
National Education Association **(744)**
National Farmers Union (Farmers Educational & Co-operative Union of America) **(747)**
National Federation of Federal Employees **(748)**
National Federation of Federal Employees, Federal Dist. 1, IAMAW, AFL-CIO **(748)**
National Football League Players Association **(752)**
National Fraternal Order of Police **(753)**
National Industrial Council - Employer Association Group **(763)**
National Industrial Council - State Associations Group **(763)**
National Labor Relations Board Professional Association **(768)**
National League of Postmasters of the United States **(768)**
National Nurses United **(775)**
National Organization of Industrial Trade Unions **(777)**
National Organization of Legal Services Workers **(777)**
National Postal Mail Handlers Union **(781)***
National Railway Labor Conference **(784)**
National Rural Letter Carriers' Association **(788)***
National Treasury Employees Union **(801)***
National Weather Service Employees Organization **(804)**
National Writers Union **(806)**
The Newspaper Guild **(810)**
North American Technician Excellence **(823)**
Office and Professional Employees International Union (OPEIU) **(826)**
Operative Plasterers and Cement Masons International Association of the United States and Canada **(829)**
Patent and Trademark Office Society **(839)**
Patent Office Professional Association **(839)***
Pharmaceutical Industry Labor Management Association (PILMA) **(844)**
Professional Aviation Safety Specialists (AFL-CIO) **(860)**
Retail, Wholesale and Department Store Union **(885)***
Rubber and Plastics Industry Conference of the United Steelworkers of America **(888)**
Screen Actors Guild - American Federation of Television and Radio Artists **(893)**
Seafarers International Union of North America **(894)**
Service Employees International Union **(897)**
Sheet Metal and Air Conditioning Contractors' National Association **(898)**
Sheet Metal Workers' International Association **(898)**
Society for Human Resource Management **(911)**
Southwest Airlines Pilots Association **(953)**
Stage Directors and Choreographers Society **(960)**
Steamfitters Local Union 449 **(962)**
Teamsters Brewery and Soft Drink Workers Conference **(969)**
Transport Workers Union of America, AFL-CIO **(978)**
Transportation Communications International Union/IAM **(978)***
Transportation Trades Department, AFL-CIO **(979)**
U. S. Airline Pilots Association **(983)**
Union Label and Service Trades Department **(985)**
Union of American Physicians and Dentists **(985)***
UNITE-HERE **(985)**
United Association for Labor Education **(985)***
United Association of Journeymen and Apprentices of the Plumbing and Pipe Fitting Industry of the U.S. and Canada **(985)**
United Auto Workers (UAW) **(986)**
United Brotherhood of Carpenters and Joiners of America **(986)***
United Electrical Radio & Machine Workers of America **(986)***
United Farm Workers of America **(986)**
United Federation of Police & Security Officers **(987)**
United Federation of Teachers **(987)**
United Food and Commercial Workers International Union **(987)**
United Mine Workers of America **(988)***
United Motorcoach Association **(988)***
United Nations Staff Union **(988)**
United States Business and Industry Council **(991)**
United Steelworkers of America **(1001)**
United Transportation Union **(1001)**

United Union of Roofers, Waterproofers and Allied Workers **(1001)**
Utility Workers Union of America **(1007)**
Visiting Nurse Associations of America **(1010)**
Workers United **(1025)**
Workers' Injury Law and Advocacy Group **(1025)***
Writers Guild of America East **(1029)***
Writers Guild of America West **(1029)***

INSTRUMENTS

American Harp Society **(129)**
American Microscopical Society **(151)**
Analytical and Life Science Systems Association **(223)**
IEEE Instrumentation and Measurement Society **(484)**
Instrumentation Testing Association **(504)**
International Double Reed Society **(541)***
International Hearing Society **(549)**
International Horn Society **(550)**
International Society of Automation **(571)**
International Trumpet Guild **(578)**
International Tuba-Euphonium Association **(578)**
Laboratory Products Association **(592)**
Microscopy Society of America **(615)**
National Association of Professional Band Instrument Repair Technicians **(686)**
Optical Imaging Association **(829)***
SPIE - The International Society for Optical Engineering **(958)**

INSURANCE INDUSTRY

ACORD - Association for Cooperative Operations Research and Development **(11)**
Alliance of Claims Assistance Professionals **(25)**
America's Health Insurance Plans **(28)**
American Academy of Actuaries **(29)**
American Agents Alliance **(43)**
American Association of Crop Insurers **(59)***
American Association of Dental Consultants **(59)**
American Association of Independent Claims Professionals **(63)**
American Association of Insurance Management Consultants **(63)**
American Association of Insurance Services **(63)**
American Association of Managing General Agents **(64)**
American Bail Coalition **(78)**
American Bankers Insurance Association **(79)**
American Benefits Council **(80)**
American Council of Life Insurers (ACLI) **(110)***
American Financial Services Association **(121)**
American Fraternal Alliance **(124)**
American Institute for CPCU - Insurance Institute of America **(136)**
American Institute of Marine Underwriters **(139)**
American Insurance Association **(141)**
American Insurance Marketing and Sales Society **(141)**
American Land Title Association **(144)**
American Nuclear Insurers **(156)**
American Prepaid Legal Services Institute **(167)**
American Risk and Insurance Association **(175)***
American Society for Healthcare Risk Management **(185)**
American Society of Law, Medicine and Ethics **(202)**
American Society of Pension Professionals & Actuaries **(206)**
American Society of Safety Engineers **(209)**
Americas Association of Cooperative/Mutual Insurance Societies **(222)**
Appraisers Association of America **(226)***
Associated Risk Managers **(237)**
Association & Society Insurance Corporation **(237)**
Association for Advanced Life Underwriting **(238)**
The Association of Average Adjusters of the United States and Canada **(268)**
Association of Defense Trial Attorneys **(278)**
Association of Finance and Insurance Professionals **(283)**
Association of Financial Guaranty Insurers **(283)**
Association of Home Office Underwriters **(287)**
Association of Insurance Compliance Professionals **(289)**
Association of Life Insurance Counsel **(291)**
Attorneys' Liability Assurance Society Inc. **(320)**
Aviation Insurance Association **(324)**
Blue Cross Blue Shield Association **(332)**
Captive Insurance Companies Association **(342)**
Casualty Actuarial Society **(344)***
Collision Industry Electronic Commerce Association **(365)***
Committee of Annuity Insurers **(368)**
Conference of Consulting Actuaries **(375)**
Consumer Credit Industry Association **(381)**
Council of Institutional Investors **(394)**
The Council of Insurance Agents and Brokers **(394)**
Council on Employee Benefits **(399)**
CPCU Society **(402)***
Crop Insurance Research Bureau **(404)**

Delta Dental Plans Association **(409)**
Direct Marketing Insurance and Financial Services Council **(413)**
Employee Benefit Research Institute **(426)**
The ERISA Industry Committee (ERIC) **(433)**
Financial & Insurance Conference Planners **(444)**
Fraternal Field Managers Association **(453)**
GAMA International **(455)**
Gamma Iota Sigma **(456)**
Incentive Manufacturers & Representatives Alliance **(487)**
Incentive Marketing Association **(487)***
Independent Automotive Damage Appraisers Association **(488)**
Independent Insurance Agents & Brokers of America, Inc. **(490)**
Inland Marine Underwriters Association **(496)**
Institute for Business & Home Safety **(496)**
Institutional Life Markets Association **(504)**
Insurance Accounting and Systems Association **(504)**
Insurance Consumer Affairs Exchange **(505)**
Insurance Information Institute **(505)***
Insurance Institute for Highway Safety **(505)**
Insurance Loss Control Association **(505)***
Insurance Marketing Communications Association **(505)**
Insured Retirement Institute **(505)**
Inter-Industry Conference on Auto Collision Repair **(506)**
Intermediaries and Reinsurance Underwriters Association **(508)**
International Association for Insurance Law - United States Chapter **(513)**
International Association of Accident Reconstruction Specialists **(514)**
International Association of Arson Investigators **(515)**
International Association of Defense Counsel **(519)**
International Association of Industrial Accident Boards and Commissions **(523)**
International Association of Insurance Receivers **(523)**
International Claim Association **(535)**
International Foundation of Employee Benefit Plans **(547)**
International Insurance Society **(552)**
Intersure, Ltd. **(583)**
Liability Insurance Research Bureau **(596)**
Life Insurance Settlement Association **(597)**
Life Insurers Council **(597)***
Lightning Protection Institute **(598)**
LOMA **(600)**
Mass Marketing Insurance Institute **(607)**
Million Dollar Round Table **(616)***
Mortgage Insurance Companies of America **(619)**
National Association of Catastrophe Adjusters **(651)**
National Association of Certified Professional Midwives **(651)**
National Association of Dental Plans **(662)**
National Association of Disability Evaluating Professionals **(663)**
National Association of Fire Investigators **(668)**
National Association of Fraternal Insurance Counsellors **(669)**
National Association of Independent Fee Appraisers **(674)**
National Association of Independent Insurance Adjusters **(674)**
National Association of Independent Insurance Auditors and Engineers **(674)**
National Association of Independent Life Brokerage Agencies **(674)**
National Association of Insurance and Financial Advisors **(675)**
National Association Of Insurance and Financial Advisors(NAIFA) **(676)**
National Association of Insurance Commissioners **(676)**
National Association of Insurance Women (International) **(676)**
National Association of Medicaid Directors **(680)**
National Association of Mutual Insurance Companies **(681)**
National Association of Professional Insurance Agents **(687)**
National Association of Professional Surplus Lines Offices, Ltd. **(688)***
National Association of Public Insurance Adjusters **(689)**
National Association of State Farm Agents **(701)**
National Association of Subrogation Professionals **(704)**
National Association of Surety Bond Producers **(704)**
National Business Group on Health **(716)**
National Cargo Bureau **(718)**
National Committee for Quality Assurance **(724)***
National Conference of Insurance Legislators **(727)**
National Coordinating Committee for Multiemployer Plans **(730)**
National Council of Self-Insurers **(736)**

National Council on Compensation Insurance, Inc. (738)
National Crop Insurance Services (741)
National Defined Contribution Council (742)*
National Health Care Anti-Fraud Association (758)*
National Insurance Crime Bureau (766)
National Organization of Life and Health Insurance Guaranty Association (777)
National Organization of Social Security Claimants' Representatives (778)
National Risk Retention Association (787)
National Society of Insurance Premium Auditors (794)
National Structured Settlements Trade Association (797)*
National Truck and Heavy Equipment Claims Council (802)
North American Bar-Related Title Insurers (814)
Organization of Flying Adjusters (832)
Physician Insurers Association of America (847)
Professional Insurance Communicators of America (862)
Professional Insurance Marketing Association (862)
Professional Liability Agents Network (863)
Professional Liability Underwriting Society (863)
Promotion Marketing Association (866)
Property Casualty Insurers Association of America (867)
Property Loss Research Bureau (867)
Public Agency Risk Managers Association (869)
Public Risk Management Association (870)
Reinsurance Association of America (879)
Risk and Insurance Management Society, Inc. (RIMS) (886)
Self-Insurance Institute of America, Inc. (896)
Shipowners Claims Bureau, Inc. (899)
Society for Risk Analysis (920)
Society of Actuaries (927)
Society of Certified Insurance Counselors (932)
Society of Financial Service Professionals (936)
Society of Insurance Financial Management (940)
Society of Insurance Research (940)
Society of Insurance Trainers and Educators (940)
Society of Professional Benefit Administrators (945)*
Society of Risk Management Consultants (947)
State Risk and Insurance Management Association (961)
The Surety and Fidelity Association of America (966)
United Food and Commercial Workers International Union (987)
University Risk Management and Insurance Association (1003)
WIFS - Women in Insurance and Financial Services (1017)

INVENTORS
National Congress of Inventor Organizations (729)

JEWELRY & GEMS
Accredited Gemologists Association (10)
The American Gem Society (125)
American Gem Trade Association (125)
American Society of Appraisers (192)
American Watch Association (219)
American Watchmakers-Clockmakers Institute (219)
Diamond Council of America (411)
Diamond Manufacturers & Importers Association of America (411)*
Fashion Jewelry and Accessories Trade Association (438)
Gemological Institute of America (457)
Independent Time and Labor Management Association (492)
Indian Arts and Crafts Association (492)
Indian Diamond and Colorstone Association (492)
Industrial Diamond Association of America (493)
Jewelers Board of Trade (587)*
Jewelers of America (587)
Jewelers Shipping Association (587)
Jeweler's Vigilance Committee (587)
Jewelers' Security Alliance of the United States (587)
Jewelry Industry Distributors Association (587)*
Leading Jewelers Guild (594)
Manufacturing Jewelers and Suppliers of America (604)*
Metal Findings Manufacturers Association (613)
National Association of Jewelry Appraisers (677)
National Ornamental Goldfish Growers Association (778)
Silver Users Association (900)
Society of North American Goldsmiths (943)*
Women's Jewelry Association (1023)*

LAW ENFORCEMENT/SECURITY
Academy of Criminal Justice Sciences (4)*
Academy of Security Educators and Trainers (9)
Airborne Law Enforcement Association (19)
Alarm Industry Communication Committee (21)
American Academy of Forensic Sciences (34)*

American Association of Motor Vehicle Administrators (65)
American Association of Police Officers (70)
American Association of Police Polygraphists (70)
American Association of State Troopers (73)
American Bail Coalition (78)
American Biological Safety Association (81)
American Catholic Correctional Chaplains Association (88)
American College of Contingency Planners (95)*
American College of Forensic Examiners Institute (96)
American Correctional Association (108)*
American Correctional Chaplains Association (108)
American Correctional Health Services Association (108)
American Criminal Justice Association Lambda Alpha Epsilon (112)
American Driver and Traffic Safety Education Association (115)
American Federation of Police and Concerned Citizens (119)
American Foreign Service Protective Association (123)
American Forensic Association (123)
American Highway Users Alliance (131)
American Jail Association (142)*
American Jewish Correctional Chaplains Association (143)
American Judicature Society (143)
American Knife & Tool Institute (144)
American Polygraph Association (166)
American Probation and Parole Association (167)
American Securitization Forum (178)
American Society of Crime Laboratory Directors (196)
American Society of Criminology (196)*
The American Society of Forensic Odontology (198)
American Society of Mechanical Engineers (ASME) (203)
American Society of Questioned Document Examiners (208)
American Society of Safety Engineers (209)
American Traffic Safety Service Association (217)
American Wood-Protection Association (222)
ASIS International (232)
Association for the Advancement of Automotive Medicine (258)*
Association of Certified Fraud Examiners (271)
Association of Civilian Technicians (273)*
Association of Correctional Food Service Affiliates (277)
Association of Firearm and Toolmark Examiners (283)
Association of Forensic Document Examiners (284)
Association of Former Agents of the U.S. Secret Service (284)
Association of Programs for Female Offenders (303)
APCO (Association of Public-Safety Communications Officials) International (304)
Association of State Correctional Administrators (310)
Association of State Dam Safety Officials (310)
ASTM International (319)*
Automatic Fire Alarm Association (321)
Automotive Safety Council (323)
Board of Certified Safety Professionals (332)*
Building Seismic Safety Council (337)
Business Executives for National Security (338)*
Campus Safety, Health and Environmental Management Association (341)*
Central Station Alarm Association (349)
Commercial Vehicle Safety Alliance (367)
Commission on Accreditation for Law Enforcement Agencies Incorporation (367)
Communications Fraud Control Association (369)
Computer Security Institute (373)*
Consortium of Forensic Science Organizations (378)
Correctional Education Association (386)
Correctional Vendors Association (386)
Corrections, U.S.A. (386)
Council of International Investigators (395)
Council on Licensure, Enforcement and Regulation (400)
Crane Certification Association of America (403)
Defense Fire Protection Association (408)
Disaster Preparedness and Emergency Response Association (413)
Document Security Alliance (415)
Electronic Security Association (424)
Energy Security Council (428)
Espionage Research Institute International (433)
Evidence Photographers International Council (434)
FBI Agents Association (438)
Federal Criminal Investigators Association (439)
Federal Judges Association (439)
Federal Law Enforcement Officers Association (439)
Federal Probation and Pre-trial Officers Association (440)
Financial and Security Products Association (444)

Fire Suppression Systems Association (446)
Flight Safety Foundation (448)
Governors' Highway Safety Association (464)
Health Information Trust Alliance (HITRUST) (470)*
High Technology Crime Investigation Association (474)
Hispanic American Police Command Officers Association (HAPCOA) (475)
Human Factors and Ergonomics Society (480)*
IFIA Americas Committee Inc. (486)
Independent Armored Car Operators Association (488)
Information Systems Audit and Control Association (495)
Information Systems Security Association (495)
Institute of Nuclear Materials Management (502)*
Institute of Nuclear Power Operations (502)
Insurance Institute for Highway Safety (505)
International Anti-Counterfeiting Coalition (511)
International Association for Correctional and Forensic Psychology (512)
International Association for Healthcare Security and Safety (512)
International Association for Identification (513)
International Association for the Study of Organized Crime (514)
International Association of Accident Reconstruction Specialists (514)
International Association of Addictions and Offender Counselors (514)*
International Association of Airport and Seaport Police (515)
International Association of Arson Investigators (515)
International Association of Auto Theft Investigators (516)
International Association of Campus Law Enforcement Administrators (517)
International Association of Chiefs of Police (517)
International Association of Dive Rescue Specialists (519)
International Association of Electrical Inspectors (520)
International Association of Fire Chiefs (521)
International Association of Forensic Nurses (521)*
The International Association of Forensic Toxicologists (522)*
The International Association of Law Enforcement Intelligence Analysts (523)
International Association of Personal Protection Agents (526)
International Association of Professional Security Consultants (527)*
International Association of Special Investigation Units (528)
International Association of Women Police (529)
International Association of Workforce Professionals (IAWP) (529)
International Brotherhood of Correctional Officers (531)
International Brotherhood of Police Officers (532)
International Cargo Security Council (533)
International Community Corrections Association (536)
International Conference of Police Chaplains (536)
International Consumer Product Health and Safety Organization (537)
International Guards Union of America (549)
International Municipal Lawyers Association (557)
International Police Mountain Bike Association (561)*
International Safety Equipment Association (ISEA) (563)
International Security Management Association (564)
International Society of Air Safety Investigators (570)
International Society of Crime Prevention Practitioners (572)
The International Stability Operations Association (575)*
International Union of Police Associations, AFL-CIO (579)
Jewelers' Security Alliance of the United States (587)
Justice Research and Statistics Association (589)
Law Enforcement Alliance of America (594)
Lightning Protection Institute (598)
Major Cities Chiefs Association (601)
Major County Sheriffs' Association (601)
MASINT Association (607)*
Mine Safety Institute of America (616)
Motorcycle Safety Foundation (620)
Mountain Rescue Association (620)
National Alarm Association of America (631)
National Armored Car Association (635)
National Association of Assistant United States Attorneys (647)
National Association of Blacks in Criminal Justice (649)
National Association of Chiefs of Police (653)

LAW/LAW FIRMS

LESBIAN/GAY/BISEXUAL/TRANSGENDER

LIBRARIES

LOCKS

MACHINERY/EQUIPMENT

National Fluid Power Association *(751)*
National Lubricating Grease Institute *(770)*
National Office Products Alliance *(776)*
National School Supply and Equipment Association *(789)*
National Tooling and Machining Association *(800)*
NIBA - The Belting Association *(810)*
North American Equipment Dealers Association *(816)*
North American Olive Oil Association *(819)*
Outdoor Power Equipment Aftermarket Association *(835)*
Outdoor Power Equipment and Engine Service Association *(835)*
Outdoor Power Equipment Institute *(835)*
Packaging Machinery Manufacturers Institute *(836)*
Power Crane and Shovel Association *(855)*
Power Tool Institute, Inc. *(855)**
Power Transmission Distributors Association *(855)**
Power Washers of North America *(855)*
Power-Motion Technology Representatives Association *(855)*
Precision Machined Products Association *(856)*
Private Label Manufacturers Association *(858)*
Process Equipment Manufacturers' Association *(858)*
Service Dealers Association *(897)*
Snow Control Equipment Manufacturers Committee *(902)*
Society of Manufacturing Engineers *(941)*
Society of Tribologists and Lubrication Engineers *(949)*
Special Interest Group for Computer-Human Interaction *(954)**
Spring Manufacturers Institute *(960)*
Submersible Wastewater Pump Association *(965)*
Sump and Sewage Pump Manufacturers Association *(965)*
Textile Care Allied Trades Association *(972)*
Tillage & Ground Engaging Equipment Product Council *(974)*
Tooling, Manufacturing and Technologies Association *(976)*
Trencher Equipment Committee *(980)*
Trenchless Equipment Committee *(980)*
Truck and Engine Manufacturers Association *(980)*
Underground Equipment Manufacturers Council *(984)*
United Auto Workers (UAW) *(986)*
United Electrical Radio & Machine Workers of America *(986)**
United States Cutting Tool Institute *(993)**
Valve Manufacturers Association of America *(1007)*
Valve Repair Council *(1007)*
Vibration Institute *(1008)*
Water and Wastewater Equipment Manufacturers Association *(1012)**
Water Systems Council *(1013)*
Western Dredging Association *(1015)*
Wire and Cable Industry Suppliers Association *(1019)**
Wood Machinery Manufacturers of America *(1024)*
Woodworking Machinery Industry Association *(1024)*

MANAGEMENT

AABC Commissioning Group *(1)**
Academy of Management *(6)**
Academy of Marketing Science *(6)**
AFCOM *(14)*
Alliance for Nonprofit Management *(23)**
AMC Institute *(28)**
American Academy of Ambulatory Care Nursing *(30)*
American Academy of Medical Management *(36)**
American Association of Healthcare Administrative Management *(61)**
American Association of Insurance Management Consultants *(63)*
American Association of Managing General Agents *(64)*
American College of Health Plan Management *(96)*
American College of Healthcare Executives *(96)*
American College of Mental Health Administration *(98)*
American Health Information Management Association *(129)*
American Management Association *(146)**
American Society for Engineering Management *(184)*
American Society for Pain Management Nursing *(188)*
The American Society for Public Administration *(189)**
American Society of Association Executives-The Center for Association Leadership *(193)*
American Society of Farm Managers and Rural Appraisers *(197)*
Analytical Laboratory Managers Association *(223)**
APICS The Association for Operations Management *(224)**
APPAM - The Association for Public Policy Analysis and Management *(225)**

ARMA International *(228)*
The Association for Consortium Leadership *(243)*
Association for Financial Professionals, Inc. *(247)*
Association for Healthcare Resource and Materials Management *(248)**
Association for Information and Image Management International *(249)**
Association for Linen Management *(251)*
Association for Management Information in Financial Services *(251)*
Association for Medical Imaging Management *(252)**
Association for Recorded Sound Collections *(255)**
Association of AE Business Leaders *(263)*
Association of Equipment Management Professionals *(281)*
Association of Information Technology Professionals *(289)*
Association of Internal Management Consultants *(289)*
Association of International Education Administrators *(289)*
Association of Management Consulting Firms *(292)*
Association of Productivity Specialists *(300)*
Association of Professional Office Managers *(302)*
Association of Proposal Management Professionals *(303)**
Association of School Business Officials International *(306)*
Association of State and Territorial Solid Waste Management Officials *(310)*
Association of Threat Assessment Professionals *(314)**
Association of University Research Parks *(316)*
Association of Woodworking and Furnishings Suppliers *(318)*
Automotive Trade Association Executives *(324)*
Building Owners and Managers Association International *(337)**
Building Owners and Managers Institute International *(337)*
Business Forms Management Association *(339)**
Case Management Society of America *(343)**
Christian Leadership Alliance *(355)*
Christian Management Association *(356)*
Cleaning Management Institute *(357)*
Clinical Laboratory Management Association *(358)**
Club Managers Association of America *(359)*
College Athletic Business Management Association *(362)**
Communications Media Management Association *(369)*
Construction Financial Management Association *(379)*
Construction Management Association of America *(379)*
Council of American Survey Research Organizations *(392)**
Council of State Retail Associations *(397)*
Council of Supply Chain Management Professionals *(398)*
Decision Sciences Institute *(407)**
Directors Guild of America *(413)*
Disaster Recovery Contractors Association (DRCA) *(413)*
Emergency Department Practice Management Association (EDPMA) *(425)**
Employee Services Management Association *(426)*
Environmental Industry Associations *(431)*
Federal Managers Association *(439)*
Financial Management Association International *(444)*
Forest Products Industry National Labor-Management Committee *(451)*
Fraternal Field Managers Association *(453)*
Fulfillment Management Association *(454)*
GAMA International *(455)*
Golf Course Superintendents Association of America *(463)**
Groundwater Management Districts Association *(466)*
Healthcare Billing and Management Association *(470)*
Healthcare Financial Management Association *(471)*
Healthcare Information and Management Systems Society *(471)*
Hospitality Institute of Technology and Management *(479)*
Hospitality Sales and Marketing Association International *(479)**
In-Plant Printing and Mailing Association *(487)**
Independent Association of Accredited Registrars *(488)*
Independent Time and Labor Management Association *(492)*
Industrial Asset Management Council *(492)*
Institute for Operations Research and the Management Sciences *(497)*
Institute for Supply Management *(497)*
Institute Management Accountants *(498)**

Institute of Behavioral and Applied Management *(498)*
Institute of Career Certification International *(498)*
Institute of Certified Professional Managers *(498)*
Institute of Certified Records Managers *(499)*
Institute of Management Consultants USA *(501)*
Institute of Real Estate Management *(503)*
International Advertising Association *(509)*
International Association of Clerks, Recorders, Election Officials and Treasurers *(518)*
International Association of Exhibitions and Events *(520)*
International Association of Healthcare Central Service Materiel Management *(522)*
International Association of Lighting Management Companies *(524)*
International Association of Venue Managers *(528)**
International City/County Management Association *(535)*
International Council for Small Business *(538)*
International Customer Service Association *(539)**
International Facility Management Association *(543)*
International Paralegal Management Association *(559)*
International Public Management Association for Human Resources *(562)*
International Security Management Association *(564)*
International Society for Performance Improvement *(567)**
International Society of Managing and Technical Editors *(573)*
International Ticketing Association *(577)*
Laboratory Animal Management Association *(592)*
Library Leadership and Management Association *(597)*
LOMA *(600)*
Management Association for Private Photogrammetric Surveyors *(602)*
Materials Handling and Management Society *(608)*
MGMA-ACMPE *(614)**
Mineral Economics and Management Society *(617)*
NAFA Fleet Management Association *(624)*
National Academy of Public Administration *(628)*
National Affordable Housing Management Association *(629)*
National Association for Environmental Management *(638)*
National Association of Corporate Directors *(658)*
National Association of County Administrators *(659)*
National Association of County Human Services Administrators *(660)*
National Association of Credit Management *(661)*
National Association of Flood and Stormwater Management Agencies *(668)*
National Association of Foster Grandparent Program Directors *(669)*
National Association of Government Defined Contribution Administrators *(670)*
National Association of Healthcare Access Management *(671)**
National Association of Postal Supervisors *(685)*
National Association of Professional Organizers *(687)*
National Association of Real Estate Investment Managers *(690)**
National Association of Retired and Senior Volunteer Program Directors *(692)*
National Association of Scientific Materials Managers *(694)**
National Association of Service Managers *(695)*
National Association of State Administrators and Supervisors of Private Schools *(697)*
National Classification Management Society *(722)*
National Contract Management Association *(729)**
National Council of Agricultural Employers *(733)*
National Council of Social Security Management Associations *(736)*
National Grants Management Association *(756)*
National Institute of Packaging, Handling and Logistics Engineers *(765)*
National Interscholastic Athletic Administrators Association *(766)*
National Management Association *(771)*
National Petroleum Management Association *(780)*
National Property Management Association *(783)**
The National Safety Management Society *(789)*
Newspaper Association Managers *(810)*
Newspaper Purchasing Management Association *(810)*
North American Performing Arts Managers and Agents *(819)**
North American Society for Sport Management *(822)*
Nuclear Information and Records Management Association *(825)*
Object Management Group *(825)*
Paper and Plastic Representatives Management Council *(838)**
Product Development and Management Association *(858)*

Professional Association of Health Care Office Management (859)
Professional Convention Management Association (861)
Professional Grounds Management Society (862)
Professional Housing Management Association (862)*
Professional Managers Association (863)
Professional Records and Information Services Management International (864)
Professional Services Council (865)
Project Management Institute (866)*
Property Records Industry Association (867)*
Public Risk Management Association (870)
Radiology Business Management Association (874)
Real Estate Management Brokers Institute (875)
Religious Conference Management Association (880)
Restaurant Facility Management Association (884)
Snow & Ice Management Association (901)*
Society for Advancement of Management (903)*
Society for Foodservice Management (909)*
Society for Human Resource Management (911)
Society for Information Management (913)
Society for Wetland Scientists (927)
Society of Competitive Intelligence Professionals (933)
Society of Risk Management Consultants (947)
Sports Turf Managers Association (959)
State Risk and Insurance Management Association (961)
Strategic Account Management Association (963)
Technology Services Industry Association (970)
Trade Promotion Management Associates (977)
Transportation and Logistics Council (978)
Turnaround Management Association (982)
University Council for Educational Administration (1002)*
University Risk Management and Insurance Association (1003)
USA Sprinkler Fitter Business Managers Association (1005)
Veterinary Hospital Managers Association (1008)*
Wildlife Management Institute (1017)
Women in Management (1021)
WorldatWork (1028)
Young Presidents' Organization (1030)

MANUFACTURERS

Adhesive and Sealant Council (12)*
Advanced Medical Technology Association (AdvaMed) (13)
Aerospace Industries Association of America (14)
Agricultural Retailers Association (16)
AIM Global (17)*
Air Diffusion Council (18)
Air Distribution Institute (18)
Alliance of Automobile Manufacturers (24)
ALMA - The International Loudspeaker Association (26)*
Aluminum Anodizers Council (27)
The Aluminum Association, Inc. (27)*
Aluminum Extruders Council (27)
Aluminum Foil Container Manufacturers Association (27)*
American Amusement Machine Association (45)
American Apparel & Footwear Association (46)
American Architectural Manufacturers Association (46)
American Association of Automatic Door Manufacturers (54)
American Bearing Manufacturers Association (80)*
American Beverage Association (80)
American Board of Industrial Hygiene (82)*
American Boat Builders and Repairers Association (84)
American Boiler Manufacturers Association (84)
American Brush Manufacturers Association (86)
American Chemistry Council (90)
American Cleaning Institute (91)
American Coatings Association (92)
American Coke and Coal Chemicals Institute (92)
American Composites Manufacturers Association (105)
American Concrete Institute (106)
American Concrete Pavement Association (106)
American Concrete Pipe Association (106)
American Concrete Pressure Pipe Association (106)
American Custom Gunmakers Guild (112)
American Edged Products Manufacturers Association (115)
American Feed Industry Association (120)
American Fence Association (120)
American Fiber Manufacturers Association (121)
American Fire Safety Council (121)
American Fire Sprinkler Association (121)
American Flock Association (122)*
American Floorcovering Alliance (122)
American Foundry Society (123)
American Galvanizers Association (124)
American Gear Manufacturers Association (125)*

American Glovebox Society (126)
American Hardware Manufacturers Association (128)
American Herbal Products Association (130)
American Home Furnishings Alliance (132)
American Institute of Aeronautics and Astronautics (136)*
American Institute of Steel Construction (140)
American Institute of Timber Construction (141)
American Iron and Steel Institute (142)
American Ladder Institute (144)*
American Lighting Association (145)*
American Measuring Tool Manufacturers Association (148)*
American Mold Builders Association (152)
American Orthotic and Prosthetic Association (159)*
American Peanut Council (162)
American Pet Products Association (163)
American Petroleum Institute (163)
American Pipe Fittings Association (165)
American Pyrotechnics Association (172)
American Road and Transportation Builders Association (175)
American Society for Quality (189)
American Solar Energy Society (211)
American Textile Machinery Association (216)*
American Walnut Manufacturers Association (219)
American Watch Association (219)
American Welding Society (220)
American Wire Cloth Institute (221)
American Wire Producers Association (221)*
AMT - The Association For Manufacturing Technology (222)
Amusement Industry Manufacturers and Suppliers International (223)
APA The Engineered Wood Association (224)
APICS The Association for Operations Management (224)*
APMI International (225)
Apple Products Research and Education Council (226)
Archery Trade Association (227)
Architectural Precast Association (228)
Architectural Woodwork Institute (228)*
The Arts and Creative Materials Institute, Inc. (229)*
Asia America MultiTechnology Association (231)*
Asphalt Emulsion Manufacturers Association (233)*
Asphalt Institute (233)
Asphalt Recycling and Reclaiming Association (233)*
Asphalt Roofing Manufacturers Association (233)
Associated Builders and Contractors (235)
Associated Cooperage Industries of America (235)
Associated Glass and Pottery Manufacturers (236)
Associated Pipe Organ Builders of America (236)
Associated Wire Rope Fabricators (237)
The Association for Manufacturing Excellence (252)
Association for Retail Environments (256)
Association for Unmanned Vehicle Systems International (261)
Association of Energy Service Companies (280)
Association of Equipment Manufacturers (281)
Association of Gaming Equipment Manufacturers (285)
Association of Home Appliance Manufacturers (287)
Association of Independent Corrugated Converters (288)
Association of Industrial Metallizers, Coaters and Laminators (288)*
Association of Medical Diagnostic Manufacturers (293)
Association of Natural Bio-Control Producers (295)*
Association of Oil Pipe Lines (296)
Association of Pool and Spa Professionals (299)
Association of Rotational Molders International (306)*
Association of Steel Distributors (311)
Association of the Wall and Ceiling Industry (314)*
Association of United States Night Vision Manufacturers (315)*
Association of Vacuum Equipment Manufacturers (316)
Auto Suppliers Benchmarking Association (321)
Automatic Guided Vehicle Systems (321)
Automatic Transmission Rebuilders Association (321)*
Automotive Aftermarket Industry Association (321)
Automotive Engine Rebuilders Association (322)
Automotive Lift Institute, Inc. (322)
Automotive Parts Remanufacturers Association (323)*
Automotive Recyclers Association (323)
Automotive Safety Council (323)
Aviation Distributors and Manufacturers Association International (324)
Awards and Recognition Association (325)
Basic Acrylic Monomer Manufacturers (326)
Battery Council International (326)
Beer Institute (327)
Belt Association (328)

BEMA - The Baking Industry Suppliers Association (328)
Billiard and Bowling Institute of America (329)
Book Manufacturers' Institute (333)
Brake Manufacturers Council (334)
Brick Industry Association (335)
Builders Hardware Manufacturers Association (337)
Business and Institutional Furniture Manufacturers Association International (338)
Calorie Control Council (341)
Can Manufacturers Institute (341)*
The Carpet and Rug Institute (343)
Carpet Cushion Council (343)*
Casket and Funeral Supply Association of America (344)
Cast Iron Soil Pipe Institute (344)
Casting Industry Suppliers Association (344)
Cedar Shake and Shingle Bureau (347)
Cellulose Insulation Manufacturers Association (347)
Cemented Carbide Producers Association (347)
Ceramic Tile Institute of America (349)
Chain Link Fence Manufacturers Institute (350)
Chemical Fabrics and Film Association (351)*
Chlorinated Paraffins Industry Association (354)
Chlorine Institute (354)
Cigar Association of America, Inc. (356)
Cleaning Equipment Trade Association (357)
Coin Laundry Association (361)*
Color Pigments Manufacturers Association, Inc. (365)
Compact Loader/Compact Excavator Council (371)
Composite Can and Tube Institute (372)
Composite Panel Association (372)*
Compressed Air and Gas Institute (372)
Computer and Communications Industry Association (372)
Concrete Anchor Manufacturers Association (373)
Concrete Plant Manufacturers Bureau (374)
Concrete Reinforcing Steel Institute (374)
Consortium for Advanced Management, International (378)
Consumer Electronics Association (381)
Consumer Healthcare Products Association (381)
Consumer Specialty Products Association (381)
Contact Lens Manufacturers Association (382)
Content Delivery and Security Association (382)
Converting Equipment Manufacturers Association (383)
Conveyor Equipment Manufacturers Association (383)
Cookware Manufacturers Association (384)
Cooling Technology Institute (384)
Copper and Brass Fabricators Council (384)
Copper and Brass Servicenter Association (384)
The Cordage Institute (385)
CoreNet Global (385)
Corn Refiners Association, Inc. (385)
Cotton Council International (387)
Council of Defense and Space Industry Associations (393)
Council of Manufacturing Associations (395)
Council of Producers & Distributors of Agrotechnology (396)
CPA Manufacturing Services Association (402)
Craft & Hobby Association (402)
Crane Manufacturers Association of America (403)
Dental Trade Alliance (410)
Diamond Manufacturers & Importers Association of America (411)*
Distilled Spirits Council of the United States, Inc. (414)
Distribution Business Management Association (414)
Diving Equipment and Marketing Association (415)
Door and Access Systems Manufacturers Association, International (415)
The Door and Hardware Institute (416)
Ductile Iron Society (417)
Earthmoving & Mining Equipment Council (418)
Electrical Generating Systems Association (422)
Electrical Manufacturing and Coil Winding Association (422)*
Electrocoat Association (423)
Electronic Distribution Show Corporation (423)*
Electronic Security Association (424)
Emergency Department Practice Management Association (EDPMA) (425)*
Energy Frontiers International (428)*
Envelope Manufacturers Association (430)
Equipment and Tool Institute (432)*
Equipment Marketing and Distribution Association (432)
Equipment Service Association (433)
Exhibit Designers and Producers Association (435)*
Expansion Joint Manufacturers Association, Inc. (436)*
Exterior Insulation and Finish Systems Industry Members Association (EIMA) (436)*
Fabricators & Manufacturers Association, International (437)

Plastics Pipe Institute *(850)**
Plumbing and Drainage Institute *(850)**
Polyisocyanurate Insulation Manufacturers
    Association *(852)*
Polyurethane Manufacturers Association *(852)**
Porcelain Enamel Institute *(853)*
Portable and Stationary Crushing Bureau *(853)*
Portable Sanitation Association International *(853)*
Portland Cement Association *(853)**
Powder Actuated Tool Manufacturers Institute *(854)**
Power Sources Manufacturers Association *(855)*
Power Tool Institute, Inc. *(855)**
Power Transmission Distributors Association *(855)**
Precision Machined Products Association *(856)*
Precision Metalforming Association *(856)*
Pressure Sensitive Tape Council *(856)*
Pressure Vessel Manufacturers Association *(857)**
Pressure Washer Manufacturers Association *(857)*
Private Label Manufacturers Association *(858)*
Product Liability Advisory Council *(859)*
Production and Operations Management Society
    (859)
Production Engine Remanufacturers Association
    (859)*
Professional Picture Framers Association *(864)*
Quarters Furniture Manufacturers Association *(872)**
QVM/CMC Vehicle Manufacturers Association *(872)*
Rack Manufacturers Institute *(872)*
RadTech *(874)*
Railway Engineering-Maintenance Suppliers
    Association *(874)**
The Railway Tie Association *(874)*
Rapid Technologies & Additive Manufacturing
    Community of SME *(875)*
Recreation Vehicle Industry Association *(877)**
The Refractories Institute *(878)*
Refractory Ceramic Fibers Coalition *(878)**
Remanufacturing Institute *(881)*
Resistance Welding Manufacturing Alliance *(883)*
Robotic Industries Association *(887)*
Robotics & Flexible Machinery Tech Group *(887)*
Roof Coatings Manufacturers Association *(888)*
Rubber Manufacturers Association *(888)*
Safe and Vault Technicians Association *(890)*
Scaffold Industry Association *(891)**
Scaffolding, Shoring and Forming Institute *(892)*
Scale Manufacturers Association *(892)*
Schiffli Lace and Embroidery Manufacturers
    Association *(892)*
Scientific Equipment and Furniture Association *(892)*
Screen Manufacturers Association *(893)*
Secondary Materials and Recycled Textiles
    Association *(894)*
Security Industry Association *(895)*
Semiconductor Equipment and Materials
    International *(896)**
Semiconductor Industry Association *(897)*
The Silver Institute *(900)*
Single Ply Roofing Institute *(900)*
SMMA - The Motor and Motion Association *(901)*
Snack Food Association *(901)*
Snow Control Equipment Manufacturers Committee
    (902)
Society for Imaging Informatics in Medicine *(912)**
Society of Chemical Manufacturers and Affiliates
    Inc. *(932)*
Society of Manufacturing Engineers *(941)*
Society of the Plastics Industry *(948)**
Solar Energy Industries Association (SEIA) *(952)*
Southern Cypress Manufacturers Association *(953)*
Space Transportation Association *(953)*
Specialty Equipment Market Association *(957)**
Sporting Arms and Ammunition Manufacturers'
    Institute Inc. *(959)*
Sports and Fitness Industry Association *(959)*
Spring Manufacturers Institute *(960)*
Steel Deck Institute *(962)**
Steel Door Institute *(962)*
Steel Founders' Society of America *(962)*
Steel Joist Institute *(962)*
Steel Manufacturers Association *(962)*
Steel Plate Fabricators Association Division of STI/
    SPFA *(962)*
Steel Shipping Container Institute *(963)*
Steel Tank Institute Division of STI/SPFA *(963)**
Steel Tube Institute of North America *(963)**
Steel Window Institute *(963)**
Storage Equipment Manufacturer's Association *(963)*
Stucco Manufacturers Association *(964)*
Submersible Wastewater Pump Association *(965)*
Sump and Sewage Pump Manufacturers Association
    (965)
Sunglass Association of America *(965)*
Tag and Label Manufacturers Institute *(968)*
Technical Association of the Pulp and Paper Industry
    (970)
Tennis Industry Association *(971)*
Textile Care Allied Trades Association *(972)*
Textile Fibers and By-Products Association *(972)**
Tile Council of North America, Inc. *(974)**

Tile Roofing Institute *(974)*
Timber Products Manufacturers Association *(975)*
Tire Industry Association *(975)*
Tooling, Manufacturing and Technologies
    Association *(976)*
Towing Equipment Manufacturers Association *(976)*
Toy Industry Association *(976)*
The Transformer Association *(977)**
Transportation Safety Equipment Institute *(979)*
Travel Goods Association *(979)**
Truck and Engine Manufacturers Association *(980)*
Truck Mixer Manufacturers Bureau *(981)*
Truck Trailer Manufacturers Association *(981)**
Tube and Pipe Association, International *(981)*
Tube Council of North America *(982)*
Tubular Exchanger Manufacturers Association *(982)*
Ultrasonic Industry Association *(983)*
Unified Abrasives Manufacturers Association *(984)*
United Producers Formulators and Distributors
    Association *(988)*
United States Beet Sugar Association *(991)*
United States Cutting Tool Institute *(993)**
United States Marine Safety Association *(996)*
User Experience Professionals Association *(1005)*
Valve Manufacturers Association of America *(1007)*
Valve Repair Council *(1007)*
Van Body Manufacturers Division *(1008)*
Vanadium Producers and Reclaimers Association
    (1008)
Variable Electronic Components Institute *(1008)*
Vibration Isolation and Seismic Control
    Manufacturers Association *(1009)**
The Vinegar Institute *(1009)**
Water Quality Association *(1013)*
Water Systems Council *(1013)*
Web Sling and Tie down Association *(1014)*
Window and Door Manufacturers Association *(1018)*
Window Covering Manufacturers Association *(1018)*
Wire and Cable Industry Suppliers Association
    (1019)*
Wire Reinforcement Institute *(1019)**
Wire Rope Technical Board *(1019)*
Wiring Harness Manufacturers Association *(1020)*
Wood Component Manufacturers Association *(1024)*
Wood Flooring Manufacturers Association *(1024)*
Wood Machinery Manufacturers of America *(1024)*
Wood Moulding and Millwork Producers Association
    (1024)
Wood Products Manufacturers Association *(1024)*
Woven Wire Products Association *(1029)*
Writing Instrument Manufacturers Association
    (1029)

MATERIAL HANDLING

AIM Global *(17)**
Alliance of Hazardous Materials Professionals *(25)*
Association of Professional Material Handling
    Consultants *(301)*
Automatic Guided Vehicle Systems *(321)*
Conveyor Equipment Manufacturers Association
    (383)
Crane Manufacturers Association of America *(403)*
Dangerous Goods Advisory Council *(407)*
Distribution Business Management Association
    (414)
Hoist Manufacturers Institute *(477)*
Industrial Metal Containers and Wire Decking
    Product Section *(494)*
Industrial Truck Association *(494)*
Institute of Caster and Wheel Manufacturers *(498)*
Institute of Hazardous Materials Management *(500)*
Lift Manufacturers Product Section - Material
    Handling Institute *(597)*
Loading Dock Equipment Manufacturers *(599)*
Material Handling Equipment Distributors
    Association *(608)*
Material Handling Industry of America *(608)**
Materials Handling and Management Society *(608)*
Monorail Manufacturers Association *(619)*
National Wooden Pallet and Container Association
    (805)
Rack Manufacturers Institute *(872)*
Scale Manufacturers Association *(892)*
Storage Equipment Manufacturer's Association *(963)*
United States Industrial Fabrics Institute *(995)*
Web Sling and Tie down Association *(1014)*

MEDICINE/HEALTH CARE/MENTAL HEALTH

AABB - American Association of Blood Banks *(1)*
AAGL - Advancing Minimally Invasive Gynecology
    Worldwide *(2)*
Abortion Care Network *(2)*
Academic Pediatric Association *(3)*
Academy for Eating Disorders *(3)**
Academy Health *(3)*
Academy of Ambulatory Foot and Ankle Surgery *(3)*
Academy of Aphasia *(4)*
Academy of Behavioral Medicine Research *(4)*
Academy of Breastfeeding Medicine *(4)*

Academy of Clinical Laboratory Physicians and
    Scientists *(4)*
Academy of Dental Materials *(5)*
Academy of Dentistry International *(5)*
Academy of Doctors of Audiology *(5)**
Academy of General Dentistry *(5)*
Academy of Laser Dentistry *(6)**
Academy of Managed Care Providers *(6)*
Academy of Medical-Surgical Nurses *(7)*
Academy of Molecular Imaging *(7)**
Academy of Nutrition and Dietetics *(7)*
Academy of Organizational and Occupational
    Psychiatry *(7)*
Academy of Osseointegration *(7)**
Academy of Physicians in Clinical Research *(8)**
Academy of Prosthodontics *(8)*
Academy of Psychosomatic Medicine *(8)*
Academy of Radiology Research *(8)**
Academy of Rehabilitative Audiology *(8)*
Academy of Surgical Research *(9)*
Academy of Veterinary Allergy and Clinical
    Immunology *(9)*
Academy of Veterinary Homeopathy *(9)*
Accreditation Association for Ambulatory Health
    Care *(9)*
Accredited Medical Equipment Providers of America
    (10)
Accrediting Bureau of Health Education Schools *(10)*
Acute Long Term Hospital Association *(12)**
ADARA *(12)*
Advanced Medical Technology Association
    (AdvaMed) *(13)*
AFT Healthcare *(15)*
Air and Surface Transport Nurses Association *(17)*
Air Medical Operators Association *(19)*
Air Medical Physician Association *(19)*
Air Movement and Control Association International
    (19)
Allergy and Asthma Network Mothers of Asthmatics
    (22)
Alliance for Aging Research *(22)*
Alliance for Children and Families *(22)*
Alliance for Continuing Medical Education *(22)*
The Alliance for Home Health Quality and
    Innovation *(23)*
Alliance for Massage Therapy Education *(23)*
Alliance for Natural Health USA *(23)**
Alliance for Quality Care *(23)*
Alliance for Regenerative Medicine *(23)*
Alliance of Cardiovascular Professionals *(25)*
Alpha Omega Alpha Honor Medical Society *(26)*
Alpha Omega International Dental Fraternity *(26)*
Alpha Tau Delta *(27)*
Ambulatory Surgery Center Association *(28)*
America's Blood Centers *(28)**
America's Health Insurance Plans *(28)*
American Academy for Cerebral Palsy and
    Developmental Medicine *(29)**
American Academy of Addiction Psychiatry *(29)**
American Academy of Allergy, Asthma, and
    Immunology *(30)**
American Academy of Ambulatory Care Nursing *(30)*
American Academy of Anesthesiologist Assistants
    (30)*
American Academy of Anti-Aging Medicine *(30)*
American Academy of Audiology *(31)**
American Academy of Child and Adolescent
    Psychiatry *(31)*
American Academy of Clinical Neuropsychology
    (31)*
American Academy of Clinical Psychiatrists *(31)*
American Academy of Cosmetic Dentistry *(31)*
American Academy of Cosmetic Surgery *(32)*
American Academy of Craniofacial Pain *(32)*
American Academy of Dental Group Practice *(32)*
American Academy of Dental Practice
    Administration *(32)*
American Academy of Dental Sleep Medicine *(32)*
American Academy of Dermatology *(32)**
American Academy of Disability Evaluating
    Physicians *(33)*
American Academy of Emergency Medicine *(33)*
American Academy of Environmental Medicine *(33)*
American Academy of Esthetic Dentistry *(33)**
American Academy of Facial Plastic and
    Reconstructive Surgery *(34)*
American Academy of Family Physicians *(34)**
American Academy of Fertility Care Professionals
    (34)
American Academy of Gnathologic Orthopedics *(34)*
American Academy of Gold Foil Operators *(34)*
American Academy of Health Care Providers-
    Addictive Disorders *(34)*
American Academy of Health Physics *(35)**
American Academy of Home Care Physicians *(35)*
American Academy of Hospice and Palliative
    Medicine *(35)*
American Academy of Implant Dentistry *(35)*
American Academy of Maxillofacial Prosthetics *(35)*
American Academy of Medical Acupuncture *(36)*

American Academy of Medical Administrators *(36)**
American Academy of Medical Hypnoanalysts *(36)*
American Academy of Medical Management *(36)**
American Academy of Neurological and Orthopaedic Surgeons *(36)**
American Academy of Neurology *(36)*
American Academy of Nurse Practitioners *(37)*
American Academy of Nursing *(37)**
American Academy of Ophthalmic Executives *(37)*
American Academy of Ophthalmology *(37)**
American Academy of Optometry *(37)*
American Academy of Oral and Maxillofacial Pathology *(37)*
American Academy of Oral and Maxillofacial Radiology *(37)*
American Academy of Oral Medicine *(38)*
American Academy of Orofacial Pain *(38)*
American Academy of Orthopaedic Surgeons *(38)*
American Academy of Orthotists and Prosthetists *(38)*
American Academy of Osteopathy *(38)*
American Academy of Otolaryngic Allergy *(38)*
American Academy of Otolaryngology-Head and Neck Surgery *(39)**
American Academy of Pain Management *(39)*
American Academy of Pain Medicine *(39)*
American Academy of Pediatric Dentistry *(39)*
American Academy of Pediatrics *(39)*
American Academy of Periodontology *(39)**
American Academy of Physical Medicine and Rehabilitation *(40)**
American Academy of Physician Assistants *(40)*
American Academy of Physician Assistants in Occupational Medicine *(40)*
American Academy of Podiatric Practice Management *(40)*
American Academy of Podiatric Sports Medicine *(40)*
American Academy of Professional Coders *(40)*
American Academy of Psychiatry and the Law *(41)*
American Academy of Psychoanalysis and Dynamic Psychiatry *(41)**
American Academy of Psychotherapists *(41)**
American Academy of Restorative Dentistry *(41)*
American Academy of Sanitarians *(41)*
American Academy of Sleep Medicine *(42)**
American Academy of Somnology *(42)*
American Academy of the History of Dentistry *(42)*
American Academy of Thermology *(42)*
American Academy of Veterinary Acupuncture *(42)*
American Academy of Veterinary and Comparative Toxicology *(42)*
American Academy of Veterinary Pharmacology and Therapeutics *(42)*
American Academy of Wound Management *(42)*
American Academy on Communication in Healthcare *(43)*
American Aging Association *(43)**
American Alliance for Health, Physical Education, Recreation and Dance *(44)**
American Ambulance Association *(44)*
American Animal Hospital Association *(45)**
American Art Therapy Association, Inc. *(46)*
American Assembly for Men in Nursing *(47)*
American Association for Accreditation of Ambulatory Surgery Facilities *(47)**
American Association for Aerosol Research *(47)*
American Association for Cancer Education *(48)*
American Association for Cancer Research *(48)**
American Association for Clinical Chemistry, Inc. *(48)*
American Association for Dental Research *(49)*
American Association for Geriatric Psychiatry *(49)*
American Association for Hand Surgery *(49)*
American Association for Health Education *(49)*
American Association for Homecare *(50)*
American Association for Laboratory Animal Science *(50)*
American Association for Marriage and Family Therapy *(50)**
American Association for Pediatric Ophthalmology and Strabismus *(50)*
American Association for Physical Activity and Recreation *(51)*
American Association for Respiratory Care *(51)*
American Association for the History of Medicine *(52)*
American Association for the History of Nursing *(52)*
American Association for the Study of Liver Diseases *(52)*
American Association for the Surgery of Trauma *(52)*
American Association of Thoracic Surgery *(53)*
American Association for Women Podiatrists *(53)*
American Association for Women Radiologists *(53)*
American Association for Wound Care Management *(53)*
American Association of Acupuncture and Oriental Medicine *(53)**
American Association of Anatomists *(54)**
American Association of Avian Pathologists *(54)*
American Association of Behavioral Therapists *(54)*

American Association of Bioanalysts *(54)*
American Association of Birth Centers *(55)**
American Association of Bovine Practitioners *(55)*
American Association of Cardiovascular and Pulmonary Rehabilitation *(55)*
American Association of Certified Allergists *(56)*
American Association of Certified Orthoptists *(56)**
American Association of Chairs of Departments of Psychiatry *(56)**
American Association of Children's Residential Centers *(56)**
American Association of Clinical Endocrinologists *(56)**
American Association of Clinical Urologists *(56)*
American Association of Colleges of Nursing *(57)**
American Association of Colleges of Osteopathic Medicine *(57)*
American Association of Colleges of Pharmacy *(57)**
American Association of Colleges of Podiatric Medicine *(58)*
American Association of Community Psychiatrists *(58)**
American Association of Corporate and Public Practice Veterinarians *(59)*
American Association of Critical-Care Nurses *(59)*
The American Association of Dental Boards *(59)*
American Association of Dental Consultants *(59)*
American Association of Dental Editors *(60)*
American Association of Diabetes Educators *(60)*
American Association of Directors of Psychiatric Residency Training *(60)*
American Association of Endodontists *(60)*
American Association of Equine Practitioners *(60)*
The American Association of Eye and Ear Centers of Excellence *(61)*
American Association of Feline Practitioners *(61)*
American Association of Food Hygiene Veterinarians *(61)*
American Association of Genitourinary Surgeons *(61)*
American Association of Healthcare Administrative Management *(61)**
American Association of Healthcare Consultants *(62)*
American Association of Heart Failure Nurses *(62)*
American Association of Hip and Knee Surgeons *(62)*
American Association of Hospital and Healthcare Podiatrists *(62)*
American Association of Immunologists *(62)**
American Association of Integrated Healthcare Delivery Systems *(63)*
American Association of International Healthcare Recruitment *(63)*
American Association of Kidney Patients *(64)**
American Association of Legal Nurse Consultants *(64)*
American Association of Managed Care Nurses *(64)*
American Association of Medical Assistants *(65)*
American Association of Medical Dosimetrists *(65)*
American Association of Medical Milk Commissions *(65)*
American Association of Medical Society Executives *(65)*
American Association of Naturopathic Physicians *(66)**
American Association of Neurological Surgeons *(66)**
American Association of Neuromuscular and Electrodiagnostic Medicine *(66)**
American Association of Neuropathologists *(66)*
American Association of Neuroscience Nurses *(66)**
American Association of Nurse Anesthetists *(67)*
The American Association of Nurse Attorneys *(67)*
American Association of Occupational Health Nurses *(67)**
American Association of Oral and Maxillofacial Surgeons *(67)*
American Association of Orthodontists *(67)**
American Association of Orthopaedic Medicine *(68)*
American Association of Osteopathic Women Physicians *(68)*
American Association of Pastoral Counselors *(68)*
American Association of Pathologists' Assistants *(68)**
American Association of Physician Specialists *(69)*
American Association of Physicians and Health Care Professionals *(69)*
American Association of Physicians of Indian Origin *(69)*
American Association of Physicists in Medicine *(69)**
American Association of Plastic Surgeons *(70)*
American Association of Poison Control Centers *(70)*
American Association of Preferred Provider Organizations *(70)*
American Association of Professional Hypnotherapists *(71)*
American Association of Psychiatric Administrators *(71)*
American Association of Psychiatric Technicians *(71)*
American Association of Public Health Dentistry *(71)*

American Association of Public Health Physicians *(72)*
American Association of Sleep Technologists *(73)**
American Association of Small Ruminant Practitioners *(73)*
American Association of Suicidology *(74)*
American Association of Surgical Physician Assistants *(74)*
American Association of Swine Veterinarians *(74)*
American Association of Tissue Banks *(75)*
American Association of Veterinary Clinicians *(76)*
American Association of Veterinary Immunologists *(76)**
American Association of Veterinary Laboratory Diagnosticians *(76)**
American Association of Veterinary Parasitologists *(76)**
American Association of Veterinary State Boards *(76)*
American Association of Wildlife Veterinarians *(77)*
American Association of Women Dentists *(77)*
American Association of Zoo Keepers *(77)*
American Association of Zoo Veterinarians *(77)*
American Auditory Society *(78)**
American Baptist Homes and Caring Ministries *(79)*
American Board for Certification in Orthotics and Prosthetics, Inc. (ABC) *(81)*
American Board of Anesthesiology *(81)*
The American Board of Facial Plastic and Reconstructive Surgery *(82)*
American Board of Family Medicine *(82)*
American Board of Health Physics *(82)*
American Board of Internal Medicine *(82)*
American Board of Medical Specialties *(82)*
American Board of Multiple Specialties in Podiatry *(82)*
American Board of Nursing Specialties *(82)*
The American Board of Opticianry and the National Contact Lens Examiners *(83)*
American Board of Perianesthesia Nursing Certification Inc. *(83)*
American Board of Periodontology *(83)*
American Board of Physical Medicine and Rehabilitation *(83)*
American Board of Podiatric Medicine *(83)*
American Board of Podiatric Surgery *(83)*
American Board of Preventive Medicine *(83)*
American Board of Professional Psychology *(83)*
American Board of Psychiatry & Neurology *(83)*
American Board of Quality Assurance and Utilization Review Physicians, Inc. *(84)**
American Board of Surgery *(84)*
American Board of Veterinary Practitioners *(84)*
American Brachytherapy Society *(85)**
American Broncho-Esophagological Association *(86)*
American Burn Association *(87)*
American Case Management Association *(88)*
American Chiropractic Association *(90)*
American Chiropractic Registry of Radiologic Technologists *(90)*
American Cleft Palate-Craniofacial Association *(91)**
American Clinical and Climatological Association *(91)*
American Clinical Laboratory Association *(91)*
American Clinical Neurophysiology Society *(92)*
American College for Advancement in Medicine *(93)**
American College Health Association *(93)**
American College of Allergy, Asthma and Immunology *(93)*
American College of Cardiology *(93)**
American College of Cardiovascular Administrators *(93)**
American College of Certified Wound Specialists *(94)**
American College of Chest Physicians *(94)**
American College of Chiropractic Orthopedists *(94)*
American College of Clinical Pharmacy *(94)*
American College of Dentists *(95)*
American College of Emergency Physicians *(95)*
American College of Epidemiology *(95)*
American College of Eye Surgeons *(95)*
American College of Foot & Ankle Orthopedics & Medicine *(95)*
American College of Foot and Ankle Surgeons *(95)*
American College of Forensic Psychiatry *(96)*
American College of Gastroenterology *(96)*
American College of Health Care Administrators *(96)**
American College of Health Plan Management *(96)*
American College of Healthcare Architects *(96)*
American College of Healthcare Executives *(96)*
American College of Healthcare Information Administrators *(97)*
American College of International Physicians *(97)*
American College of Laboratory Animal Medicine *(97)**
American College of Legal Medicine *(97)*
American College of Medical Genetics *(97)**
American College of Medical Physics *(97)**

American College of Medical Quality (97)*
American College of Medical Toxicology (98)
American College of Mental Health Administration (98)
American College of Mohs Surgeons (98)
American College of Neuropsychiatrists (98)
American College of Neuropsychopharmacology (98)
American College of Nuclear Medicine (98)
American College of Nurse Practitioners (99)*
American College of Nurse-Midwives (99)*
American College of Occupational and Environmental Medicine (99)
American College of Oral and Maxillofacial Surgeons (99)
American College of Osteopathic Emergency Physicians (99)*
American College of Osteopathic Family Physicians (100)
American College of Osteopathic Internists (100)*
American College of Osteopathic Obstetricians and Gynecologists (100)
American College of Osteopathic Pediatricians (100)
American College of Osteopathic Surgeons (100)
American College of Phlebology (100)
American College of Physician Executives (101)*
American College of Physicians (101)
American College of Physicians Services, Inc. (101)
American College of Podiatric Radiologists (101)
American College of Preventive Medicine (101)*
American College of Prosthodontists (101)
American College of Psychiatrists (102)
American College of Psychoanalysts (102)
American College of Radiation Oncology (102)*
American College of Radiology (102)
American College of Rheumatology (102)*
American College of Sports Medicine (102)*
American College of Surgeons (103)*
American College of Surgeons Professional Association (103)*
American College of Veterinary Anesthesiologists (103)
American College of Veterinary Dermatology (104)
American College of Veterinary Internal Medicine (104)
American College of Veterinary Nutrition (104)
American College of Veterinary Ophthalmologists (104)*
American College of Veterinary Pathologists (104)
American College of Veterinary Radiology (104)
American College of Veterinary Surgeons (104)*
American Congress of Obstetricians and Gynecologists (107)
American Congress of Rehabilitation Medicine (107)
American Correctional Health Services Association (108)
American Council on Science and Health (110)
American Counseling Association (111)
American Dance Therapy Association (113)*
American Dental Assistants Association (113)
American Dental Association (113)*
American Dental Education Association (113)
American Dental Hygienists' Association (114)*
American Dental Interfraternity Council (114)
American Dental Society of Anesthesiology (114)
American Dermatological Association (114)
American Diabetes Association (115)
American Embryo Transfer Association (116)
American Endodontic Society, Inc. (117)
American Epilepsy Society (117)*
American Equilibration Society (117)
American Family Therapy Academy (118)*
American Federation for Medical Research (119)
American Gastroenterological Association (125)
American Geriatrics Society (126)
American Group Psychotherapy Association (127)*
American Guild of Organists (127)
American Gynecological and Obstetrical Society (128)
American Head and Neck Society (129)*
American Headache Society (129)
American Health Care Association (129)
American Health Information Management Association (129)
American Health Lawyers Association (130)*
American Health Planning Association (130)
American Health Quality Association (130)
American Heart Association (130)*
American Heartworm Society (130)
American Herb Association (130)
American Herbal Products Association (130)
American Hernia Society (131)*
American Holistic Medical Association (132)*
American Holistic Nurses Association (132)*
American Holistic Veterinary Medical Association (132)
American Horticultural Therapy Association (133)
American Hospital Association (133)
American Industrial Hygiene Association (135)
American Institute for Medical and Biological Engineering (136)

American Institute of Biological Sciences (137)
American Institute of Homeopathy (139)
American Institute of Oral Biology (139)
American Institute of Organbuilders (139)
American Institute of Stress (140)
American Institute of Ultrasound in Medicine (141)
American Kinesiotherapy Association (144)
American Laryngological Association (144)*
American Laryngological, Rhinological and Otological Society (144)
American Lung Association (146)
American Manual Medicine Association (147)*
American Massage Therapy Association (147)*
American Medical Association (148)
American Medical Association Alliance, Inc. (149)
American Medical Directors Association (149)*
American Medical Group Association (149)*
American Medical Informatics Association (149)*
American Medical Rehabilitation Providers Association (149)
American Medical Society for Sports Medicine (149)
American Medical Student Association (150)
American Medical Technologists (150)*
American Medical Women's Association (150)
American Medical Writers Association (150)
American Men's Studies Association (150)
American Mental Health Counselors Association (151)
American Midwifery Certification Board (151)
American Mosquito Control Association (153)
American Music Therapy Association (154)
American Naprapathic Association (154)
American National Chamber of Commerce (154)
American Nephrology Nurses Association (155)
American Network of Community Options and Resources (ANCOR) (155)*
American Neurogastroenterology and Motility Society (155)
American Neurological Association (155)
American Neuropsychiatric Association (155)
American Neurotology Society (156)
American Nurses Association (156)*
American Occupational Therapy Association, Inc. (157)*
American Ophthalmological Society (157)
American Optometric Association (157)
American Optometric Student Association (157)
American Organization for Bodywork Therapies of Asia (158)
American Organization of Nurse Executives (158)*
American Orthodontic Society (158)
American Orthopaedic Association (158)*
American Orthopaedic Foot and Ankle Society (158)*
American Orthopaedic Society for Sports Medicine (159)*
American Orthopsychiatric Association (159)
American Orthotic and Prosthetic Association (159)*
American Osteopathic Academy of Addiction Medicine (159)
American Osteopathic Academy of Orthopedics (159)
American Osteopathic Academy of Sports Medicine (159)
American Osteopathic Association (160)
American Osteopathic Association of Prolotherapy Integrative Pain Management (160)
American Osteopathic Board of Physical Medicine and Rehabilitation (160)
American Osteopathic College of Allergy and Immunology (160)
American Osteopathic College of Anesthesiologists (160)
American Osteopathic College of Dermatology (160)
American Osteopathic College of Occupational and Preventive Medicine (160)
American Osteopathic College of Pathologists (160)
American Osteopathic College of Proctology (161)
American Osteopathic College of Radiology (161)
American Osteopathic College of Rheumatology, Inc. (161)
American Osteopathic Colleges of Ophthalmology and Otolaryngology - Head and Neck Surgery (161)
American Otological Society (161)*
American Pain Society (161)
American Pancreatic Association (162)
American Pathology Foundation (162)
American Pediatric Society (162)
American Pediatric Surgical Association (162)
American Pharmacists Association (163)*
American Physical Therapy Association (164)
American Physical Therapy Association - Private Practice Section (165)
American Physiological Society (165)*
American Podiatric Medical Association (166)
American Podiatric Medical Students Association (166)
American Podiatric Medical Writers Association (166)

American Polarity Therapy Association (166)
American Prosthodontic Society (168)*
American Psychiatric Association (168)
American Psychiatric Nurses Association (168)*
American Psychoanalytic Association (168)*
American Psychological Association (169)*
American Psychological Association - Division of Psychoanalysis (169)
American Psychological Association - Division of Psychotherapy (169)
American Psychological Association - Society of Clinical Psychology (169)
American Psychology-Law Society (170)
American Psychopathological Association (170)
American Psychosocial Oncology Society (170)
American Psychosomatic Society (170)
American Psychotherapy Association (170)
American Public Health Association (171)
American Radium Society (173)*
American Registry for Diagnostic Medical Sonography (174)*
American Registry of Medical Assistants (174)
American Registry of Radiologic Technologists (174)*
American Rehabilitation Counseling Association (174)
American Rhinologic Society (175)*
American Roentgen Ray Society (176)
American Running Association (176)
American Running Association/American Medical Athletic Association (176)
American School Counselor Association (177)*
American School Health Association (177)*
American Sexually Transmitted Diseases Association (178)
American Shoulder and Elbow Surgeons (179)
American Skin Association (180)*
American Sleep Apnea Association (180)
American Society for Adolescent Psychiatry (180)
American Society for Aesthetic Plastic Surgery (180)*
American Society for Apheresis (180)
American Society for Artificial Internal Organs (181)
American Society for Bioethics and Humanities (181)
American Society for Blood and Marrow Transplantation (181)*
American Society for Bone and Mineral Research (181)
American Society for Cell Biology (182)*
American Society for Clinical Investigation (182)
American Society for Clinical Laboratory Science (182)*
American Society for Clinical Pathologists (182)
American Society for Clinical Pathology (182)
American Society for Clinical Pharmacology and Therapeutics (182)*
American Society for Colposcopy and Cervical Pathology (183)
American Society for Cytotechnology (183)
American Society for Dental Aesthetics (183)*
American Society for Dermatologic Surgery (183)
American Society for Experimental NeuroTherapeutics (184)
American Society for Gastrointestinal Endoscopy (184)
American Society for Healthcare Engineering (184)
American Society for Healthcare Environmental Services (185)*
American Society for Healthcare Food Service Administrators (185)
American Society for Healthcare Human Resources Administration (185)
American Society for Healthcare Risk Management (185)
American Society for Histocompatibility and Immunogenetics (185)
American Society for Investigative Pathology (186)
American Society for Laser Medicine and Surgery (186)*
American Society for Mass Spectrometry (186)
American Society for Metabolic and Bariatric Surgery (187)*
American Society for Neurochemistry (187)
American Society for Nutrition (187)
American Society for Pain Management Nursing (188)
American Society for Parenteral and Enteral Nutrition (188)
American Society for Pharmacology and Experimental Therapeutics (188)
American Society for Precision Engineering (188)
American Society for Reconstructive Microsurgery (189)*
American Society for Reproductive Medicine (189)*
American Society for Stereotactic and Functional Neurosurgery (189)
American Society for Surgery of the Hand (189)*
American Society for the Advancement of Anesthesia and Sedation in Dentistry (190)
American Society for the Alexander Technique (190)
American Society for Therapeutic Radiology and Oncology (190)

American Society for Virology (190)
American Society of Abdominal Surgeons (190)
American Society of Addiction Medicine (191)
American Society of Andrology (192)
American Society of Anesthesia Technologists and Technicians (192)*
American Society of Anesthesiologists (192)
American Society of Bariatric Physicians (193)*
American Society of Breast Disease (193)*
American Society of Cataract and Refractive Surgery (194)
American Society of Clinical Oncology (194)*
American Society of Clinical Psychopharmacology (195)*
American Society of Colon and Rectal Surgeons (195)
American Society of Consultant Pharmacists (195)*
American Society of Cytopathology (196)
American Society of Dentist Anesthesiologists (196)*
American Society of Dermatological Retailers (196)
American Society of Dermatology (196)
American Society of Dermatopathology (197)
American Society of Echocardiography (197)*
American Society of Electroneurodiagnostic Technologists (197)*
American Society of Emergency Radiology (197)
American Society of Extra-Corporeal Technology (197)*
The American Society of Forensic Odontology (198)
American Society of General Surgeons (198)*
American Society of Group Psychotherapy and Psychodrama (198)
American Society of Hair Restoration Surgery (199)
American Society of Hand Therapists (199)*
American Society of Head and Neck Radiology (199)*
American Society of Health-System Pharmacists (199)
American Society of Hematology (199)*
American Society of Human Genetics (200)*
American Society of Hypertension, Inc. (200)
American Society of Interventional Pain Physicians (201)
American Society of Laboratory Animal Practitioners (201)
American Society of Law, Medicine and Ethics (202)
American Society of Lipo-Suction Surgery (202)*
American Society of Master Dental Technologists (202)
American Society of Maxillofacial Surgeons (202)
American Society of Medical Association Counsel (203)
American Society of Nephrology (204)
American Society of Neuroimaging (204)
American Society of Neuroradiology (204)*
American Society of Neurorehabilitation (204)*
American Society of Nuclear Cardiology (205)
American Society of Ocularists (205)
American Society of Ophthalmic Administrators (205)
American Society of Ophthalmic Plastic and Reconstructive Surgery (205)
American Society of Ophthalmic Registered Nurses (205)*
American Society of Orthopedic Physician Assistants (205)
American Society of Parasitologists (206)
The American Society of Pediatric Hematology/Oncology (206)*
American Society of Pediatric Nephrology (206)
The American Society of Pediatric Neurosurgeons (206)
American Society of PeriAnesthesia Nurses (206)
American Society of Plant Biologists (207)
American Society of Plastic Surgeons (207)
American Society of Podiatric Medical Assistants (208)
American Society of Podiatric Medicine (208)
American Society of Podiatry Executives (208)
American Society of Preventive Oncology (208)
American Society of Psychoanalytic Physicians (208)
American Society of Radiologic Technologists (208)*
American Society of Regional Anesthesia and Pain Medicine (209)
American Society of Retina Specialists (209)
American Society of Transplant Surgeons (210)*
American Society of Transplantation (210)*
American Society of Trial Consultants (210)
American Society of Tropical Medicine and Hygiene (210)
American Speech-Language-Hearing Association (212)*
American Spinal Injury Association (212)*
American Sports Medicine Association (213)
American Student Dental Association (214)
American Surgical Association (215)
American Telemedicine Association (215)*
American Therapeutic Recreation Association (216)
American Thoracic Society (216)*
American Thyroid Association (216)

American Trauma Society (217)*
American Urogynecologic Society (218)*
American Urological Association (218)*
American Venous Forum (218)
American Veterinary Dental Society (218)
American Veterinary Distributors Association (218)
American Veterinary Medical Association (219)
American Veterinary Society of Animal Behavior (219)
Animal Health Institute (223)
Anxiety Disorders Association of America (224)*
Applied Research Ethics National Association (226)
Armed Forces Optometric Society (229)
Arthroscopy Association of North America (230)*
Asian American Psychological Association (232)*
Aspirin Foundation of America, Inc. (233)
ASPSN - American Society of Plastic Surgical Nurses (234)*
Assembly of Episcopal Healthcare Chaplains (234)*
Assisted Living Federation of America (234)
Assistive Technology Industry Association (234)
Associated Air Balance Council (234)
Associated Bodywork and Massage Professionals (234)
Associated Professional Sleep Societies (237)*
The Association for Academic Surgery (237)
Association for Ambulatory Behavioral Healthcare (238)
Association for Applied and Therapeutic Humor (238)
Association for Applied Psychophysiology and Biofeedback (238)*
Association for Applied Sport Psychology (239)
Association for Behavior Analysis International (240)
Association for Behavioral and Cognitive Therapies (240)*
Association for Behavioral Health & Wellness (240)
Association for Birth Psychology (240)
Association for Chemoreception Sciences (241)
Association for Child Psychoanalysis (241)
Association for Clinical Research Training (241)
Association for Community Affiliated Plans (242)
Association for Comprehensive Energy Psychology (242)*
Association for Conflict Resolution (243)*
Association for Death Education and Counseling (244)*
Association for Electronic Healthcare Transaction (245)
Association for Equine Sports Medicine (246)
Association for Gnotobiotics (247)
Association for Healthcare Documentation Integrity (247)
Association for Healthcare Foodservice (248)
Association for Healthcare Philanthropy (248)
Association for Healthcare Resource and Materials Management (248)*
Association for Healthcare Volunteer Resource Professionals (248)
Association for Hospital Medical Education (249)*
Association for Humanistic Psychology (249)*
Association for Medical Imaging Management (252)*
The Association for Nursing Professional Development (252)
Association for Play Therapy (253)*
Association for Prevention Teaching and Research (APTR) (254)*
Association for Professionals in Infection Control and Epidemiology (254)
Association for Psychoanalytic Medicine (254)
Association for Psychological Science (254)*
Association for Psychological Type International (254)
Association for Quality Imaging (AQI) (254)
Association for Radiological and Imaging Nursing (255)
Association for Research in Nervous and Mental Disease (255)
Association for Research in Otolaryngology (255)
Association for Research in Vision and Ophthalmology (255)*
Association for Surgical Education (257)
Association for the Advancement of Automotive Medicine (258)*
Association for the Advancement of Medical Instrumentation (258)
Association for the Advancement of Psychology (258)
Association for the Advancement of Psychotherapy (258)
Association for the Advancement of Wound Care (258)
Association for the Behavioral Sciences and Medical Education (259)
Association for the Treatment of Sexual Abusers (260)
Association for Transpersonal Psychology (260)
Association for Vascular Access (261)
Association for Women in Psychology (262)*

Association for Women Veterinarians Foundation (262)
Association of Academic Chairmen of Plastic Surgery (262)
Association of Academic Health Centers (262)
Association of Academic Health Sciences Library (263)
Association of Academic Physiatrists (263)
Association of Air Medical Services (264)
Association of American Cancer Institutes (264)
Association of American Indian Physicians (265)
Association of American Medical Colleges (265)*
Association of American Physicians (265)
Association of American Physicians and Surgeons (266)
Association of American Veterinary Medical Colleges (267)
Association of Asian-Pacific Community Health Organizations (268)*
Association of Avian Veterinarians (268)
Association of Aviation Psychologists (269)
Association of Biomedical Communications Directors (269)
Association of Black Cardiologists (269)*
Association of Black Nursing Faculty (269)
The Association of Black Psychologists (270)
Association of Bone and Joint Surgeons (270)
Association of Camp Nurses (271)
Association of Children's Prosthetic-Orthotic Clinics (272)
Association of Chiropractic Colleges (272)
Association of Christian Therapists (273)
Association of Clinical Research Organizations (273)
Association of Clinical Research Professionals (273)*
Association of Clinical Scientists (273)
Association of Community Cancer Centers (275)*
Association of Community Health Nursing Educators (276)*
Association of Dermatology Administrators & Managers (278)
Association of Educational Therapists (280)*
Association of Educators in Imaging and Radiologic Sciences, Inc (280)
Association of Family Medicine Administration (282)
Association of Family Medicine Residency Directors (282)*
Association of Free Standing Radiation Oncology Centers (284)
Association of Gay and Lesbian Psychiatrists (285)
Association of Genetic Technologists (285)*
Association of Halfway House Alcoholism Programs of North America (286)
Association of Health Information Outsourcing Services (286)
Association of Healthcare Internal Auditors (287)*
Association of Hispanic Healthcare Executives (287)
Association of Jewish Family & Children's Agencies (290)
Association of Managed Care Dentists (292)
Association of Maternal and Child Health Programs (AMCHP) (293)*
Association of Medical Device Reprocessors (293)
Association of Medical Education and Research in Substance Abuse (293)*
The Association of Medical Illustrators (293)
Association of Medical School Pediatric Department Chairs (293)
Association of Mental Health Librarians (294)*
Association of Military Surgeons of the United States (294)
Association of Minority Health Professions Schools (295)
Association of Neurosurgical Physician Assistants (295)
Association of Nurses in AIDS Care (296)*
Association of Nutrition & Foodservice Professionals (296)
Association of Occupational and Environmental Clinics (296)*
Association of Occupational Health Professionals in Healthcare (296)*
Association of Oncology Social Work (297)
Association of Organ Procurement Organizations (297)
Association of Osteopathic State Executive Directors (297)
Association of Otolaryngology Administrators (297)
Association of Pathology Chairs (298)
Association of Pedestrian and Bicycle Professionals (298)*
Association of Pediatric Hematology/Oncology Nurses (298)*
Association of Pediatric Oncology Social Workers (298)
Association of Pediatric Program Directors (298)
Association of periOperative Registered Nurses (299)
Association of Physician Assistants in Cardiovascular Surgery (299)*
Association of Physician Assistants in Obstetrics and Gynecology (299)

Association of Plastic Surgery Assistants (299)
Association of Postgraduate Physician Assistant Programs (300)
Association of Professional Chaplains (301)*
Association of Professors of Gynecology and Obstetrics (302)
Association of Professors of Medicine (302)
Association of Program Directors in Internal Medicine (302)
Association of Program Directors in Radiology (303)
Association of Program Directors in Surgery (303)*
Association of Psychology Postdoctoral and Internship Centers (303)*
Association of Public Health Laboratories (304)
Association of Public Health Nurses (304)
Association of Regulatory Boards of Optometry (305)*
Association of Rehabilitation Nurses (305)
Association of Rehabilitation Programs in Computer Technology (305)
Association of Reproductive Health Professionals (305)
Association of Residents in Radiation Oncology (306)*
Association of Rheumatology Health Professionals (306)*
Association of Schools and Colleges of Optometry (307)
Association of Schools of Allied Health Professions (307)*
Association of Schools of Public Health (307)
Association of SIDS and Infant Mortality Programs (308)
Association of Specialized and Cooperative Library Agencies (309)
Association of Specialty Professors (309)
Association of State and Provincial Psychology Boards (309)
Association of State and Territorial Dental Directors (310)
Association of State and Territorial Health Officials (310)
Association of State and Territorial Public Health Nutrition Directors (310)
Association of Surgical Assistants (312)
Association of Surgical Technologists (312)
Association of Teachers of Maternal and Child Health (312)
Association of Technical Personnel in Ophthalmology (313)
Association of Telehealth Service Providers (313)
Association of Traumatic Stress Specialists (315)
Association of United States Night Vision Manufacturers (315)*
Association of University Anesthesiologists (315)
Association of University Centers on Disabilities (AUCD) (315)
Association of University Professors of Ophthalmology (315)*
Association of University Programs in Health Administration (316)*
Association of University Programs in Occupational Health and Safety (316)
Association of University Radiologists (316)
Association of Vascular and Interventional Radiographers (316)
Association of Veterinary Biologics Companies (317)
Association of Vision Science Librarians (317)*
Association of Women Surgeons (317)
Association of Women's Health, Obstetric and Neonatal Nurses (318)
Attention Deficit Disorder Association (320)*
Auxiliary to the National Medical Association (324)
Behavior Genetics Association (327)*
Billings Ovulation Method Association of the United States (329)
BioCommunications Association (329)*
Biomedical Engineering Society (330)*
Biotechnology Industry Organization (BIO) (330)
Black Mental Health Alliance (331)
Black Psychiatrists of America (331)
Blue Cross Blue Shield Association (332)
Board of Registered Polysomnographic Technologists (333)*
Board of Specialty Society (333)
Brain Injury Association of America (334)*
Cancer Immunotherapy Consortium (341)
Cancer Patient Education Network (341)
Capital Health (342)
Cardiovascular Credentialing International (342)
Care Continuum Alliance (342)
Case Management Society of America (343)*
Catecholamine Club (344)
Catholic Health Association of the United States (345)
Catholic Medical Association (346)
Center for American Nurses (348)
Certification Board for Urologic Nurses and Associates (349)
Cervical Spine Research Society (350)*

Cheiron: The International Society for the History of Behavioral and Social Sciences (351)
Chi Eta Phi Sorority, Inc. (352)
Child Life Council (353)
Child Neurology Society (353)
Child Welfare League of America (353)*
Chinese American Medical Society (354)
Christian Chiropractors Association (355)
Christian Medical & Dental Associations (356)
Civil Aviation Medical Association (357)
Clerkship Directors in Internal Medicine (358)
Clinical and Laboratory Standards Institute (358)
Clinical Immunology Society (358)*
Clinical Ligand Assay Society (358)
Clinical Orthopaedic Society (358)*
Collaborative Family Healthcare Association (362)
College of American Pathologists (363)
College of Diplomates of the American Board of Orthodontics (364)
College of Healthcare Information Management Executives (364)
College of Optometrists in Vision Development (364)
Commission on Accreditation of Allied Health Education Programs (368)
Commissioned Officers Association of the United States Public Health Service (368)
Committee of Interns and Residents/ SEIU (368)
Community Health Charities of America (371)
Computerized Medical Imaging Society (373)
Conference of Radiation Control Program Directors (375)
Conference of Research Workers in Animal Diseases (375)
Congress of Chiropractic State Associations (377)
Congress of Lung Association Staffs (377)
Congress of Neurological Surgeons (377)*
Consortium of Behavioral Health Nurses and Associates (378)
Consumer Health Alliance (381)
Consumer Healthcare Products Association (381)
Contact Lens Association of Ophthalmologists (382)*
Contact Lens Council (382)
Contact Lens Manufacturers Association (382)
Contact Lens Society of America (382)*
Continua Health Alliance (382)
Council of Chiropractic Physiological Therapeutics and Rehabilitation (392)
Council of Colleges of Acupuncture and Oriental Medicine (392)
Council of Medical Specialty Societies (395)
Council of Nephrology Nurses and Technicians (396)
Council of State Administrators of Vocational Rehabilitators (397)
Council of State and Territorial Epidemiologists (397)
Council of Teaching Hospitals (398)
Council on Chiropractic Education (399)
Council on Chiropractic Orthopedics (399)
Council on Diagnostic Imaging to the A.C.A. (399)
Council on Radionuclides and Radiopharmaceuticals (400)
Council on Renal Nutrition (400)
Delta Dental Plans Association (409)
Delta Sigma Delta (409)
Dental Trade Alliance (410)
Dermatology Foundation (410)
Dermatology Nurses' Association (410)*
Developmental Disabilities Nurses Association (411)
Diagnostic Marketing Association (411)
Directors of Health Promotion and Education (DHPE) (413)
Drug & Alcohol Testing Industry Association (416)
Drug Information Association (417)
ECRI (418)
EEG and Clinical Neuroscience Society (421)
Emdr International Association (425)
Emergency Department Practice Management Association (EDPMA) (425)*
Emergency Medicine Residents' Association (425)*
Emergency Nurses Association (425)*
Employee Assistance Professionals Association (426)
Endocrine Fellows Foundation (427)
The Endocrine Society (427)*
Entomological Society of America (429)*
The ERISA Industry Committee (ERIC) (433)
ETAD North America (433)
Eye Bank Association of America (436)
Federal Physicians Association (439)*
Federation of American Hospitals (440)*
Federation of American Societies for Experimental Biology (440)
Federation of Associations in Behavioral & Brain Sciences (441)
Federation of Behavioral, Psychological and Cognitive Sciences (441)
Federation of Podiatric Medical Boards (442)
Federation of Spine Associations (442)
Federation of State Boards of Physical Therapy (442)
Federation of State Medical Boards of the United States (442)

Federation of Straight Chiropractors and Organizations (442)
Feldenkrais Guild of North America (442)
Fleischner Society (447)
Foster Family-Based Treatment Association (452)
Foundation for Advances in Medicine and Science (452)
Friends of the National Institute of Dental and Craniofacial Research (FNIDCR) (454)
Gay and Lesbian Medical Association (457)
Genetics Society of America (458)
Gerontological Society of America (460)*
Global Health Council (462)*
Glove Shippers Association (463)*
Group for the Use of Psychology in History (466)
Gynecologic Oncology Group (467)
The Harvey Society (469)
Health and Sciences Communications Association (469)*
Health Care Administrators Association (469)
Health Care Compliance Association (469)
Health Care Education Association (469)
Health Forum (469)
Health Industry Business Communications Council (469)
Health Industry Distributors Association (469)
Health Industry Representatives Association (470)
Health Information Trust Alliance (HITRUST) (470)*
Health Ministries Association (470)*
Health Occupations Students of America (470)
Health Physics Society (470)
Healthcare Billing and Management Association (470)
Healthcare Compliance Packaging Council (470)
Healthcare Convention and Exhibitors Association (471)
Healthcare Distribution Management Association (471)
Healthcare Financial Management Association (471)
Healthcare Information and Management Systems Society (471)
Healthcare Leadership Council (471)
Healthcare Supply Chain Association (472)
Hearing Industries Association (472)
Heart Failure Society of America (472)
Heart Rhythm Society (472)
Hemophilia Federation of America (474)
Hinman Dental Society (475)
Hispanic Dental Association (475)
The Histochemical Society (476)
History of Dermatology Society (476)
Holistic Dental Association (477)
Hosa (478)
Hospice and Palliative Nurses Association (478)*
Hospice Association of America (479)
Human Anatomy and Physiology Society (480)*
Human Biology Association (480)
Human Factors and Ergonomics Society (480)*
Human Factors Society (481)
IEEE Computational Intelligence Society (483)
IEEE Engineering in Medicine and Biology Society (484)
IEEE Photonics Society (485)
Imaging and Perimetry Society (486)
Independent Medical Distributors Association (490)
Indian Dental Association (USA) (492)
Infectious Diseases Society of America (494)*
Infusion Nurses Society (496)
Institute for Credentialing Excellence (497)*
Institute of Medicine (501)*
Inter-National Association of Business Industry & Rehabilitation (506)
Inter-Society Color Council (506)
InterAmerican College of Physicians and Surgeons (507)
International Academy for Child Brain Development (509)
International Academy of Behavioral Medicine, Counseling and Psychotherapy (509)
International Academy of Gnathology - American Section (509)
International Academy of Oral Medicine and Toxicology (509)
International Anesthesia Research Society (511)*
International Association for Colon Hydrotherapy (511)
International Association for Continuing Education and Training (511)
International Association for Correctional and Forensic Psychology (512)
International Association for Dental Research (512)
International Association for Healthcare Security and Safety (512)
International Association for Near Death Studies, Inc. (513)
International Association for Orthodontics (513)
International Association for the Study of Dreams (514)
International Association for the Study of Pain (514)*

International Association of Counselors and Therapists **(519)**
International Association of Eating Disorders Professionals **(520)***
International Association of Electronic Keyboard Manufacturers **(520)**
International Association of Equine Dentists **(520)**
International Association of Flight And Critical Care Paramedics **(521)**
International Association of Forensic Nurses **(521)***
International Association of Healthcare Central Service Materiel Management **(522)**
International Association of Healthcare Practitioners **(522)**
International Association of Infant Massage **(523)**
International Association of Medical Equipment Remarketers and Servicers (IAMERS) **(524)**
International Association of Milk Control Agencies **(524)**
International Association of Oral and Maxillofacial Surgeons **(525)**
International Association of Physicians in AIDS Care **(526)***
International Association of Rehabilitation Professionals **(527)**
International Atherosclerosis Society **(529)**
International Biometric Industry Association **(530)**
International Biometric Society **(530)**
International Bone and Mineral Society **(530)**
International Brain Injury Association **(531)***
International Cadmium Association **(532)**
International Center for Study of Psychiatry and Psychology **(534)**
The International Childbirth Education Association **(534)**
International Chiropractic Pediatric Association **(534)**
International Chiropractors Association **(534)***
International College of Applied Kinesiology **(535)**
International College of Cranio-Mandibular Orthopedics **(535)**
International College of Dentists, U.S.A. Section **(535)**
International College of Surgeons **(535)**
International Communication Association **(536)***
International Community Corrections Association **(536)**
International Congress of Oral Implantologists **(537)***
International Consumer Product Health and Safety Organization **(537)**
International Council for Health, Physical, Education, Recreation, Sport and Dance **(537)**
International Council of Psychologists **(538)**
International Dyslexia Association **(541)***
International Embryo Transfer Society **(542)**
International Executive Housekeepers Association **(543)**
International Federation for Artificial Organs **(544)**
International Federation of Nurse Anesthetists **(544)**
International Fitness Professionals Association **(545)**
International Graphoanalysis Society **(548)**
International Hyperbaric Medical Association, Inc. **(551)**
International Iridology Practitioners Association **(552)**
International Lactation Consultant Association **(553)**
International Listening Association **(554)**
International Liver Transplantation Society **(554)**
International Neural Network Society **(558)***
International Neuropsychological Society **(558)**
International Newspaper Marketing Association **(558)**
International Nurses Society on Additictions **(558)**
International Pediatric Nephrology Association **(559)**
International Pediatric Transplant Association **(560)***
International Pharmaceutical Excipients Council of the Americas **(560)***
International Psycho-Oncology Society **(561)***
International Psychogeriatric Association **(561)**
International Psychohistorical Association **(562)**
International Society for Adolescent Psychiatry and Psychology **(565)**
International Society for Antiviral Research **(565)**
International Society for Computerized Electrocardiology **(566)**
International Society for Developmental Psychobiology **(566)**
International Society for Heart and Lung Transplantation **(566)**
International Society for Infectious Diseases **(566)**
International Society for Magnetic Resonance in Medicine **(567)**
International Society for Medical Publication Professionals **(567)**
The International Society for Minimally Invasive Cardiothoracic Surgery **(567)**
International Society for Neuronal Regulation **(567)**
International Society for Pharmacoeconomics and Outcomes Research **(568)***

International Society for Pharmacoepidemiology **(568)***
International Society for Prenatal Diagnosis **(568)**
International Society for Preventive Oncology **(568)**
International Society for Prosthetics and Orthotics - United States **(569)**
International Society for Quality of Life Research **(569)**
International Society for Quality-of-Life Studies **(569)**
International Society for Research on Aggression **(569)**
International Society for the Study of Dissociation **(570)**
International Society for the Study of Subtle Energies and Energy Medicine **(570)**
International Society for the Study of Trauma and Dissociation **(570)***
International Society for Traumatic Stress Studies **(570)**
International Society of Arthroscopy, Knee Surgery and Orthopaedic Sports Medicine **(571)**
International Society of Hair Restoration Surgery **(573)***
International Society of Nurses in Genetics **(573)**
International Society of Political Psychology **(573)**
International Society of Psychiatric Consultation Liaison Nurses **(574)**
International Society of Psychiatric-Mental Health Nurses **(574)**
International Society of Refractive Surgery of the American Academy of Ophthalmology **(574)**
International Society on Thrombosis and Hemostasis **(575)**
International Stress Management Association - USA **(576)***
The International Transactional Analysis Association **(578)**
International Transplant Nurses Society **(578)**
International Transplant-Skin Cancer Collaborative **(578)**
International Veterinary Academy of Pain Management **(580)**
International Veterinary Acupuncture Society **(580)**
Intersocietal Accreditation Commission **(582)**
Intersociety Council For Pathology Information **(582)**
Iroquois Healthcare Alliance **(585)**
ISEH Society for Hematology and Stem Cells **(586)**
Islamic Medical Association of North America **(586)**
JAWS Society **(586)**
Jean Piaget Society **(586)***
Joint Council of Allergy, Asthma and Immunology **(588)**
Joint Review Committee on Education in Radiologic Technology **(589)**
Kidney Care Partners **(591)**
Korean American Spine Society **(591)**
Lamaze International **(592)***
Large Urology Group Practice Association (LUGPA) **(593)**
LeadingAge (American Association of Homes and Services for the Aging) **(595)**
Malignant Hyperthermia Association of the United States **(602)**
Medicaid Health Plans of America **(611)**
Medical Device Manufacturers Association **(611)**
Medical Fitness Association **(611)***
Medical Imaging Contrast Agent Associations **(611)**
Medical Library Association **(611)***
Medical Marketing Association **(611)**
Medical Mycological Society of the Americas **(611)**
Medical Transcription Industry Association (MTIA) **(611)***
Medical-Dental-Hospital Business Associates **(612)**
Mental Health America **(612)**
MGMA-ACMPE **(614)***
Microanalysis Society **(614)**
Midwives Alliance of North America **(615)**
Movement Disorder Society **(620)***
MTM Association for Standards and Research **(620)**
Musculoskeletal Tumor Society **(621)**
National Association of Independent Review Organizations **(624)**
NANDA International **(625)**
Natco-The Organization for Transplant Professionals **(626)**
National Abortion Federation **(626)**
National Academies of Practice **(627)**
National Academy of Clinical Biochemistry **(627)**
National Academy of Neuropsychology **(628)***
National Academy of Opticianry **(628)**
National Adult Day Service Association **(629)**
National Alliance for Hispanic Health **(631)**
National Alliance for Hospice Access **(631)**
National Alliance for Specialty Healthcare Programs **(632)**
National Alliance of Medicare Set-Aside Professionals, Inc. **(632)**
National Alliance of State and Territorial AIDS Directors **(633)**

National Arab-American Medical Association **(635)***
National Association for Ambulatory Care **(636)**
National Association for Behavioral Health **(636)**
National Association for Biomedical Research **(636)**
National Association for Children's Behavioral Health (NACBH) **(637)**
National Association for Drama Therapy **(638)**
National Association for Health and Fitness **(639)***
National Association for Health Care Recruitment **(639)***
National Association for Healthcare Quality **(639)**
National Association for Home Care and Hospice **(639)**
National Association for Medical Direction of Respiratory Care **(640)**
National Association for Practical Nurse Education and Service **(641)**
National Association for Proton Therapy **(642)**
National Association of Public Health Statistics and Information Systems **(642)**
National Association for Rehabilitation Leadership **(642)**
National Association for Rural Mental Health **(642)**
National Association for the Advancement of Orthotics and Prosthetics **(643)**
National Association for the Advancement of Psychoanalysis **(643)***
The National Association for the Dually Diagnosed **(643)***
National Association for the Education of Young Children **(644)***
National Association for the Support of Long Term Care **(644)**
National Association of Medical Staff Services **(645)**
National Association of Addiction Treatment Providers **(645)**
National Association of Advisors for the Health Professions **(645)**
National Association of Air Medical Communication Specialists **(646)**
National Association for Alcoholism and Drug Abuse Counselors **(646)**
National Association of Boards of Examiners of Long Term Care Administrators **(650)**
National Association of Boards of Pharmacy **(650)**
National Association of Certified Professional Midwives **(651)**
National Association of Chain Drug Stores **(652)**
National Association of Child Care Professionals **(653)***
National Association of Children's Hospitals and Related Institutions **(653)**
National Association of Chronic Disease Directors **(653)**
National Association of City and County Health Officials **(654)**
National Association of Clinical Nurse Specialists **(654)**
National Association of Community Health Centers **(656)**
National Association of Councils on Developmental Disabilities **(658)**
National Association of County and City Health Officials **(659)**
National Association of County Behavioral Health and Developmental Disability Directors **(659)**
National Association of County Health Facility Administrators **(660)**
National Association of Dental Assistants **(662)***
National Association of Dental Laboratories **(662)**
National Association of Dental Plans **(662)**
National Association of Directors of Nursing Administration in Long Term Care **(663)**
National Association of Disability Examiners **(663)**
National Association of Emergency Medical Technicians **(665)**
National Association of EMS Educators **(665)**
National Association of EMS Physicians **(665)**
National Association of Epilepsy Centers **(666)**
National Association of Federal Veterinarians **(668)**
National Association of Free Clinics **(671)**
National Association of Health Data Organizations **(671)***
National Association of Health Education Centers **(671)**
National Association of Health Services Executives **(671)**
National Association of Health Unit Coordinators **(671)***
National Association of Healthcare Access Management **(671)***
National Association of Healthcare Education Centers **(671)**
National Association of Hispanic Nurses **(672)**
National Association of Hospital Hospitality Houses **(673)**
National Association Of Insurance and Financial Advisors(NAIFA) **(676)**
National Association of Local Boards of Health **(678)**

National Association of Long Term Care Administrator Boards **(679)**
National Association of Managed Care Physicians **(679)**
National Association of Managed Care Physicians **(679)***
National Association of Medicaid Directors **(680)**
National Association of Medical Examiners **(680)**
National Association of Medical Minority Educators, Inc. **(680)**
National Association of Mental Health Planning Advisory Council **(680)**
National Association of Neonatal Nurses **(682)**
National Association of Nephrology Technologists and Technicians **(682)**
National Association of Nurse Massage Therapists **(682)**
National Association of Nurse Practitioners in Women's Health **(682)***
National Association of Optometrics and Opticians **(683)**
National Association of Optometrists and Opticians **(683)**
National Association of Orthopedic Nurses **(683)**
National Association of Orthopaedic Technologists **(683)**
National Association of Osteopathic Foundations **(683)**
National Association of Pediatric Nurse Practitioners **(684)***
National Association of Physician Nurses **(684)***
National Association of Physician Recruiters **(684)**
National Association of Portable X-Ray Providers **(685)**
National Association of Professional Geriatric Care Managers **(687)***
National Association of Professional Pet Sitters **(687)***
National Association of Psychiatric Health Systems **(688)***
National Association of Public Hospitals and Health Systems **(688)**
National Association of Rehabilitation Providers and Agencies **(691)**
National Association of Rehabilitation Research and Training Centers **(691)**
National Association of Rural Health Clinics **(692)**
National Association of School Nurses **(693)***
National Association of School Psychologists **(693)***
National Association of Service Providers in Private Rehabilitation **(695)**
National Association of Seventh-Day Adventist Dentists **(695)**
National Association of Social Workers **(696)***
National Association of Spine Specialists **(696)**
National Association of State Alcohol and Drug Abuse Directors (NASADAD) **(697)**
National Association of State Directors of Developmental Disabilities Services, Inc. **(700)**
National Association of State Emergency Medical Services Officials **(700)***
National Association of State Head Injury Administrators **(701)**
National Association of State Mental Health Directors **(701)**
National Association of State Mental Health Program Directors **(701)**
National Association of State Veterans Homes **(702)**
National Association of Therapeutic Schools and Programs (NATSAP) **(706)**
National Association of Urban Hospitals **(708)**
National Association of Veterans Affairs Physicians and Dentists **(708)**
National Association of Veterans Research and Education Foundations **(708)***
National Association of Vision Professionals **(708)**
National Black Association for Speech, Language and Hearing **(714)**
National Black Nurses Association **(714)**
National Board for Certification in Occupational Therapy, Inc. **(715)**
National Board for Certified Counselors **(715)**
National Board for Respiratory Care **(715)**
National Board of Medical Examiners **(716)**
National Business Group on Health **(716)**
National Cancer Registrars Association **(717)***
National Center for Assisted Living **(719)**
National Center for Homeopathy **(719)**
National Certification Commission for Acupuncture and Oriental Medicine **(720)***
National Certification Council for Activity Professionals **(720)**
National Child Care Association **(721)**
National Coalition for Assistive and Rehab Technology **(723)**
National Coalition of Creative Arts Therapies Associations **(723)**
National Committee for Quality Assurance **(724)***
National Comprehensive Cancer Network **(725)**
National Conference of Executives of The ARC **(727)**

National Conference of Local Environmental Health Administrators **(727)**
National Council for Community Behavioral Healthcare **(731)***
National Council for Prescription Drug Programs **(732)**
National Council for Therapeutic Recreation Certification **(733)**
National Council of State Boards for Nursing **(736)**
National Council on Problem Gambling **(739)***
National Council on Radiation Protection and Measurement **(739)**
National Council on Rehabilitation Education **(739)**
National CPA Health Care Advisors Association **(740)***
National Dental Assistants Association **(742)**
National Dental Association **(742)***
National Dental EDI Council **(743)**
National Dental Hygienists' Association **(743)**
National Family Caregivers Association **(747)**
National Family Planning and Reproductive Health Association **(747)**
National Federation of Licensed Practical Nurses **(749)**
National Gerontological Nursing Association **(755)**
National Health Association **(758)**
National Health Care Anti-Fraud Association **(758)***
National Health Council **(758)**
National Health Federation **(758)**
National Hemophilia Foundation **(759)**
National Hispanic Medical Association **(759)**
National Home Infusion Association **(760)***
National Hospice & Palliative Care Organization **(760)***
National Human Services Assembly **(761)***
National Indian Health Board **(763)**
National Institute of Electromedical Information **(765)**
National League for Nursing **(768)**
National Mastitis Council **(772)**
National Medical Association **(772)**
National Multiple Sclerosis Society **(774)**
National Network of Depression Centers **(775)**
National Nurses United **(775)**
National Optometric Association **(776)**
National Organization for Associate Degree Nursing **(776)***
National Organization of Nurse Practitioner Faculties **(777)**
National Organization of State Offices of Rural Health **(778)**
National Pace Association **(778)**
National Perinatal Association **(780)**
National Phlebotomy Association **(781)**
National Prison Hospice Association **(782)**
National Psychological Association for Psychoanalysis **(783)***
National Register of Health Service Providers in Psychology **(785)**
National Rehabilitation Association **(785)**
National Rehabilitation Counseling Association **(785)**
National Remotivation Therapy Organization **(786)**
National Renal Administrators Association **(786)**
National Rural Health Association **(788)**
National Society of Certified Healthcare Business Consultants **(793)***
National Society of Genetic Counselors **(794)***
National Spinal Cord Injury Association **(795)***
National Stroke Association **(797)***
National Student Nurses Association **(797)**
National Student Osteopathic Medical Association **(797)***
National Student Speech Language Hearing Association **(798)***
National Surgical Assistant Association **(798)**
National Therapeutic Recreation Society **(800)**
National Tuberculosis Controllers Association **(802)**
National Wellness Institute, Inc. **(804)***
National WIC Association **(805)**
National Wildlife Rehabilitators Association **(805)**
Neuro-Developmental Treatment Association **(808)**
Neurofibromatosis, Inc., Northeast **(808)**
The Neuropathy Association **(808)**
Neurosurgical Society of America **(809)**
Neurotechnology Industry Organization **(809)**
New York E-Health Collaborative **(809)**
North American Association of Central Cancer Registries **(812)**
North American Clinical Dermatologic Society **(815)**
North American Menopause Society **(818)***
North American Neuro-Ophthalmology Society **(819)***
North American Skull Base Society **(820)**
North American Society for Cardiovascular Imaging **(821)***
North American Society for Dialysis and Transplantation **(821)**
North American Society for Pediatric Gastroenterology, Hepatology and Nutrition **(821)**

North American Society for the Psychology of Sport and Physical Activity **(822)**
North American Society of Adlerian Psychology **(822)**
North American Spine Society **(822)**
Nurses Organization of Veterans Affairs **(825)**
Obesity Society **(825)**
Omega Tau Sigma **(827)**
Omicron Kappa Upsilon **(827)**
Oncology Nursing Society **(827)**
Ophthalmic Photographers' Society **(829)***
Optical Imaging Association **(829)***
The Optical Lab Division **(829)***
Optical Society of America **(829)**
Optical Storage Technology Association **(829)**
Opticians Association of America **(829)***
Optometric Extension Program Foundation **(830)**
Organization Development Institute **(830)***
Organization for Safety and Asepsis Procedures **(831)**
Organizational Behavior Teaching Society **(832)***
Orthopaedic Research Society **(833)**
Orthopaedic Section - American Physical Therapy Association **(833)**
Orthopaedic Trauma Association **(834)**
Orthopedic Surgical Manufacturers Association **(834)**
Osteoarthritis Research Society International **(834)**
Osteopathic Cranial Academy **(834)**
Outpatient Ophthalmic Surgery Society **(835)**
Pan American Allergy Society **(837)**
Parapsychological Association **(838)**
Patient Centered Primary Care Collaborative **(840)**
Pediatric Endocrine Society **(840)**
Pediatric Nursing Certification Board **(840)***
Pediatric Orthopedic Society of North America **(840)**
Pedorthic Footwear Association **(840)**
Pet Partners **(842)***
Pharmaceutical Education and Research Institute **(844)**
Phi Rho Sigma Medical Society **(846)**
Physician Assistant Education Association **(847)**
Physician Insurers Association of America **(847)**
Pierre Fauchard Academy **(848)***
Plasma Protein Therapeutics Association **(850)**
Plastic Surgery Administrative Association **(850)**
Plastic Surgery Research Council **(850)**
Preventive Cardiovascular Nurses Association **(857)***
Professional Association of Health Care Office Management **(859)**
Psi Omega Fraternity **(868)**
Psychology Society **(868)**
Psychometric Society **(868)**
The Psychonomic Society **(868)**
Radiation Research Society **(873)**
Radiation Therapy Oncology Group **(873)**
Radiological Society of North America **(873)***
Radiology Business Management Association **(874)**
Regulatory Affairs Professionals Society **(879)***
Rehabilitation Engineering and Assistive Technology Society of North America **(879)***
Renal Physicians Association **(881)***
Research Society on Alcoholism **(882)**
Research!America **(882)**
Resolve, The National Infertility Association **(883)**
Respiratory Nursing Society **(883)**
Rheumatology Nurses Society **(886)***
Rolf Institute of Structural Integration **(887)**
Ruth Jackson Orthopaedic Society **(889)**
Ryan White Medical Providers Coalition **(889)**
Scoliosis Research Society **(893)**
Semiconductor Environmental Safety and Health Association **(896)***
Shock Society **(899)**
Sigma Epsilon Delta Dental Fraternity **(899)**
Sigma Theta Tau International **(899)**
Silicones Environmental, Health and Safety Council of North America **(900)**
Sleep Research Society **(900)***
Society for a Science of Clinical Psychology **(903)**
Society for Academic Emergency Medicine **(903)***
The Society for Adolescent Medicine **(903)***
Society for Assisted Reproductive Technology **(905)**
Society for Biomaterials **(905)**
Society for Cardiovascular Angiography and Interventions **(905)***
Society for Cardiovascular Magnetic Resonance **(905)**
Society for Chaos Theory in Psychology and Life Sciences **(905)**
Society for Clinical Trials **(906)**
Society for Clinical Vascular Surgery **(906)**
Society for Community Research and Action **(906)***
Society for Computers in Psychology **(906)**
Society for Consumer Psychology **(907)**
Society for Cross-Cultural Research **(907)***
Society for Developmental and Behavioral Pediatrics **(907)***
Society for Ear, Nose and Throat Advances in Children **(907)**
Society for Education in Anesthesia **(908)**

METALS

Metal Building Contractors and Erectors Association *(613)*
Metal Building Manufacturers Association *(613)**
Metal Construction Association *(613)*
Metal Findings Manufacturers Association *(613)*
Metal Framing Manufacturers Association *(613)**
Metal Injection Molding Association *(613)*
Metal Powder Industries Federation *(613)*
Metal Powder Producers Association *(614)*
Metal Treating Institute *(614)*
Metals Service Center Institute *(614)*
Minerals, Metals and Materials Society *(617)**
Mining and Metallurgical Society of America *(617)*
NACE International *(623)*
National Association for Surface Finishing *(643)*
National Association of Architectural Metal Manufacturers *(647)*
National Association of Graphic and Product Identification Manufacturers *(670)*
National Association of Reinforcing Steel Contractors *(691)*
National Association of Steel Pipe Distributors *(703)*
National Blacksmiths and Weldors Association *(715)*
National Certified Pipe Welding Bureau *(720)*
National Coil Coating Association *(723)*
National Corrugated Steel Pipe Association *(730)**
National Council of Erectors, Fabricators and Riggers *(734)*
National Institute of Steel Detailing *(765)*
National Ornamental and Miscellaneous Metals Association *(778)**
National Slag Association *(792)*
National Steel Bridge Alliance *(796)*
National Tooling and Machining Association *(800)*
Non-Ferrous Founders' Society *(811)*
North American Die Casting Association *(816)*
North American Metal Packaging Alliance, Inc. (NAMPA) *(818)*
Plumbing Manufacturers Institute *(851)*
Powder Coating Institute *(854)*
Powder Metallurgy Equipment Association *(854)*
Powder Metallurgy Parts Association *(854)**
Precision Machined Products Association *(856)*
Precision Metalforming Association *(856)*
Rack Manufacturers Institute *(872)*
Refractory Metals Association *(878)*
Resistance Welding Manufacturing Alliance *(883)*
Reusable Industrial Packaging Association *(885)*
Scaffolding, Shoring and Forming Institute *(892)*
Sheet Metal and Air Conditioning Contractors' National Association *(898)*
Sheet Metal Workers' International Association *(898)*
The Silver Institute *(900)*
Silver Users Association *(900)*
Society of American Silversmiths *(929)**
Society of Mineral Analysts *(942)*
Society of North American Goldsmiths *(943)**
Society of Rheology *(946)**
Specialty Steel Industry of North America *(958)*
SSPC: the Society for Protective Coatings *(960)**
Steel Deck Institute *(962)**
Steel Door Institute *(962)*
Steel Founders' Society of America *(962)*
Steel Joist Institute *(962)*
Steel Manufacturers Association *(962)*
Steel Plate Fabricators Association Division of STI/SPFA *(962)*
Steel Recycling Institute *(963)*
Steel Shipping Container Institute *(963)*
Steel Tank Institute Division of STI/SPFA *(963)**
Steel Tube Institute of North America *(963)**
Steel Window Institute *(963)**
TAUC - The Association of Union Constructors *(968)**
Tin Stabilizers Association *(975)*
Truss Plate Institute *(981)*
Tube Council of North America *(982)*
United States Cutting Tool Institute *(993)**
United Steelworkers of America *(1001)*
Vanadium Producers and Reclaimers Association *(1008)*
Welding Research Council *(1015)*
World Gold Trust Services *(1026)**

MINORITIES

African-American Library and Information Science Association *(15)*
African-American Women's Clergy Association *(15)*
Airport Minority Advisory Council (AMAC) *(21)*
American Association of Blacks in Energy *(55)*
American Association of Jewish Lawyers and Jurists *(64)*
American Association of Minority Businesses *(65)*
American Association of Physicians of Indian Origin *(69)*
American Council for Southern Asian Art *(109)**
American Hellenic Educational Progressive Association (AHEPA) *(130)*
American Indian Higher Education Consortium *(135)*
American Schools of Oriental Research *(177)*

Asian American Hotel Owners Association *(231)*
Asian American Journalists Association *(231)*
Asian Pacific American Labor Alliance, AFL-CIO *(232)*
Asian Women in Business *(232)*
ASPIRA Association, Inc. *(233)*
Association for Africanist Anthropology *(238)*
Association for Asian American Studies *(239)*
Association for Asian Studies *(239)**
Association for Multicultural Counseling and Development *(252)*
Association for the Study of African American Life and History *(259)*
Association of African American Museums *(263)*
Association of African Studies Programs *(263)*
Association of Black Anthropologists *(269)*
Association of Black Cardiologists *(269)**
Association of Black Foundation Executives *(269)*
The Association of Black Psychologists *(270)*
Association of Black Sociologists *(270)**
Association of Hispanic Healthcare Executives *(287)*
Association of Latina and Latino Anthropologists *(291)*
Association of Minority Health Professions Schools *(295)*
Association on American Indian Affairs *(319)*
BCA *(326)*
Black Caucus of the American Library Association *(331)*
Black Coaches & Administrators *(331)*
Black Entertainment and Sports Lawyers Association *(331)*
Black Farmers and Agriculturists Association *(331)*
Black Filmmaker Foundation *(331)*
Black Mental Health Alliance *(331)*
Black Retail Action Group *(332)**
Black Theatre Network *(332)*
Chinese American Medical Society *(354)*
Coalition of Black Trade Unionists *(360)*
Community Action Partnership *(369)*
Conference of Minority Public Administrators *(375)*
Conference of Minority Transportation Officials *(375)**
Conference on Asian History *(376)**
Consortium for Graduate Study in Management *(378)*
Council for Opportunity in Education *(390)*
Equal Employment Advisory Council *(432)*
Hispanic American Police Command Officers Association (HAPCOA) *(475)*
Hispanic Association of Colleges and Universities *(475)**
Hispanic Association on Corporate Responsibility *(475)*
Hispanic Dental Association *(475)*
Hispanic Elected Local Officials *(475)*
Hispanic Lobbyists Association *(475)*
Hispanic National Bar Association *(475)*
Indian Educators Federation *(492)*
InterAmerican College of Physicians and Surgeons *(507)*
International Association of Black Professional Fire Fighters *(517)*
Intertribal Monitoring Association on Indian Trust Funds *(583)*
Intertribal Timber Council *(583)*
Labor Council for Latin American Advancement (LCLAA) *(592)*
Latin Business Association *(594)*
Mexican-American Grocers Association *(614)*
Military Impacted Schools Association *(616)*
National Action Council for Minorities in Engineering (NACME) *(628)*
National Alliance for Hispanic Health *(631)*
National Alliance of Black School Educators *(632)*
National Alliance of Postal and Federal Employees *(633)*
National Alliance to Save Native Languages *(633)*
National American Indian Housing Council *(634)*
National Association for Bilingual Education *(636)*
National Association for Equal Opportunity in Higher Education *(638)*
National Association for Ethnic Studies *(638)*
National Association of Black Accountants, Inc. *(648)*
National Association of Black County Officials *(649)*
National Association of Black Journalists *(649)**
National Association of Black Professors *(649)*
National Association of Black Social Workers *(649)*
National Association of Black Suppliers *(649)*
National Association of Black Women Entrepreneurs *(649)*
National Association of Black-Owned Broadcasters *(649)*
National Association of Blacks in Criminal Justice *(649)*
National Association of Blacks In Government *(649)*
The National Association of Colored Women's Club, Inc. *(656)*

National Association of Hispanic and Latino Studies *(672)*
National Association of Hispanic Federal Executives *(672)*
National Association of Hispanic Firefighters *(672)*
National Association of Hispanic Journalists *(672)*
National Association of Hispanic Nurses *(672)*
National Association of Hispanic Publications *(672)*
National Association of Hispanic Real Estate Professionals *(672)*
National Association of Investment Companies *(676)*
National Association of Japan-America Societies *(677)*
National Association of Latino Elected and Appointed Officials *(677)**
National Association of Latino Independent Producers *(677)*
National Association of Medical Minority Educators, Inc. *(680)*
National Association of Minority and Women Owned Law Firms *(680)*
National Association of Minority Automobile Dealers *(680)*
National Association of Minority Contractors *(680)*
National Association of Multicultural Engineering Program Advocates *(681)*
National Association of Multicultural Media Executives *(681)*
National Association of Native American Studies *(681)**
National Association of Negro Business and Professional Women's Clubs *(681)**
National Association of Neighborhoods *(681)*
National Association of Real Estate Brokers *(689)*
National Association of Securities Professionals *(695)*
National Association of Tribal Historic Preservation Officers *(707)*
National Bankers Association *(712)*
National Bar Association *(712)*
National Beauty Culturists' League *(713)*
National Black Caucus of Local Elected Officials *(714)*
National Black Caucus of State Legislators *(714)*
National Black Chamber of Commerce *(714)*
National Black Farmers Association *(714)*
National Black MBA Association *(714)*
National Black Nurses Association *(714)*
National Black Police Association *(714)*
National Black Public Relations Society *(715)**
National Coalition of African American Owned Media *(723)*
National Coalition of Black Meeting Planners *(723)*
National Conference of Black Lawyers *(726)*
National Conference of Black Mayors *(726)*
National Council of Minorities in Energy *(735)*
National Dental Association *(742)**
National Economic Association *(744)**
National Forum for Black Public Administrators *(752)*
National Hispanic Corporate Council *(759)*
National Hispanic Medical Association *(759)*
National Indian Education Association *(762)*
National Indian Gaming Association *(762)**
National Indian Head Start Directors Association *(763)*
National Indian Health Board *(763)*
National Lesbian and Gay Journalists Association *(769)*
National Medical Association *(772)*
National Minority Business Council *(773)*
National Minority Supplier Development Council *(773)*
National Newspaper Publishers Association *(775)*
National Optometric Association *(776)*
National Organization for the Professional Advancement of Black Chemists and Chemical Engineers *(777)**
National Organization of Black County Officials *(777)*
National Organization of Black Law Enforcement Executives *(777)*
National Society of Black Engineers *(793)**
National Society of Black Physicists *(793)*
National Society of Hispanic MBAs *(794)*
Native American Contractors Association *(806)*
SACNAS (Society for Advancement of Chicanos and Native Americans in Science) *(889)*
Society for Asian and Comparative Philosophy *(904)*
Society of Hispanic Professional Engineers *(938)*
Society of Mexican American Engineers and Scientists *(941)*
United States Hispanic Chamber of Commerce *(995)*
Urban Financial Services Coalition *(1003)*
Women in Management *(1021)*

NATURAL RESOURCES

ADSC: The International Association of Foundation Drilling *(12)**
Advanced Biofuels Association *(12)*
Aluminum Extruders Council *(27)*

America's Natural Gas Alliance *(29)*
American Association for Aerosol Research *(47)*
American Association of Petroleum Geologists *(68)**
American Association of Professional Landmen *(71)*
American Backflow Prevention Association *(78)*
American Bureau of Metal Statistics *(86)*
American Coal Ash Association *(92)*
American Coal Council *(92)*
American Coke and Coal Chemicals Institute *(92)*
American Exploration & Production Council *(118)*
American Filtration and Separations Society *(121)**
American Fuel & Petrochemical Manufacturers *(124)*
American Gas Association *(124)*
American Ground Water Trust *(127)*
American Hydrogen Association *(134)*
American Institute of Commemorative Art *(138)*
American Institute of Hydrology *(139)*
The American Institute of Mining, Metallurgical, and Petroleum Engineers *(139)**
American Membrane Technology Association *(150)*
American Petroleum Institute *(163)*
American Public Gas Association *(170)*
American Society of Gas Engineers *(198)*
American Society of Irrigation Consultants *(201)*
American Society of Limnology and Oceanography *(202)*
American Society of Mining and Reclamation *(203)**
American Water Resources Association *(220)**
American Water Works Association *(220)*
American-European Soda Ash Shipping Association *(222)*
Association of Bituminous Contractors *(269)*
Association of Boards of Certification *(270)*
Association of Clean Water Administrators *(273)*
Association of Diving Contractors International *(279)*
Association of Energy Service Companies *(280)*
Association of Metropolitan Water Agencies *(294)*
Association of Oil Pipe Lines *(296)*
Association of State Dam Safety Officials *(310)*
Association of State Drinking Water Administrators *(311)*
Association of the Wall and Ceiling Industry *(314)**
Association of Water Technologies *(317)**
Automotive Oil Change Association *(323)**
Barre Granite Association *(326)*
Bituminous Coal Operators Association *(331)*
BP and AMOCO Marketers Association *(334)*
Brick Industry Association *(335)*
Building Stone Institute *(338)*
Caribbean Basin Ethanol Producer Association (CBEPA) *(343)*
Cast Stone Institute *(344)*
Chevron and Texaco Petroleum Marketers Association *(352)*
China Clay Producers Association *(354)*
Clay Minerals Society *(357)*
Coal Exporters Association of the U.S. *(359)*
Coal Operators and Associates *(359)*
Coal Technology Association *(359)*
Coal Trading Association *(359)*
Compressed Air and Gas Institute *(372)*
Compressed Gas Association *(372)*
Coordinating Research Council *(384)*
Council of Petroleum Accountants Societies *(396)*
DeepStar Project *(408)*
Diesel Technology Forum *(412)*
Distribution Contractors Association *(414)*
Drilling Engineering Association *(416)*
Emissions Control Technology Association (ECTA) *(426)*
Energy Security Council *(428)*
Energy Telecommunications and Electrical Association *(428)*
Energy Traffic Association *(428)*
Environmental and Water Resources Institute of the American Society of Civil Engineers *(430)*
The Evaporative Cooling Institute *(434)*
Expanded Shale, Clay and Slate Institute *(435)*
Federal Water Quality Association *(440)*
Fiberglass Tank and Pipe Institute *(443)*
Fuel Cell and Hydrogen Energy Association *(454)**
FutureGen Industrial Alliance, Inc. *(455)*
Gas Machinery Research Council *(456)*
Gas Processors Association *(456)*
Gas Processors Suppliers Association *(456)*
Gas Technology Institute *(456)*
Gas Turbine Association *(457)*
Gasification Technologies Council *(457)*
Gasoline and Automotive Service Dealers of America *(457)*
Ground Water Protection Council *(466)*
Groundwater Management Districts Association *(466)*
Gypsum Association *(467)*
Independent Fuel Terminal Operators Association *(490)*
Independent Lubricant Manufacturers Association *(490)**
Independent Petroleum Association of America *(491)*
Independent Terminal Operators Association *(492)*

Industrial Minerals Association -- North America *(494)*
Institute for Briquetting and Agglomeration *(496)**
International Association for Hydrogen Energy *(513)*
International Association of Drilling Contractors *(519)*
International Association of Geophysical Contractors *(522)*
International Association of Ice Cream Vendors *(523)*
International Association of Independent Tanker Owners *(523)*
International Bottled Water Association *(530)*
International Cast Polymer Association *(533)*
International Desalination Association *(540)*
International Energy Credit Association *(542)*
International Lead Zinc Research Organization *(553)*
International Liquid Terminals Association *(554)*
International Marine Minerals Society *(555)*
International Oil Scouts Association *(558)*
International Oxygen Manufacturers Association *(559)*
International Ozone Association-Pan American Group Branch *(559)*
International Packaged Ice Association *(559)*
International Slurry Surfacing Association *(565)**
International Waterlily and Water Gardening Society *(580)**
International Zinc Association-America *(582)*
Interstate Council on Water Policy *(582)*
Interstate Natural Gas Association of America *(583)*
Interstate Oil and Gas Compact Commission *(583)**
Irrigation Association *(585)*
Liaison Committee of Cooperating Oil and Gas Associations *(597)*
Lignite Energy Council *(598)*
Marble Institute of America *(604)*
Marine Preservation Association *(605)*
Methanol Institute *(614)*
Mine Safety Institute of America *(616)*
Mineral Economics and Management Society *(617)*
Minerals, Metals and Materials Society *(617)**
Mining and Metallurgical Society of America *(617)*
National Alliance of Forest Owners *(632)*
National Association of Clean Water Agencies *(654)*
National Association of Division Order Analysts *(663)*
National Association of Flood and Stormwater Management Agencies *(668)*
National Association of Royalty Owners *(692)*
National Association of Shell Marketers *(696)*
National Association of State Land Reclamationists *(701)*
National Association of Truck Stop Operators(NATSO) *(707)*
National Association of Wastewater Transporters *(708)*
National Association of Water Companies (NAWC) *(709)*
National BioDiesel Board *(713)*
The National Building Granite Quarries Association *(716)*
National Clay Pipe Institute *(722)**
The National Coal Council *(722)*
National Coal Transportation Association *(722)*
National Council of Coal Lessors *(734)*
National Drilling Association *(743)*
National Energy Services Association *(746)*
National Ground Water Association *(756)*
National Hydropower Association *(761)*
National Industrial Sand Association *(763)*
National Institute for Water Resources *(766)*
National Lubricating Grease Institute *(770)*
National Marine Electronics Association *(771)*
National Mining Association *(772)**
National Ocean Industries Association *(775)*
National Onsite Wastewater Recycling Association *(776)*
National Petroleum Council *(780)*
National Petroleum Management Association *(780)*
National Propane Gas Association *(783)*
National Quartz Producers Council *(783)*
National Ready Mixed Concrete Association *(784)*
National Rural Water Association *(788)*
National Slag Association *(792)*
National Stone, Sand, and Gravel Association *(796)*
National Stripper Well Association *(797)*
National Systems Contractors Association *(798)**
National Utility Contractors Association (NUCA) *(803)**
National Water Resources Association *(804)*
Natural Areas Association *(806)*
Natural Gas Supply Association *(807)*
Natural Stone Council *(807)*
NGVAmerica *(810)*
Nickel Institute *(811)*
NORA: Association of Responsible Recyclers *(811)*
North American Insulation Manufacturers Association *(817)*
North American Lake Management Society *(817)*
Northwest Natural Resource Group *(824)*

OESP - National Association of Oil and Energy Service Professionals *(826)*
Offshore Marine Service Association *(827)*
Pellet Fuels Institute *(841)*
Perlite Institute *(842)*
Petroleum Convenience Alliance for Technology Standards *(843)*
Petroleum Equipment Institute *(843)*
Petroleum Equipment Suppliers Association *(843)*
Petroleum Marketers Association of America *(843)*
Petroleum Packaging Council *(843)*
Petroleum Technology Transfer Council *(844)*
Petroleum Transportation and Storage Association *(844)*
Pipe Line Contractors Association *(849)**
Pipeline Research Council International, Inc. *(849)*
Pressure Vessel Manufacturers Association *(857)**
Process Equipment Manufacturers' Association *(858)*
Propane Engine Fuel Committee/Propane Education and Research Council *(867)*
The Refractories Institute *(878)*
Renewable Fuels Association *(881)*
River Management Society *(886)**
Salt Institute *(891)*
Service Station Dealers of America and Allied Trades *(898)*
The Silver Institute *(900)*
Snow & Ice Management Association *(901)**
Society for Free Radical Biology and Medicine *(909)*
The Society for Freshwater Science *(910)**
Society for Mining, Metallurgy and Exploration, Inc. *(915)**
Society for Organic Petrology *(917)**
Society for Range Management *(920)*
Society of Economic Geologists *(934)*
Society of Exploration Geophysicists *(935)*
Society of Independent Gasoline Marketers of America (SIGMA) *(939)*
Society of Mineral Analysts *(942)*
Society of Petroleum Engineers *(944)*
Society of Petroleum Evaluation Engineers *(944)*
Society of Petrophysicists and Well Log Analysts *(944)*
Soil and Water Conservation Society *(951)*
Solution Mining Research Institute *(952)**
Sorptive Minerals Institute *(952)*
Spill Control Association of America *(958)*
Stucco Manufacturers Association *(964)*
The Sulphur Institute *(965)*
Sump and Sewage Pump Manufacturers Association *(965)*
Tile Council of North America, Inc. *(974)**
Tubular Exchanger Manufacturers Association *(982)*
United Mine Workers of America *(988)**
United Natural Products Alliance *(988)*
United States Clay Producers Traffic Association *(991)*
United States Committee on Irrigation and Drainage *(992)*
United States Energy Association *(993)*
U.S. Oil and Gas Association *(997)*
United States Society on Dams *(999)*
Universities Council on Water Resources *(1002)*
Water and Sewer Distributors of America *(1012)*
Water and Wastewater Equipment Manufacturers Association *(1012)**
Water Environment Federation *(1013)**
Water Quality Association *(1013)*
Water Sports Industry Association *(1013)**
Water Systems Council *(1013)*
WaterJet Technology Association - Industrial and Municipal Cleaning Association *(1013)**
Waterways Council, Inc. *(1014)*
Women in Mining National *(1022)*
World Gold Trust Services *(1026)**
World Waterpark Association *(1028)*
Zoological Association of America *(1030)*

NONPROFIT

Alliance for Nonprofit Management *(23)**
Alliance of Nonprofit Mailers *(25)*
American Architectural Foundation *(46)*
American Fraternal Alliance *(124)*
American Hellenic Educational Progressive Association (AHEPA) *(130)*
American Lung Association *(146)*
American Navion Society *(155)*
Aspirin Foundation of America, Inc. *(233)*
Association for Research on Nonprofit Organizations and Voluntary Action *(255)*
Association of Fund-Raising Distributors and Suppliers *(285)*
Brain Injury Association of America *(334)**
Centerpoint for Leaders *(348)*
Council on Foundations *(399)**
Flight Safety Foundation *(448)*
Forum of Regional Associations of Grantmakers *(452)*
Georgia Charter Schools Association *(459)*
Giving USA Foundation *(461)*

Costume Society of America **(387)***
Drug, Chemical and Associated Technologies Association **(417)**
The Fragrance Foundation **(453)**
Fragrance Materials Association **(453)**
The Handcrafted Soapmakers Guild **(468)**
Independent Cosmetic Manufacturers and Distributors **(489)**
Indoor Tanning Association **(492)**
Intercoiffure America/Canada **(507)**
International Aloe Science Council **(510)**
International Association of Color Manufacturers **(518)**
International Association of Hygienic Physicians **(523)**
International Fragrance Association North America **(547)**
International SalonSpa Business Network (ISBN) **(563)**
National Beauty Culturists' League **(713)**
National Costumers Association **(730)**
National Health Association **(758)**
National Interstate Council of State Boards of Cosmetology **(766)**
Personal Care Products Council **(842)***
Professional Beauty Association | National Cosmetology Association **(861)***
Regulatory Affairs Professionals Society **(879)***
Research Institute for Fragrance Materials **(882)**
Society of Clinical and Medical Hair Removal **(933)**
Society of Cosmetic Chemists **(934)**
World International Nail and Beauty Association **(1026)**

PHARMACEUTICAL INDUSTRY

Academy of Managed Care Pharmacy **(6)***
Academy of Pharmaceutical Research and Science **(8)**
Academy of Physicians in Clinical Research **(8)***
Accreditation Council for Pharmacy Education **(10)**
Alpha Zeta Omega **(27)**
American Academy of Clinical Toxicology **(31)**
American Academy of Orthotists and Prosthetists **(38)**
American Academy of Pain Management **(39)**
American Academy of Veterinary and Comparative Toxicology **(42)**
American Academy of Veterinary Pharmacology and Therapeutics **(42)**
American Association of Colleges of Pharmacy **(57)***
American Association of Homeopathic Pharmacists **(62)**
American Association of Pharmaceutical Scientists **(68)**
American Clinical Laboratory Association **(91)**
American College of Apothecaries **(93)**
American College of Clinical Pharmacology **(94)***
American College of Clinical Pharmacy **(94)**
American College of Neuropsychopharmacology **(98)**
American Institute of the History of Pharmacy **(141)**
American Pharmacists Association **(163)***
American Society for Automation in Pharmacy **(181)**
American Society for Clinical Pharmacology and Therapeutics **(182)***
American Society for Pharmacology and Experimental Therapeutics **(188)**
American Society of Clinical Psychopharmacology **(195)***
American Society of Consultant Pharmacists **(195)***
American Society of Health-System Pharmacists **(199)**
American Society of Pharmacognosy **(207)***
American Wholesale Marketers Association **(221)***
Animal Health Institute **(223)**
Aspirin Foundation of America, Inc. **(233)**
Association of Clinical Research Professionals **(273)***
The Association of Community Pharmacists Congressional Network **(276)**
Association of Food and Drug Officials **(283)**
Biomedical Engineering Society **(330)***
Biotechnology Industry Organization (BIO) **(330)**
Cancer Immunotherapy Consortium **(341)**
Chain Drug Marketing Association **(350)***
Consumer Healthcare Products Association **(381)**
Controlled Release Society **(383)**
Drug Information Association **(417)**
Drug, Chemical and Associated Technologies Association **(417)**
Federation of American Societies for Experimental Biology **(440)**
Food and Drug Law Institute **(449)***
Generic Animal Drug Alliance **(458)**
Generic Pharmaceutical Association **(458)**
Health Industry Distributors Association **(469)**
Healthcare Compliance Packaging Council **(470)**
Healthcare Distribution Management Association **(471)**
Healthcare Leadership Council **(471)**
Inter-Society Color Council **(506)**

International Academy of Compounding Pharmacists **(509)**
International Federation of Pharmaceutical Wholesalers **(544)**
International Pharmaceutical Aerosol Consortium **(560)**
International Pharmaceutical Excipients Council of the Americas **(560)***
International Society for Pharmaceutical Engineering **(567)**
International Society for Pharmacoeconomics and Outcomes Research **(568)***
International Society for Pharmacoepidemiology **(568)***
International Veterinary Academy of Pain Management **(580)**
Kappa Psi Pharmaceutical Fraternity, Inc. **(590)**
Lambda Kappa Sigma **(593)***
National Alliance of State Pharmacy Associations **(633)**
National Association for Alcoholism and Drug Abuse Counselors **(646)**
National Association of Boards of Pharmacy **(650)**
National Association of Chain Drug Stores **(652)**
National Community Pharmacists Association **(725)**
National Council for Prescription Drug Programs **(732)**
National Home Infusion Association **(760)***
National Pharmaceutical Council **(780)**
Parenteral Drug Association **(838)**
Pharmaceutical Care Management Association **(844)**
Pharmaceutical Education and Research Institute **(844)**
Pharmaceutical Industry Labor Management Association (PILMA) **(844)**
Pharmaceutical Marketing Research Group **(844)**
Pharmaceutical Printed Literature Association **(844)**
Pharmaceutical Research and Manufacturers of America (PhRMA) **(844)***
Phi Delta Chi **(845)**
Regulatory Affairs Professionals Society **(879)***
Safety Pharmacology Society **(890)***
Society for Clinical Data Management **(906)**
Society of Infectious Diseases Pharmacists **(939)**
Society of Pharmaceutical and Biotech Trainers **(944)**
United States Pharmacopeia **(997)**

PHILOSOPHY

American Association of Philosophy Teachers **(69)**
American Catholic Philosophical Association **(88)***
American Philosophical Association **(164)***
American Philosophical Society **(164)***
American Society for Political and Legal Philosophy **(188)**
Association for Informal Logic and Critical Thinking **(249)**
Association for Philosophy of the Unconscious **(253)**
Association for Practical and Professional Ethics **(253)***
Association for Symbolic Logic **(257)***
Association of Muslim Social Scientists of North America **(295)**
Federation of State Humanities Councils **(442)**
International Association for Philosophy and Literature **(514)**
International Society for Philosophical Enquiry **(568)**
Jean Piaget Society **(586)***
Metaphysical Society of America **(614)***
North American Society for Social Philosophy **(821)**
Philosophy of Education Society **(846)**
Philosophy of Science Association **(846)***
Radical Philosophy Association **(873)**
Semiotic Society of America **(897)**
Society for Ancient Greek Philosophy **(904)**
Society for Asian and Comparative Philosophy **(904)**
Society for Business Ethics **(905)***
Society for Medieval and Renaissance Philosophy **(915)**
Society for Natural Philosophy **(916)**
Society for Phenomenology and Existential Philosophy **(918)**
Society for Philosophy and Technology **(919)**
Society for the Advancement of American Philosophy **(922)**
Society for the Philosophy of Sex and Love **(923)**
Society for the Study of Symbolic Interaction **(925)***
Society of Christian Philosophers **(932)***
Society of Philosophers in America **(944)**

PLANNING

American College of Contingency Planners **(95)***
American Health Planning Association **(130)**
American Institute of Certified Planners **(137)**
American Planning Association **(166)***
Association of Collegiate Schools of Planning **(275)***
CoreNet Global **(385)**
Council of Educational Facility Planners International **(393)**
DRI International **(416)***
Financial & Insurance Conference Planners **(444)**

Financial Planning Association **(445)**
Human Resource People and Strategy **(481)**
Institute of Store Planners **(503)***
International Association for Impact Assessment **(513)***
International Society of Meeting Planners **(573)**
Meeting Professionals International **(612)**
National Alliance of Preservation Commissions **(633)**
National Association of Development Organizations **(662)**
National Association of Environmental Professionals **(666)**
National Association of Housing and Redevelopment Officials **(673)**
National Association of Planning Councils **(685)**
National Association of Regional Councils **(690)**
National Criminal Justice Association **(740)**
National Emergency Management Association **(745)**
Project Management Institute **(866)***
Society for College and University Planning **(906)**
Society of Competitive Intelligence Professionals **(933)**
Society of Government Meeting Professionals **(938)**
Society of Outdoor Recreation Professionals **(943)**

PLASTICS INDUSTRY

Academy of Dental Materials **(5)**
Adhesive and Sealant Council **(12)***
American Composites Manufacturers Association **(105)**
Association of Rotational Molders International **(306)***
Center for the Polyurethanes Industry **(348)***
Chemical Fabrics and Film Association **(351)***
Closure and Container Manufacturers Association **(359)**
Contact Lens Manufacturers Association **(382)**
Corrugated Polyethylene Pipe Association **(386)**
EPS Industry Alliance **(432)**
Fiber Society **(443)**
Flexible Film & Bag Division **(447)**
Foil and Specialty Effects Association **(448)**
Foodservice & Packaging Institute, Inc. **(450)***
Glove Shippers Association **(463)***
INDA, Association of the Nonwoven Fabrics Industry **(488)***
Independent Sealing Distributors **(491)**
International Association of Plastics Distributors **(526)**
International Card Manufacturers Association **(532)**
International Cast Polymer Association **(533)**
International Society for Plastination **(568)***
Manufacturers Representatives of America, Inc. **(603)**
National Association for PET Container Resources **(641)***
Paper and Plastic Representatives Management Council **(838)***
Plastic Shipping Container Institute **(850)***
Plastics Pipe Institute **(850)***
Polyurethane Manufacturers Association **(852)***
Roof Coatings Manufacturers Association **(888)**
Rubber and Plastics Industry Conference of the United Steelworkers of America **(888)**
Society of Plastics Engineers **(944)**
Society of the Plastics Industry **(948)***
Spray Polyurethane Foam Alliance **(959)***
Thermoforming Institute **(973)**
Uni-Bell PVC Pipe Association **(984)***
Vinyl Institute **(1009)***
Vinyl Siding Institute, Inc. **(1009)**

POLITICS/POLITICAL SCIENCE

Academy of Political Science **(8)**
American Academy of Political and Social Science **(40)**
American Association of Political Consultants **(70)**
American College of Surgeons Professional Association **(103)***
American Enterprise Institute for Public Policy Research **(117)**
American Institute for Maghrib Studies **(136)**
American League of Lobbyists **(145)**
American Political Science Association **(166)***
American Society for Political and Legal Philosophy **(188)**
APPAM - The Association for Public Policy Analysis and Management **(225)***
The Association for Consortium Leadership **(243)**
Association for Politics and the Life Sciences **(253)**
Combat Contractor's Association **(366)**
Conference for the Study of Political Thought **(374)**
Council for European Studies **(390)***
Democratic Attorneys General Association **(410)**
Democratic Governors Association **(410)**
Election Technology Association **(421)**
Institute of Judicial Administration **(501)***
International Association of Women Ministers **(529)**
International Studies Association **(576)***
Latin American Studies Association **(594)***

National Association of Business Political Action
  Committees (651)
National Association of State Election Directors
  (700)
The National Campus Ministry Association (717)
National Conference of Black Political Scientists
  (727)
National Federation of Republican Women (750)
National Governors Association (755)
National Republican Congressional Committee (786)
Pi Gamma Mu (847)
Republican Governors Association (881)
Republican National Lawyers Association (881)
The Ripon Society (886)
Social Science History Association (902)
Union for Radical Political Economics (985)*
Women's Caucus for Political Science (1023)
World Affairs Councils of America (1025)
World Future Society (1026)
Young Presidents' Organization (1030)

POPULATION

American Public Health Association (171)
American Society for Reproductive Medicine (189)*
Association for Community Affiliated Plans (242)
Association for Population/Family Planning Libraries
  and Information Centers, International (253)
Ecological Society of America (418)
Population Action International (852)
Population Association of America (853)*
Society for the Study of Social Biology (925)

POSTAL AND MAIL SERVICES

Alliance of Nonprofit Mailers (25)
American Postal Workers Union (167)*
Association for Postal Commerce (253)
Association of Alternate Postal Systems (264)
Association of Marketing Service Providers (293)*
Direct Marketing Association (412)
Direct Selling Association (413)
Express Association of America (436)
International Warehouse Logistics Association
  (580)*
Mail Systems Management Association (601)
Messenger Courier Association of the Americas
  (612)
National Alliance of Postal and Federal Employees
  (633)
National Association of Letter Carriers (678)
National Association of Postal Supervisors (685)
National Association of Postmasters of the United
  States (685)
National League of Postmasters of the United States
  (768)
National Mail Order Association (771)
National Postal Mail Handlers Union (781)*
National Postal Policy Council (781)
National Rural Letter Carriers' Association (788)*
National Star Route Mail Contractors Association
  (796)
Parcel Shippers Association (838)
Pharmaceutical Care Management Association (844)

PRINTING INDUSTRY

Amalgamated Printer's Association (27)
American Printing History Association (167)
Association of College and University Printers (274)
Binding Industries Association (329)*
Calendar Marketing Association (340)
Checks Payment Systems Association (351)
Digital Media Association (412)*
Flexographic Prepress Platemakers Association (447)
Flexographic Technical Association (447)
Foil and Specialty Effects Association (448)
Graphic Communications Conference of the
  International Brotherhood of Teamsters (465)
Gravure Association of America (465)
Illustrator's Partnership of America (486)
Imaging Supplies Coalition (487)
In-Plant Printing and Mailing Association (487)*
International Allied Printing Trades Association (510)
International Association of Printing House
  Craftsmen (526)
International Digital Enterprise Alliance (540)
International Fine Print Dealers Association (545)*
International Metal Decorators Association (556)
International Plate Printers, Die Stampers and
  Engravers Union of North America (560)
International Society of Copier Artists (572)
International Thermographers Association (577)
Label Printing Industries of America (591)
National Association for Printing Leadership (641)
National Association of Litho Clubs (678)
National Association of Passports and Visa Services
  (683)
National Association of Printing Ink Manufacturers
  (686)
National Government Publishing Association (755)
NPES, The Association for Suppliers of Printing,
  Publishing, and Converting Technologies (824)

NPTA Alliance (824)
Online Publishers Association, Inc. (828)
Pharmaceutical Printed Literature Association (844)
Printing Brokerage/Buyers Association International
  (857)
Printing Industries of America (857)
Printing Industry Credit Executives (857)
Printing Industry Financial Executives (858)
Reprographic Services Association (881)
Retail Print Music Dealers Association (885)*
Specialty Graphic Imaging Association (957)
Tag and Label Manufacturers Institute (968)
Worldwide Printing Thermographers Association
  (1028)

PUBLIC AFFAIRS AND PUBLIC RELATIONS

Agriculture Council of America (16)*
American Association for Affirmative Action (47)
American League of Lobbyists (145)
Arthur W. Page Society (230)
Association for Conservation Information (243)
Association of Cable Communicators (270)
Association of Celebrity Personal Assistants (271)
Association of Eminent Domain Professionals (280)
Association of Image Consultants International (287)
Automotive Public Relations Council (323)*
Baptist Communicators Association (326)
The Coalition for America's Gateways and Trade
  Corridors (360)
Council for Advancement and Support of Education
  (388)*
Council of Communication Management (393)*
Customer Relations Institute Global, LLC (406)
International Association of Business
  Communicators (517)
National Association of Consumer Advocates (657)
National Association of County Information Officers
  (660)*
National Association of Schools of Public Affairs and
  Administration (694)
National Black Public Relations Society (715)*
National Conference of Personal Managers (728)
National Council for Marketing and Public Relations
  (732)
National Council on Public Polls (739)*
National Golf Foundation (755)*
National Investor Relations Institute (767)
National Research Council (786)
National School Public Relations Association (789)
PROMAX/BDA (866)
Public Affairs Council (868)
Public Notice Resource Center (869)
The Public Relations Society of America (870)
Public Relations Student Society of America (870)
React International (875)
Religion Communicators Council (880)
Section for Women in Public Administration (894)
Society for Healthcare Strategy and Market
  Development (910)*
Women in Government Relations, Inc. (1021)

PUBLIC WORKS

Alliance of Work/Life Progress (25)
American Public Works Association (172)
American Tort Reform Association (217)
Association of Eminent Domain Professionals (280)
Public Works Historical Society (870)
React International (875)
Society for the Study of Social Problems (925)*

PURCHASING

American Purchasing Society (172)
Association for Healthcare Resource and Materials
  Management (248)*
The Coalition for Government Procurement (360)
Electronic Commerce Code Management Association
  (423)
Institute for Supply Management (497)
National Association of Educational Procurement,
  Inc. (664)*
National Association of State Procurement Officials
  (702)*
National Institute of Governmental Purchasing (765)
The National Procurement Institute, Inc (783)*
Printing Brokerage/Buyers Association International
  (857)

REAL ESTATE

AIR Commercial Real Estate Association (18)
American Academy of Estate Planning Attorneys (33)
American Academy of State Certified Appraisers (42)
American Association for Geodetic Surveying (49)
American Association of Residential Mortgage
  Regulators (72)
American College of Real Estate Lawyers (102)
American Land Rights Association (144)
American Land Title Association (144)
American Real Estate and Urban Economics
  Association (173)*

American Real Estate Society (173)
American Resort Development Association (175)
American Society of Agricultural Appraisers (191)
American Society of Appraisers (192)
American Society of Equine Appraisers (197)
American Society of Farm Managers and Rural
  Appraisers (197)
Appraisal Institute (226)
Appraisers Association of America (226)*
Association for Governmental Leasing and Finance
  (247)
The Association of Average Adjusters of the United
  States and Canada (268)
Association of Commercial Real Estate (275)
Association of Foreign Investors in U.S. Real Estate
  (284)
Association of Machinery and Equipment Appraisers
  (292)
Association of Metropolitan Planning Organizations
  (294)
Association of Real Estate License Law Officials
  (305)
Association of Real Estate Women (305)
Building Owners and Managers Association
  International (337)*
Building Owners and Managers Institute
  International (337)
CCIM Institute (347)
NAIOP, The Commercial Real Estate Development
  Association (366)
Commercial Real Estate Women Network (367)
Community Associations Institute (CAI) (370)*
Consumer Mortgage Coalition (381)
CoreNet Global (385)
Corporate Facility Advisors, Inc. (386)
Council for Affordable and Rural Housing (388)
Council of Multiple Listing Services (395)
Council of Real Estate Brokerage Managers (396)
Council of Residential Specialists (396)
The Counselors of Real Estate (401)*
CRE Finance Council (403)
ECRI (418)
Hotel Brokers International (479)
Independent Automotive Damage Appraisers
  Association (488)
Institute of Business Appraisers (498)
Institute of Real Estate Management (503)
International Association of Assessing Officers
  (516)*
International Association of Attorneys and
  Executives in Corporate Real Estate (516)
International Council of Shopping Centers (538)
International Real Estate Federation - American
  Chapter (562)
International Real Estate Institute (562)
International Right of Way Association (563)
International Society of Appraisers (570)
Land Trust Alliance (593)*
Management Association for Private
  Photogrammetric Surveyors (602)
Mortgage Bankers Association of America (619)
Mortgage Insurance Companies of America (619)
National Affordable Housing Management
  Association (629)
National Alliance of Forest Owners (632)
National Apartment Association (634)
National Association of Bar-Related Title Insurers
  (648)
National Association of County Surveyors (660)
National Association of Estate Planners and
  Councils (666)*
National Association of Exclusive Buyer Agents (666)
National Association of Fire Investigators (668)
National Association of Hispanic Real Estate
  Professionals (672)
National Association of Home Builders (673)*
National Association of Housing and Redevelopment
  Officials (673)
National Association of Housing Cooperatives (673)
National Association of Independent Fee Appraisers
  (674)
National Association of Independent Insurance
  Adjusters (674)
National Association of Jewelry Appraisers (677)
The National Association of Marine Surveyors, Inc.
  (679)
National Association of Mortgage Brokers (681)
National Association of Public Insurance Adjusters
  (689)
National Association of Real Estate Appraisers (689)
National Association of Real Estate Brokers (689)
National Association of Real Estate Editors (690)
National Association of Real Estate Investment
  Managers (690)*
National Association of Real Estate Investment
  Trusts (NAREIT) (690)
National Association of Realtors (690)
National Association of Residential Property
  Managers (691)

National Association of Review Appraisers and Mortgage Underwriters **(692)**
National Business Incubation Association **(717)**
National Council of Exchangors **(734)**
National Council of Real Estate Investment Fiduciaries **(735)***
National Federal Development Association **(748)**
National Home Performance Council, Inc. **(760)**
National Housing and Rehabilitation Association **(760)***
National Institute of Building Sciences **(764)**
National Leased Housing Association **(769)**
National Multi-Housing Council **(774)**
National Network of Estate Planning Attorneys **(775)**
National Real Estate Investors Association **(784)**
National Reverse Mortgage Lenders Association **(787)**
National Society of Professional Surveyors **(794)**
National Society of Real Estate Appraisers, Inc. **(795)**
PeerSpan **(840)**
Professional Housing Management Association **(862)***
Professional Women's Appraisal Association **(866)**
Property Loss Research Bureau **(867)**
Property Owners Association **(867)**
Public Lands Council **(869)**
Real Estate Buyers Agent Council **(875)**
Real Estate Educators Association **(875)***
Real Estate Information Professionals Association **(875)**
Real Estate Investment Securities Association **(875)**
Real Estate Management Brokers Institute **(875)**
Real Estate Roundtable **(876)**
Real Estate Valuation Advocacy Association **(876)**
REALTORS Land Institute **(876)**
RESPRO (Real Estate Services Providers Council) **(883)**
Self Storage Association **(896)**
Society of Accredited Marine Surveyors **(927)**
Society of Industrial and Office Realtors **(939)***
Society of Mortgage, Appraisal, Real Estate and Title Professionals **(942)**
United States Green Building Council **(994)**
Women's Council of REALTORS **(1023)**

REFRACTORIES
Brick Industry Association **(335)**
Casting Industry Suppliers Association **(344)**
The Refractories Institute **(878)**

RELIGION
Academy of Homiletics **(5)**
African-American Women's Clergy Association **(15)**
American Academy of Ministry **(36)**
American Academy of Religion **(41)***
American Association of Christian Counselors **(56)**
American Association of Jewish Lawyers and Jurists **(64)**
American Association of Pastoral Counselors **(68)**
American Baptist Homes and Caring Ministries **(79)**
American Catholic Correctional Chaplains Association **(88)**
American Catholic Historical Association **(88)**
American Catholic Philosophical Association **(88)***
American Conference of Cantors **(107)**
American Correctional Chaplains Association **(108)**
American Council of Christian Churches **(109)**
American Jewish Correctional Chaplains Association **(143)**
The American Jewish Historical Society **(143)**
American Jewish Press Association **(143)***
American National Chamber of Commerce **(154)**
American Schools of Oriental Research **(177)**
American Society of Missiology **(203)**
American Society of Sephardic Studies **(209)**
American Theological Library Association **(216)***
Assembly of Episcopal Healthcare Chaplains **(234)***
Associated Church Press **(235)***
Association for Biblical Higher Education **(240)***
Association for Clinical Pastoral Education **(241)***
Association for Jewish Studies **(250)***
Association for Spiritual, Ethical and Religious Values in Counseling **(257)**
Association for the Sociology of Religion **(259)***
Association of Advanced Rabbinical and Talmudic Schools **(263)**
Association of Catholic Colleges and Universities **(271)***
Association of Catholic Publishers **(271)**
Association of Christian Librarians **(272)**
Association of Christian Schools International **(272)**
Association of Christian Therapists **(273)**
Association of College and University Religious Affairs **(274)**
Association of Episcopal Colleges **(281)**
Association of Jesuit Colleges and Universities **(290)**
Association of Jewish Aging Services **(290)**
Association of Jewish Family & Children's Agencies **(290)**
Association of Jewish Libraries **(290)**

Association of Lutheran Development Executives **(292)**
Association of Professional Chaplains **(301)***
Association of Professors of Mission **(302)**
Association of Statisticians of American Religious Bodies **(311)**
Baptist Communicators Association **(326)**
Canon Law Society of America **(342)***
Cantors Assembly **(342)**
Catholic Academy for Communication Arts Professionals **(345)**
Catholic Association of Diocesan Ecumenical and Interreligious Officers **(345)**
Catholic Campus Ministry Association **(345)***
Catholic Cemetery Conference **(345)**
Catholic Charities USA **(345)**
Catholic Health Association of the United States **(345)**
Catholic Library Association **(346)**
Catholic Medical Association **(346)**
Catholic Press Association **(346)**
Catholic Radio Association **(346)**
Catholic Theological Society of America **(346)**
CBA **(346)**
Center for Spiritual and Ethical Education **(348)**
Central Conference of American Rabbis **(348)**
Chief Administrators of Catholic Education **(352)**
Choristers Guild **(355)**
Christian College Consortium **(355)**
Christian Labor Association of the United States of America **(355)**
Christian Leadership Alliance **(355)**
Christian Legal Society **(356)***
Christian Management Association **(356)**
Christian Medical & Dental Associations **(356)**
Christian Meetings & Conventions Association **(356)**
Christian Schools International **(356)**
Church and Synagogue Library Association **(356)**
Church Music Publishers Association **(356)***
College Theology Society **(365)**
COMISS Network - The Network on Ministry in Specialized Settings **(366)***
Conference of Major Superiors of Men, United States of America **(375)**
Council for Christian Colleges and Universities **(389)***
Council of American Jewish Museums **(391)**
Council of Archives and Research Libraries in Jewish Studies **(392)**
Council of Societies for the Study of Religion **(397)***
Evangelical Christian Publishers Association **(434)**
Evangelical Church Library Association **(434)**
Evangelical Council for Financial Accountability **(434)**
Evangelical Press Association **(434)**
Federation of Diocesan Liturgical Commissions **(441)**
Fellowship of United Methodists in Music and Worship Arts **(442)**
Humanities Education and Research Association **(481)**
IFCA International **(486)**
Institute on Religion in an Age of Science **(504)**
Interim Ministry Network **(508)**
International Association of Baptist Colleges and Universities **(516)**
International Association of Jewish Vocational Services **(523)**
International Association of Women Ministers **(529)**
International Conference of Police Chaplains **(536)**
Jesuit Association of Student Personnel Administrators **(587)***
Jesuit Secondary Education Association **(587)**
Jewish Book Council **(587)***
Jewish Communal Service Association of North America **(588)**
Jewish Community Centers Association of North America **(588)**
Jewish Education Service of North America **(588)**
Jewish Educators Assembly **(588)**
JWB Jewish Chaplains Council **(590)**
Lutheran Education Association **(600)**
Lutheran Educational Conference of North America **(600)**
Men of Reform Judaism **(612)**
Military Chaplains Association of the U.S. **(616)**
Military Chaplains Association of the United States **(616)**
National Action Council for Minorities in Engineering (NACME) **(628)**
National Association of Baptist Professors of Religion **(648)**
National Association of Catholic Chaplains **(651)***
National Association of Catholic School Teachers **(651)**
National Association of Church Business Administration **(653)***
National Association of Church Food Service **(653)**
National Association of Church Personnel Administrators **(653)**

National Association of Congregational Christian Churches **(657)**
National Association of Diaconate Directors **(662)**
National Association of Ecumenical and Interreligious Staff **(664)**
National Association of Episcopal Schools **(666)**
National Association of Jewish Legislators **(677)**
National Association of Pastoral Musicians **(683)***
National Association of Seventh-Day Adventist Dentists **(695)**
National Association of State Catholic Conference Directors **(699)**
National Association of Temple Administrators **(705)**
National Association of Temple Educators **(705)**
The National Campus Ministry Association **(717)**
National Catholic Band Association **(718)**
National Catholic Development Conference **(718)***
National Catholic Educational Association **(718)**
National Catholic Educational Exhibitors **(718)**
National Church Goods Association **(722)**
National Church Library Association **(722)**
National Conference of Diocesan Vocation Directors **(727)**
National Conference of Yeshiva Principals **(729)**
National Federation of Priests' Councils **(749)**
National Institute of Business and Industrial Chaplaincy **(764)**
National Religious Broadcasters **(785)**
National Religious Broadcasters, Music License Committee **(785)**
National Society for Hebrew Day Schools **(792)**
North American Academy of Ecumenists **(812)***
North American Academy of Liturgy **(812)**
North American Association for the Study of Religion **(812)**
North American Association of Christians in Social Work **(813)***
North American Association of Professors of Christian Education **(813)**
North American Coalition for Christian Admissions Professionals **(815)**
Orthodox Theological Society in America **(833)**
Professional Association of Christian Educators **(859)***
Protestant Church-Owned Publishers Association **(868)***
Rabbinical Assembly **(872)**
Religion Communicators Council **(880)**
Religion Newswriters Association **(880)***
Religious Communication Association **(880)***
Religious Conference Management Association **(880)**
Religious Education Association **(880)***
Religious Research Association **(880)**
Resource Center for Religious Institutes **(883)**
Society for Buddhist-Christian Studies **(905)**
Society for Humanistic Judaism **(912)**
Society for the Scientific Study of Religion **(924)***
Society for Values in Higher Education **(926)**
Society of Biblical Literature **(931)***
Society of Christian Ethics **(932)***
United States Conference of Catholic Bishops **(992)**
United Synagogue of Conservative Judaism **(1001)**

RENTALS
American Automotive Leasing Association **(78)**
American Rental Association **(174)**
Association of Progressive Rental Organizations **(303)**
Automotive Fleet and Leasing Association **(322)**
Consortium of College and University Media Centers **(378)**
Corporate Housing Providers Association **(386)***
Equipment Leasing and Finance Association **(432)**
Institute of International Container Lessors **(501)***
National Association of Equipment Leasing Brokers **(666)**
National Association of Residential Property Managers **(691)**
National Leased Housing Association **(769)**
National Multi-Housing Council **(774)**
National Truck Leasing System **(802)**
North American Retail Dealers Association **(820)**
Office Business Center Association International **(826)**
Production Equipment Rental Association **(859)**
Real Estate Investment Securities Association **(875)**
Textile Rental Services Association of America **(973)**
Truck Renting and Leasing Association **(981)**
United Association of Equipment Leasing **(985)**
Vacation Rental Managers Association **(1007)***

RETAIL/WHOLESALE
ABC Children's Group **(2)***
Allied Trades of the Baking Industry **(26)**
American Association of Franchisees and Dealers **(61)**
American Association of Meat Processors **(64)**
American Beverage Licensees **(81)**
American Booksellers Association **(85)***
American Collegiate Retailing Association **(105)**

American Insurance Marketing and Sales Society *(141)*
American Luggage Dealers Association *(146)*
American Nursery and Landscape Association *(156)**
American Pet Products Association *(163)*
American Society of Dermatological Retailers *(196)*
American Supply Association *(214)**
American Traffic Safety Service Association *(217)*
American Wholesale Marketers Association *(221)**
Appliance Parts Distributors Association *(226)*
Archery Range and Retailers Organization *(227)*
Archery Trade Association *(227)*
Art Dealers Association of America *(229)*
AscdiNatd *(231)**
Asian American Convenience Stores Association *(231)*
Associated Equipment Distributors *(235)*
Association for High Technology Distribution *(248)*
Association for Hose and Accessories Distribution *(248)*
Association for Retail Environments *(256)*
Association for Retail Technology Standards *(256)*
Association of Coupon Professionals *(277)*
Association of Food Industries *(283)*
Association of Fund-Raising Distributors and Suppliers *(285)*
Association of Independent Manufacturers'/ Representatives, Inc. *(288)*
Association of Pool and Spa Professionals *(299)*
Association of Retail Travel Agents *(306)**
Association of Steel Distributors *(311)*
Aviation Distributors and Manufacturers Association International *(324)*
Bearing Specialist Association *(327)*
Bicycle Product Suppliers Association *(329)*
Biscuit and Cracker Manufacturers' Association *(330)**
Black Retail Action Group *(332)**
Board Retailers Association *(333)*
Building Material Dealers Association *(337)*
Business Solutions Association *(340)*
Cable & Telecommunications Association for Marketing *(340)*
Carwash Owner's and Supplier's Association *(343)**
CBA *(346)*
CIES - The Food Business Forum *(356)*
The Clearing House Association *(357)*
Commercial Vehicle Solutions Network *(367)*
Computing Technology Industry Association (CompTIA) *(373)*
Copper and Brass Servicenter Association *(384)*
Council of State Retail Associations *(397)*
Craft & Hobby Association *(402)*
Craft Retailers Association for Tomorrow *(403)*
The Door and Hardware Institute *(416)*
Electrical Equipment Representatives Association *(422)*
Electronic Components Industry Association *(423)**
Electronic Retailing Association *(423)**
Electronics Representatives Association *(424)*
Equipment Marketing and Distribution Association *(432)*
Financial and Security Products Association *(444)*
Fluid Power Distributors Association *(448)**
Food Industry Suppliers Association *(449)*
Food Marketing Institute *(449)*
Foodservice Equipment Distributors Association *(450)*
Foodservice Sales & Marketing Association *(450)*
Footwear Distributors and Retailers of America *(450)*
Ford Motor Minority Dealers Association *(451)*
Garden Centers of America *(456)*
Gases and Welding Distributors Association *(457)*
Global Market Development Center *(462)*
Health Industry Distributors Association *(469)*
Health Industry Representatives Association *(470)*
Healthcare Distribution Management Association *(471)*
Heating, Airconditioning and Refrigeration Distributors International *(473)*
Heavy Duty Representatives Association *(473)*
Home Improvement Research Institute *(478)*
Independent Laboratory Distributors Association *(490)*
Independent Medical Distributors Association *(490)*
Independent Office Products and Furniture Dealers Association *(490)*
Independent Professional Representatives Organization *(491)*
Inflatable Advertising Dealers Association *(494)*
InfoComm International *(495)*
Institute of Store Planners *(503)**
International Association of Airport Duty Free Stores *(515)*
International Association of Medical Equipment Remarketers and Servicers (IAMERS) *(524)*
International Association of Plastics Distributors *(526)*

International Bowling Pro Shop and Instructors Association *(530)*
International Council of Shopping Centers *(538)*
International Crystal Federation *(539)*
International Electronic Article Surveillance Manufacturers Association *(542)*
International Federation of Pharmaceutical Wholesalers *(544)*
International Foodservice Distributors Association *(546)*
International Formalwear Association *(546)*
International Home Furnishings Representatives Association *(550)*
International Housewares Association *(550)*
International Map Trade Association *(555)*
International Premium Cigar and Pipe Retailers *(561)*
International Sanitary Supply Association *(563)*
Jewelers of America *(587)*
Jewelry Industry Distributors Association *(587)**
Leading Jewelers Guild *(594)*
Machinery Dealers National Association *(601)*
Manufacturers' Agents Association for the Foodservice Industry *(603)*
Manufacturers' Agents National Association *(603)*
Marine Retailers Association of America *(605)*
Material Handling Equipment Distributors Association *(608)*
Materials Marketing Associates *(608)*
Metals Service Center Institute *(614)*
Monument Builders of North America *(619)*
Multi-Level Marketing International Association *(621)**
Music Distributors Association *(622)*
Mystery Shopping Providers Association *(623)*
NAGMR Consumer Product Brokers *(624)*
NAMM - The International Music Products Association *(625)*
National Alarm Association of America *(631)*
National Antique and Art Dealers Association of America *(634)*
National Appliance Parts Suppliers Association *(634)*
National Association for Retail Marketing Services *(642)*
National Association of Chain Drug Stores *(652)*
National Association of Chemical Distributors *(652)*
National Association of College Stores *(655)**
National Association of Convenience Stores *(658)*
National Association of Decorative Fabric Distributors *(662)*
National Association of Electrical Distributors *(664)*
National Association of Fire Equipment Distributors *(668)*
National Association of Flour Distributors *(668)*
National Association of Independent Publishers Representatives *(675)*
National Association of Marine Services *(679)*
National Association of Recording Merchandisers (NARM) *(690)*
National Association of Resale & Thrift Shops *(691)*
National Association of Retail Collection Attorneys *(692)**
National Association of Shell Marketers *(696)*
National Association of Sporting Goods Wholesalers *(696)**
National Association of Steel Pipe Distributors *(703)*
National Association of Ticket Brokers *(706)*
National Association of Video Distributors *(708)*
National Association of Wholesaler-Distributors *(709)*
National Automobile Dealers Association *(711)*
National Beer Wholesalers Association *(713)**
National Bicycle Dealers Association *(713)*
National Candle Association *(717)*
National Community Pharmacists Association *(725)*
National Confectionery Sales Association *(726)*
National Electrical Manufacturers Representatives Association *(745)*
National Emergency Equipment Dealers Association *(745)*
National Fastener Distributors Association *(747)*
National Field Selling Association *(750)*
National Frozen and Refrigerated Foods Association *(753)**
National Grocers Association *(756)*
National Home Furnishings Association *(759)*
National Honey Packers and Dealers Association *(760)*
National Ice Cream Retailers Association *(761)*
National Independent Flag Dealers Association *(762)*
National Kitchen and Bath Association *(767)*
National Luggage Dealers Association *(770)*
National Lumber and Building Material Dealers Association *(770)*
National Marine Distributors Association *(771)*
National Marine Representatives Association *(771)*
National Poultry and Food Distributors Association *(782)*
National Retail Federation *(786)**
National Retail Hobby Stores Association *(786)*
National Retail Tenants Association *(787)*

National School Supply and Equipment Association *(789)*
National Shoe Retailers Association *(791)*
National Ski and Snowboard Retailers Association *(791)**
National Sporting Goods Association *(796)**
National Truck Equipment Association *(802)**
National Yogurt Association *(806)*
North American Association of Floor Covering Distributors *(811)*
North American Building Material Distribution Association *(814)**
North American Flowerbulb Wholesalers Association *(816)*
North American Meat Association *(818)*
North American Retail Dealers Association *(820)*
North American Retail Hardware Association *(820)*
North American Wholesale Lumber Association *(823)*
NPTA Alliance *(824)*
Nuclear Suppliers Association *(825)**
The Optical Lab Division *(829)**
Oriental Rug Retailers of America, Inc. *(833)*
Original Equipment Suppliers Association *(833)**
Outdoor Power Equipment and Engine Service Association *(835)*
Paint and Decorating Retailers Association *(836)*
Path to Purchase Institute *(839)*
Pet Industry Distributors Association *(842)*
Petroleum Equipment Institute *(843)*
Petroleum Equipment Suppliers Association *(843)*
Pharmaceutical Research and Manufacturers of America (PhRMA) *(844)**
Power Transmission Distributors Association *(855)**
Power-Motion Technology Representatives Association *(855)*
Print Services & Distribution Association *(857)*
Professional Picture Framers Association *(864)*
Professional Retail Store Maintenance Association *(864)*
Professional Society for Sales and Marketing Training *(865)**
Quality Bakers of America Cooperative *(871)*
Radio Advertising Bureau *(873)*
Recreation Vehicle Dealers Association of North America *(876)*
The Recreational Vehicle Aftermarket Association *(877)*
Retail Advertising and Marketing Association International *(884)*
Retail Bakers of America *(884)**
Retail Confectioners International *(884)*
Retail Industry Leaders Association *(884)*
Retail Packaging Manufacturers Association *(885)*
Retail Print Music Dealers Association *(885)**
Retail Solutions Providers Association *(885)*
Retail, Wholesale and Department Store Union *(885)**
Sales and Marketing Executives International, Inc. *(890)*
Sales Association of the Chemical Industry *(890)*
Sales Association of the Paper Industry *(890)*
Sales Lead Management Association *(890)*
Sanitary Supply Wholesaling Association *(891)*
Security Hardware Distributors Association *(895)*
Sewn Products Equipment and Suppliers of the Americas *(898)*
Souvenir Wholesale Distributors Association *(953)*
Specialty Tools and Fasteners Distributors Association *(958)*
Uniform Retailers Association *(984)*
United Producers Formulators and Distributors Association *(988)*
United Shoe Retailers Association *(988)*
Used Textbook Association *(1005)*
Vacuum Dealers Trade Association/Sewing Dealers Trade Association *(1007)*
Wallcovering Association *(1012)*
Wholesale Florist and Florist Supplier Association *(1016)*
Wine and Spirits Wholesalers of America *(1018)**
WorkPlace Furnishings *(1025)*

RUBBER INDUSTRY

American Chemical Society - Rubber Division *(90)**
Carpet Cushion Council *(343)**
Fluid Sealing Association *(448)**
Independent Sealing Distributors *(491)*
International Institute of Synthetic Rubber Producers *(552)**
Rubber and Plastics Industry Conference of the United Steelworkers of America *(888)*
Rubber Manufacturers Association *(888)*
Rubber Pavements Association *(888)**
Rubber Trade Association of North America *(888)*
Scrap Tire Management Council *(893)*
Society of the Plastics Industry *(948)**
Tire and Rim Association *(975)*
Tire Industry Association *(975)*
Tire Retread and Repair Information Bureau *(975)**

SCIENCE

AASP - The Palynological Society (2)
Academy of Applied Science (4)
Academy of Clinical Laboratory Physicians and Scientists (4)
Academy of Clinical Research Professionals (4)
Academy of Molecular Imaging (7)*
Academy of Pharmaceutical Research and Science (8)
The Acoustical Society of America (11)
African Studies Association (15)
American Academy of Arts & Sciences (30)
American Academy of Clinical Toxicology (31)*
American Academy of Forensic Sciences (34)*
American Academy of Health Physics (35)*
American Academy of Somnology (42)
American Academy of Thermology (42)
American Academy of Veterinary and Comparative Toxicology (42)
American Aging Association (43)*
American Anthropological Association (45)*
American Association for Cancer Research (48)*
American Association for Clinical Chemistry, Inc. (48)
American Association for Crystal Growth (49)
American Association for Dental Research (49)
American Association for Geodetic Surveying (49)
American Association for Geriatric Psychiatry (49)
American Association for Laboratory Accreditation (50)
American Association for Physical Activity and Recreation (51)
American Association for the Advancement of Artificial Intelligence (51)
American Association for the Advancement of Science (51)*
American Association of Anatomists (54)*
American Association of Avian Pathologists (54)
American Association of Bioanalysts (54)
American Association of Immunologists (62)*
American Association of Pathologists' Assistants (68)*
American Association of Petroleum Geologists (68)*
American Association of Pharmaceutical Scientists (68)
The American Association of Phonetic Sciences (69)
American Association of Physical Anthropologists (69)
American Association of Physicists in Medicine (69)*
American Association of Physics Teachers (69)
The American Association of Radon Scientists and Technologists (72)*
American Association of State Climatologists (73)
American Association of Tissue Banks (75)
American Association of Variable Star Observers (76)
American Association of Veterinary Laboratory Diagnosticians (76)*
American Association of Veterinary Parasitologists (76)*
American Association of Wildlife Veterinarians (77)
American Association of Zoo Keepers (77)
American Association of Zoo Veterinarians (77)
American Astronautical Society (77)
American Astronomical Society (77)*
American Biological Safety Association (81)
American Bladesmith Society (81)
American Board of Health Physics (82)
American Botanical Council (85)
American Bryological and Lichenological Society (86)
American Clinical Laboratory Association (91)
American College of Laboratory Animal Medicine (97)*
American College of Medical Genetics (97)*
American College of Medical Physics (97)*
American College of Medical Toxicology (98)
American College of Toxicology (103)
American College of Veterinary Pathologists (104)
American Council of Independent Laboratories (109)*
American Council on Science and Health (110)
American Crystallographic Association (112)*
American Dairy Science Association (113)
The American Electrophoresis Society (116)
American Entomological Society (117)
American Federation for Aging Research (119)
American Federation of Astrologers, Inc. (119)
American Fern Society (121)
American Filtration and Separations Society (121)*
American Folklore Society (122)
American Genetic Association (126)
The American Geographical Society (126)
American Geological Institute (126)
American Geophysical Union (126)
American Geriatrics Society (126)
American Glovebox Society (126)
American Heartworm Society (130)
American Indian Science and Engineering Society (135)

American Institute for Maghrib Studies (136)
American Institute for Medical and Biological Engineering (136)
American Institute of Aeronautics and Astronautics (136)*
American Institute of Bangladesh Studies (137)
American Institute of Biological Sciences (137)
American Institute of Fishery Research Biologists (138)
American Institute of Indian Studies (139)
American Institute of Oral Biology (139)
American Institute of Physics (140)
American Institute of Professional Geologists (140)
American Institutes for Research (141)
American Littoral Society (146)*
American Meat Science Association (148)
American Metalcasting Consortium (151)
American Meteorological Society (151)
American Microscopical Society (151)
American National Standards Institute (154)
American Nuclear Society (156)
American Numismatic Society (156)
American Pain Society (161)
American Pathology Foundation (162)
American Peptide Society (163)*
American Physical Society (164)*
American Physiological Society (165)*
American Phytopathological Society (165)
American Political Science Association (166)*
American Psychological Association (169)*
American Psychological Association Practice Organization (170)
The American Quaternary Association (172)
American Rock Mechanics Association (176)
American Schools of Oriental Research (177)
American Scientific Glassblowers Society (178)*
American Society for Biochemistry and Molecular Biology (181)
American Society for Bone and Mineral Research (181)
American Society for Cell Biology (182)*
American Society for Clinical Laboratory Science (182)*
American Society for Clinical Pathology (182)
American Society for Cytotechnology (183)
American Society for Ethnohistory (184)*
American Society for Horticultural Science (185)
American Society for Information Science and Technology (186)*
American Society for Investigative Pathology (186)
American Society for Laser Medicine and Surgery (186)*
American Society for Mass Spectrometry (186)
American Society for Microbiology (187)*
American Society for Mohs Histotechnology (187)
American Society for Pharmacology and Experimental Therapeutics (188)
American Society for Reproductive Medicine (189)*
American Society of Animal Science (192)
American Society of Cytopathology (196)
American Society of Gene & Cell Therapy (198)*
American Society of Geolinguistics (198)
American Society of Human Genetics (200)*
American Society of Ichthyologists and Herpetologists (200)
American Society of Laboratory Animal Practitioners (201)
American Society of Limnology and Oceanography (202)
American Society of Mammalogists (202)
The American Society of Naturalists (203)
American Society of Papyrologists (205)
American Society of Parasitologists (206)
American Society of Pharmacognosy (207)*
American Society of Plant Biologists (207)
American Society of Plant Taxonomists (207)*
American Society of Primatologists (208)
American Society on Aging (211)*
American Sociological Association (211)*
American Solar Energy Society (211)
American Weather and Climate Industry Association (220)
Analytical and Life Science Systems Association (223)
Analytical Laboratory Managers Association (223)*
Animal Behavior Society (223)
Archaeological Institute of America (227)
ASFE/The Geoprofessional Business Association (231)*
ASM International (232)
ASPRS-The Imaging and Geospatial Information Society (233)
Association for Adult Development and Aging (238)*
Association for Africanist Anthropology (238)
Association for Arid Lands Studies (239)
Association for Assessment and Accreditation of Laboratory Animal Care International (239)
Association for Chemoreception Sciences (241)
Association for Clinical Research Training (241)
Association for Competitive Technology (ACT) (242)

Association for Feminist Anthropology (246)
Association for Gnotobiotics (247)
Association for Library and Information Science Education (251)
Association for Molecular Pathology (252)*
Association for Politics and the Life Sciences (253)
Association for Psychological Science (254)*
The Association for Science Teacher Education (256)
The Association for Social Anthropology in Oceania (256)
Association for the Study of Classical African Civilizations (259)
The Association for the Study of Play (260)
Association for Tropical Biology and Conservation (260)*
Association for Women Geoscientists (261)
Association for Women in Science (262)
Association of American Geographers (265)*
Association of American Pesticide Control Officials (265)
Association of American State Geologists (266)*
Association of Applied IPM Ecologists (267)
Association of Assistive Technology ACT Programs (268)
Association of Biomolecular Resource Facilities (269)
Association of Black Anthropologists (269)
Association of Cinema and Video Laboratories (273)
Association of Clinical Research Organizations (273)
Association of Clinical Scientists (273)
Association of Earth Science Editors (279)
Association of Ecosystem Research Centers (279)
Association of Environmental and Engineering Geologists (281)
Association of Independent Research Institutes (288)
Association of Latina and Latino Anthropologists (291)
Association of Management/International Association of Management (292)
Association of Medical Diagnostic Manufacturers (293)
Association of Muslim Social Scientists of North America (295)
Association of Natural Resource Enforcement Trainers (295)
Association of Old Crows (297)
Association of Pathology Chairs (298)
Association of Public Health Laboratories (304)
Association of Research Directors (306)
Association of Research Directors of 1890s Colleges and Universities (306)
Association of Science Museum Directors (307)*
Association of Science-Technology Centers (307)
Association of Senior Anthropologists (308)
Association of Third World Studies (314)
Association of Universities for Research in Astronomy, Inc. (315)*
Association of University Research Parks (316)
Association of Zoos and Aquariums (318)
AVS: Science and Technology of Materials, Interfaces, and Processing (325)
Balloon Federation of America (325)
Behavior Genetics Association (327)*
Belt Association (328)
Beta Beta Beta (328)
BioCommunications Association (329)*
Bioelectromagnetics Society (329)
Biological Stain Commission (330)*
Biomedical Engineering Society (330)*
Biophysical Society (330)*
Biotechnology Industry Organization (BIO) (330)
The Botanical Society of America (333)
Care Continuum Alliance (342)
Center for Research Libraries (348)
Chemical Sources Association (352)*
Clay Minerals Society (357)
Clinical and Laboratory Standards Institute (358)
Clinical Laboratory Management Association (358)*
Clinical Ligand Assay Society (358)
Coalition of Visionary Resources (361)
The Coastal and Estuarine Research Federation (361)
Coblentz Society (361)
COLA (362)
Coleopterists Society (362)
College of American Pathologists (363)
The Combustion Institute (366)
Commission on Professionals in Science and Technology (368)
Compressed Gas Association (372)
Conference Board of the Mathematical Sciences (374)
Conservation and Preservation Charities of America (377)*
Consortium of Social Science Associations (379)
Controlled Release Society (383)
Corporate Crisis Response Officers Association (385)
Council for Agricultural Science and Technology (388)
Council for Chemical Research, Inc. (389)
Council for Museum Anthropology (390)

Society for Psychological Anthropology (919)*
Society for Risk Analysis (920)
Society for Social Studies of Science (921)
Society for the Anthropology of Food and Nutrition (923)
Society for the Anthropology of North America (923)
Society for the Anthropology of Work (923)
Society for the History of Discoveries (923)
Society for the Science & the Public (924)
Society for the Study of Amphibians and Reptiles (925)
Society for the Study of Evolution (925)
Society for the Study of Reproduction (925)*
Society for the Study of Social Biology (925)
Society for Theriogenology (926)
Society for Vascular Medicine (926)
Society for Vector Ecology (927)
Society for Wetland Scientists (927)
Society of Biological Psychiatry (931)*
Society of Commercial Seed Technologists (933)
Society of Competitive Intelligence Professionals (933)
Society of Economic Geologists (934)
Society of Engineering Science (935)
Society of Ethnobiology (935)
Society of Exploration Geophysicists (935)
Society of Forensic Toxicologists (936)
Society of Geriatric Cardiology (937)
Society of Hispanic Professional Engineers (938)
Society of Independent Professional Earth Scientists (939)
Society of Nematologists (942)
Society of Petrophysicists and Well Log Analysts (944)
Society of Quality Assurance (946)
Society of Research Administrators International (946)
Society of Rheology (946)*
Society of Systematic Biologists (947)
Society of Toxicologic Pathologists (948)*
Society of Toxicologic Pathology (948)*
Society of Toxicology (948)*
Society of Vertebrate Paleontology (950)*
Society of Woman Geographers (950)
Society of Wood Science and Technology (950)
Soil Science Society of America (951)*
Space Transportation Association (953)
Special Interest Group for Computer Science Education (954)
TechAmerica (fka Technology Association of America) (969)
Teratology Society (971)
Toxicology Forum (976)*
Tree-Ring Society (980)
Triological Society (980)
United Lightning Protection Association (987)
United States and Canadian Academy of Pathology (989)
United States Federation for Culture Collections (994)
United States Federation of Scholars and Scientists (994)
United States-Israel Science & Technology Foundation (USISTF) (995)
Universities Research Association (1002)
Universities Space Research Association (1002)*
Veterinary Botanical Medical Association (1008)*
Vibration Isolation and Seismic Control Manufacturers Association (1009)*
Weather Modification Association (1014)
Weather Risk Management Association (1014)
Weed Science Society of America (1014)
Wilderness Education Association (1017)*
Wilderness Medical Society (1017)
Women in Cell Biology (1021)
World Aquaculture Society (1025)
World Future Society (1026)
XBRL US, Inc. (1029)

SEWING
Craft & Hobby Association (402)
Sewing and Craft Alliance (898)
Sewn Products Equipment and Suppliers of the Americas (898)
Souvenirs, Gifts and Novelties Trade Association (953)

SEX
American Association of Sexuality Educators, Counselors and Therapists (73)
American Sexually Transmitted Diseases Association (178)
American Society of Andrology (192)
Association for the Treatment of Sexual Abusers (260)
National Abstinence Education Association (626)
Society for Sex Therapy and Research (921)
Society for the Philosophy of Sex and Love (923)
Society for the Scientific Study of Sexuality (924)*

SIGNS & SIGNALS
IEEE Signal Processing Society (485)
International Marking and Identification Association (556)
International Municipal Signal Association (557)*
International Sign Association (564)*
National Association of Sign Supply Distributors (696)
Outdoor Advertising Association of America (834)
POPAI The Global Association for Marketing at Retail (852)
Railway Systems Suppliers, Inc (874)
Society for Environmental Graphic Design (908)
World Sign Associates (1027)

SOCIAL SERVICE/URBAN AFFAIRS
Advanced Transit Association (13)
AFL-CIO (American Federation of Labor and Congress of Industrial Organizations) (14)
Alliance for Children and Families (22)
Alliance of Information and Referral Systems (25)
American Association for Marriage and Family Therapy (50)*
American Association of Public Welfare Attorneys (72)
American Association of Suicidology (74)
American Benefits Council (80)
American Enterprise Institute for Public Policy Research (117)
American Institute of Certified Planners (137)
American Network of Community Options and Resources (ANCOR) (155)*
American Orthopsychiatric Association (159)
American Planning Association (166)*
American Public Health Association (171)
American Public Human Services Association (171)*
APHSA - Information Systems Management (224)
Association of Administrators of the Interstate Compact on the Placement of Children (263)
Association of Baccalaureate Social Work Program Directors (269)
Association of Christian Therapists (273)
Association of Family and Conciliation Courts (282)
Association of Jewish Family & Children's Agencies (290)
Association of Junior Leagues International (290)
Association of Oncology Social Work (297)
Association of Pediatric Oncology Social Workers (298)
Association of Social Work Boards (309)
Association of YMCA Professionals (318)
Catholic Charities USA (345)
Child Welfare League of America (353)*
Clinical Social Work Association (359)
Community Action Partnership (369)
Community Health Charities of America (371)
The Corps Network (formerly the National Association of Service and Conservation Corps) (386)
Council of Large Public Housing Authorities (395)
Council of State Community Development Agencies (397)
Council of the Great City Schools (398)*
Council on Social Work Education (400)
Cristo Rey Network (404)
Equal Justice Works (432)
Family, Career and Community Leaders of America (437)
General Federation of Women's Clubs (458)*
Independent Sector (491)
InterAction (American Council of Voluntary International Action) (506)
International Association for Truancy and Dropout Prevention (514)
International Community Corrections Association (536)
International Downtown Association (541)*
International Economic Development Council (541)*
Management Association for Private Photogrammetric Surveyors (602)
Meals on Wheels Association of America (609)
National Abortion Federation (626)
National Alliance for Hispanic Health (631)
National Alliance of Community Economic Development Associations (632)
National AMBUCS (633)
National Association for Community Mediation (637)*
National Association for Home Care and Hospice (639)
National Association for Program Information and Performance Measurement (641)
National Association for Rural Mental Health (642)
National Association of Area Agencies on Aging (647)
National Association of Black Social Workers (649)
National Association of County Human Services Administrators (660)
National Association of Foster Grandparent Program Directors (669)

National Association of Housing and Redevelopment Officials (673)
National Association of Neighborhoods (681)
National Association of Public Child Welfare Administrators (688)
National Association of Puerto Rican-Hispanic Social Workers (689)
National Association of Social Workers (696)*
National Association of State Retirement Administrators (702)
National Association of Urban Hospitals (708)
National Collaboration for Youth (723)
National Conference of State Social Security Administrators (728)
National Council of Nonprofits (735)
National Energy Assistance Directors' Association (746)
National Family Planning and Reproductive Health Association (747)
National Housing and Rehabilitation Association (760)*
National Human Services Assembly (761)*
National League of Cities (765)*
National Legal Aid and Defender Association (769)
The National Network for Social Work Managers (774)
National Organization of Social Security Claimants' Representatives (778)
National Staff Development and Training Association (796)
National WIC Association (805)
North American Association of Christians in Social Work (813)*
The Philanthropy Roundtable (846)
Population Action International (852)
Public Housing Authorities Directors Association (869)
School Social Work Association of America (892)*
Society for Social Work Leadership in Health Care (921)
TASH (968)
United States Conference of Mayors (992)
Voices for America's Children (1011)

SOCIOLOGY
African Studies Association (15)
American Association of Suicidology (74)
American Council of Learned Societies (109)
American Men's Studies Association (150)
American Real Estate and Urban Economics Association (173)*
American Society of Geolinguistics (198)
American Sociological Association (211)*
Association for Applied and Clinical Sociology (238)
Association for Humanist Sociology (249)*
Association for the Sociology of Religion (259)*
Association for the Study of Classical African Civilizations (259)
Association of Black Sociologists (270)*
Cheiron: The International Society for the History of Behavioral and Social Sciences (351)
Community Development Society (370)
Human Behavior and Evolution Society (480)
International Association for Business and Society (511)
International Rural Sociology Association (563)
International Society for Quality-of-Life Studies (569)
International Society for the Comparative Studies of Civilizations (569)
International Studies Association (576)*
The International Transactional Analysis Association (578)
Law and Society Association (594)*
National Association of Neighborhoods (681)
National Council on Family Relations (738)*
North American Society for the Sociology of Sport (822)
Population Association of America (853)*
The Rural Sociological Society (889)
Social Science History Association (902)
Society for Disability Studies (907)
Society for Social Studies of Science (921)
Society for the Advancement of Behavior Analysis (922)
Society for the Psychological Study of Science Issues (924)
Society for the Psychological Study of Social Issues (924)*
Society for the Scientific Study of Religion (924)*
Society for the Study of Social Problems (925)*
Society for the Study of Symbolic Interaction (925)*
Sociological Practice Association (950)
Special Interest Group for Computer-Human Interaction (954)*

SPEAKERS
American Institute of Parliamentarians (140)
American Seminar Leaders Association (178)
International Association of Speakers Bureaus (528)

National Association of Parliamentarians (683)
National Forensic Association (752)
National Speakers Association (795)*
Society of Armenian Studies (930)

SPORTS/LEISURE/ENTERTAINMENT

Academy of Leisure Sciences (6)
Academy of Motion Picture Arts and Sciences (7)
Aerobics and Fitness Association of America (13)
Airforwarders Association (20)
Alliance for Women in Media (24)
Alliance of Motion Picture & Television Producers (25)
America Outdoors Association (28)*
American Academy of Podiatric Sports Medicine (40)
American Alliance for Health, Physical Education, Recreation and Dance (44)*
American Amusement Machine Association (45)
American Association for Physical Activity and Recreation (51)
American Association for Vocational Instructional Materials (53)
American Baseball Coaches Association (80)
American Boat and Yacht Council (84)
American Boat Builders and Repairers Association (84)
American Bridge Teachers' Association (86)
American Camp Association (88)
American Canoe Association (88)
American Cinema Editors (91)
American College of Sports Medicine (102)*
American Council of Snowmobile Associations (110)
American Council on Exercise (110)*
American Disc Jockey Association (115)
American Entertainment Armories Association (117)
American Federation of Musicians (119)
American Fly Fishing Trade Association (122)
American Football Coaches Association (122)
American Gaming Association (124)*
American Greyhound Track Operators Association (127)
American Hiking Society (131)
The American Hockey Coaches Association (132)
American Hockey League (132)
American Kennel Club (143)
American League of Anglers and Boaters (145)
American Medical Society for Sports Medicine (149)
American Mountain Guides Association (153)
American National Chamber of Commerce (154)
American Numismatic Society (156)
American Orthopaedic Society for Sports Medicine (159)*
American Osteopathic Academy of Sports Medicine (159)
American Philatelic Society (163)
American Pyrotechnics Association (172)
American Resort Development Association (175)
American Running Association (176)
American Running Association/American Medical Athletic Association (176)
American Sand Association (177)
American Society of Cinematographers (194)*
American Society of Golf Course Architects (198)
American Society of Marine Artists (202)
American Society of Travel Agents (210)
American Sportfishing Association (212)
American Sports Builders Association (212)*
American Sports Medicine Association (213)
American Sportscasters Association (213)
American Stamp Dealers Association (213)
American Swimming Coaches Association (215)
American Therapeutic Recreation Association (216)
American Volleyball Coaches Association (219)
Amusement & Music Operators Association (223)
Amusement Industry Manufacturers and Suppliers International (223)
Archery Range and Retailers Organization (227)
Archery Trade Association (227)
The Arts and Creative Materials Institute, Inc. (229)*
Art Directors Guild/Scenic, Title and Graphic Artists (230)
Association for Applied Sport Psychology (239)
Association for Information Media and Equipment (249)
The Association for the Study of Play (260)
Association for Women in Sports Media (262)
Association of Cinema and Video Laboratories (273)
Association of Film Commissioners International (283)
Association of Gaming Equipment Manufacturers (285)
Association of Golf Merchandisers (286)
Association of Independent Commercial Producers (287)
Association of Marina Industries (293)
Association of Moving Image Archivists (295)
Association of Official Racing Chemists (296)
Association of Pool and Spa Professionals (299)
Association of Private Club Directors (300)

Association of Professional Ball Players of America (301)
Association of Public Television Stations (304)
Association of Racing Commissioners International (304)
Association of Surfing Professionals - North America (312)
Association of Talent Agents (312)*
Association of Volleyball Professionals (317)
Association of YMCA Professionals (318)
Association of Zoos and Aquariums (318)
ATP Tour, Inc. (320)
Awards and Recognition Association (325)
Balloon Federation of America (325)
Baseball Writers Association of America (326)
Billiard and Bowling Institute of America (329)
Billiard Congress of America (329)
Black Coaches & Administrators (331)
Black Entertainment and Sports Lawyers Association (331)
Black Filmmaker Foundation (331)
Board Retailers Association (333)
Boating Writers International (333)
Bowling Proprietors' Association of America (334)
Bowling Writers Association of America (334)
CALLERLAB - International Association of Square Dance Callers (341)
Central Intercollegiate Athletic Association (349)
Clowns of America International (359)
Club Managers Association of America (359)
College Athletic Business Management Association (362)*
College Gymnastics Association (363)
College Sports Information Directors of America (364)*
College Swimming Coaches Association of America (364)
Collegiate Commissioners Association (365)
Consortium of College and University Media Centers (378)
Cross Country Ski Areas Association (405)
Cruise Lines International Association (405)
Dance/USA (406)*
Delaware Standardbred Owners Association (409)
Directors Guild of America (413)
Diving Equipment and Marketing Association (415)
Division 1-A Athletic Directors Association (415)
Dramatists Guild of America (416)
Dude Ranchers' Association (417)
Employee Services Management Association (426)
Entertainment Merchants Association (429)
Entertainment Software Association (ESA) (429)*
Executive Women's Golf Association (435)
The Exercise Safety Association (435)
Football Bowl Association (450)
Football Writers Association of America (450)
Free Speech Coalition (453)
The French Film Office/UniFrance USA (453)
Game Manufacturers Association (456)*
Giant Screen Cinema Association (460)
Golf Coaches Association of America (463)
Golf Course Builders Association of America (463)
Golf Course Superintendents Association of America (463)*
Golf Range Association of America (463)*
Golf Writers Association of America (463)
Harness Tracks of America (468)
Heli Ski US Association (473)
Historians Film Committee/Film & History (476)
Hobby Manufacturers Association (477)
ICAAAA Coaches Association (482)
Ice Skating Institute (482)
IDEA, The Health and Fitness Association (482)
Independent Film and Television Alliance (489)*
Independent Filmmaker Project (489)
Industry Council on Tangible Assets (494)
Inflatable Boat Manufacturers Association (495)
Institute of Diving (499)
Interactive Gaming Council Canada (507)
Interactive Media Entertainment & Gaming Association (507)
Intercollegiate Tennis Association (507)
International Association of Amusement Parks and Attractions(IAAPA) (515)*
International Association of Approved Basketball Officials, Inc. (515)
International Association of Audio Visual Communicators (516)*
International Association of Broadcast Monitors (517)
International Association of Dive Rescue Specialists (519)
International Association of Golf Administrators (522)
International Association of Skateboard Companies (527)
International Association of Speakers Bureaus (528)
International Association of Venue Managers (528)*
International Bowling Pro Shop and Instructors Association (530)

International Boxing Federation (530)
International Brotherhood of Magicians (531)
International Cinema Technology Association (534)*
International Coach Federation (535)
International Council for Health, Physical, Education, Recreation, Sport and Dance (537)
International Entertainment Buyers Association (543)
International Family Recreation Association (544)
International Game Developers Association (548)
International Golf Associates (548)
International Health, Racquet and Sportsclub Association (549)
International Hot Rod Association (550)*
International Hunter Education Association (550)
International League of Professional Baseball Clubs (554)
International Light Transportation Vehicle Association, Inc. (554)
International Professional Rodeo Association (561)
International Sled Dog Racing Association (564)
International Snowmobile Manufacturers Association (565)
International Spa Association (575)
International Sport Show Producers Association (575)
International Sports Heritage Association (575)*
International Superyacht Society (576)
International Ticketing Association (577)
The Jockey Club (588)
The Jockeys' Guild (588)
KWPN of North America (591)
Ladies Professional Golf Association (592)
Literary Managers and Dramaturgs of the Americas (599)
Lpga Tournament Owners Association (600)
Magic Dealers Association (601)
Major Indoor Soccer League (601)
Major League Baseball Players Association (601)
Major League Soccer (601)*
Marine Retailers Association of America (605)
Minor League Baseball (617)
Motion Picture Association of America (MPAA) (619)
NAIR -- International Association of Bowling Equipment Specialists (624)
National Academy of Recording Arts and Sciences (628)
National Alliance for Accessible Golf (631)*
National Alliance for Media Arts and Culture (631)
National Alliance for Musical Theatre (632)
National Alliance for Youth Sports (632)
National Association for Campus Activities (637)
National Association for Girls and Women in Sport (639)
National Association for Kinesiology in Higher Education (640)
National Association for Sport and Physical Education (643)*
National Association of Academic Advisors for Athletes (645)*
National Association of Athletic Development Directors (647)
National Association of Basketball Coaches (648)*
National Association of Boat Manufacturers (650)
National Association of Broadcasters (650)
National Association of Casino Party Operators (651)
National Association of Charterboat Operators (652)
National Association of Collegiate Directors of Athletics (656)
National Association of Collegiate Marketing Administrators (656)
National Association of Collegiate Women Athletic Administrators (656)
National Association of Composers, USA (657)
National Association of County Park and Recreation Officials (660)
National Association of Intercollegiate Athletics (676)
National Association of Jai Alai Frontons (677)
National Association of Latino Independent Producers (677)
National Association of Marine Services (679)
National Association of Police Athletics/Activities Leagues, Inc. (685)
National Association of Professional Baseball Leagues (686)
National Association of Recording Merchandisers (NARM) (690)
National Association of RV Parks and Campgrounds (692)*
National Association of Sporting Goods Wholesalers (696)*
National Association of Sports Commissions (697)
National Association of Sports Officials (697)
National Association of Sports Public Address Announcers (697)
National Association of State Boating Law Administrators (698)
National Association of State Outdoor Recreation Liaison Officers (701)

STORAGE

SURPLUS

TAXATION

TESTING

American Council of Independent Laboratories (109)*
American Evaluation Association (118)
American Society for Histocompatibility and Immunogenetics (185)
American Society for Nondestructive Testing (187)
American Society for Quality (189)
American Society of Home Inspectors (200)
Association for Assessment in Counseling and Education (240)
Association of Forensic Document Examiners (284)
Association of Regulatory Boards of Optometry (305)*
Association of Test Publishers (313)
ASTM International (319)*
Cardiovascular Credentialing International (342)
Controlled Environment Testing Association (383)
InterNational Electrical Testing Association (542)*
International Test and Evaluation Association (577)
National Association of Disability Examiners (663)
National Association of Document Examiners (663)
National Conference of Bar Examiners (726)
National Council of Examiners for Engineering and Surveying (734)
Society for Clinical Trials (906)
Society of Experimental Test Pilots (935)
Society of Flight Test Engineers (936)

TOBACCO INDUSTRY

American Wholesale Marketers Association (221)*
Association of Dark Leaf Tobacco Dealers and Exporters (278)
Bakery, Confectionery, Tobacco Workers and Grain Millers International Union (325)
Burley Tobacco Growers Cooperative Association (338)
Cigar Association of America, Inc. (356)
International Premium Cigar and Pipe Retailers (561)
Pipe Tobacco Council, Inc. (849)
Society for Research on Nicotine and Tobacco (920)
Specialty Tobacco Council (958)
Tobacco Associates, Inc. (975)
Tobacco Merchants Association of the United States (975)*
Tobacconists' Association of America (976)
United States Tobacco Cooperative Inc (1000)

TOOLS

American Knife & Tool Institute (144)
American Ladder Institute (144)*
American Measuring Tool Manufacturers Association (148)*
Concrete Sawing and Drilling Association (374)*
Equipment and Tool Institute (432)*
Equipment Service Association (433)
Hand Tools Institute (468)
International Association of Tool Craftsmen (528)
International Saw and Knife Association (564)
International Staple, Nail and Tool Association (575)
National Tooling and Machining Association (800)
North American Punch Manufacturers Association (820)
Powder Actuated Tool Manufacturers Institute (854)*
Power Tool Institute, Inc. (855)*
Specialty Steel Industry of North America (958)
Specialty Tools and Fasteners Distributors Association (958)
Tooling, Manufacturing and Technologies Association (976)
Underground Equipment Manufacturers Council (984)
United States Cutting Tool Institute (993)*

TRADE (FOREIGN AND DOMESTIC)

Agribusiness Council (16)
Airforwarders Association (20)
American Association of Exporters & Importers (60)
American Automotive Policy Council (78)
American Chamber of Commerce Executives (89)
American Concrete Pumping Association (106)*
American Cotton Shippers Association (108)
American Factoring Association (118)
American Hardwood Export Council (129)
American Import Shippers Association (134)
American Importers and Exporters/Meat Products Group (135)
American Indonesian Chamber of Commerce (135)
American Institute for International Steel (136)
American International Automobile Dealers Association (142)
American Poultry International Ltd. (167)
American Seed Trade Association (178)
American-European Soda Ash Shipping Association (222)
American-Israel Chamber of Commerce and Industry (222)
American-Uzbekistan Chamber of Commerce (222)
Association of American Chambers of Commerce in Latin America (264)

Association of Dark Leaf Tobacco Dealers and Exporters (278)
Association of Food Industries (283)
Association of Foreign Trade Representatives (284)
Association of Global Automakers (285)*
The Association of Women in International Trade (317)
BAFT-IFSA (325)
Bicycle Product Suppliers Association (329)
Brazilian American Chamber of Commerce (334)*
BritishAmerican Business Inc. (335)
Canadian-American Business Council (341)
Cheese Importers Association of America, Inc. (351)
Chilean Avocado Importers Association (CAIA) (353)
Coal Exporters Association of the U.S. (359)
Coal Trading Association (359)
Colombian American Association (365)*
Council of the Americas (398)
Customs and International Trade Bar Association (406)
The Danish-American Chamber of Commerce (USA) (407)
Diamond Manufacturers & Importers Association of America (411)*
Directors of Health Promotion and Education (DHPE) (413)
Ecuadorean American Association (419)
Emerging Markets Private Equity Association (425)
EMTA - Trade Association for the Emerging Markets (427)
European-American Business Council (434)
Export Institute of the United States (436)
The Fair Currency Alliance (437)
Fashion Accessories Shippers Association (438)
FCIB-NACM Corporation (438)
Financial Services Forum (445)
Finnish American Chamber of Commerce (445)
Formaldehyde Council, Inc. (452)
German American Business Association (460)
German American Chamber of Commerce (460)
Global Offset and Countertrade Association (GOCA) (462)
Hellenic-American Chamber of Commerce (474)
Icelandic American Chamber of Commerce (482)
INDA, Association of the Nonwoven Fabrics Industry (488)*
Independent Distributors Association (489)
Industrial Fabrics Association International (493)
Interactive Media Entertainment & Gaming Association (507)
International Association of Independent Tanker Owners (523)
International Housewares Association (550)
International Natural Sausage Casing Association (557)
International Reciprocal Trade Association (562)
International Trade Commission Trial Lawyers Association (577)
The International Wood Products Association (581)
Ireland Chamber of Commerce in the United States (585)
Italy-America Chamber of Commerce (586)
Malaysian Rubber Export Promotion Council (USA) (602)
Meat Importers Council of America (609)
Mexico-U.S. Business Committee, U.S. Council (614)
Moroccan American Business Council (619)
National Association for the Specialty Food Trade (644)
National Association of Beverage Importers Inc. (648)
National Association of Blind Merchants (650)
National Association of Export Companies (666)*
National Association of Foreign Trade Zones (669)
National Association of Professional Surplus Lines Offices, Ltd. (688)*
National Association of Shell Marketers (696)
National Black Chamber of Commerce (714)
National Council on International Trade Development (739)
National Customs Brokers and Forwarders Association of America (741)
National Flea Market Association (751)
National Foreign Trade Council, Inc. (752)
National Treasury Employees Union (801)*
National U.S.-Arab Chamber of Commerce (803)
National Wooden Pallet and Container Association (805)
North American Export Grain Association, Inc. (816)
North American-Chilean Chamber of Commerce (823)
Northwest Fruit Exporters (824)
Organization for International Investment (831)
Organization of Women in International Trade (832)
Oriental Rug Importers Association of America (833)
Pakistan American Business Association (837)
Professional Picture Framers Association (864)
Professional Records and Information Services Management International (864)

Ranchers-Cattlemen Action Legal Fund, United Stockgrower of America (874)
Romanian-American Chamber of Commerce (888)
Small Business Exporters Association of the United States (900)
Softwood Export Council (951)
Swedish-American Chambers of Commerce of the USA, Inc. (967)
Trade Exchange of America (977)
United States-Taiwan Business Council (989)
United States-ASEAN Business Council Inc. (990)
United States Association of Importers of Textiles and Apparel (990)
United States Business and Industry Council (991)
United States Dairy Export Council (993)
United States Grains Council (994)*
United States Hispanic Chamber of Commerce (995)
United States Meat Export Federation (996)
United States Pan Asian American Chamber of Commerce (997)*
U.S.-Russia Business Council (999)
United States-Sudan Business Council (999)
United States Wheat Associates, Inc. (1000)
United States-China Business Council (1001)
United States-China Chamber of Commerce (1001)
Venezuelan American Association of the U.S. (1008)*
Wi-Fi Alliance (1016)*
Woodworking Machinery Industry Association (1024)

TRAINING

Academy of Security Educators and Trainers (9)
Accrediting Council for Continuing Education & Training (10)
American Society for Training and Development (190)
American Technical Education Association (215)
Association for Information Media and Equipment (249)
Association of Career and Technical Education (271)
The Association of Collegiate Conference and Events Directors International (275)
Automotive Training Managers Council (324)
Distance Education and Training Council (414)
Driving School Association of America (416)
International Association of Correctional Training Personnel (518)*
International Association of Culinary Professionals (519)
International Association of Round Dance Teachers (527)
International Society for Performance Improvement (567)*
International Society of Fire Service Instructors (572)
International Society of Managing and Technical Editors (573)
National Association of Junior Auxiliaries (677)
National Association of Partners in Education (683)
National Association of Professional Asian American Women (686)
The National Association of Professional Receptionists (688)
National Association of Workforce Development Professionals (710)*
National Basketball Athletic Trainers Association (712)
National Business Incubation Association (717)
National Environmental, Safety and Health Training Association (746)
National Exercise Trainers Association (747)
National Petroleum Management Association (780)
National Training and Simulation Association (801)*
North American Transportation Management Institute (823)
Professional Baseball Athletic Trainers Society (860)
Professional Football Athletic Trainers Society (861)
Professional Society for Sales and Marketing Training (865)*
Professional Tennis Registry (865)
Society of Insurance Trainers and Educators (940)
Training Directors' Forum (977)*
Training Officers Consortium (977)
The Travel Institute (979)*
United Professional Horsemen's Association (988)
United States Fencing Coaches Association (994)
Voice and Speech Trainers Association (1011)
Walking Horse Trainers Association (1012)

TRANSPORTATION

AASHTO: Transportation Center of Excellence (2)
Academy of Model Aeronautics (7)
Academy of Rail Labor Attorneys (8)
Advanced Transit Association (13)
Aeronautical Repair Station Association (14)*
Aerospace & Flight Test Radio Coordinating Council (14)
Aerospace Futures Alliance (14)
Aerospace Industries Association of America (14)
AFL-CIO - Maritime Trades Department (15)

Agricultural and Food Transporters Conference (16)
AHS International - The Vertical Flight Society (17)
Air and Expedited Motor Carriers Association (17)
Air Carrier Association of America (17)
Air Force Association (18)
Air Force Sergeants Association (19)
Air Line Pilots Association International (19)
Air Medical Operators Association (19)
Air Traffic Control Association (19)
Airborne Law Enforcement Association (19)
Aircraft Builders Council (20)
Aircraft Electronics Association (20)
Aircraft Locknut Manufacturers Association (20)*
Aircraft Owners and Pilots Association (20)
Airforwarders Association (20)
Airline Industrial Relations Conference (20)
Airlines Electronic Engineering Committee (20)
Airlines For America (21)
Airport Consultants Council (21)
Airport Ground Transportation Association (21)*
Airport Minority Advisory Council (AMAC) (21)
Airports Council International - North America (21)
Alliance of Automobile Manufacturers (24)
Alliance of Automotive Service Providers (24)*
Allied Pilots Association (26)
Alternative Fuel Vehicle Network (27)
Amalgamated Transit Union (28)
Ambulance Manufacturers Division (28)
America's Independent Truckers' Association, Inc. (29)
American Academy of Ambulatory Care Nursing (30)
American Ambulance Association (44)
American Association for Accreditation of Ambulatory Surgery Facilities (47)*
American Association of Airport Executives (53)*
American Association of Motor Vehicle Administrators (65)
American Association of Port Authorities (70)
American Association of Private Railroad Car Owners (71)
American Association of Railroad Superintendents (72)
American Astronautical Society (77)
American Automotive Leasing Association (78)
American Automotive Policy Council (78)
American Bonanza Society (85)
American Bureau of Shipping (86)
American Bus Association (87)*
American Coal Ash Association (92)
American Cotton Shippers Association (108)
American Driver and Traffic Safety Education Association (115)
American Highway Users Alliance (131)
American Import Shippers Association (134)
American Institute for Shippers' Associations (136)
American Institute of Aeronautics and Astronautics (136)*
American Institute of Marine Underwriters (139)
American International Automobile Dealers Association (142)
American Maritime Congress (147)
American Maritime Officers (147)
American Maritime Officers Plans (147)
American Maritime Officers Service (147)
American Motorcyclist Association (153)
American Moving and Storage Association (153)
American Pilots' Association (165)*
American Public Transportation Association (171)
American Railway Development Association (173)
American Railway Engineering and Maintenance-of-Way Association (173)
American Road and Transportation Builders Association (175)
American Salvage Pool Association (177)
American School Bus Council (177)
American Short Line and Regional Railroad Association (179)
American Society of Body Engineers (193)
American Society of Naval Engineers (204)
American Society of Transportation and Logistics (210)
American Traffic Safety Service Association (217)
American Train Dispatchers Association (217)
American Truck Dealers (217)
American Trucking Associations (218)
American Waterways Operators (220)*
Animal Transportation Association (223)*
Army Aviation Association of America (229)
ASME International Gas Turbine Institute (233)
Asphalt Emulsion Manufacturers Association (233)*
Asphalt Institute (233)
Asphalt Recycling and Reclaiming Association (233)*
Asphalt Roofing Manufacturers Association (233)
ASPRS-The Imaging and Geospatial Information Society (233)
Associated Equipment Distributors (235)
Association for Commuter Transportation (242)
Association for the Advancement of Automotive Medicine (258)*

Association for Unmanned Vehicle Systems International (261)
Association of Air Medical Services (264)
Association of American Railroads (266)*
Association of American Shippers (266)
Association of Asphalt Paving Technologists (268)
The Association of Average Adjusters of the United States and Canada (268)
Association of Aviation Psychologists (269)
Association of Clean Water Administrators (273)
Association of Equipment Management Professionals (281)
Association of Finance and Insurance Professionals (283)
Association of Flight Attendants - CWA (283)
Association of Global Automakers (285)*
Association of HazMat Shippers (286)
Association of Mailing, Shipping, and Office Automation Specialists (292)
Association of Marina Industries (293)
Association of Naval Aviation (295)*
Association of Oil Pipe Lines (296)
Association of Pedestrian and Bicycle Professionals (298)*
Association of Professional Flight Attendants (301)
Association of Railway Museums (305)
Association of Ship Brokers and Agents (U.S.A.) (308)*
Association of Transportation Professionals (314)
Association of Water Technologies (317)*
Atlantic intra Coastal Waterway Association (319)
Automatic Transmission Rebuilders Association (321)*
Automotive Aftermarket Industry Association (321)
Automotive Body Parts Association (322)
Automotive Communication Council (322)*
Automotive Distribution Network (322)
Automotive Engine Rebuilders Association (322)
Automotive Fleet and Leasing Association (322)
Automotive Industry Action Group (322)
Automotive Lift Institute, Inc. (322)
Automotive Maintenance and Repair Association (323)
Automotive Market Research Council (323)
Automotive Oil Change Association (323)*
Automotive Parts Remanufacturers Association (323)*
Automotive Public Relations Council (323)*
Automotive Recyclers Association (323)
Automotive Safety Council (323)
Automotive Service Association (323)
Automotive Trade Association Executives (324)
Automotive Training Managers Council (324)
Aviation Distributors and Manufacturers Association International (324)
Aviation Industry CBT Committee (324)*
Aviation Insurance Association (324)
Aviation Maintenance Foundation International (324)
The Aviation Security Services Association (324)
Aviation Suppliers Association (324)
Aviation Technician Education Council (325)*
Bearing Specialist Association (327)
Bicycle Product Suppliers Association (329)
Brake Manufacturers Council (334)
Brotherhood of Locomotive Engineers and Trainmen (336)
Brotherhood of Maintenance of Way Employees Division (336)
Brotherhood of Railroad Signalmen (336)*
Brotherhood Railway Carmen/TCU (336)
Bulk Carrier Conference (338)
C-Port (340)
Car Care Council (342)
Cargo Airline Association (343)
Carwash Owner's and Supplier's Association (343)*
Center for the Polyurethanes Industry (348)*
Certified Auto Parts Association (349)*
Certified Claims Professional Accreditation Council (349)
Chamber of Shipping of America (351)
Civil Aviation Medical Association (357)
The Coalition for Transportation Productivity (360)
The Coalition of Airline Pilots Associations (360)
The Coastal and Estuarine Research Federation (361)
Collision Industry Electronic Commerce Association (365)*
Combat Helicopter Pilots Association (366)
Commercial Space Flight Federation (367)
Commercial Vehicle Safety Alliance (367)
The Commercial Vehicle Solutions Network (367)*
Commercial Vehicle Solutions Network (367)
Commercial Vehicle Training Association (367)
Community Transportation Association of America (371)*
Conference of Minority Transportation Officials (375)*
Contractors Pump Bureau (383)
Coordinating Research Council (384)

Council of American Maritime Museums (391)*
Council of American Master Mariners (392)
Council of Supply Chain Management Professionals (398)
Council on the Safe Transportation of Hazardous Articles (401)
Cruise Lines International Association (405)
Dangerous Goods Advisory Council (407)
Delta Nu Alpha (409)
Distribution and LTL Carriers Association (414)
Dredging Contractors of America, Inc. (416)
Driver Employer Council of America (416)
Driving School Association of America (416)
Electric Drive Transportation Association (421)
Electrical Generating Systems Association (422)
Emissions Control Technology Association (ECTA) (426)
Energy Traffic Association (428)
Enhanced Protective Glass Automotive Association (429)
Equipment and Tool Institute (432)*
Express Delivery & Logistics Association (436)
FAA Managers Association, Inc. (436)
Fashion Accessories Shippers Association (438)
Filter Manufacturers Council (444)
Fleet Reserve Association (447)
Flight Safety Foundation (448)
Flying Physicians Association (448)
Ford Motor Minority Dealers Association (451)
Friction Material Standards Institute (454)
Gasoline and Automotive Service Dealers of America (457)
General Aviation Manufacturers Association (458)
Global Business Travel Association (462)
Global Cold Chain Alliance (462)
Governors' Highway Safety Association (464)
Heavy Duty Brake Manufacturers Council (473)
Heavy Duty Manufacturers Association (473)
Heavy Duty Representatives Association (473)
Helicopter Association International (473)
Independent Armored Car Operators Association (488)
Independent Automotive Damage Appraisers Association (488)
Independent Petroleum Association of America (491)
Independent Pilots Association (491)
Industrial Truck Association (494)
Inland Marine Underwriters Association (496)
Institute of International Container Lessors (501)*
Institute of Navigation (502)
Institute of Nuclear Materials Management (502)*
Institute of Transportation Engineers (503)*
Insurance Institute for Highway Safety (505)
Intelligent Transportation Society of America (506)
Inter-Industry Conference on Auto Collision Repair (506)
Interactive Travel Services Association (507)*
Intermodal Association of North America (508)
The International Air Cargo Association (509)
International Air Transport Association (510)
International Association of Airport and Seaport Police (515)
International Association of Airport Duty Free Stores (515)
International Association of Auto Theft Investigators (516)
International Association of Independent Tanker Owners (523)
International Association of Machinists and Aerospace Workers (524)
International Association of Movers (525)
International Association of Natural Resource Pilots (525)
International Association of Railway Operating Officers (527)
International Association of Structural Movers (528)
International Aviation Ground Support Association (529)
International Aviation Women's Association (529)
International Bridge, Tunnel and Turnpike Association (531)
International Brotherhood of Boilermakers, Iron Shipbuilders, Blacksmiths, Forgers and Helpers (531)
International Brotherhood of Teamsters (532)
International Brotherhood of Teamsters - Airline Division (532)
International Cargo Gear Bureau (533)
International Cargo Security Council (533)
International Carwash Association (533)
International Council of Air Shows (538)
International Door Association (541)
International Flight Services Association (545)
International Furniture Transportation and Logistics Council (548)
International Grooving & Grinding Association (549)
International Hydrofoil Society (550)*
International Liquid Terminals Association (554)
International Longshore and Warehouse Union (555)

Western Association of Industrial Distributors (1015)
Western Dredging Association (1015)
Wine and Spirits Shippers Association (1018)
Women in Aviation International (1020)
Women's Transportation Seminar (WTS International) (1024)
World Airline Entertainment Association (1025)*
World Shipping Council (1027)

TRAVEL/TOURISM/LODGING

Academy of Hospitality Industry Attorneys (5)
Adventure Travel Trade Association (13)
Africa Travel Association (15)
Airlines For America (21)
Airport Ground Transportation Association (21)*
American Bus Association (87)*
American Culinary Federation (112)
American Highway Users Alliance (131)
American Hotel & Lodging Association (AH&LA) (134)
American Public Transportation Association (171)
American Society of Travel Agents (210)
American Youth Hostels, Inc (Hostelling International USA) (222)
Asian American Hotel Owners Association (231)
Associated Luxury Hotels International (236)
Association of Corporate Travel Executives (ACTE) (277)
Association of Destination Management Executives (278)
Association of Retail Travel Agents (306)*
Association of Travel Marketing Executives (315)
BMC - A Foodservice Sales and Marketing Council (332)
Caribbean Hotel and Tourism Association (343)
Council of Hotel and Restaurant Trainers (394)
Cruise Lines International Association (405)
Destination Marketing Association International (411)
Discover America Partnership (413)
Global Business Travel Association (462)
Green Hotels Association (466)
Hospitality Financial and Technology Professionals (479)
Hospitality Sales and Marketing Association International (479)*
Hotel Brokers International (479)
Hotel Electronic Distribution Network Association (479)
Interactive Travel Services Association (507)*
International Association of Amusement Parks and Attractions(IAAPA) (515)*
International Association of Tour Managers - North American Region (528)
International Council on Hotel, Restaurant and Institutional Education (539)
The International Ecotourism Society (542)
International Executive Housekeepers Association (543)
International Family Recreation Association (544)
International Food, Wine and Travel Writers Association (546)
International Gay and Lesbian Travel Association (548)
International Society of Hospitality Consultants (573)
International Society of Hotel Association Executives (573)
International Society of Travel and Tourism Educators (574)
Latino Hotel Association (594)
Motorist Information and Services Association (620)
National Air Carrier Association (630)
National Air Transportation Association (630)
National Association of Business Travel Agents (651)
National Association of Cruise Oriented Agencies (662)
National Association of Passports and Visa Services (683)
National Association of RV Parks and Campgrounds (692)*
National Association of Truck Stop Operators(NATSO) (707)
National Caves Association (719)*
National Council for International Visitors (732)
National Council of Chain Restaurants (734)
National Council of State Tourism Directors (736)
National Council of Travel Attractions (737)
National Tour Association (800)
Network of Executive Women in Hospitality (808)
OpenTravel Alliance (828)
Passenger Vessel Association (839)
Professional Association of Innkeepers International (860)
Receptive Services Association of America (876)
Recreation Vehicle Rental Association (877)
Regional Airline Association (878)*
Resort Hotel Association (883)
Select Registry/Distinguished Inns of North America (896)*

Small Luxury Hotels of the World (901)
Society of American Travel Writers (930)*
Society of Government Travel Professionals (938)*
Society of Incentive & Travel Executives (939)
Student Youth and Travel Association (964)
The Travel and Tourism Research Association (979)
Travel Goods Association (979)*
The Travel Institute (979)*
US Travel Association (983)*
UNITE-HERE (985)
United States Tour Operators Association (1000)*

UTILITIES

American Coal Ash Association (92)
American Gas Association (124)
American Membrane Technology Association (150)
American Public Gas Association (170)
American Public Power Association (171)
American Public Works Association (172)
American Water Works Association (220)
Association of Edison Illuminating Companies (279)
Association of Metropolitan Water Agencies (294)
Edison Electric Institute (419)
Electric Power Research Institute (421)
Electric Reliability Coordinating Council (421)*
Electricity Consumers Resource Council (ELCON) (422)
EUCG, Inc. (433)
Institute of Nuclear Power Operations (502)
Institute of Public Utilities (502)*
International Right of Way Association (563)
International Utility Efficiency Partnerships (580)
Large Public Power Council (593)
Municipal Waste Management Association (621)
National Association of Energy Service Companies (665)
National Association of Regulatory Utility Commissioners (691)*
National Association of State Utility Consumer Advocates (NASUCA) (702)
National Association of Water Companies (NAWC) (709)
National Ground Water Association (756)
National Institute for Water Resources (766)
National Renderers Association (786)
National Rural Economic Developers Association (788)
National Rural Electric Cooperative Association (788)
National Utility Contractors Association (NUCA) (803)*
North American Electric Reliability Corporation (816)*
Public Utilities Risk Management Association (870)
United States Energy Association (993)
Utilities Telecom Council (1006)*
Utility Arborist Association (1006)
Utility Communicators International (1006)
Utility Management & Conservation Association (1006)
Utility Workers Union of America (1007)

VACUUM

Association of Industrial Metallizers, Coaters and Laminators (288)*
Association of Vacuum Equipment Manufacturers (316)
AVS: Science and Technology of Materials, Interfaces, and Processing (325)
Society of Vacuum Coaters (950)*
Vacuum Dealers Trade Association/Sewing Dealers Trade Association (1007)

VOLUNTEER

Association for Healthcare Volunteer Resource Professionals (248)
Association for Research on Nonprofit Organizations and Voluntary Action (255)
Independent Sector (491)
International Society for Third-Sector Research (570)*
National Association of Foster Grandparent Program Directors (669)
National Association of Retired and Senior Volunteer Program Directors (692)
National Council for International Visitors (732)
National Volunteer Fire Council (803)

WATERPROOFERS

Asphalt Roofing Manufacturers Association (233)
Sealant, Waterproofing and Restoration Institute (894)*
Spray Polyurethane Foam Alliance (959)*

WOMEN/WOMEN'S ISSUES

African-American Women's Clergy Association (15)
Alliance for Women in Media (24)
American Association for Women in Community Colleges (53)

American Association for Women Podiatrists (53)
American Association for Women Radiologists (53)
American Association of Birth Centers (55)*
American Association of Family and Consumer Sciences (61)
American Association of Occupational Health Nurses (67)*
American Association of Osteopathic Women Physicians (68)
American Association of University Women (76)
American Association of Women Dentists (77)
American Business Women's Association (87)
American Medical Women's Association (150)
American Midwifery Certification Board (151)
American National CattleWomen (154)
American Society of Women Accountants (ACC) (211)
American Woman's Society of Certified Public Accountants (221)
Asian Women in Business (232)
Association for Women Geoscientists (261)
Association for Women in Communications (261)
Association for Women in Computing (261)
Association for Women in Mathematics (261)
Association for Women in Psychology (262)*
Association for Women in Science (262)
Association for Women in Sports Media (262)
Association for Women Veterinarians Foundation (262)
Association of Girl Scout Executive Staff (285)
Association of Junior Leagues International (290)
Association of Programs for Female Offenders (303)
Association of Real Estate Women (305)
Association of Reproductive Health Professionals (305)
The Association of Women in International Trade (317)
Association of Women in the Metal Industries (317)
Association of Women Soil Scientists (317)
Association of Women Surgeons (317)
Association of Women's Business Centers (318)
Association of Women's Health, Obstetric and Neonatal Nurses (318)
Caucus for Women in Statistics (346)
Coalition of Labor Union Women (361)
Commercial Real Estate Women Network (367)
Committee of 200 (368)
Coordinating Council for Women in History (384)
Cosmetic Executive Women (387)
Credit Professionals International (403)
Delta Phi Epsilon (409)
Executive Women in Government (435)
Executive Women International (435)
Executive Women's Golf Association (435)
Fashion Group International (438)
Federally Employed Women (FEW) (440)
General Federation of Women's Clubs (458)*
Intercoiffure America/Canada (507)
The International Alliance for Women (510)
International Alliance for Women in Music (510)*
International Association of Women in Fire and Emergency Services (528)
International Association of Women Ministers (529)
International Association of Women Police (529)
International Aviation Women's Association (529)
International Council of Psychologists (538)
International Women's Writing Guild (581)*
Ladies Professional Golf Association (592)
Midwives Alliance of North America (615)
NALS (625)*
National Abortion Federation (626)
National Association for Girls and Women in Sport (639)
National Association for Practical Nurse Education and Service (641)
National Association of Black Women Entrepreneurs (649)
National Association of Collegiate Women Athletic Administrators (656)
The National Association of Colored Women's Club, Inc. (656)
National Association of Commissions for Women (656)*
National Association of Insurance Women (International) (676)
National Association of Minority and Women Owned Law Firms (680)
National Association of Negro Business and Professional Women's Clubs (681)*
National Association of Nurse Practitioners in Women's Health (682)*
National Association of Professional Asian American Women (686)
National Association of Professional Mortgage Women (687)
National Association of University Women (708)
National Association of Women Artists (709)
National Association of Women Business Owners (709)

National Association of Women Highway Safety Leaders, Inc. *(709)*
National Association of Women in Construction *(710)*
National Association of Women Judges *(710)*
National Association of Women Lawyers *(710)*
National Bankers Association *(712)*
National Conference of Women's Bar Associations *(728)**
National Council for Research on Women *(732)**
National Council on Family Relations *(738)**
National Family Planning and Reproductive Health Association *(747)*
National Federation of Press Women *(749)*
National Federation of Republican Women *(750)*
National Foundation for Women Legislators *(753)*
National Human Resources Association *(761)**
National League of American Pen Women *(768)*
National Minority Business Council *(773)*
National WIC Association *(805)*
National Women's Studies Association *(805)**
Nine to Five, National Association of Working Women *(811)*
North American Menopause Society *(818)**
Organization of Women in International Trade *(832)*
Pi Lambda Theta *(847)*
Population Action International *(852)*
Professional Association of Volleyball Officials *(860)*
Professional Women Controllers *(865)**
Professional Women in Construction *(866)**
Professional Women Photographers *(866)*
Ruth Jackson Orthopaedic Society *(889)*
Society for Maternal-Fetal Medicine *(915)**
Society for Menstrual Cycle Research *(915)*
Society of Woman Geographers *(950)*
Society of Women Engineers *(950)*
Stuntwomen's Association of Motion Pictures *(964)*
United States Conference of Catholic Bishops *(992)*
WEB: Worldwide Employee Benefits Network *(1014)**
WIFS - Women in Insurance and Financial Services *(1017)*
Women Band Directors International *(1020)*
Women Chefs and Restaurateurs *(1020)**
Women Construction Owners and Executives, USA *(1020)*
Women in Aerospace *(1020)*
Women in Agribusiness *(1020)*
Women in Cable Telecommunications, Inc. *(1020)*
Women in Endocrinology *(1021)*
Women in Energy *(1021)*
Women in Film *(1021)*
Women in Government *(1021)*
Women in Government Relations, Inc. *(1021)*
Women in International Security *(1021)**
Women in Management *(1021)*
Women in Mining National *(1022)*
Women in Packaging *(1022)*
Women in Technology International *(1022)*
Women of the Motion Picture Industry, International *(1022)*
Women's Business Enterprise National Council *(1022)*
Women's Caucus for Art *(1022)*
Women's Caucus for Political Science *(1023)*
Women's Council of REALTORS *(1023)*
Women's Foodservice Forum *(1023)**
Women's International Network of Utility Professionals *(1023)*
Women's Jewelry Association *(1023)**
Women's National Book Association *(1023)*
Women's Professional Rodeo Association *(1023)*
Women's Regional Publications of America *(1024)**
Women's Transportation Seminar (WTS International) *(1024)*
World International Nail and Beauty Association *(1026)*
WTA Tour, Inc. *(1029)*
Zonta International *(1030)*

Geographic Index

All active organizations in NTPA can be found here under the city and state where they are headquartered.

ALABAMA

Athens

National Association of Retired and Senior Volunteer Program Directors *(692)*

Auburn

American Association of Bovine Practitioners *(55)*
Industrial Electronics Society *(493)*
University Aviation Association *(1002)*

Birmingham

Alliance for Continuing Medical Education *(22)*
American Assembly for Men in Nursing *(47)*
American Association of Teachers of Arabic *(74)*
American Harp Society *(129)*
American Society for Reproductive Medicine *(189)*
American Wood-Protection Association *(222)*
Association of Edison Illuminating Companies *(279)*
Association of University Programs in Occupational Health and Safety *(316)*
Collegiate Commissioners Association *(365)*
Congress on Research in Dance *(377)*
Cookware Manufacturers Association *(384)*
Ductile Iron Pipe Research Association *(417)*
Governmental Research Association *(464)*
International Andalusian and Lusitano Horse Association *(510)*
International Iridology Practitioners Association *(552)*
National Association of Church Food Service *(653)*
Society for Assisted Reproductive Technology *(905)*
Society for Reproductive Endocrinology and Infertility *(920)*
Society of Dance History Scholars *(934)*
Society of Reproductive Surgeons *(946)*
Woven Wire Products Association *(1029)*

Daleville

United Gamefowl Breeders Association, Inc. *(987)*

Decatur

Racking Horse Breeders Association of America *(872)*

Florence

Beta Beta Beta *(328)*

Geneva

International Food & Beverage Association (IFBA) *(546)*

Hoover

National Association of School Resource Officers *(693)*

Hueytown

National Roadside Vegetation Management Association *(787)*

Huntsville

American Educational Studies Association *(116)*
National Speleological Society *(795)*

Madison

Women Chefs and Restaurateurs *(1020)*

Montgomery

American Association of Small Ruminant Practitioners *(73)*

American College of Theriogenologists *(103)*
National Young Farmers Education Association *(806)*
Real Estate Educators Association *(875)*
Society for Theriogenology *(926)*

Orange Beach

National Association of Charterboat Operators *(652)*

Spanish Ft.

Education Credit Union Council *(419)*

Tuscaloosa

Association of Ecosystem Research Centers *(279)*
Kappa Delta Epsilon *(590)*

Wemmel

The Aviation Security Services Association *(324)*

ALASKA

Cordova

Heli Ski US Association *(473)*

St. Paul Island

Central Bering Sea Fisherman's Association *(348)*

ARIZONA

Avondale

National Association of Exclusive Buyer Agents *(666)*

Chandler

American Jewish Press Association *(143)*
Association for Comparative Economic Studies *(242)*
IMAGE Society *(486)*
League for Innovation in the Community College *(595)*

Dewey

Keyboard Teachers Association International *(590)*

Flagstaff

American Holistic Nurses Association *(132)*
Distributed Wind Energy Association *(414)*

Fountain Hills

American Osteopathic College of Allergy and Immunology *(160)*
Construction Industry CPAs/Consultants Association *(379)*
United States Swim School Association *(999)*
VITA *(1011)*

Glendale

American Disc Jockey Association *(115)*

Goodyear

Casting Industry Suppliers Association *(344)*
National Association of Litho Clubs *(678)*

Mesa

American Hydrogen Association *(134)*
American Psychological Association - Division of Psychotherapy *(169)*
National Association for Community Mediation *(637)*
Society of Forensic Toxicologists *(936)*

Nogales

Fresh Produce Association of the Americas *(453)*

Phoenix

American Academy of Dental Group Practice *(32)*
American Association of Public Welfare Attorneys *(72)*
American College of Medical Toxicology *(98)*
Association of Energy Services Professionals, International *(281)*
Association of Golf Merchandisers *(286)*
Evangelical Christian Publishers Association *(434)*
Health Industry Business Communications Council *(469)*
International Academy of Trial Lawyers *(509)*
National Association for Information Destruction, Inc. *(640)*
National Association of Railroad Trial Counsel *(689)*
National Bulk Vendors Association *(716)*
National Dental EDI Council *(743)*
National Environmental, Safety and Health Training Association *(746)*
Society for American Baseball Research *(903)*
Society of American Business Editors and Writers *(928)*
Supima *(966)*

Scottsdale

Alliance of Work/Life Progress *(25)*
American Association of Cosmetology Schools *(59)*
Association of Forensic Document Examiners *(284)*
Association of Retail Travel Agents *(306)*
Council of Educational Facility Planners International *(393)*
Council on Chiropractic Education *(399)*
Information Technology Alliance *(495)*
International Ozone Association-Pan American Group Branch *(559)*
Marine Preservation Association *(605)*
National Council for Prescription Drug Programs *(732)*
Professional Beauty Association | National Cosmetology Association *(861)*
Residential Space Planners International *(883)*
The Western Red Cedar Pole Association *(1016)*
WorldatWork *(1028)*

Sedona

World Research Foundation *(1027)*

Tempe

American Federation of Astrologers, Inc. *(119)*
Institute for Supply Management *(497)*
International Association of Speakers Bureaus *(528)*
National Speakers Association *(795)*
Rubber Pavements Association *(888)*
Society of Professional Rope Access Technicians *(945)*
Special Interest Group for Teacher Educators *(955)*
Travel Journalists Guild *(980)*

Tucson

American Institute for Maghrib Studies *(136)*
Association of American Physicians and Surgeons *(266)*
Association of University Research Parks *(316)*
Consortium for North American Higher Education Collaboration *(378)*
Harness Tracks of America *(468)*
International Studies Association *(576)*
The Masonry Heater Association of North America *(607)*

Middle East Studies Association of North America **(615)**
National Association of Chain Manufacturers **(652)**
National Association of Professional Geriatric Care Managers **(687)**
National Association of Self-Instructional Language Programs **(695)**
National Elder Law Foundation **(744)**
National Shoe Retailers Association **(791)**
Society for Linguistic Anthropology **(914)**
Tree-Ring Society **(980)**

ARKANSAS

Arkadelphia

National Association of Barber Boards of America **(648)**

Fairbanks

Western History Association **(1015)**

Fayetteville

American Collegiate Retailing Association **(105)**
Chinese American Librarians Association **(354)**
International Conference of Funeral Service Examining Boards **(536)**
International Weed Science Society **(581)**
North American Membrane Society **(818)**

Gurdon

International Concatenated Order of Hoo-Hoo **(536)**

Hardy

Council of Graphological Societies **(394)**

Hot Springs Village

Aluminum Foil Container Manufacturers Association **(27)**

Jonesboro

The Herpetologists' League **(474)**

Little Rock

American Case Management Association **(88)**
Apiary Inspectors of America **(224)**
Case Management Society of America **(343)**
Communications Supply Service Association **(369)**
National Association of Supervisors for Business Education **(704)**
National Interstate Council of State Boards of Cosmetology **(766)**

Maumelle

The National Federation of Nonpublic School State Accrediting Associations **(749)**

Pine Bluff

United States Trout Farmers Association **(1000)**

Rogers

Cottage Industry Miniaturists Trade Association **(387)**

CALIFORNIA

Albany

Seismological Society of America **(895)**

Aliso Viejo

American Association of Critical-Care Nurses **(59)**
Association for Applied and Therapeutic Humor **(238)**
Council of Communication Management **(393)**
Manufacturers' Agents National Association **(603)**
NAGMR Consumer Product Brokers **(624)**
Power-Motion Technology Representatives Association **(855)**

Anaheim

Materials and Methods Standards Association **(608)**
United Applications Standards Group **(985)**
World Floor Covering Association **(1026)**
World International Nail and Beauty Association **(1026)**

Arcadia

American Sports Medicine Association **(213)**

Arnold

American Academy of Gnathologic Orthopedics **(34)**

Artesia

American Society of Gas Engineers **(198)**

Auburn

Magic Dealers Association **(601)**

Bakersfield

American Society of Ocularists **(205)**
Off-Road Business Association **(826)**
Society for the Advancement of American Philosophy **(922)**

Berkeley

The American Finance Association **(121)**
International Association for the Study of Dreams **(514)**
International Society for Magnetic Resonance in Medicine **(567)**
Iranian American Community of Northern California **(585)**
National Association of Science Writers **(694)**
Substance Abuse Librarians and Information Specialists **(965)**
United States Association for Computational Mechanics **(990)**
USENIX: The Advanced Computing Systems Association **(1005)**

Beverly Hills

Academy of Motion Picture Arts and Sciences **(7)**
Association of Film Commissioners International **(283)**
International Association for Corporate and Professional Recruitment **(511)**
National Coalition of African American Owned Media **(723)**
National Congress of Inventor Organizations **(729)**
Producers Guild of America **(858)**
The Society of Composers and Lyricists **(933)**
Women of the Motion Picture Industry, International **(1022)**

Brentwood

International Association of Home Staging Professionals **(522)**

Buena Park

Independent Distributors of Electronics Association **(489)**

Burbank

American Auto Racing Writers and Broadcasters Association **(78)**
Association of Correctional Food Service Affiliates **(277)**
Caucus for Producers, Writers & Directors **(346)**

Camarillo

National Association of Aircraft and Communication Suppliers **(646)**
National Religious Broadcasters, Music License Committee **(785)**

Camp Pendleton

American College of Contingency Planners **(95)**

Campbell

Society for Information Display **(913)**

Canoga Park

Free Speech Coalition **(453)**

Canyon Country

American Sand Association **(177)**

Carlsbad

American College of Forensic Psychiatry **(96)**
Gemological Institute of America **(457)**
NAMM - The International Music Products Association **(625)**
Viola da Gamba Society of America **(1009)**
Western Association of Industrial Distributors **(1015)**

Chino

Certified Milk Producers Association of America **(350)**

Citrus Heights

American Association of Corporate and Public Practice Veterinarians **(59)**

Claremont

Conference for the Study of Political Thought **(374)**
Society for Psychological Anthropology **(919)**

Clovis

Association for Play Therapy **(253)**
Association of Natural Bio-Control Producers **(295)**

Coarsegold

Association of Applied IPM Ecologists **(267)**

Commerce

Association of Woodworking and Furnishings Suppliers **(318)**

Concord

National Association of Stock Plan Professionals **(703)**

Corona

Society for Vector Ecology **(927)**

Costa Mesa

National Bicycle Dealers Association **(713)**

Covina

National Narcotics Officers Associations' Coalition **(774)**
Society for the Advancement of Material and Process Engineering **(922)**

Culver City

Association of African American Museums **(263)**
Ceramic Tile Institute of America **(349)**

Cupertinoc

Optical Storage Technology Association **(829)**

Cypress

AAGL - Advancing Minimally Invasive Gynecology Worldwide **(2)**

Daly City

Underwater Society of America **(984)**

Davis

American Association of Veterinary Laboratory Diagnosticians **(76)**
American Society for Enology and Viticulture **(184)**
Geothermal Resources Council **(460)**
Society for Cryobiology **(907)**

Del Mar

National Association of Credit Union Chairmen **(661)**
National Association of Credit Union Supervisory and Auditing Committees **(661)**
National Council of Postal Credit Unions **(735)**

Delano

Paramount Citrus Association **(838)**

Diamond Bar

International Food, Wine and Travel Writers Association **(546)**
Specialty Equipment Market Association **(957)**

Edwards

American College of Healthcare Information Administrators **(97)**

El Dorado Hills

International Association of Financial Crimes Investigators **(521)**

El Segundo

Alliance of Area Business Publications **(24)**
American Academy of Medical Acupuncture **(36)**
American Property Tax Counsel **(168)**
City and Regional Magazine Association **(357)**
Parenting Media Association **(838)**

El Sobrante

American Institute of Engineers, Inc. **(138)**

Elk Grove

Coleopterists Society **(362)**
National Plant Board **(781)**

Emeryville

Esperanto-USA **(433)**

Encino

Academy of Country Music **(4)**
Entertainment Merchants Association **(429)**
National Risk Retention Association **(787)**

Fair Oaks

Association of Commercial Real Estate **(275)**

Folsom

North American Blueberry Council **(814)**

Fountain Valley

Western Economic Association International **(1015)**

Fresno

Association of Field Ornithologists **(282)**
Mu Phi Epsilon **(621)**
National Council on Rehabilitation Education **(739)**
National Truck and Heavy Equipment Claims Council **(802)**
Nisei Farmers League **(811)**
Society of Armenian Studies **(930)**

Friant

Specialty Sleep Association **(958)**

Fullerton

Association of Vision Science Librarians **(317)**
National Aerosol Association **(629)**
Omega Delta **(827)**
United States Federation of Scholars and Scientists **(994)**

Garden Grove

American Society for Aesthetic Plastic Surgery **(180)**

Gardena

International Right of Way Association (563)
Korean Drycleaners-Laundry Association (591)

Glendale

American Council of Hypnotist Examiners (109)
Interagency Communications Interoperability Joint
Powers Authority (507)
React International (875)

Goleta

Asian/Pacific American Librarians Association (232)

Hermosa Beach

American Association for Career Education (48)

Hollywood

American Society of Cinematographers (194)
Association of Cinema and Video Laboratories (273)
Association of Moving Image Archivists (295)
Fur Information Council of America (454)
Stuntmen's Association of Motion Pictures (964)

Huntington Beach

Association of Surfing Professionals - North America
(312)
IEEE Instrumentation and Measurement Society
(484)

Imperial Beach

Electrical Manufacturing and Coil Winding
Association (422)

Industry

Society of Hispanic Professional Engineers (938)

Irvine

American Association for Women Podiatrists (53)
American College for Advancement in Medicine (93)
American College of Trial Lawyers (103)
Motorcycle Industry Council, Inc. (620)
Motorcycle Safety Foundation (620)
Multi-Level Marketing International Association
(621)
Office Business Center Association International
(826)
Specialty Vehicle Institute of America (958)
Stucco Manufacturers Association (964)
Thermoforming Institute (973)

Keene

United Farm Workers of America (986)

Kensington

Gas Turbine Association (457)

La Habra

Interactive Audio Special Interest Group (507)
MIDI Manufacturers Association (615)

La Jolla

Catecholamine Club (344)
Conference on Asian History (376)
International Golf Associates (548)
International Society for Computational Biology
(566)
North American Clinical Dermatologic Society (815)

La Mirada

Fresh Produce and Floral Council (453)
North American Association of Professors of
Christian Education (813)
Professional Association of Christian Educators
(859)

La Quinta

United Association of Equipment Leasing (985)

Lafayette

International Institute for Lath and Plaster (551)

Laguna Beach

American Pathology Foundation (162)
Association of Private Club Directors (300)
Healthcare Billing and Management Association
(470)
Neuro-Developmental Treatment Association (808)

Laguna Hills

Picture Archive Council of America (848)

Lake Forest

Event Planners Association (434)

Lancaster

Society of Experimental Test Pilots (935)
Society of Flight Test Engineers (936)

Landers

American Welara Pony Registry (220)

Larkspur

Conservation and Preservation Charities of America
(377)

Leucadia

Academy of Veterinary Homeopathy (9)

Livermore

National Institute of Steel Detailing (765)

Lodi

USA Sprinkler Fitter Business Managers Association
(1005)

Loma Linda

American Institute of Oral Biology (139)
National Association of Seventh-Day Adventist
Dentists (695)

Loma Rica

North American Wensleydale Sheep Association
(823)

Long Beach

Academy of Managed Care Providers (6)
American Association of Philosophy Teachers (69)
American Microscopical Society (151)
American Society of Questioned Document
Examiners (208)
Society for French Historical Studies (909)
Society for History Education (911)
Specialty Coffee Association of America (957)

Los Alamitos

National Fastener Distributors Association (747)

Los Angeles

Academy of Molecular Imaging (7)
African-American Library and Information Science
Association (15)
AIR Commercial Real Estate Association (18)
American Association of Medical Milk Commissions
(65)
American Association of Police Officers (70)
American Association of Teachers of Slavic and East
European Languages (75)
American Head and Neck Society (129)
American Radium Society (173)
The Association for Academic Surgery (237)
Association for the Study of Classical African
Civilizations (259)
Association of Celebrity Personal Assistants (271)
Association of Latino Professionals in Finance and
Accounting (291)
Association of Managed Care Dentists (292)
Association of Talent Agents (312)
Association of Volleyball Professionals (317)
Directors Guild of America (413)
Independent Film and Television Alliance (489)
International Documentary Association (541)
International Pediatric Nephrology Association (559)
Latin Business Association (594)
Leading Jewelers Guild (594)
Mexican-American Grocers Association (614)
Middle East Librarians' Association (615)
National Association of Business Travel Agents (651)
National Association of Composers, USA (657)
National Association of Latino Elected and
Appointed Officials (677)
National Association of Television Program
Executives (705)
The National Network for Social Work Managers
(774)
National Notary Association (775)
North American Skull Base Society (820)
Organization of American Kodaly Educators (832)
Screen Actors Guild - American Federation of
Television and Radio Artists (893)
Society of Allied Weight Engineers (928)
Society of American Gastrointestinal and
Endoscopic Surgeons (929)
Society of Children's Book Writers and Illustrators
(932)
Wedding and Portrait Photographers International
(1014)
Women in Film (1021)
Women in Technology International (1022)
Writers Guild of America West (1029)

Los Gatos

Alliance for Gray Market and Counterfeit Abatement
(23)

Manhattan Beach

Alpha Tau Delta (27)
The Independent Book Publishers Association (488)

Mendocino

The International Food & Beverage Forum (546)

Menlo Park

Alpha Omega Alpha Honor Medical Society (26)

Mill Valley

All-America Rose Selections (22)

Mission Viejo

Association of American Educators (264)
International Map Trade Association (555)

Modesto

Association for Healthcare Documentation Integrity
(247)
Medical Transcription Industry Association (MTIA)
(611)

Monrovia

National Health Federation (758)
World Pet Association (1027)

Monterey

National Federation of Modern Language Teachers
Associations (749)
Professional Liability Agents Network (863)

Morgan Hill

Utility Smart Network Access Port (1007)

Mountain View

German American Business Association (460)
International Society of Offshore and Polar
Engineers (573)

Nevada City

American Herb Association (130)

Newark

Video Electronics Standards Association (1009)

Newport Beach

American Society of Dermatological Retailers (196)

Oakland

American Society of Medical Association Counsel
(203)
Association for Women in Computing (261)
Association of Asian-Pacific Community Health
Organizations (268)
Council on Anthropology and Education (398)
Earthquake Engineering Research Institute (418)
ICLEI - Local Governments for Sustainability (482)
National Association of State & Local Equity Funds
(697)
National Center for Employee Ownership (719)
National Council on Crime and Delinquency (738)
National Federation of Community Broadcasters
(748)
Transpacific Stabilization Agreement (977)
Union of American Physicians and Dentists (985)

Oceanside

American Society of Architectural Illustrators (192)
National Public Employer Labor Relations
Association (783)

Ocotillo

International Association of Audio Visual
Communicators (516)

Old Station

Society of Telecommunications Consultants (948)

Ontario

International Association of Plumbing and
Mechanical Officials (526)

Orange

AFCOM (14)
Association of Aviation Psychologists (269)
USFN-America's Mortgage Banking Attorneys (1006)

Orange Park Acres

American Connemara Pony Society (107)

Oxnard

Automatic Transmission Rebuilders Association
(321)
United States Federation for Culture Collections
(994)

Pacifica

American Association of Intensive English Programs
(63)
Humanities Education and Research Association
(481)
Laser and Electro-Optics Manufacturers' Association
(593)

Palm Desert

American Association of Franchisees and Dealers
(61)
Performance Warehouse Association (841)

Palm Springs

Environmental Assessment Association (430)
International Real Estate Institute (562)
International Society of Meeting Planners (573)
National Association of Real Estate Appraisers (689)

National Association of Review Appraisers and Mortgage Underwriters **(692)**

Palo Alto

American Association for the Advancement of Artificial Intelligence **(51)**
American Broncho-Esophagological Association **(86)**
Association for Transpersonal Psychology **(260)**
Electric Power Research Institute **(421)**

Pasadena

American Construction Inspectors Association **(107)**
American Seminar Leaders Association **(178)**
International Webmasters Association **(580)**
Society of University Otolaryngologists-Head and Neck Surgeons **(949)**

Petaluma

Association for Humanistic Psychology **(249)**

Pismo Beach

American Factoring Association **(118)**
International Association for Correctional and Forensic Psychology **(512)**

Placentia

Association of Professional Ball Players of America **(301)**

Pleasant Hill

California Redwood Association **(341)**

Pleasanton

The International Transactional Analysis Association **(578)**

Plumas Lake

Society of Air Force Clinical Surgeons **(928)**

Rancho Cordova

Council for Near-Infrared Spectroscopy **(390)**

Rancho Cucamonga

International Institute of Municipal Clerks **(552)**
Used Textbook Association **(1005)**

Rancho Palos Verdes

U.S. Metric Association **(983)**

Rancho Santa Margarita

International Association of Skateboard Companies **(527)**
Professional Association of Diving Instructors **(859)**

Redding

American Buckskin Registry Association **(86)**

Redondo Beach

American Society of Picture Professionals **(207)**

Rhonert Park

Society for Philosophy and Technology **(919)**

Riverside

International Society of Chemical Ecology **(572)**

Roseville

Corporate Event Marketing Association **(386)**
High Technology Crime Investigation Association **(474)**

S. Lake Tahoe

American Institute of Inspectors **(139)**

Sacramento

American Agents Alliance **(43)**
American Association of Psychiatric Technicians **(71)**
American Criminal Justice Association Lambda Alpha Epsilon **(112)**
Association for Wedding Professionals International **(261)**
Association of Threat Assessment Professionals **(314)**
County Counsels' Association of California **(401)**
DBA International **(407)**
DBA International **(407)**
National Coalition of Public Safety Officers **(723)**
National Council on Teacher Retirement **(740)**
National Independent Flag Dealers Association **(762)**
Search - The National Consortium for Justice Information and Statistics **(894)**
Winegrape Growers of America **(1019)**

Salinas

Refrigerating Engineers and Technicians Association **(878)**

San Bernardino

Vocational Evaluation and Career Assessment Professionals **(1011)**

San Clemente

Christian Leadership Alliance **(355)**

Internet Marketing Association **(582)**
Petroleum Packaging Council **(843)**

San Diego

Academy of Prosthodontics **(8)**
Accredited Gemologists Association **(10)**
American Academy of Estate Planning Attorneys **(33)**
American Association for Cancer Education **(48)**
American College of Veterinary Dermatology **(104)**
American Council on Exercise **(110)**
Customer Relations Institute Global, LLC **(406)**
Diving Equipment and Marketing Association **(415)**
IDEA, The Health and Fitness Association **(482)**
IEEE Computational Intelligence Society **(483)**
Information Storage Industry Consortium **(495)**
International Council on Systems Engineering **(539)**
Miniature Book Society **(617)**
Mountain Rescue Association **(620)**
National Association for Year-Round Education **(645)**
National Association of Hispanic Real Estate Professionals **(672)**
Network Professional Association **(808)**
Open Mobile Alliance **(828)**
Service Industry Association **(897)**
Society for Anthropology in Community Colleges **(904)**
Society for Software Quality **(921)**
Technology Services Industry Association **(970)**

San Francisco

American Academy of Ophthalmic Executives **(37)**
American Academy of Ophthalmology **(37)**
American Association for Pediatric Ophthalmology and Strabismus **(50)**
American Board of Podiatric Surgery **(83)**
American Dehydrated Onion and Garlic Association **(113)**
American Ophthalmological Society **(157)**
American Society of Ophthalmic Registered Nurses **(205)**
American Society on Aging **(211)**
Asian American Journalists Association **(231)**
Association of AE Business Leaders **(263)**
The Association of Asian American Investment Managers **(268)**
Association of Independent Colleges of Art and Design **(287)**
Association of Mental Health Librarians **(294)**
Business for Social Responsibility **(339)**
Efficiency First **(421)**
Fibre Channel Industry Association **(443)**
International Anesthesia Research Society **(511)**
International Association of Business Communicators **(517)**
International Association of Professional Security Consultants **(527)**
International Computer Music Association **(536)**
International Longshore and Warehouse Union **(555)**
International Society of Refractive Surgery of the American Academy of Ophthalmology **(574)**
Medical Marketing Association **(611)**
National Alliance for Media Arts and Culture **(631)**
National Association of Casino Party Operators **(651)**
National Employment Lawyers Association (NELA) **(746)**
National Society of Newspaper Columnists **(794)**
Neurotechnology Industry Organization **(809)**
The Open Group **(828)**
Pacific Coast Marine Firemen, Oilers, Watertenders and Wipers Association **(836)**
Pacific Maritime Association **(836)**
Production Equipment Rental Association **(859)**
Sailors' Union of the Pacific **(890)**
SCSI Trade Association **(893)**
Social Venture Network **(902)**
Transaction Processing Performance Council **(977)**

San Jose

American Voice Input/Output Society **(219)**
Career Planning and Adult Development Network **(343)**
Christian Management Association **(356)**
EDA Consortium **(419)**
FlexTech Alliance **(447)**
International Disk Drive Equipment and Materials Association **(540)**
National Association for Chicana and Chicano Studies **(637)**
Public Agency Risk Managers Association **(869)**
Semiconductor Equipment and Materials International **(896)**

San Juan Capistrano

Glove Shippers Association **(463)**

San Leandro

American College of Phlebology **(100)**

San Lucas

United States Cattlemen's Association **(991)**

San Marcos

Retail Florist Association **(884)**

San Mateo

Asia America MultiTechnology Association **(231)**

San Pedro

International Association of Airport and Seaport Police **(515)**
National Watercolor Society **(804)**

San Rafael

National Association of Commissions for Women **(656)**
North American-Bulgarian Chamber of Commerce **(823)**

San Ramon

International Multimedia Telecommunications Consortium **(557)**
International Society of Arthroscopy, Knee Surgery and Orthopaedic Sports Medicine **(571)**

Santa Ana

Amusement Industry Manufacturers and Suppliers International **(223)**
Optometric Extension Program Foundation **(830)**

Santa Barbara

American Academy of Mechanics **(35)**
American Institute of Commemorative Art **(138)**
IT Financial Management Association **(586)**

Santa Clara

Economic History Association **(418)**
Professional and Technical Consultants Association **(859)**
Special Interest Group on Mobility of Systems, Users, Data and Computing **(956)**

Santa Clarita

American College of Veterinary Nutrition **(104)**
The National Flute Association, Inc. **(751)**

Santa Cruz

American Board of Vocational Experts **(84)**
SACNAS (Society for Advancement of Chicanos and Native Americans in Science) **(889)**

Santa Monica

Human Factors and Ergonomics Society **(480)**
Human Factors Society **(481)**
National Academy of Recording Arts and Sciences **(628)**
National Association of Latino Independent Producers **(677)**
PROMAX/BDA **(866)**
Society of Independent Show Organizers **(939)**

Santa Rosa

American Glovebox Society **(126)**
National Association of Field Training Officers **(668)**
North American Peruvian Horse Association **(819)**

Santa Ynez

American Handwriting Analysis Foundation **(128)**

Sebastopol

Surface Design Association **(966)**

Sherman Oaks

Aerobics and Fitness Association of America **(13)**
Alliance of Motion Picture & Television Producers **(25)**
Hollywood Radio & Television Society **(477)**

Sonoma

National Association for PET Container Resources **(641)**

Sonora

American Academy of Pain Management **(39)**

Soquel

Ecological Farming Association **(418)**

St. Helena

Napa Valley Vintners Association **(625)**

Stanford

Conference on Jewish Social Studies **(376)**

Studio City

Accordionists and Teachers Guild International **(9)**
Art Directors Guild/Scenic, Title and Graphic Artists **(230)**
Costume Designers Guild **(387)**
Stuntwomen's Association of Motion Pictures **(964)**

Sun City

Armed Forces Broadcasters Association **(228)**

Sunland

American Entertainment Armories Association (117)

Sutter Creek

National Association of Federal Education Program Administrators (667)

Tarzana

American Hypnosis Association (134)

Torrance

American Board of Podiatric Medicine (83)
Antenna Measurement Techniques Association (224)
Masonry Institute of America (607)

Universal City

American Cinema Editors (91)

Valley Center

National Animal Supplement Council (634)

Van Nuys

American Society of Music Arrangers and Composers (203)
National Black Public Relations Society (715)

Ventura

International Association of Infant Massage (523)
Marketing Association of Credit Unions (606)

Villa Park

Sales Lead Management Association (890)

Vista

The Society for Modeling and Simulation International (916)
Variable Electronic Components Institute (1008)

W. Hills

United Shoe Retailers Association (988)

Walnut Creek

Infrared Data Association (496)
The National Safety Management Society (789)

Woodlake

National Forest Recreation Association (752)

Woodland

The Association for International Agriculture and Rural Development (250)
Community College Journalism Association (370)
Wood Moulding and Millwork Producers Association (1024)

Yucaipa

American Mustang Association (154)

COLORADO

Arvada

National Translator Association (801)
Outpatient Ophthalmic Surgery Society (835)

Aurora

AGN International North America, Inc (15)
Aircraft Mechanics Fraternal Association (20)
American Brush Manufacturers Association (86)
American Coal Ash Association (92)
American Society of Bariatric Physicians (193)
Arabian Horse Association (227)
Geospatial Information Technology Association (459)
International Association of Correctional Training Personnel (518)
National Alliance of Medicare Set-Aside Professionals, Inc. (632)
National Association of Counsel for Children (658)
The Retired Enlisted Association (885)

Avon

International Crystal Federation (539)

Berthoud

Society of Animal Artists (930)

Boulder

Alliance of Associations of Teachers of Japanese (24)
American Homebrewers Association (133)
American Mountain Guides Association (153)
American Society for Theatre Research (190)
American Solar Energy Society (211)
Association for Experiential Education (246)
Association for Theatre in Higher Education (260)
Behavior Genetics Association (327)
The Brewers Association (335)
Geological Society of America (459)
International Alliance for Women in Music (510)
Mining and Metallurgical Society of America (617)
National American Indian Court Judges Association (634)
National Earth Science Teachers Association (743)
National Ecological Observatory Network, Inc (743)
NCSL International (808)

Outdoor Industry Association (835)
Paleontological Society (837)
Rolf Institute of Structural Integration (887)
Society for Mathematical Biology (915)
State Higher Education Executive Officers (961)

Brighton

American Highland Cattle Association (131)

Broomfield

Billiard Congress of America (329)
National Association for Retail Marketing Services (642)

Centennial

American Galvanizers Association (124)
American Institute of Timber Construction (141)
American Wool Council (222)
Cattlemen's Beef Promotion and Research Board (346)
National Association of RV Parks and Campgrounds (692)
National Cattlemen's Beef Association (718)
National Stroke Association (797)

Colorado Springs

American Academy of Forensic Sciences (34)
American Society for Engineering Management (184)
Association for the Advancement of Psychology (258)
Association of Christian Schools International (272)
CBA (346)
Global Market Development Center (462)
Help Desk Institute (474)
National Association of Blind Merchants (650)
National Association of Marine Services (679)
National Association of Media Brokers (680)
National Association of Rehabilitation Research and Training Centers (691)
National Institute for Animal Agriculture (764)
National Junior College Athletic Association (767)
National Livestock Producers Association (770)
National Strength and Conditioning Association (797)
National Wheelchair Basketball Association (804)
Professional Rodeo Cowboys Association (864)
Small Publishers Association of North America (901)
Special Interest Group on Ada Programming Language (955)
University Film and Video Association (1002)
USA Archery (1004)
USA Taekwondo (1005)
USA Volleyball (1005)
Women's Professional Rodeo Association (1023)

Denver

American Cheese Society (89)
American Society of Farm Managers and Rural Appraisers (197)
American Society of Sugar Beet Technologists (209)
American Water Works Association (220)
Association of Avian Veterinarians (268)
Association of Environmental and Engineering Geologists (281)
Association of periOperative Registered Nurses (299)
Beet Sugar Development Foundation (327)
Coalition of Visionary Resources (362)
Council of American Jewish Museums (391)
Council on Botanical and Horticultural Libraries (399)
Democratic Attorneys General Association (410)
Environmental and Engineering Geophysical Society (430)
Financial Planning Association (445)
Financial Planning Standards Board (445)
International Association of Women Police (529)
International Erosion Control Association (543)
International Sport Show Producers Association (575)
Marketing Education Association (606)
Museum Store Association (621)
National Academy of Neuropsychology (628)
National Association of Street Schools (703)
National Civic League (722)
National Conference of State Legislatures (728)
National Conference of State Social Security Administrators (728)
National Council of Supervisors of Mathematics (737)
National Environmental Health Association (746)
National Exchange Traded Fund Association (747)
North American Conference on British Studies (815)
North American Transportation Management Institute (823)
Society of Mortgage, Appraisal, Real Estate and Title Professionals (942)
United States Committee on Irrigation and Drainage (992)
United States Meat Export Federation (996)
United States Potato Board (997)
United States Society on Dams (999)

Divide

Combat Helicopter Pilots Association (366)

Englewood

American Hernia Society (131)
The American Institute of Mining, Metallurgical, and Petroleum Engineers (139)
American National CattleWomen (154)
American Sheep Industry Association (178)
American Society of General Surgeons (198)
MGMA-ACMPE (614)
North American Limousin Foundation (817)
Society for Mining, Metallurgy and Exploration, Inc. (915)

Erie

National Council on Education for the Ceramic Arts (738)

Federal Heights

International Hunter Education Association (550)

Ft. Collins

Associated Schools of Construction (237)
Association for University and College Counseling Center Directors (260)
The Association of Collegiate Conference and Events Directors International (275)
Association of Fraternity Advisors (284)
Conference of Research Workers in Animal Diseases (375)
International Firestop Council (545)
International Veterinary Acupuncture Society (580)
National Association for Ethnic Studies (638)
National Association for Interpretation (640)

Glenwood Springs

Association of Equipment Management Professionals (281)
International Association of Natural Resource Pilots (525)

Golden

Associated Bodywork and Massage Professionals (234)
Mineral Economics and Management Society (617)

Grand Junction

National Association of Private, Nontraditional Schools and Colleges (686)

Greeley

Higher Education Consortium for Special Education (474)
National Council for Marketing and Public Relations (732)
National Onion Association (776)

Greenwood Village

Air and Surface Transport Nurses Association (17)
Investment Management Consultants Association (584)

Highlands Ranch

National Health Club Association (758)

Johnstown

Irish Blacks Cattle Society (585)

Lafayette

International Society for the Study of Subtle Energies and Energy Medicine (570)
Reliability Society (880)

Lakewood

American Animal Hospital Association (45)
American College of Veterinary Internal Medicine (104)
Council of Petroleum Accountants Societies (396)
National Ski Area Association (791)
National Ski Patrol System (792)
PSIA-AASI (868)
Women in Mining National (1022)

Littleton

American Association for Crystal Growth (49)
Association of Surgical Assistants (312)
Association of Surgical Technologists (312)
National Association of Active Investment Managers (645)
National Coal Transportation Association (722)
Society of Economic Geologists (934)

Longmont

Disaster Preparedness and Emergency Response Association (413)
The Masonry Society (607)

Louisville

American Fly Fishing Trade Association (122)
Cryogenic Engineering Conference (405)
National Association for Poetry Therapy (641)

American Academy of Orthotists and Prosthetists *(38)*
American Academy of Wound Management *(42)*
American Advertising Federation *(43)*
American Architectural Foundation *(46)*
American Association for Affirmative Action *(47)*
American Association for Clinical Chemistry, Inc. *(48)*
American Association for Homecare *(50)*
American Association for Justice *(50)*
American Association for the Advancement of Science *(51)*
American Association of Bank Directors *(54)*
American Association of Blacks in Energy *(55)*
American Association of Classified School Employees *(56)*
American Association of Colleges for Teacher Education *(57)*
American Association of Colleges of Nursing *(57)*
American Association of Collegiate Registrars and Admissions Officers *(58)*
American Association of Community Colleges *(58)*
American Association of Credit Union Leagues *(59)*
American Association of Crop Insurers *(59)*
American Association of Exporters & Importers *(60)*
American Association of Jewish Lawyers and Jurists *(64)*
The American Association of Language Specialists *(64)*
American Association of Museums *(65)*
American Association of Naturopathic Physicians *(66)*
American Association of Neurological Surgeons *(66)*
American Association of Residential Mortgage Regulators *(72)*
American Association of Retired Persons *(72)*
American Association of Sexuality Educators, Counselors and Therapists *(73)*
American Association of State Colleges and Universities *(73)*
American Association of Suicidology *(74)*
American Association of University Professors *(75)*
American Association of University Women *(76)*
American Astronomical Society *(77)*
American Automotive Policy Council *(78)*
American Bakers Association *(78)*
American Bankers Association *(79)*
American Bankers Association Securities Association (ABASA) *(79)*
American Bankers Insurance Association *(79)*
The American Bar Association Rule of Law Initiative *(80)*
American Bearing Manufacturers Association *(80)*
American Benefits Council *(80)*
American Beverage Association *(80)*
American Beverage Institute *(81)*
American Bus Association *(87)*
American Chemical Society *(89)*
American Chemistry Council *(90)*
American Cleaning Institute *(91)*
American Clinical Laboratory Association *(91)*
American Coal Council *(92)*
American Coatings Association *(92)*
American Coke and Coal Chemicals Institute *(92)*
American College of Cardiology *(93)*
American College of Oral and Maxillofacial Surgeons *(99)*
American College of Preventive Medicine *(101)*
American College of Tax Counsel *(103)*
American College Personnel Association *(105)*
American Conference of Academic Deans *(107)*
American Congress of Community Supports and Employment Services *(107)*
American Congress of Obstetricians and Gynecologists *(107)*
American Corn Growers Association *(108)*
American Council of Engineering Companies *(109)*
American Council of Independent Laboratories *(109)*
American Council of Life Insurers (ACLI) *(110)*
American Council of State Savings Supervisors *(110)*
American Council on Education *(110)*
American Council on International Personnel *(110)*
American Councils for International Education *(111)*
American Dental Education Association *(113)*
American Educational Research Association *(116)*
American Enterprise Institute for Public Policy Research *(117)*
American Exploration & Production Council *(118)*
American Family Therapy Academy *(118)*
American Farm Bureau Federation *(118)*
American Farmland Trust *(118)*
American Federation of Government Employees *(119)*
American Federation of Labor & Congress of Industrial Organizations *(119)*
American Federation of School Administrators *(120)*
American Federation of State, County and Municipal Employees *(120)*
American Federation of Teachers (AFL-CIO) *(120)*
American Financial Services Association *(121)*

American Fire Safety Council *(121)*
American Foreign Service Association *(122)*
American Foreign Service Protective Association *(123)*
American Forest & Paper Association *(123)*
American Friends of Turkey *(124)*
American Fuel & Petrochemical Manufacturers *(124)*
American Gaming Association *(124)*
American Gas Association *(124)*
American Geophysical Union *(126)*
American Health Care Association *(129)*
American Health Lawyers Association *(130)*
American Health Quality Association *(130)*
American Hellenic Educational Progressive Association (AHEPA) *(130)*
American Highway Users Alliance *(131)*
American Historical Association *(131)*
American Horse Council *(133)*
American Hotel & Lodging Association (AH&LA) *(134)*
American Immigration Lawyers Association *(134)*
American Institute for Conservation of Historic and Artistic Works *(136)*
American Institute for Medical and Biological Engineering *(136)*
American Institute for Shippers' Associations *(136)*
The American Institute of Architects *(137)*
American Institute of Architecture Students *(137)*
American Institute of Building Design *(137)*
American Institute of Certified Planners *(137)*
American Institutes for Research *(141)*
American Insurance Association *(141)*
American Iron and Steel Institute *(142)*
American Land Title Association *(144)*
American League of Anglers and Boaters *(145)*
American Logistics Association *(146)*
American Lung Association *(146)*
American Maritime Congress *(147)*
American Maritime Officers Service *(147)*
American Meat Institute *(148)*
American Medical Rehabilitation Providers Association *(149)*
American Military Society *(152)*
American Mushroom Institute *(153)*
American National Chamber of Commerce *(154)*
American National Standards Institute *(154)*
American Naturopathic Association *(155)*
American Nursery and Landscape Association *(156)*
American Oilseed Coalition *(157)*
American Peanut Product Manufacturers, Inc. *(162)*
American Petroleum Institute *(163)*
American Pharmacists Association *(163)*
American Pilots' Association *(165)*
American Political Science Association *(166)*
American Postal Workers Union *(167)*
American Psychological Association *(169)*
American Psychological Association Practice Organization *(170)*
American Public Gas Association *(170)*
American Public Health Association *(171)*
American Public Human Services Association *(171)*
American Public Power Association *(171)*
American Public Transportation Association *(171)*
American Resort Development Association *(175)*
American Rights at Work *(175)*
American Road and Transportation Builders Association *(175)*
American Seniors Housing Association *(178)*
American Short Line and Regional Railroad Association *(179)*
American Sleep Apnea Association *(180)*
American Small Manufacturers' Coalition *(180)*
American Society for Bone and Mineral Research *(181)*
American Society for Engineering Education *(183)*
American Society for Microbiology *(187)*
The American Society for Public Administration *(189)*
American Society of Access Professionals *(190)*
American Society of Association Executives-The Center for Association Leadership *(193)*
American Society of Hematology *(199)*
American Society of Interior Designers *(200)*
American Society of International Law *(201)*
American Society of Landscape Architects *(201)*
American Society of Nephrology *(204)*
American Sociological Association *(211)*
American Spice Trade Association *(212)*
American Studies Association *(214)*
American Sugarbeet Growers Association *(214)*
American Telemedicine Association *(215)*
American Tort Reform Association *(217)*
American Urogynecologic Society *(218)*
American Watch Association *(219)*
American Wind Energy Association (AWEA) *(221)*
Animal Health Institute *(223)*
APHSA - Information Systems Management *(224)*
APPAM - The Association for Public Policy Analysis and Management *(225)*
Apple Processors Association *(225)*

Application Developers Alliance *(226)*
Appraisal Foundation *(226)*
Arms Control Association *(229)*
Aseptic Packaging Council *(231)*
Asian Pacific American Labor Alliance, AFL-CIO *(232)*
Asphalt Roofing Manufacturers Association *(233)*
ASPIRA Association, Inc. *(233)*
Aspirin Foundation of America, Inc. *(233)*
Associated Air Balance Council *(234)*
Associated Luxury Hotels International *(236)*
Associated Universities Inc. *(237)*
Association for Behavioral Health & Wellness *(240)*
Association for Canadian Studies in the United States *(241)*
Association for Community Affiliated Plans *(242)*
Association for Commuter Transportation *(242)*
Association for Competitive Technology (ACT) *(242)*
Association for Demand Response & Smart Grid *(244)*
Association for Enterprise Opportunity *(245)*
Association for Information Protection *(249)*
Association for Philosophy of the Unconscious *(253)*
Association for Prevention Teaching and Research (APTR) *(254)*
Association for Professionals in Infection Control and Epidemiology *(254)*
Association for Psychological Science *(254)*
Association for Quality Imaging (AQI) *(254)*
Association for Retail Technology Standards *(256)*
Association for the Accreditation of Human Research Protection Programs *(257)*
Association for the Study of African American Life and History *(259)*
Association for Tropical Biology and Conservation *(260)*
Association of Academic Health Centers *(262)*
Association of Administrators of the Interstate Compact on the Placement of Children *(263)*
Association of Alternative Newsweeklies *(264)*
Association of American Chambers of Commerce in Latin America *(264)*
Association of American Colleges and Universities *(264)*
Association of American Geographers *(265)*
Association of American Law Schools *(265)*
Association of American Medical Colleges *(265)*
Association of American Railroads *(266)*
Association of American Universities *(266)*
Association of American Veterinary Medical Colleges *(267)*
Association of Bituminous Contractors *(269)*
Association of Black Cardiologists *(269)*
Association of Cable Communicators *(270)*
Association of Career Professionals International *(271)*
Association of Catholic Colleges and Universities *(271)*
Association of Clean Water Administrators *(273)*
Association of Clinical Research Organizations *(273)*
Association of Collegiate Schools of Architecture *(275)*
Association of Community College Trustees *(276)*
The Association of Community Pharmacists Congressional Network *(276)*
Association of Corporate Counsel *(277)*
Association of Corporate Credit Unions *(277)*
Association of Defense Communities *(278)*
Association of Dermatology Administrators & Managers *(278)*
Association of Direct Response Fundraising Counsel *(279)*
Association of Environmental and Resource Economists *(281)*
Association of Farmworker Opportunity Programs *(282)*
Association of Federal Communications Consulting Engineers *(282)*
Association of Fish and Wildlife Agencies *(283)*
Association of Flight Attendants - CWA *(283)*
Association of Foreign Investors in U.S. Real Estate *(284)*
Association of Global Automakers *(285)*
Association of Governing Boards of Universities and Colleges *(286)*
Association of Graduate Schools in Association of American Universities *(286)*
Association of HazMat Shippers *(286)*
Association of Home Appliance Manufacturers *(287)*
The Association of International Photography Art Dealers *(289)*
Association of Jesuit Colleges and Universities *(290)*
Association of Jewish Aging Services *(290)*
Association of Maternal and Child Health Programs (AMCHP) *(293)*
Association of Medical Device Reprocessors *(293)*
Association of Medical Diagnostic Manufacturers *(293)*
Association of Meeting Professionals *(294)*

Healthcare Leadership Council *(471)*
Healthcare Supply Chain Association *(472)*
Hearing Industries Association *(472)*
Heart Rhythm Society *(472)*
Hemophilia Federation of America *(474)*
Hispanic Association on Corporate Responsibility *(475)*
Hispanic Elected Local Officials *(475)*
Hispanic Lobbyists Association *(475)*
Hispanic National Bar Association *(475)*
Hospice Association of America *(479)*
Hotel Electronic Distribution Network Association *(479)*
HR Policy Association *(480)*
ICAAAA Coaches Association *(482)*
IEEE Computer Society *(483)*
Incentive Federation, Inc. *(487)*
Incorporated Research Institutions for Seismology *(487)*
Independent Bakers Association *(488)*
Independent Community Bankers of America *(488)*
Independent Fuel Terminal Operators Association *(490)*
Independent Petroleum Association of America *(491)*
Independent Sector *(491)*
Independent Telephone and Telecommunications Alliance *(492)*
Independent Terminal Operators Association *(492)*
Indoor Tanning Association *(492)*
Industrial Energy Consumers of America *(493)*
Industrial Minerals Association -- North America *(494)*
Industrial Truck Association *(494)*
Information Technology Industry Council *(495)*
Institute for Credentialing Excellence *(497)*
Institute for Responsible Housing Preservation *(497)*
Institute of Clean Air Companies *(499)*
Institute of International Container Lessors *(501)*
Institute of International Finance *(501)*
Institute of Makers of Explosives *(501)*
Institute of Management Consultants USA *(501)*
Institute of Medicine *(501)*
Institute of Scrap Recycling Industries, Inc. *(503)*
Institute of Shortening and Edible Oils *(503)*
Institute of Transportation Engineers *(503)*
Institutional Life Markets Association *(504)*
Instructional Technology Council *(504)*
Insured Retirement Institute *(505)*
The Integrated Ocean Drilling Program *(505)*
Intellectual Property Owners Association *(505)*
Intelligent Transportation Society of America *(506)*
Inter-American Bar Association *(506)*
Inter-National Association of Business Industry & Rehabilitation *(506)*
InterAction (American Council of Voluntary International Action) *(506)*
Interactive Travel Services Association *(507)*
InterAmerican College of Physicians and Surgeons *(507)*
Intercollegiate Men's Choruses, an International Association of Male Choruses *(507)*
International Air Transport Association *(510)*
International Allied Printing Trades Association *(510)*
International Anti-Counterfeiting Coalition *(511)*
International Association of Airport Duty Free Stores *(515)*
International Association of Bridge, Structural, Ornamental and Reinforcing Iron Workers *(517)*
International Association of Color Manufacturers *(518)*
International Association of Fire Fighters *(521)*
International Association of Homes and Services for the Ageing *(522)*
International Association of Official Human Rights Agencies *(525)*
International Banana Association *(529)*
International Biometric Industry Association *(530)*
International Biometric Society *(530)*
International Bridge, Tunnel and Turnpike Association *(531)*
International Brotherhood of Electrical Workers *(531)*
International Brotherhood of Teamsters *(532)*
International Brotherhood of Teamsters - Airline Division *(532)*
International Cargo Security Council *(533)*
International City/County Management Association *(535)*
International Claim Association *(535)*
International Communication Association *(536)*
International Council for Small Business *(538)*
International Council of Employers of Bricklayers and Allied Craftworkers *(538)*
International Dairy Foods Association *(539)*
International Downtown Association *(541)*
International Economic Development Council *(541)*
The International Ecotourism Society *(542)*
International Electronic Article Surveillance Manufacturers Association *(542)*
International Emissions Trading Association *(542)*

International Federation of Professional and Technical Engineers *(544)*
International Franchise Association *(547)*
International Hydrolized Protein Council *(551)*
International Ice Cream Association *(551)*
International Jelly and Preserve Association *(553)*
International Labor Communications Association *(553)*
International Labor Rights Forum *(553)*
International Legal Fraternity of Phi Delta Phi *(554)*
International Life Sciences Institute *(554)*
International Microelectronics and Packaging Society - IMAPS *(556)*
International Oxygen Manufacturers Association *(559)*
International Pharmaceutical Aerosol Consortium *(560)*
International Society for Antiviral Research *(565)*
International Society for Technology in Education *(569)*
The International Stability Operations Association *(575)*
International Trade Commission Trial Lawyers Association *(577)*
International Union of Bricklayers and Allied Craftworkers *(579)*
International Union of Operating Engineers *(579)*
International Utility Efficiency Partnerships *(580)*
International Zinc Association-America *(582)*
Internet Alliance *(582)*
Internet Commerce Association (f/k/a Internet Traffic Association) *(582)*
Interstate Natural Gas Association of America *(583)*
Investment Adviser Association *(583)*
Investment Company Institute *(584)*
Jesuit Secondary Education Association *(587)*
Joint National Committee for Languages *(589)*
Joint National Committee for Languages-National Council for Languages and International Studies *(589)*
Juice Products Association *(589)*
Justice Research and Statistics Association *(589)*
Kidney Care Partners *(591)*
Knowledge Alliance *(591)*
Labor Council for Latin American Advancement (LCLAA) *(592)*
Laborers International Union of North America *(592)*
Laborers-Employers Cooperation & Education Trust *(592)*
Lamaze International *(592)*
Land Trust Alliance *(593)*
Large Public Power Council *(593)*
LeadingAge (American Association of Homes and Services for the Aging) *(595)*
Leather Industries of America *(596)*
Library Copyright Alliance *(597)*
Lighter Association *(598)*
Linguistic Society of America *(598)*
Log Homes Council *(600)*
Magnet Schools of America *(601)*
Malaysian Rubber Export Promotion Council (USA) *(602)*
Managed Funds Association *(602)*
Manufactured Housing Association for Regulatory Reform *(602)*
Marine Engineers Beneficial Association *(605)*
Marine Technology Society *(605)*
Marketing Research Association *(606)*
MASINT Association *(607)*
Masonry Veneer Manufacturers Association *(607)*
Mathematical Association of America *(609)*
Medicaid Health Plans of America *(611)*
Medical Device Manufacturers Association *(611)*
Medical Imaging Contrast Agent Associations *(611)*
Messenger Courier Association of the Americas *(612)*
Mexico-U.S. Business Committee, U.S. Council *(614)*
Midwives Alliance of North America *(615)*
Modular Building Systems Council *(618)*
Money Management Institute *(618)*
Mortgage Bankers Association of America *(619)*
Mortgage Insurance Companies of America *(619)*
Motion Picture Association of America (MPAA) *(619)*
Municipal Waste Management Association *(621)*
Museum Education Roundtable *(621)*
Museum Trustee Association *(621)*
NAFSA: Association of International Educators *(624)*
NALP - The Association for Legal Career Professionals *(624)*
National Association of Student Personnel Administrators *(626)*
National Abortion Federation *(626)*
National Abstinence Education Association *(626)*
National Academy of Clinical Biochemistry *(627)*
National Academy of Education *(627)*
National Academy of Engineering of the United States of America *(627)*
National Academy of Public Administration *(628)*
National Academy of Sciences *(628)*

National Adult Education Professional Development Consortium *(629)*
National Aeronautic Association *(629)*
National Agricultural Aviation Association *(630)*
National Air Traffic Controllers Association *(630)*
National ALEC Association/ Prepaid Communications Association *(631)*
National Alliance for Hispanic Health *(631)*
National Alliance of Black School Educators *(632)*
National Alliance of Community Economic Development Associations *(632)*
National Alliance of Forest Owners *(632)*
National Alliance of Postal and Federal Employees *(633)*
National Alliance of State and Territorial AIDS Directors *(633)*
National Alliance to Save Native Languages *(633)*
National American Indian Housing Council *(634)*
National Asian Pacific American Bar Association *(635)*
National Assembly of State Arts Agencies *(635)*
National Association for Behavioral Health *(636)*
National Association for Biomedical Research *(636)*
National Association for Business Economics *(636)*
National Association for Children's Behavioral Health (NACBH) *(637)*
National Association of County Community and Economic Development *(637)*
National Association for Environmental Management *(638)*
National Association for Equal Opportunity in Higher Education *(638)*
National Association for Gifted Children *(639)*
National Association for Home Care and Hospice *(639)*
National Association for Multicultural Education *(640)*
National Association for Olmsted Parks *(641)*
National Association for Program Information and Performance Measurement *(641)*
National Association for State Community Services Programs *(643)*
National Association for Surface Finishing *(643)*
National Association for the Advancement of Orthotics and Prosthetics *(643)*
National Association for the Education of Young Children *(644)*
National Association for the Self-Employed *(644)*
National Association for the Support of Long Term Care *(644)*
National Association of Medical Staff Services *(645)*
National Association of Affordable Housing Lenders *(646)*
National Association of Agricultural Fair Agencies *(646)*
National Association of Area Agencies on Aging *(647)*
National Association of Attorneys General *(647)*
National Association of Beverage Importers Inc. *(648)*
National Association of Black County Officials *(649)*
National Association of Black Social Workers *(649)*
National Association of Black-Owned Broadcasters *(649)*
National Association of Blacks In Government *(649)*
National Association of Boards of Examiners of Long Term Care Administrators *(650)*
National Association of Bond Lawyers *(650)*
National Association of Broadcast Employees and Technicians-Communications Workers of America, AFL-CIO (NABET-CWA) *(650)*
National Association of Broadcasters *(650)*
National Association of Business Political Action Committees *(651)*
National Association of City and County Health Officials *(654)*
National Association of Clean Air Agencies *(654)*
National Association of Clean Water Agencies *(654)*
National Association of College and University Attorneys *(654)*
National Association of College and University Business Officers *(654)*
The National Association of Colored Women's Club, Inc. *(656)*
National Association of Conservation Districts *(657)*
National Association of Consumer Advocates *(657)*
National Association of Corporate Directors *(658)*
National Association of Councils on Developmental Disabilities *(658)*
National Association of Counties *(659)*
National Association of County Administrators *(659)*
National Association of County Aging Programs *(659)*
National Association of County and City Health Officials *(659)*
National Association of County Behavioral Health and Developmental Disability Directors *(659)*
National Association of County Civil Attorneys *(659)*
National Association of County Engineers *(660)*

National Association of County Human Services Administrators *(660)*
National Association of County Information Officers *(660)*
National Association of County Information Technology Administrators *(660)*
National Association of County Intergovernmental Relations Officials *(660)*
National Association of Criminal Defense Lawyers *(661)*
National Association of Development Organizations *(662)*
National Association of Disability Representatives *(663)*
National Association of Energy Service Companies *(665)*
National Association of Enrolled Agents *(666)*
National Association of Epilepsy Centers *(666)*
National Association of Federal Veterinarians *(668)*
National Association of Federally Impacted Schools *(668)*
National Association of Flood and Stormwater Management Agencies *(668)*
National Association of Foreign Trade Zones *(669)*
National Association of Graduate-Professional Students *(670)*
National Association of Health Services Executives *(671)*
National Association of Healthcare Access Management *(671)*
National Association of Hispanic Federal Executives *(672)*
National Association of Hispanic Firefighters *(672)*
National Association of Hispanic Journalists *(672)*
National Association of Hispanic Nurses *(672)*
National Association of Hispanic Publications *(672)*
National Association of Home Builders *(673)*
National Association of Housing and Redevelopment Officials *(673)*
National Association of Housing Cooperatives *(673)*
National Association of Independent Colleges and Universities *(674)*
National Association of Independent Housing Professionals *(674)*
National Association of Independent Schools *(675)*
National Association of Insurance Commissioners *(676)*
National Association of Investment Companies *(676)*
National Association of Japan-America Societies *(677)*
National Association of Jewish Legislators *(677)*
National Association of Judiciary Interpreters and Translators *(677)*
National Association of Letter Carriers *(678)*
National Association of Local Government Environmental Professionals *(678)*
National Association of Local Housing Finance Agencies *(678)*
National Association of Long Term Care Administrator Boards *(679)*
National Association of Manufacturers *(679)*
National Association of Margarine Manufacturers *(679)*
National Association of Medicaid Directors *(680)*
National Association of Minority Contractors *(680)*
National Association of Negro Business and Professional Women's Clubs *(681)*
National Association of Neighborhoods *(681)*
National Association of Nurse Practitioners in Women's Health *(682)*
National Association of Nutrition and Aging Services Programs *(682)*
National Association of Older Worker Employment Services *(683)*
National Association of Plant Patent Owners *(685)*
National Association of Private Special Education Centers *(686)*
National Association of Psychiatric Health Systems *(688)*
National Association of Public Child Welfare Administrators *(688)*
National Association of Public Hospitals and Health Systems *(688)*
National Association of Railroad Passengers *(689)*
National Association of Real Estate Investment Trusts (NAREIT) *(690)*
National Association of Regional Councils *(690)*
National Association of Regulatory Utility Commissioners *(691)*
National Association of Rehabilitation Providers and Agencies *(691)*
National Association of Resource Conservation and Development Councils *(691)*
National Association of Retail Collection Attorneys *(692)*
National Association of Schools of Public Affairs and Administration *(694)*
National Association of Secretaries of State *(695)*
National Association of Securities Professionals *(695)*

National Association of Security Companies (NASCO) *(695)*
National Association of Shareholder and Consumer Attorneys *(696)*
National Association of Small Business Contractors *(696)*
National Association of Social Workers *(696)*
National Association of State Alcohol and Drug Abuse Directors (NASADAD) *(697)*
National Association of State Aviation Officials *(698)*
National Association of State Budget Officers *(698)*
National Association of State Catholic Conference Directors *(699)*
National Association of State Departments of Agriculture *(699)*
National Association of State Directors of Migrant Education *(700)*
National Association of State Directors of Teacher Education and Certification *(700)*
National Association of State Foresters *(701)*
National Association of State Workforce Agencies *(703)*
National Association of States United For Aging and Disabilities *(703)*
National Association of Student Financial Aid Administrators *(703)*
National Association of Surety Bond Producers *(704)*
National Association of Theatre Owners *(706)*
National Association of Towns and Townships (NATAT) *(706)*
National Association of Tribal Historic Preservation Officers *(707)*
National Association of University Women *(708)*
National Association of Veterans Program Administrators *(708)*
National Association of Vision Professionals *(708)*
National Association of Water Companies (NAWC) *(709)*
National Association of Waterfront Employers *(709)*
National Association of Wheat Growers *(709)*
National Association of Wholesaler-Distributors *(709)*
National Association of Women Business Owners *(709)*
National Association of Women Judges *(710)*
National Association of Workforce Boards (NAWB) *(710)*
National Association of Workforce Development Professionals *(710)*
National Bankers Association *(712)*
National Bar Association *(712)*
National Basketball Referees Association *(713)*
National Beauty Culturists' League *(713)*
National BioDiesel Board *(713)*
National Black Caucus of Local Elected Officials *(714)*
National Black Caucus of State Legislators *(714)*
National Black Chamber of Commerce *(714)*
The National Building Granite Quarries Association *(716)*
National Business Aviation Association *(716)*
National Business Group on Health *(716)*
National Cable & Telecommunications Association *(717)*
National Candle Association *(717)*
National Cannabis Industry Association *(717)*
National Center for Assisted Living *(719)*
National Cheese Institute *(720)*
National Chicken Council *(720)*
National Child Care Association *(721)*
National Club Association *(722)*
The National Coal Council *(722)*
National Collaboration for Youth *(723)*
National Committee for Quality Assurance *(724)*
National Communication Association *(724)*
National Community Development Association *(725)*
National Confectioners Association *(725)*
National Conference of Executives of The ARC *(727)*
National Conference of State Historic Preservation Officers *(728)*
National Conference on Public Employee Retirement Systems *(729)*
National Consumers League *(729)*
National Cooperative Business Association *(729)*
National Coordinating Committee for Multiemployer Plans *(730)*
National Council for Accreditation of Teacher Education *(731)*
National Council for Advanced Manufacturing *(731)*
National Council for Community Behavioral Healthcare *(731)*
National Council for Geographic Education *(731)*
National Council for Interior Design Qualifications *(732)*
National Council for International Visitors *(732)*
National Council for Languages and International Studies *(732)*
National Council for Science and the Environment *(733)*

National Council of Architectural Registration Boards *(733)*
National Council of Chain Restaurants *(734)*
National Council of Farmer Cooperatives *(734)*
National Council of Higher Education Loan Programs *(735)*
National Council of Minorities in Energy *(735)*
National Council of Nonprofits *(735)*
National Council of Social Security Management Associations *(736)*
National Council of State Directors of Community Colleges *(736)*
National Council of State Housing Agencies *(736)*
National Council of State Tourism Directors *(736)*
National Council of Travel Attractions *(737)*
National Council of University Research Administrators *(737)*
National Council of Urban Education Associations *(738)*
National Council on Aging *(738)*
National Council on Compensation Insurance, Inc. *(738)*
National Council on International Trade Development *(739)*
National Council on Problem Gambling *(739)*
National Counter Intelligence Corps Association *(740)*
National Criminal Justice Association *(740)*
National Customs Brokers and Forwarders Association of America *(741)*
National Dental Association *(742)*
National Education Association *(744)*
National Energy Assistance Directors' Association *(746)*
National Family Planning and Reproductive Health Association *(747)*
National Farmers Union (Farmers Educational & Co-operative Union of America) *(747)*
National Federation of Federal Employees *(748)*
National Federation of Federal Employees, Federal Dist. 1, IAMAW, AFL-CIO *(748)*
National Football League Players Association *(752)*
National Foreign Trade Council, Inc. *(752)*
National Forum for Black Public Administrators *(752)*
National Foundation for Credit Counseling *(753)*
National Foundation for Women Legislators *(753)*
National Governors Association *(755)*
National Grain and Feed Association *(755)*
National Grain Trade Council *(756)*
National Grange *(756)*
National Grants Management Association *(756)*
National Guard Association of the U.S. *(757)*
National Health Care Anti-Fraud Association *(758)*
National Health Council *(758)*
National Hispanic Corporate Council *(759)*
National Hispanic Medical Association *(759)*
National Home Performance Council, Inc. *(760)*
National Housing and Rehabilitation Association *(760)*
National Housing Conference *(761)*
National Human Services Assembly *(761)*
National Humanities Alliance *(761)*
National Hydropower Association *(761)*
National Indian Education Association *(762)*
National Indian Gaming Association *(762)*
National Indian Health Board *(763)*
National Industrial Council - Employer Association Group *(763)*
National Industrial Council - State Associations Group *(763)*
National Industrial Sand Association *(763)*
National Installment Lenders Association *(764)*
National Institute of Building Sciences *(764)*
National Institute of Oilseed Products *(765)*
National Institute of Senior Centers *(765)*
National Institute of Senior Housing *(765)*
National Labor Relations Board Professional Association *(768)*
National League of American Pen Women *(768)*
National League of Cities *(768)*
National Leased Housing Association *(769)*
National Legal Aid and Defender Association *(769)*
National Lesbian and Gay Journalists Association *(769)*
National Lesbian and Gay Law Association *(769)*
National Lumber and Building Material Dealers Association *(770)*
National Maritime Safety Association *(772)*
National Migrant and Seasonal Head Start Association *(772)*
National Mining Association *(772)*
National Mitigation Banking Association *(773)*
National Multi-Housing Council *(774)*
National Music Publishers Association *(774)*
National Newspaper Publishers Association *(775)*
National Ocean Industries Association *(775)*
National Oilseed Processors Association *(776)*
National Organization for the Professional Advancement of Black Chemists and Chemical Engineers *(777)*

Vinyl Acetate Council *(1009)*
Vinyl Siding Institute, Inc. *(1009)*
Visiting Nurse Associations of America *(1010)*
Visually Impaired Data Processors International *(1011)*
Voices for America's Children *(1011)*
Warrior Protection & Readiness Coalition *(1012)*
Waste Equipment Technology Association *(1012)*
Water and Wastewater Equipment Manufacturers Association *(1012)*
Water Systems Council *(1013)*
Weather Risk Management Association *(1014)*
Western Association for Art Conservation *(1015)*
White House Correspondents Association *(1016)*
White House News Photographers Association *(1016)*
Wine and Spirits Wholesalers of America *(1018)*
WineAmerica *(1019)*
Wireless Communications Association International *(1019)*
Women in Aerospace *(1020)*
Women in Government *(1021)*
Women in International Security *(1021)*
Women's Business Enterprise National Council *(1022)*
Women's Transportation Seminar (WTS International) *(1024)*
Working Group for Investment in Reliable and Economic Electric Systems *(1025)*
World Affairs Councils of America *(1025)*
World Federation of Public Health Associations *(1026)*
World Media Association *(1027)*
World Shipping Council *(1027)*
Writing Instrument Manufacturers Association *(1029)*

FLORIDA

Alachua
Veterinary Hospital Managers Association *(1008)*

Altamonte Springs
The Institute of Internal Auditors *(500)*
National Association of Physician Recruiters *(684)*
Society for Technological Advancement of Reporting *(922)*

Amelia Island
Smocking Arts Guild of America *(901)*

Aventura
Hedge Fund Association *(473)*

Bay Harbor
American Society of Podiatric Medicine *(208)*

Bay Lake
Health Occupations Students of America *(470)*

Boca Grande
Marine Retailers Association of America *(605)*

Boca Raton
American Academy of Anti-Aging Medicine *(30)*
American Society for Artificial Internal Organs *(181)*
Building Trades Association *(338)*
Communications Media Management Association *(369)*
Electrical Generating Systems Association *(422)*
International Electronic Commerce Association *(542)*
National Association of Real Estate Editors *(690)*
National Extension Association of Family and Consumer Sciences *(747)*

Bonita Springs
National Association of Principals of Schools for Girls *(686)*

Boynton Beach
Federation of Podiatric Medical Boards *(442)*

Bradenton
International Council of Fine Arts Deans *(538)*
National Association of Home Inspectors *(673)*

Brandon
National Independent Concessionaires Association *(762)*

Carrabelle
Association of College and University Printers *(274)*

Championsgate
International Academy of Oral Medicine and Toxicology *(509)*

Clearwater
American College of Nutrition *(99)*
Commission on Accreditation of Allied Health Education Programs *(368)*
Concrete Sawing and Drilling Association *(374)*

National High School Athletic Coaches Association *(759)*

Clermont
National Educational Broadband Services Organization *(744)*

Cleveland
Society of Pelvic Surgeons *(944)*

Clewiston
Sugar Industry Technologists *(965)*

Cocoa
Solar Rating and Certification Corporation *(952)*

Coral Gables
Academy of Behavioral Medicine Research *(4)*
Association for Communication Administration *(241)*
Caribbean Hotel and Tourism Association *(343)*
Holistic Dental Association *(477)*

Coral Springs
Academy of Laser Dentistry *(6)*

Dania Beach
American Maritime Officers *(147)*
American Maritime Officers Plans *(147)*

Davie
American Dermatological Association *(114)*

Daytona Beach
APCO (Association of Public-Safety Communications Officials) International *(304)*
Ladies Professional Golf Association *(592)*
Light Aircraft Manufacturers Association *(598)*

Delray Beach
The American Consultants League *(108)*
AscdiNatd *(231)*
Association of Service and Computer Dealers International *(308)*

Destin
International Conference of Police Chaplains *(536)*

Doral
International Federation of the Phonographic Industry *(544)*

Dunedin
International Wildlife Management Consortium *(581)*

Englewood
Clowns of America International *(359)*

Ft. Lauderdale
American Boat Builders and Repairers Association *(84)*
The American Fair Credit Council *(118)*
American Swimming Coaches Association *(215)*
College Swimming Coaches Association of America *(364)*
Cruise Lines International Association *(405)*
International Gay and Lesbian Travel Association *(548)*
International Superyacht Society *(576)*
International Turfgrass Society *(579)*
National Association of Federally Licensed Firearms Dealers *(668)*
United States Superyacht Association *(999)*

Ft. Myers
Architectural Precast Association *(228)*

Ft. Pierce
National Shellfisheries Association *(790)*
Ocean Research & Conservation Association *(826)*

Gainesville
American Psychopathological Association *(170)*
American Society for Metabolic and Bariatric Surgery *(187)*
Association of Leadership Educators *(291)*
CPAmerica International *(402)*
International Newspaper Group *(558)*
National Association of County Surveyors *(660)*
National Association of University Fisheries and Wildlife Programs *(707)*
National Block and Bridle Club *(715)*
Natural Science Collections Alliance *(807)*

Glenview
Steel Tube Institute of North America *(963)*

Gonzalez
International Family Recreation Association *(544)*

Green Cove Springs
American Association of Public Health Physicians *(72)*

Gulf Breeze
Suntanning Association for Education *(966)*

Hollywood
Association for Retail Environments *(256)*
International Association for Identification *(513)*
Phi Delta Epsilon International Medical Fraternity *(845)*

Homestead
United States Aquaculture Suppliers Association *(990)*

Inverness
Council of American Master Mariners *(392)*

Islamorada
Craft Retailers Association for Tomorrow *(403)*

Jacksonville
American Association of Avian Pathologists *(54)*
American Association of Clinical Endocrinologists *(56)*
Association of American Shippers *(266)*
Association of Pediatric Oncology Social Workers *(298)*
Certified Claims Professional Accreditation Council *(349)*
The Commercial Vehicle Solutions Network *(367)*
Commercial Vehicle Solutions Network *(367)*
Maritime Law Association of the U.S. *(606)*
Metal Treating Institute *(614)*
National Association of Teachers of Singing *(705)*
National Certification Commission for Acupuncture and Oriental Medicine *(720)*
National Independent Living Association *(762)*
National Lipid Association *(770)*
Society of Accredited Marine Surveyors *(927)*
Society of Biological Psychiatry *(931)*

Jacksonville Beach
National Center for Housing Management *(719)*

Jupiter
National Association of Police Athletics/Activities Leagues, Inc. *(685)*
National Golf Foundation *(755)*
National Tax Lien Association *(799)*

Lady Lake
Professional Association of Health Care Office Management *(859)*

Lake Mary
Lpga Tournament Owners Association *(600)*

Lakeland
National Tutoring Association *(803)*
National Watermelon Association *(804)*
Seaplane Pilots Association *(894)*

Lighthouse Point
C-Port *(340)*

Longwood
National Concrete Burial Vault Association *(725)*
National Intercollegiate Soccer Officials Association *(766)*

Lutz
Xplor International *(1029)*

Maitland
National Association of Multicultural Engineering Program Advocates *(681)*
National Cartoonists Society *(718)*
Society of University Surgeons *(949)*
Violin Society of America *(1010)*

Marco Island
Association of Internal Management Consultants *(289)*
Textile Bag and Packaging Association *(972)*

Margate
National Association of Cruise Oriented Agencies *(662)*

Miami
Abacus International *(2)*
Accredited Medical Equipment Providers of America *(10)*
American Welding Society *(220)*
Gases and Welding Distributors Association *(457)*
The International Air Cargo Association *(509)*
International Association for Hydrogen Energy *(513)*
National Association of State Administrators and Supervisors of Private Schools *(697)*
National Independent Private Schools Association *(762)*
Production and Operations Management Society *(859)*

Resistance Welding Manufacturing Alliance (883)
Society of Laparoendoscopic Surgeons (940)
United Association for Labor Education (985)

Milton

International Order of the Golden Rule (559)

Minneola

Pharmaceutical Marketing Research Group (844)

Naples

Conveyor Equipment Manufacturers Association (383)
International Society of Hospitality Consultants (573)
Mechanical Power Transmission Association (610)
North American Punch Manufacturers Association (820)
Spring Research Institute (960)

New Port Richey

American Board of Quality Assurance and Utilization Review Physicians, Inc. (84)
Association of Defense Trial Attorneys (278)
Association of Millwork Distributors (294)

New Smyrna Beach

Society of Otorhinolaryngology and Head-Neck Nurses (943)

Ocala

American Academy of Podiatric Sports Medicine (40)

Oldsmar

National Association of Ordnance and Explosive Waste Contractors (682)
National Property Management Association (783)

Orange Park

Pile Driving Contractors Association (848)

Orlando

American Academy of Optometry (37)
American Cash Flow Association (88)
Association for Biblical Higher Education (240)
Developmental Disabilities Nurses Association (411)
The Exercise Safety Association (435)
Futon Association International (455)
The Institute of Financial Operations (499)
International Laser Display Association (553)
Laser Institute of America (593)
Life Insurance Settlement Association (597)
National Center for Simulation (719)
Society for News Design (916)
Water Sports Industry Association (1013)

Ormond Beach

American Association of Behavioral Therapists (54)

Oviedo

Associated Church Press (235)

Palm Beach

Association of Eminent Domain Professionals (280)
Window Council (1018)

Palm Beach Gardens

Association for the Advancement of International Education (258)
Executive Women's Golf Association (435)
International Association of Healthcare Practitioners (522)
Library Binding Institute (597)
Professional Golfers Association of America (862)
Society for Community Research and Action (906)

Palm Coast

Book Manufacturers' Institute (333)

Palm Harbor

American College of Eye Surgeons (95)

Panama City

Association of Plastic Surgery Assistants (299)
Institute of Diving (499)

Pensacola

American Association of Occupational Health Nurses (67)
Association for Radiological and Imaging Nursing (255)
Instrumentation Testing Association (504)
International Precious Metals Institute (561)
National Organization for Associate Degree Nursing (776)
Semiotic Society of America (897)
Society of Environmental Toxicology and Chemistry (935)

Perry

Pulp and Paper Safety Association (871)

Ponte Vedra Beach

ATP Tour, Inc. (320)
The PGA Tour, Inc. (844)

Port Charlotte

National Plasterers Council (781)

Punta Gorda

Zoological Association of America (1030)

Riverview

National Association of Underwater Instructors (707)

S. Daytona

American Horse Publications (133)

Sarasota

American Accounting Association (43)
International Network of Merger and Acquisition Partners (557)
International Union of Police Associations, AFL-CIO (579)
National Association of Computerized Tax Processors (657)
National Association of Fire Investigators (668)
Retirement Industry Trust Association (885)
Wedding and Event Videographers Association International (1014)

Sebastian

American Association of Surgical Physician Assistants (74)

St. Augustine

American Culinary Federation (112)
Conference of Educational Administrators of Schools and Programs for the Deaf (375)
International Council of Psychologists (538)

St. Petersburg

Armed Forces Financial Network (229)
Minor League Baseball (617)
National Association of Jai Alai Frontons (677)
National Association of Professional Baseball Leagues (686)
National Hay Association (758)
Professional Association of Resume Writers and Career Coaches (860)
Text and Academic Authors Association (972)
WTA Tour, Inc. (1029)

Stuart

American Membrane Technology Association (150)

Suite F6-491

National Association of Extension 4-H Agents (667)

Tallahassee

American Association of Business Valuation Specialists (55)
American Association of Physicians and Health Care Professionals (69)
American Association of State Troopers (73)
American Real Estate and Urban Economics Association (173)
American Society of Notaries (204)
Association for Institutional Research (250)
Association of Collegiate Schools of Planning (275)
Association of Osteopathic State Executive Directors (297)
College Language Association (363)
National Association for Relationship and Marriage Education (642)
National Association of Dental Laboratories (662)
North American Agricultural Marketing Officials (812)
North American Cartographic Information Society (814)

Tampa

Alpha Zeta Omega (27)
American Association of Kidney Patients (64)
American Association of Physical Anthropologists (69)
American Association of Physician Specialists (69)
American College of Physician Executives (101)
American Rehabilitation Counseling Association (174)
Asian American Convenience Stores Association (231)
Association of Battery Recyclers (269)
Association of Neurosurgical Physician Assistants (295)
The Association to Advance Collegiate Schools of Business (319)
BICSI (329)
Federation of Defense and Corporate Counsel (441)
Financial Management Association International (444)
Home Improvement Research Institute (478)
Institute for Business & Home Safety (496)
International Fitness Professionals Association (545)

International Packaged Ice Association (559)
International Society for Pharmaceutical Engineering (567)
Major Indoor Soccer League (601)
National Border Patrol Council (716)
National Dental Hygienists' Association (743)
National Health Association (758)
National Mobility Equipment Dealers Association (773)
North American Academy of Ecumenists (812)
Phi Alpha Theta (845)

Tarpon Springs

American Council on Consumer Interests (110)
Southern Shrimp Alliance (953)

Titusville

American Federation of Police and Concerned Citizens (119)
National Association of Chiefs of Police (653)

Valrico

Fermenters International Trade Association (443)

Venice

Imaging Supplies Coalition (487)

Vero Beach

International Association of Dive Rescue Specialists (519)

W. Palm Beach

American Greyhound Track Operators Association (127)
National Alliance for Youth Sports (632)

Weston

National Association of Legal Search Consultants (678)

Windermere

American Society for Neurochemistry (187)

Winter Park

Outdoor Amusement Business Association (834)

Yulee

American Association of Zoo Veterinarians (77)

GEORGIA

Acworth

Veterinary Botanical Medical Association (1008)

Albany

American Peanut Shellers Association (162)
Quail Unlimited (871)

Alpharetta

Coordinating Research Council (384)
Electronic Components Industry Association (423)
United Egg Producers (986)

Athens

Council on Governmental Ethics Laws (399)
Geoscience Information Society (459)
National Alliance of Preservation Commissions (633)
National Investment Banking Association (767)

Atlanta

American Academy of Religion (41)
American Apparel Producer's Network (46)
American Beekeeping Federation (80)
American College of Rheumatology (102)
American Photographic Artists (164)
American Society of Heating, Refrigerating and Air Conditioning Engineers (ASHRAE) (199)
American Spinal Injury Association (212)
Apple Products Research and Education Council (226)
Asian American Hotel Owners Association (231)
Association for Dressings and Sauces (245)
Association for Information Systems (250)
Association for Multicultural Counseling and Development (252)
Association of Energy Engineers (280)
Association of Fund-Raising Distributors and Suppliers (285)
Association of Home Office Underwriters (287)
Association of Minority Health Professions Schools (295)
Association of Rheumatology Health Professionals (306)
Association of Senior Anthropologists (308)
Calorie Control Council (341)
Cast Iron Soil Pipe Institute (344)
Coalition for Independent Seniors (360)
The Coca-Cola Bottlers' Association (361)
Concord Grape Association (373)
Consumer Credit Industry Association (381)
CoreNet Global (385)
Council of State and Territorial Epidemiologists (397)

Council on Occupational Education *(400)*
Decision Sciences Institute *(407)*
Evidence Photographers International Council *(434)*
Federal Probation and Pre-trial Officers Association *(440)*
Forest Landowners Association *(451)*
Georgia Charter Schools Association *(459)*
GSM Association *(467)*
Healthcare Convention and Exhibitors Association *(471)*
Hinman Dental Society *(475)*
Institute for Professionals in Taxation *(497)*
Institute of Nuclear Power Operations *(502)*
International Association of Addictions and Offender Counselors *(514)*
International Association Of Pet Cemeteries and Crematories *(526)*
International Business Brokers Association *(532)*
International Flight Services Association *(545)*
International Food Additives Council *(546)*
International Formula Council *(547)*
International Light Transportation Vehicle Association, Inc. *(554)*
Life Insurers Council *(597)*
LOMA *(600)*
Lyrasis *(600)*
Manufacturers' Agents Association for the Foodservice Industry *(603)*
National Association of Chronic Disease Directors *(653)*
National Basketball Athletic Trainers Association *(712)*
National Economic Association *(744)*
National Pecan Shellers Association *(780)*
North American Electric Reliability Corporation *(816)*
Professional Baseball Athletic Trainers Society *(860)*
Professional Football Athletic Trainers Society *(861)*
Professional Photographers of America *(863)*
Research Chefs Association *(882)*
Society for Maintenance & Reliability Professionals *(914)*
Society for the Anthropology of Food and Nutrition *(923)*
Society of Biblical Literature *(931)*
Society of International Business Fellows *(940)*
Synthetic Turf Council *(967)*
The Vinegar Institute *(1009)*

Augusta

National Barrel Horse Association *(712)*
Society for Hematopathology *(910)*
Society for Pediatric Pathology *(918)*
United States and Canadian Academy of Pathology *(989)*

Austell

Construction Owners Association of America *(380)*

Avondale Estates

International Paralegal Management Association *(559)*

Canton

National Organization for Human Service *(777)*

Carrollton

Insulated Cable Engineers Association *(504)*
Society of Professors of Education *(945)*

Columbus

Independent Automotive Damage Appraisers Association *(488)*
International Premium Cigar and Pipe Retailers *(561)*

Conyers

International Association of Accident Reconstruction Specialists *(514)*
National Association of Elevator Contractors *(665)*
Tobacconists' Association of America *(976)*

Covington

Association of Railway Museums *(305)*
Tourist Railway Association Inc. *(976)*

Dalton

American Floorcovering Alliance *(122)*
The Carpet and Rug Institute *(343)*

Dawsonville

National Association of Personnel Services *(684)*

Decatur

Association for Clinical Pastoral Education *(241)*
Association of Administrative Law Judges *(263)*
National Pan-Hellenic Council *(778)*
North American Academy of Liturgy *(812)*
Pine Chemicals Association *(848)*

Duluth

IGAF Polaris *(486)*
United States Racquet Stringers Association *(998)*

East Point

National Conference of Black Mayors *(726)*

Evans

American Association of Retirement Communities *(72)*

Fayetteville

National Ornamental and Miscellaneous Metals Association *(778)*
The Railway Tie Association *(874)*
State Guard Association of the United States *(961)*

Griffin

Textile Fibers and By-Products Association *(972)*

Hoschton

American Association of Food Hygiene Veterinarians *(61)*

Jasper

Automatic Fire Alarm Association *(321)*

Kennesaw

Baptist Communicators Association *(326)*
National Franchisee Association *(753)*
Women in Packaging *(1022)*

La Grange

Human Anatomy and Physiology Society *(480)*
Resilient Floor Covering Institute *(883)*
Society for the Preservation of Oral Health *(924)*

Lawrenceville

American Academy of Sanitarians *(41)*
PKF North American Network *(849)*

Lilburn

Women's Basketball Coaches Association *(1022)*

Macon

China Clay Producers Association *(354)*

Marietta

American Association for Applied Linguistics *(47)*
American Association of Healthcare Consultants *(62)*
American Salvage Pool Association *(177)*
Association of Physician Assistants in Cardiovascular Surgery *(299)*
The Foodservice Group, Inc. *(450)*
International Society of Communication Specialists *(572)*
Network of Ingredient Marketing Specialists *(808)*
Open Applications Group *(828)*
Refrigerated Foods Association *(878)*
Wood Component Manufacturers Association *(1024)*

McDonough

Association of Technical and Supervisory Professionals *(313)*
National On-Site Testing Association *(776)*

Monroe

Association of Large Distribution Cooperatives *(291)*

Monticello

American Correctional Health Services Association *(108)*

Newnan

Health Industry Representatives Association *(470)*
Recreational Park Trailer Industry Association *(877)*

Norcross

ASME International Gas Turbine Institute *(233)*
The Association of Suppliers to the Paper Industry *(312)*
Industrial Asset Management Council *(492)*
Institute of Industrial Engineers *(500)*
International Plant Nutrition Institute *(560)*
Porcelain Enamel Institute *(853)*
Technical Association of the Pulp and Paper Industry *(970)*
United Producers Formulators and Distributors Association *(988)*

Peachtree City

Association of State and Provincial Psychology Boards *(309)*
Civil Aviation Medical Association *(357)*

Pooler

American Society for Aesthetics *(180)*

Ray City

Outfitters Association of America *(835)*

Roswell

American Academy of Medical Management *(36)*

Savannah

BP and AMOCO Marketers Association *(334)*

Smyrna

National Tuberculosis Controllers Association *(802)*

Snellville

International Association of Flight And Critical Care Paramedics *(521)*

St. Marys

National Poultry and Food Distributors Association *(782)*

Stockbridge

The Fiduciary and Investment Risk Management Association *(443)*

Suwanee

Handweavers Guild of America, Inc. *(468)*

Tifton

National Peanut Buying Point Association *(780)*

Tucker

Poultry Breeders of America *(854)*
U.S Poultry and Egg Association *(998)*

Union City

National Funeral Directors and Morticians Association *(754)*

Warner Robins

Council of Administrators of Special Education *(391)*

Watkinsville

Society of Municipal Arborists *(942)*

Winterville

American Association for Vocational Instructional Materials *(53)*

HAWAII

Hilo

International Planetarium Society *(560)*

Honolulu

International Marine Minerals Society *(555)*
Jean Piaget Society *(586)*
Pacific Telecommunications Council *(836)*
U.S. Hereditary Angioedema Association *(983)*
World History Association *(1026)*

Lanai City

International Horn Society *(550)*

Princeville

Association of Chartered Accountants in the United States *(272)*

Waikoloa

Rocky Mountain Llama & Alpaca Association *(887)*

IDAHO

Boise

American Bryological and Lichenological Society *(86)*
Association for Skilled and Technical Sciences *(256)*
Conference of Historical Journals *(375)*
International Association of Round Dance Teachers *(527)*
International Festivals and Events Association *(545)*
National Institute for Water Resources *(766)*

Caldwell

American Association of Wildlife Veterinarians *(77)*

Lewiston

Society of Mineral Analysts *(942)*

Meridian

American College of Veterinary Ophthalmologists *(104)*

Moscow

Appaloosa Horse Club *(225)*
Society of Systematic Biologists *(947)*
United States of America Dry Pea and Lentil Council, Inc. *(996)*

Pocatello

Belt Association *(328)*

Rupert

North American Colleges and Teachers of Agriculture *(815)*

Soda Springs

National Barley Growers Association *(712)*

Tendoy

American Lands Access Association *(144)*

Twin Falls

American Society of Agricultural Appraisers *(191)*
American Society of Equine Appraisers *(197)*
Epsilon Sigma Phi *(432)*

ILLINOIS

Aledo

National Hereford Hog Record Association *(759)*

Algonquin

Mason Contractors Association of America *(607)*

Alma

North American Nature Photography Association *(819)*

Alsip

NAIR -- International Association of Bowling Equipment Specialists *(624)*

Alton

Congress of Independent Unions *(377)*
Xi Psi Phi Dental Fraternity *(1029)*

Arlington Heights

Academy of Osseointegration *(7)*
Air Movement and Control Association International *(19)*
American Association of Certified Allergists *(56)*
American College of Allergy, Asthma and Immunology *(93)*
American College of Osteopathic Family Physicians *(100)*
American Society for Blood and Marrow Transplantation *(181)*
American Society of Colon and Rectal Surgeons *(195)*
American Society of Plastic Surgeons *(207)*
Association of Business Owners of America *(270)*
Audit Bureau of Circulations *(270)*
Institute of Environmental Sciences and Technology *(499)*
National Association of Personal Financial Advisors *(684)*
Society of Surgical Oncology *(947)*

Aurora

American Purchasing Society *(172)*
Chevron and Texaco Petroleum Marketers Association *(352)*

Bannockburn

International Institute of Connector and Interconnection Technology *(551)*
IPC - Association Connecting Electronics Industries *(584)*
IPC - Surface Mount Equipment Manufacturers Association *(585)*
IPC Washington Office *(585)*

Barrington

Association for the Advancement of Automotive Medicine *(258)*
Closure and Container Manufacturers Association *(359)*

Batavia

Christian Association for Psychological Studies *(355)*
Pharmaceutical Printed Literature Association *(844)*

Beecher

American Chain of Warehouses *(89)*

Bloomingdale

American Society of Clinical Hypnosis *(194)*
User Experience Professionals Association *(1005)*

Bloomington

American Rabbit Breeders Association *(172)*

Buffalo Grove

American Board of Psychiatry & Neurology *(83)*

Burr Ridge

National Association of Spine Specialists *(696)*
North American Spine Society *(822)*

Byron

Professional Reactor Operator Society *(864)*

Carbondale

American Association of Teachers of French *(74)*
American Institute of Hydrology *(139)*
National Association of State Land Reclamationists *(701)*
Society for Phenomenology and Existential Philosophy *(918)*
Universities Council on Water Resources *(1002)*

Champaign

American Dairy Science Association *(113)*
American Embryo Transfer Association *(116)*
American Meat Science Association *(148)*

American Society of Animal Science *(192)*
Association of American Feed Control Officials *(265)*
Board of Certified Safety Professionals *(332)*
Brazilian Studies Association *(335)*
International Embryo Transfer Society *(542)*
International Society of Arboriculture *(571)*
Labor and Employment Relations Association *(592)*
National Association of Advisors for the Health Professions *(645)*
Poultry Science Association *(854)*

Chicago

Academy of General Dentistry *(5)*
Academy of Nutrition and Dietetics *(7)*
Accreditation Council for Pharmacy Education *(10)*
African American Contractors Association *(15)*
American Academy of Cosmetic Surgery *(32)*
American Academy of Disability Evaluating Physicians *(33)*
American Academy of Esthetic Dentistry *(33)*
American Academy of Implant Dentistry *(35)*
American Academy of Matrimonial Lawyers *(35)*
American Academy of Neurological and Orthopaedic Surgeons *(36)*
American Academy of Pediatric Dentistry *(39)*
American Academy of Periodontology *(39)*
American Agricultural Marketing Association *(44)*
American Association for the Surgery of Trauma *(52)*
American Association of Cardiovascular and Pulmonary Rehabilitation *(55)*
The American Association of Dental Boards *(59)*
American Association of Diabetes Educators *(60)*
American Association of Endodontists *(60)*
American Association of Individual Investors *(63)*
American Association of Law Libraries *(64)*
American Association of Legal Nurse Consultants *(64)*
American Association of Medical Assistants *(65)*
American Association of School Librarians *(72)*
American Association of Women Dentists *(77)*
American Bar Association *(79)*
American Board of Medical Specialties *(82)*
American Board of Preventive Medicine *(83)*
American Burn Association *(87)*
American College of Foot and Ankle Surgeons *(95)*
American College of Healthcare Executives *(96)*
American College of Osteopathic Emergency Physicians *(99)*
American College of Prosthodontists *(101)*
American College of Psychiatrists *(102)*
American College of Surgeons *(103)*
American College of Surgeons Professional Association *(103)*
American Council for Southern Asian Art *(109)*
American Dental Assistants Association *(113)*
American Dental Association *(113)*
American Dental Hygienists' Association *(114)*
American Dental Society of Anesthesiology *(114)*
American Equilibration Society *(117)*
American Franchisee Association *(123)*
American Gynecological and Obstetrical Society *(128)*
American Health and Beauty Aids Institute *(129)*
American Health Information Management Association *(129)*
American Hospital Association *(133)*
American Institute of Indian Studies *(139)*
American Institute of Steel Construction *(140)*
American Ladder Institute *(144)*
American Library Association *(145)*
American Marketing Association *(147)*
American Medical Association *(148)*
American Medical Association Alliance, Inc. *(149)*
American Organization of Nurse Executives *(158)*
American Osteopathic Association *(160)*
American Osteopathic Board of Physical Medicine and Rehabilitation *(160)*
American Osteopathic College of Pathologists *(160)*
American Planning Association *(166)*
American Prepaid Legal Services Institute *(167)*
American Prosthodontic Society *(168)*
American Schools Association *(177)*
American Senior Benefits Association *(178)*
American Society for Clinical Pathologists *(182)*
American Society for Clinical Pathology *(182)*
American Society for Healthcare Engineering *(184)*
American Society for Healthcare Environmental Services *(185)*
American Society for Healthcare Human Resources Administration *(185)*
American Society for Healthcare Risk Management *(185)*
American Society for Reconstructive Microsurgery *(189)*
American Society for Surgery of the Hand *(189)*
American Society of Dentist Anesthesiologists *(196)*
American Society of Hair Restoration Surgery *(199)*
American Society of Lipo-Suction Surgery *(202)*
American Society of Retina Specialists *(209)*
American Specialty Toy Retailing Association *(212)*

American Student Dental Association *(214)*
American Theological Library Association *(216)*
American Veterinary Society of Animal Behavior *(219)*
APICS The Association for Operations Management *(224)*
Appliance Parts Distributors Association *(226)*
Appraisal Institute *(226)*
Assistive Technology Industry Association *(234)*
Association for Corporate Growth *(244)*
Association for Electronic Healthcare Transaction *(245)*
Association for Healthcare Resource and Materials Management *(248)*
Association for Healthcare Volunteer Resource Professionals *(248)*
Association for Library and Information Science Education *(251)*
Association for Library Collections and Technical Services *(251)*
The Association for Library Service to Children *(251)*
The Association for Nursing Professional Development *(252)*
Association of Black Sociologists *(270)*
Association of College and Research Libraries *(273)*
Association of Information Technology Professionals *(289)*
Association of Litigation Support Professionals *(292)*
Association of Professional Design Firms *(301)*
Association of Professional Researchers for Advancement *(302)*
Association of Real Estate License Law Officials *(305)*
Association of Specialized and Cooperative Library Agencies *(309)*
Association of Specialized and Professional Accreditors *(309)*
Association of Steel Distributors *(311)*
Attorneys' Liability Assurance Society Inc. *(320)*
Bank Administration Institute *(326)*
Battery Council International *(326)*
Blue Cross Blue Shield Association *(332)*
Building Service Contractors Association International *(337)*
Catholic Library Association *(346)*
Catholic Press Association *(346)*
CCIM Institute *(347)*
Center for Research Libraries *(348)*
Classification Society *(357)*
Clinical Laboratory Management Association *(358)*
Commercial Law League of America *(366)*
Committee of 200 *(368)*
Common - A Users Group *(369)*
Construction Writers Association *(380)*
Council for Adult and Experiential Learning *(388)*
Council of Medical Specialty Societies *(395)*
Council of Real Estate Brokerage Managers *(396)*
Council of Residential Specialists *(396)*
The Counselors of Real Estate *(401)*
Cristo Rey Network *(404)*
Decorative Plumbing and Hardware Association *(408)*
Defense Research Institute *(408)*
Donors Forum *(415)*
Electrical and Computer Engineering Department Heads Association *(422)*
Electronics Representatives Association *(424)*
Expanded Shale, Clay and Slate Institute *(435)*
Federal Judges Association *(439)*
Financial & Insurance Conference Planners *(444)*
Financial Managers Society *(445)*
Giving Institute *(461)*
Giving USA Foundation *(461)*
Government Finance Officers Association of the United States and Canada *(464)*
Government Finance Officers Association, Federal Liaison Center *(464)*
Health Forum *(469)*
Healthcare Information and Management Systems Society *(471)*
Human Resource People and Strategy *(481)*
Inflatable Boat Manufacturers Association *(495)*
InSight *(496)*
Institute of Food Technologists *(499)*
Institute of Real Estate Management *(503)*
International Association of Defense Counsel *(519)*
International Association of Healthcare Central Service Materiel Management *(522)*
International Association of Lighting Designers *(524)*
International Association of Physicians in AIDS Care *(526)*
International Association of School Librarianship *(527)*
International Bone and Mineral Society *(530)*
International Carwash Association *(533)*
International College of Surgeons *(535)*
International Contrast Ultrasound Society *(537)*
International Council of Library Association Executives *(538)*
International Engineering Consortium *(543)*

International Federation for Choral Music *(544)*
International Foodservice Manufacturers Association *(546)*
International Interior Design Association *(552)*
International Law Students Association *(553)*
International Magnetics Association *(555)*
International Museum Theatre Alliance *(557)*
International SalonSpa Business Network (ISBN) *(563)*
International Society of Appraisers *(570)*
International Society of Transport Aircraft Trading *(574)*
International Special Events Society *(575)*
ISEH Society for Hematology and Stem Cells *(586)*
Joint Review Committee on Education in Radiologic Technology *(589)*
Legal Marketing Association *(596)*
Legal Netlink Alliance *(596)*
Library and Information Technology Association *(597)*
Library Leadership and Management Association *(597)*
Medical Library Association *(611)*
Metal Framing Manufacturers Association *(613)*
National Alliance for Advanced Transportation Batteries *(631)*
National Association of Bar Executives *(648)*
National Association of Boat Builders *(650)*
National Association of Charter School Authorizers *(652)*
National Association of Concessionaires *(657)*
National Association of Fire Equipment Distributors *(668)*
National Association of Independent Fee Appraisers *(674)*
National Association of Orthopedic Nurses *(683)*
National Association of Osteopathic Foundations *(683)*
National Association of Real Estate Investment Managers *(690)*
National Association of Realtors *(690)*
National Association of Women Highway Safety Leaders, Inc. *(709)*
National Association of Women Lawyers *(710)*
National Automatic Merchandising Association *(711)*
National Black MBA Association *(714)*
National Conference of Bar Foundations *(726)*
National Conference of Bar Presidents *(726)*
National Conference of Commissioners on Uniform State Laws *(727)*
National Conference of Federal Trial Judges *(727)*
National Conference of Specialized Court Judges *(728)*
National Council of Real Estate Investment Fiduciaries *(735)*
National Council of State Boards for Nursing *(736)*
National Council of Structural Engineers Associations *(737)*
National Federation of Priests' Councils *(749)*
National Futures Association *(754)*
National Institute of Pension Administrators *(765)*
National Marine Manufacturers Association *(771)*
National Society of Genetic Counselors *(794)*
National Steel Bridge Alliance *(796)*
National Student Osteopathic Medical Association *(797)*
Network of Nonprofit Search Consultants *(808)*
Neurosurgical Society of America *(809)*
North American Association of Floor Covering Distributors *(811)*
North American Association of Food Equipment Manufacturers *(813)*
North American Building Material Distribution Association *(814)*
North American Retail Dealers Association *(820)*
North American Students of Cooperation *(822)*
NPTA Alliance *(824)*
Organization Development Network *(831)*
PeerSpan *(840)*
Plan Sponsor Council of America *(849)*
PlanetSpace, Inc. *(849)*
POPAI The Global Association for Marketing at Retail *(852)*
Power Transmission Distributors Association *(855)*
Precast/Prestressed Concrete Institute *(856)*
Print Services & Distribution Association *(857)*
Product Development and Management Association *(858)*
Professional Convention Management Association *(861)*
Professional Insurance Marketing Association *(862)*
Public Library Association *(869)*
Real Estate Buyers Agent Council *(875)*
Real Estate Management Brokers Institute *(875)*
REALTORS Land Institute *(876)*
Red Tag News Publications Association *(878)*
Research Council on Structural Connections *(882)*
Screen Manufacturers Association *(893)*
Serbian-American Chamber of Commerce *(897)*
Showmen's League of America *(899)*

Sigma Epsilon Delta Dental Fraternity *(899)*
Society for Buddhist-Christian Studies *(905)*
Society for Healthcare Consumer Advocacy *(910)*
Society for Healthcare Strategy and Market Development *(910)*
Society for Vascular Surgery *(926)*
Society of Architectural Historians *(930)*
Society of Gastroenterology Nurses and Associates *(937)*
Society of Gynecologic Oncologists *(938)*
Society of Incentive & Travel Executives *(939)*
Society of Thoracic Surgeons *(948)*
Society of Women Engineers *(950)*
Special Care Dentistry *(954)*
Special Care Dentistry Association *(954)*
Strategic Account Management Association *(963)*
Tile Roofing Institute *(974)*
Truck and Engine Manufacturers Association *(980)*
Turnaround Management Association *(982)*
United States Soccer Federation *(999)*
United States-China Chamber of Commerce *(1001)*
Urban Libraries Council *(1004)*
Utilimetrics/Alliance for Advanced Metering & Data Management Solutions *(1006)*
Wallcovering Association *(1012)*
Window and Door Manufacturers Association *(1018)*
Women in Municipal Government *(1022)*
Women's Council of REALTORS *(1023)*
Young Adult Library Services Association *(1030)*

Chicago Ridge

Associated Pipe Organ Builders of America *(236)*

Crystal Lake

Automotive Engine Rebuilders Association *(322)*
International Association of Diecutting and Diemaking *(519)*
Steel Founders' Society of America *(962)*

Darien

American Academy of Dental Sleep Medicine *(32)*
American Academy of Sleep Medicine *(42)*
American Association of Sleep Technologists *(73)*
Associated Professional Sleep Societies *(237)*
Sleep Research Society *(900)*

Deer Park

Independent Cosmetic Manufacturers and Distributors *(489)*

Deerfield

Academy for Eating Disorders *(3)*
American Association for Public Opinion Research *(51)*
American Pediatric Surgical Association *(162)*
American Society of Dermatopathology *(197)*
Association for Death Education and Counseling *(244)*
Association of University Technology Managers *(316)*
Institute of Nuclear Materials Management *(502)*
International Society for Traumatic Stress Studies *(570)*
Maple Flooring Manufacturers Association *(604)*
Selected Independent Funeral Homes *(896)*
The Society for Adolescent Medicine *(903)*
Society for Vascular Medicine *(926)*
Society of Vertebrate Paleontology *(950)*

DeKalb

Association for Women Veterinarians Foundation *(262)*
College Reading and Learning Association *(364)*
Coordinating Council for Women in History *(384)*

Des Plaines

American Academy of Medical Administrators *(36)*
American College of Cardiovascular Administrators *(93)*
American College of Health Plan Management *(96)*
American Society of Home Inspectors *(200)*
American Society of Plumbing Engineers *(207)*
American Society of Safety Engineers *(209)*
Emergency Nurses Association *(425)*
Gas Technology Institute *(456)*
Institute for Certification of Computing Professionals *(497)*
International Warehouse Logistics Association *(580)*
MTM Association for Standards and Research *(620)*
National Association of Bar-Related Title Insurers *(648)*
National Association of the Remodeling Industry *(705)*
National Insurance Crime Bureau *(766)*
North American Bar-Related Title Insurers *(814)*
Property Casualty Insurers Association of America *(867)*
Society for Academic Emergency Medicine *(903)*
Urban and Regional Information Systems Association *(1003)*

Downers Grove

Association of Women Surgeons *(317)*
Computing Technology Industry Association (CompTIA) *(373)*
Independent Medical Distributors Association *(490)*
Liability Insurance Research Bureau *(596)*
Property Loss Research Bureau *(867)*

Dundee

Amusement & Music Operators Association *(223)*
The Lawn Institute *(594)*
Turfgrass Producers International *(982)*
Women in Management *(1021)*

East Alton

American Dental Interfraternity Council *(114)*

East Moline

Mass Finishing Job Shops Association *(607)*

El Paso

National Association of Industrial and Technical Teacher Educators *(675)*

Elgin

American College of Chiropractic Orthopedists *(94)*
Foodservice Equipment Distributors Association *(450)*
Heavy Duty Representatives Association *(473)*
Recycled Paperboard Technical Association *(877)*
Service Specialists Association *(897)*

Elk Grove Village

American Academy of Pediatrics *(39)*
American Amusement Machine Association *(45)*
American College of Occupational and Environmental Medicine *(99)*
Fibre Box Association *(443)*
National Ice Cream Retailers Association *(761)*

Elmhurst

American Dairy Products Institute *(112)*
American Professional Society on the Abuse of Children *(168)*
Medical-Dental-Hospital Business Associates *(612)*

Elmwood Park

American Society of Podiatric Medical Assistants *(208)*

Evanston

American Massage Therapy Association *(147)*
Dermatology Foundation *(410)*
U.S.A. Toy Library Association *(983)*

Fox River Grove

Steel Deck Institute *(962)*

Frankfort

International Association of Attorneys and Executives in Corporate Real Estate *(516)*

Galena

Association of Academic Museums & Galleries *(263)*

Galesburg

International Formalwear Association *(546)*

Galva

Association for the Sociology of Religion *(259)*
Religious Research Association *(880)*

Geneva

International Society of Hair Restoration Surgery *(573)*
National Association of Independent Insurance Adjusters *(674)*

Glen Ellyn

American Endodontic Society, Inc. *(117)*
American Fence Association *(120)*
Association of Rotational Molders International *(306)*
Bearing Specialist Association *(327)*
Ceramic Tile Distributors Association *(349)*
Evangelical Church Library Association *(434)*
National Association of Architectural Metal Manufacturers *(647)*
National Association of Container Distributors *(658)*
National Church Goods Association *(722)*
Plastic Pipe and Fittings Association *(850)*
Pressure Vessel Manufacturers Association *(857)*

Glendale Heights

International Association for Healthcare Security and Safety *(512)*

Glenview

Academy of Veterinary Allergy and Clinical Immunology *(9)*
American Academy of Hospice and Palliative Medicine *(35)*
American Academy of Pain Medicine *(39)*
American Association of Neuroscience Nurses *(66)*
American Luggage Dealers Association *(146)*

American Pain Society (161)
American Society for Bioethics and Humanities (181)
The American Society of Pediatric Hematology/Oncology (206)
Association of Pediatric Hematology/Oncology Nurses (298)
Association of Rehabilitation Nurses (305)
Awards and Recognition Association (325)
International Association of Rehabilitation Professionals (527)
International Transplant Nurses Society (578)
Metal Construction Association (613)
National Association for Healthcare Quality (639)
National Association of Neonatal Nurses (682)
National Frame Building Association (753)
National Luggage Dealers Association (770)
National Registry of Environmental Professionals (785)
North American Neuromodulation Society (819)
Professional Records and Information Services Management International (864)
The Society for Freshwater Science (910)

Gurnee

American Association for Accreditation of Ambulatory Surgery Facilities (47)
National Conference of State Liquor Administrators (728)

Highland Park

International Housewares Representatives Association (550)
Submersible Wastewater Pump Association (965)

Hillside

Air Distribution Institute (18)
Catholic Cemetery Conference (345)

Hoffman Estates

Inter-Industry Conference on Auto Collision Repair (506)

Homewood

StateNets Radio (962)

Inverness

Food Shippers of America (450)

Itasca

American Supply Association (214)
Associated Risk Managers (237)
National Safety Council (789)

Jacksonville

American Dialect Society (115)

Joliet

American Association of Private Railroad Car Owners (71)

La Fox

American Association of Railroad Superintendents (72)

La Grange

American Osteopathic Academy of Addiction Medicine (159)
International Staple, Nail and Tool Association (575)

La Grange Park

American Nuclear Society (156)

Lake Bluff

Casket and Funeral Supply Association of America (344)

Lake Zurich

Insurance Consumer Affairs Exchange (505)
Steel Plate Fabricators Association Division of STI/SPFA (962)
Steel Tank Institute Division of STI/SPFA (963)

Lemont

Independent Time and Labor Management Association (492)

Libertyville

United Lightning Protection Association (987)

Lincolnshire

Association of Legal Administrators (291)

Lincolnwood

International Sanitary Supply Association (563)

Lisle

Association of Black Nursing Faculty (269)
Land Improvement Contractors of America (593)
Quality Chekd Daries (871)
United States Cross Country Coaches Association (993)
Water Quality Association (1013)

Lombard

Council of Supply Chain Management Professionals (398)
Islamic Medical Association of North America (586)

Long Grove

Conference of Consulting Actuaries (375)

Marengo

Equipment and Tool Institute (432)

Maroa

National Association of County Agricultural Agents (659)

Maywood

American Association of Genitourinary Surgeons (61)

Mokena

Radiant Panel Association (872)

Moline

American Rental Association (174)
Association of Official Seed Certifying Agencies (296)

Montgomery

National Association of Independent Public Finance Advisors (675)
Wire Fabricators Association (1019)

Morton

American Shetland Pony Club/American Miniature Horse Registry (179)
Insurance Loss Control Association (505)

Mt. Prospect

National Association of Boards of Pharmacy (650)
National Ski and Snowboard Retailers Association (791)
National Sporting Goods Association (796)
Society for Critical Care Medicine (934)

Mundelein

American Biological Safety Association (81)

N. Riverside

Mail Systems Management Association (601)

Naperville

Business Marketing Association (339)
Cable and Telecommunications Human Resources Association (340)
Contract Packaging Association (382)
Incentive Manufacturers & Representatives Alliance (487)
Incentive Marketing Association (487)
Institute of Packaging Professionals (502)
National Association of Sporting Goods Wholesalers (696)
Pressure Sensitive Tape Council (856)
The Recreational Vehicle Aftermarket Association (877)
Urgent Care Association of America (1004)

Niles

Society for Sex Therapy and Research (921)

Normal

National Association of Professional Band Instrument Repair Technicians (686)

Northbrook

American College of Chest Physicians (94)
American Society of Pharmacognosy (207)
American Society of Tropical Medicine and Hygiene (210)
Collision Industry Electronic Commerce Association (365)
Federation of Associations of Regulatory Boards (441)
Sump and Sewage Pump Manufacturers Association (965)

Northfield

Broadcast Cable Credit Association (335)
College of American Pathologists (363)
International Psychogeriatric Association (561)
Media Financial Management Association (610)

Oak Brook

American Fraternal Alliance (124)
American Society for Gastrointestinal Endoscopy (184)
American Society of Head and Neck Radiology (199)
American Society of Neuroradiology (204)
Associated Equipment Distributors (235)
Association of Program Directors in Radiology (303)
Association of University Radiologists (316)
Ceilings and Interior Systems Construction Association (347)
Children's Literature Association (353)
Delta Dental Plans Association (409)
Radiological Society of North America (873)

Spring Manufacturers Institute (960)
Warehousing Education and Research Council (1012)
Zonta International (1030)

Oak Park

Cryogenic Society of America (405)
Insurance Marketing Communications Association (505)

Oakbrook Terrace

American Association of Physicians of Indian Origin (69)
Coin Laundry Association (361)
International Association of Oral and Maxillofacial Surgeons (525)
National Truck Leasing System (802)

Ottawa

American Emu Association (117)

Palatine

American Academy of Dental Practice Administration (32)
American Chiropractic Registry of Radiologic Technologists (90)
American Society of Artists (193)
Joint Council of Allergy, Asthma and Immunology (588)

Palos Hills

University Photographers Association of America (1002)

Park Ridge

American Association of Nurse Anesthetists (67)
American Egg Board (116)
American Society of Anesthesiologists (192)
Association of University Anesthesiologists (315)
Insurance Accounting and Systems Association (504)
Million Dollar Round Table (616)
Non-Ferrous Founders' Society (811)
Society for Education in Anesthesia (908)
Society for Obstetric Anesthesia and Perinatology (917)
Society of Tribologists and Lubrication Engineers (949)

Pecatonica

Clydesdale Breeders of the United States (359)

Pekin

International Association of Eating Disorders Professionals (520)

Peoria

American Society of Dermatology (196)
Chester White Swine Record Association (352)
Employers Association (426)
National Spotted Swine Records (796)
North American Association of Summer Sessions (813)
Poland China Record Association (852)

Plainfield

Turf Equipment Technicians Association (982)

River Forest

Lutheran Education Association (600)

Rockford

Association of Christian Teachers and Schools (272)
Fabricators & Manufacturers Association, International (437)
National Association of Health Unit Coordinators (671)
Tube and Pipe Association, International (981)

Rolling Meadows

American Mold Builders Association (152)
American Society for Dermatologic Surgery (183)
The Association for Manufacturing Excellence (252)
Information Systems Audit and Control Association (495)
Metals Service Center Institute (614)
North American Fiberboard Association (816)
North American Wholesale Lumber Association (823)
Plumbing Manufacturers Institute (851)
Refrigeration Service Engineers Society (878)

Roselle

National Credit Reporting Association (740)

Rosemont

American Academy of Orthopaedic Surgeons (38)
American Academy of Physical Medicine and Rehabilitation (40)
American Association of Hip and Knee Surgeons (62)
American Association of Oral and Maxillofacial Surgeons (67)
American Concrete Pavement Association (106)

American Medical Technologists *(150)*
American Orthopaedic Association *(158)*
American Orthopaedic Foot and Ankle Society *(158)*
American Orthopaedic Society for Sports Medicine *(159)*
American Shoulder and Elbow Surgeons *(179)*
Arthroscopy Association of North America *(230)*
Association of Bone and Joint Surgeons *(270)*
Association of Children's Prosthetic-Orthotic Clinics *(272)*
Board of Specialty Society *(333)*
Cervical Spine Research Society *(350)*
Dairy Management, Inc. *(406)*
Federation of Spine Associations *(442)*
International Concrete Repair Institute *(536)*
International Housewares Association *(550)*
National Dairy Council *(741)*
National Roofing Contractors Association *(787)*
Orthopaedic Research Society *(833)*
Orthopaedic Trauma Association *(834)*
Pediatric Orthopedic Society of North America *(840)*
Ruth Jackson Orthopaedic Society *(889)*
United Dairy Industry Association *(986)*

Schaumburg

Air Diffusion Council *(18)*
American Academy of Dermatology *(32)*
American Architectural Manufacturers Association *(46)*
American Association of Clinical Urologists *(56)*
American College of Legal Medicine *(97)*
American Conference of Cantors *(107)*
American Foundry Society *(123)*
American Hardware Manufacturers Association *(128)*
American Society of Andrology *(192)*
American Society of Regional Anesthesia and Pain Medicine *(209)*
American Veterinary Medical Association *(219)*
Association of Professional Chaplains *(301)*
Concrete Reinforcing Steel Institute *(374)*
Congress of Neurological Surgeons *(377)*
Large Urology Group Practice Association (LUGPA) *(593)*
National Association of Publishers' Representatives *(689)*
Society of Actuaries *(927)*
Society of Government Service Urologists *(938)*
Society of University Urologists *(949)*

Skokie

Academy of Aphasia *(4)*
Accreditation Association for Ambulatory Health Care *(9)*
Construction Marketing Research Council *(380)*
NanoBusiness Alliance *(625)*
Parachute Industry Association *(838)*
Path to Purchase Institute *(839)*
Portland Cement Association *(853)*
United States Court Reporters Association *(993)*

Springfield

American Academy of Oral and Maxillofacial Radiology *(37)*
American Association of Public Health Dentistry *(71)*
American Neurotology Society *(156)*
American Otological Society *(161)*
Association for Preservation Technology International *(253)*
Association for Surgical Education *(257)*
Association of Artisan Business (AAB) *(268)*
Association of Assistive Technology ACT Programs *(268)*
Association of Halfway House Alcoholism Programs of North America *(286)*
Association of Science Museum Directors *(307)*
Association of Technology Act Projects *(313)*
Hispanic Dental Association *(475)*
National Association of State Agencies for Surplus Property *(697)*
North American Association of Central Cancer Registries *(812)*

St. Charles

Association of Nutrition & Foodservice Professionals *(296)*
Society for Laboratory Automation and Screening *(914)*

St. Paul

Power Washers of North America *(855)*

Sugar Grove

Immigration and Ethnic History Society *(487)*

Urbana

American Oil Chemists' Society *(157)*
Clay Minerals Society *(357)*
Conference on College Composition and Communication *(376)*
Conference on English Education *(376)*

Conference on English Leadership *(376)*
National Council of Teachers of English *(737)*
Society for the Advancement of Economic Theory *(922)*
Society for the Philosophy of Sex and Love *(923)*
Society for the Study of Symbolic Interaction *(925)*
Society of Engineering Science *(935)*
Women's Classical Caucus *(1023)*

Vernon Hills

Material Handling Equipment Distributors Association *(608)*

Wancona

Aluminum Extruders Council *(27)*

Wauconda

Aluminum Anodizers Council *(27)*
International Magnesium Association *(555)*

Westchester

Healthcare Financial Management Association *(471)*
Professional Currency Dealers Association *(861)*

Wheaton

American Academy of Oral and Maxillofacial Pathology *(37)*
American Association of Insurance Services *(63)*
American Society of Business Publication Editors *(194)*
Calendar Marketing Association *(340)*
National Association of Ticket Brokers *(706)*
National Retail Hobby Stores Association *(786)*
Society for Simulation in Healthcare *(921)*

Wheeling

Cremation Association of North America *(404)*
International Council on Education for Teaching *(539)*
North American Die Casting Association *(816)*

Willowbrook

Vibration Institute *(1008)*

Wilmette

Boating Writers International *(333)*

Winfield

American Academy of Medical Hypnoanalysts *(36)*

Woodstock

American Naprapathic Association *(154)*

INDIANA

Bedford

National Trappers Association *(801)*

Bloomington

Animal Behavior Society *(223)*
Association for Educational Communications and Technology *(245)*
Association for Practical and Professional Ethics *(253)*
Association of College Unions International *(274)*
Campus Safety, Health and Environmental Management Association *(341)*
Consortium of College and University Media Centers *(378)*
Organization of American Historians *(832)*
Phi Delta Kappa International *(845)*
Pi Lambda Theta *(847)*
Society for Computers in Psychology *(906)*
Society for Ethnomusicology *(908)*
Society for Textual Scholarship *(922)*
University Risk Management and Insurance Association *(1003)*
Wilderness Education Association *(1017)*

Carmel

Association for Management Information in Financial Services *(251)*
Fraternity Executives Association *(453)*
National Precast Concrete Association *(782)*

Evansville

Phi Mu Alpha Sinfonia *(846)*

Franklin

The American Safe Deposit Association *(176)*

Frankton

American Red Poll Association *(174)*

Ft. Wayne

North American Society of Adlerian Psychology *(822)*

Greencastle

Electronics Technicians Association International *(424)*
Tamworth Swine Association *(968)*

Greenville

American Association of Dental Consultants *(59)*

Greenwood

College Sports Information Directors of America *(364)*
National Federation of Music Clubs *(749)*

Huntington

Conference on Faith and History *(376)*
North American Coalition for Christian Admissions Professionals *(815)*

Indianapolis

Alpha Chi Sigma Fraternity, Inc. *(26)*
Alpha Kappa Psi *(26)*
American Academy of Osteopathy *(38)*
American College of Sports Medicine *(102)*
American Pianists Association *(165)*
American Society of Orthopedic Physician Assistants *(205)*
American Teleservices Association *(215)*
Associated Construction Publications *(235)*
Association for Applied Sport Psychology *(239)*
Association for Research on Nonprofit Organizations and Voluntary Action *(255)*
Association of Natural Resource Enforcement Trainers *(295)*
Association of Professional Communication Consultants *(301)*
Black Coaches & Administrators *(331)*
Corporate Housing Providers Association *(386)*
Custom Electronic Design and Installation Association *(405)*
Diagnostic Marketing Association *(411)*
Institute of Noise Control Engineering *(502)*
Interior Design Educators Council *(508)*
International Ticketing Association *(577)*
Just Plain Folks Songwriting/Musician Networking Organization *(589)*
Kappa Delta Pi *(590)*
National Association of Mutual Insurance Companies *(681)*
National Association of Orthopaedic Technologists *(683)*
National Collegiate Athletic Association *(724)*
National Costumers Association *(730)*
National Council of Acoustical Consultants *(733)*
National Council on Public History *(739)*
National Federation Coaches Association *(748)*
National Federation of State High School Associations *(750)*
National FFA Organization *(750)*
National Interscholastic Athletic Administrators Association *(766)*
National Network of Estate Planning Attorneys *(775)*
National Panhellenic Conference *(778)*
NFHS Music Association *(810)*
NFHS Speech Debate and Theatre Association *(810)*
North - American Interfraternity Conference *(812)*
North American Retail Hardware Association *(820)*
Osteopathic Cranial Academy *(834)*
Partnership for Philanthropic Planning *(839)*
Percussive Arts Society *(841)*
Phi Epsilon Kappa *(845)*
Phi Rho Sigma Medical Society *(846)*
Pony of the Americas Club *(852)*
Professional Insurance Communicators of America *(862)*
Radical Philosophy Association *(873)*
Real Estate Investment Securities Association *(875)*
Religious Conference Management Association *(880)*
Roller Skating Association International *(887)*
Sigma Theta Tau International *(899)*
Society for Free Radical Biology and Medicine *(909)*
Society for Nutrition Education and Behavior *(917)*
Society for Pediatric Dermatology *(917)*
Society for the Scientific Study of Religion *(924)*
Society of Broadcast Engineers *(931)*
Society of Professional Journalists *(945)*
United States of America Gymnastics *(997)*
United States Synchronized Swimming *(999)*
Vacation Rental Managers Association *(1007)*

Kokomo

National Appliance Service Association *(635)*

Martinsville

American Camp Association *(88)*
Association of Shareware Professionals *(308)*

Muncie

Academy of Model Aeronautics *(7)*
Association for General and Liberal Studies *(247)*
Charles Homer Haskins Society *(351)*

Noblesville

Association of Life Insurance Counsel *(291)*

Notre Dame

History of Science Society *(477)*

Plainfield

National Chimney Sweep Guild *(721)*

Richmond

Cheiron: The International Society for the History of Behavioral and Social Sciences *(351)*

Rolling Prairie

American North Country Cheviot Sheep Association *(156)*

Shelbyville

International Buckskin Horse Association *(532)*
Society of Insurance Research *(940)*

Wabash

Belgian Draft Horse Corporation of America *(327)*

Warsaw

American Association of Nutritional Consultants *(67)*

West Lafayette

American Berkshire Association *(80)*
American Society of Parasitologists *(206)*
American Walnut Manufacturers Association *(219)*
The Association of American Seed Control Officials *(266)*
Committee on History in the Classroom *(368)*
Conservation Technology Information Center *(378)*
National Association of Swine Records *(704)*
National Rural Education Association *(788)*
National Swine Registry *(798)*
Walnut Council *(1012)*

IOWA

Ames

Council for Agricultural Science and Technology *(388)*
National Farmers Organization *(747)*

Ankeny

Associated Construction Distributors International *(235)*
Association of Boards of Certification *(270)*
Association of Image Consultants International *(287)*
International Association of Lighting Management Companies *(524)*
National Postsecondary Agriculture Student Organization *(781)*
National Rural Economic Developers Association *(788)*
Soil and Water Conservation Society *(951)*

Bettendorf

Society for German-American Studies *(910)*

Buffalo

International Security Management Association *(564)*

Cedar Rapids

Association for Information Media and Equipment *(249)*
National Association of Media and Technology Centers *(680)*
National Systems Contractors Association *(798)*

Davenport

International Trumpet Guild *(578)*

Decorah

National Ballroom and Entertainment Association *(712)*

Des Moines

American Judicature Society *(143)*
Association of Former Agents of the U.S. Secret Service *(284)*
Independent Staffing Alliance *(492)*
International Association for Food Protection *(512)*
International Association of Career Consulting Firms *(517)*
National Association of State Student Grant and Aid Programs *(702)*
National Independent Fire Alarm Distributors *(762)*
North American Saxophone Alliance *(820)*
Stadium Managers Association *(960)*
Vacuum Dealers Trade Association/Sewing Dealers Trade Association *(1007)*

Dexter

Barzona Breeder's Association of America *(326)*

Dubuque

Resort and Commercial Recreation Association *(883)*

Guttenberg

American School Band Directors' Association *(177)*

Indianola

Balloon Federation of America *(325)*

Iowa City

Equipment Marketing and Distribution Association *(432)*
Imaging and Perimetry Society *(486)*
Midwest Free Community Papers *(615)*

Mason City

Employers of America *(427)*

Milo

American Hampshire Sheep Association *(128)*
American Polypay Sheep Association *(167)*
The American Rambouillet Sheep Breeders Association *(173)*
National Tunis Sheep Registry *(802)*

Mt. Vernon

Concrete Foundations Association *(373)*
Tilt-up Concrete Association *(974)*

Ottumwa

United Suffolk Sheep Association *(1001)*

Perry

American Association of Swine Veterinarians *(74)*

Sioux City

Gelatin Manufacturers Institute of America *(457)*

Urbandale

National Pork Producers Association *(781)*
National Pork Producers Council *(781)*

Waterloo

Consultant Dietitians in Health Care Facilities *(380)*

KANSAS

Abilene

National Greyhound Association *(756)*

Baldwin City

Association for Informal Logic and Critical Thinking *(249)*

Cheney

Council on Diagnostic Imaging to the A.C.A. *(399)*

Dighton

National Association for Family and Community Education *(638)*

Hutchinson

United States Custom Harvesters, Inc. *(993)*

Independence

Aerospace & Flight Test Radio Coordinating Council *(14)*

Kansas City

The Grant Professionals Association *(465)*
International Brotherhood of Boilermakers, Iron Shipbuilders, Blacksmiths, Forgers and Helpers *(531)*
National Soccer Coaches Association of America *(792)*
Piano Technicians Guild *(848)*
Society for Ear, Nose and Throat Advances in Children *(907)*

Lawrence

Accrediting Council on Education in Journalism and Mass Communications *(11)*
American Society of Ichthyologists and Herpetologists *(200)*
American Society of Mammalogists *(202)*
Association of Real Estate Women *(305)*
Commercial Real Estate Women Network *(367)*
Golf Course Superintendents Association of America *(463)*
International Association of Audio Information Services *(516)*
Mycological Society of America *(623)*
Print Council of America *(857)*
Radiation Research Society *(873)*
Society for Pediatric Psychology *(918)*
Society of Pediatric Psychology *(943)*
Sports Turf Managers Association *(959)*
Weed Science Society of America *(1014)*
Wildlife Disease Association *(1017)*

Leawood

American Medical Society for Sports Medicine *(149)*
Association of Family Medicine Administration *(282)*
Association of Family Medicine Residency Directors *(282)*
International Isotope Society *(552)*
Society of Teachers of Family Medicine *(947)*

Lecompton

American Railway Development Association *(173)*

Lenexa

The American Association of Nurse Attorneys *(67)*
American College of Clinical Pharmacy *(94)*
American College of Healthcare Architects *(96)*
American Society for Pain Management Nursing *(188)*
Association of College and University Auditors *(274)*
Association of Genetic Technologists *(285)*
International Nurses Society on Addictions *(558)*
Natco-The Organization for Transplant Professionals *(626)*
National Association for Health Care Recruitment *(639)*
National Association of EMS Physicians *(665)*
National Association of Graduate Admissions Professionals *(670)*
Transportation Lawyers Association *(978)*

Manhattan

AIB International *(17)*
Baking Industry Sanitation Standards Committee *(325)*
Fluid Fertilizer Foundation *(448)*
Journalism Education Association *(589)*
National Academic Advising Association *(626)*
World War Two Studies Association *(1028)*

Mission

American Reusable Textile Association *(175)*

Mission Woods

Allied Trades of the Baking Industry *(26)*

Olathe

National Board for Respiratory Care *(715)*

Overland Park

Agriculture Council of America *(16)*
American Academy of Veterinary Pharmacology and Therapeutics *(42)*
American Association of School Personnel Administrators *(73)*
American Business Women's Association *(87)*
Angel Capital Association *(223)*
ARMA International *(228)*
Association of Collegiate Business Schools and Programs *(275)*
Association of Professional Investment Consultants *(301)*
BEMA - The Baking Industry Suppliers Association *(328)*
Copper and Brass Servicenter Association *(384)*
Council for Learning Disabilities *(390)*
International Association of Operative Millers *(525)*
International Association of Plastics Distributors *(526)*
National Agri-Marketing Association *(629)*
National Auctioneers Association *(711)*
National Crop Insurance Services *(741)*
National Operating Committee for Standards of Athletic Equipment *(776)*
World Waterpark Association *(1028)*

Oxford

Professional Association of Volleyball Officials *(860)*

Shawnee

American Academy of Family Physicians *(34)*
International College of Applied Kinesiology *(535)*
Metal Building Contractors and Erectors Association *(613)*
Trucking Management, Inc. *(981)*

Spring Hill

Ankole Watusi International Registry *(223)*

St. George

American Cheviot Sheep Society *(90)*

Stanley

Council for Children with Behavioral Disorders *(389)*

Topeka

American Association of Zoo Keepers *(77)*
CALLERLAB - International Association of Square Dance Callers *(341)*
Foil and Specialty Effects Association *(448)*
Glass Association of North America *(461)*
Home Baking Association *(477)*
Liaison Committee of Cooperating Oil and Gas Associations *(597)*
National Association of Foster Grandparent Program Directors *(669)*
National Association of Trailer Manufacturers *(706)*
Transportation Safety Equipment Institute *(979)*

Walton

American International Marchigiana Society *(142)*

Wichita

American Academy of Environmental Medicine *(33)*
American Bonanza Society *(85)*

Congress of Chiropractic State Associations (377)
International Balloon Association (529)
National Association of Educational Office
Professionals (664)

Winfield

Pi Gamma Mu (847)

KENTUCKY

Bardstown

Substance Abuse Program Administrators
Association (965)

Berea

American Forage and Grassland Council (122)
Work Colleges Consortium (1024)

Bowling Green

American Association of State Climatologists (73)
National Association of Teacher Educators for
Family Consumer Sciences (704)
North American Thermal Analysis Society (823)

Covington

National Real Estate Investors Association (784)
Retail Packaging Manufacturers Association (885)

Crestwood

Association of Kentucky Fried Chicken Franchisees,
Inc. (290)

Elizabethtown

American Academy of Physician Assistants in
Occupational Medicine (40)

Florence

National Lieutenant Governors Association (769)

Frankfort

Conference of Radiation Control Program Directors
(375)
International Association of Personnel in
Employment Security (526)
International Association of Workforce Professionals
(IAWP) (529)

Georgetown

American Academy of Equine Art (33)
American Holsteiner Horse Association (132)

Hodgenville

Purebred Morab Horse Association (871)

Leitchfield

Ornamental Concrete Producers Association (833)

Lexington

Academy of Doctors of Audiology (5)
ACUTA – The Association for Information
Communications Technology Professionals in
Higher Education (11)
American Academy on Communication in
Healthcare (43)
American Association of Equine Practitioners (60)
American Board of Family Medicine (82)
American Farrier's Association (118)
American Hackney Horse Society (128)
American Hanoverian Society (128)
American Probation and Parole Association (167)
American Saddlebred Horse Association (176)
American Society of Mining and Reclamation (203)
American Volleyball Coaches Association (219)
Asphalt Institute (233)
Association of American Plant Food Control Officials
(266)
The Association of Medical Illustrators (293)
Association of Racing Commissioners International
(304)
Association of State Dam Safety Officials (310)
Bluegrass Tourism Marketing Association (332)
Burley Tobacco Growers Cooperative Association
(338)
Caribbean Studies Association (343)
CHA - Certified Horsemanship Association (350)
Chief Officers of State Libraries Agencies (352)
College Savings Plans Network (364)
Council of State Governments (397)
Council on Licensure, Enforcement and Regulation
(400)
International Coach Federation (535)
International Spa Association (575)
NASTD - Technology Professionals Serving State
Government (626)
National Association of Agricultural Educators (646)
National Association of Government Defined
Contribution Administrators (670)
National Association of Local Government Auditors
(678)
National Association of State Auditors, Comptrollers
and Treasurers (698)

National Association of State Boating Law
Administrators (698)
National Association of State Chief Administrators
(699)
National Association of State Chief Information
Officers (699)
National Association of State Facilities
Administrators (701)
National Association of State Personnel Executives
(702)
National Association of State Procurement Officials
(702)
National Association of State Technology Directors
(702)
National Association of State Treasurers (702)
National Association of Supervisors of Agricultural
Education (704)
National Association of Unclaimed Property
Administrators (707)
National Emergency Management Association (745)
National Gerontological Nursing Association (755)
National Horsemen's Benevolent and Protective
Association (760)
National Thoroughbred Racing Association (800)
National Tour Association (800)
National Turf Writers and Broadcasters (802)
Paso Fino Horse Association, Inc. (839)
Pyramid Society (871)
Receptive Services Association of America (876)
Society of Trauma Nurses (949)
Southeastern Livestock Network (953)
State Debt Management Network (961)
Thoroughbred Club of America (973)
Thoroughbred Owners and Breeders Association
(974)
United States Equestrian Federation (993)

Louisville

American Association of Preferred Provider
Organizations (70)
American Association of Professional Farriers (71)
American Murray Grey Association (153)
American Society for Healthcare Food Service
Administrators (185)
Associated Cooperage Industries of America (235)
Association for Healthcare Foodservice (248)
Association of Presbyterian Colleges and
Universities (300)
Digital Screenmedia Association (412)
Distillers Grains Technology Council (414)
Independent Pilots Association (491)
Mystery Shopping Providers Association (623)
National Alliance for Specialty Healthcare Programs
(632)
National Association of Equipment Leasing Brokers
(666)
National Association of Pizzeria Operators (685)
National Association of Vision Care Plans (708)
National Barbecue Association (712)
Railway Systems Suppliers, Inc (874)
Society for Foodservice Management (909)

Morehead

Organizational Systems Research Association (833)

Morning View

American Bashkir Curly Registry (80)

Nicholasville

The Jockeys' Guild (588)

Owensboro

National Association of Video Distributors (708)

Paducah

American Society of Interventional Pain Physicians
(201)

Pikesville

Coal Operators and Associates (359)

Richmond

Association for Linen Management (251)
Council on Education of the Deaf (399)

Smiths Grove

American British White Park Association (86)

Taylor Mill

Chemical Coaters Association International (351)
Industrial Heating Equipment Association (493)

Versailles

United Professional Horsemen's Association (988)

Water Valley

World Watusi Association (1028)

Wilmore

Association of Professors of Mission (302)

LOUISIANA

Baton Rouge

American Clinical and Climatological Association
(91)
Association of Commercial Finance Attorneys (275)
Association of Independent Information
Professionals (288)
Institute on Religion in an Age of Science (504)
Manuscript Society (604)
National Independent Nursery Furniture Retailers
Association (762)
Society for Social Studies of Science (921)
World Aquaculture Society (1025)

Harahan

Offshore Marine Service Association (827)

Kenner

American Guild of Hypnotherapists (127)

Metairie

American Institute of Homeopathy (139)

New Orleans

Food Sanitation Institute (450)
National Marine Representatives Association (771)

Ruston

Academy of Marketing Science (6)

Shreveport

Association of Third World Studies (314)

Slidell

National Taxidermists Association (799)
Retail Bakers of America (884)

MAINE

Bar Harbor

Society for Human Ecology (911)

Brunswick

American Musicological Society (154)
Modern Greek Studies Association (618)

Camden

Association of Women's Business Centers (318)

Kennebunk

Network Advertising Initiative (808)

Old Town

Wild Blueberry Association of North America (1017)

Orono

Chinese American Food Society (354)
Potato Association of America (854)

Readfield

International Association for the Study of
Cooperation in Education (514)

Scarborough

National Association of African American Studies
and Affiliates (646)
National Association of Hispanic and Latino Studies
(672)
National Association of Native American Studies
(681)

Windham

Association of State Wetland Managers (311)

MARYLAND

Abingdon

American Holistic Veterinary Medical Association
(132)

Annapolis

Airlines Electronic Engineering Committee (20)
American Academy of Environmental Engineers (33)
American Boat and Yacht Council (84)
Asphalt Emulsion Manufacturers Association (233)
Asphalt Recycling and Reclaiming Association (233)
Association for Hose and Accessories Distribution
(248)
Association for Recorded Sound Collections (255)
Association of Transportation Professionals (314)
Building Owners and Managers Institute
International (337)
College Athletic Business Management Association
(362)
Executive Women in Government (435)
Fluid Power Distributors Association (448)
Independent Sealing Distributors (491)
International Masonry Institute (556)
International Slurry Surfacing Association (565)
National Marine Bankers Association (771)
Organization for Safety and Asepsis Procedures
(831)
Plasma Protein Therapeutics Association (850)

Security Hardware Distributors Association *(895)*
Society for Gynecologic Investigation *(910)*
UniForum Association *(984)*
United Association of Journeymen and Apprentices of the Plumbing and Pipe Fitting Industry of the U.S. and Canada *(985)*
Wholesale Florist and Florist Supplier Association *(1016)*
Yacht Brokers Association of America *(1030)*

Arnold

International Association of Forensic Nurses *(521)*

Baltimore

Accreditation Board for Engineering and Technology Inc. *(9)*
American Cultural Resources Association (ACRA) *(112)*
American Institute of Floral Designers *(138)*
American Registry for Internet Numbers *(174)*
Association for Assessment in Counseling and Education *(240)*
Association of Career and Technical Education *(271)*
Association of Jewish Family & Children's Agencies *(290)*
Black Mental Health Alliance *(331)*
Business Solutions Association *(340)*
Council of Colleges of Acupuncture and Oriental Medicine *(392)*
Council of State Restaurant Associations *(397)*
Fire Suppression Systems Association *(446)*
Interim Ministry Network *(508)*
International Association of Ice Cream Vendors *(523)*
International Beverage Dispensing Equipment Association *(529)*
International Dyslexia Association *(541)*
International Police Mountain Bike Association *(561)*
International Society for Third-Sector Research *(570)*
Music Critics Association of North America *(622)*
National Association of Educational Procurement, Inc. *(664)*
National Association of Waterproofing and Structural Repair Contractors *(709)*
National Correctional Industries Association *(730)*
National Council of Investigative and Security Services Inc. *(735)*
National Finance Adjusters *(750)*
National Information Standards Organization *(763)*
National Sweetener and Ingredient Marketing Association *(798)*
National Women's Studies Association *(805)*
Phi Alpha Delta *(845)*
Professional Basketball Writers' Association *(860)*
Professional Grounds Management Society *(862)*
Register of Professional Archeologists *(879)*
Tissue Banks International *(975)*
Trauma Care International *(979)*
United States Lacrosse *(995)*

Bel Air

American Veterinary Distributors Association *(218)*
Flexographic Prepress Platemakers Association *(447)*
Generic Animal Drug Alliance *(458)*
League of Historic American Theatres *(595)*
Pet Industry Distributors Association *(842)*
Secondary Materials and Recycled Textiles Association *(894)*
Shippers of Recycled Textiles *(899)*
Souvenir Wholesale Distributors Association *(953)*
Special Event Sites Marketing Alliance *(954)*
Web Sling and Tie down Association *(1014)*
Wood Machinery Manufacturers of America *(1024)*

Beltsville

National Turfgrass Federation *(802)*
Operative Plasterers and Cement Masons International Association of the United States and Canada *(829)*

Bethesda

AABB - American Association of Blood Banks *(1)*
Academy of Psychosomatic Medicine *(8)*
Adhesive and Sealant Council *(12)*
Alliance for Natural Health USA *(23)*
Alliance of Hazardous Materials Professionals *(25)*
American Alliance for Theatre and Education *(44)*
American Association for Geriatric Psychiatry *(49)*
American Association of Acupuncture and Oriental Medicine *(53)*
American Association of Anatomists *(54)*
American Association of Immunologists *(62)*
American Beverage Licensees *(81)*
American College of Foot & Ankle Orthopedics & Medicine *(95)*
American College of Gastroenterology *(96)*
American College of Medical Genetics *(97)*
American College of Medical Quality *(97)*
American College of Radiation Oncology *(102)*
American College of Toxicology *(103)*
American Fisheries Society *(121)*
American Gastroenterological Association *(125)*

American Institute of Fishery Research Biologists *(138)*
American Medical Informatics Association *(149)*
American Occupational Therapy Association, Inc. *(157)*
American Physiological Society *(165)*
American Podiatric Medical Association *(166)*
American Podiatric Medical Students Association *(166)*
American Pyrotechnics Association *(172)*
American Running Association *(176)*
American Running Association/American Medical Athletic Association *(176)*
American School Health Association *(177)*
American Society for Cell Biology *(182)*
American Society for Clinical Laboratory Science *(182)*
American Society for Investigative Pathology *(186)*
American Society for Nutrition *(187)*
American Society for Pharmacology and Experimental Therapeutics *(188)*
American Society of Health-System Pharmacists *(199)*
American Society of Human Genetics *(200)*
American Society of Nuclear Cardiology *(205)*
ASPRS-The Imaging and Geospatial Information Society *(233)*
Associated Specialty Contractors *(237)*
Association for Financial Professionals, Inc. *(247)*
Association for Molecular Pathology *(252)*
Association of Biomolecular Resource Facilities *(269)*
Association of Chiropractic Colleges *(272)*
Association of Military Surgeons of the United States *(294)*
Association of Pathology Chairs *(298)*
Association of Program Directors in Surgery *(303)*
Automotive Aftermarket Industry Association *(321)*
Automotive Communication Council *(322)*
Car Care Council *(342)*
Chief Executives Organization *(352)*
EPDM Roofing Association *(432)*
Federation of American Societies for Experimental Biology *(440)*
Genetics Society of America *(458)*
Hearing Loss Association of America *(472)*
The Histochemical Society *(476)*
International Municipal Lawyers Association *(557)*
International Society for Advancement Cytometry *(565)*
International Society for Pharmacoepidemiology *(568)*
Intersociety Council For Pathology Information *(582)*
National Association of Community Health Centers *(656)*
National Association of School Psychologists *(693)*
National Association of Therapeutic Schools and Programs (NATSAP) *(706)*
National Council on Radiation Protection and Measurement *(739)*
National Electrical Contractors Association *(744)*
National Finishing Contractors Association *(751)*
Parenteral Drug Association *(838)*
Polyisocyanurate Insulation Manufacturers Association *(852)*
The Protein Society *(868)*
RadTech *(874)*
Renewable Natural Resources Foundation *(881)*
RNA Society *(887)*
Society for Developmental Biology *(907)*
Society for Leukocyte Biology *(914)*
Society for Radiation Oncology Administration *(919)*
Society of American Foresters *(928)*
Society of Fire Protection Engineers *(936)*
Society of Geriatric Cardiology *(937)*
United States Composting Council *(992)*
The Wildlife Society *(1017)*
Women in Cell Biology *(1021)*
World Future Society *(1026)*
World Jurist Association *(1027)*

Bowie

American Association for Adult and Continuing Education *(47)*
National Coalition of Black Meeting Planners *(723)*
Service Station Dealers of America and Allied Trades *(898)*
Tire Industry Association *(975)*
United States-Sudan Business Council *(999)*

Brookline

American Academy of the History of Dentistry *(42)*

Cabin John

International Hydrofoil Society *(550)*

Calverton

Intermodal Association of North America *(508)*

Cambridge

North American Gamebird Association *(817)*

Camp Springs

Seafarers International Union of North America *(894)*

Chester

Distributed Computing Industry Association *(414)*

Chevy Chase

American Association of Colleges of Osteopathic Medicine *(57)*
American Hungarian Educators Association *(134)*
American Society of Addiction Medicine *(191)*
The Endocrine Society *(427)*
The Environmental Information Association *(431)*
International Private Infrastructure Association *(561)*
National Association of Veterans Research and Education Foundations *(708)*
National Certification Commission *(720)*
Romanian-American Chamber of Commerce *(888)*
Society of Professional Benefit Administrators *(945)*

Church Hill

International Association of Conference Center Administrators *(518)*

College Park

American Association of Physicists in Medicine *(69)*
American Association of Physics Teachers *(69)*
American College of Medical Physics *(97)*
American Institute of Physics *(140)*
American Physical Society *(164)*
Association for Politics and the Life Sciences *(253)*
Association of Professional Schools of International Affairs *(302)*
Association of Reporters of Judicial Decisions *(305)*
National Association of Black Journalists *(649)*
The National Association of Professional Receptionists *(688)*
National Council for History Education *(732)*
Society for Features Journalism *(909)*

Columbia

American Dance Therapy Association *(113)*
American Medical Directors Association *(149)*
Biscuit and Cracker Manufacturers' Association *(330)*
Chain Link Fence Manufacturers Institute *(350)*
COLA *(362)*
FCIB-NACM Corporation *(438)*
International Union of Elevator Constructors *(579)*
National Association of Catering and Events *(651)*
National Association of Credit Management *(661)*
National Society for Histotechnology *(792)*
Universities Space Research Association *(1002)*
Zero Balancing Health Association *(1030)*

Crisfield

National Association of Black Professors *(649)*

Crofton

Association of Professors of Gynecology and Obstetrics *(302)*
EPS Industry Alliance *(432)*
Insulating Concrete Form Association *(504)*
International Association of Arson Investigators *(515)*

Easton

Bulk Carrier Conference *(338)*

Edgewater

International Aviation Women's Association *(529)*
National Aircraft Finance Association *(630)*

Edgewood

American Academy of Home Care Physicians *(35)*

Elkridge

Correctional Education Association *(386)*

Elkton

Thoroughbred Racing Associations of North America *(974)*

Ellicott City

American Sports Builders Association *(212)*
Association of Catholic Publishers *(271)*
Intersocietal Accreditation Commission *(582)*
Investment Program Association *(584)*

Finksburg

International Double Reed Society *(541)*

Frederick

Airborne Law Enforcement Association *(19)*
Aircraft Owners and Pilots Association *(20)*
American Association for Laboratory Accreditation *(50)*
Association for Assessment and Accreditation of Laboratory Animal Care International *(239)*
Bioelectromagnetics Society *(329)*
Diesel Technology Forum *(412)*
National Auto Auction Association *(711)*

National Seasoning Manufacturers Association **(790)**
National Society of Professional Surveyors **(794)**
Quarters Furniture Manufacturers Association **(872)**
Society for Applied Spectroscopy **(904)**

Ft. Washington

The Association of Black Psychologists **(270)**
Cable & Telecommunications Association for Marketing **(340)**
School Nutrition Association **(892)**

Gaithersburg

American Association for Geodetic Surveying **(49)**
American College of Dentists **(95)**
Association of Analytical Communities International **(267)**
Fusion Power Associates **(455)**
National Board for Certification in Occupational Therapy, Inc. **(715)**
National Environmental Balancing Bureau **(746)**
Pediatric Nursing Certification Board **(840)**
Special Interest Group for Information Retrieval **(955)**

Germantown

American College of Veterinary Surgeons **(104)**
American Society of Psychoanalytic Physicians **(208)**
Council for American Private Education **(389)**
International Society of Weighing and Measurement **(574)**
National Association of Business Owners and Entrepreneurs **(651)**
Society for Historical Archaeology **(911)**

Glen Burnie

State Education Technology Directors Association **(961)**

Glyndon

Society of Government Travel Professionals **(938)**

Great Falls

International Truck Parts Association **(578)**

Greenbelt

Academy of Criminal Justice Sciences **(4)**
Commercial Vehicle Safety Alliance **(367)**
National Association of Black Accountants, Inc. **(648)**
National Fenestration Rating Council **(750)**
National Volunteer Fire Council **(803)**

Hagerstown

American Jail Association **(142)**
American Society for Colposcopy and Cervical Pathology **(183)**
Association of State Correctional Administrators **(310)**

Hanover

American College Health Association **(93)**
Association of Academic Physiatrists **(263)**
Institute for Operations Research and the Management Sciences **(497)**
International Union of Painters and Allied Trades **(579)**
National Automotive Finance Association **(711)**
National Vehicle Leasing Association **(803)**

Hyattsville

Gypsum Association **(467)**

Kensington

American Association for Wound Care Management **(53)**
Bakery, Confectionery, Tobacco Workers and Grain Millers International Union **(325)**
National Family Caregivers Association **(747)**
Society of Eye Surgeons **(936)**

Landover

Biomedical Engineering Society **(330)**
Commissioned Officers Association of the United States Public Health Service **(368)**
Contact Lens Council **(382)**
National Academy of Opticianry **(628)**
National Phlebotomy Association **(781)**

Lanham

American Railway Engineering and Maintenance-of-Way Association **(173)**
Entomological Society of America **(429)**
International Association of Heat and Frost Insulators and Asbestos Workers **(522)**
National Asphalt Pavement Association **(635)**
National Association of Real Estate Brokers **(689)**
Society for Vascular Ultrasound **(927)**

Largo

Association of Supervisory and Administrative School Personnel **(312)**
Black Data Processing Associates **(331)**

National Association of Minority Automobile Dealers **(680)**

Laurel

American Institute of Ultrasound in Medicine **(141)**
Drycleaning & Laundry Institute **(417)**
SOLE - The International Society of Logistics **(952)**

Linthicum

American Midwifery Certification Board **(151)**
American Urological Association **(218)**
Flexible Packaging Association **(447)**
International Organization of Masters, Mates and Pilots **(559)**

Lutherville

Foodservice Sales & Marketing Association **(450)**
Rheumatology Nurses Society **(886)**

Manchester

International Association of Special Investigation Units **(528)**

Marriottsville

American Commodity Distribution Association **(105)**

Montgomery Village

IEEE Magnetics Society **(484)**

Myersville

ADARA **(12)**

N. Potomac

Coal Technology Association **(359)**

Ocean Pines

Apparel Graphics Institute **(225)**

Olney

Association for Childhood Education International **(241)**
National Food Service Security Council **(752)**
Professional Handlers Association **(862)**

Owings Mills

National Association of Sewer Service Companies **(695)**

Port Republic

The Coastal and Estuarine Research Federation **(361)**

Potomac

Society of Atherosclerosis Imaging and Prevention **(930)**

Princess Anne

Association of Research Directors **(306)**
Association of Research Directors of 1890s Colleges and Universities **(306)**

Rockville

Alpha Omega International Dental Fraternity **(26)**
American Academy of Appellate Lawyers **(30)**
American Association of Colleges of Podiatric Medicine **(58)**
American College Dance Festival Association **(92)**
American College of Clinical Pharmacology **(94)**
American College of Mortgage Attorneys **(98)**
American College of Osteopathic Internists **(100)**
American College of Real Estate Lawyers **(102)**
American Institute of Professional Bookkeepers **(140)**
American Medical Writers Association **(150)**
American Registry for Diagnostic Medical Sonography **(174)**
American Society for Biochemistry and Molecular Biology **(181)**
American Society of Consulting Arborists **(196)**
American Society of Plant Biologists **(207)**
American Speech-Language-Hearing Association **(212)**
APSE: The Network on Employment **(226)**
Association & Society Insurance Corporation **(237)**
Association for Research in Vision and Ophthalmology **(255)**
Association of Community Cancer Centers **(275)**
The Association of Language Companies **(290)**
Association of Professional Office Managers **(302)**
Association of Schools and Colleges of Optometry **(307)**
Association of Water Technologies **(317)**
Association on American Indian Affairs **(319)**
Biophysical Society **(330)**
Brotherhood Railway Carmen/TCU **(336)**
Caucus for Women in Statistics **(346)**
Child Life Council **(353)**
Council of State Administrators of Vocational Rehabilitators **(397)**
Council of Teaching Hospitals **(398)**
Employee Services Management Association **(426)**
Football Bowl Association **(450)**
Forest Resources Association **(451)**

Friends of the National Institute of Dental and Craniofacial Research (FNIDCR) **(454)**
Institute of Hazardous Materials Management **(500)**
International College of Dentists, U.S.A. Section **(535)**
International Natural Sausage Casing Association **(557)**
Mechanical Service Contractors of America **(610)**
National Association of Professional Asian American Women **(686)**
National Certified Pipe Welding Bureau **(720)**
National Federal Development Association **(748)**
National School Public Relations Association **(789)**
National Student Speech Language Hearing Association **(798)**
The Oceanography Society **(826)**
Physician Insurers Association of America **(847)**
Plumbing Contractors of America **(851)**
Regulatory Affairs Professionals Society **(879)**
Renal Physicians Association **(881)**
Restoration Industry Association **(884)**
Reusable Industrial Packaging Association **(885)**
Taxicab, Limousine & Paratransit Association **(969)**
Transportation Communications International Union/IAM **(978)**
United States Pharmacopeia **(997)**
Window Coverings Association of America **(1018)**

Salisbury

Czechoslovak Studies Association **(406)**

Severna Park

American Board of Periodontology **(83)**
American Institute of Parliamentarians **(140)**
Industry Council on Tangible Assets **(494)**
International Society for Ecological Modelling-North American Chapter **(566)**
National Marine Electronics Association **(771)**

Silver Spring

American College of Nurse-Midwives **(99)**
American Herbal Products Association **(130)**
American Hiking Society **(131)**
American Music Therapy Association **(154)**
American Nurses Association **(156)**
American Society for Information Science and Technology **(186)**
American Society for Parenteral and Enteral Nutrition **(188)**
American Youth Hostels, Inc (Hostelling International USA) **(222)**
Anxiety Disorders Association of America **(224)**
ASFE/The Geoprofessional Business Association **(231)**
Association for Information and Image Management International **(249)**
Association of Public Health Laboratories **(304)**
Association of Public Treasurers of the United States and Canada **(304)**
Association of University Centers on Disabilities (AUCD) **(315)**
Association of Zoos and Aquariums **(318)**
Auxiliary to the National Medical Association **(324)**
Center for American Nurses **(348)**
CIES - The Food Business Forum **(356)**
Concrete Plant Manufacturers Bureau **(374)**
Conference of Major Superiors of Men, United States of America **(375)**
International Aloe Science Council **(510)**
International Plate Printers, Die Stampers and Engravers Union of North America **(560)**
International Society for Performance Improvement **(567)**
National Association for Bilingual Education **(636)**
National Association for Proton Therapy **(642)**
National Association of Public Health Statistics and Information Systems **(642)**
National Association of Passports and Visa Services **(683)**
National Association of Pastoral Musicians **(683)**
National Association of School Nurses **(693)**
National Association of State Directors of Career Technical Education Consortium **(699)**
National Association of State Utility Consumer Advocates (NASUCA) **(702)**
National Black Nurses Association **(714)**
National Board for Certified Clinical Hypnotherapists **(715)**
National Coalition of Creative Arts Therapies Associations **(723)**
National Council for the Social Studies **(733)**
National Dance Education Organization **(742)**
National Lighting Bureau **(769)**
National Medical Association **(772)**
National Nurses United **(775)**
National Ready Mixed Concrete Association **(784)**
National School Supply and Equipment Association **(789)**
Obesity Society **(825)**
Population Association of America **(853)**
Resource Center for Religious Institutes **(883)**

Security Industry Association (895)
Sports and Fitness Industry Association (959)
SWANA - Solid Waste Association of North America (967)
Truck Mixer Manufacturers Bureau (981)

Solomons

International Society for Computerized Electrocardiology (566)

Suitland

Air Force Sergeants Association (19)

Takoma Park

Certified Contractors Network (349)
River Management Society (886)

Thurmont

National Ornamental Goldfish Growers Association (778)

Timonium

American Society of Trial Consultants (210)
International Metal Decorators Association (556)

Towson

Society of Military Orthopaedic Surgeons (941)

University Park

Space Transportation Association (953)

Upper Marlboro

American Trauma Society (217)
International Association of Machinists and Aerospace Workers (524)
National Association of Home Builders Research Center (673)

Westminster

Association of Independent Research Institutes (288)
Credit Research Foundation (403)

Wheaton

Association of Partners for Public Lands (298)

MASSACHUSETTS

Amherst

The Association for Environmental Health and Sciences (246)
Creative Education Foundation (403)
Union for Radical Political Economics (985)

Andover

Eastern Apicultural Society of North America (418)

Ashland

Fire Department Safety Officers Association (446)

Attleboro Falls

Manufacturing Jewelers and Suppliers of America (604)

Ayer

ALMA - The International Loudspeaker Association (26)

Bedford

IEEE Microwave Theory and Techniques Society (485)

Belmont

National Association for Armenian Studies and Research (636)
National Coalition of Girls' Schools (723)

Beverly

American Association for Hand Surgery (49)
American Association of Thoracic Surgery (53)
American Association of Plastic Surgeons (70)
American Federation for Medical Research (119)
American Society of Maxillofacial Surgeons (202)
American Surgical Association (215)
ASPSN - American Society of Plastic Surgical Nurses (234)
Association of Academic Chairmen of Plastic Surgery (262)
The International Society for Minimally Invasive Cardiothoracic Surgery (567)
Society for Clinical and Experimental Surgery (906)
Society for Pediatric Urology (918)
Society for Surgery of the Alimentary Tract (921)
Society for Vascular Nursing (926)

Boston

American Flock Association (122)
American Herbalists Guild (131)
American Institute for Afghanistan Studies (135)
The American Jewish Historical Society (143)
American Meteorological Society (151)
American Schools of Oriental Research (177)
American Society of Law, Medicine and Ethics (202)
Applied Research Ethics National Association (226)

Archaeological Institute of America (227)
Association for Computers and the Humanities (242)
Association for Textual Scholarship in Art History (257)
Association of Independents in Radio (288)
Association of Institutional Investors (289)
The Association of Literary Scholars, Critics, and Writers (291)
Cashmere and Camel Hair Manufacturers Institute (344)
Design Management Institute (410)
Family Firm Institute, Inc. (437)
Housing Partnership Network (479)
International Health, Racquet and Sportsclub Association (549)
International Reprographic Association (563)
International Society for Ecological Economics (566)
International Society of Exposure Science (572)
International Society of Hotel Association Executives (573)
Moroccan American Business Council (619)
National Immigration Project of the National Lawyers Guild (761)
National Textile Association (800)
Visual Resources Association (1010)

Boxborough

OpenTravel Alliance (828)
Special Interest Group for Data Communication (955)

Brookline

International Society for Infectious Diseases (566)
Orthodox Theological Society in America (833)

Burlington

International Association for Human Resource Information Management (512)
Neurofibromatosis, Inc., Northeast (808)
Organization for the Advancement of Structured Information Standards (831)

Cambridge

American Academy of Arts & Sciences (30)
American Association of Variable Star Observers (76)
American Society for Political and Legal Philosophy (188)
Consortium on Financing Higher Education (379)
Marketing Science Institute (606)
Medieval Academy of America (612)

Canton

Association of Strategic Alliance Professionals, Inc. (311)

Carver

Cranberry Institute (403)

Chestnut Hill

Society for Italian Historical Studies (914)

Chicopee

National Association of Power Engineers (685)

Danvers

Women in Agribusiness (1020)

E. Longmeadow

National Retail Tenants Association (787)

Essex

Newspaper Association Managers (810)

Fairhaven

American Evaluation Association (118)

Framingham

The Travel Institute (979)

Gloucester

The American Hockey Coaches Association (132)
Tag and Label Manufacturers Institute (968)

Hanson

The Arts and Creative Materials Institute, Inc. (229)
Council for Art Education (389)

Lanesborough

IEEE Education Society (484)

Leyden

American Shropshire Registry Association (179)

Lynnfield

Fire and Emergency Manufacturers and Services Association (446)
Fire Apparatus Manufacturers' Association (446)

Malden

National Association of Trade Exchanges (706)
Phycological Society of America (846)

Marshfield

Illustrator's Partnership of America (486)

Medford

International Institute of Forecasters (552)

Melrose

American Society of Abdominal Surgeons (190)

N. Andover

Plumbing and Drainage Institute (850)

N. Attleboro

Photo Chemical Machining Institute (846)

N. Scituate

Solar Alliance (951)

Needham

American Theatre and Drama Society (216)
Object Management Group (825)
WACRA - World Association for Case Method Research and Application (1011)

Norton

New England Club Managers Association (809)

Norwell

Adjutants General Association of the United States (12)
American Bluefin Tuna Association (81)

Norwood

Infusion Nurses Society (496)

Nutting Lake

American Society of Test Engineers (209)

Plympton

American Cotswold Record Association (108)

Quincy

International Brotherhood of Correctional Officers (531)
International Brotherhood of Police Officers (532)
International Fire Marshals Association (545)
National Association for Kinesiology in Higher Education (640)
National Association of Government Employees (670)
National Association of State Controlled Substances Authorities (699)
National Fire Protection Association (751)

S. Dartmouth

SMMA - The Motor and Motion Association (901)

Scituate

Strategic Marketplace Initiative (963)

Shrewsbury

International Disaster Recovery Association (540)

Somerville

Triumvirate Environmental (980)

Southborough

Society for Clinical and Experimental Hypnosis (906)

Springfield

American Hockey League (132)
Association of YMCA Professionals (318)
Paperboard Packaging Council (838)

Sudbury

Association for Medical Imaging Management (252)

Topsfield

International Desalination Association (540)

W. Tisbury

Association of Travel Marketing Executives (315)

Wakefield

International Imaging Industry Association (551)
International Technology Law Association (577)

Waltham

Ethics and Compliance Officer Association (433)
Single Ply Roofing Institute (900)

Wayland

Open Geospatial Consortium (828)

Wenham

Christian College Consortium (355)

Westborough

International District Energy Association (540)
Public Utilities Risk Management Association (870)

Westfield

American Registry of Medical Assistants (174)

Westford

National Roof Deck Contractors Association **(787)**

Westminster

Wood Products Manufacturers Association **(1024)**

Williamstown

Catalogue Raisonne Scholars Association **(344)**

Wilmington

International Association for Modular Exhibitry **(513)**

Woods Hole

International Society of Protistologists **(573)**
Society of General Physiologists **(937)**

Worcester

American Antiquarian Society **(45)**
International Society for Preventive Oncology **(568)**

MICHIGAN

Allegan

National Association of Flight Instructors **(668)**

Allendale

Council of Writing Program Administrators **(398)**
National Council of Writing Program Administrators **(738)**
Rhetoric Society of America **(886)**

Ann Arbor

American Academy of Clinical Neuropsychology **(31)**
American Oriental Society **(158)**
American Society for Clinical Investigation **(182)**
Association for Asian Studies **(239)**
Association for Population/Family Planning Libraries and Information Centers, International **(253)**
Association of Teachers of Technical Writing **(313)**
Automated Imaging Association **(321)**
College of Healthcare Information Management Executives **(364)**
Guild of Artists and Artisans **(467)**
International Society of Barristers **(571)**
National Center for Manufacturing Sciences **(719)**
National Coalition of Alternative Community Schools **(723)**
National Network of Depression Centers **(775)**
Robotic Industries Association **(887)**
Society for College and University Planning **(906)**
Society for Research in Child Development **(920)**
Society for Research on Adolescence **(920)**

Auburn Hills

Automotive Market Research Council **(323)**
Ideas America **(482)**

Belleville

American Neurogastroenterology and Motility Society **(155)**
Association of American Physicians **(265)**

Birch Run

Avko Educational Research Foundation **(325)**

Birmingham

National Arab-American Medical Association **(635)**

Bloomfield Hills

National Association of Sales Professionals **(692)**

Brighton

Automotive Safety Council **(323)**
National Trailer Dealers Association **(801)**

Brooklyn

International Furniture Transportation and Logistics Council **(548)**
Office Furniture Distribution Association **(827)**

Burton

Association for the Behavioral Sciences and Medical Education **(259)**

Clinton

Amalgamated Printer's Association **(27)**

Dearborn

Forming and Fabricating Community of SME **(452)**
North American Manufacturing Research Institution of SME **(817)**
Rapid Technologies & Additive Manufacturing Community of SME **(875)**
Robotics & Flexible Machinery Tech Group **(887)**
Society of Manufacturing Engineers **(941)**

Detroit

Association for Business Simulation and Experiential Learning **(241)**
National Association of Black Suppliers **(649)**
National Association of Black Women Entrepreneurs **(649)**
Slovak Studies Association **(900)**

United Auto Workers (UAW) **(986)**
The Wellness Plan **(1015)**

Dowling

National Lincoln Sheep Breeders Association **(770)**

East Lansing

Academy of International Business **(5)**
American Council of Snowmobile Associations **(110)**
American Osteopathic College of Anesthesiologists **(160)**
Association of College Honor Societies **(274)**
Institute of Public Utilities **(502)**
International Safe Transit Association **(563)**
Society for Historians of the Gilded Age and Progressive Era **(911)**

Farmington Hills

Ambulance Manufacturers Division **(28)**
American College of Neuropsychiatrists **(98)**
American Concrete Institute **(106)**
Independent Professional Representatives Organization **(491)**
National Dental Assistants Association **(742)**
National Truck Equipment Association **(802)**
Post-Tensioning Institute **(853)**
Slag Cement Association **(900)**
Snow Control Equipment Manufacturers Committee **(902)**
Society for Humanistic Judaism **(912)**
Tooling, Manufacturing and Technologies Association **(976)**
Towing Equipment Manufacturers Association **(976)**
Van Body Manufacturers Division **(1008)**

Flint

International Physical Fitness Association **(560)**

Fremont

National Association of Rural Health Clinics **(692)**

Garden City

Clinical Ligand Assay Society **(358)**

Grand Rapids

American Manual Medicine Association **(147)**
Business and Institutional Furniture Manufacturers Association International **(338)**
Christian Schools International **(356)**
Society of Christian Philosophers **(932)**

Grandville

Association of Sewing and Design Professionals **(308)**
IFCA International **(486)**
Professional Society for Sales and Marketing Training **(865)**
Visitor Studies Association **(1010)**

Haslett

International Cut Flower Growers Association **(539)**
International Snowmobile Manufacturers Association **(565)**

Houghton

Society for Industrial Archeology **(913)**

Ionia

Professional Aviation Maintenance Association **(860)**

Jackson

Digital Imaging Marketing Association **(412)**
National Association of Photo Equipment Technicians **(684)**
PMA - The Worldwide Community of Imaging Associations **(851)**
Professional Picture Framers Association **(864)**

Kalamazoo

American Association of Veterinary Parasitologists **(76)**
American Society for Legal History **(186)**
Association of Rehabilitation Programs in Computer Technology **(305)**
International Society for the Comparative Studies of Civilizations **(569)**
International Tuba-Euphonium Association **(578)**

Lake Orion

Society of Automotive Analysts **(930)**

Lansing

American Academy of Podiatric Practice Management **(40)**
American Board of Industrial Hygiene **(82)**
American Society of Irrigation Consultants **(201)**
Association of SIDS and Infant Mortality Programs **(308)**
Cherry Marketing Institute **(352)**
National Association of Legal Investigators **(678)**
National Organization of State Associations for Children **(778)**

Scribes-The American Society of Legal Writers **(893)**

Livonia

International Hearing Society **(549)**
Society for Nonprofit Organizations **(917)**

Madison Heights

Convenience Caterers & Food Manufacturers Association **(383)**
National Association of Investors Corporation **(677)**

Marshall

Distinguished Restaurants of North America **(414)**
Select Registry/Distinguished Inns of North America **(896)**

Midland

American Custom Gunmakers Guild **(112)**

Mt. Pleasant

American Baseball Coaches Association **(80)**
Society for the Study of Amphibians and Reptiles **(925)**

Novi

Brotherhood of Maintenance of Way Employees Division **(336)**
Chain Drug Marketing Association **(350)**
Crane Certification Association of America **(403)**

Oak Park

Trade Exchange of America **(977)**

Okemos

National Association of College and University Food Services **(655)**
Veterinary Orthopedic Society **(1008)**

Portage

Association for Behavior Analysis International **(240)**
InterNational Electrical Testing Association **(542)**
Society for the Advancement of Behavior Analysis **(922)**

Powers

National Association of County Health Facility Administrators **(660)**

Rochester

American Society of Body Engineers **(193)**

Saline

Association for Graphic Arts Training **(247)**

South Lyon

Phi Delta Chi **(845)**

Southfield

Automotive Industry Action Group **(322)**
Ford Motor Minority Dealers Association **(451)**

St. Clair Shores

International Society of Travel and Tourism Educators **(574)**
National Association of Resale & Thrift Shops **(691)**

St. Joseph

American Society of Agricultural and Biological Engineers **(191)**

Sterling Heights

National Organization of State Offices of Rural Health **(778)**

Traverse City

Association of Directory Publishers **(279)**
Local Media Association **(599)**

Troy

Automation Alley **(321)**
Automotive Public Relations Council **(323)**
Original Equipment Suppliers Association **(833)**
Visiting Physicians Association **(1010)**

W. Bloomfield

Floor Covering Installation Contractors Association **(448)**

Walled Lake

American Association of Teachers of Spanish and Portuguese **(75)**
Associated Wire Rope Fabricators **(237)**

Warren

American Guild of Music **(127)**

Whitehall

The Travel and Tourism Research Association **(979)**

Willis

National Association of Agriculture Employees **(646)**

Ypsilanti

Association for Applied and Clinical Sociology **(238)**

Zeeland

Christian Labor Association of the United States of America *(355)*

MINNESOTA

Alexandria

International Travel Writers and Editors Association *(578)*

Professional Women's Appraisal Association *(866)*

Belle Plaine

International Listening Association *(554)*

Bemidji

Association of Camp Nurses *(271)*

Blaine

Utility Arborist Association *(1006)*

Crystal

Evangelical Press Association *(434)*

Duluth

American Academy of Health Care Providers-Addictive Disorders *(34)*
Association for Consumer Research *(243)*

Eden Prairie

Academy of Surgical Research *(9)*
Energy and Environmental Building Association *(427)*
Laboratory Animal Management Association *(592)*
Utility Management & Conservation Association *(1006)*
Wiring Harness Manufacturers Association *(1020)*

Edina

Plastic Surgery Administrative Association *(850)*
Surface Mount Technology Association *(966)*

Fridley

Association of Health Information Outsourcing Services *(286)*

Hanover

Association of Cooperative Educators *(277)*

Houston

North American Clun Forest Association *(815)*

Lino Lakes

Association of Asphalt Paving Technologists *(268)*

Mankato

National Forensic Association *(752)*

Maple Grove

International Association of Printing House Craftsmen *(526)*

Merrifield

International Sled Dog Racing Association *(564)*

Minneapolis

ACA International, The Association of Credit and Collection Professionals *(2)*
Aircraft Builders Council *(20)*
Alliance of Automotive Service Providers *(24)*
American Academy of Neurology *(36)*
American Craft Council *(111)*
American Neurological Association *(155)*
American Society of Neuroimaging *(204)*
American Society of Neurorehabilitation *(204)*
American Society of Ophthalmic Plastic and Reconstructive Surgery *(205)*
American Technical Education Association *(215)*
Asian American Psychological Association *(232)*
Associated Collegiate Press *(235)*
Association for Asian American Studies *(239)*
Association for Chemoreception Sciences *(241)*
Association of Personal Historians *(299)*
Association of Waldorf Schools of North America *(317)*
Captive Insurance Companies Association *(342)*
College Gymnastics Association *(363)*
Engineering College Magazines Associated *(429)*
Export Institute of the United States *(436)*
Flexible Intermediate Bulk Container Association *(447)*
Forest Stewardship Council - United States Chapter *(451)*
Grain Elevator and Processing Society *(464)*
Health Care Compliance Association *(469)*
Human Biology Association *(480)*
International Association of Commercial Collectors *(518)*
International Society for Research on Aggression *(569)*
Marketing Agencies Association Worldwide *(606)*
National Council on Family Relations *(738)*
National Exercise Trainers Association *(747)*

National Foster Parent Association *(753)*
National Mail Order Association *(771)*
National Network of Grantmakers *(775)*
National Orientation Directors Association *(778)*
National Scholastic Press Association *(789)*
North American Neuro-Ophthalmology Society *(819)*
Portable Sanitation Association International *(853)*
Professional Liability Underwriting Society *(863)*
Visual Communications Industry Group *(1010)*

Minnetonka

National Association for Ambulatory Care *(636)*

New Prague

American Agricultural Editors Association *(43)*
Turf and Ornamental Communicators Association *(982)*

New Ulm

Archery Trade Association *(227)*

Newton

Transworld Advertising Agency Network *(979)*

Northfield

International Alliance of Technology Integrators *(510)*
National Association of Geoscience Teachers *(669)*
United Ostomy Associations of America *(988)*

Outing

International Wild Rice Association *(581)*

Preston

Algal Biomass Organization *(22)*

Prior Lake

International Ceramic Association *(534)*

Red Wing

American Federation of Violin and Bow Makers *(120)*

Richfield

American Filtration and Separations Society *(121)*

Richmond

Monument Builders of North America *(619)*

Rochester

American Association of Neuromuscular and Electrodiagnostic Medicine *(66)*
American Board of Physical Medicine and Rehabilitation *(83)*
Professional Skaters Association *(865)*
Society of Thoracic Radiology *(948)*

Roseville

American Jewish Correctional Chaplains Association *(143)*
Geosynthetic Materials Association *(459)*
Industrial Fabrics Association International *(493)*
Marine Fabricators Association *(605)*
United States Industrial Fabrics Institute *(995)*

St. Cloud

Billings Ovulation Method Association of the United States *(329)*
National Wildlife Rehabilitators Association *(805)*
Society of Christian Ethics *(932)*

St. Louis Park

Association of Art Editors *(267)*

St. Paul

American Association of Cereal Chemists International *(55)*
American Association of Pathologists' Assistants *(68)*
American Association of Woodturners *(77)*
American Composers Forum *(105)*
American Phytopathological Society *(165)*
American Registry of Radiologic Technologists *(174)*
American Society of Brewing Chemists *(193)*
Association of American State Geologists *(266)*
Association of College and University Religious Affairs *(274)*
Association of Technical Personnel in Ophthalmology *(313)*
Automotive Fleet and Leasing Association *(322)*
Child Neurology Society *(353)*
Controlled Release Society *(383)*
Council of Engineering and Scientific Society Executives *(393)*
Heart Failure Society of America *(472)*
Higher Education Consortium for Urban Affairs *(475)*
Hospitality Institute of Technology and Management *(479)*
International Society for Molecular Plant Microbe Interactions *(567)*
Leafy Greens Council *(595)*
Master Brewers Association of the Americas *(607)*
National Agricultural Alumni and Development Association *(630)*

National Alfalfa Alliance *(631)*
National Alfalfa and Forage Alliance *(631)*
National Association of Fundraising Ticket Manufacturers *(669)*
National Association of Investment Professionals *(676)*
National Association of Scientific Materials Managers *(694)*
North American Gaming Regulators Association *(817)*
Qualitative Research Consultants Association *(871)*
Recognition Professionals International *(876)*
Society of Insurance Trainers and Educators *(940)*
Surfaces in Biomaterials Foundation *(966)*

Stillwater

National Church Library Association *(722)*

Waconia

National Shippers Strategic Transportation Council *(791)*

Waite Park

National Association for Rural Mental Health *(642)*

Wayzata

Advertising and Marketing International Network *(13)*

Winona

International Society for Philosophical Enquiry *(568)*

MISSISSIPPI

Biloxi

American Shrimp Processors Association *(179)*

Brandon

American Society of Certified Engineering Technicians *(194)*

Clinton

America's Independent Truckers' Association, Inc. *(29)*
National Association of Emergency Medical Technicians *(665)*

Greenville

National Association of Junior Auxiliaries *(677)*

Hattiesburg

American Kinesiotherapy Association *(144)*
American Therapeutic Recreation Association *(216)*
National Government Publishing Association *(755)*

Indianola

Catfish Farmers of America *(344)*

Itta Bena

National Conference of Black Political Scientists *(727)*

Jackson

American Poultry International Ltd. *(167)*
The Catfish Institute *(345)*
Conference of Minority Public Administrators *(375)*
National Tile Contractors Association *(800)*
Professional School Photographers Association International *(865)*

Mississippi State

Agricultural History Society *(16)*

Ocean Springs

National Marine Educators Association *(771)*

Ridgeland

NGNP Industry Alliance *(810)*

Southaven

National Cotton Batting Institute *(730)*

Tupelo

United Methodist Association of Health and Welfare Ministries *(987)*

University

Society of Philosophers in America *(944)*

Vicksburg

Aquatic Plant Management Society, Inc. *(227)*

MISSOURI

Ava

Missouri Fox Trotting Horse Breed Association *(617)*

Ballwin

International Business Music Association *(532)*

Boonville

American Karakul Sheep Registry *(143)*

Camdenton

National Caves Association *(719)*

Chesterfield

Data Management Association International *(407)*
International Fruit Tree Association *(547)*
National Christmas Tree Association *(721)*
National Corn Growers Association *(730)*
National Wood Flooring Association *(805)*
United Soybean Board *(989)*
United States Junior Chamber (Jaycees) *(995)*

Columbia

American Education Finance Association *(116)*
American Society of News Editors *(204)*
Columbia Sheep Breeders Association of America *(365)*
Community Development Society *(370)*
Investigative Reporters and Editors *(583)*
National Association of Animal Breeders *(647)*
National Association of State Outdoor Recreation Liaison Officers *(701)*
National Newspaper Association *(775)*
Veterinary Cancer Society *(1008)*

Edwards

Production Engine Remanufacturers Association *(859)*

Fenton

North American Equipment Dealers Association *(816)*

Gladstone

National Association of Sports Public Address Announcers *(697)*

Grain Vally

Owner-Operator Independent Drivers Association, Inc. *(836)*

Grandview

International Association of Personal Protection Agents *(526)*

Greenwood

American Bridge Teachers' Association *(86)*

Independence

National Association of Parliamentarians *(683)*
Parliamentary Associates *(839)*

Jefferson City

Association of State Chamber Professionals *(310)*
National Association of Government Labor Officials *(670)*
National Conference of State Fleet Administrators *(728)*
Women in Energy *(1021)*

Joplin

International Society of Weekly Newspaper Editors *(574)*

Kansas City

Accredited Pet Cemetery Society *(10)*
Alliance of Professional Tattooists *(25)*
Alpha Gamma Rho *(26)*
American Association of Grain Inspection and Weighing Agencies *(61)*
American Association of Private Lenders *(71)*
American Association of Veterinary State Boards *(76)*
American Hereford Association *(131)*
American International Charolais Association *(142)*
American Public Works Association *(172)*
American Society of Electroneurodiagnostic Technologists *(197)*
Association of Diesel Specialists *(279)*
Association of Mailing, Shipping, and Office Automation Specialists *(292)*
Aviation Insurance Association *(324)*
Business Technology Association *(340)*
Council on Chiropractic Orthopedics *(399)*
Electrical Equipment Representatives Association *(422)*
Express Delivery & Logistics Association *(436)*
Hotel Brokers International *(479)*
International Association of Administrative Professionals *(515)*
International Association of Assessing Officers *(516)*
International Window Cleaning Association *(581)*
Investment Recovery Association *(584)*
Livestock Marketing Association *(599)*
Mass Marketing Insurance Institute *(607)*
Mutual Fund Education Alliance *(623)*
National Animal Control Association *(634)*
National Association of Basketball Coaches *(648)*
National Association of Collegiate Women Athletic Administrators *(656)*
National Association of Intercollegiate Athletics *(676)*

National Association of Professional Surplus Lines Offices, Ltd. *(688)*
National Lubricating Grease Institute *(770)*
National Portable Storage Association *(781)*
National Rural Health Association *(788)*
Public Works Historical Society *(870)*
Scaffold Industry Association *(891)*
Sealant, Waterproofing and Restoration Institute *(894)*
Tile Contractors' Association of America *(974)*
Transportation Elevator and Grain Merchants Association *(978)*

Kearney

In-Plant Printing and Mailing Association *(487)*

Kirksville

American Association of Osteopathic Women Physicians *(68)*
American Osteopathic College of Dermatology *(160)*
National Association of College Wind and Percussion Instructors *(655)*

Lee's Summit

Aircraft Electronics Association *(20)*

Lenexa

Association of Statisticians of American Religious Bodies *(311)*

Marceline

National Association of Medical Examiners *(680)*
Society for Invertebrate Pathology *(913)*

Maryland Heights

Professional Football Writers of America *(862)*

Maryville

Lightning Protection Institute *(598)*

Milan

American Osteopathic College of Radiology *(161)*

Nelson

Palomino Horse Association *(837)*

Nixa

Ophthalmic Photographers' Society *(829)*

O'Fallon

Business Products Credit Association *(339)*

Platte City

American Chianina Association *(90)*
American Maine-Anjou Association *(146)*
National Association of Farm Broadcasting *(667)*

Raytown

Stained Glass Association of America *(960)*

Rolla

Structural Stability Research Council *(964)*

Rutledge

Society of Quantitative Analysts *(946)*

Saint Louis

Energy Storage Council *(428)*

Springfield

American College of Forensic Examiners Institute *(96)*
American Psychotherapy Association *(170)*
Enactus *(427)*
International Association of Fairs and Expositions *(521)*
JAWS Society *(586)*
National Association of Air Medical Communication Specialists *(646)*
National Association of Portable X-Ray Providers *(685)*
Retail Confectioners International *(884)*
Society for Environmental Geochemistry and Health *(908)*
Sociological Practice Association *(950)*

St Louis

The American Association of Phonetic Sciences *(69)*

St. Charles

Concrete Anchor Manufacturers Association *(373)*
International Brotherhood of Magicians *(531)*
Powder Actuated Tool Manufacturers Institute *(854)*

St. Joseph

American Angus Association *(45)*
United States Animal Health Association *(989)*

St. Louis

Airport Ground Transportation Association *(21)*
American Academy of Fertility Care Professionals *(34)*
American Association of Bioanalysts *(54)*

American Association of Orthodontists *(67)*
American Fern Society *(121)*
American Optometric Association *(157)*
American Optometric Student Association *(157)*
American Society of Concrete Contractors *(195)*
American Society of Theatre Consultants *(210)*
American Soybean Association *(211)*
Association of Defensive Spray Manufacturers *(278)*
Black Caucus of the American Library Association *(331)*
The Botanical Society of America *(333)*
Catholic Health Association of the United States *(345)*
College of Diplomates of the American Board of Orthodontics *(364)*
Consortium for Graduate Study in Management *(378)*
Credit Professionals International *(403)*
Electrical Apparatus Service Association *(422)*
Geochemical Society *(458)*
International Association of Black Professional Fire Fighters *(517)*
International Association of Broadcast Monitors *(517)*
International Association of Conference Centers *(518)*
Korean American Spine Society *(591)*
Materials Technology Institute *(609)*
National Association of Electrical Distributors *(664)*
National Garden Clubs *(754)*
National Independent Laboratory Association *(762)*
National Society of Real Estate Appraisers, Inc. *(795)*
Painting and Decorating Contractors of America *(837)*
Society for Economic Botany *(908)*
Society for Medieval and Renaissance Philosophy *(915)*
Society for the Study of Evolution *(925)*
Sponge and Chamois Institute *(958)*
Tillage & Ground Engaging Equipment Product Council *(974)*
United States Basketball Writers Association *(991)*
WaterJet Technology Association - Industrial and Municipal Cleaning Association *(1013)*

St. Peters

Paint and Decorating Retailers Association *(836)*

Waynesville

Society of Army Physician Assistants *(930)*

Willow Springs

Scottish Blackface Breeders Association *(893)*

MONTANA

Big Sandy

Kamut Association of North America *(590)*

Billings

R-Calf *(872)*
Ranchers-Cattlemen Action Legal Fund, United Stockgrower of America *(874)*

Bozeman

American Independent Business Alliance *(135)*
American Simmental Association *(179)*
Housing Education and Research Association *(479)*

Havre

North American Elk Breeders Association *(816)*

Helena

National Association for Government Training and Development *(639)*
National Association of Division Order Analysts *(663)*

Kalispell

Society of Pelvic Reconstructive Surgeons *(943)*

Missoula

Association for University Business and Economic Research *(260)*
College Music Society *(363)*
International Association of Railway Operating Officers *(527)*
International Association of Wildland Fire *(528)*
Outdoor Writers Association of America *(835)*

Power

American Honey Producers Association *(133)*

St Louis

Society of Neurological Surgeons *(943)*

NEBRASKA

Arnold

National Blacksmiths and Weldors Association *(715)*

Diller

Piedmontese Association of the United States (848)

Elkhorn

American Tarentaise Association (215)
Montadale Sheep Breeders Association (619)

Gretna

Military Impacted Schools Association (616)

Hastings

Amerifax Cattle Association (222)

Lincoln

Contact Lens Manufacturers Association (382)
Golf Course Builders Association of America (463)
Human Behavior and Evolution Society (480)
International Stress Management Association - USA (576)
National Association of Housing Information Managers (673)
National Collegiate Honors Council (724)
National Conference on Weights and Measures (729)
National Council of State Agencies for the Blind (736)
Organic Crop Improvement Association International (830)
Organization of Wildlife Planners (832)

Omaha

American Academy of Maxillofacial Prosthetics (35)
American Laryngological, Rhinological and Otological Society (144)
American Shorthorn Association (179)
Association of University Professors of Ophthalmology (315)
Fraternal Field Managers Association (453)
Health and Sciences Communications Association (469)
National Science Education Leadership Association (790)
Society of Infectious Diseases Pharmacists (939)
Triological Society (980)
Wellness Councils of America (1015)

Peru

Institute of Behavioral and Applied Management (498)

Wayne

American White American Creme Horse Registry (221)

York

Groundwater Management Districts Association (466)

NEVADA

Baker

National Association of Home and Workshop Writers (672)

Gardnerville

National Indian Head Start Directors Association (763)

Henderson

Association of Gaming Equipment Manufacturers (285)
Independent Photo Imagers (491)
National Association of Heavy Equipment Training Schools (672)
National Conference of Personal Managers (728)

Las Vegas

American Academy of Somnology (42)
The American Gem Society (125)
Antique and Amusement Photographers International (224)
Association for the Study of Higher Education (259)
International Foundation for Telemetering (547)
International Imaging Technology Council (551)
National Association of Reunion Managers (692)
National Constables Association (729)
National Council of Exchangors (734)
The National Procurement Institute, Inc (783)
Society for Cross-Cultural Research (907)
Society of American Fight Directors (928)
Society of American Law Teachers (929)
Sports and Entertainment Alliance in Technology (959)
United States Air Tour Association (989)
United States Targhee Sheep Association (999)

Mesquite

Pierre Fauchard Academy (848)

Reno

National Council of Juvenile and Family Court Judges (735)

Sparks

Association of State and Territorial Dental Directors (310)

NEW HAMPSHIRE

Alstead

Timber Framers Guild (974)

Chester

American College of Laboratory Animal Medicine (97)

Concord

Academy of Applied Science (4)
American Ground Water Trust (127)

Durham

Association for Communication Excellence (242)
History of Economics Society (476)
Sea Grant Association (894)

Etna

American Academy of Gold Foil Operators (34)

Gilford

International Association of Law Enforcement Firearms Instructors, Inc. (523)

Goshen

Cleveland Bay Horse Society of North America (358)

Hanover

Plastic Surgery Research Council (850)

Hollis

Natural Stone Council (807)

Londonderry

Tree Care Industry Association (980)

Manchester

National Human Resources Association (761)

Nashua

Workers' Injury Law and Advocacy Group (1025)

New Durham

American Milking Devon Cattle Association (152)

Plymouth

American Credit and Collections Association (111)

Portsmouth

International Association of Privacy Professionals (526)
National Electrical Manufacturers Representatives Association (745)
Standards Engineering Society (961)

Spofford

Unfinished Furniture Association (984)

Warren

National Association of Academies of Science (645)

Winchester

Cross Country Ski Areas Association (405)

Windham

Nuclear Information and Records Management Association (825)

NEW JERSEY

Avon-By-the-Sea

United States Lifesaving Association (996)

Berkeley Heights

Local Search Association (fka Yellow Pages Association) (600)

Bound Brook

American Society for the Advancement of Anesthesia and Sedation in Dentistry (190)

Branchburg

Intermediaries and Reinsurance Underwriters Association (508)

Bridgewater

Alliance of Black Telecommunications Employees (24)

Butler

Hobby Manufacturers Association (477)

Canford

Used Truck Association (1005)

Chatham

American Bureau of Metal Statistics (86)

Cherry Hill

American Association of Teachers of German (74)

American Society of PeriAnesthesia Nurses (206)
Equipment Service Association (433)
The International Fluid Power Society (545)
National Association of Pediatric Nurse Practitioners (684)

Cinnaminson

Atlantic Independent Union (319)

Clifton

National Council on Public Polls (739)

Collingswood

National Association of Environmental Professionals (666)

Dumont

American Musicians Union (154)

E. Brunswick

Association for Humanist Sociology (249)

East Rutherford

National Association for Printing Leadership (641)
R & E Council of the NAPL (872)

Eatontown

Society of Marine Port Engineers (941)

Edison

American Osteopathic College of Rheumatology, Inc. (161)
International Executive Association (543)

Elizabeth

American Importers and Exporters/Meat Products Group (135)

Elmwood Park

Craft & Hobby Association (402)

Englewood Cliffs

Association of Ship Brokers and Agents (U.S.A.) (308)
National Organization of Social Security Claimants' Representatives (778)

Fairfield

Textile Care Allied Trades Association (972)

Fairview

Schiffli Lace and Embroidery Manufacturers Association (892)

Far Hills

United States Golf Association (994)

Forked River

Blue Water Fishermen's Association (332)

Hackensack

Foster Family-Based Treatment Association (452)

Hackettstown

National Kitchen and Bath Association (767)

Hainesport

Tau Epsilon Rho Law Society (968)

Hamilton

International Sculpture Center (564)

Harrington Park

International Motor Press Association (557)

Hawthorne

Deep Foundations Institute (408)

Hazlet

The Securities Transfer Association (895)

Highland Park

Historians of Netherlandish Art (476)

Highlands

American Littoral Society (146)

Hillsborough

American Association of Feline Practitioners (61)
Costume Society of America (387)
International Ombudsman Association (558)
Society for Medical Decision Making (915)

Hillside

National Commodity Supplemental Food Program Association (724)

Holmdel

Containerization and Intermodal Institute (382)

Iselin

United States Clay Producers Traffic Association (991)
United States Maritime Alliance (USMX) (996)

Jersey City

Global Association of Risk Professionals *(461)*
The Society of Naval Architects and Marine Engineers *(942)*

Lafayette

American Crossbred Pony Registry *(112)*

Lakewood

Property Owners Association *(867)*

Lawrenceville

International Society for Pharmacoeconomics and Outcomes Research *(568)*

Lincroft

American Association for Women in Community Colleges *(53)*

Logan Township

Association of Educational Publishers *(280)*

Mahwah

Foundation for Advances in Medicine and Science *(452)*
History of Earth Sciences Society *(476)*

Manalapan

Harness Horsemen International *(468)*

Mantua

International Society of Managing and Technical Editors *(573)*

Maplewood

Alliance for Quality Care *(23)*

Marlton

National Association of Recording Merchandisers (NARM) *(690)*
National Limousine Association *(770)*

Maywood

Society for Experimental Biology and Medicine *(909)*

Mendham

Power Sources Manufacturers Association *(855)*

Middlesex

American Microchemical Society *(151)*

Monroe Township

American Engineering Association *(117)*

Montclair

Celebrant Foundation and Institute *(347)*
National Music Council *(774)*

Montvale

Institute Management Accountants *(498)*
Investment Casting Institute *(584)*
Network Branded Prepaid Card Association *(808)*

Moorestown

International Hard Anodizing Association *(549)*

Morristown

Financial Executives International *(444)*

Mount Laurel

Osteoarthritis Research Society International *(834)*
Society for Information Management *(913)*

Mt. Laurel

American Association for Aerosol Research *(47)*
American Association of Heart Failure Nurses *(62)*
American Mosquito Control Association *(153)*
American Society for Histocompatibility and Immunogenetics *(185)*
American Society of Hand Therapists *(199)*
American Society of Transplantation *(210)*
Association for Accounting Marketing *(238)*
Dermatology Nurses' Association *(410)*
International Energy Credit Association *(542)*
International Liver Transplantation Society *(554)*
International Pediatric Transplant Association *(560)*
Juvenile Products Manufacturers Association *(590)*
NADCA: The HVAC Inspection, Maintenance and Restoration Association *(623)*
National Association of Professional Organizers *(687)*
National Association of Professional Pet Sitters *(687)*
Society for Biomaterials *(905)*
The Wound, Ostomy and Continence Nurses Society *(1028)*

Mt. Royal

American Association for Paralegal Education *(50)*
American Auditory Society *(78)*
American Headache Society *(129)*
Association for Governmental Leasing and Finance *(247)*
Association for Research in Otolaryngology *(255)*

Association of Women in the Metal Industries *(317)*
International Federation of Fertility Societies *(544)*
International Game Developers Association *(548)*
National Society for Experiential Education *(792)*
Society for Cardiovascular Magnetic Resonance *(905)*

Murray Hill

Association of Consulting Chemists and Chemical Engineers *(276)*

N. Bergen

International Longshoremen's Association, AFL-CIO *(555)*

Naponee

Association of Food Industries *(283)*

Neptune

Chemical Sources Association *(352)*
National Association of Flavors and Food-Ingredient Systems *(668)*
National Honey Packers and Dealers Association *(760)*
North American Olive Oil Association *(819)*
Society of Flavor Chemists *(936)*

New Providence

Ireland Chamber of Commerce in the United States *(585)*
National Council of Self-Insurers *(736)*

Newark

Committee on Lesbian and Gay History *(368)*
Community Colleges Humanities Association *(370)*
International Municipal Signal Association *(557)*
Omicron Kappa Upsilon *(827)*

Oakhurst

National Association of Health and Educational Facilities Finance Authorities *(671)*

Oceanville

American Academy of Orofacial Pain *(38)*

Parsippany

Hydraulic Institute *(481)*

Pennington

The Electrochemical Society *(423)*

Piscataway

African Studies Association *(15)*
Broadcast Technology Society *(336)*
Geoscience and Remote Sensing Society *(459)*
IEEE Aerospace and Electronic Systems Society (AESS) *(483)*
IEEE Circuits and Systems Society *(483)*
IEEE Components, Packaging, and Manufacturing Technology Society *(483)*
IEEE Control Systems Society *(484)*
IEEE Electron Devices Society *(484)*
IEEE Engineering in Medicine and Biology Society *(484)*
IEEE - Industry Applications Society *(484)*
IEEE Photonics Society *(485)*
IEEE Power and Energy Society *(485)*
IEEE Power Electronics Society *(485)*
IEEE Signal Processing Society *(485)*
IEEE Technology Management Council *(486)*
North American Calorimetry Conference *(814)*
Professional Communications Society *(861)*
Solid-State Circuits Society *(952)*

Pitman

Academy of Medical-Surgical Nurses *(7)*
American Academy of Ambulatory Care Nursing *(30)*
American Nephrology Nurses Association *(155)*
Certification Board for Urologic Nurses and Associates *(349)*
Society of Urologic Nurses and Associates *(949)*

Princeton

American Association of Teachers of Turkic Languages *(75)*
American Society of Group Psychotherapy and Psychodrama *(198)*
APMI International *(225)*
Association for Convention Marketing Executives *(244)*
Audio Publishers Association *(320)*
Construction Financial Management Association *(379)*
Event Service Professionals Association *(434)*
International Card Manufacturers Association *(532)*
International Function Point Users Group *(548)*
Metal Injection Molding Association *(613)*
Metal Powder Industries Federation *(613)*
Metal Powder Producers Association *(614)*
NAFA Fleet Management Association *(624)*
National Association of Independent Brokers Dealers *(674)*

Powder Metallurgy Equipment Association *(854)*
Powder Metallurgy Parts Association *(854)*
Refractory Metals Association *(878)*
Smart Card Alliance *(901)*
Tobacco Merchants Association of the United States *(975)*
Travel Goods Association *(979)*
United States Rowing Association *(998)*

Princeton Junction

North American Association of Commencement Officers *(813)*

Ramsey

Sales Association of the Paper Industry *(890)*

Rio Grande

Independent Free Papers of America *(490)*

River Edge

American Society of Wedding Professionals *(211)*

Robbinsville

Drug, Chemical and Associated Technologies Association *(417)*

Roseland

Communications Fraud Control Association *(369)*

Rutherford

CPA Associates International *(402)*

S. Plainfield

National Police and Security Officers Association of America *(781)*
Trade Promotion Management Associates *(977)*

Secaucus

Oriental Rug Importers Association of America *(833)*

Skillman

Intercollegiate Tennis Association *(507)*

Somerville

CPA USA Network *(402)*

Springfield

International Boxing Federation *(530)*

Swedesboro

American Society of Baking *(193)*

Teaneck

Association of Jewish Libraries *(290)*
International Association of Medical Equipment Remarketers and Servicers (IAMERS) *(524)*

Trenton

Association of Labor Relations Agencies *(290)*
Capital Health *(342)*

Tuckerton

American Mideast Business Associates *(151)*

Turnersville

Computer Measurement Group *(372)*

Upper Montclair

International Congress of Oral Implantologists *(537)*

Upper Saddle River

The Food Institute *(449)*

Verona

Association of Traumatic Stress Specialists *(315)*

W. Caldwell

American Society of Perfumers *(206)*

W. Orange

Professional Hockey Writers' Association *(862)*

W. Windsor

National Association of Noise Control Officials *(682)*

Wall Township

United States Marine Safety Association *(996)*

West Trenton

Interstate Council on Water Policy *(582)*

Westfield

Association for Spanish and Portuguese Studies *(256)*
Council of Hotel and Restaurant Trainers *(394)*
Garden Centers of America *(456)*

Westwood

Sales Association of the Chemical Industry *(890)*

Whippany

National Exchange Carrier Association *(746)*

Woodbridge

National Association of Printing Ink Manufacturers *(686)*

Woodcliff Lake

Research Institute for Fragrance Materials *(882)*

Wyckhoff

International Psychohistorical Association *(562)*

NEW MEXICO

Albuquerque

Alternative Fuel Vehicle Network *(27)*
American College of Mental Health Administration *(98)*
American Indian Science and Engineering Society *(135)*
American Peptide Society *(163)*
American Society of Radiologic Technologists *(208)*
American Theatre Critics Association *(216)*
Association of Educators in Imaging and Radiologic Sciences, Inc *(280)*
Directed Energy Professional Society *(413)*
Financial and Security Products Association *(444)*
Indian Arts and Crafts Association *(492)*
Indian Educators Federation *(492)*
Intertribal Monitoring Association on Indian Trust Funds *(583)*
National Alliance of State Broadcast Associations *(633)*
National Association of Nuclear Pharmacies *(682)*
Society of Vacuum Coaters *(950)*
Women's Regional Publications of America *(1024)*

Farmington

American Ornithologists' Union *(158)*

Hobbs

Soaring Society of America *(902)*

Las Cruces

The Evaporative Cooling Institute *(434)*
International Center for Study of Psychiatry and Psychology *(534)*

Los Alamos

IEEE - Nuclear and Plasma Sciences Society *(482)*

Portales

Council for Educational Diagnosticians *(389)*

Rio Rancho

Association for Child Psychoanalysis *(241)*

Santa Fe

American Catholic Correctional Chaplains Association *(88)*
American Society for Mass Spectrometry *(186)*
Association of Food Journalists *(283)*
Federation of Analytical Chemistry and Spectroscopy Societies *(440)*
Women In Film and Television International *(1021)*

Silver City

Spanish Barb Horse Association *(954)*

Socorro

The National Association of Dog Obedience Instructors *(663)*
Special Interest Group on Applied Computing *(956)*

NEW YORK

Albany

Academy of Certified Archivists *(4)*
Academy of Rehabilitative Audiology *(8)*
Association of Financial Guaranty Insurers *(283)*
Comparative and International Education Society *(371)*
International Association of Milk Control Agencies *(524)*
National Association for Pupil Transportation *(642)*
National Association of Government Archives and Records Administrators *(669)*
North American Association of Wardens and Superintendents *(814)*
SEMATECH *(896)*
WIFS - Women in Insurance and Financial Services *(1017)*

Amenia

American Warmblood Registry *(219)*

Amherst

Surface Engineering Coating Association *(966)*

Astoria

American Alliance of Home Modification Professionals (AAHMP) *(44)*

Avoca

International Herb Association *(550)*

Bay Terrace

National Institute of Electromedical Information *(765)*

Bayside

American Stamp Dealers Association *(213)*
Baseball Writers Association of America *(326)*
Dance Masters of America, Inc. *(406)*

Bellmore

Society of Professional Investigators *(945)*

Binghamton

American Name Society *(154)*
National Perinatal Association *(780)*
Society for Ancient Greek Philosophy *(904)*

Bohemia

Flexographic Technical Association *(447)*

Brentwood

National Association of Puerto Rican-Hispanic Social Workers *(689)*

Briarcliff Manor

Academy of Management *(6)*
International Society for Medical Publication Professionals *(567)*
United Federation of Police & Security Officers *(987)*

Brockport

Society for Medical Anthropology *(915)*

Bronx

American Catholic Historical Association *(88)*
Association for the Advancement of Psychotherapy *(258)*

Brooklyn

American Association of Hospital and Healthcare Podiatrists *(62)*
The American Geographical Society *(126)*
Association for Birth Psychology *(240)*
Association of Professional Art Advisors *(300)*
Freelancers Union *(453)*
Independent Filmmaker Project *(489)*
International Society of Copier Artists *(572)*
National Society for Hebrew Day Schools *(792)*
National Student Nurses Association *(797)*
Osborne Association *(834)*
Sculptors Guild *(894)*
Society for Asian and Comparative Philosophy *(904)*

Buffalo

American Crystallographic Association *(112)*
Association for the Bibliography of History *(259)*
Gift Associates Interchange Network *(460)*
National Association for Health and Fitness *(639)*
National Association of Independent Lighting Distributors *(674)*
National Chemical Credit Association *(720)*
National Coalition for Assistive and Rehab Technology *(723)*
Printing Industry Credit Executives *(857)*
Utility Communicators International *(1006)*

Canandaigua

The Association of Theatre Movement Educators *(314)*

Cedarhurst

Jewish Educators Assembly *(588)*

Cheektowaga

Training Directors' Forum *(977)*

Chestertown

Building Stone Institute *(338)*

Churchville

International League of Electrical Associations *(553)*

Clifton Park

Iroquois Healthcare Alliance *(585)*
National Association of Independent Insurance Auditors and Engineers *(674)*

Clinton

International Association of Auto Theft Investigators *(516)*

Cohoes

Professional Service Association *(865)*

Cortland

Automotive Lift Institute, Inc. *(322)*
National Academy of Arbitrators *(627)*

Craryville

Therapeutic Touch International Association *(973)*

Derby

American Fox Terrier Club *(123)*

East Northport

Surgical Infection Society *(967)*

Elba

American Veal Association *(218)*

Fairport

Microanalysis Society *(614)*

Farmingdale

The Association of Average Adjusters of the United States and Canada *(268)*

Floral Park

Indian Dental Association (USA) *(492)*

Forest Hills

American Podiatric Medical Writers Association *(166)*
Institute of General Semantics *(500)*

Garden City

Scientific Equipment and Furniture Association *(892)*

Great Neck

National Interscholastic Swimming Coaches Association *(766)*
The National Money Transmitters Association *(773)*

Greenwich

Agricultural Stewardship Association *(16)*

Hamilton

Association of Professional Model Makers *(302)*
Public Radio Program Directors Association *(870)*

Hauppauge

American Catalog Mailers Association *(88)*
Cosmetic Industry Buyers and Suppliers *(387)*

Hempstead

National Catholic Development Conference *(718)*

Henrietta

National Payroll Reporting Consortium *(780)*

Huntington

Independent Professional Painting Contractors Association of America *(491)*
National Conference of Diocesan Vocation Directors *(727)*
Transportation and Logistics Council *(978)*

Hyde Park

International Foodservice Editorial Council *(546)*

Ithaca

Association of African Studies Programs *(263)*
Association of Official Seed Analysts, Inc. *(296)*
North American Fuzzy Information Processing Society *(817)*
Omega Tau Sigma *(827)*
Paleontological Research Institution *(837)*
Society for Personality and Social Psychology *(918)*
Society for the Psychological Study of Lesbian and Gay Issues *(924)*
Society of Commercial Seed Technologists *(933)*

Jackson Heights

National Spinal Cord Injury Association *(795)*
United Spinal Association *(989)*

Jamaica

American Association for the Study of Hungarian History *(52)*
National Organization of Industrial Trade Unions *(777)*

Kingston

American Institute for Patristic and Byzantine Studies *(136)*
The National Association for the Dually Diagnosed *(643)*

Latham

Cleaning Management Institute *(357)*
Interstate Renewable Energy Council *(583)*

Liverpool

Association of Free Community Papers *(284)*
North American Society for Trenchless Technology *(822)*

Long Island City

Leather Apparel Association *(596)*

Machias

American Scientific Glassblowers Society *(178)*

Melville

The Acoustical Society of America *(11)*
International Association of Electronic Keyboard Manufacturers *(520)*

Society of Rheology *(946)*

Middle Island

Copywriters Council of America *(385)*

Millerton

American Border Leicester Association *(85)*

Mineola

National Conference of CPA Practitioners *(727)*

Mt. Vernon

International Association for Insurance Law - United States Chapter *(513)*
Society of Insurance Financial Management *(940)*

New City

National Council for Therapeutic Recreation Certification *(733)*

New Rochelle

Academy of Breastfeeding Medicine *(4)*
American Import Shippers Association *(134)*

New Windsor

Intercollegiate Broadcasting System *(507)*

New York

The Academy of American Poets *(3)*
Academy of Political Science *(8)*
Academy of Security Educators and Trainers *(9)*
Actors' Equity Association *(11)*
Advertising Council *(13)*
The Advertising Research Foundation *(13)*
Africa Travel Association *(15)*
Allied Artists of America *(25)*
American Abstract Artists *(29)*
American Academy of Research Historians of Medieval Spain *(41)*
American Academy of Teachers of Singing *(42)*
American Arbitration Association *(46)*
American Artists Professional League *(47)*
American Association for Chinese Studies *(48)*
American Association of Advertising Agencies *(53)*
American Association of Independent Music *(63)*
American Board of Multiple Specialties in Podiatry *(82)*
American Board of Perianesthesia Nursing Certification Inc. *(83)*
American Book Producers Association *(85)*
American Business Media *(87)*
American College of Counselors *(95)*
American College of Podiatric Radiologists *(101)*
American Composers Alliance *(105)*
American Copper Council *(108)*
American Council of Learned Societies *(109)*
American Council on Science and Health *(110)*
American Dance Guild *(113)*
American Federation for Aging Research *(119)*
American Federation of Musicians *(119)*
American Federation of Musicians and Employers Pension Fund *(119)*
American Foreign Law Association *(122)*
American Geriatrics Society *(126)*
American Group Psychotherapy Association *(127)*
American Guild of Musical Artists *(127)*
American Guild of Organists *(127)*
American Guild of Variety Artists *(128)*
American Indonesian Chamber of Commerce *(135)*
American Institute of Certified Public Accountants *(137)*
American Institute of Chemical Engineers *(138)*
American Institute of Graphic Arts *(139)*
American Institute of Marine Underwriters *(139)*
American Laryngological Association *(144)*
American Management Association *(146)*
American Montessori Society *(152)*
American Music Center *(153)*
American Numismatic Society *(156)*
American Printing History Association *(167)*
American Psychoanalytic Association *(168)*
American Securitization Forum *(178)*
American Skin Association *(180)*
American Society for Dental Aesthetics *(183)*
American Society of Composers, Authors and Publishers (ASCAP) *(195)*
American Society of Geolinguistics *(198)*
American Society of Hypertension, Inc. *(200)*
American Society of Journalists and Authors *(201)*
American Society of Magazine Editors *(202)*
American Society of Mechanical Engineers (ASME) *(203)*
American Sportscasters Association *(213)*
American Telemarketing Association *(215)*
American Thoracic Society *(216)*
American-European Soda Ash Shipping Association *(222)*
American-Israel Chamber of Commerce and Industry *(222)*
Antiquarian Booksellers Association of America *(224)*

Appraisers Association of America *(226)*
Archivists and Librarians in the History of the Health Sciences *(228)*
Argentine-American Chamber of Commerce *(228)*
Art and Antique Dealers League of America *(229)*
Art Dealers Association of America *(229)*
Art Directors Club *(229)*
Arthur W. Page Society *(230)*
Artist Rights Society *(230)*
ArtTable *(231)*
Asian Women in Business *(232)*
Associated Actors and Artistes of America *(234)*
Associated Press Managing Editors *(237)*
Association for Behavioral and Cognitive Therapies *(240)*
Association for Computing Machinery *(243)*
Association for Jewish Studies *(250)*
Association for Psychoanalytic Medicine *(254)*
Association for Research in Nervous and Mental Disease *(255)*
Association for the Study of Food and Society *(259)*
Association for the Study of Nationalities *(259)*
Association of Advanced Rabbinical and Talmudic Schools *(263)*
Association of American Publishers *(266)*
Association of American University Presses *(267)*
Association of Art Museum Directors *(267)*
Association of Authors' Representatives *(268)*
Association of Black Foundation Executives *(269)*
Association of Departments of English *(278)*
Association of Departments of Foreign Languages *(278)*
Association of Episcopal Colleges *(281)*
Association of Executive Search Consultants *(282)*
Association of Foreign Trade Representatives *(284)*
Association of Hispanic Healthcare Executives *(287)*
Association of Independent Commercial Producers *(287)*
Association of Junior Leagues International *(290)*
Association of Management Consulting Firms *(292)*
Association of National Advertisers *(295)*
Association of Productivity Specialists *(300)*
Association of Theatrical Press Agents and Managers *(314)*
Audio Engineering Society *(320)*
Authors Guild *(320)*
AVS: Science and Technology of Materials, Interfaces, and Processing *(325)*
BCA *(326)*
Belgian-American Chamber of Commerce *(327)*
Beverage Media Group, Inc *(328)*
Bibliographical Society of America *(328)*
BKR International *(331)*
Black Entertainment and Sports Lawyers Association *(331)*
Black Filmmaker Foundation *(331)*
Black Retail Action Group *(332)*
Book Industry Study Group, Inc. *(333)*
Brazilian American Chamber of Commerce *(334)*
BritishAmerican Business Inc. *(335)*
The Broadway League *(336)*
Builders Hardware Manufacturers Association *(337)*
Builders Association *(338)*
Business Council for International Understanding *(338)*
Cabletelevision Advertising Bureau *(340)*
Cancer Immunotherapy Consortium *(341)*
Center for Waste Reduction Technologies *(348)*
Central Conference of American Rabbis *(348)*
Chamber Music America *(350)*
Children's Book Council *(353)*
Chinese American Medical Society *(354)*
The Clearing House Association *(357)*
Cocoa Merchants' Association of America *(361)*
College Art Association *(362)*
Colombian American Association *(365)*
The Color Association of the United States *(365)*
Columbia Scholastic Press Association *(365)*
Commercial Finance Association *(366)*
Committee of Interns and Residents/ SEIU *(368)*
Community Development Venture Capital Alliance *(370)*
Composite Lumber Manufacturers Association *(372)*
Computer Security Institute *(373)*
The Concrete Industry Board *(373)*
The Conference Board *(374)*
Consolidated Tape Association *(378)*
Content Delivery and Security Association *(382)*
Copier Dealers Association *(384)*
Copper Development Association *(384)*
Copyright Society of the U.S.A. *(385)*
Cosmetic Executive Women *(387)*
Council for European Studies *(390)*
The Council for Trade and Economic Cooperation *(391)*
Council of Archives and Research Libraries in Jewish Studies *(392)*
Council of Fashion Designers of America *(393)*
Council of Literary Magazines and Presses *(395)*
Council of Nephrology Nurses and Technicians *(396)*

Council of Protocol Executives *(396)*
Council of the Americas *(398)*
Council on Renal Nutrition *(400)*
CRE Finance Council *(403)*
Dance Critics Association *(406)*
Dance Films Association *(406)*
The Danish-American Chamber of Commerce (USA) *(407)*
Decorative Furnishings Association *(408)*
Diamond Manufacturers & Importers Association of America *(411)*
Direct Care Alliance *(412)*
Direct Marketing Association *(412)*
Direct Marketing Insurance and Financial Services Council *(413)*
Dramatists Guild of America *(416)*
DRI International *(416)*
Econometric Society *(418)*
Ecuadorean American Association *(419)*
Editorial Freelancers Association *(419)*
EMTA - Trade Association for the Emerging Markets *(427)*
Fashion Accessories Shippers Association *(438)*
Fashion Accessories Shippers Association/Gemini Shippers Association *(438)*
Fashion Group International *(438)*
Federation of Modern Painters and Sculptors *(442)*
Finnish American Chamber of Commerce *(445)*
Fixed Income Analysts Society *(446)*
The Fragrance Foundation *(453)*
The French Film Office/UniFrance USA *(453)*
Fulfillment Management Association *(454)*
German American Chamber of Commerce *(460)*
Global Acetate Manufacturers Association *(461)*
Graphic Artists Guild *(465)*
Greater Blouse, Skirt and Undergarment Association *(466)*
Group for the Use of Psychology in History *(466)*
Guild of Book Workers *(467)*
Guild of Italian American Actors *(467)*
Guitar and Accessories Marketing Association *(467)*
The Harvey Society *(469)*
Hellenic-American Chamber of Commerce *(474)*
Hispanic Organization of Latin Actors *(476)*
Home Builders Association *(478)*
Home Fashion Products Association *(478)*
ICE Futures U.S. *(482)*
Icelandic American Chamber of Commerce *(482)*
IEEE Communications Society *(483)*
Illuminating Engineering Society of North America *(486)*
Indian Diamond and Colorstone Association *(492)*
Information Theory Society *(495)*
Inland Marine Underwriters Association *(496)*
Institute of Electrical and Electronics Engineers (IEEE) *(499)*
Institute of International Bankers *(501)*
Institute of Judicial Administration *(501)*
Insurance Information Institute *(505)*
Interactive Advertising Bureau *(506)*
International Academy of Television Arts and Sciences *(509)*
International Advertising Association *(509)*
International Alliance of Theatrical Stage Employees, Moving Picture Technicians, Artists and Allied Crafts of the U.S., Its Territories and Canada *(510)*
International Association for the Study of Organized Crime *(514)*
International Association of Art Critics *(516)*
International Association of Credit Portfolio Managers *(519)*
International Association of Culinary Professionals *(519)*
International Association of Microfinance Investors *(524)*
International Cargo Gear Bureau *(533)*
International Cinema Technology Association *(534)*
International Copper Association *(537)*
International Council of Shopping Centers *(538)*
International Federation of Accountants *(544)*
International Fine Print Dealers Association *(545)*
International Insurance Society *(552)*
International Licensing Industry Merchandisers' Association *(554)*
International Radio and Television Society Foundation Inc. *(562)*
International Society for the Performing Arts *(569)*
International Swaps and Derivatives Association *(576)*
International Tax Institute *(576)*
International Trademark Association *(577)*
International Women's Writing Guild *(581)*
Italian American Studies Association *(586)*
Italy-America Chamber of Commerce *(586)*
Jewelers of America *(587)*
Jeweler's Vigilance Committee *(587)*
Jewelers' Security Alliance of the United States *(587)*
Jewish Book Council *(587)*

Jewish Communal Service Association of North America **(588)**
Jewish Community Centers Association of North America **(588)**
Jewish Education Service of North America **(588)**
The Jockey Club **(588)**
JWB Jewish Chaplains Council **(590)**
Lawyers Committee on Nuclear Policy **(594)**
League of American Orchestras **(595)**
League of Resident Theatres **(595)**
Lipizzan Association of North America **(599)**
Literary Managers and Dramaturgs of the Americas **(599)**
Loan Syndication & Trading Association **(599)**
Major League Baseball Players Association **(601)**
Major League Soccer **(601)**
Man and Cybernetics Systems Society **(602)**
Market Technicians Association **(606)**
Materials Properties Council **(609)**
Media Credit Association **(610)**
Media Rating Council **(610)**
Men of Reform Judaism **(612)**
Modern Language Association **(618)**
MPA - The Association of Magazine Media **(620)**
Music Publishers Association of the United States **(622)**
Mystery Writers of America **(623)**
NABIM - the International Band and Orchestral Products Association **(623)**
National Academy of Television Arts and Science **(628)**
National Alliance for Musical Theatre **(632)**
National Antique and Art Dealers Association of America **(634)**
National Association for Multi-Ethnicity in Communications **(640)**
National Association for Oilheat Research and Education **(641)**
National Association for the Advancement of Psychoanalysis **(643)**
National Association for the Specialty Food Trade **(644)**
National Association of Episcopal Schools **(666)**
National Association of Export Companies **(666)**
National Association of Independent Publishers Representatives **(675)**
National Association of Temple Educators **(705)**
National Association of Women Artists **(709)**
National Basketball Association **(712)**
National Basketball Players Association **(713)**
National Book Critics Circle **(716)**
National Cargo Bureau **(718)**
National Cleaners Association **(722)**
National Coffee Association of the U.S.A. **(723)**
National Conference of Black Lawyers **(726)**
National Conference of Yeshiva Principals **(729)**
National Council for Research on Women **(732)**
National Eating Disorders Association **(743)**
National Federation of Community Development of Credit Unions **(748)**
National Football League **(752)**
National Guild for Community Arts Education **(757)**
National Hemophilia Foundation **(759)**
National Hockey League **(759)**
National Lawyers Guild **(768)**
National League for Nursing **(768)**
National Minority Business Council **(773)**
National Minority Supplier Development Council **(773)**
National Multiple Sclerosis Society **(774)**
National Organization of Legal Services Workers **(777)**
National Psychological Association for Psychoanalysis **(783)**
National Sculpture Society **(790)**
National Society for Graphology **(792)**
National Society of Film Critics **(793)**
National Society of Mural Painters **(794)**
National Writers Union **(806)**
The Neuropathy Association **(808)**
New Dramatists **(809)**
The New York Academy of Sciences **(809)**
New York E-Health Collaborative **(809)**
North American Natural Casing Association **(819)**
North American Performing Arts Managers and Agents **(819)**
North American-Chilean Chamber of Commerce **(823)**
Norwegian-American Chamber of Commerce **(824)**
Office and Professional Employees International Union (OPEIU) **(826)**
Online Audiovisual Catalogers **(827)**
Online Publishers Association, Inc. **(828)**
OPERA America **(828)**
Overseas Press Club of America **(835)**
Periodical and Book Association of America **(842)**
PET Resin Association **(843)**
Pipe Fabrication Institute **(849)**
Poetry Society of America **(851)**
Portugal-US Chamber of Commerce **(853)**

Practising Law Institute **(855)**
Private Art Dealers Association **(858)**
Private Label Manufacturers Association **(858)**
Professional Fraternity Association **(862)**
Professional Lighting and Sound Association **(863)**
Professional Women in Construction **(866)**
Professional Women Photographers **(866)**
Professional Women Singers Association **(866)**
Promotion Marketing Association **(866)**
Psychology Society **(868)**
The Public Relations Society of America **(870)**
Public Relations Student Society of America **(870)**
Publishers' Publicity Association **(870)**
Rabbinical Assembly **(872)**
Radio Advertising Bureau **(873)**
Regional Plan Association **(879)**
Religion Communicators Council **(880)**
The Renaissance Society of America **(881)**
Retail, Wholesale and Department Store Union **(885)**
Risk and Insurance Management Society, Inc. (RIMS) **(886)**
Securities Industry and Financial Markets Association (SIFMA) **(895)**
Security Traders Association **(895)**
Shipowners Claims Bureau, Inc. **(899)**
Shock Society **(899)**
Small Luxury Hotels of the World **(901)**
Society for General Music **(910)**
Society for Menstrual Cycle Research **(915)**
Society for Physical Regulation in Biology and Medicine **(919)**
Society of American Graphic Artists **(929)**
Society of American Historians **(929)**
Society of Corporate Secretaries and Governance Professionals **(933)**
Society of Cosmetic Chemists **(934)**
Society of Illustrators **(939)**
Society of Maritime Arbitrators **(941)**
Society of Publication Designers **(946)**
Society of Satellite Professionals International **(947)**
Society of Scribes **(947)**
Sommelier Society of America **(952)**
South Asian Journalists Association **(952)**
The Spain-United States Chamber of Commerce **(953)**
Special Interest Group for Algorithm and Computation Theory **(954)**
Special Interest Group for Computer-Human Interaction **(954)**
Special Interest Group for Computers and Society **(955)**
Special Interest Group for Design of Communication **(955)**
Special Interest Group for Measurement and Evaluation **(955)**
Special Interest Group for University and College Computing Services **(955)**
Special Interest Group on Accessible Computing **(955)**
Special Interest Group on Artificial Intelligence **(956)**
Special Interest Group on Hypertext/Hypermedia **(956)**
Special Interest Group on Operating Systems **(956)**
Special Interest Group on Software Engineering **(956)**
Stage Directors and Choreographers Society **(960)**
Stage Managers Association **(960)**
Station Representatives Association **(962)**
Subcontractors Trade Association **(964)**
Tea Association of the United States of America **(969)**
Tea Council of the U.S.A. **(969)**
Television Bureau of Advertising **(971)**
Textile Producers and Suppliers Association **(973)**
Theatre Communications Group **(973)**
Theatre Library Association **(973)**
Toy Industry Association **(976)**
Traffic Audit Bureau for Media Measurement, Inc. **(977)**
Trans-Atlantic American Flag Liner Operators and Trans-Pacific American Flag Berth Operators **(977)**
Type Directors Club **(983)**
UNITE-HERE **(985)**
United Federation of Teachers **(987)**
United Nations Staff Union **(988)**
United States Association of Independent Gymnastic Clubs **(990)**
United States Tour Operators Association **(1000)**
United States-Austrian Chamber of Commerce **(1001)**
United Synagogue of Conservative Judaism **(1001)**
University/Resident Theatre Association **(1003)**
Van Alen Institute **(1007)**
Vehicular Technology Society **(1008)**
Venezuelan American Association of the U.S. **(1008)**
Welding Research Council **(1015)**
Window Covering Manufacturers Association **(1018)**
Window Covering Safety Council **(1018)**
Women's Caucus for Art **(1022)**
Women's Jewelry Association **(1023)**

Women's National Book Association **(1023)**
Wood Flooring Manufacturers Association **(1024)**
Workers United **(1025)**
World Airline Entertainment Association **(1025)**
World Gold Trust Services **(1026)**
World Teleport Association **(1027)**
World Trade Centers Association **(1027)**
Writers Guild of America East **(1029)**
YMA Fashion Scholarship Fund **(1030)**

Patterson

National Fire Sprinkler Association **(751)**

Pearl River

ACORD - Association for Cooperative Operations Research and Development **(11)**

Pelham

Dance Educators of America **(406)**

Plattsburgh

American Military Retirees Association **(152)**

Port Jefferson

Council of American Survey Research Organizations **(392)**

Potsdam

Society for Consumer Psychology **(907)**

Poughkeepsie

Association for Symbolic Logic **(257)**
International Association of Outsourcing Professionals **(525)**
Organizational Behavior Teaching Society **(832)**

Queensbury

International Vessel Operators Dangerous Goods Association **(580)**

Rego Park

National Association of Jewelry Appraisers **(677)**

Rochester

American Association of Teachers of Italian **(74)**
The Association for the Study of Play **(260)**
Association Montessori International - United States of America **(262)**
Biological Stain Commission **(330)**
Collaborative Family Healthcare Association **(362)**
College English Association **(363)**
Gravure Association of America **(465)**
International Builders Exchange Executives/Builders Exchange Network **(532)**
International Fire Photographers Association **(545)**
National Braille Association **(716)**
Sportsplex Operators and Developers Association **(959)**

Rockville Centre

Rubber Trade Association of North America **(888)**

Rome

Electrostatic Discharge Association **(425)**
National Miniature Donkey Association **(772)**

Sackets Harbor

Safety Glazing Certification Council **(890)**

Salem

National Elevator Industry, Inc. **(745)**

Saratoga Springs

The Handcrafted Soapmakers Guild **(468)**

Shelter Island

National Academy of Building Inspection Engineers **(627)**

Sherburne

Malignant Hyperthermia Association of the United States **(602)**

Sparkill

North American Association for the Study of Religion **(812)**

Springville

Christian Chiropractors Association **(355)**

Staten Island

International Customer Service Association **(539)**

Stony Brook

American Association for the History of Medicine **(52)**
International Association for Philosophy and Literature **(514)**
National Association of State Veterans Homes **(702)**

Syosset

Interactive Multimedia and Collaborative Communications Alliance **(507)**

National Association of Uniform Manufacturers and Distributors **(707)**

Syracuse

Institute of Certified Records Managers **(499)**
Society for the Study of Social Biology **(925)**
United States Institute for Theatre Technology **(995)**

Tarrytown

ABC Children's Group **(2)**
American Booksellers Association **(85)**
American Wire Cloth Institute **(221)**
Capital Markets Credit Analysts Society **(342)**
Expansion Joint Manufacturers Association, Inc. **(436)**
Hand Tools Institute **(468)**
Institute of Store Planners **(503)**
Tubular Exchanger Manufacturers Association **(982)**

Troy

American Automatic Control Council **(78)**
National Conference of Insurance Legislators **(727)**
National Council of Legislators from Gaming States **(735)**

Victor

Independent Equipment Dealers Association **(489)**

W. Clarksville

Finnsheep Breeders Association **(445)**

W. Coxsackie

International Grooving & Grinding Association **(549)**

W. Seneca

National American Legion Press Association **(634)**

Warwick

American Rhinologic Society **(175)**

West Seneca

North American Serials Interest Group **(820)**

White Plains

Council for International Tax Education **(390)**
Greeting Card Association **(466)**
National Action Council for Minorities in Engineering (NACME) **(628)**
Silver Council **(900)**
Society of Motion Picture and Television Engineers **(942)**
United States Tennis Association **(1000)**

Whitestone

American Society of Master Dental Technologists **(202)**

Woodbury

Photoimaging Manufacturers and Distributors Association **(846)**

Woodmere

International Castor Oil Association **(533)**

Wykagyl

American Society of Sephardic Studies **(209)**

NORTH CAROLINA

Asheville

Association of Boarding Schools **(270)**

Carrboro

International Society on Thrombosis and Hemostasis **(575)**

Cary

Cotton Incorporated **(387)**
INDA, Association of the Nonwoven Fabrics Industry **(488)**

Chapel Hill

American Board of Professional Psychology **(83)**
American Cleft Palate-Craniofacial Association **(91)**
International Society of Psychiatric-Mental Health Nurses **(574)**

Charlotte

American Association of Minority Businesses **(65)**
American Humor Studies Association **(134)**
The Association of Career Firms North America **(271)**
Association of Professional Material Handling Consultants **(301)**
Association of Regulatory Boards of Optometry **(305)**
Automatic Guided Vehicle Systems **(321)**
Conference on Latin American History **(377)**
Council of State Retail Associations **(397)**
Crane Manufacturers Association of America **(403)**
Hoist Manufacturers Institute **(477)**
The Hosiery Association **(478)**
Industrial Metal Containers and Wire Decking Product Section **(494)**

Institute of Caster and Wheel Manufacturers **(498)**
International Marking and Identification Association **(556)**
Lift Manufacturers Product Section - Material Handling Institute **(597)**
Loading Dock Equipment Manufacturers **(599)**
Material Handling Industry of America **(608)**
Materials Handling and Management Society **(608)**
Monorail Manufacturers Association **(619)**
The National Campus Ministry Association **(717)**
National Optometric Association **(776)**
Order Fulfillment Solutions **(830)**
Professional Construction Estimators Association of America **(861)**
Rack Manufacturers Institute **(872)**
Retail Solutions Providers Association **(885)**
Storage Equipment Manufacturer's Association **(963)**
Truck Writers of North America **(981)**
U. S. Airline Pilots Association **(983)**

Clover

Synthetic Yarn and Fiber Association **(967)**

Cornelius

NAMTA - National Art Materials Trade Association **(635)**

Cullowhee

Educational Association of University Centers **(420)**

Durham

American Pancreatic Association **(162)**
American Society for Ethnohistory **(184)**
American Society of Papyrologists **(205)**
Association of Graduate Liberal Studies Programs **(286)**
Association of International Education Administrators **(289)**
Beta Alpha Psi **(328)**
Forest History Society **(451)**
International Association for Near Death Studies, Inc. **(513)**
International Lead Zinc Research Organization **(553)**
National Association of Blacks in Criminal Justice **(649)**
National Press Photographers Association **(782)**
Organization for Tropical Studies **(831)**
Social Science History Association **(902)**
Society for Thermal Medicine **(926)**
Undersea and Hyperbaric Medical Society **(984)**

Fletcher

The American Association of Radon Scientists and Technologists **(72)**

Fuquay Varina

National Adult Day Service Association **(629)**

Garner

American Academy of Psychotherapists **(41)**
American Society of Crime Laboratory Directors **(196)**
National Federation of Licensed Practical Nurses **(749)**

Gastonia

National Council of Textile Organizations **(737)**

Greensboro

American Men's Studies Association **(150)**
American Polarity Therapy Association **(166)**
Art Therapy Credentials Board **(230)**
Commercial Food Equipment Service Association **(366)**
Food Industry Suppliers Association **(449)**
International Professional Groomers **(561)**
National Board for Certified Counselors **(715)**
Psychometric Society **(868)**
Romanian Studies Association of America **(888)**
Society for Romanian Studies **(921)**
Southeastern Theatre Conference **(953)**

Greenville

National Maritime Alliance **(772)**

Henderson

American Society of Highway Engineers **(200)**

Hertford

Oceanic Engineering Society **(826)**

Hickory

ADED - The Association for Driver Rehabilitation Specialists **(12)**

High Point

American Home Furnishings Alliance **(132)**
Furniture Manufacturers Alliance **(454)**
High Point Market **(474)**
Interior Design Society **(508)**
International Casual Furnishings Association **(533)**

International Home Furnishings Representatives Association **(550)**
National AMBUCS **(633)**
National AMBUCS, Inc **(633)**
National Home Furnishings Association **(759)**

Hillsborough

BioCommunications Association **(329)**

Huntersville

Association on Higher Education and Disability **(319)**
Society for Disability Studies **(907)**

Indian Trail

Cleaning Equipment Trade Association **(357)**

King

Pet Sitters International **(843)**

Lake Toxaway

The Paddlesports Industry Association **(836)**

Lumberton

The International Compressor Remanufacturers Association **(536)**

Matthews

Federation of Internet Solution Providers of the Americas **(441)**

Morrisville

American Society of Echocardiography **(197)**
Council of Multiple Listing Services **(395)**
International Lactation Consultant Association **(553)**
National Association of County Recorders, Election Officials and Clerks **(660)**
Property Records Industry Association **(867)**
Real Estate Information Professionals Association **(875)**
United States Lactation Consultant Association **(996)**

New London

American Society of Furniture Designers **(198)**

Pembroke

American College Counseling Association **(92)**

Pittsboro

North American Raspberry & Blackberry Association **(820)**

Raleigh

Allied Finance Adjusters **(26)**
American Board of Anesthesiology **(81)**
American College of Epidemiology **(95)**
American Kennel Club **(143)**
American Society for Cytotechnology **(183)**
American Society for Precision Engineering **(188)**
American Society for Virology **(190)**
Association for Career and Technical Education Research **(241)**
Association for Clinical Research Training **(241)**
Association for Gnotobiotics **(247)**
Beef Improvement Federation **(327)**
Cardiovascular Credentialing International **(342)**
Controlled Environment Testing Association **(383)**
Delta Theta Phi **(409)**
Fiber Society **(443)**
The International Childbirth Education Association **(534)**
Multi-Housing Laundry Association **(621)**
National Association of Medical Minority Educators, Inc. **(680)**
National Association of State Park Directors **(702)**
National Weather Association **(804)**
RCI, Inc. **(875)**
Sewn Products Equipment and Suppliers of the Americas **(898)**
Society for In Vitro Biology **(912)**
Society of Invasive Cardiovascular Professionals **(940)**
Special Interest Group on Security, Audit, and Control **(956)**
Tobacco Associates, Inc. **(975)**
United States Tobacco Cooperative Inc **(1000)**
Waterproofing Contractors Association **(1013)**

Research Triangle Park

American Association of Textile Chemists and Colorists **(75)**
American Sexually Transmitted Diseases Association **(178)**
Brake Manufacturers Council **(334)**
Filter Manufacturers Council **(444)**
Heavy Duty Brake Manufacturers Council **(473)**
Heavy Duty Manufacturers Association **(473)**
International Society of Automation **(571)**
MEMA Information Services Council **(612)**
Motor and Equipment Manufacturers Association **(619)**

National Council for Air and Stream Improvement, Inc. *(731)*
Sigma Xi, The Scientific Research Society *(899)*

Salisbury

Association for Evolutionary Economics *(246)*
National Sportscasters and Sportswriters Association and Hall of Fame *(796)*

Southport

American Psychology-Law Society *(170)*

Spindale

American Dairy Goat Association *(112)*

Tillery

Black Farmers and Agriculturists Association *(331)*

West End

Wild Bird Feeding Industry *(1017)*
Wild Bird Feeding Institute *(1017)*

Wilmington

International Nanny Association *(557)*

Winston-Salem

American Psychological Association - Division of Psychoanalysis *(169)*
American Society for Eighteenth-Century Studies *(183)*
National Surgical Assistant Association *(798)*
Specialty Tobacco Council *(958)*

Wrightsville Beach

Board Retailers Association *(333)*

NORTH DAKOTA

Bismarck

Delta Waterfowl Foundation *(409)*
Lignite Energy Council *(598)*
United States Durum Growers Association *(993)*

Fargo

American Academy of Veterinary and Comparative Toxicology *(42)*
International Association for Impact Assessment *(513)*
Transportation Research Forum *(979)*

Mandan

National Sunflower Association *(798)*

OHIO

Akron

American Chemical Society - Rubber Division *(90)*
Association of Nurses in AIDS Care *(296)*
International Chemical Workers Union Council/UFCW *(534)*
National Subcontractors Alliance *(798)*
Wire and Cable Industry Suppliers Association *(1019)*

Athens

National Business Incubation Association *(717)*

Aurora

American Board of Nursing Specialties *(82)*
College of Optometrists in Vision Development *(364)*

Bay Village

Advertising Media Credit Executives Association *(13)*

Beachwood

American Academy of Advertising *(30)*
Institute of Mathematical Statistics *(501)*

Beavercreek

Society of Air Force Physician Assistants *(928)*

Bowling Green

National Association of Local Boards of Health *(678)*
Society for Industrial and Organizational Psychology Inc. *(912)*

Brecksville

Precision Machined Products Association *(856)*

Broadview Heights

Phi Beta Fraternity *(845)*

Canfield

National Association of Flour Distributors *(668)*

Canton

American Institute of Organbuilders *(139)*
North American Deer Farmers Association *(815)*

Cedarville

Association of Christian Librarians *(272)*

Chesterland

Organization Development Institute *(830)*

Cincinnati

American Conference of Governmental Industrial Hygienists *(107)*
Catholic Campus Ministry Association *(345)*
Construction Users Roundtable *(380)*
Cooperative Education and Internship Association *(384)*
Educational Theatre Association *(420)*
Electrocoat Association *(423)*
International Union of Toxicology *(579)*
Music Teachers National Association *(622)*
National Association of Church Personnel Administrators *(653)*
National Association of Directors of Nursing Administration in Long Term Care *(663)*
National Association of Sports Commissions *(697)*
National Association of Test Directors *(705)*
WorkPlace Furnishings *(1025)*

Cleveland

Academy of Accounting Historians *(3)*
American Association of Automatic Door Manufacturers *(54)*
American Association of Neuropathologists *(66)*
American Orff-Schulwerk Association *(158)*
American Train Dispatchers Association *(217)*
Aquarium and Zoo Facilities Association *(227)*
Association of Personal Computer User Groups *(299)*
Brotherhood of Locomotive Engineers and Trainmen *(336)*
Cemented Carbide Producers Association *(347)*
Chemical Fabrics and Film Association *(351)*
Compressed Air and Gas Institute *(372)*
Conference of Business Economists *(374)*
Door and Access Systems Manufacturers Association, International *(415)*
Fire Equipment Manufacturer's Association *(446)*
Fluid Controls Institute *(448)*
Forging Industry Association *(452)*
Heat Exchange Institute *(472)*
International Association for Energy Economics *(512)*
International Society of Explosives Engineers *(572)*
Machine Knife Association *(601)*
Marble Institute of America *(604)*
Metal Building Manufacturers Association *(613)*
National Academies of Practice *(627)*
National Association of Consumer Bankruptcy Attorneys *(657)*
National Association of Estate Planners and Councils *(666)*
National Association of Graphic and Product Identification Manufacturers *(670)*
National Coil Coating Association *(723)*
National Confectionery Sales Association *(726)*
National Sunroom Association *(798)*
National Tooling and Machining Association *(800)*
North American Small Business International Trade Educators *(821)*
Percussion Marketing Council *(841)*
Power Tool Institute, Inc. *(855)*
Pressure Washer Manufacturers Association *(857)*
Scaffolding, Shoring and Forming Institute *(892)*
The Society for Investigative Dermatology *(913)*
Society for Photographic Education *(919)*
Steel Window Institute *(963)*
The Transformer Association *(977)*
Unified Abrasives Manufacturers Association *(984)*
United Abrasives Manufacturers Association, Coated Division *(985)*
United States Association for Energy Economics *(990)*
United States Cutting Tool Institute *(993)*

Columbus

American Folklore Society *(122)*
American Guernsey Association *(127)*
American Neuropsychiatric Association *(155)*
American Society for Nondestructive Testing *(187)*
American Society for Stereotactic and Functional Neurosurgery *(189)*
American Society of Criminology *(196)*
Association for International Agricultural and Extension Education *(250)*
Association of College and University Housing Officers-International *(274)*
Association of University Interior Designers *(315)*
Business Professionals of America *(339)*
Council of Development Finance Agencies *(393)*
Edison Welding Institute *(419)*
The Entrepreneurship Institute *(430)*
Game Manufacturers Association *(456)*
Health Care Education Association *(469)*
Heating, Airconditioning and Refrigeration Distributors International *(473)*
Industrial Diamond Association of America *(493)*
International Community Corrections Association *(536)*
International Neuropsychological Society *(558)*

International Rural Sociology Association *(563)*
Iron Casting Research Institute *(585)*
National Association of Consumer Credit Administrators *(657)*
National Association of Diaconate Directors *(662)*
National Board of Boiler and Pressure Vessel Inspectors *(715)*
National Council of State Supervisors for Languages *(736)*
National Society of Insurance Premium Auditors *(794)*
National Tractor Pullers Association *(801)*
North American Farm Show Council *(816)*
Nursery and Landscape Association Executives of North America *(825)*
Parapsychological Association *(838)*
Scale Manufacturers Association *(892)*
Society for Historians of American Foreign Relations *(910)*
United Producers, Inc. *(988)*
United States of Ayrshire Breeders' Association *(997)*
United States Trotting Association *(1000)*

Copley

Tire and Rim Association *(975)*

Dayton

American Society for the Alexander Technique *(190)*
American Woman's Society of Certified Public Accountants *(221)*
Association for Accounting Administration *(237)*
Association of Destination Management Executives *(278)*
Catholic Academy for Communication Arts Professionals *(345)*
Cellulose Insulation Manufacturers Association *(347)*
Education Law Association *(420)*
Health Ministries Association *(470)*
International Union of Electronic, Electrical, Salaried, Machine, and Furniture Workers-CWA *(579)*
National Alarm Association of America *(631)*
National Association of Nephrology Technologists and Technicians *(682)*
National Flea Market Association *(751)*
National Guild of Professional Paperhangers *(757)*
National Institute of Packaging, Handling and Logistics Engineers *(765)*
National Management Association *(771)*
National Society of Accountants for Cooperatives *(793)*
SAVE International *(891)*
Ultrasonic Industry Association *(983)*
Urban History Association *(1004)*

Dublin

International League of Professional Baseball Clubs *(554)*
International Society for Prosthetics and Orthotics - United States *(569)*

Englewood

American Wine Society *(221)*

Fairborn

Society of United States Air Force Flight Surgeons *(949)*

Fairlawn

Cantors Assembly *(342)*

Fredericktown

Percheron Horse Association of America *(841)*

Gahanna

American Association for Employment in Education *(49)*

Geneva

North American Association of State and Provincial Lotteries *(813)*
North American Association of State and Provincial Lotteries *(813)*

Grand Rapids

American Bladesmith Society *(81)*

Grove City

Women's International Network of Utility Professionals *(1023)*

Harrison

American Watchmakers-Clockmakers Institute *(219)*

Hicksville

Academy of Dentistry International *(5)*

Hilliard

Perennial Plant Association *(841)*

Huber Heights

American Osteopathic Colleges of Ophthalmology and Otolaryngology - Head and Neck Surgery *(161)*

Independence

The Association of Concert Bands *(276)*
Industrial Fasteners Institute *(493)*
Precision Metalforming Association *(856)*

Kent

North American Society for the Sociology of Sport *(822)*

Kettering

Driving School Association of America *(416)*

Kirtland

Herb Society of America *(474)*

Lake Zurich

Fastener Industry Coalition *(438)*

Lakewood

International Society for Astrological Research *(565)*

Lewis Center

American Concrete Pumping Association *(106)*

Lewisburg

National Show Horse Registry *(791)*

Lima

Organization of Flying Adjusters *(832)*

Loudonville

Society of Nematologists *(942)*

Marblehead

National Association of Optometrics and Opticians *(683)*
National Association of Optometrists and Opticians *(683)*

Materials Park

ASM International *(232)*

Mayfield Heights

North American Menopause Society *(818)*

McComb

American and Delaine-Merino Record Association *(45)*

Mentor

American Measuring Tool Manufacturers Association *(148)*

Montpelier

Society for the Study of Male Psychology and Physiology *(925)*

N. Baltimore

Bridge Grid Flooring Manufacturers Association *(335)*

N. Bloomfield

Association for Living History, Farm and Agricultural Museums *(251)*

New Albany

Association for Financial Technology *(247)*
National Catholic College Admission Association *(718)*

Newark

American Trakehner Association *(217)*

North Canton

International Association for Language Learning Technology *(513)*

North Olmsted

United Transportation Union *(1001)*

Norwalk

International Hot Rod Association *(550)*

Oberlin

Association of Specialty Cut Flower Growers *(309)*
Campus Computer Resellers Alliance *(341)*
National Association of College Stores *(655)*

Olmsted Falls

American Aging Association *(43)*

Oxford

Academy of Legal Studies in Business *(6)*
American Classical League *(91)*
Association for Integrative Studies *(250)*
Delta Sigma Pi *(409)*

Painesville

International Federation for Artificial Organs *(544)*

Pickerington

American Motorcyclist Association *(153)*

Reynoldsburg

American Jersey Cattle Association/National All-Jersey Inc. *(142)*

Rocky River

Lake Carriers Association *(592)*

Sandusky

Wilson Ornithological Society *(1018)*

Seven Hills

Phi Gamma Nu Fraternity *(845)*

Strongsville

Ductile Iron Society *(417)*

Swanton

Sanitary Supply Wholesaling Association *(891)*

Tipp City

Inflatable Advertising Dealers Association *(494)*

Toledo

Farm Labor Organizing Committee *(437)*
International Society for Plastination *(568)*
National Exchange Club *(747)*

University Heights

Catholic Theological Society of America *(346)*

W. Alexandria

Women in Aviation International *(1020)*

W. Milton

International Door Association *(541)*
National Association of Nurse Massage Therapists *(682)*

Walbridge

The Construction Innovation Forum *(379)*

Washington

American Ceramics Society *(89)*

Waynesville

American Association of Police Polygraphists *(70)*

Westerville

Association for Middle Level Education *(252)*
Glass Manufacturing Industry Council *(461)*
International Executive Housekeepers Association *(543)*
National Ground Water Association *(756)*
National Institute of Ceramic Engineers *(764)*
Religion Newswriters Association *(880)*

Westlake

American Society of Sanitary Engineering *(209)*
Christian Educators Association International *(355)*
National Association of Athletic Development Directors *(647)*
National Association of Collegiate Directors of Athletics *(656)*
National Association of Collegiate Marketing Administrators *(656)*
Steel Door Institute *(962)*

Willoughby Hills

Council on Library-Media Technicians *(400)*

Wilmington

Rural Electricity Resource Council *(889)*

Woodmere

American Holistic Medical Association *(132)*

Youngstown

International Association of Hygienic Physicians *(523)*

Zanesville

Art Glass Association *(230)*
International Decorative Artisans League *(540)*
The Knitting Guild Association *(591)*
The National NeedleArts Association *(774)*
Society of Glass and Ceramic Decorated Products *(937)*
Uniform Retailers Association *(984)*

OKLAHOMA

Ada

Association of Independent Trust Companies *(288)*

Bethany

Pinto Horse Association of America *(848)*

Broken Arrow

International Council for Machinery Lubrication *(538)*
National Career Development Association *(717)*

Duncan

National Rural Water Association *(788)*

Edmond

American Weather and Climate Industry Association *(220)*
United States Fencing Coaches Association *(994)*

Kellyville

Natural Colored Wool Growers Association *(807)*

Maramec

The American Quaternary Association *(172)*

Muskogee

National Council for Impacted Schools *(732)*

Norman

Association for Continuing Higher Education *(243)*
Golf Coaches Association of America *(463)*
Native American Journalists Association *(806)*
Public Investors Arbitration Bar Association *(869)*
Society for Cinema and Media Studies *(905)*

Oklahoma City

American Choral Directors Association *(90)*
Association of Alternate Postal Systems *(264)*
Association of American Indian Physicians *(265)*
Association of Public Health Nurses *(304)*
Conference on Consumer Finance Law *(376)*
Domestic Energy Producers Alliance *(415)*
Ground Water Protection Council *(466)*
International Association of Clothing Designers and Executives *(518)*
International Professional Rodeo Association *(561)*
Interstate Oil and Gas Compact Commission *(583)*
National Christian School Association *(721)*
National Reining Horse Association *(785)*
National Stripper Well Association *(797)*
Professional Women Controllers *(865)*
Society for Applied Anthropology *(904)*

Shawnee

American Journalism Historians Association *(143)*

Stillwater

Food Distribution Research Society *(449)*
International Association for Computer Information Systems *(511)*
International Ground Source Heat Pump Association *(549)*
National Association of Government Guaranteed Lenders (NAGGL) *(670)*
School Science and Mathematics Association *(892)*

Tulsa

American Association of Petroleum Geologists *(68)*
American Osteopathic College of Occupational and Preventive Medicine *(160)*
Gas Processors Association *(456)*
Gas Processors Suppliers Association *(456)*
Kappa Kappa Iota-National *(590)*
Lawn and Garden Dealers' Association *(594)*
NALS *(625)*
National Association of Insurance Women (International) *(676)*
National Association of Legal Assistants *(677)*
National Association of Royalty Owners *(692)*
Palomino Horse Breeders of America *(837)*
Petroleum Equipment Institute *(843)*
SEPM - Society for Sedimentary Geology *(897)*
Society of Exploration Geophysicists *(935)*

OREGON

Beaverton

American Association of Professional Hypnotherapists *(71)*
Association for the Treatment of Sexual Abusers *(260)*
Continua Health Alliance *(382)*

Bend

Exhibitor Appointed Contractors Association *(435)*
Health Care Administrators Association *(469)*
Natural Areas Association *(806)*

Cannon Beach

International College of Cranio-Mandibular Orthopedics *(535)*

Corvallis

The American Society of Naturalists *(203)*
Council On Forest Engineering *(399)*
International Institute of Fisheries Economics and Trade *(551)*
National Intramural-Recreational Sports Association *(766)*

Creswell

SAFE Association *(890)*

Eugene

Association for Direct Instruction *(244)*
Forest Industries Telecommunications *(451)*
Society of North American Goldsmiths *(943)*

Florence

International Sports Heritage Association *(575)*

Glendale

National Judges Association *(767)*

Gresham

National Association of Hospital Hospitality Houses *(673)*

Hood River

National Cherry Growers and Industries Foundation *(720)*
Portable Computer and Communications Association *(853)*

Lake Oswego

Academy of Dental Materials *(5)*

Lebanon

National Employment Counseling Association *(745)*

Medford

Association of Insolvency and Restructuring Advisors *(289)*
Fur Commission USA *(454)*

Milwaukie

American Association of Homeopathic Pharmacists *(62)*

Newport

American Genetic Association *(126)*
International Association of Aquatic and Marine Science Libraries and Information Centers *(515)*

Otis

The Kite Trade Association International *(591)*

Portland

American Forest Resource Council *(123)*
Association of Telehealth Service Providers *(313)*
Building Commissioning Association *(337)*
Building Material Dealers Association *(337)*
Center for Spiritual and Ethical Education *(348)*
Church and Synagogue Library Association *(356)*
Feldenkrais Guild of North America *(442)*
Information Systems Security Association *(495)*
Intertribal Timber Council *(583)*
Maritime Fire and Safety Association *(605)*
National Association of Consumer Shows *(658)*
National Association of Professional Process Servers *(688)*
National Association of State Charity Officials *(699)*
National Conference of Women's Bar Associations *(728)*
Nonprofit Technology Network *(811)*
North American Snowsports Journalists Association *(821)*
Shareholder Services Association *(898)*
Society for Values in Higher Education *(926)*
Softwood Export Council *(951)*

Salem

Motorist Information and Services Association *(620)*
National Lamb Feeders Association *(768)*
North American Association of Educational Negotiators *(813)*
Oregon Farm Bureau Federation *(830)*

Sutherlin

KWPN of North America *(591)*

W. Linn

Institute of Certified Business Counselors *(498)*

Yamhill

American Romney Breeders Association *(176)*

PALAU

Lords Valley

Community Managers International Association *(371)*

PENNSYLVANIA

Allentown

Quality Bakers of America Cooperative *(871)*

Ardmore

Association for Comprehensive Energy Psychology *(242)*
Souvenirs, Gifts and Novelties Trade Association *(953)*

Bala Cynwyd

Catholic Medical Association *(346)*

Bellefonte

American Philatelic Society *(163)*
Independent Turf and Ornamental Distributors Association *(492)*
National Guardianship Association *(757)*

Bethlehem

American Council of Christian Churches *(109)*
Cement Employers Association *(347)*
Electronic Commerce Code Management Association *(423)*
National Association of Colleges and Employers *(655)*
The National Society of Painters in Casein and Acrylic *(794)*
PMCA: An International Association of Confectioners *(851)*

Bloomsburg

Philosophy of Science Association *(846)*

Blue Bell

American Society for Automation in Pharmacy *(181)*

Brookville

International Glove Association *(548)*

Broomall

International Association of Golf Administrators *(522)*

Bryn Mawr

Carpet Cushion Council *(343)*

Burgettstown

American Poultry Association *(167)*

Butler

Abrasive Engineering Society *(2)*
Jewelry Industry Distributors Association *(587)*
North American Society for Sport Management *(822)*

Carlisle

International Association of Approved Basketball Officials, Inc. *(515)*
International Plant Propagators Society *(560)*
Oral History Association *(830)*

Cheswick

Enhanced Protective Glass Automotive Association *(429)*

Clark

National Dog Groomers Association of America, Inc. *(743)*

Clarks Summit

Solution Mining Research Institute *(952)*

Coatesville

Dog Writers' Association of America *(415)*

Coopersburg

Paper Shipping Sack Manufacturers' Association, Inc. *(838)*

Cranberry Township

AIM Global *(17)*
AIM North America *(17)*

Dallastown

National Office Managers Association of America *(775)*
Physician Office Managers Association of America *(847)*

Dillsburg

National Peach Council *(780)*

Dingmans Ferry

American Nature Study Society *(155)*

Doylestown

National Demolition Association *(742)*
National Tactical Officers Association of America *(799)*

Drexel Hill

Association of Coupon Professionals *(277)*
Society for the Advancement of Education *(922)*

E. Petersburg

OESP - National Association of Oil and Energy Service Professionals *(826)*

Edinboro

American Association of University Administrators *(75)*

Elizabethtown

American Association of Meat Processors *(64)*

Ephrata

American Academy of State Certified Appraisers *(42)*

Erie

Association of Ancient Historians *(267)*
Truck-frame and Axle Repair Association *(981)*

Exton

National Freight Transportation Association *(753)*
Society of Cable Telecommunications Engineers *(931)*

Flourtown

North American Society for Pediatric Gastroenterology, Hepatology and Nutrition *(821)*

Ft. Washington

National Comprehensive Cancer Network *(725)*

Gardners

Wildlife Management Institute *(1017)*

Gettysburg

American College of Certified Wound Specialists *(94)*
Forestry Conservation Communications Association *(452)*
Timber Frame Business Council *(974)*

Gibsonia

IEEE Consumer Electronics Society *(483)*

Glen Mills

American Organization for Bodywork Therapies of Asia *(158)*

Greensburg

Associated Glass and Pottery Manufacturers *(236)*

Harrisburg

American College of Veterinary Radiology *(104)*
Association for Women in Sports Media *(262)*
Association of American Editorial Cartoonists *(264)*
Association of Opinion Journalists *(297)*
Association of Professional Landscape Designers *(301)*
Aviation Technician Education Council *(325)*
National Frozen and Refrigerated Foods Association *(753)*
The National Greenhouse Manufacturers Association *(756)*
Perlite Institute *(842)*
Society of Depreciation Professionals *(934)*

Hatfield

Association of Independent Manufacturers'/ Representatives, Inc. *(288)*

Hellertown

Federation of Straight Chiropractors and Organizations *(442)*

Homestead

National United Merchants Beverage Association *(803)*

Horsham

Drug Information Association *(417)*

Hunker

Mine Safety Institute of America *(616)*

Indiana

American Driver and Traffic Safety Education Association *(115)*

Irwin

Association for Hospital Medical Education *(249)*

Jenkintown

Society of Environmental Journalists *(935)*

Johnstown

Association of State and Territorial Public Health Nutrition Directors *(310)*

Kennett Square

American Public Gardens Association *(170)*

King of Prussia

American Association of Managing General Agents *(64)*
American Horticultural Therapy Association *(133)*
International Furnishings and Design Association *(548)*

Laceyville

International Association of Counselors and Therapists *(519)*

Lancaster

Distribution Business Management Association *(414)*

National Association of Addiction Treatment Providers (645)
Society for Archaeological Sciences (904)

Lansdale

Mobile Air Conditioning Society Worldwide (617)
National Association of Independent Review Organizations (624)

Lebanon

American Association of Chairs of Departments of Psychiatry (56)
American Association of Directors of Psychiatric Residency Training (60)
Cast Stone Institute (344)

Lemont

North American Society for Sport History (821)

Malvern

American Institute for CPCU - Insurance Institute of America (136)
American Risk and Insurance Association (175)
Association for the Advancement of Wound Care (258)
CPCU Society (402)

Manheim

National Wrestling Coaches Association (806)

Marienville

National Association of County Park and Recreation Officials (660)
Society of Outdoor Recreation Professionals (943)

Mechanicsburg

The United States Harness Writers' Association (994)

Media

Glass, Molders, Pottery, Plastics and Allied Workers International Union (461)
International Chiropractic Pediatric Association (534)

Monroeville

Sewing and Craft Alliance (898)

Montgomeryville

Bicycle Product Suppliers Association (329)

Mt. Union

National Association of Forensic Economics (669)

New Kensington

International Graphoanalysis Society (548)

New Tripoli

National Remotivation Therapy Organization (786)

Newtown Square

North American Catalysis Society (815)
Project Management Institute (866)
Society of Financial Service Professionals (936)

Norristown

Gamma Iota Sigma (456)

North Versailles

Independent Laboratory Distributors Association (490)

Norvelt

National Association of Farm Service Agency County Office Employees (667)

Pennsburg

Council of Chiropractic Physiological Therapeutics and Rehabilitation (392)

Perkiomenville

American Association of Birth Centers (55)

Philadelphia

Academy of Ambulatory Foot and Ankle Surgery (3)
AMC Institute (28)
American Academy of Political and Social Science (40)
American Association for Cancer Research (48)
American Board of Internal Medicine (82)
American Board of Surgery (84)
American College of Physicians (101)
American College of Physicians Services, Inc. (101)
American Entomological Society (117)
American Institute of Chemists (138)
American Law Institute (144)
American Medical Women's Association (150)
American Philological Association (163)
American Philosophical Society (164)
American Society of Media Photographers (203)
Association of Gay and Lesbian Psychiatrists (285)
Association of Library Trustees, Advocates, Friends and Foundations (291)

Association of Oncology Social Work (297)
Aviation Distributors and Manufacturers Association International (324)
Beta Phi Mu (328)
CEO Council for Growth (349)
Chemical Heritage Foundation (351)
Delta Phi Epsilon (409)
Gynecologic Oncology Group (467)
History of Dermatology Society (476)
International Association of Jewish Vocational Services (523)
International Brotherhood of Electrical Workers #98 (531)
International Federation of Nurse Anesthetists (544)
International Kitchen Exhaust Cleaning Association (553)
International Visual Literacy Association (580)
Jesuit Association of Student Personnel Administrators (587)
National Association of Catholic School Teachers (651)
National Association of Clinical Nurse Specialists (654)
National Board of Medical Examiners (716)
National Federation of Advanced Information Services (748)
National Field Selling Association (750)
National Railway Historical Society (784)
National Renal Administrators Association (786)
National Wood Tank Institute (805)
North American Horticultural Supply Association (817)
Opportunity Finance Network (829)
Printing Brokerage/Buyers Association International (857)
Radiation Therapy Oncology Group (873)
The Risk Management Association (886)
Society for Clinical Trials (906)
Society for Historians of the Early American Republic (911)
Society for Industrial & Applied Mathematics (912)
Society for Social Work Leadership in Health Care (921)
Society of Chemical Industry, American Section (932)
Society of Hospital Medicine (938)
Strategic Rail Finance (963)
Tin Stabilizers Association (975)
Twentieth-Century Spanish Association of America (983)
Victorian Society in America (1009)
Water and Sewer Distributors of America (1012)

Pittsburgh

Air and Waste Management Association (17)
American Association for the Advancement of Slavic Studies (52)
American Cable Association (87)
Association for Bridge Construction and Design (240)
Association for Slavic, East European, and Eurasian Studies (256)
Association of American Cancer Institutes (264)
Association of Earth Science Editors (279)
Association of Otolaryngology Administrators (297)
The Combustion Institute (385)
Council of State Speech-Language-Hearing Association Presidents (398)
Hardwood Manufacturers Association (468)
Hospice and Palliative Nurses Association (478)
International Society of Nurses in Genetics (573)
Latin American Studies Association (594)
The Learning Disabilities Association (596)
Marketing and Advertising Global Network (606)
National Association of EMS Educators (665)
National Association of Subrogation Professionals (704)
National Black Association for Speech, Language and Hearing (714)
National Federation of Municipal Analysts (749)
Oncology Nursing Society (827)
The Refractories Institute (878)
Rubber and Plastics Industry Conference of the United Steelworkers of America (888)
Southern Cypress Manufacturers Association (953)
Special Interest Group on Management of Data (956)
SSPC: the Society for Protective Coatings (960)
Steamfitters Local Union 449 (962)
Steel Recycling Institute (963)
United Electrical Radio & Machine Workers of America (986)
United Steelworkers of America (1001)

Plymouth Meeting

ECRI (418)

Portersville

Institute for Briquetting and Agglomeration (496)

Radnor

College Theology Society (365)

Richboro

American Tin Trade Association (217)

Scranton

Federal Magistrate Judges Association (439)

Sewickley

Binding Industries Association (329)
Graphic Arts Technical Foundation (465)
Label Printing Industries of America (591)
Printing Industry Financial Executives (858)
Technical Association of the Graphic Arts (969)

Shenandoah

The American Hair Loss Council (128)

Silver Spring

Herb Growing and Marketing Network (474)

Slatington

Analytical Laboratory Managers Association (223)

Solebury

National Paralegal Association (779)

Somerset

National Fellowship of Child Care Executives (750)

South Park

International Society for Respiratory Protection (569)

Stroudsburg

Association for Computational Linguistics (242)
International Association of Women Ministers (529)

University Park

American Pomological Society (167)
IEEE Ultrasonics, Ferroelectrics and Frequency Control Society (486)
National HEP-CAMP Association (759)

Villanova

National Catholic Band Association (718)

W. Chester

Graphic Arts Sales Foundation (465)
National Association of Traffic Accident Reconstructionists and Investigators (706)

W. Conshohocken

ASTM International (319)

Wampum

Colorado Ranger Horse Association (365)

Warrendale

Association for Iron and Steel Technology (250)
Materials Research Society (609)
Minerals, Metals and Materials Society (617)
SAE International (889)

Wayne

Aircraft Locknut Manufacturers Association (20)
Clinical and Laboratory Standards Institute (358)
The Cordage Institute (385)
Flag Manufacturers Association of America (446)
Fluid Sealing Association (448)
Gasket Fabricators Association (457)
National Classification Management Society (722)
Vibration Isolation and Seismic Control Manufacturers Association (1009)

Wexford

Association of Occupational Health Professionals in Healthcare (296)
NARSA-The International Heal Transfer Association (625)

Whitehall

Society for the Scientific Study of Sexuality (924)

Williamsport

National Association of Pupil Services Administrators (689)

Willow Grove

The International Association of Forensic Toxicologists (522)

Wyndmoor

International Academy for Child Brain Development (509)

Wynnewood

National Association of Town Watch (706)

York

Association of Food and Drug Officials (283)

RHODE ISLAND

Cranston

Association of Medical Education and Research in
  Substance Abuse **(293)**
Jewelers Shipping Association **(587)**

E. Greenwich

Association for the Calligraphic Arts **(259)**
Society for Advancement of Consulting **(903)**

Kingston

Fashion Jewelry and Accessories Trade Association
  (438)

N. Scituate

Continental Dorset Club **(382)**

Newport

Tall Ships America **(968)**

Providence

Alliance of Artists Communities **(24)**
American Academy of Addiction Psychiatry **(29)**
American Mathematical Society **(148)**
Coalition of Essential Schools **(360)**
Metal Findings Manufacturers Association **(613)**
National Prison Hospice Association **(782)**

Wakefield

Society for the Teaching of Psychology **(926)**

Warren

Association of Marina Industries **(293)**
Sail America **(890)**

Warwick

Jewelers Board of Trade **(587)**
Society of American Silversmiths **(929)**

Westerly

Nuclear Suppliers Association **(825)**

SOUTH CAROLINA

Anderson

American Academy of Ministry **(36)**
Tile Council of North America, Inc. **(974)**

Beaufort

Atlantic intra Coastal Waterway Association **(319)**

Chappells

National Verbatim Reporters Association **(803)**

Charleston

Association of Catholic Diocesan Archivists **(271)**
National Golf Course Owners Association **(755)**
North American Council of Automotive Teachers
  (815)
Professional Association of Innkeepers International
  (860)
Psi Omega Fraternity **(868)**
Society of School Librarians International **(947)**
Special Interest Group for Computer Science
  Education **(954)**
United States Club Soccer **(992)**

Clemson

American Association for Agricultural Education **(47)**
American Real Estate Society **(173)**
World's Poultry Science Association, U.S.A. Branch
  (1028)

Columbia

American Bandmasters Association **(78)**
American Comparative Literature Association **(105)**
Association for Education in Journalism and Mass
  Communication **(245)**
Association of Programs for Female Offenders **(303)**
Association of Schools of Journalism and Mass
  Communication **(307)**
Coblentz Society **(361)**
National Association for Campus Activities **(637)**
National Association of Bankruptcy Trustees **(647)**
National Association of Chapter Thirteen Trustees
  (NACTT) **(652)**
National Association of Produce Market Managers
  (686)
National Association of State Boards of Geology
  (698)
National Educational Telecommunications
  Association **(744)**
SEAMS Association **(894)**
Turkish Studies Association **(982)**

Darlington

National Motorsports Press Association **(773)**

Florence

Steel Joist Institute **(962)**

Ft. Mill

Association of Industrial Metallizers, Coaters and
  Laminators **(288)**

Converting Equipment Manufacturers Association
  (383)

Greenville

American Academy of Thermology **(42)**
American Orthopsychiatric Association **(159)**
Association of Pet Dog Trainers **(299)**
National Christian College Athletic Association **(721)**

Greenwood

North American Flowerbulb Wholesalers
  Association **(816)**

Hilton Head Island

Professional Tennis Registry **(865)**
Tennis Industry Association **(971)**

Irmo

National Conference of Bankruptcy Judges **(726)**

Lexington

International Association of Structural Movers **(528)**

Mauldin

Catholic Radio Association **(346)**

Mt. Pleasant

Association of Corporate Contributions
  Professionals **(277)**

Myrtle Beach

Grand Strand Business Association **(465)**

N. Charleston

American Metalcasting Consortium **(151)**

Orangeburg

National Association of Student Affairs Professionals
  (703)

Seneca

National Council of Examiners for Engineering and
  Surveying **(734)**

Simpsonville

International Society of Crime Prevention
  Practitioners **(572)**
Self-Insurance Institute of America, Inc. **(896)**

Summerville

United States Air Force Medical Service Corps
  Association **(989)**

SOUTH DAKOTA

Brookings

North American Case Research Association **(814)**

Mission

Association of Community Tribal Schools **(276)**

Pierre

Wheat Quality Council **(1016)**

Sioux Falls

American Society of Missiology **(203)**
ATM Industry Association **(320)**
Lutheran Educational Conference of North America
  (600)

Sturgis

Public Radio News Directors Incorporated **(870)**

Watertown

National Association of Tower Erectors **(706)**

TENNESSEE

Alcoa

National Safe Skies Alliance **(788)**

Bartlett

American College of Apothecaries **(93)**

Brentwood

American College of Neuropsychopharmacology **(98)**
American Society of Clinical Psychopharmacology
  (195)
National Association of Child Care Professionals
  (653)
Songwriters Guild of America **(952)**

Bristol

Christian Medical & Dental Associations **(356)**

Chattanooga

American Polygraph Association **(166)**
Association of Private Enterprise Education **(300)**

Cleveland

Cookie and Snack Bakers Association **(383)**

Collierville

National Alliance of Independent Crop Consultants
  (632)

Cordova

National Cotton Council of America **(730)**
National Cotton Ginners' Association **(730)**
National Cottonseed Products Association **(731)**

E. Ridge

American Association of Christian Schools **(56)**

Fairview

The Technology Institute for Music Educators **(970)**

Fayetteville

American Veterinary Dental Society **(218)**

Gallatin

Association of Procurement Technical Assistance
  Centers **(300)**

Germantown

American Association of International Healthcare
  Recruitment **(63)**
Automotive Distribution Network **(322)**
Orthopedic Surgical Manufacturers Association **(834)**

Goodlettsville

Society for Excellence in Eyecare **(909)**

Hendersonville

National Association of Small Trucking Companies
  (696)

Jefferson City

Delta Omicron **(409)**

Johnson City

EEG and Clinical Neuroscience Society **(421)**

Jonesborough

Artist-Blacksmiths' Association of North America
  (230)

Kingsport

Associated Funeral Directors International **(236)**

Knoxville

America Outdoors Association **(28)**
American Association of Veterinary Immunologists
  (76)
Assembly of Episcopal Healthcare Chaplains **(234)**
Association for Technology in Music Instruction
  (257)
College and University Professional Association for
  Human Resources **(362)**
Huntington College of Health Sciences **(481)**
International Association for Truancy and Dropout
  Prevention **(514)**
International Guards Union of America **(549)**
International Textile and Apparel Association **(577)**
National Association of Blind Teachers **(650)**
National Swine Improvement Federation **(798)**
North American Society for the Psychology of Sport
  and Physical Activity **(822)**
Society for the Study of Social Problems **(925)**
Tau Beta Pi Association **(968)**
TechLaw Group **(969)**
World Association of Veterinary Anatomists **(1025)**

LaFollette

National Association of Activity Professionals **(645)**

Lakeland

Opticians Association of America **(829)**

Loudon

Polyurethane Foam Association **(852)**

Memphis

American Association for Laboratory Animal Science
  (50)
American Cotton Shippers Association **(108)**
American Mathematical Association of Two Year
  Colleges **(147)**
American Society of Laboratory Animal Practitioners
  (201)
Association for Asian Performance **(239)**
The Folk Alliance International **(449)**
National Association of Crop Insurance Agents **(662)**
National Hardwood Lumber Association **(757)**

Murfreesboro

National Spotted Saddle Horse Association **(796)**
Walking Horse Owners Association of America
  (1011)

Nashville

Academy of Homiletics **(5)**
American Association for State and Local History
  (51)
American Board of Veterinary Practitioners **(84)**
American Economic Association **(115)**

American Society of Professional Estimators (208)
Church Music Publishers Association (356)
College Band Directors National Association (363)
College Media Association (363)
Community Banking Advisors Network (370)
Country Music Association (401)
Country Radio Broadcasters, Inc. (401)
CPA Auto Dealer Consultants Association (402)
CPA Manufacturing Services Association (402)
Diamond Council of America (411)
Fellowship of United Methodists in Music and Worship Arts (442)
Gospel Music Association (464)
Institute of Career Certification International (498)
International Association of Baptist Colleges and Universities (516)
International Bluegrass Music Association (530)
International Conference of Symphony and Opera Musicians (537)
International Engraved Graphics Association (543)
International Entertainment Buyers Association (543)
International Veterinary Academy of Pain Management (580)
Music and Entertainment Industry Educators Association (622)
Nashville Songwriters Association, International (625)
National Association of Consumer Agency Administrators (657)
National Association of Nonprofit Accountants & Consultants (682)
National Association of State Boards of Accountancy (698)
National CPA Health Care Advisors Association (740)
National Federation of Independent Business (NFIB) (748)
National Fraternal Order of Police (753)
Not-For-Profit Services Association (824)
Worldwide Printing Thermographers Association (1028)

Newbern

American Design Drafting Association International and American Digital Design Association (114)

Newport

Society of American Registered Architects (929)

Portland

American Romagnola Association (176)

Shelbyville

Spotted Saddle Horse Breeders' and Exhibitors' Association (959)
Walking Horse Trainers Association (1012)

Smyrna

University and College Designers Association (1002)

Springfield

Association of Dark Leaf Tobacco Dealers and Exporters (278)

TEXAS

Abilene

Society of Cleaning and Restoration Technicians (932)

Addison

International and American Associations of Clinical Nutritionists (510)
International Society for Heart and Lung Transplantation (566)
Romanian-U.S. Business Council (888)

Alvarado

American Miniature Horse Association (152)

Amarillo

American Quarter Horse Association (172)

Arlington

Billiard and Bowling Institute of America (329)
BMC - A Foodservice Sales and Marketing Council (332)
Bowling Proprietors' Association of America (334)
Bowling Writers Association of America (334)
International Bowling Pro Shop and Instructors Association (530)
Manufacturers Representatives of America, Inc. (603)
National Independent Automobile Dealers Association (761)
Pan American Association of Ophthalmology (837)
Paper and Plastic Representatives Management Council (838)
United States Bowling Congress (991)

Austin

Alliance of Claims Assistance Professionals (25)

American Academy of Nurse Practitioners (37)
American Botanical Council (85)
American College of Construction Lawyers (94)
American College of Musicians (98)
Association for Continuing Legal Education (244)
Association of Certified Fraud Examiners (271)
Association of Donor Recruitment Professionals (279)
Association of Progressive Rental Organizations (303)
Clean Technology & Sustainable Industries Organization (CTSI) (357)
Consortium for Advanced Management, International (378)
Emdr International Association (425)
Government Management Information Sciences (464)
Historians of Islamic Art Association (476)
Hospitality Financial and Technology Professionals (479)
International Association of Insurance Receivers (523)
National Association of Investigative Specialists (676)
National Council on Qualifications for the Lighting Professions (739)
National Guard Executive Directors Association (757)
National Guild of Piano Teachers (757)
The New Media Consortium (809)
Research Society on Alcoholism (882)
Service Dealers Association (897)
Society for Asian Music (904)
Society of Certified Insurance Counselors (932)
State Risk and Insurance Management Association (961)
Technology Transfer Society (970)
Theta Tau (973)
Wi-Fi Alliance (1016)

Bay City

Federation of Employers and Workers of America (441)

Belton

National Association of Baptist Professors of Religion (648)

Boerne

Industrial Foundation of America (493)

Bonham

American Agriculture Movement, Inc. (44)

Bryan

American Backflow Prevention Association (78)

Burton

American Bralers Association (86)

Canyon

National Opera Association (776)

Carrollton

Phi Chi Theta (845)

Cibolo

Hispanic American Police Command Officers Association (HAPCOA) (475)

College Station

Academy of Leisure Sciences (6)
Aerospace Department Chairs Association (14)
American Peanut Research and Education Society, Inc. (162)
Institute of Nautical Archaeology (502)
Research Association of Minority Professors (882)

Colleyville

Association of Finance and Insurance Professionals (283)
Automotive Service Association (323)

Commerce

Association for Specialists in Group Work (257)

Converse

Society of Military Otolaryngologists - Head and Neck Surgeons (941)

Coppell

International Association of Venue Managers (528)
Western Music Association (1016)

Corpus Christi

American Heartworm Society (130)
Cotton Growers Warehouse Association (387)
International Association of Marriage and Family Counselors (524)
Society for Advancement of Management (903)

Crowley

International Oil Mill Superintendents Association (558)

Cypress

Supply Chain Council (966)

Dallas

Academic Language Therapy Association (3)
Academy of Hospitality Industry Attorneys (5)
Alliance of National Staffing and Employment Resources (25)
American Academy of Restorative Dentistry (41)
American Association of Community Psychiatrists (58)
American Association of Psychiatric Administrators (71)
American Board of Trial Advocates (84)
American College of Psychoanalysts (102)
American Fire Sprinkler Association (121)
American Gem Trade Association (125)
American Heart Association (130)
American Lighting Association (145)
American Orthodontic Society (158)
American Society for Adolescent Psychiatry (180)
American Viola Society (219)
Associated Locksmiths of America (236)
Association of Attorney-Mediators (268)
Association of Firearm and Toolmark Examiners (283)
Center for Exhibition Industry Research (348)
Choristers Guild (355)
Consumer Health Alliance (381)
Embroidery Trade Association (425)
Football Writers Association of America (450)
Gas Machinery Research Council (456)
Global Semiconductor Alliance (463)
Holiday and Decorative Association (477)
Home Furnishings Independents Association (478)
Independent Distributors Association (489)
International Academy of Behavioral Medicine, Counseling and Psychotherapy (509)
International Association of Exhibitions and Events (520)
International Clarinet Association (535)
International Newspaper Marketing Association (558)
International Society for Adolescent Psychiatry and Psychology (565)
International Society of Bassists (571)
International Society of Beverage Technologists (571)
Learning Forward (596)
Meeting Professionals International (612)
Music Distributors Association (622)
National Association of Dental Plans (662)
National Association of Document Examiners (663)
National Association of Planning Councils (685)
National Association of School Music Dealers (692)
National Athletic Trainers Association (710)
National Black Police Association (714)
National Business Association (716)
National Collegiate Wrestling Association (724)
National Corrugated Steel Pipe Association (730)
National Council of Property Taxation (735)
Piano Manufacturers Association International (848)
Pipe Line Contractors Association (849)
Professional Retail Store Maintenance Association (864)
Retail Print Music Dealers Association (885)
Safe and Vault Technicians Association (890)
Society of Independent Professional Earth Scientists (939)
Southwest Airlines Pilots Association (953)
Uni-Bell PVC Pipe Association (984)
Women in Endocrinology (1021)
Women's Foodservice Forum (1023)

Denton

National Senior Corps Association (790)
Red Angus Association of America (877)
Society for the Study of Indigenous Languages of the Americas (925)
Society of Ethnobiology (935)
Women's Caucus for Political Science (1023)

Dripping Springs

American Red Brangus Association (174)

El Paso

Raptor Breeders of America (875)

Euless

Association of Professional Flight Attendants (301)
Federation of State Medical Boards of the United States (442)

Flower Mound

Hosa (478)

Fort Worth

Allied Pilots Association (26)
American Association of Community Theatre (58)

American Association of Professional Landmen *(71)*
American Institute of Stress *(140)*
American Paint Horse Association *(161)*
Association of Biomedical Communications Directors *(269)*
Human Milk Banking Association of North America *(481)*
International Society of Certified Electronics Technicians *(572)*
Livestock Publications Council *(599)*
National Association of Women in Construction *(710)*
National Cutting Horse Association *(741)*
North American Society for Oceanic History *(821)*
Texas Longhorn Breeders Association of America *(972)*
Voice and Speech Trainers Association *(1011)*

Forth Worth

Council of Societies for the Study of Religion *(397)*

Franklin

International Nubian Breeders Association *(558)*

Fredericksburg

National Terrazzo and Mosaic Association *(800)*

Fredonia

American Southdown Breeders Association *(211)*

Frisco

American Society of Breast Disease *(193)*
Health Information Trust Alliance (HITRUST) *(470)*

Ft. Worth

American College of Osteopathic Obstetricians and Gynecologists *(100)*
National Electronic Service Dealers Association *(745)*

Gainesville

National Tractor Parts Dealer Association *(801)*

Garland

Aestheticians International Association *(14)*
American Metal Detector Manufacturers Association *(151)*
National Association of Professional Mortgage Women *(687)*

Godley

Galiceno Horse Breeders Association *(455)*

Gouldbusk

National Horsemen's Association, Inc. *(760)*

Grand Saline

American Blonde D'Aquitaine Association *(81)*

Grapevine

National Aircraft Resale Association *(630)*

Hawkins

International Pet and Animal Transportation Association *(560)*

Houston

AASP - The Palynological Society *(2)*
American Association for Women Radiologists *(53)*
American Association of Insurance Management Consultants *(63)*
American Brahman Breeders Association *(85)*
American Bureau of Shipping *(86)*
American Catholic Philosophical Association *(88)*
American Society of Emergency Radiology *(197)*
Association of Clinical Scientists *(273)*
Association of Diving Contractors International *(279)*
Association of Energy Service Companies *(280)*
Association of Psychology Postdoctoral and Internship Centers *(303)*
Auto Suppliers Benchmarking Association *(321)*
Automotive Body Parts Association *(322)*
Benchmarking Network Association *(328)*
Coastal Conservation Association *(361)*
Cooling Technology Institute *(384)*
Council for Elementary Science International *(389)*
DeepStar Project *(408)*
Drilling Engineering Association *(416)*
Election Technology Association *(421)*
Energy Security Council *(428)*
Fiberglass Tank and Pipe Institute *(443)*
Golf Writers Association of America *(463)*
Green Hotels Association *(466)*
Intercoiffure America/Canada *(507)*
International Association for Mathematical Geosciences *(513)*
International Association of Clerks, Recorders, Election Officials and Treasurers *(518)*
International Association of Drilling Contractors *(519)*
International Association of Geophysical Contractors *(522)*

International Atherosclerosis Society *(529)*
International Contact Center Benchmarking Consortium *(537)*
International Facility Management Association *(543)*
International Institute of Synthetic Rubber Producers *(552)*
International Maintenance Institute *(555)*
International Oil Scouts Association *(558)*
Linguistic Association of Canada and the United States *(598)*
NACE International *(623)*
National Association for Black Geologists and Geophysicists *(636)*
National Association of Pipe Coating Applicators *(684)*
National Association of State Election Directors *(700)*
National Energy Services Association *(746)*
National Institute of Business and Industrial Chaplaincy *(764)*
North American Carbon Capture & Storage Association *(814)*
Petroleum Equipment Suppliers Association *(843)*
Railway Industrial Clearance Association *(874)*
Romance Writers of America *(888)*
Society for Natural Philosophy *(916)*
Society for Neuro-Oncology *(916)*
Society for Uroradiology *(926)*
Society of Abdominal Radiology *(927)*
Society of Mexican American Engineers and Scientists *(941)*
Society of Petroleum Evaluation Engineers *(944)*
Society of Petrophysicists and Well Log Analysts *(944)*
Society of Piping Engineers and Designers *(944)*
Telecommunications Benchmarking International Group *(971)*
United Development Council *(986)*
United States Organizations for Bankruptcy Alternatives (USOBA) *(997)*
United States Professional Tennis Association *(998)*
US Rice Producers Association *(1004)*
Wireless Industry Association *(1019)*

Huntsville

Association of Paroling Authorities International *(297)*
National Juvenile Court Services Association *(767)*

Ingram

Exotic Wildlife Association *(435)*

Iola

American Dexter Cattle Association *(114)*

Irving

ADSC: The International Association of Foundation Drilling *(12)*
American Association for Respiratory Care *(51)*
American College of Emergency Physicians *(95)*
American Concrete Pipe Association *(106)*
American Recovery Association *(174)*
Corrugated Polyethylene Pipe Association *(386)*
Electronic Security Association *(424)*
Emergency Medicine Residents' Association *(425)*
Energy Telecommunications and Electrical Association *(428)*
National Collegiate Baseball Writers Association *(724)*
National Society of Hispanic MBAs *(794)*
Plastics Pipe Institute *(850)*
Promotional Products Association International *(867)*
Society of Emergency Medicine Physician Assistants *(934)*
Young Presidents' Organization *(1030)*
YPO-WPO *(1030)*

Keller

National Pawnbrokers Association *(779)*

Kerrville

National Association of Pipe Fabricators *(684)*

Kingsville

Santa Gertrudis Breeders International *(891)*

Lago Vista

Communications Marketing Association *(369)*

League City

Latino Hotel Association *(594)*

Ledbetter

American Suffolk Horse Association *(214)*

Lewisville

American Donkey and Mule Society *(115)*

Longview

National Appliance Parts Suppliers Association *(634)*

Lousiana

National Council of the Multifamily Housing Industry *(737)*

Lubbock

American Association of Home Inspectors *(62)*
American Leather Chemists Association *(145)*
The American Society of Forensic Odontology *(198)*
Association for Arid Lands Studies *(239)*
National Sorghum Producers *(795)*
Plains Cotton Growers, Inc. *(849)*
Western Literature Association *(1016)*

Madisonville

American Pinzgauer Association *(165)*

Malakoff

Quarter Century Wireless Association *(872)*

Mansfield

International Federation of Leather Guilds *(544)*
Sigma Phi Delta *(899)*

Matador

National Association of Farmer Elected Committees (NAFEC) *(667)*

Mineral Wells

Society of Composers, Inc. *(933)*

Missouri City

International Academy of Compounding Pharmacists *(509)*

Montgomery

Flying Physicians Association *(448)*
National Association of Credit Union Service Organizations *(661)*

N. Richland Hills

National Association of Catastrophe Adjusters *(651)*

Nacogdoches

Association for Business Communication *(240)*
United Braford Breeders *(986)*

Palacios

Society of Professional Audio Recording Services *(945)*

Pasadena

National Association for Developmental Education *(638)*

Pearland

North American Society for Dialysis and Transplantation *(821)*

Pilot Point

Association for Equine Sports Medicine *(246)*

Pipe Creek

American Goat Society *(127)*

Plano

Armed Forces Optometric Society *(229)*
Exhibition Services and Contractors Association *(435)*
Ice Skating Institute *(482)*
National Association of Mortgage Brokers *(681)*
Restaurant Facility Management Association *(884)*
Society of Diagnostic Medical Sonographers *(934)*
WEB: Worldwide Employee Benefits Network *(1014)*

Ranger

American Ostrich Association *(161)*

Richardson

American Literary Translators Association *(146)*
Automotive Oil Change Association *(323)*
Distribution Contractors Association *(414)*
International Association of Electrical Inspectors *(520)*
Kappa Psi Pharmaceutical Fraternity, Inc. *(590)*
National Association of Church Business Administration *(653)*
National Student Employment Association *(797)*
The North American Rail Shippers Association *(820)*
Society of Petroleum Engineers *(944)*

Rocksprings

American Angora Goat Breeder's Association *(45)*

San Angelo

Mohair Council of America *(618)*

San Antonio

American Council for Construction Education *(109)*
American Payroll Association *(162)*
American Sesame Growers Association *(178)*
American Society of Primatologists *(208)*
Beefmaster Breeders United *(327)*
Braunvieh Association of America *(334)*

Hispanic Association of Colleges and Universities *(475)*
International Association for Colon Hydrotherapy *(511)*
International Brangus Breeders Association *(531)*
International Society for Developmental Psychobiology *(566)*
Medical Mycological Society of the Americas *(611)*
National Association of Property Tax Representatives - Transportation, Energy, Communications *(688)*
Pan American Allergy Society *(837)*
Research and Development Associates for Military Food and Packaging Systems *(881)*

San Marcos

Computer Assisted Language Instruction Consortium *(372)*
International Society of Applied Intelligence *(570)*

Schertz

Society for Physician Assistants in Pediatrics *(919)*

Seguin

International Association of Equine Dentists *(520)*

Selma

Non Commissioned Officers Association (NCOA) *(811)*

Shallowater

Progressive Gardening Trade Association *(866)*

Southlake

Division 1-A Athletic Directors Association *(415)*

Sugar Land

Energy Traffic Association *(428)*
Women Band Directors International *(1020)*

The Woodlands

American Pediatric Society *(162)*
American Society of Pediatric Nephrology *(206)*
Independent Armored Car Operators Association *(488)*
Powder Coating Institute *(854)*
Society for Pediatric Research *(918)*

Tow

The American Association of Code Enforcement *(57)*

Tyler

Religious Communication Association *(880)*

Victoria

National Association of Steel Pipe Distributors *(703)*

Waco

American Football Coaches Association *(122)*
American Society of Limnology and Oceanography *(202)*
National Association of Academic Advisors for Athletes *(645)*

Whitesboro

American Brahmousin Council *(85)*

Wichita Falls

Texas Alliance of Energy Producers *(972)*

UTAH

Clearfield

Society for Epidemiologic Research *(908)*

Draper

American Apitherapy Society *(46)*

Farmington

American Society of Podiatry Executives *(208)*

Herriman

Association for Vascular Access *(261)*

Highland

Food Industry Association Executives *(449)*

Kaysville

National Association of Arms Shows *(647)*

Layton

National EMS Pilots Association *(746)*

Midvale

Executive Women International *(435)*

Orem

International Surface Fabricators Association *(576)*

Park City

United States Ski and Snowboard Association *(999)*

Pleasant Grove

National Slag Association *(792)*

Provo

American Association of Presidents of Independent Colleges and Universities *(71)*
International Association for Business and Society *(511)*
National Dance Council of America *(741)*
The Rural Sociological Society *(889)*
Society for the Advancement of Scandinavian Study *(923)*

Riverton

Weather Modification Association *(1014)*

Salt Lake City

Academy of Clinical Laboratory Physicians and Scientists *(4)*
Air Medical Physician Association *(19)*
American Academy of Professional Coders *(40)*
Institute of Business Appraisers *(498)*
Law and Society Association *(594)*
Major Cities Chiefs Association *(601)*
National Association for Family Child Care *(638)*
National Association of Certified Valuation Analysts *(652)*
National Association of Decorative Fabric Distributors *(662)*
National Association of Health Data Organizations *(671)*
National Association of Industrial Bankers *(675)*
National Drilling Association *(743)*
United Natural Products Alliance *(988)*
United Potato Growers of America *(988)*
Utah Association of Public Charter Schools *(1006)*
Wilderness Medical Society *(1017)*

VERMONT

Barre

Barre Granite Association *(326)*

Bennington

American Cream Draft Horse Association *(111)*

Brattleboro

Holstein Association USA *(477)*
Organic Trade Association *(830)*

Danville

American Society of Dowsers *(197)*

Essex Junction

American Electrology Association *(116)*

Montpelier

International Regional Magazine Association *(562)*

Putney

National Association of Certified Professional Midwives *(651)*

S. Burlington

Funeral Consumers Alliance *(454)*

Shelburne

American Morgan Horse Association *(152)*

Swanton

International Maple Syrup Institute *(555)*

Waitsfield

National Association of State Head Injury Administrators *(701)*

White River Junction

Human Capital Institute *(480)*

Woodstock

International Furniture Rental Association *(548)*

VIRGIN ISLANDS

St. Thomas

Caribbean Cable Communications *(343)*

VIRGINIA

Alexandria

Academy of Clinical Research Professionals *(4)*
Academy of Managed Care Pharmacy *(6)*
Academy of Physicians in Clinical Research *(8)*
Accreditation Council for Accountancy and Taxation *(9)*
Aeronautical Repair Station Association *(14)*
AHS International - The Vertical Flight Society *(17)*
Air Traffic Control Association *(19)*
Airport Consultants Council *(21)*
Ambulatory Surgery Center Association *(28)*
American Academy of Facial Plastic and Reconstructive Surgery *(34)*
American Academy of Otolaryngology-Head and Neck Surgery *(39)*
American Academy of Physician Assistants *(40)*

American Art Therapy Association, Inc. *(46)*
American Association for Dental Research *(49)*
American Association for Marriage and Family Therapy *(50)*
American Association for the Study of Liver Diseases *(52)*
American Association of Airport Executives *(53)*
American Association of Colleges of Pharmacy *(57)*
American Association of Family and Consumer Sciences *(61)*
American Association of Poison Control Centers *(70)*
American Association of Port Authorities *(70)*
American Automotive Leasing Association *(78)*
American Bankruptcy Institute *(79)*
American Board for Certification in Orthotics and Prosthetics, Inc. (ABC) *(81)*
The American Board of Facial Plastic and Reconstructive Surgery *(82)*
American Chamber of Commerce Executives *(89)*
American College of Health Care Administrators *(96)*
American College of International Physicians *(97)*
American College of Nurse Practitioners *(99)*
American College of Osteopathic Surgeons *(100)*
American Correctional Association *(108)*
American Council on the Teaching of Foreign Languages *(111)*
American Counseling Association *(111)*
American Diabetes Association *(115)*
American Escrow Association *(118)*
American Gear Manufacturers Association *(125)*
American Geological Institute *(126)*
American Horticultural Society *(133)*
American Independent Writers *(135)*
American Indian Higher Education Consortium *(135)*
American Inns of Court *(135)*
American Institute of Constructors *(138)*
American International Automobile Dealers Association *(142)*
American League of Lobbyists *(145)*
American Medical Group Association *(149)*
American Mental Health Counselors Association *(151)*
American Moving and Storage Association *(153)*
American Network of Community Options and Resources (ANCOR) *(155)*
American Orthotic and Prosthetic Association *(159)*
American Peanut Council *(162)*
American Physical Therapy Association *(164)*
American Physical Therapy Association - Private Practice Section *(165)*
American Public Communications Council *(170)*
American Rock Mechanics Association *(176)*
American School Bus Council *(177)*
American School Counselor Association *(177)*
American Seed Trade Association *(178)*
American Society for Clinical Pharmacology and Therapeutics *(182)*
American Society for Horticultural Science *(185)*
American Society for Training and Development *(190)*
American Society of Clinical Oncology *(194)*
American Society of Consultant Pharmacists *(195)*
American Society of Military Comptrollers *(203)*
American Society of Naval Engineers *(204)*
American Society of Travel Agents *(210)*
American Sportfishing Association *(212)*
American Staffing Association *(213)*
American Statistical Association *(213)*
American Subcontractors Association *(214)*
American Translators Association *(217)*
American Wire Producers Association *(221)*
Analytical and Life Science Systems Association *(223)*
APPA - Leadership in Educational Facilities *(225)*
ASIS International *(232)*
Assisted Living Federation of America *(234)*
Association for Adult Development and Aging *(238)*
Association for Counselor Education and Supervision *(244)*
Association for Education and Rehabilitation of the Blind & Visually Impaired *(245)*
Association for Federal Information Resources Management *(246)*
Association for Financial Counseling and Planning Education *(246)*
Association for Gay, Lesbian, Bisexual, and Transgender Issues in Counseling *(247)*
Association for Spiritual, Ethical and Religious Values in Counseling *(257)*
Association for Supervision and Curriculum Development (ASCD) *(257)*
Association for Women in Communications *(261)*
Association for Women in Science *(262)*
Association of Air Medical Services *(264)*
Association of Baccalaureate Social Work Program Directors *(269)*
Association of College and University Clubs *(274)*
Association of Consulting Foresters of America *(276)*
Association of Corporate Travel Executives (ACTE) *(277)*

Association of Credit Union Internal Auditors *(278)*
Association of Government Accountants *(286)*
Association of Independent Corrugated Converters *(288)*
Association of Machinery and Equipment Appraisers *(292)*
Association of Marketing Service Providers *(293)*
Association of Naval Aviation *(295)*
Association of Old Crows *(297)*
Association of Pool and Spa Professionals *(299)*
Association of Postgraduate Physician Assistant Programs *(300)*
Association of Professors of Medicine *(302)*
Association of Program Directors in Internal Medicine *(302)*
Association of Specialty Professors *(309)*
Association of the United States Navy, Inc. *(314)*
Catholic Charities USA *(345)*
Clerkship Directors in Internal Medicine *(358)*
Club Managers Association of America *(359)*
Color Marketing Group *(365)*
Color Pigments Manufacturers Association, Inc. *(365)*
Community Financial Services Association of America CFSA *(370)*
Community Health Charities of America *(371)*
Composite Can and Tube Institute *(372)*
Construction Specifications Institute *(380)*
Convention Industry Council *(383)*
Council for Affordable and Rural Housing *(388)*
Council for Electronic Revenue Communication Advancement *(389)*
Council of North American Insulation Manufacturers Association *(396)*
Council of Professional Associations on Federal Statistics *(396)*
Council on Social Work Education *(400)*
Disaster Recovery Contractors Association (DRCA) *(413)*
Enlisted Association of the National Guard of the United States *(429)*
Entrepreneurs' Organization *(430)*
Envelope Manufacturers Association *(430)*
Environmental Bankers Association *(430)*
Federal Managers Association *(439)*
Federally Employed Women (FEW) *(440)*
Federation of State Boards of Physical Therapy *(442)*
Fleet Reserve Association *(447)*
Flight Safety Foundation *(448)*
Forest Landowners Tax Council *(451)*
Glass Packaging Institute *(461)*
Global Business Travel Association *(462)*
Global Cold Chain Alliance *(462)*
Health Industry Distributors Association *(469)*
Helicopter Association International *(473)*
Independent Electrical Contractors *(489)*
Independent Insurance Agents & Brokers of America, Inc. *(490)*
Independent Lubricant Manufacturers Association *(490)*
Independent Office Products and Furniture Dealers Association *(490)*
Insulation Contractors Association of America *(504)*
International Association for Cold Storage Construction *(511)*
International Association for Dental Research *(512)*
International Association of Amusement Parks and Attractions(IAAPA) *(515)*
International Association of Chiefs of Police *(517)*
International Association of Counseling Services *(518)*
International Association of Movers *(525)*
International Association of Refrigerated Warehouses *(527)*
International Bottled Water Association *(530)*
International Brain Injury Association *(531)*
International Corrugated Packaging Foundation *(537)*
International Digital Enterprise Alliance *(540)*
International Institute of Ammonia Refrigeration *(551)*
International Military Community Executives Association *(556)*
International Public Management Association for Human Resources *(562)*
International Road Federation *(563)*
International Shippers Association *(564)*
International Sign Association *(564)*
International Sleep Products Association *(565)*
The International Wood Products Association *(581)*
Judge Advocates Association *(589)*
Licensing Executives Society *(597)*
Machinery Dealers National Association *(601)*
Major County Sheriffs' Association *(601)*
Meals on Wheels Association of America *(609)*
Mental Health America *(612)*
Methanol Institute *(614)*
Midwest Dairy Coalition *(615)*
Military Officers Association of America (MOAA) *(616)*

Military Operations Research Society *(616)*
Musculoskeletal Tumor Society *(621)*
National Active and Retired Federal Employees Association *(629)*
National Affordable Housing Management Association *(629)*
National Air Transportation Association *(630)*
National Alcohol Beverage Control Association *(631)*
National Alliance for Accessible Golf *(631)*
National Association for Practical Nurse Education and Service *(641)*
National Association for Rehabilitation Leadership *(642)*
National Association for Alcoholism and Drug Abuse Counselors *(646)*
National Association of Chain Drug Stores *(652)*
National Association of Children's Hospitals and Related Institutions *(653)*
National Association of Convenience Stores *(658)*
The National Association of Crime Victim Compensation Boards *(661)*
National Association of Drug Court Professionals *(663)*
National Association of Elementary School Principals *(664)*
National Association of Farmers Market Nutrition Programs *(667)*
National Association of Free Clinics *(669)*
National Association of Mental Health Planning Advisory Council *(680)*
National Association of Partners in Education *(683)*
National Association of Police Organizations *(685)*
National Association of Postal Supervisors *(685)*
National Association of Postmasters of the United States *(685)*
National Association of Professional Employer Organizations *(687)*
National Association of Professional Insurance Agents *(687)*
National Association of Service Providers in Private Rehabilitation *(695)*
National Association of Sign Supply Distributors *(696)*
National Association of State Directors of Developmental Disabilities Services, Inc. *(700)*
National Association of State Directors of Special Education *(700)*
National Association of State Directors of Veterans Affairs *(700)*
National Association of State Energy Officials *(700)*
National Association of State Mental Health Directors *(701)*
National Association of State Mental Health Program Directors *(701)*
National Association of Telecommunications Officers and Advisors *(705)*
National Association of Truck Stop Operators(NATSO) *(707)*
National Beer Wholesalers Association *(713)*
National Biosolids Partnership *(713)*
National Cancer Registrars Association *(717)*
National Center for Homeopathy *(719)*
National Community Pharmacists Association *(725)*
National Council for Agricultural Education *(731)*
National Council of Commercial Plant Breeders *(734)*
National Defense Transportation Association *(742)*
National District Attorneys Association *(743)*
National Drug Court Institute *(743)*
National Emergency Number Association *(745)*
National Federation of Republican Women *(750)*
National Head Start Association *(758)*
National Home Infusion Association *(760)*
National Hospice & Palliative Care Organization *(760)*
National Industries for the Blind *(763)*
National Investor Relations Institute *(767)*
National League of Postmasters of the United States *(768)*
National Military Family Association, Inc. *(772)*
National Motor Freight Traffic Association, Inc. *(773)*
National Naval Officers Association *(774)*
National Office Products Alliance *(776)*
National Onsite Wastewater Recycling Association *(776)*
National Organization of Black Law Enforcement Executives *(777)*
National Pace Association *(778)*
National Parent Teachers Association *(779)*
National Rehabilitation Association *(785)*
National Renderers Association *(786)*
National Rural Letter Carriers' Association *(788)*
National School Boards Association *(789)*
National School Transportation Association *(790)*
National Sheriffs' Association *(791)*
National Society of Accountants *(793)*
National Society of Black Engineers *(793)*
National Society of Professional Engineers *(794)*
National Stone, Sand, and Gravel Association *(796)*
National Wooden Pallet and Container Association *(805)*

North American Insulation Manufacturers Association *(817)*
Office Furniture Dealers Alliance *(826)*
Online Lenders Alliance *(827)*
Operations Security Professionals Society *(828)*
The Optical Lab Division *(829)*
Outdoor Power Equipment Aftermarket Association *(835)*
Outdoor Power Equipment Institute *(835)*
Parcel Shippers Association *(838)*
Passenger Vessel Association *(839)*
PCIA - The Wireless Infrastructure Association *(840)*
Peanut and Tree Nut Processors Association *(840)*
Petroleum Convenience Alliance for Technology Standards *(843)*
Pharmaceutical Industry Labor Management Association (PILMA) *(844)*
Physician Assistant Education Association *(847)*
Plant Growth Regulation Society of America *(849)*
Power and Communications Contractors Association *(855)*
Professional Engineers in Private Practice *(861)*
Public Risk Management Association *(870)*
Registry of Interpreters for the Deaf *(879)*
Research!America *(882)*
Salt Institute *(891)*
Self Storage Association *(896)*
SOCAP International *(902)*
Society for Human Resource Management *(911)*
Society for Marketing Professional Services *(914)*
Society for the History of Discoveries *(923)*
Society of American Florists *(928)*
Society of American Military Engineers *(929)*
Society of General Internal Medicine *(937)*
Society of Government Meeting Professionals *(938)*
Special Libraries Association *(956)*
Spill Control Association of America *(958)*
State Government Affairs Council *(961)*
Sunglass Association of America *(965)*
TechServe Alliance *(971)*
TESOL International Association *(971)*
Textile Rental Services Association of America *(973)*
Towing and Recovery Association of America *(976)*
Transportation Intermediaries Association *(978)*
Truck Renting and Leasing Association *(981)*
Truckload Carriers Association *(981)*
Truss Plate Institute *(981)*
United Motorcoach Association *(988)*
United States Contract Tower Association *(992)*
The Vision Council *(1010)*
Water Environment Federation *(1013)*
Wire Rope Technical Board *(1019)*
Women Construction Owners and Executives, USA *(1020)*

Annandale

Connected International Meeting Professionals Association *(377)*
National Emergency Equipment Dealers Association *(745)*
Naval Submarine League *(807)*

Arlington

Academy of Rail Labor Attorneys *(8)*
The Accrediting Commission of Career Schools and Colleges *(10)*
Aerospace Industries Association of America *(14)*
Agricultural and Food Transporters Conference *(16)*
Air Conditioning Contractors of America *(18)*
Air Conditioning, Heating and Refrigeration Institute (AHRI) *(18)*
Air Force Association *(18)*
Airport Minority Advisory Council (AMAC) *(21)*
Alliance for Responsible Atmospheric Policy *(23)*
The Aluminum Association, Inc. *(27)*
American Anthropological Association *(45)*
American Apparel & Footwear Association *(46)*
The American Association of Eye and Ear Centers of Excellence *(61)*
American Association of Motor Vehicle Administrators *(65)*
American Association of Pharmaceutical Scientists *(68)*
American Butter Institute *(87)*
American Chiropractic Association *(90)*
American Composites Manufacturers Association *(105)*
American Court and Commercial Newspapers *(111)*
American Feed Industry Association *(120)*
American Fiber Manufacturers Association *(121)*
American Intellectual Property Law Association *(141)*
American Mobile Telecommunications Association *(152)*
American Psychiatric Association *(168)*
American Psychiatric Nurses Association *(168)*
American Society of Pension Professionals & Actuaries *(206)*
American Society of Transplant Surgeons *(210)*
American Sugar Alliance *(214)*
American Trucking Associations *(218)*

American Waterways Operators (220)
Armed Forces Special Agents Association (229)
Asbestos Cement Product Producers Association (231)
Associated Builders and Contractors (235)
Associated General Contractors of America (AGC) (236)
Association for Africanist Anthropology (238)
Association for Enterprise Information (245)
Association for Feminist Anthropology (246)
Association for Postal Commerce (253)
The Association for Social Anthropology in Oceania (256)
Association for the Advancement of Medical Instrumentation (258)
Association for Unmanned Vehicle Systems International (261)
Association of Black Anthropologists (269)
Association of Children's Museums (272)
Association of Clinical Research Professionals (273)
Association of Educational Service Agencies (280)
Association of Fundraising Professionals (285)
Association of Latina and Latino Anthropologists (291)
Association of Public Data Users (304)
Association of Public Television Stations (304)
Association of State and Territorial Health Officials (310)
Association of State Drinking Water Administrators (311)
Association of the United States Army (313)
Association of University Programs in Health Administration (316)
Casualty Actuarial Society (344)
Cement Kiln Recycling Coalition (347)
Chief Administrators of Catholic Education (352)
Child Care Aware of America (353)
Chlorine Institute (354)
Chorus America (355)
Coal Trading Association (359)
College Savings Foundation (364)
COMISS Network - The Network on Ministry in Specialized Settings (366)
Consumer Electronics Association (381)
Council for Community and Economic Research (388)
Council for Exceptional Children (390)
Council of Better Business Bureaus (392)
Council of Defense and Space Industry Associations (393)
Council on Foundations (399)
Dental Trade Alliance (410)
Distribution and LTL Carriers Association (414)
Employee Assistance Professionals Association (426)
Employee Assistance Society of North America (426)
FBI Agents Association (438)
Federal Bar Association (438)
Federation of State Humanities Councils (442)
Food Marketing Institute (449)
Formaldehyde Council, Inc. (452)
Forum of Regional Associations of Grantmakers (452)
Foundation for International Meetings (453)
Gasification Technologies Council (457)
Halogenated Solvents Industry Alliance (468)
Halon Alternatives Research Corporation (468)
Healthcare Distribution Management Association (471)
Hearth, Patio and Barbecue Association (472)
The History of Education Society (477)
IFIA Americas Committee Inc. (486)
Independent Association of Accredited Registrars (488)
Industrial Research Institute (494)
Infectious Diseases Society of America (494)
Insurance Institute for Highway Safety (505)
International Association of Independent Tanker Owners (523)
International Cast Polymer Alliance (533)
International Cast Polymer Association (533)
International Fragrance Association North America (547)
International Liquid Terminals Association (554)
International Pharmaceutical Excipients Council of the Americas (560)
International Safety Equipment Association (ISEA) (563)
Internet Security Alliance (582)
Joint Electron Device Engineering Council (589)
Manufactured Housing Institute (602)
Manufacturers Alliance/MAPI Inc. (603)
Manufacturers of Emission Controls Association (603)
Medical Imaging and Technology Alliance (611)
Military Chaplains Association of the U.S. (616)
Military Chaplains Association of the United States (616)
National Accounting and Finance Council (628)
National Air Carrier Association (630)
National Alliance for Hospice Access (631)

National Alliance of State Science and Mathematics Coalitions (633)
National Apartment Association (634)
National Association for College Admission Counseling (637)
National Association for the Practice of Anthropology (644)
National Association of Chemical Distributors (652)
National Association of Federal Credit Unions (667)
National Association of Publicly Traded Partnerships (689)
National Association of State Boards of Education (698)
National Association of State Credit Union Supervisors (699)
National Association of Veterans Affairs Physicians and Dentists (708)
National Board for Professional Teaching Standards (NBPTS) (715)
National Catholic Educational Association (718)
National Catholic Educational Exhibitors (718)
National Defense Industrial Association (742)
National Electrical Manufacturers Association (744)
National Federation of Press Women (749)
National Genealogical Society (754)
National Grocers Association (756)
National Ice Cream Mix Association (761)
The National Industrial Transportation League (763)
National Institute for State Credit Union Examination (764)
National Lime Association (769)
National Milk Producers Federation (772)
National Private Truck Council (782)
National Rural Electric Cooperative Association (788)
National Science Teachers Association (790)
National Society of Black Physicists (793)
National Tank Truck Carriers (799)
National Telecommunications Cooperative Association (799)
National Training and Simulation Association (801)
National Venture Capital Association (803)
National Water Resources Association (804)
National Waterways Conference (804)
Navy League of the United States (807)
Newspaper Association of America (810)
North American Technician Excellence (823)
Partnership for Air-Conditioning, Heating Refrigeration Accreditation (839)
Patent and Trademark Office Society (839)
Patent Office Professional Association (839)
Pellet Fuels Institute (841)
Petroleum Marketers Association of America (843)
Pharmaceutical Education and Research Institute (844)
Photoluminescent Safety Association (846)
Plastics Foodservice Packaging Group (850)
Professional Services Council (865)
Public Notice Resource Center (869)
Radio Technical Commission for Maritime Services (873)
Rehabilitation Engineering and Assistive Technology Society of North America (879)
Retail Industry Leaders Association (884)
Rice Millers' Association (886)
Ryan White Medical Providers Coalition (889)
Snack Food Association (901)
Society for Healthcare Epidemiology of America (910)
Society for the Anthropology of North America (923)
Society for the Anthropology of Work (923)
Society for the Exploration of Psychotherapy Integration (923)
Society of Federal Labor and Employee Relations Professionals (936)
Society of State Leaders of Health and Physical Education (947)
Steel Shipping Container Institute (963)
TAUC - The Association of Union Constructors (968)
Technology and Maintenance Council of American Trucking Associations (970)
Telecommunications Industry Association (971)
Tortilla Industry Association (976)
Touchstone Energy Cooperatives (976)
U.S. Rice Producers Group (983)
United States-Taiwan Business Council (989)
United States Dairy Export Council (993)
United States Wheat Associates, Inc. (1000)
USA Rice Council (1004)
USA Rice Federation (1004)
Vinyl Institute (1009)
Waterways Council, Inc. (1014)
Worldwide ERC (1028)

Ashburn

Inter-Company Marketing Group (506)
National Association for Drama Therapy (638)
National Contract Management Association (729)
National Recreation and Parks Association (784)
National Therapeutic Recreation Society (800)

Baskerville

National Black Farmers Association (714)

Blacksburg

Adhesion Society (12)
Aquacultural Engineering Society (227)
International Society for Educational Planning (566)
International Society for Quality-of-Life Studies (569)
Society of Reliability Engineers (946)

Bon Air

Healthcare Compliance Packaging Council (470)

Broadlands

Custom Tailors and Designers Association of America (406)

Burke

America's Small Business Development Center Network (29)
Association of Small Business Development Centers (308)
Defense Orientation Conference Association (408)
Pakistan American Business Association (837)

Centreville

International Society of Fire Service Instructors (572)
National Association for Search and Rescue (642)

Chantilly

Automotive Parts Remanufacturers Association (323)
Compressed Gas Association (372)
The Door and Hardware Institute (416)
Mineralogical Society of America (617)
Remanufacturing Institute (881)
Sheet Metal and Air Conditioning Contractors' National Association (898)
Women in Cable Telecommunications, Inc. (1020)

Charlottesville

American Psychosocial Oncology Society (170)
Association for Documentary Editing (245)
Cancer Patient Education Network (341)
CFA Institute (350)
Community College Business Officers (370)
International Psycho-Oncology Society (561)
International Society for Prenatal Diagnosis (568)
Modular Building Institute (618)
National Association of College Auxiliary Services (655)
North American Society for Social Philosophy (821)
Society for the History of Technology (923)
Society of Quality Assurance (946)
University Council for Educational Administration (1002)

Chesapeake

Association for the Advancement of Computing in Education (258)
Association of Girl Scout Executive Staff (285)
Independent Hardee's Franchisee Association (490)
The National Association of Marine Surveyors, Inc. (679)
National Association of Residential Property Managers (691)

Christiansburg

American Association of Veterinary Clinicians (76)
North American Mycological Association (818)

Clifton

American Association of Independent Claims Professionals (63)
National Transit Benefits Association (801)

Cullen

National Military Intelligence Association (772)

Culpeper

Association of Social Work Boards (309)

Danville

Tube Council of North America (982)

Dumfries

Society of Former Special Agents of the Federal Bureau of Investigation (937)

Fairfax

Alliance of Information and Referral Systems (25)
American Association of Attorney-Certified Public Accountants (54)
American Association of Healthcare Administrative Management (61)
American Association of Pastoral Counselors (68)
American Bail Coalition (78)
American College of Bankruptcy (93)
American Concrete Pressure Pipe Association (106)
American Conference for Irish Studies (106)
American Society for Therapeutic Radiology and Oncology (190)

American Society of Cataract and Refractive Surgery *(194)*
American Society of Ophthalmic Administrators *(205)*
American String Teachers Association *(213)*
American Wholesale Marketers Association *(221)*
Armed Forces Communications and Electronics Association *(228)*
Association for Women in Mathematics *(261)*
Association of Military Colleges and Schools of the United States *(294)*
Association of Residents in Radiation Oncology *(306)*
Association of Writers and Writing Programs *(318)*
Atlantic Seaboard Wine Association *(319)*
Contact Lens Association of Ophthalmologists *(382)*
Council on the Safe Transportation of Hazardous Articles *(401)*
Electronic Funds Transfer Association *(423)*
Independent Educational Consultants Association *(489)*
InfoComm International *(495)*
International Association of Fire Chiefs *(521)*
International Association of Women in Fire and Emergency Services *(528)*
International Test and Evaluation Association *(577)*
Laboratory Products Association *(592)*
Marine Corps Reserve Association *(605)*
National Armored Car Association *(635)*
National Association of Independent Life Brokerage Agencies *(674)*
National Association of Miscellaneous, Ornamental and Architectural Products Contractors *(681)*
National Association of Reinforcing Steel Contractors *(691)*
National Council of Erectors, Fabricators and Riggers *(734)*
National Pest Management Association *(780)*
National Rifle Association of America *(787)*
National Utility Contractors Association (NUCA) *(803)*
Optical Imaging Association *(829)*
The Propeller Club of the United States *(867)*
Radiology Business Management Association *(874)*
Recreation Vehicle Dealers Association of North America *(876)*
Recreation Vehicle Rental Association *(877)*
Silver Users Association *(900)*
Society for Industrial Microbiology *(913)*
Society for Technical Communication *(922)*
Society of Chairmen of Academic Radiology Oncology Programs *(932)*
Society of Independent Gasoline Marketers of America (SIGMA) *(939)*
Society of Interventional Radiology *(940)*
Society of Neurointerventional Surgery *(942)*
Specialized Carriers and Rigging Association *(957)*
Specialty Graphic Imaging Association *(957)*
Spray Polyurethane Foam Alliance *(959)*

Falls Church

Accrediting Bureau of Health Education Schools *(10)*
American Association for Budget and Program Analysis *(48)*
American Association of Early Childhood Educators *(60)*
American Industrial Hygiene Association *(135)*
American Institute for International Steel *(136)*
American Pipe Fittings Association *(165)*
American Textile Machinery Association *(216)*
American Thyroid Association *(216)*
Association for Healthcare Philanthropy *(248)*
Association of Executive and Administrative Professionals *(281)*
Association of the Wall and Ceiling Industry *(314)*
Association of Vacuum Equipment Manufacturers *(316)*
Automotive Maintenance and Repair Association *(323)*
Community Associations Institute (CAI) *(370)*
Consortium of Forensic Science Organizations *(378)*
Corporate Facility Advisors, Inc. *(386)*
Data Interchange Standards Association *(407)*
Defense Fire Protection Association *(408)*
Exterior Insulation and Finish Systems Industry Members Association (EIMA) *(436)*
Foodservice & Packaging Institute, Inc. *(450)*
GAMA International *(455)*
HUBZone Contractors National Council *(480)*
International Association of Emergency Managers *(520)*
International Aviation Ground Support Association *(529)*
International Chiropractors Association *(534)*
International Real Estate Federation - American Chapter *(562)*
Irrigation Association *(585)*
National Association of Dental Assistants *(662)*
National Association of Government Communicators *(670)*

National Association of Insurance and Financial Advisors *(675)*
National Association Of Insurance and Financial Advisors(NAIFA) *(676)*
National Association of Physician Nurses *(684)*
National Association of State Emergency Medical Services Officials *(700)*
National Association of University Forest Resources Programs *(707)*
Naval Enlisted Reserve Association *(807)*
Pipeline Research Council International, Inc. *(849)*
Plumbing-Heating-Cooling Contractors - National Association *(851)*
Process Equipment Manufacturers' Association *(858)*
Quality Service Contractors *(871)*
Society for Personality Assessment *(918)*
Society of Competitive Intelligence Professionals *(933)*
Society of Research Administrators International *(946)*
Tire Retread and Repair Information Bureau *(975)*
United States Clean Heat & Power Association *(992)*
Voluntary Protection Programs Participants' Association, Inc. *(1011)*

Forest

American Association of Christian Counselors *(56)*

Franklin

Peanut Growers Cooperative Marketing Association *(840)*

Fredericksburg

American Canoe Association *(88)*
American Traffic Safety Service Association *(217)*
Catholic Association of Diocesan Ecumenical and Interreligious Officers *(345)*
International Parking Institute *(559)*
National Petroleum Management Association *(780)*
Society of Medical Consultants to the Armed Forces *(941)*
United States Parachute Association *(997)*

Front Royal

Brotherhood of Railroad Signalmen *(336)*

Gainesville

Commission on Accreditation for Law Enforcement Agencies Incorporation *(367)*

Garrisonville

Clinical Social Work Association *(359)*
National Association of Shell Marketers *(696)*

Glen Allen

American Association of Integrated Healthcare Delivery Systems *(63)*
American Association of Managed Care Nurses *(64)*
National Association of Managed Care Physicians *(679)*
National Association of Managed Care Physicians *(679)*

Great Falls

Express Association of America *(436)*
International Cadmium Association *(532)*

Greenville

International Waterlily and Water Gardening Society *(580)*

Hamilton

Basic Acrylic Monomer Manufacturers *(326)*
Methacrylate Producers Association *(614)*

Hampton

Central Intercollegiate Athletic Association *(349)*

Harrisonburg

Institute of Certified Professional Managers *(498)*

Haymarket

Corporate Crisis Response Officers Association *(385)*
NORA: Association of Responsible Recyclers *(811)*

Herndon

American Association of Medical Dosimetrists *(65)*
Association for Facilities Engineering *(246)*
Association of Major City and County Building Officials *(292)*
Association of Muslim Social Scientists of North America *(295)*
NAIOP, The Commercial Real Estate Development Association *(366)*
Contact Lens Society of America *(382)*
Electronic Distribution Show Corporation *(423)*
Industrial Designers Society of America *(493)*
Interactive Media Entertainment & Gaming Association *(507)*
Interlocking Concrete Pavement Institute *(508)*
International Electronic Manufacturing Initiative *(542)*

NACHA - The Electronic Payments Association *(623)*
National Concrete Masonry Association *(725)*
National Institute of Governmental Purchasing *(765)*
National Organization of Life and Health Insurance Guaranty Association *(777)*
National Rural Telecommunications Cooperative *(788)*
Professional Landcare Network *(863)*
SCORE Association *(893)*
Silicones Environmental, Health and Safety Council of North America *(900)*
United States Army Warrant Officers Association *(990)*

Lake Anna

Giant Screen Cinema Association *(460)*

Lake Ridge

Association of Civilian Technicians *(273)*
Federal Physicians Association *(439)*
ISA -The Association of Learning Providers *(586)*
National Association of Assistant United States Attorneys *(647)*

Leesburg

American Roentgen Ray Society *(176)*
American Wood Council *(221)*
Automotive Training Managers Council *(324)*
Composite Panel Association *(372)*
International Council of Air Shows *(538)*
Professional Housing Management Association *(862)*
Society for Imaging Informatics in Medicine *(912)*

Lexington

Society for Military History *(915)*

Lorton

Black Theatre Network *(332)*
International Hyperbaric Medical Association, Inc. *(551)*

Lovettsville

Silica Fume Association *(899)*

Luray

United States Internet Industry Association *(995)*

Lynchburg

Professional Putters Association *(864)*

Manassas

Air and Expedited Motor Carriers Association *(17)*
Association of Teacher Educators *(312)*
Automotive Recyclers Association *(323)*
Express Carriers Association *(436)*
Garden Writers Association *(456)*
Institute of Navigation *(502)*
International Federation of Pharmaceutical Wholesalers *(544)*
Mulch and Soil Council *(621)*
National Rehabilitation Counseling Association *(785)*
National Religious Broadcasters *(785)*
Truck Trailer Manufacturers Association *(981)*

Martinsville

International Window Film Association *(581)*

McLean

Academic Pediatric Association *(3)*
Allergy and Asthma Network Mothers of Asthmatics *(22)*
Alliance for Massage Therapy Education *(23)*
Alliance for Women in Media *(24)*
American Academy of Clinical Toxicology *(31)*
American Academy of Health Physics *(35)*
American Ambulance Association *(44)*
American Association of Political Consultants *(70)*
American Association of Tissue Banks *(75)*
American Board of Health Physics *(82)*
American Frozen Food Institute *(124)*
American Psychosomatic Society *(170)*
American Society of Women Accountants (ACC) *(211)*
American Truck Dealers *(217)*
Americas Association of Cooperative/Mutual Insurance Societies *(222)*
AMT - The Association For Manufacturing Technology *(222)*
Associated Owners and Developers *(236)*
Association Foundation Group *(262)*
Association Media and Publishing *(262)*
Association of Christian Therapists *(273)*
Association of Former Intelligence Officers *(284)*
Association of Hispanic Advertising Agencies *(287)*
Association of Medical School Pediatric Department Chairs *(293)*
Association of Pediatric Program Directors *(298)*
Association of Veterinary Biologics Companies *(317)*
Automotive Trade Association Executives *(324)*
Board of Registered Polysomnographic Technologists *(333)*
Construction Industry Round Table, Inc. *(379)*

Construction Management Association of America **(379)**
Emergency Department Practice Management Association (EDPMA) **(425)**
Enterprise Wireless Alliance **(429)**
Environmental Design Research Association **(431)**
Food Processing Suppliers Association **(449)**
Frozen Potato Products Institute **(454)**
Health Physics Society **(470)**
Hospitality Sales and Marketing Association International **(479)**
The International Alliance for Women **(510)**
International Association for Continuing Education and Training **(511)**
International Association of Protocol Consultants **(527)**
International Foodservice Distributors Association **(546)**
International Frozen Food Association **(547)**
International Society for Neuronal Regulation **(567)**
International Society for the Study of Dissociation **(570)**
International Society for the Study of Trauma and Dissociation **(570)**
Land Mobile Communications Council **(593)**
Meat Industry Suppliers Alliance **(610)**
National After School Association **(629)**
National Association of Biology Teachers **(648)**
National Association of Development Companies **(662)**
National Association of Mortgage Bankers **(681)**
National Association of Multicultural Media Executives **(681)**
National Automobile Dealers Association **(711)**
National Child Support Enforcement Association **(721)**
National Fisheries Institute **(751)**
National Frozen Pizza Institute **(754)**
National Investment Company Service Association **(767)**
National Yogurt Association **(806)**
Pediatric Endocrine Society **(840)**
Pedorthic Footwear Association **(840)**
Public Media Business Association **(869)**
Resolve, The National Infertility Association **(883)**
Semiconductor Environmental Safety and Health Association **(896)**
SnowSports Industries America **(902)**
Society for Developmental and Behavioral Pediatrics **(907)**
Society for Integrative and Comparative Biology **(913)**
Society for Risk Analysis **(920)**
Student Youth and Travel Association **(964)**
Tuna Council **(982)**
United States Psychiatric Rehabilitation Association **(998)**
Women in Government Relations, Inc. **(1021)**
Women Networking in Electronic Transactions **(1022)**

Mechanicsville

International Association of Bedding and Furniture Law Officials **(516)**
International Microwave Power Institute **(556)**

Merrifield

Marine Corps League **(605)**
National Wildlife Federation **(805)**

Middleburg

American College of Veterinary Anesthesiologists **(103)**
American Water Resources Association **(220)**

Midlothian

Alliance of Cardiovascular Professionals **(25)**
National Association of Disability Evaluating Professionals **(663)**
Teaching-Family Association **(969)**

Mount Vernon

United Engineering Foundation **(986)**

New Kanet

American Health Planning Association **(130)**

Norfolk

The Association for Consortium Leadership **(243)**

Oak Hill

Petroleum Technology Transfer Council **(844)**

Occoquan

World Federation for Mental Health **(1026)**

Portsmouth

Association for Ambulatory Behavioral Healthcare **(238)**
International Reciprocal Trade Association **(562)**

Potomac Falls

American Edged Products Manufacturers Association **(115)**
Architectural Woodwork Institute **(228)**
National Association of Public Insurance Adjusters **(689)**

Purcellville

Newspaper Purchasing Management Association **(810)**

Quantico

Marine Corps Association **(604)**
Marine Corps Aviation Association **(604)**

Remington

American Devon Cattle Association **(114)**

Reston

American Academy of Audiology **(31)**
American Academy of Craniofacial Pain **(32)**
American Academy of Otolaryngic Allergy **(38)**
American Alliance for Health, Physical Education, Recreation and Dance **(44)**
American Association for Health Education **(49)**
American Association for Physical Activity and Recreation **(51)**
American Association of Engineering Societies **(60)**
American Brachytherapy Society **(85)**
American College of Nuclear Medicine **(98)**
American College of Radiology **(102)**
American Congress of Rehabilitation Medicine **(107)**
American Hardwood Export Council **(129)**
American Institute of Aeronautics and Astronautics **(136)**
American Institute of Biological Sciences **(137)**
American Press Institute **(167)**
American Society of Appraisers **(192)**
American Society of Civil Engineers **(194)**
Animal Transportation Association **(223)**
Architectural Engineering Institute **(227)**
Association for Advanced Life Underwriting **(238)**
Association for Conflict Resolution **(243)**
The Association for Research in Business Education - Delta Pi Epsilon **(255)**
Association of Free Standing Radiation Oncology Centers **(284)**
Association of Insurance Compliance Professionals **(289)**
Association of Investment Management Sales Executives **(289)**
Association of School Business Officials International **(306)**
Association of TeleServices International, Inc. **(313)**
Association of Vascular and Interventional Radiographers **(316)**
Brick Industry Association **(335)**
Council for Employment Law Equity (CELE) **(389)**
The Council of Landscape Architectural Registration Boards **(395)**
Council on Technology Teacher Education **(401)**
Distributive Education Clubs of America (DECA) **(415)**
Environmental and Water Resources Institute of the American Society of Civil Engineers **(430)**
Environmental Mutagen Society **(431)**
EUCG, Inc. **(433)**
Family, Career and Community Leaders of America **(437)**
Fleischner Society **(447)**
Future Business Leaders of America - Phi Beta Lambda **(455)**
Hardwood Plywood and Veneer Association **(468)**
Inter-Society Color Council **(506)**
International Council for Health, Physical, Education, Recreation, Sport and Dance **(537)**
International Graphic Arts Education Association **(548)**
International Technology and Engineering Educators Association **(576)**
Internet Society **(582)**
Kitchen Cabinet Manufacturers Association **(591)**
Management Association for Private Photogrammetric Surveyors **(602)**
Meat Importers Council of America **(609)**
Microscopy Society of America **(615)**
Music Industry Conference **(622)**
National Art Education Association **(635)**
National Association for Business Teacher Education **(636)**
National Association for Girls and Women in Sport **(639)**
The National Association for Music Education (Formerly MENC) **(641)**
National Association for Research in Science Teaching **(642)**
National Association for Sport and Physical Education **(643)**
National Association of Corporate Treasurers **(658)**
National Association of Professional Background Screeners **(686)**

National Association of Schools of Art and Design **(693)**
National Association of Schools of Dance **(693)**
National Association of Schools of Music **(694)**
National Association of Schools of Theatre **(694)**
National Association of Secondary School Principals **(694)**
National Association of Student Councils **(703)**
National Business Education Association **(716)**
National Council of Athletic Training **(734)**
National Council of Teachers of Mathematics **(737)**
National Dance Association **(741)**
National Insulation Association **(766)**
National Society of Certified Healthcare Business Consultants **(793)**
North American Meat Association **(818)**
North American Society for Cardiovascular Imaging **(821)**
NPES, The Association for Suppliers of Printing, Publishing, and Converting Technologies **(824)**
Packaging Machinery Manufacturers Institute **(836)**
Product Liability Advisory Council **(859)**
Recreation Vehicle Industry Association **(877)**
Safety Pharmacology Society **(890)**
Society for Organic Petrology **(917)**
Society for Pediatric Radiology **(918)**
Society of Computed Body Tomography and Magnetic Resonance **(933)**
Society of Financial Examiners **(936)**
Society of Nuclear Medicine **(943)**
Society of Radiologists in Ultrasound **(946)**
Society of Toxicologic Pathologists **(948)**
Society of Toxicologic Pathology **(948)**
Society of Toxicology **(948)**
Sports Lawyers Association **(959)**
Technology Student Association **(970)**
Teratology Society **(971)**
Wine and Spirits Shippers Association **(1018)**
Wireless Innovation Forum **(1019)**
Workgroup for Electronic Data Interchange **(1025)**

Richmond

American Academy of Anesthesiologist Assistants **(30)**
American College of Osteopathic Pediatricians **(100)**
American Insurance Marketing and Sales Society **(141)**
American Osteopathic Academy of Orthopedics **(159)**
American Society of Extra-Corporeal Technology **(197)**
Association for Psychological Type International **(254)**
Clinical Orthopaedic Society **(358)**
Conductors Guild **(374)**
Independent Research Libraries Association **(491)**
International Association of Law Enforcement Intelligence Analysts **(523)**
International Council on Hotel, Restaurant and Institutional Education **(539)**
International Society of Political Psychology **(573)**
Master Pools Guild, Inc. **(608)**
Medical Fitness Association **(611)**
National Alliance of State Pharmacy Associations **(633)**
Oriental Rug Retailers of America, Inc. **(833)**
Philosophy of Education Society **(846)**
Resort Hotel Association **(883)**
Respiratory Nursing Society **(883)**
Society for Neuroscience in Anesthesiology and Critical Care **(916)**
Society for Pediatric Anesthesia **(917)**
Society of Cardiovascular Anesthesiologists **(931)**
Uniformed Services Academy of Family Physicians **(984)**

Roanoke

Association of United States Night Vision Manufacturers **(315)**
Mechanical Association Railcar Technical Services **(610)**
Society of Pharmaceutical and Biotech Trainers **(944)**

Smithfield

American Society of Marine Artists **(202)**

Spotsylvania

Combat Contractor's Association **(366)**

Springfield

American Astronautical Society **(77)**
The American Board of Opticiary and the National Contact Lens Examiners **(83)**
Association of Former OSI Special Agents **(284)**
Chief Petty Officers Association **(352)**
Christian Legal Society **(356)**
Commercial Vehicle Training Association **(367)**
Law Enforcement Alliance of America **(594)**
National Association for Uniformed Services **(644)**
National Band Association **(712)**

Protestant Church-Owned Publishers Association *(868)*
Senior Army Reserve Commanders Association *(897)*
Society for Imaging Science and Technology *(912)*
Society of Military Widows *(941)*
United States Coast Guard Chief Petty Officers Association *(992)*

Stafford

National Association of Credit Specialists *(661)*
National Chief Petty Officers' Association *(721)*

Staunton

Association of College Administration Professionals *(273)*

Stephens City

Welsh Pony and Cob Society of America *(1015)*

Sterling

American Medical Student Association *(150)*
International Cemetery, Cremation and Funeral Association *(533)*
International Society of Air Safety Investigators *(570)*
Jewish Funeral Directors of America *(588)*
National Association of Urban Hospitals *(708)*
Nurses Organization of Veterans Affairs *(825)*

Triangle

United Mine Workers of America *(988)*

Unionville

System Safety Society *(967)*

Vienna

Alarm Industry Communication Committee *(21)*
American Boiler Manufacturers Association *(84)*
American League for Exports and Security Assistance *(145)*
Association of Organ Procurement Organizations *(297)*
Brain Injury Association of America *(334)*
Central Station Alarm Association *(349)*
Education Industry Association *(420)*
International Cost Estimating and Analysis Association effective *(537)*
International Institute for Energy Conservation *(551)*
Manufacturers Standardization Society of the Valve and Fitting Industry, Inc. *(603)*
Manufacturers Standardization Society of the Valve and Fittings Industry *(603)*
National Academy of Elder Law Attorneys, Inc. *(627)*
National Association for Medical Direction of Respiratory Care *(640)*
National Council of Agricultural Employers *(733)*
National Court Reporters Association *(740)*
National Glass Association *(755)*
National Woodland Owners Association *(806)*
Specialized Information Publishers Association *(957)*
United States Apple Association *(989)*

Virginia Beach

Association of Management/International Association of Management *(292)*
Espionage Research Institute International *(433)*
National Air Filtration Association *(630)*
National Certification Council for Activity Professionals *(720)*

Warrenton

American Society of Transportation and Logistics *(210)*
Association of Military Banks of America *(294)*
Caribbean Basin Ethanol Producer Association (CBEPA) *(343)*
Council of Industrial Boiler Owners (CIBO) *(394)*
Educational Book and Media Association *(420)*
Intersure, Ltd. *(583)*
QVM/CMC Vehicle Manufacturers Association *(872)*
Society for Applied Learning Technology *(904)*

Washington

American Osteopathic College of Proctology *(161)*

Williamsburg

American Judges Association *(143)*
Conference of Chief Justices *(374)*
Conference of State Court Administrators *(376)*
Council of Colleges of Arts and Sciences *(393)*
Court Information Technology Officer Consortium *(402)*
Electric Utility Fleet Managers Conference *(422)*
Measurement, Control and Automation Association *(609)*
National Association for Court Management *(637)*
National Center for State Courts *(720)*
National College of Probate Judges *(724)*
Society for Cultural Anthropology *(907)*

Winchester

Evangelical Council for Financial Accountability *(434)*

WASHINGTON

Battle Ground

American Land Rights Association *(144)*

Bellevue

International Saw and Knife Association *(564)*
Mobile Marketing Association *(618)*
National Association of Vertical Transportation Professionals *(708)*
Pet Partners *(842)*

Bellingham

National Council for Workforce Education *(733)*
Society for Economic Anthropology *(908)*
SPIE - The International Society for Optical Engineering *(958)*

Benton City

American Beefalo Association *(80)*

Blaine

Consortium of Behavioral Health Nurses and Associates *(378)*

Booragoon

National Aquaculture Council *(635)*

Bremerton

Eight Sheet Outdoor Advertising Association *(421)*

Cheney

Society of Photo-Technologists *(944)*

Covington

International Miniature Cattle Breeders Society *(556)*

Dayton

National Conference of Local Environmental Health Administrators *(727)*

Des Moines

American Baptist Homes and Caring Ministries *(79)*

Edmonds

American Academy of Oral Medicine *(38)*
American Medallic Sculpture Association *(148)*
Institute of Tax Consultants *(503)*
The National Federation of Paralegal Associations, Inc. *(749)*

Ellensburg

Family and Consumer Sciences Education Association *(437)*

Gig Harbor

International Association of Certified Thermographers *(517)*
International Thermographers Association *(577)*
Structural Insulated Panel Association *(964)*

Kelso

American Agricultural Law Association *(44)*

Kent

Aerospace Futures Alliance *(14)*

Kirkland

Association of Women Soil Scientists *(317)*
The Bluetooth Special Interest Group *(332)*

Lynnwood

American Society of Tax Professionals *(209)*

Maple Valley

Advanced Transit Association *(13)*

Moxee

Hop Growers of America *(478)*

Mukilteo

1394 Trade Association *(1)*

Ocean Shores

Transportation Clubs International *(978)*

Richland

Organic Reactions Catalysis Society *(830)*

Ridgefield

National Association of Temple Administrators *(705)*

Seattle

Adventure Travel Trade Association *(13)*
American Correctional Chaplains Association *(108)*
American Legend Cooperative *(145)*
The American Society of Pediatric Neurosurgeons *(206)*
Association for the Advancement of Baltic Studies *(258)*
Association of Academic Health Sciences Library *(263)*
At-Sea Processors Association *(319)*

Council of International Investigators *(395)*
Deep Sea Fishermen's Union *(408)*
Fishing Vessel Owners' Association *(446)*
Foundation for Russian-American Economic Cooperation *(453)*
Glass Art Society *(461)*
International Association for the Study of Pain *(514)*
International Association of Tour Managers - North American Region *(528)*
International Guild of Symphony, Opera and Ballet Musicians *(549)*
National Association of Disability Examiners *(663)*
National Association of Ecumenical and Interreligious Staff *(664)*
National Center for Asia-Pacific Economic Cooperation *(719)*
Northwest Natural Resource Group *(824)*
Professional Bowlers Association *(861)*
Society for Slovene Studies *(921)*

Shoreline

Aviation Industry CBT Committee *(324)*

Snohomish

International Academy of Gnathology - American Section *(509)*

Spokane

Metaphysical Society of America *(614)*
Timber Products Manufacturers Association *(975)*

Sumas

Cedar Shake and Shingle Bureau *(347)*
Sales and Marketing Executives International, Inc. *(890)*

Sumner

School Social Work Association of America *(892)*

Tacoma

American Society for Environmental History *(184)*
APA The Engineered Wood Association *(224)*
Guild of American Luthiers *(467)*

Tumwater

National Association of Elevator Safety Authorities International *(665)*

Vancouver

American Navion Society *(155)*
The Institute of Inspection, Cleaning and Restoration Certification *(500)*
Western Dredging Association *(1015)*

Walla Walla

Association of Seventh-Day Adventist Librarians *(308)*

Woodinville

Log Home Builders Association of North America *(600)*

Yakima

Academy of Organizational and Occupational Psychiatry *(7)*
Northwest Fruit Exporters *(824)*

WEST VIRGINIA

Charles Town

National Institute for Farm Safety, Incorporation *(764)*

Charleston

National Conference of Appellate Court Clerks *(726)*
National Council of Coal Lessors *(734)*
Wholesale Beer Association Executives of America *(1016)*

Morgantown

AACE International *(1)*
International Writing Centers Association *(581)*

WISCONSIN

Appleton

National Association of Tax Professionals *(704)*

Beloit

American Milking Shorthorn Society *(152)*
The Brown Swiss Association *(336)*

Brookfield

American Society of Golf Course Architects *(198)*
International Foundation of Employee Benefit Plans *(547)*
International Society of Certified Employee Benefit Specialists *(572)*
National Funeral Directors Association *(754)*
Society of Risk Management Consultants *(947)*

Cedarburg

Association of Pedestrian and Bicycle Professionals **(298)**

Clinton

Red and White Dairy Cattle Association **(877)**

Eau Claire

The Association for Science Teacher Education **(256)**

Elm Grove

Specialty Tools and Fasteners Distributors Association **(958)**

Germantown

Federation of Environmental Technologists, Inc. **(441)**

Hales Corners

Intermarket Agency Network **(508)**

Kaukauna

NANDA International **(625)**

Kimberly

Association of Physician Assistants in Obstetrics and Gynecology **(299)**

La Crosse

National Conference on Research in Language and Literacy **(729)**
Orthopaedic Section - American Physical Therapy Association **(833)**

LaFarge

CROPP Cooperative / Organic Valley **(405)**

Lake Delton

American Shire Horse Association **(179)**

Lake Geneva

National Clay Pipe Institute **(722)**

Luxemburg

International Silo Association **(564)**

Madison

American Academy of Cosmetic Dentistry **(31)**
American Association of Certified Orthoptists **(56)**
American College of Veterinary Pathologists **(104)**
The American Electrophoresis Society **(116)**
American Institute of Bangladesh Studies **(137)**
American Institute of the History of Pharmacy **(141)**
American Osteopathic Academy of Sports Medicine **(159)**
American Society of Agronomy (ASA, CSSA, SSSA) **(191)**
American Society of Preventive Oncology **(208)**
Association of Family and Conciliation Courts **(282)**
Association of State Energy Research and Technology Transfer Institution **(311)**
Association of State Floodplain Managers **(311)**
Association of State Supervisors of Mathematics **(311)**
Business Forms Management Association **(339)**
Credit Union Executives Society **(403)**
Credit Union National Association, Inc. **(404)**
Crop Science Society of America **(404)**
Forest Products Society **(451)**
International Association of Industrial Accident Boards and Commissions **(523)**
International Dairy-Deli-Bakery Association **(540)**
International Neural Network Society **(558)**
International Society of Psychiatric Consultation Liaison Nurses **(574)**
Media Communications Association International **(610)**
National Association of Professors of Hebrew **(688)**
National Conference of Bar Examiners **(726)**
National Council on Measurement in Education **(739)**
North American Lake Management Society **(817)**
Preventive Cardiovascular Nurses Association **(857)**
The Psychonomic Society **(868)**
Purebred Dairy Cattle Association **(871)**
Society for Psychophysiological Research **(919)**
Society for Research on Nicotine and Tobacco **(920)**
Society for the Study of Reproduction **(925)**
Society for Wetland Scientists **(927)**
Society of Clinical and Medical Hair Removal **(933)**
Soil Science Society of America **(951)**
Special Interest Group for Architecture of Computer Systems **(954)**
States Organization for Boating Access **(962)**
Structural Building Components Association **(964)**
Transportation Development Association **(978)**
Visual Artists Rights Coalition **(1010)**
World Council of Credit Unions, Inc. **(1026)**

Menasha

Pyrotechnics Guild International **(871)**

Menomonee Falls

American Society of Agricultural Consultants **(191)**

Mequon

Association of Lutheran Secondary Schools **(292)**
International Molded Fibre Association **(556)**

Middleton

International Association of Music Libraries, United States Branch **(525)**
Music Library Association **(622)**

Milwaukee

Agricultural & Applied Economics Association **(16)**
Alliance for Children and Families **(22)**
American Academy for Cerebral Palsy and Developmental Medicine **(29)**
American Academy of Allergy, Asthma, and Immunology **(30)**
American Academy of Emergency Medicine **(33)**
American Association of Children's Residential Centers **(56)**
American Association of Dental Editors **(60)**
American Association of Medical Society Executives **(65)**
American College of Mohs Surgeons **(98)**
American Malting Barley Association **(146)**
American Society for Mohs Histotechnology **(187)**
American Society for Quality **(189)**
American Society of Gene & Cell Therapy **(198)**
American Society of Photographers **(207)**
American Venous Forum **(218)**
Association of Equipment Manufacturers **(281)**
Chinese Language Teachers Association **(354)**
Clinical Immunology Society **(358)**
Compact Loader/Compact Excavator Council **(371)**
Contractors Pump Bureau **(383)**
Farm Equipment Council **(437)**
Forestry Equipment Council **(452)**
iNARTE, Inc. **(487)**
Industrial Perforators Association **(494)**
Industrial/Agricultural Mower Manufacturers Council **(494)**
International Association for Orthodontics **(513)**
International Society for Quality of Life Research **(569)**
International Transplant-Skin Cancer Collaborative **(578)**
Manufacturers Elevating and Work Platform Council **(603)**
Milking Machine Manufacturers Council **(616)**
Mounted Breakers Manufacturers Bureau **(620)**
Movement Disorder Society **(620)**
National Association for Fixed Annuities **(639)**
National Association of Catholic Chaplains **(651)**
National Association of Credential Evaluation Services, Inc. **(661)**
National Association of Health Education Centers **(671)**
National Association of Minority and Women Owned Law Firms **(680)**
National Association of School Safety and Law Enforcement Officers **(693)**
National Association of Service Managers **(695)**
National Fluid Power Association **(751)**
NIBA - The Belting Association **(810)**
Nine to Five, National Association of Working Women **(811)**
Pi Sigma Epsilon **(847)**
Polyurethane Manufacturers Association **(852)**
Portable and Stationary Crushing Bureau **(853)**
Power Crane and Shovel Association **(855)**
Scoliosis Research Society **(893)**
Snow & Ice Management Association **(901)**
Society for Mucosal Immunology **(916)**
Society of American Travel Writers **(930)**
Society of Behavioral Medicine **(930)**
Trencher Equipment Committee **(980)**
Trenchless Equipment Committee **(980)**
Underground Equipment Manufacturers Council **(984)**
Urban Affairs Association **(1003)**
World Allergy Organization **(1025)**

Monona

Society of Wood Science and Technology **(950)**

Muskego

Lambda Kappa Sigma **(593)**

Neenah

The World Umpires Association **(1027)**

Nekoosa

Delta Sigma Delta **(409)**

New Glarus

Belted Galloway Society **(328)**

Oak Creek

American Society of Anesthesia Technologists and Technicians **(192)**
Art Libraries Society of North America **(230)**

Association of Educational Therapists **(280)**
International Consumer Product Health and Safety Organization **(537)**
Literacy Research Association **(599)**
NaSPA: Networks and Systems Professional Association **(626)**
National Association of Congregational Christian Churches **(657)**
National Association of Healthcare Education Centers **(671)**
National Association of State Farm Agents **(701)**
Society of Pediatric Nurses **(943)**

Oregon

Archery Range and Retailers Organization **(227)**

Oshkosh

Historians Film Committee/Film & History **(476)**

Pewaukee

Society for Chaos Theory in Psychology and Life Sciences **(905)**

Portage

Association of Arts Administration Educators **(268)**

Princeton

American Association of Candy Technologists **(55)**

Racine

Carwash Owner's and Supplier's Association **(343)**
International Association of Tool Craftsmen **(528)**
National Association of Sports Officials **(697)**

River Falls

American Forensic Association **(123)**
Learning Resources Network **(596)**

S. Milwaukee

Delta Nu Alpha **(409)**

Shawano

Network of Executive Women in Hospitality **(808)**

Stevens Point

National Wellness Institute, Inc. **(804)**

Three Lakes

National Association of Wastewater Transporters **(708)**

Verona

Association of Lutheran Development Executives **(292)**
National Dairy Herd Information Association **(741)**
National Mastitis Council **(772)**
United States National Committee of the International Dairy Federation **(996)**

W. Bend

International Memorialization Supply Association **(556)**

Waterloo

National Association of Fraternal Insurance Counsellors **(669)**

Waukesha

Association for High Technology Distribution **(248)**
Employer Associations of America **(426)**

Wausau

American Society for Laser Medicine and Surgery **(186)**

Whitewater

Special Interest Group on Management Information Systems **(956)**

WYOMING

Basin

Aviation Maintenance Foundation International **(324)**

Cheyenne

Association for Conservation Information **(243)**
Association of Conservation Engineers **(276)**
National Association of State Fire Marshals **(701)**

Cody

American Knife & Tool Institute **(144)**
Dude Ranchers' Association **(417)**

Encampment

Western Writers of America **(1016)**

Laramie

American Society of Plant Taxonomists **(207)**

Budget Index

Every association that has provided annual budget data will be found in one of the fourteen categories below, from Under $10,000 to Over $100 Million.

OVER $100,000,000

Academy of Motion Picture Arts and Sciences *(7)*
Air Line Pilots Association International *(19)*
Amalgamated Transit Union *(28)*
American Association of Retired Persons *(72)*
American Bankers Association *(79)*
American Bar Association *(79)*
American Beverage Association *(80)*
American Bureau of Shipping *(86)*
American Chemical Society *(89)*
American Chemistry Council *(90)*
American College of Radiology *(102)*
American College of Surgeons *(103)*
American Dental Association *(113)*
American Diabetes Association *(115)*
American Federation of Labor & Congress of Industrial Organizations *(119)*
American Federation of State, County and Municipal Employees *(120)*
American Heart Association *(130)*
American Hospital Association *(133)*
American Institute of Certified Public Accountants *(137)*
American Institutes for Research *(141)*
American Medical Association *(148)*
American Petroleum Institute *(163)*
American Psychological Association *(169)*
American Psychological Association - Division of Psychoanalysis *(169)*
American Psychological Association - Division of Psychotherapy *(169)*
American Psychological Association - Society of Clinical Psychology *(169)*
American Society of Mechanical Engineers (ASME) *(203)*
American Speech-Language-Hearing Association *(212)*
ASME International Gas Turbine Institute *(233)*
Associated Universities Inc. *(237)*
Association of American Medical Colleges *(265)*
Association of Universities for Research in Astronomy, Inc. *(315)*
Biotechnology Industry Organization (BIO) *(330)*
Blue Cross Blue Shield Association *(332)*
CFA Institute *(350)*
College of American Pathologists *(363)*
Communications Workers of America *(369)*
Consumer Electronics Association *(381)*
Dairy Management, Inc. *(406)*
Edison Electric Institute *(419)*
Electric Power Research Institute *(421)*
Financial Industry Regulatory Authority (FINRA) *(444)*
Gemological Institute of America *(457)*
IEEE Education Society *(484)*
IEEE Power Electronics Society *(485)*
Institute of Electrical and Electronics Engineers (IEEE) *(499)*
Institute of Nuclear Power Operations *(502)*
International Brotherhood of Electrical Workers #98 *(531)*
International Brotherhood of Teamsters *(532)*
Lyrasis *(600)*
National Academy of Sciences *(628)*
National Association of Letter Carriers *(678)*
National Association of Realtors *(690)*
National Basketball Players Association *(713)*
National Board of Medical Examiners *(716)*

National Collegiate Athletic Association *(724)*
National Council on Compensation Insurance, Inc. *(738)*
National Fire Protection Association *(751)*
National Football League *(752)*
National Football League Players Association *(752)*
National Multiple Sclerosis Society *(774)*
National Rifle Association of America *(787)*
National Wildlife Federation *(805)*
The PGA Tour, Inc. *(844)*
Pharmaceutical Research and Manufacturers of America (PhRMA) *(844)*
Professional Golfers Association of America *(862)*
Project Management Institute *(866)*
Service Employees International Union *(897)*
Society for Human Resource Management *(911)*
UNITE-HERE *(985)*
United Federation of Teachers *(987)*
United Food and Commercial Workers International Union *(987)*
United Mine Workers of America *(988)*
United States Golf Association *(994)*
United States Tennis Association *(1000)*

$50-100,000,000

AASHTO: Transportation Center of Excellence *(2)*
Actors' Equity Association *(11)*
America's Health Insurance Plans *(28)*
America's Natural Gas Alliance *(29)*
American Academy of Arts & Sciences *(30)*
American Academy of Family Physicians *(34)*
American Academy of Pediatrics *(39)*
American Arbitration Association *(46)*
American Association for Cancer Research *(48)*
American Association for the Advancement of Science *(51)*
American College of Physicians *(101)*
American College of Rheumatology *(102)*
American Council of Learned Societies *(109)*
American Council on Education *(110)*
American Councils for International Education *(111)*
American Enterprise Institute for Public Policy Research *(117)*
American Federation of Government Employees *(119)*
American Federation of Teachers (AFL-CIO) *(120)*
American Gas Association *(124)*
American Geophysical Union *(126)*
The American Institute of Architects *(137)*
American Institute of Physics *(140)*
American Kennel Club *(143)*
American Law Institute *(144)*
American Management Association *(146)*
American Osteopathic Association *(160)*
American Philosophical Society *(164)*
American Physical Society *(164)*
American Postal Workers Union *(167)*
American Quarter Horse Association *(172)*
American Society for Engineering Education *(183)*
American Society for Microbiology *(187)*
American Society of Clinical Oncology *(194)*
Association for Computing Machinery *(243)*
Association for Supervision and Curriculum Development (ASCD) *(257)*
Association of American Railroads *(266)*
ASTM International *(319)*
ATP Tour, Inc. *(320)*
BSA | The Software Alliance *(337)*
Child Care Aware of America *(353)*

Computing Technology Industry Association (CompTIA) *(373)*
The Conference Board *(374)*
Conference of State Bank Supervisors *(376)*
Cotton Incorporated *(387)*
Credit Union National Association, Inc. *(404)*
CTIA - The Wireless Association *(405)*
Healthcare Information and Management Systems Society *(471)*
ICE Futures U.S. *(482)*
International Council of Shopping Centers *(538)*
International Union of Operating Engineers *(579)*
Investment Company Institute *(584)*
Laborers International Union of North America *(592)*
Ladies Professional Golf Association *(592)*
Military Officers Association of America (MOAA) *(616)*
Mortgage Bankers Association of America *(619)*
National Academy of Recording Arts and Sciences *(628)*
National Association of Broadcasters *(650)*
National Association of Home Builders *(673)*
National Association of Insurance Commissioners *(676)*
National Board for Professional Teaching Standards (NBPTS) *(715)*
National Cable & Telecommunications Association *(717)*
National Cattlemen's Beef Association *(718)*
National Council of State Boards for Nursing *(736)*
National Council on Aging *(738)*
National Federation of Independent Business (NFIB) *(748)*
National Futures Association *(754)*
National Hockey League *(759)*
National Industries for the Blind *(763)*
National Parks Conservation Association *(779)*
National Restaurant Association *(786)*
National Rural Electric Cooperative Association *(788)*
National Rural Water Association *(788)*
Nuclear Energy Institute *(824)*
Pacific Maritime Association *(836)*
Portland Cement Association *(853)*
Practising Law Institute *(855)*
Radiological Society of North America *(873)*
SAE International *(889)*
Securities Industry and Financial Markets Association (SIFMA) *(895)*
Sheet Metal Workers' International Association *(898)*
Specialty Equipment Market Association *(957)*
United States Chamber of Commerce *(991)*
United States Soccer Federation *(999)*
Universities Space Research Association *(1002)*
WTA Tour, Inc. *(1029)*

$25-50,000,000

AABB - American Association of Blood Banks *(1)*
Advanced Medical Technology Association (AdvaMed) *(13)*
Advertising Council *(13)*
Air Conditioning, Heating and Refrigeration Institute (AHRI) *(18)*
Aircraft Owners and Pilots Association *(20)*
Allied Pilots Association *(20)*
American Academy of Dermatology *(32)*
American Academy of Ophthalmology *(37)*
American Academy of Orthopaedic Surgeons *(38)*
American Angus Association *(45)*

$10-25,000,000

American Registry for Diagnostic Medical Sonography *(174)*
American Registry for Internet Numbers *(174)*
American Registry of Radiologic Technologists *(174)*
American Rental Association *(174)*
American Society for Biochemistry and Molecular Biology *(181)*
American Society for Bone and Mineral Research *(181)*
American Society for Cell Biology *(182)*
American Society for Reproductive Medicine *(189)*
American Society for Therapeutic Radiology and Oncology *(190)*
American Society of Cataract and Refractive Surgery *(194)*
American Society of Nephrology *(204)*
American Society of Pension Professionals & Actuaries *(206)*
American Society of Plastic Surgeons *(207)*
American Society of Safety Engineers *(209)*
American Soybean Association *(211)*
American Thoracic Society *(216)*
American Urological Association *(218)*
Appraisal Institute *(226)*
Armed Forces Communications and Electronics Association *(228)*
ASM International *(232)*
Associated Bodywork and Massage Professionals *(234)*
Association for Advanced Life Underwriting *(238)*
Association for Corporate Growth *(244)*
Association for Iron and Steel Technology *(250)*
Association for Professionals in Infection Control and Epidemiology *(254)*
Association for the Advancement of Medical Instrumentation *(258)*
Association of American Geographers *(265)*
Association of American Publishers *(266)*
Association of American Universities *(266)*
Association of Corporate Counsel *(277)*
Association of Environmental Engineering and Science Professors *(281)*
Association of Flight Attendants - CWA *(283)*
Association of Fundraising Professionals *(285)*
Association of Legal Administrators *(291)*
Association of National Advertisers *(295)*
Association of periOperative Registered Nurses *(299)*
Association of Private Sector Colleges and Universities (Career College Association) *(300)*
Association of Public and Land-Grant Universities (APLU) *(303)*
Association of Schools of Public Health *(307)*
Association of State and Territorial Health Officials *(310)*
Association of Women's Health, Obstetric and Neonatal Nurses *(318)*
The Association to Advance Collegiate Schools of Business *(319)*
Audit Bureau of Circulations *(320)*
Automotive Aftermarket Industry Association *(321)*
Automotive Industry Action Group *(322)*
The Bluetooth Special Interest Group *(332)*
BPA Worldwide *(334)*
Brotherhood of Locomotive Engineers and Trainmen *(336)*
Brotherhood of Maintenance of Way Employees Division *(336)*
Building Owners and Managers Association International *(337)*
Business for Social Responsibility *(339)*
Business Roundtable *(339)*
Catholic Charities USA *(345)*
Catholic Health Association of the United States *(345)*
CCIM Institute *(347)*
Certified Auto Parts Association *(349)*
Chemical Heritage Foundation *(351)*
Chief Executives Organization *(352)*
CIES - The Food Business Forum *(356)*
Coastal Conservation Association *(361)*
Community Associations Institute (CAI) *(370)*
Computer and Communications Industry Association *(372)*
Computing Research Association *(373)*
Congress of Neurological Surgeons *(377)*
Consortium for Graduate Study in Management *(378)*
Consumer Healthcare Products Association *(381)*
Copper Development Association *(384)*
CoreNet Global *(385)*
Council for Advancement and Support of Education *(388)*
Council for Christian Colleges and Universities *(389)*
Council for Professional Recognition *(391)*
Council of American Overseas Research Centers *(392)*
Council on Foundations *(399)*
CropLife America *(404)*
Cruise Lines International Association *(405)*

Custom Electronic Design and Installation Association *(405)*
Defense Research Institute *(408)*
Delta Dental Plans Association *(409)*
Directors Guild of America *(413)*
Distilled Spirits Council of the United States, Inc. *(414)*
Educause *(420)*
Emergency Nurses Association *(425)*
Enactus *(427)*
Entrepreneurs' Organization *(430)*
Equal Justice Works *(432)*
Fabricators & Manufacturers Association, International *(437)*
Federation of American Hospitals *(440)*
Federation of American Societies for Experimental Biology *(440)*
Federation of State Boards of Physical Therapy *(442)*
Financial Planning Association *(445)*
The Financial Services Roundtable *(445)*
FutureGen Industrial Alliance, Inc. *(455)*
Futures Industry Association *(455)*
Glass, Molders, Pottery, Plastics and Allied Workers International Union *(461)*
Global Association of Risk Professionals *(461)*
Golf Course Superintendents Association of America *(463)*
Government Finance Officers Association of the United States and Canada *(464)*
Growth Energy *(466)*
Healthcare Distribution Management Association *(471)*
Healthcare Financial Management Association *(471)*
Heart Rhythm Society *(472)*
Hispanic Association of Colleges and Universities *(475)*
Holstein Association USA *(477)*
IEEE Communications Society *(483)*
Independent Bakers Association *(488)*
Independent Film and Television Alliance *(489)*
Independent Pilots Association *(491)*
Independent Sector *(491)*
Infectious Diseases Society of America *(494)*
InfoComm International *(495)*
Institute for Supply Management *(497)*
Institute of Food Technologists *(499)*
Institute of Medicine *(501)*
Institute of Scrap Recycling Industries, Inc. *(503)*
Insurance Institute for Highway Safety *(505)*
The Integrated Ocean Drilling Program *(505)*
Inter-Industry Conference on Auto Collision Repair *(506)*
Interactive Advertising Bureau *(506)*
International Alliance of Technology Integrators *(510)*
International Anesthesia Research Society *(511)*
International Association for the Study of Pain *(514)*
International Association of Amusement Parks and Attractions(IAAPA) *(515)*
International Association of Bridge, Structural, Ornamental and Reinforcing Iron Workers *(517)*
International Association of Chiefs of Police *(517)*
International Association of Drilling Contractors *(519)*
International Association of Fire Chiefs *(521)*
International Association of Fire Fighters *(521)*
International Association of Plumbing and Mechanical Officials *(526)*
International Copper Association *(537)*
International Dairy-Deli-Bakery Association *(540)*
International Facility Management Association *(543)*
International Federation of Accountants *(544)*
International Franchise Association *(547)*
International Health, Racquet and Sportsclub Association *(549)*
International Housewares Association *(550)*
International Plant Nutrition Institute *(560)*
International Sanitary Supply Association *(563)*
International Society for Technology in Education *(569)*
International Society of Automation *(571)*
International Trademark Association *(577)*
International Union of Electronic, Electrical, Salaried, Machine, and Furniture Workers-CWA *(579)*
International Union of Elevator Constructors *(579)*
Interstate Natural Gas Association of America *(583)*
Investment Management Consultants Association *(584)*
IPC - Association Connecting Electronics Industries *(584)*
Jewish Community Centers Association of North America *(588)*
The Jockey Club *(588)*
Laborers-Employers Cooperation & Education Trust *(592)*
LeadingAge (American Association of Homes and Services for the Aging) *(595)*
Loan Syndication & Trading Association *(599)*

Local Search Association (fka Yellow Pages Association) *(600)*
LOMA *(600)*
Managed Funds Association *(602)*
Manufacturers Alliance/MAPI Inc. *(603)*
Marine Corps Association *(604)*
Marine Preservation Association *(605)*
Materials Research Society *(609)*
Meals on Wheels Association of America *(609)*
Mechanical Service Contractors of America *(610)*
Meeting Professionals International *(612)*
Modern Language Association *(618)*
Mortgage Insurance Companies of America *(619)*
Motorcycle Safety Foundation *(620)*
MPA - The Association of Magazine Media *(620)*
NACHA - The Electronic Payments Association *(623)*
NAFSA: Association of International Educators *(624)*
NAMM - The International Music Products Association *(625)*
National Academy of Engineering of the United States of America *(627)*
National Apartment Association *(634)*
National Association for College Admission Counseling *(637)*
National Association for Home Care and Hospice *(639)*
National Association for the Education of Young Children *(644)*
National Association for the Specialty Food Trade *(644)*
National Association of Children's Hospitals and Related Institutions *(653)*
National Association of College and University Business Officers *(654)*
National Association of Corporate Directors *(658)*
National Association of Counties *(659)*
National Association of Federal Credit Unions *(667)*
National Association of Independent Schools *(675)*
National Association of Insurance and Financial Advisors *(675)*
National Association of Real Estate Investment Trusts (NAREIT) *(690)*
National Association of Secondary School Principals *(694)*
National Association of Social Workers *(696)*
National Association of State Mental Health Program Directors *(701)*
National Association of Student Financial Aid Administrators *(703)*
National Association of Theatre Owners *(706)*
National Beer Wholesalers Association *(713)*
National BioDiesel Board *(713)*
National Board for Certification in Occupational Therapy, Inc. *(715)*
National Board of Boiler and Pressure Vessel Inspectors *(715)*
National Business Group on Health *(716)*
National Cargo Bureau *(718)*
National Center for Manufacturing Sciences *(719)*
National Community Pharmacists Association *(725)*
National Confectioners Association *(725)*
National Conference of Bar Examiners *(726)*
National Conference of State Legislatures *(728)*
National Conference of Women's Bar Associations *(728)*
National Cooperative Business Association *(729)*
National Corn Growers Association *(730)*
National Cotton Council of America *(730)*
National Council for Air and Stream Improvement, Inc. *(731)*
National Council of Architectural Registration Boards *(733)*
National Council of Examiners for Engineering and Surveying *(734)*
National Council of Juvenile and Family Court Judges *(735)*
National Council of Teachers of English *(737)*
National Council of Teachers of Mathematics *(737)*
National Council of the Multifamily Housing Industry *(737)*
National Crop Insurance Services *(741)*
National Federation of State High School Associations *(750)*
National FFA Organization *(750)*
National Foundation for Credit Counseling *(753)*
National Hemophilia Foundation *(759)*
National Hospice & Palliative Care Organization *(760)*
National Institute of Building Sciences *(764)*
National Kitchen and Bath Association *(767)*
National League for Nursing *(768)*
National Military Family Association, Inc. *(772)*
National Minority Supplier Development Council *(773)*
National Multi-Housing Council *(774)*
National Organization of Social Security Claimants' Representatives *(778)*
National Pork Producers Council *(781)*
National Ready Mixed Concrete Association *(784)*
National Recreation and Parks Association *(784)*

National Roofing Contractors Association *(787)*
National Rural Letter Carriers' Association *(788)*
National School Boards Association *(789)*
National Society of Black Engineers *(793)*
National Society of Professional Engineers *(794)*
National Sporting Goods Association *(796)*
National Strength and Conditioning Association *(797)*
National Telecommunications Cooperative Association *(799)*
National Treasury Employees Union *(801)*
The New York Academy of Sciences *(809)*
Newspaper Association of America *(810)*
Non Commissioned Officers Association (NCOA) *(811)*
North American Spine Society *(822)*
Operative Plasterers and Cement Masons International Association of the United States and Canada *(829)*
Organization for Tropical Studies *(831)*
Osborne Association *(834)*
Parenteral Drug Association *(838)*
Personal Care Products Council *(842)*
Pipeline Research Council International, Inc. *(849)*
Plasma Protein Therapeutics Association *(850)*
Produce Marketing Association *(858)*
Professional Liability Underwriting Society *(863)*
Professional Rodeo Cowboys Association *(864)*
Promotional Products Association International *(867)*
The Public Relations Society of America *(870)*
Recreation Vehicle Industry Association *(877)*
Retail Industry Leaders Association *(884)*
Risk and Insurance Management Society, Inc. (RIMS) *(886)*
Rubber and Plastics Industry Conference of the United Steelworkers of America *(888)*
SCORE Association *(893)*
Sigma Theta Tau International *(899)*
Society for Industrial & Applied Mathematics *(912)*
Society for the Science & the Public *(924)*
Society for Vascular Surgery *(926)*
Society of Certified Insurance Counselors *(932)*
Society of Chemical Manufacturers and Affiliates Inc. *(932)*
Society for Critical Care Medicine *(934)*
Society of Exploration Geophysicists *(935)*
Society of Hospital Medicine *(938)*
Society of Interventional Radiology *(940)*
Society of Nuclear Medicine *(943)*
Southwest Airlines Pilots Association *(953)*
Specialty Graphic Imaging Association *(957)*
SPIE - The International Society for Optical Engineering *(958)*
TechAmerica (fka Technology Association of America) *(969)*
Telecommunications Industry Association *(971)*
Toy Industry Association *(976)*
U. S. Airline Pilots Association *(983)*
US Travel Association *(983)*
United Spinal Association *(989)*
United States Dairy Export Council *(993)*
United States Grains Council *(994)*
United States Lacrosse *(995)*
United States of America Gymnastics *(997)*
United States Potato Board *(997)*
United States Telecom Association *(1000)*
United States Wheat Associates, Inc. *(1000)*
United Synagogue of Conservative Judaism *(1001)*
United Union of Roofers, Waterproofers and Allied Workers *(1001)*
USA Rice Federation *(1004)*
Utility Workers Union of America *(1007)*
Water Environment Federation *(1013)*
The Wellness Plan *(1015)*
Workers United *(1025)*
WorldatWork *(1028)*
Worldwide ERC *(1028)*
Writers Guild of America West *(1029)*

$5-10,000,000

Academy Health *(3)*
Academy of Country Music *(4)*
Academy of Management *(6)*
Academy of Model Aeronautics *(7)*
Academy of Osseointegration *(7)*
Accreditation Board for Engineering and Technology Inc. *(9)*
Accreditation Council for Pharmacy Education *(10)*
The Accrediting Commission of Career Schools and Colleges *(10)*
The Acoustical Society of America *(11)*
The Advertising Research Foundation *(13)*
Alliance for Telecommunications Industry Solutions *(23)*
The Aluminum Association, Inc. *(27)*
American Academy of Allergy, Asthma, and Immunology *(30)*
American Academy of Audiology *(31)*
American Academy of Cosmetic Dentistry *(31)*

American Academy of Hospice and Palliative Medicine *(35)*
American Academy of Medical Management *(36)*
American Accounting Association *(43)*
American Advertising Federation *(43)*
American Anthropological Association *(45)*
American Apparel & Footwear Association *(46)*
American Association for Laboratory Animal Science *(50)*
American Association for Marriage and Family Therapy *(50)*
American Association of Thoracic Surgery *(53)*
American Association of Bioanalysts *(54)*
American Association of Colleges for Teacher Education *(57)*
American Association of Endodontists *(60)*
American Association of Equine Practitioners *(60)*
American Association of Individual Investors *(63)*
American Association of Insurance Services *(63)*
American Association of Law Libraries *(64)*
American Association of Medical Assistants *(65)*
American Association of Physics Teachers *(69)*
American Association of Poison Control Centers *(70)*
American Association of Professional Landmen *(71)*
American Association of University Professors *(75)*
American Bakers Association *(78)*
American Board of Podiatric Surgery *(83)*
American Board of Surgery *(84)*
American Burn Association *(87)*
American Bus Association *(87)*
American Ceramics Society *(89)*
American Chiropractic Association *(90)*
American Cleaning Institute *(91)*
American Coatings Association *(92)*
American College of Allergy, Asthma and Immunology *(93)*
American College of Clinical Pharmacy *(94)*
American College of Foot and Ankle Surgeons *(95)*
American College of Medical Genetics *(97)*
American College of Nurse-Midwives *(99)*
American College of Occupational and Environmental Medicine *(99)*
American College of Physician Executives *(101)*
American Correctional Association *(108)*
American Craft Council *(111)*
American Dental Hygienists' Association *(114)*
American Economic Association *(115)*
American Epilepsy Society *(117)*
American Farmland Trust *(118)*
American Financial Services Association *(121)*
American Foreign Service Protective Association *(123)*
American Foundry Society *(123)*
American Gaming Association *(124)*
American Geological Institute *(126)*
American Geriatrics Society *(126)*
American Hardwood Export Council *(129)*
American Health Lawyers Association *(130)*
American Hotel & Lodging Association (AH&LA) *(134)*
American Institute of Biological Sciences *(137)*
American Institute of Ultrasound in Medicine *(141)*
American Intellectual Property Law Association *(141)*
American Land Title Association *(144)*
American Meat Institute *(147)*
American Medical Student Association *(150)*
American Neurological Association *(155)*
American Oil Chemists' Society *(157)*
American Organization of Nurse Executives *(158)*
American Orthopaedic Society for Sports Medicine *(159)*
American Orthotic and Prosthetic Association *(159)*
American Pet Products Association *(163)*
American Philatelic Society *(163)*
American Public Human Services Association *(171)*
American Resort Development Association *(175)*
American Road and Transportation Builders Association *(175)*
American Roentgen Ray Society *(176)*
American School Counselor Association *(177)*
American Society for Aesthetic Plastic Surgery *(180)*
American Society for Dermatologic Surgery *(183)*
American Society for Healthcare Engineering *(184)*
American Society for Investigative Pathology *(186)*
American Society for Metabolic and Bariatric Surgery *(187)*
American Society for Nondestructive Testing *(187)*
American Society for Nutrition *(187)*
American Society for Pharmacology and Experimental Therapeutics *(188)*
American Society for Surgery of the Hand *(189)*
American Society of Appraisers *(192)*
American Society of Colon and Rectal Surgeons *(195)*
American Society of Consultant Pharmacists *(195)*
American Society of Echocardiography *(197)*
American Society of Human Genetics *(200)*
American Society of Hypertension, Inc. *(200)*
American Society of Plant Biologists *(207)*

American Society of Transplantation *(210)*
American Sociological Association *(211)*
American Sportfishing Association *(212)*
American Staffing Association *(213)*
American Statistical Association *(213)*
American Theological Library Association *(216)*
American Tort Reform Association *(217)*
American Traffic Safety Service Association *(217)*
American Train Dispatchers Association *(217)*
American Waterways Operators *(220)*
APA The Engineered Wood Association *(224)*
Arabian Horse Association *(227)*
Archaeological Institute of America *(227)*
ARMA International *(228)*
Arthroscopy Association of North America *(230)*
Asian American Hotel Owners Association *(231)*
Asphalt Institute *(233)*
Assisted Living Federation of America *(234)*
Association for Information and Image Management International *(249)*
Association for Institutional Research *(250)*
Association for Middle Level Education *(252)*
Association for Prevention Teaching and Research (APTR) *(254)*
Association for Psychological Science *(254)*
Association for Research in Vision and Ophthalmology *(255)*
Association for Unmanned Vehicle Systems International *(261)*
Association of American Colleges and Universities *(264)*
Association of Clinical Research Professionals *(273)*
Association of Community Cancer Centers *(275)*
Association of Community College Trustees *(276)*
Association of Energy Engineers *(280)*
Association of Global Automakers *(285)*
Association of Governing Boards of Universities and Colleges *(286)*
Association of Government Accountants *(286)*
Association of Junior Leagues International *(290)*
Association of Latino Professionals in Finance and Accounting *(291)*
Association of Pool and Spa Professionals *(299)*
Association of Professional Flight Attendants *(301)*
Association of Research Libraries *(306)*
Association of School Business Officials International *(306)*
Association of Small Foundations *(309)*
Association of Social Work Boards *(309)*
Association of University Centers on Disabilities (AUCD) *(315)*
Association of Volleyball Professionals *(317)*
Association of Zoos and Aquariums *(318)*
Automation Alley *(321)*
Automotive Distribution Network *(322)*
Bank Administration Institute *(326)*
Beer Institute *(327)*
Blinded Veterans Association *(332)*
The Brewers Association *(335)*
Brick Industry Association *(335)*
The Broadway League *(336)*
Business Executives for National Security *(338)*
Cable & Telecommunications Association for Marketing *(340)*
Cabletelevision Advertising Bureau *(340)*
Case Management Society of America *(343)*
Casualty Actuarial Society *(344)*
CBA *(346)*
Center for Research Libraries *(348)*
Center for the Polyurethanes Industry *(348)*
Central Intercollegiate Athletic Association *(349)*
Child Welfare League of America *(353)*
Chlorine Chemistry Council *(354)*
Christian Medical & Dental Associations *(356)*
Clinical and Laboratory Standards Institute *(358)*
Club Managers Association of America *(359)*
COLA *(362)*
College and University Professional Association for Human Resources *(362)*
Committee of Interns and Residents/ SEIU *(368)*
Communications Supply Service Association *(369)*
Community Financial Services Association of America CFSA *(370)*
Community Transportation Association of America *(371)*
Construction Financial Management Association *(379)*
Consumer Bankers Association *(380)*
Consumer Specialty Products Association *(381)*
Coordinating Research Council *(384)*
Corporate Council on Africa *(385)*
Council for Adult and Experiential Learning *(388)*
Council for Exceptional Children *(390)*
Council for Opportunity in Education *(390)*
The Council of Insurance Agents and Brokers *(394)*
Council of Residential Specialists *(396)*
Council of State and Territorial Epidemiologists *(397)*
Council of Supply Chain Management Professionals *(398)*
Council of the Great City Schools *(398)*

Council on Social Work Education *(400)*
Craft & Hobby Association *(402)*
Credit Union Executives Society *(403)*
Delta Waterfowl Foundation *(409)*
Dermatology Foundation *(410)*
Design-Build Institute of America *(411)*
Destination Marketing Association International *(411)*
Direct Selling Association *(413)*
Distributive Education Clubs of America (DECA) *(415)*
Ecological Society of America *(418)*
Educational Theatre Association *(420)*
Electric Power Supply Association (EPSA) *(421)*
The Electrochemical Society *(423)*
Electronic Retailing Association *(423)*
Environmental Industry Associations *(431)*
Equipment Leasing and Finance Association *(432)*
Farm Credit Council *(437)*
The Fertilizer Institute *(443)*
Financial Executives International *(444)*
Food Processing Suppliers Association *(449)*
Freelancers Union *(453)*
Generic Pharmaceutical Association *(458)*
Geological Society of America *(459)*
German American Chamber of Commerce *(460)*
Gerontological Society of America *(460)*
Global Market Development Center *(462)*
Graphic Arts Technical Foundation *(465)*
Graphic Communications Conference of the International Brotherhood of Teamsters *(465)*
Health Forum *(469)*
Healthcare Leadership Council *(471)*
Helicopter Association International *(473)*
HR Policy Association *(480)*
IEEE Signal Processing Society *(485)*
Illuminating Engineering Society of North America *(486)*
INDA, Association of the Nonwoven Fabrics Industry *(488)*
Independent Petroleum Association of America *(491)*
Industrial Fabrics Association International *(493)*
Information Technology Industry Council *(495)*
Institute for Business & Home Safety *(496)*
Institute for Operations Research and the Management Sciences *(497)*
Institute of Transportation Engineers *(503)*
Insurance Information Institute *(505)*
Intelligent Transportation Society of America *(506)*
InterAction (American Council of Voluntary International Action) *(506)*
Intermodal Association of North America *(508)*
International Association of Business Communicators *(517)*
International Association of Privacy Professionals *(526)*
International Bottled Water Association *(530)*
International Brotherhood of Electrical Workers *(531)*
International Congress of Oral Implantologists *(537)*
International Economic Development Council *(541)*
International Federation of Professional and Technical Engineers *(544)*
International Foodservice Distributors Association *(546)*
International Foodservice Manufacturers Association *(546)*
International Lead Zinc Research Organization *(553)*
International Longshore and Warehouse Union *(555)*
International Maple Syrup Institute *(555)*
International Organization of Masters, Mates and Pilots *(559)*
International Sign Association *(564)*
International Society for Magnetic Resonance in Medicine *(567)*
International Society for Pharmaceutical Engineering *(567)*
International Society for Pharmacoeconomics and Outcomes Research *(568)*
International Society of Arboriculture *(571)*
International Society on Thrombosis and Hemostasis *(575)*
International Union of Police Associations, AFL-CIO *(579)*
Intersocietal Accreditation Commission *(582)*
Jewelers Shipping Association *(587)*
Land Trust Alliance *(593)*
Learning Forward *(596)*
Marine Engineers Beneficial Association *(605)*
Material Handling Industry of America *(608)*
Metals Service Center Institute *(614)*
Minerals, Metals and Materials Society *(617)*
Movement Disorder Society *(620)*
National Association of Student Personnel Administrators *(626)*
National Academy of Public Administration *(628)*
National Air Transportation Association *(630)*
National Alcohol Beverage Control Association *(631)*
National Alliance for Hispanic Health *(631)*

National Alliance of State and Territorial AIDS Directors *(633)*
National Asphalt Pavement Association *(635)*
National Association for Biomedical Research *(636)*
The National Association for Music Education (Formerly MENC) *(641)*
National Association of Basketball Coaches *(648)*
National Association of Chronic Disease Directors *(653)*
National Association of Clean Water Agencies *(654)*
National Association of Colleges and Employers *(655)*
National Association of Criminal Defense Lawyers *(661)*
National Association of Drug Court Professionals *(663)*
National Association of Electrical Distributors *(664)*
National Association of Elementary School Principals *(664)*
National Association of Housing and Redevelopment Officials *(673)*
National Association of Independent Colleges and Universities *(674)*
National Association of Intercollegiate Athletics *(676)*
National Association of Investors Corporation *(677)*
National Association of Managed Care Physicians *(679)*
National Association of Professional Surplus Lines Offices, Ltd. *(688)*
National Association of Public Hospitals and Health Systems *(688)*
National Association of Regulatory Utility Commissioners *(691)*
National Association of School Psychologists *(693)*
National Association of State Energy Officials *(700)*
National Association of State Procurement Officials *(702)*
National Association of Tax Professionals *(704)*
National Association of Television Program Executives *(705)*
National Athletic Trainers Association *(710)*
National Automatic Merchandising Association *(711)*
National Basketball Association *(712)*
National Board for Certified Counselors *(715)*
National Board for Respiratory Care *(715)*
National Catholic Educational Association *(718)*
National Contract Management Association *(729)*
National Council for Community Behavioral Healthcare *(731)*
National Council for International Visitors *(732)*
National Council for Prescription Drug Programs *(732)*
National Council of Athletic Training *(734)*
National Council of Farmer Cooperatives *(734)*
National Council of State Housing Agencies *(736)*
National Council of University Research Administrators *(737)*
National Council on Crime and Delinquency *(738)*
National Court Reporters Association *(740)*
National District Attorneys Association *(743)*
National Environmental Health Association *(746)*
National Fisheries Institute *(751)*
National Funeral Directors Association *(754)*
National Glass Association *(755)*
National Grocers Association *(756)*
National Ground Water Association *(756)*
National Guard Association of the U.S. *(757)*
National Hardwood Lumber Association *(757)*
National Head Start Association *(758)*
National Indian Gaming Association *(762)*
National Institute of Governmental Purchasing *(765)*
National Investor Relations Institute *(767)*
National Motor Freight Traffic Association, Inc. *(773)*
National Newspaper Publishers Association *(775)*
National Nurses United *(775)*
National Organization of Life and Health Insurance Guaranty Association *(777)*
National Pest Management Association *(780)*
National Pharmaceutical Council *(780)*
National Precast Concrete Association *(782)*
National Propane Gas Association *(783)*
National Railway Labor Conference *(784)*
National Reining Horse Association *(785)*
National Sheriffs' Association *(791)*
National Soccer Coaches Association of America *(792)*
National Staff Development and Training Association *(796)*
National Stone, Sand, and Gravel Association *(796)*
National Swine Registry *(798)*
National Thoroughbred Racing Association *(800)*
National Tour Association *(800)*
National Truck Equipment Association *(802)*
National Venture Capital Association *(803)*
North American Insulation Manufacturers Association *(817)*
OPERA America *(828)*
Phi Delta Kappa International *(845)*
The Philanthropy Roundtable *(846)*

PKF North American Network *(849)*
Plains Cotton Growers, Inc. *(849)*
PMA - The Worldwide Community of Imaging Associations *(851)*
Police Executive Research Forum *(852)*
POPAI The Global Association for Marketing at Retail *(852)*
Population Action International *(852)*
Precast/Prestressed Concrete Institute *(856)*
Printing Industries of America *(857)*
Private Equity Growth Capital Council *(858)*
Private Label Manufacturers Association *(858)*
Professional Bowlers Association *(861)*
Professional Convention Management Association *(861)*
Professional Photographers of America *(863)*
Professional Retail Store Maintenance Association *(864)*
Professional Services Council *(865)*
Property Loss Research Bureau *(867)*
Radio Advertising Bureau *(873)*
Real Estate Buyers Agent Council *(875)*
Regulatory Affairs Professionals Society *(879)*
Reinsurance Association of America *(879)*
Renewable Fuels Association *(881)*
Research Institute for Fragrance Materials *(882)*
Rubber Manufacturers Association *(888)*
School Nutrition Association *(892)*
Security Industry Association *(895)*
Semiconductor Industry Association *(897)*
Sigma Xi, The Scientific Research Society *(899)*
SnowSports Industries America *(902)*
Society for Applied Learning Technology *(904)*
Society for Cardiovascular Angiography and Interventions *(905)*
Society for Laboratory Automation and Screening *(914)*
Society for Mining, Metallurgy and Exploration, Inc. *(915)*
Society for Research in Child Development *(920)*
Society of American Foresters *(928)*
Society of American Gastrointestinal and Endoscopic Surgeons *(929)*
Society of American Military Engineers *(929)*
Society of Economic Geologists *(934)*
Society of Financial Service Professionals *(936)*
Society of the Plastics Industry *(948)*
Society of Women Engineers *(950)*
Software & Information Industry Association (SIIA) *(950)*
Solar Electric Power Association *(951)*
Solar Energy Industries Association (SEIA) *(952)*
Special Libraries Association *(956)*
Specialty Vehicle Institute of America *(958)*
SSPC: the Society for Protective Coatings *(960)*
Tau Beta Pi Association *(968)*
Tax Executives Institute, Inc. *(968)*
Technical Association of the Pulp and Paper Industry *(970)*
Television Bureau of Advertising *(971)*
Theatre Communications Group *(973)*
Touchstone Energy Cooperatives *(976)*
Transport Workers Union of America, AFL-CIO *(978)*
Truck and Engine Manufacturers Association *(980)*
United Association of Journeymen and Apprentices of the Plumbing and Pipe Fitting Industry of the U.S. and Canada *(985)*
United Farm Workers of America *(986)*
United Fresh Produce Association *(987)*
United Motorcoach Association *(988)*
United States and Canadian Academy of Pathology *(989)*
United States Conference of Mayors *(992)*
United States Energy Association *(993)*
United States Hispanic Chamber of Commerce *(995)*
United States Maritime Alliance (USMX) *(996)*
United States Professional Tennis Association *(998)*
United States Rowing Association *(998)*
United States Trotting Association *(1000)*
USA Rice Council *(1004)*
Utilities Telecom Council *(1006)*
The Vision Council *(1010)*
Water Quality Association *(1013)*
Wi-Fi Alliance *(1016)*
Wine and Spirits Wholesalers of America *(1018)*
Women's Business Enterprise National Council *(1022)*
Women's Foodservice Forum *(1023)*
World Floor Covering Association *(1026)*
World Gold Trust Services *(1026)*
World Trade Centers Association *(1027)*
The Wound, Ostomy and Continence Nurses Society *(1028)*

$2-5,000,000

AACE International *(1)*
ACA International, The Association of Credit and Collection Professionals *(2)*
Academy of Applied Science *(4)*
Academy of Medical-Surgical Nurses *(7)*

Academy of Molecular Imaging (7)
Academy of Nutrition and Dietetics (7)
Accrediting Bureau of Health Education Schools (10)
Accrediting Council for Continuing Education & Training (10)
ACPA College Student Educators International (11)
Acrylonitrile Group, Inc. (11)
Acute Long Term Hospital Association (12)
Adhesive and Sealant Council (12)
AFCOM (14)
Agricultural Retailers Association (16)
Air and Waste Management Association (17)
AIR Commercial Real Estate Association (18)
Air Conditioning Contractors of America (18)
Air Force Sergeants Association (19)
Air Movement and Control Association International (19)
Air Traffic Control Association (19)
Aircraft Electronics Association (20)
Aircraft Mechanics Fraternal Association (20)
Alliance for Children and Families (22)
Alliance for Continuing Medical Education (22)
Alpha Omega Alpha Honor Medical Society (26)
Ambulatory Surgery Center Association (28)
America's Blood Centers (28)
American Academy of Child and Adolescent Psychiatry (31)
American Academy of Cosmetic Surgery (32)
American Academy of Emergency Medicine (33)
American Academy of Forensic Sciences (34)
American Academy of Implant Dentistry (35)
American Academy of Neurology (36)
American Academy of Nursing (37)
American Academy of Optometry (37)
American Academy of Orthotists and Prosthetists (38)
American Academy of Pain Management (39)
American Academy of Pain Medicine (39)
American Academy of Religion (41)
American Ambulance Association (44)
American Architectural Foundation (46)
American Architectural Manufacturers Association (46)
American Association for Accreditation of Ambulatory Surgery Facilities (47)
American Association for Dental Research (49)
American Association for Health Education (49)
American Association for Homecare (50)
American Association for the Surgery of Trauma (52)
American Association of Cereal Chemists International (55)
American Association of Hip and Knee Surgeons (62)
American Association of Managing General Agents (64)
American Association of Neurological Surgeons (66)
American Association of Neuromuscular and Electrodiagnostic Medicine (66)
American Association of Physician Specialists (69)
American Association of Physicians of Indian Origin (69)
American Association of Port Authorities (70)
American Association of State Troopers (73)
American Association of Textile Chemists and Colorists (75)
American Association of Tissue Banks (75)
American Association of Variable Star Observers (76)
American Association of Veterinary State Boards (76)
American Benefits Council (80)
American Board of Physical Medicine and Rehabilitation (83)
American Board of Preventive Medicine (83)
American Board of Trial Advocates (84)
American Boat and Yacht Council (84)
American Booksellers Association (85)
American Business Media (87)
American Business Women's Association (87)
American Cable Association (87)
American Chamber of Commerce Executives (89)
American Choral Directors Association (90)
American Clinical Laboratory Association (91)
American College Health Association (93)
American College of Musicians (98)
American College of Neuropsychopharmacology (98)
American College of Osteopathic Emergency Physicians (99)
American College of Osteopathic Family Physicians (100)
American College of Osteopathic Internists (100)
American College of Phlebology (101)
American College of Physicians Services, Inc. (101)
American College of Preventive Medicine (101)
American College of Prosthodontists (101)
American College of Trial Lawyers (103)
American College of Veterinary Internal Medicine (104)
American College of Veterinary Surgeons (104)
American College Personnel Association (105)

American Composites Manufacturers Association (105)
American Concrete Pavement Association (106)
American Concrete Pipe Association (106)
American Conference of Governmental Industrial Hygienists (107)
American Cotton Shippers Association (108)
American Dairy Science Association (113)
American Dental Society of Anesthesiology (114)
American Federation for Aging Research (119)
American Federation of Police and Concerned Citizens (119)
American Feed Industry Association (120)
American Fence Association (120)
The American Finance Association (121)
American Fisheries Society (121)
American Football Coaches Association (122)
American Foreign Service Association (122)
American Fraternal Alliance (124)
American Frozen Food Institute (124)
American Gear Manufacturers Association (125)
The American Gem Society (125)
American Gem Trade Association (125)
American Guild of Musical Artists (127)
American Headache Society (129)
American Hereford Association (131)
American Historical Association (131)
American Horticultural Society (133)
American Indian Higher Education Consortium (135)
American Indian Science and Engineering Society (135)
American Inns of Court (135)
American Institute of Graphic Arts (139)
American Institute of Indian Studies (139)
American International Automobile Dealers Association (142)
American Jersey Cattle Association/National All-Jersey Inc. (142)
American Laryngological, Rhinological and Otological Society (144)
American Lighting Association (145)
American Logistics Association (146)
American Luggage Dealers Association (146)
American Medical Directors Association (149)
American Medical Informatics Association (149)
American Medical Rehabilitation Providers Association (149)
American Medical Technologists (150)
American Miniature Horse Association (152)
American Montessori Society (152)
American Moving and Storage Association (153)
American Network of Community Options and Resources (ANCOR) (155)
American Nursery and Landscape Association (156)
American Orthopaedic Association (158)
American Orthopaedic Foot and Ankle Society (158)
American Pain Society (161)
American Peanut Council (162)
American Peanut Shellers Association (162)
American Phytopathological Society (165)
American Pilots' Association (165)
American Psychiatric Nurses Association (168)
American Psychoanalytic Association (168)
American Psychological Association Practice Organization (170)
American Public Gas Association (170)
American Railway Engineering and Maintenance-of-Way Association (173)
American Seed Trade Association (178)
American Seniors Housing Association (178)
American Short Line and Regional Railroad Association (179)
American Simmental Association (179)
American Society for Blood and Marrow Transplantation (181)
American Society for Clinical Investigation (182)
American Society for Clinical Pharmacology and Therapeutics (182)
American Society for Colposcopy and Cervical Pathology (183)
American Society for Histocompatibility and Immunogenetics (185)
American Society for Horticultural Science (185)
American Society for Laser Medicine and Surgery (186)
American Society for Mass Spectrometry (186)
American Society for Parenteral and Enteral Nutrition (188)
American Society of Addiction Medicine (191)
American Society of Agricultural and Biological Engineers (191)
American Society of Agronomy (ASA, CSSA, SSSA) (191)
American Society of Animal Science (192)
American Society of Cinematographers (194)
American Society of Composers, Authors and Publishers (ASCAP) (195)
American Society of Cytopathology (196)
American Society of Home Inspectors (200)
American Society of International Law (201)

American Society of Interventional Pain Physicians (201)
American Society of Lipo-Suction Surgery (202)
American Society of Military Comptrollers (203)
American Society of Naval Engineers (204)
American Society of Neuroradiology (204)
American Society of Nuclear Cardiology (205)
American Society of PeriAnesthesia Nurses (206)
American Society of Plumbing Engineers (207)
American Society of Regional Anesthesia and Pain Medicine (209)
American Society of Transplant Surgeons (210)
American Society of Travel Agents (210)
American Society of Tropical Medicine and Hygiene (210)
American Society on Aging (211)
American Solar Energy Society (211)
American Student Dental Association (214)
American Telemedicine Association (215)
American Translators Association (217)
American Volleyball Coaches Association (219)
American Wholesale Marketers Association (221)
American Wood Council (221)
Amusement & Music Operators Association (223)
Animal Health Institute (223)
APPA - Leadership in Educational Facilities (225)
Appaloosa Horse Club (225)
Appraisal Foundation (226)
Archery Trade Association (227)
Architectural Woodwork Institute (228)
Army Aviation Association of America (229)
Art Directors Club (229)
Art Directors Guild/Scenic, Title and Graphic Artists (230)
ASPIRA Association, Inc. (233)
ASPRS-The Imaging and Geospatial Information Society (233)
Associated Builders and Contractors (235)
Associated Construction Publications (235)
Associated Equipment Distributors (235)
Associated Locksmiths of America (236)
Associated Professional Sleep Societies (237)
Association for Asian Studies (239)
Association for Assessment and Accreditation of Laboratory Animal Care International (239)
Association for Behavior Analysis International (240)
Association for Behavioral and Cognitive Therapies (240)
Association for Childhood Education International (241)
Association for Clinical Pastoral Education (241)
Association for Community Affiliated Plans (242)
Association for Competitive Technology (ACT) (242)
Association for Healthcare Documentation Integrity (247)
Association for Healthcare Philanthropy (248)
The Association for Manufacturing Excellence (252)
Association for Medical Imaging Management (252)
Association for Molecular Pathology (252)
Association for Retail Environments (256)
Association for the Accreditation of Human Research Protection Programs (257)
Association for the Advancement of Computing in Education (258)
Association of Academic Health Centers (262)
Association of Air Medical Services (264)
Association of American Indian Physicians (265)
Association of American Law Schools (265)
Association of American Veterinary Medical Colleges (267)
Association of Asian-Pacific Community Health Organizations (268)
Association of Black Cardiologists (269)
Association of Boarding Schools (270)
Association of Bone and Joint Surgeons (270)
Association of College and Research Libraries (273)
Association of College and University Housing Officers-International (274)
Association of College Unions International (274)
Association of Corporate Travel Executives (ACTE) (277)
Association of Executive Search Consultants (282)
Association of Family and Conciliation Courts (282)
Association of Family Medicine Residency Directors (282)
Association of Fish and Wildlife Agencies (283)
Association of Hispanic Healthcare Executives (287)
Association of Home Appliance Manufacturers (287)
Association of Independent Corrugated Converters (288)
Association of Jesuit Colleges and Universities (290)
Association of Maternal and Child Health Programs (AMCHP) (293)
Association of Military Banks of America (294)
Association of Military Surgeons of the United States (294)
Association of Millwork Distributors (294)
Association of Nutrition & Foodservice Professionals (296)

Association of Occupational and Environmental Clinics **(296)**
Association of Oil Pipe Lines **(296)**
Association of Old Crows **(297)**
Association of Program Directors in Internal Medicine **(302)**
Association of Public Television Stations **(304)**
APCO (Association of Public-Safety Communications Officials) International **(304)**
Association of Rehabilitation Nurses **(305)**
Association of Reproductive Health Professionals **(305)**
Association of Science-Technology Centers **(307)**
Association of Small Business Development Centers **(308)**
Association of State and Provincial Psychology Boards **(309)**
Association of State and Territorial Solid Waste Management Officials **(310)**
Association of State Dam Safety Officials **(310)**
Association of State Floodplain Managers **(311)**
Association of Surgical Technologists **(312)**
Association of the United States Navy, Inc. **(314)**
Association of the Wall and Ceiling Industry **(314)**
Association of University Professors of Ophthalmology **(315)**
Association of University Technology Managers **(316)**
Association of Writers and Writing Programs **(318)**
ATM Industry Association **(320)**
Audio Engineering Society **(320)**
Authors Guild **(320)**
Automatic Transmission Rebuilders Association **(321)**
Automotive Service Association **(323)**
AVS: Science and Technology of Materials, Interfaces, and Processing **(325)**
Awards and Recognition Association **(325)**
BAFT-IFSA **(325)**
Bank Insurance and Securities Association **(326)**
Basic Acrylic Monomer Manufacturers **(326)**
Battery Council International **(326)**
Biomedical Engineering Society **(330)**
Biophysical Society **(330)**
Board of Certified Safety Professionals **(332)**
The Botanical Society of America **(333)**
Brazilian American Chamber of Commerce **(334)**
Building Owners and Managers Institute International **(337)**
Business Council for International Understanding **(338)**
Can Manufacturers Institute **(341)**
Care Continuum Alliance **(342)**
The Carpet and Rug Institute **(343)**
Catfish Farmers of America **(344)**
The Catfish Institute **(345)**
Central Conference of American Rabbis **(348)**
Chain Drug Marketing Association **(350)**
Chamber Music America **(350)**
Cherry Marketing Institute **(352)**
Child Neurology Society **(353)**
Chilean Avocado Importers Association (CAIA) **(353)**
Chinese American Medical Society **(354)**
Chlorine Institute **(354)**
Christian Schools International **(356)**
Cigar Association of America, Inc. **(356)**
College Art Association **(362)**
College of Healthcare Information Management Executives **(364)**
Commercial Finance Association **(366)**
Commercial Real Estate Women Network **(367)**
Commercial Vehicle Safety Alliance **(367)**
Commission on Accreditation for Law Enforcement Agencies Incorporation **(367)**
Committee of 200 **(368)**
Common - A Users Group **(369)**
Community Action Partnership **(369)**
Competitive Carriers Association **(371)**
Competitive Telecommunications Association **(371)**
Composite Panel Association **(372)**
Compressed Gas Association **(372)**
Concrete Reinforcing Steel Institute **(374)**
Connected International Meeting Professionals Association **(377)**
Conservation and Preservation Charities of America **(377)**
Consortium of School Networking **(378)**
Construction Management Association of America **(379)**
Consumer Data Industry Association **(381)**
Continua Health Alliance **(382)**
Convention Industry Council **(383)**
Cosmetic Executive Women **(387)**
Council for Higher Education Accreditation **(390)**
Council for Responsible Nutrition **(391)**
Council of American Survey Research Organizations **(392)**
Council of Better Business Bureaus **(392)**
Council of Federal Home Loan Banks **(393)**
Council of Graduate Schools **(394)**

Council of Institutional Investors **(394)**
The Council of Landscape Architectural Registration Boards **(395)**
Council of Teaching Hospitals **(398)**
Council of the Americas **(398)**
Council on Occupational Education **(400)**
Council On State Taxation **(400)**
Council on Undergraduate Research **(401)**
The Counselors of Real Estate **(401)**
CPAmerica International **(402)**
CPCU Society **(402)**
Cristo Rey Network **(404)**
Crop Science Society of America **(404)**
Customer Relations Institute Global, LLC **(406)**
DBA International **(407)**
DBA International **(407)**
Defense Credit Union Council **(408)**
Delaware Standardbred Owners Association **(409)**
Dental Trade Alliance **(410)**
Directors of Health Promotion and Education (DHPE) **(413)**
Diving Equipment and Marketing Association **(415)**
Donors Forum **(415)**
The Door and Hardware Institute **(416)**
DRI International **(416)**
Earthquake Engineering Research Institute **(418)**
Electrical Apparatus Service Association **(422)**
Electrical Generating Systems Association **(422)**
Electronic Security Association **(424)**
Electronic Transactions Association **(424)**
Emerging Markets Private Equity Association **(425)**
Employee Benefit Research Institute **(426)**
EMTA - Trade Association for the Emerging Markets **(427)**
Enterprise Wireless Alliance **(429)**
Entertainment Merchants Association **(429)**
Entomological Society of America **(429)**
Environmental and Energy Study Institute **(430)**
Environmental Council of the States **(431)**
Equal Employment Advisory Council **(432)**
Ethics and Compliance Officer Association **(433)**
Evangelical Council for Financial Accountability **(434)**
Executive Women's Golf Association **(435)**
Eye Bank Association of America **(436)**
Family, Career and Community Leaders of America **(437)**
Fashion Accessories Shippers Association **(438)**
Fashion Accessories Shippers Association/Gemini Shippers Association **(438)**
Federal Bar Association **(438)**
Federal Law Enforcement Officers Association **(439)**
Federation of American Scientists **(440)**
Federation of Tax Administrators **(442)**
Fibre Box Association **(443)**
Financial Managers Society **(445)**
Financial Planning Standards Board **(445)**
Financial Services Forum **(445)**
Flavor and Extract Manufacturers Association **(446)**
Fleet Reserve Association **(447)**
Flexible Packaging Association **(447)**
FlexTech Alliance **(447)**
Flight Safety Foundation **(448)**
Food and Drug Law Institute **(449)**
The Food Institute **(449)**
Footwear Distributors and Retailers of America **(450)**
Forging Industry Association **(452)**
The Fragrance Foundation **(453)**
GAMA International **(455)**
Gas Processors Association **(456)**
Gases and Welding Distributors Association **(457)**
General Aviation Manufacturers Association **(458)**
General Federation of Women's Clubs **(458)**
Genetics Society of America **(458)**
Glass Packaging Institute **(461)**
Global Business Travel Association **(462)**
Global Health Council **(462)**
Governors' Highway Safety Association **(464)**
Grain Elevator and Processing Society **(464)**
Gridwise Alliance **(466)**
Ground Water Protection Council **(466)**
Health Industry Distributors Association **(469)**
Health Occupations Students of America **(470)**
Health Physics Society **(470)**
Heart Failure Society of America **(472)**
Hearth, Patio and Barbecue Association **(472)**
Heating, Airconditioning and Refrigeration Distributors International **(473)**
Higher Education Consortium for Urban Affairs **(475)**
Hinman Dental Society **(475)**
Hospice and Palliative Nurses Association **(478)**
Hospitality Sales and Marketing Association International **(479)**
Hydraulic Institute **(481)**
Ice Skating Institute **(482)**
IEEE Photonics Society **(485)**
The Independent Book Publishers Association **(488)**
Independent Lubricant Manufacturers Association **(490)**
Industrial Asset Management Council **(492)**

Industrial Designers Society of America **(493)**
Industrial Fasteners Institute **(493)**
Industrial Research Institute **(494)**
Industrial Truck Association **(494)**
Infusion Nurses Society **(496)**
InsideNGO **(496)**
Institute for Professionals in Taxation **(497)**
The Institute of Inspection, Cleaning and Restoration Certification **(500)**
Institute of International Bankers **(501)**
Institute of Mathematical Statistics **(501)**
Institute of Navigation **(502)**
Insurance Accounting and Systems Association **(504)**
Insured Retirement Institute **(505)**
Intellectual Property Owners Association **(505)**
Interlocking Concrete Pavement Institute **(508)**
International Academy of Television Arts and Sciences **(509)**
International Alliance of Theatrical Stage Employees, Moving Picture Technicians, Artists and Allied Crafts of the U.S., Its Territories and Canada **(510)**
International Association for Dental Research **(512)**
International Association for Food Protection **(512)**
International Association for Identification **(513)**
International Association of Administrative Professionals **(515)**
International Association of Airport Duty Free Stores **(515)**
International Association of Assessing Officers **(516)**
International Association of Credit Portfolio Managers **(519)**
International Association of Defense Counsel **(519)**
International Association of Electrical Inspectors **(520)**
International Association of Emergency Managers **(520)**
International Association of Fairs and Expositions **(521)**
International Association of Healthcare Central Service Materiel Management **(522)**
International Association of Lighting Designers **(524)**
International Association of Machinists and Aerospace Workers **(524)**
International Association of Movers **(525)**
International Association of Refrigerated Warehouses **(527)**
International Association of Venue Managers **(528)**
International Bridge, Tunnel and Turnpike Association **(531)**
International Carwash Association **(533)**
International Coach Federation **(535)**
International Corrugated Packaging Foundation **(537)**
International Dairy Foods Association **(539)**
International Digital Enterprise Alliance **(540)**
International District Energy Association **(540)**
International Documentary Association **(541)**
International Door Association **(541)**
International Dyslexia Association **(541)**
International Formula Council **(547)**
International Hot Rod Association **(550)**
International Institute of Ammonia Refrigeration **(551)**
International Insurance Society **(552)**
International Interior Design Association **(552)**
International Lactation Consultant Association **(553)**
International Licensing Industry Merchandisers' Association **(554)**
International Life Sciences Institute **(554)**
International Liver Transplantation Society **(554)**
International Parking Institute **(559)**
International Premium Cigar and Pipe Retailers **(561)**
International Public Management Association for Human Resources **(562)**
International Right of Way Association **(563)**
International Sleep Products Association **(565)**
International Society for Clinical Densitometry **(565)**
International Society for Heart and Lung Transplantation **(566)**
International Society for Infectious Diseases **(566)**
International Society of Arthroscopy, Knee Surgery and Orthopaedic Sports Medicine **(571)**
International Society of Transport Aircraft Trading **(574)**
International Spa Association **(575)**
International Studies Association **(576)**
International Union of Journeymen and Allied Trades **(579)**
International Warehouse Logistics Association **(580)**
Interstate Renewable Energy Council **(583)**
Investment Adviser Association **(583)**
Investment Program Association **(584)**
Jewelers Board of Trade **(587)**
Jewish Education Service of North America **(588)**
The Jockeys' Guild **(588)**
Joint Review Committee on Education in Radiologic Technology **(589)**
Justice Research and Statistics Association **(589)**
Lamaze International **(592)**

Large Public Power Council *(593)*
Laser Institute of America *(593)*
League for Innovation in the Community College *(595)*
Learning Resources Network *(596)*
Legal Marketing Association *(596)*
Licensing Executives Society *(597)*
Lignite Energy Council *(598)*
Manufactured Housing Institute *(602)*
Marine Technology Society *(605)*
Maritime Fire and Safety Association *(605)*
Market Technicians Association *(606)*
Marketing Research Association *(606)*
Marketing Science Institute *(606)*
Material Handling Equipment Distributors Association *(608)*
Medical Device Manufacturers Association *(611)*
Medieval Academy of America *(612)*
Mental Health America *(612)*
Metal Powder Industries Federation *(613)*
Military Impacted Schools Association *(616)*
Mineralogical Society of America *(617)*
Mobile Marketing Association *(618)*
Money Management Institute *(618)*
Motorcycle Industry Council, Inc. *(620)*
NAFA Fleet Management Association *(624)*
NALP - The Association for Legal Career Professionals *(624)*
Napa Valley Vintners Association *(625)*
NaSPA: Networks and Systems Professional Association *(626)*
National Abortion Federation *(626)*
National Academic Advising Association *(626)*
National Academy of Elder Law Attorneys, Inc. *(627)*
National Academy of Television Arts and Science *(628)*
National Action Council for Minorities in Engineering (NACME) *(628)*
National Alliance for Youth Sports *(632)*
National Alliance of Forest Owners *(632)*
National Alliance of Postal and Federal Employees *(633)*
National American Indian Housing Council *(634)*
National Art Education Association *(635)*
National Asian Pacific American Bar Association *(635)*
National Assembly of State Arts Agencies *(635)*
National Association for Campus Activities *(637)*
National Association for Equal Opportunity in Higher Education *(638)*
National Association for Healthcare Quality *(639)*
National Association for Information Destruction, Inc. *(640)*
National Association for Printing Leadership *(641)*
National Association of Public Health Statistics and Information Systems *(642)*
National Association for State Community Services Programs *(643)*
National Association for the Self-Employed *(644)*
National Association for Uniformed Services *(644)*
National Association of Medical Staff Services *(645)*
National Association of Area Agencies on Aging *(647)*
National Association of Attorneys General *(647)*
National Association of Black Accountants, Inc. *(648)*
National Association of Black Journalists *(649)*
National Association of Bond Lawyers *(650)*
National Association of Charter School Authorizers *(652)*
National Association of Chemical Distributors *(652)*
National Association of Clean Air Agencies *(654)*
National Association of College and University Attorneys *(654)*
National Association of College and University Food Services *(655)*
National Association of Conservation Districts *(657)*
National Association of Consumer Bankruptcy Attorneys *(657)*
National Association of Credit Management *(661)*
National Association of Enrolled Agents *(666)*
National Association of Government Guaranteed Lenders (NAGGL) *(670)*
National Association of Independent Life Brokerage Agencies *(674)*
National Association of Long Term Care Administrator Boards *(679)*
National Association of Mutual Insurance Companies *(681)*
National Association of Neonatal Nurses *(682)*
National Association of Nurse Practitioners in Women's Health *(682)*
National Association of Pediatric Nurse Practitioners *(684)*
National Association of Personal Financial Advisors *(684)*
National Association of Police Athletics/Activities Leagues, Inc. *(685)*
National Association of Postal Supervisors *(685)*

National Association of Postmasters of the United States *(685)*
National Association of Professional Baseball Leagues *(686)*
National Association of Professional Employer Organizations *(687)*
National Association of Professional Insurance Agents *(687)*
National Association of Psychiatric Health Systems *(688)*
National Association of Real Estate Appraisers *(689)*
National Association of Regional Councils *(690)*
National Association of Retail Collection Attorneys *(692)*
National Association of School Nurses *(693)*
National Association of Schools of Music *(694)*
National Association of State Alcohol and Drug Abuse Directors (NASADAD) *(697)*
National Association of State Boards of Education *(698)*
National Association of State Boating Law Administrators *(698)*
National Association of State Chief Information Officers *(699)*
National Association of State Directors of Developmental Disabilities Services, Inc. *(700)*
National Association of State Directors of Special Education *(700)*
National Association of State Foresters *(701)*
National Association of State Treasurers *(702)*
National Association of State Workforce Agencies *(703)*
National Association of States United For Aging and Disabilities *(703)*
National Association of Surety Bond Producers *(704)*
National Association of the Remodeling Industry *(705)*
National Association of Tower Erectors *(706)*
National Association of Truck Stop Operators(NATSO) *(707)*
National Association of Water Companies (NAWC) *(709)*
National Association of Wholesaler-Distributors *(709)*
National Association of Workforce Boards (NAWB) *(710)*
National Auctioneers Association *(711)*
National Auto Auction Association *(711)*
National Bar Association *(712)*
National Black Caucus of State Legislators *(714)*
National Business Association *(716)*
National Center for Asia-Pacific Economic Cooperation *(719)*
National Center for Housing Management *(719)*
National Certification Commission for Acupuncture and Oriental Medicine *(720)*
National Chicken Council *(720)*
National Communication Association *(724)*
National Concrete Masonry Association *(725)*
National Conference of State Historic Preservation Officers *(728)*
National Conference on Public Employee Retirement Systems *(729)*
National Consumers League *(729)*
National Coordinating Committee for Multiemployer Plans *(730)*
National Council for Accreditation of Teacher Education *(731)*
National Council for Science and the Environment *(733)*
National Council for the Social Studies *(733)*
National Council of Higher Education Loan Programs *(735)*
National Council of Real Estate Investment Fiduciaries *(735)*
National Council on Family Relations *(738)*
National Council on Radiation Protection and Measurement *(739)*
National Criminal Justice Association *(740)*
National Defense Transportation Association *(742)*
National Eating Disorders Association *(743)*
National Educational Telecommunications Association *(744)*
National Emergency Number Association *(745)*
National Exchange Club *(747)*
National Family Planning and Reproductive Health Association *(747)*
National Federation of Community Development of Credit Unions *(748)*
National Fenestration Rating Council *(750)*
National Fire Sprinkler Association *(751)*
National Fluid Power Association *(751)*
The National Flute Association, Inc. *(751)*
National Foreign Trade Council, Inc. *(752)*
National Frozen and Refrigerated Foods Association *(753)*
National Golf Foundation *(755)*
National Grain and Feed Association *(755)*
National Greyhound Association *(756)*
National Health Care Anti-Fraud Association *(758)*

National Health Council *(758)*
National Hispanic Medical Association *(759)*
National Home Infusion Association *(760)*
National Horsemen's Benevolent and Protective Association *(760)*
National Housing Conference *(761)*
National Hydropower Association *(761)*
National Indian Education Association *(762)*
National Indian Health Board *(763)*
National Insulation Association *(766)*
National Interstate Council of State Boards of Cosmetology *(766)*
National Intramural-Recreational Sports Association *(766)*
National League of Postmasters of the United States *(768)*
National Legal Aid and Defender Association *(769)*
National Lipid Association *(770)*
National Mobility Equipment Dealers Association *(773)*
National Ocean Industries Association *(775)*
National Organization of Industrial Trade Unions *(777)*
National Organization of Legal Services Workers *(777)*
National Pace Association *(778)*
National Petroleum Council *(780)*
National Potato Council *(782)*
National Private Truck Council *(782)*
National Register of Health Service Providers in Psychology *(785)*
National Religious Broadcasters *(785)*
National Renal Administrators Association *(786)*
National Renderers Association *(786)*
National Reverse Mortgage Lenders Association *(787)*
National Rural Health Association *(788)*
National Safe Skies Alliance *(788)*
National School Supply and Equipment Association *(789)*
National Ski Area Association *(791)*
National Society of Accountants *(793)*
National Speakers Association *(795)*
National Stroke Association *(797)*
National Student Nurses Association *(797)*
National Sunflower Association *(798)*
National Tactical Officers Association of America *(799)*
National Tank Truck Carriers *(799)*
National Volunteer Fire Council *(803)*
National WIC Association *(805)*
National Wood Flooring Association *(805)*
National Wooden Pallet and Container Association *(805)*
Natural Gas Supply Association *(807)*
Natural Products Association *(807)*
The New Media Consortium *(809)*
The Newspaper Guild *(810)*
North American Association of Food Equipment Manufacturers *(813)*
North American Die Casting Association *(816)*
North American Equipment Dealers Association *(816)*
North American Menopause Society *(818)*
North American Retail Dealers Association *(820)*
North American Securities Administrators Association (NASAA) *(820)*
North American Society for Pediatric Gastroenterology, Hepatology and Nutrition *(821)*
North American Technician Excellence *(823)*
NPES, The Association for Suppliers of Printing, Publishing, and Converting Technologies *(824)*
NPTA Alliance *(824)*
Obesity Society *(825)*
Object Management Group *(825)*
Online Lenders Alliance *(827)*
Online Publishers Association, Inc. *(828)*
Open Geospatial Consortium *(828)*
The Open Group *(828)*
Open Mobile Alliance *(828)*
Oregon Farm Bureau Federation *(830)*
Organic Crop Improvement Association International *(830)*
Organic Trade Association *(830)*
Organization for International Investment *(831)*
Organization for the Advancement of Structured Information Standards *(831)*
Organization for the Promotion and Advancement of Small Telecommunications Companies *(831)*
Organization of American Historians *(832)*
Original Equipment Suppliers Association *(833)*
Orthopaedic Research Society *(833)*
Orthopaedic Trauma Association *(834)*
Outdoor Advertising Association of America *(834)*
Outdoor Industry Association *(835)*
Outdoor Power Equipment Institute *(835)*
Owner-Operator Independent Drivers Association, Inc. *(836)*
Pacific Telecommunications Council *(836)*
Paleontological Research Institution *(837)*

Passenger Vessel Association *(839)*
PCIA - The Wireless Infrastructure Association *(840)*
Pediatric Nursing Certification Board *(840)*
Pension Real Estate Association *(841)*
Pet Food Institute *(842)*
Petroleum Equipment Institute *(843)*
Petroleum Equipment Suppliers Association *(843)*
Physician Assistant Education Association *(847)*
Physician Insurers Association of America *(847)*
Plastics Pipe Institute *(850)*
Plumbing Contractors of America *(851)*
Plumbing-Heating-Cooling Contractors - National
   Association *(851)*
Precision Metalforming Association *(856)*
Preventive Cardiovascular Nurses Association *(857)*
Print Services & Distribution Association *(857)*
Producers Guild of America *(858)*
Professional Aviation Safety Specialists (AFL-CIO)
   (860)
Professional Beauty Association | National
   Cosmetology Association *(861)*
Professional Landcare Network *(863)*
Professional Tennis Registry *(865)*
Public Affairs Council *(868)*
Public Housing Authorities Directors Association
   (869)
Radiation Research Society *(873)*
Radio Television Digital News Association *(873)*
Radiology Business Management Association *(874)*
RCI, Inc. *(875)*
Real Estate Roundtable *(876)*
Recreation Vehicle Dealers Association of North
   America *(876)*
Red Angus Association of America *(877)*
Refrigeration Service Engineers Society *(878)*
Regional Plan Association *(879)*
Registry of Interpreters for the Deaf *(879)*
Renal Physicians Association *(881)*
Research!America *(882)*
Reserve Officers Association of the U.S. *(882)*
Retail Florist Association *(884)*
Retail Solutions Providers Association *(885)*
The Retired Enlisted Association *(885)*
Romance Writers of America *(888)*
RTCA, Inc. *(888)*
Salt Institute *(891)*
Satellite Broadcasting and Communications
   Association *(891)*
Scoliosis Research Society *(893)*
Search - The National Consortium for Justice
   Information and Statistics *(894)*
Selected Independent Funeral Homes *(896)*
Self Storage Association *(896)*
Self-Insurance Institute of America, Inc. *(896)*
Silicones Environmental, Health and Safety Council
   of North America *(900)*
Snack Food Association *(901)*
SOCAP International *(902)*
Society for Academic Emergency Medicine *(903)*
Society for College and University Planning *(906)*
Society for Conservation Biology *(906)*
Society for Healthcare Epidemiology of America
   (910)
Society for Industrial and Organizational Psychology
   Inc. *(912)*
Society for Information Display *(913)*
Society for Information Management *(913)*
The Society for Investigative Dermatology *(913)*
Society for Marketing Professional Services *(914)*
Society for Maternal-Fetal Medicine *(915)*
Society for Pediatric Research *(918)*
Society for Public Health Education *(919)*
Society for Simulation in Healthcare *(921)*
Society for Technical Communication *(922)*
Society for the Advancement of Material and Process
   Engineering *(922)*
Society for the Study of Reproduction *(925)*
Society of American Florists *(928)*
Society of Architectural Historians *(930)*
Society of Biblical Literature *(931)*
Society of Biological Psychiatry *(931)*
Society of Cable Telecommunications Engineers
   (931)
Society of Cardiovascular Anesthesiologists *(931)*
Society of Children's Book Writers and Illustrators
   (932)
Society of Competitive Intelligence Professionals
   (933)
Society of Corporate Secretaries and Governance
   Professionals *(933)*
Society of Diagnostic Medical Sonographers *(934)*
Society of Eye Surgeons *(936)*
Society of Gastroenterology Nurses and Associates
   (937)
Society of General Internal Medicine *(937)*
Society of Gynecologic Oncologists *(938)*
Society of Hispanic Professional Engineers *(938)*
Society of Incentive & Travel Executives *(939)*
Society of Independent Gasoline Marketers of
   America (SIGMA) *(939)*

Society of Industrial and Office Realtors *(939)*
Society of International Business Fellows *(940)*
Society of Military Widows *(941)*
Society of Motion Picture and Television Engineers
   (942)
The Society of Naval Architects and Marine
   Engineers *(942)*
Society of Neurointerventional Surgery *(942)*
Society of Pharmaceutical and Biotech Trainers *(944)*
Society of Plastics Engineers *(944)*
Society of Research Administrators International
   (946)
Society of Surgical Oncology *(947)*
Society of Teachers of Family Medicine *(947)*
Society of Tribologists and Lubrication Engineers
   (949)
Softwood Export Council *(951)*
Soil Science Society of America *(951)*
Special Interest Group for Computer-Human
   Interaction *(954)*
Specialized Carriers and Rigging Association *(957)*
Specialty Coffee Association of America *(957)*
Specialty Steel Industry of North America *(958)*
Specialty Tools and Fasteners Distributors
   Association *(958)*
Sports and Fitness Industry Association *(959)*
State Higher Education Executive Officers *(961)*
Steamfitters Local Union 449 *(962)*
Steel Founders' Society of America *(962)*
Strategic Account Management Association *(963)*
Structural Building Components Association *(964)*
Sugar Association *(965)*
Supima *(966)*
Supply Chain Council *(966)*
The Surety and Fidelity Association of America *(966)*
Technology and Maintenance Council of American
   Trucking Associations *(970)*
Technology Services Industry Association *(970)*
TechServe Alliance *(971)*
TESOL International Association *(971)*
Textile Rental Services Association of America *(973)*
Tire Industry Association *(975)*
Traffic Audit Bureau for Media Measurement, Inc.
   (977)
Transportation Intermediaries Association *(978)*
Transportation Trades Department, AFL-CIO *(979)*
Travel Goods Association *(979)*
Tree Care Industry Association *(980)*
Truckload Carriers Association *(981)*
Turnaround Management Association *(982)*
U.S. Hereditary Angioedema Association *(983)*
Union of American Physicians and Dentists *(985)*
United Electrical Radio & Machine Workers of
   America *(986)*
United States Apple Association *(989)*
United States-ASEAN Business Council Inc. *(990)*
United States Beet Sugar Association *(991)*
United States Institute for Theatre Technology *(995)*
United States Parachute Association *(997)*
U.S Poultry and Egg Association *(998)*
U.S.-Russia Business Council *(999)*
United States Tour Operators Association *(1000)*
United States-China Business Council *(1001)*
US Navy Veterans Association *(1004)*
US Rice Producers Association *(1004)*
USA Taekwondo *(1005)*
USENIX: The Advanced Computing Systems
   Association *(1005)*
Valve Manufacturers Association of America *(1007)*
Vinyl Institute *(1009)*
Vinyl Siding Institute, Inc. *(1009)*
Visiting Nurse Associations of America *(1010)*
Voluntary Protection Programs Participants'
   Association, Inc. *(1011)*
Warehousing Education and Research Council
   (1012)
Waterways Council, Inc. *(1014)*
Wildlife Management Institute *(1017)*
Women in Cable Telecommunications, Inc. *(1020)*
Women's Basketball Coaches Association *(1022)*
Women's Council of REALTORS *(1023)*
World Airline Entertainment Association *(1025)*
World Allergy Organization *(1025)*
World Pet Association *(1027)*
World Shipping Council *(1027)*
Writers Guild of America East *(1029)*
Young Presidents' Organization *(1030)*
Zonta International *(1030)*

$1-2,000,000

Academic Pediatric Association *(3)*
The Academy of American Poets *(3)*
Academy of Clinical Research Professionals *(4)*
Academy of Radiology Research *(8)*
ACUTA - The Association for Information
   Communications Technology Professionals in
   Higher Education *(11)*
ADSC: The International Association of Foundation
   Drilling *(12)*
Aeronautical Repair Station Association *(14)*

AFL-CIO Working for America Institute *(15)*
AGN International North America, Inc *(15)*
Agricultural & Applied Economics Association *(16)*
AHS International - The Vertical Flight Society *(17)*
Airborne Law Enforcement Association *(19)*
Airline Industrial Relations Conference *(20)*
Allergy and Asthma Network Mothers of Asthmatics
   (22)
Alliance for Aging Research *(22)*
The Alliance for Home Health Quality and
   Innovation *(23)*
Aluminum Extruders Council *(27)*
America's Small Business Development Center
   Network *(29)*
American Academy for Cerebral Palsy and
   Developmental Medicine *(29)*
American Academy of Addiction Psychiatry *(29)*
American Academy of Anti-Aging Medicine *(30)*
American Academy of Craniofacial Pain *(32)*
American Academy of Dental Sleep Medicine *(32)*
American Academy of Diplomacy *(32)*
American Academy of Disability Evaluating
   Physicians *(33)*
American Academy of Facial Plastic and
   Reconstructive Surgery *(34)*
American Academy of Matrimonial Lawyers *(35)*
American Academy of Mechanics *(35)*
American Academy of Osteopathy *(38)*
American Academy of Otolaryngic Allergy *(38)*
American Academy of Psychiatry and the Law *(41)*
American Amusement Machine Association *(45)*
American Art Therapy Association, Inc. *(46)*
American Association for Aerosol Research *(47)*
American Association for Geriatric Psychiatry *(49)*
American Association for Pediatric Ophthalmology
   and Strabismus *(50)*
American Association for Public Opinion Research
   (51)
American Association for State and Local History
   (51)
American Association for the Advancement of
   Artificial Intelligence *(51)*
American Association of Anatomists *(54)*
American Association of Blacks in Energy *(55)*
American Association of Bovine Practitioners *(55)*
American Association of Cardiovascular and
   Pulmonary Rehabilitation *(55)*
American Association of Christian Schools *(56)*
American Association of Colleges of Podiatric
   Medicine *(58)*
American Association of Cosmetology Schools *(59)*
American Association of Crop Insurers *(59)*
American Association of Exporters & Importers *(60)*
American Association of Family and Consumer
   Sciences *(61)*
American Association of Healthcare Administrative
   Management *(61)*
American Association of Naturopathic Physicians
   (66)
American Association of Neuroscience Nurses *(66)*
American Association of Occupational Health
   Nurses *(67)*
American Association of Political Consultants *(70)*
American Association of Preferred Provider
   Organizations *(70)*
American Association of Sleep Technologists *(73)*
American Association of Suicidology *(74)*
American Association of Swine Veterinarians *(74)*
American Association of Teachers of French *(74)*
American Association of Teachers of German *(74)*
American Association of Teachers of Spanish and
   Portuguese *(75)*
American Association of Woodturners *(77)*
American Automotive Policy Council *(78)*
American Bankers Insurance Association *(79)*
American Baseball Coaches Association *(80)*
American Beverage Institute *(81)*
American Biological Safety Association *(81)*
American Board of Industrial Hygiene *(82)*
American Board of Perianesthesia Nursing
   Certification Inc. *(83)*
American Board of Professional Psychology *(83)*
American Boiler Manufacturers Association *(84)*
American Botanical Council *(85)*
American Case Management Association *(88)*
American Cheese Society *(89)*
American Chemical Society - Rubber Division *(90)*
American Classical League *(91)*
American College for Advancement in Medicine *(93)*
American College of Clinical Pharmacology *(94)*
American College of Dentists *(95)*
American College of Forensic Examiners Institute
   (96)
American College of Nurse Practitioners *(99)*
American College of Osteopathic Obstetricians and
   Gynecologists *(100)*
American College of Osteopathic Surgeons *(100)*
American College of Psychiatrists *(102)*
American College of Radiation Oncology *(102)*
American College of Toxicology *(103)*

American Composers Forum *(105)*
American Concrete Pumping Association *(106)*
American Conference of Cantors *(107)*
American Congress of Rehabilitation Medicine *(107)*
American Council on International Personnel *(110)*
American Council on Science and Health *(110)*
American Dairy Goat Association *(112)*
American Dairy Products Institute *(112)*
American Dental Assistants Association *(113)*
American Evaluation Association *(118)*
The American Fair Credit Council *(118)*
American Federation of Astrologers, Inc. *(119)*
American Federation of School Administrators *(120)*
American Forest Resource Council *(123)*
American Galvanizers Association *(124)*
American Gelbvieh Association *(125)*
American Group Psychotherapy Association *(127)*
American Health Quality Association *(130)*
American Herbal Products Association *(130)*
American Hiking Society *(131)*
American Holistic Nurses Association *(132)*
American Home Furnishings Alliance *(132)*
American Import Shippers Association *(134)*
American Institute for Conservation of Historic and
   Artistic Works *(136)*
American Institute for Maghrib Studies *(136)*
American Institute of Architecture Students *(137)*
American Institute of Floral Designers *(138)*
American Institute of Marine Underwriters *(139)*
American Institute of Professional Geologists *(140)*
American International Charolais Association *(142)*
American Jail Association *(142)*
The American Jewish Historical Society *(143)*
American Judicature Society *(143)*
American Legend Cooperative *(145)*
American Littoral Society *(146)*
American Maritime Officers Service *(147)*
American Medical Association Alliance, Inc. *(149)*
American Medical Society for Sports Medicine *(149)*
American Medical Writers Association *(150)*
American Mental Health Counselors Association
   (151)
American Morgan Horse Association *(152)*
American Mushroom Institute *(153)*
American Music Center *(153)*
American Music Therapy Association *(154)*
American Orthodontic Society *(158)*
American Osteopathic Academy of Orthopedics
   (159)
American Pediatric Society *(162)*
American Philological Association *(163)*
American Philosophical Association *(164)*
American Polygraph Association *(166)*
American Probation and Parole Association *(167)*
American Public Gardens Association *(170)*
American Recovery Association *(174)*
American Saddlebred Horse Association *(176)*
American Senior Benefits Association *(178)*
American Shetland Pony Club/American Miniature
   Horse Registry *(179)*
American Shoulder and Elbow Surgeons *(179)*
American Shrimp Processors Association *(179)*
American Skin Association *(180)*
American Society for Clinical Laboratory Science
   (182)
American Society for Enology and Viticulture *(184)*
American Society for Healthcare Human Resources
   Administration *(185)*
American Society for Healthcare Risk Management
   (185)
American Society for Information Science and
   Technology *(186)*
The American Society for Public Administration
   (189)
American Society of Bariatric Physicians *(193)*
American Society of Concrete Contractors *(195)*
American Society of Criminology *(196)*
American Society of Dermatopathology *(197)*
American Society of Farm Managers and Rural
   Appraisers *(197)*
American Society of Gene & Cell Therapy *(198)*
American Society of Hand Therapists *(199)*
American Society of Limnology and Oceanography
   (202)
American Society of Media Photographers *(203)*
American Society of Ophthalmic Administrators
   (205)
The American Society of Pediatric Hematology/
   Oncology *(206)*
American Society of Sanitary Engineering *(209)*
American Spice Trade Association *(212)*
American Stamp Dealers Association *(213)*
American String Teachers Association *(213)*
American Studies Association *(214)*
American Sugar Alliance *(214)*
American Sugarbeet Growers Association *(214)*
American Supply Association *(214)*
American Surgical Association *(215)*
American Telemarketing Association *(215)*
American Teleservices Association *(215)*

American Thyroid Association *(216)*
American Trauma Society *(217)*
American Water Resources Association *(220)*
American Wire Producers Association *(221)*
Analytical and Life Science Systems Association
   (223)
APPAM - The Association for Public Policy Analysis
   and Management *(225)*
Arms Control Association *(229)*
Art and Antique Dealers League of America *(229)*
Art Dealers Association of America *(229)*
Arthur W. Page Society *(230)*
ASFE/The Geoprofessional Business Association
   (231)
Asian American Journalists Association *(231)*
Asphalt Roofing Manufacturers Association *(233)*
Assistive Technology Industry Association *(234)*
Associated Wire Rope Fabricators *(237)*
Association for Biblical Higher Education *(240)*
Association for Dressings and Sauces *(245)*
Association for Education in Journalism and Mass
   Communication *(245)*
Association for Enterprise Information *(245)*
Association for Enterprise Opportunity *(245)*
Association for Financial Counseling and Planning
   Education *(246)*
Association for Healthcare Foodservice *(248)*
Association for Hose and Accessories Distribution
   (248)
Association for Information Systems *(250)*
Association for Play Therapy *(253)*
Association for Postal Commerce *(253)*
Association for the Treatment of Sexual Abusers
   (260)
Association for Vascular Access *(261)*
Association for Women in Science *(262)*
Association of Academic Physiatrists *(263)*
Association of American Cancer Institutes *(264)*
Association of American University Presses *(267)*
Association of Art Museum Directors *(267)*
Association of Boards of Certification *(270)*
Association of Catholic Colleges and Universities
   (271)
Association of Civilian Technicians *(273)*
Association of Clinical Research Organizations *(273)*
Association of Collegiate Business Schools and
   Programs *(275)*
Association of Collegiate Schools of Architecture
   (275)
Association of Diesel Specialists *(279)*
Association of Diving Contractors International *(279)*
Association of Educational Publishers *(280)*
Association of Farmworker Opportunity Programs
   (282)
Association of Film Commissioners International
   (283)
Association of Food Industries *(283)*
Association of Foreign Investors in U.S. Real Estate
   (284)
Association of Gaming Equipment Manufacturers
   (285)
Association of Home Office Underwriters *(287)*
Association of Industrial Metallizers, Coaters and
   Laminators *(288)*
Association of Insolvency and Restructuring
   Advisors *(289)*
The Association of International Photography Art
   Dealers *(289)*
Association of Investment Management Sales
   Executives *(289)*
Association of Jewish Family & Children's Agencies
   (290)
Association of Management/International
   Association of Management *(292)*
Association of Marketing Service Providers *(293)*
Association of Metropolitan Water Agencies *(294)*
Association of Nurses in AIDS Care *(296)*
Association of Official Seed Certifying Agencies *(296)*
Association of Organ Procurement Organizations
   (297)
Association of Pediatric Hematology/Oncology
   Nurses *(298)*
Association of Pet Dog Trainers *(299)*
Association of Professional Chaplains *(301)*
Association of Professors of Gynecology and
   Obstetrics *(302)*
Association of Professors of Medicine *(302)*
Association of Proposal Management Professionals
   (303)
Association of Real Estate License Law Officials
   (305)
Association of Schools and Colleges of Optometry
   (307)
Association of Schools of Allied Health Professions
   (307)
Association of Specialty Professors *(309)*
Association of State Correctional Administrators
   (310)
Association of State Drinking Water Administrators
   (311)

Association of Test Publishers *(313)*
Association of Theatrical Press Agents and
   Managers *(314)*
Association of University Programs in Health
   Administration *(316)*
Association of University Radiologists *(316)*
Association of Waldorf Schools of North America
   (317)
Association of Water Technologies *(317)*
Association on Higher Education and Disability
   (319)
At-Sea Processors Association *(319)*
Auto Suppliers Benchmarking Association *(321)*
Automated Imaging Association *(321)*
Automotive Engine Rebuilders Association *(322)*
Automotive Oil Change Association *(323)*
Automotive Parts Remanufacturers Association *(323)*
Automotive Recyclers Association *(323)*
Aviation Suppliers Association *(324)*
Bakery, Confectionery, Tobacco Workers and Grain
   Millers International Union *(325)*
Beet Sugar Development Foundation *(327)*
BEMA - The Baking Industry Suppliers Association
   (328)
Benchmarking Network Association *(328)*
Bibliographical Society of America *(328)*
Bituminous Coal Operators Association *(331)*
BKR International *(331)*
Board of Registered Polysomnographic Technologists
   (333)
Brain Injury Association of America *(334)*
Broadcast Cable Credit Association *(335)*
Broadcast Education Association *(335)*
Building Service Contractors Association
   International *(337)*
Burley Tobacco Growers Cooperative Association
   (338)
Business and Institutional Furniture Manufacturers
   Association International *(338)*
Business Higher Education Forum *(339)*
Business Marketing Association *(339)*
Business Professionals of America *(339)*
Business Technology Association *(340)*
Calorie Control Council *(341)*
Canadian-American Business Council *(341)*
Cardiovascular Credentialing International *(342)*
Cast Iron Soil Pipe Institute *(344)*
Cedar Shake and Shingle Bureau *(347)*
Central Station Alarm Association *(349)*
Cervical Spine Research Society *(350)*
Chamber of Shipping of America *(351)*
Child Life Council *(353)*
Choristers Guild *(355)*
Chorus America *(355)*
Christian Leadership Alliance *(355)*
Christian Legal Society *(356)*
Christian Management Association *(356)*
The Coalition for Government Procurement *(360)*
Coalition for Juvenile Justice *(360)*
Coalition of Service Industries *(361)*
Coin Laundry Association *(361)*
College Music Society *(363)*
Color Pigments Manufacturers Association, Inc.
   (365)
The Combustion Institute *(366)*
Commercial Law League of America *(366)*
Computer Security Institute *(373)*
Conference of Consulting Actuaries *(375)*
Conference of Minority Transportation Officials *(375)*
Conference of Radiation Control Program Directors
   (375)
Consortium for Advanced Management,
   International *(378)*
Construction Users Roundtable *(380)*
Consumer Credit Industry Association *(381)*
Content Delivery and Security Association *(382)*
Controlled Release Society *(383)*
Copper and Brass Fabricators Council *(384)*
The Corps Network (formerly the National
   Association of Service and Conservation Corps)
   (386)
Correctional Education Association *(386)*
Council for Community and Economic Research
   (388)
Council for Affordable and Rural Housing *(388)*
Council of Educational Facility Planners
   International *(393)*
Council of Fashion Designers of America *(393)*
Council of Industrial Boiler Owners (CIBO) *(394)*
Council of Large Public Housing Authorities *(395)*
Council of Real Estate Brokerage Managers *(396)*
Council on Chiropractic Education *(399)*
Council on Governmental Relations *(400)*
Country Radio Broadcasters, Inc. *(401)*
Credit Research Foundation *(403)*
Dance Educators of America *(406)*
Dance/USA *(406)*
Dangerous Goods Advisory Council *(407)*
Data Interchange Standards Association *(407)*
Deep Foundations Institute *(408)*

Dermatology Nurses' Association *(410)*
Design Management Institute *(410)*
Diesel Technology Forum *(412)*
Direct Care Alliance *(412)*
Directed Energy Professional Society *(413)*
Distance Education and Training Council *(414)*
Distribution Business Management Association *(414)*
Distribution Contractors Association *(414)*
Domestic Energy Producers Alliance *(415)*
Dramatists Guild of America *(416)*
Dredging Contractors of America, Inc. *(416)*
Drug & Alcohol Testing Industry Association *(416)*
Drug, Chemical and Associated Technologies Association *(417)*
Drycleaning & Laundry Institute *(417)*
Ductile Iron Pipe Research Association *(417)*
Ecological Farming Association *(418)*
Econometric Society *(418)*
Education Finance Council *(419)*
Education Writers Association *(420)*
Electric Drive Transportation Association *(421)*
Electrostatic Discharge Association *(425)*
Emdr International Association *(425)*
Emergency Medicine Residents' Association *(425)*
Employee Assistance Professionals Association *(426)*
Employers Council on Flexible Compensation *(427)*
Energy and Environmental Building Association *(427)*
Energy Bar Association *(428)*
Energy Programs Consortium *(428)*
Energy Solutions Center *(428)*
Enlisted Association of the National Guard of the United States *(429)*
Envelope Manufacturers Association *(430)*
Environmental Assessment Association *(430)*
The ERISA Industry Committee (ERIC) *(433)*
European-American Business Council *(434)*
Exotic Wildlife Association *(435)*
Exterior Insulation and Finish Systems Industry Members Association (EIMA) *(436)*
FAA Managers Association, Inc. *(436)*
Family Firm Institute, Inc. *(437)*
Fashion Group International *(438)*
FCIB-NACM Corporation *(438)*
Federal Communications Bar Association *(439)*
Federal Education Association *(439)*
Federally Employed Women (FEW) *(440)*
Federation of Employers and Workers of America *(441)*
Financial & Insurance Conference Planners *(444)*
Financial Management Association International *(444)*
Food Shippers of America *(450)*
Foodservice Sales & Marketing Association *(450)*
Forest Resources Association *(451)*
Formaldehyde Council, Inc. *(452)*
Foundation for Russian-American Economic Cooperation *(453)*
Fresh Produce and Floral Council *(453)*
Fresh Produce Association of the Americas *(453)*
Gas Machinery Research Council *(456)*
Gasification Technologies Council *(457)*
Georgia Charter Schools Association *(459)*
Geospatial Information Technology Association *(459)*
Geothermal Energy Association *(459)*
Geothermal Resources Council *(460)*
Glass Association of North America *(461)*
Gypsum Association *(467)*
Handweavers Guild of America, Inc. *(468)*
Hardwood Plywood and Veneer Association *(468)*
Health Industry Business Communications Council *(469)*
Healthcare Billing and Management Association *(470)*
Healthcare Convention and Exhibitors Association *(471)*
Hearing Industries Association *(472)*
Hearing Loss Association of America *(472)*
Hemophilia Federation of America *(474)*
Hispanic Association on Corporate Responsibility *(475)*
Hispanic National Bar Association *(475)*
Home Builders Association *(478)*
The Hosiery Association *(478)*
Hospitality Financial and Technology Professionals *(479)*
Human Factors and Ergonomics Society *(480)*
Human Relations Area Files *(481)*
Human Resource People and Strategy *(481)*
Independent Distributors Association *(489)*
Independent Educational Consultants Association *(489)*
Independent Filmmaker Project *(489)*
Independent Telephone and Telecommunications Alliance *(492)*
Indoor Tanning Association *(492)*
Industrial Minerals Association -- North America *(494)*

Information Systems Security Association *(495)*
Institute for Credentialing Excellence *(497)*
Institute of Business Appraisers *(498)*
Institute of Hazardous Materials Management *(500)*
Institute of International Container Lessors *(501)*
Institute of Makers of Explosives *(501)*
Institute of Nautical Archaeology *(502)*
Institute of Packaging Professionals *(502)*
Intercoiffure America/Canada *(507)*
International Academy of Compounding Pharmacists *(509)*
International Academy of Trial Lawyers *(509)*
International Association for Healthcare Security and Safety *(512)*
International Association for Human Resource Information Management *(512)*
International Association of Arson Investigators *(515)*
International Association of Campus Law Enforcement Administrators *(517)*
International Association of Culinary Professionals *(519)*
International Association of Exhibitions and Events *(520)*
International Association of Financial Crimes Investigators *(521)*
International Association of Forensic Nurses *(521)*
International Association of Geophysical Contractors *(522)*
International Association of Oral and Maxillofacial Surgeons *(525)*
International Association of Physicians in AIDS Care *(526)*
International Association of Plastics Distributors *(526)*
International Bone and Mineral Society *(530)*
International Boxing Federation *(530)*
International Brangus Breeders Association *(531)*
International Business Brokers Association *(532)*
International Card Manufacturers Association *(532)*
International Cargo Gear Bureau *(533)*
International Chiropractic Pediatric Association *(534)*
International Chiropractors Association *(534)*
International Communication Association *(536)*
International Concrete Repair Institute *(536)*
International Conference of Funeral Service Examining Boards *(536)*
International Contact Center Benchmarking Consortium *(537)*
International Council of Air Shows *(538)*
International Council on Hotel, Restaurant and Institutional Education *(539)*
International Council on Systems Engineering *(539)*
International Desalination Association *(540)*
International Disk Drive Equipment and Materials Association *(540)*
International Downtown Association *(541)*
InterNational Electrical Testing Association *(542)*
International Energy Credit Association *(542)*
International Erosion Control Association *(543)*
International Federation for Choral Music *(544)*
International Fine Print Dealers Association *(545)*
International Hearing Society *(549)*
International Ice Cream Association *(551)*
International Institute for Energy Conservation *(551)*
International Institute of Municipal Clerks *(552)*
International Institute of Synthetic Rubber Producers *(552)*
International Labor Rights Forum *(553)*
International League of Professional Baseball Clubs *(554)*
International Liquid Terminals Association *(554)*
International Microelectronics and Packaging Society - IMAPS *(556)*
International Municipal Lawyers Association *(557)*
International Municipal Signal Association *(557)*
International Newspaper Marketing Association *(558)*
International Order of the Golden Rule *(559)*
International Pediatric Nephrology Association *(559)*
International Pharmaceutical Excipients Council of the Americas *(560)*
International Professional Rodeo Association *(561)*
International Radio and Television Society Foundation Inc. *(562)*
International Real Estate Institute *(562)*
International Road Federation *(563)*
International Safe Transit Association *(563)*
International Safety Equipment Association (ISEA) *(563)*
International Sculpture Center *(564)*
International Security Management Association *(564)*
International Society for Advancement Cytometry *(565)*
International Society for Computational Biology *(566)*
International Society for Medical Publication Professionals *(567)*

The International Society for Minimally Invasive Cardiothoracic Surgery *(567)*
International Society for Performance Improvement *(567)*
International Society for Pharmacoepidemiology *(568)*
International Society for Traumatic Stress Studies *(570)*
International Society of Explosives Engineers *(572)*
International Society of Hair Restoration Surgery *(573)*
International Special Events Society *(575)*
International Technology and Engineering Educators Association *(576)*
International Test and Evaluation Association *(577)*
International Titanium Association *(577)*
International Window Film Association *(581)*
Internet Security Alliance *(582)*
Interstate Oil and Gas Compact Commission *(583)*
Investigative Reporters and Editors *(583)*
Investment Casting Institute *(584)*
ISEH Society for Hematology and Stem Cells *(586)*
Islamic Medical Association of North America *(586)*
Jeweler's Vigilance Committee *(587)*
Jewelers' Security Alliance of the United States *(587)*
Jewish Book Council *(587)*
Joint Electron Device Engineering Council *(589)*
Juice Products Association *(589)*
Juvenile Products Manufacturers Association *(590)*
Kidney Care Partners *(591)*
Kitchen Cabinet Manufacturers Association *(591)*
Lake Carriers Association *(592)*
Large Urology Group Practice Association (LUGPA) *(593)*
Latin American Studies Association *(594)*
Law Enforcement Alliance of America *(594)*
The Learning Disabilities Association *(596)*
Life Insurance Settlement Association *(597)*
Livestock Marketing Association *(599)*
Lutheran Education Association *(600)*
Magnet Schools of America *(601)*
Manufacturers of Emission Controls Association *(603)*
Manufacturers' Agents National Association *(603)*
Manufacturing Jewelers and Suppliers of America *(604)*
Marble Institute of America *(604)*
Master Brewers Association of the Americas *(607)*
Materials Technology Institute *(609)*
Media Financial Management Association *(610)*
Media Rating Council *(610)*
Medicaid Health Plans of America *(611)*
Messenger Courier Association of the Americas *(612)*
Metal Building Manufacturers Association *(613)*
Metal Construction Association *(613)*
Methacrylate Producers Association *(614)*
Methanol Institute *(614)*
Microscopy Society of America *(615)*
Military Operations Research Society *(616)*
Mobile Air Conditioning Society Worldwide *(617)*
Modular Building Institute *(618)*
Museum Store Association *(621)*
Mystery Writers of America *(623)*
NADCA: The HVAC Inspection, Maintenance and Restoration Association *(623)*
Nashville Songwriters Association, International *(625)*
Natco-The Organization for Transplant Professionals *(626)*
National Academy of Education *(627)*
National Affordable Housing Management Association *(629)*
National After School Association *(629)*
National Agri-Marketing Association *(629)*
National Agricultural Aviation Association *(630)*
National Alliance of Black School Educators *(632)*
National Alliance of State Pharmacy Associations *(633)*
National AMBUCS *(633)*
National AMBUCS, Inc *(633)*
National Association for Business Economics *(636)*
National Association for Court Management *(637)*
National Association for Gifted Children *(639)*
National Association for Interpretation *(640)*
National Association for Retail Marketing Services *(642)*
National Association for Surface Finishing *(643)*
National Association of Agricultural Educators *(646)*
National Association for Alcoholism and Drug Abuse Counselors *(646)*
National Association of Animal Breeders *(647)*
National Association of Bankruptcy Trustees *(647)*
National Association of Boards of Examiners of Long Term Care Administrators *(650)*
National Association of Chiefs of Police *(653)*
National Association of Church Business Administration *(653)*
National Association of College Auxiliary Services *(655)*

National Association of Collegiate Directors of
    Athletics (656)
National Association of Consumer Advocates (657)
National Association of Councils on Developmental
    Disabilities (658)
National Association of Dental Laboratories (662)
National Association of Dental Plans (662)
National Association of Development Companies
    (662)
National Association of Development Organizations
    (662)
National Association of Educational Procurement,
    Inc. (664)
National Association of Elevator Contractors (665)
National Association of Emergency Medical
    Technicians (665)
National Association of EMS Physicians (665)
National Association of Energy Service Companies
    (665)
National Association of Episcopal Schools (666)
National Association of Farm Broadcasting (667)
National Association of Federally Impacted Schools
    (668)
National Association of Fire Equipment Distributors
    (668)
National Association of Foreign Trade Zones (669)
National Association of Free Clinics (669)
National Association of Graduate Admissions
    Professionals (670)
National Association of Healthcare Access
    Management (671)
National Association of Hispanic Journalists (672)
National Association Of Insurance and Financial
    Advisors(NAIFA) (676)
National Association of Investment Companies (676)
National Association of Japan-America Societies
    (677)
National Association of Latino Independent
    Producers (677)
National Association of Legal Assistants (677)
National Association of Local Boards of Health (678)
National Association of Minority Automobile Dealers
    (680)
National Association of Partners in Education (683)
National Association of Pastoral Musicians (683)
National Association of Police Organizations (685)
National Association of Professional Background
    Screeners (686)
National Association of Publicly Traded Partnerships
    (689)
National Association of Railroad Passengers (689)
National Association of Real Estate Investment
    Managers (690)
National Association of Recording Merchandisers
    (NARM) (690)
National Association of Residential Property
    Managers (691)
National Association of Review Appraisers and
    Mortgage Underwriters (692)
National Association of RV Parks and Campgrounds
    (692)
National Association of Schools of Public Affairs and
    Administration (694)
National Association of Sporting Goods Wholesalers
    (696)
National Association of Sports Officials (697)
National Association of State Auditors, Comptrollers
    and Treasurers (698)
National Association of State Budget Officers (698)
National Association of State Credit Union
    Supervisors (699)
National Association of State Emergency Medical
    Services Officials (700)
National Association of State Fire Marshals (701)
National Association of State Retirement
    Administrators (702)
National Association of Subrogation Professionals
    (704)
National Association of Town Watch (706)
National Association of Trailer Manufacturers (706)
National Association of Underwater Instructors
    (707)
National Association of Waterfront Employers (709)
National Association of Wheat Growers (709)
National Association of Women Business Owners
    (709)
National Association of Women Judges (710)
National Border Patrol Council (716)
National Business Education Association (716)
National Business Incubation Association (717)
National Cancer Registrars Association (717)
National Center for Employee Ownership (719)
National Cheese Institute (720)
National Christian College Athletic Association (721)
National Classification Management Society (722)
National Cleaners Association (722)
National Club Association (722)
National Coffee Association of the U.S.A. (723)
National Collegiate Honors Council (724)
National Conference of Bankruptcy Judges (726)

National Conference of Commissioners on Uniform
    State Laws (727)
National Council for History Education (732)
National Council for Research on Women (732)
National Council for Therapeutic Recreation
    Certification (733)
National Council of Nonprofits (735)
National Council of Structural Engineers
    Associations (737)
National Council of Textile Organizations (737)
National Council on Education for the Ceramic Arts
    (738)
National Council on Teacher Retirement (740)
National Customs Brokers and Forwarders
    Association of America (741)
National Dairy Council (741)
National Demolition Association (742)
National Electrical Manufacturers Representatives
    Association (745)
National Employment Lawyers Association (NELA)
    (746)
National Environmental Balancing Bureau (746)
National Exercise Trainers Association (747)
National Federal Development Association (748)
National Federation of Community Broadcasters
    (748)
National Federation of Music Clubs (749)
National Federation of Republican Women (750)
National Finishing Contractors Association (751)
National Forum for Black Public Administrators (752)
National Frame Building Association (753)
National Funeral Directors and Morticians
    Association (754)
National Garden Clubs (754)
National Genealogical Society (754)
National Golf Course Owners Association (755)
National Grange (756)
National Guild for Community Arts Education (757)
National Guild of Piano Teachers (757)
National Home Furnishings Association (759)
National Housing and Rehabilitation Association
    (760)
National Human Services Assembly (761)
National Independent Automobile Dealers
    Association (761)
The National Industrial Transportation League (763)
National Institute of Pension Administrators (765)
National Interscholastic Athletic Administrators
    Association (766)
National Investment Company Service Association
    (767)
National Junior College Athletic Association (767)
National Lime Association (769)
National Music Publishers Association (774)
The National NeedleArts Association (774)
National Network of Estate Planning Attorneys (775)
National Newspaper Association (775)
National Oilseed Processors Association (776)
National Operating Committee for Standards of
    Athletic Equipment (776)
National Parking Association (779)
National Pawnbrokers Association (779)
National Press Photographers Association (782)
National Property Management Association (783)
National Railroad Construction and Maintenance
    Association, Inc. (783)
National Scholastic Press Association (789)
National School Transportation Association (790)
National Society for Histotechnology (792)
National Society of Compliance Professionals (793)
National Society of Genetic Counselors (794)
National Society of Hispanic MBAs (794)
National Speleological Society (795)
National Structured Settlements Trade Association
    (797)
National Systems Contractors Association (798)
National Terrazzo and Mosaic Association (800)
National Tile Contractors Association (800)
National Training and Simulation Association (801)
National Truck Leasing System (802)
National Turkey Federation (802)
National U.S.-Arab Chamber of Commerce (803)
National Utility Contractors Association (NUCA)
    (803)
National Watermelon Association (804)
National Wrestling Coaches Association (806)
National Writers Union (806)
Native American Contractors Association (806)
Navy League of the United States (807)
Network Advertising Initiative (808)
Network Branded Prepaid Card Association (808)
Network of Executive Women in Hospitality (808)
The Neuropathy Association (808)
New Dramatists (809)
NGVAmerica (810)
Nine to Five, National Association of Working
    Women (811)
Nonprofit Technology Network (811)
North - American Interfraternity Conference (812)

North American Association for Environmental
    Education (812)
North American Association of Central Cancer
    Registries (812)
North American Association of State and Provincial
    Lotteries (813)
North American Coalition for Christian Admissions
    Professionals (815)
North American Limousin Foundation (817)
North American Millers' Association (818)
North American Neuromodulation Society (819)
North American Wholesale Lumber Association
    (823)
Ocean Research & Conservation Association (826)
Office and Professional Employees International
    Union (OPEIU) (826)
Offshore Marine Service Association (827)
Online News Association (827)
Optometric Extension Program Foundation (830)
Osteoarthritis Research Society International (834)
Outdoor Amusement Business Association (834)
Paint and Decorating Retailers Association (836)
Painting and Decorating Contractors of America
    (837)
Paperboard Packaging Council (838)
Paso Fino Horse Association, Inc. (839)
Patient Centered Primary Care Collaborative (840)
Pediatric Endocrine Society (840)
Pediatric Orthopedic Society of North America (840)
Pedorthic Footwear Association (840)
Percussive Arts Society (841)
Personal Watercraft Industry Association (PWIA)
    (842)
Pet Industry Distributors Association (842)
Pet Industry Joint Advisory Council (842)
Pet Sitters International (843)
Petroleum Marketers Association of America (843)
Petroleum Technology Transfer Council (844)
Pharmaceutical Education and Research Institute
    (844)
Pharmaceutical Industry Labor Management
    Association (PILMA) (844)
Pharmaceutical Marketing Research Group (844)
Phi Alpha Delta (845)
Phi Mu Alpha Sinfonia (846)
Piano Technicians Guild (848)
Pinto Horse Association of America (848)
Pipe Line Contractors Association (849)
Plan Sponsor Council of America (849)
Plastic Pipe and Fittings Association (850)
Plumbing Manufacturers Institute (851)
Polyisocyanurate Insulation Manufacturers
    Association (852)
Population Association of America (853)
Post-Tensioning Institute (853)
Poultry Science Association (854)
Powder Coating Institute (854)
Power Transmission Distributors Association (855)
PRBA - The Rechargeable Battery Association (856)
Precision Machined Products Association (856)
Printing Brokerage/Buyers Association International
    (857)
Product Development and Management Association
    (858)
Product Liability Advisory Council (859)
Professional Engineers in Private Practice (861)
Professional Housing Management Association (862)
Professional Lighting and Sound Association (863)
Professional Records and Information Services
    Management International (864)
Professional Skaters Association (865)
PROMAX/BDA (866)
Promotion Marketing Association (866)
The Protein Society (868)
The Psychonomic Society (868)
Public Education Network (869)
Public Risk Management Association (870)
Quality Bakers of America Cooperative (871)
Rabbinical Assembly (872)
Railway Supply Institute (874)
Railway Systems Suppliers, Inc (874)
Real Estate Information Professionals Association
    (875)
Real Estate Investment Securities Association (875)
Recreation Vehicle Rental Association (877)
Refrigerating Engineers and Technicians Association
    (878)
Regional Airline Association (878)
Rehabilitation Engineering and Assistive Technology
    Society of North America (879)
Research Chefs Association (882)
Research Society on Alcoholism (882)
Resilient Floor Covering Institute (883)
Resolve, The National Infertility Association (883)
Restaurant Facility Management Association (884)
Restoration Industry Association (884)
Rice Millers' Association (886)
The Ripon Society (886)
RNA Society (887)
Robotic Industries Association (887)

Rolf Institute of Structural Integration *(887)*
Roller Skating Association International *(887)*
Safety Glazing Certification Council *(890)*
Sailors' Union of the Pacific *(890)*
Satellite Industry Association *(891)*
Scaffold Industry Association *(891)*
Schools Interoperability Framework Association
(892)
Seafarers International Union of North America
(894)
Security Traders Association *(895)*
Seismological Society of America *(895)*
Select Registry/Distinguished Inns of North America
(896)
SEPM - Society for Sedimentary Geology *(897)*
Sewing and Craft Alliance *(898)*
The Silver Institute *(900)*
National Association of Small Business Investment
Companies *(900)*
Smart Card Alliance *(901)*
Snow & Ice Management Association *(901)*
Soaring Society of America *(902)*
The Society for Adolescent Medicine *(903)*
Society for American Archaeology *(903)*
Society for Assisted Reproductive Technology *(905)*
Society for Biomaterials *(905)*
Society for Clinical Data Management *(906)*
Society for Developmental Biology *(907)*
Society for Gynecologic Investigation *(910)*
Society for Imaging Informatics in Medicine *(912)*
Society for Imaging Science and Technology *(912)*
Society for Industrial Microbiology *(913)*
Society for Leukocyte Biology *(914)*
Society for Maintenance & Reliability Professionals
(914)
The Society for Modeling and Simulation
International *(916)*
Society for Neuro-Oncology *(916)*
Society for Pediatric Anesthesia *(917)*
Society for Pediatric Radiology *(918)*
Society for Personality and Social Psychology *(918)*
Society for Range Management *(920)*
Society for Surgery of the Alimentary Tract *(921)*
Society for the Psychological Study of Social Issues
(924)
Society for the Study of Evolution *(925)*
Society for Vascular Ultrasound *(927)*
Society of American Travel Writers *(930)*
Society of Behavioral Medicine *(930)*
Society of Cosmetic Chemists *(934)*
Society of Environmental Toxicology and Chemistry
(935)
Society of Fire Protection Engineers *(936)*
Society of General Physiologists *(937)*
Society of Government Meeting Professionals *(938)*
Society of Illustrators *(939)*
Society of Laparoendoscopic Surgeons *(940)*
Society of Petrophysicists and Well Log Analysts
(944)
Society of Professional Benefit Administrators *(945)*
Society of Professional Journalists *(945)*
Society of Quality Assurance *(946)*
Society of Toxicologic Pathologists *(948)*
Society of Toxicologic Pathology *(948)*
Society of Urologic Nurses and Associates *(949)*
Society of Vacuum Coaters *(950)*
Society of Vertebrate Paleontology *(950)*
The Society of Wine Educators *(950)*
Soil and Water Conservation Society *(951)*
Solar Alliance *(951)*
Solar Rating and Certification Corporation *(952)*
Southeastern Theatre Conference *(953)*
Sporting Arms and Ammunition Manufacturers'
Institute Inc. *(959)*
Sports Turf Managers Association *(959)*
Spray Polyurethane Foam Alliance *(959)*
Stage Directors and Choreographers Society *(960)*
Steel Manufacturers Association *(962)*
Steel Tank Institute Division of STI/SPFA *(963)*
Student National Medical Association *(964)*
Student Youth and Travel Association *(964)*
The Sulphur Institute *(965)*
Surface Mount Technology Association *(966)*
Tag and Label Manufacturers Institute *(968)*
TAUC - The Association of Union Constructors *(968)*
Taxicab, Limousine & Paratransit Association *(969)*
Tea Council of the U.S.A. *(969)*
Technology Student Association *(970)*
Telecommunications Benchmarking International
Group *(971)*
Tennis Industry Association *(971)*
Texas Alliance of Energy Producers *(972)*
Text and Academic Authors Association *(972)*
Thoroughbred Club of America *(973)*
Tile Council of North America, Inc. *(974)*
Timber Products Manufacturers Association *(975)*
Tobacco Merchants Association of the United States
(975)
Transpacific Stabilization Agreement *(977)*
The Travel Institute *(979)*

Truck Renting and Leasing Association *(981)*
Trucking Management, Inc. *(981)*
Turfgrass Producers International *(982)*
Undersea and Hyperbaric Medical Society *(984)*
Uni-Bell PVC Pipe Association *(984)*
United Nations Staff Union *(988)*
United States Composting Council *(992)*
United States Industrial Fabrics Institute *(995)*
U.S. Oil and Gas Association *(997)*
United States Synchronized Swimming *(999)*
United States Tobacco Cooperative Inc *(1000)*
Universities Research Association *(1002)*
University Professional & Continuing Education
Association *(1003)*
University Professional & Continuing Education
Association *(1003)*
University Risk Management and Insurance
Association *(1003)*
University/Resident Theatre Association *(1003)*
Urban and Regional Information Systems
Association *(1003)*
Urban Libraries Council *(1004)*
Urgent Care Association of America *(1004)*
User Experience Professionals Association *(1005)*
Utilimetrics/Alliance for Advanced Metering & Data
Management Solutions *(1006)*
Vacation Rental Managers Association *(1007)*
Vibration Institute *(1008)*
Video Electronics Standards Association *(1009)*
Voices for America's Children *(1011)*
Water Systems Council *(1013)*
Wellness Councils of America *(1015)*
Wild Blueberry Association of North America *(1017)*
Window and Door Manufacturers Association *(1018)*
Wine and Spirits Shippers Association *(1018)*
Women in Aviation International *(1020)*
Women in Film *(1021)*
Women in Government *(1021)*
Women's Professional Rodeo Association *(1023)*
Women's Transportation Seminar (WTS
International) *(1024)*
Workgroup for Electronic Data Interchange *(1025)*
WorkPlace Furnishings *(1025)*
World Future Society *(1026)*
XBRL US, Inc. *(1029)*
YMA Fashion Scholarship Fund *(1030)*

$500-1,000,000

AABC Commissioning Group *(1)*
AAGL - Advancing Minimally Invasive Gynecology
Worldwide *(2)*
Academy for Eating Disorders *(3)*
Academy of Breastfeeding Medicine *(4)*
Academy of Criminal Justice Sciences *(4)*
Academy of Doctors of Audiology *(5)*
Academy of International Business *(5)*
Academy of Laser Dentistry *(6)*
Academy of Marketing Science *(6)*
Academy of Political Science *(8)*
Academy of Psychosomatic Medicine *(8)*
Advanced Biofuels Association *(12)*
Advertising and Marketing International Network
(13)
AFL-CIO (American Federation of Labor and
Congress of Industrial Organizations) *(14)*
African Studies Association *(15)*
Agricultural Stewardship Association *(16)*
Airforwarders Association *(20)*
Airport Consultants Council *(21)*
Airport Minority Advisory Council (AMAC) *(21)*
Algal Biomass Organization *(22)*
Alliance for Regenerative Medicine *(23)*
Alliance for Responsible Atmospheric Policy *(23)*
Alliance of Artists Communities *(24)*
Alliance of Associations of Teachers of Japanese *(24)*
Alliance of Hazardous Materials Professionals *(25)*
Alliance of Information and Referral Systems *(25)*
Alpha Omega International Dental Fraternity *(26)*
AMC Institute *(28)*
America Outdoors Association *(28)*
American Academy of Ambulatory Care Nursing *(30)*
American Academy of Environmental Engineers *(33)*
American Academy of Esthetic Dentistry *(33)*
American Academy of Medical Acupuncture *(36)*
American Academy of Medical Administrators *(36)*
American Academy of Ophthalmic Executives *(37)*
American Academy of Podiatric Practice
Management *(40)*
American Academy of Political and Social Science
(40)
American Academy of Wound Management *(42)*
American Academy on Communication in
Healthcare *(43)*
American Agents Alliance *(43)*
American Association for Hand Surgery *(49)*
American Association for the Advancement of Slavic
Studies *(52)*
American Association of Avian Pathologists *(54)*
American Association of Christian Counselors *(56)*
American Association of Clinical Urologists *(56)*

American Association of Credit Union Leagues *(59)*
American Association of Feline Practitioners *(61)*
American Association of Heart Failure Nurses *(62)*
American Association of Independent Music *(63)*
American Association of Kidney Patients *(64)*
American Association of Legal Nurse Consultants
(64)
American Association of Meat Processors *(64)*
American Association of Medical Dosimetrists *(65)*
American Association of Medical Society Executives
(65)
American Association of Pastoral Counselors *(68)*
American Association of Pathologists' Assistants
(68)
American Association of Physical Anthropologists
(69)
American Association of Plastic Surgeons *(70)*
American Association of School Personnel
Administrators *(73)*
American Association of Wildlife Veterinarians *(77)*
American Association of Zoo Veterinarians *(77)*
American Astronautical Society *(77)*
American Automatic Control Council *(78)*
American Automotive Leasing Association *(78)*
American Bearing Manufacturers Association *(80)*
American Beekeeping Federation *(80)*
American Berkshire Association *(80)*
American Beverage Licensees *(81)*
The American Board of Facial Plastic and
Reconstructive Surgery *(82)*
American Board of Periodontology *(83)*
American Board of Podiatric Medicine *(83)*
American Board of Quality Assurance and
Utilization Review Physicians, Inc. *(84)*
American Brachytherapy Society *(85)*
American Brahman Breeders Association *(85)*
American Canoe Association *(88)*
American Catalog Mailers Association *(88)*
American Chianina Association *(90)*
American Cleft Palate-Craniofacial Association *(91)*
American Clinical Neurophysiology Society *(92)*
American Coal Ash Association *(92)*
American Coal Council *(92)*
American Coke and Coal Chemicals Institute *(92)*
American College of Bankruptcy *(93)*
American College of Laboratory Animal Medicine
(97)
American College of Medical Toxicology *(98)*
American College of Mohs Surgeons *(98)*
American College of Oral and Maxillofacial Surgeons
(99)
American College of Real Estate Lawyers *(102)*
American College of Veterinary Ophthalmologists
(104)
American College of Veterinary Pathologists *(104)*
American College of Veterinary Radiology *(104)*
American Concrete Pressure Pipe Association *(106)*
American Council of Independent Laboratories *(109)*
American Crystallographic Association *(112)*
American Exploration & Production Council *(118)*
American Farrier's Association *(118)*
American Federation for Medical Research *(119)*
American Fiber Manufacturers Association *(121)*
American Fly Fishing Trade Association *(122)*
American Folklore Society *(122)*
American Genetic Association *(126)*
The American Geographical Society *(126)*
American Guernsey Association *(127)*
American Guild of Variety Artists *(128)*
American Hardware Manufacturers Association
(128)
American Head and Neck Society *(129)*
American Heartworm Society *(130)*
American Hernia Society *(131)*
American Highway Users Alliance *(131)*
American Holistic Veterinary Medical Association
(132)
American Horse Council *(133)*
American Institute for Medical and Biological
Engineering *(136)*
American Institute of Constructors *(138)*
The American Institute of Mining, Metallurgical, and
Petroleum Engineers *(139)*
American Institute of the History of Pharmacy *(141)*
American Institute of Timber Construction *(141)*
American Maine-Anjou Association *(146)*
American Malting Barley Association *(146)*
American Maritime Congress *(147)*
American Mathematical Association of Two Year
Colleges *(147)*
American Meat Science Association *(148)*
American Medical Women's Association *(150)*
American Membrane Technology Association *(150)*
American Mideast Business Associates *(151)*
American Midwifery Certification Board *(151)*
American Mosquito Control Association *(153)*
American Mountain Guides Association *(153)*
American Musicological Society *(154)*
American National CattleWomen *(154)*

American Neurogastroenterology and Motility Society (155)
American Optometric Student Association (157)
American Orff-Schulwerk Association (158)
American Ornithologists' Union (158)
American Osteopathic College of Anesthesiologists (160)
American Osteopathic College of Dermatology (160)
American Osteopathic College of Radiology (161)
American Osteopathic Colleges of Ophthalmology and Otolaryngology - Head and Neck Surgery (161)
American Ostrich Association (161)
American Pediatric Surgical Association (162)
American Peptide Society (163)
American Pianists Association (165)
American Press Institute (167)
American Professional Society on the Abuse of Children (168)
American Psychosomatic Society (170)
American Purchasing Society (172)
American Pyrotechnics Association (172)
American Rabbit Breeders Association (172)
American Real Estate Society (173)
American Rhinologic Society (175)
American Rights at Work (175)
American School Health Association (177)
American Schools of Oriental Research (177)
American Seminar Leaders Association (178)
American Sheep Industry Association (178)
American Shorthorn Association (179)
American Small Manufacturers' Coalition (180)
American Society for Aesthetics (180)
American Society for Apheresis (180)
American Society for Artificial Internal Organs (181)
American Society for Bioethics and Humanities (181)
American Society for Healthcare Environmental Services (185)
American Society for Healthcare Food Service Administrators (185)
American Society for Pain Management Nursing (188)
American Society for Reconstructive Microsurgery (189)
American Society of Access Professionals (190)
American Society of Agricultural Appraisers (191)
American Society of Andrology (192)
American Society of Baking (193)
American Society of Breast Disease (193)
American Society of Brewing Chemists (193)
American Society of Clinical Hypnosis (194)
American Society of Clinical Psychopharmacology (195)
American Society of Electroneurodiagnostic Technologists (197)
American Society of Extra-Corporeal Technology (197)
American Society of Journalists and Authors (201)
American Society of Law, Medicine and Ethics (202)
American Society of Mammalogists (202)
American Society of News Editors (204)
American Society of Ophthalmic Plastic and Reconstructive Surgery (205)
American Society of Pharmacognosy (207)
American Society of Professional Estimators (208)
American Society of Women Accountants (ACC) (211)
American Specialty Toy Retailing Association (212)
American Spinal Injury Association (212)
American Sports Builders Association (212)
American Swimming Coaches Association (215)
American Textile Machinery Association (216)
American Therapeutic Recreation Association (216)
American Venous Forum (218)
American Watchmakers-Clockmakers Institute (219)
American Youth Hostels, Inc (Hostelling International USA) (222)
Americas Association of Cooperative/Mutual Insurance Societies (222)
Anxiety Disorders Association of America (224)
APSE: The Network on Employment (226)
The Arts and Creative Materials Institute, Inc. (229)
Asphalt Emulsion Manufacturers Association (233)
Asphalt Recycling and Reclaiming Association (233)
Associated Actors and Artistes of America (234)
Associated Air Balance Council (234)
Associated Risk Managers (237)
Association for Accounting Administration (237)
Association for Accounting Marketing (238)
Association for Conflict Resolution (243)
Association for Consumer Research (243)
Association for Continuing Legal Education (244)
Association for Death Education and Counseling (244)
Association for Direct Instruction (244)
Association for Education and Rehabilitation of the Blind & Visually Impaired (245)
Association for Educational Communications and Technology (245)
Association for Experiential Education (246)

Association for Facilities Engineering (246)
Association for High Technology Distribution (248)
Association for Hospital Medical Education (249)
Association for Jewish Studies (250)
Association for Library Collections and Technical Services (251)
The Association for Library Service to Children (251)
Association for Linen Management (251)
Association for Preservation Technology International (253)
Association for Quality Imaging (AQI) (254)
Association for Research in Otolaryngology (255)
Association for Research on Nonprofit Organizations and Voluntary Action (255)
Association for Slavic, East European, and Eurasian Studies (256)
Association for the Advancement of Automotive Medicine (258)
Association for the Advancement of Baltic Studies (258)
Association for the Study of African American Life and History (259)
Association for Theatre in Higher Education (260)
Association Media and Publishing (262)
Association Montessori International - United States of America (262)
Association of Alternative Newsweeklies (264)
Association of American Educators (264)
Association of American Feed Control Officials (265)
Association of American Physicians and Surgeons (266)
Association of Assistive Technology ACT Programs (268)
Association of Avian Veterinarians (268)
Association of Battery Recyclers (269)
Association of Biomolecular Resource Facilities (269)
Association of Black Foundation Executives (269)
Association of Bridal Consultants (270)
Association of Children's Museums (272)
Association of Clean Water Administrators (273)
Association of College and University Auditors (274)
The Association of Collegiate Conference and Events Directors International (275)
Association of Collegiate Schools of Planning (275)
Association of Corporate Contributions Professionals (277)
Association of Defense Communities (278)
Association of Directory Publishers (279)
Association of Edison Illuminating Companies (279)
Association of Educational Service Agencies (280)
Association of Energy Services Professionals, International (281)
Association of Environmental and Engineering Geologists (281)
Association of Equipment Management Professionals (281)
Association of Finance and Insurance Professionals (283)
Association of Food and Drug Officials (283)
Association of Free Community Papers (284)
Association of Fund-Raising Distributors and Suppliers (285)
Association of Healthcare Internal Auditors (287)
Association of Hispanic Advertising Agencies (287)
Association of Image Consultants International (287)
Association of Independent Colleges of Art and Design (287)
Association of Independent Research Institutes (288)
Association of Information Technology Professionals (289)
Association of Insurance Compliance Professionals (289)
Association of International Education Administrators (289)
Association of Jewish Aging Services (290)
Association of Management Consulting Firms (292)
Association of Marina Industries (292)
Association of Medical Device Reprocessors (293)
The Association of Medical Illustrators (293)
Association of Metropolitan Planning Organizations (294)
Association of Minority Health Professions Schools (295)
The Association of Mortgage Investors (295)
Association of Moving Image Archivists (295)
Association of Otolaryngology Administrators (297)
Association of Partners for Public Lands (298)
Association of Pediatric Program Directors (298)
Association of Procurement Technical Assistance Centers (300)
Association of Professional Investment Consultants (301)
Association of Professional Researchers for Advancement (302)
Association of Program Directors in Surgery (303)
Association of Psychology Postdoctoral and Internship Centers (303)
Association of Racing Commissioners International (304)
Association of Regulatory Boards of Optometry (305)

Association of Rheumatology Health Professionals (306)
Association of Rotational Molders International (306)
Association of Service and Computer Dealers International (308)
Association of Ship Brokers and Agents (U.S.A.) (308)
Association of State and Territorial Dental Directors (310)
Association of Strategic Alliance Professionals, Inc. (311)
Association of Supervisory and Administrative School Personnel (312)
Association of Talent Agents (312)
Association of Teacher Educators (312)
Association of TeleServices International, Inc. (313)
Association of University Research Parks (316)
Association of YMCA Professionals (318)
Association on American Indian Affairs (319)
Automatic Fire Alarm Association (321)
Automotive Body Parts Association (322)
Automotive Fleet and Leasing Association (322)
Automotive Lift Institute, Inc. (322)
Automotive Maintenance and Repair Association (323)
Auxiliary to the National Medical Association (324)
Aviation Insurance Association (324)
Aviation Maintenance Foundation International (324)
Bearing Specialist Association (327)
Beefmaster Breeders United (327)
Billiard Congress of America (329)
Billings Ovulation Method Association of the United States (329)
Biscuit and Cracker Manufacturers' Association (330)
Black Coaches & Administrators (331)
Black Mental Health Alliance (331)
Book Industry Study Group, Inc. (333)
BritishAmerican Business Inc. (335)
The Brown Swiss Association (336)
Builders Hardware Manufacturers Association (337)
Builders Association (338)
Business Products Credit Association (339)
California Redwood Association (341)
Campus Safety, Health and Environmental Management Association (341)
Cantors Assembly (342)
Captive Insurance Companies Association (342)
Car Care Council (342)
Cargo Airline Association (343)
Casket and Funeral Supply Association of America (344)
Catholic Campus Ministry Association (345)
Catholic Cemetery Conference (345)
Catholic Medical Association (346)
Catholic Press Association (346)
Ceilings and Interior Systems Construction Association (347)
Cement Kiln Recycling Coalition (347)
Center for Waste Reduction Technologies (348)
Ceramic Tile Distributors Association (349)
Certified Contractors Network (349)
Cheese Importers Association of America, Inc. (351)
Chi Eta Phi Sorority, Inc. (352)
Children's Book Council (353)
Christian Educators Association International (355)
City and Regional Magazine Association (357)
Clinical Immunology Society (358)
Coal Operators and Associates (359)
Coalition of Black Trade Unionists (360)
Coalition of Essential Schools (360)
The Coastal and Estuarine Research Federation (361)
Cocoa Merchants' Association of America (361)
College of Optometrists in Vision Development (364)
College Sports Information Directors of America (364)
Color Marketing Group (365)
Commercial Food Equipment Service Association (366)
Commission on Accreditation of Allied Health Education Programs (368)
Commissioned Officers Association of the United States Public Health Service (368)
Commodity Markets Council (368)
Community Development Venture Capital Alliance (370)
Computer Measurement Group (372)
Concrete Foundations Association (373)
The Concrete Industry Board (373)
Concrete Sawing and Drilling Association (374)
Congress of Independent Unions (377)
Conservation Technology Information Center (378)
Consortium of Social Science Associations (379)
Construction Industry Round Table, Inc. (379)
Construction Owners Association of America (380)
Consumer Health Alliance (381)
Consumer Mortgage Coalition (381)
Contact Lens Council (382)

Contact Lens Manufacturers Association *(382)*
Contact Lens Society of America *(382)*
Conveyor Equipment Manufacturers Association *(383)*
Corporate Facility Advisors, Inc. *(386)*
Corporate Housing Providers Association *(386)*
Costume Designers Guild *(387)*
Council for Agricultural Science and Technology *(388)*
Council of Administrators of Special Education *(391)*
Council of Colleges of Arts and Sciences *(393)*
Council of Engineering and Scientific Society Executives *(393)*
Council of Medical Specialty Societies *(395)*
Council of Petroleum Accountants Societies *(396)*
Council of Producers & Distributors of Agrotechnology *(396)*
Council of Professional Associations on Federal Statistics *(396)*
Council of Science Editors *(397)*
Council of State Administrators of Vocational Rehabilitators *(397)*
Council of State Community Development Agencies *(397)*
Council on Employee Benefits *(399)*
Council on Licensure, Enforcement and Regulation *(400)*
Council on Radionuclides and Radiopharmaceuticals *(400)*
Council on the Safe Transportation of Hazardous Articles *(401)*
CPA Associates International *(402)*
Cranberry Institute *(403)*
Creative Education Foundation *(403)*
Cremation Association of North America *(404)*
Crop Insurance Research Bureau *(404)*
Dance Masters of America, Inc. *(406)*
Decision Sciences Institute *(407)*
Decorative Plumbing and Hardware Association *(408)*
Defense Orientation Conference Association *(408)*
Department for Professional Employees - AFL-CIO *(410)*
Diamond Council of America *(411)*
Digital Media Association *(412)*
Diplomatic and Consular Officers, Retired (Dacor) *(412)*
Division 1-A Athletic Directors Association *(415)*
Door and Access Systems Manufacturers Association, International *(415)*
Early Care and Education Consortium *(417)*
Economic History Association *(418)*
EDA Consortium *(419)*
Education Industry Association *(420)*
Efficiency First *(421)*
Electric Utility Fleet Managers Conference *(422)*
Electricity Consumers Resource Council (ELCON) *(422)*
Electronic Distribution Show Corporation *(423)*
Electronic Funds Transfer Association *(423)*
Electronics Technicians Association International *(424)*
Emergency Department Practice Management Association (EDPMA) *(425)*
Endocrine Fellows Foundation *(427)*
Energy Recovery Council *(428)*
Energy Telecommunications and Electrical Association *(428)*
The Entrepreneurship Institute *(430)*
Environmental Technology Council *(431)*
Equipment and Tool Institute *(432)*
Equipment Marketing and Distribution Association *(432)*
EUCG, Inc. *(433)*
Evangelical Christian Publishers Association *(434)*
Executive Women International *(435)*
Exhibit Designers and Producers Association *(435)*
Expanded Shale, Clay and Slate Institute *(435)*
Export Institute of the United States *(436)*
Farm Labor Organizing Committee *(437)*
FBI Agents Association *(438)*
Federal Facilities Council *(439)*
Federal Managers Association *(439)*
Federation of State Humanities Councils *(442)*
Feldenkrais Guild of North America *(442)*
Flexographic Technical Association *(447)*
The Folk Alliance International *(449)*
Foodservice & Packaging Institute, Inc. *(450)*
Foodservice Equipment Distributors Association *(450)*
Forest History Society *(451)*
Forest Industries Telecommunications *(451)*
Forest Landowners Association *(451)*
Forest Products Society *(451)*
Forum of Regional Associations of Grantmakers *(452)*
Foster Family-Based Treatment Association *(452)*
Fuel Cell and Hydrogen Energy Association *(454)*
Garden Writers Association *(456)*

Gasoline and Automotive Service Dealers of America *(457)*
Gay and Lesbian Medical Association *(457)*
Giant Screen Cinema Association *(460)*
Giving Institute *(461)*
Glass Art Society *(461)*
Golf Coaches Association of America *(463)*
Golf Course Builders Association of America *(463)*
The Grant Professionals Association *(465)*
Graphic Artists Guild *(465)*
Gravure Association of America *(465)*
Greeting Card Association *(466)*
Guild of Artists and Artisans *(467)*
Halogenated Solvents Industry Alliance *(468)*
The Handcrafted Soapmakers Guild *(468)*
Hardwood Manufacturers Association *(468)*
Harness Tracks of America *(468)*
Health Care Administrators Association *(469)*
Hellenic-American Chamber of Commerce *(474)*
Help Desk Institute *(474)*
High Technology Crime Investigation Association *(474)*
Hispanic Dental Association *(475)*
The Histochemical Society *(476)*
History of Science Society *(477)*
Hollywood Radio & Television Society *(477)*
Home Improvement Research Institute *(478)*
Hotel Brokers International *(479)*
Hotel Electronic Distribution Network Association *(479)*
ICOM, International Communications Agency Network *(482)*
IEEE - Industry Applications Society *(484)*
IEEE Instrumentation and Measurement Society *(484)*
IEEE Magnetics Society *(484)*
Incentive Marketing Association *(487)*
Independent Automotive Damage Appraisers Association *(488)*
Independent Cosmetic Manufacturers and Distributors *(489)*
Independent Office Products and Furniture Dealers Association *(490)*
Industrial Electronics Society *(493)*
Industrial Energy Consumers of America *(493)*
Industrial Foundation of America *(493)*
Information Technology Alliance *(495)*
Information Theory Society *(495)*
Inland Marine Underwriters Association *(496)*
InSight *(496)*
Institute of Clean Air Companies *(499)*
Institute of Environmental Sciences and Technology *(499)*
Institute of Judicial Administration *(501)*
Institute of Management Consultants USA *(501)*
Institute of Nuclear Materials Management *(502)*
Institute of Shortening and Edible Oils *(503)*
Institutional Life Markets Association *(504)*
Insulation Contractors Association of America *(504)*
Interactive Media Entertainment & Gaming Association *(507)*
Interactive Travel Services Association *(507)*
InterAmerican College of Physicians and Surgeons *(507)*
Intercollegiate Tennis Association *(507)*
Interim Ministry Network *(508)*
International Advertising Association *(509)*
International Association for Continuing Education and Training *(511)*
International Association for Energy Economics *(512)*
International Association for Impact Assessment *(513)*
International Association for Orthodontics *(513)*
International Association of Approved Basketball Officials, Inc. *(515)*
International Association of Audio Visual Communicators *(516)*
International Association of Conference Centers *(518)*
International Association of Diecutting and Diemaking *(519)*
International Association of Industrial Accident Boards and Commissions *(523)*
International Association of Jewish Vocational Services *(523)*
International Association of Lighting Management Companies *(524)*
International Association of Operative Millers *(525)*
International Association of Rehabilitation Professionals *(527)*
International Association of Special Investigation Units *(528)*
International Association of Tour Managers - North American Region *(528)*
International Banana Association *(529)*
International Biometric Society *(530)*
International Bluegrass Music Association *(530)*
International Brain Injury Association *(531)*
International Brotherhood of Magicians *(531)*

International Claim Association *(535)*
International College of Surgeons *(535)*
International Conference of Police Chaplains *(536)*
International Consumer Product Health and Safety Organization *(537)*
The International Ecotourism Society *(542)*
International Emissions Trading Association *(542)*
International Executive Housekeepers Association *(543)*
International Federation of Pharmaceutical Wholesalers *(544)*
International Festivals and Events Association *(545)*
International Flight Services Association *(545)*
The International Fluid Power Society *(545)*
International Foundation for Telemetering *(547)*
International Fragrance Association North America *(547)*
International Game Developers Association *(548)*
International Gay and Lesbian Travel Association *(548)*
International Grooving & Grinding Association *(549)*
International Ground Source Heat Pump Association *(549)*
International Imaging Industry Association *(551)*
International Law Students Association *(553)*
International Magnesium Association *(555)*
International Natural Sausage Casing Association *(557)*
International Neuropsychological Society *(558)*
International Ombudsman Association *(558)*
International Packaged Ice Association *(559)*
International Pediatric Transplant Association *(560)*
International Precious Metals Institute *(561)*
International Psychogeriatric Association *(561)*
International Reprographic Association *(563)*
International Slurry Surfacing Association *(565)*
International Snowmobile Manufacturers Association *(565)*
International Society for Prenatal Diagnosis *(568)*
International Society for Quality of Life Research *(569)*
International Society for the Study of Dissociation *(570)*
International Society of Appraisers *(570)*
International Society of Barristers *(571)*
International Society of Offshore and Polar Engineers *(573)*
The International Stability Operations Association *(575)*
International Surface Fabricators Association *(576)*
International Technology Law Association *(577)*
International Ticketing Association *(577)*
International Transplant Nurses Society *(578)*
International Travel Writers and Editors Association *(578)*
International Veterinary Acupuncture Society *(580)*
International Zinc Association-America *(582)*
Intertribal Timber Council *(583)*
Iron Casting Research Institute *(585)*
Iroquois Healthcare Alliance *(585)*
Irrigation Association *(585)*
ISA -The Association of Learning Providers *(586)*
Italy-America Chamber of Commerce *(586)*
Jewelers of America *(587)*
Joint Council of Allergy, Asthma and Immunology *(588)*
Journalism Education Association *(589)*
Knowledge Alliance *(591)*
Labor Council for Latin American Advancement (LCLAA) *(592)*
Laboratory Products Association *(592)*
Law and Society Association *(593)*
Lawn and Garden Dealers' Association *(594)*
Leather Industries of America *(596)*
Liability Insurance Research Bureau *(596)*
Linguistic Society of America *(598)*
Local Media Association *(599)*
Log Home Builders Association of North America *(600)*
Machinery Dealers National Association *(601)*
Malignant Hyperthermia Association of the United States *(602)*
Management Association for Private Photogrammetric Surveyors *(602)*
Manufacturers Standardization Society of the Valve and Fittings Industry *(603)*
Manufacturers' Agents Association for the Foodservice Industry *(603)*
Maple Flooring Manufacturers Association *(604)*
Marine Corps Aviation Association *(604)*
Maritime Law Association of the U.S. *(606)*
Mason Contractors Association of America *(607)*
The Masonry Society *(607)*
Meat Importers Council of America *(609)*
Medical Marketing Association *(611)*
Medical Transcription Industry Association (MTIA) *(611)*
Metal Treating Institute *(614)*
Middle East Studies Association of North America *(615)*

Monument Builders of North America *(619)*
Musculoskeletal Tumor Society *(621)*
Music Library Association *(622)*
Mutual Fund Education Alliance *(623)*
NALS *(625)*
NARSA-The International Heal Transfer Association *(625)*
NASTD - Technology Professionals Serving State Government *(626)*
National Academy of Arbitrators *(627)*
National Academy of Neuropsychology *(628)*
National Academy of Opticianry *(628)*
National Aeronautic Association *(629)*
National Air Carrier Association *(630)*
National Aircraft Resale Association *(630)*
National Alliance for Musical Theatre *(632)*
National Animal Control Association *(634)*
National Arab-American Medical Association *(635)*
NAMTA - National Art Materials Trade Association *(635)*
National Association for Ambulatory Care *(636)*
National Association for Bilingual Education *(636)*
National Association for Developmental Education *(638)*
National Association for Environmental Management *(638)*
National Association for Fixed Annuities *(639)*
National Association for Health Care Recruitment *(639)*
National Association for Multicultural Education *(640)*
National Association for PET Container Resources *(641)*
National Association for Pupil Transportation *(642)*
National Association for Research in Science Teaching *(642)*
The National Association for the Dually Diagnosed *(643)*
National Association for the Support of Long Term Care *(644)*
National Association of Advisors for the Health Professions *(645)*
National Association of Affordable Housing Lenders *(646)*
National Association of Architectural Metal Manufacturers *(647)*
National Association of Bar Executives *(648)*
National Association of Beverage Importers Inc. *(648)*
National Association of Black-Owned Broadcasters *(649)*
National Association of Broadcast Employees and Technicians-Communications Workers of America, AFL-CIO (NABET-CWA) *(650)*
National Association of Business Political Action Committees *(651)*
National Association of Catholic Chaplains *(651)*
National Association of Child Care Professionals *(653)*
National Association of Church Personnel Administrators *(653)*
National Association of Clinical Nurse Specialists *(654)*
National Association of Concessionaires *(657)*
National Association of Container Distributors *(658)*
National Association of Counsel for Children *(658)*
National Association of County Agricultural Agents *(659)*
National Association of County Engineers *(660)*
National Association of Credit Union Service Organizations *(661)*
National Association of EMS Educators *(665)*
National Association of Extension 4-H Agents *(667)*
National Association of Flight Instructors *(668)*
National Association of Government Defined Contribution Administrators *(670)*
National Association of Health Data Organizations *(671)*
National Association of Health Services Executives *(671)*
National Association of Hispanic Nurses *(672)*
National Association of Independent Fee Appraisers *(674)*
National Association of Insurance Women (International) *(676)*
National Association of Junior Auxiliaries *(677)*
National Association of Local Housing Finance Agencies *(678)*
National Association of Medical Examiners *(680)*
National Association of Minority and Women Owned Law Firms *(680)*
National Association of Mortgage Brokers *(681)*
National Association of Parliamentarians *(683)*
National Association of Pizzeria Operators *(685)*
National Association of Printing Ink Manufacturers *(686)*
National Association of Professional Geriatric Care Managers *(687)*
National Association of Professional Organizers *(687)*

National Association of Professional Process Servers *(688)*
National Association of Public Insurance Adjusters *(689)*
National Association of Railroad Trial Counsel *(689)*
National Association of Real Estate Brokers *(689)*
National Association of Resource Conservation and Development Councils *(691)*
National Association of Royalty Owners *(692)*
National Association of School Resource Officers *(693)*
National Association of Schools of Art and Design *(693)*
National Association of Secretaries of State *(695)*
National Association of Sewer Service Companies *(695)*
National Association of Shareholder and Consumer Attorneys *(696)*
National Association of Spine Specialists *(696)*
National Association of Sports Commissions *(697)*
National Association of State Aviation Officials *(698)*
National Association of State Departments of Agriculture *(699)*
National Association of State Directors of Career Technical Education Consortium *(699)*
National Association of State Park Directors *(702)*
National Association of State Technology Directors *(702)*
National Association of Steel Pipe Distributors *(703)*
National Association of Teachers of Singing *(705)*
National Association of Telecommunications Officers and Advisors *(705)*
National Association of Therapeutic Schools and Programs (NATSAP) *(706)*
National Association of Uniform Manufacturers and Distributors *(707)*
National Association of University Women *(708)*
National Association of Women in Construction *(710)*
National Association of Women Lawyers *(710)*
National Association of Workforce Development Professionals *(710)*
National Bankers Association *(712)*
National Bicycle Dealers Association *(713)*
National Black Chamber of Commerce *(714)*
National Candle Association *(717)*
National Catholic Development Conference *(718)*
National Center for Homeopathy *(719)*
National Child Support Enforcement Association *(721)*
National Chimney Sweep Guild *(721)*
National Christmas Tree Association *(721)*
The National Coal Council *(722)*
National Coal Transportation Association *(722)*
National Coalition for Assistive and Rehab Technology *(723)*
National Coalition of Girls' Schools *(723)*
National Coil Coating Association *(723)*
National Community Development Association *(725)*
National Conference of Black Mayors *(726)*
National Conference of Insurance Legislators *(727)*
National Conference on Weights and Measures *(729)*
National Correctional Industries Association *(730)*
National Council for Geographic Education *(731)*
National Council for Marketing and Public Relations *(732)*
National Council of Agricultural Employers *(733)*
National Council of Self-Insurers *(736)*
National Council of Supervisors of Mathematics *(737)*
National Council on Problem Gambling *(739)*
National Education Association *(744)*
National Electronic Service Dealers Association *(745)*
National Elevator Industry, Inc. *(745)*
National Emergency Management Association *(745)*
National Energy Services Association *(746)*
National Environmental, Safety and Health Training Association *(746)*
National Extension Association of Family and Consumer Sciences *(747)*
National Family Caregivers Association *(747)*
National Farmers Union (Farmers Educational & Co-operative Union of America) *(747)*
National Federation Coaches Association *(748)*
National Federation of Municipal Analysts *(749)*
The National Federation of Paralegal Associations, Inc. *(749)*
National Finance Adjusters *(750)*
National Foundation for Women Legislators *(753)*
National Fraternal Order of Police *(753)*
National Hispanic Corporate Council *(759)*
National Immigration Project of the National Lawyers Guild *(761)*
National Information Standards Organization *(763)*
National Installment Lenders Association *(764)*
National Intercollegiate Soccer Officials Association *(766)*
National Investment Banking Association *(767)*
National Leased Housing Association *(769)*

National Lieutenant Governors Association *(769)*
National Limousine Association *(770)*
National Livestock Producers Association *(770)*
National Lubricating Grease Institute *(770)*
National Luggage Dealers Association *(770)*
National Lumber and Building Material Dealers Association *(770)*
National Management Association *(771)*
National Marine Electronics Association *(771)*
National Network of Depression Centers *(775)*
National Network of Grantmakers *(775)*
National Onion Association *(776)*
National Organization of Nurse Practitioner Faculties *(777)*
National Organization of State Offices of Rural Health *(778)*
National Orientation Directors Association *(778)*
National Ornamental and Miscellaneous Metals Association *(778)*
National Pasta Association *(779)*
National Phlebotomy Association *(781)*
National Plasterers Council *(781)*
National Portable Storage Association *(781)*
National Public Employer Labor Relations Association *(783)*
National Railway Historical Society *(784)*
National Registry of Environmental Professionals *(785)*
National Rehabilitation Association *(785)*
National Religious Campaign Against Torture *(786)*
National School Public Relations Association *(789)*
National Sculpture Society *(790)*
National Shoe Retailers Association *(791)*
National Society for Hebrew Day Schools *(792)*
National Society of Accountants for Cooperatives *(793)*
National Society of Professional Surveyors *(794)*
National Sorghum Producers *(795)*
National Spinal Cord Injury Association *(795)*
National Star Route Mail Contractors Association *(796)*
National Student Speech Language Hearing Association *(798)*
National Textile Association *(800)*
National Trappers Association *(801)*
National Water Resources Association *(804)*
National Weather Service Employees Organization *(804)*
National Wellness Institute, Inc. *(804)*
National Wheelchair Basketball Association *(804)*
National Woman's Party *(805)*
National Women's Studies Association *(805)*
Naval Submarine League *(807)*
NCSL International *(808)*
Neurofibromatosis, Inc., Northeast *(808)*
NIBA - The Belting Association *(810)*
Nisei Farmers League *(811)*
Non-Ferrous Founders' Society *(811)*
NORA: Association of Responsible Recyclers *(811)*
North American Association of Floor Covering Distributors *(811)*
North American Blueberry Council *(814)*
North American Building Material Distribution Association *(814)*
North American Export Grain Association, Inc. *(816)*
North American Lake Management Society *(817)*
North American Meat Association *(818)*
North American Neuro-Ophthalmology Society *(819)*
North American Society for Trenchless Technology *(822)*
North American Transportation Management Institute *(823)*
Northwest Fruit Exporters *(824)*
The Oceanography Society *(826)*
Open Applications Group *(828)*
OpenTravel Alliance *(828)*
The Optical Lab Division *(829)*
Optoelectronics Industry Development Association *(830)*
Organization Development Network *(831)*
Outpatient Ophthalmic Surgery Society *(835)*
Paleontological Society *(837)*
Palomino Horse Breeders of America *(837)*
Pan American Association of Ophthalmology *(837)*
Peanut and Tree Nut Processors Association *(840)*
Pellet Fuels Institute *(841)*
Performance Warehouse Association *(841)*
Petroleum Convenience Alliance for Technology Standards *(843)*
Phi Alpha Theta *(845)*
Pi Lambda Theta *(847)*
Pickle Packers International *(848)*
Pierre Fauchard Academy *(848)*
Pine Chemicals Association *(848)*
Plastics Foodservice Packaging Group *(850)*
Pony of the Americas Club *(852)*
Power and Communications Contractors Association *(855)*
Power Tool Institute, Inc. *(855)*
Pressure Sensitive Tape Council *(856)*

Professional Association of Health Care Office Management *(859)*
Professional Association of Innkeepers International *(860)*
Professional Baseball Athletic Trainers Society *(860)*
Professional Insurance Marketing Association *(862)*
Public Agency Risk Managers Association *(869)*
Public Investors Arbitration Bar Association *(869)*
Public Library Association *(869)*
Public Radio Program Directors Association *(870)*
Pyramid Society *(871)*
Pyrotechnics Guild International *(871)*
Qualitative Research Consultants Association *(871)*
R & E Council of the NAPL *(872)*
Racking Horse Breeders Association of America *(872)*
The Railway Tie Association *(874)*
REALTORS Land Institute *(876)*
Recycled Paperboard Technical Association *(877)*
The Refractories Institute *(878)*
Refractory Ceramic Fibers Coalition *(878)*
Refrigerated Foods Association *(878)*
Religious Conference Management Association *(880)*
The Renaissance Society of America *(881)*
Research and Development Associates for Military Food and Packaging Systems *(881)*
Resource Center for Religious Institutes *(883)*
RESPRO (Real Estate Services Providers Council) *(883)*
Retail Advertising and Marketing Association International *(884)*
Retail Bakers of America *(884)*
Reusable Industrial Packaging Association *(885)*
Rheumatology Nurses Society *(886)*
Safety Pharmacology Society *(890)*
Sail America *(890)*
Santa Gertrudis Breeders International *(891)*
SAVE International *(891)*
Sealant, Waterproofing and Restoration Institute *(894)*
Seaplane Pilots Association *(894)*
The Securities Transfer Association *(895)*
Senior Executives Association *(897)*
Sewn Products Equipment and Suppliers of the Americas *(898)*
Sheet Metal and Air Conditioning Contractors' National Association *(898)*
Shipbuilders Council of America *(898)*
Single Ply Roofing Institute *(900)*
Sleep Research Society *(900)*
Society for American Baseball Research *(903)*
Society for Applied Spectroscopy *(904)*
Society for Cardiovascular Magnetic Resonance *(905)*
Society for Cinema and Media Studies *(905)*
Society for Clinical Vascular Surgery *(906)*
Society for Developmental and Behavioral Pediatrics *(907)*
Society for Experimental Biology and Medicine *(909)*
Society for Experimental Mechanics, Inc. *(909)*
Society for Foodservice Management *(909)*
Society for Free Radical Biology and Medicine *(909)*
Society for Historians of American Foreign Relations *(910)*
Society for Historical Archaeology *(911)*
Society for Humanistic Judaism *(912)*
Society for Integrative and Comparative Biology *(913)*
Society for Medical Decision Making *(915)*
Society for Military History *(915)*
Society for Nutrition Education and Behavior *(917)*
Society for Obstetric Anesthesia and Perinatology *(917)*
Society for Pediatric Dermatology *(917)*
Society for Personality Assessment *(918)*
Society for Photographic Education *(919)*
Society for Radiation Oncology Administration *(919)*
Society for Research on Nicotine and Tobacco *(920)*
Society for Risk Analysis *(920)*
Society for Scholarly Publishing *(921)*
Society for the Psychological Study of Science Issues *(924)*
Society for the Study of Social Problems *(925)*
Society for Vascular Medicine *(926)*
Society for Wetland Scientists *(927)*
Society of Accredited Marine Surveyors *(927)*
Society of Broadcast Engineers *(931)*
Society of Computed Body Tomography and Magnetic Resonance *(933)*
Society of Environmental Journalists *(935)*
Society of Experimental Test Pilots *(935)*
Society of Financial Examiners *(936)*
Society of Forensic Toxicologists *(936)*
Society of Former Special Agents of the Federal Bureau of Investigation *(937)*
Society of Mexican American Engineers and Scientists *(941)*
Society of Military Orthopaedic Surgeons *(941)*
Society of North American Goldsmiths *(943)*
Society of Pediatric Nurses *(943)*

Society of Publication Designers *(946)*
Society of Radiologists in Ultrasound *(946)*
Society of Rheology *(946)*
Society of Satellite Professionals International *(947)*
Society of State Leaders of Health and Physical Education *(947)*
Society of Thoracic Radiology *(948)*
Society of Trauma Nurses *(949)*
Society of Woman Geographers *(950)*
Solution Mining Research Institute *(952)*
Southeastern Livestock Network *(953)*
Souvenirs, Gifts and Novelties Trade Association *(953)*
Soyfoods Association of North America *(953)*
The Spain-United States Chamber of Commerce *(953)*
SPARC *(954)*
Special Care Dentistry *(954)*
Special Care Dentistry Association *(954)*
Special Interest Group for Design of Communication *(955)*
Specialized Information Publishers Association *(957)*
Spring Manufacturers Institute *(960)*
Stable Value Investment Association *(960)*
Stadium Managers Association *(960)*
State Education Technology Directors Association *(961)*
State Government Affairs Council *(961)*
Steel Joist Institute *(962)*
Steel Recycling Institute *(963)*
Steel Tube Institute of North America *(963)*
Strategic Marketplace Initiative *(963)*
Structural Insulated Panel Association *(964)*
Subcontractors Trade Association *(964)*
Swedish-American Chambers of Commerce of the USA, Inc. *(967)*
Synthetic Turf Council *(967)*
Tea Association of the United States of America *(969)*
Teratology Society *(971)*
Texas Longhorn Breeders Association of America *(972)*
Thoroughbred Owners and Breeders Association *(974)*
Thoroughbred Racing Associations of North America *(974)*
Tile Roofing Institute *(974)*
Timber Framers Guild *(974)*
Tobacco Associates, Inc. *(975)*
Tooling, Manufacturing and Technologies Association *(976)*
Tortilla Industry Association *(976)*
Toxicology Forum *(976)*
Transportation Lawyers Association *(978)*
Treated Wood Council *(980)*
Truck Trailer Manufacturers Association *(981)*
Truss Plate Institute *(981)*
Uniformed Services Academy of Family Physicians *(984)*
United Association of Equipment Leasing *(985)*
United Cerebral Palsy *(986)*
United Engineering Foundation *(986)*
United Methodist Association of Health and Welfare Ministries *(987)*
United States-Taiwan Business Council *(989)*
United States Association of Former Members of Congress *(990)*
United States Association of Importers of Textiles and Apparel *(990)*
United States Business and Industry Council *(991)*
United States Canola Association *(991)*
United States Custom Harvesters, Inc. *(993)*
United States High Speed Rail Association *(994)*
United States of America Dry Pea and Lentil Council, Inc. *(996)*
United States Psychiatric Rehabilitation Association *(998)*
United States Racquet Stringers Association *(998)*
University Council for Educational Administration *(1002)*
University Film and Video Association *(1002)*
Van Alen Institute *(1007)*
Vinyl Acetate Council *(1009)*
Violin Society of America *(1010)*
VITA *(1011)*
Waste Equipment Technology Association *(1012)*
Water and Wastewater Equipment Manufacturers Association *(1012)*
Weed Science Society of America *(1014)*
Western Economic Association International *(1015)*
Western History Association *(1015)*
White House Correspondents Association *(1016)*
Wholesale Florist and Florist Supplier Association *(1016)*
WIFS - Women in Insurance and Financial Services *(1017)*
Wilderness Medical Society *(1017)*
Window Covering Safety Council *(1018)*
WineAmerica *(1019)*
The Wire Association International, Inc. *(1019)*

Wireless Communications Association International *(1019)*
Wireless Industry Association *(1019)*
Wireless Innovation Forum *(1019)*
Women in International Security *(1021)*
Women's Jewelry Association *(1023)*
Woodworking Machinery Industry Association *(1024)*
World Affairs Councils of America *(1025)*
World Waterpark Association *(1028)*
Xplor International *(1029)*

$250-500,000

ABC Children's Group *(2)*
Academy of Ambulatory Foot and Ankle Surgery *(3)*
Academy of Rail Labor Attorneys *(8)*
Accreditation Council for Accountancy and Taxation *(9)*
ADED - The Association for Driver Rehabilitation Specialists *(12)*
Adventure Travel Trade Association *(13)*
Aerospace & Flight Test Radio Coordinating Council *(14)*
AFL-CIO - Maritime Trades Department *(15)*
Africa Travel Association *(15)*
Agricultural and Food Transporters Conference *(16)*
Air Medical Operators Association *(19)*
Air Medical Physician Association *(19)*
Aircraft Builders Council *(20)*
Alkylphenols and Ethoxylates Research Council *(22)*
Alliance for Natural Health USA *(23)*
Alliance for Nonprofit Management *(23)*
Alliance for Women in Media *(24)*
Alliance of Nonprofit Mailers *(25)*
Allied Finance Adjusters *(26)*
Alpha Chi Sigma Fraternity, Inc. *(26)*
American Academy of Adoption Attorneys *(30)*
American Academy of Anesthesiologist Assistants *(30)*
American Academy of Clinical Neuropsychology *(31)*
American Academy of Clinical Toxicology *(31)*
American Academy of Dental Group Practice *(32)*
American Academy of Dental Practice Administration *(32)*
American Academy of Health Physics *(35)*
American Academy of Home Care Physicians *(35)*
American Academy of Oral and Maxillofacial Pathology *(37)*
American Academy of Oral Medicine *(38)*
American Academy of Orofacial Pain *(38)*
American Academy of Psychotherapists *(41)*
American Academy of Restorative Dentistry *(41)*
American Alliance for Theatre and Education *(44)*
American Association for Adult and Continuing Education *(47)*
American Association for Applied Linguistics *(47)*
American Association for Employment in Education *(49)*
American Association for Paralegal Education *(50)*
American Association of Acupuncture and Oriental Medicine *(53)*
American Association of Attorney-Certified Public Accountants *(54)*
American Association of Automatic Door Manufacturers *(54)*
American Association of Birth Centers *(55)*
American Association of Children's Residential Centers *(56)*
American Association of Community Theatre *(58)*
The American Association of Dental Boards *(59)*
American Association of Directors of Psychiatric Residency Training *(60)*
American Association of Engineering Societies *(60)*
American Association of Franchisees and Dealers *(61)*
American Association of Managed Care Nurses *(64)*
American Association of Minority Businesses *(65)*
American Association of Neuropathologists *(66)*
American Association of Orthopaedic Medicine *(68)*
American Association of Police Officers *(70)*
American Association of Private Railroad Car Owners *(71)*
American Association of Public Health Dentistry *(71)*
The American Association of Radon Scientists and Technologists *(72)*
American Association of Residential Mortgage Regulators *(72)*
American Association of Veterinary Clinicians *(76)*
American Association of Veterinary Laboratory Diagnosticians *(76)*
American Association of Zoo Keepers *(77)*
American Backflow Prevention Association *(78)*
The American Board of Opticianry and the National Contact Lens Examiners *(83)*
American Board of Veterinary Practitioners *(84)*
American Brush Manufacturers Association *(86)*
American Cinema Editors *(91)*
American Clinical and Climatological Association *(91)*
American College of Apothecaries *(93)*

American College of Construction Lawyers *(94)*
American College of Foot & Ankle Orthopedics & Medicine *(95)*
American College of Healthcare Architects *(96)*
American College of Legal Medicine *(97)*
American College of Medical Physics *(97)*
American College of Medical Quality *(97)*
American College of Mortgage Attorneys *(98)*
American College of Neuropsychiatrists *(98)*
American College of Nutrition *(99)*
American College of Osteopathic Pediatricians *(100)*
American Comparative Literature Association *(105)*
American Copper Council *(108)*
American Council for Construction Education *(109)*
American Dermatological Association *(114)*
American Design Drafting Association International and American Digital Design Association *(114)*
American Electrology Association *(116)*
American Embryo Transfer Association *(116)*
American Equilibration Society *(117)*
American Family Therapy Academy *(118)*
American Filtration and Separations Society *(121)*
American Fire Safety Council *(121)*
American Greyhound Track Operators Association *(127)*
American Ground Water Trust *(127)*
American Hampshire Sheep Association *(128)*
American Hanoverian Society *(128)*
American Health and Beauty Aids Institute *(129)*
The American Hockey Coaches Association *(132)*
American Honey Producers Association *(133)*
American Institute for Afghanistan Studies *(135)*
American Institute for International Steel *(136)*
American Institute of Bangladesh Studies *(137)*
American Institute of Building Design *(137)*
American Judges Association *(143)*
American Ladder Institute *(144)*
American Land Rights Association *(144)*
American League of Lobbyists *(145)*
American Military Retirees Association *(152)*
American Military Society *(152)*
American Milking Shorthorn Society *(152)*
American Mobile Telecommunications Association *(152)*
American Mold Builders Association *(152)*
American Neuropsychiatric Association *(155)*
American Ophthalmological Society *(157)*
American Orthopsychiatric Association *(159)*
American Pancreatic Association *(162)*
American Pathology Foundation *(162)*
American Photographic Artists *(164)*
American Podiatric Medical Students Association *(166)*
American Property Tax Counsel *(168)*
American Psychosocial Oncology Society *(170)*
American Public Communications Council *(170)*
American Radium Society *(173)*
American Registry of Medical Assistants *(174)*
American Risk and Insurance Association *(175)*
American Rock Mechanics Association *(176)*
American Running Association *(176)*
American Running Association/American Medical Athletic Association *(176)*
American Salers Association *(176)*
American Salvage Pool Association *(177)*
American Sand Association *(177)*
American Schools Association *(177)*
American Sexually Transmitted Diseases Association *(178)*
American Society for Automation in Pharmacy *(181)*
American Society for Eighteenth-Century Studies *(183)*
American Society for Experimental NeuroTherapeutics *(184)*
American Society for Neurochemistry *(187)*
American Society for Precision Engineering *(188)*
American Society for Theatre Research *(190)*
American Society for Virology *(190)*
American Society of Anesthesia Technologists and Technicians *(192)*
American Society of Consulting Arborists *(196)*
American Society of Crime Laboratory Directors *(196)*
American Society of Dentist Anesthesiologists *(196)*
American Society of Dowsers *(197)*
American Society of Emergency Radiology *(197)*
American Society of Golf Course Architects *(198)*
American Society of Head and Neck Radiology *(199)*
American Society of Ichthyologists and Herpetologists *(200)*
American Society of Maxillofacial Surgeons *(202)*
American Society of Neuroimaging *(204)*
American Society of Ocularists *(205)*
American Society of Ophthalmic Registered Nurses *(205)*
American Society of Pediatric Nephrology *(206)*
American Society of Plant Taxonomists *(207)*
American Society of Preventive Oncology *(208)*
American Society of Transportation and Logistics *(210)*

American Urogynecologic Society *(218)*
American Veterinary Dental Society *(218)*
American Veterinary Distributors Association *(218)*
American Warmblood Registry *(219)*
American Watch Association *(219)*
American Wine Society *(221)*
American Wood-Protection Association *(222)*
Angel Capital Association *(223)*
Animal Behavior Society *(223)*
Antiquarian Booksellers Association of America *(224)*
APMI International *(225)*
Appraisers Association of America *(226)*
Aquatic Plant Management Society, Inc. *(227)*
Architectural Precast Association *(228)*
Armed Forces Optometric Society *(229)*
Art Libraries Society of North America *(230)*
Art Therapy Credentials Board *(230)*
Artist-Blacksmiths' Association of North America *(230)*
ArtTable *(231)*
AscdiNatd *(231)*
Asian Pacific American Labor Alliance, AFL-CIO *(232)*
Asian Women in Business *(232)*
ASPSN - American Society of Plastic Surgical Nurses *(234)*
Associated Collegiate Press *(235)*
Associated Press Managing Editors *(237)*
Associated Schools of Construction *(237)*
The Association for Academic Surgery *(237)*
Association for Applied Psychophysiology and Biofeedback *(238)*
Association for Applied Sport Psychology *(239)*
Association for Behavioral Health & Wellness *(240)*
Association for Business Communication *(240)*
Association for Canadian Studies in the United States *(241)*
Association for Chemoreception Sciences *(241)*
Association for Commuter Transportation *(242)*
Association for Comprehensive Energy Psychology *(242)*
Association for Continuing Higher Education *(243)*
The Association for Environmental Health and Sciences *(246)*
Association for Federal Information Resources Management *(246)*
Association for Financial Technology *(247)*
Association for Governmental Leasing and Finance *(247)*
Association for Healthcare Volunteer Resource Professionals *(248)*
Association for Library and Information Science Education *(251)*
The Association for Nursing Professional Development *(252)*
Association for Psychological Type International *(254)*
Association for Radiological and Imaging Nursing *(255)*
Association for Surgical Education *(257)*
Association for Symbolic Logic *(257)*
Association for the Advancement of International Education *(258)*
Association for the Advancement of Psychotherapy *(258)*
Association for the Advancement of Wound Care *(258)*
Association for the Study of Higher Education *(259)*
Association for the Study of Nationalities *(259)*
Association for Wedding Professionals International *(261)*
Association for Women in Communications *(261)*
Association for Women in Mathematics *(261)*
Association of Advanced Rabbinical and Talmudic Schools *(263)*
Association of American Chambers of Commerce in Latin America *(264)*
Association of American Pesticide Control Officials *(265)*
The Association of Asian American Investment Managers *(268)*
Association of Baccalaureate Social Work Program Directors *(269)*
Association of Business Owners of America *(270)*
Association of Cable Communicators *(270)*
Association of Chiropractic Colleges *(272)*
Association of Consulting Foresters of America *(276)*
Association of Credit Union Internal Auditors *(278)*
Association of Dermatology Administrators & Managers *(278)*
Association of Donor Recruitment Professionals *(279)*
Association of Educational Therapists *(280)*
Association of Former Intelligence Officers *(284)*
Association of Genetic Technologists *(285)*
Association of Golf Merchandisers *(286)*
Association of Independents in Radio *(288)*
Association of Lutheran Development Executives *(292)*

Association of Medical School Pediatric Department Chairs *(293)*
Association of Occupational Health Professionals in Healthcare *(296)*
Association of Oncology Social Work *(297)*
Association of Pathology Chairs *(298)*
Association of Pedestrian and Bicycle Professionals *(298)*
Association of Performing Arts Presenters *(298)*
Association of Physician Assistants in Cardiovascular Surgery *(299)*
Association of Professional Ball Players of America *(301)*
Association of Professional Landscape Designers *(301)*
Association of Professional Schools of International Affairs *(302)*
Association of Public Treasurers of the United States and Canada *(304)*
Association of Real Estate Women *(305)*
Association of SIDS and Infant Mortality Programs *(308)*
Association of Specialized and Professional Accreditors *(309)*
Association of State and Territorial Public Health Nutrition Directors *(310)*
Association of State Energy Research and Technology Transfer Institution *(311)*
Association of State Wetland Managers *(311)*
Association of Steel Distributors *(311)*
Association of Surfing Professionals - North America *(312)*
Association of Technical Personnel in Ophthalmology *(313)*
Association of Threat Assessment Professionals *(314)*
Association of Woodworking and Furnishings Suppliers *(318)*
Audio Publishers Association *(320)*
Automotive Safety Council *(323)*
Automotive Trade Association Executives *(324)*
Balloon Federation of America *(325)*
Beta Beta Beta *(328)*
Bicycle Product Suppliers Association *(329)*
Binding Industries Association *(329)*
Bioelectromagnetics Society *(329)*
Biomass Thermal Energy Council *(330)*
Black Retail Action Group *(332)*
Book Manufacturers' Institute *(333)*
BP and AMOCO Marketers Association *(334)*
Braunvieh Association of America *(334)*
Brotherhood of Railroad Signalmen *(336)*
Building Commissioning Association *(337)*
Building Stone Institute *(338)*
Business Solutions Association *(340)*
Cable and Telecommunications Human Resources Association *(340)*
CALLERLAB - International Association of Square Dance Callers *(341)*
Canon Law Society of America *(342)*
Carpet Cushion Council *(343)*
Casting Industry Suppliers Association *(344)*
Caucus for Producers, Writers & Directors *(346)*
Center for Exhibition Industry Research *(348)*
Center for Spiritual and Ethical Education *(348)*
CHA - Certified Horsemanship Association *(350)*
Checks Payment Systems Association *(351)*
Chemical Coaters Association International *(351)*
Chester White Swine Record Association *(352)*
Chevron and Texaco Petroleum Marketers Association *(352)*
Chief Officers of State Libraries Agencies *(352)*
Christian Labor Association of the United States of America *(355)*
Church Music Publishers Association *(356)*
Clay Minerals Society *(357)*
Cleaning Equipment Trade Association *(357)*
Cleaning Management Institute *(357)*
Clerkship Directors in Internal Medicine *(358)*
Clydesdale Breeders of the United States *(359)*
The Coalition for Transportation Productivity *(360)*
The Coalition of Airline Pilots Associations *(360)*
Coalition of Labor Union Women *(361)*
College Media Association *(363)*
College of Diplomates of the American Board of Orthodontics *(364)*
College Savings Foundation *(364)*
College Swimming Coaches Association of America *(364)*
Collision Industry Electronic Commerce Association *(365)*
The Color Association of the United States *(365)*
NAIOP, The Commercial Real Estate Development Association *(366)*
The Commercial Vehicle Solutions Network *(367)*
Commercial Vehicle Solutions Network *(367)*
Commercial Vehicle Training Association *(367)*
Communications Media Management Association *(369)*

National Alliance of Community Economic Development Associations *(632)*
National Alliance of Independent Crop Consultants *(632)*
National Alliance of State Broadcast Associations *(633)*
National American Indian Court Judges Association *(634)*
National Animal Supplement Council *(634)*
National Association for Armenian Studies and Research *(636)*
National Association for Behavioral Health *(636)*
National Association for Children's Behavioral Health (NACBH) *(637)*
National Association of County Community and Economic Development *(637)*
National Association for Family Child Care *(638)*
National Association for Girls and Women in Sport *(639)*
National Association for Medical Direction of Respiratory Care *(640)*
National Association for Olmsted Parks *(641)*
National Association for Search and Rescue *(642)*
National Association of Academic Advisors for Athletes *(645)*
National Association of Active Investment Managers *(645)*
National Association of Addiction Treatment Providers *(645)*
National Association of Athletic Development Directors *(647)*
National Association of Biology Teachers *(648)*
National Association of Black County Officials *(649)*
National Association of Black Social Workers *(649)*
National Association of Blacks in Criminal Justice *(649)*
National Association of Collegiate Marketing Administrators *(656)*
National Association of Collegiate Women Athletic Administrators *(656)*
National Association of Corporate Treasurers *(658)*
National Association of County Behavioral Health and Developmental Disability Directors *(659)*
National Association of Cruise Oriented Agencies *(662)*
National Association of Disability Evaluating Professionals *(663)*
National Association of Division Order Analysts *(663)*
National Association of Educational Office Professionals *(664)*
National Association of Elevator Safety Authorities International *(665)*
National Association of Environmental Professionals *(666)*
National Association of Epilepsy Centers *(666)*
National Association of Equipment Leasing Brokers *(666)*
National Association of Estate Planners and Councils *(666)*
National Association of Exclusive Buyer Agents *(666)*
National Association of Farm Service Agency County Office Employees *(667)*
National Association of Federal Education Program Administrators *(667)*
National Association of Fire Investigators *(668)*
National Association of Fraternal Insurance Counsellors *(669)*
National Association of Geoscience Teachers *(669)*
National Association of Hispanic Publications *(672)*
National Association of Home Inspectors *(673)*
National Association of Housing Cooperatives *(673)*
National Association of Independent Insurance Adjusters *(674)*
National Association of Independent Lighting Distributors *(674)*
National Association of Local Government Auditors *(678)*
National Association of Medicaid Directors *(680)*
National Association of Mortgage Bankers *(681)*
National Association of Negro Business and Professional Women's Clubs *(681)*
National Association of Nephrology Technologists and Technicians *(682)*
National Association of Orthopaedic Technologists *(683)*
National Association of Personnel Services *(684)*
National Association of Pipe Coating Applicators *(684)*
National Association of Principals of Schools for Girls *(686)*
National Association of Private Special Education Centers *(686)*
National Association of Professional Pet Sitters *(687)*
National Association of Public Child Welfare Administrators *(688)*
National Association of Resale & Thrift Shops *(691)*
National Association of Rural Health Clinics *(692)*
National Association of School Music Dealers *(692)*
National Association of Schools of Theatre *(694)*

National Association of Security Companies (NASCO) *(695)*
National Association of Shell Marketers *(696)*
National Association of State Agencies for Surplus Property *(697)*
National Association of State & Local Equity Funds *(697)*
National Association of State Boards of Geology *(698)*
National Association of State Controlled Substances Authorities *(699)*
National Association of State Directors of Migrant Education *(700)*
National Association of State Directors of Teacher Education and Certification *(700)*
National Association of State Farm Agents *(701)*
National Association of State Personnel Executives *(702)*
National Association of State Utility Consumer Advocates (NASUCA) *(702)*
National Association of Temple Administrators *(705)*
National Association of Ticket Brokers *(706)*
National Association of Towns and Townships (NATAT) *(706)*
National Association of Tribal Historic Preservation Officers *(707)*
National Association of Veterans Affairs Physicians and Dentists *(708)*
National Association of Veterans Research and Education Foundations *(708)*
National Association of Vision Care Plans *(708)*
National Automotive Finance Association *(711)*
National Basketball Referees Association *(713)*
National Bison Association *(713)*
National Braille Association *(716)*
National Catholic College Admission Association *(718)*
National Certification Council for Activity Professionals *(720)*
National Certified Pipe Welding Bureau *(720)*
National Chemical Credit Association *(720)*
National Child Care Association *(721)*
National Civic League *(722)*
National Clay Pipe Institute *(722)*
National Coalition of Black Meeting Planners *(723)*
National Conference of Bar Presidents *(726)*
National Conference of State Liquor Administrators *(728)*
National Corrugated Steel Pipe Association *(730)*
National Cottonseed Products Association *(731)*
National Council for Advanced Manufacturing *(731)*
National Council for Workforce Education *(733)*
National Council of Chain Restaurants *(734)*
National Council of Urban Education Associations *(738)*
National Council on Measurement in Education *(739)*
National Council on Public History *(739)*
National Council on Qualifications for the Lighting Professions *(739)*
National Credit Reporting Association *(740)*
National Dairy Herd Information Association *(741)*
National Dance Council of America *(741)*
National Dance Education Organization *(742)*
National Earth Science Teachers Association *(743)*
National Electrical Contractors Association *(744)*
National Energy Assistance Directors' Association *(746)*
National Fastener Distributors Association *(747)*
National Federation of Advanced Information Services *(748)*
National Federation of Priests' Councils *(749)*
National Food Service Security Council *(752)*
National Grain Trade Council *(756)*
National Grants Management Association *(756)*
National Guardianship Association *(757)*
National Hay Association *(758)*
National Health Association *(758)*
National Health Federation *(758)*
National Hearing Conservation Association *(758)*
National Home Performance Council, Inc. *(760)*
National Humanities Alliance *(761)*
National Ice Cream Retailers Association *(761)*
National Independent Concessionaires Association *(762)*
National Industrial Sand Association *(763)*
National Institute for Animal Agriculture *(764)*
National Institute of Oilseed Products *(765)*
National Lawyers Guild *(768)*
National Lesbian and Gay Journalists Association *(769)*
National Marine Distributors Association *(771)*
National Mastitis Council *(772)*
National Migrant and Seasonal Head Start Association *(772)*
National Minority Business Council *(773)*
National Organization for Associate Degree Nursing *(776)*

National Organization for the Professional Advancement of Black Chemists and Chemical Engineers *(777)*
National Organization of Black County Officials *(777)*
National Pan-Hellenic Council *(778)*
National Park Hospitality Association *(779)*
National Petroleum Management Association *(780)*
National Plant Board *(781)*
National Postal Policy Council *(781)*
National Real Estate Investors Association *(784)*
National Retail Tenants Association *(787)*
National Risk Retention Association *(787)*
National Shellfisheries Association *(790)*
National Slag Association *(792)*
National Society for Experiential Education *(792)*
National Society of Certified Healthcare Business Consultants *(793)*
National Solid Wastes Management Association *(795)*
National Stripper Well Association *(797)*
National Surgical Assistant Association *(798)*
National Tax Association *(799)*
National Tax Lien Association *(799)*
National Trailer Dealers Association *(801)*
National Tuberculosis Controllers Association *(802)*
National Waterways Conference *(804)*
National Weather Association *(804)*
National Wildlife Rehabilitators Association *(805)*
National Yogurt Association *(806)*
Native American Journalists Association *(806)*
Naval Enlisted Reserve Association *(807)*
Neuro-Developmental Treatment Association *(808)*
Neurosurgical Society of America *(809)*
North American Association of Commencement Officers *(813)*
North American Carbon Capture & Storage Association *(814)*
North American Deer Farmers Association *(815)*
North American Metal Packaging Alliance, Inc. (NAMPA) *(818)*
North American Nature Photography Association *(819)*
North American Peruvian Horse Association *(819)*
North American Society for Cardiovascular Imaging *(821)*
North American Students of Cooperation *(822)*
Northeast Organic Farming Association *(824)*
Northwest Natural Resource Group *(824)*
Norwegian-American Chamber of Commerce *(824)*
Nurses Organization of Veterans Affairs *(825)*
Ocean Carrier Equipment Management Association (OCEMA) *(825)*
OESP - National Association of Oil and Energy Service Professionals *(826)*
Office Business Center Association International *(826)*
Ophthalmic Photographers' Society *(829)*
Opticians Association of America *(829)*
Oral History Association *(830)*
Organization for Safety and Asepsis Procedures *(831)*
Organization of American Kodaly Educators *(832)*
Osteopathic Cranial Academy *(834)*
Outdoor Power Equipment and Engine Service Association *(835)*
Outdoor Writers Association of America *(835)*
Overseas Press Club of America *(835)*
The Paddlesports Industry Association *(836)*
Paper Shipping Sack Manufacturers' Association, Inc. *(838)*
Parachute Industry Association *(838)*
Parcel Shippers Association *(838)*
Patent Office Professional Association *(839)*
Perennial Plant Association *(841)*
Performing Arts Alliance *(841)*
Periodical and Book Association of America *(842)*
Pet Partners *(842)*
Petroleum Packaging Council *(843)*
Photoimaging Manufacturers and Distributors Association *(846)*
Phycological Society of America *(846)*
Pi Sigma Epsilon *(847)*
Piano Manufacturers Association International *(848)*
Picture Archive Council of America *(848)*
Pile Driving Contractors Association *(848)*
Pipe Fabrication Institute *(849)*
Plastic Surgery Research Council *(850)*
PMCA: An International Association of Confectioners *(851)*
Poetry Society of America *(851)*
Polyurethane Foam Association *(852)*
Polyurethane Manufacturers Association *(852)*
Porcelain Enamel Institute *(853)*
Portable Sanitation Association International *(853)*
Portfolio Management Institute *(853)*
Power-Motion Technology Representatives Association *(855)*
Process Equipment Manufacturers' Association *(858)*

Production and Operations Management Society **(859)**
Professional Association of Resume Writers and Career Coaches **(860)**
Professional Association of Volleyball Officials **(860)**
Professional Bail Agents of the United States **(860)**
Professional Grounds Management Society **(862)**
Professional Liability Agents Network **(863)**
Professional Women in Construction **(866)**
The Propeller Club of the United States **(867)**
Property Records Industry Association **(867)**
Psychology Society **(868)**
Public Employees Roundtable **(869)**
Public Utilities Risk Management Association **(870)**
Quarter Century Wireless Association **(872)**
Radiant Panel Association **(872)**
Radio Technical Commission for Maritime Services **(873)**
RadTech **(874)**
Railway Industrial Clearance Association **(874)**
Ranchers-Cattlemen Action Legal Fund, United Stockgrower of America **(874)**
Receptive Services Association of America **(876)**
Recognition Professionals International **(876)**
Recreational Park Trailer Industry Association **(877)**
Red and White Dairy Cattle Association **(877)**
Renewable Natural Resources Foundation **(881)**
Retail Confectioners International **(884)**
River Management Society **(886)**
Roof Coatings Manufacturers Association **(888)**
Rubber Pavements Association **(888)**
The Rural Sociological Society **(889)**
SACNAS (Society for Advancement of Chicanos and Native Americans in Science) **(889)**
SAFE Association **(890)**
Sales and Marketing Executives International, Inc. **(890)**
SB Latex Council **(891)**
School Social Work Association of America **(892)**
Science Fiction and Fantasy Writers of America **(892)**
Scientific Equipment and Furniture Association **(892)**
SCSI Trade Association **(893)**
Secondary Materials and Recycled Textiles Association **(894)**
Security Hardware Distributors Association **(895)**
Shareholder Services Association **(898)**
Shock Society **(899)**
Society for Applied Anthropology **(904)**
Society for Clinical Trials **(906)**
Society for Community Research and Action **(906)**
Society for Consumer Psychology **(907)**
Society for Education in Anesthesia **(908)**
Society for Epidemiologic Research **(908)**
Society for Ethnomusicology **(908)**
Society for Excellence in Eyecare **(909)**
The Society for Freshwater Science **(910)**
Society for Healthcare Consumer Advocacy **(910)**
Society for In Vitro Biology **(912)**
Society for Neuroscience in Anesthesiology and Critical Care **(916)**
Society for News Design **(916)**
Society for Pediatric Pathology **(918)**
Society for Psychophysiological Research **(919)**
Society for Reproductive Endocrinology and Infertility **(920)**
Society for Research on Adolescence **(920)**
Society for Social Studies of Science **(921)**
Society for the Scientific Study of Sexuality **(924)**
Society for the Study of Amphibians and Reptiles **(925)**
Society for Theriogenology **(926)**
Society of American Business Editors and Writers **(928)**
Society of American Magicians **(929)**
Society of Christian Philosophers **(932)**
Society of Collision Repair Specialists **(933)**
Society of Emergency Medicine Physician Assistants **(934)**
Society of Government Travel Professionals **(938)**
Society of Independent Professional Earth Scientists **(939)**
Society of Independent Show Organizers **(939)**
Society of Infectious Diseases Pharmacists **(939)**
Society of Municipal Arborists **(942)**
Society of Neurological Surgeons **(943)**
Society of Otorhinolaryngology and Head-Neck Nurses **(943)**
Society of Petroleum Evaluation Engineers **(944)**
Society of Piping Engineers and Designers **(944)**
SOLE - The International Society of Logistics **(952)**
Songwriters Guild of America **(952)**
Southern Shrimp Alliance **(953)**
Space Transportation Association **(953)**
Special Interest Group for Algorithm and Computation Theory **(954)**
Special Interest Group on Software Engineering **(956)**
Specialty Sleep Association **(958)**
Sports Lawyers Association **(959)**

Spotted Saddle Horse Breeders' and Exhibitors' Association **(959)**
StateNets Radio **(962)**
Steel Deck Institute **(962)**
Steel Door Institute **(962)**
Substance Abuse Program Administrators Association **(965)**
Suntanning Association for Education **(966)**
Surface Design Association **(966)**
Surgical Infection Society **(967)**
Sustainable Buildings Industry Council **(967)**
System Safety Society **(967)**
TASH **(968)**
Textile Care Allied Trades Association **(972)**
Theta Tau **(973)**
Tilt-up Concrete Association **(974)**
Tire and Rim Association **(975)**
Tire Retread and Repair Information Bureau **(975)**
Tobacconists' Association of America **(976)**
Towing and Recovery Association of America **(976)**
Trade Promotion Management Associates **(977)**
Training Officers Consortium **(977)**
Transportation Development Association **(978)**
The Travel and Tourism Research Association **(979)**
Treatment Communities of America **(980)**
Type Directors Club **(983)**
Unified Abrasives Manufacturers Association **(984)**
Uniform Retailers Association **(984)**
Union Label and Service Trades Department **(985)**
United Federation of Police & Security Officers **(987)**
United Ostomy Associations of America **(988)**
United Shoe Retailers Association **(988)**
United States Advanced Ceramics Association **(989)**
United States Animal Health Association **(989)**
United States Association for Energy Economics **(990)**
United States Contract Tower Association **(992)**
United States Cutting Tool Institute **(993)**
United States Lactation Consultant Association **(996)**
United States Ski and Snowboard Association **(999)**
United States Society on Dams **(999)**
United States Swim School Association **(999)**
University and College Designers Association **(1002)**
University Aviation Association **(1002)**
Urban Affairs Association **(1003)**
USA Maritime **(1004)**
USA Volleyball **(1005)**
Utility Arborist Association **(1006)**
Vacuum Dealers Trade Association/Sewing Dealers Trade Association **(1007)**
Vanadium Producers and Reclaimers Association **(1008)**
Veterinary Cancer Society **(1008)**
Veterinary Hospital Managers Association **(1008)**
Veterinary Orthopedic Society **(1008)**
Victorian Society in America **(1009)**
Viola da Gamba Society of America **(1009)**
Visual Communications Industry Group **(1010)**
Walking Horse Trainers Association **(1012)**
Wallcovering Association **(1012)**
Water and Sewer Distributors of America **(1012)**
Weather Risk Management Association **(1014)**
Web Sling and Tie down Association **(1014)**
WEB: Worldwide Employee Benefits Network **(1014)**
Wedding and Event Videographers Association International **(1014)**
Wedding and Portrait Photographers International **(1014)**
Welding Research Council **(1015)**
Welsh Pony and Cob Society of America **(1015)**
Western Dredging Association **(1015)**
Western Writers of America **(1016)**
White House News Photographers Association **(1016)**
Wildlife Disease Association **(1017)**
The Wildlife Society **(1017)**
Window Covering Manufacturers Association **(1018)**
Window Coverings Association of America **(1018)**
Wiring Harness Manufacturers Association **(1020)**
Women in Aerospace **(1020)**
Women in Government Relations, Inc. **(1021)**
Women in Technology International **(1022)**
Wood Machinery Manufacturers of America **(1024)**
Wood Products Manufacturers Association **(1024)**
World Aquaculture Society **(1025)**
World International Nail and Beauty Association **(1026)**
World Sign Associates **(1027)**
World Teleport Association **(1027)**
Yacht Brokers Association of America **(1030)**

$100-250,000

Abortion Care Network **(2)**
Academic Language Therapy Association **(3)**
Academy of Clinical Laboratory Physicians and Scientists **(4)**
Academy of Dental Materials **(5)**
Academy of Dentistry International **(5)**
Academy of Legal Studies in Business **(6)**

Academy of Pharmaceutical Research and Science **(8)**
Academy of Prosthodontics **(8)**
Academy of Surgical Research **(9)**
Accrediting Council on Education in Journalism and Mass Communications **(11)**
Adhesion Society **(12)**
Aerospace Futures Alliance **(14)**
AFT Healthcare **(15)**
Agricultural History Society **(16)**
Agriculture Council of America **(16)**
Air and Expedited Motor Carriers Association **(17)**
Air and Surface Transport Nurses Association **(17)**
Air Carrier Association of America **(17)**
Airport Ground Transportation Association **(21)**
Alliance for Gray Market and Counterfeit Abatement **(23)**
Alliance of Area Business Publications **(24)**
Alliance of Automotive Service Providers **(24)**
Alliance of Cardiovascular Professionals **(25)**
Alpha Gamma Rho **(26)**
Aluminum Anodizers Council **(27)**
Aluminum Foil Container Manufacturers Association **(27)**
American Academy of Advertising **(30)**
American Academy of Appellate Lawyers **(30)**
American Academy of Maxillofacial Prosthetics **(35)**
American Academy of Oral and Maxillofacial Radiology **(37)**
American Academy of Podiatric Sports Medicine **(40)**
American Academy of Psychoanalysis and Dynamic Psychiatry **(41)**
American Academy of State Certified Appraisers **(42)**
American Academy of Veterinary Acupuncture **(42)**
American Aging Association **(43)**
American Agricultural Editors Association **(43)**
American Agricultural Law Association **(44)**
American Apparel Producer's Network **(46)**
American Assembly for Men in Nursing **(47)**
American Association for Affirmative Action **(47)**
American Association for Agricultural Education **(47)**
American Association for Budget and Program Analysis **(48)**
American Association for the History of Medicine **(52)**
American Association for Vocational Instructional Materials **(53)**
American Association for Women in Community Colleges **(53)**
American Association for Women Radiologists **(53)**
American Association for Wound Care Management **(53)**
American Association of Candy Technologists **(55)**
American Association of Classified School Employees **(56)**
The American Association of Code Enforcement **(57)**
American Association of Community Psychiatrists **(58)**
American Association of Dental Consultants **(59)**
American Association of Genitourinary Surgeons **(61)**
American Association of Independent Claims Professionals **(63)**
American Association of Integrated Healthcare Delivery Systems **(63)**
American Association of Intensive English Programs **(63)**
American Association of International Healthcare Recruitment **(63)**
The American Association of Nurse Attorneys **(67)**
American Association of Police Polygraphists **(70)**
American Association of Sexuality Educators, Counselors and Therapists **(73)**
American Association of Small Ruminant Practitioners **(73)**
American Association of State Climatologists **(73)**
American Association of Teachers of Italian **(74)**
American Association of Teachers of Slavic and East European Languages **(75)**
American Association of Women Dentists **(77)**
American Auditory Society **(78)**
American Bail Coalition **(78)**
American Bladesmith Society **(81)**
American Board of Nursing Specialties **(82)**
American Boat Builders and Repairers Association **(84)**
American Bonanza Society **(85)**
American Bryological and Lichenological Society **(86)**
American Buckskin Registry Association **(86)**
American Bureau of Metal Statistics **(86)**
American Butter Institute **(87)**
American Chain of Warehouses **(89)**
American College Dance Festival Association **(92)**
American College of Epidemiology **(95)**
American College of Eye Surgeons **(95)**
American College of Health Care Administrators **(96)**
American College of Tax Counsel **(103)**
American College of Theriogenologists **(103)**

American College of Veterinary Anesthesiologists (103)
American College of Veterinary Dermatology (104)
American Commodity Distribution Association (105)
American Composers Alliance (105)
American Conference of Academic Deans (107)
American Construction Inspectors Association (107)
The American Consultants League (108)
American Council of Christian Churches (109)
American Council of Hypnotist Examiners (109)
American Council of Snowmobile Associations (110)
American Council on Consumer Interests (110)
American Court and Commercial Newspapers (111)
American Criminal Justice Association Lambda Alpha Epsilon (112)
American Culinary Federation (112)
American Cultural Resources Association (ACRA) (112)
American Custom Gunmakers Guild (112)
American Dance Therapy Association (113)
American Devon Cattle Association (114)
American Dexter Cattle Association (114)
American Donkey and Mule Society (115)
American Driver and Traffic Safety Education Association (115)
American Edged Products Manufacturers Association (115)
American Education Finance Association (116)
American Educational Studies Association (116)
American Escrow Association (118)
American Factoring Association (118)
American Federation of Musicians (119)
American Fire Sprinkler Association (121)
American Flock Association (122)
American Floorcovering Alliance (122)
American Forage and Grassland Council (122)
American Forensic Association (123)
American Friends of Turkey (124)
American Glovebox Society (126)
American Gynecological and Obstetrical Society (128)
American Hackney Horse Society (128)
American Harp Society (129)
American Herbalists Guild (131)
American Highland Cattle Association (131)
American Holistic Medical Association (132)
American Holsteiner Horse Association (132)
American Horse Publications (133)
American Horticultural Therapy Association (133)
American Independent Business Alliance (135)
American Indonesian Chamber of Commerce (135)
American Institute of Parliamentarians (140)
American Insurance Marketing and Sales Society (141)
American Knife & Tool Institute (144)
American Laryngological Association (144)
American Leather Chemists Association (145)
American Literary Translators Association (146)
American Medical Group Association (149)
American Navion Society (155)
American Neurotology Society (156)
American Oilseed Coalition (157)
American Organization for Bodywork Therapies of Asia (158)
American Oriental Society (158)
American Osteopathic Academy of Addiction Medicine (159)
American Osteopathic Academy of Sports Medicine (159)
American Osteopathic College of Occupational and Preventive Medicine (160)
American Otological Society (161)
American Peanut Product Manufacturers, Inc. (162)
American Peanut Research and Education Society, Inc. (162)
American Pipe Fittings Association (165)
American Prepaid Legal Services Institute (167)
American Prosthodontic Society (168)
American Psychopathological Association (170)
American Psychotherapy Association (170)
American Real Estate and Urban Economics Association (173)
American Red Brangus Association (174)
The American Safe Deposit Association (176)
American Scientific Glassblowers Society (178)
American Sleep Apnea Association (180)
American Society for Cytotechnology (183)
American Society for Dental Aesthetics (183)
American Society for Engineering Management (184)
American Society for Environmental History (184)
American Society for Indexing (186)
American Society for Mohs Histotechnology (187)
American Society for the Alexander Technique (190)
American Society of Business Publication Editors (194)
American Society of General Surgeons (198)
American Society of Group Psychotherapy and Psychodrama (198)
American Society of Highway Engineers (200)
American Society of Interior Designers (200)

American Society of Irrigation Consultants (201)
American Society of Mining and Reclamation (203)
American Society of Missiology (203)
American Society of Neurorehabilitation (204)
American Society of Notaries (204)
American Society of Orthopedic Physician Assistants (205)
American Society of Parasitologists (206)
The American Society of Pediatric Neurosurgeons (206)
American Society of Perfumers (206)
American Society of Picture Professionals (207)
American Society of Primatologists (208)
American Society of Sugar Beet Technologists (209)
American Society of Trial Consultants (210)
American Southdown Breeders Association (211)
American Subcontractors Association (214)
American Technical Education Association (215)
American Trakehner Association (217)
American Voice Input/Output Society (219)
American Woman's Society of Certified Public Accountants (221)
Analytical Laboratory Managers Association (223)
Antenna Measurement Techniques Association (224)
Apple Processors Association (225)
Apple Products Research and Education Council (226)
Appliance Parts Distributors Association (226)
Architectural Engineering Institute (227)
Aseptic Packaging Council (231)
Asia America MultiTechnology Association (231)
Aspirin Foundation of America, Inc. (233)
Associated Owners and Developers (236)
Association for Ambulatory Behavioral Healthcare (238)
Association for Applied and Therapeutic Humor (238)
Association for Asian American Studies (239)
Association for Child Psychoanalysis (241)
Association for Communication Excellence (242)
Association for Comparative Economic Studies (242)
Association for Counselor Education and Supervision (244)
Association for Evolutionary Economics (246)
Association for Management Information in Financial Services (251)
Association for Practical and Professional Ethics (253)
Association for Recorded Sound Collections (255)
The Association for Research in Business Education - Delta Pi Epsilon (255)
The Association for Science Teacher Education (256)
Association for the Advancement of Psychology (258)
Association for the Sociology of Religion (259)
Association for Transpersonal Psychology (260)
Association of Academic Chairmen of Plastic Surgery (262)
Association of Academic Health Sciences Library (263)
Association of Administrative Law Judges (263)
Association of AE Business Leaders (263)
Association of American Physicians (265)
Association of American Plant Food Control Officials (266)
Association of Asphalt Paving Technologists (268)
Association of Attorney-Mediators (268)
Association of Bituminous Contractors (269)
Association of Black Sociologists (270)
Association of Catholic Publishers (271)
Association of Children's Prosthetic-Orthotic Clinics (272)
Association of Christian Librarians (272)
Association of Christian Teachers and Schools (272)
Association of Christian Therapists (273)
Association of Clinical Scientists (273)
Association of Commercial Finance Attorneys (275)
Association of Commercial Real Estate (275)
Association of Community Health Nursing Educators (276)
Association of Cooperative Educators (277)
Association of Coupon Professionals (277)
Association of Defense Trial Attorneys (278)
Association of Destination Management Executives (278)
Association of Direct Response Fundraising Counsel (279)
Association of Educators in Imaging and Radiologic Sciences, Inc (280)
Association of Energy Service Companies (280)
Association of Environmental and Resource Economists (281)
Association of Episcopal Colleges (281)
Association of Executive and Administrative Professionals (281)
Association of Field Ornithologists (282)
Association of Former Agents of the U.S. Secret Service (284)
Association of Fraternity Advisors (284)

Association of Free Standing Radiation Oncology Centers (284)
Association of Independent Information Professionals (288)
Association of Independent Manufacturers'/ Representatives, Inc. (288)
Association of Independent Trust Companies (288)
Association of Jewish Libraries (290)
The Association of Language Companies (290)
Association of Life Insurance Counsel (291)
The Association of Literary Scholars, Critics, and Writers (291)
Association of Machinery and Equipment Appraisers (292)
Association of Medical Diagnostic Manufacturers (293)
Association of Medical Education and Research in Substance Abuse (293)
Association of Meeting Professionals (294)
Association of Military Colleges and Schools of the United States (294)
Association of Naval Aviation (295)
Association of Opinion Journalists (297)
Association of Paroling Authorities International (297)
Association of Pediatric Oncology Social Workers (298)
Association of Personal Historians (299)
Association of Plastic Surgery Assistants (299)
Association of Presbyterian Colleges and Universities (300)
Association of Private Enterprise Education (300)
Association of Professional Design Firms (301)
Association of Professional Genealogists (301)
Association of Schools of Journalism and Mass Communication (307)
Association of Sewing and Design Professionals (308)
Association of Specialty Cut Flower Growers (309)
Association of State Supervisors of Mathematics (311)
The Association of Suppliers to the Paper Industry (312)
Association of Transportation Professionals (314)
Association of Travel Marketing Executives (315)
Association of University Anesthesiologists (315)
Association of Vascular and Interventional Radiographers (316)
Association of Veterinary Biologics Companies (317)
Association of Women Surgeons (317)
Atlantic Independent Union (319)
Attention Deficit Disorder Association (320)
Aviation Distributors and Manufacturers Association International (324)
Barre Granite Association (326)
BCA (326)
Behavior Genetics Association (327)
Belgian Draft Horse Corporation of America (327)
Belted Galloway Society (328)
Biological Stain Commission (330)
Black Caucus of the American Library Association (331)
Black Entertainment and Sports Lawyers Association (331)
Black Filmmaker Foundation (331)
Blue Water Fishermen's Association (332)
Board Retailers Association (333)
Brake Manufacturers Council (334)
Business Forms Management Association (339)
C-Port (340)
Capital Markets Credit Analysts Society (342)
Career Planning and Adult Development Network (343)
Cashmere and Camel Hair Manufacturers Institute (344)
Cast Stone Institute (344)
Catholic Library Association (346)
Catholic Radio Association (346)
Cellulose Insulation Manufacturers Association (347)
Cement Employers Association (347)
Center for American Nurses (348)
Ceramic Tile Institute of America (349)
Chain Link Fence Manufacturers Institute (350)
Chemical Fabrics and Film Association (351)
Chief Petty Officers Association (352)
Children's Literature Association (353)
Chlorobenzene Producers Association (354)
Christian Association for Psychological Studies (355)
Christian Chiropractors Association (355)
Christian College Consortium (355)
Church and Synagogue Library Association (356)
Civil Aviation Medical Association (357)
Clean Technology & Sustainable Industries Organization (CTSI) (357)
Clinical Ligand Assay Society (358)
Clinical Orthopaedic Society (358)
Clowns of America International (359)
Coal Technology Association (359)
The Coalition for America's Gateways and Trade Corridors (360)

Coalition of Higher Education Assistance Organizations *(360)*
Coleopterists Society *(362)*
College Athletic Business Management Association *(362)*
College Band Directors National Association *(363)*
College Reading and Learning Association *(364)*
College Theology Society *(365)*
Columbia Sheep Breeders Association of America *(365)*
Commission on Professionals in Science and Technology *(368)*
Communications Fraud Control Association *(369)*
Community College Business Officers *(370)*
Composite Lumber Manufacturers Association *(372)*
Computer Assisted Language Instruction Consortium *(372)*
Conference of Research Workers in Animal Diseases *(375)*
Congress of Chiropractic State Associations *(377)*
Congress of Lung Association Staffs *(377)*
Consortium of College and University Media Centers *(378)*
Consortium of Forensic Science Organizations *(378)*
Consultant Dietitians in Health Care Facilities *(380)*
Contact Lens Association of Ophthalmologists *(382)*
Continental Dorset Club *(382)*
Cookware Manufacturers Association *(384)*
Copier Dealers Association *(384)*
The Cordage Institute *(385)*
Corporate Environmental Enforcement Council *(386)*
Cotton Warehouse Association of America *(387)*
Council for Children with Behavioral Disorders *(389)*
Council for Electronic Revenue Communication Advancement *(389)*
Council for Learning Disabilities *(390)*
Council for the Advancement of Standards in Higher Education *(391)*
Council of American Jewish Museums *(391)*
Council of Communication Management *(393)*
Council of International Investigators *(395)*
Council of Scientific Society Presidents *(397)*
Council of Societies for the Study of Religion *(397)*
Council of State Retail Associations *(397)*
Council on Diagnostic Imaging to the A.C.A. *(399)*
Council on Governmental Ethics Laws *(399)*
Cross Country Ski Areas Association *(405)*
Custom Tailors and Designers Association of America *(406)*
Dance Films Association *(406)*
Deep Sea Fishermen's Union *(408)*
Delta Omicron *(409)*
Delta Theta Phi *(409)*
Diagnostic Marketing Association *(411)*
Direct Marketing Insurance and Financial Services Council *(413)*
Disaster Recovery Contractors Association (DRCA) *(413)*
Distillers Grains Technology Council *(414)*
Distributed Wind Energy Association *(414)*
Eastern Apicultural Society of North America *(418)*
Educational Book and Media Association *(420)*
Electronic Commerce Code Management Association *(423)*
Electronic Components Industry Association *(423)*
Employee Assistance Society of North America *(426)*
Enhanced Protective Glass Automotive Association *(429)*
EPS Industry Alliance *(432)*
Epsilon Sigma Phi *(432)*
Esperanto-USA *(433)*
Evangelical Press Association *(434)*
Executive Women in Government *(435)*
Exhibition Services and Contractors Association *(435)*
Express Association of America *(436)*
Express Delivery & Logistics Association *(436)*
Federal Judges Association *(439)*
Federal Magistrate Judges Association *(439)*
Federation of Associations of Regulatory Boards *(441)*
Federation of Internet Solution Providers of the Americas *(441)*
Fiberglass Tank and Pipe Institute *(443)*
Fire and Emergency Manufacturers and Services Association *(446)*
Fire Apparatus Manufacturers' Association *(446)*
Fire Equipment Manufacturer's Association *(446)*
Flexible Film & Bag Division *(447)*
Flexible Intermediate Bulk Container Association *(447)*
Flexographic Prepress Platemakers Association *(447)*
Floor Covering Installation Contractors Association *(448)*
Fluid Controls Institute *(448)*
Flying Physicians Association *(448)*
Food Industry Association Executives *(449)*
Football Writers Association of America *(450)*
Friction Material Standards Institute *(454)*

Friends of the National Institute of Dental and Craniofacial Research (FNIDCR) *(454)*
Frozen Potato Products Institute *(454)*
Fulfillment Management Association *(454)*
Funeral Consumers Alliance *(454)*
Fusion Power Associates *(455)*
Futon Association International *(455)*
Gamma Iota Sigma *(456)*
Gas Turbine Association *(457)*
Generic Animal Drug Alliance *(458)*
Geothermal Heat Pump Consortium *(459)*
German American Business Association *(460)*
Giving USA Foundation *(461)*
Glove Shippers Association *(463)*
Glutamate Association (United States) *(463)*
Golf Writers Association of America *(463)*
Gospel Music Association *(464)*
Government Management Information Sciences *(464)*
Guild of Book Workers *(467)*
Guild of Natural Science Illustrators *(467)*
Guitar and Accessories Marketing Association *(467)*
Halon Alternatives Research Corporation *(468)*
Health Industry Representatives Association *(470)*
Heat Exchange Institute *(472)*
Hedge Fund Association *(473)*
Herb Growing and Marketing Network *(474)*
Hispanic Organization of Latin Actors *(476)*
Historians of Islamic Art Association *(476)*
Hobby Manufacturers Association *(477)*
Home Baking Association *(477)*
Home Fashion Products Association *(478)*
Home Furnishings Independents Association *(478)*
HUBZone Contractors National Council *(480)*
Human Milk Banking Association of North America *(481)*
IEEE Circuits and Systems Society *(483)*
IGAF Polaris *(486)*
IMAGE Society *(486)*
Imaging Supplies Coalition *(487)*
Incentive Federation, Inc. *(487)*
Independent Armored Car Operators Association *(488)*
Independent Association of Accredited Registrars *(488)*
Independent Distributors of Electronics Association *(489)*
Independent Equipment Dealers Association *(489)*
Independent Laboratory Distributors Association *(490)*
Independent Medical Distributors Association *(490)*
Independent Sealing Distributors *(491)*
Indian Arts and Crafts Association *(492)*
Indian Educators Federation *(492)*
Industrial Diamond Association of America *(493)*
Industrial Heating Equipment Association *(493)*
Industrial Perforators Association *(494)*
Infrared Data Association *(496)*
Institute of Real Estate Management *(503)*
Instructional Technology Council *(504)*
Instrumentation Testing Association *(504)*
Insulated Cable Engineers Association *(504)*
Insulating Concrete Form Association *(504)*
Insurance Marketing Communications Association *(505)*
Interactive Multimedia and Collaborative Communications Alliance *(507)*
International Academy of Gnathology - American Section *(509)*
The International Air Cargo Association *(509)*
The International Alliance for Women *(510)*
International Association for Computer Information Systems *(511)*
International Association for Hydrogen Energy *(513)*
International Association for Mathematical Geosciences *(513)*
International Association for Modular Exhibitry *(513)*
International Association for Near Death Studies, Inc. *(513)*
International Association for the Study of Dreams *(514)*
International Association of Baptist Colleges and Universities *(516)*
International Association of Black Professional Fire Fighters *(517)*
International Association of Color Manufacturers *(518)*
International Association of Commercial Collectors *(518)*
International Association of Counseling Services *(518)*
International Association of Golf Administrators *(522)*
International Association of Homes and Services for the Ageing *(522)*
International Association of Ice Cream Vendors *(523)*
International Association of Infant Massage *(523)*
International Association of Insurance Receivers *(523)*

International Association of Law Enforcement Intelligence Analysts *(523)*
International Association of Microfinance Investors *(524)*
International Association of Printing House Craftsmen *(526)*
International Association of Round Dance Teachers *(527)*
International Association of Skateboard Companies *(527)*
International Association of Speakers Bureaus *(528)*
International Association of Used Equipment Dealers *(528)*
International Association of Wildland Fire *(528)*
International Association of Women Police *(529)*
International Atherosclerosis Society *(529)*
International Aviation Women's Association *(529)*
International Biometric Industry Association *(530)*
International Bowling Pro Shop and Instructors Association *(530)*
International Brotherhood of Police Officers *(532)*
International Buckskin Horse Association *(532)*
International Builders Exchange Executives/Builders Exchange Network *(532)*
International Chemical Workers Union Council/UFCW *(534)*
The International Childbirth Education Association *(534)*
International College of Cranio-Mandibular Orthopedics *(535)*
International Conference of Symphony and Opera Musicians *(537)*
International Council of Employers of Bricklayers and Allied Craftworkers *(538)*
International Council of Fine Arts Deans *(538)*
International Customer Service Association *(539)*
International Family Recreation Association *(544)*
International Firestop Council *(545)*
The International Food & Beverage Forum *(546)*
International Formalwear Association *(546)*
International Furnishings and Design Association *(548)*
International Guards Union of America *(549)*
International Home Furnishings Representatives Association *(550)*
International Horn Society *(550)*
International Imaging Technology Council *(551)*
International Labor Communications Association *(553)*
International Light Transportation Vehicle Association, Inc. *(554)*
International Map Trade Association *(555)*
International Marking and Identification Association *(556)*
International Microwave Power Institute *(556)*
International Military Community Executives Association *(556)*
International Motor Press Association *(557)*
International Nanny Association *(557)*
International Neural Network Society *(558)*
International Nurses Society on Addititions *(558)*
International Ozone Association-Pan American Group Branch *(559)*
International Pet and Animal Transportation Association *(560)*
International Psycho-Oncology Society *(561)*
International Regional Magazine Association *(562)*
International Society for Computerized Electrocardiology *(566)*
International Society for Developmental Psychobiology *(566)*
International Society of Air Safety Investigators *(570)*
International Society of Certified Electronics Technicians *(572)*
International Society of Communication Specialists *(572)*
International Society of Exposure Science *(572)*
International Society of Fire Service Instructors *(572)*
International Society of Psychiatric-Mental Health Nurses *(574)*
International Society of Weighing and Measurement *(574)*
International Textile and Apparel Association *(577)*
International Thermographers Association *(577)*
International Truck Parts Association *(578)*
International Union of Toxicology *(579)*
International Vessel Operators Dangerous Goods Association *(580)*
International Veterinary Academy of Pain Management *(580)*
International Women's Writing Guild *(581)*
Internet Commerce Association (f/k/a Internet Traffic Association) *(582)*
Interstate Council on Water Policy *(582)*
IT Financial Management Association *(586)*
Jean Piaget Society *(586)*
Jesuit Secondary Education Association *(587)*
Jewish Educators Assembly *(588)*
Jewish Funeral Directors of America *(588)*
Joint National Committee for Languages *(589)*

Kappa Kappa Iota-National **(590)**
Kappa Psi Pharmaceutical Fraternity, Inc. **(590)**
Korean American Spine Society **(591)**
Label Printing Industries of America **(591)**
Lambda Kappa Sigma **(593)**
Laser and Electro-Optics Manufacturers' Association **(593)**
Lawyers Committee on Nuclear Policy **(594)**
Library Binding Institute **(597)**
Life Insurers Council **(597)**
Lighter Association **(598)**
Livestock Publications Council **(599)**
Major County Sheriffs' Association **(601)**
Manuscript Society **(604)**
Marine Corps League **(605)**
Marketing and Advertising Global Network **(606)**
Marketing Association of Credit Unions **(606)**
The Masonry Heater Association of North America **(607)**
Mass Marketing Insurance Institute **(607)**
Meat Industry Suppliers Alliance **(610)**
Media Communications Association International **(610)**
Media Credit Association **(610)**
Military Chaplains Association of the U.S. **(616)**
Military Chaplains Association of the United States **(616)**
Mining and Metallurgical Society of America **(617)**
Modular Building Systems Council **(618)**
Mohair Council of America **(618)**
Mu Phi Epsilon **(621)**
Museum Trustee Association **(621)**
Music Publishers Association of the United States **(622)**
NanoBusiness Alliance **(625)**
National Abstinence Education Association **(626)**
National Academies of Practice **(627)**
National Agricultural Alumni and Development Association **(630)**
National Alliance for Accessible Golf **(631)**
National Alliance of Medicare Set-Aside Professionals, Inc. **(632)**
National Alliance of Preservation Commissions **(633)**
National Armored Car Association **(635)**
National Association for Drama Therapy **(638)**
National Association for Family and Community Education **(638)**
National Association for Oilheat Research and Education **(641)**
National Association for Practical Nurse Education and Service **(641)**
National Association for Proton Therapy **(642)**
National Association for Relationship and Marriage Education **(642)**
National Association for Sport and Physical Education **(643)**
National Association for the Advancement of Orthotics and Prosthetics **(643)**
National Association for the Advancement of Psychoanalysis **(643)**
National Association of Academies of Science **(645)**
National Association of Activity Professionals **(645)**
National Association of African American Studies and Affiliates **(646)**
National Association of Assistant United States Attorneys **(647)**
National Association of Blind Merchants **(650)**
National Association of Boat Manufacturers **(650)**
National Association of Catastrophe Adjusters **(651)**
National Association of Catholic School Teachers **(651)**
National Association of Certified Professional Midwives **(651)**
National Association of Charterboat Operators **(652)**
National Association of Consumer Agency Administrators **(657)**
National Association of Consumer Shows **(658)**
National Association of County Recorders, Election Officials and Clerks **(660)**
National Association of Credit Union Chairmen **(661)**
National Association of Credit Union Supervisory and Auditing Committees **(661)**
The National Association of Crime Victim Compensation Boards **(661)**
National Association of Diaconate Directors **(662)**
National Association of Farmers Market Nutrition Programs **(667)**
National Association of Federal Veterinarians **(668)**
National Association of Flood and Stormwater Management Agencies **(668)**
National Association of Flour Distributors **(668)**
National Association of Forensic Economics **(669)**
National Association of Foster Grandparent Program Directors **(669)**
National Association of Fundraising Ticket Manufacturers **(669)**
National Association of Government Communicators **(670)**
National Association of Graphic and Product Identification Manufacturers **(670)**

National Association of Health Unit Coordinators **(671)**
National Association of Hispanic and Latino Studies **(672)**
National Association of Hospital Hospitality Houses **(673)**
National Association of Independent Insurance Auditors and Engineers **(674)**
National Association of Independent Public Finance Advisors **(675)**
National Association of Investigative Specialists **(676)**
National Association of Jewelry Appraisers **(677)**
National Association of Judiciary Interpreters and Translators **(677)**
National Association of Latino Elected and Appointed Officials **(677)**
National Association of Legal Search Consultants **(678)**
National Association of Local Government Environmental Professionals **(678)**
National Association of Margarine Manufacturers **(679)**
National Association of Marine Services **(679)**
The National Association of Marine Surveyors, Inc. **(679)**
National Association of Medical Minority Educators, Inc. **(680)**
National Association of Minority Contractors **(680)**
National Association of Miscellaneous, Ornamental and Architectural Products Contractors **(681)**
National Association of Multicultural Engineering Program Advocates **(681)**
National Association of Multicultural Media Executives **(681)**
National Association of Neighborhoods **(681)**
National Association of Nutrition and Aging Services Programs **(682)**
National Association of Optometrics and Opticians **(683)**
National Association of Optometrists and Opticians **(683)**
National Association of Physician Nurses **(684)**
National Association of Physician Recruiters **(684)**
National Association of Portable X-Ray Providers **(685)**
National Association of Power Engineers **(685)**
National Association of Real Estate Editors **(690)**
National Association of Rehabilitation Providers and Agencies **(691)**
National Association of Sales Professionals **(692)**
National Association of Science Writers **(694)**
National Association of Scientific Materials Managers **(694)**
National Association of Securities Professionals **(695)**
National Association of Sign Supply Distributors **(696)**
National Association of State Election Directors **(700)**
National Association of State Facilities Administrators **(701)**
National Association of State Veterans Homes **(702)**
National Association of Street Schools **(703)**
National Association of Swine Records **(704)**
National Association of Temple Educators **(705)**
National Association of Unclaimed Property Administrators **(707)**
National Association of University Forest Resources Programs **(707)**
National Association of Urban Hospitals **(708)**
National Association of Vertical Transportation Professionals **(708)**
National Association of Veterans Program Administrators **(708)**
National Association of Wastewater Transporters **(708)**
National Association of Waterproofing and Structural Repair Contractors **(709)**
National Association of Women Artists **(709)**
National Associations of State Directors of Pupil Transportation Services **(710)**
National Band Association **(712)**
National Barbecue Association **(712)**
National Barley Growers Association **(712)**
National Basketball Athletic Trainers Association **(712)**
National Beauty Culturists' League **(713)**
National Black Police Association **(714)**
National Board for Certified Clinical Hypnotherapists **(715)**
National Bulk Vendors Association **(716)**
National Career Development Association **(717)**
National Cartoonists Society **(718)**
National Caves Association **(719)**
National Certification Commission **(720)**
National Cherry Growers and Industries Foundation **(720)**
National Christian School Association **(721)**
National Church Goods Association **(722)**

National College of Probate Judges **(724)**
National Concrete Burial Vault Association **(725)**
National Confectionery Sales Association **(726)**
National Conference of Appellate Court Clerks **(726)**
National Conference of CPA Practitioners **(727)**
National Conference of Executives of The ARC **(727)**
National Conference of State Fleet Administrators **(728)**
National Costumers Association **(730)**
National Council for Agricultural Education **(731)**
National Council for Languages and International Studies **(732)**
National Council of Acoustical Consultants **(733)**
National Council of Postal Credit Unions **(735)**
National Council of Social Security Management Associations **(736)**
National Council of State Agencies for the Blind **(736)**
National Council on Rehabilitation Education **(739)**
National CPA Health Care Advisors Association **(740)**
National Dance Association **(741)**
National Defender Investigator Association **(742)**
National Dental Association **(742)**
National Dental EDI Council **(743)**
National Dog Groomers Association of America, Inc. **(743)**
National Drilling Association **(743)**
National Elder Law Foundation **(744)**
National Federation of Licensed Practical Nurses **(749)**
National Federation of Modern Language Teachers Associations **(749)**
National Federation of Press Women **(749)**
National Field Selling Association **(750)**
National Flea Market Association **(751)**
National Foster Parent Association **(753)**
National Freight Transportation Association **(753)**
National Frozen Pizza Institute **(754)**
National Gerontological Nursing Association **(755)**
The National Greenhouse Manufacturers Association **(756)**
National Guild of Professional Paperhangers **(757)**
National Health Club Association **(758)**
National HEP-CAMP Association **(759)**
National Human Resources Association **(761)**
National Independent Nursery Furniture Retailers Association **(762)**
National Independent Private Schools Association **(762)**
National Indian Head Start Directors Association **(763)**
National Industrial Council - Employer Association Group **(763)**
National Industrial Council - State Associations Group **(763)**
National Institute for Farm Safety, Incorporation **(764)**
National Institute for State Credit Union Examination **(764)**
National Institute of Electromedical Information **(765)**
National Institute of Steel Detailing **(765)**
National Institute for Water Resources **(766)**
National Interscholastic Swimming Coaches Association **(766)**
National League of American Pen Women **(768)**
National Mail Order Association **(771)**
National Marine Bankers Association **(771)**
National Maritime Alliance **(772)**
National Maritime Safety Association **(772)**
National Military Intelligence Association **(772)**
National Mitigation Banking Association **(773)**
The National Money Transmitters Association **(773)**
National Naval Officers Association **(774)**
The National Network for Social Work Managers **(774)**
National Onsite Wastewater Recycling Association **(776)**
National Optometric Association **(776)**
National Organization for Human Service **(777)**
National Perinatal Association **(780)**
National Postsecondary Agriculture Student Organization **(781)**
National Poultry and Food Distributors Association **(782)**
The National Procurement Institute, Inc **(783)**
National Psychological Association for Psychoanalysis **(783)**
National Recycling Coalition **(784)**
National Rural Economic Developers Association **(788)**
National Rural Education Association **(788)**
National Science Education Leadership Association **(790)**
National Show Horse Registry **(791)**
National Society of Insurance Premium Auditors **(794)**
National Spotted Swine Records **(796)**
National Student Employment Association **(797)**

$50-100,000

Red Tag News Publications Association **(878)**
Reliability Society **(880)**
Religion Communicators Council **(880)**
Religious Education Association **(880)**
Religious Research Association **(880)**
Remanufacturing Institute **(881)**
Resort and Commercial Recreation Association **(883)**
Rocky Mountain Llama & Alpaca Association **(887)**
Romanian-American Chamber of Commerce **(888)**
Sanitary Supply Wholesaling Association **(891)**
Scaffolding, Shoring and Forming Institute **(892)**
Silica Fume Association **(899)**
Silver Users Association **(900)**
Small Publishers Association of North America **(901)**
Social Science History Association **(902)**
Society for Business Ethics **(905)**
Society for Ear, Nose and Throat Advances in Children **(907)**
Society for Features Journalism **(909)**
Society for History Education **(911)**
Society for Industrial Archeology **(913)**
Society for Mathematical Biology **(915)**
Society for Occupational and Environmental Health **(917)**
Society for Phenomenology and Existential Philosophy **(918)**
Society for Physical Regulation in Biology and Medicine **(919)**
Society for Physician Assistants in Pediatrics **(919)**
Society for the History of Authorship, Reading and Publishing **(923)**
Society for the Study of Symbolic Interaction **(925)**
Society of Air Force Clinical Surgeons **(928)**
Society of American Registered Architects **(929)**
Society of Cleaning and Restoration Technicians **(932)**
Society of Composers, Inc. **(933)**
Society of Federal Labor and Employee Relations Professionals **(936)**
Society of Flavor Chemists **(936)**
Society of Invasive Cardiovascular Professionals **(940)**
Society of Maritime Arbitrators **(941)**
Society of Pelvic Surgeons **(944)**
Society of Photo-Technologists **(944)**
Society of Quantitative Analysts **(946)**
Society of University Otolaryngologists-Head and Neck Surgeons **(949)**
Sommelier Society of America **(952)**
Souvenir Wholesale Distributors Association **(953)**
Special Event Sites Marketing Alliance **(954)**
Special Interest Group on Artificial Intelligence **(956)**
Special Interest Group on Operating Systems **(956)**
State Guard Association of the United States **(961)**
Steel Window Institute **(963)**
Structural Stability Research Council **(964)**
Stuntmen's Association of Motion Pictures **(964)**
Sump and Sewage Pump Manufacturers Association **(965)**
Synthetic Yarn and Fiber Association **(967)**
Technical Association of the Graphic Arts **(969)**
The Technology Institute for Music Educators **(970)**
Textile Bag and Packaging Association **(972)**
Tourist Railway Association Inc. **(976)**
Transportation Clubs International **(978)**
Transportation Research Forum **(979)**
Tube Council of North America **(982)**
Ultrasonic Industry Association **(983)**
Unfinished Furniture Association **(984)**
United Applications Standards Group **(985)**
United Association for Labor Education **(985)**
United Lightning Protection Association **(987)**
United Producers Formulators and Distributors Association **(988)**
United Producers, Inc. **(988)**
United Professional Horsemen's Association **(988)**
United States Air Tour Association **(989)**
United States Clay Producers Traffic Association **(991)**
United States Court Reporters Association **(993)**
United States Internet Industry Association **(995)**
United States-Austrian Chamber of Commerce **(1001)**
United Steelworkers of America **(1001)**
Used Textbook Association **(1005)**
Used Truck Association **(1005)**
Utility Communicators International **(1006)**
Utility Smart Network Access Port **(1007)**
Valve Repair Council **(1007)**
Voice and Speech Trainers Association **(1011)**
Waterproofing Contractors Association **(1013)**
Weather Modification Association **(1014)**
Western Association of Industrial Distributors **(1015)**
The Western Red Cedar Pole Association **(1016)**
Wire Fabricators Association **(1019)**
Wire Rope Technical Board **(1019)**
Women's International Network of Utility Professionals **(1023)**
The World Umpires Association **(1027)**

$25-50,000

AASP - The Palynological Society **(2)**
Academy of Accounting Historians **(3)**
Academy of Behavioral Medicine Research **(4)**
Academy of Homiletics **(5)**
Academy of Veterinary Allergy and Clinical Immunology **(9)**
Aestheticians International Association **(14)**
Air Distribution Institute **(18)**
Aircraft Locknut Manufacturers Association **(20)**
Allied Trades of the Baking Industry **(26)**
American Academy of Clinical Psychiatrists **(31)**
American Academy of Equine Art **(33)**
American Academy of Ministry **(36)**
American Academy of Physician Assistants in Occupational Medicine **(40)**
American Academy of the History of Dentistry **(42)**
American Academy of Veterinary Pharmacology and Therapeutics **(42)**
American Apitherapy Society **(46)**
American Artists Professional League **(47)**
American Association for Women Podiatrists **(53)**
American Association of Behavioral Therapists **(54)**
American Association of Dental Editors **(60)**
American Association of Hospital and Healthcare Podiatrists **(62)**
American Association of Presidents of Independent Colleges and Universities **(71)**
American Association of Retirement Communities **(72)**
American Blonde D'Aquitaine Association **(81)**
American Bralers Association **(86)**
American Bridge Teachers' Association **(86)**
American College of Chiropractic Orthopedists **(94)**
American College of Counselors **(95)**
American College of Mental Health Administration **(98)**
American College of Psychoanalysts **(102)**
American Connemara Pony Society **(107)**
American Dance Guild **(113)**
American Dialect Society **(115)**
American Federation of Violin and Bow Makers **(120)**
American Fern Society **(121)**
American Fox Terrier Club **(123)**
American Guild of Organists **(127)**
The American Hair Loss Council **(128)**
American Hypnosis Association **(134)**
American Institute of Homeopathy **(139)**
American Institute of Inspectors **(139)**
American Institute of Stress **(140)**
American Marketing Association **(147)**
American Measuring Tool Manufacturers Association **(148)**
American Osteopathic College of Rheumatology, Inc. **(161)**
American Pinzgauer Association **(165)**
American Polypay Sheep Association **(167)**
American Red Poll Association **(174)**
American Romney Breeders Association **(176)**
American School Band Directors' Association **(177)**
American Shropshire Registry Association **(179)**
American Society for Ethnohistory **(184)**
American Society for Stereotactic and Functional Neurosurgery **(189)**
American Society for the Advancement of Anesthesia and Sedation in Dentistry **(190)**
American Society of Agricultural Consultants **(191)**
American Society of Dermatological Retailers **(196)**
American Society of Dermatology **(196)**
American Society of Furniture Designers **(198)**
American Society of Gas Engineers **(198)**
American Society of Podiatric Medical Assistants **(208)**
American Wire Cloth Institute **(221)**
Amerifax Cattle Association **(222)**
Aquacultural Engineering Society **(227)**
Association for Adult Development and Aging **(238)**
Association for Applied and Clinical Sociology **(238)**
Association for Assessment in Counseling and Education **(240)**
Association for Business Simulation and Experiential Learning **(241)**
The Association for Consortium Leadership **(243)**
Association for Documentary Editing **(245)**
Association for Gay, Lesbian, Bisexual, and Transgender Issues in Counseling **(247)**
Association for General and Liberal Studies **(247)**
Association for Healthcare Resource and Materials Management **(248)**
Association for Information Media and Equipment **(249)**
The Association for International Agriculture and Rural Development **(250)**
Association for Multicultural Counseling and Development **(252)**
Association for Politics and the Life Sciences **(253)**
Association for the Behavioral Sciences and Medical Education **(259)**
Association for the Calligraphic Arts **(259)**
Association for the Study of Classical African Civilizations **(259)**
Association for University and College Counseling Center Directors **(260)**
Association for Women in Psychology **(262)**
Association of American State Geologists **(266)**
Association of Applied IPM Ecologists **(267)**
The Association of Average Adjusters of the United States and Canada **(268)**
Association of Black Nursing Faculty **(269)**
The Association of Black Psychologists **(270)**
Association of Camp Nurses **(271)**
Association of Career and Technical Education **(271)**
Association of Career Professionals International **(271)**
Association of Celebrity Personal Assistants **(271)**
Association of Cinema and Video Laboratories **(273)**
Association of College and University Clubs **(274)**
Association of Eminent Domain Professionals **(280)**
Association of Food Journalists **(283)**
Association of Independent Commercial Producers **(287)**
Association of Institutional Investors **(289)**
Association of Large Distribution Cooperatives **(291)**
Association of Official Racing Chemists **(296)**
Association of Professional Art Advisors **(300)**
Association of Public Health Nurses **(304)**
Association of Railway Museums **(305)**
Association of State Chamber Professionals **(310)**
Association of Teachers of Maternal and Child Health **(312)**
Association of Technical and Supervisory Professionals **(313)**
Association of Third World Studies **(314)**
Association of University Programs in Occupational Health and Safety **(316)**
Automatic Guided Vehicle Systems **(321)**
Automotive Training Managers Council **(324)**
Aviation Industry CBT Committee **(324)**
Barzona Breeder's Association of America **(326)**
Beta Alpha Psi **(328)**
Boating Writers International **(333)**
Bowling Proprietors' Association of America **(334)**
Bulk Carrier Conference **(338)**
Cancer Patient Education Network **(341)**
Chemical Sources Association **(352)**
Coalition of Visionary Resources **(361)**
Coblentz Society **(361)**
Combat Helicopter Pilots Association **(366)**
Concord Grape Association **(373)**
Concrete Anchor Manufacturers Association **(373)**
Conference of Minority Public Administrators **(375)**
Congress on Research in Dance **(377)**
Council of Writing Program Administrators **(398)**
Council on Botanical and Horticultural Libraries **(399)**
Council on Education of the Deaf **(399)**
Craft Retailers Association for Tomorrow **(403)**
Crane Manufacturers Association of America **(403)**
Credit Professionals International **(403)**
Customs and International Trade Bar Association **(406)**
Dance Critics Association **(406)**
Disaster Preparedness and Emergency Response Association **(413)**
Dog Writers' Association of America **(415)**
Eight Sheet Outdoor Advertising Association **(421)**
Energy Traffic Association **(428)**
Family and Consumer Sciences Education Association **(437)**
Federal Physicians Association **(439)**
Federal Probation and Pre-trial Officers Association **(440)**
Federal Water Quality Association **(440)**
Flag Manufacturers Association of America **(446)**
Fleischner Society **(447)**
Food Distribution Research Society **(449)**
Forest Landowners Tax Council **(451)**
Fraternal Field Managers Association **(453)**
Free Speech Coalition **(453)**
Greater Blouse, Skirt and Undergarment Association **(466)**
The Harvey Society **(469)**
Heavy Duty Representatives Association **(473)**
Hoist Manufacturers Institute **(477)**
Human Behavior and Evolution Society **(480)**
Icelandic American Chamber of Commerce **(482)**
Ideas America **(482)**
Imaging and Perimetry Society **(486)**
Independent Time and Labor Management Association **(492)**
Indian Diamond and Colorstone Association **(492)**
Inflatable Advertising Dealers Association **(494)**
Institute for Briquetting and Agglomeration **(496)**
Institute of Career Certification International **(498)**
Institute of Diving **(499)**
Inter-Society Color Council **(506)**
International Academy of Behavioral Medicine, Counseling and Psychotherapy **(509)**

1172 National Trade and Professional Associations of the U.S. 2013 ©2013, Columbia Books, Inc.

International Association for the Study of Cooperation in Education *(514)*
International Association of Art Critics *(516)*
International Association of Career Consulting Firms *(517)*
International Association of Milk Control Agencies *(524)*
International Association of Railway Operating Officers *(527)*
International Association of School Librarianship *(527)*
International Association of Women in Fire and Emergency Services *(528)*
International Balloon Association *(529)*
International Cargo Security Council *(533)*
The International Compressor Remanufacturers Association *(536)*
International Council of Psychologists *(538)*
International Federation for Artificial Organs *(544)*
International Furniture Transportation and Logistics Council *(548)*
International Herb Association *(550)*
International Institute for Lath and Plaster *(551)*
International Iridology Practitioners Association *(552)*
International Listening Association *(554)*
International Longshoremen's Association, AFL-CIO *(555)*
International Maintenance Institute *(555)*
International Marine Minerals Society *(555)*
International Plate Printers, Die Stampers and Engravers Union of North America *(560)*
International Saw and Knife Association *(564)*
International Society for Molecular Plant Microbe Interactions *(567)*
International Society for Research on Aggression *(569)*
International Society for Respiratory Protection *(569)*
International Society of Chemical Ecology *(572)*
International Society of Psychiatric Consultation Liaison Nurses *(574)*
International Sports Heritage Association *(575)*
The International Wood Products Association *(581)*
Jewelry Industry Distributors Association *(587)*
Judge Advocates Association *(589)*
Kamut Association of North America *(590)*
The Lawn Institute *(594)*
Leafy Greens Council *(595)*
Lipizzan Association of North America *(599)*
Literary Managers and Dramaturgs of the Americas *(599)*
Marine Corps Reserve Association *(605)*
Masonry Institute of America *(607)*
Mathematical Association of America *(609)*
Miniature Book Society *(617)*
Modern Greek Studies Association *(618)*
Motorist Information and Services Association *(620)*
Music Distributors Association *(622)*
Music Industry Conference *(622)*
NABIM - the International Band and Orchestral Products Association *(623)*
NAGMR Consumer Product Brokers *(624)*
National Academy of Building Inspection Engineers *(627)*
National Academy of Clinical Biochemistry *(627)*
National Active and Retired Federal Employees Association *(629)*
National Association for Ethnic Studies *(638)*
National Association for Kinesiology in Higher Education *(640)*
National Association of Air Medical Communication Specialists *(646)*
National Association of Bar-Related Title Insurers *(648)*
National Association of Casino Party Operators *(651)*
National Association of Chain Manufacturers *(652)*
National Association of Church Food Service *(653)*
National Association of County Administrators *(659)*
National Association of County Park and Recreation Officials *(660)*
National Association of Disability Examiners *(663)*
National Association of Document Examiners *(663)*
National Association of Export Companies *(666)*
National Association of Farmer Elected Committees (NAFEC) *(667)*
National Association of Hispanic Firefighters *(672)*
National Association of Hispanic Real Estate Professionals *(672)*
National Association of Industrial Bankers *(675)*
National Association of Media and Technology Centers *(680)*
National Association of Nurse Massage Therapists *(682)*
National Association of Professional Mortgage Women *(687)*
National Association of Publishers' Representatives *(689)*
National Association of Puerto Rican-Hispanic Social Workers *(689)*

National Association of School Safety and Law Enforcement Officers *(693)*
National Association of Service Managers *(695)*
National Association of State Administrators and Supervisors of Private Schools *(697)*
National Association of State Outdoor Recreation Liaison Officers *(701)*
National Association of Supervisors of Agricultural Education *(704)*
National Association of Traffic Accident Reconstructionists and Investigators *(706)*
National Black Public Relations Society *(715)*
National Book Critics Circle *(716)*
The National Campus Ministry Association *(717)*
National Cannabis Industry Association *(717)*
National Catholic Educational Exhibitors *(718)*
National Collegiate Wrestling Association *(724)*
National Conference of Black Political Scientists *(727)*
National Conference of Federal Trial Judges *(727)*
National Conference of State Social Security Administrators *(728)*
National Conference of Yeshiva Principals *(729)*
National Conference on Research in Language and Literacy *(729)*
National Council of Commercial Plant Breeders *(734)*
National Council of Writing Program Administrators *(738)*
National Employment Counseling Association *(745)*
National EMS Pilots Association *(746)*
National Institute of American Doll Artists *(764)*
National Lesbian and Gay Law Association *(769)*
National Marine Representatives Association *(771)*
National Music Council *(774)*
National Prison Hospice Association *(782)*
The National Safety Management Society *(789)*
National Technical Association *(799)*
National Tooling and Machining Association *(800)*
National Tractor Pullers Association *(801)*
National Tunis Sheep Registry *(802)*
National Turfgrass Federation *(802)*
Newspaper Purchasing Management Association *(810)*
North American Agricultural Marketing Officials *(812)*
North American Bar-Related Title Insurers *(814)*
North American Farm Show Council *(816)*
North American Flowerbulb Wholesalers Association *(816)*
North American Manufacturing Research Institution of SME *(817)*
North American Mycological Association *(818)*
North American Performing Arts Managers and Agents *(819)*
North American Snowsports Journalists Association *(821)*
North American Society for Sport History *(821)*
Northern Nut Growers Association *(824)*
Nursery and Landscape Association Executives of North America *(825)*
Omicron Kappa Upsilon *(827)*
Organic Reactions Catalysis Society *(830)*
Organization Development Institute *(830)*
Organization of Professional Employees of the U.S. Department of Agriculture (OPEDA) *(832)*
Organization of Women in International Trade *(832)*
Oriental Rug Retailers of America, Inc. *(833)*
Paper and Plastic Representatives Management Council *(838)*
Partnership for Air-Conditioning, Heating Refrigeration Accreditation *(839)*
Partnership for Philanthropic Planning *(839)*
Percussion Marketing Council *(841)*
Phi Rho Sigma Medical Society *(846)*
Philosophy of Education Society *(846)*
Photoluminescent Safety Association *(846)*
Plant Growth Regulation Society of America *(849)*
Print Council of America *(857)*
Private Art Dealers Association *(858)*
Production Equipment Rental Association *(859)*
Professional and Technical Consultants Association *(859)*
Professional Aviation Maintenance Association *(860)*
Professional Handlers Association *(862)*
Professional Show Managers Association *(865)*
Protestant Church-Owned Publishers Association *(868)*
Public Radio News Directors Incorporated *(870)*
Public Works Historical Society *(870)*
QVM/CMC Vehicle Manufacturers Association *(872)*
React International *(875)*
Research Council on Structural Connections *(882)*
Respiratory Nursing Society *(883)*
Sales Association of the Paper Industry *(890)*
Service Dealers Association *(897)*
Shippers of Recycled Textiles *(899)*
Sigma Epsilon Delta Dental Fraternity *(899)*
Society for Chaos Theory in Psychology and Life Sciences *(905)*
Society for Environmental Graphic Design *(908)*

Society for Healthcare Strategy and Market Development *(910)*
Society for Hematopathology *(910)*
Society for Invertebrate Pathology *(913)*
Society for Light Treatment and Biological Rhythms *(914)*
Society for Social Work Leadership in Health Care *(921)*
Society for the Advancement of Behavior Analysis *(922)*
Society for the Exploration of Psychotherapy Integration *(923)*
Society for the Preservation of Oral Health *(924)*
Society of Atherosclerosis Imaging and Prevention *(930)*
Society of Dance History Scholars *(934)*
Society of Marine Port Engineers *(941)*
Society of Mortgage, Appraisal, Real Estate and Title Professionals *(942)*
Society of Reproductive Surgeons *(946)*
Society of Risk Management Consultants *(947)*
Society of Scribes *(947)*
Society of University Urologists *(949)*
Southern Cypress Manufacturers Association *(953)*
Special Interest Group for Computer Science Education *(954)*
Special Interest Group for Measurement and Evaluation *(955)*
Sportsplex Operators and Developers Association *(959)*
Storage Equipment Manufacturer's Association *(963)*
Stucco Manufacturers Association *(964)*
Stuntwomen's Association of Motion Pictures *(964)*
Substance Abuse Librarians and Information Specialists *(965)*
Tetrahydrofuran Task Force *(972)*
Therapeutic Touch International Association *(973)*
Truck Mixer Manufacturers Bureau *(981)*
Truck-frame and Axle Repair Association *(981)*
United Gamefowl Breeders Association, Inc. *(987)*
United States Association for Computational Mechanics *(990)*
The United States Harness Writers' Association *(994)*
United States Targhee Sheep Association *(999)*
United States Trout Farmers Association *(1000)*
Variable Electronic Components Institute *(1008)*
Vibration Isolation and Seismic Control Manufacturers Association *(1009)*
Vocational Evaluation and Career Assessment Professionals *(1011)*
WACRA - World Association for Case Method Research and Application *(1011)*
Walnut Council *(1012)*
Western Association for Art Conservation *(1015)*
Western Literature Association *(1016)*
Winegrape Growers of America *(1019)*
Wire and Cable Industry Suppliers Association *(1019)*
Women in Management *(1021)*
Woven Wire Products Association *(1029)*

$10-25,000

Academy of Organizational and Occupational Psychiatry *(7)*
Academy of Rehabilitative Audiology *(8)*
Accordionists and Teachers Guild International *(9)*
Advanced Transit Association *(13)*
Advertising Media Credit Executives Association *(13)*
All-America Rose Selections *(22)*
Alpha Tau Delta *(27)*
American Academy of Gold Foil Operators *(34)*
American Academy of Medical Hypnoanalysts *(36)*
American Academy of Veterinary and Comparative Toxicology *(42)*
American Angora Goat Breeder's Association *(45)*
American Association of Business Valuation Specialists *(55)*
American Association of Corporate and Public Practice Veterinarians *(59)*
American Association of Early Childhood Educators *(60)*
American Association of Food Hygiene Veterinarians *(61)*
American Association of Philosophy Teachers *(69)*
American Association of Psychiatric Administrators *(71)*
American Association of Teachers of Arabic *(74)*
American Bashkir Curly Registry *(80)*
American Book Producers Association *(85)*
American British White Park Association *(86)*
American Cheviot Sheep Society *(90)*
American College Counseling Association *(92)*
American College of Veterinary Nutrition *(104)*
American Conference for Irish Studies *(106)*
The American Electrophoresis Society *(116)*
American Entertainment Armories Association *(117)*
American Foreign Law Association *(122)*
American Health Planning Association *(130)*
American Hungarian Educators Association *(134)*

American Institute of Fishery Research Biologists *(138)*
American Journalism Historians Association *(143)*
American Microscopical Society *(151)*
American Murray Grey Association *(153)*
American Name Society *(154)*
American Naprapathic Association *(154)*
American Osteopathic Board of Physical Medicine and Rehabilitation *(160)*
American Osteopathic College of Pathologists *(160)*
American Polarity Therapy Association *(166)*
American Pomological Society *(167)*
American Poultry Association *(167)*
The American Quaternary Association *(172)*
American Society of Body Engineers *(193)*
American Society of Music Arrangers and Composers *(203)*
American Society of Theatre Consultants *(210)*
American Tarentaise Association *(215)*
American Theatre Critics Association *(216)*
American Tin Trade Association *(217)*
American Veterinary Society of Animal Behavior *(219)*
American Welara Pony Registry *(220)*
Ankole Watusi International Registry *(223)*
APHSA - Information Systems Management *(224)*
Art Glass Association *(230)*
Asian/Pacific American Librarians Association *(232)*
Assembly of Episcopal Healthcare Chaplains *(234)*
Associated Business Writers of America *(235)*
Association for Bridge Construction and Design *(240)*
Association for Communication Administration *(241)*
Association for Conservation Information *(243)*
Association for Humanist Sociology *(249)*
Association for Integrative Studies *(250)*
The Association for Social Anthropology in Oceania *(256)*
Association for Spanish and Portuguese Studies *(256)*
Association for Spiritual, Ethical and Religious Values in Counseling *(257)*
Association for the Study of Food and Society *(259)*
Association for Women in Computing *(261)*
Association of Academic Museums & Galleries *(263)*
Association of Biomedical Communications Directors *(269)*
Association of Catholic Diocesan Archivists *(271)*
Association of College and University Printers *(274)*
Association of College Honor Societies *(274)*
Association of Community Tribal Schools *(276)*
Association of Conservation Engineers *(276)*
Association of Consulting Chemists and Chemical Engineers *(276)*
Association of Earth Science Editors *(279)*
Association of Firearm and Toolmark Examiners *(283)*
Association of Halfway House Alcoholism Programs of North America *(286)*
Association of Labor Relations Agencies *(290)*
Association of Osteopathic State Executive Directors *(297)*
Association of Personal Computer User Groups *(299)*
Association of Productivity Specialists *(300)*
Association of Progressive Rental Organizations *(303)*
Association of Rehabilitation Programs in Computer Technology *(305)*
Association of Reporters of Judicial Decisions *(305)*
Association of Retail Travel Agents *(306)*
Association of Teachers of Technical Writing *(313)*
Association of University Interior Designers *(315)*
Automotive Communication Council *(322)*
Baptist Communicators Association *(326)*
Beef Improvement Federation *(327)*
Black Data Processing Associates *(331)*
Black Theatre Network *(332)*
Bowling Writers Association of America *(334)*
Brazilian Studies Association *(335)*
Carwash Owner's and Supplier's Association *(343)*
Catecholamine Club *(344)*
Catholic Association of Diocesan Ecumenical and Interreligious Officers *(345)*
Certified Claims Professional Accreditation Council *(349)*
Classification Society *(357)*
Clinical Laboratory Management Association *(358)*
Colorado Ranger Horse Association *(365)*
COMISS Network - The Network on Ministry in Specialized Settings *(366)*
Community Managers International Association *(371)*
Conference on Faith and History *(376)*
Consortium of Behavioral Health Nurses and Associates *(378)*
The Construction Innovation Forum *(379)*
Construction Marketing Research Council *(380)*
Coordinating Council for Women in History *(384)*
Council for Elementary Science International *(389)*
Council for Museum Anthropology *(390)*

Council on Chiropractic Orthopedics *(399)*
Council on Technology Teacher Education *(401)*
Delta Sigma Pi *(409)*
Driving School Association of America *(416)*
Ecuadorean American Association *(419)*
Evangelical Church Library Association *(434)*
Federal Criminal Investigators Association *(439)*
Fermenters International Trade Association *(443)*
Finnsheep Breeders Association *(445)*
Future Business Leaders of America - Phi Beta Lambda *(455)*
Geoscience Information Society *(459)*
Guild of Italian American Actors *(467)*
Harness Horsemen International *(468)*
History of Earth Sciences Society *(476)*
Housing Education and Research Association *(479)*
Humanities Education and Research Association *(481)*
Independent Staffing Alliance *(492)*
Institute of Behavioral and Applied Management *(498)*
Intermarket Agency Network *(508)*
International Alliance for Women in Music *(510)*
International Association for Language Learning Technology *(513)*
International Association for Philosophy and Literature *(514)*
International Association for Truancy and Dropout Prevention *(514)*
International Association of Electronic Keyboard Manufacturers *(520)*
International Association of Heat and Frost Insulators and Asbestos Workers *(522)*
International Association of Home Staging Professionals *(522)*
International Association of Hygienic Physicians *(523)*
International Association of Personal Protection Agents *(526)*
International Association of Tool Craftsmen *(528)*
International Association of Women Ministers *(529)*
International Business Music Association *(532)*
International Ceramic Association *(534)*
International Contrast Ultrasound Society *(537)*
International Council on Education for Teaching *(539)*
International Cut Flower Growers Association *(539)*
International Frozen Food Association *(547)*
International Guild of Candle Artisans *(549)*
International Hard Anodizing Association *(549)*
International Isotope Society *(552)*
International Memorialization Supply Association *(556)*
International Physical Fitness Association *(560)*
International Psychohistorical Association *(565)*
International Society for Adolescent Psychiatry and Psychology *(565)*
International Society for Preventive Oncology *(568)*
International Society for the Comparative Studies of Civilizations *(569)*
International Society for the Performing Arts *(569)*
International Society of Certified Employee Benefit Specialists *(572)*
International Society of Crime Prevention Practitioners *(572)*
International Society of Weekly Newspaper Editors *(574)*
International Transplant-Skin Cancer Collaborative *(578)*
International Wild Rice Association *(581)*
International Writing Centers Association *(581)*
Italian American Studies Association *(586)*
The Kite Trade Association International *(591)*
Land Mobile Communications Council *(593)*
Leather Apparel Association *(596)*
Lift Manufacturers Product Section - Material Handling Institute *(597)*
Light Aircraft Manufacturers Association *(598)*
Materials and Methods Standards Association *(608)*
MEMA Information Services Council *(612)*
Metal Framing Manufacturers Association *(613)*
Mineral Economics and Management Society *(617)*
Museum Education Roundtable *(621)*
Music Critics Association of North America *(622)*
Music Teachers National Association *(622)*
Mystery Shopping Providers Association *(623)*
National Alarm Association of America *(631)*
National Antique and Art Dealers Association of America *(634)*
National Appliance Service Association *(635)*
National Association of Baptist Professors of Religion *(648)*
National Association of Blind Teachers *(650)*
National Association of College Wind and Percussion Instructors *(655)*
National Association of Computerized Tax Processors *(657)*
National Association of County Aging Programs *(659)*

National Association of County Information Officers *(660)*
National Association of Government Employees *(670)*
National Association of Housing Information Managers *(673)*
National Association of Industrial and Technical Teacher Educators *(675)*
National Association of Litho Clubs *(678)*
National Association of Photo Equipment Technicians *(684)*
National Association of Plant Patent Owners *(685)*
National Association of Private, Nontraditional Schools and Colleges *(686)*
National Association of Reunion Managers *(692)*
National Association of Student Affairs Professionals *(703)*
National Association of Teacher Educators for Family Consumer Sciences *(704)*
National Association of University Fisheries and Wildlife Programs *(707)*
National Association of Women Highway Safety Leaders, Inc. *(709)*
National Ballroom and Entertainment Association *(712)*
National Black Nurses Association *(714)*
The National Building Granite Quarries Association *(716)*
National Conference of Black Lawyers *(726)*
National Conference of Personal Managers *(728)*
National Constables Association *(729)*
National Cotton Batting Institute *(730)*
National Council of Minorities in Energy *(735)*
National Council of State Directors of Community Colleges *(736)*
National Counter Intelligence Corps Association *(740)*
National Emergency Equipment Dealers Association *(745)*
National Forensic Association *(752)*
National Independent Fire Alarm Distributors *(762)*
National Judges Association *(767)*
National Labor Relations Board Professional Association *(768)*
National Seasoning Manufacturers Association *(790)*
National Ski and Snowboard Retailers Association *(791)*
National Society of Newspaper Columnists *(794)*
The National Society of Painters in Casein and Acrylic *(794)*
National Sportscasters and Sportswriters Association and Hall of Fame *(796)*
National Sweetener and Ingredient Marketing Association *(798)*
National Turf Writers and Broadcasters *(802)*
Natural Colored Wool Growers Association *(807)*
Network of Ingredient Marketing Specialists *(808)*
North American Calorimetry Conference *(814)*
North American Punch Manufacturers Association *(820)*
Organization of Black Designers *(832)*
Organization of Flying Adjusters *(832)*
Organization of Wildlife Planners *(832)*
Organizational Systems Research Association *(833)*
Oriental Rug Importers Association of America *(833)*
Palomino Horse Association *(837)*
Parliamentary Associates *(839)*
Phi Beta Fraternity *(845)*
Plastic Surgery Administrative Association *(850)*
Portugal-US Chamber of Commerce *(853)*
Pressure Washer Manufacturers Association *(857)*
Professional Football Writers of America *(862)*
Professional Reactor Operator Society *(864)*
Publishers' Publicity Association *(870)*
Purebred Dairy Cattle Association *(871)*
Purebred Morab Horse Association *(871)*
Radio and Television Correspondents Association *(873)*
Research Association of Minority Professors *(882)*
Sales Association of the Chemical Industry *(890)*
Schiffli Lace and Embroidery Manufacturers Association *(892)*
Scribes-The American Society of Legal Writers *(893)*
Sculptors Guild *(894)*
Senior Army Reserve Commanders Association *(897)*
Society for Archaeological Sciences *(904)*
Society for French Historical Studies *(909)*
Society for Historians of the Gilded Age and Progressive Era *(911)*
Society for Human Ecology *(911)*
Society for Organic Petrology *(917)*
Society for Textual Scholarship *(922)*
Society for the History of Discoveries *(923)*
Society for the Study of Indigenous Languages of the Americas *(925)*
Society for the Study of Social Biology *(925)*
Society of American Graphic Artists *(929)*
Society of American Historians *(929)*
Society of Medical Consultants to the Armed Forces *(941)*

International Real Estate Federation - American Chapter *(562)*
International Rural Sociology Association *(563)*
International Society for Ecological Modelling-North American Chapter *(566)*
International Society for Quality-of-Life Studies *(569)*
International Society of Copier Artists *(572)*
International Sport Show Producers Association *(575)*
International Stress Management Association - USA *(576)*
International Turfgrass Society *(579)*
International Visual Literacy Association *(580)*
International Weed Science Society *(581)*
Irish Blacks Cattle Society *(585)*
Jesuit Association of Student Personnel Administrators *(587)*
JWB Jewish Chaplains Council *(590)*
Keyboard Teachers Association International *(590)*
Latino Hotel Association *(594)*
Liaison Committee of Cooperating Oil and Gas Associations *(597)*
Linguistic Association of Canada and the United States *(598)*
Loading Dock Equipment Manufacturers *(599)*
Magic Dealers Association *(601)*
Mass Finishing Job Shops Association *(607)*
Mechanical Association Railcar Technical Services *(610)*
Metal Findings Manufacturers Association *(613)*
Metaphysical Society of America *(614)*
Middle East Librarians' Association *(615)*
Mine Safety Institute of America *(616)*
Montadale Sheep Breeders Association *(619)*
National American Legion Press Association *(634)*
National Appliance Parts Suppliers Association *(634)*
National Association for Government Training and Development *(639)*
National Association for Health and Fitness *(639)*
National Association for Year-Round Education *(645)*
National Association of Agricultural Fair Agencies *(646)*
National Association of Black Women Entrepreneurs *(649)*
National Association of Chapter Thirteen Trustees (NACTT) *(652)*
National Association of Composers, USA *(657)*
National Association of County Civil Attorneys *(659)*
National Association of County Health Facility Administrators *(660)*
National Association of County Intergovernmental Relations Officials *(660)*
National Association of Credential Evaluation Services, Inc. *(661)*
National Association of Home and Workshop Writers *(672)*
National Association of Investment Professionals *(676)*
National Association of Jai Alai Frontons *(677)*
National Association of Mental Health Planning Advisory Council *(680)*
National Association of Orthopedic Nurses *(683)*
National Association of Property Tax Representatives - Transportation, Energy, Communications *(688)*
National Association of State Archaeologists *(697)*
National Association of State Catholic Conference Directors *(699)*
National Association of State Charity Officials *(699)*
National Association of State Land Reclamationists *(701)*
National Association of Supervisors for Business Education *(704)*
National Association of Teachers' Agencies *(705)*
National Association of Test Directors *(705)*
National Blacksmiths and Weldors Association *(715)*
National Block and Bridle Club *(715)*
National Catholic Band Association *(718)*
National Coalition of Alternative Community Schools *(723)*
National Conference of Local Environmental Health Administrators *(727)*
National Council of State Supervisors for Languages *(736)*
National Council of State Tourism Directors *(736)*
National Council on Public Polls *(739)*
National Defined Contribution Council *(742)*
National Economic Association *(744)*
National Federation of Federal Employees *(748)*
The National Federation of Nonpublic School State Accrediting Associations *(749)*
National Fellowship of Child Care Executives *(750)*
National Hereford Hog Record Association *(759)*
National Independent Living Association *(762)*
National Juvenile Court Services Association *(767)*
National Lincoln Sheep Breeders Association *(770)*
National Ornamental Goldfish Growers Association *(778)*

National Party Boat Owners Alliance *(779)*
National Practitioners Network for Fathers and Family *(782)*
National Quartz Producers Council *(783)*
National Remotivation Therapy Organization *(786)*
National Society for Graphology *(792)*
National Society of Film Critics *(793)*
National Society of Mural Painters *(794)*
National Society of Real Estate Appraisers, Inc. *(795)*
National Spotted Saddle Horse Association *(796)*
National Swine Improvement Federation *(798)*
National Wood Tank Institute *(805)*
NFHS Music Association *(810)*
NFHS Speech Debate and Theatre Association *(810)*
North American Academy of Ecumenists *(812)*
North American Clun Forest Association *(815)*
North American Fuzzy Information Processing Society *(817)*
Omega Tau Sigma *(827)*
Online Audiovisual Catalogers *(827)*
Optical Storage Technology Association *(829)*
Orthodox Theological Society in America *(833)*
Poultry Breeders of America *(854)*
Professional Basketball Writers' Association *(860)*
Professional Hockey Writers' Association *(862)*
Professional Insurance Communicators of America *(862)*
Professional Women Singers Association *(866)*
Religious Communication Association *(880)*
Romanian Studies Association of America *(888)*
Scottish Blackface Breeders Association *(893)*
Screen Manufacturers Association *(893)*
Slovak Studies Association *(900)*
Social Venture Network *(902)*
Society for Ancient Greek Philosophy *(904)*
Society for Asian and Comparative Philosophy *(904)*
Society for Asian Music *(904)*
Society for Cross-Cultural Research *(907)*
Society for Environmental Geochemistry and Health *(908)*
Society for History in the Federal Government *(911)*
Society for Italian Historical Studies *(914)*
Society for Medieval and Renaissance Philosophy *(915)*
Society for Menstrual Cycle Research *(915)*
Society for Natural Philosophy *(916)*
Society for Romanian Studies *(921)*
Society for Slovene Studies *(921)*
Society for Software Quality *(921)*
Society for the Philosophy of Sex and Love *(923)*
Society for the Study of Male Psychology and Physiology *(925)*
Society of American Silversmiths *(929)*
Society of Armenian Studies *(930)*
Society of Engineering Science *(935)*
Society of Military Otolaryngologists - Head and Neck Surgeons *(941)*
Society of Philosophers in America *(944)*
Society of Professors of Education *(945)*
Society of United States Air Force Flight Surgeons *(949)*
Sociological Practice Association *(950)*
South Asian Journalists Association *(952)*
Spanish Barb Horse Association *(954)*
Sunglass Association of America *(965)*
Tamworth Swine Association *(968)*
Tin Stabilizers Association *(975)*
Tree-Ring Society *(980)*
Turkish Studies Association *(982)*
United States Cross Country Coaches Association *(993)*
United States Federation for Culture Collections *(994)*
United States Federation of Scholars and Scientists *(994)*
United States Fencing Coaches Association *(994)*
United States-Israel Science & Technology Foundation (USISTF) *(995)*
United States Junior Chamber (Jaycees) *(995)*
United States Pan Asian American Chamber of Commerce *(997)*
United States-China Chamber of Commerce *(1001)*
Urban Financial Services Coalition *(1003)*
Visually Impaired Data Processors International *(1011)*
Window Council *(1018)*
Women Band Directors International *(1020)*
Women in Agribusiness *(1020)*
Women in Energy *(1021)*
Women in Municipal Government *(1022)*

Executive Index

All Individuals appearing in the Association Index appear here, in alphabetical order by last name.

Aanderud, Jenny
Center for Spiritual and Ethical Education *(348)*

Aaronson, Mel
United Federation of Teachers *(987)*

Abashian, Marianna
Brain Injury Association of America *(334)*

Abayhan, Canan
American Association of Museums *(65)*

Abbe, Camille
Midwives Alliance of North America *(615)*

Abbey, Erin
American Pain Society *(161)*
National Association of Neonatal Nurses *(682)*
The American Society of Pediatric Hematology/
Oncology *(206)*

Abbey, Susan
National Association of Document Examiners *(663)*

Abbott, Dan G.
National Insurance Crime Bureau *(766)*

Abbott, Jennifer
Naval Enlisted Reserve Association *(807)*

Abbott, Mark
Major League Soccer *(601)*

Abbott, Marty
American Council on the Teaching of Foreign
Languages *(111)*

Abbott, MD, Rick
The American Society of Pediatric Neurosurgeons *(206)*

Abbott, CMP, Sandy
Association of periOperative Registered Nurses *(299)*

Abbott, Stephen "Steve" R.
International Society for Technology in Education *(569)*

Abbott, Turner T.
Powder Metallurgy Parts Association *(854)*
Refractory Metals Association *(878)*

Abdelsamad, Moustafa H.
Society for Advancement of Management *(903)*

Abe, Danielle S.
American League of Lobbyists *(145)*

Abebe, Betel
World Trade Centers Association *(1027)*

Abel, Debra
American Academy of Audiology *(31)*

Abel, Tracy

International College of Cranio-Mandibular
Orthopedics *(535)*

Abell, Ryan
Print Services & Distribution Association *(857)*

Abels, PhD, Arnold
Association of Psychology Postdoctoral and Internship
Centers *(303)*

Aberle, CAE, MBA, Kathryn B.
Society for Simulation in Healthcare *(921)*

Abernathy, Wayne
American Bankers Association *(79)*

Abner, Carrie
American Probation and Parole Association *(167)*

Aboid, Joe
Professional Putters Association *(864)*

Abounader, John V.
International Association of Auto Theft Investigators
(516)

Abousleman, Fred
National Association of Regional Councils *(690)*

Abraham, Michael
Professional Fraternity Association *(862)*

Abraham, Michael T.
Theta Tau *(973)*

Abraham, Rick
Foodservice Sales & Marketing Association *(450)*

Abramo, Marsha
Reliability Society *(880)*

Abramovich, Carolina
ISEH Society for Hematology and Stem Cells *(586)*

Abramowitz, PharmD, Paul W.
American Society of Health-System Pharmacists *(199)*

Abrams, Bradley
Slovak Studies Association *(900)*

Abrams, Burton
American Sleep Apnea Association *(180)*

Abrams, Greg
American Society of Medical Association Counsel *(203)*

Abrams, Holly
National School Boards Association *(789)*

Abrams, Jaclyn
National Club Association *(722)*

Abrams, Joyce

American Society of Heating, Refrigerating and Air
Conditioning Engineers (ASHRAE) *(199)*

Abrams, Lena
Stage Directors and Choreographers Society *(960)*

Abrams, Robert
Dance Critics Association *(406)*

Abrams-Bell, Martha
National Center for Housing Management *(719)*

Abrate, Jayne
American Association of Teachers of French *(74)*

Abreu, Isabel
Professional Association of Innkeepers International
(860)

Abreu, Jabneel "Jenny"
Direct Marketing Association Nonprofit Federation
(412)

Abreu, Julio
Mental Health America *(612)*

Abreu-Hernandez, Neosoty
National Council of University Research Administrators
(737)

Abril, Jennifer
International Fragrance Association North America
(547)

Abrom, CMP, Ingrid
American Coal Council *(92)*

Abroms, Ed
American Cinema Editors *(91)*

Abtahi, Allen
InterAction (American Council of Voluntary
International Action) *(506)*

Abu Rish, Ziad M.
Middle East Studies Association of North America
(615)

Abuzobaa, Shereen
Training Directors' Forum *(977)*

Acemoglu, Daron
Econometric Society *(418)*

Achelpohl, Kate
Packaging Machinery Manufacturers Institute *(836)*

Achenbach, Jr., Robert P.
American Agricultural Law Association *(44)*

Achilles, Charles A.
CCIM Institute *(347)*
Institute of Real Estate Management *(503)*

Ackerly, Tod

American Bearing Manufacturers Association *(80)*

Ackerman, David
Marketing Education Association *(606)*

Ackerman, Holly
American Association of Airport Executives *(53)*

Ackerman, CAE, Jennifer
Public Risk Management Association *(870)*

Ackerman, Julie
Packaging Machinery Manufacturers Institute *(836)*

Ackins, Cynthia D.
Consortium for Graduate Study in Management *(378)*

Ackles, Mitch
Hedge Fund Association *(473)*

Ackleson, Mary
National Association of Government Communicators *(670)*

Ackroyd, Rand
Plumbing and Drainage Institute *(850)*

Acord, David
TAUC - The Association of Union Constructors *(968)*

Acosta, Jr., CAE, Daniel
International Union of Toxicology *(579)*

Acosta, Doris
Academy of Nutrition and Dietetics *(7)*

Acosta, Evan
Ecuadorean American Association *(419)*

Acosta, Gary
National Association of Hispanic Real Estate Professionals *(672)*

Acosta-Aguilar, Veronica J.
Hispanic Association of Colleges and Universities *(475)*

Acott, Mike
National Asphalt Pavement Association *(635)*

Acquard, Charles A.
National Association of State Utility Consumer Advocates (NASUCA) *(702)*

Acunto, Stephen C.
International Association for Insurance Law - United States Chapter *(513)*

Acworth, Will
Futures Industry Association *(455)*

Adair, Aaron
Association of University Technology Managers *(316)*

Adair, Katie
Association of Academic Physiatrists *(263)*

Adam, David F.
United States Maritime Alliance (USMX) *(996)*

Adamich, Melanie
Help Desk Institute *(474)*

Adams, Aisha
International Parking Institute *(559)*

Adams, Alex
National Association of Chain Drug Stores *(652)*

Adams, Amy
Fresh Produce Association of the Americas *(453)*

Adams, Andrew A.
Special Interest Group for Computers and Society *(955)*

Adams, Bruce
International Association of Rehabilitation Professionals *(527)*

Adams, Carole
American Wool Council *(222)*

Adams, Carrie
Mathematical Association of America *(609)*

Adams, Dr. Gary
National Cotton Council of America *(730)*

Adams, James
Metal Powder Producers Association *(614)*

Adams, James P.
APMI International *(225)*
Metal Powder Industries Federation *(613)*
Powder Metallurgy Equipment Association *(854)*
Powder Metallurgy Parts Association *(854)*
Refractory Metals Association *(878)*

Adams, Jane
National Head Start Association *(758)*

Adams, Jennifer
American Council on Education *(110)*

Adams, Jim
Offshore Marine Service Association *(827)*

Adams, Joan
National Association of Teachers of Singing *(705)*

Adams, John Lawrence
International Council of Library Association Executives *(538)*

Adams, Josie
National Association of Veterans Program Administrators *(708)*

Adams, Kathy
Society for Simulation in Healthcare *(921)*

Adams, Kerry
American Institute for Maghrib Studies *(136)*

Adams, Linda
Aircraft Electronics Association *(20)*

Adams, Lou Ann
American Angus Association *(45)*

Adams, Mark
National Association of Insurance Women (International) *(676)*

Adams, SPHR, Mark R
American Association of Oral and Maxillofacial Surgeons *(67)*

Adams, Mike
Republican Governors Association *(881)*

Adams, Nevin
Employee Benefit Research Institute *(426)*

Adams, Nicholas
The Aluminum Association, Inc. *(27)*

Adams, Paige
Women's Business Enterprise National Council *(1022)*

Adams, Priscilla
Association of Former Intelligence Officers *(284)*

Adams, Rachel
Child Welfare League of America *(353)*

Adams, Shelley
Society for American Archaeology *(903)*

Adams, Sheri
Building Commissioning Association *(337)*

Adams, Stephanie
National Council of Acoustical Consultants *(733)*

Adams, Susan
International Association of Healthcare Central Service Materiel Management *(522)*

Adams, Ted
Association of Small Foundations *(309)*

Adams, Thomas
Association of Minority Health Professions Schools *(295)*

Adams, Thomas H.
American Coal Ash Association *(92)*

Adams, Tiffany N.
Council of Manufacturing Associations *(395)*

Adams-Weyant, Brenda
National Association of County Park and Recreation Officials *(660)*
Society of Outdoor Recreation Professionals *(943)*

Adamson, Daniel M.
Solar Energy Industries Association (SEIA) *(952)*

Adamson, Mike
Aircraft Electronics Association *(20)*

Adaska, John
American Association of Veterinary Laboratory Diagnosticians *(76)*

Adcock, Carol
American Leather Chemists Association *(145)*

Adcock, Cynthia Dodd
National Housing Conference *(761)*

Adcock, Dan C.
National Active and Retired Federal Employees Association *(629)*

Adcock, Sarah
American Society for Blood and Marrow Transplantation *(181)*
American Society of Colon and Rectal Surgeons *(195)*

Addington, Craig
National Sunroom Association *(798)*
The Transformer Association *(977)*

Addington, John H.
Compressed Air and Gas Institute *(372)*
Door and Access Systems Manufacturers Association, International *(415)*
Fluid Controls Institute *(448)*
Heat Exchange Institute *(472)*
National Coil Coating Association *(723)*
National Sunroom Association *(798)*
Pressure Washer Manufacturers Association *(857)*
Steel Window Institute *(963)*

Addison, Gee Cee
Society of Children's Book Writers and Illustrators *(932)*

Addy, Dawn
United Association for Labor Education *(985)*

Adelizzi, Michael
American Supply Association *(214)*

Adelman, Anna
Dental Trade Alliance *(410)*

Adelson, Robin
Children's Book Council *(353)*

Adelstein, Jonathan S.
PCIA - The Wireless Infrastructure Association *(840)*

Adem, Jenet
AASHTO: Transportation Center of Excellence *(2)*

Adere, Janet
National Association for Search and Rescue *(642)*

Aderson, Benjamin "Ben"
TechAmerica (fka Technology Association of America) *(969)*

Adey, John
American Boat and Yacht Council *(84)*

Adienge, Erick
Association of College Unions International *(274)*

Adkins, Ariel
Art Directors Club *(229)*

Adkins, David
Council of State Governments *(397)*

Adkins, Jonathan
Governors' Highway Safety Association *(464)*

Adkins, JD, Shirlyn A.
American Association of Neuromuscular and Electrodiagnostic Medicine *(66)*

Adkins, Tim
Industrial Designers Society of America *(493)*

Adkins, Troy
American Society of Interior Designers *(200)*

Adkinson, Kim
Association of Small Foundations *(309)*

Adl, Sina
International Society of Protistologists *(573)*

Adler, Dave
American Society for Therapeutic Radiology and Oncology *(190)*

Adler, Jon
Federal Law Enforcement Officers Association *(439)*

Adler, Kevin
National Association of Personal Financial Advisors *(684)*

Adler, Prudence S.
Association of Research Libraries *(306)*

Adler, Sara
National Academy of Arbitrators *(627)*

Adler, Wade
American Association of Retirement Communities *(72)*

Adona, Nadia
Society for Environmental Graphic Design *(908)*

Adranly, Rula
National Council on Crime and Delinquency *(738)*

Adriano, Ace
AIR Commercial Real Estate Association *(18)*

Adsit, Russel "Russ"
International Erosion Control Association *(543)*

Afable, Lawrence
National Ready Mixed Concrete Association *(784)*

Afremow, George
Specialty Equipment Market Association *(957)*

Aft, PE, Larry
Institute of Industrial Engineers *(500)*

Aftergood, Steven
Federation of American Scientists *(440)*

Agan, Colleen
National Community Pharmacists Association *(725)*

Agard, Kathryn E.
American Association of Medical Society Executives *(65)*

Agard, Kristin
Agricultural & Applied Economics Association *(16)*

Agarwal, Rajni
National Affordable Housing Management Association *(629)*

Agashe, Lalita
International Association for the Study of Cooperation in Education *(514)*

Agatucci, Jacob
Community Colleges Humanities Association *(370)*

Agent, Betty
International Guild of Symphony, Opera and Ballet Musicians *(549)*

Ager, Samantha
National Association of Wholesaler-Distributors *(709)*

Aggarwal, Praveen
Association for Consumer Research *(243)*

Agnew, Dominique
NAMM - The International Music Products Association *(625)*

Agnew, Dr. Jacqueline
Association of University Programs in Occupational Health and Safety *(316)*

Agnew, Jeff
The Coalition for America's Gateways and Trade Corridors *(360)*

Agnew, Peter
Chlorine Institute *(354)*

Agnew, Tom
Society of Exploration Geophysicists *(935)*

Agostini, Martha
Risk and Insurance Management Society, Inc. (RIMS) *(886)*

Agoudemos, Pat
Association of Lutheran Development Executives *(292)*

Agran, PhD, Martin
TASH *(968)*

Agrawal, Gopal
Indian Diamond and Colorstone Association *(492)*

Aguiar, Lori A.
Tall Ships America *(968)*

Aguilar, Karen
APPA - Leadership in Educational Facilities *(225)*

Aguilera, Jose
American Academy of Pain Management *(39)*

Aguirre, PhD, Edgar L.
Sugar Industry Technologists *(965)*

Aguirre, John
Winegrape Growers of America *(1019)*

ahari, Ilyana Sudani Z
Malaysian Rubber Export Promotion Council (USA) *(602)*

Ahart, Amy
National Association of Independent Schools *(675)*

Ahearn, CTIE, Cheryl
American Society of Travel Agents *(210)*

Ahearn, Jennifer
American Association of Colleges of Nursing *(57)*

Ahee, APR, Renee
National Arab-American Medical Association *(635)*

Ahern, F. Gregory
Investment Company Institute *(584)*

Ahern, Rich
Federal Criminal Investigators Association *(439)*

Ahlgrimm, Marijo
American Institutes for Research *(141)*

Ahmad, Jahan
General Aviation Manufacturers Association *(458)*

Ahmad, Jordan
Associated General Contractors of America (AGC) *(236)*

Ahmad, Sadaqat
National Association for Environmental Management *(638)*

Ahmed, MA, MS, Erica
Mental Health America *(612)*

Ahmed, Nedda H.
Art Libraries Society of North America *(230)*

Ahmed, Rasheed
Islamic Medical Association of North America *(586)*

Ahn, Emi Ochiai
Alliance of Associations of Teachers of Japanese *(24)*

Ahn, Judie
National Academy of Education *(627)*

Aho, Andrew
Geosynthetic Materials Association *(459)*

Aho, Andrew M.
Industrial Fabrics Association International *(493)*

Ahtone, Tristan
Native American Journalists Association *(806)*

Ahuja, Kelley
Institute of Food Technologists *(499)*

Aiken, Alyssa
Food Processing Suppliers Association *(449)*

Aiken, Christa
Eye Bank Association of America *(436)*

Aiken, Paul
Authors Guild *(320)*

Aiken, Peter
Data Management Association International *(407)*

Aikens, Lynn
American Statistical Association *(213)*

Ailes, Justin B.
American Land Title Association *(144)*

Aimone, Logan
Associated Collegiate Press *(235)*
National Scholastic Press Association *(789)*

Aines, CPA, MBA, Paul
American Society of Clinical Oncology *(194)*

Ainsworth, Susan L
American College Health Association *(93)*

Ainsworth, William "Bill"
International Association of Geophysical Contractors *(522)*

Airgood, Colleen
National Motor Freight Traffic Association, Inc. *(773)*

Airmet, Rebecca
Society for Applied Spectroscopy *(904)*

Aitken, A. Dawn
International Society of Travel and Tourism Educators *(574)*

Aitken, Anne Carter
International Society for Ecological Economics *(566)*

Aitken, Esq., Herve H.
North American Transportation Employee Relations Association *(823)*

Aitken, Michael P.
Society for Human Resource Management *(911)*

Akbarnia, Ladan
Historians of Islamic Art Association *(476)*

Ake, CPA, Tiffany
American Society of Hematology *(199)*

Akel, Dan
National Association of Police Athletics/Activities Leagues, Inc. *(685)*

Akers, Esq., Grace
American Immigration Lawyers Association *(134)*

Akers, John
United States Basketball Writers Association *(991)*

Akers, Joseph
National Organization of Black Law Enforcement Executives *(777)*

Akers, Robert
National Tooling and Machining Association *(800)*

Akin, Christina
Institute for Professionals in Taxation *(497)*

Aklilu, Ghennet
American Society of Hematology *(199)*

Aksamit, Ewa
Association of Professional Chaplains *(301)*

al'Absi, PhD, Mustafa
American Psychosomatic Society *(170)*

Alahouzos, Gabrielle

Natural Products Association *(807)*

Alam, Putri
United States-ASEAN Business Council Inc. *(990)*

Alampi, Rick
American Association of Feline Practitioners *(61)*

Alarcon-Yohe, MPH, Mariela
Directors of Health Promotion and Education (DHPE) *(413)*

Alavi, Afshin
American Academy of Implant Dentistry *(35)*

Alawi, Wali
American Society of Interior Designers *(200)*

Albanezi, Trier
Global Cold Chain Alliance *(462)*

Albano, Jonathan
Asian American Hotel Owners Association *(231)*

Albano, Robert A.
National Association of Heavy Equipment Training Schools *(672)*

Albert, Holly R.
Arthroscopy Association of North America *(230)*

Albert, Ida
American Guernsey Association *(127)*

Albert, Mary
Competitive Telecommunications Association *(371)*

Albert, Terri
Wire Reinforcement Institute *(1019)*

Albertani, Bevin
Laborers International Union of North America *(592)*

Alberti, Joe
Voice and Speech Trainers Association *(1011)*

Albertini, Rebecca
International Association of Eating Disorders Professionals *(520)*

Albertson, Mila
Greeting Card Association *(466)*
National Candle Association *(717)*

Albertson, Richard
National Association for Relationship and Marriage Education *(642)*

Albertson, Toni
Community College Journalism Association *(370)*

Albinder, Frank
Intercollegiate Men's Choruses, an International Association of Male Choruses *(507)*

Albizo, Joel D.
The Council of Landscape Architectural Registration Boards *(395)*

Albrecht, Bobbie
National Association of Realtors *(690)*

Albrecht, Karl
Organic Reactions Catalysis Society *(830)*

Albrecht, Richard
American Society of Plumbing Engineers *(207)*

Albright, J.
Child Care Aware of America *(353)*

Albrizzi, Lisa
American College of Physician Executives *(101)*

Alcock, Sarah
American Urogynecologic Society *(218)*
Bank Insurance and Securities Association *(326)*
Institute for Credentialing Excellence *(497)*
Institute of Clean Air Companies *(499)*

Alcorn, Kathleen
Global Association of Risk Professionals *(461)*

Alcorn, Walter

Consumer Electronics Association *(381)*

Alcott, Chris
Society of Diagnostic Medical Sonographers *(934)*

Alden, FAAP, MD, Errol R.
American Academy of Pediatrics *(39)*

Alderman, Ray
VITA *(1011)*

Alderson, Michael
National Barbecue Association *(712)*
Society for Foodservice Management *(909)*

Alderson, Patricia
Rice Millers' Association *(886)*
USA Rice Council *(1004)*
USA Rice Federation *(1004)*

Aldinger, Tim
National Association of Workforce Boards (NAWB) *(710)*

Aldred, Ingrid
Association & Society Insurance Corporation *(237)*

Aldred, Maxine
American Geophysical Union *(126)*

Aldrich, Ann
American Association of Intensive English Programs *(63)*

Aldrich, CPA, Patrick
American Association of Neuromuscular and Electrodiagnostic Medicine *(66)*

Aldrich, Rob
Land Trust Alliance *(593)*

Aldrich, Susan L.
College of Healthcare Information Management Executives *(364)*

Aldridge, Carol
Pyramid Society *(871)*

Aldridge, Linda
National Association of Extension 4-H Agents *(667)*

Aldridge, Richard
National Council of Teachers of Mathematics *(737)*

Aleman, Therese
Professional Photographers of America *(863)*

Alexander, Aisha
National Association of Workforce Boards (NAWB) *(710)*

Alexander, MD, C. Bruce
American Society for Clinical Pathologists *(182)*

Alexander, Cathy
Underwater Construction Corporation *(984)*

Alexander, Hollee
National Potato Council *(782)*

Alexander, Jackie
Energy and Environmental Building Association *(427)*

Alexander, Joe
The Clearing House Association *(357)*

Alexander, Joe L.
National Association of Composers, USA *(657)*

Alexander, Judy
International Association of Career Consulting Firms *(517)*

Alexander, Kelley
National Society of Accountants for Cooperatives *(793)*

Alexander, CAE, CRNI, MA, RN, FAAN, Mary
Infusion Nurses Society *(496)*

Alexander, Natalie
Custom Tailors and Designers Association of America *(406)*

Alexander, Rex J.

National EMS Pilots Association *(746)*

Alexander, Sarah E.
Emerging Markets Private Equity Association *(425)*

Alexander, Sharon
Intelligent Transportation Society of America *(506)*

Alexander, Sue
International Society for Clinical Densitometry *(565)*

Alexander, Tom
Advanced Biofuels Association *(12)*

Alexandrovic, Marsha
North American Transportation Employee Relations Association *(823)*

Alexis, Natasha
Gases and Welding Distributors Association *(457)*

Alfano, Holly
National Association of Truck Stop Operators(NATSO) *(707)*

Alfano, Jr., MD, Louis F.
American Society of Abdominal Surgeons *(190)*

Alfaro, Manny
Hispanic Organization of Latin Actors *(476)*

Alfieri, Jan
American Gear Manufacturers Association *(125)*

Alford, Edward
International Real Estate Federation - American Chapter *(562)*

Alford, Jr., Harry C.
National Black Chamber of Commerce *(714)*

Alford, Kay DeBow
National Black Chamber of Commerce *(714)*

Alford, Leanne
Emergency Medicine Residents' Association *(425)*

Alfred, MS, Kelly C.
Federation of State Medical Boards of the United States *(442)*

Alger, JD, Aurelie M.
American Association of Plastic Surgeons *(70)*
The International Society for Minimally Invasive Cardiothoracic Surgery *(567)*

Alger, Sallie
Association of Seventh-Day Adventist Librarians *(308)*

Alger, III, Stan
Society for Clinical Vascular Surgery *(906)*

Algrant, Lynne
Association of Black Foundation Executives *(269)*

Alguire, FACP, MD, Patrick
American College of Physicians Services, Inc. *(101)*

Alhadari, Andrea
Delta Phi Epsilon *(409)*

Ali, Hamza
Society of Chemical Industry, American Section *(932)*

Ali, PhD, Moonis
International Society of Applied Intelligence *(570)*

Alic-Batson, Roslyn
Section for Women in Public Administration *(894)*

Alin, Michael C.
American Society of Interior Designers *(200)*

Alito, Melaku
National Volunteer Fire Council *(803)*

Allar, Bruce
National Association of Pizzeria Operators *(685)*

Allard, Dave
Lignite Energy Council *(598)*

Allaster, Stacey
WTA Tour, Inc. *(1029)*

Allaway, CAE, CMP, IOM, Kent
Produce Marketing Association *(858)*

Allay, CPA, Melissa
Door and Access Systems Manufacturers Association, International *(415)*

Allegra, Richard
Association on Higher Education and Disability *(319)*

Allegretti, Thomas A.
American Waterways Operators *(220)*

Alleluia, Vincent V.
American Society of Master Dental Technologists *(202)*

Allen, Adrienne
Council of Institutional Investors *(394)*

Allen, Antoinette
Cable & Telecommunications Association for Marketing *(340)*

Allen, MD, Beverley
Black Psychiatrists of America *(331)*

Allen, CSS, Bryan
Electronics Technicians Association International *(424)*

Allen, Caroline
American Association of Colleges of Nursing *(57)*

Allen, Celeste
The National Federation of Paralegal Associations, Inc. *(749)*

Allen, Christopher "Chriss" M.
Opticians Association of America *(829)*

Allen, Cindy
Distributive Education Clubs of America (DECA) *(415)*

Allen, PhD, Dan J.
American Association of Behavioral Therapists *(54)*

Allen, Derek
Association for Informal Logic and Critical Thinking *(249)*

Allen, CAP, Dexter K.
American Anthropological Association *(45)*

Allen, Diana
Ideas America *(482)*

Allen, Diana J.
Council for Christian Colleges and Universities *(389)*

Allen, Elizabeth
National Society of Genetic Counselors *(794)*
Special Care Dentistry *(954)*
Special Care Dentistry Association *(954)*

Allen, Emily
International Association of Administrative Professionals *(515)*

Allen, Eric
Calorie Control Council *(341)*

Allen, Greg
American Craft Council *(111)*

Allen, Janice
American Association for Geriatric Psychiatry *(49)*

Allen, Jason
National Association of Black Accountants, Inc. *(648)*

Allen, Jeff
Federation of State Humanities Councils *(442)*

Allen, Jeff
National Barbecue Association *(712)*

Allen, Joan
American Gem Trade Association *(125)*

Allen, John
Spill Control Association of America *(958)*

Allen, Julie
World Council of Credit Unions, Inc. *(1026)*

Allen, Karen
American Architectural Manufacturers Association *(46)*

Allen, Karen
National Parks Conservation Association *(779)*

Allen, Katie
American Angus Association *(45)*
Architectural Woodwork Institute *(228)*

Allen, Kenny
National Greyhound Association *(756)*

Allen, Klancy
Appaloosa Horse Club *(225)*

Allen, Kristin
Electricity Consumers Resource Council (ELCON) *(422)*

Allen, Lee-Ann H.
Society for Leukocyte Biology *(914)*

Allen, Les
Financial Planning Association *(445)*

Allen, Linda
American Physiological Society *(165)*

Allen, Lisa
American Hospital Association *(133)*

Allen, Mark S.
International Foodservice Distributors Association *(546)*

Allen, Matt
Tennis Industry Association *(971)*

Allen, Michelle
Association for Childhood Education International *(241)*

Allen, Mildred
Black Data Processing Associates *(331)*

Allen, Morgan
New Dramatists *(809)*

Allen, Nancy
National Cancer Registrars Association *(717)*

Allen, Patrick
Sports Turf Managers Association *(959)*

Allen, Rachel
National Alliance for Media Arts and Culture *(631)*

Allen, Robert F.
National Railway Labor Conference *(784)*

Allen, Rock
National Network of Estate Planning Attorneys *(775)*

Allen, Rosemary
National United Merchants Beverage Association *(803)*

Allen, MBA, Sharon
American Society for Healthcare Human Resources Administration *(185)*

Allen, Stuart
Computer Ethics Institute *(372)*

Allen, Esq., Susan Au
United States Pan Asian American Chamber of Commerce *(997)*

Allen, Sylvia
International Festivals and Events Association *(545)*

Allen, Thomas H.
Association of American Publishers *(266)*

Allen, Tonya
American Meat Institute *(148)*

Allen, Van
Radio Advertising Bureau *(873)*

Allen, Veronica
American Subcontractors Association *(214)*

Allen, Wayne
American Agriculture Movement, Inc. *(44)*

Allende, Ada
CoreNet Global *(385)*

Allera, Ed
Generic Animal Drug Alliance *(458)*

Alles, Pete
National Fluid Power Association *(751)*

Allis, Kevin J.
Native American Contractors Association *(806)*

Allison, Kathy
National Association of Independent Life Brokerage Agencies *(674)*

Allison, Linda S.
National Association of Independent Colleges and Universities *(674)*

Allison, Richard
American College of Musicians *(98)*
National Guild of Piano Teachers *(757)*

Allison, Richard L.
National Board of Boiler and Pressure Vessel Inspectors *(715)*

Allmen, Lynette Van
Credit Union Executives Society *(403)*

Allmon, Warren D.
Paleontological Research Institution *(837)*

Alluisi, MA, Ed, Jennifer
American Psychosocial Oncology Society *(170)*
International Psycho-Oncology Society *(561)*

Allured, Michael
American Association of Candy Technologists *(55)*

Allynn, Jon
American Society of Photographers *(207)*

Allyson, Sandy
Society of Former Special Agents of the Federal Bureau of Investigation *(937)*

Almand, Kathleen H.
National Fire Protection Association *(751)*

Almanza, CEM, CMP, Ilse
American Society for Healthcare Engineering *(184)*

Almas, Reidar
International Rural Sociology Association *(563)*

Almdale, Dana
Association of Professional Researchers for Advancement *(302)*
InSight *(496)*
National Society of Genetic Counselors *(794)*

Almeida, Ann Marie
Association of Women's Business Centers *(318)*

Almeida, Edmar Luiz de
International Association for Energy Economics *(512)*

Almond, Carrie
National Federation of Republican Women *(750)*

Almond, Tonya
American Academy of Pediatric Dentistry *(39)*

Almstedt, CMP, Kim
American Ambulance Association *(44)*

Almy, David
Marketing Research Association *(606)*

Alongi, Deene
American Institute of Certified Planners *(137)*
American Planning Association *(166)*

Alonso, Dolores
Chlorobenzene Producers Association *(354)*
Society of Chemical Manufacturers and Affiliates Inc. *(932)*

Alonso, Luis
Employee Benefit Research Institute *(426)*

Alonzo, Julie

International Andalusian and Lusitano Horse
  Association *(510)*

Aloy, Anthony
National Association of Personal Financial Advisors
  (684)

Alper, Andy
United Association of Equipment Leasing *(985)*

Alsene, Tammy
Society of Insurance Trainers and Educators *(940)*

Alsmeyer, Richard H.
National Seasoning Manufacturers Association *(790)*

Alston, Carolyn
The Coalition for Government Procurement *(360)*

Alston, Denise
Governors' Highway Safety Association *(464)*

Alston, Nelda
Professional Retail Store Maintenance Association
  (864)

Alston, Penny
American College of Tax Counsel *(103)*
Masonry Veneer Manufacturers Association *(607)*
Roof Coatings Manufacturers Association *(888)*

Alstyne, John Van
Inter-Industry Conference on Auto Collision Repair
  (506)

Alt, Alyson
Blinded Veterans Association *(332)*

Alt, Ronald
Federation of Tax Administrators *(442)*

Alter, Stephen
League of American Orchestras *(595)*

Alter, Timothy
The Construction Innovation Forum *(379)*

Alterio, Michael
American Business Media *(87)*

Alterman, Marcia
Professional Association of Volleyball Officials *(860)*

Alterman, Stephen A.
Cargo Airline Association *(343)*

Alther, Pamela
American Sugarbeet Growers Association *(214)*

Althoff, Kimberly
International Sanitary Supply Association *(563)*

Althouse, Kristen
Sports Turf Managers Association *(959)*

Althouse, LaVonne
International Association of Women Ministers *(529)*

Altizer, Matthew
Percussive Arts Society *(841)*

Altman, Dannell (Danni)
International Association of Operative Millers *(525)*

Altman, Faith
International Parking Institute *(559)*

Altman, Jennifer
Asian American Hotel Owners Association *(231)*

Altman, Suzanna Schlesinger
American Composers Forum *(105)*

Altom, Kay
Professional Retail Store Maintenance Association
  (864)

Altschul, Michael F.
CTIA - The Wireless Association *(405)*

Altshuler, Kenneth
American Academy of Matrimonial Lawyers *(35)*

Alvare, Bethany

National Investment Company Service Association
  (767)

Alvarenga, Rosibel
Society of Toxicology *(948)*

Alvarez, Alex de
Energy Security Council *(428)*

Alvarez, David
IEEE Communications Society *(483)*

Alvarez, Denise
Retail Confectioners International *(884)*

Alvarez, Joe
American Humor Studies Association *(134)*

Alverson, Robert
Fishing Vessel Owners' Association *(446)*

Alves, Merritt
Association of Marina Industries *(293)*

Alvidrez, Laura
Intertribal Timber Council *(583)*

Am, Bibiana
National Society of Hispanic MBAs *(794)*

Amador, Marilyn
American Society for Gastrointestinal Endoscopy *(184)*

Aman, Zach
National Association of Graduate-Professional
  Students *(670)*

Amarelo, Monica
Federation of American Scientists *(440)*

Amato, Danielle Mages
Literary Managers and Dramaturgs of the Americas
  (599)

Amatulli, Lisa
American Society of Perfumers *(206)*

Ambach, Dennis
Electronic Funds Transfer Association *(423)*

Ambers, Kitty
American Insurance Marketing and Sales Society *(141)*

Ambos, Elizabeth
Council on Undergraduate Research *(401)*

Ambrose, Jodie
Plastic Surgery Research Council *(850)*

Ambrose, Katie
National Institute for Animal Agriculture *(764)*

Ambrus, Amanda
Manufacturers' Agents Association for the Foodservice
  Industry *(603)*

Amdur, Thom
National Housing and Rehabilitation Association *(760)*

Amerault, Linda
American Society of Sugar Beet Technologists *(209)*

Ames, Roger
Society for Asian and Comparative Philosophy *(904)*

Ames, Rosemary
Mu Phi Epsilon *(621)*

Amidon, Ashley
The International Wood Products Association *(581)*

Amin, Kirit
Association for Federal Information Resources
  Management *(246)*

Amitay, Stephen D.
National Association of Security Companies (NASCO)
  (695)

Amman, Sara
Resort Hotel Association *(883)*

Ammerman, Kristen
RCI, Inc. *(875)*

Ammon, Jr., Dr. Robin
North American Society for Sport Management *(822)*

Amorosi, Joanie
American Academy of Facial Plastic and Reconstructive
  Surgery *(34)*

Amos, Cindy
Transportation Intermediaries Association *(978)*

Amos, Jennie
AACE International *(1)*

Amos, Rikki D.
Public Affairs Council *(868)*

Ams, John G.
National Society of Accountants *(793)*

Amselle, Jorge
Salt Institute *(891)*

Amundsen, Chris
American Craft Council *(111)*

An, Arthur
American Society of Neuroradiology *(204)*

Anagnos, Christine
Association of Art Museum Directors *(267)*

Anagnostelis, Debbie
American Pediatric Society *(162)*
Society for Pediatric Research *(918)*

Anaman, Dana
North American Technician Excellence *(823)*

Anania, Stephen
American Mushroom Institute *(153)*

Ananian, Denise
American Academy of Estate Planning Attorneys *(33)*

Anas, CAE, Peter
Friends of the National Institute of Dental and
  Craniofacial Research (FNIDCR) *(454)*

Anawalt, Ben
National Association of Credit Management *(661)*

Ancell, Michael
Power and Communications Contractors Association
  (855)

Ancheta, Michael
International Interior Design Association *(552)*

Anciano, John
Alpha Zeta Omega *(27)*

Andeberhan, Fistume
National Alliance of Black School Educators *(632)*

Andelman, Barbara
National Association of Consumer Bankruptcy
  Attorneys *(657)*

Andenoro, Tony
Association of Leadership Educators *(291)*

Andersen, Crossan R.
Entertainment Merchants Association *(429)*

Andersen, Elizabeth
American Society of International Law *(201)*

Andersen, Jason F.
Society of Environmental Toxicology and Chemistry
  (935)

Andersen, Seth S.
American Judicature Society *(143)*

Andersen, Vicki
North American Snowsports Journalists Association
  (821)

Anderson, Alana Alissa Yoshiko
The Society of Naval Architects and Marine Engineers
  (942)

Anderson, Andrea
Forest History Society *(451)*

Anderson, Andy
American Comparative Literature Association *(105)*

Anderson, Andy
Waterproofing Contractors Association *(1013)*

Anderson, Breanna
Global Semiconductor Alliance *(463)*

Anderson, Brian
The Philanthropy Roundtable *(846)*

Anderson, CFCS, Carol
American Association of Family and Consumer Sciences *(61)*

Anderson, Carole
American Society on Aging *(211)*

Anderson, Chris
American Jail Association *(142)*

Anderson, Clay
Air Conditioning, Heating and Refrigeration Institute (AHRI) *(18)*

Anderson, Cle
American Association for Adult and Continuing Education *(47)*

Anderson, MS, Dan
Society of Forensic Toxicologists *(936)*

Anderson, CAPT Dave
American Poultry Association *(167)*

Anderson, Elayne
Association of Bridal Consultants *(270)*

Anderson, Elizabeth H.
Personal Care Products Council *(842)*

Anderson, Eric R.
Physician Insurers Association of America *(847)*

Anderson, Eugene L.
American Dental Education Association *(113)*

Anderson, USAF (Ret.), George K.
Association of Military Surgeons of the United States *(294)*

Anderson, Glaire
Historians of Islamic Art Association *(476)*

Anderson, Glen R.
Pressure Sensitive Tape Council *(856)*

Anderson, Helen
National Council on Education for the Ceramic Arts *(738)*

Anderson, James
United States Internet Industry Association *(995)*

Anderson, James E.
Printing Industry Credit Executives *(857)*

Anderson, Jason
Canola Council of Canada *(341)*

Anderson, JD, Jeannie
CFA Institute *(350)*

Anderson, Jeff
Ice Skating Institute *(482)*

Anderson, Jennifer
Museum Store Association *(621)*

Anderson, Jim
The Vision Council *(1010)*

Anderson, Joanne B.
American Academy of Actuaries *(29)*

Anderson, Joel
International Warehouse Logistics Association *(580)*

Anderson, Dr. John A.
Electricity Consumers Resource Council (ELCON) *(422)*

Anderson, Jon
Baking Industry Sanitation Standards Committee *(325)*

Anderson, CAE, Judell
Alliance of Automotive Service Providers *(24)*

Anderson, Judy
Association of Programs for Female Offenders *(303)*

Anderson, Julie
American Camp Association *(88)*

Anderson, Karen
Hydraulic Institute *(481)*

Anderson, Karl
Soil Science Society of America *(951)*

Anderson, Kathy
Acute Long Term Hospital Association *(12)*

Anderson, Katie
International Society of Arthroscopy, Knee Surgery and Orthopaedic Sports Medicine *(571)*

Anderson, Keri
National Council of Examiners for Engineering and Surveying *(734)*

Anderson, Kevin
International Council on Hotel, Restaurant and Institutional Education *(539)*

Anderson, Kirstin
Alliance for Children and Families *(22)*

Anderson, Kristin Lord
Helicopter Association International *(473)*

Anderson, Lauren J.
Association of YMCA Professionals *(318)*

Anderson, Lewis
Flexible Intermediate Bulk Container Association *(447)*

Anderson, Libby
Association of Corporate Contributions Professionals *(277)*

Anderson, Liz
International Association of Defense Counsel *(519)*

Anderson, Lori
International Sign Association *(564)*

Anderson, Louise
International Economic Development Council *(541)*

Anderson, MS, MT (ASCP), Marcy
Clinical and Laboratory Standards Institute *(358)*

Anderson, Mark
North American Limousin Foundation *(817)*

Anderson, CAE, FASAE, Mark C.
American Society for Surgery of the Hand *(189)*

Anderson, Melodie
American Academy of Periodontology *(39)*

Anderson, Michael
International Trumpet Guild *(578)*

Anderson, Michael J.
International Federation for Choral Music *(544)*

Anderson, Mindy
Women's Professional Rodeo Association *(1023)*

Anderson, CAE, CPA, MBA, Nancy L.
American College of Foot and Ankle Surgeons *(95)*

Anderson, Nicole
International Bone and Mineral Society *(530)*

Anderson, Norman B.
American Psychological Association *(169)*

Anderson, CAE, IOM, Patricia
American Association of Neurological Surgeons *(66)*

Anderson, MPA, Patricia K.
Society of State Leaders of Health and Physical Education *(947)*

Anderson, Paul
ECRI *(418)*

Anderson, Philip I.
National Cargo Bureau *(718)*

Anderson, R. Bentley
American Catholic Historical Association *(88)*

Anderson, Richard
Heavy Duty Manufacturers Association *(473)*

Anderson, Roger
Association of Theatrical Press Agents and Managers *(314)*

Anderson, Russ
National Collegiate Baseball Writers Association *(724)*

Anderson, CAE, Shaine
Professional Landcare Network *(863)*

Anderson, Sharon
National Chimney Sweep Guild *(721)*

Anderson, Shawn
PROMAX/BDA *(866)*

Anderson, Sheila
National Association of Government Employees *(670)*

Anderson, Sherry
National Association of Addiction Treatment Providers *(645)*

Anderson, Stephani
Association of Career and Technical Education *(271)*

Anderson, Steven
Forest History Society *(451)*

Anderson, CAE, Steven C.
National Association of Chain Drug Stores *(652)*

Anderson, Susan
Society of Former Special Agents of the Federal Bureau of Investigation *(937)*

Anderson, Teresa
ASIS International *(232)*

Anderson, William R.
National Association of Insurance and Financial Advisors *(675)*

Anderson, Zenitta
American Council on Education *(110)*

Anderson-Smith, AICI, Yasmin
Association of Image Consultants International *(287)*

Andersson, Jonas
International Council on Systems Engineering *(539)*

Andraza, Meg
Association for Institutional Research *(250)*

Andre, Rae
Organizational Behavior Teaching Society *(832)*

Andreassi, Shawn
SAE International *(889)*

Andrejeski, Mark
American College of Rheumatology *(102)*

Andren, Carl
Institute of Navigation *(502)*

Andres, TJ
Association of Executive Search Consultants *(282)*

Andresen, Randi V.
American Association of Oral and Maxillofacial Surgeons *(67)*

Andress, Kali
American Volleyball Coaches Association *(219)*

Andrew, Don
PCIA - The Wireless Infrastructure Association *(840)*

Andrew, Stephanie
National Institute of Steel Detailing *(765)*

Andrews, Alex
Council of the Americas *(398)*

Andrews, Anne
NACHA - The Electronic Payments Association *(623)*

Andrews, LAc, ND, Becky
American Botanical Council *(85)*

Andrews, Bill
Association of Commercial Real Estate *(275)*

Andrews, David
American Hockey League *(132)*

Andrews, Hanna
The Academy of American Poets *(3)*

Andrews, Hannah
Association Media and Publishing *(262)*

Andrews, Jean
International Association for Human Resource
Information Management *(512)*

Andrews, Kelly
Waterproofing Contractors Association *(1013)*

Andrews, Ken
National Association of Portable X-Ray Providers *(685)*

Andrews, Lanette
National Council of Property Taxation *(735)*

Andrews, Lynne
Society of Mexican American Engineers and Scientists
(941)

Andrews, Mike
Association of Community Cancer Centers *(275)*

Andrews, Tara
Coalition for Juvenile Justice *(360)*

Andrisano, JD, Kelly
National Association of County Human Services
Administrators *(660)*

Andrus, MBA, Patrick J.
American Society for Healthcare Engineering *(184)*

Anfuso, Alyssa
Association of Steel Distributors *(311)*

Ang, Sokha
Corporate Facility Advisors, Inc. *(386)*

Angel, Angie
Home Improvement Research Institute *(478)*

Angel, Gerry
American Guild of Musical Artists *(127)*

Angel, Esq., Naomi R.
Door and Access Systems Manufacturers Association,
International *(415)*

Angelastro, Deana
Truck Mixer Manufacturers Bureau *(981)*

Angelini, Andrea
International Federation for Choral Music *(544)*

Angelo, Joseph
International Association of Independent Tanker
Owners *(523)*

Angelo, Rich St.
Radiant Panel Association *(872)*

Angelo, Robin Vest
United States Potato Board *(997)*

Angelopoulos, Dr. Christos
American Academy of Oral and Maxillofacial Radiology
(37)

Anglemyer, Donna
SAE International *(889)*

Angles, Margot
International Association of Venue Managers *(528)*

Angley, Tina
American Society of Safety Engineers *(209)*

Anglim, Terri

American College of Veterinary Internal Medicine *(104)*

Angood, FACS, FCCM, FRCS, MD, Peter
American College of Physician Executives *(101)*

Angove, R. Lawrence
Association of Directory Publishers *(279)*

Angus, Bruce
National Marine Electronics Association *(771)*

Anibarro, Gustavo
Laser Institute of America *(593)*

Animasahun, Shina
National Association of State Mental Health Program
Directors *(701)*

Anis, Patricia A.
International Food, Wine and Travel Writers
Association *(546)*

Anker, Jennifer
American Amusement Machine Association *(45)*

Ankus, Esq., Joseph
National Association of Legal Search Consultants *(678)*

Ankus, Stephanie
National Association of Legal Search Consultants *(678)*

Anno-Murk, Mary Catherine
College Music Society *(363)*

Annotti, Joe
American Fraternal Alliance *(124)*

Annunziata Nicolaides, Kathleen
American Society of Questioned Document Examiners
(208)

Annunziato, Jeanine
National Association of Catholic Chaplains *(651)*

Ansaldi, Lou
National Association of State Workforce Agencies *(703)*

Anstead, Alicia
Association of Performing Arts Presenters *(298)*

Antczak, Frederick J.
Rhetoric Society of America *(886)*

Antelo, Cristina E.
Hispanic Lobbyists Association *(475)*

Anthony, Julie
Specialized Information Publishers Association *(957)*

Anthony, Theresa
National Confectioners Association *(725)*

Anthony, Virginia Q.
American Academy of Child and Adolescent Psychiatry
(31)

Antinucci, Angela
National Association of Service Managers *(695)*

Antion, Daniel
American Nuclear Insurers *(156)*

Antion-Mohr, Sherry
United States Trotting Association *(1000)*

Anto, Michael
National Athletic Trainers Association *(710)*

Antoine, Valerie
U.S. Metric Association *(983)*

Antolick, Steven
Checks Payment Systems Association *(351)*
International Association of Airport Duty Free Stores
(515)

Antonescu, Mihaela-Daniela
Geothermal Energy Association *(459)*

Antonini, Jack M.
National Association of Credit Union Service
Organizations *(661)*

Antonio, Mara

HR Policy Association *(480)*

Antoniou, Julie
National Head Start Association *(758)*

Antonucci, Mark
National Confectionery Sales Association *(726)*

Antor, CMP, Sandy J.
National Association for Home Care and Hospice *(639)*

Antrim, Debbie
Custom Electronic Design and Installation Association
(405)

Apel, Justin
Golf Course Builders Association of America *(463)*

Apgar, Jonathan
Organization of American Historians *(832)*

Aplebaum, Lowell
International Facility Management Association *(543)*

Apollonio, Susan
American Society of Landscape Architects *(201)*

Aponte, Rosie
The Advertising Research Foundation *(13)*

Apostolik, Richard
Global Association of Risk Professionals *(461)*

Apostolos, MCSD, Paul
National Roofing Contractors Association *(787)*

Appel, Heather
Committee of Interns and Residents/ SEIU *(368)*

Appel, Sherry
AASHTO: Transportation Center of Excellence *(2)*

Appelbaum, Stuart
Retail, Wholesale and Department Store Union *(885)*

Appelhans, JD, Patricia F.
Association of Professional Chaplains *(301)*

Appell, Adrienne Citrin
Toy Industry Association *(976)*

Appelton, Forrest
Chief Warrant and Warrant Officers Association,
United States Coast Guard *(352)*

Apple, Katherine Kelly
American Federation for Aging Research *(119)*

Apple, MS, RN, Kathy
National Council of State Boards for Nursing *(736)*

Apple, PhD, Martin A.
Council of Scientific Society Presidents *(397)*

Appleby, James
Gerontological Society of America *(460)*

Applegate, William
American Society of Transplantation *(210)*

Applekamp, Jeff
Gas Processors Association *(456)*
Gas Processors Suppliers Association *(456)*

Appleman, Marc
Society for American Baseball Research *(903)*

Aprigliano, Christel
Professional Photographers of America *(863)*

Aqara (Lombardini), Joyce
IEEE Electron Devices Society *(484)*

Aquiline, Laina M.
International Council of Employers of Bricklayers and
Allied Craftworkers *(538)*

Aquiline, Matthew S.
International Council of Employers of Bricklayers and
Allied Craftworkers *(538)*

Aquino, Amy Carpenter
Emergency Nurses Association *(425)*

Aragon, Benito
American Indian Science and Engineering Society *(135)*

Arai, Andrew
Society for Cardiovascular Magnetic Resonance *(905)*

Arakaki, Lisa
North American Association of Commencement Officers *(813)*

Aramanda, James
The Clearing House Association *(357)*

Aranda, III, Peter J.
Consortium for Graduate Study in Management *(378)*

Araujo, CEM, Jodi
Hobby Manufacturers Association *(477)*
NADCA: The HVAC Inspection, Maintenance and Restoration Association *(623)*

Araujo, Michael
American Council on Education *(110)*

Arawole, Joyce
American College of Oral and Maxillofacial Surgeons *(99)*

Arbes, Sarah C.
Retail Industry Leaders Association *(884)*

Arcangeli-Story, Linda
Messenger Courier Association of the Americas *(612)*

Arce, Sandy
The Coalition for Government Procurement *(360)*

Arceneaux, Michael N.
Association of Metropolitan Water Agencies *(294)*

Archambeault, Paul R.
Airlines For America *(21)*

Archer, PHR, Dennis J.
Board of Certified Safety Professionals *(332)*

Archer, Jim
Northwest Fruit Exporters *(824)*

Archer, Patrick
American Peanut Council *(162)*

Archibald, David
Association for Canadian Studies in the United States *(241)*

Archibald, Grace
American Academy of Addiction Psychiatry *(29)*

Archibald, R. Scott
Polyurethane Manufacturers Association *(852)*

Arctur, David
Open Geospatial Consortium *(828)*

Arcuri, Amy
Bowling Proprietors' Association of America *(334)*
International Bowling Pro Shop and Instructors Association *(530)*

Ardalan, Rick
Competitive Telecommunications Association *(371)*

Ardavin, Patricia
Association of Energy Engineers *(280)*

Ardelian, Dan
International Chemical Workers Union Council/UFCW *(534)*

Arden, Janet
Bearing Specialist Association *(327)*

Ardis, Mike
National Association of Professional Surplus Lines Offices, Ltd. *(688)*

Ardouny, Mary Ellen
The Corps Network (formerly the National Association of Service and Conservation Corps) *(386)*

Arel, Dominique
Association for the Study of Nationalities *(259)*

Arellano, Art
AAGL - Advancing Minimally Invasive Gynecology Worldwide *(2)*

Arenberg, Carol
National Academy of Engineering of the United States of America *(627)*

Arend, Jr., Thomas E.
American College of Cardiology *(93)*

Arends, Lindsay
American Association for Public Opinion Research *(51)*
International Society for Traumatic Stress Studies *(570)*

Arends-Kuenning, Mary
Brazilian Studies Association *(335)*

Arendt, Lucie
International Dairy-Deli-Bakery Association *(540)*

Arent, Shereen
American Diabetes Association *(115)*

Arenz, Greg
North American Lake Management Society *(817)*

Argenas, Dan
Wedding and Event Videographers Association International *(1014)*

Argiropoulos, Theresa
IEEE Signal Processing Society *(485)*

Argow, Keith A
National Woodland Owners Association *(806)*

Arguello, Jr., Julio
Association of Maternal and Child Health Programs (AMCHP) *(293)*

Arias, Luddy
American Railway Development Association *(173)*

Arias, Susan
American Rhinologic Society *(175)*

Aring, Mary Beth
Pharmaceutical Research and Manufacturers of America (PhRMA) *(844)*

Arlowe, Danielle Fagre
American Financial Services Association *(121)*

Armas-Kelly, Martha
American Agents Alliance *(43)*

Armbrust, Dan
SEMATECH *(896)*

Armentrout, Erek
American Dental Assistants Association *(113)*

Armijo, April
American Indian Science and Engineering Society *(135)*

Armistead, Shirley
American Society for Healthcare Human Resources Administration *(185)*

Armitage, Charles
American Association of Professional Landmen *(71)*

Armitage, Michael "Mike"
American College of Phlebology *(100)*

Armitage, Neil
American Academy of Dental Group Practice *(32)*

Armour, Henry
National Association of Convenience Stores *(658)*

Armour, Melissa
Oregon Farm Bureau Federation *(830)*

Arms, Anneli
Federation of Modern Painters and Sculptors *(442)*

Armstead, Quitina
National Catholic Educational Association *(718)*

Armstrong, Anthony
Learning Forward *(596)*

Armstrong, Cutler
Music and Entertainment Industry Educators Association *(622)*

Armstrong, CAE, MAM, Elizabeth B.
International Association of Emergency Managers *(520)*
National Association of Government Communicators *(670)*
National Association of State Emergency Medical Services Officials *(700)*

Armstrong, Laura
Consumer Bankers Association *(380)*

Armstrong, Malinda
Adhesive and Sealant Council *(12)*

Armstrong, Michael J.
National Council of Architectural Registration Boards *(733)*

Armstrong, Peggy
International Dairy Foods Association *(539)*

Armstrong, JD, Robert G.
American Academy of Estate Planning Attorneys *(33)*

Armstrong, Trina
American Society for Cell Biology *(182)*

Arnaiz, Sherri
Towing and Recovery Association of America *(976)*

Arnal, William
North American Association for the Study of Religion *(812)*

Arnaudet, Larry
Exhibition Services and Contractors Association *(435)*

Arnaudet, Mitt
Exhibition Services and Contractors Association *(435)*

Arnett, Jeanine H.
Association for Financial Professionals, Inc. *(247)*

Arnett, John
Copper and Brass Fabricators Council *(384)*

Arnoff, Kathie-Jo
Kappa Delta Pi *(590)*

Arnold, Brian
National Swine Registry *(798)*

Arnold, JD, PhD, David W.
Association of Test Publishers *(313)*

Arnold, Elizabeth
Oriental Rug Retailers of America, Inc. *(833)*

Arnold, Jeff
American Society of Home Inspectors *(200)*

Arnold, MAM, Jeffrey
North American Transportation Management Institute *(823)*

Arnold, Joanne
Recycled Paperboard Technical Association *(877)*

Arnold, Kelley
Council of State Governments *(397)*

Arnold, Kenneth E.
Society of Petroleum Engineers *(944)*

Arnold, Mary
Credit Union Executives Society *(403)*

Arnold, Omar
National Federation of Federal Employees *(748)*

Arnold, Peter
National Structured Settlements Trade Association *(797)*

Arnold, MA, MHPE, Roberta E.
Radiological Society of North America *(873)*

Arnold, Stevan J.
The American Society of Naturalists *(203)*

Arnone, Anna
American Society for Therapeutic Radiology and
Oncology *(190)*

Arnott, Ann
Power Transmission Distributors Association *(855)*

Arnstein, Mary
American Association for the Advancement of Slavic
Studies *(52)*
Association for Slavic, East European, and Eurasian
Studies *(256)*

Arnston-Terrell, Mary
National Concrete Masonry Association *(725)*

Arocho, Esq., Antonio "Tony"
Hispanic National Bar Association *(475)*

Arokiasamy, Charles
National Council on Rehabilitation Education *(739)*

Aron, Cathy
Picture Archive Council of America *(848)*

Aronoff, Roberta
Communications Fraud Control Association *(369)*

Aronowitz, MD, Paul B.
Association of Program Directors in Internal Medicine
(302)

Aronowitz-Jones, Michelle
Gravure Association of America *(465)*

Aronson, Beth
American Association of Colleges of Nursing *(57)*

Aronson, PhD, Rosa
TESOL International Association *(971)*

Aronson, Sherri
Owner-Operator Independent Drivers Association, Inc.
(836)

Aronson, MD, FACC, FACCP, Solomon
Society of Cardiovascular Anesthesiologists *(931)*

Arrants, Sandra T.
International Precious Metals Institute *(561)*

Arrington, Michael
International Association of Baptist Colleges and
Universities *(516)*

Arscott, Brian
National Association of Insurance Commissioners
(676)

Arsenault, Maureen
National Institute of Senior Centers *(765)*

Arslan, Kristie L.
National Association for the Self-Employed *(644)*

Arteaga, Elizabeth
The Rural Sociological Society *(889)*

Arteaga, Roland A.
Armed Forces Financial Network *(229)*
Defense Credit Union Council *(408)*

Artemakis, MD, MPH, Angelo
American Society of Neuroradiology *(204)*

Arth, Tim
Campus Safety, Health and Environmental
Management Association *(341)*

Arther, Dr. Bob
American Association of Veterinary Parasitologists *(76)*

Arthur, Dixie
American Society of Association Executives-The
Center for Association Leadership *(193)*

Arthur, Holly
Association of American Railroads *(266)*

Arthur, CMP, Kirsten
World Airline Entertainment Association *(1025)*

Arthur, Noemi C.
Society of Interventional Radiology *(940)*

Arthur, Vaughn E.
Dangerous Goods Advisory Council *(407)*

Arthur, Violet
National Housing and Rehabilitation Association *(760)*

Arthurs, Eugene G.
SPIE - The International Society for Optical
Engineering *(958)*

Arunasalam, Chitra
American Music Center *(153)*

Arvay, MBA, Sara B.
Association of American Cancer Institutes *(264)*

Arvin, Shannon
National Interscholastic Athletic Administrators
Association *(766)*

Arzt, Alvin H.
American Endodontic Society, Inc. *(117)*

Arzt, Leonard
National Association for Proton Therapy *(642)*

Asbury, Donna L.
Association of Partners for Public Lands *(298)*

Aschoff, Brenda
American Neurological Association *(155)*

Asdal, Robert K.
Hydraulic Institute *(481)*

Aselin, Don
Sportsplex Operators and Developers Association *(959)*

Asensio, Javier
International Federation of the Phonographic Industry
(544)

Ash, Charisse Bazin
American Association of Community Colleges *(58)*

Ashburn, Ronald E.
Association for Iron and Steel Technology *(250)*

Ashby, DeWitt
National Association of Agricultural Fair Agencies
(646)
National Association of State Departments of
Agriculture *(699)*

Ashe, Leah
National Defense Transportation Association *(742)*

Asher, Pranoti
American Geophysical Union *(126)*

Ashford, Nina Salerno
Corrections, U.S.A. *(386)*

Ashley, Carl
Conservation and Preservation Charities of America
(377)

Ashley, Dave
Automatic Fire Alarm Association *(321)*

Ashley, David
National Strength and Conditioning Association *(797)*

Ashley, W. Harrison
National Cotton Ginners' Association *(730)*

Ashley-Burke, Amy
National Association of Convenience Stores *(658)*

Ashmore, Kelly
International Association of Lighting Designers *(524)*

Ashpole, Barry R.
Association for Recorded Sound Collections *(255)*

Ashton, Mary S.
American Water Resources Association *(220)*

Ashurst, Anne
American Composites Manufacturers Association *(105)*
International Cast Polymer Association *(533)*

Ashurst, James
Recreation Vehicle Industry Association *(877)*

Askew, Alex
BCA *(326)*

Askew, David
National Association of Minority and Women Owned
Law Firms *(680)*

Askew, Timothy E.
Tissue Banks International *(975)*

Aslan, Barbara
National Association of Concessionaires *(657)*

Asmar, Yesmin
United States Hispanic Chamber of Commerce *(995)*

Aspinall, Judy
Chain Drug Marketing Association *(350)*

Asplen, Laure
International Union of Electronic, Electrical, Salaried,
Machine, and Furniture Workers-CWA *(579)*

Asplund, Chad
American Medical Society for Sports Medicine *(149)*

Asquith, Marcia E.
Financial Industry Regulatory Authority (FINRA) *(444)*

Assante, CAE, Carylann
Student Youth and Travel Association *(964)*

Assante, Philip
National Association for Surface Finishing *(643)*

Assef, Saeed
Instrumentation Testing Association *(504)*

Astner, Janet L.
American Sociological Association *(211)*

Astorga, Lisa
Association for Research in Otolaryngology *(255)*
International Society on Thrombosis and Hemostasis
(575)

Astorino, Joe
SAE International *(889)*

Astrachan, Eric
Tile Council of North America, Inc. *(974)*

Atchinson, Brian
Physician Insurers Association of America *(847)*

Atchison, Laura
Distinguished Restaurants of North America *(414)*
National Barbecue Association *(712)*

Atchison, Sharee
National Institute for Animal Agriculture *(764)*
National Livestock Producers Association *(770)*

Atkins, Helen Barsky
American Association for Cancer Research *(48)*

Atkins, Hilary
Air Conditioning Contractors of America *(18)*

Atkins, Jody Rosen
National Extension Association of Family and
Consumer Sciences *(747)*

Atkins, Linda
Society of Collision Repair Specialists *(933)*

Atkins, Louis M.
National Association of Postal Supervisors *(685)*

Atkins, Maria P.
American Academy of Facial Plastic and Reconstructive
Surgery *(34)*

Atkinson, Carolyn
National Association of Unclaimed Property
Administrators *(707)*

Atkinson, Dale J.
Federation of Associations of Regulatory Boards *(441)*

Atkinson, MS, RD, Joan M.
Association of State and Territorial Public Health
Nutrition Directors *(310)*

Atkinson, Laura
International Association of Culinary Professionals *(519)*

Atkinson, Rene
Academy of Psychosomatic Medicine *(8)*
American College of Medical Quality *(97)*
American College of Radiation Oncology *(102)*
International Society for Pharmacoepidemiology *(568)*

Atkinson, Teresa
American Association of Neuromuscular and Electrodiagnostic Medicine *(66)*

Aton, Neal
American Bankers Insurance Association *(79)*

Attardo, Christina
International Licensing Industry Merchandisers' Association *(554)*

Atterbury, MPA, RD, LDN, Cynthia
Association of State and Territorial Public Health Nutrition Directors *(310)*

Attey, Phil
American Hellenic Educational Progressive Association (AHEPA) *(130)*

Attoh, Jeffrey
National Association of Convenience Stores *(658)*

Atuel, Hope
Appraisal Institute *(226)*

Atwaters, Sybrina
Religious Education Association *(880)*

Atwell, Laura J.
National Council on Radiation Protection and Measurement *(739)*

Atwood, Cindy
Commercial Vehicle Training Association *(367)*

Atwood, Claudette
National Rural Water Association *(788)*

Atzenhofer, CPA, Thomas J.
Hospitality Financial and Technology Professionals *(479)*

Auberg, Jamie
Phi Beta Fraternity *(845)*

Aubin, Kristine
Attorneys' Liability Assurance Society Inc. *(320)*

Aubrey, Sam
International Association of Black Professional Fire Fighters *(517)*

Auckerman, Sharolyn R.
National Telecommunications Cooperative Association *(799)*

Audette, Kristi
American Association for Geodetic Surveying *(49)*

Audley, Lo
Association of Independents in Radio *(288)*

Auer, Gloria
State Higher Education Executive Officers *(961)*

Auer, Kenneth E.
Farm Credit Council *(437)*

Auerbach, Abby
Television Bureau of Advertising *(971)*

Auerbach, Donald C.
Investment Company Institute *(584)*

Auerbach, Dr. Elise
American Institute of Indian Studies *(139)*

Auerbach, Leslie
Energy Solutions Center *(428)*

Augello, Jeffrey
National Association of Home Builders *(673)*

Augoustakis, Antony
Women's Classical Caucus *(1023)*

Augustine, Jackie
Photoimaging Manufacturers and Distributors Association *(846)*

Augusto, Melisa
National Farmers Union (Farmers Educational & Co-operative Union of America) *(747)*

Augustosky, Frank J
National League of Postmasters of the United States *(768)*

Augustyn, John
Metal Findings Manufacturers Association *(613)*

Augustyn, Nicole
American College of Chest Physicians *(94)*

Augustyniak, Ashley
Chemical Heritage Foundation *(351)*

Auker, Joyce
BritishAmerican Business Inc. *(335)*

Aukett, Linda
United Ostomy Associations of America *(988)*

Auld, CHES, MPH, M. Elaine
Society for Public Health Education *(919)*

aurg, jones
Federal Forest Resource Coalition *(439)*

Ausloos, Ginger
The Association to Advance Collegiate Schools of Business *(319)*

Austen, Jane
Stuntwomen's Association of Motion Pictures *(964)*

Austin, Anita
Association of American Editorial Cartoonists *(264)*

Austin, Chris
Inflatable Advertising Dealers Association *(494)*

Austin, Doug
Institute of Clean Air Companies *(499)*

Austin, Elleana
Association for the Advancement of International Education *(258)*

Austin, Joe
National Association of Credit Specialists *(661)*

Austin, Jonathan
American Association of Veterinary Clinicians *(76)*

Austin, Judy
Conference of Historical Journals *(375)*

Austin, Kathy
Association of University Professors of Ophthalmology *(315)*

Austin, Michael
Paint and Decorating Retailers Association *(836)*

Austin, Saundra Johnson
National Action Council for Minorities in Engineering (NACME) *(628)*

Austin, Ski
National Basketball Association *(712)*

Austin, Stephen P.
International Association of Arson Investigators *(515)*

Austin, Susan
American Association of Community Theatre *(58)*

Auth, Kathryn
Water Systems Council *(1013)*

Autrey, CAP, CPS, Sharon
American Society for Healthcare Engineering *(184)*

Avallone, CPA, Michael
American Association of Clinical Endocrinologists *(56)*

Avdeyev, Melanie

American Chemical Society - Rubber Division *(90)*

Averett, CFP, MBA, Joanna
National Association of Estate Planners and Councils *(666)*

Averitt, Bryce
Producers Guild of America *(858)*

Avery, Christine
American Payroll Association *(162)*

Avery, Michael
National Auctioneers Association *(711)*

Avery, Mike
Society for Organic Petrology *(917)*

Avery, CAE, Susan
Copper and Brass Servicenter Association *(384)*

Avery, CAE, Susan E.
International Association of Plastics Distributors *(526)*

Avila, Maria de Pilar
New America Alliance *(809)*

Avila, Marvin
National Alliance for Musical Theatre *(632)*

Avina, Al
Blinded Veterans Association *(332)*

Aviv, Diana
Independent Sector *(491)*

Avramidis, Manny
American Management Association *(146)*

Avrit, Karen
Academic Language Therapy Association *(3)*

Awai, Keoki
International Conference of Police Chaplains *(536)*

Axelrod, Gary
American Society for Pharmacology and Experimental Therapeutics *(188)*

Ayaz, Dr. Sandi
National Tutoring Association *(803)*

Ayele, Samson
National Council for Community Behavioral Healthcare *(731)*

Ayers, Carolyn S.
Animal Health Institute *(223)*

Ayers, PhD, Gail S.
Commercial Real Estate Women Network *(367)*

Ayers, Jayne
Society for Healthcare Strategy and Market Development *(910)*

Ayers, MPA, Jennifer L.
American Institute for Medical and Biological Engineering *(136)*

Ayers, Katherine
Cattlemen's Beef Promotion and Research Board *(346)*

Ayers, Laraine H.
Recreational Park Trailer Industry Association *(877)*

Ayers, MHCM, CAE, Linda T.
Emergency Department Practice Management Association (EDPMA) *(425)*

Ayerst, Donna
American Foreign Service Association *(122)*

Aylward, Kari
North American Building Material Distribution Association *(814)*

Aylward-Cahill, Susan
American Society of Landscape Architects *(201)*

Ayman-Nolley, Saba
Jean Piaget Society *(586)*

Ayres, Debbie

American Board for Certification in Orthotics and
Prosthetics, Inc. (ABC) *(81)*

Ayres, Marilyn
Land Trust Alliance *(593)*

Ayres, Maj. Melissa
National Naval Officers Association *(774)*

Azevedo, Roberto David de
Brazilian American Chamber of Commerce *(334)*

Aznavourian, Lynette
Archaeological Institute of America *(227)*

Azzoni, Riccardo
Woodworking Machinery Industry Association *(1024)*

Baase, Charlie
American Society of Lipo-Suction Surgery *(202)*

Baazet, Suzanne Moyer
African Studies Association *(15)*

Babb, Ivar G.
National Association of Marine Laboratories *(679)*

Babbitt, Adeena
American Society for Aesthetic Plastic Surgery *(180)*

Babby, Ellen
American Council on Education *(110)*

Babiasz, Elena
Crop Insurance Research Bureau *(404)*

Babjak, Patricia M.
Academy of Nutrition and Dietetics *(7)*

Bacak, Jr., CAE, Walter W.
American Translators Association *(217)*

Baccam, Lou
American Academy of Actuaries *(29)*

Baccante, Richard
American Institute of Physics *(140)*

Baccinelli, Maggy
Association of Corporate Counsel *(277)*

Bach, Daniel N.
Book Manufacturers' Institute *(333)*

Bach, Greg
National Alliance for Youth Sports *(632)*

Bach, Susan A.
United States Pharmacopeia *(997)*

Bachenheimer, Susan
Association of Military Surgeons of the United States
(294)

Bachman, Dori
Parachute Industry Association *(838)*

Bachman, Maria
International Trademark Association *(577)*

Bachmann, John W.
American National Chamber of Commerce *(154)*

Bachner, John P.
ASFE/The Geoprofessional Business Association *(231)*
National Lighting Bureau *(769)*

Backus, Susan
Shelf-Stable Food Processors Association *(898)*

Bacon, Julia
U.S.-Russia Business Council *(999)*

Bacon, Rick
National Association of Spine Specialists *(696)*

Bacot, John
Association of Independent Corrugated Converters
(288)

Bacsinila, CPA, Arceli (Pinky)
American Gastroenterological Association *(125)*

Badame, Esq., Kristopher P.

Event Planners Association *(434)*

Badat, Mary Carol
American Society of Anesthesiologists *(192)*

Baddeliyanage, Nadira E.
International Cemetery, Cremation and Funeral
Association *(533)*

Badeen, George
Allied Finance Adjusters *(26)*

Bader, Bill
International Electronic Manufacturing Initiative *(542)*

Badger, Bruce
International Institute of Ammonia Refrigeration *(551)*

Badham, Portia E.
American Association of Advertising Agencies *(53)*

Badillo, Kelly C.
Automotive Recyclers Association *(323)*

Badley, Beverley
National Venture Capital Association *(803)*

Bae, Jean
IEEE Electron Devices Society *(484)*

Baehr, Jennifer
National Association of Stock Plan Professionals *(703)*

Baer, Greg
Loading Dock Equipment Manufacturers *(599)*
Materials Handling and Management Society *(608)*

Baerveldt, Calvin
Society of Eye Surgeons *(936)*

Baez, Ramon J.
Academy of Dentistry International *(5)*

Bagada, Valji
USFN-America's Mortgage Banking Attorneys *(1006)*

Baggett, Alphonsus
American Association of Sexuality Educators,
Counselors and Therapists *(73)*

Baggish, Jeremy
American Cleft Palate-Craniofacial Association *(91)*

Bagin, Rich D.
National School Public Relations Association *(789)*

Bagnasco, Colleen
Society of Actuaries *(927)*

Bagot, Nancy E.
Electric Power Supply Association (EPSA) *(421)*

Baguyos, Jeremy
International Society of Bassists *(571)*

Bagwell, Margarita
Consortium for Advanced Management, International
(378)

Bahr, Fredrick W.
American Institute of Organbuilders *(139)*

Bai, Simon
National Cleaners Association *(722)*

Baile, David
International Society for the Performing Arts *(569)*

Bailey, Alicia
Guild of Book Workers *(467)*

Bailey, Ambika Puniani
National Roofing Contractors Association *(787)*

Bailey, Brent K.
Coordinating Research Council *(384)*

Bailey, Bridgette
National Association of State Aviation Officials *(698)*

Bailey, Dave
GSM Association *(467)*

Bailey, Debra L.

American Osteopathic Colleges of Ophthalmology and
Otolaryngology - Head and Neck Surgery *(161)*

Bailey, Evelyn
Chemical Heritage Foundation *(351)*

Bailey, MD, Janet E.
Association of Program Directors in Radiology *(303)*

Bailey, Janet L.
Registry of Interpreters for the Deaf *(879)*

Bailey, Jerome
American Association of Kidney Patients *(64)*

Bailey, Jerry
Conference of Radiation Control Program Directors
(375)

Bailey, Katey
Laborers-Employers Cooperation & Education Trust
(592)

Bailey, Kathi
American Association of State Colleges and
Universities *(73)*

Bailey, Kieren
Association of Seventh-Day Adventist Librarians *(308)*

Bailey, Kirk A.
Outdoor Industry Association *(835)*

Bailey, Linda
National Fire Protection Association *(751)*

Bailey, Lori
Precision Metalforming Association *(856)*

Bailey, Lori A.
American Orthopsychiatric Association *(159)*

Bailey, M. Nell
Rehabilitation Engineering and Assistive Technology
Society of North America *(879)*

Bailey, Matthew W.
Association of Defense Trial Attorneys *(278)*

Bailey, Natasha
Utilities Telecom Council *(1006)*

Bailey, Pam
National Association of Certified Valuation Analysts
(652)

Bailey, Pamela G.
Grocery Manufacturers Association (GMA) *(466)*

Bailey, Paul
Secondary Materials and Recycled Textiles Association
(894)

Bailey, Rhonda
International Association for Near Death Studies, Inc.
(513)

Bailey, Steve
National Management Association *(771)*

Bailey, Tanya
The Financial Services Roundtable *(445)*

Bailey, Tracey
Association of American Educators *(264)*

Bailey, Traci
Broadcast Education Association *(335)*

Bailey-Hainer, Brenda
American Theological Library Association *(216)*

Bailley, Ruth
American Lands Access Association *(144)*

Bailor, David
National Council for the Social Studies *(733)*

Baily, Mary Lou
Association of Collegiate Schools of Architecture *(275)*

Baime, David S.
American Association of Community Colleges *(58)*

Bain, Scott
Software & Information Industry Association (SIIA) *(950)*

Bain-Selbo, Eric
Society for Values in Higher Education *(926)*

Bainwol, Mitch
Alliance of Automobile Manufacturers *(24)*

Bair, James A.
North American Millers' Association *(818)*

Bair, Kellie
Intersocietal Accreditation Commission *(582)*

Bair, Marty
American Association of Managing General Agents *(64)*

Baird, Laurel
Interstate Oil and Gas Compact Commission *(583)*

Baird, Lougene
Rocky Mountain Llama & Alpaca Association *(887)*

Baird, Robert
North American Performing Arts Managers and Agents *(819)*

Baird, Robert "Rob" W.
Independent Electrical Contractors *(489)*

Bajkowski, John
American Association of Individual Investors *(63)*

Baka, Susan
Organization of Women in International Trade *(832)*

Bakamjian, Ted
Society of Exploration Geophysicists *(935)*

Bakeman, Nancy
Energy and Environmental Building Association *(427)*

Baker, Ann Meier
Chorus America *(355)*

Baker, Bill
Recreation Vehicle Industry Association *(877)*

Baker, Brenda
National Association for Campus Activities *(637)*

Baker, Brenda
Petroleum Packaging Council *(843)*

Baker, Brian
International Brotherhood of Electrical Workers *(531)*

Baker, C. Scott
American Genetic Association *(126)*

Baker, CAE, MBA, Carla
American College of Prosthodontists *(101)*

Baker, Carolyn
American Counseling Association *(111)*

Baker, CSS, Chrissy
Electronics Technicians Association International *(424)*

Baker, Chuck
National Railroad Construction and Maintenance Association, Inc. *(783)*

Baker, David
Writing Instrument Manufacturers Association *(1029)*

Baker, David H.
International Slurry Surfacing Association *(565)*
Lighter Association *(598)*
Plastic Shipping Container Institute *(850)*

Baker, Deanna
Archaeological Institute of America *(227)*

Baker, Del
Electronic Traders Association *(424)*

Baker, Donna M.
Gemological Institute of America *(457)*

Baker, George
Esperanto-USA *(433)*

Baker, Dr. Henry
Association of American Veterinary Medical Colleges *(267)*

Baker, Jason
National District Attorneys Association *(743)*

Baker, Jenny
Society for Industrial and Organizational Psychology Inc. *(912)*

Baker, CAE, Jerome F.
Sigma Xi, The Scientific Research Society *(899)*

Baker, Kai
Association of American Law Schools *(265)*

Baker, Kara
National Tractor Pullers Association *(801)*

Baker, Kate
Science Fiction and Fantasy Writers of America *(892)*

Baker, Katelin
Forest Landowners Association *(451)*

Baker, Kay
Production Equipment Rental Association *(859)*

Baker, Ken
National Council for Interior Design Qualifications *(732)*

Baker, Laura
International Association of Women in Fire and Emergency Services *(528)*

Baker, Laurie
United Transportation Union *(1001)*

Baker, Maggie
Association of the Wall and Ceiling Industry *(314)*

Baker, SET, Michael B.
Automatic Fire Alarm Association *(321)*

Baker, Mike
International Hot Rod Association *(550)*

Baker, Mike
National Bicycle Dealers Association *(713)*

Baker, Moira Fathy
National Science Teachers Association *(790)*

Baker, Ned
National Association of Local Boards of Health *(678)*

Baker, Nick
Association of Home Appliance Manufacturers *(287)*

Baker, Paul
Music Industry Conference *(622)*
The National Association for Music Education (Formerly MENC) *(641)*

Baker, Paul M.A.
Rehabilitation Engineering and Assistive Technology Society of North America *(879)*

Baker, Peter M.
Laser Institute of America *(593)*

Baker, Rebecca
Decorative Plumbing and Hardware Association *(408)*

Baker, Rhonda
National Academic Advising Association *(626)*

Baker, Hon. Richard H.
Managed Funds Association *(602)*

Baker, Robert H. (Bob)
Amalgamated Transit Union *(28)*

Baker, Sally J.
American Association of Equine Practitioners *(60)*

Baker, Sheree
Society of Actuaries *(927)*

Baker, Timothy D.
Association for Multicultural Counseling and Development *(252)*

Baker-Batterman, Jenn
International Association for Orthodontics *(513)*

Bakker, Lesley
Project Management Institute *(866)*

Baksa, Barbara
National Association of Stock Plan Professionals *(703)*

Bakx, Marcel
National Institute of Packaging, Handling and Logistics Engineers *(765)*

Balakgie, CAE, FASAE, Carla
National Automatic Merchandising Association *(711)*

Balasa, CAE, JD, Donald A.
American Association of Medical Assistants *(65)*

Balascak, Joshua
Chemical Heritage Foundation *(351)*

Balboa, Andrea
American Association of Physician Specialists *(69)*

Balbresky, Paul
Society of Insurance Trainers and Educators *(940)*

Balch, Alan F.
American Saddlebred Horse Association *(176)*

Balchunas, Norm
Association of Old Crows *(297)*

Balcom, Marti
National Association of Workforce Boards (NAWB) *(710)*

Baldwin, Chip
Soccer Industry Council of America *(902)*
Sports and Fitness Industry Association *(959)*

Baldwin, J. David
Ecological Society of America *(418)*

Baldwin, James
International Game Developers Association *(548)*

Baldwin, John D.
National Catholic Development Conference *(718)*

Baldwin, Melissa
American Association for Aerosol Research *(47)*

Baldwin, Mike S.
Brotherhood of Railroad Signalmen *(336)*

Baldwin, Molly
American Institute of Floral Designers *(138)*
National Small Business Association *(705)*
Professional Grounds Management Society *(862)*
Small Business Exporters Association of the United States *(900)*

Baldwin, CAE, Rand A.
Aluminum Extruders Council *(27)*

Baldwin, Robert N
National Center for State Courts *(720)*

Balek, Bill
International Sanitary Supply Association *(563)*

Bales, Tracey M.
Post-Tensioning Institute *(853)*

Balice, Carmela
International Association of Defense Counsel *(519)*

Balick, Rachel
American Academy of Orthotists and Prosthetists *(38)*

Balint, CPA, Annette
INDA, Association of the Nonwoven Fabrics Industry *(488)*

Baliozian, Kevin
American Association of Legal Nurse Consultants *(64)*
International Bone and Mineral Society *(530)*
ISEH Society for Hematology and Stem Cells *(586)*

Balk, DACLAM, DVM, MS, Melvin W.
American College of Laboratory Animal Medicine *(97)*

Balkissoon, Anila
Society for the Psychological Study of Science Issues *(924)*
Society for the Psychological Study of Social Issues *(924)*

Balko, Gregg
Society for the Advancement of Material and Process Engineering *(922)*

Ball, Allison
American Psychosocial Oncology Society *(170)*
International Society for Prenatal Diagnosis *(568)*

Ball, Holly
Federation of State Boards of Physical Therapy *(442)*

Ball, Ian
International Federation of Accountants *(544)*

Ball, Lisa
Manufacturers' Agents National Association *(603)*

Ballantyne, Michele
Recording Industry Association of America (RIAA) *(876)*

Ballard, Bonnifer
American Nuclear Society *(156)*

Ballard, Julie
International Association of Exhibitions and Events *(520)*

Ballard, Lynette
Catholic Health Association of the United States *(345)*

Ballard, Shawn
Traffic Audit Bureau for Media Measurement, Inc. *(977)*

Ballard, CMP, Wanda Neal
Parenteral Drug Association *(838)*

Ballard-Wood, Aime
Association for Psychological Science *(254)*

Ballen, Debra T.
Institute for Business & Home Safety *(496)*

Ballentine, James
American Bankers Association *(79)*

Ballin, Robin
Jewish Community Centers Association of North America *(588)*

Ballinger, Amelia
Convention Industry Council *(383)*

Ballmaier, Olimpia
Radiological Society of North America *(873)*

Balmer, Tom
National Ice Cream Mix Association *(761)*
National Milk Producers Federation *(772)*

Balmford, Esq., Kathryn E.
Association of Medical Device Reprocessors *(293)*

Baloh, Diane L.
American Concrete Institute *(106)*

Balon, Maribeth
North American Skull Base Society *(820)*

Balser, Frank
International Digital Enterprise Alliance *(540)*

Balsley, PE, Jennifer
Architectural Engineering Institute *(227)*

Baltutis, Kira
National Conference of Bar Foundations *(726)*

Balz, Frank
National Association of Independent Colleges and Universities *(674)*

Balzer, Howard
Professional Football Writers of America *(862)*

Bambel, Paul
National Association of RV Parks and Campgrounds *(692)*

Bambery, Carol
Association of Fish and Wildlife Agencies *(283)*

Bamford-Rees, Diana
Council for Adult and Experiential Learning *(388)*

Banasiak, Kate
Independent Staffing Alliance *(492)*
Stadium Managers Association *(960)*

Bancells, Richie
Professional Baseball Athletic Trainers Society *(860)*

Bancheri, Salvatore
American Association of Teachers of Italian *(74)*

Bancroft, Elizabeth A
Association of Former Intelligence Officers *(284)*

Bancroft, Gina
American League of Lobbyists *(145)*

Banderas, C. Ramiro
Communications Media Management Association *(369)*

Bandler, Jeremy
Jewish Communal Service Association of North America *(588)*

Bandy, Michael
American Professional Society on the Abuse of Children *(168)*

Bandy, Michael J.
Medical-Dental-Hospital Business Associates *(612)*

Banes, Douglas
United Brotherhood of Carpenters and Joiners of America *(986)*

Bangert, Bobby
Gay and Lesbian Medical Association *(457)*

Banister, Joyse L.
Pony of the Americas Club *(852)*

Bankerd, Julia
Association of Career and Technical Education *(271)*

Bankert, Lu Anne
Association of Community Cancer Centers *(275)*

Banks, Jonathan
Sail America *(890)*

Banks, Rick
American Philatelic Society *(163)*

Banks, Steve
Association of Boarding Schools *(270)*

Banks, Thomas
American Society of Interior Designers *(200)*

Bannan, Kathryn
Knowledge Alliance *(591)*

Banning, CAE, MA, Christine
National Parking Association *(779)*

Bannister, James R.
Association for Financial Technology *(247)*

Bannon, James W.
National Electrical Manufacturers Representatives Association *(745)*

Bannon, Traci
FBI Agents Association *(438)*

Bannwarth, Mandie "Amanda"
Aviation Insurance Association *(324)*

Baptista, MD, PhD, Carlos A.C.
International Society for Plastination *(568)*

Baptiste, USAF(Ret.), Thomas L.
National Center for Simulation *(719)*

Baquerizo, Maria Rosa
Colombian American Association *(365)*
Ecuadorean American Association *(419)*
Venezuelan American Association of the U.S. *(1008)*

Baran, Krista
International Society for Traumatic Stress Studies *(570)*

Baran, Leo J.
American Foundry Society *(123)*

Baranowski, Mary
Incorporated Research Institutions for Seismology *(487)*

Baranski, James "Jim"
National Stroke Association *(797)*

Barbaccia, Tina G.
American Society of Business Publication Editors *(194)*

Barbadimos, MD, Aris
American Association of Orthopaedic Medicine *(68)*

Barbee, CMP, Lori
National Elder Law Foundation *(744)*

Barber, Tierra
National Association of Academic Advisors for Athletes *(645)*

Barbera, Brad
Product Development and Management Association *(858)*
Utilimetrics/Alliance for Advanced Metering & Data Management Solutions *(1006)*

Barbier, Cecilia
Gases and Welding Distributors Association *(457)*

Barbieri, Kelly Ann
Professional Women Photographers *(866)*

Barbour, Charlene
National Federation of Licensed Practical Nurses *(749)*

Barbour, CEO, PhD, Shaun
American Academy of Psychotherapists *(41)*

Barbudo, CPA, MS, Cristina
Association of Government Accountants *(286)*

Barcan, Myra
MPA - The Association of Magazine Media *(620)*

Barcellona, Nina
Society for Photographic Education *(919)*

Barchiesi, Robert C.
International Anti-Counterfeiting Coalition *(511)*

Barclay, Ben
International Society of Transport Aircraft Trading *(574)*

Barclay, AAE, Charles
American Association of Airport Executives *(53)*

Barclay, Lakisha
American Chemical Society - Rubber Division *(90)*

Barcroft, Ann R.
Bank Administration Institute *(326)*

Bardach, Emily M.
American Wire Producers Association *(221)*

Bardakjian, Kevork B.
Society of Armenian Studies *(930)*

Barden, Douglas E.
Men of Reform Judaism *(612)*

Barden, Todd
National Reining Horse Association *(785)*

Bardolf, PhD, Lynnette
National Hearing Conservation Association *(758)*

Bardos, Gordon N.
Association for the Study of Nationalities *(259)*

Bardzik, Jonathan
American Nursery and Landscape Association *(156)*

Barefoot, Lexie
Academic Language Therapy Association *(3)*

Barenblat, Ayesha

Business for Social Responsibility *(339)*

Barenie, Mark
Institute of Food Technologists *(499)*

Barfield, Martin
Cosmetic Executive Women *(387)*

Barfield, Thomas
American Institute for Afghanistan Studies *(135)*

Barford, CAE, Mark
National Hardwood Lumber Association *(757)*

Barger, Polly Haselton
CHA - Certified Horsemanship Association *(350)*

Barger, Shirlyn
American Thyroid Association *(216)*

Bargmann, Russ
International Longshore and Warehouse Union *(555)*

Barillaro, Laura
The Jockey Club *(588)*

Baris, Andrew
American Association of Bank Directors *(54)*

Baris, Esq., David H.
American Association of Bank Directors *(54)*

Barkalow, Tammy White
Society of Quality Assurance *(946)*

Barker, Emma
Association for Jewish Studies *(250)*

Barker, Ian
National Soccer Coaches Association of America *(792)*

Barker, Justin
National Apartment Association *(634)*

Barker, Sarah
The Association of Theatre Movement Educators *(314)*

Barkey, Pat
Association for University Business and Economic Research *(260)*

Barkley, Scott
Baptist Communicators Association *(326)*

Barkmeier, Sharon
Institute of Career Certification International *(498)*

Barksdale, ANP-BC, CNE, FAANP, FNP-BC, PhD, Debra J.
National Organization of Nurse Practitioner Faculties *(777)*

Barlag, Kim
National Business Incubation Association *(717)*

Barlow, Kathleen M.
American Hackney Horse Society *(128)*

Barlow, LeAnn
Association of Nutrition & Foodservice Professionals *(296)*

Barlow, Roger E.
The Catfish Institute *(345)*

Barna, Leah
Controlled Release Society *(383)*

Barnaby, Monica
Association of Women in the Metal Industries *(317)*

Barnard, Dale
International Society for Antiviral Research *(565)*

Barnard, Linda Garcia
Nine to Five, National Association of Working Women *(811)*

Barnard, Vickii
Global Market Development Center *(462)*

Barnes, Charles
Tooling, Manufacturing and Technologies Association *(976)*

Barnes, David
National Council of Teachers of Mathematics *(737)*

Barnes, Deborah
American Counseling Association *(111)*

Barnes, MBL, PhD, Gail
National Dairy Council *(741)*

Barnes, Heather
International Museum Theatre Alliance *(557)*

Barnes, John D.
American Physical Therapy Association *(164)*

Barnes, Joseph L.
Fleet Reserve Association *(447)*

Barnes, Kate
National Truck Leasing System *(802)*

Barnes, Luke
American College of Physician Executives *(101)*

Barnes, Lyndsi
American Printing History Association *(167)*

Barnes, Mary
GAMA International *(455)*

Barnes, Michael J.
Voice and Speech Trainers Association *(1011)*

Barnes, Nancy
National Kitchen and Bath Association *(767)*

Barnes, Shauna
American Academy of Allergy, Asthma, and Immunology *(30)*

Barnes, Sheila
Appraisal Institute *(226)*

Barnes, Sheryl
United States Ski and Snowboard Association *(999)*

Barnes, Stacey
National Association of Healthcare Access Management *(671)*
National Association of Medical Staff Services *(645)*

Barnett, Jeffrey
U.S.-Russia Business Council *(999)*

Barnett, Lauren A.
Society for Healthcare Strategy and Market Development *(910)*

Barnett, Teresa
American Association for Laboratory Accreditation *(50)*

Barnette, Carrie
American Orff-Schulwerk Association *(158)*

Barnette, Diane
National Council of Juvenile and Family Court Judges *(735)*

Barnette, Erin
International Lactation Consultant Association *(553)*

Barnette, Marcia L.
National Association for Home Care and Hospice *(639)*

Barney, Randall
World Teleport Association *(1027)*

Barnhard, John
United Union of Roofers, Waterproofers and Allied Workers *(1001)*

Barnhardt, Thomas
Radio Advertising Bureau *(873)*

Barnhart, CMP, Jaime
American Moving and Storage Association *(153)*

Barnhart, Jeffrey E.
Audio Publishers Association *(320)*
International Card Manufacturers Association *(532)*

Barnhart, Michael
Society for Asian and Comparative Philosophy *(904)*

Barnhart, Dr. Stephen R.
International Association of Personal Protection Agents *(526)*

Barnhill, PhD, Robert E.
SACNAS (Society for Advancement of Chicanos and Native Americans in Science) *(889)*

Barnhisel, Richard I.
American Society of Mining and Reclamation *(203)*

Barno, CMP, MBA, Haydee
American College of Preventive Medicine *(101)*

Barocci, Robert L.
The Advertising Research Foundation *(13)*

Baron, Barry
JWB Jewish Chaplains Council *(590)*

Baron, James Scott
American Traffic Safety Service Association *(217)*

Baron, Joyce
Directors Guild of America *(413)*

Baron, Katie
Music Publishers Association of the United States *(622)*

Baron, Stephanie
International Housewares Representatives Association *(550)*

Baroncelli, Sharon
International Association of Women in Fire and Emergency Services *(528)*

Barquin, Ramon
Computer Ethics Institute *(372)*

Barr, Janette
Concrete Foundations Association *(373)*

Barr, Janette
Tilt-up Concrete Association *(974)*

Barr, Karen L.
Investment Adviser Association *(583)*

Barr, Teri
American Society of Agronomy (ASA, CSSA, SSSA) *(191)*

Barra, Amy
Intermediaries and Reinsurance Underwriters Association *(508)*

Barrack, David W.
American Edged Products Manufacturers Association *(115)*
National Association of Public Insurance Adjusters *(689)*

Barragan, Frank
Society of Hispanic Professional Engineers *(938)*

Barranger, Kristin
ASME International Gas Turbine Institute *(233)*

Barratt, CMP, Michael E.
Automotive Aftermarket Industry Association *(321)*

Barrell, Carly
National Association of Health Data Organizations *(671)*

Barresi, PhD, Dr. Barry J.
American Optometric Association *(157)*

Barrett, MD, Anna
American Society of Neurorehabilitation *(204)*

Barrett, Chris
Marine Technology Society *(605)*

Barrett, PhD, Christopher K.
Human Biology Association *(480)*

Barrett, Grant
American Dialect Society *(115)*

Barrett, Jeanne
Association of Business Owners of America *(270)*

Barrett, Jerome A.
American Academy of Sleep Medicine *(42)*
Associated Professional Sleep Societies *(237)*
Sleep Research Society *(900)*

Barrett, Kevin N.
Pipe Line Contractors Association *(849)*

Barrett, Mark
International Association for Cold Storage
   Construction *(511)*

Barrett, Miranda
Entrepreneurs' Organization *(430)*

Barrett, Murphie
United States Chamber of Commerce *(991)*

Barrett, Sabine
Society of Environmental Toxicology and Chemistry
   (935)

Barrie, Skip
CCIM Institute *(347)*

Barrie, Thom
Information Systems Security Association *(495)*

Barrientez, CMP, Ginger
National Independent Automobile Dealers Association
   (761)

Barrientos, June J.
American Institute of Oral Biology *(139)*

Barrineau, Clark
American School Bus Council *(177)*

Barron, Margaret R.
Council on Library-Media Technicians *(400)*

Barron, Phillip
American Conference for Irish Studies *(106)*

Barron, Rena
American Society for Healthcare Risk Management
   (185)

Barroso, Donzelina A.
Portugal-US Chamber of Commerce *(853)*

Barroso, Margarida
The Histochemical Society *(476)*

Barrow, Marlyn
APSE: The Network on Employment *(226)*

Barry, Amanda
American Board of Anesthesiology *(81)*

Barry, Anne
Council on the Safe Transportation of Hazardous
   Articles *(401)*
International Vessel Operators Dangerous Goods
   Association *(580)*

Barry, Chris
Business Marketing Association *(339)*
Institute of Packaging Professionals *(502)*
National Association of Sporting Goods Wholesalers
   (696)
The Recreational Vehicle Aftermarket Association *(877)*

Barry, Jo Anne
American Thoracic Society *(216)*

Barry, Jonna
Wilderness Medical Society *(1017)*

Barry, Michael
Insurance Information Institute *(505)*

Barry, CAE, Michael A.
American College of Preventive Medicine *(101)*

Barsdate, Kelly J.
National Assembly of State Arts Agencies *(635)*

Barson, Janet
CPA USA Network *(402)*

Barsook, Beverly
Museum Store Association *(621)*

Barstnar, Kathie
Environmental and Engineering Geophysical Society
   (430)

Barstow, Bob
Automotive Distribution Network *(322)*

Barstow, Scott
American Counseling Association *(111)*

Bartanen, Jason
Inter-Industry Conference on Auto Collision Repair
   (506)

Bartecki, Garry
Associated Equipment Distributors *(235)*

Bartelik, Marek
International Association of Art Critics *(516)*

Bartelmay, Janet L.
Association of American Railroads *(266)*

Bartelse, Jurian
American Veal Association *(218)*

Barter, Loretta
Loading Dock Equipment Manufacturers *(599)*
Material Handling Industry of America *(608)*
Materials Handling and Management Society *(608)*

Barth, Cathy L.
Academy of Criminal Justice Sciences *(4)*

Bartha, Caterina
Dance Films Association *(406)*
Dramatists Guild of America *(416)*

Bartkowski, John P
Religious Research Association *(880)*

Bartlett, Barbara Walker
American Association of Poison Control Centers *(70)*

Bartlett, Charles
American Entomological Society *(117)*

Bartlett, Dennis
American Bail Coalition *(78)*

Bartlett, Emily
Human Milk Banking Association of North America
   (481)

Bartlett, Greg
Strategic Account Management Association *(963)*

Bartlett, Jodi
American Association of Meat Processors *(64)*

Bartlett, Laura J.
American Association of Advertising Agencies *(53)*

Bartlett, Megan Riccardi
National Association for Search and Rescue *(642)*

Barto, Pete
International Association of Amusement Parks and
   Attractions(IAAPA) *(515)*

Bartoletti, JoAnn
National Association of Secondary School Principals
   (694)

Barton, Alexander
Crop Science Society of America *(404)*
Soil Science Society of America *(951)*

Barton, Chip
Council of State Governments *(397)*

Barton, Mark
ASM International *(232)*

Barton, Nathan
The Rural Sociological Society *(889)*

Barton, Paul
National Association of Women in Construction *(710)*

Barton, Richard J.
American Management Association *(146)*

Barton, Shirley

ASME International Gas Turbine Institute *(233)*

Bartsch, Debby
American Optometric Association *(157)*

Bartus, PhD, Shane
Sigma Phi Delta *(899)*

Bartz, Amy
Association of Woodworking and Furnishings
   Suppliers *(318)*

Baruah, Smita
Global Health Council *(462)*

Baruch, Wayne
National Academy of Recording Arts and Sciences
   (628)

Barwick, Timi Agar
Physician Assistant Education Association *(847)*

Barylski, Mike
Alliance for Children and Families *(22)*

Barzin, Mariam
International Society for Magnetic Resonance in
   Medicine *(567)*

Basa, Eniko Molnar
American Hungarian Educators Association *(134)*

Basalla, Rich
National Tooling and Machining Association *(800)*

Basalyga, Deborah H.
Federal Magistrate Judges Association *(439)*

Basaria, Gwen
American Association of Airport Executives *(53)*

Basch, PhD, Linda
National Council for Research on Women *(732)*

Basco, Buenaventura "Ven"
Asian/Pacific American Librarians Association *(232)*

Base, Vernor
World Watusi Association *(1028)*

Baseil, Rich
IEEE Signal Processing Society *(485)*

Basev, Sevket
International Network of Merger and Acquisition
   Partners *(557)*

Basham, Michele
American Art Therapy Association, Inc. *(46)*

Basile, Carol
Mobile Marketing Association *(618)*

Baskerville, JD, Dr. Lezli
National Association for Equal Opportunity in Higher
   Education *(638)*

Baskin, Laurie
Theatre Communications Group *(973)*

Basler, David R.
Meeting Professionals International *(612)*

Basore, Irene
National Certification Commission for Acupuncture
   and Oriental Medicine *(720)*

Bass, Beth
Women's Basketball Coaches Association *(1022)*

Bass, Debra
American Association of Family and Consumer
   Sciences *(61)*

Bass, Debra
American Counseling Association *(111)*

Bass, James K.
National Telecommunications Cooperative Association
   (799)

Bass, Kristin
Pharmaceutical Care Management Association *(844)*

Bass, Marsha
Painting and Decorating Contractors of America *(837)*

Bass, Michael
National Basketball Association *(712)*

Bass, Nancy
Enactus *(427)*

Bassett, Andrew
National Association for Gifted Children *(639)*

Bassett, Patrick F.
National Association of Independent Schools *(675)*

Bassiouney, Reem
American Association of Teachers of Arabic *(74)*

Bassler, Bonnie L.
American Society for Microbiology *(187)*

Basso, Jack
AASHTO: Transportation Center of Excellence *(2)*

Basson, Sara
American Voice Input/Output Society *(219)*

Bast, CAE, MBA, Gail L.
Society for Mucosal Immunology *(916)*

Basto, Jorge
Court Information Technology Officer Consortium *(402)*

Basye, Sue
The Brown Swiss Association *(336)*

Batarla, Rob
American Physical Therapy Association *(164)*

Batcha, Laura
Organic Trade Association *(830)*

Batchelor, Debbie
Violin Society of America *(1010)*

Batchelor, Nanci K.
Society for Industrial Archeology *(913)*

Bates, Brenda
American College of Trial Lawyers *(103)*

Bates, Brenda
World Gold Trust Services *(1026)*

Bates, Brianna
Distance Education and Training Council *(414)*

Bates, Chris
Independent Office Products and Furniture Dealers Association *(490)*
National Office Products Alliance *(776)*
Office Furniture Dealers Alliance *(826)*

Bates, CAPT Dave
Allied Pilots Association *(26)*

Bates, Dr. Hudson
Nickel Institute *(811)*

Bates, Jeff
TechAmerica (fka Technology Association of America) *(969)*

Bates, Mariette
Society for Disability Studies *(907)*

Bates, Saundra
NALS *(625)*

Bates, Sterling
Association for Psychological Type International *(254)*

Bates, Terri
National Association of University Forest Resources Programs *(707)*

Bath, Jody
American Academy of Emergency Medicine *(33)*

Batheja, Renu
PCIA - The Wireless Infrastructure Association *(840)*

Batimarchi, Paulo

International Federation of the Phonographic Industry *(544)*

Batiste, Gene
National Association of Independent Schools *(675)*

Batra, Nikki
American Association of Certified Orthoptists *(56)*

Batson, Jane
Republican Governors Association *(881)*

Batson, Jim
American Bladesmith Society *(81)*

Batson, Ruth
The American Gem Society *(125)*

Batt, Anna Marie
National Emergency Number Association *(745)*

Batt, Matt
International Society of Hair Restoration Surgery *(573)*

Battaglia, Carmen
Dog Writers' Association of America *(415)*

Battaglia, Michael
International Council for Small Business *(538)*

Battaglia, Rosanne
Gift Associates Interchange Network *(460)*

Battat, Brenda
Hearing Loss Association of America *(472)*

Batteen, Carol
Fishing Vessel Owners' Association *(446)*

Batten, Susan Taylor
Association of Black Foundation Executives *(269)*

Battersby, Gregory J.
International Licensing Industry Merchandisers' Association *(554)*

Battle, Candice
National Association of Private Special Education Centers *(686)*

Battle, Felisha
National Society of Professional Engineers *(794)*

Battle, Kim
American College of Osteopathic Pediatricians *(100)*

Battles, Joey S.
American Registry of Radiologic Technologists *(174)*

Battrell, MSDH(, Ann
American Dental Hygienists' Association *(114)*

Baty, II, James
Concrete Foundations Association *(373)*
Tilt-up Concrete Association *(974)*

Baty-Chabrian, PhD, Dr. Peggy
Women in Aviation International *(1020)*

Bauchner, Howard
American Medical Association *(148)*

Bauer, Anita
National Association of Electrical Distributors *(664)*

Bauer, Anne Watson
Association for Childhood Education International *(241)*

Bauer, Bob
Association of Food Industries *(283)*
National Association of Flavors and Food-Ingredient Systems *(668)*
National Honey Packers and Dealers Association *(760)*
North American Olive Oil Association *(819)*

Bauer, Danielle
American Student Dental Association *(214)*

Bauer, David
American Road and Transportation Builders Association *(175)*

Bauer, Jane

American Cheese Society *(89)*

Bauer, MBA, Kate E.
American Association of Birth Centers *(55)*

Bauer, Mik
National Association of Housing Cooperatives *(673)*

Bauer, Rhonda
National Association for Retail Marketing Services *(642)*

Baugh, Beth
American Herb Association *(130)*

Baugh, Ginelle
Business Council for International Understanding *(338)*

Baugh, Robert
AFL-CIO Working for America Institute *(15)*

Baughman, Dutch
Division 1-A Athletic Directors Association *(415)*

Baughman, Sue
Association of Research Libraries *(306)*

Baugus, R. V.
International Association of Venue Managers *(528)*

Bauler, Randy
American Association of Critical-Care Nurses *(59)*

Baum, Hadassah
Beta Alpha Psi *(328)*

Bauman, Dawn M.
United States Psychiatric Rehabilitation Association *(998)*

Bauman, Suzanne
Organization for Safety and Asepsis Procedures *(831)*

Baumann, James
Advertising Council *(13)*
Association of College and University Housing Officers-International *(274)*

Baumann, Jennifer
Conference of Consulting Actuaries *(375)*

Baumer, Kathy
Society for Cardiovascular Magnetic Resonance *(905)*

Baumgarten, Deborah A.
Society of Abdominal Radiology *(927)*

Baumgarten, Kathy
American Military Retirees Association *(152)*

Baumgartner, Chester
Seaplane Pilots Association *(894)*

Baun, Betsey
Southeastern Theatre Conference *(953)*

Baur, Laruen
International Psycho-Oncology Society *(561)*

Bausell, Jim
Rural Electricity Resource Council *(889)*

Bautista, Linda
Association of the United States Navy, Inc. *(314)*

Bavido, Joe
Dairy Management, Inc. *(406)*
United Dairy Industry Association *(986)*

Baxter, Carrie
Association Montessori International - United States of America *(262)*

Baxter, Margaret
Original Equipment Suppliers Association *(833)*

Baxter, Mark
Vinyl Siding Institute, Inc. *(1009)*

Baxter, Parker
National Association of Charter School Authorizers *(652)*

Baxter-Bellamy, Amy L.

Society for Historians of the Early American Republic *(911)*

Bay, Bryndon
Music Publishers Association of the United States *(622)*

Bay, Sharon
Parenting Media Association *(838)*

Bay-Cheng, Sarah
American Theatre and Drama Society *(216)*

Bayard, Jean Pierre
North American Association of State and Provincial Lotteries *(813)*

Baybrook, Loren
Historians Film Committee/Film & History *(476)*

Bayer, Amy
Society for Psychophysiological Research *(919)*

Bayer, Anna
Competitive Telecommunications Association *(371)*

Bayer, PhD, Cherie L.
American Jersey Cattle Association/National All-Jersey Inc. *(142)*

Bayer, Helen
College Art Association *(362)*

Bayer, Kris
American Fiber Manufacturers Association *(121)*

Bayless, Rebecca J.
Irrigation Association *(585)*

Baylin, Desiree R.
National Office Managers Association of America *(775)*
Physician Office Managers Association of America *(847)*

Baylor, Katie
Association for Financial Counseling and Planning Education *(246)*

Bayne, Steve
Academy of Dental Materials *(5)*

Bayston, Darwin
Life Insurance Settlement Association *(597)*

Bazan, Jaime
Association of American Chambers of Commerce in Latin America *(264)*

Bazaz, Aggie Ebrahimi
National Alliance for Media Arts and Culture *(631)*

Bazinet, Michael G.
National Shooting Sports Foundation *(791)*

Bazrod, Larry
CoreNet Global *(385)*

Bazzle, CVR, Becky
National Verbatim Reporters Association *(803)*

Bazzoli, III, CAE, Fred
College of Healthcare Information Management Executives *(364)*

Bazzy, Michael
Minerals, Metals and Materials Society *(617)*

Beaber, Kevin
American School Band Directors' Association *(177)*

Beach, Carolyn
American Solar Energy Society *(211)*

Beach, Kerry
AIB International *(17)*

Beach, Maureen M.
American Beverage Association *(80)*

Beachum, CAE, Jeffrey
Interior Design Educators Council *(508)*

Beachy, Christopher
American Society of Ichthyologists and Herpetologists *(200)*

Beacom, David
National Science Teachers Association *(790)*

Beakley, PE, Josh
American Concrete Pipe Association *(106)*

Beal, Andrew
National Association of Insurance Commissioners *(676)*

Beal, Doug
USA Volleyball *(1005)*

Beal, Jason
Infusion Nurses Society *(496)*

Beal, MBA, Kathy
American College of Medical Genetics *(97)*

Beal, Mary
NALP - The Association for Legal Career Professionals *(624)*

Beales, Char
Cable & Telecommunications Association for Marketing *(340)*

Beales, Glenn
Association for Facilities Engineering *(246)*
Association of Investment Management Sales Executives *(289)*
National Association of Corporate Treasurers *(658)*

Beall, Mary Kay
Vacuum Dealers Trade Association/Sewing Dealers Trade Association *(1007)*

Beall, Mike
National Cooperative Business Association *(729)*

Beall, Stephanie
Weather Modification Association *(1014)*

Beals, CAE, Kimberly
International Pharmaceutical Excipients Council of the Americas *(560)*

Beals, Tim
National Student Osteopathic Medical Association *(797)*

Bean, Amy
National Association of Dental Laboratories *(662)*

Bean, Bransom
International Superyacht Society *(576)*

Bean, Margaret
American Supply Association *(214)*

Bean, Roger M.
American Board of Family Medicine *(82)*

Beans, Kathleen M.
The Risk Management Association *(886)*

Beard, Allison E.
American Health Lawyers Association *(130)*

Beard, Beth
National Recreation and Parks Association *(784)*

Beard, Cameron
Norwegian-American Chamber of Commerce *(824)*

Beard, Jeffrey L.
American Council of Engineering Companies *(109)*

Beardsley, Elaine
Percheron Horse Association of America *(841)*

Beardsley, Faye
American Federation of Government Employees *(119)*

Beardsley, Timothy M.
American Institute of Biological Sciences *(137)*

Beardwood, John P
International Technology Law Association *(577)*

Bearer, Donna
North American Peruvian Horse Association *(819)*

Bearse, Michael

Laborers International Union of North America *(592)*

Beasley, Barbara
National Association of Secondary School Principals *(694)*

Beasley, Tonya
Association for Clinical Pastoral Education *(241)*

Beason, Robert
Wilson Ornithological Society *(1018)*

Beaston, Lori
America's Blood Centers *(28)*

Beattie, Stephanie
GAMA International *(455)*

Beatty, Antonio T.
Commission on Accreditation for Law Enforcement Agencies Incorporation *(367)*

Beatty, Bob
American Association for State and Local History *(51)*

Beatty, Chuck
Distributive Education Clubs of America (DECA) *(415)*

Beaty, Lisa
Institute of Navigation *(502)*

Beauchemin, Patricia
Treatment Communities of America *(980)*

Beaudoin, Becky J.
Council for Art Education *(389)*
The Arts and Creative Materials Institute, Inc. *(229)*

Beaudoin, Joseph A.
National Active and Retired Federal Employees Association *(629)*

Beaudreau, Judith
International Association of Clerks, Recorders, Election Officials and Treasurers *(518)*

Beaulieu, Jamie
Hearth, Patio and Barbecue Association *(472)*

Beaumont, Jr., Guy D.
American College of Osteopathic Surgeons *(100)*

Beaupre, Steven J.
American Society of Ichthyologists and Herpetologists *(200)*

Beauvais, Christine
AASHTO: Transportation Center of Excellence *(2)*

Beauvois, Nan Marchand
National Council of State Tourism Directors *(736)*

Beaver, Allyson
Professional Bowlers Association *(861)*

Beaver, Mary
Public Affairs Council *(868)*

Beavers, Vern
North American Gamebird Association *(817)*

Beazley, William G.
Society of Piping Engineers and Designers *(944)*

Bebar, Mark
International Hydrofoil Society *(550)*

Bebchuk, Trevor
Veterinary Orthopedic Society *(1008)*

Bechard, Matthew
National Association of Real Estate Investment Trusts (NAREIT) *(690)*

Becherer, John
United Soybean Board *(989)*

Bechtel, Phil
Council of Federal Home Loan Banks *(393)*

Bechtloff, Debora
Plastics Pipe Institute *(850)*

Beck, David

American Institute of Organbuilders *(139)*

Beck, Erica
United States of America Dry Pea and Lentil Council, Inc. *(996)*

Beck, Holly
National Association of County Community and Economic Development *(637)*
National Association of Local Housing Finance Agencies *(678)*

Beck, Jane
Coordinating Research Council *(384)*

Beck, Marc
United States Dairy Export Council *(993)*

Beck, Margaret
MEMA Information Services Council *(612)*
Motor and Equipment Manufacturers Association *(619)*

Beck, Robert A.
The National Coal Council *(722)*

Beck, Ron
North American Flowerbulb Wholesalers Association *(816)*

Beck, Rosalie
National Association of Baptist Professors of Religion *(648)*

Beck, Shari
Cosmetic Executive Women *(387)*

Beck, Tabitha
National Association for State Community Services Programs *(643)*

Beck, Tina
Social Venture Network *(902)*

Beckenbaugh, Scot
Association of Labor Relations Agencies *(290)*

Becker, Catherine
American Council for Southern Asian Art *(109)*

Becker, Jr., Fred R.
National Association of Federal Credit Unions *(667)*

Becker, Maureen
International Police Mountain Bike Association *(561)*

Becker, Mila
American Society of Hematology *(199)*

Becker, Ramey
Financial Planning Standards Board *(445)*

Becker, Sandra L.
International Society of Certified Employee Benefit Specialists *(572)*

Becker, MS, Scott J.
Association of Public Health Laboratories *(304)*

Becker, Sharon
Health Ministries Association *(470)*

Becker, Tiffany
Semiconductor Environmental Safety and Health Association *(896)*

Becker, William
National Association of Clean Air Agencies *(654)*

Becker-Doyle, CAE, Eve
National Athletic Trainers Association *(710)*

Beckering, Thea
National Housing Conference *(761)*

Beckerman, Scott
Environmental Bankers Association *(430)*

Beckham, Barbara
Association of State Chamber Professionals *(310)*

Beckham, Julie
American Society for Reproductive Medicine *(189)*

Beckler, Tim

Delta Waterfowl Foundation *(409)*

Beckner, Debbie
Delta Omicron *(409)*

Beckner, Gary
Association of American Educators *(264)*

Becks, Jonathan
National Association of Women Lawyers *(710)*

Beckstead, Rick
National Conference of State Social Security Administrators *(728)*

Becktold, Susan M.
National Association for Program Information and Performance Measurement *(641)*

Beckwith, Lyle
National Association of Convenience Stores *(658)*

Becton, Mary
American Frozen Food Institute *(124)*

Beday, Summer
Automotive Oil Change Association *(323)*

Beddingfield, CPA, Laura
Society of American Travel Writers *(930)*

Beddis, Maureen
The Vision Council *(1010)*

Beddoe, Paul
National Association of County Health Facility Administrators *(660)*

Bedenbaugh, Christine
Academic Language Therapy Association *(3)*

Bedingfield, Kate
Motion Picture Association of America (MPAA) *(619)*

Beditz, Joseph
National Golf Foundation *(755)*

Bedker, Shari
American College of Bankruptcy *(93)*

Bedlin, Howard
National Council on Aging *(738)*

Bednar, Kelly
Bowling Proprietors' Association of America *(334)*

Bednarek, Janet R.
Urban History Association *(1004)*

Bednarek, Thomas
BioCommunications Association *(329)*

Bednarski, Karen
International Sports Heritage Association *(575)*

Bednash, RN, PhD, FAAN, Geraldine
American Association of Colleges of Nursing *(57)*

Beebe, Doug
Actors' Equity Association *(11)*

Beecher, Janice A.
Institute of Public Utilities *(502)*

Beel, Tina
Palomino Horse Breeders of America *(837)*

Beene, Michael
National Association for the Self-Employed *(644)*

Beer, Josh de
American College of Mohs Surgeons *(98)*

Beers, Tom
National Association for Business Economics *(636)*

Beery, Sharon
Golf Coaches Association of America *(463)*

Beeth, Harry
United States Tennis Association *(1000)*

Befumo, Phil
Photoluminescent Safety Association *(846)*

Befus, Elizabeth Feigin
National Multi-Housing Council *(774)*

Begey, Paul
Institute of International Bankers *(501)*

Beggan, Blair Marie
Association of Air Medical Services *(264)*

Beggs, Sara
Association of Small Foundations *(309)*

Begley, Rhonda
American Camp Association *(88)*

Behan, Catherine
Alliance for Aging Research *(22)*

Behar, Mina
Leather Apparel Association *(596)*

Behari, Mina
American Society of Transplant Surgeons *(210)*

Behn, Cathy J.
Clydesdale Breeders of the United States *(359)*

Behnke, Lisa
Purebred Dairy Cattle Association *(871)*

Behr, Dawn M.
National Funeral Directors Association *(754)*

Behrens, Anne
American Association for Hand Surgery *(49)*
American Society for Reconstructive Microsurgery *(189)*

Beideman, Benjamin
Blue Water Fishermen's Association *(332)*

Beighle, Vicki
American Association of Petroleum Geologists *(68)*

Beighley, Buck
American College of Emergency Physicians *(95)*

Beil, Ashley
American Volleyball Coaches Association *(219)*

Beilman, Mark
Reprographic Services Association *(881)*

Beirne, David
Election Technology Association *(421)*

Beisel, Courtney Leigh
National Association of Charter School Authorizers *(652)*

Beitelspacher, Lauren Skinner
Academy of Marketing Science *(6)*

Beiting, Laura
International Spa Association *(575)*

Beizer, Doug
Biomedical Engineering Society *(330)*

Bel, Gary
ACORD - Association for Cooperative Operations Research and Development *(11)*

Belanger, Daniele
Canadian-American Business Council *(341)*

Belanger, Debbie
Canola Council of Canada *(341)*

Belanger, Diane
Public Utilities Risk Management Association *(870)*

Belar, PhD, Cynthia D.
American Psychological Association *(169)*

Belasco, Warren
Association for the Study of Food and Society *(259)*

Belaunde, Kimberly
Society for Healthcare Epidemiology of America *(910)*

Belcher, Carol
Hardwood Manufacturers Association *(468)*

Belcher, Scott F.
Intelligent Transportation Society of America *(506)*

Belcik, Gail
National Association of Steel Pipe Distributors *(703)*

Belden, Angelisa
American Association of Neuroscience Nurses *(66)*
National Association for Healthcare Quality *(639)*

Belden, PE, PhD, David L.
United Engineering Foundation *(986)*

Belden, Joey
Women Chefs and Restaurateurs *(1020)*

Belfanti, Andrea
International Society of Hospitality Consultants *(573)*

Belford, Kevin B.
American Gas Association *(124)*

Belian, David
Generic Pharmaceutical Association *(458)*

Belk, Adrienne
Board Retailers Association *(333)*

Belkin, Kristin Lohse
Historians of Netherlandish Art *(476)*

Bell, Ann
International Microelectronics and Packaging Society -
IMAPS *(556)*

Bell, Bridgette
Public Employees Roundtable *(869)*

Bell, Cynthia
American Business Women's Association *(87)*

Bell, Dan
National Association of College Stores *(655)*

Bell, David
Technical Association of the Pulp and Paper Industry
(970)

Bell, Deb
International Association of Arson Investigators *(515)*

Bell, Don L.
National Association of Chain Drug Stores *(652)*

Bell, Duawwonna
National Association of Independent Schools *(675)*

Bell, Elaine
American Osteopathic Board of Physical Medicine and
Rehabilitation *(160)*

Bell, Ford
American Association of Museums *(65)*

Bell, Frances Roton
American Association of Community Psychiatrists *(58)*
American Association of Psychiatric Administrators
(71)
American College of Psychoanalysts *(102)*
American Society for Adolescent Psychiatry *(180)*
International Society for Adolescent Psychiatry and
Psychology *(565)*

Bell, Gloria
National United Merchants Beverage Association *(803)*

Bell, Greg
American Postal Workers Union *(167)*

Bell, James
Humanities Education and Research Association *(481)*

Bell, PhD, James T.
International Fitness Professionals Association *(545)*

Bell, Jim
National Coffee Association of the U.S.A. *(723)*

Bell, Joe
Polyurethane Manufacturers Association *(852)*

Bell, Kathy
National Association of Elevator Contractors *(665)*

Bell, Kayley
Mountain Rescue Association *(620)*

Bell, Marty
National Housing and Rehabilitation Association *(760)*
National Reverse Mortgage Lenders Association *(787)*

Bell, Peter H.
National Housing and Rehabilitation Association *(760)*
National Reverse Mortgage Lenders Association *(787)*

Bell, Robert
Society of Satellite Professionals International *(947)*

Bell, FACHE, Robert
World Teleport Association *(1027)*

Bell, Talitta
The Grant Professionals Association *(465)*

Bellaman, Michael D.
Associated Builders and Contractors *(235)*

Bellanti, Joseph A.
American Association of Certified Allergists *(56)*

Bellantone, CAE, Paul
Promotional Products Association International *(867)*

Bellantoni, Nicholas
National Association of State Archaeologists *(697)*

Bellenoit, SSJ, Sr. Suzanne
United States Conference of Catholic Bishops *(992)*

Bellet, Sarah
Information Systems Security Association *(495)*

Bellew, Norma
Public Housing Authorities Directors Association *(869)*

Bellfield, Dee
Ambulatory Surgery Center Association *(28)*

Bellias, Kerri
International Sleep Products Association *(565)*

Bellinger, Julia
American Spice Trade Association *(212)*

Bellinger, Marilyn
INDA, Association of the Nonwoven Fabrics Industry
(488)

Bellis, Elizabeth
Energy Programs Consortium *(428)*

Bellis-Jones, Hugh
American Hanoverian Society *(128)*

Bellocchio, Matthew
American Institute of Organbuilders *(139)*

Bellotti, Gene
Association for Psychological Type International *(254)*

Bellows, Thomas J.
American Association for Chinese Studies *(48)*

Bellucci, Kathryn
American Rhinologic Society *(175)*

Belmont, Linda
Drug Information Association *(417)*

Below, Stephany
Society for Industrial and Organizational Psychology
Inc. *(912)*

Belshe, Mark
Rubber Pavements Association *(888)*

Belt, Terre
National Association of Home Builders Research
Center *(673)*

Belton, Athenae
Council on Undergraduate Research *(401)*

Beltramini, Elizabeth
Association of College Unions International *(274)*

Beltran, Onofre
College Art Association *(362)*

Beltz, Nicola Vocola
The Association for Consortium Leadership *(243)*

Belvedere, DDS, Paul
American Society for Dental Aesthetics *(183)*

Belyeu, Lt. Col. Grady
National Naval Officers Association *(774)*

Ben-Yehuda, Muli
Special Interest Group on Operating Systems *(956)*

Benard, Darcie-Jo
National Limousine Association *(770)*

Benard, DPM, Marc A.
American Board of Podiatric Medicine *(83)*

Benasaraf, Russell M.
Society of Corporate Secretaries and Governance
Professionals *(933)*

Benavides, Selene
National Society of Hispanic MBAs *(794)*

Benavot, Aaron
Comparative and International Education Society *(371)*

BenAvram, CAE, Debra
American Society for Parenteral and Enteral Nutrition
(188)

Benberg, Tom
Council on Chiropractic Education *(399)*

Benbow, Ann E.
American Geological Institute *(126)*

Benbroo, Rod
International Formalwear Association *(546)*

Benchaln, CAE, Nazha
National U.S.-Arab Chamber of Commerce *(803)*

Bendell, Phyllis
American Academy of Arts & Sciences *(30)*

Bender, DeLaine
National Christmas Tree Association *(721)*

Bender, Jennifer
American Institute of Graphic Arts *(139)*

Bender, Neal
IPC - Association Connecting Electronics Industries
(584)
IPC - Surface Mount Equipment Manufacturers
Association *(585)*
IPC Washington Office *(585)*

Bendure, Vicki
Society for Maternal-Fetal Medicine *(915)*

Benedetto, FACP, Anthony V.
History of Dermatology Society *(476)*

Benedict, Lois
American Society of Heating, Refrigerating and Air
Conditioning Engineers (ASHRAE) *(199)*

Benedict, Mark
Organization of Professional Employees of the U.S.
Department of Agriculture (OPEDA) *(832)*

Benedict, Mark B.
Silica Fume Association *(899)*

Benediktsson, Jon
Geoscience and Remote Sensing Society *(459)*

Bengloff, Rich
American Association of Independent Music *(63)*

Bengston, Scott
Producers Guild of America *(858)*

Bengtson, Emily
Hispanic National Bar Association *(475)*

Benham, CPA, Amy
American Academy of Audiology *(31)*

Benigno, Christy
American Hereford Association *(131)*

Benish, Robert A.
Plan Sponsor Council of America *(849)*

Benish, Susan
National Church Library Association *(722)*

Benishek, Mark
Portable and Stationary Crushing Bureau *(853)*

Benitez, Jacqueline
Accreditation Association for Ambulatory Health Care *(9)*

Benjamin, Chuck
Association of Partners for Public Lands *(298)*

Benjamin, David A.
Intercollegiate Tennis Association *(507)*

Benjamin, FACP, MD, Georges C.
American Public Health Association *(171)*

Benjamin, Jon
American Academy of Appellate Lawyers *(30)*
American College of Mortgage Attorneys *(98)*
American Society of Consulting Arborists *(196)*
Association of Water Technologies *(317)*

Benjamin, Marc
Jewish Funeral Directors of America *(588)*

Benjamin, Margaret C.
Envelope Manufacturers Association *(430)*

Benjamin, CAE, Maynard H.
Envelope Manufacturers Association *(430)*

Benjamin, CAE, MPH, Michael L.
Family, Career and Community Leaders of America *(437)*

Benjamin, Vaughn
Media Credit Association *(610)*

Benka, Jennifer
The Academy of American Poets *(3)*

Benn, Lesley A.
International Law Students Association *(553)*

Benne, Susan
Antiquarian Booksellers Association of America *(224)*

Benner, Brendan
Medical Device Manufacturers Association *(611)*

Bennet, Caressa D.
Rural Telecommunications Group *(889)*

Bennet, James
American Society of Magazine Editors *(202)*

Bennet, DSc, PhD, Peter
Undersea and Hyperbaric Medical Society *(984)*

Bennett, Brooke
North American Limousin Foundation *(817)*

Bennett, Catherine
Council of Fashion Designers of America *(393)*

Bennett, Christopher
International Association of Assessing Officers *(516)*

Bennett, Gary
Institute for Operations Research and the Management Sciences *(497)*

Bennett, Jane
Building Stone Institute *(338)*

Bennett, Katherine Egan
American Society for Therapeutic Radiology and Oncology *(190)*

Bennett, Margie
Association of Fundraising Professionals *(285)*

Bennett, Mary
Electronic Traders Association *(424)*
Electronic Transactions Association *(424)*

Bennett, Matt

Pharmaceutical Research and Manufacturers of America (PhRMA) *(844)*

Bennett, Richard
American Orthopaedic Society for Sports Medicine *(159)*

Bennett, Robbie S.
American Polygraph Association *(166)*

Bennett, Roderick
AFL-CIO - Building and Construction Trades Department *(15)*

Bennett, S. Ray
Council on Chiropractic Education *(399)*

Bennett, Sarita
Midwives Alliance of North America *(615)*

Bennett, Severine
International Society of Political Psychology *(573)*

Bennett, Shannon
International Association of Official Human Rights Agencies *(525)*

Bennett, Sharon
American Academy of Implant Dentistry *(35)*

Bennett, Stephen
United Cerebral Palsy *(986)*

Bennett, T. Ray
American Bureau of Shipping *(86)*

Bennett, DMD, Terry R.
American Academy of Craniofacial Pain *(32)*

Benney, CAE, James C.
National Fenestration Rating Council *(750)*

Bennitt, Ian H.
Shipbuilders Council of America *(898)*

Benoit, Michael R.
Cement Kiln Recycling Coalition *(347)*

Benold, Laura
Clean Technology & Sustainable Industries Organization (CTSI) *(357)*

Benoudiz, Sondra Fry
Specialty Graphic Imaging Association *(957)*

Benowitz, CMP, Melissa R.
American Association of Attorney-Certified Public Accountants *(54)*

Bens, Cynthia
Alliance for Aging Research *(22)*

Bensen, Clara
Emdr International Association *(425)*

Benson, Amy
Risk and Insurance Management Society, Inc. (RIMS) *(886)*

Benson, Dana
ATM Industry Association *(320)*

Benson, Dianne
Society for Research on Nicotine and Tobacco *(920)*

Benson, Julie
Insured Retirement Institute *(505)*

Benson, Laura
Association of Performing Arts Presenters *(298)*

Benson, Peter
Electronic Commerce Code Management Association *(423)*

Benson, Sandra
United States Dairy Export Council *(993)*

Bensyl, MA, PhD, Diana M.
American College of Epidemiology *(95)*

Bentley, CMP, Beth
American Lighting Association *(145)*

Bentley, Holly
Building Owners and Managers Institute International *(337)*

Bentley, JoAnn F.
Artist-Blacksmiths' Association of North America *(230)*

Bentley, John
Brotherhood of Locomotive Engineers and Trainmen *(336)*

Bentley, Tracey
International Association of Privacy Professionals *(526)*

Bentley, MSW, William
Voices for America's Children *(1011)*

Benton, Jeani E.
SAFE Association *(890)*

Benton, Joe
National Association of Black Social Workers *(649)*

Benton, Karen
American Academy of Oral and Maxillofacial Pathology *(37)*

Benton, Laura N.
The Aluminum Association, Inc. *(27)*

Benton, Mack C.
America's Blood Centers *(28)*

Benton, Susan B.
Urban Libraries Council *(1004)*

Benton, Thomas C.
Society of Accredited Marine Surveyors *(927)*

Bentsen, Todd
Society for Neuroscience *(916)*

Bentz, Geoffrey
The American Bar Association Rule of Law Initiative *(80)*

Benz, CPA, Bill
Association of Schools of Public Health *(307)*

Benz, Helen
American Cleaning Institute *(91)*

Benzekri, Margo
Council for Employment Law Equity (CELE) *(389)*

Benzinger, Linda
National Exercise Trainers Association *(747)*

Berechko, Natasha
Independent Film and Television Alliance *(489)*

Berens, Kelly
Democratic Governors Association *(410)*

Berens, Michael
American Society of Interior Designers *(200)*

Berens, Patrick
National Speakers Association *(795)*

Berenson, Marsha
American Academy of Emergency Medicine *(33)*

Berenson, Terry
Professional Women Photographers *(866)*

Berg, Adam
International Licensing Industry Merchandisers' Association *(554)*

Berg, David A.
Airlines For America *(21)*

Berg, David C.
Congress of Neurological Surgeons *(377)*

Berg, Esther
American Association of Physician Specialists *(69)*

Berg, Jennifer
Association for the Study of Food and Society *(259)*

Berg, Jennifer
International Congress of Oral Implantologists *(537)*

Berg, Jordan
American Automatic Control Council *(78)*

Berg, Nancy
International Society for Pharmaceutical Engineering *(567)*

Berg-Ferguson, Amy
Plumbing Manufacturers Institute *(851)*

Bergantz, RN, Wendy
Radiation Therapy Oncology Group *(873)*

Berge, Kathi
American Association for Justice *(50)*

Bergen, Barry
Society for French Historical Studies *(909)*

Berger, B. Daniel
National Association of Federal Credit Unions *(667)*

Berger, Harris M.
American Folklore Society *(122)*

Berger, Janice
Independent Educational Consultants Association *(489)*

Berger, Jay
Earthquake Engineering Research Institute *(418)*

Berger, Jonathan
CIES - The Food Business Forum *(356)*

Berger, Madelon I.
Healthcare Billing and Management Association *(470)*

Berger, MD, Robert
North American Clinical Dermatologic Society *(815)*

Berger, Ronald S.
Subcontractors Trade Association *(964)*

Berger-Hughes, Mary Lee
National Academy of Engineering of the United States of America *(627)*

Bergeron, Margaret "Peg"
American Military Retirees Association *(152)*

Bergeron, Paul
National Apartment Association *(634)*

Bergeron, CAE, CGMP, Rob
Society of Government Meeting Professionals *(938)*

Bergeson, CAE, PhD, Dave
Professional Records and Information Services Management International *(864)*

Bergeson, CAE, PhD, David J.
Association of Pediatric Hematology/Oncology Nurses *(298)*

Bergey, Brad
National Association of Printing Ink Manufacturers *(686)*

Bergey, Paul
IEEE Technology Management Council *(486)*

Bergfeld, Ellen G.M.
American Society of Agronomy (ASA, CSSA, SSSA) *(191)*
Crop Science Society of America *(404)*
Soil Science Society of America *(951)*

Berggren, Jerry
National Association of Dental Plans *(662)*

Berggren, Todd
Geological Society of America *(459)*

Berghahn, Walter
Healthcare Compliance Packaging Council *(470)*

Berginnis, CFM, Chad
Association of State Floodplain Managers *(311)*

Bergman, PhD, Elizabeth M.
American Association of Teachers of Arabic *(74)*

Bergman, PhD, Jerry

Society for the Study of Male Psychology and Physiology *(925)*

Bergmann, James
National Association of Criminal Defense Lawyers *(661)*

Bergmann, Katie
Packaging Machinery Manufacturers Institute *(836)*

Bergmann, Stefan
Forest Products Society *(451)*

Bergquist, Gloria
Alliance of Automobile Manufacturers *(24)*

Bergren, Martha Dewey
National Association of School Nurses *(693)*

Bergseth, Karen
Surface Mount Technology Association *(966)*

Bergstresser, MD, Paul
The Society for Investigative Dermatology *(913)*

Bergstrom, Randolph
National Council on Public History *(739)*

Beri, Manny
Shipowners Claims Bureau, Inc. *(899)*

Beringer, Dennis
Association of Aviation Psychologists *(269)*

Berk, Kenneth
Object Management Group *(825)*

Berkeley, Brian
Society for Information Display *(913)*

Berkes, Joan
National Association of Student Financial Aid Administrators *(703)*

Berkland, Eric
Council of Residential Specialists *(396)*

Berkman, PhD, Harold W.
Academy of Marketing Science *(6)*

Berkofsky, Joe
Jewish Education Service of North America *(588)*

Berkowitz, Deborah
Society for Cardiovascular Magnetic Resonance *(905)*

Berkowitz, Dorrie
United Synagogue of Conservative Judaism *(1001)*

Berkowitz, Eric
American Alliance for Health, Physical Education, Recreation and Dance *(44)*

Berkowitz, Joan C.
Association for Preservation Technology International *(253)*

Berkowitz, Terri
American Society for Clinical Pathology *(182)*
Association of Rehabilitation Nurses *(305)*

Berkson, Robin
Donors Forum *(415)*

Berland, Dan
National Association of State Directors of Developmental Disabilities Services, Inc. *(700)*

Berliant, Kris
National Conference of Federal Trial Judges *(727)*
National Conference of Specialized Court Judges *(728)*

Berlin, Robert H.
Society for Military History *(915)*

Berlin, Steve
National Association of State Boards of Education *(698)*

Berlowitz, Leslie Cohen
American Academy of Arts & Sciences *(30)*

Berman, Alan
DRI International *(416)*

Berman, ABPP, PhD, Alan L.
American Association of Suicidology *(74)*

Berman, Barbara L.
American Institute of Certified Public Accountants *(137)*

Berman, Barry
American Collegiate Retailing Association *(105)*

Berman, Henry L.
Association of Small Foundations *(309)*

Berman, Howie
American Council on the Teaching of Foreign Languages *(111)*

Berman, Richard B.
American Beverage Institute *(81)*

Bernal, Erica
National Association of Latino Elected and Appointed Officials *(677)*

Bernard, Eric
National Association of Long Term Care Administrator Boards *(679)*

Bernard, Jordana
American Telemedicine Association *(215)*

Bernard, Kathy
North American Equipment Dealers Association *(816)*

Bernard, Sherry
American Academy of Professional Coders *(40)*

Bernardo, Meg
Association of Surfing Professionals - North America *(312)*

Bernat, Andrew
Computing Research Association *(373)*

Bernat, Annette Pena
American Chiropractic Association *(90)*

Bernay, Casey
Art Directors Guild/Scenic, Title and Graphic Artists *(230)*

Berner, Kornelia 'Connie'
National Association of Ordnance and Explosive Waste Contractors *(682)*

Berner, Mary G.
MPA - The Association of Magazine Media *(620)*

Bernert, MBA, John
National Intramural-Recreational Sports Association *(766)*

Bernescut, Cedric
National Catholic Educational Association *(718)*
National Catholic Educational Exhibitors *(718)*

Bernfeld, Anna
National Funeral Directors Association *(754)*

Bernhard, Dawn
Red Angus Association of America *(877)*

Bernhards, John F.
APPA - Leadership in Educational Facilities *(225)*

Bernhardt, Amanda
American String Teachers Association *(213)*

Bernhardt, Charlie
American Federation of Government Employees *(119)*

Bernhardt, Elise M.
Council of Archives and Research Libraries in Jewish Studies *(392)*

Bernhardt, Jennifer
World Council of Credit Unions, Inc. *(1026)*

Bernier, Jane
National Agricultural Alumni and Development Association *(630)*

Berning, Doreen
American Oil Chemists' Society *(157)*

Berns, Peter
National Conference of Executives of The ARC *(727)*

Bernstecker, Rachelle
American Seniors Housing Association *(178)*

Bernstein, Abby H.
Professional Aviation Safety Specialists (AFL-CIO) *(860)*

Bernstein, Brian A.
American Chemical Society *(89)*

Bernstein, Edward
Industrial Research Institute *(494)*

Bernstein, Jim
American Society for Pharmacology and Experimental Therapeutics *(188)*

Bernstein, Lynda
IEEE - Industry Applications Society *(484)*

Bernstein, Marc
Institute of Food Technologists *(499)*

Berretta, Lisa
Workgroup for Electronic Data Interchange *(1025)*

Berry, Beth-Ellen
International Life Sciences Institute *(554)*

Berry, Calvin
Real Estate Management Brokers Institute *(875)*

Berry, Clint
Red Angus Association of America *(877)*

Berry, Corrie Silvia
Manufacturing Jewelers and Suppliers of America *(604)*

Berry, David
Community Colleges Humanities Association *(370)*

Berry, Jr., PhD, Dr. Lemuel
National Association of African American Studies and Affiliates *(646)*
National Association of Hispanic and Latino Studies *(672)*
National Association of Native American Studies *(681)*

Berry, CAE, MBA, M. Suzanne C.
American Epilepsy Society *(117)*
American Society for Experimental NeuroTherapeutics *(184)*

Berry, Michael
National Association of Jai Alai Frontons *(677)*

Berry, Michael
National Ski Area Association *(791)*

Berry, Michelle
American College of Health Care Administrators *(96)*

Berry, Monique
Black Data Processing Associates *(331)*

Berry, CAE, Peter J.
International Association of Campus Law Enforcement Administrators *(517)*

Berry, Scott
Associated General Contractors of America (AGC) *(236)*

Berry, Steven K.
Competitive Carriers Association *(371)*

Berry, Travis
Democratic Attorneys General Association *(410)*

Berryhill, Jeffrey
Christian Association for Psychological Studies *(355)*

Bers, Steven
Passenger Vessel Association *(839)*

Bersani, Maribeth
Assisted Living Federation of America *(234)*

Berschauer, Candace
GAMA International *(455)*

Bersell, Sean Devlin
Entertainment Merchants Association *(429)*

Berson, Ginny Z.
National Federation of Community Broadcasters *(748)*

Bertagna, Joe
The American Hockey Coaches Association *(132)*

Bertagna, Kathy
The American Hockey Coaches Association *(132)*

Bertagna, Nancy
World Pet Association *(1027)*

Bertalmio, Genny
North American Association of Food Equipment Manufacturers *(813)*

Berthiaume, Jason
Pellet Fuels Institute *(841)*

Bertholf, PhD, Roger L
Association of Clinical Scientists *(273)*

Bertholin, Denise
Women in International Security *(1021)*

Bertolotti, Liz
Audio Publishers Association *(320)*

Bertone, Chuck
Society of Photo-Technologists *(944)*

Bertram, Whitney
National Association of County Recorders, Election Officials and Clerks *(660)*

Bertsch, Jason
American Enterprise Institute for Public Policy Research *(117)*

Bertsch, Kenneth A.
Society of Corporate Secretaries and Governance Professionals *(933)*

Bertuzzi, Stefano
American Society for Cell Biology *(182)*

Besesparis, Ted
National Association of Professional Insurance Agents *(687)*

Beshea, CFIRS, CFP, Bradley F.
The Fiduciary and Investment Risk Management Association *(443)*

Beskind, Donald
International Society of Barristers *(571)*

Besley, Bobbi
Resource Center for Religious Institutes *(883)*

Besore, CAE, MBA, Celia Trigo
National Association of Hispanic Nurses *(672)*

Bespalova, Elena
International Association for the Study of Pain *(514)*

Bess, Kindra
International Society for Pharmaceutical Engineering *(567)*

Bess, Pamela L.
BMC - A Foodservice Sales and Marketing Council *(332)*
Manufacturers Representatives of America, Inc. *(603)*
Paper and Plastic Representatives Management Council *(838)*

Bessette, Jackie
International Life Sciences Institute *(554)*

Bessette, Renee
National Hearing Conservation Association *(758)*

Bessette, Robert D.
Council of Industrial Boiler Owners (CIBO) *(394)*

Bessey, Lynda
National Council on Family Relations *(738)*

Best, Connor
Napa Valley Vintners Association *(625)*

Best, Glenna
National Defined Contribution Council *(742)*

Best, Julie
Phi Rho Sigma Medical Society *(846)*

Best, Stephen
American Photographic Artists *(164)*

Bethel, Thomas J.
American Maritime Officers Plans *(147)*

Bethke, Jennifer
Turnaround Management Association *(982)*

Bethune, William "Bill" J.
National Council of Minorities in Energy *(735)*

Beto, Amanda
Information Systems Audit and Control Association *(495)*

Betters, Gerald
National Association of County Health Facility Administrators *(660)*

Bettiga, Bart A.
National Tile Contractors Association *(800)*

Bettin, MA, Christopher
American Association of Nurse Anesthetists *(67)*

Bettman, Gary B.
National Hockey League *(759)*

Betts, ATR-BC, PhD, Donna
National Coalition of Creative Arts Therapies Associations *(723)*

Betts, CAE, Lisa R.
Employee Stock Ownership Plan Association *(426)*

Betz, PhD, Robert
The American Association of Eye and Ear Centers of Excellence *(61)*

Betzner, Claudia
Service Industry Association *(897)*

Bevans-Kerr, Bob
American Association of Avian Pathologists *(54)*

Bevans-Kerr, Janece
American Association of Avian Pathologists *(54)*

Beverage, Dick
Association of Professional Ball Players of America *(301)*

Beveridge, Richard
Alliance of Cardiovascular Professionals *(25)*

Bevilacqua, Esq., Gabriel L. I.
American Board of Surgery *(84)*

Beyer, Bruce
Gravure Association of America *(465)*

Beyer, Henry
American Mountain Guides Association *(153)*

Beyer, Irene
National Sportscasters and Sportswriters Association and Hall of Fame *(796)*

Beyer, Stephen W.
Transportation and Logistics Council *(978)*

Beza, Linda P.
National Association of College and University Attorneys *(654)*

Bezas, Sophia S.
National Association of Chemical Distributors *(652)*

Bhagat, Deepak
Indian Dental Association (USA) *(492)*

Bhagavath, MD, Bala
Society of Reproductive Surgeons *(946)*

Bhaskar, Manisha S.
American Academy of Orthotists and Prosthetists *(38)*

Bhatia, Peter
Accrediting Council on Education in Journalism and Mass Communications *(11)*

Bhatia, S. Joe
American National Standards Institute *(154)*

Bhatnagar, Supriya
Association of Writers and Writing Programs *(318)*

Biacchi, Tony
American Risk and Insurance Association *(175)*

Biagini, Alice
Italy-America Chamber of Commerce *(586)*

Biagini, Nancy
Communications Workers of America *(369)*

Bialek, Jennifer
Association of Corporate Travel Executives (ACTE) *(277)*

Bialor, Donna
International Castor Oil Association *(533)*

Bianchi, Carlos
North American-Chilean Chamber of Commerce *(823)*

Bianchi, CAE, Maria
American Ambulance Association *(44)*

Bianchini, Lori
National Council of Teachers of English *(737)*

Bianchini, Vic
Million Dollar Round Table *(616)*

Bianucci, Deborah L.
Bank Administration Institute *(326)*

Biard-Schaeffer, Vanessa
Institute of General Semantics *(500)*

Bias, Val
National Hemophilia Foundation *(759)*

Biasi, Gwen
Association of Legal Administrators *(291)*

Bibbo, ACSW, LICSW, Anthony J
The National Network for Social Work Managers *(774)*

Bibbs, Tanisha
Real Estate Investment Securities Association *(875)*

Bibbs-Sanders, Angelia
National Academy of Recording Arts and Sciences *(628)*

Bibby, Douglas M.
National Multi-Housing Council *(774)*

Bibeau, Phillip A.
Wood Products Manufacturers Association *(1024)*

Biberman, Felix
American Guild of Variety Artists *(128)*

Bice, Nicole
World Council of Credit Unions, Inc. *(1026)*

Bichler, Gail
Society of Publication Designers *(946)*

Bickett, Mari Kay
National Council of Juvenile and Family Court Judges *(735)*

Bicsak, Dennis
American Greyhound Track Operators Association *(127)*

Biddle, RiShawn
National Indian Education Association *(762)*

Biddle, Robert E.
Association for Accounting Administration *(237)*

Biddle, Steve
The American Society of Pediatric Hematology/ Oncology *(206)*

Biddle, MEd, Steve
American Pain Society *(161)*
National Association of Neonatal Nurses *(682)*

Biderman, David

Environmental Industry Associations *(431)*
National Solid Wastes Management Association *(795)*
Waste Equipment Technology Association *(1012)*

Bidermann-Roizen, Camille
International Academy of Television Arts and Sciences *(509)*

Bidstrup, W. Richard
ETAD North America *(433)*

Bieber, Elaine
United Synagogue of Conservative Judaism *(1001)*

Biegel, Douglas A.
COLA *(362)*

Biehn, Bettie
National Legal Aid and Defender Association *(769)*

Bielawski, Marcin
Jewelers of America *(587)*

Bielen, Kelly
International Economic Development Council *(541)*

Bieliauskas, PhD, Linas A.
American Academy of Clinical Neuropsychology *(31)*

Bielsker, Simone
American Staffing Association *(213)*

Biemesderfer, Chris
American Astronomical Society *(77)*

Bienacker, CAE, Bridgette
Sheet Metal and Air Conditioning Contractors' National Association *(898)*

Bier, CAE, Marilyn
ARMA International *(228)*

Bierkortte, Denise
National Ground Water Association *(756)*

Bierlein, Esq., Larry "Lawrence" W.
Association of HazMat Shippers *(286)*
Reusable Industrial Packaging Association *(885)*

Bierma, John
National Remotivation Therapy Organization *(786)*

Bierman, Lois
American Orthopaedic Foot and Ankle Society *(158)*

Biernat, Scott
Association of Metropolitan Water Agencies *(294)*

Bierria, Ray
Child Welfare League of America *(353)*

Bies, Laura
The Wildlife Society *(1017)*

Biesiada, Michele
National Roofing Contractors Association *(787)*

Biffin, Lorren
Association of Insolvency and Restructuring Advisors *(289)*

Bigge, Robert H.
Iron Casting Research Institute *(585)*

Biggins, Michael
Society for Slovene Studies *(921)*

Biggs, Elizabeth
Ecological Society of America *(418)*

Biggs, Kathe
American Academy of Podiatric Practice Management *(40)*

Biggs, Matthew
International Federation of Professional and Technical Engineers *(544)*

Bigham, Jeffrey P.
Special Interest Group on Accessible Computing *(955)*

Bikel, Theodore
Associated Actors and Artistes of America *(234)*

Bilak, Karen
Association of the Wall and Ceiling Industry *(314)*

Bilau, Geoff
International Association of Plumbing and Mechanical Officials *(526)*

Bilich, Georgeann
Society of Petroleum Engineers *(944)*

Biljetina, Richard
Energy Solutions Center *(428)*

Bilke, Darrell L.
Pinto Horse Association of America *(848)*

Billeb, Jan
American Knife & Tool Institute *(144)*

Biller, DVM, PhD, Barbara
Veterinary Cancer Society *(1008)*

Billey, Scott A.
Professional Liability Underwriting Society *(863)*

Billing, III, Frederic T.
American Clinical and Climatological Association *(91)*

Billings, Karen
Software & Information Industry Association (SIIA) *(950)*

Billings, Paul
American Lung Association *(146)*

Billings, Robert
Generic Pharmaceutical Association *(458)*

Billings, Robin
Alliance for Energy and Economic Growth *(23)*

Billingsley, Angel
Council of State Community Development Agencies *(397)*

Billingsley, Mary
American Academy of Child and Adolescent Psychiatry *(31)*

Billitzer, Barbara
International Right of Way Association *(563)*

Billman, Kimberly
American Jersey Cattle Association/National All-Jersey Inc. *(142)*

Billups, Jr., Clinton Ford
National Conference of Personal Managers *(728)*

Billups, Edith
National Organization of Black County Officials *(777)*

Billups, Robert
National School Boards Association *(789)*

Billy, J.D., Carrie L.
American Indian Higher Education Consortium *(135)*

Bilnoski, Amanda
National Juvenile Court Services Association *(767)*

Bilson, Jr., Gregg
American Entertainment Armories Association *(117)*

Bimson, Gabbe
Association for Equine Sports Medicine *(246)*

Binder, Patricia
National Garden Clubs *(754)*

Binet, David E.
National Association of Theatre Owners *(706)*

Binfa, Patricia V.
International College of Surgeons *(535)*

Bingaman, Maria
United Soybean Board *(989)*

Bingham, Tony
American Society for Training and Development *(190)*

Bingman, Karla

United States Psychiatric Rehabilitation Association **(998)**

Biniewicz, Melissa
United States Soccer Federation **(999)**

Binkley, Beth
American Association for Respiratory Care **(51)**

Binkowski, Bruce
Football Bowl Association **(450)**

Binns, Polly
Council for Resource Development **(391)**

Binns, Steve
American Cheese Society **(89)**

Binns, Susan O.
Association of Halfway House Alcoholism Programs of North America **(286)**

Binstock, Jeff
Omega Delta **(827)**

Binstock, Stuart
Construction Financial Management Association **(379)**

Binz, Jo Ann
Fulfillment Management Association **(454)**

Binzer, Howard
Catholic Campus Ministry Association **(345)**

Biordi, Michelle
International Energy Credit Association **(542)**

Bipes, Steven
United States Chamber of Commerce **(991)**

Birch, CAE, Brian K.
Snow & Ice Management Association **(901)**

Birch, Bryan
Enlisted Association of the National Guard of the United States **(429)**

Birch, Jean
Refrigeration Service Engineers Society **(878)**

Birch, Wanda
National Association of State Treasurers **(702)**

Birchard, Ethan
Association of Executive Search Consultants **(282)**

Bird, Anne
Society of Architectural Historians **(930)**

Bird, Bill
Art Glass Association **(230)**

Birdsall, Michelle S.
Institute of Transportation Engineers **(503)**

Birdsell, Bob
Mason Contractors Association of America **(607)**

Birdsell, Rob
Cristo Rey Network **(404)**

Birdsong, James R.
RCI, Inc. **(875)**

Birenbaum, PhD, Mark S.
American Association of Bioanalysts **(54)**
Association of Defensive Spray Manufacturers **(278)**
National Independent Laboratory Association **(762)**
WaterJet Technology Association - Industrial and Municipal Cleaning Association **(1013)**

Birk, Dr. Ann
Consortium on Financing Higher Education **(379)**

Birkey, Douglas
Air Force Association **(18)**

Birkey, Lyle
National Council for Science and the Environment **(733)**

Birkhauser, Mark
International Hunter Education Association **(550)**

Birkofer, Julie A.
Plasma Protein Therapeutics Association **(850)**

Birks, Heather
Broadcast Education Association **(335)**

Birmingham, Patricia
Women's Business Enterprise National Council **(1022)**

Birmingham, Sharon
American Ostrich Association **(161)**

Birnbaum, Liz
Ecological Farming Association **(418)**

Birnbaum, Robby H.
The American Fair Credit Council **(118)**

Birnie, Lauren
American Council of Learned Societies **(109)**

Birschel, Dee
International Foundation of Employee Benefit Plans **(547)**

Bisacquino, Thomas J.
NAIOP, The Commercial Real Estate Development Association **(366)**

Bisceglia, Erin Herzog
Association of College and University Clubs **(274)**

Bishop, Anna
Pyramid Society **(871)**

Bishop, Esq., Bianca L.
American Health Lawyers Association **(130)**

Bishop, Brenda
Global Market Development Center **(462)**

Bishop, Jan
American Harp Society **(129)**

Bishop, John R.
National Association of College and University Attorneys **(654)**

Bishop, Ken L.
National Association of State Boards of Accountancy **(698)**

Bishop, Paul D.
Association of Boards of Certification **(270)**

Bishop, CPA, Sandy
National Recreation and Parks Association **(784)**

Bishop, PE, Thomas
Electrical Apparatus Service Association **(422)**

Bishop, Timothy H.
National Affordable Housing Management Association **(629)**

Bishop, Toby
American Volleyball Coaches Association **(219)**

Bishophall, Rebecca
International Downtown Association **(541)**

Bishopp, Ann
Urban and Regional Information Systems Association **(1003)**

Bisson, Donald
Composite Panel Association **(372)**

Bissonnette, Jocelyn
National Association of Federally Impacted Schools **(668)**

Biswas, Gautam
Special Interest Group on Artificial Intelligence **(956)**

Bitokofer, Dwight
Independent Free Papers of America **(490)**

Bitterman, Cynthia Melton
National Leased Housing Association **(769)**

Bitting, Christina "Chris"
American Association of State Colleges and Universities **(73)**

Bittle, Amy
American Society of Hypertension, Inc. **(200)**

Bittner, Andrew
National Fraternal Order of Police **(753)**

Bittner, Gregory T.
Canon Law Society of America **(342)**

Bittner, Maggie
SnowSports Industries America **(902)**

Biuso, Sr., Gerald J.
Land Improvement Contractors of America **(593)**

Bivins, Marella
Society for Maintenance & Reliability Professionals **(914)**

Bjarkman, M.A.
Association for Humanistic Psychology **(249)**

Bjelke, Tiffany
Directed Energy Professional Society **(413)**

Bjella, Brian
United Association of Equipment Leasing **(985)**

Bjerklie, Margaret
American Academy of Pediatric Dentistry **(39)**

Bjerkness, Michelle
American Association of Cereal Chemists International **(55)**
American Phytopathological Society **(165)**
Master Brewers Association of the Americas **(607)**

Bjorling, Debra
International Association Of Pet Cemeteries and Crematories **(526)**

Black, Andrew M.
Association of Oil Pipe Lines **(296)**

Black, Barry
Society for Neuroscience **(916)**

Black, Cheryl
American Theatre and Drama Society **(216)**

Black, David
Bioelectromagnetics Society **(329)**

Black, Faye Malarkey
Regional Airline Association **(878)**

Black, Garnett
Aerospace Industries Association of America **(14)**

Black, Jacquiline
World Affairs Councils of America **(1025)**

Black, James
National Association of State Workforce Agencies **(703)**

Black, Lynne
National Subcontractors Alliance **(798)**

Black, Mike
Association of Ship Brokers and Agents (U.S.A.) **(308)**

Black, Patricia L
American Psychiatric Nurses Association **(168)**

Black, Peter D.
BPA Worldwide **(334)**

Black, Robert H.
American Society for Engineering Education **(183)**

Black, Sam
Satellite Industry Association **(891)**

Black, Willie
United States Rowing Association **(998)**

Blackburn, Allison
Council of Independent Colleges **(394)**

Blackburn, Cathy
Paleontological Research Institution **(837)**

Blackburn, Charles
Sigma Xi, The Scientific Research Society **(899)**

Blackburn, Charlie
North American Association of Central Cancer Registries *(812)*

Blackburn, Jennifer
National Sorghum Producers *(795)*

Blackburn, LaToya
American Fuel & Petrochemical Manufacturers *(124)*

Blackburn-Moreno, Ronald
ASPIRA Association, Inc. *(233)*

Blackfield, Anne
Association of Technology Act Projects *(313)*

Blackford, Jenny
American Gear Manufacturers Association *(125)*

Blackman, Marcia
American Academy of Emergency Medicine *(33)*

Blackmer, Diane
Association of Golf Merchandisers *(286)*

Blackmon, Cathy
American Connemara Pony Society *(107)*

Blackmon, Kathy
American Association for Respiratory Care *(51)*

Blacksberg, Layah
Jewish Communal Service Association of North America *(588)*

Blackstone, Jon
American Surgical Association *(215)*

Blackwelder, Challee
Association of Investment Management Sales Executives *(289)*
National Association of Corporate Treasurers *(658)*

Blackwell, Angela M
American College of Health Plan Management *(96)*

Blackwell, Carl
National Marine Manufacturers Association *(771)*

Blackwell, Kathy
Society for Features Journalism *(909)*

Blackwood, Janelle
Information Technology Industry Council *(495)*

Blackwood, Jim
Clinical and Laboratory Standards Institute *(358)*

Blackwood, Wade
American Canoe Association *(88)*

Blaese, Cindy
Institute for Certification of Computing Professionals *(497)*

Blafkin, Mark
Association for Competitive Technology (ACT) *(242)*

Blahut, Marge
Arthroscopy Association of North America *(230)*

Blair, Cecilia
American Society for Histocompatibility and Immunogenetics *(185)*

Blair, Dan G.
National Academy of Public Administration *(628)*

Blair, Jason
National Association of Flight Instructors *(668)*

Blair, Linda W.
International Association of Music Libraries, United States Branch *(525)*

Blair, Malcolm
Steel Founders' Society of America *(962)*

Blair, Michele
Heart Failure Society of America *(472)*

Blair, Monisha
Outdoor Advertising Association of America *(834)*

Blair, Paul
Council of Supply Chain Management Professionals *(398)*

Blair, Phillip 'Phil'
American Association for the Advancement of Science *(51)*

Blair, Rhonda
American Society for Theatre Research *(190)*

Blair, Rob
Steel Founders' Society of America *(962)*

Blair, Wayne
International Ombudsman Association *(558)*

Blaisdell, Lori
International Municipal Signal Association *(557)*

Blake, Catherine C.
Federal Judges Association *(439)*

Blake, Jennifer K.
American Dental Assistants Association *(113)*

Blake, Laura Lee
Asian American Hotel Owners Association *(231)*

Blake, Lissa
Women in Agribusiness *(1020)*

Blake, MSW, CDBC, Mychelle
Association of Pet Dog Trainers *(299)*

Blake, Nancy E.
Society for Experimental Biology and Medicine *(909)*

Blake, CAE, Patricia
American Society for Gastrointestinal Endoscopy *(184)*

Blakely, PhD, Eleanor A.
Radiation Research Society *(873)*

Blakely, Mack
International Society of Certified Electronics Technicians *(572)*
National Electronic Service Dealers Association *(745)*

Blakely, Stephen
Employee Benefit Research Institute *(426)*

Blakeslee, Ann
Association of Teachers of Technical Writing *(313)*

Blakeslee, Michael
The National Association for Music Education (Formerly MENC) *(641)*

Blakey, Leslie
The Coalition for America's Gateways and Trade Corridors *(360)*

Blakey, Marion C.
Aerospace Industries Association of America *(14)*

Blalock, Elizabeth
The Society for Investigative Dermatology *(913)*

Blalock, Phil A.
National Association of Farmers Market Nutrition Programs *(667)*

Blalock Keller, Kori
Professional Aviation Safety Specialists (AFL-CIO) *(860)*

Blamer, Jeff
Christian Schools International *(356)*

Blancato, Robert B.
Alliance of Information and Referral Systems *(25)*
National Association of Nutrition and Aging Services Programs *(682)*

Blanchard, Benjamin S.
SOLE - The International Society of Logistics *(952)*

Blanchard, Pat
American Association of Veterinary Laboratory Diagnosticians *(76)*

Blanchard, Sarah Ruen
Association of State Energy Research and Technology Transfer Institution *(311)*

Blanchette, Richard
Professional Association of Health Care Office Management *(859)*

Blanchfield, John
American Bankers Association *(79)*

Blanco, Pilar Rodriguez
Latin American Studies Association *(594)*

Bland, Chalyce
Emergency Medicine Residents' Association *(425)*

Bland, Kelli
National Organization of Black Law Enforcement Executives *(777)*

Bland, Rodger
Automatic Transmission Rebuilders Association *(321)*

Blandin, Giselle
IEEE Photonics Society *(485)*

Blaney, Desane
Association of Golf Merchandisers *(286)*

Blank, Janet
Independent Community Bankers of America *(488)*

Blank, Larry
American Society of Music Arrangers and Composers *(203)*

Blank, Rolf
Council of Chief State School Officers *(392)*

Blank, Thomas
Association of Independent Trust Companies *(288)*

Blanken, CMP, MBA, Heather S.
The International Childbirth Education Association *(534)*

Blankenbiller, Amy J.
National Elevator Industry, Inc. *(745)*

Blankenship, Janice
National AMBUCS *(633)*
National AMBUCS, Inc *(633)*

Blankenship, Samuel
Directed Energy Professional Society *(413)*

Blaser, Robert
Renal Physicians Association *(881)*

Blasgen, Rick
Council of Supply Chain Management Professionals *(398)*

Blatman, Judy
Council for Responsible Nutrition *(391)*

Blatzer, Bruce T.
Iron Casting Research Institute *(585)*

Blaylock, Crystal
National Stroke Association *(797)*

Blaylock, Deb
BEMA - The Baking Industry Suppliers Association *(328)*

Blazar, Betsy
American Society for Nondestructive Testing *(187)*

Blazauskas, Roman G.
Consumer Healthcare Products Association *(381)*

Blazek, Peggy
Water Quality Association *(1013)*

Blazevic, AAS, Angela
International Association of Assessing Officers *(516)*

Bleak, Chris
Utah Association of Public Charter Schools *(1006)*

Bledsoe, Thomas
Housing Partnership Network *(479)*

Blehart, Bruce
American Academy of Sleep Medicine *(42)*

Blekys, Irena
Association for the Advancement of Baltic Studies *(258)*

Blessington, Jacque
American Association of Zoo Keepers *(77)*

Blevins, Brianne
American Sugarbeet Growers Association *(214)*

Blevins, Colleen
ACPA College Student Educators International *(11)*

Blevins, Dean
Religious Education Association *(880)*

Blews, Jr., Edward O.
Council for Christian Colleges and Universities *(389)*

Blicker, Stacey
International Titanium Association *(577)*

Blietz, CAE, Jamie
American Registry for Diagnostic Medical Sonography *(174)*

Blim, Jill F.
American Society of Retina Specialists *(209)*

Bliss, Gretchen
Educause *(420)*

Blistein, PhD, Adam D.
American Philological Association *(163)*

Blixrud, Julia
Association of Research Libraries *(306)*

Blizzard, Jim
Environmental Council of the States *(431)*

Bloch, Jeffrey
Consumer Bankers Association *(380)*

Block, Barry
American Podiatric Medical Writers Association *(166)*

Block, Lara
Hedge Fund Association *(473)*

Block, CHt, Linda
International Society for the Study of Subtle Energies and Energy Medicine *(570)*

Block, CAE, CFRE, Marsha S.
American Group Psychotherapy Association *(127)*

Block, Sally
ArtTable *(231)*

Block, Sam
Wine and Spirits Wholesalers of America *(1018)*

Block, Wayne
National Ski Patrol System *(792)*

Block, William C.
Social Science History Association *(902)*

Block-Verk, Jonathan
PROMAX/BDA *(866)*

Blockstein, PhD, David E.
National Council for Science and the Environment *(733)*

Blodgett, Leslie
Geothermal Energy Association *(459)*

Bloesch, Jeanne
American Society for Surgery of the Hand *(189)*

Blom, Deborah
The Association of Collegiate Conference and Events Directors International *(275)*

Blonder, Karen
Association for Unmanned Vehicle Systems International *(261)*

Blondes, Chellie H.
American Academy of Orthotists and Prosthetists *(38)*

Blood, Barry
ADARA *(12)*

Bloodworth, Michelle
America's Natural Gas Alliance *(29)*

Bloom, John
Association of Fish and Wildlife Agencies *(283)*

Bloom, Lindsey
Association of Military Surgeons of the United States *(294)*

Bloom, Marlene
American Society of Consultant Pharmacists *(195)*

Bloom, Shawn M.
National Pace Association *(778)*

Bloomfield, Shirley A.
National Telecommunications Cooperative Association *(799)*

Bloomhuff, CAE, Esq., Amy B.
American Conference of Governmental Industrial Hygienists *(107)*

Bloomquist, Mitch
Tilt-up Concrete Association *(974)*

Bloomrosen, Meryl
American Medical Informatics Association *(149)*

Blouin, CAE, Anne
American Society of Association Executives-The Center for Association Leadership *(193)*

Blouin, Kathleen
National Business Aviation Association *(716)*

Bluhm, Mark
International Society of Arboriculture *(571)*

Blum, Alisa
National Association of City and County Health Officials *(654)*
National Association of County and City Health Officials *(659)*

Blum, Carol
Council on Governmental Relations *(400)*

Blum, Charles
The Fair Currency Alliance *(437)*

Blum, Jared O.
Polyisocyanurate Insulation Manufacturers Association *(852)*

Blum, Laura
Heart Rhythm Society *(472)*

Blum, Michael A.
Marine Corps League *(605)*

Blum, Ray
National Tutoring Association *(803)*

Blum, Richard
Marine Corps League *(605)*

Blumberg, Linda
Art Dealers Association of America *(229)*

Blume, Jane
International Association of Fire Fighters *(521)*

Blumenthal, Mark
American Botanical Council *(85)*

Blumgart, Pamela James
American Society for Healthcare Engineering *(184)*

Blumka, Anthony
National Antique and Art Dealers Association of America *(634)*

Blunt, Kenneth
Association of Public Television Stations *(304)*

Blunt, Matt
American Automotive Policy Council *(78)*

Blunt, Rebecca
Graphic Arts Technical Foundation *(465)*

Blust, Steven R.
Institute of International Container Lessors *(501)*

Bly, Robert W.
The American Consultants League *(108)*

Blyth, Myrna
American Association of Retired Persons *(72)*

Blythe, Thomas J.
American Mathematical Society *(148)*

Bo, DVM, PhD, Gabriel A.
International Embryo Transfer Society *(542)*

Boa, CAE, J. Michael
Casualty Actuarial Society *(344)*

Boal, Barb
American Philatelic Society *(163)*

Boardman, Katie
Association for Living History, Farm and Agricultural Museums *(251)*

Boatright, Grace
National Grange *(756)*

Bobb-Semple, Roxanne
American Board for Certification in Orthotics and Prosthetics, Inc. (ABC) *(81)*

Bobbino, Martha
Employee Benefit Research Institute *(426)*

Bobo, Robert
Discover America Partnership *(413)*

Bobowski, CPA, Bob
International Sleep Products Association *(565)*

Bobrow, CAE, CMM, CMP, MaryAnne P.
American Association of Corporate and Public Practice Veterinarians *(59)*

Bock, Ingeborg
The American Bar Association Rule of Law Initiative *(80)*

Bock, Lorna
Association of State Correctional Administrators *(310)*

Bock, MS, Nancy
American Cleaning Institute *(91)*

Bockel, Laurence Van
Global Offset and Countertrade Association (GOCA) *(462)*

Bockhop, CMP, Tracey
Preventive Cardiovascular Nurses Association *(857)*

Bocus, Ann Marie
American Society for Investigative Pathology *(186)*
Association for Molecular Pathology *(252)*

Bodack, Jeannine
SSPC: the Society for Protective Coatings *(960)*

Bodanyi, Stephanie
Turnaround Management Association *(982)*

Bodarky, George
Public Radio News Directors Incorporated *(870)*

Boddewyn, Noelle
Promotion Marketing Association *(866)*

Boddicker, John A.
American Maine-Anjou Association *(146)*

Boddicker, Rhonda
American Maine-Anjou Association *(146)*

Bode, Denise
American Wind Energy Association (AWEA) *(221)*

Bode, John W.
Cheese Importers Association of America, Inc. *(351)*

Boden, Natalie
Society of Thoracic Surgeons *(948)*

Bodiford, Katie

National Association of State Boards of Accountancy (698)

Bodis-Wollner, MD, Ivan
EEG and Clinical Neuroscience Society (421)

Bodkin, Lindsay
International Coach Federation (535)

Bodnar, John
Technical Association of the Graphic Arts (969)

Bodnovich, John D.
American Beverage Licensees (81)

Bodo, Beth M.
International Desalination Association (540)

Bodoff, Russell
National Home Infusion Association (760)

Bodor, Alison
National Confectioners Association (725)

Bodor, Geza S.
Academy of Clinical Laboratory Physicians and Scientists (4)

Boecker, Christie
International Association of Counselors and Therapists (519)

Boeckman, LaVerne
World Research Foundation (1027)

Boehlert, Jason
Manufactured Housing Institute (602)

Boehme, Karen
National Fluid Power Association (751)

Boehmisch, Quintin
American Miniature Horse Association (152)

Boel, Bridget A.
National Active and Retired Federal Employees Association (629)

Boer, Jolyn de
Tennis Industry Association (971)

Boer, Sandra den
International Hearing Society (549)

Boettcher, Jim
North American Society for Social Philosophy (821)

Bogacheva, Irina
Society of Quantitative Analysts (946)

Bogan, Gary
Independent Association of Accredited Registrars (488)

Bogart, Elizabethe
BP and AMOCO Marketers Association (334)

Bogart, Wendy
Council for Advancement and Support of Education (388)

Bogatz, Esq., Neil
International Association of Plumbing and Mechanical Officials (526)

Boggia, Marguerite Dar
International Society for Astrological Research (565)

Boggs, Barb
The Grant Professionals Association (465)

Boggs, Jeremy
Association for Computers and the Humanities (242)

Boggs, Julie
College and University Professional Association for Human Resources (362)

Boggs, RDH, Sharon
National Association of Seventh-Day Adventist Dentists (695)

Boghosian, Heidi
National Lawyers Guild (768)

Bogie, Patty
MPA - The Association of Magazine Media (620)

Bogl, Alan
Guild of Artists and Artisans (467)

Bogle, Hon. AIA, Ronald E
American Architectural Foundation (46)

Boglin, Felice
Commission on Professionals in Science and Technology (368)

Bognanno, Thomas G.
Community Health Charities of America (371)

Bogren, Scott
Community Transportation Association of America (371)

Bohan, Mark
Graphic Arts Technical Foundation (465)
Technical Association of the Graphic Arts (969)

Bohannan, Marcia
Promotional Products Association International (867)

Bohannon, Janiene
Association for Professionals in Infection Control and Epidemiology (254)

Bohanon, Nancy C.
National Futures Association (754)

Bohle, Suzanne
American Culinary Federation (112)

Bohlen, Stacy A.
National Indian Health Board (763)

Bohlke, Susannah
Van Alen Institute (1007)

Bohm, John
National Association of Housing and Redevelopment Officials (673)

Bohnsack, Mary
Fabricators & Manufacturers Association, International (437)

Bohon, Patricia
International Society of Certified Electronics Technicians (572)
National Electronic Service Dealers Association (745)

Bohorquez, Gayle
American Foreign Service Protective Association (123)

Bohrer, Kirk
International Association of Home Staging Professionals (522)

Bohrman, Jenny
National Association of Orthopedic Nurses (683)

Boice, Jackie
Association of Fundraising Professionals (285)

Boisseau, Robert
American Institute of Physics (140)

Boissy, Bob
North American Serials Interest Group (820)

Bojorquez, Roman
AAGL - Advancing Minimally Invasive Gynecology Worldwide (2)

Boland, James
International Union of Bricklayers and Allied Craftworkers (579)

Boland, Mary C.
American Copper Council (108)

Boland, Nancie
Production Engine Remanufacturers Association (859)

Bolden, Joanetta
National Association of Area Agencies on Aging (647)

Boldt, Juergen
Object Management Group (825)

Bolen, Edward M.
National Business Aviation Association (716)

Boles, Angela B.
Tau Beta Pi Association (968)

Boles, Jerry C.
Brotherhood of Railroad Signalmen (336)

Bolin, Kimberly
American Wholesale Marketers Association (221)

Boling, John
Council of Producers & Distributors of Agrotechnology (396)

Bolinger, Chrysta
Catholic Campus Ministry Association (345)

Bollig, Jeff
Golf Course Superintendents Association of America (463)

Bolling, Dennis
United Producers, Inc. (988)

Bollinger, III, Burton J.
American Association of Orthodontists (67)

Bolm, Sarah
American Bar Association (79)

Bolman, CAE, Tom
International Association of Conference Centers (518)

Bolos, Laura
Application Developers Alliance (226)

Bolster, Carole
Healthcare Financial Management Association (471)

Boltin, Ann
Association of Catholic Diocesan Archivists (271)

Bolton, Roger
Arthur W. Page Society (230)

Bomar, Ernest
American College of Gastroenterology (96)

Bomback, Larry
OPERA America (828)

Bomberger, Irvin E.
American Orthopaedic Society for Sports Medicine (159)

Bommarito, Paula
Catholic Health Association of the United States (345)

Bona, Alvaro Della
Academy of Dental Materials (5)

Bona, Andrea
Independent Community Bankers of America (488)

Bonacasa, Angela
Society of American Fight Directors (928)

Bonacci, Dr. John
Association of Consulting Chemists and Chemical Engineers (276)

Bonanno, Karen
International Association of School Librarianship (527)

Bonanti, Roselyn
Workers' Injury Law and Advocacy Group (1025)

Bonaparte, David
Jewelers of America (587)

Bonaventura, Philip
The Public Relations Society of America (870)

Bonavita, Laura
National League of Cities (768)

Bonbright, EdD, Jane
National Dance Education Organization (742)

Bond, Jeff
Professional Retail Store Maintenance Association (864)

Bond, Tamara
Society of Satellite Professionals International *(947)*

Bonds, CMSR, FMSD, MBA, Roger G.
American Academy of Medical Management *(36)*

Bone, David
United States Racquet Stringers Association *(998)*

Bone, David L.
Fellowship of United Methodists in Music and Worship Arts *(442)*

Bone, CPA, Matt
National Association of Tax Professionals *(704)*

Boney, Maurice W.
Irish Blacks Cattle Society *(585)*

Bonfante, Lawrence
United States Tennis Association *(1000)*

Bongiorno, Deborah
National Association of Elementary School Principals *(664)*

Bongiorno, Frank
North American Saxophone Alliance *(820)*

Bongiorno, Phillip A.
Society of Thoracic Surgeons *(948)*

Bongiovi, Larry
American Correctional Chaplains Association *(108)*
American Jewish Correctional Chaplains Association *(143)*

Boni, Marcus
Specialty Coffee Association of America *(957)*

Bonin, Pamela
American Society of Travel Agents *(210)*

Bonissone, Piero P.
North American Fuzzy Information Processing Society *(817)*

Bonk, Leslie
Outdoor Power Equipment and Engine Service Association *(835)*

Bonner, PhD, John M.
Council for Agricultural Science and Technology *(388)*

Bonner, Patti
National Association of Elevator Contractors *(665)*

Bono, Meredith
The Association for Nursing Professional Development *(252)*

Bonoff, Steve
International Digital Enterprise Alliance *(540)*

Bonofiglio, Liz
Cosmetic Executive Women *(387)*

Bonosaro, Carol A.
Senior Executives Association *(897)*

Bonsaint, Rebecca R.
American Association of Plastic Surgeons *(70)*

Bonsignore, Lisa
International Safe Transit Association *(563)*

Bonta, DMD MS MS, Dr. C. Yolanda
Hispanic Dental Association *(475)*

Bontempo, Patti
Kappa Delta Pi *(590)*

Bontjes, Christopher
Society of American Magicians *(929)*

Bontrager, Elizabeth
Money Management Institute *(618)*

Bonvillain, Jane
Construction Industry Round Table, Inc. *(379)*

Bonzell, Philip
Patent and Trademark Office Society *(839)*

Boocks, Lori
Pediatric Nursing Certification Board *(840)*

Booher, Jr., C. William
National Association of Veterans Affairs Physicians and Dentists *(708)*

Book, Stephanie
American Association of School Librarians *(72)*

Booker, Robert
United States Tobacco Cooperative Inc *(1000)*

Bookhout, Sue
North American Gamebird Association *(817)*

Bookout, William
National Animal Supplement Council *(634)*

Bookwalter, Sarah
Association of Meeting Professionals *(294)*

Boone, Chelsea
Global Semiconductor Alliance *(463)*

Boone, Jeanne
Newspaper Association of America *(810)*

Boone, Rob
The American Bar Association Rule of Law Initiative *(80)*

Boone, Tamea A.
Society of Military Widows *(941)*

Boone, Xenia "Senny"
Direct Marketing Association Nonprofit Federation *(412)*

Booth, Carol
Interstate Oil and Gas Compact Commission *(583)*

Booth, Eric
National Alliance of State and Territorial AIDS Directors *(633)*

Booth, Liz
Association for Women in Communications *(261)*

Booth, Wendy
National Dog Groomers Association of America, Inc. *(743)*

Boothby, Christina
American Orthopaedic Association *(158)*

Boothroyd, Kaaren
National Association of Professional Geriatric Care Managers *(687)*

Booze, John
American Chiropractic Association *(90)*

Bopp, Ken
United States Tobacco Cooperative Inc *(1000)*

Borato, Meghan
Society for Photographic Education *(919)*

Borawski, CAE, Paul E.
American Society for Quality *(189)*

Borchelt, PE, J. Gregg
Brick Industry Association *(335)*

Borchers, James A.
Concrete Anchor Manufacturers Association *(373)*
Powder Actuated Tool Manufacturers Institute *(854)*

Bordeaux, Ben R.
Association of Community Tribal Schools *(276)*

Bordeaux, Dr. Roger C.
Association of Community Tribal Schools *(276)*

Bordeaux, Rosa
Association of Community Tribal Schools *(276)*

Bordeianu, PhD, Fr. Radu
Orthodox Theological Society in America *(833)*

Borden, Debi
Media Financial Management Association *(610)*

Borden, Enid A.
Meals on Wheels Association of America *(609)*

Bordignon, Kristen
American Neurotology Society *(156)*

Bordignon, Kristen
American Otological Society *(161)*

Boreiko, Craig
International Crystal Federation *(539)*

Borello, Genevieve
Industrial Research Institute *(494)*

Borenstein, Corey Fabian
Council for European Studies *(390)*

Borer, David
American Federation of Government Employees *(119)*

Borges, Adilson
Academy of Marketing Science *(6)*

Borgese, Sheila
Sales Association of the Paper Industry *(890)*

Borgognoni, Gina
Armed Forces Optometric Society *(229)*

Borich, Alexis
American College of Veterinary Dermatology *(104)*

Boring, Joan
Miniature Book Society *(617)*

Borland, Joe S.
American Sports Medicine Association *(213)*

Borman, Keith T.
American Short Line and Regional Railroad Association *(179)*

Born, CMM, Darlene
Professional Association of Health Care Office Management *(859)*

Born, Matthew
American Law Institute *(144)*
Home Builders Association *(478)*

Borner, Bruce
Fashion Group International *(438)*

Bornstein, PhD, Robert A.
International Neuropsychological Society *(558)*

Bornstein, Sandy
American Neuropsychiatric Association *(155)*

Bornt, Susan
NAIOP, The Commercial Real Estate Development Association *(366)*

Borodziuk, Beth
The International Fluid Power Society *(545)*

Boros, Stephen
Plastics Pipe Institute *(850)*

Borowicz, Donna
Local Search Association (fka Yellow Pages Association) *(600)*

Borowski, Patricia A.
National Association of Professional Insurance Agents *(687)*

Borowsky, Scott C.
Souvenirs, Gifts and Novelties Trade Association *(953)*

Borozzi, John
United States Club Soccer *(992)*

Borr, Mari
National Association of Teacher Educators for Family Consumer Sciences *(704)*

Borschke, Dan
National Association of Concessionaires *(657)*

Boruff, Chet
Association of Official Seed Certifying Agencies *(296)*

Borut, Don
Hispanic Elected Local Officials *(475)*

Borut, Donald J.
National League of Cities *(768)*

Bosack, Theodore
Society for the Teaching of Psychology *(926)*

Bosak, Kathy
Optical Society of America *(829)*

Bosak, Steve
Society for Ecological Restoration International *(908)*

Bosarge, Johnette
National Marine Educators Association *(771)*

Boschert, PE, Jeff
National Clay Pipe Institute *(722)*

Boscia, Kim
Farm Credit Council *(437)*

Bosco, Cassandra
National Aeronautic Association *(629)*

Bosco, Gabrielle
Hydraulic Institute *(481)*

Bosco, Mary Lou
AIM Global *(17)*
AIM North America *(17)*

Bose, Jennifer
American Academy of Hospice and Palliative Medicine *(35)*

Bose, PhD PE, Jim
International Ground Source Heat Pump Association *(549)*

Boskey, Craig
National Marine Manufacturers Association *(771)*

Bosland, Neil
The Association to Advance Collegiate Schools of Business *(319)*

Bosley, Lowell
International Magnetics Association *(555)*

Boss, Terry D.
Interstate Natural Gas Association of America *(583)*

Bossard, Marian
Toy Industry Association *(976)*

Bossey, Robert D.
International Association of Law Enforcement Firearms Instructors, Inc. *(523)*

Bostick, Martha
American Academy of Addiction Psychiatry *(29)*

Bostley, Jean R.
Catholic Library Association *(346)*

Boston, Lauren
National Apartment Association *(634)*

Bostrom, Ann
Society for Risk Analysis *(920)*

Bostrom, Linda
Public Library Association *(869)*

Bostwick, Melinda
Association of Corporate Contributions Professionals *(277)*

Bostwick, Peg
Association of State Wetland Managers *(311)*

Boswell, Brad
Associated Cooperage Industries of America *(235)*

Boswell, Pamela L.
American Public Transportation Association *(171)*

Botana, Michelle
Healthcare Billing and Management Association *(470)*

Botbyl, Dena

Hobby Manufacturers Association *(477)*

Botens, Ted
National Association of Rehabilitation Providers and Agencies *(691)*

Boterbloem, Kees
Phi Alpha Theta *(845)*

Bott, Kimberly
National Lubricating Grease Institute *(770)*

Bottalico, Jo
U.S.-Russia Business Council *(999)*

Bottoni, Rosa
United States Composting Council *(992)*

Botts, Laura
Academy of Certified Archivists *(4)*

Boubin, Jackie
United States Meat Export Federation *(996)*

Bouchard, Lauren
Arthroscopy Association of North America *(230)*

Boucher, Andrew P.
National Register of Health Service Providers in Psychology *(785)*

Boucher, Robin
American Academy on Communication in Healthcare *(43)*

Boucouvalas, Marcie
Association for Transpersonal Psychology *(260)*

Boudreau, Tony
Electronic Security Association *(424)*

Boudrie, Joe
Institute for Supply Management *(497)*

Boughman, Joann
American Society of Human Genetics *(200)*

Boukas, Lori
American Board of Medical Specialties *(82)*

Boulanger, Jessica
Business Roundtable *(339)*

Bouley, Alice
Society of Economic Geologists *(934)*

Boulter, Spencer
American Association of Medical Dosimetrists *(65)*

Boulton, Lyndie
American Society for Enology and Viticulture *(184)*

Boumans, Marcel
History of Economics Society *(476)*

Bouraoui, Sue
The Association for Manufacturing Excellence *(252)*

Bourdon, Cathleen J.
American Library Association *(145)*

Bourelle, Isabel
Consortium on Financing Higher Education *(379)*

Bourgholtzer, Tony
Foundation for Advances in Medicine and Science *(452)*

Bourgoyne, Rusty
Combat Helicopter Pilots Association *(366)*

Bouris, Greg
Major League Baseball Players Association *(601)*

Bourland, Jonathan
National Council for Research on Women *(732)*

Bourque, Brian
Professional Retail Store Maintenance Association *(864)*

Bourque, Gary
Hospitality Financial and Technology Professionals *(479)*

Bourque, Jenny M.
American Short Line and Regional Railroad Association *(179)*

Bourquin, Laetitia
World Federation of Public Health Associations *(1026)*

Bourseau, Sandy
American Society of Home Inspectors *(200)*

Bousquet, Carol
ALMA - The International Loudspeaker Association *(26)*

Boutin, JD, Marc M.
National Health Council *(758)*

Bouton, MA, Barbara
National Hospice & Palliative Care Organization *(760)*

Bova, Steve
International Business Brokers Association *(532)*

Bova, CAE, Steve
Financial & Insurance Conference Planners *(444)*

Bove, Kellie
American Dental Education Association *(113)*

Bove, Kellie
SWANA - Solid Waste Association of North America *(967)*

Bow, Jonathan
State Risk and Insurance Management Association *(961)*

Bowden, Karen M.
The Aluminum Association, Inc. *(27)*

Bowden, Kirk
National Association of Certified Valuation Analysts *(652)*

Bowden, Ron
National High School Athletic Coaches Association *(759)*

Bowden, Scott
Automotive Distribution Network *(322)*

Bowdish, Bruce E.
American College of Medical Genetics *(97)*

Bowdring, Stacy
Power and Communications Contractors Association *(855)*

Bowen, MA, Ashley
National Association of County and City Health Officials *(659)*

Bowen, CAE, FACHE, Deborah J.
American College of Healthcare Executives *(96)*

Bowen, Nathan
National Association of Agricultural Fair Agencies *(646)*

Bowen, Patsy L.
AGN International North America, Inc *(15)*

Bowen, Richard
Future Business Leaders of America - Phi Beta Lambda *(455)*

Bowen, Sharon
Conference of Radiation Control Program Directors *(375)*

Bowen, Sr., Walter T.
University and College Designers Association *(1002)*

Bowens, Jermaine
Chamber Music America *(350)*

Bower, MBA, Andrea
AMC Institute *(28)*

Bower, Doug
Power-Motion Technology Representatives Association *(855)*

Bower, Lori

Society of Cable Telecommunications Engineers *(931)*

Bower, Steve
Newspaper Purchasing Management Association *(810)*

Bower, CAE, Tim
National Association of Environmental Professionals *(666)*

Bowers, April
Public Investors Arbitration Bar Association *(869)*

Bowers, CAE, P.G., Carol W.
American Association of Engineering Societies *(60)*

Bowers, Diane K.
Council of American Survey Research Organizations *(392)*

Bowers, Ellen
Council of Graphological Societies *(394)*

Bowers, Isaac
Equal Justice Works *(432)*

Bowers, PhD, Jan
Family and Consumer Sciences Education Association *(437)*

Bowers, Jennifer
Association of College and University Printers *(274)*

Bowers, MPH, RN, Nancy
American Society for Reproductive Medicine *(189)*

Bowers, Rita
Cable & Telecommunications Association for Marketing *(340)*

Bowles, Bill
Quail Unlimited *(871)*

Bowles, Laura
American Academy of Medical Administrators *(36)*

Bowles, Laura
American College of Cardiovascular Administrators *(93)*

Bowles, Sandra
Handweavers Guild of America, Inc. *(468)*

Bowling, Patricia
American Home Furnishings Alliance *(132)*

Bowling, Tina
American Forage and Grassland Council *(122)*

Bowman, Bill
American Angus Association *(45)*

Bowman, Bryan
Professional Services Council *(865)*

Bowman, Bryon
Scaffold Industry Association *(891)*

Bowman, Jerry M.
Institute of Food Technologists *(499)*

Bowman, Ken
Aviation Insurance Association *(324)*
International Window Cleaning Association *(581)*

Bowman, Kenneth "Ken" R.
Sealant, Waterproofing and Restoration Institute *(894)*

Bowman, Kristi
International Dyslexia Association *(541)*

Bowman, Lisa
Society for Marketing Professional Services *(914)*

Bowman, Mike
United States of America Gymnastics *(997)*

Bowman, Nicole
Global Semiconductor Alliance *(463)*

Bowman, Paul D.
National Defined Contribution Council *(742)*

Bowman, Sarah
National Society of Compliance Professionals *(793)*

Bowman, Tom
Communications Media Management Association *(369)*

Bowman, Valerie
Association for Conflict Resolution *(243)*

Bowser, Diana
AIM Global *(17)*

Bowser, Kathleen
Professional Handlers Association *(862)*

Bowyer, Brent
Independent Photo Imagers *(491)*

Bowyer, Fran
Independent Photo Imagers *(491)*

Bowzer, Melanie
National Association of State Procurement Officials *(702)*

Bowzer, Melanie
The Association of Medical Illustrators *(293)*

Boxx, W. Randy
The Association to Advance Collegiate Schools of Business *(319)*

Boyce, Brendan
Biological Stain Commission *(330)*

Boyce, Colleen
American Association for the Advancement of Artificial Intelligence *(51)*

Boyce, Jane
Society of Petroleum Engineers *(944)*

Boyce, Jessi
National Association of Home Builders *(673)*

Boyd, Cathy
National Tour Association *(800)*

Boyd, Chip
Society for Technical Communication *(922)*

Boyd, Chuck
Recreation Vehicle Rental Association *(877)*

Boyd, Dennis W
Federal Physicians Association *(439)*
National Association of Assistant United States Attorneys *(647)*

Boyd, Jr., John W.
National Black Farmers Association *(714)*

Boyd, Nancy F.
Supima *(966)*

Boyd, Robin
International Institute of Synthetic Rubber Producers *(552)*

Boyd, Ronald J.
International Association of Airport and Seaport Police *(515)*

Boyd-Douglas, Dr. Nicole
Association for Women in Psychology *(262)*

Boyer, Bailey
The Travel and Tourism Research Association *(979)*

Boyer, Carolyn
National Association of Personnel Services *(684)*

Boyer, Jan
Cast Stone Institute *(344)*

Boyer, Keyvi
Air Traffic Control Association *(19)*

Boyes, Frances
Union for Radical Political Economics *(985)*

Boyette, Warren
National Association of State Foresters *(701)*

Boyke, Debra Wendorf

United States National Committee of the International Dairy Federation *(996)*

Boykin, Brittany
National Association of County Community and Economic Development *(637)*

Boykins, Adoncia
Futures Industry Association *(455)*

Boylan, CMP, Jennifer K.
Society for Pediatric Radiology *(918)*

Boylan, Lisa
National Association of Chain Drug Stores *(652)*

Boyle, Dee
SSPC: the Society for Protective Coatings *(960)*

Boyle, Diane R.
National Association Of Insurance and Financial Advisors(NAIFA) *(676)*

Boyle, Eric
Society for History in the Federal Government *(911)*

Boyle, Heidi
Pharmaceutical Marketing Research Group *(844)*

Boyle, J. Patrick
American Meat Institute *(148)*

Boyle, J. D.
Broadcast Education Association *(335)*

Boyle, Laura
Society for Public Health Education *(919)*

Boyle, Patrick J.
Shelf-Stable Food Processors Association *(898)*

Boyle, PhD, Dr. Paul
Association of Zoos and Aquariums *(318)*

Boyle, Paul J.
Newspaper Association of America *(810)*

Boyle, Shane
Visiting Nurse Associations of America *(1010)*

Boyle, Shannon
Foodservice Sales & Marketing Association *(450)*

Boyle, Tracy
International Dairy Foods Association *(539)*

Boyles, Felicia K.
Controlled Environment Testing Association *(383)*

Boyles, Felicia Kenan
National Association of Medical Minority Educators, Inc. *(680)*

Boynes, Shawn E.
Association for Professionals in Infection Control and Epidemiology *(254)*

Boynton, Julie
The Endocrine Society *(427)*

Bozek, Robert J.
Conference of Major Superiors of Men, United States of America *(375)*

Bozeman, Gail M
American Association of Colleges for Teacher Education *(57)*

Bozzo, Tom
Association of American Universities *(266)*
Association of Graduate Schools in Association of American Universities *(286)*

Braaten, PhD, Douglas
The New York Academy of Sciences *(809)*

Brabant, Jessica
Society for Vascular Surgery *(926)*

Brabant, Lyn
International Studies Association *(576)*

Bracamontes, Icela Nahyr

National Association of Latino Independent Producers
(677)

Brace, Tom
Plan Sponsor Council of America **(849)**

Bracewell, Kelsey
American Canoe Association **(88)**

Bracey, Remy
Business Higher Education Forum **(339)**

Brach, Suzanne
American Society of Clinical Oncology **(194)**

Brachman, Sarah
Independent Educational Consultants Association
(489)

Bracken, Anne
Association of Corporate Counsel **(277)**

Brackett, MD, Bess E.
Clinical Orthopaedic Society **(358)**

Brackett, Esq., Douglas 'Tony'
Black Entertainment and Sports Lawyers Association
(331)

Brackett, L.
Society of Financial Examiners **(936)**

Brackpool, Lynn
Financial Planning Association **(445)**

Bradaric, Julie
International Anesthesia Research Society **(511)**

Bradbeer, Gayle
Council on Botanical and Horticultural Libraries **(399)**

Bradburn, Denise
National Precast Concrete Association **(782)**

Bradburn, Windora
National Association for Uniformed Services **(644)**
Society of Military Widows **(941)**

Bradbury, Candice
National Chimney Sweep Guild **(721)**

Braddock, Martha
International Association of Emergency Managers
(520)

Braden, Karolynn
Academy of Clinical Laboratory Physicians and
Scientists **(4)**

Braden, Nicholas
American Public Power Association **(171)**

Bradford, Clint
International Guild of Candle Artisans **(549)**

Bradford, Devin Anna
Institute of Career Certification International **(498)**

Bradford, PhD, E. James
Association of Analytical Communities International
(267)

Bradford, Hazel
International Masonry Institute **(556)**

Bradford, Terrence A.
National Association of Black Social Workers **(649)**

Bradham, Stefan
Federation of American Societies for Experimental
Biology **(440)**

Bradle, CAE, CMP, MA, Nicole C.
Society for Education in Anesthesia **(908)**

Bradley, Anne
American Farm Bureau Federation **(118)**

Bradley, Anne
American Farm Bureau Federation **(118)**

Bradley, Craig
Art Glass Association **(230)**

Bradley, Daniel
International Plate Printers, Die Stampers and
Engravers Union of North America **(560)**

Bradley, Deborah
Women Construction Owners and Executives, USA
(1020)

Bradley, Gregory L.
SAE International **(889)**

Bradley, Gwendolyn
American Association of University Professors **(75)**

Bradley, Heather
Institute of Industrial Engineers **(500)**

Bradley, Janet
United States Psychiatric Rehabilitation Association
(998)

Bradley, Janice Comer
Waste Equipment Technology Association **(1012)**

Bradley, Lorna
The American Association of Eye and Ear Centers of
Excellence **(61)**

Bradley, Lynne E.
American Library Association **(145)**

Bradley, Matthew
Patent and Trademark Office Society **(839)**

Bradley, Melissa
Council of American Overseas Research Centers **(392)**

Bradley, Regina
Advertising Council **(13)**

Bradley, Sandra
American Council of Learned Societies **(109)**

Bradley, Trenell
National Association for Home Care and Hospice **(639)**

Bradley, Troy
Balloon Federation of America **(325)**

Bradley-Foley, Margaret
International Association of Culinary Professionals
(519)

Bradshaw, ACC, BS, Cindy
National Certification Council for Activity Professionals
(720)

Bradshaw, Mary I.
American Association of Immunologists **(62)**

Bradshaw, Ryan Pace
Consumer Bankers Association **(380)**

Bradshaw, Teresa J.
Pan American Association of Ophthalmology **(837)**

Brady, Chery
Therapeutic Touch International Association **(973)**

Brady, Colleen
International Communication Association **(536)**

Brady, Dan
Forum of Regional Associations of Grantmakers **(452)**

Brady, Joseph
North American Securities Administrators Association
(NASAA) **(820)**

Brady, Linda
Association for Healthcare Documentation Integrity
(247)

Brady, Lori
Nuclear Energy Institute **(824)**

Brady, Marcus
American Telemedicine Association **(215)**

Brady, Meghan
Professional Grounds Management Society **(862)**

Brady, CTC, Thomas
Ceramic Tile Institute of America **(349)**

Brady, Todd
American Public Gas Association **(170)**

Brady, CPA, William M.
American Society for Dermatologic Surgery **(183)**

Braen, Beth
National Association of Television Program Executives
(705)

Braendel, Eric
American Bus Association **(87)**

Braff, Andrew
Algal Biomass Organization **(22)**

Bragaw, Dick
American Society of Colon and Rectal Surgeons **(195)**

Bragdon, Doug
Society for Information Display **(913)**

Bragg, Lynn
Glass Packaging Institute **(461)**

Bragg, Patrick
PSIA-AASI **(868)**

Bragiel, Mary Colleen
Urban Libraries Council **(1004)**

Brahms, Thomas W.
Institute of Transportation Engineers **(503)**

Brainard, Keith
National Association of State Retirement
Administrators **(702)**

Braine, Kathryn
Association of Executive Search Consultants **(282)**

Braithwaite, Marlene
Urban Financial Services Coalition **(1003)**

Braithwaite, Nancy A.
Casualty Actuarial Society **(344)**

Braja, Vilma
National Dance Education Organization **(742)**

Brake, Jennifer
National Association of Government Guaranteed
Lenders (NAGGL) **(670)**

Brakefield, Tom
National Association of Pipe Fabricators **(684)**

Brakey, Jacqueline C.
Society for Epidemiologic Research **(908)**

Bram, Jim
National Association of Underwater Instructors **(707)**

Braman, Gary
System Safety Society **(967)**

Bramble, Mark
American Society of Cytopathology **(196)**

Bramlet, Eileen
Telecommunications Industry Association **(971)**

Branch, Brian
World Council of Credit Unions, Inc. **(1026)**

Branch, Keith
National Association of Blacks in Criminal Justice **(649)**

Branch, L. Maurice
American Logistics Association **(146)**

Branch, Sarah
Offshore Marine Service Association **(827)**

Brand, Michele
The National Procurement Institute, Inc **(783)**

Brand, Tom
National Association of Farm Broadcasting **(667)**

Brandel, Norma "Dusty"
American Auto Racing Writers and Broadcasters
Association **(78)**

Brandenberger, Joel
National Turkey Federation *(802)*

Brandenburg, Vicki
United Egg Producers *(986)*

Brandhorst, Carl
Atlantic Seaboard Wine Association *(319)*

Brandi, Carolyn
Commission on Professionals in Science and
Technology *(368)*

Brandl, Philip J.
International Housewares Association *(550)*

Brando, Fran
Association of Theatrical Press Agents and Managers
(314)

Brandt, Deborah K.
Council on Social Work Education *(400)*

Brandt, CAE, Rebecca
International Society for Quality of Life Research *(569)*

Brandt, Rob
The Botanical Society of America *(333)*

Brandt, Stephanie
Consumer Credit Industry Association *(381)*

Brandt,, CAE, Rebecca
American Association of Medical Society Executives
(65)

Brandt-Meyer, Megan
CRE Finance Council *(403)*

Brandts, Jill
Thermoforming Institute *(973)*

Brandy, Roxanne
DeepStar Project *(408)*

Branham, Mary
Council of State Governments *(397)*

Braniff, Thomas M.
American Association of Insurance Management
Consultants *(63)*

Brank, Eve
American Psychology-Law Society *(170)*

Brann, Esther V.
Adhesion Society *(12)*

Branner, Melody
Institute of Certified Professional Managers *(498)*

Bransford, William L.
Senior Executives Association *(897)*

Branson, Gunnar
National Association of Real Estate Investment
Managers *(690)*

Branson, Kathy
World Pet Association *(1027)*

Brant, Rob
Accredited Medical Equipment Providers of America
(10)

Branter, Noreen
Minor League Baseball *(617)*

Brantley, Andy
College and University Professional Association for
Human Resources *(362)*

Brantley, Tom
Professional Aviation Safety Specialists (AFL-CIO) *(860)*

Brantley, Yvette
Radiation Therapy Oncology Group *(873)*

Brasacchio, Kate
Hearing Loss Association of America *(472)*

Brash, Julian
Society for the Anthropology of North America *(923)*

Brasher, Christine
American Association of State Troopers *(73)*

Brassard, Bill
National Shooting Sports Foundation *(791)*

Brasse, Sally
National Society of Accountants *(793)*

Brasseur, Georg
IEEE Instrumentation and Measurement Society *(484)*

Braswell, Robert
Technology and Maintenance Council of American
Trucking Associations *(970)*

Brattain, Shirley R.
Tamworth Swine Association *(968)*

Bratton, Adam
Public Employees Roundtable *(869)*

Bratz, Valmor A.
Brazilian American Chamber of Commerce *(334)*

Brauch, Matthew
Consumer Bankers Association *(380)*

Braun, Bill
Air and Waste Management Association *(17)*

Braun, Patrick
Society of Mineral Analysts *(942)*

Braun, Theresa C.
American Institute of Physics *(140)*

Braun, Werner
The Carpet and Rug Institute *(343)*

Braunger, Ed
American Greyhound Track Operators Association
(127)

Braunsdorf, Gerette
National Association for Home Care and Hospice *(639)*

Braus, Judy
North American Association for Environmental
Education *(812)*

Brautigam, Dwight D.
Conference on Faith and History *(376)*

Bravo, Dr. Rolando
American Institute of Hydrology *(139)*

Bravo, Simon
National Intramural-Recreational Sports Association
(766)

Brawley, Kay
National Employment Counseling Association *(745)*

Brawner, CMP, Deborah
American Society of Association Executives-The
Center for Association Leadership *(193)*

Braxton, Carly
American Alliance for Health, Physical Education,
Recreation and Dance *(44)*
National Association for Sport and Physical Education
(643)

Braxton, Joanne E.
National Association of Negro Business and
Professional Women's Clubs *(681)*

Bray, Janet
Association of Career and Technical Education *(271)*

Bray, Sarah Hardesty
Association of Governing Boards of Universities and
Colleges *(286)*

Brazeau, Ginette
Association of Labor Relations Agencies *(290)*

Brazel, CMP, Judy
Society of Nuclear Medicine *(943)*

Brazil-Nichols, Laura
North American Society for Dialysis and
Transplantation *(821)*

Brazile, Barbara
Ford Motor Minority Dealers Association *(451)*

Breach, CPA, Todd
American Association of Immunologists *(62)*

Breaux, Jeff
College Media Association *(363)*

Brebner, Linda B.
International Association of Women Ministers *(529)*

Brebner, Nancy
Insurance Consumer Affairs Exchange *(505)*

Brecht, Kirsten
American Councils for International Education *(111)*

Breden, CAE, CMP, Cathy
Center for Exhibition Industry Research *(348)*
International Association of Exhibitions and Events
(520)

Bree, Stephanie
American Society for Enology and Viticulture *(184)*

Breece, George W.
National Association for the Advancement of Orthotics
and Prosthetics *(643)*

Breeden, Christine
Association of Social Work Boards *(309)*

Breeding, Joan
American Association of State Troopers *(73)*

Breedon, Angela
Music and Entertainment Industry Educators
Association *(622)*

Breeland, Jocelyn
American Network of Community Options and
Resources (ANCOR) *(155)*

Breen, Brendan
Association for Psychological Science *(254)*

Bregman, Leah
Society for Ecological Restoration International *(908)*

Brehany, PhD, STL, Dr. John F.
Catholic Medical Association *(346)*

Breisch, Alyson
Health Ministries Association *(470)*

Breitkopf, Susan
American Association of Museums *(65)*

Brenden, Ken
American Architectural Manufacturers Association *(46)*

Brengle, Anne B.
Council of American Maritime Museums *(391)*

Brenkus, Susan
Healthcare Financial Management Association *(471)*

Brennan, CAE, Cate
National Athletic Trainers Association *(710)*

Brennan, Eileen M.
Accrediting Bureau of Health Education Schools *(10)*

Brennan, Heather
American Institute of Aeronautics and Astronautics
(136)

Brennan, Jr., Joseph
Interactive Media Entertainment & Gaming Association
(507)

Brennan, Katie
National School Boards Association *(789)*

Brennan, Madonna
Laborers International Union of North America *(592)*

Brennan, Maria
Women in Cable Telecommunications, Inc. *(1020)*

Brennan, Mary Ellen
American Industrial Hygiene Association *(135)*

Brennan, MK
American Polarity Therapy Association *(166)*

Brennan, Paul
National Board of Boiler and Pressure Vessel
Inspectors *(715)*

Brennan, Jr., MA, Richard D.
National Association for Home Care and Hospice *(639)*

Brennan, CAE, Valerie
American College of Osteopathic Obstetricians and
Gynecologists *(100)*

Brenner, Beth Fuchs
Decorative Furnishings Association *(408)*

Brenner, Ellen Terris
American Peptide Society *(163)*

Brenning, Karen
American Society of Bariatric Physicians *(193)*

Brent, Joseph
Semiotic Society of America *(897)*

Brentzel, Joe
National Association for College Admission Counseling
(637)

Bresett, Josh
National Association for Pupil Transportation *(642)*

Bresolin, CAE, Linda B.
Radiological Society of North America *(873)*

Bresson, CAE, Karen E.
Vibration Institute *(1008)*

Bretcko, Kathi
Independent Laboratory Distributors Association *(490)*

Bretthauer, Linda
Commercial Real Estate Women Network *(367)*

Brevard, Rae
RESPRO (Real Estate Services Providers Council) *(883)*

Brevitz, Karl F.
National Association of College and University
Attorneys *(654)*

Brewer, Allison
American Bus Association *(87)*

Brewer, Brent
Society for Business Ethics *(905)*

Brewer, Jason
Retail Industry Leaders Association *(884)*

Brewer, John B.
American Moving and Storage Association *(153)*

Brewer, Lynn M.
American Bus Association *(87)*

Brewer, Miriam
International Franchise Association *(547)*

Brewer, Tim
Association of State Chamber Professionals *(310)*

Brewer-Pratt, Elisa
Associated General Contractors of America (AGC) *(236)*

Brewin, Nicole
Railway Supply Institute *(874)*

Brewington, FAAN, PhD, RN, Janice
National League for Nursing *(768)*

Brewster, Amanda
Organic Crop Improvement Association International
(830)

Brewster, Bill
National Stripper Well Association *(797)*

Brewster, Chris B.
United States Lifesaving Association *(996)*

Brewster, Scott
International Warehouse Logistics Association *(580)*

Brey, Ann
Pan American Allergy Society *(837)*

Brey, James
American Meteorological Society *(151)*

Breyault, John
National Consumers League *(729)*

Brian, Dave
National Cutting Horse Association *(741)*

Brian, Kimmel
National Association of Convenience Stores *(658)*

Brice, Steve T.
National Industries for the Blind *(763)*

Brice-Rowland, Taryn
National Association of Truck Stop Operators(NATSO)
(707)

Briceno, Hazel
National Association of Negro Business and
Professional Women's Clubs *(681)*

Bricker, Megan
American Ceramics Society *(89)*

Bricker, Timothy
American Association of Private Lenders *(71)*

Brickley, Jennifer
Neurofibromatosis, Inc., Northeast *(808)*

Bridgeford, Tawny
National Mining Association *(772)*

Bridges, Jessica
United States Clean Heat & Power Association *(992)*

Bridges, Jonathan
Accrediting Bureau of Health Education Schools *(10)*

Briehl, PhD, Margaret
Society for Free Radical Biology and Medicine *(909)*

Brienza, Anita
Worldwide ERC *(1028)*

Brigati, Allison Fahrenkopf
National Academy of Public Administration *(628)*

Briggs, Don
Turf Equipment Technicians Association *(982)*

Briggs, Eli
National Association of County and City Health
Officials *(659)*

Briggs, James I.
Airports Council International - North America *(21)*

Briggs, Joe
National Football League Players Association *(752)*

Briggs, Les
American Sociological Association *(211)*

Brigham, Charles
Textile Rental Services Association of America *(973)*

Brigham, Dana A.
International Union of Elevator Constructors *(579)*

Bright, CAE, IOM, Carrie D.
American Midwifery Certification Board *(151)*

Bright, FACP, MD, Cedric M.
National Medical Association *(772)*

Bright, Charlene
American Public Health Association *(171)*

Bright, Deanna
American Association for Aerosol Research *(47)*

Bright, MPA, Jennifer
Society for Healthcare Epidemiology of America *(910)*

Bright, Richard
American Council of Independent Laboratories *(109)*
American Subcontractors Association *(214)*

Bright, Steve
Association of Industrial Metallizers, Coaters and
Laminators *(288)*
Converting Equipment Manufacturers Association
(383)

Brigner, Paul
Internet Society *(582)*

Brill, Kristen
Society of Pharmaceutical and Biotech Trainers *(944)*

Brill, Laurie
Lutheran Educational Conference of North America
(600)

Brill, Vicki
National Association of Stock Plan Professionals *(703)*

Brimer, Leslee
National Association of Police Athletics/Activities
Leagues, Inc. *(685)*

Brimsek, Tobi
Society for American Archaeology *(903)*

Brinegar, Richard S.
International Webmasters Association *(580)*

Bringardner, Chase
Association for Theatre in Higher Education *(260)*

Brink, Carolee Martin
National Collegiate Honors Council *(724)*

Brink, Linda
National Association of Trailer Manufacturers *(706)*

Brinkema, Corey
Forest Stewardship Council - United States Chapter
(451)

Brinkley, Dee
Association of Junior Leagues International *(290)*

Brinkmann, PhD, Jay
Mortgage Bankers Association of America *(619)*

Brinkmann, Kelly
Retail Confectioners International *(884)*

Brintnall, Michael A
Academy of Political Science *(8)*
American Political Science Association *(166)*

Briotta, Patty
National Association of Federal Credit Unions *(667)*

Brisach, Susanne
Smocking Arts Guild of America *(901)*

Briscoe, III, Andrew C.
Sugar Association *(965)*

Briscoe, Mark
National Association of Insurance and Financial
Advisors *(675)*

Briscoe, Scott
Association of State and Territorial Health Officials
(310)

Briseno, Valerie
Business Technology Association *(340)*

Brissett, Colette
National Association for Business Economics *(636)*

Brisson, Mary
Iroquois Healthcare Alliance *(585)*

Bristow, Danielle
National Orientation Directors Association *(778)*

Bristow, Paul
Association of Threat Assessment Professionals *(314)*

Britland, Dawn
Manufacturing Jewelers and Suppliers of America *(604)*

Britt, Tonja
American Society for Pain Management Nursing *(188)*

Britz, Joanna

Women's Basketball Coaches Association *(1022)*

Brizzie, Lorna
National Junior College Athletic Association *(767)*

Brncic, Dianne
American Academy on Communication in Healthcare *(43)*

Broad, Molly Corbett
American Council on Education *(110)*

Broadbent, Kenneth J.
Steamfitters Local Union 449 *(962)*

Broadbent, Nan
Seismological Society of America *(895)*

Broaddus, Susan
National Association of Federal Credit Unions *(667)*

Broadus, Melissa
Air Conditioning Contractors of America *(18)*

Broadway, Julie
American Morgan Horse Association *(152)*

Brocato, Kelly
National Association of Clean Water Agencies *(654)*

Brochstein, Marty
International Licensing Industry Merchandisers' Association *(554)*

Brock, Dasha Y.
National Association of Surety Bond Producers *(704)*

Brock, Heidi B.
The Aluminum Association, Inc. *(27)*

Brock, Miranda
National Association of Uniform Manufacturers and Distributors *(707)*

Brock, Sherri
American Association of Nutritional Consultants *(67)*

Brockhoff, Mark
Commercial Real Estate Women Network *(367)*

Brockles, Chris
American Society of Breast Disease *(193)*

Brockman, Andrew
National Alliance for Accessible Golf *(631)*

Brockman, MD, David Dean
American College of Psychoanalysts *(102)*

Brockman, Thomas
National Funeral Directors Association *(754)*

Brockmeyer, Chris
The Broadway League *(336)*

Brockway, Roger
IFIA Americas Committee Inc. *(486)*

Brodd, Ralph
National Alliance for Advanced Transportation Batteries *(631)*

Broderick, Carissa
National Agricultural Alumni and Development Association *(630)*

Broderick, Paul
American Osteopathic College of Proctology *(161)*

Broderson, Jeff
American School Counselor Association *(177)*

Brodie, Bridget
American College of Medical Quality *(97)*

Brodie, III, Edmund D. ("Butch")
Society for the Study of Evolution *(925)*

Brodke, MD, Darrel S.
Cervical Spine Research Society *(350)*

Brodoff, Maureen B.
National Fire Protection Association *(751)*

Brodt, Joanne
American Insurance Association *(141)*

Broek, Lindsey
American Maine-Anjou Association *(146)*

Broendel, Jane E.
National Association of Letter Carriers *(678)*

Brogan, Jim
Miniature Book Society *(617)*

Brogie, Ed
National Association of Academies of Science *(645)*

Brogus, Rob
Association of HazMat Shippers *(286)*

Brohm, Marilyn
National Lubricating Grease Institute *(770)*

Broida, Bethany
National Criminal Justice Association *(740)*

Broman, Bruce
Precision Metalforming Association *(856)*

Bromberg, Kristin
National Finishing Contractors Association *(751)*

Bronaugh, Caroline
Society for Ecological Restoration International *(908)*

Bronson, Kim Ledbetter
Winegrape Growers of America *(1019)*

Broockerd, Ashley
National Association of Collegiate Women Athletic Administrators *(656)*

Brooke, Krista
National Art Education Association *(635)*

Brookhart, Sarah
Association for Psychological Science *(254)*

Brookover, Patrick
Grocery Manufacturers Association (GMA) *(466)*

Brooks, A. Oakley
National Air Carrier Association *(630)*

Brooks, Aaron
National Organization of Black Law Enforcement Executives *(777)*

Brooks, Andrew
Society of Allied Weight Engineers *(928)*

Brooks, Arthur C.
American Enterprise Institute for Public Policy Research *(117)*

Brooks, Bridget
Industrial Designers Society of America *(493)*

Brooks, Carolyn B.
Association of Research Directors *(306)*
Association of Research Directors of 1890s Colleges and Universities *(306)*

Brooks, Chris
Academy of Model Aeronautics *(7)*

Brooks, Deirdre
Health Industry Distributors Association *(469)*

Brooks, Doug
American Society of Picture Professionals *(207)*

Brooks, Doug
The International Stability Operations Association *(575)*

Brooks, Elise
The Financial Services Roundtable *(445)*

Brooks, Gary
Community Development Venture Capital Alliance *(370)*

Brooks, Jeanne
Online News Association *(827)*

Brooks, Jerry
National Interstate Council of State Boards of Cosmetology *(766)*

Brooks, Jill
Association of State Correctional Administrators *(310)*

Brooks, Joseph
Air Movement and Control Association International *(19)*

Brooks, Mark
Utility Workers Union of America *(1007)*

Brooks, Mary Jane
Association of Research Libraries *(306)*

Brooks, Mitch
National Plasterers Council *(781)*

Brooks, Robert
Pharmaceutical Printed Literature Association *(844)*

Brooks, Stephenie
Airports Council International - North America *(21)*

Brookstein, Jane
Academy Health *(3)*

Broomall, James K.
Association for Continuing Higher Education *(243)*

Broome, Kim
Rice Millers' Association *(886)*

Brosche, Marcus
American Bralers Association *(86)*

Brosie, Denise
International Decorative Artisans League *(540)*

Brosio, Lauren
Decorative Plumbing and Hardware Association *(408)*
Organization Development Network *(831)*

Brosius, Alison
Interlocking Concrete Pavement Institute *(508)*

Brosnan, Kim
American Camp Association *(88)*

Brosnan, Michael J.
American Association of Physics Teachers *(69)*

Brostko, Bree
Resort Hotel Association *(883)*

Brotherman, Lelan
National Collegiate Wrestling Association *(724)*

Brothers, Randy
Service Specialists Association *(897)*

Brotman, CAE, Allison
Associated General Contractors of America (AGC) *(236)*

Brotons, Toni Rae
International Foodservice Distributors Association *(546)*

Brouder, Cara
Catholic Health Association of the United States *(345)*

Brough, Bill
Internet Marketing Association *(582)*

Broughton, Danette
American Society of Nephrology *(204)*

Broussard, John E.
USA Rice Federation *(1004)*

Broussard, Johnny
Rice Millers' Association *(886)*
USA Rice Council *(1004)*

Broussard, Linda
Special Libraries Association *(956)*

Brousseau, Zachary
Regulatory Affairs Professionals Society *(879)*

Brower, CCP, CMM, Susan

International Association of Exhibitions and Events
(520)

Brown, Adam
Public Education Network *(869)*

Brown, Allen
The Open Group *(828)*

Brown, Amber
Association of Correctional Food Service Affiliates
(277)

Brown, MBA, Amy L.
American Society of Dentist Anesthesiologists *(196)*

Brown, Andreason L.
Donors Forum *(415)*

Brown, Ann
Digital Media Association *(412)*

Brown, CPS, Barb
American Society for Laser Medicine and Surgery *(186)*

Brown, Bridget
National Association of Workforce Development
Professionals *(710)*

Brown, Carol S.
International Association of Women Ministers *(529)*

Brown, Dr. Cecilia Wright
National Technical Association *(799)*

Brown, Chris
National Association of Broadcasters *(650)*

Brown, CEM, CMP, Chris
The Wound, Ostomy and Continence Nurses Society
(1028)

Brown, Christie
New Dramatists *(809)*

Brown, Christopher
NALP - The Association for Legal Career Professionals
(624)

Brown, Darlene
American Society of Laboratory Animal Practitioners
(201)

Brown, David L.
America Outdoors Association *(28)*

Brown, CAE, Dennis
Equipment Leasing and Finance Association *(432)*

Brown, Diane Alicia
Association of State Floodplain Managers *(311)*

Brown, Donald O.
American Association of Community Colleges *(58)*

Brown, Donna
National Association of State Energy Officials *(700)*

Brown, Donna
Texas Alliance of Energy Producers *(972)*

Brown, Duane
Association of Professors of Mission *(302)*

Brown, CAE, Geoffrey E.
Giving Institute *(461)*

Brown, CAE, Geoffrey E.
Giving USA Foundation *(461)*

Brown, Georgia
National Independent Automobile Dealers Association
(761)

Brown, Gregory
National Apartment Association *(634)*

Brown, Gwendolyn
National Trailer Dealers Association *(801)*

Brown, CEM, Heather W.
National Association of College Auxiliary Services
(655)

Brown, Isaac
National Assembly of State Arts Agencies *(635)*

Brown, J. Rex
Petroleum Equipment Institute *(843)*

Brown, J. Noah
Association of Community College Trustees *(276)*

Brown, James D.
Commission on Accreditation for Law Enforcement
Agencies Incorporation *(367)*

Brown, CMP, Jana
Golf Course Superintendents Association of America
(463)

Brown, Jay
Combat Helicopter Pilots Association *(366)*

Brown, BA, Jay
Alliance for Continuing Medical Education *(22)*

Brown, Jim
Society for Critical Care Medicine *(934)*

Brown, Joan
American Medical Society for Sports Medicine *(149)*

Brown, Joann
Federal Managers Association *(439)*

Brown, Jodene M.
American Orthopaedic Association *(158)*

Brown, John Howard
Communications Supply Service Association *(369)*

Brown, Karen
NAMTA - National Art Materials Trade Association
(635)

Brown, Katie
The Brewers Association *(335)*

Brown, Katie Kiley
National Comprehensive Cancer Network *(725)*

Brown, Ken
National Association of Local Government
Environmental Professionals *(678)*
The Institute of Financial Operations *(499)*

Brown, Kerwin
BEMA - The Baking Industry Suppliers Association
(328)

Brown, Kevin
CPCU Society *(402)*

Brown, Kevin
Gerontological Society of America *(460)*

Brown, Kim
National Minority Supplier Development Council *(773)*

Brown, Kimberly Freeman
American Rights at Work *(175)*

Brown, Laticha
Black Retail Action Group *(332)*

Brown, Liesa
Society of Chemical Manufacturers and Affiliates Inc.
(932)

Brown, Linda
American Society of Plant Taxonomists *(207)*

Brown, Lisa
American Society of Ophthalmic Registered Nurses
(205)

Brown, Lloyd
AASHTO: Transportation Center of Excellence *(2)*

Brown, Lois
Population Association of America *(853)*

Brown, M. Eileen
Association for Psychological Type International *(254)*

Brown, Mandy
National Society of Hispanic MBAs *(794)*

Brown, Margaret B.
Association of Professional Schools of International
Affairs *(302)*

Brown, Marikay
Society of Hospital Medicine *(938)*

Brown, Mary Ellen
Association for Behavioral and Cognitive Therapies
(240)

Brown, Michael J.
National Chicken Council *(720)*

Brown, Michelle
Transportation Safety Equipment Institute *(979)*

Brown, Michelle Moskowitz
Council of Archives and Research Libraries in Jewish
Studies *(392)*

Brown, Morgan
Air Force Sergeants Association *(19)*

Brown, Nancy A.
American Heart Association *(130)*

Brown, Nancy L.
Educational Theatre Association *(420)*

Brown, Pam
American Association of Heart Failure Nurses *(62)*

Brown, Pamela
Million Dollar Round Table *(616)*

Brown, Pat
Hemophilia Federation of America *(474)*

Brown, Pat
National Association of Councils on Developmental
Disabilities *(658)*

Brown, Peter
International Society for Clinical Densitometry *(565)*

Brown, R. Steven
Environmental Council of the States *(431)*

Brown, Ralph B.
The Rural Sociological Society *(889)*

Brown, CAE, Richard
Associated General Contractors of America (AGC) *(236)*

Brown, Richard D.
American Antiquarian Society *(45)*

Brown, Robert
International Game Developers Association *(548)*

Brown, Robin Beard
America Outdoors Association *(28)*

Brown, Roger
International Society for Philosophical Enquiry *(568)*

Brown, Rosa
Council on Licensure, Enforcement and Regulation
(400)

Brown, Ryan
American Composites Manufacturers Association *(105)*

Brown, Sandra
American Jail Association *(142)*

Brown, Sara
National Association of Health Unit Coordinators *(671)*

Brown, Scott
Association of Independent Information Professionals
(288)

Brown, Scott
National Barley Growers Association *(712)*

Brown, Sean
Minor League Baseball *(617)*

Brown, Steve
National Council for Agricultural Education *(731)*

Brown, Dr. Steve A.

National FFA Organization *(750)*

Brown, Steven J.
National Business Aviation Association *(716)*

Brown, Suzy
Genetics Society of America *(458)*

Brown, Sylvia
Computerized Medical Imaging Society *(373)*

Brown, Tai M.
American Football Coaches Association *(122)*

Brown, Terry
Association of Pool and Spa Professionals *(299)*

Brown, Theresa
American Paint Horse Association *(161)*

Brown, Therese
Association of Catholic Publishers *(271)*

Brown, Timothy A.
International Organization of Masters, Mates and Pilots *(559)*

Brown, Tina
Driver Employer Council of America *(416)*

Brown, Todd
Society of Chemical Manufacturers and Affiliates Inc. *(932)*

Brown, Tyler
International Brotherhood of Boilermakers, Iron Shipbuilders, Blacksmiths, Forgers and Helpers *(531)*

Brown, Vivian
National Electrical Contractors Association *(744)*

Brown, Wanda M.
Society for Healthcare Epidemiology of America *(910)*

Brown-Hailey, Ann C.
Electric Utility Fleet Managers Conference *(422)*

Browne, Andy
Utilities Telecom Council *(1006)*

Browne, Bill
Organization of Black Designers *(832)*

Browne, Charles
National FFA Organization *(750)*

Browne, Frederica
American Society of Addiction Medicine *(191)*

Browne, Heather
Community College Business Officers *(370)*

Browne, Joe
National Football League *(752)*

Browne, III, John R.
International Brotherhood of Magicians *(531)*

Browne, Katherine E.
Society for Economic Anthropology *(908)*

Browne, Lisa
National Hardwood Lumber Association *(757)*

Browne, Pamela Ravare
Association of Latino Professionals in Finance and Accounting *(291)*

Browner, Donald
Community Transportation Association of America *(371)*

Browning, Jessica
American Enterprise Institute for Public Policy Research *(117)*

Browning, Mabel McKinney
American Bar Association *(79)*

Browning, Stephen R.
Pet Partners *(842)*

Browning, MPH, Susan M.
American Burn Association *(87)*

Brownlee, Cathy
Association of Professional Design Firms *(301)*

Brownlee, Kenny
National Peanut Buying Point Association *(780)*

Brownlee, Pam
American Association of Zoo Veterinarians *(77)*

Brownlow, Kathy
National Association of Underwater Instructors *(707)*

Brownstein, Clifford M.
National Association of Therapeutic Schools and Programs (NATSAP) *(706)*

Broyles, Scott
National Safe Skies Alliance *(788)*

Brozana, Amanda Leigh
National Grange *(756)*

Brozell, CAE, MS, Michelle D.
American College of Foot and Ankle Surgeons *(95)*

Brozick, CAE, Carla
American Rental Association *(174)*

Broznak, Leslie
American Jail Association *(142)*

Brubaker, Scott
American Association of Tissue Banks *(75)*

Bruce, Doug
Tillage & Ground Engaging Equipment Product Council *(974)*

Bruce, Heidi
American Association for the Study of Liver Diseases *(52)*

Bruce, CMP, Jennifer Hickey
National School Transportation Association *(790)*

Bruce, CAE, CEM, CMP, Jerome
Association of Government Accountants *(286)*

Bruce, Maggie
National Council for Prescription Drug Programs *(732)*

Bruce, Richard
National Truck and Heavy Equipment Claims Council *(802)*

Bruce, Shawn
Piano Technicians Guild *(848)*

Bruch, Lori
National Association for Rehabilitation Leadership *(642)*

Bruchac, Margaret M.
Council for Museum Anthropology *(390)*

Brueggeman, Brenda
Society for Disability Studies *(907)*

Bruhn, CPT, EdD, Gay E.
International Society for Performance Improvement *(567)*

Brumley, Joe
Open Geospatial Consortium *(828)*

Brummel, Debbie
National Agri-Marketing Association *(629)*

Brummett, Mary Jane
Catholic Health Association of the United States *(345)*

Brummett, Rita
The Travel and Tourism Research Association *(979)*

Brummund, Sandy
American Tarentaise Association *(215)*

Brundage, Diane
Technology Services Industry Association *(970)*

Brundage, Patricia L.
Art Dealers Association of America *(229)*

Brune, Christine W.

American Horse Publications *(133)*

Bruner, CAE, MBA, Trudie
Water and Sewer Distributors of America *(1012)*

Brungardt, CAE, Stacy
Society of Teachers of Family Medicine *(947)*

Bruno, LCSW, MSW, Julie
American Academy of Hospice and Palliative Medicine *(35)*

Brunschon, Bill
American Poultry Association *(167)*

Brunt, Donna
The Association for Research in Business Education - Delta Pi Epsilon *(255)*

Brunt, MD, L. Michael
Society of American Gastrointestinal and Endoscopic Surgeons *(929)*

Brunton, Melissa K.
Direct Selling Association *(413)*

Brusch, Matt
National Investor Relations Institute *(767)*

Brush, Sam
American Poultry Association *(167)*

Bruss, Joanne
International Society of Travel and Tourism Educators *(574)*

Brust, Haley J.
Association for Governmental Leasing and Finance *(247)*
Association of Women in the Metal Industries *(317)*
National Society for Experiential Education *(792)*

Bruzenak, Kristie
Guild of Natural Science Illustrators *(467)*

Bruzik, James P.
RNA Society *(887)*

Bryan, Jr., Dr. Charles F.
Independent Research Libraries Association *(491)*

Bryan, Mac
Recreation Vehicle Industry Association *(877)*

Bryan, Michele
The PGA Tour, Inc. *(844)*

Bryan, Scott H.S.
American College of Trial Lawyers *(103)*

Bryan, MD, Sean
American Medical Society for Sports Medicine *(149)*

Bryan, Tim
National Rural Telecommunications Cooperative *(788)*

Bryant, Dr. Anne L.
National School Boards Association *(789)*

Bryant, Bruce
American Federation of School Administrators *(120)*

Bryant, PhD, Cedric X.
American Council on Exercise *(110)*

Bryant, CMP, Desiree
Renal Physicians Association *(881)*

Bryant, Jane Quincy
Association of Management/International Association of Management *(292)*

Bryant, Jennifer
National Association of Negro Business and Professional Women's Clubs *(681)*

Bryant, Jennifer A.
American College of Osteopathic Internists *(100)*

Bryant, Julie
National Cutting Horse Association *(741)*

Bryant, LaShawne
National Dental Association *(742)*

Bryant, Laurie I.
Meat Importers Council of America **(609)**

Bryant, Matthew
American Society of Addiction Medicine **(191)**

Bryant, Michael R.
National Association of State Boards of Accountancy **(698)**

Bryant, Pat
InsideNGO **(496)**

Bryant, Tracee E.
Black Mental Health Alliance **(331)**

Bryant,, PhD, Diane P.
Council for Learning Disabilities **(390)**

Bryce, Marianna
National AMBUCS **(633)**
National AMBUCS, Inc **(633)**

Brydson, Gina
International Association of Venue Managers **(528)**

Bryer, Russ
Spring Manufacturers Institute **(960)**

Brymer, APR, CAE, N. Eugene
International Association of Structural Movers **(528)**

Bryson, Randy
Consortium of Behavioral Health Nurses and Associates **(378)**

Buado, Michelle
Radiation Therapy Oncology Group **(873)**

Bubolz, Katy
Global Offset and Countertrade Association (GOCA) **(462)**

Buccelli, Matt
International Economic Development Council **(541)**

Buchanan, Bruce
American Society of Mining and Reclamation **(203)**

Buchanan, Richard W.
National Basketball Association **(712)**

Buchanan, Shelia
American Academy of Cosmetic Surgery **(32)**

Buchanan, DO, Steve P.
American College of Osteopathic Obstetricians and Gynecologists **(100)**

Buche, Tim
Motorcycle Industry Council, Inc. **(620)**
Motorcycle Safety Foundation **(620)**
Specialty Vehicle Institute of America **(958)**

Buchenau, Jurgen
Conference on Latin American History **(377)**

Bucher, Lisa
Air and Waste Management Association **(17)**

Buck, Anna Lopez
National Association of Hispanic Journalists **(672)**

Buck, CMP, Christina
Convention Industry Council **(383)**

Buck, Diane
American Library Association **(145)**

Buck, Helen M.
Jewelers' Security Alliance of the United States **(587)**

Buck, Kevin
Association of Corporate Counsel **(277)**

Buckendahl, PhD, Chad W.
Association of Test Publishers **(313)**

Buckius, Lori
Council on the Safe Transportation of Hazardous Articles **(401)**
International Vessel Operators Dangerous Goods Association **(580)**

Buckler, Carlyn
Paleontological Research Institution **(837)**

Buckler-Bowers, Pam
National Guard Association of the U.S. **(757)**

Buckley, Ellen R.
National Field Selling Association **(750)**

Buckley, CAE, J D, George A.
Casket and Funeral Supply Association of America **(344)**

Buckley, Jean M.
Future Business Leaders of America - Phi Beta Lambda **(455)**

Buckley, John
National Association of Blind Teachers **(650)**

Buckley, Maurice A.
Ireland Chamber of Commerce in the United States **(585)**

Buckley, Mona
Professional Insurance Marketing Association **(862)**

Buckley, Sheila
National Business Incubation Association **(717)**

Buckner, Mel R.
Society of Exploration Geophysicists **(935)**

Bucy, Erik P.
Association for Politics and the Life Sciences **(253)**

Buczkiewicz, Jeff
Mason Contractors Association of America **(607)**

Budd, CPCU, Ed
Society of Insurance Research **(940)**

Budens, Robert D.
Patent Office Professional Association **(839)**

Budka, Patty
National Association of Consumer Advocates **(657)**

Budway, Robert R.
Can Manufacturers Institute **(341)**

Budzinski, Linda R.
International Cemetery, Cremation and Funeral Association **(533)**

Buehler, Greg
Open Geospatial Consortium **(828)**

Buehler, Stephanie
American Association of Sexuality Educators, Counselors and Therapists **(73)**

Buell, Sylvia
National Association of Catering and Events **(651)**

Bueno, Irene B.
National HEP-CAMP Association **(759)**

Buerkle, Mary Jane
Plains Cotton Growers, Inc. **(849)**

Buffenbarger, Thomas R.
International Association of Machinists and Aerospace Workers **(524)**

Bugden, Betty
The American Hair Loss Council **(128)**

Bui, Diana
Asian Pacific American Labor Alliance, AFL-CIO **(232)**

Buis, Tom
Growth Energy **(466)**

Bukata, Beth
American Society for Therapeutic Radiology and Oncology **(190)**

Bukovic, Mary
Association of Equipment Manufacturers **(281)**

Buksa, CAE, JD, Daniel
Academy of General Dentistry **(5)**

Bulas, Margaret
Management Association for Private Photogrammetric Surveyors **(602)**

Buley, M. Patricia
Institute of Hazardous Materials Management **(500)**

Bulger, Jim
International Brangus Breeders Association **(531)**

Bulis, Ben
American Fly Fishing Trade Association **(122)**

Bull, Yvonne
Produce Marketing Association **(858)**

Bullard, Bill
R-Calf **(872)**
Ranchers-Cattlemen Action Legal Fund, United Stockgrower of America **(874)**

Bullard, Justice Janice
Federal Administrative Law Judges Conference **(438)**

Buller, Bob
Society of Biblical Literature **(931)**

Bullington, Smith
Society of General Internal Medicine **(937)**

Bult, Jan M.
Plasma Protein Therapeutics Association **(850)**

Bumanis, Al
American Music Therapy Association **(154)**

Bumann, Dave
Association of Conservation Engineers **(276)**

Bumphus, Dr. Walter G.
American Association of Community Colleges **(58)**

Bumpous, Sue
SWANA - Solid Waste Association of North America **(967)**

Bunaes, Siobhan
American Academy of Ophthalmology **(37)**

Bunce, Col. Peter J.
General Aviation Manufacturers Association **(458)**

Bunch, Michelle
North American Insulation Manufacturers Association **(817)**

Bundy, Denise R.
Dental Trade Alliance **(410)**

Bunker, John
Association for Healthcare Foodservice **(248)**
National Barbecue Association **(712)**
Society for Foodservice Management **(909)**

Bunker-Alberts, Michele
United States Lactation Consultant Association **(996)**

Bunn, Tommy
United States Tobacco Cooperative Inc **(1000)**

Bunning, Sue
American College of Nuclear Medicine **(98)**

Bunns, Valerie
Women's Business Enterprise National Council **(1022)**

Bunse, Dr. Benno W.
German American Chamber of Commerce **(460)**

Bunt, Amy
Thoroughbred Owners and Breeders Association **(974)**

Buntain, Dr. Bonnie J.
American Association of Food Hygiene Veterinarians **(61)**

Bunte, Alexander
National Conference on Public Employee Retirement Systems **(729)**

Bunton, David S.
Appraisal Foundation **(226)**

Bunton, Jean M.

Consumer Bankers Association *(380)*

Buntrock, Julie
Network of Executive Women in Hospitality *(808)*

Bunzel, David
Optical Storage Technology Association *(829)*

Buongiorno, B.K.
Society of Petroleum Evaluation Engineers *(944)*

Bur, Diane C.
American Board of Physical Medicine and Rehabilitation *(83)*

Burak, Joseph
National Communication Association *(724)*

Burak, Susan (Zsuzsanna)
North American Society of Adlerian Psychology *(822)*

Burandt, Gary
ICOM, International Communications Agency Network *(482)*

Burch, Emily
Association for Death Education and Counseling *(244)*

Burch, Monte
National Association of Home and Workshop Writers *(672)*

Burcham, Frank
Alternative Fuel Vehicle Network *(27)*

Burchard, Renee L.
Education Finance Council *(419)*

Burchill, Laura
Association of State Wetland Managers *(311)*

Burd, Mary Ellen
Chemical Heritage Foundation *(351)*

Burdell, Seals
U.S Poultry and Egg Association *(998)*

Burden, Kathleen
Golf Course Superintendents Association of America *(463)*

Burdette, Joan
National Association for College Admission Counseling *(637)*

Burdette, Melinda
American Association of Clinical Endocrinologists *(56)*

Burdge, Carol
International Glove Association *(548)*

Burdick, Ann
Writers Guild of America East *(1029)*

Burdick, Rick
Society for Research on Adolescence *(920)*

Buresh, Dr. Robert E.
World's Poultry Science Association, U.S.A. Branch *(1028)*

Burford, Mary Catherine
Learning Forward *(596)*

burg, Jones
National Council of the Multifamily Housing Industry *(737)*

Burg, Ronald G.
American Concrete Institute *(106)*

Burgdorf, Ken
American Optometric Association *(157)*

Burger, Sharon
International Cost Estimating and Analysis Association effective *(537)*

Burger, Thomas R.
Professional Managers Association *(863)*

Burgeson, Charlene R.
National Association for Sport and Physical Education *(643)*

Burgess, Angela R.
IEEE Computer Society *(483)*

Burgess, Becky
National Association of Electrical Distributors *(664)*

Burgess, Deborah
Off-Road Business Association *(826)*

Burgess, Hilary
National Sheriffs' Association *(791)*

Burgess, Julie
American Society of Consulting Arborists *(196)*
Window Coverings Association of America *(1018)*

Burgess, Lauren
Certified Contractors Network *(349)*

Burgess, Marsha
The Association for Library Service to Children *(251)*

Burggraf, Amy
Republican Governors Association *(881)*

Burghardt, Jordan B
Congress of Neurological Surgeons *(377)*

Burgis, Eric
Energy Solutions Center *(428)*

Burgos, Nilda R.
International Weed Science Society *(581)*

Burian, Enrica
National Roofing Contractors Association *(787)*

Burin, James M.
Flight Safety Foundation *(448)*

Burk, CAE, Brett
Semiconductor Environmental Safety and Health Association *(896)*
Society for Integrative and Comparative Biology *(913)*

Burk, CMP, Marla
Family, Career and Community Leaders of America *(437)*

Burk, Jr., Richard "Brett" J.
Health Physics Society *(470)*

Burk, Tina
American College of Osteopathic Family Physicians *(100)*

Burkard, Jessica
National Organization of State Offices of Rural Health *(778)*

Burke, Angela
American Bar Association *(79)*

Burke, Camille L.
National Register of Health Service Providers in Psychology *(785)*

Burke, Carolyn
American Society for Bioethics and Humanities *(181)*

Burke, Christina
International Foodservice Manufacturers Association *(546)*

Burke, Denise M.
American Beverage Association *(80)*

Burke, Doug
Air Conditioning, Heating and Refrigeration Institute (AHRI) *(18)*

Burke, Helen
Resource Center for Religious Institutes *(883)*

Burke, Dr. Jana
National Association of Rehabilitation Research and Training Centers *(691)*

Burke, Jenny
Student Youth and Travel Association *(964)*

Burke, Jessica
International Association of Lighting Designers *(524)*

Burke, PhD, John E.
Accreditation Association for Ambulatory Health Care *(9)*

Burke, Judy
Accrediting Bureau of Health Education Schools *(10)*

Burke, Judy
The Institute of Internal Auditors *(500)*

Burke, Julie Nicholson
Mental Health America *(612)*

Burke, Karen
American Society for Artificial Internal Organs *(181)*

Burke, Kathleen
National Military Family Association, Inc. *(772)*

Burke, Kellie
National Association of Public Hospitals and Health Systems *(688)*

Burke, CPA, Kevin B.
National Council of State Housing Agencies *(736)*

Burke, Kevin M.
American Apparel & Footwear Association *(46)*

Burke, Kevin S.
American Judges Association *(143)*

Burke, Nancy M.
Direct Selling Association *(413)*

Burke, Patricia A.
International Desalination Association *(540)*

Burke, Richard
Association for Education in Journalism and Mass Communication *(245)*

Burke, Susan
Association of National Advertisers *(295)*

Burke, Tom
American Health Care Association *(129)*

Burke, Wynn
Common - A Users Group *(369)*

Burkett, Angela
Association of Professional Landscape Designers *(301)*
Perlite Institute *(842)*
The National Greenhouse Manufacturers Association *(756)*

Burkett, T. J.
United States Trotting Association *(1000)*

Burkgren, Thomas J.
American Association of Swine Veterinarians *(74)*

Burkhalter, Ernest
Commission on Professionals in Science and Technology *(368)*

Burkhart, Andrea
American Society of Appraisers *(192)*

Burkhart, PhD, Diane
American Osteopathic Association *(160)*

Burkhart, Lori
American Chiropractic Association *(90)*

Burkhart, Tammy
Educause *(420)*

Burki, Saira
American Association of Collegiate Registrars and Admissions Officers *(58)*

Burkman, Sarah
Newspaper Association of America *(810)*

Burks, Beverly
National Pan-Hellenic Council *(778)*

Burks, Catalina
International Association of Plumbing and Mechanical Officials *(526)*

Burkum, Kevin

American Egg Board (116)

Burle, CMP, Marlene
American Optometric Student Association (157)

Burleson, RPh, Michael A.
National Association of Boards of Pharmacy (650)

Burleson, Tracy
American Gas Association (124)

Burlew, William S.
Electric Power Supply Association (EPSA) (421)

Burnell, Angel
Owner-Operator Independent Drivers Association, Inc. (836)

Burner, Larry
American Academy of Child and Adolescent Psychiatry (31)

Burnett, Jeff
Open Geospatial Consortium (828)

Burnett, Jefferson G.
National Association of Independent Schools (675)

Burnett, Lani
Reserve Officers Association of the U.S. (882)

Burnett, Melissa
American Society of Animal Science (192)

Burnett, Russ
American Industrial Hygiene Association (135)

Burnett, Shirley
American Geriatrics Society (126)

Burnett, Suzanne
Association for Conflict Resolution (243)

Burnett, Tara
National Association of Home Builders (673)

Burnette, Ed
National Legal Aid and Defender Association (769)

Burnette, Megan
American Society for Healthcare Environmental Services (185)

Burney, Lou Ann
American Resort Development Association (175)

Burnham, Karen H.
Fire and Emergency Manufacturers and Services Association (446)
Fire Apparatus Manufacturers' Association (446)

Burns, CPA, MBA, CPE, Andrea
Pediatric Nursing Certification Board (840)

Burns, Anne
Academy of Pharmaceutical Research and Science (8)

Burns, Anne
Spill Control Association of America (958)

Burns, Anne Davis
American Waterways Operators (220)

Burns, Danielle
American Association of Healthcare Administrative Management (61)

Burns, Jennifer
Association of State Dam Safety Officials (310)

Burns, Kelly
Common - A Users Group (369)

Burns, Leah
College and University Professional Association for Human Resources (362)

Burns, Lillian
MTM Association for Standards and Research (620)

Burns, M. Jane
American Burn Association (87)

Burns, Michael

American Business Media (87)

Burns, Mike
College Gymnastics Association (363)

Burns, Richard
American Astronautical Society (77)

Burns, Richard
National Terrazzo and Mosaic Association (800)

Burns, Scott
National District Attorneys Association (743)

Burns, Taryn
American Society of Association Executives-The Center for Association Leadership (193)

Burns, Tom
National School Boards Association (789)

Burns, Travis
Society of Military Orthopaedic Surgeons (941)

Burns, CAE, William M.
Association for Play Therapy (253)

Burnstein, Jeffrey
Automated Imaging Association (321)
Robotic Industries Association (887)

Burr, Geoffrey
Associated Builders and Contractors (235)

Burr, Tracy
American Academy for Cerebral Palsy and Developmental Medicine (29)

Burrell, Elizabeth
American Academy of Diplomacy (32)

Burrell, Julie
American Public Works Association (172)

Burress, Dixie
International Trumpet Guild (578)

Burrger-Laskosky, Elaine F.
Tooling, Manufacturing and Technologies Association (976)

Burris-Kitchen, Deborah
Association for Humanist Sociology (249)

Burroughs, John
Lawyers Committee on Nuclear Policy (594)

Burroughs, CFRE, Kate S.
Association of American Cancer Institutes (264)

Burrows, Barbara
North American Wensleydale Sheep Association (823)

Burrows, Brian
International Brotherhood of Electrical Workers #98 (531)

Burrows, Roberta
Institute of Environmental Sciences and Technology (499)

Burruss, Christopher
Truckload Carriers Association (981)

Bursiek, Brian
Pickle Packers International (848)

Burt, Chris
National Soccer Coaches Association of America (792)

Burt, Christine
International Association of Arson Investigators (515)

Burt, John
The Association of Literary Scholars, Critics, and Writers (291)

Burt, Robin
Independent Film and Television Alliance (489)

Burton, Amy
ACUTA - The Association for Information Communications Technology Professionals in Higher Education (11)

Burton, Ann
International Facility Management Association (543)

Burton, Ann
The Coca-Cola Bottlers' Association (361)

Burton, Anne-Marie
National Association of City and County Health Officials (654)
National Association of County and City Health Officials (659)

Burton, Bill
National Association of Video Distributors (708)

Burton, David R.
National Small Business Association (792)

Burton, Haleema M.
National Association of College and University Attorneys (654)

Burton, Mat
Enactus (427)

Burton, Orisanmi
Association of Black Anthropologists (269)

Burtraw, Kim
Association of Energy Services Professionals, International (281)

Burum, Joe
Showmen's League of America (899)

Burwell, Deborah
National Association of Blacks in Criminal Justice (649)

Burwell, Todd
BAFT-IFSA (325)

Busansky, Alexander
National Council on Crime and Delinquency (738)

Busby, Dan
Evangelical Council for Financial Accountability (434)

Busby, Matthew
Professional Services Council (865)

Buscemi, Angela
AABB - American Association of Blood Banks (1)

Buscemi, Cheryl
Automation Alley (321)

Busch, Audrey
Association of Assistive Technology ACT Programs (268)

Busch, Tom
National Association of Sports Public Address Announcers (697)

Buser, Robert
Association of International Education Administrators (289)

Buser, PhD, Sam
Society for the Psychological Study of Men and Masculinity (924)

Bush, Adrienne
American Council of Independent Laboratories (109)

Bush, Beth
American Academy of Physician Assistants (40)

Bush, Bonnie
Copper and Brass Servicenter Association (384)
International Association of Plastics Distributors (526)

Bush, Keith
U.S.-Russia Business Council (999)

Bush, JD, CAE, Milton M.
American Council of Independent Laboratories (109)
IFIA Americas Committee Inc. (486)
Independent Association of Accredited Registrars (488)

Bush, Traci
Industrial Energy Consumers of America (493)

Bushaw, Bill

Phi Delta Kappa International *(845)*
Pi Lambda Theta *(847)*

Bushell, CGMP, Krystal
Society of Government Meeting Professionals *(938)*

Bushfield, Suzanne Y.
Association for the Accreditation of Human Research
Protection Programs *(257)*

Bushkell, Lee
The PGA Tour, Inc. *(844)*

Bushue, Barry
Oregon Farm Bureau Federation *(830)*

Bushway, Rob
National Junior College Athletic Association *(767)*

Bushy, FAAN, PhD, RN, Angeline
Association of Community Health Nursing Educators
(276)

Busiek, Pamela Jo
Independent Cosmetic Manufacturers and Distributors
(489)

Buskey, Rep. James
National Council of Legislators from Gaming States
(735)

Busley, Marc R.
National Quartz Producers Council *(783)*

Buss, Linda
Institute of Certified Records Managers *(499)*

Bussema, Ev
Council for Christian Colleges and Universities *(389)*

Bussey, Tadson
University and College Designers Association *(1002)*

Bustamante, Liz
Electrical Generating Systems Association *(422)*

Butcher, Deena
Hospice and Palliative Nurses Association *(478)*

Butcher, Diane
American Board of Professional Psychology *(83)*

Butcher, Kathy
National Ground Water Association *(756)*

Butcher, Meg
American Society of Farm Managers and Rural
Appraisers *(197)*

Butera, Michael A.
Music Industry Conference *(622)*
The National Association for Music Education
(Formerly MENC) *(641)*

Buterbaugh, Bruce
Council of Chief State School Officers *(392)*

Butler, Bill
Sheet Metal Workers' International Association *(898)*

Butler, Chelsie
CoreNet Global *(385)*

Butler, Chuck
Enhanced Protective Glass Automotive Association
(429)

Butler, Heather
NACE International *(623)*

Butler, Jane
National Association of Government Guaranteed
Lenders (NAGGL) *(670)*

Butler, Jean
Toy Industry Association *(976)*

Butler, Jim
American Theological Library Association *(216)*

Butler, John
American Council of Hypnotist Examiners *(109)*

Butler, John

American Institute of Fishery Research Biologists *(138)*

Butler, Kathleen
National Council for Interior Design Qualifications
(732)

Butler, Kathleen M.
American Society of Notaries *(204)*

Butler, Kelly
National Association of Professional Baseball Leagues
(686)

Butler, Kelly
Power Transmission Distributors Association *(855)*

Butler, Kim
American Association for Vocational Instructional
Materials *(53)*

Butler, Lawrence
National Association of Real Estate Brokers *(689)*

Butler, Lisa
International Society of Arboriculture *(571)*

Butler, Lisbeth Nelson
American Federation of Violin and Bow Makers *(120)*

Butler, Patrick
Association of Public Television Stations *(304)*

Butler, Paul
Heli Ski US Association *(473)*

Butler, Roscoe
Managed Funds Association *(602)*

Butler, S. Kent
Association for Multicultural Counseling and
Development *(252)*

Butler, Staci
Association for Unmanned Vehicle Systems
International *(261)*

Butler, Tony
Association for Healthcare Foodservice *(248)*
Society for Foodservice Management *(909)*

Butlin, Jennifer
American Association of Colleges of Nursing *(57)*

Buttrick, MPW, Jonathan
National Student Nurses Association *(797)*

Butts, Rose
Renal Physicians Association *(881)*

Butts, Ryan
Registry of Interpreters for the Deaf *(879)*

Buzalski, Jennifer
Association of Professional Researchers for
Advancement *(302)*
International Business Brokers Association *(532)*
Society of Incentive & Travel Executives *(939)*

Buzbee, Brent
USA Volleyball *(1005)*

Buzby, Barry
National Industrial Council - State Associations Group
(763)

Buzzerd, Jr., CAE, Jr. CAE, Harry W.
American Textile Machinery Association *(216)*
Association of Vacuum Equipment Manufacturers *(316)*
Process Equipment Manufacturers' Association *(858)*

Bybee, Tony
National Association of Intercollegiate Athletics *(676)*

Byer, Eric R
National Air Transportation Association *(630)*

Byers, Christy Baily
Accrediting Bureau of Health Education Schools *(10)*

Byers, Jacqueline
National Association of Counties *(659)*
National Association of County Intergovernmental
Relations Officials *(660)*

Byers, Mary

International Association for Orthodontics *(513)*

Byers, CAE, Michele
American College of Emergency Physicians *(95)*

Byfield, Judith A.
Association of African Studies Programs *(263)*

Byko, Maureen
Minerals, Metals and Materials Society *(617)*

Bylsma, PhD, Wayne H.
American College of Physicians *(101)*
American College of Physicians Services, Inc. *(101)*

Bynoe, Sonya
American Academy of Forensic Sciences *(34)*

Bynoe, Sylin
National Association of Blacks In Government *(649)*

Bynog, David M.
American Viola Society *(219)*

Bynum, Marjorie
SOCAP International *(902)*

Byrd, Alicia
National Council of State Boards for Nursing *(736)*

Byrd, Bart
National Association of Academic Advisors for Athletes
(645)

Byrd, David
National Ski Area Association *(791)*

Byrd, Jean
Association of the United States Navy, Inc. *(314)*

Byrd, Keisha
Association for Women in Science *(262)*

Byrd, Ricardo C
National Association of Neighborhoods *(681)*

Byrne, Florence
Chlorine Institute *(354)*

Byrne, Ian J.
World Affairs Councils of America *(1025)*

Byrne, Kelly
Capital Markets Credit Analysts Society *(342)*

Byrne, Kristina
National Association of Local Government
Environmental Professionals *(678)*

Byrne, Marianne
North American Association of Food Equipment
Manufacturers *(813)*

Byrne, Richard C.
American Wire Cloth Institute *(221)*
Expansion Joint Manufacturers Association, Inc. *(436)*
Hand Tools Institute *(468)*
Tubular Exchanger Manufacturers Association *(982)*

Byrne, Steve
Society of Petroleum Engineers *(944)*

Byrnes, Betty
Consumer Data Industry Association *(381)*

Bythrow, Cory
National Federation of Federal Employees *(748)*

Byus, Kent
Society for Advancement of Management *(903)*

Byyny, Dr. Richard L.
Alpha Omega Alpha Honor Medical Society *(26)*

C R., Fr. Gabriel
Orthodox Theological Society in America *(833)*

Caballero, MPH, Jeffrey B.
Association of Asian-Pacific Community Health
Organizations *(268)*

Cabbage, Elizabeth
Association of Veterinary Biologics Companies *(317)*

Cabe, Sue
Communications Supply Service Association *(369)*

Cabezas, Maria Soledad
Latin American Studies Association *(594)*

Cabiness, Monique
National Association for the Education of Young Children *(644)*

Cabocel, Melissa J.
Consumer Bankers Association *(380)*

Cabral, Cristina
Pediatric Orthopedic Society of North America *(840)*

Cabral, Diana
North American Skull Base Society *(820)*

Cabral, Sam A.
International Union of Police Associations, AFL-CIO *(579)*

Cabral, Samuel A.
International Union of Police Associations, AFL-CIO *(579)*

Cabrera, Tonya
American Association for Public Opinion Research *(51)*

Cabrero, Margo
Society of Medical Consultants to the Armed Forces *(941)*

Cacace, Robert
Alliance for Children and Families *(22)*

Cacanindin, Heather
Society for the Study of Evolution *(925)*
The Botanical Society of America *(333)*

Caccioppoli, Dominic
ACORD - Association for Cooperative Operations Research and Development *(11)*

Cachapero, Joanne
Free Speech Coalition *(453)*

Cacho, Tracy
Women in Government Relations, Inc. *(1021)*

Cachuela, Christine
American College of Nuclear Medicine *(98)*
Society of Nuclear Medicine *(943)*

Caddell, Tom
National Association for Retail Marketing Services *(642)*

Cadena, Eugenia
Association of Metropolitan Water Agencies *(294)*

Cadrin, Steve
American Institute of Fishery Research Biologists *(138)*

Cadwalader, Erin
Association for Women in Science *(262)*

Cadwallader, Susan
Marketing Education Association *(606)*

Caffarelli, CCS, Patrick
National Automatic Merchandising Association *(711)*

Cafferelli, Holly
AHS International - The Vertical Flight Society *(17)*

Caffey-Fleming, Dolores
Auxiliary to the National Medical Association *(324)*

Cagnoli, W. Allan
Hearth, Patio and Barbecue Association *(472)*

Cahill, Len
Community Transportation Association of America *(371)*

Cahill, Leslie C.
American Seed Trade Association *(178)*

Cahill McDonald, Dorothy
American Podiatric Medical Students Association *(166)*

Cain, Angela

CoreNet Global *(385)*

Cain, Patricia A.
Society of American Law Teachers *(929)*

Cain, Rick
American Institute of Chemical Engineers *(138)*

Cain, Sarah McCubbin
Association of State Dam Safety Officials *(310)*

Cain, Tonier
National Association of State Mental Health Directors *(701)*

Cairns, Ann
American Geophysical Union *(126)*

Cairns, Rich
International Bowling Pro Shop and Instructors Association *(530)*

Cajchun, Kimya Bailey
Air Conditioning Contractors of America *(18)*

Cakanic, Marc
American Society of Andrology *(192)*

Calabrese, Denise
Association of Professional Landscape Designers *(301)*
Perlite Institute *(842)*
The National Greenhouse Manufacturers Association *(756)*

Calabrese, CMP, Katie A.
Association of Private Sector Colleges and Universities (Career College Association) *(300)*

Calabria, Jill
American Sportfishing Association *(212)*

Calaby, Cecelia
American Bankers Association Securities Association (ABASA) *(79)*

Calambokidis, Joan Baggett
International Masonry Institute *(556)*

Calaro, Karen
REALTORS Land Institute *(876)*

Calarusse, Crystal
National Association of Schools of Public Affairs and Administration *(694)*

Calaway, Nancy
American College of Emergency Physicians *(95)*

Caldarera, Mike A.
National Propane Gas Association *(783)*

Caldeira, Stephen J.
International Franchise Association *(547)*

Calderon, Diego
National Association of Sewer Service Companies *(695)*

Calderon, Marisa
National Association of Hispanic Real Estate Professionals *(672)*

Calderon, Steve
Association of Latino Professionals in Finance and Accounting *(291)*

Caldwell, Alan
International Association of Fire Chiefs *(521)*

Caldwell, Ann Cameron
National Conference of Executives of The ARC *(727)*

Caldwell, Chris
International Foodservice Distributors Association *(546)*

Caldwell, Corey
Association of Flight Attendants - CWA *(283)*

Caldwell, Gregg
Log Homes Council *(600)*

Caldwell, Heather
National Association for College Admission Counseling *(637)*

Caldwell, Melinda
Structural Building Components Association *(964)*

Caldwell, PE, Michael R.
American Institute of Timber Construction *(141)*

Caldwell, Monica
Accredited Gemologists Association *(10)*

Caldwell, Susan M.
Information Systems Audit and Control Association *(495)*

Calhoun, A. Cedric
Alliance of Hazardous Materials Professionals *(25)*

Calhoun, David R.
Association of Theatrical Press Agents and Managers *(314)*

Calhoun, Donald (Don) B.
Monument Builders of North America *(619)*

Calhoun, Glen
International Association for Identification *(513)*

Calhoun, Harold
American Guild of Organists *(127)*

Calhoun, JD, MA, Terry
Society for College and University Planning *(906)*

Calico, CFE, Marla
International Association of Fairs and Expositions *(521)*

Caliendo, M.J.
Utility Communicators International *(1006)*

Calio, Nicholas E.
Airlines For America *(21)*

Calitz, Louis
Human Capital Institute *(480)*

Calkins, J. Scott
National Concrete Burial Vault Association *(725)*

Call, Jerry
American Foundry Society *(123)*

Callaghan, Kathy
SWANA - Solid Waste Association of North America *(967)*

Callahan, CAE, Deborah
National Fenestration Rating Council *(750)*

Callahan, Quinton
American College of Nurse-Midwives *(99)*

Callahan, CCE, Terry
Credit Research Foundation *(403)*

Callan, Bevin
Information Systems Audit and Control Association *(495)*

Callanan, Kate
America's Health Insurance Plans *(28)*

Callaway, Rev. James G.
Association of Episcopal Colleges *(281)*

Callebert, Mark
Kamut Association of North America *(590)*

Calleja, Jay
National Agricultural Aviation Association *(630)*

Callen, Cammie
Soil and Water Conservation Society *(951)*

Callen, Robin
American Board of Psychiatry & Neurology *(83)*

Callender, Mary
National Intramural-Recreational Sports Association *(766)*

Callery, T. Grant
Financial Industry Regulatory Authority (FINRA) *(444)*

Callies, Rick

United States Wheat Associates, Inc. *(1000)*

Calliotte, Cathy
Pet Industry Joint Advisory Council *(842)*

Calvani, Terry
American Economic Association *(115)*

Calvert, Bob
American and Delaine-Merino Record Association *(45)*

Calvert, Denise
American College of Medical Genetics *(97)*

Calvet, Linda A.
Colombian American Association *(365)*

Calvin, Sue
Heating, Airconditioning and Refrigeration Distributors International *(473)*

Calvo, CAE, Roque J.
The Electrochemical Society *(423)*

Calzada, Laura de la
National Association for the Support of Long Term Care *(644)*

Camacho, Rosario
National Federation of Priests' Councils *(749)*

Camara, Christina M.
Association of Government Accountants *(286)*

Camara, Wayne
The College Board *(363)*

Cameron, Jack
Brake Manufacturers Council *(334)*

Cameron, Jim
National Council for History Education *(732)*

Cameron, Karen
American Health Planning Association *(130)*

Cameron, Tonya
Nuclear Energy Institute *(824)*

Camfield, Laura
International Society for Quality-of-Life Studies *(569)*

Camillieri, IBCLC, Regina
United States Lactation Consultant Association *(996)*

Camlin, William C.
National Association of Traffic Accident Reconstructionists and Investigators *(706)*

Cammarata, Kenneth
American Society of Head and Neck Radiology *(199)*
American Society of Neuroradiology *(204)*

Cammer, Katie
American Association of Attorney-Certified Public Accountants *(54)*

Cammisa, Carol
Investment Casting Institute *(584)*

Camp, Vicki
The Hosiery Association *(478)*

Campa, Jacqueline F.
Million Dollar Round Table *(616)*

Campagne, Kelly
National Alliance of State and Territorial AIDS Directors *(633)*

Campana, Armando
American Welding Society *(220)*

Campanale, Sue
Sales Lead Management Association *(890)*

Campanella, MBA, Gail
National Network of Depression Centers *(775)*

Campbell, MS, Alisha T.
American Association of Medical Society Executives *(65)*

Campbell, Allison

Organization of Women in International Trade *(832)*

Campbell, Brian
International Labor Rights Forum *(553)*

Campbell, Bryan
American Association of Clinical Endocrinologists *(56)*

Campbell, MA, Christopher C.
National Association for Alcoholism and Drug Abuse Counselors *(646)*

Campbell, Colin
Academy of Marketing Science *(6)*

Campbell, Dana
National Association of Small Trucking Companies *(696)*

Campbell, Dorthy (Dot)
Rural Electricity Resource Council *(889)*

Campbell, Douglas P.
Automotive Safety Council *(323)*

Campbell, Erwin
American Association of Physics Teachers *(69)*

Campbell, Fred
American Criminal Justice Association Lambda Alpha Epsilon *(112)*

Campbell, Gillian
Society of Independent Show Organizers *(939)*

Campbell, Hugh
Service Station Dealers of America and Allied Trades *(898)*

Campbell, Jeannie
National Council for Community Behavioral Healthcare *(731)*

Campbell, Jim
American Professional Society on the Abuse of Children *(168)*

Campbell, CAE, Joan
American Board of Multiple Specialties in Podiatry *(82)*

Campbell, Karen K.
American Criminal Justice Association Lambda Alpha Epsilon *(112)*

Campbell, Karen Obringer
National Employment Counseling Association *(745)*

Campbell, CAE, CMP, Linda
American Association of Healthcare Consultants *(62)*

Campbell, Linda
Handweavers Guild of America, Inc. *(468)*

Campbell, Lisa
Canola Council of Canada *(341)*

Campbell, Madelyn
Oral History Association *(830)*

Campbell, Mark
National Association of Public Hospitals and Health Systems *(688)*

Campbell, Marlyne
National Association for Healthcare Quality *(639)*

Campbell, Mary Mencarini
United States Conference of Catholic Bishops *(992)*

Campbell, Michael H.
Airline Industrial Relations Conference *(20)*

Campbell, Michele
International Bottled Water Association *(530)*

Campbell, Ron
ACPA College Student Educators International *(11)*

Campbell, Steve
Association for the Advancement of Medical Instrumentation *(258)*

Campbell, MD, PhD, Steven
Society of Pelvic Surgeons *(944)*

Campbell, Susan
International Association of Infant Massage *(523)*

Campbell, Tom
ACUTA - The Association for Information Communications Technology Professionals in Higher Education *(11)*

Campbell, William J.
Chief Administrators of Catholic Education *(352)*

Campbell, William "Tommy"
National Association for Uniformed Services *(644)*

Campbelll, Millie
International Association for Colon Hydrotherapy *(511)*

Camper, Mark
American Association of Christian Counselors *(56)*

Camps, Adriano
Geoscience and Remote Sensing Society *(459)*

Canaday, Monna
National Onion Association *(776)*

Canady, Mo
National Association of School Resource Officers *(693)*

Canda, Mary
National Association for Printing Leadership *(641)*

Candan, K. Selçuk
Special Interest Group on Management of Data *(956)*

Candee, Roland
State Guard Association of the United States *(961)*

Candelaria, Tracy
Weed Science Society of America *(1014)*

Canfield, Anne C.
Consumer Mortgage Coalition *(381)*

Canfield, Cheryl
American Council of Hypnotist Examiners *(109)*

Canfield, Jill M.
National Telecommunications Cooperative Association *(799)*

Canfield, Shane
Council on Employee Benefits *(399)*

Canino, Michael
American Society of Hand Therapists *(199)*

Cannady, Richard
International Society of Crime Prevention Practitioners *(572)*

Canner, Sharon
College of Healthcare Information Management Executives *(364)*

Canniff, Teri
Hearing Loss Association of America *(472)*

Canning, Michael
North American Securities Administrators Association (NASAA) *(820)*

Canning, CAE, Esq., Michael F.
Pet Industry Joint Advisory Council *(842)*

Cannistraro, Marco
Marine Engineers Beneficial Association *(605)*

Cannon, Caren
Council on Employee Benefits *(399)*

Cannon, Charlie
Rubber Manufacturers Association *(888)*
Scrap Tire Management Council *(893)*

Cannon, Hugh
Society of Nuclear Medicine *(943)*

Cannon, CAE, Hugh "Mac"
Association for Business Simulation and Experiential Learning *(241)*

Cannon, James R.
Customs and International Trade Bar Association *(406)*

Cannon, Kathy
American Pediatric Society *(162)*

Cannon, JD, Kathy
Society for Pediatric Research *(918)*

Cano, Sharleene E.
American Thyroid Association *(216)*

Cant, Scott
College of Diplomates of the American Board of Orthodontics *(364)*

Canter, Art
Association of Strategic Alliance Professionals, Inc. *(311)*

Canter, CAE, MBA, Marianne
American Academy of Allergy, Asthma, and Immunology *(30)*

Canter, Thomas C.
National Coal Transportation Association *(722)*

Canton, Loreeta
American Association of Poison Control Centers *(70)*

Cantrell, Bill
Walking Horse Trainers Association *(1012)*

Cantrell, Joann
Association for Iron and Steel Technology *(250)*

Cantrell, Mike
Domestic Energy Producers Alliance *(415)*

Cantrill, PhD, Richard Mary
American Oil Chemists' Society *(157)*

Cantu, Amy
Community Financial Services Association of America CFSA *(370)*

Cantwell, T. J.
International Parking Institute *(559)*

Canty, Brian
American Psychoanalytic Association *(168)*

Canuteson, MA, Sue
National Hospice & Palliative Care Organization *(760)*

Cao, FSME, PhD, Jian
North American Manufacturing Research Institution of SME *(817)*

Caoile, Gloria T.
Asian Pacific American Labor Alliance, AFL-CIO *(232)*

Capcara, Linda
SCSI Trade Association *(893)*

Capece, Laurie
Weather Modification Association *(1014)*

Capelli, Cynthia Fondriest
National Transit Benefits Association *(801)*

Capie, Megan
Juvenile Products Manufacturers Association *(590)*

Capitani, Stacey Dolan
Napa Valley Vintners Association *(625)*

Capka, John
National Tooling and Machining Association *(800)*

Caplan, Erik
American Society of Hand Therapists *(199)*

Caple, Karen
Global Health Council *(462)*

Capobianco, John
Society of Illustrators *(939)*

Capon, Andy
International Society for Respiratory Protection *(569)*

Capon, Ross B.
National Association of Railroad Passengers *(689)*

Capon, Sue
International Society for Pharmacoeconomics and Outcomes Research *(568)*

Caponetti, James D.
American Fern Society *(121)*

Caponiti, James E.
American Maritime Congress *(147)*

Caponiti, John
Automotive Recyclers Association *(323)*

Caporaletti – Hoyt, Linda
Healthcare Distribution Management Association *(471)*

Capp, Joshua
American Association of School Librarians *(72)*

Cappelletti, CMP, Paula
Appraisal Institute *(226)*

Cappitell, CAE, MBA, Susan Brown
American Roentgen Ray Society *(176)*

Capps, Brandi
National Association of Insurance Women (International) *(676)*

Capps, Russ
Association of Corporate Counsel *(277)*

Capra, Angela
International College of Applied Kinesiology *(535)*

Capra, Kim
American Institute of Constructors *(138)*

Caprio, Vincent
NanoBusiness Alliance *(625)*

Captain, Timothy
National Kitchen and Bath Association *(767)*

Capuano, Eden
Society of Neurointerventional Surgery *(942)*

Caputo, RN, APRN, CDE, Dorothy
Dermatology Nurses' Association *(410)*

Caputo, Paul
National Association for Interpretation *(640)*

Caputo, Sally
Association of Management Consulting Firms *(292)*

Caputo, Sheila
National Association for Interpretation *(640)*

Caputo-Hansen, Gilda C.
American Society of Hypertension, Inc. *(200)*

Caramusa, Cathy
Independent Cosmetic Manufacturers and Distributors *(489)*

Carantit, Laurie
International Association for Human Resource Information Management *(512)*

Carbary, Erin
Drug & Alcohol Testing Industry Association *(416)*

Carbaugh, Kimberly
Association of Nurses in AIDS Care *(296)*

Carberry, Dawn
Aviation Suppliers Association *(324)*

Carbone, Nancy
National Apartment Association *(634)*

Carbone, William J.
American Association of Physician Specialists *(69)*

Carbott, Tom
Materials Handling and Management Society *(608)*

Carcone, Kimberly
Toy Industry Association *(976)*

Card, Bradford A.
National Trooper's Coalition *(802)*

Carde, Ring
International Society of Chemical Ecology *(572)*

Carden, Joe
Professional Services Council *(865)*

Carder, Rick
National Association of Federal Education Program Administrators *(667)*

Cardillo, Trisha
National Association of Disability Representatives *(663)*

Cardinal, Joanna
Applied Research Ethics National Association *(226)*

Cardinal, Lisa
Air Conditioning, Heating and Refrigeration Institute (AHRI) *(18)*

Cardinale, Kirsty
National Association for the Advancement of Psychoanalysis *(643)*

Cardinale, Vera
Association for Prevention Teaching and Research (APTR) *(254)*

Cardon, PHR, Irene E.
National Association of Federal Credit Unions *(667)*

Cardona, Jeanne L.
Association of Ship Brokers and Agents (U.S.A.) *(308)*

Cardona, Laurie Hansen
National Association of Catholic Chaplains *(651)*

Cardona, Maria
National Horsemen's Association, Inc. *(760)*

Cardone, Tina
C-Port *(340)*

Cardoza, Freddy
North American Association of Professors of Christian Education *(813)*
Professional Association of Christian Educators *(859)*

Cardoza, Jessica
New America Alliance *(809)*

Cardwell, Leanne
Medicaid Health Plans of America *(611)*

Cardwell, Melissa
National Association of Certified Valuation Analysts *(652)*

Cardwell, Nancy
International Bluegrass Music Association *(530)*

Carella, Ariana
American Association of Museums *(65)*

Carelli, Frank
International Association of Machinists and Aerospace Workers *(524)*

Carew, Heather
Snow & Ice Management Association *(901)*

Carew, Julie A.
American Philological Association *(163)*

Carey, CAE, Cheryl Kreider
American Academy of Audiology *(31)*

Carey, Jennifer
Association of Real Estate Women *(305)*

Carey, Kim
American Truck Dealers *(217)*

Carey, Laura
Cosmetic Industry Buyers and Suppliers *(387)*

Carey, Meghan
National Society of Genetic Counselors *(794)*
Special Care Dentistry *(954)*
Special Care Dentistry Association *(954)*

Carey, CAE, Paula
Association of Life Insurance Counsel *(291)*

Carey, Shelley Johnson
Association of American Colleges and Universities *(264)*

Carey, CAE, Steve
Ambulance Manufacturers Division *(28)*

Carey, CAE, Steve
National Truck Equipment Association *(802)*
Towing Equipment Manufacturers Association *(976)*

Cargile, Linda
American Association of Small Ruminant Practitioners *(73)*
American College of Theriogenologists *(103)*
Society for Theriogenology *(926)*

Cargo, Ryan
National Animal Supplement Council *(634)*

Carigan, Lin
Conference of Radiation Control Program Directors *(375)*

Carlberg, Kristina
National Association for Information Destruction, Inc. *(640)*

Carley, PhD, Wayne
Association for Facilities Engineering *(246)*

Carli, Lorraine
National Fire Protection Association *(751)*

Carlile, Greg
Association of Diesel Specialists *(279)*

Carlile, Gregory
Mass Marketing Insurance Institute *(607)*

Carlin, Kelly
National Athletic Trainers Association *(710)*

Carlisle, Aimee
National Trappers Association *(801)*

Carlisle, Kenneth
Air Traffic Control Association *(19)*

Carlitti, Rocco
CTIA - The Wireless Association *(405)*

Carlos, Kimme
African Studies Association *(15)*

Carlough, Chris E.
Sheet Metal Workers' International Association *(898)*

Carlow, Kristi
National Association of Unclaimed Property Administrators *(707)*

Carlozzi, Kayla
Building Stone Institute *(338)*

Carlsen, Donna
Association for Institutional Research *(250)*

Carlsen, Kathleen
Academic Language Therapy Association *(3)*

Carlson, Al
Photoluminescent Safety Association *(846)*

Carlson, Bonnie J.
Promotion Marketing Association *(866)*

Carlson, Chris
Asian American Hotel Owners Association *(231)*

Carlson, Dave
Fibre Box Association *(443)*

Carlson, Drew
Federation of State Medical Boards of the United States *(442)*

Carlson, Erin
National Health Care Anti-Fraud Association *(758)*

Carlson, Marla
Consultant Dietitians in Health Care Facilities *(380)*

Carlson, Matt

National Sporting Goods Association *(796)*

Carlson, Pamela
National Association of Nutrition and Aging Services Programs *(682)*

Carlson, Pamela "Pam"
National Association of Professional Geriatric Care Managers *(687)*

Carlson, Robert
Community Transportation Association of America *(371)*
Council of the Great City Schools *(398)*

Carlson, Sally
Equal Justice Works *(432)*

Carlson, Scott
National Association of Nutrition and Aging Services Programs *(682)*

Carlson, Ed, MS, Susan
Arthroscopy Association of North America *(230)*

Carlson, W. Bernard
Society for the History of Technology *(923)*

Carlson, Will
Select Registry/Distinguished Inns of North America *(896)*

Carlton, Bruce J.
The National Industrial Transportation League *(763)*

Carlton, Sarah
Council of Multiple Listing Services *(395)*

Carlton, Sarah Gillian
Real Estate Information Professionals Association *(875)*

Carman, Jody Falletta
United States Meat Export Federation *(996)*

Carmenates, CAE, CMP, Diana
International Dairy Foods Association *(539)*

Carmichael, MD, J. Kevin
Ryan White Medical Providers Coalition *(889)*

Carmichael, Kim
American Society for Metabolic and Bariatric Surgery *(187)*

Carmichael, Neil
American Arbitration Association *(46)*

Carmichael, William B.
American Bail Coalition *(78)*

Carmigiano, Christie
Precision Metalforming Association *(856)*

Carneal, George U.
National Aeronautic Association *(629)*

Carnes, Bruce
National Cable & Telecommunications Association *(717)*

Carnes, Mary
Armed Forces Broadcasters Association *(228)*

Carnes, Rick
Songwriters Guild of America *(952)*

Carnevale, Joe
Shipbuilders Council of America *(898)*

Carney, Bill
American Academy of Craniofacial Pain *(32)*

Carney, Bill
Association of TeleServices International, Inc. *(313)*

Carney, Bill
Conference of Minority Transportation Officials *(375)*

Carney, Geneva
American Tort Reform Association *(217)*

Carney, Jennifer
National Association for the Specialty Food Trade *(644)*

Carney, Joanne Padrón
American Association for the Advancement of Science *(51)*

Carney, Jordan
Plastic Surgery Research Council *(850)*

Carney, Margaret
American Management Association *(146)*

Carney, Sean
American Society of Transplantation *(210)*

Carney, Sue
American Postal Workers Union *(167)*

Carolla, Adrianne
Minerals, Metals and Materials Society *(617)*

Caron, Liz Dart
American Institute of Physics *(140)*

Caron, Louise Q.
International Licensing Industry Merchandisers' Association *(554)*

Carothers, Cathy
International Lactation Consultant Association *(553)*

Carozza, CFE, Dick
Association of Certified Fraud Examiners *(271)*

Carpenter, Barry
North American Meat Association *(818)*

Carpenter, Dennis
National Association of Black Accountants, Inc. *(648)*

Carpenter, Dennis N.
International Bottled Water Association *(530)*

Carpenter, Diane
American Sportfishing Association *(212)*

Carpenter, Glenn
University Photographers Association of America *(1002)*

Carpenter, Greg
Organization for the Advancement of Structured Information Standards *(831)*

Carpenter, Isaac
American Dental Hygienists' Association *(114)*

Carpenter, MD, James
Civil Aviation Medical Association *(357)*

Carpenter, Jr., Jot D.
CTIA - The Wireless Association *(405)*

Carpenter, Kerri
Navy League of the United States *(807)*

Carpenter, Matt
American Society of Extra-Corporeal Technology *(197)*

Carpenter, Suzanne
National Federation of Music Clubs *(749)*

Carpenter, Todd
National Information Standards Organization *(763)*

Carpenter, Todd A.
Society for Scholarly Publishing *(921)*

Carpio, Patricia
Design-Build Institute of America *(411)*

Carr, Brice
American Saddlebred Horse Association *(176)*

Carr, Chuck
Institute of Scrap Recycling Industries, Inc. *(503)*

Carr, CDFM, Claudia
American Society of Military Comptrollers *(203)*

Carr, Debbie
Mohair Council of America *(618)*

Carr, Deborah A.
American Association of Poison Control Centers *(70)*

Carr, Diane
Educational Theatre Association *(420)*

Carr, Erin
American Immigration Lawyers Association *(134)*

Carr, J.D., SPHR, J. Robert
Society for Human Resource Management *(911)*

Carr, James
National Association of Intercollegiate Athletics *(676)*

Carr, Janet
National Association of City and County Health Officials *(654)*

Carr, Lynne
Spring Manufacturers Institute *(960)*

Carr, Meredith
Aviation Insurance Association *(324)*

Carr, Shannon
Association of Lutheran Secondary Schools *(292)*

Carr, Susan
American Society of Media Photographers *(203)*

Carr, Susan
Association of Educators in Imaging and Radiologic Sciences, Inc *(280)*

Carr, Zachary
National Council for International Visitors *(732)*

Carr-Smith, Kathleen
National Ready Mixed Concrete Association *(784)*

Carranza, Yolanda
Automotive Engine Rebuilders Association *(322)*

Carravallah, Mary
Society of Women Engineers *(950)*

Carre, Daniel
American Society for Reproductive Medicine *(189)*

Carrell, Tony
National Association of Extension 4-H Agents *(667)*

Carreras, Lisa
International Association of Attorneys and Executives in Corporate Real Estate *(516)*

Carrico, PhD, Christine K.
American Society for Pharmacology and Experimental Therapeutics *(188)*

Carrier, Betsy
National Association of Public Hospitals and Health Systems *(688)*

Carrigan, Carol B.
United States Institute for Theatre Technology *(995)*

Carrington, Belvian
International Association of Movers *(525)*

Carrodeguas, Vincent
The International Air Cargo Association *(509)*

Carroll, Ann
Helicopter Association International *(473)*

Carroll, Barbara
Reinsurance Association of America *(879)*

Carroll, Brian
The Vision Council *(1010)*

Carroll, Carol
Association of Bridal Consultants *(270)*

Carroll, Cathy
National Council of Supervisors of Mathematics *(737)*

Carroll, Jr., Charles "Chuck" T.
National Association of Waterfront Employers *(709)*
National Maritime Safety Association *(772)*

Carroll, Chris
College Media Association *(363)*

Carroll, Cynthia A.

International Liquid Terminals Association *(554)*

Carroll, David
National Legal Aid and Defender Association *(769)*

Carroll, David C.
Gas Technology Institute *(456)*

Carroll, Jessica
International Society of Arboriculture *(571)*

Carroll, Kim
National Tractor Parts Dealer Association *(801)*

Carroll, Mark T.
American Law Institute *(144)*

Carroll, Michael
National Association for Black Geologists and Geophysicists *(636)*

Carroll, Patricia
American Culinary Federation *(112)*

Carroll, Payten
National Association for State Community Services Programs *(643)*

Carroll, V. Susan
American Association of Neuroscience Nurses *(66)*

Carrow, Marri
United States Grains Council *(994)*

Carruth, Catherine
Association for Healthcare Resource and Materials Management *(248)*

Carslon, PhD, Deborah L.
Institute of Nautical Archaeology *(502)*

Carson, Charles E.
American Dialect Society *(115)*

Carson, CMP, Holly
Community Associations Institute (CAI) *(370)*

Carson, Jeffrey E.
National Association of Blacks in Criminal Justice *(649)*

Carson, Madhuri
Maple Flooring Manufacturers Association *(604)*

Carson, Marlis
National Council of Farmer Cooperatives *(734)*

Carta, Laura
Urgent Care Association of America *(1004)*

Carteaux, William R.
Society of the Plastics Industry *(948)*

Carter, Barbara
Society for Human Ecology *(911)*

Carter, Bo
National Collegiate Baseball Writers Association *(724)*

Carter, Bobbi
National Career Development Association *(717)*

Carter, Bonnie
National Guard Association of the U.S. *(757)*

Carter, Brian
The American Quaternary Association *(172)*

Carter, Catherine
American Board for Certification in Orthotics and Prosthetics, Inc. (ABC) *(81)*

Carter, Cathy
System Safety Society *(967)*

Carter, Charles
Research Council on Structural Connections *(882)*

Carter, Christine L.
Organization for the Study of Sex Differences *(831)*

Carter, Dave
National Bison Association *(713)*

Carter, David

Applied Research Ethics National Association *(226)*

Carter, Donna
National Association of Environmental Professionals *(666)*

Carter, EdD, Dr. Gene R.
Association for Supervision and Curriculum Development (ASCD) *(257)*

Carter, Gennice T.
Academy Health *(3)*

Carter, Jamie
The Jockeys' Guild *(588)*

Carter, Janet
CoreNet Global *(385)*

Carter, Janie
American Botanical Council *(85)*

Carter, Jerry
National Council of Examiners for Engineering and Surveying *(734)*

Carter, Julie
American Educational Studies Association *(116)*

Carter, Katherine
Defense Orientation Conference Association *(408)*

Carter, Margaret
National Active and Retired Federal Employees Association *(629)*

Carter, Nancy
Society of Exploration Geophysicists *(935)*

Carter, Neal
Association for Canadian Studies in the United States *(241)*

Carter, Dr. Philip B.
Association for Gnotobiotics *(247)*

Carter, Scott
Professional Landcare Network *(863)*

Carter, Shirley
Phi Delta Kappa International *(845)*

Carter, Stephanie
Association for Play Therapy *(253)*

Carter, Steve
American Society of Nuclear Cardiology *(205)*

Carter, Terri
National Association for the Education of Young Children *(644)*

Carter-Eggers, SPHR, Christine
American Association of Diabetes Educators *(60)*

Cartier, CAE, Brian
National Association of College Stores *(655)*

Cartwright, Betty
American Association for Laboratory Animal Science *(50)*

Cartwright, Ian
Common - A Users Group *(369)*

Cartwright, Jan
Society of Teachers of Family Medicine *(947)*

Cartwright, Victoria
National Association of Foreign Trade Zones *(669)*

Caruso, CAE, Beth
American Railway Engineering and Maintenance-of-Way Association *(173)*

Caruso, L.
IEEE Circuits and Systems Society *(483)*

Caruso, Philip J.
Institute of Transportation Engineers *(503)*

Carver, Brent
Rheumatology Nurses Society *(886)*

Carver, David
Employers Council on Flexible Compensation *(427)*

Carver, DC, Gary L.
Council on Chiropractic Orthopedics *(399)*

Casatelli, Linda
Gravure Association of America *(465)*

Case, Barbara
Association for Applied Sport Psychology *(239)*

Case, Bettye Anne
Association for Women in Mathematics *(261)*

Case, Caci
Transportation Clubs International *(978)*

Case, David R.
Environmental Technology Council *(431)*

Case, Diane B.
State Capital Group *(961)*

Case, John
Warehousing Education and Research Council *(1012)*

Case, Susan
American Society of Criminology *(196)*

Casente, Jr., Salvador A.
Electric Power Research Institute *(421)*

Caserta, Alana
Commercial Finance Association *(366)*

Casey, Danya
Meeting Professionals International *(612)*

Casey, David
Phi Chi Theta *(845)*

Casey, Gabe
American College of Emergency Physicians *(95)*

Casey, Ike
SOCAP International *(902)*

Casey, Joanne
National Propane Gas Association *(783)*

Casey, Joanne "Joni" F.
Intermodal Association of North America *(508)*

Casey, Rob
Incorporated Research Institutions for Seismology *(487)*

Casey, Robin
Text and Academic Authors Association *(972)*

Casey, Stephanie
Alpha Gamma Rho *(26)*

Casey, Teresa M.
Association of Financial Guaranty Insurers *(283)*

Cash-Curry, Esq., Tamela R.
Black Entertainment and Sports Lawyers Association *(331)*

Cashell, Craig
Delta Sigma Pi *(409)*

Cashen, Fran
Healthcare Billing and Management Association *(470)*

Cashen, Jill
United Food and Commercial Workers International Union *(987)*

Cashill-Florio, Kayce
Association of Marina Industries *(293)*

Cashin, Cian
American Association of Motor Vehicle Administrators *(65)*

Casidy, Patty
National Defense Transportation Association *(742)*

Casillas, Jennifer
International Society for Pharmacoeconomics and Outcomes Research *(568)*

Casmatta, Dale
Phycological Society of America *(846)*

Casna, Barbara
Holstein Association USA *(477)*

Casper, Jeff
Traffic Audit Bureau for Media Measurement, Inc. *(977)*

Casper, Kathy
American Accounting Association *(43)*

Casper, Steve
National Council of Juvenile and Family Court Judges *(735)*

Caspers, CAE, Karen Dunn
American Dental Hygienists' Association *(114)*

Cassaday, Barbara
Piano Technicians Guild *(848)*

Cassarly, Jackie
American Association of Veterinary Laboratory Diagnosticians *(76)*

Cassaro, James P.
Music Library Association *(622)*

Cassata, James R.
National Council on Radiation Protection and Measurement *(739)*

Cassedy, Joe
Beef Improvement Federation *(327)*

Cassel, MD, Christine K.
American Board of Internal Medicine *(82)*

Cassel, Ron
Association of Regulatory Boards of Optometry *(305)*

Casserly, Michael D.
Council of the Great City Schools *(398)*

Cassidy, Christopher
American Academy of Actuaries *(29)*

Cassidy, Dan
American Bladesmith Society *(81)*

Cassidy, MEd, CFLE, Dawn
National Council on Family Relations *(738)*

Cassidy, Karen
Association of Nutrition & Foodservice Professionals *(296)*

Cassidy, Kathleen M.
American Short Line and Regional Railroad Association *(179)*

Cassidy, Michael "Mike" A.
Truss Plate Institute *(981)*

Casso, Mark A.
Construction Industry Round Table, Inc. *(379)*

Castaldo, Anthony
U.S. Hereditary Angioedema Association *(983)*

Castaldo, John
Barre Granite Association *(326)*

Castaneda, Jaime
National Milk Producers Federation *(772)*

Casteel, Terri Theresa
United States Army Warrant Officers Association *(990)*

Castellani, John J.
Pharmaceutical Research and Manufacturers of America (PhRMA) *(844)*

Castellano, Amy
National Alliance of Forest Owners *(632)*

Castellanos, Nathan
Association of Academic Health Centers *(262)*

Caster, Colleen
Global Cold Chain Alliance *(462)*

Castignoli, Doreen

BPA Worldwide *(334)*

Castillo, Angelica
Society for Education in Anesthesia *(908)*

Castillo, Cheryl E
American College of Trial Lawyers *(103)*

Castillo, Christie
National Art Education Association *(635)*

Castillo, Marie E.
National Association of Negro Business and Professional Women's Clubs *(681)*

Castillo, Rebecca
Columbia Scholastic Press Association *(365)*

Casto, Emily
Grocery Manufacturers Association (GMA) *(466)*

Casto, James
National Society of Newspaper Columnists *(794)*

Casto, AuD, PhD, Kristen
National Hearing Conservation Association *(758)*

Castonguay, Joan
American Management Association *(146)*

Castro, Arlynda
North American Peruvian Horse Association *(819)*

Castro, Gloria
American College of Musicians *(98)*

Castro, Johann De
Academy of Managed Care Pharmacy *(6)*

Castro, Rafael De
National Independent Nursery Furniture Retailers Association *(762)*

Castronovo, Joe
International Association of Electronic Keyboard Manufacturers *(520)*

Caswell, Anna Harrington
National Association of State Land Reclamationists *(701)*

Caswell, Kathleen A.
Orthopaedic Trauma Association *(834)*

Catalano, Diane
Surgical Infection Society *(967)*

Catalano, Liz
Clinical Laboratory Management Association *(358)*

Catalano, Patricia
Intersocietal Accreditation Commission *(582)*

Cataldo, Catherine
National Industrial Council - State Associations Group *(763)*

Catalfu, Peter
Electrical Generating Systems Association *(422)*

Catalon, Dr. Katie B.
National Beauty Culturists' League *(713)*

Catanzaro, Emily
American Thoracic Society *(216)*

Catapano, Joseph
American Association of Pharmaceutical Scientists *(68)*

Cates-Wessel, Kathryn
American Academy of Addiction Psychiatry *(29)*

Cathcart, Chris D
Consumer Specialty Products Association *(381)*

Cathcart, Marsha
American Association for Respiratory Care *(51)*

Cathcart, CAE, Sherrie
American Association for the Study of Liver Diseases *(52)*

Catherino, MD, Bill

Society for Reproductive Endocrinology and Infertility *(920)*

Catizone, DPh, MS, RPh, Carmen A.
National Association of Boards of Pharmacy *(650)*

Catlett, Athena
North American Die Casting Association *(816)*

Catling, CIPP, Wills
International Association of Privacy Professionals *(526)*

Catsimatidis, John A.
United States Air Tour Association *(989)*

Cattan, Jacques
American Institute of Steel Construction *(140)*

Cattanach, Julie A.
International Association for Food Protection *(512)*

Cattaneo, Elizabeth
American Rights at Work *(175)*

Cattaneo, Liz
American Rights at Work *(175)*

Cattel, Jennifer
Marketing Research Association *(606)*

Cattoi, Robert
American Board of Family Medicine *(82)*

Catura, Nate
Federal Law Enforcement Officers Association *(439)*

Caughlin, Jeanine
Path to Purchase Institute *(839)*

Cauldwell, Andri
Archaeological Institute of America *(227)*

Cauley, Diedra
National Shooting Sports Foundation *(791)*

Cauley, Gerry W.
North American Electric Reliability Corporation *(816)*

Caulfield, Joshua
American Institute of Architecture Students *(137)*

Caulk, Kelly S.
Association of American Law Schools *(265)*

Caulk, Marla
Catholic Charities USA *(345)*

Causey, Dawn
American Bankers Association *(79)*

Cavalli, Katrina
American Securitization Forum *(178)*

Cavallo, Cindy
International Dairy Foods Association *(539)*
International Ice Cream Association *(551)*
National Cheese Institute *(720)*

Cavanagh, Mike
Council for Electronic Revenue Communication Advancement *(389)*

Cavanaugh, Michael
Institute on Religion in an Age of Science *(504)*

Cavanaugh, DABVP, DVM, Mike
American Animal Hospital Association *(45)*

Cavanaugh, Shannon
International Business Brokers Association *(532)*

Cavarretta, CAE, Joseph S.
American Academy of Environmental Engineers *(33)*

Cavazos, Oscar
Service Dealers Association *(897)*

Cavell, Mark
National FFA Organization *(750)*

Cavender, Mike
Radio Television Digital News Association *(873)*

Cavendish, James

Society for the Scientific Study of Religion *(924)*

Cavicchia, Jeanine
National Association of Latino Elected and Appointed Officials *(677)*

Cayton, Andrew
Society for Historians of the Early American Republic *(911)*

Cazacu, Eugen
Association for Consumer Research *(243)*

CCC-A, MA, Laura Kauth
National Hearing Conservation Association *(758)*

Ceaser, Veronica
The Association for Manufacturing Excellence *(252)*

Ceballos, Jose
National Air Traffic Controllers Association *(630)*

Cecchine, CPA, Melissa
National Apartment Association *(634)*

Ceci, John
American Law Institute *(144)*

Cedarquist, Scott
American Society of Agricultural and Biological Engineers *(191)*

Ceh, MPA, Victoria
International Society of Hair Restoration Surgery *(573)*

Cehelsky, Dr. Marta
Universities Research Association *(1002)*

Cejalvo, Barbette
International League of Electrical Associations *(553)*

Cekosh, Nick
Sleep Research Society *(900)*

Celenza, CMP, Anthony
Osteoarthritis Research Society International *(834)*
Society for Biomaterials *(905)*

Cencer, Jackie
College of Optometrists in Vision Development *(364)*

Cendana, Gregory A.
Asian Pacific American Labor Alliance, AFL-CIO *(232)*

Cenedella, Matthew
WTA Tour, Inc. *(1029)*

Censky, Steve
American Soybean Association *(211)*

Censotti, Jessica
Islamic Medical Association of North America *(586)*

Centra, Catherine G.
Hearth, Patio and Barbecue Association *(472)*

Cephas, Christopher
National Association of School Nurses *(693)*

Cephas, Joseph
Independent Electrical Contractors *(489)*

Cephas, Sheila J.
International Cemetery, Cremation and Funeral Association *(533)*

Cerame, Stephen
National League for Nursing *(768)*

Cerasuola, Teresa
Italian American Studies Association *(586)*

Cerda, Alejandro
North American-Chilean Chamber of Commerce *(823)*

Cermak, Jennifer
EDA Consortium *(419)*

Cernauskas, Michael R.
National Association of Charter School Authorizers *(652)*

Cerone, Lisa
Asphalt Emulsion Manufacturers Association *(233)*

International Slurry Surfacing Association *(565)*

Certain, Chaplain Robert
Military Chaplains Association of the U.S. *(616)*

Certo, Jane
American Society of PeriAnesthesia Nurses *(206)*

Cervantes, Angeles
Construction Management Association of America *(379)*

Cervantes, Michelle
Computer Measurement Group *(372)*

Cervantes, Nicole
Sealant, Waterproofing and Restoration Institute *(894)*

Cervarich, Margaret B.
National Asphalt Pavement Association *(635)*

Cestero, George Zeppenfeldt
Association of Hispanic Healthcare Executives *(287)*

Chacon-Martinez, Marta
FCIB-NACM Corporation *(438)*

Chaconas, CMP, Dorothy
Biophysical Society *(330)*

Chaddock, Robert
American Motorcyclist Association *(153)*

Chadwick, Dave
Organization of Wildlife Planners *(832)*

Chadwick, Fran
National League of American Pen Women *(768)*

Chadwick, Philip
Bioelectromagnetics Society *(329)*

Chafe, Arlene
International Society of Explosives Engineers *(572)*

Chaffee, Judith
The Association of Theatre Movement Educators *(314)*

Chafin, Deborah
Technical Association of the Pulp and Paper Industry *(970)*

Chai, Amy
National Association of Home Builders *(673)*

Chaifetz, Peshie
Land Trust Alliance *(593)*

Chaimovich, Jason
American Hockey League *(132)*

Chairez, Salvador
Navy League of the United States *(807)*

Chait, Steven J.
National Antique and Art Dealers Association of America *(634)*

Chakerian, Aram
Napa Valley Vintners Association *(625)*

Chalabi, Jeff
Textile Bag and Packaging Association *(972)*

Chalan, Mary Zuni
Intertribal Monitoring Association on Indian Trust Funds *(583)*

Chale, Amie
American Arbitration Association *(46)*

Chalew, Gail
Jewish Communal Service Association of North America *(588)*

Chalifoux, Robert
Distance Education and Training Council *(414)*

Chalker, Bob
NACE International *(623)*

Chalko, Kasia
Association for Death Education and Counseling *(244)*
The Society for Adolescent Medicine *(903)*

Chally, Misty
National Franchisee Association *(753)*

Chalmers, Barbara
American Board of Quality Assurance and Utilization
Review Physicians, Inc. *(84)*

Chamberlain, Cathy L.
Association of Cooperative Educators *(277)*

Chamberlain, CAE, APR, FASAE, Henry H.
Building Owners and Managers Association
International *(337)*

Chamberlain, Mark
American Jersey Cattle Association/National All-Jersey
Inc. *(142)*

Chamberlin, Liz
International Security Management Association *(564)*

Chamberlin, Michael M.
EMTA - Trade Association for the Emerging Markets
(427)

Chambers, EdM, MBA, PhD, David W.
American College of Dentists *(95)*

Chambers, Elizabeth B.
SMMA - The Motor and Motion Association *(901)*

Chambers, Jane
American Association of Physics Teachers *(69)*

Chambers, John
National Educational Telecommunications Association
(744)

Chambers, Nathaniel
National Association of Black Journalists *(649)*

Chambers, Ray B.
National Railroad Construction and Maintenance
Association, Inc. *(783)*

Chambers, Reid
Multi-Housing Laundry Association *(621)*

Chambers, Richard F.
The Institute of Internal Auditors *(500)*

Chambers, Rick
Association of Mailing, Shipping, and Office
Automation Specialists *(292)*

Chambers, Shannon
National Air Transportation Association *(630)*

Chambers, Stacia-Ann
North American Electric Reliability Corporation *(816)*

Chambers, William H.
SMMA - The Motor and Motion Association *(901)*

Chamblin, Keith
National Thoroughbred Racing Association *(800)*

Chamiec-Case, MAR, MSW, PhD, Rick
North American Association of Christians in Social
Work *(813)*

Chamness, Charles M.
National Association of Mutual Insurance Companies
(681)

Champ, D. Zachary
PCIA - The Wireless Infrastructure Association *(840)*

Champney, Dawn Kristof
Water and Wastewater Equipment Manufacturers
Association *(1012)*

Chan, Donny
Malaysian Rubber Export Promotion Council (USA)
(602)

Chan, Jennifer
North American Wholesale Lumber Association *(823)*

Chan, Julie
Society for Vascular Surgery *(926)*

Chan, Susan D.
American Association of Zoo Keepers *(77)*

Chan, Yuen
IEEE Power and Energy Society *(485)*

Chance, Terry
Pet Sitters International *(843)*

Chandler, CAE, CMP, MPA, Bonnie
Hispanic Dental Association *(475)*

Chandler, Christine
American Society of Media Photographers *(203)*

Chandler, Jennifer
National Council of Nonprofits *(735)*

Chandler, Kerry D.
National Basketball Association *(712)*

Chandler, Mary
University Aviation Association *(1002)*

Chandler, CAE, MA, RHIA, Nancy Deal
American College of Prosthodontists *(101)*

Chandler, Randy
Institute for Operations Research and the Management
Sciences *(497)*

Chandler, Sage
Consumer Electronics Association *(381)*

Chandler, Terry
Diamond Council of America *(411)*

Chandler, Theodore S.
AFL-CIO Housing Investment Trust *(15)*

Chandler, Tom
American Teleservices Association *(215)*

Chandler, William
American Society of Tropical Medicine and Hygiene
(210)
Association of University Technology Managers *(316)*
The Society for Adolescent Medicine *(903)*

Chandross, Karen
American Society for Neurochemistry *(187)*

Chaney, Arthur
American Agriculture Movement, Inc. *(44)*

Chaney, Elizabeth
National Association of Sports Commissions *(697)*

Chaney, G. P. Russ
International Association of Plumbing and Mechanical
Officials *(526)*

Chaney, Gwen
The National Association of Dog Obedience Instructors
(663)

Chang, Adolph
United Association of Equipment Leasing *(985)*

Chang, Anna
American Numismatic Society *(156)*

Chang, Eleanor
American Booksellers Association *(85)*

Chang, Eun-Joo
Society for Neuroscience *(916)*

Chang, Jan Le
The Association of Asian American Investment
Managers *(268)*

Chang, Kristie
Women in Cable Telecommunications, Inc. *(1020)*

Chang, Michelle
Sailors' Union of the Pacific *(890)*

Chang, Monique
Association for Computing Machinery *(243)*

Chanin, Robert H.
National Education Association *(744)*

Chao, Wen-Lu
Physician Insurers Association of America *(847)*

Chaparro, Maggie
National Minority Supplier Development Council *(773)*

Chapeskie, Dave
International Maple Syrup Institute *(555)*

Chapin, Rene
National Association of Dental Plans *(662)*

Chaplin, Miranda
National Association of Agricultural Educators *(646)*

Chapman, Ann
National Ocean Industries Association *(775)*

Chapman, Deb
International Sleep Products Association *(565)*

Chapman, CFE, Harold
World Floor Covering Association *(1026)*

Chapman, Isaac
International Association of Business Communicators
(517)

Chapman, James
American Physiological Society *(165)*

Chapman, John
Law Enforcement Alliance of America *(594)*

Chapman, Kathy
Petroleum Technology Transfer Council *(844)*

Chapman, Maria
American Society for Healthcare Food Service
Administrators *(185)*

Chapman, Maria
Association for Healthcare Foodservice *(248)*

Chapman, Maria Manning
Technology Services Industry Association *(970)*

Chapman, Nancy
Soyfoods Association of North America *(953)*

Chapman, Sara
Deep Sea Fishermen's Union *(408)*

Chapman, Susan
American Society of Agronomy (ASA, CSSA, SSSA)
(191)
Crop Science Society of America *(404)*
Soil Science Society of America *(951)*

Chappell, Allyson
National Venture Capital Association *(803)*

Chappell, Diane
American Wine Society *(221)*

Chappell, Krista
American Probation and Parole Association *(167)*

Chappell, William
IEEE Microwave Theory and Techniques Society *(485)*

Chappuies, Dave
FAA Managers Association, Inc. *(436)*

Charbonneau, Jane
American Association of Woodturners *(77)*

Chard, Timothy
Federal Law Enforcement Officers Association *(439)*

Charest, Ashley M.
Glass Association of North America *(461)*

Chari, Rhoda
National Association of Student Personnel
Administrators *(626)*

Charlery, Delver
National Association of Wheat Growers *(709)*

Charles, Dr. Harvey
Association of International Education Administrators
(289)

Charles, III, J. Kenneth
Steel Joist Institute *(962)*

Charles, Jessica
International Society for Performance Improvement
(567)

Charles, Shelli
American Orthopsychiatric Association *(159)*

Charles, Vivian Dandridge
National Association of Independent Schools *(675)*

Charles, Yverose
World Trade Centers Association *(1027)*

Charlesworth, CITP, CPA, Jack
PKF North American Network *(849)*

Charlow, Renee
Black Theatre Network *(332)*

Charlton, Knight
American Dental Society of Anesthesiology *(114)*

Charlton, Philip
Utility Arborist Association *(1006)*

Charlton-Perrin, Geoffrey
Accreditation Association for Ambulatory Health Care
(9)

Charney, Amanda
International Association of Amusement Parks and
Attractions(IAAPA) *(515)*

Charon, Marc T.
Managed Funds Association *(602)*

Charvat, Jeffrey L.
National Association of School Psychologists *(693)*

Chase, Brooks W.
Resort Hotel Association *(883)*

Chase, Jessica
Interlocking Concrete Pavement Institute *(508)*

Chase, Lon
Reliability Society *(880)*

Chase, Loren
Organization of Wildlife Planners *(832)*

Chase, Matthew
National Association of Counties *(659)*
National Association of Development Organizations
(662)

Chase, Matthew D.
National Association of County Intergovernmental
Relations Officials *(660)*

Chase, CPA, Paul
Financial Executives International *(444)*

Chase, Ronald
Association of Federal Communications Consulting
Engineers *(282)*

Chase, Sue
National Fluid Power Association *(751)*

Chase, Tiffany
Energy Telecommunications and Electrical Association
(428)

Chastain, III, Merritt B.
National Association of Pipe Coating Applicators *(684)*

Chatara, Nathela
Association for Preservation Technology International
(253)

Chatman, Jordan
Construction Specifications Institute *(380)*

Chatman, Quintin
National Association of Criminal Defense Lawyers
(661)

Chatterjee, Emily
National Asian Pacific American Bar Association *(635)*

Chaudhry, DO, FACOI, MS, FACP, Humayun J.
Federation of State Medical Boards of the United States
(442)

Chaudhry, Khalid
National Association for the Education of Young
Children *(644)*

Chaudhuri, Nupur
National Women's Studies Association *(805)*

Chausis, Charlene
National Council of Supervisors of Mathematics *(737)*

Chavern, David C.
United States Chamber of Commerce *(991)*

Chavez, Becky
National Center for Employee Ownership *(719)*

Chavez, Edgar
American Cleaning Institute *(91)*

Chavez, Greg
The Vision Council *(1010)*

Chavez, Trenton
American Holistic Medical Association *(132)*

Chavez, Zaida
American Welding Society *(220)*

Chavis, Barbara A.
National Association of State Boards of Geology *(698)*

Chavis, CPA, Regina
Academy of Political Science *(8)*
American Political Science Association *(166)*

Chaw, Terisa E.
National Employment Lawyers Association (NELA)
(746)

Chawdry, Alyssa
American Securitization Forum *(178)*

Chawszczewski, PhD, Susanne
National Association of Catholic Chaplains *(651)*

Cheah, Stanton
ACPA College Student Educators International *(11)*
American College Personnel Association *(105)*

Cheaney, Willis
Black Coaches & Administrators *(331)*

Cheatham, Amy
American Medical Rehabilitation Providers Association
(149)

Cheatham, Demetris W.
National Bar Association *(712)*

Check, William
National Cable & Telecommunications Association
(717)

Checkley, Ann E.
Association of Reproductive Health Professionals *(305)*

Cheek, Dolores
Embroidery Trade Association *(425)*

Cheeks, Irica
Academy of Pharmaceutical Research and Science *(8)*

Cheesebrough, Charles
National Council on Family Relations *(738)*

Cheever, Nicole
Art Libraries Society of North America *(230)*

Chehak (Klamath), Gail E.
Indian Arts and Crafts Association *(492)*

Chelena, Kay
National Association of Extension 4-H Agents *(667)*

Chelf, Lauren
Association of Analytical Communities International
(267)

Chella-Nigl, Ann
American College of Clinical Pharmacy *(94)*

Chen, C. Philip
Man and Cybernetics Systems Society *(602)*

Chen, Chester
American National Chamber of Commerce *(154)*

Chen, Feng
Parenteral Drug Association *(838)*

Chen, Gregory
American Immigration Lawyers Association *(134)*

Chen, Haiqiang
Chinese American Food Society *(354)*

Chen, James
American Importers and Exporters/Meat Products
Group *(135)*

Chen, John S.
NALP - The Association for Legal Career Professionals
(624)

Chen, Lilly Lee
Linguistic Association of Canada and the United States
(598)

Chen, Yea-Fen
Chinese Language Teachers Association *(354)*

Chen, Yi-chao
Society for Natural Philosophy *(916)*

Chen, Yi-Chao
Society of Engineering Science *(935)*

Chen, Yimang
American Society of Human Genetics *(200)*
Genetics Society of America *(458)*

Chen, Yuyi
League for Innovation in the Community College *(595)*

Chenard, Lucian
Association for Biblical Higher Education *(240)*

Chenevey, Cathy
American Institute of Aeronautics and Astronautics
(136)

Cheney, Ashley
National Council of Examiners for Engineering and
Surveying *(734)*

Cheney, Liana de Girolami
Association for Textual Scholarship in Art History *(257)*

Cheng, Elaine
CFA Institute *(350)*

Cheng, MD, MPH, Tina L.
American Society of Neuroradiology *(204)*

Chenn, AICI, CIP, Helena
Association of Image Consultants International *(287)*

Cheris, Judy
Greeting Card Association *(466)*

Cherkashov, Georgy
International Marine Minerals Society *(555)*

Chernin, DMD, MLS, David A.
American Academy of the History of Dentistry *(42)*

Cherry, CEM, David
National Hospice & Palliative Care Organization *(760)*

Cherry, James
American Theatre and Drama Society *(216)*

Cherry, Julia
Society for Wetland Scientists *(927)*

Chertoff, MD, MS, Jocelyn D.
Association of Program Directors in Radiology *(303)*

Cherubini, Tim
Lyrasis *(600)*

Chervitz, Randi
Craft Retailers Association for Tomorrow *(403)*

Chesak, Chris
Adventure Travel Trade Association *(13)*

Chesebrough, Dave

Association for Enterprise Information **(245)**

Chesnais, Alain
Special Interest Group for Measurement and Evaluation **(955)**

Chesnutt, David
Manuscript Society **(604)**

Chester, Lisa
International Kitchen Exhaust Cleaning Association **(553)**
National Renal Administrators Association **(786)**

Chesterfield, Nancy
American Simmental Association **(179)**

Chetelat,, CAE, Amy
American Sports Builders Association **(212)**
Flexographic Prepress Platemakers Association **(447)**
Generic Animal Drug Alliance **(458)**
Web Sling and Tie down Association **(1014)**
Wood Machinery Manufacturers of America **(1024)**

Cheung, Brian
SOCAP International **(902)**

Chew, Emily Y.
American Ophthalmological Society **(157)**

Cheyne, Barbara
American Concrete Institute **(106)**

Cheyney, CPM, LM, PhD, Melissa
Midwives Alliance of North America **(615)**

Chezem, Amy
Juvenile Products Manufacturers Association **(590)**

Chi, Power
Global Semiconductor Alliance **(463)**

Chiappetta, Christina
International Public Management Association for Human Resources **(562)**

Chiarelli, Salvatore
Risk and Insurance Management Society, Inc. (RIMS) **(886)**

Chiasson, CFA, CAE, Jack
National Association of Independent Life Brokerage Agencies **(674)**

Chiat, Sharon
Association of Children's Museums **(272)**

Chieco, Fred
International Motor Press Association **(557)**

Chilafoe, Marisa
Maritime Fire and Safety Association **(605)**

Chilcote, MBA, PHR, Lisa
Association of Public Health Laboratories **(304)**

Chilcott, Susan M.
American Association of State Colleges and Universities **(73)**

Child, Martha
Major League Baseball Players Association **(601)**

Childers, Amy
Interstate Oil and Gas Compact Commission **(583)**

Childers, MD, Rory W.
International Society for Computerized Electrocardiology **(566)**

Childress, Kaycee
Industrial Designers Society of America **(493)**

Childress, Mary
American Public Transportation Association **(171)**

Childress, Terri
National Minority Supplier Development Council **(773)**

Childs, FAIA, FACHA, Douglas
American College of Healthcare Architects **(96)**

Childs, PE, Matt
American Concrete Pipe Association **(106)**

Chiles, Patience
American Association of Neuroscience Nurses **(66)**

Chiles, Sue
American Optometric Association **(157)**

Chill, Nancy
The Endocrine Society **(427)**

Chimenti, Linda M.
Council for Agricultural Science and Technology **(388)**

Chin, PLC, Deborah
The ERISA Industry Committee (ERIC) **(433)**

Chin, Ed
Orthopedic Surgical Manufacturers Association **(834)**

Chin, Janet
The International Transactional Analysis Association **(578)**

Chinn, Jennifer
Automation Alley **(321)**

Chionchio, John
National Association of Ordnance and Explosive Waste Contractors **(682)**

Chiralo, Robert
MASINT Association **(607)**

Chirico, CMP, Bethany Blue
National Association for College Admission Counseling **(637)**

Chiruvolu, Vikram Surya
Society for the Science & the Public **(924)**

Chisholm, CAE, CMP, Amy
Building Owners and Managers Association International **(337)**

Chisholm, Ben
Industrial Designers Society of America **(493)**

Chisholm, Bridget
North American Association for Environmental Education **(812)**

Chism, Katie
National Systems Contractors Association **(798)**

Chitester, Ken
Appraisal Institute **(226)**

Chitty, Haley
National Association of Student Financial Aid Administrators **(703)**

Chitwood, Debra
American Federation of Police and Concerned Citizens **(119)**
National Association of Chiefs of Police **(653)**

Chitwood, Jim
DeepStar Project **(408)**

Chiu, MSW, Wendy
The National Network for Social Work Managers **(774)**

Chiueh, Tzi-Dar
Solid-State Circuits Society **(952)**

Chizmadia, Richard
American Guild of Music **(127)**

Chmiel, Dorothy
Air and Waste Management Association **(17)**

Chmura, Jason
Society for Nonprofit Organizations **(917)**

Choate, Lisa
American Councils for International Education **(111)**

Chocolaad, Yvette
National Association of State Workforce Agencies **(703)**

Chodkowski, Stefan
Democratic Attorneys General Association **(410)**

Choe, Jenny
Associated Equipment Distributors **(235)**

Choe, Paul
Korean Drycleaners-Laundry Association **(591)**

Choi, CAE, Bill
Equipment Leasing and Finance Association **(432)**

Choi, Chong-Hie
APPA - Leadership in Educational Facilities **(225)**

Chokshi, Mansi
Specialty Coffee Association of America **(957)**

Chomick, Chris
National Institute of American Doll Artists **(764)**

Chomsky, Jack
Cantors Assembly **(342)**

Chongpinitchai, Anna
American Resort Development Association **(175)**

Chopak, Chuck
The Association for International Agriculture and Rural Development **(250)**

Choquette, Gary
Pipeline Research Council International, Inc. **(849)**

Chorbajian, Torcom
Society for Mathematical Biology **(915)**

Chornenky, Rae Lynne
National Federation of Republican Women **(750)**

Choudhury, Abigail
American Institute for Conservation of Historic and Artistic Works **(136)**

Choudhury, Dr. Arpita
Association of Fish and Wildlife Agencies **(283)**

Chouinard, Elizabeth
American Federation for Medical Research **(119)**

Chow, PhD, Ida
Society for Developmental Biology **(907)**

Chow, Kathy
Asian American Journalists Association **(231)**

Chow, Marc
National Renal Administrators Association **(786)**

Chow, Peter C.Y.
American Association for Chinese Studies **(48)**

Chow, Richard
Toy Industry Association **(976)**

Choy, Kam
International Association of Professional Security Consultants **(527)**

Choyke, Barbara
American Association of Oral and Maxillofacial Surgeons **(67)**

Chrapaty, Erin
American Institute of Ultrasound in Medicine **(141)**

Chrastka, John F.
American Library Association **(145)**

Chriss, Ernest
Air Force Sergeants Association **(19)**

Christensen, Annmarie
Global Health Council **(462)**

Christensen, CAE, MBA, Lynne
Cedar Shake and Shingle Bureau **(347)**

Christensen, Paul A.
Society of Professional Audio Recording Services **(945)**

Christensen, Rod
National Alfalfa and Forage Alliance **(631)**

Christensen, Todd
National Legal Aid and Defender Association **(769)**

Christensen, Valerie
Association of Educators in Imaging and Radiologic Sciences, Inc **(280)**

Christenson, Fay Gallagher
Gerontological Society of America *(460)*

Christiano, S. G. 'Sam'
National Association of State Boards of Geology *(698)*

Christiansen, Marilou
National Center for Asia-Pacific Economic Cooperation *(719)*

Christiansen, Mary Anna
National Defense Industrial Association *(742)*

Christianson, Jim
The Kite Trade Association International *(591)*

Christianson, Lori
National Head Start Association *(758)*

Christie, Jeanne
Association of State Wetland Managers *(311)*

Christie, Lisa
The National Association for the Dually Diagnosed *(643)*

Christie, Lois
Intercoiffure America/Canada *(507)*

Christie, Lorna
Produce Marketing Association *(858)*

Christison, Carol L.
International Dairy-Deli-Bakery Association *(540)*

Christman, Yvette
National Futures Association *(754)*

Christner, Beverly
Council of State and Territorial Epidemiologists *(397)*

Christner, Windy
American Pharmacists Association *(163)*

Christoffersen, Chris
National Association of Rural Health Clinics *(692)*

Christofferson, Jay P
Associated Schools of Construction *(237)*

Christopher, Andrew N.
Society for the Teaching of Psychology *(926)*

Christopher, Maia
Association for the Treatment of Sexual Abusers *(260)*

Christy, Craig
National Association of Self-Instructional Language Programs *(695)*

Christy, Pamela
Association of Pet Dog Trainers *(299)*

Chromek, Paul
Gas Technology Institute *(456)*

Chrouser, MA, PhD, Kelley
American Society for Healthcare Risk Management *(185)*

Chu, Eliza
Community Development Venture Capital Alliance *(370)*

Chu, Lailai
Association for Asian Studies *(239)*

Chu, Wilson
The Association of Asian American Investment Managers *(268)*

Chuba, Darci
International Claim Association *(535)*

Chubb, Jessica
International Executive Housekeepers Association *(543)*

Chubb, Tina
International Executive Housekeepers Association *(543)*

Chubb, Tremaine

International Executive Housekeepers Association *(543)*

Chudoba, Lauri A.
International Parking Institute *(559)*

Chumley, Pam
Association for Dressings and Sauces *(245)*
International Flight Services Association *(545)*

Chumley, Pamela A.
The Vinegar Institute *(1009)*

Chung, Alex
Exhibit Designers and Producers Association *(435)*

Chung, Brian
Piano Manufacturers Association International *(848)*

Chung, CSHM, PhD, Jeffrey Y.
The National Safety Management Society *(789)*

Chung, Prof. Jin S.
International Society of Offshore and Polar Engineers *(573)*

Chung, Sandra
National Ecological Observatory Network, Inc *(743)*

Church, Barbara
International Safe Transit Association *(563)*

Church, Doug
National Air Traffic Controllers Association *(630)*

Church, Edward A.
International Safe Transit Association *(563)*

Church, Jeff
National Association of Architectural Metal Manufacturers *(647)*
National Church Goods Association *(722)*
Pressure Vessel Manufacturers Association *(857)*

Church, Matthew
National Pawnbrokers Association *(779)*

Church, Richard W.
Bearing Specialist Association *(327)*

Church, Rick
American Fence Association *(120)*
Association of Rotational Molders International *(306)*
Ceramic Tile Distributors Association *(349)*

Churchill, Chris
National Hardwood Lumber Association *(757)*

Churchill, Deb
National Association of Produce Market Managers *(686)*

Churchill, James
American Society of Photographers *(207)*

Chustek, Roy
Association of Departments of English *(278)*
Association of Departments of Foreign Languages *(278)*

Chvotkin, Alan
Professional Services Council *(865)*

Chvotkin, Alan L.
Professional Services Council *(865)*

Chwat, John
Electronic Security Association *(424)*

Cialone, Henry J.
Edison Welding Institute *(419)*

Ciampaglia, Brandon
National Association of EMS Educators *(665)*

Ciatto, JoAnn
American Board of Medical Specialties *(82)*

Cibello, Hernan
InterAction (American Council of Voluntary International Action) *(506)*

Cibulka, James G.
National Council for Accreditation of Teacher Education *(731)*

Ciccone, John
American Society of Cataract and Refractive Surgery *(194)*

Cichello, Jan
National Agri-Marketing Association *(629)*

Cicio, Paul N.
Industrial Energy Consumers of America *(493)*

Cieck, Catherine
Conference of Consulting Actuaries *(375)*

Cienkowski, PhD, Kathleen M.
Academy of Rehabilitative Audiology *(8)*

Cieplik, Eric
National Society of Compliance Professionals *(793)*

Ciesinski, Michael
FlexTech Alliance *(447)*

Cigich, Jessica
Professional Aviation Safety Specialists (AFL-CIO) *(860)*

Cilia, MBA, Kathy
American Medical Technologists *(150)*

Cillay, Pat
Society of American Foresters *(928)*

Cimini, Toni
National Association for Uniformed Services *(644)*

Cinea, CSCS, MA, Keith E.
National Strength and Conditioning Association *(797)*

Cingari, Kelly
Exhibit Designers and Producers Association *(435)*

Cino, Angie
Audio Publishers Association *(320)*

Cinquemani, CPA, Paul
National Association of Tax Professionals *(704)*

Ciocci, Linda Church
National Hydropower Association *(761)*

Cioffari, Nancy C.
American Association of Colleges of Osteopathic Medicine *(57)*

Cioffoletti, Bill
Professional Golfers Association of America *(862)*

Cipicchio, Aimee
Steel Manufacturers Association *(962)*

Cipinko, Scott J.
Consumer Credit Industry Association *(381)*

Cipolla, Jack
American Federation of Astrologers, Inc. *(119)*

Cipriano, CMP, Laurie
American Educational Research Association *(116)*

Ciravolo, Janet
National Association of Printing Ink Manufacturers *(686)*

Ciresi, Pat
American Association of Preferred Provider Organizations *(70)*
National Alliance for Specialty Healthcare Programs *(632)*

Cirino, Eileen
American College of Medical Physics *(97)*

Cisar, John
International Turfgrass Society *(579)*

Cisar, Kathy
Museum Store Association *(621)*

Cisneros, Cindy
Public Education Network *(869)*

Cissel, John
The Coalition for Government Procurement *(360)*

Cisternino, Mark

Flexographic Technical Association *(447)*

Ciukaj, Mary Beth
Council of Residential Specialists *(396)*

Ciulla, Barbara
Business Marketing Association *(339)*
National Association of Sporting Goods Wholesalers *(696)*
The Recreational Vehicle Aftermarket Association *(877)*

Clackett, ACA, CPA, Timothy
Association of Chartered Accountants in the United States *(272)*

Claffee, Lily Fu
American National Chamber of Commerce *(154)*

Claghorn, Karey
American Polypay Sheep Association *(167)*

Clair, Kathie St.
American Physical Therapy Association - Private Practice Section *(165)*

Clair, Miki Saint
Society of Pharmaceutical and Biotech Trainers *(944)*

Clamp, Cyndi
National Association of Reunion Managers *(692)*

Clancy, Felicity Feather
American Physical Therapy Association *(164)*

Clancy, Marty
American Institute of Chemical Engineers *(138)*

Clapsadle, Barbara
Credit Research Foundation *(403)*

Clarahan, Marcia
National Association of Animal Breeders *(647)*

Clardy, Townley
Performing Arts Alliance *(841)*

Clare, Bevin
American Herbalists Guild *(131)*

Clarenbach, J D, Jane
National Association for Gifted Children *(639)*

Clarenbach, JD, Sara
SACNAS (Society for Advancement of Chicanos and Native Americans in Science) *(889)*

Clark, Allyson
Association for Accounting Marketing *(238)*

Clark, Amanda
National Association of County Intergovernmental Relations Officials *(660)*

Clark, PhD, Betsy
National Alliance for Accessible Golf *(631)*

Clark, Brad
International Association of Privacy Professionals *(526)*

Clark, Brittany
Corporate Council on Africa *(385)*

Clark, Calum
United States Ski and Snowboard Association *(999)*

Clark, Caren
National Association of City and County Health Officials *(654)*
National Association of County and City Health Officials *(659)*

Clark, Carol
Global Alcohol Producers Group *(461)*

Clark, Carolyn
Professional Convention Management Association *(861)*

Clark, Charles B.
Brick Industry Association *(335)*

Clark, Cheryl
National Association for Surface Finishing *(643)*

Clark, Cheryl A.
Union of American Physicians and Dentists *(985)*

Clark, Chris
Snack Food Association *(901)*

Clark, Cindi
APSE: The Network on Employment *(226)*

Clark, Cindy
USA Archery *(1004)*

Clark, Clayton
National Association of State Directors of Veterans Affairs *(700)*

Clark, Donna
American Traffic Safety Service Association *(217)*

Clark, Doug
National Truck Leasing System *(802)*

Clark, PhD, ACSW, MPH, II, Elizabeth J.
National Association of Social Workers *(696)*

Clark, Emily
Association of Bone and Joint Surgeons *(270)*

Clark, Fred
US Rice Producers Association *(1004)*

Clark, Heather
Association of Environmental and Engineering Geologists *(281)*

Clark, Holly
National Business Aviation Association *(716)*

Clark, J.R.
Association of Private Enterprise Education *(300)*

Clark, Jackie
National Automatic Merchandising Association *(711)*

Clark, James
National Independent Living Association *(762)*

Clark, James Bryce
Organization for the Advancement of Structured Information Standards *(831)*

Clark, Jane
National Truck Leasing System *(802)*

Clark, Jay
Helicopter Association International *(473)*

Clark, ACSW, LCSW, MSW, Jeanne
American Academy of Medical Hypnoanalysts *(36)*

Clark, Jenny
American Institute of Ultrasound in Medicine *(141)*

Clark, Jessica
Association of Independents in Radio *(288)*

Clark, Jill
Military Operations Research Society *(616)*

Clark, Jim
International Union of Electronic, Electrical, Salaried, Machine, and Furniture Workers-CWA *(579)*

Clark, CAE, Jr., John D.
BICSI *(329)*

Clark, MD, Joseph Y.
Society of Government Service Urologists *(938)*

Clark, Julia A.
International Federation of Professional and Technical Engineers *(544)*

Clark, Julie
National Legal Aid and Defender Association *(769)*

Clark, Kara
Plan Sponsor Council of America *(849)*

Clark, Kay
Lift Manufacturers Product Section - Material Handling Institute *(597)*
Material Handling Industry of America *(608)*

Clark, Kelly E
American Astronomical Society *(77)*

Clark, Kevin
American Music Center *(153)*

Clark, Kevin
American Public Works Association *(172)*

Clark, Kevin
Association of Film Commissioners International *(283)*

Clark, Lance
The International Wood Products Association *(581)*

Clark, CAE, Larry
International Association of Assessing Officers *(516)*

Clark, Lauren
National Association of Credit Union Supervisory and Auditing Committees *(661)*

Clark, Lee Ann
American Pediatric Surgical Association *(162)*
Society for Vascular Medicine *(926)*

Clark, Linda L.
Society for French Historical Studies *(909)*

Clark, Marilyn
Spill Control Association of America *(958)*

Clark, Matthew
The Association for Academic Surgery *(237)*

Clark, Megan
International Carwash Association *(533)*

Clark, Natasha
American Society for Horticultural Science *(185)*

Clark, Patricia C.
Kappa Delta Epsilon *(590)*

Clark, Randy
National Shooting Sports Foundation *(791)*

Clark, Jr., Ray L.
Leafy Greens Council *(595)*

Clark, Rick
Used Truck Association *(1005)*

Clark, Robert Cary
International Society on Thrombosis and Hemostasis *(575)*

Clark, Roland
Society for Romanian Studies *(921)*

Clark, Sarah E.
Women in Agribusiness *(1020)*

Clark, Sharon
National Association of Planning Councils *(685)*

Clark, Stan
Association of College Administration Professionals *(273)*

Clark, Ted
Tobacconists' Association of America *(976)*

Clark, Teresa
Alpha Chi Sigma Fraternity, Inc. *(26)*

Clark, Teresa
American College of Health Plan Management *(96)*

Clark, Tiffany
National Association of Scientific Materials Managers *(694)*

Clark, Tom
American Homebrewers Association *(133)*
The Brewers Association *(335)*

Clark, Valeria
National Funeral Directors and Morticians Association *(754)*

Clark, William
American Institute for Shippers' Associations *(136)*

Clark-Roland, Quiana
Southeastern Theatre Conference *(953)*

Clarke, Andrew
International Society for Quality-of-Life Studies *(569)*

Clarke, Boyd
Certified Milk Producers Association of America *(350)*

Clarke, Don
International Cost Estimating and Analysis Association
effective *(537)*

Clarke, CAE, James L. "Jim"
American Society of Association Executives-The
Center for Association Leadership *(193)*

Clarke, Jeffrey
NGVAmerica *(810)*

Clarke, Mark
Purebred Dairy Cattle Association *(871)*

Clarke, Megan
Academy of Motion Picture Arts and Sciences *(7)*

Clarke, Peggy
The Association of Women in International Trade *(317)*

Clarke, Thea
American Society for Cell Biology *(182)*

Clarke, Thomas M
National Center for State Courts *(720)*

Clarke, William
National Academy of Clinical Biochemistry *(627)*

Classen, Sara
National Hispanic Medical Association *(759)*

Claudy, Lynn D.
National Association of Broadcasters *(650)*

Clauss-Ehlers, Caroline S.
Association for Multicultural Counseling and
Development *(252)*

Clawges, Lori
American Association of Clinical Endocrinologists *(56)*

Clay, Jr., Rudolph
Black Caucus of the American Library Association
(331)

Clayback, Don
National Coalition for Assistive and Rehab Technology
(723)

Clayborne, Robert
National Council of State Boards for Nursing *(736)*

Clayman, Arnold
American Society of Consultant Pharmacists *(195)*

Claymore, Paul
Auto Suppliers Benchmarking Association *(321)*
International Contact Center Benchmarking
Consortium *(537)*

Clayton, Charles
American Society of Hematology *(199)*

Clayton, Debra
Guild of Artists and Artisans *(467)*

Clayton, JoAnn
The Institute of Internal Auditors *(500)*

Clayton, Paul
United States Meat Export Federation *(996)*

Clayton, Robin Y.
National Fenestration Rating Council *(750)*

Clayton, Susan
American Correctional Association *(108)*

Clayton-Pedersen, Alma R.
Association of American Colleges and Universities
(264)

Cleary, Dan
Society for Industrial & Applied Mathematics *(912)*

Cleary, James Chip
International Association of Amusement Parks and
Attractions(IAAPA) *(515)*

Cleary, Jennifer
Theatre Communications Group *(973)*

Cleary, Kathie
Obesity Society *(825)*

Cleary, Mary Jane
National Council on Compensation Insurance, Inc.
(738)

Cleary, Patrick J.
National Association of Professional Employer
Organizations *(687)*

Cleary, Susan
Independent Film and Television Alliance *(489)*

Cleave, Paula
American Bar Association *(79)*

Cleaveland, Brent
Fashion Jewelry and Accessories Trade Association
(438)

Cleaves, Cheryl
American Mathematical Association of Two Year
Colleges *(147)*

Clegg, Suzanne
National Association for Business Economics *(636)*

Clehane, Diane
Fashion Group International *(438)*

Clem, Sarah
Organization for Tropical Studies *(831)*

Clemans, Terry W.
National Credit Reporting Association *(740)*

Clemens, Kristen
Destination Marketing Association International *(411)*

Clemens, Therese O.
International Society for the Study of Trauma and
Dissociation *(570)*

Clemens, Thérèse O.
International Society for the Study of Dissociation
(570)

Clement, Stacey A.
Post-Tensioning Institute *(853)*

Clements, David E.
International Association of Electrical Inspectors *(520)*

Clements, Fred
National Bicycle Dealers Association *(713)*

Clements, Galen
Council of International Investigators *(395)*

Clements, Irene
National Foster Parent Association *(753)*

Clements, Janice
American Railway Engineering and Maintenance-of-
Way Association *(173)*

Clements, Julie A.
American Mental Health Counselors Association *(151)*

Clements, Lisa
Association of Litigation Support Professionals *(292)*

Clements, Col. Robert
National Naval Officers Association *(774)*

Clements, Rosemary A.
Employee Stock Ownership Plan Association *(426)*

Clements, Sarah
Society of Trauma Nurses *(949)*

Clements, CAE, Sarah
National Gerontological Nursing Association *(755)*

Clemmensen, J. Scott
Capital Health *(342)*

Clemmer, Tracie D.
International Downtown Association *(541)*

Clemmons, Ajenai S.
National Black Caucus of State Legislators *(714)*

Clemmons, Deirdre L.
Airports Council International - North America *(21)*

Clemmons, Mary Anna
Women's Professional Rodeo Association *(1023)*

Clemons, CAE, CMP, Calvin K.
Business Solutions Association *(340)*
Fire Suppression Systems Association *(446)*

Clemons, Claudia J.
National Association of Waterproofing and Structural
Repair Contractors *(709)*

Clemons, G. Scott
Bibliographical Society of America *(328)*

Clerkley, Cheretta
American Society for Parenteral and Enteral Nutrition
(188)

Cleveland, Kenneth
American Academy of Orofacial Pain *(38)*

Cleveland, Kenneth S.
American Equilibration Society *(117)*

Cleveland, Robin
Pyrotechnics Guild International *(871)*

Clevenger, Sandy
American Hanoverian Society *(128)*

Clevidence, Kristen
National Mobility Equipment Dealers Association *(773)*

Clifton, Stephen
National Council of Social Security Management
Associations *(736)*

Cliggett, Lisa
Society for Economic Anthropology *(908)*

Clime, Cathleen
American Intellectual Property Law Association *(141)*

Climo, Dagmar
International Academy of Compounding Pharmacists
(509)

Cline, Andrew R.
Coleopterists Society *(362)*

Cline, Dr. Bryan
Health Information Trust Alliance (HITRUST) *(470)*

Cline, Doug
International Society of Fire Service Instructors *(572)*

Cline, Jason
Association of College Unions International *(274)*

Cline, Korenna
Convention Industry Council *(383)*

Cline, Mark
United States Superyacht Association *(999)*

Clingman, Dustin
International Game Developers Association *(548)*

Clinton, Cindy
National Show Horse Registry *(791)*

Clinton, James D.
American Association of Christian Counselors *(56)*

Clinton, Jennifer
National Council for International Visitors *(732)*

Clinton, Larry
Internet Security Alliance *(582)*

Clinton, Shundra
Council of State and Territorial Epidemiologists *(397)*

Clinton, Tim
American Association of Christian Counselors *(56)*

Close, Jeffrey S.
Society of Professional Asset-Managers and Record Keepers *(945)*

Close, Michael
Society of American Magicians *(929)*

Cloud, Deborah
LeadingAge (American Association of Homes and Services for the Aging) *(595)*

Clough, Brenda
International Cemetery, Cremation and Funeral Association *(533)*

Clough, Jonathan
International Society for Ecological Modelling-North American Chapter *(566)*

Clougherty, Jr., Chuck
International Fire Photographers Association *(545)*

Clouse, Lynn
National Association of RV Parks and Campgrounds *(692)*

Clowers, Tammy
The Retired Enlisted Association *(885)*

Clutter, Ted
Geothermal Heat Pump Consortium *(459)*

Co, Albert
Society of Rheology *(946)*

Coakley, Peggy
American Academy of Ophthalmic Executives *(37)*

Coane, RADM, Casey
Association of the United States Navy, Inc. *(314)*

Coates, CMP, Adonia C.
American Thyroid Association *(216)*

Coates, Charlotte
Cattlemen's Beef Promotion and Research Board *(346)*

Coates, Jason
Learning Resources Network *(596)*

Coates, Julie
Learning Resources Network *(596)*

Coates, Lindsay
InterAction (American Council of Voluntary International Action) *(506)*

Coates, Monica L.
Organization for International Investment *(831)*

Coates, MBA, Vivian H.
ECRI *(418)*

Cobb, Diane
Church Music Publishers Association *(356)*

Cobb, Eleanor
Fellowship of United Methodists in Music and Worship Arts *(442)*

Cobbs, Melissa
National Association of Insurance Women (International) *(676)*

Coble, Greg
American Youth Hostels, Inc (Hostelling International USA) *(222)*

Cobuluis, Karen
National Emergency Management Association *(745)*

Coburn, Michael
Research!America *(882)*

Coburn, Michael
Society of University Urologists *(949)*

Coburn, Nancy
National Shooting Sports Foundation *(791)*

Cochenour, Paulette
American Simmental Association *(179)*

Cochin, Lisa

Women's Jewelry Association *(1023)*

Cochraham, Sharon
National Pace Association *(778)*

Cochran, David W.
Manufacturing Jewelers and Suppliers of America *(604)*

Cochran, Tom
United States Conference of Mayors *(992)*

Cochran, Wanda
American Concrete Pipe Association *(106)*

Cockey, Carolyn Davis
Association of Women's Health, Obstetric and Neonatal Nurses *(318)*

Cockroft, Carolyn
International Association of Chiefs of Police *(517)*

Codding, Fred H.
National Association of Miscellaneous, Ornamental and Architectural Products Contractors *(681)*
National Council of Erectors, Fabricators and Riggers *(734)*

Codispoti, Noelle
Gamma Iota Sigma *(456)*

Codling, Racquel
Equipment Leasing and Finance Association *(432)*

Codrington, Raymond
Association of Black Anthropologists *(269)*

Cody, Alison
Manufacturers' Agents Association for the Foodservice Industry *(603)*

Cody, Leslie Quinn
American Electrology Association *(116)*

Coe, Katherine
International Bluegrass Music Association *(530)*

Coe, Priscilla
American Apitherapy Society *(46)*

Coe, Wendy
American College of Veterinary Pathologists *(104)*

Coelho, Marco
Society of International Business Fellows *(940)*

Coffelt, Ben
The Society of Wine Educators *(950)*

Coffer, Teresa
American Coal Council *(92)*

Coffey, Bonnie J
Association of Health Information Outsourcing Services *(286)*

Coffey, C. Edward
American Neuropsychiatric Association *(155)*

Coffey, MSW, PhD, Darla Spence
Council on Social Work Education *(400)*

Coffiel, Renee
Urban Financial Services Coalition *(1003)*

Coffield, Shirley A.
International Natural Sausage Casing Association *(557)*

Coffin, Linda
Association of Personal Historians *(299)*

Coffindaffer, Matthew A.
National Council of Agricultural Employers *(733)*

Coffman, David
Business Professionals of America *(339)*

Coffman, Dianne
American Gelbvieh Association *(125)*

Coffman, Jennifer
Association for Africanist Anthropology *(238)*

Coffman, Joya

Association of State and Territorial Health Officials *(310)*

Coffman, Richard
Institute of International Bankers *(501)*

Coffman, Robert
Allied Pilots Association *(26)*

Coffman-Burke, Mary
Society of Former Special Agents of the Federal Bureau of Investigation *(937)*

Cogan, Thomas
Cruise Lines International Association *(405)*

Cogburn, Chris
National Sorghum Producers *(795)*

Cohen, MD, Alan R.
The American Society of Pediatric Neurosurgeons *(206)*

Cohen, Anna
Cleveland Bay Horse Society of North America *(358)*

Cohen, Arthur
Public Radio Program Directors Association *(870)*

Cohen, Bob
Association of Private Sector Colleges and Universities (Career College Association) *(300)*

Cohen, Bruce
Inflatable Advertising Dealers Association *(494)*

Cohen, Catherine Grealy
American Academy of Ophthalmology *(37)*

Cohen, Dan
American Association for Justice *(50)*
Association of Defense Communities *(278)*

Cohen, Dasha
American Medical Informatics Association *(149)*

Cohen, David
Department for Professional Employees - AFL-CIO *(410)*

Cohen, PhD, Deb
Society for Human Resource Management *(911)*

Cohen, Dr. Elaine
United Synagogue of Conservative Judaism *(1001)*

Cohen, Elise
Technical Association of the Graphic Arts *(969)*

Cohen, Ellen L.
Association of Reproductive Health Professionals *(305)*

Cohen, Genie
International Association of Jewish Vocational Services *(523)*

Cohen, Gregory M.
American Highway Users Alliance *(131)*

Cohen, PhD, Jeff
American Men's Studies Association *(150)*

Cohen, Jeffrey E.
Federation of American Hospitals *(440)*

Cohen, CAE, Jonathan
Air Line Pilots Association International *(19)*

Cohen, PhD, RN, Joni
Alpha Tau Delta *(27)*

Cohen, Larry
Communications Workers of America *(369)*

Cohen, Margie
American Hiking Society *(131)*

Cohen, Mark
American Academy of Actuaries *(29)*

Cohen, Marsha A.
Reinsurance Association of America *(879)*

Cohen, CAE, MPA, Megan
National Association of Medical Staff Services *(645)*

Cohen, Michele
REALTORS Land Institute *(876)*

Cohen, Paul Douglas
EDA Consortium *(419)*

Cohen, Rick
National Council of Nonprofits *(735)*

Cohen, Roger
Regional Airline Association *(878)*

Cohen, Sarah
American Association for the Surgery of Trauma *(52)*

Cohen, Sheryl
American Association of Independent Music *(63)*

Cohen, Susan
NAMTA - National Art Materials Trade Association *(635)*

Cohen-Baruch, Rosalind
Business for Social Responsibility *(339)*

Cohenour, Meriruth
Pinto Horse Association of America *(848)*

Cohn, Andy
American Association of Pharmaceutical Scientists *(68)*

Cohn, Cindy
Specialty Coffee Association of America *(957)*

Cohn, Donna
International Imaging Industry Association *(551)*

Cohn, Karen
American Advertising Federation *(43)*

Cohn, Natalie
Craft & Hobby Association *(402)*

Cohn, Sarah
Visitor Studies Association *(1010)*

Cohon, Charles
Manufacturers' Agents National Association *(603)*

Cohoon, Nikkita
National Society of Insurance Premium Auditors *(794)*

Cohrssen, Noah
Manufacturers Alliance/MAPI Inc. *(603)*

Coin, Richard E.
American Automotive Policy Council *(78)*

Cojescu, Lucian
PROMAX/BDA *(866)*

Cokely, PhD, Carol
Academy of Rehabilitative Audiology *(8)*

Coker, Carolyn
Associated General Contractors of America (AGC) *(236)*

Cokley, Nicole
Black Retail Action Group *(332)*

Colabaugh, Kathy
Robotics and Automation Society *(887)*

Colacci, Josephine
International Association of Healthcare Central Service Materiel Management *(522)*

Colamarino, Rob
Minor League Baseball *(617)*
National Association of Professional Baseball Leagues *(686)*

Colas (IBFNA), Dr. Ralph G.
American Council of Christian Churches *(109)*

Colberg, Amy C.
Brain Injury Association of America *(334)*

Colbert, Debra
Waterways Council, Inc. *(1014)*

Colbert, Holly
National Insulation Association *(766)*

Colbourne, William J.
Blue Cross Blue Shield Association *(332)*

Colburn, Jeff
Council of Manufacturing Associations *(395)*
National Association of Manufacturers *(679)*

Colburn, Loren
Association of Free Community Papers *(284)*

Colburn, Martin P.
Financial Industry Regulatory Authority (FINRA) *(444)*

Colby, Kim
Christian Legal Society *(356)*

Colby, Ralph H.
Society of Rheology *(946)*

Cole, Ashley
American Horse Council *(133)*

Cole, Betty
Women's Business Enterprise National Council *(1022)*

Cole, Christopher
Medieval Academy of America *(612)*

Cole, Dawn
Custom Electronic Design and Installation Association *(405)*

Cole, Diana
USA Volleyball *(1005)*

Cole, Donald W.
Organization Development Institute *(830)*

Cole, Jeffrey M.
Academy of General Dentistry *(5)*

Cole, John
Association of American Editorial Cartoonists *(264)*

Cole, Jon A.
Poultry Science Association *(854)*

Cole, Kenneth T.
National Guild for Community Arts Education *(757)*

Cole, Kevin
International Surface Fabricators Association *(576)*

Cole, Liz
International Council of Fine Arts Deans *(538)*

Cole, Melissa
Foster Family-Based Treatment Association *(452)*

Cole, Paul
American Institute of Building Design *(137)*

Cole, DDS, Stacy V.
American Academy of Craniofacial Pain *(32)*

Cole, Wendy
National Association of Realtors *(690)*

Colee, Missy
Society of Biblical Literature *(931)*

Colein, Carol
American Society of Irrigation Consultants *(201)*

Colella, Stephen
Literary Managers and Dramaturgs of the Americas *(599)*

Colello, Maryteresa
Interstate Renewable Energy Council *(583)*

Coleman, Byers W.
State Guard Association of the United States *(961)*

Coleman, Carolyn M.
National League of Cities *(768)*

Coleman, Clare
National Family Planning and Reproductive Health Association *(747)*

Coleman, David
The College Board *(363)*

Coleman, Dorothy
National Association of Manufacturers *(679)*

Coleman, Douglas
Linguistic Association of Canada and the United States *(598)*

Coleman, CAE, Jacquelyn T.
American Academy of Psychiatry and the Law *(41)*
American Academy of Psychoanalysis and Dynamic Psychiatry *(41)*

Coleman, Jai
Association for Facilities Engineering *(246)*

Coleman, Kelly
Ocean Stewards Institute *(826)*

Coleman, Lillian
Association for Education in Journalism and Mass Communication *(245)*

Coleman, Litika
Association for Information Systems *(250)*

Coleman, Michael
Association of the United States Army *(313)*

Coleman, Mindy L.
The Jockeys' Guild *(588)*

Coleman, Natalie
International Association of Electrical Inspectors *(520)*

Coleman, Pamela
National Association of Real Estate Investment Trusts (NAREIT) *(690)*

Coleman, Richard
Space Transportation Association *(953)*

Coleman, Rita M.
Warehousing Education and Research Council *(1012)*

Coleman-Bach, Yvonne
National Newspaper Publishers Association *(775)*

Coles, Adrienne
AFT Healthcare *(15)*

Coles, Leslie
National Coalition of Girls' Schools *(723)*

Colestock, Regan
Association of American University Presses *(267)*

Colfelt, Jennifer
Private Equity Growth Capital Council *(858)*

Colgan, Robert
National Electrical Contractors Association *(744)*

Colin, Benoit
Electric Drive Transportation Association *(421)*

Colker, Ryan
Sustainable Buildings Industry Council *(967)*

Collado, III, Emilio G.
American Watch Association *(219)*

Collamore, Thomas
American National Chamber of Commerce *(154)*

Collamore, Thomas J.
United States Chamber of Commerce *(991)*

Collatz, Mark
Adhesive and Sealant Council *(12)*

Collet, Cathy
Livestock Marketing Association *(599)*

Collette, Robert L.
Institute of Shortening and Edible Oils *(503)*

Colley, Dennis J.
Fibre Box Association *(443)*

Collier, Arlene
Joint Electron Device Engineering Council *(589)*

Collier, Claybrook

Cable & Telecommunications Association for Marketing **(340)**

Collier, Jamus
The Integrated Ocean Drilling Program **(505)**

Collier, Sandra
Intelligent Transportation Society of America **(506)**

Collier, Trish
National Association of College and University Food Services **(655)**

Colliet, Marvel
Interstate Natural Gas Association of America **(583)**

Colligan, Caitlin
PCIA - The Wireless Infrastructure Association **(840)**

Colligan, Caitlin
PCIA - The Wireless Infrastructure Association **(840)**

Collin, Barry C.
Sigma Xi, The Scientific Research Society **(899)**

Collina, Tom
Arms Control Association **(229)**

Collings, Patrick
National Corrugated Steel Pipe Association **(730)**

Collins, Blaine
Norwegian-American Chamber of Commerce **(824)**

Collins, Bob
APICS The Association for Operations Management **(224)**

Collins, Bridget
American Kinesiotherapy Association **(144)**

Collins, Cara
Electrical Generating Systems Association **(422)**

Collins, Christie
American Concrete Pumping Association **(106)**

Collins, Dan
American Public Communications Council **(170)**

Collins, David
International Association for Mathematical Geosciences **(513)**

Collins, Gail
CCIM Institute **(347)**

Collins, Ginger
National Association of Document Examiners **(663)**

Collins, Jeniffer
Georgia Charter Schools Association **(459)**

Collins, Jim
Southeastern Livestock Network **(953)**

Collins, John
American Society of Crime Laboratory Directors **(196)**

Collins, John H.
American Welara Pony Registry **(220)**

Collins, Julie
American Association for Laboratory Accreditation **(50)**

Collins, Kim
Wilderness Education Association **(1017)**

Collins, Lee
The Coalition of Airline Pilots Associations **(360)**

Collins, Linda J.
Insurance Marketing Communications Association **(505)**

Collins, Mary Beth
American College of Emergency Physicians **(95)**

Collins, Mary M.
Broadcast Cable Credit Association **(335)**
Media Financial Management Association **(610)**

Collins, Meg

Council of American Survey Research Organizations **(392)**

Collins, Mimi
National Association of Colleges and Employers **(655)**

Collins, Patricia
Equipment Marketing and Distribution Association **(432)**

Collins, Penny
Fleet Reserve Association **(447)**

Collins, Polly
National Society of Professional Engineers **(794)**

Collins, Richard
American College of Clinical Pharmacy **(94)**

Collins, Samuel
Society for the Anthropology of Work **(923)**

Collins, Stu
United Transportation Union **(1001)**

Collins, Travis
American Concrete Pumping Association **(106)**

Collison, Jim
Employers of America **(427)**

Collison, Rita Haxmeier
Employers of America **(427)**

Collot, Mélanie
Global Acetate Manufacturers Association **(461)**

Colloton, OP, Rev. Paul H.
National Association of Pastoral Musicians **(683)**

Collura, Barbara
Resolve, The National Infertility Association **(883)**

Collyer, Emilio
International Gay and Lesbian Travel Association **(548)**

Colman, Jennifer
Automotive Trade Association Executives **(324)**

Colman, Pam Colman
Society of Nuclear Medicine **(943)**

Colombini, Ken
National Corn Growers Association **(730)**

Colon, Clara
Loan Syndication & Trading Association **(599)**

Colon, Susan Esprella
National Contract Management Association **(729)**

Colot, Ginette C
Aerospace Industries Association of America **(14)**

Colquhoun, Marcia
American Crystallographic Association **(112)**

Colson, Karen
Association for Research in Vision and Ophthalmology **(255)**

Colson, Lillian
Inland Marine Underwriters Association **(496)**

Colucci, Marlene M.
American Hotel & Lodging Association (AH&LA) **(134)**

Columbaro, Norina
ASM International **(232)**

Columbel, Jennifer
National Association of Drug Court Professionals **(663)**

Colvard, Jean
American Society of Clinical Oncology **(194)**

Colville, Mary
National Chicken Council **(720)**

Colville, Stephen A.
International Association of Drilling Contractors **(519)**

Comber, Dean
Association of Real Estate License Law Officials **(305)**

Combes, Eva
IPC Washington Office **(585)**

Combest, CAE, Hannes
National Auctioneers Association **(711)**

Combest, Hon. Larry
Cotton Warehouse Association of America **(387)**

Combs, Dorothy K.
American Institute of Professional Geologists **(140)**

Combs, Kathleen
Association for Library and Information Science Education **(251)**
Medical Library Association **(611)**

Combs, Kathy
Academy of Veterinary Homeopathy **(9)**

Combs, Nancye
Heating, Airconditioning and Refrigeration Distributors International **(473)**

Comeaux, David
Academy of Hospitality Industry Attorneys **(5)**

Comer, Edward H.
Edison Electric Institute **(419)**

Comer, Jennifer L.
Workers' Injury Law and Advocacy Group **(1025)**

Comer, Stan
American Chianina Association **(90)**

Comerford, Meagan
American Pediatric Surgical Association **(162)**
Society of Vertebrate Paleontology **(950)**

Comfort, Marguerite
American College Personnel Association **(105)**

Comi, Francine
American Thoracic Society **(216)**

Comi, Tom
Self Storage Association **(896)**

Comiono, Dave
Crane Manufacturers Association of America **(403)**

Compart, Erika Pontarelli
Public Affairs Council **(868)**

Compeau, Larry D.
Society for Consumer Psychology **(907)**

Compton, Kathy
The American Institute of Architects **(137)**

Comstock, Greg
Red Angus Association of America **(877)**

Comstock, W. Stephen
American Society of Heating, Refrigerating and Air Conditioning Engineers (ASHRAE) **(199)**

Conaghan, Jim
Newspaper Association of America **(810)**

Conahan, Margot Sutton
Association of College and Research Libraries **(273)**

Conard, Linda
National Association of Student Financial Aid Administrators **(703)**

Conatser, Glenn
National Swine Improvement Federation **(798)**

Concepcion, Danilo B.
Council of Nephrology Nurses and Technicians **(396)**

Concio, Jose L.
Periodical and Book Association of America **(842)**

Condon, Edward
National Head Start Association **(758)**

Condon, Kimberly J.
Product Liability Advisory Council **(859)**

Condon, Mark

Credit Union National Association, Inc. *(404)*

Coneset, Phyllis
Institute of Real Estate Management *(503)*

Conetsco, Cherlynn
International Association of Protocol Consultants *(527)*

Coneys, Robert
American College of Foot & Ankle Orthopedics & Medicine *(95)*
Society for Radiation Oncology Administration *(919)*

Congdon, Geraldine
Surface Design Association *(966)*

Congdon, Stephen
Consumer Bankers Association *(380)*

Conheady, Mark
AABB - American Association of Blood Banks *(1)*

Conis, Kym
Foil and Specialty Effects Association *(448)*

Conklin, Charlie
United States Trout Farmers Association *(1000)*

Conklin, Henry
All-America Rose Selections *(22)*

Conklin, Jackie
Interlocking Concrete Pavement Institute *(508)*

Conklin, Lita M.
Cigar Association of America, Inc. *(356)*

Conklin, Shelley
Non Commissioned Officers Association (NCOA) *(811)*

Conlan, Mike
National Community Pharmacists Association *(725)*

Conley, Kevin
National Recreation and Parks Association *(784)*

Conley, Sharon
National Association of School Nurses *(693)*

Conley, PhD, Stephen
American School Health Association *(177)*

Conley, Suzanne
International Pediatric Nephrology Association *(559)*

Conley, Tom
High Point Market *(474)*

Conlin, Sue
Therapeutic Touch International Association *(973)*

Conlon, Joe
American Mosquito Control Association *(153)*

Conlon, Peggy
Advertising Council *(13)*

Conn, Jacki
ARMA International *(228)*

Conneely, Nancy
National Association of State Directors of Career Technical Education Consortium *(699)*

Connel, Shari
National Sorghum Producers *(795)*

Connell, Barbara
American Society for Gastrointestinal Endoscopy *(184)*

Connell, Gordon
American Boat Builders and Repairers Association *(84)*

Connell, Julia
American Art Therapy Association, Inc. *(46)*

Connelly, David M.
Open Applications Group *(828)*

Connelly, Gail
National Association of Elementary School Principals *(664)*

Connelly, John P.

National Fisheries Institute *(751)*

Connelly, Tracey DePellegrin
Genetics Society of America *(458)*

Conner, April
Academy of Model Aeronautics *(7)*

Conner, Baird
International Engraved Graphics Association *(543)*

Conner, Charles F.
National Council of Farmer Cooperatives *(734)*

Conner, Cristin
American Paint Horse Association *(161)*

Conner, Cynthia
American Health Lawyers Association *(130)*

Conner, David Michael
Association of Community College Trustees *(276)*

Conner, Diane
Association of Genetic Technologists *(285)*
National Association of EMS Physicians *(665)*

Conner, Don
National Wood Flooring Association *(805)*

Conner, Roger
Catholic Charities USA *(345)*

Conners, MBA, John
United Development Council *(986)*

Conners, Rosalind
Association for Research on Nonprofit Organizations and Voluntary Action *(255)*

Connolly, Peter
American Federation of Police and Concerned Citizens *(119)*
National Association of Chiefs of Police *(653)*

Connolly, PA, Suzanne H.
National Association for Program Information and Performance Measurement *(641)*

Connor, Michael
National Association of Criminal Defense Lawyers *(661)*

Connors, Jennifer
Acute Long Term Hospital Association *(12)*

Connors, Jerry
The United States Harness Writers' Association *(994)*

Connors, Jerry C.
Data Interchange Standards Association *(407)*

Connors, Nancy
American College of Physicians Services, Inc. *(101)*

Connors, Patrick
PeerSpan *(840)*

Connors, Stacy
Iroquois Healthcare Alliance *(585)*

Connors, Susan H
Brain Injury Association of America *(334)*

Conrad, ChFC, Donna
Society of Financial Service Professionals *(936)*

Conrad, Doug
Association of Destination Management Executives *(278)*
National Association of Nephrology Technologists and Technicians *(682)*

Conrad, John Fuher
Growth Energy *(466)*

Conrad, Ken
National Restaurant Association *(786)*

Conrad, Kraig
National Investor Relations Institute *(767)*

Conrad, Patricia

National Interscholastic Athletic Administrators Association *(766)*

Conrad, Shawn D.
International Parking Institute *(559)*

Conrardy, Chris
Edison Welding Institute *(419)*

Conroy, Kathy
National Association of Theatre Owners *(706)*

Conschafter, Michael
Aerospace Industries Association of America *(14)*

Constantine, George
Bicycle Product Suppliers Association *(329)*

Constantine, Jan F.
Authors Guild *(320)*

Constantine, Joanne
American Academy of Physical Medicine and Rehabilitation *(40)*

Constantinidis, Sylvia
National Association of Composers, USA *(657)*

Contardo, Jeanne B.
Business Higher Education Forum *(339)*

Conte, Simon
The American Bar Association Rule of Law Initiative *(80)*

Contento, DPM, Kirk M.
Federation of Podiatric Medical Boards *(442)*

Conti, Michael Robert
National Association of Composers, USA *(657)*

Conti, Nick
American Antiquarian Society *(45)*

Contre, Amy
National Bulk Vendors Association *(716)*

Contreras, Geraldine
Association of Latino Professionals in Finance and Accounting *(291)*

Contreras, Paul
American Glovebox Society *(126)*

Converse, Jim
American Bearing Manufacturers Association *(80)*

Converse, Susan
Television Bureau of Advertising *(971)*

Conway, Anne
Television Bureau of Advertising *(971)*

Conway, Anthony W.
Alliance of Nonprofit Mailers *(25)*

Conway, CADC, CPT, Catherine
National Association for Poetry Therapy *(641)*

Conway, Jane
American Urological Association *(218)*

Conway, OTR, Shaun
National Board for Certification in Occupational Therapy, Inc. *(715)*

Conway, CPA, MBA, Thomas
American Society of Anesthesiologists *(192)*

Conyers, Debbie
Electronic Components Industry Association *(423)*

Conyers, Jessica
International Association for Continuing Education and Training *(511)*

Conzelman, James K.
The Ripon Society *(886)*

Coogan, Lee
Gridwise Alliance *(466)*
Sorptive Minerals Institute *(952)*

Coogler, L. Scott

Federal Judges Association *(439)*

Cook, Amanda
Corporate Housing Providers Association *(386)*

Cook, Betty
Music Industry Conference *(622)*
The National Association for Music Education
   (Formerly MENC) *(641)*

Cook, Billy D.
Institute for Professionals in Taxation *(497)*

Cook, Bob
American Association of Christian Counselors *(56)*

Cook, Darel
Promotional Products Association International *(867)*

Cook, Erin
International Interior Design Association *(552)*

Cook, Glenn
National School Boards Association *(789)*

Cook, Gloria
American Oil Chemists' Society *(157)*

Cook, Jacqui
American Chamber of Commerce Executives *(89)*

Cook, James
Certified Claims Professional Accreditation Council
   (349)

Cook, Jeff
American Psychological Association Practice
   Organization *(170)*

Cook, Ken
National Association of Service Managers *(695)*

Cook, Kim
National Speakers Association *(795)*

Cook, CAE, Kris
National Affordable Housing Management Association
   (629)

Cook, Leslie
Help Desk Institute *(474)*

Cook, Marion
College of American Pathologists *(363)*

Cook, Mark
Tire Industry Association *(975)*

Cook, Melinda
National Operating Committee for Standards of
   Athletic Equipment *(776)*

Cook, Paula
Society of Certified Insurance Counselors *(932)*

Cook, PhD, Sue
Ocean Research & Conservation Association *(826)*

Cook, Timothy P.
Independent Community Bankers of America *(488)*

Cook, Tom M.
National Renderers Association *(786)*

Cook, Tracey
International Sign Association *(564)*

Cook, William J.
American Geophysical Union *(126)*

Cooke, Eileen
American College of Neuropsychopharmacology *(98)*

Cooke, Paula
American Society of Cataract and Refractive Surgery
   (194)

Cooke, Tina
American Society of Professional Estimators *(208)*

Cooksey, John
World Aquaculture Society *(1025)*

Cooley, Cheryl L.

American Society of Farm Managers and Rural
   Appraisers *(197)*

Cooley, Gail
Dangerous Goods Advisory Council *(407)*

Cooley, Harriet
Towing and Recovery Association of America *(976)*

Cooley, PhD, Laura
American Academy on Communication in Healthcare
   (43)

Coolsen, Peter
National Association for Court Management *(637)*

Coombs, Gary
Organizational Behavior Teaching Society *(832)*

Coon, Janice
National Grocers Association *(756)*

Coon, Sue
Women in Aviation International *(1020)*

Cooney, Brian D.
Independent Community Bankers of America *(488)*

Cooney, Kevin
American Schools of Oriental Research *(177)*

Coons, Gerry
Outdoor Power Equipment Aftermarket Association
   (835)

Coons, Julie
Electronic Retailing Association *(423)*

Coons, Nancy
Retail Packaging Manufacturers Association *(885)*

Coontz, Diane
Association of State and Territorial Health Officials
   (310)

Cooper, Adreanne
The ERISA Industry Committee (ERIC) *(433)*

Cooper, Alexander
International Association of Forensic Nurses *(521)*

Cooper, DDS, Barry
International College of Cranio-Mandibular
   Orthopedics *(535)*

Cooper, Becky
National Collegiate Athletic Association *(724)*

Cooper, Ben
Gospel Music Association *(464)*

Cooper, Beverly
Armed Forces Communications and Electronics
   Association *(228)*

Cooper, Cardell
National Community Development Association *(725)*

Cooper, Claude
Association of Major City and County Building Officials
   (292)

Cooper, Creig
International Association of Administrative
   Professionals *(515)*

Cooper, Dwanna
American Society of Radiologic Technologists *(208)*

Cooper, Geoff
Renewable Fuels Association *(881)*

Cooper, Greg
Special Interest Group on Software Engineering *(956)*

Cooper, CST, Dr. H.H.A.
Academy of Security Educators and Trainers *(9)*

Cooper, Dr. Howard
The American Society of Forensic Odontology *(198)*

Cooper, Janet
Radiological Society of North America *(873)*

Cooper, Jenelle
National Association of School Nurses *(693)*

Cooper, Jennifer
National Indian Health Board *(763)*

Cooper, Jerry L.
Assisted Living Federation of America *(234)*

Cooper, Joann
National Finance Adjusters *(750)*

Cooper, Kevin
Helicopter Association International *(473)*

Cooper, Kiwani
Association for Healthcare Volunteer Resource
   Professionals *(248)*

Cooper, Linda
American Student Dental Association *(214)*

Cooper, Matt
National Association of Graduate-Professional
   Students *(670)*

Cooper, Melissa
Professional Housing Management Association *(862)*

Cooper, Mike
National Plant Board *(781)*

Cooper, Nancy H.
National Association of Bankruptcy Trustees *(647)*

Cooper, Paige
Professional Tennis Registry *(865)*

Cooper, Patricia
Satellite Industry Association *(891)*

Cooper, Ray
Association of Firearm and Toolmark Examiners *(283)*

Cooper, Robin
National Association of State Directors of
   Developmental Disabilities Services, Inc. *(700)*

Cooper, Roger B.
American Gas Association *(124)*

Cooper, Scott P.
American National Standards Institute *(154)*

Cooper, Stephanie
National Association of Clean Air Agencies *(654)*

Cooper, Thomas A.
International Anesthesia Research Society *(511)*

Cooper, Tina
American Indian Higher Education Consortium *(135)*

Cooper, Vikki
American Counseling Association *(111)*

Coorsh, Richard P.
Federation of American Hospitals *(440)*

Cope, PE, PhD, Anne D.
Institute for Business & Home Safety *(496)*

Cope, Emily
Air and Waste Management Association *(17)*

Cope, Jessica
National Grange *(756)*

Copeland, Dannell
National AMBUCS, Inc *(633)*

Copeland, Eve
United States-Israel Science & Technology Foundation
   (USISTF) *(995)*

Copeland, J. Joseph
National AMBUCS *(633)*
National AMBUCS, Inc *(633)*

Copeland, Lisa
NACE International *(623)*

Coplan, Jodi
CCIM Institute *(347)*

Coppa, Mark
BICSI *(329)*

Coppage, Edna
National Wooden Pallet and Container Association
(805)

Copperwheat, Gabrielle
Association for Convention Marketing Executives *(244)*
North American Association of Commencement
Officers *(813)*

Coppess, James Bryan
AFL-CIO (American Federation of Labor and Congress
of Industrial Organizations) *(14)*

Coppock, Daren
Agricultural Retailers Association *(16)*

Coppola, Mary T.
Healthcare Distribution Management Association *(471)*

Copps, Mike
Healthcare Supply Chain Association *(472)*

Copps, Mike
National Association of Healthcare Access
Management *(671)*

Copus, Josh
National Association of Workforce Boards (NAWB)
(710)

Corallo, Debbie
The Railway Tie Association *(874)*

Corathers, Donald A.
Educational Theatre Association *(420)*

Coratolo, Giovanni
United States Chamber of Commerce *(991)*

Corb, Benjamin
American Society for Biochemistry and Molecular
Biology *(181)*

Corbet, Aaron
National Association of Farm Broadcasting *(667)*

Corbett, Justin R.
National Association for Community Mediation *(637)*

Corbett, Mollie
Society of Gastroenterology Nurses and Associates
(937)

Corbin, Heather
International Public Management Association for
Human Resources *(562)*

Corbin, Kimberly
National Black MBA Association *(714)*

Corbin, CAE, Lauren
Association of Private Sector Colleges and Universities
(Career College Association) *(300)*

Corbin, Robert
Council of Industrial Boiler Owners (CIBO) *(394)*

Corby, Joseph
Association of Food and Drug Officials *(283)*

Corcoran, Carol
Ladies Professional Golf Association *(592)*

Corcoran, Cassie
National Association of Dental Laboratories *(662)*

Corcoran, Darcy
Independent Sector *(491)*

Corcoran, James P.
Global Offset and Countertrade Association (GOCA)
(462)

Corcoran, Jennifer
National Association of Insurance and Financial
Advisors *(675)*

Corcoran, Joanne
National Association of Subrogation Professionals
(704)

Corcoran, John J.
Construction Industry CPAs/Consultants Association
(379)

Corcoran, Kate E.
Medical Library Association *(611)*

Corcoran, Kevin P.
Eye Bank Association of America *(436)*

Corcoran, Leila
Women Chefs and Restaurateurs *(1020)*

Corcoran, Patrick
National Association of Theatre Owners *(706)*

Cordie, Michele
American Society for Therapeutic Radiology and
Oncology *(190)*

Cordle, Adam Paul
American Viola Society *(219)*

Coren, Emily
Guild of Natural Science Illustrators *(467)*

Coren, Pat
American Littoral Society *(146)*

Corey, Lindsey
National Rural Health Association *(788)*

Corey Henry, Corey
National Yogurt Association *(806)*

Corkern, Patricia
American Recovery Association *(174)*

Corkran, Anne-Marie
American Bankruptcy Institute *(79)*

Corkrey, Meaghan
Professional Insurance Marketing Association *(862)*

Corlew, Ed
Pulp and Paper Safety Association *(871)*

Corley, Alison
International Association of Professional Security
Consultants *(527)*

Corley, Joel
Building Owners and Managers Association
International *(337)*

Corley, Tim
Alliance of Professional Tattooists *(25)*

Cormany, Dennis
Promotional Products Association International *(867)*

Cornelious, Melvin
National United Merchants Beverage Association *(803)*

Cornelius, Debbie
National Chimney Sweep Guild *(721)*

Cornell, Elisabeth
Strategic Account Management Association *(963)*

Cornell, Mary Beth
Technical Association of the Pulp and Paper Industry
(970)

Corner, Frances Clay
American Academy of Equine Art *(33)*

Cornett, Doris
American Jail Association *(142)*

Cornett, Mary Pat
American Academy of Otolaryngology-Head and Neck
Surgery *(39)*

Cornett, Troy L.
American Society of Pension Professionals & Actuaries
(206)

Corngold, Sally Marshall
Optometric Extension Program Foundation *(830)*

Cornish, Jeff
World Future Society *(1026)*

Cornish, Kent
National Alliance of State Broadcast Associations *(633)*

Cornwell, Alexandra
International Microwave Power Institute *(556)*

Coronado, David L.
Association of American Geographers *(265)*

Corpora, Cindy
National Association of Colleges and Employers *(655)*

Corr, Debbie
Alliance for Gray Market and Counterfeit Abatement
(23)

Corr, Patrick
Specialized Carriers and Rigging Association *(957)*

Corral, Gus
Government Finance Officers Association of the United
States and Canada *(464)*
Government Finance Officers Association, Federal
Liaison Center *(464)*

Correa, A.C.
Association for Arid Lands Studies *(239)*

Correll, Krystle
Society of Toxicologic Pathology *(948)*

Correll, Randall
American Astronautical Society *(77)*

Correll, Rich A.
College of Healthcare Information Management
Executives *(364)*

Corrigan, Karen
Professional Women Photographers *(866)*

Corrigan, Susan
American Art Therapy Association, Inc. *(46)*

Corro, Victor Miguel
World Council of Credit Unions, Inc. *(1026)*

Corry, Jannise
National Retail Federation *(786)*

Corry, Jannise
Association for Retail Technology Standards *(256)*

Corso, Ronald A.
United States Society on Dams *(999)*

Corson, Christopher T.
International Association of Machinists and Aerospace
Workers *(524)*

Corson, David
Association of Science-Technology Centers *(307)*

Cortelyou, Curtis
Foundation for Russian-American Economic
Cooperation *(453)*

Cortez, Kathy
Infectious Diseases Society of America *(494)*

Cortijo, Gemma
The Spain-United States Chamber of Commerce *(953)*

Cortina, Elise
National Yogurt Association *(806)*

Cortina, Elise
Frozen Potato Products Institute *(454)*

Cortina, Thomas A.
Halon Alternatives Research Corporation *(468)*

Cortis, Cynthia
International Society of Transport Aircraft Trading
(574)
The Association for Nursing Professional Development
(252)

Corts, Dr. Paul R.
Council for Christian Colleges and Universities *(389)*

Cortsen, Marie
Society for Medical Decision Making *(915)*

Corwin, Philip S.
Internet Commerce Association (f/k/a Internet Traffic Association) (582)

Corzine, Kenneth
National Cutting Horse Association (741)

Coscetta, Holly
National Conference of CPA Practitioners (727)

Cosdon, Mark
American Theatre and Drama Society (216)

Cosens, Carrie
Airborne Law Enforcement Association (19)

Cosgrove, Kathleen
Club Managers Association of America (359)

Cosgrove, Lindsey
National Guild for Community Arts Education (757)

Cosic, Mejrima-Mary
Academy of Aphasia (4)

Cosme, Manuel
United States Hispanic Chamber of Commerce (995)

Costa, Charles A.
Association of Former OSI Special Agents (284)

Costa, Frank
American Institute of Marine Underwriters (139)

Costa, Wesley
Life Insurance Settlement Association (597)

Costantin, Sandra
International Nanny Association (557)

Costanzo, Brian
Entrepreneurs' Organization (430)

Costas, Peter L.
International Precious Metals Institute (561)

Costello, Eileen
Catalogue Raisonne Scholars Association (344)

Costello, Frank J.
MPA - The Association of Magazine Media (620)

Costello, Ginny
International Housewares Association (550)

Costello, Jennifer
American Institute of Ultrasound in Medicine (141)

Costello, Lisa
American Hotel & Lodging Association (AH&LA) (134)

Costello, Megan
Association of Corporate Travel Executives (ACTE) (277)

Costello, Patti
American Society for Healthcare Environmental Services (185)

Coster, PhD, RPh, John M.
Generic Pharmaceutical Association (458)

Costigan, Andy
Association of Catholic Colleges and Universities (271)

Costin, Terry
Credit Union National Association, Inc. (404)

Costolanski, Peter
National Association of Resource Conservation and Development Councils (691)

Cot, Raj
The Aviation Security Services Association (324)

Cota, Tammy
Internet Alliance (582)

Cote, Andre F.
Enterprise Wireless Alliance (429)

Cote, Charles
Pharmaceutical Care Management Association (844)

Cote, Keri
International Carwash Association (533)

Cote, Theresa
National Association of Educational Office Professionals (664)

Cothern, Judy
American Accounting Association (43)

Cothran, Somerlyn
National Stripper Well Association (797)

Cothrun, Keith
American Association of Teachers of German (74)

Cotter, Christine
American Society of Psychoanalytic Physicians (208)

Cotter, David
Textile Care Allied Trades Association (972)

Cotter, Kathy
Material Handling Equipment Distributors Association (608)

Cottingham, Christine
Measurement, Control and Automation Association (609)

Cottler, PhD, Linda B.
American Psychopathological Association (170)

Cotton, Dell
Peanut Growers Cooperative Marketing Association (840)

Cotton-Murphy, J. Elizabeth
National Conference of Commissioners on Uniform State Laws (727)

Cottrell, Charles
North American Insulation Manufacturers Association (817)

Cottrell, CAE, Cookie
Generic Pharmaceutical Association (458)

Cottrell, Nina
Council of Residential Specialists (396)

Couch, Kristin
Association for Convention Marketing Executives (244)

Couch, Roberta (BJ)
Association for Hospital Medical Education (249)

Couch, Ryan
The International Childbirth Education Association (534)

Couch, Steve
International Plant Nutrition Institute (560)

Coufal, Nancy
American Highland Cattle Association (131)

Coughlin, Carol
National Association of Tower Erectors (706)

Coughlin, Kathy
Network of Executive Women in Hospitality (808)

Coulson, Mike
American Public Human Services Association (171)

Counce, Jeannie
National Home Infusion Association (760)

Counter, Kate
Society for Range Management (920)
Weed Science Society of America (1014)

Counts, Andy
American Home Furnishings Alliance (132)
Furniture Manufacturers Alliance (454)

Counts, Heather
American Chianina Association (90)

Coupe, Brian
National Association of Service Providers in Private Rehabilitation (695)
National Rehabilitation Association (785)

Courchaine, Lynn
Association for Management Information in Financial Services (251)

Courrier, Kathleen
American Institutes for Research (141)

Courtemanche, Dan
Major League Soccer (601)

Courter, Carol
The Conference Board (374)

Courter, Carrie
Air Traffic Control Association (19)

Courtney, PhD, John E.
American Society for Nutrition (187)

Courtney, Kurt
American Apparel & Footwear Association (46)

Courtright, Henry A.
Electric Power Research Institute (421)

Cousens, M. Bonnie
Society for Humanistic Judaism (912)

Cousin, CPA, MBA, James L.
Association of periOperative Registered Nurses (299)

Cousin, Lavinia
National Association of Women Judges (710)

Cousins, Mary
National Housing Conference (761)

Coussens, Paul
American Association of Veterinary Immunologists (76)

Cout, Jennifer
Defense Research Institute (408)

Coutinho, PhD, Savia A.
POPAI The Global Association for Marketing at Retail (852)

Couto, Jennifer
Energy Solutions Center (428)

Coutu, Mike
Associated Luxury Hotels International (236)

Couture, CPCM, Neal J.
National Contract Management Association (729)

Covall, Mark J.
National Association of Psychiatric Health Systems (688)

Cove, Brian P.
Commercial Finance Association (366)

Cove, Tom
Soccer Industry Council of America (902)
Sports and Fitness Industry Association (959)

Cover, Joni
National Alliance of State Pharmacy Associations (633)

Coverstone, Jacob
International Society for Magnetic Resonance in Medicine (567)

Covert, Dick
Master Pools Guild, Inc. (608)

Covert, Kim
International Association of Women Police (529)

Covert, Larry
American Society of Association Executives-The Center for Association Leadership (193)

Covert, Stephanie L.
Object Management Group (825)

Coviello, Mike
National Fraternal Order of Police (753)

Covington, Brian
The National Flute Association, Inc. (751)

Covino, Susan

Association for Demand Response & Smart Grid **(244)**

Cowan, Anne
Cable & Telecommunications Association for
Marketing **(340)**

Cowan, Kathy
National Association of School Psychologists **(693)**

Cowan, Kristor W.
American Federation of Teachers (AFL-CIO) **(120)**

Cowan, Lancey
Association for Research in Vision and Ophthalmology
(255)

Cowan, Melissa
Billiard Congress of America **(329)**

Cowden, Joseph L.
National Automobile Dealers Association **(711)**

Cowden, Shawn
National Association of Elevator Contractors **(665)**

Cowen, Bill
Society of Cosmetic Chemists **(934)**

Cowen, Caitlin
Association of Avian Veterinarians **(268)**

Cowen, Debbie
Association of Avian Veterinarians **(268)**

Cowger, Lexie
American Institute of Ultrasound in Medicine **(141)**

Cowl, MD, MS, Clayton T.
Civil Aviation Medical Association **(357)**

Cowles, Richard
Business Professionals of America **(339)**

Cownie, Frank
ICLEI - Local Governments for Sustainability **(482)**

Cox, Alison
Contact Lens Society of America **(382)**

Cox, Annie
Academy for Eating Disorders **(3)**

Cox, ELS, PhD, Audra E.
American Society for Investigative Pathology **(186)**
Association for Molecular Pathology **(252)**

Cox, Chris
American Association of Cosmetology Schools **(59)**

Cox, Christopher W.
National Rifle Association of America **(787)**

Cox, Ciarra
Voluntary Protection Programs Participants'
Association, Inc. **(1011)**

Cox, ABPP, PhD, David R.
American Board of Professional Psychology **(83)**

Cox, Deborah
National Association of Development Organizations
(662)

Cox, Erica Smedley
Construction Specifications Institute **(380)**

Cox, J. David
American Federation of Government Employees **(119)**

Cox, Jerry W.
Dangerous Goods Advisory Council **(407)**
Steel Shipping Container Institute **(963)**

Cox, Jim
American Association of Cosmetology Schools **(59)**

Cox, Jim
National Biosolids Partnership **(713)**

Cox, John
International Fragrance Association North America
(547)

Cox, John H.

Flavor and Extract Manufacturers Association (446)

Cox, Joseph J.
Chamber of Shipping of America **(351)**

Cox, Kathy
Women Band Directors International **(1020)**

Cox, Kelley
United States Chamber of Commerce **(991)**

Cox, Lisa
National Association of Federal Credit Unions **(667)**

Cox, Mary Elise
Association of Energy Engineers **(280)**

Cox, Merrilee
Society for Features Journalism **(909)**

Cox, Molly
Direct Selling Association **(413)**

Cox, Phil
Republican Governors Association **(881)**

Cox, Phyllis
National Tractor Parts Dealer Association **(801)**

Cox, Sharon
Flexographic Technical Association **(447)**

Cox, CPA, Thomas V.
Intelligent Transportation Society of America **(506)**

Cox-Black, Lisa
Allergy and Asthma Network Mothers of Asthmatics
(22)

Coy, Jennifer
National Contract Management Association **(729)**

Coy, Ulmer "Steven"
The Travel Institute **(979)**

Coyle, Dennis
Association of Professional Researchers for
Advancement **(302)**
Clinical Laboratory Management Association **(358)**
Decorative Plumbing and Hardware Association **(408)**
ISEH Society for Hematology and Stem Cells **(586)**
National Association of Independent Fee Appraisers
(674)

Coyle, Stephen
AFL-CIO Housing Investment Trust **(15)**

Coyne, Anabela
International Society for Clinical Densitometry **(565)**

Cozzi, Ashley
Association for Computing Machinery **(243)**

Cozzi, Lauren
United Cerebral Palsy **(986)**

Crabtree, Jill
International Bluegrass Music Association **(530)**

Crabtree-Ireland, Duncan
Screen Actors Guild - American Federation of
Television and Radio Artists **(893)**

Craciunescu, PhD, Dr. Oana I.
Society for Thermal Medicine **(926)**

Crady, Erin
Thoroughbred Owners and Breeders Association **(974)**

Craemer, Kevin
Internet Society **(582)**

Craig, Anita B.
American Association of Orthodontists **(67)**

Craig, Elizabeth
National Prison Hospice Association **(782)**

Craig, James M.
American Institute of Marine Underwriters **(139)**

Craig, Jim
United States Green Building Council **(994)**

Craig, Leah
Sports Turf Managers Association **(959)**

Craig, Lynn M.
American Waterways Operators **(220)**

Craig, Paul
National Association of County Agricultural Agents
(659)

Craig, Thomas L.
Orthopedic Surgical Manufacturers Association **(834)**

Craighead, CEM, Scott
International Association of Exhibitions and Events
(520)

Crain, Cindy
National Taxidermists Association **(799)**

Crain, Greg
National Taxidermists Association **(799)**

Cram, Marcia E.
Irrigation Association **(585)**

Cramb, Heidi
American Culinary Federation **(112)**

Cramer, Aron
Business for Social Responsibility **(339)**

Cramer, David
International Association of Machinists and Aerospace
Workers **(524)**

Cramer, Jen
Association of Professional Landscape Designers **(301)**
Perlite Institute **(842)**
The National Greenhouse Manufacturers Association
(756)

Cramer, Marie
National Hemophilia Foundation **(759)**

Cramer, William E.
National Association of County Intergovernmental
Relations Officials **(660)**

Crandall, Derrick A.
American League of Anglers and Boaters **(145)**
National Park Hospitality Association **(779)**

Crandall, Kathy
American Association of Tissue Banks **(75)**

Crandall, Matthew
Association for Enterprise Opportunity **(245)**

Crane, Angus
North American Insulation Manufacturers Association
(817)

Crane, Ann Marie
Creative Education Foundation **(403)**

Crane, CAE, CMP, Elizabeth Dooley
American Association of Thoracic Surgery **(53)**

Crane, Jennifer
Sealant, Waterproofing and Restoration Institute **(894)**

Crane, Kristin
Professional Convention Management Association
(861)

Crane, MPH, PhD, Stephen C.
American Thoracic Society **(216)**

Cranston, Ron
National Emergency Number Association **(745)**

Crassweller, Dr. Robert
American Pomological Society **(167)**

Craven, David
Federation of American Societies for Experimental
Biology **(440)**

Craven, Geoff
National Association of Media and Technology Centers
(680)

Craven, Rhonda

International Casual Furnishings Association **(533)**

Craven, Robert
Council of State Speech-Language-Hearing Association Presidents **(398)**

Crawford, Ace
National Electrical Contractors Association **(744)**

Crawford, Ann
Geological Society of America **(459)**

Crawford, Brian
American Chemical Society **(89)**

Crawford, SPHR, Calvin
American Association of Airport Executives **(53)**

Crawford, Chris
Country Music Association **(401)**

Crawford, Christopher L.
National Association of Development Companies **(662)**

Crawford, D. Sims
National Association of Chapter Thirteen Trustees (NACTT) **(652)**

Crawford, Diane C.
National Phlebotomy Association **(781)**

Crawford, Ellen
National Federation of Press Women **(749)**

Crawford, Gale
Association for Iron and Steel Technology **(250)**

Crawford, Gregory L.
Steel Recycling Institute **(963)**

Crawford, Gwen
American Shorthorn Association **(179)**

Crawford, Horace E. J.
National Phlebotomy Association **(781)**

Crawford, Ian
Geothermal Resources Council **(460)**

Crawford, Jonathan
American Foreign Service Association **(122)**

Crawford, Julie
American Association of Community Theatre **(58)**

Crawford, Kate
National Association of Independent Housing Professionals **(674)**

Crawford, Nicole
Network of Executive Women in Hospitality **(808)**

Crawford, Sara
Perennial Plant Association **(841)**

Crawford, Sydney
Society of Economic Geologists **(934)**

Crawford, Tom
PMA - The Worldwide Community of Imaging Associations **(851)**

Crawford, Winnie
National Weather Association **(804)**

Crawley, Duanne
The American Society for Public Administration **(189)**

Crawley, PE, Njemile A.
National Society of Black Engineers **(793)**

Craycraft, Bob
American Resort Development Association **(175)**

Crea, Joseph R.
Business Roundtable **(339)**

Creagan, Jane
American Music Therapy Association **(154)**

Creech, Denise
American Chemical Society **(89)**

Creeden, William

International Brotherhood of Boilermakers, Iron Shipbuilders, Blacksmiths, Forgers and Helpers **(531)**

Creelman, Wayne
American Association of Psychiatric Administrators **(71)**

Creighan, Kevin P.
Association of Flight Attendants - CWA **(283)**

Cremmins, Randi
American Urological Association **(218)**

Cremone, Ralph
Commercial Finance Association **(366)**

Creneti, Lauren
International Society of Explosives Engineers **(572)**

Crenshaw, Tonya
Roller Skating Association International **(887)**

Crenshaw, Yvette
National Association of Community Health Centers **(656)**

Crerar, Ken A.
The Council of Insurance Agents and Brokers **(394)**

Crespi, Rochelle
Association of Real Estate Women **(305)**

Crespo, Hilda
ASPIRA Association, Inc. **(233)**

Crespo, Mario
National Exercise Trainers Association **(747)**

Cress, Kristen P.
United Methodist Association of Health and Welfare Ministries **(987)**

Cressy, Dr. Peter H.
Distilled Spirits Council of the United States, Inc. **(414)**

Creswell, R. LeRoy
National Shellfisheries Association **(790)**

Crews, Dan
Association for Spanish and Portuguese Studies **(256)**

Crews, Kimberly
Society of Woman Geographers **(950)**

Crews-Anderson, Vickie
InSight **(496)**

Crews-Anderson, Victoria
NPTA Alliance **(824)**

Creyer, Mark
Association of Independent Manufacturers'/Representatives, Inc. **(288)**

Crichton, Jenny
National Organization of State Associations for Children **(778)**

Crider, Jule
American Association for Wound Care Management **(53)**

Crigger, Bill
The Association of Career Firms North America **(271)**

Crimmins, Tom
National Council for Impacted Schools **(732)**

Crippen, Dan
National Governors Association **(755)**

Criqui, Katie
Deep Foundations Institute **(408)**

Crispen, Cheryl
Securities Industry and Financial Markets Association (SIFMA) **(895)**

Crisson, Mark
American Public Power Association **(171)**

Crist, Greg
American Health Care Association **(129)**

Crist, MBA, Katrina
Association for Professionals in Infection Control and Epidemiology **(254)**

Cristol, Richard E.
Juice Products Association **(589)**
National Association of Margarine Manufacturers **(679)**
National Institute of Oilseed Products **(765)**

Cristol, Rick
National Pasta Association **(779)**

Critchlow, Charles H.
American-European Soda Ash Shipping Association **(222)**

Crites, Leon
Marine Preservation Association **(605)**

Crites, Melodie
Association of American Shippers **(266)**

Croce, Donna
National Leased Housing Association **(769)**

Croce, Ginger
Association for Education and Rehabilitation of the Blind & Visually Impaired **(245)**

Croce, Jr., Nicholas
American Psychiatric Nurses Association **(168)**

Crock, Lisa
Child Life Council **(353)**

Crocker, Chris
National Association for the Specialty Food Trade **(644)**

Crockett, Alan
American Council of Engineering Companies **(109)**

Crockett, Debbie
American Academy of Forensic Sciences **(34)**

Crockett, Kerry
United States and Canadian Academy of Pathology **(989)**

Crockett, Michelle
Federally Employed Women (FEW) **(440)**

Crockett, Stephanie
Association for Assessment in Counseling and Education **(240)**

Crolius, Amy
Association for Unmanned Vehicle Systems International **(261)**

Crolius, Robert W.
The Refractories Institute **(878)**

Cromartie, William J.
American Entomological Society **(117)**

Cronan, John J.
Society of Radiologists in Ultrasound **(946)**

Cronin, Brian P.
Professional Association of Diving Instructors **(859)**

Cronin, Jr., Edward J.
Association for Medical Imaging Management **(252)**

Crooks, Donna
Ice Skating Institute **(482)**

Croom, Barry
Association for Career and Technical Education Research **(241)**

Croom, Gelasia
American Society for Clinical Pathology **(182)**

Cropper, Cabell C.
National Criminal Justice Association **(740)**

Cropper, Janet
Women's Professional Rodeo Association **(1023)**

Cropsey, PhD, Karen
Society for Research on Nicotine and Tobacco **(920)**

Crosby, Alfred J.

Adhesion Society *(12)*

Crosby, JD, John B.
American Osteopathic Association *(160)*
National Association of Osteopathic Foundations *(683)*

Crosby, Joseph R.
Council On State Taxation *(400)*

Crosby, Mark E.
Enterprise Wireless Alliance *(429)*
Land Mobile Communications Council *(593)*

Crosby, Mary Neil
Power Transmission Distributors Association *(855)*

Crosby, Miriam
American Peanut Shellers Association *(162)*

Crosby, Susan
Society of Independent Gasoline Marketers of America (SIGMA) *(939)*

Croskey, DPM, Raymond Bazemore
American College of Counselors *(95)*

Croson, Matt
Adhesive and Sealant Council *(12)*

Cross, Dr. Don
Congress of Chiropractic State Associations *(377)*

Cross, Edward P.
Liaison Committee of Cooperating Oil and Gas Associations *(597)*

Cross, Joann Noe
Academy of Accounting Historians *(3)*

Cross, Julie
International Alliance for Women in Music *(510)*

Cross, Latressa
National Association for Alcoholism and Drug Abuse Counselors *(646)*

Cross, Lou
North American Cartographic Information Society *(814)*

Cross, CAE, Sandra
Executive Women's Golf Association *(435)*

Cross, Steve
National Religious Broadcasters *(785)*

Cross, Susan M.
National Association of Concessionaires *(657)*

Crosse, CMP, CAE, Ann Mehan
Society for Scholarly Publishing *(921)*

Crosser, Lane
Sanitary Supply Wholesaling Association *(891)*

Crossfield, Cathy
Independent Hardee's Franchisee Association *(490)*

Crossley, Mark
American Society of Agricultural and Biological Engineers *(191)*

Crossman, Paul
National Fire Protection Association *(751)*

Crosson, Carol
Insurance Consumer Affairs Exchange *(505)*

Crosson, Patrick
International Dairy Foods Association *(539)*

Crothers, Ed
American Mountain Guides Association *(153)*

Crouch, Chasity
Country Radio Broadcasters, Inc. *(401)*

Crouch, Jim
United States Parachute Association *(997)*

Crouch, John
Pellet Fuels Institute *(841)*

Crouch, Madeleine

American Viola Society *(219)*
International Clarinet Association *(535)*
International Society of Bassists *(571)*
Music Distributors Association *(622)*
National Association of School Music Dealers *(692)*
Retail Print Music Dealers Association *(885)*

Crouch, Margaret
North American Society for Social Philosophy *(821)*

Crouse, CAE, Cindy
International Association of Diecutting and Diemaking *(519)*

Crouse, Jennifer
American Seed Trade Association *(178)*

Crow, Susan H.
National Sheriffs' Association *(791)*

Crowder, April
Central Intercollegiate Athletic Association *(349)*

Crowder, Carolyn
International Center for Study of Psychiatry and Psychology *(534)*

Crowe, Gary A.
National Association of Professional Process Servers *(688)*

Crowe, Jack J.
Cristo Rey Network *(404)*

Crowe, John H.
Society for Cryobiology *(907)*

Crowe, MS, Malinda
American Public Health Association *(171)*

Crowley, Brian
Aerospace Industries Association of America *(14)*

Crowley, James M.
Society for Industrial & Applied Mathematics *(912)*

Crowley, Laureen
The Institute of Financial Operations *(499)*

Crowley, Mark
HUBZone Contractors National Council *(480)*

Crowley, Shiela
Cheese Importers Association of America, Inc. *(351)*
Document Security Alliance *(415)*

Crowly, Cory
Congressional Legislative Staff Association *(377)*

Crowne, James
American Intellectual Property Law Association *(141)*

Crowther, William
Society for Romanian Studies *(921)*

Croxall, Kathy
National Association of Teacher Educators for Family Consumer Sciences *(704)*

Croy, Donna
National Association for Alcoholism and Drug Abuse Counselors *(646)*

Crozier, Lon
Electronic Security Association *(424)*

Cruea, MPA, Renee
Academy of Radiology Research *(8)*

Cruel, Doris J.
National Association of State Boards of Education *(698)*

Cruickshank, Jill
National Environmental Health Association *(746)*

Crum, Donna
National Association of Corporate Directors *(658)*

Crum, Elisabeth
National Woman's Party *(805)*

Crum, Kevin
Association of Racing Commissioners International *(304)*

Crum, Larry
International Hot Rod Association *(550)*

Crump, Amanda
The Association for International Agriculture and Rural Development *(250)*

Crump, David
National Association of Home Builders *(673)*

Crump, CMP, CAE, John
National Coalition of Black Meeting Planners *(723)*

Crunstedt, Ashley
Automotive Fleet and Leasing Association *(322)*
Surfaces in Biomaterials Foundation *(966)*

Cruse, Denise
American Academy of Physician Assistants *(40)*

Crutchfield, Susan K.
Antique and Amusement Photographers International *(224)*

Crutchley, Josephine
North American Association of Commencement Officers *(813)*

Cruz, Franklin A.
Coalition for Juvenile Justice *(360)*

Cruz, J.R.
Vehicular Technology Society *(1008)*

Cruz, Jesus
Association for Spanish and Portuguese Studies *(256)*

Cruz, Rafael
Cosmetic Industry Buyers and Suppliers *(387)*

Cruz, Teresa
Joint Review Committee on Education in Radiologic Technology *(589)*

Cruzado, Doris Santiago
National Mobility Equipment Dealers Association *(773)*

Cryan, Teresa V.
Institute for Operations Research and the Management Sciences *(497)*

Cryer, MA, Keryl M.
Accreditation Board for Engineering and Technology Inc. *(9)*

Crystal, DDS, David
American Society for the Advancement of Anesthesia and Sedation in Dentistry *(190)*

Csepegi, John
National Council for History Education *(732)*

Cubberley, William C.
Practising Law Institute *(855)*

Cubillas, Fernando
Association of Celebrity Personal Assistants *(271)*

Cucchiara, Joe
Theatre Communications Group *(973)*

Cuccia, Charles J.
Shipowners Claims Bureau, Inc. *(899)*

Cuccia, Megan
Forest Products Society *(451)*

Cudahy, Jim
National Court Reporters Association *(740)*

Cudahy, John
International Council of Air Shows *(538)*

Cudd, Stacia
National Association of Farm Broadcasting *(667)*

Cuddihy, Kevin
Society for Technical Communication *(922)*

Cudworth, Carol
Society for Mining, Metallurgy and Exploration, Inc. *(915)*

Cueroni, Nancy

National Marine Distributors Association *(771)*
Outdoor Power Equipment and Engine Service Association *(835)*

Cuevas, Laurie
The Brown Swiss Association *(336)*

Cuevas, Zuleika
National Hispanic Corporate Council *(759)*

Cuff, Martin
Association of Film Commissioners International *(283)*

Cuitino, Alberto M.
American Academy of Mechanics *(35)*

Cuka, Gabriel
Phi Rho Sigma Medical Society *(846)*

Culkin, CAE, Doug
National Apartment Association *(634)*

Culkin, Elizabeth
Independent Sector *(491)*

Cull, Daniel
Western Association for Art Conservation *(1015)*

Cullather, Kevin
American Public Power Association *(171)*

Cullen, Genevieve
Electric Drive Transportation Association *(421)*

Cullen, Mary E.
Association of American Law Schools *(265)*

Cullen, CAE, Tracy H.
Society of the Plastics Industry *(948)*

Cullison, Linda
American Society of Colon and Rectal Surgeons *(195)*

Culliton, Kate
American Pediatric Society *(162)*

Culliton, Kate
Society for Pediatric Research *(918)*

Cullman, Erica Johnson
The New York Academy of Sciences *(809)*

Culpepper, S. Todd
World Affairs Councils of America *(1025)*

Cumber, Carol
North American Case Research Association *(814)*

Cumming, Ann Marie
National Association of Broadcasters *(650)*

Cummings, Joe
National Soccer Coaches Association of America *(792)*

Cummings, Karen
American Phytopathological Society *(165)*
American Society of Brewing Chemists *(193)*
Master Brewers Association of the Americas *(607)*

Cummings, Kathy
International Labor Communications Association *(553)*

Cummings, Lauren
National Association of State Budget Officers *(698)*

Cummings, Robert "Bob" E.
USA Rice Federation *(1004)*

Cummings, Tavia
American Association of Community Colleges *(58)*

Cummins, Bob
American Brahmousin Council *(85)*

Cummins, CMP, Jenna
American Gynecological and Obstetrical Society *(128)*

Cummins, CMP, Jenna
Society of Gynecologic Oncologists *(938)*

Cummins, Tracy
National Energy Services Association *(746)*

Cummiskey, Melissa

Geological Society of America *(459)*

Cumpston, Andrea
National Cooperative Business Association *(729)*

Cundiff, Dave
American Association of Public Health Physicians *(72)*

Cunha, Jr., Manuel
Nisei Farmers League *(811)*

Cunic, Jocelyn
American Academy of Nursing *(37)*

Cunnar, Christiane
Human Relations Area Files *(481)*

Cunneen, Elizabeth
National Conference of Commissioners on Uniform State Laws *(727)*

Cunnick, Christine
National Grocers Association *(756)*

Cunningham, Amy Gray
Lift Manufacturers Product Section - Material Handling Institute *(597)*

Cunningham, Ann Marie
Door and Access Systems Manufacturers Association, International *(415)*

Cunningham, Beth A.
American Association of Physics Teachers *(69)*

Cunningham, Candace
ASM International *(232)*

Cunningham, Cheryl Dungan
American Harp Society *(129)*

Cunningham, AA, BS, MS, Gary
National Academic Advising Association *(626)*

Cunningham, Glinda
American Ostrich Association *(161)*

Cunningham, MHA, Greg L.
American Case Management Association *(88)*

Cunningham, Jesse
American Academy for Cerebral Palsy and Developmental Medicine *(29)*
Clinical Immunology Society *(358)*

Cunningham, Julie A.
Conference of Minority Transportation Officials *(375)*

Cunningham, Keri
Craft & Hobby Association *(402)*

Cunningham, Kim
American Medical Student Association *(150)*

Cunningham, Leigh
National Academic Advising Association *(626)*

Cunningham, Mary
International Swaps and Derivatives Association *(576)*

Cunningham, Michelle
Association of Healthcare Internal Auditors *(287)*

Cunningham, Mike
American Nephrology Nurses Association *(155)*

Cunningham, Ralph
International Association of Accident Reconstruction Specialists *(514)*

Cunningham, Rebecca
RCI, Inc. *(875)*

Cunningham, Sean
Cabletelevision Advertising Bureau *(340)*

Cunningham, Terry
CCIM Institute *(347)*

Cunnngham, Cassandra
Financial Industry Regulatory Authority (FINRA) *(444)*

Cupo, Al
Local Media Association *(599)*

Cupo, Robert E. (Bob)
National Catholic Development Conference *(718)*

Cupp, CMP, Julie
National Insulation Association *(766)*

Cuppernull, Carolyn
Ocean Stewards Institute *(826)*

Curcuruto, Jim
National Shooting Sports Foundation *(791)*

Curd, Corine
National Association of Emergency Medical Technicians *(665)*

Cure, Michael
Point of Purchase Advertising Institute *(851)*

Curlee, Jesse W.
Supima *(966)*

Curley, Jim
United States Tennis Association *(1000)*

Curran, John
American Registry for Internet Numbers *(174)*

Curran, Laurie
Opportunity Finance Network *(829)*

Curran, PE, Sullivan "Sully" D.
Fiberglass Tank and Pipe Institute *(443)*

Currie, John V.
Council on the Safe Transportation of Hazardous Articles *(401)*
International Vessel Operators Dangerous Goods Association *(580)*

Currie, Kevin
Association of State Floodplain Managers *(311)*

Currie, Lara Mehr
Council on the Safe Transportation of Hazardous Articles *(401)*
International Vessel Operators Dangerous Goods Association *(580)*

Currie, Lindsay
Council on Undergraduate Research *(401)*

Curro, Dr. Tom
American Association of Zoo Veterinarians *(77)*

Curry, Andrea
American Society of Association Executives-The Center for Association Leadership *(193)*

Curry, George E.
National Newspaper Publishers Association *(775)*

Curry, Jennifer
Association for Spiritual, Ethical and Religious Values in Counseling *(257)*

Curry, Jon
International Documentary Association *(541)*

Curtice, Melissa
Music Teachers National Association *(622)*

Curtis, Chester
Air Force Association *(18)*

Curtis, Debbie
Association of Legal Administrators *(291)*

Curtis, Janice
SEPM - Society for Sedimentary Geology *(897)*

Curtis, Jill
Vacation Rental Managers Association *(1007)*

Curtis, AAP, John
American Association of University Professors *(75)*

Curtis, Joyce
The National Safety Management Society *(789)*

Curtis, Kerry
American Society for Colposcopy and Cervical Pathology *(183)*

Curtis, Kerry
Society for Cardiovascular Angiography and
Interventions *(905)*

Curtis, Michael P.
American Councils for International Education *(111)*

Curtis, Michelle
National Insurance Crime Bureau *(766)*

Curtis, Millie
Intersure, Ltd. *(583)*

Curtis, MBA, SPHR, Sara
American Society of Anesthesiologists *(192)*

Curtis, Tom
American Water Works Association *(220)*

Curtiss, CEBS, PhD, RPh, Fred
Academy of Managed Care Pharmacy *(6)*

Cusack, Dorothy
Independent Sealing Distributors *(491)*
Wholesale Florist and Florist Supplier Association
(1016)
Yacht Brokers Association of America *(1030)*

Cusack, Dot
Fluid Power Distributors Association *(448)*

Cushman, Charles S.
American Land Rights Association *(144)*

Cushman, Diane L.
National Council on Family Relations *(738)*

Cushnie, PhD, Michele
International Association of Business Communicators
(517)

Cusimano, Frankie
Strategic Account Management Association *(963)*

Custer, Judy
Therapeutic Touch International Association *(973)*

Custer, Katrina
National Association of Wheat Growers *(709)*

Cutcher, Anthony
National Federation of Priests' Councils *(749)*

Cuter, Fabienne
Professional Women Photographers *(866)*

Cuthbert, Patricia
American Psychosocial Oncology Society *(170)*
International Psycho-Oncology Society *(561)*
International Society for Prenatal Diagnosis *(568)*

Cutler, Dr. Peter
Nickel Institute *(811)*

Cutsforth-Huber, Bonnie
National Opera Association *(776)*

Cutshaw, Stacey McCarroll
Society for Photographic Education *(919)*

Cutting, Vickie
American Society for Eighteenth-Century Studies *(183)*

Cvikota, Kris
Healthcare Billing and Management Association *(470)*

Cypher, Lauren
Association of Insolvency and Restructuring Advisors
(289)

Cyphers, Frank
International Chemical Workers Union Council/UFCW
(534)

Cyr, CAE, MBA, Dale R.
American Registry for Diagnostic Medical Sonography
(174)

Cyr, Thomas E.
International Academy of Gnathology - American
Section *(509)*

Cyrill, Charles
American Truck Dealers *(217)*

Cyrus, Sylvia Y.
Association for the Study of African American Life and
History *(259)*

Czajkowski, Ginger
American Academy of Emergency Medicine *(33)*

Czarnecki, Mark T.
Benchmarking Network Association *(328)*
Telecommunications Benchmarking International
Group *(971)*

Czarnecki, Paul
NASTD - Technology Professionals Serving State
Government *(626)*
National Association of State Technology Directors
(702)

Czech, Debbie
American Orthopaedic Society for Sports Medicine
(159)

Czeropski, Anne
Institute of Nuclear Materials Management *(502)*

Czosek, Michelle
International Association for Human Resource
Information Management *(512)*

Czubaruk, Kim
American Academy of Nursing *(37)*

Czuhajewski, Stephanie
Society of Trauma Nurses *(949)*

Czuhajewski, CAE, Stephanie
Academy of Doctors of Audiology *(5)*
National Gerontological Nursing Association *(755)*

D'Agostino, Bellinda
American Association for Geriatric Psychiatry *(49)*

D'Agostino, FCMAA, CAE, Bruce
Construction Management Association of America
(379)

D'Agostino, Judith A.
American Council on Science and Health *(110)*

D'Amato, Sally-Ann
Society of Motion Picture and Television Engineers
(942)

D'Ambrosi, Dean
National Association for Printing Leadership *(641)*
R & E Council of the NAPL *(872)*

D'Amelio, Patsy
Employee Benefit Research Institute *(426)*

D'Angelo, Barbara
Association for Business Communication *(240)*

D'Aniello, Charles A.
Association for the Bibliography of History *(259)*

D'Antonio, PhD, RN, CAE, IOM, Patricia
American Association for the History of Nursing *(52)*

D'Apolito, PhD, Karen
National Perinatal Association *(780)*

D'arelli, Mike
American Agents Alliance *(43)*

D'Costa, William J.
APPA - Leadership in Educational Facilities *(225)*

D'Elia, Joe
United States Coast Guard Chief Petty Officers
Association *(992)*

D'Errico, Deanna
American Association of Community Colleges *(58)*

D'Imperio, Alexandra
Association of Free Standing Radiation Oncology
Centers *(284)*

D'Ippolito, Mary Ann
American Guernsey Association *(127)*

D'Orazio, Ann
Metals Service Center Institute *(614)*

D'Orazio, Micah
American Society of Safety Engineers *(209)*

D'Uva, CAE, Matthew R.
SOCAP International *(902)*

D'Allaird, Michelle
Aestheticians International Association *(14)*

D'Aoust, Cynthia
Meeting Professionals International *(612)*

Dabel, Jane
Society for History Education *(911)*

Dacey, Ralph G.
Society of Neurological Surgeons *(943)*

Dacre, Debbie
American Veterinary Distributors Association *(218)*
Pet Industry Distributors Association *(842)*
Secondary Materials and Recycled Textiles Association
(894)
Souvenir Wholesale Distributors Association *(953)*

Dacus, Corie
Council of Engineering and Scientific Society
Executives *(393)*

Dad, MD, Luqman K.
Association of Residents in Radiation Oncology *(306)*

Daddow, Maryann
Automation Alley *(321)*

Dade, Michael
BICSI *(329)*

Dadgar, Nina
National Community Pharmacists Association *(725)*

Dadisman, Ellen C.
American Academy of Actuaries *(29)*

Daeger, Rachel
Interior Design Educators Council *(508)*

Daeger, Rachel
Society for Nutrition Education and Behavior *(917)*

Daggett, Harold J.
International Longshoremen's Association, AFL-CIO
(555)

Daggs, Jim
Amalgamated Printer's Association *(27)*

Dahl, Bill
The Botanical Society of America *(333)*

Dahl, Eric R.
World Trade Centers Association *(1027)*

Dahl, Mary
National Association of Container Distributors *(658)*

Dahl, William M.
Society for the Study of Evolution *(925)*

Dahlen, CAE, Robin E.
American Beekeeping Federation *(80)*

Dahlman, Gayle
Consortium of School Networking *(378)*

Dahlroth, CEM, CMP, Jane
American College of Medical Genetics *(97)*

Dahne, Melissa
National Association of Student Personnel
Administrators *(626)*

Daigle, Leslie
Internet Society *(582)*

Daikh, MD, PhD, David
Association of Specialty Professors *(309)*

Dailey, Cheryl
National Council of Juvenile and Family Court Judges
(735)

Dailey, Kathy
National Association of Electrical Distributors *(664)*

Dailing, Clifford D.
National Rural Letter Carriers' Association *(788)*

Daily, Kimberly J.
Phi Mu Alpha Sinfonia *(846)*

Daisey, Jason R.
Associated Builders and Contractors *(235)*

Dalal, Jagdish
International Association of Outsourcing Professionals *(525)*

Dale, AAC, Dmin, LMFT, Diana C.
National Institute of Business and Industrial Chaplaincy *(764)*

Dale, James R.
Metal Injection Molding Association *(613)*
Metal Powder Industries Federation *(613)*
Powder Metallurgy Equipment Association *(854)*
Powder Metallurgy Parts Association *(854)*
Refractory Metals Association *(878)*

Dale, Rick
Society for Computers in Psychology *(906)*

Dale, Terry L.
United States Tour Operators Association *(1000)*

Daleske, Nicolette
National Association of Children's Hospitals and Related Institutions *(653)*

Dalewitz, Michael
Association of Litigation Support Professionals *(292)*

Dalhouse, Scott
American Academy of Pediatric Dentistry *(39)*

Dalition, Mitch
The Open Group *(828)*

Dallara, Charles H.
Institute of International Finance *(501)*

Dallas, Bill
International Test and Evaluation Association *(577)*

Dallas, Stewart
International Facility Management Association *(543)*

Dalling, Derek
American Academy of Podiatric Practice Management *(40)*

Dallstream, CMP, CMM, Pamela S.
Society for Critical Care Medicine *(934)*

Dally, Jessica
Society of Professional Audio Recording Services *(945)*

Dalonges, Anthony J.
United States Maritime Alliance (USMX) *(996)*

Dalsky, Dianne
American Society for Laser Medicine and Surgery *(186)*

Dalton, Dawn
Quality Service Contractors *(871)*

Daly, Alicia
American Rights at Work *(175)*

Daly, Candace
American Society of Podiatry Executives *(208)*

Daly, Kenneth
National Association of Corporate Directors *(658)*

Daly, Linda
National Fire Sprinkler Association *(751)*

Daly, Pat
National Association of Recording Merchandisers (NARM) *(690)*

Daly, Timothy
National Council for the Social Studies *(733)*

Dameron, Patricia
Professional Retail Store Maintenance Association *(864)*

Damewood, Megan
American Board for Certification in Orthotics and Prosthetics, Inc. (ABC) *(81)*

Damewood, MD, Richard
Association of Program Directors in Surgery *(303)*

Damiano, Jr., MD, Ralph J.
The International Society for Minimally Invasive Cardiothoracic Surgery *(567)*

Damjanovic, Stevan
International Society for Philosophical Enquiry *(568)*

Dammrich, Thomas J.
National Marine Manufacturers Association *(771)*

Damon, Carole
Tile Contractors' Association of America *(974)*

Damon, JD, Christopher A.
American Medical Technologists *(150)*

Damon, PhD, Lorie
Building Owners and Managers Association International *(337)*

daMota, Gail
Education Finance Council *(419)*

Dana, Charles
Farm Credit Council *(437)*

Dana, Robert
Parenteral Drug Association *(838)*

Danback, Gary
Institute of International Container Lessors *(501)*

Dancy, Chris
Helicopter Association International *(473)*

Dancy, David
American Public Works Association *(172)*

Dancy, Jon
American Association of Occupational Health Nurses *(67)*

Dando, Kate
Council of Chief State School Officers *(392)*

Dandrea, Joel M.
Specialized Carriers and Rigging Association *(957)*

Dandridge, Ed
National Association of Investment Companies *(676)*

Daniel, Amanda
Interlocking Concrete Pavement Institute *(508)*

Daniel, Channing
American Composites Manufacturers Association *(105)*

Daniel, Chris
American College of Veterinary Ophthalmologists *(104)*

Daniel, Geraldine
National Fisheries Institute *(751)*

Daniel, J. Todd
National Ornamental and Miscellaneous Metals Association *(778)*

Daniel, Jerlean
National Association for the Education of Young Children *(644)*

Daniel, Larry
America's Independent Truckers' Association, Inc. *(29)*

Daniel, Linda M.
National Association of Independent Lighting Distributors *(674)*

Daniel, Reva
Association of Professional Communication Consultants *(301)*

Daniel, Stacee
American College of Veterinary Ophthalmologists *(104)*

Daniel, Wesley
America's Independent Truckers' Association, Inc. *(29)*

Danielewicz, Wes
Turf Equipment Technicians Association *(982)*

Daniels, Ann
American Public Works Association *(172)*

Daniels, Anovia
SnowSports Industries America *(902)*

Daniels, Ariane
Association of Professional Researchers for Advancement *(302)*
International Carwash Association *(533)*

Daniels, Christopher
American Dental Education Association *(113)*

Daniels, Eva
National Association for Family Child Care *(638)*

Daniels, Grayson
American Beekeeping Federation *(80)*

Daniels, Janet
American Horticultural Society *(133)*

Daniels, John
Navy League of the United States *(807)*

Daniels, John Y.
American Association of Textile Chemists and Colorists *(75)*

Daniels, Lindy
International Facility Management Association *(543)*

Daniels, MPA, Lisa
International Association of Assessing Officers *(516)*

Daniels, Margery Berg
International Society for Third-Sector Research *(570)*

Daniels, Russell
American Society of Home Inspectors *(200)*

Daniels, MD, Sarah
Society of Pelvic Reconstructive Surgeons *(943)*

Daniels, Sue
American Mold Builders Association *(152)*

Daniels, Tera
State Education Technology Directors Association *(961)*

Danielson, Karen V.
Shareholder Services Association *(898)*

Danielsson, Lotta
United States-Taiwan Business Council *(989)*

Danish, Susan E.
Association of Junior Leagues International *(290)*

Danjczek, Thomas A.
Steel Manufacturers Association *(962)*

Danko, Danielle
Health Industry Distributors Association *(469)*

Danley, Robert J.
United Union of Roofers, Waterproofers and Allied Workers *(1001)*

Dann, BCET, MA, Marcy
Association of Educational Therapists *(280)*

Dannahey, Mary W.
Association of Consulting Foresters of America *(276)*

Dannenberg, Klaus
American Institute of Aeronautics and Astronautics *(136)*

Dannenfeldt, Paula
National Association of Clean Water Agencies *(654)*

Danner, Donald "Dan"
National Federation of Independent Business (NFIB) *(748)*

Danner, Pamela Beck
International Association of Lighting Designers *(524)*

Danner-Knight, Beth
American String Teachers Association *(213)*

Dansby, Angela
United States Canola Association *(991)*

Dansereau, Jennifer Zukowski
National Turkey Federation *(802)*

Dantzic, Cynthia
Society of Scribes *(947)*

Dapson, Richard
Biological Stain Commission *(330)*

Darby, MBA, Keith
American College of Phlebology *(100)*

Darcy, Bill
National Kitchen and Bath Association *(767)*

Darcy, Keith T.
Ethics and Compliance Officer Association *(433)*

Darden, Geraldene
Physician Assistant Education Association *(847)*

Darden, CMP, Robert
Distribution Contractors Association *(414)*

Dare, Jack
Path to Purchase Institute *(839)*

Darensburg, Oletha
The Society for Modeling and Simulation International *(916)*

Darisse, Justin
National Council of Farmer Cooperatives *(734)*

Darkangelo, Anthony "Tony"
National Finishing Contractors Association *(751)*

Darling, Bruce B.
National Research Council *(786)*

Darling, Helen
National Business Group on Health *(716)*

Darmohraj, CAE, Andrew
American Pet Products Association *(163)*

Darnell, Lucas R.
American Frozen Food Institute *(124)*
Frozen Potato Products Institute *(454)*

Darr, Linda Bauer
American Moving and Storage Association *(153)*

Darras, Katherine Tew
International Swaps and Derivatives Association *(576)*

Darrow, Diane
National Association of Retail Collection Attorneys *(692)*

Das, Parthavi
Women in Cable Telecommunications, Inc. *(1020)*

Dashiell, Judy
National Fisheries Institute *(751)*

DaSilva, Jessica
Community Colleges Humanities Association *(370)*

Dasso, III, Edward
National Futures Association *(754)*

Dasti, Ahsun
Association of Muslim Social Scientists of North America *(295)*

Dathorne, PhD, O.R.
Caribbean Studies Association *(343)*

Dato, Virginia
American Association of Public Health Physicians *(72)*

Datri, James Edmund
American Advertising Federation *(43)*

Daub, Eugene
American Medallic Sculpture Association *(148)*

Dauber, Miri Pomerantz
Jewish Book Council *(587)*

Daucher, MS, Rachelle R.
Accreditation Board for Engineering and Technology Inc. *(9)*

Daudelin, Marcia
International Society of Transport Aircraft Trading *(574)*

Daudlin, Sandra
International Society for Magnetic Resonance in Medicine *(567)*

Daudt, Janis
International Institute of Municipal Clerks *(552)*

Daugherty, Dianne
Malignant Hyperthermia Association of the United States *(602)*

Daugherty, Terresa
Society of Environmental Toxicology and Chemistry *(935)*

Daughetee, Autumn
National Association of Women in Construction *(710)*

Daughton, Dr. William
American Society for Engineering Management *(184)*

Daughtrey, Clay
Marketing Education Association *(606)*

Daughtry, Jr., Sylvester
Commission on Accreditation for Law Enforcement Agencies Incorporation *(367)*

Daum, Helen
International Ceramic Association *(534)*

Dauphin-Fletcher, Aurelie
International Academy of Television Arts and Sciences *(509)*

Dauphinais, David
American College of Preventive Medicine *(101)*

Dautenhahn, Mallorie
ARMA International *(228)*

Dauth, Pam Rodgers
Associated Luxury Hotels International *(236)*

Dauzier, Jennifer S.
International Association of Law Enforcement Intelligence Analysts *(523)*

Davalos, Rafael
The American Electrophoresis Society *(116)*

Davenport, Bill
American Concrete Pavement Association *(106)*

Davenport, Charles
National Association of Intercollegiate Athletics *(676)*

Davenport, Keely
University Risk Management and Insurance Association *(1003)*

Davenport, Linda Ruiz
National Council of Supervisors of Mathematics *(737)*

Davenport, Maureen
National Association of Manufacturers *(679)*

Davenport, Patrice
Society of Competitive Intelligence Professionals *(933)*

Davey, Dena
Association of Bridal Consultants *(270)*

Davey, Lauren
Society for Physician Assistants in Pediatrics *(919)*

Davey, Tara
Council of Hotel and Restaurant Trainers *(394)*

David, Kathy Boyd
Society for Cardiovascular Angiography and Interventions *(905)*

David, CMT, Mary
American Translators Association *(217)*

Davidge, Catherine
Association for Molecular Pathology *(252)*

Davidian, Ken
American Astronautical Society *(77)*

Davidow, Sally
American Postal Workers Union *(167)*

Davidshofer, PhD, Charles
Association for University and College Counseling Center Directors *(260)*

Davidson, Betty
National Association of Division Order Analysts *(663)*

Davidson, Beverly
American Academy of Clinical Psychiatrists *(31)*
National Defender Investigator Association *(742)*

Davidson, Cheryl. A
Congress of Neurological Surgeons *(377)*

Davidson, PhD, Dr. Dan E.
American Councils for International Education *(111)*

Davidson, Janet
Women In Film and Television International *(1021)*

Davidson, Jill
Coalition of Essential Schools *(360)*

Davidson, June
American Seminar Leaders Association *(178)*

Davidson, Lily
National Family Planning and Reproductive Health Association *(747)*

Davidson, Lynne
Society of Laparoendoscopic Surgeons *(940)*

Davidson, Mary Beth
National Association of County Intergovernmental Relations Officials *(660)*

Davidson, Paula
American Association of Law Libraries *(64)*

Davie, Bruce S.
Special Interest Group for Data Communication *(955)*

Davies, Catherine
Chorus America *(355)*

Davies, Damon
Meeting Professionals International *(612)*

Davies, David R.
American Journalism Historians Association *(143)*

Davies, Erika
Association of Black Foundation Executives *(269)*

Davies, Marcia
Mortgage Bankers Association of America *(619)*

Davies, PhD, Marshall
Public Risk Management Association *(870)*

Davies, CPA, P. Stratton
American College of Chest Physicians *(94)*

Davies, Richard
1394 Trade Association *(1)*

Dávila, Carlos
National Association of Area Agencies on Aging *(647)*

Davin, Laurie
National Association of EMS Educators *(665)*

Davin, Tom
Software & Information Industry Association (SIIA) *(950)*

Davis, Alan B.
National Association for Campus Activities *(637)*

Davis, JD, MPH, Amy L.
Applied Research Ethics National Association *(226)*

Davis, Angela
American Association for Women Radiologists *(53)*
American Society of Emergency Radiology *(197)*

Davis, CAE, April
International Society for Performance Improvement *(567)*

Davis, Aubree
American Public Gardens Association *(170)*

Davis, Bill
American Anthropological Association *(45)*

Davis, Bill
Association of Latina and Latino Anthropologists *(291)*

Davis, Bobby
Violin Society of America *(1010)*

Davis, Brenda
Society of Insurance Trainers and Educators *(940)*

Davis, Brendan
Ambulatory Surgery Center Association *(28)*

Davis, Brett
Association for Unmanned Vehicle Systems International *(261)*

Davis, Bruce
National Association of Orthopaedic Technologists *(683)*

Davis, Candice
International Entertainment Buyers Association *(543)*

Davis, Cathy Futrell
Association for Healthcare Resource and Materials Management *(248)*

Davis, Cheryle
United States-ASEAN Business Council Inc. *(990)*

Davis, Chip
Pharmaceutical Research and Manufacturers of America (PhRMA) *(844)*

Davis, Christopher L.
Money Management Institute *(618)*

Davis, Colette
Christian Medical & Dental Associations *(356)*

Davis, Cynthia
National Association for Retail Marketing Services *(642)*

Davis, Dawn M
Congress of Neurological Surgeons *(377)*

Davis, Deb
National Military Intelligence Association *(772)*

Davis, Debra
American Society of Pension Professionals & Actuaries *(206)*

Davis, Diane
Chemical Sources Association *(352)*
National Association of Flavors and Food-Ingredient Systems *(668)*

Davis, Don
Air Conditioning, Heating and Refrigeration Institute (AHRI) *(18)*
American Society of Interior Designers *(200)*

Davis, Donald L.
National Association of Older Worker Employment Services *(683)*

Davis, Donna
U.S. Hereditary Angioedema Association *(983)*

Davis, USMC (Ret.), MAJ Drew
Reserve Officers Association of the U.S. *(882)*

Davis, Dylan
National U.S.-Arab Chamber of Commerce *(803)*

Davis, PhD, Edward L.
Distributive Education Clubs of America (DECA) *(415)*

Davis, Elizabeth (Betsy)
Institute of Electrical and Electronics Engineers (IEEE) *(499)*

Davis, Erika
National Association of Blacks In Government *(649)*

Davis, Erin
Association of Industrial Metallizers, Coaters and Laminators *(288)*
Converting Equipment Manufacturers Association *(383)*

Davis, Franklin
American Subcontractors Association *(214)*

Davis, Gayle
Association of periOperative Registered Nurses *(299)*

Davis, Gerald E.
Mine Safety Institute of America *(616)*

Davis, Harrison
Association for Multicultural Counseling and Development *(252)*

Davis, Hester
National Association of State Archaeologists *(697)*

Davis, Jeanette
Rice Millers' Association *(886)*
USA Rice Council *(1004)*
USA Rice Federation *(1004)*

Davis, Jeffrey
American Association of Retired Persons *(72)*

Davis, Joel
International Studies Association *(576)*

Davis, John
Professional Rodeo Cowboys Association *(864)*

Davis, John R.
Fleet Reserve Association *(447)*

Davis, Jon
National Cheese Institute *(720)*

Davis, Joseph A.
Society of Environmental Journalists *(935)*

Davis, CSI, Joy
Construction Specifications Institute *(380)*

Davis, Julie
National Cutting Horse Association *(741)*

Davis, Karen
American Society of Home Inspectors *(200)*

Davis, Kathie
IDEA, The Health and Fitness Association *(482)*

Davis, Kathleen
International Bridge, Tunnel and Turnpike Association *(531)*

Davis, Kathryn
Council on Anthropology and Education *(398)*

Davis, Kelly
SnowSports Industries America *(902)*

Davis, CAE, Laura
American Academy of Hospice and Palliative Medicine *(35)*

Davis, Leigh Ann
National Conference of Executives of The ARC *(727)*

Davis, Lessie
National Wildlife Rehabilitators Association *(805)*

Davis, Linda
Academy of Political Science *(8)*
American Political Science Association *(166)*

Davis, MSN, RN, Lois
Association for Vascular Access *(261)*

Davis, Lynn
The PGA Tour, Inc. *(844)*

Davis, Marcy
Association of Personal Historians *(299)*

Davis, Margaret
International Association of Bedding and Furniture Law Officials *(516)*

Davis, Mary Ellen K.
Association of College and Research Libraries *(273)*

Davis, Michael
National Association of Convenience Stores *(658)*

Davis, Michael J.
Academy of Management *(6)*

Davis, Michael P
American Malting Barley Association *(146)*

Davis, Mike
United States Golf Association *(994)*

Davis, Nanette
American Society of Questioned Document Examiners *(208)*

Davis, Pat
American Association of Legal Nurse Consultants *(64)*

Davis, Paula
Ideas America *(482)*

Davis, Peter
IDEA, The Health and Fitness Association *(482)*

Davis, R. R.
Congress of Independent Unions *(377)*

Davis, Randall "Randy" P. K.
International Association of Amusement Parks and Attractions(IAAPA) *(515)*

Davis, Rebecca
Cotton Warehouse Association of America *(387)*

Davis, Rhondi
National Association of Rural Health Clinics *(692)*

Davis, Robert
The Broadway League *(336)*

Davis, Robin
National Association of Clean Water Agencies *(654)*

Davis, Samantha
American Academy of Podiatric Practice Management *(40)*

Davis, Scoop
Non Commissioned Officers Association (NCOA) *(811)*

Davis, Scott
International Alliance of Technology Integrators *(510)*

Davis, Seth
Geochemical Society *(458)*

Davis, Sharon
Home Baking Association *(477)*

Davis, Sharon
Texas Alliance of Energy Producers *(972)*

Davis, Steven H.
Society of Exploration Geophysicists *(935)*

Davis, Sue
Society of American Business Editors and Writers *(928)*

Davis, Tara
Society for Mining, Metallurgy and Exploration, Inc. *(915)*

Davis, Terry
American Association for State and Local History *(51)*

Davis, Theresa
Meeting Professionals International *(612)*

Davis, Tiffany
International Entertainment Buyers Association *(543)*

Davis, Tim

Davis, Tinsley
International Waterlily and Water Gardening Society *(580)*

Davis, Tinsley
National Association of Science Writers *(694)*

Davis, Tricia
American Society for Nondestructive Testing *(187)*

Davis, Will
Society of Mexican American Engineers and Scientists *(941)*

Davis, Will
Chester White Swine Record Association *(352)*

Davis, William
American Society of Consultant Pharmacists *(195)*

Davis II, John K.
American Board of Internal Medicine *(82)*

Davis III, Arthur E.
American Escrow Association *(118)*

Davis-Felner, Kelly
Wi-Fi Alliance *(1016)*

Davis-Runyan, Natalie
Alliance of National Staffing and Employment Resources *(25)*

Davison, Hamilton
American Catalog Mailers Association *(88)*

Davison, Shannon
Truck Renting and Leasing Association *(981)*

Davison, Yoshie
American Academy of Child and Adolescent Psychiatry *(31)*

Davisson, Donna
North American Small Business International Trade Educators *(821)*

Daw, Ann
National Association for the Specialty Food Trade *(644)*

Dawirs, Morgan
Picture Archive Council of America *(848)*

Dawkins, Diana
Society of American Military Engineers *(929)*

Dawson, MBA, Janene
Natco-The Organization for Transplant Professionals *(626)*

Dawson, Kay
National Scholastic Press Association *(789)*

Dawson, Kay
Associated Collegiate Press *(235)*

Dawson, Sandra
Coordinating Council for Women in History *(384)*

Day, Bret C.
United Professional Horsemen's Association *(988)*

Day, Craig
American Institute of Aeronautics and Astronautics *(136)*

Day, Marley
National Association for Information Destruction, Inc. *(640)*

Day, Rich
National Association of Home and Workshop Writers *(672)*

Day, Robert D.
Renewable Natural Resources Foundation *(881)*

Day, Susan
North American Nature Photography Association *(819)*

Day, Takaro J.
AASHTO: Transportation Center of Excellence *(2)*

Day, PhD, CAE, CMP, William H.
Gas Turbine Association *(457)*

Dayak, MA, Meena
National Council for Community Behavioral Healthcare *(731)*

Dayton, Adrienne Watts
National School Supply and Equipment Association *(789)*

Dayton, Beth
American Meteorological Society *(151)*

Dayton, CPA, Sandra
Justice Research and Statistics Association *(589)*

Dayton, Steve
American Association for Paralegal Education *(50)*

de Raismes III, JD, Joseph N.
Mental Health America *(612)*

De Angelis, Franco
Italy-America Chamber of Commerce *(586)*

de Bernardo, Mark A.
Council for Employment Law Equity (CELE) *(389)*

De Cagna, Meeghan
American Medical Student Association *(150)*

de Candolle, Gabriel
International Federation of Fertility Societies *(544)*

De Jong, Daniel B.
Tax Executives Institute, Inc. *(968)*

De Koker, Neil
Original Equipment Suppliers Association *(833)*

De La Paz, Katie
International Technology and Engineering Educators Association *(576)*

de la Vega, Alessandra
Society for Experimental Mechanics, Inc. *(909)*

de Leede, Gihis
Phi Delta Kappa International *(845)*

de Lemos, Anne Ornelas
American Society on Aging *(211)*

de los Santos, Gerardo E.
League for Innovation in the Community College *(595)*

De Luca, Alessandro
Robotics and Automation Society *(887)*

de Mars, J D, Susan S.
United States Pharmacopeia *(997)*

de Mause, Lloyd
International Psychohistorical Association *(562)*

De Pas, Penney
Society of Invasive Cardiovascular Professionals *(940)*

de Perre, Pol Van
Society for Clinical Data Management *(906)*

de Ramos, Cynthia Allen
American Network of Community Options and Resources (ANCOR) *(155)*

De Sadier Walker, LaKimba
National Black Caucus of State Legislators *(714)*

de Sousa, CAE, Mary S.
National Council of Architectural Registration Boards *(733)*

De Vinay, Paula
Association of Community Health Nursing Educators *(276)*

de Vries, Gerda
Society for Mathematical Biology *(915)*

De Vroomen, Jack
North American Flowerbulb Wholesalers Association *(816)*

de Vroomen, Patricia
North American Flowerbulb Wholesalers Association *(816)*

De Weese, Kirk
International Brotherhood of Magicians *(531)*

de Zarate, Guillermo Ortiz
National Council of Architectural Registration Boards *(733)*

Dea, CAE, Francesca M.
Obesity Society *(825)*

Deal, Brenda
Creative Education Foundation *(403)*

Dean, DO, Amy
American Academy of Environmental Medicine *(33)*

Dean, Christine
Strategic Marketplace Initiative *(963)*

Dean, Colleen Hearn
National Dance Association *(741)*

Dean, Gabrielle
Society for Textual Scholarship *(922)*

Dean, Heather
National Parent Teachers Association *(779)*

Dean, Kate
United States Internet Service Provider Association *(995)*

Dean, CMP, Kathleen R.
Casualty Actuarial Society *(344)*

Dean, Keisha
Society of Publication Designers *(946)*

Dean, Mandy
American Association of Clinical Endocrinologists *(56)*

Dean, Mary
American Society of Gene & Cell Therapy *(198)*

Dean, Meredith
National Association for Drama Therapy *(638)*

Dean, Stephanie
American Pediatric Society *(162)*
Society for Pediatric Research *(918)*

Dean, PhD, Stephen O.
Fusion Power Associates *(455)*

Dean, Virginia
American Bankers Association *(79)*

Deane, Gordon
National Organization of Legal Services Workers *(777)*

Deane, Michael
National Association of Water Companies (NAWC) *(709)*

DeAngelis, ACSW, LICSW, Donna
Association of Social Work Boards *(309)*

DeAngelo, Edward W.
CRE Finance Council *(403)*

DeAngelo, Raymond J.
CFA Institute *(350)*

Deans, Candice
National Association of College and University Business Officers *(654)*

Deans, Donna
American Association of Occupational Health Nurses *(67)*
ASPSN - American Society of Plastic Surgical Nurses *(234)*
Association for Radiological and Imaging Nursing *(255)*

Deans, Rebecca
Association of Independent Colleges of Art and Design *(287)*

Dearborn, Karen
American College Dance Festival Association *(92)*

Deardorff, Dr. Darla K.
Association of International Education Administrators *(289)*

Dearie, John
Financial Services Forum *(445)*

Dease, Martin
National Recreation and Parks Association *(784)*

Deason, Lauren
The PGA Tour, Inc. *(844)*

Deasy, Esq., Robert P.
American Immigration Lawyers Association *(134)*

DeAvegno, Amy
International Natural Sausage Casing Association *(557)*

Deavy, Shelly
Public Affairs Council *(868)*

DeBaker, April
American Water Works Association *(220)*

DeBardi, Lonna
Healthcare Distribution Management Association *(471)*

Debarry, Christina
Allied Artists of America *(25)*

Debatin, Gloria
Mu Phi Epsilon *(621)*

DeBeaumont, Gael
Plastic Surgery Research Council *(850)*

DeBoda, PE, Ted
National Association of Sewer Service Companies *(695)*

DeBoe, Meg C.
Chief Administrators of Catholic Education *(352)*

DeBoer, Jeffrey D.
Real Estate Roundtable *(876)*

DeBoer, Kathy
American Volleyball Coaches Association *(219)*

DeBoer, Roxanne
Business and Institutional Furniture Manufacturers Association International *(338)*

DeBoer-Langworthy, Carol
Association for Documentary Editing *(245)*

DeBolt, Dave
Country Radio Broadcasters, Inc. *(401)*

DeBolt, Don J.
American Orthotic and Prosthetic Association *(159)*

DeBolt, Sally Ann
Association for Middle Level Education *(252)*

DeBry, Ronald W.
Society of Systematic Biologists *(947)*

Debus, Tim
International Banana Association *(529)*

Dec, MD, Katherine
American Medical Society for Sports Medicine *(149)*

DeCaprio, Robert
Messenger Courier Association of the Americas *(612)*

DeCarlo, Jennifer
The Association of International Photography Art Dealers *(289)*

DeCherney, MD, Alan H.
American Society for Reproductive Medicine *(189)*

Deck, III, Frederick W.
Airline Industrial Relations Conference *(20)*

Decker, Jan
Arabian Horse Association *(227)*

Decker, Maribeth C.
Federation of State Boards of Physical Therapy *(442)*

Decker, Sabra L.
International Safety Equipment Association (ISEA) *(563)*

Decker, Susan M.

American College of Apothecaries *(93)*

DeClark, Cindy
Care Continuum Alliance *(342)*

DeCourcey, Susan
Association for the Advancement of Medical Instrumentation *(258)*

DeCrane, Sean
International Firestop Council *(545)*

DeCrappeo, Tony
Council on Governmental Relations *(400)*

Dedovic, Milos
Serbian-American Chamber of Commerce *(897)*

Dee, Kevin
National Association of Intercollegiate Athletics *(676)*

Dee, Kristin
American Association of Legal Nurse Consultants *(64)*
Society of Gastroenterology Nurses and Associates *(937)*

Deeds, PhD, Jan
American Men's Studies Association *(150)*

Deeds, Meredith
International Association of Culinary Professionals *(519)*

Deegan, John
Military Impacted Schools Association *(616)*

Deegan, Mike
Council of Educational Facility Planners International *(393)*

Deegan-Krause, Kevin
Slovak Studies Association *(900)*

Deely, John
Semiotic Society of America *(897)*

Deem, Cheryl A.
American Spice Trade Association *(212)*

Deemer, Joe
Graphic Arts Technical Foundation *(465)*

Deems, Joseph E.
National Risk Retention Association *(787)*

Deere, William R.
United States Telecom Association *(1000)*

Deering, Anne-Lise
American Medallic Sculpture Association *(148)*

Deerr, Terri
American Association of Naturopathic Physicians *(66)*

Deesawala, Huzefa
International Swaps and Derivatives Association *(576)*

Deeter, Tom
American Teleservices Association *(215)*

DeFeo, Nicole
Delta Phi Epsilon *(409)*

Deffner, Darren
Solar Electric Power Association *(951)*

Deffner, Faithe
American Accordionists Association *(43)*

Defibaugh, Cara
Association for Financial Counseling and Planning Education *(246)*

DeFiglia, Joseph
American Society of Civil Engineers *(194)*

Defilippi, Aldo
Association of American Chambers of Commerce in Latin America *(264)*

DeFillipi, CUDE, Pablo
National Federation of Community Development of Credit Unions *(748)*

DeFlorian, Terri A.
Orthopaedic Section - American Physical Therapy Association *(833)*

DeForest, Alice
American Academy of Periodontology *(39)*

DeFrancis, Leane
American Choral Directors Association *(90)*

DeFrehn, Randy G.
National Coordinating Committee for Multiemployer Plans *(730)*

DeFries, Diane
American College Dance Festival Association *(92)*

DeGennaro, Jeannette
AVS: Science and Technology of Materials, Interfaces, and Processing *(325)*

Degg, Kenneth W.
National Agricultural Aviation Association *(630)*

DeGirolamo, Nicole
Illuminating Engineering Society of North America *(486)*

Degli-Angeli, Helen
Manufacturers' Agents National Association *(603)*

Degnon, CAE, George K.
American Psychosomatic Society *(170)*
Pediatric Endocrine Society *(840)*

Degnon, Laura
Association of Medical School Pediatric Department Chairs *(293)*

Degnon, CAE, Laura E.
Association of Pediatric Program Directors *(298)*
Society for Developmental and Behavioral Pediatrics *(907)*

Degnon, Marge
Academic Pediatric Association *(3)*

DeGolyer, Lisa
Construction Owners Association of America *(380)*

DeGraaf, Rita K.
Conference of Consulting Actuaries *(375)*

DeGroot, Doug
Special Interest Group for Architecture of Computer Systems *(954)*

DeGroote, Michael
Institute of Diving *(499)*

Degryse, Patrick
Society for Archaeological Sciences *(904)*

DeHaan, Robert
National Fisheries Institute *(751)*

DeHaan, Steve
National Home Furnishings Association *(759)*

DeHaven, Dr. W. Ron
American Veterinary Medical Association *(219)*

Dehner, Ilse
United States Equestrian Federation *(993)*

Dehoney, Catherine
Chorus America *(355)*

Deighton, Bruce
Association for Hospital Medical Education *(249)*

Deighton, John
Marketing Science Institute *(606)*

Deitch, Janis
American Coke and Coal Chemicals Institute *(92)*

Dejonge, Katie
Transportation Clubs International *(978)*

Dekdebrun, Greg
National Ski and Snowboard Retailers Association *(791)*

Del Polito, PhD, Gene A.
Association for Postal Commerce **(253)**

Del Valle, Casilda
National Minority Supplier Development Council **(773)**

Delacourt, John
Plasma Protein Therapeutics Association **(850)**

Delacruz, Charles M.
National Grain and Feed Association **(755)**

Delagrange, Annette
American Solar Energy Society **(211)**

Delahanty, James L.
Omicron Kappa Upsilon **(827)**

Delahanty, Patricia
National Sculpture Society **(790)**

Delaney, Cathe
National Association of Professional Pet Sitters **(687)**

Delaney, Patrick
American Soybean Association **(211)**

Delaney, Paul
Federation of State Boards of Physical Therapy **(442)**

Delaney, Timothy
National Council of Nonprofits **(735)**

Delaney, Valerie
Construction Owners Association of America **(380)**

DelaRosa, Michelle
Alliance for Women in Media **(24)**
American Society of Women Accountants (ACC) **(211)**
Public Media Business Association **(869)**

Delaurier, Rachelle
Alpha Gamma Rho **(26)**

DeLauro, Danielle
Cabletelevision Advertising Bureau **(340)**

Delavan, John
Print Services & Distribution Association **(857)**
Product Development and Management Association **(858)**

Delene, David
Weather Modification Association **(1014)**

Delgado, Deborah Denard
National Black Caucus of Local Elected Officials **(714)**

Delgado, Hector L.
Society for the Study of Social Problems **(925)**

Delgado, PhD, MS, Dr. Jane L.
National Alliance for Hispanic Health **(631)**

DelGreco, Kristen
Exhibit Designers and Producers Association **(435)**

Delhey, Karen
Guild of Artists and Artisans **(467)**

Delio, Kathy
International Association of Machinists and Aerospace Workers **(524)**

Delis, Dimitrios
Professional Picture Framers Association **(864)**

DeLisle, Annette
The Association to Advance Collegiate Schools of Business **(319)**

Delk, Wade
American Society for Pain Management Nursing **(188)**
International Nurses Society on Additictions **(558)**

Dell, Mia
United Food and Commercial Workers International Union **(987)**

DellaCorte, DPM, Michael P.
American Board of Podiatric Medicine **(83)**
American College of Podiatric Radiologists **(101)**

DellaPietra, Mark

Society for Marketing Professional Services (914)

Dellario, Bernie
Eye Bank Association of America **(436)**

Dellert, MBA, RN, Ed
American College of Chest Physicians **(94)**

Dellinger, Cari
International Bridge, Tunnel and Turnpike Association **(531)**

Delman, Farrell
Tobacco Merchants Association of the United States **(975)**

Delmonico, Katherine
Council for Affordable and Rural Housing **(388)**

DeLoach, Roy
National Association of Mortgage Brokers **(681)**

DeLorenzo, David
National Association of College and University Business Officers **(654)**

Delorie, Mary
Higher Education Consortium for Urban Affairs **(475)**

Delta, Esq., CMP, George B.
Incentive Federation, Inc. **(487)**

DeLuca, Lorena
Loan Syndication & Trading Association **(599)**

DeLuca, Peter
Minerals, Metals and Materials Society **(617)**

DeLucia, Robert J.
Airline Industrial Relations Conference **(20)**

DeLucia-Waack, Janice
Association for Specialists in Group Work **(257)**

Delurey, Dan
Association for Demand Response & Smart Grid **(244)**

Delventhal, Bruce
The American Hockey Coaches Association **(132)**

DeMarchi, Jane
National Association of Wheat Growers **(709)**

DeMarco, Darren
International Brotherhood of Electrical Workers **(531)**

DeMarco, Edward J.
The Risk Management Association **(886)**

DeMarco, Kathleen A.
Generic Animal Drug Alliance **(458)**

Demarco, Kathy
Web Sling and Tie down Association **(1014)**

DeMarco, Mary
Quality Chekd Dairies **(871)**

DeMarco, Maryanne
The Coalition of Airline Pilots Associations **(360)**

DeMarco-Barrett, Barbara
American Society of Journalists and Authors **(201)**

Demarest, Sarah Tinsley
Mortgage Bankers Association of America **(619)**

DeMaria, JoAnna
American Lung Association **(146)**

DeMartino, Janice
American Academy of Nurse Practitioners **(37)**

DeMasters, Carol
Association of Food Journalists **(283)**

Demchuk, Thomas D.
AASP - The Palynological Society **(2)**

DeMellier, Dan
Society of Exploration Geophysicists **(935)**

Demerath, Ellen W.
Human Biology Association **(480)**

DeMercado, George
Caribbean Hotel and Tourism Association **(343)**

Demers, EdD, Stephen T.
Association of State and Provincial Psychology Boards **(309)**

Demicoli, Bernadette "Bennie"
International Hearing Society **(549)**

Deming, Mary Ann
International Association of Assessing Officers **(516)**

Deming, Nicole
Children's Book Council **(353)**

DeMiranda, Michael
Council on Technology Teacher Education **(401)**

Demko, DMD, B. Gail
American Academy of Dental Sleep Medicine **(32)**

Demkowicz, Leszek
United States Association for Computational Mechanics **(990)**

DeMoraes, Keila
Resistance Welding Manufacturing Alliance **(883)**

DeMoro, Rose Ann
National Nurses United **(775)**

Dempsey, Kevin M.
American Iron and Steel Institute **(142)**

Dempsey, Tony
American Association of Colleges of Nursing **(57)**

DeNardo, Gina
Building Stone Institute **(338)**

Denault, Pat
Business History Conference **(339)**

Denbow, Rich
Association of Metropolitan Planning Organizations **(294)**

Denchfield, Teresa
American Sportfishing Association **(212)**

Dencker, Tim
National Association of Electrical Distributors **(664)**

Denecke, Daniel
Council of Graduate Schools **(394)**

Denenberg, David
National Basketball Association **(712)**

Dengler, Erin
National Association of Collegiate Directors of Athletics **(656)**

Denham, CAE, PLS, Laurie
American Society of Transportation and Logistics **(210)**

denHartog, Tim
International Association of Plumbing and Mechanical Officials **(526)**

DenHollander, Katie
National Association of Orthopedic Nurses **(683)**

DeNies, Sam
Council of Development Finance Agencies **(393)**

Denis, MA, Ingrid
Association of Occupational and Environmental Clinics **(296)**

Denis, Maurice
National Association of Community Health Centers **(656)**

Denison, Carletta
Petroleum Equipment Institute **(843)**

Deniz, Crista
Association for Women in Computing **(261)**

Denkler, Jim
American Culinary Federation **(112)**

Denkova, Reneta
North American-Bulgarian Chamber of Commerce *(823)*

Denman, Barbara L.
Baptist Communicators Association *(326)*

Dennett, Diana
America's Health Insurance Plans *(28)*

Denney, Josh
Mortgage Bankers Association of America *(619)*

Dennie, Dawn
American Health Information Management Association *(129)*

Denning, Anita
The American Bar Association Rule of Law Initiative *(80)*

Dennis, Aliesha
National Association of Advisors for the Health Professions *(645)*

Dennis, Cindy
American Inns of Court *(135)*

Dennis, Debbie
Iroquois Healthcare Alliance *(585)*

Dennis, Elease
United States-ASEAN Business Council Inc. *(990)*

Dennis, Kathy B.
American Correctional Association *(108)*

Dennis, Mo
Grain Elevator and Processing Society *(464)*

Dennison, Hazel
American Nephrology Nurses Association *(155)*

Denny, Beth
American Society for Cytotechnology *(183)*

Denny, Mark
National Association of County Park and Recreation Officials *(660)*

Densa, Steve
Minor League Baseball *(617)*
National Association of Professional Baseball Leagues *(686)*

Denston, Susan A.
American Textile Machinery Association *(216)*
International Association of Emergency Managers *(520)*
National Association of State Emergency Medical Services Officials *(700)*
Process Equipment Manufacturers' Association *(858)*

Dentali, PhD, Steven
American Herbal Products Association *(130)*

Dentel, PhD, Steve K.
Association of Environmental Engineering and Science Professors *(281)*

Denton, Angie Stump
American Hereford Association *(131)*

Denton, Bryce
Forest Stewardship Council - United States Chapter *(451)*

Denton, Jeremy
Filter Manufacturers Council *(444)*

Deomano, PhD, Edgar
National Wooden Pallet and Container Association *(805)*

DePaolo, Anthony R.
International Foodservice Manufacturers Association *(546)*

DePaso, Thomas
National Football League Players Association *(752)*

DePass, Joyce
American Society of Landscape Architects *(201)*

Deponzi-Haas, CMP, Dana

American College of Phlebology *(100)*

Derby, Mike
Professional Aviation Safety Specialists (AFL-CIO) *(860)*

Deringis, Sheila
American Public Gas Association *(170)*

Derkacz, Karin
Electronics Representatives Association *(424)*

Derkay, CAE, Lori
University Professional & Continuing Education Association *(1003)*

Derks, Paula
Aircraft Electronics Association *(20)*

DeRosa, Anthony
Association of State Drinking Water Administrators *(311)*

DeRosa, II, Ed
National Turf Writers and Broadcasters *(802)*

Derouin, Cherie
International Pet and Animal Transportation Association *(560)*

DeRoxtra, Ron
Bowling Writers Association of America *(334)*
International Bowling Pro Shop and Instructors Association *(530)*

Derr, John
Telecommunications Industry Association *(971)*

Derrick, Phyllis
The Association of Women in International Trade *(317)*

Derry, Thomas W.
Association for Financial Professionals, Inc. *(247)*
Institute for Supply Management *(497)*

Derting, Libby
Women in Government *(1021)*

DeRupo, Joe
National Coffee Association of the U.S.A. *(723)*

DeRusha, Al
Outdoor Amusement Business Association *(834)*

Desai, Anuj
New York E-Health Collaborative *(809)*

Desai, Viresh
American Society of Consultant Pharmacists *(195)*

DeSalvio, Joe
Association for Financial Professionals, Inc. *(247)*

DeSalvio, Lars M.
Tax Executives Institute, Inc. *(968)*

DeSantis, Karen
American Society of Nuclear Cardiology *(205)*

DeServi, KariAnn
American Biological Safety Association *(81)*

Deshong, Richard Todd
National Association of Disability Examiners *(663)*

Desigan, Shyam
American Academy of Physician Assistants *(40)*

DeSirant, Cindy
American Society for Colposcopy and Cervical Pathology *(183)*

Desjardins, Emily
Joint Electron Device Engineering Council *(589)*

Desmarais, Maurice A.
National Association of Sporting Goods Wholesalers *(696)*

Despins, Abby
Preventive Cardiovascular Nurses Association *(857)*

Desrosiers, Mary Catherine
Association for Supervision and Curriculum Development (ASCD) *(257)*

Desy, Pierre
Emergency Nurses Association *(425)*

DeTemple, Matthew
National Association of Towns and Townships (NATAT) *(706)*

Dethloff, Lauren
American College of Prosthodontists *(101)*

Detmer, MD, Don E.
American Medical Informatics Association *(149)*

DeTrapani, Jenna
National Mobility Equipment Dealers Association *(773)*

Dettor, John
United States Professional Tennis Association *(998)*

Detweiler, Joan
National Tactical Officers Association of America *(799)*

Detwiler, Sandra
American Gear Manufacturers Association *(125)*

Deuel, RAC, RN, Margaret A.
American Association of Tissue Banks *(75)*

Deuschle, Karen
American Association of Cereal Chemists International *(55)*
Controlled Release Society *(383)*
Master Brewers Association of the Americas *(607)*

Deuschle, Mark
Global Market Development Center *(462)*

Deutsch, Christopher
National Association of Drug Court Professionals *(663)*

Deutsch, Jennifer
Interactive Advertising Bureau *(506)*

Deutsch, Tom
American Securitization Forum *(178)*

Deutsch-Layne, Erika
American Society for Precision Engineering *(188)*

DeVaan, Gary
Health Care Compliance Association *(469)*

Develen, Carolyn
North American Menopause Society *(818)*

DeVeny-Edwards, CPM, Janet
Association of Public Health Nurses *(304)*

Dever, Trish
Association for Healthcare Foodservice *(248)*

Devereaux, BC-DMT, NCC, PhD, Christina
American Dance Therapy Association *(113)*

Devereux, Renee
Society for Values in Higher Education *(926)*

Deverman, CAE, Arlene C.
American Society of Addiction Medicine *(191)*

Devey, Kathy
International Foodservice Distributors Association *(546)*

Devi, MD, Gayatri
American Medical Women's Association *(150)*

Devick, Tim
Vacuum Dealers Trade Association/Sewing Dealers Trade Association *(1007)*

DeVille, Chris
National Lipid Association *(770)*

Devine, Ann
Pi Sigma Epsilon *(847)*

Devine, Debbie
International Association of Credit Portfolio Managers *(519)*

Devine, James R,
Chain Drug Marketing Association *(350)*

Devine, John
Chain Drug Marketing Association *(350)*

DeVinney, Sheri
Medical Device Manufacturers Association *(611)*

DeVita, Lili
Financial Executives International *(444)*

DeVivo, Frank
Practising Law Institute *(855)*

Devlin, Matthew
American Association of Public Welfare Attorneys *(72)*

Devlin, Shannon
College Music Society *(363)*

Devney, John
Delta Waterfowl Foundation *(409)*

Devor, Christine
The Transformer Association *(977)*

DeVries, Christine
American Association for Geriatric Psychiatry *(49)*

Devroey, Paul
International Federation of Fertility Societies *(544)*

Dew, PhD, Brian
Association for Counselor Education and Supervision *(244)*

Dew, Carolyn
Phi Delta Kappa International *(845)*
Pi Lambda Theta *(847)*

DeWeese, Judy
National Association of Women in Construction *(710)*

Dewey, Ady
National Association of State Retirement Administrators *(702)*

Dewey, W. Dennis
National Assembly of State Arts Agencies *(635)*

Dewhirst, Kaitlin
National Student Osteopathic Medical Association *(797)*

Dewhirst, DVM, PhD, Mark W.
Society for Thermal Medicine *(926)*

Dewine, Debbie A.
Tau Beta Pi Association *(968)*

Dewire, Nancy
National Indian Education Association *(762)*

Dewitt, Allison
North American Retail Hardware Association *(820)*

DeWitt, Cindy
American Association of Airport Executives *(53)*

DeWitt, John W.
Association of Strategic Alliance Professionals, Inc. *(311)*

DeWitt, Larry
Paint and Decorating Retailers Association *(836)*

Dewyngaert, Brian
American Federation of Government Employees *(119)*

Dexter, Justin
American Glovebox Society *(126)*

Dexter, Sandy L.
Association for Assessment and Accreditation of Laboratory Animal Care International *(239)*

Dexter-Smith, Michael J.
Association of Chartered Accountants in the United States *(272)*

DeYoung, Jean
American College of Surgeons *(103)*

Dezio, Kathleen
Personal Care Products Council *(842)*

DeZur, Samantha
Education Finance Council *(419)*

Dhakal, Binaya
Association of Science-Technology Centers *(307)*

Dhariwal, CCP, ISP, Kewal
Institute for Certification of Computing Professionals *(497)*

Dhepyasuwan, Nui
Academic Pediatric Association *(3)*

Dhillon, PhD, Major S.
Society for Vector Ecology *(927)*

Di Corpo, Joe
Specialty Vehicle Institute of America *(958)*

Di Pierri, Marleda C.
International Association for the Study of Pain *(514)*

Di Polvere, Edward J.
National Association of Noise Control Officials *(682)*

Diagne, Malick
National Forum for Black Public Administrators *(752)*

Diamond, Carrie
National Society for Histotechnology *(792)*

Diamond, Marvin
American Board of Quality Assurance and Utilization Review Physicians, Inc. *(84)*

Diamond, Pamela
American Craft Council *(111)*

Diamond, Paula
Council of Colleges of Acupuncture and Oriental Medicine *(392)*

Diana, Cathy
American Institute of Chemical Engineers *(138)*

Diana, Tom
Credit Research Foundation *(403)*

Diane, Mori
National Black Caucus of State Legislators *(714)*

DiAngelo, Deborah
American Association of Teachers of German *(74)*

Diaz, Lidia
Craft & Hobby Association *(402)*

Diaz, Paula
Special Libraries Association *(956)*

DiBari, Shannon
American National Chamber of Commerce *(154)*
United States Chamber of Commerce *(991)*

DiBartolo, Susan M.
Consumer Healthcare Products Association *(381)*

Dibble, Carol
Association for Biblical Higher Education *(240)*

Dibblee, Robert
National Association of Real Estate Investment Trusts (NAREIT) *(690)*

DiBitetto, Andrea Zuniga
Hispanic Lobbyists Association *(475)*

DiBitetto, Frank
Laborers-Employers Cooperation & Education Trust *(592)*

DiCampli, Edward F.
Helicopter Association International *(473)*

DiCarlo, Sam
Food Marketing Institute *(449)*

Dicato, Amy
National Wrestling Coaches Association *(806)*

Dichter, Evelyn
National Association of Recording Merchandisers (NARM) *(690)*

Dichtl, John
National Council on Public History *(739)*

DiCicco, Ashley
National Property Management Association *(783)*

Dick, Kerry
American Institute of Building Design *(137)*

Dicke, Julie
American Morgan Horse Association *(152)*

Dicker, Eli J.
Tax Executives Institute, Inc. *(968)*

Dickerhoof, Edward
Organization of Professional Employees of the U.S. Department of Agriculture (OPEDA) *(832)*

Dickerson, Cristalle Hinkle
American Board of Anesthesiology *(81)*

Dickerson, David
Personal Watercraft Industry Association (PWIA) *(842)*

Dickerson, Dawn D.
National Student Speech Language Hearing Association *(798)*

Dickerson, Guadalupe
Rubber Pavements Association *(888)*

Dickerson, Ken
Ecological Farming Association *(418)*

Dickerson, Phillis
National Dental Hygienists' Association *(743)*

Dickerson, Spencer
United States Contract Tower Association *(992)*

Dickey, Keith W.
American Dental Interfraternity Council *(114)*

Dickey, Dr. Keith W.
Xi Psi Phi Dental Fraternity *(1029)*

Dickey, Sarah
Angel Capital Association *(223)*

Dickey, Trina
National Defense Industrial Association *(742)*

Dickinson, Q. Todd
American Intellectual Property Law Association *(141)*

Dickison, Anne
USENIX: The Advanced Computing Systems Association *(1005)*

Dickison, Philip
National Council of State Boards for Nursing *(736)*

Dickson, Bruce
Aspirin Foundation of America, Inc. *(233)*

Dickson, Eileen
National Ready Mixed Concrete Association *(784)*

Dickson, Margaret
Institute for Professionals in Taxation *(497)*

Dickstein, Jason
Aircraft Electronics Association *(20)*

Dickstein, Jason
Aviation Suppliers Association *(324)*

Dickstein, Michele
Aviation Suppliers Association *(324)*

DiCostanzo, Steven J.
Golf Range Association of America *(463)*

Didawick, Scott
American Association of Pharmaceutical Scientists *(68)*

Didia, Diana
American Institute of Certified Public Accountants *(137)*

Didiano, Mark
Association for Iron and Steel Technology *(250)*

Didion, Catherine
National Academy of Engineering of the United States of America *(627)*

Didlot, Tammi
American National CattleWomen *(154)*

Diebold, Doug
American Blonde D'Aquitaine Association *(81)*

Diebold, Steve
Wire Fabricators Association *(1019)*

Diehl, Erika A.
United Transportation Union *(1001)*

Diehl, Nicholas
International Ombudsman Association *(558)*

Diemand, Mariellen
Applied Research Ethics National Association *(226)*

DiEnna, Jack
Geothermal Heat Pump National and International Initiative *(460)*

Diepstra, Jan
National Council of Structural Engineers Associations *(737)*

Dierig, Emily
National Emergency Management Association *(745)*

Dierking, Dan
National Council of Real Estate Investment Fiduciaries *(735)*

Dierks, Neil
National Pork Producers Association *(781)*
National Pork Producers Council *(781)*

Diers, Christine Paige
Public Radio News Directors Incorporated *(870)*

Dieterich, Carrie
Entertainment Merchants Association *(429)*

Dietl, Greg
Paleontological Research Institution *(837)*

Dietrich, Becca
Electricity Storage Association *(422)*

Dietrich, CAE, CPA, Joe
American College of Healthcare Executives *(96)*

Dietsche, Erica
The Food Institute *(449)*

Dietz, Brian
National Cable & Telecommunications Association *(717)*

Dietz, Donna
Clinical Social Work Association *(359)*

Dietz, Francis
Air Conditioning, Heating and Refrigeration Institute (AHRI) *(18)*

Dietz, Michele R
Oncology Nursing Society *(827)*

Dietz, CTE, PHR, Sallie
Global Business Travel Association *(462)*

Dietz, Timothy J.
Self Storage Association *(896)*

Difatta, Mary Anne
American Society of Retina Specialists *(209)*

Diffendaffer, Gary
Investment Management Consultants Association *(584)*

DiFrisco, Michael
American Academy of Cosmetic Dentistry *(31)*

Diganci, Todd T.
Financial Industry Regulatory Authority (FINRA) *(444)*

DiGangi, Christine
Society of Professional Journalists *(945)*

Digges, Cheryl
Sugar Association *(965)*

Diggs, CaSandra
Council of Fashion Designers of America *(393)*

DiGiacomo, Derek
Society of Cable Telecommunications Engineers *(931)*

DiGiacomo, CPA, Kelly
Steel Founders' Society of America *(962)*

DiGiovanni, Carvin
Association of Pool and Spa Professionals *(299)*

Dikter, David
Assistive Technology Industry Association *(234)*

Dilbeck, Donna
Electronic Components Industry Association *(423)*

DiLenge, Tom
Biotechnology Industry Organization (BIO) *(330)*

DiLeonardo, Melissa C.
Association of Jesuit Colleges and Universities *(290)*

Dilka, Karen
Council on Education of the Deaf *(399)*

Dill, Chris
Sports and Entertainment Alliance in Technology *(959)*

Dill, Kevin
American Society of PeriAnesthesia Nurses *(206)*

Dillard, Felicia
Association for Information and Image Management International *(249)*

Dillard, Kevin
American Association of Orthodontists *(67)*

Dillard, Shane
American Backflow Prevention Association *(78)*

Dillen, J. Ardie (Butch)
Materials Research Society *(609)*

Dilley, Denise
Council on Renal Nutrition *(400)*

Dillhyon, Mike
National Association of Police Athletics/Activities Leagues, Inc. *(685)*

Dillingham, Tim
American Littoral Society *(146)*

Dillmon, Kathy
Association of Conservation Engineers *(276)*

Dillner, Sandra L.
SAE International *(889)*

Dillon, PHR, Ashleigh
College and University Professional Association for Human Resources *(362)*

Dillon, Bill "William"
National Association of College and University Business Officers *(654)*

Dillon, David B.
Oregon Farm Bureau Federation *(830)*

Dillon, Joanna
Ecological Farming Association *(418)*

Dillon, Joseph E.
Council of Better Business Bureaus *(392)*

Dillon, Kevin
Association of Cinema and Video Laboratories *(273)*

Dillon, Dr. Kristine E.
Consortium on Financing Higher Education *(379)*

Dillon, Naomi
National School Boards Association *(789)*

Dillon, Pam
National Association of State Boating Law Administrators *(698)*

Dillon, Tracy
Association for Retail Environments *(256)*

DiMarco, Marlene
National Earth Science Teachers Association *(743)*

DiMickele, Andrea
National Speakers Association *(795)*

Dimino, Resa
National Association for PET Container Resources *(641)*

Dimitroff, Emil A.
North American-Bulgarian Chamber of Commerce *(823)*

Dimitt, Heather
Learning Resources Network *(596)*

Dimmitt, Cindy
National Environmental Health Association *(746)*

Dinan, Esq., Donald R.
National Tax Lien Association *(799)*

Dindo, Kathe
German American Chamber of Commerce *(460)*

Dine, Philip
National Association of Letter Carriers *(678)*

Dineen, Kristen
ASFE/The Geoprofessional Business Association *(231)*

Dineen, Mark
Women in Agribusiness *(1020)*

Dinegar, Chris
Association for the Advancement of Medical Instrumentation *(258)*

DiNello, Stacie
BPA Worldwide *(334)*

Dinges, David F.
Associated Professional Sleep Societies *(237)*

Dingman, Rob
American Motorcyclist Association *(153)*

Dingwall, Robert
Society for the Study of Symbolic Interaction *(925)*

Dinkel, Devin
National Association of School Nurses *(693)*

Dinneen, Bob
Renewable Fuels Association *(881)*

Dinozo, Cristina
MPA - The Association of Magazine Media *(620)*

Dintrone, Patricia
Association of Ancient Historians *(267)*

Dionne, Chris
Association of University Anesthesiologists *(315)*

Diop, Mbayang Diouf
Corporate Council on Africa *(385)*

DiOrio, Peg
Society of Quantitative Analysts *(946)*

DiPaola, Steve
Actors' Equity Association *(11)*

DiPasquale, Frank
School Nutrition Association *(892)*

DiPiro, PharmD, Joseph
American Association of Colleges of Pharmacy *(57)*

DiPrimo, Kathy
American Association of Orthodontists *(67)*

DiProva, Vicky
National Association of Women Lawyers *(710)*

DiRenzo, Angel
Delta Phi Epsilon *(409)*

DiRienzo, Michael
The Silver Institute *(900)*

DiRocco, Barbara
American Hotel & Lodging Association (AH&LA) *(134)*

Dirst, Michelle
National Association of State Alcohol and Drug Abuse Directors (NASADAD) *(697)*

DiSanto, Larry
Capital Health *(342)*

Disbrow, Kate
National Council of Farmer Cooperatives *(734)*

Disbrow, Lynn M.
Institute of Real Estate Management *(503)*

Dischler, Mark
International Documentary Association *(541)*

Dishart, Pete
Enhanced Protective Glass Automotive Association *(429)*

Dishaw, Michelle
American Academy of Podiatric Practice Management *(40)*

Dismuke, Laisha C.
CropLife America *(404)*

Disney, Peggy
National Stone, Sand, and Gravel Association *(796)*

Dispensa, Paul C.
Liability Insurance Research Bureau *(596)*
Property Loss Research Bureau *(867)*

Dispenza, CPA, Sara
American Society of International Law *(201)*

Dissinger, Deanne
American Law Institute *(144)*

Distelhorst, Garen P.
Marble Institute of America *(604)*

Distelhorst, CAE, Garis F.
Marble Institute of America *(604)*

Distelhorst, Helen
Marble Institute of America *(604)*

Ditmeyer, Betty Jo
Western History Association *(1015)*

Dittmann, Roger
United States Federation of Scholars and Scientists *(994)*

Divelbiss, Jennifer
Radiological Society of North America *(873)*

Dively, Lindsay J.
Association of Public Treasurers of the United States and Canada *(304)*

DiVenere, Lucia
American Congress of Obstetricians and Gynecologists *(107)*

DiVincenzo, Brenda
Independent Photo Imagers *(491)*

DiVirgilio, MNM, Debbie
The Grant Professionals Association *(465)*

DiVirgilio, Michael
Containerization and Intermodal Institute *(382)*

Dix , Dave
National Association of Certified Valuation Analysts *(652)*

Dixon, Andrea L.
Association of American Cancer Institutes *(264)*

Dixon, Cindy
National Conference of State Fleet Administrators *(728)*

Dixon, Janet L.
Associated Equipment Distributors *(235)*

Dixon, Janice
Commission on Accreditation for Law Enforcement Agencies Incorporation *(367)*

Dixon, Laurie
American Neurological Association *(155)*

Dixon, Suzanne
National Parks Conservation Association *(779)*

Dixon, MD, MPH, Suzanne D.
Society for Developmental and Behavioral Pediatrics *(907)*

Djerrouf, Connie
Information Systems Audit and Control Association *(495)*

Djordjevic, Diane
National Association of Home Builders *(673)*

Dluzynski, Janice
American Association of Motor Vehicle Administrators *(65)*

Do, Tri
Association on Higher Education and Disability *(319)*

Doak, PhD, Dr. Gordon A
National Association of Animal Breeders *(647)*

Doak, Ivy
Society for the Study of Indigenous Languages of the Americas *(925)*

Doan, Violet S.
IEEE Computer Society *(483)*

Doane, Craig
American Academy of Family Physicians *(34)*

Doane, E. David
International Liquid Terminals Association *(554)*

Dobbins, Steve
YPO-WPO *(1030)*

Dobbins, Thomas
American Composites Manufacturers Association *(105)*
International Cast Polymer Association *(533)*

Dobbs, Dan
National Reining Horse Association *(785)*

Dobbs, Madeline
American Public Gardens Association *(170)*

Dobkin, MD, Bruce
American Society of Neurorehabilitation *(204)*

Dobkin, Jon
National Association of Television Program Executives *(705)*

Dobmeier, Robert
Association for Adult Development and Aging *(238)*

Dobrez, Tom
StateNets Radio *(962)*

Dobrott, Steve
Spanish Barb Horse Association *(954)*

Dobrowolski, Mary Ellen
Air Force Association *(18)*

Dobry, Misty
Seafarers International Union of North America *(894)*

Docampo, Roberto
International Society of Protistologists *(573)*

Dochstader, Jennifer
Tag and Label Manufacturers Institute *(968)*

Dockery, Sonia
Cotton Council International *(387)*

Dockins, Patrick M.
Warehousing Education and Research Council *(1012)*

Dockter, Keven
American Mathematical Association of Two Year Colleges *(147)*

Docter, Linda
Association for Canadian Studies in the United States *(241)*

Dodd, Carri
Flexographic Technical Association *(447)*

Dodd, Hon. Christopher J.
Motion Picture Association of America (MPAA) *(619)*

Dodd, Dan
Costume Designers Guild *(387)*

Dodd, Donna
Association of Collegiate Schools of Planning *(275)*

Dodd, Kate
American Society for Therapeutic Radiology and Oncology *(190)*

Dodd, Kelly
National Association of Corporate Directors *(658)*

Dodd, Michael
The Endocrine Society *(427)*

Dodd, Stacy
National Association of Secretaries of State *(695)*

Doddridge, Kathy
Risk and Insurance Management Society, Inc. (RIMS) *(886)*

Dodds, Barbara
Ladies Professional Golf Association *(592)*

Dodds, Christopher
Council of Independent Colleges *(394)*

Dodds, Diane
American Society for Laser Medicine and Surgery *(186)*

Dodds, Peter
International Society for Molecular Plant Microbe Interactions *(567)*

Dodenhoff, Richard
American Society for Pharmacology and Experimental Therapeutics *(188)*

Dodge, Brian A.
Retail Industry Leaders Association *(884)*

Dodge, Garen
Council for Employment Law Equity (CELE) *(389)*

Dodge, Gary
Forest Stewardship Council - United States Chapter *(451)*

Dodge, Laurie
Association of Junior Leagues International *(290)*

Dodge, Sarah
International Academy of Compounding Pharmacists *(509)*

Dodia, Pooja K.
Decision Sciences Institute *(407)*

Dodson, Kathleen A.
American Orthotic and Prosthetic Association *(159)*

Dodson, Mike
Association of Educational Publishers *(280)*

Dodson, Sylvia
Owner-Operator Independent Drivers Association, Inc. *(836)*

Dodson, Veronigue
National Association of Black Journalists *(649)*

Dodson-Chambers, Shae
Ranchers-Cattlemen Action Legal Fund, United Stockgrower of America *(874)*

Doell, Paul
National Air Carrier Association *(630)*

Doerfler, Steve
National Association of Graphic and Product Identification Manufacturers *(670)*

Doezema, Kathy
Christian Schools International *(356)*

Dogan, Stacey
Copyright Society of the U.S.A. *(385)*

Doggett, Enid
American Federation of Government Employees *(119)*

Doggett, CCP, Marc G.
National Glass Association *(755)*

Doherty, Mark G.
Emdr International Association *(425)*

Doherty, Peter
Microscopy Society of America *(615)*

Dohrmann, Deb
National Wildlife Rehabilitators Association *(805)*

Dolan, Christine
National Association of Elementary School Principals *(664)*

Dolan, Connor
Fuel Cell and Hydrogen Energy Association *(454)*

Dolan, Dan
Electric Power Supply Association (EPSA) *(421)*

Dolan, Dana
Bank Administration Institute *(326)*

Dolan, Gregory A.
Methanol Institute *(614)*

Dolan, Jack F.
American Council of Life Insurers (ACLI) *(110)*

Dolan, Karen
International Council of Air Shows *(538)*

Dolan, Patrick
Interactive Advertising Bureau *(506)*

Dolan, Sean P.
Catholic Academy for Communication Arts Professionals *(345)*

Dolan, CAE, FACHE, PhD, Thomas C.
American College of Healthcare Executives *(96)*

Dolet, Peggy
American Society for Engineering Education *(183)*

Dolibois, CAE, Robert J.
American Nursery and Landscape Association *(156)*

Dolim, Barbara A.
Mechanical Service Contractors of America *(610)*

Dolim, Mike
Association of Old Crows *(297)*

Dolin, Matt
United Transportation Union *(1001)*

Doll, Linda A.
National Watercolor Society *(804)*

Dollar, Stephanie S. Baron
Women's Basketball Coaches Association *(1022)*

Dollins, Sallie C.
Institute of Transportation Engineers *(503)*

Dolnack, Chris
National Shooting Sports Foundation *(791)*

Domagalski, Deb
Women in Management *(1021)*

Doman, Janet
International Academy for Child Brain Development *(509)*

Dombi, William A.
National Association for Home Care and Hospice *(639)*

Domboski, Kristy L.
Construction Financial Management Association *(379)*

Domine, Victor

Craft & Hobby Association *(402)*

Dominique, A. J.
United States Rowing Association *(998)*

Donadio, Brian J.
American College of Osteopathic Internists *(100)*

Donahey, PE, Rex C.
American Concrete Institute *(106)*

Donahoe, Patrick W.
Associated Universities Inc. *(237)*

Donahue, George
Association of Flight Attendants - CWA *(283)*

Donald, Ian Mc
National Association of Publishers' Representatives *(689)*

Donald, Illyce Mac
National Genealogical Society *(754)*

Donaldson, Ann
Trauma Care International *(979)*

Donaldson, Elaine
Music Teachers National Association *(622)*

Donaldson, Eric
International Foodservice Manufacturers Association *(546)*

Donaldson, J. Mark
Stuntmen's Association of Motion Pictures *(964)*

Donaldson, MD, Jim
Society for Pediatric Radiology *(918)*

Donaldson, John
TESOL International Association *(971)*

Donaldson, Joseph
National Association of Extension 4-H Agents *(667)*

Donaldson, Lydia L.
American College of Veterinary Anesthesiologists *(103)*

Donaldson, Randall P.
Society for German-American Studies *(910)*

Donato, Kathleen
National Association for the Education of Young Children *(644)*

Donato, Sheila
Association for the Advancement of Wound Care *(258)*

Dones, Bles
Public Risk Management Association *(870)*

Donfor, Anthony
Conference of State Bank Supervisors *(376)*

Donham, Tammy
Country Music Association *(401)*

Donio, Jim
National Association of Recording Merchandisers (NARM) *(690)*

Donlon, Sandy
American Holistic Nurses Association *(132)*

Donn, Valerie
Association of Directory Publishers *(279)*
Local Media Association *(599)*

Donnellan, Kevin J.
American Association of Retired Persons *(72)*

Donnelly, Christina
Environmental Markets Association *(431)*

Donnelly, Christina
Hotel Electronic Distribution Network Association *(479)*

Donnelly, Christina
Weather Risk Management Association *(1014)*

Donnelly, MS, Christine

International Society of Crime Prevention Practitioners *(572)*

Donnelly, Drei
Association of Celebrity Personal Assistants *(271)*

Donnelly, John L
National Association of Vertical Transportation Professionals *(708)*

Donnelly, Marlene Hill
Guild of Natural Science Illustrators *(467)*

Donnelly, PhD, Maureen A.
American Society of Ichthyologists and Herpetologists *(200)*

Donnelly, Patrick J.
American Oil Chemists' Society *(157)*

Donnelly, Thomas F.
National Water Resources Association *(804)*

Donner, Martin
International Newspaper Group *(558)*

Donofrio, Rachel
National Catholic Development Conference *(718)*

Donoghue, Edward A.
National Elevator Industry, Inc. *(745)*

Donohoe, Susan K.
TechServe Alliance *(971)*

Donohue, Jay
International Association of Administrative Professionals *(515)*

Donohue, Michele
American Society for Therapeutic Radiology and Oncology *(190)*

Donohue, CMSRN, CPP, MN, Regina
American Academy of Ambulatory Care Nursing *(30)*

Donohue, Sharon King
National Committee for Quality Assurance *(724)*

Donohue, Thomas J.
American National Chamber of Commerce *(154)*
United States Chamber of Commerce *(991)*

Donor, Lisa
Air Force Sergeants Association *(19)*

Donovan, Claudine
American Statistical Association *(213)*

Donovan, CAE, Kristi
Association of University Programs in Health Administration *(316)*

Donovan, Lois
ISA -The Association of Learning Providers *(586)*

Donovan, Mary
Messenger Courier Association of the Americas *(612)*

Donovan, Patricia
The Open Group *(828)*

Donovan, Tricia
Library Copyright Alliance *(597)*

Doodeman, Karen
Association for Retail Environments *(256)*

Dooley, Austin L.
Society of Maritime Arbitrators *(941)*

Dooley, Calvin M.
American Chemistry Council *(90)*
Chlorine Chemistry Council *(354)*

Dooley, Connie
Petroleum Equipment Institute *(843)*

Dooley, Dennis
Capital Health *(342)*

Dooling, Kelly
League for Innovation in the Community College *(595)*

Doolittle, Sondra
American Academy of Forensic Sciences *(34)*

Doomanis, Stefan
Mystery Shopping Providers Association *(623)*

Doornbosch, Trisha
Equipment and Tool Institute *(432)*

Dopp, Mark
American Meat Institute *(148)*

Dopp, Mark
Shelf-Stable Food Processors Association *(898)*

Doran, Ashlie
Association of Pathology Chairs *(298)*

Doran, Dennis
Construction Management Association of America *(379)*

Doran, John
National Coalition of Public Safety Officers *(723)*

Doresca, Annie
Jewelers of America *(587)*

Dorgan, Kimberly Olsen
American Council of Life Insurers (ACLI) *(110)*

Doria, Gabi
Caribbean Hotel and Tourism Association *(343)*

Doria, Guy
Club Managers Association of America *(359)*

Doringo, Lowell
Health Occupations Students of America *(470)*

Doris, Susanne K.
American Guild of Variety Artists *(128)*

Dorn, Jennifer (Jenna) L.
American Academy of Physician Assistants *(40)*

Dorn, Susan E.
United States Green Building Council *(994)*

Dornan, James
American Society of Pension Professionals & Actuaries *(206)*

Dornberger, Sherrie
National Association of Directors of Nursing Administration in Long Term Care *(663)*

Dorning, Jennifer
Department for Professional Employees - AFL-CIO *(410)*

Dorning, Melinda
Association of Collegiate Business Schools and Programs *(275)*

Dorr, Jackie
Women in Mining National *(1022)*

Dorrough, Carol
The Fertilizer Institute *(443)*

Dorsano, Sofia
World Allergy Organization *(1025)*

Dorsey, Darlene D.
North American Association for Environmental Education *(812)*

Dorsey, Mark
PSIA-AASI *(868)*

Dorsey, Pamela
The Aluminum Association, Inc. *(27)*

Dorsey, Dr. Scott W.
American Choral Directors Association *(90)*

Dorsey, Susan
Council for Opportunity in Education *(390)*

Dort, DDS, Leslie C.
American Academy of Dental Sleep Medicine *(32)*

Dosik, Anita

APPA - Leadership in Educational Facilities *(225)*

Doss, Joseph
International Bottled Water Association *(530)*

Doss, Karl
National Legal Aid and Defender Association *(769)*

Dossin, Lia
State Education Technology Directors Association *(961)*

Dotchin, Susan
National Governors Association *(755)*

Dotolo, PhD, Dr. Lawrence G.
The Association for Consortium Leadership *(243)*

Dotson, Jennifer
Organization Development Network *(831)*

Doty, Brian
Bluegrass Tourism Marketing Association *(332)*
National Gerontological Nursing Association *(755)*

Doty, Brian
Society of Trauma Nurses *(949)*

Doty, David
Interactive Advertising Bureau *(506)*

Doty, Kate
American Society of International Law *(201)*

Doubet, Sherry
American Salers Association *(176)*
North American South Devon Association *(822)*
United States Beef Breeds Council *(991)*

Douce, Denise
International Dyslexia Association *(541)*

Doucet, Tony
Association for Psychological Type International *(254)*

Doucette, Lucille
American Society of Limnology and Oceanography *(202)*

Doud, Dustin
American Astronautical Society *(77)*

Dougan, William R.
National Federation of Federal Employees *(748)*
National Federation of Federal Employees, Federal Dist. 1, IAMAW, AFL-CIO *(748)*

Dougherty, Caitlin
International Energy Credit Association *(542)*
National Association of Professional Pet Sitters *(687)*

Dougherty, Colleen
American Academy of Child and Adolescent Psychiatry *(31)*

Dougherty, Diane
Chief Officers of State Libraries Agencies *(352)*

Dougherty, Douglas
Geothermal Heat Pump Consortium *(459)*

Dougherty, John J.
International Brotherhood of Electrical Workers #98 *(531)*

Dougherty, Matthew S.
National Association of Foreign Trade Zones *(669)*

Dougherty, Meredith
International Safe Transit Association *(563)*

Dougherty, Michael
American Society of Human Genetics *(200)*

Dougherty, Patrick
National Community Pharmacists Association *(725)*

Douglas, Brian
Association of Energy Engineers *(280)*

Douglas, James S.
Association for Molecular Pathology *(252)*

Douglas, CPA, James S.

American Society for Investigative Pathology *(186)*

Douglas, Jan Eric
American Academy of Teachers of Singing *(42)*

Douglas, Joy
Truckload Carriers Association *(981)*

Douglas, Lonnie
International Association of Official Human Rights Agencies *(525)*

Douglas, Patricia
National Coordinating Committee for Multiemployer Plans *(730)*

Douglas, Scott
National Strength and Conditioning Association *(797)*

Douglas, Stacey L.
Used Textbook Association *(1005)*

Douglass, Laurie
American Chiropractic Association *(90)*

Douin, David A.
National Board of Boiler and Pressure Vessel Inspectors *(715)*

Douthit, Rhonda
University Council for Educational Administration *(1002)*

Douvris, Mara
Institute of Environmental Sciences and Technology *(499)*

Dove, G. Timothy
National Association of Flour Distributors *(668)*

Dove, Greg
National Flea Market Association *(751)*

Dove, Susan
Nurses Organization of Veterans Affairs *(825)*

Dover, CAE, Marge
National Association of Legal Assistants *(677)*

Dow, Roger J.
US Travel Association *(983)*

Dow, Thomas A.
American Society for Precision Engineering *(188)*

Dowd, Christopher G.
Shareholder Services Association *(898)*

Dowd, Verna
United Gamefowl Breeders Association, Inc. *(987)*

Dowdell, John
Correctional Education Association *(386)*

Dowden, James C.
Alliance of Area Business Publications *(24)*
American Academy of Medical Acupuncture *(36)*
City and Regional Magazine Association *(357)*
Parenting Media Association *(838)*

Dowden, Tracey
American Academy of Medical Acupuncture *(36)*
Parenting Media Association *(838)*

Dowdy, Angie
National Conference of State Social Security Administrators *(728)*

Dowdy, Carrie
National Council on Public History *(739)*

Dowling, Jennifer Connell
National Venture Capital Association *(803)*

Dowling, Theodora
Public Lands Council *(869)*

Dowling, Valerie
National Federation of Republican Women *(750)*

Downard, CGMP, Michael
Society of Government Meeting Professionals *(938)*

Downey, CAE, David T.

International Downtown Association (541)

Downey, Linda
Women's Foodservice Forum (1023)

Downey, Pat "Patrick"
Gas Machinery Research Council (456)

Downey, Paul
National Association of Nutrition and Aging Services Programs (682)

Downham, Max C.
International College of Surgeons (535)

Downing, CMP, Denise
International Hard Anodizing Association (549)

Downing, MBA, G. Daniel
ECRI (418)

Downing, John
American Society of Limnology and Oceanography (202)

Downs, Chris
Society for the Psychological Study of Lesbian and Gay Issues (924)

Downs, JD, MHA, Gov. Christian G.
Association of Community Cancer Centers (275)

Downs, David H.
American Real Estate and Urban Economics Association (173)

Downs, Linda
College Art Association (362)

Downs, Mary E.
American Academy of Actuaries (29)

Downs, Paul D.
American Foreign Law Association (122)

Doxey, Nichole
National Association of Health and Educational Facilities Finance Authorities (671)

Doyle, Ashley
American College of Osteopathic Family Physicians (100)

Doyle, Beth
Council for Adult and Experiential Learning (388)

Doyle, APR, Chris
Adventure Travel Trade Association (13)

Doyle, Christina
Association of Schools and Colleges of Optometry (307)

Doyle, Elizabeth Z.
Meals on Wheels Association of America (609)

Doyle, Frank
IEEE Control Systems Society (484)

Doyle, Frank
NAFSA: Association of International Educators (624)

Doyle, J. Andrew
American Coatings Association (92)

Doyle, Jeff
Society of Economic Geologists (934)

Doyle, Jennifer
Health Industry Distributors Association (469)

Doyle, MBA, John J.
Project Management Institute (866)

Doyle, Jr., John S.
Waterways Council, Inc. (1014)

Doyle, CAE, Kenneth A.
Society of Independent Gasoline Marketers of America (SIGMA) (939)

Doyle, Kevin
Society for Marketing Professional Services (914)

Doyle, Krissy
Society of American Florists (928)

Doyle, Michele
United States Composting Council (992)

Doyle, Rick
Synthetic Turf Council (967)

Doyle, Stephen P.
Alarm Industry Communication Committee (21)
Central Station Alarm Association (349)

Doyle, Walter
National Association for Black Geologists and Geophysicists (636)

Doyle, William
Marine Engineers Beneficial Association (605)

Doyle, Zanetta
National Association of Development Organizations (662)

Doyle-Kimball, Mary
National Association of Real Estate Editors (690)

Dozier, Damon A.
American Anthropological Association (45)

Dozier, Tom
National Auto Auction Association (711)

Dozier-Brame, Monica
National Center for Employee Ownership (719)

Drabek, Steve
Quality Chekd Dairies (871)

Drabon, Lysan
Society for Clinical Data Management (906)

Draeger, Justin
National Association of Student Financial Aid Administrators (703)

Drafta, CIH, CSP, SPHR, Ron
American Board of Industrial Hygiene (82)

Drager, Kris
American Foundry Society (123)

Dragon, Margaret
Health Care Compliance Association (469)

Drain, David
Digital Screenmedia Association (412)

Drake, Chris
Employee Assistance Professionals Association (426)

Drake, Clay
National Lamb Feeders Association (768)

Drake, James M.
The American Society of Pediatric Neurosurgeons (206)

Drake, Janie
Society for the Advancement of Material and Process Engineering (922)

Drake, Kymberly
NAMM - The International Music Products Association (625)

Drake, Marta Perez
National Association of College and University Business Officers (654)

Drake, MBA, Stephanie H.
American Society for Healthcare Human Resources Administration (185)

Drapeau, Kathryn Porter
American Homebrewers Association (133)

Draper, Timothy D.
Immigration and Ethnic History Society (487)

Draves, CAE, IV, William A.
Learning Resources Network (596)

Drax, Dr. DJ
American Disc Jockey Association (115)

Drea, Dan
National Association of Congregational Christian Churches (657)

Drebin, MD, PhD, Jeffrey A.
Society of Surgical Oncology (947)

Drechsler Sharp, Marybeth
Council for the Advancement of Standards in Higher Education (391)

Drees, Carey
Alliance for Children and Families (22)

Dreger, Marianne
American College of Occupational and Environmental Medicine (99)

Dreher, Michael
National Forensic Association (752)

Dreier, CMP, Brenda
Society for Laboratory Automation and Screening (914)

Drennan, Andy
Food Processing Suppliers Association (449)

Drennan, Brittni
International Brangus Breeders Association (531)

Dreskin, Joan
Interstate Natural Gas Association of America (583)

Dress, Kara
American Urogynecologic Society (218)
Association of Professional Researchers for Advancement (302)
Bank Insurance and Securities Association (326)
National Association of Medical Staff Services (645)
National Association of Orthopedic Nurses (683)

Dresselhaus, Angela
North American Serials Interest Group (820)

Drevna, Charles T.
American Fuel & Petrochemical Manufacturers (124)

Drew, MD, Denis W.
International Society for Computerized Electrocardiology (566)

Drew, James
Radiological Society of North America (873)

Drew, Mark
American Association of Wildlife Veterinarians (77)

Drewry, Brett
Marine Preservation Association (605)

Drewsen, Alan C.
International Trademark Association (577)

Drexler, Diane
American College of Neuropsychopharmacology (98)

Dreyer, CMP, Johnny
Gas Processors Association (456)
Gas Processors Suppliers Association (456)

Dreyfus, Blair
National Association of Litho Clubs (678)

Dreyfus, Susan
Alliance for Children and Families (22)

Driggs, Kathi
Club Managers Association of America (359)

Drinan, JD, James M.
American Association of Endodontists (60)

Drioane, Gina
Consortium of Social Science Associations (379)

Dripps, CAE, John N.
National Association of Secondary School Principals (694)

Driscoll, Danielle
Organization Development Network (831)

Driscoll, Leah

International Executive Housekeepers Association *(543)*

Driscoll, Phillip
Amalgamated Printer's Association *(27)*

Driscoll, Terry
National Air Filtration Association *(630)*

Driskill, Jimmy
Appraisal Institute *(226)*

Driver, Riley
Southeastern Theatre Conference *(953)*

Driver-Barstow, Susannah
Editorial Freelancers Association *(419)*

Drobins, Barbara
American Society of Landscape Architects *(201)*

Drobnis, Michael
Society of Neurointerventional Surgery *(942)*

Drohan, CAE, William M
Sports Lawyers Association *(959)*

Drollinger, Darrin J.
American Society of Agricultural and Biological Engineers *(191)*

Drotar, Stephanie
League of Resident Theatres *(595)*

Droz, Fred
Council of Communication Management *(393)*

Drozdek, Jenni
American Philosophical Society *(164)*

Drozdowski, Rob
Electronic Transactions Association *(424)*

Drudy, Michael A.
Railway Systems Suppliers, Inc *(874)*

Drulis, Jean
Human Milk Banking Association of North America *(481)*

Drum, Bob
Society of Architectural Historians *(930)*

Drummer, Betsy
International Society for the Comparative Studies of Civilizations *(569)*

Drummond, Erin
The Association for Academic Surgery *(237)*

Drummond, PhD, Sean P.A.
Sleep Research Society *(900)*

Drupa, David A.
National Association of Biology Teachers *(648)*
Society for Risk Analysis *(920)*

Drupa, Jill
National Association of Biology Teachers *(648)*

Drury, Jr., Charles W.
Council On State Taxation *(400)*

Drury, Margaret
Society of Flight Test Engineers *(936)*

Du Teil, Jack John
United States Army Warrant Officers Association *(990)*

Duane, Patricia
American Institute of Certified Public Accountants *(137)*

Duarte, PhD, Cynthia
National Association for Chicana and Chicano Studies *(637)*

Duarte, Gloria A.
Union of American Physicians and Dentists *(985)*

Duax, William L.
American Crystallographic Association *(112)*

DuBeau, Gretchen

Alliance for Natural Health USA *(23)*

Dubiel, Holly
National Association of EMS Educators *(665)*

Dubinsky, Jim
Association for Business Communication *(240)*

Dubnansky, Erin
American Gastroenterological Association *(125)*

Dubnicka, Thomas J.
Bank Administration Institute *(326)*

DuBois, CMP, CAE, FASAE, CTA, David
International Association of Exhibitions and Events *(520)*

Dubois, MPS, Deacon Thomas MPS R.
National Association of Diaconate Directors *(662)*

Dubois, Deborah E.
National Legal Aid and Defender Association *(769)*

DuBois, Dee
National Junior College Athletic Association *(767)*

DuBois, MBA, PHR, Maureen
American Academy of Child and Adolescent Psychiatry *(31)*

Dubois, Robert W.
National Pharmaceutical Council *(780)*

Dubord, Taylor
International Association of Ice Cream Vendors *(523)*

Dubow, Eric
International Society for Research on Aggression *(569)*

Dubroff, Rich
Professional Basketball Writers' Association *(860)*

Dubrowski, Ken
Illustrator's Partnership of America *(486)*

Ducate, CEM, CMP, Douglas L.
Center for Exhibition Industry Research *(348)*

DuChateau, Brandan
National Wellness Institute, Inc. *(804)*

Duck, Leah
American Concrete Pumping Association *(106)*

Ducker, Crystal
International Spa Association *(575)*

Ducker, Valerie
Society of Research Administrators International *(946)*

Duckler, Cheryl
International Society of Hair Restoration Surgery *(573)*

Duckworth, James 'Rusty"
American Trucking Associations *(218)*

Duda, Kathleen
Patent Office Professional Association *(839)*

Dudley, Hubert T.
National Roof Deck Contractors Association *(787)*

Dudley, Lynn
American Benefits Council *(80)*

Dudley, Stephanie D.
Population Association of America *(853)*

Dudley, Susan
Society for the Psychological Study of Science Issues *(924)*
Society for the Psychological Study of Social Issues *(924)*

Duduit, Michael
American Academy of Ministry *(36)*

Dudzik, Joseph
National Council of State Boards for Nursing *(736)*

Duenow, Peg
Association of Kentucky Fried Chicken Franchisees, Inc. *(290)*

Duensing, MEd, Lennie
American Academy of Pain Management *(39)*

Duensing, Tiffiny J.
Arthroscopy Association of North America *(230)*

Duerdoth, CAE, Katherine J.
American Society for Dermatologic Surgery *(183)*

Duesing, Bill
Northeast Organic Farming Association *(824)*

Duesterhaus, Rich
National Association of Conservation Districts *(657)*

Duff, Michael J.
Analytical and Life Science Systems Association *(223)*

Duffin, Michael B.
Precision Machined Products Association *(856)*

Duffy, Bill
National School Supply and Equipment Association *(789)*

Duffy, Christine
Cruise Lines International Association *(405)*

Duffy, Deb
WIFS - Women in Insurance and Financial Services *(1017)*

Duffy, Patrick
Union for Radical Political Economics *(985)*

Duffy, Stephen C.
American Academy of Facial Plastic and Reconstructive Surgery *(34)*

Duffy, Susan Day
American Beverage Licensees *(81)*

Dugan, Lesa
American Osteopathic College of Anesthesiologists *(160)*

Dugan, MBA, Michael
Federation of State Medical Boards of the United States *(442)*

Dugard, Dr. Paul
Halogenated Solvents Industry Alliance *(468)*

Dugas, Jennifer
American Bankruptcy Institute *(79)*

Duggan, Diane
The College Board *(363)*

Duggan, Michael P.
National American Legion Press Association *(634)*

Duggan, Noreene
American Council on Education *(110)*

Duggan, Tomiko
World Media Association *(1027)*

Duginske, Sara B.
United States Psychiatric Rehabilitation Association *(998)*

Duguay, Linda
Sea Grant Association *(894)*

Duke, Diane C.
Free Speech Coalition *(453)*

Duke, CAE, Robert
International Association of Fire Chiefs *(521)*

Dukes, Brooke
National Association of Sales Professionals *(692)*

Dukes, CMP, Diane
Professional Liability Underwriting Society *(863)*

Dulli, Zachary R.
National Council for Geographic Education *(731)*

Dumaresq, EdD, Dr. Richard
Aviation Technician Education Council *(325)*

Dummer, CAE, Greg

Society for Laboratory Automation and Screening *(914)*

Dummett, Bridget
Museum Store Association *(621)*

Dumont, Peter F.
Air Traffic Control Association *(19)*

Dumont, Robert J.
Tooling, Manufacturing and Technologies Association *(976)*

Dunavant, Kathy
National Association of Junior Auxiliaries *(677)*

Dunbar, Anne
National Marine Manufacturers Association *(771)*

Dunbar, Linda
International Association of Correctional Training Personnel *(518)*

Dunbar, Peter
National Exchange Carrier Association *(746)*

Dunbar, Susan
American Industrial Hygiene Association *(135)*

Duncan, Andy
National Hospice & Palliative Care Organization *(760)*

Duncan, SPHR, Brenda A.
Healthcare Information and Management Systems Society *(471)*

Duncan, Claudia
National Tour Association *(800)*

Duncan, Daniel
AFL-CIO - Maritime Trades Department *(15)*

Duncan, Jessica
American Gastroenterological Association *(125)*

Duncan, Joanne
Biotechnology Industry Organization (BIO) *(330)*

Duncan, Jovan
National Association of Postal Supervisors *(685)*

Duncan, Mallory B.
National Retail Federation *(786)*

Duncan, Mike
Board Retailers Association *(333)*

Duncan, Patricia
American Spinal Injury Association *(212)*

Duncan, Renee
Undersea and Hyperbaric Medical Society *(984)*

Duncan, PE, PhD, Rick
Spray Polyurethane Foam Alliance *(959)*

Duncan, Shan D.
Animal Behavior Society *(223)*

Duncan-Jones, Geri
American Health and Beauty Aids Institute *(129)*

Dundas, Bill
International Sign Association *(564)*

Dunford, Ron
National Cheese Institute *(720)*

Dungey, Rick
International Fruit Tree Association *(547)*
National Christmas Tree Association *(721)*

Dungy, Gwendolyn J.
National Association of Student Personnel Administrators *(626)*

Dunham, Louise
National Tunis Sheep Registry *(802)*

Dunham, Rodney
The National Federation of Paralegal Associations, Inc. *(749)*

Dunipace, Laura
National Association of Disability Examiners *(663)*

Dunkel, Alexander
National Association of Self-Instructional Language Programs *(695)*

Dunkelberger, Dona
Ornamental Concrete Producers Association *(833)*

Dunkelberger, Scott
Ornamental Concrete Producers Association *(833)*

Dunlap, CPA, Brian E.
National Propane Gas Association *(783)*

Dunlap, Dennis
American Marketing Association *(147)*

Dunlap, Ellen S.
American Antiquarian Society *(45)*

Dunlap, John
Self Storage Association *(896)*

Dunlap, Peter
American Bankers Insurance Association *(79)*

Dunleavey, Jennifer
Direct Selling Association *(413)*

Dunlop, Jodi
American Society of Heating, Refrigerating and Air Conditioning Engineers (ASHRAE) *(199)*

Dunmire, Linda
The American Safe Deposit Association *(176)*

Dunn, Esq., Alexandra
Association of Clean Water Administrators *(273)*

Dunn, Amy
American Watchmakers-Clockmakers Institute *(219)*

Dunn, Ben M.
American Peptide Society *(163)*

Dunn, USA (Ret.), BG Malinda E.
American Inns of Court *(135)*

Dunn, Bill
National Shooting Sports Foundation *(791)*

Dunn, Carol
International Association of Forensic Nurses *(521)*

Dunn, Dan
National Drilling Association *(743)*

Dunn, CAE, Donna French
Association of YMCA Professionals *(318)*

Dunn, Eric
American Association of Motor Vehicle Administrators *(65)*

Dunn, Heather
Society of Professional Journalists *(945)*

Dunn, James
Union Label and Service Trades Department *(985)*

Dunn, Karen
Child Welfare League of America *(353)*

Dunn, Katrina
American Society for Nutrition *(187)*

Dunn, Laura
The Society of Composers and Lyricists *(933)*

Dunn, Marcus
Security Industry Association *(895)*

Dunn, Martha
National Association of Physician Recruiters *(684)*

Dunn, Michelle
American Credit and Collections Association *(111)*

Dunn, Rob
American Resort Development Association *(175)*

Dunn, Sidney N.
Fraternity Executives Association *(453)*
Osteopathic Cranial Academy *(834)*

Dunn, Susan
Hydraulic Institute *(481)*

Dunn-Rankin, Derek
The Combustion Institute *(366)*

Dunnaway-McIntire, Nora
Sports Turf Managers Association *(959)*

Dunne, Diane
American College of Radiology *(102)*

Dunne, Leslie
Society of General Internal Medicine *(937)*

Dunnick, Kim
International Trumpet Guild *(578)*

Duntley, Janey
National Agricultural Alumni and Development Association *(630)*

Duong, Thanh
Medicaid Health Plans of America *(611)*

Duplinsky, Annette C.
Helicopter Association International *(473)*

DuPont, Rose
International Franchise Association *(547)*

Dupree, Jeff
National Exchange Carrier Association *(746)*

Dupree, Lindley "Lil"
Community Action Partnership *(369)*

Duran, Catherine L.
American Institute of Professional Geologists *(140)*

Duran, Kathy
International Brotherhood of Boilermakers, Iron Shipbuilders, Blacksmiths, Forgers and Helpers *(531)*

Duran, Mishaela
National Parent Teachers Association *(779)*

Durand, Tracey
American Logistics Association *(146)*

Durante, Anthony
American Association of Physician Specialists *(69)*

Durante, Bill
American Intellectual Property Law Association *(141)*

Durband, Heather
American College of Phlebology *(100)*

Durbin, Martin J.
American Petroleum Institute *(163)*

Durcsak, Connie
Utilities Telecom Council *(1006)*

Durden, Daniel
National Association of Home Builders *(673)*

Duren, Steve
Adhesive and Sealant Council *(12)*

Durfee, Don
Society for Industrial Archeology *(913)*

Durham, Alexis
American Herbalists Guild *(131)*

Durham, Judy B.
NPES, The Association for Suppliers of Printing, Publishing, and Converting Technologies *(824)*

Durham, Maria Garcia
Association of Performing Arts Presenters *(298)*

Durham, Melody
Federation of American Hospitals *(440)*

Durie, Chelsie
Technical Association of the Pulp and Paper Industry *(970)*

Duris, Mark
IPC - Association Connecting Electronics Industries *(584)*

IPC - Surface Mount Equipment Manufacturers Association **(585)**

Durkee, David B.
Bakery, Confectionery, Tobacco Workers and Grain Millers International Union **(325)**

Durkin, CEM, Amy
National Catholic Educational Association **(718)**
National Catholic Educational Exhibitors **(718)**

Durkin, Ashley
Wine and Spirits Wholesalers of America **(1018)**

Durkin, Hap
Catholic Campus Ministry Association **(345)**

Durkin, J D, Helen
International Health, Racquet and Sportsclub Association **(549)**

Durkin, Patrick
Archery Trade Association **(227)**

Durniak, Anthony J.
Institute of Electrical and Electronics Engineers (IEEE) **(499)**

Durst, Cheryl
International Interior Design Association **(552)**

Durst, PhD, Elizabeth
American Association of Teachers of Slavic and East European Languages **(75)**

Durst, Karl W.
Society for Simulation in Healthcare **(921)**

Durston, Deryck
Association for Clinical Pastoral Education **(241)**

Duryea, Michele
Population Action International **(852)**

Duse, Kathy
National Art Education Association **(635)**

Dussor, William
International Health, Racquet and Sportsclub Association **(549)**

Dustman, Karl
Percussion Marketing Council **(841)**

Dutcher, Heather
Native American Journalists Association **(806)**

Dutra, Geri
American Classical League **(91)**

Dutton, MD, PhD, Jonathan J.
American Society of Ophthalmic Plastic and Reconstructive Surgery **(205)**

Dutton, PhD, Rennie
Voices for America's Children **(1011)**

Duty, Kimberly D.
National Multi-Housing Council **(774)**

Duval, Jill
Women's Regional Publications of America **(1024)**

Duval, Lisa
Custom Electronic Design and Installation Association **(405)**

Duvall, Henry
Council of the Great City Schools **(398)**

Duvic, Philip
Architectural Woodwork Institute **(228)**

Dux, Rob
Council of Residential Specialists **(396)**

Dvorak, Darin
Health Care Compliance Association **(469)**

Dvorak, CAE, MS, Mitchell
National Association of Housing Cooperatives **(673)**

Dwamena, Dei
American Association of Community Colleges **(58)**

Dweck, Jake
Canadian-American Business Council **(341)**

Dwyer, Jeanette P.
National Rural Letter Carriers' Association **(788)**

Dwyer, John W.
Lignite Energy Council **(598)**

Dwyer, Lauren
National Multi-Housing Council **(774)**

Dwyer, CAE, Michael
Juvenile Products Manufacturers Association **(590)**

Dwyer, Pat
Decorative Plumbing and Hardware Association **(408)**

Dwyer, Saralyn
System Safety Society **(967)**

Dwyer, Esq., Stephen C.
American Staffing Association **(213)**

Dwyer, Tom
Association of College and University Auditors **(274)**

Dyck, Zoë
International Academy of Television Arts and Sciences **(509)**

Dye, Carl M.
American Schools Association **(177)**

Dye, Jane
Society for Cinema and Media Studies **(905)**

Dye, Mary Jane
American String Teachers Association **(213)**

Dye, Morgan
Airports Council International - North America **(21)**

Dyekman, Larry A.
National Futures Association **(754)**

Dyer, Carolina Cordero
Osborne Association **(834)**

Dyer, Connie
American Hardware Manufacturers Association **(128)**

Dyer, Don
Center for Research Libraries **(348)**

Dyer, Lynn M.
Foodservice & Packaging Institute, Inc. **(450)**

Dyer, Mark
Independent Equipment Dealers Association **(489)**

Dyer, CAE, Randy
International Electronic Article Surveillance Manufacturers Association **(542)**

Dyer, Susan
National Volunteer Fire Council **(803)**

Dyke, Christina Van
Society of Christian Philosophers **(932)**

Dyke, Ted Van
Public Housing Authorities Directors Association **(869)**

Dykema, CAE, Sue
American Society for Aesthetic Plastic Surgery **(180)**

Dykers, Craig
Norwegian-American Chamber of Commerce **(824)**

Dykes, Barb
Institute of Packaging Professionals **(502)**

Dykes, Joseph (Joe) R.
North American Equipment Dealers Association **(816)**

Dykstra, Gregg
National Association of Mutual Insurance Companies **(681)**

Dykstra, Leslie
American Society of Consultant Pharmacists **(195)**

Dylkiewicz, Stephanie

American Pain Society **(161)**
The American Society of Pediatric Hematology/ Oncology **(206)**

Dylla, H. Frederick
American Institute of Physics **(140)**

Dyreson, Curtis
Special Interest Group on Management of Data **(956)**

Dysart, Katie
Generic Pharmaceutical Association **(458)**

Dyson, Debbie L.
National Training and Simulation Association **(801)**

Dyson, CMP, Lisa
TESOL International Association **(971)**

Dyson, Peter
American Society of Media Photographers **(203)**

Dyson, Sue
The International Fluid Power Society **(545)**

Dyson, Susan
Equipment Service Association **(433)**

Dzanis, David
American College of Veterinary Nutrition **(104)**

Dzime-Assison, Roosevelt
Directors of Health Promotion and Education (DHPE) **(413)**

Dzimian, Thomas
German American Chamber of Commerce **(460)**

Dzuban, Mark
Society of Cable Telecommunications Engineers **(931)**

E., Ernesto Acuña
Academy of Dentistry International **(5)**

Eaddy, Suzette
National Minority Supplier Development Council **(773)**

Eadie, Wayne
MPA - The Association of Magazine Media **(620)**

Eads, Katie
American Association of Managed Care Nurses **(64)**
National Association of Managed Care Physicians **(679)**

Eads, CAE, Kip
Professional Retail Store Maintenance Association **(864)**

Eagan, Jill
International Dyslexia Association **(541)**

Eagen, Jim
Financial Executives International **(444)**

Eagle, Jane
National Notary Association **(775)**

Eagles, Kate
National Association for PET Container Resources **(641)**

Eames, Charles
American Institute of Organbuilders **(139)**

Earey, Carol
Psychometric Society **(868)**

Earl, Charles N.
National Council of State Directors of Community Colleges **(736)**

Earl, Sharon
International Municipal Signal Association **(557)**

Earle, Kim
American Astronomical Society **(77)**

Earle, Kristen
National Council of Higher Education Loan Programs **(735)**

Earle, Sydney
Consortium on Financing Higher Education **(379)**

Earle, William T.
National Association of Beverage Importers Inc. *(648)*

Early, RN, Barbara J.
Academy of Clinical Research Professionals *(4)*

Early, Carole A.
The National Association of Colored Women's Club, Inc. *(656)*

Earnest, CMP, Carla
National Association of Residential Property Managers *(691)*

Earp, Wendy
Motor and Equipment Manufacturers Association *(619)*

Earthman, Dr. Glen I.
International Society for Educational Planning *(566)*

Earwood, Janeen
National Spinal Cord Injury Association *(795)*
United Spinal Association *(989)*

Easley, Jr., Cliff R.
American Blonde D'Aquitaine Association *(81)*

Easley, Emily
Solar Electric Power Association *(951)*

Easley, Hugh
National Association of College Stores *(655)*

Easley, Thomas
American Medical Association *(148)*

Eason, Damon
National Athletic Trainers Association *(710)*

Eason, Michael
American Board of Anesthesiology *(81)*

Eason, CPA, Mike
Association of Fundraising Professionals *(285)*

Eason, Tracee
Education Writers Association *(420)*

East, Bill
National Association of State Directors of Special Education *(700)*

East, Kenneth
American Planning Association *(166)*

East, Lisa
Society for the Study of Social Problems *(925)*

East, Wayne
International Hunter Education Association *(550)*

Easterling, Cindi
Undersea and Hyperbaric Medical Society *(984)*

Eastlack, Darla
American Society of Baking *(193)*

Eastlack, Darla
Association for Research in Otolaryngology *(255)*

Eastlack, Darla M.
American Auditory Society *(78)*

Eastlee, Christopher
Air Medical Operators Association *(19)*

Eastman, Michael J.
Equal Employment Advisory Council *(432)*

Eastmann, Frieda
National Association of Psychiatric Health Systems *(688)*

Easton, CPA, FACMPE, MD, Dana D.
American College of Apothecaries *(93)*

Easton, Drew
Outdoor Writers Association of America *(835)*

Easton, Jr., John J.
Edison Electric Institute *(419)*

Eastwood, Barbara
International Association of Electrical Inspectors *(520)*

Eaton, Christopher J.
Accrediting Bureau of Health Education Schools *(10)*

Eaton, Judith S.
Council for Higher Education Accreditation *(390)*

Ebbert, Clark
American Society of Landscape Architects *(201)*

Ebel, Johnna
Marine Corps Association *(604)*

Ebene, Eric
Biophysical Society *(330)*

Eberle, Dee Dee
National Conference of Executives of The ARC *(727)*

Eberle, Diane
American Institute of Ultrasound in Medicine *(141)*

Eberle, Francis Q.
National Science Teachers Association *(790)*

Eberle, MD, Gareth A
Flying Physicians Association *(448)*

Eberlein, Timothy J.
American College of Surgeons *(103)*

Ebersole, MD, John S.
American Clinical Neurophysiology Society *(92)*

Ebert, Jeff
American Cheviot Sheep Society *(90)*

Eble, Brian
Video Electronics Standards Association *(1009)*

Eble, Michelle
Association of Teachers of Technical Writing *(313)*

Eby, Debbie
International Society of Automation *(571)*

Echard, CAE, IOM, REF, Steve
Association of Rheumatology Health Professionals *(306)*

Echeverri, Natalia
International Federation of the Phonographic Industry *(544)*

Echeverria, Ginny
Physician Insurers Association of America *(847)*

Echo-Hawk, Lael
Native American Contractors Association *(806)*

EchoHawk, Bernadette BC
National American Indian Housing Council *(634)*

Echols, MA, Karylinn
National Association of Hospital Hospitality Houses *(673)*

Echols, CMP, Kim
Reserve Officers Association of the U.S. *(882)*

Eckebrecht, CAE, Betty
BICSI *(329)*

Eckenrode, Melissa
National Council on Problem Gambling *(739)*

Ecker, Robert H.
Aircraft Locknut Manufacturers Association *(20)*
Fluid Sealing Association *(448)*
Gasket Fabricators Association *(457)*
Vibration Isolation and Seismic Control Manufacturers Association *(1009)*

Ecker, Sarah
American Society of Electroneurodiagnostic Technologists *(197)*

Eckhardt, Greg
National Honey Packers and Dealers Association *(760)*

Eckhart, Julie
Geospatial Information Technology Association *(459)*

Eckhoff, Michael
National Association of Academies of Science *(645)*

Edans, CPA, Phyllis
American College of Emergency Physicians *(95)*

Eddy, Dan
The National Association of Crime Victim Compensation Boards *(661)*

Eddy, Melissa
Mu Phi Epsilon *(621)*

Edelman, Esq., Doreen
American Friends of Turkey *(124)*

Edelman, Phyllis
Genetics Society of America *(458)*

Edelman, Victoria
Association of Litigation Support Professionals *(292)*

Edelson, David
Association of Public and Land-Grant Universities (APLU) *(303)*

Edelson, Gilbert S.
Art Dealers Association of America *(229)*

Edelson, Richard L.
Dermatology Foundation *(410)*

Edelstein, Edward
Jewish Educators Assembly *(588)*

Edgar, Charity
Alliance for Energy and Economic Growth *(23)*

Edgell, Dawn
Professional Engineers in Private Practice *(861)*

Edmonds, Jenifer
American Association of Veterinary Parasitologists *(76)*

Edmonds, Valerie A.
Library and Information Technology Association *(597)*

Edmonson, Adrienne
Association for Applied and Therapeutic Humor *(238)*

Edmundowicz, Cara
Republican Governors Association *(881)*

Edson, Guy
American Swimming Coaches Association *(215)*

Edson, Phil
MASINT Association *(607)*

Edusei, Kellee
Dance/USA *(406)*

Edwards, Bill
American Association of Integrated Healthcare Delivery Systems *(63)*

Edwards, Carol
United States Conference of Mayors *(992)*

Edwards, CAE, Carol
TESOL International Association *(971)*

Edwards, Dana
American Academy of Optometry *(37)*

Edwards, Deborah L.
Academy Health *(3)*

Edwards, Ret., COL Dennis
National Defense Transportation Association *(742)*

Edwards, Emily
Professional Aviation Safety Specialists (AFL-CIO) *(860)*

Edwards, Gary
Allied Trades of the Baking Industry *(26)*

Edwards, Gary
American Backflow Prevention Association *(78)*

Edwards, Jennifer
American College of Preventive Medicine *(101)*

Edwards, Jennifer
Biomedical Engineering Society *(330)*

Edwards, Karen Gray
American Sociological Association *(211)*

Edwards, Ken
Contractors Pump Bureau *(383)*

Edwards, Ken
Mounted Breakers Manufacturers Bureau *(620)*

Edwards, Lee
Data Management Association International *(407)*

Edwards, Lisa
International Society for Heart and Lung
Transplantation *(566)*

Edwards, PhD, Marigold A.
International Stress Management Association - USA
(576)

Edwards, III, Martin E.
Interstate Natural Gas Association of America *(583)*

Edwards, Maury L.
National Council of State Housing Agencies *(736)*

Edwards, CMP, Melissa
Association of Corporate Travel Executives (ACTE)
(277)

Edwards, Mike
United States Soccer Federation *(999)*

Edwards, Patricia
American Saddlebred Horse Association *(176)*

Edwards, DDS, MSc, Paul C.
American Academy of Oral and Maxillofacial Pathology
(37)

Edwards, Peggy
Professional Tennis Registry *(865)*

Edwards, III, R. A. "Gus"
National Stone, Sand, and Gravel Association *(796)*

Edwards, Rich
American Forensic Association *(123)*

Edwards, Sandra
American Association of Colleges of Pharmacy *(57)*

Edwards, Savannah
Association of Consulting Foresters of America *(276)*

Edwards, Sylvia
United States Lactation Consultant Association *(996)*

Edwards, Tony M.
National Association of Real Estate Investment Trusts
(NAREIT) *(690)*

Edwards, Vicki
American Farmland Trust *(118)*

Eelman, Peter R.
AMT - The Association For Manufacturing Technology
(222)

Egan, Jennifer
Powder Coating Institute *(854)*

Egan, Tom
Packaging Machinery Manufacturers Institute *(836)*

Egan-Blahna, Pam
Industrial Fabrics Association International *(493)*

Egbert, Cindy
Association for Vascular Access *(261)*

Egeland, Jr., Andrew M.
Association of Military Banks of America *(294)*

Eger, Jeff
Water Environment Federation *(1013)*

Egerstedt, Magnus
IEEE Control Systems Society *(484)*

Eget, Susan M.
American Academy of Medical Administrators *(36)*
American College of Cardiovascular Administrators
(93)

Eggeman, Debra
Independent Distributors of Electronics Association
(489)

Eggleston, DVM, Victor
Belted Galloway Society *(328)*

Egly, Lysa
Independent Electrical Contractors *(489)*

Egner, David
American Fuel & Petrochemical Manufacturers *(124)*

Ehalt, Elaine
Association of Otolaryngology Administrators *(297)*

Ehle, Lauren
Selected Independent Funeral Homes *(896)*

Ehlers, Suzanne
Population Action International *(852)*

Ehlinger, Betty Gorsegner
Association for Information Media and Equipment
(249)
National Association of Media and Technology Centers
(680)

Ehmke, Miranda
Committee of 200 *(368)*

Ehrenberg, Jr., Dr. Rudy
Association of Military Colleges and Schools of the
United States *(294)*

Ehresman, Nate
National Council on Measurement in Education *(739)*

Ehret, Debby
Materials Technology Institute *(609)*

Ehrig, John
International Multimedia Telecommunications
Consortium *(557)*

Ehrle, Bruce
American Health Quality Association *(130)*

Ehrlich, Joel
National Council on Crime and Delinquency *(738)*

Ehrlich, Laurie
Solar Electric Power Association *(951)*

Ehsanyar, Mariam
InterAction (American Council of Voluntary
International Action) *(506)*

Eichel, Ann
Association for Middle Level Education *(252)*

Eichenbrenner, Paula
American Society for Nutrition *(187)*

Eichler, Mark
The Society of Naval Architects and Marine Engineers
(942)

Eidbo, Elling
Association of Organ Procurement Organizations *(297)*

Eidemiller, PhD, Betty
Society of Toxicology *(948)*

Eidenmuller, Michael E.
Religious Communication Association *(880)*

Eiken, Doug
National Association of State Outdoor Recreation
Liaison Officers *(701)*

Eiken, MS, Mary
Society of Gynecologic Oncologists *(938)*

Eimer, CAE, Mary Jane
Association for Behavioral and Cognitive Therapies
(240)

Eisaman, Connie
Association for Prevention Teaching and Research
(APTR) *(254)*

Eisbrenner, Lauren
Society of Automotive Analysts *(930)*

Eisen, Debora
American Pet Products Association *(163)*

Eisen, Dennis
National Federal Development Association *(748)*

Eisen, Jonathan B.
International Foodservice Distributors Association
(546)

Eisenbarth, Natalie
InterAction (American Council of Voluntary
International Action) *(506)*

Eisenberg, CAE, MA, Barry S.
American College of Occupational and Environmental
Medicine *(99)*

Eisenberg, Dennis Me.
National Society for Hebrew Day Schools *(792)*

Eisenberg, Scott
International Network of Merger and Acquisition
Partners *(557)*

Eisenberger, Rona
Renal Physicians Association *(881)*

Eisenman, Wilma
Health Care Compliance Association *(469)*

Eisenstadt, Matthew
ASPIRA Association, Inc. *(233)*

Eisinger, Teryl
National Organization of State Offices of Rural Health
(778)

Eisman, Mitchell
Independent Sector *(491)*

Eisner, Bill
Intermarket Agency Network *(508)*

Ek, Kay
Billings Ovulation Method Association of the United
States *(329)*

Ek, Sue
Billings Ovulation Method Association of the United
States *(329)*

Ekart, Imola
American Society for Therapeutic Radiology and
Oncology *(190)*

Ekdahl, Jon N.
American Medical Association *(148)*

Ekedahl, Duane
Pet Food Institute *(842)*

Eker, Tamra
BritishAmerican Business Inc. *(335)*

Ekman, Richard
Council of Independent Colleges *(394)*

Ekstrom, Michelle
International Association of Wildland Fire *(528)*

Elacqua, Daniel
American Specialty Toy Retailing Association *(212)*

Elbin, Kelly
Professional Golfers Association of America *(862)*

Elder, Catherine A.
SOLE - The International Society of Logistics *(952)*

Elder, Christina
American Association for Clinical Chemistry, Inc. *(48)*

Elder, Harry
American Miniature Horse Association *(152)*

Elder, Jack
Independent Armored Car Operators Association *(488)*

Elder, Lynn W.
Electricity Consumers Resource Council (ELCON) *(422)*

Elder, Nancy L.
Destination Marketing Association International *(411)*

Elderkin, PA, Ann L.
American Society for Bone and Mineral Research *(181)*

Eldredge, Nancy
National Association of Forensic Economics *(669)*

Eldridge, COI, CPP, Ashley
National Chimney Sweep Guild *(721)*

Eldridge, Dianna
Professional Women Controllers *(865)*

Elehwany, Maggie
National Rural Health Association *(788)*

Elert, Debbie
Visiting Physicians Association *(1010)*

Elfand, Julie
American Society of Access Professionals *(190)*
Employers Council on Flexible Compensation *(427)*
National Association of Boards of Examiners of Long
   Term Care Administrators *(650)*
National Association of Long Term Care Administrator
   Boards *(679)*

Elfstrom, Paul
Promotional Products Association International *(867)*

Elias, Diana
American Association for Laboratory Accreditation *(50)*

Elias, Jennine J.
Native American Contractors Association *(806)*

Elie, Vitoria
Power and Communications Contractors Association
   (855)

Eline, Mindy Kaplan
National Association of Student Financial Aid
   Administrators *(703)*

Elipani, Jeanne
Society of Women Engineers *(950)*

Elish, Herb
The College Board *(363)*

Elizondo, Amy L.
National Rural Health Association *(788)*

Elkin, PhD, T. David
Society of Pediatric Psychology *(943)*

Elkins, Angie
American Music Therapy Association *(154)*

Ellek, Jenn
National Confectioners Association *(725)*

Elleman, Jessica
National Association of Public Insurance Adjusters
   (689)

Eller, Julia
Water Environment Federation *(1013)*

Eller, Suzannah
Society for Industrial Microbiology *(913)*

Ellery, Caitlin
International Flight Services Association *(545)*

Elling, Terry
American Society of Military Comptrollers *(203)*

Elliot, Bob
Interagency Communications Interoperability Joint
   Powers Authority *(507)*

Elliot, Jacqueline
International Union of Journeymen and Allied Trades
   (579)

Elliot, Joanne P.
North American Bar-Related Title Insurers *(814)*

Elliot, CAE, MBA, RPh, Victoria E.
Dermatology Nurses' Association *(410)*

Elliott, Beth
American Society of Brewing Chemists *(193)*
Master Brewers Association of the Americas *(607)*

Elliott, Craig
Parenteral Drug Association *(838)*

Elliott, Diane
American Association of Private Railroad Car Owners
   (71)

Elliott, Dorinda
Overseas Press Club of America *(835)*

Elliott, CAE, Helene
Professional Hockey Writers' Association *(862)*

Elliott, Joanne
Naval Enlisted Reserve Association *(807)*

Elliott, Joanne P.
National Association of Bar-Related Title Insurers
   (648)

Elliott, Mary
Arthur W. Page Society *(230)*

Elliott, Monica
Institute of Industrial Engineers *(500)*

Elliott, MA, Robin A.
American Society for Experimental NeuroTherapeutics
   (184)

Elliott, Steven R.
International Union of Journeymen and Allied Trades
   (579)

Elliott, Susan
Music Critics Association of North America *(622)*

Elliott-Ortega, Kara
Society of Architectural Historians *(930)*

Ellis, Aaron
American Association of Port Authorities *(70)*

Ellis, Alicia
Independent Office Products and Furniture Dealers
   Association *(490)*
National Office Products Alliance *(776)*
Office Furniture Dealers Alliance *(826)*

Ellis, Beth
National Electrical Contractors Association *(744)*

Ellis, Bob
American Logistics Association *(146)*

Ellis, David J.
American Horticultural Society *(133)*

Ellis, MD, Dorothy
International Foundation of Employee Benefit Plans
   (547)

Ellis, Edythe
SEPM - Society for Sedimentary Geology *(897)*

Ellis, Eric W.
Association of Collegiate Schools of Architecture *(275)*

Ellis, Jim
International Guild of Candle Artisans *(549)*

Ellis, Joseph
Business Professionals of America *(339)*

Ellis, Mark G.
Industrial Minerals Association -- North America *(494)*
National Industrial Sand Association *(763)*

Ellis, Robert P.
Conference of Research Workers in Animal Diseases
   (375)

Ellis, Wanda J.
American Floorcovering Alliance *(122)*

Ellison, B. J.
American Donkey and Mule Society *(115)*

Ellison, Dionne
National Association for Campus Activities *(637)*

Ellison, Michael
Fiber Society *(443)*

Ellman, Pamela
Business for Social Responsibility *(339)*

Ellsworth, Sarah
Technical Association of the Pulp and Paper Industry
   (970)

Elluru, MD, Ravindhra
Society for Ear, Nose and Throat Advances in Children
   (907)

Elman, Janet Rice
Association of Children's Museums *(272)*

Elman, Julie
Society for News Design *(916)*

Elmendorf, Edward M.
American Association of State Colleges and
   Universities *(73)*

Elmore, Kelly
American Historical Association *(131)*
Historians of American Communism *(476)*

Elmore, Scott
American Apparel & Footwear Association *(46)*

Eloranta, Jari
Economic History Association *(418)*

Elsasser, John
The Public Relations Society of America *(870)*

Elsbree, Amy
National League of Cities *(768)*

Elswick, Heidi
White House News Photographers Association *(1016)*

Elwood, Dr. P.H., Thomas W.
Association of Schools of Allied Health Professions
   (307)

Ely, CAE, Karl
American Society of Association Executives-The
   Center for Association Leadership *(193)*

Emamali, Bernadeen
National Association of Beverage Importers Inc. *(648)*

Emancipator, MD, Kenneth
American Society for Clinical Pathologists *(182)*

Ember, Carol R.
Human Relations Area Files *(481)*

Embler, Brittany
AFCOM *(14)*

Embrey, Mary Louise
National Association of School Nurses *(693)*

Embrick, David
Association for Humanist Sociology *(249)*

Emely, CAE, CMP, PhD, Charles H.
American Railway Engineering and Maintenance-of-
   Way Association *(173)*

Emely, CAE, Mary Ann
American Council of Engineering Companies *(109)*

Emershaw, George
American Board of Multiple Specialties in Podiatry *(82)*

Emerson, Charles H.
American Thyroid Association *(216)*

Emerson, Marvin
United States Trout Farmers Association *(1000)*

Emery, Bob
Institute of Scrap Recycling Industries, Inc. *(503)*

Emmert, Mark A.
National Collegiate Athletic Association *(724)*

Emmitte, John
The Integrated Ocean Drilling Program *(505)*

Emms, Abbie
Interior Design Society *(508)*

Ems, Leslie
University Risk Management and Insurance
Association *(1003)*

Emshoff, Jim
Society for Community Research and Action *(906)*

Emson, Kenny
National Multi-Housing Council *(774)*

Enders, Rene
American Association of Managed Care Nurses *(64)*

Endres, Maggie
American Academy of Cosmetic Surgery *(32)*

Endsley, Bill
International Real Estate Federation - American
Chapter *(562)*

Endsley, Rikki
USENIX: The Advanced Computing Systems
Association *(1005)*

Eng, Derek
National Truck Equipment Association *(802)*

Eng, Linda
National Center for Asia-Pacific Economic Cooperation
(719)

Engberg, Richard A.
American Water Resources Association *(220)*

Engebretson, Jacquelynn
National Indian Health Board *(763)*

Engebretson, Peter R.
InterAction (American Council of Voluntary
International Action) *(506)*

Engel, Gerald
IEEE Society on Social Implications of Technology
(485)

Engel, Timothy
American Academy of Neurology *(36)*

Engelhardt, James F.
Manufacturers Alliance/MAPI Inc. *(603)*

Engelland, DVM, Glenn
American Embryo Transfer Association *(116)*

Engelmann, Anita
FAA Managers Association, Inc. *(436)*

Engelson, Irv
Man and Cybernetics Systems Society *(602)*

Engelson, Irving
IEEE Technology Management Council *(486)*

Engen, Katie
American Society of Plant Biologists *(207)*

Engerman, David
Society for Historians of American Foreign Relations
(910)

Enget, Aaron
Professional Rodeo Cowboys Association *(864)*

Engh, Fred C.
National Alliance for Youth Sports *(632)*

Engh, Jeremy Anderson
American Devon Cattle Association *(114)*

Engh, John
National Alliance for Youth Sports *(632)*

Engle, Carey
National Association Of Insurance and Financial
Advisors(NAIFA) *(676)*

Engle, Mark
Metal Construction Association *(613)*

Engle, William
Association of Telehealth Service Providers *(313)*

Englebrecht, CAE, Kaye
National Association of Orthopedic Nurses *(683)*

The Association for Nursing Professional Development
(252)

Engler, Christie
National Society of Insurance Premium Auditors *(794)*

Engler, Hon. John M.
Business Roundtable *(339)*

Engler, Maggie
Spanish Barb Horse Association *(954)*

Englert, James
International Police Mountain Bike Association *(561)*

Englert, Shelby
American Pharmacists Association *(163)*

Engleson, Eric
The Academy of American Poets *(3)*

English, Glenn L.
National Rural Electric Cooperative Association *(788)*

English, James D.
Rubber and Plastics Industry Conference of the United
Steelworkers of America *(888)*

Engquist, Christopher P.
Laborers-Employers Cooperation & Education Trust
(592)

Engstrom, Rob
United States Chamber of Commerce *(991)*

Enloe, Elise
Association of Bridal Consultants *(270)*

Enlow, Jr., Dr. Ralph E.
Association for Biblical Higher Education *(240)*

Ennis, Erin
United States-China Business Council *(1001)*

Ennis, Greg
Wi-Fi Alliance *(1016)*

Ennis, Lori
American Neurogastroenterology and Motility Society
(155)
Association of American Physicians *(265)*

Enns, Barbara
Cedar Shake and Shingle Bureau *(347)*

Enright, Ame
Child Life Council *(353)*

Enriquez, Jocelyn V
Public Media Business Association *(869)*

Ensign, Thomas
Million Dollar Round Table *(616)*

Ensor, Patti
Standards Engineering Society *(961)*

Enyart, Chris
American Association of Exporters & Importers *(60)*

Epperly, Joe
North American Limousin Foundation *(817)*

Epperly, BSN, RN, Trisha
Alpha Tau Delta *(27)*

Epperson, Charlie
Property Records Industry Association *(867)*

Epperson, Damon
North American Electric Reliability Corporation *(816)*

Epperson, CAE, Gary L.
Alpha Kappa Psi *(26)*

Epperson, Keith
American Feed Industry Association *(120)*

Eppler, Erin
National Association of Health Data Organizations
(671)

Eppley, Donnie

International Association of Approved Basketball
Officials, Inc. *(515)*

Epstein, Mark Alan
National Health Association *(758)*

Epstein, ScD, Mark H.
International Society for Pharmacoepidemiology *(568)*
Society for Radiation Oncology Administration *(919)*

Equihua, Xavier Fco
Chilean Avocado Importers Association (CAIA) *(353)*

Erb, Penny
National Wood Flooring Association *(805)*

Erbaugh, J. Mark
Association for International Agricultural and
Extension Education *(250)*

Erbe, Tom
International Computer Music Association *(536)*

Erbes, Barbara
Organization for the Advancement of Structured
Information Standards *(831)*

Erceg, MS, PHN, RN, Linda Ebner
Association of Camp Nurses *(271)*

Ercison, II, Clifton A.
System Safety Society *(967)*

Ercolino, Jess
American Society of Hand Therapists *(199)*

Erdheim, Ric
National Electrical Manufacturers Association *(744)*

Erdner, Lisa
Label Printing Industries of America *(591)*

Erickson, Audrae
Corn Refiners Association, Inc. *(385)*

Erickson, Donald R.
Security Industry Association *(895)*

Erickson, Erin
National Hearing Conservation Association *(758)*

Erickson, Jenna
Investment Program Association *(584)*

Erickson, Kathleen
Association for Humanistic Psychology *(249)*

Erickson, L. Eileen
Society of American Military Engineers *(929)*

Erickson, Nancy
American Society for Theatre Research *(190)*
Association for Theatre in Higher Education *(260)*

Ericson, Brad
American Academy of Professional Coders *(40)*

Ericson, PhD, Kris
American College of Mental Health Administration *(98)*

Eriksen, Jamie
Specialty Equipment Market Association *(957)*

Eriksson, Berit
Sailors' Union of the Pacific *(890)*

Erker, Sherry
American Academy on Communication in Healthcare
(43)

Erman, Reha
The International Air Cargo Association *(509)*

Ernst, Charles A.S.
College English Association *(363)*

Ernst, Gordon J.
National Association of Vertical Transportation
Professionals *(708)*

Ernst, Margaret
National Chicken Council *(720)*

Ernst, Mary Fran

National Association of Medical Examiners **(680)**

Erthal, Dr. Margaret
The Association for Research in Business Education - Delta Pi Epsilon **(255)**

Ervin, Gerard
National Federation of Modern Language Teachers Associations **(749)**

Ervin, Jeannie
Composite Panel Association **(372)**

Erwin, Lisa
Pet Partners **(842)**

Erwin, Randy
National Federation of Federal Employees **(748)**

Erwin, Sandra
National Defense Industrial Association **(742)**

Esbeck, Mark
International Network of Merger and Acquisition Partners **(557)**

Escalante, Miguel
International Studies Association **(576)**

Esch, Emily
American Association of Philosophy Teachers **(69)**

Escobar, Barbara E.
American Society of Hypertension, Inc. **(200)**

Escobar, Candace
APPAM - The Association for Public Policy Analysis and Management **(225)**

Escutia, Noemi
Association for Healthcare Volunteer Resource Professionals **(248)**

Esenwein, Jan
Society for Neuro-Oncology **(916)**

Esguerra, Jorge
Society of American Foresters **(928)**

Esheley, Don
Association for Skilled and Technical Sciences **(256)**

Eshelman, Jeffrey
Independent Petroleum Association of America **(491)**

Esher, Cynthia A.
Measurement, Control and Automation Association **(609)**

Eshkenazi, CAE, Abe
APICS The Association for Operations Management **(224)**

Eshleman, Amy
Urban Libraries Council **(1004)**

Eshleman, Ronald L.
Vibration Institute **(1008)**

Eshoo, Jeanette
Marine Corps League **(605)**

Eskandar, MD, Emad
American Society for Stereotactic and Functional Neurosurgery **(189)**

Eskew, Jame
Association of American Indian Physicians **(265)**

Eskew, Kimberly
ISEH Society for Hematology and Stem Cells **(586)**

Esmond, Jeanne
American Society of News Editors **(204)**

Esp, Jim
Digital Imaging Marketing Association **(412)**
PMA - The Worldwide Community of Imaging Associations **(851)**
Professional Picture Framers Association **(864)**

Esp, Jim
Professional School Photographers Association International **(865)**

Espinosa, Horacio
Society of Engineering Science **(935)**

Espinosa, Rhodonna
Strategic Account Management Association **(963)**

Espinoza, Manny
Association of Latino Professionals in Finance and Accounting **(291)**

Esposito, Dawn
Italian American Studies Association **(586)**

Esposito, MCC, Donna Kaye
National Association of Cruise Oriented Agencies **(662)**

Esposito, Sante J.
National Independent Automobile Dealers Association **(761)**

Esposito, Tess
American Association of University Professors **(75)**

Esposito-Montanez, Genaro
Optical Society of America **(829)**

Essenmacher, Erin
National Association of Corporate Directors **(658)**

Esser, Jeffrey L.
Government Finance Officers Association of the United States and Canada **(464)**
Government Finance Officers Association, Federal Liaison Center **(464)**

Essig, Joseph
Society of American Graphic Artists **(929)**

Esslinger, Tom
Marine Corps Association **(604)**

Estep, Janet O.
NACHA - The Electronic Payments Association **(623)**

Estep, Sandy
National Abstinence Education Association **(626)**

Estergard, Pam
Association for High Technology Distribution **(248)**
Employer Associations of America **(426)**

Estersohn, Shelley
Society of American Florists **(928)**

Estes, Chris
National Housing Conference **(761)**

Estes, Cristin
Association of Family Medicine Administration **(282)**

Estes, Jon-Paul
United States Bowling Congress **(991)**

Estes, FNP BC, PhD, RN, Tracy
Respiratory Nursing Society **(883)**

Esteves, Martin
Satellite Broadcasting and Communications Association **(891)**

Estock, Margaret
Wilderness Education Association **(1017)**

Estok, Paul J.
Harness Tracks of America **(468)**

Estrada, Eric
SACNAS (Society for Advancement of Chicanos and Native Americans in Science) **(889)**

Estrada, Victoria
The New Media Consortium **(809)**

Estrada-Portales, Isabel M.
Care Continuum Alliance **(342)**

Eswein, Larry
American Society of Orthopedic Physician Assistants **(205)**

Etheridge, Todd
National Funeral Directors Association **(754)**

Ethier, Donald

American Traffic Safety Service Association **(217)**

Etka, Steve
Midwest Dairy Coalition **(615)**

Etkin, CAE, Steven A.
Association of the Wall and Ceiling Industry **(314)**

Ettenson, Donna
America's Small Business Development Center Network **(29)**

Ettington, Deborah
North American Case Research Association **(814)**

Etzkorn, Lars
National League of Cities **(768)**

Euart, JCD, RSM, Sharon
Canon Law Society of America **(342)**

Eubanks, CAE, Colleen Delaney
National Child Support Enforcement Association **(721)**

Euker, Farasha
American Fisheries Society **(121)**

Eustice, Jessica
American Association of Cardiovascular and Pulmonary Rehabilitation **(55)**

Evanko, George
EPDM Roofing Association **(432)**

Evans, Alison
Perlite Institute **(842)**
The National Greenhouse Manufacturers Association **(756)**

Evans, Arlene C.
Wedding and Portrait Photographers International **(1014)**

Evans, B.J.
USA Volleyball **(1005)**

Evans, Chris
Petroleum Equipment Suppliers Association **(843)**

Evans, Christine
American Society of Furniture Designers **(198)**

Evans, Connie
Association for Enterprise Opportunity **(245)**

Evans, Craig A.
National Association of Women Judges **(710)**

Evans, David
Laser Institute of America **(593)**

Evans, Donald D.
American Chemistry Council **(90)**

Evans, Douglas L.
National Cattlemen's Beef Association **(718)**

Evans, Hope S.
American Society of Farm Managers and Rural Appraisers **(197)**

Evans, Jennifer
Association of Woodworking and Furnishings Suppliers **(318)**

Evans, Jeremy M.
Phi Mu Alpha Sinfonia **(846)**

Evans, John
American Hospital Association **(133)**

Evans, Kelly
American Therapeutic Recreation Association **(216)**

Evans, Kelly
Obesity Society **(825)**

Evans, Lamar
American Therapeutic Recreation Association **(216)**

Evans, Lamar
National Government Publishing Association **(755)**

Evans, Larry H.

Allergy and Asthma Network Mothers of Asthmatics *(22)*

Evans, Nicholas W.
Intellectual Property Owners Association *(505)*

Evans, Nicole
Emdr International Association *(425)*

Evans, Pat
Credit Professionals International *(403)*

Evans, Raissa
Association for Accounting Marketing *(238)*

Evans, Rhett
Golf Course Superintendents Association of America *(463)*

Evans, Sarah
Society of Piping Engineers and Designers *(944)*

Evans, Sarah
Water Environment Federation *(1013)*

Evans, Scott
Federation of Employers and Workers of America *(441)*

Evans, Stephen
National Marine Manufacturers Association *(771)*

Evans, Steven
Railway Industrial Clearance Association *(874)*

Evans-Lombe, Monica
International Nurses Society on Additictions *(558)*
National Association of Graduate Admissions Professionals *(670)*

Evans-Richey, Elfriede
Keyboard Teachers Association International *(590)*

Evanson, Tim
Association of American Veterinary Medical Colleges *(267)*

Evarts, Amanda
United Suffolk Sheep Association *(1001)*

Evener, David
National Ground Water Association *(756)*

Everbach, Wayne
College and University Professional Association for Human Resources *(362)*

Everett, Anita
American Association of Community Psychiatrists *(58)*

Everett, Brian
National Shippers Strategic Transportation Council *(791)*

Everett, David
BICSI *(329)*

Everett, Diane
Association of Nutrition & Foodservice Professionals *(296)*

Everett, Donna R.
Organizational Systems Research Association *(833)*

Everett, Karen
National Shippers Strategic Transportation Council *(791)*

Everhart, Lori
The Association of Collegiate Conference and Events Directors International *(275)*

Everly, Robin
Council on Botanical and Horticultural Libraries *(399)*

Everly, Ron
National Association for Home Care and Hospice *(639)*

Eversole, Amanda Engstrom
American National Chamber of Commerce *(154)*

Evert, Teresa
National Exchange Carrier Association *(746)*

Evola, Vito M.

Delta Theta Phi *(409)*

Evtuch, Scott
Professional Convention Management Association *(861)*

Ewig, MHA, Brent
Association of Maternal and Child Health Programs (AMCHP) *(293)*

Ewing, Allison
American College of Physicians *(101)*
American College of Physicians Services, Inc. *(101)*

Ewing, CMP, Carol
Association of College and University Auditors *(274)*

Ewing, Suzanne D.
National Association for Home Care and Hospice *(639)*

Ewoldt, Kriston
Business Marketing Association *(339)*
Pressure Sensitive Tape Council *(856)*

Exner, Gwen
Psychometric Society *(868)*

Eyet, Teresa
American Health Care Association *(129)*

Eyles, PhD, RN, Mary
National Association for Practical Nurse Education and Service *(641)*

Eyring , Teresa
Theatre Communications Group *(973)*

Ezaki, Ayako
The International Ecotourism Society *(542)*

Ezell, Lynn
National Art Education Association *(635)*

Faaborg, MS, Nicole
American College of Veterinary Internal Medicine *(104)*

Fabel, PhD, Kirk
Worldwide ERC *(1028)*

Faber, Jo Ann
American College of Allergy, Asthma and Immunology *(93)*

Faber, Stuart J.
National Association of Business Travel Agents *(651)*

Faberman, Edward P.
Air Carrier Association of America *(17)*

Fabian, Craig
Aeronautical Repair Station Association *(14)*

Fabian, Lawrence J.
Advanced Transit Association *(13)*

Fabian, Mark
ICE Futures U.S. *(482)*

Fabian, Nelson E.
National Environmental Health Association *(746)*

Fabiano, Michelle
FlexTech Alliance *(447)*

Fabrizio-Clontz, Jodi
National Association of Broadcast Employees and Technicians-Communications Workers of America, AFL-CIO (NABET-CWA) *(650)*

Fadin, Gina
Million Dollar Round Table *(616)*

Faenza, Kate
Federal Bar Association *(438)*

Faerber, Charles N.
National Notary Association *(775)*

Fagan, Beth
National Council for Prescription Drug Programs *(732)*

Fagan, James F.
Research and Development Associates for Military Food and Packaging Systems *(881)*

Fagan, Marygene
Research and Development Associates for Military Food and Packaging Systems *(881)*

Fagan, Shannon
International Liver Transplantation Society *(554)*

Fagen, PhD, Adam
Genetics Society of America *(458)*

Faherty, Rebecca
International Association of Privacy Professionals *(526)*

Fahey, Brian
Association of Catholic Diocesan Archivists *(271)*

Fahey, Jim
Association for Accounting Administration *(237)*

Fahrenkopf, Jr., Frank J.
American Gaming Association *(124)*

Faight, Ian
Southern Cypress Manufacturers Association *(953)*

Faiman-Silva, Sandra
Association for Feminist Anthropology *(246)*

Fain, James
American Association of Diabetes Educators *(60)*

Fairbairn, Kyle
Military Impacted Schools Association *(616)*

Fairbank, Ben
International Warehouse Logistics Association *(580)*

Fairbank, Dennis
Catholic Cemetery Conference *(345)*

Fairbanks, Linda
Association for Linen Management *(251)*

Fairbrother, Jeffrey T.
North American Society for the Psychology of Sport and Physical Activity *(822)*

Fairclough, Aimee
Archaeological Institute of America *(227)*

Fairhall, PhD, Gail
American Academy of Cosmetic Surgery *(32)*

Fairhurst, Ann
American Collegiate Retailing Association *(105)*

Fairweather, Virginia
Deep Foundations Institute *(408)*

Faison, Pat
Juice Products Association *(589)*

Fajnor, Paul J.
Audit Bureau of Circulations *(320)*

Falardeau, John
American Chiropractic Association *(90)*

Falco, Elisa
Georgia Charter Schools Association *(459)*

Falcon, MPP, Adolph P.
National Alliance for Hispanic Health *(631)*

Falcone, Mary
Entomological Society of America *(429)*

Falgione, Christie
American Driver and Traffic Safety Education Association *(115)*

Falk, Diane M.
World Media Association *(1027)*

Falkenstein, Donald
Council for Advancement and Support of Education *(388)*

Fall, Awa
National Forum for Black Public Administrators *(752)*

Falla, Carlos de
Human Factors and Ergonomics Society *(480)*
Human Factors Society *(481)*

Fallert, Rachel
Chain Drug Marketing Association *(350)*

Fallon, Laena E.
Financial Services Forum *(445)*

Fallon, Molly
Jewelers of America *(587)*

Falls, Susan
Society for the Anthropology of North America *(923)*

Falls, Warren
Ocean Research & Conservation Association *(826)*

Fan, Henry
Women in Technology International *(1022)*

Fancher, Mac
American Association for Clinical Chemistry, Inc. *(48)*

Fancher, Mark
National Conference of Black Lawyers *(726)*

Fanella, Kelly
American Society of Safety Engineers *(209)*

Fanelli, Duke
Association of National Advertisers *(295)*

Fanning, CAE, Deborah M.
Council for Art Education *(389)*
The Arts and Creative Materials Institute, Inc. *(229)*

Fanning, Mark
American Institutes for Research *(141)*

Fanning, Rich
United States Professional Tennis Association *(998)*

Fanning, Victoria B.
Educause *(420)*

Fano, Erin
American Ambulance Association *(44)*

Fantaci, Kim
National Society of Accountants for Cooperatives *(793)*

Fantaci, Kimberly
American Woman's Society of Certified Public
Accountants *(221)*
Association for Accounting Administration *(237)*
National Guild of Professional Paperhangers *(757)*
SAVE International *(891)*

Fantetti, Elizabeth
Professional Beauty Association | National
Cosmetology Association *(861)*

Farabi, Dianne
International Society for Prosthetics and Orthotics -
United States *(569)*

Farach, Frank
Society for a Science of Clinical Psychology *(903)*

Farber, Erica
Radio Advertising Bureau *(873)*

Farber, MA, Matthew
Association of Community Cancer Centers *(275)*

Farber, Rebecca
Society of Scribes *(947)*

Farberman, APR, Rhea K.
American Psychological Association *(169)*

Farbman, EdD, Andrea H.
American Music Therapy Association *(154)*

Fardy, Ian
Health Industry Distributors Association *(469)*

Fargo, Cristine Z.
International Safety Equipment Association (ISEA)
(563)

Farhoumand, Rouzbeh
International Multimedia Telecommunications
Consortium *(557)*

Faris, Lesa

Women in Cable Telecommunications, Inc. *(1020)*

Fariss-Newman, Gwen
American Evaluation Association *(118)*

Farley, Beth
American Meteorological Society *(151)*

Farley, Donald "Don"
Forging Industry Association *(452)*

Farley, James
International Brotherhood of Police Officers *(532)*

Farley, James
National Association of Government Employees *(670)*

Farmakidis, Anne
Association of American Medical Colleges *(265)*

Farmakis, William D.
National Association of Publishers' Representatives
(689)

Farmer, Gary
American Association for Vocational Instructional
Materials *(53)*

Farmer, Pam
Institute of Environmental Sciences and Technology
(499)

Farmer, FAICP, Paul
American Institute of Certified Planners *(137)*
American Planning Association *(166)*

Farmer, BS, MCP, Scott
Society of Diagnostic Medical Sonographers *(934)*

Farmwald, Janice
ASM International *(232)*

Farner, Jr., John R.
Irrigation Association *(585)*

Farnsley, II, Arthur E.
Society for the Scientific Study of Religion *(924)*

Farnsworth, Tim
Arms Control Association *(229)*

Farquhar, Thomas
American Society for Indexing *(186)*

Farquharson, Phil
Association of Earth Science Editors *(279)*

Farr, Carl
National Association of Wholesaler-Distributors *(709)*

Farr, Dagmar
Food Marketing Institute *(449)*

Farr, Glenn
National Association for Campus Activities *(637)*

Farr, SPHR, Jo Anne
Motor and Equipment Manufacturers Association *(619)*

Farr, Rachel
North American Gaming Regulators Association *(817)*

Farrace, Robert
National Association of Secondary School Principals
(694)

Farrar, Carlena
Federal Bar Association *(438)*

Farrar, Hank
The Clearing House Association *(357)*

Farrel, Susan
Product Development and Management Association
(858)

Farrell, Anne
Distributive Education Clubs of America (DECA) *(415)*

Farrell, Bob
American Trucking Associations *(218)*

Farrell, CAE, Brian
Edison Electric Institute *(419)*

Farrell, Christopher
The Society of Composers and Lyricists *(933)*

Farrell, Dianne
Recreation Vehicle Industry Association *(877)*

Farrell, Donald
National Commodity Supplemental Food Program
Association *(724)*

Farrell, USN (Ret.), Gerard
Commissioned Officers Association of the United
States Public Health Service *(368)*

Farrell, Jay
National Association of State Foresters *(701)*

Farrell, Kathleen M.
Housing Partnership Network *(479)*

Farrell, Jr. USAF (Ret.), Lt. Gen. Lawrence P.
National Defense Industrial Association *(742)*

Farrell, Margaret
National Association of Hispanic Nurses *(672)*

Farrell, Paula
Executive Women in Government *(435)*

Farrell, Rick
Council of Infrastructure Financing Authorities *(394)*

Farrell, Robert P.
Distribution and LTL Carriers Association *(414)*

Farrell, Ryan
The Brewers Association *(335)*

Farrell, Scott
American Association of Oral and Maxillofacial
Surgeons *(67)*

Farrell, Susan
Clinical Laboratory Management Association *(358)*
Society of Gastroenterology Nurses and Associates
(937)

Farrell, Timothy S.
American Hardware Manufacturers Association *(128)*

Farrell-Stevenson, JD, Maureen
National Association of Counsel for Children *(658)*

Farrenkopf, Tina M.
National American Indian Court Judges Association
(634)

Farrey, Patrick
Business Marketing Association *(339)*
Institute of Packaging Professionals *(502)*
National Association of Sporting Goods Wholesalers
(696)
The Recreational Vehicle Aftermarket Association *(877)*

Farrey, Patrick M.
Pressure Sensitive Tape Council *(856)*

Farrington, Kate
Association for Healthcare Philanthropy *(248)*

Farris, Amy
American Statistical Association *(213)*

Farris, Jeff
Consortium for Graduate Study in Management *(378)*

Farris, Melinda
International Association of Operative Millers *(525)*

Farrow, Gloria J.
American Dance Therapy Association *(113)*

Farrow, Jill
Nonprofit Technology Network *(811)*

Farrow, Rik
USENIX: The Advanced Computing Systems
Association *(1005)*

Farthing, Penny
American League of Lobbyists *(145)*

Fasheh, Alexa
Academy of Country Music *(4)*

Fassler, Joe K.
National Park Hospitality Association *(779)*

Fassold, James
American Society of Perfumers *(206)*

Fasulo, John
Actors' Equity Association *(11)*

Fattahi, Parva
The Association of Women in International Trade *(317)*

Fatter, CFA, CPA, Marianne
Association of Certified Fraud Examiners *(271)*

Fatz, Kathy
Bearing Specialist Association *(327)*

Faught, Jeff
International Association of Natural Resource Pilots *(525)*

Faul, Nikki
International Association of Diecutting and Diemaking *(519)*

Faulconer, J. Walter
American Astronautical Society *(77)*

Faulds, John
Association of Retail Travel Agents *(306)*

Faulkner, Christian D.
International Association of Chiefs of Police *(517)*

Faulkner, MD, Larry R.
American Board of Psychiatry & Neurology *(83)*

Faulkner, Tom
International Association for Human Resource Information Management *(512)*

Faulkner, Vonetta
International Labor Rights Forum *(553)*

Faulstick, Scott
Accrediting Council for Continuing Education & Training *(10)*

Faurer, Sybil
Museum Store Association *(621)*

Fausnaught, Wayne D.
National Association of Pupil Services Administrators *(689)*

Faust, Kristin
Society for Nutrition Education and Behavior *(917)*

Faustino, Erlinda
The Society of Naval Architects and Marine Engineers *(942)*

Fay, Carrie
International Spa Association *(575)*

Fay, Joan
American Wholesale Marketers Association *(221)*

Fay, MA, Joseph
Society for the Scientific Study of Sexuality *(924)*

Fay, Kevin J.
Alliance for Responsible Atmospheric Policy *(23)*

Fayad, Elizabeth
National Parks Conservation Association *(779)*

Faye, Monique
National Association of Clean Air Agencies *(654)*

Fayton, Kimberly
American Society of Hematology *(199)*

Fazzari, Rebecca
American Association of Political Consultants *(70)*

Fazzari, CMP, Rebecca I.
Emergency Department Practice Management Association (EDPMA) *(425)*

Fazzi, Joe
International Digital Enterprise Alliance *(540)*

Feagan, BSN, MA, RN, Marlene
Health Ministries Association *(470)*

Feal, Rosemary G.
Modern Language Association *(618)*

Fears, Charles (Chip)
National Association of Women Artists *(709)*

Feasby, Judy
Financial Planning Association *(445)*

Feather-Gannon, Susan
Organizational Systems Research Association *(833)*

Featherston, Julie
North American Coalition for Christian Admissions Professionals *(815)*

Featherstone, CAE, Eric
American Academy of Oral Medicine *(38)*

Featherstone, Jerry
Association of the United States Navy, Inc. *(314)*

Feavel, Kurt
International Police Mountain Bike Association *(561)*

Fechter, Tricia
Association of Fraternity Advisors *(284)*

Fedchock, Bonnie
National Association of Catering and Events *(651)*

Feddema, Marissa
Van Alen Institute *(1007)*

Fedder, Alan
UniForum Association *(984)*

Feder, Dr. Theodore H.
Artist Rights Society *(230)*

Federinko, Patricia
American Psychiatric Nurses Association *(168)*

Federwitz, Diane
Network of Executive Women in Hospitality *(808)*

Fedich, Nancy
National Credit Reporting Association *(740)*

Fedor, Stefanie
ArtTable *(231)*

Fedrich, Ginny
Association for Accounting Administration *(237)*

Fedrizzi, S. Richard
United States Green Building Council *(994)*

Fee, Everett
American Society of Limnology and Oceanography *(202)*

Fee, Lynn
Mobile Air Conditioning Society Worldwide *(617)*

Fee, Patti
Packaging Machinery Manufacturers Institute *(836)*

Feehan, Brian
Industrial Truck Association *(494)*

Feeser, Melissa
American Resort Development Association *(175)*

Fege, Arnold
Public Education Network *(869)*

Fegley, Matt
Strategic Account Management Association *(963)*

Feher, PhD, Leslie
Association for Birth Psychology *(240)*

Fehling, David
Association of Diesel Specialists *(279)*

Fehlings, MD, PhD, Michael G.
Cervical Spine Research Society *(350)*

Fehr, Roz
Music Industry Conference *(622)*

Fehr, Steve
Major League Baseball Players Association *(601)*

Fehrenbach, MPH, Lacy M.
Association of State and Territorial Health Officials *(310)*

Feibel, Fredrick
Academy of Veterinary Allergy and Clinical Immunology *(9)*

Feibusch, Morris D.
Bituminous Coal Operators Association *(331)*

Feidler, USAR (Ret.), Lt. Col. Robert E.
Reserve Officers Association of the U.S. *(882)*

Feidt, Ray
Crane Certification Association of America *(403)*

Feig, MD, Stephen A.
American Society of Breast Disease *(193)*

Feild, Dave
Multi-Housing Laundry Association *(621)*

Feild, David
The International Childbirth Education Association *(534)*

Feinberg, Jonathan
American Institute of Graphic Arts *(139)*

Feinsod, Eryn
Association of Executive Search Consultants *(282)*

Feinstein, Steven B.
International Contrast Ultrasound Society *(537)*

Feirtag, Kate
Society of Illustrators *(939)*

Feit, David
The Acoustical Society of America *(11)*

Felcyn, George
Furniture Retailers of America *(454)*

Felder, Anthony L.
Concrete Reinforcing Steel Institute *(374)*

Felder, Herk
American Microchemical Society *(151)*

Felder, Robin E.
American Association for Cancer Research *(48)*

Feldman, Alexander
United States-ASEAN Business Council Inc. *(990)*

Feldman, Bob
International Association of Medical Equipment Remarketers and Servicers (IAMERS) *(524)*

Feldman, CAE, MPA, IOM, Brad L.
National Society of Insurance Premium Auditors *(794)*

Feldman, David
ADARA *(12)*

Feldman, Douglas A.
Society for Medical Anthropology *(915)*

Feldman, Gabe
Sports Lawyers Association *(959)*

Feldman, Esq., John
Transworld Advertising Agency Network *(979)*

Feldman, Paul H.
General Aviation Manufacturers Association *(458)*

Feldman, Robin
National Association for Gifted Children *(639)*

Feldman, Steven
Association of Zoos and Aquariums *(318)*

Feldman, Timothy
International Society of Automation *(571)*

Feldmann, Anne Tyler
National Housing and Rehabilitation Association *(760)*

Feldmann, Holly
National Postsecondary Agriculture Student Organization *(781)*

Feldpush, Beth
National Association of Public Hospitals and Health Systems *(688)*

Feldt, Laura
National Association of Neonatal Nurses *(682)*

Felesena, Nancy
International Association for Healthcare Security and Safety *(512)*

Felker, Caitlin
International Cast Polymer Association *(533)*

Fellin, Eileen M.
The Association of Average Adjusters of the United States and Canada *(268)*

Fells, Robert M.
International Cemetery, Cremation and Funeral Association *(533)*

Felstead, Brent
International Society of Meeting Planners *(573)*
National Association of Real Estate Appraisers *(689)*

Felten, Paula
Association of periOperative Registered Nurses *(299)*

Felton, Daniel
International Bottled Water Association *(530)*

Felton, Dianne
Mental Health America *(612)*

Felton, Rob
Air Distribution Institute *(18)*

Fenaughty, William D.
National Federation of Federal Employees *(748)*
National Federation of Federal Employees, Federal Dist. 1, IAMAW, AFL-CIO *(748)*

Feng, Jinjuan Heidi
Special Interest Group on Accessible Computing *(955)*

Feniger, Jr., Jerome R.
Station Representatives Association *(962)*

Fenn, Scott
Solar Energy Industries Association (SEIA) *(952)*

Fennal, CNS, PhD, RN, Dr. Mildred D.
Chi Eta Phi Sorority, Inc. *(352)*

Fennell, Lisa
Association of Regulatory Boards of Optometry *(305)*

Fenner, Linda
Society of Environmental Toxicology and Chemistry *(935)*

Fenner, Michael
Council of Residential Specialists *(396)*

Fennig, IOM, Elise
Grocery Manufacturers Association (GMA) *(466)*

Fenolio, Kim
Coin Laundry Association *(361)*

Fenselau, Megan
American Numismatic Society *(156)*

Fensterheim, CAE, Robert J.
Acrylonitrile Group, Inc. *(11)*
Alkylphenols and Ethoxylates Research Council *(22)*
Chlorinated Paraffins Industry Association *(354)*
Emulsion Polymers Council *(427)*
North American Polyelectrolyte Producers Association *(819)*
SB Latex Council *(891)*
Vinyl Acetate Council *(1009)*

Fenza, David W.
Association of Writers and Writing Programs *(318)*

Fera, Lei Lani
Internet Marketing Association *(582)*

Ferch, Roger

National Steel Bridge Alliance *(796)*

Ferch, Roger E.
American Institute of Steel Construction *(140)*

Ferdinand, Marilyn
National Parent Teachers Association *(779)*

Ferdowsyan, Mahsheed Rouhani
National Concrete Masonry Association *(725)*

Ferebee, MPH, Annette
American Public Health Association *(171)*

Ferenc, Dr. Susan
Council of Producers & Distributors of Agrotechnology *(396)*

Ference, Gregory C.
Czechoslovak Studies Association *(406)*

Ferensic, Rori
Electronic Traders Association *(424)*
Electronic Transactions Association *(424)*

Ferer, Kenneth
Oceanic Engineering Society *(826)*

Ferguson, Carroy U. "Cuf"
Association for Humanistic Psychology *(249)*

Ferguson, Charles D.
Federation of American Scientists *(440)*

Ferguson, Cindy
Association of Progressive Rental Organizations *(303)*

Ferguson, Edward E.
National Association of County Aging Programs *(659)*

Ferguson, Mark
American Institute of Certified Planners *(137)*
American Planning Association *(166)*

Ferguson, Neil
Association of Progressive Rental Organizations *(303)*

Ferguson, Sarah
Academy of Rehabilitative Audiology *(8)*

Ferguson, Tom
Council on the Safe Transportation of Hazardous Articles *(401)*

Fermanis, Alexis
Society of Industrial and Office Realtors *(939)*

Fernandes, John J.
The Association to Advance Collegiate Schools of Business *(319)*

Fernandes, Lourdes
Aerospace Industries Association of America *(14)*

Fernandes, Sangeeta
American Academy of Ophthalmic Executives *(37)*
American Academy of Ophthalmology *(37)*

Fernandez, Carla
American Anthropological Association *(45)*

Fernandez, Dan
Masonry Veneer Manufacturers Association *(607)*

Fernandez, Dana
Alliance of Black Telecommunications Employees *(24)*

Fernandez, Daniel C.
The International Air Cargo Association *(509)*

Fernandez, Enrique
National Academy of Recording Arts and Sciences *(628)*

Fernandez, George
American Institute of Graphic Arts *(139)*

Fernandez, Jennifer
Mexico-U.S. Business Committee, U.S. Council *(614)*

Fernandez, MS, Karina
American Society of Hematology *(199)*

Fernandez, Kim

International Parking Institute *(559)*

Fernandez, Maria
National Association of Latino Elected and Appointed Officials *(677)*

Fernandez, Pamela
American Architectural Foundation *(46)*

Fernandez, Susan J.
Academy of Management *(6)*

Fernando, Mark
National Communication Association *(724)*

Fernando, Wendy
American Association of Colleges of Osteopathic Medicine *(57)*

Fernley, G.A. Taylor
National Field Selling Association *(750)*

Fernley, Kyle
Society for Social Work Leadership in Health Care *(921)*

Ferrante, Anne
American Pet Products Association *(163)*

Ferrante, Maria
Packaging Machinery Manufacturers Institute *(836)*

Ferrante, Mark
Coalition for Juvenile Justice *(360)*

Ferranto, Marcia
Women's Transportation Seminar (WTS International) *(1024)*

Ferrara, Cecilia
National Customs Brokers and Forwarders Association of America *(741)*

Ferrara, Dave
Hollywood Radio & Television Society *(477)*

Ferrara, Gregory B.
National Grocers Association *(756)*

Ferrarello, Debi Page
United States Lactation Consultant Association *(996)*

Ferrari, Serge
International Bone and Mineral Society *(530)*

Ferraris, Laura
Audit Bureau of Circulations *(320)*

Ferraro, John
Masonry Veneer Manufacturers Association *(607)*

Ferraro, Susan
International Association of Venue Managers *(528)*

Ferree, Wesley
Professional Construction Estimators Association of America *(861)*

Ferreira, Donald M.
Electrical Generating Systems Association *(422)*

Ferrell, Ellen C.
National Cotton Council of America *(730)*

Ferrell, Linda
Academy of Marketing Science *(6)*

Ferrell, O. C.
Academy of Marketing Science *(6)*

Ferrell, Roger
American Custom Gunmakers Guild *(112)*

Ferrenz, Denise
National Association of School Psychologists *(693)*

Ferrese, Justin
American Association of Suicidology *(74)*

Ferri, Annette
The International Wood Products Association *(581)*

Ferris, Frank D.
National Treasury Employees Union *(801)*

Ferruggia, Rosanne
American Beverage Licensees *(81)*

Ferrugia, Tom
The Broadway League *(336)*

Ferry, Julie
InSight *(496)*

Ferry, CAE, MPA, Julie
Legal Marketing Association *(596)*

Ferryman, Kadija
National Council for Research on Women *(732)*

Ferstl, DC, Joseph F.
American College of Chiropractic Orthopedists *(94)*

Fertel, Marvin S.
Nuclear Energy Institute *(824)*

Fertig, Bill
National Spinal Cord Injury Association *(795)*

Ferzoco, Jeff
Regional Plan Association *(879)*

Fesler, Douglas
American Society for Bone and Mineral Research *(181)*

Festo, Donna
International Society of Arthroscopy, Knee Surgery and Orthopaedic Sports Medicine *(571)*

Fetgatter, James A.
Association of Foreign Investors in U.S. Real Estate *(284)*

Fetrow, Jaqueline
The Protein Society *(868)*

Fetsko, Bonnie
Association of Professors of Gynecology and Obstetrics *(302)*

Fetterhoff, Mark
National Association of Area Agencies on Aging *(647)*

Fetterman, John
National Association of State Boating Law Administrators *(698)*

Fetteroll, Steven J.
The Wire Association International, Inc. *(1019)*

Fetz, Brian
Video Electronics Standards Association *(1009)*

Ffolkes, Suzanne
Research!America *(882)*

Ficek, Melissa
American Association of Collegiate Registrars and Admissions Officers *(58)*

Fick, Janel
North American Neuro-Ophthalmology Society *(819)*

Fick, Lisa
Association for Unmanned Vehicle Systems International *(261)*

Fickenscher, CPE, FAAFP, FACPE, MD, Kevin M.
American Medical Informatics Association *(149)*

Ficklin, Eddy
American Music Center *(153)*

Field, Alexander J.
Economic History Association *(418)*

Field, Corey
Copyright Society of the U.S.A. *(385)*

Field, Theresa "TC"
International Pediatric Transplant Association *(560)*

Fielder, Amy
Gay and Lesbian Medical Association *(457)*

Fielding, MD, Julia R.
American Association for Women Radiologists *(53)*

Fields, Adrienne

Artist Rights Society *(230)*

Fields, Carl M.
Electrical Apparatus Service Association *(422)*

Fields, Fletcher
National Association for Environmental Management *(638)*

Fields, Jana
American Bus Association *(87)*

Fields, Laurel
American College of Eye Surgeons *(95)*

Fields, Lisa Marie
National Student Speech Language Hearing Association *(798)*

Fields, Marko
National Council on Education for the Ceramic Arts *(738)*

Fields, Stana
National Association for Multi-Ethnicity in Communications *(640)*

Fields, Tim
International Association of Baptist Colleges and Universities *(516)*

Fields, MBA, Sr., Vincent A.
Association of Academic Physiatrists *(263)*

Fiels, Keith Michael
American Library Association *(145)*

Fienberg, Howard
Marketing Research Association *(606)*

Fienberg, Dr. Rick
American Astronomical Society *(77)*

Fier, Candace
American Academy of Fertility Care Professionals *(34)*

Fier, DDS, Marvin A.
American Society for Dental Aesthetics *(183)*

Fierro, Adrienne
Parenteral Drug Association *(838)*

Fiesler, Amada
Product Development and Management Association *(858)*

Fife, Sharon Postigo
Driving School Association of America *(416)*

Fifer, Joseph J.
Healthcare Financial Management Association *(471)*

Figi, Alison
National Association of Private Special Education Centers *(686)*

Figoten, CAE, Jeremy
National Apartment Association *(634)*

Figueroa, Dante
Inter-American Bar Association *(506)*

Figueroa, Edgar
Wi-Fi Alliance *(1016)*

Figueroa, Gloria
American Rhinologic Society *(175)*

Figueroa, Miguel
American Theological Library Association *(216)*

Fike, Greg
United States Soccer Federation *(999)*

Fikes, Dana
Professional Housing Management Association *(862)*

Fildes, PhD, Brian N.
Association for the Advancement of Automotive Medicine *(258)*

File, Jayma
Environmental and Engineering Geophysical Society *(430)*

Filion, Diane
Society for Psychophysiological Research *(919)*

Filippelli, Patrick
Professional Records and Information Services Management International *(864)*

Filipski, Tina Berres
Promotional Products Association International *(867)*

Filko, Jordan
International Association of Microfinance Investors *(524)*

Fillebrown , David
Incorporated Research Institutions for Seismology *(487)*

Filler, Larry
National Transit Benefits Association *(801)*

Filler, Marshall S.
Aeronautical Repair Station Association *(14)*

Filling, Constance
American Academy of Orthopaedic Surgeons *(38)*

Filling, Constance
College of American Pathologists *(363)*

Filson, Tim
Corrections, U.S.A. *(386)*

Filz, Susan
IPC - Surface Mount Equipment Manufacturers Association *(585)*

Finan, Amy
Biotechnology Industry Organization (BIO) *(330)*

Financial, Palomar
International Association of Insurance Receivers *(523)*

Finch, Jim
Regional Plan Association *(879)*

Finch, Liz
Accordionists and Teachers Guild International *(9)*

Finco, Susan
NANDA International *(625)*

Finders, PhD, Margaret J.
National Conference on Research in Language and Literacy *(729)*

Findley, Stephanie
Allied Finance Adjusters *(26)*

Fine, Camden R.
Independent Community Bankers of America *(488)*

Fine, Frank
American Luggage Dealers Association *(146)*

Fine, MBA, MS, CAE, Glen
Clinical and Laboratory Standards Institute *(358)*

Fine, CAE, Gregory J.
Turnaround Management Association *(982)*

Fine, Robert C.
American Nuclear Society *(156)*

Fine, Steven
Materials and Methods Standards Association *(608)*

Finerfrock, William A.
Healthcare Billing and Management Association *(470)*

Finger, David
National Volunteer Fire Council *(803)*

Finizio, J. Joseph
Retail Solutions Providers Association *(885)*

Fink, Mark
International Double Reed Society *(541)*

Finke, PhD, Wayne H.
American Society of Geolinguistics *(198)*

Finkel, Adam
National Court Reporters Association *(740)*

Finkel, Louis Andrew
Grocery Manufacturers Association (GMA) *(466)*

Finkelstein, Allan
Jewish Community Centers Association of North
America *(588)*

Finkelstein, Kate
National Association of Urban Hospitals *(708)*

Finkle, Jillian
International Museum Theatre Alliance *(557)*

Finley, David
American Society of Gene & Cell Therapy *(198)*

Finley, CMP, Diana L.
American Academy of Osteopathy *(38)*

Finley, Diane
Society for the Teaching of Psychology *(926)*

Finley, CML, CMST, Fred B.
Rubber Trade Association of North America *(888)*

Finley, Katherine M.
Organization of American Historians *(832)*

Finley, Patrick
Operative Plasterers and Cement Masons International
Association of the United States and Canada *(829)*

Finley, Robert "Bob" L.
Fire Department Safety Officers Association *(446)*

Finley, Saundra
Phi Chi Theta *(845)*

Finn, Buffy
American Society of Tropical Medicine and Hygiene
(210)

Finn, Candice
National Council on Education for the Ceramic Arts
(738)

Finn, Genevieve
Child Life Council *(353)*

Finn, Terry
Electrostatic Discharge Association *(425)*

Finn, Wendy
National Association of School Psychologists *(693)*

Finn, Will
International Health, Racquet and Sportsclub
Association *(549)*

Finnegan, Joe
Council on Education of the Deaf *(399)*

Finnegan, Jr., Joseph P.
Conference of Educational Administrators of Schools
and Programs for the Deaf *(375)*

Finnegan, Meegan
Agricultural Stewardship Association *(16)*

Finnell, Megan
National Association of EMS Physicians *(665)*

Finnerty, James
American Association of Immunologists *(62)*

Finnerty, Linda
Council on Social Work Education *(400)*

Finnerty, Pete
Association for Gay, Lesbian, Bisexual, and
Transgender Issues in Counseling *(247)*

Finneseth, Cindy
Association of Official Seed Analysts, Inc. *(296)*

Finnessy, CMP, John
National Portable Storage Association *(781)*

Finney, Adam
Food Processing Suppliers Association *(449)*

Finney, John
American Roentgen Ray Society *(176)*

Finney, Mike
Travel Journalists Guild *(980)*

Finno, Ariel
National Investor Relations Institute *(767)*

Fins, MD, Joseph J.
American Society for Bioethics and Humanities *(181)*

Finstrom, Diane M.
Society of Independent Professional Earth Scientists
(939)

Fiola, Carole
National Retail Tenants Association *(787)*

Fiorato, Tony
Slag Cement Association *(900)*

Fiordi, Heidi Buttner
American Academy of Child and Adolescent Psychiatry
(31)

Fiore, James F.
American Board of Surgery *(84)*

Fiore, Paul
Tire Industry Association *(975)*

Fiore, Taryn
Academy of Management *(6)*

Fiorentino, Donna M.
International Society for Clinical Densitometry *(565)*

Fiorentino, Margaret
Beta Alpha Psi *(328)*

Fiorilla, John
National Railway Historical Society *(784)*

Fiorito, Susan S.
American Collegiate Retailing Association *(105)*

Fiorletta, Carlo
Guild of Italian American Actors *(467)*

Firestone, Naomi
Jewish Book Council *(587)*

Firman, James
National Institute of Senior Housing *(765)*

Firman, EdD, James P.
National Council on Aging *(738)*

Firschein, Ben
United States Pharmacopeia *(997)*

Fisch, JD, LLM, Sanford M.
American Academy of Estate Planning Attorneys *(33)*

Fischer, Charles
American Gear Manufacturers Association *(125)*

Fischer, Craig
Police Executive Research Forum *(852)*

Fischer, Dawn Elissa
Association of Black Anthropologists *(269)*

Fischer, John
American Red Brangus Association *(174)*

Fischer, Kurt H.
The International Food & Beverage Forum *(546)*

Fischer, Mike
Composite Lumber Manufacturers Association *(372)*
Masonry Veneer Manufacturers Association *(607)*

Fischer, Timothy
R & E Council of the NAPL *(872)*

Fise, JD, Thomas F.
American College of Gastroenterology *(96)*
American Orthotic and Prosthetic Association *(159)*

Fish, Jon
Advertising Council *(13)*

Fish, Kendra
National Systems Contractors Association *(798)*

Fish, Marty
International Balloon Association *(529)*

Fishback, Price
Economic History Association *(418)*

Fishburn, Ashley
Health Industry Distributors Association *(469)*

Fisher, Colleen M.
Council for Affordable and Rural Housing *(388)*

Fisher, BA, Debrah
Alliance for Continuing Medical Education *(22)*

Fisher, Dennis
United States Trotting Association *(1000)*

Fisher, Diane J.
National Association for Business Teacher Education
(636)

Fisher, CAE, PhD, Donald W.
American Medical Group Association *(149)*

Fisher, Donna J.
American Bankers Association *(79)*

Fisher, Ellen
Women's Regional Publications of America *(1024)*

Fisher, Erin N.
Irrigation Association *(585)*

Fisher, Gary
Association for Graphic Arts Training *(247)*

Fisher, Jenny
International Association for Orthodontics *(513)*

Fisher, Jim
National Association of Towns and Townships (NATAT)
(706)

Fisher, John
Industrial/Agricultural Mower Manufacturers Council
(494)

Fisher, Katy
Refrigerated Foods Association *(878)*

Fisher, Kurt
Power-Motion Technology Representatives Association
(855)

Fisher, M. Patricia
Association of Forensic Document Examiners *(284)*

Fisher, Nancy
United States Wheat Associates, Inc. *(1000)*

Fisher, Randy W.
American Society of Interior Designers *(200)*

Fisher, Ron
Defense Fire Protection Association *(408)*

Fisher, Rory Mohar
American Animal Hospital Association *(45)*

Fisher, Vickie
American Railway Engineering and Maintenance-of-
Way Association *(173)*

Fisher, Will
Institute of Food Technologists *(499)*

Fishkin, Richard A.
Men of Reform Judaism *(612)*

Fishman, Dan
The Philanthropy Roundtable *(846)*

Fisk, Royce
Food Shippers of America *(450)*

Fister, Nancy
Association of Woodworking and Furnishings
Suppliers *(318)*

Fistolera, John
Distributive Education Clubs of America (DECA) *(415)*

Fitch, George

Caribbean Basin Ethanol Producer Association
(CBEPA) *(343)*

Fite, CPA, Kathleen
The Door and Hardware Institute *(416)*

Fithian, John
National Association of Theatre Owners *(706)*

Fitterer, Amy
Dance/USA *(406)*

Fitzgerald, Amanda
American School Counselor Association *(177)*

Fitzgerald, CEM, Brian
National Association of Neonatal Nurses *(682)*

Fitzgerald, Brian
Professional Records and Information Services
Management International *(864)*

Fitzgerald, Brian K.
Business Higher Education Forum *(339)*

Fitzgerald, CAE, DABFE, FACFE, Frank S.
Window Council *(1018)*

Fitzgerald, Gary
Allergy and Asthma Network Mothers of Asthmatics
(22)

Fitzgerald, Gary J.
Iroquois Healthcare Alliance *(585)*

Fitzgerald, Jennifer
American Schools of Oriental Research *(177)*

Fitzgerald, Jennifer
Real Estate Investment Securities Association *(875)*

FitzGerald, John K.
Interactive Gaming Council Canada *(507)*

Fitzgerald, Judith M.
National Insurance Crime Bureau *(766)*

Fitzgerald, Karen
United States Junior Chamber (Jaycees) *(995)*

Fitzgerald, Kathleen
Association for Humanist Sociology *(249)*

Fitzgerald, Kathryn R.
Screen Manufacturers Association *(893)*

Fitzgerald, Michael
American Osteopathic Association *(160)*

Fitzgerald, Pamela "Pam"
Society of Industrial and Office Realtors *(939)*

Fitzgerald-Redd, Stacy
Rice Millers' Association *(886)*
USA Rice Council *(1004)*
USA Rice Federation *(1004)*

Fitzhugh, Lynne
Academic Language Therapy Association *(3)*

Fitzmier, John R.
American Academy of Religion *(41)*

Fitzpatrick, Joy
Standards Engineering Society *(961)*

Fitzpatrick, Lise
Association for Information Systems *(250)*

Fitzpatrick, Shelly
International Ground Source Heat Pump Association
(549)

Fitzpatrick, Susan
Association for Women in Science *(262)*

Fitzpatrick, CAE, JD, Z. Kay
The Technology Institute for Music Educators *(970)*

Fitzpatrick-Navarro, CPRP, CPSI, CTRS, Tara
National Recreation and Parks Association *(784)*

Fitzsimmons, David
National Association of Chain Drug Stores *(652)*

Fiveash, Chuck
Technical Association of the Pulp and Paper Industry
(970)

Fix, Dr. Justin
National Swine Registry *(798)*

Fix-Lanes, Whitney
National Student Osteopathic Medical Association
(797)

Fjerstad, Adrianne
Grain Elevator and Processing Society *(464)*

Flahaven, Brian
Council for Advancement and Support of Education
(388)

Flaherty, CAE, Catherine
Photo Chemical Machining Institute *(846)*

Flaherty, Kate
American Epilepsy Society *(117)*

Flaherty, Maggi
National Eating Disorders Association *(743)*

Flaherty, Richard M.
International Corrugated Packaging Foundation *(537)*

Flaherty, Ryan
Surface Mount Technology Association *(966)*

Flake, Denise
Case Management Society of America *(343)*

Flam, Deborah
Risk and Insurance Management Society, Inc. (RIMS)
(886)

Flamm, Steve
International Association of Venue Managers *(528)*

Flanagan, Art
Council of American Survey Research Organizations
(392)

Flanagan, Jim
Educational Theatre Association *(420)*

Flanagan, Maureen
Society for Historians of the Gilded Age and
Progressive Era *(911)*

Flanagan, Sarah A.
National Association of Independent Colleges and
Universities *(674)*

Flanary, Dick
National Association of Secondary School Principals
(694)

Flango, Carol R
National Center for State Courts *(720)*

Flanigan, James
Society for Critical Care Medicine *(934)*

Flanigan, Jim
American Veterinary Medical Association *(219)*

Flanigan, MD, Robert C.
American Association of Genitourinary Surgeons *(61)*

Flannery, Tim
National Federation Coaches Association *(748)*

Flatley, John
Corporate Environmental Enforcement Council *(386)*
Performance Track Participants Association *(841)*

Flaum, Jackie
Associated Collegiate Press *(235)*

Flaum, Jackie
National Scholastic Press Association *(789)*

Flax, Margery L.
Mystery Writers of America *(623)*

Fleck, Maelu
American Association of Orthopaedic Medicine *(68)*

Fleenor, C. J.

National Young Farmers Education Association *(806)*

Fleet, Bill
National FFA Organization *(750)*

Flegler, Saundra
Society for Public Health Education *(919)*

Fleischer, Elizabeth
Materials Research Society *(609)*

Fleischmann, Mary Walker
The Counselors of Real Estate *(401)*

Fleishell, Sherri
ADARA *(12)*

Fleisher, JD, PhD, Lynn D.
American Academy of Wound Management *(42)*

Fleishman, Amy
American College of Preventive Medicine *(101)*

Fleiss, MD, Paul M.
American Association of Medical Milk Commissions
(65)

Fleming, A.V.
Ford Motor Minority Dealers Association *(451)*

Fleming, Michael
American Chamber of Commerce Executives *(89)*

Fleming, Robin
Charles Homer Haskins Society *(351)*

Fleming, Russ
National Fire Sprinkler Association *(751)*

Fleming, Shane
Capital Health *(342)*

Flemma, Jr., Robert J.
Conference on Consumer Finance Law *(376)*

Flemming, Barbara
Computer Measurement Group *(372)*

Flemming, Kristen
Academy of Psychosomatic Medicine *(8)*
Society for Radiation Oncology Administration *(919)*

Flesch, Megan
Commercial Law League of America *(366)*

Flesher, Patti
Portland Cement Association *(853)*

Fletcher, Bill
American Federation of Government Employees *(119)*

Fletcher, Jill
Association of Boarding Schools *(270)*

Fletcher, Kimberly
National Association of States United For Aging and
Disabilities *(703)*

Fletcher, Marion
American Association for Vocational Instructional
Materials *(53)*

Fletcher, Meghan
Information Technology Industry Council *(495)*

Fletcher, Nancy J.
Outdoor Advertising Association of America *(834)*

Fletcher, DSW, Robert J.
The National Association for the Dually Diagnosed
(643)

Fletty, Eric
The Association of Suppliers to the Paper Industry
(312)

Flick, Rebecca
Resolve, The National Infertility Association *(883)*

Flint, Alex
Nuclear Energy Institute *(824)*

Flint, Jeff

National Association of Security Companies (NASCO) *(695)*

Flint, Thomas
Society of Christian Philosophers *(932)*

Flinton, Michelle
Family, Career and Community Leaders of America *(437)*

Flippen-Anderson, Judy
American Crystallographic Association *(112)*

Flood, Colleen
Airport Consultants Council *(21)*

Flood, Scott
United States Soccer Federation *(999)*

Flora, Brad
Small Publishers Association of North America *(901)*

Flora, Debi
Small Publishers Association of North America *(901)*

Flora, Diane
The American Gem Society *(125)*

Floreancig, Lisa
National Association of Mutual Insurance Companies *(681)*

Florek, Donna M.
IEEE Power Electronics Society *(485)*

Flores, PhD, Antonio R.
Hispanic Association of Colleges and Universities *(475)*

Flores, Betsy
National Milk Producers Federation *(772)*

Flores, Milena
Flexographic Technical Association *(447)*

Flores, Tina
Global Health Council *(462)*

Florez, John
Society of Mexican American Engineers and Scientists *(941)*

Florian, Michele
American Jail Association *(142)*

Florio, Elijah
United States Parachute Association *(997)*

Florio, Kayce
Sail America *(890)*

Florita, Rose Marie
Search - The National Consortium for Justice Information and Statistics *(894)*

Flory, Mary
American Mustang Association *(154)*

Flowe, PE, Charles L.
American Society of Highway Engineers *(200)*

Flower, Lenore
American Academy of Diplomacy *(32)*

Flower, Nancy
Compressed Gas Association *(372)*

Flowers, Carl
National Association for Rehabilitation Leadership *(642)*

Flowers, Claudia
American Business Media *(87)*

Flowers, Lucinda
Association of University Programs in Health Administration *(316)*

Floyd-Thomas, Stacey M.
Society of Christian Ethics *(932)*

Fluharty, Mackenzie
Power and Communications Contractors Association *(855)*

Flyee, Thomas
United Brotherhood of Carpenters and Joiners of America *(986)*

Flynn, Amanda
American Nursery and Landscape Association *(156)*

Flynn, PhD, RPh, Arlene A.
American Association of Colleges of Pharmacy *(57)*

Flynn, Betty Stone
Thoroughbred Club of America *(973)*

Flynn, Daniel "Dan" T.
United States Soccer Federation *(999)*

Flynn, CFSP, Deirdre
North American Association of Food Equipment Manufacturers *(813)*

Flynn, Edward J.
The Association of Average Adjusters of the United States and Canada *(268)*

Flynn, James F.
CPA Associates International *(402)*

Flynn, Jeannie
National Association of Home Inspectors *(673)*

Flynn, PhD, Marilyn Sheldon
The National Network for Social Work Managers *(774)*

Flynn, Sean
Ice Skating Institute *(482)*

Flynn, Simon A.
American Academy of Veterinary Acupuncture *(42)*

Flynn, Sue
International Institute of Synthetic Rubber Producers *(552)*

Flynn, Taylor
National Association of Sign Supply Distributors *(696)*

Flynn, Jr., William J.
National Postal Mail Handlers Union *(781)*

Fobes, Alexis
Independent Bakers Association *(488)*

Foeder, Denise
Iroquois Healthcare Alliance *(585)*

Foehl, Angela
American Art Therapy Association, Inc. *(46)*

Foerster, Maureen
Text and Academic Authors Association *(972)*

Fofona, Amadou
Association of African Studies Programs *(263)*

Fogarty, Sharie
Jewelers of America *(587)*

Fogel, Gary
IEEE Computational Intelligence Society *(483)*

Fogel, Robert
National Association of County Engineers *(660)*

Fogerty, Paul
American Society for Apheresis *(180)*

Fogle, II, Leanne
Belted Galloway Society *(328)*

Fogleman, PhD, Guy
Federation of American Societies for Experimental Biology *(440)*

Fogleman, Ken
The International Transactional Analysis Association *(578)*

Folds, Felicia
Women's Basketball Coaches Association *(1022)*

Foleno, Kassi
Coin Laundry Association *(361)*

Foley, David

American Association of Equine Practitioners *(60)*

Foley, Georgia H.
Specialty Tools and Fasteners Distributors Association *(958)*

Foley, Jen
Harness Tracks of America *(468)*

Foley, Patricia T.
American Bureau of Metal Statistics *(86)*

Foley, CMP, Roselle
National Association of Chemical Distributors *(652)*

Foley, Teresa Hayden
Commissioned Officers Association of the United States Public Health Service *(368)*

Folino, Brian
Golf Range Association of America *(463)*

Folk, Sara
IGAF Polaris *(486)*

Folstein, Steve
American Academy of Allergy, Asthma, and Immunology *(30)*

Fondario, Jessica
Interior Design Society *(508)*

Fong, Arleen
Television Bureau of Advertising *(971)*

Fong, Jim
University Professional & Continuing Education Association *(1003)*

Fontaine, MD, PhD, Magali J.
Association of Clinical Scientists *(273)*

Fontana, Gregory P.
The International Society for Minimally Invasive Cardiothoracic Surgery *(567)*

Fontes, Brian
National Emergency Number Association *(745)*

Foor, Brian
Consortium of School Networking *(378)*

Foor, Carrie
American Association of Railroad Superintendents *(72)*

Foose, Scott W.
Regional Airline Association *(878)*

Foote, Mary Ann
Forging Industry Association *(452)*

Foote, William
American Psychology-Law Society *(170)*

Foraker, Brian
Professional Bowlers Association *(861)*

Foran, Bree J.
General Aviation Manufacturers Association *(458)*

Foran, Will
North - American Interfraternity Conference *(812)*

Forbes, Kathleen
Association of Graduate Liberal Studies Programs *(286)*

Forbes, Michael
International Association of Outsourcing Professionals *(525)*

Forbes, Rick
Brotherhood of Maintenance of Way Employees Division *(336)*

Forburger, Melissa T.
American College of Medical Genetics *(97)*

Forbus, Tonia
Professional and Technical Consultants Association *(859)*

Ford, Amy
National Society of Accountants for Cooperatives *(793)*

Ford, Annie M.
Black Caucus of the American Library Association *(331)*

Ford, Betty
American Association of Cereal Chemists International *(55)*
American Phytopathological Society *(165)*

Ford, Brian
Organization for the Promotion and Advancement of Small Telecommunications Companies *(831)*

Ford, Carmen
National Alcohol Beverage Control Association *(631)*

Ford, Christine
American Society of Cataract and Refractive Surgery *(194)*

Ford, Janice
National Cancer Registrars Association *(717)*

Ford, Jeanine
Accrediting Council for Independent Colleges and Schools *(10)*

Ford, John E.
Santa Gertrudis Breeders International *(891)*

Ford, Karla A.
American Poultry International Ltd. *(167)*

Ford, Leslie
National Council for Interior Design Qualifications *(732)*

Ford, Lisa Nye
American Teleservices Association *(215)*

Ford, Pamela
National Cable & Telecommunications Association *(717)*

Ford, Suzy
ASFE/The Geoprofessional Business Association *(231)*

Ford, Tim
Association of Defense Communities *(278)*

Ford, Walt
Marine Corps Association *(604)*

Forde, Kevin M.
Federal Judges Association *(439)*

Forde, Winston J.
International Society of Explosives Engineers *(572)*

Fordham, Jennifer "Jenny"
Natural Gas Supply Association *(807)*

Fordyce, Lauren
Association for Feminist Anthropology *(246)*

Fore, Anita
Authors Guild *(320)*

Fore, Troy
American Beekeeping Federation *(80)*

Foreman, Kathy
International Ticketing Association *(577)*

Foresman, Sarah
Association for Corporate Growth *(244)*

Forest, Tom
American College of Veterinary Pathologists *(104)*

Forger, Gary
Automatic Guided Vehicle Systems *(321)*
Material Handling Industry of America *(608)*
Materials Handling and Management Society *(608)*

Forgeron, Sandrine
American Law Institute *(144)*

Forgit, Susan
American Antiquarian Society *(45)*

Forister, Jill E.
American Association of Endodontists *(60)*

Forkenbrock, John B.
National Association of Federally Impacted Schools *(668)*

Forlenza, James
National Food Service Security Council *(752)*

Forman, CIPP, Alison
International Association of Privacy Professionals *(526)*

Forman, David
Human Capital Institute *(480)*

Forman, PhD, Henry
Society for Free Radical Biology and Medicine *(909)*

Forman, Michelle
Association of Public Health Laboratories *(304)*

Formwalt, Lance
North American Equipment Dealers Association *(816)*

Fornaro, John
Association of Private Club Directors *(300)*

Forrest, Sandy
Materials Research Society *(609)*

Forrest, Wayne
American Indonesian Chamber of Commerce *(135)*

Forrester, Kimberly
United States Professional Tennis Association *(998)*

Forristell, Tom
Society of Insurance Research *(940)*

Forsbach, Eric
International Conference of Funeral Service Examining Boards *(536)*

Forsberg, CPA, George
The Financial Services Roundtable *(445)*

Forsberg, Philip
North American Lake Management Society *(817)*

Forstag, Benjamin R.
American Telemedicine Association *(215)*

Forster, Marthe Lyngås
American Society for Healthcare Environmental Services *(185)*

Forster, PhD, Michael J.
American Aging Association *(43)*

Forster-Smith, Lucy
Association of College and University Religious Affairs *(274)*

Fort, Andrew O.
Council of Societies for the Study of Religion *(397)*

Fort, Jane
American School Counselor Association *(177)*

Fort, Taryn
National Stroke Association *(797)*

Forte, Paula
American Academy of Religion *(41)*

Fortenberry, ScD, Dr. Norman
American Society for Engineering Education *(183)*

Fortenberry, Norman L.
Commission on Professionals in Science and Technology *(368)*

Fortin, Andrew S.
Community Associations Institute (CAI) *(370)*

Fortin, Guy
Pipe Fabrication Institute *(849)*

Fortman, Jr., Fred
American Society of Safety Engineers *(209)*

Fortney, Mary Martha
National Association of State Credit Union Supervisors *(699)*

Forton, Dale

Professional Aviation Maintenance Association *(860)*

Fortuna, Nina
American Society of Magazine Editors *(202)*
MPA - The Association of Magazine Media *(620)*

Fortune, Hank
Recreation Vehicle Dealers Association of North America *(876)*
Recreation Vehicle Rental Association *(877)*

Fortune, Mickey
RadTech *(874)*

Foscue, Amy
National Industrial Council - Employer Association Group *(763)*

Foshee, D. Scott
National Investment Banking Association *(767)*

Foshee, Emily
National Investment Banking Association *(767)*

Foss, Catherine
Plastic Surgery Research Council *(850)*

Foss, Vanessa O
American Society for Information Science and Technology *(186)*

Foster, Alec
Piano Technicians Guild *(848)*

Foster, CAE, MBA, Allison J.
Association of Schools of Public Health *(307)*

Foster, Corbi
American College of Medical Physics *(97)*

Foster, Jack
Manufacturers' Agents National Association *(603)*

Foster, FACS, MD, Jill A.
American Society of Ophthalmic Plastic and Reconstructive Surgery *(205)*

Foster, Maurice
National Association of Black Journalists *(649)*

Foster, Michelle
Young Presidents' Organization *(1030)*

Foster, Nancy E.
United States Apple Association *(989)*

Foster, Richard J.
American Swimming Coaches Association *(215)*

Foster, Robert
National Association of Drug Court Professionals *(663)*

Foster, Robert E.
The Evaporative Cooling Institute *(434)*

Foster, Sarah B.
United States Coast Guard Chief Petty Officers Association *(992)*

Foster, Shelagh E.
American Society of Clinical Oncology *(194)*

Foster, PhD, Stuart A.
American Association of State Climatologists *(73)*

Fothergill, MA, MBA, Annette W.
Medical Mycological Society of the Americas *(611)*

Foti, MD, PhD, Margaret
American Association for Cancer Research *(48)*

Fotis, James J.
Law Enforcement Alliance of America *(594)*

Fotre, Margit
Water Quality Association *(1013)*

Foulger, Teresa
Special Interest Group for Teacher Educators *(955)*

Foulk, Susan
Council for Near-Infrared Spectroscopy *(390)*

Fountain, Thomas

Church and Synagogue Library Association *(356)*

Fountain-Allen, Vanessa
National Association of Small Business Investment Companies *(900)*

Fouse, David
American Public Health Association *(171)*

Fouts, Matt
Zoological Association of America *(1030)*

Foutz, Ginger
Organization of American Historians *(832)*

Fowler, CAE, Jim
International Flight Services Association *(545)*
Research Chefs Association *(882)*

Fowler, Melissa
Cheese Importers Association of America, Inc. *(351)*

Fowlkes, PhD, Brian J.
American Institute of Ultrasound in Medicine *(141)*

Fox, Alissa
Blue Cross Blue Shield Association *(332)*

Fox, CPA, Amy
Society of Neurointerventional Surgery *(942)*

Fox, Bev Meyers
Society of Financial Service Professionals *(936)*

Fox, Carson
National Association of Drug Court Professionals *(663)*

Fox, Christine
State Education Technology Directors Association *(961)*

Fox, Christopher H.
American Association for Dental Research *(49)*
International Association for Dental Research *(512)*

Fox, Derek
Veterinary Orthopedic Society *(1008)*

Fox, Desiree
American College of Veterinary Internal Medicine *(104)*

Fox, Frank
Professional Association of Resume Writers and Career Coaches *(860)*

Fox, Gary C.
MGMA-ACMPE *(614)*

Fox, John G.
Society for Applied Learning Technology *(904)*

Fox, Lawrence
Society of American Graphic Artists *(929)*

Fox, Leisa
Association of State Chamber Professionals *(310)*

Fox, PhD, Marilyn L.
American Academy of Orthopaedic Surgeons *(38)*

Fox, Michael J.
Gasoline and Automotive Service Dealers of America *(457)*

Fox, Norma S.
Stucco Manufacturers Association *(964)*

Fox, Patricia
Interstate Renewable Energy Council *(583)*

Fox, Roxanne R.
Helicopter Association International *(473)*

Fox, Russell H.
Forestry Conservation Communications Association *(452)*

Fox, Stephenie
International Federation of Accountants *(544)*

Fox, Steven A.
Central Conference of American Rabbis *(348)*

Foxgrover, Chick

American Association of Advertising Agencies *(53)*

Foxworthy, Madelyn
Alliance for Telecommunications Industry Solutions *(23)*

Foy, John
National Reining Horse Association *(785)*

Foy, Kim
The Exercise Safety Association *(435)*

Foy, Sharon
The Exercise Safety Association *(435)*

Foye, Brittany
The Council of Insurance Agents and Brokers *(394)*

Frack, CPA, Joseph E.
Society of Financial Service Professionals *(936)*

Frado, Chris
Cross Country Ski Areas Association *(405)*

Fraga, Suzanne G.
Manufacturers' Agents Association for the Foodservice Industry *(603)*

Fraidenburg, Keith
College of Healthcare Information Management Executives *(364)*

Frame, James W.
National Exchange Carrier Association *(746)*

Frampton-Brown, Paula
American Association for Cancer Education *(48)*

Francesconi, Edi
Council of Educational Facility Planners International *(393)*

Francesconi, Peter
Tennis Industry Association *(971)*

Francese, Joseph
American Geriatrics Society *(126)*

Francis, Andrew B.
American Academy of Orthotists and Prosthetists *(38)*

Francis, Carl
National Football League Players Association *(752)*

Francis, Christina
National Football League Players Association *(752)*

Francis, Dave
American Farm Bureau Federation *(118)*

Francis, Fara
Associated General Contractors of America (AGC) *(236)*

Francis, John
National Bicycle Dealers Association *(713)*

Francis, Joseph
Supply Chain Council *(966)*

Francis, Micki
Association of Investment Management Sales Executives *(289)*
Conference of Minority Transportation Officials *(375)*
National Association of Corporate Treasurers *(658)*

Francis, Patricia
Urban and Regional Information Systems Association *(1003)*

Francis, Rosalie
International Hearing Society *(549)*

Francis, Ryan R.
National Conference on Public Employee Retirement Systems *(729)*

Francis, Shari L.
National Council for Accreditation of Teacher Education *(731)*

Francisco, Melody
Mineral Economics and Management Society *(617)*

Franco, Adolfo

Direct Selling Association *(413)*

Franco, CIA, CPA, Barbara
Association of Credit Union Internal Auditors *(278)*

Francois, Carol
Learning Forward *(596)*

Francois, DuWvaughn Pierre
National WIC Association *(805)*

Francois, Mary
Beefmaster Breeders United *(327)*

Frandanisa, Karen
Herb Society of America *(474)*

Frank, Abe L.
National Collegiate Athletic Association *(724)*

Frank, Cynthia
Copper Development Association *(384)*

Frank, Heidi
Online Audiovisual Catalogers *(827)*

Frank, Jay A.
Legal Netlink Alliance *(596)*

Frank, Kathy
International Society of Certified Employee Benefit Specialists *(572)*

Frank, Luke
American Society of Irrigation Consultants *(201)*

Frank, PhD, Dr. Martin
American Physiological Society *(165)*

Frank, Paul D.
Information Storage Industry Consortium *(495)*

Frank, Peter
Association of Home Appliance Manufacturers *(287)*

Frank, Rachel
Professional Records and Information Services Management International *(864)*

Frankel, Noralee
American Historical Association *(131)*

Franken, Jessica E.
INDA, Association of the Nonwoven Fabrics Industry *(488)*

Frankenstein, Geri
American College of Trial Lawyers *(103)*

Franklin, Bobby
CTIA - The Wireless Association *(405)*

Franklin, Jim
Red Tag News Publications Association *(878)*

Franklin, Kelly
Asphalt Roofing Manufacturers Association *(233)*
Masonry Veneer Manufacturers Association *(607)*

Franklin, Sheila
American Hiking Society *(131)*

Franko, Mark
Congress on Research in Dance *(377)*

Frankovich, Nicholas
Society for American Baseball Research *(903)*

Franks, Audra
American Dental Education Association *(113)*

Franks, MTA, Audra
Association of Academic Health Centers *(262)*

Franks, Carli
Print Services & Distribution Association *(857)*

Franks, Elizabeth
Society for Clinical Trials *(906)*

Fransioli, Timothy
International Association of Geophysical Contractors *(522)*

Frantz, Pamela
National Conference of State Liquor Administrators
(728)

Franz, DVM, Charles
American College of Theriogenologists *(103)*

Franz, DVM, Charles F.
Society for Theriogenology *(926)*

Franzen, Pamela W.
Sump and Sewage Pump Manufacturers Association
(965)

Franzenburg, Emily
American Association of School Personnel
Administrators *(73)*

Frary, Casey
American Foreign Service Association *(122)*

Fraser, David
United States Potato Board *(997)*

Fraser, Don
National Association for College Admission Counseling
(637)

Fraser, CAE, PhD, Michael
Association of Maternal and Child Health Programs
(AMCHP) *(293)*

Fratt, Justin
Gospel Music Association *(464)*

Frawley, Irene
Special Interest Group for University and College
Computing Services *(955)*
Special Interest Group on Accessible Computing *(955)*
Special Interest Group on Artificial Intelligence *(956)*
Special Interest Group on Hypertext/Hypermedia *(956)*

Frawley, Kourtney
Society of Industrial and Office Realtors *(939)*

Frazer, Angelyn
National Association of Criminal Defense Lawyers
(661)

Frazier, Cynthia
National School Public Relations Association *(789)*

Frazier, Dawn
Association of Analytical Communities International
(267)

Frazier-Lindsey, Lorna
Commission on Accreditation of Allied Health
Education Programs *(368)*

Frazine, Jeff
Professional Picture Framers Association *(864)*

Fread, Dorothy
Pinto Horse Association of America *(848)*

Frede, Candace
American Council of Learned Societies *(109)*

Frede, Lauren
Society of Laparoendoscopic Surgeons *(940)*

Fredell, Eric
Software & Information Industry Association (SIIA)
(950)

Frederick, Allison
United States Rowing Association *(998)*

Frederick, Amanda
American Chemical Society *(89)*

Frederick, Brenda
Orthopaedic Research Society *(833)*

Frederick, Carrie
Phi Beta Fraternity *(845)*

Frederick, Julie
Association of Professional Flight Attendants *(301)*

Frederick, Kenneth "Ken"
Sunglass Association of America *(965)*

Frederick, Shirley
Auxiliary to the National Medical Association *(324)*

Fredericks, Dr. Jim
National Pest Management Association *(780)*

Fredette, Gabrielle
International Foodservice Editorial Council *(546)*

Fredette, CAE, Marie
International Association of Speakers Bureaus *(528)*

Fredrickson, Sheila
International Society of Certified Electronics
Technicians *(572)*
National Electronic Service Dealers Association *(745)*

Free, David
Association of College and Research Libraries *(273)*

Free, Miles K.
Precision Machined Products Association *(856)*

Freedenberg, Paul
United Abrasives Manufacturers Association, Coated
Division *(985)*

Freedenberg, Paul
AMT - The Association For Manufacturing Technology
(222)

Freedland, Ken
Academy of Behavioral Medicine Research *(4)*

Freedlund, Kurt
North American Association of State and Provincial
Lotteries *(813)*

Freedman, CAE, Adina Rae
Association of Avian Veterinarians *(268)*

Freedman, Allan
Society of Fire Protection Engineers *(936)*

Freedman, Fred A.
Dental Trade Alliance *(410)*

Freedman, Holly
Emerging Markets Private Equity Association *(425)*

Freedman, Michael A.
United States Internet Industry Association *(995)*

Freedman, Ronald
American College of Radiology *(102)*

Freel, Joann
National Association of EMS Educators *(665)*

Freelon, Byron
National Society of Black Physicists *(793)*

Freeman, Brad
Major Indoor Soccer League *(601)*

Freeman, Elaine
Chain Drug Marketing Association *(350)*

Freeman, Geoffrey
Discover America Partnership *(413)*

Freeman, James
Association for Informal Logic and Critical Thinking
(249)

Freeman, Linda
Alliance for Children and Families *(22)*

Freeman, Lisa C.
Association for Women Veterinarians Foundation *(262)*

Freeman, Marc
National Business Aviation Association *(716)*

Freeman, Mark
The National Society of Painters in Casein and Acrylic
(794)

Freeman, Melanie
National Association of Educational Procurement, Inc.
(664)

Freeman, Michael
Healthcare Leadership Council *(471)*

Freeman, Michael
American Society of Test Engineers *(209)*

Freeman, Murray
Association of Legal Administrators *(291)*

Freeman, Tita
Business Roundtable *(339)*

Freeman, Trisha
National Ground Water Association *(756)*

Frehill, PhD, Dr. Lisa
National Action Council for Minorities in Engineering
(NACME) *(628)*

Freibrun, Susan
Material Handling Equipment Distributors Association
(608)

Freiburg, Natha
Flexible Film & Bag Division *(447)*
Foodservice & Packaging Institute, Inc. *(450)*

Freitas, Stephen
Outdoor Advertising Association of America *(834)*

French, Catherine
American Association of Neuromuscular and
Electrodiagnostic Medicine *(66)*

French, Christopher
International Association of Art Critics *(516)*

French, Connie
Professional Records and Information Services
Management International *(864)*

French, David
American Massage Therapy Association *(147)*

French, David G.
National Retail Federation *(786)*

French, Donald "Don"
Black Data Processing Associates *(331)*

French, MD, Jacqueline A.
American Society for Experimental NeuroTherapeutics
(184)

French, June
Diving Equipment and Marketing Association *(415)*

Frenchak, Dawn
SAE International *(889)*

Frendak, Diane
Association of Science-Technology Centers *(307)*

Frendt, Donna
Sanitary Supply Wholesaling Association *(891)*

Frentz, Peter W.
Institute of Transportation Engineers *(503)*

Freshman, Phil
Association of Art Editors *(267)*

Fresvik, Michael K.
Association of American Pesticide Control Officials
(265)

Freudenberg, Dr. Heino ,
International Association of Clothing Designers and
Executives *(518)*

Freundel, Erika
American Association of Residential Mortgage
Regulators *(72)*

Freundlich, Carrie
Learning Forward *(596)*

Frey, PhD, Camille
International Stress Management Association - USA
(576)

Frey, Cara
Professional Bowlers Association *(861)*

Frey, Christie
International Association of Airport Duty Free Stores
(515)

Frey, James S.
National Association of Credential Evaluation Services, Inc. *(661)*

Frey, Jane
American Association of Meat Processors *(64)*

Frey, Kelly
American School Counselor Association *(177)*

Frey, CST, MS, Kevin
Association of Surgical Technologists *(312)*

Frey, Michele
Association of Surgical Technologists *(312)*

Frey, Tom
Automotive Distribution Network *(322)*

Freyn, Liz
American Pediatric Surgical Association *(162)*
American Society of Dermatopathology *(197)*
Association for Death Education and Counseling *(244)*
Society of Vertebrate Paleontology *(950)*

Freysinger, Carol
International Jelly and Preserve Association *(553)*
Juice Products Association *(589)*
National Pasta Association *(779)*

Fri, Perry
Healthcare Distribution Management Association *(471)*

Friberg, Andrea
Public Utilities Risk Management Association *(870)*

Frick, MS, Neil
National Hemophilia Foundation *(759)*

Fricke, Doug
National Pork Producers Association *(781)*
National Pork Producers Council *(781)*

Fricke, Jim
National Association of Consumer Shows *(658)*

Fridy, Sandy V.
Irrigation Association *(585)*

Fried, Brandon
Airforwarders Association *(20)*

Fried, Linda
Association of American Physicians *(265)*

Friedberg, Josh
International Association of Skateboard Companies *(527)*

Friedlander, Andy
National Independent Automobile Dealers Association *(761)*

Friedman, Avner
Society for Mathematical Biology *(915)*

Friedman, Barbara
American Journalism Historians Association *(143)*

Friedman, Gary
American Correctional Chaplains Association *(108)*
American Jewish Correctional Chaplains Association *(143)*

Friedman, Jessica
National Contract Management Association *(729)*

Friedman, Kirk
Independent Petroleum Association of America *(491)*

Friedman, Mark
Sales Lead Management Association *(890)*

Friedman, Neil H.
Association of Gaming Equipment Manufacturers *(285)*

Friedman, Ronald J.
Diamond Manufacturers & Importers Association of America *(411)*

Friedman, Sara Y.
SEAMS Association *(894)*

Friedmann, Kaitlin

Association for Convention Marketing Executives *(244)*

Friedmann, Kaitlin
Audio Publishers Association *(320)*
International Card Manufacturers Association *(532)*
National Association of Independent Brokers Dealers *(674)*

Friedmann, Lynne
National Association of Science Writers *(694)*

Friel, Erin
National Association of State Fire Marshals *(701)*

Friel, Mia
Cremation Association of North America *(404)*
Society of Gastroenterology Nurses and Associates *(937)*

Friend, Sandy
American Culinary Federation *(112)*

Fries, Valerie J.
International Right of Way Association *(563)*

Frigo, Debra
American Academy of Disability Evaluating Physicians *(33)*

Friis, Jan
Council for Higher Education Accreditation *(390)*

Frilow, Michelle
Help Desk Institute *(474)*

Frinton, Sandy
International Association of Outsourcing Professionals *(525)*

Frinzi, Dominic H.
Harness Horsemen International *(468)*

Frisbie, John
United States-China Business Council *(1001)*

Frisby, Bradford V.
National Mining Association *(772)*

Frisby, Cheryl L.
National Association of Independent Colleges and Universities *(674)*

Frisby, Michele
International City/County Management Association *(535)*

Friske, Jason
Zonta International *(1030)*

Fritsch, Julie
National Association of Agricultural Educators *(646)*

Fritsche, Rick
Texas Longhorn Breeders Association of America *(972)*

Fritter, Bunny
National Electrical Contractors Association *(744)*

Fritz, Gerry
Associated Builders and Contractors *(235)*

Fritz, CHES, MPH, Josel Bernardo
National Association of Public Hospitals and Health Systems *(688)*

Fritz, Kathryn "Kate" E.
AMT - The Association For Manufacturing Technology *(222)*

Fritzlen, Susan M.
Association of Government Accountants *(286)*

Frjelich, Amanda
Metal Framing Manufacturers Association *(613)*

Froelich, F.E. Win
National Association of Waterfront Employers *(709)*
National Maritime Safety Association *(772)*

Froetscher, Janet P.
National Safety Council *(789)*

Frohlich, Michael
Growth Energy *(466)*

Froling, Deborah S.
National Association of Women Lawyers *(710)*

Frommeyer, Donald J.
National Association of Mortgage Bankers *(681)*

Fromyer, Mary O.
Global Offset and Countertrade Association (GOCA) *(462)*

Fronstin, Paul
Employee Benefit Research Institute *(426)*

Frontino, Caitlin
International Pediatric Transplant Association *(560)*

Frooman, Jeff
Society for Business Ethics *(905)*

Frosh, Dan
Family Firm Institute, Inc. *(437)*

Frost, Michaelle
Infusion Nurses Society *(496)*

Frost, Shelley
Association of Old Crows *(297)*

Frueh, Robert
World Trade Centers Association *(1027)*

Fruth, Larry
Schools Interoperability Framework Association *(892)*

Fry, CPA, CSA, Angela
The American Gem Society *(125)*

Fry, Erin
Romance Writers of America *(888)*

Fry, Sonya K.
Overseas Press Club of America *(835)*

Fry, Stephani
Romance Writers of America *(888)*

Frye, CMM, Jim
Association of Marina Industries *(293)*

Frye, Lisa
Association of Professional Landscape Designers *(301)*

Frye, Mary
Home Furnishings Independents Association *(478)*

Frye, Tamara
Opportunity Finance Network *(829)*

Fryer, Robin
The International Transactional Analysis Association *(578)*

Frykman, Joanie
National Asphalt Pavement Association *(635)*

Fryman, Jeff
Automated Imaging Association *(321)*

Fryshman, PhD, Bernard
Association of Advanced Rabbinical and Talmudic Schools *(263)*

Fu, Lois
Independent Sector *(491)*

Fu, Yan
Association for Population/Family Planning Libraries and Information Centers, International *(253)*

Fuchs, Celeste
North American Association of Food Equipment Manufacturers *(813)*

Fuchs, George
National Association of Printing Ink Manufacturers *(686)*

Fuchs, Jennifer
Garden Writers Association *(456)*

Fuchs, Lauren
Equal Justice Works *(432)*

Fuchs, Rachel

Society for French Historical Studies *(909)*

Fuehrer, Aaron
ACUTA – The Association for Information Communications Technology Professionals in Higher Education *(11)*

Fuentes, Sara
Navy League of the United States *(807)*

Fuhrer, Bob
National Rural Telecommunications Cooperative *(788)*

Fuhrman, LD, MS, RD, Trisha
Council on Renal Nutrition *(400)*

Fujita, Masayuki
IEEE Control Systems Society *(484)*

Fukuda, Neva
American Association of Certified Orthoptists *(56)*

Fulambarker, Sam
American Association of Physicians of Indian Origin *(69)*

Fulbright, Dennis
Northern Nut Growers Association *(824)*

Fulcher, Robert
Academy of Managed Care Pharmacy *(6)*

Fulford, Wayne
Heavy Duty Manufacturers Association *(473)*

Fulgency, Bob
North American Mycological Association *(818)*

Fulghum, Tracy
Vehicular Technology Society *(1008)*

Fulk, H. Roger
National Association of Supervisors for Business Education *(704)*

Fulkerson, Gregory
National Council of State Supervisors for Languages *(736)*

Fullagar, FACEP, MD, Christopher J.
Air Medical Physician Association *(19)*

Fullenbaum, Matt
American Tort Reform Association *(217)*

Fuller, Beth
Cristo Rey Network *(404)*

Fuller, Craig L.
Aircraft Owners and Pilots Association *(20)*

Fuller, CAE, Erin M.
Alliance for Women in Media *(24)*

Fuller, Lauren
Academy of Managed Care Pharmacy *(6)*

Fuller, Lee O.
Independent Petroleum Association of America *(491)*

Fuller, Robert
Cruise Lines International Association *(405)*

Fuller, Rogers
American Association of Physics Teachers *(69)*

Fuller, Truman S.
Association of Reporters of Judicial Decisions *(305)*

Fuller-Bertrand, MPA, Ivonne
National Medical Association *(772)*

Fullmer, Judy
National Association for Family and Community Education *(638)*

Fullwood, P. Catlin
Workers United *(1025)*

Fulmer, Brian
The Endocrine Society *(427)*

Fulmer, Rise
The National NeedleArts Association *(774)*

Fulmer, Sherry
National Barrel Horse Association *(712)*

Fulton, Jim
Retail Bakers of America *(884)*

Fulton, Kenneth R.
National Academy of Sciences *(628)*

Fults, Carla
Association of Administrators of the Interstate Compact on the Placement of Children *(263)*

Funderburk, Elizabeth A.
Consumer Healthcare Products Association *(381)*

Funderburk, Olga
American Choral Directors Association *(90)*

Fung, Maria
Chinese American Librarians Association *(354)*

Funk, Carla
International Association of School Librarianship *(527)*

Funk, Carla J.
Medical Library Association *(611)*

Funk, Pat
Association of Retail Travel Agents *(306)*

Fuqua, Chuck
American Forest & Paper Association *(123)*
American Wood Council *(221)*

Fuqua, John
SCORE Association *(893)*

Furgeson, Jr., W. Royal
Federal Judges Association *(439)*

Furlong, Cathy
Caucus for Women in Statistics *(346)*

Furlong, Robin
National Management Association *(771)*

Furman, Allan
Oriental Rug Retailers of America, Inc. *(833)*

Furman, Debbie
American Society of Consultant Pharmacists *(195)*

Furman, Nelly
Association of Departments of Foreign Languages *(278)*

Furman, Phillip
International Society for Antiviral Research *(565)*

Furnas, Kelly
Journalism Education Association *(589)*

Furneaux, Pamela
Electronic Traders Association *(424)*
Electronic Transactions Association *(424)*

Furness, Roger K.
Audio Engineering Society *(320)*

Furnish, Brian
Burley Tobacco Growers Cooperative Association *(338)*

Furnish, Melonie
Palomino Horse Breeders of America *(837)*

Furr, Bruce
American Association of Certified Orthoptists *(56)*

Fursland, Richard
BritishAmerican Business Inc. *(335)*

Furth, Daniel
National Tank Truck Carriers *(799)*

Furth, John
Association of Management Consulting Firms *(292)*

Fusco, Barbara
American Homebrewers Association *(133)*
The Brewers Association *(335)*

Fuss, Babette
American Society for Neurochemistry *(187)*

Futchko, Rose
Institute for Operations Research and the Management Sciences *(497)*

Futhey, Jr., Malcolm B.
United Transportation Union *(1001)*

Gabay, Jeannette
Laser Institute of America *(593)*

Gabay, Julio
Abacus International *(2)*

Gabbard, Abigail
Expanded Shale, Clay and Slate Institute *(435)*

Gabel, Diane
Information Systems Audit and Control Association *(495)*

Gabel-Onkels, Sandra
Academy of Organizational and Occupational Psychiatry *(7)*

Gabert, Susan
Family Firm Institute, Inc. *(437)*

Gabilaia, Tamuna
Organization of Women in International Trade *(832)*

Gabin, Jan
Capital Health *(342)*

Gable, Denise
National Parking Association *(779)*

Gable, CAE, Ty E.
National Precast Concrete Association *(782)*

Gabri, David
Associated Luxury Hotels International *(236)*

Gabriel, Pam
Fiber Society *(443)*

Gabriele, Erin
Beta Phi Mu *(328)*

Gacek, Josh
American Securitization Forum *(178)*

Gacs, David
Council of the Americas *(398)*

Gaddis, Evan R.
National Electrical Manufacturers Association *(744)*

Gady, Cynthia (Cindy)
National Association of Community Health Centers *(656)*

Gaede, Stan D.
Christian College Consortium *(355)*

Gaffney, Carol A.
The Securities Transfer Association *(895)*

Gaffney, Deborah K.
Tax Executives Institute, Inc. *(968)*

Gaffney, Jonathan
National Aeronautic Association *(629)*

Gage, John
American Federation of Government Employees *(119)*

Gage, Kevin
National Association of Broadcasters *(650)*

Gage, Matt
Association of Volleyball Professionals *(317)*

Gager, William C.
Automotive Parts Remanufacturers Association *(323)*
Remanufacturing Institute *(881)*

Gagliano, James L.
The Jockey Club *(588)*

Gagliardi, Robert
National Chemical Credit Association *(720)*

Gagne, Dawn
Automotive Communication Council *(322)*

Gagnon, Andrea
Association of Specialty Cut Flower Growers (309)

Gagnon, David
Organic Trade Association (830)

Gagnon, Heather
Maple Flooring Manufacturers Association (604)

Gagnon, Marc
International Health, Racquet and Sportsclub Association (549)

Gagnon, Patricia J.
The Travel Institute (979)

Gagu, Luana
Romanian-U.S. Business Council (888)

Gaido, Esq., Peter
Society for Laboratory Automation and Screening (914)

Gaidry, CAE, James M.
International Test and Evaluation Association (577)

Gainer, Bill
National Governors Association (755)

Gaines, Ann
Seaplane Pilots Association (894)

Gaines, Barry
American Theatre Critics Association (216)

Gaines, Jenny
Society of Chemical Manufacturers and Affiliates Inc. (932)

Gaines, Kitty L.
National Dental Association (742)

Gainey, Linda K.
American Pharmacists Association (163)

Gainor, Dia
National Association of State Emergency Medical Services Officials (700)

Gainyard, Daniel
American Osteopathic Academy of Orthopedics (159)

Gaitan, Laressa
Association of Independent Corrugated Converters (288)

Gaitan, Patricia
Women in Government Relations, Inc. (1021)

Gajare, Aniket
The Wildlife Society (1017)

Gajdosik, Stephen
Catholic Radio Association (346)

Galante, Diane
Audio Publishers Association (320)
Event Service Professionals Association (434)

Galanter, MD, Marc
Association of Medical Education and Research in Substance Abuse (293)

Galaska, Jason
National Association of Athletic Development Directors (647)
National Association of Collegiate Marketing Administrators (656)

Galassi, Janice
American Federation of Musicians (119)

Galblum, Amy
International Society for Infectious Diseases (566)

Galbraith, Bruce W.
National Association of Principals of Schools for Girls (686)

Galbraith, James
Association for Evolutionary Economics (246)

Galdamez, Karen A.
Council On State Taxation (400)

Galderisi, MD, PhD, Silvana
EEG and Clinical Neuroscience Society (421)

Gale, Darryl
National Wooden Pallet and Container Association (805)

Gale, David B.
North American Association of State and Provincial Lotteries (813)

Galen, Christopher
National Milk Producers Federation (772)

Galeone, Richard J.
International College of Dentists, U.S.A. Section (535)

Galimore, Ron
United States of America Gymnastics (997)

Galindo, Gerardo
AAGL - Advancing Minimally Invasive Gynecology Worldwide (2)

Galioto, Kristin
Glass Art Society (461)

Galis, George
International Union of Painters and Allied Trades (579)

Gallagher, Brian
Academy of Pharmaceutical Research and Science (8)
American Pharmacists Association (163)

Gallagher, Edward G.
The Surety and Fidelity Association of America (966)

Gallagher, Janne
Council on Foundations (399)

Gallagher, Jim
Medical Fitness Association (611)

Gallagher, Kurt
Pet Food Institute (842)

Gallagher, Lisa M.
Healthcare Distribution Management Association (471)

Gallagher, Mary
Directors Guild of America (413)

Gallagher, Michael D.
Entertainment Software Association (ESA) (429)

Gallagher, Sean
American Institute for Medical and Biological Engineering (136)

Gallagher, Teri
Strategic Marketplace Initiative (963)

Gallagher, Terrence V.
American Hardware Manufacturers Association (128)

Gallanis, Peter G.
National Organization of Life and Health Insurance Guaranty Association (777)

Gallegos, Al
National Association of Hispanic Federal Executives (672)

Gallegos, Cynthia
World Trade Centers Association (1027)

Gallegos, Leticia
International Association of Plumbing and Mechanical Officials (526)

Galleher, Caroline B.
Council On State Taxation (400)

Gallenagh, Elizabeth A.
Healthcare Distribution Management Association (471)

Galler, CMP, Sharon R.
Alliance of Information and Referral Systems (25)
American Association of Healthcare Administrative Management (61)

Galli, Marlo
American Association of Certified Orthoptists (56)

Galligan-Stierle, PhD, Michael
Association of Catholic Colleges and Universities (271)

Gallinger, Matt
Cleaning Management Institute (357)

Gallisdorfer, James
Community Health Charities of America (371)

Galloway, Flip
ATP Tour, Inc. (320)

Galloway, Greg
American Booksellers Association (85)

Galloway, Leslie
American Society for Metabolic and Bariatric Surgery (187)

Galloway, Pam
Texas Longhorn Breeders Association of America (972)

Gallt, Jack
National Association of State Procurement Officials (702)

Galves, PhD, Albert
International Center for Study of Psychiatry and Psychology (534)

Galvin, Susan
American Horticultural Society (133)

Gamache, Dr. Gerald L.
International Council of Psychologists (538)

Gamba, Brenda
Jewelers Board of Trade (587)

Gamber, Wendy
Society for Historians of the Gilded Age and Progressive Era (911)

Gamberini, Brian
Society of American Florists (928)

Gambino, Joyce A.
Society of Thoracic Surgeons (948)

Gamble, Chuck
North American Farm Show Council (816)

Gamble, Vickie
American Society for Reproductive Medicine (189)

Gambrell, Stefanie
American Farm Bureau Federation (118)

Gamel, Esq., Jason C.
American Resort Development Association (175)

Gamelli, Adele
National Association of Power Engineers (685)

Gammel, CAE, C. David
Entomological Society of America (429)

Gammer, Elyse
Association of Film Commissioners International (283)

Gammonley, Kevin
North American Building Material Distribution Association (814)
NPTA Alliance (824)

Gamperl, Karen
Association of Real Estate License Law Officials (305)

Ganapathy-Coleman, Hemalatha
Society for Cross-Cultural Research (907)

Gandorf, CAE, Jim
National Glass Association (755)

Ganey, Laurella
Plasma Protein Therapeutics Association (850)

Ganey, Michael J.
American Kennel Club (143)

Gangel, Mike
Wedding and Portrait Photographers International (1014)

Gangi, Ted
National Collegiate Baseball Writers Association *(724)*
United States Basketball Writers Association *(991)*

Gangone, CEM, Angelo
Association of Woodworking and Furnishings Suppliers *(318)*

Ganino, Pat
International Decorative Artisans League *(540)*

Gann, Ben
National Lumber and Building Material Dealers Association *(770)*

Gannon, Dawn
Resolve, The National Infertility Association *(883)*

Gannon, PhD, John L.
International Association for Correctional and Forensic Psychology *(512)*

Gannon, Leo J.
Laborers-Employers Cooperation & Education Trust *(592)*

Gant, Dean
International Association of Drilling Contractors *(519)*

Gant, Paula
American Gas Association *(124)*

Ganta, Arthur
National Association of Conservation Districts *(657)*

Gantenberg, FACHE, James B.
American Society of Neuroradiology *(204)*

Ganter, Lissa
Law and Society Association *(594)*

Garber, Jan
International Association of Golf Administrators *(522)*

Garber, Judy
OESP - National Association of Oil and Energy Service Professionals *(826)*

Garber, Marion
Creative Education Foundation *(403)*

Garber, Paula J.
Society for Personality Assessment *(918)*

Garbini, PE, Robert A.
Concrete Plant Manufacturers Bureau *(374)*
National Ready Mixed Concrete Association *(784)*
Truck Mixer Manufacturers Bureau *(981)*

Garcia, Aida
Labor Council for Latin American Advancement (LCLAA) *(592)*

Garcia, Apollo
American College of Veterinary Internal Medicine *(104)*

Garcia, Beatriz
Society of Hispanic Professional Engineers *(938)*

Garcia, Carla
Association of American Railroads *(266)*

Garcia, Cindy
INDA, Association of the Nonwoven Fabrics Industry *(488)*

Garcia, Claudia
International Webmasters Association *(580)*

Garcia, Donna
National Association of Realtors *(690)*

Garcia, Eric
The Folk Alliance International *(449)*

Garcia, Jr., Gilberto
National Association of Hispanic Federal Executives *(672)*

Garcia, PhD, Jaime
National Association for Chicana and Chicano Studies *(637)*

Garcia, Jeneen

The Public Relations Society of America *(870)*

Garcia, CAE, Jeneen
Public Relations Student Society of America *(870)*

Garcia, Joshua
American Gem Trade Association *(125)*

Garcia, Karina Pena
Direct Marketing Association *(412)*

Garcia, Laura
Interlocking Concrete Pavement Institute *(508)*

Garcia, Leo
United States Club Soccer *(992)*

Garcia, Marcela
US Rice Producers Association *(1004)*

Garcia, Margie
American Payroll Association *(162)*

Garcia, Meridyth
International Academy of Compounding Pharmacists *(509)*

Garcia, Sarah
National Association of Professional Geriatric Care Managers *(687)*

Garcia, Socorro
National Association of Fire Equipment Distributors *(668)*

Gardiner, Eileen
Medieval Academy of America *(612)*

Gardner, Benton W.
Sewn Products Equipment and Suppliers of the Americas *(898)*

Gardner, Bob
National Federation of State High School Associations *(750)*
NFHS Music Association *(810)*

Gardner, Butch
American Football Coaches Association *(122)*

Gardner, Catherine
The Advertising Research Foundation *(13)*

Gardner, Cecilia L.
Jeweler's Vigilance Committee *(587)*

Gardner, Chris
MEMA Information Services Council *(612)*

Gardner, Crispina
American Boat and Yacht Council *(84)*

Gardner, Dave
Sewn Products Equipment and Suppliers of the Americas *(898)*

Gardner, Debbie
Society for Maternal-Fetal Medicine *(915)*

Gardner, Debora
American Accounting Association *(43)*

Gardner, Den
American Agricultural Editors Association *(43)*
Turf and Ornamental Communicators Association *(982)*

Gardner, Gail
American Association of Orthodontists *(67)*

Gardner, Kelly
Global Health Council *(462)*

Gardner, PhD, Kent
Governmental Research Association *(464)*

Gardner, Lori B.
Association of Community Cancer Centers *(275)*

Gardner, Marilyn
American Association of Physics Teachers *(69)*

Gardner, Mark A.
National Postal Mail Handlers Union *(781)*

Gardner, Michael A.
Gypsum Association *(467)*

Gardner, Robert
EDA Consortium *(419)*

Gardner, Robert
NFHS Speech Debate and Theatre Association *(810)*

Gardner, PhD, Scott Lyell
American Society of Parasitologists *(206)*

Gardner, Stacey
Eye Bank Association of America *(436)*

Gardner, Stephen
The Aluminum Association, Inc. *(27)*

Garello, Rene
Oceanic Engineering Society *(826)*

Garfein, Carolyn H.
American Association of University Women *(76)*

Garfield, Dean C.
Information Technology Industry Council *(495)*

Garfield, Robert L.
National Yogurt Association *(806)*

Garfinkel, Jennifer
AABB - American Association of Blood Banks *(1)*

Garfinkel, John
International Sanitary Supply Association *(563)*

Gargano, Lisa L.
Rice Millers' Association *(886)*
USA Rice Council *(1004)*
USA Rice Federation *(1004)*

Gargiulo, Sabina
American Association of Heart Failure Nurses *(62)*
American Society of Hand Therapists *(199)*

Gariepy, Tambria
Aeronautical Repair Station Association *(14)*

Garland, Kristine J
Composite Can and Tube Institute *(372)*

Garlich, Heather
Food Marketing Institute *(449)*

Garlock, Stephanie
National Sheriffs' Association *(791)*

Garlock, Vincent E.
American Intellectual Property Law Association *(141)*

Garman, Elizabeth
Association for Professionals in Infection Control and Epidemiology *(254)*

Garmezy, Kathy
Directors Guild of America *(413)*

Garnant, Bev
American Society of Concrete Contractors *(195)*

Garner, Amber
American Society of Nephrology *(204)*

Garner, Jennifer
Information Technology Industry Council *(495)*
The Institute of Financial Operations *(499)*

Garner, Keith
National Association of Realtors *(690)*

Garner, Ken
Association of Marketing Service Providers *(293)*

Garner, Perry
National Farmers Organization *(747)*

Garneski, Christina
Institute of Transportation Engineers *(503)*

Garnett, Mary
Graphic Arts Technical Foundation *(465)*

Garnett, Terry W.
Association of Civilian Technicians *(273)*

Garnick, Jennifer
Independent Film and Television Alliance *(489)*

Garnier, Jacqueline
International Association of Fire Chiefs *(521)*

Garpow, Bill
Recreational Park Trailer Industry Association *(877)*

Garrett, Charles
American Metal Detector Manufacturers Association *(151)*

Garrett, MD, Gaelyn C.
American Laryngological Association *(144)*

Garrett, Janella H.
American Blonde D'Aquitaine Association *(81)*

Garrett, Karen
Direct Selling Association *(413)*

Garrett, Laura
Veterinary Cancer Society *(1008)*

Garrett, CMP, Marlene
American Fire Sprinkler Association *(121)*

Garrido, Anna
IPC - Surface Mount Equipment Manufacturers Association *(585)*
IPC Washington Office *(585)*

Garrigan, Snoa
Interior Design Society *(508)*

Garriott, Gale
Federation of Tax Administrators *(442)*

Garrison, Clinton
National Hospice & Palliative Care Organization *(760)*

Garrison, Gwen
American Dental Education Association *(113)*

Garrison, Dr. Howard
Federation of American Societies for Experimental Biology *(440)*

Garrison, Ken
Society of Competitive Intelligence Professionals *(933)*

Garson, Elaine
National Board for Certified Clinical Hypnotherapists *(715)*

Garst, Barry
American Camp Association *(88)*

Garten, Sarajane
Society of General Internal Medicine *(937)*

Gartside, Robert
American Academy of Teachers of Singing *(42)*

Garver, Al
Enlisted Association of the National Guard of the United States *(429)*

Garver, Peter
Society for American Baseball Research *(903)*

Garver, Vanessa
Appraisers Association of America *(226)*

Garverick, USN (Ret.), CAPT Michael C.
Naval Submarine League *(807)*

Garvey, Heather
American Society for Microbiology *(187)*

Garvey, Melissa
American College of Nurse-Midwives *(99)*

Garvin, Mark
Tree Care Industry Association *(980)*

Garvin, Victoria
Association of Children's Museums *(272)*

Gary, Dawn
National Automatic Merchandising Association *(711)*

Garza, Alejandra Ally

The Coastal and Estuarine Research Federation *(361)*

Garza, Jose Luis B.
National Association of Hispanic Publications *(672)*

Garza, PhD, Dr. Kristine (Tina)
SACNAS (Society for Advancement of Chicanos and Native Americans in Science) *(889)*

Garza, Pam
National Collaboration for Youth *(723)*

Garza, Robert
National Organization of Legal Services Workers *(777)*

Gascho, Eric
National Health Council *(758)*

Gasda, Heather Hartz
American Philological Association *(163)*

Gashaw, Brukie
National Association of State Budget Officers *(698)*

Gaskey, Kathy
American Psychology-Law Society *(170)*

Gaskill, Debra
National Systems Contractors Association *(798)*

Gaskill, Laura
Urgent Care Association of America *(1004)*

Gaskin, CAE, William E.
Precision Metalforming Association *(856)*

Gaskins III, Herman "Trace"
National Association of College Auxiliary Services *(655)*

Gasperini, Jr., CAE, Frank A.
National Council of Agricultural Employers *(733)*

Gass, MD, Margery L.S.
North American Menopause Society *(818)*

Gasser, Heather
Resolve, The National Infertility Association *(883)*

Gaston, Kate
Mental Health America *(612)*

Gastwirth, DPM, Glenn B.
American Podiatric Medical Association *(166)*

Gatewood, Maurice
The Accrediting Commission of Career Schools and Colleges *(10)*

Gatilao, Arnold
USENIX: The Advanced Computing Systems Association *(1005)*

Gatlin, Dede
American Saddlebred Horse Association *(176)*

Gatson, Stephanie M.
ACPA College Student Educators International *(11)*
American College Personnel Association *(105)*

Gattari, Lynn
National Miniature Donkey Association *(772)*

Gatti, Mike
National Retail Federation *(786)*
Retail Advertising and Marketing Association International *(884)*

Gatti, Peter J.
The National Industrial Transportation League *(763)*

Gatto, Carolyn
American Psychoanalytic Association *(168)*

Gatty, Bob
American Wholesale Marketers Association *(221)*

Gaudet, Brian
Independent Pilots Association *(491)*

Gaudet, Christine
Society of Pharmaceutical and Biotech Trainers *(944)*

Gaughan, CET, Phil L.

American Society of Certified Engineering Technicians *(194)*

Gaughran, Eileen
American Payroll Association *(162)*

Gauldin, Deb
Association for Applied and Therapeutic Humor *(238)*

Gaumond, Ruth
American Society for Horticultural Science *(185)*

Gauntt, Jim
The Railway Tie Association *(874)*

Gaus, Eve
Young Adult Library Services Association *(1030)*

Gaus, Judy
Association of Equipment Manufacturers *(281)*

Gauthier, Stella
Ruth Jackson Orthopaedic Society *(889)*

Gauthier, Stephen
Government Finance Officers Association of the United States and Canada *(464)*
Government Finance Officers Association, Federal Liaison Center *(464)*

Gautschy, Sharon
American Association for the Surgery of Trauma *(52)*

Gaver, Wayne
International Double Reed Society *(541)*

Gavier-Widen, Dolores
Wildlife Disease Association *(1017)*

Gavilan, Horacio
Association of Hispanic Advertising Agencies *(287)*

Gavin, Jim
Turnaround Management Association *(982)*

Gavlin, Nancy
American Institute of Steel Construction *(140)*

Gavrilos , James T
American Equilibration Society *(117)*

Gawell, Karl
Geothermal Energy Association *(459)*

Gawronski, Daphne
Radiology Business Management Association *(874)*

Gay, Brian
Midwest Free Community Papers *(615)*

Gayle, Brenda
National Association of Investors Corporation *(677)*

Gaylinn, Daniel
Association for Transpersonal Psychology *(260)*

Gaynes, Elizabeth
Osborne Association *(834)*

Gaynor, Charlene F.
Association of Educational Publishers *(280)*

Gaynor, Gerard H. (Gus)
IEEE Technology Management Council *(486)*

Ge, Liang
Association of Corporate Counsel *(277)*

Ge, Shuzhi Sam
IEEE Control Systems Society *(484)*

Geagan, Michael
Radiant Panel Association *(872)*

Gearhart, Judy
International Labor Rights Forum *(553)*

Geary, Doreen
APCO (Association of Public-Safety Communications Officials) International *(304)*

Geary, CAE, Michael V.
Nursery and Landscape Association Executives of North America *(825)*

Geary, Robin
Dermatology Nurses' Association *(410)*

Geary, Susan
National Association of Home and Workshop Writers *(672)*

Gebhart, Karen
Helicopter Association International *(473)*

Gecawicz, Jennifer
Society for Clinical Vascular Surgery *(906)*

Gecker, Dana
Plastics Pipe Institute *(850)*

Gedris, Mark
United States Apple Association *(989)*

Geduldig, Courtney
Financial Services Forum *(445)*

Gee, Sharon
National Assembly of State Arts Agencies *(635)*

Gee, Talbot H.
Heating, Airconditioning and Refrigeration Distributors International *(473)*

Geegan, Kelly
Society of Incentive & Travel Executives *(939)*

Geenen, Bob
Association of State Floodplain Managers *(311)*

Geenen, Mark
International Disk Drive Equipment and Materials Association *(540)*

Gehani, Chad P.
Indian Dental Association (USA) *(492)*

Gehring, Jill
Zonta International *(1030)*

Gehrisch, Michael D.
Destination Marketing Association International *(411)*

Gehrmann, Gunnar
National Association of Clean Water Agencies *(654)*

Geib, Laura Mowawd
Consumer Specialty Products Association *(381)*

Geier-Horan, MPP, Alexis
American Society of Addiction Medicine *(191)*

Geiger, Greg
American Ceramics Society *(89)*

Geiger, Mike
Chief Executives Organization *(352)*

Geigle, Linda
National Association for Family Child Care *(638)*

Geiling, Joan
American Society for Biochemistry and Molecular Biology *(181)*

Geismann, Mary
Society for Laboratory Automation and Screening *(914)*

Geisz, Steve
Resort and Commercial Recreation Association *(883)*

Gelder, Craig van
Association of Professors of Mission *(302)*

Gelhaus, Lisa
National Center for Assisted Living *(719)*

Gelhausen, Marvin
AACE International *(1)*

Geller, Harold
American Association of Advertising Agencies *(53)*

Geller, Sr., Perry K.
Brotherhood of Maintenance of Way Employees Division *(336)*

Gellert, Susanne
German American Chamber of Commerce *(460)*

Gellici, Janet
American Coal Council *(92)*

Gellman, Olivia Baeza
CCIM Institute *(347)*

Gelman-Kipnis, George
International Association of Law Enforcement Intelligence Analysts *(523)*

Gelwicks, Maureen
Educational Book and Media Association *(420)*

Gemeinhardt, Robin
National Association of Personal Financial Advisors *(684)*

Gemelaris, Rich
National Concrete Masonry Association *(725)*

Genadio, Joanne
National Fire Sprinkler Association *(751)*

Genberg, Ira
Associated Owners and Developers *(236)*

Gencarella, Laura Beth
International Fine Print Dealers Association *(545)*

Gendron, Cheryl
National Fenestration Rating Council *(750)*

Genova, Gina
American Composers Alliance *(105)*

Genovese, Ilse
American Association for Geodetic Surveying *(49)*

Gensburg, Bret
Special Interest Group for Technology Coordinators *(955)*

Genter, PhD, Mary Beth
American College of Toxicology *(103)*

Gentil, Ryan
Coal Trading Association *(359)*

Gentili, Jason
National Association of State Boards of Education *(698)*

Gentry, Keith
Society of Diagnostic Medical Sonographers *(934)*

Gentry, Tom
ACPA College Student Educators International *(11)*
American College Personnel Association *(105)*

Genzer, Jeffrey C.
National Association of State Energy Officials *(700)*

Georgakis, Molly
Eye Bank Association of America *(436)*

Georgantas, Althea
World Affairs Councils of America *(1025)*

George, Ann
Hop Growers of America *(478)*

George, Elizabeth M.
American Academy of Health Care Providers-Addictive Disorders *(34)*

George, Francis
Association for Research in Vision and Ophthalmology *(255)*

George, Jim
Institute of Packaging Professionals *(502)*

George, John
Association of Federal Communications Consulting Engineers *(282)*

George, Karen
American Council of Engineering Companies *(109)*

George, Kelly
American Gem Trade Association *(125)*

George, MEd, RRT, Kerry E.
National Board for Respiratory Care *(715)*

George, Lee Anne
Association of Research Libraries *(306)*
Library Copyright Alliance *(597)*

George, Michele
American Society of Home Inspectors *(200)*

George, Richard
American Society of Body Engineers *(193)*

George, Sheri
Institute for Supply Management *(497)*

Gepfert, Larry
International Association of Natural Resource Pilots *(525)*

Gephart, Jim
SCORE Association *(893)*

Geraci, Anthony
American Association of Private Lenders *(71)*

Geraghty, Katie
Home Fashion Products Association *(478)*

Geramian, Sue R.E.
Direct Marketing Association *(412)*

Gerard, Diane
Association of Professional Chaplains *(301)*

Gerard, Jack N.
American Petroleum Institute *(163)*

Gerard, Leo W.
Rubber and Plastics Industry Conference of the United Steelworkers of America *(888)*
United Steelworkers of America *(1001)*

Gerber, Jan
National Credit Reporting Association *(740)*

Gerber, Joe
American Society of Consultant Pharmacists *(195)*

Gerber, Liz
Association of Writers and Writing Programs *(318)*

Gerber, Michael
National Association of Insurance and Financial Advisors *(675)*

Gerdano, Samuel J.
American Bankruptcy Institute *(79)*

Gerding, Alethea
American College of Prosthodontists *(101)*

Gerfen, Sarah
Anxiety Disorders Association of America *(224)*

Gergely, MBA, Susan
American Organization of Nurse Executives *(158)*

Gerhardt, Michael
Dredging Contractors of America, Inc. *(416)*

Gerhart, Laura
National Tactical Officers Association of America *(799)*

Gerlak, Andrea K.
International Studies Association *(576)*

Gerlinger, MD, Tad
Society of Military Orthopaedic Surgeons *(941)*

Germain, Kelly
Giant Screen Cinema Association *(460)*

Germain, Scott St.
Associated Wire Rope Fabricators *(237)*

Germann, Laura
Universities Council on Water Resources *(1002)*

Germano, Elaine
American College of Nurse-Midwives *(99)*

Germano, Ken
Medical Fitness Association *(611)*

Germek, Paul
Suntanning Association for Education *(966)*

Geroux, Megan
WIFS - Women in Insurance and Financial Services *(1017)*

Gerow, John
American Murray Grey Association *(153)*

Gerrard, Paul
Blue Cross Blue Shield Association *(332)*

Gerrish, John
National Institute of Packaging, Handling and Logistics Engineers *(765)*

Gerritsen, Peter
Transworld Advertising Agency Network *(979)*

Gerrone, Marc
Institute Management Accountants *(498)*

Gerrow, Angela
Africa Travel Association *(15)*

Gerry, Rich
National Council for Prescription Drug Programs *(732)*

Gershman, David
National Home Infusion Association *(760)*

Gerson, David
American Enterprise Institute for Public Policy Research *(117)*

Gerspacher, Julie
American Association of Police Polygraphists *(70)*

Gerstell, Glenn
American Academy of Diplomacy *(32)*

Gerstler, Cheryl
WIFS - Women in Insurance and Financial Services *(1017)*

Gerstner, Joanne C.
Association for Women in Sports Media *(262)*

Gervasi, Ralph
Common - A Users Group *(369)*

Gervasi, Rosetta
American Medical Association Alliance, Inc. *(149)*

Gesaman, Krista
Exterior Insulation and Finish Systems Industry Members Association (EIMA) *(436)*

Gesner, Lisa
Educause *(420)*

Gessert, Bill
International Customer Service Association *(539)*

Gessert, Lisa
International Customer Service Association *(539)*

Gestram, Iris
National Association for Olmsted Parks *(641)*

Gettemy, Jim
International Association for Identification *(513)*

Getty, Linda
Society for Sex Therapy and Research *(921)*

Getzin, Leonard
Society of Nuclear Medicine *(943)*

Gev, Alon
American-Israel Chamber of Commerce and Industry *(222)*

Gevertz, Brenda
Jewish Communal Service Association of North America *(588)*

Gewolb, Lauren
Appraisers Association of America *(226)*

Geyer, Carol
Organization for the Advancement of Structured Information Standards *(831)*

Geyer, Wayne B.

Steel Plate Fabricators Association Division of STI/SPFA *(962)*
Steel Tank Institute Division of STI/SPFA *(963)*

Geylin, Mike
International Motor Press Association *(557)*

Geylin, Rachel
International Motor Press Association *(557)*

Gfroerer, Shawna A.
Business Professionals of America *(339)*

Ghafar, Michelle
National Council on Crime and Delinquency *(738)*

Gharzai, Fatema
American Society for Horticultural Science *(185)*

Ghaussy, CMP, Mariam
Construction Management Association of America *(379)*

Ghelani, Rahim
Phi Gamma Nu Fraternity *(845)*

Gherke, Shannon
Credit Union Executives Society *(403)*

Ghorbani, Daniel D.
Manufactured Housing Association for Regulatory Reform *(602)*

Giacalone, Sara
Legal Marketing Association *(596)*
Organization Development Network *(831)*

Giacomin, A. Jeffrey
Society of Rheology *(946)*

Giallorenzi, Tom G.
Optical Society of America *(829)*

Giamanco, Jan
Accredited Gemologists Association *(10)*

Giamberardino, Marco
National Electrical Contractors Association *(744)*

Gianino, Adele
Catholic Health Association of the United States *(345)*

Giannakos, Carrie
National Appliance Service Association *(635)*

Giannini, Patricia
APCO (Association of Public-Safety Communications Officials) International *(304)*

Giannoulias, CMP, Sara
American Society for Healthcare Risk Management *(185)*

Giano, SPHR, Sheila
National Association of College Stores *(655)*

Gibb, Bryan
National Council for Community Behavioral Healthcare *(731)*

Gibb, Steve
Society for Risk Analysis *(920)*

Gibbons, Gavin
Tuna Council *(982)*

Gibbons, Heather W.
American School Health Association *(177)*

Gibbs, Betty L.
Mining and Metallurgical Society of America *(617)*

Gibbs, Bill
National District Attorneys Association *(743)*

Gibbs, Christopher
Global Health Council *(462)*

Gibbs, Kevin
Council of State and Territorial Epidemiologists *(397)*

Gibbs, Laura
American Society of Health-System Pharmacists *(199)*

Gibbs, Tonya
Truck Renting and Leasing Association *(981)*

Gibian, Karen
Investment Company Institute *(584)*

Gibney, CPA, Cathy
National Hospice & Palliative Care Organization *(760)*

Gibson, Alice
International Association of Eating Disorders Professionals *(520)*

Gibson, MS, RN, Amy
Patient Centered Primary Care Collaborative *(840)*

Gibson, CDRS, OTR/L, Beth Anderson
ADED - The Association for Driver Rehabilitation Specialists *(12)*

Gibson, Cassey
Architectural Woodwork Institute *(228)*

Gibson, Cherie
Intelligent Transportation Society of America *(506)*

Gibson, Claudia
National Association of Community Health Centers *(656)*

Gibson, Colin
The Broadway League *(336)*

Gibson, Dan
International Franchise Association *(547)*

Gibson, Dana
Society of Cardiovascular Anesthesiologists *(931)*

Gibson, Jaclyn Kerper
International Economic Development Council *(541)*

Gibson, Jennifer C.
National Association of Chemical Distributors *(652)*

Gibson, Jodi
American Association of Port Authorities *(70)*

Gibson, John
National Association of Flight Instructors *(668)*

Gibson, John
National Cotton Council of America *(730)*

Gibson, Linda
Forest Resources Association *(451)*

Gibson, Melissa
Association for Research on Nonprofit Organizations and Voluntary Action *(255)*

Gibson, Roberta
American Correctional Association *(108)*

Gibson, Sharon
Association for Community Affiliated Plans *(242)*

Gibson, Susan Baxter
Institute for Business & Home Safety *(496)*

Gibson, Talton
Women in Cable Telecommunications, Inc. *(1020)*

Gibson, Thomas J. J.
American Iron and Steel Institute *(142)*

Gideon, Kelly
Pony of the Americas Club *(852)*

Gidley, Debbie
American Association of Women Dentists *(77)*

Gidman, John
Association of Institutional Investors *(289)*

Gielen, Nina
American Council of Learned Societies *(109)*

Gieminiani, Marcela
Allergy and Asthma Network Mothers of Asthmatics *(22)*

Giertz, J. Fred
National Tax Association *(799)*

Giese, James
Crop Science Society of America *(404)*

Giese, Theodore L.
Abrasive Engineering Society *(2)*

Giesecke, Anne
Underwater Society of America *(984)*

Gieseke, Ken
National Frame Building Association *(753)*

Gieseman, Oksana
Soil and Water Conservation Society *(951)*

Giesen, James C.
Agricultural History Society *(16)*

Giesey, Deborah C.
Tax Executives Institute, Inc. *(968)*

Giffin, Abby
American Medical Directors Association *(149)*

Gifford, David
American Health Care Association *(129)*

Gifford, MBA, Kim
American Society of Transplant Surgeons *(210)*

Gifford, Kristen
Diesel Technology Forum *(412)*

Gift, Stephen
Retail Solutions Providers Association *(885)*

Giganti, Ed
Catholic Health Association of the United States *(345)*

Gigantiello, Steve
Healthcare Convention and Exhibitors Association *(471)*

Giglio, Diane
National Association of Colleges and Employers *(655)*

Gikas, Stamatis A.
Hellenic-American Chamber of Commerce *(474)*

Gil, Armando M.
Independent Filmmaker Project *(489)*

Gilanshah, Ellie
The National Industrial Transportation League *(763)*

Gilberg, Steven
American Leather Chemists Association *(145)*

Gilbert, Jacqueline
Community Financial Services Association of America CFSA *(370)*

Gilbert, PsyD, Michael
International Center for Study of Psychiatry and Psychology *(534)*

Gilbert, Nichole
Young Adult Library Services Association *(1030)*

Gilbert, Rachel
General Aviation Manufacturers Association *(458)*

Gilbert, CHME, CHA, Robert A.
Hospitality Sales and Marketing Association International *(479)*

Gilbert, Sherry
SnowSports Industries America *(902)*

Gilcher, Emily
Drug & Alcohol Testing Industry Association *(416)*

Gilchrist, Jon W.
Sealant, Waterproofing and Restoration Institute *(894)*

Gildersleeve, Linda
Society for Gynecologic Investigation *(910)*

Giles, Chris
Galiceno Horse Breeders Association *(455)*

Giles, Jason
National Indian Gaming Association *(762)*

Giles, Kim
Electrical Generating Systems Association *(422)*

Giles, Miriam
American Academy of Addiction Psychiatry *(29)*

Giles, Tali
Nashville Songwriters Association, International *(625)*

Gilfoyle, JD, Nathalie
American Psychological Association *(169)*

Gilhooly, Maureen
The Association for Manufacturing Excellence *(252)*

Gill, G.C. Chip
International Association of Geophysical Contractors *(522)*

Gill, CFE, JD, John D.
Association of Certified Fraud Examiners *(271)*

Gill, CAE, L. Diane
Council on Governmental Ethics Laws *(399)*

Gill, Rick
Disaster Recovery Contractors Association (DRCA) *(413)*

Gill, Sarah
International Conference of Funeral Service Examining Boards *(536)*

Gill, Susan
American Association for Respiratory Care *(51)*

Gill, Tim
American Statistical Association *(213)*

Gill, Tom
United States Lifesaving Association *(996)*

Gillan, Steven
American Alliance of Home Modification Professionals (AAHMP) *(44)*

Gilland, CCS, Dean R.
National Automatic Merchandising Association *(711)*

Gilland, Eloise
Earthquake Engineering Research Institute *(418)*

Gillengerten, Yvonne
National Public Employer Labor Relations Association *(783)*

Gilles, Nicole
American Sand Association *(177)*

Gillespie, Annelise
American Pyrotechnics Association *(172)*

Gillespie, Glynnis
Telework Advisory Group for World at Work *(971)*

Gillespie, Gwendolyn K.
Society for the Science & the Public *(924)*

Gillespie, Jen
National Swine Registry *(798)*

Gillespie, John
National Cooperative Business Association *(729)*

Gillespie, Vickie
Art Glass Association *(230)*

Gillett, Belinda
Partnership for Philanthropic Planning *(839)*

Gillette, Jennifer
Mulch and Soil Council *(621)*

Gillette, Lisa
Investment Adviser Association *(583)*

Gillette, Melissa
Aestheticians International Association *(14)*

Gilliam, Elaine
Society for Technical Communication *(922)*

Gilliam, Ken
Meeting Professionals International *(612)*

Gilligan, Daniel
Petroleum Marketers Association of America *(843)*

Gilligan, Donald
National Association of Energy Service Companies *(665)*

Gilligan, MA, Kandace
University Professional & Continuing Education Association *(1003)*
University Professional & Continuing Education Association *(1003)*

Gilligan, Paige
American Society of Agricultural Consultants *(191)*

Gillihan, Scott W.
American Ornithologists' Union *(158)*

Gillin, Colin
American Association of Wildlife Veterinarians *(77)*

Gillinson, CAE, Brenda
Independent Lubricant Manufacturers Association *(490)*

Gillis, Jack
Certified Auto Parts Association *(349)*

Gillispie, Susan
Organization for Tropical Studies *(831)*

Gillman, Dorothy
National Association of Veterans Program Administrators *(708)*

Gillmeiste, Robert
American Academy of Pediatric Dentistry *(39)*

Gilman, Maureen
National Treasury Employees Union *(801)*

Gilmartin, Denise
Association of Independent Commercial Producers *(287)*

Gilmer, LouAnn
National Association of State Foresters *(701)*

Gilmer, Ray
United Fresh Produce Association *(987)*

Gilmore, Jon
ACPA College Student Educators International *(11)*

Gilmore, Jr., Jon
American College Personnel Association *(105)*

Gilmore, Kelly
Retail Advertising and Marketing Association International *(884)*

Gilmore, Nina
Alliance of Hazardous Materials Professionals *(25)*

Gilmore, Terry
National Rural Telecommunications Cooperative *(788)*

Gilmore, Ursula
American Public Human Services Association *(171)*

Gilpin, Andrew
North American Performing Arts Managers and Agents *(819)*

Gilpin, Carmella
International Council for Health, Physical, Education, Recreation, Sport and Dance *(537)*

Gilpin, Don
Custom Electronic Design and Installation Association *(405)*

Gilsdorf, Michael
National Association of Federal Veterinarians *(668)*

Gilsenan, Dianne
American Orthopaedic Foot and Ankle Society *(158)*

Gilson, PhD, Dr. Erika H.
American Association of Teachers of Turkic Languages *(75)*

Gilson, Susan E.

National Association of Flood and Stormwater Management Agencies **(668)**

Gimer, Richard H.
Carpet Cushion Council **(343)**

Giner, Robin
Outdoor Writers Association of America **(835)**

Gingerich, Philip D.
Paleontological Society **(837)**

Ginn, Bryan
SnowSports Industries America **(902)**

Ginsbach, Pam
National Association for Business Economics **(636)**

Ginsberg, Ellen C.
Nuclear Energy Institute **(824)**

Ginsberg, Matt
National Railroad Construction and Maintenance Association, Inc. **(783)**

Ginsburg, Amy
American College Dance Festival Association **(92)**

Ginter, Kim
National Strength and Conditioning Association **(797)**

Ginter, Lisa
American Probation and Parole Association **(167)**

Ginther, Charles
North American Council of Automotive Teachers **(815)**

Gioe, Tim
Refrigeration Service Engineers Society **(878)**

Gioielli, Ellen
The International Childbirth Education Association **(534)**

Giometti, Anthony
American Society of Heating, Refrigerating and Air Conditioning Engineers (ASHRAE) **(199)**

Giordani, Pattie
National Association of Colleges and Employers **(655)**

Giordano, Kelly
Children's Book Council **(353)**

Gioseffi, Andrew R.
Construction Financial Management Association **(379)**

Giovanetti, Geoffrey N.
Wine and Spirits Shippers Association **(1018)**

Gipper, Jerry
VITA **(1011)**

Giracca, Shaughna
National Child Support Enforcement Association **(721)**

Girado, Sandra
National Association for Multi-Ethnicity in Communications **(640)**

Girard, Meghan
International Society for Clinical Densitometry **(565)**

Girard, Michael A.
North American Maple Syrup Council **(818)**

Girard, Stephan
Packaging Machinery Manufacturers Institute **(836)**

Giraudo, James
National Independent Flag Dealers Association **(762)**

Giroux, Teresa
Automotive Parts Remanufacturers Association **(323)**

Giroux, CMP, William
Truckload Carriers Association **(981)**

Gishler, Kimberley
Corporate Event Marketing Association **(386)**

Githens, William F.
The Risk Management Association **(886)**

Gitlin, MD, Scott D.
Association of Specialty Professors **(309)**

Gitomer, David L.
Association of Graduate Liberal Studies Programs **(286)**

Gittens, Joe
Security Industry Association **(895)**

Gittinger, Michael
Quarters Furniture Manufacturers Association **(872)**

Gittings, Nico
American Rights at Work **(175)**

Gittins, Naomi
National School Boards Association **(789)**

Giuda, Ashley
American Nursery and Landscape Association **(156)**

Giuffre, Jon
Family, Career and Community Leaders of America **(437)**

Giunta, Jim
National Collegiate Wrestling Association **(724)**

Givens, Todd
Nashville Songwriters Association, International **(625)**

Givler, Peter J.
Association of American University Presses **(267)**

Giznik, Caryn
American Specialty Toy Retailing Association **(212)**

Gizzi, Amanda
Jewelers of America **(587)**

Glaccum, Katy
Delta Sigma Pi **(409)**

Glad, CMP, CAE, Linda A.
National Association of Episcopal Schools **(666)**

Gladden, Linda L.
American Association of Orthodontists **(67)**

Glade, Brian J.
Association of Executive Search Consultants **(282)**

Glading, Laura
Association of Professional Flight Attendants **(301)**

Glaittli, Shannon
Executive Women International **(435)**

Glanz, Susan
American Association for the Study of Hungarian History **(52)**

Glanz, William
International Association of Fire Fighters **(521)**

Glas, Bradley J.
National Party Boat Owners Alliance **(779)**

Glasby, M. J.
Association of Pet Dog Trainers **(299)**

Glasener, Karl
Crop Science Society of America **(404)**

Glaser, Matthew T.
National Association of Chemical Distributors **(652)**

Glaser, Tamara B.
Resort Hotel Association **(883)**

Glasgow, Roger
Association of Halfway House Alcoholism Programs of North America **(286)**

Glashow, Andi
National Council for Science and the Environment **(733)**

Glasmann, J. Reed
Clay Minerals Society **(357)**

Glaspie, Amy D.
Society for Research in Child Development **(920)**
Society for Research on Adolescence **(920)**

Glass, Erin
The Brewers Association **(335)**

Glass, Gary
American Homebrewers Association **(133)**

Glass, CAE, FACHE, Maureen C
American College of Healthcare Executives **(96)**

Glass, Vicki
National Association of Development Organizations **(662)**

Glasscock, Kim
Automotive Recyclers Association **(323)**

Glasser, Mike
Antique and Amusement Photographers International **(224)**

Glasser, Roberta
Holistic Dental Association **(477)**

Glavin, JD, Kristin Olds
American Orthopaedic Association **(158)**

Glazer, DDS, Howard S.
American Society for Dental Aesthetics **(183)**

Glazer, Julia
Association of Real Estate Women **(305)**

Glazier, Mitch
Recording Industry Association of America (RIAA) **(876)**

Glazner, Steve
APPA - Leadership in Educational Facilities **(225)**

Gleason, Alan
Soaring Society of America **(902)**

Gleason, Diane
National Air Transportation Association **(630)**

Gleason, Kathryn L.
National Pharmaceutical Council **(780)**

Gleason, BS, Teresa
Academy of Surgical Research **(9)**

Gleberman, Ellen J.
Association of Global Automakers **(285)**

Gleed, Carlton
Society of American Foresters **(928)**

Gleesing, Kathryn
International Foundation of Employee Benefit Plans **(547)**

Gleit, Morton B.
National Confectionery Sales Association **(726)**

Glendening, Jr., Dale D.
Association of Administrative Law Judges **(263)**

Glendinning, David
Armed Forces Special Agents Association **(229)**

Glenn, Debbie
Society of Cleaning and Restoration Technicians **(932)**

Glenn, Doug
Forging Industry Association **(452)**

Glenn, Gary
Society of Cleaning and Restoration Technicians **(932)**

Glenn, Heather
Association for Governmental Leasing and Finance **(247)**

Glenn, Ken
Transpacific Stabilization Agreement **(977)**

Glenn, Phyllis
International Society for Heart and Lung Transplantation **(566)**

Glick, Andrea
United Synagogue of Conservative Judaism **(1001)**

Glickman, Lauren

American Wind Energy Association (AWEA) *(221)*

Glicoes, Jennifer
National Communication Association *(724)*

Glidden, Michele
Society for the Science & the Public *(924)*

Gliedman, Michael S.
National Basketball Association *(712)*

Glispie, Jeff
Association of Reproductive Health Professionals *(305)*

Glmartin, Ed
Association of Flight Attendants - CWA *(283)*

Glossa, Dawn M.
American Society of Anesthesiologists *(192)*

Glover, Denise
Society of Ethnobiology *(935)*

Glover, Jeanne
Marine Technology Society *(605)*

Glover, Rhonda A.
National Association of Black Suppliers *(649)*

Glover, PhD, Robert W.
National Association of State Mental Health Directors *(701)*
National Association of State Mental Health Program Directors *(701)*

Glowacki, Elaine
Forest Products Society *(451)*

Glowacki, Ian
Hearth, Patio and Barbecue Association *(472)*

Glowacki, Jeri
Non Commissioned Officers Association (NCOA) *(811)*

Glowinski, Robert W.
American Wood Council *(221)*

Gluck, Joel
Wireless Innovation Forum *(1019)*

Glucksman, Daniel I.
International Safety Equipment Association (ISEA) *(563)*

Glyptis, Stephanie
Air and Waste Management Association *(17)*

Gmiter, Cheri D.
Marketing and Advertising Global Network *(606)*

Gnass, Stephen Paul
National Congress of Inventor Organizations *(729)*

Gnos, Don
National Lamb Feeders Association *(768)*

Goad, Liz
Filter Manufacturers Council *(444)*

Goad, Sandi
American Hotel & Lodging Association (AH&LA) *(134)*

Goberman, Claire C.
International Association for Philosophy and Literature *(514)*

Goble, Michelle
Academy of Country Music *(4)*

Goble, Todd
National Association of Street Schools *(703)*

Goch, David
Industrial Heating Equipment Association *(493)*

Godaire, PHR, Dawn
Heart Rhythm Society *(472)*

Godbout, Theodore C.
The ERISA Industry Committee (ERIC) *(433)*

Goddard, Carol A.
American Hernia Society *(131)*
American Society of General Surgeons *(198)*

Goddard, Christie
Commission on Accreditation for Law Enforcement Agencies Incorporation *(367)*

Goddard, Stephen
Print Council of America *(857)*

Godden, David
Association for Informal Logic and Critical Thinking *(249)*

Goddin, Lesley A.
National Tile Contractors Association *(800)*

Godes, Cynthia
American Society for Cell Biology *(182)*

Godfrey, Jonathan
Association for Competitive Technology (ACT) *(242)*

Godin, Darlene
Tall Ships America *(968)*

Godinez, Lauren
Calorie Control Council *(341)*

Godlewski, Philip
American Board of Perianesthesia Nursing Certification Inc. *(83)*

Godsberg, Alicia
Federation of American Scientists *(440)*

Godsman, Bonnie
GAMA International *(455)*

Godwin, Jean C.
American Association of Port Authorities *(70)*

Godwin, Kathy
CoreNet Global *(385)*

Goedkoop, Annie
The Electrochemical Society *(423)*

Goekler, PhD, Susan
Directors of Health Promotion and Education (DHPE) *(413)*

Goeks, Debra
Association of Pedestrian and Bicycle Professionals *(298)*

Goergen, Jr., Michael T.
Society of American Foresters *(928)*

Goertz, Elena
American Society of Media Photographers *(203)*

Goessel, Lydia
Financial & Insurance Conference Planners *(444)*
Print Services & Distribution Association *(857)*
Society of Incentive & Travel Executives *(939)*

Goettl, Elizabeth Stewart
Cristo Rey Network *(404)*

Goetz, Amy
American Society for Bone and Mineral Research *(181)*

Goetz, Meg
American Indian Higher Education Consortium *(135)*

Goetz, Tom
Associated Construction Distributors International *(235)*

Goetze, PhD, David B.
Association for Politics and the Life Sciences *(253)*

Goff, Linda
Community Action Partnership *(369)*

Goff, Michael
Independent Sector *(491)*

Goff, PE, Ron
American Institute of Timber Construction *(141)*

Goffi-Fynn, Jeanne
American Academy of Teachers of Singing *(42)*

Goffin, Vincent

National Association of Recording Merchandisers (NARM) *(690)*

Gogal, Laura
American Society for Therapeutic Radiology and Oncology *(190)*

Goguen, LEED AP, PE, Claude
National Precast Concrete Association *(782)*

Goh, Edward Whistler
Association of Productivity Specialists *(300)*

Goheen, John
National Guard Association of the U.S. *(757)*

Goik-Kurn, Sheri
National Organization for Human Service *(777)*

Goin, Carma
In-Plant Printing and Mailing Association *(487)*

Goins, Elizabeth Kasper
User Experience Professionals Association *(1005)*

Goins, Pam
Council of State Governments *(397)*

Golan, Shachar
Phi Gamma Nu Fraternity *(845)*

Golanski, Susan B.
American Academy of Physician Assistants in Occupational Medicine *(40)*

Gold, Alan
National Cutting Horse Association *(741)*

Gold, Brett
Diplomatic and Consular Officers, Retired (Dacor) *(412)*

Gold, Irisa
Society of Hospital Medicine *(938)*

Gold, Jerry
Society for the Exploration of Psychotherapy Integration *(923)*

Gold, Jody
American Medical Society for Sports Medicine *(149)*

Gold, Josh
The Institute of Financial Operations *(499)*

Gold, Lori
Association of Strategic Alliance Professionals, Inc. *(311)*

Gold, Peter
National Center for Homeopathy *(719)*

Gold, Rhonda
National Association of Public Hospitals and Health Systems *(688)*

Gold, Roberta
Association for Applied and Therapeutic Humor *(238)*

Gold, Rosalind
National Association of Latino Elected and Appointed Officials *(677)*

Gold, Stephen V.
Manufacturers Alliance/MAPI Inc. *(603)*

Gold, Virginia
Association for Computing Machinery *(243)*

Goldberg, Alan
Jewish Community Centers Association of North America *(588)*

Goldberg, Allison
Association of State and Territorial Solid Waste Management Officials *(310)*

Goldberg, Bert
American Factoring Association *(118)*

Goldberg, Bob
National Association of Realtors *(690)*
North American Retail Dealers Association *(820)*

Goldberg, CPA, CTA, Bruce K.
The Fiduciary and Investment Risk Management Association *(443)*

Goldberg, Cait
Society for the Science & the Public *(924)*

Goldberg, Casey Ward
United States Psychiatric Rehabilitation Association *(998)*

Goldberg, Dan
Turnaround Management Association *(982)*

Goldberg, James M.
National Alcohol Beverage Control Association *(631)*

Goldberg, MD, Jeffrey
Society of Reproductive Surgeons *(946)*

Goldberg, Jim
North American Meat Association *(818)*

Goldberg, Joan R.
International Society for Advancement Cytometry *(565)*

Goldberg, Jodi
National Society of Accountants *(793)*

Goldberg, Linda
NACE International *(623)*

Goldberg, Michael I
American Society for Microbiology *(187)*

Goldberg, Robert C.
Business Technology Association *(340)*

Goldberg, Todd
National Association of Computerized Tax Processors *(657)*

Goldberger, PhD, Bruce
Society of Forensic Toxicologists *(936)*

Goldbetter, Larry
National Writers Union *(806)*

Goldbrum, Larry H.
Society of Professional Asset-Managers and Record Keepers *(945)*

Golden, Bobbie
The Coca-Cola Bottlers' Association *(361)*

Golden, Camille
International Warehouse Logistics Association *(580)*

Golden, Charity
ASME International Gas Turbine Institute *(233)*

Golden, David
National Association of Surety Bond Producers *(704)*

Golden, Joseph
Weather Modification Association *(1014)*

Golden, Kathie Stromile
National Conference of Black Political Scientists *(727)*

Golden, Nikki
National Association of the Remodeling Industry *(705)*

Goldensohn, Ellen
Chamber Music America *(350)*

Goldfarb, Barry
National Association of University Forest Resources Programs *(707)*

Goldfarb, Ronald
Association of Writers and Writing Programs *(318)*

Goldfield, David
Urban History Association *(1004)*

Goldfine, Jill
Automotive Trade Association Executives *(324)*

Goldie, Crystal B.
Joint National Committee for Languages *(589)*

Goldin, Kimberly

International Society for Medical Publication Professionals *(567)*

Goldman, Jack
Hearth, Patio and Barbecue Association *(472)*

Goldman, Jennifer
Foodservice & Packaging Institute, Inc. *(450)*

Goldman, Kathy
National Association for Information Destruction, Inc. *(640)*

Goldman, Mark
Interactive Advertising Bureau *(506)*

Goldman, Nina
American Council of Engineering Companies *(109)*

Goldman, Trudy
American Society of Safety Engineers *(209)*

Goldmann, Hilary
International Society for Technology in Education *(569)*

Goldner, James
International Association of Medical Equipment Remarketers and Servicers (IAMERS) *(524)*

Goldrich, Mike
The New York Academy of Sciences *(809)*

Goldsby, Cheryl
Regional Airline Association *(878)*

Goldsby, Terry
Aquatic Plant Management Society, Inc. *(227)*

Goldschmidt, Andrew
National Association of County Intergovernmental Relations Officials *(660)*

Goldschmidt, CAE, Andrew
National Association of Counties *(659)*

Goldsmith, PhD, Barbara
Clinical and Laboratory Standards Institute *(358)*

Goldsmith, Helene
Parliamentary Associates *(839)*

Goldsmith, Patricia J.
National Comprehensive Cancer Network *(725)*

Goldsmith, Thomas D.
Electronic Transactions Association *(424)*

Goldspiel, Eileen G.
American Association of Museums *(65)*

Goldstein, Alanna
American Geriatrics Society *(126)*

Goldstein, Beth McGettigan
American Law Institute *(144)*

Goldstein, Debbie
Association for Professionals in Infection Control and Epidemiology *(254)*

Goldstein, Gail
AscdiNatd *(231)*

Goldstein, Jack
Actors' Equity Association *(11)*

Goldstein, Josh
AFL-CIO (American Federation of Labor and Congress of Industrial Organizations) *(14)*

Goldstein, Justin
Binding Industries Association *(329)*
Label Printing Industries of America *(591)*

Goldstein, Justin
Printing Industry Financial Executives *(858)*

Goldstein, Nick
American Road and Transportation Builders Association *(175)*

Goldstein, Pamela
National Immigration Project of the National Lawyers Guild *(761)*

Goldstein, Stephen
Association of Litigation Support Professionals *(292)*

Goldstone, Robyn
AFCOM *(14)*

Goldstrom, Mort
Newspaper Association of America *(810)*

Golladay-Davis, April
Federal Bar Association *(438)*

Gollos, Hal
American Association of Motor Vehicle Administrators *(65)*

Golonka, CPA, Catherine
Surface Engineering Coating Association *(966)*

Golson, E. Palmer
United States-China Business Council *(1001)*

Goltry, Scott
American Meat Institute *(148)*

Gomes, Cheryl
Fiber Society *(443)*

Gomes-Koizumi, Agnes
International Association for Corporate and Professional Recruitment *(511)*

Gomez, Kristin
American Public Gas Association *(170)*

Gomez, Luis
American Academy of Cosmetic Surgery *(32)*

Gomez, Matthew
American Society of International Law *(201)*

Gomez, Pete
Cantors Assembly *(342)*

Gomez-Zormelo, Dulce
National Wildlife Federation *(805)*

Gomulinski, Curtis D.
Tau Beta Pi Association *(968)*

Goncalves, Chris
ICE Futures U.S. *(482)*

Goncalves, Marie
Manufacturing Jewelers and Suppliers of America *(604)*

Gondl, Vinai
Association of Residents in Radiation Oncology *(306)*

Gondles, Jr., CAE, James A
American Correctional Association *(108)*

Gongliewski, Nancy J.
Society of Quality Assurance *(946)*

Gonner, Sylvia
The Institute of Internal Auditors *(500)*

Gono, Rowena
International Downtown Association *(541)*

Gonsalves, Rennie
Linguistic Association of Canada and the United States *(598)*

Gonzales, Esther Moreno
Society of Mexican American Engineers and Scientists *(941)*

Gonzales, Gil
National Indian Head Start Directors Association *(763)*

Gonzales, Karen M.
Destination Marketing Association International *(411)*

Gonzales, Magda
Hispanic Association of Colleges and Universities *(475)*

Gonzales, Robyn
National Council on Teacher Retirement *(740)*

Gonzales, Tricia
Environmental Design Research Association *(431)*

Gonzalez, Amanda
American Society of Baking *(193)*

Gonzalez, Anna
Association for Asian American Studies *(239)*

Gonzalez, David
AIR Commercial Real Estate Association *(18)*

Gonzalez, Diana
Society for Imaging Science and Technology *(912)*

Gonzalez, Elvia
Hollywood Radio & Television Society *(477)*

Gonzalez, Gil
Association of Performing Arts Presenters *(298)*

Gonzalez, Jack
American Public Transportation Association *(171)*

Gonzalez, Julia
World Trade Centers Association *(1027)*

Gonzalez, Laura
Society for Anthropology in Community Colleges *(904)*

Gonzalez, Manny
National Society of Hispanic MBAs *(794)*

Gonzalez, Miguel A.
National Education Association *(744)*

Gonzalez, CFLE, MEd, Nancy
National Council on Family Relations *(738)*

Gonzalez, Rene A.
Hispanic Association of Colleges and Universities *(475)*

Gonzalez, MPS, RN, Rose
American Nurses Association *(156)*

Gonzalez, Thanya
Utility Management & Conservation Association *(1006)*

Gonzalez, Valerie
American Association of Kidney Patients *(64)*

Gonzalez, DMD, Jr., W. Edward
American Orthodontic Society *(158)*

Gonzalez del Valle, Luis T.
Twentieth-Century Spanish Association of America *(983)*

Gonzalez-Micklin, Gloria
United States-China Business Council *(1001)*

Gonzalez-Rowe, Angela
Latino Hotel Association *(594)*

Gonze, Robert
Associated Glass and Pottery Manufacturers *(236)*

Gooch, Dan
National Association of County Park and Recreation Officials *(660)*

Gooch, David A.
Coal Operators and Associates *(359)*

Gooch, Katrina
National Board for Certified Counselors *(715)*

Good, Carl
National Roofing Contractors Association *(787)*

Good, Greg
History of Earth Sciences Society *(476)*

Good, Kathie
Council for Educational Diagnosticians *(389)*

Good, Laura
Million Dollar Round Table *(616)*

Good, Lisa
National Federation of Municipal Analysts *(749)*

Good, Shane
American Association of Zoo Keepers *(77)*

Good, CAE, William
National Roofing Contractors Association *(787)*

Goodbred, Tracy
American Association of Occupational Health Nurses *(67)*

Goode, Ron
Truckload Carriers Association *(981)*

Goode, Thomas
Alliance for Telecommunications Industry Solutions *(23)*

Goodell, Pam
Association of Strategic Alliance Professionals, Inc. *(311)*

Goodermuth, Annlouise
Association for Research in Nervous and Mental Disease *(255)*

Goodfellow, Julianne
National Multi-Housing Council *(774)*

Goodhart, Jessi
Painting and Decorating Contractors of America *(837)*

Goodhart, Scot
Strategic Account Management Association *(963)*

Goodhope, Randy
American Resort Development Association *(175)*

Goodill, BC-DMT, LPC, NCC, PhD, Sharon
American Dance Therapy Association *(113)*

Goodin, Colleen
National Employment Lawyers Association (NELA) *(746)*

Goodin, Kathy
International Nubian Breeders Association *(558)*

Goodin-Mitchell, Kathy
Promotional Products Association International *(867)*

Gooding, Jean
Distilled Spirits Council of the United States, Inc. *(414)*

Goodlander, Jennifer
Association for Asian Performance *(239)*

Goodman, Amy L.
Delta Theta Phi *(409)*

Goodman, Esq., Brian S.
National Association of Public Insurance Adjusters *(689)*

Goodman, Katie
American Institute for Medical and Biological Engineering *(136)*

Goodman, Kimberly
The Environmental Information Association *(431)*

Goodman, Meg
Business Marketing Association *(339)*

Goodman, Michele
National Wildlife Rehabilitators Association *(805)*

Goodman, Paul
Tube Council of North America *(982)*

Goodman, Ronald P.
Sales Lead Management Association *(890)*

Goodman, PhD, Steven R.
Society for Experimental Biology and Medicine *(909)*

Goodman, Tom
National Association of County Civil Attorneys *(659)*

Goodnight, Lisa
American Association of University Women *(76)*

Goodrich, Angela B.
Urban Libraries Council *(1004)*

Goodrich, David
American Printing History Association *(167)*

Goodrich, Lorraine
Automotive Industry Action Group *(322)*

Goodson, ABA, ATA, CPA, Wanda
Accreditation Council for Accountancy and Taxation *(9)*

Goodwin, Andrea J.
Manufacturers Alliance/MAPI Inc. *(603)*

Goodwin, Brian
American Boat and Yacht Council *(84)*

Goodwin, Brooke
Independent Hardee's Franchisee Association *(490)*

Goodwin, Frank
International Lead Zinc Research Organization *(553)*

Goodwin, Jennifer
Institute for Professionals in Taxation *(497)*

Goodwin, CAE, Jill
Society for Vascular Surgery *(926)*

Goodwin, Kelly
United States Trout Farmers Association *(1000)*

Goodwin, Lane
National Association of State Administrators and Supervisors of Private Schools *(697)*

Goodwin, Tammy
Salt Institute *(891)*

Goodwin, Virginia McHugh
Association Montessori International - United States of America *(262)*

Goodwin, William
Institute of International Bankers *(501)*

Goold, James
Institute of Nautical Archaeology *(502)*

Goosen, EdD, MS, Rebecca
National Association for Developmental Education *(638)*

Goosman, Gary
American Congress of Community Supports and Employment Services *(107)*

Goozen, Linda
National Association of Geoscience Teachers *(669)*

Gopalakrishnan, Ganesh
Optoelectronics Industry Development Association *(830)*

Gorajczyk, John
Association of Forensic Document Examiners *(284)*

Goraleski, Karen A.
American Society of Tropical Medicine and Hygiene *(210)*

Gordillo, Ariana
National Association of Free Clinics *(669)*

Gordley, John D.
United States Canola Association *(991)*

Gordon, Alan S.
American Guild of Musical Artists *(127)*

Gordon, Andrew
National Association of Resource Conservation and Development Councils *(691)*

Gordon, Barbara
National Association of Student Financial Aid Administrators *(703)*

Gordon, Barbara A.
American Society for Biochemistry and Molecular Biology *(181)*

Gordon, Christina
American Academy of Oral and Maxillofacial Radiology *(37)*

Gordon, Clayton
Illuminating Engineering Society of North America *(486)*

Gordon, Donna

American Society of Plant Biologists *(207)*

Gordon, Eric
Ecological Society of America *(418)*

Gordon, Frank
Materials Research Society *(609)*

Gordon, Harris
Association Montessori International - United States of America *(262)*

Gordon, Heidi
American Society of Bariatric Physicians *(193)*

Gordon, Holly
Solar Alliance *(951)*

Gordon, CMP, Julie A.
Society of Fire Protection Engineers *(936)*

Gordon, Kate
ATP Tour, Inc. *(320)*

Gordon, Kelly Carolyn
Association for Theatre in Higher Education *(260)*

Gordon, Lee
American Meteorological Society *(151)*

Gordon, FACHE, MBA, RHIA, Lynne Thomas
American Health Information Management Association *(129)*

Gordon, Nancy L.
Health Care Compliance Association *(469)*

Gordon, Randall C.
National Grain and Feed Association *(755)*

Gordon, Sandra R.
American Academy of Orthopaedic Surgeons *(38)*

Gordon, Stephanie
National Association of Student Personnel Administrators *(626)*

Gordon-Troy, Esq., Tatia L.
American Immigration Lawyers Association *(134)*

Gore, Brian
MASINT Association *(607)*

Gore, Lenay
American Public Transportation Association *(171)*

Gorelick, Richard
Graphic Arts Sales Foundation *(465)*

Gorell, Nancy
Society for Industrial Microbiology *(913)*

Goren, Dave
National Sportscasters and Sportswriters Association and Hall of Fame *(796)*

Gorg, Brian
Educational Book and Media Association *(420)*

Gorham, Doug
Institute of Electrical and Electronics Engineers (IEEE) *(499)*

Gorham, Millicent
National Black Nurses Association *(714)*

Gorin, CAE, Susan
National Association of School Psychologists *(693)*

Gorman, Abigail W.
American Dental Education Association *(113)*

Gorman, Charlie
Equipment and Tool Institute *(432)*

Gorman, Hugh
Society for the History of Technology *(923)*

Gorman, John S.
Conference of State Bank Supervisors *(376)*

Gorman, Kim
American Board of Quality Assurance and Utilization Review Physicians, Inc. *(84)*

Gorman, Mark S.
Distilled Spirits Council of the United States, Inc. *(414)*

Gorman, Mary
National Association of Children's Hospitals and Related Institutions *(653)*

Gorman, Maryann
ASTM International *(319)*

Gorman, Roberta
Society of Motion Picture and Television Engineers *(942)*

Gornal, Joy
Society of Interventional Radiology *(940)*

Gorski, Claudia
American Meteorological Society *(151)*

Gorski, Jonah
American Association of Cardiovascular and Pulmonary Rehabilitation *(55)*

Gorski, Lisa
Care Continuum Alliance *(342)*

Goryl, Carey
International Association of Forensic Nurses *(521)*

Gosain, Arun K.
American Society of Maxillofacial Surgeons *(202)*

Gosciniak, Heather
Society of Cable Telecommunications Engineers *(931)*

Goshgarian, Katie
Home Fashion Products Association *(478)*
World Airline Entertainment Association *(1025)*

Goss, Edward A.
Arthroscopy Association of North America *(230)*

Goss, Ron
United States Meat Export Federation *(996)*

Gosselin, Jamison
Assisted Living Federation of America *(234)*

Gosser, Lisa
International Association of Healthcare Central Service Materiel Management *(522)*

Gossett, Bruce
American Society of Civil Engineers *(194)*

Gossett, Kathie
Special Interest Group for Design of Communication *(955)*

Gotsick, Katherine
Strategic Account Management Association *(963)*

Gottemoeller, EdD, Meg
The Conference Board *(374)*

Gotthardt, Craig
Air Conditioning Contractors of America *(18)*

Gottheim, Steve
American Land Title Association *(144)*

Gottlieb, Bonnie
National Association of Real Estate Investment Trusts (NAREIT) *(690)*

Gottlieb, Martin S.
American Institute of Engineers, Inc. *(138)*

Gottmann, MBA, Ruth A.
American Society of Andrology *(192)*
Large Urology Group Practice Association (LUGPA) *(593)*

Gottschalk, Simon
Society for the Study of Symbolic Interaction *(925)*

Gottwald, Rich
International Sign Association *(564)*

Gotwals, Amy E.
National Association of Area Agencies on Aging *(647)*

Goudeseune, Scott
American Council on Exercise *(110)*

Goudy, Ellen
Interim Ministry Network *(508)*

Gough, Dale
American Association of Collegiate Registrars and Admissions Officers *(58)*

Gouhin, Patrick
International Society of Automation *(571)*

Gouin, MBA, Holly
Society for Academic Emergency Medicine *(903)*

Gould, Marc
Real Estate Buyers Agent Council *(875)*

Gould, Mark R.
American Library Association *(145)*

Gould, Mimi
National League of American Pen Women *(768)*

Gould, Patrick
Society of Actuaries *(927)*

Gould, Randy
Glass, Molders, Pottery, Plastics and Allied Workers International Union *(461)*

Gould, Sarah
Society for Nutrition Education and Behavior *(917)*

Gould, Steven
Council on Diagnostic Imaging to the A.C.A. *(399)*

Goulding, Judy
Modern Language Association *(618)*

Goulding, CAE, CMP, Tressa
Scoliosis Research Society *(893)*

Gourley, Sue
National Association of Realtors *(690)*

Goury, Yaniv
Public Housing Authorities Directors Association *(869)*

Govert, MaryAnn
Financial Managers Society *(445)*

Govindan, MD, Srini
American Academy of Thermology *(42)*

Gowan, Jo Dee
North American Blueberry Council *(814)*

Goyer, Anne
Chemical Coaters Association International *(351)*
Industrial Heating Equipment Association *(493)*

Goyert, PhD, Sonna
Shock Society *(899)*

Graber, Dennis W.
National Concrete Masonry Association *(725)*

Grable-Grant, Lenora
National Association of Blacks In Government *(649)*

Grabowski, Steve
National Foundation for Credit Counseling *(753)*

Grace, Eve
Conference for the Study of Political Thought *(374)*

Grace, Mark
American Society of Farm Managers and Rural Appraisers *(197)*

Grace, CAE, MS, Paul
National Board for Certification in Occupational Therapy, Inc. *(715)*

Grace, Suzanne
Association of Railway Museums *(305)*

Grace, Suzanne
Tourist Railway Association Inc. *(976)*

Gracey, Melissa
PKF North American Network *(849)*

Grachek, CNHA, FACHCA, MSN, Marianna Kern
American College of Health Care Administrators *(96)*

Gradwohl, Emeritus Richard
International Miniature Cattle Breeders Society *(556)*

Grady, Brittany
National Student Osteopathic Medical Association *(797)*

Grady, Chris
American Institute of Aeronautics and Astronautics *(136)*

Grady, Erin K.
AASHTO: Transportation Center of Excellence *(2)*

Grady, James P.
Association of American Railroads *(266)*

Grady, Mary Tucker
Independent Office Products and Furniture Dealers Association *(490)*

Grady, Perry
American Association of Textile Chemists and Colorists *(75)*

Graeber, DMD, John J.
Academy of Laser Dentistry *(6)*

Graf, Cheryl
American Student Dental Association *(214)*

Graf, Marguerite L.
National Air Traffic Controllers Association *(630)*

Graf, Mary
American Association of Nurse Anesthetists *(67)*

Graff, Esq., APM, Brian H.
American Society of Pension Professionals & Actuaries *(206)*

Graff, Troy
National Independent Automobile Dealers Association *(761)*

Graham, Aaron
Society of Flavor Chemists *(936)*

Graham, Adam
American Gem Trade Association *(125)*

Graham, Beverly
Association of Moving Image Archivists *(295)*

Graham, Chrystal
America Outdoors Association *(28)*

Graham, Dan
Internet Society *(582)*

Graham, Dianne
American Association of Motor Vehicle Administrators *(65)*

Graham, Don
Baptist Communicators Association *(326)*

Graham, Elliott
International Psycho-Oncology Society *(561)*
International Society for Prenatal Diagnosis *(568)*

Graham, Gail
Lpga Tournament Owners Association *(600)*

Graham, Joe
National Rifle Association of America *(787)*

Graham, John
Materials Marketing Associates *(608)*

Graham, IV, CAE, John
American Society of Association Executives-The Center for Association Leadership *(193)*

Graham, Lawrence T.
National Confectioners Association *(725)*

Graham, Marilyn
American Apitherapy Society *(46)*

Graham, Meredith

American College of Nurse-Midwives *(99)*

Graham, Michael H.
Phycological Society of America *(846)*

Graham, Penny
National Agri-Marketing Association *(629)*

Graham, Robert
National Association of State Veterans Homes *(702)*

Graham, CMPE, MA, Scott E.
CBA *(346)*

Graham, Sherry
Vacuum Dealers Trade Association/Sewing Dealers Trade Association *(1007)*

Graham, Tanya
American Society of Professional Estimators *(208)*

Graham, Terri
National Association of County Information Officers *(660)*

Graham, Dr. Wallace
American Heartworm Society *(130)*

Graham, Wendy
American Academy of Psychotherapists *(41)*

Grahek, Greg
American Association of Cereal Chemists International *(55)*
Controlled Release Society *(383)*
International Society for Molecular Plant Microbe Interactions *(567)*
Master Brewers Association of the Americas *(607)*

Grainawi, Lorri
Steel Plate Fabricators Association Division of STI/SPFA *(962)*
Steel Tank Institute Division of STI/SPFA *(963)*

Grainger, Allen
Santa Gertrudis Breeders International *(891)*

Grainger, Nessa
The National Society of Painters in Casein and Acrylic *(794)*

Gralen, Mark E.
Attorneys' Liability Assurance Society Inc. *(320)*

Gram, Wendy
National Ecological Observatory Network, Inc *(743)*

Gramlich, Robert
American Wind Energy Association (AWEA) *(221)*

Gramm, Stefanie
National Council of Higher Education Loan Programs *(735)*

Granade, Ginny
Federal Judges Association *(439)*

Granados, CAE, Kim "Kimberly" Shoop
Professional Engineers in Private Practice *(861)*

Granahan, Marcie
American Alliance for Theatre and Education *(44)*

Granath, CAE, CMP, Kay
Professional Records and Information Services Management International *(864)*

Granato, LLM, MBA, Matt J.
America's Blood Centers *(28)*

Granberg, Griffin
Association of Educators in Imaging and Radiologic Sciences, Inc *(280)*

Grande, MD, MPH, Christopher M.
Trauma Care International *(979)*

Grande, Eileen
Visiting Nurse Associations of America *(1010)*

Grande, Tina
Healthcare Leadership Council *(471)*

Grandi, Edward
American Sleep Apnea Association *(180)*

Grandin, Steve
Academy of Certified Archivists *(4)*
National Association of Government Archives and Records Administrators *(669)*

Grandy, Kelly
American Association of Insurance Services *(63)*

Granen, MT (ASCP), Linette
Association of Public Health Laboratories *(304)*

Granger, Rebecca C.
Educause *(420)*

Granger, Ron
American Choral Directors Association *(90)*

Granitto, Diana
Institute of Environmental Sciences and Technology *(499)*

Grannis, Kathy
Association for Retail Technology Standards *(256)*
Retail Advertising and Marketing Association International *(884)*

Granskog, Sharon Curtis
American Veterinary Medical Association *(219)*

Grant, Elizabeth
National Association of State Charity Officials *(699)*

Grant, Eric
American Angus Association *(45)*

Grant, Evelyn
EUCG, Inc. *(433)*

Grant, Gary R.
Black Farmers and Agriculturists Association *(331)*

Grant, Geraldine
National Association for Black Geologists and Geophysicists *(636)*

Grant, Idris
National Association of Sales Professionals *(692)*

Grant, John
Society of the Plastics Industry *(948)*

Grant, Marcus D.
Central Intercollegiate Athletic Association *(349)*

Grant, Michael A.
National Bankers Association *(712)*

Grant, Patricia Goodspeed
Association for Adult Development and Aging *(238)*

Grant, Rachel
National Propane Gas Association *(783)*

Grant, Rob
American Academy of Child and Adolescent Psychiatry *(31)*

Grant, Teresa
American Bakers Association *(78)*

Graper, Randy
National Frame Building Association *(753)*

Grapin, Mark W.
Army Aviation Association of America *(229)*

Grass, CAE, P E, Peter T.
Asphalt Institute *(233)*

Grassi, Terri L.
Pan American Association of Ophthalmology *(837)*

Grasty, Leisa
Tile Council of North America, Inc. *(974)*

Grater, Elizabeth
Institute for Credentialing Excellence *(497)*

Gratton, Peter
Radical Philosophy Association *(873)*

Grau, John M.
National Electrical Contractors Association *(744)*

Grau, Jonathan
American Medical Informatics Association *(149)*

Graul, Jr., Donald O.
American Independent Writers *(135)*

Graul, Faye
Halogenated Solvents Industry Alliance *(468)*

Gravatt, Laurie Bendall
Disaster Recovery Contractors Association (DRCA) *(413)*

Gravatt, Nancy
American Iron and Steel Institute *(142)*

Graves, Bill
American Trucking Associations *(218)*

Graves, Brianna
Art Directors Club *(229)*

Graves, David G.
National Parks Conservation Association *(779)*

Graves, David R.
American Association of Crop Insurers *(59)*

Graves, Gregory D.
National Onsite Wastewater Recycling Association *(776)*

Graves, Karen
The History of Education Society *(477)*

Graves, Linda
AASHTO: Transportation Center of Excellence *(2)*

Graves, Orim
National Association of Securities Professionals *(695)*

Graves, Susan B.
American Psychological Association *(169)*

Graves, Thomas J.
American Coatings Association *(92)*

Graves, Wayne S.
Association for Computing Machinery *(243)*

Gravesmill, Meg
Accreditation Association for Ambulatory Health Care *(9)*

Gravholt, Molly
Community Health Charities of America *(371)*

Gravley, Dolores
American Gelbvieh Association *(125)*

Gray, PhD, Albert C.
Accrediting Council for Independent Colleges and Schools *(10)*

Gray, Beverly
The National Federation of Nonpublic School State Accrediting Associations *(749)*

Gray, Bonnie
International Right of Way Association *(563)*

Gray, Brian
National Catholic Educational Exhibitors *(718)*

Gray, Carol
Association of Biomedical Communications Directors *(269)*

Gray, Charles D
National Association of Regulatory Utility Commissioners *(691)*

Gray, Cynthia
American Judicature Society *(143)*

Gray, Ethan
National Association of Clinical Nurse Specialists *(654)*
Society of Hospital Medicine *(938)*

Gray, LPC, NCC, PhD, Geneva M.
International Association of Addictions and Offender Counselors *(514)*

Gray, John M.

Healthcare Distribution Management Association *(471)*

Gray, Karen R.
International Cemetery, Cremation and Funeral Association *(533)*

Gray, Kathryn
Association for Enterprise Opportunity *(245)*

Gray, Kia
United States and Canadian Academy of Pathology *(989)*

Gray, Lauren
Public Relations Student Society of America *(870)*

Gray, Lesli
National Association of Consumer Shows *(658)*

Gray, Mary Ann
Institute of Certified Business Counselors *(498)*

Gray, Melissa
Greeting Card Association *(466)*

Gray, Neil A.
International Bridge, Tunnel and Turnpike Association *(531)*

Gray, Patricia
National Black Nurses Association *(714)*

Gray, Jr., Robin B.
Electronic Components Industry Association *(423)*

Gray, CAE, Sandra Trice
Centerpoint for Leaders *(348)*

Gray, Stephanie
American Academy of Religion *(41)*

Gray, Therese
American Society for Gastrointestinal Endoscopy *(184)*

Gray, Tom
American Wind Energy Association (AWEA) *(221)*

Graybill, Thea
National Association of Clean Water Agencies *(654)*

Grayson, Amie Garrett
International Council on Hotel, Restaurant and Institutional Education *(539)*

Grayson, Mary
Health Forum *(469)*

Grayson, Matt
National Tour Association *(800)*
Receptive Services Association of America *(876)*

Graziano, Carl
National Association of Public Hospitals and Health Systems *(688)*

Graziano, Stephen
National Kitchen and Bath Association *(767)*

Greabell, Lynne
National Alliance of State and Territorial AIDS Directors *(633)*

Grealis, Allison
Precision Metalforming Association *(856)*

Grealy, Jane
American Society of Architectural Illustrators *(192)*

Grealy, Mary R.
Healthcare Leadership Council *(471)*

Greaney, Carrie
Pipeline Research Council International, Inc. *(849)*

Grear, Sandra B
College of American Pathologists *(363)*

Greasley, Corrinne
International Swaps and Derivatives Association *(576)*

Greaves, Jeri
National Housing and Rehabilitation Association *(760)*

Greaves, William W.

American Board of Preventive Medicine *(83)*

Greberman, Sharyn Bowman
National League of American Pen Women *(768)*

Greco, CAE, Dana
Society of Teachers of Family Medicine *(947)*

Greco, Greg
International Graphoanalysis Society *(548)*

Greco, Kathleen R.
American Frozen Food Institute *(124)*
Frozen Potato Products Institute *(454)*
International Frozen Food Association *(547)*

Greco, Krista A.
American Society for Reconstructive Microsurgery *(189)*

Greco, Marian
American Concrete Pavement Association *(106)*

Greco, Robert "Bob" A.
Direct Marketing Association *(412)*

Green, Allen
American College for Advancement in Medicine *(93)*

Green, Artisia
Black Theatre Network *(332)*

Green, Bart
Association of Chiropractic Colleges *(272)*

Green, Bonnie
American Association of Textile Chemists and Colorists *(75)*

Green, Bret
American Beefalo Association *(80)*

Green, Brian
International Plant Nutrition Institute *(560)*

Green, CAE, CFO, CPA, Brian
Building Owners and Managers Association International *(337)*

Green, Candace
Distribution Contractors Association *(414)*

Green, Chris
Application Developers Alliance *(226)*

Green, Chris
Producers Guild of America *(858)*

Green, Deborah
Xplor International *(1029)*

Green, CDRS, OTR/L, Elizabeth
ADED - The Association for Driver Rehabilitation Specialists *(12)*

Green, Ed, MS, Evelyn Polk
Attention Deficit Disorder Association *(320)*

Green, AIA, Henry L.
National Institute of Building Sciences *(764)*

Green, Jenna
Caucus for Women in Statistics *(346)*

Green, Jennifer
American Society for Parenteral and Enteral Nutrition *(188)*

Green, John
Investigative Reporters and Editors *(583)*

Green, Josh
National Council on Education for the Ceramic Arts *(738)*

Green, Judy L.
Family Firm Institute, Inc. *(437)*

Green, Karen
Women's Regional Publications of America *(1024)*

Green, Karen L.
Association for Radiological and Imaging Nursing *(255)*

Green, Katherine
Electronics Representatives Association *(424)*

Green, Kimberly A.
National Association of State Directors of Career
Technical Education Consortium *(699)*

Green, Laura Gayle
Music Library Association *(622)*

Green, Lee
Professional Skaters Association *(865)*

Green, Marcia
Humanities Education and Research Association *(481)*

Green, Marilyn
International Food, Wine and Travel Writers
Association *(546)*

Green, Marissa K.
Alliance for Continuing Medical Education *(22)*

Green, CAE, Nancy
National Association for Gifted Children *(639)*

Green, Parman
National Association of County Agricultural Agents
(659)

Green, Peggy
American Society of Radiologic Technologists *(208)*

Green, Peter
National Association of Schools of Public Affairs and
Administration *(694)*

Green, Richard M.
National Guard Association of the U.S. *(757)*

Green, Robert J.
National Council of Chain Restaurants *(734)*

Green, Samatha
National Foundation for Women Legislators *(753)*

Green, Shanna
PROMAX/BDA *(866)*

Green, Terri
Palomino Horse Breeders of America *(837)*

Green, William H.
International Tax Institute *(576)*

Greenagel, John
Semiconductor Industry Association *(897)*

Greenan, Hattie
Plan Sponsor Council of America *(849)*

Greenawalt, Patricia
American Society for Engineering Education *(183)*

Greenaway, MArch, Rev. Douglas A.
National WIC Association *(805)*

Greenaway, Kathy
National Association of Secondary School Principals
(694)

Greenback, Laura
Software & Information Industry Association (SIIA)
(950)

Greenbaum, Amy
Jeweler's Vigilance Committee *(587)*

Greenbaum, Edna Fine
Council of Protocol Executives *(396)*

Greenberg, MPA, Janice
Utilimetrics/Alliance for Advanced Metering & Data
Management Solutions *(1006)*

Greenberg, MPP, Pamela
Association for Behavioral Health & Wellness *(240)*

Greenberg, Sally
National Consumers League *(729)*

Greenberg, Susannah
Women's National Book Association *(1023)*

Greenberg, Wendy
Association of Women Soil Scientists *(317)*

Greenberger, Jim
National Alliance for Advanced Transportation
Batteries *(631)*

Greenblatt, Andrea
National Council for Research on Women *(732)*

Greenblatt, Melissa
National Dance Education Organization *(742)*

Greene, Brighid
Dance Films Association *(406)*

Greene, Cary
WineAmerica *(1019)*

Greene, Dale
Council On Forest Engineering *(399)*

Greene, Debra Illingworth
National Council on Crime and Delinquency *(738)*

Greene, CAE, P E, Don H.
Institute of Industrial Engineers *(500)*

Greene, Ed
The Vision Council *(1010)*

Greene, Elizabeth R.
NAIOP, The Commercial Real Estate Development
Association *(366)*

Greene, Holly M.
Association for Equine Sports Medicine *(246)*

Greene, Jeff
National Society of Mural Painters *(794)*

Greene, Joel
International District Energy Association *(540)*

Greene, Mike
Council for Responsible Nutrition *(391)*

Greene, Ramona
Commercial Vehicle Solutions Network *(367)*

Greene, CAE, MBA, Richard
Painting and Decorating Contractors of America *(837)*

Greene, Steven
International Microelectronics and Packaging Society -
IMAPS *(556)*

Greene, Susan
American Solar Energy Society *(211)*

Greene, Tenikka
National Conference on Public Employee Retirement
Systems *(729)*

Greene, Tom
American Academy of Ambulatory Care Nursing *(30)*
American Nephrology Nurses Association *(155)*

Greenfield, Barden
American Veterinary Dental Society *(218)*

Greenfield, Heather
Computer and Communications Industry Association
(372)

Greenfield, CMP, Julie
American School Health Association *(177)*

Greenlee, Esq., Bob
International Association of Defense Counsel *(519)*

Greenlee, Merrill
National Association of Junior Auxiliaries *(677)*

Greenman, Gail
Oregon Farm Bureau Federation *(830)*

Greenrose, Karen
American Association of Preferred Provider
Organizations *(70)*

Greenslade, Joe
Industrial Fasteners Institute *(493)*

Greenspan, Owen M.
Search - The National Consortium for Justice
Information and Statistics *(894)*

Greenstreet, Charlene
Water Systems Council *(1013)*

Greenville, Jennifer
International College of Dentists, U.S.A. Section *(535)*

Greenwald, CAE, P E, Jeffrey H.
Institute of Hazardous Materials Management *(500)*

Greenwald, Kay
American Conference of Cantors *(107)*

Greenwalt, Pamela
Screen Actors Guild - American Federation of
Television and Radio Artists *(893)*

Greenway, FAWM, FCCP, PhD, Loren
Wilderness Medical Society *(1017)*

Greenwood, Jr., Allen B. "Beau"
CropLife America *(404)*

Greenwood, Hon. James C.
Biotechnology Industry Organization (BIO) *(330)*

Greenwood, Karen E.
American Medical Informatics Association *(149)*

Greenwood, Maryscott "Scotty"
Canadian-American Business Council *(341)*

Greenwood, Vickie
Association of Family Medicine Residency Directors
(282)

Greer, Collins
National Association for Program Information and
Performance Measurement *(641)*

Greer, Eddie
Board of Certified Safety Professionals *(332)*

Greer, Laura
Financial & Insurance Conference Planners *(444)*

Greer, Linda
Society for Neuro-Oncology *(916)*

Greer, Mary
The American Bar Association Rule of Law Initiative
(80)

Greer, Richard
Laborers International Union of North America *(592)*

Greer, Trineka
National Association of Black Accountants, Inc. *(648)*

Grefe, MA, Lynn S.
National Eating Disorders Association *(743)*

Grefe, Richard
American Institute of Graphic Arts *(139)*

Gregg, Jerrold D.
United States Committee on Irrigation and Drainage
(992)

Gregg, Michael
Society for Archaeological Sciences *(904)*

Gregg, Michael
Christian Medical & Dental Associations *(356)*

Grego, Tony
Real Estate Investment Securities Association *(875)*

Gregori, Tara
Council of State Speech-Language-Hearing Association
Presidents *(398)*

Gregorio, Cesaltine
Portugal-US Chamber of Commerce *(853)*

Gregory, Chad
United Egg Producers *(986)*

Gregory, RPSGT, David
American Association of Sleep Technologists *(73)*

Gregory, Gene
United Egg Producers *(986)*

Gregory, MD, Richard O.
American Society for Laser Medicine and Surgery *(186)*

Gregory, Steven
Council of State Governments *(397)*

Gregory, Vicki L
American Society for Information Science and
Technology *(186)*

Greiner, Philip
Photo Chemical Machining Institute *(846)*

Greissing, Christopher K.
Industrial Minerals Association -- North America *(494)*
National Industrial Sand Association *(763)*

Greketis, CMP, Maryanne
Society for Academic Emergency Medicine *(903)*

Gremer, Carrie
American Pain Society *(161)*
National Association of Neonatal Nurses *(682)*
The American Society of Pediatric Hematology/
Oncology *(206)*

Grenache, David
Academy of Clinical Laboratory Physicians and
Scientists *(4)*

Greninger, Marie
National Association of Legal Assistants *(677)*

Grepps, Lisa S.
Association of Pool and Spa Professionals *(299)*

Gresham, Kisha
Association of Energy Services Professionals,
International *(281)*

Gresham, Dr. Robert
Society of Tribologists and Lubrication Engineers *(949)*

Gresham-Fiegel, Carolyn
United States Fencing Coaches Association *(994)*

Greskiewicz, Michael
Institute of Packaging Professionals *(502)*
The Recreational Vehicle Aftermarket Association *(877)*

Gressley, Kim
National Association of Extension 4-H Agents *(667)*

Gressley, Trudy
International Disk Drive Equipment and Materials
Association *(540)*

Grettenberger, Susan
Association of Baccalaureate Social Work Program
Directors *(269)*

Gretter, Bradley
National Council on Aging *(738)*

Grever, Kim
Electric Drive Transportation Association *(421)*

Grevsmuehl, Marie
American Academy for Cerebral Palsy and
Developmental Medicine *(29)*

Grewe, Nina Agbayani
Association of Asian-Pacific Community Health
Organizations *(268)*

Greyson, MD, Bruce
International Association for Near Death Studies, Inc.
(513)

Gribbin, Mike
National Retail Federation *(786)*

Gribble, Jan
The National Association of Dog Obedience Instructors
(663)

Grider, Jody
American Association of Cereal Chemists International
(55)

Griesbach, Mary Ann
American Littoral Society *(146)*

Griesser, Emily
Associated Collegiate Press *(235)*
National Scholastic Press Association *(789)*

Grifferty, John
The New York Academy of Sciences *(809)*

Griffin, MS, Carol
American Medical Writers Association *(150)*

Griffin, Deanie
National Health Care Anti-Fraud Association *(758)*

Griffin, Drew P.
American Hockey League *(132)*

Griffin, Erin
Screen Actors Guild - American Federation of
Television and Radio Artists *(893)*

Griffin, Glenn
American Public Health Association *(171)*

Griffin, Kelly
County Executives of America *(402)*

Griffin, Kelly Foster
Organization of American Kodaly Educators *(832)*

Griffin, Lori
Council of Development Finance Agencies *(393)*

Griffin, Michael G.
County Executives of America *(402)*

Griffin, Nancy
Balloon Federation of America *(325)*

Griffin, Patricia
Green Hotels Association *(466)*

Griffin, Paul M.
Destination Marketing Association International *(411)*

Griffin, Steve
American Dairy Products Institute *(112)*

Griffin, Susan
National Council for the Social Studies *(733)*

Griffin, Tara M.
American Equilibration Society *(117)*

Griffin-Rossi, CAE, Theresa J.
American Association for Accreditation of Ambulatory
Surgery Facilities *(47)*

Griffis, Sharon
Color Marketing Group *(365)*

Griffith, Becky
Phi Delta Chi *(845)*

Griffith, Carlsen
Hispanic Elected Local Officials *(475)*
National League of Cities *(768)*

Griffith, Cathy
Wedding and Portrait Photographers International
(1014)

Griffith, David
National Association of State Boards of Education
(698)

Griffith, MD, CAE, Ezra E.H.
American Academy of Psychiatry and the Law *(41)*

Griffith, Jennifer
Urban and Regional Information Systems Association
(1003)

Griffith, Jim
American Medical Society for Sports Medicine *(149)*

Griffith, Mary
American Counseling Association *(111)*

Griffiths, Matthew
Professional Lighting and Sound Association *(863)*

Grigg, Bill
American Dehydrated Onion and Garlic Association
(113)

Grigg, Melissa
Osborne Association *(834)*

Griggs, Ashley
Standards Engineering Society *(961)*

Griggs, USN (Ret.), CAPT Earl N.
Naval Submarine League *(807)*

Griggs, Harris B.
International Engraved Graphics Association *(543)*

Griggs, Jr., James L.
Armed Forces Communications and Electronics
Association *(228)*

Griggs, Karen
International Aviation Women's Association *(529)*
National Aircraft Finance Association *(630)*

Griggs, Megan
Intellectual Property Owners Association *(505)*

Griggs, Mindy
The Association of Collegiate Conference and Events
Directors International *(275)*

Grigonis, Paul
Precast/Prestressed Concrete Institute *(856)*

Grigorian, Christopher H.
Transportation Safety Equipment Institute *(979)*

Grigsby, Anthony
National Association of Broadcast Employees and
Technicians-Communications Workers of America,
AFL-CIO (NABET-CWA) *(650)*

Grimes, Betty
National Garden Clubs *(754)*

Grimes, Larry B.
The National Coal Council *(722)*

Grimes, CAE, Richard P.
Assisted Living Federation of America *(234)*

Grimes, Susan
National Association of Independent Life Brokerage
Agencies *(674)*

Grimes, Thao
American Meat Institute *(148)*

Grimm, Blake
The Financial Services Roundtable *(445)*

Grimm, Craig
International Society for Performance Improvement
(567)

Grimm, Don
International Oil Scouts Association *(558)*

Grimm, Kim
National Association of Catering and Events *(651)*

Grimm, Linda
Financial Management Association International *(444)*

Grimm, CPPO, CPPB, Rick
National Institute of Governmental Purchasing *(765)*

Grinder, David
National Association of Power Engineers *(685)*

Grindle, David
United States Institute for Theatre Technology *(995)*

Grinnan, Suzanne E.
Society for Imaging Science and Technology *(912)*

Grippi, Carolyn
National Academy of Television Arts and Science *(628)*

Grisaitis, Olga
Art Directors Club *(229)*

Griswold, Britt
Guild of Natural Science Illustrators *(467)*

Griswold, Daniel T.
National Association of Foreign Trade Zones *(669)*

Grizzard, Matt
Food Marketing Institute *(449)*

Grizzard, Susan R.
National Association of Teachers of Singing *(705)*

Groah, CNAA, MSN, RN, FAAN, Linda K.
Association of periOperative Registered Nurses *(299)*

Grochala, Eugene
Capital Health *(342)*

Grodner, R. Marshall
Association of Commercial Finance Attorneys *(275)*

Groeneveld, Susan J.
CCIM Institute *(347)*

Groenjes, LuAnne
National Conference on Weights and Measures *(729)*

Groenke, Susan L.
Conference on English Leadership *(376)*

Groff, Courtney
American Automotive Leasing Association *(78)*

Groff, Lindsay
Society for Social Work Leadership in Health Care
(921)

Grogan, James A.
International Association of Heat and Frost Insulators
and Asbestos Workers *(522)*

Grogg, Matt
Association of American Veterinary Medical Colleges
(267)

Grogg, Shelley
Roller Skating Association International *(887)*

Groh, Al W.
Union of American Physicians and Dentists *(985)*

Groh, Mark de
American Architectural Foundation *(46)*

Groh, Michael
Academy of Veterinary Allergy and Clinical
Immunology *(9)*

Groh, Monica
American Institute of Certified Planners *(137)*

Grohe, Bill
United Association of Equipment Leasing *(985)*

Gromling, Dr. Tom
The American Society of Forensic Odontology *(198)*

Grommons, Debra L.
GAMA International *(455)*

Gromoll, Peggy
Association of Official Seed Certifying Agencies *(296)*

Grone, Lynn
American Gastroenterological Association *(125)*

Groner, Sheldon M.
National Association of Real Estate Investment Trusts
(NAREIT) *(690)*

Gronlund, Gail
National Association for Home Care and Hospice *(639)*

Gronlund, Nancy
Association of Legal Administrators *(291)*

Gronstal, Donna
International Association for Food Protection *(512)*

Groome, PhD, Meghan
The New York Academy of Sciences *(809)*

Grooms, Lynn
Turfgrass Producers International *(982)*

Grosmann, James R.
National Tooling and Machining Association *(800)*

Gross, CMM, Brad
Association of Marina Industries *(293)*

Gross, Dee
American Association of Public Welfare Attorneys *(72)*
National Staff Development and Training Association
(796)

Gross, Donna
High Point Market *(474)*

Gross, Elaine
Materials Research Society *(609)*

Gross, Elina
Plumbing-Heating-Cooling Contractors - National
Association *(851)*

Gross, Jim
Mortgage Bankers Association of America *(619)*

Gross, Julien
International Society for Developmental Psychobiology
(566)

Gross, Katherine "Katei" E.
Stained Glass Association of America *(960)*

Gross, JD, Lauren G.
American Association of Immunologists *(62)*

Gross, Renita
International Liquid Terminals Association *(554)*

Gross, Richard
Stained Glass Association of America *(960)*

Gross, Ursula
Association of Governing Boards of Universities and
Colleges *(286)*

Gross-Harmon, Leah
World Floor Covering Association *(1026)*

Grosse, Larry
Associated Schools of Construction *(237)*

Grossfeld, Robin
Association of Corporate Counsel *(277)*

Grossgart, Chris
International Association of Business Communicators
(517)

Grossman, Beth
ACORD - Association for Cooperative Operations
Research and Development *(11)*

Grossman, Ian
American Association of Motor Vehicle Administrators
(65)

Grossman, Jerry
Photoimaging Manufacturers and Distributors
Association *(846)*

Grossman, Jim
American Historical Association *(131)*
Historians of American Communism *(476)*

Grossman, Lee
International Dyslexia Association *(541)*

Grosso, Elise
Point of Purchase Advertising Institute *(851)*

Grosswirth, Adam
National Alliance for Musical Theatre *(632)*

Grost, Gregg
Golf Coaches Association of America *(463)*

Grote, Paul
The Electrochemical Society *(423)*

Groth, Nancy
National Council for Accreditation of Teacher
Education *(731)*

Grotrian, Sheri A.
Institute of Behavioral and Applied Management *(498)*

Groundwater, John
Passenger Vessel Association *(839)*

Grove, Andrea
International Society of Political Psychology *(573)*

Grove, Liza L.
BMC - A Foodservice Sales and Marketing Council
(332)

Grove, Stephanie
Sail America *(890)*

Grove, Susan Evans
The Society of Naval Architects and Marine Engineers
(942)

Grover, Kim
United States Energy Association *(993)*

Groves, Ed
Council for Advancement and Support of Education
(388)

Groves, Jacquie
Pi Lambda Theta *(847)*

Groves, Wallace K.
American Association of Private Lenders *(71)*

Grubb, Mike
Gas Machinery Research Council *(456)*

Grubb, Sloane
National Safety Council *(789)*

Grubbe, Frederick H.
Appraisal Institute *(226)*

Grubbs, Rebecca
National Grain and Feed Association *(755)*

Grubbs, Shawn
Academy of Model Aeronautics *(7)*

Grube, LLD, Edward "Ed"
Lutheran Education Association *(600)*

Gruber, A.J.
International Safe Transit Association *(563)*

Gruber, CPO, Beverly
National Remotivation Therapy Organization *(786)*

Gruber, Loraine
Outdoor Industry Association *(835)*

Gruber, Maurice
Association of Eminent Domain Professionals *(280)*

Grudnik, Lynn
National Health Association *(758)*

Grudzinski, Phil
American Teleservices Association *(215)*

Gruen, Nancy
Enterprise Wireless Alliance *(429)*

Gruenburg, Drew N.
Society of American Florists *(928)*

Grueskin, Mark
Water and Sewer Distributors of America *(1012)*

Gruet, Racha
Association of Christian Librarians *(272)*

Grummitt, Adam
Computer Measurement Group *(372)*

Grummon, PhD, Phyllis
Society for College and University Planning *(906)*

Grundahl, PE, Kirk
Structural Building Components Association *(964)*

Grundahl, Suzanne
Structural Building Components Association *(964)*

Grundy, Jeff
American Society of Body Engineers *(193)*

Grundy, Scott M.
International Atherosclerosis Society *(529)*

Gruszkowski, Ann Marie
American Nuclear Society *(156)*

Grutzkuhn, William
National Association of Enrolled Agents *(666)*

Gryde, Brandon
Dance/USA *(406)*

Grygny, Joseph
International Molded Fibre Association *(556)*

Guard, Linda
United States Pharmacopeia *(997)*

Guarino, Cindy
Association of Independent Corrugated Converters *(288)*

Guarnaccia, Kim
Paperboard Packaging Council *(838)*

Guaspari, Mary Beth
RTCA, Inc. *(888)*

Guastella, Michael J.
Council on Radionuclides and Radiopharmaceuticals *(400)*

Guastello, Stephen J.
Society for Chaos Theory in Psychology and Life Sciences *(905)*

Guccione, Gary
National Greyhound Association *(756)*

Gudjonsson, Hlynur
Icelandic American Chamber of Commerce *(482)*

Guenther, Robert L.
United Fresh Produce Association *(987)*

Guerrero, Carol
Association for Play Therapy *(253)*

Guerrero, Cathi
American Society of Ocularists *(205)*

Guerrero, Diana
American Society for Aesthetic Plastic Surgery *(180)*

Guerrero, Victoria
International Interior Design Association *(552)*

Guerrieri, Gale
American Academy of Nursing *(37)*

Guess, Adam
American Football Coaches Association *(122)*

Guess, Deborah L.
National Association of Teachers of Singing *(705)*

Guess, Kay
North American Case Research Association *(814)*

Guess, Radious
Kappa Kappa Iota-National *(590)*

Gueye, Paul
National Society of Black Physicists *(793)*

Gueziel, Meriam
United Nations Staff Union *(988)*

Guffain, Pamela D.
The Fertilizer Institute *(443)*

Guffey, Cliff
American Postal Workers Union *(167)*

Guggolz, Rick A
American Brachytherapy Society *(85)*
Association of Insurance Compliance Professionals *(289)*
Sports Lawyers Association *(959)*

Guida, George
Italian American Studies Association *(586)*

Guidi, Pete
Ductile Iron Society *(417)*

Guidice, Donna
Cabletelevision Advertising Bureau *(340)*

Guido, Leanne

Technology Student Association *(970)*

Guidos, J D, Robert J.
Infectious Diseases Society of America *(494)*

Guidry, Janelle
National Association of Basketball Coaches *(648)*

Guidry, PhD, Jeffrey J.
Research Association of Minority Professors *(882)*

Guilbeau, Merlin J.
Electronic Security Association *(424)*

Guilfoyle, Dana
MGMA-ACMPE *(614)*

Guinn, Jim
USA Rice Council *(1004)*

Guiot, Philippe
American Association of Motor Vehicle Administrators *(65)*

Guirguis, Karim
American Bankruptcy Institute *(79)*

Guitar, Monte C.
Precision Machined Products Association *(856)*

Guiterman, Anthony
League for Innovation in the Community College *(595)*

Gulati, Sunil K.
United States Soccer Federation *(999)*

Gulick, Kelly
American Trakehner Association *(217)*

Gulick, Mathew
International Association of Color Manufacturers *(518)*

Gulick, Sharon
Community Development Society *(370)*

Gulino, Mary Ann
National Business Incubation Association *(717)*

Gulka, Craig
NCSL International *(808)*

Gulledge, Theresa
Professional Association of Diving Instructors *(859)*

Gulliford, Jim
Soil and Water Conservation Society *(951)*

Gumeny, Katie
Lake Carriers Association *(592)*

Gump, Jason
National Association of Community Health Centers *(656)*

Gumpert, Eric
American Thoracic Society *(216)*

Gunderson, Barbara
Association of University Technology Managers *(316)*

Gunderson, David E.
Associated Schools of Construction *(237)*

Gunderson, Jackie
American Association of Neuromuscular and Electrodiagnostic Medicine *(66)*

Gunderson, Hon. Steve
Association of Private Sector Colleges and Universities (Career College Association) *(300)*

Gunn, Esq., Brian
Intertribal Monitoring Association on Indian Trust Funds *(583)*

Gunn, Briana
Plastic Pipe and Fittings Association *(850)*
Pressure Vessel Manufacturers Association *(857)*

Gunn, Tomi
Medical Library Association *(611)*

Gunstream, Robby D.
College Music Society *(363)*

Guo, X. Edward
Society for Physical Regulation in Biology and Medicine *(919)*

Gupta, Raghav
Intercollegiate Broadcasting System *(507)*

Gupta, Sarita
American Rights at Work *(175)*

Gupta, PhD, Sushil K.
Production and Operations Management Society *(859)*

Guptill, Rhonda
American Academy of Medical Administrators *(36)*
American College of Cardiovascular Administrators *(93)*

Gupton, Richard
Agricultural Retailers Association *(16)*

Guran, Letitia
Romanian Studies Association of America *(888)*

Gurfel, Diana
International Aviation Women's Association *(529)*

Gurley, Daniel
National Air Transportation Association *(630)*

Gurley, Sarah
National Golf Course Owners Association *(755)*

Gurmu, Wosene
American Intellectual Property Law Association *(141)*

Gurney, Bonnie T.
AMT - The Association For Manufacturing Technology *(222)*

Gusdorf, CAE, Lori
Association of Fundraising Professionals *(285)*

Gust, Tina
Minor League Baseball *(617)*

Gustafson, Andrew
USENIX: The Advanced Computing Systems Association *(1005)*

Gustafson, Deborah S.
Council for Art Education *(389)*
The Arts and Creative Materials Institute, Inc. *(229)*

Gustafson, Douglas
International Association of Lighting Designers *(524)*

Gustafson, Elyse R.
Institute of Mathematical Statistics *(501)*

Gustafson, Judy
Women in Energy *(1021)*

Gustafson, Mary
Plasma Protein Therapeutics Association *(850)*

Gustafsson, Jimmy
Swedish-American Chambers of Commerce of the USA, Inc. *(967)*

Gustavson, Maggie
Leather Industries of America *(596)*

Gustavsson, Einar
Icelandic American Chamber of Commerce *(482)*

Gustis, CMP, MEd, Barbara A.
American Association of Colleges of Pharmacy *(57)*

Gustufson, Wendy
Religion Newswriters Association *(880)*

Guth, Gail
Guild of Natural Science Illustrators *(467)*

Guthrie, Jackie
Pony of the Americas Club *(852)*

Guthrie, Ken
Society of Actuaries *(927)*

Guthrie, Larry
American Academy of Cosmetic Surgery *(32)*

Guthrie, Russell
International Federation of Accountants *(544)*

Guthrie, Tony
Association of Independent Trust Companies *(288)*

Gutierrez, Anna
National Council of Social Security Management
Associations *(736)*

Gutierrez, Ingrid
National Drug Court Institute *(743)*

Gutierrez, John Paul
International Communication Association *(536)*

Gutierrez, Rob
National Truck Equipment Association *(802)*

Gutierrez-Richards, ACSW, LCSW, Helena
Association of Pediatric Oncology Social Workers *(298)*

Gutknecht, Mike
Amusement Industry Manufacturers and Suppliers
International *(223)*

Gutowski, Sharon
United States Junior Chamber (Jaycees) *(995)*

Guy, Claiborne
National Association of Therapeutic Schools and
Programs (NATSAP) *(706)*

Guy, Jerryl
National Association of County Information
Technology Administrators *(660)*
National Association of County Intergovernmental
Relations Officials *(660)*

Guy, Nicole
Microscopy Society of America *(615)*

Guy, Phyllis R.
Dance Masters of America, Inc. *(406)*

Guyer, Dana
American Philatelic Society *(163)*

Guyer, Paul
American Society for Aesthetics *(180)*

Guyton, Shep
Grand Strand Business Association *(465)*

Guzman, Jessica
World Pet Association *(1027)*

Guzman, Marisela
The Council of Landscape Architectural Registration
Boards *(395)*

Guzman, PHR, Rhina
American Thoracic Society *(216)*

Guzman, Sergio
United Farm Workers of America *(986)*

Guzman, Vivianna
American Management Association *(146)*

Gwaltney, Lisa
Association for Institutional Research *(250)*

Gwiazdowski, Amy E.
Employee Stock Ownership Plan Association *(426)*

Gwin, Meloney
Association of Real Estate License Law Officials *(305)*

Gwin, Meloney
Real Estate Educators Association *(875)*

Gwyn, Mike
American Metalcasting Consortium *(151)*

Gyovai, Norma
American Moving and Storage Association *(153)*

Haack, Susan
The Counselors of Real Estate *(401)*

Haag, CAE, MSM, David
Association of Rheumatology Health Professionals
(306)

Haag, Thomas
United States Cutting Tool Institute *(993)*

Haaland, Paul
National Association of Affordable Housing Lenders
(646)

Haas, Bill
Automotive Service Association *(323)*

Haas, Ernestine
National Association of Church Business
Administration *(653)*

Haas, Gail
American Association of Heart Failure Nurses *(62)*
The Wound, Ostomy and Continence Nurses Society
(1028)

Haas, Jeff
American Public Power Association *(171)*

Haas, Laurie
Association of Jewish Libraries *(290)*

Haas-Stapleton, Eric
Society for Invertebrate Pathology *(913)*

Haase, Kenneth F.
National Futures Association *(754)*

Haase, Nanette
Cremation Association of North America *(404)*

Haaser, Barry
Utility Smart Network Access Port *(1007)*

Haataja, Dave
Water Quality Association *(1013)*

Habash, CIO, Tony
American Psychological Association *(169)*

Haber, PhD, Pierre C.
Psychology Society *(868)*

Haberkamp, Randy
Academy of Motion Picture Arts and Sciences *(7)*

Haberstro, Philip
National Association for Health and Fitness *(639)*

Haberthier, Thomas H.
Geological Society of America *(459)*

Habura, Andrea
International Society of Protistologists *(573)*

Hacke, Kevin
International Special Events Society *(575)*
National Association of Independent Fee Appraisers
(674)

Hackel, Robert A
Association of Labor Relations Agencies *(290)*

Hackemann, Marisa
American Board of Veterinary Practitioners *(84)*

Hacker, Neville
Society of Pelvic Surgeons *(944)*

Hacker CMP, Perry
The Association of Collegiate Conference and Events
Directors International *(275)*

Hackett, Bruce
Air Movement and Control Association International
(19)

Hackett, Frank
National Auto Auction Association *(711)*

Hackett, CAE, FACHE, Karen L.
American Academy of Orthopaedic Surgeons *(38)*

Hackett, Vicki
Plastics Pipe Institute *(850)*

Hackler, Cullen L.
Porcelain Enamel Institute *(853)*

Hackley, Paul
Society for Organic Petrology *(917)*

Hackman, Michelle
International Food Service Executives' Association
(546)

Hackney, VT
Van Body Manufacturers Division *(1008)*

Hadden, Amilde
Modern Language Association *(618)*

Hadden, Sally
American Society for Legal History *(186)*

Haddox, Cindy
Outdoor Industry Association *(835)*

Hadel, James
United Union of Roofers, Waterproofers and Allied
Workers *(1001)*

Haderer, Russell G.
BPA Worldwide *(334)*

Haders, Donna
Machine Knife Association *(601)*

Hadley, Craig
Society for the Anthropology of Food and Nutrition
(923)

Hadley, CAE CMP, Sherry W.
Airborne Law Enforcement Association *(19)*

Haendler, Jessica
American Association of Veterinary State Boards *(76)*

Hagan, Kate
American Association of Law Libraries *(64)*

Hagan, Sara
Environmental and Water Resources Institute of the
American Society of Civil Engineers *(430)*

Hagans, Robert R.
American Association of Retired Persons *(72)*

Hagberg, Meghan
Business Council for International Understanding *(338)*

Hageman-Apol, Magda
Meals on Wheels Association of America *(609)*

Hagemo, Ted
International Association of Railway Operating Officers
(527)

Hagen, Elizabeth
National Association of Professional Organizers *(687)*

Hager, Amy
Satellite Broadcasting and Communications
Association *(891)*

Hager, Mike
Brotherhood of Locomotive Engineers and Trainmen
(336)

Hagerty, Denise
American Medical Association *(148)*

Haggerty, Nicole
Association of Direct Response Fundraising Counsel
(279)

Hagler, June M.
National Student Employment Association *(797)*

Hague, Terri
American Society of Transplantation *(210)*

Hagy, Sarah
International Kitchen Exhaust Cleaning Association
(553)

Hagy, CAE, Sarah
Water and Sewer Distributors of America *(1012)*

Hahn, FACHE, Cynthia
American College of Healthcare Executives *(96)*

Hahn, Greg
Academy of Model Aeronautics *(7)*

Hahn, Hannelore

International Women's Writing Guild *(581)*

Hahn, Karla
Association of Research Libraries *(306)*

Hahn, Lynnette
Pi Sigma Epsilon *(847)*

Hahn, Martin J.
Glutamate Association (United States) *(463)*
International Hydrolized Protein Council *(551)*

Hahn, Paige
Republican Governors Association *(881)*

Hahn, Peter L.
Society for Historians of American Foreign Relations
(910)

Hahn, MD, Stephen M.
Society of Chairmen of Academic Radiology Oncology
Programs *(932)*

Hahn, Theodore
Society for Software Quality *(921)*

Haidar, Ali
American Correctional Association *(108)*

Haider, Shahzad
Satellite Broadcasting and Communications
Association *(891)*

Haidle, Gina
North American Securities Administrators Association
(NASAA) *(820)*

Haigh, Liz
American Water Works Association *(220)*

Haile-Selassie, Zerihun
American Council on the Teaching of Foreign
Languages *(111)*

Hailey, CAE, Tammy
NALS *(625)*

Hain, Julie
International Sculpture Center *(564)*

Haines, Becky
American College of Radiology *(102)*

Haines, G. William
Carpet Cushion Council *(343)*

Hair, Bonnie
Interior Design Society *(508)*

Hair, Ray
American Federation of Musicians *(119)*

Haire, Jennifer
National Center for State Courts *(720)*

Hairston, Rod
National Association of Sales Professionals *(692)*

Hairston, Valerie
National Apartment Association *(634)*

Haisman, Roger
Competitive Telecommunications Association *(371)*

Haitz, Lynda
Technology Student Association *(970)*

Hajigeorgiou, Jen
Information Systems Audit and Control Association
(495)

Hake, Eric R.
Association for Evolutionary Economics *(246)*

Hakemian, John
National Employment Counseling Association *(745)*

Hakenholz, CMP, Diana
The Association of Collegiate Conference and Events
Directors International *(275)*

Hakimian, Behrooz
Oriental Rug Importers Association of America *(833)*

Halal, , Anne
American Meat Institute *(148)*

Halal, Ernie
National Association of Insurance and Financial
Advisors *(675)*

Halamandaris, Val J.
National Association for Home Care and Hospice *(639)*

Halaszynski, Christopher
American Association of Professional Landmen *(71)*

Halataei, Allison
National Music Publishers Association *(774)*

Halbert, Julie Beth Wright
Council of the Great City Schools *(398)*

Halbert, Stacy L.
Academy Health *(3)*

Halbur, PhD, Bernie
Alliance for Continuing Medical Education *(22)*

Halden, LoAnn
International Gay and Lesbian Travel Association *(548)*

Hale, April
National American Indian Housing Council *(634)*

Hale, Dale L.
American Jewish Correctional Chaplains Association
(143)

Hale, Donna Sizemore
American String Teachers Association *(213)*

Hale, Glen
International Council of Shopping Centers *(538)*

Hale, MS, RN, Kathleen A.
Association of Women's Health, Obstetric and
Neonatal Nurses *(318)*

Hale, Mark
Automotive Service Association *(323)*

Hale, Marquie
National Fraternal Order of Police *(753)*

Hales, Lucy
Steel Plate Fabricators Association Division of STI/
SPFA *(962)*

Hales, Stuart C.
Special Libraries Association *(956)*

Halevy, Tammy A.
Association for Enterprise Opportunity *(245)*

Haley, Kathleen
National Association of Pastoral Musicians *(683)*

Haley, Kelly A.
Brotherhood of Railroad Signalmen *(336)*

Haley, Michael L.
International Communication Association *(536)*

Haley, Monica J.
AMT - The Association For Manufacturing Technology
(222)

Haliday, CRM, MBA, Rae Lynn
Institute of Certified Records Managers *(499)*

Halim, Magda
Environmental Design Research Association *(431)*

Hall, Anita
Association of Official Seed Analysts, Inc. *(296)*
Society of Commercial Seed Technologists *(933)*

Hall, Becca
Society of Neurointerventional Surgery *(942)*

Hall, Billye
American Council for Construction Education *(109)*

Hall, Candy
North American Association of Summer Sessions *(813)*

Hall, Chris

International Association of Business Communicators
(517)

Hall, Christel
Sales Lead Management Association *(890)*

Hall, Darwin
Western Economic Association International *(1015)*

Hall, Donna
ACUTA - The Association for Information
Communications Technology Professionals in Higher
Education *(11)*

Hall, Doreen
Society of Rheology *(946)*

Hall, Dorothy
National Council of Juvenile and Family Court Judges
(735)

Hall, Gary
National Basketball Players Association *(713)*

Hall, Gloria
International Society for Pharmaceutical Engineering
(567)

Hall, Jan
ADSC: The International Association of Foundation
Drilling *(12)*

Hall, Jone
International Manganese Institute *(555)*

Hall, PhD, Judy E.
National Register of Health Service Providers in
Psychology *(785)*

Hall, Karen
Fuel Cell and Hydrogen Energy Association *(454)*

Hall, Kathryn
Geochemical Society *(458)*

Hall, Ken
International Brotherhood of Teamsters - Airline
Division *(532)*
Teamsters Brewery and Soft Drink Workers Conference
(969)

Hall, Kim
Pinto Horse Association of America *(848)*

Hall, Kirsten
American Book Producers Association *(85)*

Hall, Linda A.
Society of Professional Journalists *(945)*

Hall, Lisa
American Railway Engineering and Maintenance-of-
Way Association *(173)*

Hall, Mary
Health Information Trust Alliance (HITRUST) *(470)*

Hall, Mike
The Society of Naval Architects and Marine Engineers
(942)

Hall, Nicole
Cristo Rey Network *(404)*

Hall, Raymond
NaSPA: Networks and Systems Professional
Association *(626)*

Hall, Reggie
NAMTA - National Art Materials Trade Association
(635)

Hall, CAE, MEd, Robert A.
American Association of Hip and Knee Surgeons *(62)*

Hall, Robert E.
Air and Waste Management Association *(17)*

Hall, Robyn
The Association to Advance Collegiate Schools of
Business *(319)*

Hall, Rosemary
Association of Diesel Specialists *(279)*
Aviation Insurance Association *(324)*

International Window Cleaning Association *(581)*

Hall, Stephen
American Correctional Chaplains Association *(108)*

Hall, Stevan A.
Pile Driving Contractors Association *(848)*

Hall, Tamara
Graphic Artists Guild *(465)*

Hall, Terry
Napa Valley Vintners Association *(625)*

Hall, Tommy
Walking Horse Owners Association of America *(1011)*

Hall, Tricia
Association for Child Psychoanalysis *(241)*

Hallada, Nicole
Association of Equipment Manufacturers *(281)*

Hallaway, Rashid
Disaster Recovery Contractors Association (DRCA) *(413)*

Hallen, Laura
National Association of Sporting Goods Wholesalers *(696)*
The Recreational Vehicle Aftermarket Association *(877)*

Haller, Cindy
Guild of Book Workers *(467)*

Haller, Joan
Professional Landcare Network *(863)*

Haller, Matthew
International Franchise Association *(547)*

Haller, Ralph
Forestry Conservation Communications Association *(452)*

Halley, Geoffrey
American Boiler Manufacturers Association *(84)*

Halley-Boyce, FACHE, PhD, RN, Jamesetta A.
Chi Eta Phi Sorority, Inc. *(352)*

Halliday, Tracey A.
American Beverage Association *(80)*

Hallion, Dennis
National Trooper's Coalition *(802)*

Hallman, Jill A.
American Board of Physical Medicine and Rehabilitation *(83)*

Hallman, Linda D.
American Association of University Women *(76)*

Hallock, Nan
Society for Laboratory Automation and Screening *(914)*

Halloran, Charles
Community Financial Services Association of America CFSA *(370)*

Halm, Karen
American Society of Neuroradiology *(204)*

Halm, Sherry
American College of Osteopathic Obstetricians and Gynecologists *(100)*

Halperin, Meredith
International Society of Transport Aircraft Trading *(574)*
Legal Marketing Association *(596)*

Halpern, Keith
The Broadway League *(336)*

Halpert, Samantha Burch
Federation of American Hospitals *(440)*

Halpin, Amy
International Documentary Association *(541)*

Halpin, Jonathan
Association of Collegiate Schools of Architecture *(275)*

Halsey, Debra
National Council for Marketing and Public Relations *(732)*

Halstead, Donna G.
American Concrete Institute *(106)*

Halstead, Todd R.
National Association of Theatre Owners *(706)*

Halsted, Amy
International Superyacht Society *(576)*

Halter, Don
NGNP Industry Alliance *(810)*

Halterman, Debby
American Indian Science and Engineering Society *(135)*

Halverson, Megan
Preventive Cardiovascular Nurses Association *(857)*

Halverson, Tracy
National Association for Family Child Care *(638)*

Halvorson, MD, Lisa M.
Women in Endocrinology *(1021)*

Hamacher, CFA, Theresa
National Investment Company Service Association *(767)*

Hamaker, Christian A.
National Telecommunications Cooperative Association *(799)*

Haman, D.J.
American Association of Orthodontists *(67)*

Hamann, Rachel
Physician Assistant Education Association *(847)*

Hamberger, Edward R.
Association of American Railroads *(266)*

Hambley, Dr. Dora (Holly)
Organization of Professional Employees of the U.S. Department of Agriculture (OPEDA) *(832)*

Hamblin, Sarah
International Trade Commission Trial Lawyers Association *(577)*

Hambrick, Jr., George W.
American Skin Association *(180)*

Hamel, John
American Psychosocial Oncology Society *(170)*

Hamel, PhD, Willem Arthur
Association of Management/International Association of Management *(292)*

Hamershock, Christine
NAFA Fleet Management Association *(624)*

Hames, John
American Wine Society *(221)*

Hames, Raymond
Human Behavior and Evolution Society *(480)*

Hamidi, Jeff
Materials Research Society *(609)*

Hamidzada, Fred
National Active and Retired Federal Employees Association *(629)*

Hamill, Deborah L.
International Association of Outsourcing Professionals *(525)*

Hamill, Linda
Cemented Carbide Producers Association *(347)*

Hamill, Matthew
National Association of College and University Business Officers *(654)*

Hamill, Stephanie
Wireless Innovation Forum *(1019)*

Hamilton, Adnée

Council of State Governments *(397)*

Hamilton, Carol M.
American Association for the Advancement of Artificial Intelligence *(51)*

Hamilton, Dawn
American College of Sports Medicine *(102)*

Hamilton, Ellen
North American Corriente Association *(815)*

Hamilton, George
American College of Nurse-Midwives *(99)*

Hamilton, CAE, Jenifer
American Society of Hematology *(199)*

Hamilton, Jim
National Truck Equipment Association *(802)*

Hamilton, Karen
American Guild of Organists *(127)*

Hamilton, Kathryn George
NAIOP, The Commercial Real Estate Development Association *(366)*

Hamilton, Lydia
Association for the Study of Nationalities *(259)*

Hamilton, MD, Lynn
American Society of Breast Disease *(193)*

Hamilton, Sara
Association for Molecular Pathology *(252)*
Association of Pathology Chairs *(298)*

Hamilton, PhD, Steven
Society for Laboratory Automation and Screening *(914)*

Hamilton, Rev. Thomas
American Council of Christian Churches *(109)*

Hamilton, Veronica
National Association of Service Providers in Private Rehabilitation *(695)*

Hamilton, PhD, W. Mark
American Mental Health Counselors Association *(151)*

Hamlin, CAE, FASAE, Deborah M.
Irrigation Association *(585)*

Hamlin, Lise
Hearing Loss Association of America *(472)*

Hamlin, Pam
Manufacturers' Agents National Association *(603)*

Hamlin, Tina
Independent Petroleum Association of America *(491)*

Hamlin-Smith, Stephan J.
Society for Disability Studies *(907)*

Hamm, Julia
Solar Electric Power Association *(951)*

Hamm, Rita R.
International Association for Impact Assessment *(513)*

Hamm, William E.
Lutheran Educational Conference of North America *(600)*

Hamme, Frankie
Society for Vascular Ultrasound *(927)*

Hammer, Andrew
American Beefalo Association *(80)*

Hammer, Diana
Society for Healthcare Consumer Advocacy *(910)*

Hammer, Philip "Bo"
American Institute of Physics *(140)*

Hammer, Taylor
International Association for Philosophy and Literature *(514)*

Hammer, Thomas A.
American Oilseed Coalition *(157)*

National Oilseed Processors Association *(776)*

Hammerberg, Jeanne
Automatic Fire Alarm Association *(321)*

Hammerberg, CFSP, SET, Thomas P.
Automatic Fire Alarm Association *(321)*

Hammerman, Ira D.
Securities Industry and Financial Markets Association (SIFMA) *(895)*

Hammersla, Jason
American Benefits Council *(80)*

Hammersley, Clarke
BICSI *(329)*

Hammond, Bruce
National Sporting Goods Association *(796)*

Hammond, John
United States Energy Association *(993)*

Hammond, Kate
International Association of Outsourcing Professionals *(525)*

Hammond, Keli
American Society of Hematology *(199)*

Hammond, Laura
American Institute of Bangladesh Studies *(137)*

Hammond, Mark
American Beverage Association *(80)*

Hammond, Norah
National Systems Contractors Association *(798)*

Hammond, Robert
Society of Industrial and Office Realtors *(939)*

Hammond, Susan G.
National Association of Women Artists *(709)*

Hammond-Chambers, Rupert J.
United States-Taiwan Business Council *(989)*

Hammonds, Dana
National Football League Players Association *(752)*

Hammontree, Hannah
Equipment Marketing and Distribution Association *(432)*

Hamod, David
National U.S.-Arab Chamber of Commerce *(803)*

Hamor, Kathy V.
College Savings Foundation *(364)*

Hamoudia, Mohsen
International Institute of Forecasters *(552)*

Hamp, Eric
Military Operations Research Society *(616)*

Hampshire, Frank
Motor and Equipment Manufacturers Association *(619)*

Hampson, Anne
IGAF Polaris *(486)*

Hampton, Beth T.
Optical Society of America *(829)*

Hampton, Erica
American Land Title Association *(144)*

Hampton, LeAnn
Association of Defensive Spray Manufacturers *(278)*
WaterJet Technology Association - Industrial and Municipal Cleaning Association *(1013)*

Hampton, Mike
Electronic Security Association *(424)*

Hampton, Pamela
Academy of Applied Science *(4)*

Hamre, Julie P.
NALP - The Association for Legal Career Professionals *(624)*

Han, Charles
American Association of Collegiate Registrars and Admissions Officers *(58)*

Han, Elena
American College of Radiology *(102)*

Han, Jin Ki
Korean Drycleaners-Laundry Association *(591)*

Han, Liebao
International Turfgrass Society *(579)*

Hanafin, Tracy
Club Managers Association of America *(359)*

Hancher, Justin
NORA: Association of Responsible Recyclers *(811)*

Hancock, Amy E.
American Beverage Association *(80)*

Hancock, DNP, RN-BC, Beverly
American Organization of Nurse Executives *(158)*

Hancock, Christopher
Design Management Institute *(410)*

Hancock, Jill
National Christian College Athletic Association *(721)*

Hancock, Ross
American Welding Society *(220)*

Hancock, Wendy
Association of Science-Technology Centers *(307)*

Hand, Delicia Reynolds
National Association of Consumer Advocates *(657)*

Handcock, Ben
Wheat Quality Council *(1016)*

Handeli, Larry A.
Ireland Chamber of Commerce in the United States *(585)*

Handelman, Ethan
National Housing Conference *(761)*

Handler, Howard
Major League Soccer *(601)*

Handley, Cathy
American Registry for Internet Numbers *(174)*

Handley, Jeff
Marble Institute of America *(604)*

Handley, Lynn
National Society of Hispanic MBAs *(794)*

Handley, Tiffany
National Fraternal Order of Police *(753)*

Handrich, PhD, Rita R.
American Society of Trial Consultants *(210)*

Handschuh, Steve
MEMA Information Services Council *(612)*

Handy, Angela
Investment Program Association *(584)*

Handy, Femida
Association for Research on Nonprofit Organizations and Voluntary Action *(255)*

Handzo, Kim
International Anti-Counterfeiting Coalition *(511)*

Hanen, Laura
National Association of City and County Health Officials *(654)*

Hanes, Greg
United States Meat Export Federation *(996)*

Haney, Carol
National Association of Basketball Coaches *(648)*

Haney, James A.
National Association of Basketball Coaches *(648)*

Haney, Michael L.
American Professional Society on the Abuse of Children *(168)*

Haney, Regina M.
National Catholic Educational Exhibitors *(718)*

Haney, EdD, Regina M.
National Catholic Educational Association *(718)*

Hanf, Susan
American Medical Directors Association *(149)*

Hanhisalo, Markus
International Multimedia Telecommunications Consortium *(557)*

Hanifi, Shah Mahmoud
American Institute for Afghanistan Studies *(135)*

Haning, CEM, CMP, Susan D.
National Association of Independent Life Brokerage Agencies *(674)*

Hanis, Monique
Solar Energy Industries Association (SEIA) *(952)*

Hanisch, Douglas
American Society of PeriAnesthesia Nurses *(206)*

Hankin, PhD, Robert A.
Health Industry Business Communications Council *(469)*

Hankins, Danny
Aerospace & Flight Test Radio Coordinating Council *(14)*

Hanks, Neal
Southwest Airlines Pilots Association *(953)*

Hanlen, Terry
American Translators Association *(217)*

Hanley, Chris
American Association of Zoo Veterinarians *(77)*

Hanley, Christopher
International Union of Operating Engineers *(579)*

Hanley, Darcy
National Ski Patrol System *(792)*

Hanley, Edward
American Maritime Officers Service *(147)*

Hanley, Kristin
Public Affairs Council *(868)*

Hanley, Lawrence J.
Amalgamated Transit Union *(28)*

Hanley, CAE, William H.
Illuminating Engineering Society of North America *(486)*

Hann, Victoria
United States and Canadian Academy of Pathology *(989)*

Hanna, Betty
International Association of Healthcare Central Service Materiel Management *(522)*

Hanna, Craig
American Academy of Actuaries *(29)*

Hanna, Dennis L.
American School Band Directors' Association *(177)*

Hanna, MD, Ehab
American Head and Neck Society *(129)*

Hanna, John
United States Racquet Stringers Association *(998)*

Hanna, Libby
Geospatial Information Technology Association *(459)*

Hannah, Geri
The Lawn Institute *(594)*

Hannahs, Michelle

Association of American Colleges and Universities *(264)*

Hannaway, Jane
American Institutes for Research *(141)*

Hanni, CAE, Jr., M. John
American Society of Dermatology *(196)*

Hannigan, Philip
Conveyor Equipment Manufacturers Association *(383)*

Hannum, Jane
Nuclear Information and Records Management Association *(825)*

Hanrahan, Philip
National Horsemen's Benevolent and Protective Association *(760)*

Hanreich, Franziska
Alliance for Gray Market and Counterfeit Abatement *(23)*

Hansard, Kelly
American Roentgen Ray Society *(176)*

Hanschen, John
Showmen's League of America *(899)*

Hanscom, Paul
Automotive Fleet and Leasing Association *(322)*

Hansell, David M.
Fleischner Society *(447)*

Hansen, Angie
International Association Of Pet Cemeteries and Crematories *(526)*

Hansen, Bob
University Professional & Continuing Education Association *(1003)*

Hansen, Chris
Association of Litigation Support Professionals *(292)*

Hansen, Cynthia
American Academy of Pediatric Dentistry *(39)*

Hansen, Dain
Radiant Panel Association *(872)*

Hansen, Ed
American Association of Zoo Keepers *(77)*

Hansen, Glenn J.
BPA Worldwide *(334)*

Hansen, Jennie Chin
American Geriatrics Society *(126)*

Hansen, Joseph T.
United Food and Commercial Workers International Union *(987)*

Hansen, Judy
Laboratory Animal Management Association *(592)*

Hansen, Kate
Democratic Governors Association *(410)*

Hansen, Kathleen M.
Modern Language Association *(618)*

Hansen, Mike
Calendar Marketing Association *(340)*

Hansen, Robert
National Opera Association *(776)*

Hansen, Dr. Robert J.
University Professional & Continuing Education Association *(1003)*

Hansen, Sarah
MPA - The Association of Magazine Media *(620)*

Hansen, Stephanie
National Organization of State Offices of Rural Health *(778)*

Hansen, Susan
National Translator Association *(801)*

Hansom-Pitt, Tela
Association of Public Television Stations *(304)*

Hanson, Bonnie J.
Industrial Fabrics Association International *(493)*

Hanson, Caroline E.
Poultry Breeders of America *(854)*

Hanson, Christy
American Geophysical Union *(126)*

Hanson, Deb
American Society for Reproductive Medicine *(189)*

Hanson, Dr. Frances
Connected International Meeting Professionals Association *(377)*

Hanson, Jessica
American Council of Life Insurers (ACLI) *(110)*

Hanson, USNR (Ret.), Capt. Marshall A.
Reserve Officers Association of the U.S. *(882)*

Hanson, Matt
National Association of Intercollegiate Athletics *(676)*

Hanson, Paul
American Composers Forum *(105)*

Hanson, Rich
Academy of Model Aeronautics *(7)*

Hanson, CPA, S. John
American Academy of Cosmetic Dentistry *(31)*

Hanzel, Amy
Retail Solutions Providers Association *(885)*

Hanzich, Kim
Art Directors Club *(229)*

Happ, CAE, Pamela R.
College of Optometrists in Vision Development *(364)*

Haran, Ann
American Association for the Study of Liver Diseases *(52)*

Harashinski, Christine
American Bureau of Metal Statistics *(86)*

Harbonic, Jason
International Kitchen Exhaust Cleaning Association *(553)*

Harbonic, Jason
North American Horticultural Supply Association *(817)*

Harcrow, Richard
Corrections, U.S.A. *(386)*

Hardcastle, Gary
Philosophy of Science Association *(846)*

Harden, Kim
Association of Nutrition & Foodservice Professionals *(296)*

Harder, David N.
American Herbalists Guild *(131)*

Harder, Lorene
American Society of Andrology *(192)*

Hardigan, PhD, Patrick C.
Association for the Behavioral Sciences and Medical Education *(259)*

Hardiman, CAE, Tom
Modular Building Institute *(618)*

Hardin, Amy
Congress of Chiropractic State Associations *(377)*

Hardin, Carolyn
National Drug Court Institute *(743)*

Hardin, Neal
Society for Academic Emergency Medicine *(903)*

Hardin, BA, Raven

Natco-The Organization for Transplant Professionals *(626)*

Hardin, BA, Raven
National Association for Health Care Recruitment *(639)*

Hardin, III, William G.
American Real Estate Society *(173)*

Harding, Ian
AASP - The Palynological Society *(2)*

Harding, Juliet
National Active and Retired Federal Employees Association *(629)*

Hardison, Keith
Association of Paroling Authorities International *(297)*

Hardman, Dennis J.
APA The Engineered Wood Association *(224)*

Hardman, Sharon
AACE International *(1)*

Hardock, Randolf H.
American Seniors Housing Association *(178)*

Hardulak, Ann Marie
Phi Beta Fraternity *(845)*

Hardwick, Maureen Donahue
International Pharmaceutical Aerosol Consortium *(560)*

Hardy, Bernadette
American College of Phlebology *(100)*

Hardy, Connie
ARMA International *(228)*

Hardy, DeLania
Association of Metropolitan Planning Organizations *(294)*

Hardy, Jacqueline
National Council on Education for the Ceramic Arts *(738)*

Hardy, Lee
Society of Christian Philosophers *(932)*

Hardy, Patricia
Eye Bank Association of America *(436)*

Hardy, Rick
National Barrel Horse Association *(712)*

Hardy, Robert B.
Council on Governmental Relations *(400)*

Hardy, Roy W.
Forging Industry Association *(452)*

Hare, Jill
National Stroke Association *(797)*

Harger, Jeffrey
United Lightning Protection Association *(987)*

Harget, Jackie
National Association of Educational Procurement, Inc. *(664)*

Hargett, CAE, CPA, Brenda
American Academy of Otolaryngology-Head and Neck Surgery *(39)*

Hargett, Caitlin
Education Finance Council *(419)*

Hargett, Ret. Maj. Gen. Gus
National Guard Association of the U.S. *(757)*

Hargis, Eric
National Parent Teachers Association *(779)*

Hargrave, Jacqueline
NADCA: The HVAC Inspection, Maintenance and Restoration Association *(623)*

Hargrove, Joshua
American Dental Education Association *(113)*

Hargrove, Monica R.

Airports Council International - North America *(21)*

Hariston, CMP, Michelle A.
Taxicab, Limousine & Paratransit Association *(969)*

Harken, Bonnie
International Association of Eating Disorders Professionals *(520)*

Harker, Roy
Association of Gay and Lesbian Psychiatrists *(285)*

Harkin, Lynn M.
National Rural Economic Developers Association *(788)*

Harkins, Barbara
Association of Arts Administration Educators *(268)*

Harkins, Betsy
National Federation of Municipal Analysts *(749)*

Harkins, Mina
National Committee for Quality Assurance *(724)*

Harkins, Ryan
International Energy Credit Association *(542)*

Harklau, Linda
American Association for Applied Linguistics *(47)*

Harles, Charles W.
Inter-National Association of Business Industry & Rehabilitation *(506)*

Harley, Janet
Association for Education in Journalism and Mass Communication *(245)*

Harley, Tonya
Association of Community College Trustees *(276)*

Harlow, D. Brooke
Managed Funds Association *(602)*

Harlow, Krystal
American Indian Science and Engineering Society *(135)*

Harlow, Marc
Enhanced Protective Glass Automotive Association *(429)*

Harlow, Stephanie
Burley Tobacco Growers Cooperative Association *(338)*

Harlow, CAE, CPA, Tom
Conference of State Bank Supervisors *(376)*

Harmacek, Marilyn
Association of Independent Information Professionals *(288)*

Harman, Donna Akers
American Forest & Paper Association *(123)*

Harman, Patricia L.
Restoration Industry Association *(884)*

Harmon, MPH, Linda L.
Lamaze International *(592)*

Harmon, Rick
American Water Works Association *(220)*

Harmon, Susan
National Association of Blacks In Government *(649)*

Harms, Dena
National Rural Water Association *(788)*

Harnad, Jane
Organization for the Advancement of Structured Information Standards *(831)*

Harned, CCM, Stephen W
National Weather Association *(804)*

Harnik, Esq., Stephen M.
United States-Austrian Chamber of Commerce *(1001)*

Harold, Catherine
American Land Title Association *(144)*

Haroz, Sam
American Society for Gastrointestinal Endoscopy *(184)*

Harp, Missy
The American Board of Facial Plastic and Reconstructive Surgery *(82)*

Harper, MA, Carol
American Academy of Pain Management *(39)*

Harper, CAE, Colleen
ASFE/The Geoprofessional Business Association *(231)*

Harper, Donna
International Hot Rod Association *(550)*

Harper, Georgia
Theatre Library Association *(973)*

Harper, Glenn
International Sculpture Center *(564)*

Harper, Dr. Howard
SEPM - Society for Sedimentary Geology *(897)*

Harper, Joel
United States Junior Chamber (Jaycees) *(995)*

Harper, Monica
National Association of Equipment Leasing Brokers *(666)*

Harper, Terry
United States Synchronized Swimming *(999)*

Harper, Tranis
National Barrel Horse Association *(712)*

Harpine, William
Association for Communication Administration *(241)*

Harpster, Tyra
American Association of Airport Executives *(53)*

Harr, Kathy
National Alliance for Media Arts and Culture *(631)*

Harr, Wendy
American Optometric Association *(157)*

Harrah, Janet
Association for University Business and Economic Research *(260)*

Harrell, Alvin C.
Conference on Consumer Finance Law *(376)*

Harrell, MD, Heather E.
Clerkship Directors in Internal Medicine *(358)*

Harrell, Jennifer
Alliance for Telecommunications Industry Solutions *(23)*

Harrell, Marti
National Precast Concrete Association *(782)*

Harrell, Sherry
National Appliance Parts Suppliers Association *(634)*

Harrell, Stan
American National Chamber of Commerce *(154)*

Harrell, Stan
United States Chamber of Commerce *(991)*

Harrelson, Beverly
American Accounting Association *(43)*

Harreys, Miranda
U.S. Hereditary Angioedema Association *(983)*

Harrier, Peggy
Cooperative Education and Internship Association *(384)*

Harriett, Sylvester
National Society of Black Engineers *(793)*

Harrington, Ellen
Academy of Motion Picture Arts and Sciences *(7)*

Harrington, Jack
Risk and Insurance Management Society, Inc. (RIMS) *(886)*

Harrington, ARP, CPCU, Joseph S.

American Association of Insurance Services *(63)*

Harrington, PhD, Leslie
The Color Association of the United States *(365)*

Harrington, Page
National Woman's Party *(805)*

Harrington, Tiffany
Association for Psychological Science *(254)*

Harris, Allan
National Technical Association *(799)*

Harris, Esq., Allan M.
Society for Photographic Education *(919)*

Harris, Bill
American Architectural Foundation *(46)*

Harris, Caroline
United States Chamber of Commerce *(991)*

Harris, Chuck
Southern Cypress Manufacturers Association *(953)*

Harris, Cindy
International Society of Arboriculture *(571)*

Harris, Danny
National Association of Fire Equipment Distributors *(668)*

Harris, David
United States Equestrian Federation *(993)*

Harris, Deborah
International Reading Association *(562)*

Harris, Deirdre
American Accounting Association *(43)*

Harris, Heather
American Board for Certification in Orthotics and Prosthetics, Inc. (ABC) *(81)*

Harris, James
Propane Engine Fuel Committee/Propane Education and Research Council *(867)*

Harris, Jeff
International Association of Black Professional Fire Fighters *(517)*

Harris, Joan D.
National Association for State Community Services Programs *(643)*

Harris, Judith L.
US Travel Association *(983)*

Harris, Karen
International Association of Speakers Bureaus *(528)*

Harris, Kelly
World Waterpark Association *(1028)*

Harris, Lynne R.
Consumer Specialty Products Association *(381)*

Harris, USAF (Ret.), Col. Marvin J.
Military Officers Association of America (MOAA) *(616)*

Harris, CAE, Mary Busey
National Association of the Remodeling Industry *(705)*

Harris, Maurice
American Health Lawyers Association *(130)*

Harris, Melanie
Livestock Marketing Association *(599)*

Harris, Michael
Mineralogical Society of America *(617)*

Harris, Michelle
Electric Drive Transportation Association *(421)*

Harris, Natasha Mandigo
Women's Foodservice Forum *(1023)*

Harris, CAE, Nicole
National Glass Association *(755)*

Harris, Nikki
National Speakers Association *(795)*

Harris, Pam
International Association of Conference Center Administrators *(518)*

Harris, Pamela Q.
National Association for Court Management *(637)*

Harris, Peggy
American Association of Neuropathologists *(66)*

Harris, Phillip
Association for Educational Communications and Technology *(245)*

Harris, Rick
Association of Proposal Management Professionals *(303)*

Harris, Robert
Air Movement and Control Association International *(19)*

Harris, Robert J.
Industrial Fasteners Institute *(493)*

Harris, Dr. Ron
National Religious Broadcasters *(785)*

Harris, Russell
Association for Computing Machinery *(243)*

Harris, Scott
American Council on Education *(110)*

Harris, Susan
Institute of Food Technologists *(499)*

Harris, Taylor S.
International Society for the Performing Arts *(569)*

Harris, Tom
International Police Mountain Bike Association *(561)*

Harris, Tonya
Council of the Great City Schools *(398)*

Harris, PhD, Dr. William G.
Association of Test Publishers *(313)*

Harris, Jr., William R.
Army Aviation Association of America *(229)*

Harris, Yvette
National Forum for Black Public Administrators *(752)*

Harrison, Alisa
International Franchise Association *(547)*

Harrison, Andre
National Asian Pacific American Bar Association *(635)*

Harrison, Andrea
National Association of Black County Officials *(649)*
National Organization of Black County Officials *(777)*

Harrison, Beth
The Academy of American Poets *(3)*

Harrison, Bonita
National Council of Farmer Cooperatives *(734)*

Harrison, Bridget
American Horse Council *(133)*

Harrison, Ce
The Council of Insurance Agents and Brokers *(394)*

Harrison, Emily
Alpha Gamma Rho *(26)*

Harrison, MD, George
Association of Gay and Lesbian Psychiatrists *(285)*

Harrison, Ginger L.
Institute of Hazardous Materials Management *(500)*

Harrison, Guy
National Republican Congressional Committee *(786)*

Harrison, Jennifer
Intelligent Transportation Society of America *(506)*

Harrison, Jim
Maritime Fire and Safety Association *(605)*

Harrison, Joel
American Pianists Association *(165)*

Harrison, CAE, CMP, MBA, John P.
Real Estate Investment Securities Association *(875)*

Harrison, Jonathan M.
Product Liability Advisory Council *(859)*

Harrison, CMP, MTA, Laura
National Association of City and County Health Officials *(654)*
National Association of County and City Health Officials *(659)*

Harrison, Lisa
Association of Academic Health Centers *(262)*

Harrison, Lisa
Federation of American Hospitals *(440)*

Harrison, Lori
Council of State Retail Associations *(397)*

Harrison, Lori
Water Environment Federation *(1013)*

Harrison, MS, RN, Peg
Pediatric Nursing Certification Board *(840)*

Harrison, Jr., Robert Harry
YMA Fashion Scholarship Fund *(1030)*

Harrison, Robyn
National Football League Players Association *(752)*

Harrison, Roger R.
Manufacturers Alliance/MAPI Inc. *(603)*

Harrison, CAE, Sheilah J.
American Financial Services Association *(121)*

Harrison, CUDE, Valerie
National Federation of Community Development of Credit Unions *(748)*

Harrold, Mary Jo
Orthopaedic Research Society *(833)*

Harrold, Rita
Illuminating Engineering Society of North America *(486)*

Harrouk, PhD, Wafa A.
Teratology Society *(971)*

Harrow, Richard
Leather Apparel Association *(596)*

Harsh, Ed
American Music Center *(153)*

Harsha, Barbara
Governors' Highway Safety Association *(464)*

Harsha, Peter
Computing Research Association *(373)*

Hart, Alan
United Electrical Radio & Machine Workers of America *(986)*

Hart, Amy
Division I-A Athletic Directors Association *(415)*

Hart, Beverly G.
International Society of Psychiatric Consultation Liaison Nurses *(574)*

Hart, Jr., Clyde J.
American Bus Association *(87)*

Hart, Helen
National Blacksmiths and Weldors Association *(715)*

Hart, J.D., Henry A.
Society for Human Resource Management *(911)*

Hart, Lauren
National Network of Depression Centers *(775)*

Hart, Laurence
Association for Information and Image Management International *(249)*

Hart, Lucinda
Hospitality Financial and Technology Professionals *(479)*

Hart, Michele Spilberg
Society for Clinical and Experimental Hypnosis *(906)*

Hart, Ron
University Professional & Continuing Education Association *(1003)*

Hart, Sandy
Association of Personal Computer User Groups *(299)*

Hart, Stan
Mystery Shopping Providers Association *(623)*

Hart, Esq., Thomas
United States High Speed Rail Association *(994)*

Hart-Davidson, Bill
Association of Teachers of Technical Writing *(313)*

Harte, Carri
Conservation and Preservation Charities of America *(377)*

Hartgen, Paul
Council of Manufacturing Associations *(395)*

Harth, Joe
Object Management Group *(825)*

Hartig, Kate
National Institute for State Credit Union Examination *(764)*

Hartke, Jason
United States Green Building Council *(994)*

Hartl, Charles
United States Lifesaving Association *(996)*

Hartle, Allison
Academic Pediatric Association *(3)*

Hartle, Jill
American Academy of Ophthalmology *(37)*

Hartle, Terry W.
American Council on Education *(110)*

Hartley, Angela
National Industries for the Blind *(763)*

Hartline, Connie
American Public Works Association *(172)*

Hartlove, Michelle D.
National Association of Vision Professionals *(708)*

Hartman, Bobbie
Association of Social Work Boards *(309)*

Hartman, Janelle
The Newspaper Guild *(810)*

Hartman, Stanley I.
American Institute of Professional Bookkeepers *(140)*

Hartmann, Barbara
Academy of Osseointegration *(7)*

Hartnett, Daniel
Association of Metropolitan Water Agencies *(294)*

Hartogs, David
American Public Health Association *(171)*

Hartquist, David A.
Specialty Steel Industry of North America *(958)*

Hartranft, Jim
Electronics Representatives Association *(424)*

Hartranft, MBA, Scott
National Committee for Quality Assurance *(724)*

Hartsough, Jeff
Percussive Arts Society *(841)*

Hartwell, Keith
National Railroad Construction and Maintenance Association, Inc. *(783)*

Hartwick, Ken F
Police Executive Research Forum *(852)*

Hartwig, Bobbi
North American Limousin Foundation *(817)*

Hartwig, CPCU, Dr. Robert P.
Insurance Information Institute *(505)*

Hartz, Carrie
Air and Waste Management Association *(17)*

Harvey, De
American Registry for Internet Numbers *(174)*

Harvey, Glynis
American Institute of Ultrasound in Medicine *(141)*

Harvey, LTCOL Jerry A.
American College of Healthcare Information Administrators *(97)*

Harvey, Jerusha
International Society for Pharmacoeconomics and Outcomes Research *(568)*

Harvey, Karen
American Association for the Advancement of Artificial Intelligence *(51)*

Harvey, Karen W.
American Public Transportation Association *(171)*

Harvey, R. C.
Association of American Editorial Cartoonists *(264)*

Harvieux, MSW, Anne
Association of SIDS and Infant Mortality Programs *(308)*

Harwell, Ken
American Red Poll Association *(174)*

Harwick, Dennis P.
Captive Insurance Companies Association *(342)*

Harwood, Rick
National Association of State Alcohol and Drug Abuse Directors (NASADAD) *(697)*

Harwood, CMP, Sandra Vura
Infectious Diseases Society of America *(494)*

Harwood Mattox, Vivienne
Society of Vacuum Coaters *(950)*

Hasbrouck, Robert C.
International Association of Auto Theft Investigators *(516)*

Haselden, Nancy
Society of International Business Fellows *(940)*

Haselwander, Stephanie
American Miniature Horse Association *(152)*

Hasemann, John W.
American Hardware Manufacturers Association *(128)*

Hasenfeld, Hertz
Diamond Manufacturers & Importers Association of America *(411)*

Hashmi, Akrama
Islamic Medical Association of North America *(586)*

Haskard, Tom
TechServe Alliance *(971)*

Haskin, Kris
American Association for Hand Surgery *(49)*

Haskins, Vickie
Alliance of Hazardous Materials Professionals *(25)*

Hassan, Rizwan
American Immigration Lawyers Association *(134)*

Hassassian, Sima

International Public Management Association for Human Resources *(562)*

Hassett, CMP, Crista
National Association of Mutual Insurance Companies *(681)*

Hassett, Kim
Antenna Measurement Techniques Association *(224)*

Hassmiller, CAE, Bob
National Association of College Auxiliary Services *(655)*

Hastings, Annamarie
International Society of Refractive Surgery of the American Academy of Ophthalmology *(574)*

Hastings, Patricia A.
Materials Research Society *(609)*

Hata, Nobu
National Association of Realtors *(690)*

Hatch, Robert
The Financial Services Roundtable *(445)*

Hatchell, Jason
Association for Healthcare Documentation Integrity *(247)*

Hatcher, Donald L.
Association for Informal Logic and Critical Thinking *(249)*

Hatcher, Jennifer L.
Food Marketing Institute *(449)*

Hatcher, Yvette
National Legal Aid and Defender Association *(769)*

Haterius, Stephen
National Association of Agricultural Fair Agencies *(646)*
National Association of State Departments of Agriculture *(699)*

Hatfield, Jennifer
Association of Pool and Spa Professionals *(299)*

Hatfield, Krissa
Association for Management Information in Financial Services *(251)*

Hatfield-Goldman, Jan
Worldwide ERC *(1028)*

Hathaway, Hannah
Appaloosa Horse Club *(225)*

Hathaway, Kristen
National Association of Dental Plans *(662)*

Hatherill, William A.
Federation of State Boards of Physical Therapy *(442)*

Hathorne, Debbie
International Sport Show Producers Association *(575)*

Hathorne, Nancy
Writers Guild of America East *(1029)*

Hatton, Karolyn
ArtTable *(231)*

Hatton, Melinda Reid "Mindy"
American Hospital Association *(133)*

Hatzakos, Janice
American Society for Information Science and Technology *(186)*

Hauck, Ben
Institute of General Semantics *(500)*

Hauck, Graham
International Cargo Security Council *(533)*

Hauck-Lawson, Annie
Association for the Study of Food and Society *(259)*

Hauge, Heidi
Rolf Institute of Structural Integration *(887)*

Haughey, Helen
Association of Sewing and Design Professionals *(308)*

Haughey, Rick
National Multi-Housing Council *(774)*

Haught, Robert
National Society of Newspaper Columnists *(794)*

Haughton, CMP, Alexis A.
USFN-America's Mortgage Banking Attorneys *(1006)*

Haughton, Jeff
International Sport Show Producers Association *(575)*

Hauglie, Paul
Automotive Engine Rebuilders Association *(322)*

Haugstad, Kimberly
Hemophilia Federation of America *(474)*

Hauk, Janet
Equipment Service Association *(433)*

Haukap, Sarah
North American Association of Floor Covering Distributors *(811)*
North American Building Material Distribution Association *(814)*

Haumann, Barbara
Organic Trade Association *(830)*

Haunroth, Gregg
Society of Pharmaceutical and Biotech Trainers *(944)*

Haupt, Susan
Trade Promotion Management Associates *(977)*

Hauptli, Todd J
American Association of Airport Executives *(53)*

Hauser, Karen
The Broadway League *(336)*

Hauser, Melanie
Golf Writers Association of America *(463)*

Hauser, Ronna
National Community Pharmacists Association *(725)*

Hausken, Tom
Optical Society of America *(829)*

Hausman, Shawn
American Council of Life Insurers (ACLI) *(110)*

Hausmann, Lauren
National Small Business Association *(792)*

Hausner, MBA, Laurence
American Diabetes Association *(115)*

Hauss, Linda
United Shoe Retailers Association *(988)*

Haut, Judith
Publishers' Publicity Association *(870)*

Hauth, Russell R.
National Religious Broadcasters, Music License Committee *(785)*

Haveles, Kayla
American Antiquarian Society *(45)*

Havenga, Tara
American Society for Surgery of the Hand *(189)*

Havens, Kris
AFT - Public Employees *(15)*
AFT Healthcare *(15)*

Havens, Robin
National Cancer Registrars Association *(717)*

Havlik, MD, Robert J.
American Society of Maxillofacial Surgeons *(202)*

Havlina, Ernest
American Backflow Prevention Association *(78)*

Havsy, Jeffrey

National Council of Real Estate Investment Fiduciaries *(735)*

Haward, Richard "Dick" J.
Scottish Blackface Breeders Association *(893)*

Hawarden, Vicki
International Association of Venue Managers *(528)*

Hawbaker, Scott
National Association of County Agricultural Agents *(659)*

Hawbecker, CPA, Mary
National Association of Community Health Centers *(656)*

Hawes, Jean
Outdoor Power Equipment Institute *(835)*

Hawes, Kay
National Association of Intercollegiate Athletics *(676)*

Hawk, Andy
PSIA-AASI *(868)*

Hawk, Darlene
National Propane Gas Association *(783)*

Hawke, Catherine E.
American Bar Association *(79)*

Hawkins, Alison
The Philanthropy Roundtable *(846)*

Hawkins, Bethany
American Association for State and Local History *(51)*
Organization for Tropical Studies *(831)*

Hawkins, PhD, Bill
Mathematical Association of America *(609)*

Hawkins, Cheri
National Intramural-Recreational Sports Association *(766)*

Hawkins, Cheryl
American Clinical Laboratory Association *(91)*

Hawkins, Jr., Daniel R.
National Association of Community Health Centers *(656)*

Hawkins, David A
National Association for College Admission Counseling *(637)*

Hawkins, SPHR, Diane M.
Meeting Professionals International *(612)*

Hawkins, Jennifer
United States Synchronized Swimming *(999)*

Hawkins, John
American Farm Bureau Federation *(118)*

Hawkins, John
American Society of Addiction Medicine *(191)*

Hawkins, Julie
American Soybean Association *(211)*

Hawkins, Justin
Commercial Real Estate Women Network *(367)*

Hawkins, Paul
PeerSpan *(840)*

Hawkins, Perry
American Institute of Inspectors *(139)*

Hawkins, FACP, MD, Richard E.
American Board of Medical Specialties *(82)*

Hawkins, Ronald
Security Industry Association *(895)*

Hawkins, Shanon
Paso Fino Horse Association, Inc. *(839)*

Hawkinson, Deborah
Forest Resources Association *(451)*

Hawkinson, Mary

Bearing Specialist Association *(327)*

Hawkos, Lise
Visual Resources Association *(1010)*

Hawks, Jeff
Sump and Sewage Pump Manufacturers Association *(965)*

Hawks, Troy
National Ski Area Association *(791)*

Hawley, John
American Society for Clinical Investigation *(182)*

Hawley, Ronald P.
Search - The National Consortium for Justice Information and Statistics *(894)*

Hawrelko, Donna
Accredited Gemologists Association *(10)*

Hawrysz, David L.
National Futures Association *(754)*

Haws, Jean
Outdoor Power Equipment Aftermarket Association *(835)*

Hawthorne, Kristy
Liaison Committee of Cooperating Oil and Gas Associations *(597)*

Hawthorne, Matthew
National Religious Campaign Against Torture *(786)*

Haxton, Elizabeth
Association of Meeting Professionals *(294)*

Hay, Duncan
Society for Industrial Archeology *(913)*

Hay, Kelley
Association of Surgical Technologists *(312)*

Hayashi, Annie Carpenter
Orthopaedic Research Society *(833)*

Hayden, Christopher
Ocean Research & Conservation Association *(826)*

Hayden, Irene
AGN International North America, Inc *(15)*

Hayden, J. Jolly
Working Group for Investment in Reliable and Economic Electric Systems *(1025)*

Hayden, John
Society for Mining, Metallurgy and Exploration, Inc. *(915)*

Hayden, Katharine S.
Federal Judges Association *(439)*

Hayden, Lisa
College and University Professional Association for Human Resources *(362)*

Hayden, Patrick
North American Export Grain Association, Inc. *(816)*

Hayden, Thomas K.
National Notary Association *(775)*

Haydon, CAE, Donald F.
Society of Diagnostic Medical Sonographers *(934)*

Hayes, Brian
CropLife America *(404)*

Hayes, Christine
Tax Executives Institute, Inc. *(968)*

Hayes, Deb
Chain Drug Marketing Association *(350)*

Hayes, Fred
Packaging Machinery Manufacturers Institute *(836)*

Hayes, Garry
National Association of Heavy Equipment Training Schools *(672)*

Hayes, Jason
American Coal Council *(92)*

Hayes, Jessica
Association of Halfway House Alcoholism Programs of North America *(286)*

Hayes, Jim
College Media Association *(363)*

Hayes, Dr. John
National Association of University Fisheries and Wildlife Programs *(707)*

Hayes, MD, John R.
National Network of Depression Centers *(775)*

Hayes, Margaret
Fashion Group International *(438)*

Hayes, Michael J.
International Dyslexia Association *(541)*

Hayes, Nicole
Outdoor Advertising Association of America *(834)*

Hayes, Pamela
National Association of Truck Stop Operators(NATSO) *(707)*

Hayes, Peggy
American College Health Association *(93)*

Hayes, Phillip W.
American Sugar Alliance *(214)*

Hayes, Robert G.
Coastal Conservation Association *(361)*

Hayes, Robin
American Counseling Association *(111)*

Hayes, Roderick
Urban Financial Services Coalition *(1003)*

Hayes, Roger A.
Casting Industry Suppliers Association *(344)*

Hayes, Shirley
National Spotted Saddle Horse Association *(796)*

Hayes, Stephen
Corporate Council on Africa *(385)*

Hayes, Tiffany
American Association of Physics Teachers *(69)*

Hayes, Tim
AIR Commercial Real Estate Association *(18)*

Haygood, Courtney
The Association to Advance Collegiate Schools of Business *(319)*

Haylock, Ph.D. R.N., Pamela J.
Association for Vascular Access *(261)*

Haynes, Alexandra
Airport Minority Advisory Council (AMAC) *(21)*

Haynes, Carline
American Society for Information Science and Technology *(186)*

Haynes, Gail C.
Pension Real Estate Association *(841)*

Haynes, JD, J. Charles
Society for Neuro-Oncology *(916)*

Haynes, John
American Institute of Physics *(140)*

Haynes, Milt
Black Data Processing Associates *(331)*

Haynes, Robin
National Council of Textile Organizations *(737)*

Haynes, W. Thomas
The Coca-Cola Bottlers' Association *(361)*

Haynie, Mark
International Trumpet Guild *(578)*

Hays, Angela
NFHS Music Association *(810)*
NFHS Speech Debate and Theatre Association *(810)*

Hays, Cathy
Travel Goods Association *(979)*

Hays, Cheryl
American Culinary Federation *(112)*

Hays, Fred
Alberta Beef Producers *(21)*

Hays, John J.
Farm Credit Council *(437)*

Hays, Nancy
Educause *(420)*

Hays, Susan
Wild Bird Feeding Industry *(1017)*

Hays, Susan M.
Wild Bird Feeding Institute *(1017)*

Hays, William E.
Society of Toxicology *(948)*

Hayward, Phil
National Recreation and Parks Association *(784)*

Hayward, Tom
National Association of State Boating Law
Administrators *(698)*

Haywood, Sara
Association for Professionals in Infection Control and
Epidemiology *(254)*

Hazard, CAE, PhD, Diane
American Accounting Association *(43)*

Hazeltine, CAE, Derek B.
Professional Liability Underwriting Society *(863)*

Hazelwood, Rya Hobart
Industrial Asset Management Council *(492)*

Hazzard, Stephanie
National Junior College Athletic Association *(767)*

Head, Ian
National Lawyers Guild *(768)*

Head, Terry R.
International Association of Movers *(525)*
International Shippers Association *(564)*

Headings-Bemis, Renee
Society of Animal Artists *(930)*

Headley, Annette
Accrediting Council for Independent Colleges and
Schools *(10)*

Headley, Jubi
Municipal Waste Management Association *(621)*

Headtke, Dawn
Real Estate Buyers Agent Council *(875)*

Healey, Patrick T.
Friction Material Standards Institute *(454)*

Healy, Cindy
Paperboard Packaging Council *(838)*

Healy, Jr., Esq., Robert L.
American Public Transportation Association *(171)*

Healy, Suzanne M.
APPA - Leadership in Educational Facilities *(225)*

Heany, Juliene
Consortium of School Networking *(378)*

Heard, Belinda
Association of Dark Leaf Tobacco Dealers and
Exporters *(278)*

Hearn, Carmel
Association of Physician Assistants in Cardiovascular
Surgery *(299)*

Hearn, Gordon
Transportation Lawyers Association *(978)*

Hearn, Maureen
Association for Information and Image Management
International *(249)*

Hearn, Ted
American Cable Association *(87)*

Heasley, PhD, Robert
American Men's Studies Association *(150)*

Heater, Rob
Vacuum Dealers Trade Association/Sewing Dealers
Trade Association *(1007)*

Heatley, Tammye F.
Association of Public Television Stations *(304)*

Heaton, Deb
American Classical League *(91)*

Heaton, John
The Association of American Seed Control Officials
(266)
Western History Association *(1015)*

Heaton, Linda
Object Management Group *(825)*

Heaton, Tim
Society for the Study of Social Biology *(925)*

Heberlein, John R.
The Endocrine Society *(427)*

Hebert, David E.
American College of Nurse Practitioners *(99)*

Hebert, Marc
Society for Light Treatment and Biological Rhythms
(914)

Hebert, Tamara
Institute of Nautical Archaeology *(502)*

Hebron, Elizabeth
National Conference of State Historic Preservation
Officers *(728)*

Hecht, Helen
Federation of Tax Administrators *(442)*

Hecht, Stuart J.
American Theatre and Drama Society *(216)*

Hechter, Michael
National Cancer Registrars Association *(717)*

Heck, Dorothea
National Association of Retail Collection Attorneys
(692)

Heck, Kimberly "Kim"
Sports Turf Managers Association *(959)*

Heck, Timothy
National Air Transportation Association *(630)*

Heck, Timothy J.
Design-Build Institute of America *(411)*

Hecker, Cheryl
National Association of Directors of Nursing
Administration in Long Term Care *(663)*

Heckler, Tim
United States Professional Tennis Association *(998)*

Heckman, Julie L.
American Pyrotechnics Association *(172)*

Hecquet, Beth
National Association of Sports Commissions *(697)*

Hecsh, Janet
Council on Anthropology and Education *(398)*

Hedge, Rachel
National Association of Police Organizations *(685)*

Hedge, Russ

Hearn, Gordon — *see above*

American Youth Hostels, Inc (Hostelling International
USA) *(222)*

Hedges, Jane T.
American Association for the Advancement of Slavic
Studies *(52)*

Hedges, Mike
Society for Mining, Metallurgy and Exploration, Inc.
(915)

Hedinger, Barb
American Society of Breast Disease *(193)*

Hedland, Kathleen L.
Council of Supply Chain Management Professionals
(398)

Hedland, Merle
American Academy of Medical Administrators *(36)*
American College of Cardiovascular Administrators
(93)
Society of Tribologists and Lubrication Engineers *(949)*

Hedrick, Diana
Association of Military Surgeons of the United States
(294)

Hedrick, Janet
American Foreign Service Association *(122)*

Hedrick, Jennifer
Hearth, Patio and Barbecue Association *(472)*
Pellet Fuels Institute *(841)*

Hedstrom, Karl
Nonprofit Technology Network *(811)*

Heeke, CAE, Melissa
National Chimney Sweep Guild *(721)*

Heenan, Jr., William M.
Steel Recycling Institute *(963)*

Heesen, Mark G.
National Venture Capital Association *(803)*

Heffelfinger, K.
EUCG, Inc. *(433)*

Hefferan, Ellen
Loan Syndication & Trading Association *(599)*

Heffes, Ellen
Financial Executives International *(444)*

Heffner, Jennifer Davis
American Society of Picture Professionals *(207)*

Heffner, Susan R.
Healthcare Distribution Management Association *(471)*

Heflin, Mary Jo
Orthopaedic Research Society *(833)*

Hefner, Brian
Truck Renting and Leasing Association *(981)*

Hefner, Lauren
Laboratory Products Association *(592)*
Optical Imaging Association *(829)*

Hegarty, John F.
National Postal Mail Handlers Union *(781)*

Hegel, Stacy
Delta Waterfowl Foundation *(409)*

Hegmann, Bill
National Exchange Carrier Association *(746)*

Hegre, Connie
National Association of Casino Party Operators *(651)*

Hegyi, Agnes
Computer Ethics Institute *(372)*

Hehn, Brian
Choristers Guild *(355)*

Hehn, Eve
Choristers Guild *(355)*

Heideman, Ken

American Meteorological Society *(151)*

Heidemann, Sylvia
National Concrete Burial Vault Association *(725)*

Heider, Claret M.
Building Seismic Safety Council *(337)*
National Institute of Building Sciences *(764)*

Heiderscheit, Tess
Agricultural & Applied Economics Association *(16)*

Heidorn, Dave
American Society of Safety Engineers *(209)*

Heidrich, Greg
Society of Actuaries *(927)*

Heighton, Rachel
American Farrier's Association *(118)*

Heilbrunn, Janel
Ethics and Compliance Officer Association *(433)*

Heilman, Craig W.
Warrior Protection & Readiness Coalition *(1012)*

Heilman, Susan
Alliance of Cardiovascular Professionals *(25)*

Heim, Tami
Christian Leadership Alliance *(355)*

Heimbecker, Paula
Text and Academic Authors Association *(972)*

Heimberg, Richard
Society for a Science of Clinical Psychology *(903)*

Heimlich, John P.
Airlines For America *(21)*

Heimowitz, Mike
American Fire Safety Council *(121)*

Hein, Jessica
American Paint Horse Association *(161)*

Hein, Rebecca
Material Handling Equipment Distributors Association *(608)*

Hein, Steve
National Association for Uniformed Services *(644)*
Society of Military Widows *(941)*

Heinbokel, Jr., Raymond J.
National Association of Photo Equipment Technicians *(684)*

Heine, Margaret
Organization of Women in International Trade *(832)*

Heine, Roberta
Voices for America's Children *(1011)*

Heinecke, Jason
National Indian Health Board *(763)*

Heinecke, Stu
Sales Lead Management Association *(890)*

Heinen, Kayla
Society of Children's Book Writers and Illustrators *(932)*

Heiner, Sean
Association of State Chamber Professionals *(310)*

Heinonen, Cheryl
Pacific Maritime Association *(836)*

Heinrich, Pamela M.
National Association for Fixed Annuities *(639)*

Heins, Mary
National Tactical Officers Association of America *(799)*

Heinsch, Karen
National Association of Pastoral Musicians *(683)*

Heinz, Alecia
Barzona Breeder's Association of America *(326)*

Heinze, Esq., Bernd G.
American Association of Managing General Agents *(64)*

Heinze, Kelsey
Association of Dermatology Administrators & Managers *(278)*

Heinze, Lynn
Cattlemen's Beef Promotion and Research Board *(346)*

Heinze, CMP, Martha A.
American Association of Managing General Agents *(64)*
American Horticultural Therapy Association *(133)*
International Furnishings and Design Association *(548)*

Heinzeroth, Dennis
Association of Professional Model Makers *(302)*

Heischman, Dmin, Daniel R.
National Association of Episcopal Schools *(666)*

Heisel, Scott E
American Malting Barley Association *(146)*

Heiser, Stuart
National Association of Schools of Public Affairs and Administration *(694)*

Heisler, Mary Kate
Lamaze International *(592)*

Heisler, DDS, William H.
National Association of Seventh-Day Adventist Dentists *(695)*

Heisse, Bob
Associated Press Managing Editors *(237)*

Heitz, Carly
American Society of Notaries *(204)*

Heitzman, MA, MD, Amy
University Professional & Continuing Education Association *(1003)*

Heitzman, MA, MEd, Amy
University Professional & Continuing Education Association *(1003)*

Heitzman, Lynn
Association of Postgraduate Physician Assistant Programs *(300)*

Heitzman, Lynn
Physician Assistant Education Association *(847)*

Helbach, Randy
Disaster Preparedness and Emergency Response Association *(413)*

Helberg, CMP, Beth
American Payroll Association *(162)*

Helein, Ruth
American Psychological Association - Division of Psychoanalysis *(169)*
National Surgical Assistant Association *(798)*

Heleniak, Timothy
The American Geographical Society *(126)*

Helfat, Jonathan N.
Commercial Finance Association *(366)*

Helfrich, Jeanette L.
National Retail Hobby Stores Association *(786)*

Helgerson, Lance
Professional Liability Underwriting Society *(863)*

Hellem, Steve
Corporate Environmental Enforcement Council *(386)*

Heller, Christian
AACE International *(1)*

Heller, Dave
Truckload Carriers Association *(981)*

Heller, Theresia
National Association of Attorneys General *(647)*

Helling, CAPT Randolph
Air Line Pilots Association International *(19)*

Hellstein, DDS, MS, John W.
American Academy of Oral and Maxillofacial Pathology *(37)*

Hellwig, Kirstin
American Society of Interior Designers *(200)*

Helm, Elizabeth
National Sculpture Society *(790)*

Helm, MBA, Kevin
Association of Family Medicine Residency Directors *(282)*

Helmbrecht, Greg
The Association of American Seed Control Officials *(266)*

Helmes, PhD, C. Tucker
Chlorobenzene Producers Association *(354)*
Dibasic Esters Group *(412)*
ETAD North America *(433)*

Helmes, PhD, C. Tucker
Tributyl Phosphate Task Force *(980)*

Helmling, Gayle
Council of Colleges of Arts and Sciences *(393)*

Helmrich, Susan
The Coastal and Estuarine Research Federation *(361)*

Helms, Sherry
Cleaning Equipment Trade Association *(357)*

Heltzel, Lucy
Beet Sugar Development Foundation *(327)*

Helwig, Debra
IGAF Polaris *(486)*

Helwig, H. Kurt
Electronic Funds Transfer Association *(423)*

Helzer, Zach
Medical Imaging and Technology Alliance *(611)*

Hembree, Allie
International Spa Association *(575)*

Hemingway, Dr. Claire
The Botanical Society of America *(333)*

Hemmelgarn, Jacelyn
American Society of Animal Science *(192)*

Hemminger, Carlyn
Society of Hispanic Professional Engineers *(938)*

Hemond, Roland
Association of Professional Ball Players of America *(301)*

Hempel, Katherine
American Society for Cell Biology *(182)*

Hemphill, Jana
American Cheese Society *(89)*

Hemphill, Jean
National District Attorneys Association *(743)*

Hendee, Ric
Cotton Incorporated *(387)*

Henden, PhD, Arne
American Association of Variable Star Observers *(76)*

Hendershot, Heather
Society for Cinema and Media Studies *(905)*

Hendershot, Peggy
National Thoroughbred Racing Association *(800)*

Hendershot, Sherlynn
WEB: Worldwide Employee Benefits Network *(1014)*

Henderson, Allen
National Association of Teachers of Singing *(705)*

Henderson, Alma C.
Service Employees International Union *(897)*

Henderson, Bob

Associated Equipment Distributors *(235)*

Henderson, Dan
American Radio Relay League *(172)*

Henderson, Daniel "Dan"
Produce Marketing Association *(858)*

Henderson, Deborah
Data Management Association International *(407)*

Henderson, Donna
Beefmaster Breeders United *(327)*

Henderson, Doug
Women in Aviation International *(1020)*

Henderson, Edwin M.
Society of Eye Surgeons *(936)*

Henderson, Harold W.
Lake Carriers Association *(592)*

Henderson, Jasmine
Wine and Spirits Wholesalers of America *(1018)*

Henderson, Jean
International Association of Women Ministers *(529)*

Henderson, John
American Councils for International Education *(111)*

Henderson, John
International Association of Amusement Parks and
Attractions(IAAPA) *(515)*

Henderson, Julie W.
National Frozen and Refrigerated Foods Association
(753)

Henderson, Kalen
American Society of Photographers *(207)*

Henderson, Lavette C.
National Dental Association *(742)*

Henderson, Mihisha
Design-Build Institute of America *(411)*

Henderson, Nancy
Ladies Professional Golf Association *(592)*

Henderson, Robin
Association of Administrators of the Interstate
Compact on the Placement of Children *(263)*

Henderson, Robin
National Association of Public Child Welfare
Administrators *(688)*

Henderson, MS, Scott
Refrigerating Engineers and Technicians Association
(878)
United States Pharmacopeia *(997)*

Henderson, Sky
American String Teachers Association *(213)*

Hendlass, Tim
International Society of Applied Intelligence *(570)*

Hendle, Kate
Receptive Services Association of America *(876)*

Hendon, Jori
Midwest Free Community Papers *(615)*

Hendrick, Melissa
Promotional Products Association International *(867)*

Hendricks, Donald H.
Organization of Flying Adjusters *(832)*

Hendricks, Marina
Newspaper Association of America *(810)*

Hendricks, Tom
National Air Transportation Association *(630)*

Hendrickson, Amy
National Association of State Departments of
Agriculture *(699)*

Hendrickson, B. J.

International Association of Chiefs of Police *(517)*

Hendrickson, Dan
Aerospace Industries Association of America *(14)*

Hendrickson, Jed A.
American Institute of Commemorative Art *(138)*

Hendrickson, Marlene L.
American Staffing Association *(213)*

Hendrickx, Mary
IEEE Photonics Society *(485)*

Hendrie, Caroline W.
Education Writers Association *(420)*

Hendrie, Jeri
American Nephrology Nurses Association *(155)*

Hendrix, Brent
National Association for Environmental Management
(638)

Hendrix, MS, Brian L.
United States Pharmacopeia *(997)*

Hendry, Jamie
International Association for Business and Society
(511)

Henebry, Martha
American Association of Collegiate Registrars and
Admissions Officers *(58)*

Henegar, Bob
National Board for Certified Counselors *(715)*

Heney, Daniel
Maple Flooring Manufacturers Association *(604)*

Henk, Chad
Xplor International *(1029)*

Henk, Skip
Xplor International *(1029)*

Henke, Dr. Janice
International Wildlife Management Consortium *(581)*

Henke, W. Kurt
Crop Insurance Research Bureau *(404)*

Henkel, Dan
American College of Sports Medicine *(102)*

Henkin, Alan
Central Conference of American Rabbis *(348)*

Henley, Ann
National Association of Elementary School Principals
(664)

Henley, FAAFP, MD, Douglas E.
American Academy of Family Physicians *(34)*

Henley, Lara
Country Music Association *(401)*

Henmueller, Joseph M.
Automotive Maintenance and Repair Association *(323)*

Henneberry, Mike
International Labor Communications Association *(553)*

Hennerberg, Dennis
Piedmontese Association of the United States *(848)*

Hennessey, Chris
League for Innovation in the Community College *(595)*

Hennessey, Debbie
Society of Broadcast Engineers *(931)*

Hennessey, Mary C.
American Society of Clinical Oncology *(194)*

Hennessey, Nicole
National Association of Recording Merchandisers
(NARM) *(690)*

Hennessey, Scott
Solar Energy Industries Association (SEIA) *(952)*

Hennessy, Dina
American Society of Radiologic Technologists *(208)*

Hennessy, Larry
Traffic Audit Bureau for Media Measurement, Inc. *(977)*

Hennessy, Mary J.
Industrial Fabrics Association International *(493)*

Henning, Brian G.
Metaphysical Society of America *(614)*

Henning, Laura
Dance/USA *(406)*

Henninger, Elaine
The Association for Academic Surgery *(237)*

Henrich, Jean
American Association of Individual Investors *(63)*

Henrici, Jane
Association for Feminist Anthropology *(246)*

Henricksen, Ron
Independent Time and Labor Management Association
(492)

Henriksen, Jeff
National Association of Real Estate Investment Trusts
(NAREIT) *(690)*

Henriksen, Missy
National Pest Management Association *(780)*

Henriquez, Santa
American College of Nutrition *(99)*

Henry, Corey
American Frozen Food Institute *(124)*
National Frozen Pizza Institute *(754)*

Henry, Dawn
Association of Corporate Contributions Professionals
(277)

Henry, Dorothy
Society for Clinical Data Management *(906)*

Henry, Heather Feldmann
Investigative Reporters and Editors *(583)*

Henry, James L.
USA Maritime *(1004)*

Henry, Jeff
American Association of Managing General Agents *(64)*

Henry, Kevin P.
International and American Associations of Clinical
Nutritionists *(510)*

Henry, CMDSM, Linda
Mail Systems Management Association *(601)*

Henry, Mary Kay
Service Employees International Union *(897)*

Henry, CFE, CPA, Michele
International Association of Chiefs of Police *(517)*

Henry, Robert
World Association of Veterinary Anatomists *(1025)*

Henry, Scott
Antique and Amusement Photographers International
(224)

Henry, Scott
ASM International *(232)*

Hensch, Joachim
International Association of Clothing Designers and
Executives *(518)*

Henschel, Kira
Underground Equipment Manufacturers Council *(984)*

Hensen, Katie
American Guernsey Association *(127)*

Hensinger, Barbara
National Independent Concessionaires Association
(762)

Hensley, Brandon
National Association of Sign Supply Distributors *(696)*

Hensley, Jason
Piano Technicians Guild *(848)*

Hensley, Karen
BioCommunications Association *(329)*

Henson, Katie
The Brown Swiss Association *(336)*

Henson, Mary
United States Equestrian Federation *(993)*

Henson, Ray
National Council for Impacted Schools *(732)*

Henson, Shannon
International Association of Operative Millers *(525)*

Hentges, PhD, Eric
International Life Sciences Institute *(554)*

Henze, Roxann
Industrial Designers Society of America *(493)*

Henzi, Pia
National Association of Flavors and Food-Ingredient Systems *(668)*

Heon, Tricia
National Auto Auction Association *(711)*

Hepp, CAE, Ronnie
Recreation Vehicle Dealers Association of North America *(876)*

Heppenheimer, Susan
American Society of Master Dental Technologists *(202)*

Heppes, CAE, Sr., Jerry
The Door and Hardware Institute *(416)*

Herald, Adriana
Museum Store Association *(621)*

Herberghs, Todd
Association of Defense Communities *(278)*

Herbert, Jane
International Society for Developmental Psychobiology *(566)*

Herbertson, Kara
National Association of State Directors of Career Technical Education Consortium *(699)*

Herbison, Bart
Nashville Songwriters Association, International *(625)*

Herbolsheimer, Robert T.
Meals on Wheels Association of America *(609)*

Herd, Michael
NACHA - The Electronic Payments Association *(623)*

Herdman, PhD, RN, T. Heather
NANDA International *(625)*

Herdrich, Peter R.
Archaeological Institute of America *(227)*

Herendeen, Jennifer
Academy of Nutrition and Dietetics *(7)*

Herfkens, John
International Society for Traumatic Stress Studies *(570)*

Hergenrather, Ken
National Council on Rehabilitation Education *(739)*

Herian, Victoria L.
Society of Wood Science and Technology *(950)*

Herlensky, Doug
Association for Middle Level Education *(252)*

Herlihy, Jim
United States Meat Export Federation *(996)*

Herlihy, CMP, Kelley
American Schools of Oriental Research *(177)*

Herman, Chris
Gas Technology Institute *(456)*

Herman, Hattie
American Federation for Aging Research *(119)*

Herman, Jeffrey "Jeff"
Society of American Silversmiths *(929)*

Herman, Jerry
United Synagogue of Conservative Judaism *(1001)*

Herman, Jonathan
National Guild for Community Arts Education *(757)*

Herman, Nate
American Apparel & Footwear Association *(46)*
Fashion Accessories Shippers Association *(438)*

Herman, Nate
Travel Goods Association *(979)*

Herman, PhD, SPHR, Rebecca
Institute of Behavioral and Applied Management *(498)*

Herman, Roberta
American College of Veterinary Internal Medicine *(104)*

Herman, Susan T.
American Clinical Neurophysiology Society *(92)*

Herman, MD, Susan T.
National Association of Epilepsy Centers *(666)*

Herman, Terry
United States Wheat Associates, Inc. *(1000)*

Herman-Betzen, Marsha
Association of College Unions International *(274)*

Hermansen, CPA, Scott M.
National Board for Respiratory Care *(715)*

Hermberg, Kevin
American Association of Philosophy Teachers *(69)*

Hermsen, Elizabeth
Society of Infectious Diseases Pharmacists *(939)*

Hernandez, Anna
American Independent Business Alliance *(135)*

Hernandez, Carolina
American Academy of Implant Dentistry *(35)*

Hernandez, Cesar
National Wheelchair Basketball Association *(804)*

Hernandez, David Perez
Human Resource People and Strategy *(481)*

Hernandez, Eli
National Association of Enrolled Agents *(666)*

Hernandez, Elizabeth
American Society for Horticultural Science *(185)*

Hernandez, Fred
CoreNet Global *(385)*

Hernandez, Jennifer
Defense Credit Union Council *(408)*

Hernandez, Jetheda
National Association of Consumer Advocates *(657)*

Hernandez, John P.
Council for Opportunity in Education *(390)*

Hernandez, Maria
American Society for Biochemistry and Molecular Biology *(181)*

Hernandez, Paola
American Association of Feline Practitioners *(61)*

Hernandez, Sara
USENIX: The Advanced Computing Systems Association *(1005)*

Hernick, Mark E.
American Geophysical Union *(126)*

Herold, Eve

American Psychiatric Association *(168)*

Heron, Alison
Alliance of Hazardous Materials Professionals *(25)*

Heron, Kathleen
National Council of Farmer Cooperatives *(734)*

Herrejon, Theresa
American Society for Gastrointestinal Endoscopy *(184)*

Herrera, David
Religion Newswriters Association *(880)*

Herrera, Kelly
Association of Private Club Directors *(300)*

Herrera, Laura
IEEE Engineering in Medicine and Biology Society *(484)*

Herrera, Lori
Outdoor Industry Association *(835)*

Herrera, Manuel
Hispanic Organization of Latin Actors *(476)*

Herrera, Patricia
Geospatial Information Technology Association *(459)*

Herrick, Charles
International Association of Business Communicators *(517)*

Herrick, Ned
Graphic Arts Technical Foundation *(465)*

Herrick, CAE, II, Raymond "Ray" W.
Foodservice Equipment Distributors Association *(450)*

Herrick, Steve
American Academy of Religion *(41)*

Herrin, Deborah C.
Optical Society of America *(829)*

Herrington, TyAnna
Association of Teachers of Technical Writing *(313)*

Herrmann, Katrina Renee
Stage Managers Association *(960)*

Herrod-Jeter, Sheryl
National Association of Regulatory Utility Commissioners *(691)*

Herron, Amy
Institute of Noise Control Engineering *(502)*

Herron, Daniel J.
Academy of Legal Studies in Business *(6)*

Herron, Tom
National Fenestration Rating Council *(750)*

Herselius, CMP, Nancy
Associated Construction Distributors International *(235)*

Hershey, David
American Trucking Associations *(218)*
National Accounting and Finance Council *(628)*

Hershey, Jane
Viola da Gamba Society of America *(1009)*

Hershey, Jill
The Clearing House Association *(357)*

Hershman, Richard
National Association of College Stores *(655)*

Hertlein, Ralph
Open Applications Group *(828)*

Hertz, Marcia
Housing Partnership Network *(479)*

Hertzberg, Lisa
National Consumers League *(729)*

Heru, Nzinga Ratibisha
Association for the Study of Classical African Civilizations *(259)*

Hesbacher, Gretchen
National Institute of Building Sciences *(764)*

Heselbarth, Kim
Refrigeration Service Engineers Society *(878)*

Heske, Edward J.
American Society of Mammalogists *(202)*

Heslop, Wil
National Correctional Industries Association *(730)*

Hess, Curt
Association of University Research Parks *(316)*

Hess, Jean
American Society of PeriAnesthesia Nurses *(206)*

Hess, John W.
Geological Society of America *(459)*

Hess, Rick
National Frame Building Association *(753)*

Hess, Stephanie
National Association for Court Management *(637)*

Hessel, Carolyn Starman
Jewish Book Council *(587)*

Hession, Audra
National Elevator Industry, Inc. *(745)*

Hestekin, Jamie
North American Membrane Society *(818)*

Hester, John
National Hardwood Lumber Association *(757)*

Hesterlee, PharmD, Edward J.
American College of Apothecaries *(93)*

Heston, Judi
National Bulk Vendors Association *(716)*

Heston-Demirel, Vivienne
National Council for Research on Women *(732)*

Hetherington, Britt
National Military Family Association, Inc. *(772)*

Hetherington, Lisa
Association of Biomolecular Resource Facilities *(269)*

Hetzel, Joseph R.
Door and Access Systems Manufacturers Association, International *(415)*

Hetzel, Nancy
National Institute for Farm Safety, Incorporation *(764)*

Heuer, Greg
Architectural Woodwork Institute *(228)*

Heuett, Will
Society for Mathematical Biology *(915)*

Heun, PhD, Linda
American Association of Colleges of Osteopathic Medicine *(57)*

Heuser, Patricia E.
Independent Turf and Ornamental Distributors Association *(492)*
International Plant Propagators Society *(560)*
National Guardianship Association *(757)*

Heusser, EdD, H. Earl
National Association of Private, Nontraditional Schools and Colleges *(686)*

Heusser, PsyD, Irene L.
National Association of Private, Nontraditional Schools and Colleges *(686)*

Heuvelmans, Toine
International Computer Music Association *(536)*

Hewett, John
United States of America Gymnastics *(997)*

Hewitt, Chiquitta
United Cerebral Palsy *(986)*

Hewitt, CAE, Dan
Entertainment Software Association (ESA) *(429)*

Hewitt, Kimberly
Catholic Health Association of the United States *(345)*

Hewitt, Sean
National Institute of Oilseed Products *(765)*

Hewitt, CMP, Sean
Healthcare Convention and Exhibitors Association *(471)*

Hewitt, Sherry
Building Owners and Managers Institute International *(337)*

Hewitt, Steve
International Marking and Identification Association *(556)*

Hewlett, Marcy
Association of TeleServices International, Inc. *(313)*

Hews, Laurie
International Association for Food Protection *(512)*

Heyda, Kathy
American Agricultural Editors Association *(43)*
Turf and Ornamental Communicators Association *(982)*

Heydasch, Jason
College and University Professional Association for Human Resources *(362)*

Heydrick, EdD, Kenneth W.
National Alliance of State Science and Mathematics Coalitions *(633)*

Heymann, Harald O.
American Academy of Esthetic Dentistry *(33)*

Heymann, Thomas A.
National Notary Association *(775)*

Hiatt, Jonathan P.
AFL-CIO (American Federation of Labor and Congress of Industrial Organizations) *(14)*

Hiatt, Capt. Kevin L.
Flight Safety Foundation *(448)*

Hiatt, PE, Richard S.
Rural Electricity Resource Council *(889)*

Hiatt, Tammie
International Professional Rodeo Association *(561)*

Hibbard, Debra
American Association of Textile Chemists and Colorists *(75)*

Hibbs, CPA, Jr., MBA, Ralph L.
American College of Physicians *(101)*
American College of Physicians Services, Inc. *(101)*

Hickey, Dan
American Massage Therapy Association *(147)*

Hickey, David T.
International Sign Association *(564)*

Hickey, Gary
Working Group for Investment in Reliable and Economic Electric Systems *(1025)*

Hickey, Jr., James J.
American Horse Council *(133)*

Hickey, Karen
Association for Iron and Steel Technology *(250)*

Hickey, CMP, Marci
Pet Industry Distributors Association *(842)*

Hickey, CMP, Marci L.
Souvenir Wholesale Distributors Association *(953)*

Hickey, Ryan
Pharmaceutical Care Management Association *(844)*

Hickling, Ken
International Superyacht Society *(576)*

Hickman, J. Whitney
American Bonanza Society *(85)*

Hickman, Meryl
TechAmerica (fka Technology Association of America) *(969)*

Hickman, CAE, CMP, Sabeena
Professional Landcare Network *(863)*

Hickox, Aimee
Academy of Managed Care Pharmacy *(6)*

Hicks, Artis
American Society for Engineering Education *(183)*

Hicks, Christina
National Association of Bankruptcy Trustees *(647)*

Hicks, Darlene
National Sheriffs' Association *(791)*

Hicks, Darryl
National Reverse Mortgage Lenders Association *(787)*

Hicks, Gloria N.
National Association of State Boards of Geology *(698)*

Hicks, Janet
Artist Rights Society *(230)*

Hicks, Jim
1394 Trade Association *(1)*

Hicks, Lisa
International Association of Administrative Professionals *(515)*

Hicks, Mark
United Lightning Protection Association *(987)*

Hicks, Melissa
Cable and Telecommunications Human Resources Association *(340)*

Hicks, Paul
The New Media Consortium *(809)*

Hicks, Rush
Church Music Publishers Association *(356)*

Hicks, Sabrina
International Bottled Water Association *(530)*

Hicks, Shawn
International Door Association *(541)*
National Association of Nurse Massage Therapists *(682)*

Hicks, Sonia
National Parent Teachers Association *(779)*

Hicks, William
The National Association for the Dually Diagnosed *(643)*

Hidalgo, Kenita
Resource Center for Religious Institutes *(883)*

Hiebert, Holly
American Chianina Association *(90)*

Hiebert, Dr. Ronald
Natural Areas Association *(806)*

Hieronymus, Harry
Exhibition Services and Contractors Association *(435)*

Higby, PhD, Gregory J.
American Institute of the History of Pharmacy *(141)*

Higdem, Jann
Women in Mining National *(1022)*

Higgens, Barbara C.
Plumbing Manufacturers Institute *(851)*

Higginbotham, Andrea Brusca
SPARC *(954)*

Higginbotham, Charles
International Association of Chiefs of Police *(517)*

Higginbotham, Patricia G.

Higginbottom, Dr. Frank L. *(cont.)*
Global Business Travel Association *(462)*

Higginbottom, Dr. Frank L.
American Academy of Restorative Dentistry *(41)*

Higgins, Becky
Object Management Group *(825)*

Higgins, Geary
National Electrical Contractors Association *(744)*

Higgins, J. Kim
Wild Blueberry Association of North America *(1017)*

Higgins, Meghan
Event Service Professionals Association *(434)*
International Card Manufacturers Association *(532)*

Higgins, Meghan
North American Association of Commencement Officers *(813)*

Higgins, Tom
The College Board *(363)*

Higgins, DO, William
American Osteopathic College of Allergy and Immunology *(160)*

Higgs, Cathy
International Association of Electrical Inspectors *(520)*

High, Casey
Aviation Insurance Association *(324)*
International Window Cleaning Association *(581)*

Hight, Marlene
American Economic Association *(115)*

Hightower, Gracie
National Dental Assistants Association *(742)*

Hightower, Shonda
United States-China Business Council *(1001)*

Higley, Taylor
American Federation of Government Employees *(119)*

Higman, Susan
Global Health Council *(462)*

Hilbert, III, John W.
Vanadium Producers and Reclaimers Association *(1008)*

Hildebolt, Charles
American Academy of Oral and Maxillofacial Radiology *(37)*

Hildebrand, Stephen R.
The Door and Hardware Institute *(416)*

Hildreth, Anna B.
Bank Insurance and Securities Association *(326)*

Hildreth, Erin
Health Industry Distributors Association *(469)*

Hiles, Abigail
Transportation Elevator and Grain Merchants Association *(978)*

Hilger, Aaron
International Builders Exchange Executives/Builders Exchange Network *(532)*

Hilgers, Kenneth R.
International Society of Automation *(571)*

Hilke, CG, Ann
National Genealogical Society *(754)*

Hill, Alan
Competitive Telecommunications Association *(371)*

Hill, Andrea
Association of Specialized and Cooperative Library Agencies *(309)*

Hill, Annie
Communications Workers of America *(369)*

Hill, Candy S.
Catholic Charities USA *(345)*

Hill, Courtney
National Structured Settlements Trade Association *(797)*

Hill, Cynthia M.
National Collegiate Honors Council *(724)*

Hill, Dave
Associated Construction Distributors International *(235)*

Hill, Debbie
National Association of Professional Surplus Lines Offices, Ltd. *(688)*

Hill, Dennis
Association of Official Racing Chemists *(296)*

Hill, Edwin D.
International Brotherhood of Electrical Workers *(531)*

Hill, Eric
Enterprise Wireless Alliance *(429)*

Hill, Gary
National Association of Stock Plan Professionals *(703)*

Hill, Geoff
Aircraft Electronics Association *(20)*

Hill, Graham
National Coffee Association of the U.S.A. *(723)*

Hill, Jacqueline
InSight *(496)*

Hill, Jean
Society for Community Research and Action *(906)*

Hill, Johanna
Marine Corps League *(605)*

Hill, John
National On-Site Testing Association *(776)*

Hill, Dr. John
National Rural Education Association *(788)*

Hill, John
International Executive Association *(543)*

Hill, Julie
American Society of Consulting Arborists *(196)*
Association of Water Technologies *(317)*
Window Coverings Association of America *(1018)*

Hill, Katie
Spill Control Association of America *(958)*

Hill, Ken
Society for Human Ecology *(911)*

Hill, Laura
American College of Neuropsychopharmacology *(98)*

Hill, Laurie
Association of Progressive Rental Organizations *(303)*

Hill, Lee
Passenger Vessel Association *(839)*
Spill Control Association of America *(958)*

Hill, Linda
International Map Trade Association *(555)*

Hill, Lucille
American Advertising Federation *(43)*

Hill, Matt
Museum Education Roundtable *(621)*

Hill, Michael
United Cerebral Palsy *(986)*

Hill, Michelle
North American Society for Trenchless Technology *(822)*

Hill, Nancy
American Association of Advertising Agencies *(53)*

Hill, Nate
American Public Gas Association *(170)*

Hill, Penny
National Watercolor Society *(804)*

Hill, Richard B
American Society for Information Science and Technology *(186)*

Hill, Sanford J.
International Map Trade Association *(555)*

Hill, Steven
Satellite Broadcasting and Communications Association *(891)*

Hill, Tess
Electronics Representatives Association *(424)*

Hill, Tom
The Institute of Inspection, Cleaning and Restoration Certification *(500)*

Hill, Vickie L.
American Institute of Professional Geologists *(140)*

Hill, Wendy
National Society of Compliance Professionals *(793)*

Hilla, Elizabeth B
Health Industry Distributors Association *(469)*

Hilleary, Dan
United Fresh Produce Association *(987)*

Hiller, Larry
Potato Association of America *(854)*

Hiller, Paul M.
Orthopaedic Trauma Association *(834)*

Hilliard, Melanie
College of Healthcare Information Management Executives *(364)*

Hilliard, Ramona
Association of Rheumatology Health Professionals *(306)*

Hillier, Sian
American Society of Ophthalmic Registered Nurses *(205)*

Hilliker, Matthew
American Society for Pharmacology and Experimental Therapeutics *(188)*

Hillis, Sharon
Cleaning Management Institute *(357)*

Hillman, Allan
International Association of Airport Duty Free Stores *(515)*

Hillman, Jack
National Wood Tank Institute *(805)*

Hillman, Renee
Federation of Straight Chiropractors and Organizations *(442)*

Hillmuth, Billy
Service Station Dealers of America and Allied Trades *(898)*

Hillsman, Sally T.
American Sociological Association *(211)*

Hilmer, Kelly
Automatic Transmission Rebuilders Association *(321)*

Hilpert "Oelkers", Maddie
American Dental Hygienists' Association *(114)*

Hilsenroth, Robert
American Association of Zoo Veterinarians *(77)*

Hilser, Karin
Universities Space Research Association *(1002)*

Hilson, CAE, Amy C.
Association of State and Provincial Psychology Boards *(309)*

Hiltabidle, Beth

Association for Hose and Accessories Distribution **(248)**
Fluid Power Distributors Association **(448)**

Hilton, Cynthia
Institute of Makers of Explosives **(501)**

Hilton, Deanna
Academy of Dental Materials **(5)**

Hilton, Thomas
Academy of Dental Materials **(5)**

Hilvers, Anthony
IPC - Association Connecting Electronics Industries **(584)**

Himes, Christine
Society for the Study of Social Biology **(925)**

Himrod, CAE, CDM, CFPP, RD, Pam
Association of Nutrition & Foodservice Professionals **(296)**

Hinchcliffe, Bill
Truck-frame and Axle Repair Association **(981)**

Hinchman, James F.
National Research Council **(786)**

Hinchman, Joan
National Society of Compliance Professionals **(793)**

Hinchman, Theodore S.
National Counter Intelligence Corps Association **(740)**

Hinckley, CG, Kathleen W.
Association of Professional Genealogists **(301)**

Hinckley, Stewart A.
Society for Neuroscience in Anesthesiology and Critical Care **(916)**

Hinckley, CMP, Stewart A.
American College of Osteopathic Pediatricians **(100)**
American Osteopathic Academy of Orthopedics **(159)**
American Society of Extra-Corporeal Technology **(197)**

Hinde, John
International Biometric Society **(530)**

Hinds, Emma
Women in Aerospace **(1020)**

Hinds, W. Scott
National Association for Fixed Annuities **(639)**

Hine, Thompson
Tobacco Vapor Electronic Cigarette Association **(975)**

Hinen, CAE, IOM, CMP, Karen R.
Association of College and University Auditors **(274)**

Hines, Carrie
American Small Manufacturers' Coalition **(180)**

Hines, Debbie
Owner-Operator Independent Drivers Association, Inc. **(836)**

Hines, JoAnn R.
Women in Packaging **(1022)**

Hines, Susan
Design-Build Institute of America **(411)**

Hing, Sokhan
ASPRS-The Imaging and Geospatial Information Society **(233)**

Hingston-Oliver, Angela
Valve Manufacturers Association of America **(1007)**
Valve Repair Council **(1007)**

Hinkle, Bob
Institute for Briquetting and Agglomeration **(496)**

Hinkle, MS, Lisa
Association for Healthcare Volunteer Resource Professionals **(248)**

Hinners, John
United States Meat Export Federation **(996)**

Hinojosa, Amy
National Association of Hispanic Publications **(672)**

Hinrichs, Kimberly
World Council of Credit Unions, Inc. **(1026)**

Hinton, Jr., Henry (Butch) L.
Business Executives for National Security **(338)**

Hinton, Pam
Timber Frame Business Council **(974)**

Hinton, Skip
National Educational Telecommunications Association **(744)**

Hinton, Thomas
Customer Relations Institute Global, LLC **(406)**

Hipes, CMP, Charlene
Alliance of Information and Referral Systems **(25)**

Hipkins, Al
American Musicological Society **(154)**

Hipschman, David
National Association of Flight Instructors **(668)**

Hirn, Richard J.
National Weather Service Employees Organization **(804)**

Hirsch, Andrea S.
United States Tennis Association **(1000)**

Hirsch, Bob
Associated Builders and Contractors **(235)**

Hirsch, David G.
Middle East Librarians' Association **(615)**

Hirschbeck, John
The World Umpires Association **(1027)**

Hirschberg, Mike
AHS International - The Vertical Flight Society **(17)**

Hirschenfang, Gail P.
American Conference of Cantors **(107)**

Hirschfeld, Audrey R.
ICE Futures U.S. **(482)**

Hirschhaut, Jaclyn C.
American Home Furnishings Alliance **(132)**

Hirsh, Brooke
Optoelectronics Industry Development Association **(830)**

Hirsh, Stephanie
Learning Forward **(596)**

Hirst, Robert R.
International Bottled Water Association **(530)**

Hirt, James
American Society of Appraisers **(192)**

Hiscock, Bev
Select Registry/Distinguished Inns of North America **(896)**

Hissong, Candace
National Judges Association **(767)**

Hitchcock, Christina
Blinded Veterans Association **(332)**

Hitchcock, Reed
Hotel Electronic Distribution Network Association **(479)**

Hitchcock, Reed B.
Asphalt Roofing Manufacturers Association **(233)**
Roof Coatings Manufacturers Association **(888)**

Hitchen, Russell
Concrete Sawing and Drilling Association **(374)**

Hite, Carol
Association for Financial Counseling and Planning Education **(246)**

Hite, William P.
United Association of Journeymen and Apprentices of the Plumbing and Pipe Fitting Industry of the U.S. and Canada **(985)**

Hitt, Carrie Cullen
Solar Alliance **(951)**

Hitt, Julie
American Academy of Anesthesiologist Assistants **(30)**

Hitt, Perry
Association of Internal Management Consultants **(289)**

Hittle, Todd
American Business Media **(87)**

Hitz, C. Breck
Laser and Electro-Optics Manufacturers' Association **(593)**

Hitzig, Sara
Association for Psychological Science **(254)**

Hix, Bradley
American Society of Electroneurodiagnostic Technologists **(197)**

Hixon, Marion
Air Traffic Control Association **(19)**

Hixon, Tom
National Electrical Manufacturers Association **(744)**

Hixson, Roger
National Emergency Number Association **(745)**

Hjalmquist, Jennifer
Heavy Duty Manufacturers Association **(473)**

Hlavacek, Chelsea
National Association of Tower Erectors **(706)**

Hlibka, Nadia
Middle East Studies Association of North America **(615)**

Hnatiuk, CAE, EdD, RN, Cynthia R. Nowicki
Academy of Medical-Surgical Nurses **(7)**
American Academy of Ambulatory Care Nursing **(30)**

Ho, Peter
Association of Asian-Pacific Community Health Organizations **(268)**

Hoagland, CAE, SPHR, Michael P.
American Geophysical Union **(126)**

Hoal, Brian
Society of Economic Geologists **(934)**

Hoang, Linh
National Association of Workforce Development Professionals **(710)**

Hoang, Mai
United States-China Chamber of Commerce **(1001)**

Hoang, Trinh
The National Association for Music Education (Formerly MENC) **(641)**

Hoarle, CAE, MBA, Kimberly
American Society for Healthcare Risk Management **(185)**

Hoban, Rachel
Children's Book Council **(353)**

Hoban, Roseanne M.
National Association of Independent Public Finance Advisors **(675)**
Wire Fabricators Association **(1019)**

Hobart, Mary
American Radio Relay League **(172)**

Hobbie, PhD, Richard A.
National Association of State Workforce Agencies **(703)**

Hobbs, Aaron
RISE (Responsible Industry for a Sound Environment) **(886)**

Hobbs, David
American International Charolais Association *(142)*

Hobbs, Larry
International Society of Beverage Technologists *(571)*

Hobbs, Stephanie
Local Search Association (fka Yellow Pages
Association) *(600)*

Hobby, Karen
National Plasterers Council *(781)*

Hobby, Michelle
National Industries for the Blind *(763)*

Hoberman, Henry
Motion Picture Association of America (MPAA) *(619)*

Hoboy, CAE, MBA, Lance K.
Accreditation Board for Engineering and Technology
Inc. *(9)*

Hobson, Melissa
American Mental Health Counselors Association *(151)*

Hoch, Corinne
ACUTA - The Association for Information
Communications Technology Professionals in Higher
Education *(11)*

Hoch, Leo H.
American Council of Engineering Companies *(109)*

Hochberg, Tina
American College of Oral and Maxillofacial Surgeons
(99)
American Urogynecologic Society *(218)*

Hochgraf, Lisa
Credit Union Executives Society *(403)*

Hochstetler, Debbie
Religious Conference Management Association *(880)*

Hochstetler, Paula P.
Airport Consultants Council *(21)*

Hock, Charles
National Association of Independent Insurance
Auditors and Engineers *(674)*

Hockaday, Robin
Soil and Water Conservation Society *(951)*

Hockridge, Aleah
The Society for Modeling and Simulation International
(916)

Hodell, Jason
Association of Volleyball Professionals *(317)*

Hodes, CAE, Carol
National Institute of Governmental Purchasing *(765)*

Hodes, Joe
National Corn Growers Association *(730)*

Hodge, Beth
American Society of Nuclear Cardiology *(205)*

Hodge, Tracy
Incentive Marketing Association *(487)*

Hodgen, Rachael
National Association of Consumer Bankruptcy
Attorneys *(657)*

Hodges, Chiquita
American Society for Healthcare Engineering *(184)*

Hodges, Deborah
Leather Industries of America *(596)*

Hodges, Deborah J.
Construction Writers Association *(380)*

Hodges, James H.
Shelf-Stable Food Processors Association *(898)*

Hodges, Jeannie Shaughnessy
Peanut and Tree Nut Processors Association *(840)*

Hodges, Jeff

College Sports Information Directors of America *(364)*

Hodges, Joanne
National Council of Teachers of Mathematics *(737)*

Hodgson, Anya
United States Cutting Tool Institute *(993)*

Hodgson, Barbara
AAGL - Advancing Minimally Invasive Gynecology
Worldwide *(2)*

Hodgson, Cynthia
National Information Standards Organization *(763)*

Hodgson, CAE, Kristin
Clinical and Laboratory Standards Institute *(358)*

Hodgson, Lucy
Sculptors Guild *(894)*

Hodor, Elizabeth
National Student Osteopathic Medical Association
(797)

Hodson, PhD, Colleen
Dude Ranchers' Association *(417)*

Hoehling, Annaliese
Nonprofit Technology Network *(811)*

Hoehn, Michael
Case Management Society of America *(343)*

Hoehns Wright, Sylvia
National League of American Pen Women *(768)*

Hoekman, Anne
Academy of International Business *(5)*

Hoeksema, Mary Jo
Population Association of America *(853)*

Hoekstra, Nicole
American Boat Builders and Repairers Association *(84)*

Hoelter, Matt
The American Electrophoresis Society *(116)*

Hoelzel, Chris
Air Conditioning Contractors of America *(18)*

Hoenninger, PhD, A.R. "Dick"
International Association for Colon Hydrotherapy *(511)*

Hoey, MBA, RPh, B. Douglas
National Community Pharmacists Association *(725)*

Hofacker, BSN, MS, RN, Janie K.
Association of American Cancer Institutes *(264)*

Hofberger, Randy
American Association of Candy Technologists *(55)*

Hofelich, Andrea
National Pharmaceutical Council *(780)*

Hofer, Johannes P.
United States-Austrian Chamber of Commerce *(1001)*

Hofer, Scott Michael
Society of Multivariate Experimental Psychology *(942)*

Hoff, Brandon Van
Independent Bakers Association *(488)*

Hoff, Kelly
American Thyroid Association *(216)*

Hoff, LeAnn
National Conference of State Legislatures *(728)*

Hoff, Tammy
Academy of Pharmaceutical Research and Science *(8)*
American Pharmacists Association *(163)*

Hoffa, James P.
International Brotherhood of Teamsters *(532)*
International Brotherhood of Teamsters - Airline
Division *(532)*

Hoffer, Larry
Association of Science-Technology Centers *(307)*

Hoffert, Barbara
National Book Critics Circle *(716)*

Hoffman, Becki
Society of Experimental Test Pilots *(935)*

Hoffman, Bill
Object Management Group *(825)*

Hoffman, Candi
National Organization of Nurse Practitioner Faculties
(777)

Hoffman, Carrie
Association for Information Protection *(249)*
National Association for Surface Finishing *(643)*

Hoffman, Carrie L.
American Academy of Wound Management *(42)*

Hoffman, Chris
National Conference of State Fleet Administrators *(728)*

Hoffman, Chuck
Family, Career and Community Leaders of America
(437)

Hoffman, Colleen M.
Association of Consulting Foresters of America *(276)*

Hoffman, APM, Craig P.
American Society of Pension Professionals & Actuaries
(206)

Hoffman, Deborah
American Lung Association *(146)*

Hoffman, Dennis
Reliability Society *(880)*

Hoffman, MA, Donna
Society of University Otolaryngologists-Head and Neck
Surgeons *(949)*

Hoffman, Erin
Society for Physician Assistants in Pediatrics *(919)*

Hoffman, Jeff
American Society of Pension Professionals & Actuaries
(206)

Hoffman, Jena L.
International Ticketing Association *(577)*

Hoffman, Jennifer
Association of Social Work Boards *(309)*

Hoffman, John
GSM Association *(467)*

Hoffman, Karen
Training Officers Consortium *(977)*

Hoffman, Kathy J. Mapes
National Association of Surety Bond Producers *(704)*

Hoffman, Ken W.
Consumer Healthcare Products Association *(381)*

Hoffman, CPA, CMA, Kenneth L.
American Association of Nurse Anesthetists *(67)*

Hoffman, Kurt
Specialized Carriers and Rigging Association *(957)*

Hoffman, Dr. Lawrence M.
American Association of Dental Consultants *(59)*

Hoffman, MA, Miles
American College of Occupational and Environmental
Medicine *(99)*

Hoffman, J D, RN, Nancy
The American Association of Nurse Attorneys *(67)*

Hoffman, Nina
American Society of Hematology *(199)*

Hoffman, Robert
Information Technology Industry Council *(495)*

Hoffman, Steve
United States Soccer Federation *(999)*

Hoffman, Thomas
American College of Radiology *(102)*

Hoffman, III, William
American Society of Maxillofacial Surgeons *(202)*

Hoffman, Yossi
Rabbinical Assembly *(872)*

Hoffman-Kahl, Karen
Security Hardware Distributors Association *(895)*

Hoffmann, Claudette
National Kitchen and Bath Association *(767)*

Hoffmann, Heinz K.
Independent Professional Painting Contractors
Association of America *(491)*

Hoffmann, Lauren
National Recreation and Parks Association *(784)*

Hoffmann, Richard
Interstate Natural Gas Association of America *(583)*

Hoffner, Darin R.
UWC - Strategic Services on Unemployment and
Workers' Compensation *(1007)*

Hoffpauir, Elvis L.
Mobile Air Conditioning Society Worldwide *(617)*

Hofland, Andrew
American Montessori Society *(152)*

Hofland, MBA, Carla
American Montessori Society *(152)*

Hofman, Julie
American College of Occupational and Environmental
Medicine *(99)*

Hofmann, Angela Marshall
Organization of Women in International Trade *(832)*

Hofmann, Janice
Resilient Floor Covering Institute *(883)*

Hofmann, John
Society for Psychophysiological Research *(919)*
Society for Research on Nicotine and Tobacco *(920)*

Hofmann, Steven
Public Library Association *(869)*

Hogan, Christopher
International Bottled Water Association *(530)*

Hogan, Cyndy
National League of Cities *(768)*

Hogan, David
National Retail Federation *(786)*

Hogan, Kevin
Investment Program Association *(584)*

Hogan, PhD, M. Michele
American Association of Immunologists *(62)*

Hogan, Susan
American Fox Terrier Club *(123)*

Hogan, Wanda
National Association of Catastrophe Adjusters *(651)*

Hoggard, CAE, PAHM, Kerry B.
American Health Lawyers Association *(130)*

Hogle, Maureen Chinn
Association of State Dam Safety Officials *(310)*

Hogsett, Heather
National Governors Association *(755)*

Hohenhaus, MA, RN, Susan M.
Emergency Nurses Association *(425)*

Hohimer, Colette Iocca
Association of Bone and Joint Surgeons *(270)*

Hohler, Karen
Craft Retailers Association for Tomorrow *(403)*

Hohman, Tom
Cruise Lines International Association *(405)*

Hohman, MS, Violet
American Public Health Association *(171)*

Hoiberg, Paul
Society for Mining, Metallurgy and Exploration, Inc.
(915)

Hoil, Jennifer
Women in Aerospace *(1020)*

Hoke, Jared
American Academy of Child and Adolescent Psychiatry
(31)

Hoke, PhD, Mary
Association of Community Health Nursing Educators
(276)

Hokimi, K. Jai
SCORE Association *(893)*

Holaday, Gerald W.
American Poultry International Ltd. *(167)*

Holbus, Ed
Carwash Owner's and Supplier's Association *(343)*

Holcomb, Alison
Cancer Patient Education Network *(341)*
International Psycho-Oncology Society *(561)*

Holcomb, Beth
Architectural Woodwork Institute *(228)*

Holcomb, Rodney
Food Distribution Research Society *(449)*

Hold, CIC, CLU, CPU, PhD, William T.
Society of Certified Insurance Counselors *(932)*

Holden, Connie
International Function Point Users Group *(548)*

Holder, Carlyle I.
National Association of Blacks in Criminal Justice *(649)*

Holder, Charles
American Moving and Storage Association *(153)*

Holder, Gerard
Council of Large Public Housing Authorities *(395)*

Holder, Jeannette
Entertainment Software Association (ESA) *(429)*

Holder, Pat
Competitive Carriers Association *(371)*

Holder, Roy
National Band Association *(712)*

Holder, Sandra
American Society for Information Science and
Technology *(186)*

Holdt, Erin von
Independent Photo Imagers *(491)*

Holeman, Scott
National Association of Insurance Commissioners
(676)

Holen, Margo
American Congress of Rehabilitation Medicine *(107)*

Holguin, Julieta
LeadingAge (American Association of Homes and
Services for the Aging) *(595)*

Holizna, Kim
Organization of Women in International Trade *(832)*

Holl, Joyce
National Orientation Directors Association *(778)*

Holladay, Blair E.
American Society for Clinical Pathology *(182)*

Holland, Aileen
Modular Building Institute *(618)*

Holland, Danielle
Insured Retirement Institute *(505)*

Holland, Erica
Society of Interventional Radiology *(940)*

Holland, John J.
International Copper Association *(537)*

Holland, Julie
International Association of Eating Disorders
Professionals *(520)*

Holland, Kevin W.
Air Conditioning Contractors of America *(18)*

Holland, Kimberly T.
Professional Liability Underwriting Society *(863)*

Holland, Lisa
Community Action Partnership *(369)*

Holland, AIC, CPC, Michael M.
American Council for Construction Education *(109)*

Holland, CCM, AAP, Priscilla C.
NACHA - The Electronic Payments Association *(623)*

Holland, Renee
National Association of Realtors *(690)*

Holland, Rosemary
Association of International Education Administrators
(289)

Holland, Stuart
International Association of Audio Information Services
(516)

Hollander, Richard E.
Society of Industrial and Office Realtors *(939)*

Hollands, Bruce
Uni-Bell PVC Pipe Association *(984)*

Hollein, CTP, Marie N.
Financial Executives International *(444)*

Holler, Richard
Association of Shareware Professionals *(308)*

Holleyman, II, Robert W.
BSA | The Software Alliance *(337)*

Holliday, Barry
Dredging Contractors of America, Inc. *(416)*

Holliday, Evonne
National Bankers Association *(712)*

Holliday, Jenny
International Association of Diecutting and Diemaking
(519)

Holliday, Tyler
Internet Marketing Association *(582)*

Holliday, Wayne
American Society for Nondestructive Testing *(187)*

Holliday, Wendy
National Association of College Stores *(655)*

Hollingsworth, Carroll
Communications Marketing Association *(369)*

Hollingsworth, Karen
Communications Marketing Association *(369)*

Hollingsworth, Roger
Managed Funds Association *(602)*

Hollingsworth, Tracy
Manufacturers Alliance/MAPI Inc. *(603)*

Hollis, David
Public Radio Program Directors Association *(870)*

Hollis, Jim
Federation of Internet Solution Providers of the
Americas *(441)*

Hollis, Nicholas E.
Agribusiness Council *(16)*

Holloman, Bridget
National Motorsports Press Association *(773)*

Hollon, Bob
The Association for Science Teacher Education *(256)*

Holloway, Anne
American Wholesale Marketers Association *(221)*

Holloway, Robinson
Golf Writers Association of America *(463)*

Holly, Richard
National Association for the Education of Young Children *(644)*

Holman, James E.
National Blacksmiths and Weldors Association *(715)*

Holman, Stephen
Association of Private Sector Colleges and Universities (Career College Association) *(300)*

Holmbeck, Grayson
Society of Pediatric Psychology *(943)*

Holmberg, Martha
International Association of Culinary Professionals *(519)*

Holmes, Ann
Marine Engineers Beneficial Association *(605)*

Holmes, Bruce
National Association for the Education of Young Children *(644)*

Holmes, Dawn
Association of Family and Conciliation Courts *(282)*

Holmes, Dawn
Association of Family and Conciliation Courts *(282)*

Holmes, Devin
Business Executives for National Security *(338)*

Holmes, Jessica
Council on Social Work Education *(400)*

Holmes, Karen
Professional Services Council *(865)*

Holmes, Kristen
National Frozen Pizza Institute *(754)*

Holmes, Michele
Stage Directors and Choreographers Society *(960)*

Holmes, Rob
Travel Goods Association *(979)*

Holmes, Wanda
American Inns of Court *(135)*

Holmgren, Hoag
Professional and Organizational Development Network in Higher Education *(859)*

Holmsten, Linda
Association of State and Territorial Health Officials *(310)*

Holnes, Darrel Alejandro
Poetry Society of America *(851)*

Holsinger, Ann
Red Angus Association of America *(877)*

Holstein, Robert
American Institutes for Research *(141)*

Holston, Kelly
The Environmental Information Association *(431)*

Holt, Dorothy
Handweavers Guild of America, Inc. *(468)*

Holt, Jan
National Wooden Pallet and Container Association *(805)*

Holt, Joey
Lift Manufacturers Product Section - Material Handling Institute *(597)*

Material Handling Industry of America *(608)*

Holt, Lawrence J.
National Council of Self-Insurers *(736)*

Holt, Phillip
National Installment Lenders Association *(764)*

Holt, Dr. Rex D.
American Association of Food Hygiene Veterinarians *(61)*

Holt, Sid
American Society of Magazine Editors *(202)*

Holtmann, Peter
iNARTE, Inc. *(487)*

Holton, Ann K.
American Academy of Facial Plastic and Reconstructive Surgery *(34)*

Holtzapple, Dr. Elizabeth
National Association of Test Directors *(705)*

Holverstott, Cherie
American Society for Reproductive Medicine *(189)*

Holway, David J.
International Brotherhood of Correctional Officers *(531)*
International Brotherhood of Police Officers *(532)*
National Association of Government Employees *(670)*

Homa, Jessica
American Society for Biochemistry and Molecular Biology *(181)*

Homayounpour, Cyrus K.
University Professional & Continuing Education Association *(1003)*

Homer, Jennifer
American Society for Training and Development *(190)*

Hon, Brandon Chan Siew
Malaysian Rubber Export Promotion Council (USA) *(602)*

Hon, Teresa
Public Works Historical Society *(870)*

Honaker, PhD, Michael
American Psychological Association *(169)*

Honaman, John
National Athletic Trainers Association *(710)*

Hone, Mitchel
Women in Municipal Government *(1022)*

Honea, Garrett
Investment Adviser Association *(583)*

Honeycutt, Gina
National Correctional Industries Association *(730)*

Honeycutt, Kellie
ArtTable *(231)*

Honeycutt, CAE, Nancy R.
American Student Dental Association *(214)*

Hong, Betty
Physician Insurers Association of America *(847)*

Honigsberg, Catherine
Certified Contractors Network *(349)*

Honley, Steve
American Foreign Service Association *(122)*

Honour, Sandy
Technology Student Association *(970)*

Hood, Blair E
National Electrical Contractors Association *(744)*

Hood, CPA, Dave
American Society for Surgery of the Hand *(189)*

Hood, PhD, Linda
Association for Research in Otolaryngology *(255)*

Hood, Linda
American Auditory Society *(78)*

Hood, Melanie
National Ski Patrol System *(792)*

Hood, Phil
Percussion Marketing Council *(841)*

Hood, Rita J.
AGN International North America, Inc *(15)*

Hood, CWE, Shields
The Society of Wine Educators *(950)*

Hook III,, MD, Edward
American Sexually Transmitted Diseases Association *(178)*

Hooks, Norma R.
International Double Reed Society *(541)*

Hoolsema, Jason
American Society for Therapeutic Radiology and Oncology *(190)*

Hooper, David
Federation of State Medical Boards of the United States *(442)*

Hooper, Donna
American Academy of Estate Planning Attorneys *(33)*

Hooper, CMP, Kartraice D.
Environmental Design Research Association *(431)*

Hooper, Kenneth W.
National Electrical Manufacturers Representatives Association *(745)*

Hooper, Matt
College Swimming Coaches Association of America *(364)*

Hoover, Anne H.
American Health Lawyers Association *(130)*

Hoover, Bill
Walnut Council *(1012)*

Hoover, Carrie
National Association of Children's Hospitals and Related Institutions *(653)*

Hoover, Lisa
Association of College and University Printers *(274)*

Hoover, Mark
American Society of Radiologic Technologists *(208)*

Hope, Amy
American Association of Cereal Chemists International *(55)*
American Phytopathological Society *(165)*
Controlled Release Society *(383)*
International Society for Molecular Plant Microbe Interactions *(567)*
Master Brewers Association of the Americas *(607)*

Hope, Darrell L.
Directors Guild of America *(413)*

Hope, Elizabeth Liz
National Black MBA Association *(714)*

Hope, Patrick
American College of Cardiology *(93)*

Hope, Samuel
National Association of Schools of Art and Design *(693)*
National Association of Schools of Dance *(693)*
National Association of Schools of Music *(694)*
National Association of Schools of Theatre *(694)*

Hoper, Mark
Fabricators & Manufacturers Association, International *(437)*
Tube and Pipe Association, International *(981)*

Hopkins, Christy
Electronic Retailing Association *(423)*

Hopkins, D.J.

Literary Managers and Dramaturgs of the Americas **(599)**

Hopkins, Debra
Continental Dorset Club **(382)**

Hopkins, Don
Apiary Inspectors of America **(224)**

Hopkins, CMP, Jennifer
American Academy of Implant Dentistry **(35)**

Hopkins, Marian E.
Business Roundtable **(339)**

Hopkins, Mary
Business Technology Association **(340)**

Hopkins, Melanie
International Society for the Performing Arts **(569)**

Hopkins, Patricia
Independent Community Bankers of America **(488)**

Hopkins, Ramona
Professional Insurance Marketing Association **(862)**

Hopkins, Susan
Resistance Welding Manufacturing Alliance **(883)**

Hopkins, Tom
American Society of Pension Professionals & Actuaries **(206)**

Hopper, PhD, David L.
American Academy of Somnology **(42)**

Hopper, Jonathan
National Council on Education for the Ceramic Arts **(738)**

Hopper, Linda
National Association of Educational Office Professionals **(664)**

Hopper, Regina
America's Natural Gas Alliance **(29)**

Horan, CPA, Beth
American Council of Independent Laboratories **(109)**

Horan, Pam
Online Publishers Association, Inc. **(828)**

Horch-Prezioso, Tamara
American Society of Architectural Illustrators **(192)**

Hord, Suzanne
Competitive Carriers Association **(371)**

Horgan, Candace
National Ski Patrol System **(792)**

Horn, Andrew
Academy of Motion Picture Arts and Sciences **(7)**

Horn, Ashley
American Association of Clinical Endocrinologists **(56)**

Horn, Brian
Society of Financial Service Professionals **(936)**

Horn, Esther
Computer Assisted Language Instruction Consortium **(372)**

Horn, PE, Gregg L.
Ductile Iron Pipe Research Association **(417)**

Horn, Jeffrey A.
Building Owners and Managers Institute International **(337)**

Horn, Kerrie
Pipe Line Contractors Association **(849)**

Horn, Michael
The Philanthropy Roundtable **(846)**

Horn, Thomas W.
American Philatelic Society **(163)**

Horn, Vernon
American Historical Association **(131)**

Horn, Vernon
Historians of American Communism **(476)**

Hornback, Chris
National Association of Clean Water Agencies **(654)**

Hornberger, Nancy Gannon
Coalition for Juvenile Justice **(360)**

Horne, Janet
Council on Licensure, Enforcement and Regulation **(400)**

Horne, Scott J.
Institute of Scrap Recycling Industries, Inc. **(503)**

Horne-Lawlor, Anita
International Health, Racquet and Sportsclub Association **(549)**

Horner, Barbara
American Thoracic Society **(216)**

Horner, Cornelia
American Land Title Association **(144)**

Horner, Daniel
Arms Control Association **(229)**

Horner, Michael J.
National Association of Water Companies (NAWC) **(709)**

Horner, Robert
Illuminating Engineering Society of North America **(486)**

Horning, Alice
National Council of Writing Program Administrators **(738)**

Horning, Brian
National Association of Athletic Development Directors **(647)**
National Association of Collegiate Directors of Athletics **(656)**
National Association of Collegiate Marketing Administrators **(656)**

Hornsby, Renee
National Hardwood Lumber Association **(757)**

Hornstein (FIU), Joe
College Sports Information Directors of America **(364)**

Hornung, Susan
Association of Specialized and Cooperative Library Agencies **(309)**

Horowitz, Roger
Business History Conference **(339)**

Horowitz, Sara
Freelancers Union **(453)**

Horowitz, Sara
Association for Jewish Studies **(250)**

Horowitz, Stacey
Foster Family-Based Treatment Association **(452)**

Horowitz, Trish
Financial Services Forum **(445)**

Horsley, John C.
AASHTO: Transportation Center of Excellence **(2)**

Horsley, Laura
Building Owners and Managers Association International **(337)**

Horstman, Amy
Western History Association **(1015)**

Horstman, Pat
American Poultry Association **(167)**

Hortenstine, Jaysen
National Franchisee Association **(753)**

Hortert, Larry
Association of Technical and Supervisory Professionals **(313)**

Horton , Martha R.
International Society for Computerized Electrocardiology **(566)**

Horton, Elizabeth
CROPP Cooperative / Organic Valley **(405)**

Horton, Kim Gallagher
Association of Natural Bio-Control Producers **(295)**

Horton, Michelle
Ecological Society of America **(418)**

Horton, Paige (Purdum)
The Door and Hardware Institute **(416)**

Horton, Rose L.
Association of Women's Health, Obstetric and Neonatal Nurses **(318)**

Horton, Wayne
American Association of Community Colleges **(58)**

Horton-Parker, Radha
Association for Adult Development and Aging **(238)**

Horvath, Grace
CPAmerica International **(402)**

Horvath, Peter
Quality Chekd Dairies **(871)**

Horvath, R. Skip
Natural Gas Supply Association **(807)**

Horvath, Ralph E.
Natural Gas Supply Association **(807)**

Horvit, Mark
Investigative Reporters and Editors **(583)**

Horwitz, Howard J.
American College of Healthcare Executives **(96)**

Horwitz, Michele
American Association for Clinical Chemistry, Inc. **(48)**

Horwitz, Pamela S.
American Corn Growers Association **(108)**

Horzepa, Joseph "Joe"
Power Sources Manufacturers Association **(855)**

Horzepa, Judy
Power Sources Manufacturers Association **(855)**

Hoseney, R. Carl
American Association of Cereal Chemists International **(55)**

Hoskin, Patti
Health Care Compliance Association **(469)**

Hoskins, Angela
National Association of Pizzeria Operators **(685)**

Hoskins, Brent
Business Technology Association **(340)**

Hoskins, Harvey
National Association of Nonprofit Accountants & Consultants **(682)**

Hoskins, Kathy
Association of Investment Management Sales Executives **(289)**
National Association of Corporate Treasurers **(658)**

Hosler, DACBR, DC, Bryan K.
Council on Diagnostic Imaging to the A.C.A. **(399)**

Hoss, Robert J.
International Association for the Study of Dreams **(514)**

Hostetler, Dan
Association of Business Owners of America **(270)**

Houchins, Susan
American Society of Appraisers **(192)**

Hough, Clayton L.
International Dairy Foods Association **(539)**

Hough, Harry E.

American Purchasing Society *(172)*

Hough, Richard H.
American Purchasing Society *(172)*

Houghton, David
National Association of Pipe Fabricators *(684)*

Houghton, Lorraine
Association for Healthcare Foodservice *(248)*
Society for Foodservice Management *(909)*

Houk, Adriana
Association of Maternal and Child Health Programs
(AMCHP) *(293)*

Houk, Bob
Trade Promotion Management Associates *(977)*

Hould, Danielle
International Society for Pharmaceutical Engineering
(567)

Hourahan, PE, Glenn
Air Conditioning Contractors of America *(18)*

House, Chuck
Grain Elevator and Processing Society *(464)*

House, Tim
PCIA - The Wireless Infrastructure Association *(840)*

Houseman, Larry
International Guild of Candle Artisans *(549)*

Houser, Edward
American Catholic Philosophical Association *(88)*

Houser, Erica
Correctional Education Association *(386)*

Houser, Robert
Utility Workers Union of America *(1007)*

Houston, Betsy
Federation of Materials Societies *(441)*

Houston, Carol
American Osteopathic College of Radiology *(161)*

Houston, Ian M.
American Foreign Service Association *(122)*

Houston, Katherine
Institutional Life Markets Association *(504)*

Houston, Kenya
Association of the United States Navy, Inc. *(314)*

Hovde, Nia
International Festivals and Events Association *(545)*

Hovermale, David J.
American Oilseed Coalition *(157)*
National Oilseed Processors Association *(776)*

Hovey, Adrienne
Association of Pet Dog Trainers *(299)*

Hovis, Joanne
National Association of Telecommunications Officers
and Advisors *(705)*

Hovis, Jr., John H.
United Electrical Radio & Machine Workers of America
(986)

Howard, Anita
National Wood Flooring Association *(805)*

Howard, Bruce
National Federation of State High School Associations
(750)

Howard, Delores
National Science Teachers Association *(790)*

Howard, Elaine
Mortgage Bankers Association of America *(619)*

Howard, III, Eli P.
Sheet Metal and Air Conditioning Contractors'
National Association *(898)*

Howard, Gerald M.
Building Systems Councils of the National Association
of Home Builders *(338)*
Modular Building Systems Council *(618)*

Howard, Gerald "Jerry" M.
National Association of Home Builders *(673)*
Panelized Home Building Council *(837)*

Howard, Jessica
Professional Landcare Network *(863)*

Howard, Jim
IEEE Aerospace and Electronic Systems Society (AESS)
(483)

Howard, Karen
National Animal Supplement Council *(634)*

Howard, Kimberly A.
Association of Corporate Counsel *(277)*

Howard, CMP, Leslie N.
United Fresh Produce Association *(987)*

Howard, Marvin "Marv"
International Beverage Dispensing Equipment
Association *(529)*

Howard, Michael W.
Electric Power Research Institute *(421)*

Howard, Monique
National Association of Conservation Districts *(657)*

Howard, Muriel A.
American Association of State Colleges and
Universities *(73)*

Howard, Peter
American Classical League *(91)*

Howard, Robin
Council on Undergraduate Research *(401)*

Howard, Susie
Professional Beauty Association | National
Cosmetology Association *(861)*

Howard, Tracy
Wi-Fi Alliance *(1016)*

Howard, MBA, Vernice L.
Independent Electrical Contractors *(489)*

Howard-Hammack, Winnifred
The American Safe Deposit Association *(176)*

Howards, Stuart, S.
Society for Reproductive Endocrinology and Infertility
(920)

Howe, Brenda
American Society of Dermatopathology *(197)*
Association for Death Education and Counseling *(244)*

Howe, Caroline Van
Assistive Technology Industry Association *(234)*

Howe, Hassana
Parenteral Drug Association *(838)*

Howe, William H.
Association of Bituminous Contractors *(269)*

Howell, Amber
ATM Industry Association *(320)*

Howell, Clinton
Art and Antique Dealers League of America *(229)*

Howell, Jack
IEEE Communications Society *(483)*

Howell, Jane
American Society of Civil Engineers *(194)*

Howell, Jennifer
International Association for Impact Assessment *(513)*

Howell, Jill
InterNational Electrical Testing Association *(542)*

Howell, Kay

Propane Engine Fuel Committee/Propane Education
and Research Council *(867)*

Howell, Steve
American Institute of Aeronautics and Astronautics
(136)

Howell, Teri
Wilderness Medical Society *(1017)*

Howells-Tierney, Janet
Technology and Maintenance Council of American
Trucking Associations *(970)*

Howerton, Melissa
Association of Zoos and Aquariums *(318)*

Howes, Ken
American Association of State Troopers *(73)*

Howie, Allan
Loading Dock Equipment Manufacturers *(599)*

Howie, Allan M.
Industrial Metal Containers and Wire Decking Product
Section *(494)*
Institute of Caster and Wheel Manufacturers *(498)*

Howlett, Kip
Hardwood Plywood and Veneer Association *(468)*

Howlett, Thomas LPM
Marine Corps Reserve Association *(605)*

Hoyem, Martin
Society for the Anthropology of North America *(923)*

Hoyler, Maureen
Council for Opportunity in Education *(390)*

Hoyne, Donna
American College of Rheumatology *(102)*

Hoyne, Wendy
Lutheran Educational Conference of North America
(600)

Hoyt, MD, Dr. David B.
American College of Surgeons *(103)*

Hoyt, Peter W.
Path to Purchase Institute *(839)*

Hoyt, Rose
Life Insurers Council *(597)*

Hreben, Jill C.
United Methodist Association of Health and Welfare
Ministries *(987)*

Hritz, Gary
Federal Education Association *(439)*

Hromiak, Amy
Golf Course Builders Association of America *(463)*

Hronek, Jill
Institute of Nuclear Materials Management *(502)*

Hrubec, Rick
Appraisal Institute *(226)*

Hruska, Cindy
United States Dairy Export Council *(993)*

Hsiung, Jack
Society for the Advancement of Material and Process
Engineering *(922)*

Hsu, Pi-Lan
CPCU Society *(402)*

Huang, Alexander
Association for Asian Performance *(239)*

Huang, Frank
National Council for Accreditation of Teacher
Education *(731)*

Huang, Guangwei
Chinese American Food Society *(354)*

Huang, Jing
Construction Specifications Institute *(380)*

Huang, Yao-Wen
Chinese American Food Society *(354)*

Hubbard, April
American Subcontractors Association *(214)*

Hubbard, Christine
Progressive Gardening Trade Association *(866)*

Hubbard, Dan
National Business Aviation Association *(716)*

Hubbard, Darrin
Qualitative Research Consultants Association *(871)*

Hubbard, Dave
National Mobility Equipment Dealers Association *(773)*

Hubbard, Esq., Jr., Edward S.
Renewable Fuels Association *(881)*

Hubbard, Mike
National Council of Textile Organizations *(737)*

Hubbard, Steve
National Fellowship of Child Care Executives *(750)*

Hubbell, Tom
American Rental Association *(174)*

Huber, Amy
The American Society for Public Administration *(189)*

Huber, Cathy
Association for Healthcare Documentation Integrity *(247)*

Huber, Erin
Property Records Industry Association *(867)*

Huber, James R.
National Association of Chain Drug Stores *(652)*

Huber, Janet
International Society of Arboriculture *(571)*

Huber, Jen
Associated Builders and Contractors *(235)*

Huber, Patricia
Business Higher Education Forum *(339)*

Huber, Valerie
National Abstinence Education Association *(626)*

Huberman, Mark A.
International Association of Hygienic Physicians *(523)*

Hucker, Douglas K.
American Gem Trade Association *(125)*

Huckestein, Donna
National Association of State Head Injury Administrators *(701)*

Huckle, Vincent
American Society of Pension Professionals & Actuaries *(206)*

Huddleston, C. West
National Association of Drug Court Professionals *(663)*

Huddleston, Kearsten
Black Coaches & Administrators *(331)*

Hudelson, Wess
Copper and Brass Servicenter Association *(384)*
International Association of Plastics Distributors *(526)*

Hudgins, Christopher
International Sleep Products Association *(565)*

Hudgins, Michelle
National Education Association *(744)*

Hudlin, Warrington
Black Filmmaker Foundation *(331)*

Hudson, Carol
National Ski Patrol System *(792)*

Hudson, Dawn
Academy of Motion Picture Arts and Sciences *(7)*

Hudson, Don
International Physical Fitness Association *(560)*

Hudson, J. William (Bill)
International Association of Refrigerated Warehouses *(527)*

Hudson, J.William
Global Cold Chain Alliance *(462)*

Hudson, Jennifer
American Association of Physicists in Medicine *(69)*

Hudson, Joan
National Finance Adjusters *(750)*

Hudson, Lesley M.
American Spinal Injury Association *(212)*

Hudson, Lori
National Real Estate Investors Association *(784)*

Hudson, Marianne
Angel Capital Association *(223)*

Hudson, Matt
Society of Professional Rope Access Technicians *(945)*

Hudson, Sandy
NAIOP, The Commercial Real Estate Development Association *(366)*

Hudson, Scott
Federal Probation and Pre-trial Officers Association *(440)*

Hudson, Scott
International Brotherhood of Electrical Workers *(531)*

Hudson, Sharon L.
Accreditation Council for Pharmacy Education *(10)*

Hudson, Tom
National Automotive Finance Association *(711)*

Hudson, Tricia
COLA *(362)*

Hudson-Matuszak, Ellie
Specialty Coffee Association of America *(957)*

Huenecke, Art
IPC - Surface Mount Equipment Manufacturers Association *(585)*
IPC Washington Office *(585)*

Huether, David
US Travel Association *(983)*

Huey, Erik V.
Entertainment Software Association (ESA) *(429)*

Huff, Charlie
International Association of Milk Control Agencies *(524)*

Huff, Elizabeth
Appraisers Association of America *(226)*

Huff, Jim
Health and Sciences Communications Association *(469)*

Huff, Robert
American Water Works Association *(220)*

Huffaker, Lucinda
Religious Education Association *(880)*

Huffhines, Craig
American Hereford Association *(131)*

Huffman, Wes
Coalition of Higher Education Assistance Organizations *(360)*

Hufford, Steve
Society for Information Management *(913)*

Huffy, Morgan
International Society of Arthroscopy, Knee Surgery and Orthopaedic Sports Medicine *(571)*

Hugelmeyer, Frank

Outdoor Industry Association *(835)*

Huget, Laurie
Cryogenic Society of America *(405)*

Huggins, Jim
Solar Rating and Certification Corporation *(952)*

Huggins, Paige
Industrial Minerals Association -- North America *(494)*
National Industrial Sand Association *(763)*

Huggins, PE, Roland
American Fire Sprinkler Association *(121)*

Hughes, Carolyn
American Bladesmith Society *(81)*

Hughes, Colleen
Computing Technology Industry Association (CompTIA) *(373)*

Hughes, Elizabeth
Underwater Society of America *(984)*

Hughes, Gary E.
American Council of Life Insurers (ACLI) *(110)*

Hughes, J. Trevor
International Association of Privacy Professionals *(526)*

Hughes, Jeffrey R.
GAMA International *(455)*

Hughes, Jessica
International Dairy-Deli-Bakery Association *(540)*

Hughes, John P.
Electricity Consumers Resource Council (ELCON) *(422)*

Hughes, Joseph E.M.
Shipowners Claims Bureau, Inc. *(899)*

Hughes, Julia K.
United States Association of Importers of Textiles and Apparel *(990)*

Hughes, Kathleen Marie
American Library Association *(145)*
Public Library Association *(869)*

Hughes, Ken
American Rental Association *(174)*

Hughes, PE, Mark
International Concrete Repair Institute *(536)*

Hughes, Mary
Fluid Fertilizer Foundation *(448)*

Hughes, Michael
Institute of Industrial Engineers *(500)*

Hughes, Esq., Michael J.
American Artists Professional League *(47)*

Hughes, Mike
National Golf Course Owners Association *(755)*

Hughes, APR, Nancy
National Health Council *(758)*

Hughes, Paula
American Dairy Goat Association *(112)*

Hughes, Sandy
HR Policy Association *(480)*

Hughes, MSN, RN, Suzanne
Preventive Cardiovascular Nurses Association *(857)*

Hughes, Thomas
Strategic Marketplace Initiative *(963)*

Hughes, Dr. Vicki L.
National Optometric Association *(776)*

Hughley, Corey
Association of State and Territorial Health Officials *(310)*

Huheey, CAE, Cynthia
Interim Ministry Network *(508)*

Huisken, Duane
International Association of Plumbing and Mechanical
Officials *(526)*

Huisken, Duane
Radiant Panel Association *(872)*

Hulbert, Terence
American Institute of Physics *(140)*

Huleatt, Bill
Child Care Aware of America *(353)*

Hulett, Karla
American Trucking Associations *(218)*

Hull, Angela M.
American Education Finance Association *(116)*

Hull, Donna M.
American Society of Agricultural and Biological
Engineers *(191)*

Hull, Jennifer
American Association for Pediatric Ophthalmology and
Strabismus *(50)*

Hull, Kate
National Conference of Executives of The ARC *(727)*

Hull, Kathleen
Law and Society Association *(594)*

Hull, Richard T.
Text and Academic Authors Association *(972)*

Huls, Carol
The Corps Network (formerly the National Association
of Service and Conservation Corps) *(386)*

Hult, G. Tomas M.
Academy of International Business *(5)*

Hultman, CAE, Alberta E.
USFN-America's Mortgage Banking Attorneys *(1006)*

Hultman, C. Scott
Association of Academic Chairmen of Plastic Surgery
(262)

Hultz, Gloria
North American Association of Wardens and
Superintendents *(814)*

Hume, Barbara
Insured Retirement Institute *(505)*

Humes, Paul
National Ground Water Association *(756)*

Humfeld, CAE, Terry
Cranberry Institute *(403)*

Hummel, Captain Gary
U. S. Airline Pilots Association *(983)*

Hummel, Mary Ellen
American Hereford Association *(131)*

Hummel, Michelle
Agricultural Retailers Association *(16)*

Hummer, Anne
Society for Conservation Biology *(906)*

Hummer, Clayton
National Association of Air Medical Communication
Specialists *(646)*

Hummert, Josie
North American Association of Educational
Negotiators *(813)*

Humphrey, Beth
College and University Professional Association for
Human Resources *(362)*

Humphrey, Cliff
National Rural Electric Cooperative Association *(788)*

Humphrey, Liz
National Organization of Black County Officials *(777)*

Humphrey, Mindy

Council of American Jewish Museums *(391)*

Humphrey, Tyler
American Chianina Association *(90)*

Humphreys, Brian
National Association of Children's Hospitals and
Related Institutions *(653)*

Humphreys, Debbie
American Business Media *(87)*

Humphreys, Dr. Debra
Association of American Colleges and Universities
(264)

Humphreys, Kenneth K.
FutureGen Industrial Alliance, Inc. *(455)*

Hundley, Matthew
Association for Women in Mathematics *(261)*

Hune, Jackie
NACE International *(623)*

Huney, Kathy
Mobile Air Conditioning Society Worldwide *(617)*

Hung, John
Industrial Electronics Society *(493)*

Hungiville, Beth L.
Marine Fabricators Association *(605)*

Hunnicutt, PhD, David M.
Wellness Councils of America *(1015)*

Hunsche, Caspar
Supply Chain Council *(966)*

Hunsucker, Christy
American Mathematical Association of Two Year
Colleges *(147)*

Hunt, Amy
Selected Independent Funeral Homes *(896)*

Hunt, Esq., Carrie
National Association of Federal Credit Unions *(667)*

Hunt, Christopher
Educational Theatre Association *(420)*

Hunt, Christopher
Infusion Nurses Society *(496)*

Hunt, David
Family, Career and Community Leaders of America
(437)

Hunt, CAE, Elizabeth K.
Basic Acrylic Monomer Manufacturers *(326)*

Hunt, CAE, Elizabeth "Betty"
Methacrylate Producers Association *(614)*

Hunt, Geoff
American Society for Biochemistry and Molecular
Biology *(181)*

Hunt, Jayne Ellen
Consumer Bankers Association *(380)*

Hunt, MD, John R.
Flying Physicians Association *(448)*

Hunt, Mercedes
The International Ecotourism Society *(542)*

Hunt, DO, FACOP, CMP, Michael
American College of Osteopathic Pediatricians *(100)*

Hunt, Richard
Consumer Bankers Association *(380)*

Hunt, Scott
The Endocrine Society *(427)*

Hunt, Tonya
Alliance for Responsible Atmospheric Policy *(23)*

Hunt Batjer, MD, H.
Neurosurgical Society of America *(809)*

Hunt,, AAC, Barry
American Academy of Anesthesiologist Assistants *(30)*

Hunter, Cecilia A.
American Association of Physicists in Medicine *(69)*

Hunter, Cheryl
American Academy of Forensic Sciences *(34)*

Hunter, Chris
College Savings Plans Network *(364)*

Hunter, Claudia
National Precast Concrete Association *(782)*

Hunter, David
International Emissions Trading Association *(542)*

Hunter, G. William
National Basketball Players Association *(713)*

Hunter, Garry E.
World Jurist Association *(1027)*

Hunter, Joan
Institute on Religion in an Age of Science *(504)*

Hunter, MD, John G.
Society for Surgery of the Alimentary Tract *(921)*

Hunter, Kathleen
Association of National Advertisers *(295)*

Hunter, Kirk
The Lawn Institute *(594)*
Turfgrass Producers International *(982)*

Hunter, Leah R.
International Licensing Industry Merchandisers'
Association *(554)*

Hunter, CMP, Rebecca
American Association of Tissue Banks *(75)*

Hunter, Scott
International Association Of Pet Cemeteries and
Crematories *(526)*

Hunter, Valerie
Cardiovascular Credentialing International *(342)*

Huntington, Suzanne
Costume Designers Guild *(387)*

Huntley, Jery Y.
Vinyl Siding Institute, Inc. *(1009)*

Huot, Andrew
Guild of Book Workers *(467)*

Hupp, Bill
Delta Dental Plans Association *(409)*

Hurd, Carly
American Institute of Steel Construction *(140)*

Hurd, Earl F.
Operative Plasterers and Cement Masons International
Association of the United States and Canada *(829)*

Hurdle, Delicia
American Bearing Manufacturers Association *(80)*
Institute for Credentialing Excellence *(497)*
National Association of County Community and
Economic Development *(637)*

Hurey, III, Howard L.
American Inns of Court *(135)*

Hurlbut, Millie
Association of the United States Army *(313)*

Hurlbutt, Lorraine
Joint Electron Device Engineering Council *(589)*

Hurley, Ellie
Clinical Laboratory Management Association *(358)*
Financial & Insurance Conference Planners *(444)*

Hurley, MA, Karen A.
Society for Obstetric Anesthesia and Perinatology *(917)*

Hurley, Kevin
Healthcare Supply Chain Association *(472)*

The Association of International Photography Art Dealers *(289)*

Hurley, Kimberly
Air Conditioning Contractors of America *(18)*

Hurley, PE, Morgan J.
Society of Fire Protection Engineers *(936)*

Hurns, Diane
American Society of Safety Engineers *(209)*

Hurocy, Jerry
International Chemical Workers Union Council/UFCW *(534)*

Hursh, Shannon
American Academy of Health Care Providers-Addictive Disorders *(34)*

Hurson, John A.
Personal Care Products Council *(842)*

Hurst, Edward A.
Sigma Phi Delta *(899)*

Hurst, Elizabeth
Natural Products Association *(807)*

Hurst, Julia
National Lieutenant Governors Association *(769)*

Hurst, Mark
National Institute of Pension Administrators *(765)*

Hurst, Robin
Human Anatomy and Physiology Society *(480)*

Hurston, Patrick
Chlorine Chemistry Council *(354)*

Hurt, Billie
Forging Industry Association *(452)*

Hurt, Carrie A.
Council of Better Business Bureaus *(392)*

Hurt, Frank
Bakery, Confectionery, Tobacco Workers and Grain Millers International Union *(325)*

Hurter, Bill
Wedding and Portrait Photographers International *(1014)*

Hurtgen, Nancy
BioCommunications Association *(329)*

Hurtt, Erica
The Clearing House Association *(357)*

Hurula, Barbara
Federation of Environmental Technologists, Inc. *(441)*

Hurwit, Nick
American College of Foot & Ankle Orthopedics & Medicine *(95)*

Hurwitz, Janet
Clinical Ligand Assay Society *(358)*

Hurwitz, Lissa
Brain Injury Association of America *(334)*

Huschka, Denis
International Society for Quality-of-Life Studies *(569)*

Huse, Brian
Robotic Industries Association *(887)*

Huseman, Wenda
National Ski Area Association *(791)*

Huskey, Julia
Online Audiovisual Catalogers *(827)*

Huskey, Samuel J.
American Philological Association *(163)*

Huson, Julie
International Association of Outsourcing Professionals *(525)*

Huss, Claudia

Huss, Matthew
American Psychology-Law Society *(170)*

Hussey, Patricia
Consolidated Tape Association *(378)*

Hustick, Jr., Gerald
National Organization of Industrial Trade Unions *(777)*

Huston, Andy
North - American Interfraternity Conference *(812)*

Huston, Melissa
American Society for Bone and Mineral Research *(181)*
Bank Insurance and Securities Association *(326)*
Institute for Credentialing Excellence *(497)*

Hutcherson, Christine
Environmental Industry Associations *(431)*
National Solid Wastes Management Association *(795)*
Waste Equipment Technology Association *(1012)*

Hutcherson, Victor
Society for Applied Spectroscopy *(904)*

Hutcheson, Susanna K.
Copywriters Council of America *(385)*

Hutchings, Carol
High Technology Crime Investigation Association *(474)*

Hutchins, Donna
North American Die Casting Association *(816)*

Hutchins, Jonathan
National Association of Local Housing Finance Agencies *(678)*

Hutchins, Michael
The Wildlife Society *(1017)*

Hutchinson, Alexxis
Central Intercollegiate Athletic Association *(349)*

Hutchinson, Kim J.
Association of Global Automakers *(285)*

Hutchinson, Mindy
National Press Photographers Association *(782)*

Hutchinson, Robert
Wireless Industry Association *(1019)*

Hutchinson, Roy S.
North American Maple Syrup Council *(818)*

Hutchinson, Suzanne C.
Mortgage Insurance Companies of America *(619)*

Hutchinson, Ted
American Society of Law, Medicine and Ethics *(202)*

Hutchison, Barbara
Student Youth and Travel Association *(964)*

Hutchison, Jeannie
Association of Progressive Rental Organizations *(303)*

Hutchison, Johannah
International Sculpture Center *(564)*

Hutchison, Karen
International Society of Weighing and Measurement *(574)*

Hutchison, CAE, Karen
Society for Historical Archaeology *(911)*

Hutchison, Roy
International Maple Syrup Institute *(555)*

Hutt, Katherine R.
Council of Better Business Bureaus *(392)*

Hutton, Greg
United States Club Soccer *(992)*

Hutton, Steve
National Association of Plant Patent Owners *(685)*

Hutton, Terrence

Pressure Sensitive Tape Council *(856)*

Hutya, Mary
Recreation Vehicle Industry Association *(877)*

Huver, Lois
Select Registry/Distinguished Inns of North America *(896)*

Huynh, Janet
American Association of Sexuality Educators, Counselors and Therapists *(73)*

Hvidhyld, Patti
Surface Mount Technology Association *(966)*

Hvidston, Patricia
Catholic Charities USA *(345)*

Hwang, Ronnie
NPTA Alliance *(824)*

Hwong, Henry
Air Conditioning, Heating and Refrigeration Institute (AHRI) *(18)*

Hyatt, David F.
National Automobile Dealers Association *(711)*

Hyatt, Janet
National Association of School Resource Officers *(693)*

Hyde, Barbara
American Society for Microbiology *(187)*

Hyde, Judy
Mohair Council of America *(618)*

Hydo, Lynn
Surgical Infection Society *(967)*

Hyers, Suzanne
Association of American Colleges and Universities *(264)*

Hyett, Becky
National Hereford Hog Record Association *(759)*

Hyink, Ron
National Precast Concrete Association *(782)*

Hyland, Carl
Council for Responsible Nutrition *(391)*

Hyland, Duane
American Institute of Aeronautics and Astronautics *(136)*

Hyland, PE, Michael
American Public Power Association *(171)*

Hyman, Alex
National Association of School Psychologists *(693)*

Hyman, Deborah
National Black Public Relations Society *(715)*

Hyman, Marc
Association for the Advancement of Baltic Studies *(258)*

Hymans, LCSW, Dwight
Association of Social Work Boards *(309)*

Hymes, Kimberly
Council for Exceptional Children *(390)*

Hysaw, Guillermo L.
National Association of Black Accountants, Inc. *(648)*

Hyslop, Carol
Academy of Applied Science *(4)*

Hyun, Rhee Soo
Behavior Genetics Association *(327)*

Iacino, Dawn
International Association of Fire Fighters *(521)*

Iacuzzi, Judith Q.
U.S.A. Toy Library Association *(983)*

Ian, MBA, Jennifer A.
American Thoracic Society *(216)*

Iannone, Gail
American Radio Relay League *(172)*

Iannuzzi, John Nicholas
Lipizzan Association of North America *(599)*

Iantorno, Fred
Collision Industry Electronic Commerce Association *(365)*

Iasiello, Angelo
American Institute of Aeronautics and Astronautics *(136)*

Iasiello, Mark
Heavy Duty Brake Manufacturers Council *(473)*

Ibach, Greg
National Association of Agricultural Fair Agencies *(646)*

Ibarra, Armelinda
American Brahman Breeders Association *(85)*

Iciek, Brian
National Academy of Opticianry *(628)*

Ickert-Bond, Steffi
American Society of Plant Taxonomists *(207)*

Ickes-Jefferson, Julie
College of Optometrists in Vision Development *(364)*

Ickowicz, Elvy
American Geriatrics Society *(126)*

Idem, Scott
American Astronomical Society *(77)*

Idleman, Shirley
American Dental Assistants Association *(113)*

Ienna, Jack
InterAmerican College of Physicians and Surgeons *(507)*

Ifft, Desiree
Association of Schools and Colleges of Optometry *(307)*

Ignagni, CAE, Karen M.
America's Health Insurance Plans *(28)*

Ignatiev, Tina
American Therapeutic Recreation Association *(216)*

Ignatz, Kerry
Academy of Management *(6)*

Igoe, Kim
American Association of Museums *(65)*

Ihde, Tom
American Institute of Fishery Research Biologists *(138)*

Ikemire, Heather
National Guild for Community Arts Education *(757)*

Ilozor, Doreen
Association for Asian Studies *(239)*

Imbert, Bev
American Luggage Dealers Association *(146)*

Imes, CCHt., Katin B.
American Association of Professional Hypnotherapists *(71)*

Imran, Kashif
Association for Institutional Research *(250)*

Inaba, Megan
National Basketball Players Association *(713)*

Inchauteguiz, Peter
American Association of Pharmaceutical Scientists *(68)*

Indence, John
National Hemophilia Foundation *(759)*

Inderbitzen, Bob
American Radio Relay League *(172)*

Ingemie, David J.

SnowSports Industries America *(902)*

Ingenito, Victoria L.
Care Continuum Alliance *(342)*

Ingle, Gary L.
Music Teachers National Association *(622)*

Inglesby, Beverly
Professional Lighting and Sound Association *(863)*

Ingley, Kathryn P.
International Association of Electrical Inspectors *(520)*

Ingley, Stephen J.
Airborne Law Enforcement Association *(19)*

Inglis, Brian
Society of Independent Gasoline Marketers of America (SIGMA) *(939)*

Inglis, Joan
International Association of Home Staging Professionals *(522)*

Ingoglia, Charles
National Council for Community Behavioral Healthcare *(731)*

Ingraham, Peggy
Meals on Wheels Association of America *(609)*

Ingram, Allison
National Society of Accountants *(793)*

Ingram, Charles W.
National Association of State Departments of Agriculture *(699)*

Ingram, Charlie
National Association of Agricultural Fair Agencies *(646)*

Ingram, Daniel
United States Dairy Export Council *(993)*

Ingram, Douglas H.
American Academy of Psychoanalysis and Dynamic Psychiatry *(41)*

Ingram, CCC-SLP, MA, Kellie E.
National Black Association for Speech, Language and Hearing *(714)*

Ingram, Kwana
American Translators Association *(217)*

Ingram, Marc
Community Associations Institute (CAI) *(370)*

Ingram, Margaret
Zonta International *(1030)*

Ingram, Steve
Vacation Rental Managers Association *(1007)*

Ingram, Tom
Diving Equipment and Marketing Association *(415)*

Ingram, Tracey
Association of Industrial Metallizers, Coaters and Laminators *(288)*
Converting Equipment Manufacturers Association *(383)*

Ingrams, Alex
Society for the Psychological Study of Science Issues *(924)*

Ingrassia, CAE, Phil
Recreation Vehicle Dealers Association of North America *(876)*
Recreation Vehicle Rental Association *(877)*

Ingrum, Bob
Men of Reform Judaism *(612)*

Ingwersen, Jim
Wilderness Medical Society *(1017)*

Inman, Kathleen
Beta Phi Mu *(328)*

Inman, Suzi
Federally Employed Women (FEW) *(440)*

Inniss, Yvonne
Council for Resource Development *(391)*

Inoue, Atsushi
North American Fuzzy Information Processing Society *(817)*

Intorre, Ben
American Musicians Union *(154)*

Iocco, Stephanie
Society for Applied Spectroscopy *(904)*

Iovino, Molly
Quality Chekd Daries *(871)*

Ireland, CAE, Evelyn F.
National Association of Dental Plans *(662)*

Ireland, Michael
ASME International Gas Turbine Institute *(233)*

Irish, Kelsey
Council for Adult and Experiential Learning *(388)*

Irish, Sean
Association of Surgical Technologists *(312)*

Irizarry, Myra Y.
Professional Beauty Association | National Cosmetology Association *(861)*

Irlbeck, Alicia
National Pork Producers Association *(781)*
National Pork Producers Council *(781)*

Ironfield, Susan B.
Mortgage Insurance Companies of America *(619)*

Irtenkauf, Erin
Society of Quality Assurance *(946)*

Irvine, James
Vehicular Technology Society *(1008)*

Irvine, CMRS, CPC, Melody S.
American Academy of Professional Coders *(40)*

Irving, Diane
American Wind Energy Association (AWEA) *(221)*

Irwin, April-Marie
National Telecommunications Cooperative Association *(799)*

Irwin, MD, Michael R
American Psychosomatic Society *(170)*

Irwin, Steve
National Reverse Mortgage Lenders Association *(787)*

Isaac, Katherine
American Association of University Professors *(75)*

Isaac, Steven
Charles Homer Haskins Society *(351)*

Isaacs, Caliene
OpenTravel Alliance *(828)*

Isaacs, David
Semiconductor Industry Association *(897)*

Isaacs, Leora
Jewish Education Service of North America *(588)*

Isaacs, CAE, Marla
Association of Nutrition & Foodservice Professionals *(296)*

Isaacson, Walter
Society of American Historians *(929)*

Isaak, Flash
Composite Panel Association *(372)*

Isard, Susan
Petroleum Marketers Association of America *(843)*

Isayama, Maki
Copper Development Association *(384)*

Isberg, Pete
National Payroll Reporting Consortium *(780)*

Ischiropoulos, PhD, Harry
Society for Free Radical Biology and Medicine *(909)*

Isenschmid, DABFT, PhD, Daniel S.
The International Association of Forensic Toxicologists *(522)*

Isham, Jennifer
Tree Care Industry Association *(980)*

Ishee, Angie
American Association of State Troopers *(73)*

Ishikawa, Yoshiyuki
International Double Reed Society *(541)*

Iskowitz, Candace
Institute for Business & Home Safety *(496)*

Isler, Elaine Dickey
Government Management Information Sciences *(464)*

Isley, Victoria
Destination Marketing Association International *(411)*

Israel, Lillian
Association for Computing Machinery *(243)*

Israel, Nehmesah
The Environmental Information Association *(431)*

Israel, Robert
Ethics and Compliance Officer Association *(433)*

Israelite, David M.
National Music Publishers Association *(774)*

Israelsen, Loren D.
United Natural Products Alliance *(988)*

Issing, David A.
Association of Independent Research Institutes *(288)*

Itow, Candace
American Guild of Musical Artists *(127)*

Iturralde, Elsie
National Association of the Remodeling Industry *(705)*

Iuculano, Russel
North American Securities Administrators Association (NASAA) *(820)*

Iuliano, Matt F.
The Jockey Club *(588)*

Ivanauski, Beverly
Catholic Cemetery Conference *(345)*

Ivanova, Rossana
Regional Plan Association *(879)*

Iverson, Corene
National Association of Tower Erectors *(706)*

Ives, Bill
Ceramic Tile Distributors Association *(349)*

Ives, Ralph
Advanced Medical Technology Association (AdvaMed) *(13)*

Ives, William C.
Association of Rotational Molders International *(306)*
Bearing Specialist Association *(327)*
North American Fiberboard Association *(816)*

Ivester, PhD, Robert W.
North American Manufacturing Research Institution of SME *(817)*

Ivey, Annette
Association of Clean Water Administrators *(273)*

Ivey, Rick
National Cutting Horse Association *(741)*

Ivey, W. Marion
Cleaning Management Institute *(357)*

Ivicevic, Tom
Aerobics and Fitness Association of America *(13)*

Ivie, George W.

Media Rating Council *(610)*

Ivory, Shanda Thomas
National Association for College Admission Counseling *(637)*

Ivy, Jennifer
Self-Insurance Institute of America, Inc. *(896)*

Ivy, Jermaine
National Alliance of State and Territorial AIDS Directors *(633)*

Ivy, Joanne C.
American Egg Board *(116)*

Ivy, Robert
The American Institute of Architects *(137)*

Iwanski, Veronica
Turfgrass Producers International *(982)*

Iyengar, Malini
Caucus for Women in Statistics *(346)*

Izaguirre, Terry
Association for Clinical Pastoral Education *(241)*

Izquierdo, Jorge
Packaging Machinery Manufacturers Institute *(836)*

Izzi, Cathy
Plasma Protein Therapeutics Association *(850)*

Izzo, Laura
Wood Machinery Manufacturers of America *(1024)*

Jablonski, Karol
Delta Waterfowl Foundation *(409)*

Jachnicki, Bob
National Insurance Crime Bureau *(766)*

Jacinto, Julie
Office Business Center Association International *(826)*

Jackman, Frank
Flight Safety Foundation *(448)*

Jackman, Jay
National Association of Supervisors of Agricultural Education *(704)*

Jackman, CAE, PhD, William Jay
National Association of Agricultural Educators *(646)*

Jackobson, Carlotta
Cosmetic Executive Women *(387)*

Jackson, Alisa
The Association of Black Psychologists *(270)*

Jackson, Andrew
International Regional Magazine Association *(562)*

Jackson, Andrew
Society for Information Management *(913)*

Jackson, Ann Stephens
International Atherosclerosis Society *(529)*

Jackson, Ashley
American Association for Homecare *(50)*

Jackson, Benjamin
ICE Futures U.S. *(482)*

Jackson, Candace
Association of Collegiate Business Schools and Programs *(275)*

Jackson, Carol
Ice Skating Institute *(482)*

Jackson, CFCS, Carolyn W.
American Association of Family and Consumer Sciences *(61)*

Jackson, Cheryl
LeadingAge (American Association of Homes and Services for the Aging) *(595)*

Jackson, Dayna

National Frozen and Refrigerated Foods Association *(753)*

Jackson, Debby
Transportation Development Association *(978)*

Jackson, Gayle
Surface Mount Technology Association *(966)*

Jackson, Gwen
TAUC - The Association of Union Constructors *(968)*

Jackson, CPA, Henry G.
Society for Human Resource Management *(911)*

Jackson, Holley
American Association of Suicidology *(74)*

Jackson, Jennifer
Cotton Council International *(387)*

Jackson, Jennifer
National Association of Educational Office Professionals *(664)*

Jackson, Jennifer L.
National Association of Student Financial Aid Administrators *(703)*

Jackson, CMP, Jill
National Association of Dental Laboratories *(662)*

Jackson, Jody
American Warmblood Registry *(219)*

Jackson, John "Jack"
Catholic Charities USA *(345)*

Jackson, Jonathan
Alliance for Energy and Economic Growth *(23)*

Jackson, CAE, Joseph M.
American Academy of Esthetic Dentistry *(33)*
American Prosthodontic Society *(168)*
International Society of Appraisers *(570)*

Jackson, Keya
Council of Federal Home Loan Banks *(393)*

Jackson, Kristine
Touchstone Energy Cooperatives *(976)*

Jackson, Liz
American Walnut Manufacturers Association *(219)*

Jackson, Liz
Walnut Council *(1012)*

Jackson, Marcella
Federation of American Societies for Experimental Biology *(440)*

Jackson, Marth
Clinical Ligand Assay Society *(358)*

Jackson, III, Maxie C.
National Federation of Community Broadcasters *(748)*

Jackson, Melinda
International Society of Political Psychology *(573)*

Jackson, Melissa
Water Environment Federation *(1013)*

Jackson, Michel
International Sign Association *(564)*

Jackson, Mike
Napa Valley Vintners Association *(625)*

Jackson, Nancy
American Academy of Forensic Sciences *(34)*

Jackson, Patrice
Quality Service Contractors *(871)*

Jackson, Paula
American Association of Blacks in Energy *(55)*

Jackson, Rhonda
National Association of State Aviation Officials *(698)*

Jackson, Ronald G.

National Association of State Catholic Conference
Directors *(699)*

Jackson, MBA, Sandra
Association for the Accreditation of Human Research
Protection Programs *(257)*

Jackson, Sandra Y.
Natural Products Association *(807)*

Jackson, Sarah
American Association for Applied Linguistics *(47)*

Jackson, Simon
International Pet and Animal Transportation
Association *(560)*

Jackson, Steve
Independent Terminal Operators Association *(492)*

Jackson, Steve
National Auctioneers Association *(711)*

Jackson, Steve
The American Quaternary Association *(172)*

Jackson, Vera R.
American Society of Consultant Pharmacists *(195)*

Jackson, Willa
National Human Services Assembly *(761)*

Jackson-McNeill, Cynthia
Commission on Accreditation of Allied Health
Education Programs *(368)*

Jacob, Kristin
Association of Program Directors in Radiology *(303)*

Jacobs, Christiane P.
Association of Military Banks of America *(294)*

Jacobs, Christopher
Society for Physical Regulation in Biology and
Medicine *(919)*

Jacobs, Clifford
National Association of Drug Court Professionals *(663)*

Jacobs, David
Eight Sheet Outdoor Advertising Association *(421)*

Jacobs, Emily
Association of Administrators of the Interstate
Compact on the Placement of Children *(263)*

Jacobs, George M.
International Association for the Study of Cooperation
in Education *(514)*

Jacobs, Hal
Decision Sciences Institute *(407)*

Jacobs, Jane
Association for Facilities Engineering *(246)*

Jacobs, Jill E.
North American Society for Cardiovascular Imaging
(821)

Jacobs, John
Telecommunications Industry Association *(971)*

Jacobs, Livia A.
The Wire Association International, Inc. *(1019)*

Jacobs, Madeleine
American Chemical Society *(89)*

Jacobs, Ronald M.
Information Technology Industry Council *(495)*

Jacobs, Stacy
American College of Osteopathic Family Physicians
(100)

Jacobs, Stephen
National Association of Manufacturers *(679)*

Jacobsberg, MD, PhD, Lawrence
Association for Psychoanalytic Medicine *(254)*

Jacobsen, Dawn
Investment Program Association *(584)*

Jacobsen, Marie
American Theological Library Association *(216)*

Jacobsen, Melissa
American Association of School Librarians *(72)*

Jacobsen, Melissa
American Association of School Librarians *(72)*

Jacobshagen, CAE, Rosemary
Appliance Parts Distributors Association *(226)*

Jacobsohn, Alice
Environmental Industry Associations *(431)*
National Solid Wastes Management Association *(795)*

Jacobson, Craig
Association for Computing Machinery *(243)*

Jacobson, David
Association for Applied and Therapeutic Humor *(238)*

Jacobson, Dena
Alliance for Gray Market and Counterfeit Abatement
(23)

Jacobson, Douglas N.
National Council on International Trade Development
(739)

Jacobson, CAE, Eric
American Lighting Association *(145)*

Jacobson, Fay
Asian American Hotel Owners Association *(231)*

Jacobson, Gretchen
NACE International *(623)*

Jacobson, Lawrence A.
National Society of Professional Engineers *(794)*

Jacobson, Susan Kaplan
Art and Antique Dealers League of America *(229)*

Jacobson, Trudy R.
National Conference of Executives of The ARC *(727)*

Jacoby, Alexandra
Society for Menstrual Cycle Research *(915)*

Jacoby, Jackie
Environmental and Engineering Geophysical Society
(430)

Jacoby, Jake
Truck Renting and Leasing Association *(981)*

Jacques, Cheryl
International District Energy Association *(540)*

Jaeger, Hallie
American Association of Legal Nurse Consultants *(64)*
The Association for Nursing Professional Development
(252)

Jaeger, Julia
International Association of Women Police *(529)*

Jaffe, Betsy
InfoComm International *(495)*

Jaffe, David
National Association of Home Builders *(673)*

Jaffe, Michael
Fiber Society *(443)*

Jaffe, Miranda
American Pet Products Association *(163)*

Jaffe, Rosann
Air Movement and Control Association International
(19)

Jaffeson, ACA, AICP, Richard C.
National Certification Commission *(720)*

Jagoe, John R.
Export Institute of the United States *(436)*

Jagtiani, Patricia
Natural Gas Supply Association *(807)*

Jahn, Christopher L.
National Association of Chemical Distributors *(652)*

Jahn, Gina
AFCOM *(14)*

Jahn, Madeline
Wellness Councils of America *(1015)*

Jahnke, Kimberly
Society for Clinical Data Management *(906)*

Jahrling, James O.
American Board of Medical Specialties *(82)*

Jaimes, Juan
Donors Forum *(415)*

Jakhelln, Samantha Grover
Intellectual Property Owners Association *(505)*

Jaksa, Katy
Association of Family Medicine Residency Directors
(282)

Jakub, Paula S.
American Foreign Service Protective Association *(123)*

Jakulevicius, John
Corporate Council on Africa *(385)*

Jallow, Pa
American Intellectual Property Law Association *(141)*

Jamall, Cheryl
American Boiler Manufacturers Association *(84)*

Jame, Breggie
Association of Minority Health Professions Schools
(295)

James, Anita
National Athletic Trainers Association *(710)*
National Council of Athletic Training *(734)*

James, Annie N.
Association of Traumatic Stress Specialists *(315)*

James, Barbara
Association for Education and Rehabilitation of the
Blind & Visually Impaired *(245)*

James, Bonnie
National Council of Art Administrators *(734)*

James, Brenda
International Ground Source Heat Pump Association
(549)

James, Catherine
International Technology and Engineering Educators
Association *(576)*

James, Dennis
Healthcare Information and Management Systems
Society *(471)*

James, Derek
Video Electronics Standards Association *(1009)*

James, Jerry
Competitive Telecommunications Association *(371)*

James, Kerrick
Travel Journalists Guild *(980)*

James, Larry H.
National Fraternal Order of Police *(753)*

James, CDE, Linda
National Association of Document Examiners *(663)*

James, CNS, MS, RN, Michelle
International Transplant Nurses Society *(578)*

James, CAE, Philip J.
National Glass Association *(755)*

James, Thomas M.
Truck Renting and Leasing Association *(981)*

James, Timothy P.
International Union of Operating Engineers *(579)*

James, Trudy
American Association of State Colleges and
Universities *(73)*

James A., Capo
United States Maritime Alliance (USMX) *(996)*

James-Brown, Christine
Child Welfare League of America *(353)*

James-Simpson, Fachon
National Association of State Alcohol and Drug Abuse
Directors (NASADAD) *(697)*

Jamie, Linda
National Confectioners Association *(725)*

Jamieson, Rick
Friction Material Standards Institute *(454)*

Jamieson, Suzy
International Council for Machinery Lubrication *(538)*

Jamison, Carla
Urgent Care Association of America *(1004)*

Jamison, Dixie
National Alcohol Beverage Control Association *(631)*

Jamison, RN, Sharon
Society of Otorhinolaryngology and Head-Neck Nurses
(943)

Jamison, Stephanie
American Oriental Society *(158)*

Jamison, Terrance
Alliance of Black Telecommunications Employees *(24)*

Jan, CMP, Grace
American College of Mortgage Attorneys *(98)*

Jan, CAE, CMP, Grace L
Association of Water Technologies *(317)*

Jan, CAE, CMP, Grace L.
American Academy of Appellate Lawyers *(30)*
American Society of Consulting Arborists *(196)*

Janata, Michelle
Open Mobile Alliance *(828)*

Jancewicz, Anna
National Air Traffic Controllers Association *(630)*

Jancius, Angela
Society for the Anthropology of Work *(923)*

Janda, Pat
American Board of Psychiatry & Neurology *(83)*

Jane Purvis, Sarah
CFA Institute *(350)*

Janela, Joseph J.
Academy of Pharmaceutical Research and Science *(8)*
American Pharmacists Association *(163)*

Janes, David C.
Food and Drug Law Institute *(449)*

Janevski, Kendra L.
Generic Pharmaceutical Association *(458)*

Janicek, Kelly
United States Animal Health Association *(989)*

Janicki, Greg
Automotive Public Relations Council *(323)*
Original Equipment Suppliers Association *(833)*

Janik, Laurene K.
National Association of Realtors *(690)*

Janin, Melanie
Business for Social Responsibility *(339)*

Janis, Denis
Association of Professional Researchers for
Advancement *(302)*
Cremation Association of North America *(404)*
International Business Brokers Association *(532)*
Lamaze International *(592)*

Utilimetrics/Alliance for Advanced Metering & Data
Management Solutions *(1006)*

Janis, Jeffrey E.
Association of Academic Chairmen of Plastic Surgery
(262)

Janis, Lenore
Professional Women in Construction *(866)*

Jankowiak, William R.
Society for Cross-Cultural Research *(907)*

Jankowski, Daniel
Intercollegiate Tennis Association *(507)*

Jankowski, Rachael D.
American Society of Agronomy (ASA, CSSA, SSSA)
(191)

Jannuzzi, Christopher J.
IEEE Electron Devices Society *(484)*

Janowiak, John R.
Electrical and Computer Engineering Department
Heads Association *(422)*

Janowski, Ken
American Society of Gene & Cell Therapy *(198)*

Jansen, Judith
Society for the Study of Reproduction *(925)*

Jansen, CPA, Sarah
National Conference of CPA Practitioners *(727)*

Jansett, Julie
Federation of Environmental Technologists, Inc. *(441)*

Janssen, Rita
International Test and Evaluation Association *(577)*

Janszen, Elizabeth
American Watchmakers-Clockmakers Institute *(219)*

Janzen, Judith M.
Church and Synagogue Library Association *(356)*

Jaquet, Michael
United States Ski and Snowboard Association *(999)*

Jardin, Bonny Des
Woven Wire Products Association *(1029)*

Jardine, Elizabeth
Coalition of Essential Schools *(360)*

Jarmin, Jennifer
Physician Assistant Education Association *(847)*

Jarrahy, Reza
American Society of Maxillofacial Surgeons *(202)*

Jarrett, Cheryl
United States of America Gymnastics *(997)*

Jarris, MBA, MD, Paul E.
Association of State and Territorial Health Officials
(310)

Jarschke, Carolyn
Health Care Administrators Association *(469)*

Jarvis, Ann
International Coach Federation *(535)*

Jarvis, Bernard K.
Association of American Medical Colleges *(265)*

Jarvis, Bob
Independent Petroleum Association of America *(491)*

Jarvis, David
Aquarium and Zoo Facilities Association *(227)*

Jarvis, Virginia 'Gigi'
National Association of Enrolled Agents *(666)*

Jarzabek, Jeff
International Association of Oral and Maxillofacial
Surgeons *(525)*

Javidi, Tara
Information Theory Society *(495)*

Jawanda, Suke
The Bluetooth Special Interest Group *(332)*

Jaworksi, Dawn
National Association of Sewer Service Companies *(695)*

Jaworski, CMP, Janet L.
American Membrane Technology Association *(150)*

Jayankura-Jones, Liz
Association of Hispanic Advertising Agencies *(287)*

Jayaram, Geetha
American Association of Psychiatric Administrators
(71)

Jayne, Deborah
Society for American Baseball Research *(903)*

JD, Liz Schumacher
Large Urology Group Practice Association (LUGPA)
(593)

Jean Sauerman, Jean
System Safety Society *(967)*

Jeans-Gail, Sean
National Association of Railroad Passengers *(689)*

Jeavons, Thomas
Association for Research on Nonprofit Organizations
and Voluntary Action *(255)*

Jeffers, Shelley
Timber Products Manufacturers Association *(975)*

Jefferson, Kelley
Society for Assisted Reproductive Technology *(905)*

Jefferson, Patrick
National Association of Black County Officials *(649)*

Jefferson, Rich
Association of Equipment Manufacturers *(281)*

Jefferson, Teri
AACE International *(1)*

Jefferson, Tiffany
Child Welfare League of America *(353)*

Jefferson, Wallace B.
Conference of Chief Justices *(374)*

Jeffery, CAE, Blake
Association of Medical Diagnostic Manufacturers *(293)*

Jeffress, Charles
American Association for Justice *(50)*

Jeffries, Laikisha
Friends of the National Institute of Dental and
Craniofacial Research (FNIDCR) *(454)*

Jehn, Paul
Ground Water Protection Council *(466)*

Jelenko, Amy
International Documentary Association *(541)*

Jelinek, Miloslav
International Society of Bassists *(571)*

Jelley, Deacon Michael
National Association of Diaconate Directors *(662)*

Jenkins, Ashley D.
Council on Social Work Education *(400)*

Jenkins, Barbara
Poultry Breeders of America *(854)*
U.S Poultry and Egg Association *(998)*

Jenkins, Debbie
Coordinating Research Council *(384)*

Jenkins, Elizabeth
American Society of Cytopathology *(196)*

Jenkins, Jacques
National Ready Mixed Concrete Association *(784)*

Jenkins, James
Asian American Hotel Owners Association *(231)*

Jenkins, Jennifer
Distributed Wind Energy Association *(414)*

Jenkins, JoAnn
American Society of Cytopathology *(196)*

Jenkins, Kareem D.
American Sociological Association *(211)*

Jenkins, Kimberly
National Association of State Boating Law
Administrators *(698)*

Jenkins, Lewis
American Academy of Orthopaedic Surgeons *(38)*

Jenkins, Esq., Monique
Professional Housing Management Association *(862)*

Jenkins, Nancy
American Reusable Textile Association *(175)*

Jenkins, Nina
Society for Invertebrate Pathology *(913)*

Jenkins, Renee
National Barrel Horse Association *(712)*

Jenkins, Tamara
American Association for the Surgery of Trauma *(52)*

Jenkins, Tyshawn
Market Technicians Association *(606)*

Jenkins-Gibson, CMP, Ozzie
National Coalition of Black Meeting Planners *(723)*

Jennings, Brandon
National Society of Hispanic MBAs *(794)*

Jennings, Catherine
Wine and Spirits Shippers Association *(1018)*

Jennings, CAE, SPHR, Dave
Community Associations Institute (CAI) *(370)*

Jennings, Debbie
Natco-The Organization for Transplant Professionals
(626)

Jennings, , CMP, Debbie
National Association of Graduate Admissions
Professionals *(670)*

Jennings, Liz
Retail Industry Leaders Association *(884)*

Jennings, Matthew
International Air Transport Association *(510)*

Jennings, Shirley
National Association for Year-Round Education *(645)*

Jennison, Richard
Manufactured Housing Institute *(602)*

Jenny, Margaret
RTCA, Inc. *(888)*

Jensen, Amy
National Stroke Association *(797)*

Jensen, Andrew
Coalition of Service Industries *(361)*

Jensen, Bente
Harness Tracks of America *(468)*

Jensen, Chris
IEEE Computer Society *(483)*

Jensen, James E.
National Research Council *(786)*

Jensen, Jason
International Association of Natural Resource Pilots
(525)

Jensen, Kyle
Alliance for Aging Research *(22)*

Jensen, Mark
American Honey Producers Association *(133)*

Jensen, Mary
American Sheep Industry Association *(178)*

Jensen, Richard L.
Society for the Advancement of Scandinavian Study
(923)

Jensen, Ron
National Guard Association of the U.S. *(757)*

Jensen, Sara
Aircraft Builders Council *(20)*

Jensen, Steven
American Catholic Philosophical Association *(88)*

Jenson, Laura
The Brown Swiss Association *(336)*

Jeon, CAE, CPA, Joori
American Hotel & Lodging Association (AH&LA) *(134)*

Jeppesen-Wigelsworth, Alison
Women's Classical Caucus *(1023)*

Jepson, Terry
Association of Shareware Professionals *(308)*

Jerdonek, Andrew
American College of Medical Quality *(97)*

Jeric, Andrea J.
Precision Machined Products Association *(856)*

Jernigan, Bryan
National Association of Federally Impacted Schools
(668)

Jernigan, Jerry
Braunvieh Association of America *(334)*

Jervert, Karin
International Sculpture Center *(564)*

Jesien, PhD, George S.
Association of University Centers on Disabilities
(AUCD) *(315)*

Jessee, Valera B.
United Producers Formulators and Distributors
Association *(988)*

Jessup, Eric
Transportation Research Forum *(979)*

Jeste, MD, Dilip V.
American Association for Geriatric Psychiatry *(49)*

Jester, Denise
International Sculpture Center *(564)*

Jesuele, Neil J.
American Hospital Association *(133)*
Health Forum *(469)*

Jeter, Lisa
National Association of Attorneys General *(647)*

Jetton, Francine
Society of General Internal Medicine *(937)*

Jetton, Shellie
Association of Talent Agents *(312)*

Jewart, Sheilah
American Society for Neurochemistry *(187)*

Jewell, Mike
Marine Engineers Beneficial Association *(605)*

Jewett, Tony
National Parks Conservation Association *(779)*

Jewler, MA, Don
Association of Community Cancer Centers *(275)*

Jezierski, Carol
Association for Corporate Growth *(244)*

Jiang, He
International Society of Applied Intelligence *(570)*

Jibson, MD, PhD, Micheal

American Association of Directors of Psychiatric
Residency Training *(60)*

Jilani, Nasreen
Nine to Five, National Association of Working Women
(811)

Jill, Nowak
American Association of Orthodontists *(67)*

Jilly, Julie
Professional Tennis Registry *(865)*

Jimenez, Astrid
National Hispanic Medical Association *(759)*

Jimenez, Denise
National Conference of Federal Trial Judges *(727)*

Jimenez, Hector
Alliance for Women in Media *(24)*

Jimenez, CCM, Marisu
Association of College and University Clubs *(274)*

Jimenez, Natalia
American Association of Collegiate Registrars and
Admissions Officers *(58)*

Jimenez, Reese
American Rights at Work *(175)*

Jimenez, Yadira
National Association of Hispanic Real Estate
Professionals *(672)*

Jirdeh, Hussein D.
Universities Space Research Association *(1002)*

Joanis, Marie
National Potato Council *(782)*

Jobe, Joe
National BioDiesel Board *(713)*

Jobes, Linda
International Flight Services Association *(545)*

Joblin, Nathan
Social Venture Network *(902)*

Joe, Stephanie
American Rhinologic Society *(175)*

Joehari, Julisa
Malaysian Rubber Export Promotion Council (USA)
(602)

jog, Mark
American Agricultural Marketing Association *(44)*

Johannes, Mary
International Swaps and Derivatives Association *(576)*

Johanns, Patrick J.
Alpha Chi Sigma Fraternity, Inc. *(26)*

Johanson, MN, RN, Wanda L.
American Association of Critical-Care Nurses *(59)*

Johansson, Erin
American Rights at Work *(175)*

John, Bridget
International Association for Impact Assessment *(513)*

John, Brittany
International Studies Association *(576)*

Johns, Allie
National Christian College Athletic Association *(721)*

Johns, Barbara
American Society for Enology and Viticulture *(184)*

Johns, Bethany
American Astronomical Society *(77)*

Johns, Brad
Association of Academic Physiatrists *(263)*

Johns, Cheryl
Association of Home Office Underwriters *(287)*

Johns, Gregory
National Association of Federal Credit Unions *(667)*

Johns, Joe
Radio and Television Correspondents Association *(873)*

Johns, Kevin
American Academy of Anesthesiologist Assistants *(30)*
American Osteopathic Academy of Orthopedics *(159)*

Johns, Marc
Society for College and University Planning *(906)*

Johns, Robert S.
National Dental Association *(742)*

Johnsen, CMC, Lissa
Information Technology Alliance *(495)*

Johnson, Adrian
National Association for Rehabilitation Leadership *(642)*

Johnson, Akili M.
Urban Financial Services Coalition *(1003)*

Johnson, Amy
Society of Financial Service Professionals *(936)*

Johnson, CAE, Anna
American Association of Medical Assistants *(65)*

Johnson, Arley
National Association for State Community Services Programs *(643)*

Johnson, B.J.
Automotive Service Association *(323)*

Johnson, Beth
The Association of Theatre Movement Educators *(314)*

Johnson, Bill
The Door and Hardware Institute *(416)*

Johnson, BJ
International Association of Home Staging Professionals *(522)*

Johnson, Brett
United States Rowing Association *(998)*

Johnson, Brian
National Postsecondary Agriculture Student Organization *(781)*

Johnson, Bridget
American Enterprise Institute for Public Policy Research *(117)*

Johnson, Candice
Communications Workers of America *(369)*

Johnson, Carla
School Science and Mathematics Association *(892)*

Johnson, Carol
North American Limousin Foundation *(817)*

Johnson, Carrie
Association of Professional Researchers for Advancement *(302)*
Society of Incentive & Travel Executives *(939)*

Johnson, MA, MT (ASCP), Catherine
COLA *(362)*

Johnson, Cathy
Appraisal Foundation *(226)*

Johnson, Chanda
National Black Public Relations Society *(715)*

Johnson, Chris
American Association of Automatic Door Manufacturers *(54)*

Johnson, PhD, Chris
Imaging and Perimetry Society *(486)*

Johnson, Chris
Heat Exchange Institute *(472)*

Johnson, CNM, MS, Christina

American College of Nurse-Midwives *(99)*

Johnson, Christine
Cardiovascular Credentialing International *(342)*

Johnson, Cliff
Pipeline Research Council International, Inc. *(849)*

Johnson, Dan
Light Aircraft Manufacturers Association *(598)*

Johnson, Dane
The American Society of Forensic Odontology *(198)*

Johnson, David
Conference of Historical Journals *(375)*

Johnson, APR, CEBS, Deanna
American Benefits Council *(80)*

Johnson, CPA, Debbie
American Diabetes Association *(115)*

Johnson, Deborah S.
Professional Women's Appraisal Association *(866)*

Johnson, Diane
American Biological Safety Association *(81)*

Johnson, Diane E.
Livestock Publications Council *(599)*

Johnson, Donald
Hearth, Patio and Barbecue Association *(472)*

Johnson, Elena
International Masonry Institute *(556)*

Johnson, Elizabeth
Parachute Industry Association *(838)*

Johnson, Eric
American Association of Cardiovascular and Pulmonary Rehabilitation *(55)*
Print Services & Distribution Association *(857)*
Product Development and Management Association *(858)*

Johnson, CMM, CMP, Eric
Society of Incentive & Travel Executives *(939)*

Johnson, Everett L.
Mineralogical Society of America *(617)*

Johnson, Felicia
National Property Management Association *(783)*

Johnson, Frances Brigham
Agribusiness Council *(16)*

Johnson, Frank
National Association of County Intergovernmental Relations Officials *(660)*

Johnson, Fred
Credit Union Executives Society *(403)*

Johnson, Gay
National Association of Nurse Practitioners in Women's Health *(682)*

Johnson, Georgette
National Association of Women Lawyers *(710)*

Johnson, Glenda G.
National Association of State Auditors, Comptrollers and Treasurers *(698)*

Johnson, III, J. Cliff
Council of Manufacturing Associations *(395)*
National Association of Manufacturers *(679)*

Johnson, Jacqueline
Association of Travel Marketing Executives *(315)*

Johnson, Jr., James W.
United States Beet Sugar Association *(991)*

Johnson, Jane
Association for Accounting Administration *(237)*

Johnson, Jeanne
Association of American Veterinary Medical Colleges *(267)*

Johnson, Jeffery
International Facility Management Association *(543)*

Johnson, Jen
American Swimming Coaches Association *(215)*

Johnson, Jennifer
Society for Industrial Microbiology *(913)*

Johnson, Jennifer J.
National Council of Teachers of Mathematics *(737)*

Johnson, Jill
American Gear Manufacturers Association *(125)*

Johnson, Jim
American Securitization Forum *(178)*

Johnson, Joey C.
National Rural Letter Carriers' Association *(788)*

Johnson, John K.
National Association of State Boating Law Administrators *(698)*

Johnson, John W.
National Association of State Boards of Accountancy *(698)*

Johnson, Judith M.
American Astronomical Society *(77)*

Johnson, Judy
American Philatelic Society *(163)*

Johnson, Julie
National Association of Heavy Equipment Training Schools *(672)*

Johnson, Katie Kenney
American Society of Law, Medicine and Ethics *(202)*

Johnson, Kevin
Association of Government Accountants *(286)*

Johnson, Kim
International Association of Lighting Management Companies *(524)*

Johnson, Kirk
National Rural Electric Cooperative Association *(788)*

Johnson, Kristi
Research Chefs Association *(882)*

Johnson, Ladd
North American Gamebird Association *(817)*

Johnson, Lanee
International Association of Movers *(525)*

Johnson, Laura
American Psychotherapy Association *(170)*

Johnson, Laura R.
American Society of Cataract and Refractive Surgery *(194)*

Johnson, PhD, Laurence F.
The New Media Consortium *(809)*

Johnson, Lee
United States of America Gymnastics *(997)*

Johnson, Lenora
National School Boards Association *(789)*

Johnson, Lin
Evangelical Church Library Association *(434)*

Johnson, Lisa M.
American Association of Colleges for Teacher Education *(57)*

Johnson, Liz
National Ornamental and Miscellaneous Metals Association *(778)*

Johnson, Lorretta
AFT - Public Employees *(15)*
American Federation of Teachers (AFL-CIO) *(120)*

Johnson, Lyndon B.
Silver Council *(900)*

Johnson, Lynnecia
Electric Drive Transportation Association *(421)*

Johnson, AICI, CIP, Magoe
Association of Image Consultants International *(287)*

Johnson, Marlene M.
NAFSA: Association of International Educators *(624)*

Johnson, Mary
American Composites Manufacturers Association *(105)*
International Cast Polymer Alliance *(533)*
International Cast Polymer Association *(533)*

Johnson, Mary Ann
Columbia Sheep Breeders Association of America *(365)*

Johnson, Melinda
Evangelical Council for Financial Accountability *(434)*

Johnson, CMP, Melissa Faubel
Public Library Association *(869)*

Johnson, Michael W.
National Beer Wholesalers Association *(713)*

Johnson, Michele C.
International Society of Arthroscopy, Knee Surgery and Orthopaedic Sports Medicine *(571)*

Johnson, Michelle R.
Design-Build Institute of America *(411)*

Johnson, Nancy
Aluminum Anodizers Council *(27)*
Aluminum Extruders Council *(27)*

Johnson, Nancy
American Board of Health Physics *(82)*

Johnson, Nancy
American Homebrewers Association *(133)*
The Brewers Association *(335)*

Johnson, Nancy
American Academy of Health Physics *(35)*

Johnson, Pam
NASTD - Technology Professionals Serving State Government *(626)*
National Association of State Technology Directors *(702)*

Johnson, Patricia Kiernan
OPERA America *(828)*

Johnson, Paul
The PGA Tour, Inc. *(844)*

Johnson, Peggie
American Voice Input/Output Society *(219)*

Johnson, PhD, Pete
The Brewers Association *(335)*

Johnson, R. Craig
International Congress of Oral Implantologists *(537)*

Johnson, R. Wayne
IEEE Components, Packaging, and Manufacturing Technology Society *(483)*

Johnson, R. Christopher
Scaffolding, Shoring and Forming Institute *(892)*

Johnson, Rae Ann S.
Manufacturers Alliance/MAPI Inc. *(603)*

Johnson, Ramsay
American Association of Community Colleges *(58)*

Johnson, Randy
AHS International - The Vertical Flight Society *(17)*

Johnson, Randy
International Business Music Association *(532)*

Johnson, Richard A.
Brotherhood Railway Carmen/TCU *(336)*
Transportation Communications International Union/IAM *(978)*

Johnson, Richard M.
Parenteral Drug Association *(838)*

Johnson, Rob
Billiard Congress of America *(329)*

Johnson, Robert
Outdoor Amusement Business Association *(834)*

Johnson, Robert G.
International Real Estate Institute *(562)*
International Travel Writers and Editors Association *(578)*
National Association of Review Appraisers and Mortgage Underwriters *(692)*

Johnson, Robert J.
National Association for Information Destruction, Inc. *(640)*

Johnson, Robert K.
National Rural Water Association *(788)*

Johnson, CFA, PhD, Robert R.
CFA Institute *(350)*

Johnson, Roberta
National Earth Science Teachers Association *(743)*

Johnson, Roger
National Farmers Union (Farmers Educational & Co-operative Union of America) *(747)*

Johnson, Roxanne
National Association of Professional Insurance Agents *(687)*

Johnson, Ryan M
WorldatWork *(1028)*

Johnson, Sarah
National Organization of Black Law Enforcement Executives *(777)*

Johnson, Sarah
National Tactical Officers Association of America *(799)*

Johnson, Seth
American Guernsey Association *(127)*

Johnson, Shane
National Alfalfa and Forage Alliance *(631)*

Johnson, Sharon
Society of Petrophysicists and Well Log Analysts *(944)*

Johnson, Shelly
American Massage Therapy Association *(147)*

Johnson, Sheri
AASHTO: Transportation Center of Excellence *(2)*

Johnson, Sonjya
American College of Osteopathic Surgeons *(100)*
American Osteopathic College of Proctology *(161)*

Johnson, Stacey
Business Solutions Association *(340)*

Johnson, Stephen G.
American Correctional Chaplains Association *(108)*
American Jewish Correctional Chaplains Association *(143)*

Johnson, Steve
American Association of Bovine Practitioners *(55)*
Bowling Proprietors' Association of America *(334)*

Johnson, Susan E.
RESPRO (Real Estate Services Providers Council) *(883)*

Johnson, Susan M.
Forest Landowners Association *(451)*

Johnson, Susan R.
American Foreign Service Association *(122)*

Johnson, Suzanne
Owner-Operator Independent Drivers Association, Inc. *(836)*

Johnson, CAE, Tanya Howe
Partnership for Philanthropic Planning *(839)*

Johnson, Teddi
American Public Health Association *(171)*

Johnson, Teresa
National Adult Day Service Association *(629)*

Johnson, Teresa
Solar Rating and Certification Corporation *(952)*

Johnson, Thomas L.
Medicaid Health Plans of America *(611)*

Johnson, Timothy "Tim"
National Electrical Contractors Association *(744)*

Johnson, LPN, Tina
National Federation of Licensed Practical Nurses *(749)*

Johnson, DVM, Tom
American Association of Small Ruminant Practitioners *(73)*

Johnson, Tracy
Financial Industry Regulatory Authority (FINRA) *(444)*

Johnson, Travis D.
International Anti-Counterfeiting Coalition *(511)*

Johnson, Troy
Society for History Education *(911)*

Johnson, Troy E.
Environmental Assessment Association *(430)*

Johnson, Wanda
National Indian Education Association *(762)*

Johnson, Wanda
The Endocrine Society *(427)*

Johnson, William A.
American Society of Papyrologists *(205)*

Johnson, William J.
National Association of Police Organizations *(685)*

Johnson-Curiskis, Nanette
International Listening Association *(554)*

Johnston, Dave
Vinyl Siding Institute, Inc. *(1009)*

Johnston, David A.
Exterior Insulation and Finish Systems Industry Members Association (EIMA) *(436)*

Johnston, Debby
The Knitting Guild Association *(591)*

Johnston, Gordon
Generic Pharmaceutical Association *(458)*

Johnston, James J.
Owner-Operator Independent Drivers Association, Inc. *(836)*

Johnston, Mara
International Association of Chiefs of Police *(517)*

Johnston, Melissa Zack
Council of Chief State School Officers *(392)*

Johnston, Neela
American Association of School Librarians *(72)*

Johnston, Pat
National Association for Children's Behavioral Health (NACBH) *(637)*

Johnston, Peter
WTA Tour, Inc. *(1029)*

Johnston, Sam
Showmen's League of America *(899)*

Johnston, Shawn
American Fisheries Society *(121)*

Johnston, Susan Whealler
Association of Governing Boards of Universities and Colleges *(286)*

Johnston, Therese
American Society of Golf Course Architects *(198)*

Johnston-Robledo, Ingrid
Society for Menstrual Cycle Research *(915)*

Johnstone, Jennifer J.
International Association of Law Enforcement
Intelligence Analysts **(523)**

Joiner, Susan
Energy Telecommunications and Electrical Association
(428)

Jolkovski, Martha
Independent Lubricant Manufacturers Association
(490)

Jolley, Ben
American Academy of Professional Coders **(40)**

Jolliffe-Henry, Mary
The Accrediting Commission of Career Schools and
Colleges **(10)**

Jolly, Barbara
Association of Supervisory and Administrative School
Personnel **(312)**

Jolly, Gina
Insurance Accounting and Systems Association **(504)**

Jolly, PhD, Jennifer
National Association for Gifted Children **(639)**

Jon, Sankalp
Visual Artists Rights Coalition **(1010)**

Jonas, Chris
National Association for Business Economics **(636)**

Joncich, Lisa
International Lactation Consultant Association **(553)**

jone, Alan
International Food & Beverage Association (IFBA) **(546)**

jone, glyn
National Aquaculture Council **(635)**

Jones , Brien
National Association of Certified Valuation Analysts
(652)

Jones, Aislinn
American Academy of Religion **(41)**

Jones, Alan
Boating Writers International **(333)**

Jones, Alison
Association of College and University Housing
Officers-International **(274)**

Jones, Allison
National Alliance of Independent Crop Consultants
(632)

Jones, April
Incorporated Research Institutions for Seismology
(487)

Jones, April
National Board for Professional Teaching Standards
(NBPTS) **(715)**

Jones, Bethany H.
National Association of Surety Bond Producers **(704)**

Jones, Brenda
Association for Healthcare Resource and Materials
Management **(248)**

Jones, Brian
American Academy of Cosmetic Surgery **(32)**

Jones, Brian Mondragón
Agricultural & Applied Economics Association **(16)**

Jones, Brigitte
Blinded Veterans Association **(332)**

Jones, Brittany
Executive Women International **(435)**

Jones, Bryce
Growth Energy **(466)**

Jones, CAE, Charlie
Heart Rhythm Society **(472)**

Jones, Coulter
Investigative Reporters and Editors **(583)**

Jones, Cynthia
The Securities Transfer Association **(895)**

Jones, Dale
Association of Statisticians of American Religious
Bodies **(311)**

Jones, Dannie
National Association of State Park Directors **(702)**

Jones, David
National Association of Service Managers **(695)**

Jones, Dean
Religious Conference Management Association **(880)**

Jones, Desyreé
Society of American Military Engineers **(929)**

Jones, CAE, EdD, RN, Dolores C.
National Association of Pediatric Nurse Practitioners
(684)

Jones, Donald C.
American Association of Clinical Endocrinologists **(56)**

Jones, Earla
National Association of College and University
Business Officers **(654)**

Jones, Erin M.
Food and Drug Law Institute **(449)**

Jones, Gary
Money Management Institute **(618)**

Jones, Georgi
American Buckskin Registry Association **(86)**

Jones, Gerard A.
National Organization of Industrial Trade Unions **(777)**

Jones, Gloriatine
American Association of Colleges for Teacher
Education **(57)**

jones, Glyn
Tetrahydrofuran Task Force **(972)**

Jones, LMSW, SPHR, Gregory A.
American Montessori Society **(152)**

Jones, Hillary
American Cleft Palate-Craniofacial Association **(91)**

Jones, Holli
National Association of Enrolled Agents **(666)**

Jones, Isabel
Visiting Nurse Associations of America **(1010)**

Jones, James C.
National Association for Multi-Ethnicity in
Communications **(640)**

Jones, James "Jim"
Rolf Institute of Structural Integration **(887)**

Jones, Jason
American Volleyball Coaches Association **(219)**

Jones, Jennifer
International Association of Lighting Designers **(524)**

Jones, MD, PhD, Judith K.
Pharmaceutical Education and Research Institute **(844)**

Jones, Kate
National Council of State Boards for Nursing **(736)**

Jones, Katenna
Association of Pet Dog Trainers **(299)**

Jones, Kathleen
ADSC: The International Association of Foundation
Drilling **(12)**

Jones, Kaye
International Association of Career Consulting Firms
(517)

Jones, Keith
American Academy of Actuaries **(29)**

Jones, Kelly
Agricultural Retailers Association **(16)**

Jones, Kim
National Institute of Pension Administrators **(765)**

Jones, Larry
Consumer Specialty Products Association **(381)**

Jones, Leslie
National Association of Catering and Events **(651)**

Jones, Linda
American Society on Aging **(211)**

Jones, Lindsay
Council for Exceptional Children **(390)**

Jones, Liz
Online Lenders Alliance **(827)**

Jones, Mandisa
American Association of Naturopathic Physicians **(66)**

Jones, Marshall
National Association of Councils on Developmental
Disabilities **(658)**

Jones, Melva
National Legal Aid and Defender Association **(769)**

Jones, Michael
National Apartment Association **(634)**

Jones, Michael
Lignite Energy Council **(598)**

Jones, CMP, Michele M.
National Insulation Association **(766)**

Jones, CMP, Michelle W.
International Parking Institute **(559)**

Jones, Mike
Association on American Indian Affairs **(319)**

Jones, Newton B.
International Brotherhood of Boilermakers, Iron
Shipbuilders, Blacksmiths, Forgers and Helpers **(531)**

Jones, Nori
American Association for Clinical Chemistry, Inc. **(48)**

Jones, Olivia
National Association of Student Personnel
Administrators **(626)**

Jones, P. David
Society of Wood Science and Technology **(950)**

jones, Palm
Worldwide Printing Thermographers Association
(1028)

Jones, Pamela K.
Council for Christian Colleges and Universities **(389)**

Jones, Patrick D.
International Bridge, Tunnel and Turnpike Association
(531)

Jones, Paul
Truck-frame and Axle Repair Association **(981)**

Jones, Paul C.
Mining and Metallurgical Society of America **(617)**

Jones, Penelope
American Association for Clinical Chemistry, Inc. **(48)**
National Academy of Clinical Biochemistry **(627)**

Jones, Randall D.
National Association of Professional Surplus Lines
Offices, Ltd. **(688)**

Jones, CPA, Richard
American Academy of Optometry **(37)**

Jones, Richard A.
National Association for Uniformed Services **(644)**

Jones, Richard A.
Radical Philosophy Association *(873)*

Jones, Rick
Society of Military Widows *(941)*

Jones, Robyn
Association for Asian Studies *(239)*

Jones, Rochelle
National Association of Black Accountants, Inc. *(648)*

Jones, CCC-A, COI, PhD, Dr. Ronald
National Black Association for Speech, Language and Hearing *(714)*

Jones, Russell
League of American Orchestras *(595)*

Jones, Salita
Textile Rental Services Association of America *(973)*

Jones, Sam
Phi Beta Fraternity *(845)*

Jones, Scott
Society of Broadcast Engineers *(931)*

Jones, Scott P.
Forest Landowners Association *(451)*

Jones, Sherard
Radiant Panel Association *(872)*

Jones, Stella
Food Industry Suppliers Association *(449)*

Jones, Steven R.
Association of Cable Communicators *(270)*

Jones, Suzanne M
Association of Energy Services Professionals, International *(281)*

Jones, Tambra
Specialty Sleep Association *(958)*

Jones, Tanneka
United Cerebral Palsy *(986)*

Jones, Ted
Stucco Manufacturers Association *(964)*

Jones, Terry
Association of Insolvency and Restructuring Advisors *(289)*

Jones, CG, CGL, Thomas W.
National Genealogical Society *(754)*

Jones, Tim
American Society for Nondestructive Testing *(187)*

Jones, Tommy
National School Public Relations Association *(789)*

Jones, Wendi
Commission on Accreditation for Law Enforcement Agencies Incorporation *(367)*

Jones, William
National Council of Exchangors *(734)*

Joneson, Kathy A.
International Safe Transit Association *(563)*

Jonker, Jamie
National Ice Cream Mix Association *(761)*

Jonson, Urban
National Motor Freight Traffic Association, Inc. *(773)*

Jopp, Alexandra
American Institute for International Steel *(136)*

Jopp, EdD, Devin A.
Workgroup for Electronic Data Interchange *(1025)*

Jordan, Andrew
Cotton Growers Warehouse Association *(387)*

Jordan, Cole
Stage Directors and Choreographers Society *(960)*

Jordan, Cynthia
American Sports Builders Association *(212)*
Web Sling and Tie down Association *(1014)*

Jordan, PA-C, Damon
Association of Neurosurgical Physician Assistants *(295)*

Jordan, Dawn
National Environmental Health Association *(746)*

Jordan, Deborah
Council for Professional Recognition *(391)*

Jordan, Dr. Don M.
National Association of Academies of Science *(645)*

Jordan, Jackie
Envelope Manufacturers Association *(430)*

Jordan, CTRS, PhD, Jerry
National Therapeutic Recreation Society *(800)*

Jordan, Keith
Association of Old Crows *(297)*

Jordan, Kenneth
Association of Energy Service Companies *(280)*

Jordan, Kyle
Association of Fraternity Advisors *(284)*

Jordan, MS, Linda
Federation of State Medical Boards of the United States *(442)*

Jordan, Lisa
National Association of College and University Business Officers *(654)*

Jordan, Lori
Water Environment Federation *(1013)*

Jordan, Margaret Ann
Society of Actuaries *(927)*

Jordan, USAF (Ret.), Col. Michael
Military Officers Association of America (MOAA) *(616)*

Jordan, Michelle
The National Association for the Dually Diagnosed *(643)*

Jordan, Patty
Association of Energy Service Companies *(280)*

Jordan, CAE, CPSM, FSMPS, Roger
Professional Services Council *(865)*

Jordan, Steve
National Independent Automobile Dealers Association *(761)*

Jordan, Thomas
International Union of Police Associations, AFL-CIO *(579)*

Jordan, Thomas J.
Consolidated Tape Association *(378)*

Jordan, Tina
Association of American Publishers *(266)*

Jordan-Carr, Melody
American Society of Association Executives-The Center for Association Leadership *(193)*

Jorden, Jay
National Speleological Society *(795)*

Jorgensen, Amy
Grain Elevator and Processing Society *(464)*

Jorgensen, Mandie
Hospitality Sales and Marketing Association International *(479)*

Jorgensen, Mark
Mining and Metallurgical Society of America *(617)*

Jørgensen, Sven E.
International Society for Ecological Modelling-North American Chapter *(566)*

Jorgenson, Jane
The Wildlife Society *(1017)*

Jorss, Ann
National Council of Commercial Plant Breeders *(734)*

Joselow, Thea
Association of Opinion Journalists *(297)*

Joseph, Bruce
National Religious Broadcasters, Music License Committee *(785)*

Joseph, Casey
Shippers of Recycled Textiles *(899)*

Joseph, Heather
SPARC *(954)*

Joseph, Jacqueline A.
National Association of Document Examiners *(663)*

Joseph, Jeff
Biotechnology Industry Organization (BIO) *(330)*

Joseph, Jeff
Consumer Electronics Association *(381)*

Joseph, Steven
International Cast Polymer Alliance *(533)*

Joseph, CAE, MPS, Thomas L.
American Society for Blood and Marrow Transplantation *(181)*

Joseph, Wavel
Interlocking Concrete Pavement Institute *(508)*

Joseph-Biddle, Jacqui
National Council of Teachers of English *(737)*

Josephs, Katherine
Association for Retail Environments *(256)*

Josephson, CMP, Barbra
American Dental Society of Anesthesiology *(114)*

Josephson, Philip
Alpha Gamma Rho *(26)*

Josh, Steven
National Association of Boat Manufacturers *(650)*

Joshi, Anita
National Investor Relations Institute *(767)*

Joshi, Maulik S.
American Hospital Association *(133)*

Joshipura, Sanjeev
Commodity Markets Council *(368)*

Joslin, Amanda
International Lactation Consultant Association *(553)*

Joslin, Randy
Electrical Apparatus Service Association *(422)*

Joslin, Rick
Help Desk Institute *(474)*

Joslyn, Tammy
Management Association for Private Photogrammetric Surveyors *(602)*

Josman, Cathy
Association of Governing Boards of Universities and Colleges *(286)*

Josten, R. Bruce
American National Chamber of Commerce *(154)*
North American Transportation Employee Relations Association *(823)*

Jouben, Elona M.
American Association of University Professors *(75)*

Jourdain, Charles
California Redwood Association *(341)*

Jourdain, Christine
American Council of Snowmobile Associations *(110)*

Jovanovich, Linda

Hardwood Manufacturers Association *(468)*

Jowyk, Xenia ("Ksen'ya")
Real Estate Roundtable *(876)*

Joy, Julene
National Society of Accountants *(793)*

Joy-Rodgers, Cindy
National Newspaper Association *(775)*

Joyce, CAE, Alana
American Association of Political Consultants *(70)*

Joyce, Francesca
CropLife America *(404)*

Joyce, James
National Association of Broadcast Employees and
Technicians-Communications Workers of America,
AFL-CIO (NABET-CWA) *(650)*

Joyce, Kathleen
National Beer Wholesalers Association *(713)*

Joyce, Sherman
American Tort Reform Association *(217)*

Joyce, Stephanie
International Brotherhood of Boilermakers, Iron
Shipbuilders, Blacksmiths, Forgers and Helpers *(531)*

Joye, Bridgette
International Newspaper Marketing Association *(558)*

Joyner, Brad
The International Childbirth Education Association
(534)

Joyner, Brady
Controlled Environment Testing Association *(383)*

Joyner, Michelle
National Military Family Association, Inc. *(772)*

Joyner, Terry
National Association for State Community Services
Programs *(643)*

Jubb, Stephen
National Alliance for Accessible Golf *(631)*

Juchno, Wayne
NARSA-The International Heal Transfer Association
(625)

Judd, Harlan E
American Hackney Horse Society *(128)*

Judd, Robert
American Musicological Society *(154)*

Judge, Tricia
International Imaging Technology Council *(551)*

Judson, CMP, Bennett
National Roofing Contractors Association *(787)*

Judson, Roger
Precision Metalforming Association *(856)*

Judy Estus, Judy
Society of Financial Examiners *(936)*

Juhl, Jan
Automotive Engine Rebuilders Association *(322)*

Julia, Thomas A.
Composite Panel Association *(372)*

Julian, Larry
National Association of Legal Investigators *(678)*

Julian, Philip
American Assembly for Men in Nursing *(47)*

Juliano, Perry
Utilimetrics/Alliance for Advanced Metering & Data
Management Solutions *(1006)*

Julyan, Seth
Opportunity Finance Network *(829)*

Juneau, James J.

Fire and Emergency Manufacturers and Services
Association *(446)*

Juneau, Nici
American Lighting Association *(145)*

Junemann, Gregory J.
International Federation of Professional and Technical
Engineers *(544)*

Jung, CPA, MST, Marlene D.
Society of Professional Asset-Managers and Record
Keepers *(945)*

Jungmeyer, Lance
Fresh Produce Association of the Americas *(453)*

Jupin, Bob
National Society of Professional Surveyors *(794)*

Jurd, Lindsey
American Association of Colleges of Osteopathic
Medicine *(57)*

Jurgonis, Charlie
American Federation of State, County and Municipal
Employees *(120)*

Jurich, Steve
National Home Infusion Association *(760)*

Jurigian, Sandra L.
National Association for Armenian Studies and
Research *(636)*

Jurkash, John
Government Finance Officers Association of the United
States and Canada *(464)*
Government Finance Officers Association, Federal
Liaison Center *(464)*

Jurmain, Trish
Association of Celebrity Personal Assistants *(271)*

Jurus, William L.
American Chain of Warehouses *(89)*

Just, Marilee
Retail Florist Association *(884)*

Jutchenko, Ashley R.
American Skin Association *(180)*

Jutten, Julie
Professional Rodeo Cowboys Association *(864)*

Juul, Dorthea
American Board of Psychiatry & Neurology *(83)*

Juzwik, Mary
National Conference on Research in Language and
Literacy *(729)*

Kaatz, Kraig
National Trappers Association *(801)*

Kabadian, CMP, MA, Melissa
American College of Prosthodontists *(101)*

Kabak, Edward M.
Promotion Marketing Association *(866)*

Kabati, Pamela Geurds
National Association of Realtors *(690)*

Kabbani, Jim
Tortilla Industry Association *(976)*

Kabin, CCP, Bonnie
WorldatWork *(1028)*

Kabnick, MD, Lowell S.
American Venous Forum *(218)*

Kabo, Teresa
National Association of Schools of Dance *(693)*

Kachel, Pamela K.
AMT - The Association For Manufacturing Technology
(222)

Kachelski, CAE, Barbara
Credit Union Executives Society *(403)*

Kaczinski, PE, Mark
Bridge Grid Flooring Manufacturers Association *(335)*

Kaczmar, Maria
National Association of Colleges and Employers *(655)*

Kaczorowski, Katie
Communications Fraud Control Association *(369)*

Kadas, Katie
Seismological Society of America *(895)*

Kadash, Richard
NAFA Fleet Management Association *(624)*

Kadi, Arpad A.
Shipowners Claims Bureau, Inc. *(899)*

Kadzis, CAE, Richard
CoreNet Global *(385)*

Kaffes, Andrew
Friends of the National Institute of Dental and
Craniofacial Research (FNIDCR) *(454)*

Kafka, Kim
North American Elk Breeders Association *(816)*

Kagan, Eve Gamzu
American College of Toxicology *(103)*

Kagarise, Leslie
Passenger Vessel Association *(839)*

Kahan, Alan
Entomological Society of America *(429)*

Kahan, Marlene
American Society of Magazine Editors *(202)*

Kahl, MBA, Alexander
American Society of Anesthesiologists *(192)*

Kahl, CAE, Kimberly
National Association of Exclusive Buyer Agents *(666)*

Kahl, Nathan
American Society for Engineering Education *(183)*

Kahler, Brenda
Business for Social Responsibility *(339)*

Kahler, Denise
Commercial Real Estate Women Network *(367)*

Kahn, Brad
Forest Stewardship Council - United States Chapter
(451)

Kahn, III, Charles N. "Chip"
Federation of American Hospitals *(440)*

Kahn, Chris
The Independent Book Publishers Association *(488)*

Kahn, David L.
International Association for the Study of Dreams *(514)*

Kahn, Drummond
National Association of Local Government Auditors
(678)

Kahn, Jerry
International Physical Fitness Association *(560)*

Kahn, Louis
American Friends of Turkey *(124)*

Kahn, Lynn
American College of Surgeons *(103)*

Kahn, Jr., MD, Norman B.
Council of Medical Specialty Societies *(395)*

Kahn, Polly
League of American Orchestras *(595)*

Kahn, Ray
IEEE Computer Society *(483)*

Kaible, Jay
Flexographic Technical Association *(447)*

Kail, Greg

American Water Works Association *(220)*

Kaiser, Don
EUCG, Inc. *(433)*

Kaiser, Don
Wireless Innovation Forum *(1019)*

Kaiser, John
American Association of Advertising Agencies *(53)*

Kaiser, Michael
WineAmerica *(1019)*

Kaiser, Timothy G.
Public Housing Authorities Directors Association *(869)*

Kaitz, James A.
Association for Financial Professionals, Inc. *(247)*

Kalacevic, Tamara
National Association of Criminal Defense Lawyers *(661)*

Kalata, Emily
Society for Vascular Surgery *(926)*

Kalata, Jane
National Association of Minority and Women Owned Law Firms *(680)*

Kalavar, Gopi
Materials Research Society *(609)*

Kaledin, Nick
Association of Theatrical Press Agents and Managers *(314)*

Kaleida, Brian
SAE International *(889)*

Kalen, Pamela J.
National Business Group on Health *(716)*

Kalentsits, Maria
International Association of Aquatic and Marine Science Libraries and Information Centers *(515)*

Kalert, Jane
AAGL - Advancing Minimally Invasive Gynecology Worldwide *(2)*

Kalinga, Ronna
Society for Vascular Surgery *(926)*

Kalisch, Bert
American Public Gas Association *(170)*

Kalish, Jana
United States Association of Importers of Textiles and Apparel *(990)*

Kalish, Susan
Automotive Aftermarket Industry Association *(321)*

Kalkunte, Sheila J
American Academy of Actuaries *(29)*

Kalkwarf, Jonathan
Metals Service Center Institute *(614)*

Kallas, Anmarie
Council for Exceptional Children *(390)*

Kaller, Richard
Certified Contractors Network *(349)*

Kallstrom, MBA, RRT, Thomas J.
American Association for Respiratory Care *(51)*

Kallushi, Kastriot
Diplomatic and Consular Officers, Retired (Dacor) *(412)*

Kalmus, Elizabeth
Industrial Research Institute *(494)*

Kalogeridis, Carla
Association Media and Publishing *(262)*

Kalokitis, Stacy M.
Metal Powder Industries Federation *(613)*

Kalutkiewicz, Michael J.

Academy of Radiology Research *(8)*

Kam, Karl
International Advertising Association *(509)*

Kamara, Tamara
College of Healthcare Information Management Executives *(364)*

Kamhong Thompson, Brittaney R.
National Concrete Masonry Association *(725)*

Kaminskas, Pete
TechAmerica (fka Technology Association of America) *(969)*

Kaminsky, Harry
American Arbitration Association *(46)*

Kamm, Justin
Association of Volleyball Professionals *(317)*

Kammerer, Michelle Tigard
Country Radio Broadcasters, Inc. *(401)*

Kamon, Leah
Radio Advertising Bureau *(873)*

Kamoun, Sophien
International Society for Molecular Plant Microbe Interactions *(567)*

Kampman, Rosalba
Biophysical Society *(330)*

Kamszik, Micki
RCI, Inc. *(875)*

Kana, Bill
American Academy of Audiology *(31)*

Kanagy, David L.
Society for Mining, Metallurgy and Exploration, Inc. *(915)*

Kanapeaux, Kate
Information Systems Security Association *(495)*

Kane, PhD, Anthony R.
AASHTO: Transportation Center of Excellence *(2)*

Kane, Christopher M.
American Geological Institute *(126)*

Kane, Coleman J.
Tax Executives Institute, Inc. *(968)*

Kane, Daniel J.
United Mine Workers of America *(988)*

Kane, Frances
Association of Waldorf Schools of North America *(317)*

Kane, Gerry
Association for Iron and Steel Technology *(250)*

Kane, MD, John M.
American Society of Clinical Psychopharmacology *(195)*

Kane, Mary Reynolds
Professional Convention Management Association *(861)*

Kane, Meg
National Association of Waterfront Employers *(709)*
National Maritime Safety Association *(772)*

Kane, Sanford
National Alliance for Advanced Transportation Batteries *(631)*

Kane, Sarah
Agricultural Stewardship Association *(16)*

Kane, Terry M.
Industrial Diamond Association of America *(493)*

Kane-Lee, Emily
Gay and Lesbian Medical Association *(457)*

Kanefield, Karen
American Association of Suicidology *(74)*

Kanich, Jack
American College of Prosthodontists *(101)*

Kanis, Jim
American Library Association *(145)*

Kanon, Carolyn
American Bankruptcy Institute *(79)*

Kantrowitz, Michele
International Society for Medical Publication Professionals *(567)*

Kantsios, Victoria
National Association of Ordnance and Explosive Waste Contractors *(682)*

Kanwit, Stephanie W.
America's Health Insurance Plans *(28)*

Kanya, D. Theresa
American College of Physicians *(101)*

Kao, Andrew
Interactive Advertising Bureau *(506)*

Kapfer, Greg
Internet Society *(582)*

Kapinos, Maggie
Amusement & Music Operators Association *(223)*

Kaplan, CMP, Ellen
International Society for Performance Improvement *(567)*

Kaplan, Keith
Fur Information Council of America *(454)*

Kaplan, Lorrie Kline
American College of Nurse-Midwives *(99)*

Kaplan, Marianne
American Spinal Injury Association *(212)*

Kaplan, Mark
Ceilings and Interior Systems Construction Association *(347)*

Kaplan, Stephanie
Pet Industry Distributors Association *(842)*

Kapler, Robert
America's Blood Centers *(28)*

Kaplowitz, MS, Jessica Marino
Association of Schools of Allied Health Professions *(307)*

Kaplowitz, Karen
Distributed Computing Industry Association *(414)*

Kappas, MA, MFT, George J.
American Hypnosis Association *(134)*

Kappel, Dawn
National Council of State Boards for Nursing *(736)*

Kappel, Ellen S.
The Oceanography Society *(826)*

Kappeler, Sue
National Management Association *(771)*

Kappmeier, Kelly
Association for Healthcare Documentation Integrity *(247)*

Kara, Paula
Society for Neuroscience *(916)*

Karadbil, Jenna
International Technology Law Association *(577)*

Karamanos, Rigas
Soil and Plant Analysis Council *(951)*

Karamat, Sherrif
Professional Convention Management Association *(861)*

Karamyar, Tina
Decorative Plumbing and Hardware Association *(408)*

Karasov, Phyllis
International Association for Identification *(513)*

Karasu, MD, T. Byram
Association for the Advancement of Psychotherapy *(258)*

Karch, Elizabeth H.
Real Estate Roundtable *(876)*

Karcher, David A.
American Society of Cataract and Refractive Surgery *(194)*

Karcher, Michael
United States Superyacht Association *(999)*

Karchner, CMP, Paula J.
The Council of Insurance Agents and Brokers *(394)*

Karczewski, Joel
Automotive Industry Action Group *(322)*

Kardos, Zorica
International Federation of Nurse Anesthetists *(544)*

Karen, Jay
Professional Association of Innkeepers International *(860)*

Karges, Matthew
Builders Association *(338)*

Karhuse, Amanda
National Association of Secondary School Principals *(694)*

Karl, Susan
Council of Residential Specialists *(396)*

Karlin, W. Michael
Veterinary Orthopedic Society *(1008)*

Karlson, PhD, David
Society of General Internal Medicine *(937)*

Karnani Bonjour, Shalini 'Shelly'
SCORE Association *(893)*

Karoff, Paul
American Academy of Arts & Sciences *(30)*

Karolak, Eric
Early Care and Education Consortium *(417)*

Karp, Donna N.
Society of Professional Investigators *(945)*

Karp, Jonathan
The American Jewish Historical Society *(143)*

Karp, Stacey
Association of Public Television Stations *(304)*

Karp, Stacey
Association of Public Television Stations *(304)*

Karpowicz, CAE, Pauline
American Political Science Association *(166)*

Karpowicz, Polly
Academy of Political Science *(8)*

Karr, Gary
Advanced Medical Technology Association (AdvaMed) *(13)*

Karras, Terry
American Society for Therapeutic Radiology and Oncology *(190)*

Karsnak, Emily
International Communication Association *(536)*

Karson, CAE, Jennifer
Association of Nutrition & Foodservice Professionals *(296)*

Karstaedt, Todd
American Society for Therapeutic Radiology and Oncology *(190)*

Kart, Suzanne
Learning Resources Network *(596)*

Kasabian, Robert J.
American Jail Association *(142)*

Kasbaum, Diana
Association of State Supervisors of Mathematics *(311)*

Kase, Kirsten
Automotive Parts Remanufacturers Association *(323)*

Kasekamp, Andres
Association for the Advancement of Baltic Studies *(258)*

Kasen, Dan
National Sporting Goods Association *(796)*

Kasendorf, Christina
The Association for Academic Surgery *(237)*

Kasinitz, Barry
International Association of Fire Fighters *(521)*

Kaskas, Safi
Association of Muslim Social Scientists of North America *(295)*

Kaslow, D. Carlos
Self Storage Association *(896)*

Kasmark, Chris
LeadingAge (American Association of Homes and Services for the Aging) *(595)*

Kasmer, Donna Lee
National Chimney Sweep Guild *(721)*

Kasmer, Joyce
Inter-Industry Conference on Auto Collision Repair *(506)*

Kasowicz, Jennifer
National Society of Genetic Counselors *(794)*
Society of Gastroenterology Nurses and Associates *(937)*

Kasper, Elizabeth
American Society of Clinical Hypnosis *(194)*

Kasper, Evie
Grocery Manufacturers Association (GMA) *(466)*

Kasper, CAE, PhD, John E.
American Society of Clinical Hypnosis *(194)*
User Experience Professionals Association *(1005)*

Kassalen, MBA, Beth
International Society of Nurses in Genetics *(573)*
International Transplant Nurses Society *(578)*

Kassimatis, Yvonne
American Association for the Study of Liver Diseases *(52)*

Kasson, Janet
American Concrete Pumping Association *(106)*

Kassouf, Kass
Consumer Healthcare Products Association *(381)*

Kastigar, Elizabeth (Beth)
Consumer Credit Industry Association *(381)*

Kasuyi, Ditu
Urban Financial Services Coalition *(1003)*

Kaswell, Stuart J.
Managed Funds Association *(602)*

Katanick, CAE, Sandra L.
Intersocietal Accreditation Commission *(582)*

Kato, Erin
American Student Dental Association *(214)*

Katopis, Christopher J.
The Association of Mortgage Investors *(295)*

Kator, Chris
American Society of Safety Engineers *(209)*

Kats, Natalia
University Professional & Continuing Education Association *(1003)*

Katsikeas, Constantine
Academy of Marketing Science *(6)*

Katterjohn, Chris
Alliance of Area Business Publications *(24)*

Katto, Cireena
American Canoe Association *(88)*

Katz, Irv
National Human Services Assembly *(761)*

Katz, Jonathan
National Assembly of State Arts Agencies *(635)*

Katz, MD, Karen
Phi Delta Epsilon International Medical Fraternity *(845)*

Katz, Marc
National Association of State Workforce Agencies *(703)*

Katz, Mia
International Association of Plastics Distributors *(526)*

Katz, ChFC, CLU, Richard S.
Inter-Company Marketing Group *(506)*

Katzman, David
International Labor Communications Association *(553)*

Kauffman, Sue
American Geophysical Union *(126)*

Kauffman, Tim
American Federation of Government Employees *(119)*

Kauffmann, Peter
The College Board *(363)*

Kaufman, Alan P.
Toy Industry Association *(976)*

Kaufman, Betsy
America's Small Business Development Center Network *(29)*
Association of Small Business Development Centers *(308)*

Kaufman, James
National Association of Children's Hospitals and Related Institutions *(653)*

Kaufman, Kristie
American Society for Metabolic and Bariatric Surgery *(187)*

Kaufman, Larry
Electronics Representatives Association *(424)*

Kaufman, Rabbi Jan Caryl
Rabbinical Assembly *(872)*

Kaufman, CAE, Rita Schauer
Association of Professional Chaplains *(301)*

Kaufman, Roxanne
Marine Corps Aviation Association *(604)*

Kaumaya, Biljana
The American Institute of Architects *(137)*

Kaumaya, Pravin T.P.
American Peptide Society *(163)*

Kaur, Mandy
National Environmental Balancing Bureau *(746)*

Kautter, CAE, Bill
National Association of Physician Recruiters *(684)*

Kautter, CAE, Tina
Society for Technological Advancement of Reporting *(922)*

Kautzman, Kim
International Association of Railway Operating Officers *(527)*

Kauvar, Joanne Marks
Council of American Jewish Museums *(391)*

Kavanagh, Lawrence
American Iron and Steel Institute *(142)*

Kavanagh, Malachy
International Council of Shopping Centers **(538)**

Kavanagh, Shayne
Government Finance Officers Association of the United States and Canada **(464)**

Kavanaugh, Meegan
American Spice Trade Association **(212)**

Kaveny, Donald B.
American College of Osteopathic Surgeons **(100)**

Kavinoky, Janet F.
United States Chamber of Commerce **(991)**

Kawamura, Yoshi
The Integrated Ocean Drilling Program **(505)**

Kawano, Sandy
Society of United States Air Force Flight Surgeons **(949)**

Kay, Ann
AFL-CIO Housing Investment Trust **(15)**

Kay, David
Women in Film **(1021)**

Kay, Richard S.
American Society of Comparative Law **(195)**

Kay, Sally
The Hosiery Association **(478)**

Kay, Sara
New York E-Health Collaborative **(809)**

Kaye, David
Association for Theatre in Higher Education **(260)**

Kaye, Lori
American Feed Industry Association **(120)**

Kaye, Marty
National Intramural-Recreational Sports Association **(766)**

Kaylie, Tracy
Resolve, The National Infertility Association **(883)**

Kaylor, Debbie
National Cattlemen's Beef Association **(718)**

Kaylor, Susan
Global Market Development Center **(462)**

Kays, B. Thomas
Psi Omega Fraternity **(868)**

Kayser, Adele
Equipment Service Association **(433)**
The International Fluid Power Society **(545)**

Kazakoff, Lois
Association of Opinion Journalists **(297)**

Kazi, Olympia
Van Alen Institute **(1007)**

Kazim, Yvonne
American Public Health Association **(171)**

Kazimir, Gina
Special Event Sites Marketing Alliance **(954)**

Kazmark, Karen
Kitchen Cabinet Manufacturers Association **(591)**

Kean, David A.
Resort Hotel Association **(883)**

Keane, Alison
American Coatings Association **(92)**

Keane, CAE, Anthony J.
International Facility Management Association **(543)**

Keane, Kevin P.
International Association of Printing House Craftsmen **(526)**

Keane, Kevin W.
American Beverage Association **(80)**

Keane, Laura B.
Society for Maintenance & Reliability Professionals **(914)**

Keane, Lawrence G.
National Shooting Sports Foundation **(791)**

Keane, Susan
Marketing Science Institute **(606)**

Keaney, Elizabeth
International Museum Theatre Alliance **(557)**

Kearney, Lisa K.
Association of Psychology Postdoctoral and Internship Centers **(303)**

Kearney, Susan
Council of Better Business Bureaus **(392)**

Kearney, Tom
American Frozen Food Institute **(124)**

Kearns, Brian
United States Energy Association **(993)**

Kearns, Heather
Women in Government **(1021)**

Kearns, John J.
Copper Development Association **(384)**

Kearns, Kevin L.
United States Business and Industry Council **(991)**

Kearns, Stacie
USA Volleyball **(1005)**

Keathley, Karen Marie
American Society of Podiatric Medical Assistants **(208)**

Keating, Frank
American Bankers Association **(79)**

Keating, Gail
International Reading Association **(562)**

Keating, Patricia H.
Air Distribution Institute **(18)**

Keating, Sonja
United States Equestrian Federation **(993)**

Keaton, Michael
Natural Products Association **(807)**

Kebede, Kebret
Human Anatomy and Physiology Society **(480)**

Kechichian, Joseph
Society of Armenian Studies **(930)**

Keck, Daniel
Healthcare Financial Management Association **(471)**

Kecskemethy, Tom
American Academy of Political and Social Science **(40)**

Kedia, Satish
National Association for the Practice of Anthropology **(644)**

Keebler, Barbara A.
National Catholic Educational Association **(718)**
National Catholic Educational Exhibitors **(718)**

Keefe, COl, USAF (Ret.), Joseph
National Military Intelligence Association **(772)**

Keefe, Pamela J.
Electric Power Research Institute **(421)**

Keefer, Kerri
International Spa Association **(575)**

Keegan, Tom
American Institute of Fishery Research Biologists **(138)**

Keegstra, Jennifer
Christian Labor Association of the United States of America **(355)**

Keehan, Jenny
Retail Industry Leaders Association **(884)**

Keehnen, Jenna
United States Organizations for Bankruptcy Alternatives (USOBA) **(997)**

Keel, Judith K.
Association of Women Surgeons **(317)**
Independent Medical Distributors Association **(490)**

Keel, Katie
Association of Women Surgeons **(317)**
Independent Medical Distributors Association **(490)**

Keel, William D.
Society for German-American Studies **(910)**

Keeler, Honor
Association on American Indian Affairs **(319)**

Keeling, Carol
Professional Landcare Network **(863)**

Keeling, CAE, J. Michael
Employee Stock Ownership Plan Association **(426)**

Keeling, John
National Potato Council **(782)**

Keen, David
National Association of Counties **(659)**
National Association of County Intergovernmental Relations Officials **(660)**

Keen, Mary Lou
American Gem Trade Association **(125)**

Keenan, CAE, Barbara Byrd
Institute of Food Technologists **(499)**

Keenan, EdD, Derek
Association of Christian Schools International **(272)**

Keenan, Kara
International Institute of Fisheries Economics and Trade **(551)**

Keenan, William
Craft & Hobby Association **(402)**

Keene, Michael
International Union of Police Associations, AFL-CIO **(579)**

Keene, Dr. Robert C.
American Academy of Gold Foil Operators **(34)**

Keener, Ray
Bicycle Product Suppliers Association **(329)**

Keeney, Tyler T.
Association of Marketing Service Providers **(293)**

Keese, Bill
Association of Progressive Rental Organizations **(303)**

Keesler, David C
Federal Magistrate Judges Association **(439)**

Keesler, James
National Electronic Service Dealers Association **(745)**

Kegerreis, Michael W.
North American Society for Oceanic History **(821)**

Kegley, Jacquelyn
Society for the Advancement of American Philosophy **(922)**

Kehlbeck, Keith
Distinguished Restaurants of North America **(414)**

Kehn, Tisha
American Society of Neuroimaging **(204)**
Association for Chemoreception Sciences **(241)**

Kehnemui, Sharon
American Enterprise Institute for Public Policy Research **(117)**

Kehoe, Peter
NAFSA: Association of International Educators **(624)**

Keilitz, Dave
American Baseball Coaches Association **(80)**

Keilman, Nan
Trade Exchange of America *(977)*

Keilty, Mike
Society for the Advancement of Material and Process Engineering *(922)*

Keim, Chris
American Embryo Transfer Association *(116)*

Keim, Jessica Clark
Gerontological Society of America *(460)*

Keippel, Judy
National Association of Women Highway Safety Leaders, Inc. *(709)*

Keiser, Jennette
Society for Environmental Graphic Design *(908)*

Keister, Jane
Shareholder Services Association *(898)*

Keith, David
National Religious Broadcasters *(785)*

Keith, Floyd A.
Black Coaches & Administrators *(331)*

Keith, Gary S.
National Fire Protection Association *(751)*

Keith, Heather
Association of Oil Pipe Lines *(296)*

Keith, Karen
Association of College Unions International *(274)*

Keith, MD, MSPH, Stephen N.
American College of Clinical Pharmacology *(94)*

Keith-Hoffman, Kristi
National Franchisee Association *(753)*

Keithley, Carter E.
Toy Industry Association *(976)*

Kelemen, Danna
National Agricultural Aviation Association *(630)*

Kelemen, Kim
Association of Clinical Research Professionals *(273)*

Kelemen, Kim
National Insulation Association *(766)*

Kelham, Tiffany
International Ticketing Association *(577)*

Kell, Brian
American Thoracic Society *(216)*

Kelleher, Amber
Association of Corporate Travel Executives (ACTE) *(277)*

Kelleher, Jack
Amusement & Music Operators Association *(223)*

Kelleher, Roger
American Management Association *(146)*

Kelleher, Sean
Society of Fire Protection Engineers *(936)*

Kellenberger, David
World International Nail and Beauty Association *(1026)*

Keller, Alice S.
Gemological Institute of America *(457)*

Keller, Alison
National Association of State Chief Information Officers *(699)*

Keller, Elizabeth
International Microelectronics and Packaging Society - IMAPS *(556)*

Keller, Jeff
Academy for Eating Disorders *(3)*
American Society of Tropical Medicine and Hygiene *(210)*

Keller, Kaaryn
National Association of Student Personnel Administrators *(626)*

Keller, Karen
Graphic Arts Technical Foundation *(465)*

Keller, Kit
Association of Pedestrian and Bicycle Professionals *(298)*

Keller, Marthe
American Abstract Artists *(29)*

Keller, Michael E.
American Society of Test Engineers *(209)*

Keller, Tracy
Association of Girl Scout Executive Staff *(285)*

Kellermann, Kim
American Stamp Dealers Association *(213)*

Kellermann, Tad
National Lipid Association *(770)*

Kelley, CAE, Allison
Romance Writers of America *(888)*

Kelley, Barbara
Hearing Loss Association of America *(472)*

Kelley, Brady
National Association of Insurance Commissioners *(676)*
National Association of Professional Surplus Lines Offices, Ltd. *(688)*

Kelley, Bryan
National FFA Organization *(750)*

Kelley, Colleen M.
National Treasury Employees Union *(801)*

Kelley, Dave
National Recreation and Parks Association *(784)*

Kelley, Elizabeth
Real Estate Valuation Advocacy Association *(876)*

Kelley, Jodie L.
BSA | The Software Alliance *(337)*

Kelley, Lisa
National Council of Farmer Cooperatives *(734)*

Kelley, Megan
Scoliosis Research Society *(893)*

Kelley, Paul L.
International Economic Development Council *(541)*

Kelley, Peter
National Association of Japan-America Societies *(677)*

Kelley, Rae
ASPRS-The Imaging and Geospatial Information Society *(233)*

Kelley, Tom
Truck Writers of North America *(981)*

Kellick, Bill
USA Taekwondo *(1005)*

Kelliher, Rita M.
Association of Schools of Public Health *(307)*

Kellman, Brian M.
Railway Supply Institute *(874)*

Kellmeyer, Peachy
WTA Tour, Inc. *(1029)*

Kellner, Debbi
International Health, Racquet and Sportsclub Association *(549)*

Kellough, Jalane
Electrical Generating Systems Association *(422)*

Kelly, Andrea
International Association of Infant Massage *(523)*

Kelly, Brendan
National Forensic Association *(752)*

Kelly, Carol A.
National Association of Chain Drug Stores *(652)*

Kelly, Charles L.
American Association of Minority Businesses *(65)*

Kelly, Chris
National Marine Representatives Association *(771)*

Kelly, Craig L.
National Association for Home Care and Hospice *(639)*

Kelly, Donald E.
Real Estate Valuation Advocacy Association *(876)*

Kelly, Edmund J.
American Association of Insurance Services *(63)*

Kelly, Jack A.
Institutional Life Markets Association *(504)*

Kelly, James F.
National Sculpture Society *(790)*

Kelly, John
Geothermal Heat Pump Consortium *(459)*

Kelly, John
Joint Electron Device Engineering Council *(589)*
Metal Construction Association *(613)*

Kelly, Esq., John J.
Book Manufacturers' Institute *(333)*

Kelly, Karla
National Recreation and Parks Association *(784)*

Kelly, Kevin
Electronic Retailing Association *(423)*

Kelly, Laura
Sewn Products Equipment and Suppliers of the Americas *(898)*

Kelly, Lauren
National Apartment Association *(634)*

Kelly, Lee Norton
New England Club Managers Association *(809)*

Kelly, Linda
Water Environment Federation *(1013)*

Kelly, Michael A.
International Society of Barristers *(571)*

Kelly, Mike
Solid-State Circuits Society *(952)*

Kelly, Patrick
Healthcare Distribution Management Association *(471)*

Kelly, Rhoda L.
National Association of Chain Drug Stores *(652)*

Kelly, Richelle
Voluntary Protection Programs Participants' Association, Inc. *(1011)*

Kelly, Robert D.
Jesuit Association of Student Personnel Administrators *(587)*

Kelly, Shannon
Cotton Council International *(387)*

Kelly, Sharon L.
International Association of Emergency Managers *(520)*
National Association of State Emergency Medical Services Officials *(700)*

Kelly, Susan
American Public Power Association *(171)*

Kelly, Teresa C.
American Translators Association *(217)*

Kelly, Tom
United States Ski and Snowboard Association *(999)*

Kelly, William
American Society for Engineering Education *(183)*

Kelly Ball, Erin E.
Commodity Markets Council *(368)*

Kelly,, MSN, RN, Glenda
Association of Public Health Nurses *(304)*

Kelman, Lori
Beta Beta Beta *(328)*

Kelso, Heather
PMA - The Worldwide Community of Imaging
Associations *(851)*

Keltner, Stephen
Sculptors Guild *(894)*

Kemerling, Karen
Association of periOperative Registered Nurses *(299)*

Kemmerer, Kristél Pfeil
Music and Entertainment Industry Educators
Association *(622)*

Kemmis, Barbara
Cremation Association of North America *(404)*

Kemnitz, D'Arcy
National Lesbian and Gay Law Association *(769)*

Kemp, Ellen
National Immigration Project of the National Lawyers
Guild *(761)*

Kemp, Lauren
Bank Insurance and Securities Association *(326)*
National Association of Local Housing Finance
Agencies *(678)*

Kemp, CAE, Steven C
American College of Oral and Maxillofacial Surgeons
(99)

Kemp, Todd E.
National Grain and Feed Association *(755)*

Kemp, Yakini B.
College Language Association *(363)*

Kemper, ARM, Coletta I.
The Council of Insurance Agents and Brokers *(394)*

Kempis-Persons, Jen
North American Meat Association *(818)*

Kempthorne, Dirk
American Council of Life Insurers (ACLI) *(110)*

Kendall, Anna Mariae
Material Handling Equipment Distributors Association
(608)

Kendall, David
The Brown Swiss Association *(336)*

Kendall, David J.
American Milking Shorthorn Society *(152)*

Kendall, Kurt
Guild of American Luthiers *(467)*

Kendall, Patrick
American Frozen Food Institute *(124)*

Kendall, Steve
American Jail Association *(142)*

Kendall, Tip Tucker
Women's Basketball Coaches Association *(1022)*

Kendall-Ellis, PT, Laurie
American Physical Therapy Association - Private
Practice Section *(165)*

Kendrick, James
Independent Community Bankers of America *(488)*

Kendrick, James M.
American Society of Composers, Authors and
Publishers (ASCAP) *(195)*

Kendrick, Nancy C.

The American Electrophoresis Society *(116)*

Kendrick, Robyn
American Association of Veterinary State Boards *(76)*

Kendrick, Stephen
National Lumber and Building Material Dealers
Association *(770)*

Kendrick, Stephen
Window and Door Manufacturers Association *(1018)*

Kendzel, CAE, MPH, Jim
American Society of Plumbing Engineers *(207)*

Kennard, Aaron D.
National Sheriffs' Association *(791)*

Kennedy, Carol
Research!America *(882)*

Kennedy, Colleen
BAFT-IFSA *(325)*

Kennedy, David
Council on Governmental Relations *(400)*

Kennedy, David W.
American Rhinologic Society *(175)*

Kennedy, Debra
American Society for Dermatologic Surgery *(183)*

Kennedy, Eileen
American Littoral Society *(146)*

Kennedy, Erica
American Academy of Actuaries *(29)*

Kennedy, Jr., Gerard J.
Plumbing-Heating-Cooling Contractors - National
Association *(851)*

Kennedy, Hank
American Management Association *(146)*

Kennedy, Jason
The International Stability Operations Association
(575)

Kennedy, John
International Society of Bassists *(571)*

Kennedy, John
National Association of Fire Investigators *(668)*

Kennedy, John
National Association of Student Personnel
Administrators *(626)*

Kennedy, John J.
Jewelers' Security Alliance of the United States *(587)*

Kennedy, Judith A.
National Association of Affordable Housing Lenders
(646)

Kennedy, Kay
International Association for Corporate and
Professional Recruitment *(511)*

Kennedy, Lindsay
National Sorghum Producers *(795)*

Kennedy, Lisa
National Swine Registry *(798)*

Kennedy, Mark
AMT - The Association For Manufacturing Technology
(222)

Kennedy, Michael E.
Associated General Contractors of America (AGC) *(236)*

Kennedy, Miki
Professional Association of Volleyball Officials *(860)*

Kennedy, Richard
International Federation of Fertility Societies *(544)*

Kennedy, Rozella
American Indian Science and Engineering Society *(135)*

Kennedy, Sandra L.

Retail Industry Leaders Association *(884)*

Kennedy, Shannon
High Point Market *(474)*

Kennedy, Sharonda
International Association of Lighting Designers *(524)*

Kennedy, Sheena
Association of Boards of Certification *(270)*

Kennedy, Steven
International Swaps and Derivatives Association *(576)*

Kennedy-Sutherland, Elaine
Tree-Ring Society *(980)*

Kennelly, Edward J.
American Society of Pharmacognosy *(207)*

Kennemore, MS, Wes
Association of Public Health Laboratories *(304)*

Kenner, LAc, PhD, Dan
National Health Federation *(758)*

Kennett, Earle W.
National Institute of Building Sciences *(764)*

Kenney, SPHR, Deb
National Shooting Sports Foundation *(791)*

Kenney, Jamila
International Association of Movers *(525)*

Kenney, Jeffrey F.
National Council for Interior Design Qualifications
(732)

Kenney, Jo
Women's Council of REALTORS *(1023)*

Kenney, P E, Thomas
National Association of Home Builders Research
Center *(673)*

Kenniff, Thomas
National Press Photographers Association *(782)*

Kennison, Silvia
Hispanic Association of Colleges and Universities *(475)*

Kenny, Maura
The Renaissance Society of America *(881)*

Kenny, Rhenda Mayo
American Welding Society *(220)*

Kensell, Debi
Restaurant Facility Management Association *(884)*

Kent, Alan
American Institute of Building Design *(137)*

Kent, Bill
Chevron and Texaco Petroleum Marketers Association
(352)

Kent, David L.
Amalgamated Printer's Association *(27)*

Kent, Jeanette
Oncology Nursing Society *(827)*

Kent, John G.
Safety Glazing Certification Council *(890)*

Kent, Jonathan
International Association of Airport Duty Free Stores
(515)

Kent, Kathy
Geothermal Energy Association *(459)*

Kent, Norma G.
American Association of Community Colleges *(58)*

Kenyon, Dione D.
Jewelers Board of Trade *(587)*

Kenyon, John
Nonprofit Technology Network *(811)*

Kenyon, PhD, Kaylene J.

American Association of Immunologists **(62)**

Kenyon, Michael
Percussive Arts Society **(841)**

Keogh, Miles
National Association of Regulatory Utility
    Commissioners **(691)**

Keough, Katherine
National Association of State Controlled Substances
    Authorities **(699)**

Keough, Matthew
American Historical Association **(131)**

Kephart, Amy
The American Society of Pediatric Hematology/
    Oncology **(206)**

Kepler, Brynn
American Association of Meat Processors **(64)**

Kepner, MEd, Susan
Association for Surgical Education **(257)**

Keppler, Stephen A.
Commercial Vehicle Safety Alliance **(367)**

Keppler, CMP, Trish
Society for Social Work Leadership in Health Care
    (921)
Water and Sewer Distributors of America **(1012)**

Keramidas, PhD, CAE, Sherry
Regulatory Affairs Professionals Society **(879)**

Keran, Christopher M
American Academy of Neurology **(36)**

Kerans, Stacey
Glass Packaging Institute **(461)**

Kerby, MBA, Zane
Global Business Travel Association **(462)**

Kerchner, George A.
PRBA - The Rechargeable Battery Association **(856)**

Kerchval, Michael P.
International Council of Shopping Centers **(538)**

Kerester, Alison
Gasification Technologies Council **(457)**

Kerezy, John
Community College Journalism Association **(370)**

Kerg, Fran
American Polarity Therapy Association **(166)**

Kerhin, Jennifer
Association for Vascular Access **(261)**

Kerker, Kim
National Council of Architectural Registration Boards
    (733)

Kerkhoven, Paul
NGVAmerica **(810)**

Kerkuska, Gabe
Construction Financial Management Association **(379)**

Kerley, Michael L.
National Association of Insurance and Financial
    Advisors **(675)**
National Association Of Insurance and Financial
    Advisors(NAIFA) **(676)**

Kern, Joseph D.
International Association of Color Manufacturers **(518)**

Kernick, Stevie Hughes
Property Records Industry Association **(867)**

Kerns, Bill
National Tunis Sheep Registry **(802)**

Kerns, CAE, Donald E.
Society of Diagnostic Medical Sonographers **(934)**

Kerns, Gladys
State Higher Education Executive Officers **(961)**

Kerns, Ruth
American Student Dental Association **(214)**

Kerns, Samuel
American Forest & Paper Association **(123)**

Kerns, Tracey
Agricultural Retailers Association **(16)**

Kerr, Camille
National Center for Employee Ownership **(719)**

Kerr, Jill K.
Physician Insurers Association of America **(847)**

Kerr, John W.
Atlantic Independent Union **(319)**

Kerr, Kenneth
American Backflow Prevention Association **(78)**

Kerr, Michael R.
National Conference of Commissioners on Uniform
    State Laws **(727)**

Kerr, Paula
American Salvage Pool Association **(177)**

Kerr, Robert
National Association of Enrolled Agents **(666)**

Kerrigan, Steve
Multi-Housing Laundry Association **(621)**

Kersels, Kristina
Association of Moving Image Archivists **(295)**

Kersting, CAE, Christopher J.
Specialty Equipment Market Association **(957)**

Kerzner, ChFC, CLU, Robert A.
LOMA **(600)**

Kesinger, Lori
International Association of Audio Information Services
    (516)

Kesler, Linda
American Simmental Association **(179)**

Kesler, Zachary
American Society of Nuclear Cardiology **(205)**

Kesselbrenner, Dan
National Immigration Project of the National Lawyers
    Guild **(761)**

Kessler, Brett
American North Country Cheviot Sheep Association
    (156)

Kessler, Drew
National Foundation for Credit Counseling **(753)**

Kessler, Greg
Computer Assisted Language Instruction Consortium
    (372)

Kessler, Melissa George
National Association of Wheat Growers **(709)**

Kessler, Robin
The Ripon Society **(886)**

Kessler, Theresa
International Foodservice Distributors Association
    (546)

Kessler, Wayne
American Arbitration Association **(46)**

Kestler, Eric
Construction Specifications Institute **(380)**

Ketch, Todd D.
American Health Quality Association **(130)**

Ketchum, Jim
Association of American Geographers **(265)**

Ketchum, Kevin
North American Wholesale Lumber Association **(823)**

Ketchum, Lauren

International Sanitary Supply Association **(563)**

Ketchum, Richard G.
Financial Industry Regulatory Authority (FINRA) **(444)**

Ketevong, Samlane
American Board for Certification in Orthotics and
    Prosthetics, Inc. (ABC) **(81)**

Kettering, Carolyn
American Society of Heating, Refrigerating and Air
    Conditioning Engineers (ASHRAE) **(199)**

Kettering, Maureen
Environmental Mutagen Society **(431)**
Society of Toxicologic Pathologists **(948)**
Society of Toxicologic Pathology **(948)**

Ketterling, Dana
American Chamber of Commerce Executives **(89)**

Keuneke, Kathryn F.
Million Dollar Round Table **(616)**

Keuren, Carol Van
Theatre Communications Group **(973)**

Kevil, PhD, Chris
Society for Free Radical Biology and Medicine **(909)**

Keville, Kathi
American Herb Association **(130)**

Kevorkian, Christopher
MPA - The Association of Magazine Media **(620)**

Key, Joanne
Environmental Council of the States **(431)**

Key, Linda
National Association of Steel Pipe Distributors **(703)**

Key, Sidney "Louie " L.
Aircraft Mechanics Fraternal Association **(20)**

Keydash, Mary
International Society for Magnetic Resonance in
    Medicine **(567)**

Keyes, Elizabeth
American Pharmacists Association **(163)**

Keyes, Hayley
International Professional Groomers **(561)**

Keys, John
National Institute of Building Sciences **(764)**

Keys, Lynda
Cotton Incorporated **(387)**

Keyser, Angela R.
American Association of Physicists in Medicine **(69)**

Keyser, Christopher
Writers Guild of America West **(1029)**

Keyser, Jenny
Higher Education Consortium for Urban Affairs **(475)**

Keyserling, JD, Jonathan
National Hospice & Palliative Care Organization **(760)**

Kezios, Susan
American Franchisee Association **(123)**

Khalsa, Karta "K.P." Purkh
American Herbalists Guild **(131)**

Khan, Farzin A.
National Association of Securities Professionals **(695)**

Khan, MD, Jemshed A.
American Society of Ophthalmic Plastic and
    Reconstructive Surgery **(205)**

Khan, Sajjad
Canola Council of Canada **(341)**

Khan, Zahrah
American Sheep Industry Association **(178)**
American Wool Council **(222)**

Kharecha, Shilpa

Association for Asian Studies *(239)*

Khatchadourian, Erica
AFL-CIO Housing Investment Trust *(15)*

Kheradmand, Bahman
Association of the Wall and Ceiling Industry *(314)*

Khirallah, Ernest
American Academy of Ophthalmic Executives *(37)*

Khomina, Irina
Jewish Community Centers Association of North America *(588)*

Khoo, Michael
Population Action International *(852)*

Khoury, Lynda
National Tooling and Machining Association *(800)*

Kibble, Mark
National Ground Water Association *(756)*

Kibler, Mary Ann
American Art Therapy Association, Inc. *(46)*

Kibort, Toni
Center for Research Libraries *(348)*

Kichler, Florrie Binford
The Independent Book Publishers Association *(488)*

Kicker, Tammy
Association for Enterprise Information *(245)*

Kidd, Nancy
National Communication Association *(724)*

Kidd, Stacey A.
American Society of Plumbing Engineers *(207)*

Kidder, Christopher
Energy Frontiers International *(428)*

Kidder, Ralph
The History of Education Society *(477)*

Kidera, Steve
Consumer Electronics Association *(381)*

Kidwai, Sabrina
American Society of Association Executives-The Center for Association Leadership *(193)*

Kidwell, Arlene
National Association of Student Personnel Administrators *(626)*

Kiefer, Tim
International Society for Clinical Densitometry *(565)*

Kieffer, Donald F.
National Hay Association *(758)*

Kieffer, Joanne
American Society for Parenteral and Enteral Nutrition *(188)*

Kieley, Jennifer
Association of Public Television Stations *(304)*

Kiene, Jacquelyn Beamon
American Physical Society *(164)*

Kiener, Robert C.
Precision Machined Products Association *(856)*

Kiernan, John A.
Biological Stain Commission *(330)*

Kiernan, Thomas C.
National Parks Conservation Association *(779)*

Kierstein, Resa
SCORE Association *(893)*

Kiew, Low Yoke
Malaysian Rubber Export Promotion Council (USA) *(602)*

Kiff, Stacy
American Society of Retina Specialists *(209)*

Kiggins, Karen
National Slag Association *(792)*

Kight, Kimberly
Association of Marketing Service Providers *(293)*

Kiker, Jason
Association of Career and Technical Education *(271)*

Kiklas, Thomas R.
Tobacco Vapor Electronic Cigarette Association *(975)*

Kilbourne, Brett
Utilities Telecom Council *(1006)*

Kilbourne, Kym
Plasma Protein Therapeutics Association *(850)*

Kilbride, Patrick
Association of American Chambers of Commerce in Latin America *(264)*

Kilcawley, Mackenzie
National Association of Real Estate Investment Trusts (NAREIT) *(690)*

Kileff, Heather
Association of Schools of Public Health *(307)*

Kiley, Shannon
Association for Iron and Steel Technology *(250)*

Kilfeather, Stephanie A.
Association of American Railroads *(266)*

Kilgore, Stephanie
Association of Energy Services Professionals, International *(281)*

Kilkelly, Maureen B.
American Federation of Musicians and Employers Pension Fund *(119)*

Kilkenny, Sara
Academy of Physicians in Clinical Research *(8)*

Kill, Debra
Marine Technology Society *(605)*

Killackey, III, James F.
National Association of Postal Supervisors *(685)*

Killalea, Mike
Drilling Engineering Association *(416)*

Killgore, Lucille
American Association of Clinical Endocrinologists *(56)*

Killingsworth, Wanda
Federally Employed Women (FEW) *(440)*

Killion, Diane
AABB - American Association of Blood Banks *(1)*

Killmer, Rev. Richard
National Religious Campaign Against Torture *(786)*

Killmer, William
Mortgage Bankers Association of America *(619)*

Killmeyer, Amy
Hospice and Palliative Nurses Association *(478)*

Killpack, Karen
National Sheriffs' Association *(791)*

Kilner, Pat
Geological Society of America *(459)*

Kilpatrick, Dona
American Institutes for Research *(141)*

Kilstein, Deborah
Association for Community Affiliated Plans *(242)*

Kim, Charles
American Council of Engineering Companies *(109)*

Kim, Charlie
Commercial Vehicle Training Association *(367)*

Kim, Esq., Hank H.
National Conference on Public Employee Retirement Systems *(729)*

Kim, Jin Soo
American Society of Nephrology *(204)*

Kim, Joanne
National Association of Catering and Events *(651)*

Kim, Kelly
Association for Healthcare Philanthropy *(248)*

Kim, Luenna H.
National Society of Newspaper Columnists *(794)*

Kim, Peter
Accrediting Council for Independent Colleges and Schools *(10)*

Kim, Songi
American College of Healthcare Executives *(96)*

Kim, Soo Ryun
Accrediting Council for Independent Colleges and Schools *(10)*

Kim, MA, Vivian C.
National Association of Professional Asian American Women *(686)*

Kim, Yong-Seog
Society for Information Display *(913)*

Kimball, Daryl G.
Arms Control Association *(229)*

Kimball, Marcus
Equipment Marketing and Distribution Association *(432)*

Kimball, CAE, Philip H.
North American Meat Association *(818)*

Kimball, Shannon
Association for Corporate Growth *(244)*

Kimble, Joseph
Scribes-The American Society of Legal Writers *(893)*

Kimble, Mark C.
Solar Electric Power Association *(951)*

Kimble, Vicki
Dance/USA *(406)*

Kimbrell, Meredith
American Wholesale Marketers Association *(221)*

Kimbro, Lisa G.
National Comprehensive Cancer Network *(725)*

Kimbrough-Melton, JD, Robin
American Orthopsychiatric Association *(159)*

Kimmel, Brent
Association of American Law Schools *(265)*

Kimmel, Doug
Society for the Psychological Study of Lesbian and Gay Issues *(924)*

Kimmel, III, Harry A.
Drycleaning & Laundry Institute *(417)*

Kimmel, Kathryn
Gemological Institute of America *(457)*

Kimmet, Haley
TASH *(968)*

Kimmich, Allison
National Women's Studies Association *(805)*

Kimnach, Kim
American Society of Plant Biologists *(207)*

Kimsal, Bob
Jewish Community Centers Association of North America *(588)*

Kimura-Fay, CMP, Ayuko
American Society of Hematology *(199)*

Kinard, Lauren A.
Flexible Packaging Association *(447)*

Kincaid, Ashley McDonald

Phi Delta Kappa International *(845)*
Pi Lambda Theta *(847)*

Kincaid, Diane
American Probation and Parole Association *(167)*

Kincaid, Larry
American Sheep Industry Association *(178)*
American Wool Council *(222)*

Kincaid, Lee
American Maritime Congress *(147)*

Kind, Jerrie Lynn
American Society for Pain Management Nursing *(188)*
National Association of EMS Physicians *(665)*

Kinder, Fred
Pinto Horse Association of America *(848)*

Kindsvatter, Christian
American Society of Podiatry Executives *(208)*

King, Amatullah
American Cleft Palate-Craniofacial Association *(91)*

King, Anika
Software & Information Industry Association (SIIA) *(950)*

King, FACHE, MHSA, Anthony V.
The Wellness Plan *(1015)*

King, Bob
United Auto Workers (UAW) *(986)*

King, Brian
Council of International Investigators *(395)*

King, Catherine
Paso Fino Horse Association, Inc. *(839)*

King, EdD, Dan L.
American Association of University Administrators *(75)*

King, Diana
United States Dairy Export Council *(993)*

King, Don
Association for Conservation Information *(243)*

King, Gail Remy
Hispanic Elected Local Officials *(475)*

King, Irwin
International Neural Network Society *(558)*

King, Jackie
American Veterinary Distributors Association *(218)*
Secondary Materials and Recycled Textiles Association *(894)*

King, Jamie
National Association for Interpretation *(640)*

King, CMP, Jennifer
NALS *(625)*

King, Jerry N.
Synthetic Yarn and Fiber Association *(967)*

King, Joanna
American College of Nurse-Midwives *(99)*

King, Joseph
Institute for Business & Home Safety *(496)*

King, Judy
Bowling Proprietors' Association of America *(334)*
International Bowling Pro Shop and Instructors Association *(530)*

King, Julianna
Dermatology Nurses' Association *(410)*

King, Karen
American Society for Nutrition *(187)*

King, Kim
United Association of Equipment Leasing *(985)*

King, Leslie
Consumer Electronics Association *(381)*

King, Leslie
United States of America Gymnastics *(997)*

King, Linda
Single Ply Roofing Institute *(900)*

King, Mark
National Association of Teachers' Agencies *(705)*

King, Melissa
The Coalition for Government Procurement *(360)*

King, Michael
Mental Health America *(612)*

King, Ophelia
Society of Corporate Secretaries and Governance Professionals *(933)*

King, Patti
National Funeral Directors Association *(754)*

King, Peter B.
American Public Works Association *(172)*

King, Rachel Diamond
Independent Educational Consultants Association *(489)*

King, Rayma
Perennial Plant Association *(841)*

King, CAE, Robin R.
Alliance for Continuing Medical Education *(22)*

King, Roland H.
National Association of Independent Colleges and Universities *(674)*

King, Sheila
Vacation Rental Managers Association *(1007)*

King, Teri
National Collegiate Honors Council *(724)*

King, Tom
Financial Managers Society *(445)*

King, Toshia
Council on Chiropractic Education *(399)*

King,, CAE, Steven T.
Pet Industry Distributors Association *(842)*

King-Gamble, PHR, Marcia
Association for Retail Environments *(256)*

Kingsley, Lynne
Association of Performing Arts Presenters *(298)*

Kingsley, Robert B.
United Electrical Radio & Machine Workers of America *(986)*

Kington, Janet
Association of Girl Scout Executive Staff *(285)*

Kinkade, Michael D.
Accreditation Council for Accountancy and Taxation *(9)*

Kinkade, Tamiko
Hispanic Dental Association *(475)*

Kinlaw, Ruby
International Conference of Police Chaplains *(536)*

Kinnaird, Jula J.
National Grain Trade Council *(756)*

Kinnarney, Kathy
Computer Measurement Group *(372)*

Kinne, Michael B.
United Spinal Association *(989)*

Kinne, Richard "Doc"
American Association of Variable Star Observers *(76)*

Kinnear, Victoria R.
National Information Standards Organization *(763)*

Kinney, Brenda
American Institute of Ultrasound in Medicine *(141)*

Kinney, Emily
Women's Transportation Seminar (WTS International) *(1024)*

Kinney, Linda
Motion Picture Association of America (MPAA) *(619)*

Kinney, Paul
National Retail Tenants Association *(787)*

Kinsman, Matthew
American Business Media *(87)*

Kinter, Marcia
Specialty Graphic Imaging Association *(957)*

Kintz, Justin
European-American Business Council *(434)*

Kinzler, Ben
Diamond Manufacturers & Importers Association of America *(411)*

Kinzler, Jan
Association for Vascular Access *(261)*

Kipley, Richard "Kip"
WorldatWork *(1028)*

Kipper, CJ
Association of Sewing and Design Professionals *(308)*

Kipping, Kelly
International Association of Lighting Management Companies *(524)*

Kirbabas, Chris
American Massage Therapy Association *(147)*

Kirby, Craig A.
Recreation Vehicle Industry Association *(877)*

Kirby, Kenneth
Intersocietal Accreditation Commission *(582)*

Kirch, MD, Darrell G.
Association of American Medical Colleges *(265)*

Kirchhoff, Elizabeth
International Chiropractic Pediatric Association *(534)*

Kirchhoff, Mary
American Chemical Society *(89)*

Kirchner, Joy
National Association of Government Defined Contribution Administrators *(670)*

Kirchner, Paul G.
American Pilots' Association *(165)*

Kireta, Jr., Andrew G.
Copper Development Association *(384)*

Kireta, Sr., Andrew G.
Copper Development Association *(384)*

Kirk, Carl
Technology and Maintenance Council of American Trucking Associations *(970)*

Kirk, Ken
National Association of Clean Water Agencies *(654)*

Kirk, Krista
Academy of Managed Care Pharmacy *(6)*

Kirk, Linda D.
Institute for Responsible Housing Preservation *(497)*

Kirk, Nancye J.
Institute of Real Estate Management *(503)*

Kirk, Esq., Ronda Robinson
Black Entertainment and Sports Lawyers Association *(331)*

Kirk, Sheila
Independent Educational Consultants Association *(489)*

Kirkland, Bradley
Marine Corps Association *(604)*

Kirkland, Chira
National Association of Schools of Art and Design *(693)*
National Association of Schools of Dance *(693)*
National Association of Schools of Music *(694)*

Kirkland, Elizabeth
International Public Management Association for Human Resources *(562)*

Kirkland, Dr. P.H., Katherine
Association of Occupational and Environmental Clinics *(296)*

Kirkland, DrPH, MPH, Katherine H.
Society for Occupational and Environmental Health *(917)*

Kirkland, Lydia
Real Estate Management Brokers Institute *(875)*

Kirkman, Alyssa
Corporate Facility Advisors, Inc. *(386)*

Kirkman, Ellen
Association for Women in Mathematics *(261)*

Kirkpatrick, Charles
National Association of Barber Boards of America *(648)*

Kirkpatrick, James R.
American Astronautical Society *(77)*

Kirkpatrick, Lynn
American Agriculture Movement, Inc. *(44)*

Kirksey-Walcott, Sharon
National Head Start Association *(758)*

Kirrane, Dr. Barbara
American Academy of Clinical Toxicology *(31)*

Kirsch, David
Business History Conference *(339)*

Kirsch, Jonathan
The Independent Book Publishers Association *(488)*

Kirsch, Karl
International Business Brokers Association *(532)*

Kirschner, Celeste
American Society of Anesthesiologists *(192)*

Kirsh, Steven M.
American Academy of Adoption Attorneys *(30)*

Kischak, Peter S.
Service Station Dealers of America and Allied Trades *(898)*

Kiser, Gayle
College and University Professional Association for Human Resources *(362)*

Kiser, Kent
Institute of Scrap Recycling Industries, Inc. *(503)*

Kiser, Kris
Outdoor Power Equipment Aftermarket Association *(835)*
Outdoor Power Equipment Institute *(835)*

Kiser, Melissa
Association of Information Technology Professionals *(289)*

Kish, Keri
National Association of Professional Surplus Lines Offices, Ltd. *(688)*

Kisha, Mike
National Religious Broadcasters *(785)*

Kiskaddon, Sarah H.
Association for the Accreditation of Human Research Protection Programs *(257)*

Kiso, John
National Association of Electrical Distributors *(664)*

Kissel, Kimberly
Society of Broadcast Engineers *(931)*

Kissinger, Courtney
Scoliosis Research Society *(893)*

Kissinger, Tammy
Association of State Correctional Administrators *(310)*

Kistler, Matt
The Council of Insurance Agents and Brokers *(394)*

Kistler, Susan
American Evaluation Association *(118)*

Kitchell, Sharon
StateNets Radio *(962)*

Kitchen, Michelle L.
National Affordable Housing Management Association *(629)*

Kitchene, Gregory
Optometric Extension Program Foundation *(830)*

Kitchens, Esq., William
National Frozen and Refrigerated Foods Association *(753)*

Kite, Angela
Controlled Environment Testing Association *(383)*

Kite, Angela L.
Association for Clinical Research Training *(241)*

Kittner, Alyse
American Organization of Nurse Executives *(158)*

Kittredge, Lloyd E.
Society of Accredited Marine Surveyors *(927)*

Kitts, Tracy
National Business Incubation Association *(717)*

Kitzmiller, W. John
Association of Academic Chairmen of Plastic Surgery *(262)*

Kiva, Jeff
American Society for Blood and Marrow Transplantation *(181)*
American Society of Colon and Rectal Surgeons *(195)*

Kivikko, Renee
Land Trust Alliance *(593)*

Kiyak, Tunga
Academy of International Business *(5)*

Kizart, Vanessa
American Society for Gastrointestinal Endoscopy *(184)*

Kizer, Jr., MBA, William
Wellness Councils of America *(1015)*

Kjaer, Lars
World Shipping Council *(1027)*

Klabacka, Matt
National Association of Heavy Equipment Training Schools *(672)*

Klafeta, Jennifer A.
Delta Omicron *(409)*

Klafter, Craig Evan
American Society for Legal History *(186)*

Klahn, Jennifer
Archaeological Institute of America *(227)*

Klaiber, Pete
United States of America Dry Pea and Lentil Council, Inc. *(996)*

Klapstein, Jessica
American Bearing Manufacturers Association *(80)*

Klapstein, Jessica
Healthcare Supply Chain Association *(472)*

Klapstein, Jessica
National Association of Local Housing Finance Agencies *(678)*

Klatt, Ryan
Golf Coaches Association of America *(463)*

Klatz, DO, MD, Ronald
American Academy of Anti-Aging Medicine *(30)*

Klaus, Kathy
American College of Veterinary Internal Medicine *(104)*

Klausner, Brian
United States Rowing Association *(998)*

Klee, Caro
National Federation of Modern Language Teachers Associations *(749)*

Kleiman, Mary Ellen
National Association of Chain Drug Stores *(652)*

Klein, Alisa
Association for the Treatment of Sexual Abusers *(260)*

Klein, Bill
Alliance for Telecommunications Industry Solutions *(23)*

Klein, Brigid
Consumer Specialty Products Association *(381)*

Klein, Christina
International Association of Industrial Accident Boards and Commissions *(523)*

Klein, CMP, Christine M.
Institute of Food Technologists *(499)*

Klein, Dan
USENIX: The Advanced Computing Systems Association *(1005)*

Klein, Gary J.
National Association of Theatre Owners *(706)*

Klein, CMA, Dr. Hans E.
WACRA - World Association for Case Method Research and Application *(1011)*

Klein, James A.
American Benefits Council *(80)*

Klein, Janice
National Society for Graphology *(792)*

Klein, Jessica
American Association of Veterinary State Boards *(76)*

Klein, Jody
Association of Authors' Representatives *(268)*

Klein, Kathie
Society of Biblical Literature *(931)*

Klein, Ken
Outdoor Advertising Association of America *(834)*

Klein, Kim
PeerSpan *(840)*

Klein, Kolleen
Radiological Society of North America *(873)*

Klein, Lisa
Cosmetic Executive Women *(387)*

Klein, PhD, Nanci
Association for the Advancement of Psychology *(258)*

Klein, Philip
Consumer Specialty Products Association *(381)*

Klein, Randy
Renewable Fuels Association *(881)*

Klein, Capt. Richard
Council of American Master Mariners *(392)*

Klein, DDS, Richard E.
American Academy of Craniofacial Pain *(32)*

Klein, Richard I.
National Association of Manufacturers *(679)*

Klein, Ron
National Board for Certified Clinical Hypnotherapists *(715)*

Kleine, John

BP and AMOCO Marketers Association *(334)*

Kleinman, Pamela
ASM International *(232)*

Kleinman, Ron
Schools Interoperability Framework Association *(892)*

Kleinz, APR, Karen H.
National School Public Relations Association *(789)*

Kleitman, Tobias
National Aircraft Finance Association *(630)*

Klenke, Karin
Association of Management/International Association of Management *(292)*

Klepic, Tracey
National Rural Telecommunications Cooperative *(788)*

Klepser, Colleen B.
The Electrochemical Society *(423)*

Kleso, Mavis E.
Appraisal Foundation *(226)*

Klestzick, Karen R.
National League for Nursing *(768)*

Klett, Janeil
American Association for the Study of Liver Diseases *(52)*

Klich, Kevin
Hispanic Association on Corporate Responsibility *(475)*

Klieforth, Linda
Internet Society *(582)*

Klim, ScD, Edward J.
International Snowmobile Manufacturers Association *(565)*

Klimek, John
National Council for Prescription Drug Programs *(732)*

Klimova, MSc, Oksana
Association of University Centers on Disabilities (AUCD) *(315)*

Klimp, Jack W.
National Association for Uniformed Services *(644)*
Society of Military Widows *(941)*

Kline, Dusty
ARMA International *(228)*

Kline, MD, Lanning B.
North American Neuro-Ophthalmology Society *(819)*

Kline, Michael E.
SSPC: the Society for Protective Coatings *(960)*

Kline, Missy
College and University Professional Association for Human Resources *(362)*

Kline, Richard
Union Label and Service Trades Department *(985)*

Kline, Ron
Society for the History of Technology *(923)*

Kline, Tim
Research Chefs Association *(882)*
Society for Maintenance & Reliability Professionals *(914)*

Klinedinst, CPHIMS, FHIMSS, PMP, JoAnn W.
Healthcare Information and Management Systems Society *(471)*

Klingensmith, MD, Mary
Association for Surgical Education *(257)*

Klinger, Judith
International Association of Culinary Professionals *(519)*

Klinger, Raymond W.
National Ornamental Goldfish Growers Association *(778)*

Klingner, CPM, Gary
Portfolio Management Institute *(853)*

Klink, Angela
AVS: Science and Technology of Materials, Interfaces, and Processing *(325)*

Klinke, Kristi
American Association for the History of Nursing *(52)*
American Society for Indexing *(186)*

Klinski, Sharon
Orthopaedic Section - American Physical Therapy Association *(833)*

Klipple, Bruce J.
United Electrical Radio & Machine Workers of America *(986)*

Klipstein, Richard W.
National Organization of Life and Health Insurance Guaranty Association *(777)*

Kloeppel, Julianna
Public Library Association *(869)*

Klonoski, Grace
Optical Society of America *(829)*

Kloos, Charlene
Alliance of Information and Referral Systems *(25)*

Klose, Jack F.
National Association of Managed Care Physicians *(679)*

Klotzbach, Karl
Farm Equipment Council *(437)*

Klug, Cheryl
Accrediting Council on Education in Journalism and Mass Communications *(11)*

Klugel, Jeff
Association of Surfing Professionals - North America *(312)*

Klugh, Karen
American Financial Services Association *(121)*

Kluss, Todd
Gerontological Society of America *(460)*

Klyberg, Kim
American Association for the Advancement of Science *(51)*

Knaan, Idit
Coalition for Juvenile Justice *(360)*

Knapp, Don
ICLEI - Local Governments for Sustainability *(482)*

Knapp, CAE, Jolene L
Society for College and University Planning *(906)*

Knapp, Kevin
Balloon Federation of America *(325)*

Knapp, Mark
National Blacksmiths and Weldors Association *(715)*

Knapp, Pat Matson
Society for Environmental Graphic Design *(908)*

Kneebone, CAE, Sharon
Institute of Food Technologists *(499)*

Kneiss, Sharon H.
Environmental Industry Associations *(431)*
National Solid Wastes Management Association *(795)*
Waste Equipment Technology Association *(1012)*

Knerr, Andrew
The Society of Wine Educators *(950)*

Knettel, JD, Anthony J.
Association of Academic Health Centers *(262)*

Knezovich, CAE, Jeffrey P.
American Society of Lipo-Suction Surgery *(202)*

Knife, Lee
Digital Media Association *(412)*

Knight, David
American Association of Medical Assistants *(65)*

Knight, CMP, Desiree
American Railway Engineering and Maintenance-of-Way Association *(173)*

Knight, Jack
American Society for Political and Legal Philosophy *(188)*

Knight, Jacque
Association for Dressings and Sauces *(245)*

Knight, Laurie
National Association of Broadcasters *(650)*

Knight, Margaret
Association of American Indian Physicians *(265)*

Knight, Nancy Nicolaides
Association of Foreign Investors in U.S. Real Estate *(284)*

Knight, Sheila
American Morgan Horse Association *(152)*

Knight, Sue
Center for Spiritual and Ethical Education *(348)*

Knight, Susan
National After School Association *(629)*

Knight, Yvonne
American Dental Education Association *(113)*

Knights, Derek E.
Self Storage Association *(896)*

Knipp, Anna Marie
American Hackney Horse Society *(128)*

Knobbe, Jeanne
International Ground Source Heat Pump Association *(549)*

Knoblauch, Jenna
National Alfalfa Alliance *(631)*
National Alfalfa and Forage Alliance *(631)*

Knoetgen, Peter
North American Electric Reliability Corporation *(816)*

Knopes, Carol
Radio Television Digital News Association *(873)*

Knopp, Greg
American Council of Engineering Companies *(109)*

Knopp, Linda
National Business Incubation Association *(717)*

Knott, Mary
Residential Space Planners International *(883)*

Knott, Vicki
Belgian Draft Horse Corporation of America *(327)*

Knouse, Janice
The American Board of Facial Plastic and Reconstructive Surgery *(82)*

Knowdell, Richard L.
Career Planning and Adult Development Network *(343)*

Knowles, Brian
Fulfillment Management Association *(454)*

Knowles, David
Corn Refiners Association, Inc. *(385)*

Knowles, Janet R.
American Fire Sprinkler Association *(121)*

Knowlton, Gretchen
National Association for State Community Services Programs *(643)*

Knox, CMP, Bridgitti
Consortium for Graduate Study in Management *(378)*

Knox, Debbie
American Council on Education *(110)*

Knox, Jill
Association for Applied and Therapeutic Humor *(238)*

Knox, Laurie A.
Electronic Security Association *(424)*

Knudson, Angela
International Association of Physicians in AIDS Care *(526)*

Knudson, Jeff
National Farmers Union (Farmers Educational & Co-operative Union of America) *(747)*

Knuerr, Jillian
American Foundry Society *(123)*

Knusden, Scott
International Institute for Energy Conservation *(551)*

Knutson, John F.
International Society for Research on Aggression *(569)*

Knutson, Nancy
Pet Industry Joint Advisory Council *(842)*

Knutson, Shane
National Center for Housing Management *(719)*

Koba, Susan
National Science Education Leadership Association *(790)*

Kobert, Charlotte
IEEE Consumer Electronics Society *(483)*

Kobetz, CST, Dr. Richard W.
Academy of Security Educators and Trainers *(9)*

Koblenz, Andrew D.
National Automobile Dealers Association *(711)*

Koblich, Joseph
American Nuclear Society *(156)*

Kobrinetz, Jim
Spring Manufacturers Institute *(960)*

Kocak, Donna
Marine Technology Society *(605)*

Kocak, Mike
Polyurethane Manufacturers Association *(852)*

Kocelko, Larissa
National Association of EMS Educators *(665)*

Koch, Christopher L.
World Shipping Council *(1027)*

Koch, Diane
Graphic Arts Technical Foundation *(465)*

Koch, Drew
Institute of Certified Professional Managers *(498)*

Koch, DO, FACOEP, Drew A.
American College of Osteopathic Emergency Physicians *(99)*

Koch, Greeley S.
Association of Corporate Travel Executives (ACTE) *(277)*

Koch, CAE, Julie
Produce Marketing Association *(858)*

Koch, Mandy
National Wellness Institute, Inc. *(804)*

Kochie, Stephanie
Delta Phi Epsilon *(409)*

Kocinski, MPP, Jacqueline M.
American Academy of Hospice and Palliative Medicine *(35)*

Kocmieroski, Matthew
International Guild of Symphony, Opera and Ballet Musicians *(549)*

Koczak, Kelly
Produce Marketing Association *(858)*

Koczka, Susan
International Association of Campus Law Enforcement Administrators *(517)*

Kodali, Vijaya
American Association of Physicians of Indian Origin *(69)*

Koeber, Chuck
Association for Humanist Sociology *(249)*

Koehler, Jordan
Executive Women International *(435)*

Koehler, Shari
Golf Course Superintendents Association of America *(463)*

Koehn-Pike, Jodi
Council for Opportunity in Education *(390)*

Koelling, Peter
National Conference of Federal Trial Judges *(727)*
National Conference of Specialized Court Judges *(728)*

Koen, A. D.
Texas Alliance of Energy Producers *(972)*

Koenig, Carl H.
International Council of Fine Arts Deans *(538)*

Koenig, Stephen E.
Poultry Science Association *(854)*

Koenigsfeld, PhD, Jason
Club Managers Association of America *(359)*

Koeninger, Jeff
Hosa *(478)*

Koeninger, Dr. Jim
Hosa *(478)*

Koenst, Lizzy
Society of Industrial and Office Realtors *(939)*

Koepke, Rick
Association for Death Education and Counseling *(244)*
International Society for Traumatic Stress Studies *(570)*

Koerber, Amy
Association of Teachers of Technical Writing *(313)*

Koeser, Ross
International Consumer Product Health and Safety Organization *(537)*

Koetje, David
Christian Schools International *(356)*

Koetje, MD, Jeff
American Medical Student Association *(150)*

Koff, Eileen
National Association of Professional Organizers *(687)*

Kofinas, Adam
United Synagogue of Conservative Judaism *(1001)*

Kofke, MD, William A.
Association of University Anesthesiologists *(315)*

Kogon, Diana J.
Quail Unlimited *(871)*

Kohlbeck, Dana
Fire Equipment Manufacturer's Association *(446)*

Kohler, CTR, MPH, Betsy
North American Association of Central Cancer Registries *(812)*

Kohler, Sarah
Building Service Contractors Association International *(337)*

Kohlmoos, James W.
Knowledge Alliance *(591)*
National Association of State Boards of Education *(698)*

Kohlrieser, Greg
American Trucking Associations *(218)*

Kohn, Catherine
Associated Church Press *(235)*

Kohn, Rita
Dance Critics Association *(406)*

Kohn, Susan
Controlled Release Society *(383)*

Kohoutek, Perla
Institute of Packaging Professionals *(502)*

Kohr, Beth
American Medical Association Alliance, Inc. *(149)*

Kohr, Leah
Edison Welding Institute *(419)*

Kohse-Höinghaus, Katharina
The Combustion Institute *(366)*

Kohut, Christine
Catholic Cemetery Conference *(345)*

Kohut, Kathryn
American Association of Intensive English Programs *(63)*

Kohut, Tania
American Chamber of Commerce Executives *(89)*

Kok, Kristin
Choristers Guild *(355)*

Kokalis-Burelle, Nancy
Society of Nematologists *(942)*

Kokes, Marvin
National Cattlemen's Beef Association *(718)*

Kolakowski, Gail
American Bankers Association *(79)*

Kolar, CAE, Mary Jane
National Council on Qualifications for the Lighting Professions *(739)*

Kolata, William
Society for Industrial & Applied Mathematics *(912)*

Kolb, Daniela
Global Acetate Manufacturers Association *(461)*

Kolb, Michael T.
National Public Employer Labor Relations Association *(783)*

Kolb, Steven
Council of Fashion Designers of America *(393)*

Kolbe, David L.
International Association of Bridge, Structural, Ornamental and Reinforcing Iron Workers *(517)*

Kolbe, Lisa R.
Conference Board of the Mathematical Sciences *(374)*

Kolbe, Sherry L.
National Association of Private Special Education Centers *(686)*

Kolberg, Maarja
BICSI *(329)*

Kolding, Betty
Society of Professional Asset-Managers and Record Keepers *(945)*

Kolev, Daniela
Employee Services Management Association *(426)*

Koliander, Christina
American Morgan Horse Association *(152)*

Kolias, Nick
IEEE Microwave Theory and Techniques Society *(485)*

Kolin, Dr. Irwin
College of Diplomates of the American Board of Orthodontics *(364)*

Kolly, Tim
Defense Research Institute *(408)*

Kolmaister, Valerie
Biomedical Engineering Society *(330)*

Kolodgy, Robert
Blue Cross Blue Shield Association *(332)*

Kolodziej, CMP, Amie
Craft & Hobby Association *(402)*

Kolodziej, Richard R.
NGVAmerica *(810)*

Kolpak, Dorothy
Professional Convention Management Association *(861)*

Koltai, MD, Dr. Peter J.
American Broncho-Esophagological Association *(86)*

Kolton, Anne Womack
American Chemistry Council *(90)*
Chlorine Chemistry Council *(354)*

Kolus, Cheryl
American Veterinary Society of Animal Behavior *(219)*

Komadel, Peter
Clay Minerals Society *(357)*

Komisar, Marie
National Association of Women Judges *(710)*

Komives, Stephen
Society for News Design *(916)*

Komorowski, Art
International Door Association *(541)*

Konapelsky, Kathy
ASPRS-The Imaging and Geospatial Information Society *(233)*

Kondapeta, Padma
Ireland Chamber of Commerce in the United States *(585)*

Konetschni, Lynn Millar
National Industries for the Blind *(763)*

Kong, Cindy
Destination Marketing Association International *(411)*

kong, Hong
World Federation for Mental Health *(1026)*

Konicki, MHS, Doris L.
American College of Occupational and Environmental Medicine *(99)*

Konieczny, Jeannine
National Association of Government Labor Officials *(670)*

Konikow, Kim
Dance/USA *(406)*

Konopasek, Alice
North American Association of Food Equipment Manufacturers *(813)*

Konopka, Lauren A.
Association of School Business Officials International *(306)*

Konrath, Jessica
Public Risk Management Association *(870)*

Kontak, Dot
School Social Work Association of America *(892)*

Koob, MPA, Sue
Preventive Cardiovascular Nurses Association *(857)*

Kool, BSc, Paul
American Society for Apheresis *(180)*

Koon, Cathy
National Federation of Press Women *(749)*

Koon, Samantha
International Society of Arboriculture *(571)*

Koonce, Kevin

Council of North American Insulation Manufacturers Association *(396)*
North American Insulation Manufacturers Association *(817)*

Koontz, Michele Smith
Society for the Study of Social Problems *(925)*

Kop, Willem J.
American Psychosomatic Society *(170)*

Kopasz, Diane
Association of Children's Museums *(272)*

Kopaz, Kristin
Manufacturing Jewelers and Suppliers of America *(604)*

Kopchinski, Robert
Society of Behavioral Medicine *(930)*

Kopcinski, Ray
Million Dollar Round Table *(616)*

Kopelman, Meredith
Plan Sponsor Council of America *(849)*

Kopernick, James L.
International Plate Printers, Die Stampers and Engravers Union of North America *(560)*

Koperski, MD, Judith A.
North American Clinical Dermatologic Society *(815)*

Kopf, David
Motorcycle Industry Council, Inc. *(620)*

Kopfer, Maryann
World Trade Centers Association *(1027)*

Kopinski, Jason
American Academy of Neurology *(36)*

Kopp, Amanda
National Association of Women Artists *(709)*

Koppal, Cori
Convenience Caterers & Food Manufacturers Association *(383)*

Koppel, Allison
American Fraternal Alliance *(124)*

Koppes, Bill
National Tooling and Machining Association *(800)*

Koppes, William
Precision Metalforming Association *(856)*

Kopple, Chrissy
National Association of Chain Drug Stores *(652)*

Kopriva, Dan
United States Cross Country Coaches Association *(993)*

Kopycki, William
Middle East Librarians' Association *(615)*

Koralek, Derry
National Association for the Education of Young Children *(644)*

Koran, J. J.
Institute of Industrial Engineers *(500)*

Koranda, Amy B
National Air Transportation Association *(630)*

Korbel, Kimberly A.
Wire Rope Technical Board *(1019)*
Women in Government Relations, Inc. *(1021)*

Korber, Kenneth
American College of Osteopathic Family Physicians *(100)*

Korch, David J.
National Alliance of Medicare Set-Aside Professionals, Inc. *(632)*

Korduner, David
Directors Guild of America *(413)*

Korieocha, Dr. Stella
National Optometric Association *(776)*

Koriouchkina, Lisa
Association for the Study of Nationalities *(259)*

Kormoi, Sam
American Association for Accreditation of Ambulatory Surgery Facilities *(47)*

Korn, Cliff
International Association of Healthcare Practitioners *(522)*

Korn, Jeff
Drug Information Association *(417)*

Kornbluh, Harvey L.
Associated Owners and Developers *(236)*

Kornegay, Glenda
National Association of School Psychologists *(693)*

Kornet, Lou
Paperboard Packaging Council *(838)*

Korngold, PhD, Robert
American Society for Blood and Marrow Transplantation *(181)*

Kornhauser, PhD, Stanley H.
National Institute of Electromedical Information *(765)*

Kornstein, Jeffrey
The American Jewish Historical Society *(143)*

Korosec, Jessie
Equipment and Tool Institute *(432)*

Korotky, Kenneth
American College of Radiology *(102)*

Korsmo, Michelle Larson
American Land Title Association *(144)*

Korson, Koula
National Association of Surety Bond Producers *(704)*

Korson, Teri M.
Distribution Contractors Association *(414)*

Kortenhaus, Robert J.
Distribution and LTL Carriers Association *(414)*

Korzen, Mary
Air and Waste Management Association *(17)*

Kos, Karleen
International Society for Pharmaceutical Engineering *(567)*

Kosar, Chris
The Advertising Research Foundation *(13)*

Koshy, Sheron
Electronic Commerce Code Management Association *(423)*

Koshy, Susan
Ruth Jackson Orthopaedic Society *(889)*

Kosior, Laurel
Colorado Ranger Horse Association *(365)*

Kositzky, Tom
APA The Engineered Wood Association *(224)*

Koski, Mark
National Federation of State High School Associations *(750)*

Kosky, Rachelle
Generic Pharmaceutical Association *(458)*

Kosmark, Gene
American Federation of Musicians *(119)*

Kosmatka, Steven H.
Portland Cement Association *(853)*

Kosmetatos, Sofia
American Health Quality Association *(130)*

Kosowski, Meg
Health Care Compliance Association *(469)*

Koss, Joseph

North American Gaming Regulators Association *(817)*

Koss, Pamela Figenshow
Glass Art Society *(461)*

Kossak, Shelley
National Council for Science and the Environment *(733)*

Kost, Richard S.
Aviation Maintenance Foundation International *(324)*

Kostantenaco, Linda
National Child Care Association *(721)*

Kostantin, Brian
Marketing Science Institute *(606)*

Kostecki, PhD, Dr. Paul T.
The Association for Environmental Health and Sciences *(246)*

Kostelny, Sandy
National Public Employer Labor Relations Association *(783)*

Koster, Janet Bandows
Association for Women in Science *(262)*

Kosto, Adam J.
American Academy of Research Historians of Medieval Spain *(41)*

Kostopoulos, Angelo
HR Policy Association *(480)*

Kotak, Dilip
IEEE Technology Management Council *(486)*

Kotche, Kelly
American Bakers Association *(78)*

Koth, Jessica A.
National Funeral Directors Association *(754)*

Kothe, Mark
Automotive Parts Remanufacturers Association *(323)*

Kotowski, CAE, CMP, Karen
Convention Industry Council *(383)*

Kotrba, Linda
American Association of Surgical Physician Assistants *(74)*

Kottler, Alan
American Association of Professional Landmen *(71)*

Kotz, Nancy
Association of Partners for Public Lands *(298)*

Kotzé, Frances
Society of Economic Geologists *(934)*

Kotzur, Joslyn
Beefmaster Breeders United *(327)*

Kouris, John R.
Defense Research Institute *(408)*

Kovach, Pat
American Orthopaedic Society for Sports Medicine *(159)*

Koval, Susan
IEEE Power and Energy Society *(485)*

Kovaleski, John
National Cartoonists Society *(718)*

Kovalik, Sandy
National Council for Prescription Drug Programs *(732)*

Kovats, CMP, Diane E.
American Association of Immunologists *(62)*

Kowal, CGMP, Kimberly
Society of Government Meeting Professionals *(938)*

Kowalczyk, Leslie
Learning Resources Network *(596)*

Kowalik, Amy Y.
American Goat Society *(127)*

Kowalski, Christine
International Council on Systems Engineering *(539)*

Kowalski, David
American Knife & Tool Institute *(144)*

Kowalski, CAE, Michael J.
American Water Resources Association *(220)*

Kowalski, Richard J.
American Association of Occupational Health Nurses *(67)*

Kozak, Jerry
American Butter Institute *(87)*
National Milk Producers Federation *(772)*

Kozal, Judith D.
Pierre Fauchard Academy *(848)*

Kozel, Tanya
International District Energy Association *(540)*

Koziol, Patricia S.
Hobby Manufacturers Association *(477)*

Kozlik, Ted
National Association of Pupil Services Administrators *(689)*

Kozloff, Jeff
Pharmaceutical Marketing Research Group *(844)*

Kozlowski, Carol
Society of Actuaries *(927)*

Kozlowski, Jeanne M.
National Fire Sprinkler Association *(751)*

Kozlowski, Kelly
Automation Alley *(321)*

Kraar, CMP, Donna M.
Association of Professional Chaplains *(301)*

Krabill, Ryan
National Potato Council *(782)*

Kracke, Annette
Golf Course Builders Association of America *(463)*

Kradz, Kendyl
International Psycho-Oncology Society *(561)*

Kraemer, Carol
American Society of Tax Professionals *(209)*
Institute of Tax Consultants *(503)*

Kraemer, Donna
Association of Corporate Contributions Professionals *(277)*

Kraemer, Suzette
MPA - The Association of Magazine Media *(620)*

Kraft, Heather
Glass Art Society *(461)*

Kraft, Lisa
American Association of Intensive English Programs *(63)*

Kraft, Melissa
American Association of Anatomists *(54)*

Kraft, Rory
American Association of Philosophy Teachers *(69)*

Krajcik, Joseph
National Association for Research in Science Teaching *(642)*

Kral, Jami
Urgent Care Association of America *(1004)*

Kral, Steve
Society for Mining, Metallurgy and Exploration, Inc. *(915)*

Kralka, Peter
American College of Epidemiology *(95)*

Kram, Joan
American Association of Neuroscience Nurses *(66)*

Kramer, MD, Janet
Attention Deficit Disorder Association *(320)*

Kramer, Jessica
Association for Adult Development and Aging *(238)*

Kramer, SPHR, Julia Gregg
American Fuel & Petrochemical Manufacturers *(124)*

Kramer, Katie
Council of Development Finance Agencies *(393)*

Kramer, Kelly
Society of Hispanic Professional Engineers *(938)*

Kramer, Mitchell
Independent Medical Distributors Association *(490)*
Power-Motion Technology Representatives Association *(855)*

Kramer, Russ
American Society of Marine Artists *(202)*

Kramer, Shaun
American Society of Gene & Cell Therapy *(198)*

Kramer, Steven M.
Association of Oil Pipe Lines *(296)*

Kramer, Tammy
International Pharmaceutical Excipients Council of the Americas *(560)*

Kramer-Beddo, Stephanie
North American Limousin Foundation *(817)*

Kranov, PhD, Ashley Ater
Accreditation Board for Engineering and Technology Inc. *(9)*

Krant, CMP, Deborah
National Center for Employee Ownership *(719)*

Krantz, Adam
Federal Water Quality Association *(440)*

Kranz, Leslie
National Council on Teacher Retirement *(740)*

Krapohl, Donald
American Polygraph Association *(166)*

Krasner, Barry
National Air Traffic Controllers Association *(630)*

Krasner, David
Securities Industry and Financial Markets Association (SIFMA) *(895)*

Krassner, Kathy
Greeting Card Association *(466)*

Krassner, Kaye
Small Publishers Association of North America *(901)*

Kraus, D. Bambi
National Association of Tribal Historic Preservation Officers *(707)*

Kraus, Deb
Natural Areas Association *(806)*

Kraus, Maribeth T.
Modern Language Association *(618)*

Kraus, Timothy R.
Heavy Duty Manufacturers Association *(473)*

Krause, Frank
American Geophysical Union *(126)*

Krause, Kari
American Veterinary Society of Animal Behavior *(219)*

Kraut, Alan G.
Association for Psychological Science *(254)*

Krautheim, LD, MA, RD, Ann Marie
National Dairy Council *(741)*

Kravitz, Rhonda Rios
National Association for Chicana and Chicano Studies *(637)*

Kravitz, Roberta A.
International Society for Magnetic Resonance in
Medicine *(567)*

Krawutschke, Dr. Peter
Joint National Committee for Languages-National
Council for Languages and International Studies
(589)

Kraynack, Bethany
Alliance for Regenerative Medicine *(23)*

Krebsbach, Sandra
American Technical Education Association *(215)*

Krehbiel, Ken
National Council of Teachers of Mathematics *(737)*

Kreiner, David
Society for the Teaching of Psychology *(926)*

Kreinovich, Vladik
North American Fuzzy Information Processing Society
(817)

Kreiter, Amber
Association for Play Therapy *(253)*

Kreiter, Kathy
International Association for the Study of Pain *(514)*

Kreizman, Janet B.
The Endocrine Society *(427)*

Krejci, David
Grain Elevator and Processing Society *(464)*

Kremer, Jolene
American Society for Dermatologic Surgery *(183)*

Krempa, Aaron
International Association for Philosophy and Literature
(514)

Krese, Christopher
National Association of Chain Drug Stores *(652)*

Kresge, Brandy
PMCA: An International Association of Confectioners
(851)

Kress, John W.
Association for Tropical Biology and Conservation
(260)

Kret, Dot
Association of Rehabilitation Programs in Computer
Technology *(305)*

Kreuzburg, Paula
Business Solutions Association *(340)*

Krever, Marcy K.
American Montessori Society *(152)*

Krewson, Pamela
National Wooden Pallet and Container Association
(805)

Krichbaum, JD, John A.
American Burn Association *(87)*

Krigstein, Alex
National Register of Health Service Providers in
Psychology *(785)*

Kriner, Scott
Metal Construction Association *(613)*

Krisko, John J.
AMT - The Association For Manufacturing Technology
(222)

Krissoff, Mike
Asphalt Emulsion Manufacturers Association *(233)*
Asphalt Recycling and Reclaiming Association *(233)*
International Slurry Surfacing Association *(565)*

Krivanek, Jenny
American Institute of Physics *(140)*

Kriz, Danielle
Information Technology Industry Council *(495)*

Krizel, Lauren
Society for Conservation Biology *(906)*

Krochta, Tanya J.
ACORD - Association for Cooperative Operations
Research and Development *(11)*

Krock, Rich
Vinyl Institute *(1009)*

Krock, Trista
Society of Biblical Literature *(931)*

Kroeger, Ken
Brotherhood of Locomotive Engineers and Trainmen
(336)

Kroh, Lerrene
National Sunflower Association *(798)*

Krohm, Greg
International Association of Industrial Accident Boards
and Commissions *(523)*

Krohn, PE, Jason J.
Precast/Prestressed Concrete Institute *(856)*

Krolikowski, Anne
Clinical Immunology Society *(358)*

Kroll, Deborah
American Society for Bone and Mineral Research *(181)*

Kroll, Kevin
Steel Plate Fabricators Association Division of STI/
SPFA *(962)*
Steel Tank Institute Division of STI/SPFA *(963)*

Krolman, Walter
ICAAAA Coaches Association *(482)*

Krome, Paul
United States Lacrosse *(995)*

Kron, Kathy
American Society of Plant Taxonomists *(207)*

Krone, Judith P.
Handweavers Guild of America, Inc. *(468)*

Kronshage, Alisa
NanoBusiness Alliance *(625)*

Krot, Marna
National Association of Physician Recruiters *(684)*

Kroupa, Cheryl
National Cherry Growers and Industries Foundation
(720)

Kroussakis, Pam
Association of Dermatology Administrators &
Managers *(278)*

Kruchten, Cheryl
Controlled Release Society *(383)*
Master Brewers Association of the Americas *(607)*

Kruchten, Katheleen
Professional Managers Association *(863)*

Krucoff, Carole
Museum Education Roundtable *(621)*

Krueger, Jon
Association of Fund-Raising Distributors and Suppliers
(285)
Society for Maintenance & Reliability Professionals
(914)

Krueger, CAE, Keith R.
Consortium of School Networking *(378)*

Krueger, Tracy
Pi Sigma Epsilon *(847)*

Krug, Mark
National Junior College Athletic Association *(767)*

Krug, CAE, Susan
American Medical Writers Association *(150)*

Krulik, Brenda O.

**National Action Council for Minorities in Engineering
(NACME) *(628)***

Krum, Libby
American International Automobile Dealers
Association *(142)*

Krupa, Daniel
Maple Flooring Manufacturers Association *(604)*

Krupa, Donna
American Physiological Society *(165)*

Krupansky, Stella
Tooling, Manufacturing and Technologies Association
(976)

Krupica,, BS, Angela
American Holistic Nurses Association *(132)*

Krupnick, Susan L.W.
International Society of Psychiatric Consultation
Liaison Nurses *(574)*

Kruse, USN (Ret.), Capt. Dennis K.
American Society of Naval Engineers *(204)*

Kruse, Kevin
Society of Pharmaceutical and Biotech Trainers *(944)*

Kruse, Megan
American Registry for Internet Numbers *(174)*

Krutsch, Kim
Automation Alley *(321)*

Krutz, Rev. C. Dana
National Association of Ecumenical and Interreligious
Staff *(664)*

Krysler, CAE, Gary
Women's Council of REALTORS *(1023)*

Kubarth, Michael
International Association of Tool Craftsmen *(528)*

Kubek, Karen
American Massage Therapy Association *(147)*

Kubicki, Jeri
National Association of Manufacturers *(679)*

Kubik, Marianne
The Association of Theatre Movement Educators *(314)*

Kubis, Dianne K.
American College of Allergy, Asthma and Immunology
(93)

Kubler, Caitlin
National Association Of Insurance and Financial
Advisors(NAIFA) *(676)*

Kubota, Lily
Specialty Coffee Association of America *(957)*

Kubsh, Joseph E.
Manufacturers of Emission Controls Association *(603)*

Kuchuris, Paul
The Association for Manufacturing Excellence *(252)*

Kudlas, Myke
American Society of Radiologic Technologists *(208)*

Kudrin, Rena J.
Central Bering Sea Fisherman's Association *(348)*

Kuehn, Kathy
The Psychonomic Society *(868)*

Kuenn, Neil
American Veterinary Distributors Association *(218)*
Business Solutions Association *(340)*
National Association of Sign Supply Distributors *(696)*

Kueser, Bill
Pet Partners *(842)*

Kugler, Esq., Ellen J.
National Association of Urban Hospitals *(708)*

Kuhar, Laura J.
International Anesthesia Research Society *(511)*

Kuhlmann, Jenny
National Association of Schools of Art and Design *(693)*
National Association of Schools of Dance *(693)*

Kuhn, Amy
National Franchisee Association *(753)*

Kuhn, Earle F.
American Endodontic Society, Inc. *(117)*

Kuhn, Linda
International Longshore and Warehouse Union *(555)*

Kuhn, Thomas R.
Edison Electric Institute *(419)*

Kuhrt, Linda
National Stroke Association *(797)*

Kukawka, Stan
Variable Electronic Components Institute *(1008)*

Kukoda, Steve L.
International Copper Association *(537)*

Kulakowski, Elliott
Society of Research Administrators International *(946)*

Kulinski, Anna
International Society of Travel and Tourism Educators *(574)*

Kulish, Mark
United States Telecom Association *(1000)*

Kullman, Cecilia
Swedish-American Chambers of Commerce of the USA, Inc. *(967)*

Kulp, MS, Amy J.
American Association of Suicidology *(74)*

Kumar, Kristina
American Board of Physical Medicine and Rehabilitation *(83)*

Kumar, Rakesh
Solid-State Circuits Society *(952)*

Kumbaroglu, Gürkan
International Association for Energy Economics *(512)*

Kummer, Markus
Internet Society *(582)*

Kump, Gail
Association of American Publishers *(266)*

Kun, Paula K.
National Association for Sport and Physical Education *(643)*

Kuna, Lauryn
Drug, Chemical and Associated Technologies Association *(417)*

Kuniyuki, Janice
Pacific Telecommunications Council *(836)*

Kunkel, Christoph M.
Council of Independent Colleges *(394)*

Kunkle, Laura A.
Nursery and Landscape Association Executives of North America *(825)*

Kunoff, MBA, Martin S.
United Synagogue of Conservative Judaism *(1001)*

Kunz, Andy
United States High Speed Rail Association *(994)*

Kunz, Karen
American Association for Budget and Program Analysis *(48)*

Kunz, Marie L
American Association of Birth Centers *(55)*

Kupfer, Ruth
Design Management Institute *(410)*

Kupferschmid, Keith
Software & Information Industry Association (SIIA) *(950)*

Kupferschmid, CPA, Lana
National Conference of CPA Practitioners *(727)*

Kupta, Frank
Insulated Cable Engineers Association *(504)*

Kuranz, Mark
American School Counselor Association *(177)*

Kurdakul, Sheri
Trade Promotion Management Associates *(977)*

Kurec, Dianne S.
SOLE - The International Society of Logistics *(952)*

Kurek, Rob
Academy of Model Aeronautics *(7)*

Kuriger, Nicholas J.
Equal Employment Advisory Council *(432)*

Kurilecz, CA, CRM, Peter A.
Institute of Certified Records Managers *(499)*

Kuris, Armand M.
American Society of Parasitologists *(206)*

Kurkian, CAE, CPA, Scott
Professional Photographers of America *(863)*

Kurkjy, Fay
National Association of Local Government Auditors *(678)*

Kurklis, Ted
Association of Energy Engineers *(280)*

Kurland, Rachel
Association of Sewing and Design Professionals *(308)*

Kurnick, Judith
League of American Orchestras *(595)*

Kurowski, Jeff
Recreation Vehicle Dealers Association of North America *(876)*

Kurowski, Kerry
Biscuit and Cracker Manufacturers' Association *(330)*

Kurrle, Diane
United States Apple Association *(989)*

Kurrle, Jonathan
Society of the Plastics Industry *(948)*

Kurtis, Dean
International Housewares Association *(550)*

Kurtz, JD, Carolyn
Accreditation Association for Ambulatory Health Care *(9)*

Kurtz, Jana
American Academy of Optometry *(37)*

Kurtz, Jessica
National Frozen and Refrigerated Foods Association *(753)*

Kurtz, John
International Staple, Nail and Tool Association *(575)*

Kurtzman, Andrew
Telecommunications Industry Association *(971)*

Kuryluk, Jayne
Christian Meetings & Conventions Association *(356)*

Kurzak, Mary Beth
International Association of Defense Counsel *(519)*

Kurzeja, Richard E.
International Buckskin Horse Association *(532)*

Kurzweil, Jenny
SACNAS (Society for Advancement of Chicanos and Native Americans in Science) *(889)*

Kushma, Rachel
Intercollegiate Tennis Association *(507)*

Kushner, Gary J.
National Pasta Association *(779)*

Kusinski, Greg
DeepStar Project *(408)*

Kusler, Jon
Association of State Wetland Managers *(311)*

Kusnic, Rick
United Transportation Union *(1001)*

Kutac, Paul
American Association of Police Officers *(70)*

Kutscher, DeVere
United States Hispanic Chamber of Commerce *(995)*

Kutska, Helen M.
American Fuel & Petrochemical Manufacturers *(124)*

Kutsko, John
Society of Biblical Literature *(931)*

Kutt, Pat
NACE International *(623)*

Kuty, Gary
National Council of Investigative and Security Services Inc. *(735)*

Kutyn, Mary Alice
Society of Independent Gasoline Marketers of America (SIGMA) *(939)*

Kutz, Trish
Structural Building Components Association *(964)*

Kuvin, Brad
Precision Metalforming Association *(856)*

Kuvshinova, Anna
American Society on Aging *(211)*

Kuwitzky, Carl
The Coalition of Airline Pilots Associations *(360)*

Kuykendall, Ron
National Association of Real Estate Investment Trusts (NAREIT) *(690)*

Kuyper, Mark W.
Evangelical Christian Publishers Association *(434)*

Kuzler, Jen Larkin
Art Directors Club *(229)*

Kuznetsov, Vladimir F.
American Society of Master Dental Technologists *(202)*

Kvitkovich, Gina
GAMA International *(455)*

Kvitkovich, Gina
Helicopter Association International *(473)*

Kwang, Helen
International Executive Association *(543)*

Kwart, Michael
Insulation Contractors Association of America *(504)*

Kyger, Jim
Printing Industries of America *(857)*

Kyger, Sarah
Society for Maternal-Fetal Medicine *(915)*

Kyle, Lesley
Society of Plastics Engineers *(944)*

Kyle, Shirlee
Distributive Education Clubs of America (DECA) *(415)*

Kyle, Jr., William C.
National Association for Research in Science Teaching *(642)*

Kyles, CMP, Sandra
Air Conditioning Contractors of America *(18)*

Kyllo, Rachel
International Ice Cream Association *(551)*

Kynoch, Brent
The Environmental Information Association *(431)*

Kyriacopoulos, Peter
Association of Public Health Laboratories *(304)*

Kysilko, David
National Association of State Boards of Education *(698)*

L'Orange, Hans P.
State Higher Education Executive Officers *(961)*

La Moy, William T.
American Printing History Association *(167)*

La Rosa, Diane
American Society of Ophthalmic Registered Nurses *(205)*

Laabs, EdD, Jonathan C.
Lutheran Education Association *(600)*

Laager, Maryanne
National Association of College and University Business Officers *(654)*

Laatsch, Shawn
International Planetarium Society *(560)*

LaBella, Jeanne
American Public Power Association *(171)*

Labelle, Daniel
Professional Association of Health Care Office Management *(859)*

LaBennett, Oneka
Association of Black Anthropologists *(269)*

Labiner, MD, David M.
National Association of Epilepsy Centers *(666)*

Laboda, Amy
Women in Aviation International *(1020)*

LaBoda, Larry
American Massage Therapy Association *(147)*

LaBorde, Jo E.
The Institute of Financial Operations *(499)*

LaBoube, Roger
Structural Stability Research Council *(964)*

LaBouff, Michele
LOMA *(600)*

LaBranche, CAE, Gary A.
Association for Corporate Growth *(244)*

Labrie, Marie
Society for Information Display *(913)*

Labrinidis, Alexandros
Special Interest Group on Management of Data *(956)*

LaBue, Jason
Association of Film Commissioners International *(283)*

Labuskes, David
InfoComm International *(495)*

LaBute, Susan
American Ceramics Society *(89)*

Lacasella, Dale
American Construction Inspectors Association *(107)*

LaCava, Patricia K.
National Alcohol Beverage Control Association *(631)*

Lacayo, Anamarcia
Pacific Telecommunications Council *(836)*

Lacey, ARP, Catherine
American Resort Development Association *(175)*

Lacey, Robert
International Allied Printing Trades Association *(510)*

Lach, Eileen M.
Institute of Electrical and Electronics Engineers (IEEE) *(499)*

Lachance, Janice R.
Special Libraries Association *(956)*

Lachapelle, Jeanne
Society of Financial Examiners *(936)*

Lachapelle, Pete
National Association of Pizzeria Operators *(685)*

Lack, Lillian
Hospitality Financial and Technology Professionals *(479)*

Lack, Timothy W.
International Food, Wine and Travel Writers Association *(546)*

Lackey, Nancy
American Society of Naval Engineers *(204)*

Laconi, Teresa
USA Archery *(1004)*

Lacoss, Lisa
American Society of Dowsers *(197)*

Lacy, Connie
American Jail Association *(142)*

Lacy, Peggy
Fibre Box Association *(443)*

Lacy, USA-Ret., COL Warren C.
Military Officers Association of America (MOAA) *(616)*

Laddbush, Kathleen
Association of Catholic Colleges and Universities *(271)*

LaDier, Tovah
International Biometric Industry Association *(530)*

Ladner, Kathy
United States Professional Tennis Association *(998)*

Ladouceur, Jill
Association for Financial Counseling and Planning Education *(246)*

LaFave, Holland
Society of Behavioral Medicine *(930)*

Lafey, Dawn
International Masonry Institute *(556)*

Lafferty, Marty
Distributed Computing Industry Association *(414)*

Lafferty, Sari
Distributed Computing Industry Association *(414)*

Laffin, Mary Anne
National Perinatal Association *(780)*

Laffman-Johnson, Elise
American Society for Clinical Pharmacology and Therapeutics *(182)*

Laffy, Kurt
American Association of Clinical Endocrinologists *(56)*

LaFlair, Suzanne
American Councils for International Education *(111)*

LaFleche, David
Educational Theatre Association *(420)*

Laflin, Katrina
Women in Management *(1021)*

Laforgia, Tony
Association of American Publishers *(266)*

LaFountain, Becky
North American Society of Adlerian Psychology *(822)*

LaFrance, David B.
American Water Works Association *(220)*

Lagace, Nettie
National Information Standards Organization *(763)*

LaGasse, Alfred B.
Taxicab, Limousine & Paratransit Association *(969)*

LaGasse, CAE, Robert C.
Garden Writers Association *(456)*
Mulch and Soil Council *(621)*
Progressive Gardening Trade Association *(866)*

Lagershausen, Jack L.
Air Diffusion Council *(18)*

LaGesse, Lilia
Council of Independent Colleges *(394)*

LaGoe, Terri
Worldwide ERC *(1028)*

Lagos, Nancy
Cabletelevision Advertising Bureau *(340)*

Lagoudas, Prof. Dimitris C.
Aerospace Department Chairs Association *(14)*

Lah, Thomas
Technology Services Industry Association *(970)*

LaHaie, CAE, Jerri J.
Society of Municipal Arborists *(942)*

Lahaie, Ute S
International Association for Language Learning Technology *(513)*

Laher, Douglas
American Association for Respiratory Care *(51)*

Lahmers, Kevin
American Association of Veterinary Immunologists *(76)*

Lai, Loi Lei
Man and Cybernetics Systems Society *(602)*

Lai, Loi Lei
Man and Cybernetics Systems Society *(602)*

Lai, Teddy
Greater Blouse, Skirt and Undergarment Association *(466)*

Laible, Myron
Outdoor Advertising Association of America *(834)*

Laidlaw, Kent G.
Association of Traumatic Stress Specialists *(315)*

Laine, Christine
American College of Physicians Services, Inc. *(101)*

Laing, Don M.
American Diabetes Association *(115)*

Laing, Ellen
Society of North American Goldsmiths *(943)*

Lair, Bridget
National Business Incubation Association *(717)*

Laird, Betsy
International Council of Shopping Centers *(538)*

Laird, Erica
Builders Association *(338)*

Lakas, Mike
American Society for Surgery of the Hand *(189)*

Lake, Carrie S.
Professional Services Council *(865)*

Lake, Jim
National Fire Sprinkler Association *(751)*

Lake, Lauren
Association of Energy Engineers *(280)*

Lakhani, Neeta
Wedding and Portrait Photographers International *(1014)*

Lakine, Schwanna C.
National Association of Chronic Disease Directors *(653)*

Lalain, Dave A.
Automotive Industry Action Group *(322)*

Lally, Carol

International Foodservice Editorial Council **(546)**

Lally, Rosemary
Council of Institutional Investors **(394)**

Lam, Teresa
Omega Delta **(827)**

Lamangan, Joshua
American Staffing Association **(213)**

LaMarre, Rachel
Association of Marina Industries **(293)**
Sail America **(890)**

Lamay, Stephanie
RTCA, Inc. **(888)**

Lamb, Elsa
Association for the Advancement of International Education **(258)**

Lamb, James A.
American Board of Podiatric Surgery **(83)**

Lamb, Scott
Society of Government Travel Professionals **(938)**

Lamb, Shawn Douglas
Society of Toxicology **(948)**

Lambe, CAE, Maureen
National Apartment Association **(634)**

Lambert, Adeline
International Labor Rights Forum **(553)**

Lambert, Jean
Specialty Graphic Imaging Association **(957)**

Lambert, LeRoy
Hellenic-American Chamber of Commerce **(474)**

Lambert, Malinda
Association of Performing Arts Presenters **(298)**

Lambert, Michael
International Association of Marriage and Family Counselors **(524)**

Lambert, Michael P.
Distance Education and Training Council **(414)**

Lambert, Mike
Automotive Distribution Network **(322)**

Lambert, Paul R.
American Otological Society **(161)**

Lambert, Richelle
International Imaging Technology Council **(551)**

Lambert, Susan J.
Iron Casting Research Institute **(585)**

Lambert, Teres
National Institute for Animal Agriculture **(764)**

Lambert, William C.
Phi Mu Alpha Sinfonia **(846)**

Lambright, Megan
National Association of Independent Lighting Distributors **(674)**

Lamond, Joe
NAMM - The International Music Products Association **(625)**

Lamoureux, Nicole D.
National Association of Free Clinics **(669)**

Lampart, Karen
Conveyor Equipment Manufacturers Association **(383)**

Lampe, Frank
American Herbal Products Association **(130)**

Lampe, Klaus von
International Association for the Study of Organized Crime **(514)**

Lampe, Mark
United States Ski and Snowboard Association **(999)**

Lampert, Eric
Society of American Magicians **(929)**

Lampeter, Walter
National Surgical Assistant Association **(798)**

Lampl, DO, Barry A.
American Osteopathic College of Allergy and Immunology **(160)**

Lampron, Bruce
National Retail Federation **(786)**

Lamude, COL Douglas J.
Senior Army Reserve Commanders Association **(897)**

LaMura, Renee
Polyisocyanurate Insulation Manufacturers Association **(852)**

Lamy, Jonathan
Recording Industry Association of America (RIAA) **(876)**

Lancaster, Ally
American Cultural Resources Association (ACRA) **(112)**

Lancaster, Ally
Register of Professional Archeologists **(879)**

Lancaster, Clint
National Association of Trailer Manufacturers **(706)**

Lancaster, Joyce
Weed Science Society of America **(1014)**

Lance, Lisa
International Professional Rodeo Association **(561)**

Lance, Peter M.
The Cordage Institute **(385)**

Land, Carol
Glass Association of North America **(461)**

Land, Mark
American Association of Homeopathic Pharmacists **(62)**

Land, Steve
Uniform Retailers Association **(984)**

Landacre, Jessica K.
Intellectual Property Owners Association **(505)**

Landau, Elizabeth
American Geophysical Union **(126)**

Landau, Michael
Association of Litigation Support Professionals **(292)**

Landeck, Dolores
American Society of Agricultural and Biological Engineers **(191)**

Landen, Libby
Retail Advertising and Marketing Association International **(884)**

Landers, Valerie
Illuminating Engineering Society of North America **(486)**

Landfare, Jeremy
Healthcare Information and Management Systems Society **(471)**

Landicho, Tom
American Society for Nutrition **(187)**

Landis, Alicia A.
Fleet Reserve Association **(447)**

Landis, Lisa L.
Welsh Pony and Cob Society of America **(1015)**

Landry, Catherine J.
Interstate Natural Gas Association of America **(583)**

Landry, Lori
Network Professional Association **(808)**

Landsburg, Alex

The Society of Naval Architects and Marine Engineers **(942)**

Landseadel, Matthew "Matt"
Hemophilia Federation of America **(474)**

Landsman, David
The National Money Transmitters Association **(773)**

Landwehr, Christy
CHA - Certified Horsemanship Association **(350)**

Lane, Amy
American Gear Manufacturers Association **(125)**

Lane, Becky
Alarm Industry Communication Committee **(21)**
Central Station Alarm Association **(349)**

Lane, Brian
American Telemedicine Association **(215)**

Lane, Carol S.
American Astronautical Society **(77)**

Lane, Carolyn
Society for Hematopathology **(910)**
Society for Pediatric Pathology **(918)**
United States and Canadian Academy of Pathology **(989)**

Lane, Carrie
Society for the Anthropology of Work **(923)**

Lane, Dylan
Tau Beta Pi Association **(968)**

Lane, Joe
Crane Certification Association of America **(403)**

Lane, Joni
Modular Building Institute **(618)**

Lane, Juliane
Earthquake Engineering Research Institute **(418)**

Lane, Marshall
National Foreign Trade Council, Inc. **(752)**

Lane, Mary Ellen
Council of American Overseas Research Centers **(392)**

Lane, Michele
American Medical Society for Sports Medicine **(149)**

Lane, Nancy
Local Media Association **(599)**

Lane, Neil
The College Board **(363)**

Lane, Pamela
National Association of Emergency Medical Technicians **(665)**

Lane, Ray
American Society of Interventional Pain Physicians **(201)**

Lane, Sharon
ATM Industry Association **(320)**

Lane, Susan
National Association of Independent Fee Appraisers **(674)**

Lane, T. C.
United States Trotting Association **(1000)**

Laner, Ken
NAGMR Consumer Product Brokers **(624)**

Lanese, CMP, Ginenne
Society for Photographic Education **(919)**

Laney, Jason
American Seed Trade Association **(178)**

Laney, Kate
Korean American Spine Society **(591)**

Lang, David
American Association of Private Lenders **(71)**

Lang, Julie
Forest Products Society *(451)*

Lang, LaToya Rembert
Marketing Research Association *(606)*

Lang, Nancy
American Dental Education Association *(113)*

Lang, Sandra
Professional Photographers of America *(863)*

Lang, AAP, Scott
NACHA - The Electronic Payments Association *(623)*

Lang, MPH, William G.
American Association of Colleges of Pharmacy *(57)*

Langager, Steve
Printing Industry Credit Executives *(857)*

Langdon, Lynn O.
American Board of Internal Medicine *(82)*

Lange, Barbara
Society of Motion Picture and Television Engineers *(942)*

Lange, David R.
American Association of Petroleum Geologists *(68)*

Lange, Greg
United Motorcoach Association *(988)*

Lange, Janet
North American Association of Summer Sessions *(813)*

Lange, USMC (Ret.), Col. Lee
Military Officers Association of America (MOAA) *(616)*

Lange, Dr. Mark D.
National Cotton Council of America *(730)*

Langerman, Brian
InSight *(496)*

Langerman, Kari
Wine and Spirits Wholesalers of America *(1018)*

Langford, Jason
Aeronautical Repair Station Association *(14)*

Langham, Anna
Hispanic Elected Local Officials *(475)*
National League of Cities *(768)*

Langham, Ray
American Sesame Growers Association *(178)*

Langhenry, Jr., Ed
Resistance Welding Manufacturing Alliance *(883)*

Langill, PhD, Thomas J.
American Galvanizers Association *(124)*

Langley, Cheryl
Manufactured Housing Institute *(602)*

Langley, Kathy
American Association of Medical Assistants *(65)*

Langley, CPA, Mark
Project Management Institute *(866)*

Langley, Reece
Rice Millers' Association *(886)*
USA Rice Council *(1004)*
USA Rice Federation *(1004)*

Langsdorf, Karin
American Academy of Cosmetic Dentistry *(31)*

Langseth, Debra
American Network of Community Options and Resources (ANCOR) *(155)*

Langston, Chelsea
National Association of Consumer Advocates *(657)*

Langstraat, Laura A.
National Crop Insurance Services *(741)*

Lanham, Carolyn C.
American Society of Addiction Medicine *(191)*

Lanham, Linda
Aerospace Futures Alliance *(14)*

Lanier, Robin
National Association of Judiciary Interpreters and Translators *(677)*
National Council on International Trade Development *(739)*

Lanigan, Diane
National Organization of Legal Services Workers *(777)*

Lanke, CAE, Eric
National Fluid Power Association *(751)*

Lannan, Connie
American Rental Association *(174)*

Lanning, CMP, Megan
Precast/Prestressed Concrete Institute *(856)*

Lanning, Sarah
ASFE/The Geoprofessional Business Association *(231)*

Lanning, Tom
Financial Managers Society *(445)*

Lano, June
Indian Educators Federation *(492)*

Lansdown, Cathy
Missouri Fox Trotting Horse Breed Association *(617)*

Lansing, Carol
Society for Italian Historical Studies *(914)*

Lant, PhD, Christopher L.
Universities Council on Water Resources *(1002)*

Lanter, Amy
ARMA International *(228)*

Lanzano, Steve
Television Bureau of Advertising *(971)*

Lanzer, Nicholas
International Association of Privacy Professionals *(526)*

Lapetina, Susan
American Apparel & Footwear Association *(46)*

LaPierre, Jr., Wayne R.
National Rifle Association of America *(787)*

Lapka, Heidi
National Association of Boards of Examiners of Long Term Care Administrators *(650)*
National Association of Long Term Care Administrator Boards *(679)*

LaPlante, Alane
Manufacturers' Agents National Association *(603)*

LaPlante, Shelli
International Association for Impact Assessment *(513)*

LaPorta, Jim
Quarter Century Wireless Association *(872)*

Laporte, Amaury
Environmental and Energy Study Institute *(430)*

LaPorte, Mary
American Association of Insurance Management Consultants *(63)*

Laporte, Paul
Military Operations Research Society *(616)*

Lapsansky, Mary Ellen
The Fragrance Foundation *(453)*

Lapus, Dominic
American Institute of Aeronautics and Astronautics *(136)*

Lara, Martha
American Association of Neurological Surgeons *(66)*

Lara, BA, Rebecca
American Holistic Nurses Association *(132)*

Larabee, Kelly
Distributed Computing Industry Association *(414)*

LaRacuente, MBA, Joan
American Montessori Society *(152)*

Larco-Murzyn, PhD, Carol
LOMA *(600)*

Lard, Todd A.
Council On State Taxation *(400)*

Lardner-Stone, Anne
Promotional Products Association International *(867)*

Large, Daphne
National Credit Reporting Association *(740)*

Largent, Hon. Steve
CTIA - The Wireless Association *(405)*

Larkin, Jim
International Association of Fire Fighters *(521)*

Larkin, Peter S.
National Grocers Association *(756)*

Larkin, Wendy
Motorcycle Industry Council, Inc. *(620)*
Specialty Vehicle Institute of America *(958)*

Larmett, Kathleen M.
National Council of University Research Administrators *(737)*

Larner, Jayson C.
American Waterways Operators *(220)*

Laroche, Deborah
American Mathematical Society *(148)*

LaRoche, Joyce
Association of State Chamber Professionals *(310)*

LaRoche, Nancy
National Shippers Strategic Transportation Council *(791)*

LaRoe, Lisa Moore
The Wildlife Society *(1017)*

LaRowe, Michelle
International Nanny Association *(557)*

Larrisey, MA, Megan
Clinical and Laboratory Standards Institute *(358)*

Larsen, Christian B.
Electric Power Research Institute *(421)*

Larsen, CFP, Craig L.
Softwood Export Council *(951)*

Larsen, Dana B.
International Studies Association *(576)*

Larsen, David
National Funeral Directors Association *(754)*

Larsen, JD, LPN, Helen M.
National Association for Practical Nurse Education and Service *(641)*

Larsen, Jody
Custom Electronic Design and Installation Association *(405)*

Larsen, Kelsey
Women's Professional Rodeo Association *(1023)*

Larsen, Mike
National Association of Consumer Credit Administrators *(657)*

Larsen, Paul J.
Pharmaceutical Research and Manufacturers of America (PhRMA) *(844)*

Larsen, Scott
Industrial Asset Management Council *(492)*

Larsen, Wanda
Association of Equipment Manufacturers *(281)*

Larson, Esq., Amy W
National Waterways Conference *(804)*

Larson, Anita
Association of State Floodplain Managers *(311)*

Larson, Brian
National Lincoln Sheep Breeders Association *(770)*

Larson, Chad
Research Council on Structural Connections *(882)*

Larson, Chelsea
Application Developers Alliance *(226)*

Larson, Dave
International Association for Food Protection *(512)*

Larson, Erin
American Society of Gene & Cell Therapy *(198)*

Larson, Hannah
Alpines International Club *(27)*

Larson, John
National Association of Conservation Districts *(657)*

Larson, Judy
Society for Simulation in Healthcare *(921)*

Larson, Mary
Oral History Association *(830)*

Larson, Melora
Cryogenic Engineering Conference *(405)*

Larson, MS, Mina
National Certification Commission for Acupuncture
and Oriental Medicine *(720)*

Larson, BC, RN, Neal
National Association of Directors of Nursing
Administration in Long Term Care *(663)*

Larson, Oscar
Association of American Geographers *(265)*

Larson, Roger
Child Neurology Society *(353)*

Larson, Sandra
National Automatic Merchandising Association *(711)*

Larson, Terry
Mass Finishing Job Shops Association *(607)*

LaRusch, James
American Public Transportation Association *(171)*

LaRussa, PE, Joe
Society of Manufacturing Engineers *(941)*

LaRusso, Dan
National Association of Credit Management *(661)*

LaRusso, Mary
American Hospital Association *(133)*
American Society for Healthcare Risk Management
(185)

Lasaki, Folayo
Independent Filmmaker Project *(489)*

LaSala, Ken
International Association of Fire Chiefs *(521)*

Laser, Cindy
Broadcast Cable Credit Association *(335)*

Laser, Cindy
Media Financial Management Association *(610)*

Lasher, Craig
Population Action International *(852)*

Lasko, Elizabeth W.
The National Association for Music Education
(Formerly MENC) *(641)*

Laskowski, Ann
Alliance for Quality Care *(23)*

Laskowski, Jeff
Automotive Public Relations Council *(323)*

Lasner, Stacy
The Academy of American Poets *(3)*

Lassanske, Donna J.
Purebred Morab Horse Association *(871)*

Lasser, CMP, Stephanie Lifland
Investment Management Consultants Association *(584)*

Laszlo, Arp
The New Media Consortium *(809)*

Late, Michele
American Public Health Association *(171)*

Latham, Ann
National Association of Surety Bond Producers *(704)*

Latham, Tim
American Society of Certified Engineering Technicians
(194)

Latimer, Steve
International Association of Counselors and Therapists
(519)

Latimore, Linda
National Housing and Rehabilitation Association *(760)*
National Reverse Mortgage Lenders Association *(787)*

Latin, Gary A.
American Bureau of Shipping *(86)*

Latko, Mary Ann
American Industrial Hygiene Association *(135)*

Latoff, Blair
United States Chamber of Commerce *(991)*

Latta, Carol J.
Decision Sciences Institute *(407)*

Lattimer, BSN, RN, Cheri
Case Management Society of America *(343)*

Lattimore, Bernie
The American Rambouillet Sheep Breeders Association
(173)

Lattimore, Burk
The American Rambouillet Sheep Breeders Association
(173)

Latza, Esq., William D.
Society of Financial Examiners *(936)*

Lau, Frederick
Society for Asian Music *(904)*

Lau, Susan
National Health Council *(758)*

Lau, PhD, Yuen-Sum (Vincent)
American Association of Colleges of Pharmacy *(57)*

Laube, Trina
National Wellness Institute, Inc. *(804)*

Lauber, MD, Jeffrey
American Society of Dermatological Retailers *(196)*

Lauck, W. Larry "Lawrence"
American Lighting Association *(145)*

Laudadio, Natalie
Government Finance Officers Association of the United
States and Canada *(464)*
Government Finance Officers Association, Federal
Liaison Center *(464)*

Lauderdale, Casey
Social Venture Network *(902)*

Laudon, Matthew
Clean Technology & Sustainable Industries
Organization (CTSI) *(357)*

Lauer, Betsy
Association for Enterprise Information *(245)*

Lauer, Dianne
American Maritime Congress *(147)*

Lauer, Kimberly
Institute of Management Consultants USA *(501)*

Laufer, Lucille J.

Oriental Rug Importers Association of America *(833)*

Laughlin, Alice
American Hotel & Lodging Association (AH&LA) *(134)*

Laughlin, Don
American Angus Association *(45)*

Laughman, J. Jacob
American College of Veterinary Radiology *(104)*

Laughner, John
Magnet Schools of America *(601)*

Laughton, Dave
Teamsters Brewery and Soft Drink Workers Conference
(969)

Launchbaugh, Cyndy
Copper and Brass Servicenter Association *(384)*

Laur, Elizabeth
Movement Disorder Society *(620)*

Laurence, David E.
Association of Departments of English *(278)*
Modern Language Association *(618)*

Laurent, Gina
United States Conference of Catholic Bishops *(992)*

Laurent, Keith
American Resort Development Association *(175)*

Laurent, Michael
Lift Manufacturers Product Section - Material Handling
Institute *(597)*
Loading Dock Equipment Manufacturers *(599)*
Material Handling Industry of America *(608)*
Materials Handling and Management Society *(608)*

Laurie, AIA, Barbara G.
Organization of Black Designers *(832)*

Lauriers, Kristen Des
Association of Free Community Papers *(284)*

Laurin, Katie
International Erosion Control Association *(543)*

Laursen, Finn
Christian Educators Association International *(355)*

Lausch, Susan M.
Flight Safety Foundation *(448)*

Laushman, Judy M.
Association of Specialty Cut Flower Growers *(309)*

Lauth, Rosemary S.
American Association of State Colleges and
Universities *(73)*

Lauwers, BA, IBCLC, Judith
International Lactation Consultant Association *(553)*

Lauzon, Nicole
Smart Card Alliance *(901)*

Lavach, Beth
Consortium of Forensic Science Organizations *(378)*

LaValley, CAE, Alison
National Roofing Contractors Association *(787)*

LaValley, David
The Wire Association International, Inc. *(1019)*

Lavan, Cary Sue
Women in Management *(1021)*

Lavandero, Ramon
American Association of Critical-Care Nurses *(59)*

Lavelle, Peggy
Association of Catholic Diocesan Archivists *(271)*

Lavender, Gary
Crane Certification Association of America *(403)*

Laverty, Katie Burnham
Society for Nonprofit Organizations *(917)*

Lavery, Michael J.

Audit Bureau of Circulations *(320)*

Lavietes, Jon
Association of Strategic Alliance Professionals, Inc. *(311)*

LaVigne, Andrew
American Seed Trade Association *(178)*
National Council of Commercial Plant Breeders *(734)*

Lavigne, Patrick
National Rural Electric Cooperative Association *(788)*

Lavilla, Stacy K.
Association of Asian-Pacific Community Health Organizations *(268)*

Lavin, Jack
National Petroleum Management Association *(780)*

Lavin, Ruth
National Petroleum Management Association *(780)*

Lavoie, Julien
Entertainment Software Association (ESA) *(429)*

Lavoine, Sean
American Hockey League *(132)*

Law, Dick
Association of Former OSI Special Agents *(284)*

Law, AICI, CIP, Kimberly
Association of Image Consultants International *(287)*

Law, Reagan
America's Independent Truckers' Association, Inc. *(29)*

Law, Rebekah
Association for Continuing Higher Education *(243)*

Lawhon, Lance
American Botanical Council *(85)*

Lawhun, Richard E.
American Concrete Pressure Pipe Association *(106)*

Lawler, CMP, Nancy
National Asphalt Pavement Association *(635)*

Lawler, CEM, Sarah
American Association of Community Colleges *(58)*
American Health Information Management Association *(129)*

Lawler, Tom
International Emissions Trading Association *(542)*

Lawlor, Bonnie
National Federation of Advanced Information Services *(748)*

Lawlor, Jen
United Inventors Association of the U.S.A. *(987)*

Lawlor, Kevin
Institute of Scrap Recycling Industries, Inc. *(503)*

Lawlor, Marilyn
Friends of the National Institute of Dental and Craniofacial Research (FNIDCR) *(454)*

Lawlor, CPM, Mary
National Association of Certified Professional Midwives *(651)*

Lawlor, Ronit
Path to Purchase Institute *(839)*

Lawniczak, Jonathan
National Association of State Treasurers *(702)*

Lawrence, Brandon
The Conference Board *(374)*

Lawrence, Brian
iNARTE, Inc. *(487)*

Lawrence, Brian D.
American Society of Wedding Professionals *(211)*

Lawrence, Carey
Environmental Industry Associations *(431)*
National Solid Wastes Management Association *(795)*

Waste Equipment Technology Association *(1012)*

Lawrence, Carly
Eye Bank Association of America *(436)*

Lawrence, Carol
Association for Facilities Engineering *(246)*

Lawrence, Carolyn
Supply Chain Council *(966)*

Lawrence, Connie
Women in Aviation International *(1020)*

Lawrence, Dan
Arabian Horse Association *(227)*

Lawrence, Francine
AFT Healthcare *(15)*

Lawrence, Francine
Department for Professional Employees - AFL-CIO *(410)*

Lawrence, Frederick
Independent Petroleum Association of America *(491)*

Lawrence, III, Hal C.
American Congress of Obstetricians and Gynecologists *(107)*

Lawrence, Hannah
Healthcare Supply Chain Association *(472)*

Lawrence, Jeff
Ocean Carrier Equipment Management Association (OCEMA) *(825)*

Lawrence, Lisa
Delta Waterfowl Foundation *(409)*

Lawrence, Lori
American School Health Association *(177)*

Lawrence, Marilyn
International Municipal Signal Association *(557)*

Lawrence, Melissa
Aestheticians International Association *(14)*

Lawrence, Pam
Marine Corps Aviation Association *(604)*

Lawrence, Rachel
International Nanny Association *(557)*

Lawrence, MD, PhD, Theodore S.
Society of Chairmen of Academic Radiology Oncology Programs *(932)*

Lawrie-Munro, L. Michele
The American Institute of Mining, Metallurgical, and Petroleum Engineers *(139)*

Lawry, Angie
Chief Executives Organization *(352)*

Laws, Tajuanna
International Society for Traumatic Stress Studies *(570)*

Laws, Toni F.
National Association of Multicultural Media Executives *(681)*

Laws, Tracey W.
Reinsurance Association of America *(879)*

Lawser, CAE, Erik
Refrigerated Foods Association *(878)*

Lawser, CAE, Steven V.
Wood Component Manufacturers Association *(1024)*

Lawson, Caroline
International Nubian Breeders Association *(558)*

Lawson, Emily
American Staffing Association *(213)*

Lawson, LPC, PhD, Gerard
Association for Counselor Education and Supervision *(244)*

Lawson, Kirk

American Translators Association *(217)*

Lawson, Kirk
Business Professionals of America *(339)*

Lawson, Larry
American Society of Agricultural Appraisers *(191)*
American Society of Equine Appraisers *(197)*

Lawson, Lynn
National Council of Coal Lessors *(734)*

Lawson, Melissa
National Association of Therapeutic Schools and Programs (NATSAP) *(706)*

Lawson, Quentin R.
National Alliance of Black School Educators *(632)*

Lawson, Randy
International Guards Union of America *(549)*

Lawson, Richard
Marine Technology Society *(605)*

Lawson, DFAPA, MD, PhD, William B.
Black Psychiatrists of America *(331)*

Lawton, Henry W.
International Psychohistorical Association *(562)*

Laxmi, John
South Asian Journalists Association *(952)*

Lay, Anh
Geothermal Resources Council *(460)*

Laycock, Steve
Amusement Industry Manufacturers and Suppliers International *(223)*

Laycox, Sandy
National Association of Public Hospitals and Health Systems *(688)*

Layman, Lauren
Alliance for Telecommunications Industry Solutions *(23)*

Layne, Jerry
The World Umpires Association *(1027)*

Layne, R. Davis
Voluntary Protection Programs Participants' Association, Inc. *(1011)*

Layton, Denise
Soaring Society of America *(902)*

Lazar, Jodi
Urban Libraries Council *(1004)*

Lazarewicz, Matt
Electricity Storage Association *(422)*

Lazaroski, Irene K.
Catholic Cemetery Conference *(345)*

Lazcano, Diane
American Massage Therapy Association *(147)*

Lazdowski, Yvette
Academy of Accounting Historians *(3)*

Lazear, Angela
Mortgage Bankers Association of America *(619)*

Lazenby, Estella
National Black Nurses Association *(714)*

Lazic, Djurdja
American Society of International Law *(201)*

Lazo, Robert
National Academy of Television Arts and Science *(628)*

Lazowski, Karen
Women's Foodservice Forum *(1023)*

Le, Anthony
United States High Speed Rail Association *(994)*

Le, Hanh
Association of Small Foundations *(309)*

Le, Sean
Board of Certified Safety Professionals *(332)*

Lea, Daniel
Cellulose Insulation Manufacturers Association *(347)*
Inflatable Advertising Dealers Association *(494)*

Lea, Russ
National Ecological Observatory Network, Inc *(743)*

Leach, Edward J.
League for Innovation in the Community College *(595)*

Leach, Jeff
Special Libraries Association *(956)*

Leach, Len
National Minority Supplier Development Council *(773)*

Leach, Robyn M.
Railway Supply Institute *(874)*

Leadbeater, Cher
National Association of Residential Property Managers *(691)*

Leader, Mark
American Society for Cell Biology *(182)*

Leadingham, Scott
Society of Professional Journalists *(945)*

Leaf, Michael M.
Steamfitters Local Union 449 *(962)*

Leahey, Jeffrey A.
National Hydropower Association *(761)*

Leahey, Esp., Mark B.
Medical Device Manufacturers Association *(611)*

Leahy, Caitlin
Association for Experiential Education *(246)*

Leahy, Deirdre
Consumer Bankers Association *(380)*

Leahy, P. Patrick
American Geological Institute *(126)*

Leahy, Patricia
National Association of Service Providers in Private Rehabilitation *(695)*
National Rehabilitation Association *(785)*

Leahy, Patricia E
Society of Maritime Arbitrators *(941)*

Leake, David B.
American Association for the Advancement of Artificial Intelligence *(51)*

Leal, Gloria
Texas Alliance of Energy Producers *(972)*

Leal, Melissa
Wood Moulding and Millwork Producers Association *(1024)*

LeaMond, Nancy
American Association of Retired Persons *(72)*

Lear, Diane C.
National Hydropower Association *(761)*

Learmonth, Bruce
Forest Products Society *(451)*

Learner, Neal
Academy of Managed Care Pharmacy *(6)*

Leary, Dan
United States Trotting Association *(1000)*

Leary, Lou Ann
American Nephrology Nurses Association *(155)*

Leary, Susan
National Academy of Recording Arts and Sciences *(628)*

Leasure, Greg
American Academy of Anesthesiologist Assistants *(30)*
American Osteopathic Academy of Orthopedics *(159)*

American Society of Extra-Corporeal Technology *(197)*

LeaSure, J. D.
Espionage Research Institute International *(433)*

Leasure, Mark A.
Infectious Diseases Society of America *(494)*

Leatherman, Sandra E.
Metal Powder Industries Federation *(613)*
Powder Metallurgy Equipment Association *(854)*
Powder Metallurgy Parts Association *(854)*
Refractory Metals Association *(878)*

Leatherwood, Shayne
National Association of Dental Plans *(662)*

Leaton, Mary
International Ticketing Association *(577)*

Leavens, PhD, Donald R.
National Electrical Manufacturers Association *(744)*

Leavitt, Steven W.
Tree-Ring Society *(980)*

Lebano, Edoardo
American Association of Teachers of Italian *(74)*

LeBaron, Robin
National Home Performance Council, Inc. *(760)*

Lebby, CAE, CMP, Kathryn
Association for Play Therapy *(253)*

LeBeau, PhD, Marc
Society of Forensic Toxicologists *(936)*

Lebeau, Patricia S.
Association of Former Intelligence Officers *(284)*

LeBeck, Lynn
Association of Natural Bio-Control Producers *(295)*

LeBedz, Peggy
Metal Powder Industries Federation *(613)*
Powder Metallurgy Parts Association *(854)*
Refractory Metals Association *(878)*

Lebegue, Arnaud
Joint Electron Device Engineering Council *(589)*

Lebens, Grant
Association for Advanced Life Underwriting *(238)*

Lebensorger, Mitzi
National Center for Homeopathy *(719)*

LeBlanc, Albert
Association for Graphic Arts Training *(247)*

Leblond, Norm
Association of Home Office Underwriters *(287)*

LeBoeuf, CAE, Jeffrey J.
American Osteopathic College of Occupational and Preventive Medicine *(160)*

Lebron, Andrea
Power Transmission Distributors Association *(855)*

Lebron, Andy
Institute of International Bankers *(501)*

Lechner, PhD, Anat
The Color Association of the United States *(365)*

Lecker, Barbara
American Speech-Language-Hearing Association *(212)*

LeClair, Daniel R.
The Association to Advance Collegiate Schools of Business *(319)*

LeClair, Lawrence E.
National Association of Surety Bond Producers *(704)*

LeConte, Phil
American Association of Police Officers *(70)*

Ledbetter, Angela
National Independent Automobile Dealers Association *(761)*

Ledbetter, Mark
Society of Government Economists *(937)*

Leddy, Janay
Professional Bowlers Association *(861)*

Leddy, Rick
National Association of Basketball Coaches *(648)*

Lederer, Jr., Robert F.
National Pest Management Association *(780)*

Lederman, Geralyn
American Psychoanalytic Association *(168)*

Lederman, EdM, Stephanie
American Federation for Aging Research *(119)*

Ledesma, Vanessa
Caribbean Hotel and Tourism Association *(343)*

Ledger, Karen A.
Attorneys' Liability Assurance Society Inc. *(320)*

Ledgerwood, Melanie
Professional Bail Agents of the United States *(860)*

Ledoux, CAE, CMP, Amy
American Society of Association Executives-The Center for Association Leadership *(193)*

LeDoux, Diana
United States Potato Board *(997)*

Ledoux, Maria
Alliance of Information and Referral Systems *(25)*
American Association of Healthcare Administrative Management *(61)*

Lee, Allan
American Association of Colleges of Pharmacy *(57)*

Lee, Amanda
Fire Suppression Systems Association *(446)*

Lee, April
American Beverage Association *(80)*

Lee, Aretha
Resolve, The National Infertility Association *(883)*

Lee, Bill
Consolidated Tape Association *(378)*
North American Retail Hardware Association *(820)*

Lee, Brad
National Mail Order Association *(771)*

Lee, Connie
American Association of Pharmaceutical Scientists *(68)*

Lee, D. Ronnie
Association of Large Distribution Cooperatives *(291)*

Lee, Danny
American Assembly for Men in Nursing *(47)*

Lee, David
Tree Care Industry Association *(980)*

Lee, David
Local Media Association *(599)*

Lee, Dianne
American Society for Clinical Pharmacology and Therapeutics *(182)*

Lee, Emily
Pacific Telecommunications Council *(836)*

Lee, Emily McCracken
Society for Healthcare Strategy and Market Development *(910)*

Lee, Fulvia
Association of Hispanic Advertising Agencies *(287)*

Lee, H.S.
Solid-State Circuits Society *(952)*

Lee, Heather
CTIA - The Wireless Association *(405)*

Lee, Ilka

American Society for Precision Engineering *(188)*

Lee, James
American Stamp Dealers Association *(213)*
Association for Advanced Life Underwriting *(238)*

Lee, Jee Hang
Association of Community College Trustees *(276)*

Lee, Jennifer
Hospitality Financial and Technology Professionals *(479)*

Lee, Jenny
Subcontractors Trade Association *(964)*

Lee, Jim
International Association of Fire Fighters *(521)*

Lee, MD, PhD, Kendall H.
American Society for Stereotactic and Functional Neurosurgery *(189)*

Lee, Kevin
American Society of Hypertension, Inc. *(200)*

Lee, Luise
American Bridge Teachers' Association *(86)*

Lee, Mary K.
American Registry for Internet Numbers *(174)*

Lee, Melanie
Urban Financial Services Coalition *(1003)*

Lee, Melissa
Association for Competitive Technology (ACT) *(242)*

Lee, Michelle
American Cheese Society *(89)*

Lee, Mike
ATM Industry Association *(320)*

Lee, Missy
National Association of Junior Auxiliaries *(677)*

Lee, Najean
League of American Orchestras *(595)*

Lee, Pat
Fabricators & Manufacturers Association, International *(437)*
Tube and Pipe Association, International *(981)*

Lee, Paula
International Trademark Association *(577)*

Lee, Rebekah
International Association of Fairs and Expositions *(521)*

Lee, Reginald
Alliance of Black Telecommunications Employees *(24)*

Lee, PhD, Richard M.
Asian American Psychological Association *(232)*

Lee, Robb
American Society of Association Executives-The Center for Association Leadership *(193)*

Lee, Robert A.
National WIC Association *(805)*

Lee, Robin
World Gold Trust Services *(1026)*

Lee, Samantha
National WIC Association *(805)*

Lee, Seong-Whan
Man and Cybernetics Systems Society *(602)*

Lee, Seong-Whan
Man and Cybernetics Systems Society *(602)*

Lee, J.D., MPH, Teresa L.
The Alliance for Home Health Quality and Innovation *(23)*

Lee, Victor
National Association of County Community and Economic Development *(637)*

Lee Cole, Dana
Hardwood Federation *(468)*

Leech, Garth
AACE International *(1)*

Leech, Stacey DeLisio
American Cable Association *(87)*

Leeds, Diane
Aviation Suppliers Association *(324)*

Leenders, Thijs
North American Flowerbulb Wholesalers Association *(816)*

Leeper, Julie
National Association of State Student Grant and Aid Programs *(702)*

Leeson, Shirley
American Lands Access Association *(144)*

Lefebvre, Lauren
Association for Prevention Teaching and Research (APTR) *(254)*

Leffel, Terry
Thoroughbred Owners and Breeders Association *(974)*

Leffelman, MS, Brittanie
Wellness Councils of America *(1015)*

Lefko, MHA, Jeff
American Academy of Thermology *(42)*

Legaspi, CMP, Angie
American Society for Surgery of the Hand *(189)*

Leger, Diane
American Accounting Association *(43)*

Leggett, Anne
Association for Women in Mathematics *(261)*

Leggs, Brad
American Association of Psychiatric Technicians *(71)*

Legon, Richard D.
Association of Governing Boards of Universities and Colleges *(286)*

LeGrand, CMP, CAE, Crista
Council of State Restaurant Associations *(397)*
Fire Suppression Systems Association *(446)*
International Association of Ice Cream Vendors *(523)*

Lehman, Donna
PRBA - The Rechargeable Battery Association *(856)*

Lehman, Lisa
National Educational Telecommunications Association *(744)*

Lehman, Sherri
North American Millers' Association *(818)*

Lehmann, PhD, Ruth
The Harvey Society *(469)*

Lehmann-Bench, Aleya
Appraisers Association of America *(226)*

Lehmuth, OSF, Georgette
National Catholic Development Conference *(718)*

Lehnerer, Melodye G.
Sociological Practice Association *(950)*

Lehr, Cheryl
American Society for Cell Biology *(182)*
Women in Cell Biology *(1021)*

Lehrer, Barney
National Association of Export Companies *(666)*

Lehrfeld, Jodi
Metal Construction Association *(613)*

Lehrich, Christopher
North American Association for the Study of Religion *(812)*

Lehto, Nancy

American Polarity Therapy Association *(166)*

Leibbrand, Jane
National Council for Accreditation of Teacher Education *(731)*

Leibman, Mark
Associated Builders and Contractors *(235)*

Leibold, Esq., Peter M.
American Health Lawyers Association *(130)*

Leibowitz, David
Conductors Guild *(374)*

Leicht, Mary Ellen
National Junior College Athletic Association *(767)*

Leight, Elizabeth Ysla
Society of Professional Benefit Administrators *(945)*

Leighton, Daniel
Women in Technology International *(1022)*

Leighton, David
Women in Technology International *(1022)*

Leighton, Emma
American Society of Clinical Hypnosis *(194)*

Leighton, Emma J.
User Experience Professionals Association *(1005)*

Leighton, Russell
American Association for Respiratory Care *(51)*

Leikam, Dale
Fluid Fertilizer Foundation *(448)*

Leimbach, Jill
National Association of Credit Management *(661)*

Leininger, John
International Graphic Arts Education Association *(548)*

Leininger, Kerri
National Ready Mixed Concrete Association *(784)*

Leininger, Robert H.
Music Critics Association of North America *(622)*

Leino, MA, PhD, Victor E
American College Health Association *(93)*

Leipold, James G.
NALP - The Association for Legal Career Professionals *(624)*

Leishman, Marguerite
Association of Career and Technical Education *(271)*

Leistner, Stacy
Toy Industry Association *(976)*

Lemacks, Emily W.
Psi Omega Fraternity *(868)*

LeMaitre, Kim
Association of Community Cancer Centers *(275)*

LeMaster, Lynn
Edison Electric Institute *(419)*

Lemay, Helen Schneider
American Society of Limnology and Oceanography *(202)*

Lemay, PE, SE, Lionel
National Ready Mixed Concrete Association *(784)*

LeMay, Rosemary
American Academy of Pain Management *(39)*

Lembesis, Felicia
National Association of Professional Pet Sitters *(687)*

Lemek, MA, Cindy
Society of American Travel Writers *(930)*

LeMeur, Bill
Institute of Caster and Wheel Manufacturers *(498)*

Lemick, Stacie
SPARC *(954)*

Lemieux, Russ
Association of Fund-Raising Distributors and Suppliers *(285)*
Society for Maintenance & Reliability Professionals *(914)*

Lemieux, Russ
World Airline Entertainment Association *(1025)*

Lemire, Carol L.
American College of Toxicology *(103)*

Lemire, Franc
American Academy of Addiction Psychiatry *(29)*

LeMire, William A.
International Association of Arson Investigators *(515)*

Lemke, Lee R.
China Clay Producers Association *(354)*

Lemke, Rocio
International Warehouse Logistics Association *(580)*

Lemmon, Regina
Council of State Speech-Language-Hearing Association Presidents *(398)*

Lemon, Terrie
Society of Insurance Research *(940)*

LeMond, Leslie
Society for Cinema and Media Studies *(905)*

Lemos, Jain
American Society of Picture Professionals *(207)*

Lempesis, Bill
Video Electronics Standards Association *(1009)*

Lemyre, Daniel "Dan"
Society for Biomaterials *(905)*

Lenane, Pamela
National Association of Health and Educational Facilities Finance Authorities *(671)*

Lenard, Jeff
National Association of Convenience Stores *(658)*

Lenczycki, Julie
Association of University Interior Designers *(315)*

Leneway, Robert
Association of Rehabilitation Programs in Computer Technology *(305)*

Lengerman, Michele L
Congress of Neurological Surgeons *(377)*

Lenhart, Mark
Decorative Plumbing and Hardware Association *(408)*

Lenker, Ashley L.
Joint National Committee for Languages-National Council for Languages and International Studies *(589)*

Lennan, Anne C.
Society of Professional Benefit Administrators *(945)*

Lennard, Ian J.
National Cargo Bureau *(718)*

Lennon, Maureen
International Association of Business Communicators *(517)*

Lennon, Shane
Human Capital Institute *(480)*

Lennon, Susan
Society for Research in Child Development *(920)*
Society for Research on Adolescence *(920)*

Lenosky, Chuck
Health and Sciences Communications Association *(469)*

Lent, Julia
American Society of Landscape Architects *(201)*

Lenth, Charles S.
State Higher Education Executive Officers *(961)*

Lentz, Linda
Society for Industrial and Organizational Psychology Inc. *(912)*

Lenz, Esq., Edward A.
American Staffing Association *(213)*

Leo, Jennifer
Electronic Traders Association *(424)*
Electronic Transactions Association *(424)*

Leo, Linda
American Culinary Federation *(112)*

Leon, Diane
Association for Play Therapy *(253)*

Leon, Jason
Hispanic Association on Corporate Responsibility *(475)*

Leon, Suzanne
Object Management Group *(825)*

Leonard, Chris
American Association of Textile Chemists and Colorists *(75)*

Leonard, Dan
National Pharmaceutical Council *(780)*

Leonard, Ed
Gospel Music Association *(464)*

Leonard, Iris R.
Commercial Vehicle Safety Alliance *(367)*

Leonard, CAE, Jeanne
National Association of Secondary School Principals *(694)*

Leonard, John
American Swimming Coaches Association *(215)*

Leonard, John
International Association of Campus Law Enforcement Administrators *(517)*

Leonard, Jose E.
American Maritime Officers *(147)*

Leonard, Kate
Correctional Vendors Association *(386)*

Leonard, Kim
International Institute of Forecasters *(552)*

Leonard, Megan
Open Mobile Alliance *(828)*

Leonard, Thomas
History of Economics Society *(476)*

Leonardo, Arthur A.
North American Association of Wardens and Superintendents *(814)*

Leonardo, Ed
Association for the Advancement of Medical Instrumentation *(258)*

Leone, Rosalie
Association of Millwork Distributors *(294)*

Leong, Lawrence H.
Society of Atherosclerosis Imaging and Prevention *(930)*

Leongini, Marybeth
Consumer Bankers Association *(380)*

Leonhard, CPA, Raymond W.
Brick Industry Association *(335)*

LePage, Keith
National Association of Reinforcing Steel Contractors *(691)*

Lependorf, Jeffrey
Council of Literary Magazines and Presses *(395)*

Leppin, Pam
American Speech-Language-Hearing Association *(212)*

Lerit, Lindsey

Association of YMCA Professionals *(318)*

Lerman, CCM, Richard J.
National Association of Uniform Manufacturers and Distributors *(707)*

Lerner, Aaron
American Fisheries Society *(121)*

Lerner, PhD, Jeffrey C.
ECRI *(418)*

Lerner-Levine, Marion
Society of American Graphic Artists *(929)*

Leroy, Daphne
National Association for Multi-Ethnicity in Communications *(640)*

LeRoy, Russ
Independent Distributors Association *(489)*

LeSane, Melissa
Latin Business Association *(594)*

Lesemann, Mara
Guild of Italian American Actors *(467)*

Leshner, Alan I.
American Association for the Advancement of Science *(51)*

Lesieur, Michelle P.
American Registry of Medical Assistants *(174)*

Leslie, Ande
Human Resource People and Strategy *(481)*

Leslie, CMP, Melissa
Distribution Contractors Association *(414)*

Leslie, Michelle
Airports Council International - North America *(21)*

Leslie, Thomas G.
American Bandmasters Association *(78)*

Lesnewich, Steve
AMT - The Association For Manufacturing Technology *(222)*

Lessin, Stuart R.
Dermatology Foundation *(410)*

Lessley, William
National Association of Dental Laboratories *(662)*

Lestenkof, Phillip
Central Bering Sea Fisherman's Association *(348)*

Lester, Damon
National Association of Minority Automobile Dealers *(680)*

Lester, MBA CAE, Vickie
National Fastener Distributors Association *(747)*

Lestition, CAE, Amy E.
Association Media and Publishing *(262)*

Leth, Jerry
Manufacturers' Agents National Association *(603)*

Letourneau, Allison
Council of Hotel and Restaurant Trainers *(394)*

Lettieri, John
Organization for International Investment *(831)*

Letto, Jay
Society of Environmental Journalists *(935)*

Leubecker, Vernon
Marine Corps Reserve Association *(605)*

Leung, Jessica
International Interior Design Association *(552)*

Leung, Rosemarie
National Association of Professional Asian American Women *(686)*

Leung, Som-lok

International Association of Credit Portfolio Managers **(519)**

LeValdo, Rhonda
Native American Journalists Association **(806)**

LeVan, William H.
Cast Iron Soil Pipe Institute **(344)**

Levar, Bryce
Coalition of Visionary Resources **(361)**

Leve, Jay
National Council on Public Polls **(739)**

Levene, Nate
American Glovebox Society **(126)**

Levenick, Christopher
The Philanthropy Roundtable **(846)**

Levenstein, Lauren
National Family Planning and Reproductive Health Association **(747)**

Leventhal, Ivy
American College of Veterinary Internal Medicine **(104)**

Levesque, Carl
American Wind Energy Association (AWEA) **(221)**

Levesque, Katrina
American Society of Appraisers **(192)**

Levesque, Merril
National Association of Development Companies **(662)**

Levet, Jenny
APSE: The Network on Employment **(226)**

Levi, JD, Bruce
American Academy of Neurology **(36)**

Levi, Ed
Apiary Inspectors of America **(224)**

Levi, Robert
National Association of Postmasters of the United States **(685)**

LeVie, Jeanette
Association of Certified Fraud Examiners **(271)**

Levin, Bertha
National Association of Public Child Welfare Administrators **(688)**

Levin, Douglas A.
State Education Technology Directors Association **(961)**

Levin, Dova
Academy of Molecular Imaging **(7)**

Levin, Jason
American Radium Society **(173)**

Levin, Mark
Chain Link Fence Manufacturers Institute **(350)**

Levin, Megan
Refrigerated Foods Association **(878)**

Levin, APRN, PhD, RN, Pamela
Association of Community Health Nursing Educators **(276)**

Levin, Sheri
Association for Childhood Education International **(241)**

Levin, Esq., Stephen
International Society for Philosophical Enquiry **(568)**

Levin-Epstein, Michael
Food and Drug Law Institute **(449)**

Levin-Reisman, MBA, Rika
Jewish Education Service of North America **(588)**

Levinas, Randi B.
U.S.-Russia Business Council **(999)**

Levine, Andrea

National Exchange Carrier Association (746)

Levine, Ellen
Association of Graduate Liberal Studies Programs **(286)**

Levine, Dr. Felice J.
American Educational Research Association **(116)**

Levine, GG, Gail Brett
National Association of Jewelry Appraisers **(677)**

Levine, Jeremy
Delta Sigma Pi **(409)**

Levine, Joseph A.
Cantors Assembly **(342)**

Levine, Melissa
American Society of Hypertension, Inc. **(200)**

Levine, Paul
National Motor Freight Traffic Association, Inc. **(773)**

Levine, Raleigh
Society of American Law Teachers **(929)**

Levine, Richard
International Conference of Symphony and Opera Musicians **(537)**

Levine, Ronn
Specialized Information Publishers Association **(957)**

Levine, Ronni
North American Society for Cardiovascular Imaging **(821)**

Levine-Clark, Marjorie
North American Conference on British Studies **(815)**

Levinson, Martin H.
Institute of General Semantics **(500)**

Levison, Steve
American Society for Neurochemistry **(187)**

Levit, Gabriela
Association for Women in Computing **(261)**

Levitt, Alan
United States Dairy Export Council **(993)**

Levitt, Debi
American Membrane Technology Association **(150)**

Levitz, Hillary
United States Rowing Association **(998)**

Levrio, PhD, Jay
American Podiatric Medical Association **(166)**

Levy, Allison
International Interior Design Association **(552)**

Levy, Arthur J.
American Management Association **(146)**

Levy, Barbara A.
Pharmaceutical Care Management Association **(844)**

Levy, CAE, Beverly I.
American College of Mortgage Attorneys **(98)**

Levy, Buffy
North American Association of Food Equipment Manufacturers **(813)**

Levy, David M.
Alliance of Nonprofit Mailers **(25)**

Levy, Donna
Institute of Packaging Professionals **(502)**

Levy, Eileen
Land Improvement Contractors of America **(593)**

Levy, Howard A.
Trans-Atlantic American Flag Liner Operators and Trans-Pacific American Flag Berth Operators **(977)**

Levy, Jill
Risk and Insurance Management Society, Inc. (RIMS) **(886)**

Levy, Kathy
Association of Sewing and Design Professionals **(308)**

Levy, Krista L.
American College of Clinical Pharmacology **(94)**

Levy, Neomi
Environmental Council of the States **(431)**

Levy, PhD, Richard
Parenteral Drug Association **(838)**

Levy, Robert
North American Neuromodulation Society **(819)**

Levy, Staci B.
American Nuclear Society **(156)**

Levy, Tracy
Society for Vascular Surgery **(926)**

Lew, Michael
National Alliance for Advanced Transportation Batteries **(631)**

Lewin, Alyza
American Association of Jewish Lawyers and Jurists **(64)**

Lewin, Barton
American Student Dental Association **(214)**

Lewin, Cynthia M.
American Association of Retired Persons **(72)**

Lewis, PhD, Alison M.
Beta Phi Mu **(328)**

Lewis, Allison L.
Association for Prevention Teaching and Research (APTR) **(254)**

Lewis, Anisha N.
The Association of Black Psychologists **(270)**

Lewis, Ben
National Association of Personal Financial Advisors **(684)**

Lewis, Bill
American Society of Home Inspectors **(200)**

Lewis, Brad
Professional Convention Management Association **(861)**

Lewis, CAE, Brian
International Society for Technology in Education **(569)**

Lewis, Carrie
National Education Association **(744)**

Lewis, Chris
Association of Professional Model Makers **(302)**

Lewis, MSN, RN, Cindy
Society for Vascular Nursing **(926)**

Lewis, D'Renda
United Gamefowl Breeders Association, Inc. **(987)**

Lewis, Dean
American Architectural Manufacturers Association **(46)**

Lewis, Deanna
Local Media Association **(599)**

Lewis, Debbie
National Association of Retail Collection Attorneys **(692)**

Lewis, Denny L.
Association of Zoos and Aquariums **(318)**

Lewis, Faith
Footwear Distributors and Retailers of America **(450)**

Lewis, Flint H.
American Chemical Society **(89)**

Lewis, Jr. MD, Frank R.
American Board of Surgery **(84)**

Lewis, Gary

Geological Society of America *(459)*

Lewis, Howard A.
Institute of Business Appraisers *(498)*

Lewis, Jackie
National Association of Schools of Public Affairs and
Administration *(694)*

Lewis, Jason
Association for Institutional Research *(250)*

Lewis, John J.
Association of Clinical Research Organizations *(273)*

Lewis, Karen S.
Forging Industry Association *(452)*

Lewis, Karla
American Psychiatric Nurses Association *(168)*

Lewis, Kevin
Council of Engineering and Scientific Society
Executives *(393)*

Lewis, Kim
American Pianists Association *(165)*

Lewis, Kimberly
United States Green Building Council *(994)*

Lewis, Kristine B.
National Council of State Housing Agencies *(736)*

Lewis, Laura
National Association of Collegiate Women Athletic
Administrators *(656)*

Lewis, Laura
National Ski Area Association *(791)*

Lewis, Louise A.
Phycological Society of America *(846)*

Lewis, Maeceon
National Association of Public Hospitals and Health
Systems *(688)*

Lewis, APR, CAE, Mark F.
Society of Mineral Analysts *(942)*

Lewis, Megan
Network of Nonprofit Search Consultants *(808)*

Lewis, Michael S.
International Order of the Golden Rule *(559)*

Lewis, Peter
The American Geographical Society *(126)*

Lewis, Reed
Belt Association *(328)*

Lewis, CMP, Renee J.
American Concrete Institute *(106)*

Lewis, Reta Jo
Executive Women in Government *(435)*

Lewis, Rita M.
Linguistic Society of America *(598)*
National Cable & Telecommunications Association
(717)

Lewis, Sandra
The National Association of Colored Women's Club,
Inc. *(656)*

Lewis, Steve
Data Management Association International *(407)*

Lewis, Steve
Society of Flight Test Engineers *(936)*

Lewis, Suford
Institute for Certification of Computing Professionals
(497)

Lewis, Sylvia
American Institute of Certified Planners *(137)*
American Planning Association *(166)*

Lewis, Teresa

Lewis, Venise
National Pace Association *(778)*

Lewis, Vera
National Black MBA Association *(714)*

Lewis, Vivian
United Synagogue of Conservative Judaism *(1001)*

Lewis-Alim, Marilyn
National League of American Pen Women *(768)*

Lewkowitz, Marc A.
Supima *(966)*

Lewnard, Jack
Gas Technology Institute *(456)*

Lewris, Alinda
International Association of Protocol Consultants *(527)*

Lewthwaite, MA, Tim
Association of Zoos and Aquariums *(318)*

Li, Aimee
Patent and Trademark Office Society *(839)*

Li, Haipeng
Chinese American Librarians Association *(354)*

Li, Qi
American Dental Education Association *(113)*

Li, Xiangdong
Society for Environmental Geochemistry and Health
(908)

Liang, Dawna
ICLEI - Local Governments for Sustainability *(482)*

Liang, Hui-Ling
International Association of Emergency Managers
(520)
National Association of Government Communicators
(670)

Liao, Lola
National Council for Interior Design Qualifications
(732)

Libarkin, Julie
National Association of Geoscience Teachers *(669)*

Liberman, DSc, PhD, Jacob
International Society for the Study of Subtle Energies
and Energy Medicine *(570)*

Liberti, Rita
North American Society for Sport History *(821)*

Liberto, Donna
Business Solutions Association *(340)*
Council of State Restaurant Associations *(397)*
Fire Suppression Systems Association *(446)*
International Association of Ice Cream Vendors *(523)*
Register of Professional Archeologists *(879)*

Libunao, Ferdinand
American Society for Healthcare Human Resources
Administration *(185)*

Licata, John
National Wrestling Coaches Association *(806)*

Licht, Barbara
American College of Physicians *(101)*

Lichtenberger, Mark
Radiological Society of North America *(873)*

Lichtenstein, AUS (Ret.), Col. Jack D. P.
ASIS International *(232)*

Lichtenstein, Mark
National Recycling Coalition *(784)*

Lichter, MD, Allen Sollie
American Society of Clinical Oncology *(194)*

Lichter, Dmin, David A.
National Association of Catholic Chaplains *(651)*

Lichthardt, Kanika
The College Board *(363)*

Lichwick, Nicole
Women's Jewelry Association *(1023)*

Licina-Tubbs, Darleen
Hardwood Manufacturers Association *(468)*

Licitra, Tim
Market Technicians Association *(606)*

Liddle, David
Association of the United States Army *(313)*

Liddle, MD, Rodger
American Pancreatic Association *(162)*

Lieber, CAE, H. Stephen
Healthcare Information and Management Systems
Society *(471)*

Lieberman, Ross
American Cable Association *(87)*

Lieberman, Sandy
American Dental Society of Anesthesiology *(114)*

Liebhoff, Emilie
National Coalition of Girls' Schools *(723)*

Liebrock, Lorie M.
Special Interest Group on Applied Computing *(956)*

Liebschutz, Ann
United States-Israel Science & Technology Foundation
(USISTF) *(995)*

Liefer, D.J.
Tile Council of North America, Inc. *(974)*

Lien, Magnhild
Association for Women in Mathematics *(261)*

Lier, Leo van
National Federation of Modern Language Teachers
Associations *(749)*

Lies, Valerie S.
Donors Forum *(415)*

Lieske, CPA, MBA, John A.
American Podiatric Medical Association *(166)*

Lieu, Lisa
Specialized Carriers and Rigging Association *(957)*

Lieurance, Laury
American Judicature Society *(143)*

Liew, Dustin Van
Public Lands Council *(869)*

Liggett, Esq., Martha L.
American Society of Hematology *(199)*

Light, Anita
National Association of Public Child Welfare
Administrators *(688)*

Light, MPA, CAE, Mark W.
International Association of Fire Chiefs *(521)*

Light, Nancy
American Medical Informatics Association *(149)*

Lightfield, Michael
Council of State Community Development Agencies
(397)

Lighthill, Stephen
American Society of Cinematographers *(194)*

Lightle, Susan
American Academy of Osteopathy *(38)*

Lightman, Bernard V.
History of Science Society *(477)*

Ligon, MPA, Tamika R.
North American Association of State and Provincial
Lotteries *(813)*

Likis, CNM, NP, Frances

American College of Nurse-Midwives *(99)*

Liles, Rutledge R.
International Society of Barristers *(571)*

Liley, Thomas
North American Saxophone Alliance *(820)*

Lilja, Christy
American Farm Bureau Federation *(118)*

Lilja, Scott
National Independent Automobile Dealers Association *(761)*

Lillich, Mike
Labor and Employment Relations Association *(592)*

Lillico, Scherr
American Society of Music Arrangers and Composers *(203)*

Lilly, Cindi
American Society for Mass Spectrometry *(186)*
Federation of Analytical Chemistry and Spectroscopy Societies *(440)*

Lilly, Keri
Association of Nutrition & Foodservice Professionals *(296)*

Lilly, Patricia A
Fluid Power Distributors Association *(448)*
Security Hardware Distributors Association *(895)*

Lily, Patricia "Trish" A.
Wholesale Florist and Florist Supplier Association *(1016)*

Lim, Hyung
Association of Surgical Technologists *(312)*

Lim, James
Coalition of Service Industries *(361)*

Lim, Kevin
Special Interest Group for Architecture of Computer Systems *(954)*

Lim, Maribel
American Thoracic Society *(216)*

Lim, Sopha
National Association of Dental Plans *(662)*

Lim, Steve
American Council of Engineering Companies *(109)*

Limperopulos, Brian
International Association of Movers *(525)*

Lin, Sissie
IEEE Power and Energy Society *(485)*

Lin, Stacy
Society of Actuaries *(927)*

Linas, MD, Stuart L.
American Board of Internal Medicine *(82)*

Lincoln, MA, Elizabeth
Drug Information Association *(417)*

Lincoln, Judy
American Horse Publications *(133)*

Lincoln, Ryan
Latin American Studies Association *(594)*

Lind, Brenda
Professional Managers Association *(863)*

Lind, Natalie
International Association of Healthcare Central Service Materiel Management *(522)*

Lindahl, Joe
American Association of Neuroscience Nurses *(66)*

Lindamood, Cherry
North American Association of Wardens and Superintendents *(814)*

Lindauer, Martha

Society of Toxicology *(948)*

Lindauer, Stephen R.
TAUC - The Association of Union Constructors *(968)*

Lindberg, Jon W.
American Congress of Rehabilitation Medicine *(107)*

Linde, Therese
Swedish-American Chambers of Commerce of the USA, Inc. *(967)*

Lindeman, CMP, Kent
Association for Applied Sport Psychology *(239)*

Lindeman, CMP, Kent
Society for Free Radical Biology and Medicine *(909)*
Society for Pediatric Dermatology *(917)*

Lindemann, Todd V.
Industrial Fabrics Association International *(493)*

Linden, Bob
American Association of Advertising Agencies *(53)*

Linden, Danny
National Council for Community Behavioral Healthcare *(731)*

Linden, Harry van der
Radical Philosophy Association *(873)*

Linden, Lisa
Resort and Commercial Recreation Association *(883)*

Linden, Septimus van der
Energy Storage Council *(428)*

Linden, Stacy
American Petroleum Institute *(163)*

Linderer, Mike
International Brotherhood of Boilermakers, Iron Shipbuilders, Blacksmiths, Forgers and Helpers *(531)*

Linderman, Bob
The American Fair Credit Council *(118)*

Lindholm, Douglas L.
Council On State Taxation *(400)*

Lindner, CAE, Randy
National Association of Boards of Examiners of Long Term Care Administrators *(650)*
National Association of Long Term Care Administrator Boards *(679)*

Lindner, CAE, Ray
National Guard Executive Directors Association *(757)*

Lindsay, David
Society for American Archaeology *(903)*

Lindsay, Lisa
National Association of Emergency Medical Technicians *(665)*

Lindsay, Mike
International Saw and Knife Association *(564)*

Lindsay, Russell
Petroleum Technology Transfer Council *(844)*

Lindsey, Joy
National Parent Teachers Association *(779)*

Lindsey, Marcie Gerrietts
Music Teachers National Association *(622)*

Lindsley, Melissa
American Galvanizers Association *(124)*

Lindstrom, Wayne
Mental Health America *(612)*

Lineberger, Judson
International Association for Continuing Education and Training *(511)*

Lineberry, Quentin
North American Thermal Analysis Society *(823)*

Linenthal, Edward T.
Organization of American Historians *(832)*

Lingenfelter, Paul E.
State Higher Education Executive Officers *(961)*

Lingle, Ted
Specialty Coffee Association of America *(957)*

Lingofelter, Stephanie
Heating, Airconditioning and Refrigeration Distributors International *(473)*

Link, Geraldine
National Ski Area Association *(791)*

Link, Kevin W.
Association for Management Information in Financial Services *(251)*

Linke, Lisa
National Association of Retail Collection Attorneys *(692)*

Linke, Richard
IEEE Photonics Society *(485)*

Linkous, Frank
Mine Safety Institute of America *(616)*

Linkous, Jonathan D.
American Telemedicine Association *(215)*

Linn, Jim
American Gas Association *(124)*

Linn, John
National Institute of Steel Detailing *(765)*

Linn, Leslie
Incorporated Research Institutions for Seismology *(487)*

Linn, CPP, Michael R.
National Independent Automobile Dealers Association *(761)*

Linney, Barbara
American College of Physician Executives *(101)*

Linquist, Scott
Gospel Music Association *(464)*

Linsky, Norm
Society for Cardiovascular Angiography and Interventions *(905)*

Linthicum, Kenneth
Society for Vector Ecology *(927)*

Linton, David
American Association of Insurance Services *(63)*

Lintvet, Don
Solar Electric Power Association *(951)*

Lintz, Kimber L.
Mutual Fund Education Alliance *(623)*

Linville, PE, Jeffrey
American Institute of Timber Construction *(141)*

Linville, Tina
The Jockeys' Guild *(588)*

Liodice, Bob
Association of National Advertisers *(295)*

Lioi, Margaret M.
Chamber Music America *(350)*

Lione, Susan B.
The Institute of Internal Auditors *(500)*

Liotta, Donna R.
American Hardware Manufacturers Association *(128)*

Lipartito, Kenneth
Business History Conference *(339)*

Lipetz, Robert Weisenburger
Glass Manufacturing Industry Council *(461)*

Lipkin, Steve
University Film and Video Association *(1002)*

Lipman, Ellen

American Society of Radiologic Technologists *(208)*

Lipner, Jennifer
American Society of Interior Designers *(200)*

Lipner, PhD, Rebecca S.
American Board of Internal Medicine *(82)*

Lipowicz, Agnes
Association for Healthcare Resource and Materials Management *(248)*

Lippert, Gerald
National Association of Criminal Defense Lawyers *(661)*

Lippert, Valerie
Society for Simulation in Healthcare *(921)*

Lippincott, Erin
New York E-Health Collaborative *(809)*

Lippincott, John
Council for Advancement and Support of Education *(388)*

Lippitt, Barry L.
Tau Epsilon Rho Law Society *(968)*

Lipscomb, CMP, Fiona
National Association for Retail Marketing Services *(642)*

Lipscomb, Joseph B.
American Real Estate Society *(173)*

Lipscomb, Tina
1394 Trade Association *(1)*

Lipsen, Linda A.
American Association for Justice *(50)*

Lipsey, Dawn R.
International Association of Special Investigation Units *(528)*

Lipsey, PhD, Dr. Jerry
American Simmental Association *(179)*

Lipson, Beth
Opportunity Finance Network *(829)*

Lipson, CLU, Marshall
Society of Financial Service Professionals *(936)*

Lipson, Merna
Association of the United States Army *(313)*

Liptak, Elisabeth
International Dyslexia Association *(541)*

Lipton, Don
American Farm Bureau Federation *(118)*

Lipton, Karen Shoos
AABB - American Association of Blood Banks *(1)*

Lira, Robyn
American Society of Retina Specialists *(209)*

Lira, Tonya
Association of Military Surgeons of the United States *(294)*

Lisack, Jr., CAE, John
American Association of Pharmaceutical Scientists *(68)*

Lisboa, Robin
National Association of State Directors of Migrant Education *(700)*

Liscia, Laurent
Organization for the Advancement of Structured Information Standards *(831)*

Liskar, Jeff
Appraisal Institute *(226)*

Lisner, Stephen
League of American Orchestras *(595)*

List, Barry
Institute for Operations Research and the Management Sciences *(497)*

Liston, CMP, CFE, Dianne
Association of Certified Fraud Examiners *(271)*

Litch, CAE, Esq., C. Scott
American Academy of Pediatric Dentistry *(39)*

Litchford, Tom
National Retail Federation *(786)*

Litewski, Andrea
American Fraternal Alliance *(124)*

Litke, S. Scot
ADSC: The International Association of Foundation Drilling *(12)*

Little, Caroline H.
Newspaper Association of America *(810)*

Little, Daniel
Intertribal Monitoring Association on Indian Trust Funds *(583)*

Little, Elaine H.
Helicopter Association International *(473)*

Little, Joseph M.
Steamfitters Local Union 449 *(962)*

Little, Julie
Educause *(420)*

Little, Melanie
American Craft Council *(111)*

Little, Phil
National Narcotics Officers Associations' Coalition *(774)*

Little, Robin
NAFSA: Association of International Educators *(624)*

Little, Sherwin
American Classical League *(91)*

Little, Susan
Consumer Specialty Products Association *(381)*

Little, Susan
Heating, Airconditioning and Refrigeration Distributors International *(473)*

Littlefield, Amy
Service Station Dealers of America and Allied Trades *(898)*

Littlefield, Cynthia A.
Association of Jesuit Colleges and Universities *(290)*

Littlefield, Darcy
National Conference of Executives of The ARC *(727)*

Littlefield, Roy E.
Service Station Dealers of America and Allied Trades *(898)*
Tire Industry Association *(975)*

Littman, Juliane Sarry
International Association of Credit Portfolio Managers *(519)*

Littrell, Jill
International Center for Study of Psychiatry and Psychology *(534)*

Littrell, Wade
Council of State Governments *(397)*

Litvinova, Luba
Nurses Organization of Veterans Affairs *(825)*

Litz, Michael
Forum of Regional Associations of Grantmakers *(452)*

Liu, B. Y. J.
American Association for Aerosol Research *(47)*

Liu, Jaymee
Asia America MultiTechnology Association *(231)*

Liu, Junhua (Lucy)
American Association of Colleges of Osteopathic Medicine *(57)*

Liu, RN, MS, Karen
National Association for Medical Direction of Respiratory Care *(640)*

Liu, Phoebe
The Door and Hardware Institute *(416)*

Liu, Sherry
National Alfalfa and Forage Alliance *(631)*

Liu, Siyuan "Steven"
Association for Asian Performance *(239)*

Liu, Tori Miller
Global Cold Chain Alliance *(462)*

Liu, Yiman
German American Business Association *(460)*

Livaudais, Jeff
American Fire Sprinkler Association *(121)*

Lively, Nancy H.
American Cream Draft Horse Association *(111)*

Lively, Philip
ASTM International *(319)*

Liveoak, Jerrod
American Academy of Hospice and Palliative Medicine *(35)*

Liverpool, Deighton E.
American Association for Cancer Research *(48)*

Livingston, Dave
American Society of Consultant Pharmacists *(195)*

Livingston, Ed
National Association of Industrial and Technical Teacher Educators *(675)*

Livingston, Kimmy
American Association of Attorney-Certified Public Accountants *(54)*

Livingston, Nancy
Truck Trailer Manufacturers Association *(981)*

Livingstone, Jed
National Association of Underwater Instructors *(707)*

Livinski, Pamela
TAUC - The Association of Union Constructors *(968)*

Livolsi, Nikki
Producers Guild of America *(858)*

Livsey, Jake
Institute of Nuclear Materials Management *(502)*

Ljungren, Doug
American Kennel Club *(143)*

Llabre, Maria
Academy of Behavioral Medicine Research *(4)*

Llewellyn, John
Mason Contractors Association of America *(607)*

Lloyd, Gina
Institute for Operations Research and the Management Sciences *(497)*

Lloyd, John G.
National Institute of Building Sciences *(764)*

Lloyd, Randi
Cosmetic Executive Women *(387)*

Lloyd, Timothy
American Folklore Society *(122)*

Lo, Stanley
National Academy of Clinical Biochemistry *(627)*

Loalbo, Dennis
Biscuit and Cracker Manufacturers' Association *(330)*

Loar, Granville
Scaffold Industry Association *(891)*

Loayza, Angel
American Society of Hypertension, Inc. *(200)*

Lobato, Patricia
National Exchange Traded Fund Association *(747)*

Lobban, Nicole
American Public Human Services Association *(171)*

Lobley, Joseph B.
Society of Accredited Marine Surveyors *(927)*

Lobovsky, Rachel
The American Jewish Historical Society *(143)*

Loburk, Shannon
Federation of State Humanities Councils *(442)*

Lockhart, Monica
National Association of Real Estate Investment Managers *(690)*

Lockhart, Nina K.
National Association of Energy Service Companies *(665)*

Locklear, Ken
International Hyperbaric Medical Association, Inc. *(551)*

Lockridge, Jack
Federal Bar Association *(438)*

Lockwood, Bill A.
American Society for Automation in Pharmacy *(181)*

Lockwood, Lisa
Marketing Research Association *(606)*

Lockwood, Stephanie
International Council of Shopping Centers *(538)*

Lockwood, PhD, Thomas
Design Management Institute *(410)*

Loeb, Matthew D.
International Alliance of Theatrical Stage Employees, Moving Picture Technicians, Artists and Allied Crafts of the U.S., Its Territories and Canada *(510)*

Loeb, Matthew S.
Institute of Electrical and Electronics Engineers (IEEE) *(499)*

Loeber, Gayle
National Educational Telecommunications Association *(744)*

Loew, CAE, EdM, Ann T.
American College of Veterinary Surgeons *(104)*

Loffer, MD, Franklin D.
AAGL - Advancing Minimally Invasive Gynecology Worldwide *(2)*

Lofgreen, Tirza N.
Healthcare Distribution Management Association *(471)*

Lofgren, CAE, Lousanne (Zan)
American Orthopaedic Foot and Ankle Society *(158)*

Lofland, L. Keith
International Association of Electrical Inspectors *(520)*

Loflin, Michael W.
Marble Institute of America *(604)*

Loflin, Stacey
Self Storage Association *(896)*

Lofquist, Dr. Les
IFCA International *(486)*

LoFrumento, John
American Society of Composers, Authors and Publishers (ASCAP) *(195)*

Lofstrom, Joyce A.
Healthcare Information and Management Systems Society *(471)*

Loftus, Jerome C.
QVM/CMC Vehicle Manufacturers Association *(872)*

Loftus, Kristy
National Child Support Enforcement Association *(721)*

Logan, Barbara
US Travel Association *(983)*

Logan, Joseph P.
International Casual Furnishings Association *(533)*

Logan, Leah
National Housing Conference *(761)*

Logan, PCS, PhD, PT, Lynne Romeiser
American Academy for Cerebral Palsy and Developmental Medicine *(29)*

Logan, Mary K.
Association for the Advancement of Medical Instrumentation *(258)*

Logan, Quan O.
Special Libraries Association *(956)*

Logan, MBA, RHIA, Richard C.
Association of Health Information Outsourcing Services *(286)*

Logan, Sheila
National Association of Electrical Distributors *(664)*

Logan, Steven
National Association of Criminal Defense Lawyers *(661)*

Loger, Debi
American Association of Psychiatric Technicians *(71)*

Loggia, Rosemary
Society for the Advancement of Material and Process Engineering *(922)*

Logue, Brian
United States Lacrosse *(995)*

Logue, Paul
Society of Accredited Marine Surveyors *(927)*

Lohmander, MD, PhD, Stefan
Osteoarthritis Research Society International *(834)*

Lohmann, Dorothy
Infusion Nurses Society *(496)*

Lohmiller, Sheila
Network of Executive Women in Hospitality *(808)*

Lohr, John
National Association of Farm Service Agency County Office Employees *(667)*

Loiacono, Gail
Laser Institute of America *(593)*

Loise, CAE, CMP, Vicki
Association of University Technology Managers *(316)*

Lojanica, Ana
Patient Centered Primary Care Collaborative *(840)*

Lok, Kevin Cheah Kal
Malaysian Rubber Export Promotion Council (USA) *(602)*

Lok, Wayne
College Art Association *(362)*

Lokerson, Sarah
Council for Exceptional Children *(390)*

Lokken, Sherri
National Association of Reunion Managers *(692)*

LoMaglio, Shapri
Council for Christian Colleges and Universities *(389)*

Lomas, Jane
National Textile Association *(800)*

Lomas, Jane
National Textile Association *(800)*

Lomax, Mark
National Tactical Officers Association of America *(799)*

Lomax, Samantha
Association for Women in Science *(262)*

Lomax, Sheila
Catholic Press Association *(346)*

Lomazzi, Marta
World Federation of Public Health Associations *(1026)*

Lombardi, Candice
International Sculpture Center *(564)*

Lombardi, Joanne
Society for Clinical Trials *(906)*

Lombardi, Sarah
National Society of Genetic Counselors *(794)*

Lombardo, Anna W.
Propane Engine Fuel Committee/Propane Education and Research Council *(867)*

Lomeli, Adriana
American Association for Accreditation of Ambulatory Surgery Facilities *(47)*

Lonbardini, Carol
Alliance of Motion Picture & Television Producers *(25)*

London, Jennifer
Institute of Food Technologists *(499)*

London, Jessica W.
Society for Environmental Graphic Design *(908)*

London, Judy
Gas Processors Association *(456)*
Gas Processors Suppliers Association *(456)*

London, CEAP, LCSW, Marina
Employee Assistance Professionals Association *(426)*

Long, Barbara
Association for Professionals in Infection Control and Epidemiology *(254)*

Long, Christopher S.
International Door Association *(541)*

Long, Clinton E.
Business Executives for National Security *(338)*

Long, Connie
Forging Industry Association *(452)*

Long, Deborah
Southern Shrimp Alliance *(953)*

Long, DeVera
International Computer Music Association *(536)*

long, Dustin
National Motorsports Press Association *(773)*

Long, Erick
Academy of Country Music *(4)*

Long, Holly
American Society of Interventional Pain Physicians *(201)*

Long, Janell
DeepStar Project *(408)*

Long, Janet
National Fluid Power Association *(751)*

Long, John
United States Equestrian Federation *(993)*

Long, Khalilah
NAFSA: Association of International Educators *(624)*

Long, Kirk
Business for Social Responsibility *(339)*

Long, Kristen
American Society of Human Genetics *(200)*

Long, Kristi
BAFT-IFSA *(325)*

Long, Lahoma
American Association of Professional Landmen *(71)*

Long, CMP, Marian
American Association of Diabetes Educators *(60)*

Long, Terri
North American Millers' Association *(818)*

Long, Thayer
Independent Electrical Contractors *(489)*

Long, MBA CAE, Therese
Organization for Safety and Asepsis Procedures *(831)*

Long Crow, Kelly
North American Transportation Management Institute *(823)*

Long-Wagner, Roe
International Door Association *(541)*
National Association of Nurse Massage Therapists *(682)*

Longcor, Charles
Building Owners and Managers Association International *(337)*

Longcor, Megan
SACNAS (Society for Advancement of Chicanos and Native Americans in Science) *(889)*

Longendorfer, D O, Lillian Hynes
American Osteopathic College of Pathologists *(160)*

Longfellow, Dr. David G.
Toxicology Forum *(976)*

Longfield, Christine
Resort Hotel Association *(883)*

Longhofer, Susan L.
American Academy of Veterinary Pharmacology and Therapeutics *(42)*

Longie, Joanne
National Council for Prescription Drug Programs *(732)*

Longley, Jim
MASINT Association *(607)*

Longly, Chris
National Auctioneers Association *(711)*

Longo, Gerald F.
American Association of Advertising Agencies *(53)*

Longo, Jena
General Aviation Manufacturers Association *(458)*

Longton, Kyle
Diplomatic and Consular Officers, Retired (Dacor) *(412)*

Longvall, Emily
National Association of Nurse Practitioners in Women's Health *(682)*

Longwell, Sarah
American Beverage Institute *(81)*

Loomis, Bob
Reliability Society *(880)*

Loomis, Laura
Diving Equipment and Marketing Association *(415)*

Loomis, Libby
Painting and Decorating Contractors of America *(837)*

Loomis, FBCA, Susanne
BioCommunications Association *(329)*

Loos, Elizabeth
Delta Waterfowl Foundation *(409)*

Loos, Kaitlyn
National Independent Concessionaires Association *(762)*

Loper, William
Association of the United States Army *(313)*

Lopes, Tommy
International Association of Approved Basketball Officials, Inc. *(515)*

Lopez, Aiyana
Concrete Reinforcing Steel Institute *(374)*

Lopez, Amy
Electric Drive Transportation Association *(421)*

Lopez, Carlos
American Fuel & Petrochemical Manufacturers *(124)*

Lopez, Cindy
Institute of Makers of Explosives *(501)*

Lopez, Lourdes
National Academy of Recording Arts and Sciences *(628)*

Lopez, Luisa
National Association of Social Workers *(696)*

Lopez, Marlene
Fresh Produce Association of the Americas *(453)*

Lopez, Orly Konig
Society of Satellite Professionals International *(947)*
World Teleport Association *(1027)*

Lopez, Teresa
College Art Association *(362)*

López, Ray
Hispanic Association of Colleges and Universities *(475)*

Lopez-Bautista, Juan M.
Phycological Society of America *(846)*

Lopez-Tello, Erika
Hispanic National Bar Association *(475)*

Lopinsky, CAE, Lisa
General Federation of Women's Clubs *(458)*

Lopofsky, Lisa
Independent Cosmetic Manufacturers and Distributors *(489)*

Lopresti, Dr. James "Jim"
Community Action Partnership *(369)*

Lorberau, Karen
Natural Areas Association *(806)*

Lord, Chad
National Parks Conservation Association *(779)*

Lord, Jennifer
Academy of Homiletics *(5)*

Lord, John
American Association of Family and Consumer Sciences *(61)*

Lord-Toof, Melissa
American Pathology Foundation *(162)*

Lordan, Tim
Congressional Internet Caucus Advisory Committee *(377)*

Lords, Curtis
National Strength and Conditioning Association *(797)*

Lore, Heather
International Association of Industrial Accident Boards and Commissions *(523)*

Lore, Ken
National Housing and Rehabilitation Association *(760)*

Lorence, Chris
Independent Community Bankers of America *(488)*

Lorenzo, Frank
International Home Furnishings Representatives Association *(550)*

Loria, Olivia C.
National Coalition of Alternative Community Schools *(723)*

Lorms, CAE, David C
American Osteopathic College of Anesthesiologists *(160)*

Lorsbach, Barbara Z.
American Hospital Association *(133)*

Lorusso, RN, Michelle

Institute of Industrial Engineers *(500)*

Losey, Barbara
Alkylphenols and Ethoxylates Research Council *(22)*

Losey, Marshall
International Nubian Breeders Association *(558)*

Loshbough, Bill
National Association for Pupil Transportation *(642)*

Losi, Robert P.
National Postal Mail Handlers Union *(781)*

Losi, Ryan
Society of International Business Fellows *(940)*

Losinski, Mickey
Council for Children with Behavioral Disorders *(389)*

Losos, Elizabeth
Organization for Tropical Studies *(831)*

Lospaluto, Dawn
R & E Council of the NAPL *(872)*

Lospaluto, Dawn A.
National Association for Printing Leadership *(641)*

Lostrom, Martha M.
National League of Postmasters of the United States *(768)*

Lotito, CMP, Jessica
IEEE Engineering in Medicine and Biology Society *(484)*

Lotridge, Larry
National Association of Chain Drug Stores *(652)*

Lott, Laura
American Association of Museums *(65)*

Lott, Savanna
American Society of Emergency Radiology *(197)*

Lott, Timothy
Search - The National Consortium for Justice Information and Statistics *(894)*

Lotz, CAE, Amy B.
Alliance for Women in Media *(24)*
Association Foundation Group *(262)*

Lotz, David
Actors' Equity Association *(11)*

Lou, Elvie
International Electronic Article Surveillance Manufacturers Association *(542)*

Loubier, Andrea
International Newspaper Marketing Association *(558)*

Louden, Allan D.
American Forensic Association *(123)*

Loudy, Elizabeth A.
State Government Affairs Council *(961)*

Lough, Dan
United Transportation Union *(1001)*

Lough, Leah
Association for the Advancement of Medical Instrumentation *(258)*

Loughin, Thomas G.
American Society of Mechanical Engineers (ASME) *(203)*

Loughlin, Sean
Association for the Advancement of Medical Instrumentation *(258)*

Loughne, Carol
Air Conditioning, Heating and Refrigeration Institute (AHRI) *(18)*

Loughney, Kerry
Federal Communications Bar Association *(439)*

Louie, Emy
United States High Speed Rail Association *(994)*

Louis, Katie
Golf Coaches Association of America *(463)*

Lounsbury, Dave
The Open Group *(828)*

Loutinsky, MaryBeth
Marine Technology Society *(605)*

Lovan, Wanda
The Botanical Society of America *(333)*

Love, Cindy
National Marine Electronics Association *(771)*

Love, Denise
National Association of Health Data Organizations *(671)*

Loveday, David
Water Quality Association *(1013)*

Lovelace, III, Plumer
National Council on Measurement in Education *(739)*

Loveland, Catherine
North American Bar-Related Title Insurers *(814)*

Loveless, Charles M.
American Federation of State, County and Municipal Employees *(120)*

Lovell, Deanna
INDA, Association of the Nonwoven Fabrics Industry *(488)*

Lovell, Jarrett
United States Federation of Scholars and Scientists *(994)*

Lovell, CVN, MEd, RN, Marge
Society for Vascular Nursing *(926)*

Lovendahl, Kristi
Petroleum Technology Transfer Council *(844)*

Loving, Dennis L.
Combat Contractor's Association *(366)*

Loving, Susan J.
International Cemetery, Cremation and Funeral Association *(533)*

Lovingood, Mark
National Military Intelligence Association *(772)*

Lovingood, Vivian
American Public Gardens Association *(170)*

Lovoy, Casey
Association for Psychological Type International *(254)*

LoVullo, Lisa
Plasma Protein Therapeutics Association *(850)*

Low, Barbara M.
National Insurance Crime Bureau *(766)*

Low, Melissa
Club Managers Association of America *(359)*

Lowden, Joan
American Association of Airport Executives *(53)*

Lowder, Kate
Natural Colored Wool Growers Association *(807)*

Lowder, Mark J.
Middle East Studies Association of North America *(615)*

Lowe, Amanda
National Association of State Directors of Special Education *(700)*

Lowe, Charles
National Council of Writing Program Administrators *(738)*

Lowe, Christine
Society for Industrial Microbiology *(913)*

Lowe, Deborah
Real Estate Investment Securities Association *(875)*

Lowe, Harriet
American Camp Association *(88)*

Lowe, Joshua
American Association for the Study of Liver Diseases *(52)*

Lowe, PhD, Mary Martin
Alliance for Continuing Medical Education *(22)*

Lowe, Paul W.
Society of Army Physician Assistants *(930)*

Lowe, Robert R.
American Society on Aging *(211)*

Lowe, CG, Sheila
American Handwriting Analysis Foundation *(128)*

Lowe, Steven W.
Business Executives for National Security *(338)*

Lowe, Ted
Radiant Panel Association *(872)*

Lowe, Zack
International Security Management Association *(564)*

Lowell, CML, CAE, David M.
Associated Locksmiths of America *(236)*
Safe and Vault Technicians Association *(890)*

Lowenfish, Sonja
American Warmblood Registry *(219)*

Lowenstein, Ludwig
International Council of Psychologists *(538)*

Lowery, Dax
United States Synchronized Swimming *(999)*

Lowery, Lee K.
American Society of Women Accountants (ACC) *(211)*

Lowery, Nancy
Society of Mexican American Engineers and Scientists *(941)*

Lowhorn, Wade
North - American Interfraternity Conference *(812)*

Lowinski, Jeff
Window and Door Manufacturers Association *(1018)*

Lowrance, Jessica
Association for Postal Commerce *(253)*

Lowrie, Kathy
Choristers Guild *(355)*

Lowry, Charles B.
Association of Research Libraries *(306)*
Library Copyright Alliance *(597)*

Lowry, Kimberly
Sustainable Buildings Industry Council *(967)*

Lowry, Marcia
International Council of Air Shows *(538)*

Lowry, Mark
Refrigeration Service Engineers Society *(878)*

Loya, Brenda
AFL-CIO (American Federation of Labor and Congress of Industrial Organizations) *(14)*

Lozada, Laura
National Association for the Specialty Food Trade *(644)*

Lozito, John P.
Academy of Management *(6)*

Lu, Nancy
Association Media and Publishing *(262)*

Lu, Wilson
International Executive Association *(543)*

Lubell, Andy
American Luggage Dealers Association *(146)*

Lubic, James E.
American Watchmakers-Clockmakers Institute *(219)*

Lubkin, Sharon
Society for Mathematical Biology *(915)*

Lubner, PhD, Tanya
Water Quality Association *(1013)*

Lubold, Jennifer
National Association of Drug Court Professionals *(663)*

Luby, Corey
National Tactical Officers Association of America *(799)*

Lucas, Annie
National Association of Negro Business and Professional Women's Clubs *(681)*

Lucas, Anthony
Information Technology Industry Council *(495)*

Lucas, Barbara E.R.
United States Institute for Theatre Technology *(995)*

Lucas, Hillary
Corporate Council on Africa *(385)*

Lucas, Jim
United States Institute for Theatre Technology *(995)*

Lucas, Kathy
American Connemara Pony Society *(107)*

Lucas, Marsha
Society for Developmental Biology *(907)*

Lucas, Michael
Paleontological Research Institution *(837)*

Lucas, Michele
Farm Credit Council *(437)*

Lucas, Pat
Marine Retailers Association of America *(605)*

Lucca, Frank
Entertainment Merchants Association *(429)*

Lucero, Ada
National Lime Association *(769)*

Lucey, SJ, Gregory
Association of Jesuit Colleges and Universities *(290)*

Luchtefeld, Jason M
American Equilibration Society *(117)*

Luciani, Lisa
National Weather Service Employees Organization *(804)*

Luciano, S.
International Cargo Gear Bureau *(533)*

Lucius, Susan
National Association of Tax Professionals *(704)*

Luckado, Amy
Association for Hose and Accessories Distribution *(248)*
Fluid Power Distributors Association *(448)*
Independent Sealing Distributors *(491)*
Security Hardware Distributors Association *(895)*
Wholesale Florist and Florist Supplier Association *(1016)*
Yacht Brokers Association of America *(1030)*

Luckett, AAP, Scott
Automotive Aftermarket Industry Association *(321)*

Lucy, CPA, JD, Cecil B.
National Black MBA Association *(714)*

Lucy, Rebecca
American Society of Sugar Beet Technologists *(209)*
Beet Sugar Development Foundation *(327)*

Lucy, William
Coalition of Black Trade Unionists *(360)*

Ludeman, Ruth
Association of Executive and Administrative Professionals *(281)*
National Association of Dental Assistants *(662)*

Ludgate, Evelyn

The American Safe Deposit Association *(176)*

Ludlam, Jay
Defense Research Institute *(408)*

Ludlum, Scott
International Society for Pharmaceutical Engineering *(567)*

Ludwick, Beth
Grocery Manufacturers Association (GMA) *(466)*

Ludwig, Dorothy
The Council of Landscape Architectural Registration Boards *(395)*

Ludwig, BA, Karen
Association of Surgical Technologists *(312)*

Ludwig, Kristin
American Society of Clinical Oncology *(194)*

Ludwig, Mary Ann
National Hemophilia Foundation *(759)*

Luebbe, Linda
Groundwater Management Districts Association *(466)*

Luebking, Will
American Federation of Musicians and Employers Pension Fund *(119)*

Lueck, Therese
American Journalism Historians Association *(143)*

Luedeka, Robert J.
Polyurethane Foam Association *(852)*

Luehrsen, Mary
NAMM - The International Music Products Association *(625)*

Luen, Sheryl Van der
Motorcycle Industry Council, Inc. *(620)*

Lueth, Brian
Scoliosis Research Society *(893)*

Lugar, Katherine
Retail Industry Leaders Association *(884)*

Lugo, Armando
International Federation of the Phonographic Industry *(544)*

Lugo, Carlos
Association of University Interior Designers *(315)*

Lugo, Fred
National Senior Corps Association *(790)*

Luhr, Gary W.
Association of Presbyterian Colleges and Universities *(300)*

Lui, Adeline
Association of Energy Services Professionals, International *(281)*

Lukacs, George
Society for Wetland Scientists *(927)*

Lukas, Lisamarie
Society of Actuaries *(927)*

Luke, Anne Forristall
Association of Equipment Manufacturers *(281)*

Lukens, David R.
Associated General Contractors of America (AGC) *(236)*

Lukins, David
National Speleological Society *(795)*

Lukken, Walter
Futures Industry Association *(455)*

Lukoff, David
Association for Transpersonal Psychology *(260)*

Lula, Brain
SPIE - The International Society for Optical Engineering *(958)*

Lull, Kenny
National Association of School Nurses *(693)*

Lulofs, Neal
Audit Bureau of Circulations *(320)*

Lum, Alisa
Pacific Telecommunications Council *(836)*

Lumia, Crislyn
State Government Affairs Council *(961)*

Lumia, Ronald
Robotics and Automation Society *(887)*

Lumme, Dale
Navy League of the United States *(807)*

Lummis, Adair
Religious Research Association *(880)*

Lumpkin, Michael
International Documentary Association *(541)*

Luna, Andrea
Police Executive Research Forum *(852)*

Luna, Carl A.
National Association of Publicly Traded Partnerships *(689)*

Luna, Jacqueline
American Architectural Manufacturers Association *(46)*

Luna, Sam
International Communication Association *(536)*

Lunceford, Jeneva Stene
American Simmental Association *(179)*

Lund, PhD, Adrian K.
Insurance Institute for Highway Safety *(505)*

Lund, Bradley J.
American Pathology Foundation *(162)*
Healthcare Billing and Management Association *(470)*
Neuro-Developmental Treatment Association *(808)*

Lund, Elizabeth
Medical Library Association *(611)*

Lund, Gregory W.
Brotherhood of Locomotive Engineers and Trainmen *(336)*

Lundahl, Annie
Association of Boarding Schools *(270)*

Lundberg, Elizabeth
Human Capital Institute *(480)*

Lundberg, Jr., Rolf
United States Chamber of Commerce *(991)*

Lundgren, Elizabeth
Ankole Watusi International Registry *(223)*

Lundgren, Holly
National Retail Hobby Stores Association *(786)*

Lundgren, Linda
The National Association of Dog Obedience Instructors *(663)*

Lundmark, Torbjorn
International Society for Respiratory Protection *(569)*

Luner, Karin
Women's Caucus for Art *(1022)*

Lung, Christine
American Society of Radiologic Technologists *(208)*

Lunsford, Laura G.
Society for the Teaching of Psychology *(926)*

Lunsford, Sandra
American Jail Association *(142)*

Lunzer, Bernard J.
The Newspaper Guild *(810)*

Luo, Sarah
Registry of Interpreters for the Deaf *(879)*

Luper, CAE, Brenda
National Council for the Social Studies *(733)*

Lupinski, Ellen
Society of Research Administrators International *(946)*

Lupo, Phil
American Board of Family Medicine *(82)*

Lupson, Warren
Air Conditioning, Heating and Refrigeration Institute (AHRI) *(18)*

Lupson, Warren
Partnership for Air-Conditioning, Heating Refrigeration Accreditation *(839)*

Lureman, Tandance
Exhibition Services and Contractors Association *(435)*

Lurie, Thad
American Wind Energy Association (AWEA) *(221)*

Lurker, Renee
International Association of Airport Duty Free Stores *(515)*

Luscher, Dan
Business for Social Responsibility *(339)*

Lush (Yankton Sioux), Brian
Indian Arts and Crafts Association *(492)*

Lusis, Sheila
National Certification Commission for Acupuncture and Oriental Medicine *(720)*

Lusk, MA, Aisha
Association for Spiritual, Ethical and Religious Values in Counseling *(257)*

Lusk, Christine
American Academy of Clinical Toxicology *(31)*

Lusk, Cody
American International Automobile Dealers Association *(142)*

Lusk, Eileen
American Association of Hip and Knee Surgeons *(62)*

Lusk, Michelle
Cement Kiln Recycling Coalition *(347)*

Lust, Tim
National Sorghum Producers *(795)*

Luster, Ashley
American Farrier's Association *(118)*

Lustig, Edgar L.
American Society of Theatre Consultants *(210)*

Luther, Julie
Concrete Plant Manufacturers Bureau *(374)*

Luther, Megan
Investigative Reporters and Editors *(583)*

Luthi, Randal
National Ocean Industries Association *(775)*

Lutschaunig, Mark
American Veterinary Medical Association *(219)*

Lutsenko, Olga
The Council for Trade and Economic Cooperation *(391)*

Lutterman, CPA, Angie
Investment Management Consultants Association *(584)*

Lutton, Alison
National Association for the Education of Young Children *(644)*

Lutton, Jessica
Gerontological Society of America *(460)*

Luttrell, Ed
National Grange *(756)*

Lutz, Christian
American Society of Professional Estimators *(208)*

Lutz, Drew
United States Pharmacopeia *(997)*

Lutz, Jonathan
Institute of Certified Professional Managers *(498)*

Lutz, Linda
Organic Trade Association *(830)*

Luu, Mai
Society for Academic Emergency Medicine *(903)*

Luzier, Michael
National Association of Home Builders Research Center *(673)*

Lybrand, Kim
Professional Construction Estimators Association of America *(861)*

Lycett, Robbi
Biotechnology Industry Organization (BIO) *(330)*

Lyckberg, Todd
International Society of Refractive Surgery of the American Academy of Ophthalmology *(574)*

Lyda, Gwen
Public Housing Authorities Directors Association *(869)*

Lyddane, Pat
National Solid Wastes Management Association *(795)*

Lyle, Judy
Association of Occupational Health Professionals in Healthcare *(296)*

Lyle, Virginia
EPS Industry Alliance *(432)*

Lyles, Jenn
American Association of Cosmetology Schools *(59)*

Lyman, Mary S.
National Association of Publicly Traded Partnerships *(689)*

Lyman, Robert H.
Association of the United States Navy, Inc. *(314)*

Lymn, Nadine
Ecological Society of America *(418)*

Lynch, Annmarie
Society of Cosmetic Chemists *(934)*

Lynch, Candace
American Association for Crystal Growth *(49)*

Lynch, Elaine
American Anthropological Association *(45)*

Lynch, Elizabeth
National Conference of Bar Foundations *(726)*

Lynch, Jean
Academy of Osseointegration *(7)*
American Association of Medical Assistants *(65)*
American Society of Colon and Rectal Surgeons *(195)*

Lynch, CAE, MPS, Jean
American Society for Blood and Marrow Transplantation *(181)*

Lynch, CAE, Jennifer
American Immigration Lawyers Association *(134)*
Association for Tropical Biology and Conservation *(260)*

Lynch, Jim
Association of Professional Office Managers *(302)*

Lynch, USAF (Ret.), MGEN Joseph G.
Military Officers Association of America (MOAA) *(616)*

Lynch, Kelly
Campus Computer Resellers Alliance *(341)*

Lynch, Kevin
American Fisheries Society *(121)*

Lynch, Kevin A.
National Industries for the Blind *(763)*

Lynch, Lara
Airport Consultants Council *(21)*

Lynch, Michelle
Promotion Marketing Association *(866)*

Lynch, Mike
United States Tobacco Cooperative Inc *(1000)*

Lynch, Monique C.
National Council for Accreditation of Teacher Education *(731)*
National Council of Teachers of Mathematics *(737)*

Lynch, Rosie
International Society for Medical Publication Professionals *(567)*

Lynch, Sam
National Association of State Boating Law Administrators *(698)*

Lynch, Sandy
American Moving and Storage Association *(153)*

Lynch, Scott
American Bearing Manufacturers Association *(80)*

Lynch, Susan
American Public Power Association *(171)*

Lynch, Susan
Association for Assessment and Accreditation of Laboratory Animal Care International *(239)*

Lynch, Ted
American Gaming Association *(124)*

Lynch, Theodore D.
United States Advanced Ceramics Association *(989)*

Lynch, Thomas E.
National Auto Auction Association *(711)*

Lynch, Zack
Neurotechnology Industry Organization *(809)*

Lyndon, Elizabeth
National Precast Concrete Association *(782)*

Lyndrup, Anne
National Golf Course Owners Association *(755)*

Lynes, Katie
American College of Health Care Administrators *(96)*

Lynn, Denis
International Society of Protistologists *(573)*

Lynn, Don
American Trucking Associations *(218)*

Lynne, Sherrie
Sculptors Guild *(894)*

Lynskey, Greg
Association of Air Medical Services *(264)*

Lyon, Chris
Fibre Channel Industry Association *(443)*
SCSI Trade Association *(893)*

Lyon, CAE, Jasmine C.
Veterinary Botanical Medical Association *(1008)*

Lyon, Jonathan
Federation of Tax Administrators *(442)*

Lyon, Margot
American Theological Library Association *(216)*

Lyon, Sarah
Society for the Anthropology of Work *(923)*

Lyons, Catherine
International Sleep Products Association *(565)*

Lyons, Christopher
Archivists and Librarians in the History of the Health Sciences *(228)*

Lyons, Gregory
The American Gem Society *(125)*

Lyons, DVM, James
American Romagnola Association *(176)*

Lyons, Lisbeth
Printing Industries of America *(857)*

Lyons, Jr., Robert P.
IEEE Aerospace and Electronic Systems Society (AESS) *(483)*

Lyons, FACI, III, William J.
The Concrete Industry Board *(373)*

Lytle, Jessica
National Recreation and Parks Association *(784)*

Ma, Hong
Chinese American Librarians Association *(354)*

Maak, Joshua C.
The Sulphur Institute *(965)*

Maas, Brent
National Institute of Governmental Purchasing *(765)*

Maas, Corey S.
American Academy of Facial Plastic and Reconstructive Surgery *(34)*

Maatz, Lisa M.
American Association of University Women *(76)*

Maaza, Illeny
International Digital Enterprise Alliance *(540)*

Mabarak, Fadi
National Plasterers Council *(781)*

Mabarak, Natalya
National Plasterers Council *(781)*

Mabry, Deidreax
American Meat Science Association *(148)*

Mabry, Michael R.
Radiology Business Management Association *(874)*

Mabry, Vickie
National Pecan Shellers Association *(780)*

Macalindong, Tony
American Association of Neurological Surgeons *(66)*

Macaluso, Katie
National Association of Neonatal Nurses *(682)*

Macander, Jamie
American Society for Healthcare Human Resources Administration *(185)*

Macanufo, Elizabeth
Consortium for Graduate Study in Management *(378)*

Macaulay, Scott
Independent Filmmaker Project *(489)*

Maccabe, Dr. Andrew
Association of American Veterinary Medical Colleges *(267)*

MacCarthy, PhD, Mark
Software & Information Industry Association (SIIA) *(950)*

Macchio, Ralph
National Association of Wastewater Transporters *(708)*

MacCullough, Don
National Educational Broadband Services Organization *(744)*

MacCutcheon, Colleen
American Brachytherapy Society *(85)*

MacDonald, Mary Lehman
AFT Healthcare *(15)*

MacDonald, Nora K.
American Horticultural Society *(133)*

MacDonald, Tamara
International Technology and Engineering Educators Association *(576)*

MacDougall, Carol A.
Institute of Transportation Engineers *(503)*

MacDougall, Mia
Motorcycle Industry Council, Inc. *(620)*

Mace, Carissa
Fresh Produce and Floral Council *(453)*

Macedo, Sarah
Formaldehyde Council, Inc. *(452)*

Macek, Kara
Governors' Highway Safety Association *(464)*

MacFarland, Karen
American Association of Physicists in Medicine *(69)*

MacGillivray, Peter
Specialty Equipment Market Association *(957)*

MacGregor, Paul
At-Sea Processors Association *(319)*

MacGregor, Shannon
Construction Specifications Institute *(380)*

Machado, Jackie
American Fisheries Society *(121)*

Machado, Michiale
Self-Insurance Institute of America, Inc. *(896)*

Machel, Mary-Jo
Marketing Research Association *(606)*

Maciag, Gregory A.
ACORD - Association for Cooperative Operations Research and Development *(11)*

Macias, Natalie
Softwood Export Council *(951)*

Maciejewski, Anthony
Robotics and Automation Society *(887)*

Macikas, Barb
Public Library Association *(869)*

MacInnes, Erin
American Association of Suicidology *(74)*

MacIntyre, Deborah
American Society of Cytopathology *(196)*

Maciog, Greg
American College of Oral and Maxillofacial Surgeons *(99)*

Mack, Bonnie
American Society of Head and Neck Radiology *(199)*

Mack, Carl B.
National Society of Black Engineers *(793)*

Mack, Caroline M.
Manufacturers Alliance/MAPI Inc. *(603)*

Mack, Dale
National Organization for the Professional Advancement of Black Chemists and Chemical Engineers *(777)*

Mack, Peter
Association of Professional Model Makers *(302)*

Mack, Rachel
American College Health Association *(93)*

Mack, Timothy C.
World Future Society *(1026)*

Mack, Toby
Associated Equipment Distributors *(235)*

Mack, Wendy L.
American College of Health Plan Management *(96)*

Macke, Mimi
Society of Biological Psychiatry *(931)*

MacKelvie, Tressa
American Radium Society *(173)*

MacKelvie, Tressa
North American Skull Base Society *(820)*

Mackenzie, Iain
International Sign Association *(564)*

MacKenzie, Ian
Investment Management Consultants Association *(584)*

Mackes, PhD, Marilyn F.
National Association of Colleges and Employers *(655)*

Mackey, Cameron L.
Manufacturers Alliance/MAPI Inc. *(603)*

Mackey, Carol-Ann P.
American Antiquarian Society *(45)*

Mackey, Linda
Investment Adviser Association *(583)*

Mackey, Mark
Livestock Marketing Association *(599)*

Mackey, Maureen
Association of Junior Leagues International *(290)*

MacKie, II, Robb S.
American Bakers Association *(78)*

Mackie, Sue
United States Swim School Association *(999)*

Mackintosh, Esther
Federation of State Humanities Councils *(442)*

Macklin, Nancy
Hearing Loss Association of America *(472)*

MacLane-Baeder, Doreen
Association of Medical Education and Research in Substance Abuse *(293)*

MacLaren, Kimberly
Conveyor Equipment Manufacturers Association *(383)*

MacLean, Laura
Association of Fish and Wildlife Agencies *(283)*

MacLeod, Laurel
National Religious Broadcasters *(785)*

MacLeod, Sarah
Aeronautical Repair Station Association *(14)*

MacMullin, Glenda
Consumer Electronics Association *(381)*

MacNab, Clare
American Society for Histocompatibility and Immunogenetics *(185)*
Juvenile Products Manufacturers Association *(590)*
NADCA: The HVAC Inspection, Maintenance and Restoration Association *(623)*

MacNab, CEM, CMP, Clare
American Association of Heart Failure Nurses *(62)*

Macotto, Jennifer
SACNAS (Society for Advancement of Chicanos and Native Americans in Science) *(889)*

MacPhee, Norma Jean
Engineering College Magazines Associated *(429)*

MacPherson, Bruce
International Trademark Association *(577)*

MacPherson, Jim
America's Blood Centers *(28)*

MacPherson, Kelly
National Golf Course Owners Association *(755)*

MacRae, Nancy
American College of Chest Physicians *(94)*

MacWilliams, CHSP, Leeann
National Frozen and Refrigerated Foods Association *(753)*

Madara, Dr. James
American Medical Association *(148)*

Madara, Susan
Society of Biblical Literature *(931)*

Madaus, Carolyn
American Academy of Cosmetic Dentistry *(31)*

Madden, Dennis
Automatic Transmission Rebuilders Association *(321)*

Madden, Jesse
The Door and Hardware Institute *(416)*

Madden, Lee
National Strength and Conditioning Association *(797)*

Madden, Sally
American Society of Safety Engineers *(209)*

Madden, Susan
Competitive Carriers Association *(371)*

Madden, Suzanne
American Forest & Paper Association *(123)*

Madden, Suzanne
American Wood Council *(221)*

Madden, Esq., Turner
International Association of Venue Managers *(528)*

Madden Charles, Janet
International Association for Cold Storage Construction *(511)*

Maddox, Elizabeth
Insured Retirement Institute *(505)*

Maddox, Kimberley
Instructional Technology Council *(504)*

Maddox, Lyn
American Society of Tropical Medicine and Hygiene *(210)*
Institute of Nuclear Materials Management *(502)*
The Society for Adolescent Medicine *(903)*

Maddox, Michael
Pet Industry Joint Advisory Council *(842)*

Maddux, Daniel J.
American Payroll Association *(162)*

Maddux, FCCP, PharmD, Michael S.
American College of Clinical Pharmacy *(94)*

Maddy, Jim
Association of Zoos and Aquariums *(318)*

Mader, Meg
Natural Products Association *(807)*

Mader, Richard E.
Association for Retail Technology Standards *(256)*

Madigan, cj
Association of Personal Historians *(299)*

Madoff, Larry
International Society for Infectious Diseases *(566)*

Madon, Stephanie
American Psychology-Law Society *(170)*

Madrid, Robert
National Humanities Alliance *(761)*

Madrigal, Lorena
American Association of Physical Anthropologists *(69)*

Madsen, Kristen
National Academy of Recording Arts and Sciences *(628)*

Madsen, Stephanie
At-Sea Processors Association *(319)*

Maeder, Krista J.
American Judicature Society *(143)*

Mael, Barry
United Synagogue of Conservative Judaism *(1001)*

Maenner, Anna

National Association of Fraternal Insurance
Counsellors *(669)*

Maes, CAE, Majel
National Association of College and University Food
Services *(655)*

Maffei, Patricia
Fashion Group International *(438)*

Mafrica, CAE, Leonard
American Society of Regional Anesthesia and Pain
Medicine *(209)*

Magali, Mario
Cosmetic Industry Buyers and Suppliers *(387)*

Magalnick, Barbara
Editorial Freelancers Association *(419)*

Magee, Earl
Society of Professors of Child and Adolescent
Psychiatry *(945)*

Magee, James
AABC Commissioning Group *(1)*

Magee, Jeff
NACE International *(623)*

Mages, Marilyn
Independent Cosmetic Manufacturers and Distributors
(489)

Maggard, Ann
Touchstone Energy Cooperatives *(976)*

Maggard, Emily
International Institute of Municipal Clerks *(552)*

Maggi, CAE, Dennis J.
American College of Trial Lawyers *(103)*

Maggi, Sara
National Society of Professional Surveyors *(794)*

Maggio, Christine
International Technology and Engineering Educators
Association *(576)*

Maggio, CMP, Maria
National Property Management Association *(783)*

Maggitt, Shalonda
Real Estate Information Professionals Association *(875)*

Maghazehe, PhD, CHE, Al
Capital Health *(342)*

Maghraoui, Lisa
Telecommunications Industry Association *(971)*

Magid, Donni
Metal Powder Industries Federation *(613)*
Powder Metallurgy Equipment Association *(854)*
Powder Metallurgy Parts Association *(854)*
Refractory Metals Association *(878)*

Magill, Julie
American College of Neuropsychopharmacology *(98)*

Maginn, Marjorie
Women in Government *(1021)*

Maglio, Capt. Ron
National Association of Charterboat Operators *(652)*

Magnani, Pamela
International Association of Fire Chiefs *(521)*

Magness, Rita Chua
American Academy of Facial Plastic and Reconstructive
Surgery *(34)*

Magnus, Sandra H.
American Institute of Aeronautics and Astronautics
(136)

Magnuson, Cynthia
National Federation of Independent Business (NFIB)
(748)

Magnuson, John R.
National Home Infusion Association *(760)*

Magnuson, Mary
National Association of Fundraising Ticket
Manufacturers *(669)*

Magnuson, Peter
Association of Career and Technical Education *(271)*

Magnuson, Stew
National Defense Industrial Association *(742)*

Magnussen, Anke
American Holsteiner Horse Association *(132)*

Magrath, Anne
American College of Surgeons Professional Association
(103)

Magrogan, Mary T.
Institute for Operations Research and the Management
Sciences *(497)*

Magruder, Elicia
Plumbing-Heating-Cooling Contractors - National
Association *(851)*

Magruder, Jim
Board of Registered Polysomnographic Technologists
(333)

Magruder, Lora Ann
American Chemistry Council *(90)*

Maguire, Crystal
Aeronautical Repair Station Association *(14)*

Maguire, Debbie
Optical Storage Technology Association *(829)*

Maguire, Deborah
World Federation for Mental Health *(1026)*

Maguire, DDS, John J.
Association of Managed Care Dentists *(292)*

Magyar, CHES, MEd, Sandra F.
American Association of Public Health Physicians *(72)*

Mahaffey, Ashley J.
International Paralegal Management Association *(559)*

Mahaffey, CAE, MS, J. C. (Chris)
American College of Foot and Ankle Surgeons *(95)*

Mahan, Tripp
PROMAX/BDA *(866)*

Mahanna, Mike
National Association for Environmental Management
(638)

Mahar, Jennifer
Society for the Study of Evolution *(925)*

Mahar, Paula
Materials Research Society *(609)*

Maher, Elizabeth
American Society of Transplantation *(210)*

Maher, Mary
Association of Children's Museums *(272)*

Maher, Nicole R.
Concrete Plant Manufacturers Bureau *(374)*
Truck Mixer Manufacturers Bureau *(981)*

Maher, Peter
National Association of Pastoral Musicians *(683)*

Maher, CSS, Teresa
Electronics Technicians Association International *(424)*

Mahler, Bryan
Outdoor Industry Association *(835)*

Mahmoud, Seif A.
Federation of State Boards of Physical Therapy *(442)*

Mahon, James
International Association of Conference Centers *(518)*

Mahon, John
React International *(875)*

Mahoney, Ann
International City/County Management Association
(535)

Mahoney, Cathleen M.
National Abortion Federation *(626)*

Mahoney, Justice J. Jeremiah
Federal Administrative Law Judges Conference *(438)*

Mahoney, Jaime
American Road and Transportation Builders
Association *(175)*

Mahoney, CPA, Jeffrey P.
Council of Institutional Investors *(394)*

Mahoney, Jim
American Association of Independent Music *(63)*

Mahoney, John
NGNP Industry Alliance *(810)*

Mahoney, Karin
International Sleep Products Association *(565)*

Mahoney, APN, Kathleen
Association of Women's Health, Obstetric and
Neonatal Nurses *(318)*

Mahoney, Katie
National Association for Information Destruction, Inc.
(640)

Mahoney, Mike
The American Hair Loss Council *(128)*

Mahoney, Patrick
Institute of Electrical and Electronics Engineers (IEEE)
(499)

Mahurin, Ronald P.
Council for Christian Colleges and Universities *(389)*

Maibach, Michael C.
European-American Business Council *(434)*

Maier, Kimberly
Association of Professional Art Advisors *(300)*

Maietta, Sarah
American Public Gardens Association *(170)*

Mailman, Dan
Linguistic Association of Canada and the United States
(598)

Maiman, Janice
American Institute of Certified Public Accountants
(137)

Maimon, Catherine
Environmental Industry Associations *(431)*
National Solid Wastes Management Association *(795)*
Waste Equipment Technology Association *(1012)*

Maimone, Heather
American Chemical Society - Rubber Division *(90)*

Main, Ellen
Society for Conservation Biology *(906)*

Main, Michael
International Contrast Ultrasound Society *(537)*

Maine, Lucinda L.
American Association of Colleges of Pharmacy *(57)*

Mainelli, Andrea
The College Board *(363)*

Maino, FAAO, MEd, Dominick M.
College of Optometrists in Vision Development *(364)*

Mainor, Trena
Council of Large Public Housing Authorities *(395)*

Mais, Gretchen
American Farmland Trust *(118)*

Maison, Perry
National Grocers Association *(756)*

Majdalany, Michael

Transaction Processing Performance Council **(977)**

Majette, Sheena
American Medical Directors Association **(149)**

Majkowski, Edward J.
Society of Insurance Financial Management **(940)**

Majkowski, Vivian
Voice and Speech Trainers Association **(1011)**

Major, Chris
Angel Capital Association **(223)**

Major, Doreatha
Air Force Association **(18)**

Major, Mary Jo
National Associations of State Directors of Pupil
Transportation Services **(710)**

Majors, Mary
Semiconductor Environmental Safety and Health
Association **(896)**

Makansi, Jason
Energy Storage Council **(428)**

Maki, Michelle
Original Equipment Suppliers Association **(833)**

Maki, PhD, Dr. Sonja L.
Plant Growth Regulation Society of America **(849)**

Makin, Michael
Graphic Arts Technical Foundation **(465)**

Makin, Michael
Label Printing Industries of America **(591)**

Makowka, Norbert W.
National Association of Fire Equipment Distributors
(668)

Makowski, Ann
Society for Environmental Graphic Design **(908)**

Malaise, Richard E.
National Automobile Dealers Association **(711)**

Malak, Clark
Wood Moulding and Millwork Producers Association
(1024)

Malakoff, Deborah
The Vision Council **(1010)**

Malaman, Roberto
International Association for Energy Economics **(512)**

Malamis, Alexia
The Association for Nursing Professional Development
(252)

Malay, DPM, FACFAS, D. Scot
American College of Foot and Ankle Surgeons **(95)**

Malbin, Susan
The American Jewish Historical Society **(143)**

Malcom, Denver L.
National Association of Student Affairs Professionals
(703)

Malcom, Shirley M.
American Association for the Advancement of Science
(51)

Malcos, Jenelle
Human Anatomy and Physiology Society **(480)**

Malcuit, Pam
American Dexter Cattle Association **(114)**

Maldonado, Gilbert
Consortium for North American Higher Education
Collaboration **(378)**

Male, CAE, Jane
Electrical Equipment Representatives Association **(422)**
Investment Recovery Association **(584)**

Malek, Paul
Association of Equipment Manufacturers **(281)**

Malenfant, Kara
Association of College and Research Libraries **(273)**

Malesardi, Maryann
Association of Government Accountants **(286)**

Malesh, Rae
National Association of Mutual Insurance Companies
(681)

Malgire, Sharon
American Public Gardens Association **(170)**

Malgrande, Michael
Academy of Management **(6)**

Malicki, Mary
National Council for History Education **(732)**

Maline, Karen F.
Justice Research and Statistics Association **(589)**

Malinich, Katie
Defense Research Institute **(408)**

Malisch, Ward
American Society of Concrete Contractors **(195)**

Malkin, Vanessa
International Studies Association **(576)**

Mallardi, CMC, MBA, Vincent
Printing Brokerage/Buyers Association International
(857)

Malleck, Liz
AHS International - The Vertical Flight Society **(17)**

Mallernee, II, Rollin E.
National Basketball Athletic Trainers Association **(712)**
Professional Baseball Athletic Trainers Society **(860)**

Malliarakis, CNP, MAc, MSM, RN, Kate Driscoll
Association of Medical Education and Research in
Substance Abuse **(293)**

Mallice, Charles
International Association of Personal Protection Agents
(526)

Mallin, CPCU, JD, Thomas W.
Property Loss Research Bureau **(867)**

Mallison, Andy
National Plasterers Council **(781)**

Mallon, Linda
American Academy of Actuaries **(29)**

Mallory, RD, Georgeann
American Society for Metabolic and Bariatric Surgery
(187)

Mallory, CAE, James L.
Non-Ferrous Founders' Society **(811)**

Mallory, Larry
American Artists Professional League **(47)**

Mallory, BA, Lauren
Alliance for Continuing Medical Education **(22)**

Malloy, Maureen
Society for American Archaeology **(903)**

Malloy, CAE, CMP, Michelle
National Association of Regulatory Utility
Commissioners **(691)**

Malloy, Thomas J.
Intermodal Association of North America **(508)**

Malmberg, Ingrid
Outdoor Industry Association **(835)**

Malmstrom, Allison
National Association of Trailer Manufacturers **(706)**

Malone, FAAN, PhD, RN, Beverly
National League for Nursing **(768)**

Malone, Deborah
International Advertising Association **(509)**

Malone, Jerry
National Christian College Athletic Association **(721)**

Malone, Judy
American Sheep Industry Association **(178)**
American Wool Council **(222)**

Malone, Karen
Healthcare Information and Management Systems
Society **(471)**

Malone, Malena
Public Housing Authorities Directors Association **(869)**

Malone, Robert J.
History of Science Society **(477)**

Maloney, Barry C.
Foodservice Sales & Marketing Association **(450)**

Maloney, Colleen
BritishAmerican Business Inc. **(335)**

Maloney, Janet
National FFA Organization **(750)**

Maloney, Patrick
Hydraulic Institute **(481)**

Malott, PhD, Maria E.
Association for Behavior Analysis International **(240)**
Society for the Advancement of Behavior Analysis
(922)

Malott, Richard W.
Society for the Advancement of Behavior Analysis
(922)

Malottke, Brenda
American Society for Bone and Mineral Research **(181)**
United Soybean Board **(989)**

Maloy, CMP, Donna
National Association of Local Government Auditors
(678)
National Association of State Auditors, Comptrollers
and Treasurers **(698)**

Maloy, Rita
Art Therapy Credentials Board **(230)**

Malry, Jr., Charles
Association for Professionals in Infection Control and
Epidemiology **(254)**

Mamdani, Tahera
National Council on Family Relations **(738)**

Mamigonian, Marc A.
National Association for Armenian Studies and
Research **(636)**

Mamone, Allie
Snack Food Association **(901)**

Mamone, Gina
Assisted Living Federation of America **(234)**

Manacap-Johnson, Mae
International Spa Association **(575)**

Manak, Denise
National Association of Collegiate Directors of
Athletics **(656)**

Manak, Pat
College Athletic Business Management Association
(362)
National Association of Athletic Development Directors
(647)

Mance, Dianne
National Black Nurses Association **(714)**

Mancera, Mary
National Association of Hispanic Real Estate
Professionals **(672)**

Mancini, Dawn
Plant Growth Regulation Society of America **(849)**

Mancini, John F.
Association for Information and Image Management
International **(249)**

Mancino, CAE, EdD, RN, Diane J.
National Student Nurses Association *(797)*

Mancuso, Tony
Association of Regulatory Boards of Optometry *(305)*

Mandel, Jed R.
Truck and Engine Manufacturers Association *(980)*

Mandel, Joyce
International Magnesium Association *(555)*

Mandelbaum, Mark
American Society of Agronomy (ASA, CSSA, SSSA) *(191)*
Soil Science Society of America *(951)*

Mandell, David
Aerospace Industries Association of America *(14)*

Mandell, Missy
Large Public Power Council *(593)*

Manderscheid, PhD, Ron
National Association of County Behavioral Health and Developmental Disability Directors *(659)*

Mandes, Vincent J.
American Board of Internal Medicine *(82)*

Mandeville, Lawrence L.
Antenna Measurement Techniques Association *(224)*

Mandigo, Glenton
United States Advanced Ceramics Association *(989)*

Mandlawitz, Myrna
School Social Work Association of America *(892)*

Mandlawitz, J D, MEd, Myrna R.
American Dance Therapy Association *(113)*

Mandrier, Brian
International Cargo Security Council *(533)*

Mandt, David
International Association of Amusement Parks and Attractions(IAAPA) *(515)*

Manduca, Cathryn
National Association of Geoscience Teachers *(669)*

Manelli, Megan
Association of Jewish Family & Children's Agencies *(290)*

Manetta, Rob
International Association of Medical Equipment Remarketers and Servicers (IAMERS) *(524)*

Manfredini, Rose
Metals Service Center Institute *(614)*

Manfredo, Jen
NPTA Alliance *(824)*

Mang, Crystal
American Military Retirees Association *(152)*

Mangan, Andrew
United States-Sudan Business Council *(999)*

Mangan, Dan
International Reading Association *(562)*

Mangano, Mary Ann
Ice Skating Institute *(482)*

Mangicaro, Maria
International Center for Study of Psychiatry and Psychology *(534)*

Mangol, CMP, Lynn
International Society of Explosives Engineers *(572)*

Mangram, Kermett
Seafarers International Union of North America *(894)*

Mangual, Dennis
Textile Rental Services Association of America *(973)*

Maniatis, Stephanie
American Hellenic Educational Progressive Association (AHEPA) *(130)*

Manigat, Ana
National Immigration Project of the National Lawyers Guild *(761)*

Manion-Leone, Maureen
Association of Executive Search Consultants *(282)*

Maniscalcony, John
National Association for Oilheat Research and Education *(641)*

Manke, David
United States Psychiatric Rehabilitation Association *(998)*

Manke, Jeff
International Balloon Association *(529)*

Manke, CAE, Jim
Laboratory Animal Management Association *(592)*

Manley, Jillian
American Academy of Pain Management *(39)*

Manley, Jody
American Council on Science and Health *(110)*

Manley, Justin
Marine Technology Society *(605)*

Mann, Anne
National Institute for Animal Agriculture *(764)*

Mann, April
National Orientation Directors Association *(778)*

Mann, Caitlin
American Correctional Association *(108)*

Mann, Felisa
Conference on English Leadership *(376)*

Mann, Kevin
American Water Works Association *(220)*

Mann, Kim
National Association of Agriculture Employees *(646)*

Mann, Esq., Kim D.
Glass Association of North America *(461)*

Mann, Niki
Metal Treating Institute *(614)*

Mann, Wendy
National Telecommunications Cooperative Association *(799)*

Manna, Christine
Association of National Advertisers *(295)*

Manna, Mary
National Interstate Council of State Boards of Cosmetology *(766)*

Manning, Marybeth
SPIE - The International Society for Optical Engineering *(958)*

Manning, Tom
Society for Laboratory Automation and Screening *(914)*

Mannozzi, Candida
Association of American Geographers *(265)*

Mano, Barry
National Association of Sports Officials *(697)*

Manolescu, Ioana
Special Interest Group on Management of Data *(956)*

Manross, Dede
International Society of Explosives Engineers *(572)*

Mansell, Dana
American Society of Bariatric Physicians *(193)*

Manser, Virginia A.
Cooling Technology Institute *(384)*

Mansfield, Karen
American Society of Neuroradiology *(204)*

Mansfield, Richard H.
Worldwide ERC *(1028)*

Mansfield, Rodger
National Corn Growers Association *(730)*

Manship, Greg
Council of Multiple Listing Services *(395)*

Manson, Margaret
National Federation of Advanced Information Services *(748)*

Manspeaker, Barbara
American Association of Zoo Keepers *(77)*

Mansur, Bernadette
National Hockey League *(759)*

Mantel, Eileen R.
Heating, Airconditioning and Refrigeration Distributors International *(473)*

Mantz, John
National Labor Relations Board Professional Association *(768)*

Manuck, Stephen
Academy of Behavioral Medicine Research *(4)*

Manuel, Aubrey
National Foster Parent Association *(753)*

Many Horses, Danielle Her
National Indian Gaming Association *(762)*

Manzi, Merle
International Association of Law Enforcement Intelligence Analysts *(523)*

Mara, Emil
Association of Public Television Stations *(304)*

Maraney, John V. "Skip"
National Star Route Mail Contractors Association *(796)*

Maraney, Tracy
National Association of Schools of Art and Design *(693)*
National Association of Schools of Dance *(693)*
National Association of Schools of Music *(694)*
National Association of Schools of Theatre *(694)*

Marans, David
The Advertising Research Foundation *(13)*

Marans, Jerrold
Sheet Metal and Air Conditioning Contractors' National Association *(898)*

Maranuk, BA, Marybeth
International Association for Near Death Studies, Inc. *(513)*

Marburger, Megan
American College for Advancement in Medicine *(93)*

Marcavage, Kelly
Spray Polyurethane Foam Alliance *(959)*

Marcec, Dan
Asian American Hotel Owners Association *(231)*

Marcellus, Simona
Technical Association of the Pulp and Paper Industry *(970)*

Marchant, Alan
Universities Space Research Association *(1002)*

Marchbanks, Rachael
American Indian Higher Education Consortium *(135)*

Marchena, Suzi
The Philanthropy Roundtable *(846)*

Marchese, Edward
Fluid Sealing Association *(448)*

Marchesi, Maria
American Society of Andrology *(192)*

Marchetti, Deanna
Association for Death Education and Counseling *(244)*

Marchiondo, Alan
American Association of Veterinary Parasitologists *(76)*

Marchyshyn, Jim
International Hot Rod Association *(550)*

Marchyshyn, Pam
International Hot Rod Association *(550)*

Marcial, Matthew
American Association of Clinical Endocrinologists *(56)*

Marcuccilli, Kim . M
Congress of Neurological Surgeons *(377)*

Marcum, Larry
National Environmental Health Association *(746)*

Marcus, Adam
Distributed Computing Industry Association *(414)*

Marcus, Alan I.
Agricultural History Society *(16)*

Marcus, Donald
International Organization of Masters, Mates and Pilots *(559)*

Marcus, Jesse
Propane Engine Fuel Committee/Propane Education and Research Council *(867)*

Marcus, Peter J.
World Jurist Association *(1027)*

Marcus, Ralph J.
National Association of Housing Cooperatives *(673)*

Marczak, Janine
Composite Can and Tube Institute *(372)*

Marden, CFP, MA, Jean Marie
American Society for Clinical Pathology *(182)*

Mardis, James
Rural Telecommunications Group *(889)*

Mare, Doris
National Psychological Association for Psychoanalysis *(783)*

Marecheau, Eppie
Council for Affordable and Rural Housing *(388)*

Marek, Sue
International Society for Medical Publication Professionals *(567)*

Marema, Lenore
The Surety and Fidelity Association of America *(966)*

Mareno, Noel
International Imaging Industry Association *(551)*

Maresca, Andrea
Association for Community Affiliated Plans *(242)*

Maresca, Andrea
National Association of Medicaid Directors *(680)*

Margaritis, John
Independent Armored Car Operators Association *(488)*

Margolin, MBA, Robert
Alliance for Regenerative Medicine *(23)*

Margolis, Garry
Audio Engineering Society *(320)*

Margula, CPA, MBA, George
Association for Professionals in Infection Control and Epidemiology *(254)*

Margulies, Beth
National Electrical Contractors Association *(744)*

Marhevko, Thomas
National Marine Manufacturers Association *(771)*

Mariano, Joseph N.
Direct Selling Association *(413)*

Maric, Tara
Council of Real Estate Brokerage Managers *(396)*

Marie Smith, MBA, Anne
Alliance for Continuing Medical Education *(22)*

Marin, Octavio
National Association of Latino Independent Producers *(677)*

Marin-Pilgrim, Kris
Jewish Education Service of North America *(588)*

Marinac, PharmD, BCPS, Jaque
American College of Clinical Pharmacy *(94)*

Marincola, Elizabeth
Society for the Science & the Public *(924)*

Marineau, CMP, Rachel
National Association of Independent Life Brokerage Agencies *(674)*

Marinho, John
CTIA - The Wireless Association *(405)*

Marino, Denisha
Society for Range Management *(920)*

Marino, Paul J.
Airborne Law Enforcement Association *(19)*

Marino, Robert
National Marine Manufacturers Association *(771)*

Marinucci, MBA, P E, PhD, Antonio
ADSC: The International Association of Foundation Drilling *(12)*

Marinucci, BSN, CRNI, RN, Kathy
Infusion Nurses Society *(496)*

Marion, Joseph
AscdiNatd *(231)*
Association of Service and Computer Dealers International *(308)*

Marion, Ruth
AscdiNatd *(231)*
Association of Service and Computer Dealers International *(308)*

Marion, Shelia
AFL-CIO Working for America Institute *(15)*

Mariutto, Ron
Tooling, Manufacturing and Technologies Association *(976)*

Mark, Carol
Seismological Society of America *(895)*

Markano, Andrew
Delaware Standardbred Owners Association *(409)*

Markee, Neil
National Association of Educational Procurement, Inc. *(664)*

Markel, Julia
Association for Wedding Professionals International *(261)*

Markel, Liz
Association of Specialized and Cooperative Library Agencies *(309)*

Markel, Richard
Association for Wedding Professionals International *(261)*

Markelis, Daiva
Association for the Advancement of Baltic Studies *(258)*

Markens, Ben
Paperboard Packaging Council *(838)*

Marker, Lori
National Athletic Trainers Association *(710)*

Markey, John
American Board of Anesthesiology *(81)*

Markey, Kathleen
Irrigation Association *(585)*

Markey, Patrick

United States Conference of Catholic Bishops *(992)*

Markham, Diane
Reserve Officers Association of the U.S. *(882)*

Markle, R. L.
Radio Technical Commission for Maritime Services *(873)*

Marklin, Ed
American Society for Biochemistry and Molecular Biology *(181)*

Markovchick, Kathryn
International Association for the Study of Cooperation in Education *(514)*

Markovic, Lisa
International Association of Oral and Maxillofacial Surgeons *(525)*

Markovsky, Sharon
Society of Insurance Research *(940)*

Markowitz, Barrie
United States Tennis Association *(1000)*

Markowitz, Morry B.
Fuel Cell and Hydrogen Energy Association *(454)*

Markowski, CAE, Paul A.
American College of Chest Physicians *(94)*

Marks, Gary H.
Association for the Advancement of Computing in Education *(258)*

Marks, PhD, JD, MPH, Howard
National Asphalt Pavement Association *(635)*

Marks, Kelly
Conference of Minority Transportation Officials *(375)*
National Association of Medical Staff Services *(645)*

Marks, PhD, Lori
American Gastroenterological Association *(125)*

Marks, Steven M.
Recording Industry Association of America (RIAA) *(876)*

Marksberry, Kellie
American Institute of Stress *(140)*

Markt, D.D.S., Jeffery C.
American Academy of Maxillofacial Prosthetics *(35)*

Markwart, Luther A
American Sugarbeet Growers Association *(214)*

Markwood, CAE, Priscilla S.
American Society for Investigative Pathology *(186)*
Association of Pathology Chairs *(298)*

Markwood, Sandy
National Association of Area Agencies on Aging *(647)*

Marlo, Leslie R.
Casualty Actuarial Society *(344)*

Marlor, Lynne M.
American Purchasing Society *(172)*

Marlowe, CAE, CSI, PE, Walter T.
Construction Specifications Institute *(380)*

Marmer, Fran
International Council of Shopping Centers *(538)*

Marmion, Rosemarie
American Academy of Ambulatory Care Nursing *(30)*

Marmolejo, Francisco J.
Consortium for North American Higher Education Collaboration *(378)*

Marneris, Mandy
American Gynecological and Obstetrical Society *(128)*

Marolt, Bill
United States Ski and Snowboard Association *(999)*

Maron, CAE, Rebecca
Society for Vascular Surgery *(926)*

Maroney, Dennis
American Society of Perfumers *(206)*

Maroney, Michael
School Science and Mathematics Association *(892)*

Marotta, Jamie R.
National Music Publishers Association *(774)*

Marovec, Lisa
Council of Hotel and Restaurant Trainers *(394)*

Marple, Cynthia
American Gas Association *(124)*

Marquardt, Gail
National Funeral Directors Association *(754)*

Marquart, Stephanie
Medical Fitness Association *(611)*

Marques, Michel
Society for Clinical Data Management *(906)*

Marquis, Damon K.
Society of Thoracic Surgeons *(948)*

Marriott, Candler
Council of Industrial Boiler Owners (CIBO) *(394)*

Marriott, Farrah
National Correctional Industries Association *(730)*

Marriott, Liz
Military Operations Research Society *(616)*

Marrone, Mike
TAUC - The Association of Union Constructors *(968)*

Marrs, Becky
National Association of Development Companies *(662)*

Marrs, Summer
National Truck Equipment Association *(802)*

Mars, Gil
Association of African American Museums *(263)*

Marschner, Susan
Human Factors and Ergonomics Society *(480)*
Human Factors Society *(481)*

Marselli, Mark A.
The Wire Association International, Inc. *(1019)*

Marsh, Bridget
Loan Syndication & Trading Association *(599)*

Marsh, Cheryl
Association of Christian Therapists *(273)*

Marsh, Debi
American College of Physician Executives *(101)*

Marsh, Jeff
Association of American Railroads *(266)*

Marsh, Joanne
NAFA Fleet Management Association *(624)*

Marsh, Kathleen
Music Publishers Association of the United States *(622)*

Marsh, Molly
Council on Licensure, Enforcement and Regulation *(400)*

Marsh, Semaj
National AMBUCS *(633)*

Marshall, Brennan
Organization for International Investment *(831)*

Marshall, Cheryl
Academy of Motion Picture Arts and Sciences *(7)*
Costume Designers Guild *(387)*

Marshall, David K.
Society for Industrial & Applied Mathematics *(912)*

Marshall, Debbie
Smart Card Alliance *(901)*

Marshall, Donna

CFA Institute *(350)*

Marshall, Dr. Edwin C.
National Optometric Association *(776)*

Marshall, Jessi
Professional Beauty Association | National Cosmetology Association *(861)*

Marshall, Kate
American Alliance for Theatre and Education *(44)*

Marshall, Lynne
American College of Veterinary Surgeons *(104)*

Marshall, Michelle
Women in Agribusiness *(1020)*

Marshall, Ricky
APCO (Association of Public-Safety Communications Officials) International *(304)*

Marshall, Robert
Society for Economic Anthropology *(908)*

Marshall, Stephanie
American Council on Education *(110)*

Marshall, Susan
Feldenkrais Guild of North America *(442)*

Marshall, Thomas A.
American Association of Neurological Surgeons *(66)*

Marshall, Wade
National Catholic Educational Association *(718)*
National Catholic Educational Exhibitors *(718)*

Marsico, CCTM, Dale J.
Community Transportation Association of America *(371)*

Marsoni, Jennifer
North American Securities Administrators Association (NASAA) *(820)*

Marston , Steve
National Association of Certified Valuation Analysts *(652)*

Marston, Linda
International Dyslexia Association *(541)*

Marsyada, Buddy
National Trappers Association *(801)*

Mart, Warren L.
International Association of Machinists and Aerospace Workers *(524)*

Marteeny, Annette
DBA International *(407)*

Martell, Peter
Ice Skating Institute *(482)*

Martello, Marsha
National Tactical Officers Association of America *(799)*

Martens, Margaret
Water Systems Council *(1013)*

Marti, Chris
Metals Service Center Institute *(614)*

Martin, Abigail
Organization for International Investment *(831)*

Martin, Adam
Society for Research in Child Development *(920)*
Society for Research on Adolescence *(920)*

Martin, Andrea L.
Caribbean Cable Communications *(343)*

Martin, Angela
IEEE Engineering in Medicine and Biology Society *(484)*

Martin, Ann L.
American Association of Pastoral Counselors *(68)*

Martin, Anna
National Information Standards Organization *(763)*

Martin, Ashley
National Indian Education Association *(762)*

Martin, Bev
National Academic Advising Association *(626)*

Martin, Beverly
National Community Pharmacists Association *(725)*

Martin, Bill
Gravure Association of America *(465)*

Martin, Carrie
American Lung Association *(146)*

Martin, Cecilia
Society of Exploration Geophysicists *(935)*

Martin, Charlotte St.
The Broadway League *(336)*

Martin, Chris
National Council of Higher Education Loan Programs *(735)*

Martin, Cooper
The American Institute of Architects *(137)*

Martin, Craig
North American Association for the Study of Religion *(812)*

Martin, Danny C.
American Society of Naval Engineers *(204)*

Martin, Dave
Electronic Retailing Association *(423)*

Martin, David
Council on Foundations *(399)*

Martin, CAE, David Julian
Society for Critical Care Medicine *(934)*

Martin, DeAnna
Scaffold Industry Association *(891)*

Martin, Debbie
Promotion Marketing Association *(866)*

Martin, Debra
National Conference of Bar Examiners *(726)*

Martin, Dee
FBI Agents Association *(438)*

Martin, Edward J.
Association of Racing Commissioners International *(304)*

Martin, Fonda
Association for Applied and Clinical Sociology *(238)*

Martin, Gary C.
North American Export Grain Association, Inc. *(816)*

Martin, George R.
United Potato Growers of America *(988)*

Martin, Heather
Christian Leadership Alliance *(355)*

Martin, Janell
American College of Rheumatology *(102)*

Martin, John
American Lands Access Association *(144)*

Martin, Joleen
Cabletelevision Advertising Bureau *(340)*

Martin, Ken
American Philatelic Society *(163)*

Martin, APA, CPC, QPA, Kimberly B.
National Institute of Pension Administrators *(765)*

Martin, Krista
American Medical Informatics Association *(149)*

Martin, Laura
American Cotton Shippers Association *(108)*

Martin, Laura

Martin, Leland D. (cont.)
Association of University Centers on Disabilities (AUCD) *(315)*

Martin, Leland D.
Investment Casting Institute *(584)*

Martin, Lisa
Association of College and University Housing Officers-International *(274)*

Martin, Lonnie
North American Securities Administrators Association (NASAA) *(820)*

Martin, FAAP, FCCM, MBA, MD, Lynn D.
Society for Pediatric Anesthesia *(917)*

Martin, Lynn M.
National Association for Pupil Transportation *(642)*

Martin, Marc
League of American Orchestras *(595)*

Martin, MSN, RNC, Marylouise
National Perinatal Association *(780)*

Martin, Matt
American Academy of Anesthesiologist Assistants *(30)*

Martin, Melinda
American Society of Interventional Pain Physicians *(201)*

Martin, Michael
National Wood Flooring Association *(805)*

Martin, Michael J.
National Association for Pupil Transportation *(642)*

Martin, Michele
United Auto Workers (UAW) *(986)*

Martin, Michelle
American Society of Cataract and Refractive Surgery *(194)*

Martin, Mike
Alliance of Professional Tattooists *(25)*

Martin, Pat
Association of Ship Brokers and Agents (U.S.A.) *(308)*

Martin, Patricia A.
American Educational Research Association *(116)*

Martin, Patrick
Society for Industrial Archeology *(913)*

Martin, Penny
American Conference of Governmental Industrial Hygienists *(107)*

Martin, Prescott
American Sugar Alliance *(214)*

Martin, Robin
Communications Media Management Association *(369)*

Martin, Sandra
The Spain-United States Chamber of Commerce *(953)*

Martin, Sherry
American Association of Pharmaceutical Scientists *(68)*

Martin, Steve
Society of Flight Test Engineers *(936)*

Martin, Susan
American Society of Women Accountants (ACC) *(211)*

Martin, Teri
Association of American Geographers *(265)*

Martin, Terrill D.
North American Thermal Analysis Society *(823)*

Martin, Tracey A.
American Psychological Association - Division of Psychotherapy *(169)*

Martin, Tracy
The Society for Investigative Dermatology *(913)*

Martinek, CMP, Shelley
Association of Progressive Rental Organizations *(303)*

Martinelli, Ruzzo
Hollywood Radio & Television Society *(477)*

Martinez, Alicia
Hispanic Association of Colleges and Universities *(475)*

Martinez, Amber
Association of Latino Professionals in Finance and Accounting *(291)*

Martinez, CMP, Anne R.
American Podiatric Medical Association *(166)*

Martinez, Dan
Professional Rodeo Cowboys Association *(864)*

Martinez, Danny
Packaging Machinery Manufacturers Institute *(836)*

Martinez, Dean
APICS The Association for Operations Management *(224)*

Martinez, Dorothy
The Philanthropy Roundtable *(846)*

Martinez, BA, CFCP, Elizabeth
American Academy of Fertility Care Professionals *(34)*

Martinez, Emmy
National Alliance for Youth Sports *(632)*

Martinez, Estela
SWANA - Solid Waste Association of North America *(967)*

Martinez, James
National Parent Teachers Association *(779)*

Martinez, Kate
Special Care Dentistry *(954)*
Special Care Dentistry Association *(954)*

Martinez, Nubia
International Advertising Association *(509)*

Martinez, Pat
National Hispanic Corporate Council *(759)*

Martinez, Rheanna
Council for Opportunity in Education *(390)*

Martinez, Samanthi
Association of Professional Model Makers *(302)*

Martinez, Walter
Joint National Committee for Languages *(589)*
Joint National Committee for Languages-National Council for Languages and International Studies *(589)*
National Council for Languages and International Studies *(732)*

Martinez-Alvarez, Paco
Society of Federal Labor and Employee Relations Professionals *(936)*

Martinez-Ebers, Valerie
Women's Caucus for Political Science *(1023)*

Martini, Lisa
Association of American Shippers *(266)*

Martino, Beth
American Association of Colleges of Osteopathic Medicine *(57)*

Martino, Donna
Outdoor Industry Association *(835)*

Martino, Melinda
American Bashkir Curly Registry *(80)*

Martino, Salvatore
American Society of Radiologic Technologists *(208)*

Martins, Susan
Paperboard Packaging Council *(838)*

Martins, Veronica
Tobacco Associates, Inc. *(975)*

Martinson, Greg
Independent Community Bankers of America *(488)*

Martis, CAE, Sarah
Society of American Travel Writers *(930)*

Martonik, Joanne
National Association for Olmsted Parks *(641)*

Marturet, Juan Luis
International Federation of the Phonographic Industry *(544)*

Martusewicz, Rebecca
American Educational Studies Association *(116)*

Martz, Peggy
Special Event Sites Marketing Alliance *(954)*

Marullo, Tom
Meals on Wheels Association of America *(609)*

Maruschak, Janine
Association of Official Seed Analysts, Inc. *(296)*

Marvel, PhD, CAE, Kevin B
American Astronomical Society *(77)*

Marvin, Christie
Society for Personality and Social Psychology *(918)*

Mary Caligiure, MA, RDT, LCAT, Mary
National Association for Drama Therapy *(638)*

Marzano, James H.
American Association of Physician Specialists *(69)*

Marzano, Suzy
College of Healthcare Information Management Executives *(364)*

Marzette, Mario
Workgroup for Electronic Data Interchange *(1025)*

Mascarenhas, Sheryl
Phi Rho Sigma Medical Society *(846)*

Masche, Sarah
National Golf Course Owners Association *(755)*

Mascone, Cynthia
American Institute of Chemical Engineers *(138)*

Masdeu, Joseph
American Society of Neuroimaging *(204)*

Masek, Joyce
National Catholic College Admission Association *(718)*

Masenior, Michael
International Metal Decorators Association *(556)*

Mashima, Ted
Association of American Veterinary Medical Colleges *(267)*

Masia, Seth
American Solar Energy Society *(211)*

Maskiell, Aisyah
Reusable Industrial Packaging Association *(885)*

Maslyn, Mark A.
American Farm Bureau Federation *(118)*

Mason, Amy
American Society for Colposcopy and Cervical Pathology *(183)*

Mason, Anna
Women's Foodservice Forum *(1023)*

Mason, Anna Marie
Society for Imaging Informatics in Medicine *(912)*

Mason, CAE, Caron
American Translators Association *(217)*

Mason, Christine
National Association of Elementary School Principals *(664)*

Mason, David
Association for Asian Performance *(239)*

Mason, Deborah A
National Center for State Courts *(720)*

Mason, Debra L.
Religion Newswriters Association *(880)*

Mason, Deirdre
Association of State Drinking Water Administrators *(311)*

Mason, Diane
Society of Animal Artists *(930)*

Mason, Gwynn
American Association of Family and Consumer Sciences *(61)*

Mason, Jocelyn
APPAM - The Association for Public Policy Analysis and Management *(225)*

Mason, Juliet
National Association of College and University Business Officers *(654)*

Mason, Lori
National Association of College and University Food Services *(655)*

Mason, Mike
Farm Credit Council *(437)*

Mason, CPA, Robert
American Association of Independent Claims Professionals *(63)*

Mason, Sandra L.
Mortgage Insurance Companies of America *(619)*

Mason, Sylviene
Forest Resources Association *(451)*

Massad, John
National Association for the Practice of Anthropology *(644)*

Massare, PhD, John S.
Contact Lens Association of Ophthalmologists *(382)*

Massello, Carolyn S.
International Stress Management Association - USA *(576)*

Massenburg, USN (Ret.), VADM Walter B.
Association of Naval Aviation *(295)*

Massengile, Andrea
Association of Catholic Publishers *(271)*

Masset, Jennifer
American Association of Independent Music *(63)*

Massey, Carrie
American Polarity Therapy Association *(166)*

Massey, Erica
Self-Insurance Institute of America, Inc. *(896)*

Massey, Frank
United Union of Roofers, Waterproofers and Allied Workers *(1001)*

Massey, CPA, Jan C.
American Association of Immunologists *(62)*

Massey, Joseph M.
International Brangus Breeders Association *(531)*

Massie, James D.
Medical Imaging Contrast Agent Associations *(611)*

Massoff, Nathan
Sigma Epsilon Delta Dental Fraternity *(899)*

Masson, Tonia M.
Environmental Mutagen Society *(431)*
Teratology Society *(971)*

Mast, Austin R.
American Society of Plant Taxonomists *(207)*

Masters, Amanda
Council of State and Territorial Epidemiologists *(397)*

Masterson, Laurel
R-Calf *(872)*
Ranchers-Cattlemen Action Legal Fund, United Stockgrower of America *(874)*

Masterson, Maggie
United Motorcoach Association *(988)*

Mastrogiuseppe, Alexandra
Alliance for Telecommunications Industry Solutions *(23)*

Mastrolia, Barbara
Catholic Press Association *(346)*

Mat, Joha
American Naturopathic Association *(155)*

Mata, Laarni V.
Asian American Hotel Owners Association *(231)*

Mataac, Celso
National Association of Japan-America Societies *(677)*

Matacio, Lauren
Association of Seventh-Day Adventist Librarians *(308)*

Matanis, Jacque
Society of Vacuum Coaters *(950)*

Matarazzo, Linda
IEEE Photonics Society *(485)*

Matarazzo, Steven
IEEE Power and Energy Society *(485)*

Matarrese, Melissa
National Council of Structural Engineers Associations *(737)*

Mate, Hon
National Association of Crop Insurance Agents *(662)*

Matei, Alina
Academy of Management *(6)*

Material, Jury
American Society of Artists *(193)*

Math, Sabri
American Society of Appraisers *(192)*

Mathe, Jennifer
International Society of Certified Employee Benefit Specialists *(572)*

Matheis, Christine
Center for Research Libraries *(348)*

Mather, Dean
American Orthotic and Prosthetic Association *(159)*

Mathers, Kathleen O.
The Fertilizer Institute *(443)*

Mathers, BS, Tom
National Customs Brokers and Forwarders Association of America *(741)*

Matheson, Michelle
Pet Partners *(842)*

Mathew, Erin
American Academy of Estate Planning Attorneys *(33)*

Mathew, Jon
Raptor Breeders of America *(875)*

Mathews, Alexander S.
Animal Health Institute *(223)*

Mathews, Bill
National Association of Professional Band Instrument Repair Technicians *(686)*

Mathews, Bobbye
Worldwide ERC *(1028)*

Mathews, Dan
National Automatic Merchandising Association *(711)*

Mathews, David
National Collegiate Wrestling Association *(724)*

Mathews, Leslie
American Hereford Association *(131)*

Mathews, Michelle
Music Industry Conference *(622)*

Mathews, Nancy Mowll
Catalogue Raisonne Scholars Association *(344)*

Mathewson, Dave
Academy of Model Aeronautics *(7)*

Mathieson, Elaine
American Society of Sanitary Engineering *(209)*

Mathis, Donald W.
Community Action Partnership *(369)*

Mathis, Jerrica
Society for Public Health Education *(919)*

Mathis, Wesley
Federation of Employers and Workers of America *(441)*

Mathison, Louvenia
National Black Caucus of Local Elected Officials *(714)*

Mathur, Praneet
PCIA - The Wireless Infrastructure Association *(840)*

Matias, Bienvenida
National Association of Latino Independent Producers *(677)*

Matikonis, Kathleen
Infectious Diseases Society of America *(494)*

Matlack, Larry
American Agriculture Movement, Inc. *(44)*

Matlick, CAE, Sam
National Association of Enrolled Agents *(666)*

Matlon, PhD, Ronald J.
American Society of Trial Consultants *(210)*

Matney, Sheryl
National Association of Councils on Developmental Disabilities *(658)*

Matraku, Brunilda
American Philosophical Society *(164)*

Matris, Gwyn
Building Material Dealers Association *(337)*

Matson, Brandon
Association of Medical Device Reprocessors *(293)*

Matson, Jodi
Text and Academic Authors Association *(972)*

Matsuda, Catherine
Congressional Internet Caucus Advisory Committee *(377)*

Matsumura, MD, Jon S.
Independent Fuel Terminal Operators Association *(490)*

Matsuoka, Tina
National Asian Pacific American Bar Association *(635)*

Matt, Meg
Association of Energy Services Professionals, International *(281)*

Matter, John
National Ballroom and Entertainment Association *(712)*

Matternas, John J.
American Academy of State Certified Appraisers *(42)*

Matterson, Charlie
Accrediting Council for Continuing Education & Training *(10)*

Matteson, Jennifer
National Association of Veterans Program Administrators *(708)*

Matthes, CAE, MS, Nancy
Association for the Accreditation of Human Research Protection Programs *(257)*

Matthews, Amy
Association of Partners for Public Lands *(298)*

Matthews, Anita
Association of Regulatory Boards of Optometry *(305)*

Matthews, Cheryl
American Coatings Association *(92)*

Matthews, D.J.
Association of Vision Science Librarians *(317)*

Matthews, Dale
Church Music Publishers Association *(356)*

Matthews, Henry
Capital Markets Credit Analysts Society *(342)*

Matthews, Hilary
International Society of Arthroscopy, Knee Surgery and
Orthopaedic Sports Medicine *(571)*

Matthews, Katy
American Academy of Pediatrics *(39)*

Matthews, Kelly
Reserve Officers Association of the U.S. *(882)*

Matthews, Kevin
Insurance Loss Control Association *(505)*

Matthews, Maria D.
Professional Photographers of America *(863)*

Matthews, Mark
American Society for Engineering Education *(183)*

Matthews, CPA, Richard
United States and Canadian Academy of Pathology
(989)

Matthews, Russ
International Furniture Transportation and Logistics
Council *(548)*
Office Furniture Distribution Association *(827)*

Matthews, Sallie
Society of American Gastrointestinal and Endoscopic
Surgeons *(929)*

Matthews, Shari
Society for Experimental Mechanics, Inc. *(909)*

Matthews, Sparky
Society of United States Air Force Flight Surgeons *(949)*

Matthews, Steven
National Council of Examiners for Engineering and
Surveying *(734)*

Matthews, Tamara
National Association of Fire Equipment Distributors
(668)

Matthiesen, Karen
American College of Dentists *(95)*

Mattingly, Ed
International Decorative Artisans League *(540)*

Mattingly, Joseph
Air Conditioning, Heating and Refrigeration Institute
(AHRI) *(18)*

Mattingly, Rick
Percussive Arts Society *(841)*

Mattison, Jay
National Dairy Herd Information Association *(741)*

Mattison, PhD, Julie
American Aging Association *(43)*

Mattocks, Ron
Council for Advancement and Support of Education
(388)

Mattos, Jaime
TESOL International Association *(971)*

Mattox, Tim
International Firestop Council *(545)*

Mattson-Erimm, CAE, Kristina

Credit Union Executives Society *(403)*

Matusek, Melissa
American College of Foot and Ankle Surgeons *(95)*

Matyas, Jaime Berman
National Wildlife Federation *(805)*

Matyas, PhD, Marsha Lakes
American Physiological Society *(165)*

Matz, Marshall L.
School Nutrition Association *(892)*

Mauder, Ashley
Public Relations Student Society of America *(870)*

Mauer, Tricia
Brick Industry Association *(335)*

Maul, Mary
National Cancer Registrars Association *(717)*

Maull, MA, PhD, Fleet
National Prison Hospice Association *(782)*

Maulsby, Erin
American Osteopathic College of Radiology *(161)*

Maultsby, Doris K.
American Seniors Housing Association *(178)*

Maupin, Katie
National Swine Registry *(798)*

Mauras, Kelly J.
USFN-America's Mortgage Banking Attorneys *(1006)*

Maurelus, Melynda
American College of Medical Quality *(97)*
Society for Radiation Oncology Administration *(919)*

Maurer, Robert S.
American Osteopathic College of Rheumatology, Inc.
(161)

Mauriello, David A
International Society for Ecological Modelling-North
American Chapter *(566)*

Maurizi, Sarah
World Affairs Councils of America *(1025)*

Mauro, Flo
American Nature Study Society *(155)*

Maury, Marilynn
American Health Care Association *(129)*

Maves, Tom
Association of State Drinking Water Administrators
(311)

Mavreshko, Lana
Promotion Marketing Association *(866)*

Mavris, Jen
Organic Trade Association *(830)*

Mawson, Janice
National Venture Capital Association *(803)*

Mawyer, Gary
The Wound, Ostomy and Continence Nurses Society
(1028)

Mawyer, Tracy
Association for Advanced Life Underwriting *(238)*

Maxey, Rebecca
Society of Nuclear Medicine *(943)*

Maxwell, Adam
iNARTE, Inc. *(487)*

Maxwell, MD, Edward J.
American Association of Community Psychiatrists *(58)*

Maxwell, Kathy
Piano Technicians Guild *(848)*

Maxwell, Susan
Association of Business Owners of America *(270)*

May, Christian
Federal Network for Sustainability *(439)*

May, David
Appraisal Institute *(226)*

May, Debra Cox
North American Agricultural Marketing Officials *(812)*

May, J. Thomas
Society for Applied Anthropology *(904)*

May, PhD, MPH, Jeanette C.
Care Continuum Alliance *(342)*

May, John P.
American Military Society *(152)*

May, Ken
American Agents Alliance *(43)*

May, Mary
Associated Locksmiths of America *(236)*

May, Mike
Soccer Industry Council of America *(902)*
Sports and Fitness Industry Association *(959)*

May, Paul
National Certification Commission for Acupuncture
and Oriental Medicine *(720)*

May, Paula
National Hardwood Lumber Association *(757)*

May, Richard
Association of Progressive Rental Organizations *(303)*

May, Robert
North American Punch Manufacturers Association
(820)

May, Sara Cameron
American Academy of Implant Dentistry *(35)*

May, CAE, CCA, CPA, Simeon
National Association of Church Business
Administration *(653)*

May, Stacey
American Association of Pharmaceutical Scientists *(68)*

May, Stephen B.
United States Internet Industry Association *(995)*

May, III, Virgil Robert
National Association of Disability Evaluating
Professionals *(663)*

May, William E.
American Cotton Shippers Association *(108)*

Maya, Beatriz
Farm Labor Organizing Committee *(437)*

Mayberry, Rob
Gelatin Manufacturers Institute of America *(457)*

Maye, CAE, Noel
Financial Planning Standards Board *(445)*

Mayer, Ana
American Health Lawyers Association *(130)*

Mayer, Brett
Nonprofit Technology Network *(811)*

Mayer, David
Art and Antique Dealers League of America *(229)*

Mayes, Brenda J.
American Board of Periodontology *(83)*

Mayes, Sara
Fashion Accessories Shippers Association/Gemini
Shippers Association *(438)*

Mayeux, Sally
Plant Growth Regulation Society of America *(849)*

Mayfield, CMP, Karin
National Home Furnishings Association *(759)*

Mayfield, Lindsey J.E.

American College of Trial Lawyers *(103)*

Mayhew, Ed
Red Tag News Publications Association *(878)*

Maylett, Nicole
American Association for the Advancement of Science *(51)*

Maynard, Ashley
Jean Piaget Society *(586)*

Maynard, CEAP, PhD, John
Employee Assistance Professionals Association *(426)*

Maynard, Patrice
Council for American Private Education *(389)*

Maynard, Tami
Council on Occupational Education *(400)*

Mayne, Bill
Country Radio Broadcasters, Inc. *(401)*

Mayo, Tiffany
Association of Diesel Specialists *(279)*
Aviation Insurance Association *(324)*

Mayor, Christine
National Association for Drama Therapy *(638)*

Mayor, Vincent
Soccer Industry Council of America *(902)*

Mayor, VJ
Sports and Fitness Industry Association *(959)*

Mayorga, CHES, MPH, Lina
Cancer Patient Education Network *(341)*

Mays, John W.
National Animal Control Association *(634)*

Mays, Linda
The Association for Library Service to Children *(251)*

Mays, Meredith
International Association of Chiefs of Police *(517)*

Maytham, Peter
American Society of Marine Artists *(202)*

Maza, Harriet
Society for Humanistic Judaism *(912)*

Maza, Lauren
Obesity Society *(825)*

Mazanec, Lauren
Design-Build Institute of America *(411)*

Mazard, Camelia
Organization of Women in International Trade *(832)*

Mazarei, Rakhshan
International Right of Way Association *(563)*

Maze, Joshua
NACHA - The Electronic Payments Association *(623)*

Mazelin, Janelle
Association of Christian Librarians *(272)*

Mazelin, John
Contract Packaging Association *(382)*

Mazon, Alison
Society of Accredited Marine Surveyors *(927)*

Mazur, Jr., Michael J.
International Paralegal Management Association *(559)*

Mazyck, MS, RN, Donna J.
National Association of School Nurses *(693)*

Mazza, Lorraine
International Council of Shopping Centers *(538)*

Mc Burney, Ruth E.
Conference of Radiation Control Program Directors *(375)*

McAbee, Linda
The Fertilizer Institute *(443)*

McAdams, Michael
Advanced Biofuels Association *(12)*

McAdow, Sam
National Wooden Pallet and Container Association *(805)*

McAfee, Kelli
American Correctional Association *(108)*

McAlister, David
University Aviation Association *(1002)*

McAlister, Roy E.
American Hydrogen Association *(134)*

McAlister, Trish
National Council of Examiners for Engineering and Surveying *(734)*

McAllister, Brett
Airports Council International - North America *(21)*

McAllister, Margaret
Publishers' Publicity Association *(870)*

McAllister, Mike
The PGA Tour, Inc. *(844)*

McAllister, Patricia
Council of Graduate Schools *(394)*

McAnally, Loren
Combat Helicopter Pilots Association *(366)*

McAndrew, John
Association of Corporate Counsel *(277)*

McArdle, Bernice
Inflatable Boat Manufacturers Association *(495)*

McArdle, Melissa
Association of Information Technology Professionals *(289)*

McArthur, Cory
Canola Council of Canada *(341)*

McAuliffe, Heidi
American Coatings Association *(92)*

McAuliffe, Sherry
American Osteopathic Association *(160)*

McBarnet, Alec
Chevron and Texaco Petroleum Marketers Association *(352)*

McBride, Jerry L.
International Association of Music Libraries, United States Branch *(525)*
Music Library Association *(622)*

McBride, John J.
Livestock Marketing Association *(599)*

McBride, Lisa
The Risk Management Association *(886)*

McBride, Regina
United States Court Reporters Association *(993)*

McBride, Sean
Grocery Manufacturers Association (GMA) *(466)*

McBride, Verlanda
Urban and Regional Information Systems Association *(1003)*

McCabe, Bridget
National Human Services Assembly *(761)*

McCabe, Don
Avko Educational Research Foundation *(325)*

McCabe, John J.
Association of Foreign Trade Representatives *(284)*

McCabe, Lisa Volpe
Satellite Broadcasting and Communications Association *(891)*

McCabe, CMP, T. J.
American Public Health Association *(171)*

McCabe-Leche, Pat
National Guild of Piano Teachers *(757)*

McCafferty, Therese
Independent Petroleum Association of America *(491)*

McCain, CAE, Byron W.
American Assembly for Men in Nursing *(47)*

McCall, Deborah
American Society for Cell Biology *(182)*

McCall, Linda
Association of American University Presses *(267)*

McCalley, Barbara S.
Ophthalmic Photographers' Society *(829)*

McCallister, Cheri
Council of Petroleum Accountants Societies *(396)*

McCallum, Mark
National Association of Surety Bond Producers *(704)*

McCamant, Robert
American Printing History Association *(167)*

McCandless, Jerri
American Network of Community Options and Resources (ANCOR) *(155)*

McCann, Cory
International Society for Prenatal Diagnosis *(568)*

McCann, F. L.
American Train Dispatchers Association *(217)*

McCann, Jett
Association of Academic Health Sciences Library *(263)*

McCann, RN, PhD, Kathleen
American Academy of Sleep Medicine *(42)*
National Association of Psychiatric Health Systems *(688)*

McCann, Nancey Kaplan
American Society of Cataract and Refractive Surgery *(194)*

McCannon, Melinda "Mindy"
Organizational Systems Research Association *(833)*

McCarns, Paula
American Camp Association *(88)*

McCarren, Helen
Society of Cosmetic Chemists *(934)*

McCarroll, Ollie
American Osteopathic Association *(160)*

McCarron, Douglas J.
United Brotherhood of Carpenters and Joiners of America *(986)*

McCartan, Dr. Anne-Marie
Council of Colleges of Arts and Sciences *(393)*

McCarter, Katherine S.
Ecological Society of America *(418)*

McCarthy, Becky
National Society of Professional Engineers *(794)*

McCarthy, Ben
International Emissions Trading Association *(542)*

McCarthy, Berry
National Pace Association *(778)*

McCarthy, Brian
National Football League *(752)*

McCarthy, Brian
Pharmaceutical Care Management Association *(844)*

McCarthy, Eli S.
Conference of Major Superiors of Men, United States of America *(375)*

McCarthy, Jack
International Association of Broadcast Monitors *(517)*

McCarthy, James A.

Snack Food Association *(901)*

McCarthy, Kelley
Professional Beauty Association | National Cosmetology Association *(861)*

McCarthy, Kristin
The American Finance Association *(121)*

McCarthy, Mike
Fulfillment Management Association *(454)*

McCarthy, MBA, MSc, Sarah
American Society for Apheresis *(180)*

McCarthy, Sean
Traffic Audit Bureau for Media Measurement, Inc. *(977)*

McCarthy, Susan
American Society of Gas Engineers *(198)*

McCarthy, Tracy
Pi Sigma Epsilon *(847)*

McCarty, James K.
Manufacturing Jewelers and Suppliers of America *(604)*

McCarty, Joel
Timber Framers Guild *(974)*

McCarty, Kathy
International Council on Hotel, Restaurant and Institutional Education *(539)*

McCarty, Willard
Association for Computers and the Humanities *(242)*

McCaughey, Steve
Seaplane Pilots Association *(894)*

McCauley, Gail R.
Institute of Management Consultants USA *(501)*

McCauley, Kelly
Council of Fashion Designers of America *(393)*

McCauley, CPM, Paul
Portfolio Management Institute *(853)*

McCauley, Renee
Special Interest Group for Computer Science Education *(954)*

McCaulley, Rebecca
National Association of Computerized Tax Processors *(657)*

McCaulsin, Doc, John R. "Doc"
Air Force Sergeants Association *(19)*

McCausland, Dan
American Meat Institute *(148)*

McClain, Debbie
American Society for Colposcopy and Cervical Pathology *(183)*

McClain, Joe
Beer Institute *(327)*

McClain, Pamela K.
American Academy of Periodontology *(39)*

McClain, Sheresa
International Warehouse Logistics Association *(580)*

McClanahan, Merida
Appaloosa Horse Club *(225)*

McClary, Joe
Real Estate Educators Association *(875)*

McCleary, ChFC, CLU, MSFS, Clark B.
National Association of Estate Planners and Councils *(666)*

McCleary, Rose Ella
National Association of Church Business Administration *(653)*

McClelland, Meghan
Air Force Association *(18)*

McClendon, CAE, Brent J.

The International Wood Products Association *(581)*

Mcclendon, Kelley
Retail Bakers of America *(884)*

McClintock, Mary
Law and Society Association *(594)*

McClintock, Paul
United States Clay Producers Traffic Association *(991)*

McCloskey, Abby
The Financial Services Roundtable *(445)*

McCloskey, Bill
National Agricultural Alumni and Development Association *(630)*

McCloskey, Guy
Society for Buddhist-Christian Studies *(905)*

McCloskey, Kimberly
Containerization and Intermodal Institute *(382)*

McCloskey, Lynn A.
International Association of Law Enforcement Intelligence Analysts *(523)*

McClughen, Judy
American Society of Animal Science *(192)*

McClung, CAE, CMA, MBA, Harriet
Association for Radiological and Imaging Nursing *(255)*
National Organization for Associate Degree Nursing *(776)*

McClure, David P.
United States Internet Industry Association *(995)*

McClure, Denise
American Camp Association *(88)*

McClure, Donald E.
American Mathematical Society *(148)*

McClure, Joan S.
National Comprehensive Cancer Network *(725)*

McClure, John S.
Academy of Homiletics *(5)*

McClure, DVM, JD, Dr. Kent D.
Animal Health Institute *(223)*

McClure, Linda
American Chemical Society - Rubber Division *(90)*

McClure, Orla
Plastic Surgery Administrative Association *(850)*

McClure, IOM, Robert (Bob)
Building Owners and Managers Association International *(337)*

McClure, Tom
Educational Association of University Centers *(420)*

McCluskey, III, MD, George M.
American Shoulder and Elbow Surgeons *(179)*

McCluskey, Meghan
APCO (Association of Public-Safety Communications Officials) International *(304)*

McColl, Mary
Actors' Equity Association *(11)*

McColloch, John
National Association of Insurance Women (International) *(676)*

McCollor, Heather
National Association of Scientific Materials Managers *(694)*

McCollough, Mark
Asphalt Emulsion Manufacturers Association *(233)*

McCollum, Leah
National Association of Equipment Leasing Brokers *(666)*

McComis, EdD, Michale S

The Accrediting Commission of Career Schools and Colleges *(10)*

McConkie, Aimee
National Association of Industrial Bankers *(675)*

McConnaughey, Steve
National Auto Auction Association *(711)*

McConnaughy, James
National Antique and Art Dealers Association of America *(634)*

McConnell, Ann
Global Market Development Center *(462)*

McConnell, Christine
Association for Library Collections and Technical Services *(251)*

McConnell, Jr., David T.
Global Market Development Center *(462)*

McConnell, Hayley
National Grocers Association *(756)*

McConnon, Pat
Council of State and Territorial Epidemiologists *(397)*

McCook, Darrel
Environmental Markets Association *(431)*
Juice Products Association *(589)*

McCook, Darrel
Research Chefs Association *(882)*

McCook, Monica
National Watermelon Association *(804)*

McCook, Patsy
American Apitherapy Society *(46)*

McCord, Mark
NASTD - Technology Professionals Serving State Government *(626)*
National Association of State Technology Directors *(702)*

McCorkle, Betty
International Customer Service Association *(539)*

McCorkle, MSN, RN, Michele R.
Oncology Nursing Society *(827)*

McCormack, Mary
Fire Department Safety Officers Association *(446)*

McCormack, Maryanne
Intercoiffure America/Canada *(507)*

McCormack, Michael
American Society for Cell Biology *(182)*

McCormick, Connie
National Association of Student Financial Aid Administrators *(703)*

McCormick, Gail Rodgers
General Federation of Women's Clubs *(458)*

McCormick, George
Stadium Managers Association *(960)*

McCormick, Jennifer
Transportation Trades Department, AFL-CIO *(979)*

McCormick, Michael W.
Global Business Travel Association *(462)*

McCormick, Mike
Plasma Protein Therapeutics Association *(850)*

McCormick, Jr., Walter B.
United States Telecom Association *(1000)*

McCort, Gregg A.
International Council of Shopping Centers *(538)*

McCourt, James "Bud"
International Association of Heat and Frost Insulators and Asbestos Workers *(522)*

McCown, Colin
American Wood-Protection Association *(222)*

McCoy, Beth
Association for Healthcare Resource and Materials Management *(248)*

McCoy, Gary
Spring Manufacturers Institute *(960)*

McCoy, Jody
National Association of Media Brokers *(680)*

McCoy, Keith
National Association of Manufacturers *(679)*

McCoy, Timothy S.
Corporate Council on Africa *(385)*

McCrabb, Barbara Humphrey
United States Conference of Catholic Bishops *(992)*

McCracken, Jacqueline
National Propane Gas Association *(783)*

McCracken, Keith
Marketing Agencies Association Worldwide *(606)*

McCracken, Todd
National Small Business Association *(792)*

McCrackin, Leah
American Society of Dermatopathology *(197)*

McCraken, Amy
National Stroke Association *(797)*

McCrary, PhD, Victor
National Organization for the Professional Advancement of Black Chemists and Chemical Engineers *(777)*

McCrath, C. Cliff
National Intercollegiate Soccer Officials Association *(766)*

McCray, CAE, Kevin B.
National Ground Water Association *(756)*

McCray, Tonya
American Geophysical Union *(126)*

McCreary, Sarah
National Association of State Foresters *(701)*

McCrehin, Christine
American Water Resources Association *(220)*

McCrehin, Christine Jewett
The American Society for Public Administration *(189)*

McCreight, James L.
Museum Trustee Association *(621)*

McCreight, Tim
American Institute of Chemical Engineers *(138)*

McCrensky, PhD, Jay
International Private Infrastructure Association *(561)*
Romanian-American Chamber of Commerce *(888)*

McCroddan, CPA, Steve
Grocery Manufacturers Association (GMA) *(466)*

McCrudden, Charlie
Air Conditioning Contractors of America *(18)*

McCubbin, Elaine
American College of Gastroenterology *(96)*

McCubbin, III, George
National Border Patrol Council *(716)*

McCubbrey, Janis
National Association of Counsel for Children *(658)*

McCuistion, Jeanene
Red Angus Association of America *(877)*

McCuller, Janet
National Association of Drug Court Professionals *(663)*

McCullough, Cassandra
Association of Black Cardiologists *(269)*

McCullough, Cristy
Women's Business Enterprise National Council *(1022)*

McCullough, Lynn
Event Service Professionals Association *(434)*

McCurdy, Hon. David K.
American Gas Association *(124)*

McCurrie, Tom
International Special Events Society *(575)*

McCutcheon, Mary
The Association for Social Anthropology in Oceania *(256)*

McCutcheon, Megan
Gerontological Society of America *(460)*

McDade, Marci
Surface Design Association *(966)*

McDaniel, Barbara
National Training and Simulation Association *(801)*

McDaniel, Beth
Painting and Decorating Contractors of America *(837)*

McDaniel, Christopher
Insured Retirement Institute *(505)*

McDaniel, Joe
American Salers Association *(176)*

McDaniel, Patricia B.
Tau Beta Pi Association *(968)*

McDaniel, Susan
National Tour Association *(800)*

McDaniels, Robyn
Association for Prevention Teaching and Research (APTR) *(254)*

McDannell, Libby
American Society of Transplantation *(210)*

McDermott, Erin C.
United Union of Roofers, Waterproofers and Allied Workers *(1001)*

McDermott, Jane
Promotion Marketing Association *(866)*

McDermott, John J.
National Apartment Association *(634)*

McDermott, Lara
National Association of Shareholder and Consumer Attorneys *(696)*

Mcdermott, Phil
Underwater Construction Corporation *(984)*

McDevitt, Jo-Ann
Association of Educational Publishers *(280)*

McDevitt, Kate
Association of Writers and Writing Programs *(318)*

McDonald, Catherine
Data Interchange Standards Association *(407)*

McDonald, PBVM, PhD, Sr. Dale
National Catholic Educational Association *(718)*

McDonald, Donna
Women in Cable Telecommunications, Inc. *(1020)*

McDonald, Gavin
International Union of Painters and Allied Trades *(579)*

McDonald, Jarom
Association for Computers and the Humanities *(242)*

McDonald, John
Alarm Industry Communication Committee *(21)*
Central Station Alarm Association *(349)*

McDonald, Mary C.
American Philosophical Society *(164)*

McDonald, Nancy
American Board of Professional Psychology *(83)*

McDonald, Phil
American Association of Woodturners *(77)*

McDonald, Robert
Association for Management Information in Financial Services *(251)*

McDonald, Sister Dale
National Catholic Educational Exhibitors *(718)*

McDonald, Stephen B.
Specialty Equipment Market Association *(957)*

McDonald, Todd
Academy of Pharmaceutical Research and Science *(8)*
American Pharmacists Association *(163)*

McDonnell, Ben
National Association of Housing Cooperatives *(673)*

McDonnell, Jane
Online News Association *(827)*

McDonnell, Kevin
International Ticketing Association *(577)*

McDonnough, Paul A.
Direct Marketing Association *(412)*

McDonough, Audrey
American Academy of Home Care Physicians *(35)*

McDonough, Colleen
Independent Sealing Distributors *(491)*
Yacht Brokers Association of America *(1030)*

McDonough, Douglas J.
American Dental Assistants Association *(113)*

McDonough, Frank
American Society of Cataract and Refractive Surgery *(194)*

McDonough, Kristen
Association of National Advertisers *(295)*

McDonough, Maureen
Semiconductor Equipment and Materials International *(896)*

McDonough, Timothy J.
American Council on Education *(110)*

McDonough, William T.
United Food and Commercial Workers International Union *(987)*

McDougal, Claudia A.
Outpatient Ophthalmic Surgery Society *(835)*

McDougal, Laura
Catholic Press Association *(346)*

McDougall, John
Waterproofing Contractors Association *(1013)*

McDowell, CSEP, Cynthia
National Stone, Sand, and Gravel Association *(796)*

McDowell, David
Society of Engineering Science *(935)*

McDuffie, Kate
American Association for Geriatric Psychiatry *(49)*

McDuffie, Nicole
Equal Employment Advisory Council *(432)*

McElgunn, Peggy
Alliance of Cardiovascular Professionals *(25)*
Teaching-Family Association *(969)*

McEllrath, Robert
International Longshore and Warehouse Union *(555)*

McElrath, Heather
National Grain and Feed Association *(755)*

McElroy, Arvel
National Interscholastic Swimming Coaches Association *(766)*

McElroy, Carole
American Bureau of Shipping *(86)*

McElroy, Deborah C.
Airports Council International - North America *(21)*

McElroy, Karen
RCI, Inc. *(875)*

Mcelvain, Guy
American Holsteiner Horse Association *(132)*

McElvaine, PhD, Allison T.
Society for Public Health Education *(919)*

McElveny, Ceela
American Society of Radiologic Technologists *(208)*

McEnany, Craig A.
National Postsecondary Agriculture Student
    Organization *(781)*

McEnelly, Casey
Dance/USA *(406)*

McEntee, Christine W.
American Geophysical Union *(126)*

McEntire, Donna
Joint Electron Device Engineering Council *(589)*

McEntire, Kip
Red Angus Association of America *(877)*

McEvoy, Maggie
Business Executives for National Security *(338)*

McEvoy, Robert "Bob"
National Association of County Administrators *(659)*

McEwan, Katrina
Association for Facilities Engineering *(246)*

McEwen, Bill
Masonry Institute of America *(607)*

McEwen, Darryl D.
International Association of Used Equipment Dealers
    (528)

McEwen, Ellen
Safe and Vault Technicians Association *(890)*

McEwen, Jane
International Packaged Ice Association *(559)*

McFadden, Heather
Society for Ethnomusicology *(908)*

McFadden, Kristin
Educational Theatre Association *(420)*

McFadden, MBA, Lawrence D.
National Parking Association *(779)*

McFadden, Lisa
American Society for Investigative Pathology *(186)*
Association for Molecular Pathology *(252)*

McFadyen, Buffie
Corrections, U.S.A. *(386)*

McFarland, Belle
National Association of Healthcare Access
    Management *(671)*

McFarland, Debra A.
Aircraft Electronics Association *(20)*

McFarland, Jason
International Association of Drilling Contractors *(519)*

McFarland, Laurel
National Association of Schools of Public Affairs and
    Administration *(694)*

McFarland, Lauren
Aircraft Electronics Association *(20)*

McFarlin, Adam
International Tuba-Euphonium Association *(578)*

McFarlin, Denise
American Theological Library Association *(216)*

McFee, John
Window and Door Manufacturers Association *(1018)*

McGarry, Dennis

National Telecommunications Cooperative Association
    (799)

McGarry, Jim
National School Supply and Equipment Association
    (789)

McGarry, Kevin
United States Wheat Associates, Inc. *(1000)*

McGaughey, William
International Society for the Comparative Studies of
    Civilizations *(569)*

McGavic, Claude
National Association of Home Inspectors *(673)*

McGavic, Judi
National Association of Home Inspectors *(673)*

McGavin, Joe
National Association for Sport and Physical Education
    (643)

McGee, Becki
United States Equestrian Federation *(993)*

McGee, Emily
Flight Safety Foundation *(448)*

McGee, Fred L.
Architectural Precast Association *(228)*

McGee, James M.
National Alliance of Postal and Federal Employees
    (633)

McGee, Esq., Karen
Water and Wastewater Equipment Manufacturers
    Association *(1012)*

McGee, Laura
International Window Film Association *(581)*

McGee, Paul
American Health Care Association *(129)*

McGehee, Doris
Women of the Motion Picture Industry, International
    (1022)

McGehee, Elton
Cement Employers Association *(347)*

McGeoch, Leslie
International Society of Managing and Technical
    Editors *(573)*

McGeorge, Scott
Federation of Analytical Chemistry and Spectroscopy
    Societies *(440)*

McGhee, Shon
National Society of Black Engineers *(793)*

McGhee, Sylvia
American Association for State and Local History *(51)*

McGhiey, CAE, Anne
Movement Disorder Society *(620)*

McGibbon, Patrick W.
AMT - The Association For Manufacturing Technology
    (222)

McGill, Erica
SEMATECH *(896)*

McGill, Jennifer H.
Association for Education in Journalism and Mass
    Communication *(245)*
Association of Schools of Journalism and Mass
    Communication *(307)*

McGill, Sharon
American Osteopathic Association *(160)*

McGillicuddy, Linda
American Headache Society *(129)*

McGinly, PhD, CAE, William C
Association for Healthcare Philanthropy *(248)*

McGinn, Patrick
Clinical and Laboratory Standards Institute *(358)*

McGinness, Jody L.
The Protein Society *(868)*

McGinnis, CFCS, Gay Nell
American Association of Family and Consumer
    Sciences *(61)*

McGinnis, Jon
Society for Medieval and Renaissance Philosophy *(915)*

McGinty, Casey
Church Music Publishers Association *(356)*

McGivney, William T.
National Comprehensive Cancer Network *(725)*

McGlaughlin, Jerry
American Psychological Association *(169)*

McGlone, Ecedra
American Association of Kidney Patients *(64)*

McGlothin, Karen
Electrocoat Association *(423)*

McGlothlin, Charles W.
The National Safety Management Society *(789)*

McGlotten, Tivona
Gynecologic Oncology Group *(467)*

McGlynn, Marcie
International Association of Rehabilitation
    Professionals *(527)*

McGoff, Michael F.
American Name Society *(154)*

McGorry, Joan
United Ostomy Associations of America *(988)*

McGough, Michael
National Corrugated Steel Pipe Association *(730)*

McGough, Michael C.
National Investor Relations Institute *(767)*

McGowan, Kitty
United States Superyacht Association *(999)*

McGowan, MA, Meghan
Federation of Associations in Behavioral & Brain
    Sciences *(441)*
Federation of Behavioral, Psychological and Cognitive
    Sciences *(441)*

McGrady, Laura
Million Dollar Round Table *(616)*

McGrat, Katie
Association of Seventh-Day Adventist Librarians *(308)*

McGrath, CAE, Charles A.
Interlocking Concrete Pavement Institute *(508)*

McGrath, Isabel
Recreation Vehicle Dealers Association of North
    America *(876)*

McGrath, Julie
International Anesthesia Research Society *(511)*

McGrath, Kelly
Association for the Treatment of Sexual Abusers *(260)*

McGrath, Matthew T.
Meat Importers Council of America *(609)*

McGrath, Michael
National Civic League *(722)*

McGrath, Scott
Organization for the Advancement of Structured
    Information Standards *(831)*

McGrath, Shaun
American Solar Energy Society *(211)*

McGraw, James L.
International Institute of Synthetic Rubber Producers
    (552)

McGraw, Judy
Air Force Sergeants Association *(19)*

McGraw, Paula
American Association for the Study of Liver Diseases *(52)*

McGraw, Scott
International Association of Tour Managers - North American Region *(528)*

McGraw, Timothy Y.
American-Uzbekistan Chamber of Commerce *(222)*

McGreevey, John D.
Tin Stabilizers Association *(975)*

McGreevy, III, James A.
American Beverage Association *(80)*

McGreevy, Shane
Professional Lighting and Sound Association *(863)*

McGreevy, Tim D.
United States of America Dry Pea and Lentil Council, Inc. *(996)*

McGrew, Portia
Independent Film and Television Alliance *(489)*

McGroder, Patrick J.
International Academy of Trial Lawyers *(509)*

McGuffin, Michael
American Herbal Products Association *(130)*

McGuigan, Jake
National Shooting Sports Foundation *(791)*

McGuiness, Jeffrey C.
HR Policy Association *(480)*

McGuinness, Nargis A.
The Danish-American Chamber of Commerce (USA) *(407)*

McGuire, Christian
Art Directors Guild/Scenic, Title and Graphic Artists *(230)*

McGuire, Dorothy
Employee Services Management Association *(426)*

McGuire, Jan Martin
Society of Animal Artists *(930)*

McGuire, Jim
BPA Worldwide *(334)*

McGuire, Joseph M.
Association of Home Appliance Manufacturers *(287)*

McGuire, Leigh A.
ASIS International *(232)*

McGuire, Margaret
Nursery and Landscape Association Executives of North America *(825)*

McGuire, PhD, Richard A.
The American Association of Phonetic Sciences *(69)*

McGuire, Sean
Plumbing Contractors of America *(851)*

McGuire, Steve
American Simmental Association *(179)*

McGuire-Kueltz, Maureen
National Council on Rehabilitation Education *(739)*

McGuirk, Dennis P.
Semiconductor Equipment and Materials International *(896)*

McGury, Carol
Utilimetrics/Alliance for Advanced Metering & Data Management Solutions *(1006)*

McHale, Jean
Institute for Supply Management *(497)*

McHenry, Irene
Council for American Private Education *(389)*

McHugh, Ella
International Interior Design Association *(552)*

McHugh, John
Organization for the Promotion and Advancement of Small Telecommunications Companies *(831)*

McHugh, CAE, Kathleen
American Specialty Toy Retailing Association *(212)*

McIlvaine, Rob
American Nephrology Nurses Association *(155)*

McIlwaith, Tad
Society for Anthropology in Community Colleges *(904)*

McInerney, USAF (Ret.), Jim
National Defense Industrial Association *(742)*

McInerney, CHA, Joseph A.
American Hotel & Lodging Association (AH&LA) *(134)*

McIntire-Strasburg, PhD, Janice
American Humor Studies Association *(134)*

McIntosh, Jennifer
The Association to Advance Collegiate Schools of Business *(319)*

McIntosh, Maxine
National Association of Consumer Advocates *(657)*

McIntosh-Peters, Alcenia
Association of Academic Health Centers *(262)*

McIntyre, Corey
National Association of Independent Schools *(675)*

McIntyre, Jeanne
American Academy of Otolaryngology-Head and Neck Surgery *(39)*

McIntyre, Jim
National Council for Prescription Drug Programs *(732)*

McIntyre, Malcolm
Alliance for Children and Families *(22)*

McIntyre, Marcia
American Orthopaedic Association *(158)*

McIntyre, Stephanie N.
American Association of Poison Control Centers *(70)*

McIrvin, Michelle
Educause *(420)*

McIver, Krystyna
Association of Analytical Communities International *(267)*

McJury, Stephanie
National Council of University Research Administrators *(737)*

McKay, BJ Morrison
International Society for Computational Biology *(566)*

McKay, Carol
National Consumers League *(729)*

McKechnie, J. Kevin
American Bankers Insurance Association *(79)*

McKee, Allison A.
Consumer Healthcare Products Association *(381)*

McKee, Linda
Manufacturers' Agents National Association *(603)*

McKee, Melanie
American Traffic Safety Service Association *(217)*

McKeever, III, Joseph F.
Committee of Annuity Insurers *(368)*

McKelvy, MA, SPHR, Dorothy
Project Management Institute *(866)*

McKemie, Catherine
American Folklore Society *(122)*

McKenna, James C.
Pacific Maritime Association *(836)*

McKenna, Leigh
National Health Care Anti-Fraud Association *(758)*

McKenna, Robert
Heavy Duty Manufacturers Association *(473)*

McKenna, Robert Bob
Motor and Equipment Manufacturers Association *(619)*

McKenney, Dr. James F.
American Association of Community Colleges *(58)*

McKenzie, Alyce
Academy of Homiletics *(5)*

McKenzie, Christine
America's Independent Truckers' Association, Inc. *(29)*

McKenzie, Gary
National Pest Management Association *(780)*

McKenzie, Shirley C.
American Dairy Goat Association *(112)*

McKeon, John J.
Construction Management Association of America *(379)*

McKeon, Margaret
Insurance Accounting and Systems Association *(504)*

McKeown, Caitlin
Fibre Box Association *(443)*

McKernon, Carol
Society of American Foresters *(928)*

McKether, Willie Lewis
Association of Black Anthropologists *(269)*

McKibben, Judith
American Society for Enology and Viticulture *(184)*

McKiernan, Kristen
National Conference of Executives of The ARC *(727)*

McKiernan, Patricia
Graphic Artists Guild *(465)*

McKinley, Craig R.
Air Force Association *(18)*

McKinley, Ron
National Network of Grantmakers *(775)*

McKinney, April
Federation of Employers and Workers of America *(441)*

McKinney, Craig
Technical Association of the Pulp and Paper Industry *(970)*

McKinney, Darren
American Tort Reform Association *(217)*

McKinney, J. Andrew
ALMA - The International Loudspeaker Association *(26)*

McKinney, MD, J. Mark
Association of Program Directors in Radiology *(303)*

McKinnish, Kim
National Beer Wholesalers Association *(713)*

McKinnon, Kerry
National Contract Management Association *(729)*

McKinnon, Monette
American Dental Education Association *(113)*

McKinzie, Melissa
American Nuclear Society *(156)*

McKissen, Dustin
National Speakers Association *(795)*

McKnelly, Philip K.
National Association of State Park Directors *(702)*

McKnight, Rodney
National Associations of State Directors of Pupil Transportation Services *(710)*

McKnight, Sharon
American Society of Agricultural and Biological Engineers *(191)*

McKnight (EMC), Dr. John
American Council of Christian Churches *(109)*

McKown, Jennie
Association of Postgraduate Physician Assistant Programs *(300)*

McKuen, Rod
American Guild of Variety Artists *(128)*

McLafferty, MD, Rob
American Venous Forum *(218)*

McLain, Ret., USN, Joseph S.
Beer Institute *(327)*

McLane, Annette
Student National Medical Association *(964)*

McLane, Kathleen
Council for Exceptional Children *(390)*

McLaughlin, Brenna
Association of American University Presses *(267)*

McLaughlin, Bridget
Human Resource People and Strategy *(481)*
National Institute of Pension Administrators *(765)*

McLaughlin, Janet
Association of American Colleges and Universities *(264)*

McLaughlin, Julie A.
National Insulation Association *(766)*

McLaughlin, Linda
American Fraternal Alliance *(124)*

McLaughlin, Margaret
African Studies Association *(15)*

McLaughlin, Matt
Utilimetrics/Alliance for Advanced Metering & Data Management Solutions *(1006)*

McLaughlin, Rachael
Sigma Theta Tau International *(899)*

McLaughlin, Scott
International Computer Music Association *(536)*

McLaughlin, Tara
Airforwarders Association *(20)*
Messenger Courier Association of the Americas *(612)*

McLaughlin, CFA, CPA, Timothy G.
CFA Institute *(350)*

McLean, Bob
Employee Assistance Society of North America *(426)*

McLean, Bob
Promotional Products Association International *(867)*

McLean, Diana K.
National Association for Poetry Therapy *(641)*

McLean, Gloria
American Dance Guild *(113)*

McLean, Kari E.
American Orthopaedic Association *(158)*

McLean, Missi
Society for Vascular Ultrasound *(927)*

McLean, Rebecca
National Real Estate Investors Association *(784)*

McLean, CAE, Robert E.
Coal Trading Association *(359)*

McLear, Dr. Rob
American College of Veterinary Radiology *(104)*

McLemore, Laura Lyons
Academy of Certified Archivists *(4)*

McLendon, Dr. Lennox
National Adult Education Professional Development Consortium *(629)*

McLeod, Andrew

National Cooperative Business Association *(729)*

McLeod, CAE, CEM, Ann
Society of American Military Engineers *(929)*

McLeod, CMP, Barbara
Society of Thoracic Radiology *(948)*

McLeod, Cindy
Association of Edison Illuminating Companies *(279)*

McLeod, Michael R.
American Association of Crop Insurers *(59)*

McLeod, Mike
American Peanut Product Manufacturers, Inc. *(162)*

McLernon, Nancy L.
Organization for International Investment *(831)*

McLin, Joyce A.
The American Safe Deposit Association *(176)*

McLuckie, Jr., Frederick P.
International Brotherhood of Teamsters *(532)*

McMackin, Michael
American Society of Theatre Consultants *(210)*

McMahan, Michelle
International Academy of Compounding Pharmacists *(509)*

McMahan, Dr. Robert Young
American Accordionists Association *(43)*

McMahen, Nancy
National Rural Electric Cooperative Association *(788)*

McMahon, Colleen
Council of Residential Specialists *(396)*

McMahon, Diane
The International Fluid Power Society *(545)*

McMahon, J. Michael
National Association of Pastoral Musicians *(683)*

McMahon, Lawrence
American Studies Association *(214)*

McMahon, Madeline Fullerton
Alarm Industry Communication Committee *(21)*
Central Station Alarm Association *(349)*

McMahon, Megan
National Chimney Sweep Guild *(721)*

McMahon, Siobhan
Association of School Business Officials International *(306)*

McMahon, Stacy
National Association of Schools of Dance *(693)*

McManamay, Mary Ann
International Council of Air Shows *(538)*

McManimon, Erin
National Association of Attorneys General *(647)*

Mcmanus, Mike
American Society of Anesthesia Technologists and Technicians *(192)*

McManus, Siobhan
Cosmetic Executive Women *(387)*

McManus-White, Etienne
Forest Stewardship Council - United States Chapter *(451)*

McMillan, Dafina
Theatre Communications Group *(973)*

McMillan, Karrie
Investment Company Institute *(584)*

McMillan, Meredith L.
National Association of College and University Attorneys *(654)*

McMillen, Heather
Society for Economic Botany *(908)*

McMonigle, Amy
Building Owners and Managers Institute International *(337)*

McMorris, Lamell J.
National Basketball Referees Association *(713)*

McMullen, Hollis
National Association of State Alcohol and Drug Abuse Directors (NASADAD) *(697)*

McMurrey, Nancy
American Academy of Nurse Practitioners *(37)*

McMurry, Stephen
Association of American Plant Food Control Officials *(266)*

McNalis, Kelly
Inter-Industry Conference on Auto Collision Repair *(506)*

McNall, Faye
American Society of Electroneurodiagnostic Technologists *(197)*

McNally, Caroline
American Mountain Guides Association *(153)*

McNally, Denise D.
National Association of Medical Examiners *(680)*

McNally, Hannah
Women in Mining National *(1022)*

McNally, Ian
American Massage Therapy Association *(147)*

McNamara, Cathy
Academy of General Dentistry *(5)*

McNamara, Jody
American String Teachers Association *(213)*

McNamara, Mary
American Nurses Association *(156)*
Meals on Wheels Association of America *(609)*

McNamara, Sean
Association of Public Data Users *(304)*

McNamara, Sean A.
Council for Community and Economic Research *(388)*

Mcnamee, Katherine
American Association of Museums *(65)*

McNamee, Marie
InsideNGO *(496)*

McNamee, Mike
Investment Company Institute *(584)*

McNatt, CMP, Claudia V.
Commercial Vehicle Safety Alliance *(367)*

McNeal, CFE, CPA, Andi
Association of Certified Fraud Examiners *(271)*

McNealy, Katie
National Investment Company Service Association *(767)*

McNees, Lynne Walker
International Spa Association *(575)*

McNees, Pat
Association of Personal Historians *(299)*

McNeil, Catherine Masterson
International Health, Racquet and Sportsclub Association *(549)*

McNeil, Eddy
Turnaround Management Association *(982)*

McNeil, Jim
Bank Insurance and Securities Association *(326)*

McNeil, Marcus
Student National Medical Association *(964)*

McNeil, Regina
National Exchange Carrier Association *(746)*

McNeill, DeeDee
Nuclear Suppliers Association *(825)*

McNeill, Derek
National Institute of Governmental Purchasing *(765)*

McNeill, Gail
Certified Contractors Network *(349)*

McNeill, MD, Diana B.
Association of Program Directors in Internal Medicine *(302)*

McNerney, John
National Certified Pipe Welding Bureau *(720)*

McNerney, Keely
American Psychiatric Nurses Association *(168)*

McNevin, Anthony J.
American College of Certified Wound Specialists *(94)*

McNormally, Timothy J.
Tax Executives Institute, Inc. *(968)*

McNulty, Michael J.
Wire and Cable Industry Suppliers Association *(1019)*

McPeek, Mark A.
The American Society of Naturalists *(203)*

McPhail, Irving Pressley
National Action Council for Minorities in Engineering (NACME) *(628)*

McPhaul, MD, Michael J.
American Federation for Medical Research *(119)*

McPherson, Amy
The Botanical Society of America *(333)*

McPherson, Casey
Contact Lens Society of America *(382)*

McPherson, Elizabeth
American Indian Science and Engineering Society *(135)*

McPherson, James
National Association of Attorneys General *(647)*

McPherson, BA, JD, MBA, M. Peter
Association of Public and Land-Grant Universities (APLU) *(303)*

McPherson, PhD, Susan
American Academy of Clinical Neuropsychology *(31)*

McQuaid, John A.
Steel Shipping Container Institute *(963)*

McQueen, Mary Campbell
National Center for State Courts *(720)*

McQuilkin, Andrew R.
Institute of Store Planners *(503)*

McQuillan, John
Triumvirate Environmental *(980)*

McQuillan, Larry
American Institutes for Research *(141)*

McQuiston, Cathie
American Federation of Government Employees *(119)*

McRae, Arnetta
American Association of Blacks in Energy *(55)*

McRae, Meghan
Committee of 200 *(368)*

McRary, Kristen
Country Radio Broadcasters, Inc. *(401)*

McReynolds, Connie
Vocational Evaluation and Career Assessment Professionals *(1011)*

McRoberts, Alan
International Association for Identification *(513)*

McRunnel, Karen
National Association of County Civil Attorneys *(659)*

McShay, Frank
The Risk Management Association *(886)*

McSheffrey, Brian F.
Commissioned Officers Association of the United States Public Health Service *(368)*

McSorley, Kelly
The Advertising Research Foundation *(13)*

McSorley, Susan
American Academy of Orthopaedic Surgeons *(38)*

McSweeney, CAE, Mark
National Chimney Sweep Guild *(721)*

McSwiggen, James
RNA Society *(887)*

McTernan, Joseph "Joe"
American Orthotic and Prosthetic Association *(159)*

McVay, Christina
Black Theatre Network *(332)*

McVay, Robert G.
National Rural Health Association *(788)*

McWhorter, Kristin
National Poultry and Food Distributors Association *(782)*

McWilliams, MD, Charles A.
American Association of Clinical Urologists *(56)*

Mead, Chris
American Chamber of Commerce Executives *(89)*

Mead, Dean Michael
Governmental Research Association *(464)*

Mead, George (Fritz)
National Tank Truck Carriers *(799)*

Mead, Kevin
IGAF Polaris *(486)*

Mead, Pat
Accreditation Association for Ambulatory Health Care *(9)*

Meade, Carla Burgman
National Association of State Directors of Special Education *(700)*

Meade, Denys
Physician Office Managers Association of America *(847)*

Meade, Elizabeth
American Staffing Association *(213)*

Meade, Michelle
Receptive Services Association of America *(876)*

Meadows, Rod
Minor League Baseball *(617)*
National Association of Professional Baseball Leagues *(686)*

Meadows, Tim
Cremation Association of North America *(404)*
Organization Development Network *(831)*

Meadows, Veronica
The Council of Landscape Architectural Registration Boards *(395)*

Meals, Torian
National ALEC Association/ Prepaid Communications Association *(631)*

Mealy, PhD, Kimberly
Academy of Political Science *(8)*
American Political Science Association *(166)*

Mealy, Lynne
International Association for Human Resource Information Management *(512)*

Mealy, Marc
United States-ASEAN Business Council Inc. *(990)*

Means, Antionette

Mental Health America *(612)*

Means, Katherine "Kathy" A.
Produce Marketing Association *(858)*

Measel, Michelle
American Association of Exporters & Importers *(60)*

Mechelse, Mark
Global Market Development Center *(462)*

Mechem, John T.
Mortgage Bankers Association of America *(619)*

Mechler, CAE, CMP, Pamela
American College of Radiology *(102)*

Mecklenborg, Mark
American Ceramics Society *(89)*

Meckley, Lacey
Association of University Programs in Health Administration *(316)*

Medard, Muriel
Information Theory Society *(495)*

Medbery, Shirley
National Council for Marketing and Public Relations *(732)*

Medders, Dr. David
Association for Biblical Higher Education *(240)*

Meddock, Larry
Water Sports Industry Association *(1013)*

Medich, Cathy
Smart Card Alliance *(901)*

Medick, CAE, CPA, Susan
Automotive Aftermarket Industry Association *(321)*

Medina, Connie
Society of Mexican American Engineers and Scientists *(941)*

Medina, Jean
Airlines For America *(21)*

Medina, FACS, MD, Jesus E.
American Laryngological, Rhinological and Otological Society *(144)*
Triological Society *(980)*

Medina, Nikki Smith
Society for Imaging Informatics in Medicine *(912)*

Medley, Carlos
Associated Church Press *(235)*

Medley, Debbie
American Board of Family Medicine *(82)*

Medley, Larry J.
National Concrete Masonry Association *(725)*

Medlin, E. Lander
APPA - Leadership in Educational Facilities *(225)*

Medlock, Marilyn
American Membrane Technology Association *(150)*

Medrano, Maria
Association of American Chambers of Commerce in Latin America *(264)*

Medwin, Daniel B.
Central Conference of American Rabbis *(348)*

Meehan, Thomas
American Association of Zoo Veterinarians *(77)*

Meek, CPA, MBA, Jay
National Association of State Mental Health Directors *(701)*
National Association of State Mental Health Program Directors *(701)*

Meek, Jennifer
The Association of Women in International Trade *(317)*

Meek, Robert
Indian Arts and Crafts Association *(492)*

Meek-Barker, Jean
Fashion Group International *(438)*

Meeker, Mary
United States Federation for Culture Collections *(994)*

Meeks, Jim
National Tax Lien Association *(799)*

Meeks, Regina
Community Health Charities of America *(371)*

Meers, Esq., James
Sugar Association *(965)*

Meesarapu, Jacob
Association for Assessment and Accreditation of Laboratory Animal Care International *(239)*

Megivern, Kathleen
Commission on Accreditation of Allied Health Education Programs *(368)*

Mehaffy, George L.
American Association of State Colleges and Universities *(73)*

Mehren, David F.
National Association of Independent Insurance Adjusters *(674)*

Mehrotra, Kishan
International Society of Applied Intelligence *(570)*

Mehta, Nimish
Indian Diamond and Colorstone Association *(492)*

Meier, Gina
Professional Convention Management Association *(861)*

Meier, Jyl
American Escrow Association *(118)*

Meier, MSEd, CAE, Sara
International Association for Continuing Education and Training *(511)*

Meier, Virginia
National Strength and Conditioning Association *(797)*

Meigs, Montgomery C.
Business Executives for National Security *(338)*

Meijer, Jon
Drycleaning & Laundry Institute *(417)*

Meincke, Brian
ASTM International *(319)*

Meinecke, Dana
National Pawnbrokers Association *(779)*

Meinig, Kristina
Audit Bureau of Circulations *(320)*

Meinrath, Eliza Guyol
Association of Collegiate Business Schools and Programs *(275)*

Meinsler, Lucille F.
American Association of Chairs of Departments of Psychiatry *(56)*
American Association of Directors of Psychiatric Residency Training *(60)*

Meisinger, Jessica
National Renderers Association *(786)*

Meixelsperger, Wes
American Society of Agronomy (ASA, CSSA, SSSA) *(191)*
Crop Science Society of America *(404)*
Soil Science Society of America *(951)*

Melancon, Barry C.
American Institute of Certified Public Accountants *(137)*

Melancon, Reena
Wood Moulding and Millwork Producers Association *(1024)*

Melanio, Grace-Sonia

Association of Asian-Pacific Community Health Organizations *(268)*

Melaniphy, Margie
International SalonSpa Business Network (ISBN) *(563)*

Melaniphy, Michael P.
American Public Transportation Association *(171)*

Melanson, Peter
National Strength and Conditioning Association *(797)*

Melby, Alan
Linguistic Association of Canada and the United States *(598)*

Melchi, Jonathan
Heating, Airconditioning and Refrigeration Distributors International *(473)*

Meldrum, Dave
Eastern Apicultural Society of North America *(418)*

Meldrum, CWDP, MS, Patti
National Association of Workforce Development Professionals *(710)*

Meldrum, Tom
Software & Information Industry Association (SIIA) *(950)*

Mele, Chris
National Association of Regulatory Utility Commissioners *(691)*

Melenchuk, Susan
Roller Skating Association International *(887)*

Melendes, Christine
Association for Corporate Growth *(244)*

Meleney, Margaret
Club Managers Association of America *(359)*

Melgosa, Annette
Association of Seventh-Day Adventist Librarians *(308)*

Meli, Laura
ArtTable *(231)*

Melillo, DPM, Thomas V.
American Association of Colleges of Podiatric Medicine *(58)*

Melin, CMP, MEd, Jeffrey
American Epilepsy Society *(117)*

Melkerson-Kirby, Penny
College of Optometrists in Vision Development *(364)*

Mella, Jeanne L.
Association of American Medical Colleges *(265)*

Mello, PhD, Brad
National Communication Association *(724)*

Mello, Jack
Art Directors Club *(229)*

Mellor, Peter
Major Indoor Soccer League *(601)*

Melloy, Kris
Council for Children with Behavioral Disorders *(389)*

Melnick, Donald E.
National Board of Medical Examiners *(716)*

Melnick, Scott
American Institute of Steel Construction *(140)*

Melnicove, Susan A.
ASIS International *(232)*

Melnykovich, George O.
Food Processing Suppliers Association *(449)*
Meat Industry Suppliers Alliance *(610)*

Melon, Sean
Portable Sanitation Association International *(853)*

Melone, Linda
American Society of Journalists and Authors *(201)*

Melovidov, Ray
Central Bering Sea Fisherman's Association *(348)*

Meloy, Ada
American Council on Education *(110)*

Melsop, Michelle
Telecommunications Industry Association *(971)*

Melton, Dana
National Indian Gaming Association *(762)*

Melton, Diane
IEEE Magnetics Society *(484)*

Melton, Gary B.
American Orthopsychiatric Association *(159)*

Melton, Gary L.
American Train Dispatchers Association *(217)*

Melton, Tiffany
American College of Nurse Practitioners *(99)*

Meltzer, Shelley
North - American Interfraternity Conference *(812)*

Melville, Lanette
American Board of Professional Psychology *(83)*

Melville, Scott M.
Consumer Healthcare Products Association *(381)*

Melvin, CAE, CMP, Leslie
Association for Retail Environments *(256)*

Melvin, Patrick
International Society of Hair Restoration Surgery *(573)*

Melvin, Sharon C.
Auxiliary to the National Medical Association *(324)*

Melvin, Stephanie
Council for Resource Development *(391)*

Melzer, Sharon
International Association for the Study of Organized Crime *(514)*

Melzi, Randy
Council of the Americas *(398)*

Mena, Jr., Eliseo
Institute of International Container Lessors *(501)*

Menard, CPP, Robert
American Purchasing Society *(172)*

Mencher, Jordan
American Association of Wildlife Veterinarians *(77)*

Menchey, Joel
National Association of School Music Dealers *(692)*

Mendell, Emily
National Venture Capital Association *(803)*

Mendelsohn, Paul
The American Institute of Architects *(137)*

Mendelson, Jeanne
Lamaze International *(592)*

Mendenhall, Anne
National Association of College Stores *(655)*

Mendenhall, Keith
Aeronautical Repair Station Association *(14)*

Mendes, David
American Subcontractors Association *(214)*

Mendes, MA, Joel
Utilimetrics/Alliance for Advanced Metering & Data Management Solutions *(1006)*

Mendez, Kenneth
Advanced Medical Technology Association (AdvaMed) *(13)*

Mendez, Paul
Council for Chemical Research, Inc. *(389)*

Mendonca, Marc S.

Radiation Research Society *(873)*

Mendoza, Carol M.
World Aquaculture Society *(1025)*

Mendoza, Trisha
BICSI *(329)*

Mendoza, Zenaida Avelar
Association of Latino Professionals in Finance and Accounting *(291)*

Mendoza-Denton, Norma
Society for Linguistic Anthropology *(914)*

Mendys, Alison
Heavy Duty Manufacturers Association *(473)*

Menefee, Jennifer
American Academy of Gnathologic Orthopedics *(34)*

Meneley, Nicki
National Panhellenic Conference *(778)*

Menendz, April
Intercoiffure America/Canada *(507)*

Menezes, Will
Life Insurance Settlement Association *(597)*

Meng, Michele
Ceilings and Interior Systems Construction Association *(347)*

Menighan, Thomas E.
Academy of Pharmaceutical Research and Science *(8)*
American Pharmacists Association *(163)*

Mennillo, MBA, Kathleen
International Hearing Society *(549)*

Mennite, Mary Anne
Society of Financial Service Professionals *(936)*

Menotti, Esq., David E.
American Coke and Coal Chemicals Institute *(92)*

Menser, Laurie S.
American Society for Investigative Pathology *(186)*

Mentel, Eva
Hardwood Plywood and Veneer Association *(468)*

Menyo, PhD, Laurie
ECRI *(418)*

Menzies, Charles
Society for the Anthropology of Work *(923)*

Merbs, Shannath L.
American Society of Ophthalmic Plastic and Reconstructive Surgery *(205)*

Mercado, Catalina
Association for Conflict Resolution *(243)*

Mercado, Jeff
Jeweler's Vigilance Committee *(587)*

Mercardo, CEM, Tina Lynn
Craft & Hobby Association *(402)*

Mercer, Aaron
National Religious Broadcasters *(785)*

Mercer, Anne L.
Endocrine Fellows Foundation *(427)*

Mercer, Steve
United States Wheat Associates, Inc. *(1000)*

Mercier, Kathleen
Public Education Network *(869)*

Mercill, Alan M
International Pharmaceutical Excipients Council of the Americas *(560)*

Merculief, Marva
Central Bering Sea Fisherman's Association *(348)*

Mercurio, Ashley
Association of Diesel Specialists *(279)*

Mercurio, David
CoreNet Global *(385)*

Meredith, Mimi
Society of Environmental Toxicology and Chemistry *(935)*

Merenda, Daniel W.
National Association of Partners in Education *(683)*

Merfeld, Patrick
Earthmoving & Mining Equipment Council *(418)*

Meric, Linda
Nine to Five, National Association of Working Women *(811)*

Mericsko, John
National Association of City and County Health Officials *(654)*
National Association of County and City Health Officials *(659)*

Merkel, Rachelle J.
Kappa Delta Pi *(590)*

Merkley, MBA, Terry
American Association of Diabetes Educators *(60)*

Merklinger, James 'Jim"
Association of Corporate Counsel *(277)*

Merkord, Chris
American Ornithologists' Union *(158)*

Merkx, Dr. Gilbert W.
Association of International Education Administrators *(289)*

Merlie, Maria
National Association of Psychiatric Health Systems *(688)*

Merlo, Beth
Defense Credit Union Council *(408)*

Merola, Marci
American Library Association *(145)*

Merrell, CAE, Billy
The Academy of American Poets *(3)*

Merrell, Sam
American Society of Picture Professionals *(207)*

Merrick, Michael J.
International Council of Shopping Centers *(538)*

Merrifield, Jeff F.
Marine Engineers Beneficial Association *(605)*

Merrifield, Shawn
Produce Marketing Association *(858)*

Merrihew, Jason
American Animal Hospital Association *(45)*

Merrilees, Craig
International Longshore and Warehouse Union *(555)*

Merrill, Chris
Council on Technology Teacher Education *(401)*

Merrill, Clarence
Christian Labor Association of the United States of America *(355)*

Merrill, Leslie J.
International Desalination Association *(540)*

Merrill, Shannon
American Mold Builders Association *(152)*

Merrill, Susan
United States Bowling Congress *(991)*

Merrill, Wayne J.
The American Safe Deposit Association *(176)*

Merriman, Klein S.
Association for Retail Environments *(256)*

Merriman, Tim
National Association for Interpretation *(640)*

Merritt, Franklin
Global Health Council *(462)*

Merritt, Joseph F.
American Society of Mammalogists *(202)*

Merritt, Mark
Pharmaceutical Care Management Association *(844)*

Merritt, Meryem
National Pork Producers Association *(781)*

Merritt, Monica L.
United States Institute for Theatre Technology *(995)*

Merritt, Nicole
International Society for the Performing Arts *(569)*

Merritt, PhD, Rob
National Association for Poetry Therapy *(641)*

Merry, Carroll
American Society of Agricultural Consultants *(191)*

Merry, Glenn
United States Rowing Association *(998)*

Mertz, Alan
American Clinical Laboratory Association *(91)*

Merzon, Steven
International Trademark Association *(577)*

Mesaris, Kelly
American Institute of Floral Designers *(138)*
Professional Grounds Management Society *(862)*

Meserve, CHPA, Evelyn F.
International Association for Healthcare Security and Safety *(512)*

Mesiano, Vincent
Schiffli Lace and Embroidery Manufacturers Association *(892)*

Mesirow, Robert
CTIA - The Wireless Association *(405)*

Mesis, Jimmie
National Council of Investigative and Security Services Inc. *(735)*

Meskan, Peggy
Structural Building Components Association *(964)*

Meslener, Chrissy
American Payroll Association *(162)*

Mesones, Amanda
American Association of Motor Vehicle Administrators *(65)*

Messer, Theresa Clark
National Basketball Players Association *(713)*

Messick, Christine Kupfer
United States-Taiwan Business Council *(989)*

Messick, Donald L.
The Sulphur Institute *(965)*

Messner, Kevin
Association of Home Appliance Manufacturers *(287)*

Mestas, Melanie
American Academy of Professional Coders *(40)*

Mester, John C.
Associated Universities Inc. *(237)*

Mesterharm, Tracy
Investment Program Association *(584)*

Metcalf, Allan
American Dialect Society *(115)*

Metcalf, Ben
Democratic Governors Association *(410)*

Metcalf, MBA, Jill
Society for Medical Decision Making *(915)*

Metroff, Ken
National Postal Policy Council *(781)*

Metropulos, Karen
Healthcare Financial Management Association *(471)*

Metteauer, Michael
International Trademark Association *(577)*

Metter, Kristine
Visiting Nurse Associations of America *(1010)*

Metz, Dale
National Animal Supplement Council *(634)*

Metz, Lloyd
National Association of Investment Companies *(676)*

Metz, Marie
Guild of Natural Science Illustrators *(467)*

Metzgar, Jodi
Institute of Nuclear Materials Management *(502)*

Metzger, Bill
Fermenters International Trade Association *(443)*

Metzger, Daniel J.
Thoroughbred Owners and Breeders Association *(974)*

Metzger, Jeanne Lazarus
National Venture Capital Association *(803)*

Metzger, Kristen L.
International Association of Aquatic and Marine Science Libraries and Information Centers *(515)*

Metzger, Thom
Environmental Industry Associations *(431)*
National Solid Wastes Management Association *(795)*
Waste Equipment Technology Association *(1012)*

Metzler, DACVO, DVM, MS, Anne Gemensky
Omega Tau Sigma *(827)*

Metzler, Carol
National Park Hospitality Association *(779)*

Metzler, Christina A.
American Occupational Therapy Association, Inc. *(157)*

Metzner, Mary
National Aerosol Association *(629)*

Metzner, Tervia
National Association of Uniform Manufacturers and Distributors *(707)*

Mewawalla, Anuneha S.
Arthur W. Page Society *(230)*

Mewhiney, Kate
Anxiety Disorders Association of America *(224)*

Meyer, Adele R.
National Association of Resale & Thrift Shops *(691)*

Meyer, Amy
American Society of Andrology *(192)*

Meyer, Angela
National Association of Educational Office Professionals *(664)*

Meyer, Brian M.
American Society of Health-System Pharmacists *(199)*

Meyer, CHP, Charles R. (Russ)
Conference of Radiation Control Program Directors *(375)*

Meyer, Dan
American Dairy Products Institute *(112)*

Meyer, Darlene
Orthopaedic Trauma Association *(834)*

Meyer, Deborah
Ceilings and Interior Systems Construction Association *(347)*

Meyer, Donna
National Organization for Associate Degree Nursing *(776)*

Meyer, Eve R.

International Alliance for Women in Music *(510)*

Meyer, Francine
National Electrical Manufacturers Association *(744)*

Meyer, Jan
Independent Community Bankers of America *(488)*

Meyer, John M.
Holstein Association USA *(477)*

Meyer, Kathy
United States Equestrian Federation *(993)*

Meyer, Margot
Association of Corporate Credit Unions *(277)*

Meyer, Marvin
American Choral Directors Association *(90)*

Meyer, Michal
Chemical Heritage Foundation *(351)*

Meyer, Michelle
Electronic Components Industry Association *(423)*

Meyer, Nina
American Society of Travel Agents *(210)*

Meyer, Reginald
National Confectioners Association *(725)*

Meyer, Russell L.
North American Academy of Ecumenists *(812)*

Meyer, Scott
National Association of Home Builders *(673)*

Meyer, Sheila
Association of College and University Housing Officers-International *(274)*

Meyer, Steve
The College Board *(363)*

Meyer, Suzanne
National Association of Corporate Directors *(658)*

Meyer, Theresa
National Association for Fixed Annuities *(639)*

Meyer, Warren
National Forest Recreation Association *(752)*

Meyering, Stephanie
Juice Products Association *(589)*

Meyers, Elizabeth
National Parks Conservation Association *(779)*

Meyers, Louis Jay
The Folk Alliance International *(449)*

Meyers, Mary V.
American College of Foot and Ankle Surgeons *(95)*

Meyers, Michael
Printing Industry Credit Executives *(857)*

Meyers, Nicholas
American Psychiatric Association *(168)*

Meyers, Richard
Office Business Center Association International *(826)*

Meyerson, Adam
The Philanthropy Roundtable *(846)*

Meyocks, Terence J.
The Jockeys' Guild *(588)*

Mialot, Laurence
International Society for Infectious Diseases *(566)*

Mica, J. Clark
The Fertilizer Institute *(443)*

Michael, Karen
National Association of Bond Lawyers *(650)*

Michael, Laura
American Osteopathic College of Pathologists *(160)*

Michael, Michele

Association of Insolvency and Restructuring Advisors *(289)*

Michael, Scott
American Moving and Storage Association *(153)*

Michael-Lee, Kim
Concrete Reinforcing Steel Institute *(374)*

Michaels, Edward "Ted"
Energy Recovery Council *(428)*

Michaels, Jonathan
Soccer Industry Council of America *(902)*

Michaels, Jonathan
Sports and Fitness Industry Association *(959)*

Michaelson, Juliette
Regional Plan Association *(879)*

Michal, Rick
American Nuclear Society *(156)*

Michalek, Jennifer
American Society for Gastrointestinal Endoscopy *(184)*

Michalek, Nancy
The Association of Concert Bands *(276)*

Michalski, Lauren
Association of Transportation Professionals *(314)*

Micheal, Emebet G.
Association for Childhood Education International *(241)*

Michel, John
American Composers Forum *(105)*

Michel, Nancy
Justice Research and Statistics Association *(589)*

Michel, Ruth
American Association of Neuromuscular and Electrodiagnostic Medicine *(66)*

Michels, Esq., Dina
American Society of Clinical Oncology *(194)*

Michels, Harold T.
Copper Development Association *(384)*

Michels, Linda
AAGL - Advancing Minimally Invasive Gynecology Worldwide *(2)*

Michels, Nicola
German American Chamber of Commerce *(460)*

Michelson, Paul E.
Conference on Faith and History *(376)*

Michielsen, Stephen
Fiber Society *(443)*

Michlig, Greg
Credit Union Executives Society *(403)*

Mickley, CPBD, Steven
American Institute of Building Design *(137)*

Micklos, Jeffrey G.
Federation of American Hospitals *(440)*

Micou, Matt
Strategic Account Management Association *(963)*

Middleton, Fred
National Cotton Batting Institute *(730)*

Middleton, Jean R.
Association of Public and Land-Grant Universities (APLU) *(303)*

Middleton, Kim
American Academy of Facial Plastic and Reconstructive Surgery *(34)*

Middleton, Esq., Matthew J.
Black Entertainment and Sports Lawyers Association *(331)*

Midland, David

National Association of Health Education Centers *(671)*

Midman, Joy
National Association for Children's Behavioral Health (NACBH) *(637)*

Midyette, Buxton S.
Supima *(966)*

Miedema, Amy
American Academy of Audiology *(31)*

Miedema, Wyatt
National Contract Management Association *(729)*

Mielcarek, Kimberly
North American Electric Reliability Corporation *(816)*

Mifsud, Paul
Academy of Nutrition and Dietetics *(7)*

Migala, Chris
Organization Development Network *(831)*

Migdol, Marvin
Consumer Health Alliance *(381)*

Miggins, Ida
Council for Higher Education Accreditation *(390)*

Mighetto, Lisa
American Society for Environmental History *(184)*

Mihelich, Kathleen
International Association of Plumbing and Mechanical Officials *(526)*

Mikell, SAP, Shirley Beckett
National Association for Alcoholism and Drug Abuse Counselors *(646)*

Mikita, Lisa J.
Association of Legal Administrators *(291)*

Mikitka, CAE, CMP, Michael J.
Warehousing Education and Research Council *(1012)*

Mikkelsen, Paula
Paleontological Research Institution *(837)*

Mikola, Gary
Society of Manufacturing Engineers *(941)*

Miksch, Ann
Professional Skaters Association *(865)*

Miksch, Karen
Association for the Study of Higher Education *(259)*

Mikstay, John
BPA Worldwide *(334)*

Mikula, Brian
Federation of Straight Chiropractors and Organizations *(442)*

Milam, Rene
Newspaper Association of America *(810)*

Milanese, Jody
Small Business Exporters Association of the United States *(900)*

Milar, Kathy
Cheiron: The International Society for the History of Behavioral and Social Sciences *(351)*

Milbrandt, Peggy
Path to Purchase Institute *(839)*

Milburn, Malvin
Association of Community Cancer Centers *(275)*

Milburn, Trisha
American Association for Geodetic Surveying *(49)*
National Society of Professional Surveyors *(794)*

Miles, CMP, Gretchen L.
American College of Clinical Pharmacy *(94)*

Miles, Karen
US Rice Producers Association *(1004)*

Mileski, Denise

The Coalition for Government Procurement *(360)*

Milewski, Jeannie
Concord Grape Association *(373)*
The Vinegar Institute *(1009)*

Milgram, Lisa
Interactive Advertising Bureau *(506)*

Milhouse, Tinia
National Educational Telecommunications Association *(744)*

Militello, Betsy King
National Alliance for Musical Theatre *(632)*

Milizzo, Joe
IEEE Communications Society *(483)*

Milla, Jay
PROMAX/BDA *(866)*

Millage, Anne
The Institute of Internal Auditors *(500)*

Millan, Leanna
National Writers Union *(806)*

Millan, Ran
National Alliance for Hospice Access *(631)*

Millar, BSN, RN, Dorice
American Academy of Fertility Care Professionals *(34)*

Millar, Helen
World Federation for Mental Health *(1026)*

Millar, Sheila A.
Fashion Jewelry and Accessories Trade Association *(438)*

Millar, William W.
American Public Transportation Association *(171)*

Millard, Dean
American Chiropractic Association *(90)*

Miller, Andy
World Waterpark Association *(1028)*

Miller, Anelle
Society of Illustrators *(939)*

Miller, Angelica
North American Mycological Association *(818)*

Miller, Anita
Materials Research Society *(609)*

Miller, Barbara
Greeting Card Association *(466)*

Miller, CCC-SLP, MA, Barbara
National Candle Association *(717)*

Miller, Belinda
Association for Unmanned Vehicle Systems International *(261)*

Miller, Bonnie
Intersocietal Accreditation Commission *(582)*

Miller, Brad
Association of Corporate Credit Unions *(277)*

Miller, Brad
Business and Institutional Furniture Manufacturers Association International *(338)*

Miller, AP, LEED, PE, Brian
Precast/Prestressed Concrete Institute *(856)*

Miller, Brian
Type Directors Club *(983)*

Miller, Brooke
Society for Psychophysiological Research *(919)*

Miller, Bruce W.
American Society of Journalists and Authors *(201)*

Miller, Cameron
Phi Mu Alpha Sinfonia *(846)*

Miller, Carol
Lift Manufacturers Product Section - Material Handling Institute *(597)*
Loading Dock Equipment Manufacturers *(599)*
Material Handling Industry of America *(608)*
Materials Handling and Management Society *(608)*

Miller, Caroline
Association for Postal Commerce *(253)*

Miller, Carrie
National Association for Interpretation *(640)*

Miller, Charla
AACE International *(1)*

Miller, Christine
American Agriculture Movement, Inc. *(44)*

Miller, Curtis
American Farm Bureau Federation *(118)*

Miller, Cynthia
American Association of University Women *(76)*

Miller, Darlene G.
National Council for Workforce Education *(733)*

Miller, David
Society of United States Air Force Flight Surgeons *(949)*

Miller, David G.
International Academy of Compounding Pharmacists *(509)*

Miller, Debbie
American College of Forensic Psychiatry *(96)*

Miller, Deborah
Society for the Psychological Study of Lesbian and Gay Issues *(924)*

Miller, Debra
International Association of Arson Investigators *(515)*

Miller, Denise
International Sign Association *(564)*

Miller, Diane
Institute of Real Estate Management *(503)*

Miller, Dillon
International Swaps and Derivatives Association *(576)*

Miller, PE, Edward L.
American Chemical Society - Rubber Division *(90)*

Miller, Eleanor
National Rural Electric Cooperative Association *(788)*

Miller, Elisa
White House News Photographers Association *(1016)*

Miller, Elizabeth
Stage Directors and Choreographers Society *(960)*

Miller, Eric
National Association of Federal Credit Unions *(667)*

Miller, Fanny
National Association of Hispanic Publications *(672)*

Miller, Fred
Home Improvement Research Institute *(478)*

Miller, PhD, Gregory A
American Hiking Society *(131)*

Miller, MACN, PhD, Gregory D.
National Dairy Council *(741)*

Miller, Holly
The Accrediting Commission of Career Schools and Colleges *(10)*

Miller, Jane
The Knitting Guild Association *(591)*

Miller, Jeffrey
International Society of Hair Restoration Surgery *(573)*

Miller, Jeffrey T.
Treated Wood Council *(980)*

Miller, Jim
National Tractor Pullers Association **(801)**

Miller, MHA, Joan M.
Association for Healthcare Volunteer Resource Professionals **(248)**

Miller, Joby
Game Manufacturers Association **(456)**

Miller, John G.
IEEE Computer Society **(483)**

Miller, CMP, Joyce
American Society for Pain Management Nursing **(188)**

Miller, Judy
The American Society for Public Administration **(189)**

Miller, Judy M.
Graphic Arts Sales Foundation **(465)**

Miller, Jule
Academy of Pharmaceutical Research and Science **(8)**
American Pharmacists Association **(163)**

Miller, Julie
Society for Maternal-Fetal Medicine **(915)**

Miller, Julie
USENIX: The Advanced Computing Systems Association **(1005)**

Miller, Julie Simon
America's Health Insurance Plans **(28)**

Miller, Justin
Self-Insurance Institute of America, Inc. **(896)**

Miller, Katie
National Association of City and County Health Officials **(654)**

Miller, Kellsey
Delta Sigma Pi **(409)**

Miller, Kenneth
Association of Old Crows **(297)**

Miller, Kim
Association of American University Presses **(267)**

Miller, Kimberly
International Society of Hair Restoration Surgery **(573)**

Miller, Kimberly
National Board of Boiler and Pressure Vessel Inspectors **(715)**

Miller, Lee
Caucus for Producers, Writers & Directors **(346)**

Miller, Leslie
National Fluid Power Association **(751)**

Miller, Leslie D.
Manufacturers Alliance/MAPI Inc. **(603)**

Miller, CAE, Lexie
Association of Foreign Investors in U.S. Real Estate **(284)**

Miller, Lindsay
The Philanthropy Roundtable **(846)**

Miller, Lisa
Society of Nematologists **(942)**

Miller, CAE, Lois
Association for Comprehensive Energy Psychology **(242)**

Miller, Louise S.
Association of Academic Health Sciences Library **(263)**

Miller, Maggie
Intermodal Association of North America **(508)**

Miller, Mallory
Small Luxury Hotels of the World **(901)**

Miller, Maria
National Farmers Union (Farmers Educational & Co-operative Union of America) **(747)**

Miller, Marsha
Evangelical Council for Financial Accountability **(434)**

Miller, Mary
Edison Electric Institute **(419)**

Miller, Mary
Professional Association of Health Care Office Management **(859)**

Miller, Matt
Association of Independent Commercial Producers **(287)**

Miller, Matthew
Petroleum Packaging Council **(843)**

Miller, Meg
Produce Marketing Association **(858)**

Miller, Meghan
Building Service Contractors Association International **(337)**

Miller, Michael
Council of Institutional Investors **(394)**
National Community Pharmacists Association **(725)**

Miller, Michelle Parrilli
North American Association of Floor Covering Distributors **(811)**

Miller, Midori
Infrared Data Association **(496)**

Miller, Mona
Society for Neuroscience **(916)**

Miller, Nancy
National Council of Juvenile and Family Court Judges **(735)**

Miller, Patti
Canola Council of Canada **(341)**

Miller, Patty
World Waterpark Association **(1028)**

Miller, Paul
American Catalog Mailers Association **(88)**

Miller, PLC, Paul
Independent Office Products and Furniture Dealers Association **(490)**

Miller, Paul A.
Silver Users Association **(900)**

Miller, Peter L.
American Institute for CPCU - Insurance Institute of America **(136)**

Miller, Rachel
The Association for Manufacturing Excellence **(252)**

Miller, Radhika Singh
Equal Justice Works **(432)**

Miller, Rex
International Association of Conference Center Administrators **(518)**

Miller, Rich
Combat Helicopter Pilots Association **(366)**

Miller, Richard
American Institute of Certified Public Accountants **(137)**

Miller, Rob
American Association for Laboratory Accreditation **(50)**

Miller, Robert
National Fellowship of Child Care Executives **(750)**

Miller, Robert
Soil and Plant Analysis Council **(951)**

Miller, Robert H.
American Laryngological, Rhinological and Otological Society **(144)**

Miller, Roberta

American Association of Teachers of Spanish and Portuguese **(75)**

Miller, Rod
Western Writers of America **(1016)**

Miller, Rosyln
National Academies of Practice **(627)**

Miller, CAE, MBA, Sara
American Public Health Association **(171)**

Miller, Sarah "Sally"
Institute of International Bankers **(501)**

Miller, Scott
Academy of Motion Picture Arts and Sciences **(7)**

Miller, Shannon
National Association of Trailer Manufacturers **(706)**

Miller, Stephanie
Direct Marketing Association **(412)**

Miller, Steve
Trucking Management, Inc. **(981)**

Miller, CPA, Steve
American Society for Biochemistry and Molecular Biology **(181)**

Miller, Steven W.
States Organization for Boating Access **(962)**

Miller, Susan M.
Alliance for Telecommunications Industry Solutions **(23)**

Miller, Susanna
National Action Council for Minorities in Engineering (NACME) **(628)**

Miller, Teka
National Bar Association **(712)**

Miller, Teresa
Contact Lens Society of America **(382)**

Miller, Thomas A.
American Bureau of Shipping **(86)**

Miller, Tierre
Society of Toxicologic Pathologists **(948)**
Society of Toxicologic Pathology **(948)**

Miller, Tim
Allied Trades of the Baking Industry **(26)**

Miller, Tom
Associated Wire Rope Fabricators **(237)**

Miller, Tonya
Association for Vascular Access **(261)**

Miller, Troy
National Real Estate Investors Association **(784)**

Miller, Wayne
American Health Lawyers Association **(130)**

Miller, William "Bud"
American Public Gas Association **(170)**

Miller, Zandra
American Society of Landscape Architects **(201)**

Miller, Zipporah
National Science Teachers Association **(790)**

Miller Thorpe, Michelle
National Association of Railroad Trial Counsel **(689)**

Miller-Holodnicki, Madeleine
Council of Supply Chain Management Professionals **(398)**

Millett, MD, MPH, David P.
Civil Aviation Medical Association **(357)**

Millette, Marijo
Radiological Society of North America **(873)**

Milligan, ACS, FLMI, Kathy
LOMA **(600)**

Milligan, Melinda
Society for the Study of Symbolic Interaction *(925)*

Milligan, MBA, PE, PhD, Michael K. J.
Accreditation Board for Engineering and Technology Inc. *(9)*

Milligan, Renee
Association of African Studies Programs *(263)*

Milligan, Sherry
American Association for Respiratory Care *(51)*

Milliron, Matthew
Educause *(420)*

Millman, Diane
Association of Free Standing Radiation Oncology Centers *(284)*

Mills, Alex
Texas Alliance of Energy Producers *(972)*

Mills, Amy
Turkish Studies Association *(982)*

Mills, Ashley
Council on Foundations *(399)*

Mills, D.T.J
Association of Management/International Association of Management *(292)*

Mills, Joanie
Newspaper Association of America *(810)*

Mills, Kathreja A.
Jesuit Secondary Education Association *(587)*

Mills, Kevin
National Legal Aid and Defender Association *(769)*

Mills, Lee Ann
International Society for Heart and Lung Transplantation *(566)*

Mills, Megan
University Professional & Continuing Education Association *(1003)*
University Professional & Continuing Education Association *(1003)*

Mills, MBA, Penny S.
American Society of Addiction Medicine *(191)*

Mills, Stephanie
National Certification Commission for Acupuncture and Oriental Medicine *(720)*

Milman, Erik
Corrections, U.S.A. *(386)*

Milman, Mila
Copper Development Association *(384)*

Milne, David
Automotive Training Managers Council *(324)*

Milner, Debbie
Child Welfare League of America *(353)*

Milstein, Donna
Craft Retailers Association for Tomorrow *(403)*

Milthrope, Kathy
Ladies Professional Golf Association *(592)*

Milton, Bayley
The American Association of Dental Boards *(59)*

Milton, Marisa L.
HR Policy Association *(480)*

Milz, Phyllis
American Academy of Hospice and Palliative Medicine *(35)*

Mimm, David
US Travel Association *(983)*

Mimms, David
Air Force Sergeants Association *(19)*

Mims, Jo Anne

Associated Locksmiths of America *(236)*

Minami, Prof. Masahiko
Alliance of Associations of Teachers of Japanese *(24)*

Minard, Pamela
Original Equipment Suppliers Association *(833)*

Minassian, Catherine
National Association for Armenian Studies and Research *(636)*

Minchak, Gregory
Hispanic Elected Local Officials *(475)*

Minchak, Gregory N.
National League of Cities *(768)*

Minchella, Dennis J.
American Society of Parasitologists *(206)*

Minder, Jessica
American Podiatric Medical Students Association *(166)*

Miner, Alise
Specialty Equipment Market Association *(957)*

Miner, Anuja
American Butter Institute *(87)*
National Milk Producers Federation *(772)*

Miner, Daran
United States Tennis Association *(1000)*

Miner, MLS, Sherry
American Society for Clinical Laboratory Science *(182)*

Miner, Stephen
American Wind Energy Association (AWEA) *(221)*

Minetti, Conceicao A.S.A
North American Calorimetry Conference *(814)*

Minges, Sara
North American Electric Reliability Corporation *(816)*

Minhinnett, CMP, Pauline
American Society of Human Genetics *(200)*

Mininger, Wayne
National Onion Association *(776)*

Minjack, Svetlana
U.S.-Russia Business Council *(999)*

Minnen, Peter van
American Society of Papyrologists *(205)*

Minner, Thom
American Architectural Foundation *(46)*

Minnich, Chris
Council of Chief State School Officers *(392)*

Minnich, Nelson H.
American Catholic Historical Association *(88)*

Minnillo, MPA, Becky "Rebecca"
The Society for Investigative Dermatology *(913)*

Minnix, Jr., William "Larry"
International Association of Homes and Services for the Ageing *(522)*
LeadingAge (American Association of Homes and Services for the Aging) *(595)*

Mino, Courtney
AGN International North America, Inc *(15)*

Minor, Deborah
American Academy of Religion *(41)*

Minor, PhD, Robert N.
American Men's Studies Association *(150)*

Minor, Tanisha
American Association of Acupuncture and Oriental Medicine *(53)*

Minter, Khara L.
Food and Drug Law Institute *(449)*

Mintier, Robyn
Phi Delta Kappa International *(845)*

Pi Lambda Theta *(847)*

Minton, Barbara
Society of American Graphic Artists *(929)*

Mintz, Alex
International Society of Political Psychology *(573)*

Mintz, Suzanne G
National Family Caregivers Association *(747)*

Miorin, CPA, Pat
Armed Forces Communications and Electronics Association *(228)*

Mirabella, Mike
AMC Institute *(28)*

Miranda, Fausto
American College of Nurse-Midwives *(99)*

Miranda, Kathy
American Society for Histocompatibility and Immunogenetics *(185)*

Miranda, Paulo de
Inter-American Bar Association *(506)*

Mirau, Tammy
National Association of Church Business Administration *(653)*

Mirman, Marlene
Biophysical Society *(330)*

Mirmelstein, CMP, MA, Ross F.
National Sheriffs' Association *(791)*

Mirnezam, MBA, Alex
American Council on Exercise *(110)*

Mishkin, Erin
Association of Independents in Radio *(288)*

Mishler, Katie
Artist Rights Society *(230)*

Mishra, Anita
Association of Analytical Communities International *(267)*

Miskow, Rosanne
Council of Protocol Executives *(396)*

Misner, Lloyd
American Sand Association *(177)*

Misovic, Kathleen
American Society for Healthcare Risk Management *(185)*

Misra, Pradeep
IEEE Control Systems Society *(484)*

Mister, Esq., Steven M.
Council for Responsible Nutrition *(391)*

Mitch, Joe
United States Basketball Writers Association *(991)*

Mitchell, Alex
American Society for Surgery of the Hand *(189)*

Mitchell, Alicia
American Hospital Association *(133)*

Mitchell, Andrea
Substance Abuse Librarians and Information Specialists *(965)*

Mitchell, Ann
American Association for Aerosol Research *(47)*

Mitchell, Beverly
National Grange *(756)*

Mitchell, SPHR, Carla
Grocery Manufacturers Association (GMA) *(466)*

Mitchell, Jr., Debbie
Independent Sealing Distributors *(491)*

Mitchell, Debbie K.

Mitchell, Douglas *(cont'd)*
National Association of County and City Health
Officials *(659)*

Mitchell, Douglas
National Association of Health and Educational
Facilities Finance Authorities *(671)*

Mitchell, Gina
Stable Value Investment Association *(960)*

Mitchell, Greg
Writers Guild of America West *(1029)*

Mitchell, Gregory L.
Society for the Science & the Public *(924)*

Mitchell, Janice
Media Credit Association *(610)*

Mitchell, Jeff
American Dental Hygienists' Association *(114)*

Mitchell, Jennifer
National Wellness Institute, Inc. *(804)*

Mitchell, Jenny
Frozen Potato Products Institute *(454)*

Mitchell, Jere R
National Association of Animal Breeders *(647)*

Mitchell, Joette
Credit Union Executives Society *(403)*

Mitchell, BA, MSBA, John E.
American Association of Pathologists' Assistants *(68)*

Mitchell, John W.
IPC - Association Connecting Electronics Industries
(584)
IPC - Surface Mount Equipment Manufacturers
Association *(585)*
IPC Washington Office *(585)*

Mitchell, Judy
American Paint Horse Association *(161)*

Mitchell, Keith
AVS: Science and Technology of Materials, Interfaces,
and Processing *(325)*

Mitchell, Kelcey
Flight Safety Foundation *(448)*

Mitchell, Kevin
Association of Collegiate Schools of Architecture *(275)*

Mitchell, Lora
Truckload Carriers Association *(981)*

Mitchell, Margaret
National Association of Enrolled Agents *(666)*

Mitchell, Mark
Violin Society of America *(1010)*

Mitchell, Marsena
National Black Caucus of Local Elected Officials *(714)*

Mitchell, Megan
Sugar Association *(965)*

Mitchell, Melinda
Christian Medical & Dental Associations *(356)*

Mitchell, Michael
National Conference of Black Political Scientists *(727)*

Mitchell, Michelle
Council of Educational Facility Planners International
(393)

Mitchell, Nancy
American Academy of Advertising *(30)*

Mitchell, PE, Nathan
American Public Power Association *(171)*

Mitchell, Peter
International Union of Electronic, Electrical, Salaried,
Machine, and Furniture Workers-CWA *(579)*

Mitchell, Regina
Truck Writers of North America *(981)*

Mitchell, Robert B.
The Association for Research in Business Education -
Delta Pi Epsilon *(255)*

Mitchell, Ruth
American Supply Association *(214)*

Mitchell, Suzanne
National Council of Supervisors of Mathematics *(737)*

Mitchell, CAE, Trevor
ARMA International *(228)*

Mitchell, Vernetta J.
American Association for Cancer Research *(48)*

Mitchell-Grooms, Amanda
Professional Tennis Registry *(865)*

Mitchem, PhD, Dr. Arnold L.
Council for Opportunity in Education *(390)*

Mitchem, Lily A.
Art Dealers Association of America *(229)*

Miti, Zangose
American College of Clinical Pharmacy *(94)*

Mitrovic, Barb
American Society for Quality *(189)*

Mitstifer, Dorothy I.
Association of College Honor Societies *(274)*
Council for the Advancement of Standards in Higher
Education *(391)*

Mittelsteadt, Tina
National Sunflower Association *(798)*

Miyamoto, Suzanne
American Association of Colleges of Nursing *(57)*

Miyasato, Evelyn
American Press Institute *(167)*

Miyazaki, Emily
American Association of Certified Orthoptists *(56)*

Mize, MS, Mitzi
American Society for Reproductive Medicine *(189)*

Mizell, Amanda
National Association of Professional Geriatric Care
Managers *(687)*

Mizell, Jessica
Transportation Intermediaries Association *(978)*

Mizgata, Jennifer
Online News Association *(827)*

Mlutkowski, Kevin P.
American Concrete Institute *(106)*

Mlynarski, Rick
National Catholic Band Association *(718)*

Moakler, Kathleen
National Military Family Association, Inc. *(772)*

Mobley, Gail
National Ice Cream Mix Association *(761)*
National Milk Producers Federation *(772)*

Mobley, Randy A.
International League of Professional Baseball Clubs
(554)

Mobley, Sid
National Exchange Club *(747)*

Mobley, Terri
Society for Maternal-Fetal Medicine *(915)*

Mobley, CMP, Vanessa
American Academy of Hospice and Palliative Medicine
(35)
National Association for Healthcare Quality *(639)*

Mobley,, CMP, Vanessa
American Association of Neuroscience Nurses *(66)*

Mocanu, MD, Edgar
International Federation of Fertility Societies *(544)*

Mock, Barbara
American Association of Cereal Chemists International
(55)
American Phytopathological Society *(165)*
American Society of Brewing Chemists *(193)*
Controlled Release Society *(383)*
Master Brewers Association of the Americas *(607)*

Mock, Dee
Council for Elementary Science International *(389)*

Modarelli, III, Robert
National Center for Asia-Pacific Economic Cooperation
(719)

Moden, Rebecca
The Council of Landscape Architectural Registration
Boards *(395)*

Modesitt, Carol Ann
National Opera Association *(776)*

Modiano, Albert L.
U.S. Oil and Gas Association *(997)*

Modrak, Deborah
Society for Ancient Greek Philosophy *(904)*

Moebius, Wanda
Advanced Medical Technology Association (AdvaMed)
(13)

Moein, Ahmad
Iranian American Community of Northern California
(585)

Moen, Ron
Society for Academic Emergency Medicine *(903)*

Moeser, Erica
National Conference of Bar Examiners *(726)*

Moffat, Jane
Canadian-American Business Council *(341)*

Moffett, Frances
Association of Steel Distributors *(311)*

Moffett, CMP, Janis
International Association of Financial Crimes
Investigators *(521)*

Moffett, Sharon
AABB - American Association of Blood Banks *(1)*

Moffitt, Larry
World Media Association *(1027)*

Mogensen, Angie
Intermodal Association of North America *(508)*

Mogerman, Cary
American Academy of Matrimonial Lawyers *(35)*

Mohammed, PhD, Linton A.
American Society of Questioned Document Examiners
(208)

Mohan, Barry
American Meteorological Society *(151)*

Mohan, Sachin
Tree Care Industry Association *(980)*

Mohn, Frosty
National Association of Insurance Commissioners
(676)

Mohn, MD, Kimball
Association for Hospital Medical Education *(249)*

Mohney, Mary
Society for Human Resource Management *(911)*

Mohney, Ron
Independent Photo Imagers *(491)*

Mohr, JD, MBA, Mary L.
Retirement Industry Trust Association *(885)*

Mohr, Monique
Society for Physician Assistants in Pediatrics *(919)*

Mohr, Robin

National Association of Optometrists and Opticians
(683)

Mohr, Rodney
Violin Society of America *(1010)*

Mohsin, MBA, Rita H.
Federation of State Medical Boards of the United States
(442)

Molchan, Andrew
National Association of Federally Licensed Firearms
Dealers *(668)*

Molenda, Adam
Timber Products Manufacturers Association *(975)*

Molick, Christine J.
National Conference of Bankruptcy Judges *(726)*

Molina, Angelica
National Indian Gaming Association *(762)*

Molina, Chuck
The Door and Hardware Institute *(416)*

Molina, Joanna
Society of Competitive Intelligence Professionals *(933)*

Molinari, Audrey
National Association of Professional Background
Screeners *(686)*

Molinari, Cara
American Society of Clinical Oncology *(194)*

Moll, Anne Von
Electrocoat Association *(423)*

Moll, Barbara M.
National Automatic Merchandising Association *(711)*

Molle, PhD, Mary
Association of Community Health Nursing Educators
(276)

Mollet, Petra
American Public Transportation Association *(171)*

Mollo, Barbara
Government Finance Officers Association of the United
States and Canada *(464)*

Molloy, Gregory P.
National Railway Historical Society *(784)*

Molloy, Justin
Society for Environmental Graphic Design *(908)*

Molloy, Mary
Society of Illustrators *(939)*

Molnar, Amy
American College of Rheumatology *(102)*

Molnar, Shanan
Human Anatomy and Physiology Society *(480)*

Molnar, Theresa
The Fragrance Foundation *(453)*

Molyneaux, Angel
National Association for Government Training and
Development *(639)*

Molyneux, Beverly
American Association of Petroleum Geologists *(68)*

Monahan, Jan
National Concrete Burial Vault Association *(725)*

Monahan, Kevin
Public Relations Student Society of America *(870)*

Monahan, CAE, Thomas A.
National Concrete Burial Vault Association *(725)*

Monckton, Michelle M.
Catholic Press Association *(346)*

Monday, Tom
National Association of Convenience Stores *(658)*

Moneymaker, Carol A.

Accrediting Bureau of Health Education Schools *(10)*

Moneypenny, Una
National Fenestration Rating Council *(750)*

Monier, Michael Le
American Association of International Healthcare
Recruitment *(63)*

Moninghoff, Lara
Society for Neuroscience *(916)*

Monismith, Alaina
The International Stability Operations Association
(575)

Monk, Kim
United States of America Dry Pea and Lentil Council,
Inc. *(996)*

Monk, Rick
American Farmland Trust *(118)*

Monkhouse, PMP, Peter
Project Management Institute *(866)*

Monreale, Eileen
Inland Marine Underwriters Association *(496)*

Monroe, PhD, Eric G.
IMAGE Society *(486)*

Monroe, Nora
American Philosophical Society *(164)*

Monroe, Raymond W.
Steel Founders' Society of America *(962)*

Monroe, Terry
International Association of Fire Chiefs *(521)*

Monsen, Vincent
American Philosophical Association *(164)*

Monson, Barbara M.
Envelope Manufacturers Association *(430)*

Monson, Eric
Structural Building Components Association *(964)*

Montagni, Patricia
International Council of Shopping Centers *(538)*

Montague, Larry N.
Technical Association of the Pulp and Paper Industry
(970)

Montalvo, Ileana
Association of Independent Commercial Producers
(287)

Montana, Liz
American Academy of Mechanics *(35)*

Montanaro, Kristina
International Anti-Counterfeiting Coalition *(511)*

Montavy, Debbie
National Association of Parliamentarians *(683)*

Montazzoli, Mallory
Association for Experiential Education *(246)*

Monte, Brent Del
Biotechnology Industry Organization (BIO) *(330)*

Montealegre, Grace
Organization of Women in International Trade *(832)*

Monteith, Bette
International Festivals and Events Association *(545)*

Montemayor, Angel
Market Technicians Association *(606)*

Montemurro, Anthony
Federation of Environmental Technologists, Inc. *(441)*

Montesa, Esperanza
Society for Industrial Microbiology *(913)*

Monteverde, Susan J.
American Association of Port Authorities *(70)*

Montfort, Linda G.
AMT - The Association For Manufacturing Technology
(222)

Montgomery, Adryon
Association of Professors of Gynecology and Obstetrics
(302)

Montgomery, Christine
Specialized Carriers and Rigging Association *(957)*

Montgomery, Jennifer
WineAmerica *(1019)*

Montgomery, Jodi Pais
International Documentary Association *(541)*

Montgomery, Ken
Investment Program Association *(584)*

Montgomery, Megan
American Association of Exporters & Importers *(60)*

Montgomery, Michael
The Association of Concert Bands *(276)*

Montgomery, Michelle
Society for Industrial & Applied Mathematics *(912)*

Montgomery, Nada Vencl
The Association of Concert Bands *(276)*

Montgomery, Pamela "Pam"
Society for Values in Higher Education *(926)*

Montgomery, Regina
American Economic Association *(115)*

Montgomery, Sonja
American College of Emergency Physicians *(95)*

Monti, PhD, Michael J.
Association of Collegiate Schools of Architecture *(275)*

Montiel, Sherry
Electrical Generating Systems Association *(422)*

Montoya, Pilar
Society of Hispanic Professional Engineers *(938)*

Monzon, Cesar
International Association of Plumbing and Mechanical
Officials *(526)*

Moody, Barbara
American Society for Therapeutic Radiology and
Oncology *(190)*

Moody, Gretchen
American Philatelic Society *(163)*

Moody, Meisha
National Association of Drug Court Professionals *(663)*

Moody, Robert S.
Sommelier Society of America *(952)*

Moody, Sally
Society for Developmental Biology *(907)*

Moody, William J.
American Bandmasters Association *(78)*

Mook, Magda
International Coach Federation *(535)*

Moon, Lori
National Volunteer Fire Council *(803)*

Moon, Suzanne
Society for the History of Technology *(923)*

Moon, W. Jay
American Society of Missiology *(203)*

Moon, Wooil M.
Geoscience and Remote Sensing Society *(459)*

Mooney, Collin
Commercial Vehicle Safety Alliance *(367)*

Mooney, Kathleen
National Watercolor Society *(804)*

Mooney, Ted
Internet Society *(582)*

Moore, Allison
Fresh Produce Association of the Americas *(453)*

Moore, Andrew D.
National Agricultural Aviation Association *(630)*

Moore, Anne
Specialized Information Publishers Association *(957)*

Moore, Antonio
American Beverage Association *(80)*

Moore, Artesha
Association for Professionals in Infection Control and
Epidemiology *(254)*

Moore, Aubrey
International Association of Assessing Officers *(516)*

Moore, Dr. Bert
American Shorthorn Association *(179)*

Moore, CAE, MA, Bob
Institute of Food Technologists *(499)*

Moore, Bonnie
Public Affairs Council *(868)*

Moore, Carlos F. J.
American Textile Machinery Association *(216)*

Moore, Carrie Sampson
National Association for Kinesiology in Higher
Education *(640)*

Moore, Cindy
National Lipid Association *(770)*

Moore, Courtney
Forum of Regional Associations of Grantmakers *(452)*

Moore, Crystal
American Chamber of Commerce Executives *(89)*

Moore, D'Nese
IEEE Power and Energy Society *(485)*

Moore, David
Energy Security Council *(428)*

Moore, David
National Educational Broadband Services Organization
(744)

Moore, David B.
Association of American Medical Colleges *(265)*

Moore, Dawn
Institute of Scrap Recycling Industries, Inc. *(503)*

Moore, Detlef B.
American Association of Dental Editors *(60)*
International Association for Orthodontics *(513)*

Moore, Diane
Society of Marine Port Engineers *(941)*

Moore, Frank
National Association of Healthcare Access
Management *(671)*
National Lumber and Building Material Dealers
Association *(770)*

Moore, Gavin
Association of Boards of Certification *(270)*

Moore, Jackie
North American Society for the Psychology of Sport
and Physical Activity *(822)*

Moore, James E.
Institute of Industrial Engineers *(500)*

Moore, James F.
United States Golf Association *(994)*

Moore, PhD, Jan
Academy of Rehabilitative Audiology *(8)*

Moore, Jason
Women's Business Enterprise National Council *(1022)*

Moore, Jay
NALS *(625)*

Moore, Jennifer
Restaurant Facility Management Association *(884)*

Moore, Jennifer
AFCOM *(14)*

Moore, Jerry
American Society of Gas Engineers *(198)*

Moore, Joe
International Health, Racquet and Sportsclub
Association *(549)*

Moore, Joel
American Solar Energy Society *(211)*

Moore, John R.
National Police and Security Officers Association of
America *(781)*

Moore, DHD, Jon R.
Professional Housing Management Association *(862)*

Moore, PT, DPT, Justin
American Physical Therapy Association *(164)*

Moore, Karin
Wine and Spirits Wholesalers of America *(1018)*

Moore, Kathryn
National Athletic Trainers Association *(710)*

Moore, Kristy
National Association of State Boating Law
Administrators *(698)*

Moore, Kristy
Renewable Fuels Association *(881)*

Moore, Latisha
National Association of Multicultural Engineering
Program Advocates *(681)*

Moore, Melissa
Institute for Operations Research and the Management
Sciences *(497)*

Moore, Michael
International Conference of Symphony and Opera
Musicians *(537)*

Moore, Michael
North American Carbon Capture & Storage Association
(814)

Moore, Michael D.
ADSC: The International Association of Foundation
Drilling *(12)*

Moore, Mildred E.
Montadale Sheep Breeders Association *(619)*

Moore, Mindy
Ladies Professional Golf Association *(592)*

Moore, LPN, Missy
National Federation of Licensed Practical Nurses *(749)*

Moore, PhD, Nancy Gordon
American Psychological Association *(169)*

Moore, Odell J.
Chamber of Shipping of America *(351)*

Moore, Paula
Association of Catholic Colleges and Universities *(271)*

Moore, Rebecca
National Association of Congregational Christian
Churches *(657)*

Moore, Rick
National Committee for Quality Assurance *(724)*

Moore, Roni
National Automatic Merchandising Association *(711)*

Moore, CAE, Ryan J.
Non-Ferrous Founders' Society *(811)*

Moore, Sabrina

North American Meat Association *(818)*

Moore, Scott
Society for Neuroscience *(916)*

Moore, Sharlyn
National Club Association *(722)*

Moore, Sharon
Orthopaedic Trauma Association *(834)*

Moore, Sonja
American Institute of Aeronautics and Astronautics
(136)

Moore, Steve
Country Music Association *(401)*

Moore, Susie
American Association of Petroleum Geologists *(68)*

Moore, Tess
National Association of Medicaid Directors *(680)*

Moore, Tina
International Natural Sausage Casing Association *(557)*

Moore, Tom
National Ski Area Association *(791)*

Moore, CTP, Tom
National Private Truck Council *(782)*

Moore, Tracye
National Dental Hygienists' Association *(743)*

Moore, Trudi
American Beverage Association *(80)*

Moore, Virginia Rollet
Interactive Advertising Bureau *(506)*

Moore, Walter
Chlorine Chemistry Council *(354)*

Moore, Walter K.
American Chemistry Council *(90)*

Moore, William H.
Shipowners Claims Bureau, Inc. *(899)*

Moore-Adams, Melvin A.
Council of Producers & Distributors of Agrotechnology
(396)

Moore-Keish, Martha
North American Academy of Liturgy *(812)*

Moore-Merrell, Lori
International Association of Fire Fighters *(521)*

Moorhead, Joanna
National Railway Labor Conference *(784)*

Moorhead, Tracey
Care Continuum Alliance *(342)*

Mooring, John E.
National Association of Housing Information Managers
(673)

Moorman, Amy F.
Dental Trade Alliance *(410)*

Moos, BS, Martha Finch
Association of Technical Personnel in Ophthalmology
(313)

Moose, Cathy
Materials Handling and Management Society *(608)*

Mopsik, Eugene
American Society of Media Photographers *(203)*

Moquin, PhD, Barbara E.
Association for the Behavioral Sciences and Medical
Education *(259)*

Morabito, Lisa
Radiation Therapy Oncology Group *(873)*

Morahg, Gilead
National Association of Professors of Hebrew *(688)*

Morales, MEd, Alex
Precast/Prestressed Concrete Institute *(856)*

Morales, Edrick
North American Catalysis Society *(815)*

Morales, Linda
Private Label Manufacturers Association *(858)*

Morales-Caramella, Joyce
Association of Battery Recyclers *(269)*

Moran, Brian
Association of Private Sector Colleges and Universities (Career College Association) *(300)*

Moran, James David
American Antiquarian Society *(45)*

Moran, Lena
International Foundation for Telemetering *(547)*

Moran, III, Martine O.
Catholic Campus Ministry Association *(345)*

Moran, Mary
Association of Women Surgeons *(317)*
Independent Medical Distributors Association *(490)*

Moran, PhD, SPHR, Mary Jo
National Association of Church Personnel Administrators *(653)*

Moran, Medina
Waterways Council, Inc. *(1014)*

Moran, Neil
International Dairy Foods Association *(539)*

Moran, Patti J.
Pet Sitters International *(843)*

Moran, Peter J.
Society of American Florists *(928)*

Moran, Robert
Flexographic Technical Association *(447)*

Moran, Sally
International Society for Magnetic Resonance in Medicine *(567)*

Moran, CMP, Tina M.
American Orthotic and Prosthetic Association *(159)*

Moran, Tom
International Foodservice Distributors Association *(546)*

Morano, Linda
American Mental Health Counselors Association *(151)*

Morano, Tom
American Financial Services Association *(121)*

Moravec, COL Joseph
Senior Army Reserve Commanders Association *(897)*

Mordell, Scott
YPO-WPO *(1030)*

Mordhorst, Klaus C.J.
Society of Maritime Arbitrators *(941)*

More, John "Chip"
United States Lifesaving Association *(996)*

Morelli, Genevieve
Independent Telephone and Telecommunications Alliance *(492)*

Morelli, Joe
American Legend Cooperative *(145)*

Moreno, Antonio
American Pediatric Society *(162)*
Society for Pediatric Research *(918)*

Moreno, Laura
American Foundry Society *(123)*

Moreno, Marianella
Percussive Arts Society *(841)*

Moreton, Leonard J.
Modern Language Association *(618)*

Morgan, Allison Conway
Grocery Manufacturers Association (GMA) *(466)*

Morgan, Ann
Marketing Research Association *(606)*

Morgan, Becky
Bank Insurance and Securities Association *(326)*

Morgan, BS, MBA, Ben
National Cottonseed Products Association *(731)*

Morgan, Carolyn
PKF North American Network *(849)*

Morgan, Cheryl
Pine Chemicals Association *(848)*

Morgan, Clark
National Lipid Association *(770)*

Morgan, Crystal
Alliance for Children and Families *(22)*

Morgan, Diane
Tree Care Industry Association *(980)*

Morgan, Donna M.
American Board of Physical Medicine and Rehabilitation *(83)*

Morgan, Elaina
Malignant Hyperthermia Association of the United States *(602)*

Morgan, Fiona
Express Carriers Association *(436)*

Morgan, Fiona J.
Air and Expedited Motor Carriers Association *(17)*

Morgan, Harold
Taxicab, Limousine & Paratransit Association *(969)*

Morgan, James
Professional Association of Diving Instructors *(859)*

Morgan, Jeffrey D.
National Investor Relations Institute *(767)*

Morgan, John
Association of Coupon Professionals *(277)*

Morgan, Karynne Chong
International Marine Minerals Society *(555)*

Morgan, Katrinka
Herb Society of America *(474)*

Morgan, Kevin
American Football Coaches Association *(122)*

Morgan, Kristina
International Federation of Professional and Technical Engineers *(544)*

Morgan, Madelaine
American Gear Manufacturers Association *(125)*

Morgan, Mark S.
Petroleum Transportation and Storage Association *(844)*

Morgan, Russell
American Society of Agricultural Consultants *(191)*

Morgan, Sandy
Educational Theatre Association *(420)*

Morgan, Scott
Professional Photographers of America *(863)*

Morgan, Staci
Regional Airline Association *(878)*

Morgan, PhD, Stephanie S.
Alarm Industry Communication Committee *(21)*

Morgan, Stephanie S.
Central Station Alarm Association *(349)*

Morgan, Susan
National Association of Mutual Insurance Companies *(681)*

Morgan, Tammy
Consumer Bankers Association *(380)*

Morgan, Taryn
Renewable Fuels Association *(881)*

Morgenstern, Lanie
Cruise Lines International Association *(405)*

Moriarty, Fred
Unfinished Furniture Association *(984)*

Morillo, Ursula
Rabbinical Assembly *(872)*

Morin, Ted
The Association of Theatre Movement Educators *(314)*

Morishita, Dr. Teresa
American Association of Zoo Veterinarians *(77)*

Morisseau, Stephen B.
Gemological Institute of America *(457)*

Mork, Grodon R.
Committee on History in the Classroom *(368)*

Mork, Jamie
Local Media Association *(599)*

Mork, Stan
Information Technology Alliance *(495)*

Morley, Fran
Association of Personal Historians *(299)*

Morman, Suzette
Society for Environmental Geochemistry and Health *(908)*

Mormile, Eugenia
Contact Lens Society of America *(382)*

Morozzi, James
Gridwise Alliance *(466)*

Morr, Thomas G.
CEO Council for Growth *(349)*

Morrell, Mike
Standards Engineering Society *(961)*

Morri, Rachelle
Diving Equipment and Marketing Association *(415)*

Morris, Alan R.
American Institute of Certified Public Accountants *(137)*

Morris, Bill
American Teleservices Association *(215)*

Morris, Cara
United States Lacrosse *(995)*

Morris, Charlie
Pine Chemicals Association *(848)*

Morris, Christa
National Reining Horse Association *(785)*

Morris, Dan
Retail, Wholesale and Department Store Union *(885)*

Morris, David
Sculptors Guild *(894)*

Morris, David W.
Defense Orientation Conference Association *(408)*

Morris, Deborah W.
National Concrete Masonry Association *(725)*

Morris, Dianne
Book Manufacturers' Institute *(333)*

Morris, Eboni
Hemophilia Federation of America *(474)*

Morris, Elizabeth

Tag and Label Manufacturers Institute *(968)*

Morris, Emily
American Health Lawyers Association *(130)*

Morris, Jackki
International Microelectronics and Packaging Society -
IMAPS *(556)*

Morris, Jeff
American Association of Physician Specialists *(69)*

Morris, Jennifer W.
Public Risk Management Association *(870)*

Morris, John "Scooter"
Special Interest Group for Computer-Human
Interaction *(954)*

Morris, Katy
National Council of State Agencies for the Blind *(736)*

Morris, Kevin
Competitive Telecommunications Association *(371)*

Morris, Kevin
National Turfgrass Federation *(802)*

Morris, Margretta "Meg"
National Recycling Coalition *(784)*

Morris, Mary
College Savings Foundation *(364)*

Morris, Mike
American Philosophical Association *(164)*

Morris, Mitchell
International Association of Plumbing and Mechanical
Officials *(526)*

Morris, Randy
National Business Incubation Association *(717)*

Morris, Rick
Consumer Aerosol Products Council *(380)*

Morris, Robert C.
Society of Professors of Education *(945)*

Morris, Roger
National Insurance Crime Bureau *(766)*

Morris, Sharon R.
Railway Systems Suppliers, Inc *(874)*

Morris, Skip
International League of Electrical Associations *(553)*

Morris, Susan
American Medical Rehabilitation Providers Association
(149)

Morris, Taylor A.
American Land Title Association *(144)*

Morris, III, Walter L.
Parenteral Drug Association *(838)*

Morris, Wayne
Association of Home Appliance Manufacturers *(287)*

Morris-Stilwell, Kathy
International Veterinary Academy of Pain Management
(580)

Morrison, CAE, IOM, Barbara
International Association of Oral and Maxillofacial
Surgeons *(525)*

Morrison, Colleen
NACHA - The Electronic Payments Association *(623)*

Morrison, James
American College of Radiology *(102)*

Morrison, Jeff M.
Substance Abuse Program Administrators Association
(965)

Morrison, MD, Jeffrey
American College for Advancement in Medicine *(93)*

Morrison, Linda

Society for the Study of Symbolic Interaction *(925)*

Morrison, Madeline
Council of Chief State School Officers *(392)*

Morrison, Marvin
International Council of Shopping Centers *(538)*

Morrison, Megan
Building Service Contractors Association International
(337)

Morrison, Meghan
National Association of Energy Service Companies
(665)

Morrison, Ric
Wood Moulding and Millwork Producers Association
(1024)

Morrison, Robert
National Association of State Alcohol and Drug Abuse
Directors (NASADAD) *(697)*

Morrison, Tom
Metal Treating Institute *(614)*

Morrison, Virginia
Society for Photographic Education *(919)*

Morrison, William
Association of Boards of Certification *(270)*

Morriss, Robyn L.
Reinsurance Association of America *(879)*

Morrissey, Bob
National Watermelon Association *(804)*

Morrissey, Michael J.
International Insurance Society *(552)*

Morrow, Diane
CBA *(346)*

Morrow, Hugh
International Cadmium Association *(532)*

Morrow, James R.
Intermodal Association of North America *(508)*

Morrow, Leigh
Potato Association of America *(854)*

Morrow, Michael
Society of Surgical Oncology *(947)*

Morrow, Tara C.
National Religious Campaign Against Torture *(786)*

Morrow, Thomas
National Association of Managed Care Physicians
(679)

Morrow, Tom
Semiconductor Equipment and Materials International
(896)

Morrow, Wade
CALLERLAB - International Association of Square
Dance Callers *(341)*

Morse, Cristina
International Masonry Institute *(556)*

Morse, Jesse
NCSL International *(808)*

Morse, Stephen
American Academy of Optometry *(37)*

Mortan, Simone
International Museum Theatre Alliance *(557)*

Mortensen, Amber
American Association of Cosmetology Schools *(59)*

Mortenson, Deb
National Wildlife Rehabilitators Association *(805)*

Mortenson, Gary
International Trumpet Guild *(578)*

Morton, CAE, Cynthia

National Association for the Support of Long Term
Care *(644)*

Morton, Susan E.
American Society of Questioned Document Examiners
(208)

Moscato, Cathie
Society of American Registered Architects *(929)*

Moscicki, Eve
American Psychiatric Association *(168)*

Moseley, Karen
Care Continuum Alliance *(342)*

Moseley-Bennett, Meredith
Professional Lighting and Sound Association *(863)*

Moser, Brenda
National Affordable Housing Management Association
(629)

Moser, Charles
National Association of Postmasters of the United
States *(685)*

Moses, Bob
Audio Engineering Society *(320)*

Moses, Ellery
Home Fashion Products Association *(478)*

Moses, Ginnah
American Highland Cattle Association *(131)*

Moses, Kim
Envelope Manufacturers Association *(430)*

Moses, Max G.
American Academy of Implant Dentistry *(35)*

Moses, Monica
American Craft Council *(111)*

Moses, Dr. Napoleon
National Association for Equal Opportunity in Higher
Education *(638)*

Moses, Thomas M.
Gemological Institute of America *(457)*

Moses, Timothy
American Academy of Dermatology *(32)*

Mosher-Williams, Rachel
Council on Foundations *(399)*

Mosier, Terry
ASM International *(232)*

Moskos, Rini
United States Trotting Association *(1000)*

Moskowitz, Kenneth
Practising Law Institute *(855)*

Moskowitz, Rich
American Fuel & Petrochemical Manufacturers *(124)*

Mosley, Audrey Byrd
National Research Council *(786)*

Mosley, Erin Smith
National Humanities Alliance *(761)*

Mosley, Janel
American College of Clinical Pharmacy *(94)*

Mosman, Jim
National Council on Teacher Retirement *(740)*

Moss, Anne Marie
Oregon Farm Bureau Federation *(830)*

Moss, Dan
Manufacturers Elevating and Work Platform Council
(603)

Moss, Debra A.
International Franchise Association *(547)*

Moss, Donna
Produce Marketing Association *(858)*

Moss, PHR, Donna
National Council of Examiners for Engineering and Surveying *(734)*

Moss, Hazel E.
National Alliance for Hispanic Health *(631)*

Moss, Jennifer Sheridan
American Society of Papyrologists *(205)*

Mossaidis, Basil
American Hellenic Educational Progressive Association (AHEPA) *(130)*

Mosser, Amy
Health Forum *(469)*

Mossman, MD, Douglass
American Academy of Psychiatry and the Law *(41)*

Mosteller, Donna
Gift Associates Interchange Network *(460)*

Mostrom, Michelle S.
American Academy of Veterinary and Comparative Toxicology *(42)*

Motanic, Don
Intertribal Timber Council *(583)*

Moten, Beth
American Federation of Government Employees *(119)*

Moter, Polly
Lawn and Garden Dealers' Association *(594)*

Motley, III, John J.
North American Perishable Agricultural Receivers *(819)*

Motola, Jeanne
Drug, Chemical and Associated Technologies Association *(417)*

Mott, Sophy
American Association of Family and Consumer Sciences *(61)*

Motter, Robbie
American Seminar Leaders Association *(178)*

Mottley, Tanya Hodge
Executive Women in Government *(435)*

Motyka, Konrad
FBI Agents Association *(438)*

Moulden, Yolanda Y.
American Academy of Environmental Engineers *(33)*

Moulton, Candy
Western Writers of America *(1016)*

Moulton, Jack
American Association of Legal Nurse Consultants *(64)*

Moulton, Jennifer
American Wholesale Marketers Association *(221)*

Mounce, Dave
Concrete Reinforcing Steel Institute *(374)*

Mount, Michele
General Federation of Women's Clubs *(458)*

Mount, Mike
Distributive Education Clubs of America (DECA) *(415)*
Motorcycle Industry Council, Inc. *(620)*

Mountford, Mardi K.
International Formula Council *(547)*

Mountjoy, E. Leo
The North American Rail Shippers Association *(820)*

Mounts, Keith
American Society for Engineering Education *(183)*

Mourad, Teresa
Ecological Society of America *(418)*

Moustis, Linda
Emergency Nurses Association *(425)*

Mouzount, Maryam

Conference of State Bank Supervisors *(376)*

Mower-Payne, Julie
Refrigerating Engineers and Technicians Association *(878)*

Moxley, Jr., Charles J.
Lawyers Committee on Nuclear Policy *(594)*

Moxley, Fred
American College of Oral and Maxillofacial Surgeons *(99)*

Moye, Chantay Parks
American Society of Transplant Surgeons *(210)*

Moye, Dorothy
Surface Design Association *(966)*

Moyer, Ann E.
The Renaissance Society of America *(881)*

Moyer, Bruce
National Association of Postal Supervisors *(685)*

Moyer, Bruce L.
Federal Bar Association *(438)*
National Association of Assistant United States Attorneys *(647)*

Moyer, Chrissi
Automotive Recyclers Association *(323)*

Moyer, RN, MS, Diane
Health Care Education Association *(469)*

Moyer, Glen
Balloon Federation of America *(325)*

Moyer, Mike
National Wrestling Coaches Association *(806)*

Moylan, Dan
NAMM - The International Music Products Association *(625)*

Mpunga, Susan
Association of Women's Business Centers *(318)*

Mroczka, Victor S.
Customs and International Trade Bar Association *(406)*

Mrosko, Cathy
National Systems Contractors Association *(798)*

Mucci, Karen
American Probation and Parole Association *(167)*

Muck, Larry
American Association of Private Lenders *(71)*

Muck, Leslie
Chemical Coaters Association International *(351)*

Muckian, Mike
World Council of Credit Unions, Inc. *(1026)*

Muehlbauer, Charles
Marble Institute of America *(604)*

Muehlbauer, CAE, Eric
National Association of Spine Specialists *(696)*

Muehlbauer, CAE, Eric J.
North American Spine Society *(822)*

Muehrcke, Jill
Society for Nonprofit Organizations *(917)*

Mueller, Dawn
Association of College and Research Libraries *(273)*

Mueller, Jessica
The International Stability Operations Association *(575)*

Mueller, Lorin
Federation of State Boards of Physical Therapy *(442)*

Mueller, Mary
National League of Postmasters of the United States *(768)*

Mueller, Michael

Society of American Fight Directors *(928)*

Mueller, CMP, Rhonda E.
Catholic Health Association of the United States *(345)*

Mueller, Shannon
American Society of Ophthalmic Administrators *(205)*

Muench, Lynn M.
American Waterways Operators *(220)*

Muffoletto, Jessica
Foodservice Sales & Marketing Association *(450)*

Muha, Denise B.
National Leased Housing Association *(769)*

Muirheid, Sara
Professional Rodeo Cowboys Association *(864)*

Mula, Renee M.
Employee Services Management Association *(426)*

Mulcahy, Charles F.
Sheet Metal Workers' International Association *(898)*

Mulcahy, Geri
American Medical Technologists *(150)*

Mulcahy, Tammy
Point of Purchase Advertising Institute *(851)*

Mulder, Gary
Protestant Church-Owned Publishers Association *(868)*

Mulder, Kristie
InterNational Electrical Testing Association *(542)*

Mulder, Stephannie
Historians of Islamic Art Association *(476)*

Muleta, Kenatu
Family, Career and Community Leaders of America *(437)*

Mulgrew, Michael
United Federation of Teachers *(987)*

Mullally, Sonia
National Sunflower Association *(798)*

Mullaly, Cynthia A.
Restoration Industry Association *(884)*

Mullan, Kathryn
American Resort Development Association *(175)*

Mullaney, Helen M.
National Finance Adjusters *(750)*

Mullen, Bruce
National Fire Protection Association *(751)*

Mullen, Mark
International Reading Association *(562)*

Mullen, Michael C.
Express Association of America *(436)*

Mullen, Shawna
Society of Experimental Test Pilots *(935)*

Mullender, Pam
Women's Transportation Seminar (WTS International) *(1024)*

Mullenix, Steve
National Council for Prescription Drug Programs *(732)*

Mullennix, Berry
Domestic Energy Producers Alliance *(415)*

Muller, J. Gisele
Society of Laparoendoscopic Surgeons *(940)*

Muller, Joyce
National Association of Independent Review Organizations *(624)*

Mullhausen, Vince
Council of State Restaurant Associations *(397)*
Fire Suppression Systems Association *(446)*

Mulligan, CAE, Clark

Laboratory Products Association **(592)**
Optical Imaging Association **(829)**

Mulligan, Sam
Professional Bowlers Association **(861)**

Mullin, Matthew
International Economic Development Council **(541)**

Mulliner, Sandra
National Association of Service Providers in Private
Rehabilitation **(695)**

Mullings, Lisa J.
National Association of Truck Stop Operators(NATSO)
(707)

Mullins, Christine
Instructional Technology Council **(504)**

Mullins, Margaret
Women's Transportation Seminar (WTS International)
(1024)

Mullins, Whitney
Delta Omicron **(409)**

Mulloy-Bonn, Nancy
American Law Institute **(144)**

Mulvaney, Kevin
Vinyl Institute **(1009)**

Mulvaney, Richard E.
National Trooper's Coalition **(802)**

Mulvihill, Jason
Private Equity Growth Capital Council **(858)**

Mulvihill, Jason
United States Aquaculture Suppliers Association **(990)**

Mulvihill, Patrick
Higher Education Consortium for Urban Affairs **(475)**

Mumey, Brendan
Special Interest Group for Algorithm and Computation
Theory **(954)**

Muncaster, Alice L.
The Counselors of Real Estate **(401)**

Muncy, Jacque
Association of American Indian Physicians **(265)**

Muncy, Janet
Forestry Conservation Communications Association
(452)

Muncy, CAE, Steve A.
American Fire Sprinkler Association **(121)**

Munday, Donna
IGAF Polaris **(486)**

Mundell, George
National Private Truck Council **(782)**

Mundhenke, Rachel
International Association of Fairs and Expositions
(521)

Mundschenk, Chris
Building Service Contractors Association International
(337)
Wallcovering Association **(1012)**

Mundt, Cassie
Paleontological Research Institution **(837)**

Mundt, Megan
Defense Credit Union Council **(408)**

Mundy, Ray
Airport Ground Transportation Association **(21)**

Mundy, Sandra
Airport Ground Transportation Association **(21)**

Muniak, Chuck
System Safety Society **(967)**

Munisteri, Rick

NAMTA - National Art Materials Trade Association
(635)

Muniz, Alexander
Association for Radiological and Imaging Nursing **(255)**

Munk, Laurie
AABB - American Association of Blood Banks **(1)**

Munke, Peggy
Association of Baccalaureate Social Work Program
Directors **(269)**

Munley, Laura
National Academy of Elder Law Attorneys, Inc. **(627)**

Munoz, Raul
Society of Mexican American Engineers and Scientists
(941)

Munro, John
American Concrete Pressure Pipe Association **(106)**

Munro, Stuart
American Association of Chairs of Departments of
Psychiatry **(56)**

Munroe, Debbie J.
Council for Art Education **(389)**
The Arts and Creative Materials Institute, Inc. **(229)**

Munroe, Jamie
National Lawyers Guild **(768)**

Munroe, Tara
National Association for Business Economics **(636)**

Munson, Anne
Association for Institutional Research **(250)**

Munson, MEd, Anne P.
National Association of College Auxiliary Services
(655)

Munster, Aileen Dullaghan
National Grocers Association **(756)**

Muntean, Helen
International Association of Plastics Distributors **(526)**

Munyon, James
AIB International **(17)**

Murakami, Angela
National Association of Veterans Research and
Education Foundations **(708)**

Murakawa, Haru
Association for Transpersonal Psychology **(260)**

Murat, Chantelle
Accreditation Board for Engineering and Technology
Inc. **(9)**

Muratore, Chris
International Society for Pharmaceutical Engineering
(567)

Muratore, Robert
Ultrasonic Industry Association **(983)**

Murdoch, Jay
Efficiency First **(421)**

Murdock, Amber
Retail Solutions Providers Association **(885)**

Murdock, Deborah L.
National Network of Estate Planning Attorneys **(775)**

Murdock, Susan
American Association of Independent Claims
Professionals **(63)**

Murdock, Susan
Kidney Care Partners **(591)**

Murgueitio, Bruce
Society of Tribologists and Lubrication Engineers **(949)**

Murin, Christopher
American Supply Association **(214)**

Murman, Deborah Rothstein

National Basketball Players Association **(713)**

Murnane, Jr., Robert
National Conference on Weights and Measures **(729)**

Murner, Doreen
National Association of Educational Procurement, Inc.
(664)

Murno, Jonathan R.
EMTA - Trade Association for the Emerging Markets
(427)

Murphrey, Theresa
Association for International Agricultural and
Extension Education **(250)**

Murphy, Anne
Association of Professors of Gynecology and Obstetrics
(302)

Murphy, Ashley
National Intramural-Recreational Sports Association
(766)

Murphy, Barbara
Association for Technology in Music Instruction **(257)**

Murphy, Calvin
The American Association of Radon Scientists and
Technologists **(72)**

Murphy, Christopher
NAFSA: Association of International Educators **(624)**

Murphy, Christopher M.
American Academy of Wound Management **(42)**
International Claim Association **(535)**
National Mitigation Banking Association **(773)**

Murphy, Debra
Association for Medical Imaging Management **(252)**

Murphy, Dennis
Electric Power Research Institute **(421)**

Murphy, Eileen
Fleet Reserve Association **(447)**

Murphy, Ellie
Vibration Institute **(1008)**

Murphy, Emmett
National Pawnbrokers Association **(779)**

Murphy, BS, DDS, Gerald J.
American Academy of Craniofacial Pain **(32)**

Murphy, James A.
Glove Shippers Association **(463)**

Murphy, Jessica Russell
Coalition for Juvenile Justice **(360)**

Murphy, Jill
Association of Government Accountants **(286)**

Murphy, Jim
National Fire Sprinkler Association **(751)**

Murphy, John C.
National Association of County Community and
Economic Development **(637)**
National Association of Local Housing Finance
Agencies **(678)**

Murphy, Kathy
Women's Foodservice Forum **(1023)**

Murphy, Kelly
Regional Airline Association **(878)**

Murphy, Kevin
POPAI The Global Association for Marketing at Retail
(852)
Security Industry Association **(895)**

Murphy, Kimberly
National Customs Brokers and Forwarders Association
of America **(741)**

Murphy, Lisa
National Tile Contractors Association **(800)**

Murphy, Lynn

Association for Healthcare Philanthropy *(248)*

Murphy, Marie
HR Policy Association *(480)*

Murphy, Maureen
American Association for Women in Community Colleges *(53)*

Murphy, CMP, Maureen
Federation of American Societies for Experimental Biology *(440)*

Murphy, Megan
National Coalition of Girls' Schools *(723)*

Murphy, Megan
American Statistical Association *(213)*

Murphy, Patrick
International Laser Display Association *(553)*

Murphy, Patrick
National Association of Elementary School Principals *(664)*

Murphy, Peggy
American Automotive Policy Council *(78)*

Murphy, MS, Penny
American Congress of Obstetricians and Gynecologists *(107)*

Murphy, Peter
Association of the United States Army *(313)*

Murphy, Priscilla
Chi Eta Phi Sorority, Inc. *(352)*

Murphy, Ryan
Radio Television Digital News Association *(873)*

Murphy, Sarah
Association of Professional Researchers for Advancement *(302)*

Murphy, Scott
ASTM International *(319)*

Murphy, Shannon
Electronic Security Association *(424)*

Murphy, Stephanie
Air Conditioning, Heating and Refrigeration Institute (AHRI) *(18)*

Murphy, Steve
Cottage Industry Miniaturists Trade Association *(387)*

Murphy, Sue
National Human Resources Association *(761)*

Murphy, Tim
Association for Community Affiliated Plans *(242)*

Murphy, Tom
National Association for Home Care and Hospice *(639)*

Murphy, Yvette
Association for Childhood Education International *(241)*

Murphy, Zell
Cable & Telecommunications Association for Marketing *(340)*

Murphy Peck, Chris
National Association of Medical Staff Services *(645)*

Murphy-Love, CAE, Dana J.
The National Federation of Paralegal Associations, Inc. *(749)*

Murrain, Noel V.S.
National Alliance of Postal and Federal Employees *(633)*

Murray, Bette
National Pork Producers Association *(781)*

Murray, Candace
International Association for Identification *(513)*

Murray, Carole

American Society of Association Executives-The Center for Association Leadership *(193)*

Murray, Charlotte
Phi Beta Fraternity *(845)*

Murray, Chip
National Alliance of Forest Owners *(632)*

Murray, Deb
UniForum Association *(984)*

Murray, Donald
National Association of County Civil Attorneys *(659)*

Murray, Jackie
Book Manufacturers' Institute *(333)*

Murray, Jane
Thoroughbred Racing Associations of North America *(974)*

Murray, Jo Ann
American Board of Trial Advocates *(84)*

Murray, Karen
International Association for Human Resource Information Management *(512)*

Murray, Kimberly
National Football League Players Association *(752)*

Murray, Marc L.
The Wire Association International, Inc. *(1019)*

Murray, Margaret A.
Association for Community Affiliated Plans *(242)*

Murray, Marrilyn
National Luggage Dealers Association *(770)*

Murray, Molly
Independent Office Products and Furniture Dealers Association *(490)*

Murray, Ottis
Association for Humanist Sociology *(249)*

Murray, Patrick D.
Coastal Conservation Association *(361)*

Murray, Penny
Schools Interoperability Framework Association *(892)*

Murray, Rebecca M.
Academy of General Dentistry *(5)*

Murray, Roxanne
Association of American Universities *(266)*

Murray, Sarah
Association for Medical Imaging Management *(252)*

Murray, Tara
American Philatelic Society *(163)*

Murray, Lt. Gov. Tim
Democratic Lieutenant Governors' Association (DLGA) *(410)*

Murray, DDS, William
The Public Relations Society of America *(870)*

Murrell, Debra
National American Legion Press Association *(634)*

Murtaugh, Courtney
North American Academy of Liturgy *(812)*

Murton, Susan "Suzy"
Association of Otolaryngology Administrators *(297)*

Musacchio, Robert A.
American Medical Association *(148)*

Musante, Susan
American Institute of Biological Sciences *(137)*

Musheno, Kim E.
Association of University Centers on Disabilities (AUCD) *(315)*

Musick, Marjorie

National Association of Public Insurance Adjusters *(689)*

Muskett, Nancy
Society of Independent Gasoline Marketers of America (SIGMA) *(939)*

Muskin, Alies
Anxiety Disorders Association of America *(224)*

Musso, CAE, RSBA, John D.
Association of School Business Officials International *(306)*

Mustafa, Suela
International Studies Association *(576)*

Mustard, Todd R.
TAUC - The Association of Union Constructors *(968)*

Mustello, Randi
International Trademark Association *(577)*

Muth, Barbara
American Society for Therapeutic Radiology and Oncology *(190)*

Muth, Michael
National Trooper's Coalition *(802)*

Mutnik, Gail E.
American Association for Clinical Chemistry, Inc. *(48)*

Mutrux, Eric P.
American Association of Orthodontists *(67)*

Mutter, Reginald
Bulk Carrier Conference *(338)*

Myatt, Leslie
Society for Gynecologic Investigation *(910)*

Mycka, Mary
Stadium Managers Association *(960)*

Mydland, Kimberly
Radiology Business Management Association *(874)*

Myers, April
National League of American Pen Women *(768)*

Myers, Arthur J.
International Military Community Executives Association *(556)*

Myers, David
American Institutes for Research *(141)*

Myers, Dawn
National Rural Water Association *(788)*

Myers, Diana
WTA Tour, Inc. *(1029)*

Myers, Heather
National Association of Sewer Service Companies *(695)*

Myers, Jim
American Industrial Hygiene Association *(135)*

Myers, Kathryn
American Association for Paralegal Education *(50)*

Myers, Kirt
National Association of Exclusive Buyer Agents *(666)*

Myers, Lisa
American Anthropological Association *(45)*

Myers, Mary Kate
Association for Research on Nonprofit Organizations and Voluntary Action *(255)*

Myers, Meredith
United States Potato Board *(997)*

Myers, Molly M.
National Venture Capital Association *(803)*

Myers, Patty
Association of Food and Drug Officials *(283)*

Myers, Paul
Healthcare Billing and Management Association *(470)*

Myers, Pierce
Parcel Shippers Association *(838)*

Myers, Randy
Patent Office Professional Association *(839)*

Myers, Sara
National Adult Day Service Association *(629)*

Myers, Shannon
National Association of Collegiate Women Athletic Administrators *(656)*

Myers, Stephen
College of American Pathologists *(363)*

Myers, Theresa
National Association for the Education of Young Children *(644)*

Myers, CAE, Tina M.
Society for Marketing Professional Services *(914)*

Myers, Tony
American Association of Psychiatric Technicians *(71)*

Myers, Vickie
National Watercolor Society *(804)*

Myers, Vickie Rideout
American Sugar Alliance *(214)*

Myers, Vivian
National Foreign Trade Council, Inc. *(752)*

Myers, William
RCI, Inc. *(875)*

Myers-Carpenter, Lori
National Association of Housing and Redevelopment Officials *(673)*

Myler, Paul
PMCA: An International Association of Confectioners *(851)*

Mylin, Wayne
American Organization for Bodywork Therapies of Asia *(158)*

Mynatt, Daniel S.
National Association of Baptist Professors of Religion *(648)*

Myrick, Angela
Common - A Users Group *(369)*

Myrick, Prof. Michael L.
Coblentz Society *(361)*

Myroniak, Tom
Specialty Equipment Market Association *(957)*

Mzamo, Brenda
Board of Registered Polysomnographic Technologists *(333)*

Naas, Gail
International Association for Colon Hydrotherapy *(511)*

Naasz, Kraig R.
American Frozen Food Institute *(124)*
Frozen Potato Products Institute *(454)*
International Frozen Food Association *(547)*
National Yogurt Association *(806)*

Naber, Tom
National Association of Electrical Distributors *(664)*

Nabi, Sabina
Internet Society *(582)*

Nabors, Lyn O'Brien
International Food Additives Council *(546)*

Nacarato, Kara
International Hearing Society *(549)*

Nacario, Julio
National Correctional Industries Association *(730)*

Naccarato, F. Anthony
American Maritime Officers Service *(147)*

Nachlas, Dr. J. A.
Society of Reliability Engineers *(946)*

Nachlis, Gayle
Women in Film *(1021)*

Nachtway, Brenda
Direct Care Alliance *(412)*

Nadeau, Elizabeth A.
International Union of Operating Engineers *(579)*

Nader, Cecelia M.
National Association of Colleges and Employers *(655)*

Nader, Larry
Society for Industrial and Organizational Psychology Inc. *(912)*

Nadler, Kirsten
Society for Academic Emergency Medicine *(903)*

Nadler, Molly
The American Association of Dental Boards *(59)*

Naegele, Ray
Medical Library Association *(611)*

Naegelin, Sara
Society for Environmental Graphic Design *(908)*

Naftel, MD, A. Jack
Society of Professors of Child and Adolescent Psychiatry *(945)*

Nagel, Donna
Missouri Fox Trotting Horse Breed Association *(617)*

Nagem, Tammy Covington
High Point Market *(474)*

Naglak, Gigi
Chemical Heritage Foundation *(351)*

Nagle, Kurt J.
American Association of Port Authorities *(70)*

Nagle, Richard
National Cargo Bureau *(718)*

Nagle, Teri
American Association of Port Authorities *(70)*

Nagorsky, Esq., Edward S.
National Kitchen and Bath Association *(767)*

Nahin, Linda
American Gas Association *(124)*

Nail, Leanna
American Feed Industry Association *(120)*

Naiman, Jeanette
Association of Military Surgeons of the United States *(294)*

Naismith, Sylvia
Cosmetic Executive Women *(387)*

Najduch, Jennifer
The Association for Library Service to Children *(251)*

Nakama, Sharon
Pacific Telecommunications Council *(836)*

Nakatani, MD, PhD, Takeshi
International Federation for Artificial Organs *(544)*

Nakon, Sara
PSIA-AASI *(868)*

Namazi, Jennifer
National Association of Stock Plan Professionals *(703)*

Namenek, Amanda
National Tooling and Machining Association *(800)*

Nammo, David
Christian Legal Society *(356)*

Nance, Jeff
Academy of Model Aeronautics *(7)*

Nance, Mary A.

North American Menopause Society *(818)*

Nance, Reggie
Public Affairs Council *(868)*

Nania, Roseanna
Warehousing Education and Research Council *(1012)*

Nanof, Jillian
Association for Medical Imaging Management *(252)*

Nanof, Tim
American Occupational Therapy Association, Inc. *(157)*

Nanou, Chryssie
International Computer Music Association *(536)*

Napelenok, Yuriy
American Institute of Architecture Students *(137)*

Napier, CAE, Bennett E.
National Association of Dental Laboratories *(662)*

Nappi, Ralph J.
NPES, The Association for Suppliers of Printing, Publishing, and Converting Technologies *(824)*

Nappier, Sherry A.
American Association of Orthodontists *(67)*

Naranjo, Erica
American Association of Cardiovascular and Pulmonary Rehabilitation *(55)*

Narcisso, Deborah
Association of Universities for Research in Astronomy, Inc. *(315)*

Nardone, CMP, Natalie
American Salvage Pool Association *(177)*

Narducci, Mike
Object Management Group *(825)*

Narr, Tony
Police Executive Research Forum *(852)*

Narug, Scott
North American Association of Floor Covering Distributors *(811)*

Narva, James
National Association of State Fire Marshals *(701)*

Naser, Cristeena G.
American Bankers Association Securities Association (ABASA) *(79)*

Naser, Deborah
American Board of Quality Assurance and Utilization Review Physicians, Inc. *(84)*

Nash, MBA, MD, David B.
American College of Medical Quality *(97)*

Nash, CMP, Heather
American College of Chest Physicians *(94)*

Nash, Marlo
Voices for America's Children *(1011)*

Nash, R. Scott
National Association of Baptist Professors of Religion *(648)*

Nash, Shoshana
American Association for Crystal Growth *(49)*

Nash, Susan
American Association of Petroleum Geologists *(68)*

Naso, Markisan
American Association of School Librarians *(72)*

Naspinski, Marissa E.
American Association for Dental Research *(49)*
International Association for Dental Research *(512)*

Nasri, CAE, CPA, Fred
International Right of Way Association *(563)*

Nassirian, Barmak

American Association of Collegiate Registrars and Admissions Officers (58)

Natale, PE, CAE, Patrick J
American Society of Civil Engineers (194)

Natchipolsky, Mike
Fire and Emergency Manufacturers and Services Association (446)

Nathan, Greg
National Golf Foundation (755)

Nathan, Sonja
Neurofibromatosis, Inc., Northeast (808)

Nathan, Terry
The Independent Book Publishers Association (488)

Nation, Larry M.
American Association of Petroleum Geologists (68)

Natz, Betsy
Formaldehyde Council, Inc. (452)

Natz, Betsy
Institute of Clean Air Companies (499)

Natz, Kevin
National Council of Farmer Cooperatives (734)

Nau, Larry
International Waterlily and Water Gardening Society (580)

Nauflett, Shari
Utilities Telecom Council (1006)

Naugle, Bonnie
American Institute for Conservation of Historic and Artistic Works (136)

Naugle, James
Laser Institute of America (593)

Naumann, Bonnie
American Angora Goat Breeder's Association (45)

Naurocki, Gloria
American Nuclear Society (156)

Nauser, Lauren
Fixed Income Analysts Society (446)

Navar, B. Nichole
Academy of Molecular Imaging (7)

Navarro, Sheryl
Wedding and Portrait Photographers International (1014)

Navarro-McElhaney, Kristine
National Council on Public History (739)

Navone, Jay
National Association of School Safety and Law Enforcement Officers (693)

Nawalinski, Beth
Association of Library Trustees, Advocates, Friends and Foundations (291)

Naylor, Brooke N.
Healthcare Distribution Management Association (471)

Nazareth, Maria
Association of Governing Boards of Universities and Colleges (286)

Neaderland, Louise
International Society of Copier Artists (572)

Neal, Derek
Association for Middle Level Education (252)

Neal, Gerald
National Association of Real Estate Brokers (689)

Neal, Sandra
International Computer Music Association (536)

Neale, JoAnn
Major League Soccer (601)

Nealis, Libby Kuffner
School Social Work Association of America (892)

Nealis, Nora
National Cleaners Association (722)

Nealon, Caroline
American Forest & Paper Association (123)

Nearon, John
Power Washers of North America (855)

Neary, Erin J.
National Association of Episcopal Schools (666)

Neas, Cheryl
Opportunity Finance Network (829)

Neas, Ralph G.
Generic Pharmaceutical Association (458)

Nease, Linda
Council for Learning Disabilities (390)

Nebesky, Radka Z.
National Academy of Engineering of the United States of America (627)

Neckorcuk, Carrie
The Financial Services Roundtable (445)

Nedbal, Karen
Solar Energy Industries Association (SEIA) (952)

Needham, Joanne
Global Health Council (462)

Neel, Carolyn
World History Association (1026)

Neely, Nancy
Association of Woodworking and Furnishings Suppliers (318)

Neely, Susan K.
American Beverage Association (80)

Nees, Larry
The Association of American Seed Control Officials (266)

Neff, Barbara
National Association of Scientific Materials Managers (694)

Neff, Brian
Cleveland Bay Horse Society of North America (358)

Neff, Michael W.
American Society for Horticultural Science (185)

Neff, PE, Theodore L.
Post-Tensioning Institute (853)

Neff, Tish
Society for Education in Anesthesia (908)

Negron, Barbara
North American Natural Casing Association (819)

Negron, Jr., Francisco M.
National School Boards Association (789)

Negron, Nidia
Craft & Hobby Association (402)

Negroni, Peter
The College Board (363)

Negus, PhD, Susan J.
National Health Federation (758)

Nehasil, John W.
American Concrete Institute (106)

Nehl, Jim
Utility Management & Conservation Association (1006)

Nehls, PhD, Kim
Association for the Study of Higher Education (259)

Neiburgs, MD, Herbert E.
International Society for Preventive Oncology (568)

Neigh, Janet E.
Hospice Association of America (479)
National Association for Home Care and Hospice (639)

Neighbors, Margaret A.
American Society of Ichthyologists and Herpetologists (200)

Neikirk, John
Society for American Archaeology (903)

Neil, Randy L.
American Stamp Dealers Association (213)

Neill, SPHR, Gene D.
Mortgage Bankers Association of America (619)

Neill, Kim
American Association of Clinical Endocrinologists (56)

Neilson, Todd
International Brotherhood of Electrical Workers #98 (531)

Neiman, MD, Harvey
American College of Radiology (102)

Neimiller, Rick
American Jail Association (142)

Neitch, Deborah
International Association of Arson Investigators (515)

Neitzel, Vicki
Professional Tennis Registry (865)

Nekvasil, Glen G.
Lake Carriers Association (592)

Nelesen, Drew
National Council on Measurement in Education (739)

Nellenbach, Michael
Truckload Carriers Association (981)

Nelli, Vincenzo
Society for Information Management (913)

Nellinger, Margie
Corporate Housing Providers Association (386)

Nellis, Kirk K.
Lawn and Garden Dealers' Association (594)

Nellor, Dale
American Meat Institute (148)
Shelf-Stable Food Processors Association (898)

Nellson, Shirley
Middle East Studies Association of North America (615)

Nelsen-Oyervides, Elisa
Literacy Research Association (599)

Nelson, Amy
SPIE - The International Society for Optical Engineering (958)

Nelson, Beth
National Alfalfa Alliance (631)
National Alfalfa and Forage Alliance (631)

Nelson, Bill
WineAmerica (1019)

Nelson, Bob
National Candle Association (717)

Nelson, Bobbie
Women's Council of REALTORS (1023)

Nelson, Carolyn
National Federation of Music Clubs (749)

Nelson, Claudia
Children's Literature Association (353)

Nelson, Deb
Social Venture Network (902)

Nelson, Douglas T.
CropLife America (404)

Nelson, E. Colette
American Subcontractors Association *(214)*

Nelson, Elizabeth
Vinyl Siding Institute, Inc. *(1009)*

Nelson, Genny
Center for Exhibition Industry Research *(348)*

Nelson, Ivar
International Association for the Study of Pain *(514)*

Nelson, Johnathan "Mark"
American Association of Community Colleges *(58)*

Nelson, Jon
Association of Lutheran Development Executives *(292)*

Nelson, Joyce M.
National Multiple Sclerosis Society *(774)*

Nelson, Kathryn
Garden Writers Association *(456)*

Nelson, Kelly
American Society of Interior Designers *(200)*

Nelson, Kristy
American Culinary Federation *(112)*

Nelson, Ligita
Institute of Public Utilities *(502)*

Nelson, Lisa
Data Management Association International *(407)*

Nelson, Lisa M.
Society of Clinical and Medical Hair Removal *(933)*

Nelson, Lorraine
American Association of Franchisees and Dealers *(61)*

Nelson, CAE, MPH, Mariah Burton
American Society of Association Executives-The
Center for Association Leadership *(193)*

Nelson, Matt
AIR Commercial Real Estate Association *(18)*

Nelson, Matthew
Council on Foundations *(399)*

Nelson, CAE, Michael S.
National Association of Enrolled Agents *(666)*

Nelson, Patricia A.
National Limousine Association *(770)*

Nelson, Paula
International Association of Wildland Fire *(528)*

Nelson, Dr. R. Jay
Association of Christian Teachers and Schools *(272)*

Nelson, CAE, FACE, MBA, Robert
American Health Information Management Association
(129)

Nelson, Robert F.
National Coffee Association of the U.S.A. *(723)*

Nelson, Ryan
National Council of Social Security Management
Associations *(736)*

Nelson, PhD, Sally
Society for Free Radical Biology and Medicine *(909)*

Nelson, Steve
International Society for Molecular Plant Microbe
Interactions *(567)*

Nelson, Steve C.
American Association of Cereal Chemists International
(55)
American Phytopathological Society *(165)*
American Society of Brewing Chemists *(193)*
Controlled Release Society *(383)*
Master Brewers Association of the Americas *(607)*

Nelson, Stuart
Blinded Veterans Association *(332)*

Nelson, Thomas

CBA *(346)*

Nelson, Wendy
Urban and Regional Information Systems Association
(1003)

Nelson Gallagher, Ruth
Clinical Laboratory Management Association *(358)*

Nelson-Hogan, Debra
American Academy of Pain Management *(39)*

Nemec, Kelly
Express Delivery & Logistics Association *(436)*

Nemeth, Lynne
American Holistic Nurses Association *(132)*

Nendza, Carol
Women Band Directors International *(1020)*

Nephews, Dr. Melantha
National Optometric Association *(776)*

Nershi, David
Society for Industrial and Organizational Psychology
Inc. *(912)*

Nesbitt, CPP, Paul
National Property Management Association *(783)*

Nesemann, MD, Michael E.
Federal Physicians Association *(439)*

Nesper, Larry
American Society for Ethnohistory *(184)*

Ness, Jeff Van
Association for Community Affiliated Plans *(242)*

Nessle, Elaine
The Coalition for America's Gateways and Trade
Corridors *(360)*

Nester, Dawn
Federally Employed Women (FEW) *(440)*

Nestor, Michele
National Recycling Coalition *(784)*

Netterville, Lawrence
National Society of Real Estate Appraisers, Inc. *(795)*

Neuburger, Rebecca
Police Executive Research Forum *(852)*

Neufeld, Kelsey
National Student Osteopathic Medical Association
(797)

Neumann, Christopher
American Association for Physical Activity and
Recreation *(51)*

Neumann, Madeline
The National Flute Association, Inc. *(751)*

Neumann, Mark D.
Association of Federal Communications Consulting
Engineers *(282)*

Neumann, Ronald E.
American Academy of Diplomacy *(32)*

Neun, Jean
National Pest Management Association *(780)*

Neuvelt, Carol Singer
National Association for Environmental Management
(638)

Nevels, Tondanisha
National Association of Bar Executives *(648)*

Neville, James A.
The National Association of Marine Surveyors, Inc.
(679)

Neville, Esq., Martin J.
The Arts and Creative Materials Institute, Inc. *(229)*

Neville, Mary Cecile
SnowSports Industries America *(902)*

Nevin, Jennie
Hollywood Radio & Television Society *(477)*

Nevin, Kit
American Dairy Goat Association *(112)*

Nevins, Kate
Lyrasis *(600)*

Nevius, Anna
Caucus for Women in Statistics *(346)*

New, Leah
Taxicab, Limousine & Paratransit Association *(969)*

Newbauer, EdD, John F.
North American Society of Adlerian Psychology *(822)*

Newbern, MEd, RDH, T. Carla
National Dental Hygienists' Association *(743)*

Newberry, Lauren
Environmental Markets Association *(431)*
Weather Risk Management Association *(1014)*

Newberry, Lauren LeMunyan
National Institute of Oilseed Products *(765)*

Newberry, Seth
Open Mobile Alliance *(828)*

Newberry, Susan
The Carpet and Rug Institute *(343)*

Newborn, Tangie
Alliance for Nonprofit Management *(23)*

Newbourne, Nancy
Food Shippers of America *(450)*

Newbry, Chris
Cigar Association of America, Inc. *(356)*

Newchurch, Donna
National Association for Behavioral Health *(636)*

Newcomb, Bill
International Society for Respiratory Protection *(569)*

Newcomer, Dr. Christian E.
Association for Assessment and Accreditation of
Laboratory Animal Care International *(239)*

Newell, Gillian
Association of Correctional Food Service Affiliates
(277)

Newell, Mark E.
United States Golf Association *(994)*

Newell, Tricia
American Society of Agronomy (ASA, CSSA, SSSA)
(191)

Newell, William "Bill" H.
Association for Integrative Studies *(250)*

Newhall, Amy W.
Middle East Studies Association of North America
(615)

Newhouse, Aric
National Association of Manufacturers *(679)*

Newhouse, Teri
American Public Works Association *(172)*

Newkirk, Merle Lee
Arms Control Association *(229)*

Newman, Debbie Butler
American Association of Tissue Banks *(75)*

Newman, Edward
American Society for Cell Biology *(182)*

Newman, Jeffrey L.
American Oil Chemists' Society *(157)*

Newman, Jennifer
Dance Films Association *(406)*

Newman, Jhoesel
Society of Thoracic Radiology *(948)*

Newman, Joel
American Feed Industry Association *(120)*

Newman, Libby
American International Automobile Dealers
Association *(142)*

Newman, Max
International Academy of Television Arts and Sciences
(509)

Newman, Monica
International Association of Flight And Critical Care
Paramedics *(521)*

Newman, Rachel
Society of Gynecologic Oncologists *(938)*

Newman, Richard
Academy of Nutrition and Dietetics *(7)*

Newman, Robert
Independent Film and Television Alliance *(489)*

Newman, Susan
National Retail Federation *(786)*

Newman, Susan
Seismological Society of America *(895)*

Newman, Susan S.
Corporate Facility Advisors, Inc. *(386)*

Newport, Sharon
The Door and Hardware Institute *(416)*

Newsum, Phil
Association of Diving Contractors International *(279)*

Newton, Debbi
Association of Kentucky Fried Chicken Franchisees,
Inc. *(290)*

Newton, PhD, Grant W.
Association of Insolvency and Restructuring Advisors
(289)

Newton, Susan
American Association of Credit Union Leagues *(59)*

Newton, Susie
International Society for Heart and Lung
Transplantation *(566)*

Newton, Tom
Clowns of America International *(359)*

Newton-Dunn, Susan
American Institute of Chemical Engineers *(138)*

Nexon, David H.
Advanced Medical Technology Association (AdvaMed)
(13)

Nezbeth, Mary
North American Blueberry Council *(814)*

Ng, FACS, MD, John D.
American Society of Ophthalmic Plastic and
Reconstructive Surgery *(205)*

Ngo, Tai
American Board of Podiatric Surgery *(83)*

Nguyen, An Di H
American Hardwood Export Council *(129)*

Nguyen, Chi
Society of Scribes *(947)*

Nguyen, H. T.
Federal Education Association *(439)*

Nguyen, Jennifer
Generic Pharmaceutical Association *(458)*

Nguyen, Linh
Data Interchange Standards Association *(407)*

Nguyen, Loan
National Association of Professional Insurance Agents
(687)

Nguyen, Quang

Xplor International *(1029)*

Nguyen, Robert
Music Industry Conference *(622)*

Nguyen, Sally
Alliance for Gray Market and Counterfeit Abatement
(23)

Nguyen, Sandy T.
American Institute for Conservation of Historic and
Artistic Works *(136)*

Nguyen, Thu
National Association of Development Companies *(662)*

Nguyen, Vicky
American Society on Aging *(211)*

Ngwenyama, Nokuthula
American Viola Society *(219)*

Ni, Sophie
National Association of Graduate-Professional
Students *(670)*

Niami, Farhad
Society of Government Economists *(937)*

Nichol, John
North American Saxophone Alliance *(820)*

Nicholas, Deborah
International Sleep Products Association *(565)*

Nicholls, Pam
Land Trust Alliance *(593)*

Nichols, Jon
Association of Correctional Food Service Affiliates
(277)

Nichols, Karen J.
National Association of Osteopathic Foundations *(683)*

Nichols, Mark
American Booksellers Association *(85)*

Nichols, Marshall W.
National Petroleum Council *(780)*

Nichols, Mike
National Business Aviation Association *(716)*

Nichols, Pam
National Association of Government Guaranteed
Lenders (NAGGL) *(670)*

Nichols, Rebecca
American Statistical Association *(213)*

Nichols, Robert S.
Financial Services Forum *(445)*

Nichols, Tom
American Association of International Healthcare
Recruitment *(63)*

Nichols, Willard "Randy"
American Public Communications Council *(170)*

Nicholson, MD, Brandi T.
Association of Program Directors in Radiology *(303)*

Nicholson, Bryan
Electricity Storage Association *(422)*

Nicholson, Christine
Association of Black Foundation Executives *(269)*

Nicholson, Kathy
AFT - Public Employees *(15)*

Nicholson, Kim
American Association of Textile Chemists and Colorists
(75)

Nicholson, Kirsten
Society for the Study of Amphibians and Reptiles *(925)*

Nicholson, Maggie
International Business Brokers Association *(532)*

Nicholson, Natasha

International Association of Business Communicators
(517)

Nicholson, Robert
National Association of Police Athletics/Activities
Leagues, Inc. *(685)*

Nichtern, Laurie R.
Association of Independent Commercial Producers
(287)

Nick, DDS, MS, Doyle
National Association of Seventh-Day Adventist
Dentists *(695)*

Nickerson - Goldstein, Amy
Copyright Society of the U.S.A. *(385)*

Nicklos, Linda
Woodworking Machinery Industry Association *(1024)*

Nicklow, Heather
The Learning Disabilities Association *(596)*

Nicolais, CAE, Susan
Retail Bakers of America *(884)*

Nicolaou, Noni
National Telecommunications Cooperative Association
(799)

Nicoletti, Lilia
The Fragrance Foundation *(453)*

Nicoletti, Susan
American Society for Reconstructive Microsurgery
(189)

Nicolici, Florence
American Architectural Manufacturers Association *(46)*

Nicoll, Jill
Association of Zoos and Aquariums *(318)*

Nieber, John L.
American Institute of Hydrology *(139)*

Niebrzydowski, Richard
American College of Osteopathic Family Physicians
(100)

Niebuhr, CAE, RN, MS, Bonnie
American Board of Nursing Specialties *(82)*
American Board of Perianesthesia Nursing Certification
Inc. *(83)*

Niegoski, Joseph
American Public Transportation Association *(171)*

Niehaus, John
National Association of Flight Instructors *(668)*

Niel, Laura
National Tank Truck Carriers *(799)*

Nielsen, MD, David R.
American Academy of Otolaryngology-Head and Neck
Surgery *(39)*

Nielsen, Dori
National Council on Education for the Ceramic Arts
(738)

Nielsen, Jeff
Society of Interventional Radiology *(940)*

Nielsen, MPH, PhD, Marci
Patient Centered Primary Care Collaborative *(840)*

Niem, Tiffany W.
Appraisers Association of America *(226)*

Nieman, Bob
Coin Laundry Association *(361)*

Niemeyer, Ray
Lift Manufacturers Product Section - Material Handling
Institute *(597)*
Material Handling Industry of America *(608)*

Niemi, Susan R.
Industrial Fabrics Association International *(493)*

Nienaber, Kelli
Equipment Leasing and Finance Association *(432)*

Niepoth, Curt
Financial Planning Association *(445)*

Nies, Diane
International Dyslexia Association *(541)*

Niesing, Cassandra
International Molded Fibre Association *(556)*

Niespodziewanski, Felix
American College of Surgeons *(103)*

Nightingale, John T.
Magic Dealers Association *(601)*

Nigohosian, Debra
American Association of Teachers of Spanish and Portuguese *(75)*

Nigrelli, Amy
Credit Union National Association, Inc. *(404)*

Nigro, Joseph J.
Sheet Metal Workers' International Association *(898)*

Nikkel, Donna K.
Arthroscopy Association of North America *(230)*

Nikkel, Sally
Radiological Society of North America *(873)*

Nikolis, Chris
American Hockey League *(132)*

Nikpourfand, Dariush "Nick"
National Certified Pipe Welding Bureau *(720)*

Niles, Andrew
American Urological Association *(218)*

Nilsen, Michael
Association of Fundraising Professionals *(285)*

Nilssen, Lauren
Institute of Makers of Explosives *(501)*

Niman, Neil B.
History of Economics Society *(476)*

Nimchuk, Cindy
Association of Ancient Historians *(267)*

Nimitz, Jack L.
US Navy Veterans Association *(1004)*

Nimrick, Matt
Roller Skating Association International *(887)*

Niner, Maryann
American Chamber of Commerce Executives *(89)*

Nines, Larry
National Association of Health and Educational Facilities Finance Authorities *(671)*

Ning, Peng
Special Interest Group on Security, Audit, and Control *(956)*

Nipper, James
American Public Power Association *(171)*

Nisankarao, Raj
National Business Association *(716)*

Nisenson, Aaron
International Union of Police Associations, AFL-CIO *(579)*

Nissen, Alanna
American Craft Council *(111)*

Nistal, Martin Llamas
IEEE Education Society *(484)*

Niswander, Kate
Alliance for Women in Media *(24)*

Nix, Troy
American Mold Builders Association *(152)*

Nixon, MD, L. James
Clerkship Directors in Internal Medicine *(358)*

Nixon, Michael
Association of Professional Model Makers *(302)*

Nixon, Patrick B.
American Logistics Association *(146)*

Nizza, CPA, Jane
National Association of College Stores *(655)*

Nkemgnu, Edna
Appraisal Foundation *(226)*

Noa, Ernie
International Society of Arboriculture *(571)*

Noakes, Natalie
Chief Executives Organization *(352)*

Nobel, Steve
Decorative Furnishings Association *(408)*

Noble, Charles
International Conference of Symphony and Opera Musicians *(537)*

Noble, PE, PTOE, Douglas E.
Institute of Transportation Engineers *(503)*

Noble, Jennifer
Red Angus Association of America *(877)*

Noble, Sandy
International Chemical Workers Union Council/UFCW *(534)*

Noblett, Cecilia
Society of Nuclear Medicine *(943)*

Nocella, Matthew
National Hydropower Association *(761)*

Nocera, John
Academy of Osseointegration *(7)*
American Society of Colon and Rectal Surgeons *(195)*

Nochimson, David
Theatre Library Association *(973)*

Nochlin, Debbie
Investment Management Consultants Association *(584)*

Nocitra, Sue
American College of Veterinary Surgeons *(104)*

Nodland, Sean
Training Directors' Forum *(977)*

Noel, Elana
National Environmental Balancing Bureau *(746)*

Noel, James
InterNational Electrical Testing Association *(542)*

Noel, Jerel
Cardiovascular Credentialing International *(342)*

Nofsinger, John
Rack Manufacturers Institute *(872)*

Nofsinger, John
Storage Equipment Manufacturer's Association *(963)*

Noguerón-Liu, Silvia
Council on Anthropology and Education *(398)*

Nojowitz, Dovid
National Society for Hebrew Day Schools *(792)*

Nokes, Pamela
National Association for Girls and Women in Sport *(639)*

Nolan, Becky
Armed Forces Communications and Electronics Association *(228)*

Nolan, Cathy
Data Management Association International *(407)*

Nolan, CAE, Debra S.
Library Binding Institute *(597)*

Nolan, Justin M.
Society of Ethnobiology *(935)*

Nolan, Lynn
International Society for Technology in Education *(569)*

Nolan, M. Richardson "Rich"
National Mining Association *(772)*

Nolan, Mike
International Surface Fabricators Association *(576)*

Nolan, Rich
Coal Exporters Association of the U.S. *(359)*

Nolan, Sheri
National Alfalfa and Forage Alliance *(631)*

Nolan, Susan F.
National Conference of Insurance Legislators *(727)*

Noland, Kathi
The American Institute of Mining, Metallurgical, and Petroleum Engineers *(139)*

Noland, Paul
International Association of Amusement Parks and Attractions(IAAPA) *(515)*

Noland, Priscilla
Society of Teachers of Family Medicine *(947)*

Noll, Ann
Battery Council International *(326)*

Noll, Kay
American Society of Clinical Oncology *(194)*

Nolt, Katie
American Association of Meat Processors *(64)*

Nolte, John
American Institute of Organbuilders *(139)*

Nolte, Renee
Paint and Decorating Retailers Association *(836)*

Nolte, CAE, Traci
Society of Teachers of Family Medicine *(947)*

Noncek, Matthew D.
Conference of Consulting Actuaries *(375)*

Noon, Sara
United States Lacrosse *(995)*

Noonan, Gary P.
American Academy of Sanitarians *(41)*

Noonan, Heather C.
League of American Orchestras *(595)*

Noonan, Patty
The Travel Institute *(979)*

Nootz, Tressie
American Society for Pain Management Nursing *(188)*
National Association for Health Care Recruitment *(639)*

Nora, J D, MBA, MD, Lois Margaret
American Board of Medical Specialties *(82)*

Norberg, Tracey
Rubber Manufacturers Association *(888)*

Norbut, Jennifer
CCIM Institute *(347)*

Nord, G. Daryl
International Association for Computer Information Systems *(511)*

Nord, Jeretta Horn
International Association for Computer Information Systems *(511)*

Nordal, Katherine C
American Psychological Association Practice Organization *(170)*

Nordin, Kerstin E.
Finnish American Chamber of Commerce *(445)*

Nordlinger, Michelle
Women in Packaging *(1022)*

Nordvig, O. Kent

Association for Prevention Teaching and Research (APTR) *(254)*

Norenberg, Jeffrey P.
National Association of Nuclear Pharmacies *(682)*

Noriega, Arlene
Society for the Psychological Study of Lesbian and Gay Issues *(924)*

Noriega, Yahaira
National Federation of Priests' Councils *(749)*

Norlander, Susan
Timber Framers Guild *(974)*

Norman, Dr. Bill M.
National Cotton Council of America *(730)*

Norman, Janice
Association of Directory Publishers *(279)*
Local Media Association *(599)*

Norman, Mark Van
National Indian Gaming Association *(762)*

Normandin, CAE, MPA, Joni
Society for Experimental Mechanics, Inc. *(909)*

Normandin, Kyle
Association for Preservation Technology International *(253)*

Norris, Amy
Association of Partners for Public Lands *(298)*

Norris, Daniel
Organizational Systems Research Association *(833)*

Norris, Gail
Competitive Telecommunications Association *(371)*

Norris, Jeffrey A.
Equal Employment Advisory Council *(432)*

Norris, Nina
National Council of Examiners for Engineering and Surveying *(734)*

Norris, Roberta
American Association of Small Ruminant Practitioners *(73)*
American College of Theriogenologists *(103)*
Society for Theriogenology *(926)*

North, Carrie
International Carwash Association *(533)*

North, Dewite
Independent Community Bankers of America *(488)*

North, Tristan M.
American Ambulance Association *(44)*

Northcutt, Sally
American Angus Association *(45)*

Northrop, Jeff
International Association of Privacy Professionals *(526)*

Northrup, Judi
American Orthopaedic Foot and Ankle Society *(158)*

Northup, Larry
Automotive Aftermarket Industry Association *(321)*

Norton, Debra
National Interstate Council of State Boards of Cosmetology *(766)*

Norton, Judy
American Composites Manufacturers Association *(105)*

Norton, Judy
International Cast Polymer Alliance *(533)*
International Cast Polymer Association *(533)*

Norton, Lee Ann
Bowling Proprietors' Association of America *(334)*
International Bowling Pro Shop and Instructors Association *(530)*

Norton, Negley
Local Search Association (fka Yellow Pages Association) *(600)*

Norton, Ryan
The Society for Adolescent Medicine *(903)*

Norton, Ryan
National Association of Private Special Education Centers *(686)*

Norton, Sue
The Society for Freshwater Science *(910)*

Norwig, John
Professional Football Athletic Trainers Society *(861)*

Noseworthy, Susan
Association of Performing Arts Presenters *(298)*

Nosil, Mike
Child Care Aware of America *(353)*

Nosko, Michele
United Motorcoach Association *(988)*

Notaris, David De
National Council of State Agencies for the Blind *(736)*

Noth, Robin
Midwest Free Community Papers *(615)*

Notini, Jill A.
Association of Home Appliance Manufacturers *(287)*

Novak, Eileen Kiley
Materials Research Society *(609)*

Novak, Jim
Turfgrass Producers International *(982)*

Novak, John M.
Society of Professors of Education *(945)*

Novak, Liz
Copper and Brass Servicenter Association *(384)*
International Association of Plastics Distributors *(526)*

Novak, Marcy
American Association of Teachers of Spanish and Portuguese *(75)*

Novak, Pat
Associated Equipment Distributors *(235)*

Novak, Richard
Association of Governing Boards of Universities and Colleges *(286)*

Novak, Sarah
American Feed Industry Association *(120)*

Novak, Stephen E.
Archivists and Librarians in the History of the Health Sciences *(228)*

Novelli, Thomas C.
Medical Device Manufacturers Association *(611)*

Noverini, Donald
Million Dollar Round Table *(616)*

Novey, Levi
The Corps Network (formerly the National Association of Service and Conservation Corps) *(386)*

Novick, Sylvia
Society of Thoracic Surgeons *(948)*

Novy, Steven B.
Transportation Lawyers Association *(978)*

Nowak, John
Association of Equipment Manufacturers *(281)*

Nowak, Steven
Aircraft Mechanics Fraternal Association *(20)*

Nowak, Vincent
Livestock Marketing Association *(599)*

Nowicki, Susan A.
International Association of Oral and Maxillofacial Surgeons *(525)*

Nowviskie, Bethany
Association for Computers and the Humanities *(242)*

Nozette, Mark D.
Attorneys' Liability Assurance Society Inc. *(320)*

Ntarangwi, Mwenda
Association for Africanist Anthropology *(238)*

Ntsomi, Miriam
National Health Care Anti-Fraud Association *(758)*

Nucci, Larry
Jean Piaget Society *(586)*

Nuckolls, Randy
Society of International Business Fellows *(940)*

Nuechterlein, John
American Composers Forum *(105)*

Nuessel, Dr. Frank
American Name Society *(154)*

Nugent, PhD, Rebecca
Classification Society *(357)*

Nuhn, Peter J.
National Weather Service Employees Organization *(804)*

Nuland, Esq., Christopher L.
American Association of Clinical Endocrinologists *(56)*

Nunes, David
National Association of Professional Baseball Leagues *(686)*

Nunes, Frank E.
International Institute for Lath and Plaster *(551)*

Nunez, Anita
Association of Latino Professionals in Finance and Accounting *(291)*

Nunez, Jane
Association of Independent Commercial Producers *(287)*

Nunez, Marcelo
National Science Teachers Association *(790)*

Nunn, Steve
The Open Group *(828)*

Nunnally-Olsen, Timothy M.
Council of Defense and Space Industry Associations *(393)*

Nunnery, Dawn
European-American Business Council *(434)*

Nunnery, Ron
Shelf-Stable Food Processors Association *(898)*

Nunnery, Ronald L.
American Meat Institute *(148)*

NuQuay, Celena T.
Society for Public Health Education *(919)*

Nurnberg, Paula
National Association of Tower Erectors *(706)*

Nurse, Jonathan
International Association for Dental Research *(512)*

Nusbaum, Howard C.
American Resort Development Association *(175)*

Nuss, Katherine
United States Conference of Catholic Bishops *(992)*

Nussle, Jim
Growth Energy *(466)*

Nussman, Chris
National Emergency Number Association *(745)*

Nussman, J. Michael
American Sportfishing Association *(212)*

Nutkis, Daniel
Health Information Trust Alliance (HITRUST) *(470)*

Nutley, Chris
Contract Packaging Association *(382)*

Nutt, AA, BSEd, EdD, MEd, Charlie L.
National Academic Advising Association *(626)*

Nutt, AIA, CAE, Stephen
National Council of Architectural Registration Boards *(733)*

Nutter, Franklin W.
Reinsurance Association of America *(879)*

Nuxoll, Dennis R.
American Farmland Trust *(118)*

Nuzum, Russ
National Association of Medical Staff Services *(645)*

Nuzum, Russell
Lamaze International *(592)*

Nuzzaco, Mark J.
NPES, The Association for Suppliers of Printing,
  Publishing, and Converting Technologies *(824)*

Nybro, Ruth
National Association of Counties *(659)*

Nye, Heidi
American Evaluation Association *(118)*

Nye, Nicolette
National Ocean Industries Association *(775)*

Nye, Sharon
Federal Water Quality Association *(440)*

Nygren, Marcus
Swedish-American Chambers of Commerce of the USA,
  Inc. *(967)*

Nykwest, Beverly C.
National Association of Regional Councils *(690)*

Nyman, Barbara
American Association of Pastoral Counselors *(68)*

Nyman, Karen
Miniature Book Society *(617)*

Nysewander, Dorette
Aerobics and Fitness Association of America *(13)*

Nystrom, Karen
National Association of Personal Financial Advisors
  (684)

O, Ken
Solid-State Circuits Society *(952)*

O' Mara, Stephen
Association of Food Industries *(283)*

O'Beirne, Kim
National Customs Brokers and Forwarders Association
  of America *(741)*

O'Block, PhD, Robert L.
American College of Forensic Examiners Institute *(96)*

O'Brian, Betty Sue
International Iridology Practitioners Association *(552)*

O'Brien, Alice
National Education Association *(744)*

O'Brien, Barbara E.
National Confectioners Association *(725)*

O'Brien, Bruce
Charles Homer Haskins Society *(351)*

O'Brien, Charlie
Milking Machine Manufacturers Council *(616)*

O'Brien, Cindy L.
National Council on Radiation Protection and
  Measurement *(739)*

O'Brien, Claire
American Association of Motor Vehicle Administrators
  (65)

O'Brien, Hugh Aodh
Stuntmen's Association of Motion Pictures *(964)*

O'Brien, James
Military Officers Association of America (MOAA) *(616)*

O'Brien, Jennifer
Society for Imaging Science and Technology *(912)*

O'Brien, DNP, RN, Karen
Association of Public Health Nurses *(304)*

O'Brien, Kelly
Writers Guild of America East *(1029)*

O'Brien, Kevin
Inland Marine Underwriters Association *(496)*

O'Brien, Lieann
Women Chefs and Restaurateurs *(1020)*

O'Brien, Lisa
United Soybean Board *(989)*

O'Brien, Maggie
American Society of Naval Engineers *(204)*

O'Brien, SPHR, Margaret K
American College of Healthcare Executives *(96)*

O'Brien, Michael
American Geophysical Union *(126)*

O'Brien, CAE, Michael
National Lumber and Building Material Dealers
  Association *(770)*
Window and Door Manufacturers Association *(1018)*

O'Brien, Patrick
Concrete Sawing and Drilling Association *(374)*

O'Brien, Tami
American String Teachers Association *(213)*

O'Bryan, Raymond J.
American Chemistry Council *(90)*

O'Bryon, CAE, David S.
Association of Chiropractic Colleges *(272)*

O'Connell, Bill
National Rural Water Association *(788)*

O'Connell, Edward L
American Association of Port Authorities *(70)*

O'Connell, Jack
Baseball Writers Association of America *(326)*

O'Connell, K. Michael
Commercial Vehicle Training Association *(367)*

O'Connell, Patricia
Association of Management Consulting Firms *(292)*

O'Connell, Patricia R.
National Guard Association of the U.S. *(757)*

O'Connell, Susan N.
American Board of Medical Specialties *(82)*

O'Connell, Veronica
Consumer Electronics Association *(381)*

O'Connell, William K.
American Chiropractic Association *(90)*

O'Conner, Pat
Minor League Baseball *(617)*
National Association of Professional Baseball Leagues
  (686)

O'Connor, Barbara
Association of Litigation Support Professionals *(292)*
Print Services & Distribution Association *(857)*

O'Connor, Daniel T.
Catecholamine Club *(344)*

O'Connor, David
United States Equestrian Federation *(993)*

O'Connor, Julia
International Association of Movers *(525)*

O'Connor, Margaret

Council of Supply Chain Management Professionals
  (398)

O'Connor, Mary Kay
International Dairy-Deli-Bakery Association *(540)*

O'Connor, MBA, Mike
Industrial Asset Management Council *(492)*

O'Connor, Pat
International Warehouse Logistics Association *(580)*

O'Connor, Shannon
ABC Children's Group *(2)*

O'Connor, Steve
Mortgage Bankers Association of America *(619)*

O'Connor, Tabatha
Custom Electronic Design and Installation Association
  (405)

O'Connor, Timothy
United States Potato Board *(997)*

O'Connor, William
American Association of Colleges of Nursing *(57)*

O'Day, Miriam
American Association for Respiratory Care *(51)*

O'Day, Paul T.
American Fiber Manufacturers Association *(121)*

O'Dell, HCCP, John
Certified Claims Professional Accreditation Council
  (349)

O'Dell, Mollie
National Propane Gas Association *(783)*

O'Donnell, Brenda
Insurance Institute for Highway Safety *(505)*

O'Donnell, Brian
Tennis Industry Association *(971)*

O'Donnell, Dr. Frank
Inter-Society Color Council *(506)*

O'Donnell, Julia
American Association of Law Libraries *(64)*

O'Donnell, Kate
Environmental Design Research Association *(431)*

O'Donnell, Kirk
AIB International *(17)*

O'Donnell, Leigh
The Handcrafted Soapmakers Guild *(468)*

O'Donnell, CIH, Lynn C.
American Board of Industrial Hygiene *(82)*

O'Donnell, Michael
Acute Long Term Hospital Association *(12)*

O'Donnell, Stacey
Society for Technical Communication *(922)*

O'Donnell, Whitney
American College of Health Care Administrators *(96)*

O'Donnell-Tormey, PhD, Jill
Cancer Immunotherapy Consortium *(341)*

O'Donoghue, Michael
International Microelectronics and Packaging Society -
  IMAPS *(556)*

O'Donohue, Mary
United States Canola Association *(991)*

O'Dowd, Kyle
National Association of Criminal Defense Lawyers
  (661)

O'Dowd, Mary Nell
Federation of Defense and Corporate Counsel *(441)*

O'Dowd, Tom
Property Loss Research Bureau *(867)*

O'Gorman, James
Society of Telecommunications Consultants *(948)*

O'Gorman, R. W.
Automotive Lift Institute, Inc. *(322)*

O'Grady, Felice
Society for Experimental Biology and Medicine *(909)*

O'Grady, Lorraine
Society for Pediatric Urology *(918)*

O'Grady, PhD, Dr. Richard T.
American Institute of Biological Sciences *(137)*

O'Hanley, Sarah
National Association of Independent Life Brokerage
Agencies *(674)*

O'Hanlon, Brenden
Chamber Music America *(350)*
International Sculpture Center *(564)*

O'Hara, Kevin
American Society of Landscape Architects *(201)*

O'Hara, MS, Matthew
Registry of Interpreters for the Deaf *(879)*

O'Hara, Sara
The Association for Manufacturing Excellence *(252)*

O'Hare, Don
World Shipping Council *(1027)*

O'Hora, CPA, Thomas
International Society for Pharmacoepidemiology *(568)*

O'Kane, Margaret E.
National Committee for Quality Assurance *(724)*

O'Keefe, Billy
Society of Professional Journalists *(945)*

O'Keefe, Dave
Appaloosa Horse Club *(225)*

O'Keefe, John
International Union of Police Associations, AFL-CIO
(579)

O'Keefe, Stephanie Matthews
American Bankers Association *(79)*

O'Keefe, Tom Sheridan
National Association of Investment Professionals *(676)*

O'Keeffe, Amy
Committee of 200 *(368)*

O'Krongly, Erin
American College of Mohs Surgeons *(98)*

O'Leary, Donna K.
National Health Council *(758)*

O'Leary, John
American Society for Aesthetic Plastic Surgery *(180)*

O'Leary, Michael
Motion Picture Association of America (MPAA) *(619)*

O'Leary, Nancy
American Federation for Aging Research *(119)*

O'Leary, Shannon
National Lipid Association *(770)*

O'Liddy, Nancy
Transportation Intermediaries Association *(978)*

O'Loughlin, John
Association for Corporate Growth *(244)*

O'Loughlin, Kathleen T.
American Dental Association *(113)*

O'Loughlin, Linda
The Risk Management Association *(886)*

O'Maley, Esq., Amy
International Association of Defense Counsel *(519)*

O'Meara, James

International Council on Education for Teaching *(539)*

O'Melveny, Mary K.
Communications Workers of America *(369)*

O'Neal, Katie W.
American Association of Bovine Practitioners *(55)*

O'Neil, Jim
Society for the Psychological Study of Men and
Masculinity *(924)*

O'Neil, Linda
National Electrical Contractors Association *(744)*

O'Neil, CAE, Peter J.
American Industrial Hygiene Association *(135)*

O'Neil, Sarah
Association of Consulting Foresters of America *(276)*

O'Neilin, Glorianne
Association of Old Crows *(297)*

O'Neill, Carol
Association of Organ Procurement Organizations *(297)*

O'Neill, Eileen
Water Environment Federation *(1013)*

O'Neill, Eric J.
American Short Line and Regional Railroad Association
(179)

O'Neill, Hugh J.
Civil Aviation Medical Association *(357)*

O'Neill, Jill
National Federation of Advanced Information Services
(748)

O'Neill, Nancy
Association of Physician Assistants in Cardiovascular
Surgery *(299)*

O'Neill, Robert
Manufacturers Standardization Society of the Valve
and Fitting Industry, Inc. *(603)*

O'Neill, Robert
Manufacturers Standardization Society of the Valve
and Fittings Industry *(603)*

O'Neill, Robert J.
International City/County Management Association
(535)

O'Quinn, Jim
Theatre Communications Group *(973)*

O'Reilly, Caroline
Organization for the Promotion and Advancement of
Small Telecommunications Companies *(831)*

O'Reilly, Joanne
American Bar Association *(79)*

O'Rourke, Brian
Directors Guild of America *(413)*

O'Rourke, Dina M.
Construction Financial Management Association *(379)*

O'Rourke, Julie
Coin Laundry Association *(361)*

O'Rourke, Morgan
Risk and Insurance Management Society, Inc. (RIMS)
(886)

O'Rourke, Patricia
Council of Supply Chain Management Professionals
(398)

O'Rourke, Ryan
Association of Fraternity Advisors *(284)*

O'Shea, Jennifer
American Gas Association *(124)*

O'Shea, Patrick M.
International Society for Philosophical Enquiry *(568)*

O'Steen, Heather

American Association of Feline Practitioners *(61)*

O'Sullivan, Allyson
Composite Panel Association *(372)*

O'Sullivan, Kevin
Laborers International Union of North America *(592)*

O'Sullivan, Kimberly
American Speech-Language-Hearing Association *(212)*

O'Sullivan, Laurel
Donors Forum *(415)*

O'Sullivan, Sue
American College of Legal Medicine *(97)*

O'Sullivan, Susan
Concrete Reinforcing Steel Institute *(374)*

O'Sullivan, Terence M.
Laborers International Union of North America *(592)*

O'Sullivan, William P.
National Organization of Life and Health Insurance
Guaranty Association *(777)*

O'Toole, Michael
American Society for Nondestructive Testing *(187)*

O'Toole, Pam
National Association of Trailer Manufacturers *(706)*

O'Toole, Timothy "Tim" W.
Mason Contractors Association of America *(607)*

O'Brien, Gabriella Ferraro
United States Lacrosse *(995)*

O'Brien, Kerry
Equal Justice Works *(432)*

O'Brien, CFP, MBA, Kim
National Association for Fixed Annuities *(639)*

O'Brien, Kristen
US Rice Producers Association *(1004)*

O'Brien, Mike
Growth Energy *(466)*

O'Brien, Teresa
Independent Sector *(491)*

O'Bryan, Raymond J.
Chlorine Chemistry Council *(354)*

O'Comartun, Colm
Democratic Governors Association *(410)*

O'Connor, Emily
Association of Meeting Professionals *(294)*

O'Grady, Susan
Sump and Sewage Pump Manufacturers Association
(965)

O'Hara, Brendan
Association of Defense Communities *(278)*

O'Hara, Michael
GSM Association *(467)*

O'Kane, Megan
Manufactured Housing Institute *(602)*

O'Keefe, Denis J.
International Psychohistorical Association *(562)*

O'Leary, Rachel
The Public Relations Society of America *(870)*

O'Malley, Timothy C.
National Association of Letter Carriers *(678)*

O'Neal, Sheila
National Association for Health Care Recruitment *(639)*

Oakes, Cathy
Society of Cable Telecommunications Engineers *(931)*

Oakes, Phil
National Association of State Fire Marshals *(701)*

Oakes-Locascio, Valerie
National Association of Export Companies *(666)*

Oakley, Bill
National Association of Pizzeria Operators *(685)*

Oakley, Janet
AASHTO: Transportation Center of Excellence *(2)*

Oakley, Marcia
National Association of College Auxiliary Services *(655)*

Oakley, Paul C.
American Moving and Storage Association *(153)*

Oakman, Laurie
National Auto Auction Association *(711)*

Oaks, Sarah
Association for Healthcare Resource and Materials Management *(248)*

Oaks, Ursula
NAFSA: Association of International Educators *(624)*

Oathout, Russell C.
Transportation Communications International Union/IAM *(978)*

Obadia, Eva
International Academy of Television Arts and Sciences *(509)*

Obalil, Deborah
Association of Independent Colleges of Art and Design *(287)*

Oberbeck, Helen
American College of Osteopathic Obstetricians and Gynecologists *(100)*

Oberbeck, Paul B.
International Magnetics Association *(555)*

Oberkfell, Larry
International Foodservice Manufacturers Association *(546)*

Oberlander, Kristin
National Association for the Self-Employed *(644)*

Obermayer, James W.
Sales Lead Management Association *(890)*

Oberski, Sally
Catholic Academy for Communication Arts Professionals *(345)*

Oblinger, Diana G.
Educause *(420)*

Obrinsky, Mark H.
National Multi-Housing Council *(774)*

Obston, Andrea
Messenger Courier Association of the Americas *(612)*

Obuchowski, Col. Al
United States Air Force Medical Service Corps Association *(989)*

Obuchowski, Alex
Renewable Fuels Association *(881)*

Ocampo, Ryan
Association for Medical Imaging Management *(252)*

Ocampo-Guzman, Antonio
Voice and Speech Trainers Association *(1011)*

Ocejo, Michele
Commercial Finance Association *(366)*

Ochs, MS, Luann
Clinical and Laboratory Standards Institute *(358)*

Ochsenreiter, Glenn
National Ready Mixed Concrete Association *(784)*

Octubre, Barbara
Deep Foundations Institute *(408)*

Ocwieja, Mary

North American Association for Environmental Education *(812)*

Odegard, Tim
Academic Language Therapy Association *(3)*

Odell, Andrew
American Indonesian Chamber of Commerce *(135)*

Oderkirk, Kimberly
Floor Covering Installation Contractors Association *(448)*

Odessky, Julie
American Dermatological Association *(114)*

Odett, Tony
Edison Electric Institute *(419)*

Odle, Jack
North American Equipment Dealers Association *(816)*

Odle, Sharon
National Association of Blacks In Government *(649)*

Oehmke, Dan
NASTD - Technology Professionals Serving State Government *(626)*

Oetjen, Stephanie
National Association of Professional Employer Organizations *(687)*

Oeuvray, Nicole
Art Directors Guild/Scenic, Title and Graphic Artists *(230)*

Offord, Jr., Jerome
Black Caucus of the American Library Association *(331)*

Offringa, Kate
Council of North American Insulation Manufacturers Association *(396)*
North American Insulation Manufacturers Association *(817)*

Ofuokwu, Rosalind
American Hellenic Educational Progressive Association (AHEPA) *(130)*

Ogborn, Mary
Defense Research Institute *(408)*

Ogburn, Jacqueline
American Association of Physicists in Medicine *(69)*

Ogden, B. J.
Council of Industrial Boiler Owners (CIBO) *(394)*

Ogden, Denise
American Collegiate Retailing Association *(105)*

Ogden, Sarah E.
National Society of Professional Engineers *(794)*

Ogg, Jody
Soil and Water Conservation Society *(951)*

Oghlidos, Sasan
National Defense Industrial Association *(742)*

Ogle, James A.
American Academy of Orthopaedic Surgeons *(38)*

Ogle, Mike
Lift Manufacturers Product Section - Material Handling Institute *(597)*
Loading Dock Equipment Manufacturers *(599)*
Material Handling Industry of America *(608)*
Materials Handling and Management Society *(608)*
Order Fulfillment Solutions *(830)*

Ogle, Steve
INDA, Association of the Nonwoven Fabrics Industry *(488)*

Oglesby, Keisha L.
American College of Osteopathic Internists *(100)*

Oglesby Cook, Jacqueline
American Health Quality Association *(130)*

Ogrodzinski, Henry M
National Association of State Aviation Officials *(698)*

Oguzhan, Errol
Society of Allied Weight Engineers *(928)*

Ohlensehlen, Bob
Epsilon Sigma Phi *(432)*

Ohlhorst, Sarah D.
American Society for Nutrition *(187)*

Ohm, DC, Jeanne
International Chiropractic Pediatric Association *(534)*

Ohmori, AICI, CIP, Hitomi
Association of Image Consultants International *(287)*

Ohnstad, Krissy
Surface Mount Technology Association *(966)*

Oie, Gretchen A.
Electronic Distribution Show Corporation *(423)*

Oilar, Walt
International Wild Rice Association *(581)*

Oken, Wilda
Professional Photographers of America *(863)*

Okolita, Kelley
DRI International *(416)*

Okoro, Elizabeth
International Association of Defense Counsel *(519)*

Oksala, Steve
Society of Cable Telecommunications Engineers *(931)*

Okunseri, BDS, Christopher
American Association of Public Health Dentistry *(71)*

Olaes, Amanda
Air and Surface Transport Nurses Association *(17)*

Oldak, Mike
Utilities Telecom Council *(1006)*

Oldes, Terry
National Federation of Priests' Councils *(749)*

Oldham, Olivea
Association of College and University Housing Officers-International *(274)*

Oldham, Sheryl
American Escrow Association *(118)*

Olding, Robert (Rob)
National Organization for Human Service *(777)*

Olea, Rose
American Orthopaedic Foot and Ankle Society *(158)*

Olean, Kirsten
Association of American Medical Colleges *(265)*

Oleck, Richard
Building Trades Association *(338)*

Olek, Meggan
American Academy of Audiology *(31)*

Olentine, PhD, Charles
Poultry Breeders of America *(854)*
U.S Poultry and Egg Association *(998)*

Oleson, Alexandra
American Academy of Arts & Sciences *(30)*

Oleson, Kristen
Retail Solutions Providers Association *(885)*

Oleszczak, Andrea
Automation Alley *(321)*

Olewnik, PhD, Maureen C.
AIB International *(17)*

Oliff, Athena
The Coalition for Government Procurement *(360)*

Oliff, Kevin
Association for Commuter Transportation *(242)*

Olinger, Pat

Orem, Kathleen
Satellite Industry Association *(891)*

Orenick, Esq., Racquel R.
Healthcare Information and Management Systems
Society *(471)*

Orfanos, Joanne
Property Casualty Insurers Association of America
(867)

Orff, Debby
Alpha Kappa Psi *(26)*

Orgovan, Joseph
The Surety and Fidelity Association of America *(966)*

Orient, MD, Jane M.
Association of American Physicians and Surgeons
(266)

Orin, David
Robotics and Automation Society *(887)*

Orlet, Ed
National Association of Electrical Distributors *(664)*

Orlova, Svetlana
Object Management Group *(825)*

Orman, Michelle
Women's Jewelry Association *(1023)*

Orms, CAE, FACHE, R. Norris
Healthcare Information and Management Systems
Society *(471)*

Ornelas, Christopher D.
National Association of Broadcasters *(650)*

Ornstein, Karen B.
The Electrochemical Society *(423)*

Orozco, Lisa
American Society for Aesthetic Plastic Surgery *(180)*

Orr, CAE, Cindy Challis
Association of Equipment Management Professionals
(281)

Orr, Jill
Museum Education Roundtable *(621)*

Orr, CAE, Stan
Association of Equipment Management Professionals
(281)

Orrico, JD, Katie O.
American Association of Neurological Surgeons *(66)*

Orris, Tim
Air Movement and Control Association International
(19)

Orrock, Regina Satagaj
International Health, Racquet and Sportsclub
Association *(549)*

Orsi, Meg
National Society of Genetic Counselors *(794)*

Orta, Carlos F.
Hispanic Association on Corporate Responsibility *(475)*

Ortberg, Barton
Alliance of Area Business Publications *(24)*
American Academy of Medical Acupuncture *(36)*
City and Regional Magazine Association *(357)*
Parenting Media Association *(838)*

Orth, J. Neil
American International Charolais Association *(142)*

Orthman, Dennis
Strategic Marketplace Initiative *(963)*

Ortisi, Russ
Automotive Industry Action Group *(322)*

Ortiz, Jr., Prof. David
Association for Spanish and Portuguese Studies *(256)*

Ortiz, AAP, Jennifer
Automotive Aftermarket Industry Association *(321)*

Car Care Council *(342)*

Ortiz, KC
Catholic Charities USA *(345)*

Ortiz, Maggie
Earthquake Engineering Research Institute *(418)*

Ortiz, Miquela
American Society for Mass Spectrometry *(186)*

Ortiz, Suzette
EMTA - Trade Association for the Emerging Markets
(427)

Ortiz-Davis, MBA CAE, Rosario
American Society of Association Executives-The
Center for Association Leadership *(193)*

Orwick, Peter
American Sheep Industry Association *(178)*
American Wool Council *(222)*

Orwig, MBA, Janet Pippin
Association of State and Provincial Psychology Boards
(309)

Orza, Gene
Major League Baseball Players Association *(601)*

Osafo, Jacqueline Price
American Society for Gastrointestinal Endoscopy *(184)*

Osborn, J.R.
Association for Africanist Anthropology *(238)*

Osborn, Nancy
National Association of Multicultural Media Executives
(681)

Osborne, Andrew
Special Event Sites Marketing Alliance *(954)*

Osborne, Charmaine
American Society for Healthcare Engineering *(184)*

Osborne, J. Glenn
National Association of County Human Services
Administrators *(660)*

Osborne, Patrick
American Association of Airport Executives *(53)*

Osborne, Shane
National Center for Assisted Living *(719)*

Osborne, Sis
Walking Horse Owners Association of America *(1011)*

Osburm, LPC, NCC, PhD, Monica Z.
American College Counseling Association *(92)*

Osburn, Greg
Association of American Geographers *(265)*

Oser, Lee
The Association of Literary Scholars, Critics, and
Writers *(291)*

Oser, Scott
National Housing and Rehabilitation Association *(760)*

Oseth, Jane
International Sleep Products Association *(565)*

Osgood, Alicia
Direct Marketing Association Nonprofit Federation
(412)

Osgood, Barbara
International Brotherhood of Correctional Officers
(531)

Osgood, Kirstin
Precast/Prestressed Concrete Institute *(856)*

Oshins, Cary
United States Composting Council *(992)*

Oshobukola, Femi
American Foreign Service Association *(122)*

Oshry, Gary
National Association of Trade Exchanges *(706)*

Osman, Todd
Materials Research Society *(609)*

Osman, CTIS, Vicki
American Bus Association *(87)*

Osnower, Anna
Society of Independent Show Organizers *(939)*

Ospina, John
Gases and Welding Distributors Association *(457)*

Ossolinski, Rita
National Association of County Administrators *(659)*

Osten, Joslyn
American Anthropological Association *(45)*

Oster, Christine
Air Traffic Control Association *(19)*

Oster, Gary A.
US Travel Association *(983)*

Oster, CAE, Susan M.
International Psychogeriatric Association *(561)*

Osterhout, James
American Society for Metabolic and Bariatric Surgery
(187)

Osterhout, Mitzi
American Traffic Safety Service Association *(217)*

Ostermann, Eric
Association of Physician Assistants in Obstetrics and
Gynecology *(299)*

Ostrich, Lisa
National Association of Schools of Theatre *(694)*

Ostrich, Lisa A.
National Association of Schools of Art and Design
(693)

Ostroman, Emily
Cotton Council International *(387)*

Ostrowski, Gordon
National Opera Association *(776)*

Ostrowski, PT, Jeff
American Physical Therapy Association - Private
Practice Section *(165)*

Oswald, Barbara
Federal Probation and Pre-trial Officers Association
(440)

Oswald, Julie
Society for Critical Care Medicine *(934)*

Oswald, Susan
American Society of Consultant Pharmacists *(195)*

Oswell, Michelle
International Association of Music Libraries, United
States Branch *(525)*

Oteri, Frank J.
American Music Center *(153)*

Otero, Dario R.
United States Tennis Association *(1000)*

Otis, DEE, P E, PhD, Dick
National Onsite Wastewater Recycling Association
(776)

Otomo, Miyuki
The Integrated Ocean Drilling Program *(505)*

OToole, Johanna
National Air Transportation Association *(630)*

Ott, Chris
State Higher Education Executive Officers *(961)*

Ott, Daniela
American Watchmakers-Clockmakers Institute *(219)*

Ott, James M.
American College of Physicians *(101)*

Ott, MS, Matt
National Grocers Association *(756)*

Ott, Melanie S.
National Council of Teachers of Mathematics *(737)*

Ott-Barnett, Annette
Managed Funds Association *(602)*

Otte, Daniel
American Entomological Society *(117)*

Otte, Marinus L.
Society for Wetland Scientists *(927)*

Otter, Richard C.
Independent Armored Car Operators Association *(488)*

Otterson, Brenda
American Maritime Officers Service *(147)*

Ottinger, Randy
United States Parachute Association *(997)*

Otto, Christa
International Association of Counselors and Therapists *(519)*

Otto, Linda
International Association of Counselors and Therapists *(519)*

Otto, Lindsay
National Lipid Association *(770)*

Otto, Robert
International Association of Counselors and Therapists *(519)*

Ouellet, Kathi
Indian Arts and Crafts Association *(492)*

Oury, Cameron
Golf Course Superintendents Association of America *(463)*

Outhuse, Heather
Women in Government Relations, Inc. *(1021)*

Outlay, Christina
Special Interest Group on Management Information Systems *(956)*

Outler, Shawn R.
Black Retail Action Group *(332)*

Ouzts, Elbert
National Association of College and University Business Officers *(654)*

Overbeck, Paul
International Ozone Association-Pan American Group Branch *(559)*

Overby, Tami
United States Chamber of Commerce *(991)*

Overcash, Sharon
International Society on Thrombosis and Hemostasis *(575)*

Overman, Gregg
Allied Pilots Association *(26)*

Overstreet, Jason
United States Bowling Congress *(991)*

Overstreet, John
Indoor Tanning Association *(492)*

Overstreet, Judge Morris
Auxiliary to the National Medical Association *(324)*

Overstreet, Timothy H.
SOLE - The International Society of Logistics *(952)*

Overton, Cheri
National Ski Patrol System *(792)*

Overton, Pam
Division I-A Athletic Directors Association *(415)*

Overturf, Dwight
The Risk Management Association *(886)*

Ovington, Kay
Society of General Internal Medicine *(937)*

Owczarczak, Allison
American Nature Study Society *(155)*

Owen, Cliff
Council on Occupational Education *(400)*

Owen, David
National Association of Small Trucking Companies *(696)*

Owen, Elizabeth
National Association of Consumer Agency Administrators *(657)*

Owen, Hunter
National Association of Small Trucking Companies *(696)*

Owen, Keith
National Association of Small Trucking Companies *(696)*

Owen, Marc
Senior Executives Association *(897)*

Owen, Richard D.
National Institute of Packaging, Handling and Logistics Engineers *(765)*

Owens, Alexandra
American Society of Journalists and Authors *(201)*

Owens, Brigett
Family Firm Institute, Inc. *(437)*

Owens, David
International Association of Dive Rescue Specialists *(519)*

Owens, David K.
Edison Electric Institute *(419)*

Owens, Dolores Y.
National Association of University Women *(708)*

Owens, Erika
National Bar Association *(712)*

Owens, Felice
National Prison Hospice Association *(782)*

Owens, Gerald R.
Electric Utility Fleet Managers Conference *(422)*

Owens, Jim
Edison Electric Institute *(419)*

Owens, Kitty
American Federation of Teachers (AFL-CIO) *(120)*

Owens, Laura A.
APSE: The Network on Employment *(226)*

Owens, Lisa L.
Editorial Freelancers Association *(419)*

Owens, Marilla
American Psychosocial Oncology Society *(170)*
International Psycho-Oncology Society *(561)*
International Society for Prenatal Diagnosis *(568)*

Owens, Oscar
Amalgamated Transit Union *(28)*

Owens, Pam
National Association of Professional Background Screeners *(686)*

Owens, CUDE, Pamela
National Federation of Community Development of Credit Unions *(748)*

Owens, Redd
Paramount Citrus Association *(838)*

Owens, Scott
Paramount Citrus Association *(838)*

Owens, Sheila
National Association of Insurance and Financial Advisors *(675)*

Owens, Tom
Professional Liability Agents Network *(863)*

Owens, Tory
WIFS - Women in Insurance and Financial Services *(1017)*

Oxford, Donna
American Horticultural Therapy Association *(133)*

Oxman, Jason
Electronic Traders Association *(424)*
Electronic Transactions Association *(424)*

Ozuna, Reda
American Association of Veterinary Laboratory Diagnosticians *(76)*

Ozzanto, Arianna
Screen Actors Guild - American Federation of Television and Radio Artists *(893)*

Pa, Khunteang
International Association for Continuing Education and Training *(511)*

Pace, Jill H.
American College of Real Estate Lawyers *(102)*

Pace, John
ASTM International *(319)*

Pacheco, Donna
National Coffee Association of the U.S.A. *(723)*

Pacheco, Lawrence
FutureGen Industrial Alliance, Inc. *(455)*

Pack, CPA, Thomas
American Watchmakers-Clockmakers Institute *(219)*

Packard, Leslie
International Association of Drilling Contractors *(519)*

Packard, Nathan
American Studies Association *(214)*

Packard-Milam, CAE, Michele
Emergency Medicine Residents' Association *(425)*

Packer, Jerry
Association for Applied and Therapeutic Humor *(238)*

Packer, Trevor
The College Board *(363)*

Pacuit, J.F.
Tire and Rim Association *(975)*

Paddock, Carol A.
Kappa Delta Pi *(590)*

Padelford, Patricia
Society for the Advancement of Material and Process Engineering *(922)*

Paden, Vicki
American Dairy Science Association *(113)*

Padilla, Jennifer
Academic Pediatric Association *(3)*

Padilla, Mapy
Pan American Association of Ophthalmology *(837)*

Padilla, Maria
The Spain-United States Chamber of Commerce *(953)*

Pagano, Jennie Berg
Security Hardware Distributors Association *(895)*

Page, Cynthia
Council of Independent Colleges *(394)*

Page, MPA, Janice
American Academy of Pediatrics *(39)*

Page, Janie
Bioelectromagnetics Society *(329)*

Page, Kelly
International Concrete Repair Institute *(536)*

Page, Lawrence

Natural Science Collections Alliance *(807)*

Page, Lina
Opportunity Finance Network *(829)*

Page, Tami
North American Neuro-Ophthalmology Society *(819)*

Pagel, Alison
North American Limousin Foundation *(817)*

Pagel, Megan
Controlled Release Society *(383)*

Pagels, Nancy T.
International Desalination Association *(540)*

Paget, Mike
Council for Children with Behavioral Disorders *(389)*

Paine, Elizabeth
Federation of State Humanities Councils *(442)*

Paine, Jonathan
Window and Door Manufacturers Association *(1018)*

Paine, Jonathan M.
National Lumber and Building Material Dealers Association *(770)*

Paine, Richard
National Forensic Association *(752)*

Painter, Bill
American Baptist Homes and Caring Ministries *(79)*

Painter, Jerry M.
The Masonry Society *(607)*

Painter, Ron
National Association of Workforce Boards (NAWB) *(710)*

Paisner, Susan
American Public Transportation Association *(171)*

Paiva, Ricardo
Institute for Business & Home Safety *(496)*

Pak, Frances
Pet Partners *(842)*

Pak, Natalie
Federation of State Humanities Councils *(442)*

Palacio-Grottola, LCSW, Sonia
National Association of Puerto Rican-Hispanic Social Workers *(689)*

Palank, Melissa
Society of Insurance Trainers and Educators *(940)*

Palantino, Susan A.
Society for Industrial & Applied Mathematics *(912)*

Palatiello, John M.
Management Association for Private Photogrammetric Surveyors *(602)*

Palatiello, Nick
Management Association for Private Photogrammetric Surveyors *(602)*

Palatiello, Sally
Management Association for Private Photogrammetric Surveyors *(602)*

Palazzo, Daniel
National Constables Association *(729)*

Palcanis, Kent G.
American Board of Periodontology *(83)*

Palcher-Silliman, Jennifer
Healthcare Convention and Exhibitors Association *(471)*

Palermo, PhD, Tonya
Society of Pediatric Psychology *(943)*

Paley, Susan
National Association of Corporate Directors *(658)*

Palkovich, Mark

Miniature Book Society *(617)*

Pallasch, CAE, Brian T.
American Society of Civil Engineers *(194)*

Palm, Julie
International Sleep Products Association *(565)*

Palmarini, James
Educational Theatre Association *(420)*

Palmateer, Cathy
Office Business Center Association International *(826)*

Palmer, Brenda W.
Pharmaceutical Care Management Association *(844)*

Palmer, Brett
National Association of Small Business Investment Companies *(900)*

Palmer, Craig A.
American Dental Association *(113)*

Palmer, Ellen S.
Jesuit Secondary Education Association *(587)*

Palmer, MBA, Heather
American Podiatric Medical Association *(166)*

Palmer, Jeffrey B.
Vinyl Institute *(1009)*

Palmer, Kathy
The Travel and Tourism Research Association *(979)*

Palmer, Lynn
Caucus for Women in Statistics *(346)*

Palmer, Mark
North American Wholesale Lumber Association *(823)*

Palmer, Michael
The Travel and Tourism Research Association *(979)*

Palmer, Ross B.
Veterinary Orthopedic Society *(1008)*

Palmer, Sara L.
Middle East Studies Association of North America *(615)*

Palmer, Victoria
Association of University Research Parks *(316)*

Palomarez, Javier
United States Hispanic Chamber of Commerce *(995)*

Palombizio, Cheryl L.
Defense Research Institute *(408)*

Palonis, Margery
Academy of General Dentistry *(5)*

Paloutzian, Brent
American College of Clinical Pharmacy *(94)*

Pals, Tony
National Association of Independent Colleges and Universities *(674)*

Paltsios, Karol
Deep Foundations Institute *(408)*

Paltz, BA, FCP, Minette
American Academy of Fertility Care Professionals *(34)*

Palusci, Vincent J.
American Professional Society on the Abuse of Children *(168)*

Palys, CAE, Beth W.
American Academy of Appellate Lawyers *(30)*
American Society of Consulting Arborists *(196)*
The Association of Language Companies *(290)*

Pampel, Haydee
International Association of Oral and Maxillofacial Surgeons *(525)*

Pan, Michael T.
National Action Council for Minorities in Engineering (NACME) *(628)*

Pan, Weike
Special Interest Group on Artificial Intelligence *(956)*

Pancrazi, Elsbeth
Poetry Society of America *(851)*

Pandit, Nitin
International Institute for Energy Conservation *(551)*

Panjabi, Chitra
National Woman's Party *(805)*

Pankey, Hazel J.
Industrial Asset Management Council *(492)*

Pankey, Patricia
Society of United States Air Force Flight Surgeons *(949)*

Pankonin, Mike
Forestry Equipment Council *(452)*

Pankov, Andrey
International Public Management Association for Human Resources *(562)*

Pankow, Sara
National Association of Insurance Commissioners *(676)*

Panneton, FLMI, Roland L.
National Association of Insurance and Financial Advisors *(675)*

Pannier, Wendy
International Association for the Study of Dreams *(514)*

Pantaleon, Janet
International Institute of Municipal Clerks *(552)*

Pantaleone, Michael
National Association of Corporate Directors *(658)*

Pantuso, CTIS, Peter J.
American Bus Association *(87)*

Panvini, Vincent A.
Sheet Metal Workers' International Association *(898)*

Papa, Joseph
National Research Council *(786)*

Papacosma, Prof. S. Victor
Modern Greek Studies Association *(618)*

Papadakis, Alec
Major Indoor Soccer League *(601)*

Papageorge, Lauren
Association of Investment Management Sales Executives *(289)*

Papandon, Alexi
National Association of Professional Insurance Agents *(687)*

Papanikolopoulos, Nikos
Robotics and Automation Society *(887)*

Papasadero, Otto
North American Retail Dealers Association *(820)*

Papazian, Charlie
The Brewers Association *(335)*

Pape, Carol A.
Association of Professional Chaplains *(301)*

Pape, John
IEEE Communications Society *(483)*

Papineau-Basaria, Gwen
American Association of Airport Executives *(53)*

Papp, Courtney
American Society of PeriAnesthesia Nurses *(206)*

Papp, Sharon
American Foreign Service Association *(122)*

Pappas, Christina
International Society of Hotel Association Executives *(573)*

Pappas, James P.

Association for Continuing Higher Education *(243)*

Pappas, Lisa
Marine Corps Association *(604)*

Pappas, CAE, Virginia
American College of Nuclear Medicine *(98)*

Pappas, CAE, Virginia M.
Society of Nuclear Medicine *(943)*

Paque, CAE, Mike
Ground Water Protection Council *(466)*

Paradis, Todd
American Society of Appraisers *(192)*

Paradise, Vicki A.
Shipowners Claims Bureau, Inc. *(899)*

Paradowski, Philip
National Association of Catholic Chaplains *(651)*

Parassio, Anthony "Tony"
Produce Marketing Association *(858)*

Pardoe, CDC, CDT, Keith
The Door and Hardware Institute *(416)*

Pare, Paul F.
Automotive Market Research Council *(323)*

Paredes, J. Anthony
Association of Senior Anthropologists *(308)*

Paredes, Mario J.
North American-Chilean Chamber of Commerce *(823)*

Parente, Genilee
Valve Repair Council *(1007)*

Parenti, Marietta
American Medical Association *(148)*

Parfitt, Adam
Council on Licensure, Enforcement and Regulation *(400)*

Parikh, P. Divya
Physician Insurers Association of America *(847)*

Parillo, Jane
Association for the Calligraphic Arts *(259)*

Parillo, Mark
World War Two Studies Association *(1028)*

Paris, Cheryl Van
National Interscholastic Athletic Administrators Association *(766)*

Pariseau, MSSW, Crystal K.
Association of University Centers on Disabilities (AUCD) *(315)*

Parish, MD, Lawrence Charles
History of Dermatology Society *(476)*

Parish, Wendy Jo
Federal Communications Bar Association *(439)*

Parisien, Lia
Environmental Council of the States *(431)*

Park, Brenda
Council of Engineering and Scientific Society Executives *(393)*

Park, Carmen
American Telemedicine Association *(215)*

Park, Christy
Dance Films Association *(406)*

Park, Lynda
American Association for the Advancement of Slavic Studies *(52)*
Association for Slavic, East European, and Eurasian Studies *(256)*

Park, Peter S.
College Music Society *(363)*

Park, Sae

American Society for Engineering Education *(183)*

Park, Tae Hong
International Computer Music Association *(536)*

Parke, Ann
National Coalition of Girls' Schools *(723)*

Parke, Beth
Society of Environmental Journalists *(935)*

Parke, II, David
American Academy of Ophthalmology *(37)*

Parker, MS, RD, Allison
Apple Products Research and Education Council *(226)*
United States Apple Association *(989)*

Parker, Ashley
Association of Career and Technical Education *(271)*

Parker, Brian D.
Alpha Kappa Psi *(26)*

Parker, Casey
NORA: Association of Responsible Recyclers *(811)*

Parker, Chuck
Continua Health Alliance *(382)*

Parker, Corinne "Cory"
Society of Otorhinolaryngology and Head-Neck Nurses *(943)*

Parker, Denise
USA Archery *(1004)*

Parker, Doug
International Institute of Connector and Interconnection Technology *(551)*

Parker, Erich
Aseptic Packaging Council *(231)*

Parker, Jennifer
Caucus for Women in Statistics *(346)*

Parker, Joel
Industrial Asset Management Council *(492)*

Parker, Karen
National Community Development Association *(725)*

Parker, MA, Kathy
National Association of State Mental Health Directors *(701)*
National Association of State Mental Health Program Directors *(701)*

Parker, CAE, Kerry
International Association of Professional Security Consultants *(527)*

Parker, Marilyn B.
North American Colleges and Teachers of Agriculture *(815)*

Parker, Michael A.
American Society of Anesthesiologists *(192)*

Parker, Michelle
Society of Emergency Medicine Physician Assistants *(934)*

Parker, Michelle J.
National Association of College and University Attorneys *(654)*

Parker, DDS, Mitchell S.
American Orthodontic Society *(158)*

Parker, Nancy
Association of Rheumatology Health Professionals *(306)*

Parker, Olen K.
American Design Drafting Association International and American Digital Design Association *(114)*

Parker, Penny
National Property Management Association *(783)*

Parker, Ray
United States Fencing Coaches Association *(994)*

Parker, Rick
North American Colleges and Teachers of Agriculture *(815)*

Parker, Scott D.
NORA: Association of Responsible Recyclers *(811)*

Parker, Wade R.
National Chicken Council *(720)*

Parkin, Scott L.
National Council on Aging *(738)*

Parkinson, Mark
American Health Care Association *(129)*
National Center for Assisted Living *(719)*

Parks, Ayrianne
Association of Farmworker Opportunity Programs *(282)*

Parks, Elizabeth
American Society for Therapeutic Radiology and Oncology *(190)*

Parks, Kathy
International Home Furnishings Representatives Association *(550)*

Parks, Michele
Council of Chief State School Officers *(392)*

Parks, Prudence
Utilities Telecom Council *(1006)*

Parks, CMP, Tracy
Society of Thoracic Radiology *(948)*

Parman, Ann
Manufactured Housing Institute *(602)*

Parman, Kristen
Livestock Marketing Association *(599)*

Paroline, Pamela S.
National Glass Association *(755)*

Parr, Adam
Steel Manufacturers Association *(962)*

Parr, Andrea
Association for Healthcare Foodservice *(248)*
National Barbecue Association *(712)*
Society for Foodservice Management *(909)*

Parr, Danielle LaBossiere
Entertainment Software Association (ESA) *(429)*

Parr, David C.
American Brush Manufacturers Association *(86)*

Parra, Victor S.
United Motorcoach Association *(988)*

Parraway, Andre
National Association of Regulatory Utility Commissioners *(691)*

Parrington-Murchison, Kimberly N.
American Shire Horse Association *(179)*

Parrish, Craig S.
Cookie and Snack Bakers Association *(383)*

Parrish, Jamie
Investment Management Consultants Association *(584)*

Parrish, Mark W.
International Federation of Pharmaceutical Wholesalers *(544)*

Parrish, Melissa
American Association for the Study of Liver Diseases *(52)*

Parrish, Patty
The National NeedleArts Association *(774)*

Parrish, Richard K.
American Ophthalmological Society *(157)*

Parrish, Robert B.
Maritime Law Association of the U.S. *(606)*

Parrish, Robin
International Association of Assessing Officers *(516)*

Parscale, Steve
Association of Collegiate Business Schools and Programs *(275)*

Parshall, Craig
National Religious Broadcasters *(785)*

Parshall, Vickie
National Association for Medical Direction of Respiratory Care *(640)*

Parson, Tom
Intermodal Association of North America *(508)*

Parsons, Bob
The Western Red Cedar Pole Association *(1016)*

Parsons, PE, Brian K.
Environmental and Water Resources Institute of the American Society of Civil Engineers *(430)*

Parsons, Jr., Earl B.
Association of Edison Illuminating Companies *(279)*

Parsons, Laura
Marketing Association of Credit Unions *(606)*

Parsons, Linda
National Active and Retired Federal Employees Association *(629)*

Parsons, Patrice
ICLEI - Local Governments for Sustainability *(482)*

Parsons, Sandi
Association for Hospital Medical Education *(249)*

Parsons, Tracy
American Board of Industrial Hygiene *(82)*

Parthasarathy, Valli
American Veterinary Society of Animal Behavior *(219)*

Parthen, Eric
USA Taekwondo *(1005)*

Partin, Tom
American Forest Resource Council *(123)*

Partyke, Sue
Valve Manufacturers Association of America *(1007)*

Parus, Barbara
National Speakers Association *(795)*

Pasakarnis, Pamela
Diagnostic Marketing Association *(411)*

Pasceri, Patricia
American Association for Wound Care Management *(53)*

Paschal, Jeanette Diana
National Association of Small Business Investment Companies *(900)*

Paschal, Michael
Association for Asian Studies *(239)*

Paschall, CAE, CMP, Joyce
American College of Occupational and Environmental Medicine *(99)*

Pasciak, Kristine
American Board of Preventive Medicine *(83)*

Pashalek, Jeanne
International Association of Women in Fire and Emergency Services *(528)*

Pasik, Alexander
Institute of Electrical and Electronics Engineers (IEEE) *(499)*

Paskun, Ali
Association of Proposal Management Professionals *(303)*

Pasquale, Carla
Society for Photographic Education *(919)*

Pasquale, Kim
Club Managers Association of America *(359)*

Pass, Martina L.
National Association of State Workforce Agencies *(703)*

Passariello, Jennifer
National Association of Insurance Commissioners *(676)*

Passerell, Wendy
American Society of Nuclear Cardiology *(205)*

Passi, CAE, Mary Ann
Corporate Housing Providers Association *(386)*

Passiment, CLS, Elissa
American Society for Clinical Laboratory Science *(182)*

Passons, Donna J.
Association for Continuing Legal Education *(244)*

Paster, Mark
Association of Organ Procurement Organizations *(297)*

Pasternak, Marc
Valve Repair Council *(1007)*

Pastore, Diane
Council for International Tax Education *(390)*

Pat-McKay, MD, MPH, Mary
Association for the Advancement of Automotive Medicine *(258)*

Pate, Allison
Association of Nutrition & Foodservice Professionals *(296)*

Pate, Barbara A.
American Seniors Housing Association *(178)*

Pate, Vicki M.
The Society for Modeling and Simulation International *(916)*

Patel, Amita
American Industrial Hygiene Association *(135)*

Patel, Ashvin
American College of Cardiology *(93)*

Patel, Bhavika
Association of Educational Publishers *(280)*

Patel, Champak
Association of Conservation Engineers *(276)*

Patel, Chayal
American Society of Retina Specialists *(209)*

Patel, Sejal
Society for History in the Federal Government *(911)*

Patel, Sunny
American College of Oral and Maxillofacial Surgeons *(99)*

Patella, Lawrence M.
Western Dredging Association *(1015)*

Patera, Mike
Aquarium and Zoo Facilities Association *(227)*

Paterkiewicz, CAE, Robert
Selected Independent Funeral Homes *(896)*

Pates, Stephanie
American Animal Hospital Association *(45)*

Patillo, Jackie
Gospel Music Association *(464)*

Patin, Catherine
National Institute of Governmental Purchasing *(765)*

Patrias, Tressa
American Association of Cereal Chemists International *(55)*

Patrick, Amanda T.
Railway Supply Institute *(874)*

Patrick, Don

Nisei Farmers League *(811)*

Patrick, Ken
Technical Association of the Pulp and Paper Industry *(970)*

Patrick, MD, MS, Kevin
Association for Prevention Teaching and Research (APTR) *(254)*

Patrick, Mary
Independent Educational Consultants Association *(489)*

Patrick, Susanna
Text and Academic Authors Association *(972)*

Patrick, Trishonda
National Home Furnishings Association *(759)*

Pattavina, Chris
Tile Contractors' Association of America *(974)*

Patten, Jr., Ezekiel
National Council of Minorities in Energy *(735)*

Patterson, Bill
Association for Iron and Steel Technology *(250)*

Patterson, Carrolyn
Academy of Nutrition and Dietetics *(7)*

Patterson, Cathy
International Association of Physicians in AIDS Care *(526)*

Patterson, Charlena
Chlorobenzene Producers Association *(354)*
Society of Chemical Manufacturers and Affiliates Inc. *(932)*

Patterson, Dave
National Shooting Sports Foundation *(791)*

Patterson, Jeff
Air and Expedited Motor Carriers Association *(17)*

Patterson, Jeremiah
Online News Association *(827)*

Patterson, Judy
Vacuum Dealers Trade Association/Sewing Dealers Trade Association *(1007)*

Patterson, Judy L.
American Gaming Association *(124)*

Patterson, Karrie
American Paint Horse Association *(161)*

Patterson, Kathy
Society for Pediatric Pathology *(918)*

Patterson, Lisa
Anxiety Disorders Association of America *(224)*

Patterson, Natasha
Towing and Recovery Association of America *(976)*

Patterson, Dr. Philip
National Christian School Association *(721)*

Patterson, Rhonda
American Bureau of Shipping *(86)*

Patterson, Richard
Sporting Arms and Ammunition Manufacturers' Institute Inc. *(959)*

Patterson, JD, Robert
Surface Engineering Coating Association *(966)*

Patterson, Robert "Rusty"
National Council for Advanced Manufacturing *(731)*

Patterson, Sheryl
Incentive Manufacturers & Representatives Alliance *(487)*

Patterson, Tammie W.
National Association of Emergency Medical Technicians *(665)*

Patterson, Tammy M.

RCI, Inc. *(875)*

Pattie, Kenton
National Emergency Equipment Dealers Association *(745)*

Pattison, Betty
GAMA International *(455)*

Pattison, Scott D.
National Association of State Budget Officers *(698)*

Patton, Bethany
National Council of Acoustical Consultants *(733)*

Patton, Charlene
Home Baking Association *(477)*

Patton, CMDSM, Jane
Mail Systems Management Association *(601)*

Patton, Jeannie
American Institute of Certified Public Accountants *(137)*

Patton, John
National Association of Chronic Disease Directors *(653)*

Patton, Kate
American Business Media *(87)*

Patton, Leah
American Donkey and Mule Society *(115)*

Patton, Susan
Association of American University Presses *(267)*

Paukert, Linda
International Oil Mill Superintendents Association *(558)*

Paul, Kenneth M.
Institute of Real Estate Management *(503)*

Paul, Mike
National Association of Swine Records *(704)*
National Swine Registry *(798)*

Paul, Traci
American Academy of Estate Planning Attorneys *(33)*

Paulen, Lisa
International Trademark Association *(577)*

Paulet, Rochelle
National Association of RV Parks and Campgrounds *(692)*

Pauline, Janice
Hispanic Elected Local Officials *(475)*

Pauline, Janice
National League of Cities *(768)*

Paulino, Dana
Information Systems Security Association *(495)*

Paulk, Liz
The American Association of Nurse Attorneys *(67)*

Paull, Dalene
International Conference of Funeral Service Examining Boards *(536)*

Paull, Judy
Society of Exploration Geophysicists *(935)*

Paulos, MBA, Gregory
Alliance for Continuing Medical Education *(22)*

Paulsen, Lucille Berrill
Allied Artists of America *(25)*

Paulsgrove, Jason
Uniform Retailers Association *(984)*

Paulson, MD, Erik K.
Society of Computed Body Tomography and Magnetic Resonance *(933)*

Paulson, Mary
The American Society of Pediatric Hematology/Oncology *(206)*

Pavick, Cathy
International Facility Management Association *(543)*

Pavina, Linda J.
American Osteopathic Association of Prolotherapy Integrative Pain Management *(160)*

Pavletich, CAE, MHA, James "Jim"
Accreditation Association for Ambulatory Health Care *(9)*

Pavlik, OFM, John A.
Conference of Major Superiors of Men, United States of America *(375)*

Pavlovich, Aimee
Concrete Sawing and Drilling Association *(374)*

Pavon, Efren
Society for the Advancement of Material and Process Engineering *(922)*

Pawelski, Meg
National Association of Sporting Goods Wholesalers *(696)*
The Recreational Vehicle Aftermarket Association *(877)*

Pawicz, Mary T.
National Association of Catholic Chaplains *(651)*

Pawlak, Kim
Text and Academic Authors Association *(972)*

Pawlenty, Gov. Tim
The Financial Services Roundtable *(445)*

Pawlowski, Ursula
American Society for Healthcare Human Resources Administration *(185)*

Paxton, Linda
Alliance of Cardiovascular Professionals *(25)*

Paxton, Matthew
Coastal Conservation Association *(361)*
Shipbuilders Council of America *(898)*

Paxton, Sharon
United Applications Standards Group *(985)*

Payaslyan, Anush
PROMAX/BDA *(866)*

Payn, Bob
National Institute of Building Sciences *(764)*

Payne, Annie
Association of Personal Historians *(299)*

Payne, Antonio
National Office Products Alliance *(776)*
Office Furniture Dealers Alliance *(826)*

Payne, August
Association of Dark Leaf Tobacco Dealers and Exporters *(278)*

Payne, Becky
United States of Ayrshire Breeders' Association *(997)*

Payne, David
Association of Government Accountants *(286)*

Payne, Larry
International Wild Rice Association *(581)*

Payne, Laura
Money Management Institute *(618)*

Payne, Michael L.
International Association of Airport Duty Free Stores *(515)*

Payne, Natalie
Association of Paroling Authorities International *(297)*

Payne, Patricia (Pat)
International Nurses Society on Addicitions *(558)*
Natco-The Organization for Transplant Professionals *(626)*

Payne, Tom
Alliance for Telecommunications Industry Solutions *(23)*

Payne, Tom
Home Baking Association *(477)*

Paynich, Vi
Electronic Retailing Association *(423)*

Payton, Christiane
American Romney Breeders Association *(176)*

Paz, Jobert
AIR Commercial Real Estate Association *(18)*

Peabody, Nixon
Council for Affordable and Rural Housing *(388)*

Peacock, Allison
International Society on Thrombosis and Hemostasis *(575)*

Peacock, Randy
American Miniature Horse Association *(152)*

Peacock, Sue
Urban Affairs Association *(1003)*

Peacy, CAE CMP, Kelly
Professional Convention Management Association *(861)*

Pearce, Dorcas
Financial Markets Association *(445)*

Pearce, Ryan
Senior Executives Association *(897)*

Pearce, Sue M.
Society of Military Otolaryngologists - Head and Neck Surgeons *(941)*

Pearcey, Chris
National Pawnbrokers Association *(779)*

Pearcy, Connie
American Kennel Club *(143)*

Pearcy, CAE, MPA, Jeff
American Association for Accreditation of Ambulatory Surgery Facilities *(47)*

Pearl, Kelly
American Small Manufacturers' Coalition *(180)*

Pearl, Scott
Association of Fundraising Professionals *(285)*

Pearl, Wendy
Country Music Association *(401)*

Pearsall, Kitty
IEEE Components, Packaging, and Manufacturing Technology Society *(483)*

Pearson, Eddie
National Association of Blacks in Criminal Justice *(649)*

Pearson, Jane
APICS The Association for Operations Management *(224)*

Pearson, CLU, LUTCF, Jim
Fraternal Field Managers Association *(453)*

Pearson, PhD, Judy
National Board for Certified Clinical Hypnotherapists *(715)*

Pearson, Lori
American Society of Orthopedic Physician Assistants *(205)*
Society for Free Radical Biology and Medicine *(909)*

Pearson, Michael
Mathematical Association of America *(609)*

Pearson, Shawn
Security Industry Association *(895)*

Pearson, Todd
PeerSpan *(840)*

Pearson, Wayne
Outfitters Association of America *(835)*

Peart, Sandra
History of Economics Society *(476)*

Pease, Doug
Information Systems Security Association *(495)*

Pease, Katey
National Tour Association *(800)*

Pease, Robert
The Brewers Association *(335)*

Peat, Brenda
American Pediatric Society *(162)*

Peavy, Elizabeth
Board Retailers Association *(333)*

Pechman, Jr., Dr. Robert D.
American College of Veterinary Radiology *(104)*

Pechmann, Cornelia (Connie)
Society for Consumer Psychology *(907)*

Pechous, Cindy
National Marine Manufacturers Association *(771)*

Peck, Barbara
American Society for Metabolic and Bariatric Surgery *(187)*

Peck, Brianne L.
National Association for Pupil Transportation *(642)*

Peck, Chris
American Urogynecologic Society *(218)*
Lamaze International *(592)*

Peck, Donna
Marketing Science Institute *(606)*

Peck, Emily
Online Publishers Association, Inc. *(828)*

Peck, Eric C.
National Association of Mortgage Brokers *(681)*

Peckham, Karen
International Dairy-Deli-Bakery Association *(540)*

Peddicord, Douglas
Association of Clinical Research Organizations *(273)*

Peddicord, Karen
Association of Women's Health, Obstetric and Neonatal Nurses *(318)*

Peddicord, Kyle
Association of Clinical Research Organizations *(273)*

Pede, David
Radiological Society of North America *(873)*

Peden, Doug
American Association for Employment in Education *(49)*

Pedersen, Michelle
Council on Licensure, Enforcement and Regulation *(400)*

Pederson, Shannon
The Wildlife Society *(1017)*

Pederson, Dr. William D.
Association of Third World Studies *(314)*

Pedigo, Christopher
Online Publishers Association, Inc. *(828)*

Pedigo, Dave
Custom Electronic Design and Installation Association *(405)*

Pedroza, Dorothy
Society of Actuaries *(927)*

Pedrycz, Witold
Man and Cybernetics Systems Society *(602)*

Peebles, Eleanor

American Association of Acupuncture and Oriental Medicine *(53)*

Peery, Larry
Society of Teachers of Family Medicine *(947)*

Peguero, Carolina
National Eating Disorders Association *(743)*

Peifer, Gary
Newspaper Association of America *(810)*

Peiffer, Claude
The International Food & Beverage Forum *(546)*

Peithman, Stephen
American Association of Community Theatre *(58)*

Pelegrin, Tony
American Financial Services Association *(121)*

Pelish, Alyssa
American Council on Science and Health *(110)*

Pellegrino, Cindy
American Federation of Musicians *(119)*

Pelleu, Bruce
National Council for Community Behavioral Healthcare *(731)*

Pelliccia, Lydia
Board of Registered Polysomnographic Technologists *(333)*

Pellom, Renee
Council on Occupational Education *(400)*

Pelta, Maureen
Association for Textual Scholarship in Art History *(257)*

Peltason, Timothy
The Association of Literary Scholars, Critics, and Writers *(291)*

Pelton, Betty
American Association of Bank Directors *(54)*

Peltz, Elin
United States Beet Sugar Association *(991)*

Peluso, Karen
Neurofibromatosis, Inc., Northeast *(808)*

Peluso, Rick
American Society of Interior Designers *(200)*

Pemberton, Phyllis T.
The National Flute Association, Inc. *(751)*

Pembroke Callihan, Le'ann
American Association of Professional Landmen *(71)*

Pena, Edna Dela
American Import Shippers Association *(134)*

Pena, Fred dela
American Import Shippers Association *(134)*

Peña, Roanne
Inter-American Bar Association *(506)*

Penafiel, CAE, Karen
Building Owners and Managers Association International *(337)*

Penaranda, Ana C.
Society of Chemical Manufacturers and Affiliates Inc. *(932)*

Pencak, MA, Lawrence C.
Association of Academic Physiatrists *(263)*

Penczek, Kristen
International Dyslexia Association *(541)*

Pendarvis, Donna
American Society of Extra-Corporeal Technology *(197)*

Pender, Annemarie B.
Association of Global Automakers *(285)*

Pendergrast, E. James

IEEE Ultrasonics, Ferroelectrics and Frequency Control Society *(486)*

Pendleton, Andrea
American Association of Anatomists *(54)*

Pendley, Tamara
National Council of Real Estate Investment Fiduciaries *(735)*

Pendola, Ellen M.
Warehousing Education and Research Council *(1012)*

Pener, Sam
Association of Family Medicine Residency Directors *(282)*

Penio, Steven
American Association of Nurse Anesthetists *(67)*

Penn, Kate
Society of American Florists *(928)*

Penn, Laura
Stage Directors and Choreographers Society *(960)*

Pennacchia, Rina
National Council on Aging *(738)*

Pennavaria, Geri S. Armstrong
Federation of Internet Solution Providers of the Americas *(441)*

Pennello, Joan
WTA Tour, Inc. *(1029)*

Penner, Bruce W.
National Sweetener and Ingredient Marketing Association *(798)*

Penney, Brad A.
National Association for State Community Services Programs *(643)*

Penney, MBA, Leah
American Group Psychotherapy Association *(127)*

Penney, Mary
County Counsels' Association of California *(401)*

Pennington, Deneen
National Career Development Association *(717)*

Pennington, PhD, Floyd
American Society of Transplantation *(210)*

Pennington, Jason J.
American Concrete Institute *(106)*

Pennington, Kathleen A.
National Oilseed Processors Association *(776)*

Pennington, CAE, Kathleen A.
American Oilseed Coalition *(157)*

Pennington, Martha
National Ornamental and Miscellaneous Metals Association *(778)*

Pennock, Jonathan
Sea Grant Association *(894)*

Penny, Piper
Gas Processors Association *(456)*
Gas Processors Suppliers Association *(456)*

Penny, Steve
United States of America Gymnastics *(997)*

Penoyar, Melanie
American Water Works Association *(220)*

Penrose, Dave
The Society for Freshwater Science *(910)*

Pensak, Myles L.
Triological Society *(980)*

Pensak, MD, FACS, Myles L.
American Laryngological, Rhinological and Otological Society *(144)*

Pensoneau, Shawn
National American Indian Housing Council *(634)*

Penza, Marie
Market Technicians Association *(606)*

Peoples, Arnold D.
International Boxing Federation *(530)*

Peoples, Daryl J.
International Boxing Federation *(530)*

Peoples, Gabriel
American Studies Association *(214)*

Pepito, MBA, Andrew
Drug Information Association *(417)*

Peppel, Alan
American Edged Products Manufacturers Association *(115)*

Pepper, Eric
SPIE - The International Society for Optical Engineering *(958)*

Pepper, Samuel J.
National Association for Year-Round Education *(645)*

Pepperman, Scott E.
National Association of State Agencies for Surplus Property *(697)*

Peppin, Richard J.
Institute of Noise Control Engineering *(502)*

Pequignot, Steven
Brotherhood Railway Carmen/TCU *(336)*

Peral, Tony
The Association to Advance Collegiate Schools of Business *(319)*

Perales, Roberto
Association of Writers and Writing Programs *(318)*

Peralta, Carmen
Society of Hispanic Professional Engineers *(938)*

Perbix, Mark
Search - The National Consortium for Justice Information and Statistics *(894)*

Percebois, Jacques
International Association for Energy Economics *(512)*

Perch, Liz
Smocking Arts Guild of America *(901)*

Perdu, Anne
Society for Research on Adolescence *(920)*

Perdue, Dr. Bobbiejean
Association of Black Nursing Faculty *(269)*

Perdue, Bruce
Professional Currency Dealers Association *(861)*

Perdue, MCC, Sandra
National Association of Cruise Oriented Agencies *(662)*

Perdziola, Stephen
National Association of EMS Educators *(665)*

Perea, Sally
American College of Veterinary Nutrition *(104)*

Peregonov, Keith
Council of Graduate Schools *(394)*

Pereira, Eduardo
United States Hispanic Chamber of Commerce *(995)*

Perel, DDS, MScD, Morton L.
International Congress of Oral Implantologists *(537)*

Perelman, Dell
American Chemistry Council *(90)*
Chlorine Chemistry Council *(354)*

Perera, Rey
American Karakul Sheep Registry *(143)*

Pereyra-Rojas, Milagros
Latin American Studies Association *(594)*

Perez, Cynthia

American College Health Association *(93)*

Perez, Diana
Market Technicians Association *(606)*

Perez, Hely
Black Theatre Network *(332)*

Perez, Kim
United States Maritime Alliance (USMX) *(996)*

Perez, Marisol
International Pharmaceutical Excipients Council of the Americas *(560)*

Perez, Melanie
National Federation of Music Clubs *(749)*

Perez, Stella
League for Innovation in the Community College *(595)*

Perez, Wendi
American Rhinologic Society *(175)*

Perez, Wendy
International Society for Pharmaceutical Engineering *(567)*

Perez Young, Wendy
The American Institute of Architects *(137)*

Perfetto, Pat
Council for the Advancement of Standards in Higher Education *(391)*

Perhac, Joyce
Sewing and Craft Alliance *(898)*

Perham, Charlotte R.
Plumbing-Heating-Cooling Contractors - National Association *(851)*

Peri, Ric
Aircraft Electronics Association *(20)*

Perillo, Patti
Association of Women Surgeons *(317)*
Independent Medical Distributors Association *(490)*

Perilstein, Michael
International Society for Philosophical Enquiry *(568)*

Perini, Geri
Petroleum Equipment Suppliers Association *(843)*

Perini, Valyn
OpenTravel Alliance *(828)*

Perkins, Catherine
National Institute of Pension Administrators *(765)*
The Association for Nursing Professional Development *(252)*

Perkins, III, Charles S.
Bituminous Coal Operators Association *(331)*

Perkins, Christina
American College of Veterinary Surgeons *(104)*

Perkins, Dee
Land Trust Alliance *(593)*

Perkins, Donald
Society for the History of Discoveries *(923)*

Perkins, Jennifer
National Emergency Management Association *(745)*

Perkins, Kim
Coalition of Visionary Resources *(361)*

Perkins, CFCP, Maria
American Academy of Fertility Care Professionals *(34)*

Perkins, Dr. Tommy
Beefmaster Breeders United *(327)*

Perkins-Roberts, Cynthia
Cabletelevision Advertising Bureau *(340)*

Perla, Jill
American Association for the Advancement of Science *(51)*

Perlberg, Dean
Association of Equipment Manufacturers *(281)*

Perle, Sylvia
American Medallic Sculpture Association *(148)*

Perlman, Camille
Association of College and University Housing Officers-International *(274)*

Perlman, MPH, Eva
Association of Public Health Laboratories *(304)*

Perlman, Sarah
Federal Bar Association *(438)*

Perlman, Tracy
National Football League *(752)*

Perlman, Victor
American Society of Media Photographers *(203)*

Perlov, Israel R.
Latin American Studies Association *(594)*

Perlroth, Mort
Association & Society Insurance Corporation *(237)*

Perlstein, Jill
American Booksellers Association *(85)*

Perlstein, William J.
American College of Bankruptcy *(93)*

Perner, Lars
Marketing Education Association *(606)*

Pernet, Dr. Bruno
American Microscopical Society *(151)*

Pernik, Audrey
American Public Health Association *(171)*

Perodin, CEM, CMP, Elisa
Alliance for Women in Media *(24)*
American Society of Women Accountants (ACC) *(211)*
Association Media and Publishing *(262)*

Perrell, CMP, Teresa
American College of Veterinary Surgeons *(104)*

Perricone, Deborah
Institute for Business & Home Safety *(496)*

Perrin, Dan
North American Council of Automotive Teachers *(815)*

Perrin, CAE, MA, Nancy
American College of Clinical Pharmacy *(94)*

Perrine, Nathan
American Coatings Association *(92)*

Perrone, Anthony M.
United Food and Commercial Workers International Union *(987)*

Perrone, Michael J.
National League of Postmasters of the United States *(768)*

Perry, Armilda
Wholesale Beer Association Executives of America *(1016)*

Perry, Brian
International Ice Cream Association *(551)*

Perry, Charles
The Retired Enlisted Association *(885)*

Perry, Daniel P.
Alliance for Aging Research *(22)*

Perry, Gail Monroe
Black Retail Action Group *(332)*

Perry, John
NACE International *(623)*

Perry, Karen
Society of Actuaries *(927)*

Perry, Luanne

Institute of Store Planners **(503)**

Perry, Michael C.
Investment Casting Institute **(584)**

Perry, Amb. Robert C.
Corporate Council on Africa **(385)**

Perry, Robert E.
American Board of Podiatric Surgery **(83)**

Perry, Robin L.
Chorus America **(355)**

Perry, Rory
National Conference of Appellate Court Clerks **(726)**

Perry, Shawn
Amalgamated Transit Union **(28)**

Perry, Sherry
Credit Professionals International **(403)**

Perry, Stacey
GAMA International **(455)**

Perry, Susan
International Technology and Engineering Educators
Association **(576)**

Perry, Teresa
Audit Bureau of Circulations **(320)**

Perry, Victoria J.
American College of Tax Counsel **(103)**

Perry, PhD, William
National Academy of Neuropsychology **(628)**

Person, Joseph
Association for Community Affiliated Plans **(242)**

Persons, Richard
National Football League Players Association **(752)**

Persson, Emily
Meals on Wheels Association of America **(609)**

Persuit, Dr. Jeanne
Association for Communication Administration **(241)**

Perth, Rod
National Association of Television Program Executives
(705)

Perusek, Anne
Society of Women Engineers **(950)**

Perveiler, Fran
Healthcare Information and Management Systems
Society **(471)**

Pesanelli, Jennifer
Federation of American Societies for Experimental
Biology **(440)**
Society for Leukocyte Biology **(914)**

Peschges, Elizabeth
Professional Skaters Association **(865)**

Peskin, Matt
National Association of Town Watch **(706)**

Pestino, Joseph
College English Association **(363)**

Pestronk, MPH, Robert M.
National Association of City and County Health
Officials **(654)**
National Association of County and City Health
Officials **(659)**

Peterman, Adam J.
ACA International, The Association of Credit and
Collection Professionals **(2)**

Peterman, Erin
Precision Metalforming Association **(856)**

Peterman, Patrick
AFCOM **(14)**

Peters, Caitlin
Academy of Nutrition and Dietetics **(7)**

Peters, David
Jewelers of America **(587)**

Peters, Dr. George
American Auto Racing Writers and Broadcasters
Association **(78)**

Peters, Linda A.
National Business Aviation Association **(716)**

Peters, Michael
Risk and Insurance Management Society, Inc. (RIMS)
(886)

Peters, Rebecca Knowles
American Council on International Personnel **(110)**

Peters, Stephanie
Museum Store Association **(621)**

Peters, Susan
North American Case Research Association **(814)**

Peters, Traci
American Automotive Leasing Association **(78)**

Petersen, Beth
International Festivals and Events Association **(545)**

Petersen, Bob
American Association of Grain Inspection and
Weighing Agencies **(61)**

Petersen, Brian
The Coca-Cola Bottlers' Association **(361)**

Petersen, David A
National Academy of Arbitrators **(627)**

Petersen, Patricia
Air Medical Physician Association **(19)**

Petersen, Robert R.
Transportation Elevator and Grain Merchants
Association **(978)**

Petersen, Shaun
National Independent Automobile Dealers Association
(761)

Peterson, PhD, Ashley
National Chicken Council **(720)**

Peterson, Becky
American Shropshire Registry Association **(179)**

Peterson, Carolyn
Association of Metropolitan Water Agencies **(294)**

Peterson, Courtney
National Association of Wastewater Transporters **(708)**

Peterson, Dana
National Association of Wheat Growers **(709)**

Peterson, Eli
The Clearing House Association **(357)**

Peterson, Faye
American Astronomical Society **(77)**

Peterson, Gayla
Foil and Specialty Effects Association **(448)**

Peterson, Gregory
International Council of Shopping Centers **(538)**

Peterson, Ivars
Mathematical Association of America **(609)**

Peterson, J. Scott
Nuclear Energy Institute **(824)**

Peterson, Jada L.
Association for Healthcare Volunteer Resource
Professionals **(248)**

Peterson, Jeff
Foil and Specialty Effects Association **(448)**

Peterson, Jennifer
Movement Disorder Society **(620)**

Peterson, Jess

Society for Range Management **(920)**

Peterson, Jodi
National Science Teachers Association **(790)**

Peterson, John
Casting Industry Suppliers Association **(344)**
Land Improvement Contractors of America **(593)**

Peterson, Joyce
National Auctioneers Association **(711)**

Peterson, CAE, SPHR, Karen
American Society of Hand Therapists **(199)**

Peterson, Lida
Connected International Meeting Professionals
Association **(377)**

Peterson, Lisa
American Kennel Club **(143)**

Peterson, Lowell
Writers Guild of America East **(1029)**

Peterson, CAE, Lynell "Lynn" G.
American Psychological Association - Society of
Clinical Psychology **(169)**

Peterson, MBA, Maggie
Society of Biological Psychiatry **(931)**

Peterson, Marina
Society for the Anthropology of North America **(923)**

Peterson, Mark G.
American Institute of Certified Public Accountants
(137)

Peterson, Michael D.
HR Policy Association **(480)**

Peterson, MA, RHIA, Patt
American Health Information Management Association
(129)

Peterson, Paul A.
National Organization of Life and Health Insurance
Guaranty Association **(777)**

Peterson, JD, Richard N.
American Academy of Orthopaedic Surgeons **(38)**

Peterson, Stacey
International Society of Automation **(571)**

Peterson, Susan
Incentive Marketing Association **(487)**

Peterson, Theodore L.
Consumer Healthcare Products Association **(381)**

Peterson, William
National Speakers Association **(795)**

Petherick, Glenn
National Housing and Rehabilitation Association **(760)**

Petit, Kim
Synthetic Yarn and Fiber Association **(967)**

Petkanas, Bill
Institute of General Semantics **(500)**

Petras, CMP, CTIE, Diane
The Travel Institute **(979)**

Petras, Donna
Child Welfare League of America **(353)**

Petrella, Vincent J.
Yacht Brokers Association of America **(1030)**

Petrelli, Dave
Nashville Songwriters Association, International **(625)**

Petri, Jessica
Association for Corporate Growth **(244)**

Petricone, Michael D.
Consumer Electronics Association **(381)**

Petrilli, Diane
American Radio Relay League **(172)**

Petrillo-Smith, Kathryn
Association of Small Foundations *(309)*

Petroskey, Dennis
US Travel Association *(983)*

Petrovic, John
American Educational Studies Association *(116)*

Petrowski, Mary Jane
Association of College and Research Libraries *(273)*

Petrulla, Maraina
American Pediatric Surgical Association *(162)*

Petrus, Sara
Retail Solutions Providers Association *(885)*

Petrush, Jessica
Association of Teachers of Maternal and Child Health *(312)*

Petrush, Jessica H.
Association of Schools of Public Health *(307)*

Petruska, Dr. George K.
Council of Chiropractic Physiological Therapeutics and Rehabilitation *(392)*

Petruzzo, Frank
Council of American Survey Research Organizations *(392)*

Pettigrew, Jennifer
Self Storage Association *(896)*

Pettigrew, Kelly L.
Offshore Marine Service Association *(827)*

Pettinger, Roger A.
American Hardware Manufacturers Association *(128)*

Pettingill, Meg
International Surface Fabricators Association *(576)*

Pettit, C. L.
Reusable Industrial Packaging Association *(885)*

Pettit, Clark
American Business Media *(87)*

Pettit, Esq., David H.
American Sports Builders Association *(212)*

Pettit, PhD, Dr. Raymond
The Advertising Research Foundation *(13)*

Pettit, Jason L.
Southwest Airlines Pilots Association *(953)*

Pettit, Lorren
Healthcare Information and Management Systems Society *(471)*

Petto, Mary
Women's Transportation Seminar (WTS International) *(1024)*

Petty, Cissy
Jesuit Association of Student Personnel Administrators *(587)*

Petty, Gary F.
National Private Truck Council *(782)*

Petty, Jacqueline
International Flight Services Association *(545)*

Petty, Jason Hawthorne
Gerontological Society of America *(460)*

Petzke, Christina
Zonta International *(1030)*

Peurifoy, Rae
Research Society on Alcoholism *(882)*

Pew, Reed
American Academy of Professional Coders *(40)*

Pezold, George
Certified Claims Professional Accreditation Council *(349)*

Pezold, George Carl
Transportation and Logistics Council *(978)*

Pezzillo, Rich
Hemophilia Federation of America *(474)*

Pezzullo, Ted J.
Healthcare Distribution Management Association *(471)*

Pfaendtner, Donna
National Organization of State Offices of Rural Health *(778)*

Pfaff, Marion
MGMA-ACMPE *(614)*

Pfaff, Sherry
National Agri-Marketing Association *(629)*

Pfeffer, Linda D.
Aerobics and Fitness Association of America *(13)*

Pfeffer, Mitchell
Souvenirs, Gifts and Novelties Trade Association *(953)*

Pfeifer, Katie
American Geological Institute *(126)*

Pfeiffenberger, BSN, CCTC, RN, Patrice
International Transplant Nurses Society *(578)*

Pfeiffer, Michael
American Nurses Association *(156)*

Pfeiffer, PhD, Stephen M.
Association for the Advancement of Psychology *(258)*

Pfenninger, Shelly
Vacation Rental Managers Association *(1007)*

Pfingst, CPA, Linda
Gravure Association of America *(465)*

Pfuhl, Jamie
Food Industry Association Executives *(449)*

Pham, Kim
American Council of Engineering Companies *(109)*

Pham, Michel Tuan
Society for Consumer Psychology *(907)*

Phan, Philip
National Association of Biology Teachers *(648)*

Phares, Liz
American Association of Anatomists *(54)*

Pharr, Jeff
Association of Professional Flight Attendants *(301)*

Phelan, Kim
Associated Equipment Distributors *(235)*

Phelan, Michael
International Society for Pharmaceutical Engineering *(567)*

Phelan, Tina
Association of Oncology Social Work *(297)*
International Kitchen Exhaust Cleaning Association *(553)*
National Renal Administrators Association *(786)*

Phelleps, Moya
Coal Exporters Association of the U.S. *(359)*
National Mining Association *(772)*

Phelps, Christine E.
American Academy of Neurology *(36)*

Phelps, David H.
American Institute for International Steel *(136)*

Phelps, George R.
Council of North American Insulation Manufacturers Association *(396)*

Phelps, Greg
National Ground Water Association *(756)*

Phelps, Kathy K.
Biscuit and Cracker Manufacturers' Association *(330)*

Phelps, Laura
American Mushroom Institute *(153)*

Phelps, Mike
National American Legion Press Association *(634)*

Phelps, Richard
Association of Boarding Schools *(270)*

Phelus, Dean
American Association of Museums *(65)*

Philbin, Eileen
American Senior Benefits Association *(178)*

Philippart, David
National Federation of Priests' Councils *(749)*

Philipps, Jim
National Association of County Intergovernmental Relations Officials *(660)*

Philips, Chris Ann
American Association of Neurological Surgeons *(66)*

Philips, Christie
NAFSA: Association of International Educators *(624)*

Philips, Dan
Operations Security Professionals Society *(828)*

Philips, Kat
Association of Directory Publishers *(279)*

Philips, Mary
American Trucking Associations *(218)*

Phillips, Alvin K.
Council for Opportunity in Education *(390)*

Phillips, Becky
American Medical Writers Association *(150)*

Phillips, Carl
Mystery Shopping Providers Association *(623)*

Phillips, Carolyn
Association of Assistive Technology ACT Programs *(268)*
Association of Technology Act Projects *(313)*

Phillips, Dr. Cheryl
LeadingAge (American Association of Homes and Services for the Aging) *(595)*

Phillips, Dan
International Horn Society *(550)*

Phillips, Debbie
Canadian-American Business Council *(341)*

Phillips, Elizabeth
Interactive Media Entertainment & Gaming Association *(507)*

Phillips, III, Fred J.
National Black MBA Association *(714)*

Phillips, CAE, Gail S.
National Association of Residential Property Managers *(691)*

Phillips, Ginger
American Council on Consumer Interests *(110)*

Phillips, Heather
Equipment Service Association *(433)*

Phillips, James
National Council of Acoustical Consultants *(733)*

Phillips, James
National Council of Acoustical Consultants *(733)*

Phillips, Jay
American Public Human Services Association *(171)*

Phillips, Jim
Association of Equipment Management Professionals *(281)*

Phillips, John
International Society for Pharmaceutical Engineering *(567)*

Phillips, John M.
American Society of Pension Professionals & Actuaries *(206)*

Phillips, Katesha
Cardiovascular Credentialing International *(342)*

Phillips, PhD, Kimberley
American Society of Primatologists *(208)*

Phillips, Larisa
The Counselors of Real Estate *(401)*

Phillips, LaRita
League for Innovation in the Community College *(595)*

Phillips, Leonard A.
International District Energy Association *(540)*

Phillips, Linda L.
Commission on Accreditation for Law Enforcement Agencies Incorporation *(367)*

Phillips, Mark
American Association of Homeopathic Pharmacists *(62)*

Phillips, Melissa
Professional Services Council *(865)*

Phillips, Meridith
American Society of Nuclear Cardiology *(205)*

Phillips, Nick
American Baseball Coaches Association *(80)*

Phillips, Pat
Professional Skaters Association *(865)*

Phillips, Patti
National Association of Collegiate Women Athletic Administrators *(656)*

Phillips, Paulette
Professional Convention Management Association *(861)*

Phillips, Ronald B.
Animal Health Institute *(223)*

Phillips, Tina
State Government Affairs Council *(961)*

Phillips, Todd
Federation of State Medical Boards of the United States *(442)*

Phillips, Tricia
National Independent Living Association *(762)*

Phillips, Will
International Association of Equine Dentists *(520)*

Phillips, Esq., William L.
Brotherhood of Railroad Signalmen *(336)*

Phillps, Nancy
American Cream Draft Horse Association *(111)*

Philp, Julie
The Association of Community Pharmacists Congressional Network *(276)*

Philp, Steve
The Open Group *(828)*

Philport, Joseph C.
Traffic Audit Bureau for Media Measurement, Inc. *(977)*

Phipps, Anthony
Emergency Nurses Association *(425)*

Phipps, Karl
Society of Tribologists and Lubrication Engineers *(949)*

Phipps, Linda
Associated Construction Distributors International *(235)*

Phipps, Robert "Bobby"
American Society for Pharmacology and Experimental Therapeutics *(188)*

Photiadis, Katie

National Insulation Association *(766)*

Photos, Bob
International Chiropractors Association *(534)*

Piacento, Ed
American Humor Studies Association *(134)*

Piacenza, Joanne
Material Handling Equipment Distributors Association *(608)*

Piatak, Karen
Conservation and Preservation Charities of America *(377)*

Piatkiewicz, Mariola
IEEE Electron Devices Society *(484)*

Piccione, Lisa
National Business Aviation Association *(716)*

Piccirilli, Robin
League for Innovation in the Community College *(595)*

Pichon, Sharon R.
American Association of Pharmaceutical Scientists *(68)*

Picillo, Anne
International District Energy Association *(540)*

Pickel, Brad
Atlantic intra Coastal Waterway Association *(319)*

Pickel, Robert G.
International Swaps and Derivatives Association *(576)*

Pickett, Jenny
Agriculture Council of America *(16)*
National Agri-Marketing Association *(629)*

Pickett, Peggy J.
American Association of Textile Chemists and Colorists *(75)*

Pickett, Teresa
Organization of Professional Employees of the U.S. Department of Agriculture (OPEDA) *(832)*

Pickett, Willard D.
Brotherhood of Railroad Signalmen *(336)*

Pickholtz, Sarajoy
IPC Washington Office *(585)*

Pickus, Michael
American Society of Military Comptrollers *(203)*

Picone, Brian
National Association of Foreign Trade Zones *(669)*

Piening, Robert
Professional Services Council *(865)*

Pier, Gwen
National Sculpture Society *(790)*

Pierce, Allan D.
The Acoustical Society of America *(11)*

Pierce, Carol
National Federation of Press Women *(749)*

Pierce, Cathy
Industrial Asset Management Council *(492)*

Pierce, Dennis R.
Brotherhood of Locomotive Engineers and Trainmen *(336)*

Pierce, Jared
American Society of Naval Engineers *(204)*

Pierce, Jason R.
Alpha Kappa Psi *(26)*

Pierce, Ken
Society of Dance History Scholars *(934)*

Pierce, Kim
Academy of Molecular Imaging *(7)*

Pierce, Lori
Animal Behavior Society *(223)*

Pierce, Monica
SSPC: the Society for Protective Coatings *(960)*

Pierce, Rob
Special Interest Group for Design of Communication *(955)*

Pierce, Russell
American Court and Commercial Newspapers *(111)*

Pierce, Valerie
American Board of Psychiatry & Neurology *(83)*

Pierno, Theresa
National Parks Conservation Association *(779)*

Pierson, DDS, Ken W.
National Association of Seventh-Day Adventist Dentists *(695)*

Pierson, Lloyd
National Basketball Referees Association *(713)*

Pierson, Michelle
Society for College and University Planning *(906)*

Pietrangelo, Anthony "Tony" R.
Nuclear Energy Institute *(824)*

Pietrangelo, Renee L.
American Network of Community Options and Resources (ANCOR) *(155)*

Pietranton, PhD, CAE, Arlene A.
American Speech-Language-Hearing Association *(212)*

Pietrykowski, Laura
Association of College and University Housing Officers-International *(274)*

Pietrzak, Allison
Turnaround Management Association *(982)*

Pietrzak, Ron
Association of Steel Distributors *(311)*
International Society of Transport Aircraft Trading *(574)*

Pietrzyk, Susan
Association for Africanist Anthropology *(238)*

Pietsch, Paul
Association for Demand Response & Smart Grid *(244)*
Demand Response and Smart Grid Coalition *(410)*

Pigg, Bob J.
Asbestos Cement Product Producers Association *(231)*

Pigg, Mark
AGN International North America, Inc *(15)*

Pighetti, Gina
American Association of Veterinary Immunologists *(76)*

Pignanelli, Frank
National Association of Industrial Bankers *(675)*

Pignato, IOM, Robert
American Wholesale Marketers Association *(221)*

Pihos, MA, Diana
American Association of Diabetes Educators *(60)*

Pike, Angela
Association of Water Technologies *(317)*

Pike, Dean
American Salers Association *(176)*

Pike, Lisa
American Academy of Environmental Engineers *(33)*

Pike, Michelle
GAMA International *(455)*

Pike, Sarah
Association of Cooperative Educators *(277)*

Pilbeam, Chad
Warehousing Education and Research Council *(1012)*

Pilkington, John
National Stripper Well Association *(797)*

Pille, CAE, SPHR, Mary
Employers Association *(426)*

Pillsworth, CMP, Elizabeth
American Epilepsy Society *(117)*
International Association of Campus Law Enforcement
Administrators *(517)*

Pilson, CAE, Barry
TESOL International Association *(971)*

Pimental, Jane
American Association of Thoracic Surgery *(53)*

Pimentel, Arcelia
Media Financial Management Association *(610)*

Pimpinella, Lisa
Electrostatic Discharge Association *(425)*

Pina, CMP, Penny
American Mathematical Society *(148)*

Pinch, Trevor
Society for Social Studies of Science *(921)*

Pinchock, George
National Catholic Band Association *(718)*

Pincus, Shirley
Inter-Industry Conference on Auto Collision Repair
(506)

Pindell, Lakisha
Tire Industry Association *(975)*

Pinero-Kluge, CAE, Liane
Association of University Programs in Health
Administration *(316)*

Pines, Steven
Education Industry Association *(420)*

Pinholster, Ginger
American Association for the Advancement of Science
(51)

Pinizzotto, Nick
Delta Waterfowl Foundation *(409)*

Pinkham, Doug G.
Public Affairs Council *(868)*

Pinkston, Anthony
International Decorative Artisans League *(540)*

Pinniger, Jennifer Joy
National Stone, Sand, and Gravel Association *(796)*

Pinsky, Mark
Opportunity Finance Network *(829)*

Pinsoneault, Laura
Alliance for Children and Families *(22)*

Pinto, Anna
Society of Scribes *(947)*

Pinto, Sara
Association of American Publishers *(266)*

Pinto-Bailey, A. Cristina
Brazilian Studies Association *(335)*

Pintozzi, Bonnie
Association of Directory Publishers *(279)*

Pinyo, June
American Pain Society *(161)*
Metal Construction Association *(613)*
National Association for Healthcare Quality *(639)*

Piper, Morley L.
Newspaper Association Managers *(810)*

Piper, Nancy
Accredited Pet Cemetery Society *(10)*

Pipinou, Jennifer
National Rehabilitation Counseling Association *(785)*

Pipkin, Ronald M.
Law and Society Association *(594)*

Pippen, Randy
National Council of Supervisors of Mathematics *(737)*

Pirolt, Katie
United States Conference of Mayors *(992)*

Pirrello, Lee Anne
American Society of Consultant Pharmacists *(195)*

Pirro, Erin
American Society of Agricultural Consultants *(191)*

Pisano, Paul
National Beer Wholesalers Association *(713)*

Pisano, Susan
America's Health Insurance Plans *(28)*

Piscatelli, Kat
American Academy of Nursing *(37)*

Piscitelli, Ralph
The Conference Board *(374)*

Pisner, Lauren
AABB - American Association of Blood Banks *(1)*

Pistilli, Vince
American College of Nuclear Medicine *(98)*

Pistilli, Vincent
Society of Nuclear Medicine *(943)*

Pitcher, Nancy G.
Real Estate Roundtable *(876)*

Pitman, Brian K.
Glass Association of North America *(461)*

Pitsch, Sue
Society of Toxicologic Pathologists *(948)*
Society of Toxicologic Pathology *(948)*

Pitsor, Kyle
National Electrical Manufacturers Association *(744)*

Pitt, Elena
National Alliance for Advanced Transportation
Batteries *(631)*

Pitt, Phil
INDA, Association of the Nonwoven Fabrics Industry
(488)

Pitt, Stephen R.
National Automobile Dealers Association *(711)*

Pittampalli, Eshwar
Open Mobile Alliance *(828)*

Pittard, CMP, Brandice
Association for Institutional Research *(250)*

Pittenger, Michele Marini
Travel Goods Association *(979)*

Pitter, Robert
North American Society for the Sociology of Sport
(822)

Pittman, Moira
Directors Guild of America *(413)*

Pittman, Suzanne Kay
Vinyl Siding Institute, Inc. *(1009)*

Pitts, Chris
National Federation of Independent Business (NFIB)
(748)

Pitts, Devri
National Aircraft Resale Association *(630)*

Pitts, Greg
National Association of Television Program Executives
(705)

Pitz, Julie
Neuro-Developmental Treatment Association *(808)*

Pizzano, CMP, Terry
Institute for Supply Management *(497)*

Placher, David

American Court and Commercial Newspapers *(111)*

Placher, David
Public Notice Resource Center *(869)*

Plack, Janice
Accreditation Association for Ambulatory Health Care
(9)

Planzer, Paul
Air Traffic Control Association *(19)*

Plasker, James R.
ASPRS-The Imaging and Geospatial Information
Society *(233)*

Plaskett, Ayesha
Taxicab, Limousine & Paratransit Association *(969)*

Plassa, Stephanie
The Electrochemical Society *(423)*

Plate, Norman E.
Scribes-The American Society of Legal Writers *(893)*

Platek, Esq., Todd L.
International Cargo Gear Bureau *(533)*

Plater, Pamela
Society of Computed Body Tomography and Magnetic
Resonance *(933)*
Society of Radiologists in Ultrasound *(946)*

Plato, Laura
National Horsemen's Benevolent and Protective
Association *(760)*

Platt, Nathan
American Society of Dowsers *(197)*

Plaugher, Zoe
InterAction (American Council of Voluntary
International Action) *(506)*

Plaut, Peg
National Barbecue Association *(712)*
Society for Foodservice Management *(909)*

Plavnik, La Tosha
Consortium of Social Science Associations *(379)*

Pleiman, Judy
Education Law Association *(420)*

Pleming, Sue
InterAction (American Council of Voluntary
International Action) *(506)*

Plenge, William H.
National Concrete Masonry Association *(725)*

Plenkovich, Krisinda
SPIE - The International Society for Optical
Engineering *(958)*

Pless, CAE, CPA, Dana M.
SAE International *(889)*

Pleteher, Christine J.
Congress of Lung Association Staffs *(377)*

Pletka, Danielle
American Enterprise Institute for Public Policy
Research *(117)*

Plienis, Robert
Association on Higher Education and Disability *(319)*

Plizka, Laura
Delta Nu Alpha *(409)*

Plog, Renee
National Council on Crime and Delinquency *(738)*

Plonski, Renie
American Philological Association *(163)*

Plotnick, Amy
American Public Human Services Association *(171)*

Plough, Greg
Scaffold Industry Association *(891)*

Plumlee, Lawrence

American Academy of Environmental Medicine **(33)**

Plumley, Thad
National Ground Water Association **(756)**

Plummer, Leslie
Phi Alpha Delta **(845)**

Plummer, Matt
American Federation of Musicians **(119)**

Plummer, Roger
International Engineering Consortium **(543)**

Plunkett, Chris
Audio Engineering Society **(320)**

Plunkett, Darlene
National Sporting Goods Association **(796)**

Plush, Kate
National Marine Manufacturers Association **(771)**

Pluvinage, Marie-Pierre
Satellite Industry Association **(891)**

Plybon, Andrea
National Association of Schools of Theatre **(694)**

Poarch, Geno
National Rural Health Association **(788)**

Pochelski, CMP, Louise
Utilimetrics/Alliance for Advanced Metering & Data
   Management Solutions **(1006)**

Pochter, Marisa
Commercial Law League of America **(366)**

Podany, Jon
Ladies Professional Golf Association **(592)**

Podgorski, Jr., Dennis
Government Finance Officers Association of the United
   States and Canada **(464)**

Podolak, Patricia
Organization for Safety and Asepsis Procedures **(831)**

Podos, Lisa
ArtTable **(231)**

Podosek, Frank
Geochemical Society **(458)**

Poe, Marianne
Association of Professors of Gynecology and Obstetrics
   (302)

Poehling, MD, Gary G.
Arthroscopy Association of North America **(230)**

Poehlman, Colleen
League of Historic American Theatres **(595)**

Poethig, Dr. Eunice B.
International Association of Women Ministers **(529)**

Pogue-Geile, Michael
Behavior Genetics Association **(327)**

Pohland, Liz
Society for Technical Communication **(922)**

Pohlmann, Susan W.
International Security Management Association **(564)**

Poindexter, CAE, Douglas L.
World Pet Association **(1027)**

Poindexter, Margaret H.
American Kennel Club **(143)**

Poinelli, Michelle
American Hotel & Lodging Association (AH&LA) **(134)**

Pointer, Duke
Natural Stone Council **(807)**

Poire, Marie-Laure
Women in International Security **(1021)**

Poisant, Molly
International Microwave Power Institute **(556)**

Poisson, Esq., David E.
State Capital Group **(961)**

Poisson, Pam
American Wind Energy Association (AWEA) **(221)**

Pojanowski, Sarah
Selected Independent Funeral Homes **(896)**

Pokharel, Roshan
American Translators Association **(217)**

Pokorny, Mercedes
American Association of Teachers of German **(74)**

Polakow, Mark
National Association of Educational Procurement, Inc.
   (664)

Polakowski, Bach
National Lesbian and Gay Journalists Association **(769)**

Polan, PhD, Susan L.
American Public Health Association **(171)**

Polburn, Aaron
International Hot Rod Association **(550)**

Poley, Scott
Minor League Baseball **(617)**
National Association of Professional Baseball Leagues
   (686)

Policano, Chris
American Federation of State, County and Municipal
   Employees **(120)**

Polikoff, Stuart
Organization for the Promotion and Advancement of
   Small Telecommunications Companies **(831)**

Poling, Charles
American Society of Radiologic Technologists **(208)**

Poling, Janet A.
American Forest & Paper Association **(123)**

Poling, CAE, Ronald D.
Holiday and Decorative Association **(477)**

Polio, Charlene
American Association for Applied Linguistics **(47)**

Polite, Christine
American Geriatrics Society **(126)**

Polka, Matthew M.
American Cable Association **(87)**

Pollack, Bridget Weston
SCORE Association **(893)**

Pollack, Richard J.
American Hospital Association **(133)**

Pollack, Wendy
Regional Plan Association **(879)**

Pollander, Donna
Equipment Service Association **(433)**

Pollander, Donna
The International Fluid Power Society **(545)**

Pollard, Diane
Society of Petroleum Evaluation Engineers **(944)**

Pollard, III, Jeff
National Association of State Boards of Education
   (698)

Pollard, Margie
Thoroughbred Racing Associations of North America
   (974)

Pollett, Jessica
Outdoor Writers Association of America **(835)**

Polley, Catherine M.
Food Marketing Institute **(449)**

Pollini, Alison
United States Rowing Association **(998)**

Pollitt, CHC, USN, Gary R.
Military Chaplains Association of the United States
   (616)

Pollitt, Kelly Duquin
National Association of Elementary School Principals
   (664)

Pollock, Ben
National Society of Newspaper Columnists **(794)**

Pollock, Denise
Native American Contractors Association **(806)**

Pollock, Lance
Professional Construction Estimators Association of
   America **(861)**

Pollock, Susan
American Society of Animal Science **(192)**

Pollock, Susan M.
Poultry Science Association **(854)**

Polls, Irwin
The Society for Freshwater Science **(910)**

Polly, Kris D.
National Water Resources Association **(804)**

Polonio, EdD, Narcisa
Association of Community College Trustees **(276)**

Polowy, Carolyn I.
National Association of Social Workers **(696)**

Polskin, Howard
MPA - The Association of Magazine Media **(620)**

Poltrack, Terry
American Society of Landscape Architects **(201)**

Polvinale, CMP, Bonnie
American Physical Therapy Association **(164)**

Pomerance, Robin
North American Performing Arts Managers and Agents
   (819)

Pomerantz, CAE, Paul
Drug Information Association **(417)**

Pomerantz-Boro, Alisa
Cantors Assembly **(342)**

Pomerene, Melissa
American Brachytherapy Society **(85)**

Pomilia, Joseph
Insurance Accounting and Systems Association **(504)**

Pomilio, Pete
American Association of Heart Failure Nurses **(62)**
Association for Accounting Marketing **(238)**
The Wound, Ostomy and Continence Nurses Society
   (1028)

Pompei, Penny
Women Construction Owners and Executives, USA
   (1020)

Pomrenke, Jacob
Society for American Baseball Research **(903)**

Pon, Jeff
Society for Human Resource Management **(911)**

Ponci, Ferdinanda
IEEE Instrumentation and Measurement Society **(484)**

Ponder, Jeffrey D.
Post-Tensioning Institute **(853)**

Ponder, Kenda
Red Angus Association of America **(877)**

Ponder, Steve
Geothermal Resources Council **(460)**

Pons, Ted E
American Arbitration Association **(46)**

Ponta, Stephanie
Society for Gynecologic Investigation **(910)**

Ponyik, Mary Jane
Catholic Theological Society of America *(346)*

Poodiack, Anne
International Franchise Association *(547)*

Pool, James W
Professional School Photographers Association
International *(865)*

Poole, Bill
National Rifle Association of America *(787)*

Poole, Hardy
National Textile Association *(800)*

Poole, PhD, Dr. Kenneth E.
Council for Community and Economic Research *(388)*

Popadziuk, Kelly
Employers Association *(426)*

Pope, Janice Prince
Spotted Saddle Horse Breeders' and Exhibitors'
Association *(959)*

Pope, Kyler
National Frame Building Association *(753)*

Pope, Lauren-Ashley
National Tour Association *(800)*

Pope, Lee Ann
National Association of State Procurement Officials
(702)

Pope, Megan
American Association of Veterinary State Boards *(76)*

Popham, Susan
Association of Teachers of Technical Writing *(313)*

Popielnicki, BA, Ana
International Society for Quality of Life Research *(569)*

Popkewitz, Ian
American Society of Agronomy (ASA, CSSA, SSSA)
(191)
Crop Science Society of America *(404)*
Soil Science Society of America *(951)*

Popkin, Marla
Outdoor Power Equipment Institute *(835)*

Poplawski, Anthony
Pacific Coast Marine Firemen, Oilers, Watertenders
and Wipers Association *(836)*

Popovic, James
American Measuring Tool Manufacturers Association
(148)

Popovich, Jeff
American Public Transportation Association *(171)*

Popovich, Luke
National Mining Association *(772)*

Popp, Jay A
National Association of Vertical Transportation
Professionals *(708)*

Popper, Virginia
Society of Ethnobiology *(935)*

Popwell, Anita
Consumer Data Industry Association *(381)*

Poray, CAE, John L.
Society of Broadcast Engineers *(931)*

Porcaro, Marissa
Professional Beauty Association | National
Cosmetology Association *(861)*

Porch, Jason
Association of Procurement Technical Assistance
Centers *(300)*

Porempski, Joe
National American Legion Press Association *(634)*

Porinchak, Laura M.
Association of the Wall and Ceiling Industry *(314)*

Porr, Susannah F.
National Association of Steel Pipe Distributors *(703)*

Porreca, Beth
United States Lacrosse *(995)*

Porreca, Michael
Society of Hospital Medicine *(938)*

Portalatin, Maria
Labor Council for Latin American Advancement
(LCLAA) *(592)*

Porte, Phillip
National Association for Medical Direction of
Respiratory Care *(640)*

Porter, Barry
National Environmental Health Association *(746)*

Porter, Cynthia
The American Society of Pediatric Hematology/
Oncology *(206)*

Porter, Dennis
Credit Union Executives Society *(403)*

Porter, Doug
Blue Cross Blue Shield Association *(332)*

Porter, Gregg
National Head Start Association *(758)*

Porter, MBA, RPh, Johnny W.
Kappa Psi Pharmaceutical Fraternity, Inc. *(590)*

Porter, Martin
Content Delivery and Security Association *(382)*

Porter, Richard
Tire Industry Association *(975)*

Porter, Samantha
Golf Course Builders Association of America *(463)*

Porter, Sandra
National Association of Supervisors for Business
Education *(704)*

Porter, Sara
American Academy of Esthetic Dentistry *(33)*
American Prosthodontic Society *(168)*
Giving Institute *(461)*
Giving USA Foundation *(461)*
International Society of Appraisers *(570)*

Porter, Serena
National Private Truck Council *(782)*

Porter, Shannon
National Association of Student Councils *(703)*

Portillo, Anthony
Society of Neurointerventional Surgery *(942)*

Portman, Robert M.
American Academy of Dermatology *(32)*

Portnow, Neil
National Academy of Recording Arts and Sciences
(628)

Porzio, Stephen
American Statistical Association *(213)*

Posadas, Aurelio
National Plant Board *(781)*

Posen, Marion J.
Mobile Air Conditioning Society Worldwide *(617)*

Posluszny, Susan
American Institute of Floral Designers *(138)*

Possick, A. Moshe
National Conference of Yeshiva Principals *(729)*

Possumato, John
Automotive Fleet and Leasing Association *(322)*

Post, Ana M. Chiquillo
National Council for the Social Studies *(733)*

Post, Gretchen S.

American Tort Reform Association *(217)*

Post, Jeff
Chemical Fabrics and Film Association *(351)*

Post, Marcie Craig
International Reading Association *(562)*

Post, Mary
American Board of Anesthesiology *(81)*

Post, Patrick
National Small Business Association *(792)*

Postava, John
National Association of Catastrophe Adjusters *(651)*

Postilion, Rita
American Burn Association *(87)*

Postone, Zach
Van Alen Institute *(1007)*

Potchoiba, Linda
Society for Research on Nicotine and Tobacco *(920)*
The Psychonomic Society *(868)*

Poteet, Gay
BEMA - The Baking Industry Suppliers Association
(328)

Potegal, Michael
International Society for Research on Aggression *(569)*

Potillo, Ed
National Alliance of Black School Educators *(632)*

Potochniak, Alicia
American Society for Aesthetic Plastic Surgery *(180)*

Potrzebowski, PhD, Patricia
National Association of Public Health Statistics and
Information Systems *(642)*

Potter, Chris
National Reining Horse Association *(785)*

Potter, CAE, Edward L.
Americas Association of Cooperative/Mutual Insurance
Societies *(222)*

Potter, James G.
American Academy of Physician Assistants *(40)*

Potter, John
Radio Advertising Bureau *(873)*

Potter, Jonathan
Application Developers Alliance *(226)*

Potter, Kathryn
American Hotel & Lodging Association (AH&LA) *(134)*

Potter, Lori
National Federation of Press Women *(749)*

Potter, Mary
American Society for Nondestructive Testing *(187)*

Potter, Sheri
American Institute of Biological Sciences *(137)*

Potts, Billye
Association for Healthcare Foodservice *(248)*

Potts, Julie Anna
American Farm Bureau Federation *(118)*

Potts, Liza
Special Interest Group for Design of Communication
(955)

Poulakidas, Jennifer
Association of Public and Land-Grant Universities
(APLU) *(303)*

Poulson, Brad
Small Publishers Association of North America *(901)*

Pound, William T.
National Conference of State Legislatures *(728)*

Povhe, Lynne
North American Menopause Society *(818)*

Povich, David J.
United States Cutting Tool Institute *(993)*

Povich, Harris
Biophysical Society *(330)*

Powell, MD, Amy
American Medical Society for Sports Medicine *(149)*

Powell, Ann
American Society for Colposcopy and Cervical Pathology *(183)*

Powell, Claudia
Women's International Network of Utility Professionals *(1023)*

Powell, Debbie
Quail Unlimited *(871)*

Powell, Devon
American Herbal Products Association *(130)*
International Aloe Science Council *(510)*

Powell, CMP, Diane
American Medical Technologists *(150)*

Powell, Elizabeth
American Postal Workers Union *(167)*

Powell, Greg
American British White Park Association *(86)*

Powell, John T.
American Peanut Shellers Association *(162)*

Powell, Judson B.
Ford Motor Minority Dealers Association *(451)*

Powell, Katie
American Dental Hygienists' Association *(114)*

Powell, Lisa E.
American Pilots' Association *(165)*

Powell, MBA, Lynn S.
Institute of Certified Professional Managers *(498)*

Powell, Marion
National Association of Professional Employer Organizations *(687)*

Powell, SPHR, Marita A.
American Academy of Orthopaedic Surgeons *(38)*

Powell, Mark
The Bluetooth Special Interest Group *(332)*

Powell, Marlon
Association for Commuter Transportation *(242)*

Powell, Marquita
American Bankers Association *(79)*

Powell, Melissa
American Miniature Horse Association *(152)*

Powell, Michael
National Cable & Telecommunications Association *(717)*

Powell, Pam
National Council of Examiners for Engineering and Surveying *(734)*

Powell, Russell
Energy Traffic Association *(428)*

Powell, Scott
Property Loss Research Bureau *(867)*

Powell, Sharon
National Association of Clean Water Agencies *(654)*

Powell, Teasha
Academy Health *(3)*

Powell, CAE, PhD, Thomas
American Meat Science Association *(148)*

Powell, PA-C, Thomas
American Academy of Physician Assistants in Occupational Medicine *(40)*

Powers, CAE, Celeste M.
Independent Lubricant Manufacturers Association *(490)*

Powers, Diane
National Association of Insurance and Financial Advisors *(675)*

Powers, Janene Chan
International Bone and Mineral Society *(530)*

Powers, Jenny
National Council for Prescription Drug Programs *(732)*

Powers, Joshua
Association of Black Foundation Executives *(269)*

Powers, Kate
Risk and Insurance Management Society, Inc. (RIMS) *(886)*

Powers, Lisa
Personal Care Products Council *(842)*

Powers, Normalyn
National Senior Corps Association *(790)*

Powery, Luke
Academy of Homiletics *(5)*

Powills, Suzanne
National Safety Council *(789)*

Poynter, PharmD, Jon
American College of Clinical Pharmacy *(94)*

Poynter, CPA, R. Kinney
National Association of State Auditors, Comptrollers and Treasurers *(698)*

Pozsik, Carol
National Tuberculosis Controllers Association *(802)*

Prado, Eileen
Solar Rating and Certification Corporation *(952)*

Prager, PhD, Dr. Martin
Materials Properties Council *(609)*
Welding Research Council *(1015)*

Prager, Susan Westerberg
Association of American Law Schools *(265)*

Pramstaller, CAE, Michael E.
American Council of Engineering Companies *(109)*

Prange, Heidi
Society of Toxicology *(948)*

Praschil, Roy
National Association of State Mental Health Directors *(701)*

Prater, Carmen
Society of Flight Test Engineers *(936)*

Prater, Marcus
Association of Gaming Equipment Manufacturers *(285)*

Prather, Catherine
National Tour Association *(800)*

Prather, Stella
Baptist Communicators Association *(326)*

Prather, Victoria
Copper Development Association *(384)*

Prats, CAE, Lisa M.
Building Owners and Managers Association International *(337)*

Pratt, Anthony
Society of Automotive Analysts *(930)*

Pratt, Frances
Women in Agribusiness *(1020)*

Pratt, James W.
American Forensic Association *(123)*

Pratt, Jane
NPES, The Association for Suppliers of Printing, Publishing, and Converting Technologies *(824)*

Obesity Society *(825)*

Pratt, Stuart K.
Consumer Data Industry Association *(381)*

Pray, Dianne
United States Racquet Stringers Association *(998)*

Preble, Jay
Major Indoor Soccer League *(601)*

Precht, Ron
American Massage Therapy Association *(147)*

Preece, Ashley
Utilities Telecom Council *(1006)*

Prendergast, E. James
Institute of Electrical and Electronics Engineers (IEEE) *(499)*

Prendergast, Sean
Major League Soccer *(601)*

Prenovost, Gary
Professional Association of Diving Instructors *(859)*

Prentice, Joshua
National Council for Interior Design Qualifications *(732)*

Prentice, Melissa
Library and Information Technology Association *(597)*

Prentice, William M.
Ambulatory Surgery Center Association *(28)*

Presser, PharmD, Arthur M.
Huntington College of Health Sciences *(481)*

Pressley, Erin
National Association of Convenience Stores *(658)*

Pressley, James A.
International Brotherhood of Boilermakers, Iron Shipbuilders, Blacksmiths, Forgers and Helpers *(531)*

Prest, Art
Rural Telecommunications Group *(889)*

Prest, George
Lift Manufacturers Product Section - Material Handling Institute *(597)*
Loading Dock Equipment Manufacturers *(599)*
Material Handling Industry of America *(608)*
Materials Handling and Management Society *(608)*

Prestel, Kelly
American Alliance for Theatre and Education *(44)*

Preston, Diana
American Bankers Association Securities Association (ABASA) *(79)*

Preston, CRNA, DNS.c, John
American Association of Nurse Anesthetists *(67)*

Preston, CMP, Katey
American Institute of Steel Construction *(140)*

Preston, Mark
United States Tennis Association *(1000)*

Preston, Robin
National School Boards Association *(789)*

Preston, Tonda
National Gerontological Nursing Association *(755)*
Society of Trauma Nurses *(949)*

Prestwood, Troy Donté
Association of Public and Land-Grant Universities (APLU) *(303)*

Pretlow, Ashanti
American Harp Society *(129)*

Prettyman, Sandra Spickard
American Educational Studies Association *(116)*

Prettyman, Ty
National Air Carrier Association *(630)*

Preus, Anthony

Society for Ancient Greek Philosophy *(904)*

Preuss, CNS, MACN, MD, Harry G.
American College of Nutrition *(99)*

Preuss, Marisa
Future Business Leaders of America - Phi Beta Lambda *(455)*

Prewitt, MA, Elizabeth
National Association of State Mental Health Program Directors *(701)*

Prewitt, Jean M.
Independent Film and Television Alliance *(489)*

Prewitt, Terry J.
Semiotic Society of America *(897)*

Prey, John H.
Delta Sigma Delta *(409)*

Pribyl, Katie
General Aviation Manufacturers Association *(458)*

Price, Bonny F.
American Society of Appraisers *(192)*

Price, Brennan
American Radio Relay League *(172)*

Price, Caitlin
Association of Otolaryngology Administrators *(297)*

Price, Christy
National Association of Extension 4-H Agents *(667)*

Price, Deborah
Minerals, Metals and Materials Society *(617)*

Price, Diana
NALS *(625)*

Price, CMP, Doug
Destination Marketing Association International *(411)*

Price, Ellen
Pet Sitters International *(843)*

Price, Gary W.
Dental Trade Alliance *(410)*

Price, Grant
American Water Works Association *(220)*

Price, Hayling
National Human Services Assembly *(761)*

Price, Heather
Commercial Food Equipment Service Association *(366)*

Price, Jennifer
American Academy of Estate Planning Attorneys *(33)*

Price, Kelly
American Public Works Association *(172)*

Price, Leigh
National Coffee Association of the U.S.A. *(723)*

Price, Margo
International Society on Thrombosis and Hemostasis *(575)*

Price, Michelle
Pi Gamma Mu *(847)*

Price, Pamela
Association for Education in Journalism and Mass Communication *(245)*

Price, Patricia K.
National Association for Family Child Care *(638)*

Price, Perry
American Craft Council *(111)*

Price, Peter O.
National Academy of Television Arts and Science *(628)*

Price, CAE, Rand C.
Security Industry Association *(895)*

Price, Rebecca

American Association for State and Local History *(51)*

Price, Robert
American Physiological Society *(165)*

Price, Robert H.
Air Force Sergeants Association *(19)*

Price, Suzanne
American Society for Nutrition *(187)*

Price-Baugh, Dr. Ricki
Council of the Great City Schools *(398)*

Price-Carter, FACHE, Andrea R.
National Association for the Support of Long Term Care *(644)*
National Association of Health Services Executives *(671)*

Price-Shehan, Julie
TechServe Alliance *(971)*

Prichard, Marcia
National Society of Professional Engineers *(794)*

Priddy, Dana
American Public Works Association *(172)*

Pride, John
National Practitioners Network for Fathers and Family *(782)*

Pridgen, Cindi
Zero Balancing Health Association *(1030)*

Priebe, Sharon
American Society of Heating, Refrigerating and Air Conditioning Engineers (ASHRAE) *(199)*

Priest, Matt
Footwear Distributors and Retailers of America *(450)*

Prikazky, Joseph
Argentine-American Chamber of Commerce *(228)*

Prillaman, Hunter
National Lime Association *(769)*

Primavera, Leslie
Association for Comprehensive Energy Psychology *(242)*

Primero, Brooke
Academy of Country Music *(4)*

Primus, Kelly
Women's Foodservice Forum *(1023)*

Prince, Christopher
National Council for Science and the Environment *(733)*

Prince, Karen
National School Supply and Equipment Association *(789)*

Prince, Lilly
International Health, Racquet and Sportsclub Association *(549)*

Prince-Eason, Pamela
Women's Business Enterprise National Council *(1022)*

Principato, Gregory O.
Airports Council International - North America *(21)*

Prine, Kristin
International Special Events Society *(575)*

Pringle, Rebecca "Becky"
National Education Association *(744)*

Prinsloo, Alta
International Federation of Accountants *(544)*

Printz, Erica
Gemological Institute of America *(457)*

Prinz, Deborah
Central Conference of American Rabbis *(348)*

Prior, Kevin J.
Catholic Health Association of the United States *(345)*

Priori, Stephen
International Society for Pharmacoeconomics and Outcomes Research *(568)*

Prisaznuk, Paul
Airlines Electronic Engineering Committee *(20)*

Priscilla, Linda
Laborers-Employers Cooperation & Education Trust *(592)*

Prisco, Marie-Clare
American Society for Healthcare Human Resources Administration *(185)*

Priser, Michael
Federal Education Association *(439)*

Pritchard, Breann
Beefmaster Breeders United *(327)*

Pritchard, Fred
Common - A Users Group *(369)*

Pritchett, Bill
Academy of Model Aeronautics *(7)*

Prober, Josh
American Osteopathic Association *(160)*

Probert, MS, RD, Karen L.
Association of State and Territorial Public Health Nutrition Directors *(310)*

Probst, Maralyn R.
Veterinary Orthopedic Society *(1008)*

Procope, Jeanne
American Academy of Otolaryngic Allergy *(38)*

Proctor, Elizabeth
International Academy of Compounding Pharmacists *(509)*

Proctor, Lisa
Society for the Science & the Public *(924)*

Proctor, Penny
Association for Specialists in Group Work *(257)*

Procunier, Laura
Alberta Beef Producers *(21)*

Proetto, Maria
IEEE Power and Energy Society *(485)*

Proffitt, Helen
Thoroughbred Owners and Breeders Association *(974)*

Prokes, Donald R.
National High School Athletic Coaches Association *(759)*

Prokopchak, Mary Lou
American Boat and Yacht Council *(84)*

Proost, Jay
American Society of Agricultural Appraisers *(191)*

Proost, Jay
American Society of Equine Appraisers *(197)*

Properzio, Paul
American Classical League *(91)*

Prosser, Cynthia
Geoscience Information Society *(459)*

Proteau, Gregory
Boating Writers International *(333)*

Proulx, Thomas "Tom"
Society for Experimental Mechanics, Inc. *(909)*

Prouty, David
Major League Baseball Players Association *(601)*

Provenzano, CPP, Jenny
American Payroll Association *(162)*

Provost, Jeff
Exhibit Designers and Producers Association *(435)*

Provost, Justin

United States Equestrian Federation *(993)*

Provost, Mary
Council for Learning Disabilities *(390)*

Prucha, Thomas
American Foundry Society *(123)*

Prudden, Amanda
Energy Telecommunications and Electrical Association *(428)*

Pruden, James
Cotton Incorporated *(387)*

Pruett, Patrick
Community Banking Advisors Network *(370)*
CPA Auto Dealer Consultants Association *(402)*
CPA Manufacturing Services Association *(402)*
National Association of Nonprofit Accountants & Consultants *(682)*
National CPA Health Care Advisors Association *(740)*
Not-For-Profit Services Association *(824)*

Pruitt, Jennifer
Historians of Islamic Art Association *(476)*

Prusa, Jennifer
BEMA - The Baking Industry Suppliers Association *(328)*

Pruss, Mary Beth
Case Management Society of America *(343)*

Pruss, MCP, MCSD, Robert
Case Management Society of America *(343)*

Prutsman, Sharon
International Municipal Signal Association *(557)*

Pruyn, Christie
Society of Incentive & Travel Executives *(939)*

Pry, CFE, Ross
Association of Certified Fraud Examiners *(271)*

Pryde, Campbell
XBRL US, Inc. *(1029)*

Pryor, Ann Looper
American Society of Landscape Architects *(201)*

Pryor, Eileen
National Retail Federation *(786)*

Pryor, Kathryn H.
Health Physics Society *(470)*

Prysock, Mark
Risk and Insurance Management Society, Inc. (RIMS) *(886)*

Przygodzki, Eva
American Fisheries Society *(121)*

Przykucki, Anne
Society for College and University Planning *(906)*

Ptacek, Teri
Agricultural Stewardship Association *(16)*

Ptak, Lisa
International Foodservice Manufacturers Association *(546)*

Ptakowski, Kristin Kroeger
American Academy of Child and Adolescent Psychiatry *(31)*

Pucker, Lee
Wireless Innovation Forum *(1019)*

Puckerin, Rory
American Hellenic Educational Progressive Association (AHEPA) *(130)*

Puckett, Eric
Association for Linen Management *(251)*

Puckett, Gary
Council on Occupational Education *(400)*

Puckett, Robert
American Academy of Religion *(41)*

Pudlewski, Bob
National School Transportation Association *(790)*

Puente, Mark A.
Association of Research Libraries *(306)*

Puffer, MD, James C.
American Board of Family Medicine *(82)*

Pugh, Marsha
Dog Writers' Association of America *(415)*

Pugh, Mary
Association of Postgraduate Physician Assistant Programs *(300)*

Pugliese, Anthony
American Institute of Certified Public Accountants *(137)*

Pugno, MD, MPH, Perry A.
American Academy of Family Physicians *(34)*

Pulaski, Jane
Interstate Renewable Energy Council *(583)*

Pulchiné, Kay
American Society of Civil Engineers *(194)*

Pullen, Lindsay
Bank Insurance and Securities Association *(326)*
National Association of Healthcare Access Management *(671)*

Pullen, MSW, Tiffani
National Association of Mental Health Planning Advisory Council *(680)*

Pulliam, Mel
American Football Coaches Association *(122)*

Pumphrey, Kristen
Pharmaceutical Care Management Association *(844)*

Pupo, Vivian
American Welding Society *(220)*

Purcell, Denise
National Association for the Specialty Food Trade *(644)*

Purcell, BS, Frank J.
American Association of Nurse Anesthetists *(67)*

Purcell, Kathryn
Association of Field Ornithologists *(282)*

Purcell, Luann
Council of Administrators of Special Education *(391)*

Purcell, Marsha
National Institute for Farm Safety, Incorporation *(764)*

Purdon-Turnbow, Jennifer
Nashville Songwriters Association, International *(625)*

Purdy, Ralph M.
United Federation of Police & Security Officers *(987)*

Purewal, Jazz
Fashion Group International *(438)*

Purger, Tibor
Computer Ethics Institute *(372)*

Puri, Bhupinder
Vibration Institute *(1008)*

Puri, Divya
Geological Society of America *(459)*

Puriefoy, Wendy D.
Public Education Network *(869)*

Purnell, Harold
American Greyhound Track Operators Association *(127)*

Purnell, Parthenia
American Public Human Services Association *(171)*

Purrier, Dianne
Society of Motion Picture and Television Engineers *(942)*

Pursch, Sheryl
Institute of Scrap Recycling Industries, Inc. *(503)*

Purser, CAE, Craig A.
National Beer Wholesalers Association *(713)*

Pursglove, Sheila
Professional Picture Framers Association *(864)*

Purvin, Jr., Robert L.
American Association of Franchisees and Dealers *(61)*

Purvis, David
American Home Furnishings Alliance *(132)*

Purvis, Shawna
National Council of Chain Restaurants *(734)*

Puryear, Adrian
National Association of State Auditors, Comptrollers and Treasurers *(698)*

Pusey, Leigh Ann
American Insurance Association *(141)*

Pusey, Stacey
Association of Educational Publishers *(280)*

Putman, Mark
National Council of Higher Education Loan Programs *(735)*

Putnam, Rob
International Lead Zinc Research Organization *(553)*

Putt, Twyla R.
Search - The National Consortium for Justice Information and Statistics *(894)*

Puyvelde, Sophie Van
Plasma Protein Therapeutics Association *(850)*

Pye, Christopher W.
Alpha Kappa Psi *(26)*

Pye, David
Metal Treating Institute *(614)*

Pyhrr, Stephen A.
American Real Estate Society *(173)*

Pyke, Elizabeth
National Criminal Justice Association *(740)*

Pylant, Linda
Marketing Research Association *(606)*

Pyle, Chris
Delta Dental Plans Association *(409)*

Pyle, David H.
The American Finance Association *(121)*

Pyle, Ellen S.
Independent Bakers Association *(488)*

Pyle, Nicholas A.
Independent Bakers Association *(488)*

Pyle, Ron
Automotive Service Association *(323)*

Pyle, Taryn
Association of Independent Corrugated Converters *(288)*

Pyles, Aisha
National Association of School Nurses *(693)*

Pysarchuk, Jackie
American Council of Engineering Companies *(109)*

Pysarchuk, Jocelyn
American Massage Therapy Association *(147)*

Pyster, CAE, Phil
National Association of Multicultural Engineering Program Advocates *(681)*
National Cartoonists Society *(718)*
Society of University Surgeons *(949)*
Violin Society of America *(1010)*

Pytluk, Scott D.

American Psychological Association - Division of
Psychoanalysis *(169)*

Pyzik, Dr. Lawrence
American Chiropractic Registry of Radiologic
Technologists *(90)*

Quackenbush, Margery
National Association for the Advancement of
Psychoanalysis *(643)*

Qualen, Mary Von
National Association of Container Distributors *(658)*

Quam, David C.
National Governors Association *(755)*

Quam-Wickham, Nancy
Society for History Education *(911)*

Quancard, Bernard
Strategic Account Management Association *(963)*

Quarles, Diane
American Real Estate Society *(173)*

Quarles, Roger F.
Burley Tobacco Growers Cooperative Association *(338)*

Quarles, Susan D.
American Immigration Lawyers Association *(134)*

Quarles, Tenez
Association for Information Systems *(250)*

Quattrone, Barbara
Society for Pediatric Radiology *(918)*

Quebbeman, Jenny
Movement Disorder Society *(620)*

Queen, Jimmy
American Association of Christian Counselors *(56)*

Queen, Kristina
Drug & Alcohol Testing Industry Association *(416)*

Queen, Pam
International Professional Rodeo Association *(561)*

Queen, Susanne
National Association of Government Guaranteed
Lenders (NAGGL) *(670)*

Queeney, Lisa
Health Industry Distributors Association *(469)*

Querol, Cecilia de
American Society of Picture Professionals *(207)*

Quick, Angela
Academy of Radiology Research *(8)*

Quigg, Mary
International Council of Air Shows *(538)*

Quigley, Colleen
Association of Educational Publishers *(280)*

Quimby, Carla
Metal Treating Institute *(614)*

Quimby, Michael
Associated Pipe Organ Builders of America *(236)*

Quine, Meg
Academy of International Business *(5)*

Quinlan, Kevin
Archaeological Institute of America *(227)*

Quinlan, Terence A.
IT Financial Management Association *(586)*

Quinlan, Trevor
National Independent Living Association *(762)*

Quinlin, Martha
ASME International Gas Turbine Institute *(233)*

Quinn, Alice
Poetry Society of America *(851)*

Quinn, Anthony

ASTM International *(319)*

Quinn, Caroline
Council for European Studies *(390)*

Quinn, Jr., Harold P.
Coal Exporters Association of the U.S. *(359)*
National Mining Association *(772)*

Quinn, James
Association of Productivity Specialists *(300)*

Quinn, Jessica
Heli Ski US Association *(473)*

Quinn, Kathleen
American Association of Advertising Agencies *(53)*

Quinn, Esq., Kenneth P.
Flight Safety Foundation *(448)*

Quinn, Kevin
Heli Ski US Association *(473)*

Quinn, Kevin
National Association of School Resource Officers *(693)*

Quinn, Lynn Grossman
Women's Business Enterprise National Council *(1022)*

Quinn, Peggy
Council for Advancement and Support of Education
(388)

Quinn, Robert M.
Kamut Association of North America *(590)*

Quinsey, Bryan
American Association of Professional Farriers *(71)*

Quintero, Fatima
American College for Advancement in Medicine *(93)*

Quirk, John F.
Amerifax Cattle Association *(222)*

Quirk, Lisa
NALP - The Association for Legal Career Professionals
(624)

Quiros, Kimberly
National Volunteer Fire Council *(803)*

Quiroz, Arelis
Venezuelan American Association of the U.S. *(1008)*

Qureshi, Farah M.
Healthcare Distribution Management Association *(471)*

Ra'anan, Alice Hellerstein
American Physiological Society *(165)*

Raak, Paul
Independent Telephone and Telecommunications
Alliance *(492)*

Rabin, Tal
Special Interest Group for Algorithm and Computation
Theory *(954)*

Rabor, Sam
National Student Osteopathic Medical Association
(797)

Rachlin, JD, MPH, Joan
Applied Research Ethics National Association *(226)*

Rachuig, Brenda
Association of Attorney-Mediators *(268)*

Rack, Hon
American Telemarketing Association *(215)*

rack, Jon
Hinman Dental Society *(475)*

Rack, Jon
Wood Flooring Manufacturers Association *(1024)*

Racz, Gary
American Literary Translators Association *(146)*

Raczkowski, Bill
American Knife & Tool Institute *(144)*

Radar, Jack S.
Financial Management Association International *(444)*

Radavich, Megan
Zonta International *(1030)*

Radcliff, CMP, Kelly
American Academy of Cosmetic Dentistry *(31)*

Radcliff, Laurie
American Society for Enology and Viticulture *(184)*

Radde, Thomas
Giving Institute *(461)*
Giving USA Foundation *(461)*
International Society of Appraisers *(570)*

Radding, Cynthia
Conference on Latin American History *(377)*

Radell, Michele
American Health Lawyers Association *(130)*

Rademacher, Nicholas
College Theology Society *(365)*

Rader, Jon
Food Sanitation Institute *(450)*

Rader, Kevin
International Association of Fire Fighters *(521)*

Rader, Rebecca H.
North American Mycological Association *(818)*

Rader, Rob
American Medical Informatics Association *(149)*

Rader, Russ
Insurance Institute for Highway Safety *(505)*

Radoszewski, Tony
Corrugated Polyethylene Pipe Association *(386)*
Plastics Pipe Institute *(850)*

Radoulovitch, Constantine "Connie"
National Association of County Engineers *(660)*

Radulovic, MA, Jon
National Hospice & Palliative Care Organization *(760)*

Rae, Emily
Paperboard Packaging Council *(838)*

Rae, AICI, CIP, Joanne
Association of Image Consultants International *(287)*

Raef, Susan
American Society of Retina Specialists *(209)*

Rael, Denise
FlexTech Alliance *(447)*

Rael, Teodoro
American Catholic Correctional Chaplains Association
(88)

Raeve, James de
The Open Group *(828)*

Raezer, Joyce Wessel
National Military Family Association, Inc. *(772)*

Rafal, Emilie
The Corps Network (formerly the National Association
of Service and Conservation Corps) *(386)*

Raff, Brian
National Steel Bridge Alliance *(796)*

Raffel, Sara
Book Industry Study Group, Inc. *(333)*

Rafol, Giles
Association of Collegiate Business Schools and
Programs *(275)*

Rag, Jon
Society for General Music *(910)*

Ragan, Lorri
American Intellectual Property Law Association *(141)*

Rager, CAE, Shari

American Medical Writers Association *(150)*

Raghunath, Krishna
FlexTech Alliance *(447)*

Ragland, Linda B.
United States Animal Health Association *(989)*

Ragnetti, Michelle
The Accrediting Commission of Career Schools and Colleges *(10)*

Ragnow, Marguerite
Society for the History of Discoveries *(923)*

Ragsdale, John
Technology Services Industry Association *(970)*

Ragusa, Diane M.
American Academy of Orthotists and Prosthetists *(38)*

Rahman, Nabil
Cold-Formed Steel Engineers Institute *(362)*

Rahn, Roy
National Association of Security Companies (NASCO) *(695)*

Rahn, Wendy
United States Rowing Association *(998)*

Raible, Robert
American Dental Association *(113)*

Railing, Ann Marie
Workgroup for Electronic Data Interchange *(1025)*

Rainbolt, Karen
Passenger Vessel Association *(839)*

Raines, John
American Society of Military Comptrollers *(203)*

Rainey, Anthony
American Association for Budget and Program Analysis *(48)*

Rainey, Cassaundra
Child Welfare League of America *(353)*

Rainforth, Emma C.
History of Earth Sciences Society *(476)*

Rainforth, Michele
Marketing Science Institute *(606)*

Rains, Laurie D.
Association of Small Business Development Centers *(308)*

Rajabiun, Sheila
American Association for Budget and Program Analysis *(48)*

Rajan, Abhilash
Appraisal Foundation *(226)*

Rajsky, CAE, Gregory T.
Aluminum Extruders Council *(27)*

Rajwany, Nur
National Council of State Boards for Nursing *(736)*

Raker, Jacky Sher
American Association of Airport Executives *(53)*

Rakers, Rebecca
Associated Equipment Distributors *(235)*

Rakestraw, Kathleen M
American School Counselor Association *(177)*

Rakestraw, Rachael Murray
Population Action International *(852)*

Rakestraw, Terry T.
Aquacultural Engineering Society *(227)*

Rakovan, Dick
Radio Advertising Bureau *(873)*

Rakowsky, Sophia
InsideNGO *(496)*

Raleigh, Lori E.
International Society of Hospitality Consultants *(573)*

Ralenkotter, Terri
American Hanoverian Society *(128)*

Raley, Bill
ASM International *(232)*

Raley, Nancy
National Association of Independent Schools *(675)*

Rallo, Jim
Automotive Fleet and Leasing Association *(322)*

Ralls, DDS, Dr. Stephen A.
American College of Dentists *(95)*

Ralston, Angie
CBA *(346)*

Ramakrishnan, Gitta
German American Business Association *(460)*

Ramamurthy, Sibu
American Association of Colleges of Pharmacy *(57)*

Ramanujam, Mahesh
United States Green Building Council *(994)*

Ramarui, Jennifer
The Oceanography Society *(826)*

Ramazzini, Regina
Clean Technology & Sustainable Industries Organization (CTSI) *(357)*

Ramirez, Armando
International Association of Lighting Designers *(524)*

Ramirez, Bruce
Council for Exceptional Children *(390)*

Ramirez, Evelyn
EMTA - Trade Association for the Emerging Markets *(427)*

Ramirez, Justin
Percussive Arts Society *(841)*

Ramirez, Lisa
Equipment Leasing and Finance Association *(432)*

Ramirez, Magdalena
American Medical Rehabilitation Providers Association *(149)*

Ramirez, Maggie
American Society for Histocompatibility and Immunogenetics *(185)*

Ramirez, Rosario Michelle
National Association of Graduate-Professional Students *(670)*

Ramirez, Sarah E.
Hispanic National Bar Association *(475)*

Ramirez, Jr., Saul N.
National Association of Housing and Redevelopment Officials *(673)*

Ramljak, Suzanne
Society of North American Goldsmiths *(943)*

Ramlogan, Nikki
TechServe Alliance *(971)*

Ramlow, Sharon
International Hot Rod Association *(550)*

Ramm, Steven I
Association for Recorded Sound Collections *(255)*

Ramminger, Scott
American Wholesale Marketers Association *(221)*

Ramos, Adela
Foodservice Equipment Distributors Association *(450)*

Ramos, Christine
Loan Syndication & Trading Association *(599)*

Ramos, Diane

National Association of Insurance and Financial Advisors *(675)*

Rampersad, Mia
International Housewares Association *(550)*

Ramsay, James Bradford
National Association of Regulatory Utility Commissioners *(691)*

Ramsey, Dan
National Association of Home and Workshop Writers *(672)*

Ramsey, Faye
American Society for Clinical Pathology *(182)*

Ramsey, John
Federal Law Enforcement Officers Association *(439)*

Ramsey, CAE, John K.
Council of Educational Facility Planners International *(393)*

Ramsey, Judith
American Boat and Yacht Council *(84)*

Ramus, Robert L.
Academy of Dentistry International *(5)*

Rancourt, Linda M.
National Parks Conservation Association *(779)*

Rand, A. Barry
American Association of Retired Persons *(72)*

Randall, Gregg
National Tractor Pullers Association *(801)*

Randall, Jennifer
International Society for the Study of Dissociation *(570)*
International Society for the Study of Trauma and Dissociation *(570)*

Randall, Michele E.
Bibliographical Society of America *(328)*

Randall, Michelle
Health Ministries Association *(470)*

Randall, CMP, Michelle
National Communication Association *(724)*

Randall, Richard
National Network of Estate Planning Attorneys *(775)*

Randall, Sue B.
American Milking Devon Cattle Association *(152)*

Randazzo, Catherine A.
The Sulphur Institute *(965)*

Randazzo, Jessica
National Catholic Educational Exhibitors *(718)*

Randazzo, Richard
American Association of Retired Persons *(72)*

Randleman, MD, J. Bradley
International Society of Refractive Surgery of the American Academy of Ophthalmology *(574)*

Randol, USA (Ret.), Doyle E
American College Health Association *(93)*

Randolph, Heather
Wine and Spirits Shippers Association *(1018)*

Randolph, Jeff
ARMA International *(228)*

Randolph, Melissa
North American Society for Cardiovascular Imaging *(821)*

Ranieri, Paul
Association for General and Liberal Studies *(247)*

Ranieri, Robert
Society of Dance History Scholars *(934)*

Ranker, Tom
American Society of Plant Taxonomists *(207)*

Rankin, Gary
American Navion Society *(155)*

Rankin, Janet Walberg
American College of Sports Medicine *(102)*

Rankin, Natasha
Employers Council on Flexible Compensation *(427)*

Rankin, Paul W.
Reusable Industrial Packaging Association *(885)*

Rankin, Russ
Baptist Communicators Association *(326)*

Rankin, Scott
Spring Manufacturers Institute *(960)*

Ransdell, Teresa
Organization of American Historians *(832)*

Rao, S. N.
American Crystallographic Association *(112)*

Raola, Orlando
Esperanto-USA *(433)*

Raper, Kellie
Food Distribution Research Society *(449)*

Rapp, Ann-Cathrine
American Antiquarian Society *(45)*

Rapp, Barbara
Musculoskeletal Tumor Society *(621)*

Rapp, Janet
American Ladder Institute *(144)*
Association of Professional Researchers for
Advancement *(302)*

Rapp, Rhonda
Association on Higher Education and Disability *(319)*

Rappaport, Theresa
Deep Foundations Institute *(408)*

Raptakis, Angelique
American Society for Pharmacology and Experimental
Therapeutics *(188)*

Raquet, Donna
American Crossbred Pony Registry *(112)*

Rarick, Michelle
Society for Obstetric Anesthesia and Perinatology *(917)*

Rasanen, John
American Geological Institute *(126)*

Rasanen, John P.
American Geological Institute *(126)*

Rasar, Kaylin
The National Federation of Paralegal Associations, Inc.
(749)

Rascoe, Michelle
Open Applications Group *(828)*

Rasmussen, Becky
National Christmas Tree Association *(721)*

Rasmussen, Brian
American Association for Marriage and Family
Therapy *(50)*

Rasmussen, Jeffery P.
Tax Executives Institute, Inc. *(968)*

Rasmussen, Mark
Professional Reactor Operator Society *(864)*

Rasmussen, Priscilla
Association for Computational Linguistics *(242)*

Rasmussen, Shannon
National Council of Urban Education Associations
(738)

Rasoulzadeh, Hesam
Internet Marketing Association *(582)*

Rassam, Dr. Gus

American Fisheries Society *(121)*

Rasul, Christine T.
AMT - The Association For Manufacturing Technology
(222)

Ratcliffe, Dolores
National Association of Black Women Entrepreneurs
(649)

Rathai, Kenna
American Agricultural Editors Association *(43)*

Rathbone, Joel
National Portable Storage Association *(781)*

Rathbone, Robert
Association of Analytical Communities International
(267)

Rathbun, Frank
Community Associations Institute (CAI) *(370)*

Rathburn, Cindy
Delta Sigma Pi *(409)*

Rathje, Lori
Society for Mucosal Immunology *(916)*

Ratley, CFE, CPA, James D.
Association of Certified Fraud Examiners *(271)*

Ratliff-Garrison, Tonya
American Quarter Horse Association *(172)*

Ratner, CAE, CMP, Nicole E.
American Association of Attorney-Certified Public
Accountants *(54)*

Ratsabout, Saengmany
Association for Asian American Studies *(239)*

Rattie, Alfred
United States Composting Council *(992)*

Ratyniak, Jayne
NAFA Fleet Management Association *(624)*

Rauch, Bill
Association for Unmanned Vehicle Systems
International *(261)*

Rauglas, Dirk
MTM Association for Standards and Research *(620)*

Raulston, Carol
Coal Exporters Association of the U.S. *(359)*
National Mining Association *(772)*

Raun, Linda
U.S. Rice Producers Group *(983)*

Rausch, Jeff
Association for Information Systems *(250)*

Rauscher, Samantha
International Sculpture Center *(564)*

Rauschke, Gena
Rolf Institute of Structural Integration *(887)*

Ravas, Tammy
International Association of Music Libraries, United
States Branch *(525)*

Rave, Marley
Meals on Wheels Association of America *(609)*

Ravelo, MD, Ramon E.
InterAmerican College of Physicians and Surgeons
(507)

Raven, Greg
United States Racquet Stringers Association *(998)*

Ravenscroft, Paul
National Association of Educational Procurement, Inc.
(664)

Rawdon, CPA, Lyn
American Staffing Association *(213)*

Rawlings, Hunter R.
Association of American Universities *(266)*

Rawlins, Bridget
American Pianists Association *(165)*

Rawlins, MS, NP, Susan
National Association of Nurse Practitioners in
Women's Health *(682)*

Rawls, Lori
United States Equestrian Federation *(993)*

Rawn, Carrie
National Institute of Governmental Purchasing *(765)*

Rawn-Schatzinger, Viola
Petroleum Technology Transfer Council *(844)*

Rawson, Chris
American Theatre Critics Association *(216)*

Rawson, W. Randall
American Boiler Manufacturers Association *(84)*

Ray, Deborah A.
Alliance for Natural Health USA *(23)*

Ray, Jennifer
The Jockeys' Guild *(588)*

Ray, Joanne
American Association of Cardiovascular and
Pulmonary Rehabilitation *(55)*
Urgent Care Association of America *(1004)*

Ray, Lisa
CBA *(346)*

Ray, Mark
American Driver and Traffic Safety Education
Association *(115)*

Ray, Melinda Mercer
National Association of Clinical Nurse Specialists *(654)*

Ray, Melissa
National Rural Letter Carriers' Association *(788)*

Ray, Sandra
Association for Research on Nonprofit Organizations
and Voluntary Action *(255)*

Ray, Shannon
Association for Spiritual, Ethical and Religious Values
in Counseling *(257)*

Rayfield, Mary Anne
Federation of Internet Solution Providers of the
Americas *(441)*

Raymond, David A.
American Council of Engineering Companies *(109)*

Raymond, Leo
Association of Marketing Service Providers *(293)*

Raymond, Melody
Association of Children's Prosthetic-Orthotic Clinics
(272)

Raymond, Rosalind P.
Sheet Metal and Air Conditioning Contractors'
National Association *(898)*

Raynaud, Caroline
German American Business Association *(460)*

Raynes, CAE, Linda J.
Electrical Apparatus Service Association *(422)*

Raza, Sanna
Voluntary Protection Programs Participants'
Association, Inc. *(1011)*

Razeghi, Marc
Edison Electric Institute *(419)*

Razzano, Douglas
IEEE Photonics Society *(485)*

Rea, Tina
Appaloosa Horse Club *(225)*

Reachmack, Tim
American Association for Laboratory Accreditation *(50)*

Read, Douglas E.
American Society of Heating, Refrigerating and Air
Conditioning Engineers (ASHRAE) *(199)*

Read, Mary Margaret
American Suffolk Horse Association *(214)*

Read, Robin
National Foundation for Women Legislators *(753)*

Reading, RN, Nancy
American Academy of Professional Coders *(40)*

Ready, Sindy
Women's Council of REALTORS *(1023)*

Reagan, James
National Cattlemen's Beef Association *(718)*

Reagan, Tim
National Stone, Sand, and Gravel Association *(796)*

Ream, Michael
American Judicature Society *(143)*

Reaman, MBA, Darren
Custom Electronic Design and Installation Association
(405)

Reamer, Terry
Association of Public Health Laboratories *(304)*

Reams, Heather
Association of American Educators *(264)*

Reamy, Kristen
Outdoor Power Equipment Aftermarket Association
(835)
Outdoor Power Equipment Institute *(835)*

Reardon, Alison
Service Employees International Union *(897)*

Reardon, Brian
S-Corporation Association *(889)*

Reardon, Karen
RISE (Responsible Industry for a Sound Environment)
(886)

Reardon, Susan K.
Military Operations Research Society *(616)*

Reardon, Thomas
Business and Institutional Furniture Manufacturers
Association International *(338)*

Reaves, Danielle
Motorcycle Industry Council, Inc. *(620)*

Rebar, Robert W.
Society for Reproductive Endocrinology and Infertility
(920)

Rebar, MD, Robert W.
American Society for Reproductive Medicine *(189)*

Rebel, Nick
American Academy of Neurological and Orthopaedic
Surgeons *(36)*

Reblando, Joe
Medicaid Health Plans of America *(611)*

Rebman, Lawrence (Larry) G.
National Association of Government Labor Officials
(670)

Rebmann, Kerrie
National Association of Elevator Contractors *(665)*

Rebuck, Patricia
Palomino Horse Association *(837)*

Recht, MBA, Scott
American College of Foot & Ankle Orthopedics &
Medicine *(95)*

Recht, Scott A.
International Society for Pharmacoepidemiology *(568)*

Recke, Lisa
American Association of Birth Centers *(55)*

Rector, Clark E.
American Advertising Federation *(43)*

Rector, Yvette
Society of Research Administrators International *(946)*

Reda, Susan
National Retail Federation *(786)*

Redburn, Dr. Michael
American Association of School Personnel
Administrators *(73)*

Redd, Eileen G.
International Test and Evaluation Association *(577)*

Reddell, Mari
American Academy of Pain Management *(39)*

Redder, Brandy
Safety Glazing Certification Council *(890)*

Reddersen, Cynthia
National Association of Consumer Advocates *(657)*

Reddin, Kim
National Onion Association *(776)*

Redding, J. Gregory
Society for German-American Studies *(910)*

Redding, Jill
American Homebrewers Association *(133)*

Reddington, John
United States Hide, Skin and Leather Association *(994)*

Reddish, Shannon
Health Industry Representatives Association *(470)*

Reder, Tammy
National Soccer Coaches Association of America *(792)*

Redman, Michael T.
American Beverage Association *(80)*

Redrick, Rosalind
The National Association of Professional Receptionists
(688)

Redstone, Leanne H.
Small Business Council of America *(900)*

Reeb, John
National Parent Teachers Association *(779)*

Reebs, Sarah
International Association for the Study of Pain *(514)*

Reed, Alyson W.
Linguistic Society of America *(598)*

Reed, CSS, Cindy
Electronics Technicians Association International *(424)*

Reed, Cynthia
Celebrant Foundation and Institute *(347)*

Reed, Dale
International Institute of Connector and
Interconnection Technology *(551)*

Reed, Doris A.
Association of Supervisory and Administrative School
Personnel *(312)*

Reed, Doug
National Association of Convenience Stores *(658)*

Reed, Jo
National Association of Area Agencies on Aging *(647)*

Reed, MBA, Keith A.
Air Force Sergeants Association *(19)*

Reed, Kenneth
CRE Finance Council *(403)*

Reed, Linda Soley
American Accordionists Association *(43)*

Reed, CAE, MBA, Lydia Middleton
Association of University Programs in Health
Administration *(316)*

Reed, Marny
International Society for Pharmaceutical Engineering
(567)

Reed, Michael
Association of Pool and Spa Professionals *(299)*

Reed, III, Morgan W.
Association for Competitive Technology (ACT) *(242)*

Reed, Sally Gardner
Association of Library Trustees, Advocates, Friends
and Foundations *(291)*

Reed, Sloane
American Association of Integrated Healthcare
Delivery Systems *(63)*

Reed, Valerie
National Forum for Black Public Administrators *(752)*

Reeder, Katie
Executive Women International *(435)*

Reedy, Bets
North American Clun Forest Association *(815)*

Reef, Grace
Child Care Aware of America *(353)*

Rees, Mandy
Voice and Speech Trainers Association *(1011)*

Rees, Susan M.
American Osteopathic Academy of Sports Medicine
(159)
Society for Psychophysiological Research *(919)*

Rees, Teresa
Label Printing Industries of America *(591)*

Rees, Vicki Lane
American Kennel Club *(143)*

Reese, Altonese
National Phlebotomy Association *(781)*

Reese, Julie
Association for Library Collections and Technical
Services *(251)*

Reese, Marily
National Forest Recreation Association *(752)*

Reeson, Amanda
American Shorthorn Association *(179)*

Reeve, EdD, Deborah B.
National Art Education Association *(635)*

Reeve, PhD, Edward M.
Council on Technology Teacher Education *(401)*

Reeves, Evelyn
Real Estate Management Brokers Institute *(875)*

Reeves, J. David
National Association of Blacks In Government *(649)*

Reeves, CMP, Nancy
The New Media Consortium *(809)*

Reeves-Pepin, Jaclyn
National Association of Biology Teachers *(648)*

Reffett, CAE, Trey
Congressional Legislative Staff Association *(377)*

Regan, Celeste E.
American Association of State Colleges and
Universities *(73)*

Regan, David W.
National Automobile Dealers Association *(711)*

Regan, Elizabeth A.
Organizational Systems Research Association *(833)*

Regan, Jillaine K.
Metal Powder Industries Federation *(613)*
Powder Metallurgy Equipment Association *(854)*
Powder Metallurgy Parts Association *(854)*
Refractory Metals Association *(878)*

Regan, Patrick
The PGA Tour, Inc. *(844)*

Regan, Paul
Christian Association for Psychological Studies *(355)*

Regan, Ron
Association of Fish and Wildlife Agencies *(283)*

Regan, Timothy J.
Emissions Control Technology Association (ECTA) *(426)*

Regelbrugge, Craig J.
American Nursery and Landscape Association *(156)*
National Association of Plant Patent Owners *(685)*

Regennitter, Michael
CBA *(346)*

Reger, Jeremy
National Petroleum Management Association *(780)*

Regnier, Dale
International Concrete Repair Institute *(536)*

Regoli, Michael
Organization of American Historians *(832)*

Regotti, Barbara
American Institute of Professional Bookkeepers *(140)*

Reh, Brian
Monorail Manufacturers Association *(619)*

Rehan, Kelly
The Association for Nursing Professional Development *(252)*

Rehberg, Sarah
National Association of Agriculture Employees *(646)*

Rehfeld, Edward
Laborers-Employers Cooperation & Education Trust *(592)*

Rehm, Rebecca
Ethics and Compliance Officer Association *(433)*

Rehm, Susan
American Association of Veterinary State Boards *(76)*

Reich, Kate
National Catholic Educational Association *(718)*

Reich, Louise
Brotherhood of Locomotive Engineers and Trainmen *(336)*

Reichardt, Mark
Open Geospatial Consortium *(828)*

Reichart, Pat
American Academy of Ambulatory Care Nursing *(30)*

Reichelt-Pepper, CAE, Christine
National Funeral Directors Association *(754)*

Reichenberg, Neil E.
International Public Management Association for Human Resources *(562)*

Reichert, Kathleen
American Skin Association *(180)*

Reichert, Monica
American Academy of Orthopaedic Surgeons *(38)*

Reichle, Donna
Modular Building Systems Council *(618)*

Reid, Amanda
Organization for International Investment *(831)*

Reid, David E.
DBA International *(407)*

Reid, Gloria
The Wellness Plan *(1015)*

Reid, PhD, Jerry B.
American Registry of Radiologic Technologists *(174)*

Reid, Kathy

National Association of Professional Surplus Lines Offices, Ltd. *(688)*

Reid, CAE, Kenneth D.
American Water Resources Association *(220)*

Reid, Kia
North American Society for Cardiovascular Imaging *(821)*
Society of Computed Body Tomography and Magnetic Resonance *(933)*

Reid, Matthew
BSA | The Software Alliance *(337)*

Reid, Michelle M.
Real Estate Roundtable *(876)*

Reid, Myke
American Postal Workers Union *(167)*

Reid, Neal
Professional Rodeo Cowboys Association *(864)*

Reid, Pamela
Entomological Society of America *(429)*

Reid, Pamela J.
Association of Machinery and Equipment Appraisers *(292)*

Reid, Proctor
National Academy of Engineering of the United States of America *(627)*

Reid, Randy
Chief Petty Officers Association *(352)*

Reid, Randy
United States Coast Guard Chief Petty Officers Association *(992)*

Reidenberg, Daniel J.
American Psychotherapy Association *(170)*

Reider, MD, Bruce
American Orthopaedic Society for Sports Medicine *(159)*

Reidy, Mike
National Cheese Institute *(720)*

Reidy, Sarah
Population Action International *(852)*

Reidy, Tom
National Academy of Public Administration *(628)*

Reiff, Barbara Finnegan
The Surety and Fidelity Association of America *(966)*

Reiff, Linda
Napa Valley Vintners Association *(625)*

Reifsteck, Adam
Chamber Music America *(350)*

Reigel, Sandy
American Association of School Personnel Administrators *(73)*

Reighart, CAE, CMP, Glenn M.
National Association of School Psychologists *(693)*

Reihl, Kathy
Association of Nurses in AIDS Care *(296)*

Reilley, Nicole
Gas Machinery Research Council *(456)*

Reilly, CAE, Barbara
National Customs Brokers and Forwarders Association of America *(741)*

Reilly, Bernard
Center for Research Libraries *(348)*

Reilly, Chad
Hospice and Palliative Nurses Association *(478)*

Reilly, Christine
Automotive Aftermarket Industry Association *(321)*

Reilly, Colleen

Theatre Library Association *(973)*

Reilly, Daniel
Society for Marketing Professional Services *(914)*

Reilly, Deborah Sykes
National Association of Independent Colleges and Universities *(674)*

Reilly, Edward T.
American Management Association *(146)*

Reilly, Elizabeth
National Confectioners Association *(725)*

Reilly, Lin
Therapeutic Touch International Association *(973)*

Reilly, Liz
Council for Advancement and Support of Education *(388)*

Reilly, Jr., Matthew B.
American Short Line and Regional Railroad Association *(179)*

Reilly, Michael
American Association of Collegiate Registrars and Admissions Officers *(58)*

Reilly, Patricia
Association of American Railroads *(266)*

Reilly, Peter
Council of the Americas *(398)*

Reilly, Philip
National Catholic Educational Exhibitors *(718)*

Reilly, EdD, Rob
IEEE Education Society *(484)*

Reimann, Mathias W.
American Society of Comparative Law *(195)*

Reimer, Chris
National Ground Water Association *(756)*

Reimer, Norman L.
National Association of Criminal Defense Lawyers *(661)*

Reimers, Laura
National Industries for the Blind *(763)*

Reimnitz, Arlen
American Society of Electroneurodiagnostic Technologists *(197)*

Reinagel, Shelly
United Soybean Board *(989)*

Reinardy, Cindy
Accrediting Council on Education in Journalism and Mass Communications *(11)*

Reinecke, Peter
United Natural Products Alliance *(988)*

Reiner, Frank
Chlorine Institute *(354)*

Reinerman, Alan J.
Society for Italian Historical Studies *(914)*

Reinfried, Robert A.
Conveyor Equipment Manufacturers Association *(383)*
Mechanical Power Transmission Association *(610)*
Scale Manufacturers Association *(892)*

Reinhard, Karen
US Travel Association *(983)*

Reinhardt, CAE, MEM, Ann
American Philosophical Society *(164)*

Reinhardt, Cheryl
American Society for Therapeutic Radiology and Oncology *(190)*

Reinhold, PhD, Timothy A.
Institute for Business & Home Safety *(496)*

Reinovsky, Robert E.

IEEE - Nuclear and Plasma Sciences Society *(482)*

Reinsch, William A.
National Foreign Trade Council, Inc. *(752)*

Reis, Cliff
American Society of Plumbing Engineers *(207)*

Reis, Jennifer
American Society of Group Psychotherapy and Psychodrama *(198)*

Reisen, Matthias
International Herb Association *(550)*

Reiser, Thomas "Tom"
International Society on Thrombosis and Hemostasis *(575)*

Reisinger, Becky
American College of Health Care Administrators *(96)*

Reisinger, Brenda
Public Agency Risk Managers Association *(869)*

Reisinger, Pamela
American Association of Law Libraries *(64)*

Reitter, CAE, Mary S
Brain Injury Association of America *(334)*

Reitz, John C.
American Society of Comparative Law *(195)*

Reitzel, Todd
American Association of Pharmaceutical Scientists *(68)*

Rekdal, Scott
National Defense Industrial Association *(742)*

Remaley, Jeffrey
Precision Machined Products Association *(856)*

Remedios, Christine
Health Forum *(469)*

Remines, Theresa
American Gastroenterological Association *(125)*

Rempe, Heather
National Auctioneers Association *(711)*

Remsberg, Dale
American Mountain Guides Association *(153)*

Remson, Mary
American Institute of Parliamentarians *(140)*

Rendall, Dave
Chevron and Texaco Petroleum Marketers Association *(352)*

Rendely, Robert
The Coalition for Government Procurement *(360)*

René, Tiffany
Romance Writers of America *(888)*

Reneau, Ryan
Society for Vector Ecology *(927)*

Renfro, Cari
Architectural Precast Association *(228)*

Renk, CAE, Karen
Incentive Manufacturers & Representatives Alliance *(487)*
Incentive Marketing Association *(487)*

Renken, Alice Brin
Viola da Gamba Society of America *(1009)*

Renkes, Robert N.
Petroleum Equipment Institute *(843)*

Renn, Nicole
American Society for Surgery of the Hand *(189)*

Renner, Dennis W.
Association of American Colleges and Universities *(264)*

Renner, Judy
National Eating Disorders Association *(743)*

Renner, Megan
American College of Osteopathic Pediatricians *(100)*

Renner, Melanie
Electronic Funds Transfer Association *(423)*

Rennie, Criss
International Association of Geophysical Contractors *(522)*

Rennie-Sanchez, Stephanie
American Society of Safety Engineers *(209)*

Rensberger, Judith
Commissioned Officers Association of the United States Public Health Service *(368)*

Renshof, Barbara
National American Indian Housing Council *(634)*

Rensing, Bernadette M.
Association of Academic Physiatrists *(263)*

Rentsch, Rusty
Aerospace Industries Association of America *(14)*

Renwall, Candace
Closure and Container Manufacturers Association *(359)*

Renzetti, CAE, Kathy
Association for Healthcare Philanthropy *(248)*

Renzi, David M.
AHS International - The Vertical Flight Society *(17)*

Repko, Michael "Mike"
National Fire Sprinkler Association *(751)*

Repp, Shelly
National Council of Higher Education Loan Programs *(735)*

Reppas, John
Neurotechnology Industry Organization *(809)*

Reppell, Jordan
Retail Confectioners International *(884)*

Resch, Mary
National Academy of Engineering of the United States of America *(627)*

Resch, Rhone
Solar Energy Industries Association (SEIA) *(952)*

Rescigno, Luca
Controlled Release Society *(383)*

Resner, Andre
Academy of Homiletics *(5)*

Resnick, Michael A.
National School Boards Association *(789)*

Ressler, John
Petroleum Packaging Council *(843)*

Retford, Lynn
Society for Critical Care Medicine *(934)*

Rethmeier, Blain
US Travel Association *(983)*

Rettich, Jon
Federation of Modern Painters and Sculptors *(442)*

Retting, Leah
Association for Conflict Resolution *(243)*

Retzlaff, Jon G.
American Association for Cancer Research *(48)*

Reuland, Fred
Library Leadership and Management Association *(597)*

Reuland, Rick
Ceilings and Interior Systems Construction Association *(347)*

Reuter, Amy
International Fragrance Association North America *(547)*

Reuter, Rachel
Contact Lens Society of America *(382)*

Reveal, Judith
American Society for Indexing *(186)*

Revere, Tonia
National Association of Sales Professionals *(692)*

Revilla-Garcia, Norma Jean
Hispanic Association of Colleges and Universities *(475)*

Rew, Mike
Communications Supply Service Association *(369)*

Rewey, Frederic
American Cash Flow Association *(88)*

Reyes, Charles
Association of State and Territorial Solid Waste Management Officials *(310)*

Reyes, Etta
North American Meat Association *(818)*

Reyes, Frank
IEEE Instrumentation and Measurement Society *(484)*

Reyes, Kathleen
International Society of Arthroscopy, Knee Surgery and Orthopaedic Sports Medicine *(571)*

Reyes, Laura
American Federation of State, County and Municipal Employees *(120)*

Reyland, Mark T.
United Inventors Association of the U.S.A. *(987)*

Reynders, Stephanie
Pharmaceutical Marketing Research Group *(844)*

Reynolds, Alicia
Association of Pet Dog Trainers *(299)*

Reynolds, Allan
National Ecological Observatory Network, Inc *(743)*

Reynolds, Christopher
American Musicological Society *(154)*

Reynolds, Dennis
American Littoral Society *(146)*

Reynolds, CAE, MA, Dennis
Child Life Council *(353)*

Reynolds, Jeff
National Franchisee Association *(753)*

Reynolds, Jeffrey L.
National Dog Groomers Association of America, Inc. *(743)*

Reynolds, John B.
Airport Consultants Council *(21)*

Reynolds, CAE, John R.
National Roadside Vegetation Management Association *(787)*

Reynolds, Kenneth W.
Network of Ingredient Marketing Specialists *(808)*

Reynolds, Kenneth W.
The Foodservice Group, Inc. *(450)*

Reynolds, Laurie
Label Printing Industries of America *(591)*

Reynolds, Leslie
National Association of Secretaries of State *(695)*

Reynolds, Lori
INDA, Association of the Nonwoven Fabrics Industry *(488)*

Reynolds, Mark
Society for Imaging Science and Technology *(912)*

Reynolds, Mary Clare
The Learning Disabilities Association *(596)*

Reynolds, Nancy

Advertising Media Credit Executives Association *(13)*
Institute of Scrap Recycling Industries, Inc. *(503)*

Reynolds, Perry
International Housewares Association *(550)*

Reynolds, Sandy
Turfgrass Producers International *(982)*

Reynolds, Shannon
Women's Basketball Coaches Association *(1022)*

Reynolds, Sonia
International Association of Physicians in AIDS Care *(526)*

Reynolds, Thomas G.
IEEE Components, Packaging, and Manufacturing Technology Society *(483)*

Reynolds-Moehrle, Jennifer
Academy of Accounting Historians *(3)*

Reynoso, Martha
International Sanitary Supply Association *(563)*

Rezai, MD, Ali R.
American Society for Stereotactic and Functional Neurosurgery *(189)*

Rhame, Lt. Gen Thomas G.
Association of the United States Army *(313)*

Rheingold, Ira
National Association of Consumer Advocates *(657)*

Rhett, Candace M.
International Federation of Professional and Technical Engineers *(544)*

Rhine, Thomas
National Communication Association *(724)*

Rhinehart, Myrna
American Shire Horse Association *(179)*

Rhinehart, R. Russell
American Automatic Control Council *(78)*

Rhinehart, Ric
Specialty Coffee Association of America *(957)*

Rhinehart, Robert S.
American Association of Business Valuation Specialists *(55)*
American Association of Physicians and Health Care Professionals *(69)*

Rhoades, Becki
National Association of Farm Broadcasting *(667)*

Rhoades, Emily B
American Association for Agricultural Education *(47)*

Rhoden, Joyce
International Maintenance Institute *(555)*

Rhoderick, CMP, Heather
American Composites Manufacturers Association *(105)*
International Cast Polymer Alliance *(533)*
International Cast Polymer Association *(533)*

Rhodes, Andrea
American Architectural Manufacturers Association *(46)*

Rhodes, BA, MS, C. Harker
American Association of Neuropathologists *(66)*

Rhodes, Carl M.
Human Capital Institute *(480)*

Rhodes, Keith
Council of Writing Program Administrators *(398)*
National Council of Writing Program Administrators *(738)*

Rhodes, APR, Marcia
Alliance of Work/Life Progress *(25)*
WorldatWork *(1028)*

Rhodes, Taylor
Mental Health America *(612)*

Rials, MS, Sandra

American Society for Healthcare Environmental Services *(185)*

Ribera, Andrea
Violin Society of America *(1010)*

Riccards, Patrick R.
American Institutes for Research *(141)*

Riccetti-Andrikos, Rose
American Fraternal Alliance *(124)*

Ricci, Bonnie
InsideNGO *(496)*

Ricci, Joseph
Textile Rental Services Association of America *(973)*

Riccio, Karen
AFCOM *(14)*

Rice, Alexis
National School Boards Association *(789)*

Rice, Barbara
American Association for the Advancement of Science *(51)*

Rice, Deborah
Obesity Society *(825)*

Rice, Fred
International Association of Accident Reconstruction Specialists *(514)*

Rice, Joe
National Golf Course Owners Association *(755)*

Rice, LuAnn
National Association for Rural Mental Health *(642)*

Rice, Norm
Sportsplex Operators and Developers Association *(959)*

Rice, Patricia N.
National Association of Health Unit Coordinators *(671)*

Rice, Quione
Society of General Internal Medicine *(937)*

Rice, Sharon
APICS The Association for Operations Management *(224)*

Rice, Teresa
National Energy Services Association *(746)*

Rice, Tina
International Association of Plumbing and Mechanical Officials *(526)*

Rice, Tondi
Intercollegiate Tennis Association *(507)*

Rice-Conboy, Liz
International Society of Hair Restoration Surgery *(573)*

Rich, Jerusha
International Society for Magnetic Resonance in Medicine *(567)*

Rich, CAE, EdD, RN, Nancy
Fastener Industry Coalition *(438)*

Rich, Phyllis M.
Nuclear Energy Institute *(824)*

Rich, R. Bruce
Association of American Publishers *(266)*

Rich, Terry
North American Association of State and Provincial Lotteries *(813)*
North American Association of State and Provincial Lotteries *(813)*

Rich, CAE, Todd
Design-Build Institute of America *(411)*

Rich, Tom
Technology Services Industry Association *(970)*

Richard, Erica
American Morgan Horse Association *(152)*

Richard, Jenny
American Congress of Rehabilitation Medicine *(107)*

Richard, Melissa
InterNational Electrical Testing Association *(542)*

Richards, Adrienne
American Frozen Food Institute *(124)*
National Frozen Pizza Institute *(754)*

Richards, Chris
National Stone, Sand, and Gravel Association *(796)*

Richards, H. West
Coalition for Independent Seniors *(360)*

Richards, Jay
NALP - The Association for Legal Career Professionals *(624)*

Richards, Jennifer
Anxiety Disorders Association of America *(224)*

Richards, Jennifer
National Association of Shell Marketers *(696)*

Richards, Kaelan
United Cerebral Palsy *(986)*

Richards, Katie
Canon Law Society of America *(342)*

Richards, Kevin
Information Systems Security Association *(495)*

Richards, Liz
Material Handling Equipment Distributors Association *(608)*

Richards, Rachel
American Podiatric Medical Association *(166)*

Richards, Ray
American Staffing Association *(213)*

Richards, Tina M.
National Stone, Sand, and Gravel Association *(796)*

Richardson, Allison
Communications Supply Service Association *(369)*

Richardson, Ashley
American Egg Board *(116)*

Richardson, CAE, Esq., Brett
Recreation Vehicle Rental Association *(877)*

Richardson, MS RD LD, Cecilia
National WIC Association *(805)*

Richardson, Charles L.
National Environmental, Safety and Health Training Association *(746)*

Richardson, Cheryl
National Association for Sport and Physical Education *(643)*

Richardson, Christine
Financial Planning Association *(445)*

Richardson, Dan
Environmental Bankers Association *(430)*

Richardson, Doris
Independent Petroleum Association of America *(491)*

Richardson, Douglas B.
Association of American Geographers *(265)*

Richardson, Jr., Jesse
Water Systems Council *(1013)*

Richardson, Jill
Industrial Designers Society of America *(493)*

Richardson, John
National Association of Medical Staff Services *(645)*
National Society of Genetic Counselors *(794)*

Richardson, Julia
American Council on the Teaching of Foreign Languages *(111)*

Richardson, Kelly
National Air Traffic Controllers Association *(630)*

Richardson, Mavis
American Journalism Historians Association *(143)*

Richardson, Rob
Aquatic Plant Management Society, Inc. *(227)*

Richardson, Robert
Computer Security Institute *(373)*

Richardson, Shawn
Extruded Polystyrene Foam Association *(436)*
Roof Coatings Manufacturers Association *(888)*

Richardson, Stephen
Environmental Bankers Association *(430)*

Richardson, Steve
Football Writers Association of America *(450)*

Richardson, Veta T
Association of Corporate Counsel *(277)*

Richarson, CAE, Esq., Brett
Recreation Vehicle Dealers Association of North
America *(876)*

Richelson, MD, Elliott
Society of Biological Psychiatry *(931)*

Richer, Steve
National Tour Association *(800)*

Richerson, Ginny
National Association for Business Teacher Education
(636)

Richert, Allyn
Quarters Furniture Manufacturers Association *(872)*

Richert, David
American Judicature Society *(143)*

Riches, Robert
National Health Club Association *(758)*

Richetti, Donald N.
Association of Old Crows *(297)*

Richey, Benjamin
United States Animal Health Association *(989)*

Richie, Scott
World Trade Centers Association *(1027)*

Richison, Sindie
International Brotherhood of Magicians *(531)*

Richison, Terry
International Brotherhood of Magicians *(531)*

Richland, Jud
American Association of Naturopathic Physicians *(66)*

Richmond, Bethany
The Carpet and Rug Institute *(343)*

Richmond, Cary
Bowling Proprietors' Association of America *(334)*

Richmond, Emily
Education Writers Association *(420)*

Richmond, Greg
National Association of Charter School Authorizers
(652)

Richmond, Judith K.
United States Chamber of Commerce *(991)*

Richmond, Ryan L.
Association of Universities for Research in Astronomy,
Inc. *(315)*

Richmond, Tom
National Cartoonists Society *(718)*

Richter, Christian
National Association for Surface Finishing *(643)*

Richter, Colleen
Urgent Care Association of America *(1004)*

Richter, Daniel K.
Society for Historians of the Early American Republic
(911)

Richter, Lisa
Association of University Technology Managers *(316)*

Richwine, Larry
National Tractor Pullers Association *(801)*

Rickard, Al
Global Cold Chain Alliance *(462)*

Rickard, Al
National Investor Relations Institute *(767)*

Rickbeil, Mallory
Wilderness Education Association *(1017)*

Rickenbach, CAE, IOM, Francine "Fran" W.
Association of Destination Management Executives
(278)
National Association of Nephrology Technologists and
Technicians *(682)*
Ultrasonic Industry Association *(983)*

Ricker, Kathy
American College of Psychiatrists *(102)*

Ricker, Kelly
Computing Technology Industry Association
(CompTIA) *(373)*

Ricker, Timothy
Water Environment Federation *(1013)*

Rickwalder, Janay
National Pest Management Association *(780)*

Rico, Edgar Gil
National Alliance for Hispanic Health *(631)*

Riddell, Jr., Dr. M. Gatz
American Association of Bovine Practitioners *(55)*

Riddell, Mary
International Association of Personnel in Employment
Security *(526)*
International Association of Workforce Professionals
(IAWP) *(529)*

Riddiough, Timothy J.
American Real Estate and Urban Economics
Association *(173)*

Riddlebaugh, Gene
National Alarm Association of America *(631)*

Rideau, Natalie
World Trade Centers Association *(1027)*

Ridenour, Robert
Society of Allied Weight Engineers *(928)*

Rideout, Tonya
National Association of Telecommunications Officers
and Advisors *(705)*

Rider, Eddie
Forest Landowners Association *(451)*

Rider, CITP, CMA, CPA, Steven C.
Industrial Fabrics Association International *(493)*

Ridgeway, Nan Bayster
Distance Education and Training Council *(414)*

Ridgley, Lisa
Voluntary Protection Programs Participants'
Association, Inc. *(1011)*

Riding, James B.
AASP - The Palynological Society *(2)*

Ridnouer, Nathan
Specialty Equipment Market Association *(957)*

Ridolfi, Michelle
American College of Mohs Surgeons *(98)*

Riebel, Karen Hanson
National Association of Shareholder and Consumer
Attorneys *(696)*

Rieck, Mark
International Right of Way Association *(563)*

Riedel, Daniel Todd
American Shire Horse Association *(179)*

Riedesel, Rebecca "Becky"
Society for Biomaterials *(905)*

Riegel, Quentin
National Association of Manufacturers *(679)*

Rieger, Penny S.
Caucus for Producers, Writers & Directors *(346)*

Riegler, Garlon
Association of Analytical Communities International
(267)

Riehl, Maureen B.
Council On State Taxation *(400)*

Riello, Laura J.
IEEE Electron Devices Society *(484)*

Rieman, Garth B.
National Council of State Housing Agencies *(736)*

Riemer, Brenda
North American Society for the Sociology of Sport
(822)

Rieple, Tricia
Financial Planning Association *(445)*

Ries, Matt
Water Environment Federation *(1013)*

Ries, Roxanne
Performance Warehouse Association *(841)*

Riesenberg, Kurt
Spray Polyurethane Foam Alliance *(959)*

Rieser, CCP, SPHR, Bill
American College of Chest Physicians *(94)*

Riesett, Kathleen Kelley
Organization for the Promotion and Advancement of
Small Telecommunications Companies *(831)*

Riess, Warren
North American Society for Oceanic History *(821)*

Riester, Andrew
The Propeller Club of the United States *(867)*

Riethmaier, Jonathan
TASH *(968)*

Riew, MD, K. Daniel
Korean American Spine Society *(591)*

Rigas, Laura Keehner
Business Executives for National Security *(338)*

Rigby, Emma C.
Canadian-American Business Council *(341)*

Rigby, Kelly
Communications Supply Service Association *(369)*

Rigby, Paul
Fleet Reserve Association *(447)*

Rigel, Christine
Society of Environmental Journalists *(935)*

Rigel, Vicki
American Cotswold Record Association *(108)*

Riggan, Tracy
IPC - Association Connecting Electronics Industries
(584)
IPC - Surface Mount Equipment Manufacturers
Association *(585)*
IPC Washington Office *(585)*

Riggleman, Erin
Intersocietal Accreditation Commission *(582)*

Riggott, Brenda L.
American Association of Neuromuscular and
Electrodiagnostic Medicine *(66)*

Riggs, Carol
Select Registry/Distinguished Inns of North America *(896)*

Riggs, David
National Conference of Local Environmental Health Administrators *(727)*

Righter, Elisabeth
Phi Rho Sigma Medical Society *(846)*

Righthouse, Jerry L.
World Sign Associates *(1027)*

Rigmaiden, Kenneth E.
International Union of Painters and Allied Trades *(579)*

Rigney, Anne M.
Society of Financial Service Professionals *(936)*

Rigney, Jr., P. Robert
American Association of Tissue Banks *(75)*

Riley, Bob
National Associations of State Directors of Pupil Transportation Services *(710)*

Riley, CTRS, PhD, Bob
National Council for Therapeutic Recreation Certification *(733)*

Riley, Carol
National Association of Elementary School Principals *(664)*

Riley, Craig
National Association of Electrical Distributors *(664)*

Riley, Emily D.
American Mathematical Society *(148)*

Riley, Jamie
Custom Electronic Design and Installation Association *(405)*

Riley, Janet
American Meat Institute *(148)*

Riley, Janet
Shelf-Stable Food Processors Association *(898)*

Riley, Kimberly T.
American Association of Colleges for Teacher Education *(57)*

Riley, Lindsey
National Association of Regional Councils *(690)*

Riley, Lynne F.
National Association of Bankruptcy Trustees *(647)*

Riley, Mark
National Association of Children's Hospitals and Related Institutions *(653)*

Riley, Melissa
International Spa Association *(575)*

Riley, Patrick
Sheet Metal Workers' International Association *(898)*

Riley, Ron
New Dramatists *(809)*

Riley, Shawna
United States Professional Tennis Association *(998)*

Riley, Zane
Public Relations Student Society of America *(870)*

Rill, Julianne
International Society for Pharmaceutical Engineering *(567)*

Rimm, Poornima
United States Professional Tennis Association *(998)*

Rimmer, Pat
American Board of Preventive Medicine *(83)*

Rinaldi, DPM, CAE, Dr. Frank
American Association of Hospital and Healthcare Podiatrists *(62)*

Rinaldi, Kara Saul
National Home Performance Council, Inc. *(760)*

Rinaldi, CAE, PhD, Robert C.
American Association of Oral and Maxillofacial Surgeons *(67)*

Rinaudo, Paula W.
International College of Dentists, U.S.A. Section *(535)*

Rinck, Greg
Global Cold Chain Alliance *(462)*

Rindelaub, Jim
Choristers Guild *(355)*

Rindfield, Tracie
Academy of Surgical Research *(9)*

Rinehart, Rebecca
The Endocrine Society *(427)*

Ring, Richard
Association for the Bibliography of History *(259)*

Ringhofer, Curt W
American Equilibration Society *(117)*

Ringo, Lori
National Association of Catastrophe Adjusters *(651)*

Ringo, Robin S.
Public Investors Arbitration Bar Association *(869)*

Ringo, Stefanie
International Society of Beverage Technologists *(571)*

Rinholm, Rodney "Rod"
Gas Technology Institute *(456)*

Rini, Lauren
International Special Events Society *(575)*

Rinkenberger, Kathy
Association of Former Agents of the U.S. Secret Service *(284)*

Riordan-Butterworth, Brendan
Interactive Advertising Bureau *(506)*

Rios, MD, MSPH, Elena V.
National Hispanic Medical Association *(759)*

Riotto, Charles M.
International Licensing Industry Merchandisers' Association *(554)*

Ripley, Barry
National Textile Association *(800)*

Ripley, Barry
National Textile Association *(800)*

Ripley, Doré
Humanities Education and Research Association *(481)*

Ripperger, Sharon
Balloon Federation of America *(325)*

Rising, Evelyn
The National Association of Colored Women's Club, Inc. *(656)*

Risinger, Amy
Foodservice Equipment Distributors Association *(450)*

Risinger, Beth B.
International Executive Housekeepers Association *(543)*

Risk, James L.
Assembly of Episcopal Healthcare Chaplains *(234)*

Riske, Kris Brandt
American Federation of Astrologers, Inc. *(119)*

Riskey, Curtis
CBA *(346)*

Riskind, Arlyn G.
National Communication Association *(724)*

Riso, Guy

SWANA - Solid Waste Association of North America *(967)*

Riso, Mark
Plumbing-Heating-Cooling Contractors - National Association *(851)*

Risser, Jr., PE, Robert J.
Concrete Reinforcing Steel Institute *(374)*

Rissler, Jennifer
ArtTable *(231)*

Ristau, EdD, Karen M.
National Catholic Educational Association *(718)*

Ristau, Louise
Awards and Recognition Association *(325)*

Risteen, Eric
National Association of States United For Aging and Disabilities *(703)*

Ristic, Meredith
National Association of Clean Water Agencies *(654)*

Ritchey, PhD, CAE, David A.
Association of Teacher Educators *(312)*

Ritchie, Gary
Council for Near-Infrared Spectroscopy *(390)*

Ritchie, John
National Association of Home Builders *(673)*

Ritchlin, Lance
Financial Planning Association *(445)*

Ritenour, Jordan
United Union of Roofers, Waterproofers and Allied Workers *(1001)*

Ritter, Barbara W.
National Telecommunications Cooperative Association *(799)*

Ritter, Brandi
Society of Air Force Physician Assistants *(928)*

Ritter, Carol
Romance Writers of America *(888)*

Ritter, Dave
Professional Tennis Registry *(865)*

Ritter, Gordon L.
Civil Aviation Medical Association *(357)*

Ritter, Stephanie
North American Horticultural Supply Association *(817)*

Ritter, Vern
Lyrasis *(600)*

Ritterbusch, Chad
American Society of Golf Course Architects *(198)*

Rittner, Toby
Council of Development Finance Agencies *(393)*

Ritz, Amanda
National Association of Sales Professionals *(692)*

Rivard, Karen
Association for the Advancement of Psychology *(258)*

Rivellese, Kristyn
Industrial Designers Society of America *(493)*

Rivenburg, Michele
International Grooving & Grinding Association *(549)*

Rivera, Alba
Association of National Advertisers *(295)*

Rivera, Dawn
Retail Bakers of America *(884)*

Rivera, Jason
Poultry Breeders of America *(854)*
U.S Poultry and Egg Association *(998)*

Rivera, Madeline
Jewelers of America *(587)*

Rivera, Margaret
American Association of Community Colleges *(58)*

Rivera, Sandra
American White American Creme Horse Registry *(221)*

Rivers, Dr. James A.
Psi Omega Fraternity *(868)*

Rivers, Patti
American Board of Quality Assurance and Utilization Review Physicians, Inc. *(84)*

Rivers, Dr. William P.
Joint National Committee for Languages-National Council for Languages and International Studies *(589)*
National Council for Languages and International Studies *(732)*

Rives, Caroline
Special Libraries Association *(956)*

Rives, Jack L
American Bar Association *(79)*

Rives, Teresa
Society of Animal Artists *(930)*

Rives-DeWitt, Alecia
American Association of Political Consultants *(70)*

Riviere, Jim E.
American Academy of Veterinary Pharmacology and Therapeutics *(42)*

Riviere, Monique
Independent Sector *(491)*

Riviere, Nancy
National Association of Secondary School Principals *(694)*

Rivin, Gabriel
National Cooperative Business Association *(729)*

Rizley, Ross
Marketing Science Institute *(606)*

Rizza, Kathleen O'Keefe
Council for Exceptional Children *(390)*

Rizzuto, CAE, A. Anthony
American Conference of Governmental Industrial Hygienists *(107)*

Roach, Betsi
Legal Marketing Association *(596)*

Roach, Erin
Social Venture Network *(902)*

Roach, Michelle
Clinical Immunology Society *(358)*

Roady, Sandy
Piano Technicians Guild *(848)*

Roark, Louanne
Personal Care Products Council *(842)*

Roark, Trent
Society for Excellence in Eyecare *(909)*

Roath, Alissa
National Center for Manufacturing Sciences *(719)*

Roba, William
Society for German-American Studies *(910)*

Robart, Andy
Gas Turbine Association *(457)*

Robb, Dawn
Professional Photographers of America *(863)*

Robb, RADM James A.
National Training and Simulation Association *(801)*

Robbins, MBA, Beth
Association of Reproductive Health Professionals *(305)*

Robbins, Dan
Motion Picture Association of America (MPAA) *(619)*

Robbins, Jeremy S.
The Catfish Institute *(345)*

Robbins, Lynn
Xplor International *(1029)*

Robbins, Mark E.
Association of Private Sector Colleges and Universities (Career College Association) *(300)*

Robbins, Michael
Air Line Pilots Association International *(19)*

Roberson, David
Specialty Coffee Association of America *(957)*

Roberson, Dee
Fermenters International Trade Association *(443)*

Roberson, CSS, Lora
Electronics Technicians Association International *(424)*

Roberson, PhD, Rodney L.
United Braford Breeders *(986)*

Robert, Stephanie
International Association of Amusement Parks and Attractions(IAAPA) *(515)*

Roberts, Becky
American Academy of Sleep Medicine *(42)*
Associated Professional Sleep Societies *(237)*

Roberts, Beth
National Trappers Association *(801)*

Roberts, Brad
Electricity Storage Association *(422)*

Roberts, Brandon
American College of Osteopathic Surgeons *(100)*

Roberts, Brian C.
National Association of County Engineers *(660)*

Roberts, Cassandra
National Council for the Social Studies *(733)*

Roberts, Cecil E.
United Mine Workers of America *(988)*

Roberts, David
National Trappers Association *(801)*

Roberts, David
Society of Professional Investigators *(945)*

Roberts, David J.
International Association of Chiefs of Police *(517)*

Roberts, Dwight
US Rice Producers Association *(1004)*

Roberts, Lt. Gov. Elizabeth
Democratic Lieutenant Governors' Association (DLGA) *(410)*

Roberts, Forrest
National Cattlemen's Beef Association *(718)*

Roberts, Grady
American Association for Agricultural Education *(47)*

Roberts, Gregory
ACPA College Student Educators International *(11)*
American College Personnel Association *(105)*

Roberts, Jacquelyn
Federation of American Societies for Experimental Biology *(440)*

Roberts, Jennifer
National Safe Skies Alliance *(788)*

Roberts, Jessica
American Osteopathic College of Radiology *(161)*

Roberts, John
Center for Spiritual and Ethical Education *(348)*

Roberts, John H.
International Grooving & Grinding Association *(549)*

Roberts, Jonathan

International Cast Polymer Association *(533)*

Roberts, Julian
American Association of Preferred Provider Organizations *(70)*
National Alliance for Specialty Healthcare Programs *(632)*
National Association of Vision Care Plans *(708)*

Roberts, Karen
Society for Pediatric Psychology *(918)*

Roberts, ChFC, CLU, Karen
WIFS - Women in Insurance and Financial Services *(1017)*

Roberts, Kimberly
Airlines For America *(21)*

Roberts, Kimberly
National Association of Truck Stop Operators(NATSO) *(707)*

Roberts, Lauren D.
Food and Drug Law Institute *(449)*

Roberts, Liz
American Photographic Artists *(164)*

Roberts, Margaret
International Brain Injury Association *(531)*

Roberts, Mark
TechServe Alliance *(971)*

Roberts, Matthew
Methanol Institute *(614)*

Roberts, Michael
American Gastroenterological Association *(125)*

Roberts, Michael
Society of Industrial and Office Realtors *(939)*

Roberts, ACE, Randy C.
American Cinema Editors *(91)*

Roberts, Rebecca
Association of Diving Contractors International *(279)*

Roberts, Rodney
Man and Cybernetics Systems Society *(602)*

Roberts, Roger
National Mining Association *(772)*

Roberts, MBA, Sedric
National Bar Association *(712)*

Roberts, Susan
Society of Radiologists in Ultrasound *(946)*

Roberts, BSN, JD, Terri
American Holistic Nurses Association *(132)*

Roberts, Dr. Terry L.
International Plant Nutrition Institute *(560)*

Roberts, Tony
Georgia Charter Schools Association *(459)*

Roberts, Vonceil
North American Association of Food Equipment Manufacturers *(813)*

Robertson, Baldwin
International Association of Fire Fighters *(521)*

Robertson, MA, IBCLC, Barbara
United States Lactation Consultant Association *(996)*

Robertson, David Alan
Association of Academic Museums & Galleries *(263)*

Robertson, David N.
Association of Finance and Insurance Professionals *(283)*

Robertson, Deborah
The Association of Theatre Movement Educators *(314)*

Robertson, Deborah L.
Phycological Society of America *(846)*

Robertson, Janet
American Football Coaches Association *(122)*

Robertson, John
Mechanical Association Railcar Technical Services *(610)*

Robertson, Kathleen
North American Metal Packaging Alliance, Inc. (NAMPA) *(818)*

Robertson, CPA, Kimberly
American Osteopathic Academy of Orthopedics *(159)*

Robertson, Larry
American Society for Gastrointestinal Endoscopy *(184)*

Robertson, Maria
School Nutrition Association *(892)*

Robertson, Michael
Specialty Graphic Imaging Association *(957)*

Robertson, Michael R.
Measurement, Control and Automation Association *(609)*

Robertson, Peter D.
America's Natural Gas Alliance *(29)*

Robertson, Scott
NAMM - The International Music Products Association *(625)*

Robertson, Stacey
Society for Historians of the Early American Republic *(911)*

Robey, Heidi
American Society of Association Executives-The Center for Association Leadership *(193)*

Robey, Michael H.
The American Board of Opticianry and the National Contact Lens Examiners *(83)*

Robichaux, Chris
Mortgage Insurance Companies of America *(619)*

Robichaux, Stephanie
The Surety and Fidelity Association of America *(966)*

Robie, Ed
Technical Association of the Pulp and Paper Industry *(970)*

Robinette, Barbara
American Board of Periodontology *(83)*

Robins, Nicki
National Association of Chain Drug Stores *(652)*

Robinson, Adele
National Association for the Education of Young Children *(644)*

Robinson, PhD, Allen
American Driver and Traffic Safety Education Association *(115)*

Robinson, APR, Amy M.
Direct Selling Association *(413)*

Robinson, Barbara
American Truck Dealers *(217)*

Robinson, PhD, Bean
Society for the Scientific Study of Sexuality *(924)*

Robinson, Bill
North American Maple Syrup Council *(818)*

Robinson, Blades
International Association of Dive Rescue Specialists *(519)*

Robinson, Bri
National Emergency Number Association *(745)*

Robinson, Charles L.
Alliance of Automobile Manufacturers *(24)*

Robinson, Cheryl

UWC - Strategic Services on Unemployment and Workers' Compensation *(1007)*

Robinson, Christie L.
American Chemical Society - Rubber Division *(90)*

Robinson, Christopher
Private Art Dealers Association *(858)*

Robinson, Cindy
American Congress of Rehabilitation Medicine *(107)*

Robinson, David
Linguistic Society of America *(598)*

Robinson, Del Baker
Electronic Transactions Association *(424)*

Robinson, Donna
Council of Educational Facility Planners International *(393)*

Robinson, Donna May
National Institute of American Doll Artists *(764)*

Robinson, Doris
American Poultry Association *(167)*

Robinson, Doug
National Association of State Chief Information Officers *(699)*

Robinson, Gail
American Association of Community Colleges *(58)*

Robinson, Ginny
Powder Coating Institute *(854)*

Robinson, Gregg
American Association of Medical Dosimetrists *(65)*

Robinson, CAE, J. Lawrence
Color Pigments Manufacturers Association, Inc. *(365)*

Robinson, James J.
Minerals, Metals and Materials Society *(617)*

Robinson, Jamisen
American Miniature Horse Association *(152)*

Robinson, Jason
American Jersey Cattle Association/National All-Jersey Inc. *(142)*

Robinson, Jena
National Association for Information Destruction, Inc. *(640)*

Robinson, Jessica
National BioDiesel Board *(713)*

Robinson, Jessie
Professional Association of Innkeepers International *(860)*

Robinson, DDS, John D.
The Public Relations Society of America *(870)*

Robinson, John F.
National Minority Business Council *(773)*

Robinson, Josh
Republican Governors Association *(881)*

Robinson, Joyce B.
American Postal Workers Union *(167)*

Robinson, Kathy
National Association of State Emergency Medical Services Officials *(700)*

Robinson, Katie
National Conference of Commissioners on Uniform State Laws *(727)*

Robinson, Kelly
American Association of Professional Landmen *(71)*

Robinson, Kesha
Equipment Leasing and Finance Association *(432)*

Robinson, Keshia
National Association of Emergency Medical Technicians *(665)*

Robinson, Kiesha
NaSPA: Networks and Systems Professional Association *(626)*

Robinson, Kinsey M.
United Union of Roofers, Waterproofers and Allied Workers *(1001)*

Robinson, Leslie
American Driver and Traffic Safety Education Association *(115)*

Robinson, Lovelyn M.
American Medical Rehabilitation Providers Association *(149)*

Robinson, JD, Lynn P.
American Gastroenterological Association *(125)*

Robinson, Lysa
Environmental Markets Association *(431)*

Robinson, Marcia
Central Intercollegiate Athletic Association *(349)*

Robinson, Mark
Machinery Dealers National Association *(601)*

Robinson, Megan
Certified Contractors Network *(349)*

Robinson, Mike
Council of State Governments *(397)*

Robinson, Mikel
International Association of Wildland Fire *(528)*

Robinson, Mitzie A.
Chief Warrant and Warrant Officers Association, United States Coast Guard *(352)*

Robinson, Nicole
Log Homes Council *(600)*

Robinson, Pamela
National Association of Bar Executives *(648)*

Robinson, Rabbi Harold
JWB Jewish Chaplains Council *(590)*

Robinson, Ross
National Association for Search and Rescue *(642)*

Robinson, Roxanne M.
American Association for Laboratory Accreditation *(50)*

Robinson, Scott
International Society for Developmental Psychobiology *(566)*

Robinson, Sharon P.
American Association of Colleges for Teacher Education *(57)*

Robinson, Sherry
Chamber Music America *(350)*

Robinson, Shirley
Material Handling Equipment Distributors Association *(608)*

Robinson, Sue
National Association of Intercollegiate Athletics *(676)*

Robinson, Terence
American Pomological Society *(167)*

Robinson, CFA, CFP, CPA, PhD, Thomas R.
CFA Institute *(350)*

Robinson, William L.
National Association of Marine Services *(679)*

Robinson-Carroll, Cornell W.
National Funeral Directors and Morticians Association *(754)*

Robison, Angelica
International Studies Association *(576)*

Robison, David
Environmental and Energy Study Institute *(430)*

Robison, Jane E.

American Association of Intensive English Programs
(63)

Robison, Pam
National Cutting Horse Association *(741)*

Robitscher, MPH, John W.
National Association of Chronic Disease Directors
(653)

Robotti, Lisa
Open Mobile Alliance *(828)*

Robuck, Eric
International Memorialization Supply Association
(556)

Roby, Don
Airborne Law Enforcement Association *(19)*

Roby, Karen Wells
Federal Magistrate Judges Association *(439)*

Rocchio, Paul
International Franchise Association *(547)*

Roch, John Michael
Association for Clinical Pastoral Education *(241)*

Rocha, Josie
Diesel Technology Forum *(412)*

Rocha, Kelly
DBA International *(407)*
DBA International *(407)*

Roche, David
Jewelers Shipping Association *(587)*

Roche, Kathy
Jewelers Shipping Association *(587)*

Roche, Robyn
Food Processing Suppliers Association *(449)*

Rocheleau, Natasha
Society of American Military Engineers *(929)*

Rochell, Judy
American College of Physician Executives *(101)*

Rochet, Jean Charles
Econometric Society *(418)*

Rochman, Julie
Institute for Business & Home Safety *(496)*

Rock, Anthony (Bud)
Association of Science-Technology Centers *(307)*

Rock, Ed
National Science Teachers Association *(790)*

Rock, Paul
Asian American Convenience Stores Association *(231)*

Rock, Sherry Barndollar
Diplomatic and Consular Officers, Retired (Dacor)
(412)

Rocke, Carol
National Association for Printing Leadership *(641)*
R & E Council of the NAPL *(872)*

Rockey, MD, Don C.
Clerkship Directors in Internal Medicine *(358)*

Rockhill, Denise
National Fluid Power Association *(751)*

Rockman, Howard A.
American Society for Clinical Investigation *(182)*

Rockne, Jennifer
American Independent Business Alliance *(135)*

Rockwell, Robin
Future Business Leaders of America - Phi Beta Lambda
(455)

Rockwell, Shelley
Conference of State Court Administrators *(376)*
National College of Probate Judges *(724)*

Rockwell, Tim
Operations Security Professionals Society *(828)*

Rod, Ed
American Pet Products Association *(163)*

Rod, Pascal
International Federation of Nurse Anesthetists *(544)*

Rodela, Kim
International Association for Business and Society
(511)

Rodger, David
United States Institute for Theatre Technology *(995)*

Rodgers, Chris
National Association of County Civil Attorneys *(659)*

Rodgers, Jim
National Association of Forensic Economics *(669)*

Rodgers, Jonathan
American Oriental Society *(158)*

Rodgers, Joseph L.
Society of Multivariate Experimental Psychology *(942)*

Rodgers, Lisa
National Association of Mutual Insurance Companies
(681)

Rodgers, Loren
National Center for Employee Ownership *(719)*

Rodgers, Paul
American Sheep Industry Association *(178)*

Rodgers, Paul
American Wool Council *(222)*

Rodgers, Robert
Visually Impaired Data Processors International *(1011)*

Rodgers-Fox, De
American Academy of Environmental Medicine *(33)*

Rodgriguez, Vince
Antenna Measurement Techniques Association *(224)*

Rodiger, Ann
American Society for the Alexander Technique *(190)*

Rodman, Myrna
Automotive Body Parts Association *(322)*

Rodman, Stanley A.
Automotive Body Parts Association *(322)*

Rodman, Terry
National Blacksmiths and Weldors Association *(715)*

Rodman, Veronique
American Enterprise Institute for Public Policy
Research *(117)*

Rodnan, Nancy
American Society for Biochemistry and Molecular
Biology *(181)*

Rodolfa, PhD, Emil
Association of Psychology Postdoctoral and Internship
Centers *(303)*

Rodrick, Scott
National Center for Employee Ownership *(719)*

Rodrigue, Kellie
American Optometric Association *(157)*

Rodrigue, MA, Phara Georges
Registry of Interpreters for the Deaf *(879)*

Rodrigues, John
National Association of Independent Schools *(675)*

Rodriguez, Antonio
Columbia Scholastic Press Association *(365)*

Rodriguez, Arturo S.
United Farm Workers of America *(986)*

Rodriguez, Jr., Cleofas "Cleo"

National Migrant and Seasonal Head Start Association
(772)

Rodriguez, Dania
Association of State and Territorial Solid Waste
Management Officials *(310)*

Rodriguez, Gail
Medical Imaging and Technology Alliance *(611)*
National Electrical Manufacturers Association *(744)*

Rodriguez, Guadalupe
Art Libraries Society of North America *(230)*

Rodriguez, Jacqueline
National Society of Hispanic MBAs *(794)*

Rodriguez, Jenny
Industrial Perforators Association *(494)*

Rodriguez, PhD, Julia E. Curry
National Association for Chicana and Chicano Studies
(637)

Rodriguez, Lisa
New America Alliance *(809)*

Rodriguez, Lysa
International Society for the Study of Subtle Energies
and Energy Medicine *(570)*

Rodriguez, Manon
Society of American Magicians *(929)*

Rodriguez, Manuel
Institute of Real Estate Management *(503)*

Rodriguez, CAE, Mary
Society of Diagnostic Medical Sonographers *(934)*

Rodriguez, Melissa
International Health, Racquet and Sportsclub
Association *(549)*

Rodriguez, Nancy
American Dental Assistants Association *(113)*

Rodriguez, Priscilla
International Liver Transplantation Society *(554)*
Osteoarthritis Research Society International *(834)*

Rodriguez, MD, Rene F.
InterAmerican College of Physicians and Surgeons
(507)

Rodriguez, Tina
National Association of State Agencies for Surplus
Property *(697)*

Rodriquez, Randy
National Association of Hispanic Firefighters *(672)*

Roe, Cindy L.
American Society of News Editors *(204)*

Roe, Cynthia
Women in Technology International *(1022)*

Roe, Elizabeth
International Card Manufacturers Association *(532)*

Roe, Jason
International Society of Transport Aircraft Trading
(574)
Print Services & Distribution Association *(857)*

Roebuck, Gary
Association of Research Libraries *(306)*
Library Copyright Alliance *(597)*

Roebuck, Vicki
National Organization of Legal Services Workers *(777)*

Roecklein, Jennifer
The National Network for Social Work Managers *(774)*

Roehrig, Steven A.
Steel Deck Institute *(962)*

Roelike, LuAnne A.
Independent Community Bankers of America *(488)*

Roemer, III, Henry C
Specialty Tobacco Council *(958)*

Roen, Duane
National Council of Writing Program Administrators *(738)*

Roenigk, William P.
National Chicken Council *(720)*

Roepke, Kevin
United States Grains Council *(994)*

Roesener, Rick
American Academy of Dental Practice Administration *(32)*

Roessler, Bryan
Association for High Technology Distribution *(248)*

Roetert, LTGEN Paul
American Alliance for Health, Physical Education, Recreation and Dance *(44)*

Rogala, Christine
Electric Drive Transportation Association *(421)*

Rogala, CAE, IOM, Joan E.
Lambda Kappa Sigma *(593)*

Rogan, Elizabeth A.
Optical Society of America *(829)*

Rogers, Anthony
Gerontological Society of America *(460)*

Rogers, Barry
Air and Waste Management Association *(17)*

Rogers, Bert
Tall Ships America *(968)*

Rogers, Bonnie
American Association of Legal Nurse Consultants *(64)*

Rogers, Carol Sue
AACE International *(1)*

Rogers, Catherine
Applied Research Ethics National Association *(226)*

Rogers, Catherine S.
Association of Management/International Association of Management *(292)*

Rogers, Cindy
American Society of Interventional Pain Physicians *(201)*

Rogers, Darrell
Alliance for Natural Health USA *(23)*

Rogers, James
Global Cold Chain Alliance *(462)*

Rogers, James
International Association for Cold Storage Construction *(511)*

Rogers, Jan
National Association of Tax Professionals *(704)*

Rogers, Jen
Plan Sponsor Council of America *(849)*

Rogers, Jim
National Association for the Advancement of Orthotics and Prosthetics *(643)*

Rogers, CFA, John D.
CFA Institute *(350)*

Rogers, Joseph E.L.
Center for Waste Reduction Technologies *(348)*

Rogers, Ken
Automation Alley *(321)*

Rogers, Maureen
Herb Growing and Marketing Network *(474)*

Rogers, Mekel
American School Band Directors' Association *(177)*

Rogers, Dr. Phillip
National Association of State Directors of Teacher Education and Certification *(700)*

Rogers, Rebecca
National Conference on Research in Language and Literacy *(729)*

Rogers, Sandy
National Family Caregivers Association *(747)*

Rogers, ABC, APR, Susan K.
Society for College and University Planning *(906)*

Rogers, CAE, Todd P.
Casualty Actuarial Society *(344)*

Rogg, Kathy
National Real Estate Investors Association *(784)*

Roggero, Jim
Court Information Technology Officer Consortium *(402)*

Rogin, Carole M.
Hearing Industries Association *(472)*

Roherty, Martha
National Association of States United For Aging and Disabilities *(703)*

Rohland, Heide
Semiconductor Environmental Safety and Health Association *(896)*
Society for Integrative and Comparative Biology *(913)*

Rohlwing, Kevin
Tire Industry Association *(975)*

Rohm, Halley
Ocean Research & Conservation Association *(826)*

Rohrbach, Heidi J.
Healthcare Distribution Management Association *(471)*

Rohrs, Alvin
Enactus *(427)*

Roise, Joe
Council On Forest Engineering *(399)*

Rojas, Buffy
DRI International *(416)*

Rojas, Verena
American College of Epidemiology *(95)*

Rojas, Verena
American Society for Cytotechnology *(183)*

Rojas, Verena
Society of Invasive Cardiovascular Professionals *(940)*

Rokvic, Vladimir
Serbian-American Chamber of Commerce *(897)*

Roland, Becky
Association of Environmental and Engineering Geologists *(281)*

Roland, Catherine B.
Association for Adult Development and Aging *(238)*

Rolando, Fredric V.
National Association of Letter Carriers *(678)*

Roldan, Richard R.
National Propane Gas Association *(783)*

Role, JD, MSLS, Susan Eads
American Association of Colleges of Osteopathic Medicine *(57)*

Rolfe, Kathy
American Bridge Teachers' Association *(86)*

Rolland, Sean
Association of Clean Water Administrators *(273)*

Roller, Debbie
American Society of Andrology *(192)*

Rollins, Barbara
National Council on Problem Gambling *(739)*

Rollins, III, CPA, Jack B.
American Association of Private Lenders *(71)*

Rollins, IOM, Wendy E.
American Lighting Association *(145)*

Rollm, Allisa
American Dehydrated Onion and Garlic Association *(113)*

Rolph, Karen Sue
Society for the Study of Indigenous Languages of the Americas *(925)*

Romain, James
North American Saxophone Alliance *(820)*

Romaine, Laura
Registry of Interpreters for the Deaf *(879)*

Roman, Karen
Technical Association of the Pulp and Paper Industry *(970)*

Roman, Lisa
American Coatings Association *(92)*

Roman, Lori
Salt Institute *(891)*

Roman, Natividad
BCA *(326)*

Roman, William J.
New England Club Managers Association *(809)*

Romanek, Broc
National Association of Stock Plan Professionals *(703)*

Romanenko, Nick
University Photographers Association of America *(1002)*

Romano, BS, Bud J.
American College of Occupational and Environmental Medicine *(99)*

Romano, Gerry
American Association of Colleges of Pharmacy *(57)*

Romano, Jorge
NAIOP, The Commercial Real Estate Development Association *(366)*

Romano, Lisa Marie
American Society of Ophthalmic Administrators *(205)*

Romano, Michael R.
National Telecommunications Cooperative Association *(799)*

Romano, Neil
Professional Baseball Athletic Trainers Society *(860)*

Romano, Rosina
Entomological Society of America *(429)*

Romanucci, MD, Demostene
American Society of Abdominal Surgeons *(190)*

Romanyshyn, Gregg
Hydraulic Institute *(481)*

Rome, Martin J.
American Speech-Language-Hearing Association *(212)*

Romeo, Anthony
International Institute of Connector and Interconnection Technology *(551)*

Romeo, Bob
Academy of Country Music *(4)*

Romeo, Joan
Bowling Writers Association of America *(334)*

Romeo, CAE, Kelly Lyn
American Land Title Association *(144)*

Romero, Jesus A.
NPES, The Association for Suppliers of Printing, Publishing, and Converting Technologies *(824)*

Romero, Kelli
The Grant Professionals Association *(465)*

Romero, Michelle

Association for Healthcare Foodservice *(248)*

Romero, Rita
Federation of Employers and Workers of America *(441)*

Romero, Teresa
United Farm Workers of America *(986)*

Romine, Phillip
Higher Education Consortium for Urban Affairs *(475)*

Rommel, Jackie
Certified Contractors Network *(349)*

Romney, Ari
Council of Large Public Housing Authorities *(395)*

Romney, Lynthia
College Savings Foundation *(364)*

Ronaldson, Christy
National Association of Home Builders *(673)*

Ronan, Dan
American Bus Association *(87)*

Ronay, Christopher J.
Institute of Makers of Explosives *(501)*

Roncketti, MS, Nancy E.
International Association of Counseling Services *(518)*

Rondeau, Deborah
International Association of Campus Law Enforcement Administrators *(517)*

Roney, John C. "Jack"
American Sugar Alliance *(214)*

Ronkin, Bruce
Music and Entertainment Industry Educators Association *(622)*

Ronsheim, Dmin, Douglas M.
American Association of Pastoral Counselors *(68)*

Ronzello, Gina C.
Cargo Airline Association *(343)*

Rood, Brian
International Conference of Symphony and Opera Musicians *(537)*

Roode, Carl
American Dairy Products Institute *(112)*

Roof, Harry
American Coal Ash Association *(92)*

Roogow, Buddy
North American Association of State and Provincial Lotteries *(813)*

Rooks, Richard
Automotive Engine Rebuilders Association *(322)*

Rooney, Curtis
Healthcare Supply Chain Association *(472)*

Rooney, Fr. Don
Catholic Association of Diocesan Ecumenical and Interreligious Officers *(345)*

Rooney, Laura
Association of Moving Image Archivists *(295)*

Rooney, Robert
National Association of Independent Publishers Representatives *(675)*

Roorda, Marten
Association of Test Publishers *(313)*

Roose, David
National Association of Police Athletics/Activities Leagues, Inc. *(685)*

Roosendaal, B. Denise
Institute for Credentialing Excellence *(497)*

Root, Jameson
North - American Interfraternity Conference *(812)*

Root, Jenay

American Radium Society *(173)*

Root, Jennifer
Association of Marketing Service Providers *(293)*

Root, Rick
World Waterpark Association *(1028)*

Root, CCM, Steven A.
American Weather and Climate Industry Association *(220)*

Roozen, David
Religious Research Association *(880)*

Ropelewski, ARM, AU, CPCU, CPIW, Deborah
Professional Liability Underwriting Society *(863)*

Roper, Christopher
Literacy Research Association *(599)*

Rosa, Maria V.
The American Geographical Society *(126)*

Rosado, Edwin S.
National Association of Counties *(659)*

Rosalsky, Jeffrey
American Nature Study Society *(155)*

Rosandich, Eric
Pi Sigma Epsilon *(847)*

Rosario, Freshta
Air Conditioning, Heating and Refrigeration Institute (AHRI) *(18)*

Rosario, Holly
Christian Leadership Alliance *(355)*

Rosario, Holly
Christian Management Association *(356)*

Rosas, Christina
Professional Women Singers Association *(866)*

Rosato, IOM, Edith
Academy of Managed Care Pharmacy *(6)*

Rosch, FACP, MA, MD, Paul J.
American Institute of Stress *(140)*

Roscoe, Lori E.
American Correctional Health Services Association *(108)*

Rose, Ahniwake
National Indian Education Association *(762)*

Rose, Bernice
American Congress of Obstetricians and Gynecologists *(107)*

Rose, Brenda
International Plant Nutrition Institute *(560)*

Rose, Carol
Underwater Society of America *(984)*

Rose, Elizabeth
Open Mobile Alliance *(828)*

Rose, Judy
Law and Society Association *(594)*

Rose, Kay
Mycological Society of America *(623)*
Wildlife Disease Association *(1017)*

Rose, Kim
North American Society for Pediatric Gastroenterology, Hepatology and Nutrition *(821)*

Rose, Matthew
National Lesbian and Gay Journalists Association *(769)*

Rose, Mattie
American Association for State and Local History *(51)*

Rose, Megan
National Association for Home Care and Hospice *(639)*

Rose, Patricia B.
American Academy of Advertising *(30)*

Rose, Rhonda
National Pace Association *(778)*

Rose, Theodore
Society for the Anthropology of Work *(923)*

Rose, Yvette A.
Cargo Airline Association *(343)*

Rose Hermel, Shauna
American Angus Association *(45)*

Roseman, Walda W.
Internet Society *(582)*

Rosen, Cindy
National Extension Association of Family and Consumer Sciences *(747)*

Rosen, Jennifer
National Foundation for Women Legislators *(753)*

Rosen, Jesse
League of American Orchestras *(595)*

Rosen, Jody
National Association of Extension 4-H Agents *(667)*

Rosen, APR, Jody B.
Communications Media Management Association *(369)*

Rosen, Karen
International Association of Jewish Vocational Services *(523)*

Rosen, Richard D.
American Meteorological Society *(151)*

Rosenbaum, Adam
Council for Advancement and Support of Education *(388)*

Rosenbaum, Lauren
Public Relations Student Society of America *(870)*

Rosenbaum, Ron
Sports and Fitness Industry Association *(959)*

Rosenberg, Brian
Software & Information Industry Association (SIIA) *(950)*

Rosenberg, Donald
Music Critics Association of North America *(622)*

Rosenberg, Ernie
American Cleaning Institute *(91)*

Rosenberg, Jean
American Society of Plant Biologists *(207)*

Rosenberg, Jeffrey
Amalgamated Transit Union *(28)*

Rosenberg, MSW, Linda
National Council for Community Behavioral Healthcare *(731)*

Rosenberg, PhD, Richard
Associated Professional Sleep Societies *(237)*

Rosenberg, Robert
National Pest Management Association *(780)*

Rosenblat, Arney
National Multiple Sclerosis Society *(774)*

Rosenblatt, Carol
Coalition of Labor Union Women *(361)*

Rosenblatt, Daniel N.
International Association of Chiefs of Police *(517)*

Rosenblatt, Sherrie L.
Can Manufacturers Institute *(341)*
National Turkey Federation *(802)*

Rosenblum, Nancy
American Society for Political and Legal Philosophy *(188)*

Rosenbrook, Olga
Corporate Event Marketing Association *(386)*

Rosencrance, CMP, Debra
American Academy of Ophthalmology *(37)*

Rosendahl, Tanya
APA The Engineered Wood Association *(224)*

Rosenfeld, Dawn
American Society of Consulting Arborists *(196)*
Association of Water Technologies *(317)*

Rosengren, Kristin
Academy Health *(3)*

Rosenkoetter, Eric
National Association of Retail Collection Attorneys *(692)*

Rosenstein, Peter D.
American Academy of Orthotists and Prosthetists *(38)*

Rosenstein, Robin L.
ISEH Society for Hematology and Stem Cells *(586)*

Rosenthal, Gwenn E.
Employee Stock Ownership Plan Association *(426)*

Rosenthal, Ileane F.
Securities Industry and Financial Markets Association (SIFMA) *(895)*

Rosenthal, Jay
National Music Publishers Association *(774)*

Rosenthal, Lisa
International Organization of Masters, Mates and Pilots *(559)*

Rosenthal, Mary
Algal Biomass Organization *(22)*

Rosenthal, CAE, CMM, CMP, Steve
American Flock Association *(122)*

Rosenthall, Melinda
Alpha Kappa Psi *(26)*

Rosentreter, Roger
American Bryological and Lichenological Society *(86)*

Rosetta, CMP, Ray
Society of Teachers of Family Medicine *(947)*

Rosier, RaShonda
American Association of Physics Teachers *(69)*

Rosier, Dr. Ronald C.
Conference Board of the Mathematical Sciences *(374)*

Roske, Bob
Quarter Century Wireless Association *(872)*

Roskos, Jackie
Specialized Carriers and Rigging Association *(957)*

Roskowski, Scott
Television Bureau of Advertising *(971)*

Roslund, Sid
National Ski Area Association *(791)*

Rosman, Lori
Association for Population/Family Planning Libraries and Information Centers, International *(253)*

Rosol, Mark
American Medical Writers Association *(150)*

Ross, Bev
National Tractor Pullers Association *(801)*

Ross, Chad M.
Association of State Floodplain Managers *(311)*

Ross, Charles
National Football League Players Association *(752)*

Ross, Christie
American Society for Pain Management Nursing *(188)*

Ross, CAE, Christie
Association of Genetic Technologists *(285)*
Natco-The Organization for Transplant Professionals *(626)*

Ross, David G.
Attorneys' Liability Assurance Society Inc. *(320)*

Ross, David J.
The Coalition of Airline Pilots Associations *(360)*

Ross, Donna
National Black Police Association *(714)*

Ross, MD, Gilbert
American Council on Science and Health *(110)*

Ross, Greg
Brotherhood of Locomotive Engineers and Trainmen *(336)*

Ross, Hedy
Obesity Society *(825)*

Ross, Holly
Nonprofit Technology Network *(811)*

Ross, Jan
Physician Insurers Association of America *(847)*

Ross, Jerry
North American Performing Arts Managers and Agents *(819)*

Ross, Justin
American Securitization Forum *(178)*

Ross, Esq., Kevin
American Association of Insurance Services *(63)*

Ross, Kim
Association of Public Health Laboratories *(304)*

Ross, Laura
International Conference of Symphony and Opera Musicians *(537)*

Ross, EIT, Loren
American Wood Council *(221)*

Ross, Marc A.
United States-China Business Council *(1001)*

Ross, CMP, Natasha
Association of Air Medical Services *(264)*

Ross, Phyllis
Water Environment Federation *(1013)*

Ross, PhD, Sara Nora
Society for Chaos Theory in Psychology and Life Sciences *(905)*

Ross, Sheldon
American Simmental Association *(179)*

Ross, Sherry J.
Professional Hockey Writers' Association *(862)*

Ross, Steven A.
World Research Foundation *(1027)*

Ross, MD, Steven Douglas K.
Board of Specialty Society *(333)*

Ross, T. Carter
National Asphalt Pavement Association *(635)*

Ross, Ted
National Association of Power Engineers *(685)*

Ross, Theodora S.
American Society for Clinical Investigation *(182)*

Ross, Velvet A.
Traffic Audit Bureau for Media Measurement, Inc. *(977)*

Ross Melton, Lori
Local Search Association (fka Yellow Pages Association) *(600)*

Rossabi, Judi
Southeastern Theatre Conference *(953)*

Rosselli-Verrico, Jackie
National Association of Uniform Manufacturers and Distributors *(707)*

Rosseter, Robert

American Association of Colleges of Nursing *(57)*

Rossi, Jospehine
Electronic Transactions Association *(424)*

Rossi, Roger
Allied Artists of America *(25)*

Rossignol, Carol
Professional Skaters Association *(865)*

Rossiter, Walter J.
RCI, Inc. *(875)*

Rossman, DVM, Richard J.
Academy of Veterinary Allergy and Clinical Immunology *(9)*

Rossmann, Paul
International Consumer Product Health and Safety Organization *(537)*

Rosso, Corey
The Accrediting Commission of Career Schools and Colleges *(10)*

Rosso, J. P.
International Precious Metals Institute *(561)*

Rostescu, Mike
American Society of Home Inspectors *(200)*

Roswurm, Sue
Institute for Supply Management *(497)*

Roszman, Beth
SACNAS (Society for Advancement of Chicanos and Native Americans in Science) *(889)*

Rotar, Ana
Internet Marketing Association *(582)*

Roth, Daniel J.
National Futures Association *(754)*

Roth, Jay D.
Directors Guild of America *(413)*

Roth, FAS, PE, Lawrence H.
American Society of Civil Engineers *(194)*

Roth, MD, Malcolm Z.
American Society of Plastic Surgeons *(207)*

Roth, Mark
Insurance Accounting and Systems Association *(504)*

Roth, Mary
Risk and Insurance Management Society, Inc. (RIMS) *(886)*

Roth, Mitch
National Academy of Recording Arts and Sciences *(628)*

Roth, Mitchell
American Teleservices Association *(215)*

Roth, Rachel B.
American Conference of Cantors *(107)*

Roth, Robin
CBA *(346)*

Roth, Ruth Gleason
American Association for the History of Nursing *(52)*
American Society for Indexing *(186)*

Roth, Scott
Art Directors Guild/Scenic, Title and Graphic Artists *(230)*

Roth, Jr., Toby
American League for Exports and Security Assistance *(145)*

Rothe, Robert
Association of National Advertisers *(295)*

Rothenberg, Marc
Society for History in the Federal Government *(911)*

Rothenberg, Randall
Interactive Advertising Bureau *(506)*

Rother, Franklyn
National Organization for Human Service *(777)*

Rothert, Nathalie
Association for Psychological Science *(254)*

Rothfuss, Bill
Association of Applied IPM Ecologists *(267)*

Rothman, Carol D.
The Newspaper Guild *(810)*

Rothrock, MD, John Farr
American Headache Society *(129)*

Rothschild, Richard
American Book Producers Association *(85)*

Rougvie, Carol
International Society of Exposure Science *(572)*

Rounds, Cindy
Healthcare Billing and Management Association *(470)*

Rountree, Ann
Environmental and Water Resources Institute of the American Society of Civil Engineers *(430)*

Rourke, Kelley
OPERA America *(828)*

Rouse, Bernard
Association for Computing Machinery *(243)*

Rouse, Bob
National Tour Association *(800)*

Rouse, Bob
Tree Care Industry Association *(980)*

Rouse, MPS, Michael J.
Accreditation Council for Pharmacy Education *(10)*

Roush, Don
Beta Beta Beta *(328)*

Roush, Kathy
Beta Beta Beta *(328)*

Roush, Kimberly
Academy of Motion Picture Arts and Sciences *(7)*

Rousse, David
INDA, Association of the Nonwoven Fabrics Industry *(488)*

Rousseau, Peter L.
American Economic Association *(115)*

Roussel, Charles
College of American Pathologists *(363)*

Roussel, Lissa
Diamond Council of America *(411)*

Rouzie, Patti
National Beer Wholesalers Association *(713)*

Rovelli, Veronica
American Feed Industry Association *(120)*

Row, FACHE, Constance F.
American Academy of Home Care Physicians *(35)*

Rowan, Linda
American Geological Institute *(126)*

Rowan, Matthew
Health Industry Distributors Association *(469)*

Rowden, Marianne
American Association of Exporters & Importers *(60)*

Rowe, Amanda W.
International Society for Heart and Lung Transplantation *(566)*

Rowe, Andrea E.
Society for Mucosal Immunology *(916)*

Rowe, III, Charles Edward
America's Small Business Development Center Network *(29)*

Rowe, Charles "Tee"
Association of Small Business Development Centers *(308)*

Rowe, Darrell
Automotive Training Managers Council *(324)*

Rowe, Michele Weston
Path to Purchase Institute *(839)*

Rowe, Patrick
National Training and Simulation Association *(801)*

Rowello, Trudie Bruner
Aviation Distributors and Manufacturers Association International *(324)*

Rower, Ken
Timber Framers Guild *(974)*

Rowland, James A.
Wine and Spirits Wholesalers of America *(1018)*

Rowland, Laureen
American Society of Ophthalmic Administrators *(205)*

Rowley, Craig
The National Procurement Institute, Inc *(783)*

Rowley, George
Electrical Generating Systems Association *(422)*

Rowson, Sharon
National Aerosol Association *(629)*

Roxburgh, Scotty
Association of Natural Resource Enforcement Trainers *(295)*

Roxbury, Lavon
National Association of Home Builders *(673)*

Roxson, Randy D.
USA Sprinkler Fitter Business Managers Association *(1005)*

Roxtra, Ron De
Bowling Proprietors' Association of America *(334)*

Roy, Michelle
Industrial Asset Management Council *(492)*

Royal, Erica
American College of Dentists *(95)*

Royce, Brenda
National Society for Histotechnology *(792)*

Royer, Janna
Lamaze International *(592)*

Royer, Joe
Heli Ski US Association *(473)*

Royer, Kyle H.
Council for Christian Colleges and Universities *(389)*

Rozak, Franklin D
National Association of Optometrics and Opticians *(683)*

Ruais, Kathy
Blinded Veterans Association *(332)*

Ruais, Rich
American Bluefin Tuna Association *(81)*

Ruane, CAES, Peter T.
American Road and Transportation Builders Association *(175)*

Ruark, Joel K.
New Dramatists *(809)*

Rubacky, Bill
United States Lacrosse *(995)*

Rubeiz, PE, Camille
Plastics Pipe Institute *(850)*

Ruben, Jeffrey M.
American Association for Cancer Research *(48)*

Ruberto, Marie A.

American Manual Medicine Association *(147)*

Rubin, Amanda
USA Taekwondo *(1005)*

Rubin, Amy
The Fragrance Foundation *(453)*

Rubin, Emma
North American Students of Cooperation *(822)*

Rubin, Gary K.
Society for Human Resource Management *(911)*

Rubin, MD, Geoffrey D
North American Society for Cardiovascular Imaging *(821)*

Rubin, Joe
Consumer Data Industry Association *(381)*

Rubin, Joe
Interactive Travel Services Association *(507)*

Rubin, Mark A.
Society of Petroleum Engineers *(944)*

Rubin, Matthew
American Welding Society *(220)*

Rubin, Michele
American Coal Council *(92)*

Rubin, Nina
Georgia Charter Schools Association *(459)*

Rubin, MPH, Susan
American Society for Healthcare Engineering *(184)*

Rubinger, David
DBA International *(407)*

Rubinger, Karla Shepard
Academy of Breastfeeding Medicine *(4)*

Rubino, Victor J.
Practising Law Institute *(855)*

Rubinstein, Ellis
The New York Academy of Sciences *(809)*

Rubinstein, Lori
Professional Lighting and Sound Association *(863)*

Rubinstein, Thomas N.
Vehicular Technology Society *(1008)*

Rubio-Cortes, Gloria
National Civic League *(722)*

Ruble, Noukla
Radio Television Digital News Association *(873)*

Rubrecht, Robert
Marine Corps Association *(604)*

Rubsamen, John
Healthcare Supply Chain Association *(472)*

Rubsamen, John
National Lumber and Building Material Dealers Association *(770)*

Ruby, Jeanette
International Bone and Mineral Society *(530)*
ISEH Society for Hematology and Stem Cells *(586)*

Ruby, Kathy
Council for Professional Recognition *(391)*

Ruby, Kristen
National Environmental Health Association *(746)*

Ruch, Emily
National Panhellenic Conference *(778)*

Ruchelman, Harold
American Engineering Association *(117)*

Ruckdeschel, Sharon L.
Child Life Council *(353)*

Ruckman, Cindy
National Association of College Stores *(655)*

Ruddock, Mandy
National Association of Teachers of Singing *(705)*

Ruddy, CCP, CPCU, Anne C
WorldatWork *(1028)*

Rude, Dan
The Association for Library Service to Children *(251)*

Rude, Harvey
Higher Education Consortium for Special Education *(474)*

Rude, Lois
Alliance for Telecommunications Industry Solutions *(23)*

Rudeen, Aleta
Society for Range Management *(920)*

Ruden, Paul M.
American Society of Travel Agents *(210)*

Ruder, Karen
Optometric Extension Program Foundation *(830)*

Rudham, Darren
FCIB-NACM Corporation *(438)*

Rudig, Jacqueline J.
Institute of General Semantics *(500)*

Rudin, Tom
The College Board *(363)*

Rudman, PhD, RHIA, William J.
American Health Information Management Association *(129)*

Rudolph, Coby
Efficiency First *(421)*

Rudominer, Ryan
Edison Electric Institute *(419)*

Rudowski, Julie
Association of the United States Army *(313)*

Rudy, Gary
Independent Free Papers of America *(490)*

Rudzin, Dave
United Ostomy Associations of America *(988)*

Rudzinski, Laura J.
National Institute of Pension Administrators *(765)*
Organization Development Network *(831)*

Ruedi, PhD, Elizabeth
Genetics Society of America *(458)*

Ruediger, Dan
KWPN of North America *(591)*

Ruf, Cathy
Pi Lambda Theta *(847)*

Rufe, Mary
American Public Power Association *(171)*

Ruff, Kathy
American Embryo Transfer Association *(116)*

Ruffin, Jackie
National Council of Juvenile and Family Court Judges *(735)*

Ruffner, Gary M.
Utility Workers Union of America *(1007)*

Rufo, Cynthia
American Schools of Oriental Research *(177)*

Ruggieri, Marina
IEEE Aerospace and Electronic Systems Society (AESS) *(483)*

Rugh, Lori
American Wind Energy Association (AWEA) *(221)*

Ruhe, Kate
International Association of Fire Chiefs *(521)*

Ruhland, Polly
Cattlemen's Beef Promotion and Research Board *(346)*

Ruiter, Rene
Association of Natural Bio-Control Producers *(295)*

Ruiz, Diana L.
Santa Gertrudis Breeders International *(891)*

Ruiz, Eduardo A.
Association of Schools of Public Health *(307)*

Ruling, Karl G.
Professional Lighting and Sound Association *(863)*

Rumachik, Jeff
National Frozen and Refrigerated Foods Association *(753)*

Rumbaugh, Matthew
International Sign Association *(564)*

Rumberger, Nick
American College of Nurse Practitioners *(99)*

Rumble, Brad
National Association of Sports Public Address Announcers *(697)*

Rummel, MEd, Chad
Society for the Psychological Study of Ethnic Minority Issues *(924)*

Rumpf, Morgan
Directors Guild of America *(413)*

Rumsey, Jim
The Society for Investigative Dermatology *(913)*

Runci, Matthew A.
Jewelers of America *(587)*

Rundgren, CPO, USN, Herb
United States Army Warrant Officers Association *(990)*

Rundle, Kim
American Association of Law Libraries *(64)*

Rundquist, Kristina
American Society of Travel Agents *(210)*

Runnels, Al
American Society of Military Comptrollers *(203)*

Runsdorf, PhD, N. Blithe
International Stress Management Association - USA *(576)*

Runyan, John
The Coalition for Transportation Productivity *(360)*

Runyard, Mitzi
National Writers Union *(806)*

Runyeon, Vicki
Tag and Label Manufacturers Institute *(968)*

Ruparel, Jiten
Technology Transfer Society *(970)*

Rupe, Jason
Reliability Society *(880)*

Rupert, Stacy
Undersea and Hyperbaric Medical Society *(984)*

Rupp, Byron
Phi Alpha Delta *(845)*

Ruppert, Terri
Automotive Service Association *(323)*

Rupprecht, Sandi
National Association of Division Order Analysts *(663)*

Rusbuldt, Robert A.
Independent Insurance Agents & Brokers of America, Inc. *(490)*

Rush, Debbie
Society for Cinema and Media Studies *(905)*

Rush, CAE, Iris M.
Association for Research in Vision and Ophthalmology *(255)*

Rush, Michael J.
Association of American Railroads *(266)*

Rush, Peter S
Window Covering Safety Council *(1018)*

Rush, Robin
Professional Women Controllers *(865)*

Rush, Tonda F.
American Court and Commercial Newspapers *(111)*
National Newspaper Association *(775)*

Rushford, Susan
The Council of Insurance Agents and Brokers *(394)*

Rushing, Hugh J.
Cookware Manufacturers Association *(384)*

Rushton, MD, MPH, Jerry
Association of Pediatric Program Directors *(298)*

Rusignuolo, Judy
USA Rice Federation *(1004)*

Rusk, Claire
Air Traffic Control Association *(19)*

Ruskin, Ann Marie
National Child Support Enforcement Association *(721)*

Ruskin, Glenn S.
American Chemical Society *(89)*

Russ, Richard
American Society for Metabolic and Bariatric Surgery *(187)*

Russell, Barbara
Casket and Funeral Supply Association of America *(344)*

Russell, Barry
Independent Petroleum Association of America *(491)*

Russell, Chad
American Polygraph Association *(166)*

Russell, Chelsea
National Alfalfa Alliance *(631)*
National Alfalfa and Forage Alliance *(631)*

Russell, Denis M.
National Foundation for Credit Counseling *(753)*

Russell, Erik
Computing Research Association *(373)*

Russell, John G.
American Society of Appraisers *(192)*

Russell, CEAP, PhD, John K.
Academy of Managed Care Providers *(6)*

Russell, CPA, Mark
Association of State and Provincial Psychology Boards *(309)*

Russell, Michelle
Professional Convention Management Association *(861)*

Russell, Michelle
Women's Foodservice Forum *(1023)*

Russell, Monica
AASHTO: Transportation Center of Excellence *(2)*

Russell, Pamela
Council for Advancement and Support of Education *(388)*

Russell Wilson, Clarissa
Safety Pharmacology Society *(890)*

Russo, Annie
APCO (Association of Public-Safety Communications Officials) International *(304)*

Russo, Dane
American Medical Writers Association *(150)*

Russo, CAE, Phillip E.
NAFA Fleet Management Association *(624)*

Rust, David
North American Mycological Association *(818)*

Rust, Susan
JAWS Society *(586)*

Rustin, Bill
The Association of Community Pharmacists
Congressional Network *(276)*

Rutenberg, Sara
Society of Children's Book Writers and Illustrators
(932)

Ruth, Betty M.
National Association of Retired and Senior Volunteer
Program Directors *(692)*

Ruth, Mark
International Coach Federation *(535)*

Ruthenberg, Karen
National Association of College and University Food
Services *(655)*

Rutherford, Al
National Society of Black Engineers *(793)*

Rutherford, Alan
International Advertising Association *(509)*

Rutherford, Alicia
POPAI The Global Association for Marketing at Retail
(852)

Rutherford, Diane
Society of Vertebrate Paleontology *(950)*

Rutherford, PhD, Nancy
International Textile and Apparel Association *(577)*

Ruthford, Eric
Northwest Natural Resource Group *(824)*

Rutkauskas, CA, CAE, DDS, John S.
American Academy of Pediatric Dentistry *(39)*

Rutkowski, Ed
American Industrial Hygiene Association *(135)*

Rutledge, Jesse
National Center for State Courts *(720)*

Rutledge, Mardy
United States Targhee Sheep Association *(999)*

Rutt, Kelly
The Environmental Information Association *(431)*

Rutter, Timothy
American Association of Nurse Anesthetists *(67)*

Rutz, Jared
Patent and Trademark Office Society *(839)*

Ruyak, Doreen Kelly
National Association of Corporate Directors *(658)*

Ryals, Karen E.
American Association of Kidney Patients *(64)*

Ryan, Benjamin
American Society of Sanitary Engineering *(209)*

Ryan, Dave
International Institute of Connector and
Interconnection Technology *(551)*

Ryan, Diane
Council of American Overseas Research Centers *(392)*

Ryan, Elizabeth
National Association for Environmental Management
(638)

Ryan, Ginny
International Writing Centers Association *(581)*

Ryan, Gloria Gaemsey
International Association of Arson Investigators *(515)*

Ryan, Jim
Insulated Cable Engineers Association *(504)*

Ryan, John W.
Conference of State Bank Supervisors *(376)*

Ryan, Kate
Public Relations Student Society of America *(870)*

Ryan, Kate
Travel Goods Association *(979)*

Ryan, Mary Wynn
National Home Furnishings Association *(759)*

Ryan, Marya
International Society of Arboriculture *(571)*

Ryan, Michael
Association of HazMat Shippers *(286)*

Ryan, PhD CHP, Michael T.
Health Physics Society *(470)*

Ryan, Jr., USN (Ret.), VADM, VADM Norbert R.
Military Officers Association of America (MOAA) *(616)*

Ryan, Patrick P.
IEEE Power and Energy Society *(485)*

Ryan, Paul D.
Association of Global Automakers *(285)*

Ryan, Rachel
National Retail Federation *(786)*

Ryan, Rebecka
Natco-The Organization for Transplant Professionals
(626)

Ryan, Jr., T. Timothy
Securities Industry and Financial Markets Association
(SIFMA) *(895)*

Rybarczyk, Karena
American Society of Hair Restoration Surgery *(199)*

Rybicki, Steven
American Orthotic and Prosthetic Association *(159)*

Ryczaj, Maureen
American Association for the Advancement of Slavic
Studies *(52)*
Association for Slavic, East European, and Eurasian
Studies *(256)*

Rydell, Catherine M.
American Academy of Neurology *(36)*

Ryden, Brett
Powder Coating Institute *(854)*

Ryder, CPA, Harry
National Roofing Contractors Association *(787)*

Ryder, Jordan
National Association of Television Program Executives
(705)

Rydzik, Pat
Printing Industry Credit Executives *(857)*

Ryerson, Mark
American Society of Radiologic Technologists *(208)*

Ryley, Linda
WTA Tour, Inc. *(1029)*

Rynearson, John
VITA *(1011)*

Rynerson, Diane
National Conference of Women's Bar Associations
(728)

Rysavy, Peter
Portable Computer and Communications Association
(853)

Rytkonen, Catherine
Toxicology Forum *(976)*

Rytlewski, Jamie
Academy of International Business *(5)*

Ryzner, Melisa
North American Die Casting Association *(816)*

Rzepka, Jennifer
NIBA - The Belting Association *(810)*

Rzepka, Laura A.
American Conference of Academic Deans *(107)*

Saal, Dana
Association for Preservation Technology International
(253)

Saalsaa, Jerry
Credit Union Executives Society *(403)*

Saar, Sarah
Association for Healthcare Foodservice *(248)*

Saathoff, David
SEMATECH *(896)*

Saavedra, Anais
Caribbean Hotel and Tourism Association *(343)*

Sabal, Rob
University Film and Video Association *(1002)*

Sabanske, Sandra
Association of Professional Investment Consultants
(301)

Sabbath, Lawrence E.
National Armored Car Association *(635)*

Sabitoni, Armand E.
Laborers International Union of North America *(592)*

Sablone, Frank A.
Tag and Label Manufacturers Institute *(968)*

Sabo, Martina
Salt Institute *(891)*

Sabo, Peter
American Boat Builders and Repairers Association *(84)*

Sabol, Steve
Association for the Study of Nationalities *(259)*

Sabourin, Dennis
National Association for PET Container Resources
(641)

Sabur, Sue
American Physiological Society *(165)*

Sacchetti, Maureen
Human Relations Area Files *(481)*

Sacco, Michael
AFL-CIO - Maritime Trades Department *(15)*

Saccoccio, Louis
National Health Care Anti-Fraud Association *(758)*

Sacerdote, John
National Association of Personnel Services *(684)*

Sachais, MD, PhD, Bruce
American Society for Apheresis *(180)*

Sachdeva, MD, FACS, Ajit K.
American College of Surgeons *(103)*

Sacher-Brown, Christina
Home Improvement Research Institute *(478)*

Sachs, Harold
Fashion Accessories Shippers Association *(438)*

Sachs, William
Northern Nut Growers Association *(824)*

Sachse-Vasquez, Christen
Research Institute for Fragrance Materials *(882)*

Sack, Nancy
National Aeronautic Association *(629)*

Sack, Esq., Steven M.
National Association of Independent Publishers
Representatives *(675)*

Sackler, Art
National Postal Policy Council *(781)*

Sackman, Bruce
Society of Professional Investigators *(945)*

Sacks, Irving
International Association for Modular Exhibitry *(513)*

Sacks, Susan
IEEE Power and Energy Society *(485)*

Sader, Leila
Sheet Metal and Air Conditioning Contractors'
National Association *(898)*

Sadler, Dennis
AABB - American Association of Blood Banks *(1)*

Sadler, Mya
American College of Veterinary Internal Medicine *(104)*

Sadoff, CPA, Carol
National Health Council *(758)*

Sadowski, John
Analytical Laboratory Managers Association *(223)*

Sadowski, Susan
American College of Mohs Surgeons *(98)*

Sadowsky, Jessica
American Network of Community Options and
Resources (ANCOR) *(155)*

Saeman, Anne
National Mastitis Council *(772)*

Saenz, Gil
Society of Mexican American Engineers and Scientists
(941)

SaFranko, James
Tissue Banks International *(975)*

Sagan, Andrew D.
Phi Alpha Delta *(845)*

Sagara, Randy
American Intellectual Property Law Association *(141)*

Sage, Bill
United States Club Soccer *(992)*

Saggese, Marty
Society for Neuroscience *(916)*

Saglam, Kismet
Association for Death Education and Counseling *(244)*
International Society for Traumatic Stress Studies *(570)*
The Society for Adolescent Medicine *(903)*

Saglam, Marianne
Institute of Transportation Engineers *(503)*

Saglio, Janet
Housing Partnership Network *(479)*

Sahel, Heidi A.
American Society of Preventive Oncology *(208)*

Sahlein, Stephen
American Institute of Professional Bookkeepers *(140)*

Sahli, Wendy
Directors of Health Promotion and Education (DHPE)
(413)

Saier, Mary
International Society for Clinical Densitometry *(565)*

Saigh, Jr., Phillip A.
American Academy of Pain Medicine *(39)*

Saikeld, Heidi
Society of Computed Body Tomography and Magnetic
Resonance *(933)*

Saitta, Mark
American Association of Motor Vehicle Administrators
(65)

Sajnani, PhD, RDT, Nisha
National Association for Drama Therapy *(638)*

Sakamoto, James
Geospatial Information Technology Association *(459)*

Sakkestad, Barbara A.
Coal Technology Association *(359)*

Saks, Pat
Corn Refiners Association, Inc. *(385)*

Saladino, Mary Katherine
International Association for Continuing Education and
Training *(511)*

Saladino, CMP, Mary Katherine
Public Media Business Association *(869)*

Salam, Abdul
Satellite Broadcasting and Communications
Association *(891)*

Salam, Amin
National U.S.-Arab Chamber of Commerce *(803)*

Salamone, Lee
Center for the Polyurethanes Industry *(348)*

Salas, MA, Antonio M.
Asian American Journalists Association *(231)*

Salas, Tony
Association of Diesel Specialists *(279)*

Salazar, Carmen
Association for Specialists in Group Work *(257)*

Salazar, Jeanette
International Boxing Federation *(530)*

Salazar, Jesse
United States Hispanic Chamber of Commerce *(995)*

Salberg, Karen
American Tin Trade Association *(217)*

Sale, JD, LLM, David M.
Council of Colleges of Acupuncture and Oriental
Medicine *(392)*

Salehi, Jennifer
American Medical Student Association *(150)*

Salek, Edward P.
Society of Tribologists and Lubrication Engineers *(949)*

Salem, Abdel
United States Fencing Coaches Association *(994)*

Salem, MA, Peter
Association of Family and Conciliation Courts *(282)*

Salerno, David
National Accounting and Finance Council *(628)*

Salerno, Diane
Producers Guild of America *(858)*

Salerno, Judith A.
Institute of Medicine *(501)*

Salhi, Raushanna
National Structured Settlements Trade Association
(797)

Saliba, Susan
Moroccan American Business Council *(619)*

Salifou, Jeanine
Association for Facilities Engineering *(246)*

Saliga, Pauline
Society of Architectural Historians *(930)*

Saline, Earl
PSIA-AASI *(868)*

Salisbury, Dallas L.
Employee Benefit Research Institute *(426)*

Salisbury, Judith "Judy" K.
American Association of Dental Consultants *(59)*

Salkeld, Heidi
American College of Radiology *(102)*

Salkin, Lou Ann Csaszar
American Guild of Variety Artists *(128)*

Sall, Kevin
American Coatings Association *(92)*

Sallay, Raymond
Center for Research Libraries *(348)*

Salmoiraghi, Jessica
The American Institute of Architects *(137)*

Salmon, Greg
Association of Surgical Assistants *(312)*

Salmon, Mary "Didi"
National Research Council *(786)*

Salmon, Patti
American Poultry Association *(167)*

Salo, Matt
National Association of Medicaid Directors *(680)*

Salomone Testa, Mary Beth
Early Care and Education Consortium *(417)*

Salsman, Richard
Semiconductor Equipment and Materials International
(896)

Salt, Matt
Specialized Information Publishers Association *(957)*

Saltman, Alex
Commercial Space Flight Federation *(367)*

Saltzman, Josh
CropLife America *(404)*

Salus, Joel
International Reprographic Association *(563)*

Salus, Larry
U.S. Hereditary Angioedema Association *(983)*

Salusky, MD, Isidro B.
International Pediatric Nephrology Association *(559)*

Salyer, Danielle
National Flea Market Association *(751)*

Salzman, Russell C.
Institute of Real Estate Management *(503)*

Sama, Hilary
European-American Business Council *(434)*

Samb, John
COMISS Network - The Network on Ministry in
Specialized Settings *(366)*

Samborski, Robert "Bob" M.
Geospatial Information Technology Association *(459)*

Samet, Sean
NPTA Alliance *(824)*

Samm, Terry
National Venture Capital Association *(803)*

Sammis, Jack
Foundation for International Meetings *(453)*

Sammon, John
American Rental Association *(174)*

Sammons-Posey, Doreleena
Directors of Health Promotion and Education (DHPE)
(413)

Samorian, Harold
Community Health Charities of America *(371)*

Samoylin, Tatiana
Recreation Vehicle Industry Association *(877)*

Sample, Janet
American Philosophical Association *(164)*

Sample, Stephen
National Press Photographers Association *(782)*

Sampson, Burke
National American Indian Housing Council *(634)*

Sampson, David A.

Property Casualty Insurers Association of America (867)

Sampson, Eric
American Statistical Association (213)

Sampson, Fred
Special Interest Group for Computer-Human Interaction (954)

Sampson, CMP, Heather
Infusion Nurses Society (496)

Sampson, Robert
American Society of Criminology (196)

Sampson, Robin
American Logistics Association (146)

Sampson, Rodney
American Diabetes Association (115)

Sampson, Vince
Education Finance Council (419)

Samson, Jon
Agricultural and Food Transporters Conference (16)

Samuel, CAE, MPA, Antoinette A.
The American Society for Public Administration (189)

Samuel, Esther
American Physiological Society (165)

Samuel, William
AFL-CIO (American Federation of Labor and Congress of Industrial Organizations) (14)

Samuels, Jason A.
National Council on Family Relations (738)

Samuels, Sara M.
WIFS - Women in Insurance and Financial Services (1017)

Samuelson, Kathleen
CBA (346)

Samuelson, Rita Kourlis
American Sheep Industry Association (178)

Sanchez, Andrea E.
International Facility Management Association (543)

Sanchez, Carleen D.
National Association for Ethnic Studies (638)

Sanchez, Carolina
National Action Council for Minorities in Engineering (NACME) (628)

Sanchez, Christina
Employee Services Management Association (426)

Sanchez, Christine
Chlorobenzene Producers Association (354)
Society of Chemical Manufacturers and Affiliates Inc. (932)

Sanchez, Elizabeth
United States Soccer Federation (999)

Sanchez, Jennifer
AAGL - Advancing Minimally Invasive Gynecology Worldwide (2)

Sanchez, Juana
Society for Healthcare Strategy and Market Development (910)

Sanchez, Sylvia
American Payroll Association (162)

Sandahl, Jennifer
IPC - Surface Mount Equipment Manufacturers Association (585)

SandBakken, John
National Sunflower Association (798)

Sandberg, Glen
Automation Alley (321)

Sandberg, Mark

Society for the Advancement of Scandinavian Study (923)

Sander, Nancy
Allergy and Asthma Network Mothers of Asthmatics (22)

Sanders, Alisa
United States Lactation Consultant Association (996)

Sanders, Barbra
Society for Technical Communication (922)

Sanders, CAE, Bruce A.
American College of Phlebology (100)

Sanders, Camille
American College of Preventive Medicine (101)

Sanders, Charlene
National Association of Church Personnel Administrators (653)

Sanders, Corrine
National Association of Chain Drug Stores (652)

Sanders, Cortney
Beta Alpha Psi (328)

Sanders, PhD, Dr. David
National Music Council (774)

Sanders, Erin
Drug, Chemical and Associated Technologies Association (417)
Kappa Delta Pi (590)

Sanders, Gene
Society of the Plastics Industry (948)

Sanders, John
National Association of Federal Veterinarians (668)

Sanders, MD, Kathy
American Association of Directors of Psychiatric Residency Training (60)

Sanders, CAE, Lee
American Bakers Association (78)

Sanders, Peggy
National Association of Nurse Massage Therapists (682)

Sanders, Seiche
American Society for Quality (189)

Sanderson, Kelly
International Swaps and Derivatives Association (576)

Sanderson, Ken
Country Music Association (401)

Sanderson, Matt
Print Services & Distribution Association (857)

Sanderson, Patti
Workgroup for Electronic Data Interchange (1025)

Sandherr, Stephen E.
Associated General Contractors of America (AGC) (236)

Sandla, Robert
League of American Orchestras (595)

Sandler, Ed
The Broadway League (336)

Sandler, Jeffery A.
Tissue Banks International (975)

Sandler, Leland
The Conference Board (374)

Sandler, CAE, William "Bill" S.
Valve Manufacturers Association of America (1007)

Sandlin, Beth
Center for Spiritual and Ethical Education (348)

Sandlin, Diane
Surface Design Association (966)

Sandor, Doug

Educational Theatre Association (420)

Sandoval, Celinda
USFN-America's Mortgage Banking Attorneys (1006)

Sandoval, Dennis
American Academy of Estate Planning Attorneys (33)

Sands, Dr. Shirley J.
Manuscript Society (604)

Sands, Theron R.
National Association of Advisors for the Health Professions (645)

Sandusky, Vincent R.
Sheet Metal and Air Conditioning Contractors' National Association (898)

Sandy, David
International Brotherhood of Magicians (531)

Sandy, DCCM, USNR, Stephen R.
Naval Enlisted Reserve Association (807)

Sanetti, Stephen L.
National Shooting Sports Foundation (791)

Sanfacon, Jeff
American Translators Association (217)

Sanford, Kathy
Burley Tobacco Growers Cooperative Association (338)

Sankey, Greg
Collegiate Commissioners Association (365)

Sankey, Patrick C
International Road Federation (563)

Sanner, Ed
International Society of Communication Specialists (572)

Sanny, Tom
University Film and Video Association (1002)

Sanquinetti, Alec
Caribbean Hotel and Tourism Association (343)

Sansalone, Nancy
American Society for Microbiology (187)

Sansone, Alicia
Loan Syndication & Trading Association (599)

Sansone, CAE, David C.
Precision Metalforming Association (856)

Sansone, Peter
Golf Range Association of America (463)

Sansone, Torry Mark
American Society of Hypertension, Inc. (200)

Sansoni, Brian T.
American Cleaning Institute (91)

Sant, Bradley
American Road and Transportation Builders Association (175)

Santa, Jr., Donald F.
Interstate Natural Gas Association of America (583)

Santa, Sue
The Philanthropy Roundtable (846)

Santalla, Anne
The Accrediting Commission of Career Schools and Colleges (10)

Santaniello, Kim
American Society for Dermatologic Surgery (183)

Santaniello, Vicki
American Alliance for Health, Physical Education, Recreation and Dance (44)
American Association for Health Education (49)

Santantonio, CTE, Wendy
Global Business Travel Association (462)

Santaromita, Kristen

National Home Infusion Association *(760)*

Santee, Jimmie
Professional Skaters Association *(865)*

Santell, Amanda
International Municipal Signal Association *(557)*

Santelli, Angela
International Congress of Oral Implantologists *(537)*

Santerfeit, Marvin
North American Electric Reliability Corporation *(816)*

Santi, Pat
Dog Writers' Association of America *(415)*

Santiago, Clemente
United States Dairy Export Council *(993)*

Santiago, Michele
Society for Marketing Professional Services *(914)*

Santiago, Tina
Professional Women Controllers *(865)*

Santini, Stephanie A.
The Sulphur Institute *(965)*

Santis, Lon
Institute of Makers of Explosives *(501)*

Santora, Kathleen C.
National Association of College and University
Attorneys *(654)*

Santore, Marcia
Women's Caucus for Art *(1022)*

Santore, Richard A.
Associated Funeral Directors International *(236)*

Santoro, Amanda
American Institute of Architecture Students *(137)*

Santoro, Christopher
Judge Advocates Association *(589)*

Santoro, Matthew
American Association of Naturopathic Physicians *(66)*

Santoro, Susan
Society for News Design *(916)*

Santorum, Dan
Professional Tennis Registry *(865)*

Santos, Antonio
Manufacturers of Emission Controls Association *(603)*

Santos, Barb De Los
The Handcrafted Soapmakers Guild *(468)*

Santos, Kendra
Professional Rodeo Cowboys Association *(864)*

Santos, Rosario
CIES - The Food Business Forum *(356)*

Sanyer, Chris Anne
National Association of Federal Credit Unions *(667)*

Sanzio, JD, MPA, RN, Teressa M.
The American Association of Nurse Attorneys *(67)*

Saper, Joel R.
American Headache Society *(129)*

Saphier, Brian
Association & Society Insurance Corporation *(237)*

Saphire, Daniel
Association of American Railroads *(266)*

Sapienza, Paul
Retail Bakers of America *(884)*

Sapir, Glenn
National Shooting Sports Foundation *(791)*

Saporta, Vicki A.
National Abortion Federation *(626)*

Sapp, Ben

International Sports Heritage Association *(575)*

Sapp, Joseph
American Institute of Constructors *(138)*

Saracco, Christa
American College of Veterinary Internal Medicine *(104)*

Sarasin, CAE, Leslie G.
Food Marketing Institute *(449)*

Sarazen, John
PSIA-AASI *(868)*

Sargent, Amy
Public Library Association *(869)*

Sargent, Walter
National Interscholastic Athletic Administrators
Association *(766)*

Sargetakis, Ted
National Association of Decorative Fabric Distributors
(662)

Sari, Virginia
National Association of Scientific Materials Managers
(694)

Saricos, Christine
Interior Design Educators Council *(508)*

Saringer, Jo Ann
National Conference of Federal Trial Judges *(727)*
National Conference of Specialized Court Judges *(728)*

Saris, Andrea
Society for Imaging Informatics in Medicine *(912)*

Sarkady, Kim
American Association of Motor Vehicle Administrators
(65)

Sarkisian, George
American Gas Association *(124)*

Sarkissian, Nellie
American Association for the Study of Liver Diseases
(52)

Sarma, Gaile
Celebrant Foundation and Institute *(347)*

Sarmiento, Adriano
American Statistical Association *(213)*

Sarmiento, Susy
National HEP-CAMP Association *(759)*

Sarode, MD, Ravi
American Society for Apheresis *(180)*

Sarreal, Ruth
Office Business Center Association International *(826)*

Sarton, Craig
International Festivals and Events Association *(545)*

Sarver, CAE, Ron
National Association of State Boating Law
Administrators *(698)*

Sas, Deborah
International Gay and Lesbian Travel Association *(548)*

Sasala, Raymond J.
National Association of Consumer Credit
Administrators *(657)*

Sashi, Claire
Econometric Society *(418)*

Satagaj, John S.
Small Business Legislative Council *(901)*

Satcher, Jamie
National Rehabilitation Counseling Association *(785)*

Sater, Dan
American Institute of Building Design *(137)*

Satin, Mort
Salt Institute *(891)*

Satlof, Ellen
National Athletic Trainers Association *(710)*

Satterfield, Marnie
Industrial Energy Consumers of America *(493)*

Sattler, JoDee
National Dairy Herd Information Association *(741)*

Satyamurthy, Nadiya
Emerging Markets Private Equity Association *(425)*

Saucedo, Tomas
National Education Association *(744)*

Saucier, Karen
National Wooden Pallet and Container Association
(805)

Sauer, Holly
Pipeline Research Council International, Inc. *(849)*

Saul, Krista
National Society of Accountants for Cooperatives *(793)*

Sault, Samantha
United States Association of Importers of Textiles and
Apparel *(990)*

Saunders, David A
American Association of Residential Mortgage
Regulators *(72)*
International Oxygen Manufacturers Association *(559)*

Saunders, Jenece
In-Plant Printing and Mailing Association *(487)*

Saunders, III, CAE, John E.
National Forum for Black Public Administrators *(752)*

Saunders, Lee A.
American Federation of State, County and Municipal
Employees *(120)*

Saunders, Linda
American Geriatrics Society *(126)*

Saunders, Marsha
Futures Industry Association *(455)*

Saunders, Mary J.
Beer Institute *(327)*

Saunders, Ruth
National Cheese Institute *(720)*

Saunders, Stacey
Financial Managers Society *(445)*

Saunders, William E.
Network Branded Prepaid Card Association *(808)*

Saundry, PhD, Peter D
National Council for Science and the Environment
(733)

Sause, Brian
Hardwood Plywood and Veneer Association *(468)*

Sausedo, Anjeanette
National Federation of Licensed Practical Nurses *(749)*

Sauter, J. Edward
Concrete Foundations Association *(373)*
Tilt-up Concrete Association *(974)*

Sauter, Joanne
Joint Review Committee on Education in Radiologic
Technology *(589)*

Sauve, RPh, Scott
Society of Pharmaceutical and Biotech Trainers *(944)*

Savage, Cole
ADSC: The International Association of Foundation
Drilling *(12)*

Savage, Julie
American Biological Safety Association *(81)*

Savage, Karen
American Biological Safety Association *(81)*

Savage, Marjorie

National Association of Church Food Service **(653)**

Savage, Michelle
XBRL US, Inc. **(1029)**

Savage, Shirley
Weather Risk Management Association **(1014)**

Savarese, Jean
Society of North American Goldsmiths **(943)**

Savarese, Joseph B.
American Stamp Dealers Association **(213)**

Saveriano, Tori
Delta Phi Epsilon **(409)**

Saverine, Lauren
National Academy of Television Arts and Science **(628)**

Savidge, Chip
The Clearing House Association **(357)**

Savigliano, PhD, Marta
Congress on Research in Dance **(377)**

Saville, Kathryn
American Council on International Personnel **(110)**

Saville, Marinell
United Fresh Produce Association **(987)**

Saving, Emily
Heating, Airconditioning and Refrigeration Distributors International **(473)**

Savitsky, Linda R.
National Association of State Retirement Administrators **(702)**

Savitt, Marc
National Association of Independent Housing Professionals **(674)**

Savitz, Jessica
National Association of Mortgage Brokers **(681)**

Savoie, Kelly
American Meteorological Society **(151)**

Savoie, Michelle
Process Equipment Manufacturers' Association **(858)**

Sawyer, Barbara
National Association for Family Child Care **(638)**

Sawyer, Barry
American Land Title Association **(144)**

Sawyer, Chris
American College of Sports Medicine **(102)**

Sawyer, Gina
American Association for State and Local History **(51)**

Sawyer, Ron
Professional Service Association **(865)**

Sawyer, Steven F.
International Fire Marshals Association **(545)**

Sawyer, Thomas H.
Phi Epsilon Kappa **(845)**

Sawyer, Thomas J.
American College of Contingency Planners **(95)**

Saxton, FACME, CCMEP, MEd, Mike
American Academy of Physician Assistants **(40)**

Sayar, AIA, CAE, Zerrin
National Council of Architectural Registration Boards **(733)**

Sayenga, Donald
National Association of Chain Manufacturers **(652)**

Sayles, Michelle
American Viola Society **(219)**

Saylor, Bonnie
Society for Applied Spectroscopy **(904)**

Sayre, Margaret

Association for Quality Imaging (AQI) **(254)**

Sayre, Steven
International Anesthesia Research Society **(511)**

Scaduto, Abigail
Paleontological Research Institution **(837)**

Scala, Gina
Direct Marketing Association **(412)**

Scalco, Mary
Drycleaning & Laundry Institute **(417)**

Scales, Aileen
Consortium of College and University Media Centers **(378)**

Scales, Shelby
Airport Minority Advisory Council (AMAC) **(21)**

Scalise, LMFT, LPC, Eric
American Association of Christian Counselors **(56)**

Scalzi, John
Science Fiction and Fantasy Writers of America **(892)**

Scango, Shelby
University Professional & Continuing Education Association **(1003)**
University Professional & Continuing Education Association **(1003)**

Scanlan, DVM, Nancy
American Holistic Veterinary Medical Association **(132)**

Scanlon, Elise
Distance Education and Training Council **(414)**

Scanlon, Karen A.
Conservation Technology Information Center **(378)**

Scanlon, Megan
Clinical and Laboratory Standards Institute **(358)**

Scanlon, Jr., Mike T.
Self Storage Association **(896)**

Scantlebury, Leslie
Romance Writers of America **(888)**

Scapp, Ron
National Association for Ethnic Studies **(638)**

Scarano, Gerard
International Union of Bricklayers and Allied Craftworkers **(579)**

Scarborough, J D, William
Project Management Institute **(866)**

Scardelletti, Robert A.
Transportation Communications International Union/ IAM **(978)**

Scarp, Mark J.
Society of American Business Editors and Writers **(928)**

Schaaf, Alexandra
Art Directors Guild/Scenic, Title and Graphic Artists **(230)**

Schaaf, Brian
The Cordage Institute **(385)**

Schable, Kelly Griswold
Society of Women Engineers **(950)**

Schadle, Lauren
Financial Planning Association **(445)**

Schaefer, Gretchen
National Alliance of Forest Owners **(632)**

Schaefer, Jeff
Society for Critical Care Medicine **(934)**

Schaefer, Maggie
National Lipid Association **(770)**

Schaefer, Miriam Fisher
Chemical Heritage Foundation **(351)**

Schaefer, CAE, IOM, Ruth

International Society of Explosives Engineers **(572)**

Schaefer-Farre, Claudia
Argentine-American Chamber of Commerce **(228)**

Schaeffer, Allen R.
Diesel Technology Forum **(412)**

Schaeffer, Anne
American Institute of Chemical Engineers **(138)**

Schaeffer, Jennifer Mock
Association of Fish and Wildlife Agencies **(283)**

Schafer, David E.
College Music Society **(363)**

Schafer, CMP, Diane
Flexographic Prepress Platemakers Association **(447)**
Wood Machinery Manufacturers of America **(1024)**

Schafer, CAE, Heather
National Volunteer Fire Council **(803)**

Schafer, Jeffrey L.
SOLE - The International Society of Logistics **(952)**

Schafer, Julie
American Society of Orthopedic Physician Assistants **(205)**

Schafer, Julie
National Association of Orthopaedic Technologists **(683)**

Schafer, Kathryn
American Association of Legal Nurse Consultants **(64)**
National Society of Genetic Counselors **(794)**

Schafer, Sandra Lee
Hospice and Palliative Nurses Association **(478)**

Schafer, Shawn
North American Deer Farmers Association **(815)**

Schaffer, Amy
Recycled Paperboard Technical Association **(877)**

Schaffer, Michelle
American Orthopaedic Society for Sports Medicine **(159)**

Schaffer, Stephanie
Internet Security Alliance **(582)**

Schaffner, Karen
Association for Retail Environments **(256)**

Schagrin, Megan
American Academy of Otolaryngology-Head and Neck Surgery **(39)**

Schaitberger, Harold A.
International Association of Fire Fighters **(521)**

Schalin, Gunnar
Association of Procurement Technical Assistance Centers **(300)**

Schall, Brandon
National Court Reporters Association **(740)**

Schaller, Debby
American Rental Association **(174)**

Schalue, PhD, Tammy
American Association of Bioanalysts **(54)**

Schamu, Nancy
National Conference of State Historic Preservation Officers **(728)**

Schank, Joshua
Transportation Research Forum **(979)**

Schanke, Robert "Bob"
Association for Theatre in Higher Education **(260)**

Schankel, Bill
Society of Cable Telecommunications Engineers **(931)**

Schantz, Lory
Association for Vascular Access **(261)**

Schantz, Victoria
National Grain Trade Council *(756)*

Schaper, Nick
United States Chamber of Commerce *(991)*

Schapiro, Saul A.
AFL-CIO Housing Investment Trust *(15)*

Schardin, CAE, MBA, Kim
American College of Mohs Surgeons *(98)*
American Society for Mohs Histotechnology *(187)*
International Transplant-Skin Cancer Collaborative *(578)*

Schardt, Martin
American Association of Professional Landmen *(71)*

Schardt, Sue
Association of Independents in Radio *(288)*

Schardt, Therese Gustavsson
Swedish-American Chambers of Commerce of the USA, Inc. *(967)*

Scharf, DC, Brian K.
Christian Chiropractors Association *(355)*

Scharff, Sherri
National Crop Insurance Services *(741)*

Scharpe, Jennifer
American Gelbvieh Association *(125)*

Schascheck, Richard
National Sporting Goods Association *(796)*

Schatz, Katrina
The Vision Council *(1010)*

Schatz, Stephen
National Council of Chain Restaurants *(734)*

Schatz, Stephen
National Retail Federation *(786)*

Schatzki, Jeff
Society for American Baseball Research *(903)*

Schatzman, Leigha
Association for High Technology Distribution *(248)*

Schaubach, Kurt
National Rural Telecommunications Cooperative *(788)*

Schauer, Tonya
Music Teachers National Association *(622)*

Schaumann, Lisa
Professional Landcare Network *(863)*

Schauseil, CAE, Robin
National Association of Credit Management *(661)*

Schaver, Rhonda
National Conference of Executives of The ARC *(727)*

Schechner, Steve
National Bulk Vendors Association *(716)*

Scheck, Cathy L.
Heart Rhythm Society *(472)*

Scheck, MA, Debby
Utilimetrics/Alliance for Advanced Metering & Data Management Solutions *(1006)*

Schecter, Joanne
American Advertising Federation *(43)*

Schecter, Marvin E.
Society of Professional Investigators *(945)*

Schedel, Margaret
International Computer Music Association *(536)*

Schedler, Michael F.
National Association for PET Container Resources *(641)*

Schee, Carolyn Vander
American Educational Studies Association *(116)*

Scheeberger, Jason

Association of State Floodplain Managers *(311)*

Scheer, Jeremy
CPAmerica International *(402)*

Scheevel, Barb
Algal Biomass Organization *(22)*

Scheff, Helene
National Dance Education Organization *(742)*

Scheib, Lauren
Association of Test Publishers *(313)*

Scheib, Melissa
Electronic Commerce Code Management Association *(423)*

Scheible, Ann
International Magnesium Association *(555)*

Scheller, Cindy
International Society for Molecular Plant Microbe Interactions *(567)*

Scheman, Rita
American Physiological Society *(165)*

Schember, Dora L
APMI International *(225)*

Schembs, Stephen
Communications Workers of America *(369)*

Schenck, William S.
National Association of State Boards of Geology *(698)*

Schendell, Bonnie
International Test and Evaluation Association *(577)*

Schenk, Julia "Jules"
National Panhellenic Conference *(778)*

Schenk, Pamela W.
Gravure Association of America *(465)*

Schenk, Tom
American Camp Association *(88)*

Scher, Linda
American Neurological Association *(155)*

Scheraga, Carl A.
Transportation Research Forum *(979)*

Scherer, Allison
American Academy of Dermatology *(32)*

Scherer, Ashley
Juvenile Products Manufacturers Association *(590)*

Scherf, Christopher N.
Thoroughbred Racing Associations of North America *(974)*

Schermoly, Mike
Owner-Operator Independent Drivers Association, Inc. *(836)*

Scherr, Robert
Cantors Assembly *(342)*

Scherzer, MPH, Eric
Committee of Interns and Residents/ SEIU *(368)*

Scherzinger, Pat
National Coal Transportation Association *(722)*

Schescke, Ramona
National Association of State Directors of Career Technical Education Consortium *(699)*

Schettini, MBA, Frank
Project Management Institute *(866)*

Scheuerman, Katherine
NAIOP, The Commercial Real Estate Development Association *(366)*

Scheuing, Laurie
Association for Women Geoscientists *(261)*

Scheurer, Danielle
Society of Hospital Medicine *(938)*

Schewbly, Brian
American Guernsey Association *(127)*

Scheyer, Patrice D.
Association of Proposal Management Professionals *(303)*

Schiave, Scott
The Association for Manufacturing Excellence *(252)*

Schick, Kim
Alliance for Children and Families *(22)*

Schick, Timothy
The Newspaper Guild *(810)*

Schickler, RJE, Rabbi Stan
National Association of Temple Educators *(705)*

Schiefer, Greg
Society of Environmental Toxicology and Chemistry *(935)*

Schieman, Brian
International Microelectronics and Packaging Society - IMAPS *(556)*

Schiemann, Scott
Association for the Sociology of Religion *(259)*

Schierholz, Stephanie
Women in Aerospace *(1020)*

Schiff, JD, Philip D.
AABB - American Association of Blood Banks *(1)*

Schiffhauer, Karen
AFT - Public Employees *(15)*

Schiffman, Marc
National Council of University Research Administrators *(737)*

Schild, David
Foster Family-Based Treatment Association *(452)*

Schilfgaarde, Elizabeth Van
American Foreign Law Association *(122)*

Schiller, Carole
Institute of Packaging Professionals *(502)*

Schilling, III, Edward L.
Biomedical Engineering Society *(330)*
Contact Lens Council *(382)*

Schilling, Kellie
National Funeral Directors Association *(754)*

Schilling, Melissa
National Shooting Sports Foundation *(791)*

Schilling, William C.
Delta Sigma Pi *(409)*

Schilling, William J.
National Association of Professional Employer Organizations *(687)*

Schindel, Geary
National Speleological Society *(795)*

Schindler, Barbara
ASTM International *(319)*

Schindler, George
Society of American Magicians *(929)*

Schipper, Diana
Industrial Research Institute *(494)*

Schipper, Janine
Association for Humanist Sociology *(249)*

Schirmer, Dana
CALLERLAB - International Association of Square Dance Callers *(341)*

Schiska, Amy
Religion Newswriters Association *(880)*

Schjenken, Denise
Society for Marketing Professional Services *(914)*

Schlatter, Terry
National Operating Committee for Standards of Athletic Equipment *(776)*

Schlecht, Shannon
United States Wheat Associates, Inc. *(1000)*

Schlegel, Randy
National Association of Chemical Distributors *(652)*

Schleicher, CAE, Renee S.
American Academy of Medical Administrators *(36)*
American College of Cardiovascular Administrators *(93)*

Schlein, Steven
Community Financial Services Association of America CFSA *(370)*

Schleinzer, Jessica
Association for Library and Information Science Education *(251)*

Schlekeway, Todd
National Association of Tower Erectors *(706)*

Schlenker, John
Edison Electric Institute *(419)*

Schlenker, John S.
Edison Electric Institute *(419)*

Schlesinger, Keith
American Society of Agronomy (ASA, CSSA, SSSA) *(191)*
Crop Science Society of America *(404)*
Soil Science Society of America *(951)*

Schlesinger, Kenneth
Theatre Library Association *(973)*

Schlesinger, Robin
National Association of Professional Employer Organizations *(687)*

Schless, David S.
American Seniors Housing Association *(178)*

Schleyer, CMP, Lynae
National Automatic Merchandising Association *(711)*

Schlichte, Kristan
Catholic Charities USA *(345)*

Schlieff, Kathi
Laboratory Animal Management Association *(592)*

Schlinger, Robin
Theatre Communications Group *(973)*

Schloss, Howard M.
Financial Industry Regulatory Authority (FINRA) *(444)*

Schlotterbeck, Beverly
National Association of Counties *(659)*
National Association of County Intergovernmental Relations Officials *(660)*

Schlueter, Chuck
Association for Conservation Information *(243)*

Schmader, CFEE, Steven Wood
International Festivals and Events Association *(545)*

Schmale, Lin
Society of American Florists *(928)*

Schmarder, Evanne
National Association of RV Parks and Campgrounds *(692)*

Schmatz, Kathleen
Automotive Aftermarket Industry Association *(321)*
Car Care Council *(342)*

Schmedake, Robert
System Safety Society *(967)*

Schmelzer, Brad
International Association of Machinists and Aerospace Workers *(524)*

Schmelzer, CAE, Peter L.
American College of Osteopathic Family Physicians *(100)*

Schmid, PhD, Charles E.
The Acoustical Society of America *(11)*

Schmid, Oona
American Anthropological Association *(45)*

Schmid, Sandra
German American Business Association *(460)*

Schmidt, Charlie
National Association of College Stores *(655)*

Schmidt, Deb
Association of Home Office Underwriters *(287)*

Schmidt, Harry
Religious Conference Management Association *(880)*

Schmidt, Jacqueline
National Court Reporters Association *(740)*

Schmidt, John
Alliance for Children and Families *(22)*

Schmidt, Kim
International Chemical Workers Union Council/UFCW *(534)*

Schmidt, Klaus
National Association of Industrial and Technical Teacher Educators *(675)*

Schmidt, Lois
Clinical and Laboratory Standards Institute *(358)*

Schmidt, Madeline McCurry
American Society of Animal Science *(192)*

Schmidt, Mary Ann
Association of Earth Science Editors *(279)*

Schmidt, Pamela J.
ISA -The Association of Learning Providers *(586)*

Schmidt, Sanford
National Association of Computerized Tax Processors *(657)*

Schmidt, Steven L.
National Alcohol Beverage Control Association *(631)*

Schmidt, Susan
Alliance of Associations of Teachers of Japanese *(24)*

Schmit, Kerry Marshall
National Association of Professional Employer Organizations *(687)*

Schmitt, CMP, Karen
National Defense Transportation Association *(742)*
Society for Pediatric Radiology *(918)*

Schmitt, Melinda Madsen
At-Sea Processors Association *(319)*

Schmitz, Carl
Catalogue Raisonne Scholars Association *(344)*

Schmitz, Michael
ICLEI - Local Governments for Sustainability *(482)*

Schmitz, Nancy Brooks
National Dance Association *(741)*

Schmoldt, Eric
Professional Rodeo Cowboys Association *(864)*

Schmucker, C. David
Business Products Credit Association *(339)*

Schmucker, Cliff
Parachute Industry Association *(838)*

Schmuecker, Judy
Alpha Gamma Rho *(26)*

Schmuff, Robin
National Finishing Contractors Association *(751)*

Schmukler, Anita
Association for Child Psychoanalysis *(241)*

Schmutz, Catherine

National Association of Professional Employer Organizations *(687)*

Schnabel, CAE, David J.
National Association of Episcopal Schools *(666)*

Schnabel, Lisa
National Association of Secondary School Principals *(694)*

Schnare, Carolyn
National Association of Convenience Stores *(658)*

Schneider, Carol Geary
Association of American Colleges and Universities *(264)*

Schneider, Cary M.
Insurance Information Institute *(505)*

Schneider, Craig R.
Health Ministries Association *(470)*

Schneider, Douglas
World Shipping Council *(1027)*

Schneider, Holly
Association for the Study of Higher Education *(259)*

Schneider, Jerry
Professional Bowlers Association *(861)*

Schneider, Kent
Armed Forces Communications and Electronics Association *(228)*

Schneider, Lori
Amusement & Music Operators Association *(223)*

Schneider, Lori L.
Pile Driving Contractors Association *(848)*

Schneider, Lynn
Association for Professionals in Infection Control and Epidemiology *(254)*

Schneider, Melissa
National Livestock Producers Association *(770)*

Schneider, Paula K.
American Society of Cataract and Refractive Surgery *(194)*

Schneider, Rebecca Dinan
National Association of Emergency Medical Technicians *(665)*

Schneider, Richard C.
Non Commissioned Officers Association (NCOA) *(811)*

Schneider, Sven
Society for the Exploration of Psychotherapy Integration *(923)*

Schneider, Tina
Associated Builders and Contractors *(235)*
National Society of Accountants for Cooperatives *(793)*

Schneider, Wendy Caruso
The New York Academy of Sciences *(809)*

Schneider, Zona J.
American Shetland Pony Club/American Miniature Horse Registry *(179)*

Schnider, Ken
Association of Applied IPM Ecologists *(267)*

Schnitzer, Diane
American Law Institute *(144)*

Schnoor, Larry
National Forensic Association *(752)*

Schnorf, Rebecca
American Medical Rehabilitation Providers Association *(149)*

Schochet, Ira
National Association of Shareholder and Consumer Attorneys *(696)*

Schochet, Peggy
NORA: Association of Responsible Recyclers *(811)*

Schoen, Ingrid
National Safety Council *(789)*

Schoen, Molly
American International Charolais Association *(142)*

Schoenberg, Susan
National Association for Sport and Physical Education *(643)*

Schoenberg, Tammy
International Association of Commercial Collectors *(518)*

Schoenbrun, Dan
Independent Filmmaker Project *(489)*

Schoenbrun, CAE, FAAO, Lois
American Academy of Optometry *(37)*

Schoenfeld, Kirsten
Catholic Charities USA *(345)*

Schoening, Paul
Association of Academic Health Sciences Library *(263)*

Schoessler, Christine K.
National Association of Truck Stop Operators(NATSO) *(707)*

Schoettger, Trish
National Association of Insurance Commissioners *(676)*

Schofer, Lucinda A.
National Association of Chemical Distributors *(652)*

Scholl, Jon
American Farmland Trust *(118)*

Scholl, Linda
Gemological Institute of America *(457)*

Scholl, Louis
American Association of Kidney Patients *(64)*

Scholle, Sarah Hudson
National Committee for Quality Assurance *(724)*

Scholz, K. W.
American Voice Input/Output Society *(219)*

Scholz, Todd
United States of America Dry Pea and Lentil Council, Inc. *(996)*

Schommer, CPA, Jay
Legal Marketing Association *(596)*
Utilimetrics/Alliance for Advanced Metering & Data Management Solutions *(1006)*

Schonfeld, Jodey
American Oil Chemists' Society *(157)*

Schonfeld, Rabbi Julie
Rabbinical Assembly *(872)*

Schongalla, Samantha
Association of Independents in Radio *(288)*

Schooley, Michael L.
National Association of Elementary School Principals *(664)*

Schooling, Sean
Recognition Professionals International *(876)*

Schoppmann, Kenneth
Licensing Executives Society *(597)*

Schorr, Sara
Scaffold Industry Association *(891)*

Schott, PHR, Amy
Society of Certified Insurance Counselors *(932)*

Schott, Kristen
National Association of Affordable Housing Lenders *(646)*

Schott, Tina M.
Contact Lens Society of America *(382)*

Schrade, Jeff

Natural Gas Supply Association *(807)*

Schrader, Bruce A.
The American Society of Forensic Odontology *(198)*

Schrader, Carol
Associated Equipment Distributors *(235)*

Schrader, David
Protestant Church-Owned Publishers Association *(868)*

Schrader, David E.
American Philosophical Association *(164)*

Schrader, Marleen
Minerals, Metals and Materials Society *(617)*

Schraff, Leslie
National Coil Coating Association *(723)*

Schreader, Jessica
American Board of Surgery *(84)*

Schreiber, Brent
American Association of Professional Landmen *(71)*

Schreiber, Linda
Society of Christian Ethics *(932)*

Schreibman, CAE, Ron
National Association of Wholesaler-Distributors *(709)*

Schreier, David P.
National Tractor Pullers Association *(801)*

Schreier, Ethan J.
Associated Universities Inc. *(237)*

Schreyer, Fred
Professional Bowlers Association *(861)*

Schrimpf, Mike
Republican Governors Association *(881)*

Schrock, Vicki
North American Transportation Management Institute *(823)*

Schroeder, Amy
American and Delaine-Merino Record Association *(45)*

Schroeder, Anaise
Council of Better Business Bureaus *(392)*

Schroeder, Ashley
Outdoor Writers Association of America *(835)*

Schroeder, Bill
National Insurance Crime Bureau *(766)*

Schroeder, Craig
Academy of Model Aeronautics *(7)*

Schroeder, Franceska O.
American Astronautical Society *(77)*

Schroeder, Gary
Marine Corps Reserve Association *(605)*

Schroeder, Holly
Consumer Specialty Products Association *(381)*

Schroeder, Kellie A.
Wood Moulding and Millwork Producers Association *(1024)*

Schroeder, Levy
Association of Farmworker Opportunity Programs *(282)*

Schroedl, Lisa
Organic Crop Improvement Association International *(830)*

Schrupp, Wendy
PSIA-AASI *(868)*

Schryver, David
American Public Gas Association *(170)*

Schryver, Ursula
American Public Power Association *(171)*

Schubert, Dallas

Abortion Care Network *(2)*

Schubert, Lynn M.
The Surety and Fidelity Association of America *(966)*

Schubert, Randy
National Wheelchair Basketball Association *(804)*

Schuchardt, PhD, Jane
Association of Public and Land-Grant Universities (APLU) *(303)*

Schuchart, Cathy
School Nutrition Association *(892)*

Schuele, Stephan
American Clinical Neurophysiology Society *(92)*

Schuermann, Bill
American Soybean Association *(211)*

Schuessler, Maryanne
National Educational Telecommunications Association *(744)*

Schulenburg, Aaron
Society of Collision Repair Specialists *(933)*

Schull, Amy
Society for Developmental and Behavioral Pediatrics *(907)*

Schull, Ann
International Society of Air Safety Investigators *(570)*

Schulman, Ellen
National Organization of Legal Services Workers *(777)*

Schulman, Gail
American Artists Professional League *(47)*

Schulte, Chandelle
National Association for Girls and Women in Sport *(639)*

Schulte, Cindy
National Mail Order Association *(771)*

Schulte, Darren
National Association of Truck Stop Operators(NATSO) *(707)*

Schulte, John D.
National Mail Order Association *(771)*

Schulte, John M.
National Environmental Balancing Bureau *(746)*

Schulte, Sherrie
Irrigation Association *(585)*

Schulte, CAE, Terrence
Uniformed Services Academy of Family Physicians *(984)*

Schulte-Cooper, Laura
The Association for Library Service to Children *(251)*

Schultz, Belienda
American Society of Home Inspectors *(200)*

Schultz, Betty
ASTM International *(319)*

Schultz, Bryan
Child Care Aware of America *(353)*

Schultz, Catherine G.
National Foreign Trade Council, Inc. *(752)*

Schultz, Eric
American Correctional Association *(108)*

Schultz, Greg
Academy for Eating Disorders *(3)*

Schultz, John
American Amusement Machine Association *(45)*

Schultz, Mark
National Association of Local Boards of Health *(678)*

Schultz, Michele
Society for In Vitro Biology *(912)*

Schultz, Monica Nesbit
The Association of Collegiate Conference and Events Directors International *(275)*

Schultz, Nicole
National Council for Prescription Drug Programs *(732)*

Schultz, Peggy L.
Association of Defense Trial Attorneys *(278)*

Schultz, Tamara
Council for Affordable and Rural Housing *(388)*

Schultz, Tina Maggio
Registry of Interpreters for the Deaf *(879)*

Schulz, Andrew
Council on Foundations *(399)*

Schulz, Craig
Construction Marketing Research Council *(380)*

Schulz, CAE, Monika
Association for Healthcare Philanthropy *(248)*

Schulz, T. J.
Airport Consultants Council *(21)*

Schulze, Brenda
Cristo Rey Network *(404)*

Schulze, James
Council of Supply Chain Management Professionals *(398)*

Schulze, Mat
Computer Assisted Language Instruction Consortium *(372)*

Schumacher, Don
National Association of Sports Commissions *(697)*

Schumacher, PsyD, Donald J.
National Hospice & Palliative Care Organization *(760)*

Schumacher, Heather
Professional Association of Health Care Office Management *(859)*

Schumacher, Joyce
Association of Analytical Communities International *(267)*

Schumacher, Sue
American Concrete Pumping Association *(106)*

Schumann, Bryce
American Angus Association *(45)*

Schunemann, Peter
American Association for Crystal Growth *(49)*

Schunn, MSW, Christy
Association of SIDS and Infant Mortality Programs *(308)*

Schupp, Tracy
National Association of Local Boards of Health *(678)*

Schur, Dee
Organization for the Advancement of Structured Information Standards *(831)*

Schuring, Martin
International Double Reed Society *(541)*

Schurk, Michele
International Association of Conference Centers *(518)*

Schurman, Lynn
Retail Bakers of America *(884)*

Schuster, Emily
Association of Science-Technology Centers *(307)*

Schuster, Neil D.
American Association of Motor Vehicle Administrators *(65)*

Schute, Diane
Council of Producers & Distributors of Agrotechnology *(396)*

Schutt, PhD, David L.

SAE International *(889)*

Schutz, Glenn
BPA Worldwide *(334)*

Schutz, Judy
National Council on Family Relations *(738)*

Schuyler, Chuck
National Shoe Retailers Association *(791)*

Schwalb, Kevin
Textile Rental Services Association of America *(973)*

Schwalbach, Chad
Music Teachers National Association *(622)*

Schwan, Deb
International Door Association *(541)*

Schwartz, Adam
National Cooperative Business Association *(729)*

Schwartz, Andy
International Association for Continuing Education and Training *(511)*
National Child Support Enforcement Association *(721)*

Schwartz, CAE, Arthur Edward
National Society of Professional Engineers *(794)*

Schwartz, Jr., Arthur L.
American Real Estate Society *(173)*

Schwartz, Eric
Copyright Society of the U.S.A. *(385)*

Schwartz, Fred
Asian American Hotel Owners Association *(231)*

Schwartz, H. Andrew
Women in International Security *(1021)*

Schwartz, MD, Henry
Association for Psychoanalytic Medicine *(254)*

Schwartz, Jacalyn
American Federation for Aging Research *(119)*

Schwartz, Jamie
Council of Literary Magazines and Presses *(395)*

Schwartz, Jeanne
Society of School Librarians International *(947)*

Schwartz, Jennifer
National Association of RV Parks and Campgrounds *(692)*

Schwartz, Joshua
Patent and Trademark Office Society *(839)*

Schwartz, Kathy
American Rental Association *(174)*

Schwartz, Lea
SCSI Trade Association *(893)*

Schwartz, Linda
American Association of Cardiovascular and Pulmonary Rehabilitation *(55)*
Clinical Laboratory Management Association *(358)*
Decorative Plumbing and Hardware Association *(408)*
Product Development and Management Association *(858)*

Schwartz, Louis O.
American Sportscasters Association *(213)*

Schwartz, Maureen M.
BKR International *(331)*

Schwartz, Neil
Soccer Industry Council of America *(902)*

Schwartz, Nina
Association of Pool and Spa Professionals *(299)*

Schwartz, ATP, Paul J.
Rehabilitation Engineering and Assistive Technology Society of North America *(879)*

Schwartz, Peter W.
North American Technician Excellence *(823)*

Schwartz, Rita C.
National Association of Catholic School Teachers *(651)*

Schwartz, MD, Robert G.
American Academy of Thermology *(42)*

Schwartz, MS, RN, Sandra
Society of Otorhinolaryngology and Head-Neck Nurses *(943)*

Schwartz, Stan
National Newspaper Association *(775)*

Schwartz, Stanley A.
American Court and Commercial Newspapers *(111)*

Schwartz, Stephanie
Association for Behavioral and Cognitive Therapies *(240)*

Schwartz, Thomas K.
American Society of Sugar Beet Technologists *(209)*
Beet Sugar Development Foundation *(327)*

Schwartz, Tina
American Amusement Machine Association *(45)*

Schwarz, Andy
Alliance for Women in Media *(24)*
Public Media Business Association *(869)*
Resolve, The National Infertility Association *(883)*

Schwarz, Barb
International Association of Home Staging Professionals *(522)*

Schwarz, Herbert
Aviation Industry CBT Committee *(324)*

Schwarz, Joyce Burgess
Association of Public Television Stations *(304)*

Schwarz, Lisa
Business Marketing Association *(339)*

Schwarz, PsyD, DCEP, Robert
Association for Comprehensive Energy Psychology *(242)*

Schwarzbach, Daniel B.
Airborne Law Enforcement Association *(19)*

Schwarzbek, Lisa
IEEE Signal Processing Society *(485)*

Schwarzwald, Melvin
Office and Professional Employees International Union (OPEIU) *(826)*

Schweers, Kevin
National Community Pharmacists Association *(725)*

Schweigardt, Andrew
Thoroughbred Owners and Breeders Association *(974)*

Schweiger, Larry J.
National Wildlife Federation *(805)*

Schweinzger, CMP, Jacky
Association of University Technology Managers *(316)*

Schweinzger, Jacky
Academy for Eating Disorders *(3)*
American Association for Public Opinion Research *(51)*
International Society for Traumatic Stress Studies *(570)*

Schweitzer, John
American Composites Manufacturers Association *(105)*

Schweitzer, Esq., Richard P.
Council on the Safe Transportation of Hazardous Articles *(401)*

Schweitzer, Rick
National Private Truck Council *(782)*

Schweitzer, Sheila
Association for Electronic Healthcare Transaction *(245)*

Schwenk, Julie
Turnaround Management Association *(982)*

Schwenke, Brett A.
American Custom Gunmakers Guild *(112)*

Schwickrath, CEM, Carol
American Academy of Cosmetic Dentistry *(31)*

Schwieger, Robert
Energy Storage Council *(428)*

Schwingshakl, Jan
International Brotherhood of Electrical Workers *(531)*

Scimeca, Marie
Steel Plate Fabricators Association Division of STI/SPFA *(962)*
Steel Tank Institute Division of STI/SPFA *(963)*

Sciullo, Alessia
International Association for Insurance Law - United States Chapter *(513)*

Sciuto, Bernie
American Academy of Home Care Physicians *(35)*

Sclar, Casey
American Public Gardens Association *(170)*

Sclove, PhD, Stanley L.
Classification Society *(357)*

Scofield, Julie M.
National Alliance of State and Territorial AIDS Directors *(633)*

Scofield, Larry
International Grooving & Grinding Association *(549)*

Scoggin, Sean
Association for Conservation Information *(243)*

Scolnik, Alvin
National Electrical Manufacturers Association *(744)*

Scorca, Marc A.
OPERA America *(828)*

Scordato, Krissy
Council of Supply Chain Management Professionals *(398)*

Scott, Amanda
Association of Baccalaureate Social Work Program Directors *(269)*

Scott, CMP, Anita L.
Association of State and Provincial Psychology Boards *(309)*

Scott, BarBara M.
Association of Black Sociologists *(270)*

Scott, Bill
American Society of Consulting Arborists *(196)*

Scott, CAE, Bill
Window Coverings Association of America *(1018)*

Scott, Christy
American Miniature Horse Association *(152)*

Scott, Dr. Daryl Michael
Association for the Study of African American Life and History *(259)*

Scott, Rep. David A.
Academy of Leisure Sciences *(6)*

Scott, Deborah
National Association of Regulatory Utility Commissioners *(691)*

Scott, Edward "Ed"
United States Parachute Association *(997)*

Scott, Ian
American Chamber of Commerce Executives *(89)*

Scott, James
The Open Group *(828)*

Scott, Janet
Viola da Gamba Society of America *(1009)*

Scott, Jennifer
American Entertainment Armories Association *(117)*

Scott, Jodi

American Society of Heating, Refrigerating and Air Conditioning Engineers (ASHRAE) *(199)*

Scott, John H
College of American Pathologists *(363)*

Scott, Judy
Romance Writers of America *(888)*

Scott, Keith
SCORE Association *(893)*

Scott, Kristin
Society of Hospital Medicine *(938)*

Scott, Leslie
National Association of State Personnel Executives *(702)*

Scott, Lisa W.
Periodical and Book Association of America *(842)*

Scott, Lorraine A.
Phi Gamma Nu Fraternity *(845)*

Scott, Mary Carroll
The College Board *(363)*

Scott, Michael R.
Railway Industrial Clearance Association *(874)*

Scott, Pat
ACUTA - The Association for Information Communications Technology Professionals in Higher Education *(11)*

Scott, Robert
National Horsemen's Benevolent and Protective Association *(760)*

Scott, Rochelle Cinque
Pharmaceutical Marketing Research Group *(844)*

Scott, Theresa L.
SEPM - Society for Sedimentary Geology *(897)*

Scott, Thomas A.
Association of Christian Schools International *(272)*

Scott, Timothy A.
International Union of Police Associations, AFL-CIO *(579)*

Scott, Wayne
American Association of Classified School Employees *(56)*

Scott-Perez, Myrna
Society of Tribologists and Lubrication Engineers *(949)*

Scott-Pinkney, Pamela
American Historical Association *(131)*
Historians of American Communism *(476)*

Scotti, Marie J.
International Advertising Association *(509)*

Scozzafava, Lori
SWANA - Solid Waste Association of North America *(967)*

Scramlin, L.C.
American Southdown Breeders Association *(211)*

Scribner, Bryan
National Auctioneers Association *(711)*

Scribner, Julie
American Law Institute *(144)*

Scrimsher, Natalie
National Career Development Association *(717)*

Scrivens, Amy
International Society for Clinical Densitometry *(565)*

Scroggs, Kimberly
Academy of Osseointegration *(7)*

Scully, Sean
American Society of Civil Engineers *(194)*

Scungio, Jennifer
Financial Services Forum *(445)*

Scussa, Frank
American Society for Histocompatibility and Immunogenetics *(185)*

Sczudlo, Walter
Association of Fundraising Professionals *(285)*

Seaborn, Corey M.
American Society of Professional Estimators *(208)*

Seabrook, David
Council for Professional Recognition *(391)*

Seabrooks, Joi
Society of Hospital Medicine *(938)*

Seal, Candace
Oregon Farm Bureau Federation *(830)*

Seal, Donald
Glass, Molders, Pottery, Plastics and Allied Workers International Union *(461)*

Seale, Charly
Exotic Wildlife Association *(435)*

Seaman, Don
Television Bureau of Advertising *(971)*

Seaman, Jr., Capt. William F.
Law Enforcement Alliance of America *(594)*

Searight, Lee Ann
National Association of Independent Fee Appraisers *(674)*

Searle, Travis
Manufacturing Jewelers and Suppliers of America *(604)*

Searles, Prentiss
American Petroleum Institute *(163)*

Sears, Rebecca
American Institute of Graphic Arts *(139)*

Sears, Stephen
Brick Industry Association *(335)*

Seaton, Amelia (Amy)
National Academy of Elder Law Attorneys, Inc. *(627)*

Seay, Rhoda
National Association of Area Agencies on Aging *(647)*

Sebastian, MD, PhD, Irene
American Institute of Homeopathy *(139)*

Sebastian, Sarah E.
American Academy of Audiology *(31)*

Sebert, John A.
National Conference of Commissioners on Uniform State Laws *(727)*

Sebesta, Stephen
Association of Certified Fraud Examiners *(271)*

Sebor, Sheila
Independent Cosmetic Manufacturers and Distributors *(489)*

Sebring, Teresa L.
Measurement, Control and Automation Association *(609)*

Seckman, David
Food Processing Suppliers Association *(449)*

Secrist, Beth
Association of Research Libraries *(306)*

Sederholm, Pamela
American Automotive Leasing Association *(78)*

Sedlacek, Audrey
Association of Meeting Professionals *(294)*

Sedlak, Matt
Packaging Machinery Manufacturers Institute *(836)*

Sedlak, Richard I.
American Cleaning Institute *(91)*

Sedory Holzer, CAE, MA, Susan E.

Society of Interventional Radiology **(940)**

See, Karen
Coalition of Labor Union Women **(361)**

Seeger, Arline M.
National Lime Association **(769)**

Seegers, Gina
Academy of Osseointegration **(7)**
American Society of Colon and Rectal Surgeons **(195)**
Society of Surgical Oncology **(947)**

Seelinger, Helena
NACE International **(623)**

Seely, Janet Cave
International Association of Movers **(525)**

Seely, Valorie D.
Restoration Industry Association **(884)**

Seeman, Phil
Association of Performing Arts Presenters **(298)**

Seery, Adam
American Industrial Hygiene Association **(135)**

Seery, Megan
National Lipid Association **(770)**

Segal, Adam
National Alliance for Hispanic Health **(631)**

Segal, Allen
Society for Neuroscience **(916)**

Segal, Scott
Electric Reliability Coordinating Council **(421)**

Segal, Susan L.
Council of the Americas **(398)**

Segelken, Bill
United States Coast Guard Chief Petty Officers Association **(992)**

Seger, Dennis
National Foster Parent Association **(753)**

Segota, John
TESOL International Association **(971)**

Seguin, Brian
Association of Mental Health Librarians **(294)**

Segundo, Adrienne
National Association of Dental Laboratories **(662)**

Seibel, Jena
Network of Executive Women in Hospitality **(808)**

Seibert, Jill
Voices for America's Children **(1011)**

Seidel, Jennifer
American Association of Advertising Agencies **(53)**

Seidel, Mary Z.
Reinsurance Association of America **(879)**

Seidel, Paula Douglas
Appraisal Foundation **(226)**

Seifert, Paul J.
Council of State Administrators of Vocational Rehabilitators **(397)**

Seiffert, Grant E.
Telecommunications Industry Association **(971)**

Seiffert, Marcia
Association of Otolaryngology Administrators **(297)**

Seiler, Amy
American Association of Preferred Provider Organizations **(70)**

Seiler, Dr. Harold J.
American Association of Dental Consultants **(59)**

Seiple, Debra
National Society of Insurance Premium Auditors **(794)**

Seiss, Nancy
United States Psychiatric Rehabilitation Association **(998)**

Seiter, Ken
National Association for the Specialty Food Trade **(644)**

Seither, Erik
The Society of Naval Architects and Marine Engineers **(942)**

Seitter, Keith L.
American Meteorological Society **(151)**

Seitz, Connie
Western Association of Industrial Distributors **(1015)**

Seitz, Jessica R.
Alpha Kappa Psi **(26)**

Selby, Steve
International Maple Syrup Institute **(555)**

Selgado, Maria
International Association of Venue Managers **(528)**

Selhi, Christine Rath
Private Art Dealers Association **(858)**

Selig, Eliza R.
Hospitality Financial and Technology Professionals **(479)**

Sellenriek, Steve
Power and Communications Contractors Association **(855)**

Sellers, PhD, Dr. Eric W.
EEG and Clinical Neuroscience Society **(421)**

Sellers, Melanie
Society for Public Health Education **(919)**

Sellheim, Amy
Captive Insurance Companies Association **(342)**
Visual Communications Industry Group **(1010)**

Sellier, Alain
United States Wheat Associates, Inc. **(1000)**

Sells, Bill
Soccer Industry Council of America **(902)**
Sports and Fitness Industry Association **(959)**

Selva, Megan
Help Desk Institute **(474)**

Selvaggio, Raymond A.
Transportation and Logistics Council **(978)**

Selvitelle, Marilyn
Society of Independent Gasoline Marketers of America (SIGMA) **(939)**

Selvitelli, CAE, Marc
NAIOP, The Commercial Real Estate Development Association **(366)**

Selwyn, Eric
Council for Higher Education Accreditation **(390)**

Semadeni, Melinda
American Society of Pension Professionals & Actuaries **(206)**

Semler, Robert C.
American Society of Marine Artists **(202)**

Semon, Chris
SnowSports Industries America **(902)**

Semore, Melanie
National Christian School Association **(721)**

Senecal, Michele T.
International Fine Print Dealers Association **(545)**

Senechal, Bethany
Ethics and Compliance Officer Association **(433)**

Senese, Victor P.
Certification Board for Urologic Nurses and Associates **(349)**

Senff, Jenny Cross
Association for Demand Response & Smart Grid **(244)**

Seng, Philip M.
United States Meat Export Federation **(996)**

Sennett, Anita
Milking Machine Manufacturers Council **(616)**

Sennett, Michael
Plumbing Manufacturers Institute **(851)**

Sentelle, David
American Society for Nondestructive Testing **(187)**

Sepel, George J.
Society of Accredited Marine Surveyors **(927)**

Sepin, Lawrence H.
American Dental Assistants Association **(113)**

Sequeira, Vivienne
Corporate Council on Africa **(385)**

Serafin, Glenn
National Association of Media Brokers **(680)**

Serels, PhD, M. Mitchell
American Society of Sephardic Studies **(209)**

Serena, CPA, MBA, Thomas J.
American Gastroenterological Association **(125)**

Serfass, Jeffrey A.
Biomass Thermal Energy Council **(330)**

Sermak, R. M.
American Train Dispatchers Association **(217)**

Serna, Phillip
Viola da Gamba Society of America **(1009)**

Sernoffsky, Erin
American College of Osteopathic Emergency Physicians **(99)**

Serota, Scott P.
Blue Cross Blue Shield Association **(332)**

Serrano, Antonia
International Gay and Lesbian Travel Association **(548)**

Serrano, Carol
Council for Exceptional Children **(390)**

Serrano, Ric
Gay and Lesbian Medical Association **(457)**

Serres, Melissa
Grain Elevator and Processing Society **(464)**

Seta, Darlene A.
International Desalination Association **(540)**

Seth, III, Andy
National Association of Towns and Townships (NATAT) **(706)**

Setlak, Ken
CCIM Institute **(347)**

Setter, Tara
BP and AMOCO Marketers Association **(334)**

Settlemire, Ian
United Ostomy Associations of America **(988)**

Setzen, Michael
American Rhinologic Society **(175)**

Sever, Megan
American Geological Institute **(126)**

Severance, Janie
National Alliance of State Pharmacy Associations **(633)**

Severin, Christina
Association for Community Affiliated Plans **(242)**

Severini, Justin
National Council of University Research Administrators **(737)**

Sevilla, Carmen

The Optical Lab Division *(829)*

Sevin, Hope
National Franchisee Association *(753)*

Sevush, Ralph
Dramatists Guild of America *(416)*

Sew, Dennis H.
Professional Bail Agents of the United States *(860)*

Seward, Bell
American College of Construction Lawyers *(94)*

Sewell, Jeremy
GSM Association *(467)*

Sewell, Summer
National Federation of Community Broadcasters *(748)*

Sewell, Jr., William H.
Social Science History Association *(902)*

Sexson, Diana
Digital Screenmedia Association *(412)*

Sexton, Cathy
Association for Institutional Research *(250)*

Sexton, Curt
American Scientific Glassblowers Society *(178)*

Sexton, CAE, Deborah
Professional Convention Management Association *(861)*

Sexton, Kathy Greenler
Software & Information Industry Association (SIIA) *(950)*

Sexton, P E, Michael
Association of Eminent Domain Professionals *(280)*

Sexton, Phill
Snow & Ice Management Association *(901)*

Sexton, III, Thomas W.
National Futures Association *(754)*

Seyler, Ruth
American Institute for Conservation of Historic and Artistic Works *(136)*

Seymour, Christeen
International Facility Management Association *(543)*

Seymour, MBA, Christopher R.
National Lipid Association *(770)*

Seymour, Claudia
Allied Artists of America *(25)*

Seymour, Debi
American Society of Animal Science *(192)*

Seymour, Joseph
Biomass Thermal Energy Council *(330)*

Seymour, Laurel
Construction Financial Management Association *(379)*

Sganga, Fred
National Association of State Veterans Homes *(702)*

Sgrignoli, David
American College of Physicians *(101)*

Sgrignoli, David L.
American College of Physicians Services, Inc. *(101)*

Sgrignoli, Dianne
American Swimming Coaches Association *(215)*

Sgueo, James M.
National Alcohol Beverage Control Association *(631)*

Shaak, Teresa
Association of American Editorial Cartoonists *(264)*

Shabahang, DDS, MS, PhD, Shahrokh
American Institute of Oral Biology *(139)*

Shackelford, Tiffany
Association of Alternative Newsweeklies *(264)*

Shackelford-Campbell, CMP, Sharon
National Hospice & Palliative Care Organization *(760)*

Shade, Dora
American Welding Society *(220)*

Shade, Valerie P.
Center for American Nurses *(348)*

Shadley, Bobby
Association of Surfing Professionals - North America *(312)*

Shafer, Francis
Chlorobenzene Producers Association *(354)*
Society of Chemical Manufacturers and Affiliates Inc. *(932)*

Shafer, Joe
Professional Rodeo Cowboys Association *(864)*

Shafer, Mark
The Risk Management Association *(886)*

Shafer, PhD, Dr. Wade
American Simmental Association *(179)*

Shaffer, David
National Braille Association *(716)*

Shaffer, Willa J.
National Association of Schools of Art and Design *(693)*
National Association of Schools of Music *(694)*
National Association of Schools of Theatre *(694)*

Shafiq, Asim
National Association of Home Builders *(673)*

Shah, CG, Aashish
The American Gem Society *(125)*

Shah, Chirag
Associated Equipment Distributors *(235)*

Shah, Hema
Global Business Travel Association *(462)*

Shah, Neha
Utilities Telecom Council *(1006)*

Shah, MD, Udayan
Society for Ear, Nose and Throat Advances in Children *(907)*

Shaham, Lauren
LeadingAge (American Association of Homes and Services for the Aging) *(595)*

Shahan, Buzz
United Potato Growers of America *(988)*

Shahdadi, Simone
International Business Brokers Association *(532)*

Shahrak, Soraya
American Academy of Religion *(41)*

Shak, Amie
Cremation Association of North America *(404)*

Shaklee, Kim
American Society of Marine Artists *(202)*

Shakleford, Sonya
Airport Minority Advisory Council (AMAC) *(21)*

Shalby, Chris
International Institute of Municipal Clerks *(552)*

Shalgian, Christian
American College of Surgeons Professional Association *(103)*

Shamapande, Katherine
Association for Healthcare Philanthropy *(248)*

Shambarger, Peter
Association for Recorded Sound Collections *(255)*

Shames, Rebecca
Association of Medical Diagnostic Manufacturers *(293)*

Shamley, Mark W.

Association of Corporate Contributions Professionals *(277)*

Shampine, Dave
System Safety Society *(967)*

Shampine, Hilary B.
Society of Former Special Agents of the Federal Bureau of Investigation *(937)*

Shanahan, CAE, Betty A.
Society of Women Engineers *(950)*

Shanahan, Chris
Association of Family and Conciliation Courts *(282)*

Shanahan, Thomas J.
Electronics Representatives Association *(424)*

Shands-Gradijan, Celina
National Association of Workforce Boards (NAWB) *(710)*

Shane, Larry I.
Federation of Podiatric Medical Boards *(442)*

Shaner, Arlene
Archivists and Librarians in the History of the Health Sciences *(228)*

Shaner, Monica
American Institute of Floral Designers *(138)*
Professional Grounds Management Society *(862)*

Shaner, APR, CAE, Thomas C.
American Institute of Floral Designers *(138)*
Professional Grounds Management Society *(862)*

Shank, Brendon
Society of Hospital Medicine *(938)*

Shank, Heidi
Council of Graduate Schools *(394)*

Shankel, Carol
International Association of Operative Millers *(525)*

Shanks, Roger
American Dairy Science Association *(113)*

Shanley, Claire
American Society of Access Professionals *(190)*
International Biometric Society *(530)*

Shanley, Mitch
National Ski Patrol System *(792)*

Shanley, Stephen
Association for Bridge Construction and Design *(240)*

Shannon, James M.
National Fire Protection Association *(751)*

Shannon, CMP, Michele
Association of Strategic Alliance Professionals, Inc. *(311)*

Shannon, Staci
National Association of Legal Assistants *(677)*

Shannon, DO, MPH, Stephen C.
American Association of Colleges of Osteopathic Medicine *(57)*

Shannon, Susan
American Shoulder and Elbow Surgeons *(179)*

Shapiro, Amanda
Assisted Living Federation of America *(234)*

Shapiro, Gary J.
Consumer Electronics Association *(381)*

Shapiro, Josh
National Coordinating Committee for Multiemployer Plans *(730)*

Shapiro, Maxine
Association of Managed Care Dentists *(292)*

Shapiro, Maxine
Textile Bag and Packaging Association *(972)*

Shapiro, Nancy

National Academy of Recording Arts and Sciences *(628)*

Shapiro, Robert A.
IEEE Technology Management Council *(486)*

Shapiro, Robert C.
Vehicular Technology Society *(1008)*

Shapiro, Steven J.
National Association of Forensic Economics *(669)*

Shapland, Kim
Association of Physician Assistants in Cardiovascular Surgery *(299)*

Shappet, Aspasia
National Association of Vision Care Plans *(708)*

Sharak, Robert L.
Cruise Lines International Association *(405)*

Sharan, Yael
International Association for the Study of Cooperation in Education *(514)*

Sharbaugh, Justin
The Fertilizer Institute *(443)*

Shareef, Omar S.
African American Contractors Association *(15)*

Shareefy, Helly
American Public Communications Council *(170)*

Shariati, Noushin
American Society of Addiction Medicine *(191)*

Sharif, Pamela D.
National Society of Black Engineers *(793)*

Shark, Alan
American Mobile Telecommunications Association *(152)*

Sharkey, Pat
Specialized Carriers and Rigging Association *(957)*

Sharland, J. Scot
Automotive Industry Action Group *(322)*

Sharma, Saloni
Research Institute for Fragrance Materials *(882)*

Sharoff, Brian
Private Label Manufacturers Association *(858)*

Sharp, Christy
American Health Care Association *(129)*

Sharp, Debra
Research Society on Alcoholism *(882)*

Sharp, George W.
EUCG, Inc. *(433)*

Sharp, Laura
United States Parachute Association *(997)*

Sharp, Mike
Aviation Industry CBT Committee *(324)*

Sharp, Norman F.
Cigar Association of America, Inc. *(356)*

Sharp, Dr. Tim
American Choral Directors Association *(90)*

Sharpe, Paul
American Federation of Musicians *(119)*

Sharpe, Ruth
AMT - The Association For Manufacturing Technology *(222)*

Sharpless, Stacey
Biscuit and Cracker Manufacturers' Association *(330)*

Sharts-Hopko, Nancy
Sigma Theta Tau International *(899)*

Shattuck, Christine
National Electrical Manufacturers Association *(744)*

Shaub, Beth
American Podiatric Medical Association *(166)*

Shavalay, Pete
American Society of Civil Engineers *(194)*

Shaver, Nick
National Association of Photo Equipment Technicians *(684)*
Professional Picture Framers Association *(864)*

Shaw, Al
International Association of Round Dance Teachers *(527)*

Shaw, Beth Portnoi
Professional Women Photographers *(866)*

Shaw, MCP, Carlos
American Society of Association Executives-The Center for Association Leadership *(193)*

Shaw, Deb
Local Media Association *(599)*

Shaw, Deborah L.
NACHA - The Electronic Payments Association *(623)*

Shaw, Eric
The International Stability Operations Association *(575)*

Shaw, Jr., H. V. "Skip"
National Frozen and Refrigerated Foods Association *(753)*

Shaw, Jeannie
United States of America Gymnastics *(997)*

Shaw, ChFC, CLU, Jeffrey S.
Life Insurers Council *(597)*

Shaw, John
Natural Products Association *(807)*

Shaw, Kimberly Maiers
Songwriters Guild of America *(952)*

Shaw, Marie M.
Conference of Consulting Actuaries *(375)*

Shaw, Mary
Cable & Telecommunications Association for Marketing *(340)*

Shaw, Montgomery T.
Society of Rheology *(946)*

Shaw, Pam
American Polygraph Association *(166)*

Shaw, Patricia
Society for the Study of Indigenous Languages of the Americas *(925)*

Shaw, Rachael
National Society of Certified Healthcare Business Consultants *(793)*

Shaw, Satya
Asian American Convenience Stores Association *(231)*

Shaw, Susanne
Accrediting Council on Education in Journalism and Mass Communications *(11)*

Shaw, Timothy
Restoration Industry Association *(884)*

Shaw-Olson, Mary
National Tile Contractors Association *(800)*

Shay, Jeffrey P.
North American Case Research Association *(814)*

Shay, Matthew
National Retail Federation *(786)*

Shay, Russell
Land Trust Alliance *(593)*

Shay-Downer, Chris
International Transplant Nurses Society *(578)*

Shayka, David M.
National Council of Teachers of Mathematics *(737)*

Shchupak, Leo
Society for Software Quality *(921)*

Shea, Jessica Welch
Health Industry Distributors Association *(469)*

Shea, Rachel Hartigan
National Communication Association *(724)*

Shea, Rhea
Society of Accredited Marine Surveyors *(927)*

Shea-Joyce, Tep
Appraisal Institute *(226)*

Sheaffer, Gale
Association for Theatre in Higher Education *(260)*

Shealey, Gloria
National Association of Minority Contractors *(680)*

Shealy, Margie
Christian Medical & Dental Associations *(356)*

Shearer, Edward L.
The National Association of Marine Surveyors, Inc. *(679)*

Shearon, Paul
International Federation of Professional and Technical Engineers *(544)*

Shearon, Wendy
American Society for Precision Engineering *(188)*

Shedd, Sherry
United Egg Producers *(986)*

Sheehan, Dan
Association of Social Work Boards *(309)*

Sheehan, Daniel
Association of Farmworker Opportunity Programs *(282)*

Sheehan, Denise M.
National Glass Association *(755)*

Sheehan, Jay
Ultrasonic Industry Association *(983)*

Sheehan, Kathleen
Visiting Nurse Associations of America *(1010)*

Sheehan, Kathy
American Bankruptcy Institute *(79)*

Sheehan, Tara
APPAM - The Association for Public Policy Analysis and Management *(225)*

Sheehan, Valerie
National Association for the Education of Young Children *(644)*

Sheehy, Jeanne
Professional Insurance Marketing Association *(862)*
Tile Roofing Institute *(974)*

Sheely, Cindy
American Bladesmith Society *(81)*

Sheer, Vickie
Dance Educators of America *(406)*

Sheerin, Geoff
PlanetSpace, Inc. *(849)*

Sheets, Brock
Association of Old Crows *(297)*

Sheets, Christie
National Association of Rehabilitation Providers and Agencies *(691)*

Sheets, Rick
Electronic Security Association *(424)*

Sheets, Susan L.
National Aircraft Resale Association *(630)*

Sheets, Trina R.
National Emergency Management Association *(745)*

Sheetz, Guy
Futures Industry Association *(455)*

Shefchik, Leroy
International Silo Association *(564)*

Sheffield, Victoria M.
Society of Eye Surgeons *(936)*

Sheffield-Saylor, Shannon
American Holistic Nurses Association *(132)*

Sheflett, Sharon A.
American Association of Pastoral Counselors *(68)*

Sheheen, Jr., Austin M.
Professional Currency Dealers Association *(861)*

Sheibley, Diane Despopoulos
National Costumers Association *(730)*

Sheikh, Faraz
Society for the Advancement of Education *(922)*

Sheine, Sandy
North American Mycological Association *(818)*

Shelby, John
Association of Commercial Real Estate *(275)*

Shelby, Mike
National Corn Growers Association *(730)*

Sheldon, Cindy
Council on Occupational Education *(400)*

Sheldrick, PhD, Dr. Reg
American Guild of Hypnotherapists *(127)*

Shelford, Heather
American Association of Colleges of Nursing *(57)*

Shelhorse, Joseph
United States High Speed Rail Association *(994)*

Shelk, John E.
Electric Power Supply Association (EPSA) *(421)*

Shelko, Kate
NAFA Fleet Management Association *(624)*

Shell, Johnny
Specialty Graphic Imaging Association *(957)*

Shellabarger, R. E.
National Cotton Council of America *(730)*

Sheller, Chip
Aerospace Industries Association of America *(14)*

Shelley, Anne
Music Library Association *(622)*

Shelley, Barb
United Potato Growers of America *(988)*

Shelley, Barry J.
American Radio Relay League *(172)*

Shellhammer, Louise M.
Door and Access Systems Manufacturers Association, International *(415)*
Heat Exchange Institute *(472)*

Shelly, Don
National Wrestling Coaches Association *(806)*

Shelp, Andy
Surfaces in Biomaterials Foundation *(966)*

Shelton, Betty
The Wellness Plan *(1015)*

Shelton, Celeste
National Association of Credit Union Supervisory and Auditing Committees *(661)*

Shelton, Celeste A.
National Association of Credit Union Chairmen *(661)*

Shelton, Darryl

Christian Schools International *(356)*

Shelton, Dr. Elizabeth W.
American Friends of Turkey *(124)*

Shelton, Haley
Association for Radiological and Imaging Nursing *(255)*

Shelton, Jason
National Home Infusion Association *(760)*

Shelton, Jodi
Global Semiconductor Alliance *(463)*

Shelton, CAE, EdD, Jody
National Association for Health Care Recruitment *(639)*

Shelton, CMP, Laura E.
Drug & Alcohol Testing Industry Association *(416)*

Shelton, Shelley
Insurance Institute for Highway Safety *(505)*

Shelton-Slappy, Shaunte
National Association of Educational Procurement, Inc. *(664)*

Shema, Robert E.
American Cable Association *(87)*

Shen, Judy
Magnet Schools of America *(601)*

Shenson, Tara
Specialty Coffee Association of America *(957)*

Shep, Sydney
Society for the History of Authorship, Reading and Publishing *(923)*

Shepard, Brian
Music Teachers National Association *(622)*

Shepard, Jane
American College of Veterinary Pathologists *(104)*
Society for Research on Nicotine and Tobacco *(920)*

Shepard, Lisa
American Dairy Goat Association *(112)*

Sheperis, Carl
Association for Assessment in Counseling and Education *(240)*

Shephard, Susan
Society of General Physiologists *(937)*

Shepherd, Barry
American Federation of Police and Concerned Citizens *(119)*
National Association of Chiefs of Police *(653)*

Shepherd, Brent
American Federation of Police and Concerned Citizens *(119)*

Shepherd, Brent
National Association of Chiefs of Police *(653)*

Shepherd, Brett
Chain Drug Marketing Association *(350)*

Shepherd, Donna M.
American Federation of Police and Concerned Citizens *(119)*
National Association of Chiefs of Police *(653)*

Shepherd, Erin
American Philosophical Association *(164)*

Shepherd, Gerry
American Handwriting Analysis Foundation *(128)*

Shepherd, Jamie
American Federation of Police and Concerned Citizens *(119)*
National Association of Chiefs of Police *(653)*

Shepherd, Ron
FCIB-NACM Corporation *(438)*

Sheppard, Craig
Association of Industrial Metallizers, Coaters and Laminators *(288)*

Converting Equipment Manufacturers Association *(383)*

Sheppard, CAE, CPA, Michael
American Urological Association *(218)*

Sher, Ira
Council of Literary Magazines and Presses *(395)*

Sheramy, PhD, Rona
Association for Jewish Studies *(250)*

Sherer, Preston
National Association of State Farm Agents *(701)*

Sheridan, Karen
American Association of Insurance Services *(63)*

Sheridan, Kathleen
American Society of Hypertension, Inc. *(200)*

Sheridan, Robert M.
Association of Vascular and Interventional Radiographers *(316)*

Sheridan, Rosemary
American Public Transportation Association *(171)*

Sheridan, William R.
National Foreign Trade Council, Inc. *(752)*

Sherlick, Zoe
National Association of Independent Schools *(675)*

Sherlock, Rick
Association of Air Medical Services *(264)*

Sherman, Cary
Recording Industry Association of America (RIAA) *(876)*

Sherman, Getmansky
Society of Quantitative Analysts *(946)*

Sherman, Jamie
Association for Feminist Anthropology *(246)*

Sherman, Janice
United States Synchronized Swimming *(999)*

Sherman, ARM, CPCU, Jill
Society of Risk Management Consultants *(947)*

Sherman, Lee
Association of Jewish Family & Children's Agencies *(290)*

Sherman, CAE, MHA, RRT, Rebecca
American Cheese Society *(89)*

Sherman, PhD, Dr. Rex
American Association of Port Authorities *(70)*

Sherman, Robert
Internet Alliance *(582)*

Sherman, Robin
American Society of Business Publication Editors *(194)*

Sherrard, Kelly
American Bearing Manufacturers Association *(80)*

Sherrill, Joy
Society for the Scientific Study of Religion *(924)*

Sherrill, Marlene
Student National Medical Association *(964)*

Sherrill, Sharon
National Association of Housing and Redevelopment Officials *(673)*

Sherrod, Elizabeth
NAIOP, The Commercial Real Estate Development Association *(366)*

Sherrod, PhD, Lonnie
Society for Research in Child Development *(920)*

Sherry, Barbara
American Society for Virology *(190)*

Sherry, Julie
Association of Commercial Real Estate *(275)*

Sherwood, Bonnie
Association for Women in Computing *(261)*

Sherwood, Patricia
Security Industry Association *(895)*

Sherwood, Scott
Real Estate Roundtable *(876)*

Sherwood, Scott
United States Lactation Consultant Association *(996)*

Sheth, Yogendra
Association of Air Medical Services *(264)*

Sheviakhova, Alesia
American Society on Aging *(211)*

Shevitz, Elisa
The Broadway League *(336)*

Shevlin, Eleanor F.
Society for the History of Authorship, Reading and
  Publishing *(923)*

Shewan, Cynthia M.
Society of Thoracic Surgeons *(948)*

Shick, Dora
National Assembly of State Arts Agencies *(635)*

Shick, Jon
Heli Ski US Association *(473)*

Shick, Maureen D.
American College of Psychiatrists *(102)*

Shideler, Beverly
American Society of Pension Professionals & Actuaries
  (206)

Shidlauski, Kristina
National Conference of Commissioners on Uniform
  State Laws *(727)*

Shields, Amy
Marketing Research Association *(606)*

Shields, David
Therapeutic Touch International Association *(973)*

Shields, Donna
Burley Tobacco Growers Cooperative Association *(338)*

Shields, Maggie
Human Resource People and Strategy *(481)*

Shields, Mike
National Republican Congressional Committee *(786)*

Shields, Tim
League of Resident Theatres *(595)*

Shields, Wayne C.
Association of Reproductive Health Professionals *(305)*

Shields, William
American College of Radiology *(102)*

Shiffer, Christine
American Board of Surgery *(84)*

Shiffert, Sarah
American Academy of Clinical Toxicology *(31)*

Shiffert, Sarah
American Psychosomatic Society *(170)*

Shifflet, Debi
American Chamber of Commerce Executives *(89)*

Shifflett, Erin
National Genealogical Society *(754)*

Shifflett, Ken
American Commodity Distribution Association *(105)*

Shifflett, Michael
Council for Exceptional Children *(390)*

Shiflett, Jr., Ronald C.
International Utility Efficiency Partnerships *(580)*

Shih, Mary
American Society of Human Genetics *(200)*
Genetics Society of America *(458)*

Shiley, CAE, MAM, Dawn M.
Association of Vacuum Equipment Manufacturers *(316)*
National Association of State Emergency Medical
  Services Officials *(700)*

Shiley-Danzeisen, Dawn M.
International Association of Emergency Managers
  (520)
National Association of Government Communicators
  (670)
Process Equipment Manufacturers' Association *(858)*

Shilling, MD, Joel M.
American Society for Clinical Pathology *(182)*

Shilton, Mary
International Community Corrections Association *(536)*

Shimada, Allen
American Institute of Fishery Research Biologists *(138)*

Shimanek, Donna
Texas Longhorn Breeders Association of America *(972)*

Shimoda, Risa
River Management Society *(886)*

Shimpi, Arun
National Industries for the Blind *(763)*

Shimron, Yonat
Religion Newswriters Association *(880)*

Shin, Candy
Incorporated Research Institutions for Seismology
  (487)

Shinholster, Beverly
Association for Clinical Pastoral Education *(241)*

Shinn, Diane
Council for Exceptional Children *(390)*

Shinofield, Joel
College Swimming Coaches Association of America
  (364)

Shipe, CAE, Ginny
Council of Real Estate Brokerage Managers *(396)*

Shipley, Lisa
Women Networking in Electronic Transactions *(1022)*

Shipp, Daniel K.
International Safety Equipment Association (ISEA)
  (563)

Shipp, Jeffry William
Farm Credit Council *(437)*

Shire, Meriel
Association of Farmworker Opportunity Programs
  (282)

Shirk, John
Automation Alley *(321)*

Shirley, Kathy
EUCG, Inc. *(433)*

Shirley, Teresa M.
National Association of Elevator Contractors *(665)*

Shirude, Sanjay
Data Management Association International *(407)*

Shishido, Colleen
Pacific Telecommunications Council *(836)*

Shishmanian, Aram
World Gold Trust Services *(1026)*

Shively, Bethany
National Association of Conservation Districts *(657)*

Shiver, Farrell C.
American Society of Questioned Document Examiners
  (208)

Shivers, Chris
American Brahman Breeders Association *(85)*

Shivers, Tony
National Association of State Boards of Education
  (698)

Shmaeff, MPA, RPh, CAE, JD, Robert T.
Huntington College of Health Sciences *(481)*

Shmidl, Pam
United States Custom Harvesters, Inc. *(993)*

Shoaf, Jeffrey D.
Associated General Contractors of America (AGC) *(236)*

Shockey, Jarvis
National Dental EDI Council *(743)*

Shockley, Carolyn R.
Electric Power Research Institute *(421)*

Shoemaker, Janet
American Society for Microbiology *(187)*

Shoemaker, John
American Bonanza Society *(85)*

Shoemaker, Jolynn
Women in International Security *(1021)*

Shoemaker, PhD PE, Lee w
Metal Building Manufacturers Association *(613)*

Shoemaker, Liz
Recreation Vehicle Rental Association *(877)*

Shoemaker, Priscilla
American Health Care Association *(129)*

Shoenig, Andrew Loeb
United States Association of Former Members of
  Congress *(990)*

Shomaker, Rob
College and University Professional Association for
  Human Resources *(362)*

Shomer, Lew R.
Society of Independent Show Organizers *(939)*

Shomers, Suzanne
American Apparel & Footwear Association *(46)*

Shook, Ray
American Welding Society *(220)*

Shook, Veda
Association of Flight Attendants - CWA *(283)*

Shor, Nancy G.
National Organization of Social Security Claimants'
  Representatives *(778)*

Shore, Nicole
Society of Invasive Cardiovascular Professionals *(940)*

Shore, Richard A.
Association for Symbolic Logic *(257)*

Shorenstein, Stuart
International Radio and Television Society Foundation
  Inc. *(562)*

Shores, Melanie
School Science and Mathematics Association *(892)*

Short, Adam
Alliance of Artists Communities *(24)*

Short, Jeff
National Customs Brokers and Forwarders Association
  of America *(741)*

Short, Loretta
International Association of Healthcare Central Service
  Materiel Management *(522)*

Short, Marsha
Western Music Association *(1016)*

Short, Nancy
Society of Pediatric Nurses *(943)*

Shorter, Tasha

Catholic Charities USA (345)

Shortsleeve, Toni
International Military Community Executives
Association (556)

Shosteck, Eron
American Bus Association (87)

Shott, Christine
American Mathematical Association of Two Year
Colleges (147)

Shotwell, Linda
Air Line Pilots Association International (19)

Shotwell, Lynn Frendt
American Council on International Personnel (110)

Shoup, William L.
SSPC: the Society for Protective Coatings (960)

Showalter, PE, John "Buddy"
American Wood Council (221)

Shreck, Ben R.
Tax Executives Institute, Inc. (968)

Shrestha, CAE, Prabhash
Association of Fundraising Professionals (285)

Shreve, Mary Anne
Recreation Vehicle Dealers Association of North
America (876)
Recreation Vehicle Rental Association (877)

Shrewsbury, Wm
National Speleological Society (795)

Shrivastava, Anusha
South Asian Journalists Association (952)

Shrivastava, Vaibhav
International Association for Philosophy and Literature
(514)

Shriver, Ann L.
International Institute of Fisheries Economics and
Trade (551)

Shriver, Sarah
American College of Dentists (95)

Shropshire-Paschal, Trina
International Municipal Lawyers Association (557)

Shrum, Wesley
Society for Social Studies of Science (921)

Shtogrin, Igor
Capital Markets Credit Analysts Society (342)

Shuart, Lori
American Kinesiotherapy Association (144)

Shubin, Evan
Electronic Retailing Association (423)

Shue, J. Christopher
Reinsurance Association of America (879)

Shue, Michael
United States-ASEAN Business Council Inc. (990)

Shuey, CMP, Tawnee
American Society of Baking (193)

Shuford, Valerie
National Organization of Black Law Enforcement
Executives (777)

Shug, Philip N.
International Association of Audio Visual
Communicators (516)

Shugart-Bethune, Donna
International Association Of Pet Cemeteries and
Crematories (526)

Shuler, Elizabeth
AFL-CIO (American Federation of Labor and Congress
of Industrial Organizations) (14)
American Federation of Labor & Congress of Industrial
Organizations (119)

Shulin, MarySue
Council of State and Territorial Epidemiologists (397)

Shulman, MPH, Joni
American Association of Neurological Surgeons (66)

Shults, Heath
Bowling Proprietors' Association of America (334)

Shultz, Colby
American Association of Anatomists (54)

Shultz, Michaelle
Association of Corporate Counsel (277)

Shumaker, Kathy
Gynecologic Oncology Group (467)

Shuman, Elizabeth
United States-Austrian Chamber of Commerce (1001)

Shumate, John P.
American Foreign Service Protective Association (123)

Shumpert, Shea
The Counselors of Real Estate (401)

Shunn-King, Martha
American Postal Workers Union (167)

Shupe, CAE, Christine Quinn
Veterinary Hospital Managers Association (1008)

Shur, Mike
Association for Psychological Type International (254)

Shure, Jane
American Chemical Society (89)

Shurney, MBA, MD, MPH, Dexter W.
National Association of Managed Care Physicians
(679)

Shutak, Robyn
National Association of Stock Plan Professionals (703)

Shuter, CMP, Dale W.
Electrical Apparatus Service Association (422)

Shutt, Alan
American Association of Pharmaceutical Scientists (68)

Shwalb, David
Society for Cross-Cultural Research (907)

Shymoniak, Douglas P.
NARSA-The International Heal Transfer Association
(625)

Sibio, Mike
Community Managers International Association (371)

Sibley, Frank
National Association of Realtors (690)

Sidbury, Lashawn
Association of Schools and Colleges of Optometry
(307)

Siddiqui, Manzoor
Common - A Users Group (369)

Sidla, Emily
International Association for Dental Research (512)

Sieben, Inez
New York E-Health Collaborative (809)

Sieber, CAE, MA, Heather
National Parking Association (779)

Siegal, Nancy L.
The Corps Network (formerly the National Association
of Service and Conservation Corps) (386)

Siegel, Adam
Retail Industry Leaders Association (884)

Siegel, J D, PhD, Alex M.
Association of State and Provincial Psychology Boards
(309)

Siegel, Bruce
National Association of Public Hospitals and Health
Systems (688)

Siegel, Cathi
American Society of Tropical Medicine and Hygiene
(210)

Siegel, David
National Society of Professional Engineers (794)

Siegel, Donald
Technology Transfer Society (970)

Siegel, Elisa K.
Association of American Medical Colleges (265)

Siegel, Gail A.
National Association of Resale & Thrift Shops (691)

Siegel, Howard
Navy League of the United States (807)

Siegel, Richard A.
Council of Archives and Research Libraries in Jewish
Studies (392)

Siegert, Evan
American Securitization Forum (178)

Siegert, Thomas
Institute of Electrical and Electronics Engineers (IEEE)
(499)

Siegfried, AIP, Angela
Society of Insurance Trainers and Educators (940)

Siegrist, Wes
Society of Animal Artists (930)

Sieh, Linda
Rice Millers' Association (886)
USA Rice Council (1004)
USA Rice Federation (1004)

Sieli, Shirl V.
American Institute of Timber Construction (141)

Sielicki, Jennifer
American Society for the Alexander Technique (190)

Sienaski-Lancia, Laura
American Academy on Communication in Healthcare
(43)

Sierra, Elena
Association of Air Medical Services (264)

Siever, Steve
International Association of Fairs and Expositions
(521)

Sieverling, Joseph B.
Reinsurance Association of America (879)

Sievert, Steven
National Dairy Herd Information Association (741)

Siffringer, Leah
NAMTA - National Art Materials Trade Association
(635)

Sifuentes, USMC (Ret.), LTCOL Raul A.
Marine Corps Aviation Association (604)

Sigfusson, Asgeir
American Foreign Service Association (122)

Sigillo, Eric
Clinical Ligand Assay Society (358)

Sigler, MNEd, RN, Barbara A.
Oncology Nursing Society (827)

Sigloh, Kirstine
University Council for Educational Administration
(1002)

Sigman, MD, Mark
Society of Reproductive Surgeons (946)

Sigmon, CAE, Joyce
American Academy of Implant Dentistry (35)

Siikamäki, Dr. Juha

Association of Environmental and Resource Economists **(281)**

Sikes, Weldon
American Association of Home Inspectors **(62)**

Sikora, Lisa
Mine Safety Institute of America **(616)**

Silberberg, Jason
National Association of Boards of Examiners of Long Term Care Administrators **(650)**
National Association of Long Term Care Administrator Boards **(679)**

Silberfeld, Dafna
National Association of Hispanic Federal Executives **(672)**

Silberglied, Gail Ravnitzky
American Association of Museums **(65)**

Silberman, DO, Dr. Arlin
American Osteopathic Academy of Addiction Medicine **(159)**

Silbermann, CAE, Bryan E.
Produce Marketing Association **(858)**

Silbermann, Sandy
National Board for Certified Clinical Hypnotherapists **(715)**

Silcox, Clark R.
National Electrical Manufacturers Association **(744)**

Silins, Andris J.
United Brotherhood of Carpenters and Joiners of America **(986)**

Sillard, Kevin
National Governors Association **(755)**

Silnes, Andrea
American Ceramics Society **(89)**

Silva, Cesar
National Stone, Sand, and Gravel Association **(796)**

Silva, Dilma Da
Special Interest Group on Operating Systems **(956)**

Silva, Michael D.
Jewelers Shipping Association **(587)**

Silva, Mike
National Association of Reunion Managers **(692)**

Silvanik, Jackson
American Volleyball Coaches Association **(219)**

Silver, Edward
Global Business Travel Association **(462)**

Silver, Ellen
American Gastroenterological Association **(125)**

Silver, Dr. Howard J.
Consortium of Social Science Associations **(379)**

Silver, Jennifer
Association of Strategic Alliance Professionals, Inc. **(311)**

Silver, Martha
Organization for the Promotion and Advancement of Small Telecommunications Companies **(831)**

Silver, Mary
Hydraulic Institute **(481)**

Silver, Sue
Ecological Society of America **(418)**

Silverberg, Esq., James Lorin
White House News Photographers Association **(1016)**

Silvergleit, Ira T.
Society of American Florists **(928)**

Silverio, Craig
Packaging Machinery Manufacturers Institute **(836)**

Silverman, Hope

Fluid Sealing Association **(448)**

Silverman, Hugh J.
International Association for Philosophy and Literature **(514)**

Silverman, Richard S.
Juice Products Association **(589)**

Silverman, Riitta
American Society of Military Comptrollers **(203)**

Silverman, JD, MPH, Ross D.
American College of Legal Medicine **(97)**

Silverman, Stephanie E.
S-Corporation Association **(889)**

Silvers, Curt
National U.S.-Arab Chamber of Commerce **(803)**

Silvers, Faith
National Grain and Feed Association **(755)**

Silverstein, Ken
SOCAP International **(902)**

Silverstrin, Debra
Association of Alternative Newsweeklies **(264)**

Silvestri, Melissa
Dance Films Association **(406)**

Silvey, Amber
Adventure Travel Trade Association **(13)**

Silvia, Josh
Hispanic Association on Corporate Responsibility **(475)**

Sim, May
Metaphysical Society of America **(614)**

Simchak, Steve
Coalition of Service Industries **(361)**

Simdars, Brian
Controlled Release Society **(383)**

Sime, Brian
Association of Educational Publishers **(280)**

Simek, James A.
Professional Currency Dealers Association **(861)**

Simeone, Ed
American Academy of Cosmetic Dentistry **(31)**

Simeone, Marie
Building Owners and Managers Association International **(337)**

Simerling, Jeffrey "Jeff"
Council of the Great City Schools **(398)**

Simian, George
American Photographic Artists **(164)**

Siminovsky, CAE, Gail S.
Academy of Laser Dentistry **(6)**

Simkins, Betty J.
Financial Management Association International **(444)**

Simkins, Geradine
Midwives Alliance of North America **(615)**

Simmonds, Warren L.
American Society of Podiatric Medicine **(208)**

Simmons, Amy
National Association of Community Health Centers **(656)**

Simmons, Anita
American Association of Motor Vehicle Administrators **(65)**

Simmons, Brian S.
Association of Christian Schools International **(272)**

Simmons, Cindy
American Society of Heating, Refrigerating and Air Conditioning Engineers (ASHRAE) **(199)**

Simmons, Debora
Association for University Business and Economic Research **(260)**

Simmons, Diane
Healthcare Financial Management Association **(471)**

Simmons, Emily
Employers Council on Flexible Compensation **(427)**

Simmons, Jerry
National Association of Royalty Owners **(692)**

Simmons, Julie
American Association of Petroleum Geologists **(68)**

Simmons, Laurie
Society of Experimental Test Pilots **(935)**

Simmons, Rod
System Safety Society **(967)**

Simmons, Susan
Council for Exceptional Children **(390)**

Simms, Ann
American Institute of Certified Planners **(137)**
American Planning Association **(166)**

Simms, Brandi
Country Music Association **(401)**

Simms, Nigel
Delta Waterfowl Foundation **(409)**

Simon, Argie
International Association of Credit Portfolio Managers **(519)**

Simon, Betty Jo
Accordionists and Teachers Guild International **(9)**

Simon, Brett
Zonta International **(1030)**

Simon, Dan
Paint and Decorating Retailers Association **(836)**

Simon, David
Fibre Box Association **(443)**

Simon, Elizabeth
Council on Social Work Education **(400)**

Simon, Joel
Council for Adult and Experiential Learning **(388)**

Simon, Kathleen Archibald
Therapeutic Touch International Association **(973)**

Simon, Kelly
National Lesbian and Gay Law Association **(769)**

Simon, CTP, Lisa
National Tour Association **(800)**

Simon, Neil A.
Investment Adviser Association **(583)**

Simon, Robert
Private Art Dealers Association **(858)**

Simon, Sandi
Texas Alliance of Energy Producers **(972)**

Simon, Scott
ARMA International **(228)**

Simoneau, Bob
National Association of State Workforce Agencies **(703)**

Simonelli, Andrew
American Academy of Actuaries **(29)**

Simonetti, Lon
Society for Cardiovascular Magnetic Resonance **(905)**

Simonian, Hovann
Society of Armenian Studies **(930)**

Simons, Robert F.
Society for Psychophysiological Research **(919)**

Simons, Wiley

American Society of Association Executives-The Center for Association Leadership *(193)*

Simonsen, Mike
American Association of Variable Star Observers *(76)*

Simonson, Elizabeth
United States Synchronized Swimming *(999)*

Simonson, Julie
Campus Computer Resellers Alliance *(341)*

Simonton, Holly
Society for Simulation in Healthcare *(921)*

Simpao, Kim
Electrical and Computer Engineering Department Heads Association *(422)*

Simpson, Burney
Propane Engine Fuel Committee/Propane Education and Research Council *(867)*

Simpson, Chelsea
Association of University Research Parks *(316)*

Simpson, MBA, PhD, Cheri
University Professional & Continuing Education Association *(1003)*

Simpson, CMP, Christine
Gas Processors Association *(456)*
Gas Processors Suppliers Association *(456)*

Simpson, Cindy
Association for Women in Science *(262)*

Simpson, David
Incorporated Research Institutions for Seismology *(487)*

Simpson, Freddie N.
Brotherhood of Maintenance of Way Employees Division *(336)*

Simpson, Jennifer
International Titanium Association *(577)*

Simpson, Joe Leigh
International Federation of Fertility Societies *(544)*

Simpson, John
The Aluminum Association, Inc. *(27)*

Simpson, Judy
American Music Therapy Association *(154)*

Simpson, Kirsten Brown
National Academy of Elder Law Attorneys, Inc. *(627)*

Simpson, Larnell
American Association for Laboratory Accreditation *(50)*

Simpson, CFE, Leslie
Association of Certified Fraud Examiners *(271)*

Simpson, Lisa
American Staffing Association *(213)*

Simpson, FAAP, MPH, Lisa
Academy Health *(3)*

Simpson, Lynn
Emdr International Association *(425)*

Simpson, Marianna Shreve
Historians of Islamic Art Association *(476)*

Simpson, Marissa
American Society for Aesthetic Plastic Surgery *(180)*

Simpson, Michael
National Council for the Social Studies *(733)*

Simpson, Sharhonda
African Studies Association *(15)*

Simpson, Sheila
The Hosiery Association *(478)*

Simpson, Stephanie
Building Service Contractors Association International *(337)*

Simpson, Thomas D.
Railway Supply Institute *(874)*

Simrany, Joseph P.
Tea Association of the United States of America *(969)*
Tea Council of the U.S.A. *(969)*

Sims, Anita
National Educational Telecommunications Association *(744)*

Sims, Brenda
Association of Teachers of Technical Writing *(313)*

Sims, Christopher A.
American Economic Association *(115)*

Sims, Helena
Association of Government Accountants *(286)*

Sims, Jeff
National Association of RV Parks and Campgrounds *(692)*

Sims, Jeff N.
Truck Trailer Manufacturers Association *(981)*

Sims, Lisa
International Association of Official Human Rights Agencies *(525)*

Sims-Wood, Dr. Janet
Association for the Study of African American Life and History *(259)*

Sinclair, Alex
GSM Association *(467)*

Sinclair, Andrew
National Association of Residential Property Managers *(691)*

Sinclair, Jack
Mexican-American Grocers Association *(614)*

Sinder, Scott
The Council of Insurance Agents and Brokers *(394)*

Sing, Michael
Intercollegiate Tennis Association *(507)*

Singer, Andrew W.
Bank Insurance and Securities Association *(326)*

Singer, MHA, Dale
Renal Physicians Association *(881)*

Singer, Dana
Society of North American Goldsmiths *(943)*

Singer, Madine
Insurance Information Institute *(505)*

Singer, Richard
National Golf Foundation *(755)*

Singer, Rick
Society of Government Travel Professionals *(938)*

Singer, Terry E.
National Association of Energy Service Companies *(665)*

Singerling, CCM, CEC, James B.
Club Managers Association of America *(359)*

Singh, Abhilasha
Industrial Research Institute *(494)*

Singh, Conchita
Fresh Produce Association of the Americas *(453)*

Singh, Daisy
American Highway Users Alliance *(131)*

Singh, Daniel
Association of American Colleges and Universities *(264)*

Singh, Sajai
International Technology Law Association *(577)*

Singh-Corcoran, Nathalie
International Writing Centers Association *(581)*

Singhal, Ram
Flexible Packaging Association *(447)*

Singler-Adams, Laura
Chief Officers of State Libraries Agencies *(352)*

Singleterry, Wynona
National Conference of Black Mayors *(726)*

Singleton, Nicole
National Council on Student Development *(740)*

Singleton, Sarah
International Sign Association *(564)*

Singleton, Tammy
National Religious Broadcasters *(785)*

Sink, Debbie
National Structured Settlements Trade Association *(797)*

Sinkhorn, Sam
American Architectural Manufacturers Association *(46)*

Sinks, Clair O'Neil
American Association of Immunologists *(62)*

Sinn, Stephanie
Investigative Reporters and Editors *(583)*

Sinnett, William
Financial Executives International *(444)*

Siok, Andrea Ball
Apple Processors Association *(225)*

Siok, William J.
American Institute of Professional Geologists *(140)*

Siradas, Sue
Appraisal Institute *(226)*

Siress, Kathy
National Rural Health Association *(788)*

Sirgy, M. Joseph
International Society for Quality-of-Life Studies *(569)*

Sirkel, Cindy
National Independent Automobile Dealers Association *(761)*

Sirman, Eva
National Association of Disability Representatives *(663)*

Sirvello, III, Tony J.
International Association of Clerks, Recorders, Election Officials and Treasurers *(518)*

Sirvet, Ene
Society of American Historians *(929)*

Sisco, Casady
National Association of Government Guaranteed Lenders (NAGGL) *(670)*

Sisemore, Teddi
American Therapeutic Recreation Association *(216)*

Siske, Blaine
Energy Telecommunications and Electrical Association *(428)*

Siske, Blaine
International Association for Human Resource Information Management *(512)*

Sisley, Todd R.
American Guild of Organists *(127)*

Sisneros, Theresa
Commission on Accreditation of Allied Health Education Programs *(368)*

Sison, Virgie
International Franchise Association *(547)*

Sisson, Joanne
International Public Management Association for Human Resources *(562)*

Sisson, Kari

American Association of Children's Residential Centers *(56)*

Sistare, Carolyn
Environmental Council of the States *(431)*

Sistler, Pat
International Association of Rehabilitation Professionals *(527)*

Sitar, FCP, PhD, Daniel S.
American College of Clinical Pharmacology *(94)*

Sitek, Greg
Associated Construction Publications *(235)*

Sitler, Penny
International Decorative Artisans League *(540)*
The Knitting Guild Association *(591)*

Sitton, Ron B.
American-Israel Chamber of Commerce and Industry *(222)*

Sitzman, MD, MPH, B. Todd
North American Neuromodulation Society *(819)*

Sivels, Jessica
Association of Real Estate License Law Officials *(305)*

Siverling, Jonathan
American Radio Relay League *(172)*

Sivertsen, Kim
APA The Engineered Wood Association *(224)*

Siwa, Chris
American Association of Law Libraries *(64)*

Sizelove, Kristen
National Association of Mutual Insurance Companies *(681)*

Sizemore, Gregory L.
Construction Users Roundtable *(380)*

Sizemore, Jennifer
American Society of Military Comptrollers *(203)*

Sizemore, PhD, Ray B.
College and University Professional Association for Human Resources *(362)*

Sjoberg, Judith A.
American Society for Mass Spectrometry *(186)*

Sjoberg, William
Customs and International Trade Bar Association *(406)*

Sjoblom, Kriss S.
Governmental Research Association *(464)*

Skalko, CTRS, MS, Diane
American Therapeutic Recreation Association *(216)*

Skalla, Mary Jane
National Federation of Press Women *(749)*

Skallas, Michael
Society of Thoracic Surgeons *(948)*

Skarstedt, Jennifer
National Costumers Association *(730)*

Skea, Melinda
American Composites Manufacturers Association *(105)*

Skeberdis, Kara
Zero Balancing Health Association *(1030)*

Sked, Janet
Defense Credit Union Council *(408)*

Skedsvold, JD, PhD, Paula R.
Federation of Associations in Behavioral & Brain Sciences *(441)*
Federation of Behavioral, Psychological and Cognitive Sciences *(441)*

Skeel, Joe
Society of Professional Journalists *(945)*

Skeffington, Joseph
Federation of Diocesan Liturgical Commissions *(441)*

Skelley, Jennifer
American Pet Products Association *(163)*

Skellhammer, Louise M.
Scaffolding, Shoring and Forming Institute *(892)*

Skelton, Caitlin
American Association of Managing General Agents *(64)*

Skelton, CAE, Robert
American Society of Association Executives-The Center for Association Leadership *(193)*

Skenandore, Tracy
American Academy of Cosmetic Dentistry *(31)*

Skewes, Barb
Association of Zoos and Aquariums *(318)*

Skiba, CAE, Thomas M.
Community Associations Institute (CAI) *(370)*

Skiera, Jim
International Society of Arboriculture *(571)*

Skiles, James H.
Grocery Manufacturers Association (GMA) *(466)*

Skillingberg, Michael
The Aluminum Association, Inc. *(27)*

Skillman, CAE, Keith
American Society of Association Executives-The Center for Association Leadership *(193)*

Skinner, Frank R.
Healthcare Convention and Exhibitors Association *(471)*

Skinner, Jake
Red and White Dairy Cattle Association *(877)*

Skinner, John H.
SWANA - Solid Waste Association of North America *(967)*

Skinner, Lisa
TechLaw Group *(969)*

Skinner, Ronald A.
Association of School Business Officials International *(306)*

Skinner, Ronald D.
American Railway Development Association *(173)*

Skipper, Sandy
Society of Competitive Intelligence Professionals *(933)*

Skjekkeland, Atle
Association for Information and Image Management International *(249)*

Skjervem, Harley
Credit Union National Association, Inc. *(404)*

Skjoldager, MBA, MS, Shawntay
International Association of Exhibitions and Events *(520)*

Skjothaug, Jolene
Timber Products Manufacturers Association *(975)*

Sklar, David P.
Association of American Medical Colleges *(265)*

Sklarow, Mark H
Independent Educational Consultants Association *(489)*

Skok, Eugene L.
Association of Asphalt Paving Technologists *(268)*

Skolnick, Marci
Stage Managers Association *(960)*

Skor, Emily
Consumer Healthcare Products Association *(381)*

Skorupskas, Erika H.
American Academy of Pediatric Dentistry *(39)*

Skotek, Denise M.

National Telecommunications Cooperative Association *(799)*

Skrdlant, Gary
AIB International *(17)*

Skrinde, Karen
Glass Art Society *(461)*

Skully, Terrie
National Truck Equipment Association *(802)*
Snow Control Equipment Manufacturers Committee *(902)*

Skurski, Daniel
National Trappers Association *(801)*

Skwarek, Shane
Market Technicians Association *(606)*

Skyba, Richard
Society of Insurance Research *(940)*

Skyler, Meryl
National Association for the Specialty Food Trade *(644)*

Slabach, Brock
National Rural Health Association *(788)*

Slade, Carolyn
The Society for Investigative Dermatology *(913)*

Slade, Karen E.
National Association of Black-Owned Broadcasters *(649)*

Sladic, Clare
Education Industry Association *(420)*

Slagle, Sheryl
National Cattlemen's Beef Association *(718)*

Slakie, Marcia
The Door and Hardware Institute *(416)*

Slam, Lisa
National Association of Real Estate Appraisers *(689)*

Slass, Lorie
American Board of Internal Medicine *(82)*

Slate, II, William K
American Arbitration Association *(46)*

Slater, Dennis J.
Association of Equipment Manufacturers *(281)*

Slater, Eric C.
American Chemical Society *(89)*

Slater, Samantha
Renewable Fuels Association *(881)*

Slatkin, PhD, David J.
American Society of Pharmacognosy *(207)*

Slatten, Bradley
Air Conditioning, Heating and Refrigeration Institute (AHRI) *(18)*

Slatton, Suzee
Association for Medical Imaging Management *(252)*

Slaughter, Tom
National Sculpture Society *(790)*

Slavin, Rose-Ella
Association of State and Territorial Health Officials *(310)*

Slavkin, Heather
AFL-CIO (American Federation of Labor and Congress of Industrial Organizations) *(14)*

Slawny, Rick
American Association of Certified Allergists *(56)*
American College of Allergy, Asthma and Immunology *(93)*
American Society of Colon and Rectal Surgeons *(195)*

Slayden, Kelli R.
Post-Tensioning Institute *(853)*

Slayden, Leigh

National Farmers Union (Farmers Educational & Co-operative Union of America) **(747)**

Slaydon, Lisa G.
National Association of Small Business Investment Companies **(900)**

Slayen, Anthony
Jewish Community Centers Association of North America **(588)**

Slazer, Frank A.
American Astronautical Society **(77)**

Slebrch, Shelly
National Grants Management Association **(756)**

Sledd, Charlie
National Association of State Boating Law Administrators **(698)**

Sleeper, CAE, CPA, Steve
Professional Beauty Association | National Cosmetology Association **(861)**

Sleight, Thomas N.
United States Grains Council **(994)**

Slesinger, Phyllis K.
Mortgage Bankers Association of America **(619)**

Slesinger, Scott
Environmental Technology Council **(431)**

Sligar, Steven R.
Vocational Evaluation and Career Assessment Professionals **(1011)**

Sliwa, James
American Society for Microbiology **(187)**

Sloan, Catherine R.
Computer and Communications Industry Association **(372)**

Sloan, Cathie
The Food Institute **(449)**

Sloan, Gerald
National Tile Contractors Association **(800)**

Sloan, Katie Smith
International Association of Homes and Services for the Ageing **(522)**

Sloan, Larry
Chlorobenzene Producers Association **(354)**
Society of Chemical Manufacturers and Affiliates Inc. **(932)**

Sloan, Lawrence D.
Society of Chemical Manufacturers and Affiliates Inc. **(932)**

Sloan, Pat
International Advertising Association **(509)**

Sloan, Rich
Association of Real Estate License Law Officials **(305)**

Sloan, Richard M.
National Narcotics Officers Associations' Coalition **(774)**

Sloan, Richard S.
International Association of Machinists and Aerospace Workers **(524)**

Sloane, Leigh Morris
Association of Professional Schools of International Affairs **(302)**

Sloat, Alice
Roller Skating Association International **(887)**

Sloat, Caroline F.
American Antiquarian Society **(45)**

Sloboda, Brian W.
Society of Government Economists **(937)**

Slocum, Joshua
Funeral Consumers Alliance **(454)**

Slocumb, Dennis J.

International Union of Police Associations, AFL-CIO **(579)**

Slogar, Elizabeth K.
North American Menopause Society **(818)**

Slominski, Jerry
National Cheese Institute **(720)**

Slominski, Jerry D.
International Dairy Foods Association **(539)**

Slone, Jody
Beverage Media Group, Inc **(328)**

Sloper, Tamara
Intersocietal Accreditation Commission **(582)**

Slotznick, Mike
Pharmaceutical Marketing Research Group **(844)**

Sloyan, Peggy
Association of Litigation Support Professionals **(292)**

Sluss, Dorothy
The Association for the Study of Play **(260)**

Slutsky, Bernice
American Seed Trade Association **(178)**

Sly, Melissa
Council for Agricultural Science and Technology **(388)**

Smaalders, Karen
International Association for the Study of Pain **(514)**

Small, Barbara
Future Business Leaders of America - Phi Beta Lambda **(455)**

Small, Dennis
National Association of City and County Health Officials **(654)**
National Association of County and City Health Officials **(659)**

Small, Kathy
National Association of Temple Administrators **(705)**

Small, Tony
National Council for Agricultural Education **(731)**
National FFA Organization **(750)**

Smallbrook, Linda
American Philosophical Association **(164)**

Smarr, Kay
Council on Occupational Education **(400)**

Smartt, Amy
Country Music Association **(401)**

Smazik, Jennie
World Allergy Organization **(1025)**

Smeallie, Peter H.
American Rock Mechanics Association **(176)**

Smee, Susan
American Association of University Professors **(75)**

Smekens, Olivier
Belgian-American Chamber of Commerce **(327)**

Smeltzer, Petra M.
National Association of Water Companies (NAWC) **(709)**

Smid, Diane
Transportation and Logistics Council **(978)**

Smidt, Mathew
Council On Forest Engineering **(399)**

Smigel, Libby
Congress on Research in Dance **(377)**

Smiley, Julie
Infusion Nurses Society **(496)**

Smiley, Valerie
United States Grains Council **(994)**

Smilor, Lisa

Council of Fashion Designers of America **(393)**

Smirnow, John
Solar Energy Industries Association (SEIA) **(952)**

Smith, Aileen
American Society of Golf Course Architects **(198)**

Smith, MA, Alex
American Association of Christian Counselors **(56)**

Smith, Alice
National Council on Public History **(739)**

Smith, Alison N.
InsideNGO **(496)**

Smith, Amy
American Berkshire Association **(80)**

Smith, Amy
Competitive Telecommunications Association **(371)**

Smith, Andrew
American Gaming Association **(124)**

Smith, Andy
Paso Fino Horse Association, Inc. **(839)**

Smith, Anne E.
American Fox Terrier Club **(123)**

Smith, ChFC, CLU, Anthony
Society of Financial Service Professionals **(936)**

Smith, Ashley M.
American Waterways Operators **(220)**

Smith, B. D.
ADSC: The International Association of Foundation Drilling **(12)**

Smith, CAE, Barbara R.
American Thyroid Association **(216)**

Smith, CAE, CHES, PhD, Becky J.
American Association for Health Education **(49)**

Smith, Bergitta E.
Association of Professors of Medicine **(302)**

Smith, CMP, Bethany
Brick Industry Association **(335)**

Smith, Bill
Industrial Foundation of America **(493)**

Smith, Billy
American Paint Horse Association **(161)**

Smith, Brad
Percussion Marketing Council **(841)**

Smith, Bradley T.
American Sociological Association **(211)**

Smith, Bram
Loan Syndication & Trading Association **(599)**

Smith, Branden
Online News Association **(827)**

Smith, Brandon
National Association of Waterproofing and Structural Repair Contractors **(709)**

Smith, Brandy
Association for the Study of Higher Education **(259)**

Smith, Breanna
Professional Housing Management Association **(862)**

Smith, Brian M.
Mutual Fund Education Alliance **(623)**

Smith, Brian T.
Association of American Veterinary Medical Colleges **(267)**

Smith, Bruce R.
Glass, Molders, Pottery, Plastics and Allied Workers International Union **(461)**

Smith, Candace M.

Smith, Carla
National Association of Professional Mortgage Women *(687)*

Smith, Carla
The Travel Institute *(979)*

Smith, Carolyn
International Titanium Association *(577)*

Smith, J.D., Cate K.
Education Law Association *(420)*

Smith, Catharine
Society of Hospital Medicine *(938)*

Smith, Celeste
American Association of Law Libraries *(64)*

Smith, Cinda
American Real Estate and Urban Economics Association *(173)*

Smith, Cindy
International Society for Philosophical Enquiry *(568)*

Smith, Connie
National Funeral Directors Association *(754)*

Smith, Courtney
National Association of Charter School Authorizers *(652)*

Smith, Craig A.
Alliance for Natural Health USA *(23)*

Smith, Curtis
International Brotherhood of Boilermakers, Iron Shipbuilders, Blacksmiths, Forgers and Helpers *(531)*

Smith, Dan
Amalgamated Transit Union *(28)*

Smith, Dan
National Forensic Association *(752)*

Smith, Darrell K.
Industrial Minerals Association -- North America *(494)*

Smith, CIH, PhD, Darrell K.
International Window Film Association *(581)*
National Industrial Sand Association *(763)*

Smith, David
International Federation of Leather Guilds *(544)*

Smith, David
Trucking Management, Inc. *(981)*

Smith, David A.
Society for a Science of Clinical Psychology *(903)*

Smith, David R.
Interlocking Concrete Pavement Institute *(508)*

Smith, FAIA, Deke
Building Seismic Safety Council *(337)*

Smith, DeMaurice
National Football League Players Association *(752)*

Smith, Denise
American Midwifery Certification Board *(151)*

Smith, Denise
Association for Governmental Leasing and Finance *(247)*

Smith, Dianna
North American Mycological Association *(818)*

Smith, Don
Association of the Wall and Ceiling Industry *(314)*

Smith, Donna
Concord Grape Association *(373)*
The Vinegar Institute *(1009)*

Smith, Ed
American Council of State Savings Supervisors *(110)*

Smith, Edward
Conference of State Bank Supervisors *(376)*

Smith, Eileen

ASIS International *(232)*

Smith, Elizabeth A.
Casualty Actuarial Society *(344)*

Smith, Eric K.
Attorneys' Liability Assurance Society Inc. *(320)*

Smith, Erin
United States Lacrosse *(995)*

Smith, Estela M.
Geothermal Resources Council *(460)*

Smith, F. Aaron
National Cannabis Industry Association *(717)*

Smith, Felicia
Association of Public Treasurers of the United States and Canada *(304)*

Smith, Gary L.
National Board for Respiratory Care *(715)*

Smith, JD, Gib
National Association of Independent Review Organizations *(624)*

Smith, Hon. Gordon
National Association of Broadcasters *(650)*

Smith, Gordon
United States Tennis Association *(1000)*

Smith, Graham
Foundation for International Meetings *(453)*

Smith, Greg
Council of the Americas *(398)*

Smith, Gregg
American Pyrotechnics Association *(172)*

Smith, Gregory
Point of Purchase Advertising Institute *(851)*

Smith, CAE, Gregory
POPAI The Global Association for Marketing at Retail *(852)*

Smith, Gregory V.
Association of Programs for Female Offenders *(303)*

Smith, Harry
International Bridge, Tunnel and Turnpike Association *(531)*

Smith, Ileane
ASTM International *(319)*

Smith, J. W.
American Fox Terrier Club *(123)*

Smith, James R.
National Association for Business Teacher Education *(636)*

Smith, Jamie
Broadcast Cable Credit Association *(335)*

Smith, Jamie L.
Media Financial Management Association *(610)*

Smith, Janet E.
NALP - The Association for Legal Career Professionals *(624)*

Smith, Jason
Hospitality Sales and Marketing Association International *(479)*

Smith, Jason Roland
International Tuba-Euphonium Association *(578)*

Smith, Jeanette
Physician Assistant Education Association *(847)*

Smith, Jeff
United States of America Gymnastics *(997)*

Smith, Jeffery L.
National Federation of Independent Business (NFIB) *(748)*

Smith, Jessica Keenan
American Society of Hand Therapists *(199)*

Smith, Jill
The Association for Academic Surgery *(237)*

Smith, Jillian
National Association of Chronic Disease Directors *(653)*

Smith, Jodi
American Society of Cytopathology *(196)*

Smith, Joseph
Association of Biomedical Communications Directors *(269)*

Smith, Joshua
International Fire Photographers Association *(545)*

Smith, Joyce E.
National Association for College Admission Counseling *(637)*

Smith, Justin
Professional Records and Information Services Management International *(864)*

Smith, Kaity
Alberta Beef Producers *(21)*

Smith, Karen L.
CCIM Institute *(347)*

Smith, Katherine Jarvis
The Council of Insurance Agents and Brokers *(394)*

Smith, CMP, Kathryn J.
American Association of Neuromuscular and Electrodiagnostic Medicine *(66)*

Smith, Katie
National Lipid Association *(770)*

Smith, Ken
Association of Graduate Liberal Studies Programs *(286)*

Smith, Kendra E.
American College of Osteopathic Surgeons *(100)*

Smith, Kevin P.
Academy of Osseointegration *(7)*

Smith, Kim L.
Institute of Hazardous Materials Management *(500)*

Smith, Kristi
National Collegiate Honors Council *(724)*

Smith, CMP, Kristi
Society of Exploration Geophysicists *(935)*

Smith, Kym
International Academy of Oral Medicine and Toxicology *(509)*

Smith, L. Kim
AHS International - The Vertical Flight Society *(17)*

Smith, CFRE, Laura
National Assembly of State Arts Agencies *(635)*

Smith, Letitia
Young Adult Library Services Association *(1030)*

Smith, CCC-SLP, PhD, Dr. Linda McCabe
National Black Association for Speech, Language and Hearing *(714)*

Smith, Linda W.
National Religious Broadcasters *(785)*

Smith, Lisa
Spray Polyurethane Foam Alliance *(959)*

Smith, Lois
Human Factors and Ergonomics Society *(480)*
Human Factors Society *(481)*

Smith, Loretta
Data Management Association International *(407)*

Smith, Lori Madeline

Technical Association of the Pulp and Paper Industry **(970)**

Smith, Luther
American Society of Agronomy (ASA, CSSA, SSSA) **(191)**
Crop Science Society of America **(404)**
Soil Science Society of America **(951)**

Smith, Lynn
American Foundry Society **(123)**

Smith, CMP, Lynn
Association of Fundraising Professionals **(285)**

Smith, Marcia
American Astronautical Society **(77)**

Smith, Margo
American Society of Law, Medicine and Ethics **(202)**

Smith, Marian
American Crossbred Pony Registry **(112)**

Smith, PhD, Marilyn Dix
International Society for Pharmacoeconomics and Outcomes Research **(568)**

Smith, CAE, PhD, Mark A.
American Society of Hematology **(199)**

Smith, Mary
Association for Information Systems **(250)**

Smith, Maureen
NAFA Fleet Management Association **(624)**

Smith, Maureen
North American Society for the Sociology of Sport **(822)**

Smith, Meg Z.
American Booksellers Association **(85)**

Smith, Michael
National Telecommunications Cooperative Association **(799)**

Smith, Michael
Interstate Oil and Gas Compact Commission **(583)**

Smith, Michelle
Association of College Unions International **(274)**

Smith, Michelle A.
Mutual Fund Education Alliance **(623)**

Smith, Neal
American Jersey Cattle Association/National All-Jersey Inc. **(142)**

Smith, Noreen
American Society of Ophthalmic Registered Nurses **(205)**

Smith, Ollie M.
Child Care Aware of America **(353)**

Smith, Pam
Mobile Air Conditioning Society Worldwide **(617)**

Smith, Pamela
Association of Private Sector Colleges and Universities (Career College Association) **(300)**

Smith, Pamela
National Association of Advisors for the Health Professions **(645)**

Smith, Pamela A.
American Osteopathic College of Radiology **(161)**

Smith, Patsy
American Society of Professional Estimators **(208)**

Smith, Paula S.
Society of Experimental Test Pilots **(935)**

Smith, Peg L.
American Camp Association **(88)**

Smith, Peggy
Worldwide ERC **(1028)**

Smith, Pete
Independent Distributors Association **(489)**

Smith, Peter
Christian Legal Society **(356)**

Smith, Peter
Mathematical Association of America **(609)**

Smith, Phil
United Mine Workers of America **(988)**

Smith, Philip
American Association for Laboratory Accreditation **(50)**

Smith, Randy
PROMAX/BDA **(866)**

Smith, Rebecca
Society for the Preservation of Oral Health **(924)**

Smith, Rich
Alberta Beef Producers **(21)**

Smith, Richard (Dick)
The Masonry Heater Association of North America **(607)**

Smith, Robert G.
American Management Association **(146)**

Smith, Jr., Robert L.
National Association of Passports and Visa Services **(683)**

Smith, PhD, Dr. Robert L.
International Association of Marriage and Family Counselors **(524)**

Smith, Robert Michael
Sculptors Guild **(894)**

Smith, Robin
Council of Administrators of Special Education **(391)**

Smith, Rodney B.
American Glovebox Society **(126)**

Smith, CHMM, CIH, Roger
American Board of Industrial Hygiene **(82)**

Smith, Ron
American Public Human Services Association **(171)**

Smith, Ronald A.
North American Society for Sport History **(821)**

Smith, Sally
International Pet and Animal Transportation Association **(560)**

Smith, CPA, Sam
National Contract Management Association **(729)**

Smith, Samuel Patrick
International Brotherhood of Magicians **(531)**

Smith, Sandra L.
National Association of College and University Food Services **(655)**

Smith, Scott
Accredited Telematics Providers Association **(10)**

Smith, Sean
Association of Science-Technology Centers **(307)**

Smith, Sean
Hearing Loss Association of America **(472)**

Smith, Sean
North American Society for the Sociology of Sport **(822)**

Smith, Sharon
National Conference of State Historic Preservation Officers **(728)**

Smith, Simon
International Society for Respiratory Protection **(569)**

Smith, Simone
National Conference of Insurance Legislators **(727)**

Smith, Stacey
National Association for Court Management **(637)**

Smith, Stephan J.
Association on Higher Education and Disability **(319)**

Smith, Stephen
Technology Services Industry Association **(970)**

Smith, Steve
International Door Association **(541)**

Smith, Steve
Motorcycle Industry Council, Inc. **(620)**

Smith, CAE, Steve R.
American Academy of Hospice and Palliative Medicine **(35)**

Smith, MBA, Steven M.
Association of Residents in Radiation Oncology **(306)**

Smith, Steven "Steve" M.
Society for Imaging Informatics in Medicine **(912)**

Smith, Sue
Conference of Radiation Control Program Directors **(375)**

Smith, Susan S.
National Confectioners Association **(725)**

Smith, Suzi
International Society for Computational Biology **(566)**

Smith, Theresa
American Trauma Society **(217)**

Smith, Thomas
National Golf Course Owners Association **(755)**

Smith, CAE, Thomas
American Society of Civil Engineers **(194)**

Smith, Thomas J.
Airports Council International - North America **(21)**

Smith, Tobin
Association of American Universities **(266)**

Smith, CSCS, MA, Torrey
National Strength and Conditioning Association **(797)**

Smith, Tracy
American Culinary Federation **(112)**

Smith, Verenda
Federation of Tax Administrators **(442)**

Smith, Wade
Air Movement and Control Association International **(19)**

Smith, Wanda Kenton
Sail America **(890)**

Smith, Wendy
Academy Health **(3)**

Smith, Capt. Whit
American Pilots' Association **(165)**

Smith, William B.
Accredited Telematics Providers Association **(10)**

Smith, William J.
Society for In Vitro Biology **(912)**

Smith, Jr., William S.
Association of Universities for Research in Astronomy, Inc. **(315)**

Smith, Yolanda
Appraisal Institute **(226)**

Smither, Aaron
Chief Officers of State Libraries Agencies **(352)**

Smither, BSEE, Brian
American Association of Acupuncture and Oriental Medicine **(53)**

Smithey, Debbie
American College of Emergency Physicians **(95)**

Smithhisler, Peter
North - American Interfraternity Conference *(812)*

Smitley, Vicky
Contract Packaging Association *(382)*

Smoke, Victoria
International Society for Pharmaceutical Engineering *(567)*

Smoot, CMP, Cassandra T.
National Conference on Public Employee Retirement Systems *(729)*

Smoot, Richard
International Society for Astrological Research *(565)*

Smoot, Sean
National Association of Police Organizations *(685)*

Smothers, Lisa Frye
Future Business Leaders of America - Phi Beta Lambda *(455)*

Smrcina, Geraldine
Million Dollar Round Table *(616)*

Smtih, Jean E.
Computing Research Association *(373)*

Smulik, Johnny
American Association of Christian Counselors *(56)*

Smurthwaite, Lex
American Paint Horse Association *(161)*

Smythe, USMC (Ret.), Col. Ana R.
Military Officers Association of America (MOAA) *(616)*

Smythe, Nancy C.
American Cleft Palate-Craniofacial Association *(91)*

Smythe, Jr., William K.
NPES, The Association for Suppliers of Printing, Publishing, and Converting Technologies *(824)*

Snapp, Barbara
Christian Medical & Dental Associations *(356)*

Snead, Rebecca P.
National Alliance of State Pharmacy Associations *(633)*

Snebold, Lorraine
Independent Sector *(491)*

Snedeker, Lee Anne
International Association of Business Communicators *(517)*

Sneed, Peter J.
American Society of Ophthalmic Plastic and Reconstructive Surgery *(205)*

Snell, David
National Active and Retired Federal Employees Association *(629)*

Snell, Roy
Health Care Compliance Association *(469)*

Snelson, Harry
American Association of Swine Veterinarians *(74)*

Snethen, CAE, CMP, Tara
Association for Molecular Pathology *(252)*

Snethen, CAE, CMP, Tara A.
American Society for Investigative Pathology *(186)*

Snider, Beth
Marine Corps League *(605)*

Snider, Emily
Association for Comprehensive Energy Psychology *(242)*

Snider, Jennie
Society of Incentive & Travel Executives *(939)*

Snider, Jennifer
Association of Professional Researchers for Advancement *(302)*
The Association for Nursing Professional Development *(252)*

Sniegowski, Kara
Society of Tribologists and Lubrication Engineers *(949)*

Snipes, Stacey
National Association of Elevator Contractors *(665)*

Snodgress, CAE, Faye
Kappa Delta Pi *(590)*

Snook, Randy
Securities Industry and Financial Markets Association (SIFMA) *(895)*

Snook, Sam
OPERA America *(828)*

Snow, Michael S.
American Hardwood Export Council *(129)*

Snow, Nancy
North American Society for Social Philosophy *(821)*

Snow, Nick
Intercollegiate Tennis Association *(507)*

Snowden, Lee
National Association of City and County Health Officials *(654)*
National Association of County and City Health Officials *(659)*

Snowiss, Sharon N.
Conference for the Study of Political Thought *(374)*

Snyder, Annie
Council of Real Estate Brokerage Managers *(396)*

Snyder, Cindy
Welsh Pony and Cob Society of America *(1015)*

Snyder, Elizabeth
American Fraternal Alliance *(124)*

Snyder, Eric M.
Cantors Assembly *(342)*

Snyder, Erin
Consumer Bankers Association *(380)*

Snyder, MHA, RRT, CFAAMA, Guy
American Academy of Medical Administrators *(36)*
American College of Cardiovascular Administrators *(93)*

Snyder, Jessica
American Nature Study Society *(155)*

Snyder, Katherine Karol
National Association of State Directors of Developmental Disabilities Services, Inc. *(700)*

Snyder, Larry
Catholic Charities USA *(345)*

Snyder, Dr. Lisa Gueldenzoph
National Association for Business Teacher Education *(636)*

Snyder, Mark
Southeastern Theatre Conference *(953)*

Snyder, Martin D
American Association of University Professors *(75)*

Snyder, Michael
National Association of State Chief Administrators *(699)*

Snyder, Mike
Telecommunications Industry Association *(971)*

Snyder, Jr., PhD, O. Peter
Hospitality Institute of Technology and Management *(479)*

Snyder, Seth
Council for Chemical Research, Inc. *(389)*

Snyder, CPA, Terry L.
PKF North American Network *(849)*

Sobczyk, Kevin M.
OPERA America *(828)*

Sobeck, Janine
Literary Managers and Dramaturgs of the Americas *(599)*

Sobel, MD, PhD, Mark E.
American Society for Investigative Pathology *(186)*
Intersociety Council For Pathology Information *(582)*

Sobien, Daniel "Dan"
National Weather Service Employees Organization *(804)*

Sobieraj, James
Licensing Executives Society *(597)*

Soboroff, Ian
Special Interest Group for Information Retrieval *(955)*

Sobota, Lori
Association of College and University Housing Officers-International *(274)*

Sobrito, June Marie
Society of Motion Picture and Television Engineers *(942)*

Soch, Karen
National Genealogical Society *(754)*

Socha, Michael
Adhesive and Sealant Council *(12)*

Sochacki, BA, MS, Stacy
National Association for Healthcare Quality *(639)*

Sockwell, Linda
National Association of Educational Office Professionals *(664)*

Soddy, Brian
AIB International *(17)*

Soehnlein, Kimberly E.
American College of Veterinary Surgeons *(104)*

Soendker, Sandi
Owner-Operator Independent Drivers Association, Inc. *(836)*

Soepangkat, Ina
American Association of State Colleges and Universities *(73)*

Sogueco, Renato Cruz
Society of American Florists *(928)*

Sohl, Bruce
Illuminating Engineering Society of North America *(486)*

Sohmer, Sy
Society for Economic Botany *(908)*

Sohn, Lisa
American Chamber of Commerce Executives *(89)*

Sojourner, Ted
Tube Council of North America *(982)*

Sok, Michelle
American Association of Pathologists' Assistants *(68)*

Sokaris, Louiza
Laborers-Employers Cooperation & Education Trust *(592)*

Sokol, Jacob
American Association of Neuromuscular and Electrodiagnostic Medicine *(66)*

Sokol, Marta
Society for Technical Communication *(922)*

Sol, John
Loan Syndication & Trading Association *(599)*

Solanki, Smita
ASME International Gas Turbine Institute *(233)*

Solarino, Vincent J.
Shipowners Claims Bureau, Inc. *(899)*

Solee, A. Kathryn
National Association of State Aviation Officials *(698)*

Solem, Michael
Association of American Geographers *(265)*

Soler, Eileen
Association of Asphalt Paving Technologists *(268)*

Soles, Jr., Thomas J.
Sheet Metal and Air Conditioning Contractors'
National Association *(898)*

Soley, Richard
Object Management Group *(825)*

Solie, Candice
APCO (Association of Public-Safety Communications
Officials) International *(304)*

Solloway, Earl
Employee Assistance Professionals Association *(426)*

Solomon, Barry
Academic Pediatric Association *(3)*

Solomon, PhD, George T.
International Council for Small Business *(538)*

Solomon, Herbert W.
National Association of Publishers' Representatives
(689)

Solomon, JD, Ronni P.
ECRI *(418)*

Solomon, Whitney
Independent Photo Imagers *(491)*

Solon, Chezka
International Association of Professional Security
Consultants *(527)*

Solorio, Season
Council for Responsible Nutrition *(391)*

Solov, Rachel
Association of Threat Assessment Professionals *(314)*

Solovyov, Elena
International Fragrance Association North America
(547)

Soloway, Stan Z.
Professional Services Council *(865)*

Solsby, Jeff L.
Wine and Spirits Wholesalers of America *(1018)*

Soltis, Rene
The Vision Council *(1010)*

Soltis- Jarrett, Victoria
International Society of Psychiatric-Mental Health
Nurses *(574)*

Soltz, Barry
Automotive Maintenance and Repair Association *(323)*

Solway, Caitlin
Cherry Marketing Institute *(352)*

Somer, Andrew
Direct Marketing Association *(412)*

Somers, CMP, Darlene
National Association of Neonatal Nurses *(682)*

Somers, Deborah
National Fire Sprinkler Association *(751)*

Somers, Jr., Fred L.
International Light Transportation Vehicle Association,
Inc. *(554)*

Somers, Frederick P.
American Occupational Therapy Association, Inc.
(157)

Somers, Nick
National Association of Postmasters of the United
States *(685)*

Somerville, Laura
Institute of Clean Air Companies *(499)*

Somerville, Nancy C.

American Society of Landscape Architects *(201)*

Somerville, Robert D.
American Bureau of Shipping *(86)*

Sommer, Craig
The Association of Collegiate Conference and Events
Directors International *(275)*

Sommer, David
Computing Technology Industry Association
(CompTIA) *(373)*

Sommer, Doris
American Montessori Society *(152)*

Sommerville, William
Vehicular Technology Society *(1008)*

Sondrup, Steven P.
Society for the Advancement of Scandinavian Study
(923)

Song, Min
Association for Asian American Studies *(239)*

Song, Wei
Council of Independent Colleges *(394)*

Sonin, S. Maria
Ethics and Compliance Officer Association *(433)*

Sonnenschein, Bonnie
World Airline Entertainment Association *(1025)*

Sontag, Julie
National Association of State & Local Equity Funds
(697)

Soppelsa, Betty
NAFSA: Association of International Educators *(624)*

Soppelsa, Elizabeth F.
NAFSA: Association of International Educators *(624)*

Sordyl, Douglas J.
American Concrete Institute *(106)*

Sorek, Chris
International Association of Business Communicators
(517)

Sorensen, Ann
American Farmland Trust *(118)*

Sorensen, Bailey
National Association for Fixed Annuities *(639)*

Sorensen, CAE, C. Mitchell
Professional Show Managers Association *(865)*

Sorenson, Tasha
Council of Literary Magazines and Presses *(395)*

Sorgenfrei, Carol Fisher
Association for Asian Performance *(239)*

Sornson, Shawn
Association of Physician Assistants in Obstetrics and
Gynecology *(299)*

Sorrell, Susan Amato
Association of State Dam Safety Officials *(310)*

Sosa, Teri
International Visual Literacy Association *(580)*

Sosby, Brian
United States Equestrian Federation *(993)*

Sosnowski, Andrew J.
National Insurance Crime Bureau *(766)*

Sosnowski, Carolyn
Special Libraries Association *(956)*

Soto, Chris
Land Trust Alliance *(593)*

Soto, Nicholas
Construction Management Association of America
(379)

Soto, Sonia

Society for Vascular Surgery *(926)*

Sou, Leang K.
National Conference of Commissioners on Uniform
State Laws *(727)*

Soucie, Urszula
Railway Engineering-Maintenance Suppliers
Association *(874)*

Souders, Shelly M.
National League of Postmasters of the United States
(768)

Souhrada, Charlie
North American Association of Food Equipment
Manufacturers *(813)*

Soule, David
Railway Engineering-Maintenance Suppliers
Association *(874)*

Soule, Dick
International Association of Privacy Professionals *(526)*

Souliere, Trish
National Collegiate Honors Council *(724)*

Sousa, Lori
The American Institute of Architects *(137)*

South-Winter, Carole
Association of Educators in Imaging and Radiologic
Sciences, Inc *(280)*

Southerland, Mittie D.
Academy of Criminal Justice Sciences *(4)*

Southworth, Jennifer
Osteopathic Cranial Academy *(834)*

Souza, Caryn R.
Association for Commuter Transportation *(242)*
Community Transportation Association of America
(371)

Souza, Richard
Materials Research Society *(609)*

Sova, Jennifer
International Home Furnishings Representatives
Association *(550)*

Sovinski, David
International Masonry Institute *(556)*

Sow, Elijah
Registry of Interpreters for the Deaf *(879)*

Sowell, PE, Urmilla
Glass Association of North America *(461)*

Sower, Suzanne
American Filtration and Separations Society *(121)*

Sowers, Terry
SSPC: the Society for Protective Coatings *(960)*

Soyster Fizgerald, CAE, CMP, Karin M.
American Bakers Association *(78)*

Spada, Alfred
American Foundry Society *(123)*

Spadaro, Mary Bakke
United States Association of Independent Gymnastic
Clubs *(990)*

Spadaro, Paul
United States Association of Independent Gymnastic
Clubs *(990)*

Spaedy, Kerry
Appraisal Institute *(226)*

Spafford, Jackie
Visual Resources Association *(1010)*

Spagnolo, MD, Samuel V.
National Association of Veterans Affairs Physicians
and Dentists *(708)*

Spahr, Brian
SSPC: the Society for Protective Coatings *(960)*

Spahr, Charles
American Ceramics Society *(89)*

Spahr, CAE, Joanna
Society of Nuclear Medicine *(943)*

Spain, Cathy
National League of Cities *(768)*

Spain, Cynnamon
Directed Energy Professional Society *(413)*

Spain, Ken
Private Equity Growth Capital Council *(858)*

Spalding, Malissa
Commissioned Officers Association of the United
States Public Health Service *(368)*

Spalding, Stacy
Neuro-Developmental Treatment Association *(808)*

Spalter-Roth, Roberta
American Sociological Association *(211)*

Spangenburg, MS, RD, Michelle
American Society for Parenteral and Enteral Nutrition
(188)

Spangler, David C.
Consumer Healthcare Products Association *(381)*

Spangler, Rob
National Finance Adjusters *(750)*

Spangler, Scott
Associated Risk Managers *(237)*

Spann, APR, CPRC, Judi
National Lipid Association *(770)*

Spann, William S.
International Premium Cigar and Pipe Retailers *(561)*

Spanos, John
Society of Depreciation Professionals *(934)*

Spar, Edward J.
Council of Professional Associations on Federal
Statistics *(396)*

Sparapani, Tim
Application Developers Alliance *(226)*

Sparhawk, Bud
Science Fiction and Fantasy Writers of America *(892)*

Sparkman, JD, Catherine
Association of Surgical Technologists *(312)*

Sparkman, David
International Warehouse Logistics Association *(580)*

Sparkman, Jerry
National Association of Tax Professionals *(704)*

Sparks, Deborah
Truckload Carriers Association *(981)*

Sparks, Jennifer
Society of American Florists *(928)*

Sparks, Margaret "Peggy"
International Association of Clerks, Recorders, Election
Officials and Treasurers *(518)*

Sparks, Richard A.
IEEE Microwave Theory and Techniques Society *(485)*

Sparrow, Donna
Commissioned Officers Association of the United
States Public Health Service *(368)*

Sparrow, G. Scott
International Association for the Study of Dreams *(514)*

Spassiani, MA, Rachel
American Medical Writers Association *(150)*

Spates, Vanessa
Heating, Airconditioning and Refrigeration Distributors
International *(473)*

Spath, Martie

American College of Gastroenterology *(96)*

Spaulding, Leanne
United States Composting Council *(992)*

Spaulding, PhD, Marc
Association of Business Owners of America *(270)*

Spaulding, Mark
Association of Industrial Metallizers, Coaters and
Laminators *(288)*
Converting Equipment Manufacturers Association
(383)

Spaulding, CAE, Stacy
American Railway Engineering and Maintenance-of-
Way Association *(173)*

Spawn, James A.
North American Corriente Association *(815)*

Spear, Caile E.
American Association for Health Education *(49)*

Spear, Gretchen
American Chemical Society - Rubber Division *(90)*

Spear, Paula Reynolds
American Society of Interventional Pain Physicians
(201)

Spearman, Tyron
National Peanut Buying Point Association *(780)*

Spears, Alice
Women's Business Enterprise National Council *(1022)*

Spears, Hillary
National Association of Councils on Developmental
Disabilities *(658)*

Spears, Jimmie
Cabletelevision Advertising Bureau *(340)*

Spears, Linda
Child Welfare League of America *(353)*

Spears, Valerie
Association on Higher Education and Disability *(319)*

Spector, Jonathan
The Conference Board *(374)*

Spector, Morris
Automotive Parts Remanufacturers Association *(323)*

Spector, Nancy
National Council of State Boards for Nursing *(736)*

Spector, S. Stuart
National Council on Aging *(738)*

Spector, Sandy
Internet Society *(582)*

Speedling, Amanda Tate
Costume Society of America *(387)*

Speer, PhD, Dr. J. Alexander
Mineralogical Society of America *(617)*

Speer, DO, Robert
American Osteopathic College of Rheumatology, Inc.
(161)

Speer, Sandra K.
Brick Industry Association *(335)*

Speers, PhD, Marjorie A.
Association for the Accreditation of Human Research
Protection Programs *(257)*

Speers, Peter
Association of Home Office Underwriters *(287)*

Speich, Margaret
United States Dairy Export Council *(993)*

Speight, MD, Mark O'Neal
American College for Advancement in Medicine *(93)*

Speil, JD, MPH, Steven
Federation of American Hospitals *(440)*

Spellane, James "Jim"
International Brotherhood of Electrical Workers *(531)*

Spena-Bosch, Mary
International Society of Explosives Engineers *(572)*

Spenard, Beth
National Association of Student Financial Aid
Administrators *(703)*

Spence, Janet
American College of Health Care Administrators *(96)*

Spence, Suzanne
National Council of Farmer Cooperatives *(734)*

Spence, Tara
American Beverage Association *(80)*

Spencer, Alanna
American Association for the Advancement of Artificial
Intelligence *(51)*

Spencer, Brian
Waterproofing Contractors Association *(1013)*

Spencer, David
North American-Chilean Chamber of Commerce *(823)*

Spencer, David B.
American Astronautical Society *(77)*

Spencer, DeShuna
National School Supply and Equipment Association
(789)

Spencer, CPH, MD, MPH, Dr. Harrison C.
Association of Schools of Public Health *(307)*

Spencer, Leticia
National Association of Bar Executives *(648)*

Spencer, Lisa
Board of Certified Safety Professionals *(332)*

Spencer, Rachael
American College of Radiation Oncology *(102)*

Spencer, CMP, Ramona
Child Life Council *(353)*

Spencer, Shemika
National Association of State Energy Officials *(700)*

Spencer, Todd
Owner-Operator Independent Drivers Association, Inc.
(836)

Sperati, Shannon
American Society of Consulting Arborists *(196)*
Window Coverings Association of America *(1018)*

Sperlich, CVA, DVM, Liane
American Academy of Veterinary Acupuncture *(42)*

Sperling, Gilbert P.
Institute of Makers of Explosives *(501)*

Sperling, Tanya
Central Conference of American Rabbis *(348)*

Sperry, Keri
American Roentgen Ray Society *(176)*

Spicer, Rebecca
National Beer Wholesalers Association *(713)*

Spielberger, PhD, Charles D.
International Academy of Behavioral Medicine,
Counseling and Psychotherapy *(509)*

Spielvogel, MD, Richard L.
North American Clinical Dermatologic Society *(815)*

Spier, Howard
Academy of Rail Labor Attorneys *(8)*

Spiess, Arthur E.
National Association of State Archaeologists *(697)*

Spiess, Heather A.
American Academy of Anesthesiologist Assistants *(30)*

Spiess, Tom

PSIA-AASI *(868)*

Spilhaus, Karl H.
Cashmere and Camel Hair Manufacturers Institute *(344)*
National Textile Association *(800)*

Spillman, Nathan
Society for Conservation Biology *(906)*

Spina, CAE, PhD, Joseph H.
National Association of College and University Food Services *(655)*

Spina, Nick
American Federation of School Administrators *(120)*

Spindler, Bob
National Council of Postal Credit Unions *(735)*

Spinella, Jeff
Senior Executives Association *(897)*

Spinelli, Emily
American Association of Teachers of Spanish and Portuguese *(75)*

Spinola, Fran
Special Interest Group on Operating Systems *(956)*

Spirrison, Seth
AAGL - Advancing Minimally Invasive Gynecology Worldwide *(2)*

Spitler, Paula
National Cancer Registrars Association *(717)*

Spitzer, Ben
International Brangus Breeders Association *(531)*

Spitzer, Eric D.
Academy of Clinical Laboratory Physicians and Scientists *(4)*

Spitzer, Steve
National Marine Electronics Association *(771)*

Splaver, Ted
American Institute of Oral Biology *(139)*

Sponberg, Adrienne
American Society of Limnology and Oceanography *(202)*

Spooner, David M.
United States Association of Importers of Textiles and Apparel *(990)*

Sporkin, Andi
Association of American Publishers *(266)*

Spracher, PhD, William C.
National Military Intelligence Association *(772)*

Spragens, Lori Cannon
Association of State Dam Safety Officials *(310)*

Sprankle, Kathryn
Association of AE Business Leaders *(263)*

Spratt, Dave
American Neurological Association *(155)*

Sprecher, Mary Helen
Wood Machinery Manufacturers of America *(1024)*

Sprenger, Nathan
National Council for Community Behavioral Healthcare *(731)*

Spriggs, Jill
American Society of Crime Laboratory Directors *(196)*

Sprigler, CPA, MBA, Melaine L.
Construction Management Association of America *(379)*

Sprindzunas, Deborah
Association for Healthcare Resource and Materials Management *(248)*

Spring, Melinda
Supply Chain Council *(966)*

Springer, Alex
Association for Research in Otolaryngology *(255)*

Springer, Alexandra
International Game Developers Association *(548)*

Springer, Jeff
American Gastroenterological Association *(125)*

Springer, Kathy
American Association of Motor Vehicle Administrators *(65)*

Springer, Michael
American Dental Association *(113)*

Springfloat, Shirley
Employee Assistance Professionals Association *(426)*

Springsteen, Art
Council for Near-Infrared Spectroscopy *(390)*

Sprinkel, Elizabeth A.
American Institute for CPCU - Insurance Institute of America *(136)*

Sproat, Kourtney
American Organization of Nurse Executives *(158)*

Sproat, Kourtney
Society for Healthcare Consumer Advocacy *(910)*

Sprott, Michael M.
Food and Drug Law Institute *(449)*

Spruill, Mittie
Textile Rental Services Association of America *(973)*

Spruill, Vikki
Council on Foundations *(399)*

Sprung, Dennis B.
American Kennel Club *(143)*

Sprynczynatyk, Maj. Gen. Dave
Adjutants General Association of the United States *(12)*

Spuhler, Eleanor M.
National Association of Estate Planners and Councils *(666)*

Spurgeon, Sara
Western Literature Association *(1016)*

Spurr, Mark
International District Energy Association *(540)*

Squair, Philip A.
National Propane Gas Association *(783)*

Squiccimari, Larry
Schiffli Lace and Embroidery Manufacturers Association *(892)*

Squier, Suzie
Retail Industry Leaders Association *(884)*

Squillante, Tina
American Society of Transplantation *(210)*

Squires, CFA, PhD, DBA, Jan
CFA Institute *(350)*

Squitiro, Natalie
American Society for Metabolic and Bariatric Surgery *(187)*

Sralla, Rosanne
International Brangus Breeders Association *(531)*

Sreenivasan, Sreenath
South Asian Journalists Association *(952)*

Sroka, Natalie
International Lactation Consultant Association *(553)*

Sroufe, PhD, Gerald E.
American Educational Research Association *(116)*

St. Amour, Lynn
Internet Society *(582)*

St. Gerard, Nneka

National Association of Public Hospitals and Health Systems *(688)*

St. John, CAE, William
Association of Nutrition & Foodservice Professionals *(296)*

Stableski, Robert
NAFSA: Association of International Educators *(624)*

Stacey, Barbara
The Railway Tie Association *(874)*

Stachelski, Kaydene
Audit Bureau of Circulations *(320)*

Stacho, Michelle
Religion Newswriters Association *(880)*

Stachowiak, Kara
International Society of Arboriculture *(571)*

Stack, Anne C.
Council for Affordable and Rural Housing *(388)*

Stack, Lauren
Association of Pool and Spa Professionals *(299)*

Stack, Michael J.
ASIS International *(232)*

Stack, MD, Richard Steven
Society of Government Service Urologists *(938)*

Stacks, Don W.
Association for Communication Administration *(241)*

Stacy, Susan B.
American College of Osteopathic Internists *(100)*

Stadnyk, Sophia M.
International Municipal Lawyers Association *(557)*

Staff, Charlie
Distillers Grains Technology Council *(414)*

Stafford, Beverlee
National Association of Service Providers in Private Rehabilitation *(695)*
National Rehabilitation Association *(785)*

Stafford, Cassie N.
National Association of Black Suppliers *(649)*

Stafne, Marcos
International Museum Theatre Alliance *(557)*

Stagg, Bill
National FFA Organization *(750)*

Stahl, Jr., Jim
International Firestop Council *(545)*

Stahl, Norm
College Reading and Learning Association *(364)*

Stahr, Patricia D.
Society for Maternal-Fetal Medicine *(915)*

Stahr, CAE, Stephen P.
Million Dollar Round Table *(616)*

Staib, George
American College Dance Festival Association *(92)*

Stalder, Susan
Military Officers Association of America (MOAA) *(616)*

Staley, Mary
TASH *(968)*

Stalknecht, Julie
National Multi-Housing Council *(774)*

Stalknecht, Paul T.
Air Conditioning Contractors of America *(18)*

Stallcup, Jackie
Children's Literature Association *(353)*

Stallings, Margaret K.
North American Society for Pediatric Gastroenterology, Hepatology and Nutrition *(821)*

Stallman, Robert
American Farm Bureau Federation *(118)*

Stallworth, Shauna D.
Organization of Black Designers *(832)*

Stambaugh, Perry A.
National Rural Electric Cooperative Association *(788)*

Stamm, Anna L.
Structural Building Components Association *(964)*

Stamm, CG, CGL, Pat
National Genealogical Society *(754)*

Stamm, Shannon
International Association of Ice Cream Vendors *(523)*

Stamp, Larry
American Institute of Inspectors *(139)*

Stanard, Mina
National Parks Conservation Association *(779)*

Standaert, Jan
Deep Sea Fishermen's Union *(408)*

Standley, Laura
Texas Longhorn Breeders Association of America *(972)*

Stanek, Kathy
National Association of Tax Professionals *(704)*

Stanfield, Clara Li
Intellectual Property Owners Association *(505)*

Stanford, Barbara A.
Council On State Taxation *(400)*

Stanford, Greg
Federal Managers Association *(439)*

Stanford, Kelly
National Association of Community Health Centers *(656)*

Stange, PhD, Judy
National Association of Mental Health Planning Advisory Council *(680)*

Stankiewicz, Carrie
American Association for Geriatric Psychiatry *(49)*

Stankiewicz, Ewa
Society for Critical Care Medicine *(934)*

Stanlaske, Dotty
National Association of Elevator Safety Authorities International *(665)*

Stanley, Angela
Water Systems Council *(1013)*

Stanley, Joan
American Association of Colleges of Nursing *(57)*

Stanley, Kathleen
Water Systems Council *(1013)*

Stanley, Lynda
Federal Facilities Council *(439)*

Stanley, Rachael M.
Costume Designers Guild *(387)*

Stanley, Richie
Association of Statisticians of American Religious Bodies *(311)*

Stanley, Teshaka
Association of the United States Army *(313)*

Stannard, Shelia
American Angus Association *(45)*

Stanton, Brent
National Academy of Television Arts and Science *(628)*

Stanton, John
National Structured Settlements Trade Association *(797)*

Stanton, John M.
Solar Energy Industries Association (SEIA) *(952)*

Stanton, Michael J.
Association of Global Automakers *(285)*

Stanton, Scott
International Association of Exhibitions and Events *(520)*

Stanzel, Katharina
International Association of Independent Tanker Owners *(523)*

Staples, Erin
National Academy of Opticianry *(628)*

Star, Jake
LOMA *(600)*

Stare, Diana L.
Institute of Shortening and Edible Oils *(503)*

Stark, Amy
Organization of American Historians *(832)*

Stark, Angie
Selected Independent Funeral Homes *(896)*

Stark, Chad
Optical Society of America *(829)*

Stark, Chris
Path to Purchase Institute *(839)*

Stark, Karl
American Federation of State, County and Municipal Employees *(120)*

Stark, Lauren
Retail Solutions Providers Association *(885)*

Starkey, John
Poultry Breeders of America *(854)*
U.S Poultry and Egg Association *(998)*

Starkey, Keith
Professional Women's Appraisal Association *(866)*

Starkey, Michelle
Association for Financial Counseling and Planning Education *(246)*

Starks, Kimberly
Association of University Programs in Health Administration *(316)*

Starkweather, DTE, PhD, Kendall N.
International Technology and Engineering Educators Association *(576)*

Starner, Ronald
Industrial Asset Management Council *(492)*

Starowicz, Sharon
Orthopedic Surgical Manufacturers Association *(834)*

Starr, Deanne L
Congress of Neurological Surgeons *(377)*

Starr, Denielle
Hydraulic Institute *(481)*

Starr, Jacqueline
International Labor Rights Forum *(553)*

Starr, James L.
American Peanut Research and Education Society, Inc. *(162)*

Starr, Jay
International Council of Shopping Centers *(538)*

Starr, Rhonda
Association of Fundraising Professionals *(285)*

Starr, Scott
Radiation Research Society *(873)*

Starr, Sharon
IPC - Association Connecting Electronics Industries *(584)*

Stasch, Jacqueline
Association of Legal Administrators *(291)*

Stashko, Ed

Organization for Tropical Studies *(831)*

Stasonis, Bob
American Society of Test Engineers *(209)*

Staton, Susan
Association of American Universities *(266)*

Stauder, Jen
Association for Psychological Science *(254)*

Stauffer, Jessica
American Society of Agricultural and Biological Engineers *(191)*

Stauffer, Marlene
PMCA: An International Association of Confectioners *(851)*

Stautzenbach, CAE, Thomas E.
American Academy of Physical Medicine and Rehabilitation *(40)*

Stave, Blake
Association of Defense Communities *(278)*

Staverman, Heather
ASPRS-The Imaging and Geospatial Information Society *(233)*

Staviski, William R.
National Trooper's Coalition *(802)*

Stawarz, Jay
International Cut Flower Growers Association *(539)*

Stawick, Edmund
Chorus America *(355)*

Stayton, H. Grier
Association of American Pesticide Control Officials *(265)*

Steach, Bob
American Paint Horse Association *(161)*

Steadman, Tracy
Association for Clinical Research Training *(241)*

Steadman, Tracy
Society of Invasive Cardiovascular Professionals *(940)*

Stearns, Paul
Gerontological Society of America *(460)*

Stebbins, Chad D.
International Society of Weekly Newspaper Editors *(574)*

Stebbins, Kirsty
National Electrical Manufacturers Representatives Association *(745)*

Stec, Christopher
American Canoe Association *(88)*

Stech, Teri
Pediatric Orthopedic Society of North America *(840)*

Steckel, Anne
National BioDiesel Board *(713)*

Steed, Navar
Society of Biblical Literature *(931)*

Steeg, Rhonda
American Association of Advertising Agencies *(53)*

Steele, Alexis
American Organization of Nurse Executives *(158)*

Steele, Amy
National Ski Area Association *(791)*

Steele, Esq., Brad D.
National Club Association *(722)*

Steele, Dave
International Sled Dog Racing Association *(564)*

Steele, Heather
International Life Sciences Institute *(554)*

Steele, Kathryn

National Hydropower Association *(761)*

Steele, Marc
Society for Ear, Nose and Throat Advances in Children *(907)*

Steele, Mark
Financial Executives International *(444)*

Steele, Dr. Robert
Special Interest Group on Mobility of Systems, Users, Data and Computing *(956)*

Steele, Scott L.
University/Resident Theatre Association *(1003)*

Steele, Susan
Society of Scribes *(947)*

Steele-Browne, Nerissa
American Psychoanalytic Association *(168)*

Steen, Alan
National Cutting Horse Association *(741)*

Steen, Dave
American Maine-Anjou Association *(146)*

Steenshorne, Jennifer E.
Association for Documentary Editing *(245)*

Steenstra, Michael
Dangerous Goods Advisory Council *(407)*

Stefaniak, CAE, Thomas L.
Society for Vascular Ultrasound *(927)*

Stefanini, Leah
Emergency Medicine Residents' Association *(425)*

Stefanoff, Lisa
National Association for the Specialty Food Trade *(644)*

Steffens, Ron
American Neurological Association *(155)*

Steffes, Pete
National Defense Industrial Association *(742)*

Stegeman, Greg
Committee of 200 *(368)*

Steger, William
Collaborative Family Healthcare Association *(362)*

Stegman, Melanie Ann
Federation of American Scientists *(440)*

Steier, Angela
Fresh Produce and Floral Council *(453)*

Steiger, Bill
American College of Physician Executives *(101)*

Steil, Peter
National Council of Real Estate Investment Fiduciaries *(735)*

Steimer, Jamie
National Association for Information Destruction, Inc. *(640)*

Stein, Allison
National Federation of Press Women *(749)*

Stein, Dean K.
American Psychoanalytic Association *(168)*

Stein, Dieter
Linguistic Society of America *(598)*

Stein, Ken
League of Historic American Theatres *(595)*

Stein, Melissa
National Association of County Behavioral Health and Developmental Disability Directors *(659)*

Stein, Norman R.
International Society for Infectious Diseases *(566)*

Stein, Peter
American Podiatric Medical Association *(166)*

Stein, CAE, MBA, Robert G.
American Society on Aging *(211)*

Stein, Stephen J.
Cantors Assembly *(342)*

Steinbach, Dianna
International Sanitary Supply Association *(563)*

Steinbach, Doris
International Society for Infectious Diseases *(566)*

Steinbach, MS, RN, Pamela
American Dental Hygienists' Association *(114)*

Steinberg, Mark D.
Association for Slavic, East European, and Eurasian Studies *(256)*

Steinbock, Anthony
Society for Phenomenology and Existential Philosophy *(918)*

Steinemann, Anne
Fragrance Materials Association *(453)*

Steiner, Betsy
EPS Industry Alliance *(432)*

Steiner, Betsy
Insulating Concrete Form Association *(504)*

Steiner, Bruce A.
American Coke and Coal Chemicals Institute *(92)*

Steiner, Eric
National Association of Wheat Growers *(709)*

Steiner, Jimmy
American Society of International Law *(201)*

Steinert, Ulrike
Kappa Delta Pi *(590)*

Steinhardt, David J.
International Digital Enterprise Alliance *(540)*

Steinhorn, Charles I.
Association for Symbolic Logic *(257)*

Steinman, Susan
American Association for Justice *(50)*

Steinmetz, Joshua
National Tractor Pullers Association *(801)*

Steinmiller, Gretchen
College Savings Plans Network *(364)*

Steiro, Lindsey
International Association of Fairs and Expositions *(521)*

Stekol, Daniel
International Right of Way Association *(563)*

Stelivan, MBA, Starr
Federation of State Medical Boards of the United States *(442)*

Stember, Lee Ann
National Council for Prescription Drug Programs *(732)*

Stemhagen, Kurt
Philosophy of Education Society *(846)*

Stemme, Fred O.
National Corn Growers Association *(730)*

Stenaka, Betty
National Motor Freight Traffic Association, Inc. *(773)*

Stenemann, Keri
National Orientation Directors Association *(778)*

Stenersen, Steve
United States Lacrosse *(995)*

Stengel, Ginny
American Society for Clinical Pharmacology and Therapeutics *(182)*

Stenitzer, George
Business Marketing Association *(339)*

Stennett, Carolyn
National Head Start Association *(758)*

Stenson, Justin
Trade Exchange of America *(977)*

Stenzel, Denise
International Coach Federation *(535)*

Stenzel, Thomas E.
United Fresh Produce Association *(987)*

Stepanek, Richard
National Association of Children's Hospitals and Related Institutions *(653)*

Stepaniuk, Kevin
American Veterinary Dental Society *(218)*

Stepano, Daniel E.
Operative Plasterers and Cement Masons International Association of the United States and Canada *(829)*

Stephen, Chris
National Rural Electric Cooperative Association *(788)*

Stephens, CAE, Angela Moore
American Group Psychotherapy Association *(127)*

Stephens, Benjamin
American Supply Association *(214)*

Stephens, Darrel W.
Major Cities Chiefs Association *(601)*

Stephens, Jennifer
Society for the Advancement of Material and Process Engineering *(922)*

Stephens, Jo Lynne
International Ground Source Heat Pump Association *(549)*

Stephens, PhD, John F.
American Studies Association *(214)*

Stephens, K.W.
International Family Recreation Association *(544)*

Stephens, Larry D.
United States Committee on Irrigation and Drainage *(992)*
United States Society on Dams *(999)*

Stephens, Lisa
Technical Association of the Pulp and Paper Industry *(970)*

Stephens, Princess
The Institute of Financial Operations *(499)*

Stephens, Ruth
United States Industrial Fabrics Institute *(995)*

Stephens, Sherry A.
Petroleum Equipment Suppliers Association *(843)*

Stephens, Sonya
American College of Osteopathic Emergency Physicians *(99)*

Stephens, Toni Messer
Association of College and University Auditors *(274)*

Stephens, Whitney
Precast/Prestressed Concrete Institute *(856)*

Stephenson, Patricia
International Downtown Association *(541)*

Stephenson, Rebecca
Alliance of Claims Assistance Professionals *(25)*

Stephenson, Severine
National Society of Hispanic MBAs *(794)*

Steranka, Joe
Professional Golfers Association of America *(862)*

Stergar, Debra L.
Industrial Truck Association *(494)*

Sterling, Cord
Aerospace Industries Association of America *(14)*

Sterling, Erica
General Federation of Women's Clubs **(458)**

Sterling, Kim
IPC - Association Connecting Electronics Industries **(584)**
IPC - Surface Mount Equipment Manufacturers Association **(585)**
IPC Washington Office **(585)**

Sterling, Lesley
Equipment Leasing and Finance Association **(432)**

Sterman, Deborah
American Public Communications Council **(170)**

Stern, David
Equal Justice Works **(432)**

Stern, David
National Basketball Association **(712)**

Stern, Debbie
Association of Jewish Libraries **(290)**

Stern, MS, Diann
International Liver Transplantation Society **(554)**
Osteoarthritis Research Society International **(834)**

Stern, Jerry
Association of Shareware Professionals **(308)**

Stern, Michelle J.
Post-Tensioning Institute **(853)**

Stern, FAPM, MD, Theodore A.
Academy of Psychosomatic Medicine **(8)**

Sternberg, Rob
Society for Archaeological Sciences **(904)**

Sternicki, Vicky
Society of Economic Geologists **(934)**

Sterrett-O'Neill, Jennifer
National Association of Government Guaranteed Lenders (NAGGL) **(670)**

Sterritt, David
National Society of Film Critics **(793)**

Stertz, Marc H.
National Automobile Dealers Association **(711)**

Stertzer, Jennifer
Association for Documentary Editing **(245)**

Stetson, Karl F.
Wi-Fi Alliance **(1016)**

Stetson, Leah
Association of State Wetland Managers **(311)**

Stetter, Patsy
Associated Equipment Distributors **(235)**

Steukers, Dr. Veronique
Nickel Institute **(811)**

Steurer, Stephen J.
Correctional Education Association **(386)**

Stevener, Sarah
Equipment Marketing and Distribution Association **(432)**

Stevens, Cindy
Consumer Electronics Association **(381)**

Stevens, David
Tire Retread and Repair Information Bureau **(975)**

Stevens, MA, MD, David
Christian Medical & Dental Associations **(356)**

Stevens, David H.
Mortgage Bankers Association of America **(619)**

Stevens, Donna
Utilimetrics/Alliance for Advanced Metering & Data Management Solutions **(1006)**

Stevens, Jr., Ernest L.
National Indian Gaming Association **(762)**

Stevens, Glenn
Automotive Public Relations Council **(323)**
Original Equipment Suppliers Association **(833)**

Stevens, Glenn W.
National Center for Housing Management **(719)**

Stevens, James T.
American Kennel Club **(143)**

Stevens, Leslie
Association for Experiential Education **(246)**

Stevens, Maj Randy
Society of Air Force Physician Assistants **(928)**

Stevens, Melissa
Women's Basketball Coaches Association **(1022)**

Stevens, CEIC, Michael
Conference of State Bank Supervisors **(376)**

Stevens, Nancy
American Association of Meat Processors **(64)**

Stevens, Paul Schott
Investment Company Institute **(584)**

Stevens, CMP, Sandy M.
Society for Maintenance & Reliability Professionals **(914)**

Stevens, Tami
American College of Clinical Pharmacology **(94)**

Stevenson, Allen
International Executive Association **(543)**

Stevenson, Bill
Association of Marketing Service Providers **(293)**

Stevenson, Emily
Alliance for Natural Health USA **(23)**

Stevenson, Jillian
National Agricultural Alumni and Development Association **(630)**

Stevenson, Robin
The American Institute of Architects **(137)**

Stevenson, Sharon
National Center for Homeopathy **(719)**

Stevenson, Terry
National Association of Ticket Brokers **(706)**

Steves, Kirstie
International League of Electrical Associations **(553)**

Steward, David
Association of Personal Computer User Groups **(299)**

Steward, Lisa
Nuclear Energy Institute **(824)**

Stewart, Anna Marie
Society of Government Meeting Professionals **(938)**

Stewart, Audra
Association for Applied Sport Psychology **(239)**

Stewart, Barbara Duffy
Association of American Cancer Institutes **(264)**

Stewart, Bill
Association of Ship Brokers and Agents (U.S.A.) **(308)**

Stewart, Connie
National Association of Foster Grandparent Program Directors **(669)**

Stewart, Dana
American Gelbvieh Association **(125)**

Stewart, Danielle
Public Relations Student Society of America **(870)**

Stewart, David
Association of Independent Commercial Producers **(287)**

Stewart, Debra W.
Council of Graduate Schools **(394)**

Stewart, Denise
National Hardwood Lumber Association **(757)**

Stewart, Edith
National Association of County Intergovernmental Relations Officials **(660)**

Stewart, Eric
American Rabbit Breeders Association **(172)**

Stewart, Erin
American Society of Pension Professionals & Actuaries **(206)**

Stewart, Frank
Forest Landowners Tax Council **(451)**

Stewart, Freda
National Association of Housing and Redevelopment Officials **(673)**

Stewart, Imagene B.
African-American Women's Clergy Association **(15)**

Stewart, MD, James
North American Clinical Dermatologic Society **(815)**

Stewart, Joye
American Academy of Anesthesiologist Assistants **(30)**

Stewart, Krista
American Association of Hip and Knee Surgeons **(62)**

Stewart, Mary
American Academy of Otolaryngology-Head and Neck Surgery **(39)**

Stewart, FACS, MD, MPH, Michael G.
Triological Society **(980)**

Stewart, Michael K.
American Association for Cancer Research **(48)**

Stewart, Natalie
HR Policy Association **(480)**

Stewart, Richard J.
American Academy of Orthopaedic Surgeons **(38)**

Stewart, Santianna
APPA - Leadership in Educational Facilities **(225)**

Stewart, Steve
American Foreign Service Protective Association **(123)**

Stewart, Valeria
International Pharmaceutical Excipients Council of the Americas **(560)**

Stewart-Loudis, Gaye
Cruise Lines International Association **(405)**

Stewart-Winter, Timothy
Committee on Lesbian and Gay History **(368)**

Stibelman, Maria
The National Flute Association, Inc. **(751)**

Stickles, Cindy
American Peanut Council **(162)**

Stidger, Kayla
American Neurological Association **(155)**

Stieger, Jan
DBA International **(407)**
DBA International **(407)**

Stiegman, Rod
Clinical Laboratory Management Association **(358)**

Stiegman, Rodney
American Association of Cardiovascular and Pulmonary Rehabilitation **(55)**

Stika, CMP, Marilyn
Institute of Career Certification International **(498)**

Stiklestad, Lynn
Archery Range and Retailers Organization **(227)**

Still, Carolyn
Perennial Plant Association **(841)**

Still, Linda M.
American Association for Cancer Research *(48)*

Still, PhD, Steven M.
Perennial Plant Association *(841)*

Stillman, Bradley C.
American College of Gastroenterology *(96)*

Stillman, Hal
International Copper Association *(537)*

Stillman, Tricia
Insurance Accounting and Systems Association *(504)*

Stillwell, Cynthia Fritts
International Women's Writing Guild *(581)*

Stilp, Paul A.
Equipment Leasing and Finance Association *(432)*

Stilson, Janet
Media Financial Management Association *(610)*

Stimson, Kay
National Association of Secretaries of State *(695)*

Stimson, Robin
International Society for Performance Improvement *(567)*

Stinchcomb, James
National Organization for Human Service *(777)*

Stine, Sandi
National Cottonseed Products Association *(731)*

Stine, BA, Sharon Hartson
Radiation Therapy Oncology Group *(873)*

Stine, LEED, PE, SE, Tabitha
American Institute of Steel Construction *(140)*

Stine, Vince
American Association for Clinical Chemistry, Inc. *(48)*

Stinebert, Christopher
American Financial Services Association *(121)*

Stinger, Amy
Catholic Charities USA *(345)*

Stinson, Mike
Physician Insurers Association of America *(847)*

Stinton, CAE, Dale A.
National Association of Realtors *(690)*

Stirpe, David J.
Alliance for Responsible Atmospheric Policy *(23)*

Stirrup, John T.
Transportation Intermediaries Association *(978)*

Stites, Anne E.
Search - The National Consortium for Justice Information and Statistics *(894)*

Stivers, Donna
Intersociety Council For Pathology Information *(582)*

Stockdell, Taylor
National Association of Counsel for Children *(658)*

Stocker, Frederick T.
Manufacturers Alliance/MAPI Inc. *(603)*

Stockinger, Charles (Chuck) M.
Chemical Fabrics and Film Association *(351)*
Metal Building Manufacturers Association *(613)*
Power Tool Institute, Inc. *(855)*

Stockman, Brian
American Society of Farm Managers and Rural Appraisers *(197)*

Stocks, Joey
Dramatists Guild of America *(416)*

Stocks, John C.
National Education Association *(744)*

Stocksdale, Joy
Surface Design Association *(966)*

Stockton, Rick
International Association of Medical Equipment Remarketers and Servicers (IAMERS) *(524)*

Stockton, CAE, Stephanie
American Nursery and Landscape Association *(156)*

Stockwell, Mads
United States-ASEAN Business Council Inc. *(990)*

Stoddard, Derick W.
Association of Natural Resource Enforcement Trainers *(295)*

Stoddard, Pamela
Guild of Artists and Artisans *(467)*

Stoddard, Rob
National Cable & Telecommunications Association *(717)*

Stodghill, Paige
International Association of Personnel in Employment Security *(526)*
International Association of Workforce Professionals (IAWP) *(529)*

Stodola, LaVonne
Credit Union Executives Society *(403)*

Stoeckigt, Jerry
Health Forum *(469)*

Stoeckiht, AICI, CIP, Cecelia
Association of Image Consultants International *(287)*

Stoeger, SJ, James A.
Jesuit Secondary Education Association *(587)*

Stoever, Henry
National Association of Corporate Directors *(658)*

Stoffel, Christine
Sports and Entertainment Alliance in Technology *(959)*

Stoger, Phaedre
National Council of State Housing Agencies *(736)*

Stogran, Johanne
The Botanical Society of America *(333)*

Stohlton, John B.
American Association of Presidents of Independent Colleges and Universities *(71)*

Stohner, Esq., George A.
Association of Talent Agents *(312)*

Stoia, Jenna
Association of American Feed Control Officials *(265)*

Stolberg, Adam
Submersible Wastewater Pump Association *(965)*

Stolberg, Carol
Submersible Wastewater Pump Association *(965)*

Stolk, Ronald
American Guild of Organists *(127)*

Stoll, Robert
Power Tool Institute, Inc. *(855)*

Stolpen, Alan
American Engineering Association *(117)*

Stone, Alec
Oncology Nursing Society *(827)*

Stone, Amy
Society of Behavioral Medicine *(930)*

Stone, Andrew
American Ground Water Trust *(127)*

Stone, Brenton C.
Association of the Wall and Ceiling Industry *(314)*

Stone, Cheryl
National Association of Government Guaranteed Lenders (NAGGL) *(670)*

Stone, Denise

American Academy of Podiatric Practice Management *(40)*

Stone, CEM, CPM, Denise
National Parking Association *(779)*

Stone, Jordan
NAGMR Consumer Product Brokers *(624)*

Stone, Marcia
National Association of State Chief Administrators *(699)*
National Association of State Facilities Administrators *(701)*

Stone, Mark
American Association of Physicians of Indian Origin *(69)*

Stone, Mark
International Tax Institute *(576)*

Stone, Michael R.
Belgian Draft Horse Corporation of America *(327)*

Stone, Sherri
Petroleum Marketers Association of America *(843)*

Stone, Sissy
Seismological Society of America *(895)*

Stone-Rogers, Jennifer
Association of Fund-Raising Distributors and Suppliers *(285)*

Stoner, MD, PhD, Bradley
American Sexually Transmitted Diseases Association *(178)*

Stones, Jason
Grain Elevator and Processing Society *(464)*

Stong, Pam
Association of Legal Administrators *(291)*

Stonington, Dan
Northwest Natural Resource Group *(824)*

Stonis, BSN, RN, Nancy
Society for Critical Care Medicine *(934)*

Stoody, John
Association of Oil Pipe Lines *(296)*

Storat, Gregory
Paper Shipping Sack Manufacturers' Association, Inc. *(838)*

Storat, Richard E.
Paper Shipping Sack Manufacturers' Association, Inc. *(838)*

Storat, Wendy
Paper Shipping Sack Manufacturers' Association, Inc. *(838)*

Storch, Maureen
American Apparel & Footwear Association *(46)*

Storey, Amy
CTIA - The Wireless Association *(405)*

Storey, Mark
Society for Neuroscience *(916)*

Storey, PhD, Maureen
American Beverage Association *(80)*

Storie, MS, Misti
National Association for Alcoholism and Drug Abuse Counselors *(646)*

Stork, Dennis G.
AACE International *(1)*

Stormes, Marc
Clinical and Laboratory Standards Institute *(358)*

Storms, Justin
American Guild of Organists *(127)*

Story, Gloria M.
Society for Applied Spectroscopy *(904)*

Story, Ray
Tobacco Vapor Electronic Cigarette Association *(975)*

Stotlar, Keely
National Council on Crime and Delinquency *(738)*

Stott, Suzanne
Academy of Medical-Surgical Nurses *(7)*

Stotts, Michael L.
National Academy of Building Inspection Engineers *(627)*

Stoumen, Elizabeth Julia
International Women's Writing Guild *(581)*

Stoupa, CPA, Steve
American Chiropractic Association *(90)*

Stout, BS, Jessica Romano
Alliance for Continuing Medical Education *(22)*

Stout, Marcia
National Institute of Ceramic Engineers *(764)*

Stout, PhD, Peter
Society of Forensic Toxicologists *(936)*

Stout, Stephanie
Red and White Dairy Cattle Association *(877)*

Stout, CAE, Steven
Hospitality Financial and Technology Professionals *(479)*

Stoutamire, Deborah
National Association of County Intergovernmental Relations Officials *(660)*

Stovall, LaTanya
American Academy of Cosmetic Surgery *(32)*

Stover, Amy
National Association of Intercollegiate Athletics *(676)*

Stover, Carole
National School Boards Association *(789)*

Stover, Dennis
Association of Surgical Assistants *(312)*

Stover, Jean
American Society of Crime Laboratory Directors *(196)*

Stowe, James
Sales Association of the Chemical Industry *(890)*

Stowell, Shannon
Adventure Travel Trade Association *(13)*

Strachan, Dan
American Fuel & Petrochemical Manufacturers *(124)*

Stracher, Patti
Greeting Card Association *(466)*

Strader, Bob
Entrepreneurs' Organization *(430)*

Stramigioli, Stefano
Robotics and Automation Society *(887)*

Strand, Brad
American Association for Physical Activity and Recreation *(51)*

Strand, Jeanne A.
National Council on Family Relations *(738)*

Strand, John
American Association of Museums *(65)*

Strang, Sallie
National Association of Children's Hospitals and Related Institutions *(653)*

Strange, Michael
National Federation of Community Development of Credit Unions *(748)*

Strassel, Annemarie
UNITE-HERE *(985)*

Stratford, Nadine

National Association of Health Unit Coordinators *(671)*

Stratico, Felicia
Hospice and Palliative Nurses Association *(478)*

Stratigos, CAE, Nicholas G.
Label Printing Industries of America *(591)*

Stratman, Christina
Structural Stability Research Council *(964)*

Stratman, Michael
International Brotherhood of Magicians *(531)*

Stratos, Cheryl
Architectural Woodwork Institute *(228)*

Stratton, Bob
American Registry for Internet Numbers *(174)*

Stratton, Bridget
American Health Information Management Association *(129)*

Stratton, Christa
Geological Society of America *(459)*

Stratton, CPA, Iris V.
Food and Drug Law Institute *(449)*

Stratton, Jake
Managed Funds Association *(602)*

Stratton, Mark
Society of Manufacturing Engineers *(941)*

Stratton, Tari
Dramatists Guild of America *(416)*

Straub, Mary
Plasma Protein Therapeutics Association *(850)*

Straus, Daphna
American Kennel Club *(143)*

Straus, Nicole
The Association of International Photography Art Dealers *(289)*

Strauss, Claudia
Society for Psychological Anthropology *(919)*

Strauss, Esq., Stephen D.
InfoComm International *(495)*

Streeck, Frederick
School Social Work Association of America *(892)*

Streeper, Martha J.
Federation of Defense and Corporate Counsel *(441)*

Streeper, Michael W.
Federation of Defense and Corporate Counsel *(441)*

Streepey, Michael
National Association of State Budget Officers *(698)*

Street, Bill
Forest Products Industry National Labor-Management Committee *(451)*

Street, Rene
American Business Women's Association *(87)*

Streeter, Barbara
Association for Child Psychoanalysis *(241)*

Streeter, Erin
National Association of Manufacturers *(679)*

Streiff, Andy
Association for Management Information in Financial Services *(251)*

Streiff, Chris
Society of Mortgage, Appraisal, Real Estate and Title Professionals *(942)*

Streight, David
Center for Spiritual and Ethical Education *(348)*

Strelecki, Heather
American Institute of Graphic Arts *(139)*

Strell, Bruce
Alpha Zeta Omega *(27)*

Strell, Jay
Writers Guild of America East *(1029)*

Streng, Hanna
The International Stability Operations Association *(575)*

Stressman, Karl
Professional Rodeo Cowboys Association *(864)*

Streszoff, Denise S.
American Association for Dental Research *(49)*
International Association for Dental Research *(512)*

Stretch, CA, NA, Dona A.
American Naprapathic Association *(154)*

Striano, Elizabeth
National Association of Clean Water Agencies *(654)*

Strich, DPM, Sheryl
American Association for Women Podiatrists *(53)*

Stricker, Beth
Paleontological Research Institution *(837)*

Stricker, PhD, George
Society for the Exploration of Psychotherapy Integration *(923)*

Strickland, Bryant
Investment Management Consultants Association *(584)*

Strickland, Carla
Commercial Food Equipment Service Association *(366)*

Strickland, Shawna
American Association for Respiratory Care *(51)*

Strickland, Sue C.
American Apparel Producer's Network *(46)*

Stricklin, Gail
American Home Furnishings Alliance *(132)*

Stringer, Elizabeth
Association of College Unions International *(274)*

Stringer, Kevin P.
International Union of Elevator Constructors *(579)*

Stringfellow, CAE, Fred
American Sports Builders Association *(212)*
Web Sling and Tie down Association *(1014)*
Wood Machinery Manufacturers of America *(1024)*

Stripnieks, Aldi
Legal Marketing Association *(596)*

Strittmatter, Aimee
The Association for Library Service to Children *(251)*

Strittmatter, CPA, Scott
Global Semiconductor Alliance *(463)*

Strobel, Eric
Council for Professional Recognition *(391)*

Strobridge, USAF (Ret.), Col. Steven P.
Military Officers Association of America (MOAA) *(616)*

Strodtbeck, Tom
National Business Incubation Association *(717)*

Strohl, Lisa
Association of Opinion Journalists *(297)*

Strokosch, Caitlin
Alliance of Artists Communities *(24)*

Stromberg, Bert
American Association of Veterinary Parasitologists *(76)*

Stromberg, JoAnn
Surface Mount Technology Association *(966)*

Stromberg, Roger L.
Conference of State Bank Supervisors *(376)*

Strong, Amy
National Association of Academies of Science *(645)*

Strong, Beth
Society of Vacuum Coaters *(950)*

Strong, Chris
National Business Aviation Association *(716)*

Strong, Jr., Harold
Association of University Research Parks *(316)*

Strong, Lori
National Association of Biology Teachers *(648)*
Semiconductor Environmental Safety and Health
Association *(896)*
Society for Integrative and Comparative Biology *(913)*

Strong, Mark W.
National League of Postmasters of the United States
(768)

Strother, Jay
International Warehouse Logistics Association *(580)*

Strother, CAE, Lynn
Human Factors and Ergonomics Society *(480)*
Human Factors Society *(481)*

Strother, Sandy
Veterinary Cancer Society *(1008)*

Stroud, Pamela
International Institute of Forecasters *(552)*

Stroud, Shannon
Emerging Markets Private Equity Association *(425)*

Strouhal, Daniel
Arthur W. Page Society *(230)*

Stroup, Jr., USA (Ret.), Lt. Gen Theodore G.
Association of the United States Army *(313)*

Strouse, Susan
Manufacturers' Agents National Association *(603)*

Strowger, Ryan
International Association of Amusement Parks and
Attractions(IAAPA) *(515)*

Strozier, Charles B.
Group for the Use of Psychology in History *(466)*

Struble, Kim
National Association of Counties *(659)*
National Association of County Intergovernmental
Relations Officials *(660)*

Strueder-Kypke, Michaela
International Society of Protistologists *(573)*

Struglinski, Suzanne
American Health Care Association *(129)*

Strunk, Patricia
Aestheticians International Association *(14)*

Struve, Sue
National Assembly of State Arts Agencies *(635)*

Strype, James S.
Institute of International Bankers *(501)*

Stuart, Eric J.
Steel Manufacturers Association *(962)*

Stuart, Greg
Mobile Marketing Association *(618)*

Stuart, Karen
Association of Talent Agents *(312)*

Stuart, R. Scott
National Livestock Producers Association *(770)*

Stuart, Vanessa
International Superyacht Society *(576)*

Stubbs, PhD, Margaret L. (Peggy)
Society for Menstrual Cycle Research *(915)*

Stuber, Laura E.
Crane Manufacturers Association of America *(403)*
Monorail Manufacturers Association *(619)*

Stuck, Janine M.

Council of Supply Chain Management Professionals
(398)

Stucker, Dale
Ethylene Oxide Sterilization Association, Inc. *(433)*

Stucki, Joseph W
Clay Minerals Society *(357)*

Stucky, Stacie C.
American Association of Neuromuscular and
Electrodiagnostic Medicine *(66)*

Studebaker, Chris
American Massage Therapy Association *(147)*

Studelska, Jana
Midwives Alliance of North America *(615)*

Studenmund, Barbara A.
Association of American Law Schools *(265)*

Studney, CAE, MBA, Peter
American Dairy Science Association *(113)*

Stueber, Ross E.
Association of Lutheran Secondary Schools *(292)*

Stuebing, Diane
Recreation Vehicle Industry Association *(877)*

Stuempfle, Steve
Society for Ethnomusicology *(908)*

Stuhlmacher, AP, LEED, Lynette
Association for Preservation Technology International
(253)

Stukey, Richard
Association for Facilities Engineering *(246)*

Stultz, Beth
Pet Sitters International *(843)*

Stump, Leanne
Automotive Oil Change Association *(323)*

Stumpf, Benjamin
Society of Behavioral Medicine *(930)*

Stumpf, CMP, Dominique
National Pest Management Association *(780)*

Stumph, David
American Society for Indexing *(186)*

Stumph, CAE, IOM, David L.
American Association for the History of Nursing *(52)*
Association for Applied Psychophysiology and
Biofeedback *(238)*
Association of Healthcare Internal Auditors *(287)*
Council of Science Editors *(397)*

Stuntz, Franki K
National Ocean Industries Association *(775)*

Sturdevant, Kenton E.
Forest Industries Telecommunications *(451)*

Sturke, Cynthia
Inter-Society Color Council *(506)*

Sturm, Jean
International Federation for Choral Music *(544)*

Sturm, Kathy
Society of Architectural Historians *(930)*

Sturzl, APP, CPM, CPSM, Scott
Institute for Supply Management *(497)*

Stutts, Ronnie W.
National Rural Letter Carriers' Association *(788)*

Stutzbach, Alisa Rata
Music Library Association *(622)*

Stybel, Laurence J.
Institute of Career Certification International *(498)*

Stygar, CAE, III, MBA, Edward J.
American Biological Safety Association *(81)*

Styles, Bonnie W.

Association of Science Museum Directors *(307)*

Su, Brian
Association of Artisan Business (AAB) *(268)*

Su, Yi-Cheng
Chinese American Food Society *(354)*

Suarez, Aquiles F.
NAIOP, The Commercial Real Estate Development
Association *(366)*

Suarez, Maria
American Literary Translators Association *(146)*

Suarez, Ysabel
American Gas Association *(124)*

Suárez-Ruiz, Isabel
Society for Organic Petrology *(917)*

Subbarao, Dr. Saligrama
American Institute of Chemists *(138)*

Suber, Tom
United States Dairy Export Council *(993)*

Sublett, James L.
Joint Council of Allergy, Asthma and Immunology *(588)*

Subramanian, Arthi
Journalism Education Association *(589)*

Substalae, Maggie
American Society of Dermatopathology *(197)*

Suchecki, Joseph L.
Truck and Engine Manufacturers Association *(980)*

Suddendorf, Mike
Association for Medical Imaging Management *(252)*

Sudhalkar, Amruta
ICLEI - Local Governments for Sustainability *(482)*

Sueur, Janine Le
Association of Junior Leagues International *(290)*

Suffern, Erika
The Renaissance Society of America *(881)*

Suffes, Dana
American Society of Heating, Refrigerating and Air
Conditioning Engineers (ASHRAE) *(199)*

Sufka, Kenneth M.
Associated Air Balance Council *(234)*

Sufranski, Bruce
American Society of Safety Engineers *(209)*

Sukup, Alicia
Society of Behavioral Medicine *(930)*

Sulewski, Gavin D.
International Plant Nutrition Institute *(560)*

Suleymanova, Dinara
American Congress of Rehabilitation Medicine *(107)*

Sulkow, Robert
Guitar and Accessories Marketing Association *(467)*
NABIM - the International Band and Orchestral
Products Association *(623)*

Sullins, John
Society for Philosophy and Technology *(919)*

Sullivan, Cheryl G.
American Academy of Nursing *(37)*

Sullivan, Edmund J.
Columbia Scholastic Press Association *(365)*

Sullivan, Edward C.
AFL-CIO - Building and Construction Trades
Department *(15)*

Sullivan, Ellen
Society of Gynecologic Oncologists *(938)*

Sullivan, USA(Ret), Gen. Gordon R.
Association of the United States Army *(313)*

Sullivan, Helen
International Parking Institute *(559)*

Sullivan, Holly
National Association of School Psychologists *(693)*

Sullivan, Isabel "Mimi"
National Wooden Pallet and Container Association *(805)*

Sullivan, Jack
National Association of Television Program Executives *(705)*

Sullivan, Jack
Society of Systematic Biologists *(947)*

Sullivan, John
American Chemical Society *(89)*

Sullivan, Julie
Association of Professional Landscape Designers *(301)*

Sullivan, Kaye
American Public Works Association *(172)*

Sullivan, Kelly
Council for Chemical Research, Inc. *(389)*

Sullivan, Kerry
International Association of Chiefs of Police *(517)*

Sullivan, Kim S.
Event Planners Association *(434)*

Sullivan, Lisa Rose
American Association of Physicists in Medicine *(69)*

Sullivan, Lucy
American Society of Electroneurodiagnostic Technologists *(197)*

Sullivan, Mike
American Society for Therapeutic Radiology and Oncology *(190)*

Sullivan, Patricia
American Society of Dermatopathology *(197)*
Institute of Nuclear Materials Management *(502)*

Sullivan, Robert
American Institute of Organbuilders *(139)*

Sullivan, Rosemary C.
National Conference of Diocesan Vocation Directors *(727)*

Sullivan, Sharon
LeadingAge (American Association of Homes and Services for the Aging) *(595)*

Sullivan, Stephen M.
American Short Line and Regional Railroad Association *(179)*

Sullivan, Susan J.
American Financial Services Association *(121)*

Sullivan, Tanya
Rural Telecommunications Group *(889)*

Sullivan, Thomas J.
Event Planners Association *(434)*

Sullivan, Vance
United Federation of Police & Security Officers *(987)*

Sullivan, William J.
Linguistic Association of Canada and the United States *(598)*

Sumanis, Barbara
Human Capital Institute *(480)*

Sumilas, Giorgia
Retail Industry Leaders Association *(884)*

Sumimoto, Mark
Society of Nuclear Medicine *(943)*

Summers, Allison
Society of Incentive & Travel Executives *(939)*

Summers, Angela
Association of Community College Trustees *(276)*

Summers, Annette
Association of Career Professionals International *(271)*
Cheese Importers Association of America, Inc. *(351)*
Women in Aerospace *(1020)*

Summers, Brian
Construction Financial Management Association *(379)*

Summers, C.J.
American Cultural Resources Association (ACRA) *(112)*

Summers, Donald R.
American Society of Sanitary Engineering *(209)*

Summers, Eric F.
International Society for Infectious Diseases *(566)*

Summers, Rick
Golf Range Association of America *(463)*

Sumner, Curtis W.
National Society of Professional Surveyors *(794)*

Sumner, David
American Radio Relay League *(172)*

Sumner, Robert
America's Natural Gas Alliance *(29)*

Sumner, Sandra
American Alliance for Health, Physical Education, Recreation and Dance *(44)*

Sumner, Vicki
National Association for Uniformed Services *(644)*

Sundaram, Sam
League of American Orchestras *(595)*

Sundby, Janna Sperry
Advertising and Marketing International Network *(13)*

Sunderland, Janice
Association for Hose and Accessories Distribution *(248)*
Fluid Power Distributors Association *(448)*
Security Hardware Distributors Association *(895)*
Wholesale Florist and Florist Supplier Association *(1016)*

Sunderland, John
Pulp and Paper Safety Association *(871)*

Sunshine, CMP, Gail
American Pathology Foundation *(162)*

Sunshine, CMP, Gail
Healthcare Billing and Management Association *(470)*

Sunshine, CMP, Gail
Neuro-Developmental Treatment Association *(808)*

Sunshine, Robert H.
International Cinema Technology Association *(534)*

Super, Tom
American Meat Institute *(148)*
National Chicken Council *(720)*

Supervielle, Joe
Wireless Communications Association International *(1019)*

Supko, Matt
American Booksellers Association *(85)*

Supovitz, Frank
National Football League *(752)*

Suppa, Matthew
Academy of Management *(6)*

Suppe, Frederick
Charles Homer Haskins Society *(351)*

Supper, Bill
Billiard and Bowling Institute of America *(329)*
International Bowling Pro Shop and Instructors Association *(530)*

Surak, Chris
Composite Panel Association *(372)*

Surian, Barbara
American Seed Trade Association *(178)*

Suriani, CMP, Annette
Pedorthic Footwear Association *(840)*

Suriani, CMP, Annette M.
Emergency Department Practice Management Association (EDPMA) *(425)*

Surillo, Samantha
National Association of Minority and Women Owned Law Firms *(680)*

Suritz, Chuck
National Sporting Goods Association *(796)*

Surprenant, Nancy
NAIR -- International Association of Bowling Equipment Specialists *(624)*

Surricchio, Michele
Biomedical Engineering Society *(330)*

Sury, Mark
National Association for Campus Activities *(637)*

Susan, Dr. Alexander
International Isotope Society *(552)*

Susano, Maria
American College of Gastroenterology *(96)*

Suskavcevic, Andrej
Craft & Hobby Association *(402)*

Susser, Peter A.
Driver Employer Council of America *(416)*

Sussman, Gretchen
Women's Foodservice Forum *(1023)*

Sussman, PhD, Joseph L.
Accreditation Board for Engineering and Technology Inc. *(9)*

Sussman, Michael
Strategic Rail Finance *(963)*

Sutela, Pekka
Association for Comparative Economic Studies *(242)*

Sutermaster, Dena Jean
Hospice and Palliative Nurses Association *(478)*

Sutermaster, Sandra
SAE International *(889)*

Sutherland, Laura
National Business Education Association *(716)*

Sutherland, Melanie
National Association of State Mental Health Program Directors *(701)*

Sutherland, Nancy
Substance Abuse Librarians and Information Specialists *(965)*

Sutherland, Tracey
American Accounting Association *(43)*

Sutich, Stefan
National Federation of Federal Employees *(748)*

Sutter, Julie
American Association of Orthodontists *(67)*

Suttles, Jill
Society for Leukocyte Biology *(914)*

Sutton, Beth
American Dairy Products Institute *(112)*

Sutton, Claudia Mansfield
Insured Retirement Institute *(505)*

Sutton, Danita
International Society for Medical Publication Professionals *(567)*

Sutton, CAE, JD, David J.
Scientific Equipment and Furniture Association *(892)*

Sutton, Debra
Entomological Society of America *(429)*

Sutton, Mark
Gas Processors Association *(456)*
Gas Processors Suppliers Association *(456)*

Sutton, Sondra
Petroleum Equipment Institute *(843)*

Sutton, CAE, William G.
Equipment Leasing and Finance Association *(432)*

Suver, Bob
National Association of County Human Services Administrators *(660)*

Suwanski, Dorothy J.
Society for Critical Care Medicine *(934)*

Suyehiro, Kiyoshi
The Integrated Ocean Drilling Program *(505)*

Suzich, Norm
SSPC: the Society for Protective Coatings *(960)*

Suzuki, Takao
IEEE Magnetics Society *(484)*

Svazas, Janet
American Academy of Oral and Maxillofacial Pathology *(37)*
American Society of Business Publication Editors *(194)*
National Retail Hobby Stores Association *(786)*

Svendsen, Eric
North American Natural Casing Association *(819)*

Svendsen, Jan
The Broadway League *(336)*

Svinicki, CAE, Jane A.
Industrial Perforators Association *(494)*

Svoboda, Deb
In-Plant Printing and Mailing Association *(487)*

Svochak, Jan
Contact Lens Manufacturers Association *(382)*

Swain, Amanda
Association for the Advancement of Baltic Studies *(258)*

Swain, John
Association for Asian Performance *(239)*

Swain, Lori
National Cancer Registrars Association *(717)*

Swan, Debra
American College of Nurse Practitioners *(99)*

Swan, Glenda
Professional Liability Underwriting Society *(863)*

Swan, CAE, Sharon J.
American Society for Clinical Pharmacology and Therapeutics *(182)*

Swaney, Julie
National Foundation for Women Legislators *(753)*

Swanhorst, Suzanne
Institute of Makers of Explosives *(501)*

Swann, MA, Amy M.
Association of Reproductive Health Professionals *(305)*

Swann, Bettyjane
National Shooting Sports Foundation *(791)*

Swann, Debra
Society of Cable Telecommunications Engineers *(931)*

Swanson, Chris
National Agricultural Alumni and Development Association *(630)*

Swanson, Emily
Visiting Nurse Associations of America *(1010)*

Swanson, Lisa
Sugar Association *(965)*

Swanson, Lynn
Free Speech Coalition *(453)*

Swanson, Rita
National Association of Subrogation Professionals *(704)*

Swanström, Justin
Coalition of Visionary Resources *(361)*

Sward, Ricky E.
Special Interest Group on Ada Programming Language *(955)*

Sward, Scott
SAE International *(889)*

Swarner, Bill
Association of Home Office Underwriters *(287)*

Swartz, Bridget
Biophysical Society *(330)*

Swartz, Cathy
National Academic Advising Association *(626)*

Swartz, Helen
National Tractor Pullers Association *(801)*

Swartz, Larry
International Association of Milk Control Agencies *(524)*

Swartz, Paul
National Rural Letter Carriers' Association *(788)*

Swartzberg, Murray
WTA Tour, Inc. *(1029)*

Swartzentrover, Kathy
National Truck Equipment Association *(802)*

Swatkowski, Len
Plumbing Manufacturers Institute *(851)*

Swatos, Jr., PhD, William H.
Association for the Sociology of Religion *(259)*
Religious Research Association *(880)*

Swearingen, Gladys
Food Marketing Institute *(449)*

Swearingen, Shawn J.
Messenger Courier Association of the Americas *(612)*

Sweazy, Caleb
The Folk Alliance International *(449)*

Sween, Nancy M.
National Academy of Elder Law Attorneys, Inc. *(627)*

Sweeney, Jerry L.
National Chief Petty Officers' Association *(721)*

Sweeney, Jill
Association for Women in Computing *(261)*

Sweeney, Julie
Housing Partnership Network *(479)*

Sweeney, Kara
National Council for Community Behavioral Healthcare *(731)*

Sweeney, Katie
Coal Exporters Association of the U.S. *(359)*
National Mining Association *(772)*

Sweeney, Les
Associated Bodywork and Massage Professionals *(234)*

Sweeney, Wiiliam
International Union of Journeymen and Allied Trades *(579)*

Sweeting, Terry
National Dance Association *(741)*

Sweetland, Barb
Alberta Beef Producers *(21)*

Sweigart, Nicole
Incentive Manufacturers & Representatives Alliance *(487)*

Incentive Marketing Association *(487)*

Swender, Elvira
American Council on the Teaching of Foreign Languages *(111)*

Swendiman, Steve
National Association of Counties *(659)*

Swenor, Patty
Professional Women Controllers *(865)*

Swensen, Pamela
Executive Women's Golf Association *(435)*

Swenson, Kurt M.
The National Building Granite Quarries Association *(716)*

Swensson, Cheri L.
American Academy of Health Care Providers-Addictive Disorders *(34)*

Swetnam, Terri
American Psychiatric Association *(168)*

Swetnam, Thomas W.
Tree-Ring Society *(980)*

Swets, Bill
International Furniture Rental Association *(548)*

Swets, Mark
Financial & Insurance Conference Planners *(444)*
North American Building Material Distribution Association *(814)*

Swett, Sherry
Funeral Consumers Alliance *(454)*

Swiderski, Jonathon
American Association for the Advancement of Slavic Studies *(52)*
Association for Slavic, East European, and Eurasian Studies *(256)*

Swientek, Bob
Institute of Food Technologists *(499)*

Swift, Deborah
Association of Donor Recruitment Professionals *(279)*

Swift, Dr. Roy
American National Standards Institute *(154)*

Swift, Susan Drake
Independent Sector *(491)*

Swinburn, CAE, John S.
Embroidery Trade Association *(425)*

Swindall, Godfrey
Public Housing Authorities Directors Association *(869)*

Swindells, Janice E.
The Wire Association International, Inc. *(1019)*

Swing, PhD, Randy
Association for Institutional Research *(250)*

Swingle, Ruth
National Association of Church Business Administration *(653)*

Swinney, Kami S.
American Gem Trade Association *(125)*

Swisher, Randi
American Fly Fishing Trade Association *(122)*

Switchenko, Katie
Radio Television Digital News Association *(873)*

Swithers, Susan
International Society for Developmental Psychobiology *(566)*

Switzer, Kristi
The Brewers Association *(335)*

Switzer, Matt
Association for Corporate Growth *(244)*

Switzer, Thomas

American Foreign Service Association *(122)*

Swoboda, Deanna
International Tuba-Euphonium Association *(578)*

Swoyer, Margie
National Pawnbrokers Association *(779)*

Sydor, MaryLou
National Association of Subrogation Professionals *(704)*

Syen, Michelle
Association for Information Systems *(250)*

Sykes, Lisa M.
Defense Research Institute *(408)*

Sylla, Julia
Council of American Overseas Research Centers *(392)*

Sylvan, PhD, Donald A.
Jewish Education Service of North America *(588)*

Sylvester, Diane A.
Society of Fire Protection Engineers *(936)*

Symelidis, CMP, Nicole Kokolakis
Council of American Survey Research Organizations *(392)*

Symons, CAE, Rameka
Association of Private Club Directors *(300)*

Syrenne, Simone
North American Gaming Regulators Association *(817)*

Szabo, Sarah
Consumer Electronics Association *(381)*

Szabunio, MD, Margaret
American Association for Women Radiologists *(53)*

Szafraniec, Alan
National Federation of Priests' Councils *(749)*

Szasz, Patricia
American Association of Intensive English Programs *(63)*

Szczepanski, Chester John
Casualty Actuarial Society *(344)*

Szmajchel, Anna
Refrigeration Service Engineers Society *(878)*

Szmurlo, Cathy
Metal Construction Association *(613)*

Sznaier, Mario
IEEE Control Systems Society *(484)*

Szpak, Carole
National Association of Psychiatric Health Systems *(688)*

Szrom, Edward M.
Institute of Scrap Recycling Industries, Inc. *(503)*

Szurgot, Karyn
American Osteopathic Association *(160)*

Szymanski, Mark
National Potato Council *(782)*

Szymaszek, Charles (Chuck)
The Wire Association International, Inc. *(1019)*

Szyper, Paula
Society for Healthcare Strategy and Market Development *(910)*

Tabat, PE, Lawrence M.
The Concrete Industry Board *(373)*

Tabbot, Milton
Independent Filmmaker Project *(489)*

Taber, John
Incorporated Research Institutions for Seismology *(487)*

Tabor, Sandi
Lignite Energy Council *(598)*

Tabor, Terry
Council of the Great City Schools *(398)*

Taborda, Cynthia
Voluntary Protection Programs Participants' Association, Inc. *(1011)*

Tacheny, Jackie
Power Washers of North America *(855)*

Tackett, Terri
National Association of Development Companies *(662)*

Tackitt, Judy
Association for Educational Communications and Technology *(245)*

Taddei, Dan
National Association of the Remodeling Industry *(705)*

Tadken, Sara
Professional Rodeo Cowboys Association *(864)*

Tadlock, Michael
American Culinary Federation *(112)*

Tadokoro, Satoshi
Robotics and Automation Society *(887)*

Taffel, Lenore
Professional Photographers of America *(863)*

Taffet, Richard S.
Textile Producers and Suppliers Association *(973)*

Taffler, Robin
Work Colleges Consortium *(1024)*

Tafoya, Nicole A.
User Experience Professionals Association *(1005)*

Taft, Charlotte
Abortion Care Network *(2)*

Taft, James
Association of State Drinking Water Administrators *(311)*

Taft, Meg
Aviation Distributors and Manufacturers Association International *(324)*

Tagler, John
Association of American Publishers *(266)*

Tagliareni, EdD, RN, M.Elaine
National League for Nursing *(768)*

Tahir, Rasheed
Federal Law Enforcement Officers Association *(439)*

Tahirkheli, Sharon N.
American Geological Institute *(126)*

Tahtinen, Mark
United States Coast Guard Chief Petty Officers Association *(992)*

Tajat, Peter
Association of Small Foundations *(309)*

Takahashi, Cheryl
Society of Ethnobiology *(935)*

Takeuchi, Lori
Pacific Telecommunications Council *(836)*

Talbert, Leslie
American Academy of Medical Administrators *(36)*

Talbert, Leslie
American College of Cardiovascular Administrators *(93)*

Talbot, IOM, Monique C
Alarm Industry Communication Committee *(21)*

Talbot, Monique C.
Central Station Alarm Association *(349)*

Talbott, Breanne
Roller Skating Association International *(887)*

Talbott, Debra

National Association of Agricultural Fair Agencies *(646)*

Talbott, Scott E.
The Financial Services Roundtable *(445)*

Talbott-Field, Mary
American Association of Legal Nurse Consultants *(64)*

Talentino, Rachel E.
Appraisers Association of America *(226)*

Talis, BA, Natalie
American Holistic Medical Association *(132)*

Tallaksen, Inger M.
Norwegian-American Chamber of Commerce *(824)*

Talley, Jodi
Association of University Technology Managers *(316)*

Talley, Max
American College of Veterinary Internal Medicine *(104)*

Talley, Ric
National Electrical Manufacturers Association *(744)*

Tallsalt, Verna
Indian Educators Federation *(492)*

Tally, Joseph
Association of Mental Health Librarians *(294)*

Tally, Sharon
Journalism Education Association *(589)*

Tally, Susan
National Association of Farm Broadcasting *(667)*

Tamang, Julia King
Learning Resources Network *(596)*

Tamasi, Jessica S.
Powder Metallurgy Equipment Association *(854)*

Tammen, Abby
National Association of College Auxiliary Services *(655)*

Tamminga, CAE, Heather
International Association of Lighting Management Companies *(524)*

Tan, Cecilia
Society for American Baseball Research *(903)*

Tanaka, Greg
Council on Anthropology and Education *(398)*

Tanaka, Kris
Information Systems Security Association *(495)*

Tanaka, Stefan
Conference on Asian History *(376)*

Tanel, Megan
Association of Equipment Manufacturers *(281)*

Tang, Calvin
NACE International *(623)*

Tangwall, Liliana
World Council of Credit Unions, Inc. *(1026)*

Tannahill, Sharon K.
Flag Manufacturers Association of America *(446)*
National Classification Management Society *(722)*

Tannehill, CMP, Lora
American Society of Neuroradiology *(204)*

Tannenbaum, CMP, Gail
American Cleaning Institute *(91)*

Tanner, Barbara
International Nurses Society on Addictions *(558)*
National Association for Health Care Recruitment *(639)*

Tanner, Christine
Construction Specifications Institute *(380)*

Tanner, Mike
United States Trotting Association *(1000)*

Tanner, Ron
National Association for the Specialty Food Trade *(644)*

Tanz, Jayne M.
InterNational Electrical Testing Association *(542)*

Tanzella, John
International Gay and Lesbian Travel Association *(548)*

Tanzman, Howard
American College of Surgeons *(103)*

Tao, Emily
International Alliance of Theatrical Stage Employees, Moving Picture Technicians, Artists and Allied Crafts of the U.S., Its Territories and Canada *(510)*

Taparauskas, Kevin
Association of Certified Fraud Examiners *(271)*

Taplinger, Susan
Direct Marketing Association *(412)*

Tappin, Donna
Democratic Governors Association *(410)*

Tapscott, Brandie
The Institute of Financial Operations *(499)*

Tapscott, Eleanore
American Society of Hematology *(199)*

Tarabishy, Ayman El
International Council for Small Business *(538)*

Tarantino, Dr. Frederick A.
Universities Space Research Association *(1002)*

Tarazon, Jennifer
United States Hispanic Chamber of Commerce *(995)*

Tarbert, Jeffrey
American Public Power Association *(171)*

Taren, PhD, Douglas
Association of Teachers of Maternal and Child Health *(312)*

Targowski, Dr. Andrew
International Society for the Comparative Studies of Civilizations *(569)*

Tarim, Tuna
IEEE Technology Management Council *(486)*

Tarker, Lisa A.
Federation of Diocesan Liturgical Commissions *(441)*

Tarlton, Tracy
National Association for Information Destruction, Inc. *(640)*

Tarnapoll, Murray R
Museum Trustee Association *(621)*

Tarrant, Edward
American Road and Transportation Builders Association *(175)*

Tarricone, Paul
Illuminating Engineering Society of North America *(486)*

Tartaglia, CSP, MBA, Benjamin W.
International Disaster Recovery Association *(540)*

Tarter, James B.
National Defender Investigator Association *(742)*

Tarulis, Jennifer
International Foodservice Manufacturers Association *(546)*

Tarver, Liz
Aircraft Owners and Pilots Association *(20)*

Tarvestad, Anthony M.
American Board of Physical Medicine and Rehabilitation *(83)*

Tashman, Len
International Institute of Forecasters *(552)*

Tastle, Bill

North American Fuzzy Information Processing Society *(817)*

Tate, Leslie
National Motor Freight Traffic Association, Inc. *(773)*

Tate, Pamela
Council for Adult and Experiential Learning *(388)*

Tate, Rose
National Association of Basketball Coaches *(648)*

Tate, Sarah
North American Society for Cardiovascular Imaging *(821)*
Society of Computed Body Tomography and Magnetic Resonance *(933)*

Tate-Beaver, Bette
National Association for Multicultural Education *(640)*

Tatevian, MD, PhD, Nina MD, PhD
Association of Clinical Scientists *(273)*

Taticek, Tiffany
NIBA - The Belting Association *(810)*

Tauriello, David
XBRL US, Inc. *(1029)*

Tauss, Roger
Transport Workers Union of America, AFL-CIO *(978)*

Taussig, Michele
Industrial Research Institute *(494)*

Taussig, Randy
Food Processing Suppliers Association *(449)*

Tauvaa, Junior
Meeting Professionals International *(612)*

Tavara, Janet
Association for Facilities Engineering *(246)*

Tavares, Nicola
Institute of Transportation Engineers *(503)*

Tavora-Jainchill, Barbara
United Nations Staff Union *(988)*

Tax, Richard F.
American Engineering Association *(117)*

Taylor, Alice
Metal Construction Association *(613)*

Taylor, Betty
American Academy of Optometry *(37)*

Taylor, Bonnie
National Systems Contractors Association *(798)*

Taylor, Carrie
American Hampshire Sheep Association *(128)*

Taylor, Charlotte
American Board of Industrial Hygiene *(82)*

Taylor, Christy
International Association of Law Enforcement Intelligence Analysts *(523)*

Taylor, Crispin
American Society of Plant Biologists *(207)*

Taylor, Esq., David
HUBZone Contractors National Council *(480)*

Taylor, Dianne
Council of State Community Development Agencies *(397)*

Taylor, Donna
National Parent Teachers Association *(779)*

Taylor, Earl
Marketing Science Institute *(606)*

Taylor, BA, Felicia K.
National Association of Pediatric Nurse Practitioners *(684)*

Taylor, Gena

National Conference of Specialized Court Judges *(728)*

Taylor, Gordon
Automotive Oil Change Association *(323)*

Taylor, Gray
Petroleum Convenience Alliance for Technology Standards *(843)*

Taylor, ACC, MS, Irene
National Association of Activity Professionals *(645)*

Taylor, J. Stewart
Association of Old Crows *(297)*

Taylor, Jacquelyn
Association of Black Cardiologists *(269)*

Taylor, James C
Academy of Prosthodontics *(8)*

Taylor, Jim
Mobile Air Conditioning Society Worldwide *(617)*

Taylor, John S
National Venture Capital Association *(803)*

Taylor, Leona
Association of Pool and Spa Professionals *(299)*

Taylor, Libby
National Confectioners Association *(725)*

Taylor, Mark
Walking Horse Owners Association of America *(1011)*

Taylor, Mary C.
Library and Information Technology Association *(597)*

Taylor, Melanie
Synthetic Turf Council *(967)*

Taylor, Melisa L.
Racking Horse Breeders Association of America *(872)*

Taylor, CAE, Michael R.
National Demolition Association *(742)*

Taylor, Mike
Solar Electric Power Association *(951)*

Taylor, Noemi
National Association of Division Order Analysts *(663)*

Taylor, Norita
Owner-Operator Independent Drivers Association, Inc. *(836)*

Taylor, Paul G.
American Society of Clinical Hypnosis *(194)*

Taylor, Phyllis M.
Consumer Healthcare Products Association *(381)*

Taylor, Richard C.
American Catholic Philosophical Association *(88)*

Taylor, Scott
Path to Purchase Institute *(839)*

Taylor, Stacey
American Society for Investigative Pathology *(186)*

Taylor, Stephanie
Association of Program Directors in Radiology *(303)*

Taylor, Stephanie
Association of University Radiologists *(316)*

Taylor, Steve
Appaloosa Horse Club *(225)*

Taylor, Susan M.
KWPN of North America *(591)*

Taylor, PhD, Sushma D.
Treatment Communities of America *(980)*

Taylor, Tammy
Conservation Technology Information Center *(378)*

Taylor, Thomas D
Academy of Prosthodontics *(8)*

Tayman, Ava Ann
Society for Gynecologic Investigation *(910)*

Teaff, Grant
American Football Coaches Association *(122)*

Teaford, Jon
Urban History Association *(1004)*

Teague, Carlotta M.
National Council on Radiation Protection and Measurement *(739)*

Teague, John
Society of American Fight Directors *(928)*

Teague, Leslie
Society of Incentive & Travel Executives *(939)*

Tearle, David J.
Gemological Institute of America *(457)*

Tebes, Jacob Kraemer
Society for Community Research and Action *(906)*

Tec, Roland
Dramatists Guild of America *(416)*

Tecle, Menges
Recreation Vehicle Industry Association *(877)*

Tedeschi, George
Graphic Communications Conference of the International Brotherhood of Teamsters *(465)*

Tedeschi, Paul
Association of Volleyball Professionals *(317)*

Tedesco, Tom
Futon Association International *(455)*

Teed, Christine
Cable and Telecommunications Human Resources Association *(340)*

Teel, Brandi
International Municipal Lawyers Association *(557)*

Teel, Leesa
International Association of Drilling Contractors *(519)*

Teeler, Patti
International Brangus Breeders Association *(531)*

Teeler, Patty
Braunvieh Association of America *(334)*

Teeter, JD, Frederick J.
Surface Engineering Coating Association *(966)*

Teeter, Shirley
Surface Engineering Coating Association *(966)*

Tefferi, Esq., Tessema
National Association of Federal Credit Unions *(667)*

Tegge, BS, Tim
National Association of Local Boards of Health *(678)*

Teghtmeyer, Suzi
Council on Botanical and Horticultural Libraries *(399)*

Teich, Albert H.
American Association for the Advancement of Science *(51)*

Teicher, Oren
American Booksellers Association *(85)*

Teichroew, Jean Kaplan
Anxiety Disorders Association of America *(224)*

Teisler, CAE, David
Association for Behavioral and Cognitive Therapies *(240)*

Teitelbaum, Sharon
National Association of Secondary School Principals *(694)*

Tejada, Roma
Regional Plan Association *(879)*

Tekrony, Dennis
Society of Commercial Seed Technologists *(933)*

Telego, D. J.
Environmental Bankers Association *(430)*

Telego, Tacy
Environmental Bankers Association *(430)*

Telep, Judy
Printing Industry Credit Executives *(857)*

Tellez, Augustin "Augie"
Seafarers International Union of North America *(894)*

Tellez, Jose
American Choral Directors Association *(90)*

Telling, Chris
Association of International Education Administrators *(289)*

Tellis, Jeff
Intercollegiate Broadcasting System *(507)*

Tellmann, Ron
Partnership for Philanthropic Planning *(839)*

Tempchin, Richard "Rick"
Edison Electric Institute *(419)*

Tempey, Nathan
National Lawyers Guild *(768)*

Temple, Amanda
Broadcast Technology Society *(336)*

Temple, Elena
United States Conference of Mayors *(992)*

Temple, Nancy
Armed Forces Communications and Electronics Association *(228)*

Templeton, Don
National Association of Health and Educational Facilities Finance Authorities *(671)*

Templeton, Matthew
American Association of Variable Star Observers *(76)*

Templeton, Peter
United States Green Building Council *(994)*

Templeton, Robert
National Association of Arms Shows *(647)*

Tenali, Neel
National Certification Commission for Acupuncture and Oriental Medicine *(720)*

TenBrink, Nikole
Risk and Insurance Management Society, Inc. (RIMS) *(886)*

Tendering, Karen
Automotive Engine Rebuilders Association *(322)*

Tendler, Elain
National Maritime Safety Association *(772)*

Tendler, Elaine
National Association of Waterfront Employers *(709)*

Tenenholz, Drew
International Society for Infectious Diseases *(566)*

TenEyck, Martie
American International Marchigiana Society *(142)*

Tennberg, Chris
Society for Ancient Greek Philosophy *(904)*

Tenny, David
National Alliance of Forest Owners *(632)*

Tennyson, Charlie
Intelligent Transportation Society of America *(506)*

Tenorio, Norman
American Educational Research Association *(116)*

Tente, David
ATM Industry Association *(320)*

Teplitz, Janice
American Association of Oral and Maxillofacial Surgeons *(67)*

Tepp, Brain
Association of periOperative Registered Nurses *(299)*

Tepper, Esq., Alan M.
Tau Epsilon Rho Law Society *(968)*

Terada, Kyoko
Emerging Markets Private Equity Association *(425)*

Terek, Richard
Musculoskeletal Tumor Society *(621)*

Teresi, Christian
Association of Writers and Writing Programs *(318)*

Teresi, Peter
ACORD - Association for Cooperative Operations Research and Development *(11)*

Terhaar, Allen A.
Cotton Council International *(387)*

Terhune, Jan
Child Care Aware of America *(353)*

Termechi, Na'ama
United States-Israel Science & Technology Foundation (USISTF) *(995)*

Termuhlen, MD, Paula
Association of Program Directors in Surgery *(303)*

Terner, Michele
National Business Aviation Association *(716)*

Ternieden, Marie D.
Shelf-Stable Food Processors Association *(898)*

Ternieden, PhD, Marie D.
American Meat Institute *(148)*

Terpstra, Nicholas
The Renaissance Society of America *(881)*

Terrana, Annika
Forest Stewardship Council - United States Chapter *(451)*

Terranova, Thomas "Tom" S.
American Association for Accreditation of Ambulatory Surgery Facilities *(47)*

Terrell, Charlie
National Association of State Workforce Agencies *(703)*

Terrell, Daphne
Infrared Data Association *(496)*

Terrell, Kenneth
Education Writers Association *(420)*

Terrell, Thomas T.
International Association of Drilling Contractors *(519)*

Terreri, Frank
Federal Law Enforcement Officers Association *(439)*

Terris, Bruce D.
IEEE Magnetics Society *(484)*

Terry, Agnes
Visiting Nurse Associations of America *(1010)*

Terry, David
Association of State Energy Research and Technology Transfer Institution *(311)*

Terry, David
National Association of State Energy Officials *(700)*

Terry, Gene
American Association for Paralegal Education *(50)*

Terry, Gisele
International Society for Astrological Research *(565)*

Terry, Karen
Association for Jewish Studies *(250)*

Terry, Kevin

United States Bowling Congress **(991)**

Terry, Kirk
Movement Disorder Society **(620)**

Terry-Sharp, Kathleen
American Anthropological Association **(45)**

Terven, Rick
United Association of Journeymen and Apprentices of the Plumbing and Pipe Fitting Industry of the U.S. and Canada **(985)**

Terwilliger, Connie
Media Communications Association International **(610)**

Terwilliger, Jason
National Tour Association **(800)**

Tesauro, Sue
The International Fluid Power Society **(545)**

Tesch, Julie
ARMA International **(228)**

Teschke, Deborah
International Housewares Association **(550)**

Tesdell, Kerwin
Community Development Venture Capital Alliance **(370)**

Tessel, Natalie M.
Pipeline Research Council International, Inc. **(849)**

Teter, Harry
American Trauma Society **(217)**

Tetreault, Mark
American Federation of Musicians **(119)**

Tetschner, CAE, Stacy
National Speakers Association **(795)**

Tettambel, DO, Melicien A.
American Association of Osteopathic Women Physicians **(68)**

Tetz, Scott
International Truck Parts Association **(578)**

Teutsch, BA, CAE, William J.
Association of Surgical Technologists **(312)**

Tewell, Deb
National Association for Interpretation **(640)**

Thacker, Carrie
American Heart Association **(130)**

Thacker, Jimmie
International Association for Truancy and Dropout Prevention **(514)**

Thackston, Chris
American Bankruptcy Institute **(79)**

Thaler, Nancy
National Association of State Directors of Developmental Disabilities Services, Inc. **(700)**

Thames, Marie
American Indian Science and Engineering Society **(135)**

Thames, Terry Boykin
United States Conference of Catholic Bishops **(992)**

Thanagosol, Rattana
International Association of Counseling Services **(518)**

Tharp, Barbara
Council for Elementary Science International **(389)**

Tharp, Cara
American Dairy Science Association **(113)**

Tharp, Charles G.
HR Policy Association **(480)**

Tharp, David W.
International Association for Food Protection **(512)**

Tharp, Marjorie
National Association of Attorneys General **(647)**

Thatcher, Caroline
Delta Theta Phi **(409)**

Thayer, Jamie
American Medical Student Association **(150)**

Thayer, Jennifer
Audio Publishers Association **(320)**

Theien, Sherry
National Ornamental and Miscellaneous Metals Association **(778)**

Theil, Brian
Oncology Nursing Society **(827)**

Theiler, Michelle
American Society for Laser Medicine and Surgery **(186)**

Theissen, Joe
Voices for America's Children **(1011)**

Thelmo, Joanne
American Cleaning Institute **(91)**

Theobald, Amy
International Society of Arboriculture **(571)**

Theobald, Shirley C.
ASM International **(232)**

Theodore, Michael
Interactive Advertising Bureau **(506)**

Theodorobeakos, Michael
Hellenic-American Chamber of Commerce **(474)**

Theofilos, Angela
American Health Quality Association **(130)**

Theriaque, Tia
National Health Care Anti-Fraud Association **(758)**

Theroit, Diane
National Academy of Recording Arts and Sciences **(628)**

Thevenot, Laura
American Society for Therapeutic Radiology and Oncology **(190)**

Thibeault, Melanie
League of American Orchestras **(595)**

Thibodeau, PhD, Linda
Academy of Rehabilitative Audiology **(8)**

Thibodeaux, Todd
Computing Technology Industry Association (CompTIA) **(373)**

Thielen, Michael B.
Republican National Lawyers Association **(881)**

Thielsen, Marian
American Pet Products Association **(163)**

Thiem, Charlie
Health Care Compliance Association **(469)**

Thill, Janet
Copper and Brass Servicenter Association **(384)**

Thill, Mark
Independent Medical Distributors Association **(490)**

Thiry, Maria
American Association of Textile Chemists and Colorists **(75)**

Thissen, Richard G.
National Active and Retired Federal Employees Association **(629)**

Thocher, Adam
Association of American Geographers **(265)**

Thoma, Joe
Associated Church Press **(235)**

Thoma, Leanne
Cattlemen's Beef Promotion and Research Board **(346)**

Thoman, Leslie

National Dairy Herd Information Association **(741)**

Thomas, Annette
International Association of Electrical Inspectors **(520)**

Thomas, Ashley
National Council for Geographic Education **(731)**

Thomas, Beth
International Concatenated Order of Hoo-Hoo **(536)**

Thomas, Beverly V.
National Independent Fire Alarm Distributors **(762)**

Thomas, Bill
Association of Private Club Directors **(300)**

Thomas, Bill
InfoComm International **(495)**

Thomas, Bob
National Governors Association **(755)**

Thomas, Brad
Enlisted Association of the National Guard of the United States **(429)**

Thomas, Brenner
YMA Fashion Scholarship Fund **(1030)**

Thomas, Caitlin
National Association of Disability Representatives **(663)**

Thomas, Cheryl
Association of State and Territorial Dental Directors **(310)**

Thomas, Chris
National Association of State Election Directors **(700)**

Thomas, Chris
Young Presidents' Organization **(1030)**

Thomas, Chrishelle M.
National Conference of Bar Presidents **(726)**

Thomas, Courtney
Property Casualty Insurers Association of America **(867)**

Thomas, Dana
National Family Planning and Reproductive Health Association **(747)**

Thomas, David
American Dairy Products Institute **(112)**

Thomas, Dawn
National Association for Campus Activities **(637)**

Thomas, Frederick George
National Black Nurses Association **(714)**

Thomas, Gerrie
National Fisheries Institute **(751)**

Thomas, Ingrid L.
American Association for Dental Research **(49)**
International Association for Dental Research **(512)**

Thomas, Jackie
AABB - American Association of Blood Banks **(1)**

Thomas, James
The American Geographical Society **(126)**

Thomas, James A.
ASTM International **(319)**

Thomas, MD, James D.
American Society of Echocardiography **(197)**

Thomas, Jeffery
Special Interest Group for Technology Coordinators **(955)**

Thomas, Jody
International Executive Housekeepers Association **(543)**

Thomas, John
Association of Veterinary Biologics Companies **(317)**

Thomas, Judy
American Association for Budget and Program
Analysis *(48)*

Thomas, Judy
Home Furnishings Independents Association *(478)*

Thomas, Julie
Dental Trade Alliance *(410)*

Thomas, Julie
School Science and Mathematics Association *(892)*

Thomas, Karen Kruse
Society for History in the Federal Government *(911)*

Thomas, Karen M.
Independent Community Bankers of America *(488)*

Thomas, Karluss
Silicones Environmental, Health and Safety Council of
North America *(900)*

Thomas, Karnel
Utilities Telecom Council *(1006)*

Thomas, Kathleen E.
American Nephrology Nurses Association *(155)*

Thomas, Kathy
American Society for Therapeutic Radiology and
Oncology *(190)*

Thomas, Kathy
National Garden Clubs *(754)*

Thomas, Kathy
Society of Chairmen of Academic Radiology Oncology
Programs *(932)*

Thomas, Lilly
Independent Community Bankers of America *(488)*

Thomas, Linda
American Roentgen Ray Society *(176)*

Thomas, Lori
National Association of Intercollegiate Athletics *(676)*

Thomas, Matt
National Academy of Public Administration *(628)*

Thomas, Nancy
Consortium for Advanced Management, International
(378)

Thomas, Peter W.
American Congress of Community Supports and
Employment Services *(107)*
National Association for the Advancement of Orthotics
and Prosthetics *(643)*

Thomas, Ralph D.
National Association of Investigative Specialists *(676)*

Thomas, Rebecca
International Iridology Practitioners Association *(552)*

Thomas, Richard
American Anthropological Association *(45)*

Thomas, Richard
Design-Build Institute of America *(411)*

Thomas, Robert D.
National Concrete Masonry Association *(725)*

Thomas, Roger W.
North American-Chilean Chamber of Commerce *(823)*

Thomas, SPHR, Ronda V.
BICSI *(329)*

Thomas, Rosa
National Immigration Project of the National Lawyers
Guild *(761)*

Thomas, Rose A.
Society of Air Force Clinical Surgeons *(928)*

Thomas, Sarah
National Committee for Quality Assurance *(724)*

Thomas, Scott

Contract Packaging Association *(382)*

Thomas, Sheri
Medical Marketing Association *(611)*

Thomas, Steven E.
American Correctional Chaplains Association *(108)*
American Jewish Correctional Chaplains Association
(143)

Thomas, Susan
American Optometric Association *(157)*

Thomas, Susan
Audit Bureau of Circulations *(320)*

Thomas, Tina
Association for the Advancement of Wound Care *(258)*

Thomas, Yvette
PMCA: An International Association of Confectioners
(851)

Thomas-French, Maria
Medical Transcription Industry Association (MTIA)
(611)

Thomas-Hall, Talisa
Association for Facilities Engineering *(246)*

Thomasell, James D.
Academy of Clinical Research Professionals *(4)*

Thomasell, CPA, James D.
Academy of Physicians in Clinical Research *(8)*
Association of Clinical Research Professionals *(273)*

Thomashower, James E.
American Guild of Organists *(127)*

Thomchick, Evelyn
American Society of Transportation and Logistics *(210)*

Thommen, Brian
American College of Osteopathic Emergency
Physicians *(99)*

Thompson, Alan
National Society of Professional Engineers *(794)*

Thompson, BS, RDH, Barbara
National Dental Hygienists' Association *(743)*

Thompson, Barbara J.
National Council of State Housing Agencies *(736)*

Thompson, Bobette
National Association of Child Care Professionals *(653)*

Thompson, Cecelia
American Botanical Council *(85)*

Thompson, Chant
North American Coalition for Christian Admissions
Professionals *(815)*

Thompson, Jr., Charles W.
International Municipal Lawyers Association *(557)*

Thompson, Charles "Chuck"
Cabletelevision Advertising Bureau *(340)*

Thompson, Cheryl
School Nutrition Association *(892)*

Thompson, CAE, Cici
Worldwide ERC *(1028)*

Thompson, Cindy
Academy of Aphasia *(4)*

Thompson, Craig
Transportation Development Association *(978)*

Thompson, CAE, CMP, David
National Council of Nonprofits *(735)*

Thompson, DeJuana
Student National Medical Association *(964)*

Thompson, Dick
Society for Chaos Theory in Psychology and Life
Sciences *(905)*

Thompson, Dionne
National Alcohol Beverage Control Association *(631)*

Thompson, Greg W.
American Association for Agricultural Education *(47)*

Thompson, I Ling
Outdoor Industry Association *(835)*

Thompson, CPA, James P.
United States Pharmacopeia *(997)*

Thompson, Jill
Association for Applied Sport Psychology *(239)*

Thompson, Jon
Republican Governors Association *(881)*

Thompson, Jr., Joseph M.
Association for Hose and Accessories Distribution
(248)
Independent Sealing Distributors *(491)*
Yacht Brokers Association of America *(1030)*

Thompson, Karen
International Association of Emergency Managers
(520)
National Association of Government Communicators
(670)

Thompson, Karen
International Aviation Ground Support Association
(529)

Thompson, Karen S.
National Association of State Emergency Medical
Services Officials *(700)*

Thompson, MD, Kenneth "Ken"
American Association of Community Psychiatrists *(58)*

Thompson, Kim
United Transportation Union *(1001)*

Thompson, Kristin
Wholesale Florist and Florist Supplier Association
(1016)

Thompson, Kristin B.
Association for Hose and Accessories Distribution
(248)
Fluid Power Distributors Association *(448)*
Independent Sealing Distributors *(491)*
Security Hardware Distributors Association *(895)*
Yacht Brokers Association of America *(1030)*

Thompson, Laura
Packaging Machinery Manufacturers Institute *(836)*

Thompson, Laurie
National Association of Development Organizations
(662)

Thompson, Linda
Council of State Community Development Agencies
(397)

Thompson, Linda
Women Band Directors International *(1020)*

Thompson, Lisa
American Academy on Communication in Healthcare
(43)
American Society of Pediatric Nephrology *(206)*

Thompson, Lisa
National Association of State Procurement Officials
(702)

Thompson, FTA, Livia
National Association of Temple Administrators *(705)*

Thompson, Lonna
Association of Public Television Stations *(304)*

Thompson, Dr. Malcolm J.
FlexTech Alliance *(447)*

Thompson, Marilyn
APA The Engineered Wood Association *(224)*

Thompson, Maureen C.
Association of School Business Officials International
(306)

Thompson, Melissa J.
American Council of Engineering Companies *(109)*

Thompson, Michael
BCA *(326)*

Thompson, Michael "Mickey" O.
Domestic Energy Producers Alliance *(415)*

Thompson, Molly
Council of State Speech-Language-Hearing Association Presidents *(398)*

Thompson, Molly
Security Hardware Distributors Association *(895)*

Thompson, Nanice Noie
American Society for Clinical Pathology *(182)*

Thompson, EdD, FAAN, RN, Patricia E.
Sigma Theta Tau International *(899)*

Thompson, Rebecca
Competitive Carriers Association *(371)*

Thompson, Robin
Association of Litigation Support Professionals *(292)*

Thompson, USA (Ret.), Lt. Gen Roger G.
Association of the United States Army *(313)*

Thompson, Sarah
BritishAmerican Business Inc. *(335)*

Thompson, Shannon Pfarr
Qualitative Research Consultants Association *(871)*

Thompson, Stephanie
Council on Licensure, Enforcement and Regulation *(400)*

Thompson, Steve
National Caves Association *(719)*

Thompson, Stuart
United States Tobacco Cooperative Inc *(1000)*

Thompson, Susan M.
American Academy of Pain Medicine *(39)*

Thompson, (USCG Ret.), Capt. Ted
Cruise Lines International Association *(405)*

Thompson, Tom
United States Marine Safety Association *(996)*

Thompson, V. Bruce
American Exploration & Production Council *(118)*

Thompson, Vince
American Football Coaches Association *(122)*

Thompson, Whitney
American Spice Trade Association *(212)*

Thompson, William S.
Microanalysis Society *(614)*

Thoms, Anna
Society of Economic Geologists *(934)*

Thomson, Chris
United Cerebral Palsy *(986)*

Thomson, Elizabeth
Spring Research Institute *(960)*

Thomson, Jeffrey C.
Institute Management Accountants *(498)*

Thomson, John D.
Spring Research Institute *(960)*

Thomson, Keith
American Philosophical Society *(164)*

Thomson, Pete
American Medical Student Association *(150)*

Thorland, Karen
Motion Picture Association of America (MPAA) *(619)*

Thorleifson, Harvey
Association of American State Geologists *(266)*

Thorman, Judith
International Franchise Association *(547)*

Thormas, Debbie
Association of Legal Administrators *(291)*

Thormeyer, Robert Julius
National Association of Regulatory Utility Commissioners *(691)*

Thorn, Amy Z.
Distribution Business Management Association *(414)*

Thornburg, Erin
InSight *(496)*

Thornburg, Jody
Education Law Association *(420)*

Thornburg, John
National Governors Association *(755)*

Thornburg, Linda
Society of Satellite Professionals International *(947)*

Thorne, Bill
National Retail Federation *(786)*

Thorne, Chris
Beer Institute *(327)*

Thorner, CAE, JD, John A.
American Society of Anesthesiologists *(192)*

Thornton, Annette
The Association of Theatre Movement Educators *(314)*

Thornton, Brian
National Association of Heavy Equipment Training Schools *(672)*

Thornton, Jennifer
Airborne Law Enforcement Association *(19)*

Thornton, Jennifer L.
National Association of School Resource Officers *(693)*

Thornton, Joseph P.
American Medical Association *(148)*

Thornton, Lau'ren
National Association of Free Clinics *(669)*

Thornton, Laura
Association of Children's Museums *(272)*

Thornton, CMP, Lisa
ACUTA - The Association for Information Communications Technology Professionals in Higher Education *(11)*

Thornton, Mark
Theatre Communications Group *(973)*

Thornton, Robert P.
International District Energy Association *(540)*

Thorp, Ellen
EPDM Roofing Association *(432)*

Thorpe, Caroline
Organization of Professional Employees of the U.S. Department of Agriculture (OPEDA) *(832)*

Thorpe, Jonathan
Central Bering Sea Fisherman's Association *(348)*

Thorpe, Ronald
National Board for Professional Teaching Standards (NBPTS) *(715)*

Thorpe, Willie
International Union of Electronic, Electrical, Salaried, Machine, and Furniture Workers-CWA *(579)*

Thorsby, Mark
Human Resource People and Strategy *(481)*

Thorsby, Mark
Metal Framing Manufacturers Association *(613)*

Thorsen, Stevie
American Littoral Society *(146)*

Thorson, Ingrid
Professional Association of Innkeepers International *(860)*

Thorstensen, Liz
International Economic Development Council *(541)*

Thorstensen, Shelley
Society of American Graphic Artists *(929)*

Thorstenson, Luke
Alliance for Regenerative Medicine *(23)*

Thorton, Stephen
EUCG, Inc. *(433)*

Thrall, DVM, PhD, Donald E.
American College of Veterinary Radiology *(104)*

Thralls, Richard
Reserve Officers Association of the U.S. *(882)*

Thrasher, Fred E.
NALP - The Association for Legal Career Professionals *(624)*

Thrasher, Holly
Pi Lambda Theta *(847)*

Thress, MS, PA-C, J. Randy
American Association of Surgical Physician Assistants *(74)*

Thrift, Joe
Napa Valley Vintners Association *(625)*

Thrower, David
Council for Exceptional Children *(390)*

Thrush, Nancy
Tissue Banks International *(975)*

Thuermer, Kitty
National Association of Independent Schools *(675)*

Thull, Karen
Energy and Environmental Building Association *(427)*

Thumann, CEM, PE, Albert
Association of Energy Engineers *(280)*

Thurber, Kenneth J.
Small Business Technology Coalition (SBTC) *(901)*

Thurgood, Meg
National Association of School Psychologists *(693)*

Thurman, Charles E.
Electrical Manufacturing and Coil Winding Association *(422)*

Thurman, F. Anthony
American Guild of Organists *(127)*

Thurman, Kevin
Direct Marketing Insurance and Financial Services Council *(413)*

Thurman, Linda
National Association of Electrical Distributors *(664)*

Thurmon, Tammy
Giant Screen Cinema Association *(460)*

Thurner, Donald
American Society of Plumbing Engineers *(207)*

Thurston, Glenna
International Lactation Consultant Association *(553)*

Tibbals, Stephen
Women in Mining National *(1022)*

Tibbitts, Susan L.
American Association for Public Opinion Research *(51)*
The Society for Adolescent Medicine *(903)*

Tibbles, April
Association for Middle Level Education *(252)*

Tibbs, Drita
American Society of Nuclear Cardiology *(205)*

Tibbs, Judith

Valve Manufacturers Association of America *(1007)*

Tichansky, Peter
Business Council for International Understanding *(338)*

Tick, Dean
American Cream Draft Horse Association *(111)*

Tickman, Marsha
IEEE Components, Packaging, and Manufacturing
Technology Society *(483)*

Ticoalu, Alfred D.
American College of Foot and Ankle Surgeons *(95)*

Tidd, Lisa
Undersea and Hyperbaric Medical Society *(984)*

Tidwell, Claudia
United States Beet Sugar Association *(991)*

Tidwell, Nicole
American College of Emergency Physicians *(95)*

Tie, Sam
United States Tobacco Cooperative Inc *(1000)*

Tieberg, Donna
American Association for Public Opinion Research *(51)*

Tielborg, J. Patrick
Pipe Line Contractors Association *(849)*

Tiemann, Becky
Academy of Hospitality Industry Attorneys *(5)*

Tiemann, Becky
National Corrugated Steel Pipe Association *(730)*

Tiemann, CPA, Alice K.
National Precast Concrete Association *(782)*

Tien, Jackie
Professional Lighting and Sound Association *(863)*

Tierney, Nancy
National Council of Juvenile and Family Court Judges
(735)

Tierney, Shawn
Association for Experiential Education *(246)*

Tighe, Jim
Edison Welding Institute *(419)*

Tigner, Robert
Association of Direct Response Fundraising Counsel
(279)
Direct Marketing Association Nonprofit Federation
(412)

Tignino, Joyce
American Association of Insurance Services *(63)*

Tignor, Keith
Apiary Inspectors of America *(224)*

Tignor, Kimberly
National Bar Association *(712)*

Tilden, Flor
Society of Laparoendoscopic Surgeons *(940)*

Tillack, Mark
Fusion Power Associates *(455)*

Tillapaugh, Tom
National Association of Street Schools *(703)*

Tiller, Lee
National Cotton Ginners' Association *(730)*

Tiller, Michael
Compressed Gas Association *(372)*

Tiller, Michelle S.
International Bottled Water Association *(530)*

Tillett, Laura
Council for Higher Education Accreditation *(390)*

Tilley, Kimberly A.
ASPRS-The Imaging and Geospatial Information
Society *(233)*

Tillinghast, Shelvia (Shelly)
Urban Affairs Association *(1003)*

Tillipman, Harvey
American Medical Directors Association *(149)*

Tillisch, Gwen
National Association of Produce Market Managers
(686)

Tillison, Jim
National Milk Producers Federation *(772)*

Tillman, Bob
ARMA International *(228)*

Tillman, Wallace F.
National Rural Electric Cooperative Association *(788)*

Tillou, Gre
National Educational Telecommunications Association
(744)

Tilstone, David
National Tooling and Machining Association *(800)*

Tilton, Donald
Quail Unlimited *(871)*

Timm, Bryan
American Institute of Organbuilders *(139)*

Timmins, Andrew M.
American Feed Industry Association *(120)*

Timmons, Deborah
American Society for Parenteral and Enteral Nutrition
(188)

Timmons, Jay W.
National Association of Manufacturers *(679)*

Timmons, Richard F.
American Short Line and Regional Railroad Association
(179)

Timmons, Tim
National Home Furnishings Association *(759)*

Timony, Margaret M.
Drug, Chemical and Associated Technologies
Association *(417)*

Timpko, Chuck
United States Dairy Export Council *(993)*

Tinch, Jennifer
National Academy of Education *(627)*

Tindell, Kathleen
Hospitality Sales and Marketing Association
International *(479)*

Tingets, Jennifer
Society for Experimental Mechanics, Inc. *(909)*

Tingley, Staci
Partnership for Philanthropic Planning *(839)*

Tinjacá, Mabel
American Public Works Association *(172)*

Tinkle, Blair
National Association of Attorneys General *(647)*

Tinkleman, MPA, Alan
American Podiatric Medical Association *(166)*

Tinsley, Deanna
American Watch Association *(219)*

Tinsley, CAE, Pete
Association for Information Systems *(250)*

Tinsley, Sharon
National Alliance of State Broadcast Associations *(633)*

Tips, JD, Scott
National Health Federation *(758)*

Tipton, Connie
International Dairy Foods Association *(539)*

Tipton, Jeanna

Delta Sigma Pi *(409)*

Tipton, Ron
National Parks Conservation Association *(779)*

Tipton, Sean B.
American Society for Reproductive Medicine *(189)*

Tirado, CAE, Martin B.
Snow & Ice Management Association *(901)*

Tiras, CMP, Lynne K.
Society for Uroradiology *(926)*
Society of Abdominal Radiology *(927)*

Tisdall, Tony
FAA Managers Association, Inc. *(436)*

Tise, Angela
Financial Executives International *(444)*

Titman, Sheridan
The American Finance Association *(121)*

Tittsworth, David G.
Investment Adviser Association *(583)*

Titus, C. Richard
Kitchen Cabinet Manufacturers Association *(591)*

Titus, Janet
Kitchen Cabinet Manufacturers Association *(591)*

Tizzano, Steve
Association of Home Office Underwriters *(287)*

Toaspern, John
United States Potato Board *(997)*

Toberman, Geri
Council of Residential Specialists *(396)*

Tobias, Karen
National Management Association *(771)*

Tobin, John
Design Management Institute *(410)*

Tobin, Margaret M.
National Coordinating Committee for Multiemployer
Plans *(730)*

Tobin, Paul J.
National Spinal Cord Injury Association *(795)*

Tobin, Paul J.
United Spinal Association *(989)*

Tobin, PhD, Dr. William J.
American Association of Early Childhood Educators
(60)

Tobolic, Timothy
Academy of Breastfeeding Medicine *(4)*

Tocci, Pat
National Wrestling Coaches Association *(806)*

Tockarshewsky, Tina M.
The Neuropathy Association *(808)*

Todaro, Mike
American Apparel Producer's Network *(46)*

Todd, Brian L.
The Food Institute *(449)*

Todd, Kristen
National Private Truck Council *(782)*

Todd, Stephanie
The American Institute of Architects *(137)*

Todd, Stuart
Shipowners Claims Bureau, Inc. *(899)*

Todd, Sue
National Electrical Manufacturers Representatives
Association *(745)*

Todd, Terry
Society of Exploration Geophysicists *(935)*

Todd, Tracy

American Association for Marriage and Family Therapy (50)

Tode, Donna
International Sanitary Supply Association (563)

Toepper, Kelly
Association of Professors of Gynecology and Obstetrics (302)

Toes, James
Security Traders Association (895)

Togliatti, Alan
Society for Simulation in Healthcare (921)

Tohle, Katrina
Asphalt Institute (233)

Toiv, Barry
Association of American Universities (266)

Tokoro, Shoko
Asian/Pacific American Librarians Association (232)

Tokuhashi, Naoki
Sigma Phi Delta (899)

Tolan, Barbara
American Society of Extra-Corporeal Technology (197)

Toland, Sarah
National Tractor Pullers Association (801)

Tolbert, Christina
Commercial Food Equipment Service Association (366)

Tolbert, Jovita
National Association for State Community Services Programs (643)

Toledo-Pereyra, Luis
Academy of Surgical Research (9)

Tolentino, Charissa
International Interior Design Association (552)

Tolino, Sarah
Emdr International Association (425)

Toll, Ray
Marine Technology Society (605)

Tolliver, Denver
Transportation Research Forum (979)

Tolliver, James A.
NAIOP, The Commercial Real Estate Development Association (366)

Tolliver, Lynetta
National Association of Housing and Redevelopment Officials (673)

Tolman, Richard S.
National Corn Growers Association (730)

Tolson, Brianne
National Association of Development Companies (662)

Tolson, CAE, Pamela J.
American Association of Public Health Dentistry (71)

Toman, Erika
Industrial Research Institute (494)

Tomaselli, Marcia
International Association of Forensic Nurses (521)

Tomaselli, Valerie
American Book Producers Association (85)

Tomaszewski, Alicia
IEEE Engineering in Medicine and Biology Society (484)

Tomayko, Larry
Meals on Wheels Association of America (609)

Tomb, Diane Lenegham
National Association of Women Business Owners (709)

Tomb, CMP, Jennifer
National Propane Gas Association (783)

Tomczynski, Linda
American College of Chest Physicians (94)

Tomeldan, Lambert
Golf Course Superintendents Association of America (463)

Tomes, Nancy
American Association for the History of Medicine (52)

Tomkins, James A.
National Association of Urban Hospitals (708)

Tomlin, Valerie
Office Business Center Association International (826)

Tomlins, Leah
National Council for International Visitors (732)

Tomlinson, Mark C.
Forming and Fabricating Community of SME (452)
Society of Manufacturing Engineers (941)

Tomlinson, CMfgE, EMCP, Mark C.
Robotics & Flexible Machinery Tech Group (887)

Tomlinson, CEM, Megan
National Association of Consumer Shows (658)

Tomlinson, Michele
SEPM - Society for Sedimentary Geology (897)

Tompkins, Deanna
American String Teachers Association (213)

Tompkins, Todd
Kappa Delta Pi (590)

Tompkins, Jr., William G.
National Newspaper Publishers Association (775)

Toms, Courtney
Association of Steel Distributors (311)

Tomson, Tracy
Restaurant Facility Management Association (884)

Toner, Amy "Carle"
National Association of Truck Stop Operators(NATSO) (707)

Toney, LaWanda
National Parent Teachers Association (779)

Toney, Dr. Myrna
National Association of State Directors of Migrant Education (700)

Tong, John
National Association of Independent Life Brokerage Agencies (674)

Tongue, John R.
Federation of Spine Associations (442)

Toof, Mark
Neuro-Developmental Treatment Association (808)

Toohey, Brian
Semiconductor Industry Association (897)

Toohey, Michael J.
Waterways Council, Inc. (1014)

Tooker, Lisa
National Marine Educators Association (771)

Toombs, Debi
American Society for Aesthetic Plastic Surgery (180)

Toombs, Susan
Women's International Network of Utility Professionals (1023)

Topp, Michael T.
Society of Industrial and Office Realtors (939)

Torbert, Frank L.
National Council of Minorities in Energy (735)

Torda, Phyllis
National Committee for Quality Assurance (724)

Torma, Carolyn

American Planning Association (166)

Tormoehlen, Roger
American Association for Agricultural Education (47)

Toro, Nilda
Scoliosis Research Society (893)

Toronto, Shannon
The Philanthropy Roundtable (846)

Torrance, Gaye L.
Mortgage Insurance Companies of America (619)

Torre, Mel
American Society of Mechanical Engineers (ASME) (203)

Torres, PhD, Alicia
American Educational Research Association (116)

Torres, Amada
National Association of Independent Schools (675)

Torres, Claudia L.
National Hispanic Corporate Council (759)

Torres, Emily
National Ski Area Association (791)

Torres, Manuel
National Association of Black Accountants, Inc. (648)

Torres, Richelle
Association for Radiological and Imaging Nursing (255)

Torres-Sobers, Celia
National Association for Bilingual Education (636)

Torreson, Jeff
International Association for Impact Assessment (513)

Torrey, Michael K.
Crop Insurance Research Bureau (404)

Torrez, Adria
Association of Woodworking and Furnishings Suppliers (318)

Torrez, Sam
American Society of Radiologic Technologists (208)

Toscano, Michael
Association for Unmanned Vehicle Systems International (261)

Toscas, PE, James G.
Precast/Prestressed Concrete Institute (856)

Toscas, Mariana
Institute of Real Estate Management (503)

Toso, Tavi
Council of Residential Specialists (396)

Toth, Christopher
National Association of Attorneys General (647)

Toth, Dr. Delphi
Lipizzan Association of North America (599)

Toth, Jenny
Brain Injury Association of America (334)

Toth, Lisa
International Interior Design Association (552)

Toth, Max
American Society of Master Dental Technologists (202)

Toth, Nadege
American Society for Histocompatibility and Immunogenetics (185)

Toth, Nadège
Association for Accounting Marketing (238)

Toth, Simone
American Society of Military Comptrollers (203)

Totilo, Michelle
Ethics and Compliance Officer Association (433)

Totzke, Becci

American Peptide Society *(163)*

Tough, Dave
Music and Entertainment Industry Educators
Association *(622)*

Touhill, Nancy
PCIA - The Wireless Infrastructure Association *(840)*

Touney, Jan
Associated Press Managing Editors *(237)*

Toussaint, Jason
World Gold Trust Services *(1026)*

Tovey, Pat
Pet Food Institute *(842)*

Towfigh, Payam
Polyurethane Manufacturers Association *(852)*

Towle, John
Performance Warehouse Association *(841)*

Towner, Jacque
American Water Resources Association *(220)*

Townes, Michele
Air Traffic Control Association *(19)*

Townes, Nancy
The National Association for Music Education
(Formerly MENC) *(641)*

Towns, Crystal
American Crystallographic Association *(112)*

Towns, Pamela R.
National Institute of Building Sciences *(764)*

Townsend, Dabney
American Society for Aesthetics *(180)*

Townsend, Robert B.
American Historical Association *(131)*

Townsley, Simon C.
International Association of Women Police *(529)*

Towse, Yvonne
AVS: Science and Technology of Materials, Interfaces,
and Processing *(325)*

Towson, Heath
Percussive Arts Society *(841)*

Tracey, Ed
Plastic Surgery Research Council *(850)*

Tracey, CAE, Jack
National Automotive Finance Association *(711)*
National Vehicle Leasing Association *(803)*

Tracey, CAE, Terri
Institute for Supply Management *(497)*

Trachtenberg, MS, Robert M.
National Association of Healthcare Education Centers
(671)

Tracy, Alan T.
United States Wheat Associates, Inc. *(1000)*

Tracy, CMP, CMM, Cara
National Speakers Association *(795)*

Tracy, Dr. John C.
National Institute for Water Resources *(766)*

Tracy, Karen
American Pharmacists Association *(163)*

Tracy, Karen K.
Academy of Pharmaceutical Research and Science *(8)*

Tracy, Lauren
Ocean Research & Conservation Association *(826)*

Tracy, Linda
Association of Pedestrian and Bicycle Professionals
(298)

Tracy, Richard
Global Cold Chain Alliance *(462)*

Tracz, Will
Special Interest Group on Software Engineering *(956)*

Trader, Barbara
TASH *(968)*

Tradewell, Steve
Napa Valley Vintners Association *(625)*

Traetow, CPA, MAc, Laurie
American Society of Bariatric Physicians *(193)*

Tragethon, Don
Refrigerating Engineers and Technicians Association
(878)

Tragethon, Jan
Refrigerating Engineers and Technicians Association
(878)

Trahan Rieger, Paula
Oncology Nursing Society *(827)*

Traiger, Lisa
Dance/USA *(406)*

Trainer, Lyn
Information Systems Security Association *(495)*

Trainer, Ryan T.
International Sleep Products Association *(565)*

Trainor, Megan
National Association of Mutual Insurance Companies
(681)

Trainor, Sonja
National School Boards Association *(789)*

Traister, Rob
Security Industry Association *(895)*

Trajkovic, Ljiljana
Man and Cybernetics Systems Society *(602)*

Trajkovic, Ljiljana
Man and Cybernetics Systems Society *(602)*

Tramantano, Michelle
Photoimaging Manufacturers and Distributors
Association *(846)*

Tran, Hoang-Tram
The Association of Women in International Trade *(317)*

Tran, Jennifer
International College of Surgeons *(535)*

Tran, Meghan
Commodity Markets Council *(368)*

Trant, Joan
International Association of Microfinance Investors
(524)

Trapp, Norm
Quality Bakers of America Cooperative *(871)*

Trasatti, Rose
National Association of Public Health Statistics and
Information Systems *(642)*

Trask, Susan
COLA *(362)*

Tratensek, Dan
North American Retail Hardware Association *(820)*

Trauger, Joe
Council of Manufacturing Associations *(395)*

Trauth, Stanley E.
The Herpetologists' League *(474)*

Trautwein, Paul
Evangelical Church Library Association *(434)*

Traver, Jeffery H.
AMT - The Association For Manufacturing Technology
(222)

Traver, Kevin
Navy League of the United States *(807)*

Traver, Tracie
Cleveland Bay Horse Society of North America *(358)*

Travers, Joe
Association for Chemoreception Sciences *(241)*

Traverse, Maureen
Direct Care Alliance *(412)*

Travis, Emily
Association of Performing Arts Presenters *(298)*

Travis, Irene
American Society for Information Science and
Technology *(186)*

Travis, Nancy
The Association of Women in International Trade *(317)*

Travis, Pat
National Military Family Association, Inc. *(772)*

Travis, Robert
Independent Pilots Association *(491)*

Travis, Sheila
National Association of Certified Valuation Analysts
(652)

Travis, MD, William D.
Fleischner Society *(447)*

Traxler, Sallie
Association of College and University Housing
Officers-International *(274)*

Traylor, Julie
National Association of College Stores *(655)*

Traylor, Steve
National Association of Telecommunications Officers
and Advisors *(705)*

Treadway, CPA, Anne
The New Media Consortium *(809)*

Treadway, Barbara
Association of Diving Contractors International *(279)*

Treadway, Don
American Quarter Horse Association *(172)*

Treby, Jill
American Geophysical Union *(126)*

Trecartin, Cathy
Travel Goods Association *(979)*

Tredwell, Jennifer
National Comprehensive Cancer Network *(725)*

Tredwell, Pete
United States Bowling Congress *(991)*

Treece, Joan
Employee Assistance Professionals Association *(426)*

Treiber, Jane
International Door Association *(541)*

Treichel, Janet M.
National Association for Business Teacher Education
(636)
National Business Education Association *(716)*

Treisman, PhD, Jessica E
The Harvey Society *(469)*

Tremain, Scott
National BioDiesel Board *(713)*

Tremel, Frank
American Cream Draft Horse Association *(111)*

Trentham, Barbara
The Society of Naval Architects and Marine Engineers
(942)

Trentham-Dietz, PhD, Amy
American Society of Preventive Oncology *(208)*

Trenti, JD, Nancy R.
National Association of Psychiatric Health Systems
(688)

Tresky, MA, Peggy
American Podiatric Medical Association *(166)*

Trevino, Jaime
American Association for Accreditation of Ambulatory Surgery Facilities *(47)*

Trewhella, Jean
IEEE Components, Packaging, and Manufacturing Technology Society *(483)*

Trewin, Shari
Special Interest Group on Accessible Computing *(955)*

Trey, Liza
Association of Corporate Counsel *(277)*

Treyens, Cliff
National Ground Water Association *(756)*

Tribble, Dr. Romie
National Economic Association *(744)*

Triebwasser, James
National Association of Agriculture Employees *(646)*

Trien, Susan
The Association for the Study of Play *(260)*

Trim, Pamela J.
American Board of Industrial Hygiene *(82)*

Trimarchi, CAE, MEM, Lori
Cocoa Merchants' Association of America *(361)*

Trimble, RPSGT, Melinda
American Association of Sleep Technologists *(73)*

Trimillos, Ricardo
Society for Asian Music *(904)*

Trimmer, Carol
National Reining Horse Association *(785)*

Trimmer, Joy
American Academy of Otolaryngology-Head and Neck Surgery *(39)*

Trimyer, Meaghan
American Psychiatric Nurses Association *(168)*

Trine, Cheryl L.
American Ornithologists' Union *(158)*

Trinidad, Amy
American Sheep Industry Association *(178)*

Triolo, Esq., Priscilla J.
Professional Women in Construction *(866)*

Trippler, Aaron K.
American Industrial Hygiene Association *(135)*

Tristan, Vicky
United States Professional Tennis Association *(998)*

Tristani, Nina
American Public Health Association *(171)*

Tristano, Keith
Council of Residential Specialists *(396)*

Trittipoe, Ben
Automotive Maintenance and Repair Association *(323)*

Tritton, Tom
Chemical Heritage Foundation *(351)*

Trivette, Amy
American Association of Airport Executives *(53)*

Troiano, Amy L.
Self-Insurance Institute of America, Inc. *(896)*

Troike, Michael
American Society of Extra-Corporeal Technology *(197)*

Troilo, Adrianne
Society for Neuroscience *(916)*

Trojan, Robert
Commercial Finance Association *(366)*

Trojano, Kate
Academy of Applied Science *(4)*

Trombino, CAE, C. James
APMI International *(225)*
Metal Powder Industries Federation *(613)*
Powder Metallurgy Equipment Association *(854)*
Powder Metallurgy Parts Association *(854)*
Refractory Metals Association *(878)*

Tronchetti, Roberto
International Golf Associates *(548)*

Trope, Jack F.
Association on American Indian Affairs *(319)*

Trope, Jim
TESOL International Association *(971)*

Trosin, Thomas N.
American Farrier's Association *(118)*

Trostle, Karen
National Marine Bankers Association *(771)*

Trota, Michi
American Dental Assistants Association *(113)*

Trotman, Stephen D.
Competitive Telecommunications Association *(371)*

Trott, Roger
Society of Former Special Agents of the Federal Bureau of Investigation *(937)*

Trotter, Margaret
Society for Clinical Data Management *(906)*

Trouten, Doug
Evangelical Press Association *(434)*

Trouten, Lis
Evangelical Press Association *(434)*

Troutman, Douglas M.
American Cleaning Institute *(91)*

Troutt, Chris
International Association of Certified Thermographers *(517)*

Trowbridge, Hannah
Society of Broadcast Engineers *(931)*

Trownsell, Ann
Mason Contractors Association of America *(607)*

Troxel, David
Computer Measurement Group *(372)*

Troy, Donna Grace
Catholic Health Association of the United States *(345)*

Troyan, Danielle
Business Higher Education Forum *(339)*

Troyer, Heather
Delta Sigma Pi *(409)*

Troyer, Joy
Seismological Society of America *(895)*

Trudeau, Paul
National Alliance of Preservation Commissions *(633)*

Trueblood, Debbie
Society of Vertebrate Paleontology *(950)*

Truesdale, Susan
National Association of Active Investment Managers *(645)*

Truitt, Alexis
American Alliance for Theatre and Education *(44)*

Truitt, Dr. Gordon E.
National Association of Pastoral Musicians *(683)*

Truitt, Rhonda
National Auctioneers Association *(711)*

Trujillo, Daniel
National Association of Counsel for Children *(658)*

Trujillo, Mitch
International Police Mountain Bike Association *(561)*

Trull, Frankie L
National Association for Biomedical Research *(636)*

Truman, Elaine
Professional Picture Framers Association *(864)*

Trumbull, David
National Textile Association *(800)*

Trumka, Richard L.
AFL-CIO (American Federation of Labor and Congress of Industrial Organizations) *(14)*
American Federation of Labor & Congress of Industrial Organizations *(119)*

Trummel, Linda
National Association of Orthopedic Nurses *(683)*

Trump, Kati
Professional Housing Management Association *(862)*

Trumpeter, Janice
American Animal Hospital Association *(45)*

Truncale, CAE, Joseph P.
National Association for Printing Leadership *(641)*

Trunzo, Janet
Advanced Medical Technology Association (AdvaMed) *(13)*

Truong, Hang
American College of Radiology *(102)*

Trusiak, Lori
Healthcare Financial Management Association *(471)*

Trusko, Kirsten
Network Branded Prepaid Card Association *(808)*

Truslow, III, Henry
National Textile Association *(800)*

Trust, CAE, David
Professional Photographers of America *(863)*

Tryon, Sharon L.
Mathematical Association of America *(609)*

Tsai, Sharlyne
American Society of Appraisers *(192)*

Tsegaye, Sihin
POPAI The Global Association for Marketing at Retail *(852)*

Tsimis, George J.
Shipowners Claims Bureau, Inc. *(899)*

Tsirpanlis, Constantine N.
American Institute for Patristic and Byzantine Studies *(136)*

Tsoflias, Sarah Lindsay
International Association of Geophysical Contractors *(522)*

Tu, Janice
United States Pan Asian American Chamber of Commerce *(997)*

Tubb, Michelle
Society for the Advancement of Material and Process Engineering *(922)*

Tucci, MD, Debara L.
American Otological Society *(161)*

Tuccitto, Joe
Flexographic Technical Association *(447)*

Tucher, Andie
Society of American Historians *(929)*

Tuchscher, Alex
Delta Waterfowl Foundation *(409)*

Tuck, Maryscott
American Moving and Storage Association *(153)*

Tucker, Adrienne
American Prepaid Legal Services Institute *(167)*

Tucker, MA, Charlotte
American Public Health Association *(171)*

Tucker, Cindy
National Academy of Opticianry *(628)*

Tucker, Debra
Biomedical Engineering Society *(330)*

Tucker, Herb
Finnsheep Breeders Association *(445)*

Tucker, Jim
International Association of Fairs and Expositions *(521)*

Tucker, Kay
Ambulatory Surgery Center Association *(28)*

Tucker, Kaylen
National Association of Elementary School Principals *(664)*

Tucker, Lloyd
Society for Technical Communication *(922)*

Tucker, Mary
International Association of Exhibitions and Events *(520)*

Tucker, Nancy
National Association of State Directors of Special Education *(700)*

Tucker, Patrick
World Future Society *(1026)*

Tucker, Puja
International Technology and Engineering Educators Association *(576)*

Tucker, Thelma
Society for Research in Child Development *(920)*

Tucker, Tim
National Association of Professional Employer Organizations *(687)*

Tucker, Tom
National School Supply and Equipment Association *(789)*

Tucker, Tracy
National Association of Government Defined Contribution Administrators *(670)*
The Association of Medical Illustrators *(293)*

Tucker-Allen, FAAN, RN, Dr. Sallie
Association of Black Nursing Faculty *(269)*

Tudor, Bob
Interstate Council on Water Policy *(582)*

Tudryn, Joyce M.
International Radio and Television Society Foundation Inc. *(562)*

Tufail, Shakeel
Pakistan American Business Association *(837)*

Tuffin, Michelle
US Travel Association *(983)*

Tufts, Julie
American Association of Poison Control Centers *(70)*

Tulipane, CAE, Barbara
National Recreation and Parks Association *(784)*

Tulipane, CMP, Jeanie
Personal Care Products Council *(842)*

Tulley, David
United States Chamber of Commerce *(991)*

Tulloch, Thomas C.
North American Association of State and Provincial Lotteries *(813)*

Tumang, Sergio
Accreditation Association for Ambulatory Health Care *(9)*

Tuncy, JoAnne

American Border Leicester Association *(85)*

Tune, Amaya
AFL-CIO (American Federation of Labor and Congress of Industrial Organizations) *(14)*

Tune, Michael
National Lesbian and Gay Journalists Association *(769)*

Tune, Sharon K.
American Historical Association *(131)*
Historians of American Communism *(476)*

Tung, Donna
The Fair Currency Alliance *(437)*

Tunner, Timothy
National Association of State Mental Health Directors *(701)*

Tunstall, Jr., Graydon (Jack) A.
Phi Alpha Theta *(845)*

Tuohy, SAP, Cynthia Moreno
National Association for Alcoholism and Drug Abuse Counselors *(646)*

Turek, Judi
Evangelical Church Library Association *(434)*

Turell, BM, MA, Sarah
American Holistic Medical Association *(132)*

Turf, Ellen
National Association of Personal Financial Advisors *(684)*

Turkheimer, Andrea
The Learning Disabilities Association *(596)*

Turman, Nikki
Society of Environmental Toxicology and Chemistry *(935)*

Turnau, Lindsey
International Academy of Compounding Pharmacists *(509)*

Turnbeaugh, Treasa
Board of Certified Safety Professionals *(332)*

Turner, CAE, PhD, Ann T.
American Association for Laboratory Animal Science *(50)*

Turner, Aprill O.
National Association of Black Journalists *(649)*

Turner, Archie L.
American Psychological Association *(169)*

Turner, Bennie L.
National Association of Black-Owned Broadcasters *(649)*

Turner, Bobbie
American College of Physicians Services, Inc. *(101)*

Turner, Craig
National Association of Farmer Elected Committees (NAFEC) *(667)*

Turner, David C.
American Council of Life Insurers (ACLI) *(110)*

Turner, Elena
Retail Solutions Providers Association *(885)*

Turner, George
National Freight Transportation Association *(753)*

Turner, George D.
American Nuclear Insurers *(156)*

Turner, III, James M.
Employee Stock Ownership Plan Association *(426)*

Turner, Janet
American Burn Association *(87)*

Turner, Jennifer
American Association of Managed Care Nurses *(64)*

Turner, Kate

International Association of Fairs and Expositions *(521)*

Turner, Laura
National League of Cities *(768)*

Turner, Lynn
American Academy of Appellate Lawyers *(30)*
American College of Mortgage Attorneys *(98)*

Turner, CAE, Marsha L.
International Association of Lighting Designers *(524)*

Turner, PhD, Matt
Association of State and Provincial Psychology Boards *(309)*

Turner, Patricia L.
American College of Surgeons *(103)*

Turner, Rebecca
American Association of Variable Star Observers *(76)*

Turner, Robin
Animal Transportation Association *(223)*
Association of Free Standing Radiation Oncology Centers *(284)*

Turner, CAE, CSE, Willis H.
Sales and Marketing Executives International, Inc. *(890)*

Turner-Lee, PhD, Nicol
National Association for Multi-Ethnicity in Communications *(640)*

Turney, PHR, SPHR, Ellen
Society for Critical Care Medicine *(934)*

Turney, MD, Susan L.
MGMA-ACMPE *(614)*

Turowski, Anamyn
Association of Waldorf Schools of North America *(317)*

Turpen, Judy
Christian Educators Association International *(355)*

Turrentine, Colleen
Democratic Lieutenant Governors' Association (DLGA) *(410)*

Turrisi, Kim
Society of Children's Book Writers and Illustrators *(932)*

Turteltaub, Adam
Health Care Compliance Association *(469)*

Turturro, Patrick
American Sportscasters Association *(213)*

Tusa, Johnny
American Football Coaches Association *(122)*

Tushie, David
International Card Manufacturers Association *(532)*

Tusler, FACHA, FAIA, Wilbur "Tib"
American College of Healthcare Architects *(96)*

Tutka, Richard
Electrical Apparatus Service Association *(422)*

Tutt, Lou
Association for Education and Rehabilitation of the Blind & Visually Impaired *(245)*

Tuttle, Cassie
Editorial Freelancers Association *(419)*

Tutwiler, Lucy
Competitive Carriers Association *(371)*

Twal, PhD, RN, Marie
International Society of Nurses in Genetics *(573)*

Twarog, Daniel L.
North American Die Casting Association *(816)*

Twiggs, Korie
Association of Children's Museums *(272)*

Twiggs, MS, PhD CHP, RHIA, Mariela

Association of Health Information Outsourcing
Services **(286)**

Twillman, Gwen
American Society for Nutrition **(187)**

Twining, Dane
Private Label Manufacturers Association **(858)**

Twitty, Moira
American Academy of Esthetic Dentistry **(33)**
American Prosthodontic Society **(168)**
American Society of Lipo-Suction Surgery **(202)**

Twitty, Moria
International Society of Appraisers **(570)**

Twombly, Mark
Seaplane Pilots Association **(894)**

Twombly, Sean
American Political Science Association **(166)**

Tyeryar, CAE, MAM, Clay D.
American Pipe Fittings Association **(165)**
American Textile Machinery Association **(216)**
Association of Vacuum Equipment Manufacturers **(316)**
International Aviation Ground Support Association
(529)

Tyler, Allen
National Young Farmers Education Association **(806)**

Tyler, MA, RN, Judith
National Student Nurses Association **(797)**

Tyler, Meghan
Society for American Archaeology **(903)**

Tyler, Tony
International Air Transport Association **(510)**

Tynan, CAE, Caryl G.
American College of Phlebology **(100)**

Tyree, Ketti
Hardwood Plywood and Veneer Association **(468)**

Tyree, Shane
Billiard Congress of America **(329)**

Tyson, Brian
American Board of Trial Advocates **(84)**

Tyson, Dave N.
ASIS International **(232)**

Tyson, Jackie
National Association of Graduate-Professional
Students **(670)**

Tyson, Jill
National Agricultural Alumni and Development
Association **(630)**

Tyson, FRCS, MD, John
Society for Gynecologic Investigation **(910)**

Tyson, Karen
National Association of Federal Credit Unions **(667)**

Tysse, G. John
Equal Employment Advisory Council **(432)**

Tzamaras, George P.
American Immigration Lawyers Association **(134)**

Ubl, Stephen J.
Advanced Medical Technology Association (AdvaMed)
(13)

Uddfolk, CMP, Jule
International Society of Hair Restoration Surgery **(573)**

Udell, DPM, Elliot T.
American Society of Podiatric Medicine **(208)**

Udo-O'Malley, Annabelle A.
Asian American Journalists Association **(231)**

Udvardy, Steve
North American Die Casting Association **(816)**

Udy, Brenda

United States of America Dry Pea and Lentil Council,
Inc. **(996)**

Uebel, Kathleen S.
American Academy of Dental Practice Administration
(32)

Ugbomah, Elizabeth
Hispanic National Bar Association **(475)**

Ugoji, Angela
American Academy of Audiology **(31)**

Ugoretz, Mark J.
The ERISA Industry Committee (ERIC) **(433)**

Uher, Jerome
American Public Human Services Association **(171)**
APHSA - Information Systems Management **(224)**

Uher, Jerome
Association of Administrators of the Interstate
Compact on the Placement of Children **(263)**

Uherek, Amanda
Healthcare Leadership Council **(471)**

Uhlir, Allison
American Society for Horticultural Science **(185)**

Uhrenholt, Debbie
Association of Commercial Real Estate **(275)**

Ullman, Eloise
Industry Council on Tangible Assets **(494)**

Ullman, Josh
College and University Professional Association for
Human Resources **(362)**

Ullrich, Nina
American Boat and Yacht Council **(84)**

Ulmer, Bonnie
The Institute of Internal Auditors **(500)**

Ulschmid, Barbara
American Agricultural Editors Association **(43)**

Ulsh, Patrick
National Interstate Council of State Boards of
Cosmetology **(766)**

Umbdenstock, Richard
American Hospital Association **(133)**

Umsted, Keith
American Public Works Association **(172)**

Underkoffler, Chad
Alliance for Telecommunications Industry Solutions
(23)

Understiller, Lynn
Society of Animal Artists **(930)**

Underwood, CAE, MBA, Catherine
American Pain Society **(161)**
National Association of Neonatal Nurses **(682)**

Underwood, Elnora
International Association of Healthcare Central Service
Materiel Management **(522)**

Underwood, Jack
Association of Management Consulting Firms **(292)**

Underwood, Karen
National Maritime Alliance **(772)**

Underwood, Katherine
National Council of Urban Education Associations
(738)

Underwood, Lee
ICE Futures U.S. **(482)**

Underwood, Tom
American Horticultural Society **(133)**

Unger, Jerome
American Association for Accreditation of Ambulatory
Surgery Facilities **(47)**

Unger, CWS-VI, Mark T.
Water Quality Association **(1013)**

Unger, Peter S.
American Association for Laboratory Accreditation **(50)**

Ungerer, Richard A.
American Montessori Society **(152)**

Upham, Peter
Association of Boarding Schools **(270)**

Upson, Stu
United States Bowling Congress **(991)**

Upton, Diana
International Association of Medical Equipment
Remarketers and Servicers (IAMERS) **(524)**

Upton, CCE, Richard D.
American Lighting Association **(145)**

Urban, Lindsey
REALTORS Land Institute **(876)**

Urbanowicz, Nancy
Academy of Management **(6)**

Urbaytis, Cindy
Institute for Supply Management **(497)**

Urgolites, Charlotte
Zero Balancing Health Association **(1030)**

Urian, Richard
Consolidated Tape Association **(378)**

Ursino, Brian
American Association of Motor Vehicle Administrators
(65)

Urso, Paul
The Electrochemical Society **(423)**

Usher, Catherine P.
Specialty Tools and Fasteners Distributors Association
(958)

Usher, USMC (Ret.), MajGen Edward
Marine Corps Association **(604)**

Usher, Todd
Physician Assistant Education Association **(847)**

Usumi, Ugur
American Cleaning Institute **(91)**

Utano, Julie
Specialized Information Publishers Association **(957)**

Uthus, Charles D.
American Automotive Policy Council **(78)**

Uttech, Sara
Soil Science Society of America **(951)**

Utterbach, Lee
Production Equipment Rental Association **(859)**

Utterback, CPA, Lois
Association of Community Cancer Centers **(275)**

Utterback, Lynda
National Ice Cream Retailers Association **(761)**

Uusimaki, Mary Helen
International Sleep Products Association **(565)**

Uy, Erin
National Association of State Directors of Career
Technical Education Consortium **(699)**

Vachon, Chris
Society of Professional Journalists **(945)**

Vachon, Jennifer
Blue Cross Blue Shield Association **(332)**

Vactor, Lynn Van
Inter-National Association of Business Industry &
Rehabilitation **(506)**

Vadala, Chris
USA Volleyball **(1005)**

Vadgama, Ashok
Consortium for Advanced Management, International *(378)*

Vaidyanathan, Rajiv
Association for Consumer Research *(243)*

Vail, Cathy
Conference of Minority Transportation Officials *(375)*

Vaillancourt, Kelly
National Association of School Psychologists *(693)*

Vaille, Kelly
Cedar Shake and Shingle Bureau *(347)*

Vajda, LCSW, DCEP, Debby
Association for Comprehensive Energy Psychology *(242)*

Valachovic, DMD, MPH, Richard W.
American Dental Education Association *(113)*

Valanide, Nicos
International Visual Literacy Association *(580)*

Valant, Angel
National Cancer Registrars Association *(717)*

Valastyan, Lynn
Society of Gastroenterology Nurses and Associates *(937)*

Valdez, Donna
American Welara Pony Registry *(220)*

Valdez, Jr., Mario R.
American Telemedicine Association *(215)*

Valdivia, Justin
Information Systems Security Association *(495)*

Vale, Chadwick
United States Hispanic Chamber of Commerce *(995)*

ValeCruz, Teresita T.
Council of the Great City Schools *(398)*

Valencia, Alicia
American Association of Credit Union Leagues *(59)*

Valenta, Judy
Religious Conference Management Association *(880)*

Valente, PhD, CAE, Carmine. M
American Institute of Ultrasound in Medicine *(141)*

Valenti, Thomas
Allied Artists of America *(25)*

Valenti, Toni
National Association of Educational Procurement, Inc. *(664)*

Valentic, Lynne
American Psychosocial Oncology Society *(170)*

Valentin, Alba
International Health, Racquet and Sportsclub Association *(549)*

Valentin, Carlos
ASPIRA Association, Inc. *(233)*

Valentine, Bruce
Association of Woodworking and Furnishings Suppliers *(318)*

Valentine, Daren
American Association for Laboratory Accreditation *(50)*

Valentine, H. Jeffrey
National Paralegal Association *(779)*

Valentine, Heather
Council for Opportunity in Education *(390)*

Valentine, Jon
National Council of State Supervisors for Languages *(736)*

Valentine, P E, Victoria
National Fire Sprinkler Association *(751)*

Valentini, MPP, Mark
National Association of Independent Life Brokerage Agencies *(674)*

Valentino, Russell
American Literary Translators Association *(146)*

Valentzas, Anne
Women's Jewelry Association *(1023)*

Valenzuela, Daniel
National Association of Hispanic Firefighters *(672)*

Valenzuela, PhD, Ed
National Association of Hispanic Federal Executives *(672)*

Valenzuela, Mandy
American College Health Association *(93)*

Valenzuela, CAE, Pamela
Association for Women in Communications *(261)*

Valenzuela, Valerie
Society of Hispanic Professional Engineers *(938)*

Valerio, Gina M.
Restoration Industry Association *(884)*

Valerio, Marcie
Legal Marketing Association *(596)*
Print Services & Distribution Association *(857)*

Valero, Cristie
Association for Women Geoscientists *(261)*

Valiga, George
National Association of Wholesaler-Distributors *(709)*

Vallarta, Ludita
Industrial Research Institute *(494)*

Valle, Jay
American Lands Access Association *(144)*

Vallee, Brenda
International Association for Truancy and Dropout Prevention *(514)*

Vallely, Patrick
American Association for Budget and Program Analysis *(48)*

Valles-Hall, Arminda
Security Industry Association *(895)*

Vallesillas, Meshack
Hollywood Radio & Television Society *(477)*

Vallimont, Jenna
National Organization for Associate Degree Nursing *(776)*

Valponi, Donna
American Academy of Family Physicians *(34)*

Valverde, Pedro A.
National Employment Lawyers Association (NELA) *(746)*

Vambreck, Marian
Air Movement and Control Association International *(19)*

Van Allen, Barbera
Mortgage Bankers Association of America *(619)*

Van Alstyne, Stacy
International Foundation of Employee Benefit Plans *(547)*

Van Amburg, Kent
American Society of Baking *(193)*

Van Amerongen, Jerry
National Cartoonists Society *(718)*

Van Beckum, Cindy
National Association of Tax Professionals *(704)*

Van Buren, Lynn
International Society for the Study of Subtle Energies and Energy Medicine *(570)*

Van Coverden, Thomas
National Association of Community Health Centers *(656)*

Van Dale, Martha
National Farmers Union (Farmers Educational & Co-operative Union of America) *(747)*

Van Daniker, CPA, DBA, Relmond P.
Association of Government Accountants *(286)*

Van De Vaarst, John
National Intercollegiate Soccer Officials Association *(766)*

Van de Velde, Gerry R.
American Fuel & Petrochemical Manufacturers *(124)*

Van Den Bussche, Ronald A.
American Society of Mammalogists *(202)*

Van der Zalm, CPA, Jeannie
National Council of Examiners for Engineering and Surveying *(734)*

Van Dermark, Kelly
Hearth, Patio and Barbecue Association *(472)*

Van Dongen, Dirk
National Association of Wholesaler-Distributors *(709)*

Van Drunen, John
Evangelical Council for Financial Accountability *(434)*

Van Dyke, Steve
Lignite Energy Council *(598)*

Van Gunten, Marjie
American Orff-Schulwerk Association *(158)*

Van Horn, Catherine
National Association of Pediatric Nurse Practitioners *(684)*

Van Loo, William
Marine Engineers Beneficial Association *(605)*

Van Ostrand, Andrew
Health Industry Distributors Association *(469)*

Van Petten, Vance
Producers Guild of America *(858)*

van Reenen, Christine
National Pace Association *(778)*

Van Riper, A. Bowdoin
Historians Film Committee/Film & History *(476)*

Van Roekel, Dennis
National Education Association *(744)*

Van Tubergen, Mike
Christian Labor Association of the United States of America *(355)*

Vance, Adam
US Travel Association *(983)*

Vance, B. Wayne
Composite Can and Tube Institute *(372)*

Vance, Beverly S.
American Mathematical Association of Two Year Colleges *(147)*

Vandall, Rebecca
Society of Research Administrators International *(946)*

VanDe Hei, Diane
Association of Metropolitan Water Agencies *(294)*

Vandegrift, Loren
Patient Centered Primary Care Collaborative *(840)*

VandenBos, PhD, Gary R.
American Psychological Association *(169)*

VanderBand, Hillary
Consumer Aerosol Products Council *(380)*

VanderBush, Emily
Airport Consultants Council *(21)*

Vanderhoef, Peter
National Fluid Power Association *(751)*

Vanderhoof, Randy
Smart Card Alliance *(901)*

Vanderkay, Judith
International Imaging Industry Association *(551)*

Vanderkleed, Anna
American Society of Bariatric Physicians *(193)*

Vanderlin, Molly
American College of Veterinary Pathologists *(104)*

Vanderlinden, Ronnie
Diamond Manufacturers & Importers Association of America *(411)*

Vanderlinden, Shauna
United States Ski and Snowboard Association *(999)*

Vandermeer, Philip
Social Science History Association *(902)*
Society for Historians of the Gilded Age and Progressive Era *(911)*

Vanderpoel, PHR, JoAnna
World Council of Credit Unions, Inc. *(1026)*

Vandervoort, Mona
Society for Mining, Metallurgy and Exploration, Inc. *(915)*

Vanderwater, Dave
American Association for Crystal Growth *(49)*

VanDeusen, Geoff
National Soccer Coaches Association of America *(792)*

Vandevort, Jake
Ethylene Oxide Sterilization Association, Inc. *(433)*

Vandeyar, David J.
National Fire Sprinkler Association *(751)*

VanDine, PE, Michael
National Clay Pipe Institute *(722)*

Vandiver, Hal F.
Hoist Manufacturers Institute *(477)*

Vandivier, Dianne
American Association for Clinical Chemistry, Inc. *(48)*

VanDuyne, Nick
New York E-Health Collaborative *(809)*

Vang, Nao
Asian American Journalists Association *(231)*

VanHooser, Ernest H.
Livestock Marketing Association *(599)*

vanMeenen, CPT, MA, Karen
National Association for Poetry Therapy *(641)*

VanMeerhaeghe, Dana
National Association of Graduate Admissions Professionals *(670)*

Vann, Kimberly
National Conference of Bar Presidents *(726)*

Vann, Rae T.
Equal Employment Advisory Council *(432)*

Vann, Shannon
North American Association of Central Cancer Registries *(812)*

Vanneman, Tracy
Society for Industrial and Organizational Psychology Inc. *(912)*

Vannoy, Darrel
North American Association of Wardens and Superintendents *(814)*

VanPutten, April
Association of Christian Librarians *(272)*

Vanscoyoc, Rob
American Folklore Society *(122)*

VanSickle, III, Harold "Bud"
Lightning Protection Institute *(598)*

VanWieren, Joyce
National Council of Structural Engineers Associations *(737)*

Varanakis, George
Wedding and Portrait Photographers International *(1014)*

Varden, Helga
Society for the Philosophy of Sex and Love *(923)*

Vargas, Arturo
National Association of Latino Elected and Appointed Officials *(677)*

Vargas, Felix
World Trade Centers Association *(1027)*

Vargas, Hector
Gay and Lesbian Medical Association *(457)*

Vargas, Juan C.
National Association of Latino Elected and Appointed Officials *(677)*

Vargas, Juliet
American Association for Budget and Program Analysis *(48)*

Vargas, Sara
Society for Pediatric Pathology *(918)*

Vargas, Veronica
US Rice Producers Association *(1004)*

Vargo, Franklin J.
National Association of Manufacturers *(679)*

Vargulich, Terri
Academy of Osseointegration *(7)*

Varley, Michael R
American Equilibration Society *(117)*

Varmecky, Stacy
Association for Iron and Steel Technology *(250)*

Varnado, Jack
Driving School Association of America *(416)*

Vartanian, Martin A.
AIR Commercial Real Estate Association *(18)*

Vasami, Ralph
Builders Hardware Manufacturers Association *(337)*
Composite Lumber Manufacturers Association *(372)*
Masonry Veneer Manufacturers Association *(607)*
PET Resin Association *(843)*
Window Covering Manufacturers Association *(1018)*

Vasil, Vicki
Board Retailers Association *(333)*

Vasilaros, Nicole
Personal Watercraft Industry Association (PWIA) *(842)*

Vasilievas, Valerie
American Nuclear Society *(156)*

Vaske, Al
Contact Lens Manufacturers Association *(382)*

Vasquez, Rene
National Association of Latino Elected and Appointed Officials *(677)*

Vasquez-Guzman, Valerie
Independent Educational Consultants Association *(489)*

Vassalli, Katie
International Liquid Terminals Association *(554)*

Vassallo, Nadine
Book Industry Study Group, Inc. *(333)*

Vassilikos, Margaret
Newspaper Association of America *(810)*

Vassos, MPA, Sandra

National Association of Pediatric Nurse Practitioners *(684)*

Vastine, Bob
Coalition of Service Industries *(361)*

Vasvari, Louise
American Hungarian Educators Association *(134)*

Vaugh, Tammy
Special Interest Group for Technology Coordinators *(955)*

Vaughan, Gordon L.
American Polygraph Association *(166)*

Vaughan, Janet
American Association of Museums *(65)*

Vaughan, Patricia Magee
American Beverage Association *(80)*

Vaughan, PhD, Therese M.
National Association of Insurance Commissioners *(676)*

Vaughn, PhD, Andrew G.
American Schools of Oriental Research *(177)*

Vaughn, Eric
National Structured Settlements Trade Association *(797)*

Vaughn, Janet
WorkPlace Furnishings *(1025)*

Vaughn, Jeanette
Public Education Network *(869)*

Vaughn, John C.
Association of American Universities *(266)*

Vaughn, Shawn
National Association of State Chief Administrators *(699)*
National Association of State Chief Information Officers *(699)*

Vaughn-Flam, Eric
International Advertising Association *(509)*

Vaught, Brian
American Soybean Association *(211)*

Vaught, Donna L
National Association of Corporate Directors *(658)*

Vazquez, Alicia
American Academy of Podiatric Practice Management *(40)*

Vazquez, Jesus C.
American Society of Podiatric Medical Assistants *(208)*

Vazquez, Margaret
International Society of Certified Electronics Technicians *(572)*

Vazquez, Margaret
National Electronic Service Dealers Association *(745)*

Vazquez, Nancy
American Association of Physicists in Medicine *(69)*

Veach, Kenny
Associated Construction Publications *(235)*

Veal, C. David
American Shrimp Processors Association *(179)*

Veal, Steve
National Soccer Coaches Association of America *(792)*

Veal, Tina
National Agricultural Alumni and Development Association *(630)*

Veale, Paula
Advertising Council *(13)*

Vecchione, Bob
National Association of Collegiate Directors of Athletics *(656)*
National Association of Collegiate Marketing Administrators *(656)*

Vechten, Allyn Van
Professional Aviation Safety Specialists (AFL-CIO) *(860)*

Vedder, Nicholas B.
Association of Academic Chairmen of Plastic Surgery *(262)*

Veeck, CAFS, Alan C
National Air Filtration Association *(630)*

Veeck, Lisa
International Sanitary Supply Association *(563)*

Veed, Mary Cannon
International Association of Insurance Receivers *(523)*

Veer, Ekant
Association for Consumer Research *(243)*

Veer, Gerrit van der
Special Interest Group for Computer-Human Interaction *(954)*

Veerappan, Venkatachlam
Association for Research in Vision and Ophthalmology *(255)*

Vega, Annete
Twentieth-Century Spanish Association of America *(983)*

Vega, CPA, Ephraim
Alliance for Aging Research *(22)*

Vega, Esq., Leonila
Direct Care Alliance *(412)*

Veglia, Toni
USENIX: The Advanced Computing Systems Association *(1005)*

Vegso, Jay
Heart Rhythm Society *(472)*

Vehar, Randy
International Chemical Workers Union Council/UFCW *(534)*

Vehrs, Kristin L.
Association of Zoos and Aquariums *(318)*

Veigle, Anne
United States Telecom Association *(1000)*

Vejvoda, MBA, PE, Miroslav F.
Post-Tensioning Institute *(853)*

Velasco, Anna
Canadian-American Business Council *(341)*

Velasco, Maria
Association of University Centers on Disabilities (AUCD) *(315)*

Velasquez, Baldemar
Farm Labor Organizing Committee *(437)*

Velasquez, Vanessa
Automatic Transmission Rebuilders Association *(321)*

Velazquez, Jennifer M.
Professional Records and Information Services Management International *(864)*

Velazquez, MSW, Pauline
National Association of Puerto Rican-Hispanic Social Workers *(689)*

Velde, Dave
National Farmers Union (Farmers Educational & Co-operative Union of America) *(747)*

Velo, Chris
Club Managers Association of America *(359)*

Veloz, Rafael A.
Inter-American Bar Association *(506)*

Velzen, Deb Van
National Association of School Resource Officers *(693)*

Vembu, Anna
Information Systems Security Association *(495)*

Vena, Debbie
American Society of Anesthesiologists *(192)*

Venable, Gwen
Poultry Breeders of America *(854)*
U.S Poultry and Egg Association *(998)*

Venables, Jeff
American Running Association *(176)*
American Running Association/American Medical Athletic Association *(176)*

Venancio, Erica
American Association of Grain Inspection and Weighing Agencies *(61)*
Transportation Elevator and Grain Merchants Association *(978)*

Venechanos, Troy
Intercollegiate Tennis Association *(507)*

Veney, Beth
Association for Women in Communications *(261)*

Venit, Mark L.
Apparel Graphics Institute *(225)*

Venkateswar, PhD, Shyama
National Council for Research on Women *(732)*

Venker, Ted
Coastal Conservation Association *(361)*

Venson, John N.
American Board of Podiatric Surgery *(83)*

Ventola, Annalisa
Parapsychological Association *(838)*

Ventura, Jack
Transportation Research Forum *(979)*

Venturelli, Anne
Specialty Tools and Fasteners Distributors Association *(958)*

Venturin, Dean E.
Refractory Ceramic Fibers Coalition *(878)*

Venzor, Mark
Society of Mexican American Engineers and Scientists *(941)*

Ver Eecke, Wilfried
Association for Philosophy of the Unconscious *(253)*

Verbanic, Michael
Construction Financial Management Association *(379)*

Verberg, Kelly G.
American Staffing Association *(213)*

Verd, Amy
Workgroup for Electronic Data Interchange *(1025)*

Verdegaal, Mary
International Licensing Industry Merchandisers' Association *(554)*

Verdin, Maria
AIR Commercial Real Estate Association *(18)*

Verdoliva, Steve
Game Manufacturers Association *(456)*

Verett, Steve
Plains Cotton Growers, Inc. *(849)*

Vergara, Christina
Women in Cable Telecommunications, Inc. *(1020)*

Verhalen, Liz
Association of Boarding Schools *(270)*

Verhey, CMP, Karen
Society for College and University Planning *(906)*

Verity, Suzanne
CoreNet Global *(385)*

Vermeer, Isabel
The Institute of Financial Operations *(499)*

Vermette, Elizabeth

Automotive Recyclers Association *(323)*

Vernon, Bernadette
Society of Cable Telecommunications Engineers *(931)*

Vernon, David
National Air Transportation Association *(630)*

Vernon, Irene
National Association for Ethnic Studies *(638)*

Vernon, Larry
Association for Educational Communications and Technology *(245)*

Verona, Edward S.
U.S.-Russia Business Council *(999)*

Verret, Catherine
The French Film Office/UniFrance USA *(453)*

Verrico, John S.
National Association of Government Communicators *(670)*

Verrier, Thomas
College Band Directors National Association *(363)*

Verrillo, Maryann
Society of Interventional Radiology *(940)*

Versfelt, David
American Association of Advertising Agencies *(53)*

Verstraete, Alain G.
The International Association of Forensic Toxicologists *(522)*

Vertino, Sheila K.
NAIOP, The Commercial Real Estate Development Association *(366)*

Vertullo, Jayme
The Learning Disabilities Association *(596)*

Verzella, Sue
Victorian Society in America *(1009)*

Vessely, Jeff
Phi Epsilon Kappa *(845)*

Vest, Charles M.
National Academy of Engineering of the United States of America *(627)*

Vetere, Bob
American Pet Products Association *(163)*

Vetrovec, Diane
Orthopaedic Trauma Association *(834)*

Vetterlein, Rachel
American Canoe Association *(88)*

Vetterling, Mary-Anne
American Association of Teachers of Spanish and Portuguese *(75)*

Vetzner, Steve
Mental Health America *(612)*

Veys, Richard
Society of Actuaries *(927)*

Vezina, John
Writers Guild of America West *(1029)*

Veziroglu, Ayfer
International Association for Hydrogen Energy *(513)*

Veziroglu, Emre A.
International Association for Hydrogen Energy *(513)*

Veziroglu, PhD, T. Nejat
International Association for Hydrogen Energy *(513)*

Vial, Vanessa
Biscuit and Cracker Manufacturers' Association *(330)*

Vialpando, Angelica
Council for Opportunity in Education *(390)*

Vialva, Maureen
National Minority Supplier Development Council *(773)*

Viancos, Fred
United States Professional Tennis Association *(998)*

Viands, Michael
Organization for the Promotion and Advancement of Small Telecommunications Companies *(831)*

Viar, Holly
Accrediting Bureau of Health Education Schools *(10)*

Viator, Jessica
National Council of Chain Restaurants *(734)*
Retail Advertising and Marketing Association International *(884)*

Vibert, Joseph
Association of Specialized and Professional Accreditors *(309)*

Vichness, Stephanie
American Industrial Hygiene Association *(135)*

Vickers, Amy
Human Milk Banking Association of North America *(481)*

Vickers, MD, Selwyn M.
Society for Surgery of the Alimentary Tract *(921)*

Vickers, Shannon
Voice and Speech Trainers Association *(1011)*

Victorson, Ret., COL Mark
National Defense Transportation Association *(742)*

Vidal, Dona
Certified Claims Professional Accreditation Council *(349)*

Vidal, Rebecca
United States Dairy Export Council *(993)*

Vidmer, Nina Albano
American Osteopathic Academy of Addiction Medicine *(159)*

Vied, Madeline
National Tour Association *(800)*

Vieder, Deborah B.
NPES, The Association for Suppliers of Printing, Publishing, and Converting Technologies *(824)*

Viehland, Doug
Association of Collegiate Business Schools and Programs *(275)*

Vieira, Isabel
American Academy of Addiction Psychiatry *(29)*

Vieira, Leda
Association for Gnotobiotics *(247)*

Vienken, Joerg
International Federation for Artificial Organs *(544)*

Vienna, Lisa
Heart Rhythm Society *(472)*

Viera, Nicole
Malignant Hyperthermia Association of the United States *(602)*

Vierhaus, Rebecca
League of American Orchestras *(595)*

Vierra, Stephanie
Sustainable Buildings Industry Council *(967)*

Vigilante, Dr. Richard
Association of Jesuit Colleges and Universities *(290)*

Vigne, Toya
Women in Government Relations, Inc. *(1021)*

Viksnins, Helen
American Academy of Optometry *(37)*

Viktor, Cary F.
Global Offset and Countertrade Association (GOCA) *(462)*

Vil, Capri St.

The Corps Network (formerly the National Association of Service and Conservation Corps) *(386)*

Villabon, Jeanine
Physician Office Managers Association of America *(847)*

Villafañe, Marco Antonio
ASPIRA Association, Inc. *(233)*

Villamil-Casanova, John
ASPIRA Association, Inc. *(233)*

Villani, David
American Society of Appraisers *(192)*

Villani, Joseph S.
National School Boards Association *(789)*

Villanova, Greg
International Chemical Workers Union Council/UFCW *(534)*

Villanueva, Carlos
National Association of Water Companies (NAWC) *(709)*

Villareal, Lee Roy
Hispanic American Police Command Officers Association (HAPCOA) *(475)*

Villata, Mark
North American Blueberry Council *(814)*

Villegas, Gesana
American Welding Society *(220)*

Vincent, Clint
United States Parachute Association *(997)*

Vincent, Debbie
Association of Vacuum Equipment Manufacturers *(316)*

Vincent, Fran
International Hearing Society *(549)*

Vincent, Gay L.
American College of Surgeons *(103)*

Vincent, Keith
Promotional Products Association International *(867)*

Vincent, Steven D.
American Academy of Oral and Maxillofacial Pathology *(37)*

Vincente, Joana
Independent Filmmaker Project *(489)*

Vinci, Yasmina S.
National Head Start Association *(758)*

Vinson, Scott
National Council of Chain Restaurants *(734)*

Vinson, Stephen L.
United Methodist Association of Health and Welfare Ministries *(987)*

Vipperman, Carol
Foundation for Russian-American Economic Cooperation *(453)*

Vira, Varun
The International Stability Operations Association *(575)*

Virga, Michael
United States Composting Council *(992)*

Virgin, Melissa
Pyramid Society *(871)*

Virzi, Tammy
Pony of the Americas Club *(852)*

Visbal, Mark A.
Security Industry Association *(895)*

Viscomi, Randy
Ethylene Oxide Sterilization Association, Inc. *(433)*

Visconti, Charles G.
International Cargo Gear Bureau *(533)*

Viscovich, Melissa
National Association of Professional Employer Organizations *(687)*

Visocan, LDN, MS, RD, Barbara
Academy of Nutrition and Dietetics *(7)*

Visone, Jamison
American Society of Transplant Surgeons *(210)*

Vissicchio, Gino
American Academy of Actuaries *(29)*

Vitale, Ben
National Association of Produce Market Managers *(686)*

Vitale, Connie
National Environmental Balancing Bureau *(746)*

Vitale, Gary
North American Wholesale Lumber Association *(823)*

Vitale, Paul
Toy Industry Association *(976)*

Vitale, Rock J.
American Institute of Chemists *(138)*

Vitiritto, Beth
Vacuum Dealers Trade Association/Sewing Dealers Trade Association *(1007)*

Vitrak, Aimee
Overseas Press Club of America *(835)*

Vitrano, Paul
Specialty Vehicle Institute of America *(958)*

Vitti-Alexander, Maria Rosaria
American Association of Teachers of Italian *(74)*

Vivian, Cynthia
American Library Association *(145)*

Vizi, Don
Paso Fino Horse Association, Inc. *(839)*

Vizza, Cindy
National Club Association *(722)*

Vlaanderen, Vicky
National Bison Association *(713)*

Vlahos, Len
Book Industry Study Group, Inc. *(333)*

Vlasses, BCPS, PharmD, FCCP, DSc, Peter H.
Accreditation Council for Pharmacy Education *(10)*

Vlietstra, Katie
National Association for the Self-Employed *(644)*

Vodoor, Ramesh
International Association of Venue Managers *(528)*

Voegtlin, Gene
International Association of Chiefs of Police *(517)*

Voeks, PhD, Bob
Society for Economic Botany *(908)*

Voelker, Victoria
Pi Lambda Theta *(847)*

Vogel, Anne
Electrical Apparatus Service Association *(422)*

Vogel, Brian
Industrial Designers Society of America *(493)*

Vogel, Carolyn Gibb
Population Action International *(852)*

Vogel, Grace B.
Financial Industry Regulatory Authority (FINRA) *(444)*

Vogel, Heidi
International Horn Society *(550)*

Vogel, ABPP, PhD, Mark
Association for the Behavioral Sciences and Medical Education *(259)*

Vogel, Michael P.
Housing Education and Research Association *(479)*

Vogel-Marr, Anne
Performance Track Participants Association *(841)*

Vogelsang, Eleanor M.
The College Board *(363)*

Vogelsang, John
Organization Development Network *(831)*

Vogelsang, Karen
German American Chamber of Commerce *(460)*

Vogelzang, Jeanne M.
National Council of Structural Engineers Associations *(737)*

Vogen, Abby
Association of State Energy Research and Technology Transfer Institution *(311)*

Vogl, Michael
Society of Gynecologic Oncologists *(938)*

Vogt, Amy
Equipment Leasing and Finance Association *(432)*

Vohasek, Deborah
Information Systems Audit and Control Association *(495)*

Vohs, CAE, Maggie
The Kite Trade Association International *(591)*

Voicheck, Kelly
Property Owners Association *(867)*

Voight, Gerald F.
American Concrete Pavement Association *(106)*

Voigt, Abbe
Medical Fitness Association *(611)*

Voigt, John
Solution Mining Research Institute *(952)*

Voigt, Marilyn M.
Association of Environmental and Resource Economists *(281)*

Voisine, Don
American Abstract Artists *(29)*

Volakis, Georgia
International Digital Enterprise Alliance *(540)*

Volgy, Thomas J.
International Studies Association *(576)*

Volk, Kim E.
Delta Dental Plans Association *(409)*

Volner, Ian D.
Association for Postal Commerce *(253)*

Volpe, Angelo
Commercial Vehicle Solutions Network *(367)*
The Commercial Vehicle Solutions Network *(367)*

Volpe, Kate
American Society of Addiction Medicine *(191)*

Volpp, MD, Serena
Association of Gay and Lesbian Psychiatrists *(285)*

Voltmann, Robert A.
Transportation Intermediaries Association *(978)*

von Bernuth, CID, PE, PhD, Robert D.
Irrigation Association *(585)*

Von Deak, CAE, MBA, Todd
Society of Hospital Medicine *(938)*

Von Domitz, Annie
Motorist Information and Services Association *(620)*

Von Haden, Ronald
National Association of Professional Insurance Agents *(687)*

von Seggern, John L.

Council of Federal Home Loan Banks *(393)*

Vonada, Nancy
Chemical Heritage Foundation *(351)*

Vondrasek, Robert J.
National Fire Protection Association *(751)*

Vonier, Pascale J.
Association of Collegiate Schools of Architecture *(275)*

Voorhees, Jack
Campus Safety, Health and Environmental Management Association *(341)*

Voorhies, Karen
National Grocers Association *(756)*

Voorhis, Bill Van
The Propeller Club of the United States *(867)*

Vorck, Frederick
National Society of Compliance Professionals *(793)*

Vorel, Jan
International Association of Oral and Maxillofacial Surgeons *(525)*

Vorhaus, Kate
National Council on Education for the Ceramic Arts *(738)*

Voros, Jane Emily
American Economic Association *(115)*

Vos, Willem De
Society of Plastics Engineers *(944)*

Voskuhl, Jared
National Association of Graduate-Professional Students *(670)*

Voss, Anne
German American Chamber of Commerce *(460)*

Voss, William R.
Flight Safety Foundation *(448)*

Vossburg, Don
National Association of the Remodeling Industry *(705)*

Vossen, Pim
Creative Education Foundation *(403)*

Votaw, Kathy
Radiation Research Society *(873)*

Voth, Karla
The Public Relations Society of America *(870)*

Vought, Vicki
Employer Associations of America *(426)*

Vrabec, John M.
Financial and Security Products Association *(444)*

Vranas, CAE, Chris P.
American Association of Orthodontists *(67)*

Vroom, Jay J.
CropLife America *(404)*

Vukelich, Esq., Daniel J.
Association of Medical Device Reprocessors *(293)*

Vukovljak, Lana
American Association for Clinical Chemistry, Inc. *(48)*

Vulgamore, Patrick
Water and Sewer Distributors of America *(1012)*

Vunderink, Todd
Music Publishers Association of the United States *(622)*

Vuuren, Mark Van
International Society for Philosophical Enquiry *(568)*

Waagen, Elizabeth O.
American Association of Variable Star Observers *(76)*

Waak-Pearce, Judy
Committee of 200 *(368)*

Wacasey, Lydia

Society of Petrophysicists and Well Log Analysts *(944)*

Wachowicz, Mark
Audit Bureau of Circulations *(320)*

Wachs, Faye
North American Society for the Sociology of Sport *(822)*

Wacht, CAE, Peter G.
National Academy of Elder Law Attorneys, Inc. *(627)*

Wachter, Donna
Association of Professors of Gynecology and Obstetrics *(302)*

Wachtler, Janice
American College of Osteopathic Emergency Physicians *(99)*

Wachtler, William "Bill"
Structural Insulated Panel Association *(964)*

Wackler, Josh H.
Alpha Gamma Rho *(26)*

Waddell, Aimee
Strategic Account Management Association *(963)*

Waddington, Maureen
Bicycle Product Suppliers Association *(329)*

Wade, Alison
Association of Art Museum Directors *(267)*

Wade, CIC, CPCU, Bill
Service Specialists Association *(897)*

Wade, PhD, Jay
Society for the Psychological Study of Men and Masculinity *(924)*

Wade, Kelly
Association of Celebrity Personal Assistants *(271)*

Wade, Kerri C.
Association of Women's Health, Obstetric and Neonatal Nurses *(318)*

Wade, Shawn
Plains Cotton Growers, Inc. *(849)*

Wade, Stewart H.
American Bureau of Shipping *(86)*

Wade, Terri E.
American College of Apothecaries *(93)*

Wade, Tonya
American College of Physician Executives *(101)*

Wade, William
Heavy Duty Representatives Association *(473)*

Wadsworth, III, Harrison M.
Coalition of Higher Education Assistance Organizations *(360)*

Wadsworth, Thomas R.
Door and Access Systems Manufacturers Association, International *(415)*

Waff, Razz
Assembly of Episcopal Healthcare Chaplains *(234)*

wage, john
National Council of Travel Attractions *(737)*

Wagenblast, Jill
American Soybean Association *(211)*

Waggoner, Lee
Data Interchange Standards Association *(407)*

Wagner, Alan
Comparative and International Education Society *(371)*

Wagner, Arlene
Association of Former Intelligence Officers *(284)*

Wagner, Bo
Society for Range Management *(920)*

Wagner, Doug

North American Farm Show Council *(816)*

Wagner, E. Timothy
American College of Nurse Practitioners *(99)*

Wagner, Emanuel
Biomass Thermal Energy Council *(330)*

Wagner, Gail
Society for Economic Botany *(908)*

Wagner, Gloria
Council for Adult and Experiential Learning *(388)*

Wagner, John
Compact Loader/Compact Excavator Council *(371)*
Power Crane and Shovel Association *(855)*
Trencher Equipment Committee *(980)*
Trenchless Equipment Committee *(980)*

Wagner, Julie
National Association of Professional Geriatric Care
  Managers *(687)*

Wagner, Ken Van
American Society of Sanitary Engineering *(209)*

Wagner, Leona
Perlite Institute *(842)*

Wagner, Louis A.
National Association of Self-Instructional Language
  Programs *(695)*

Wagner, Louis E.
North American Fiberboard Association *(816)*

Wagner, Marianne Van
International Society for Developmental Psychobiology
  (566)

Wagner, Phil
Association of Zoos and Aquariums *(318)*

Wagner, Polly
Associated Cooperage Industries of America *(235)*

Wagner, Ralia
Jewish Education Service of North America *(588)*

Wagner, CMPE, COPM, Robin L.
Association of Otolaryngology Administrators *(297)*

Wagner, Rosalie
Baking Industry Sanitation Standards Committee *(325)*

Wagner, Russell
Viola da Gamba Society of America *(1009)*

Wagner, Taren
American Association of Colleges of Nursing *(57)*

Wagner, Timothy
Power and Communications Contractors Association
  (855)

Wagner-Renner, Sue
Associated Schools of Construction *(237)*

Wagoner, USN (Ret.), CAPT Robert C.
Naval Submarine League *(807)*

Wagonseller, Elizabeth
The Institute of Financial Operations *(499)*

Wahl, Bill
International Society of Explosives Engineers *(572)*

Wahler, Carol
Type Directors Club *(983)*

Wahler, Tracy
Futures Industry Association *(455)*

Wahlert, Christie
University Risk Management and Insurance
  Association *(1003)*

Wahlert, Sarah
American Board of Trial Advocates *(84)*

Wahlquist, Richard A.
American Staffing Association *(213)*

Wahnon, Carla
Alliance of Artists Communities *(24)*

Wahoski-Hufford, Natasha
Mohair Council of America *(618)*

Waidelich, EdD, William D.
Association for Middle Level Education *(252)*

Wailes, MBA, Richard
United States Pharmacopeia *(997)*

Wainberg, David
Network Advertising Initiative *(808)*

Wainwright, Lisa
Retail Confectioners International *(884)*

Wainwright, Liz
Maritime Fire and Safety Association *(605)*

Wait, Paul
Delta Waterfowl Foundation *(409)*

Waite, Jacqueline
National Council for Geographic Education *(731)*

Waite, Jennifer
National Organization for Human Service *(777)*

Waite, Leslie
American Gastroenterological Association *(125)*

Waite, Philip A.
National Association of Scientific Materials Managers
  (694)

Wakeford, Tracy
Exhibit Designers and Producers Association *(435)*

Wakeman, Brandy
African Studies Association *(15)*

Walchuk, Mary
Society for Risk Analysis *(920)*

Wald, Alan
International Association of Plumbing and Mechanical
  Officials *(526)*

Wald, Alan
Radiant Panel Association *(872)*

Wald, CAE, MBA, MS, William
Association of Real Estate License Law Officials *(305)*

Walda, John
National Association of College and University
  Business Officers *(654)*

Walden, Vince
Internet Marketing Association *(582)*

Waldman, Rep. James
National Council of Legislators from Gaming States
  (735)

Waldman, Martin
Dental Trade Alliance *(410)*

Waldman, Susan
National Association for Multi-Ethnicity in
  Communications *(640)*

Waldron, Roger
The Coalition for Government Procurement *(360)*

Waldrop, Alex
National Thoroughbred Racing Association *(800)*

Waldrup, Courtney L.C
National Association of Chapter Thirteen Trustees
  (NACTT) *(652)*

Wales, Matthew J.
American Association of Colleges for Teacher
  Education *(57)*

Waley, Robin
National Association of Negro Business and
  Professional Women's Clubs *(681)*

Walgenbach, Jessica
National Ready Mixed Concrete Association *(784)*

Walhberg, Howard
National Science Teachers Association *(790)*

Walke, Lawrence
National Association of Broadcasters *(650)*

Walker, Andrew
WTA Tour, Inc. *(1029)*

Walker, Bobbi M.
National Association of Charterboat Operators *(652)*

Walker, Brenda
National Conference of Executives of The ARC *(727)*

Walker, Carolyn
National Association of Children's Hospitals and
  Related Institutions *(653)*

Walker, Carolyn
National Foster Parent Association *(753)*

Walker, Charles
National Peach Council *(780)*
United States Equestrian Federation *(993)*

Walker, Colleen
The Association of Suppliers to the Paper Industry
  (312)

Walker, P E, Dan J.
Metal Building Manufacturers Association *(613)*

Walker, Daniel J.
National Sunroom Association *(798)*

Walker, Deborah
National Lipid Association *(770)*

Walker, Dee Ann
American Association of Sexuality Educators,
  Counselors and Therapists *(73)*

Walker, Donald
American Council of Life Insurers (ACLI) *(110)*

Walker, Eileen
Association of University Research Parks *(316)*

Walker, Greg A.
FutureGen Industrial Alliance, Inc. *(455)*

Walker, Gregg
Propane Engine Fuel Committee/Propane Education
  and Research Council *(867)*

Walker, CEOE, Gretchen
Human Behavior and Evolution Society *(480)*

Walker, Holly
American Automotive Leasing Association *(78)*

Walker, Jacki
American Counseling Association *(111)*

Walker, John
International Military Community Executives
  Association *(556)*

Walker, III, Joseph L.
International Safety Equipment Association (ISEA)
  (563)

Walker, Julie A.
American Association of School Librarians *(72)*

Walker, Kate
International Association of Emergency Managers
  (520)

Walker, Leah A.
Association of Reporters of Judicial Decisions *(305)*

Walker, Lisa A.
International Imaging Industry Association *(551)*

Walker, Marianne M.
American Law Institute *(144)*

Walker, Marin
American Society for Mass Spectrometry *(186)*

Walker, Marjory L.
National Cotton Council of America *(730)*

Walker, Michelle
Distributive Education Clubs of America (DECA) *(415)*

Walker, Miranda
Institute for Operations Research and the Management Sciences *(497)*

Walker, Monty W.
Institute of Certified Business Counselors *(498)*

Walker, Norma
Council for Advancement and Support of Education *(388)*

Walker, Pam
National Association of State Chief Information Officers *(699)*

Walker, Rachel
Society for Organic Petrology *(917)*

Walker, Richard G.
American Architectural Manufacturers Association *(46)*

Walker, Rick
Society of International Business Fellows *(940)*

Walker, Sandra
The International Compressor Remanufacturers Association *(536)*

Walker, Shane
Federation of Straight Chiropractors and Organizations *(442)*

Walker, Sharon
National Marine Educators Association *(771)*

Walker, Siovahn A.
Council for European Studies *(390)*

Walker, Steven
National Association of Corporate Directors *(658)*

Walker, Sue
National Association of Catholic Chaplains *(651)*

Walker, Suzanne
Military Officers Association of America (MOAA) *(616)*
Society of Corporate Secretaries and Governance Professionals *(933)*

Walker, Tamara
AABB - American Association of Blood Banks *(1)*

Walker, Tarra
Association for Continuing Higher Education *(243)*

Walker, MAAA, Todd
Society of Insurance Research *(940)*

Walker, Valerie
National Indian Health Board *(763)*

Walker, Wade
Newspaper Purchasing Management Association *(810)*

Walker, Wendy
American Association for the Advancement of Slavic Studies *(52)*
Association for Slavic, East European, and Eurasian Studies *(256)*

Walker, Yanin
The Wildlife Society *(1017)*

Walkos, Beth
National Association of Bond Lawyers *(650)*

Walkup, Kenny
Phi Delta Chi *(845)*

Wall, Bruce
International Society of Crime Prevention Practitioners *(572)*

Wall, Dan
National Reining Horse Association *(785)*

Wall, Eboni
Produce Marketing Association *(858)*

Wall, Jack
Chester White Swine Record Association *(352)*

National Spotted Swine Records *(796)*
Poland China Record Association *(852)*

Wall, Kristin
Association for Healthcare Documentation Integrity *(247)*

Wall, Lucas
AASHTO: Transportation Center of Excellence *(2)*

Wall, CAE, Martin A.
Association of Schools and Colleges of Optometry *(307)*

Wall, Seana
Surface Mount Technology Association *(966)*

Wall, Sharon
National Investor Relations Institute *(767)*

Wall, Vernon
American College Personnel Association *(105)*

Wall, Vernon A.
ACPA College Student Educators International *(11)*

Wallace, Allanna
American Society for Nutrition *(187)*

Wallace, Angela
National Association of Professional Organizers *(687)*

Wallace, Anne
The Financial Services Roundtable *(445)*

Wallace, Barbara
InterAction (American Council of Voluntary International Action) *(506)*

Wallace, Brian
Coin Laundry Association *(361)*

Wallace, Catherine O'Mara
Association for Canadian Studies in the United States *(241)*

Wallace, Charlie
Quality Service Contractors *(871)*

Wallace, Dave
Promotion Marketing Association *(866)*

Wallace, David
The Brown Swiss Association *(336)*

Wallace, Derwin A.
National Association of Investors Corporation *(677)*

Wallace, Evan
Juvenile Products Manufacturers Association *(590)*

Wallace, Eve
American Bankers Association *(79)*

Wallace, James (Tim)
Society for Applied Anthropology *(904)*

Wallace, Jo-Ann
National Legal Aid and Defender Association *(769)*

Wallace, Kevin
Council of State Governments *(397)*

Wallace, Lauren
Soccer Industry Council of America *(902)*
Sports and Fitness Industry Association *(959)*

Wallace, Mirta
Association for Radiological and Imaging Nursing *(255)*
National Organization for Associate Degree Nursing *(776)*

Wallace, Nicole
Association of Pediatric Hematology/Oncology Nurses *(298)*
Professional Records and Information Services Management International *(864)*

Wallace, Paul K.
International Society for Advancement Cytometry *(565)*

Wallace, Terri
Medicaid Health Plans of America *(611)*

Wallace, Tim
National Association for the Practice of Anthropology *(644)*

Wallach, CMP, Louise
Minerals, Metals and Materials Society *(617)*

Wallentin, CMP, Debbie
Society for Vascular Surgery *(926)*

Waller, Eric
Craft & Hobby Association *(402)*

Waller, Marianne
Association of Personal Historians *(299)*

Wallerstein, Lisa
National Association of Export Companies *(666)*

Walley, Paul
The National Campus Ministry Association *(717)*

Wallin, Jason
Receptive Services Association of America *(876)*

Wallingford, Shelly
National Environmental Health Association *(746)*

Wallington, Chris J.
American Society for Investigative Pathology *(186)*

Wallington, Kenneth L.
Institute of Transportation Engineers *(503)*

Wallis, Alison
American Institute of Parliamentarians *(140)*

Wallis, Anthony A.
Association of the United States Navy, Inc. *(314)*

Wallis, Lyle
Credit Research Foundation *(403)*

Wallis, PhD, Norman E.
Academy of Psychosomatic Medicine *(8)*
American College of Foot & Ankle Orthopedics & Medicine *(95)*
American College of Radiation Oncology *(102)*

Walls, Chris
Society of Trauma Nurses *(949)*

Walls, John
CTIA - The Wireless Association *(405)*

Walls, Matthew
Society of American Foresters *(928)*

Walls, Melissa
National Conference of Commissioners on Uniform State Laws *(727)*

Walls, Michael P.
American Chemistry Council *(90)*

Waln, Donna
Evangelical Church Library Association *(434)*

Walner, Cookie
American Hardware Manufacturers Association *(128)*

Waloff, Harriet
Academy of Ambulatory Foot and Ankle Surgery *(3)*

Waloff, Richard
American Jewish Press Association *(143)*

Walpert, William C.
Brotherhood of Locomotive Engineers and Trainmen *(336)*

Walrath, Brian J.
Society of Research Administrators International *(946)*

Walsemann, Gary
International Chiropractors Association *(534)*

Walsh, CAE, Angela M.
Metal Building Contractors and Erectors Association *(613)*

Walsh, David
American Society of Mechanical Engineers (ASME) *(203)*

Walsh, CMP, Dee
Catholic Health Association of the United States *(345)*

Walsh, Francis
International Brotherhood of Electrical Workers #98 *(531)*

Walsh, Gerri
Financial Industry Regulatory Authority (FINRA) *(444)*

Walsh, Jack
National Alliance for Media Arts and Culture *(631)*

Walsh, Jim
United States Association of Former Members of Congress *(990)*

Walsh, John
Special Libraries Association *(956)*

Walsh, Katie
Organization Development Network *(831)*

Walsh, Kim
Financial & Insurance Conference Planners *(444)*

Walsh, Kim
International Association of Audio Information Services *(516)*

Walsh, Kristen
International Health, Racquet and Sportsclub Association *(549)*

Walsh, Lisl
Women's Classical Caucus *(1023)*

Walsh, Sr. Mary Ann
United States Conference of Catholic Bishops *(992)*

Walsh, Megan L.
Tire Industry Association *(975)*

Walsh, Melinda
The Association of American Seed Control Officials *(266)*

Walsh, CAP, MS, Michael E.
National Association of Addiction Treatment Providers *(645)*

Walsh, Patrick J
Food Marketing Institute *(449)*

Walsh, R. Darin
American Association for Dental Research *(49)*
International Association for Dental Research *(512)*

Walsh, Rachel
American Prosthodontic Society *(168)*
Giving USA Foundation *(461)*

Walsh, CMP, Rachel
Giving Institute *(461)*

Walsh, Sara
American Prepaid Legal Services Institute *(167)*

Walsh, Sara
National Newspaper Association *(775)*

Walsh, Sarah
American Society of Home Inspectors *(200)*

Walsh, Stephen J.
International Fire Photographers Association *(545)*

Walsh, Taly
Telecommunications Industry Association *(971)*

Walske, Ynez
Association for Continuing Higher Education *(243)*

Walten, Kurt
National Association of Real Estate Investment Trusts (NAREIT) *(690)*

Walter, Daniel "Dan" G.
Associated Specialty Contractors *(237)*
National Electrical Contractors Association *(744)*

Walter, Darryl
The Wildlife Society *(1017)*

Walter, Lindsey
Registry of Interpreters for the Deaf *(879)*

Walter, Timothy M.
Catholic Press Association *(346)*

Walters, Chris
National Association of Small Business Investment Companies *(900)*

Walters, Jay
American Composers Forum *(105)*

Walters, Lance
Arabian Horse Association *(227)*

Walters, CAE, Sean
Investment Management Consultants Association *(584)*

Walters, William E.
Acute Long Term Hospital Association *(12)*

Walther, DVM, G'94, Ann
Omega Tau Sigma *(827)*

Walther, Martina
German American Business Association *(460)*

Walther, Robert
Association of Applied IPM Ecologists *(267)*

Walton, Bob
Transportation Research Forum *(979)*

Walton, Emily
National Association for Olmsted Parks *(641)*

Walton, Jeff
American Association of Christian Schools *(56)*

Walton, Jennifer D.
Casualty Actuarial Society *(344)*

Walton, Mae S.
Auxiliary to the National Medical Association *(324)*

Walton, Marcus F.
Association of Black Foundation Executives *(269)*

Walton, Marty
Association of Personal Historians *(299)*

Walton, Mia Kelly
United States Chamber of Commerce *(991)*

Walton, Ray
National Association of State Chief Administrators *(699)*

Walton, Theresa
North American Society for the Sociology of Sport *(822)*

Walton, RT, Tony
Association of Vascular and Interventional Radiographers *(316)*

Walz, Renee
Lignite Energy Council *(598)*

Wamsley, Herbert C.
Intellectual Property Owners Association *(505)*

Wamsley, Lisa
American Pinzgauer Association *(165)*

Wan-Lopaz, Jamie
Pacific Telecommunications Council *(836)*

Wanamaker, Karen
National Wooden Pallet and Container Association *(805)*

Wanca-Daniels, Margaret
LeadingAge (American Association of Homes and Services for the Aging) *(595)*

Wang, Alice
Recreation Vehicle Industry Association *(877)*

Wang, Christine
Society for Maintenance & Reliability Professionals *(914)*

Wang, Crystal
Global Semiconductor Alliance *(463)*

Wang, Hsiao-Lan
International Alliance for Women in Music *(510)*

Wang, MD, Hsueh-hwa
Chinese American Medical Society *(354)*

Wang, MD, Jeffrey
National Association of Spine Specialists *(696)*

Wang, Kinglen L.
Modern Language Association *(618)*

Wang, Scott
World Trade Centers Association *(1027)*

Wang, Tina
Asia America MultiTechnology Association *(231)*

Wangman, Brett
International Association of Rehabilitation Professionals *(527)*

Wangman, CAE, Carl A.
International Association of Rehabilitation Professionals *(527)*

Wanits, Denise
Association Montessori International - United States of America *(262)*

Wanna, Monchaya
National Association of Schools of Public Affairs and Administration *(694)*

Wannen, David
North American Performing Arts Managers and Agents *(819)*

Wanner, Aubrey M.J.
National Society for Histotechnology *(792)*

Warberg, Jim
Institute of Tax Consultants *(503)*

Warburton, Jennifer
National Association of Letter Carriers *(678)*

Warchot, Louis P.
Association of American Railroads *(266)*

Ward, Aaron
Aircraft Electronics Association *(20)*

Ward, Amelia K.
Association of Ecosystem Research Centers *(279)*

Ward, Amy Sample
Nonprofit Technology Network *(811)*

Ward, Angela
Game Manufacturers Association *(456)*

Ward, Betsy
Rice Millers' Association *(886)*
USA Rice Council *(1004)*
USA Rice Federation *(1004)*

Ward, Brendan
Association of Strategic Alliance Professionals, Inc. *(311)*

Ward, Buzz
League of Resident Theatres *(595)*

Ward, Carolyn
National Council of Investigative and Security Services Inc. *(735)*

Ward, CAE, MS, Chrissy
Society of Gynecologic Oncologists *(938)*

Ward, Christine
German American Chamber of Commerce *(460)*

Ward, Cynthia A.
Precast/Prestressed Concrete Institute *(856)*

Ward, DDS, Daniel H.
American Society for Dental Aesthetics *(183)*

Ward, J D, OSB, Daniel J.

Resource Center for Religious Institutes *(883)*

Ward, David
American Council on Education *(110)*

Ward, Elizabeth
Federation of American Hospitals *(440)*

Ward, Jack
American Hereford Association *(131)*

Ward, Jake Michael
Application Developers Alliance *(226)*

Ward, Jan
National Association of Directors of Nursing Administration in Long Term Care *(663)*

Ward, Janet
American Society of Andrology *(192)*

Ward, Jennifer
Association of Social Work Boards *(309)*

Ward, Jennifer
Council of American Survey Research Organizations *(392)*

Ward, Jennifer
International Institute of Municipal Clerks *(552)*

Ward, Joelle
American Society of Naval Engineers *(204)*

Ward, John
American Coal Ash Association *(92)*

Ward, John
Game Manufacturers Association *(456)*

Ward, Kerry
Library Leadership and Management Association *(597)*

Ward, Lynne
College Savings Plans Network *(364)*

Ward, Matt
National Association of Towns and Townships (NATAT) *(706)*

Ward, Meredith
International Association of Chiefs of Police *(517)*

Ward, Michael
American Bar Association *(79)*

Ward, Neil
Forest Resources Association *(451)*

Ward, Sheila
American Society of International Law *(201)*

Ward, Stacy L.
Automotive Industry Action Group *(322)*

Ward, Stephanie
Footwear Distributors and Retailers of America *(450)*

Ward, Tanisha
International Association of Exhibitions and Events *(520)*

Ward, Terrie
Synthetic Turf Council *(967)*

Ward, Thomas
National Association of Home Builders *(673)*

Ward-Cook, CAE, PhD, Kory
National Certification Commission for Acupuncture and Oriental Medicine *(720)*

Wardell, Debra Steinke
American Psychoanalytic Association *(168)*

Wardell, Dwight
American Society for Engineering Education *(183)*

Warden, April
International Society of Arthroscopy, Knee Surgery and Orthopaedic Sports Medicine *(571)*

Wardlow, Dustin

International Conference of Funeral Service Examining Boards *(536)*

Ware, Bill
National Association of Property Tax Representatives - Transportation, Energy, Communications *(688)*

Ware, John
National Association of State Administrators and Supervisors of Private Schools *(697)*

Wareing, Tracy
American Public Human Services Association *(171)*
APHSA - Information Systems Management *(224)*

Warens, Nora
National Association of Bar Executives *(648)*

Warfield, Gerald
Society of Composers, Inc. *(933)*

Warfield, Timothy R.
National Association for State Community Services Programs *(643)*

Warfield, William R.
Electronics Representatives Association *(424)*

Wargo, RN, Lorraine
National Association of State Head Injury Administrators *(701)*

Warhola, Kelly
The Association to Advance Collegiate Schools of Business *(319)*

Warnat, Deb
Association for the Calligraphic Arts *(259)*

Warndorf, Paul R.
AMT - The Association For Manufacturing Technology *(222)*

Warne, Lee
Association of Educational Service Agencies *(280)*

Warne, Myra
Society of Glass and Ceramic Decorated Products *(937)*

Warne, Susan
Academy of Clinical Research Professionals *(4)*

Warner, Ann
American Institute of Parliamentarians *(140)*

Warner, Briana
National Association for Environmental Management *(638)*

Warner, Charlie
Media Financial Management Association *(610)*

Warner, David
National Aircraft Finance Association *(630)*

Warner, CMDSM, Erik
Mail Systems Management Association *(601)*

Warner, Gina
National After School Association *(629)*

Warner, James
Fuel Cell and Hydrogen Energy Association *(454)*

Warner, MD, Jon J.P.
American Shoulder and Elbow Surgeons *(179)*

Warner, Judy
Social Science History Association *(902)*

Warner, Kevin
United States Synchronized Swimming *(999)*

Warner, Lance
National Council of Exchangors *(734)*

Warner, Michael
Society of Insurance Research *(940)*

Warner, Rachel
National Association of College and University Food Services *(655)*

Warner, S. Chrissy

Institute of Hazardous Materials Management *(500)*

Warner, Sarah
World Future Society *(1026)*

Warner, Shelley
Professional Rodeo Cowboys Association *(864)*

Warner, Tommy
America's Independent Truckers' Association, Inc. *(29)*

Warner, MD, William C.
Clinical Orthopaedic Society *(358)*

Warnik, John
Turnaround Management Association *(982)*

Warnke, Sheri
Country Music Association *(401)*

Warren, Anne
American Academy of Forensic Sciences *(34)*

Warren, David L.
National Association of Independent Colleges and Universities *(674)*

Warren, Elliott
Medical Device Manufacturers Association *(611)*

Warren, Jeff
International Association of Healthcare Central Service Materiel Management *(522)*

Warren, Jim
American Association of Tissue Banks *(75)*

Warren, Jim
Fabricators & Manufacturers Association, International *(437)*

Warren, Jim
Tube and Pipe Association, International *(981)*

Warren, CFE, JD, John
Association of Certified Fraud Examiners *(271)*

Warren, Laurie
Copper and Brass Servicenter Association *(384)*
International Association of Plastics Distributors *(526)*

Warren, Penny
USA Taekwondo *(1005)*

Warren, Peter
Education Finance Council *(419)*

Warren, Sharon L.
Society for Healthcare Strategy and Market Development *(910)*

Wartenberg Kagan, PhD, Ute
American Numismatic Society *(156)*

Wartman, MD, PhD, Steven
Association of Academic Health Centers *(262)*

Wasch, Kenneth
Software & Information Industry Association (SIIA) *(950)*

Washburn, Sarah
Business Marketing Association *(339)*
Institute of Packaging Professionals *(502)*
National Association of Sporting Goods Wholesalers *(696)*
The Recreational Vehicle Aftermarket Association *(877)*

Washburn, Wendy
The American Finance Association *(121)*

Washburne, Phillip
American Geriatrics Society *(126)*

Washington, Danielle V.
Association of Collegiate Schools of Architecture *(275)*

Washington, Fayton
Association & Society Insurance Corporation *(237)*

Washington, Irving
National Association of Black Journalists *(649)*

Washington, Jeff

American Correctional Association *(108)*

Washington, Kristen
American Public Human Services Association *(171)*

Washington, CAE, Lisa
Design-Build Institute of America *(411)*

Washington, III, Raymond
American Public Human Services Association *(171)*

Washington, Stanley E.
National Coalition of African American Owned Media *(723)*

Washington, Valora
Council for Professional Recognition *(391)*

Washmera, Raymond A.
National Sweetener and Ingredient Marketing Association *(798)*

Wasielewski, Dave
Society for Laboratory Automation and Screening *(914)*

Wasserman, Dan
National Basketball Players Association *(713)*

Wasserman, Karen
Textile Bag and Packaging Association *(972)*

Wasserman, Margery
National Association of Personal Financial Advisors *(684)*

Wasserstein, Ronald L.
American Statistical Association *(213)*

Waszak, Angel
American College of Psychiatrists *(102)*

Watchinski, CPA, Robert I.
American Academy of Family Physicians *(34)*

Waterfield, Don
Association of Shareware Professionals *(308)*

Waterhouse, Jim
Association of Career and Technical Education *(271)*

Waterman, Amy E.
Council of American Jewish Museums *(391)*

Waters, Bud
International Business Music Association *(532)*

Waters, John
Knowledge Alliance *(591)*

Waters, Kathryn D.
American Public Transportation Association *(171)*

Waters, Mary K.
North American Millers' Association *(818)*

Waters, Mary Piper
Telecommunications Industry Association *(971)*

Waters, CAE, Richard
American College of Chest Physicians *(94)*

Waters, RSM, Rita
Resource Center for Religious Institutes *(883)*

Waters, Susan
Sponge and Chamois Institute *(958)*

Waters, CAE, Dr. Susan B.
National Association of Insurance and Financial Advisors *(675)*

Waters, Theresa A.
American Immigration Lawyers Association *(134)*

Watford, Jack
Women's Basketball Coaches Association *(1022)*

Watkins, CAE, Carol
National Dental EDI Council *(743)*

Watkins, Edward
American Association of Public Welfare Attorneys *(72)*

Watkins, Gloria J.

American Court and Commercial Newspapers *(111)*

Watkins, Jason G.
American Anthropological Association *(45)*

Watkins, Lori
Water Quality Association *(1013)*

Watkins, Lynn
National Association of Federally Impacted Schools *(668)*

Watkins, Michael
National Funeral Directors Association *(754)*

Watkins, Ross
National Association of Professional Band Instrument Repair Technicians *(686)*

Watkins, Ruth A.
Fusion Power Associates *(455)*

Watkins, Sranda
Community Action Partnership *(369)*

Watland, Alice J.
American Telemedicine Association *(215)*

Watner, P.J.
Association of Plastic Surgery Assistants *(299)*

Watrous, Rebecca
ASME International Gas Turbine Institute *(233)*

Watson, Andrew
Object Management Group *(825)*

Watson, Brendan
Art Directors Club *(229)*

Watson, Brent
American Society for Mass Spectrometry *(186)*

Watson, Brian
AASHTO: Transportation Center of Excellence *(2)*

Watson, Carol
American Institute of Professional Bookkeepers *(140)*

Watson, Darcy
International Association of Lighting Management Companies *(524)*

Watson, Donna
Missouri Fox Trotting Horse Breed Association *(617)*

Watson, Felicia
National Association of Home Builders *(673)*

Watson, Fran Katz
Democratic Attorneys General Association *(410)*

Watson, PE, Ian C.
American Membrane Technology Association *(150)*

Watson, Jennifer
American Society for Mass Spectrometry *(186)*

Watson, Karen
Commercial Real Estate Women Network *(367)*

Watson, Linda E.
American Society of Plant Taxonomists *(207)*

Watson, Mark G.
Radiological Society of North America *(873)*

Watson, Capt. Michael R.
American Pilots' Association *(165)*

Watson, PhD, Michael S.
American College of Medical Genetics *(97)*

Watson, CMP, Pat
American Society for Metabolic and Bariatric Surgery *(187)*

Watson, Pete
Association for Living History, Farm and Agricultural Museums *(251)*

Watson, CMP, CAE, Shannon M.
Solar Energy Industries Association (SEIA) *(952)*

Watson, Tom
National Lamb Feeders Association *(768)*

Watson, Vicki
National Community Development Association *(725)*

Watson, Warren
Society of American Business Editors and Writers *(928)*

Watt, Andrew
Association of Fundraising Professionals *(285)*

Watt, David
American Running Association *(176)*

Watt, David
American Running Association/American Medical Athletic Association *(176)*

Watters, Sue
Pi Gamma Mu *(847)*

Wattonville, Kristin
American College of Osteopathic Emergency Physicians *(99)*

Watts, Bonnie L.
International Parking Institute *(559)*

Watts, David
Academy of Dental Materials *(5)*

Watts, Jennifer
Electric Drive Transportation Association *(421)*

Watts, MPH, RD, Mary Lee
American Association for Cancer Research *(48)*

Watts, Pam
National Intramural-Recreational Sports Association *(766)*

Watts-Taylor, Ernestine
National Alliance of Postal and Federal Employees *(633)*

Watzman, Bruce
Coal Exporters Association of the U.S. *(359)*

Waugerman, Stephanie
National Independent Living Association *(762)*

Waugh, Jennifer
National Home Infusion Association *(760)*

Waugh, Kenneth
United States Maglev Coalition (USMC) *(996)*

Waugh, Seth
Enlisted Association of the National Guard of the United States *(429)*

Wawrzusin, Dianne
American Music Therapy Association *(154)*

Wax, MD, Mark
American Head and Neck Society *(129)*

Wax, FACMT, MD, Paul M.
American College of Medical Toxicology *(98)*

Way, Jim
Association of Corporate Counsel *(277)*

Waybright, Elizabeth
American Jail Association *(142)*

Waylett, Bill
Navy League of the United States *(807)*

Wayne, Kirk
Tobacco Associates, Inc. *(975)*

Weakley, James H.I.
Lake Carriers Association *(592)*

Weart, Walter
Transportation Intermediaries Association *(978)*

Weatherford, Aaron
International Association of Assessing Officers *(516)*

Weatherford, Catherine J.
Insured Retirement Institute *(505)*

Weaver, Andy
Land Trust Alliance *(593)*

Weaver, Angela
Theatre Library Association *(973)*

Weaver, CMP, Brenda L.
American Geophysical Union *(126)*

Weaver, Brian L.
Association for Psychological Science *(254)*

Weaver, Glenda F.
Defense Research Institute *(408)*

Weaver, Jay
International Test and Evaluation Association *(577)*

Weaver, CAE, Jerrod A.
Non-Ferrous Founders' Society *(811)*

Weaver, MBA, Kelsey
Society of American Travel Writers *(930)*

Weaver, CMP, Laura
Society of American Florists *(928)*

Weaver, Rachel
American College for Advancement in Medicine *(93)*

Weaver, Robert "Bob"
National Finishing Contractors Association *(751)*

Weaver, Robert "Peter"
International Liquid Terminals Association *(554)*

Weaver, Sharon
Association of State Wetland Managers *(311)*

Weaver, Terri
CHA - Certified Horsemanship Association *(350)*

Weaverling, Cheryl
Credit Research Foundation *(403)*

Webb, PhD, RN, Adele A.
Association of Nurses in AIDS Care *(296)*

Webb, Corey
Consortium for Graduate Study in Management *(378)*

Webb, Debbie
Phi Delta Kappa International *(845)*

Webb, Elaine
Women of the Motion Picture Industry, International *(1022)*

Webb, Glenda J.
Hotel Brokers International *(479)*

Webb, Heather
Restaurant Facility Management Association *(884)*

Webb, Jeffrey B.
Conference on Faith and History *(376)*

Webb, John
Direct Selling Association *(413)*

Webb, Judith
United States Green Building Council *(994)*

Webb, Laura
Chain Drug Marketing Association *(350)*

Webb, Rod
Council of International Investigators *(395)*

Webb, Teresa
Society of Corporate Secretaries and Governance Professionals *(933)*

Webb, Thomas
American Academy of Nursing *(37)*

Webb, Tom B.
National Judges Association *(767)*

Webb, Vicki
Fabricators & Manufacturers Association, International *(437)*
Tube and Pipe Association, International *(981)*

Webber, E. Jean
Real Estate Management Brokers Institute *(875)*

Webber, Kate
Council of Independent Colleges *(394)*

Webber, Nicki
Association of Film Commissioners International *(283)*

Webendorfer, Stephanie
Cremation Association of North America *(404)*

Weber, Anjali
Rehabilitation Engineering and Assistive Technology Society of North America *(879)*

Weber, Barbara
Gas Technology Institute *(456)*

Weber, Becky B.
National School Transportation Association *(790)*

Weber, Beth
National Auto Auction Association *(711)*

Weber, Bill
Association of Pool and Spa Professionals *(299)*

Weber, David O.
Armed Forces Financial Network *(229)*

Weber, Eric
US Travel Association *(983)*

Weber, Dr. Eric Thomas
Society of Philosophers in America *(944)*

Weber, Greta
International Carwash Association *(533)*

Weber, Heidi
Alpha Omega International Dental Fraternity *(26)*

Weber, Jackie
International Guild of Candle Artisans *(549)*

Weber, Jordan
The Association of Collegiate Conference and Events Directors International *(275)*

Weber, Laurie
Scaffold Industry Association *(891)*

Weber, Nicole
Independent Sealing Distributors *(491)*

Weber, Nicole Tierney
Yacht Brokers Association of America *(1030)*

Weber, Ronna Sable
National School Transportation Association *(790)*

Weber, Tracy
International Sanitary Supply Association *(563)*

Weber, MBA, Vikki
International Veterinary Acupuncture Society *(580)*

Weber, FInstAM, CAE, Pam
Association of School Business Officials International *(306)*

Webster, Bob
North American Securities Administrators Association (NASAA) *(820)*

Webster, Dr. Carl
World Aquaculture Society *(1025)*

Webster, Diane
International Card Manufacturers Association *(532)*

Webster, Duane
National Humanities Alliance *(761)*

Webster, Elishia
American Family Therapy Academy *(118)*

Webster, Hugh K.
American Boiler Manufacturers Association *(84)*

Webster, Janet
International Association of Aquatic and Marine Science Libraries and Information Centers *(515)*

Webster, Mary
International College of Dentists, U.S.A. Section *(535)*

Webster, Steve
Pakistan American Business Association *(837)*

Wechsler, Debby
North American Raspberry & Blackberry Association *(820)*

Wechsler, Steven A.
National Association of Real Estate Investment Trusts (NAREIT) *(690)*

Weed, Laurie
Professional Society for Sales and Marketing Training *(865)*

Weed, Robert D.
Copper Development Association *(384)*

Weekes, Leslie
Association of American Universities *(266)*

Weekes, Pamela Antoine
Association of Junior Leagues International *(290)*

Weekley, Mary E.
American Gas Association *(124)*

Weeks, Melissa (McElroy)
American Society for Histocompatibility and Immunogenetics *(185)*

Weerts, Richard K.
National Association of College Wind and Percussion Instructors *(655)*

Weeter, Gregory B.
The National Association of Marine Surveyors, Inc. *(679)*

Weeth, Lisa
American College of Veterinary Nutrition *(104)*

Wegener, Alan
American Association of Petroleum Geologists *(68)*

Wegrzyn, Susanne R.
National Club Association *(722)*

Wehking, CMP, Christopher J.
American Society of Anesthesiologists *(192)*

Wehri, Ann
Columbia Sheep Breeders Association of America *(365)*

Wehrle, Jr., Joseph H.
National Insurance Crime Bureau *(766)*

Wehrlin, Robin
International Society for Third-Sector Research *(570)*

Wehrman, Christine
American Rental Association *(174)*

Wei, Chi
Association for Research in Vision and Ophthalmology *(255)*

Weichlein, Peter M.
United States Association of Former Members of Congress *(990)*

Weickert, Brent
Natural Products Association *(807)*

Weidlich, Joseph
Airports Council International - North America *(21)*

Weidner, Bob
Metals Service Center Institute *(614)*

Weigel, Brenda
America's Health Insurance Plans *(28)*

Weigel, Dr. Kent
National Association of Animal Breeders *(647)*

Weihl, Cindy
Gases and Welding Distributors Association *(457)*

Weil, Dave

The Association of International Photography Art Dealers *(289)*

Weil, Lynne
International Business Brokers Association *(532)*

Weiland, Carla
Association for Middle Level Education *(252)*

Weiland, Cindy
Intersocietal Accreditation Commission *(582)*

Weiland, Lois
Media Communications Association International *(610)*

Weimer, Angela
National Association of Latino Elected and Appointed Officials *(677)*

Weimer, Jr., Carroll A.
Conveyor Equipment Manufacturers Association *(383)*

Weimer, Jr., David B.
International Fire Photographers Association *(545)*

Weinberg, Carl
National Psychological Association for Psychoanalysis *(783)*

Weinberg, Esq., David B.
Battery Council International *(326)*

Weinberg, Frank M.
Defense Orientation Conference Association *(408)*

Weinberg, Mitch
Aviation Suppliers Association *(324)*

Weinberg, CAE, Myrl
National Health Council *(758)*

Weinberg, Steve
Investigative Reporters and Editors *(583)*

Weinberger, FACP, MD, Steven E.
American College of Physicians *(101)*
American College of Physicians Services, Inc. *(101)*

Weinbrecht, Kenneth
Society of Accredited Marine Surveyors *(927)*

Weindruch, CAE, Larry
National Ski and Snowboard Retailers Association *(791)*

Weiner, Jeffrey J.
American Bureau of Shipping *(86)*

Weiner, Meredith
International Pediatric Transplant Association *(560)*

Weiner, CMP, Meredith
American Society of Hand Therapists *(199)*

Weiner, Michael
Major League Baseball Players Association *(601)*

Weiner, Myra
International Housewares Representatives Association *(550)*

Weiner, William
International Housewares Representatives Association *(550)*

Weinfurter, Amy
Instructional Technology Council *(504)*

Weingarten, Randi
AFT - Public Employees *(15)*
American Federation of Teachers (AFL-CIO) *(120)*

Weinglass, PhD, Daniel
Jewelry Industry Distributors Association *(587)*

Weinman, Kendra Bridel
Women's Jewelry Association *(1023)*

Weinraub, Ellen
National Investment Company Service Association *(767)*

Weinrauch, Jaclyn

The Association for Nursing Professional Development *(252)*

Weinshel, Kristy
Society for Healthcare Epidemiology of America *(910)*

Weinstein, Jaclyn
American Radium Society *(173)*
North American Skull Base Society *(820)*

Weinstein, Jay
Association for Applied and Clinical Sociology *(238)*

Weinstein, Mindy
Institute of Food Technologists *(499)*

Weinstein, MD, Robert
American Society for Apheresis *(180)*

Weinstock, Daniel
National Frame Building Association *(753)*

Weintraub, Andrew
Society for Asian Music *(904)*

Weintraub, Rachel
Retail Advertising and Marketing Association International *(884)*

Weintraub, Esq., Richard
National Sheriffs' Association *(791)*

Weir, Daniel
National Association of Criminal Defense Lawyers *(661)*

Weir, Don
American Cultural Resources Association (ACRA) *(112)*

Weir, Sherry
Association for Federal Information Resources Management *(246)*

Weis, BSN, CCTC, RN, Karla
International Transplant Nurses Society *(578)*

Weisbarth, Jeff
United Transportation Union *(1001)*

Weisberg, Steve
The Coastal and Estuarine Research Federation *(361)*

Weisenbach, Phillip
Edison Welding Institute *(419)*

Weisenberger, Lisa
American Orthopaedic Society for Sports Medicine *(159)*

Weiser, Nora
American Cheese Society *(89)*

Weiser, Wendy J.
American Association of Clinical Urologists *(56)*
American College of Legal Medicine *(97)*
American Society of Andrology *(192)*
Society of Government Service Urologists *(938)*
Society of University Urologists *(949)*

Weisman, Avril
Community Action Partnership *(369)*

Weisman, Michael
Community Action Partnership *(369)*

Weisman, Rick
National Fraternal Order of Police *(753)*

Weiss, Alan
Society for Advancement of Consulting *(903)*

Weiss, Andrea
American Academy of Neurology *(36)*

Weiss, Arthur
Association of Independent Information Professionals *(288)*

Weiss, Audrey
Institute of Mathematical Statistics *(501)*

Weiss, Brad
Society for Cultural Anthropology *(907)*

Weiss, David
Energy Solutions Center *(428)*

Weiss, Ellen
Biophysical Society *(330)*

Weiss, Erica
Conference of Minority Transportation Officials *(375)*

Weiss, Erica
Healthcare Supply Chain Association *(472)*

Weiss, Gerard
COLA *(362)*

Weiss, Heidi
International Foodservice Distributors Association *(546)*

Weiss, Heidi
National Concrete Masonry Association *(725)*

Weiss, CAE, Jim
American Orthopaedic Association *(158)*

Weiss, MSW, Joan C.
Justice Research and Statistics Association *(589)*

Weiss, Katrina
USA Archery *(1004)*

Weiss, Larry
Copier Dealers Association *(384)*

Weiss, CMP, Leonard
National Cleaners Association *(722)*

Weiss, Marshall
American Jewish Press Association *(143)*

Weiss, Peter
American Geophysical Union *(126)*

Weiss, CAE, MS, Sharon
International Life Sciences Institute *(554)*

Weiss, Steven P.
The National Association of Marine Surveyors, Inc. *(679)*

Weissenbach, Jenny
Commercial Real Estate Women Network *(367)*

Weisser, Randy
Off-Road Business Association *(826)*

Weissman, Dana
Writers Guild of America East *(1029)*

Weissman, Jane
Interstate Renewable Energy Council *(583)*

Weissman, Juliet
The College Board *(363)*

Weist, CPH, MA, MPH, Elizabeth M.
Association of Schools of Public Health *(307)*

Weitkamp, MHS, James G.
Caribbean Hotel and Tourism Association *(343)*

Weitzenfeld, JoAnn
The Association for Manufacturing Excellence *(252)*

Welber, Chris
North American Neuromodulation Society *(819)*

Welber, MBA, Chris
American Society for Bioethics and Humanities *(181)*

Welch, Cindy
American Counseling Association *(111)*

Welch, Edmund B.
Passenger Vessel Association *(839)*

Welch, Jill
NAFSA: Association of International Educators *(624)*

Welch, Joel E.
Society of Motion Picture and Television Engineers *(942)*

Welch, Michael

Chamber Music America *(350)*

Welch, Sally R.
Distance Education and Training Council *(414)*

Welch, Stephen J.
American College of Chest Physicians *(94)*

Welch, Todd
Academy of Certified Archivists *(4)*

Welch, MSN, Valre W.
Certification Board for Urologic Nurses and Associates *(349)*
Society of Urologic Nurses and Associates *(949)*

Welch, Victoria
Healthcare Compliance Packaging Council *(470)*

Welch, ChFC, CLU, Winston
World History Association *(1026)*

Weldon, E. J.
American Association of Plastic Surgeons *(70)*

Weldon, Timothy
Council of State Governments *(397)*

Weller, Keith
Reserve Officers Association of the U.S. *(882)*

Weller, Jr., Paul S.
Apple Processors Association *(225)*

Wellikson, MD, Laurence
Society of Hospital Medicine *(938)*

Wellington, Dawn
American Recovery Association *(174)*

Wellington, Jane
Rapid Technologies & Additive Manufacturing Community of SME *(875)*

Wellmon, Jan
High Point Market *(474)*

Wells, Alicia
Nursery and Landscape Association Executives of North America *(825)*

Wells, Ann
North American Meat Association *(818)*

Wells, Barbara
International Association Of Pet Cemeteries and Crematories *(526)*

Wells, Byron R.
American Society for Eighteenth-Century Studies *(183)*

Wells, Crystal
Interim Ministry Network *(508)*

Wells, Damon
National Turkey Federation *(802)*

Wells, Donna
Professional Skaters Association *(865)*

Wells, Elizabeth
Snack Food Association *(901)*

Wells, Gary
American Judicature Society *(143)*

Wells, Ivone
National Council of University Research Administrators *(737)*

Wells, Jana
Society for Pediatric Research *(918)*

Wells, Kennedy D.
Black Coaches & Administrators *(331)*

Wells, Monique
National Association for Multi-Ethnicity in Communications *(640)*

Wells, Paula D.
Labor and Employment Relations Association *(592)*

Wells, Thomas

Society of Composers, Inc. *(933)*

Wells, Todd V.
Federal Managers Association *(439)*

Wells, Ynez
Amalgamated Transit Union *(28)*

Welsbacher, Anne
The National Flute Association, Inc. *(751)*

Welsh, Bryan
National Marine Manufacturers Association *(771)*

Welsh, Sally
Hospice and Palliative Nurses Association *(478)*

Welsh, Thomas F.
National Insurance Crime Bureau *(766)*

Welsh, Tim
Independent Electrical Contractors *(489)*

Welty, Caleb
National Association of College Auxiliary Services *(655)*

Wendel, Erin
American Physical Therapy Association *(164)*

Wendorf, Elmo
Red and White Dairy Cattle Association *(877)*

Wendy, Michael
Computing Technology Industry Association (CompTIA) *(373)*

Wener, Jim
Association of Business Owners of America *(270)*

Wenger, Lisa
Association for Childhood Education International *(241)*

Wenmark, William H.
National Association for Ambulatory Care *(636)*

Wenning, Sarah
Clean Technology & Sustainable Industries Organization (CTSI) *(357)*

Wenning, Thomas F.
National Grocers Association *(756)*

Wensel, Deborah
Property Casualty Insurers Association of America *(867)*

Wenther, PhD, Jay
American Association of Meat Processors *(64)*

Wentworth, Eryl P.
American Institute for Conservation of Historic and Artistic Works *(136)*

Wentworth, Liza
National Society of Compliance Professionals *(793)*

Wentworth, Rand
Land Trust Alliance *(593)*

Wentz, Marilyn
National Bison Association *(713)*

Wentz, Roger
American Traffic Safety Service Association *(217)*

Wentzel, Fred
National Council for Advanced Manufacturing *(731)*

Wenzel, Jean
Society for Clinical Data Management *(906)*

Wenzel, Jean M.
American Association of Medical Society Executives *(65)*

Wenzing, Claudia
United Fresh Produce Association *(987)*

Weprin, Mark
National Association of Jewish Legislators *(677)*

Weps, Ferdinand

The International Ecotourism Society *(542)*

Werbos, Kim
National Limousine Association *(770)*

Werfelmann, Andrew
Organization Development Network *(831)*

Weritz, John
The Aluminum Association, Inc. *(27)*

Werkheiser, Sandra
American Hanoverian Society *(128)*

Werlinich, Marci
Outdoor Advertising Association of America *(834)*

Werner, Aviva
EMTA - Trade Association for the Emerging Markets *(427)*

Werner, Carol
Environmental and Energy Study Institute *(430)*

Werner, Jill
American Bar Association *(79)*

Werner, Katrien
Association of State Floodplain Managers *(311)*

Werner, Kelly
Association for Linen Management *(251)*

Werner, MPA, Kitty
National Organization of Nurse Practitioner Faculties *(777)*

Werner, J D, Michael
Alliance for Regenerative Medicine *(23)*

Wernick, Rabbi Steven
United Synagogue of Conservative Judaism *(1001)*

Wernli, PHR, CFE, SPHR, LaDonna
Association of Certified Fraud Examiners *(271)*

Wert, Barbara
Architectural Woodwork Institute *(228)*

Wert, Kathleen
American Statistical Association *(213)*

Wertheim, Judith "Judy"
Council for Adult and Experiential Learning *(388)*

Wescott, Alec
HR Policy Association *(480)*

Wesley, Paige
International Association of Business Communicators *(517)*

Wesloh, Karen
Visual Communications Industry Group *(1010)*

Wesolowski, Kevin
Consortium of School Networking *(378)*

Wesolowski, Michael
Malignant Hyperthermia Association of the United States *(602)*

Wessel, Paul C.
National Association of Insurance and Financial Advisors *(675)*

Wesserling, Sue
American College of Neuropsychiatrists *(98)*

Wessling, Janet
National Association of Student Financial Aid Administrators *(703)*

West, Ashley
National Mining Association *(772)*

West, Barbara F.
National Association of Veterans Research and Education Foundations *(708)*

West, Bonnie
American National CattleWomen *(154)*

West, Bonnie M.

National Association of County Engineers *(660)*

West, Christy
American Horse Publications *(133)*

West, CAE, Dale
Society of Gastroenterology Nurses and Associates *(937)*

West, Ford B.
The Fertilizer Institute *(443)*

West, Gretchen
Association for Unmanned Vehicle Systems International *(261)*

West, Jade
National Association of Wholesaler-Distributors *(709)*

West, James
Leading Jewelers Guild *(594)*

West, PhD, Dr. Jane E.
American Association of Colleges for Teacher Education *(57)*

West, Jay
National Society of Accountants *(793)*

West, Jill W.
National Fellowship of Child Care Executives *(750)*

West, Jo-Ann
Producers Guild of America *(858)*

West, Lauren
Academy of Political Science *(8)*
American Political Science Association *(166)*

West, Michael J.
International Communication Association *(536)*

West, Michele
ACUTA - The Association for Information Communications Technology Professionals in Higher Education *(11)*

West, Michele
State Debt Management Network *(961)*

West, Nancy
United States and Canadian Academy of Pathology *(989)*

West, Roxy
Association of Destination Management Executives *(278)*
National Association of Nephrology Technologists and Technicians *(682)*

West, Sarah
Petroleum Equipment Institute *(843)*

West, Vicki L.
American Academy of Matrimonial Lawyers *(35)*

West, Wanda M.
Association of Black Sociologists *(270)*

West, William
Computing Technology Industry Association (CompTIA) *(373)*

West-Barker, Patricia
Association of Food Journalists *(283)*

West-Evans, Kathy
Council of State Administrators of Vocational Rehabilitators *(397)*

Westaway, Maxine
The International Alliance for Women *(510)*

Westbrook, Gay
Brick Industry Association *(335)*

Westcott, Ann S.
American Philosophical Society *(164)*

Westcott, Kathi
American Association of University Professors *(75)*

Westcott, Michael E.
National Alliance of Medicare Set-Aside Professionals, Inc. *(632)*

Wester, Suzanne A.
American Academy of Pediatric Dentistry *(39)*

Westercamp, Amy
Product Development and Management Association *(858)*

Westerfield, Allen D.
Imaging Supplies Coalition *(487)*

Westerman, CAE, CMP, Amy
Society of Diagnostic Medical Sonographers *(934)*

Westfield, Bentley
International Association of Fire Fighters *(521)*

Westgeest, Alfons
Global Acetate Manufacturers Association *(461)*

Westine, Lezlee
Personal Care Products Council *(842)*

Westman, David A
Congress of Neurological Surgeons *(377)*

Westmoreland, Dianna
American Ostrich Association *(161)*

Weston, Allison
Efficiency First *(421)*

Weston, PhD, RN, Marla J.
American Nurses Association *(156)*

Westover, Bradley P.
National Tax Lien Association *(799)*

Wetherbee, Angela
Society for Vascular Nursing *(926)*

Wetherby, Catherine
Technology Student Association *(970)*

Wetherington, R. Wade
The Propeller Club of the United States *(867)*

Wetmore, Kevin J.
Association for Asian Performance *(239)*

Wetter, Janis Chinnock
Society of Laparoendoscopic Surgeons *(940)*

Wetzel, F. Todd
National Association of Spine Specialists *(696)*

Wetzel, Heather
World Airline Entertainment Association *(1025)*

Wetzel, Holly
American Gaming Association *(124)*

Wetzel, Karen A.
National Information Standards Organization *(763)*

Wetzel, Marc
American Agriculture Movement, Inc. *(44)*

Wetzel, Tom
Insurance Marketing Communications Association *(505)*

Wexler, Chuck
Police Executive Research Forum *(852)*

Weyant, Robert
American Association of Public Health Dentistry *(71)*

Weygandt, Kristen
Building Service Contractors Association International *(337)*

Weymouth, Melissa
USA Volleyball *(1005)*

Weyrauch, Judy
National Academic Advising Association *(626)*

Whalen, Catherine
National Stone, Sand, and Gravel Association *(796)*

Whalen, Deb
American Society of Retina Specialists *(209)*

Whalen, Glenda
FBI Agents Association *(438)*

Whalen, Jessica
American Society of Emergency Radiology *(197)*

Whalen, CAE, MBA, Kay A.
American Academy of Allergy, Asthma, and Immunology *(30)*
American Academy of Emergency Medicine *(33)*

Whalen, Sara
National Association of Counsel for Children *(658)*

Whaley, Joy
Institute for Business & Home Safety *(496)*

Whaley, Monica Hardy
National Center for Asia-Pacific Economic Cooperation *(719)*

Whalls, Dana
Automated Imaging Association *(321)*

Wharton, Dennis
National Association of Broadcasters *(650)*

Whatley, Allison
Commercial Food Equipment Service Association *(366)*

Whatley, Warren
National Economic Association *(744)*

Wheat, Tim
International Legal Fraternity of Phi Delta Phi *(554)*

Wheatley, Carolyn
National Investor Relations Institute *(767)*

Wheeler, Bruce
Society for Research on Nicotine and Tobacco *(920)*

Wheeler, Duvall
Association of Former Intelligence Officers *(284)*

Wheeler, Ginger
Power Transmission Distributors Association *(855)*

Wheeler, Jason
Piano Technicians Guild *(848)*

Wheeler, Jim
Federal Water Quality Association *(440)*

Wheeler, Julie
Plains Cotton Growers, Inc. *(849)*

Wheeler, Leslie G.
Hearth, Patio and Barbecue Association *(472)*

Wheeler, Lollie
VITA *(1011)*

Wheeler, Pamela
National Basketball Players Association *(713)*

Wheeler, Victoria
Rack Manufacturers Institute *(872)*

Whelan, Cheryl
International College of Applied Kinesiology *(535)*

Whelan, MPH, ScD, Elizabeth M.
American Council on Science and Health *(110)*

Whelan, Michael
Fur Commission USA *(454)*

Whelchel, Sandy
Associated Business Writers of America *(235)*
National Writers Association *(806)*

Wherry, Jeffrey J.
Machine Knife Association *(601)*
Steel Door Institute *(962)*
Unified Abrasives Manufacturers Association *(984)*

Whicker, Amy
Society of Financial Service Professionals *(936)*

Whipple, Terry L.
American Fraternal Alliance *(124)*

Whipple-Struchen, Shirley

Religion Communicators Council **(880)**

Whisonant, Dolly
International Window Film Association **(581)**

Whiston, Julia
White House Correspondents Association **(1016)**

Whitaker, Betty
Academy of Managed Care Pharmacy **(6)**

Whitaker, Michelle H.
Electronic Security Association **(424)**

Whitaker, Scott
Biotechnology Industry Organization (BIO) **(330)**

Whitaker, Sherry
Aquatic Plant Management Society, Inc. **(227)**

Whitaker, Wayne
American Moving and Storage Association **(153)**

Whitby, Tahitia
Measurement, Control and Automation Association **(609)**

Whitcher, Stephanie
National Association of Basketball Coaches **(648)**

White, Aaron
Cardiovascular Credentialing International **(342)**

White, Andrea
International Titanium Association **(577)**

White, Andy
North American Association of State and Provincial Lotteries **(813)**

White, Bruce
Tree Care Industry Association **(980)**

White, Charles (Chuck)
International Association of Movers **(525)**

White, Christopher L.
Advanced Medical Technology Association (AdvaMed) **(13)**

White, Chuck
Plumbing-Heating-Cooling Contractors - National Association **(851)**

White, Claire
Evidence Photographers International Council **(434)**

White, Dave
Association of Private Club Directors **(300)**

White, David
Screen Actors Guild - American Federation of Television and Radio Artists **(893)**

White, Deborah
American Public Power Association **(171)**

White, Deborah R.
Retail Industry Leaders Association **(884)**

White, Denny
ASIS International **(232)**

White, Gary
American Institute of Physics **(140)**

White, Gregory
National Academy of Education **(627)**

White, Jeameeka
iNARTE, Inc. **(487)**

White, Jeanne
International Studies Association **(576)**

White, Jeremy
National Association of Pizzeria Operators **(685)**

White, Jerry L.
International Association of Conference Centers **(518)**

White, Jessica
Real Estate Buyers Agent Council **(875)**

White, Joan
Video Electronics Standards Association **(1009)**

White, John
Association of Alternate Postal Systems **(264)**

White, John M.
Practising Law Institute **(855)**

White, John R.
Association for Computing Machinery **(243)**

White, Johnny
International Digital Enterprise Alliance **(540)**

White, Kristen
Destination Marketing Association International **(411)**

White, LaKesha
Women's Business Enterprise National Council **(1022)**

White, Lesyllee M.
AFL-CIO Housing Investment Trust **(15)**

White, PhD, Dr. Mark
Council for Community and Economic Research **(388)**

White, Mary Lindsay
Uniformed Services Academy of Family Physicians **(984)**

White, Melanie
National Association for the Education of Young Children **(644)**

White, Nicole
American Medical Student Association **(150)**

White, Patricia
International Alliance of Theatrical Stage Employees, Moving Picture Technicians, Artists and Allied Crafts of the U.S., Its Territories and Canada **(510)**

White, Paul
Environmental Mutagen Society **(431)**

White, MCP, Phil
Society of Interventional Radiology **(940)**

White, Randy
National Association of Graphic and Product Identification Manufacturers **(670)**

White, Richard
Automotive Aftermarket Industry Association **(321)**

White, Richard
Car Care Council **(342)**

White, Robert
Renewable Fuels Association **(881)**

White, Robert F.
American Leather Chemists Association **(145)**

White, Ronald F.
Association for Politics and the Life Sciences **(253)**

White, Rosanne T.
Technology Student Association **(970)**

White, Sandra
Health Physics Society **(470)**
Society for Integrative and Comparative Biology **(913)**

White, Shera L.
Central Intercollegiate Athletic Association **(349)**

White, Terri
Association for Healthcare Documentation Integrity **(247)**

White, Terry
Specialized Carriers and Rigging Association **(957)**

White, Thomas
International Documentary Association **(541)**

White, Thornton
American Metalcasting Consortium **(151)**

White, Tiffany Barnett
Society for Consumer Psychology **(907)**

White, Tim
National Association of University Forest Resources Programs **(707)**

White, Tim
National Ski Patrol System **(792)**

White, Tom
Interactive Audio Special Interest Group **(507)**
MIDI Manufacturers Association **(615)**

White, Vickie
American Jersey Cattle Association/National All-Jersey Inc. **(142)**

Whited, Brandy
The Association to Advance Collegiate Schools of Business **(319)**

Whited, Christopher
Society of American Foresters **(928)**

Whitehead, Bruce
National Interscholastic Athletic Administrators Association **(766)**

Whitehead, Diane
Association for Childhood Education International **(241)**

Whitehead, Donna
Futures Industry Association **(455)**

Whitehead, Doug
National BioDiesel Board **(713)**

Whitehead, James R.
American College of Sports Medicine **(102)**

Whitehouse, CCP, Jr., John
Institute for Certification of Computing Professionals **(497)**

Whitehouse, CAE, Susan
Society for Industrial & Applied Mathematics **(912)**

Whiteside, Susan Fussell
National Confectioners Association **(725)**

Whitfield, Jim
Materials and Methods Standards Association **(608)**

Whiting, Richard M.
The Financial Services Roundtable **(445)**

Whitis, Russ
The Coca-Cola Bottlers' Association **(361)**

Whitley, Joshua
North American Association of Central Cancer Registries **(812)**

Whitley, Rhonda
Association of Corporate Credit Unions **(277)**

Whitlinger, Dave
New York E-Health Collaborative **(809)**

Whitlow, Joy
National Association of Broadcasters **(650)**

Whitman, Debra Bailey
American Association of Retired Persons **(72)**

Whitman, Jacqueline
National Forum for Black Public Administrators **(752)**

Whitman, Jim A.
National Association of Chain Drug Stores **(652)**

Whitman, Penny
National Tour Association **(800)**

Whitman, Torrey L.
Institute of Judicial Administration **(501)**

Whitman, Will
National Association of Public Health Statistics and Information Systems **(642)**

Whitmer, Pattye
American Society of Cataract and Refractive Surgery **(194)**

Whitmer, Sharon K.
Christian Medical & Dental Associations *(356)*

Whitmire, Debi
The Paddlesports Industry Association *(836)*

Whitmore, Bob
National Precast Concrete Association *(782)*

Whitney, Brian Austin
Just Plain Folks Songwriting/Musician Networking Organization *(589)*

Whitney, Dennis
Institute Management Accountants *(498)*

Whitney, Elizabeth
Steel Plate Fabricators Association Division of STI/SPFA *(962)*
Steel Tank Institute Division of STI/SPFA *(963)*

Whitney, Fran
Association for Symbolic Logic *(257)*

Whitney, Liz
International Warehouse Logistics Association *(580)*

Whitney, Mary Y
American College of Trial Lawyers *(103)*

Whitney, Ron
International Reciprocal Trade Association *(562)*

Whitt, Donna
National Council on Aging *(738)*

Whitt, Erin
Modular Building Institute *(618)*

Whittaker, Erin
International Cost Estimating and Analysis Association effective *(537)*

Whittaker, Rick
Office Business Center Association International *(826)*

Whittaker, Stephanie
United States Parachute Association *(997)*

Whittall-Scherfee, Ken
American Navion Society *(155)*

Whitten, Dan
America's Natural Gas Alliance *(29)*

Whittington, Jenny
University Risk Management and Insurance Association *(1003)*

Whittington, Paul
American Board of Psychiatry & Neurology *(83)*

Whittle, Don
International Coach Federation *(535)*

Whitworth, Anna
American Property Tax Counsel *(168)*

Whorton, David C.
American Short Line and Regional Railroad Association *(179)*

Whyde, Bridget
Association of Old Crows *(297)*

Whyms, Robin
National Council of Juvenile and Family Court Judges *(735)*

Whyte, Keith
National Council on Problem Gambling *(739)*

Wible, Robert
Association of Major City and County Building Officials *(292)*

Wible, Tori Jo
American Prepaid Legal Services Institute *(167)*

Wiblin, Eleanor
National Dance Council of America *(741)*

Wice, Jeffrey M
National Association of Jewish Legislators *(677)*

Wickert, Victoria
National Academy of Public Administration *(628)*

Wickham, Laurie
Craft Retailers Association for Tomorrow *(403)*

Wickline, Beth
National Recreation and Parks Association *(784)*

Wicklund, Carl
American Probation and Parole Association *(167)*

Wicklund, Michael
American Institute of Inspectors *(139)*

Wickman, Bryan
Association for Direct Instruction *(244)*

Wicks, Kristen
InterNational Electrical Testing Association *(542)*

Wicks, Stephanie J.
American School Counselor Association *(177)*

Wickstrom, Emily
American Oil Chemists' Society *(157)*

Wickwire, PhD, Pat Nellor
American Association for Career Education *(48)*

Widaman, Dwight
Evangelical Press Association *(434)*

Widder, Dr. Edith "Edie"
Ocean Research & Conservation Association *(826)*

Widelka, CAE, CPA, Ken
American Association of Diabetes Educators *(60)*

Widing, Jessica
Association of Oncology Social Work *(297)*

Widmaier, Chris
United States Tennis Association *(1000)*

Widmer, CAE, M. Eileen
Society of Surgical Oncology *(947)*

Widness, Eric
National Association of Police Athletics/Activities Leagues, Inc. *(685)*

Widoff, Joseph
Satellite Broadcasting and Communications Association *(891)*

Wie, Matt Van
American Academy of Anesthesiologist Assistants *(30)*
American Society of Extra-Corporeal Technology *(197)*

Wiederhoeft, Phyllis Castens
Association of Lutheran Development Executives *(292)*

Wiegerink, CAE, Robin L.
American Society of Echocardiography *(197)*

Wieland, James
Healthcare Billing and Management Association *(470)*

Wielgus, Magen
Association of Nutrition & Foodservice Professionals *(296)*

Wieman, BA, Carly
Association of Family and Conciliation Courts *(282)*

Wien, Gary
NAFA Fleet Management Association *(624)*

Wiener, Robin K.
Institute of Scrap Recycling Industries, Inc. *(503)*

Wierman, Tom
Council of Petroleum Accountants Societies *(396)*

Wiermanski, David
Healthcare Leadership Council *(471)*

Wiernicki, Christopher J.
American Bureau of Shipping *(86)*

Wiernik, Elle
National Association of Subrogation Professionals *(704)*

Wiernik, Leslie S.
National Association of Subrogation Professionals *(704)*

Wierzynski, Barbara
Futures Industry Association *(455)*

Wiese, Deana
United States Durum Growers Association *(993)*

Wiese, Verne
Women in Aviation International *(1020)*

Wiesenmaier, Hubert
American Import Shippers Association *(134)*

Wiesenmaier, Kurt
American Import Shippers Association *(134)*

Wietecha, Mark
National Association of Children's Hospitals and Related Institutions *(653)*

Wieting, DO, J. Michael
American Osteopathic Board of Physical Medicine and Rehabilitation *(160)*

Wigbels, Lyn D.
American Astronautical Society *(77)*

Wigen, Wendy
Educause *(420)*

Wiggans, Bob
Wine and Spirits Wholesalers of America *(1018)*

Wiggins, Beth
American Psychology-Law Society *(170)*

Wiggins, Harry
Pakistan American Business Association *(837)*

Wiggins, Jim
American College of Medical Toxicology *(98)*

Wiggins, Lance
Automatic Transmission Rebuilders Association *(321)*

Wiggins, Missy
Association for Institutional Research *(250)*

Wiggins, Rebecca
Association for Financial Counseling and Planning Education *(246)*

Wigglesworth, Robert W.
National Association of County Surveyors *(660)*

Wiggs Harris, Wylecia
Center for American Nurses *(348)*

Wigren, Melanie
American Swimming Coaches Association *(215)*

Wilber, Kathryn
American Benefits Council *(80)*

Wilber, PhD, Laura Ann
Academy of Rehabilitative Audiology *(8)*

Wilborne-Davis, CHES, MPH, Paula
Association of Occupational and Environmental Clinics *(296)*

Wilbur, Kim
National Association of College Auxiliary Services *(655)*

Wilburn, Ruth
Welsh Pony and Cob Society of America *(1015)*

Wilcha, Kristin
Association of Independent Commercial Producers *(287)*

Wilcher, Shirley J.
American Association for Affirmative Action *(47)*

Wilcox, PhD, David K.
Research Institute for Fragrance Materials *(882)*

Wilcox, Ellen
American Society of Health-System Pharmacists *(199)*

Wilcox, Kory
Pyramid Society *(871)*

Wilcox, Kristin Pearson
American Frozen Food Institute *(124)*
National Frozen Pizza Institute *(754)*

Wilcox, Laura A.
Council of Independent Colleges *(394)*

Wilczynski, Ron
High Technology Crime Investigation Association *(474)*

Wilde, Caroline
American Rehabilitation Counseling Association *(174)*

Wilde, Cathy
SWANA - Solid Waste Association of North America *(967)*

Wilde, Thomas
Wireless Communications Association International *(1019)*

Wilder, Margaret
Urban Affairs Association *(1003)*

Wilder, Mike
Log Home Builders Association of North America *(600)*

Wilding, Holly L.
National Organization of Life and Health Insurance Guaranty Association *(777)*

Wilds, Donna
Infectious Diseases Society of America *(494)*

Wile, Cameron
Human Factors and Ergonomics Society *(480)*
Human Factors Society *(481)*

Wiler, Vicki
ARMA International *(228)*

Wiles, Adriane
National Association for Gifted Children *(639)*

Wiles, Lori Joseph
National Association of Intercollegiate Athletics *(676)*

Wiley, Carol
National Association of Nurse Practitioners in Women's Health *(682)*

Wiley, Fred
Off-Road Business Association *(826)*

Wiley, Maureen
International Technology and Engineering Educators Association *(576)*

Wiley, Thomas
American Philosophical Association *(164)*

Wilhelm, John W.
UNITE-HERE *(985)*

Wilhoit, Gene
Council of Chief State School Officers *(392)*

Wilk, Ed
National Association of Aircraft and Communication Suppliers *(646)*

Wilk, Jennifer
Passenger Vessel Association *(839)*

Wilkening, Erica
International Cost Estimating and Analysis Association effective *(537)*

Wilkerson, CAE, JD, MBA, Dean
American College of Emergency Physicians *(95)*

Wilkerson, CPA, Larry J.
Federation of State Boards of Physical Therapy *(442)*

Wilkerson, Richard
International Association for the Study of Dreams *(514)*

Wilkerson, Sheryl
Automotive Aftermarket Industry Association *(321)*

Wilkerson, Steve

Professional Beauty Association | National Cosmetology Association *(861)*

Wilkes, Jenna
American Society of Nuclear Cardiology *(205)*

Wilkeson, Sheryl
American Indian Science and Engineering Society *(135)*

Wilkie, Alex J.
Association for Symbolic Logic *(257)*

Wilkins, Joy
International Hearing Society *(549)*

Wilkins, Laura
Research Chefs Association *(882)*

Wilkins, Randy
Copper and Brass Servicenter Association *(384)*
International Association of Plastics Distributors *(526)*

Wilkins, EdD, Ronnie D
American College of Neuropsychopharmacology *(98)*

Wilkins, Stephanie
National Grange *(756)*

Wilkinson, Anthony R.
National Association of Government Guaranteed Lenders (NAGGL) *(670)*

Wilkinson, Earl J.
International Newspaper Marketing Association *(558)*

Wilkinson, Felicity
National Association of Elevator Safety Authorities International *(665)*

Wilkinson, Leah
American Feed Industry Association *(120)*

Wilkinson, Richard "Lisl"
Produce Marketing Association *(858)*

Wilkinson, Stephen
International Lead Zinc Research Organization *(553)*
International Zinc Association-America *(582)*

Wilkolaski, Sherrie A.
International Food, Wine and Travel Writers Association *(546)*

Wilks, Tom
Association of Dark Leaf Tobacco Dealers and Exporters *(278)*

Will, Emily J.
Association of Forensic Document Examiners *(284)*

Will, Katherine
Society for Public Health Education *(919)*

Willams, Marcus
Alliance of Black Telecommunications Employees *(24)*

Willard, Robert "Bob" F.
Institute of Nuclear Power Operations *(502)*

Willard, Timothy
Council for Higher Education Accreditation *(390)*

Willett, Cora
Phi Beta Fraternity *(845)*

Willett, Michael
American Association of Critical-Care Nurses *(59)*

Willett, Esq., R. Hillary
USFN-America's Mortgage Banking Attorneys *(1006)*

Willett, Teresa G.
The American Association of Language Specialists *(64)*

Willey, Bruce
Association of Professional Model Makers *(302)*

Willey, Kim
National Assembly of State Arts Agencies *(635)*

Williams, Alicia
Association for Asian Studies *(239)*

Williams, Amy

Society for Information Management *(913)*

Williams, Andre D.
Association of Black Cardiologists *(269)*

Williams, Arlanda J.
National Association of Black County Officials *(649)*

Williams, Ashley
Special Interest Group for Design of Communication *(955)*

Williams, PhD, Bernard O.
International Society for the Study of Subtle Energies and Energy Medicine *(570)*

Williams, Blanche
International Association of Eating Disorders Professionals *(520)*

Williams, Bob
National Collegiate Athletic Association *(724)*

Williams, Bonnie
National Utility Contractors Association (NUCA) *(803)*

Williams, Brendan E.
American Fuel & Petrochemical Manufacturers *(124)*

Williams, C. Donald
Academy of Organizational and Occupational Psychiatry *(7)*

Williams, Jr., C.E. "Chubby"
Textile Fibers and By-Products Association *(972)*

Williams, CSS, Carla J.
The Society of Wine Educators *(950)*

Williams, Carol T.
National Funeral Directors and Morticians Association *(754)*

Williams, Carolyn
International Brotherhood of Electrical Workers *(531)*

Williams, Carolyn M.
Sheet Metal and Air Conditioning Contractors' National Association *(898)*

Williams, PhD, Carolyn Sue
HUBZone Contractors National Council *(480)*

Williams, Catherine
American Society of Pension Professionals & Actuaries *(206)*

Williams, Charlie
American Bridge Teachers' Association *(86)*

Williams, Chris
International Electronic Commerce Association *(542)*

Williams, Christy
National Franchisee Association *(753)*

Williams, Coke
Aluminum Foil Container Manufacturers Association *(27)*

Williams, Connie
Associated Universities Inc. *(237)*

Williams, Esq., Crystal
American Immigration Lawyers Association *(134)*

Williams, Cynthia
International Electronic Manufacturing Initiative *(542)*

Williams, Damaris
Association for Behavioral and Cognitive Therapies *(240)*

Williams, Dave
World Pet Association *(1027)*

Williams, David
Council of American Master Mariners *(392)*

Williams, David
Garden Centers of America *(456)*

Williams, David
Institute of Tax Consultants *(503)*

Williams, David L.
Conference of Business Economists *(374)*
International Association for Energy Economics *(512)*
United States Association for Energy Economics *(990)*

Williams, Demi
The Advertising Research Foundation *(13)*

Williams, Diane
International Association of Amusement Parks and Attractions(IAAPA) *(515)*

Williams, MA, Erika A.
Accreditation Board for Engineering and Technology Inc. *(9)*

Williams, Fiona
American Congress of Rehabilitation Medicine *(107)*

Williams, Fred
Association for Education in Journalism and Mass Communication *(245)*

Williams, CAE, Gay F.
American Accounting Association *(43)*

Williams, George
American Association of Classified School Employees *(56)*

Williams, Gloria
American Public Human Services Association *(171)*

Williams, Grace
Association of Maternal and Child Health Programs (AMCHP) *(293)*

Williams, Gwen W
National Center for State Courts *(720)*

Williams, Holly
American College Dance Festival Association *(92)*

Williams, Jacqueline
American Public Power Association *(171)*

Williams, Jacquetta
The Council of Insurance Agents and Brokers *(394)*

Williams, James F.M. E.
National Independent Private Schools Association *(762)*

Williams, Jeanette
American Institute of Parliamentarians *(140)*

Williams, Jeremy
American Association of Integrated Healthcare Delivery Systems *(63)*
American Association of Managed Care Nurses *(64)*
National Association of Managed Care Physicians *(679)*

Williams, John
Algal Biomass Organization *(22)*

Williams, John
Independent Automotive Damage Appraisers Association *(488)*

Williams, John
Southern Shrimp Alliance *(953)*

Williams, Joyce
American Society of Transplant Surgeons *(210)*

Williams, Julia
Professional Communications Society *(861)*

Williams, Keith A.
Irrigation Association *(585)*

Williams, Kelly
Phi Alpha Delta *(845)*

Williams, Dr. Kemp
American Name Society *(154)*

Williams, Sgt. Kimber
National Association of Field Training Officers *(668)*

Williams, Kris
International Newspaper Marketing Association *(558)*

Williams, Kris
International Association of Venue Managers *(528)*

Williams, Kristen
Independent Equipment Dealers Association *(489)*

Williams, Kyle
Association of Schools of Allied Health Professions *(307)*

Williams, Latrice
National Association for Campus Activities *(637)*

Williams, Lauren
Association of Proposal Management Professionals *(303)*

Williams, Lauren
National Black Caucus of State Legislators *(714)*

Williams, Len
American Logistics Association *(146)*

Williams, Libby
American Brahman Breeders Association *(85)*

Williams, Mantill
American Public Transportation Association *(171)*

Williams, Marcia
Association of Independent Trust Companies *(288)*

Williams, CAE, Marie
Society of Neurointerventional Surgery *(942)*

Williams, Martha
American Association of Teachers of German *(74)*

Williams, Mary
Wilderness Education Association *(1017)*

Williams, MT (ASCP), Mary Steele
Association for Molecular Pathology *(252)*

Williams, Matt
Standards Engineering Society *(961)*

Williams, Melissa
Association of School Business Officials International *(306)*

Williams, Melissa
The American Society for Public Administration *(189)*

Williams, Michael
North American Equipment Dealers Association *(816)*

Williams, Michael T.
National Health Care Anti-Fraud Association *(758)*

Williams, Naddia
SWANA - Solid Waste Association of North America *(967)*

Williams, Onenetta
American Association for Affirmative Action *(47)*

Williams, CAE, Pamela V.
Cable and Telecommunications Human Resources Association *(340)*

Williams, Patricia
Major Cities Chiefs Association *(601)*

Williams, Ret., COL Randy
National Guard Association of the U.S. *(757)*

Williams, Rob
United States Lifesaving Association *(996)*

Williams, PhD, Robert
American International Charolais Association *(142)*

Williams, Robert A.
Optometric Extension Program Foundation *(830)*

Williams, Robert D.
Screen Manufacturers Association *(893)*

Williams, Robert G.
Association of United States Night Vision Manufacturers *(315)*

Williams, MBA, PhD, Rodney

International Association of Venue Managers *(528)*

Williams, Roger
American Montessori Society *(152)*

Williams, Roger J.
Accrediting Council for Continuing Education & Training *(10)*

Williams, MD, Roger L.
United States Pharmacopeia *(997)*

Williams, Rowena
American Dental Education Association *(113)*

Williams, Sarah
U.S Poultry and Egg Association *(998)*

Williams, Stephanie
Association of University Programs in Health Administration *(316)*

Williams, Steven
Modular Building Institute *(618)*

Williams, Steven A.
Wildlife Management Institute *(1017)*

Williams, Tamasha
American Society for Gastrointestinal Endoscopy *(184)*

Williams, TaNisha
Association for Healthcare Resource and Materials Management *(248)*

Williams, Terry
National Association of Small Business Contractors *(696)*

Williams, Timothy S.
Water Environment Federation *(1013)*

Williams, Tina
Midwives Alliance of North America *(615)*

Williams, Tisha
Life Insurance Settlement Association *(597)*

Williams, Tonya Bessillieu
National Association of Securities Professionals *(695)*

Williams, Trudie
Standards Engineering Society *(961)*

Williams, Vanessa R.
National Conference of Black Mayors *(726)*

Williams, Virginia
Technology Student Association *(970)*

Williams, Yolanda
National Alliance for Youth Sports *(632)*

Williams,, CPA, Jackie
National Council of Acoustical Consultants *(733)*
Society for Nutrition Education and Behavior *(917)*

Williams-Jones, Kanisha
National School Boards Association *(789)*

Williams-Martinez, Deborah
Society of Geriatric Cardiology *(937)*

Williams-Nickelson, PsyD, Carol
American Medical Student Association *(150)*

Williamson, Bradford
Electronic Traders Association *(424)*

Williamson, CAE, Carolyn
University Aviation Association *(1002)*

Williamson, Craig P.
Cigar Association of America, Inc. *(356)*
Pipe Tobacco Council, Inc. *(849)*

Williamson, Gail
American Academy of Oral and Maxillofacial Radiology *(37)*

Williamson, PHR, Jeff
National Hospice & Palliative Care Organization *(760)*

Williamson, Jeffrey

American Medical Informatics Association *(149)*

Williamson, Jennifer
Electronic Retailing Association *(423)*

Williamson, Julie
International Association of Healthcare Central Service Materiel Management *(522)*

Williamson, Kent D.
Conference on College Composition and Communication *(376)*
Conference on English Education *(376)*
National Council of Teachers of English *(737)*

Williamson, Mary Jane
American Sportfishing Association *(212)*

Williamson, Mia
International Council on Hotel, Restaurant and Institutional Education *(539)*

Williamson, Michelle
U.S. Hereditary Angioedema Association *(983)*

Williamson, Dr. Scot
Universities Space Research Association *(1002)*

Williamson, Scott
American Society for Engineering Education *(183)*

Williamson, Val
American Press Institute *(167)*

Williamson, Vanessa
National Association of Legal Assistants *(677)*

Williamson, W. Scott
Reinsurance Association of America *(879)*

Williamson-Smith, Sandy
National Soccer Coaches Association of America *(792)*

Willie, Mellor C.
National American Indian Housing Council *(634)*

Willie, Pete
The American Rambouillet Sheep Breeders Association *(173)*

Williford, Melissa
American Association of Small Ruminant Practitioners *(73)*
American College of Theriogenologists *(103)*
Society for Theriogenology *(926)*

Willingham, Christal
National Family Caregivers Association *(747)*

Willis, Dave
The Commercial Vehicle Solutions Network *(367)*

Willis, Elaine
National School Public Relations Association *(789)*

Willis, Haley
National Council for International Visitors *(732)*

Willis, Jim
National Association of State Directors of Veterans Affairs *(700)*

Willis, Larry I.
Transportation Trades Department, AFL-CIO *(979)*

Willis, MSN, RN, Mary Alice
Developmental Disabilities Nurses Association *(411)*

Willis, Max
International Association of Fairs and Expositions *(521)*

Willis, Robert
Electronic Components Industry Association *(423)*

Willis, Roy W.
Propane Engine Fuel Committee/Propane Education and Research Council *(867)*

Willis, Tobey
Association for Clinical Pastoral Education *(241)*

Willison, Nichole
Interstate Natural Gas Association of America *(583)*

Willison, Scott
National HEP-CAMP Association *(759)*

Willocks, Penny
Association of Water Technologies *(317)*

Willoughby, Laura
Business Executives for National Security *(338)*

Willoughby, Neil
Entomological Society of America *(429)*

Wills, Ronald K.
National Association of Business Owners and Entrepreneurs *(651)*

Wills-Herrera, Eduardo
International Society for Quality-of-Life Studies *(569)*

Willson, Crissy
American Glovebox Society *(126)*

Wilmot, Joyce
U.S. Hereditary Angioedema Association *(983)*

Wilmot, Tom
American Mosquito Control Association *(153)*

Wilmoth, Claire
National Guild for Community Arts Education *(757)*

Wilson, Allyson
Chlorine Chemistry Council *(354)*

Wilson, Allyson
Plastics Foodservice Packaging Group *(850)*

Wilson, Angie
Automotive Service Association *(323)*

Wilson, Ann
Motor and Equipment Manufacturers Association *(619)*

Wilson, Ann
Original Equipment Suppliers Association *(833)*

Wilson, Ashley
United States Chamber of Commerce *(991)*

Wilson, Bascombe J.
Disaster Preparedness and Emergency Response Association *(413)*

Wilson, Bob
American Farm Bureau Federation *(118)*

Wilson, Bradley
Journalism Education Association *(589)*

Wilson, Butch
Catfish Farmers of America *(344)*

Wilson, Cameron
Association for Computing Machinery *(243)*

Wilson, Carolyn
National Asphalt Pavement Association *(635)*

Wilson, Chris
National Rural Water Association *(788)*

Wilson, Christine
American Association for Cancer Research *(48)*

Wilson, Christine
Worldwide ERC *(1028)*

Wilson, Christopher "Chris" E.
TechAmerica (fka Technology Association of America) *(969)*

Wilson, Chuck
National Systems Contractors Association *(798)*

Wilson, MPH, Courtney
American Association of Poison Control Centers *(70)*

Wilson, Cynthia
League for Innovation in the Community College *(595)*

Wilson, Dalton
International Society of Automation *(571)*

Wilson, Dan

United States Professional Tennis Association *(998)*

Wilson, David
Futures Industry Association *(455)*

Wilson, David P.
International Cinema Technology Association *(534)*

Wilson, Debra
National Association of Independent Schools *(675)*

Wilson, Glee
College and University Professional Association for Human Resources *(362)*

Wilson, Glenda K.
Black Coaches & Administrators *(331)*

Wilson, James
National Association of Blacks In Government *(649)*

Wilson, James
United States Lacrosse *(995)*

Wilson, Janet
American Academy of Emergency Medicine *(33)*

Wilson, Jonathan
Association for Asian Studies *(239)*

Wilson, CAE, Joyanna
American Academy of Audiology *(31)*

Wilson, Juliette
Organization of Wildlife Planners *(832)*

Wilson, CPA, Kathleen
Society of American Military Engineers *(929)*

Wilson, Katie
National Retail Federation *(786)*

Wilson, Keisha
National Association of Wholesaler-Distributors *(709)*

Wilson, Keith
Petroleum Equipment Institute *(843)*

Wilson, Dr. Kenneth
National Association of University Fisheries and Wildlife Programs *(707)*

Wilson, Kenyon
International Tuba-Euphonium Association *(578)*

Wilson, Kevin J.D.
Disaster Preparedness and Emergency Response Association *(413)*

Wilson, Kevin M
American Society for Cell Biology *(182)*

Wilson, Kim R.
National Black MBA Association *(714)*

Wilson, LaDauna
APA The Engineered Wood Association *(224)*

Wilson, Lakeesha
American Association of Blacks in Energy *(55)*

Wilson, Latorea
Federal Managers Association *(439)*

Wilson, LeAnn
Association of Career and Technical Education *(271)*

Wilson, LeAnne Redick
Business Roundtable *(339)*

Wilson, Lindsay
National Pawnbrokers Association *(779)*

Wilson, Lorna
Energy Bar Association *(428)*

Wilson, Lynn
Association of Consulting Foresters of America *(276)*

Wilson, Mark A.
Paleontological Society *(837)*

Wilson, Mark A.
Phi Mu Alpha Sinfonia *(846)*

Wilson, Marthea
American College of Cardiology *(93)*

Wilson, CMPE, MBA, Michael
International Foundation of Employee Benefit Plans *(547)*

Wilson, Michael E.
Automotive Recyclers Association *(323)*

Wilson, Mitch
Insurance Consumer Affairs Exchange *(505)*

Wilson, MD, MHP, Modena H.
American Medical Association *(148)*

Wilson, Neil
Association of Internal Management Consultants *(289)*

Wilson, Paul
LOMA *(600)*

Wilson, Richard
American Angus Association *(45)*

Wilson, Roger G.
Blue Cross Blue Shield Association *(332)*

Wilson, Ron
North American Association of Educational Negotiators *(813)*

Wilson, Ryan
National Alliance to Save Native Languages *(633)*

Wilson, Sarah
American Phytopathological Society *(165)*

Wilson, Stacey
American Association of Medical Dosimetrists *(65)*

Wilson, Sue
Union of American Physicians and Dentists *(985)*

Wilson, Terry
National Communication Association *(724)*

Wilson, Terry
YPO-WPO *(1030)*

Wilson, Wanda
ARMA International *(228)*

Wilson, PhD, CRNA, Wanda
American Association of Nurse Anesthetists *(67)*

Wilson, Wendy
International Association of Women Police *(529)*

Wilt, Charles
Association for Library Collections and Technical Services *(251)*

Wilton, Frank S.
Advanced Medical Technology Association (AdvaMed) *(13)*

Wiltse, Dave
Fellowship of United Methodists in Music and Worship Arts *(442)*

Wiltse, Tim
Visiting Nurse Associations of America *(1010)*

Wiltshire, John C.
International Marine Minerals Society *(555)*

Wiltshire, Sharon
American Association of Family and Consumer Sciences *(61)*

Wimberly, PhD, George
American Educational Research Association *(116)*

Winawer, LCSW, MSW, Hinda
American Family Therapy Academy *(118)*

Winbush, Chauncey
College Athletic Business Management Association *(362)*

Winch, Jesse
ASPRS-The Imaging and Geospatial Information Society *(233)*

Winchester, Nancy
American Society of Plant Biologists *(207)*

Winckler, Esq., RPh, Susan C.
Food and Drug Law Institute *(449)*

Windham, Michael D.
American Fern Society *(121)*

Windle, Chuck
Genetics Society of America *(458)*

Windsor, Cpt. Dave
Association of Natural Resource Enforcement Trainers *(295)*

Windsor, Duane
International Association for Business and Society *(511)*

Wines, Angie
American Student Dental Association *(214)*

Wing, Eric
National Thoroughbred Racing Association *(800)*

Wing, Lori
Potato Association of America *(854)*

Wingate, Martha
Association of Teachers of Maternal and Child Health *(312)*

Wingate-Bey, Sandra
American Society for Engineering Education *(183)*

Winger, Amanda Burton
Conductors Guild *(374)*

Winger, Jessica
American College of Veterinary Radiology *(104)*

Winger, Scott
Conductors Guild *(374)*

Wingerd, Ellen
National Association for Search and Rescue *(642)*

Wingerter, Ryan
Society for Range Management *(920)*

Wingertsahn, Ginny
Hospice and Palliative Nurses Association *(478)*

Wingrove, Brian
Society for Physician Assistants in Pediatrics *(919)*

Winkler, Kathryn
American Fisheries Society *(121)*

Winkler, Margitta
American Academy of Pediatric Dentistry *(39)*

Winkler, Steve
C-Port *(340)*

Winn, III, Ed
Association of Progressive Rental Organizations *(303)*

Winn, Karen
American Saddlebred Horse Association *(176)*

Winn, CMP, CAE, Michelle
Association of Osteopathic State Executive Directors *(297)*

Winship, Scott
American Music Center *(153)*

Winslow, Bill
International Sign Association *(564)*

Winslow, Celia
American Financial Services Association *(121)*

Winslow, Donald R.
National Press Photographers Association *(782)*

Winslow, Linda R.
National Association of Health Unit Coordinators *(671)*

Winslow, Ron
National Association of Science Writers *(694)*

Winsor, John
National Association of Composers, USA *(657)*

Winstel, Lisa
National Family Caregivers Association *(747)*

Winston, Denise
American Academy of Actuaries *(29)*

Winston, James L.
National Association of Black-Owned Broadcasters *(649)*

Winston, Kionna
National Council for History Education *(732)*

Winston, Lashonda M.
National Society of Black Engineers *(793)*

winston "jw", J. McGill
Association of Celebrity Personal Assistants *(271)*

Winter, Betsy
American Mountain Guides Association *(153)*

Winter, Delorise
Cotton Council International *(387)*

Winter, MS, RT (R), Leslie F.
Joint Review Committee on Education in Radiologic Technology *(589)*

Winter, Patty
National Reverse Mortgage Lenders Association *(787)*

Winter, Richard
Point of Purchase Advertising Institute *(851)*

Winter, Richard
POPAI The Global Association for Marketing at Retail *(852)*

Winter, Susan
Rolf Institute of Structural Integration *(887)*

Winterbottom, Michael
Global Market Development Center *(462)*

Winters, Patrick
The Institute of Inspection, Cleaning and Restoration Certification *(500)*

Winton, Peggy
Association for Information and Image Management International *(249)*

Wiramidjaja, Yan
American Council of Engineering Companies *(109)*

Wirt, CCM, CRP, RN, Susan
Association of Rehabilitation Nurses *(305)*

Wirth, Jerry D.
American Association of Colleges for Teacher Education *(57)*

Wirth, Laurie
The American Board of Facial Plastic and Reconstructive Surgery *(82)*

Wirth, Lawrence R.
American Council of Learned Societies *(109)*

Wisch, Kathryn J.
North American Menopause Society *(818)*

Wische, Jerry
Jewish Community Centers Association of North America *(588)*

Wischmeyer, CFSP, Oliver J.
Business Forms Management Association *(339)*

Wise, Beth
National Society for Histotechnology *(792)*

Wise, Carol
American Polypay Sheep Association *(167)*

Wise, Kristina
International Aviation Ground Support Association *(529)*

Wise, BS, Marsha A.

American Osteopathic College of Dermatology *(160)*

Wise, Walter
International Association of Bridge, Structural, Ornamental and Reinforcing Iron Workers *(517)*
Pharmaceutical Industry Labor Management Association (PILMA) *(844)*

Wisecup, Megan
International Hunter Education Association *(550)*

Wisel, Lee
Association of Seventh-Day Adventist Librarians *(308)*

Wisely, Stephen
APCO (Association of Public-Safety Communications Officials) International *(304)*

Wishneff, Jane
International Fragrance Association North America *(547)*

Wisnefski, Paul
International Surface Fabricators Association *(576)*

Wisniewski, Claire
Southeastern Theatre Conference *(953)*

Wisniewski, Donna
The American Association of Code Enforcement *(57)*

Wisniewski, Kira
National Women's Studies Association *(805)*

Wispelwey, June
American Institute of Chemical Engineers *(138)*

Witek, David
United States Green Building Council *(994)*

Witham, Pamela B.
Contact Lens Manufacturers Association *(382)*

Witherell, Edward C.
Institute of Career Certification International *(498)*

Witherington, Kim
American Swimming Coaches Association *(215)*

Witherow, Wendy
National Board of Boiler and Pressure Vessel Inspectors *(715)*

Withers, Arlis
American Institute of Certified Planners *(137)*

Withers, Chuck
National Board of Boiler and Pressure Vessel Inspectors *(715)*

Witiw, Sharon
United States Association of Former Members of Congress *(990)*

Witkop, MBA, Lois A.
American Diabetes Association *(115)*

Witkowski, CAE, Susan
National Association for Retail Marketing Services *(642)*

Witt, Carrie
American Society for Healthcare Environmental Services *(185)*

Witt, Evans
National Council on Public Polls *(739)*

Witt, Lynn
Corrections, U.S.A. *(386)*

Witte, Holly
International Council on Systems Engineering *(539)*

Wittenberg, MD, PhD, George
American Society of Neurorehabilitation *(204)*

Wittenberg, MA, Hope R.
Society of Teachers of Family Medicine *(947)*

Wittenburg, Audrey S.
Inter-Company Marketing Group *(506)*

Wittenhagen, Mike

Powder Coating Institute *(854)*

Witter, Susan
Timber Framers Guild *(974)*

Witters, Kristin
National Association of College and University Business Officers *(654)*

Wittich, Karin
American Association of Oral and Maxillofacial Surgeons *(67)*

Wittling, Michele
North American Society for Cardiovascular Imaging *(821)*
Society of Computed Body Tomography and Magnetic Resonance *(933)*

Wittman, Jennifer
International Association of Equine Dentists *(520)*

Wixson, Kelly
National Association of Housing Cooperatives *(673)*

Wizauer, Anne
College of Healthcare Information Management Executives *(364)*

Wlazlowski, Tiffany
National Association of Truck Stop Operators(NATSO) *(707)*

Wleklinski, Joann M.
Association of Independent Information Professionals *(288)*

Wo, Gayle E.
Orthodox Theological Society in America *(833)*

Wodiska, Joan
National Governors Association *(755)*

Wodynski, Shirley
Ceilings and Interior Systems Construction Association *(347)*

Woehrle, Lori
Council for Advancement and Support of Education *(388)*

Woehrle, MariAnne
Cable & Telecommunications Association for Marketing *(340)*

Woestehoff, Michael
National Indian Gaming Association *(762)*

Woffington, Julie
Educational Theatre Association *(420)*

Wofford, Maj. Gen. William D.
Adjutants General Association of the United States *(12)*

Wogelius, Linda
Information Systems Audit and Control Association *(495)*

Wohlhueter, Dave
College Sports Information Directors of America *(364)*

Wohlschlegel, Eric
American Petroleum Institute *(163)*

Woike, Theresa A.
American Academy of Pediatrics *(39)*

Wojcik, Chris
Society of General Internal Medicine *(937)*

Wojcik, Steve
National Business Group on Health *(716)*

Wojdyla, Karen M.
Air and Surface Transport Nurses Association *(17)*

Wojslawowicz, Tom
National Interscholastic Swimming Coaches Association *(766)*

Wojtalewicz, Theresa
Human Resource People and Strategy *(481)*
National Institute of Pension Administrators *(765)*

Wojtalwicz, Theresa

Legal Marketing Association *(596)*

Wojtas, Yajayra
Association for Retail Environments *(256)*

Wojtaszek, Meri Beth
SWANA - Solid Waste Association of North America *(967)*

Wojtkielo Snyder, Tina
Manufacturing Jewelers and Suppliers of America *(604)*

Wolahan, Ed
International Association of Correctional Training Personnel *(518)*

Woldt, Alice M.
National Association of Ecumenical and Interreligious Staff *(664)*

Woldt, CMP, Stacey M.
North American Wholesale Lumber Association *(823)*

Woletz, Paula
American Institute of Ultrasound in Medicine *(141)*

Wolf, Andrew
Association for Healthcare Documentation Integrity *(247)*

Wolf, Craig
Wine and Spirits Wholesalers of America *(1018)*

Wolf, Elroy H.
National Association of Video Distributors *(708)*

Wolf, Jason
North American Securities Administrators Association (NASAA) *(820)*

Wolf, Krysten
Electronic Commerce Code Management Association *(423)*

Wolf, CMM, Laura J.
IEEE Engineering in Medicine and Biology Society *(484)*

Wolf, Sandra DeVincent
Materials Research Society *(609)*

Wolf, Steve
The United States Harness Writers' Association *(994)*

Wolf, Valerie
American Association of Oral and Maxillofacial Surgeons *(67)*

Wolf-Armstrong, Mark
The Coastal and Estuarine Research Federation *(361)*

Wolfe, Cari
American Jersey Cattle Association/National All-Jersey Inc. *(142)*

Wolfe, Erik
ASM International *(232)*

Wolfe, CAE, Frank I.
Hospitality Financial and Technology Professionals *(479)*

Wolfe, Jody
National Council of Teachers of Mathematics *(737)*

Wolfe, John
American Philosophical Society *(164)*

Wolfe, Jonathan
United States Racquet Stringers Association *(998)*

Wolfe, Joy D.
Tax Executives Institute, Inc. *(968)*

Wolfe, Mark
Energy Programs Consortium *(428)*
National Energy Assistance Directors' Association *(746)*

Wolfe, Monica
Association of Jewish Aging Services *(290)*

Wolfe, BA, Renee
American Dance Therapy Association *(113)*

Wolfe, William A.
Steel Tube Institute of North America *(963)*

Wolfer, Autumn
Financial Managers Society *(445)*

Wolff, Esquire, Elroy H.
National Oilseed Processors Association *(776)*

Wolff, Kathy
American Society of Electroneurodiagnostic
Technologists *(197)*

Wolff, Mark
Credit Union National Association, Inc. *(404)*

Wolff, PE, PhD, Robert D.
Society of American Military Engineers *(929)*

Wolfinger, Joseph R.
Major County Sheriffs' Association *(601)*

Wolfla, Christopher E.
Congress of Neurological Surgeons *(377)*

Wolin, Jessica
Advertising Council *(13)*

Wolinetz, Carrie
Association of Graduate Schools in Association of
American Universities *(286)*

Wolk, CAE, Miriam Miller
United Fresh Produce Association *(987)*

Wolkoff, Barbara
Stage Directors and Choreographers Society *(960)*

Wollam-Nichols, Erika
Nashville Songwriters Association, International *(625)*

Wollman, Rebecca
IEEE Signal Processing Society *(485)*

Woloski, Beth
Beta Alpha Psi *(328)*

Wolotsky, Paul
American Federation of School Administrators *(120)*

Wolski, Mary
Academy of Nutrition and Dietetics *(7)*

Wolter, PhD, Bonny
Preventive Cardiovascular Nurses Association *(857)*

Wolters, Caroline
Women's Foodservice Forum *(1023)*

Wolters, John
Christian Schools International *(356)*

Wolverton, Steve
Society of Ethnobiology *(935)*

Womack, Kelly
Refrigeration Service Engineers Society *(878)*

Wong, Bonnie
Asian Women in Business *(232)*

Wong, Eddie
Council on Social Work Education *(400)*

Wong, Henry M.
Association of Public and Land-Grant Universities
(APLU) *(303)*

Wong, Kim
Travel Goods Association *(979)*

Wong, Philip
United States-China Chamber of Commerce *(1001)*

Wong, CAE, EdD, Richard
American School Counselor Association *(177)*

Wong, BS, CAE, Susan
National Student Nurses Association *(797)*

Wong, W. Eric
Reliability Society *(880)*

Wood, Jr., A. Bailey

National Automobile Dealers Association *(711)*

Wood, Al
The Clearing House Association *(357)*

Wood, Amanda
Institute for Credentialing Excellence *(497)*

Wood, Amanda
Institute of Clean Air Companies *(499)*

Wood, Amanda
Product Development and Management Association
(858)

Wood, Bryan
Hospitality Financial and Technology Professionals
(479)

Wood, Carl
Utility Workers Union of America *(1007)*

Wood, Carolyn
Recreation Vehicle Industry Association *(877)*

Wood, BS, RDH, Christine
Association of State and Territorial Dental Directors
(310)

Wood, Dan
National Christian College Athletic Association *(721)*

Wood, David
American Society of Gene & Cell Therapy *(198)*

Wood, David A.
Special Interest Group for Architecture of Computer
Systems *(954)*

Wood, Denise
American Institute of Graphic Arts *(139)*

Wood, Doris
Multi-Level Marketing International Association *(621)*

Wood, Douglas
Association of National Advertisers *(295)*

Wood, Emily
American Academy of Political and Social Science *(40)*

Wood, Glenn
Therapeutic Touch International Association *(973)*

Wood, Greg
Internet Society *(582)*

Wood, J. B.
Technology Services Industry Association *(970)*

Wood, James N.
Ductile Iron Society *(417)*

Wood, Janet
Electronic Components Industry Association *(423)*

Wood, Jayne
Association of Social Work Boards *(309)*

Wood, Jeffrey
American Institute of Chemical Engineers *(138)*

Wood, Joel
The Council of Insurance Agents and Brokers *(394)*

Wood, Katharine Calhoun
American League of Lobbyists *(145)*

Wood, Kelly
National Christian College Athletic Association *(721)*

Wood, Laura
National Association of Conservation Districts *(657)*

Wood, Lloyd
The Fair Currency Alliance *(437)*

Wood, Marc
Associated Collegiate Press *(235)*
National Scholastic Press Association *(789)*

Wood, EdD, Santiago V.
National Association for Bilingual Education *(636)*

Wood, Sarah
Society for the Science & the Public *(924)*

Wood, Scott
International Thermographers Association *(577)*

Wood, Shane
American Homebrewers Association *(133)*
The Brewers Association *(335)*

Wood, Tamika
BAFT-IFSA *(325)*

Wood, Tamiqua
National Home Infusion Association *(760)*

Wood, Tyler
Market Technicians Association *(606)*

Wood, Jr., William
American Saddlebred Horse Association *(176)*

Wood 'McLafferty', Amanda
Lamaze International *(592)*

Wood-Thomas, Bryan
World Shipping Council *(1027)*

Woodard, Diann
American Federation of School Administrators *(120)*

Woodard, Julie
National FFA Organization *(750)*

Woodburn, Laura
Health Forum *(469)*

Wooden, Heather
Institute of Environmental Sciences and Technology
(499)

Wooderson, Steve A.
Council of State Administrators of Vocational
Rehabilitators *(397)*

Woodin, CHFM, FASHE, Dale
American Society for Healthcare Engineering *(184)*

Woodley, Joe
United Association of Equipment Leasing *(985)*

Woodring, Donna
Religious Conference Management Association *(880)*

Woodruff, Frank
National Alliance of Community Economic
Development Associations *(632)*

Woodruff, Rosemarie
College Reading and Learning Association *(364)*

Woods, Dana
American Association of Critical-Care Nurses *(59)*

Woods, III, David M.
Association of Bridal Consultants *(270)*

Woods, Doris
American Kinesiotherapy Association *(144)*

Woods, Douglas K.
AMT - The Association For Manufacturing Technology
(222)

Woods, Eddie
Society of Neurointerventional Surgery *(942)*

Woods, DO, Ellen
American Osteopathic Board of Physical Medicine and
Rehabilitation *(160)*

Woods, Faith
Marine Corps Association *(604)*

Woods, Fritzi
Women's Foodservice Forum *(1023)*

Woods, James
Futures Industry Association *(455)*

Woods, James
Steel Recycling Institute *(963)*

Woods, Richard

Council of Better Business Bureaus *(392)*

Woods, PhD, S. Miles
National Association of Black Professors *(649)*

Woods, Scott
International Association of Certified Thermographers *(517)*

Woods, Tim
National Sheriffs' Association *(791)*

Woodside, Chuck
National Contract Management Association *(729)*

Woodward, James
Philosophy of Science Association *(846)*

Woodward, Michael
American Association of Physicists in Medicine *(69)*

Woodward, Tiffany
Council of Industrial Boiler Owners (CIBO) *(394)*

Woodworth, Brad
Association for the Advancement of Baltic Studies *(258)*

Woody, Catherine
Conference of State Bank Supervisors *(376)*

Woody, Linda
Dermatology Nurses' Association *(410)*

Wooldridge, John
Boating Writers International *(333)*

Wooldridge, John
Destination Marketing Association International *(411)*

Woolfolk, James "Rusty"
Military Officers Association of America (MOAA) *(616)*

Woolley, Mary
Research!America *(882)*

Woolridge, Russell
DRI International *(416)*

Woolsey, Laura
Council for Christian Colleges and Universities *(389)*

Woon, Robert
Man and Cybernetics Systems Society *(602)*

Woon, Robert
Man and Cybernetics Systems Society *(602)*

Wooster, Jon
United States Cattlemen's Association *(991)*

Wooster, Viki
American Institute of Building Design *(137)*

Wooten, Mike
Grand Strand Business Association *(465)*

Worch, Anthony
National Association of Pastoral Musicians *(683)*

Work, Julie
National Association of Athletic Development Directors *(647)*
National Association of Collegiate Marketing Administrators *(656)*

Workman, Dennis
The Aluminum Association, Inc. *(27)*

Workman, Mark E.
National Council of Teachers of Mathematics *(737)*

Works, Beth
Association for Practical and Professional Ethics *(253)*

Worley, Clay
National FFA Organization *(750)*

Worley, Darlene
American Holistic Veterinary Medical Association *(132)*

Worley, Kevan
National Association of Blind Merchants *(650)*

Wormley, Cheryl

International Society of Weekly Newspaper Editors *(574)*

Woroniecki, Jeff
Association of Professional Material Handling Consultants *(301)*
Material Handling Industry of America *(608)*
Materials Handling and Management Society *(608)*

Worsham, Berrye
Cotton Incorporated *(387)*

Worster, Carol
Gas Technology Institute *(456)*

Worters, Loretta
Insurance Information Institute *(505)*

Worth, Barbara C.
Council of Educational Facility Planners International *(393)*

Worth, Ronald D.
Society for Marketing Professional Services *(914)*

Worthington, Barry K.
United States Energy Association *(993)*

Worthington, Caryl Herrington
American Academy of Facial Plastic and Reconstructive Surgery *(34)*

Worthington, Sam
InterAction (American Council of Voluntary International Action) *(506)*

Worthman, Bruce
IEEE Communications Society *(483)*

Wortman, John
Zoological Association of America *(1030)*

Wraga, William G.
Society of Professors of Education *(945)*

Wrasse, Kimberly
American Academy of Forensic Sciences *(34)*

Wray, Dick
International Council on Systems Engineering *(539)*

Wray, Peter
American Ceramics Society *(89)*

Wrenn, Jesse
American Composites Manufacturers Association *(105)*

Wright, Brandon
Petroleum Marketers Association of America *(843)*

Wright, Carole
National Waterways Conference *(804)*

Wright, Caroline
International Bluegrass Music Association *(530)*

Wright, Christine
National Dental Assistants Association *(742)*

Wright, Don
Interagency Communications Interoperability Joint Powers Authority *(507)*

Wright, Frank
National Religious Broadcasters *(785)*

Wright, Gladys Stone
Women Band Directors International *(1020)*

Wright, Janeen
Herb Society of America *(474)*

Wright, ABC, APR, Jr., Janet E. H.
Professional Insurance Communicators of America *(862)*

Wright, Jennifer
Corporate Council on Africa *(385)*

Wright, Jerry P.
United Potato Growers of America *(988)*

Wright, Joann

International Association of Counselors and Therapists *(519)*

Wright, John
National Government Publishing Association *(755)*

Wright, Joset B.
National Minority Supplier Development Council *(773)*

Wright, Karan
American Board of Trial Advocates *(84)*

Wright, Karen
Financial Management Association International *(444)*

Wright, Kristen
Agricultural & Applied Economics Association *(16)*

Wright, Linda
Association for Governmental Leasing and Finance *(247)*
Association of Women in the Metal Industries *(317)*

Wright, Lindsay
United Natural Products Alliance *(988)*

Wright, Lisa
The Vision Council *(1010)*

Wright, Lisa C.
University Council for Educational Administration *(1002)*

Wright, Mark A.
American Waterways Operators *(220)*

Wright, Matthew
The Integrated Ocean Drilling Program *(505)*

Wright, Mickey
Association for Ambulatory Behavioral Healthcare *(238)*

Wright, Paquita
Lyrasis *(600)*

Wright, Rachel
Pet Partners *(842)*

Wright, Ray
Independent Professional Representatives Organization *(491)*

Wright, Reniece R.
National Black MBA Association *(714)*

Wright, Robert
Association of Biomedical Communications Directors *(269)*

Wright, Rosa
National Small Business Association *(792)*

Wright, JAGC, USN Ret., CAPT Samuel F.
Reserve Officers Association of the U.S. *(882)*

Wright, Scott
North American Retail Hardware Association *(820)*

Wright, Shelia B.
National Research Council *(786)*

Wright, Susan
American Emu Association *(117)*

Wright, CMP, CAE, Susan
APMI International *(225)*

Wright, Thomas K.
Regional Plan Association *(879)*

Wright, Walter
National Wellness Institute, Inc. *(804)*

Wrigley, Michelle
National Reining Horse Association *(785)*

Wrisky, Anna
North American Gaming Regulators Association *(817)*

Wrobel, Leo A.
NaSPA: Networks and Systems Professional Association *(626)*

Wroblewski, Celeste
Donors Forum *(415)*

Wu, Amos
Chinese American Food Society *(354)*

Wu, Michael C.
Asia America MultiTechnology Association *(231)*

Wu, Ming-Jen Daniel
American College of Radiology *(102)*

Wu, Dr. Vivian
Chinese American Food Society *(354)*

Wubbe, Eileen
Commercial Finance Association *(366)*

Wuelfing, Robert G.
Society of Professional Asset-Managers and Record Keepers *(945)*

Wulf, CAE, Eric
International Carwash Association *(533)*

Wulf, Matthew T.
Reinsurance Association of America *(879)*

Wulster-Radcliffe, PhD, Meghan C.
American Society of Animal Science *(192)*

Wurm, Jack
Retail, Wholesale and Department Store Union *(885)*

Wurm, Jim
Exhibitor Appointed Contractors Association *(435)*

Wuster, Tracy
American Humor Studies Association *(134)*

Wyandt, Esq., Deborah A.
Sheet Metal and Air Conditioning Contractors' National Association *(898)*

Wyatt, John
Mathematical Association of America *(609)*

Wyatt, Robert
Society of Petroleum Engineers *(944)*

Wyatt, Rosalie J.
Corporate Crisis Response Officers Association *(385)*

Wyatt, Tamera A.
Association of Public and Land-Grant Universities (APLU) *(303)*

Wybenga, Frits
Dangerous Goods Advisory Council *(407)*

Wykle, USA(Ret), Lt. Gen. Kenneth R.
National Defense Transportation Association *(742)*

Wylie, Denise
National Property Management Association *(783)*

Wyman, Joanne Stone
SOLE - The International Society of Logistics *(952)*

Wyman, Linda H.
National Association of Bond Lawyers *(650)*

Wynbrandt, Robert A.
Society of Thoracic Surgeons *(948)*

Wynn, Jr., H. Montee
National Rural Electric Cooperative Association *(788)*

Wynne, Brian P
Electric Drive Transportation Association *(421)*

Wynne, Carol
Association of Vascular and Interventional Radiographers *(316)*
National Association of Professional Background Screeners *(686)*
National Society of Certified Healthcare Business Consultants *(793)*

Wynot, Debbie
Association of Independent Information Professionals *(288)*

Wypyszynski, Keith
Global Market Development Center *(462)*

Wytkind, Edward
Transportation Trades Department, AFL-CIO *(979)*

Wyzlic, Lisa
Association on American Indian Affairs *(319)*

Xia, Patricia
Center for Research Libraries *(348)*

Xu, Jin
American Board of Family Medicine *(82)*

Xue, Jie
IEEE Components, Packaging, and Manufacturing Technology Society *(483)*

Yablonski, Cindy A.
International Society for Neuronal Regulation *(567)*

Yackel, Barb
Professional Skaters Association *(865)*

Yacker, Marc D.
Electricity Consumers Resource Council (ELCON) *(422)*

Yacobucci, Margaret (Peg)
Paleontological Society *(837)*

Yadao, Alex
American College of International Physicians *(97)*

Yaeger, April
National BioDiesel Board *(713)*

Yager, Daniel V.
HR Policy Association *(480)*

Yager, Don
International Customer Service Association *(539)*

Yager, Martha
American Educational Research Association *(116)*

Yaghoubi, Roxanne
Academy of Radiology Research *(8)*

Yakush, Christine M.
Council on the Safe Transportation of Hazardous Articles *(401)*
International Vessel Operators Dangerous Goods Association *(580)*

Yancey, Jr., W. Kenneth
SCORE Association *(893)*

Yanchulis, Phil
National Air Traffic Controllers Association *(630)*

Yanders, Miriam
American Academy on Communication in Healthcare *(43)*

Yandle, CAE, Oliver P.
Association of Legal Administrators *(291)*
Commercial Law League of America *(366)*

Yanek, William M.
Glass Association of North America *(461)*

Yang, Cherrie
United States Composting Council *(992)*

Yang, Dr. Dong Ja
International Council for Health, Physical, Education, Recreation, Sport and Dance *(537)*

Yang, Felix
The Advertising Research Foundation *(13)*

Yang, Kichoon
National Council of Teachers of Mathematics *(737)*

Yang, Stephanie
Association of Children's Museums *(272)*

Yaniszewski, Linda
Medical Transcription Industry Association (MTIA) *(611)*

Yann, Arthur
The Public Relations Society of America *(870)*

Yannelis, Nicholas C.
Society for the Advancement of Economic Theory *(922)*

Yanni, Pam
National Academy of Elder Law Attorneys, Inc. *(627)*

Yanson, Matt
Quarters Furniture Manufacturers Association *(872)*

Yaoz, Jill
AFCOM *(14)*

Yarboro, Elizabeth
American College of Radiology *(102)*

Yarborough, Laura
National Association of Corporate Treasurers *(658)*

Yarbrough, Chelle Honiker
The Travel Institute *(979)*

Yarbrough, Eric
Association of Gay and Lesbian Psychiatrists *(285)*

Yarde, Lisa
Association for Behavioral and Cognitive Therapies *(240)*

Yarussi, Lisa A.
National Fire Protection Association *(751)*

Yashinskie, Susan
American Fuel & Petrochemical Manufacturers *(124)*

Yasumura, Karen
Women in Aerospace *(1020)*

Yates, Ben
Associated Equipment Distributors *(235)*

Yates, Cathy
National District Attorneys Association *(743)*

Yates, Daniel
Ground Water Protection Council *(466)*

Yates, Gail
National Association of County Intergovernmental Relations Officials *(660)*

Yates, Rita J.
American Academy of Podiatric Sports Medicine *(40)*

Yates, Russell
Association of Corporate Travel Executives (ACTE) *(277)*

Yatskievych, George
American Fern Society *(121)*

Yaufman, II, James R.
National Association of Underwater Instructors *(707)*

Ybarra, Juanita
Petroleum Equipment Suppliers Association *(843)*

Yborra, Stephe
NGVAmerica *(810)*

Yeager, Barbara
Partnership for Philanthropic Planning *(839)*

Yeager, Robert T. (Tim)
National Organization of Legal Services Workers *(777)*

Yearicks, Lani A.
Delta Omicron *(409)*

Yearwood, Patricia
The American Society for Public Administration *(189)*

Yee, MD, Judy
Society of Abdominal Radiology *(927)*

Yeldell, Kathy R.
American Foreign Service Protective Association *(123)*

Yelich, Joel V.
National Block and Bridle Club *(715)*

Yen Tsen, Sylvia Wei
International Federation of Accountants *(544)*

Yeninas, Barbara Spector

Containerization and Intermodal Institute *(382)*

Yep, Richard
American Counseling Association *(111)*

Yerger, Ann
Council of Institutional Investors *(394)*

Yerigan, Dale
International Professional Rodeo Association *(561)*

Yeske, PhD, Dr. Ronald
National Council for Air and Stream Improvement, Inc.
(731)

Yess, Mary E.
The Electrochemical Society *(423)*

Yew, Linda
Neurofibromatosis, Inc., Northeast *(808)*

Yezbick, Frank
Automotive Market Research Council *(323)*

Yglesias, Janice
American Architectural Manufacturers Association *(46)*

Yieh, Nancy
Asian Women in Business *(232)*

Yin, L. Roger
Organizational Systems Research Association *(833)*

Ying, Phillip
Chamber Music America *(350)*

Yingst, Richard "Dick" A.
Financial Managers Society *(445)*

Ylitalo, Saaraliisa
Surface Design Association *(966)*

Yoak, Dr. Stuart
Association for Practical and Professional Ethics *(253)*

Yochum, Karen D.
American Cable Association *(87)*

Yocum, Alisha
Biophysical Society *(330)*

Yoder, Amy
Distribution Business Management Association *(414)*

Yoder, Chris
Gerontological Society of America *(460)*

Yoder, Donald G.
Accreditation Council for Accountancy and Taxation
(9)

Yoes, Patrick
National Fraternal Order of Police *(753)*

Yohe, Jeremy
American Land Title Association *(144)*

Yoho, CAE, Karen
National Association for Gifted Children *(639)*

Yoke, Beth
Young Adult Library Services Association *(1030)*

Yonkers, CMP, Lisa
American Academy of Audiology *(31)*

Yoo, Jinnie
American Society of Plumbing Engineers *(207)*

Yoong, Jade
International Right of Way Association *(563)*

York, Dennis
National Reining Horse Association *(785)*

York, PhD, Elaine
National Association of Physician Recruiters *(684)*

Yorkshire, Ted
Air Force Association *(18)*

Yoshikane, Pauleen
Fresh Produce and Floral Council *(453)*

Yost, Ellen
Choristers Guild *(355)*

Yost, Joe
Consumer Specialty Products Association *(381)*

Yost, M. Lauren
National Recreation and Parks Association *(784)*

Yost, MBA, Sandra L.
American Academy of Disability Evaluating Physicians
(33)

You, Angela
National Association of Public Child Welfare
Administrators *(688)*

Youdell, Ed
Fabricators & Manufacturers Association, International
(437)
Tube and Pipe Association, International *(981)*

Youkhanis, James
American Society for Blood and Marrow
Transplantation *(181)*

Youmans, Barb
National Association of RV Parks and Campgrounds
(692)

Youmans, Rich
Manufacturing Jewelers and Suppliers of America *(604)*

Youn, Steve
American Institute of Chemical Engineers *(138)*

Young, A. Steve
Association of Independent Corrugated Converters
(288)

Young, A. Steven
International Corrugated Packaging Foundation *(537)*

Young, Andrew T.
American Inns of Court *(135)*

Young, Angela
Human Capital Institute *(480)*

Young, Anthony
American Herbal Products Association *(130)*

Young, Charla
National Rural Electric Cooperative Association *(788)*

Young, Charlene E.
American Water Resources Association *(220)*

Young, Christopher
Distributive Education Clubs of America (DECA) *(415)*
National Registry of Environmental Professionals *(785)*

Young, Connie
Society for Industrial & Applied Mathematics *(912)*

Young, Cris
National Association of Small Business Contractors
(696)

Young, David
Bituminous Coal Operators Association *(331)*

Young, Deborah
National Association of Elementary School Principals
(664)

Young, Diane
Global Business Travel Association *(462)*

Young, Ella M.
National Funeral Directors and Morticians Association
(754)

Young, Erin
Phi Delta Kappa International *(845)*
Pi Lambda Theta *(847)*

Young, Francine
National Pan-Hellenic Council *(778)*

Young, Gretchen K.
The ERISA Industry Committee (ERIC) *(433)*

Young, Holly

Association for Communication Excellence *(242)*

Young, Jr., Hugh F.
Product Liability Advisory Council *(859)*

Young, James
Log Homes Council *(600)*

Young, Jeanette
Market Technicians Association *(606)*

Young, John K.
Society for Textual Scholarship *(922)*

Young, Jon
American Council of Hypnotist Examiners *(109)*

Young, Judith
American Alliance for Health, Physical Education,
Recreation and Dance *(44)*

Young, PhD, Judy C.
American Association for Health Education *(49)*

Young, Leonard M.
National Association of Parliamentarians *(683)*

Young, Linda
AIM Global *(17)*

Young, CEOE, Lola
National Association of Educational Office
Professionals *(664)*

Young, Mark
ATP Tour, Inc. *(320)*

Young, Mary Emma
CropLife America *(404)*

Young, Melanie
Society for Healthcare Epidemiology of America *(910)*

Young, Meredith
The Association of International Photography Art
Dealers *(289)*

Young, CMP, Meredith
Association of Meeting Professionals *(294)*

Young, MBA, Michelle
International Health, Racquet and Sportsclub
Association *(549)*

Young, Michelle D.
University Council for Educational Administration
(1002)

Young, Myrna A.
National Council on Radiation Protection and
Measurement *(739)*

Young, Penny
Plumbing-Heating-Cooling Contractors - National
Association *(851)*

Young, Penny L.
Flight Safety Foundation *(448)*

Young, Peter C.
Association of Educational Service Agencies *(280)*

Young, Ralph
Association of Independent Corrugated Converters
(288)

Young, Randy
Association of Food and Drug Officials *(283)*

Young, PE, PhD, REM, Richard A.
National Registry of Environmental Professionals *(785)*

Young, S.
National Association of Physician Nurses *(684)*

Young, Shannon
United Fresh Produce Association *(987)*

Young, Sharon K.
International Real Estate Federation - American
Chapter *(562)*

Young, Stan
Advanced Transit Association *(13)*

Young, MS, Stephanie Jackson
National Register of Health Service Providers in Psychology **(785)**

Young, Stephen
CPCU Society **(402)**

Young, Teresa
Air Force Sergeants Association **(19)**

Young, Tracey
Employee Benefit Research Institute **(426)**

Young, Tracy B.
American Educational Research Association **(116)**

Youngblood, CAE, James H.
Heart Rhythm Society **(472)**

Youngblood, Liz
National Lesbian and Gay Law Association **(769)**

Youngblood, Rena
Georgia Charter Schools Association **(459)**

Youngblut, April
America's Small Business Development Center Network **(29)**
Association of Small Business Development Centers **(308)**

Youngen, Doug
Triumvirate Environmental **(980)**

Younger, Andrew
Organization Development Network **(831)**

Younger, Andy
North American Association of Floor Covering Distributors **(811)**
North American Building Material Distribution Association **(814)**

Younger, CMP, Melanie Hughes
BICSI **(329)**

Younker, Susan
American Society of Ophthalmic Administrators **(205)**

Yourd, Hannah
Northwest Natural Resource Group **(824)**

Yourell, Diana
Rolf Institute of Structural Integration **(887)**

Ysasi, Rosie
International Aloe Science Council **(510)**

Yu, Ed, MD, MS, Jack C.
American Cleft Palate-Craniofacial Association **(91)**

Yu, Pauline
American Council of Learned Societies **(109)**

Yu, Tony
American Network of Community Options and Resources (ANCOR) **(155)**

Yun, Hanna
National Association of Professional Asian American Women **(686)**

Yun, Regina
International Legal Fraternity of Phi Delta Phi **(554)**

Yunas, Akram
Automotive Industry Action Group **(322)**

Yung, DPM, Jeffrey
American Association of Colleges of Podiatric Medicine **(58)**
Council of Teaching Hospitals **(398)**

Yungmann, George
National Association of Real Estate Investment Trusts (NAREIT) **(690)**

Yurek, Stephen R.
Air Conditioning, Heating and Refrigeration Institute (AHRI) **(18)**

Yushkevich, Sergey
International Right of Way Association **(563)**

Yusif, CAE, I.F.
American Mideast Business Associates **(151)**

Yuska, Charles (Chuck) D.
Packaging Machinery Manufacturers Institute **(836)**

Yusko, Jason
International Franchise Association **(547)**

Zabello, Irina
General Federation of Women's Clubs **(458)**

Zabinski, Lawrence E.
Attorneys' Liability Assurance Society Inc. **(320)**

Zablocky, Kim
Trade Promotion Management Associates **(977)**

Zaborowski, Bob
Flexible Packaging Association **(447)**

Zabriskie, Laura M.
Commercial Vehicle Safety Alliance **(367)**

Zabrosky, Esq., Alex W.
Institute of Management Consultants USA **(501)**

Zacharias, Thomas "Tom" P.
National Crop Insurance Services **(741)**

Zacharilla, Louis
Society of Satellite Professionals International **(947)**
World Teleport Association **(1027)**

Zachary, Tiffany
Public Investors Arbitration Bar Association **(869)**

Zackery, MeLisa
Council on Undergraduate Research **(401)**

Zader, Karen
Society for Information Management **(913)**

Zadnik, Kurt
American Academy of Optometry **(37)**

Zafrin, Vika
Association for Computers and the Humanities **(242)**

Zagar, Karen S.
Association for Hospital Medical Education **(249)**

Zagoria, MD, Ronald J.
American Society of Emergency Radiology **(197)**

Zahn, PhD, Susan Brown
American Orthopaedic Society for Sports Medicine **(159)**

Zahory, Robin Burke
Women in Cable Telecommunications, Inc. **(1020)**

Zahralddin, Moayad
American Association of Healthcare Administrative Management **(61)**

Zahralddin, Moyad
Alliance of Information and Referral Systems **(25)**

Zaid, Susan
Academy of Management **(6)**

Zaiser, Stephanie
International Brotherhood of Police Officers **(532)**
National Association of Government Employees **(670)**

Zak, Leah
American Montessori Society **(152)**

Zak, Noel
Steel Plate Fabricators Association Division of STI/SPFA **(962)**
Steel Tank Institute Division of STI/SPFA **(963)**

Zales, II, Captain Bob
National Association of Charterboat Operators **(652)**

Zalewksi, Mark
American Financial Services Association **(121)**

Zalewski, David
Association for Evolutionary Economics **(246)**

Zamanigan, Ryan

Omega Delta **(827)**

Zamora, Cecilia
National Association of Commissions for Women **(656)**

Zamora, Luis
Association of Technical and Supervisory Professionals **(313)**

Zampieri, Thomas
Blinded Veterans Association **(332)**

Zamudio, BSN, RN, Ashley
Alpha Tau Delta **(27)**

Zande, Jill
Marine Technology Society **(605)**

Zande, Katie Vande
World Allergy Organization **(1025)**

Zando, Kate
Adhesive and Sealant Council **(12)**

Zandt, Pearl Van
National Council of State Agencies for the Blind **(736)**

Zaner, Jordan
Swedish-American Chambers of Commerce of the USA, Inc. **(967)**

Zapalik, Kyle
Human Resource People and Strategy **(481)**
North American Association of Floor Covering Distributors **(811)**

Zappala, Fern
American Society of Health-System Pharmacists **(199)**

Zappas, Paul
Minerals, Metals and Materials Society **(617)**

Zapple, Alex
National Association of Healthcare Access Management **(671)**

Zapple, Alexandra
Institute of Clean Air Companies **(499)**

Zapple, Alexandra
International Bone and Mineral Society **(530)**

Zappone, Heidi
International and American Associations of Clinical Nutritionists **(510)**

Zarafshar, Tony
Telecommunications Industry Association **(971)**

Zaragoza, Jason
Association of Alternative Newsweeklies **(264)**

Zarda, Lisa
American Association of Cosmetology Schools **(59)**

Zarling, Lori
International Sanitary Supply Association **(563)**

Zarski, Mike
American Osteopathic Association **(160)**

Zartman-Ball, Eve
The Vision Council **(1010)**

Zassenhaus, Harold R.
Wood Machinery Manufacturers of America **(1024)**

Zastrow, Ann
Metals Service Center Institute **(614)**

Zaterman, Sunia
Council of Large Public Housing Authorities **(395)**

Zatkulak, Tom
Sanitary Supply Wholesaling Association **(891)**

Zaug, Dale
National Woodland Owners Association **(806)**

Zavatsky, Candice
Society for Foodservice Management **(909)**

Zawacki, Anna

United States Pan Asian American Chamber of Commerce (997)

Zawad, Amanda
American Specialty Toy Retailing Association (212)

Zawaski, Mary
National Association of Charter School Authorizers (652)

Zayner, Chris
Academy of General Dentistry (5)

Zazza, Heidi
IEEE Circuits and Systems Society (483)

Zazzera, Liz
International Swaps and Derivatives Association (576)

Zdanowicz, Mary
Association of State and Territorial Solid Waste Management Officials (310)

Zecca, Ann
Petroleum Convenience Alliance for Technology Standards (843)

Zeck, Leslie
American Association for Dental Research (49)
International Association for Dental Research (512)

Zeeman, BSN, RN, Lynn
Alpha Tau Delta (27)

Zegarek, Meryl
Mystery Writers of America (623)

Zeger, Jordana
National Hemophilia Foundation (759)

Zehme, Richard
Federal Criminal Investigators Association (439)

Zeiger, Eileen
American Society of PeriAnesthesia Nurses (206)

Zeilinger, Chris
Community Transportation Association of America (371)

Zeimetz, Greta
National Association of Tax Professionals (704)

Zein, Tamara
AABB - American Association of Blood Banks (1)

Zeisel, Steven I.
Consumer Bankers Association (380)

Zeisset, CCS, CCSP, RHIT, Ann
American Health Information Management Association (129)

Zeldow, Debbie
Alliance for Aging Research (22)

Zelkin, Carol
Interactive Multimedia and Collaborative Communications Alliance (507)

Zeller, Al
Cryogenic Engineering Conference (405)

Zeller, Ann
Association of Jewish Family & Children's Agencies (290)

Zelman, Shawn Taylor
Women Networking in Electronic Transactions (1022)

Zelner, Susan
National Association of Bond Lawyers (650)

Zeman, Jan
National Association of Publishers' Representatives (689)

Zemrani, Aziza
Conference of Minority Public Administrators (375)

Zengel, William
Association of National Advertisers (295)

Zenor, Stanley D.

Federal Communications Bar Association (439)

Zeravsky, CMP, Tara
American Beekeeping Federation (80)

Zerfas, Bart
Land Trust Alliance (593)

Zerfas, Lorraine B.
Education Credit Union Council (419)

Zern, Kristin
Association of Travel Marketing Executives (315)

Zettler, Erik R.
International Society of Protistologists (573)

Zewers, Kirsten E.
Intellectual Property Owners Association (505)

Zhang, Andy
Jewish Community Centers Association of North America (588)

Zhang, Cheng
Society for American Archaeology (903)

Zhang, Feng
National Conference of Executives of The ARC (727)

Zhang, Linjun
International Executive Association (543)

Zhao, MPH, Weiyi
American Society for Biochemistry and Molecular Biology (181)

Zhuang, PhD, Ziqing
International Society for Respiratory Protection (569)

Zicchino, Eileen
Business Marketing Association (339)

Zickar, Lou
The Ripon Society (886)

Zidar, Ellen
Society for Laboratory Automation and Screening (914)

Zidek, Billie
Independent Office Products and Furniture Dealers Association (490)
National Office Products Alliance (776)
Office Furniture Dealers Alliance (826)

Ziebart, Geoff C.
National Association of Business Political Action Committees (651)

Ziegler, Carole
Association of Earth Science Editors (279)

Ziegler, AAI, ARM, CAE, CPCU, Cynthia R.
Casualty Actuarial Society (344)

Ziegler, Julie
American Medical Association Alliance, Inc. (149)

Ziegler, Patricia
American Coatings Association (92)

Ziegler, Ron
American Association of Community Theatre (58)

Ziegler, Scott
American Philosophical Society (164)

Zielezienski, J. Stephen
American Insurance Association (141)

Zielinski, Daniel
Rubber Manufacturers Association (888)
Scrap Tire Management Council (893)

Zielinski, David E.
International Cargo Gear Bureau (533)

Zielke, Mark D.
American Society of Agricultural and Biological Engineers (191)

Ziemann, Larissa
Republican Governors Association (881)

Ziemnik, MEd, Suzanne
American Society for Clinical Pathology (182)

Zieser, Jane
Associated Construction Distributors International (235)

Zietz, Lew
National Air Traffic Controllers Association (630)

Zilleruelo, Geraldine
Wine and Spirits Shippers Association (1018)

Zillig, Rachel
Phi Alpha Delta (845)

Zillo, Joseph A.
NAFSA: Association of International Educators (624)

Zimar, Heather
American Association of Collegiate Registrars and Admissions Officers (58)

Zimecki, Lorrie
National Alcohol Beverage Control Association (631)

Zimini, Nancy
Airports Council International - North America (21)

Zimmer, Lydia
Art Directors Guild/Scenic, Title and Graphic Artists (230)

Zimmerman, Bob
Automotive Communication Council (322)

Zimmerman, Caroline
National Association of Credit Management (661)

Zimmerman, CAE, Heidi J.
Association of Water Technologies (317)

Zimmerman, CCP, Jean
Certified Claims Professional Accreditation Council (349)

Zimmerman, June F.
American Concrete Institute (106)

Zimmerman, Katie
National Association of Public Hospitals and Health Systems (688)

Zimmerman, Maggie
Association of Professional Researchers for Advancement (302)

Zimmerman, Rita Denniston
American Inns of Court (135)

Zimmerman, Esq., Scott
Pipe Fabrication Institute (849)

Zimmerman, Stacy
Association of Professional Landscape Designers (301)

Zimmermann, Bill
Appraisal Institute (226)

Zimmermann, BA, Esq., Glenn
American Board of Vocational Experts (84)

Zimmermann, PhD, Merle
American Herbal Products Association (130)

Zimmermann, Rudy
National Soccer Coaches Association of America (792)

Zink, John
Plumbing-Heating-Cooling Contractors - National Association (851)

Zinn, Terry W.
Kitchen Cabinet Manufacturers Association (591)

Zinna, Betty
International Association of Marriage and Family Counselors (524)

Zinna, Diane
Association of Writers and Writing Programs (318)

Zinnert, Michelle
American Urogynecologic Society (218)

Zinno, Rebekah
National Correctional Industries Association *(730)*

Zipperlen, Robert A.
Society of Hospital Medicine *(938)*

Zipperstein, Steven J.
Conference on Jewish Social Studies *(376)*

Zipser, Neal
Society of Automotive Analysts *(930)*

Ziriax, Lisa
National Federation of Republican Women *(750)*

Zirkel, Marie
Beefmaster Breeders United *(327)*

Zirkle, Deb
Society for Pediatric Research *(918)*

Zissis, Carin
Council of the Americas *(398)*

Zitowsky, CPA, MSA, Marcia
Healthcare Information and Management Systems
Society *(471)*

Zizer, Roland
National Association of Student Financial Aid
Administrators *(703)*

Zobaa, Mohamed K.
AASP - The Palynological Society *(2)*

Zobel, Mary Lou
Professional Women Singers Association *(866)*

Zoephel, Denise
Selected Independent Funeral Homes *(896)*

Zohdi, Tarek
United States Association for Computational
Mechanics *(990)*

Zoks, Lisa
Drug Information Association *(417)*

Zolde, Morten
The Danish-American Chamber of Commerce (USA)
(407)

Zona, Leigh A.
Theatre Communications Group *(973)*

Zoretich, Marion
Society for Imaging Science and Technology *(912)*

Zorich, Luke
American Academy of Wound Management *(42)*
National Association for Surface Finishing *(643)*

Zorrilla, Vicky
Senior Executives Association *(897)*

Zosh-McLean, Wendy
American Association of Anatomists *(54)*

Zoshak, John
Generic Pharmaceutical Association *(458)*

Zouboff, CAE, IOM, Tamara
Belgian-American Chamber of Commerce *(327)*

Zuccaro, Matthew S.
Helicopter Association International *(473)*

Zucker, Heather
Secondary Materials and Recycled Textiles Association
(894)

Zuckerman, Joanne
Association of Schools and Colleges of Optometry
(307)

Zuecca, Nicolette
The Wound, Ostomy and Continence Nurses Society
(1028)

Zuengler, Jane
American Association for Applied Linguistics *(47)*

Zulaski, Kate
Alliance for Massage Therapy Education *(23)*

Zuleg, Matt
Orthopaedic Research Society *(833)*

Zulli, Jeri
Church and Synagogue Library Association *(356)*

Zulu, CAE, CPA, Itibari M.
African-American Library and Information Science
Association *(15)*

Zuluaga, Wendy
American Securitization Forum *(178)*

Zung, Jody
American Society for Investigative Pathology *(186)*

Zuniga, MPH, PhD, Jose M.
International Association of Physicians in AIDS Care
(526)

Zupnick, Jan
The Entrepreneurship Institute *(430)*

Zurawsky, Chris
Association of American Cancer Institutes *(264)*

Zurcher, Rebecca
International Association of Defense Counsel *(519)*

Zvonkovich, Stephenie
Design-Build Institute of America *(411)*

Zwiefelhofer, Cody
Surfaces in Biomaterials Foundation *(966)*

Zwischenberger, MD, Joseph B.
American Society for Artificial Internal Organs *(181)*

Zychowicz, James L.
International Association of Music Libraries, United
States Branch *(525)*

Zygmont, Joanna
Red Tag News Publications Association *(878)*

Zywczuk, Jorja
Society of Petrophysicists and Well Log Analysts *(944)*

Association Acronym Index

Associations are often referred to by their acronyms and are listed here under the acronym with which they are most closely identified.

IA	Division I-A Athletic Directors Association *(415)*	**AAAI**	American Association for the Advancement of Artificial Intelligence *(51)*	
4As	Associated Actors and Artistes of America *(234)*	**AAAIM**	The Association of Asian American Investment Managers *(268)*	
4S	Society for Social Studies of Science *(921)*	**AAAL**	American Academy of Appellate Lawyers *(30)*	
9to5	Nine to Five, National Association of Working Women *(811)*		American Association for Applied Linguistics *(47)*	
A&WMA	Air and Waste Management Association *(17)*	**AAALAC**	Association for Assessment and Accreditation of Laboratory Animal Care International *(239)*	
A.P.L.U	Association of Public and Land-Grant Universities (APLU) *(303)*	**AAAM**	Association for the Advancement of Automotive Medicine *(258)*	
A2IM	American Association of Independent Music *(63)*		Association of African American Museums *(263)*	
A2LA	American Association for Laboratory Accreditation *(50)*	**AAAOM**	American Association of Acupuncture and Oriental Medicine *(53)*	
A4A	Airlines For America *(21)*	**AAAP**	American Academy of Addiction Psychiatry *(29)*	
A4M	American Academy of Anti-Aging Medicine *(30)*		American Association of Avian Pathologists *(54)*	
AA	Academy of Aphasia *(4)*	**AAAR**	American Association for Aerosol Research *(47)*	
AAA	Allied Artists of America *(25)*	**AAAS**	American Academy of Arts & Sciences *(30)*	
	American Abstract Artists *(29)*		American Association for the Advancement of Science *(51)*	
	American Academy of Actuaries *(29)*		Association for Asian American Studies *(239)*	
	American Academy of Advertising *(30)*	**AAB**	American Association of Bioanalysts *(54)*	
	American Academy of Audiology *(31)*		Association of Artisan Business (AAB) *(268)*	
	American Accordionists Association *(43)*	**AABB**	AABB – American Association of Blood Banks *(1)*	
	American Accounting Association *(43)*	**AABC**	American Association of Birth Centers *(55)*	
	American Ambulance Association *(44)*		Associated Air Balance Council *(234)*	
	American Angus Association *(45)*	**AABD**	American Association of Bank Directors *(54)*	
	American Anthropological Association *(45)*	**AABE**	American Association of Blacks in Energy *(55)*	
	American Arbitration Association *(46)*	**AABH**	Association for Ambulatory Behavioral Healthcare *(238)*	
	American Association of Anatomists *(54)*	**AABP**	Alliance of Area Business Publications *(24)*	
	Appraisers Association of America *(226)*		American Association of Bovine Practitioners *(55)*	
	Association for Accounting Administration *(237)*	**AABPA**	American Association for Budget and Program Analysis *(48)*	
AAA-CPA	American Association of Attorney-Certified Public Accountants *(54)*	**AABS**	Association for the Advancement of Baltic Studies *(258)*	
AAAA	American Academy of Adoption Attorneys *(30)*	**AABT**	American Association of Behavioral Therapists *(54)*	
	American Academy of Anesthesiologist Assistants *(30)*		Association for Behavioral and Cognitive Therapies *(240)*	
	American Association for Affirmative Action *(47)*	**AABVS**	American Association of Business Valuation Specialists *(55)*	
	American Association of Advertising Agencies *(53)*	**AAC**	Alliance of Artists Communities *(24)*	
	Army Aviation Association of America *(229)*		Aluminum Anodizers Council *(27)*	
AAAAI	American Academy of Allergy, Asthma, and Immunology *(30)*	**AAC&U**	Association of American Colleges and Universities *(264)*	
AAAASF	American Association for Accreditation of Ambulatory Surgery Facilities *(47)*	**AACA**	African American Contractors Association *(15)*	
AAACE	American Association for Adult and Continuing Education *(47)*		American Association of Certified Allergists *(56)*	
AAACN	American Academy of Ambulatory Care Nursing *(30)*	**AACAP**	American Academy of Child and Adolescent Psychiatry *(31)*	
AAADM	American Association of Automatic Door Manufacturers *(54)*	**AACC**	American Association for Clinical Chemistry, Inc. *(48)*	
AAAE	American Association for Agricultural Education *(47)*			
	American Association of Airport Executives *(53)*			
	Association of Arts Administration Educators *(268)*			
AAAHC	Accreditation Association for Ambulatory Health Care *(9)*			

	American Association of Cereal Chemists International *(55)*
	American Association of Christian Counselors *(56)*
	American Association of Community Colleges *(58)*
	American Automatic Control Council *(78)*
	Argentine-American Chamber of Commerce *(228)*
AACCLA	Association of American Chambers of Commerce in Latin America *(264)*
AACD	American Academy of Cosmetic Dentistry *(31)*
AACDP	American Association of Chairs of Departments of Psychiatry *(56)*
AACE	American Association for Cancer Education *(48)*
	American Association for Career Education *(48)*
	American Association of Clinical Endocrinologists *(56)*
	The American Association of Code Enforcement *(57)*
	Association for Assessment in Counseling and Education *(240)*
	Association for the Advancement of Computing in Education *(258)*
AACEI	AACE International *(1)*
AACG	American Association for Crystal Growth *(49)*
AACH	American Academy on Communication in Healthcare *(43)*
AACI	American Association of Crop Insurers *(59)*
	Association of American Cancer Institutes *(264)*
AACN	American Academy of Clinical Neuropsychology *(31)*
	American Association of Colleges of Nursing *(57)*
	American Association of Critical-Care Nurses *(59)*
AACO	American Association of Certified Orthoptists *(56)*
AACOM	American Association of Colleges of Osteopathic Medicine *(57)*
AACP	American Academy of Clinical Psychiatrists *(31)*
	American Academy of Craniofacial Pain *(32)*
	American Association of Colleges of Pharmacy *(57)*
	American Association of Community Psychiatrists *(58)*
AACPDM	American Academy for Cerebral Palsy and Developmental Medicine *(29)*
AACPM	American Association of Colleges of Podiatric Medicine *(58)*
AACPPV	American Association of Corporate and Public Practice Veterinarians *(58)*
AACR	American Association for Cancer Research *(48)*
AACRAO	American Association of Collegiate Registrars and Admissions Officers *(58)*
AACRC	American Association of Children's Residential Centers *(56)*

AACS American Academy of Cosmetic Surgery (32)

American Association for Chinese Studies (48)

American Association of Christian Schools (56)

American Association of Cosmetology Schools (59)

Association for Applied and Clinical Sociology (238)

AACSA Asian American Convenience Stores Association (231)

AACSB The Association to Advance Collegiate Schools of Business (319)

AACSE American Association of Classified School Employees (56)

AACT American Academy of Clinical Toxicology (31)

American Association of Candy Technologists (55)

American Association of Community Theatre (58)

AACTE American Association of Colleges for Teacher Education (57)

AACU American Association of Clinical Urologists (56)

AACUL American Association of Credit Union Leagues (59)

AACVPR American Association of Cardiovascular and Pulmonary Rehabilitation (55)

AAD American Academy of Dermatology (32)

American Academy of Diplomacy (32)

AADA Association for Adult Development and Aging (238)

AADB The American Association of Dental Boards (59)

AADC American Association of Dental Consultants (59)

AADE American Association of Dental Editors (60)

American Association of Diabetes Educators (60)

AADEP American Academy of Disability Evaluating Physicians (33)

AADGP American Academy of Dental Group Practice (32)

AADLA Art and Antique Dealers League of America (229)

AADPA American Academy of Dental Practice Administration (32)

AADPRT American Association of Directors of Psychiatric Residency Training (60)

AADR American Association for Dental Research (49)

AADSM American Academy of Dental Sleep Medicine (32)

AAE American Association of Endodontists (60)

Association of American Educators (264)

Association of Art Editors (267)

AAEA Agricultural & Applied Economics Association (16)

American Academy of Equine Art (33)

American Agricultural Editors Association (43)

AAEC Association of American Editorial Cartoonists (264)

AAECE American Association of Early Childhood Educators (60)

AAED American Academy of Esthetic Dentistry (33)

AAEE American Academy of Environmental Engineers (33)

American Association for Employment in Education (49)

AAEECE The American Association of Eye and Ear Centers of Excellence (57)

AAEI American Association of Exporters & Importers (60)

AAEM American Academy of Emergency Medicine (33)

American Academy of Environmental Medicine (33)

AAEP American Association of Equine Practitioners (60)

AAEPA American Academy of Estate Planning Attorneys (33)

AAES American Association of Engineering Societies (60)

AAF American Advertising Federation (43)

American Architectural Foundation (46)

AAFA American Apparel & Footwear Association (46)

AAFAS Academy of Ambulatory Foot and Ankle Surgery (3)

AAFCO Association of American Feed Control Officials (265)

AAFCP American Academy of Fertility Care Professionals (34)

AAFCS American Association of Family and Consumer Sciences (61)

AAFD American Association of Franchisees and Dealers (61)

AAFHV American Association of Food Hygiene Veterinarians (61)

AAFP American Academy of Family Physicians (34)

American Association of Feline Practitioners (61)

AAfPE American Association for Paralegal Education (50)

AAFPRS American Academy of Facial Plastic and Reconstructive Surgery (34)

AAFS American Academy of Forensic Sciences (34)

AAG Association of American Geographers (265)

AAGBA American Angora Goat Breeder's Association (45)

AAGFO American Academy of Gold Foil Operators (34)

AAGIWA American Association of Grain Inspection and Weighing Agencies (61)

AAGL AAGL - Advancing Minimally Invasive Gynecology Worldwide (2)

AAGO American Academy of Gnathologic Orthopedics (34)

AAGP American Association for Geriatric Psychiatry (49)

AAGS American Association for Geodetic Surveying (49)

AAGUS American Association of Genitourinary Surgeons (61)

AAH Academy of Accounting Historians (3)

Association of Ancient Historians (267)

AAHA American Animal Hospital Association (45)

AAHAM American Association of Healthcare Administrative Management (61)

AAHC American Association of Healthcare Consultants (62)

Association of Academic Health Centers (262)

AAHCP American Academy of Home Care Physicians (35)

AAHCPAD American Academy of Health Care Providers-Addictive Disorders (34)

AAHD American Academy of the History of Dentistry (42)

AAHE American Association for Health Education (49)

AAHFN American Association of Heart Failure Nurses (62)

AAHHP American Association of Hospital and Healthcare Podiatrists (62)

AAHI American Association of Home Inspectors (62)

AAHKS American Association of Hip and Knee Surgeons (62)

AAHM American Association for the History of Medicine (52)

AAHMP American Alliance of Home Modification Professionals (AAHMP) (44)

AAHN American Association for the History of Nursing (52)

AAHOA Asian American Hotel Owners Association (231)

AAHomecare American Association for Homecare (50)

AAHP American Academy of Health Physics (35)

American Association of Homeopathic Pharmacists (62)

American Board of Health Physics (82)

AAHPERD American Alliance for Health, Physical Education, Recreation and Dance (44)

AAHPM American Academy of Hospice and Palliative Medicine (35)

AAHRPP Association for the Accreditation of Human Research Protection Programs (257)

AAHS American Association for Hand Surgery (49)

AAHSL Association of Academic Health Sciences Library (263)

AAI American Association of Immunologists (62)

AAIA Association on American Indian Affairs (319)

Automotive Aftermarket Industry Association (321)

AAICP American Association of Independent Claims Professionals (63)

AAICPC Association of Administrators of the Interstate Compact on the Placement of Children (263)

AAID American Academy of Implant Dentistry (35)

AAIE Association for the Advancement of International Education (258)

Association of Applied IPM Ecologists (267)

AAIEP American Association of Intensive English Programs (63)

AAIHDS American Association of Integrated Healthcare Delivery Systems (63)

AAIHR American Association of International Healthcare Recruitment (63)

AAII American Association of Individual Investors (63)

AAIMCo American Association of Insurance Management Consultants (63)

AAIP Association of American Indian Physicians (265)

AAIS American Association of Insurance Services (63)

AAJ American Association for Justice (50)

AAJA Asian American Journalists Association (231)

AAJLJ American Association of Jewish Lawyers and Jurists (64)

AAKP American Association of Kidney Patients (64)

AALA American Agricultural Law Association (44)

American Automotive Leasing Association (78)

AALAS American Association for Laboratory Animal Science (50)

AALISA African-American Library and Information Science Association (15)

AALJ Association of Administrative Law Judges (263)

AALL American Association of Law Libraries (64)

AALNC American Association of Legal Nurse Consultants (64)

AALS Association of American Law Schools (265)

AALU Association for Advanced Life Underwriting (238)

AAM American Academy of Mechanics (35)

American Academy of Ministry (36)

American Agriculture Movement, Inc. (44)

American Association of Museums (65)

Association for Accounting Marketing (238)

Association of Attorney-Mediators (268)

AAMA American Academy of Medical Acupuncture (36)

American Academy of Medical Administrators (36)

American Amusement Machine Association (45)

American Architectural Manufacturers Association (46)

American Association of Medical Assistants (65)

American College of Cardiovascular Administrators (93)

Asia America MultiTechnology Association (231)

AAMB American Association of Minority Businesses (65)

AAMC Association of American Medical Colleges (265)

AAMCN American Association of Managed Care Nurses (64)

AAMD American Association of Medical Dosimetrists (65)

Association of Art Museum Directors (267)

AAMFT American Association for Marriage and Family Therapy (50)

AAMG Association of Academic Museums & Galleries (263)

AAMGA American Association of Managing General Agents (64)

AAMH American Academy of Medical Hypnoanalysts (36)

AAMI Association for the Advancement of Medical Instrumentation (258)

AAML American Academy of Matrimonial Lawyers (35)

AAMM American Academy of Medical Management (36)

AAMMC American Association of Medical Milk Commissions (65)

AAMN American Assembly for Men in Nursing (47)

AAMP American Academy of Maxillofacial Prosthetics (35)

American Association of Meat Processors (64)

AAMS Association of Air Medical Services (264)

AAMSE American Association of Medical Society Executives (65)

AAMVA American Association of Motor Vehicle Administrators (65)

AAN American Academy of Neurology (36)

American Academy of Nursing (37)

Association of Alternative Newsweeklies (264)

AANA American Association of Nurse Anesthetists (67)

Arthroscopy Association of North America (230)

AANC American Association of Nutritional Consultants (67)

AANEM American Association of Neuromuscular and Electrodiagnostic Medicine (66)

AANMA	Allergy and Asthma Network Mothers of Asthmatics *(22)*	
AANN	American Association of Neuroscience Nurses *(66)*	
AANOS	American Academy of Neurological and Orthopaedic Surgeons *(36)*	
AANP	American Academy of Nurse Practitioners *(37)*	
	American Association of Naturopathic Physicians *(66)*	
	American Association of Neuropathologists *(66)*	
AANS	American Association of Neurological Surgeons *(66)*	
AAO	American Academy of Ophthalmology *(37)*	
	American Academy of Optometry *(37)*	
	American Academy of Osteopathy *(38)*	
	American Association of Orthodontists *(67)*	
AAO-HNS	American Academy of Otolaryngology-Head and Neck Surgery *(39)*	
AAOA	American Academy of Otolaryngic Allergy *(38)*	
AAOE	American Academy of Ophthalmic Executives *(37)*	
AAOHN	American Association of Occupational Health Nurses *(67)*	
AAOM	American Academy of Oral Medicine *(38)*	
	American Association of Orthopaedic Medicine *(68)*	
AAOMP	American Academy of Oral and Maxillofacial Pathology *(37)*	
AAOMR	American Academy of Oral and Maxillofacial Radiology *(37)*	
AAOMS	American Association of Oral and Maxillofacial Surgeons *(67)*	
AAOP	American Academy of Orofacial Pain *(38)*	
	American Academy of Orthotists and Prosthetists *(38)*	
AAOS	American Academy of Orthopaedic Surgeons *(38)*	
AAOWP	American Association of Osteopathic Women Physicians *(68)*	
AAP	American Academy of Pediatrics *(39)*	
	American Academy of Periodontology *(39)*	
	American Academy of Psychotherapists *(41)*	
	Association for Asian Performance *(239)*	
	Association for the Advancement of Psychology *(258)*	
	Association for the Advancement of Psychotherapy *(258)*	
	Association of Academic Physiatrists *(263)*	
	Association of American Physicians *(265)*	
	Association of American Publishers *(266)*	
	Association of Aviation Psychologists *(269)*	
AAPA	American Academy of Physician Assistants *(40)*	
	American Association of Pathologists' Assistants *(68)*	
	American Association of Physical Anthropologists *(69)*	
	American Association of Port Authorities *(70)*	
	American Association of Psychiatric Administrators *(71)*	
	Asian American Psychological Association *(232)*	
AAPA-OM	American Academy of Physician Assistants in Occupational Medicine *(40)*	
AAPB	Association for Applied Psychophysiology and Biofeedback *(238)*	
AAPC	American Academy of Professional Coders *(40)*	
	American Association of Pastoral Counselors *(68)*	
	American Association of Political Consultants *(70)*	
	American Automotive Policy Council *(78)*	
AAPCC	American Association of Poison Control Centers *(70)*	
AAPCHO	Association of Asian-Pacific Community Health Organizations *(268)*	
AAPCO	Association of American Pesticide Control Officials *(265)*	
AAPD	American Academy of Pediatric Dentistry *(39)*	
AAPDP	American Academy of Psychoanalysis and Dynamic Psychiatry *(41)*	
AAPF	American Association of Professional Farriers *(71)*	
AAPFCO	Association of American Plant Food Control Officials *(266)*	
AAPG	American Association of Petroleum Geologists *(68)*	

AAPH	American Association of Professional Hypnotherapists *(71)*	
AAPHD	American Association of Public Health Dentistry *(71)*	
AAPHP	American Association of Public Health Physicians *(72)*	
AAPI	American Association of Physicians of Indian Origin *(69)*	
	Antique and Amusement Photographers International *(224)*	
AAPICU	American Association of Presidents of Independent Colleges and Universities *(71)*	
AAPL	American Academy of Psychiatry and the Law *(41)*	
	American Artists Professional League *(47)*	
	American Association of Private Lenders *(71)*	
	American Association of Professional Landmen *(71)*	
AAPM	American Academy of Pain Management *(39)*	
	American Academy of Pain Medicine *(39)*	
	American Association of Physicists in Medicine *(69)*	
AAPM&R	American Academy of Physical Medicine and Rehabilitation *(40)*	
AAPN	American Apparel Producer's Network *(46)*	
AAPOR	American Association for Public Opinion Research *(51)*	
AAPOS	American Association for Pediatric Ophthalmology and Strabismus *(50)*	
AAPP	American Association of Police Polygraphists *(70)*	
AAPPM	American Academy of Podiatric Practice Management *(40)*	
AAPPO	American Association of Preferred Provider Organizations *(70)*	
AAPRCO	American Association of Private Railroad Car Owners *(71)*	
AAPS	American Association of Pharmaceutical Scientists *(68)*	
	The American Association of Phonetic Sciences *(69)*	
	American Association of Physician Specialists *(69)*	
	American Association of Plastic Surgeons *(70)*	
	Association of Alternate Postal Systems *(264)*	
	Association of American Physicians and Surgeons *(266)*	
AAPSM	American Academy of Podiatric Sports Medicine *(40)*	
AAPSS	American Academy of Political and Social Science *(40)*	
AAPT	American Association of Philosophy Teachers *(69)*	
	American Association of Physics Teachers *(69)*	
	American Association of Psychiatric Technicians *(71)*	
	Association of Asphalt Paving Technologists *(268)*	
AAPWA	American Association of Public Welfare Attorneys *(72)*	
AAR	Alliance for Aging Research *(22)*	
	American Academy of Religion *(41)*	
	Association of American Railroads *(266)*	
	Association of Authors' Representatives *(268)*	
AARC	American Association for Respiratory Care *(51)*	
	American Association of Retirement Communities *(72)*	
AARD	American Academy of Restorative Dentistry *(41)*	
AARHMS	American Academy of Research Historians of Medieval Spain *(41)*	
AARMR	American Association of Residential Mortgage Regulators *(72)*	
AARP	American Association of Retired Persons *(72)*	
AARS	All-America Rose Selections *(22)*	
	American Association of Railroad Superintendents *(72)*	
AARST	The American Association of Radon Scientists and Technologists *(72)*	
AARTS	Association of Advanced Rabbinical and Talmudic Schools *(263)*	
AARWBA	American Auto Racing Writers and Broadcasters Association *(78)*	
AAS	Academy of Applied Science *(4)*	
	American Academy of Sanitarians *(41)*	
	American Academy of Somnology *(42)*	
	American Antiquarian Society *(45)*	

	American Apitherapy Society *(46)*	
	American Association of Suicidology *(74)*	
	American Astronautical Society *(77)*	
	American Astronomical Society *(77)*	
	American Auditory Society *(78)*	
	The Association for Academic Surgery *(237)*	
	Association for Asian Studies *(239)*	
AASC	American Association of State Climatologists *(73)*	
AASCO	The Association of American Seed Control Officials *(266)*	
AASCU	American Association of State Colleges and Universities *(73)*	
AASECT	American Association of Sexuality Educators, Counselors and Therapists *(73)*	
AASG	Association of American State Geologists *(266)*	
AASHH	American Association for the Study of Hungarian History *(52)*	
AASHTO	AASHTO: Transportation Center of Excellence *(2)*	
AASL	American Association of School Librarians *(72)*	
AASLD	American Association for the Study of Liver Diseases *(52)*	
AASLH	American Association for State and Local History *(51)*	
AASM	American Academy of Sleep Medicine *(42)*	
AASP	AASP - The Palynological Society *(2)*	
	Alliance of Automotive Service Providers *(24)*	
	Association for Applied Sport Psychology *(239)*	
	Association of African Studies Programs *(263)*	
AASPA	American Association of School Personnel Administrators *(73)*	
	American Association of Surgical Physician Assistants *(74)*	
AASRP	American Association of Small Ruminant Practitioners *(73)*	
AAST	American Association for the Surgery of Trauma *(52)*	
	American Association of Sleep Technologists *(73)*	
	American Association of State Troopers *(73)*	
AASV	American Association of Swine Veterinarians *(74)*	
AAT	American Academy of Thermology *(42)*	
AATA	American Art Therapy Association, Inc. *(46)*	
	American Association of Teachers of Arabic *(74)*	
AATB	American Association of Tissue Banks *(75)*	
AATCC	American Association of Textile Chemists and Colorists *(75)*	
AATE	American Alliance for Theatre and Education *(44)*	
	Esperanto-USA *(433)*	
AATF	American Association of Teachers of French *(74)*	
AATG	American Association of Teachers of German *(74)*	
AATH	Association for Applied and Therapeutic Humor *(238)*	
AATI	American Association of Teachers of Italian *(74)*	
AATJ	Alliance of Associations of Teachers of Japanese *(24)*	
AATS	American Academy of Teachers of Singing *(42)*	
	American Association of Thoracic Surgery *(53)*	
AATSEEL	American Association of Teachers of Slavic and East European Languages *(75)*	
AATSP	American Association of Teachers of Spanish and Portuguese *(75)*	
AATT	American Association of Teachers of Turkic Languages *(75)*	
AAU	Association of American Universities *(266)*	
AAUA	American Association of University Administrators *(75)*	
AAUP	American Association of University Professors *(75)*	
	Association of American University Presses *(267)*	
AAUW	American Association of University Women *(76)*	
AAV	Association of Avian Veterinarians *(268)*	
AAVA	American Academy of Veterinary Acupuncture *(42)*	
AAVC	American Association of Veterinary Clinicians *(76)*	
AAVCT	American Academy of Veterinary and Comparative Toxicology *(42)*	
AAVI	American Association of Veterinary Immunologists *(76)*	

ACCI	American Council on Consumer Interests *(110)*
ACCL	American College of Construction Lawyers *(94)*
ACCO	American College of Chiropractic Orthopedists *(94)*
ACCP	American College of Chest Physicians *(94)*
	American College of Clinical Pharmacology *(94)*
	American College of Clinical Pharmacy *(94)*
	American College of Contingency Planners *(95)*
	Association of Corporate Contributions Professionals *(277)*
ACCSC	The Accrediting Commission of Career Schools and Colleges *(10)*
ACCSES	American Congress of Community Supports and Employment Services *(107)*
ACCT	Association of Community College Trustees *(276)*
ACCU	Association of Catholic Colleges and Universities *(271)*
	Association of Corporate Credit Unions *(277)*
ACCWS	American College of Certified Wound Specialists *(94)*
ACD	American College of Dentists *(95)*
	Associated Construction Distributors International *(235)*
ACDA	American Choral Directors Association *(90)*
	American Commodity Distribution Association *(105)*
	Association of Catholic Diocesan Archivists *(271)*
ACDFA	American College Dance Festival Association *(92)*
ACDHA	American Cream Draft Horse Association *(111)*
ACE	American Cinema Editors *(91)*
	American College of Epidemiology *(95)*
	American Council on Education *(110)*
	American Council on Exercise *(110)*
	Association for Communication Excellence *(242)*
	Association of Conservation Engineers *(276)*
	Association of Cooperative Educators *(277)*
ACEC	American Council of Engineering Companies *(109)*
ACEI	Association for Childhood Education International *(241)*
ACEJMC	Accrediting Council on Education in Journalism and Mass Communications *(11)*
ACEP	American College of Emergency Physicians *(95)*
	Association for Comprehensive Energy Psychology *(242)*
ACerS	American Ceramics Society *(89)*
ACES	American College of Eye Surgeons *(95)*
	Association for Comparative Economic Studies *(242)*
	Association for Counselor Education and Supervision *(244)*
ACF	American Composers Forum *(105)*
	American Culinary Federation *(112)*
	The Association of Career Firms North America *(271)*
	Association of Consulting Foresters of America *(276)*
ACFA	American Cash Flow Association *(88)*
	Association of Commercial Finance Attorneys *(275)*
ACFAOM	American College of Foot & Ankle Orthopedics & Medicine *(95)*
ACFAS	American College of Foot and Ankle Surgeons *(95)*
ACFE	Association of Certified Fraud Examiners *(271)*
ACFEI	American College of Forensic Examiners Institute *(96)*
ACFP	American College of Forensic Psychiatry *(96)*
ACFSA	Association of Correctional Food Service Affiliates *(277)*
ACG	AABC Commissioning Group *(1)*
	American College of Gastroenterology *(96)*
	Association for Corporate Growth *(244)*
ACGA	American Corn Growers Association *(108)*
ACGG	American Custom Gunmakers Guild *(112)*
ACGIH	American Conference of Governmental Industrial Hygienists *(107)*
ACH	Association for Computers and the Humanities *(242)*
ACHA	American Catholic Historical Association *(88)*

	American College Health Association *(93)*
	American College of Healthcare Architects *(96)*
ACHCA	American College of Health Care Administrators *(96)*
ACHE	American College of Healthcare Executives *(96)*
	American Council of Hypnotist Examiners *(109)*
	Association for Continuing Higher Education *(243)*
AChemS	Association for Chemoreception Sciences *(241)*
ACHIA	American College of Healthcare Information Administrators *(97)*
ACHNE	Association of Community Health Nursing Educators *(276)*
ACHPM	American College of Health Plan Management *(96)*
ACHS	Association of College Honor Societies *(274)*
ACHSA	American Correctional Health Services Association *(108)*
ACI	American Cleaning Institute *(91)*
	American Concrete Institute *(106)*
	Association for Conservation Information *(243)*
ACI-NA	Airports Council International - North America *(21)*
ACIA	American Construction Inspectors Association *(107)*
	Associated Cooperage Industries of America *(235)*
ACICS	Accrediting Council for Independent Colleges and Schools *(10)*
ACIL	American Council of Independent Laboratories *(109)*
ACIP	American College of International Physicians *(97)*
	American Council on International Personnel *(110)*
ACIS	American Conference for Irish Studies *(106)*
ACJA/LAE	American Criminal Justice Association Lambda Alpha Epsilon *(112)*
ACJS	Academy of Criminal Justice Sciences *(4)*
ACL	American Classical League *(91)*
	The American Consultants League *(108)*
	Association for Computational Linguistics *(242)*
	The Association for Consortium Leadership *(243)*
	Association of Christian Librarians *(272)*
ACLA	American Clinical Laboratory Association *(91)*
	American Comparative Literature Association *(105)*
ACLAM	American College of Laboratory Animal Medicine *(97)*
ACLEA	Association for Continuing Legal Education *(244)*
ACLI	American Council of Life Insurers (ACLI) *(110)*
ACLM	American College of Legal Medicine *(97)*
ACLPS	Academy of Clinical Laboratory Physicians and Scientists *(4)*
ACLS	American Council of Learned Societies *(109)*
ACM	Academy of Country Music *(4)*
	American College of Musicians *(98)*
	Association for Computing Machinery *(243)*
	Association of Children's Museums *(272)*
ACMA	American Case Management Association *(88)*
	American Catalog Mailers Association *(88)*
	American College of Mortgage Attorneys *(98)*
	American Composites Manufacturers Association *(105)*
ACME	Association for Convention Marketing Executives *(244)*
ACMG	American College of Medical Genetics *(97)*
ACMHA	American College of Mental Health Administration *(98)*
ACMI	The Arts and Creative Materials Institute, Inc. *(229)*
ACMP	American College of Medical Physics *(97)*
ACMQ	American College of Medical Quality *(97)*
ACMS	American College of Mohs Surgeons *(98)*
ACMT	American College of Medical Toxicology *(98)*
ACN	Abortion Care Network *(2)*
	American College of Neuropsychiatrists *(98)*
	American College of Nutrition *(99)*
	Association of Camp Nurses *(271)*
ACNM	American College of Nuclear Medicine *(98)*
	American College of Nurse-Midwives *(99)*
ACNP	American College of Neuropsychopharmacology *(98)*

	American College of Nurse Practitioners *(99)*
ACNS	American Clinical Neurophysiology Society *(92)*
ACOEM	American College of Occupational and Environmental Medicine *(99)*
ACOEP	American College of Osteopathic Emergency Physicians *(99)*
ACOFP	American College of Osteopathic Family Physicians *(100)*
ACOG	American Congress of Obstetricians and Gynecologists *(107)*
ACOI	American College of Osteopathic Internists *(100)*
ACOMS	American College of Oral and Maxillofacial Surgeons *(99)*
ACOOG	American College of Osteopathic Obstetricians and Gynecologists *(100)*
ACOP	American College of Osteopathic Pediatricians *(100)*
ACOPSA	American College of Psychoanalysts *(102)*
ACORD	ACORD - Association for Cooperative Operations Research and Development *(11)*
ACOS	American College of Osteopathic Surgeons *(100)*
ACP	American College of Phlebology *(100)*
	American College of Physicians *(101)*
	American College of Physicians Services, Inc. *(101)*
	American College of Prosthodontists *(101)*
	American College of Psychiatrists *(102)*
	Associated Church Press *(235)*
	Associated Collegiate Press *(235)*
	Associated Construction Publications *(235)*
	Association for Child Psychoanalysis *(241)*
	Association of Catholic Publishers *(271)*
	Association of Coupon Professionals *(277)*
ACPA	ACPA College Student Educators International *(11)*
	American Catholic Philosophical Association *(88)*
	American Cleft Palate-Craniofacial Association *(91)*
	American College Personnel Association *(105)*
	American Concrete Pavement Association *(106)*
	American Concrete Pipe Association *(106)*
	American Concrete Pumping Association *(106)*
	Association of Celebrity Personal Assistants *(271)*
ACPCN	The Association of Community Pharmacists Congressional Network *(276)*
ACPE	Accreditation Council for Pharmacy Education *(10)*
	American College of Physician Executives *(101)*
	Association for Clinical Pastoral Education *(241)*
ACPI	Association of Career Professionals International *(271)*
ACPM	American College of Preventive Medicine *(101)*
ACPOC	Association of Children's Prosthetic-Orthotic Clinics *(272)*
ACPPA	American Concrete Pressure Pipe Association *(106)*
	Asbestos Cement Product Producers Association *(231)*
ACPR	American College of Podiatric Radiologists *(101)*
	American Crossbred Pony Registry *(112)*
ACPS	American Connemara Pony Society *(107)*
ACR	American College of Radiology *(102)*
	American College of Rheumatology *(102)*
	Association for Conflict Resolution *(243)*
	Association for Consumer Research *(243)*
ACRA	American Collegiate Retailing Association *(105)*
	American Cotswold Record Association *(108)*
	American Cultural Resources Association (ACRA) *(112)*
	Association of Commercial Real Estate *(275)*
ACRE	American College of Real Estate Lawyers *(102)*
ACREL	
ACRL	Association of College and Research Libraries *(273)*
ACRM	American Congress of Rehabilitation Medicine *(107)*
ACRO	American College of Radiation Oncology *(102)*

AETA	American Embryo Transfer Association *(116)*	**AFM-EPF**	American Federation of Musicians and Employers Pension Fund *(119)*	**AGB**	Association of Governing Boards of Universities and Colleges *(286)*
AF&PA	American Forest & Paper Association *(123)*	**AFMA**	American Fiber Manufacturers Association *(121)*	**AGC**	Associated General Contractors of America (AGC) *(236)*
AFA	Aerospace Futures Alliance *(14)*		Association of Family Medicine Administration *(282)*	**AGD**	Academy of General Dentistry *(5)*
	Air Force Association *(18)*	**AFMR**	American Federation for Medical Research *(119)*	**AGE**	American Aging Association *(43)*
	Airforwarders Association *(20)*	**AFMRD**	Association of Family Medicine Residency Directors *(282)*	**AGEM**	Association of Gaming Equipment Manufacturers *(285)*
	American Factoring Association *(118)*	**AFMTE**	Alliance for Massage Therapy Education *(23)*	**AGH**	American Guild of Hypnotherapists *(127)*
	American Farrier's Association *(118)*	**AFO**	Association of Field Ornithologists *(282)*	**AGI**	American Geological Institute *(126)*
	American Federation of Astrologers, Inc. *(119)*	**AFOP**	Association of Farmworker Opportunity Programs *(282)*		Apparel Graphics Institute *(225)*
	American Fence Association *(120)*	**AFOS**	Armed Forces Optometric Society *(229)*	**AGLBIC**	Association for Gay, Lesbian, Bisexual, and Transgender Issues in Counseling *(247)*
	The American Finance Association *(121)*	**AFOSISA**	Association of Former OSI Special Agents *(284)*	**AGLF**	Association for Governmental Leasing and Finance *(247)*
	American Flock Association *(122)*	**AFOT**	American Friends of Turkey *(124)*	**AGLP**	Association of Gay and Lesbian Psychiatrists *(285)*
	American Floorcovering Alliance *(122)*	**AFP**	Association for Financial Professionals, Inc. *(247)*	**AGLS**	Association for General and Liberal Studies *(247)*
	American Forensic Association *(123)*		Association of Fundraising Professionals *(285)*	**AGLSP**	Association of Graduate Liberal Studies Programs *(286)*
	American Franchisee Association *(123)*	**AFP&CC**	American Federation of Police and Concerned Citizens *(119)*	**AGM**	American Guild of Music *(127)*
	American Fraternal Alliance *(124)*	**AFPM**	American Fuel & Petrochemical Manufacturers *(124)*		Association of Golf Merchandisers *(286)*
	Aspirin Foundation of America, Inc. *(233)*	**AFQC**	Alliance for Quality Care *(23)*	**AGMA**	Alliance for Gray Market and Counterfeit Abatement *(23)*
	Association for Feminist Anthropology *(246)*	**AFRC**	American Forest Resource Council *(123)*		American Gear Manufacturers Association *(125)*
	Association of Fraternity Advisors *(284)*	**AFRDS**	Association of Fund-Raising Distributors and Suppliers *(285)*		American Guild of Musical Artists *(127)*
	North American Fiberboard Association *(816)*	**AFROC**	Association of Free Standing Radiation Oncology Centers *(284)*	**AGN-NA**	AGN International North America, Inc *(15)*
AFA-CWA	Association of Flight Attendants - CWA *(283)*	**AFS**	American Fern Society *(121)*	**AGO**	American Guild of Organists *(127)*
AFAA	Aerobics and Fitness Association of America *(13)*		American Filtration and Separations Society *(121)*	**AGPA**	American Group Psychotherapy Association *(127)*
	Association for Africanist Anthropology *(238)*		American Fisheries Society *(121)*	**AGPM**	Associated Glass and Pottery Manufacturers *(236)*
	Automatic Fire Alarm Association *(321)*		American Folklore Society *(122)*	**AGR**	Alpha Gamma Rho *(26)*
AFAC	Allied Finance Adjusters *(26)*		American Foundry Society *(123)*	**AGS**	The American Gem Society *(125)*
AFAR	American Federation for Aging Research *(119)*	**AFSA**	Air Force Sergeants Association *(19)*		The American Geographical Society *(126)*
AFAUSSS	Association of Former Agents of the U.S. Secret Service *(284)*		American Federation of School Administrators *(120)*		American Geriatrics Society *(126)*
AFBA	Armed Forces Broadcasters Association *(228)*		American Financial Services Association *(121)*		American Glovebox Society *(126)*
AFBF	American Farm Bureau Federation *(118)*		American Fire Sprinkler Association *(121)*		American Goat Society *(127)*
AFCA	American Football Coaches Association *(122)*		American Foreign Service Association *(122)*		Association of Graduate Schools in Association of American Universities *(286)*
AFCC	The American Fair Credit Council *(118)*	**AFSAA**	Armed Forces Special Agents Association *(229)*	**AGSES**	Association of Girl Scout Executive Staff *(285)*
	Association of Family and Conciliation Courts *(282)*	**AFSC**	American Fire Safety Council *(121)*	**AGT**	Association of Genetic Technologists *(285)*
AFCCE	Association of Federal Communications Consulting Engineers *(282)*	**AFSCME**	American Federation of State, County and Municipal Employees *(120)*	**AGTA**	Airport Ground Transportation Association *(21)*
AFCEA	Armed Forces Communications and Electronics Association *(228)*	**AFSPA**	American Foreign Service Protective Association *(123)*		American Gem Trade Association *(125)*
AFCI	Association of Film Commissioners International *(283)*	**AFT**	American Farmland Trust *(118)*	**AGTOA**	American Greyhound Track Operators Association *(127)*
AFCMA	Aluminum Foil Container Manufacturers Association *(27)*		American Federation of Teachers (AFL-CIO) *(120)*	**AGU**	American Geophysical Union *(126)*
AFCP	Association of Free Community Papers *(284)*		Association for Financial Technology *(247)*	**AGVA**	American Guild of Variety Artists *(128)*
AFCPE	Association for Financial Counseling and Planning Education *(246)*	**AFTA**	American Family Therapy Academy *(118)*	**AGVS**	Automatic Guided Vehicle Systems *(321)*
AFDE	Association of Forensic Document Examiners *(284)*	**AFTC**	Agricultural and Food Transporters Conference *(16)*	**AGWT**	American Ground Water Trust *(127)*
AFDI	Associated Funeral Directors International *(236)*		American Fox Terrier Club *(123)*	**AH**	Academy Health *(3)*
AFDO	Association of Food and Drug Officials *(283)*	**AFTE**	Association of Firearm and Toolmark Examiners *(283)*		Academy of Homiletics *(5)*
AFE	Association for Facilities Engineering *(246)*	**AFTHC**	AFT Healthcare *(15)*	**AH&LA**	American Hotel & Lodging Association (AH&LA) *(134)*
AFEE	Association for Evolutionary Economics *(246)*	**AFTR**	Association of Foreign Trade Representatives *(284)*	**AHA**	American Heart Association *(130)*
AFEHCT	Association for Electronic Healthcare Transaction *(245)*	**AFTRCC**	Aerospace & Flight Test Radio Coordinating Council *(14)*		American Herb Association *(130)*
AFEI	Association for Enterprise Information *(245)*	**AFVBM**	American Federation of Violin and Bow Makers *(120)*		American Hereford Association *(131)*
AFFI	American Frozen Food Institute *(124)*	**AFVN**	Alternative Fuel Vehicle Network *(27)*		American Historical Association *(131)*
AFFIRM	Association for Federal Information Resources Management *(246)*	**AFWA**	Association of Fish and Wildlife Agencies *(283)*		American Homebrewers Association *(133)*
AFFN	Armed Forces Financial Network *(229)*	**AFWPI**	Association for Wedding Professionals International *(261)*		American Hospital Association *(133)*
AFFTA	American Fly Fishing Trade Association *(122)*	**AG**	Association for Gnotobiotics *(247)*		American Hydrogen Association *(134)*
AFG	Association Foundation Group *(262)*		Authors Guild *(320)*		American Hypnosis Association *(134)*
AFGC	American Forage and Grassland Council *(122)*	**AGA**	Accredited Gemologists Association *(10)*		Arabian Horse Association *(227)*
AFGE	American Federation of Government Employees *(119)*		American Galvanizers Association *(124)*		Historians of American Communism *(476)*
AFGI	Association of Financial Guaranty Insurers *(283)*		American Gaming Association *(124)*	**AHAA**	Association of Hispanic Advertising Agencies *(287)*
AFI	Association of Food Industries *(283)*		American Gas Association *(124)*	**AHAF**	American Handwriting Analysis Foundation *(128)*
AFIA	American Feed Industry Association *(120)*		American Gastroenterological Association *(125)*	**AHAM**	Association of Home Appliance Manufacturers *(287)*
AFIO	Association of Former Intelligence Officers *(284)*		American Gelbvieh Association *(125)*	**AHBAI**	American Health and Beauty Aids Institute *(129)*
AFIP	Association of Finance and Insurance Professionals *(283)*		American Genetic Association *(126)*	**AHC**	American Horse Council *(133)*
AFIRE	Association of Foreign Investors in U.S. Real Estate *(284)*		American Guernsey Association *(127)*	**AHCA**	American Health Care Association *(129)*
AFJ	Association of Food Journalists *(283)*		Art Glass Association *(230)*		American Highland Cattle Association *(131)*
AFL-CIO	AFL-CIO (American Federation of Labor and Congress of Industrial Organizations) *(14)*		Association of Global Automakers *(285)*		The American Hockey Coaches Association *(132)*
	American Federation of Labor & Congress of Industrial Organizations *(119)*		Association of Government Accountants *(286)*	**AHDI**	Association for Healthcare Documentation Integrity *(247)*
AFL-CIO HIT	AFL-CIO Housing Investment Trust *(15)*	**AGAT**	Association for Graphic Arts Training *(247)*	**AHEA**	American Hungarian Educators Association *(134)*
AFLA	American Foreign Law Association *(122)*	**AGAUS**	Adjutants General Association of the United States *(12)*	**AHEAD**	Association on Higher Education and Disability *(319)*
	Automotive Fleet and Leasing Association *(322)*			**AHEC**	American Hardwood Export Council *(129)*
AFM	American Federation of Musicians *(119)*			**AHEPA**	American Hellenic Educational Progressive Association (AHEPA) *(130)*
				AHF	Association for Healthcare Foodservice *(248)*
				AHFA	American Home Furnishings Alliance *(132)*
				AHG	American Herbalists Guild *(131)*
				AHHA	American Holsteiner Horse Association *(132)*

AHHAP	Association of Halfway House Alcoholism Programs of North America (286)	AIBD	American Institute of Building Design (137)		American International Marchigiana Society (142)
AHHE	Association of Hispanic Healthcare Executives (287)	AIBS	American Institute of Bangladesh Studies (137)		Amusement Industry Manufacturers and Suppliers International (223)
AHHS	American Hackney Horse Society (128)		American Institute of Biological Sciences (137)	AIMSE	Association of Investment Management Sales Executives (289)
AHI	Animal Health Institute (223)	AIC	Alpines International Club (27)		American Institute of Marine Underwriters (139)
AHIA	Academy of Hospitality Industry Attorneys (5)		American Inns of Court (135)	AIMU	
	Association of Healthcare Internal Auditors (287)		American Institute for Conservation of Historic and Artistic Works (136)	AIO	American Institute of Organbuilders (139)
AHIMA	American Health Information Management Association (129)		American Institute of Chemists (138)	AIOB	American Institute of Oral Biology (139)
AHIOS	Association of Health Information Outsourcing Services (286)		American Institute of Constructors (138)	AIP	American Institute of Parliamentarians (140)
AHIP	America's Health Insurance Plans (28)	AICA	American Institute of Commemorative Art (138)		American Institute of Physics (140)
AHL	American Hockey League (132)		American International Charolais Association (142)		Association for Information Protection (249)
AHLA	American Health Lawyers Association (130)		International Association of Art Critics (516)	AIPAD	The Association of International Photography Art Dealers (289)
AHLC	The American Hair Loss Council (128)	AICAD	Association of Independent Colleges of Art and Design (287)	AIPB	American Institute of Professional Bookkeepers (140)
AHMA	American Hardware Manufacturers Association (128)	AICC	Alarm Industry Communication Committee (21)	AIPBS	American Institute for Patristic and Byzantine Studies (136)
	American Holistic Medical Association (132)		American Indonesian Chamber of Commerce (135)	AIPG	American Institute of Professional Geologists (140)
AHME	Association for Hospital Medical Education (249)		Association of Independent Corrugated Converters (288)	AIPLA	American Intellectual Property Law Association (141)
AHMP	Alliance of Hazardous Materials Professionals (25)		Aviation Industry CBT Committee (324)	AIR	AIR Commercial Real Estate Association (18)
AHNA	American Holistic Nurses Association (132)	AICCI	American-Israel Chamber of Commerce and Industry (222)		American Institutes for Research (141)
AHNS	American Head and Neck Society (129)	AIChE	American Institute of Chemical Engineers (138)		Association for Institutional Research (250)
AHOU	Association of Home Office Underwriters (287)	AICI	Association of Image Consultants International (287)		Association of Independents in Radio (288)
AHP	American Horse Publications (133)	AICP	American Institute of Certified Planners (137)	AIRA	Association of Insolvency and Restructuring Advisors (289)
	Association for Healthcare Philanthropy (248)		Association of Independent Commercial Producers (287)	AIRCON	Airline Industrial Relations Conference (20)
	Association for Humanistic Psychology (249)		Association of Insurance Compliance Professionals (289)	AIRI	Association of Independent Research Institutes (288)
AHPA	American Health Planning Association (130)	AICPA	American Institute of Certified Public Accountants (137)	AIRS	Alliance of Information and Referral Systems (25)
	American Herbal Products Association (130)	AICPCU/ IIA	American Institute for CPCU - Insurance Institute of America (136)	AIS	American Institute of Stress (140)
	American Honey Producers Association (133)	AIDA-US	International Association for Insurance Law - United States Chapter (513)		Association for Information Systems (250)
AHQA	American Health Quality Association (130)	AIE	American Institute of Engineers, Inc. (138)		Association for Integrative Studies (250)
AHRA	Association for Medical Imaging Management (252)	AIEA	Association of International Education Administrators (289)	AISA	American Import Shippers Association (134)
AHRI	Air Conditioning, Heating and Refrigeration Institute (AHRI) (18)	AIEMPG	American Importers and Exporters/Meat Products Group (135)		American Institute for Shippers' Associations (136)
AHRMM	Association for Healthcare Resource and Materials Management (248)	AIFD	American Institute of Floral Designers (138)	AISC	American Institute of Steel Construction (140)
AHS	Agricultural History Society (16)		The Food Institute (449)	AISES	American Indian Science and Engineering Society (135)
	AHS International - The Vertical Flight Society (17)	AIFRB	American Institute of Fishery Research Biologists (138)	AISI	American Iron and Steel Institute (142)
	American Hanoverian Society (128)	AIGA	American Institute of Graphic Arts (139)	AIST	Association for Iron and Steel Technology (250)
	American Harp Society (129)	AIH	American Institute of Homeopathy (139)	AITA	America's Independent Truckers' Association, Inc. (29)
	American Headache Society (129)		American Institute of Hydrology (139)	AITC	American Institute of Timber Construction (141)
	American Heartworm Society (130)	AIHA	American Industrial Hygiene Association (135)	AITP	Association of Information Technology Professionals (289)
	American Hernia Society (131)	AIHEC	American Indian Higher Education Consortium (135)	AIUM	American Institute of Ultrasound in Medicine (141)
	American Hiking Society (131)	AIHP	American Institute of the History of Pharmacy (141)	AIW	American Independent Writers (135)
	American Horticultural Society (133)	AII	American Institute of Inspectors (139)	AIWA	Atlantic intra Coastal Waterway Association (319)
	Association for Humanist Sociology (249)	AIIM	Association for Information and Image Management International (249)	AJA	American Jail Association (142)
	Association of HazMat Shippers (286)	AIIP	Association of Independent Information Professionals (288)		American Judges Association (143)
AHSA	American Hampshire Sheep Association (128)	AIIS	American Institute for International Steel (136)	AJAS	Association of Jewish Aging Services (290)
	American Humor Studies Association (134)		American Institute of Indian Studies (139)	AJCA-NAJ	American Jersey Cattle Association/National All-Jersey Inc. (142)
AHTA	American Horticultural Therapy Association (133)	AILA	American Immigration Lawyers Association (134)	AJCCA	American Jewish Correctional Chaplains Association (290)
AHTD	Association for High Technology Distribution (248)	AILACT	Association for Informal Logic and Critical Thinking (249)	AJCU	Association of Jesuit Colleges and Universities (290)
AHVMA	American Holistic Veterinary Medical Association (132)	AIM	AIM Global (17)	AJFCA	Association of Jewish Family & Children's Agencies (290)
AHVRP	Association for Healthcare Volunteer Resource Professionals (248)		AIM North America (17)	AJHA	American Journalism Historians Association (143)
AI	Appraisal Institute (226)	AIM/R	Association of Independent Manufacturers'/ Representatives, Inc. (288)	AJHS	The American Jewish Historical Society (143)
	Asphalt Institute (233)	AIMBE	American Institute for Medical and Biological Engineering (136)	AJL	Association of Jewish Libraries (290)
AIA	Aerospace Industries Association of America (14)	AIMC	Association of Internal Management Consultants (289)	AJLI	Association of Junior Leagues International (290)
	Aestheticians International Association (14)		Foundation for International Meetings (453)	AJPA	American Jewish Press Association (143)
	The American Institute of Architects (137)	AIMCAL	Association of Industrial Metallizers, Coaters and Laminators (288)	AJS	American Judicature Society (143)
	American Insurance Association (141)	AIME	The American Institute of Mining, Metallurgical, and Petroleum Engineers (139)		Association for Jewish Studies (250)
	Apiary Inspectors of America (224)		Association for Information Media and Equipment (249)	AKC	American Kennel Club (143)
	Archaeological Institute of America (227)	AIMED	Association of Mailing, Shipping, and Office Automation Specialists (292)	AKFCF	Association of Kentucky Fried Chicken Franchisees, Inc. (290)
	Automated Imaging Association (321)	AIMS	American Institute for Maghrib Studies (136)	AKPsi	Alpha Kappa Psi (26)
	Aviation Insurance Association (324)		American Insurance Marketing and Sales Society (141)	AKSR	American Karakul Sheep Registry (143)
AIAA	American Institute of Aeronautics and Astronautics (136)			AKTA	American Kinesiotherapy Association (144)
AIADA	American International Automobile Dealers Association (142)			AKTI	American Knife & Tool Institute (144)
AIAEE	Association for International Agricultural and Extension Education (250)			ALA	American Laryngological Association (144)
AIAG	Automotive Industry Action Group (322)				American Library Association (145)
AIARD	The Association for International Agriculture and Rural Development (250)				American Lighting Association (145)
AIAS	American Institute for Afghanistan Studies (135)				American Logistics Association (146)
	American Institute of Architecture Students (137)				American Lung Association (146)
AIB	Academy of International Business (5)				Association of Legal Administrators (291)
	AIB International (17)			ALAA	American Lands Access Association (144)
				ALAS	Attorneys' Liability Assurance Society Inc. (320)
				ALC	American Legend Cooperative (145)

ANSS	American Nature Study Society *(155)*	**AOU**	American Ornithologists' Union *(158)*	**APG**	Association of Professional Genealogists *(301)*
ANVM	Association of United States Night Vision Manufacturers *(315)*	**AP**	Academy of Prosthodontics *(8)*		American Public Gardens Association *(170)*
AO	Academy of Osseointegration *(7)*	**AP-LS**	American Psychology-Law Society *(170)*	**APGA**	American Public Gas Association *(170)*
	Alpha Omega International Dental Fraternity *(26)*	**APA**	Academic Pediatric Association *(3)*	**APGO**	Association of Professors of Gynecology and Obstetrics *(302)*
AOA	America Outdoors Association *(28)*		Allied Pilots Association *(26)*	**APH**	Association of Personal Historians *(299)*
	American Optometric Association *(157)*		Amalgamated Printer's Association *(27)*	**APHA**	American Paint Horse Association *(161)*
	American Orthopaedic Association *(158)*		American Pancreatic Association *(162)*		American Pharmacists Association *(163)*
	American Osteopathic Association *(160)*		American Payroll Association *(162)*		American Printing History Association *(167)*
	American Ostrich Association *(161)*		American Philological Association *(163)*		American Public Health Association *(171)*
	Association of Otolaryngology Administrators *(297)*		American Philosophical Association *(164)*	**APhA-APRS**	Academy of Pharmaceutical Research and Science *(8)*
	National Association of Osteopathic Foundations *(683)*		American Photographic Artists *(164)*	**ApHC**	Appaloosa Horse Club *(225)*
AOAAM	American Osteopathic Academy of Addiction Medicine *(159)*		American Pianists Association *(165)*	**APHL**	Association of Public Health Laboratories *(304)*
AOAC	Association of Analytical Communities International *(267)*		American Pilots' Association *(165)*	**APHON**	Association of Pediatric Hematology/ Oncology Nurses *(298)*
AOAO	American Osteopathic Academy of Orthopedics *(159)*		American Pinzgauer Association *(165)*	**APHSA**	American Public Human Services Association *(171)*
AOAPIPM	American Osteopathic Association of Prolotherapy Integrative Pain Management *(160)*		American Planning Association *(166)*		APHSA - Information Systems Management *(224)*
AOASM	American Osteopathic Academy of Sports Medicine *(159)*		American Polygraph Association *(166)*	**API**	American Petroleum Institute *(163)*
AOBOA	Association of Business Owners of America *(270)*		American Poultry Association *(167)*		American Poultry International Ltd. *(167)*
AOBPMR	American Osteopathic Board of Physical Medicine and Rehabilitation *(160)*		American Psychiatric Association *(168)*		American Prepaid Legal Services Institute *(167)*
AOBTA	American Organization for Bodywork Therapies of Asia *(158)*		American Psychological Association *(169)*		American Press Institute *(167)*
AOC	American Oilseed Coalition *(157)*		American Pyrotechnics Association *(172)*		Center for the Polyurethanes Industry *(348)*
	Association of Old Crows *(297)*		APA The Engineered Wood Association *(224)*	**APIC**	Association for Professionals in Infection Control and Epidemiology *(254)*
AOCA	American Osteopathic College of Anesthesiologists *(160)*		Apple Processors Association *(225)*		Association of Professional Investment Consultants *(301)*
	Automotive Oil Change Association *(323)*		Architectural Precast Association *(228)*	**APICS**	APICS The Association for Operations Management *(224)*
AOCAI	American Osteopathic College of Allergy and Immunology *(160)*		At-Sea Processors Association *(319)*	**APLD**	Association of Professional Landscape Designers *(301)*
AOCD	American Osteopathic College of Dermatology *(160)*		Audio Publishers Association *(320)*	**APLIC**	Association for Population/Family Planning Libraries and Information Centers, International *(253)*
AOCOO-HNS	American Osteopathic Colleges of Ophthalmology and Otolaryngology - Head and Neck Surgery *(161)*	**APA-DP**	American Psychological Association - Division of Psychotherapy *(169)*	**APLS**	Association for Politics and the Life Sciences *(253)*
AOCOPM	American Osteopathic College of Occupational and Preventive Medicine *(160)*	**APA/CP**	American Psychological Association - Society of Clinical Psychology *(169)*	**APM**	Academy of Psychosomatic Medicine *(8)*
AOCP	American Osteopathic College of Pathologists *(160)*	**APAA**	Association of Professional Art Advisors *(300)*		Association for Psychoanalytic Medicine *(254)*
AOCPr	American Osteopathic College of Proctology *(161)*	**APACVS**	Association of Physician Assistants in Cardiovascular Surgery *(299)*		Association of Professors of Medicine *(302)*
AOCR	American Osteopathic College of Radiology *(161)*	**APAI**	Association of Paroling Authorities International *(297)*		Association of Professors of Mission *(302)*
AOCS	American Oil Chemists' Society *(157)*	**APALA**	Asian Pacific American Labor Alliance, AFL-CIO *(232)*	**APMA**	American Podiatric Medical Association *(166)*
AOD	Associated Owners and Developers *(236)*		Asian/Pacific American Librarians Association *(232)*	**APME**	Associated Press Managing Editors *(237)*
AOEC	Association of Occupational and Environmental Clinics *(296)*	**APAOG**	Association of Physician Assistants in Obstetrics and Gynecology *(299)*	**APMHC**	Association of Professional Material Handling Consultants *(301)*
AOFAS	American Orthopaedic Foot and Ankle Society *(158)*	**APAP**	Association of Performing Arts Presenters *(298)*	**APMI**	APMI International *(225)*
AOHP	Association of Occupational Health Professionals in Healthcare *(296)*	**APAPO**	American Psychological Association Practice Organization *(170)*	**APMM**	Association of Professional Model Makers *(302)*
AOJ	Association of Opinion Journalists *(297)*	**APBP**	Association of Pedestrian and Bicycle Professionals *(298)*	**APMP**	Association of Proposal Management Professionals *(303)*
AOM	Academy of Management *(6)*	**APBPA**	Association of Professional Ball Players of America *(301)*	**APMS**	Aquatic Plant Management Society, Inc. *(227)*
AoM/IAoM	Association of Management/International Association of Management *(292)*	**APC**	American Peanut Council *(162)*	**APMSA**	American Podiatric Medical Students Association *(166)*
AONE	American Organization of Nurse Executives *(158)*		Aseptic Packaging Council *(231)*	**APMWA**	American Podiatric Medical Writers Association *(166)*
AOOP	Academy of Organizational and Occupational Psychiatry *(7)*		Association of Pathology Chairs *(298)*	**APNA**	American Psychiatric Nurses Association *(168)*
AOPA	Aircraft Owners and Pilots Association *(20)*	**APCC**	Association of Professional Chaplains *(301)*	**APOBA**	Associated Pipe Organ Builders of America *(236)*
	American Orthotic and Prosthetic Association *(159)*		American Public Communications Council *(170)*	**APOM**	Association of Professional Office Managers *(302)*
AOPL	Association of Oil Pipe Lines *(296)*		Association of Professional Communication Consultants *(301)*	**APOS**	American Psychosocial Oncology Society *(170)*
AOPO	Association of Organ Procurement Organizations *(297)*	**APCD**	Association of Private Club Directors *(300)*	**APOSW**	Association of Pediatric Oncology Social Workers *(298)*
AORC	Association of Official Racing Chemists *(296)*	**APCO**	APCO (Association of Public-Safety Communications Officials) International *(304)*	**APPA**	American Pet Products Association *(163)*
AORN	Association of periOperative Registered Nurses *(299)*	**APCR**	Academy of Physicians in Clinical Research *(8)*		American Probation and Parole Association *(167)*
AOS	American Ophthalmological Society *(157)*	**APCS**	Accredited Pet Cemetery Society *(10)*		American Psychopathological Association *(170)*
	American Oriental Society *(158)*	**APCU**	Association of Presbyterian Colleges and Universities *(300)*		American Public Power Association *(171)*
	American Orthodontic Society *(158)*	**APCUG**	Association of Personal Computer User Groups *(299)*		APPA - Leadership in Educational Facilities *(225)*
	American Otological Society *(161)*	**APDA**	Appliance Parts Distributors Association *(226)*	**APPAM**	APPAM - The Association for Public Policy Analysis and Management *(225)*
AOSA	American Optometric Student Association *(157)*	**APDF**	Association of Professional Design Firms *(301)*	**APPAP**	Association of Postgraduate Physician Assistant Programs *(300)*
	American Orff-Schulwerk Association *(158)*	**APDIM**	Association of Program Directors in Internal Medicine *(302)*	**APPD**	Association of Pediatric Program Directors *(298)*
	Association of Official Seed Analysts, Inc. *(296)*	**APDR**	Association of Program Directors in Radiology *(303)*	**APPE**	Association for Practical and Professional Ethics *(253)*
AOSCA	Association of Official Seed Certifying Agencies *(296)*	**APDS**	Association of Program Directors in Surgery *(303)*	**APPIC**	Association of Psychology Postdoctoral and Internship Centers *(303)*
AOSED	Association of Osteopathic State Executive Directors *(297)*	**APDT**	Association of Pet Dog Trainers *(299)*	**APPL**	Association of Partners for Public Lands *(298)*
AOSSM	American Orthopaedic Society for Sports Medicine *(159)*	**APDU**	Association of Public Data Users *(304)*	**APPMI**	American Peanut Product Manufacturers, Inc. *(162)*
AOSW	Association of Oncology Social Work *(297)*	**APEE**	Association of Private Enterprise Education *(300)*		
AOTA	American Occupational Therapy Association, Inc. *(157)*	**APERC**	Alkylphenols and Ethoxylates Research Council *(22)*		
		APEX	World Airline Entertainment Association *(1025)*		
		APF	American Pathology Foundation *(162)*		
		APFA	American Pipe Fittings Association *(165)*		
			Association of Professional Flight Attendants *(301)*		
		APFO	Association of Programs for Female Offenders *(303)*		

ASBMR	American Society for Bone and Mineral Research *(181)*	**ASDSO**	Association of State Dam Safety Officials *(310)*

ASBMR American Society for Bone and Mineral Research *(181)*

ASBMT American Society for Blood and Marrow Transplantation *(181)*

ASBO Association of School Business Officials International *(306)*

ASBP American Society of Bariatric Physicians *(193)*

ASBPE American Society of Business Publication Editors *(194)*

ASC Adhesive and Sealant Council *(12)*

American Society of Cinematographers *(194)*

American Society of Criminology *(196)*

American Society of Cytopathology *(196)*

Associated Schools of Construction *(237)*

Associated Specialty Contractors *(237)*

Automotive Safety Council *(323)*

ASCA Ambulatory Surgery Center Association *(28)*

American School Counselor Association *(177)*

American Society of Consulting Arborists *(196)*

American Swimming Coaches Association *(215)*

Association of State Correctional Administrators *(310)*

ASCAC Association for the Study of Classical African Civilizations *(259)*

ASCAP American Society of Composers, Authors and Publishers (ASCAP) *(195)*

ASCB American Society for Cell Biology *(182)*

ASCC American Society of Concrete Contractors *(195)*

ASCCP American Society for Colposcopy and Cervical Pathology *(183)*

ASCD Association for Supervision and Curriculum Development (ASCD) *(257)*

ASCDINATD AscdiNatd *(231)*

Association of Service and Computer Dealers International *(308)*

ASCE American Society of Civil Engineers *(194)*

ASCET American Society of Certified Engineering Technicians *(194)*

ASCFG Association of Specialty Cut Flower Growers *(309)*

ASCH American Society of Clinical Hypnosis *(194)*

ASCI American Society for Clinical Investigation *(182)*

ASCL American Society of Comparative Law *(195)*

ASCLA Association of Specialized and Cooperative Library Agencies *(309)*

ASCLD American Society of Crime Laboratory Directors *(196)*

ASCLS American Society for Clinical Laboratory Science *(182)*

ASCO American Society of Clinical Oncology *(194)*

Association of Schools and Colleges of Optometry *(307)*

ASCP American Society for Clinical Pathologists *(182)*

American Society for Clinical Pathology *(182)*

American Society of Clinical Psychopharmacology *(195)*

American Society of Consultant Pharmacists *(195)*

Association of State Chamber Professionals *(310)*

ASCPT American Society for Clinical Pharmacology and Therapeutics *(182)*

ASCRS American Society of Cataract and Refractive Surgery *(194)*

American Society of Colon and Rectal Surgeons *(195)*

ASCT American Society for Cytotechnology *(183)*

ASD American Society of Dermatology *(196)*

American Society of Dowsers *(197)*

Association of Steel Distributors *(311)*

ASDA American Society for Dental Aesthetics *(183)*

American Society of Dentist Anesthesiologists *(196)*

American Stamp Dealers Association *(213)*

American Student Dental Association *(214)*

ASDAL Association of Seventh-Day Adventist Librarians *(308)*

ASDP American Society of Dermatopathology *(197)*

Association of Sewing and Design Professionals *(308)*

ASDR American Society of Dermatological Retailers *(196)*

ASDS American Society for Dermatologic Surgery *(183)*

ASDSO Association of State Dam Safety Officials *(310)*

ASDWA Association of State Drinking Water Administrators *(311)*

ASE American Society for Ethnohistory *(184)*

American Society of Echocardiography *(197)*

Association for Surgical Education *(257)*

ASEA American Society of Equine Appraisers *(197)*

ASECS American Society for Eighteenth-Century Studies *(183)*

ASEE American Society for Engineering Education *(183)*

ASEEES American Association for the Advancement of Slavic Studies *(52)*

Association for Slavic, East European, and Eurasian Studies *(256)*

ASEH American Society for Environmental History *(184)*

ASEM American Society for Engineering Management *(184)*

ASENT American Society for Experimental NeuroTherapeutics *(184)*

ASER American Society of Emergency Radiology *(197)*

ASERTTI Association of State Energy Research and Technology Transfer Institution *(311)*

ASERVIC Association for Spiritual, Ethical and Religious Values in Counseling *(257)*

ASES American Shoulder and Elbow Surgeons *(179)*

American Solar Energy Society *(211)*

ASET Academy of Security Educators and Trainers *(9)*

American Society of Electroneurodiagnostic Technologists *(197)*

ASEV American Society for Enology and Viticulture *(184)*

ASF American Securitization Forum *(178)*

Association of Small Foundations *(309)*

ASFA American Society for Apheresis *(180)*

ASFD American Society of Furniture Designers *(198)*

ASFE ASFE/The Geoprofessional Business Association *(231)*

ASFMRA American Society of Farm Managers and Rural Appraisers *(197)*

ASFO The American Society of Forensic Odontology *(198)*

ASFPM Association of State Floodplain Managers *(311)*

ASFS Association for the Study of Food and Society *(259)*

ASG American Society of Geolinguistics *(198)*

ASGA American Sesame Growers Association *(178)*

American Sugarbeet Growers Association *(214)*

ASGCA American Society of Golf Course Architects *(198)*

ASGCT American Society of Gene & Cell Therapy *(198)*

ASGE American Society for Gastrointestinal Endoscopy *(184)*

American Society of Gas Engineers *(198)*

ASGPP American Society of Group Psychotherapy and Psychodrama *(198)*

ASGS American Scientific Glassblowers Society *(178)*

American Society of General Surgeons *(198)*

ASGW Association for Specialists in Group Work *(257)*

ASH American Society of Hematology *(199)*

American Society of Hypertension, Inc. *(200)*

ASHA American Saddlebred Horse Association *(176)*

American School Health Association *(177)*

American Seniors Housing Association *(178)*

American Shire Horse Association *(179)*

American Speech-Language-Hearing Association *(212)*

American Suffolk Horse Association *(214)*

ASHE American Society for Healthcare Engineering *(184)*

American Society of Highway Engineers *(200)*

Association for the Study of Higher Education *(259)*

ASHES American Society for Healthcare Environmental Services *(185)*

ASHFSA American Society for Healthcare Food Service Administrators *(185)*

ASHG American Society of Human Genetics *(200)*

ASHHRA American Society for Healthcare Human Resources Administration *(185)*

ASHI American Society for Histocompatibility and Immunogenetics *(185)*

ASHNR American Society of Home Inspectors *(200)*

American Society of Head and Neck Radiology *(199)*

ASHP American Society of Health-System Pharmacists *(199)*

ASHRAE American Society of Heating, Refrigerating and Air Conditioning Engineers (ASHRAE) *(199)*

ASHRM American Society for Healthcare Risk Management *(185)*

ASHRS American Society of Hair Restoration Surgery *(199)*

ASHS American Society for Horticultural Science *(185)*

ASHT American Society of Hand Therapists *(199)*

ASI American Sheep Industry Association *(178)*

American Society for Indexing *(186)*

Association & Society Insurance Corporation *(237)*

American Spinal Injury Association *(212)*

ASIA American Society of Irrigation Consultants *(201)*

ASIC American Society of Irrigation Consultants *(201)*

ASID American Society of Interior Designers *(200)*

ASIH American Society of Ichthyologists and Herpetologists *(200)*

American Society of International Law *(201)*

ASIL American Society for Investigative Pathology *(186)*

ASIP Association of SIDS and Infant Mortality Programs *(308)*

ASIPP American Society of Interventional Pain Physicians *(201)*

ASIS ASIS International *(232)*

ASIS&T American Society for Information Science and Technology *(186)*

ASJA American Society of Journalists and Authors *(201)*

ASJMC Association of Schools of Journalism and Mass Communication *(307)*

ASL Association for Symbolic Logic *(257)*

ASLA American Seminar Leaders Association *(178)*

American Society of Landscape Architects *(201)*

ASLAP American Society of Laboratory Animal Practitioners *(201)*

ASLH American Society for Legal History *(186)*

ASLME American Society of Law, Medicine and Ethics *(202)*

ASLMS American Society for Laser Medicine and Surgery *(186)*

ASLO American Society of Limnology and Oceanography *(202)*

ASLRRA American Short Line and Regional Railroad Association *(179)*

ASLSS American Society of Lipo-Suction Surgery *(202)*

ASLW Scribes-The American Society of Legal Writers *(893)*

ASM American Society for Microbiology *(187)*

American Society of Mammalogists *(202)*

American Society of Missiology *(203)*

ASM International *(232)*

ASMA American Society of Marine Artists *(202)*

American Sports Medicine Association *(213)*

ASMAC American Society of Medical Association Counsel *(203)*

American Society of Music Arrangers and Composers *(203)*

ASMBS American Society for Metabolic and Bariatric Surgery *(187)*

ASMC American Small Manufacturers' Coalition *(180)*

American Society of Military Comptrollers *(203)*

ASMD Association of Science Museum Directors *(307)*

ASMDT American Society of Master Dental Technologists *(202)*

ASME American Society of Magazine Editors *(202)*

American Society of Mechanical Engineers (ASME) *(203)*

ASMEIGTI ASME International Gas Turbine Institute *(233)*

ASMH American Society for Mohs Histotechnology *(187)*

ASMP American Society of Media Photographers *(203)*

ASMR American Society of Mining and Reclamation *(203)*

ASMS American Society for Mass Spectrometry *(186)*

American Society of Maxillofacial Surgeons *(202)*

ASN American Society for Neurochemistry *(187)*

American Society for Nutrition *(187)*

The American Society of Naturalists *(203)*

CADCA CPA Auto Dealer Consultants Association *(402)*

CADEIO Catholic Association of Diocesan Ecumenical and Interreligious Officers *(345)*

CAE Council on Anthropology and Education *(398)*

CAEL Council for Adult and Experiential Learning *(388)*

CAFS Chinese American Food Society *(354)*

CAGI Compressed Air and Gas Institute *(372)*

CAGTC The Coalition for America's Gateways and Trade Corridors *(360)*

CAH Conference on Asian History *(376)*

CAI Committee of Annuity Insurers *(368)*

Community Associations Institute (CAI) *(370)*

CAJM Council of American Jewish Museums *(391)*

CALA Chinese American Librarians Association *(354)*

CALCON North American Calorimetry Conference *(814)*

CALEA Commission on Accreditation for Law Enforcement Agencies Incorporation *(367)*

CALICO Computer Assisted Language Instruction Consortium *(372)*

CALLERLAB CALLERLAB - International Association of Square Dance Callers *(341)*

CAM-I Consortium for Advanced Management, International *(378)*

CAMA Civil Aviation Medical Association *(357)*

Concrete Anchor Manufacturers Association *(373)*

CAMM Council of American Maritime Museums *(391)*

Council of American Master Mariners *(392)*

CAMS Chinese American Medical Society *(354)*

CANA Cremation Association of North America *(404)*

CAORC Council of American Overseas Research Centers *(392)*

CAP College of American Pathologists *(363)*

Community Action Partnership *(369)*

CAPA Certified Auto Parts Association *(349)*

The Coalition of Airline Pilots Associations *(360)*

CAPCO Consumer Aerosol Products Council *(380)*

CAPE Council for American Private Education *(389)*

CARH Council for Affordable and Rural Housing *(388)*

CARLJS Council of Archives and Research Libraries in Jewish Studies *(392)*

CAS Casualty Actuarial Society *(344)*

Council for the Advancement of Standards in Higher Education *(391)*

CASBA Cookie and Snack Bakers Association *(383)*

CASE Council for Advancement and Support of Education *(388)*

Council of Administrators of Special Education *(391)*

CASRO Council of American Survey Research Organizations *(392)*

CAST Council for Agricultural Science and Technology *(388)*

CAUS The Color Association of the United States *(365)*

CBA Consumer Bankers Association *(380)*

CBAN Community Banking Advisors Network *(370)*

CBB Cattlemen's Beef Promotion and Research Board *(346)*

CBBB Council of Better Business Bureaus *(392)*

CBC Children's Book Council *(353)*

CBDNA College Band Directors National Association *(363)*

CBE Conference of Business Economists *(374)*

CBEPA Caribbean Basin Ethanol Producer Association (CBEPA) *(343)*

CBFC Copper and Brass Fabricators Council *(384)*

CBHL Council on Botanical and Horticultural Libraries *(399)*

CBHNA Consortium of Behavioral Health Nurses and Associates *(378)*

CBHSNA Cleveland Bay Horse Society of North America *(358)*

CBMS Conference Board of the Mathematical Sciences *(374)*

CBSA Copper and Brass Servicenter Association *(384)*

CBSFA Central Bering Sea Fisherman's Association *(348)*

CBTU Coalition of Black Trade Unionists *(360)*

CBUSA Clydesdale Breeders of the United States *(359)*

CC Catecholamine Club *(344)*

CCA Christian Chiropractors Association *(355)*

Coastal Conservation Association *(361)*

Collegiate Commissioners Association *(365)*

CCAA Conference of Consulting Actuaries *(375)*

Copywriters Council of America *(385)*

Corporate Council on Africa *(385)*

Crane Certification Association of America *(403)*

CCAI Chemical Coaters Association International *(351)*

CCAOM Council of Colleges of Acupuncture and Oriental Medicine *(392)*

CCAR Central Conference of American Rabbis *(348)*

CCAS Council of Colleges of Arts and Sciences *(393)*

CCBA The Coca-Cola Bottlers' Association *(361)*

CCBD Council for Children with Behavioral Disorders *(389)*

CCBO Community College Business Officers *(370)*

CCC Calorie Control Council *(341)*

Canola Council of Canada *(341)*

Car Care Council *(342)*

Carpet Cushion Council *(343)*

Catholic Cemetery Conference *(345)*

Christian College Consortium *(355)*

CCCC Conference on College Composition and Communication *(376)*

CCCU Council for Christian Colleges and Universities *(389)*

CCE Council on Chiropractic Education *(399)*

CCFL Conference on Consumer Finance Law *(376)*

CCFMA Convenience Caterers & Food Manufacturers Association *(383)*

CCHA Community Colleges Humanities Association *(370)*

CCI Cardiovascular Credentialing International *(342)*

Cotton Council International *(387)*

CCIA Computer and Communications Industry Association *(372)*

Consumer Credit Industry Association *(381)*

CCIM CCIM Institute *(347)*

CCJ Conference of Chief Justices *(374)*

CCJA Community College Journalism Association *(370)*

CCM Council of Communication Management *(393)*

CCMA Catholic Campus Ministry Association *(345)*

Closure and Container Manufacturers Association *(359)*

CCMI Cashmere and Camel Hair Manufacturers Institute *(344)*

CCN Certified Contractors Network *(349)*

CCO Council on Chiropractic Orthopedics *(399)*

CCPA Cemented Carbide Producers Association *(347)*

China Clay Producers Association *(354)*

CCPAC Certified Claims Professional Accreditation Council *(349)*

CCPTR Council of Chiropractic Physiological Therapeutics and Rehabilitation *(392)*

CCR Council for Chemical Research, Inc. *(389)*

CCRA Campus Computer Resellers Alliance *(341)*

CCROA Corporate Crisis Response Officers Association *(385)*

CCSAA Cross Country Ski Areas Association *(405)*

CCSSO Council of Chief State School Officers *(392)*

CCTI Composite Can and Tube Institute *(372)*

CCUMC Consortium of College and University Media Centers *(378)*

CCWH Coordinating Council for Women in History *(384)*

CDA Copier Dealers Association *(384)*

Copper Development Association *(384)*

CDABO College of Diplomates of the American Board of Orthodontics *(364)*

CDC Continental Dorset Club *(382)*

CDFA Council of Development Finance Agencies *(393)*

CDG Costume Designers Guild *(387)*

CDHCF Consultant Dietitians in Health Care Facilities *(380)*

CDI Council on Diagnostic Imaging to the A.C.A. *(399)*

CDIA Consumer Data Industry Association *(381)*

Medical Transcription Industry Association (MTIA) *(611)*

CDIM Clerkship Directors in Internal Medicine *(358)*

CDMA Chain Drug Marketing Association *(350)*

CDS Community Development Society *(370)*

CDSA Content Delivery and Security Association *(382)*

CDVCA Community Development Venture Capital Alliance *(370)*

CEA Cement Employers Association *(347)*

Coal Exporters Association of the U.S. *(359)*

College English Association *(363)*

Consumer Electronics Association *(381)*

Correctional Education Association *(386)*

County Executives of America *(402)*

CEAI Christian Educators Association International *(355)*

CEASD Conference of Educational Administrators of Schools and Programs for the Deaf *(375)*

CEB Council on Employee Benefits *(399)*

CEC Council for Exceptional Children *(390)*

Cryogenic Engineering Conference *(405)*

CECPR Council for Professional Recognition *(391)*

CED Council on Education of the Deaf *(399)*

CEDIA Custom Electronic Design and Installation Association *(405)*

CEDS Council for Educational Diagnosticians *(389)*

CEE Conference on English Education *(376)*

CEEC Corporate Environmental Enforcement Council *(389)*

Creative Education Foundation *(403)*

CEF Council of Educational Facility Planners International *(393)*

CEFPI Computer Ethics Institute *(372)*

CEI Cooperative Education and Internship Association *(384)*

CEIA Center for Exhibition Industry Research *(348)*

CEIR Conference on English Leadership *(376)*

CEL Converting Equipment Manufacturers Association *(383)*

CEMA Conveyor Equipment Manufacturers Association *(383)*

Corporate Event Marketing Association *(386)*

CEO Chief Executives Organization *(352)*

CERCA Council for Electronic Revenue Communication Advancement *(389)*

CERF The Coastal and Estuarine Research Federation *(361)*

CES Coalition of Essential Schools *(360)*

Council for European Studies *(390)*

CESI Council for Elementary Science International *(389)*

CESSE Council of Engineering and Scientific Society Executives *(393)*

CETA Cleaning Equipment Trade Association *(357)*

Controlled Environment Testing Association *(383)*

CEW Cosmetic Executive Women *(387)*

CFA Catfish Farmers of America *(344)*

Commercial Finance Association *(366)*

Concrete Foundations Association *(373)*

Council for Art Education *(389)*

CFAE Communications Fraud Control Association *(369)*

CFCA Council of Fashion Designers of America *(393)*

CFDA Commercial Food Equipment Service Association *(366)*

CFESA Chemical Fabrics and Film Association *(351)*

CFFA Conference on Faith and History *(376)*

CFH Collaborative Family Healthcare Association *(362)*

CFHA Construction Financial Management Association *(379)*

CFMA Casket and Funeral Supply Association of America *(344)*

CFSA Community Financial Services Association of America CFSA *(370)*

CFSEI Cold-Formed Steel Engineers Institute *(362)*

CFSO Consortium of Forensic Science Organizations *(378)*

CG Choristers Guild *(355)*

Conductors Guild *(374)*

CGA College Gymnastics Association *(363)*

Compressed Gas Association *(372)*

Concord Grape Association *(373)*

CGCS Council of the Great City Schools *(398)*

CGP The Coalition for Government Procurement *(360)*

CGS Council of Graduate Schools *(394)*

CGSM Consortium for Graduate Study in Management *(378)*

CGWA Cotton Growers Warehouse Association *(387)*

CH Capital Health *(342)*

CHA Catholic Health Association of the United States *(345)*

CHA - Certified Horsemanship Association *(350)*

Consumer Health Alliance *(381)*

Craft & Hobby Association *(402)*

CHART Council of Hotel and Restaurant Trainers *(394)*

CHC Committee on History in the Classroom *(368)*

Community Health Charities of America *(371)*

CHEA	Council for Higher Education Accreditation *(390)*	CLEAR	Council on Licensure, Enforcement and Regulation *(400)*	CODSIA	Council of Defense and Space Industry Associations *(393)*
CHF	Chemical Heritage Foundation *(351)*	CLFMI	Chain Link Fence Manufacturers Institute *(350)*	COE	Council for Opportunity in Education *(390)*
CHHS	Charles Homer Haskins Society *(351)*	CLGBTH	Committee on Lesbian and Gay History *(368)*		Council on Occupational Education *(400)*
CHIME	College of Healthcare Information Management Executives *(364)*	CLIA	Cruise Lines International Association *(405)*	COF	Council on Foundations *(399)*
CHJ	Conference of Historical Journals *(375)*	CLLA	Commercial Law League of America *(366)*	COFE	Council On Forest Engineering *(399)*
ChLA	Children's Literature Association *(353)*	CLMA	Clinical Laboratory Management Association *(358)*	COFHE	Consortium on Financing Higher Education *(379)*
CHPA	Combat Helicopter Pilots Association *(366)*		Composite Lumber Manufacturers Association *(372)*	COGEL	Council on Governmental Ethics Laws *(399)*
	Consumer Healthcare Products Association *(381)*		Contact Lens Manufacturers Association *(382)*	COGR	Council on Governmental Relations *(400)*
	Corporate Housing Providers Association *(386)*	CLMP	Council of Literary Magazines and Presses *(395)*	COGS	Council of Graphological Societies *(394)*
CHTA	Caribbean Hotel and Tourism Association *(343)*	CLPHA	Council of Large Public Housing Authorities *(395)*	COHEAO	Coalition of Higher Education Assistance Organizations *(360)*
CI	Chlorine Institute *(354)*	CLS	Christian Legal Society *(356)*	COLA	COLA *(362)*
	The Combustion Institute *(366)*	CLSA	Canon Law Society of America *(342)*	COLT	Council on Library-Media Technicians *(400)*
	The Cordage Institute *(385)*		Congressional Legislative Staff Association *(377)*	COMISS Network	COMISS Network - The Network on Ministry in Specialized Settings *(366)*
	Cranberry Institute *(403)*		Contact Lens Society of America *(382)*	COMPA	Conference of Minority Public Administrators *(375)*
CIAA	Central Intercollegiate Athletic Association *(349)*	CLSI	Clinical and Laboratory Standards Institute *(358)*	COMPTEL	Competitive Telecommunications Association *(371)*
	Cheese Importers Association of America, Inc. *(351)*	CLTA	Chinese Language Teachers Association *(354)*	CompTIA	Computing Technology Industry Association (CompTIA) *(373)*
CIAB	The Council of Insurance Agents and Brokers *(394)*	CLUW	Coalition of Labor Union Women *(361)*	COMSOC	IEEE Communications Society *(483)*
CIB	The Concrete Industry Board *(373)*	CMA	Calendar Marketing Association *(340)*	COMTO	Conference of Minority Transportation Officials *(375)*
CIBO	Council of Industrial Boiler Owners (CIBO) *(394)*		Catholic Medical Association *(346)*	CONAHEC	Consortium for North American Higher Education Collaboration *(378)*
CIBS	Cosmetic Industry Buyers and Suppliers *(387)*		Chamber Music America *(350)*	COPAFS	Council of Professional Associations on Federal Statistics *(396)*
CIC	Convention Industry Council *(383)*		Christian Management Association *(356)*	COPAS	Council of Petroleum Accountants Societies *(396)*
	Council of Independent Colleges *(394)*		College Media Association *(363)*	COPE	Council of Protocol Executives *(396)*
CICA	Captive Insurance Companies Association *(342)*		Communications Marketing Association *(369)*	CORAR	Council on Radionuclides and Radiopharmaceuticals *(400)*
CICAC	Congressional Internet Caucus Advisory Committee *(377)*		Cookware Manufacturers Association *(384)*	CORD	Congress on Research in Dance *(377)*
CICPAC	Construction Industry CPAs/Consultants Association *(379)*		Council for Museum Anthropology *(390)*	CORFAC	Corporate Facility Advisors, Inc. *(386)*
CIECA	Collision Industry Electronic Commerce Association *(365)*		Council of Manufacturing Associations *(395)*	COS	Clinical Orthopaedic Society *(358)*
CIES	CIES - The Food Business Forum *(356)*		Country Music Association *(401)*	COSA	Carwash Owner's and Supplier's Association *(343)*
	Comparative and International Education Society *(371)*	CMAA	Club Managers Association of America *(359)*	COSCA	Conference of State Court Administrators *(376)*
CIF	The Construction Innovation Forum *(379)*		Cocoa Merchants' Association of America *(361)*	COSCDA	Council of State Community Development Agencies *(397)*
CIFA	Council of Infrastructure Financing Authorities *(394)*		Construction Management Association of America *(379)*	CoSIDA	College Sports Information Directors of America *(364)*
CII	Containerization and Intermodal Institute *(382)*		Crane Manufacturers Association of America *(403)*	COSLA	Chief Officers of State Libraries Agencies *(352)*
	Council of Institutional Investors *(394)*	CMC	Commodity Markets Council *(368)*	CoSN	Consortium of School Networking *(378)*
	Council of International Investigators *(395)*		Consumer Mortgage Coalition *(381)*	COSSA	Consortium of Social Science Associations *(379)*
CIMA	Cellulose Insulation Manufacturers Association *(347)*	CMCA	Christian Meetings & Conventions Association *(356)*	COST	Council On State Taxation *(400)*
CIMPA	Connected International Meeting Professionals Association *(377)*	CMCAS	Capital Markets Credit Analysts Society *(342)*	COSTHA	Council on the Safe Transportation of Hazardous Articles *(401)*
CIMTA	Cottage Industry Miniaturists Trade Association *(387)*	CMDA	Christian Medical & Dental Associations *(356)*	COTH	Council of Teaching Hospitals *(398)*
CIR/SEIU	Committee of Interns and Residents/ SEIU *(368)*	CMG	Color Marketing Group *(365)*	COVD	College of Optometrists in Vision Development *(364)*
CIRB	Crop Insurance Research Bureau *(404)*		Computer Measurement Group *(372)*	COVR	Coalition of Visionary Resources *(361)*
CIRT	Construction Industry Round Table, Inc. *(379)*	CMI	Can Manufacturers Institute *(341)*	CPA	Catholic Press Association *(346)*
CIS	Clinical Immunology Society *(358)*		Cherry Marketing Institute *(352)*		Chlorobenzene Producers Association *(354)*
	Coalition for Independent Seniors *(360)*		Cleaning Management Institute *(357)*		Composite Panel Association *(372)*
CISA	Casting Industry Suppliers Association *(344)*	CMIA	Community Managers International Association *(371)*		Contract Packaging Association *(382)*
CISCA	Ceilings and Interior Systems Construction Association *(347)*	CMIS	Computerized Medical Imaging Society *(373)*	CPAAI	CPA Associates International *(402)*
CISPI	Cast Iron Soil Pipe Institute *(344)*	CMLS	Council of Multiple Listing Services *(395)*	CPADN	Career Planning and Adult Development Network *(343)*
CITBA	Customs and International Trade Bar Association *(406)*	CMMA	Communications Media Management Association *(369)*	CPAI	CPAmerica International *(402)*
CITE	Council for International Tax Education *(390)*	CMPA	Church Music Publishers Association *(356)*	CPB	Contractors Pump Bureau *(383)*
CITOC	Court Information Technology Officer Consortium *(402)*	CMPAA	Certified Milk Producers Association of America *(350)*	CPCA	Conservation and Preservation Charities of America *(377)*
CJJ	Coalition for Juvenile Justice *(360)*	CMRC	Construction Marketing Research Council *(380)*	CPCU	CPCU Society *(402)*
CJSS	Conference on Jewish Social Studies *(376)*	CMS	Clay Minerals Society *(357)*	CPDA	Council of Producers & Distributors of Agrotechnology *(396)*
CKRC	Cement Kiln Recycling Coalition *(347)*		College Music Society *(363)*	CPEN	Cancer Patient Education Network *(341)*
CLA	Catholic Library Association *(346)*	CMSA	Case Management Society of America *(343)*	CPI	Credit Professionals International *(403)*
	Christian Leadership Alliance *(355)*	CMSM	Conference of Major Superiors of Men, United States of America *(375)*	CPIA	Chlorinated Paraffins Industry Association *(354)*
	Coin Laundry Association *(361)*	CMSS	Council of Medical Specialty Societies *(395)*	CPMA	Color Pigments Manufacturers Association, Inc. *(365)*
	College Language Association *(363)*	CNAIMA	Council of North American Insulation Manufacturers Association *(396)*	CPMB	Concrete Plant Manufacturers Bureau *(374)*
	CropLife America *(404)*	CNIRS	Council for Near-Infrared Spectroscopy *(390)*	CPMT	IEEE Components, Packaging, and Manufacturing Technology Society *(483)*
CLA-USA	Christian Labor Association of the United States of America *(355)*	CNNT	Council of Nephrology Nurses and Technicians *(396)*	CPOA	Chief Petty Officers Association *(352)*
CLAH	Conference on Latin American History *(377)*	CNS	Child Neurology Society *(353)*		United States Coast Guard Chief Petty Officers Association *(992)*
CLAO	Contact Lens Association of Ophthalmologists *(382)*		Congress of Neurological Surgeons *(377)*	CPPA	Corrugated Polyethylene Pipe Association *(386)*
CLARB	The Council of Landscape Architectural Registration Boards *(395)*	COA	Coal Operators and Associates *(359)*	CPSA	Checks Payment Systems Association *(351)*
CLAS	Clinical Ligand Assay Society *(358)*		Commissioned Officers Association of the United States Public Health Service *(368)*	CPST	Commission on Professionals in Science and Technology *(352)*
	Congress of Lung Association Staffs *(377)*		Council of the Americas *(398)*	CPWD	Caucus for Producers, Writers & Directors *(346)*
CLC	Child Life Council *(353)*	COAA	Construction Owners Association of America *(380)*	CRA	California Redwood Association *(341)*
	Contact Lens Council *(382)*	COAI	Clowns of America International *(359)*		Catholic Radio Association *(346)*
CLCE	Compact Loader/Compact Excavator Council *(371)*	COCSA	Congress of Chiropractic State Associations *(377)*		Computing Research Association *(373)*
CLD	Council for Learning Disabilities *(390)*				Corn Refiners Association, Inc. *(385)*
				CRAFT	Craft Retailers Association for Tomorrow *(403)*

CRB	Council of Real Estate Brokerage Managers *(396)*	CTAM	Cable & Telecommunications Association for Marketing *(340)*	DG	Dramatists Guild of America *(416)*
	Country Radio Broadcasters, Inc. *(401)*	CTDA	Ceramic Tile Distributors Association *(349)*	DGA	Democratic Governors Association *(410)*
CRC	Coordinating Research Council *(384)*		Custom Tailors and Designers Association of America *(406)*		Directors Guild of America *(413)*
CRCPD	Conference of Radiation Control Program Directors *(375)*	CTHRA	Cable and Telecommunications Human Resources Association *(340)*	DGAC	Dangerous Goods Advisory Council *(407)*
CRD	Council for Resource Development *(391)*			DGTC	Distillers Grains Technology Council *(414)*
CRE	The Counselors of Real Estate *(401)*	CTI	Cooling Technology Institute *(384)*	DHI	The Door and Hardware Institute *(416)*
CREFC	CRE Finance Council *(403)*	CTIA	CTIA - The Wireless Association *(405)*	DHPE	Directors of Health Promotion and Education (DHPE) *(413)*
CREW	Commercial Real Estate Women Network *(367)*	CTIC	Conservation Technology Information Center *(378)*	DIA	Drug Information Association *(417)*
CRF	Credit Research Foundation *(403)*	CTIOA	Ceramic Tile Institute of America *(349)*	DiMA	Digital Imaging Marketing Association *(412)*
CRHA	Colorado Ranger Horse Association *(365)*	CTP	The Coalition for Transportation Productivity *(360)*		Digital Media Association *(412)*
CRI	The Carpet and Rug Institute *(343)*			DINA	Select Registry/Distinguished Inns of North America *(896)*
CRI Global	Customer Relations Institute Global, LLC *(406)*	CTPMA	Chevron and Texaco Petroleum Marketers Association *(352)*	DIPRA	Ductile Iron Pipe Research Association *(417)*
CRL	Center for Research Libraries *(348)*	CTS	College Theology Society *(365)*	DiRoNA	Distinguished Restaurants of North America *(414)*
CRLA	College Reading and Learning Association *(364)*	CTSA	Catholic Theological Society of America *(346)*	DIS	Ductile Iron Society *(417)*
CRMA	City and Regional Magazine Association *(357)*	CTSI	Clean Technology & Sustainable Industries Organization (CTSI) *(357)*	DISA	Data Interchange Standards Association *(407)*
CRN	Council for Responsible Nutrition *(391)*	CTTE	Council on Technology Teacher Education *(401)*	DISCUS	Distilled Spirits Council of the United States, Inc. *(414)*
	Council on Renal Nutrition *(400)*	CUES	Credit Union Executives Society *(403)*	DLCA	Distribution and LTL Carriers Association *(414)*
CRS	Controlled Release Society *(383)*	CUNA	Credit Union National Association, Inc. *(404)*	DLGA	Democratic Lieutenant Governors' Association (DLGA) *(410)*
	Council of Residential Specialists *(396)*	CUPA-HR	College and University Professional Association for Human Resources *(362)*	DLI	Drycleaning & Laundry Institute *(417)*
CRSA	Catalogue Raisonne Scholars Association *(344)*	CUR	Council on Undergraduate Research *(401)*	DMA	Dance Masters of America, Inc. *(406)*
CRSI	Concrete Reinforcing Steel Institute *(374)*	CURT	Construction Users Roundtable *(380)*		Direct Marketing Association *(412)*
CRWAD	Conference of Research Workers in Animal Diseases *(375)*	CVA	Correctional Vendors Association *(386)*	DMAI	Destination Marketing Association International *(411)*
CS	Classification Society *(357)*	CVSA	Commercial Vehicle Safety Alliance *(367)*	DMANF	Direct Marketing Association Nonprofit Federation *(412)*
	Coblentz Society *(361)*	CVSN	Commercial Vehicle Solutions Network *(367)*	DMI	Dairy Management, Inc. *(406)*
	Coleopterists Society *(362)*		The Commercial Vehicle Solutions Network *(367)*		Design Management Institute *(410)*
CSA	Chamber of Shipping of America *(351)*	CVTA	Commercial Vehicle Training Association *(367)*	DMIA	Diamond Manufacturers & Importers Association of America *(411)*
	Chemical Sources Association *(352)*	CWA	Communications Workers of America *(369)*	DMIFSC	Direct Marketing Insurance and Financial Services Council *(413)*
	Costume Society of America *(387)*		Construction Writers Association *(380)*	DNA	Delta Nu Alpha *(409)*
	Cryogenic Society of America *(405)*	CWAA	Cotton Warehouse Association of America *(387)*		Dermatology Nurses' Association *(410)*
	Czechoslovak Studies Association *(406)*	CWIS	Caucus for Women in Statistics *(346)*	DO	Delta Omicron *(409)*
CSAA	Central Station Alarm Association *(349)*	CWLA	Child Welfare League of America *(353)*	DOCA	Defense Orientation Conference Association *(408)*
CSAP	Council of State Speech-Language-Hearing Association Presidents *(398)*	CWOA	Chief Warrant and Warrant Officers Association, United States Coast Guard *(352)*	DPE	Department for Professional Employees - AFL-CIO *(410)*
CSAVR	Council of State Administrators of Vocational Rehabilitators *(397)*	CWPA	Council of Writing Program Administrators *(398)*	DPHA	Decorative Plumbing and Hardware Association *(408)*
CSBA	Columbia Sheep Breeders Association of America *(365)*	CWRT	Center for Waste Reduction Technologies *(348)*	DPhiE	Delta Phi Epsilon *(409)*
CSBS	Conference of State Bank Supervisors *(376)*	CWSRA	Chester White Swine Record Association *(352)*	DRA	Dude Ranchers' Association *(417)*
CSCAA	College Swimming Coaches Association of America *(364)*	DACC	The Danish-American Chamber of Commerce (USA) *(407)*	DRCA	Disaster Recovery Contractors Association (DRCA) *(413)*
CSCMP	Council of Supply Chain Management Professionals *(398)*	DACOR	Diplomatic and Consular Officers, Retired (Dacor) *(412)*	DRI	Defense Research Institute *(408)*
CSDA	Concrete Sawing and Drilling Association *(374)*	DAMA	Data Management Association International *(407)*	DRII	DRI International *(416)*
CSE	Council of Science Editors *(397)*	DASMA	Door and Access Systems Manufacturers Association, International *(415)*	DRSG	Demand Response and Smart Grid Coalition *(410)*
CSEE	Center for Spiritual and Ethical Education *(348)*	DATIA	Drug & Alcohol Testing Industry Association *(416)*	DSA	Digital Screenmedia Association *(412)*
CSF	College Savings Foundation *(364)*	DBA	DBA International *(407)*		Direct Selling Association *(413)*
CSFF	Commercial Space Flight Federation *(367)*	DBE	Dibasic Esters Group *(412)*		Document Security Alliance *(415)*
CSG	Council of State Governments *(397)*	DBIA	Design-Build Institute of America *(411)*	DSAA	Driving School Association of America *(416)*
CSHEMA	Campus Safety, Health and Environmental Management Association *(341)*	DBM	Distribution Business Management Association *(414)*	DSD	Delta Sigma Delta *(409)*
CSI	Cast Stone Institute *(344)*	DCA	Dance Critics Association *(406)*	DSFU	Deep Sea Fishermen's Union *(408)*
	Christian Schools International *(356)*		Diamond Council of America *(411)*	DSI	Decision Sciences Institute *(407)*
	Coalition of Service Industries *(361)*		Direct Care Alliance *(412)*	DSOA	Delaware Standardbred Owners Association *(409)*
	Computer Security Institute *(373)*		Distribution Contractors Association *(414)*	DSP	Delta Sigma Pi *(409)*
	Construction Specifications Institute *(380)*		Dredging Contractors of America, Inc. *(416)*	DTA	Dental Trade Alliance *(410)*
CSLA	Church and Synagogue Library Association *(356)*	DCAT	Drug, Chemical and Associated Technologies Association *(417)*	DTF	Diesel Technology Forum *(412)*
CSPA	Columbia Scholastic Press Association *(365)*	DCIA	Distributed Computing Industry Association *(414)*	DTP	Delta Theta Phi *(409)*
	Consumer Specialty Products Association *(381)*	DCUC	Defense Credit Union Council *(408)*	DWAA	Dog Writers' Association of America *(415)*
CSPN	College Savings Plans Network *(364)*	DDNA	Developmental Disabilities Nurses Association *(411)*	DWEA	Distributed Wind Energy Association *(414)*
CSPT	Conference for the Study of Political Thought *(374)*	DDPA	Delta Dental Plans Association *(409)*	DWF	Delta Waterfowl Foundation *(409)*
CSRA	Council of State Restaurant Associations *(397)*	DEA	Dance Educators of America *(406)*	DxMA	Diagnostic Marketing Association *(411)*
	Council of State Retail Associations *(397)*		Drilling Engineering Association *(416)*	EA	Employers Association *(426)*
CSRS	Cervical Spine Research Society *(350)*	DECA	Distributive Education Clubs of America (DECA) *(415)*	EAA	Ecuadorean American Association *(419)*
CSSA	Communications Supply Service Association *(369)*		Driver Employer Council of America *(416)*		Employer Associations of America *(426)*
	Crop Science Society of America *(404)*	DEMA	Diving Equipment and Marketing Association *(415)*		Environmental Assessment Association *(430)*
CSSB	Cedar Shake and Shingle Bureau *(347)*	DEPA	Domestic Energy Producers Alliance *(415)*		Express Association of America *(436)*
CSSP	Council of Scientific Society Presidents *(397)*	DEPS	Directed Energy Professional Society *(413)*	EABC	European-American Business Council *(434)*
CSSR	Council of Societies for the Study of Religion *(397)*	DERA	Disaster Preparedness and Emergency Response Association *(413)*	EACA	Exhibitor Appointed Contractors Association *(435)*
CSTE	Council of State and Territorial Epidemiologists *(397)*	DETC	Distance Education and Training Council *(414)*	EANGUS	Enlisted Association of the National Guard of the United States *(429)*
CSUSA	Copyright Society of the U.S.A. *(385)*	DF	Dermatology Foundation *(410)*	EAPA	Employee Assistance Professionals Association *(426)*
CSWA	Clinical Social Work Association *(359)*	DFA	Dance Films Association *(406)*	EAS	Eastern Apicultural Society of North America *(418)*
CSWE	Council on Social Work Education *(400)*		Decorative Furnishings Association *(408)*	EASA	Electrical Apparatus Service Association *(422)*
CTA	Coal Technology Association *(359)*	DFI	Deep Foundations Institute *(408)*	EASNA	Employee Assistance Society of North America *(426)*
	Coal Trading Association *(359)*	DFPA	Defense Fire Protection Association *(408)*	EAUC	Educational Association of University Centers *(420)*
	Consolidated Tape Association *(378)*			EBA	Energy Bar Association *(428)*
CTAA	Community Transportation Association of America *(371)*				Environmental Bankers Association *(430)*
				EBAA	Eye Bank Association of America *(436)*
				EBMA	Educational Book and Media Association *(420)*

FLTC Forest Landowners Tax Council *(451)*
FMA Fabricators & Manufacturers Association, International *(437)*

Federal Managers Association *(439)*

Financial Management Association International *(444)*

Financial Markets Association *(445)*

Fulfillment Management Association *(454)*
FMAA Flag Manufacturers Association of America *(446)*
FMC Filter Manufacturers Council *(444)*

United States Association of Former Members of Congress *(990)*
FMI Food Marketing Institute *(449)*
FMMDA Ford Motor Minority Dealers Association *(451)*
FMPS Federation of Modern Painters and Sculptors *(442)*
FMS Federation of Materials Societies *(441)*

Financial Managers Society *(445)*
FMSI Friction Material Standards Institute *(454)*
FNIDCR Friends of the National Institute of Dental and Craniofacial Research (FNIDCR) *(454)*
FNS Federal Network for Sustainability *(439)*
FOSA Federation of Spine Associations *(442)*
FPA Federal Physicians Association *(439)*

Financial Planning Association *(445)*

Flexible Packaging Association *(447)*

Flying Physicians Association *(448)*

Fusion Power Associates *(455)*
FPAA Fresh Produce Association of the Americas *(453)*
FPDA Fluid Power Distributors Association *(448)*
FPFC Fresh Produce and Floral Council *(453)*
FPI Foodservice & Packaging Institute, Inc. *(450)*
FPMB Federation of Podiatric Medical Boards *(442)*
FPPA Flexographic Prepress Platemakers Association *(447)*
FPPI Frozen Potato Products Institute *(454)*
FPPOA Federal Probation and Pre-trial Officers Association *(440)*
FPS Forest Products Society *(451)*
FPSA Food Processing Suppliers Association *(449)*
FPSB Financial Planning Standards Board *(445)*
FRA Fleet Reserve Association *(447)*

Forest Resources Association *(451)*

Furniture Retailers of America *(454)*
FRAEC Foundation for Russian-American Economic Cooperation *(453)*
FS Fiber Society *(443)*

Fleischner Society *(447)*
FSA Fluid Sealing Association *(448)*

Food Shippers of America *(450)*
FSBPT Federation of State Boards of Physical Therapy *(442)*
FSC Free Speech Coalition *(453)*
FSC-US Forest Stewardship Council - United States Chapter *(451)*
FSEA Foil and Specialty Effects Association *(448)*
FSF Flight Safety Foundation *(448)*
FSG The Foodservice Group, Inc. *(450)*
FSHC Federation of State Humanities Councils *(442)*
FSMA Foodservice Sales & Marketing Association *(450)*
FSMB Federation of State Medical Boards of the United States *(442)*
FSP Society of Financial Service Professionals *(936)*
FSPA Financial and Security Products Association *(444)*
FSR The Financial Services Roundtable *(445)*
FSSA Fire Suppression Systems Association *(446)*
FTA Federation of Tax Administrators *(442)*

Flexographic Technical Association *(447)*
FTPI Fiberglass Tank and Pipe Institute *(447)*
FUMMWA Fellowship of United Methodists in Music and Worship Arts *(442)*
FVOA Fishing Vessel Owners' Association *(446)*
FWAA Football Writers Association of America *(450)*
FWQA Federal Water Quality Association *(440)*
GA Gypsum Association *(467)*
GAA Gravure Association of America *(465)*
GABA German American Business Association *(460)*
GACC German American Chamber of Commerce *(460)*
GADA Generic Animal Drug Alliance *(458)*
GAG Graphic Artists Guild *(465)*
GAIN Gift Associates Interchange Network *(460)*
GAL Guild of American Luthiers *(467)*
GAMA GAMA International *(455)*

Game Manufacturers Association *(456)*

General Aviation Manufacturers Association *(458)*

Global Acetate Manufacturers Association *(461)*

Guitar and Accessories Marketing Association *(467)*
GANA Glass Association of North America *(461)*
GAP Global Alcohol Producers Group *(461)*
GARP Global Association of Risk Professionals *(461)*
GAS Glass Art Society *(461)*
GASDA Gasoline and Automotive Service Dealers of America *(457)*
GASF Graphic Arts Sales Foundation *(465)*
GATF Graphic Arts Technical Foundation *(465)*
GAWDA Gases and Welding Distributors Association *(457)*
GBSUA Greater Blouse, Skirt and Undergarment Association *(466)*
GBTA Global Business Travel Association *(462)*
GBW Guild of Book Workers *(467)*
GCA Garden Centers of America *(456)*

Greeting Card Association *(466)*
GCAA Golf Coaches Association of America *(463)*
GCBAA Golf Course Builders Association of America *(463)*
GCC/IBT Graphic Communications Conference of the International Brotherhood of Teamsters *(465)*
GCCA Global Cold Chain Alliance *(462)*
GCSAA Golf Course Superintendents Association of America *(463)*
GEA Geothermal Energy Association *(459)*
GEAPS Grain Elevator and Processing Society *(464)*
GEO Geothermal Heat Pump Consortium *(459)*
Geo-nii Geothermal Heat Pump National and International Initiative *(460)*
GFA Gasket Fabricators Association *(457)*
GFOA Government Finance Officers Association of the United States and Canada *(464)*

Government Finance Officers Association, Federal Liaison Center *(464)*
GFWC General Federation of Women's Clubs *(458)*
GHBA Galiceno Horse Breeders Association *(455)*
GHC Global Health Council *(462)*
GHSA Governors' Highway Safety Association *(464)*
GIA Gemological Institute of America *(457)*
GIAA Guild of Italian American Actors *(467)*
GIS Gamma Iota Sigma *(456)*
GITA Geospatial Information Technology Association *(459)*
GLMA Gay and Lesbian Medical Association *(457)*
GMA Geosynthetic Materials Association *(459)*

Gospel Music Association *(464)*

Grocery Manufacturers Association (GMA) *(466)*
GMDA Groundwater Management Districts Association *(466)*
GMDC Global Market Development Center *(462)*
GMIA Gelatin Manufacturers Institute of America *(457)*
GMIC Glass Manufacturing Industry Council *(461)*
GMIS Government Management Information Sciences *(464)*
GMP Glass, Molders, Pottery, Plastics and Allied Workers International Union *(461)*
GMRC Gas Machinery Research Council *(456)*
GNSI Guild of Natural Science Illustrators *(467)*
GOCA Global Offset and Countertrade Association (GOCA) *(462)*
GOG Gynecologic Oncology Group *(467)*
GPA Gas Processors Association *(456)*

The Grant Professionals Association *(465)*
GPhA Generic Pharmaceutical Association *(458)*
GPI Glass Packaging Institute *(461)*

National Association of Graphic and Product Identification Manufacturers *(670)*
GPSA Gas Processors Suppliers Association *(456)*
GRA Governmental Research Association *(464)*
GRAA Golf Range Association of America *(463)*
GRC Geothermal Resources Council *(460)*
GRSS Geoscience and Remote Sensing Society *(459)*
GS Geochemical Society *(458)*
GSA Genetics Society of America *(458)*

Geological Society of America *(459)*

Gerontological Society of America *(460)*

Global Semiconductor Alliance *(463)*

Glove Shippers Association *(463)*
GSCA Giant Screen Cinema Association *(460)*
GSIS Geoscience Information Society *(459)*
GSMA GSM Association *(467)*
GTA Gas Turbine Association *(457)*
GTC Gasification Technologies Council *(457)*
GTI Gas Technology Institute *(456)*

GUPH Group for the Use of Psychology in History *(466)*
GWA Garden Writers Association *(456)*

Office Business Center Association International *(826)*
GWAA Golf Writers Association of America *(463)*
GWPC Ground Water Protection Council *(466)*
H-SHGAPE Society for Historians of the Gilded Age and Progressive Era *(911)*
HAA Hospice Association of America *(479)*
HACC Hellenic-American Chamber of Commerce *(474)*
HACR Hispanic Association on Corporate Responsibility *(475)*
HACU Hispanic Association of Colleges and Universities *(475)*
HAEA U.S. Hereditary Angioedema Association *(983)*
HAI Helicopter Association International *(473)*
HAPCOA Hispanic American Police Command Officers Association (HAPCOA) *(475)*
HAPS Human Anatomy and Physiology Society *(480)*
HARC Halon Alternatives Research Corporation *(468)*
HARDI Heating, Airconditioning and Refrigeration Distributors International *(473)*
HBA Home Baking Association *(477)*

Human Biology Association *(480)*
HBES Human Behavior and Evolution Society *(480)*
HBI Hotel Brokers International *(479)*
HBMA Healthcare Billing and Management Association *(471)*
HBPA National Horsemen's Benevolent and Protective Association *(760)*
HCAA Health Care Administrators Association *(469)*

National CPA Health Care Advisors Association *(740)*
HCCA Health Care Compliance Association *(469)*
HCEA Health Care Education Association *(469)*

Healthcare Convention and Exhibitors Association *(471)*
HCHS Huntington College of Health Sciences *(481)*
HCI Human Capital Institute *(480)*
HCPC Healthcare Compliance Packaging Council *(470)*
HCS The Histochemical Society *(476)*
HDA Hispanic Dental Association *(475)*

Holiday and Decorative Association *(477)*

Holistic Dental Association *(477)*
HDBMC Heavy Duty Brake Manufacturers Council *(473)*
HDI Help Desk Institute *(474)*
HDMA Healthcare Distribution Management Association *(471)*

Heavy Duty Manufacturers Association *(473)*
HDRA Heavy Duty Representatives Association *(473)*
HDS History of Dermatology Society *(476)*
HECSE Higher Education Consortium for Special Education *(474)*
HECUA Higher Education Consortium for Urban Affairs *(475)*
HEDNA Hotel Electronic Distribution Network Association *(479)*
HEI Heat Exchange Institute *(472)*
HERA Housing Education and Research Association *(479)*

Humanities Education and Research Association *(481)*
HES History of Economics Society *(476)*

The History of Education Society *(477)*
HeSCA Health and Sciences Communications Association *(469)*
HESS History of Earth Sciences Society *(476)*
HF Hardwood Federation *(468)*

Health Forum *(469)*
HFA Hedge Fund Association *(473)*

Hemophilia Federation of America *(474)*
HFES Human Factors and Ergonomics Society *(480)*

Human Factors Society *(481)*
HFIA Home Furnishings Independents Association *(478)*
HFMA Healthcare Financial Management Association *(471)*
HFPA Home Fashion Products Association *(478)*
HFSA Heart Failure Society of America *(472)*
HFTP Hospitality Financial and Technology Professionals *(480)*
HGA Handweavers Guild of America, Inc. *(468)*

Hop Growers of America *(478)*
HGMN Herb Growing and Marketing Network *(474)*
HHI Harness Horsemen International *(468)*

ISHBSS	Cheiron: The International Society for the History of Behavioral and Social Sciences (351)
ISHC	International Society of Hospitality Consultants (573)
ISHLT	International Society for Heart and Lung Transplantation (566)
ISHRS	International Society of Hair Restoration Surgery (573)
ISI	Ice Skating Institute (482)
ISID	International Society for Infectious Diseases (566)
ISKA	International Saw and Knife Association (564)
ISM	Institute for Supply Management (497)
ISMA	International Security Management Association (564)
	International Snowmobile Manufacturers Association (565)
ISMA-USA	International Stress Management Association - USA (576)
ISMICS	The International Society for Minimally Invasive Cardiothoracic Surgery (567)
ISMP	International Society of Meeting Planners (573)
ISMPP	International Society for Medical Publication Professionals (567)
ISMRM	International Society for Magnetic Resonance in Medicine (567)
ISMTE	International Society of Managing and Technical Editors (573)
ISNR	International Society for Neuronal Regulation (567)
ISOA	The International Stability Operations Association (575)
ISOB	International Society of Barristers (571)
ISOC	Internet Society (582)
ISONG	International Society of Nurses in Genetics (573)
ISOP	International Society of Protistologists (573)
ISOPE	International Society of Offshore and Polar Engineers (573)
ISOQOL	International Society for Quality of Life Research (569)
ISP	Institute of Store Planners (503)
	International Society for Plastination (568)
ISPA	International Sleep Products Association (565)
	International Society for the Performing Arts (569)
	International Spa Association (575)
ISPCLN	International Society of Psychiatric Consultation Liaison Nurses (574)
ISPD	International Society for Prenatal Diagnosis (568)
ISPE	International Society for Pharmaceutical Engineering (567)
	International Society for Pharmacoepidemiology (568)
	International Society for Philosophical Enquiry (568)
ISPI	International Society for Performance Improvement (567)
ISPN	International Society of Psychiatric-Mental Health Nurses (574)
ISPO	International Society for Preventive Oncology (568)
ISPOR	International Society for Pharmacoeconomics and Outcomes Research (568)
ISPP	International Society of Political Psychology (573)
ISQOLS	International Society for Quality-of-Life Studies (569)
ISRA	International Society for Research on Aggression (569)
ISRI	Institute of Scrap Recycling Industries, Inc. (503)
ISRP	International Society for Respiratory Protection (569)
ISRS	International Society of Refractive Surgery of the American Academy of Ophthalmology (574)
ISS	International Superyacht Society (576)
ISSA	Information Systems Security Association (495)
	International Slurry Surfacing Association (565)
ISSPA	International Sport Show Producers Association (575)
ISSSEEM	International Society for the Study of Subtle Energies and Energy Medicine (570)
ISSTD	International Society for the Study of Dissociation (570)
	International Society for the Study of Trauma and Dissociation (570)
ISTA	International Safe Transit Association (563)

ISTAT	International Society of Transport Aircraft Trading (574)
ISTE	International Society for Technology in Education (569)
ISTH	International Society on Thrombosis and Hemostasis (575)
ISTR	International Society for Third-Sector Research (570)
ISTSS	International Society for Traumatic Stress Studies (570)
ISTTE	International Society of Travel and Tourism Educators (574)
ISWM	International Society of Weighing and Measurement (574)
ISWNE	International Society of Weekly Newspaper Editors (574)
ITA	Indoor Tanning Association (492)
	Industrial Truck Association (494)
	Information Technology Alliance (495)
	Instrumentation Testing Association (504)
	Intercollegiate Tennis Association (507)
	International Thermographers Association (577)
	International Titanium Association (577)
ITAA	International Textile and Apparel Association (577)
	The International Transactional Analysis Association (578)
ITAC	Telework Advisory Group for World at Work (971)
ITACCS	Trauma Care International (979)
ITC	Institute of Tax Consultants (503)
	Instructional Technology Council (504)
	Intertribal Timber Council (583)
ITCTLA	International Trade Commission Trial Lawyers Association (577)
ITE	Institute of Transportation Engineers (503)
ITEA	International Test and Evaluation Association (577)
	International Tuba-Euphonium Association (578)
ITechLaw	International Technology Law Association (577)
ITEEA	International Technology and Engineering Educators Association (576)
ITFMA	IT Financial Management Association (586)
ITG	International Trumpet Guild (578)
ITI	Information Technology Industry Council (495)
	International Tax Institute (576)
ITLMA	Independent Time and Labor Management Association (492)
ITMA	Intertribal Monitoring Association on Indian Trust Funds (583)
ITNS	International Transplant Nurses Society (578)
ITODA	Independent Turf and Ornamental Distributors Association (492)
ITPA	International Truck Parts Association (578)
ITS	Information Theory Society (495)
	International Turfgrass Society (579)
ITS America	Intelligent Transportation Society of America (506)
ITSA	Interactive Travel Services Association (507)
ITSCC	International Transplant-Skin Cancer Collaborative (578)
ITTA	Independent Telephone and Telecommunications Alliance (492)
ITWEA	International Travel Writers and Editors Association (578)
IUE-CWA	International Union of Electronic, Electrical, Salaried, Machine, and Furniture Workers-CWA (579)
IUEC	International Union of Elevator Constructors (579)
IUEP	International Utility Efficiency Partnerships (580)
IUJAT	International Union of Journeymen and Allied Trades (579)
IUOE	International Union of Operating Engineers (579)
IUPA	International Union of Police Associations, AFL-CIO (579)
IUPAT	International Union of Painters and Allied Trades (579)
IUTOX	International Union of Toxicology (579)
IVAPM	International Veterinary Academy of Pain Management (580)
IVAS	International Veterinary Acupuncture Society (580)
IVLA	International Visual Literacy Association (580)
IVODGA	International Vessel Operators Dangerous Goods Association (580)
IWA	International Webmasters Association (580)
IWCA	International Window Cleaning Association (581)

	International Writing Centers Association (581)
IWFA	International Window Film Association (581)
IWGS	International Waterlily and Water Gardening Society (580)
IWLA	International Warehouse Logistics Association (580)
IWMC	International Wildlife Management Consortium (581)
iWomen	International Association of Women in Fire and Emergency Services (528)
IWPA	The International Wood Products Association (581)
IWRA	International Wild Rice Association (581)
IWSA	Energy Recovery Council (428)
IWSS	International Weed Science Society (581)
IWWG	International Women's Writing Guild (581)
IZA	International Zinc Association-America (582)
JA	Jewelers of America (587)
JAA	Judge Advocates Association (589)
JASPA	Jesuit Association of Student Personnel Administrators (587)
JBC	Jewish Book Council (587)
JBT	Jewelers Board of Trade (587)
JCAAI	Joint Council of Allergy, Asthma and Immunology (588)
JCC	Jewish Community Centers Association of North America (588)
JCSA	Jewish Communal Service Association of North America (588)
JEA	Jewish Educators Assembly (588)
	Journalism Education Association (589)
JEDEC	Joint Electron Device Engineering Council (589)
JESNA	Jewish Education Service of North America (588)
JFDA	Jewish Funeral Directors of America (588)
JG	The Jockeys' Guild (588)
JIDA	Jewelry Industry Distributors Association (587)
JNCL-NCLIS	Joint National Committee for Languages-National Council for Languages and International Studies (589)
JPA	Juice Products Association (589)
JPF	Just Plain Folks Songwriting/Musician Networking Organization (589)
JPMA	Juvenile Products Manufacturers Association (590)
JPS	Jean Piaget Society (586)
JRCERT	Joint Review Committee on Education in Radiologic Technology (589)
JRSA	Justice Research and Statistics Association (589)
JSA	Jewelers Shipping Association (587)
JSA-US	Jewelers' Security Alliance of the United States (587)
JSEA	Jesuit Secondary Education Association (587)
JVC	Jeweler's Vigilance Committee (587)
JWBJCC	JWB Jewish Chaplains Council (590)
KANA	Kamut Association of North America (590)
KCMA	Kitchen Cabinet Manufacturers Association (591)
KDE	Kappa Delta Epsilon (590)
KDLA	Korean Drycleaners-Laundry Association (591)
KDP	Kappa Delta Pi (590)
KKI	Kappa Kappa Iota-National (590)
KTAI	The Kite Trade Association International (591)
KWPN-NA	KWPN of North America (591)
LA	Lighter Association (598)
LAA	Leather Apparel Association (596)
LACUS	Linguistic Association of Canada and the United States (598)
LAMA	Laboratory Animal Management Association (592)
	Light Aircraft Manufacturers Association (598)
LANA	Lipizzan Association of North America (599)
LASA	Latin American Studies Association (594)
LBA	Latin Business Association (594)
LBI	Library Binding Institute (597)
LCA	Lake Carriers Association (592)
	Library Copyright Alliance (597)
LCLAA	Labor Council for Latin American Advancement (LCLAA) (592)
LCNP	Lawyers Committee on Nuclear Policy (594)
LDA	The Learning Disabilities Association (596)
LEA	Lutheran Education Association (600)
LEAA	Law Enforcement Alliance of America (594)
LEC	Lignite Energy Council (598)
LECET	Laborers-Employers Cooperation & Education Trust (592)
LECNA	Lutheran Educational Conference of North America (600)
LEOMA	Laser and Electro-Optics Manufacturers' Association (593)

MSTS	Musculoskeletal Tumor Society *(621)*					
MTA	Market Technicians Association *(606)*					
	Museum Trustee Association *(621)*					
MTAI	Keyboard Teachers Association International *(590)*					
MTI	Materials Technology Institute *(609)*					
	Metal Treating Institute *(614)*					
MTMA	MTM Association for Standards and Research *(620)*					
MTNA	Music Teachers National Association *(622)*					
MTS	Marine Technology Society *(605)*					
MTT-S	IEEE Microwave Theory and Techniques Society *(485)*					
MVMA	Masonry Veneer Manufacturers Association *(607)*					
MWA	Mystery Writers of America *(623)*					
MWMA	Municipal Waste Management Association *(621)*					
N-OADN	National Organization for Associate Degree Nursing *(776)*					
N4A	National Association of Academic Advisors for Athletes *(645)*					
	National Association of Area Agencies on Aging *(647)*					
NAA	National Academy of Arbitrators *(627)*					
	National Aeronautic Association *(629)*					
	National Aerosol Association *(629)*					
	National After School Association *(629)*					
	National Apartment Association *(634)*					
	National Auctioneers Association *(711)*					
	Natural Areas Association *(806)*					
	New America Alliance *(809)*					
	Newspaper Association of America *(810)*					
NAAA	National Agricultural Aviation Association *(630)*					
	National Alarm Association of America *(631)*					
	National Auto Auction Association *(711)*					
NAAAS	National Association of African American Studies and Affiliates *(646)*					
	National Association of Hispanic and Latino Studies *(672)*					
NAAB	National Association of Animal Breeders *(647)*					
NAACCR	North American Association of Central Cancer Registries *(812)*					
NAACO	North American Association of Commencement Officers *(813)*					
NAACS	National Association of Air Medical Communication Specialists *(646)*					
	National Association of Aircraft and Communication Suppliers *(646)*					
NAADA	National Agricultural Alumni and Development Association *(630)*					
NAADAA	National Antique and Art Dealers Association of America *(634)*					
NAADAC	National Association for Alcoholism and Drug Abuse Counselors *(646)*					
NAADD	National Association of Athletic Development Directors *(647)*					
NAAE	National Association of Agricultural Educators *(646)*					
	National Association of Agriculture Employees *(646)*					
	North American Academy of Ecumenists *(812)*					
NAAEE	North American Association for Environmental Education *(812)*					
NAAFA	National Association of Agricultural Fair Agencies *(646)*					
NAAG	National Association of Attorneys General *(647)*					
NAAHL	National Association of Affordable Housing Lenders *(646)*					
NAAHP	National Association of Advisors for the Health Professions *(645)*					
NAAIM	National Association of Active Investment Managers *(645)*					
NAAL	North American Academy of Liturgy *(812)*					
NAAMA	National Arab-American Medical Association *(635)*					
NAAMM	National Association of Architectural Metal Manufacturers *(647)*					
NAAMO	North American Agricultural Marketing Officials *(812)*					
NAAOP	National Association for the Advancement of Orthotics and Prosthetics *(643)*					
NAAP	National Association for the Advancement of Psychoanalysis *(643)*					
	National Association of Activity Professionals *(645)*					
NAAS	National Association of Academies of Science *(645)*					
	National Association of Arms Shows *(647)*					
NAASR	National Association for Armenian Studies and Research *(636)*					

North American Association for the Study of Religion *(812)*

NAASS North American Association of Summer Sessions *(813)*

NAATBatt National Alliance for Advanced Transportation Batteries *(631)*

NAATP National Association of Addiction Treatment Providers *(645)*

NAAUSA National Association of Assistant United States Attorneys *(647)*

NAAWS North American Association of Wardens and Superintendents *(814)*

NAB National Association of Boards of Examiners of Long Term Care Administrators *(650)*

National Association of Broadcasters *(650)*

National Association of Long Term Care Administrator Boards *(679)*

NABA National Association of Black Accountants, Inc. *(648)*

NABBA National Association of Barber Boards of America *(648)*

NABC National Association of Basketball Coaches *(648)*

North American Blueberry Council *(814)*

NABCA National Alcohol Beverage Control Association *(631)*

NABCC North American-Bulgarian Chamber of Commerce *(823)*

NABCJ National Association of Blacks in Criminal Justice *(649)*

NABCO National Association of Black County Officials *(649)*

NABE National Association for Bilingual Education *(636)*

National Association for Business Economics *(636)*

National Association of Bar Executives *(648)*

NABET-CWA National Association of Broadcast Employees and Technicians-Communications Workers of America, AFL-CIO (NABET-CWA) *(650)*

NABGG National Association for Black Geologists and Geophysicists *(636)*

NABH National Association for Behavioral Health *(636)*

NABI National Association of Beverage Importers Inc. *(648)*

NABIE National Academy of Building Inspection Engineers *(627)*

NABIM NABIM - the International Band and Orchestral Products Association *(623)*

NABJ National Association of Black Journalists *(649)*

NABL National Association of Bond Lawyers *(650)*

NABM National Association of Blind Merchants *(650)*

National Association of Boat Manufacturers *(650)*

NABOB National Association for Black-Owned Broadcasters *(649)*

NABOE National Association of Business Owners and Entrepreneurs *(651)*

NABP National Association of Black Professors *(649)*

National Association of Boards of Pharmacy *(650)*

NABPAC National Association of Business Political Action Committees *(651)*

NABPR National Association of Baptist Professors of Religion *(648)*

NABR National Association for Biomedical Research *(636)*

NABRTI National Association of Bar-Related Title Insurers *(648)*

North American Bar-Related Title Insurers *(814)*

NABS National Association of Black Suppliers *(649)*

NABSE National Alliance of Black School Educators *(632)*

NABSW National Association of Black Social Workers *(649)*

NABT National Association of Bankruptcy Trustees *(647)*

National Association of Biology Teachers *(648)*

National Association of Blind Teachers *(650)*

NABTA National Association of Business Travel Agents *(651)*

NABTE National Association for Business Teacher Education *(636)*

NABWE National Association of Black Women Entrepreneurs *(649)*

NAC National Aquaculture Council *(635)*

National Association of Concessionaires *(657)*

NACA National Air Carrier Association *(630)*

National Animal Control Association *(634)*

National Armored Car Association *(635)*

National Association for Campus Activities *(637)*

National Association of Catastrophe Adjusters *(651)*

National Association of Consumer Advocates *(657)*

National Association of County Administrators *(659)*

Native American Contractors Association *(806)*

North American Corriente Association *(815)*

NACAA National Association of Clean Air Agencies *(654)*

National Association of Consumer Agency Administrators *(657)*

National Association of County Agricultural Agents *(659)*

NACAC National Association for College Admission Counseling *(637)*

NACADA National Academic Advising Association *(626)*

NACAP National Association of County Aging Programs *(659)*

NACAS National Association of College Auxiliary Services *(655)*

NACAT North American Council of Automotive Teachers *(815)*

NACB National Academy of Clinical Biochemistry *(627)*

NACBA National Association of Church Business Administration *(653)*

National Association of Consumer Bankruptcy Attorneys *(657)*

NACBH National Association for Children's Behavioral Health (NACBH) *(637)*

NACBHD National Association of County Behavioral Health and Developmental Disability Directors *(659)*

NACBS North American Conference on British Studies *(815)*

NACC National Association of Catholic Chaplains *(651)*

National Association of Counsel for Children *(658)*

Norwegian-American Chamber of Commerce *(824)*

NACCA National Association of Consumer Credit Administrators *(657)*

National Association of County Civil Attorneys *(659)*

NACCAP North American Coalition for Christian Admissions Professionals *(815)*

NACCC National Association of Congregational Christian Churches *(657)*

North American-Chilean Chamber of Commerce *(823)*

NACCED National Association of County Community and Economic Development *(637)*

NACCHO National Association of City and County Health Officials *(654)*

National Association of County and City Health Officials *(659)*

NACCP National Association of Child Care Professionals *(653)*

NACCRRA Child Care Aware of America *(353)*

NACCS National Association for Chicana and Chicano Studies *(637)*

NACCSA North American Carbon Capture & Storage Association *(814)*

NACD National Association of Chemical Distributors *(652)*

National Association of Conservation Districts *(657)*

National Association of Container Distributors *(658)*

National Association of Corporate Directors *(658)*

NACDA National Association of Collegiate Directors of Athletics *(656)*

NACDD National Association of Chronic Disease Directors *(653)*

National Association of Councils on Developmental Disabilities *(658)*

NACDL National Association of Criminal Defense Lawyers *(661)*

NACDS National Association of Chain Drug Stores *(652)*

North American Clinical Dermatologic Society *(815)*

NACE National Association of Catering and Events *(651)*

National Association of Colleges and Employers (655)

National Association of County Engineers (660)

NACEDA National Alliance of Community Economic Development Associations (632)

NACES National Association of Credential Evaluation Services, Inc. (661)

NACFA North American Clun Forest Association (815)

NACFAM National Council for Advanced Manufacturing (731)

NACFS National Association of Church Food Service (653)

NACHA NACHA - The Electronic Payments Association (623)

NACHC National Association of Community Health Centers (656)

NACHFA National Association of County Health Facility Administrators (660)

NACHRI National Association of Children's Hospitals and Related Institutions (653)

NACHSA National Association of County Human Services Administrators (660)

NACIO National Association of County Information Officers (660)

NACIRO National Association of County Intergovernmental Relations Officials (660)

NACIS North American Cartographic Information Society (814)

NACITA National Association of County Information Technology Administrators (660)

NACM National Association for Court Management (637)

National Association of Chain Manufacturers (652)

National Association of Credit Management (661)

NACMA National Association of Collegiate Marketing Administrators (656)

NACME National Action Council for Minorities in Engineering (NACME) (628)

NACNS National Association of Clinical Nurse Specialists (654)

NACO National Association of Charterboat Operators (652)

National Association of Counties (659)

NACOA National Association of Cruise Oriented Agencies (662)

NACOP National Association of Chiefs of Police (653)

NACPA National Association of Church Personnel Administrators (653)

NACPM National Association of Certified Professional Midwives (651)

NACPO National Association of Casino Party Operators (651)

NACPRO National Association of County Park and Recreation Officials (660)

NACRA North American Case Research Association (814)

NACRC National Association of County Recorders, Election Officials and Clerks (660)

NACS National Association of College Stores (655)

National Association of Consumer Shows (658)

National Association of Convenience Stores (658)

National Association of County Surveyors (660)

North American Catalysis Society (815)

NACSA National Association of Charter School Authorizers (652)

NACST National Association of Catholic School Teachers (651)

NACSW North American Association of Christians in Social Work (813)

NACT National Association of Corporate Treasurers (658)

NACTA North American Colleges and Teachers of Agriculture (815)

NACTP National Association of Computerized Tax Processors (657)

NACTT National Association of Chapter Thirteen Trustees (NACTT) (652)

NACUA National Association of College and University Attorneys (654)

NACUBO National Association of College and University Business Officers (654)

NACUC National Association of Credit Union Chairmen (661)

NACUFS National Association of College and University Food Services (655)

NACUSA National Association of Composers, USA (657)

NACUSAC National Association of Credit Union Supervisory and Auditing Committees (661)

NACUSO National Association of Credit Union Service Organizations (661)

NACVA National Association of Certified Valuation Analysts (652)

NACVCB The National Association of Crime Victim Compensation Boards (661)

NACW National Association of Commissions for Women (656)

NACWA National Association of Clean Water Agencies (654)

NACWAA National Association of Collegiate Women Athletic Administrators (656)

NACWC The National Association of Colored Women's Club, Inc. (656)

NACWPI National Association of College Wind and Percussion Instructors (655)

NADA National Association of Dental Assistants (662)

National Automobile Dealers Association (711)

NADCA NADCA: The HVAC Inspection, Maintenance and Restoration Association (623)

North American Die Casting Association (816)

NADCO National Association of Development Companies (662)

NADCP National Association of Drug Court Professionals (663)

NADD The National Association for the Dually Diagnosed (643)

National Association of Diaconate Directors (662)

NADE National Association for Developmental Education (638)

National Association of Disability Examiners (663)

National Association of Document Examiners (663)

NADeFA North American Deer Farmers Association (815)

NADEP National Association of Disability Evaluating Professionals (663)

NADFD National Association of Decorative Fabric Distributors (662)

NADL National Association of Dental Laboratories (662)

NADO National Association of Development Organizations (662)

NADOA National Association of Division Order Analysts (663)

NADOI The National Association of Dog Obedience Instructors (663)

NADONA National Association of Directors of Nursing Administration in Long Term Care (663)

NADP National Association of Dental Plans (662)

NADR National Association of Disability Representatives (663)

NADSA National Adult Day Service Association (629)

NADT National Association for Drama Therapy (638)

NAE National Academy of Engineering of the United States of America (627)

NAE4-HA National Association of Extension 4-H Agents (667)

NAEA National Abstinence Education Association (626)

National Art Education Association (635)

National Association of Enrolled Agents (666)

NAEBA National Association of Exclusive Buyer Agents (666)

North American Elk Breeders Association (816)

NAEC National Association of Elevator Contractors (665)

National Association of Epilepsy Centers (666)

NAEd National Academy of Education (627)

National Association of Electrical Distributors (664)

NAEDA North American Equipment Dealers Association (816)

NAEGA North American Export Grain Association, Inc. (816)

NAEIS National Association of Ecumenical and Interreligious Staff (664)

NAELA National Academy of Elder Law Attorneys, Inc. (627)

NAELB National Association of Equipment Leasing Brokers (666)

NAEM National Association for Environmental Management (638)

NAEMSE National Association of EMS Educators (665)

NAEMSP National Association of EMS Physicians (665)

NAEMT National Association of Emergency Medical Technicians (665)

NAEN North American Association of Educational Negotiators (813)

NAEOP National Association of Educational Office Professionals (664)

NAEP National Association of Educational Procurement, Inc. (664)

National Association of Environmental Professionals (666)

National Association of Estate Planners and Councils (666)

NAEPDC National Adult Education Professional Development Consortium (629)

NAES National Association for Ethnic Studies (638)

National Association of Episcopal Schools (666)

NAESA National Association of Elevator Safety Authorities International (665)

NAESCO National Association of Energy Service Companies (665)

NAESP National Association of Elementary School Principals (664)

NAEYC National Association for the Education of Young Children (644)

NAF National Abortion Federation (626)

National Automotive Finance Association (711)

NAFA NAFA Fleet Management Association (624)

National Air Filtration Association (630)

National Aircraft Finance Association (630)

National Alfalfa Alliance (631)

National Alfalfa and Forage Alliance (631)

National Association for Fixed Annuities (639)

NAFAC National Association for Ambulatory Care (636)

NAFB National Association of Farm Broadcasting (667)

NAFC National Accounting and Finance Council (628)

National Association of Free Clinics (669)

NAFCC National Association for Family Child Care (638)

NAFCD North American Association of Floor Covering Distributors (811)

NAFCE National Association for Family and Community Education (638)

NAFCM National Association for Community Mediation (637)

NAFCU National Association of Federal Credit Unions (667)

NAFD National Association of Flour Distributors (668)

NAFE National Association of Forensic Economics (669)

NAFEC National Association of Farmer Elected Committees (NAFEC) (667)

NAFED National Association of Fire Equipment Distributors (668)

NAFEM North American Association of Food Equipment Manufacturers (813)

NAFEO National Association for Equal Opportunity in Higher Education (638)

NAFEPA National Association of Federal Education Program Administrators (667)

NAFFS National Association of Flavors and Food-Ingredient Systems (668)

NAFGPD National Association of Foster Grandparent Program Directors (669)

NAFI National Association of Fire Investigators (668)

National Association of Flight Instructors (668)

NAFIC National Association of Fraternal Insurance Counsellors (669)

NAFIPS North American Fuzzy Information Processing Society (817)

NAFIS National Association of Federally Impacted Schools (668)

NAFLFD National Association of Federally Licensed Firearms Dealers (668)

NAfME The National Association for Music Education (Formerly MENC) (641)

NAFMNP National Association of Farmers Market Nutrition Programs (667)

NAFO National Alliance of Forest Owners (632)

NAFSA NAFSA: Association of International Educators (624)

NAFSC North American Farm Show Council (816)

NAFSMA National Association of Flood and Stormwater Management Agencies (668)

NAFTM National Association of Fundraising Ticket Manufacturers (669)

NAFTO National Association of Field Training Officers (669)

NAFTZ National Association of Foreign Trade Zones (669)

National Association of Healthcare Education Centers *(671)*

NAOC National Association of Ordnance and Explosive Waste Contractors *(682)*

NAON National Association of Orthopedic Nurses *(683)*

NAOO National Association of Optometrics and Opticians *(683)*

NAOOA North American Olive Oil Association *(819)*

NAOP National Association for Olmsted Parks *(641)*

NAOSMM National Association of Scientific Materials Managers *(694)*

NAOT National Association of Orthopaedic Technologists *(683)*

NAOWES National Association of Older Worker Employment Services *(683)*

NAP National Academies of Practice *(627)*

National Association of Parliamentarians *(683)*

NAPA National Academy of Public Administration *(628)*

National Asphalt Pavement Association *(635)*

National Association for the Practice of Anthropology *(644)*

NAPABA National Asian Pacific American Bar Association *(635)*

NAPAMA North American Performing Arts Managers and Agents *(819)*

NAPAR North American Perishable Agricultural Receivers *(819)*

NAPAW National Association of Professional Asian American Women *(686)*

NAPBIRT National Association of Professional Band Instrument Repair Technicians *(686)*

NAPBS National Association of Professional Background Screeners *(686)*

NAPC National Alliance of Preservation Commissions *(633)*

National Association of Planning Councils *(685)*

NAPCA National Association of Pipe Coating Applicators *(684)*

NAPCE North American Association of Professors of Christian Education *(813)*

NAPCOR National Association for PET Container Resources *(641)*

NAPCWA National Association of Public Child Welfare Administrators *(688)*

NAPE National Association of Partners in Education *(683)*

National Association of Power Engineers *(685)*

NAPEO National Association of Professional Employer Organizations *(687)*

NAPET National Association of Photo Equipment Technicians *(684)*

NAPF National Association of Pipe Fabricators *(684)*

NAPFA National Association of Personal Financial Advisors *(684)*

NAPFE National Alliance of Postal and Federal Employees *(633)*

NAPGCM National Association of Professional Geriatric Care Managers *(687)*

NAPH National Association of Professors of Hebrew *(688)*

National Association of Public Hospitals and Health Systems *(688)*

NAPHA North American Peruvian Horse Association *(819)*

NAPHS National Association of Psychiatric Health Systems *(688)*

NAPHSIS National Association of Public Health Statistics and Information Systems *(642)*

NAPIA National Association of Public Insurance Adjusters *(689)*

NAPIM National Association of Printing Ink Manufacturers *(686)*

NAPIPM National Association for Program Information and Performance Measurement *(641)*

NAPL National Association for Printing Leadership *(641)*

NAPMA North American Punch Manufacturers Association *(820)*

NAPMM National Association of Produce Market Managers *(686)*

NAPMW National Association of Professional Mortgage Women *(687)*

NAPN National Association of Physician Nurses *(684)*

NAPNAP National Association of Pediatric Nurse Practitioners *(684)*

NAPNES National Association for Practical Nurse Education and Service *(641)*

NAPNSC National Association of Private, Nontraditional Schools and Colleges *(686)*

NAPO National Association of Pizzeria Operators *(685)*

National Association of Police Organizations *(685)*

National Association of Professional Organizers *(687)*

NAPPA North American Polyelectrolyte Producers Association *(819)*

NAPPO National Association of Plant Patent Owners *(685)*

NAPPS National Association of Professional Pet Sitters *(687)*

National Association of Professional Process Servers *(688)*

NAPR National Association of Physician Recruiters *(684)*

The National Association of Professional Receptionists *(688)*

National Association of Publishers' Representatives *(689)*

NAPRHSW National Association of Puerto Rican-Hispanic Social Workers *(689)*

NAPS National Association of Personnel Services *(684)*

National Association of Postal Supervisors *(685)*

NAPSA National Appliance Parts Suppliers Association *(634)*

National Association of Pupil Services Administrators *(689)*

NAPSEC National Association of Private Special Education Centers *(686)*

NAPSG National Association of Principals of Schools for Girls *(686)*

NAPSLO National Association of Professional Surplus Lines Offices, Ltd. *(686)*

NAPT National Association for Poetry Therapy *(641)*

National Association for Proton Therapy *(642)*

National Association for Pupil Transportation *(642)*

NAPTP National Association of Publicly Traded Partnerships *(689)*

NAPTR-TEC National Association of Property Tax Representatives - Transportation, Energy, Communications *(688)*

NAPUS National Association of Postmasters of the United States *(685)*

NAPVS National Association of Passports and Visa Services *(683)*

NAPXP National Association of Portable X-Ray Providers *(685)*

NAR National Association of Realtors *(690)*

NARA National Aircraft Resale Association *(630)*

National Association of Rehabilitation Providers and Agencies *(690)*

NARA/MU National Association of Review Appraisers and Mortgage Underwriters *(692)*

NARAS National Academy of Recording Arts and Sciences *(628)*

NARBA North American Raspberry & Blackberry Association *(820)*

NARC National Association of Regional Councils *(690)*

NARC&DC National Association of Resource Conservation and Development Councils *(691)*

NARCA National Association of Retail Collection Attorneys *(692)*

NARDA North American Retail Dealers Association *(820)*

NAREA National Association of Real Estate Appraisers *(689)*

NAREB National Association of Real Estate Brokers *(689)*

NAREE National Association of Real Estate Editors *(690)*

NAREIM National Association of Real Estate Investment Managers *(690)*

NAREIT National Association of Real Estate Investment Trusts (NAREIT) *(690)*

NARFE National Active and Retired Federal Employees Association *(629)*

NARHC National Association of Rural Health Clinics *(692)*

NARI National Association of the Remodeling Industry *(705)*

NARM National Association of Recording Merchandisers (NARM) *(690)*

National Association of Reunion Managers *(692)*

NARME National Association for Relationship and Marriage Education *(642)*

NARMH National Association for Rural Mental Health *(642)*

NARMS National Association for Retail Marketing Services *(642)*

NARO National Association of Royalty Owners *(692)*

NARP National Association of Railroad Passengers *(689)*

NARPM National Association of Residential Property Managers *(691)*

NARRTC National Association of Rehabilitation Research and Training Centers *(691)*

NARS The North American Rail Shippers Association *(820)*

NARSA NARSA-The International Heal Transfer Association *(625)*

NARSC National Association of Reinforcing Steel Contractors *(691)*

NARST National Association for Research in Science Teaching *(642)*

NARSVPD National Association of Retired and Senior Volunteer Program Directors *(692)*

NARTC National Association of Railroad Trial Counsel *(689)*

NARTS National Association of Resale & Thrift Shops *(691)*

NARUC National Association of Regulatory Utility Commissioners *(691)*

NAS National Academy of Sciences *(628)*

NASA National Appliance Service Association *(635)*

National Association of State Archaeologists *(697)*

North American Saxophone Alliance *(820)*

NASAA National Assembly of State Arts Agencies *(635)*

North American Securities Administrators Association (NASAA) *(820)*

NASACT National Association of State Auditors, Comptrollers and Treasurers *(698)*

NASAD National Association of Schools of Art and Design *(693)*

NASADAD National Association of State Alcohol and Drug Abuse Directors (NASADAD) *(697)*

NASAE National Association of Supervisors of Agricultural Education *(704)*

NASAO National Association of State Aviation Officials *(698)*

NASAP National Association of Student Affairs Professionals *(703)*

North American Society of Adlerian Psychology *(822)*

NASAR National Association for Search and Rescue *(642)*

NASASP National Association of State Agencies for Surplus Property *(697)*

NASASPS National Association of State Administrators and Supervisors of Private Schools *(697)*

NASBA National Alliance of State Broadcast Associations *(633)*

National Association of State Boards of Accountancy *(698)*

NASBC National Association of Small Business Contractors *(696)*

NASBE National Association of State Boards of Education *(698)*

National Association of Supervisors for Business Education *(704)*

NASBG National Association of State Boards of Geology *(698)*

NASBITE North American Small Business International Trade Educators *(821)*

NASBLA National Association of State Boating Law Administrators *(698)*

NASBO National Association of State Budget Officers *(698)*

NASBP National Association of Surety Bond Producers *(704)*

NASBS North American Skull Base Society *(820)*

NASC National Animal Supplement Council *(634)*

National Association of Sports Commissions *(697)*

National Association of Student Councils *(703)*

NASCA National Association of State Chief Administrators *(699)*

NASCAT National Association of Shareholder and Consumer Attorneys *(696)*

NASCCD National Association of State Catholic Conference Directors *(698)*

NASCI North American Society for Cardiovascular Imaging *(821)*

NASCIO National Association of State Chief Information Officers *(699)*

NASCO National Association of Security Companies (NASCO) *(695)*

National Association of State Charity Officials *(699)*

North American Students of Cooperation *(822)*

NCQLP	National Council on Qualifications for the Lighting Professions *(739)*		National Demolition Association *(742)*
NCRA	National Cancer Registrars Association *(717)*		National Dental Association *(742)*
	National Court Reporters Association *(740)*		National Drilling Association *(743)*
	National Credit Reporting Association *(740)*	**NDAA**	National Dental Assistants Association *(742)*
NCRE	National Council on Rehabilitation Education *(739)*	**NDC**	National District Attorneys Association *(743)*
		NDCA	National Dairy Council *(741)*
NCREIF	National Council of Real Estate Investment Fiduciaries *(735)*	**NDCC**	National Dance Council of America *(741)*
		NDCI	National Defined Contribution Council *(742)*
NCRLL	National Conference on Research in Language and Literacy *(729)*	**NDEDIC**	National Drug Court Institute *(743)*
		NDEO	National Dental EDI Council *(743)*
NCRP	National Council on Radiation Protection and Measurement *(739)*		National Dance Education Organization *(742)*
NCRW	National Council for Research on Women *(732)*	**NDGAA**	National Dog Groomers Association of America, Inc. *(743)*
NCS	National Cartoonists Society *(718)*	**NDHA**	National Dental Hygienists' Association *(743)*
	National Center for Simulation *(719)*	**NDHIA**	National Dairy Herd Information Association *(741)*
NCSA	National Christian School Association *(721)*	**NDI**	Nickel Institute *(811)*
	National Confectionery Sales Association *(726)*	**NDIA**	National Defender Investigator Association *(742)*
NCSAB	National Council of State Agencies for the Blind *(736)*		National Defense Industrial Association *(742)*
NCSBN	National Council of State Boards for Nursing *(736)*	**NDTA**	National Defense Transportation Association *(742)*
NCSC	National Center for State Courts *(720)*		
NCSCJ	National Conference of Specialized Court Judges *(728)*		Neuro-Developmental Treatment Association *(808)*
NCSD	National Council on Student Development *(740)*	**NEA**	National Economic Association *(744)*
NCSDCC	National Council of State Directors of Community Colleges *(736)*		National Education Association *(744)*
		NEADA	National Energy Assistance Directors' Association *(746)*
NCSE	National Council for Science and the Environment *(733)*	**NEAFCS**	National Extension Association of Family and Consumer Sciences *(747)*
NCSEA	National Child Support Enforcement Association *(721)*	**NEBB**	National Environmental Balancing Bureau *(746)*
	National Council of Structural Engineers Associations *(737)*	**NEBSA**	National Educational Broadband Services Organization *(744)*
NCSFA	National Conference of State Fleet Administrators *(728)*	**NECA**	National Electrical Contractors Association *(744)*
NCSFPA	National Commodity Supplemental Food Program Association *(724)*		National Employment Counseling Association *(745)*
NCSG	National Chimney Sweep Guild *(721)*		National Exchange Carrier Association *(746)*
NCSHA	National Council of State Housing Agencies *(736)*	**NECMA**	New England Club Managers Association *(809)*
NCSHPO	National Conference of State Historic Preservation Officers *(728)*	**NEDA**	Electronic Components Industry Association *(423)*
NCSI	National Council of Self-Insurers *(736)*		National Eating Disorders Association *(743)*
NCSL	National Conference of State Legislatures *(728)*	**NEEDA**	National Emergency Equipment Dealers Association *(745)*
NCSLA	National Conference of State Liquor Administrators *(728)*	**NEHA**	National Environmental Health Association *(746)*
NCSLI	NCSL International *(808)*	**NEI**	Nuclear Energy Institute *(824)*
NCSM	National Council of Supervisors of Mathematics *(737)*	**NEII**	National Elevator Industry, Inc. *(745)*
NCSPA	National Corrugated Steel Pipe Association *(730)*	**NELA**	National Employment Lawyers Association (NELA) *(746)*
NCSS	National Council for the Social Studies *(733)*	**NELF**	National Elder Law Foundation *(744)*
NCSSFL	National Council of State Supervisors for Languages *(736)*	**NEMA**	National Electrical Manufacturers Association *(744)*
NCSSMA	National Council of Social Security Management Associations *(736)*		National Emergency Management Association *(745)*
NCSSSA	National Conference of State Social Security Administrators *(728)*	**NEMRA**	National Electrical Manufacturers Representatives Association *(745)*
NCSTD	National Council of State Tourism Directors *(736)*	**NEMSPA**	National EMS Pilots Association *(746)*
NCTA	National Cable & Telecommunications Association *(717)*	**NENA**	National Emergency Number Association *(745)*
	National Christmas Tree Association *(721)*	**NEON**	National Ecological Observatory Network, Inc *(743)*
	National Coal Transportation Association *(722)*	**NERA**	Naval Enlisted Reserve Association *(807)*
NCTE	National Council of Teachers of English *(737)*	**NERC**	North American Electric Reliability Corporation *(816)*
NCTM	National Council of Teachers of Mathematics *(737)*	**NESA**	National Energy Services Association *(746)*
NCTO	National Council of Textile Organizations *(737)*	**NESDA**	National Electronic Service Dealers Association *(745)*
NCTR	National Council on Teacher Retirement *(740)*	**NESHTA**	National Environmental, Safety and Health Training Association *(746)*
NCTRC	National Council for Therapeutic Recreation Certification *(733)*	**NESTA**	National Earth Science Teachers Association *(743)*
NCUEA	National Council of Urban Education Associations *(738)*	**NETA**	InterNational Electrical Testing Association *(542)*
NCURA	National Council of University Research Administrators *(737)*		National Educational Telecommunications Association *(744)*
NCWA	National Collegiate Wrestling Association *(724)*		National Exercise Trainers Association *(747)*
NCWBA	National Conference of Women's Bar Associations *(728)*	**NETFA**	National Exchange Traded Fund Association *(747)*
NCWE	National Council for Workforce Education *(733)*	**NEWH**	Network of Executive Women in Hospitality *(808)*
NCWGA	Natural Colored Wool Growers Association *(807)*	**NEXCO**	National Association of Export Companies *(666)*
NCWM	National Conference on Weights and Measures *(729)*	**NFA**	National Finance Adjusters *(750)*
NCY	National Collaboration for Youth *(723)*		The National Flute Association, Inc. *(751)*
NCYP	National Conference of Yeshiva Principals *(729)*		National Forensic Association *(752)*
			National Franchisee Association *(753)*
NDA	National Dance Association *(741)*		National Futures Association *(754)*
		NFAIS	National Federation of Advanced Information Services *(748)*
		NFBA	National Frame Building Association *(753)*

NFBPA	National Forum for Black Public Administrators *(752)*
NFCA	National Family Caregivers Association *(747)*
	National Federation Coaches Association *(748)*
	National Finishing Contractors Association *(751)*
NFCB	National Federation of Community Broadcasters *(748)*
NFCC	National Foundation for Credit Counseling *(753)*
NFCCE	National Fellowship of Child Care Executives *(750)*
NFCDCU	National Federation of Community Development of Credit Unions *(748)*
NFD&MA	National Funeral Directors and Morticians Association *(754)*
NFDA	National Fastener Distributors Association *(747)*
	National Funeral Directors Association *(754)*
NFE	Northwest Fruit Exporters *(824)*
NFFE	National Federation of Federal Employees *(748)*
	National Federation of Federal Employees, Federal Dist. 1, IAMAW, AFL-CIO *(748)*
NFFS	Non-Ferrous Founders' Society *(811)*
NFHS	National Federation of State High School Associations *(750)*
NFHS MA	NFHS Music Association *(810)*
NFHS SDTA	NFHS Speech Debate and Theatre Association *(810)*
NFI	National Fisheries Institute *(751)*
NFIB	National Federation of Independent Business (NFIB) *(748)*
NFL	National Football League *(752)*
	Nisei Farmers League *(811)*
NFLPA	National Football League Players Association *(752)*
NFLPN	National Federation of Licensed Practical Nurses *(749)*
NFMA	National Federation of Municipal Analysts *(749)*
	National Flea Market Association *(751)*
NFMC	National Federation of Music Clubs *(749)*
NFMLTA	National Federation of Modern Language Teachers Associations *(749)*
NFNSSAA	The National Federation of Nonpublic School State Accrediting Associations *(749)*
NFO	National Farmers Organization *(747)*
NFOP	National Fraternal Order of Police *(753)*
NFPA	The National Federation of Paralegal Associations, Inc. *(749)*
	National Fire Protection Association *(751)*
	National Fluid Power Association *(751)*
	National Foster Parent Association *(753)*
NFPC	National Federation of Priests' Councils *(749)*
NFPI	National Frozen Pizza Institute *(754)*
NFPRHA	National Family Planning and Reproductive Health Association *(747)*
NFPW	National Federation of Press Women *(749)*
NFRA	National Forest Recreation Association *(752)*
	National Frozen and Refrigerated Foods Association *(753)*
NFRC	National Fenestration Rating Council *(750)*
NFRW	National Federation of Republican Women *(750)*
NFSA	National Field Selling Association *(750)*
	National Fire Sprinkler Association *(751)*
NFSSC	National Food Service Security Council *(752)*
NFTA	National Freight Transportation Association *(753)*
NFTC	National Foreign Trade Council, Inc. *(752)*
NFU	National Farmers Union (Farmers Educational & Co-operative Union of America) *(747)*
NFWL	National Foundation for Women Legislators *(753)*
NGA	National Glass Association *(755)*
	National Governors Association *(755)*
	National Greyhound Association *(756)*
	National Grocers Association *(756)*
	National Guardianship Association *(757)*
NGAUS	National Guard Association of the U.S. *(757)*
NGC	National Garden Clubs *(754)*
NGCOA	National Golf Course Owners Association *(755)*
NGEDA	National Guard Executive Directors Association *(757)*
NGF	National Golf Foundation *(755)*
NGFA	National Grain and Feed Association *(755)*
NGMA	National Grants Management Association *(756)*
	The National Greenhouse Manufacturers Association *(756)*

NGNA	National Gerontological Nursing Association *(755)*	**NIHSDA**	National Indian Head Start Directors Association *(763)*
NGNP	NGNP Industry Alliance *(810)*	**NILA**	National Independent Laboratory Association *(762)*
NGPA	National Government Publishing Association *(755)*		National Independent Living Association *(762)*
NGPP	National Guild of Professional Paperhangers *(757)*	**NIMS**	Network of Ingredient Marketing Specialists *(808)*
NGPT	National Guild of Piano Teachers *(757)*	**NINFRA**	National Independent Nursery Furniture Retailers Association *(762)*
NGS	National Genealogical Society *(754)*	**NIO**	Neurotechnology Industry Organization *(809)*
NGSA	Natural Gas Supply Association *(807)*	**NIOP**	National Institute of Oilseed Products *(765)*
NGTC	National Grain Trade Council *(756)*	**NIPA**	National Institute of Pension Administrators *(765)*
NGVA	NGVAmerica *(810)*		
NGWA	National Ground Water Association *(756)*	**NIPHLE**	National Institute of Packaging, Handling and Logistics Engineers *(765)*
NH&RA	National Housing and Rehabilitation Association *(760)*	**NIPSA**	National Independent Private Schools Association *(762)*
NHA	National Hay Association *(758)*	**NIRI**	National Investor Relations Institute *(767)*
	National Health Association *(758)*	**NIRMA**	Nuclear Information and Records Management Association *(825)*
	National Humanities Alliance *(761)*	**NIRSA**	National Intramural-Recreational Sports Association *(766)*
	National Hydropower Association *(761)*	**NISA**	National Industrial Sand Association *(763)*
NHC	National Health Council *(758)*	**NISC**	National Institute of Senior Centers *(765)*
	National Housing Conference *(761)*	**NISCA**	National Interscholastic Swimming Coaches Association *(766)*
NHCA	National Health Club Association *(758)*	**NISCUE**	National Institute for State Credit Union Examination *(764)*
	National Hearing Conservation Association *(758)*	**NISD**	National Institute of Steel Detailing *(765)*
NHCAA	National Health Care Anti-Fraud Association *(758)*	**NISH**	National Institute of Senior Housing *(765)*
NHCC	National Hispanic Corporate Council *(759)*	**NISO**	National Information Standards Organization *(763)*
NHF	National Health Federation *(758)*	**NISOA**	National Intercollegiate Soccer Officials Association *(766)*
	National Hemophilia Foundation *(759)*	**NITL**	The National Industrial Transportation League *(763)*
NHFA	National Home Furnishings Association *(759)*	**NIWR**	National Institute for Water Resources *(766)*
NHHRA	National Hereford Hog Record Association *(759)*	**NJA**	National Judges Association *(767)*
NHIA	National Home Infusion Association *(760)*	**NJCAA**	National Junior College Athletic Association *(767)*
NHL	National Hockey League *(759)*	**NJCSA**	National Juvenile Court Services Association *(767)*
NHLA	National Hardwood Lumber Association *(757)*	**NKBA**	National Kitchen and Bath Association *(767)*
NHMA	National Hispanic Medical Association *(759)*	**NLA**	National Lime Association *(769)*
NHPC	National Home Performance Council, Inc. *(760)*		National Limousine Association *(770)*
NHPCO	National Hospice & Palliative Care Organization *(760)*		National Lipid Association *(770)*
NHPDA	National Honey Packers and Dealers Association *(760)*	**NLADA**	National Legal Aid and Defender Association *(769)*
NHRA	National Human Resources Association *(761)*	**NLAE**	Nursery and Landscape Association Executives of North America *(825)*
NHSA	National Head Start Association *(758)*	**NLAPW**	National League of American Pen Women *(768)*
	National Human Services Assembly *(761)*	**NLB**	National Lighting Bureau *(769)*
NHSACA	National High School Athletic Coaches Association *(759)*	**NLBMDA**	National Lumber and Building Material Dealers Association *(770)*
NIA	National Insulation Association *(766)*	**NLC**	Hispanic Elected Local Officials *(475)*
NIAA	National Institute for Animal Agriculture *(764)*		National League of Cities *(768)*
NIAAA	National Interscholastic Athletic Administrators Association *(766)*	**NLDA**	National Luggage Dealers Association *(770)*
NIADA	National Independent Automobile Dealers Association *(761)*	**NLFA**	National Lamb Feeders Association *(768)*
	National Institute of American Doll Artists *(764)*	**NLG**	National Lawyers Guild *(768)*
NIB	National Industries for the Blind *(763)*	**NLGA**	National Lieutenant Governors Association *(769)*
NIBA	National Investment Banking Association *(767)*	**NLGI**	National Lubricating Grease Institute *(770)*
	NIBA - The Belting Association *(810)*	**NLGJA**	National Lesbian and Gay Journalists Association *(769)*
NIBIC	National Institute of Business and Industrial Chaplaincy *(764)*	**NLHA**	National Leased Housing Association *(769)*
NIBS	National Institute of Building Sciences *(764)*	**NLN**	National League for Nursing *(768)*
NIC	National Industrial Council - Employer Association Group *(763)*	**NLPA**	National Livestock Producers Association *(770)*
	North - American Interfraternity Conference *(812)*	**NLPM**	National League of Postmasters of the United States *(768)*
NIC/SAG	National Industrial Council - State Associations Group *(763)*	**NLRBPA**	National Labor Relations Board Professional Association *(768)*
NICA	National Independent Concessionaires Association *(762)*	**NLSBA**	National Lincoln Sheep Breeders Association *(770)*
NICB	National Insurance Crime Bureau *(766)*	**NLUS**	Navy League of the United States *(807)*
NICE	National Institute of Ceramic Engineers *(764)*	**NMA**	National Management Association *(771)*
NICMA	National Ice Cream Mix Association *(761)*		National Maritime Alliance *(772)*
NICRA	National Ice Cream Retailers Association *(761)*		National Medical Association *(772)*
NICSA	National Investment Company Service Association *(767)*		National Mining Association *(772)*
NICSBC	National Interstate Council of State Boards of Cosmetology *(766)*	**NMBA**	National Marine Bankers Association *(771)*
NIEA	National Indian Education Association *(762)*		National Mitigation Banking Association *(773)*
NIEI	National Institute of Electromedical Information *(765)*	**NMBC**	National Minority Business Council *(773)*
NIFAD	National Independent Fire Alarm Distributors *(762)*	**NMC**	National Mastitis Council *(772)*
NIFDA	National Independent Flag Dealers Association *(762)*		National Music Council *(774)*
NIFS	National Institute for Farm Safety, Incorporation *(764)*		The New Media Consortium *(809)*
NIGA	National Indian Gaming Association *(762)*	**NMDA**	National Marine Distributors Association *(771)*
NIGP	National Institute of Governmental Purchasing *(765)*		National Miniature Donkey Association *(772)*
		NMEA	National Marine Educators Association *(771)*
			National Marine Electronics Association *(771)*

NMEDA	National Mobility Equipment Dealers Association *(773)*
NMFTA	National Motor Freight Traffic Association, Inc. *(773)*
NMHC	National Multi-Housing Council *(774)*
NMIA	National Military Intelligence Association *(772)*
NMMA	National Marine Manufacturers Association *(771)*
NMOA	National Mail Order Association *(771)*
NMPA	National Motorsports Press Association *(773)*
	National Music Publishers Association *(774)*
NMPF	National Milk Producers Federation *(772)*
NMRA	National Marine Representatives Association *(771)*
NMSA	National Maritime Safety Association *(772)*
NMSDC	National Minority Supplier Development Council *(773)*
NMSHSA	National Migrant and Seasonal Head Start Association *(772)*
NMSS	National Multiple Sclerosis Society *(774)*
NNA	National Newspaper Association *(775)*
	National Notary Association *(775)*
NNDC	National Network of Depression Centers *(775)*
NNEPA	National Network of Estate Planning Attorneys *(775)*
NNG	National Network of Grantmakers *(775)*
NNGA	Northern Nut Growers Association *(824)*
NNOA	National Naval Officers Association *(774)*
NNOAC	National Narcotics Officers Associations' Coalition *(774)*
NNPA	National Newspaper Publishers Association *(775)*
NNRG	Northwest Natural Resource Group *(824)*
NNSC	Network of Nonprofit Search Consultants *(808)*
NNSWM	The National Network for Social Work Managers *(774)*
NNU	National Nurses United *(775)*
NOA	National Onion Association *(776)*
	National Opera Association *(776)*
	National Optometric Association *(776)*
NOBCChE	National Organization for the Professional Advancement of Black Chemists and Chemical Engineers *(777)*
NOBCO	National Organization of Black County Officials *(777)*
NOBLE	National Organization of Black Law Enforcement Executives *(777)*
NOCSAE	National Operating Committee for Standards of Athletic Equipment *(776)*
NODA	National Orientation Directors Association *(778)*
NOFA	Northeast Organic Farming Association *(824)*
NOGGA	National Ornamental Goldfish Growers Association *(778)*
NOHS	National Organization for Human Service *(777)*
NOIA	National Ocean Industries Association *(775)*
NOITU	National Organization of Industrial Trade Unions *(777)*
NOLHGA	National Organization of Life and Health Insurance Guaranty Association *(777)*
NOLSW	National Organization of Legal Services Workers *(777)*
NOMAA	National Office Managers Association of America *(775)*
NOMMA	National Ornamental and Miscellaneous Metals Association *(778)*
NONPF	National Organization of Nurse Practitioner Faculties *(777)*
NOPA	National Office Products Alliance *(776)*
	National Oilseed Processors Association *(776)*
NORA	NORA: Association of Responsible Recyclers *(811)*
NOSAC	National Organization of State Associations for Children *(778)*
NOSORH	National Organization of State Offices of Rural Health *(778)*
NOSSCR	National Organization of Social Security Claimants' Representatives *(778)*
NOST	National On-Site Testing Association *(776)*
NOVA	Nurses Organization of Veterans Affairs *(825)*
NOWRA	National Onsite Wastewater Recycling Association *(776)*
NPA	National Pace Association *(778)*
	National Paralegal Association *(779)*
	National Parking Association *(779)*
	National Pasta Association *(779)*
	National Pawnbrokers Association *(779)*
	National Perinatal Association *(780)*
	National Phlebotomy Association *(781)*

	Natural Products Association **(807)**		National Retail Federation **(786)**	**NSNA**	National Student Nurses Association **(797)**
	Network Professional Association **(808)**	**NRHA**	National Reining Horse Association **(785)**	**NSNC**	National Society of Newspaper Columnists **(794)**
NPAC	National Association of Nonprofit Accountants & Consultants **(682)**		National Rural Health Association **(788)**	**NSP**	National Ski Patrol System **(792)**
	Not-For-Profit Services Association **(824)**		North American Retail Hardware Association **(820)**		National Sorghum Producers **(795)**
NPAP	National Psychological Association for Psychoanalysis **(783)**	**NRHS**	National Railway Historical Society **(784)**	**NSPA**	National Scholastic Press Association **(789)**
NPB	National Plant Board **(781)**	**NRHSA**	National Retail Hobby Stores Association **(786)**	**NSPCA**	The National Society of Painters in Casein and Acrylic **(794)**
NPBOA	National Party Boat Owners Alliance **(779)**	**NRHSPP**	National Register of Health Service Providers in Psychology **(785)**	**NSPE**	National Society of Professional Engineers **(794)**
NPBPA	National Peanut Buying Point Association **(780)**	**NRLC**	National Railway Labor Conference **(784)**	**NSPRA**	National School Public Relations Association **(789)**
NPC	National Panhellenic Conference **(778)**	**NRLCA**	National Rural Letter Carriers' Association **(788)**	**NSPS**	National Society of Professional Surveyors **(794)**
	National Peach Council **(780)**	**NRMCA**	National Ready Mixed Concrete Association **(784)**	**NSR**	National Swine Registry **(798)**
	National Petroleum Council **(780)**	**NRMLA**	National Reverse Mortgage Lenders Association **(787)**	**NSRA**	National Shoe Retailers Association **(791)**
	National Pharmaceutical Council **(780)**	**NRPA**	National Recreation and Parks Association **(784)**	**NSREA**	National Society of Real Estate Appraisers, Inc. **(795)**
	National Plasterers Council **(781)**	**NRRA**	National Risk Retention Association **(787)**	**NSRMCA**	National Star Route Mail Contractors Association **(796)**
	National Potato Council **(782)**	**NRTA**	National Retail Tenants Association **(787)**	**NSS**	National Sculpture Society **(790)**
NPCA	National Parks Conservation Association **(779)**	**NRTC**	National Rural Telecommunications Cooperative **(788)**		National Speleological Society **(795)**
	National Precast Concrete Association **(782)**	**NRTO**	National Remotivation Therapy Organization **(786)**	**NSSA**	National Sportscasters and Sportswriters Association and Hall of Fame **(796)**
NPELRA	National Public Employer Labor Relations Association **(783)**	**NRVMA**	National Roadside Vegetation Management Association **(787)**	**NSSEA**	National School Supply and Equipment Association **(789)**
NPES	NPES, The Association for Suppliers of Printing, Publishing, and Converting Technologies **(824)**	**NRWA**	National Rural Water Association **(788)**	**NSSF**	National Shooting Sports Foundation **(791)**
NPFDA	National Poultry and Food Distributors Association **(782)**	**NSA**	National Shellfisheries Association **(790)**	**NSSGA**	National Stone, Sand, and Gravel Association **(796)**
NPGA	National Propane Gas Association **(783)**		National Sheriffs' Association **(791)**	**NSSHA**	National Spotted Saddle Horse Association **(796)**
NPHA	National Park Hospitality Association **(779)**		National Slag Association **(792)**	**NSSLHA**	National Student Speech Language Hearing Association **(796)**
	National Prison Hospice Association **(782)**		National Society of Accountants **(793)**	**NSSR**	National Spotted Swine Records **(796)**
NPHC	National Pan-Hellenic Council **(778)**		National Speakers Association **(795)**	**NSSRA**	National Ski and Snowboard Retailers Association **(791)**
NPI	The National Procurement Institute, Inc **(783)**		National Stroke Association **(797)**	**NSSTA**	National Structured Settlements Trade Association **(797)**
NPM	National Association of Pastoral Musicians **(683)**		National Subcontractors Alliance **(798)**	**NSTA**	National School Transportation Association **(790)**
NPMA	National Pest Management Association **(780)**		National Sunflower Association **(798)**		National Science Teachers Association **(790)**
	National Petroleum Management Association **(780)**		National Sunroom Association **(798)**	**NSWA**	National Stripper Well Association **(797)**
	National Property Management Association **(783)**		Neurosurgical Society of America **(809)**	**NSWMA**	National Solid Wastes Management Association **(795)**
	Newspaper Purchasing Management Association **(810)**		Nuclear Suppliers Association **(825)**	**NTA**	National Tax Association **(799)**
NPMHU	National Postal Mail Handlers Union **(781)**	**NSAA**	National Ski Area Association **(791)**		National Taxidermists Association **(799)**
NPNFF	National Practitioners Network for Fathers and Family **(782)**		National Surgical Assistant Association **(798)**		National Technical Association **(799)**
NPPA	National Press Photographers Association **(782)**	**NSAC**	National Society of Accountants for Cooperatives **(793)**		National Textile Association **(800)**
NPPC	National Pork Producers Association **(781)**	**NSAI**	Nashville Songwriters Association, International **(625)**		National Tour Association **(800)**
	National Pork Producers Council **(781)**	**NSBA**	National School Boards Association **(789)**		National Translator Association **(801)**
	National Postal Policy Council **(781)**		National Small Business Association **(792)**		National Trappers Association **(801)**
NPRC	National Payroll Reporting Consortium **(780)**		National Steel Bridge Alliance **(796)**		National Tutoring Association **(803)**
NPSA	National Pecan Shellers Association **(780)**	**NSBE**	National Society of Black Engineers **(793)**	**NTBA**	National Transit Benefits Association **(801)**
	National Portable Storage Association **(781)**	**NSBP**	National Society of Black Physicists **(793)**	**NTC**	National Trooper's Coalition **(802)**
NPSOAA	National Police and Security Officers Association of America **(781)**	**NSC**	National Safety Council **(789)**	**NTCA**	National Telecommunications Cooperative Association **(799)**
NPSS	IEEE - Nuclear and Plasma Sciences Society **(482)**		Natural Science Collections Alliance **(807)**		National Tile Contractors Association **(800)**
NPTA	NPTA Alliance **(824)**	**NSCA**	National Senior Corps Association **(790)**		National Tuberculosis Controllers Association **(802)**
NPTC	National Private Truck Council **(782)**		National Strength and Conditioning Association **(797)**	**NTDA**	National Trailer Dealers Association **(801)**
NPWH	National Association of Nurse Practitioners in Women's Health **(682)**		National Systems Contractors Association **(798)**	**NTEA**	National Truck Equipment Association **(802)**
NQPC	National Quartz Producers Council **(783)**	**NSCAA**	National Soccer Coaches Association of America **(792)**	**NTEN**	Nonprofit Technology Network **(811)**
NRA	National Rehabilitation Association **(785)**	**NSCHBC**	National Society of Certified Healthcare Business Consultants **(793)**	**NTERTANKO**	International Association of Independent Tanker Owners **(523)**
	National Renderers Association **(786)**	**NSCIA**	National Spinal Cord Injury Association **(795)**	**NTEU**	National Treasury Employees Union **(801)**
	National Restaurant Association **(786)**	**NSCP**	National Society of Compliance Professionals **(793)**	**NTF**	National Turfgrass Federation **(802)**
	National Rifle Association of America **(787)**	**NSDC**	Learning Forward **(596)**		National Turkey Federation **(802)**
NRAA	National Renal Administrators Association **(786)**	**NSDTA**	National Staff Development and Training Association **(796)**	**NTHECC**	National Truck and Heavy Equipment Claims Council **(802)**
NRAL	National Association for Rehabilitation Leadership **(642)**	**NSEA**	National Student Employment Association **(797)**	**NTLA**	National Tax Lien Association **(799)**
NRB	National Religious Broadcasters **(785)**	**NSEE**	National Society for Experiential Education **(792)**	**NTLS**	National Truck Leasing System **(802)**
NRBMLC	National Religious Broadcasters, Music License Committee **(785)**	**NSFC**	National Society of Film Critics **(793)**	**NTMA**	National Terrazzo and Mosaic Association **(800)**
NRC	National Railroad Construction and Maintenance Association, Inc. **(783)**	**NSG**	National Society for Graphology **(792)**		National Tooling and Machining Association **(800)**
	National Recycling Coalition **(784)**	**NSGA**	National Sporting Goods Association **(796)**	**NTOA**	National Tactical Officers Association of America **(799)**
NRCA	National Rehabilitation Counseling Association **(785)**	**NSGC**	National Society of Genetic Counselors **(794)**	**NTPA**	National Tractor Pullers Association **(801)**
	National Roofing Contractors Association **(787)**	**NSH**	National Society for Histotechnology **(792)**	**NTPDA**	National Tractor Parts Dealer Association **(801)**
NRCAT	National Religious Campaign Against Torture **(786)**	**NSHDS**	National Society for Hebrew Day Schools **(792)**	**NTRA**	National Thoroughbred Racing Association **(800)**
NRCC	National Republican Congressional Committee **(786)**	**NSHMBA**	National Society of Hispanic MBAs **(794)**	**NTRS**	National Therapeutic Recreation Society **(800)**
NRDCA	National Roof Deck Contractors Association **(787)**	**NSHR**	National Show Horse Registry **(791)**	**NTSA**	National Training and Simulation Association **(801)**
NREA	National Rural Education Association **(788)**	**NSIF**	National Swine Improvement Federation **(798)**	**NTSRI**	National Tunis Sheep Registry **(802)**
NRECA	National Rural Electric Cooperative Association **(788)**	**NSIMA**	National Sweetener and Ingredient Marketing Association **(798)**	**NTTC**	National Tank Truck Carriers **(799)**
NREDA	National Rural Economic Developers Association **(788)**	**NSIPA**	National Society of Insurance Premium Auditors **(794)**	**NTWA**	National Turf Writers and Broadcasters **(802)**
NREP	National Registry of Environmental Professionals **(785)**	**NSL**	Naval Submarine League **(807)**	**NUCA**	National Utility Contractors Association (NUCA) **(803)**
NRF	National Research Council **(786)**	**NSLEA**	National Science Education Leadership Association **(790)**	**NUMBA**	National United Merchants Beverage Association **(803)**
		NSMA	National Seasoning Manufacturers Association **(790)**	**NUSACC**	National U.S.-Arab Chamber of Commerce **(803)**
		NSMP	National Society of Mural Painters **(794)**		
		NSMS	The National Safety Management Society **(789)**		

NVCA	National Venture Capital Association *(803)*	OPASTCO	Organization for the Promotion and Advancement of Small Telecommunications Companies *(831)*	PAUS	Piedmontese Association of the United States *(848)*	

National Venture Capital Association *(803)*
NVCA
NVFC National Volunteer Fire Council *(803)*
NVLA National Vehicle Leasing Association *(803)*
NVRA National Verbatim Reporters Association *(803)*
NVV Napa Valley Vintners Association *(625)*
NWA National Watermelon Association *(804)*
National Weather Association *(804)*
National WIC Association *(805)*
National Writers Association *(806)*
NWBA National Wheelchair Basketball Association *(804)*
NWC National Waterways Conference *(804)*
NWCA National Wrestling Coaches Association *(806)*
NWF National Wildlife Federation *(805)*
NWFA National Wood Flooring Association *(805)*
NWI National Wellness Institute, Inc. *(804)*
NWOA National Woodland Owners Association *(806)*
NWP National Woman's Party *(805)*
NWPCA National Wooden Pallet and Container Association *(805)*
NWRA National Water Resources Association *(804)*
National Wildlife Rehabilitators Association *(805)*
NWS National Watercolor Society *(804)*
NWSA National Women's Studies Association *(805)*
NWSEO National Weather Service Employees Organization *(804)*
NWTI National Wood Tank Institute *(805)*
NWU National Writers Union *(806)*
NYA National Yogurt Association *(806)*
NYAS The New York Academy of Sciences *(809)*
NYFEA National Young Farmers Education Association *(806)*
OA Osborne Association *(834)*
OAA Opticians Association of America *(829)*
OAAA Outdoor Advertising Association of America *(834)*
OABA Outdoor Amusement Business Association *(834)*
OAGi Open Applications Group *(828)*
OAH Organization of American Historians *(832)*
OAKE Organization of American Kodaly Educators *(832)*
OAOA Outfitters Association of America *(835)*
OARSI Osteoarthritis Research Society International *(834)*
OASIS Organization for the Advancement of Structured Information Standards *(831)*
OBD Organization of Black Designers *(832)*
OBTS Organizational Behavior Teaching Society *(832)*
OCEMA Ocean Carrier Equipment Management Association (OCEMA) *(825)*
OCIA Organic Crop Improvement Association International *(830)*
OCPA Ornamental Concrete Producers Association *(833)*
OD Omega Delta *(827)*
OD Network Organization Development Network *(831)*
ODI Organization Development Institute *(830)*
OEP Optometric Extension Program Foundation *(830)*
OES Oceanic Engineering Society *(826)*
OESA Original Equipment Suppliers Association *(833)*
OESP OESP - National Association of Oil and Energy Service Professionals *(826)*
OFA Organization of Flying Adjusters *(832)*
OFB Oregon Farm Bureau Federation *(830)*
OFDA Office Furniture Dealers Alliance *(826)*
Office Furniture Distribution Association *(827)*
OFII Organization for International Investment *(831)*
OFN Opportunity Finance Network *(829)*
OFS Order Fulfillment Solutions *(830)*
OGC Open Geospatial Consortium *(828)*
OGR International Order of the Golden Rule *(559)*
OHA Oral History Association *(830)*
OIA Outdoor Industry Association *(835)*
OIDA Optoelectronics Industry Development Association *(830)*
OKU Omicron Kappa Upsilon *(827)*
OLA Online Lenders Alliance *(827)*
The Optical Lab Division *(829)*
OLAC Online Audiovisual Catalogers *(827)*
OMA Open Mobile Alliance *(828)*
OMG Object Management Group *(825)*
OMSA Offshore Marine Service Association *(827)*
ONA Online News Association *(827)*
ONS Oncology Nursing Society *(827)*
OOIDA Owner-Operator Independent Drivers Association, Inc. *(836)*
OOSS Outpatient Ophthalmic Surgery Society *(835)*
OPA Online Publishers Association, Inc. *(828)*

OPC Overseas Press Club of America *(835)*
OPCMIA Operative Plasterers and Cement Masons International Association of the United States and Canada *(829)*
OPEAA Outdoor Power Equipment Aftermarket Association *(835)*
OPEDA Organization of Professional Employees of the U.S. Department of Agriculture (OPEDA) *(832)*
OPEESA Outdoor Power Equipment and Engine Service Association *(835)*
OPEI Outdoor Power Equipment Institute *(835)*
OPEIU Office and Professional Employees International Union (OPEIU) *(826)*
OPIA Optical Imaging Association *(829)*
OPS Ophthalmic Photographers' Society *(829)*
OPSEC Operations Security Professionals Society *(828)*
ORBA Off-Road Business Association *(826)*
ORCA Ocean Research & Conservation Association *(826)*
ORCS Organic Reactions Catalysis Society *(830)*
ORIA Oriental Rug Importers Association of America *(833)*
ORRA Oriental Rug Retailers of America, Inc. *(833)*
ORS Orthopaedic Research Society *(833)*
ORTHO American Orthopsychiatric Association *(159)*
OSA Optical Society of America *(829)*
OSAP Organization for Safety and Asepsis Procedures *(831)*
OSMA Orthopedic Surgical Manufacturers Association *(834)*
OSRA Organizational Systems Research Association *(833)*
OSSD Organization for the Study of Sex Differences *(831)*
OSTA Optical Storage Technology Association *(829)*
OTA Organic Trade Association *(830)*
Orthopaedic Trauma Association *(834)*
OTS Omega Tau Sigma *(827)*
Organization for Tropical Studies *(831)*
OTSA Orthodox Theological Society in America *(833)*
OWAA Outdoor Writers Association of America *(835)*
OWIT Organization of Women in International Trade *(832)*
OWP Organization of Wildlife Planners *(832)*
P2PI Path to Purchase Institute *(839)*
PA Parapsychological Association *(838)*
Parliamentary Associates *(839)*
PAA Performing Arts Alliance *(841)*
Population Association of America *(853)*
Potato Association of America *(854)*
PAAO Pan American Association of Ophthalmology *(837)*
PAAS Pan American Allergy Society *(837)*
PABA Pakistan American Business Association *(837)*
PAC Public Affairs Council *(868)*
PACA Picture Archive Council of America *(848)*
PACE Professional Association of Christian Educators *(859)*
PAD Phi Alpha Delta *(845)*
PADA Private Art Dealers Association *(858)*
PADI Professional Association of Diving Instructors *(859)*
PAEA Physician Assistant Education Association *(847)*
PAHCOM Professional Association of Health Care Office Management *(859)*
PAHRA Partnership for Air-Conditioning, Heating Refrigeration Accreditation *(839)*
PAI Population Action International *(852)*
PAII Professional Association of Innkeepers International *(860)*
PAL National Association of Police Athletics/ Activities Leagues, Inc. *(685)*
PAMA Professional Aviation Maintenance Association *(860)*
PARMA Public Agency Risk Managers Association *(859)*
PARW/CC Professional Association of Resume Writers and Career Coaches *(860)*
PAS National Postsecondary Agriculture Student Organization *(781)*
Percussive Arts Society *(841)*
PASS Professional Aviation Safety Specialists (AFL-CIO) *(860)*
PAT Phi Alpha Theta *(845)*
PATCA Professional and Technical Consultants Association *(859)*
PATMI Powder Actuated Tool Manufacturers Institute *(854)*

PAUS Piedmontese Association of the United States *(848)*
PAVO Professional Association of Volleyball Officials *(860)*
PBA Poultry Breeders of America *(854)*
Professional Bowlers Association *(861)*
PBA | NCA Professional Beauty Association | National Cosmetology Association *(861)*
PBAA Periodical and Book Association of America *(842)*
PBATS Professional Baseball Athletic Trainers Society *(860)*
PBBAI Printing Brokerage/Buyers Association International *(857)*
PBUS Professional Bail Agents of the United States *(860)*
PBWA Professional Basketball Writers' Association *(860)*
PCA Pine Chemicals Association *(848)*
Plumbing Contractors of America *(851)*
Portland Cement Association *(853)*
Print Council of America *(857)*
PCATS Petroleum Convenience Alliance for Technology Standards *(843)*
PCCA Portable Computer and Communications Association *(853)*
Power and Communications Contractors Association *(855)*
PCDA Professional Currency Dealers Association *(861)*
PCEA Professional Construction Estimators Association of America *(861)*
PCG Plains Cotton Growers, Inc. *(849)*
PCI Powder Coating Institute *(854)*
Precast/Prestressed Concrete Institute *(856)*
Property Casualty Insurers Association of America *(867)*
PCIA PCIA - The Wireless Infrastructure Association *(840)*
PCMA Pharmaceutical Care Management Association *(844)*
Professional Convention Management Association *(861)*
PCMI Photo Chemical Machining Institute *(846)*
PCNA Preventive Cardiovascular Nurses Association *(857)*
PCPA Protestant Church-Owned Publishers Association *(868)*
PCPC Personal Care Products Council *(842)*
PCRA Poland China Record Association *(852)*
PCS Professional Communications Society *(861)*
PCSA Power Crane and Shovel Association *(855)*
PCT Phi Chi Theta *(845)*
PCUS The Propeller Club of the United States *(867)*
PDA Parenteral Drug Association *(838)*
PDC Phi Delta Chi *(845)*
PDCA Painting and Decorating Contractors of America *(837)*
Pile Driving Contractors Association *(848)*
Purebred Dairy Cattle Association *(871)*
PDI Plumbing and Drainage Institute *(850)*
PDK Phi Delta Kappa International *(845)*
PDMA Product Development and Management Association *(858)*
PDP International Legal Fraternity of Phi Delta Phi *(554)*
PDRA Paint and Decorating Retailers Association *(836)*
PEGCC Private Equity Growth Capital Council *(858)*
PEI Petroleum Equipment Institute *(843)*
Porcelain Enamel Institute *(853)*
PEMA Process Equipment Manufacturers' Association *(858)*
PEN Public Education Network *(869)*
PEPP Professional Engineers in Private Practice *(861)*
PER Public Employees Roundtable *(869)*
PERA Production Engine Remanufacturers Association *(859)*
Production Equipment Rental Association *(859)*
PERC Propane Engine Fuel Committee/Propane Education and Research Council *(867)*
PERF Police Executive Research Forum *(859)*
PERI Pharmaceutical Education and Research Institute *(844)*
PES Pediatric Endocrine Society *(840)*
Philosophy of Education Society *(846)*
PESA Petroleum Equipment Suppliers Association *(843)*
PETRA PET Resin Association *(843)*
PFA Pedorthic Footwear Association *(840)*
Pierre Fauchard Academy *(848)*
Polyurethane Foam Association *(852)*
Professional Fraternity Association *(862)*

RCC	Research Chefs Association *(882)*
	Religion Communicators Council *(880)*
RCFC	Refractory Ceramic Fibers Coalition *(878)*
RCI	Association of Racing Commissioners International *(304)*
	RCI, Inc. *(875)*
	Retail Confectioners International *(884)*
RCMA	Religious Conference Management Association *(880)*
	Roof Coatings Manufacturers Association *(888)*
RCRA	Resort and Commercial Recreation Association *(883)*
RCRI	Resource Center for Religious Institutes *(883)*
RCSC	Research Council on Structural Connections *(882)*
REA	Religious Education Association *(880)*
REACT	React International *(875)*
REBAC	Real Estate Buyers Agent Council *(875)*
REEA	Real Estate Educators Association *(875)*
REIPA	Real Estate Information Professionals Association *(875)*
REISA	Real Estate Investment Securities Association *(875)*
REMBI	Real Estate Management Brokers Institute *(875)*
REMSA	Railway Engineering-Maintenance Suppliers Association *(874)*
RER	Real Estate Roundtable *(876)*
RERC	Rural Electricity Resource Council *(889)*
RESNA	Rehabilitation Engineering and Assistive Technology Society of North America *(879)*
RESOLVE	Resolve, The National Infertility Association *(883)*
RESPRO	RESPRO (Real Estate Services Providers Council) *(883)*
RETA	Refrigerating Engineers and Technicians Association *(878)*
REVAA	Real Estate Valuation Advocacy Association *(876)*
RFA	Refrigerated Foods Association *(878)*
	Renewable Fuels Association *(881)*
	Retail Florist Association *(884)*
RFCI	Resilient Floor Covering Institute *(883)*
RFMA	Restaurant Facility Management Association *(884)*
RGA	Republican Governors Association *(881)*
RHA	Resort Hotel Association *(883)*
RHBAA	Racking Horse Breeders Association of America *(872)*
RI/SME	Robotics & Flexible Machinery Tech Group *(887)*
RIA	Restoration Industry Association *(884)*
	Robotic Industries Association *(887)*
RIAA	Recording Industry Association of America (RIAA) *(876)*
RICA	Railway Industrial Clearance Association *(874)*
RID	Registry of Interpreters for the Deaf *(879)*
RIFM	Research Institute for Fragrance Materials *(882)*
RILA	Retail Industry Leaders Association *(884)*
RIMS	Risk and Insurance Management Society, Inc. (RIMS) *(886)*
RIPA	Reusable Industrial Packaging Association *(885)*
RISE	RISE (Responsible Industry for a Sound Environment) *(886)*
RISI	Rolf Institute of Structural Integration *(887)*
RITA	Retirement Industry Trust Association *(885)*
RJOS	Ruth Jackson Orthopaedic Society *(889)*
RLI	REALTORS Land Institute *(876)*
RMA	Refractory Metals Association *(878)*
	Rice Millers' Association *(886)*
	The Risk Management Association *(886)*
	Rubber Manufacturers Association *(888)*
	Scrap Tire Management Council *(893)*
RMI	Rack Manufacturers Institute *(872)*
RMLA	Rocky Mountain Llama & Alpaca Association *(887)*
RMS	River Management Society *(886)*
RNA	Religion Newswriters Association *(880)*
	RNA Society *(887)*
RNLA	Republican National Lawyers Association *(881)*
RNRF	Renewable Natural Resources Foundation *(881)*
RNS	Respiratory Nursing Society *(883)*
	Rheumatology Nurses Society *(886)*
ROA	Reserve Officers Association of the U.S. *(882)*
ROUNDALAB	International Association of Round Dance Teachers *(527)*
RPA	Radiant Panel Association *(872)*
	Radical Philosophy Association *(873)*

	Regional Plan Association *(879)*
	Register of Professional Archeologists *(879)*
	Renal Physicians Association *(881)*
	Rubber Pavements Association *(888)*
RPI	Recognition Professionals International *(876)*
RPIC	Rubber and Plastics Industry Conference of the United Steelworkers of America *(888)*
RPMA	Retail Packaging Manufacturers Association *(885)*
RPMDA	Retail Print Music Dealers Association *(885)*
RPTA	Recycled Paperboard Technical Association *(877)*
RPTIA	Recreational Park Trailer Industry Association *(877)*
RRA	Religious Research Association *(880)*
RRS	Radiation Research Society *(873)*
RS	Reliability Society *(880)*
RSA	Receptive Services Association of America *(876)*
	The Renaissance Society of America *(881)*
	Reprographic Services Association *(881)*
	Research Society on Alcoholism *(882)*
	Rhetoric Society of America *(886)*
	Roller Skating Association International *(887)*
RSAA	Romanian Studies Association of America *(888)*
RSES	Refrigeration Service Engineers Society *(878)*
RSI	Railway Supply Institute *(874)*
RSNA	Radiological Society of North America *(873)*
RSPA	Retail Solutions Providers Association *(885)*
RSPI	Residential Space Planners International *(883)*
RSS	The Rural Sociological Society *(889)*
RSSI	Railway Systems Suppliers, Inc *(874)*
RTA	The Railway Tie Association *(874)*
	Rubber Trade Association of North America *(888)*
RTAM/ SME	Rapid Technologies & Additive Manufacturing Community of SME *(875)*
RTCA	Radio and Television Correspondents Association *(873)*
	RTCA, Inc. *(888)*
RTCM	Radio Technical Commission for Maritime Services *(873)*
RTDNA	Radio Television Digital News Association *(873)*
RTG	Rural Telecommunications Group *(889)*
RTNPA	Red Tag News Publications Association *(878)*
RTOG	Radiation Therapy Oncology Group *(873)*
RVAA	The Recreational Vehicle Aftermarket Association *(877)*
RVDA	Recreation Vehicle Dealers Association of North America *(876)*
RVIA	Recreation Vehicle Industry Association *(877)*
RVRA	Recreation Vehicle Rental Association *(877)*
RWA	Romance Writers of America *(888)*
RWDCA	Red and White Dairy Cattle Association *(877)*
RWDSU	Retail, Wholesale and Department Store Union *(885)*
RWMA	Resistance Welding Manufacturing Alliance *(883)*
RWMPC	Ryan White Medical Providers Coalition *(889)*
S-Corp	S-Corporation Association *(889)*
SAA	Society for American Archaeology *(903)*
	Society of Animal Artists *(930)*
	Society of Automotive Analysts *(930)*
	Sunglass Association of America *(965)*
SAAMI	Sporting Arms and Ammunition Manufacturers' Institute Inc. *(959)*
SAAP	Society for the Advancement of American Philosophy *(922)*
SABA	Society for the Advancement of Behavior Analysis *(922)*
SABEW	Society of American Business Editors and Writers *(928)*
SABR	Society for American Baseball Research *(903)*
SAC	Society for Advancement of Consulting *(903)*
SACC	Serbian-American Chamber of Commerce *(897)*
	Society for Anthropology in Community Colleges *(904)*
SACC-USA	Swedish-American Chambers of Commerce of the USA, Inc. *(967)*
SACI	Sales Association of the Chemical Industry *(890)*
SACNAS	SACNAS (Society for Advancement of Chicanos and Native Americans in Science) *(904)*
SACP	Society for Asian and Comparative Philosophy *(904)*
SAE	SAE International *(889)*

SAEM	Suntanning Association for Education *(966)*
	Society for Academic Emergency Medicine *(903)*
SAET	Society for the Advancement of Economic Theory *(922)*
SAF	Society of American Florists *(928)*
	Society of American Foresters *(928)*
SAFCS	Society of Air Force Clinical Surgeons *(928)*
SAFD	Society of American Fight Directors *(928)*
SAFE	SAFE Association *(890)*
SAFN	Society for the Anthropology of Food and Nutrition *(923)*
SAFPA	Society of Air Force Physician Assistants *(928)*
SAG-AFTRA	Screen Actors Guild - American Federation of Television and Radio Artists *(893)*
SAGA	Smocking Arts Guild of America *(901)*
	Society of American Graphic Artists *(929)*
SAGES	Society of American Gastrointestinal and Endoscopic Surgeons *(929)*
SAGP	Society for Ancient Greek Philosophy *(904)*
SAH	Society of American Historians *(929)*
	Society of Architectural Historians *(930)*
SAHM	The Society for Adolescent Medicine *(903)*
SAI	Sugar Association *(965)*
SAIP	Society of Atherosclerosis Imaging and Prevention *(930)*
SAJA	South Asian Journalists Association *(952)*
SALIS	Substance Abuse Librarians and Information Specialists *(965)*
SALT	Society for Applied Learning Technology *(904)*
	Society of American Law Teachers *(929)*
SAM	Society for Advancement of Management *(903)*
	Society for Asian Music *(904)*
	Society of American Magicians *(929)*
SAMA	Strategic Account Management Association *(963)*
SAME	Society of American Military Engineers *(929)*
SAMP	Stuntmen's Association of Motion Pictures *(964)*
SAMPE	Society for the Advancement of Material and Process Engineering *(922)*
SAMS	Society of Accredited Marine Surveyors *(927)*
SANA	Society for the Anthropology of North America *(923)*
SANTA	Soyfoods Association of North America *(953)*
	Souvenirs, Gifts and Novelties Trade Association *(953)*
SAPA	Society of Army Physician Assistants *(930)*
SAPAA	Substance Abuse Program Administrators Association *(965)*
SAPI	Sales Association of the Paper Industry *(890)*
SAR	Society of Abdominal Radiology *(927)*
SARA	Society of American Registered Architects *(929)*
SARCA	Senior Army Reserve Commanders Association *(897)*
SART	Society for Assisted Reproductive Technology *(905)*
SAS	Society for Applied Spectroscopy *(904)*
	Society for Archaeological Sciences *(904)*
	Society of American Silversmiths *(929)*
	Society of Armenian Studies *(930)*
SASS	Society for the Advancement of Scandinavian Study *(923)*
SATW	Society of American Travel Writers *(930)*
SAVE	SAVE International *(891)*
	Society for the Advancement of Education *(922)*
SAVTA	Safe and Vault Technicians Association *(890)*
SAW	Society for the Anthropology of Work *(923)*
SAWE	Society of Allied Weight Engineers *(928)*
SB	American Society of Wedding Professionals *(211)*
SBCA	Satellite Broadcasting and Communications Association *(891)*
	Small Business Council of America *(900)*
	Structural Building Components Association *(964)*
SBCS	Society for Buddhist-Christian Studies *(905)*
SBE	Society for Business Ethics *(905)*
	Society of Broadcast Engineers *(931)*
SBEA	Small Business Exporters Association of the United States *(900)*
SBHA	Spanish Barb Horse Association *(954)*
SBIA	National Association of Small Business Investment Companies *(900)*
SBIC	Sustainable Buildings Industry Council *(967)*
SBL	Society of Biblical Literature *(931)*
SBLC	SB Latex Council *(891)*
	Small Business Legislative Council *(901)*
SBM	Society of Behavioral Medicine *(930)*
SBSBA	Scottish Blackface Breeders Association *(893)*

SIGMA	Society of Independent Gasoline Marketers of America (SIGMA) *(939)*	**SME**	Society for Mining, Metallurgy and Exploration, Inc. *(915)*	**SPARK**	Society of Professional Asset-Managers and Record Keepers *(945)*

SIGMA Society of Independent Gasoline Marketers of America (SIGMA) *(939)*
SIGMIS Special Interest Group on Management Information Systems *(956)*
SIGMOBILE Special Interest Group on Mobility of Systems, Users, Data and Computing *(956)*
SIGMOD Special Interest Group on Management of Data *(956)*
SIGOPS Special Interest Group on Operating Systems *(956)*
SIGSAC Special Interest Group on Security, Audit, and Control *(956)*
SIGSOFT Special Interest Group on Software Engineering *(956)*
SIGTC Special Interest Group for Technology Coordinators *(955)*
SIGUCCS Special Interest Group for University and College Computing Services *(955)*
SIGWEB Special Interest Group on Hypertext/ Hypermedia *(956)*
SIHS Society for Italian Historical Studies *(914)*
SIIA Self-Insurance Institute of America, Inc. *(896)*
Software & Information Industry Association (SIIA) *(950)*
SIIM Society for Imaging Informatics in Medicine *(912)*
SIM Society for Industrial Microbiology *(913)*
Society for Information Management *(913)*
SIMA Snow & Ice Management Association *(901)*
SIOP Society for Industrial and Organizational Psychology Inc. *(912)*
SIOR Society of Industrial and Office Realtors *(939)*
SIP Society for Invertebrate Pathology *(913)*
SIPA Specialized Information Publishers Association *(957)*
Structural Insulated Panel Association *(964)*
SIPES Society of Independent Professional Earth Scientists *(939)*
SIR Society of Insurance Research *(940)*
Society of Interventional Radiology *(940)*
SIS Surgical Infection Society *(967)*
SISO Society of Independent Show Organizers *(939)*
SIT Sugar Industry Technologists *(965)*
SITE Society of Incentive & Travel Executives *(939)*
Society of Insurance Trainers and Educators *(940)*
SIU Seafarers International Union of North America *(894)*
SIVB Society for In Vitro Biology *(912)*
SJI Steel Joist Institute *(962)*
SLA Showmen's League of America *(899)*
Society for Linguistic Anthropology *(914)*
Special Libraries Association *(956)*
Sports Lawyers Association *(959)*
SLAS Society for Laboratory Automation and Screening *(914)*
SLB Society for Leukocyte Biology *(914)*
SLEMA Schiffli Lace and Embroidery Manufacturers Association *(892)*
SLH Small Luxury Hotels of the World *(901)*
SLMA Sales Lead Management Association *(890)*
SLN Southeastern Livestock Network *(953)*
SLS Society of Laparoendoscopic Surgeons *(940)*
SLTBR Society for Light Treatment and Biological Rhythms *(914)*
SMA Scale Manufacturers Association *(892)*
Screen Manufacturers Association *(893)*
Society for Medical Anthropology *(915)*
Society of Maritime Arbitrators *(941)*
Society of Mineral Analysts *(942)*
Society of Municipal Arborists *(942)*
Stadium Managers Association *(960)*
Stage Managers Association *(960)*
Steel Manufacturers Association *(962)*
Storage Equipment Manufacturer's Association *(963)*
Stucco Manufacturers Association *(964)*
SMACNA Sheet Metal and Air Conditioning Contractors' National Association *(898)*
SMART Secondary Materials and Recycled Textiles Association *(894)*
SMARTP Society of Mortgage, Appraisal, Real Estate and Title Professionals *(942)*
SMB Society for Mathematical Biology *(915)*
SMCAF Society of Medical Consultants to the Armed Forces *(941)*
SMCR Society for Menstrual Cycle Research *(915)*
SMCS Man and Cybernetics Systems Society *(602)*
SMDM Society for Medical Decision Making *(915)*

SME Society for Mining, Metallurgy and Exploration, Inc. *(915)*
Society of Manufacturing Engineers *(941)*
SMEI Sales and Marketing Executives International, Inc. *(890)*
SMEMA IPC - Surface Mount Equipment Manufacturers Association *(585)*
SMEP Society of Multivariate Experimental Psychology *(942)*
SMFM Society for Maternal-Fetal Medicine *(915)*
SMH Society for Military History *(915)*
SMI Society for Mucosal Immunology *(916)*
Sorptive Minerals Institute *(952)*
Spring Manufacturers Institute *(960)*
Strategic Marketplace Initiative *(963)*
SMMA SMMA - The Motor and Motion Association *(901)*
SMO Society of Military Otolaryngologists - Head and Neck Surgeons *(941)*
SMPE Society of Marine Port Engineers *(941)*
SMPS Society for Marketing Professional Services *(914)*
SMPTE Society of Motion Picture and Television Engineers *(942)*
SMRI Solution Mining Research Institute *(952)*
SMRP Society for Maintenance & Reliability Professionals *(914)*
Society for Medieval and Renaissance Philosophy *(915)*
SMT Professional Society for Sales and Marketing Training *(865)*
SMTA Surface Mount Technology Association *(966)*
SMWIA Sheet Metal Workers' International Association *(898)*
SNA School Nutrition Association *(892)*
SNACC Society for Neuroscience in Anesthesiology and Critical Care *(916)*
SNAG Society of North American Goldsmiths *(943)*
SNAME The Society of Naval Architects and Marine Engineers *(942)*
SND Society for News Design *(916)*
SNEB Society for Nutrition Education and Behavior *(917)*
SNIS Society of Neurointerventional Surgery *(942)*
SNM Society of Nuclear Medicine *(943)*
SNMA Student National Medical Association *(964)*
SNO Society for Neuro-Oncology *(916)*
SNP Society for Natural Philosophy *(916)*
SNPO Society for Nonprofit Organizations *(917)*
SNS Society of Neurological Surgeons *(943)*
SOA Society of Actuaries *(927)*
SOAP Society for Obstetric Anesthesia and Perinatology *(917)*
SOBA States Organization for Boating Access *(962)*
SOBP Society of Biological Psychiatry *(931)*
SOCAP SOCAP International *(902)*
SOCMA Society of Chemical Manufacturers and Affiliates Inc. *(932)*
Tetrahydrofuran Task Force *(972)*
SODA Sportsplex Operators and Developers Association *(959)*
SoE Society of Ethnobiology *(935)*
SOEH Society for Occupational and Environmental Health *(917)*
SOFE Society of Financial Examiners *(936)*
SOFT Society of Forensic Toxicologists *(936)*
SOHN Society of Otorhinolaryngology and Head-Neck Nurses *(943)*
SOLE SOLE - The International Society of Logistics *(952)*
SOMA National Student Osteopathic Medical Association *(797)*
SOMOS Society of Military Orthopaedic Surgeons *(941)*
SON Society of Nematologists *(942)*
SOPHE Society for Public Health Education *(919)*
SOPHIA Society of Philosophers in America *(944)*
SoR Society of Rheology *(946)*
SORP Society of Outdoor Recreation Professionals *(943)*
SORT Shippers of Recycled Textiles *(899)*
SOS Society of Scribes *(947)*
SOT Society of Toxicology *(948)*
SoUSAFFS Society of United States Air Force Flight Surgeons *(949)*
SOVE Society for Vector Ecology *(927)*
SPA Seaplane Pilots Association *(894)*
Society for Pediatric Anesthesia *(917)*
Society for Personality Assessment *(918)*
Society for Psychological Anthropology *(919)*
Sociological Practice Association *(950)*
Soil and Plant Analysis Council *(951)*
SPAC Small Publishers Association of North America *(901)*
SPAN
SPAP Society for Physician Assistants in Pediatrics *(919)*

SPARK Society of Professional Asset-Managers and Record Keepers *(945)*
SPARS Society of Professional Audio Recording Services *(945)*
SPBA Society of Professional Benefit Administrators *(945)*
SPBT Society of Pharmaceutical and Biotech Trainers *(945)*
SPCAP Society of Professors of Child and Adolescent Psychiatry *(945)*
SPD Sigma Phi Delta *(899)*
Society for Pediatric Dermatology *(917)*
Society of Publication Designers *(946)*
SPE Society for Photographic Education *(919)*
Society of Petroleum Engineers *(944)*
Society of Plastics Engineers *(944)*
Society of Professors of Education *(945)*
SPED Society of Piping Engineers and Designers *(944)*
SPEE Society of Petroleum Evaluation Engineers *(944)*
SPEP Society for Phenomenology and Existential Philosophy *(918)*
SPESA Sewn Products Equipment and Suppliers of the Americas *(898)*
SPFA Spray Polyurethane Foam Alliance *(959)*
SPI Society of Professional Investigators *(945)*
Society of the Plastics Industry *(948)*
SPIE SPIE - The International Society for Optical Engineering *(958)*
SPJ Society of Professional Journalists *(945)*
SPN Society of Pediatric Nurses *(943)*
SPOH Society for the Preservation of Oral Health *(924)*
SPP Society for Pediatric Pathology *(918)*
Society for Pediatric Psychology *(918)*
Society of Pediatric Psychology *(943)*
Society of Pediatric Radiology *(918)*
SPR Society for Pediatric Research *(918)*
Society for Psychophysiological Research *(919)*
SPRAT Society of Professional Rope Access Technicians *(945)*
SPRBM Society for Physical Regulation in Biology and Medicine *(919)*
SPRI Single Ply Roofing Institute *(900)*
SPRS Society of Pelvic Reconstructive Surgeons *(943)*
SPS IEEE Signal Processing Society *(485)*
Safety Pharmacology Society *(890)*
Society of Pelvic Surgeons *(944)*
SPSL Society for the Philosophy of Sex and Love *(923)*
SPSMM Society for the Psychological Study of Men and Masculinity *(924)*
SPSP Society for Personality and Social Psychology *(918)*
SPSSI Society for the Psychological Study of Science Issues *(924)*
Society for the Psychological Study of Social Issues *(924)*
SPT Society for Philosophy and Technology *(919)*
Society of Photo-Technologists *(944)*
SPU Society for Pediatric Urology *(918)*
SPWLA Society of Petrophysicists and Well Log Analysts *(944)*
SQA Society of Quality Assurance *(946)*
Society of Quantitative Analysts *(946)*
SRA Society for Research on Adolescence *(920)*
Society for Risk Analysis *(920)*
Society of Research Administrators International *(946)*
Station Representatives Association *(962)*
SRCC Solar Rating and Certification Corporation *(952)*
SRCD Society for Research in Child Development *(920)*
SRE Society of Reliability Engineers *(946)*
SREI Society for Reproductive Endocrinology and Infertility *(920)*
SRF Strategic Rail Finance *(963)*
SRI Spring Research Institute *(960)*
Steel Recycling Institute *(963)*
SRM Society for Range Management *(920)*
SRMC Society of Risk Management Consultants *(947)*
SRNT Society for Research on Nicotine and Tobacco *(920)*
SROA Society for Radiation Oncology Administration *(919)*
SRS Scoliosis Research Society *(893)*
Sleep Research Society *(900)*
Society for Romanian Studies *(921)*
Society of Reproductive Surgeons *(946)*

SRU	Society of Radiologists in Ultrasound *(946)*	**STN**	Society of Trauma Nurses *(949)*	**TCAA**	Tile Contractors' Association of America *(974)*
SS	Shock Society *(899)*	**STP**	Society for the Teaching of Psychology *(926)*	**TCATA**	Textile Care Allied Trades Association *(972)*
SSA	Seismological Society of America *(895)*		Society of Toxicologic Pathologists *(948)*	**TCG**	Theatre Communications Group *(973)*
	Self Storage Association *(896)*	**STR**	Society of Toxicologic Pathology *(948)*	**TCH**	The Clearing House Association *(357)*
	Semiotic Society of America *(897)*	**STRIMA**	Society of Thoracic Radiology *(948)*	**TCI**	The Catfish Institute *(345)*
	Service Specialists Association *(897)*		State Risk and Insurance Management Association *(961)*		Transportation Clubs International *(978)*
	Shareholder Services Association *(898)*	**STS**	Society for Textual Scholarship *(922)*	**TCIA**	Tree Care Industry Association *(980)*
	Slovak Studies Association *(900)*		Society of Thoracic Surgeons *(948)*	**TCNA**	Tile Council of North America, Inc. *(974)*
	Soaring Society of America *(902)*	**STTI**	Sigma Theta Tau International *(899)*		Tube Council of North America *(982)*
	Sommelier Society of America *(952)*	**SUA**	Silver Users Association *(899)*	**TCSAA**	Twentieth-Century Spanish Association of America *(983)*
	Southern Shrimp Alliance *(953)*	**SUNA**	Certification Board for Urologic Nurses and Associates *(349)*	**TCU**	Transportation Communications International Union/IAM *(978)*
	Specialty Sleep Association *(958)*		Society of Urologic Nurses and Associates *(949)*	**TDA**	Transportation Development Association *(978)*
SSAR	Society for the Study of Amphibians and Reptiles *(925)*	**SUO-HNS**	Society of University Otolaryngologists-Head and Neck Surgeons *(949)*	**TDC**	Type Directors Club *(983)*
SSAT	Society for Surgery of the Alimentary Tract *(921)*	**SUP**	Sailors' Union of the Pacific *(890)*	**TEC**	Trenchless Equipment Committee *(980)*
SSB	Society of Systematic Biologists *(947)*	**SUR**	Society for Uroradiology *(926)*	**TEGMA**	Transportation Elevator and Grain Merchants Association *(978)*
SSCI	Steel Shipping Container Institute *(963)*	**SUS**	Society of University Surgeons *(949)*	**TEI**	The Entrepreneurship Institute *(430)*
SSCP	Society for a Science of Clinical Psychology *(903)*	**SUU**	Society of University Urologists *(949)*		Tax Executives Institute, Inc. *(968)*
SSCS	Solid-State Circuits Society *(952)*	**SVC**	Society of Vacuum Coaters *(950)*	**TEMA**	Towing Equipment Manufacturers Association *(976)*
SSDA-AT	Service Station Dealers of America and Allied Trades *(898)*	**SVHE**	Society for Values in Higher Education *(926)*		Tubular Exchanger Manufacturers Association *(982)*
SSE	Society for the Study of Evolution *(925)*	**SVIA**	Specialty Vehicle Institute of America *(958)*	**TER**	Tau Epsilon Rho Law Society *(968)*
SSFI	Scaffolding, Shoring and Forming Institute *(892)*		Stable Value Investment Association *(960)*	**TESOL**	TESOL International Association *(971)*
SSH	Society for Simulation in Healthcare *(921)*	**SVM**	Society for Vascular Medicine *(926)*	**TETA**	Turf Equipment Technicians Association *(982)*
SSHA	Social Science History Association *(902)*	**SVN**	Social Venture Network *(902)*	**TFA**	Teaching-Family Association *(969)*
SSHBEA	Spotted Saddle Horse Breeders' and Exhibitors' Association *(959)*		Society for Vascular Nursing *(926)*	**TFBC**	Timber Frame Business Council *(974)*
SSILA	Society for the Study of Indigenous Languages of the Americas *(925)*	**SVP**	Society of Vertebrate Paleontology *(950)*	**TFBPA**	Textile Fibers and By-Products Association *(972)*
SSINA	Specialty Steel Industry of North America *(958)*	**SVS**	Society for Vascular Surgery *(926)*	**TFF**	The Fragrance Foundation *(453)*
SSLHPE	Society of State Leaders of Health and Physical Education *(947)*	**SVU**	Society for Vascular Ultrasound *(927)*	**TFG**	Timber Framers Guild *(974)*
SSLI	Society of School Librarians International *(947)*	**SWAMP**	Stuntwomen's Association of Motion Pictures *(964)*	**TFI**	The Fertilizer Institute *(443)*
SSMA	School Science and Mathematics Association *(892)*	**SWANA**	SWANA - Solid Waste Association of North America *(967)*	**TGA**	Travel Goods Association *(979)*
SSMPP	Society for the Study of Male Psychology and Physiology *(925)*	**SWAPA**	Southwest Airlines Pilots Association *(953)*	**TGA-US**	Glutamate Association (United States) *(463)*
SSO	Society of Surgical Oncology *(947)*	**SWCS**	Soil and Water Conservation Society *(951)*	**THA**	The Hosiery Association *(478)*
SSP	Society for Scholarly Publishing *(921)*	**SWDA**	Souvenir Wholesale Distributors Association *(953)*	**Ti**	Thermoforming Institute *(973)*
	Society for the Science & the Public *(924)*	**SWE**	The Society of Wine Educators *(950)*	**TI:ME**	The Technology Institute for Music Educators *(970)*
SSPC	SSPC: the Society for Protective Coatings *(960)*		Society of Women Engineers *(950)*	**TIA**	Telecommunications Industry Association *(971)*
SSPI	Society of Satellite Professionals International *(947)*	**SWG**	Society of Woman Geographers *(950)*		Tennis Industry Association *(971)*
SSPMA	Sump and Sewage Pump Manufacturers Association *(965)*	**SWI**	Steel Window Institute *(963)*		Tire Industry Association *(975)*
SSQ	Society for Software Quality *(921)*	**SWPA**	Section for Women in Public Administration *(894)*		Tortilla Industry Association *(976)*
SSR	Society for the Study of Reproduction *(925)*		Submersible Wastewater Pump Association *(965)*		Toy Industry Association *(976)*
SSRC	Structural Stability Research Council *(964)*	**SWRI**	Sealant, Waterproofing and Restoration Institute *(894)*		Transportation Intermediaries Association *(978)*
SSS	Society for Slovene Studies *(921)*	**SWS**	Society for Wetland Scientists *(927)*	**TIACA**	The International Air Cargo Association *(509)*
	System Safety Society *(967)*	**SWST**	Society of Wood Science and Technology *(950)*	**TIAFT**	The International Association of Forensic Toxicologists *(522)*
SSSA	Soil Science Society of America *(951)*	**SYFA**	Synthetic Yarn and Fiber Association *(967)*	**TIAW**	The International Alliance for Women *(510)*
SSSB	Society for the Study of Social Biology *(925)*	**SYTA**	Student Youth and Travel Association *(964)*	**TIES**	The International Ecotourism Society *(542)*
SSSI	Society for the Study of Symbolic Interaction *(925)*	**T&LC**	Transportation and Logistics Council *(978)*	**TJC**	The Jockey Club *(588)*
SSSP	Society for the Study of Social Problems *(925)*	**T2S**	Technology Transfer Society *(970)*	**TJG**	Travel Journalists Guild *(980)*
SSSR	Society for the Scientific Study of Religion *(924)*	**TA**	Tea Association of the United States of America *(969)*	**TKGA**	The Knitting Guild Association *(591)*
SSSS	Society for the Scientific Study of Sexuality *(924)*		Tobacco Associates, Inc. *(975)*	**TLA**	Theatre Library Association *(973)*
SSTAR	Society for Sex Therapy and Research *(921)*	**TAA**	Text and Academic Authors Association *(972)*		Transportation Lawyers Association *(978)*
SSWA	Sanitary Supply Wholesaling Association *(891)*		Tobacconists' Association of America *(976)*	**TLBAA**	Texas Longhorn Breeders Association of America *(972)*
SSWAA	School Social Work Association of America *(892)*	**TAAFLO/ TPAFBO**	Trans-Atlantic American Flag Liner Operators and Trans-Pacific American Flag Berth Operators *(977)*	**TLMI**	Tag and Label Manufacturers Institute *(968)*
SSWLHC	Society for Social Work Leadership in Health Care *(921)*	**TAALS**	The American Association of Language Specialists *(64)*	**TLPA**	Taxicab, Limousine & Paratransit Association *(969)*
STA	The Securities Transfer Association *(895)*	**TAAN**	Transworld Advertising Agency Network *(979)*	**TMA**	Tobacco Merchants Association of the United States *(975)*
	Security Traders Association *(895)*	**TAANA**	The American Association of Nurse Attorneys *(67)*		Turnaround Management Association *(982)*
	Space Transportation Association *(953)*	**TAB**	Traffic Audit Bureau for Media Measurement, Inc. *(977)*	**TMC**	Technology and Maintenance Council of American Trucking Associations *(970)*
	Subcontractors Trade Association *(964)*	**TABS**	Association of Boarding Schools *(270)*	**TMI**	Trucking Management, Inc. *(981)*
STAFDA	Specialty Tools and Fasteners Distributors Association *(922)*	**TAGA**	Technical Association of the Graphic Arts *(969)*	**TMMB**	Truck Mixer Manufacturers Bureau *(981)*
STAR	Society for Technological Advancement of Reporting *(922)*	**TAPPI**	Technical Association of the Pulp and Paper Industry *(970)*	**TMS**	The Masonry Society *(607)*
STC	Society for Technical Communication *(922)*	**TARA**	Truck-frame and Axle Repair Association *(981)*		Minerals, Metals and Materials Society *(617)*
	Society of Telecommunications Consultants *(948)*	**TARF**	The Advertising Research Foundation *(13)*	**TMTA**	Tooling, Manufacturing and Technologies Association *(976)*
	Specialty Tobacco Council *(958)*	**TASDA**	The American Safe Deposit Association *(176)*	**TNG-CWA**	The Newspaper Guild *(810)*
STFM	Society of Teachers of Family Medicine *(947)*	**TASH**	TASH *(968)*	**TNNA**	The National NeedleArts Association *(774)*
STI	Steel Tank Institute Division of STI/SPFA *(963)*	**TASP**	The Association for the Study of Play *(260)*	**TOBA**	Thoroughbred Owners and Breeders Association *(974)*
	Steel Tube Institute of North America *(963)*	**TAUC**	TAUC - The Association of Union Constructors *(968)*	**TOC**	Training Officers Consortium *(977)*
STI/SPFA	Steel Plate Fabricators Association Division of STI/SPFA *(962)*	**TBI**	Tissue Banks International *(975)*	**TOCA**	Turf and Ornamental Communicators Association *(982)*
STLE	Society of Tribologists and Lubrication Engineers *(949)*	**TBIG**	Telecommunications Benchmarking International Group *(971)*	**TOS**	The Oceanography Society *(826)*
STM	Society for Thermal Medicine *(926)*	**TBP**	Tributyl Phosphate Task Force *(980)*	**TPA**	Tube and Pipe Association, International *(981)*
STMA	Sports Turf Managers Association *(959)*	**TBPA**	Textile Bag and Packaging Association *(972)*	**TPC**	Transaction Processing Performance Council *(977)*
		TC	Tea Council of the U.S.A. *(969)*	**TPI**	Truss Plate Institute *(981)*
		TCA	Thoroughbred Club of America *(973)*		Turfgrass Producers International *(982)*
			Tilt-up Concrete Association *(974)*	**TPM**	Timber Products Manufacturers Association *(975)*
			Treatment Communities of America *(980)*	**TPMA**	Trade Promotion Management Associates *(977)*
			Truckload Carriers Association *(981)*	**TPR**	The Philanthropy Roundtable *(846)*

TPSA   Textile Producers and Suppliers Association *(973)*

TRA   Thoroughbred Racing Associations of North America *(974)*

Tire and Rim Association *(975)*

TRAA   Towing and Recovery Association of America *(976)*

TRAIN   Tourist Railway Association Inc. *(976)*

TRALA   Truck Renting and Leasing Association *(981)*

TREA   The Retired Enlisted Association *(885)*

TREN   Trencher Equipment Committee *(980)*

TRF   Transportation Research Forum *(979)*

TRI   The Refractories Institute *(878)*

Remanufacturing Institute *(881)*

Tile Roofing Institute *(974)*

TRIB   Tire Retread and Repair Information Bureau *(975)*

TriBeta   Beta Beta Beta *(328)*

TRS   Tree-Ring Society *(980)*

TRSA   Textile Rental Services Association of America *(973)*

TS   Teratology Society *(971)*

TSA   Tamworth Swine Association *(968)*

Technology Student Association *(970)*

TechServe Alliance *(971)*

Tin Stabilizers Association *(975)*

Transpacific Stabilization Agreement *(977)*

Turkish Studies Association *(982)*

TSDA   Service Dealers Association *(897)*

TSEI   Transportation Safety Equipment Institute *(979)*

TSI   The Sulphur Institute *(965)*

TSIA   Technology Services Industry Association *(970)*

TSOP   Society for Organic Petrology *(917)*

TT   Theta Tau *(973)*

TTA   The Transformer Association *(977)*

TTD   Transportation Trades Department, AFL-CIO *(979)*

TTIA   Therapeutic Touch International Association *(973)*

TTMA   Truck Trailer Manufacturers Association *(981)*

TTRA   The Travel and Tourism Research Association *(979)*

TVB   Television Bureau of Advertising *(971)*

TVECA   Tobacco Vapor Electronic Cigarette Association *(975)*

TWC   Treated Wood Council *(980)*

TWNA   Truck Writers of North America *(981)*

TWP   The Wellness Plan *(1015)*

TWS   The Wildlife Society *(1017)*

TWU   Transport Workers Union of America, AFL-CIO *(978)*

U/RTA   University/Resident Theatre Association *(1003)*

UA   United Association of Journeymen and Apprentices of the Plumbing and Pipe Fitting Industry of the U.S. and Canada *(985)*

UAA   University Aviation Association *(1002)*

Urban Affairs Association *(1003)*

Utility Arborist Association *(1006)*

UAEL   United Association of Equipment Leasing *(985)*

UALE   United Association for Labor Education *(985)*

UAMA   Unified Abrasives Manufacturers Association *(984)*

United Abrasives Manufacturers Association, Coated Division *(985)*

UAPCS   Utah Association of Public Charter Schools *(1006)*

UAPD   Union of American Physicians and Dentists *(985)*

UASG   United Applications Standards Group *(985)*

UAW   United Auto Workers (UAW) *(986)*

UBB   United Braford Breeders *(986)*

UBC   United Brotherhood of Carpenters and Joiners of America *(986)*

UCAA   Urgent Care Association of America *(1004)*

UCC   Underwater Construction Corporation *(984)*

UCDA   University and College Designers Association *(1002)*

UCEA   University Council for Educational Administration *(1002)*

UCI   Utility Communicators International *(1006)*

UCOWR   Universities Council on Water Resources *(1002)*

UCP   United Cerebral Palsy *(986)*

UDC   United Development Council *(986)*

UE   United Electrical Radio & Machine Workers of America *(986)*

UEF   United Engineering Foundation *(986)*

UEMC   Underground Equipment Manufacturers Council *(984)*

UEP   United Egg Producers *(986)*

UFA   Unfinished Furniture Association *(984)*

UFCW   United Food and Commercial Workers International Union *(987)*

UFFCS   IEEE Ultrasonics, Ferroelectrics and Frequency Control Society *(486)*

UFPA   United Fresh Produce Association *(987)*

UFSC   Urban Financial Services Coalition *(1003)*

UFSPSO   United Federation of Police & Security Officers *(987)*

UFT   United Federation of Teachers *(987)*

UFVA   University Film and Video Association *(1002)*

UFW   United Farm Workers of America *(986)*

UGBA   United Gamefowl Breeders Association, Inc. *(987)*

UHA   Urban History Association *(1004)*

UHMS   Undersea and Hyperbaric Medical Society *(984)*

UIA   Ultrasonic Industry Association *(983)*

United Inventors Association of the U.S.A. *(987)*

UL&STD   Union Label and Service Trades Department *(985)*

ULC   Urban Libraries Council *(1004)*

ULPA   United Lightning Protection Association *(987)*

UMA   United Methodist Association of Health and Welfare Ministries *(987)*

United Motorcoach Association *(988)*

UMCA   Utility Management & Conservation Association *(1006)*

UMWA   United Mine Workers of America *(988)*

UNIFORUM   UniForum Association *(984)*

UNITE   UNITE-HERE *(985)*

UNPA   United Natural Products Alliance *(988)*

UNSU   United Nations Staff Union *(988)*

UOA   United Ostomy Associations of America *(988)*

UPAA   University Photographers Association of America *(1002)*

UPCEA   University Professional & Continuing Education Association *(1003)*

University Professional & Continuing Education Association *(1003)*

UPFDA   United Producers Formulators and Distributors Association *(988)*

UPGA   United Potato Growers of America *(988)*

UPHA   United Professional Horsemen's Association *(988)*

UPI   United Producers, Inc. *(988)*

URA   Uniform Retailers Association *(984)*

Universities Research Association *(1002)*

URISA   Urban and Regional Information Systems Association *(1003)*

URMIA   University Risk Management and Insurance Association *(1003)*

URPE   Union for Radical Political Economics *(985)*

US-IDF   United States National Committee of the International Dairy Federation *(996)*

US-ISPO   International Society for Prosthetics and Orthotics - United States *(569)*

USA-ITA   United States Association of Importers of Textiles and Apparel *(990)*

USA-TBC   United States-Taiwan Business Council *(989)*

USA-TLA   U.S.A. Toy Library Association *(983)*

USABC   United States-ASEAN Business Council Inc. *(990)*

USACA   United States Advanced Ceramics Association *(989)*

USACC   United States-Austrian Chamber of Commerce *(1001)*

USACM   United States Association for Computational Mechanics *(990)*

USADPLC   United States of America Dry Pea and Lentil Council, Inc. *(996)*

USAEE   United States Association for Energy Economics *(990)*

USAF MSC   United States Air Force Medical Service Corps Association *(989)*

USAFP   Uniformed Services Academy of Family Physicians *(984)*

USAHA   United States Animal Health Association *(989)*

USAIGC   United States Association of Independent Gymnastic Clubs *(990)*

USAPA   U. S. Airline Pilots Association *(983)*

USApple   United States Apple Association *(989)*

USARF   USA Rice Federation *(1004)*

USASA   United States Aquaculture Suppliers Association *(990)*

USAT   USA Taekwondo *(1005)*

USAV   USA Volleyball *(1005)*

USAWOA   United States Army Warrant Officers Association *(990)*

USB   United Soybean Board *(989)*

USBBC   United States Beef Breeds Council *(991)*

USBC   United States Bowling Congress *(991)*

USBIC   United States Business and Industry Council *(991)*

USBSA   United States Beet Sugar Association *(991)*

USBWA   United States Basketball Writers Association *(991)*

USCA   United States Canola Association *(991)*

United States Cattlemen's Association *(991)*

USCAP   United States and Canadian Academy of Pathology *(989)*

USCBC   United States-China Business Council *(1001)*

USCC   United States Chamber of Commerce *(991)*

United States Composting Council *(992)*

USCCB   United States Conference of Catholic Bishops *(992)*

USCCC   United States-China Chamber of Commerce *(1001)*

USCCCA   United States Cross Country Coaches Association *(993)*

USCHI   United States Custom Harvesters, Inc. *(993)*

USCHPA   United States Clean Heat & Power Association *(992)*

USCID   United States Committee on Irrigation and Drainage *(992)*

USCJ   United Synagogue of Conservative Judaism *(1001)*

USCM   United States Conference of Mayors *(992)*

USCRA   United States Court Reporters Association *(993)*

USCTA   United States Contract Tower Association *(992)*

USCTI   United States Cutting Tool Institute *(993)*

USDEC   United States Dairy Export Council *(993)*

USDGA   United States Durum Growers Association *(993)*

USEA   United States Energy Association *(993)*

USEF   United States Equestrian Federation *(993)*

USENIX   USENIX: The Advanced Computing Systems Association *(1005)*

USFCA   United States Fencing Coaches Association *(994)*

USFCC   United States Federation for Culture Collections *(994)*

USFN   USFN-America's Mortgage Banking Attorneys *(1006)*

USFSS   United States Federation of Scholars and Scientists *(994)*

USGA   United States Golf Association *(994)*

USGBC   United States Green Building Council *(994)*

USGC   United States Grains Council *(994)*

USHCC   United States Hispanic Chamber of Commerce *(995)*

USHSLA   United States Hide, Skin and Leather Association *(994)*

USHSR   United States High Speed Rail Association *(994)*

USHWA   The United States Harness Writers' Association *(994)*

USIFI   United States Industrial Fabrics Institute *(995)*

USIIA   United States Internet Industry Association *(995)*

USISPA   United States Internet Service Provider Association *(995)*

USISTF   United States-Israel Science & Technology Foundation (USISTF) *(995)*

USITT   United States Institute for Theatre Technology *(995)*

USJC   United States Junior Chamber (Jaycees) *(995)*

USLA   United States Lifesaving Association *(996)*

USLCA   United States Lactation Consultant Association *(996)*

USMA   U.S. Metric Association *(983)*

USMC   United States Maglev Coalition (USMC) *(996)*

USMEF   United States Meat Export Federation *(996)*

USMSA   United States Marine Safety Association *(996)*

USNAP   Utility Smart Network Access Port *(1007)*

USOA   Underwater Society of America *(984)*

USOBA   United States Organizations for Bankruptcy Alternatives (USOBA) *(997)*

USOGA   U.S. Oil and Gas Association *(997)*

USP   United States Pharmacopeia *(997)*

USPA   United States Parachute Association *(997)*

USPAACC   United States Pan Asian American Chamber of Commerce *(997)*

USPB   United States Potato Board *(997)*

USPRA   United States Psychiatric Rehabilitation Association *(998)*

USPTA   United States Professional Tennis Association *(998)*

USRA   United Shoe Retailers Association *(988)*

Universities Space Research Association *(1002)*

USRBC   U.S.-Russia Business Council *(999)*

USROBC   Romanian-U.S. Business Council *(888)*

USRPA   US Rice Producers Association *(1004)*

USRSA   United States Racquet Stringers Association *(998)*

USSA   United States Ski and Snowboard Association *(999)*

United States Superyacht Association *(999)*

United Suffolk Sheep Association *(1001)*
USSD United States Society on Dams *(999)*
USSS United States Synchronized Swimming *(999)*
USTA United States Telecom Association *(1000)*

United States Tennis Association *(1000)*

United States Trotting Association *(1000)*
USTC United States Tobacco Cooperative Inc *(1000)*
USTF Tuna Council *(982)*
USTFA United States Trout Farmers Association *(1000)*
USTOA United States Tour Operators Association *(1000)*
USTSA United States Targhee Sheep Association *(999)*
USW United States Wheat Associates, Inc. *(1000)*
USWA United Steelworkers of America *(1001)*
UTA Used Textbook Association *(1005)*

Used Truck Association *(1005)*
UTC Utilities Telecom Council *(1006)*
UTU United Transportation Union *(1001)*
UURWAW United Union of Roofers, Waterproofers and Allied Workers *(1001)*
UWC UWC - Strategic Services on Unemployment and Workers' Compensation *(1007)*
UWUA Utility Workers Union of America *(1007)*
UXPA User Experience Professionals Association *(1005)*
VAAUS Venezuelan American Association of the U.S. *(1008)*
VAC Vinyl Acetate Council *(1009)*
VAI Van Alen Institute *(1007)*
VASTA Voice and Speech Trainers Association *(1011)*
VBMA Veterinary Botanical Medical Association *(1008)*
VCA The Vision Council *(1010)*
VCI-Group Visual Communications Industry Group *(1010)*
VCS Veterinary Cancer Society *(1008)*
VdGSA Viola da Gamba Society of America *(1009)*
VDTA/SDTA Vacuum Dealers Trade Association/Sewing Dealers Trade Association *(1007)*
VECAP Vocational Evaluation and Career Assessment Professionals *(1011)*
VECI Variable Electronic Components Institute *(1008)*
VESA Video Electronics Standards Association *(1009)*
VHMA Veterinary Hospital Managers Association *(1008)*
VI Vibration Institute *(1008)*

The Vinegar Institute *(1009)*

Vinyl Institute *(1008)*
VIDPI Visually Impaired Data Processors International *(1011)*
VISCMA Vibration Isolation and Seismic Control Manufacturers Association *(1009)*
VITA VITA *(1011)*
VMA Valve Manufacturers Association of America *(1007)*
VNAA Visiting Nurse Associations of America *(1010)*
VOS Veterinary Orthopedic Society *(1008)*
VPA Visiting Physicians Association *(1010)*
VPPPA Voluntary Protection Programs Participants' Association, Inc. *(1011)*
VPRA Vanadium Producers and Reclaimers Association *(1008)*
VRA Visual Resources Association *(1010)*
VRC Valve Repair Council *(1007)*
VRMA Vacation Rental Managers Association *(1007)*
VSA Victorian Society in America *(1009)*

Violin Society of America *(1010)*

Visitor Studies Association *(1010)*
VSI Vinyl Siding Institute, Inc. *(1009)*
VTS Vehicular Technology Society *(1008)*
W.net Women Networking in Electronic Transactions *(1022)*
WA Wallcovering Association *(1012)*
WAAC Western Association for Art Conservation *(1015)*
WACA World Affairs Councils of America *(1025)*
WACRA WACRA - World Association for Case Method Research and Application *(1011)*
WAI AFL-CIO Working for America Institute *(15)*

The Wire Association International, Inc. *(1019)*

Women in Aviation International *(1020)*
WAID Western Association of Industrial Distributors *(1015)*
WAO World Allergy Organization *(1025)*
WAS World Aquaculture Society *(1025)*
WASDA Water and Sewer Distributors of America *(1012)*
WASTEC Waste Equipment Technology Association *(1012)*

WAVA World Association of Veterinary Anatomists *(1025)*
WAW WorldatWork *(1028)*
WBAE Wholesale Beer Association Executives of America *(1016)*
WBANA Wild Blueberry Association of North America *(1017)*
WBCA Women's Basketball Coaches Association *(1022)*
WBDI Women Band Directors International *(1020)*
WBENC Women's Business Enterprise National Council *(1022)*
WBFI Wild Bird Feeding Industry *(1017)*

Wild Bird Feeding Institute *(1017)*
WC Walnut Council *(1012)*
WCA Waterproofing Contractors Association *(1013)*

Women's Caucus for Art *(1022)*
WCAA Window Coverings Association of America *(1018)*
WCAI Wireless Communications Association International *(1019)*
WCC Women's Classical Caucus *(1023)*
WCI Waterways Council, Inc. *(1014)*
WCISA Wire and Cable Industry Suppliers Association *(1019)*
WCMA Window Covering Manufacturers Association *(1018)*

Wood Component Manufacturers Association *(1024)*
WCOE Women Construction Owners and Executives, USA *(1020)*
WCPS Women's Caucus for Political Science *(1023)*
WCR Women Chefs and Restaurateurs *(1020)*

Women's Council of REALTORS *(1023)*
WCSC Window Covering Safety Council *(1018)*
WDA Wildlife Disease Association *(1017)*
WDMA Window and Door Manufacturers Association *(1018)*
WE Women in Endocrinology *(1021)*

Women in Energy *(1021)*
WEA Wilderness Education Association *(1017)*
WEAI Western Economic Association International *(1015)*
WEB WEB: Worldwide Employee Benefits Network *(1014)*
WEDA Western Dredging Association *(1015)*
WEDI Workgroup for Electronic Data Interchange *(1025)*
WEF Water Environment Federation *(1013)*
WELCOA Wellness Councils of America *(1015)*
WERC Warehousing Education and Research Council *(1012)*
WEVA Wedding and Event Videographers Association International *(1014)*
WF&FSA Wholesale Florist and Florist Supplier Association *(1012)*
WFA Wire Fabricators Association *(1019)*
WFCA World Floor Covering Association *(1026)*
WFF Women's Foodservice Forum *(1023)*
WFMH World Federation for Mental Health *(1026)*
WFPHA World Federation of Public Health Associations *(1026)*
WFS World Future Society *(1026)*
WGA Winegrape Growers of America *(1019)*
WGAE Writers Guild of America East *(1029)*
WGAW Writers Guild of America West *(1029)*
WGR Women in Government Relations, Inc. *(1021)*
WHA Western History Association *(1015)*

World History Association *(1026)*
WHCA White House Correspondents Association *(1016)*
WHMA Wiring Harness Manufacturers Association *(1020)*
WHNPA White House News Photographers Association *(1016)*
WHOA Walking Horse Owners Association of America *(1011)*
WHTA Walking Horse Trainers Association *(1012)*
Wi-Fi Wi-Fi Alliance *(1016)*
WIA Wireless Industry Association *(1019)*

Women in Aerospace *(1020)*

Women in Agribusiness *(1020)*
WICB Women in Cell Biology *(1021)*
WICT Women in Cable Telecommunications, Inc. *(1020)*
WIF Women in Film *(1021)*
WIFS WIFS - Women in Insurance and Financial Services *(1017)*
WIFTI Women In Film and Television International *(1021)*
WIG Women in Government *(1021)*
WIIS Women in International Security *(1021)*
WIIT The Association of Women in International Trade *(317)*
WILG Workers' Injury Law and Advocacy Group *(1025)*
WIM Women in Management *(1021)*

WIMA Women in Mining National *(1022)*

Writing Instrument Manufacturers Association *(1029)*
WIMG Women in Municipal Government *(1022)*
WINBA World International Nail and Beauty Association *(1026)*
WINUP Women's International Network of Utility Professionals *(1023)*
WIRES Working Group for Investment in Reliable and Economic Electric Systems *(1025)*
WITI Women in Technology International *(1022)*
WJA Women's Jewelry Association *(1023)*

World Jurist Association *(1027)*
WJTA-IMCA WaterJet Technology Association - Industrial and Municipal Cleaning Association *(1013)*
WLA Western Literature Association *(1016)*
WMA Weather Modification Association *(1014)*

Western Music Association *(1016)*

World Media Association *(1027)*
WMI Wildlife Management Institute *(1017)*
WMIA Woodworking Machinery Industry Association *(1024)*
WMMA Wood Machinery Manufacturers of America *(1024)*
WMS Wilderness Medical Society *(1017)*
WNBA Women's National Book Association *(1023)*
WOCCU World Council of Credit Unions, Inc. *(1026)*
WOCN The Wound, Ostomy and Continence Nurses Society *(1028)*
WOMPI Women of the Motion Picture Industry, International *(1022)*
WOS Wilson Ornithological Society *(1018)*
WP Women in Packaging *(1022)*
WPA National Council of Writing Program Administrators *(738)*
WPCSA Welsh Pony and Cob Society of America *(1015)*
WPF WorkPlace Furnishings *(1025)*
WPMA Wood Products Manufacturers Association *(1024)*
WPO YPO-WPO *(1030)*
WPPI Wedding and Portrait Photographers International *(1014)*
WPRA Women's Professional Rodeo Association *(1023)*
WPRC Warrior Protection & Readiness Coalition *(1012)*
WPSA World's Poultry Science Association, U.S.A. Branch *(1028)*
WPT Worldwide Printing Thermographers Association *(1028)*
WQA Water Quality Association *(1013)*
WQC Wheat Quality Council *(1016)*
WRC Welding Research Council *(1015)*
WRCPA The Western Red Cedar Pole Association *(1016)*
WRF World Research Foundation *(1027)*
WRI Wire Reinforcement Institute *(1019)*
WRMA Weather Risk Management Association *(1014)*
WRPA Women's Regional Publications of America *(1024)*
WRTB Wire Rope Technical Board *(1019)*
WSA World Sign Associates *(1027)*
WSC Water Systems Council *(1013)*

World Shipping Council *(1027)*
WSIA Water Sports Industry Association *(1013)*
WSSA Weed Science Society of America *(1014)*

Wine and Spirits Shippers Association *(1018)*
WSTDA Web Sling and Tie down Association *(1014)*
WSWA Wine and Spirits Wholesalers of America *(1018)*
WTA World Teleport Association *(1027)*

WTA Tour, Inc. *(1029)*
WTCA World Trade Centers Association *(1027)*
WTS Women's Transportation Seminar (WTS International) *(1024)*
WUA The World Umpires Association *(1027)*
WWA Western Writers of America *(1016)*

World Waterpark Association *(1028)*

World Watusi Association *(1028)*
WWEMA Water and Wastewater Equipment Manufacturers Association *(1012)*
WWPA Woven Wire Products Association *(1029)*
WWPIA World Pet Association *(1027)*
WWTSA World War Two Studies Association *(1028)*
XI Xplor International *(1029)*
XLA Express Delivery & Logistics Association *(436)*
XPSA Extruded Polystyrene Foam Association *(436)*
YALSA Young Adult Library Services Association *(1030)*
YBAA Yacht Brokers Association of America *(1030)*
YMAFSF YMA Fashion Scholarship Fund *(1030)*

YPA	Local Search Association (fka Yellow Pages Association) *(600)*
YPO	Young Presidents' Organization *(1030)*
ZAA	Zoological Association of America *(1030)*
ZBHA	Zero Balancing Health Association *(1030)*
ZI	Zonta International *(1030)*

2013 National Trade and Professional Associations of the United States

Certification Acronym Index

Associations offering certification programs are listed here under the acronym of the certificate they confer.

8-VSB	Society of Broadcast Engineers (931)
A-620	Wiring Harness Manufacturers Association (1020)
AA	American Academy of Anesthesiologist Assistants (30)
AABC	United States Pan Asian American Chamber of Commerce (997)
AAC	American Society of Farm Managers and Rural Appraisers (197)
	National Certification Council for Activity Professionals (720)
AACEPC	The American Association of Code Enforcement (57)
AACRN	Association of Nurses in AIDS Care (296)
AAE	Association of Free Community Papers (284)
AAEP	American Association of Airport Executives (53)
AAFCS	Society for Nutrition Education and Behavior (917)
AAI	American Association of Immunologists (62)
AANPCP	American Academy of Nurse Practitioners (37)
AAPA	LOMA (600)
AAPA/PPM	American Association of Port Authorities (70)
AARE	National Auctioneers Association (711)
AAS	International Association of Assessing Officers (516)
AASECTCSE	American Association of Sexuality Educators, Counselors and Therapists (73)
AAT	American Academy of Thermology (42)
AAVSB	Conference of Research Workers in Animal Diseases (375)
ABA	American Academy of Audiology (31)
ABAAHP	American Academy of Anti-Aging Medicine (30)
ABAARM	American Academy of Anti-Aging Medicine (30)
ABAI	American Academy of Allergy, Asthma, and Immunology (30)
ABAM	American Society of Addiction Medicine (191)
ABAR	Institute of Business Appraisers (498)
ABAT	American Academy of Clinical Toxicology (31)
ABBA F-I	American Brahman Breeders Association (85)
ABC	Association of Bridal Consultants (270)
ABCASC	International Fitness Professionals Association (545)
ABCL	National Lipid Association (770)
ABCP	DRI International (416)
ABE	American Association of Endodontists (60)
ABEM	American Association of Neuromuscular and Electrodiagnostic Medicine (66)
ABHI	American Society for Histocompatibility and Immunogenetics (185)
ABID	Energy and Environmental Building Association (427)
ABIM	American Board of Internal Medicine (82)
	American College of Physicians (101)
ABMA	American Academy of Medical Acupuncture (36)
ABMP	International Society for Magnetic Resonance in Medicine (567)

ABMS	American Academy of Hospice and Palliative Medicine (35)
ABOC-AC	The American Board of Opticianry and the National Contact Lens Examiners (83)
ABOO-HNS	American College of Osteopathic Surgeons (100)
ABPM	American Academy of Pain Medicine (39)
	American College of Occupational and Environmental Medicine (99)
ABPN	American Academy of Psychiatry and the Law (41)
ABPN MOC	American Board of Psychiatry & Neurology (83)
ABPP	American Board of Professional Psychology (83)
ABR	National Association of Realtors (690)
ABT	National Certification Commission for Acupuncture and Oriental Medicine (720)
ABVE/D	American Board of Vocational Experts (84)
ABVE/F	American Board of Vocational Experts (84)
AC	American Institute of Constructors (138)
	International Society of Transport Aircraft Trading (574)
ACA	Business Professionals of America (339)
	National Certification Commission (720)
ACASP	American Academy of Anti-Aging Medicine (30)
ACC	American Physical Therapy Association - Private Practice Section (165)
	Cruise Lines International Association (405)
	National Certification Council for Activity Professionals (720)
ACCCA-CC	American Catholic Correctional Chaplains Association (88)
ACCL	National Lipid Association (770)
	Preventive Cardiovascular Nurses Association (857)
ACCME	American Academy of Environmental Medicine (33)
	American Congress of Obstetricians and Gynecologists (107)
	American Society of Health-System Pharmacists (199)
	Association for Psychoanalytic Medicine (254)
ACCP	American Society for Nondestructive Testing (187)
ACE	American Association of Airport Executives (53)
	Associated Locksmiths of America (236)
	Entomological Society of America (429)
	National Association of Concessionaires (657)
ACE NCCA	American Council on Exercise (110)
ACET	Association of Equipment Manufacturers (281)
ACF	Drug & Alcohol Testing Industry Association (416)
ACGME	Academy of Psychosomatic Medicine (8)
	American Osteopathic Board of Physical Medicine and Rehabilitation (160)
ACHA	American College of Healthcare Architects (96)

ACI	International Association for Orthodontics (513)
	Portland Cement Association (853)
ACISE	Conference of State Bank Supervisors (376)
ACJS	Academy of Criminal Justice Sciences (4)
ACLAM	American Society of Laboratory Animal Practitioners (201)
ACLAMCE	American College of Laboratory Animal Medicine (97)
ACM	American Case Management Association (88)
	American College of Musicians (98)
	Manufactured Housing Institute (602)
	National Guild of Piano Teachers (757)
ACMA	American Case Management Association (88)
ACMI	Council for Art Education (389)
ACMPE	MGMA-ACMPE (614)
ACNM	Association of Women's Health, Obstetric and Neonatal Nurses (318)
ACNPC	American Association of Critical-Care Nurses (59)
ACoM	Institute of Real Estate Management (503)
ACP	Association of Insurance Compliance Professionals (289)
	Building Commissioning Association (337)
	Council of Producers & Distributors of Agrotechnology (396)
	Institute for Certification of Computing Professionals (497)
ACPE	American Society of Health-System Pharmacists (199)
	Drug Information Association (417)
ACPFA	Association of Public Treasurers of the United States and Canada (304)
ACR	Rolf Institute of Structural Integration (887)
ACRN	Association of Nurses in AIDS Care (296)
ACS	LOMA (600)
ACSW	National Association of Social Workers (696)
ACVA-PC	American College of Veterinary Anesthesiologists (103)
ACVM	American Association of Veterinary Parasitologists (76)
ACVP	American College of Veterinary Pathologists (104)
AD	American Design Drafting Association International and American Digital Design Association (114)
ADA	American Academy of Dental Sleep Medicine (32)
	International Congress of Oral Implantologists (537)
	Society for Nutrition Education and Behavior (917)
ADA CERP	American College of Dentists (95)
ADBIA	Design-Build Institute of America (411)
ADC	National Certification Council for Activity Professionals (720)
	Professional Tennis Registry (865)
ADCNS	Art Directors Club (229)
ADDA	American Design Drafting Association International and American Digital Design Association (114)
ADPC	National Certification Council for Activity Professionals (720)

AEA	Association of Machinery and Equipment Appraisers **(292)**	**AMD**	International Council of Shopping Centers **(538)**	**APR**	National Institute of Pension Administrators **(765)**
AECCP	Association of Real Estate License Law Officials **(305)**		Society of Broadcast Engineers **(931)**		National School Public Relations Association **(789)**
AEM	International Association of Emergency Managers **(520)**	**AMDC**	Association of Millwork Distributors **(294)**		The Public Relations Society of America **(870)**
	International Fitness Professionals Association **(545)**	**AME**	American Psychiatric Association **(168)**		
AEP	National Association of Estate Planners and Councils **(666)**		Professional Aviation Maintenance Association **(860)**	**APS**	Association of Productivity Specialists **(300)**
	National Registry of Environmental Professionals **(785)**	**AMLP**	Bank Administration Institute **(326)**		Pet Sitters International **(843)**
AES	Society of Financial Examiners **(936)**	**AMLS**	National Association of Emergency Medical Technicians **(665)**	**ARA**	Accreditation Council for Accountancy and Taxation **(9)**
AESC CRA	Association of Executive Search Consultants **(282)**	**AMO**	Institute of Real Estate Management **(503)**		American Society of Farm Managers and Rural Appraisers **(197)**
AETAC	American Embryo Transfer Association **(116)**	**AMP**	American Case Management Association **(88)**		LOMA **(600)**
AF SFFP	American Society for Engineering Education **(183)**		International Foundation of Employee Benefit Plans **(547)**	**ArchiMate**	The Open Group **(828)**
AFA CF	American Farrier's Association **(118)**	**AMRT**	The Institute of Inspection, Cleaning and Restoration Certification **(500)**	**ARE**	National Council of Architectural Registration Boards **(733)**
AFA CJF	American Farrier's Association **(118)**	**AMS**	Health Industry Distributors Association **(469)**	**AREMO**	Real Estate Management Brokers Institute **(875)**
AFA CTF	American Farrier's Association **(118)**		Professional Aviation Maintenance Association **(860)**	**ARI**	Amusement Industry Manufacturers and Suppliers International **(223)**
AFC	American College of Forensic Examiners Institute **(96)**		Society of Accredited Marine Surveyors **(927)**	**ARM**	Institute of Real Estate Management **(503)**
	American Kennel Club **(143)**	**ANCC**	American Nurses Association **(156)**	**ARR**	International Society for Magnetic Resonance in Medicine **(567)**
	Association for Financial Counseling and Planning Education **(246)**		Association of Occupational Health Professionals in Healthcare **(296)**	**ARRT**	Joint Review Committee on Education in Radiologic Technology **(589)**
AFE	Society of Financial Examiners **(936)**		Association of Women's Health, Obstetric and Neonatal Nurses **(318)**	**ARRTCP**	United States Lifesaving Association **(996)**
AFIP	Association of Finance and Insurance Professionals **(283)**		Preventive Cardiovascular Nurses Association **(857)**	**ASA**	American Society of Appraisers **(192)**
AFM	American Society of Farm Managers and Rural Appraisers **(197)**	**ANCE**	American Academy of Ambulatory Care Nursing **(30)**	**ASAM**	American Society of Addiction Medicine **(191)**
AFO	National Recreation and Parks Association **(784)**	**ANSF**	Marble Institute of America **(604)**	**ASATT**	American Society of Anesthesia Technologists and Technicians **(192)**
AFPh	Antique and Amusement Photographers International **(224)**	**ANSI**	Automotive Lift Institute, Inc. **(322)**	**ASBASAM**	Association of Ship Brokers and Agents (U.S.A.) **(308)**
AFPO	Flexographic Technical Association **(447)**		International Association for Continuing Education and Training **(511)**	**ASC**	American College of Forensic Examiners Institute **(96)**
AFS	International Fitness Professionals Association **(545)**	**ANSI/KCMA**	Kitchen Cabinet Manufacturers Association **(591)**		Distribution Contractors Association **(414)**
AFTC	International Fitness Professionals Association **(545)**	**AOA**	American Academy of Hospice and Palliative Medicine **(35)**	**ASCA**	American Swimming Coaches Association **(215)**
AFTE	Association of Firearm and Toolmark Examiners **(283)**		American Osteopathic Board of Physical Medicine and Rehabilitation **(160)**	**ASCLS**	Association of Public Health Laboratories **(304)**
AGC	National Glass Association **(755)**	**AOA-CME**	American Osteopathic College of Allergy and Immunology **(160)**	**ASCP**	American Society of Clinical Psychopharmacology **(195)**
	Potato Association of America **(854)**	**AOBOG**	American College of Osteopathic Surgeons **(100)**	**ASCPi**	American Society for Clinical Pathology **(182)**
AGOC	American Guild of Organists **(127)**	**AOBOS**	American College of Osteopathic Surgeons **(100)**	**ASCS**	NADCA: The HVAC Inspection, Maintenance and Restoration Association **(623)**
AH + FSC	American Council on Exercise **(110)**	**AOBPM**	American College of Occupational and Environmental Medicine **(99)**	**ASD**	The Institute of Inspection, Cleaning and Restoration Certification **(500)**
AHC	The Door and Hardware Institute **(416)**		American Osteopathic College of Occupational and Preventive Medicine **(160)**	**ASDT**	The Institute of Inspection, Cleaning and Restoration Certification **(500)**
AHDI-F	Association for Healthcare Documentation Integrity **(247)**	**AOBS**	American College of Osteopathic Surgeons **(100)**	**ASE**	National Association for Alcoholism and Drug Abuse Counselors **(646)**
AHFI	National Health Care Anti-Fraud Association **(758)**	**AOC**	Association of Old Crows **(297)**		National Association of Service Managers **(695)**
AHI	American Medical Technologists **(150)**		The Door and Hardware Institute **(416)**	**ASEP**	International Council on Systems Engineering **(539)**
AHIP	Medical Library Association **(611)**	**AOCD/AOA**	American Osteopathic College of Dermatology **(160)**	**ASGS**	American Society of General Surgeons **(198)**
AHWD	National Association of Realtors **(690)**	**AOE**	Drycleaning & Laundry Institute **(417)**	**ASHA**	American Cleft Palate-Craniofacial Association **(91)**
AI	Maple Flooring Manufacturers Association **(604)**	**AOSC**	Event Planners Association **(434)**	**ASM**	International Council of Shopping Centers **(538)**
	National Association of Underwater Instructors **(707)**		Local Media Association **(599)**	**ASNC**	International Fitness Professionals Association **(545)**
AIA	Energy and Environmental Building Association **(427)**	**AOSSM-SC**	American Orthopaedic Society for Sports Medicine **(159)**	**ASNR**	American Society of Neurorehabilitation **(204)**
	Insulating Concrete Form Association **(504)**	**AP**	Association for Conflict Resolution **(243)**	**ASNT**	American Society for Nondestructive Testing **(187)**
	Modular Building Institute **(618)**	**APA**	National Institute of Pension Administrators **(765)**	**ASP**	Association for High Technology Distribution **(248)**
	Radiant Panel Association **(872)**		National Society of Insurance Premium Auditors **(794)**		Board of Certified Safety Professionals **(332)**
	Society of Architectural Historians **(930)**	**APAPCP**	Architectural Precast Association **(228)**	**ASPE**	Professional Construction Estimators Association of America **(861)**
	Society of Fire Protection Engineers **(936)**	**APC**	Academy of Laser Dentistry **(6)**	**ASPPB/NR**	Association of State and Provincial Psychology Boards **(309)**
AIAA	LOMA **(600)**		The American Consultants League **(108)**	**ASTC**	American Polygraph Association **(166)**
AIAF	LOMA **(600)**		National Association of Legal Assistants **(677)**	**AStd**	Standards Engineering Society **(961)**
AICC	American Institute of Constructors **(138)**		Society of Actuaries **(927)**	**ASTM**	Glove Shippers Association **(463)**
AICI FLC	Association of Image Consultants International **(287)**		United States Professional Tennis Association **(998)**	**AT**	American Society for Clinical Pathology **(182)**
AII	American Institute of Inspectors **(139)**	**APCO**	APCO (Association of Public-Safety Communications Officials) International **(304)**	**ATA**	Accreditation Council for Accountancy and Taxation **(9)**
AIM	American College of Rheumatology **(102)**	**APESCS**	International Fitness Professionals Association **(545)**	**ATCN**	Society of Trauma Nurses **(949)**
AIMS	American Angus Association **(45)**	**APFTC**	International Fitness Professionals Association **(545)**	**ATCP**	American Concrete Institute **(106)**
AIO	American Institute of Organbuilders **(139)**	**APICS**	APICS The Association for Operations Management **(224)**	**ATCS**	Art Therapy Credentials Board **(230)**
AIR	International Association of Insurance Receivers **(523)**	**APIQR**	American Petroleum Institute **(163)**	**ATMS**	International Foundation of Employee Benefit Plans **(547)**
AIRC	LOMA **(600)**	**APLDC**	Association of Professional Landscape Designers **(301)**	**ATP**	Accreditation Council for Accountancy and Taxation **(9)**
AIS	American Institute for CPCU - Insurance Institute of America **(136)**	**APM**	American Society of Pension Professionals & Actuaries **(206)**		Rehabilitation Engineering and Assistive Technology Society of North America **(879)**
	American Institute of Stress **(140)**	**APN**	National Association of Orthopedic Nurses **(683)**	**ATR**	Art Therapy Credentials Board **(230)**
ALAT	American Association for Laboratory Animal Science **(50)**	**APQP/PPAP**	Automotive Industry Action Group **(322)**	**ATR-BC**	Art Therapy Credentials Board **(230)**
ALC	REALTORS Land Institute **(876)**			**ATS**	National Auctioneers Association **(711)**
ALI/ETL	Automotive Lift Institute, Inc. **(322)**				
ALISE	Association for Library and Information Science Education **(251)**				
ALS	NALS **(625)**				
AM	IT Financial Management Association **(586)**				
AMA	National Exchange Carrier Association **(746)**				
AMA PRA	American Congress of Obstetricians and Gynecologists **(107)**				
	Orthopaedic Trauma Association **(834)**				

	Promotional Products Association International (867)	**CBTE**	Society of Broadcast Engineers (931)	**CChE**	American Institute of Chemists (138)

Promotional Products Association International (867)

SSPC: the Society for Protective Coatings (960)

CASCUE National Association of State Credit Union Supervisors (699)

CASS Ideas America (482)

CAT American Society of Anesthesia Technologists and Technicians (192)

Electronic Security Association (424)

National Association of Elevator Contractors (665)

National Athletic Trainers Association (710)

CATIAV5rI2 American Society of Body Engineers (193)

CATN-II Emergency Nurses Association (425)

CATT American Society of Anesthesia Technologists and Technicians (192)

CAVS American Hospital Association (133)

American Society of Appraisers (192)

Association for Healthcare Volunteer Resource Professionals (248)

CAWI American Welding Society (220)

CAWM Irrigation Association (585)

CAWS National Association of Waterproofing and Structural Repair Contractors (709)

CB American Institute of Professional Bookkeepers (140)

Retail Bakers of America (884)

CBA American Society for Quality (189)

Bank Administration Institute (326)

Institute of Business Appraisers (498)

National Association of Credit Management (661)

Professional Bail Agents of the United States (860)

CBB Retail Bakers of America (884)

CBBC American Boat and Yacht Council (84)

CBC Institute of Certified Business Counselors (498)

National Court Reporters Association (740)

Specialty Coffee Association of America (957)

CBCA Common - A Users Group (369)

DRI International (416)

CBCCT American Society of Nuclear Cardiology (205)

CBCLA DRI International (416)

CBCP Association of Energy Engineers (280)

CBCV DRI International (416)

CBDT International Society for Clinical Densitometry (565)

CBE Professional Beauty Association | National Cosmetology Association (861)

CBET Association for the Advancement of Medical Instrumentation (258)

CBF National Association of Credit Management (661)

CBI International Business Brokers Association (532)

National Fire Protection Association (751)

CBIP Institute for Certification of Computing Professionals (497)

CBJ Jewelers of America (587)

CBJT Jewelers of America (587)

CBM American Meteorological Society (151)

CBN American Society for Metabolic and Bariatric Surgery (187)

CBNC American Society of Nuclear Cardiology (205)

CBNT Society of Broadcast Engineers (931)

CBP Association of Pool and Spa Professionals (299)

Institute of Electrical and Electronics Engineers (IEEE) (499)

Research and Development Associates for Military Food and Packaging Systems (881)

WorldatWork (1028)

CBPE National Fire Protection Association (751)

CBRE Society of Broadcast Engineers (931)

CBS Bearing Specialist Association (327)

Brick Industry Association (335)

CBSE Building Service Contractors Association International (337)

CBSM American Academy of Sleep Medicine (42)

CBSP American Biological Safety Association (81)

CBT American Bankers Association (79)

Society of Broadcast Engineers (931)

Specialty Coffee Association of America (957)

Vibration Institute (1008)

CBTE
CBUNA Society of Broadcast Engineers (931)

Certification Board for Urologic Nurses and Associates (349)

Society of Urologic Nurses and Associates (949)

CC American Association of Bioanalysts (54)

American Watchmakers-Clockmakers Institute (219)

Marine Fabricators Association (605)

National Association of Catholic Chaplains (651)

Professional Aviation Maintenance Association (860)

CCA American Culinary Federation (112)

American Health Information Management Association (129)

American Moving and Storage Association (153)

American Society of Agronomy (ASA, CSSA, SSSA) (191)

Associated Air Balance Council (234)

Crop Science Society of America (404)

International Plant Nutrition Institute (560)

National Certification Commission (720)

Plant Growth Regulation Society of America (849)

Soil Science Society of America (951)

CCAI Chemical Coaters Association International (351)

CCAM American Association of Healthcare Administrative Management (61)

CCAP Community Action Partnership (369)

CCAT American Association of Healthcare Administrative Management (61)

CCBCP Common - A Users Group (369)

CCC American Correctional Chaplains Association (108)

Cruise Lines International Association (405)

American Speech-Language-Hearing Association (212)

CCC-A American Speech-Language-Hearing Association (212)

CCC-SLP AACE International (1)

CCC/CCE Construction Specifications Institute (380)

CCCA American Correctional Chaplains Association (108)

CCCC Catholic Cemetery Conference (345)

CCCE National Contract Management Association (729)

CCCM International Association of Conference Center Administrators (518)

CCCP Conference of State Bank Supervisors (376)

CCCS International Society for Clinical Densitometry (565)

CCD Society for Clinical Data Management (906)

CCDM American Association of Motor Vehicle Administrators (65)

CCE American Chamber of Commerce Executives (89)

American Correctional Association (108)

American Culinary Federation (112)

Club Managers Association of America (359)

International Cemetery, Cremation and Funeral Association (533)

National Association of Credit Management (661)

National Independent Concessionaires Association (762)

Society of Clinical and Medical Hair Removal (933)

CCEA International Cost Estimating and Analysis Association effective (537)

CCEM American College of Osteopathic Emergency Physicians (99)

CCEP The Association of Collegiate Conference and Events Directors International (275)

CCES American College of Sports Medicine (102)

CCET American College of Sports Medicine (102)

CCFC American Cash Flow Association (88)

CCFE International Cemetery, Cremation and Funeral Association (533)

CCFP Association of Correctional Food Service Affiliates (277)

CCG International Window Cleaning Association (581)

CCGP American Society of Consultant Pharmacists (195)

CCGRP Association of Community College Trustees (276)

CCH American Council of Hypnotist Examiners (109)

CChE American Institute of Chemists (138)

CCHP Corporate Housing Providers Association (386)

CCHT American Nephrology Nurses Association (155)

CCI SSPC: the Society for Protective Coatings (960)

CCIM Institute (347)

CCIM Espionage Research Institute International (433)

CCISM United States Lifesaving Association (996)

CCLA Child Life Council (353)

CCLS American Correctional Association (108)

CCM American Meteorological Society (151)

Club Managers Association of America (359)

Construction Management Association of America (379)

National Association of Concessionaires (657)

National Association of Professional Geriatric Care Managers (687)

Office Business Center Association International (826)

CCM, CCE New England Club Managers Association (809)

CCMC America's Health Insurance Plans (28)

American Board of Anesthesiology (81)

Biscuit and Cracker Manufacturers' Association (330)

CCMHC National Board for Certified Counselors (715)

CCMT The Institute of Inspection, Cleaning and Restoration Certification (500)

National Concrete Masonry Association (725)

CCN American Academy of Ambulatory Care Nursing (30)

American Correctional Association (108)

International and American Associations of Clinical Nutritionists (510)

Research and Development Associates for Military Food and Packaging Systems (881)

CCNE National Council of State Boards for Nursing (736)

CCNS American Association of Critical-Care Nurses (59)

CCNT Telecommunications Industry Association (971)

CCO American Correctional Association (108)

Water Quality Association (1013)

CCP American Cheese Society (89)

American Correctional Association (108)

American Concrete Institute (106)

American Society of Consultant Pharmacists (195)

American Society of Extra-Corporeal Technology (197)

Association for Information and Image Management International (249)

Association of Energy Engineers (280)

Association of Insurance Compliance Professionals (289)

Building Commissioning Association (337)

Care Continuum Alliance (342)

Celebrant Foundation and Institute (347)

Certified Claims Professional Accreditation Council (349)

Commercial Food Equipment Service Association (356)

Controlled Environment Testing Association (383)

Custom Electronic Design and Installation Association (405)

Data Management Association International (407)

Institute for Certification of Computing Professionals (497)

International Association of Clerks, Recorders, Election Officials and Treasurers (518)

International Association of Culinary Professionals (519)

Land Improvement Contractors of America (593)

Life Insurance Settlement Association (597)

National Child Care Association (721)

National Court Reporters Association (740)

National Foundation for Credit Counseling (753)

WorldatWork (1028)

CCPA International Association of Personal Protection Agents (526)

CCPES National Association of Catholic Chaplains (651)

CCPI Interlocking Concrete Pavement Institute (508)

CCPO American Concrete Pumping Association (106)

CCPR Construction Specifications Institute (380)

CCR Council for Community and Economic Research (388)

The Council of Landscape Architectural Registration Boards (395)

National Association of College Stores (655)

CCRA Association of Clinical Research Professionals (273)

National Association of Real Estate Appraisers (689)

CCrE International Cemetery, Cremation and Funeral Association (533)

CCRN American Association of Critical-Care Nurses (59)

CCRN-E American Association of Critical-Care Nurses (59)

CCRS American Recovery Association (174)

National Finance Adjusters (750)

CCRT The Institute of Inspection, Cleaning and Restoration Certification (500)

CCS American Construction Inspectors Association (107)

American Correctional Association (108)

American Health Information Management Association (129)

Construction Specifications Institute (380)

Crane Certification Association of America (403)

Heating, Airconditioning and Refrigeration Distributors International (473)

National Customs Brokers and Forwarders Association of America (741)

Pet Industry Joint Advisory Council (842)

Professional Service Association (865)

Research Chefs Association (882)

CCS-P American Health Information Management Association (129)

CCSA The Institute of Internal Auditors (500)

CCSM Community Transportation Association of America (371)

CCSP Communications Fraud Control Association (369)

National Ready Mixed Concrete Association (784)

National Ready Mixed Concrete Association (784)

North American Transportation Management Institute (823)

CCSR American Bankers Association (79)

CCST International Society of Automation (571)

CCT AACE International (1)

American Association of Healthcare Administrative Management (61)

American College for Advancement in Medicine (93)

American Jail Association (142)

American Society for Quality (189)

Cardiovascular Credentialing International (342)

The Institute of Inspection, Cleaning and Restoration Certification (500)

CCT-C American Composites Manufacturers Association (105)

CCT-CM American Composites Manufacturers Association (105)

CCT-CP American Composites Manufacturers Association (105)

International Cast Polymer Alliance (533)

CCT-I American Composites Manufacturers Association (105)

CCT-M American Composites Manufacturers Association (105)

CCT-SS American Composites Manufacturers Association (105)

International Cast Polymer Alliance (533)

CCTC International Transplant Nurses Society (578)

CCTE Association for Skilled and Technical Sciences (256)

Global Business Travel Association (462)

CCTM Community Transportation Association of America (371)

CCTN International Transplant Nurses Society (578)

CCTS American Bankers Association (79)

Ceramic Tile Distributors Association (349)

Community Transportation Association of America (371)

CCUE Credit Union National Association, Inc. (404)

CCVD Vacuum Dealers Trade Association/Sewing Dealers Trade Association (1007)

CCWS Water Quality Association (1013)

CD American Design Drafting Association International and American Digital Design Association (114)

Retail Bakers of America (884)

CDA Council for Professional Recognition (391)

CDAM Professional Housing Management Association (862)

CDBV Association of Insolvency and Restructuring Advisors (289)

CDC American Association of Dental Consultants (59)

Black Retail Action Group (332)

The Door and Hardware Institute (416)

Print Services & Distribution Association (857)

BAFT-IFSA (325)

CDCS
CDCT North American Die Casting Association (816)

CDCUs National Federation of Community Development of Credit Unions (748)

CDD American Design Drafting Association International and American Digital Design Association (114)

Developmental Disabilities Nurses Association (411)

CDDN
CDE American Association of Dental Editors (60)

American Association of Motor Vehicle Administrators (65)

Christian Medical & Dental Associations (356)

National Association of Document Examiners (663)

Special Care Dentistry Association (954)

CDF Career Planning and Adult Development Network (343)

CDFI Career Planning and Adult Development Network (343)

National Federation of Community Development of Credit Unions (748)

CDFM American Society of Military Comptrollers (203)

CDI American Health Information Management Association (129)

Registry of Interpreters for the Deaf (879)

CDI-P Registry of Interpreters for the Deaf (879)

CDL Delta Sigma Pi (409)

CDM Association of Nutrition & Foodservice Professionals (296)

National Defense Industrial Association (742)

North American Transportation Management Institute (823)

CDM/E Radio Advertising Bureau (873)

CDMC
CDME Destination Marketing Association International (411)

CDMM National Association of Pastoral Musicians (683)

CDMP Data Management Association International (407)

Institute for Certification of Computing Professionals (497)

CDN American Nephrology Nurses Association (155)

CDOA National Association of Division Order Analysts (663)

CDON/LTC National Association of Directors of Nursing Administration in Long Term Care (663)

CDP Association for Conflict Resolution (243)

Institute for Certification of Computing Professionals (497)

International Council of Shopping Centers (538)

National Poultry and Food Distributors Association (782)

Society of Depreciation Professionals (934)

CDPC National Ready Mixed Concrete Association (784)

CDPM Professional Housing Management Association (862)

CDPT Community Transportation Association of America (371)

CDR National Association for Pupil Transportation (642)

National Association for Search and Rescue (642)

CDRS ADED - The Association for Driver Rehabilitation Specialists (12)

Professional Housing Management Association (862)

CDS North American Transportation Management Institute (823)

CDSM Association of Energy Engineers (280)

CDT Construction Specifications Institute (380)

International Society for Clinical Densitometry (565)

National Association of Dental Laboratories (662)

North American Transportation Management Institute (823)

CDT/CSD American Design Drafting Association International and American Digital Design Association (114)

CDUHM Professional Housing Management Association (862)

CE American Academy of Clinical Neuropsychology (31)

American Academy of Pain Management (39)

The American Association of Radon Scientists and Technologists (72)

American College Health Association (93)

American College of Cardiology (93)

American Institute of Engineers, Inc. (138)

American Optometric Association (157)

Association for Transpersonal Psychology (260)

Association of Insurance Compliance Professionals (289)

Association of Zoos and Aquariums (318)

Financial Industry Regulatory Authority (FINRA) (444)

National Association of Corporate Directors (658)

National Association of Social Workers (696)

National Marine Manufacturers Association (771)

National Register of Health Service Providers in Psychology (785)

Society for Personality Assessment (918)

Society of Pediatric Nurses (943)

CEA Association of Energy Engineers (280)

Association of Machinery and Equipment Appraisers (292)

National Registry of Environmental Professionals (785)

Society of Broadcast Engineers (931)

CEAB American Nephrology Nurses Association (155)

CEAP Employee Assistance Professionals Association (426)

CEBA National Association of Exclusive Buyer Agents (666)

CEBS International Society of Certified Employee Benefit Specialists (572)

CEBT Eye Bank Association of America (436)

CEC American Chemical Society (89)

American Culinary Federation (112)

American Psychological Association - Division of Psychotherapy (169)

Association of Catholic Colleges and Universities (271)

Council of Residential Specialists (396)

The International Childbirth Education Association (534)

National Academy of Opticianry (628)

Restoration Industry Association (884)

CEcD International Economic Development Council (541)

CECP WorldatWork (1028)

CECS Association for Humanistic Psychology (249)

International Kitchen Exhaust Cleaning Association (553)

CECT International Kitchen Exhaust Cleaning Association (553)

CED Council on Education of the Deaf (399)

CEDA Drycleaning & Laundry Institute (417)

International Association of Eating Disorders Professionals (520)

CEDAN International Association of Eating Disorders Professionals (520)

CEDIR	American Academy of Disability Evaluating Physicians (33)
CEDP	National Center for State Courts (720)
CEDRD	International Association of Eating Disorders Professionals (520)
CEDS	International Association of Eating Disorders Professionals (520)
CEDSN	International Association of Eating Disorders Professionals (520)
CEE	National Alliance of Preservation Commissions (633)
CEF	National Concrete Masonry Association (725)
CEF/MSF	National Association for Surface Finishing (643)
CEFP	APPA - Leadership in Educational Facilities (225)
CEH	International Executive Housekeepers Association (543)
CEHP	Association for Comprehensive Energy Psychology (242)
CEHT	National Environmental Health Association (746)
CEI	Association of the Wall and Ceiling Industry (314)
	Environmental Assessment Association (430)
CEI-M	International Association of Electrical Inspectors (520)
CEI-R	International Association of Electrical Inspectors (520)
CEIP	Professional Association of Resume Writers and Career Coaches (860)
CEL	United States Rowing Association (998)
CELA	National Academy of Elder Law Attorneys, Inc. (627)
	National Elder Law Foundation (744)
CEM	Association of Energy Engineers (280)
	Association of Equipment Management Professionals (281)
	Association of the Wall and Ceiling Industry (314)
	Environmental Assessment Association (430)
	Export Institute of the United States (436)
	International Association of Emergency Managers (520)
	International Association of Exhibitions and Events (520)
	North American Manufacturing Research Institution of SME (817)
CEMS	International Fitness Professionals Association (545)
CEMT	Microscopy Society of America (615)
CEN	Emergency Nurses Association (425)
CENP	American Organization of Nurse Executives (158)
CEO	National Association of Temple Educators (705)
CEOE	American Hotel & Lodging Association (AH&LA) (134)
	National Association of Educational Office Professionals (664)
CEP	AACE International (1)
	Association of Energy Engineers (280)
	Association of the Wall and Ceiling Industry (314)
	Evidence Photographers International Council (434)
	International and American Associations of Clinical Nutritionists (510)
	International Function Point Users Group (548)
	Learning Resources Network (596)
	National Association of Electrical Distributors (664)
	Professional Photographers of America (863)
	United States Lacrosse (995)
CEPC	American Culinary Federation (112)
CEPM	IPC - Association Connecting Electronics Industries (584)
	IPC - Surface Mount Equipment Manufacturers Association (585)
CEPR	Public Relations Student Society of America (870)
CERP	American Dental Education Association (113)
	International Congress of Oral Implantologists (537)
CERS	National Association of Personnel Services (684)
CERTA	National Roofing Contractors Association (787)

CES	Environmental Assessment Association (430)
	National Auctioneers Association (711)
	National Customs Brokers and Forwarders Association of America (741)
	National Registry of Environmental Professionals (785)
	Society of Architectural Historians (930)
CESI	International Kitchen Exhaust Cleaning Association (553)
CESM	Association for Linen Management (251)
	National Registry of Environmental Professionals (785)
CESP	Association of Equipment Management Professionals (281)
	Employee Services Management Association (426)
CET	International Society of Certified Electronics Technicians (572)
	National Association of Elevator Contractors (665)
	National Electronic Service Dealers Association (745)
	National Environmental, Safety and Health Training Association (746)
CETA-DCP	Cleaning Equipment Trade Association (357)
CETA-MCP	Cleaning Equipment Trade Association (357)
CETP	National Propane Gas Association (783)
CEU	American Academy of Audiology (31)
	American Association of Petroleum Geologists (68)
	American Cleft Palate-Craniofacial Association (91)
	American Society of Group Psychotherapy and Psychodrama (198)
	American Therapeutic Recreation Association (216)
	American Water Resources Association (220)
	Conference of Minority Transportation Officials (375)
	International Order of the Golden Rule (559)
	National Association of Addiction Treatment Providers (645)
	National Funeral Directors and Morticians Association (754)
	Society for the Exploration of Psychotherapy Integration (923)
	Sump and Sewage Pump Manufacturers Association (965)
CEUs	American Management Association (146)
	Association of Environmental and Engineering Geologists (281)
CEV	Society of Broadcast Engineers (931)
CF	American Institute for Conservation of Historic and Artistic Works (136)
	International Institute of Forecasters (552)
	CFA Institute (350)
CFA	International Association of Credit Portfolio Managers (519)
CFAP	International Executive Housekeepers Association (543)
CFAT	Electronic Security Association (424)
CFB	American Sports Builders Association (212)
CFBA	Family Firm Institute, Inc. (437)
CFBE	American Hotel & Lodging Association (AH&LA) (134)
CFC	American College of Forensic Examiners Institute (96)
	Association of Film Commissioners International (283)
	Employers Council on Flexible Compensation (427)
	National Association of Air Medical Communication Specialists (646)
	North American Retail Dealers Association (820)
CFCC	AACE International (1)
	American Speech-Language-Hearing Association (212)
CFCD	Society for Research in Child Development (920)
	Vacuum Dealers Trade Association/Sewing Dealers Trade Association (1007)
CFCI	Employers Council on Flexible Compensation (427)
	International Association of Financial Crimes Investigators (521)

CFCM	National Contract Management Association (729)
CFCP	DRI International (416)
CFCS	American Association of Family and Consumer Sciences (61)
CFCS-HDFS	American Association of Family and Consumer Sciences (61)
CFCS-HNFS	American Association of Family and Consumer Sciences (61)
CFD	Learning Resources Network (596)
CFDC	AIB International (17)
CFDI	Associated Locksmiths of America (236)
CFE	Association of Certified Fraud Examiners (271)
	International Association of Venue Managers (528)
	International Food Service Executives' Association (546)
	International Franchise Association (547)
	Society of American Foresters (928)
	Society of Financial Examiners (936)
	World Floor Covering Association (1026)
CFEE	International Festivals and Events Association (545)
CFEI	National Association of Fire Investigators (668)
CFFM	Fraternal Field Managers Association (453)
CFGS	National Association of Small Business Contractors (696)
CFHI	International Association of Official Human Rights Agencies (525)
CFI	International Association of Arson Investigators (515)
	National Fire Protection Association (751)
CFI-II	National Fire Protection Association (751)
CFII	National Association of Fire Investigators (668)
CFLE	National Council on Family Relations (738)
CFLEPE	American Association of Police Polygraphists (70)
CFM	Association of State Floodplain Managers (311)
	International Facility Management Association (543)
	International Food Service Executives' Association (546)
CFMP	American Bankers Association (79)
CFN	American College of Forensic Examiners Institute (96)
CFP	American College of Forensic Examiners Institute (96)
	American Fence Association (120)
	Financial Planning Association (445)
	Financial Planning Standards Board (445)
	Society of American Foresters (928)
	World Floor Covering Association (1026)
CFPE	National Fire Protection Association (751)
CFPIM	APICS The Association for Operations Management (224)
CFPP	Association of Nutrition & Foodservice Professionals (296)
CFPS	International Function Point Users Group (548)
	National Fire Protection Association (751)
CFRE	Association for Healthcare Philanthropy (248)
	National Catholic Development Conference (718)
CFRN	Air and Surface Transport Nurses Association (17)
	Emergency Nurses Association (425)
CFS	American Association of Suicidology (74)
	American Cash Flow Association (88)
	Personal Care Products Council (842)
	Pet Industry Joint Advisory Council (842)
	Restoration Industry Association (884)
	The Institute of Internal Auditors (500)
CFSA	National Association of Church Food Service (653)
CFSC	World Floor Covering Association (1026)
CFSD	National Association of Church Food Service (653)
CFSM	Association of Correctional Food Service Affiliates (277)
CFSP	Business Forms Management Association (339)
	Credit Union National Association, Inc. (404)
	North American Association of Food Equipment Manufacturers (813)
CFSS	The Fragrance Foundation (453)
CFSSP	American Bankers Association (79)

CFSW	American College of Forensic Examiners Institute (96)
CFT	Concrete Foundations Association (373)
	The Concrete Industry Board (373)
CFuE	International Cemetery, Cremation and Funeral Association (533)
CFV	Alpha Kappa Psi (26)
CFWA	Family Firm Institute, Inc. (437)
CG	The American Gem Society (125)
CG, CMG	American Handwriting Analysis Foundation (128)
CGA	The American Gem Society (125)
	International Graphoanalysis Society (548)
CGAP	The Institute of Internal Auditors (500)
CGAS	American Academy of Health Care Providers-Addictive Disorders (34)
CGBP	North American Small Business International Trade Educators (821)
CGBSC	National Ready Mixed Concrete Association (784)
CGC	American Kennel Club (143)
	National Guardianship Association (757)
CGCIO	Government Management Information Sciences (464)
CGCM	In-Plant Printing and Mailing Association (487)
CGCS	Golf Course Superintendents Association of America (463)
CGD	Association of Energy Engineers (280)
	International Ground Source Heat Pump Association (549)
CGDIT	Association of Energy Engineers (280)
CGE	American Society of Gas Engineers (198)
CGEIT	Information Systems Audit and Control Association (495)
CGFM	Association of Government Accountants (286)
CGFNS	National Council of State Boards for Nursing (736)
CGI	Choristers Guild (355)
	National Glass Association (755)
CGIA	Irrigation Association (585)
CGIS/LIST	ASPRS-The Imaging and Geospatial Information Society (233)
CGK	Professional Grounds Management Society (862)
CGM	Professional Grounds Management Society (862)
CGMP	Connected International Meeting Professionals Association (377)
	Society of Government Meeting Professionals (938)
CGMS	National Grants Management Association (756)
CGP	American Forage and Grassland Council (122)
	American Group Psychotherapy Association (127)
	American Society of Consultant Pharmacists (195)
	National Cotton Ginners' Association (730)
CGPM	National Affordable Housing Management Association (629)
CGRN	Society of Gastroenterology Nurses and Associates (937)
CGS	Giant Screen Cinema Association (460)
CGT	Professional Grounds Management Society (862)
	Professional Service Association (865)
	Society of Commercial Seed Technologists (933)
CGTP	Gas Technology Institute (456)
	Society of Government Travel Professionals (938)
CGWP	National Ground Water Association (756)
	National Systems Contractors Association (798)
CH	American Council of Hypnotist Examiners (109)
CH&EM	Automotive Engine Rebuilders Association (322)
CHA	American Hotel & Lodging Association (AH&LA) (134)
	American Society for Quality (189)
	Latino Hotel Association (594)
CHAA	National Association of Healthcare Access Management (671)
CHAE	Hospitality Financial and Technology Professionals (479)
CHAM	National Association of Healthcare Access Management (671)
CHBA	Medical-Dental-Hospital Business Associates (612)
CHBC	National Society of Certified Healthcare Business Consultants (793)

CHBME	Healthcare Billing and Management Association (470)
CHC	American Hospital Association (133)
	American Society for Healthcare Engineering (184)
	Association for Financial Counseling and Planning Education (246)
	Association for Healthcare Resource and Materials Management (248)
	Health Care Compliance Association (469)
	Medical-Dental-Hospital Business Associates (612)
CHC-F	Health Care Compliance Association (469)
CHCC	National Alliance of Medicare Set-Aside Professionals, Inc. (632)
CHCE	Hospice Association of America (479)
	National Association for Home Care and Hospice (639)
CHCIO	College of Healthcare Information Management Executives (364)
CHCQM	American Board of Quality Assurance and Utilization Review Physicians, Inc. (84)
CHCR	National Association for Health Care Recruitment (639)
CHCSR	Professional Housing Management Association (862)
CHD	EDA Consortium (419)
CHDA	American Health Information Management Association (129)
CHES	American School Health Association (177)
	Society for Public Health Education (919)
CHESP	American Hospital Association (133)
	American Society for Healthcare Engineering (184)
	American Society for Healthcare Environmental Services (185)
	Association for Healthcare Resource and Materials Management (248)
	American Hospital Association (133)
	American Society for Healthcare Engineering (184)
	Association for Healthcare Resource and Materials Management (248)
CHFN	American Association of Heart Failure Nurses (62)
CHFP	Healthcare Financial Management Association (471)
CHFS	American College of Sports Medicine (102)
CHHE	American Hotel & Lodging Association (AH&LA) (134)
CHI	American Association of Home Inspectors (62)
	National Association for Interpretation (640)
CHITS	Physician Office Managers Association of America (847)
CHL	International Association of Healthcare Central Service Materiel Management (522)
CHME	Hospitality Sales and Marketing Association International (479)
CHMM	Alliance of Hazardous Materials Professionals (25)
	Institute of Hazardous Materials Management (500)
CHMP	Institute of Hazardous Materials Management (500)
CHO	Asian American Hotel Owners Association (231)
CHP	American Board of Health Physics (82)
	Research and Development Associates for Military Food and Packaging Systems (881)
CHPA	International Association for Healthcare Security and Safety (512)
CHPA(F)	International Association for Healthcare Security and Safety (512)
CHPAS	International Fitness Professionals Association (545)
CHPC	Health Care Compliance Association (469)
CHPS	American Health Information Management Association (129)
CHR	International Home Furnishings Representatives Association (550)
CHRC	Health Care Compliance Association (469)
CHRE	American Hotel & Lodging Association (AH&LA) (134)
CHRM	American Hotel & Lodging Association (AH&LA) (134)
CHRN	Undersea and Hyperbaric Medical Society (984)
CHRS	International Window Cleaning Association (581)
	Physician Office Managers Association of America (847)

CHS	American Hotel & Lodging Association (AH&LA) (134)
CHSE	Hospitality Sales and Marketing Association International (479)
CHSO	International Association for Healthcare Security and Safety (512)
CHSP	American Hotel & Lodging Association (AH&LA) (134)
	National Organization for Human Service (777)
CHST	Board of Certified Safety Professionals (332)
CHSWCP	Portable Sanitation Association International (853)
CHT	American Hotel & Lodging Association (AH&LA) (134)
	American Society of Hand Therapists (199)
	Undersea and Hyperbaric Medical Society (984)
CHTP	Hospitality Financial and Technology Professionals (479)
CI	American College of Forensic Examiners Institute (96)
	American Registry of Radiologic Technologists (174)
	International Association of Arson Investigators (515)
	International Iridology Practitioners Association (552)
	Registry of Interpreters for the Deaf (879)
	SWANA - Solid Waste Association of North America (967)
	Water Quality Association (1013)
CIA	The Institute of Internal Auditors (500)
CIAQM	National Registry of Environmental Professionals (785)
	Association of Energy Engineers (280)
CIAQP	Association of Energy Engineers (280)
CIAQT	Association of Energy Engineers (280)
CIC	Association for Professionals in Infection Control and Epidemiology (254)
	Institute of International Container Lessors (501)
	Investment Adviser Association (583)
	Irrigation Association (585)
	Society of Certified Insurance Counselors (932)
CICA	FCIB-NACM Corporation (438)
	International Association of Law Enforcement Intelligence Analysts (523)
CICE	FCIB-NACM Corporation (438)
CICMHE	Material Handling Industry of America (608)
CICP	FCIB-NACM Corporation (438)
CID	IPC - Association Connecting Electronics Industries (584)
	Irrigation Association (585)
CIDM	Data Management Association International (407)
CIE	The Environmental Information Association (431)
CIEC	The Environmental Information Association (431)
CIER	The Environmental Information Association (431)
CIES	The Environmental Information Association (431)
CIET	National Registry of Environmental Professionals (785)
CIFI	International Association of Special Investigation Units (528)
CIFT	American College of Sports Medicine (102)
CIG	National Association for Interpretation (640)
CIGC	Gas Technology Institute (456)
CIH	American Board of Industrial Hygiene (82)
	American Conference of Governmental Industrial Hygienists (107)
	American Industrial Hygiene Association (135)
CIHT	National Association for Interpretation (640)
CII	Council of International Investigators (395)
CIM	Association of Image Consultants International (287)
	Internet Marketing Association (582)
	Library Binding Institute (597)
	National Association for Interpretation (640)
CIMA	Investment Management Consultants Association (584)
CIMC	Investment Management Consultants Association (584)

CIMI	International Association of Infant Massage *(523)*	CKS	International Fitness Professionals Association *(545)*
CIMP	Connected International Meeting Professionals Association *(377)*	CLA	The Council of Landscape Architectural Registration Boards *(395)*
CIMS	International Sanitary Supply Association *(563)*		National Association of Legal Assistants *(677)*
CIOWTS	National Environmental Health Association *(746)*	CLAS	Clinical Ligand Assay Society *(358)*
CIP	Association for Information and Image Management International *(249)*	CLB	Library Binding Institute *(597)*
		CLBB	American Bankers Association *(79)*
	Association of Image Consultants International *(287)*	CLC	American Lighting Association *(145)*
			American Medical Technologists *(150)*
	NACE International *(623)*	CLCS	Board of Certified Safety Professionals *(332)*
	National Association for Interpretation *(640)*	CLE	American Association for Justice *(50)*
	Society of Competitive Intelligence Professionals *(933)*		American Association of Attorney-Certified Public Accountants *(54)*
CIPA	National Society of Insurance Premium Auditors *(794)*		American Foreign Law Association *(122)*
CIPFA	National Association of Independent Public Finance Advisors *(675)*		American Health Lawyers Association *(130)*
CIPM	CFA Institute *(350)*		American Intellectual Property Law Association *(141)*
CIPP	International Association of Privacy Professionals *(526)*		Association of Corporate Counsel *(277)*
CIPP/C	International Association of Privacy Professionals *(526)*		Copyright Society of the U.S.A. *(385)*
CIPP/E	International Association of Privacy Professionals *(526)*		Council for International Tax Education *(390)*
CIPP/G	International Association of Privacy Professionals *(526)*		Federal Bar Association *(438)*
CIPP/IT	International Association of Privacy Professionals *(526)*		International Aviation Women's Association *(529)*
CIR	International Association of Insurance Receivers *(523)*		International Municipal Lawyers Association *(557)*
CIRA	Association of Insolvency and Restructuring Advisors *(289)*		Maritime Law Association of the U.S. *(606)*
CIRCC	American Academy of Professional Coders *(40)*		National Employment Lawyers Association (NELA) *(746)*
CIRM	APICS The Association for Operations Management *(224)*	CLEC	American Prepaid Legal Services Institute *(167)*
CIRP	International Society for Quality-of-Life Studies *(569)*	CLEP	Association of Energy Engineers *(280)*
CIRS	Alliance of Information and Referral Systems *(25)*	CLES	Association for the Advancement of Medical Instrumentation *(258)*
CIRS-A	Alliance of Information and Referral Systems *(25)*		National Association of Chiefs of Police *(653)*
CIS	International Association of Healthcare Central Service Materiel Management *(522)*	CLEW	Association of Commercial Finance Attorneys *(275)*
		CLFC:R	International Fitness Professionals Association *(545)*
	Investment Management Consultants Association *(584)*	CLG	National Alliance of Preservation Commissions *(633)*
	IPC - Association Connecting Electronics Industries *(584)*	CLGS	National Lubricating Grease Institute *(770)*
CISA	Information Systems Audit and Control Association *(495)*	CLHRP	Society of Clinical and Medical Hair Removal *(933)*
	Information Systems Security Association *(495)*	CLI	National Association of Legal Investigators *(678)*
CISE	Conference of State Bank Supervisors *(376)*	CLIA	Irrigation Association *(585)*
CISM	Information Systems Audit and Control Association *(495)*	CLIP-R	Registry of Interpreters for the Deaf *(879)*
		CLLM	Association for Linen Management *(251)*
	Information Systems Security Association *(495)*	CLM	Association of Legal Administrators *(291)*
CISP	American Bankers Association *(79)*		Latino Hotel Association *(594)*
CISR	Society of Certified Insurance Counselors *(932)*		North American Lake Management Society *(817)*
CISSP	Black Data Processing Associates *(331)*	CLMC	International Association of Lighting Management Companies *(524)*
CIT	IPC - Association Connecting Electronics Industries *(584)*	CLMR	American Lighting Association *(145)*
	National Association for Interpretation *(640)*	CLP	American League of Lobbyists *(145)*
	National Environmental, Safety and Health Training Association *(746)*		Association of University Technology Managers *(316)*
CITC	Institute for Certification of Computing Professionals *(497)*		International Listening Association *(554)*
CITCP	Institute for Certification of Computing Professionals *(497)*		International Warehouse Logistics Association *(580)*
CITE	Society of Incentive & Travel Executives *(939)*		Licensing Executives Society *(597)*
CITGC	CHA - Certified Horsemanship Association *(350)*		North American Lake Management Society *(817)*
CITPA	National Society of Insurance Premium Auditors *(794)*		Professional Landcare Network *(863)*
CIW	American Association of Managing General Agents *(64)*		United Association of Equipment Leasing *(985)*
	Future Business Leaders of America - Phi Beta Lambda *(455)*	CLRE	The American Board of Opticianry and the National Contact Lens Examiners *(83)*
CJB	Retail Bakers of America *(884)*	CLS	International Council of Shopping Centers *(538)*
CJE	Journalism Education Association *(589)*		International Licensing Industry Merchandisers' Association *(554)*
CJLC	Specialty Coffee Association of America *(957)*		Society of Tribologists and Lubrication Engineers *(949)*
CJM	American Jail Association *(142)*	CLSD	American Hotel & Lodging Association (AH&LA) *(134)*
CJO	American Jail Association *(142)*	CLSMDS	International Fitness Professionals Association *(545)*
CKAS	International Fitness Professionals Association *(545)*	CLSO	American Hotel & Lodging Association (AH&LA) *(134)*
CKPP	American Society for Engineering Management *(184)*	CLSS	American Hotel & Lodging Association (AH&LA) *(134)*
		CLT	Association for Linen Management *(251)*
		CLT-E	Professional Landcare Network *(863)*
		CLT-I	Professional Landcare Network *(863)*

CLTC	National Association for Practical Nurse Education and Service *(641)*
	National Association Of Insurance and Financial Advisors(NAIFA) *(676)*
CLVS	National Court Reporters Association *(740)*
CLWM	Irrigation Association *(585)*
CM	American Association of Airport Executives *(53)*
	American Institute for Conservation of Historic and Artistic Works *(136)*
	American Midwifery Certification Board *(151)*
	Institute of Certified Professional Managers *(498)*
	International City/County Management Association *(535)*
	Laboratory Animal Management Association *(592)*
	Monument Builders of North America *(619)*
	National Association of Jewelry Appraisers *(677)*
	National Management Association *(771)*
	Refrigeration Service Engineers Society *(878)*
	SWANA - Solid Waste Association of North America *(967)*
CMA	American Management Association *(146)*
	Institute Management Accountants *(498)*
	Institute of Career Certification International *(498)*
	National Association of Jewelry Appraisers *(677)*
CMA (AAMA)	American Association of Medical Assistants *(65)*
CMAA	National Interscholastic Athletic Administrators Association *(766)*
CMAGT	National Glass Association *(755)*
CMAR	American Association for Laboratory Animal Science *(50)*
	Institute of Certified Professional Managers *(498)*
	Laboratory Animal Management Association *(592)*
CMAS	American Medical Technologists *(150)*
CMB	Retail Bakers of America *(884)*
CMBB	American Society for Quality *(189)*
CMBE	Conference of State Bank Supervisors *(376)*
CMBJ	Jewelers of America *(587)*
CMBM	Physician Office Managers Association of America *(847)*
CMC	American Association of Critical-Care Nurses *(59)*
	American Culinary Federation *(112)*
	American Moving and Storage Association *(153)*
	American Watchmakers-Clockmakers Institute *(219)*
	Institute of Management Consultants USA *(501)*
	International Institute of Municipal Clerks *(552)*
	National Association of Concessionaires *(657)*
	National Association of Mortgage Brokers *(681)*
	National Association of Professional Geriatric Care Managers *(687)*
CMCE	International Military Community Executives Association *(556)*
CMCN	National Association of Managed Care Physicians *(679)*
CMD	American Medical Directors Association *(149)*
	International Council of Shopping Centers *(538)*
	National Independent Automobile Dealers Association *(761)*
CMDD	Dance Masters of America, Inc. *(406)*
CMDSM	Mail Systems Management Association *(601)*
CMDSS	Mail Systems Management Association *(601)*
CME	American Academy of Family Physicians *(34)*
	American Academy of Medical Acupuncture *(36)*
	American Academy of Orthopaedic Surgeons *(38)*
	American Academy of Pain Management *(39)*

American Academy of Physician Assistants *(40)*

American Academy of Podiatric Practice Management *(40)*

American Association for Hand Surgery *(49)*

American Association of Clinical Endocrinologists *(56)*

American Association of Integrated Healthcare Delivery Systems *(63)*

American Association of Motor Vehicle Administrators *(65)*

American Association of Neuromuscular and Electrodiagnostic Medicine *(66)*

American Association of Physician Specialists *(69)*

American Cleft Palate-Craniofacial Association *(91)*

American College for Advancement in Medicine *(93)*

American College of Cardiology *(93)*

American College of Chest Physicians *(94)*

American College of Osteopathic Family Physicians *(100)*

American College of Phlebology *(100)*

American College of Rheumatology *(102)*

American College of Surgeons *(103)*

American Orthopaedic Association *(158)*

American Osteopathic Association *(160)*

American School Health Association *(177)*

American Society for Adolescent Psychiatry *(180)*

American Society for Aesthetic Plastic Surgery *(180)*

American Society for Clinical Pathology *(182)*

American Society for Dermatologic Surgery *(183)*

American Society for Investigative Pathology *(186)*

American Society for Reconstructive Microsurgery *(189)*

American Society of Abdominal Surgeons *(190)*

American Society of Bariatric Physicians *(193)*

American Society of Cataract and Refractive Surgery *(194)*

American Society of Clinical Oncology *(194)*

American Society of Echocardiography *(197)*

American Society of Hypertension, Inc. *(200)*

American Society of Nephrology *(204)*

American Society of Nuclear Cardiology *(205)*

American Society of Retina Specialists *(209)*

American Society of Transplant Surgeons *(210)*

Association for Research in Vision and Ophthalmology *(255)*

Association of Neurosurgical Physician Assistants *(295)*

Association of Physician Assistants in Obstetrics and Gynecology *(299)*

Association of Reproductive Health Professionals *(305)*

Child Neurology Society *(353)*

Christian Medical & Dental Associations *(356)*

Drug Information Association *(417)*

The Endocrine Society *(427)*

The International Society for Minimally Invasive Cardiothoracic Surgery *(567)*

LeadingAge (American Association of Homes and Services for the Aging) *(595)*

National Abortion Federation *(626)*

National Arab-American Medical Association *(635)*

National Association of Housing and Redevelopment Officials *(673)*

National Association of Professional Mortgage Women *(687)*

National Medical Association *(772)*

Obesity Society *(825)*

Orthopaedic Research Society *(833)*

Sales and Marketing Executives International, Inc. *(890)*

Society for Cardiovascular Angiography and Interventions *(905)*

Society for Pediatric Anesthesia *(917)*

Society of Air Force Physician Assistants *(928)*

Society of Army Physician Assistants *(930)*

Society of Clinical and Medical Hair Removal *(933)*

Society of Emergency Medicine Physician Assistants *(934)*

Society of Interventional Radiology *(940)*

Society of Radiologists in Ultrasound *(946)*

United States and Canadian Academy of Pathology *(989)*

CME/CE American Academy of Pain Medicine *(39)*

CMET National Comprehensive Cancer Network *(725)*

CMF National Marine Electronics Association *(771)*

American Boat Builders and Repairers Association *(84)*

Institute of Career Certification International *(498)*

CMfgE North American Manufacturing Research Institution of SME *(817)*

Society of Manufacturing Engineers *(941)*

CMfgT North American Manufacturing Research Institution of SME *(817)*

Society of Manufacturing Engineers *(941)*

CMFS Society of Tribologists and Lubrication Engineers *(949)*

CMGA American Association of Managing General Agents *(64)*

CMH Restoration Industry Association *(884)*

CMI American College of Forensic Examiners Institute *(96)*

American Watchmakers-Clockmakers Institute *(219)*

The Association of Medical Illustrators *(293)*

Institute for Professionals in Taxation *(497)*

National Association of Professional Mortgage Women *(687)*

National Registry of Environmental Professionals *(785)*

CMIR Investment Recovery Association *(584)*

CML Associated Locksmiths of America *(236)*

SOLE - The International Society of Logistics *(952)*

CMLA American Medical Technologists *(150)*

CMM Association of Marina Industries *(293)*

Custom Tailors and Designers Association of America *(406)*

In-Plant Printing and Mailing Association *(487)*

International Maintenance Institute *(555)*

Meeting Professionals International *(612)*

Professional Association of Health Care Office Management *(859)*

CMMO National Association of Housing and Redevelopment Officials *(673)*

CMO Association of Marina Industries *(293)*

CMOS Physician Office Managers Association of America *(847)*

CMP American Society for Clinical Pathology *(182)*

Convention Industry Council *(383)*

Institute of Career Certification International *(498)*

International Maintenance Institute *(555)*

International Special Events Society *(575)*

Jewelers of America *(587)*

Meeting Professionals International *(612)*

National Center for State Courts *(720)*

National Management Association *(771)*

National Society for Histotechnology *(792)*

Religious Conference Management Association *(880)*

Restoration Industry Association *(884)*

University/Resident Theatre Association *(1003)*

CMP II Laboratory Animal Management Association *(592)*

CMPC International Digital Enterprise Alliance *(540)*

CMPCS Physician Office Managers Association of America *(847)*

CMPE MGMA-ACMPE *(614)*

CMPO National Association of Housing and Redevelopment Officials *(673)*

CMPP International Society for Medical Publication Professionals *(567)*

CMQ American College of Medical Quality *(97)*

CMQ/OE American Society for Quality *(189)*

CMRP American Hospital Association *(133)*

American Society for Healthcare Engineering *(184)*

Association for Healthcare Resource and Materials Management *(248)*

Society for Maintenance & Reliability Professionals *(914)*

CMRT Society for Maintenance & Reliability Professionals *(914)*

CMS American College of Nurse-Midwives *(99)*

Environmental Assessment Association *(430)*

International Association of Assessing Officers *(516)*

International Decorative Artisans League *(540)*

International Society of Certified Employee Benefit Specialists *(572)*

National Minority Supplier Development Council *(773)*

Refrigeration Service Engineers Society *(878)*

U.S. Metric Association *(983)*

CMS-GIS/ LIS ASPRS-The Imaging and Geospatial Information Society *(233)*

CMS-RS ASPRS-The Imaging and Geospatial Information Society *(233)*

CMSP National Training and Simulation Association *(801)*

CMSR American Academy of Medical Management *(36)*

CMSRN Academy of Medical-Surgical Nurses *(7)*

CMST Associated Locksmiths of America *(236)*

International Decorative Artisans League *(540)*

CMT Amusement Industry Manufacturers and Suppliers International *(223)*

Association for Healthcare Documentation Integrity *(247)*

International Association of Counselors and Therapists *(519)*

International Maintenance Institute *(555)*

Market Technicians Association *(606)*

Professional Service Association *(865)*

CMT-R Association for Healthcare Documentation Integrity *(247)*

CMTE American Music Therapy Association *(154)*

Association of Air Medical Services *(264)*

Flag Manufacturers Association of America *(446)*

CMUSA National Association of Housing and Redevelopment Officials *(673)*

CMVO Association of Energy Engineers *(280)*

CMVP CMW American Watchmakers-Clockmakers Institute *(219)*

CNAP Not-For-Profit Services Association *(824)*

CNE American School Health Association *(177)*

National League for Nursing *(768)*

CNHA American College of Health Care Administrators *(96)*

CNM American Association of Birth Centers *(55)*

American Midwifery Certification Board *(151)*

CNMI National Association of State Boards of Accountancy *(698)*

CNML American Association of Critical-Care Nurses *(59)*

American Organization of Nurse Executives *(158)*

CNMs American College of Nurse-Midwives *(99)*

CNN American Nephrology Nurses Association *(155)*

CNN-NP American Nephrology Nurses Association *(155)*

CNP Network Professional Association *(808)*

CNRN American Association of Neuroscience Nurses *(66)*

CNS American College of Nutrition *(99)*

National Association of Clinical Nurse Specialists *(654)*

CNT Council of Colleges of Acupuncture and Oriental Medicine *(392)*

CNU School Nutrition Association *(892)*

Academy of Physicians in Clinical Research (8)

Association of Clinical Research Professionals (273)

Ceramic Tile Institute of America (349)

Cooling Technology Institute (384)

The Institute of Inspection, Cleaning and Restoration Certification (500)

CTIA CTIA - The Wireless Association (405)

CTIE The Travel Institute (979)

CTIS American Bus Association (87)

CTL American Society of Transportation and Logistics (210)

CTM Cruise Lines International Association (405)

CTN American Academy of Ambulatory Care Nursing (30)

CTO Society of Broadcast Engineers (931)

CTP Association for Financial Professionals, Inc. (247)

Institute of Tax Consultants (503)

National Private Truck Council (782)

Professional Landcare Network (863)

Telecommunications Industry Association (971)

Turnaround Management Association (982)

CTP-CSL Professional Landcare Network (863)

CTPA Association for Financial Professionals, Inc. (247)

Community Transportation Association of America (371)

Community Transportation Association of America (371)

CTPS Institute of Tax Consultants (503)

CTR Association of Traumatic Stress Specialists (315)

National Cancer Registrars Association (717)

CTRN Air and Surface Transport Nurses Association (17)

CTropMed American Society of Tropical Medicine and Hygiene (210)

CTRS International Fitness Professionals Association (545)

National Council for Therapeutic Recreation Certification (733)

CTS Association of Traumatic Stress Specialists (315)

Ceramic Tile Institute of America (349)

Environmental Assessment Association (430)

InfoComm International (495)

National Association of Personnel Services (684)

Tire Industry Association (975)

CTS-D InfoComm International (495)

CTS-I InfoComm International (495)

CTSP Tree Care Industry Association (980)

CTSS Association of Traumatic Stress Specialists (315)

CTT American Association of Motor Vehicle Administrators (65)

CTW Structural Building Components Association (964)

CUA Certification Board for Urologic Nurses and Associates (349)

CUCNS Certification Board for Urologic Nurses and Associates (349)

CUDEs National Federation of Community Development of Credit Unions (748)

CUNP Certification Board for Urologic Nurses and Associates (349)

CUPA Certification Board for Urologic Nurses and Associates (349)

CURN Certification Board for Urologic Nurses and Associates (349)

CVA National Association of Certified Valuation Analysts (652)

Vibration Institute (1008)

CVC Association of Finance and Insurance Professionals (283)

Vibration Institute (1008)

CVCHM International Veterinary Acupuncture Society (580)

CVFI National Association of Fire Investigators (668)

CVH Academy of Veterinary Homeopathy (9)

CVI NADCA: The HVAC Inspection, Maintenance and Restoration Association (623)

Vacuum Dealers Trade Association/Sewing Dealers Trade Association (1007)

CVLA National Vehicle Leasing Association (803)

CVLE National Vehicle Leasing Association (803)

CVN Society for Vascular Nursing (926)

CVO National Committee for Quality Assurance (724)

CVP Automated Imaging Association (321)

CVPM Veterinary Hospital Managers Association (1008)

CVPP International Veterinary Academy of Pain Management (580)

CVS SAVE International (891)

CVT Society of Commercial Seed Technologists (933)

CW American Watchmakers-Clockmakers Institute (219)

American Welding Society (220)

National Certified Pipe Welding Bureau (720)

CWB The Wildlife Society (1017)

CWCA American Academy of Wound Management (42)

CWD National Ground Water Association (756)

National Systems Contractors Association (798)

CWD/PI National Ground Water Association (756)

National Systems Contractors Association (798)

CWDP National Association of Workforce Development Professionals (710)

CWE American Welding Society (220)

The Society of Wine Educators (950)

CWF American Welding Society (220)

CWI American Mountain Guides Association (153)

American Welding Society (220)

CWIS American Association of Managing General Agents (64)

CWLS National Association of Counsel for Children (658)

CWP International Society of Weighing and Measurement (574)

International Webmasters Association (580)

National Wellness Institute, Inc. (804)

Window Coverings Association of America (1018)

CWPC National Wellness Institute, Inc. (804)

CWPD National Wellness Institute, Inc. (804)

CWPM National Wellness Institute, Inc. (804)

CWR American Short Line and Regional Railroad Association (179)

CWS American Academy of Wound Management (42)

American College of Certified Wound Specialists (94)

American Welding Society (220)

International Association of Personnel in Employment Security (526)

International Association of Workforce Professionals (IAWP) (529)

International Society of Weighing and Measurement (574)

National Association of Waterproofing and Structural Repair Contractors (709)

Water Quality Association (1013)

CWT Association for Linen Management (251)

Association of Water Technologies (317)

International Society of Weighing and Measurement (574)

CWTC Window Coverings Association of America (1018)

CWWMT International Maintenance Institute (555)

CxA AABC Commissioning Group (1)

CxT AABC Commissioning Group (1)

D and A American Short Line and Regional Railroad Association (179)

DAAS American Academy of Sanitarians (41)

DACP National Institute of Pension Administrators (765)

DACVO American College of Veterinary Ophthalmologists (104)

DACVS American College of Veterinary Surgeons (104)

DAE National Association of Insurance Women (International) (676)

DAPA American Psychotherapy Association (170)

DASMA-PCP Door and Access Systems Manufacturers Association, International (415)

DATIA National Association of Professional Background Screeners (686)

DC The International Childbirth Education Association (534)

DCA National Certification Commission (720)

DCC Conference of Educational Administrators of Schools and Programs for the Deaf (375)

DCCP National Community Pharmacists Association (725)

DCDC BICSI (329)

DCEP Association for Comprehensive Energy Psychology (242)

DCK American Driver and Traffic Safety Education Association (115)

DCNP Dermatology Nurses' Association (410)

DCSW National Association of Social Workers (696)

DD American Design Drafting Association International and American Digital Design Association (114)

DDCLPN Developmental Disabilities Nurses Association (411)

DDSC American Driver and Traffic Safety Education Association (115)

DEC National Cleaners Association (722)

DES Building Stone Institute (338)

DESSC American Boat and Yacht Council (84)

DFASHRM American Society for Healthcare Risk Management (185)

DFPh Antique and Amusement Photographers International (224)

DFS Professional Housing Management Association (862)

DGCP Association of Energy Engineers (280)

DHD Professional Housing Management Association (862)

DHM Professional Housing Management Association (862)

DHP Professional Housing Management Association (862)

DHS Institute for Business & Home Safety (496)

DIDC CHA - Certified Horsemanship Association (350)

Dipl.Ac. American Manual Medicine Association (147)

Diplomate American Academy of Periodontology (39)

DIS Lightning Protection Institute (598)

DIT American Design Drafting Association International and American Digital Design Association (114)

DLP American Society of Transportation and Logistics (210)

DM National Association of Underwater Instructors (707)

National Committee for Quality Assurance (724)

DML SOLE - The International Society of Logistics (952)

DNC Dermatology Nurses' Association (410)

DoDSMC Industrial Fasteners Institute (493)

DPA National Association for Sport and Physical Education (643)

DPC International Digital Enterprise Alliance (540)

DPM National Beauty Culturists' League (713)

American Society of Podiatric Medical Assistants (208)

DPT American Society for Clinical Pathology (182)

DQC The American Gem Society (125)

DRB Society of Broadcast Engineers (931)

DREI Real Estate Educators Association (875)

DS The Travel Institute (979)

DSC American Institute of Homeopathy (139)

American Swimming Coaches Association (215)

Association of Diving Contractors International (279)

DSGC National Drilling Association (743)

DTA American Driver and Traffic Safety Education Association (115)

DTC Association of Pet Dog Trainers (299)

SAE International (889)

DTR Academy of Nutrition and Dietetics (7)

DVEP Society of Cable Telecommunications Engineers (931)

E-PRO National Association of Realtors (690)

E2.0 Association for Information and Image Management International (249)

EAP Employee Assistance Society of North America (426)

EBCP Association of Energy Engineers (280)

EBPF Society for Research in Child Development (920)

EC American Short Line and Regional Railroad Association (179)

National Association of Disability Examiners (663)

ECC American Heart Association (130)

Association of Real Estate License Law Officials (305)

Cruise Lines International Association (405)

ECCS Cruise Lines International Association (405)

ECEC — The International Childbirth Education Association (534)

ECM — Association for Information and Image Management International (249)

ECM — National Association of Concessionaires (657)

ECP — Writing Instrument Manufacturers Association (1029)

ECT — International Association of Arson Investigators (515)

Ed: K-12 — Registry of Interpreters for the Deaf (879)

EDDA — LeadingAge (American Association of Homes and Services for the Aging) (595)

EDI — International Association of Black Professional Fire Fighters (517)

EDP — Xplor International (1029)

EE — North American Association for Environmental Education (812)

EEA — National Society for Experiential Education (792)

EEC — Association of Christian Schools International (272)

EEMCP — American Public Power Association (171)

EESA — National Council of Architectural Registration Boards (733)

EETC — Outdoor Power Equipment and Engine Service Association (835)

EFP — APPA - Leadership in Educational Facilities (225)

EFPM — American Academy of Medical Management (36)

EFT — Association for Comprehensive Energy Psychology (242)

EGCP — American Society for Ethnohistory (184)

EGSA — Electrical Generating Systems Association (422)

EHC — The Door and Hardware Institute (416)

EIFS-I — Association of the Wall and Ceiling Industry (314)

EIFS-IP — Association of the Wall and Ceiling Industry (314)

EIFS-M — Association of the Wall and Ceiling Industry (314)

ELD — American Association of Bioanalysts (54)

EMC — iNARTE, Inc. (487)

EMC — Minerals, Metals and Materials Society (617)

EMCP — Institute of Industrial Engineers (500)

EMDR — Emdr International Association (425)

EMI — iNARTE, Inc. (487)

EMIT — Association of Energy Engineers (280)

EMM — Association for Information and Image Management International (249)

eMPC — American Society for Engineering Management (184)

eMPC — International Digital Enterprise Alliance (540)

EMPs — AABC Commissioning Group (1)

EMS — Association of Equipment Management Professionals (281)

EMS — National Council of Exchangors (734)

ENP — National Emergency Number Association (745)

ENPC — Emergency Nurses Association (425)

EOLCS — American Petroleum Institute (163)

EPA — Air Conditioning Contractors of America (18)

EPA — American Boat and Yacht Council (84)

EPC — National Association of Emergency Medical Technicians (665)

EPC — National Ready Mixed Concrete Association (784)

EPIC — Air Conditioning Contractors of America (18)

EPIQ MOC — American Board of Preventive Medicine (83)

EPLS — National Association of Estate Planners and Councils (666)

EPP — Composite Panel Association (372)

EPPP — Association of State and Provincial Psychology Boards (309)

EPSM — American Society of Safety Engineers (209)

ERM — Association for Information and Image Management International (249)

ERP — Global Association of Risk Professionals (461)

ESA — Ecological Society of America (418)

ESA — The Exercise Safety Association (435)

ESA — International Society of Certified Electronics Technicians (572)

ESD — iNARTE, Inc. (487)

ESEP — International Council on Systems Engineering (539)

ESS — BICSI (329)

EST — Custom Electronic Design and Installation Association (405)

ETA — Electronics Technicians Association International (424)

ETB — American Embryo Transfer Association (116)

ETCP — Professional Lighting and Sound Association (863)

ETS — Tire Industry Association (975)

ETT — InterNational Electrical Testing Association (542)

EUC — National Association of Aircraft and Communication Suppliers (646)

EVP — AACE International (1)

F&AS — American Board of Podiatric Surgery (83)

FA — American Architectural Manufacturers Association (46)

FAAO — American Academy of Osteopathy (38)

FAAVA — American Academy of Veterinary Acupuncture (42)

FAC — International Association for Identification (513)

FAC — Society of Actuaries (927)

FACCP — American College of Contingency Planners (95)

FACHE — American College of Healthcare Executives (96)

FACM — American Medical Informatics Association (149)

FACMPE — MGMA-ACMPE (614)

FACTA — Consumer Data Industry Association (381)

FAHP — Association for Healthcare Philanthropy (248)

FAHRMM — Association for Healthcare Resource and Materials Management (248)

FALU — Association of Home Office Underwriters (287)

FAP — Society of Actuaries (927)

FAPA — American Psychotherapy Association (170)

FASAM — American Society of Addiction Medicine (191)

FASHRM — American Society for Healthcare Risk Management (185)

FC — American Forest & Paper Association (123)

FC — International Association for Identification (513)

FCBA — National Association of Church Business Administration (653)

FCC-COLE — iNARTE, Inc. (487)

FCL — International Shippers Association (564)

FCP — American Academy of Fertility Care Professionals (34)

FCP — Post-Tensioning Institute (853)

FCRA — Consumer Data Industry Association (381)

FCRAC — National Credit Reporting Association (740)

FCRR — United States Court Reporters Association (993)

FCS — Employers Council on Flexible Compensation (427)

FCT — The Institute of Inspection, Cleaning and Restoration Certification (500)

FCUSA — Fur Commission USA (454)

FD — National Association for the Specialty Food Trade (644)

FDSC — SAE International (889)

FE — National Association of Fire Equipment Distributors (668)

FE — National Council of Examiners for Engineering and Surveying (734)

FFSI — LOMA (600)

FHC — National Affordable Housing Management Association (629)

FIC — Fraternal Field Managers Association (453)

FICF — Fraternal Field Managers Association (453)

FIT — American Traffic Safety Service Association (217)

FIT — International Association of Arson Investigators (515)

FK — National Association of Fire Equipment Distributors (668)

FLMI — LOMA (600)

FM — American Architectural Manufacturers Association (46)

FMA — IT Financial Management Association (586)

FMC — Building Owners and Managers Institute International (337)

FMC — IT Financial Management Association (586)

FMC — National Ready Mixed Concrete Association (784)

FMEA — Automotive Industry Action Group (322)

FMM — National Registry of Environmental Professionals (785)

FMP — Federal Managers Association (439)

FMP — International Facility Management Association (543)

FMP — National Restaurant Association (786)

FMSD — American Academy of Medical Management (36)

FMT — American Foundry Society (123)

FMTS — International Fitness Professionals Association (545)

FN — National Association of Fire Equipment Distributors (668)

FOA — Glove Shippers Association (463)

FOC — Flexographic Technical Association (447)

FPBR — IT Financial Management Association (586)

FPC — American Fisheries Society (121)

FPC — American Payroll Association (162)

FPC — International Association for Identification (513)

FPCC — The International Fluid Power Society (545)

FPCM — The International Fluid Power Society (545)

FPCT — The International Fluid Power Society (545)

FPE — The International Fluid Power Society (545)

FPGEC — National Association of Boards of Pharmacy (650)

FPGEE — National Association of Boards of Pharmacy (650)

FPh — Antique and Amusement Photographers International (224)

FPMNSM — International Fitness Professionals Association (545)

FPMRS — American Urogynecologic Society (218)

FPO — Flexographic Technical Association (447)

FPS — The International Fluid Power Society (545)

FRAEC — Foundation for Russian-American Economic Cooperation (453)

FRM — Global Association of Risk Professionals (461)

FS — American Board of Podiatric Surgery (83)

FS — National Council of Examiners for Engineering and Surveying (734)

FSAB — Association of Forensic Document Examiners (284)

FSC — Forest Stewardship Council - United States Chapter (451)

FSC — National Association of Concessionaires (657)

FSC — Wood Products Manufacturers Association (1024)

FSCC — Cleaning Management Institute (357)

FSDRT — The Institute of Inspection, Cleaning and Restoration Certification (500)

FT — Association for Death Education and Counseling (244)

FTA — National Association of Temple Administrators (705)

FTCP — American Concrete Institute (106)

FWC — Power Washers of North America (855)

G7C — International Digital Enterprise Alliance (540)

G7SC — International Digital Enterprise Alliance (540)

GA — National Association of Minority Contractors (680)

GAA POCP — Gravure Association of America (465)

GASMC — Global Semiconductor Alliance (463)

GBA — International Society of Certified Employee Benefit Specialists (572)

GBE — Association of Energy Engineers (280)

GC — Lignite Energy Council (598)

GCBAA CP — Golf Course Builders Association of America (463)

GCC — International Society of Nurses in Genetics (573)

GCDF — National Employment Counseling Association (745)

GCFP — Feldenkrais Guild of North America (442)

GCFT — Feldenkrais Guild of North America (442)

GCSAS — International Society for Technology in Education (569)

GESSC — American Boat and Yacht Council (84)

GFIC — American Council on Exercise (110)

GFIC — International Fitness Professionals Association (545)

GFM — IT Financial Management Association (586)

GFSI — AIB International (17)

GFT — American Foundry Society (123)

GIC — National Glass Association (755)

GISPC — Urban and Regional Information Systems Association (1003)

GKC — National Drilling Association (743)

GLA — American Society of Transportation and Logistics (210)

GLRP — HR Policy Association (480)

GMA — National Association of Mortgage Brokers (681)

GMLC — SAE International (889)

GMS — Worldwide ERC (1028)

GMTA — National Criminal Justice Association (740)

GN National Gerontological Nursing Association *(755)*

GPC American Society for Engineering Management *(184)*

The Grant Professionals Association *(465)*

GPHR Society for Human Resource Management *(911)*

GPPA National Auctioneers Association *(711)*

GPPA-M National Auctioneers Association *(711)*

GRP WorldatWork *(1028)*

GS American Association of Bioanalysts *(54)*

American Board of Surgery *(84)*

GSA The American Gem Society *(125)*

GSCARP Automotive Recyclers Association *(323)*

GSCP National Ready Mixed Concrete Association *(784)*

GSP Board of Certified Safety Professionals *(332)*

GTC Electrical Generating Systems Association *(422)*

GTCCP ASME International Gas Turbine Institute *(233)*

GTFC National Woodland Owners Association *(806)*

GTP Global Business Travel Association *(462)*

H&PMC American Board of Anesthesiology *(81)*

HACCP Association of Food and Drug Officials *(283)*

Hospitality Institute of Technology and Management *(479)*

HBDP American Society of Heating, Refrigerating and Air Conditioning Engineers (ASHRAE) *(199)*

HC Window and Door Manufacturers Association *(1018)*

HCCP Institute of Industrial Engineers *(500)*

HCLD American Association of Bioanalysts *(54)*

HCMA Fur Commission USA *(454)*

HFDP American Society of Heating, Refrigerating and Air Conditioning Engineers (ASHRAE) *(199)*

HFMA Healthcare Financial Management Association *(471)*

HGW American Institute of Hydrology *(139)*

HHS National Environmental Health Association *(746)*

HIP National Committee for Quality Assurance *(724)*

HMIC Hoist Manufacturers Institute *(477)*

HMOC National Center for Housing Management *(719)*

HNIP Hispanic Association of Colleges and Universities *(475)*

HOTS International Bowling Pro Shop and Instructors Association *(530)*

HRCI American Management Association *(146)*

HRIP International Association for Human Resource Information Management *(512)*

HSC American Hotel & Lodging Association (AH&LA) *(134)*

HSCC National Society of Professional Surveyors *(794)*

HSO Fire Department Safety Officers Association *(446)*

HSQE American Bureau of Shipping *(86)*

HST The Institute of Inspection, Cleaning and Restoration Certification *(500)*

HSW American Institute of Hydrology *(139)*

HT American Horticultural Therapy Association *(133)*

American Society for Clinical Pathology *(182)*

HTC American Institute of Hydrology *(139)*

HTCFP American Society for Engineering Education *(183)*

HTL American Society for Clinical Pathology *(182)*

HVAC/R North American Technician Excellence *(823)*

HVACR Air Conditioning, Heating and Refrigeration Institute (AHRI) *(18)*

HWC Power Washers of North America *(855)*

HWQ American Institute of Hydrology *(139)*

I-ACT International Association for Colon Hydrotherapy *(511)*

IAAS American Association of Advertising Agencies *(53)*

IABA Accreditation Council for Accountancy and Taxation *(9)*

IAC Interactive Advertising Bureau *(506)*

IACET American Association of Petroleum Geologists *(68)*

American Institute of Timber Construction *(141)*

American Management Association *(146)*

Association of Environmental and Engineering Geologists *(281)*

Drug Information Association *(417)*

IAIM International Association of Infant Massage *(523)*

IAIMI International Association of Infant Massage *(523)*

IAP Association for High Technology Distribution *(248)*

IAPDPCP International Association of Plastics Distributors *(526)*

IAPMO International Association of Plumbing and Mechanical Officials *(526)*

IASC International Aloe Science Council *(510)*

IATA International Air Transport Association *(510)*

IBDE American Association of Bank Directors *(54)*

IBPO-SP International Brotherhood of Police Officers *(532)*

IC Tile Roofing Institute *(974)*

IC/TC Registry of Interpreters for the Deaf *(879)*

ICALP Academic Language Therapy Association *(3)*

ICB American Bankers Insurance Association *(79)*

ICC International Fitness Professionals Association *(545)*

National Association of Pastoral Musicians *(683)*

National Association of Underwater Instructors *(707)*

ICCIFP Construction Financial Management Association *(379)*

ICCP Association for Computing Machinery *(243)*

ICE Independent Distributors of Electronics Association *(489)*

ICEA Association of Women's Health, Obstetric and Neonatal Nurses *(318)*

ICGA The American Gem Society *(125)*

ICGC National Council on Problem Gambling *(739)*

ICHRC Society of Clinical and Medical Hair Removal *(933)*

ICLA Association of Women's Health, Obstetric and Neonatal Nurses *(318)*

ICMG International Professional Groomers *(561)*

ICP American Concrete Institute *(106)*

American Petroleum Institute *(163)*

International Masonry Institute *(556)*

Writing Instrument Manufacturers Association *(1029)*

ICPS International Society of Crime Prevention Practitioners *(572)*

ICRM Nuclear Information and Records Management Association *(825)*

ICS Investment Casting Institute *(584)*

ICSA International Customer Service Association *(539)*

IDC Association of Finance and Insurance Professionals *(283)*

National Institute of Steel Detailing *(765)*

IDEA American Association of Classified School Employees *(56)*

IDEC American Association of Motor Vehicle Administrators *(65)*

IDP National Council of Architectural Registration Boards *(733)*

IEEE-EPP IEEE Communications Society *(483)*

IEPSCP Institute of Industrial Engineers *(500)*

IFA National Association of Independent Fee Appraisers *(674)*

IFAA National Association of Independent Fee Appraisers *(674)*

IFAC National Association of Independent Fee Appraisers *(674)*

IFAS National Association of Independent Fee Appraisers *(674)*

IFCCE ACA International, The Association of Credit and Collection Professionals *(2)*

IFM Industrial Fabrics Association International *(493)*

Marine Fabricators Association *(605)*

IFOAM Organic Crop Improvement Association International *(830)*

IFPA PTC International Fitness Professionals Association *(545)*

IFPACFCSC International Fitness Professionals Association *(545)*

IFPSAEPC International Fitness Professionals Association *(545)*

IGA International Glove Association *(548)*

IGC National Fenestration Rating Council *(750)*

ILDAP International Laser Display Association *(553)*

IMCP National Business Incubation Association *(717)*

IMICC International Council of Employers of Bricklayers and Allied Craftworkers *(538)*

IMSA International Municipal Signal Association *(557)*

iNAE iNARTE, Inc. *(487)*

iNARTE Electrostatic Discharge Association *(425)*

iNAT iNARTE, Inc. *(487)*

INFRE National Association of Government Defined Contribution Administrators *(670)*

IOA Association for Information and Image Management International *(249)*

IPC Association of State and Provincial Psychology Boards *(309)*

IPEP Society of Cable Telecommunications Engineers *(931)*

IPMA-CP International Public Management Association for Human Resources *(562)*

IPMA-CS International Public Management Association for Human Resources *(562)*

IPMA-HR International Public Management Association for Human Resources *(562)*

IPMBA-EMS International Police Mountain Bike Association *(561)*

IPMBA-IC International Police Mountain Bike Association *(561)*

IPMBA-MOC International Police Mountain Bike Association *(561)*

IPMBA-PCC International Police Mountain Bike Association *(561)*

IPMBA-PSC International Police Mountain Bike Association *(561)*

IPMBA-SCC International Police Mountain Bike Association *(561)*

IQEX National Association of State Boards of Accountancy *(698)*

IQPP Plasma Protein Therapeutics Association *(850)*

IR Conference of Radiation Control Program Directors *(375)*

IRDC CHA - Certified Horsemanship Association *(350)*

IRRSP American Society for Nondestructive Testing *(187)*

ISA Institute for Certification of Computing Professionals *(497)*

International Society of Arboriculture *(571)*

ISC TechAmerica (fka Technology Association of America) *(969)*

ISEECP International Society of Explosives Engineers *(572)*

ISFA CP International Surface Fabricators Association *(576)*

ISM American Bureau of Shipping *(86)*

ISO Fire Department Safety Officers Association *(446)*

Spring Manufacturers Institute *(960)*

Data Management Association International *(407)*

ISP Institute for Certification of Computing Professionals *(497)*

National Classification Management Society *(722)*

ISPQ Interstate Renewable Energy Council *(583)*

ISPS American Bureau of Shipping *(86)*

ISSI The Institute of Inspection, Cleaning and Restoration Certification *(500)*

ITC National Association of Underwater Instructors *(707)*

ITCP National Association of Sewer Service Companies *(695)*

ITIL IT Financial Management Association *(586)*

ITP Society of Insurance Trainers and Educators *(940)*

ITTPC College Reading and Learning Association *(364)*

IVT National Association for Practical Nurse Education and Service *(641)*

IWCASC International Window Cleaning Association *(581)*

JCDC Career Planning and Adult Development Network *(343)*

JCP Ice Skating Institute *(482)*

JCT The Institute of Inspection, Cleaning and Restoration Certification *(500)*

JCTC Career Planning and Adult Development Network *(343)*

JDC Professional Tennis Registry *(865)*

JDFEC International Digital Enterprise Alliance *(540)*

JEP National Lesbian and Gay Journalists Association *(769)*

JFSRT The Institute of Inspection, Cleaning and Restoration Certification *(500)*

JOPDS Reserve Officers Association of the U.S. *(882)*

JPMA	Juvenile Products Manufacturers Association (590)
JWDRT	The Institute of Inspection, Cleaning and Restoration Certification (500)
K-12C	Association of Christian Schools International (272)
KBC	Aerobics and Fitness Association of America (13)
KEC	Power Washers of North America (855)
KPPAE	American Public Power Association (171)
L + WMCC	American Council on Exercise (110)
LA	American Lighting Association (145)
LAC	Association of Boards of Certification (270)
LACP	National Association of Sewer Service Companies (695)
	National Institute of Pension Administrators (765)
	United States Lifesaving Association (996)
LAT	American Association for Laboratory Animal Science (50)
LATG	American Association for Laboratory Animal Science (50)
LBAI	Latin Business Association (594)
LC	National Council on Qualifications for the Lighting Professions (739)
LCCE	Lamaze International (592)
LCEC	Lamaze International (592)
LCL	International Shippers Association (564)
LCLP	Land Trust Alliance (593)
LCP	Academy of Laser Dentistry (6)
	American League of Lobbyists (145)
LCS	Cruise Lines International Association (405)
LCSW-MFT	American Schools Association (177)
LCT	The Institute of Inspection, Cleaning and Restoration Certification (500)
LDAP	The Open Group (828)
LEAN	The Association for Manufacturing Excellence (252)
LEAP	Smart Card Alliance (901)
LECP	Institute of Industrial Engineers (500)
LEED	Hardwood Manufacturers Association (468)
	Portland Cement Association (853)
	Steel Recycling Institute (963)
LEMPCP	Institute of Industrial Engineers (500)
LES	Licensing Executives Society (597)
LIFE	Tag and Label Manufacturers Institute (968)
LJC	Professional Association of Volleyball Officials (860)
LLA	International Council for Machinery Lubrication (538)
LMC	American Alliance of Home Modification Professionals (AAHMP) (44)
LMCP	American College of Clinical Pharmacy (94)
LMTC	National Lipid Association (770)
LNCC	American Association of Legal Nurse Consultants (64)
LPC	International Association for Identification (513)
	Retail Industry Leaders Association (884)
LPN-CLTC	National Association of Directors of Nursing Administration in Long Term Care (663)
LRP	HR Policy Association (480)
LRQA	American Concrete Pressure Pipe Association (106)
LS	American Lighting Association (145)
	International Fitness Professionals Association (545)
	The Travel Institute (979)
LS I	National Association of Independent Lighting Distributors (674)
LS II	National Association of Independent Lighting Distributors (674)
LSSC	The Association for Library Service to Children (251)
LSSFC	Institute of Industrial Engineers (500)
LSSGB	Institute of Industrial Engineers (500)
LTCP	American Concrete Institute (106)
LVN	Developmental Disabilities Nurses Association (411)
LWIC	National Roof Deck Contractors Association (787)
M+CSP	Fluid Power Distributors Association (448)
MAC	National Association for Alcoholism and Drug Abuse Counselors (646)
	National Board for Certified Counselors (715)
MACE	National Council of State Boards for Nursing (736)
MACP	National Association of Sewer Service Companies (695)
MACS	Mobile Air Conditioning Society Worldwide (617)

MAE	Association of Free Community Papers (284)
MAFF	Organic Crop Improvement Association International (830)
MAG	Organic Crop Improvement Association International (830)
MAI	Appraisal Institute (226)
MALDEF	Mexican-American Grocers Association (614)
MAM	American Registry of Radiologic Technologists (174)
MaRC	POPAI The Global Association for Marketing at Retail (852)
MAS	National Registry of Environmental Professionals (785)
	Promotional Products Association International (867)
MBC	Association of Bridal Consultants (270)
	Eastern Apicultural Society of North America (418)
MBCP	DRI International (416)
MBE	National Conference of Bar Examiners (726)
MC	Association of Sewing and Design Professionals (308)
	National Association of Disability Examiners (663)
MCBA	Institute of Business Appraisers (498)
MCBC	Institute of Certified Business Counselors (498)
MCC	American Boat and Yacht Council (84)
	American Boat and Yacht Council (84)
	Cruise Lines International Association (405)
MCD	Custom Tailors and Designers Association of America (406)
MCE	ACA International, The Association of Credit and Collection Professionals (2)
MCFP	Research and Development Associates for Military Food and Packaging Systems (881)
MCH	Association of State and Territorial Public Health Nutrition Directors (310)
MCI	SSPC: the Society for Protective Coatings (960)
MCLE	American Association of Attorney-Certified Public Accountants (54)
MCM	Club Managers Association of America (359)
MCP	World Council of Credit Unions, Inc. (1026)
MCPF	PMA - The Worldwide Community of Imaging Associations (851)
	Professional Picture Framers Association (864)
MCPM	American Academy of Medical Management (36)
MCR	CoreNet Global (385)
MCRI	National Court Reporters Association (740)
MCSC	Registry of Interpreters for the Deaf (879)
MCT	American Foundry Society (123)
MDCM	North American Die Casting Association (816)
MDCP	North American Die Casting Association (816)
MDCT	North American Die Casting Association (816)
MDP	NPTA Alliance (824)
MDQM	Electronic Commerce Code Management Association (423)
MDT	American Society of Master Dental Technologists (202)
MDTC	Asphalt Institute (233)
MECP	Consumer Electronics Association (381)
MEE	National Conference of Bar Examiners (726)
MEI	National Marine Electronics Association (771)
MEP	Media Rating Council (610)
MERC	Association of American Medical Colleges (265)
MFC	Industrial Fabrics Association International (493)
	Marine Fabricators Association (605)
MFE	Building Owners and Managers Institute International (337)
MFFC	Medical Fitness Association (611)
MFS	International Fitness Professionals Association (545)
MGWC	National Ground Water Association (756)
	National Systems Contractors Association (798)
MIC	Flexible Intermediate Bulk Container Association (447)
	Lightning Protection Institute (598)
	Marine Retailers Association of America (605)
MID	Lightning Protection Institute (598)

	North American Building Material Distribution Association (814)
MIS	Society for Surgery of the Alimentary Tract (921)
MJE	Journalism Education Association (589)
ML	National Lipid Association (770)
MLA	International Council for Machinery Lubrication (538)
MLBPA	Major League Baseball Players Association (601)
MLC	American Bureau of Shipping (86)
MLPS	International Fitness Professionals Association (545)
MLT	American Association of Bioanalysts (54)
	American Medical Technologists (150)
	American Society for Clinical Pathology (182)
	International Council for Machinery Lubrication (538)
MMA-C	Monorail Manufacturers Association (619)
MMC	International Institute of Municipal Clerks (552)
	Mobile Marketing Association (618)
MOC	Alliance for Continuing Medical Education (22)
	American Academy of Otolaryngology-Head and Neck Surgery (29)
	The American Board of Facial Plastic and Reconstructive Surgery (82)
	American Board of Medical Specialties (82)
	American College of Cardiology (93)
	American College of Physicians (101)
	American Roentgen Ray Society (176)
	American Society for Clinical Pathology (182)
	American Society of Clinical Oncology (194)
	Society of Interventional Radiology (940)
MOC, CME	American Board of Physical Medicine and Rehabilitation (83)
MOC-IC	College of American Pathologists (363)
MOC-MK	College of American Pathologists (363)
MOC-PB	College of American Pathologists (363)
MOC-PC	College of American Pathologists (363)
MOC-PR	College of American Pathologists (363)
MOC-SB	College of American Pathologists (363)
MOCA	American Board of Anesthesiology (81)
MOCP	American Association of Neuromuscular and Electrodiagnostic Medicine (66)
MP	American Society for Clinical Pathology (182)
MPCE	Credit Professionals International (403)
MPFTS	International Fitness Professionals Association (545)
MPJE	National Association of Boards of Pharmacy (650)
MPM	National Association of Residential Property Managers (691)
MPPA	National Auctioneers Association (711)
MPRE	National Conference of Bar Examiners (726)
	Practising Law Institute (855)
MPS	Association of Productivity Specialists (300)
MPT	National Conference of Bar Examiners (726)
MRCP	Metal Construction Association (613)
MREA	National Society of Real Estate Appraisers, Inc. (795)
MRI	American Registry of Radiologic Technologists (174)
	American Registry of Radiologic Technologists (174)
MRT	United States Racquet Stringers Association (998)
MS/A	Business Marketing Association (339)
MS/B	Business Marketing Association (339)
MS/C	Business Marketing Association (339)
MSA	Automotive Industry Action Group (322)
MSC	American Boat and Yacht Council (84)
	Mulch and Soil Council (621)
MSCA STAR	Mechanical Service Contractors of America (610)
MSCC	National Alliance of Medicare Set-Aside Professionals, Inc. (632)
MSFRT	The Institute of Inspection, Cleaning and Restoration Certification (500)
MSI	The Institute of Inspection, Cleaning and Restoration Certification (500)
MSM	American Boat Builders and Repairers Association (84)
MSMC	Association of Marina Industries (293)
	Local Media Association (599)
MSPA	Mystery Shopping Providers Association (623)

OIC:C	Registry of Interpreters for the Deaf (879)
OIC:S/V	Registry of Interpreters for the Deaf (879)
OIC:V/S	Registry of Interpreters for the Deaf (879)
OLA	Wilderness Education Association (1017)
OLIA	Wilderness Education Association (1017)
OLMC	Training Directors' Forum (977)
OMA	Society of Tribologists and Lubrication Engineers (949)
OMC	Association of Professional Office Managers (302)
ONC	National Association of Orthopedic Nurses (683)
ONR	American Society for Engineering Education (183)
OPA-C	American Society of Orthopedic Physician Assistants (205)
OPCAT	National Association of Heavy Equipment Training Schools (672)
OPMP	American Society of Heating, Refrigerating and Air Conditioning Engineers (ASHRAE) (199)
OPPSC	International Digital Enterprise Alliance (540)
OS	Structural Building Components Association (964)
OSP	BICSI (329)
OTC	National Association of Orthopaedic Technologists (683)
	Registry of Interpreters for the Deaf (879)
OTR	National Board for Certification in Occupational Therapy, Inc. (715)
P.Ac.	American Manual Medicine Association (147)
PA(ASCP)	American Association of Pathologists' Assistants (68)
PAC	American Board of Anesthesiology (81)
	Building Owners and Managers Institute International (337)
PAC, CNE	American Association of Occupational Health Nurses (67)
PACE	American Academy of Dental Group Practice (32)
	American Society for Dental Aesthetics (183)
	The National Federation of Paralegal Associations, Inc. (749)
	Professional Skaters Association (865)
PACP	National Association of Sewer Service Companies (695)
PADISD	Professional Association of Diving Instructors (859)
PAJ	Public Affairs Council (868)
PAPHS	American College of Sports Medicine (102)
PASS	Community Transportation Association of America (371)
PAVE	American Association of Veterinary State Boards (76)
PBA	National Beauty Culturists' League (713)
PBC	Association of Bridal Consultants (270)
PBT	American Association of Bioanalysts (54)
	American Society for Clinical Pathology (182)
PC	International Association of Hygienic Physicians (523)
	Professional Tennis Registry (865)
PCA	Credit Professionals International (403)
	Plant Growth Regulation Society of America (849)
PCC	Association of Professional Chaplains (301)
	National Ready Mixed Concrete Association (784)
	Training Directors' Forum (977)
PCCN	American Association of Critical-Care Nurses (59)
PCCP	SSPC: the Society for Protective Coatings (960)
PCE	Credit Professionals International (403)
PCI	ASIS International (232)
	SSPC: the Society for Protective Coatings (960)
PCI 3000	Powder Coating Institute (854)
PCI 4000	Powder Coating Institute (854)
PCID	North American Building Material Distribution Association (814)
PCIwise	Retail Solutions Providers Association (885)
PCMH	Material Handling Industry of America (608)
PCP	National Petroleum Management Association (780)
	Post-Tensioning Institute (853)
	Writing Instrument Manufacturers Association (1029)
PCS	American Society for the Advancement of Anesthesia and Sedation in Dentistry (190)

	Credit Professionals International (403)
	LOMA (600)
	SSPC: the Society for Protective Coatings (960)
PDBIA	Design-Build Institute of America (411)
PDC	American Medical Writers Association (150)
	The Wildlife Society (1017)
PDCP	Book Industry Study Group, Inc. (333)
PDH	Deep Foundations Institute (408)
PDM	Destination Marketing Association International (411)
PDP	National Business Aviation Association (716)
PDS	Community Transportation Association of America (371)
	International Fitness Professionals Association (545)
	Licensing Executives Society (597)
PE	National Council of Examiners for Engineering and Surveying (734)
PEC	The International Childbirth Education Association (534)
PEECP	American Society of Appraisers (192)
PEI	American Society of Agricultural and Biological Engineers (191)
PERICP	Pharmaceutical Education and Research Institute (844)
PFEC	The International Childbirth Education Association (534)
PFPM	American Academy of Medical Management (36)
PFT	American Council on Exercise (110)
	International Fitness Professionals Association (545)
PG	American College of Counselors (95)
PGEC	Aerobics and Fitness Association of America (13)
PGI-DOC	Pyrotechnics Guild International (871)
PgMP	Project Management Institute (866)
PGY-I	The American Association of Dental Boards (59)
Ph.D Cert.	EEG and Clinical Neuroscience Society (421)
PHC	Manufactured Housing Institute (602)
PHQ	National Committee for Quality Assurance (724)
PHR	Society for Human Resource Management (911)
PHTLS	National Association of Emergency Medical Technicians (665)
PIM	Gas Technology Institute (456)
PIPE	American College of Psychiatrists (102)
PJJA	National Juvenile Court Services Association (767)
PJJM	National Juvenile Court Services Association (767)
PLA	Council for Adult and Experiential Learning (388)
PLIC	SAE International (889)
PLMA	Private Label Manufacturers Association (858)
PLR	American Hypnosis Association (134)
PLS	American Society of Transportation and Logistics (210)
	NALS (625)
PMA	National Beauty Culturists' League (713)
PMAC	American Society of Podiatric Medical Assistants (208)
PMB	IT Financial Management Association (586)
PMC	American Board of Anesthesiology (81)
	National Ready Mixed Concrete Association (784)
PME	Marine Corps Reserve Association (605)
PMI	American Management Association (146)
	Drug Information Association (417)
PMI-RMPSM	Project Management Institute (866)
PMI-SPSM	Project Management Institute (866)
PMMICT	Packaging Machinery Manufacturers Institute (836)
PMN	Women's Council of REALTORS (1023)
PMNC	American Society for Pain Management Nursing (188)
PMP	American Moving and Storage Association (153)
	Project Management Institute (866)
PMT	APMI International (225)
PMTC	Association of Boards of Certification (270)
PO	National Committee for Quality Assurance (724)
POA	Pet Sitters International (843)
POLT	American Association of Bioanalysts (54)
POM	Association of Professional Office Managers (302)
POSIX	The Open Group (828)
PP	NALS (625)

PPA	American Society of Agricultural Appraisers (191)
PPC	American Association of Cardiovascular and Pulmonary Rehabilitation (55)
PPCSM	American Public Power Association (171)
PPD	Society of Piping Engineers and Designers (944)
PPMCP	American Public Power Association (171)
PPMS	ACA International, The Association of Credit and Collection Professionals (2)
PPNC	International Fitness Professionals Association (545)
PPS	International Association of Assessing Officers (516)
PPT	Institute of Medicine (501)
PQC	National Concrete Masonry Association (725)
PQI	Radiological Society of North America (873)
PQPC	Precast/Prestressed Concrete Institute (856)
PRC	Marketing Research Association (606)
	National Association of Personnel Services (684)
PRDP	Association of Real Estate Women (305)
PRI	Amusement Industry Manufacturers and Suppliers International (223)
PRITE	American College of Psychiatrists (102)
PRP	Associated Locksmiths of America (236)
	National Association of Parliamentarians (683)
PS	National Council of Examiners for Engineering and Surveying (734)
PSC	International Digital Enterprise Alliance (540)
	Society for Pediatric Urology (918)
PSCP	Carpet Cushion Council (343)
PSEC	iNARTE, Inc. (487)
	iNARTE, Inc. (487)
PSMO	Fabricators & Manufacturers Association, International (437)
PSNA	American Association of Birth Centers (55)
PSP	AACE International (1)
	ASIS International (232)
	Pet Industry Distributors Association (842)
PSRS	International Fitness Professionals Association (545)
PSTC	iNARTE, Inc. (487)
PTC	Aerobics and Fitness Association of America (13)
	American Council on Exercise (110)
	National Ready Mixed Concrete Association (784)
	Tile Council of North America, Inc. (974)
PTCA	Institute of Transportation Engineers (503)
PTOE	Institute of Transportation Engineers (503)
PTP	Ceramic Tile Distributors Association (349)
PTS	National Mobility Equipment Dealers Association (773)
QAP	American Health Care Association (129)
QAPI	Structural Building Components Association (964)
QC	American Concrete Pipe Association (106)
QCAST	Architectural Woodwork Institute (228)
QCC	National Automatic Merchandising Association (711)
QCCP	Architectural Woodwork Institute (228)
QCP	National Association of Social Workers (696)
QCSW	PMA - The Worldwide Community of Imaging Associations (851)
QDPC	National Association of Elevator Safety Authorities International (665)
QEI	Institute of Clean Air Companies (499)
QEP	Academic Language Therapy Association (3)
QI	American Society of Pension Professionals & Actuaries (206)
QKA	American Registry of Radiologic Technologists (174)
QM	Automotive Industry Action Group (322)
QMD	COLA (362)
QMS	American Society of Pension Professionals & Actuaries (206)
QPA	American Society of Pension Professionals & Actuaries (206)
QPFC	American Association for Paralegal Education (50)
QPP	Spring Manufacturers Institute (960)
QS	Plasma Protein Therapeutics Association (850)
QSEAL	Therapeutic Touch International Association (973)
QTTP, QTTT	American Dance Therapy Association (113)
R-DMT	Rack Manufacturers Institute (872)
R-Mark	American Chiropractic Registry of Radiologic Technologists (90)
R.T. (ACRRT)	

RA	American Registry of Radiologic Technologists *(174)*
	National Society of Real Estate Appraisers, Inc. *(795)*
RAA	National Association of Realtors *(690)*
	National Interscholastic Athletic Administrators Association *(766)*
RAC	American Boat and Yacht Council *(84)*
	Regulatory Affairs Professionals Society *(879)*
RACE	American Association of Veterinary State Boards *(76)*
	Conference of Research Workers in Animal Diseases *(375)*
RAD	American Registry of Radiologic Technologists *(174)*
RBSM	Building Service Contractors Association International *(337)*
RC	Retail Solutions Providers Association *(885)*
RCA	American Society of Consulting Arborists *(196)*
RCAL	National Association of Long Term Care Administrator Boards *(679)*
RCAPPM	American Academy of Medical Management *(36)*
RCC	International Association of Career Consulting Firms *(517)*
RCCB	Radiology Business Management Association *(874)*
RCCP	National Community Pharmacists Association *(725)*
RCCS	Cardiovascular Credentialing International *(342)*
RCDD	BICSI *(329)*
RCE	National Association of Realtors *(690)*
RCEP	American College of Sports Medicine *(102)*
RCES	Cardiovascular Credentialing International *(342)*
RCGC	Gas Technology Institute *(456)*
RCI	American Construction Inspectors Association *(107)*
RCIS	Cardiovascular Credentialing International *(342)*
RCMSR	American Academy of Medical Management *(36)*
RCS	Cardiovascular Credentialing International *(342)*
RCSC	Polyurethane Manufacturers Association *(852)*
RCT	The Institute of Inspection, Cleaning and Restoration Certification *(500)*
RD	Academy of Nutrition and Dietetics *(7)*
RDA	American Medical Technologists *(150)*
RDCP	National Automatic Merchandising Association *(711)*
RDCS	American Registry for Diagnostic Medical Sonography *(174)*
RDMS	American Registry for Diagnostic Medical Sonography *(174)*
RDR	National Court Reporters Association *(740)*
RDT	National Association for Drama Therapy *(638)*
REBC	RCI, Inc. *(875)*
REFP	Council of Educational Facility Planners International *(393)*
REH	International Executive Housekeepers Association *(543)*
REHS/RS	National Environmental Health Association *(746)*
RELT	National Registry of Environmental Professionals *(785)*
REM	National Registry of Environmental Professionals *(785)*
REP	Association of Energy Engineers *(280)*
	National Registry of Environmental Professionals *(785)*
REPA	National Registry of Environmental Professionals *(785)*
REREX	American Registry of Radiologic Technologists *(174)*
RES	International Association of Assessing Officers *(516)*
RESD	Association for Linen Management *(251)*
RET	National Association of Dental Laboratories *(662)*
	National Environmental Health Association *(746)*
	Rehabilitation Engineering and Assistive Technology Society of North America *(879)*
RFCO	Organic Crop Improvement Association International *(830)*
RFI	The Institute of Inspection, Cleaning and Restoration Certification *(500)*
RFID	AIM North America *(17)*
RFMP	Professional Retail Store Maintenance Association *(864)*

RFMT	The Institute of Inspection, Cleaning and Restoration Certification *(500)*
	Fabricators & Manufacturers Association, International *(437)*
RG	National Association of Dental Laboratories *(662)*
RGDP	Gas Technology Institute *(456)*
RGT	Society of Commercial Seed Technologists *(933)*
RHCMM	National Registry of Environmental Professionals *(785)*
RHIA	American Health Information Management Association *(129)*
RHIT	American Health Information Management Association *(129)*
RHSP	National Environmental Health Association *(746)*
RHSS	National Environmental Health Association *(746)*
RI	American College of Forensic Examiners Institute *(96)*
	American Welding Society *(220)*
RIM	American Moving and Storage Association *(153)*
	ARMA International *(228)*
RIMC	Training Directors' Forum *(977)*
RIMS	Risk and Insurance Management Society, Inc. (RIMS) *(886)*
RITP	BICSI *(329)*
RJ	The American Gem Society *(125)*
RJE	National Association of Temple Educators *(705)*
RL	American Association of Professional Landmen *(71)*
	Associated Locksmiths of America *(236)*
RLLD	Association for Linen Management *(251)*
RLO	American Hypnosis Association *(134)*
RLT	American Hypnosis Association *(134)*
RMA	American Medical Technologists *(150)*
	American Registry of Medical Assistants *(174)*
RMC	Professional Aviation Maintenance Association *(860)*
RMCC	Association of Rheumatology Health Professionals *(306)*
RMP	National Association of Residential Property Managers *(691)*
	Rolf Institute of Structural Integration *(887)*
RMR	National Court Reporters Association *(740)*
RMT	Association for Healthcare Documentation Integrity *(247)*
RNCB	Association for Radiological and Imaging Nursing *(255)*
ROM	Walking Horse Owners Association of America *(1011)*
RP	National Association of Parliamentarians *(683)*
RPA	International Society of Certified Employee Benefit Specialists *(572)*
RPhS	Cardiovascular Credentialing International *(342)*
RPL	American Association of Professional Landmen *(71)*
RPLU	Professional Liability Underwriting Society *(863)*
RPM	National Association of Real Estate Appraisers *(689)*
RPR	National Court Reporters Association *(740)*
RPRA	American Society of Farm Managers and Rural Appraisers *(197)*
RPSGT	Board of Registered Polysomnographic Technologists *(333)*
RPT	American Medical Technologists *(150)*
	Association for Play Therapy *(253)*
RPT-S	Association for Play Therapy *(253)*
RPVI	American Registry for Diagnostic Medical Sonography *(174)*
	Society for Vascular Ultrasound *(927)*
RRAS	American Board of Podiatric Surgery *(83)*
RRC	RCI, Inc. *(875)*
RRO	RCI, Inc. *(875)*
RRT	The Institute of Inspection, Cleaning and Restoration Certification *(500)*
RSC	Registry of Interpreters for the Deaf *(879)*
RSIG	Allied Finance Adjusters *(26)*
RSPA	Retail Solutions Providers Association *(885)*
RSPS	National Association of Realtors *(690)*
	Women's Council of REALTORS *(1023)*
RST	Society of Commercial Seed Technologists *(933)*
RTA	National Association of Real Estate Appraisers *(689)*
RTB	International Reciprocal Trade Association *(562)*
	National Association of Trade Exchanges *(706)*
RTM	Pressure Sensitive Tape Council *(856)*

RTPM	BICSI *(329)*
RTTDC	American College of Surgeons *(103)*
RVS	Cardiovascular Credentialing International *(342)*
RVT	American Registry for Diagnostic Medical Sonography *(174)*
RWC	RCI, Inc. *(875)*
RWFCP	Unfinished Furniture Association *(984)*
RWP	American Short Line and Regional Railroad Association *(179)*
S and EF	American Society for Engineering Education *(183)*
S&F	National Wood Flooring Association *(805)*
S20	Electrostatic Discharge Association *(425)*
SA	Wilderness Education Association *(1017)*
SAC	International Society of Transport Aircraft Trading *(574)*
SAM-MOC	American Radium Society *(173)*
SANE-A	International Association of Forensic Nurses *(521)*
SANE-P	International Association of Forensic Nurses *(521)*
SAP	National Association for Alcoholism and Drug Abuse Counselors *(646)*
SAPSC	Association for Retail Technology Standards *(256)*
SARTECH I	National Association for Search and Rescue *(642)*
SARTECH II	National Association for Search and Rescue *(642)*
SARTECH III	National Association for Search and Rescue *(642)*
SASP	National Automobile Dealers Association *(711)*
SBCA	Satellite Broadcasting and Communications Association *(891)*
SBE	Distributive Education Clubs of America (DECA) *(415)*
SBMP	Association of School Business Officials International *(306)*
SBTS	International Fitness Professionals Association *(545)*
SC	Aerobics and Fitness Association of America *(13)*
	Professional Association of Volleyball Officials *(860)*
	Tile Roofing Institute *(974)*
SC(OT&OTA)	American Occupational Therapy Association, Inc. *(157)*
SC:L	Registry of Interpreters for the Deaf *(879)*
SCC	Help Desk Institute *(474)*
	National Association of State Boards of Accountancy *(698)*
SCCP	Solar Rating and Certification Corporation *(952)*
SCEH-ACE	Society for Clinical and Experimental Hypnosis *(906)*
SCI	American Backflow Prevention Association *(78)*
	The Institute of Inspection, Cleaning and Restoration Certification *(500)*
SCMD	International Council of Shopping Centers *(538)*
SCOP	Manufacturing Jewelers and Suppliers of America *(604)*
SCOR-P	Supply Chain Council *(966)*
SCOR-S	Supply Chain Council *(966)*
SCORE	Structural Building Components Association *(964)*
SCP	American Institute of the History of Pharmacy *(141)*
	Builders Hardware Manufacturers Association *(337)*
	International Masonry Institute *(556)*
SCPro	Council of Supply Chain Management Professionals *(398)*
SCPS	Sales and Marketing Executives International, Inc. *(890)*
SCS	International Fitness Professionals Association *(545)*
	National Association of Manufacturers *(679)*
SCSC	American Association of Woodturners *(77)*
SCSM	International Council of Shopping Centers *(538)*
SCSP	Marine Retailers Association of America *(605)*
SCT	The Institute of Inspection, Cleaning and Restoration Certification *(500)*
SCWI	American Welding Society *(220)*
SDI	National Association of Underwater Instructors *(707)*
SE	National Council of Examiners for Engineering and Surveying *(734)*
SEAP	American Society for Engineering Education *(183)*
SEBA	National Business Aviation Association *(716)*

SECB	National Council of Structural Engineers Associations (737)
SEE	National Dog Groomers Association of America, Inc. (743)
SEFA8CTL	Scientific Equipment and Furniture Association (892)
SEL	The Exercise Safety Association (435)
SERF	Association for Surgical Education (257)
SESAP	American College of Surgeons (103)
SESC	CHA - Certified Horsemanship Association (350)
SF	Medieval Academy of America (612)
SFO	Association of School Business Officials International (306)
SFR	American Society for Engineering Education (183)
	National Association of Realtors (690)
SFS	International Fitness Professionals Association (545)
SGCC	Safety Glazing Certification Council (890)
SGM	Professional Grounds Management Society (862)
SHCM	National Affordable Housing Management Association (629)
SIA	Wilderness Education Association (1017)
SIC	CHA - Certified Horsemanship Association (350)
SIF	The Open Group (828)
	Schools Interoperability Framework Association (892)
SIM	National Registry of Environmental Professionals (785)
SIOR	Society of Industrial and Office Realtors (939)
SIT	National Association of Judiciary Interpreters and Translators (677)
SLCR	CoreNet Global (385)
SLP	American Society for Engineering Education (183)
SM	Recreation Vehicle Dealers Association of North America (876)
SMART	American Society for Engineering Education (183)
	National Clay Pipe Institute (722)
SMAT-CE	Surface Mount Technology Association (966)
SMC	American Board of Anesthesiology (81)
	Building Owners and Managers Institute International (337)
SMCTC	The Institute of Inspection, Cleaning and Restoration Certification (500)
SMT	The Institute of Inspection, Cleaning and Restoration Certification (500)
	Professional Society for Sales and Marketing Training (865)
SN	American Concrete Institute (106)
SNA	Society for Nutrition Education and Behavior (917)
SNC	National Association of School Nurses (693)
SNS	International Fitness Professionals Association (545)
SOC	North American Electric Reliability Corporation (816)
SOLAS	American Bureau of Shipping (86)
SON	American Registry of Radiologic Technologists (174)
SP	National Association of Disability Examiners (663)
SPC	Academy of Laser Dentistry (6)
	Automotive Industry Action Group (322)
	International Magnetics Association (555)
	National Association of Pastoral Musicians (683)
	Training Directors' Forum (977)
SPCE	Society of Satellite Professionals International (947)
SPDC	International Society for Molecular Plant Microbe Interactions (567)
SPE	Society of Petroleum Engineers (944)
SPFE	PMA - The Worldwide Community of Imaging Associations (851)
SPHR	Society for Human Resource Management (911)
SPI	American Mountain Guides Association (153)
SPPA	National Association of Public Insurance Adjusters (690)
SPRAT	Society of Professional Rope Access Technicians (945)
SPS	International Fitness Professionals Association (545)
SRA	Academy of Surgical Research (9)
	Appraisal Institute (226)
SRAS	National Abstinence Education Association (626)
SRES	National Association of Realtors (690)

SRPA	Appraisal Institute (226)
SRS	Academy of Surgical Research (9)
SRT	Academy of Surgical Research (9)
SS	Retail Solutions Providers Association (885)
SSI0IC	American Hypnosis Association (134)
SSBBC	Institute of Industrial Engineers (500)
SSCP	Institute of Industrial Engineers (500)
	Solar Rating and Certification Corporation (952)
SSGBC	Institute of Industrial Engineers (500)
SSI	The Exercise Safety Association (435)
SSM	The Open Group (828)
SSPA	American Association of Suicidology (74)
SSSC	Specialty Steel Industry of North America (958)
ST	Recreation Vehicle Dealers Association of North America (876)
STA	The International Transactional Analysis Association (578)
STS	Board of Certified Safety Professionals (332)
	International Fitness Professionals Association (545)
SW/A	Recreation Vehicle Dealers Association of North America (876)
TADS	Association of State Dam Safety Officials (310)
TAS	National Association for Alcoholism and Drug Abuse Counselors (646)
TATO	Structural Building Components Association (964)
TBE	Associated Air Balance Council (234)
TBM	BioCommunications Association (329)
TC	International Association of Correctional Training Personnel (518)
TCEC	The International Childbirth Education Association (534)
TCI	American Backflow Prevention Association (78)
TCP	American Concrete Institute (106)
	Tea Association of the United States of America (969)
TCS	American Traffic Safety Service Association (217)
TCT	American Traffic Safety Service Association (217)
TDC	National Association of Underwater Instructors (707)
TFA	Teaching-Family Association (969)
TFC	International Association for Identification (513)
TFCCP	National Community Pharmacists Association (725)
TFM	IT Financial Management Association (586)
TGC	CHA - Certified Horsemanship Association (350)
	National Federation of Licensed Practical Nurses (749)
TGPC	American Society of Pension Professionals & Actuaries (206)
THR	American Registry of Radiologic Technologists (174)
TI:ME IA	The Technology Institute for Music Educators (970)
TI:ME 2A	The Technology Institute for Music Educators (970)
TIAPC	Transportation Intermediaries Association (978)
TIC	National Association of Underwater Instructors (707)
TIT	American Hypnosis Association (134)
TKGA	The Knitting Guild Association (591)
TLE	Professional Aviation Maintenance Association (860)
TLS	Professional Aviation Maintenance Association (860)
TMP	International Foundation of Employee Benefit Plans (547)
TNC	American Academy of Ambulatory Care Nursing (30)
TNCC	Emergency Nurses Association (425)
TOC	Suntanning Association for Education (966)
TOE	Tile Contractors' Association of America (974)
TOGAF	The Open Group (828)
TOPIC	Society of Trauma Nurses (949)
TOPS	Institute of Transportation Engineers (503)
TPA	American Telemedicine Association (215)
TPCP	Air Diffusion Council (18)
	American Petroleum Institute (163)
TPSAE	American Association of Neuromuscular and Electrodiagnostic Medicine (66)
TS	American Association of Bioanalysts (54)
	Spring Manufacturers Institute (960)
TSC	American Staffing Association (213)
TSCP	Toy Industry Association (976)

TSFC	National Community Pharmacists Association (725)
TSOS	Institute of Transportation Engineers (503)
TSTA	The International Transactional Analysis Association (578)
TTA	The International Transactional Analysis Association (578)
TTCP	Dance Educators of America (406)
TTP	National Automatic Merchandising Association (711)
TTS	Licensing Executives Society (597)
TTT	Structural Building Components Association (964)
UA STAR	Mechanical Service Contractors of America (610)
UC	Association of University Programs in Health Administration (316)
	National Swine Improvement Federation (798)
UDCC	United Development Council (986)
UDX	American Kennel Club (143)
UEP	United Egg Producers (986)
UFCT	The Institute of Inspection, Cleaning and Restoration Certification (500)
UFT	The Institute of Inspection, Cleaning and Restoration Certification (500)
UID	North American Building Material Distribution Association (724)
UM/CR	National Committee for Quality Assurance (724)
UNIX	The Open Group (828)
UPPCC	National Institute of Governmental Purchasing (765)
USFCA	United States Fencing Coaches Association (994)
USPAACC	United States Pan Asian American Chamber of Commerce (997)
UWSIC	iNARTE, Inc. (487)
VAC	International Veterinary Acupuncture Society (580)
VACC	Association for Vascular Access (261)
VBMA	Veterinary Botanical Medical Association (1008)
VC	American Association of Orthodontists (67)
	Retail Solutions Providers Association (885)
VCC	CHA - Certified Horsemanship Association (350)
VDC	SAE International (889)
VEE	Society of Actuaries (927)
VI	American Registry of Radiologic Technologists (174)
VIVA	American Association of Veterinary State Boards (76)
VMMI	Community Transportation Association of America (371)
VMP	SAVE International (891)
VQA	American Veal Association (218)
VS	American Board of Surgery (84)
	American Registry of Radiologic Technologists (174)
VSMR	NADCA: The HVAC Inspection, Maintenance and Restoration Association (623)
VTNE	American Association of Veterinary State Boards (76)
WA	Recreation Vehicle Dealers Association of North America (876)
WAP	The Open Group (828)
WBE	Independent Staffing Alliance (492)
	Women's Business Enterprise National Council (1022)
WCC	Medical Fitness Association (611)
WCET	Institute of Electrical and Electronics Engineers (IEEE) (499)
WD	BICSI (329)
WDRT	The Institute of Inspection, Cleaning and Restoration Certification (500)
WFI	National Wood Flooring Association (805)
WFI,S&C	National Wood Flooring Association (805)
WFS	International Fitness Professionals Association (545)
WFSC	National Wood Flooring Association (805)
WHC	National Wildlife Federation (805)
Wi-Fi	Wi-Fi Alliance (1016)
WIE	iNARTE, Inc. (487)
WIT	iNARTE, Inc. (487)
WLI0I	American Hypnosis Association (134)
WLCP	WorldatWork (1028)
WLFI	The Institute of Inspection, Cleaning and Restoration Certification (500)
WLS	Restoration Industry Association (884)
WMM	Weather Modification Association (1014)
WMO	Weather Modification Association (1014)
WOCNCB	The Wound, Ostomy and Continence Nurses Society (1028)
WOSB	Women's Business Enterprise National Council (1022)

WPDP	International Association of Workforce Professionals (IAWP) *(529)*
WRC	American Staffing Association *(213)*
	Power Washers of North America *(855)*
WS	American Watchmakers-Clockmakers Institute *(219)*
WSC	International Webmasters Association *(580)*
WT	American Watchmakers-Clockmakers Institute *(219)*
WTC	The Wildlife Society *(1017)*
WTCA	World Trade Centers Association *(1027)*
WWU	Wellness Councils of America *(1015)*
YEDP	American Road and Transportation Builders Association *(175)*
YFI	International Fitness Professionals Association *(545)*
YSFI	International Fitness Professionals Association *(545)*
ZB CP	Zero Balancing Health Association *(1030)*

Meetings Index

Association meetings and conferences scheduled for 2013 and beyond are detailed below under the city where the meeting is to be held.

USA

ALABAMA

Auburn
American Meat Science Association/Auburn University/June 16 - 19, 2013
Professional Landcare Network/March 7 - 10, 2013/1-10 exhibitors

Birmingham
Federation of State Humanities Councils/Nov. 7 - 10, 2013

Huntsville
National Speleological Society/NSS Headquarters/July 14 - 18, 2014

Mobile
National Association of County Agricultural Agents/July 20 - 24, 2014
National Barbecue Association/Renaissance Mobile Riverview Plaza Hotel/Feb. 20 - 23, 2013
National Marine Educators Association/Spring Hill College/July 22 - 26, 2013
Society for Cross-Cultural Research/The Battle House Renaissance Mobile Hotel and Spa/Feb. 20 - 23, 2013

Montgomery
American Bandmasters Association/The Renaissance Hotel/March 5 - 8, 2014
Society for Military History/Renaissance Montgomery Hotel and Spa at the Convention Center/April 9 - 12, 2015

Point Clear
American Association of State Colleges and Universities/Feb. 7 - 9, 2013
Interstate Oil and Gas Compact Commission/Grand Hotel Marriott Resort, Golf Club and Spa/May 20 - 22, 2013

Tuscaloosa
Pipe Fabrication Institute/Hotel Capstone/March 29 - April 1, 2014

ALASKA

Anchorage
Cryogenic Engineering Conference/Denaina Civic and Convention Center/June 17 - 21, 2013
International Association for Energy Economics/Hotel Captain Cook/July 28 - 31, 2013
International Society of Offshore and Polar Engineers/Anchorage Convention Center/June 30 - July 4, 2013
National Association of State Budget Officers/Hotel Captain Cook/July 21 - 24, 2013
National Indian Education Association/Oct. 16 - 19, 2014
National Railway Historical Society/Hilton Anchorage/Sept. 18 - 22, 2013
Scoliosis Research Society/Sept. 10 - 14, 2014
Scoliosis Research Society/Sept. 10 - 13, 2014
Seismological Society of America/April 30 - May 2, 2014
United States Association for Energy Economics/July 28 - 31, 2013

ARIZONA

Glendale
American Water Works Association/Renaissance Phoenix Glendale Hotel and Spa/March 10 - 13, 2013
Association of Image Consultants International/Renaissance Glendale Hotel and Spa/May 16 - 19, 2013
Precision Machined Products Association/Renaissance Glendale Hotel and Spa/Feb. 15 - 17, 2013

Litchfield Park
Mechanical Power Transmission Association/The Wigwam Resort/April 7 - 10, 2013

Marana
National Oilseed Processors Association/Ritz-Carlton, Dove Mountain/Feb. 10 - 14, 2013
Spring Manufacturers Institute/Ritz-Carlton Dove Mountain/April 4 - 9, 2013

Phoenix
AHS International - The Vertical Flight Society/Phoenix Convention Center/May 21 - 23, 2013
Alliance of Area Business Publications/Arizona Biltmore/Jan. 25 - 27, 2013

American Academy of Implant Dentistry/JW Marriott Phoenix Desert Ridge Resort and Spa/Oct. 23 - 26, 2013/over 100 exhibitors
American Advertising Federation/Arizona Biltmore Resort and Spa/June 5 - 8, 2013
American Animal Hospital Association/Phoenix Convention Center/March 14 - 17, 2013
American Association for Laboratory Animal Science/Nov. 1 - 5, 2015
American Association for Paralegal Education/Nov. 6 - 9, 2013
American Association of Clinical Endocrinologists/May 1 - 5, 2013
American Association of Collegiate Registrars and Admissions Officers/Phoenix Convention Center/March 20 - 23, 2016
American Association of Collegiate Registrars and Admissions Officers/JW Marriott Phoenix Desert Ridge Resort and Spa/Oct. 29 - Nov. 1, 2017
American Association of Orthopaedic Medicine/Arizona Grand Resort/April 24 - 27, 2013
American Backflow Prevention Association/May 6 - 8, 2013
American Board of Veterinary Practitioners/Rennaissance Glendale Hotel & Spa/Oct. 31 - Nov. 3, 2013
American College of Medical Genetics/March 19 - 23, 2013/1-10 exhibitors
American College of Medical Quality/Feb. 20 - 23, 2013
American College of Mohs Surgeons/JW Marriott Desert Ridge Resort/May 1 - 4, 2014
American College of Neuropsychopharmacology/JW Marriott Phoenix Desert Ridge Resort and Spa/Dec. 7 - 11, 2014
American College of Phlebology/JW Marriott Desert Ridge Resort/Nov. 6 - 9, 2014
American College of Preventive Medicine/Pointe Hilton Tapatio Cliffs Resort/Feb. 20 - 23, 2013
American Concrete Institute/Hyatt Regency Phoenix/Oct. 20 - 24, 2013
American Gas Association/Arizona Biltmore Resort and Spa/April 19 - 21, 2016
The American Gem Society/Arizona Biltmore Resort and Spa/April 24 - 27, 2013
American Health Care Association/Oct. 6 - 9, 2013
American Intellectual Property Law Association/Sheraton Wild Horse Pass Resort and Spa/Jan. 29 - Feb. 1, 2014
American Meteorological Society/Jan. 4 - 8, 2015
American Meteorological Society/Jan. 6 - 10, 2019
American Organization of Nurse Executives/April 15 - 18, 2015
American Osteopathic College of Occupational and Preventive Medicine/Phoenix Sheraton Downtown/Feb. 13 - 17, 2013
American Pediatric Surgical Association/JW Marriott Phoenix Desert Ridge Resort and Spa/May 29 - June 1, 2014
American Public Gardens Association/May 20 - 24, 2013
American Public Works Association/Aug. 30 - Sept. 2, 2015
American Registry for Internet Numbers/Oct. 10 - 11, 2013
American Seniors Housing Association/JW Marriott Desert Ridge Resort/Jan. 20 - 22, 2014
American Society for Laser Medicine and Surgery/Phoenix Convention Center/April 2 - 6, 2014
American Society for Parenteral and Enteral Nutrition/Phoenix Convention Center/Feb. 9 - 13, 2013/2000 attendees/over 100 exhibitors
American Society for Quality/Pointe at Tapatio Cliffs/March 4 - 5, 2013/500 attendees
American Society of Agronomy (ASA, CSSA, SSSA)/Nov. 6 - 9, 2016
American Society of Agronomy (ASA, CSSA, SSSA)/Nov. 8 - 11, 2020
American Society of Colon and Rectal Surgeons/Phoenix Convention Center/April 27 - May 1, 2013
American Society of Consultant Pharmacists/JW Marriott Desert Ridge Resort/June 12 - 14, 2014
American Society of Ocularists/The Wigwam Hotel/April 25 - May 1, 2015
American Society of Plumbing Engineers/Oct. 27 - Nov. 4, 2016
American Society of Regional Anesthesia and Pain Medicine/Nov. 21 - 24, 2013
American Traffic Safety Service Association/Phoenix Convention Center/Feb. 10 - 14, 2017
American Venous Forum/Wigwam Resort/Feb. 27 - March 2, 2013
Assisted Living Federation of America/May 20 - 22, 2014
Association for Hose and Accessories Distribution/JW Marriott Desert Ridge Resort/April 26 - 30, 2014

Association for Molecular Pathology/Phoenix Convention Center/Nov. 14 - 16, 2013/over 100 exhibitors

Association of Governing Boards of Universities and Colleges/Sugarloaf Animal Clinic/April 10 - 12, 2015

Association of Home Office Underwriters/The Arizona Baltimore/April 7 - 10, 2013

Association of Insurance Compliance Professionals/JW Marriott Desert Ridge Resort/Sept. 14 - 17, 2014

Association of Jewish Family & Children's Agencies/Biltmore Hotel/May 19 - 21, 2013

Association of Professors of Gynecology and Obstetrics/JW Marriott Desert Ridge Resort/Feb. 27 - March 2, 2013

Association of Teacher Educators/Hyatt Regency and Phoenix Convention Center/Feb. 13 - 17, 2015

Automotive Aftermarket Industry Association/Embassy Suites Phoenix-Scottsdale/May 14 - 16, 2013

Chlorine Chemistry Council/Sept. 23 - 25, 2013

Construction Financial Management Association/JW Marriott Phoenix Desert Ridge Resort and Spa/June 3 - 7, 2017

Conveyor Equipment Manufacturers Association/Arizona Biltmore Resort and Spa/March 15 - 19, 2013

Corporate Housing Providers Association/Arizona Biltmore Resort and Spa/Feb. 4 - 6, 2013

Council of State Speech-Language-Hearing Association Presidents/Nov. 18, 2015

Crop Science Society of America/Nov. 6 - 9, 2016

Crop Science Society of America/Nov. 8 - 11, 2020

Dairy Management, Inc./Arizona Biltmore Resort and Spa/Nov. 11 - 13, 2013

Direct Selling Association/JW Marriott Phoenix Desert Ridge Resort and Spa/June 9 - 11, 2013/900 attendees

Drug & Alcohol Testing Industry Association/Arizona Biltmore Resort and Spa/May 28 - 30, 2013

Edison Electric Institute/JW Marriott Desert Ridge Resort/Nov. 6 - 9, 2016

Enlisted Association of the National Guard of the United States/Phoenix Convention Center/Aug. 10 - 13, 2014

FlexTech Alliance/Phoenix Convention Center/Jan. 29 - Feb. 1, 2013/300 attendees

Food Shippers of America/JW Marriott Phoenix Desert Ridge Resort and Spa/Feb. 24 - 26, 2013

Foodservice Equipment Distributors Association/JW Marriott Phoenix Desert Ridge Resort and Spa/March 25 - 29, 2015

Global Market Development Center/JW Marriott Desert Ridge Resort/Sept. 6 - 10, 2013

Global Market Development Center/JW Marriott Desert Ridge Resort/Sept. 18 - 22, 2015

Health Forum/Pointe Hilton Tapation Cliffs Resort/Feb. 10 - 13, 2013

Heating, Airconditioning and Refrigeration Distributors International/JW Marriott Phoenix Desert Ridge Resort and Spa/Dec. 7 - 10, 2013

Hydraulic Institute/The Wigwam/Feb. 6 - 11, 2014

IEEE Signal Processing Society/Sept. 25 - 28, 2016

Illuminating Engineering Society of North America/JW Marriott Phoenix Desert Ridge Resort and Spa/Sept. 8 - 11, 2013

Institute for Professionals in Taxation/JW Marriott Phoenix Desert Ridge Resort and Spa/June 29 - July 2, 2014

Institute for Supply Management/May 3 - 6, 2015

Inter-Company Marketing Group/Talking Stick Resort/Feb. 4 - 6, 2014

International Association of Outsourcing Professionals/JW Marriott Phoenix Desert Ridge/Feb. 18 - 20, 2013

International Brotherhood of Magicians/Hyatt Regency and Phoenix Convention Center/July 17 - 20, 2013

International Lactation Consultant Association/JW Marriott Desert Ridge Resort/July 23 - 26, 2014

International Precious Metals Institute/JW Marriott Phoenix Desert Ridge Resort and Spa/June 22 - 25, 2013

International Technology Law Association/Westin Kierland Resort and Spa/May 1 - 3, 2013

International Union of Toxicology/Phoenix Convention Center/March 23 - 27, 2014

Investment Program Association/Arizona Grand Hotel/Oct. 28 - 30, 2014

Mortgage Bankers Association of America/Arizona Biltmore Resort and Spa/May 19 - 22, 2013

National Association of Boards of Pharmacy/Sheraton Phoenix Downtown Hotel/May 17 - 20, 2014

National Association of Private Special Education Centers/Jan. 27 - 30, 2013

National Association of Private Special Education Centers/Camelback Inn/March 27 - 30, 2013

National Association of Professional Organizers/Westin Kierland Resort and Spa/May 28 - 31, 2014

National Association of Professional Process Servers/Hyatt Regency Phoenix/April 18 - 20, 2013

National Association of Tax Professionals/JW Marriott Desert Ridge Resort/July 8 - 11, 2013

National Council for Prescription Drug Programs/Arizona Biltmore Resort & Spa/May 5 - 9, 2013/1-10 exhibitors

National Council of Real Estate Investment Fiduciaries/Arizona Biltmore/Feb. 27 - March 1, 2013

National Indian Gaming Association/Phoenix Convention Center/March 24 - 27, 2013/over 100 exhibitors

National League for Nursing/Hyatt Regency Phoenix/Sept. 17 - 20, 2014

National Milk Producers Federation/Arizona Biltmore Resort and Spa/Nov. 11 - 13, 2013

National Operating Committee for Standards of Athletic Equipment/Royal Palms Resort and Spa/Jan. 25 - 26, 2013

National Systems Contractors Association/Arizona Grand Resort/Feb. 21 - 23, 2013

National Telecommunications Cooperative Association/Phoenix Convention Center and Hyatt Regency/March 8 - 11, 2015

National Utility Contractors Association (NUCA)/Sheraton Phoenix Downtown Hotel/Feb. 11 - 15, 2013

Orthopaedic Trauma Association/JW Marriott Phoenix Desert Ridge Resort and Spa/Oct. 10 - 12, 2013/1100 attendees

Performance Warehouse Association/Sept. 21 - 25, 2013

Performance Warehouse Association/Sept. 13 - 17, 2014

Performance Warehouse Association/Sept. 26 - 30, 2015

Professional Photographers of America/Jan. 12 - 14, 2014

Security Hardware Distributors Association/Pointe Hilton Squaw Peak Resort/April 30 - May 3, 2013

Shelf-Stable Food Processors Association/Arizona Biltmore/March 9 - 11, 2014

Society for American Baseball Research/Hilton Phoenix East/Mesa/March 7 - 9, 2013

Society for Critical Care Medicine/Phoenix Convention Center/Feb. 3 - 7, 2018

Society of Surgical Oncology/March 12 - 15, 2014/1500 attendees/over 100 exhibitors

Society of Surgical Oncology/March 13, 2014

Soil Science Society of America/Nov. 6 - 9, 2016

Soil Science Society of America/Nov. 8 - 11, 2020

Specialty Tools and Fasteners Distributors Association/Phoenix Convention Center/Nov. 8 - 10, 2015

United Shoe Retailers Association/Wigwam Resort/May 5 - 7, 2013

United States Committee on Irrigation and Drainage/April 16 - 19, 2013

United States Society on Dams/Feb. 11 - 15, 2013

University Risk Management and Insurance Association/Arizona Biltmore Resort and Spa/Oct. 12 - 16, 2013

Water Environment Federation/Renaissance Phoenix Glendale Hotel and Spa/March 10 - 13, 2013

Woodworking Machinery Industry Association/Phoenix Marriott Tempe at The Buttes/April 23 - 26, 2013

Scottsdale

American Association for Hand Surgery/Westin Kierland Hotel/Jan. 13 - 26, 2016

American Association of Managing General Agents/Scottsdale Plaza Resort/March 2 - 5, 2013

American Association of Managing General Agents/J.W. Marriott Desert Ridge Resort/May 22 - 25, 2016

American Association of Motor Vehicle Administrators/Westin Kierland Resort and Spa/Aug. 26 - 28, 2013

American Association of Presidents of Independent Colleges and Universities/Scottsdale Plaza Hotel/Feb. 21 - 23, 2013

American Association of Tissue Banks/Westin Kierland Resort and Spa/Sept. 15 - 19, 2015

American Auditory Society/Chaparral Suites Resort Scottsdale/March 7 - 9, 2013

American Bakers Association/The Phoenician/March 14 - 19, 2014

American Board of Vocational Experts/FireSky Resort and Spa/April 12 - 14, 2013

American College of Oral and Maxillofacial Surgeons/Phoenician Resort/April 20 - 22, 2013

American Council of Engineering Companies/Fairmont Scottsdale Princess/Oct. 27 - 30, 2013

American Dermatological Association/Four Seasons Resort Scottsdale at Troon North/Sept. 18 - 22, 2013

American Headache Society/Camelback Inn Resort and Spa/Nov. 15 - 17, 2013

American Headache Society/Camelback Inn Resort and Spa/Nov. 14 - 16, 2014

American Headache Society/Camelback Inn Resort and Spa/Nov. 13 - 15, 2015

American Institute of Constructors/April 24 - 27, 2013

American Laryngological, Rhinological and Otological Society/Westin Kierland Resort and Spa/Jan. 24 - 26, 2013

American Osteopathic Colleges of Ophthalmology and Otolaryngology - Head and Neck Surgery/JW Marriott Camelback Inn Scottsdale Resort and Spa/May 7 - 11, 2013

American Radium Society/The Phoenician/April 27 - May 1, 2013

American Seed Trade Association/The Fairmont/Jan. 26 - 29, 2013

American Society for Cytotechnology/Hotel Valley Ho/April 19 - 21, 2013

American Society of Irrigation Consultants/Hilton Scottsdale Resort and Villas/April 20 - 22, 2013

American Sports Builders Association/Fairmont Scottsdale Princess/Dec. 4 - 8, 2015

American Veterinary Distributors Association/Fairmont Scottsdale Princess/April 27 - 29, 2014

Association for Women in Sports Media/Montelucia Resort and Spa/June 20 - 23, 2013

Association of Donor Recruitment Professionals/Talking Stick Resort/May 15 - 17, 2013/11-25 exhibitors

Association of Family Medicine Residency Directors/Hotel Valley Ho/Jan. 24 - 27, 2013

Association of Investment Management Sales Executives/Fairmont Scottsdale Princess/April 28 - 30, 2013

Association of Real Estate License Law Officials/DoubleTree Resort by Hilton Hotel Paradise Valley-Scottsdale/April 10 - 13, 2013

ATM Industry Association/Golf Club Scottsdale/Feb. 19 - 21, 2013

Bearing Specialist Association/Fairmont Scottsdale Princess/May 2 - 6, 2014

Captive Insurance Companies Association/Westin Kierland Resort and Spa/March 9 - 11, 2014

Clinical Laboratory Management Association/Phoenician Resort/May 5 - 7, 2013

Commercial Real Estate Women Network/JW Marriott Camelback Inn Scottsdale Resort and Spa/June 13 - 14, 2013

Compressed Gas Association/Hyatt Regency Scottsdale Resort and Spa at Gainey Ranch/April 7 - 12, 2013

Concrete Reinforcing Steel Institute/InterContinental Montelucia Resort and Spa/April 27 - 30, 2013

Electronic Transactions Association/Montelucia Resort and Spa/Oct. 15 - 17, 2013

Environmental Council of the States/FireSky Resort and Spa/March 4 - 6, 2013

The Fertilizer Institute/Westin Kierland Resort and Spa/Feb. 9 - 11, 2015

Financial and Security Products Association/Fairmont Scottsdale Princess Hotel and Resort/May 30 - June 1, 2013

Fluid Fertilizer Foundation/Scottsdale Plaza Resort/Feb. 18 - 20, 2013

Food Marketing Institute/The Phoenician/Jan. 20 - 22, 2013

Food Processing Suppliers Association/Westin Kierland Resort & Spa/March 6 - 9, 2013
Health Physics Society/Doubletree Paradise Valley Resort/Jan. 27 - 30, 2013
IMAGE Society/June 3 - 6, 2013
Institute of Real Estate Management/Westin Kierland Resort and Spa/Oct. 15 - 19, 2013
International Anti-Counterfeiting Coalition/Oct. 16 - 18, 2013
International Dairy Foods Association/The Boulders/May 4 - 6, 2013
International Municipal Signal Association/Westin Kierland Resort and Spa/July 18 - 25, 2013
ISA -The Association of Learning Providers/Marriott's Camelback Inn Resort/March 17 - 20, 2013
Messenger Courier Association of the Americas/The Westin Kierland/May 14 - 17, 2014
Metals Service Center Institute/Fairmont Scottsdale Princess/May 4 - 6, 2014
Million Dollar Round Table/Oct. 9 - 12, 2013
Modular Building Institute/Westin Kierland Resort and Spa/March 16 - 19, 2013
National Asphalt Pavement Association/The Phoenician/Feb. 9 - 13, 2013
National Association for Court Management/Westin Kierland Resort and Spa/July 13 - 17, 2014
National Association for Family Child Care/Fairmont Scottsdale Princess Hotel/July 18 - 20, 2013
National Association for Retail Marketing Services/Scottsdale Plaza Resort/April 27 - 30, 2013
National Association of Flour Distributors/The Phoenician/May 15 - 19, 2013
National Association of Independent Lighting Distributors/Hilton Scottsdale Resort and Villas/March 17 - 20, 2013
National Association of Professional Background Screeners/JW Marriott Phoenix Desert Ridge Resort and Spa/Sept. 15 - 17, 2013
National Association of Schools of Music/Westin Kierland Resort and Spa/Nov. 21 - 25, 2014
National Council of Farmer Cooperatives/Westin Kierland Resort and Spa/Feb. 6 - 8, 2013
National Court Reporters Association/DoubleTree Resort by Hilton Hotel Paradise Valley-Scottsdale/April 19 - 21, 2013
National Crop Insurance Services/Westin Kierland Resort and Spa/Feb. 9 - 12, 2014/3000 attendees
National Fluid Power Association/Montelucia Resort and Spa/March 5 - 8, 2013
National Institute of Oilseed Products/The Camelback Inn/March 10 - 12, 2013
National Institute of Oilseed Products/The Camelback Inn/March 15 - 17, 2015
National Ocean Industries Association/The Phoenician/Oct. 22 - 24, 2015
National Pest Management Association/Phoenician Resort/Oct. 23 - 26, 2013
National Telecommunications Cooperative Association/Phoenician Resort/Feb. 1 - 4, 2015
Non-Ferrous Founders' Society/Talking Stick Resort/Oct. 11 - 14, 2013
Pipe Line Contractors Association/Hyatt Regency Scottsdale Resort and Spa/Feb. 12 - 16, 2013
Plan Sponsor Council of America/Fairmont Scottsdale Princess/Sept. 9 - 12, 2013
Post-Tensioning Institute/Hilton Scottsdale Resort and Villas/May 5 - 7, 2013
Real Estate Investment Securities Association/DoubleTree Resort by Hilton Hotel Paradise Valley-Scottsdale/April 10 - 13, 2013
Sealant, Waterproofing and Restoration Institute/Montelucia Resort and Spa/March 3 - 6, 2013
The Society for Investigative Dermatology/Westin Kierland Resort and Spa/May 11 - 14, 2016
Society of Independent Gasoline Marketers of America (SIGMA)/Hyatt Regency Scottsdale Resort and Spa at Gainey Ranch/May 2 - 5, 2013
Society of Toxicology/Phoenician Resort/March 23 - 27, 2014
Specialized Carriers and Rigging Association/Westin Kierland Resort and Spa/April 2 - 6, 2013
Toy Industry Association/Hyatt Regency Scottsdale Resort and Spa/May 15 - 17, 2013
Transportation Elevator and Grain Merchants Association/Montelucia Resort and Spa/Jan. 24 - 25, 2013
Triological Society/Westin Kierland Resort and Spa/Jan. 24 - 26, 2013
United States Tour Operators Association/Fairmont Scottsdale Princess/Dec. 5 - 7, 2013
Water and Sewer Distributors of America/Westin Kierland Resort and Spa/Feb. 23 - 26, 2013
Wood Moulding and Millwork Producers Association/Talking Stick Resort/March 5 - 9, 2013

Tempe
AMC Institute/The Buttes Resort/Feb. 26 - 28, 2014
American Federation of Astrologers, Inc./Embassy Suites/May 2 - 4, 2013
Concrete Reinforcing Steel Institute/Tempe Mission Palms Hotel and Conference Center/March 12 - 15, 2013
International Association of Equine Dentists/Fiesta Inn Resort/Feb. 15 - 17, 2013
Society for Mathematical Biology/Tempe Mission Palms Hotel and Conference Center/June 10 - 13, 2013

Tucson
Accredited Gemologists Association/Feb. 6, 2013
American Architectural Manufacturers Association/Loews Ventana Canyon Resort/Feb. 24 - 27, 2013
American Association of Collegiate Registrars and Admissions Officers/JW Marriott Tucson Starr Pass Resort and Spa/July 14 - 16, 2013
American Association of Directors of Psychiatric Residency Training/Hilton El Conquistador/March 12 - 15, 2014
American Association of Tissue Banks/Westin La Paloma Resort and Spa/April 6 - 9, 2013
American Gem Trade Association/Tucson Convention Center/Feb. 5 - 10, 2013/11-25 exhibitors
Association of Energy Service Companies/Loews Ventana Canyon Resort/Feb. 20 - 22, 2013
Association of Universities for Research in Astronomy, Inc./April 17 - 20, 2013
Conference of Educational Administrators of Schools and Programs for the Deaf/April 11 - 13, 2013

Electrostatic Discharge Association/Westin La Paloma Resort and Spa/Feb. 11 - 16, 2014
Foodservice Equipment Distributors Association/JW Marriott Tucson Starr Pass Resort and Spa/March 30 - April 3, 2016
Institute of Transportation Engineers/Westin La Paloma Resort and Spa/March 29 - April 1, 2015
Jeweler's Vigilance Committee/Tucson Convention Center/Feb. 5 - 10, 2013
National Association of County Community and Economic Development/Oct. 18 - 23, 2013
National Association of EMS Physicians/JW Marriott Tucson Starr Pass Resort and Spa/Jan. 16 - 18, 2014
National Association of Jewelry Appraisers/Tucson Convention Center/Feb. 3 - 4, 2013
National Coal Transportation Association/Westin La Paloma Resort and Spa/April 14 - 17, 2013
National Coil Coating Association/Loews Ventana Canyon Resort/April 20 - 22, 2015
National Cottonseed Products Association/JW Marriott Tucson Starr Pass Resort and Spa/May 4 - 7, 2013
The National Greenhouse Manufacturers Association/April 14 - 16, 2013
National Motor Freight Traffic Association, Inc./Omni Tucson National Golf Resort and Spa/Jan. 26 - 29, 2014
NPES, The Association for Suppliers of Printing, Publishing, and Converting Technologies/March 10 - 13, 2013
Petroleum Equipment Suppliers Association/Loews Ventana Canyon Resort/April 2 - 5, 2014
Society of Computed Body Tomography and Magnetic Resonance/Hilton El Conquistador Resort/Oct. 12 - 16, 2013/350 attendees
Society of Financial Service Professionals/Westward Look Wyndham Grand Resort and Spa/Jan. 27 - 31, 2013
Teratology Society/Loews Ventana Canyon Resort/June 22 - 26, 2013
Textile Bag and Packaging Association/Loews Ventana Canyon Resort/March 17 - 19, 2013
Transportation Intermediaries Association/April 2 - 5, 2014
Transportation Intermediaries Association/March 21 - 24, 2018
Tree-Ring Society/May 13 - 18, 2013
Western History Association/Westin La Paloma Resort and Spa/Oct. 9 - 12, 2013

Wickenburg
Dude Ranchers' Association/Rancho de los Caballeros/Jan. 24 - 28, 2013

ARKANSAS
Little Rock
American Fisheries Society/Sept. 8 - 12, 2013
National Association of Blacks in Criminal Justice/The Peabody Hotel/July 21 - 25, 2013
National Association of Sporting Goods Wholesalers/Little Rock Convention Center/Oct. 14 - 17, 2014
National Tractor Parts Dealer Association/The Peabody Little Rock/Jan. 30 - Feb. 2, 2013
Rogers
National Taxidermists Association/Embassy Suites NorthWest Arkansas-Hotel, Spa and Convention Center/July 15 - 20, 2014

CALIFORNIA
Anaheim
AABB - American Association of Blood Banks/Oct. 24 - 27, 2015
Academy of Management/Aug. 5 - 9, 2016
American Academy of Optometry/Anaheim Convention Center/Nov. 16 - 19, 2016
American Association for Public Opinion Research/Anaheim Marriott/May 15 - 18, 2014
American Association for Respiratory Care/Nov. 16 - 19, 2013/5000 attendees/over 100 exhibitors
American Association of Physicists in Medicine/July 12 - 16, 2015
American Baseball Coaches Association/Anaheim Marriott/Jan. 5 - 8, 2017
American Frozen Food Institute/Hilton Anaheim/Feb. 23 - 27, 2013
American Mathematical Association of Two Year Colleges/Oct. 31 - Nov. 3, 2013
American Nuclear Society/Disneyland Hotel/Nov. 9 - 14, 2014
American Society for Clinical Laboratory Science/July 26 - 30, 2022
American Society of Health-System Pharmacists/Dec. 7 - 11, 2014
American Society of Sanitary Engineering/Nov. 5 - 9, 2013
American Society of Sugar Beet Technologists/Disneyland Resort/Feb. 27 - March 2, 2013
Association for Professionals in Infection Control and Epidemiology/June 6 - 9, 2014
Association of periOperative Registered Nurses/April 2 - 7, 2016
APCO (Association of Public-Safety Communications Officials) International/Aug. 18 - 21, 2013
Beta Alpha Psi/Hyatt Regency- Orange County/Aug. 8 - 10, 2013
BICSI/Anaheim Convention Center/Sept. 28 - Oct. 2, 2014
Business Professionals of America/May 6 - 10, 2015
Catholic Health Association of the United States/Anaheim Marriott/June 2 - 4, 2013
Christian Leadership Alliance/Hilton Anaheim/April 4 - May 2, 2013
CPCU Society/Sept. 20 - 23, 2014/26-50 exhibitors
Craft & Hobby Association/Anaheim Convention Center/Jan. 11 - 15, 2013
Distributive Education Clubs of America (DECA)/April 24 - 27, 2013
Educause/Oct. 15 - 18, 2013
Ethylene Oxide Sterilization Association, Inc./Anaheim Marriott/Feb. 11, 2013
Fresh Produce Association of the Americas/Oct. 17 - 20, 2014
Fresh Produce Association of the Americas/Oct. 17 - 19, 2014
Future Business Leaders of America - Phi Beta Lambda/June 22 - 25, 2013
Future Business Leaders of America - Phi Beta Lambda/June 27 - 30, 2013
Health Care Administrators Association/Disney's Grand Californian Hotel and Spa/July 10 - 12, 2014
Health Occupations Students of America/Hilton Anaheim/June 24 - 27, 2015
Hosa/Hilton Anaheim/June 24 - 27, 2015

Institute of Transportation Engineers/Anaheim Convention Center/Aug. 14 - 17, 2016

International Association of Administrative Professionals/Hilton Anaheim/ March 17 - 20, 2013

International Association of Administrative Professionals/Anaheim Marriott/ July 27 - 31, 2013

League for Innovation in the Community College/Anaheim Marriott/March 2 - 5, 2014

The Learning Disabilities Association/Feb. 19 - 22, 2014

Music Teachers National Association/Disneyland Hotel/March 9 - 13, 2013/2000 attendees

NAMM - The International Music Products Association/Anaheim Convention Center/Jan. 24 - 27, 2013/11-25 exhibitors

National Association for Relationship and Marriage Education/Anaheim Marriott/June 22 - 27, 2013

National Association of College Auxiliary Services/Anaheim Marriott/Oct. 27 - 30, 2013/51-100 exhibitors

National Association of Colleges and Employers/Anaheim Marriott/June 2 - 5, 2015

National Association of Drug Court Professionals/Anaheim Convention Center/ May 28 - 31, 2014

National Association of Episcopal Schools/Anaheim Marriott/Nov. 20 - 22, 2014

National Federation Coaches Association/Hilton Anaheim/Dec. 13 - 17, 2013

The National Industrial Transportation League/Nov. 14 - 18, 2015

National Interscholastic Athletic Administrators Association/Anaheim Marriott/Dec. 13 - 17, 2013

North American Association of Food Equipment Manufacturers/Anaheim Convention Center/Feb. 19 - 21, 2015

Produce Marketing Association/Oct. 17 - 20, 2014

Produce Marketing Association/Oct. 17 - 19, 2014/18500 attendees/over 100 exhibitors

Resource Center for Religious Institutes/Oct. 20 - 25, 2013

Resource Center for Religious Institutes/Oct. 9 - 14, 2016

Sewn Products Equipment and Suppliers of the Americas/Hilton Anaheim/ March 19 - 21, 2013

Society for Industrial and Organizational Psychology Inc./Disney's Grand Californian Hotel and Spa/April 14 - 16, 2016

Society of Professional Rope Access Technicians/Disney's Paradise Pier Hotel/ Feb. 6 - 9, 2013

World Airline Entertainment Association/Sept. 9 - 12, 2013

World Airline Entertainment Association/Sept. 15 - 18, 2014

Berkeley

National Association for Multicultural Education/University Of California, Berkeley/Jan. 12, 2013

Society for Clinical and Experimental Hypnosis/Oct. 2 - 6, 2013

Western Literature Association/DoubleTree by Hilton Berkeley Marina/Oct. 9 - 12, 2013

Beverly Hills

Association of Jewish Aging Services/March 3 - 6, 2013

Broomfield

International Builders Exchange Executives/Builders Exchange Network/Omni Interlocken Resort/June 12 - 14, 2013

Carlsbad

American Association of Women Dentists/LaCosta Resort and Spa/July 18 - 21, 2013

American Bearing Manufacturers Association/Park Hyatt Aviara/April 25 - 27, 2013

American Gear Manufacturers Association/Park Hyatt Aviara/April 25 - 27, 2013

Exhibition Services and Contractors Association/La Costa Resort and Spa/June 23 - 26, 2013

Independent Lubricant Manufacturers Association/Park Hyatt Aviara Resort/ April 18 - 20, 2013

International Association of Defense Counsel/Four Seasons Hotels and Resorts/Feb. 18 - 23, 2014

Pet Industry Distributors Association/Park Hyatt Aviara Resort/Jan. 21 - 24, 2013

Pipe Line Contractors Association/Park Hyatt Aviara/Feb. 24 - 28, 2015

Society for Clinical Vascular Surgery/La Costa Resort and Spa/March 17 - 22, 2014

Chico

Hop Growers of America/Jan. 22 - 25, 2013

Concord

American Thyroid Association/Sheraton Portland Airport Hotel/Oct. 29 - Nov. 2, 2014/1000 attendees/11-25 exhibitors

Coronado

American Academy of Psychiatry and the Law/Hotel del Coronado/Oct. 24 - 27, 2013

National Association of Development Companies/Hotel del Coronado/May 15 - 18, 2013

National Association of Legal Search Consultants/Hotel del Coronado/April 18 - 20, 2013

National Water Resources Association/Hotel del Coronado/Nov. 12 - 14, 2014

National Water Resources Association/Hotel del Coronado/Nov. 30 - Dec. 2, 2016

Costa Mesa

Healthcare Billing and Management Association/The Westin, South Coast Plaza/March 5 - 7, 2013

Dana Point

American College of Apothecaries/St. Regis Monarch Beach Resort/Feb. 6 - 9, 2013

Association for Financial Technology/Ritz-Carlton, Laguna Niguel/Sept. 22 - 24, 2013

Council on Employee Benefits/Ritz Carlton Laguna Niquel/April 7 - 10, 2013

National Association of Elevator Contractors/Ritz Carlton Laguna Niquel/April 13 - 16, 2013

National Court Reporters Association/Ritz-Carlton, Laguna Niguel/Feb. 3 - 5, 2013

Tag and Label Manufacturers Institute/St. Regis Monarch Beach Resort/Oct. 12 - 15, 2014

Garden Grove

Society for Experimental Mechanics, Inc./Hyatt Regency Orange County/Feb. 11 - 14, 2013

Half Moon Bay

Steel Founders' Society of America/Sept. 7 - 10, 2013

Hollywood

American Academy of Disability Evaluating Physicians/Loews Hollywood Hotel/Jan. 18 - 19, 2013/300 attendees

American Fraternal Alliance/Westin Diplomat Resort and Spa/Sept. 5 - 7, 2013

Association for Death Education and Counseling/Renaissance Hollywood Hotel and Spa/April 24 - 27, 2013

The Fertilizer Institute/Westin Diplomat Resort and Spa/Feb. 1 - 3, 2016

Huntington Beach

American College of Psychiatrists/Hyatt Regency Huntington Beach Resort and Spa/Feb. 18 - 22, 2015

American Neurogastroenterology and Motility Society/Sept. 20 - 22, 2013

American Psychosocial Oncology Society/Feb. 14 - 16, 2013/400 attendees

Association for Chemoreception Sciences/Hyatt Regency/April 17 - 21, 2013

Automotive Aftermarket Industry Association/Hyatt Regency Huntington Beach Resort and Spa/April 23 - 25, 2014

Illuminating Engineering Society of North America/Hyatt Regency Huntington Beach Resort and Spa/Oct. 27 - 29, 2013

National Dental EDI Council/Hilton Waterfront Resort/April 30 - May 2, 2013

Incline Village

Water Quality Association/Hyatt Regency Lake Tahoe Resort, Spa and Casino/ Sept. 4 - 6, 2013

Indian Wells

American College of Osteopathic Internists/Renaissance Esmeralda Indian Wells Resort and Spa/Oct. 9 - 13, 2013

Asphalt Emulsion Manufacturers Association/Renaissance Esmeralda Indian Wells Resort and Spa/Feb. 19 - 22, 2013

Asphalt Recycling and Reclaiming Association/Renaissance Esmeralda Indian Wells Resort and Spa/Feb. 19 - 22, 2013

Crop Insurance Research Bureau/Renaissance Esmeralda Indian Wells Resort and Spa/Feb. 6 - 8, 2013

Dental Trade Alliance/Hyatt Grand Champions Resort, Villas and Spa/Nov. 4 - 7, 2014

Foodservice Equipment Distributors Association/Renaissance Esmeralda Indian Wells Resort and Spa/March 26 - 30, 2014

Independent Lubricant Manufacturers Association/Hyatt Grand Champions Resort, Villas and Spa/March 18 - 21, 2014

Institute for Professionals in Taxation/Hyatt Grand Champions Resort, Villas and Spa/Nov. 3 - 6, 2013

International Slurry Surfacing Association/Renaissance Esmeralda Indian Wells Resort and Spa/Feb. 19 - 23, 2013

National Association of Pipe Coating Applicators/Renaissance Esmeralda Indian Wells Resort and Spa/April 24 - 28, 2013

National Crop Insurance Services/Feb. 11 - 13, 2013

National Insulation Association/Hyatt Grand Champions Resort, Villas and Spa/April 2 - 5, 2014/100 attendees/51-100 exhibitors

National Leased Housing Association/Renaissance Esmeralda Indian Wells Resort and Spa/Jan. 29 - 31, 2014

Plastic Pipe and Fittings Association/Hyatt Grand Champions Resort, Villas and Spa/March 2 - 5, 2013

Single Ply Roofing Institute/Miramonte Resort and Spa/Jan. 11 - 13, 2013

Irvine

National Association of Therapeutic Schools and Programs (NATSAP)/Hyatt Regency Irvine/Feb. 7 - 9, 2013

La Jolla

American Association for Clinical Chemistry, Inc./April 28 - May 2, 2013

American Ophthalmological Society/Lodge at Torrey Pines/May 16 - 19, 2013

Anxiety Disorders Association of America/Hyatt Regency La Jolla at Aventine/ April 4 - 7, 2013

Association of Professional Investment Consultants/Hilton La Jolla Torrey Pines/June 4 - 7, 2013

National Association of Graphic and Product Identification Manufacturers/The Lodge at Torrey Pines/April 9 - 12, 2013

National Council on Teacher Retirement/Hilton La Jolla Torrey Pines/Oct. 10 - 14, 2015

La Quinta

American College of Trial Lawyers/La Quinta Resort and Club/March 6 - 9, 2014

Association for High Technology Distribution/La Quinta Resort and Club/April 24 - 27, 2013

Conveyor Equipment Manufacturers Association/La Quinta Resort and Club/ March 14 - 18, 2014

Conveyor Equipment Manufacturers Association/La Quinta Resort and Club, A Waldorf Astoria Resort/March 11 - 15, 2016

National Association of Real Estate Investment Trusts (NAREIT)/La Quinta Resort and Club, A Waldorf Astoria Resort/March 20 - 22, 2013

National Watermelon Association/La Quinta Resort and Club, A Waldorf Astoria Resort/Feb. 18 - 22, 2015

Society for Vector Ecology/La Quinta Resort & Club/Sept. 22 - 29, 2013

Laguna

American Association of Preferred Provider Organizations/Ritz-Carlton/Jan. 19 - 21, 2014

Laguna Beach

PeerSpan/Montage Laguna Beach/June 18 - 21, 2013

Laguna Nigel

Independent Petroleum Association of America/The Ritz-Carlton/June 24 - 25, 2013

Lake Tahoe

Universities Council on Water Resources/June 11 - 13, 2013

Long Beach

Academy of Political Science/Renaissance Long Beach Hotel/Feb. 8 - 10, 2013

American Astronomical Society/Long Beach Convention and Entertainment Center/Jan. 6 - 10, 2013
American Astronomical Society/Jan. 8 - 12, 2017
American Society for Neurochemistry/March 8 - 14, 2014
American Society of Agronomy (ASA, CSSA, SSSA)/Nov. 2 - 5, 2014
American Sugarbeet Growers Association/Westin Long Beach/Feb. 1 - 3, 2015
Association for Institutional Research/Long Beach Convention and Entertainment Center/May 18 - 22, 2014
Association for the Advancement of Medical Instrumentation/June 1 - 3, 2013
Association of State Drinking Water Administrators/Hilton Long Beach and Executive Meeting Center/Oct. 27 - 31, 2013
AVS: Science and Technology of Materials, Interfaces, and Processing/Long Beach Convention and Entertainment Center/Oct. 27 - Nov. 1, 2013
Ceilings and Interior Systems Construction Association/Renaissance Long Beach Hotel/April 27 - 30, 2015/over 100 exhibitors
Ceilings and Interior Systems Construction Association/April 29 - 30, 2015
Central Conference of American Rabbis/Westin Long Beach/March 3 - 7, 2013
Conference of Minority Public Administrators/Historic Queen Mary Resort and Hotel/Feb. 20 - 24, 2013
Crop Science Society of America/Nov. 2 - 5, 2014
IEEE Power Electronics Society/Long Beach Convention Center/March 17 - 21, 2013
International Balloon Association/Hilton Long Beach & Executive Meeeting Center/July 25 - 28, 2013
Interstate Oil and Gas Compact Commission/Renaissance Long Beach Hotel/Nov. 4 - 6, 2013
National Foster Parent Association/Renaissance Long Beach Hotel/June 5 - 8, 2013
The National NeedleArts Association/Long Beach Convention Center/Feb. 2 - 4, 2013
National Science Teachers Association/Dec. 4 - 6, 2014
Navy League of the United States/Hilton Long Beach and Executive Meeting Center/June 19 - 23, 2013
Professional Beauty Association | National Cosmetology Association/Long Beach Convention and Entertainment Center/Jan. 26 - 28, 2013
The Psychonomic Society/Nov. 20 - 22, 2014
The Psychonomic Society/Nov. 20 - 23, 2014
Public Risk Management Association/Long Beach Convention and Entertainment Center/June 8 - 11, 2014
Semiconductor Environmental Safety and Health Association/Queen Mary/March 18 - 22, 2013
Society for Imaging Informatics in Medicine/Long Beach Convention and Entertainment Center/May 15 - 17, 2014
Society for the Advancement of Material and Process Engineering/Long Beach Convention Center/May 6 - 9, 2013
Soil Science Society of America/Nov. 2 - 6, 2014/3200 attendees/over 100 exhibitors
SWANA - Solid Waste Association of North America/Sept. 17, 2013
VITA/Jan. 23 - 24, 2013

Los Angeles
Academy of Pharmaceutical Research and Science/Los Angeles Convention Center/March 1 - 4, 2013
American Academy of Allergy, Asthma, and Immunology/March 4 - 8, 2016
American Academy of Oral and Maxillofacial Radiology/The Beverly Hilton, Beverly Hills/Oct. 1 - 5, 2013
American Association for Geriatric Psychiatry/Los Angeles Convention Center/March 14 - 17, 2013
American Association of Collegiate Registrars and Admissions Officers/JW Marriott Los Angeles L.A. LIVE/Oct. 26 - 29, 2014
American Association of Heart Failure Nurses/Westin Bonaventure Hotel and Suites, Los Angeles/June 26 - 28, 2014
American Association of Suicidology/April 9 - 12, 2014
American Diabetes Association/Los Angeles Convention Center/May 4, 2013
American Federation of Teachers (AFL-CIO)/Claremont Mckenna College/July 11 - 14, 2014
American Headache Society/Hyatt Regency Century Plaza/June 26 - 29, 2014
American Institute of Aeronautics and Astronautics/Hyatt Regency Century Plaza/Aug. 12 - 14, 2013
American Pharmacists Association/Los Angeles Convention Center/March 1 - 4, 2013/over 100 exhibitors
American Physical Society/March 12 - 16, 2018
American Society for Eighteenth-Century Studies/Webb Schools/March 17 - 22, 2015
American Society for Metabolic and Bariatric Surgery/Nov. 1 - 7, 2015
American Society of Composers, Authors and Publishers (ASCAP)/Loews Hollywood Hotel/April 18 - 20, 2013
American Society of Pension Professionals & Actuaries/Sheraton Los Angeles Downtown/Jan. 30 - Feb. 1, 2013
American Studies Association/Westin Bonaventure Hotel and Suites, Los Angeles/Nov. 6 - 9, 2014
American Telemedicine Association/May 1 - 3, 2015
American Telemedicine Association/May 3 - 5, 2015
American Volleyball Coaches Association/University of California, Los Angeles/May 2 - 4, 2013
Arthroscopy Association of North America/April 23 - 25, 2015
Associated Wire Rope Fabricators/Century Plaza Hyatt Regency/Oct. 20 - 23, 2013
Association of American Geographers/Los Angeles Marriott Downtown/April 9 - 13, 2013
Association of Analytical Communities International/Hyatt Regency Century Plaza/Sept. 27 - 30, 2015
Association of Family and Conciliation Courts/JW Marriott Los Angeles L.A. LIVE/May 29 - June 1, 2013
Association of Legal Administrators/Los Angeles Convention Center/May 22 - 25, 2016
Association of Physician Assistants in Cardiovascular Surgery/Jan. 23 - 27, 2013
Association of Physician Assistants in Cardiovascular Surgery/Sheraton Los Angeles Downtown Hotel/Jan. 24 - 27, 2013

Association of University Radiologists/JW Marriott Los Angeles L.A. LIVE/April 9 - 12, 2013
Association of Writers and Writing Programs/JW Marriott Los Angeles L.A. LIVE/March 30 - April 2, 2016/9000 attendees
Building Owners and Managers Association International/June 28 - 30, 2015
Commercial Finance Association/JW Marriott Los Angeles L.A. LIVE/Nov. 13 - 17, 2013
NAIOP, The Commercial Real Estate Development Association/Omni Los Angeles Hotel at California Plaza/June 5 - 6, 2013
Congress on Research in Dance/University of California, Los Angeles/April 19 - 21, 2013
Credit Research Foundation/Manhattan Beach Marriott/March 18 - 20, 2013
Entertainment Software Association (ESA)/Los Angeles Convention Center/June 11 - 13, 2013
Exhibition Services and Contractors Association/Dec. 8, 2014
Human Factors and Ergonomics Society/JW Marriott Los Angeles L.A. LIVE/Oct. 26 - 30, 2015/1500 attendees
Human Factors Society/JW Marriott Los Angeles L.A. LIVE/Oct. 26 - 30, 2015
IDEA, The Health and Fitness Association/Aug. 7 - 11, 2013
IEEE Control Systems Society/Dec. 15 - 17, 2014
Institute Management Accountants/New Orleans/June 22 - 26, 2013/11-25 exhibitors
International Cinema Technology Association/Jan. 14 - 16, 2013
International Facility Management Association/April 2 - 4, 2013
International Health, Racquet and Sportsclub Association/Los Angeles Convention Center/Jan. 19 - 20, 2013
International Health, Racquet and Sportsclub Association/Los Angeles Convention Center/March 11 - 14, 2013
International Trademark Association/Los Angeles Convention Center/April 29 - May 3, 2017
Medieval Academy of America/UCLA campus/April 10 - 12, 2014
Museum Store Association/Los Angeles Convention Center/April 13 - 15, 2013
National Alliance of State Pharmacy Associations/March 1 - 3, 2013
National Association for Court Management/Westin Bonaventure Hotel and Suites, Los Angeles/Feb. 10 - 12, 2013
National Association of Environmental Professionals/JW Marriott Los Angeles L.A. LIVE/April 1 - 5, 2013
National Association of Letter Carriers/The Los Angeles Convention Center/Aug. 15 - 19, 2016
National Association of Professional Organizers/Westin Bonaventure Hotel and Suites, Los Angeles/April 15 - 18, 2015
National Business Education Association/JW Marriott Los Angeles L.A. LIVE/April 15 - 19, 2014
National Council of State Housing Agencies/JW Marriott Los Angeles L.A. LIVE/June 1 - 4, 2015
National Legal Aid and Defender Association/Westin Bonaventure Hotel and Suites, Los Angeles/Nov. 7 - 10, 2013
National Soccer Coaches Association of America/Jan. 11 - 15, 2017/9000 attendees
National Tour Association/Feb. 16 - 20, 2014
Pediatric Orthopedic Society of North America/Renaissance Hollywood Hotel and Spa/April 30 - May 3, 2014
Risk and Insurance Management Society, Inc. (RIMS)/Los Angeles Convention Center/April 21 - 25, 2013
Society for Critical Care Medicine/Los Angeles Convention Center/Feb. 8 - 12, 2014
Society for Critical Care Medicine/Los Angeles Convention Center/Jan. 23 - 27, 2021
Society of Gynecologic Oncologists/Los Angeles Convention Center/March 9 - 13, 2013
Society of Thoracic Surgeons/Jan. 26 - 30, 2013
Society of Vertebrate Paleontology/Westin Bonaventure Hotel and Suites, Los Angeles/Oct. 30 - Nov. 2, 2013
Student Youth and Travel Association/Aug. 23 - 27, 2013

Mammoth Mountain
North American Snowsports Journalists Association/March 7 - 12, 2013
North American Snowsports Journalists Association/April 7 - 11, 2013

Monterey
Academy of Marketing Science/May 14 - 18, 2013
American Society for Enology and Viticulture/Portola Hotel and Spa/June 24 - 28, 2013
Association of University Programs in Health Administration/Portola Hotel and Spa/June 20 - 23, 2013
County Counsels' Association of California/Monterey Plaza Hotel and Spa/April 17 - 18, 2013
County Counsels' Association of California/Monterey Plaza Hotel and Spa/April 9 - 11, 2014
Directed Energy Professional Society/Hyatt Regency Monterey Hotel And Spa/April 8 - 12, 2013
Environmental Mutagen Society/Hyatt Regency Monterey Hotel And Spa/Sept. 20 - 26, 2013
Institute for Professionals in Taxation/Hyatt Regency Monterey Hotel And Spa/Sept. 29 - Oct. 2, 2013
National Council on Public History/Monterey Conference Center/March 19 - 22, 2014

Napa
Adhesive and Sealant Council/Westin Verasa Napa/June 25 - 26, 2013
American Sugar Alliance/Silverado Resort and Spa/Aug. 2 - 7, 2013
Association for Financial Technology/The Meritage Resort and Spa/Sept. 20 - 22, 2015
Association of Applied IPM Ecologists/Embassy Suites Napa Valley/Feb. 3 - 5, 2013/1-10 exhibitors
County Counsels' Association of California/Silverado Resort and Spa/Sept. 11 - 13, 2013
Federation of Defense and Corporate Counsel/Silverado Resort and Spa/July 26 - Aug. 2, 2014
Financial Management Association International/Cakebread Cellars/April 6, 2013
International Association of Professional Security Consultants/The Meritage Resort and Spa/April 21 - 24, 2013

National Maritime Safety Association/Silverado Resort and Spa/June 26 - 28, 2013

Pet Industry Joint Advisory Council/Meritage Resort and Spa/April 23 - 25, 2013/26-50 exhibitors

Plastic Pipe and Fittings Association/Silverado Resort and Spa /Oct. 5 - 8, 2013

Transportation Lawyers Association/The Meritage Resort and Spa/April 30 - May 4, 2013

Web Sling and Tie down Association/The Meritage Resort and Spa/May 6 - 9, 2013

Newport Beach

Alpha Tau Delta/Aug. 7 - 10, 2013

Council for Advancement and Support of Education/Newport Beach Marriott Hotel and Spa/April 24 - 26, 2013

Council for Advancement and Support of Education/Newport Beach Marriott Hotel and Spa/June 5 - 6, 2013

Council for Advancement and Support of Education/Newport Beach Marriott Hotel and Spa/June 7, 2013

IGAF Polaris/Island Hotel Newport Beach/Jan. 6 - 9, 2013

International Academy of Trial Lawyers/Pelican Hill/April 3 - 7, 2013

The Open Group/Jan. 28 - 31, 2013

Tag and Label Manufacturers Institute/The Resort at Pelican Hill/March 9 - 12, 2014

Western History Association/Newport Beach Marriott Hotel and Spa/Oct. 15 - 18, 2014

Ontario

Academy of Model Aeronautics/Ontario Convention Center/Jan. 11 - 13, 2013

International Association of Structural Movers/DoubleTree by Hilton/March 20 - 24, 2013

Pacific Grove

The American Society of Naturalists/Asilomar Conference Center/Jan. 13 - 15, 2014

Ecological Farming Association/Asilomar Conference Grounds/Jan. 23 - 26, 2013

Genetics Society of America/Asilomar Conference Center/March 12 - 17, 2013

Palm Desert

American Society for Horticultural Science/JW Marriott Desert Springs Resort and Spa/July 22 - 25, 2013

Institute of Nuclear Materials Management/JW Marriott Desert Springs Resort and Spa/July 14 - 18, 2013/11-25 exhibitors

International Energy Credit Association/JW Marriott Desert Springs Resort/ Oct. 6 - 9, 2014

Material Handling Equipment Distributors Association/JW Marriott Desert Springs Resort and Spa/May 4 - 8, 2013

National Association of Children's Hospitals and Related Institutions/JW Marriott Desert Springs Resort and Spa/Oct. 11 - 14, 2014

National Railroad Construction and Maintenance Association, Inc./Jan. 5 - 8, 2014

Physician Insurers Association of America/JW Marriott Desert Springs Resort and Spa/May 15 - 17, 2013

Power Transmission Distributors Association/JW Marriott Desert Springs Resort and Spa/Oct. 3 - 5, 2013

Palm Spring

American Academy of Dental Practice Administration/Hyatt Grand Champions Resort and Spa/March 5 - 8, 2014

American Academy of Periodontology/JW Marriott Desert Springs Resort/Feb. 8 - 10, 2013

American Association for Justice/JW Marriott Desert Springs Resort and Spa/ Feb. 14 - 18, 2015

American Association of Orthodontists/JW Marriott Desert Springs Resort and Spa/Feb. 8 - 10, 2013

American Burn Association/Palm Springs Convention Center/April 23 - 26, 2013

American College of Neuropsychopharmacology/JW Marriott Desert Springs Resort/Dec. 3 - 7, 2017

American Society of Consulting Arborists/Westin Mission Hills Resort and Spa/ Dec. 2 - 5, 2014

Associated General Contractors of America (AGC)/JW Marriott Desert Springs Resort/March 6 - 9, 2013

Association of Biomolecular Resource Facilities/Renaissance Palm Springs Hotel/March 2 - 5, 2013

Captive Insurance Companies Association/Westin Mission Hills Resort and Spa/March 10 - 13, 2013

Community College Business Officers/Westin Mission Hills Resort and Spa/ Sept. 28 - Oct. 1, 2013

Foodservice Sales & Marketing Association/La Quinta Resort and Club/Feb. 12 - 14, 2013

National Association of Seventh-Day Adventist Dentists/Oct. 24 - 27, 2013

National Multi-Housing Council/La Quinta Resort and Club, A Waldorf Astoria Resort/Jan. 22 - 24, 2013

National Multi-Housing Council/La Quinta Resort and Club, A Waldorf Astoria Resort/Jan. 20 - 22, 2015

National Ski Area Association/Westin Mission Hills Resort and Spa/April 30 - May 3, 2014

Society of Industrial and Office Realtors/May 2 - 4, 2013

Society of Nuclear Medicine/Palm Springs Renaissance at the Convention Center/Feb. 6 - 9, 2014

Pasadena

American Astronomical Society/June 1 - 5, 2014

American Institute of Aeronautics and Astronautics/Pasadena Convention Center/May 5 - 9, 2014

Art Libraries Society of North America/Sheraton Pasadena Hotel/April 25 - 29, 2013

Council of State and Territorial Epidemiologists/June 9 - 13, 2013

IEEE - Nuclear and Plasma Sciences Society/Sept. 29 - Oct. 4, 2013

National Contract Management Association/Pasadena Convention Center/July 21 - 24, 2013

Society of Rheology/CBD/Feb. 10 - 14, 2013

Paso Robles

American Navion Society/June 23 - 28, 2013

Pebble Beach

International Association of Defense Counsel/Lodge at Pebble Beach/Feb. 20 - 25, 2016

Rancho Mirage

Academy of Laser Dentistry/Rancho Las Palmas Resort and Spa/Feb. 7 - 9, 2013

American Academy of Actuaries/The Westin Mission Hills/Oct. 19 - 22, 2014

American Association for Pediatric Ophthalmology and Strabismus/Westin Mission Hills Resort and Spa/April 2 - 6, 2014

American Brush Manufacturers Association/Westin Mission Hills Resort and Spa/March 26 - 29, 2014

Association for Play Therapy/Westin Mission Hills Resort and Spa/Oct. 8 - 13, 2013

Association of Industrial Metallizers, Coaters and Laminators/Rancho Las Palmas Resort and Spa/March 9 - 13, 2013

Conference of Consulting Actuaries/Westin Mission Hills Resort and Spa/Oct. 19 - 22, 2014

Education Finance Council/March 7 - 8, 2013

Metal Construction Association/Rancho Las Palmas/Jan. 27 - 29, 2013

National Conference on Public Employee Retirement Systems/Oct. 6 - 9, 2013

National Customs Brokers and Forwarders Association of America/The Western Mission Hills Resort & Spa/April 7 - 10, 2013

Peanut and Tree Nut Processors Association/The Westin Mission Hills/Jan. 19 - 21, 2013/26-50 exhibitors

Public Agency Risk Managers Association/The Westin Mission Hills/Feb. 3 - 6, 2013

Society of Independent Gasoline Marketers of America (SIGMA)/Westin Mission Hills Resort and Spa/April 10 - 13, 2014

Rancho Palos Verdes

Pharmaceutical Care Management Association/Terranea Resort in Rancho Palos Verdes/Oct. 28 - 30, 2013

The Philanthropy Roundtable/Terranea Resort/Oct. 17 - 19, 2013

Redlands

International Double Reed Society/University of Redlands/June 25 - 29, 2013

Riverside

American Philatelic Society/Jan. 24 - 26, 2014

Congress on Research in Dance/Mission Inn Hotel and Spa/Nov. 14 - 17, 2013

Society of Dance History Scholars/Mission Inn Hotel and Spa/Nov. 14 - 17, 2013

Sacramento

Airports Council International - North America/Hyatt Regency Sacramento/ Nov. 11 - 13, 2013

Association on Higher Education and Disability/July 14 - 19, 2014

Canon Law Society of America/Hyatt Regency Sacramento/Oct. 14 - 17, 2013

Ecological Society of America/Aug. 10 - 15, 2014

Geochemical Society/Fountain Suites Hotel/June 9 - 13, 2014/3000 attendees/51-100 exhibitors

International Association of Assessing Officers/Aug. 24 - 27, 2014

National Association of State Administrators and Supervisors of Private Schools/Hilton Sacramento Arden West/April 21 - 24, 2013

North American Society for Trenchless Technology/Hyatt Regency Sacramento/March 3 - 7, 2013

Religious Conference Management Association/Feb. 4 - 7, 2014

Society for Range Management/Jan. 30 - Feb. 7, 2015

United States Army Warrant Officers Association/Radisson Hotel Colonia del Sacramento/Oct. 14 - 18, 2013

Water Environment Federation/Sacramento Convention Center/June 9 - 12, 2013

San Antonio

Professional Photographers of America/Jan. 18 - 20, 2015

San Diego

AABB - American Association of Blood Banks/Oct. 7 - 10, 2017

Academy Health/June 8 - 10, 2014/2400 attendees/26-50 exhibitors

Academy of Managed Care Pharmacy/San Diego Convention Center/April 3 - 5, 2013

Academy of Osseointegration/Feb. 18 - 20, 2016

Academy of Pharmaceutical Research and Science/March 27 - 30, 2015

Accrediting Bureau of Health Education Schools/Manchester Grand Hyatt/Feb. 13 - 15, 2013

ACUTA - The Association for Information Communications Technology Professionals in Higher Education/Manchester Grand Hyatt San Diego/April 14 - 17, 2013

African Studies Association/Sheraton San Diego Hotel and Marina/Nov. 19 - 22, 2015

Aircraft Builders Council/Park Hyatt Aviara Resort/Sept. 22 - 24, 2013

Airport Minority Advisory Council (AMAC)/June 8 - 11, 2013

Alliance of Associations of Teachers of Japanese/March 21, 2013

American Academy of Allergy, Asthma, and Immunology/Feb. 28 - March 4, 2014

American Academy of Child and Adolescent Psychiatry/Manchester Grand Hyatt San Diego/Oct. 21 - 26, 2014

American Academy of Hospice and Palliative Medicine/March 12 - 15, 2014

American Academy of Neurology/San Diego Convention Center/March 16 - 23, 2013

American Academy of Pediatrics/San Diego Convention and Visitors Bureau/ Oct. 11 - 14, 2014

American Academy of Physical Medicine and Rehabilitation/Marriott Convention Center/Nov. 13 - 16, 2014

American Academy of Religion/Nov. 22 - 25, 2014/10000 attendees/over 100 exhibitors

American Academy of Religion/Nov. 23 - 26, 2019/10000 attendees/over 100 exhibitors

American Accounting Association/Westin San Diego/Jan. 11 - 12, 2013

American Accounting Association/DoubleTree San Diego Mission Valley/Feb. 10 - 12, 2014

American Association for Cancer Research/Manchester Grand Hyatt San Diego/Feb. 27 - March 2, 2013

American Association for Cancer Research/April 5 - 9, 2014

American Association for Clinical Chemistry, Inc./July 30 - Aug. 3, 2017/18000 attendees

American Association for the Surgery of Trauma/Manchester Grand Hyatt San Diego/Sept. 9 - 12, 2015/1000 attendees

American Association of Anatomists/April 26 - 30, 2014

American Association of Anatomists/April 2 - 6, 2016

American Association of Anatomists/April 21 - 25, 2018

American Association of Colleges of Nursing/Hotel del Coronado/Jan. 23 - 26, 2013

American Association of Colleges of Nursing/Hotel del Coronado/Jan. 24, 2013

American Association of Colleges of Nursing/Omni San Diego Hotel/April 5 - 6, 2013

American Association of Critical-Care Nurses/May 16 - 21, 2015

American Association of Orthodontists/April 21 - 25, 2017

American Association of Pharmaceutical Scientists/Sheraton San Diego Hotel and Marina/May 20 - 22, 2013

American Association of Pharmaceutical Scientists/Sheraton San Diego Hotel and Marina/May 19 - 21, 2014

American Association of Pharmaceutical Scientists/San Diego Convention and Visitors Bureau/Nov. 2 - 6, 2014

American Association of Pharmaceutical Scientists/San Diego Convention Center/Nov. 12 - 16, 2017

American Association of Swine Veterinarians/Manchester Grand Hyatt San Diego/March 2 - 5, 2013/900 attendees/51-100 exhibitors

American Association of Tissue Banks/Hilton San Diego Bayfront/Sept. 16 - 20, 2014

American Association of Veterinary Laboratory Diagnosticians/Town and Country Resort Hotel/Oct. 17 - 23, 2013

American Bar Association/Feb. 3 - 9, 2016

American Brachytherapy Society/Manchester Grand Hyatt San Diego/April 3 - 5, 2014

American Case Management Association/Manchester Hyatt San Diego/April 8 - 11, 2013

American Chemical Society/March 13 - 17, 2016

American Chemical Society/Aug. 25 - 29, 2019

American College of Gastroenterology/Oct. 11 - 16, 2013

American College of Sports Medicine/May 27 - 30, 2015

American College of Veterinary Surgeons/San Diego Convention Center/Oct. 16 - 18, 2014

American Correctional Association/Jan. 10 - 15, 2020

American Council on Education/Manchester Grand Hyatt San Diego/March 8 - 11, 2014

American Economic Association/Manchester Grand Hyatt San Diego/Jan. 4 - 6, 2013/11-25 exhibitors

American Farm Bureau Federation/Jan. 11 - 14, 2015

The American Finance Association/Jan. 4 - 6, 2013

The American Finance Association/Marriot Marquis and Marina Hotel/Jan. 4 - 6, 2013

American Hanoverian Society/Hyatt Regency Mission Bay Spa and Marina-San Diego/Jan. 18 - 20, 2013

American Health Information Management Association/Sept. 27 - Oct. 2, 2014

American Health Lawyers Association/June 30 - July 3, 2013

American Honey Producers Association/Sheraton San Diego Hotel and Marina/Jan. 8 - 13, 2013

American Hospital Association/Manchester Grand Hyatt San Diego/July 25 - 27, 2013

American Hospital Association/Manchester Grand Hyatt San Diego/July 20 - 22, 2014

American Hospital Association/Manchester Grand Hyatt San Diego/July 17 - 19, 2016

American Hospital Association/Manchester Grand Hyatt San Diego/July 27 - 29, 2017

American Institute of Aeronautics and Astronautics/Sheraton San Diego Hotel and Marina/June 24 - 27, 2013

American Institute of Aeronautics and Astronautics/Hilton San Diego Bayfront/ Sept. 10 - 12, 2013

American Mathematical Association of Two Year Colleges/Nov. 9 - 12, 2017

American Mathematical Society/San Diego Convention and Visitors Bureau/ Jan. 9 - 12, 2013

American Medical Society for Sports Medicine/Manchester Grand/April 17 - 21, 2013

American Moving and Storage Association/Manchester Grand/Feb. 9 - 12, 2014

American Nuclear Society/Town and Country Resort Hotel/Nov. 13 - 17, 2016

American Occupational Therapy Association, Inc./San Diego Convention Center/April 25 - 28, 2013/5000 attendees/over 100 exhibitors

American Optometric Association/June 26 - 30, 2013

American Optometric Student Association/June 26 - 30, 2013

American Osteopathic Academy of Orthopedics/Sheraton San Diego Hotel and Marina/Oct. 17 - 20, 2014

American Pediatric Society/April 25 - 28, 2015

American Pharmacists Association/March 27 - 30, 2015

American Philological Association/Jan. 7 - 11, 2016

American Philological Association/Jan. 3 - 6, 2019

American Philosophical Association/April 14 - 19, 2014

American Physiological Society/April 26 - 30, 2014

American Real Estate and Urban Economics Association/San Diego Marriott Marquis and Marina/Jan. 4 - 6, 2013

American Real Estate Society/Marriott Coronado/April 1 - 5, 2014

American Roentgen Ray Society/Manchester Grand Hyatt San Diego/May 4 - 9, 2014

American Short Line and Regional Railroad Association/Hilton San Diego Bayfront/April 22 - 25, 2014/1500 attendees/51-100 exhibitors

American Society for Aesthetic Plastic Surgery/San Diego Convention Center/ April 27 - May 1, 2017

American Society for Blood and Marrow Transplantation/Feb. 11 - 15, 2015

American Society for Cell Biology/Dec. 12 - 16, 2015

American Society for Clinical Laboratory Science/July 30 - Aug. 3, 2017/19000 attendees/over 100 exhibitors

American Society for Clinical Laboratory Science/Aug. 1 - 4, 2017

American Society for Clinical Pharmacology and Therapeutics/The Bayfront Hilton/March 9 - 12, 2016

American Society for Dermatologic Surgery/Manchester Grand/Nov. 6 - 9, 2014

American Society for Investigative Pathology/April 26 - 30, 2014

American Society for Investigative Pathology/April 2 - 6, 2016

American Society for Investigative Pathology/April 18 - 22, 2018

American Society for Nutrition/April 26 - 30, 2014

American Society for Nutrition/April 2 - 6, 2016

American Society for Pain Management Nursing/Sept. 17 - 21, 2014

American Society for Pharmacology and Experimental Therapeutics/April 26 - 30, 2014

American Society for Pharmacology and Experimental Therapeutics/April 2 - 6, 2016

American Society for Pharmacology and Experimental Therapeutics/April 21 - 25, 2018

American Society for Therapeutic Radiology and Oncology/Hilton San Diego Bayfront/Nov. 8 - 9, 2013

American Society of Anesthesiologists/Oct. 24 - 28, 2015

American Society of Bariatric Physicians/April 24 - 28, 2013

American Society of Dentist Anesthesiologists/Hard Rock Hotel San Diego/ April 4 - 6, 2013

American Society of Human Genetics/Oct. 18 - 22, 2014

American Society of Human Genetics/Oct. 16 - 20, 2018

American Society of Human Genetics/Oct. 27 - 31, 2020

American Society of Neuroradiology/San Diego Convention and Visitors Bureau/May 18 - 23, 2013

American Society of Pediatric Nephrology/April 25 - 28, 2015

American Society on Aging/Manchester Grand Hyatt San Diego/March 11 - 15, 2014

American Sugarbeet Growers Association/Hilton San Diego Bayfront/Feb. 3 - 5, 2013/350 attendees

American Thoracic Society/May 16 - 21, 2014

American Traffic Safety Service Association/San Diego Convention and Visitors Bureau/Feb. 22 - 26, 2013

American Trucking Associations/San Diego Convention Center/Oct. 17 - 20, 2014

American Urological Association/San Diego Convention Center/May 4 - 8, 2013

ASPSN - American Society of Plastic Surgical Nurses/San Diego Sheraton Hotel and Marina/Oct. 11 - 14, 2013

Associated Collegiate Press/Feb. 27 - March 2, 2014

Association for Applied and Therapeutic Humor/Westin San Diego/April 4 - 7, 2013

Association for Asian Studies/Manchester Grand Hyatt San Diego/March 21 - 24, 2013/11-25 exhibitors

Association for Child Psychoanalysis/May 3 - 5, 2013

Association for Comparative Economic Studies/Jan. 4 - 6, 2013

Association for Evolutionary Economics/San Diego Marriott Marquis and Marina/Jan. 4 - 6, 2013

Association for Healthcare Resource and Materials Management/July 28 - 31, 2013/1200 attendees

Association for Research in Otolaryngology/Manchester Grand Hyatt San Diego/Feb. 22 - 26, 2014

Association for Research in Otolaryngology/Manchester Grand Hyatt San Diego/Feb. 20 - 24, 2016

Association for Symbolic Logic/Jan. 11 - 12, 2013

Association for the Treatment of Sexual Abusers/Manchester Grand/Oct. 28 - Nov. 1, 2014

Association of Boards of Certification/San Diego Marriott Mission Valley/Jan. 22 - 25, 2014

Association of Christian Librarians/Point Loma Nazarene University/June 10 - 13, 2013

Association of Community Cancer Centers/Sheraton San Diego Hotel and Marina/Oct. 8 - 11, 2014

Association of Community Cancer Centers/Sheraton San Diego Hotel and Marina/March 16 - 18, 2015

Association of Community College Trustees/Oct. 14 - 17, 2015

Association of Diesel Specialists/Manchester Hyatt San Diego/July 30 - Aug. 2, 2013

Association of Fundraising Professionals/April 7 - 10, 2013

Association of Fundraising Professionals/April 7 - 9, 2013

Association of Oncology Social Work/Loews Coronado Bay Resort/June 5 - 7, 2013

Association of Pathology Chairs/Rancho Bernardo Inn/July 15 - 17, 2015

Association of Pathology Chairs/Rancho Bernardo Inn/July 13 - 15, 2016

Association of periOperative Registered Nurses/March 2 - 7, 2013/5500 attendees/over 100 exhibitors

Association of Regulatory Boards of Optometry/San Diego Mariott Marquis and Marina/June 23 - 25, 2013

Association of Schools of Allied Health Professions/Catamaran Resort Hotel and Spa/March 19 - 20, 2013

Association of Schools of Allied Health Professions/Catamaran Resort Hotel and Spa/March 21 - 22, 2013

Association of State Dam Safety Officials/San Diego Convention Center/Sept. 20 - 25, 2014

Association of University Professors of Ophthalmology/Loews Coronado Bay Resort/Jan. 31 - Feb. 2, 2013

Association of University Technology Managers/Manchester Grand Hyatt San Diego/Feb. 14 - 17, 2016

Association of Water Technologies/Omni San Diego Hotel/Sept. 7 - 10, 2016

Association of Zoos and Aquariums/Sept. 6 - 11, 2016

Automotive Aftermarket Industry Association/Hyatt Regency Mission Bay Spa and Marina-San Diego/Sept. 9 - 13, 2014

AVS: Science and Technology of Materials, Interfaces, and Processing/San Diego Marriott Marquis and Marina/July 28 - 31, 2013

Biotechnology Industry Organization (BIO)/March 25 - 27, 2013

Building Owners and Managers Association International/June 23 - 25, 2013

Catholic Health Association of the United States/San Diego Marriott /June 5 - 7, 2016

Club Managers Association of America/San Diego Convention Center/Feb. 7 - 11, 2013

Club Managers Association of America/San Diego Convention Center/Feb. 8 - 9, 2013

The Coastal and Estuarine Research Federation/San Diego Convention Center/ Nov. 3 - 7, 2013

College of Optometrists in Vision Development/Four Points by Sheraton San Diego/Oct. 21 - 25, 2014

NAIOP, The Commercial Real Estate Development Association/Manchester Grand Hyatt San Diego/Oct. 7 - 10, 2013

Community Associations Institute (CAI)/Hilton San Diego Bayfront/April 17 - 20, 2013/26-50 exhibitors

Composite Panel Association/Loews Coronado Bay Resort/May 5 - 7, 2013

Computer Measurement Group/La Jolla/Nov. 4 - 8, 2013

Consortium of School Networking/Sheraton San Diego Hotel and Marina/ March 11 - 13, 2013

Construction Financial Management Association/Hilton San Diego Bayfront/ June 22 - 26, 2013

Construction Management Association of America/DoubleTree by Hilton/Oct. 9 - 11, 2016/1000 attendees

Construction Owners Association of America/Hilton Torrey Pines/Oct. 30 - Nov. 1, 2013

Council for Exceptional Children/April 8 - 11, 2015

Council of Colleges of Arts and Sciences/Manchester Grand Hyatt San Diego/ Nov. 2 - 5, 2016

Council of Hotel and Restaurant Trainers/Westin San Diego/Feb. 23 - 26, 2013

Council on the Safe Transportation of Hazardous Articles/The Westin San Diego/April 21 - 24, 2013

CPA USA Network/Paradise Point Hotel/June 19 - 21, 2013

Division 1-A Athletic Directors Association/Jan. 15 - 18, 2014

Drug Information Association/June 15 - 19, 2014/8000 attendees/over 100 exhibitors

Education Law Association/Sheraton San Diego Hotel and Marina/Nov. 8 - 11, 2014

The Endocrine Society/March 5 - 8, 2015

Equipment and Tool Institute/Hyatt Mission Bay/April 23 - 25, 2013

Family, Career and Community Leaders of America/July 3 - 7, 2016

Federation of Associations of Regulatory Boards/Omni San Diego Hotel/Jan. 25 - 27, 2013

The Fertilizer Institute/Manchester Grand/Feb. 3 - 5, 2014

The Fertilizer Institute/Westgate Hotel/Sept. 7 - 9, 2014

The Fertilizer Institute/Manchester Grand Hyatt San Diego/Sept. 25 - 27, 2016

Financial Management Association International/Hilton San Diego Bayfront Hotel/Oct. 10 - 13, 2018

Flexographic Technical Association/April 28 - May 1, 2013

Flight Safety Foundation/Sheraton San Diego Hotel and Marina/April 15 - 17, 2014

Fluid Sealing Association/Oct. 15 - 17, 2013

Forging Industry Association/Hotel del Coronado/May 4 - 6, 2013

GAMA International/Manchester Grand/March 17 - 20, 2013

Genetics Society of America/Town and Country Resort Hotel/March 26 - 30, 2014

Glass Association of North America/Jan. 21 - 25, 2013

Global Business Travel Association/Aug. 4 - 7, 2013/1400 attendees/26-50 exhibitors

Global Cold Chain Alliance/The Manchester Grand Hyatt/April 26 - 30, 2014

Golf Course Builders Association of America/Hilton San Diego Bayfront/Feb. 5 - 7, 2013

Golf Course Superintendents Association of America/San Diego Convention Center/Feb. 6 - 7, 2013

Governors' Highway Safety Association/Manchester Grand Hyatt San Diego/ Aug. 25 - 28, 2013

Gynecologic Oncology Group/Manchester Grand Hyatt San Diego/Jan. 24 - 27, 2013

Gynecologic Oncology Group/Manchester Grand Hyatt San Diego/Jan. 23 - 26, 2014

Gynecologic Oncology Group/Manchester Grand Hyatt San Diego/Jan. 22 - 25, 2015

Health Forum/July 25 - 28, 2013

Hispanic Association of Colleges and Universities/Hilton San Diego Bayfront/ Oct. 28 - 30, 2017

Hospice and Palliative Nurses Association/March 12 - 15, 2014

Human Factors and Ergonomics Society/Hyatt Regency Mission Bay Spa and Marina-San Diego/Sept. 30 - Oct. 4, 2013/1500 attendees

Human Factors Society/Hilton San Diego Bayfront/Sept. 30 - Oct. 4, 2013

Independent Educational Consultants Association/Nov. 13 - 16, 2013

Institute of Environmental Sciences and Technology/San Diego Marriot Del Mar/April 29 - May 2, 2014

Institute of Navigation/Catamaran Resort Hotel and Spa/Jan. 28 - 30, 2013

Institute of Navigation/Catamaran Resort Hotel and Spa/Jan. 27 - 29, 2014

Institute of Real Estate Management/Hilton San Diego Bayfront/Oct. 18 - 22, 2016

Institute of Transportation Engineers/Sheraton San Diego Hotel and Marina/ March 3 - 6, 2013

International Anesthesia Research Society/Sheraton San Diego Hotel and Marina/May 4 - 7, 2013

International Association of Healthcare Central Service Materiel Management/ Town and Country Resort Hotel/May 5 - 8, 2013/11-25 exhibitors

International Association of Industrial Accident Boards and Commissions/ Westin Gaslamp Quarter, San Diego/Sept. 30 - Oct. 3, 2013

International District Energy Association/Sheraton San Diego Hotel and Marina/Feb. 18 - 22, 2013

International Dyslexia Association/Hilton San Diego Bayfront/Nov. 12 - 15, 2014

International Erosion Control Association/Town and Country Resort and Convention Center/Feb. 10 - 13, 2013/2000 attendees/over 100 exhibitors

International Foundation of Employee Benefit Plans/Oct. 20 - 23, 2019

International Health, Racquet and Sportsclub Association/San Diego Convention Center/March 12 - 15, 2014

International Society for Heart and Lung Transplantation/Manchester Grand/ April 9 - 12, 2014

International Society for Pharmaceutical Engineering/San Diego Marriott Marris and Marina/Nov. 9 - 12, 2014

International Technology Law Association/May 1, 2015

International Trademark Association/Hilton San Diego Bayfront/May 2 - 6, 2015

International Trademark Association/May 17 - 21, 2021

International Trademark Association/May 17 - 21, 2025

International Union of Toxicology/San Diego Convention Center/March 22 - 26, 2015

IPC - Surface Mount Equipment Manufacturers Association/San Diego Convention Center/Feb. 19 - 21, 2013/over 100 exhibitors

Journalism Education Association/April 10 - 13, 2014

Labor and Employment Relations Association/La Meridian/Jan. 6 - 8, 2013

Man and Cybernetics Systems Society/Oct. 5 - 8, 2014

Manufactured Housing Institute/La Costa Spa/Sept. 29 - Oct. 1, 2013

Marine Technology Society/Sept. 23 - 27, 2013

Mathematical Association of America/San Diego Convention Center/Jan. 9 - 12, 2013/7200 attendees

Mortgage Bankers Association of America/Manchester Grand Hyatt San Diego/ Feb. 3 - 6, 2013

Movement Disorder Society/June 14 - 18, 2015

NACHA - The Electronic Payments Association/San Diego Convention Center/ April 21 - 24, 2013/11-25 exhibitors

NAFSA: Association of International Educators/Convention Center/May 25 - 30, 2014

Natco-The Organization for Transplant Professionals/Manchester Grand Hyatt San Diego/Aug. 11 - 14, 2013

National Academy of Neuropsychology/Manchester Grand/Oct. 16 - 19, 2013

National Affordable Housing Management Association/San Diego Convention Center/June 19, 2013

National Alliance for Youth Sports/San Diego Convention Center/Nov. 21 - 23, 2013

National Apartment Association/San Diego Convention Center/June 20 - 22, 2013

National Apartment Association/San Diego Convention Center/June 14 - 16, 2018

National Association for Bilingual Education/Feb. 12 - 15, 2014

National Association for Bilingual Education/San Diego Convention Center/ Feb. 13 - 15, 2014

National Association for College Admission Counseling/Oct. 1 - 3, 2015

National Association for Medical Direction of Respiratory Care/US Grant Hotel/March 21 - 23, 2013

National Association of Consumer Bankruptcy Attorneys/April 25 - 28, 2013

National Association of Graduate Admissions Professionals/Manchester Grand Hyatt San Diego/April 30 - May 3, 2014

National Association of Insurance and Financial Advisors/Sept. 6 - 9, 2014

The National Association of Marine Surveyors, Inc./Catamaran Resort Hotel and Spa/March 3 - 5, 3013

National Association of Personal Financial Advisors/Manchester Grand/April 29 - May 4, 2013/800 attendees/over 100 exhibitors

National Association of Personal Financial Advisors/Manchester Grand/May 11 - 15, 2015

National Association of Professional Surplus Lines Offices, Ltd./Sept. 30 - Oct. 3, 2013

National Association of Realtors/Nov. 13 - 16, 2015

National Association of Resale & Thrift Shops/Westin Gaslamp Quarter, San Diego/June 28 - July 1, 2013

National Association of Residential Property Managers/Hyatt Regency La Jolla/ Oct. 15 - 18, 2013

National Association of State Facilities Administrators/June 9 - 12, 2013

National Association of Subrogation Professionals/Hilton San Diego Bayfront/ Nov. 3 - 6, 2013

National Association of Surety Bond Producers/Manchester Grand Hyatt San Diego/April 19 - 22, 2015

National Collegiate Athletic Association/Jan. 15 - 18, 2014

National Contract Management Association/Westin San Diego/March 14 - 15, 2013

National Council of Self-Insurers/Rancho Bernardo Inn/May 19 - 22, 2013

National Demolition Association/San Diego Convention Center/March 23 - 26, 2013/over 100 exhibitors

National Economic Association/La Jolla, Marriot Marquis and Marina/Jan. 3 - 5, 2013

National Electrical Manufacturers Representatives Association/Hilton San Diego Bayfront/Jan. 28 - 31, 2015

National Federation of Municipal Analysts/Westin Gaslamp Quarter, San Diego/April 30 - May 3, 2013

National Frozen and Refrigerated Foods Association/Hilton San Diego Bayfront/Oct. 19 - 22, 2013

National Golf Course Owners Association/Feb. 4 - 8, 2013

National League of Postmasters of the United States/Town and Country Resort Hotel/July 21 - 25, 2013

National Mastitis Council/Omni San Diego Hotel/Jan. 27 - 29, 2013

National Motor Freight Traffic Association, Inc./Westin San Diego/Jan. 27, 2013

National Multi-Housing Council/Hilton San Diego Bayfront/Nov. 17 - 19, 2015

National Organization of Social Security Claimants' Representatives/ Manchester Grand Hyatt/Oct. 9 - 12, 2013

National Railroad Construction and Maintenance Association, Inc./Jan. 6 - 9, 2016

National Retail Federation/San Diego Convention Center/June 12 - 14, 2013

National Scholastic Press Association/Hilton Bayfront Hotel/April 10 - 13, 2014

National School Boards Association/San Diego Convention Center/April 13 - 15, 2013/26-50 exhibitors

National School Boards Association/April 14, 2013

National Speakers Association/San Diego Marriott Marquis and Marina/June 29 - July 2, 2014

National Telecommunications Cooperative Association/Manchester Grand/Feb. 5 - 8, 2017

Navy League of the United States/Sheraton San Diego Hotel and Marina/June 18 - 22, 2014

North American Society of Adlerian Psychology/Hyatt Regency/June 20 - 23, 2013

Oceanic Engineering Society/Sept. 22 - 28, 2013

Optometric Extension Program Foundation/June 26 - 30, 2013

Organization for Safety and Asepsis Procedures/Hyatt Regency Mission Bay Spa and Marina-San Diego/June 13 - 15, 2013

Orthopaedic Trauma Association/Oct. 7 - 10, 2015

Pediatric Endocrine Society/April 25 - 28, 2015

Petroleum Equipment Suppliers Association/The Grand Del Mar/April 3 - 6, 2013

Pi Sigma Epsilon/Town and Country Resort Hotel/April 1 - 7, 2013

Population Association of America/Hilton San Diego Bayfront/April 30 - May 2, 2015

Poultry Science Association/Town and Country Resort Hotel/July 21 - 25, 2013

Powder Metallurgy Parts Association/May 17 - 20, 2015

Professional Insurance Marketing Association/Hotel del Coronado/Feb. 7 - 10, 2013

The Protein Society/July 26 - 30, 2014

The Protein Society/July 9 - 13, 2016

Public Housing Authorities Directors Association/Hilton San Diego Bayfront/Jan. 13 - 16, 2013

Radiation Therapy Oncology Group/Manchester Grand Hyatt/Jan. 24 - 27, 2013

Radio Technical Commission for Maritime Services/Sheraton San Diego Hotel and Marina/Sept. 22 - 27, 2013

The Renaissance Society of America/San Diego Sheraton Hotel and Marina/April 4 - 6, 2013/1500 attendees/over 100 exhibitors

Romance Writers of America/San Diego Marriott Marquis and Marina/July 13 - 16, 2016/2100 attendees

School Social Work Association of America/Sheraton San Diego Hotel and Marina/March 20 - 23, 2013

Shock Society/Sheraton San Diego Hotel and Marina/June 1 - 4, 2013

Society for Academic Emergency Medicine/May 13 - 16, 2015

Society for Cardiovascular Angiography and Interventions/Hilton Bayfront Hotel/May 6 - 9, 2015

Society for College and University Planning/Hilton San Diego Bayfront/July 27 - 31, 2013

Society for Industrial & Applied Mathematics/Town and Country Resort Hotel/July 8 - 12, 2013

Society for Industrial Microbiology/Sheraton San Diego/Aug. 11 - 15, 2013

Society for Information Display/June 1 - 6, 2014

Society for Laboratory Automation and Screening/Jan. 18 - 22, 2014

Society for Laboratory Automation and Screening/Jan. 23 - 27, 2016

Society for Laboratory Automation and Screening/Feb. 3 - 7, 2018

Society for Marketing Professional Services/Aug. 12 - 14, 2015

Society for Maternal-Fetal Medicine/Hilton San Diego Bayfront/Feb. 2 - 7, 2015

The Society for Modeling and Simulation International/Bahia Resort Hotel/April 7 - 10, 2013

Society for Neuroscience/Nov. 9 - 13, 2013

Society for Pediatric Dermatology/Feb. 15, 2018

Society for Pediatric Research/April 25 - 28, 2015

Society for Pediatric Urology/May 3 - 5, 2013

Society for Personality Assessment/Westin Gaslamp Quarter, San Diego/March 20 - 24, 2013/500 attendees

Society for Psychological Anthropology/Hyatt Regency Mission Bay Spa and Marina-San Diego/April 4 - 7, 2013

Society for Social Studies of Science/Town and Country Resort Hotel/Oct. 9 - 12, 2013

Society for the Scientific Study of Sexuality/Paradise Point Resort and Spa/Nov. 14 - 17, 2013

Society of Actuaries/San Diego Convention and Visitors Bureau/Oct. 20 - 23, 2013

Society of American Military Engineers/San Diego Convention Center/May 21 - 24, 2013/1-10 exhibitors

Society of Behavioral Medicine/Hilton San Diego Bayfront/March 29 - April 1, 2017

Society of Biblical Literature/Nov. 22 - 25, 2014

Society of Biblical Literature/Nov. 23 - 26, 2019

Society of Biological Psychiatry/May 18 - 20, 2017

Society for Critical Care Medicine/San Diego Convention Center/Feb. 16 - 20, 2019

Society of General Internal Medicine/Manchester Grand/April 23 - 26, 2014

Society of Government Economists/Jan. 4 - 6, 2013

Society of Gynecologic Oncologists/San Diego Convention and Visitors Bureau/March 20 - 23, 2016

Society of Interventional Radiology/March 23 - 28, 2014

Society of Nuclear Medicine/June 11 - 15, 2016

Society of Toxicology/San Diego Convention and Visitors Bureau/March 22 - 26, 2015

Society of University Surgeons/Hyatt Regency La Jolla/Feb. 4 - 6, 2014

Society of University Urologists/May 3, 2013

Special Libraries Association/June 9 - 12, 2013

Special Libraries Association/June 9 - 11, 2013

SPIE - The International Society for Optical Engineering/Town & Country Resort and Convention center/March 10 - 14, 2013

Sports Turf Managers Association/Jan. 19 - 22, 2016

System Safety Society/Manchester Grand Hyatt San Diego/Aug. 21 - 29, 2015

Textile Care Allied Trades Association/Rancho Bernardo Inn/July 31 - Aug. 3, 2013

Transportation and Logistics Council/April 22 - 24, 2013

Union for Radical Political Economics/Jan. 4 - 6, 2013

United Cerebral Palsy/April 24 - 27, 2013/11-25 exhibitors

United Fresh Produce Association/San Diego Convention Center/May 14 - 16, 2013

United States and Canadian Academy of Pathology/Convention Center/March 1 - 7, 2014/4880 attendees/51-100 exhibitors

United States Animal Health Association/Town and Country Resort Hotel/Oct. 17 - 23, 2013

United States Association for Computational Mechanics/July 27 - 30, 2015

Veterinary Hospital Managers Association/Feb. 8 - 10, 2013

Worldwide ERC/Manchester Grand/May 15 - 17, 2013

San Francisco

AASP - The Palynological Society/Oct. 20 - 24, 2013

Academy for Eating Disorders/Hyatt Regency San Francisco/May 5 - 7, 2016

Academy of Osseointegration/March 12 - 14, 2015

Academy of Osseointegration/Sept. 12 - 14, 2015

Academy of Political Science/Hilton San Francisco Union Square/Sept. 3 - 6, 2015

The Acoustical Society of America/Dec. 2 - 6, 2013

Agricultural & Applied Economics Association/July 26 - 28, 2015

Alliance for Continuing Medical Education/San Francisco Marriott Marquis/Jan. 30 - Feb. 1, 2013

Alliance for Regenerative Medicine/Jan. 7 - 9, 2013

American Academy of Cosmetic Dentistry/May 6 - 9, 2015

American Academy of Dermatology/March 20 - 24, 2015

American Academy of Ophthalmic Executives/Moscone Center/Oct. 12 - 15, 2019

American Academy of Optometry/Moscone West-Moscone Center/Nov. 14 - 18, 2018

American Academy of Periodontology/Sept. 19 - 22, 2014

American Academy of Physician Assistants/May 20 - 23, 2015

American Academy of Psychoanalysis and Dynamic Psychiatry/May 16 - 18, 2013

American Association for Justice/Hilton San Francisco/July 20 - 24, 2013

American Association for the Surgery of Trauma/Hotel Adagio/Sept. 18 - 21, 2013/1000 attendees

American Association of Collegiate Registrars and Admissions Officers/Moscone Center/April 14 - 17, 2013

American Association of Community Colleges/Moscone Center/April 20 - 23, 2013/2000 attendees

The American Association of Dental Boards/Oct. 17 - 18, 2013

American Association of Endodontists/Moscone Center/April 6 - 9, 2016

American Association of Intensive English Programs/Jan. 24 - 25, 2013

American Association of Neurological Surgeons/April 5 - 9, 2014

American Association of Orthodontists/May 15 - 20, 2013

American Association of Orthodontists/May 15 - 19, 2015

American Association of Pharmaceutical Scientists/Marriott Marquis San Francisco/June 8 - 10, 2015

American Bar Association/Aug. 8 - 13, 2013

American Bar Association/Aug. 4 - 9, 2016

American Chemical Society/Aug. 10 - 14, 2014

American Chemical Society/April 2 - 6, 2017

American College Health Association/San Francisco Marriott Marquis/May 31 - June 4, 2016

American College of Allergy, Asthma and Immunology/Nov. 10 - 15, 2016/51-100 exhibitors

American College of Allergy, Asthma and Immunology/Nov. 10 - 15, 2016

American College of Clinical Pharmacy/Hilton San Francisco Union Square/Oct. 18 - 21, 2015

American College of Physicians/The Moscone Center/April 11 - 13, 2013/1-10 exhibitors

American College of Physicians Services, Inc./April 11 - 13, 2013/7000 attendees

American College of Trial Lawyers/San Francisco Marriott Marquis/Oct. 24 - 27, 2013

American Craft Council/Aug. 2 - 4, 2013

American Dental Association/The Moscone Center/Sept. 27 - Oct. 2, 2018

American Economic Association/Hilton San Francisco Union Square/Jan. 3 - 5, 2016

American Educational Research Association/April 27 - May 1, 2013

The American Finance Association/Jan. 3 - 5, 2016

American Hospital Association/San Francisco Marriott Marquis/July 23 - 25, 2015

American Immigration Lawyers Association/Hilton San Francisco Union Square/June 26 - 29, 2013

American Institute of Chemical Engineers/Hilton/Nov. 3 - 8, 2013

American Library Association/June 25 - 30, 2015

American Medical Informatics Association/Hilton San Francisco Union Square/Nov. 14 - 18, 2015

American Medical Informatics Association/Hilton San Francisco Union Square/Oct. 27 - 31, 2018

American Microscopical Society/Hilton San Francisco Union Square/Jan. 3 - 7, 2013

American Nuclear Society/Hyatt Regency San Francisco/June 11 - 15, 2017

American Pediatric Society/May 6 - 9, 2017

American Philological Association/Jan. 7 - 10, 2016

American Philosophical Association/March 27 - 31, 2013

American Political Science Association/Hilton San Francisco Union Square/Sept. 3 - 6, 2015

American Psychiatric Association/May 18 - 22, 2013

American Psychosomatic Society/Hyatt Regency Embarcadero Hotel/March 12 - 15, 2014

American Public Transportation Association/Oct. 4 - 7, 2015

American Railway Development Association/Marines Memorial Club Hotel/June 2 - 5, 2013

American Rock Mechanics Association/The Westin Milbrae/June 23 - 26, 2013

American Society for Aesthetic Plastic Surgery/Moscone Center/April 24 - 29, 2014/2600 attendees

American Society for Environmental History/March 12 - 16, 2014

American Society for Surgery of the Hand/Moscone West-Moscone Center/Oct. 2, 2013

American Society for Surgery of the Hand/Oct. 3 - 5, 2013

American Society for Surgery of the Hand/Sept. 7 - 9, 2017

American Society of Anesthesiologists/Oct. 12 - 16, 2013

American Society of Anesthesiologists/Oct. 13 - 17, 2018
American Society of Cataract and Refractive Surgery/April 19 - 23, 2013
American Society of Cataract and Refractive Surgery/April 20 - 24, 2013
American Society of Criminology/San Francisco Marriott Marquis/Nov. 19 - 22, 2014
American Society of Criminology/San Francisco Marriott Marquis/Nov. 20 - 23, 2019
American Society of Criminology/San Francisco Marriott Marquis/Nov. 13 - 16, 2024
American Society of Dermatopathology/Hilton San Francisco Union Square/ Oct. 8 - 11, 2015
American Society of Hypertension, Inc./San Francisco Marriott Hotel/May 15 - 18, 2013
American Society of Ophthalmic Administrators/Moscone Center/San Francisco Marriott Marquis/April 19 - 23, 2013
American Society of Ophthalmic Administrators/April 25 - 29, 2013
American Society of Pediatric Nephrology/May 6 - 9, 2017
American Society of Transplant Surgeons/July 26 - 31, 2014
American Society of Transplantation/July 26 - 31, 2014
American Thoracic Society/May 13 - 18, 2016
American Translators Association/Grand Hyatt San Francisco/Nov. 2 - 5, 2016
Angel Capital Association/April 17 - 19, 2013
Antiquarian Booksellers Association of America/Concourse Exhibition Center/ Feb. 15 - 17, 2013
Associated Collegiate Press/Westin San Francisco Airport/Feb. 28 - March 3, 2013
Association for Commuter Transportation/Grand Hyatt San Francisco/Aug. 2 - 6, 2014
Association for Education in Journalism and Mass Communication/Marriott San Francisco Marquis/Aug. 5 - 9, 2013
Association for Psychological Science/Hilton San Francisco/May 22 - 25, 2014
Association for Research in Vision and Ophthalmology/May 2 - 6, 2021
Association for the Advancement of International Education/Hyatt Regency/ Feb. 14 - 17, 2013
Association of Collegiate Schools of Architecture/California College of the Arts/ March 21 - 24, 2013
Association of Credit Union Internal Auditors/Grand Hyatt San Francisco/June 25 - 28, 2013
Association of Dermatology Administrators & Managers/March 17 - 22, 2015
Association of Foreign Investors in U.S. Real Estate/Ritz-Carlton/Sept. 9 - 11, 2013
Association of Governing Boards of Universities and Colleges/Hyatt Regency San Francisco/April 21 - 23, 2013
Association of Procurement Technical Assistance Centers/Westin San Francisco Market Street/March 24 - 27, 2014
Association of Schools of Journalism and Mass Communication/Marriott San Francisco Marquis/Aug. 5 - 9, 2015
Association of University Technology Managers/Moscone West-Moscone Center/Feb. 19 - 22, 2014
Automotive Aftermarket Industry Association/June 1 - 5, 2013
Building Owners and Managers Association International/Westin St. Francis Union Square/May 1 - 3, 2013
Business for Social Responsibility/Nov. 5 - 8, 2013
Closure and Container Manufacturers Association/Grand Hyatt San Francisco/ March 20 - 22, 2013
Congress of Neurological Surgeons/Oct. 19 - 24, 2013
Congress of Neurological Surgeons/Oct. 19 - 23, 2013
Construction Management Association of America/Marriott San Francisco Marquis/Oct. 19 - 21, 2014/1000 attendees
Council for Advancement and Support of Education/Hyatt Regency San Francisco/May 6 - 8, 2013
Council for Advancement and Support of Education/Hyatt Regency San Francisco/May 8 - 9, 2013
Council for Advancement and Support of Education/Moscone Center/San Francisco Marriott Marquis/June 5 - 7, 2013
Council for Advancement and Support of Education/Embarcadero, San Francisco/July 14 - 16, 2013
Council of American Survey Research Organizations/Westin San Francisco/ March 7 - 8, 2013/250 attendees
Council on Foundations/Jan. 27 - 29, 2013
The Counselors of Real Estate/Ritz Carlton Hotel/Oct. 20 - 23, 2013
Distance Education and Training Council/Fairmont San Francisco/April 14 - 16, 2013/200 attendees
Edison Electric Institute/San Francisco Marriott Marquis/June 9 - 12, 2013
The Electrochemical Society/Hilton San Francisco Union Square/Oct. 27 - Nov. 1, 2013
Endocrine Fellows Foundation/June 15 - 18, 2013
The Endocrine Society/June 15 - 18, 2013
Environmental Bankers Association/June 9 - 11, 2013
The Fertilizer Institute/Westin St. Francis/Sept. 21 - 23, 2014
Government Finance Officers Association of the United States and Canada/ June 2 - 5, 2013/over 100 exhibitors
Government Finance Officers Association, Federal Liaison Center/June 2 - 5, 2013
Heart Rhythm Society/Fairmont San Francisco/May 7 - 10, 2014
IEEE Engineering in Medicine and Biology Society/The Westin Hotel/April 7 - 11, 2013
Institute for Operations Research and the Management Sciences/Hilton San Francisco Union Square/Nov. 16 - 19, 2014
International Association of Business Communicators/San Francisco Marriott Marquis/June 14 - 17, 2015
International Association of Culinary Professionals/Hyatt Embarcadero Hotel/ April 6 - 9, 2013
International Brain Injury Association/Hyatt Embarcadero Hotel/March 19 - 23, 2014
International Fine Print Dealers Association/Fort Mason Center/Jan. 18 - 20, 2013
International Municipal Lawyers Association/Sept. 29 - Oct. 2, 2013
International Society for Antiviral Research/Hyatt Regency Embarcadero Hotel/ May 11 - 15, 2013

International Society of Hair Restoration Surgery/Oct. 23 - 27, 2013
International Society of Hair Restoration Surgery/Oct. 23 - 27, 2013
International Studies Association/Hilton San Francisco Union Square/April 3 - 6, 2013/5000 attendees
International Studies Association/San Francisco Hotels/April 4 - 7, 2018
International Trademark Association/April 24 - 28, 2021
Journalism Education Association/San Francisco Marriott Marquis/April 25 - 28, 2013
Linguistic Society of America/Hilton San Francisco Union Square/Jan. 8 - 11, 2015/1000 attendees
LOMA/Hyatt Regency San Francisco/Sept. 7 - 9, 2014
Materials Research Society/Moscone Center/April 1 - 5, 2013
Materials Research Society/April 21 - 25, 2014
NAFSA: Association of International Educators/May 28 - June 2, 2017
National Apartment Association/Moscone Center/June 9 - 11, 2016
National Association for Business Economics/San Francisco Hyatt Regency/ Sept. 7 - 10, 2013
National Association for the Specialty Food Trade/Jan. 20 - 22, 2013/1-10 exhibitors
National Association for the Specialty Food Trade/Jan. 19 - 21, 2014
National Association of Advisors for the Health Professions/Hilton San Francisco Union Square/June 25 - 29, 2014
National Association of Bar Executives/Aug. 6 - 8, 2013
National Association of Criminal Defense Lawyers/Westin San Francisco/July 24 - 27, 2013
National Association of Development Organizations/Hilton San Francisco Union Square/Aug. 24 - 27, 2013
National Association of Electrical Distributors/San Francisco Marriott Marquis/April 26 - 29, 2014
National Association of Real Estate Investment Trusts (NAREIT)/San Francisco Marriott Marquis/Nov. 13 - 15, 2013
National Association of Realtors/Nov. 8 - 11, 2013
National Association of Realtors/Nov. 8 - 11, 2019
National Association of Regulatory Utility Commissioners/San Francisco Marriott Marquis/Nov. 16 - 19, 2014
National Association of Spine Specialists/Nov. 12 - 15, 2014
National Association of Surety Bond Producers/Fairmont San Francisco/April 21 - 24, 2013
National Association of Veterans Research and Education Foundations/Hilton San Francisco Financial District/Sept. 14 - 17, 2013
National Automobile Dealers Association/Jan. 23 - 26, 2015
National Cancer Registrars Association/May 29 - June 1, 2013/26-50 exhibitors
National Cancer Registrars Association/Hilton Union Square/May 30 - June 2, 2013
National Coffee Association of the U.S.A./Palace Hotel-San Francisco/March 21 - 23, 2013
National Conference of Bankruptcy Judges/Oct. 26 - 29, 2016
National Conference of Bar Foundations/Aug. 8 - 10, 2013
National Conference of Insurance Legislators/Grand Hyatt in Union Square/ Nov. 20 - 23, 2014
National Council for the Social Studies/Moscone West-Moscone Center/Nov. 17 - 19, 2017
National Council of State Housing Agencies/San Francisco Marriott Marquis/ June 24 - 27, 2013
National Council of Supervisors of Mathematics/April 11 - 13, 2016
National Council of Teachers of Mathematics/April 13 - 16, 2016
National Council on Measurement in Education/April 26 - 30, 2013
National Council on Rehabilitation Education/SFO Airport Marriott Hotel/April 17 - 19, 2013
National Court Reporters Association/Hilton San Francisco Union Square/July 31 - Aug. 3, 2014
National Electrical Contractors Association/Oct. 3 - 6, 2015
National Electrical Contractors Association/Oct. 3 - 6, 2015
National Federation of Community Broadcasters/Parc 55 Hotel/May 29 - June 1, 2013
National Grain and Feed Association/Westin St. Francis/March 17 - 19, 2013
National Scholastic Press Association/San Francisco Marriott Marquis/April 25 - 28, 2013
National Telecommunications Cooperative Association/Hilton San Francisco Union Square/Sept. 21 - 24, 2014
Network of Executive Women in Hospitality/Grand Hyatt Union Square/Jan. 25 - 26, 2013
Neurotechnology Industry Organization/May 23 - 24, 2013/250 attendees
Nonprofit Technology Network/March 22 - 24, 2016/11-25 exhibitors
North American Catalysis Society/Sept. 7 - 11, 2014
North American Spine Society/Nov. 12 - 15, 2014
Organization of American Historians/Hilton San Francisco Union Square/April 11 - 14, 2013
Pediatric Endocrine Society/May 6 - 9, 2017
Society for American Archaeology/April 15 - 19, 2015
Society for Cardiovascular Magnetic Resonance/Hilton San Francisco Union Square/Jan. 31 - Feb. 3, 2013
Society for Education in Anesthesia/Oct. 11, 2013
Society for Environmental Graphic Design/June 6 - 8, 2013
Society for Free Radical Biology and Medicine/Hyatt Regency Embarcadero Hotel/Nov. 17 - 20, 2016
Society for Gynecologic Investigation/March 25 - 28, 2015
Society for Imaging Science and Technology/Feb. 3 - 7, 2013
Society for Integrative and Comparative Biology/Hilton San Francisco Union Square/Jan. 3 - 7, 2013
Society for Maternal-Fetal Medicine/Hilton San Francisco Union Square/Feb. 11 - 16, 2013
Society for Neuroscience in Anesthesiology and Critical Care/Oct. 10 - 11, 2013
Society for Pediatric Anesthesia/Oct. 11, 2013
Society for Pediatric Dermatology/March 19, 2015
Society for Pediatric Research/May 6 - 9, 2017
Society for Radiation Oncology Administration/Sept. 14 - 18, 2014
Society for Scholarly Publishing/San Francisco Marriott Marquis/June 5 - 7, 2013

Society for Scholarly Publishing/San Francisco Marriott Marquis/July 5 - 7, 2013
Society for the Advancement of Scandinavian Study/May 2 - 4, 2013
Society for the Philosophy of Sex and Love/March 27 - 31, 2013
Society for the Study of Social Problems/Hilton San Francisco Union Square/Aug. 15 - 17, 2014
Society for Vascular Surgery/Doubletree Hotel San Francisco/May 30 - June 1, 2013
Society for Vascular Ultrasound/Moscone Center West/May 30 - June 1, 2013
Society of Behavioral Medicine/Hilton San Francisco Union Square/March 20 - 23, 2013
Society of Biological Psychiatry/Hilton San Francisco Union Square/May 18 - 22, 2013
Society of Biological Psychiatry/May 16 - 19, 2019
Society of Biological Psychiatry/May 16 - 18, 2019
Society for Critical Care Medicine/Moscone Center/Jan. 9 - 13, 2014
Solid-State Circuits Society/Feb. 17 - 21, 2013/4000 attendees
Solid-State Circuits Society/Feb. 9 - 13, 2014/3000 attendees
Solid-State Circuits Society/Feb. 22 - 26, 2015/4000 attendees
Solid-State Circuits Society/Feb. 21 - 25, 2016/3500 attendees
Solid-State Circuits Society/Feb. 5 - 9, 2017/3000 attendees
Urban Affairs Association/The Fairmont Hotel/April 3 - 6, 2013
Women Chefs and Restaurateurs/Sir Francis Drake/Jan. 16 - 18, 2013

San Jose
Airports Council International - North America/Sept. 22 - 25, 2013
American Association for the Advancement of Science/Feb. 12 - 16, 2015
American Institute of Aeronautics and Astronautics/San Jose Convention Center/July 15 - 17, 2013
American Society for Training and Development/Jan. 30 - Feb. 1, 2013/1200 attendees
IEEE Signal Processing Society/The Fairmont Hotel/July 15 - 19, 2013
International Association of Music Libraries, United States Branch/Feb. 27 - March 3, 2013
International Society for Computerized Electrocardiology/Dolce Hayes Mansion/April 17 - 21, 2013
Music Library Association/Feb. 27 - March 3, 2013
Optical Society of America/San Jose Convention Center/June 9 - 14, 2013/1-10 exhibitors
SPIE - The International Society for Optical Engineering/San Jose Convention Center/Feb. 24 - 28, 2013
USENIX: The Advanced Computing Systems Association/Fairmont San Jose/Feb. 12 - 15, 2013
USENIX: The Advanced Computing Systems Association/June 25 - 28, 2013
USENIX: The Advanced Computing Systems Association/Fairmont San Jose/June 26 - 28, 2013

San Mateo
In-Plant Printing and Mailing Association/San Mateo Marriott San Francisco Airport/June 2 - 5, 2013

San Ramon
The Association of Concert Bands/April 3 - 7, 2013

Santa Barbara
Catholic Medical Association/Fess Parker's DoubleTree Resort by Hilton Santa Barbara/Oct. 24 - 26, 2013

Santa Clara
Association for Women in Mathematics/Santa Clara University/March 16 - 17, 2013
Electricity Storage Association/Santa Clara Convention Center/May 20 - 22, 2013
Society of Vacuum Coaters/Santa Clara Convention Center/April 25 - 30, 2015

Santa Monica
Democratic Attorneys General Association/Feb. 1 - 2, 2013
National Fisheries Institute/Loews Santa Monica Beach Hotel/Jan. 29 - 31, 2013
Plastic Surgery Research Council/Loews Santa Monica Beach Hotel/May 2 - 4, 2013

Savannah
American College of Veterinary Radiology/Oct. 8, 2013

Shell Beach
Associated Schools of Construction/Cliffs Resort/April 9 - 13, 2013

Sonoma
National Association of Federal Credit Unions/Fairmont Sonoma Mission Inn and Spa/April 24 - 26, 2013
Textile Rental Services Association of America/Fairmont Sonoma Mission Inn and Spa/Sept. 22 - 25, 2013

Squaw Valley
Exhibition Services and Contractors Association/Resort at Squaw Creek/June 28 - July 1, 2015

Stanford
American Association for the Advancement of Artificial Intelligence/Stanford University/March 25 - 27, 2013
Association of University Anesthesiologists/April 24 - 26, 2014
International Association of Defense Counsel/Stanford Law School/July 25 - Aug. 2, 2013

Universal City
International Association for Orthodontics/Sheraton Universal Hotel/April 11 - 14, 2013

Westlake Village
Council of American Survey Research Organizations/Four Seasons Hotel Westlake Village/Oct. 7 - 10, 2013

Yountville
Plastic Shipping Container Institute/Hotel Yountville/April 21 - 22, 2013

COLORADO

Avon
Distribution Contractors Association/Park Hyatt Beaver Creek Resort and Spa/July 17 - 21, 2013
Society of Gynecologic Oncologists/Westin Riverfront/Feb. 7 - 9, 2013

Beaver Creek
Self Storage Association/The Westin Riverfront Resort & Spa/Feb. 4 - 7, 2013

Boulder
American Academy of Psychotherapists/The Millennium Harvest House Hotel/June 5 - 9, 2013
Animal Behavior Society/July 28 - Aug. 1, 2013
Institute of Mathematical Statistics/July 29 - Aug. 2, 2013

Breckenridge
Wilderness Medical Society/Beaver Run Resort and Conference Center/July 11 - 17, 2013

Broomfield
American Institute of Professional Geologists/Omni Interlocken Resort/Oct. 23 - 26, 2013
Collaborative Family Healthcare Association/Omni Interlocken Resort/Oct. 10 - 12, 2013

Colorado Springs
American Academy of Osteopathy/The Broadmoor/March 19 - 23, 2014
American Boiler Manufacturers Association/Broadmoor/June 21 - 24, 2013
American Chemistry Council/June 3 - 5, 2013
American Council of Engineering Companies/The Broadmoor/Oct. 19 - 22, 2016
American Osteopathic Academy of Sports Medicine/The Broadmoor/March 6 - 9, 2013
American Physical Therapy Association - Private Practice Section/Antlers Hilton Colorado Springs/Nov. 5 - 8, 2014
American Society of Association Executives-The Center for Association Leadership/Broadmoor/March 10 - 12, 2013/616 attendees
Associated General Contractors of America (AGC)/Antlers Hilton Colorado Springs/Oct. 16 - 19, 2013
BEMA - The Baking Industry Suppliers Association/Broadmoor Resort/June 20 - 25, 2013
Casualty Actuarial Society/The Broadmoor/May 17 - 20, 2015
Chlorine Chemistry Council/June 3 - 5, 2013
Federation of Defense and Corporate Counsel/Antlers Hilton Colorado Springs/July 28 - Aug. 4, 2013
International Association of Defense Counsel/The Broadmoor/July 5 - 10, 2015
International Institute of Ammonia Refrigeration/March 17 - 20, 2013
Metals Service Center Institute/Broadmoor/May 15 - 17, 2013
National Association of College Auxiliary Services/The Broadmoor/Nov. 5 - 8, 2017
National Association of Development Companies/Broadmoor/April 30 - May 3, 2014
National Association of Surety Bond Producers/The Broadmoor/May 15 - 18, 2016
National Board of Boiler and Pressure Vessel Inspectors/The Broadmoor/April 27 - May 1, 2015
National Ocean Industries Association/The Broadmoor/Oct. 2 - 4, 2013
Power and Communications Contractors Association/The Broadmoor/July 10 - 13, 2013
Radiology Business Management Association/Broadmoor/May 19 - 22, 2013
The Retired Enlisted Association/DoubleTree by Hilton Hotel Colorado Springs/Sept. 23, 2013
Society for Obstetric Anesthesia and Perinatology/Broadmoor/May 13 - 17, 2015
Society of Insurance Trainers and Educators/June 20 - 23, 2015
United States Potato Board/The Broadmoor/March 12 - 15, 2013
USA Taekwondo/Cheyenne Mountain Resort/Jan. 12 - 13, 2013

Denver
AABB - American Association of Blood Banks/Oct. 12 - 15, 2013
AASHTO: Transportation Center of Excellence/Sheraton Denver West Hotel/Oct. 16 - 21, 2013
Academy of Criminal Justice Sciences/Sheraton Denver Downtown Hotel/March 29 - April 2, 2016
Airport Minority Advisory Council (AMAC)/June 7 - 10, 2014
American Academy of Dermatology/March 21 - 25, 2014
American Academy of Optometry/Oct. 12 - 15, 2014
American Academy of Optometry/Colorado Convention Center/Nov. 12 - 15, 2014
American Academy of Religion/Nov. 17 - 20, 2018/10000 attendees/over 100 exhibitors
American Anthropological Association/Colorado Convention Center/Nov. 18 - 22, 2015
American Association of Collegiate Registrars and Admissions Officers/Colorado Convention Center/March 30 - April 2, 2014
American Association of Critical-Care Nurses/May 17 - 22, 2014
American Association of Endodontists/Colorado Convention Center/April 25 - 28, 2018
American Association of Petroleum Geologists/May 31 - June 3, 2015
American Association of Pharmaceutical Scientists/Colorado Convention Center/Nov. 12 - 17, 2016
American Association of Residential Mortgage Regulators/Sheraton Downtown Denver Hotel/Aug. 6 - 9, 2013
American Association of Veterinary Parasitologists/July 26 - 29, 2014
American Chemical Society/March 22 - 26, 2015
American College of Nurse-Midwives/May 12 - 17, 2014
American College of Veterinary Internal Medicine/June 8 - 11, 2016
American Concrete Institute/Scanticon Denver Inc/Nov. 8 - 12, 2015
American Dental Association/Four Seasons/July 18 - 20, 2013
American Diabetes Association/Colorado Convention Center/Feb. 9, 2013
American Gelbvieh Association/Red Lion Hotel on Quebec Street/Jan. 9 - 14, 2013
American Highland Cattle Association/Jan. 22 - 27, 2013
American Institute of Floral Designers/Denver Downtown Sheraton/June 30 - July 4, 2015
American Institute of Physics/Nov. 4 - 8, 2013
American Massage Therapy Association/Colorado Convention Center/Sept. 17 - 19, 2014
American Mathematical Association of Two Year Colleges/Nov. 17 - 20, 2016
American Meteorological Society/Jan. 8 - 12, 2023

American Meteorological Society/Jan. 10 - 14, 2027
American Meteorological Society/Jan. 12 - 16, 2031
American Orff-Schulwerk Association/Nov. 13 - 16, 2013
American Organization of Nurse Executives/March 19 - 22, 2013
American Organization of Nurse Executives/Colorado Convention Center/
  March 20 - 23, 2013
American Orthopaedic Association/Sheraton Denver Downtown Hotel/June 12
  - 15, 2013
American Physical Society/Sheraton Denver Downtown Hotel/April 13 - 16,
  2013
American Physical Society/Nov. 11 - 15, 2013
American Physical Society/March 3 - 7, 2014
American Public Power Association/Jan. 21 - 25, 2014
American Salers Association/Holiday Inn Denver East-Stapleton/Jan. 19 - 22,
  2013
American Society for Apheresis/Sheraton Downtown Denver Hotel/May 22 -
  25, 2013
American Society for Healthcare Engineering/July 10 - 13, 2016/1-10
  exhibitors
American Society for Histocompatibility and Immunogenetics/Sheraton Denver
  Downtown Hotel/Oct. 20 - 24, 2014
American Society for Neurochemistry/March 19 - 23, 2016
American Society of Heating, Refrigerating and Air Conditioning Engineers
  (ASHRAE)/June 22 - 26, 2013
American Society of Landscape Architects/Colorado Convention Center/Nov.
  21 - 24, 2014/over 100 exhibitors
American Theological Library Association/June 17 - 20, 2015
American Thoracic Society/May 15 - 20, 2015
American Thyroid Association/Sheraton Denver Downtown Hotel/Sept. 21 -
  26, 2016/11-25 exhibitors
American Veterinary Medical Association/July 26 - 29, 2014
American Water Works Association/Colorado Convention Center/June 9 - 13,
  2013
Associated Builders and Contractors/Westin Tabor Center/July 31 - Aug. 2,
  2013
Association for Counselor Education and Supervision/Hyatt Regency Denver at
  Colorado Convention Center/Oct. 17 - 20, 2013
Association for Research in Vision and Ophthalmology/May 3 - 7, 2015
Association of Asphalt Paving Technologists/Westin Denver Downtown/April 7
  - 10, 2013
Association of Dermatology Administrators & Managers/March 19 - 22, 2014
Association of Environmental and Engineering Geologists/May 16 - 17, 2013
Association of Free Community Papers/Denver Marriott City Center/April 25 -
  27, 2013
Association of Independent Information Professionals/Westin Denver
  Downtown/April 3 - 7, 2013
Association of Insolvency and Restructuring Advisors/June 4 - 7, 2014
Association of periOperative Registered Nurses/March 7 - 12, 2015
Association of Procurement Technical Assistance Centers/Denver Marriott City
  Center/March 16 - 19, 2015
Association of Surgical Technologists/Hyatt Regency Denver at Colorado
  Convention Center/May 26 - 30, 2014
Catholic Press Association/Denver Marriott Tech Center/June 19 - 21, 2013
Child Life Council/Sheraton Denver Downtown Hotel/May 16 - 19, 2013
NAIOP, The Commercial Real Estate Development Association/Sheraton
  Denver Downtown Hotel/Oct. 27 - 30, 2014
Commercial Vehicle Safety Alliance/Hyatt Regency Denver at Colorado
  Convention Center/Sept. 16 - 19, 2013
Council for Advancement and Support of Education/Grand Hyatt Denver/April
  24 - 26, 2013
Council for Advancement and Support of Education/Grand Hyatt Denver/June
  5 - 7, 2013
Council of Colleges of Arts and Sciences/Sheraton Denver Downtown Hotel/
  Nov. 1 - 4, 2017
Council on Anthropology and Education/Colorado Convention Center/Nov. 18
  - 22, 2015
Council on Social Work Education/Sheraton Denver Downtown Hotel/Oct. 15
  - 18, 2015
Educause/Sheraton Denver Downtown Hotel/Feb. 4 - 6, 2013
Emdr International Association/Hyatt Regency Denver Convention Center/
  Sept. 18 - 21, 2014
Environmental and Engineering Geophysical Society/Denver Marriott Tech
  Center/March 17 - 21, 2013
Federation of State Medical Boards of the United States/Hyatt Regency Denver
  at Colorado Convention Center/April 24 - 26, 2014
Geological Society of America/Oct. 27 - 30, 2013
Government Finance Officers Association of the United States and Canada/
  May 21 - 24, 2017/over 100 exhibitors
Government Finance Officers Association, Federal Liaison Center/May 21 - 24,
  2017
Gynecologic Oncology Group/Sheraton Hotel/July 15 - 19, 2015
Heart Rhythm Society/Colorado Convention Center/May 8 - 11, 2013
Hispanic Association of Colleges and Universities/Sheraton Denver Downtown
  Hotel/Oct. 4 - 6, 2014
Human Resource People and Strategy/Denver Marriott City Center/April 14 -
  17, 2013
IEEE Magnetics Society/Nov. 4 - 7, 2013
INDA, Association of the Nonwoven Fabrics Industry/Grand Hyatt Denver/
  Sept. 30 - Oct. 3, 2013
Information Storage Industry Consortium/Nov. 4 - 8, 2013
Institute of Noise Control Engineering/Marriott Denver City Center downtown/
  Aug. 26 - 28, 2013
International Balloon Association/March 26 - 30, 2014
International Dairy-Deli-Bakery Association/June 1 - 3, 2014
International Oil Mill Superintendents Association/June 16 - 18, 2013
International Test and Evaluation Association/Sept. 16 - 20, 2013
Journalism Education Association/April 16 - 19, 2015
Messenger Courier Association of the Americas/The Sheraton Downtown/Oct.
  1 - 3, 2015
Metal Construction Association/Oct. 1 - 3, 2014

Middle East Librarians' Association/Sheraton Denver Downtown Hotel/Nov. 21
  - 24, 2015
Middle East Studies Association of North America/Sheraton Denver Downtown
  Hotel/Nov. 21 - 24, 2015
Mineralogical Society of America/Oct. 27 - 30, 2013
Mining and Metallurgical Society of America/Feb. 24 - 25, 2013
NAFSA: Association of International Educators/Denver Metro Convention and
  Visitors Bureau/May 29 - June 3, 2016
National Affordable Housing Management Association/Colorado Convention
  Center/June 18, 2014
National Apartment Association/Colorado Convention Center/June 19 - 21,
  2014
National Apartment Association/Colorado Convention Center/June 27 - 29,
  2019
National Association for Developmental Education/Sheraton Denver
  Downtown Hotel/Feb. 27 - March 2, 2013
National Association for Interpretation/Nov. 18 - 22, 2014
National Association for Interpretation/Nov. 19 - 23, 2019
National Association of Active Investment Managers/Westin Denver
  Downtown/April 28 - May 1, 2013
National Association of Catering and Events/Hyatt Regency Denver at
  Colorado Convention Center/Sept. 15 - 16, 2013
National Association of College and University Attorneys/Hyatt Regency
  Denver at Colorado Convention Center/June 22 - 25, 2014
National Association of Graphic and Product Identification Manufacturers/The
  Sheraton Downtown/Sept. 22 - 24, 2013
National Association of Professional Background Screeners/Hyatt Regency
  Denver at Colorado Convention Center/Sept. 7 - 9, 2014
National Association of State Energy Officials/Curtis Hotel/Sept. 15 - 18, 2013
National Association of Workforce Development Professionals/May 4 - 6, 2014
National Bison Association/Renaissance Denver Hotel/Jan. 23 - 26, 2013
National Coal Transportation Association/The Brown Palace Hotel /Sept. 16 -
  18, 2013
National Council for Geographic Education/Denver Marriott City Center/Aug.
  1 - 4, 2013
National Council of Acoustical Consultants/Denver Marriott City Center/Aug.
  24 - 25, 2013
National Council of Supervisors of Mathematics/Denver Downtown Hyatt
  Regency/April 15 - 17, 2013
National Council of Teachers of Mathematics/April 17 - 19, 2013
National Council of Teachers of Mathematics/Colorado Convention Center/
  April 17 - 20, 2013
National Dog Groomers Association of America, Inc./Crowne Plaza Hotel
  Denver-International Airport/June 7 - 9, 2013
National Education Association/July 1 - 6, 2014
National Federation Coaches Association/Hyatt Regency Denver Tech Center/
  June 23 - 27, 2013
National Federation of State High School Associations/Hyatt Regency Denver
  at Colorado Convention Center/June 23 - 27, 2013
National Organization of Nurse Practitioner Faculties/April 3 - 6, 2014
National Orientation Directors Association/Oct. 23 - 27, 2015
National Scholastic Press Association/Sheraton/April 16 - 20, 2015
National Science Teachers Association/Dec. 12 - 14, 2013
National Ski Patrol System/Grand Hyatt Denver/Jan. 31 - Feb. 3, 2013
Production and Operations Management Society/Denver Marriott City Center/
  May 3 - 6, 2013
Public Library Association/April 5 - 9, 2016
Red Angus Association of America/Jan. 10 - 14, 2013
Religious Education Association/Nov. 6 - 8, 2015
SnowSports Industries America/Colorado Convention Center/Jan. 31 - Feb. 3,
  2013
Society for Applied Anthropology/Denver Marriott City Center Hotel/March 19
  - 23, 2013
Society for Epidemiologic Research/June 15 - 18, 2015
Society for Italian Historical Studies/Hyatt Regency Denver Tech Center/Jan. 5
  - 8, 2017
Society for Mining, Metallurgy and Exploration, Inc./Colorado Convention
  Center/Feb. 24 - 27, 2014
Society for Mining, Metallurgy and Exploration, Inc./Colorado Convention
  Center/Feb. 22 - 25, 2015
Society for Pediatric Dermatology/March 20, 2014
Society of Biblical Literature/Nov. 17 - 20, 2018
Society of Exploration Geophysicists/Oct. 26 - 31, 2014
Society of General Internal Medicine/Sheraton Denver Downtown Hotel/April
  24 - 27, 2014
Society of Infectious Diseases Pharmacists/Sept. 10 - 13, 2013
Society of Nuclear Medicine/June 10 - 14, 2017
Society of Radiologists in Ultrasound/The Denver Marriott City Center/Oct. 24
  - 26, 2014
Special Interest Group for Computer Science Education/The Sheraton
  Downtown/March 6 - 9, 2013
Sports Turf Managers Association/Jan. 13 - 16, 2015
Water and Sewer Distributors of America/Grand Hyatt Denver/Oct. 21 - 23,
  2013
Western Economic Association International/June 27 - July 1, 2014
Wildlife Management Institute/Sheraton Downtown Denver Hotel/March 9 -
  14, 2014

Durango
International Society of Weekly Newspaper Editors/Fort Lewis College/June 25
  - 29, 2014

Englewood
ASFE/The Geoprofessional Business Association/Inverness Hotel and
  Conference Center/Jan. 25 - 26, 2013
Automotive Training Managers Council/Inverness Hotel and Conference
  Center/April 15 - 17, 2013

Estes Park
American Ornithologists' Union/Sept. 24 - 27, 2014

Ft. Collins
American Society for Virology/Colorado State University/June 21 - 25, 2014

National Association for Ethnic Studies/Colorado State University/April 12 - 13, 2013

Grand Junction

River Management Society/Colorado Mesa University/March 11 - 15, 2013

Keystone

American Association for Crystal Growth/Keystone Resort and Conference Center/July 21 - 26, 2013

Loveland

National Onion Association/July 17 - 20, 2013

Orlando

Restaurant Facility Management Association/Gaylord Palms Resort and Convention Center-Orlando/March 10 - 12, 2013

Snowmass Village

American College of Cardiology/Westin Snowmass Resort/Jan. 14 - 18, 2013

Steamboat Springs

Institute for Operations Research and the Management Sciences/Sheraton Steamboat Resort,/Feb. 7 - 10, 2013

International Society of Protistologists/Steamboat Grand Resort/July 7 - 12, 2013

Telluride

Society of Independent Gasoline Marketers of America (SIGMA)/Peaks Resort and Spa/Jan. 27 - 30, 2013

Vail

ACA International, The Association of Credit and Collection Professionals/Vail Cascade Resort and Spa/Jan. 5 - 8, 2013

American Institute of Aeronautics and Astronautics/Vail Marriott Mountain Resort/July 14 - 18, 2013

Westminster

American Network of Community Options and Resources (ANCOR)/Westin Westminster/Nov. 3, 2013

Education Law Association/Westin Westminster/Nov. 13 - 16, 2013

Winter Park

American Osteopathic College of Dermatology/Winter Park Mountain Lodge/ Jan. 23 - 26, 2013

CONNECTICUT

Hamden

North American Society for Social Philosophy/Quinnipiac University/July 11 - 13, 2013

Hartford

American Association of School Librarians/Nov. 14 - 17, 2013

American Council for Construction Education/Hartford Marriott Downtown/ July 24 - 27, 2013

American Philatelic Society/Aug. 8 - 10, 2014

American Philatelic Society/Aug. 21 - 24, 2014

Association of State Floodplain Managers/Connecticut Convention Center/June 9 - 14, 2013

International Institute of Municipal Clerks/May 17 - 20, 2015

Mathematical Association of America/Aug. 1 - 3, 2013

Microanalysis Society/Aug. 3 - 7, 2014

Microanalysis Society/Aug. 8 - 11, 2014

Microscopy Society of America/Aug. 3 - 7, 2014

Music Industry Conference/April 4 - 7, 2013

National Society of Newspaper Columnists/June 27 - 30, 2013

Organization of American Kodaly Educators/March 21 - 23, 2013

New Haven

American Association for the History of Medicine/April 29 - May 3, 2015

Association for the Advancement of Baltic Studies/Yale University/March 13 - 15, 2014

Society for the Advancement of Scandinavian Study/March 13 - 15, 2014

Uncasville

American Society of Consulting Arborists/Mohegan Sun Conference Center/ Dec. 4 - 7, 2013

Association of Water Technologies/Mohegan Sun/Oct. 30 - Nov. 2, 2013

DELAWARE

Dover

American Association of Motor Vehicle Administrators/Dover Downs Hotel and Casino/Aug. 25 - 27, 2014

National Electronic Service Dealers Association/Dover Downs Hotel and Casino/June 5 - 8, 2013

Newark

The Association for the Study of Play/University of Delaware & The Embassy Suite/March 6 - 9, 2013

Wilmington

National Conference of Black Political Scientists/March 12 - 15, 2014

DISTRICT OF COLUMBIA

Washington

AACE International/Washington Marriott Wardman Park/June 30 - July 3, 2013

Academic Pediatric Association/May 4 - 7, 2013

Academy of Political Science/Washington Marriott Wardman Park/Aug. 28 - 31, 2014

Agricultural & Applied Economics Association/Aug. 4 - 6, 2013

Air Conditioning, Heating and Refrigeration Institute (AHRI)/March 21 - 22, 2013

Air Force Association/Gaylord National-Washington/March 14 - 15, 2013

Air Force Association/Gaylord National-Washington/Sept. 14 - 15, 2013

Air Force Association/Gaylord National-Washington/Sept. 16 - 18, 2013

Air Force Association/Gaylord National-Washington/March 27 - 29, 2014

Air Force Association/Gaylord National-Washington/Sept. 13 - 14, 2014

Air Force Association/Gaylord National-Washington/Sept. 15 - 17, 2014

Air Force Association/Gaylord National-Washington/March 12 - 14, 2015

Air Force Association/Gaylord National-Washington/Sept. 12, 2015

Air Force Association/Gaylord National-Washington/Sept. 14 - 16, 2015

Air Force Association/Gaylord National-Washington/Sept. 17 - 18, 2016

Air Force Association/Gaylord National-Washington/Sept. 19 - 21, 2016

Air Force Association/Gaylord National-Washington/Sept. 16 - 17, 2017

Air Force Association/Gaylord National-Washington/Sept. 18 - 20, 2017

Air Force Association/Gaylord National-Washington/Sept. 15 - 16, 2018

Air Force Association/Gaylord National-Washington/Sept. 17 - 19, 2018

Airports Council International - North America/Washington Court Hotel/ March 20 - 21, 2013

Alliance for Regenerative Medicine/May 7 - 8, 2013

Ambulatory Surgery Center Association/Gaylord National Resort and Convention Center/May 18 - 21, 2016/2500 attendees

America's Health Insurance Plans/March 13 - 14, 2013

America's Health Insurance Plans/March 5 - 6, 2014

American Academy of Child and Adolescent Psychiatry/Marriott Wardman Park/Omni Shoreham/Oct. 24 - 29, 2017

American Academy of Dermatology/March 4 - 8, 2016

American Academy of Esthetic Dentistry/The Ritz-Carlton/Aug. 7 - 10, 2013

American Academy of Forensic Sciences/Washington Marriott Wardman Park/ Feb. 18 - 23, 2013/over 100 exhibitors

American Academy of Neurology/April 18 - 25, 2015

American Academy of Nursing/Hyatt Regency on Capitol Hill/Oct. 17 - 19, 2013

American Academy of Physical Medicine and Rehabilitation/Gaylord National-Washington/Oct. 3 - 6, 2013

American Academy of Physician Assistants/May 25 - 30, 2013

American Academy of Sanitarians/July 9 - 11, 2013

American Anthropological Association/Washington Marriott Wardman Park/ Dec. 3 - 7, 2014

American Architectural Foundation/Andrew W. Mellon Auditorium/March 22, 2013

American Association for Cancer Research/Walter E. Washington Convention Center/April 6 - 10, 2013

American Association for Homecare/Capital Hilton/May 22 - 23, 2013

American Association for the Study of Liver Diseases/Nov. 1 - 5, 2013

American Association of Anatomists/April 22 - 26, 2017

American Association of Clinical Urologists/Hyatt Regency Washington on Capitol Hill/March 10 - 12, 2013

American Association of Colleges of Nursing/Fairmont Washington/March 16 - 19, 2013

American Association of Colleges of Nursing/Fairmont Washington/March 17 - 19, 2013

American Association of Colleges of Nursing/JW Marriott Washington, D.C./ Oct. 26 - 29, 2013

American Association of Colleges of Nursing/Fairmont Washington/March 22 - 25, 2014

American Association of Colleges of Nursing/JW Marriott Washington, D.C./ Oct. 25 - 28, 2014

American Association of Colleges of Nursing/Fairmont Washington/March 21 - 24, 2015

American Association of Colleges of Nursing/JW Marriott Washington, D.C./ Oct. 24 - 27, 2015

American Association of Colleges of Nursing/Fairmont Washington/March 19 - 22, 2016

American Association of Colleges of Nursing/JW Marriott Washington, D.C./ Oct. 29 - Nov. 1, 2016

American Association of Colleges of Nursing/Fairmont Washington/March 18 - 21, 2017

American Association of Colleges of Osteopathic Medicine/Capital Hilton/April 2 - 5, 2014

American Association of Community Colleges/Marriott Wardman Park Hotel/ Feb. 11 - 13, 2013

American Association of Community Colleges/Marriott Wardman Park Hotel/ Feb. 10 - 13, 2014

American Association of Community Colleges/Marriott Wardman Park/Omni Shoreham/April 5 - 8, 2014

American Association of Endodontists/Gaylord National Resort and Convention Center/April 30 - May 3, 2014/400 attendees/over 100 exhibitors

American Association of Exporters & Importers/June 16 - 18, 2013/11-25 exhibitors

American Association of Neurological Surgeons/May 2 - 6, 2015

American Association of Oral and Maxillofacial Surgeons/Renaissance Mayflower/April 16 - 17, 2013/140 attendees

American Association of Oral and Maxillofacial Surgeons/Walter E. Washington Convention Center/Sept. 28 - Oct. 3, 2015

American Association of Pharmaceutical Scientists/Washington Hilton/Nov. 3 - 8, 2018

American Association of Physicians of Indian Origin/April 4 - 6, 2013

American Association of Physicists in Medicine/July 31 - Aug. 4, 2016

American Association of Poison Control Centers/Crystal City Marriott at Reagan National Airport/Feb. 24 - 26, 2013

American Association of Political Consultants/Hyatt Regency Washington on Capitol Hill/April 3 - 5, 2013

American Association of Professional Landmen/Grand Hyatt Washington/June 5 - 8, 2013

American Association of University Professors/Mayflower Renaissance Hotel/ June 12 - 16, 2013

American Association of University Professors/Mayflower Renaissance Washington, D.C. Hotel/June 11 - 15, 2014

American Astronomical Society/Jan. 5 - 9, 2014

American Astronomical Society/Jan. 7 - 11, 2018

American Astronomical Society/Jan. 8 - 13, 2022

American Automatic Control Council/Renaissance Washington/June 17 - 19, 2013/1100 attendees

American Cable Association/Grand Hyatt Washington/March 12 - 15, 2013

American Catholic Historical Association/Jan. 2 - 5, 2014

American Clinical Laboratory Association/Grand Hyatt Washington/April 3 - 4, 2013

American College of Cardiology/Heart House/Feb. 8 - 9, 2013

American College of Emergency Physicians/Omni Shoreham/May 19 - 22, 2013

American College of Mohs Surgeons/Omni Shoreham/May 2 - 5, 2013
American College of Nurse Practitioners/The Westin Georgetown/Feb. 23 - 26, 2013
American College of Nurse-Midwives/June 25 - 30, 2015
American College of Nurse-Midwives/May 31 - June 5, 2019
American College of Physicians/May 5 - 7, 2016
American College of Radiology/Washington Hilton/May 4 - 8, 2013
American College of Surgeons/Mandarin Oriental Hotel/April 13 - 16, 2013
American College of Surgeons Professional Association/Mandarin Oriental Hotel/April 13 - 16, 2013
American College of Veterinary Internal Medicine/June 7 - 10, 2017
American Concrete Institute/Heart House/Oct. 26 - 30, 2014
American Concrete Pipe Association/Washington Marriott Wardman Park/Jan. 13 - 17, 2013
American Congress of Obstetricians and Gynecologists/March 3 - 5, 2013
American Correctional Association/Gaylord National-Washington/Aug. 9 - 14, 2013
American Council of Engineering Companies/George Washington University/April 21 - 24, 2013
American Council of Engineering Companies/George Washington University/April 27 - 30, 2014
American Council of Life Insurers (ACLI)/June 19 - 20, 2013
American Council on Education/Omni Shoreham Hotel/March 2 - 5, 2013
American Council on Education/Washington Hilton/March 14 - 17, 2015
American Cultural Resources Association (ACRA)/Hyatt Regency Washington/Oct. 10 - 13, 2013
American Dental Association/Walter E. Washington Convention Center/Nov. 5 - 10, 2015
American Diabetes Association/Omni Shoreham/March 5 - 7, 2013
American Education Finance Association/Marriott Wardman Park Hotel/Feb. 26 - 28, 2015
American Epilepsy Society/Walter E Washington Convention Center/Dec. 6 - 9, 2013
American Federation for Medical Research/Omni Shoreham Hotel/April 17 - 19, 2013
American Federation of Teachers (AFL-CIO)/Washington Marriott/July 22 - 24, 2013
American Gas Association/Washington Court Hotel/Nov. 11, 2013
American Health Care Association/Oct. 5 - 8, 2014
American Historical Association/Washington Marriott Wardman Park/Jan. 2 - 5, 2014
American Historical Association/Marriott Wardman Park/Omni Shoreham/Jan. 4 - 7, 2018
American Hospital Association/Heart House/April 28 - May 1, 2013
American Hospital Association/Heart House/May 4 - 7, 2014
American Intellectual Property Law Association/Washington Marriott/Oct. 24 - 26, 2013
American Intellectual Property Law Association/Washington Marriott/Oct. 23 - 25, 2014
American Library Association/Liaison Capitol Hill/May 7 - 8, 2013
American Medical Association/Grand Hyatt Washington/Feb. 11 - 13, 2013
American Medical Informatics Association/Washington Hilton/Nov. 16 - 20, 2013
American Medical Informatics Association/Washington Hilton/Nov. 15 - 19, 2014
American Medical Informatics Association/Washington Hilton/Nov. 4 - 8, 2017
American Medical Student Association/March 14 - 17, 2013/1-10 exhibitors
American Neurotology Society/Walter E. Washington Convention Center/April 12 - 14, 2013
American Nuclear Society/Omni Shoreham Hotel, Washington D.C./Nov. 10 - 14, 2013
American Nuclear Society/Omni Shoreham Hotel, Washington D.C./Nov. 8 - 12, 2015
American Nuclear Society/Omni Shoreham Hotel, Washington D.C./Nov. 12 - 16, 2017
American Osteopathic Association/March 14, 2013
American Osteopathic College of Anesthesiologists/Omni Shoreham Hotel/Sept. 22 - 25, 2013
American Payroll Association/Westin Hotels and Resorts/March 11 - 13, 2013
American Pediatric Society/May 4 - 7, 2013
American Physical Therapy Association/Liaison Capitol Hill/April 14 - 16, 2013/250 attendees
American Podiatric Medical Association/March 18 - 20, 2013
American Podiatric Medical Association/March 17 - 19, 2014
American Political Science Association/Washington Marriott Wardman Park/Aug. 28 - 31, 2014
American Public Power Association/Grand Hyatt Washington/March 11 - 14, 2013
American Real Estate and Urban Economics Association/NAHB headquarters/May 30 - 31, 2013
American Resort Development Association/Fairmont Hotel/Nov. 13 - 15, 2013
American Risk and Insurance Association/Washington Court Hotel on Capitol Hill/Aug. 4 - 7, 2013
American Roentgen Ray Society/Washington Marriott Wardman Park/April 14 - 19, 2013
American Seniors Housing Association/Park Hyatt Washington/April 25 - 26, 2013
American Short Line and Regional Railroad Association/Renaissance Washington/March 14, 2013
American Short Line and Regional Railroad Association/Renaissance Washington/March 13, 2014
American Small Manufacturers' Coalition/Grand Hyatt Washington/March 5 - 6, 2013
American Society for Investigative Pathology/April 21 - 25, 2017
American Society for Mohs Histotechnology/Omni Shoreham/May 3 - 4, 2013
American Society for Pharmacology and Experimental Therapeutics/April 22 - 26, 2017
The American Society for Public Administration/Mayflower Renaissance Hotel/March 14 - 18, 2014

American Society for Therapeutic Radiology and Oncology/Washington Marriott at Metro Center/April 29 - 30, 2013
American Society for Training and Development/May 4 - 7, 2014
American Society of Anesthesiologists/JW Marriott Washington, D.C./April 29 - May 1, 2013
American Society of Anesthesiologists/JW Marriott Washington, D.C./May 5 - 7, 2014
American Society of Anesthesiologists/JW Marriott Washington, D.C./May 4 - 6, 2015
American Society of Association Executives-The Center for Association Leadership/Walter E. Washington Convention Center/May 16, 2013
American Society of Association Executives-The Center for Association Leadership/Walter E. Washington Convention Center/June 4 - 5, 2013
American Society of Criminology/Washington Hilton/Nov. 18 - 21, 2015
American Society of Criminology/Washington Hilton/Nov. 18 - 21, 2020
American Society of Dermatopathology/Washington Marriott Wardman Park/Oct. 3 - 6, 2013
The American Society of Forensic Odontology/Marriot Wardham Park/Feb. 19, 2013
American Society of Gene & Cell Therapy/May 21 - 24, 2014
American Society of International Law/Marriott Renaissance Hotel/April 3 - 6, 2013/1200 attendees
American Society of International Law/April 7 - 12, 2014
American Society of News Editors/Jurys Washington Hotel/April 14 - 17, 2013
American Society of Pediatric Nephrology/May 4 - 7, 2013
American Society of Podiatry Executives/JW Marriott Hotel - Washington/March 15, 2013
American Society of Tropical Medicine and Hygiene/Washington Marriott Wardman Park/Nov. 13 - 17, 2013
American Society on Aging/Washington Marriott Wardman Park/March 20 - 24, 2016
American Staffing Association/Oct. 8 - 11, 2013
American Student Dental Association/April 15 - 16, 2013
American Studies Association/Hilton Washington/Nov. 21 - 24, 2013
American Supply Association/Renaissance Washington, D.C. Downtown Hotel/Oct. 2 - 4, 2013
American Thoracic Society/May 17 - 24, 2017
American Thoracic Society/May 19 - 24, 2017
American Waterways Operators/Mandarin Oriental Washington D.C./April 16 - 19, 2013
APPAM - The Association for Public Policy Analysis and Management/Washington Marriott/Nov. 7 - 9, 2013
Appraisal Institute/L'Enfant Plaza Hotel/May 21 - 23, 2013
Armed Forces Communications and Electronics Association/Defense Intelligence Analysis Center/April 17 - 18, 2013
Associated Builders and Contractors/Capital Hilton/June 11 - 13, 2013
Associated Builders and Contractors/Capital Hilton/June 10 - 12, 2014
Association for Advanced Life Underwriting/Washington Marriott Wardman Park/April 28 - May 1, 2013
Association for Clinical Research Training/Omni Shoreham Hotel/April 17 - 19, 2013
Association for Convention Marketing Executives/Carnegie Library/March 12 - 13, 2013
Association for Demand Response & Smart Grid/Ronald Reagan Building and International Trade Center/July 9 - 11, 2013
Association for Education in Journalism and Mass Communication/Renaissance Washington/Aug. 8 - 11, 2013
Association for Hose and Accessories Distribution/Gaylord National Resort and Convention Center/April 20 - 24, 2013
Association for Psychological Science/Washington Marriott Wardman Park/May 23 - 26, 2013/11-25 exhibitors
Association for Supervision and Curriculum Development (ASCD)/National Harbor Marina/June 28 - 30, 2013
Association for the Study of Higher Education/Washington Hilton/Nov. 19 - 22, 2014
Association for Unmanned Vehicle Systems International/Walter E. Washington Convention Center/Aug. 13 - 16, 2013/8000 attendees/over 100 exhibitors
Association for Vascular Access/Gaylord National-Washington/Sept. 7 - 10, 2014
Association Foundation Group/FHI 360 Conference Center/May 9, 2013
Association of Academic Health Centers/Fairmont Hotel/April 22 - 23, 2013
Association of Air Medical Services/March 13, 2013
Association of American Cancer Institutes/May 16, 2013
Association of American Cancer Institutes/Sept. 29 - Oct. 1, 2013
Association of American Colleges and Universities/Jan. 22 - 24, 2014
Association of American Colleges and Universities/Jan. 22 - 25, 2014/1800 attendees
Association of American Colleges and Universities/Jan. 21 - 24, 2015/1800 attendees
Association of American Colleges and Universities/Jan. 20 - 23, 2016/1800 attendees
Association of American Law Schools/Jan. 2 - 6, 2015
Association of American State Geologists/March 10 - 13, 2013
Association of Catholic Colleges and Universities/Ritz-Carlton Hotel Company, L.L.C./Feb. 2 - 4, 2013
Association of Chiropractic Colleges/March 14 - 16, 2013
Association of Chiropractic Colleges/March 14 - 16, 2014
Association of College and University Housing Officers-International/June 28 - July 1, 2014
Association of Community Cancer Centers/Washington Marriott Wardman Park/March 6 - 8, 2013
Association of Community College Trustees/Feb. 11 - 14, 2013
Association of Community College Trustees/Feb. 10 - 13, 2014
Association of Independent Research Institutes/Sept. 8 - 11, 2013
Association of International Education Administrators/JW Marriott Washington, D.C./Feb. 16 - 19, 2014
Association of International Education Administrators/JW Marriott Washington, D.C./Feb. 15 - 18, 2015
Association of Latino Professionals in Finance and Accounting/Aug. 3 - 7, 2013

Association of Maternal and Child Health Programs (AMCHP)/Omni Shoreham Hotel/Feb. 9 - 12, 2013

Association of Metropolitan Water Agencies/Washington Court Hotel/March 17 - 20, 2013

Association of Old Crows/Marriott Wardman Park Hotel/Oct. 27 - 30, 2013

Association of Procurement Technical Assistance Centers/Hyatt Regency Washington/Nov. 11 - 13, 2013

Association of Procurement Technical Assistance Centers/Hyatt Regency Washington/Nov. 10 - 12, 2014

Association of Progressive Rental Organizations/L'Enfant Plaza Hotel/April 14 - 16, 2013

Association of Public and Land-Grant Universities (APLU)/Washington Marriott Wardman Park/Nov. 10 - 12, 2013

Association of Research Libraries/Oct. 8 - 11, 2013

Association of Schools of Journalism and Mass Communication/Renaissance Washington/Aug. 8 - 11, 2013

Association of Specialized and Professional Accreditors/March 30 - April 1, 2014

Association of Specialized and Professional Accreditors/March 29 - 30, 2015

Association of Specialized and Professional Accreditors/April 3 - 5, 2016

Association of Specialized and Professional Accreditors/April 8 - 10, 2018

Association of State and Provincial Psychology Boards/Aug. 7 - 10, 2014

Association of State Energy Research and Technology Transfer Institution/Fairmont Hotel/Feb. 5 - 8, 2013

Association of Teacher Educators/Hyatt Regency Capitol Hill/Aug. 2 - 6, 2013

Association of the United States Army/Walter E. Washington Convention Center/Oct. 21 - 23, 2013

Association of the United States Army/Walter E. Washington Convention Center/Oct. 13 - 15, 2014

Association of the United States Army/Walter E. Washington Convention Center/Oct. 12 - 14, 2015

Association of the United States Army/Walter E. Washington Convention Center/Oct. 10 - 12, 2016

Association of the United States Army/Walter E. Washington Convention Center/Oct. 9 - 11, 2017

Association of the United States Army/Walter E. Washington Convention Center/Oct. 8 - 10, 2018

Association of the United States Army/Walter E. Washington Convention Center/Oct. 14 - 16, 2019

Association of the United States Army/Walter E. Washington Convention Center/Oct. 12 - 14, 2020

Association of University Centers on Disabilities (AUCD)/Washington, DC, Renaissance Hotel/Nov. 16 - 20, 2013

Association of University Centers on Disabilities (AUCD)/Washington, DC, Renaissance Hotel/Nov. 9 - 12, 2014

Association of Writers and Writing Programs/Washington Convention Center and Washington Marriott Marquis/Feb. 8 - 11, 2017

Board of Specialty Society/April 30 - May 5, 2013

Board of Specialty Society/April 29 - May 4, 2014

Board of Specialty Society/April 28 - May 3, 2015

Board of Specialty Society/May 4 - 7, 2016

Board of Specialty Society/April 26 - 29, 2017

Brake Manufacturers Council/April 10 - 12, 2013

The Brewers Association/Washington Convention Center/March 26 - 29, 2013

Building Owners and Managers Association International/Feb. 3 - 6, 2014

Building Owners and Managers Association International/June 26 - 28, 2016

Business Higher Education Forum/Feb. 21 - 22, 2013

Business Higher Education Forum/June 10 - 11, 2013

Catholic Health Association of the United States/Washington Marriott Wardman Park/June 7 - 9, 2015

Child Welfare League of America/Hyatt Regency Crystal City at Reagan National Airport/April 14 - 17, 2013

The Coalition for America's Gateways and Trade Corridors/April 9 - 10, 2013

Commercial Finance Association/Washington Marriott Wardman Park/Nov. 12 - 14, 2014

NAIOP, The Commercial Real Estate Development Association/Capital Hilton/Feb. 11 - 14, 2013

NAIOP, The Commercial Real Estate Development Association/Capital Hilton/Feb. 10 - 13, 2014

Communications Workers of America/May 6 - 8, 2014

Conference on English Education/Nov. 20 - 23, 2014

Conference on Latin American History/Jan. 2 - 5, 2014

Congressional Internet Caucus Advisory Committee/Hyatt Regency Hotel/Jan. 22 - 23, 2013

Consortium of School Networking/Washington Hilton/March 18 - 20, 2014

Construction Industry Round Table, Inc./Fairmont Washington/April 30 - May 2, 2013

Construction Management Association of America/Hilton/Oct. 8 - 10, 2017/1000 attendees

The Corps Network (formerly the National Association of Service and Conservation Corps)/Washington Court Hotel/Feb. 12 - 15, 2013

Council for Advancement and Support of Education/Gaylord National Hotel and Convention Center/Jan. 13 - 15, 2013

Council for Advancement and Support of Education/Crowne Plaza/Feb. 6 - 8, 2013

Council for Christian Colleges and Universities/Jan. 30 - Feb. 1, 2013/11-25 exhibitors

Council for European Studies/March 14 - 16, 2014

Council for Opportunity in Education/Renaissance Washington, D.C. Downtown Hotel/March 10 - 12, 2013

Council for Resource Development/Hyatt Regency Washington on Capitol Hill/Nov. 4 - 11, 2013

Council for Resource Development/Hyatt Regency Washington on Capitol Hill/Nov. 3 - 10, 2014

Council of Chief State School Officers/Washington Marriott at Metro Center/March 17 - 19, 2013

Council of Colleges of Arts and Sciences/Washington Hilton/Nov. 4 - 7, 2015

Council of Development Finance Agencies/Aug. 6 - 9, 2013

Council of Institutional Investors/Capital Hilton/April 17 - 19, 2013

The Council of Insurance Agents and Brokers/Mandarin Oriental Hotel/Feb. 5 - 7, 2013

The Council of Insurance Agents and Brokers/Mandarin Oriental Hotel/Feb. 4 - 6, 2014

Council of Medical Specialty Societies/Washington Court Hotel/Nov. 22 - 23, 2013

Council of the Great City Schools/Mayflower Renaissance Hotel/March 9 - 12, 2013

Council on Anthropology and Education/Marriott Wardman Park and Omni Shoreham/Dec. 3 - 7, 2014

Council on Governmental Relations/Washington Marriott/Feb. 21 - 23, 2013

Council on Governmental Relations/Washington Marriott/June 6 - 7, 2013

Credit Union National Association, Inc./Washington Hilton/Feb. 24 - 28, 2013

Credit Union National Association, Inc./Washington Hilton/Feb. 23 - 27, 2014

Direct Marketing Association Nonprofit Federation/Renaissance/Feb. 7 - 8, 2013

Direct Marketing Association Nonprofit Federation/Renaissance/Feb. 13 - 14, 2014

Division 1-A Athletic Directors Association/Jan. 14 - 17, 2015

Drug Information Association/June 14 - 18, 2015/8000 attendees/over 100 exhibitors

Education Finance Council/Washington Marriott at Metro Center/July 11 - 12, 2013

Education Industry Association/Liasion Hotel/Feb. 20 - 22, 2013

Electric Drive Transportation Association/Washington Marriott Wardman Park/June 11 - 12, 2013

Employee Stock Ownership Plan Association/Renaissance Washington Hotel/May 9 - 10, 2013

Employers Council on Flexible Compensation/Hyatt Regency Washington on Capitol Hill/March 6 - 8, 2013

Family, Career and Community Leaders of America/July 5 - 9, 2015

Federal Bar Association/Ronald Reagan Building and International Trade Center /March 1, 2013

Federal Managers Association/Mayflower Renaissance Hotel/March 3 - 6, 2013

Federation of American Hospitals/Washington Marriott Wardman Park/March 3 - 5, 2013/26-50 exhibitors

Federation of American Hospitals/Washington Marriott Wardman Park/March 2 - 4, 2014/26-50 exhibitors

Federation of American Hospitals/Washington Marriott Wardman Park/March 1 - 3, 2015/26-50 exhibitors

Financial Industry Regulatory Authority (FINRA)/Renaissance Washington/May 20 - 22, 2013

Food and Drug Law Institute/Jan. 28 - 31, 2013

Food and Drug Law Institute/April 23 - 24, 2013

Genetics Society of America/Washington Marriott Wardman Park/April 3 - 7, 2013/2000 attendees/51-100 exhibitors

Geosynthetic Materials Association/Sept. 12 - 13, 2013

Gerontological Society of America/Nov. 5 - 9, 2014

Health Industry Distributors Association/Gaylord National-Washington/Sept. 25 - 27, 2013

Healthcare Supply Chain Association/Oct. 16 - 18, 2013

Heating, Airconditioning and Refrigeration Distributors International/Hyatt Regency Washington on Capitol Hill/May 22 - 23, 2013

Hispanic Association of Colleges and Universities/Westin Washington, D.C. City Center/April 15 - 16, 2013

Hispanic Elected Local Officials/Washington Marriott Wardman Park/March 9 - 13, 2013

Hispanic Elected Local Officials/Washington Marriott Wardman Park/March 8 - 12, 2014

Historians of American Communism/Washington Marriott/Jan. 2 - 5, 2014

Human Factors and Ergonomics Society/Washington Marriott Wardman Park/Sept. 19 - 23, 2016/1500 attendees

Human Factors Society/Washington Hilton/Sept. 19 - 23, 2016

IEEE Control Systems Society/Renaissance Washington, D.C. Downtown Hotel/June 17 - 19, 2013

IEEE Power and Energy Society/Feb. 24 - 28, 2013

Independent Insurance Agents & Brokers of America, Inc./Grand Hyatt Washington/April 17 - 19, 2013

Independent Insurance Agents & Brokers of America, Inc./Hyatt Regency Washington on Capitol Hill/April 9 - 11, 2014

Independent Insurance Agents & Brokers of America, Inc./Hyatt Regency Washington on Capitol Hill/April 22 - 24, 2015

Independent Insurance Agents & Brokers of America, Inc./Renaissance Washington, D.C. Downtown Hotel/April 13 - 15, 2016

Industrial Research Institute/Omni Shoreham Hotel, Washington D.C./May 21 - 23, 2013

Industrial Truck Association/Four Seasons Hotel Washington, D.C./March 11 - 13, 2013

Institute of International Bankers/Four Seasons Hotel Washington, D.C./March 3 - 5, 2013

Institute of Real Estate Management/Omni Shoreham Hotel, Washington D.C./April 6 - 10, 2013

Institute of Real Estate Management/Omni Shoreham Hotel, Washington D.C./April 5 - 9, 2014

Institute of Real Estate Management/Omni Shoreham Hotel/April 11 - 15, 2015

Insurance Accounting and Systems Association/Gaylord National Hotel and Convention Center/June 2 - 5, 2013

Insured Retirement Institute/Washington Hilton/Feb. 16 - 19, 2013

International Association of Attorneys and Executives in Corporate Real Estate/April 25 - 27, 2013

International Association of Fire Fighters/March 17 - 20, 2013

International Association of Fire Fighters/March 17 - 21, 2013

International Association of Fire Fighters/March 16 - 19, 2014

International Association of Privacy Professionals/March 6 - 8, 2013

International Card Manufacturers Association/Washington Marriott Wardman Park/June 4 - 7, 2013/11-25 exhibitors

International Foodservice Distributors Association/Hyatt Regency Washington on Capitol Hill/April 17 - 18, 2013

International Franchise Association/JW Marriott Washington, D.C./May 5 - 7, 2013

International Franchise Association/OW Marriott/May 7 - 8, 2013

International Franchise Association/Jurys Washington Hotel/Sept. 15 - 18, 2013

International Franchise Association/JW Marriott Washington, D.C./May 15 - 17, 2016

International Health, Racquet and Sportsclub Association/Top of the Hill Conference Center/May 14 - 15, 2013

International Lactation Consultant Association/Washington Marriott Wardman Park/July 22 - 25, 2015

International Museum Theatre Alliance/Smithsonian Institution/Oct. 6 - 10, 2013

International Nurses Society on Addictions/Madison Hotel/Oct. 9 - 12, 2013

International Nurses Society on Addictions/Madison Hotel/Oct. 15 - 18, 2014

International Society for Pharmaceutical Engineering/Washington Marriott Wardman Park/Nov. 3 - 6, 2013

International Society for Pharmacoeconomics and Outcomes Research/May 21 - 25, 2016

Investment Program Association/Capital Hilton/May 8 - 9, 2013

Investment Program Association/April 2 - 3, 2014

Journalism Education Association/Nov. 6 - 9, 2014

Latin American Studies Association/Washington Marriott Wardman Park/May 29 - June 1, 2013

LeadingAge (American Association of Homes and Services for the Aging)/ Washington Marriott Wardman Park/March 18 - 20, 2013

LeadingAge (American Association of Homes and Services for the Aging)/ Washington Marriott Wardman Park/March 17 - 19, 2014

Linguistic Society of America/Washington Marriott Marquis/Jan. 7 - 10, 2016/1000 attendees

Magnet Schools of America/The Hamilton Crowne Plaza Hotel/Feb. 3 - 6, 2013

Management Association for Private Photogrammetric Surveyors/Westin Washington, D.C. City Center/March 12 - 13, 2013

Mathematical Association of America/Aug. 5 - 8, 2015

Medical Device Manufacturers Association/JW Marriott Hotel - Washington/ May 21 - 23, 2013

Middle East Librarians' Association/Washington Marriott/Nov. 22 - 25, 2014

Middle East Librarians' Association/Washington Marriott/Nov. 18 - 21, 2017

Middle East Studies Association of North America/Washington Marriott Wardman Park/Nov. 22 - 25, 2014

Middle East Studies Association of North America/Washington Marriott Wardman Park/Nov. 18 - 21, 2017

NAFSA: Association of International Educators/May 26 - 31, 2019

National Academy of Elder Law Attorneys, Inc./Omni Shoreham Hotel, Washington D.C./Nov. 5 - 9, 2013

National Affordable Housing Management Association/Fairmont Washington/ March 24 - 26, 2013

National Affordable Housing Management Association/Fairmont Washington/ Oct. 27 - 29, 2013

National Affordable Housing Management Association/Washington Court Hotel/March 9 - 11, 2014

National Affordable Housing Management Association/Fairmont Washington/ Oct. 26 - 28, 2014

National Apartment Association/Omni Shoreham/March 10 - 13, 2013

National Association for Business Economics/Washington Court Hotel/March 3 - 5, 2013

National Association for Olmsted Parks/National Building Museum/March 27 - 28, 2014

National Association for Proton Therapy/The Washington Marriott Hotel/Feb. 11 - 14, 2013

National Association for the Support of Long Term Care/The Madison Hotel/ Feb. 11 - 13, 2013

National Association of Area Agencies on Aging/April 22 - 23, 2013

National Association of Certified Valuation Analysts/June 5 - 8, 2013

National Association of Chain Drug Stores/Liaison Capitol Hill/March 13 - 14, 2013/300 attendees

National Association of Chapter Thirteen Trustees (NACTT)/The Mayflower Renaissance/Jan. 23 - 25, 2014

National Association of Church Business Administration/Gaylord National-Washington/July 3 - 7, 2017

National Association of City and County Health Officials/Omni Shoreham Hotel/July 10 - 12, 2013

National Association of Counties/Washington Hilton/March 2 - 6, 2013

National Association of Counties/Washington Hilton/March 1 - 5, 2014

National Association of Counties/Washington Marriott Wardman Park/Feb. 21 - 25, 2015

National Association of Counties/Washington Marriott Wardman Park/Feb. 20 - 24, 2016

National Association of Counties/Washington Marriott Wardman Park/Feb. 25 - March 1, 2017

National Association of County Civil Attorneys/Washington Hilton/March 2 - 6, 2013

National Association of County Recorders, Election Officials and Clerks/ Washington Marriott/March 2 - 3, 2013

National Association of EMS Educators/Omni Shoreham Hotel/Aug. 5 - 10, 2013

National Association of Federal Credit Unions/Mayflower Renaissance Hotel/ Sept. 11 - 14, 2013

National Association of Federally Impacted Schools/Hyatt Regency Bethesda, near Washington, D.C./March 3 - 5, 2013

National Association of Foreign Trade Zones/Madison Hotel/Feb. 12 - 13, 2013/90 attendees

National Association of Housing and Redevelopment Officials/Renaissance Washington, D.C. Downtown Hotel/March 17 - 20, 2013

National Association of Independent Colleges and Universities/Hyatt Regency Bethesda, near Washington, D.C./Feb. 3 - 6, 2013

National Association of Independent Colleges and Universities/Washington Court Hotel/Nov. 13 - 15, 2013

National Association of Independent Colleges and Universities/Hyatt Regency Bethesda, near Washington, D.C./Feb. 2 - 5, 2014

National Association of Insurance Commissioners/Washington Marriott/Oct. 28 - 31, 2013

National Association of Pastoral Musicians/Marriott Wardman Park Hotel/July 29 - Aug. 3, 2013/1-10 exhibitors

National Association of Police Organizations/May 13 - 14, 2013

National Association of Psychiatric Health Systems/Mandarin Oriental Washington D.C./March 11 - 13, 2013

National Association of Public Hospitals and Health Systems/March 19 - 20, 2013

National Association of Realtors/May 13 - 18, 2013

National Association of Realtors/May 15 - 17, 2013

National Association of Realtors/May 12 - 17, 2014

National Association of Realtors/May 14 - 16, 2014

National Association of Realtors/May 11 - 17, 2015

National Association of Realtors/May 13 - 15, 2015

National Association of Realtors/May 9 - 14, 2016

National Association of Realtors/May 11 - 13, 2016

National Association of Realtors/May 15 - 20, 2017

National Association of Realtors/May 17 - 19, 2017

National Association of Realtors/May 14 - 19, 2018

National Association of Realtors/May 16 - 18, 2018

National Association of Realtors/May 13 - 15, 2019

National Association of Realtors/May 15 - 17, 2019

National Association of Regional Councils/Feb. 10 - 12, 2013

National Association of Rehabilitation Providers and Agencies/Renaissance Washington, D.C. Downtown Hotel/May 15 - 17, 2013

National Association of Retail Collection Attorneys/Washington, DC, Renaissance Hotel/Oct. 16 - 19, 2013

National Association of School Psychologists/Marriott Wardman Park/Omni Shoreham/Feb. 18 - 23, 2014

National Association of Secretaries of State/JW Marriott Hotel - Washington/ Jan. 24 - 27, 2013

National Association of State Chief Information Officers/Capital Hilton/April 28 - May 1, 2013

National Association of State Election Directors/JW Marriott Hotel - Washington/Jan. 24 - 26, 2013

National Association of State Energy Officials/Fairmont Hotel/Feb. 5 - 8, 2013

National Association of State Energy Officials/Fairmont Hotel/Feb. 4 - 7, 2014

National Association of State Personnel Executives/The Dupont Circle Hotel/ Jan. 25 - 27, 2013

National Association of State Student Grant and Aid Programs/Hilton Garden Inn/Oct. 15 - 18, 2013

National Association of State Treasurers/Mandarin Oriental Hotel/March 18 - 20, 2013

National Association of Student Financial Aid Administrators/March 10 - 12, 2013

National Association of Student Financial Aid Administrators/March 9 - 11, 2014

National Association of Student Financial Aid Administrators/July 10 - 13, 2016

National Association of Veterans Research and Education Foundations/ Washington Marriott Wardman Park/Sept. 14 - 17, 2014

National Association of Wholesaler-Distributors/Fairmont Washington/Jan. 29 - 31, 2013

National Athletic Trainers Association/Feb. 25, 2013

National Beer Wholesalers Association/Hyatt Regency Washington on Capitol Hill/April 14 - 17, 2013

National Beer Wholesalers Association/Hyatt Regency Washington on Capitol Hill/March 23 - 26, 2014

National Black Association for Speech, Language and Hearing/L'Enfant Plaza Hotel/April 18 - 21, 2013

National Braille Association/Hilton Washington DC North/Gaithersburg/April 18 - 20, 2013

National Cable & Telecommunications Association/June 10 - 12, 2013

National Child Support Enforcement Association/Washington Court Hotel/Feb. 7 - 9, 2013

National Collegiate Athletic Association/Jan. 14 - 17, 2015

National Community Pharmacists Association/Gaylord National Harbor/Oct. 10 - 14, 2013

National Conference of Insurance Legislators/Hyatt Regency Washington on Capitol Hill/March 8 - 10, 2013

National Conference on Public Employee Retirement Systems/Capital Hilton Hotel/Jan. 27 - 29, 2013

National Contract Management Association/Gaylord National Harbor/July 27 - 30, 2014

National Cotton Council of America/JW Marriott Washington, D.C./Feb. 6 - 9, 2014

National Council for Community Behavioral Healthcare/Gaylord Hotel/May 5 - 7, 2014

National Council for Geographic Education/JW Marriott Washington, D.C./ Aug. 6 - 9, 2015

National Council for Science and the Environment/Ronald Reagan Building and International Trade Center/Jan. 15 - 17, 2013

National Council for the Social Studies/Walter E. Washington Convention Center/Dec. 2 - 4, 2016

National Council of Agricultural Employers/Hotel Monaco Washington D.C./ Feb. 5 - 6, 2013

National Council of Farmer Cooperatives/L'Enfant Plaza Hotel/June 10 - 12, 2013

National Council of State Housing Agencies/Marriott Hotel - Washington/Jan. 13 - 18, 2013

National Council of State Housing Agencies/Hyatt Regency Washington on Capitol Hill/March 4 - 6, 2013

National Council of State Housing Agencies/JW Marriott Hotel - Washington/ Jan. 12 - 17, 2014

National Council of State Housing Agencies/Hyatt Regency Washington on Capitol Hill/March 3 - 5, 2014

National Council of State Housing Agencies/JW Marriott Washington, D.C./ Jan. 11 - 16, 2015

National Council of State Housing Agencies/Hyatt Regency Washington on Capitol Hill/March 2 - 4, 2015

National Council of Teachers of English/Nov. 20 - 23, 2014/1-10 exhibitors

National Council of University Research Administrators/Aug. 4 - 7, 2013

National Council on Teacher Retirement/Omni Shoreham Hotel, Washington D.C./Oct. 5 - 9, 2013

National Defense Transportation Association/Sept. 19 - 23, 2015

National Defense Transportation Association/Sept. 26 - 30, 2015

National Dental Hygienists' Association/July 17 - 23, 2013

National Education Association/July 3 - 8, 2016

National Electrical Contractors Association/Oct. 12 - 15, 2013

National Electrical Contractors Association/Walter E. Washington Convention Center/Oct. 12 - 15, 2013

The National Flute Association, Inc./Washington Marriott/Aug. 13 - 15, 2015

National Grocers Association/Hyatt Regency on Capitol Hill/April 17 - 18, 2013

National Head Start Association/Omni Shoreham Hotel/Jan. 28 - Feb. 1, 2013

National Hispanic Medical Association/Marriott Wardman Park Hotel/April 25 - 28, 2013

National Housing and Rehabilitation Association/Hyatt Regency Hotel/April 2 - 3, 2013

National Humanities Alliance/The George Washington University campus and Capitol Hill./March 18 - 19, 2013

National Hydropower Association/Capitol Hilton/April 22 - 24, 2013

National Institute of Building Sciences/Washington Marriott at Metro Center/Jan. 7 - 10, 2013/1-10 exhibitors

National Institute for Water Resources/Feb. 11 - 13, 2013

National League for Nursing/Washington Marriott/Sept. 18 - 21, 2013

National League of Cities/March 9 - 13, 2013

National League of Cities/March 8 - 12, 2014

National Leased Housing Association/The Washington Marriott Hotel/June 19 - 21, 2013

National Leased Housing Association/The Washington Marriott Hotel/June 18 - 20, 2014

National Migrant and Seasonal Head Start Association/Gaylord National Resort and Convention Center/April 28 - May 3, 2013

National Ocean Industries Association/The Ritz-Carlton/April 17 - 19, 2013

National Ocean Industries Association/Mandarin Oriental Washington D.C./April 9 - 11, 2014

National Ocean Industries Association/The Ritz-Carlton/April 15 - 17, 2015

National Organization of Social Security Claimants' Representatives/The JW Marriott/May 15 - 18, 2013

National Potato Council/Madison Hotel/Feb. 25 - 28, 2013

National Potato Council/Madison Hotel/Feb. 24 - 27, 2014

National Recreation and Parks Association/Grand Hyatt Washington/March 19 - 21, 2013

National Restaurant Association/April 17 - 18, 2013

National Scholastic Press Association/Marriott Wardman Park Hotel/Nov. 6 - 9, 2014

National Sheriffs' Association/JW Marriott Washington, D.C./Jan. 30 - Feb. 2, 2013

National Sheriffs' Association/JW Marriott Washington, D.C./Jan. 22 - 25, 2014

National Sheriffs' Association/JW Marriott Washington, D.C./Jan. 21 - 24, 2015

National Society for Histotechnology/Aug. 28 - Sept. 2, 2015

National Speakers Association/Marriott Wardman Park Hotel/July 18 - 21, 2015

National Telecommunications Cooperative Association/Hyatt Regency Capitol Hill/April 21 - 24, 2013

National Telecommunications Cooperative Association/Hyatt on Capitol Hill/April 6 - 9, 2014

National Telecommunications Cooperative Association/Hyatt on Capitol Hill/April 19 - 22, 2015

National Water Resources Association/Washington Court Hotel/April 15 - 17, 2013

National Water Resources Association/Washington Court Hotel/March 31 - April 2, 2014

National Water Resources Association/Washington Court Hotel/April 13 - 15, 2015

National Water Resources Association/Washington Court Hotel/April 11 - 13, 2016

National Waterways Conference/The Madison/March 11 - 13, 2013

Nonprofit Technology Network/March 13 - 15, 2014/11-25 exhibitors

North American Association of Commencement Officers/Mayflower Renaissance Hotel/Feb. 17 - 19, 2013

North American Catalysis Society/March 16 - 20, 2014

North American Menopause Society/Gaylord National-Washington/Oct. 15 - 18, 2014

North American Millers' Association/Hotel Sofitel Washington D.C. Lafayette Square/Oct. 28 - 30, 2013

North American Society for Trenchless Technology/Gaylord National Hotel and Convention Center/April 9 - 13, 2017

Nuclear Energy Institute/Grand Hyatt Washington/May 20 - 22, 2013

Oncology Nursing Society/April 25 - 28, 2013

The Open Group/July 15 - 18, 2013

Pediatric Endocrine Society/May 4 - 7, 2013

Pension Real Estate Association/March 13, 2013

Pension Real Estate Association/March 14 - 15, 2013

Petroleum Marketers Association of America/Washington Court Hotel/May 15 - 17, 2013

Population Association of America/Marriott Wardman Park Hotel/March 31 - April 2, 2016

Precast/Prestressed Concrete Institute/Gaylord National-Washington/Sept. 6 - 10, 2014

Property Records Industry Association/The Washington Marriott Hotel/Feb. 27 - March 1, 2013

Public Housing Authorities Directors Association/Washington Court Hotel/Sept. 8 - 10, 2013

Public Lands Council/April 15 - 16, 2013

RESPRO (Real Estate Services Providers Council)/March 25 - 27, 2013

RTCA, Inc./Washington Convention Center/June 5 - 6, 2013

School Nutrition Association/JW Marriott Washington, D.C./March 3 - 6, 2013

Schools Interoperability Framework Association/Sheraton Crystal City Hotel/Jan. 15 - 17, 2013

Soccer Industry Council of America/Capitol Hill/March 12 - 13, 2013

Society for College and University Planning/July 8 - 12, 2017

Society for Imaging Informatics in Medicine/Gaylord National Resort and Convention Center/May 28 - 31, 2015

Society for Imaging Informatics in Medicine/Gaylord National Resort and Convention Center/May 30 - June 2, 2019

Society for Imaging Science and Technology/April 2 - 5, 2013

Society for Italian Historical Studies/Washington Marriott Wardman Park/Jan. 2 - 5, 2014

Society for Italian Historical Studies/Marriott Wardman Park and Omni Shoreham/Jan. 4 - 7, 2018

Society for Laboratory Automation and Screening/Feb. 7 - 11, 2015

Society for Laboratory Automation and Screening/Feb. 4 - 8, 2017

Society for Laboratory Automation and Screening/Feb. 2 - 6, 2019

Society for Pediatric Dermatology/March 3, 2016

Society for Pediatric Dermatology/Feb. 28, 2019

Society for Pediatric Radiology/JW Marriott Washington, D.C./May 13 - 17, 2014

Society for Pediatric Research/Walter E Washington Convention Center/May 4 - 7, 2013

Society for Public Health Education/March 2 - 4, 2013

Society for Technological Advancement of Reporting/Liaison Capitol Hill/Oct. 3 - 5, 2013

Society of American Business Editors and Writers/The George Washington University/April 4 - 6, 2013

Society of Behavioral Medicine/Washington Hilton/March 30 - April 2, 2016

Society of Independent Gasoline Marketers of America (SIGMA)/Embassy Suites Washington D.C./July 16 - 17, 2013

Society of Infectious Diseases Pharmacists/Sept. 5 - 8, 2014

Society of International Business Fellows/St. Regis Washington, D.C./May 5 - 7, 2013

Society of Mexican American Engineers and Scientists/Feb. 13 - 16, 2013

Society of Professional Asset-Managers and Record Keepers/The Mandarin Oriental/June 16 - 18, 2013

Society of Professors of Child and Adolescent Psychiatry/Hyatt Regency Washington on Capitol Hill/May 9 - 11, 2013

Society of Surgical Oncology/March 7 - 10, 2013/1500 attendees/over 100 exhibitors

Society of Toxicologic Pathologists/Marriott Wardman Park Hotel/June 22 - 26, 2014

Society of Toxicologic Pathology/Washington Marriott Wardman Park/June 22 - 26, 2014

State Education Technology Directors Association/April 10 - 13, 2013

Tax Executives Institute, Inc./Grand Hyatt Washington/March 17 - 20, 2013

Telecommunications Industry Association/Gaylord National-Washington/Oct. 8 - 10, 2013

Textile Rental Services Association of America/Fairmont Hotel/March 17, 2013

Toxicology Forum/Jan. 29 - 31, 2013

Transportation Development Association/Grand Hyatt Washington/April 10 - 11, 2013

Turnaround Management Association/Marriott Wardman Park Hotel/Oct. 3 - 5, 2013

United States Chamber of Commerce/Capitol Hill/April 29 - May 1, 2013

United States Conference of Mayors/Jan. 17 - 19, 2013

United States Wheat Associates, Inc./Hyatt Regency Washington on Capitol Hill/Jan. 27 - 30, 2013

United States Wheat Associates, Inc./Hyatt Regency Washington on Capitol Hill/Jan. 29 - Feb. 1, 2014

University Council for Educational Administration/Washington Hilton/Nov. 20 - 24, 2014/1-10 exhibitors

USENIX: The Advanced Computing Systems Association/Nov. 3 - 8, 2013

USENIX: The Advanced Computing Systems Association/Dec. 6 - 11, 2015

Winegrape Growers of America/Holiday Inn Capitol/March 17 - 20, 2013

FLORIDA

Amelia Island

American Association of Preferred Provider Organizations/The Ritz-Carlton/Jan. 27 - 29, 2013

American Business Media/Omni Amelia Island Plantation Resort/April 28 - May 1, 2013

American Feed Industry Association/Omni Amelia Island Plantation Resort/Nov. 7 - 9, 2013

American Society for Automation in Pharmacy/Ritz-Carlton, Amelia Island/Jan. 16 - 18, 2013

American Society of Breast Disease/Ritz-Carlton, Amelia Island/Feb. 14 - 17, 2013

Association of Life Insurance Counsel/The Ritz-Carlton, Amelia Island/May 5 - 7, 2013

Copper and Brass Servicenter Association/April 9 - 13, 2013

Institute for Credentialing Excellence/Omni Amelia Island Plantation Resort/Nov. 11 - 14, 2013/11-25 exhibitors

Lutheran Educational Conference of North America/The Ritz-Carlton, Amelia Island/Feb. 9 - 11, 2013

National Aircraft Resale Association/Amelia Island Ritz-Carlton/April 3 - 5, 2013

Propane Engine Fuel Committee/Propane Education and Research Council/Dec. 10 - 11, 2013

Research and Development Associates for Military Food and Packaging Systems/Villas of Amelia Island Plantation/May 20 - 22, 2013/26-50 exhibitors

United States Cutting Tool Institute/Omni Amelia Island Plantation Resort/May 3 - 5, 2014

Aventura

American Bakers Association/Fairmont Resort/April 20 - 24, 2013

American Society of Ophthalmic Administrators/Turnberry Isle Miami/Feb. 14
- 18, 2013
Asphalt Emulsion Manufacturers Association/Fairmont Turnberry Isle Resort
and Club/Feb. 24 - 27, 2014
Independent Lubricant Manufacturers Association/Turnberry Isle Aventura/
April 9 - 12, 2014

Biscayne

Managed Funds Association/The Ritz-Carlton, Miami Key/Jan. 28 - 30, 2013

Boca Raton

Association for Financial Technology/Boca Raton Resort and Club/March 17 -
19, 2013
Association of Analytical Communities International/Boca Raton Resort and
Club/Sept. 7 - 10, 2014
Association of Investment Management Sales Executives/Boca Raton Resort
and Club/April 27 - 29, 2014
Futures Industry Association/Boca Raton Resort and Club/March 12 - 15, 2013
Futures Industry Association/Boca Raton Resort and Club/March 11 - 14, 2014
Futures Industry Association/Boca Raton Resort and Club/March 10 - 13, 2015
Futures Industry Association/Boca Raton Resort and Club/March 8 - 11, 2016
Global Offset and Countertrade Association (GOCA)/Boca Raton Resort and
Club/May 18 - 22, 2013
Independent Lubricant Manufacturers Association/Boca Raton Resort and
Club/Oct. 17 - 20, 2015
International Association of Defense Counsel/Boca Raton Resort and Club/Feb.
9 - 14, 2013
Mortgage Bankers Association of America/Boca Raton Hotel/May 19 - 22,
2013
National Association of Real Estate Investment Trusts (NAREIT)/Boca Raton
Resort and Club/April 2 - 4, 2014
National Multi-Housing Council/Boca Raton Resort and Club/Jan. 21 - 23,
2014
National Multi-Housing Council/Boca Raton Resort and Club/Jan. 19 - 21,
2016
Society of Abdominal Radiology/Boca Raton Resort and Club/March 23 - 28,
2014
United States Tour Operators Association/Boca Raton Resort and Club/Dec. 5
- 7, 2014

Bonita Springs

Academy of Doctors of Audiology/Hyatt Regency Coconut Point Resort and
Spa/Nov. 7 - 9, 2013
American Brush Manufacturers Association/Hyatt Coconut Point/March 2 - 5,
2016
American Veterinary Distributors Association/Hyatt Coconut Point/April 28 -
30, 2013
Automotive Aftermarket Industry Association/Hyatt Regency Coconut Point
Resort and Spa/May 1 - 3, 2013
Fire Suppression Systems Association/Hyatt Regency Coconut Point Resort and
Spa/Feb. 22 - 26, 2013
National Association of EMS Physicians/Hyatt Regency Coconut Point Resort
and Spa/Jan. 10 - 12, 2013
National Association of Pipe Coating Applicators/Hyatt Regency Coconut Point
Resort and Spa/April 23 - 26, 2014
National Insulation Association/Hyatt Regency Coconut Point Resort and Spa/
April 17 - 20, 2013/100 attendees
National School Transportation Association/Jan. 12 - 16, 2013
Pipe Line Contractors Association/Hyatt Regency Coconut Point Resort and
Spa/Feb. 18 - 22, 2014
Pressure Vessel Manufacturers Association/Hyatt Regency Coconut Point
Resort and Spa/March 24 - 25, 2013
Professional Records and Information Services Management International/
Hyatt Regency Coconut Point/May 13 - 17, 2013
Society of Insurance Trainers and Educators/Hyatt Regency Coconut Point
Resort and Spa/June 21 - 24, 2014
Steel Plate Fabricators Association Division of STI/SPFA/Hyatt Regency
Coconut Point/March 23 - 26, 2013
Steel Tank Institute Division of STI/SPFA/March 23 - 26, 2013

Boynton Beach

American Stamp Dealers Association/The Marriot Courtyard Hotel/Feb. 8 - 10,
2013

Cape Coral

Marine Fabricators Association/Resort at Marina Village/Jan. 18 - 20, 2013

Clearwater

Academy of Surgical Research/Sandpearl Resort/Sept. 26 - 28, 2013
Alliance for Children and Families/Clearwater Beach/Feb. 16 - 19, 2013
American College of Osteopathic Obstetricians and Gynecologists/Hilton
Clearwater Beach/April 7 - 12, 2013
American Greyhound Track Operators Association/Sheraton Sand Key Resort/
Oct. 1 - 3, 2013
American Society of Sugar Beet Technologists/Hilton Hotel/Feb. 23 - 26, 2015
Association for Continuing Legal Education/Sheraton Sand Key Resort/Feb. 2 -
5, 2013
C-Port/Hilton Clearwater Beach/Jan. 13 - 15, 2013
Catholic Campus Ministry Association/Hilton Clearwater Beach/Jan. 8 - 11,
2013
Coal Technology Association/Sheraton Sand Key Resort/June 2 - 6, 2013
Independent Turf and Ornamental Distributors Association/Clearwater Beach
Marriott Suites on Sand Key/Feb. 27 - March 1, 2013
Laboratory Animal Management Association/Hilton Clearwater Beach Resort/
April 24 - 26, 2013
National Horsemen's Benevolent and Protective Association/Sheraton Sand
Key Resort/Feb. 20 - 24, 2013
National Organization of Life and Health Insurance Guaranty Association/Jan.
8 - 10, 2013
Petroleum Equipment Institute/Sheraton Sand Key Resort/Feb. 6 - 8, 2013
Wallcovering Association/Sandpearl Resort/Jan. 27 - 29, 2013

Cocoa Beach

International Bottled Water Association/Holiday Inn Express Hotel and Suites
Cocoa Beach/Jan. 28 - 31, 2013

Coral Gables

American Association for Women Podiatrists/Biltmore Resort/April 26 - 28,
2013
Society for Community Research and Action/University of Miami/June 26 - 29,
2013

Dania Beach

International Association of Aquatic and Marine Science Libraries and
Information Centers/Oct. 20 - 24, 2013

Daytona Beach

Adhesion Society/Hilton Daytona Beach Oceanfront Resort/March 3 - 6, 2013
American Ceramics Society/Jan. 27 - Feb. 1, 2013
American Ceramics Society/Jan. 26 - 31, 2014
American Ceramics Society/Jan. 25 - 30, 2015
American Ceramics Society/Jan. 24 - 29, 2016
American Ceramics Society/Jan. 22 - 27, 2017
American Institute of Aeronautics and Astronautics/Hilton Daytona Beach
Resort/Ocean Walk Village/March 25 - 28, 2013
International Association of Counselors and Therapists/Daytona Hilton/May
17 - 19, 2013
National Association of County Engineers/Hilton Daytona Beach Resort/Ocean
Walk Village/April 19 - 23, 2015
National Mobility Equipment Dealers Association/Hilton Daytona Beach
Resort/Ocean Walk Village/Feb. 6 - 8, 2013
Sports Turf Managers Association/Hilton Daytona Beach Resort/Ocean Walk
Village/Jan. 14 - 19, 2013

Deerfield Beach

National Society of Insurance Premium Auditors/Hilton Deerfield Beach/Boca
Raton/May 5 - 7, 2013

Delray Beach

The Vinegar Institute/Seagate Hotel & Spa/March 9 - 12, 2013

Duck Key

Concrete Sawing and Drilling Association/Hawks Cay Island Resort/Feb. 28 -
March 2, 2013
National Association of Sewer Service Companies/Hawks Cay Island Resort/
Feb. 13 - 16, 2013

Florida City

Personal Care Products Council/The Breakers in Palm Beach/Feb. 25 - 27, 2013

Ft. Lauderdale

Airport Minority Advisory Council (AMAC)/June 6 - 9, 2015
American Academy of Pain Medicine/Greater Fort Lauderdale/Broward County
Convention Center/April 11 - 14, 2013/1-10 exhibitors
American Accounting Association/Bahia Mar - Fort Lauderdale Beach/Jan. 10
- 12, 2013
American Association of Directors of Psychiatric Residency Training/Hilton Ft.
Lauderdale Airport/March 6 - 9, 2013
American Boat Builders and Repairers Association/Jan. 16 - 18, 2013
American College of Osteopathic Emergency Physicians/Marriott Harbor Beach
Resort & Spa/April 2 - 6, 2013
American Institute of Chemical Engineers/Hyatt Pier/Jan. 13 - 16, 2013
American Pediatric Surgical Association/Harbor Beach Marriott Resort and
Spa/April 30 - May 3, 2015
Associated Builders and Contractors/Marriott Harbor Beach Resort & Spa/Feb.
19 - 20, 2013
Association for Professionals in Infection Control and Epidemiology/June 7 -
10, 2013
Association for Professionals in Infection Control and Epidemiology/June 8 -
10, 2013
Association of Marina Industries/Greater Fort Lauderdale/Broward County
Convention Center/Jan. 30 - Feb. 1, 2013/over 100 exhibitors
Association of Marina Industries/Greater Fort Lauderdale/Broward County
Convention Center/Jan. 29 - 31, 2014
Association of Test Publishers/The Westin Diplomat Resort and Spa/Feb. 3 - 6,
2013
Association of the United States Army/Greater Fort Lauderdale/Broward
County Convention Center/Feb. 20 - 22, 2013
Credit Research Foundation/Marriott Harbor Beach Fort Lauderdale Resort and
Spa/Oct. 21 - 23, 2013
Institute for Professionals in Taxation/Harbor Beach Marriott Resort and Spa/
Nov. 9 - 12, 2014
International Association of Healthcare Central Service Materiel Management/
Broward Country Convention Center/May 3 - 6, 2015
The International Childbirth Education Association/Royal Caribbean's Liberty
of the Seas/Nov. 9 - 14, 2013
International Parking Institute/May 19 - 22, 2013
International Parking Institute/May 19 - July 22, 2013/over 100 exhibitors
Media Financial Management Association/Atlantic Hotel/Feb. 21 - 22, 2013
Men of Reform Judaism/Ft Lauderdale Westin Beach Resort/June 27 - 30, 2013
Metal Treating Institute/Harbor Beach Marriott Resort and Spa/April 18 - 20,
2013
National Association for Kinesiology in Higher Education/Hilton Fort
Lauderdale Marina Hotel/Jan. 2 - 5, 2013
National Association of Healthcare Access Management/Westin Diplomat
Resort and Spa/May 13 - 16, 2014
National Association of Independent Brokers Dealers/Manchester Grand
Hyatt/May 8 - 10, 2013
National Association of Pipe Coating Applicators/Marriott Harbor Beach
Resort & Spa/April 13 - 16, 2016
National Center for Assisted Living/Westin Beach Resort and Spa/March 12 -
13, 2013
National Chemical Credit Association/The Westin Beach Resort/Feb. 16 - 17,
2013
National Ice Cream Mix Association/Lago Mar Resort and Club/Jan. 20 - 23,
2013
The National Industrial Transportation League/Nov. 15 - 19, 2014
National Motor Freight Traffic Association, Inc./Lago Mar Resort and Club/
May 18 - 21, 2014
National Wooden Pallet and Container Association/Marriott Harbor Beach Fort
Lauderdale Resort and Spa/March 1 - 4, 2014
Society for Pediatric Anesthesia/Marriott Harbor Beach Resort & Spa/March 6
- 9, 2014

Society for Technological Advancement of Reporting/Marriott Harbor Beach Resort & Spa/March 7 - 9, 2013

Water and Sewer Distributors of America/Hyatt Regency/Feb. 24 - 27, 2013

Ft. Myers

American Real Estate Society/Sanibel Harbour Marriott Resort and Spa/April 14 - 18, 2015

Automatic Fire Alarm Association/Sanibel Harbour Marriott Resort and Spa/ May 1 - 4, 2013

Hydraulic Institute/Sanibel Harbour Marriott Resort and Spa/Feb. 7 - 12, 2013

National Association of Elevator Contractors/Sanibel Harbour Resort and Spa/ March 29 - April 1, 2014

Gainesville

National Association of Science Writers/Nov. 1 - 5, 2013

Grande Lakes

American Head and Neck Society/JW Marriott Orlando Grande Lakes/April 10 - 11, 2013

Hammock Beach

Distance Education and Training Council/Hammock Beach Resort/April 6 - 8, 2014

Hollywood

American Association for Public Opinion Research/Westin Diplomat Resort and Spa/May 14 - 17, 2015

American Association of Collegiate Registrars and Admissions Officers/Westin Diplomat Resort/Nov. 1 - 4, 2015

American College of Neuropsychopharmacology/Westin Diplomat Resort and Spa/Dec. 8 - 12, 2013

American College of Neuropsychopharmacology/Westin Diplomat Resort and Spa/Dec. 6 - 10, 2015

American College of Neuropsychopharmacology/Westin Diplomat Resort and Spa/Dec. 4 - 8, 2016

American Medical Society for Sports Medicine/Westin Diplomat Resort and Spa/April 15 - 19, 2015

American Orthopaedic Foot and Ankle Society/Westin Diplomat Resort/July 17 - 20, 2013

American Resort Development Association/Westin Diplomat Resort/April 7 - 11, 2013

American Society of Clinical Psychopharmacology/Westin Diplomat Resort and Spa/May 28 - 31, 2013/1200 attendees

American Society of Clinical Psychopharmacology/Westin Diplomat Resort and Spa/June 16 - 19, 2014

American Society of Colon and Rectal Surgeons/Westin Diplomat Resort and Spa/May 17 - 21, 2014

Arthroscopy Association of North America/May 1 - 3, 2014

Association of University Technology Managers/Westin Diplomat Resort and Spa/March 12 - 15, 2017

Bank Insurance and Securities Association/The Westin Diplomat Resort and Spa/March 10 - 12, 2013

Edison Electric Institute/Westin Diplomat Resort and Spa/Nov. 8 - 11, 2015

Global Cold Chain Alliance/The Westin Diplomat/May 4 - 8, 2013

Institute of Transportation Engineers/Westin Diplomat Resort and Spa/Aug. 2 - 5, 2015

Mortgage Bankers Association of America/Westin Diplomat Resort/April 14 - 17, 2013

National Association of Medical Staff Services/Westin Diplomat Resort and Spa/Sept. 21 - 25, 2013/11-25 exhibitors

National Association of Independent Life Brokerage Agencies/Westin Diplomat Resort and Spa/Nov. 20 - 22, 2014

National Association of Independent Life Brokerage Agencies/Westin Diplomat Resort and Spa/Nov. 16 - 18, 2017

National Association of Schools of Music/Westin Diplomat Resort/Nov. 22 - 26, 2013

National Candle Association/July 8 - 11, 2013

National Comprehensive Cancer Network/Westin Diplomat Resort and Spa/ March 13 - 17, 2013/1700 attendees

National Comprehensive Cancer Network/Westin Diplomat Resort and Spa/ March 12 - 16, 2014

National Investor Relations Institute/June 9 - 12, 2013

National Railroad Construction and Maintenance Association, Inc./Jan. 7 - 10, 2015

Society of General Internal Medicine/Westin Diplomat Resort and Spa/May 11 - 15, 2016

Strategic Account Management Association/Westin Diplomat Resort and Spa/ May 20 - 23, 2013

Jacksonville

The Acoustical Society of America/Nov. 2 - 6, 2015

American Academy of Neurological and Orthopaedic Surgeons/June 5 - 8, 2013

American Association of Colleges of Nursing/Omni Jacksonville Hotel/Feb. 7 - 9, 2013

American Quarter Horse Association/Hyatt Regency Jacksonville Riverfront/ March 4 - 7, 2016

The Association for Manufacturing Excellence/Nov. 10 - 14, 2014

Association for the Study of African American Life and History/Hyatt/Oct. 2 - 6, 2013

Association of Avian Veterinarians/Aug. 3 - 7, 2013

Association of Equipment Management Professionals/March 17 - 19, 2013

Association of Research Directors/Hyatt Regency Jacksonville Riverfront/April 6 - 10, 2013

Association of Research Directors of 1890s Colleges and Universities/Hyatt Regency Jacksonville Riverfront/April 6 - 10, 2013

Conference of Minority Transportation Officials/Hyatt Regency Jacksonville Riverfront/July 13 - 17, 2013

Council of Colleges of Arts and Sciences/Hyatt Regency Jacksonville Riverfront/ Nov. 6 - 9, 2013

Human Anatomy and Physiology Society/May 24 - 29, 2014

NALP - The Association for Legal Career Professionals/Feb. 28 - March 2, 2013

National Alliance of Independent Crop Consultants/Hyatt Regency Jacksonville Riverfront/Jan. 23 - 26, 2013

National Association of Academic Advisors for Athletes/Hyatt Regency Jacksonville Riverfront/June 6 - 9, 2013

National Association of Black Social Workers/Hyatt Regency Jacksonville Riverfront/April 2 - 6, 2013

National Exchange Club/Hyatt Regency Jacksonville Riverfront/July 12 - 15, 2017

National Shellfisheries Association/March 29 - April 2, 2014

North American Nature Photography Association/Feb. 27 - March 2, 2013

North American Nature Photography Association/Hyatt Regency Jacksonville Riverfront/Feb. 28 - March 3, 2013

Passenger Vessel Association/Hyatt Regency Jacksonville Riverfront/Feb. 16 - 19, 2013

The Society for Freshwater Science/Hyatt Regency Jacksonville Riverfront/May 19 - 23, 2013

Spray Polyurethane Foam Alliance/Jacksonville Hyatt/Feb.12, 2015

United Ostomy Associations of America/Hyatt Regency Jacksonville Riverfront/ Aug. 7 - 10, 2013

Vibration Institute/Wyndham Jacksonville Riverwalk/June 19 - 21, 2013/11-25 exhibitors

Key Largo

Council for Affordable and Rural Housing/Ocean Reef Club/Jan. 28 - 30, 2013

Kissimmee

American Orthotic and Prosthetic Association/Gaylord Palms Resort and Convention Center-Kissimmee/Sept. 18 - 21, 2013

American Society for Laser Medicine and Surgery/Gaylord Palms Resort and Convention Center-Kissimmee/April 22 - 26, 2015

Association of School Business Officials International/Gaylord Palms Resort and Convention Center-Kissimmee/Sept. 19 - 22, 2014

International Spa Association/Gaylord Palms Resort and Convention Center-Kissimmee/Oct. 27 - 29, 2014

National Hospice & Palliative Care Organization/Gaylord Palms Resort and Convention Center-Kissimmee/Nov. 3 - 5, 2016

North American Society for Trenchless Technology/Gaylord Palms Hotel and Convention Center, Orlando Florida/April 13 - 17, 2014

Truckload Carriers Association/Gaylord Palms Resort and Convention Center-Kissimmee/March 8 - 11, 2015

Voluntary Protection Programs Participants' Association, Inc./Gaylord Palms Resort and Convention Center-Kissimmee/Aug. 29 - Sept. 1, 2016

Lake Buena Vista

American Academy of Orofacial Pain/Disney's Contemporary Resort/April 23 - 28, 2013

American Association of Dental Consultants/Disney's BoardWalk Resort/May 15 - 18, 2013

American Cleft Palate-Craniofacial Association/Hilton Orlando Lake Buena Vista/May 5 - 10, 2013/1200 attendees

Association of Program Directors in Internal Medicine/Disney's Coronado Springs Resort/April 21 - 24, 2013

College Swimming Coaches Association of America/Walt Disney World Resort/ May 15 - 17, 2013

Council of Chiropractic Physiological Therapeutics and Rehabilitation/Swan Hotel/April 19 - 21, 2013

Edison Electric Institute/Walt Disney World Swan and Dolphin/Nov. 5 - 8, 2017

National Association for Bilingual Education/Coronado Springs Resort/Feb. 7 - 9, 2013/2000 attendees

National Telecommunications Cooperative Association/Disney's Yacht and Beach Club/Feb. 3 - 6, 2013

National Telecommunications Cooperative Association/Disney's Yacht and Beach Club/Jan. 31 - Feb. 3, 2013

NCSL International/Walt Disney World Swan and Dolphin/Aug. 3 - 4, 2014/51-100 exhibitors

Organization for the Promotion and Advancement of Small Telecommunications Companies/Walt Disney World Dolphin Resort/Feb. 3 - 6, 2013

Romance Writers of America/Walt Disney World Swan and Dolphin/July 26 - 29, 2017

Society of Tribologists and Lubrication Engineers/Disneys Contemporary Resorts/May 18 - 22, 2014

Society of Urologic Nurses and Associates/Disney's Board Walk Inn/Oct. 31 - Nov. 3, 2014

Ultrasonic Industry Association/Hilton Orlando Lake Buena Vista/April 22 - 24, 2013

Uniformed Services Academy of Family Physicians/Swan and Dolphin Resorts/ March 21 - 26, 2013

United States Composting Council/Buena Vista Palace Hotel and Spa/Jan. 28 - 31, 2013/26-50 exhibitors

Writing Instrument Manufacturers Association/Hyatt Regency Grand Cypress/ May 21 - 23, 2013

Longboat Key

American Coke and Coal Chemicals Institute/Longboat Key Club and Resort/ May 3 - 4, 2013

Manalapan

Aircraft Builders Council/The Ritz-Carlton Palm Beach/Sept. 21 - 23, 2014

American Dental Society of Anesthesiology/Ritz Carlton Palm Beach/April 25 - 27, 2013

American Spice Trade Association/Ritz-Carlton, Palm Beach Manalapan/April 28 - May 1, 2013

Marco Island

American Pediatric Surgical Association/Marco Island Marriott Beach Resort, Golf Club and Spa/May 2 - 5, 2013

Association of Internal Management Consultants/Marco Island Hilton Beach Resort and Spa/April 21 - 24, 2013

Book Manufacturers' Institute/Marco Island Marriott Beach Resort, Golf Club and Spa/Nov. 1 - 6, 2013

Federation of Defense and Corporate Counsel/Marco Island Marriott Beach Resort, Golf Club and Spa/March 1 - 8, 2014

International Association of Defense Counsel/Marriot Marco Island/Feb. 14 - 19, 2015

International Builders Exchange Executives/Builders Exchange Network/Hilton Marco Island Beach Resort and Spa/Feb. 6 - 8, 2013

Manufacturers Standardization Society of the Valve and Fitting Industry, Inc./ Marco Island beach Resort/April 23 - May 3, 2013

National Association of Collegiate Directors of Athletics/Hilton Marco Island Beach Resort and Spa/Jan. 25 - 28, 2013

National Association of Collegiate Directors of Athletics/Hilton Marco Island Beach Resort and Spa/Jan. 24 - 27, 2014

National Association of Collegiate Directors of Athletics/Hilton Marco Island Beach Resort and Spa/Jan. 23 - 26, 2015

National Association of Collegiate Directors of Athletics/Hilton Marco Island Beach Resort and Spa/Jan. 29 - Feb. 1, 2016

National Association of Collegiate Directors of Athletics/Hilton Marco Island Beach Resort and Spa/Jan. 27 - 30, 2017

National Association of Collegiate Directors of Athletics/Hilton Marco Island Beach Resort and Spa/Jan. 26 - 29, 2018

National Association of Collegiate Marketing Administrators/Hilton Marco Island Beach Resort and Spa/Jan. 25 - 28, 2013

National Association of Collegiate Marketing Administrators/Hilton Marco Island Beach Resort and Spa/Jan. 24 - 27, 2014

National Association of Collegiate Marketing Administrators/Hilton Marco Island Beach Resort and Spa/Jan. 23 - 26, 2015

National Association of Collegiate Marketing Administrators/Hilton Marco Island Beach Resort and Spa/Jan. 29 - Feb. 1, 2016

National Association of Collegiate Marketing Administrators/Hilton Marco Island Beach Resort and Spa/Jan. 27 - 30, 2017

National Association of Collegiate Marketing Administrators/Hilton Marco Island Beach Resort and Spa/Jan. 26 - 29, 2018

Peanut and Tree Nut Processors Association/Marco Island Marriott Beach Resort, Golf Club and Spa/Jan. 18 - 21, 2014/26-50 exhibitors

Wire Fabricators Association/Jan. 24 - 26, 2013

Miami

American Academy of Dermatology/Miami Beach Convention Center/March 1 - 5, 2013

American Apparel Producer's Network/Eden Roc Renaissance Hotel/May 5 - 7, 2013

American Association for Justice/Fountainebleau Hotel/Feb. 9 - 13, 2013

American Association of Sexuality Educators, Counselors and Therapists/ Hilton/June 5 - 9, 2013

American Bar Association/Feb. 1 - 7, 2017

American Brush Manufacturers Association/Eden Roc Renaissance Miami Beach/March 13 - 16, 2013

American Clinical Neurophysiology Society/Miami Marriott Biscayne Bay/Feb. 5 - 20, 2013

American Medical Association/Turnberry Isle Miami/Jan. 3 - 5, 2013

American Psychosomatic Society/InterContinental Miami/March 13 - 16, 2013

American Society for Legal History/Hyatt Regency Miami/Nov. 7 - 10, 2013

The American Society of Pediatric Hematology/Oncology/Hyatt Regency/April 24 - 27, 2013

American Society of Transplant Surgeons/Jan. 31 - Feb. 2, 2013

American Translators Association/Hyatt Regency Coral Gables/Nov. 4 - 7, 2015

American Waterways Operators/Fountainebleau Hotel/Oct. 16 - 19, 2013

Anxiety Disorders Association of America/Hyatt Regency Miami/April 9 - 12, 2015

Associated Builders and Contractors/Eden Roc Renaissance Miami Beach/Nov. 11 - 13, 2014

Association for Psychological Type International/Hyatt Regency/July 10 - 14, 2013

Association for the Accreditation of Human Research Protection Programs/ Hyatt Regency Miami/April 3 - 5, 2013

Association of Dermatology Administrators & Managers/Feb. 27 - March 2, 2013

Association of Dermatology Administrators & Managers/Hyatt Regency/Feb. 27 - March 1, 2013

Association of University Anesthesiologists/JW Marriott Marquis/April 4 - 6, 2013

Automotive Aftermarket Industry Association/Dec. 7 - 11, 2013

Business History Conference/June 24 - 27, 2014

Business History Conference/June 24 - 27, 2015

Catholic Theological Society of America/Hyatt Regency/June 6 - 9, 2013

Chlorine Chemistry Council/May 5 - 8, 2013

Clinical Immunology Society/JW Marriott Marquis/April 25 - 28, 2013

Commodity Markets Council/St. Regis Bal Harbour Resort/Jan. 27 - 29, 2013

Council of Hotel and Restaurant Trainers/InterContinental Miami/July 20 - 23, 2013

Fibre Box Association/Ritz-Carlton, South Beach/April 8 - 10, 2013

IFCA International/DoubleTree by Hilton/June 24 - 28, 2013

INDA, Association of the Nonwoven Fabrics Industry/Miama Beach resort and Spa/April 12 - 14, 2013

INDA, Association of the Nonwoven Fabrics Industry/Miama Beach resort and Spa/April 23 - 25, 2013

Institute of Certified Business Counselors/Hilton Miami Downtown/Jan. 14 - 17, 2013

Institute of Transportation Engineers/Hyatt Regency Miami/March 9 - 12, 2014

International Association of Physicians in AIDS Care/June 2 - 4, 2013

International Bone and Mineral Society/Nov. 7 - 9, 2013

International District Energy Association/Hyatt Regency Miami/June 23 - 26, 2013

International Foundation of Employee Benefit Plans/Nov. 13 - 16, 2016

International Life Sciences Institute/InterContinental Miami/Jan. 18 - 23, 2013

International Ombudsman Association/Hyatt Regency Miami/April 21 - 24, 2013

International Society for Quality of Life Research/Oct. 9 - 12, 2013

International Society for Traumatic Stress Studies/InterContinental/Nov. 6 - 8, 2014/1-10 exhibitors

International Technology Law Association/May 1, 2016

International Transplant-Skin Cancer Collaborative/Feb. 28, 2013

Juice Products Association/Ritz Carlton Key Biscayne/April 12 - 17, 2013

Laser Institute of America/Hyatt Regency Miami/Oct. 6 - 10, 2013

Natco-The Organization for Transplant Professionals/Loews Miami Beach Hotel/Feb. 1 - 3, 2013

National Apartment Association/Celebrity Cruises/June 22 - 24, 2017

National Association of Clean Water Agencies/Hyatt Regency Miami/Feb. 3 - 6, 2013

National Association of Retail Collection Attorneys/Loews Miami Beach Hotel/ May 12 - 15, 2014

National Association of Television Program Executives/Fontainebleau Resort/ Jan. 28 - 30, 2013

National Board of Boiler and Pressure Vessel Inspectors/Hyatt Regency Miami/ May 13 - 17, 2013

National Confectioners Association/Fontainebleau Resort/Feb. 24 - 27, 2013

National Conference of Bankruptcy Judges/Sept. 27 - 30, 2015

National Education Association/July 1 - 6, 2015

National Investment Company Service Association/Doral Golf Resort and Spa/ Feb. 10 - 13, 2013

National Oilseed Processors Association/Ritz-Carlton Coconut Grove/Feb. 10 - 14, 2014

National Pace Association/Loews Miami Beach Hotel/Oct. 21 - 24, 2013

North American Skull Base Society/Sugarloaf Elementary School/Feb. 15 - 17, 2013

Railway Engineering-Maintenance Suppliers Association/Jan. 9 - 12, 2013/800 attendees

Refrigerated Foods Association/Doral Golf Resort and Spa/Feb. 24 - 27, 2013

Society for Medical Decision Making/Doral Golf Resort and Spa Miami/Oct. 19 - 22, 2014/600 attendees

Society for Pediatric Dermatology/Feb. 28, 2013

Society of Neurointerventional Surgery/Loews Miami Beach Hotel/July 29 - Aug. 1, 2013

Urban and Regional Information Systems Association/Hyatt Regency Miami/ June 17 - 20, 2013

Wholesale Florist and Florist Supplier Association/Doral/Oct. 23 - 25, 2013

Wholesale Florist and Florist Supplier Association/Doral/Oct. 22 - 24, 2014

Wholesale Florist and Florist Supplier Association/Doral/Oct. 21 - 23, 2015

Miami Beach

Association of Ship Brokers and Agents (U.S.A.)/Eden Roc Renaissance Hotel/ Oct. 2 - 4, 2013

CRE Finance Council/Loews Miami Beach Hotel/Jan. 14 - 16, 2013

Distribution Contractors Association/Loews Miami Beach Hotel/March 5 - 10, 2013

Electronic Retailing Association/Fontainebleau Miami Beach/Feb. 25 - 27, 2013

Hispanic Association of Colleges and Universities/Fontainebleau Miami Beach/ Oct. 10 - 12, 2015

Human Behavior and Evolution Society/Loews Hotel/July 17 - 20, 2013

International Association of Commercial Collectors/Eden Roc Renaissance Miami Beach/Jan. 16 - 18, 2013

National Association of Convenience Stores/Fontainebleau Miami Beach/Feb. 11 - 13, 2013

National Association of Manufacturers/Eden Roc Renaissance Miami Beach/ April 14 - 16, 2013/1-10 exhibitors

National Housing and Rehabilitation Association/The Loews Miami Beach Hotel/March 6 - 9, 2013

National Railroad Construction and Maintenance Association, Inc./Loews Miami Beach Hotel/Jan. 9 - 12, 2013

Professional Insurance Marketing Association/Eden Roc Renaissance Miami Beach/Jan. 23 - 26, 2014

Public Affairs Council/Eden Roc Renaissance Miami Beach/March 4 - 7, 2013

Society for Clinical Vascular Surgery/Fontainebleau Miami Beach/March 13 - 16, 2013

Society of Cardiovascular Anesthesiologists/Fontainebleau Miami Beach/April 6 - 10, 2013

Stadium Managers Association/Eden Roc Renaissance Miami Beach/Feb. 3 - 7, 2013

Naples

American Association for Hand Surgery/Naples Grande Resort and Club/Jan. 9 - 12, 2013/26-50 exhibitors

American College of Real Estate Lawyers/Grande Resort/March 14 - 17, 2013

American College of Trial Lawyers/The Ritz - Carlton/Feb. 28 - March 3, 2013

The American Hockey Coaches Association/The Naples Beach Hotel and Golf Club/May 1 - 5, 2013

American Society for Reconstructive Microsurgery/Napels Beach Hotel and Golf Club/Jan. 12 - 15, 2013

Consumer Healthcare Products Association/Ritz-Carlton Golf Resort, Naples/ March 11 - 13, 2013

Contract Packaging Association/Waldorf Astoria Naples/Feb. 21 - 24, 2013

Conveyor Equipment Manufacturers Association/La Playa Beach and Racquet/ June 23 - 26, 2013

Conveyor Equipment Manufacturers Association/La Playa Beach and Racquet/ June 22 - 25, 2014

Conveyor Equipment Manufacturers Association/Waldorf Astoria Naples/ March 13 - 17, 2015

Council for Advancement and Support of Education/Naples Grande Beach Resort/Feb. 25 - 27, 2013

Flexible Packaging Association/The Ritz-Carlton Golf Resort/Feb. 26 - 28, 2013

Institute of Clean Air Companies/Waldorf Astoria Naples/April 25 - 27, 2013

International Brotherhood of Electrical Workers/The Naples Beach Hotel and Golf Club/Jan. 31 - Feb. 1, 2013

International Kitchen Exhaust Cleaning Association/Hilton Naples/April 17 - 20, 2013

National Association of Flour Distributors/The Ritz Carlton/May 14 - 18, 2014

National Electrical Contractors Association/Naples Beach Hotel and Golf Club/ Jan. 31 - Feb. 1, 2013

National Leased Housing Association/Naples Beach Hotel and Golf Club/Jan. 23 - 25, 2013

National Ocean Industries Association/Ritz Carlton Golf Resort/Nov. 5 - 7, 2014

NPTA Alliance/The Ritz-Carlton Golf Resort/Jan. 15 - 17, 2013

Power and Communications Contractors Association/Naples Beach Hotel and Golf Club/March 1 - 6, 2013

Truck Renting and Leasing Association/The Naples Grande Beach Resort/
March 11 - 15, 2013

Nashville

Hearth, Patio and Barbecue Association/March 4 - 7, 2015/12000 attendees/
over 100 exhibitors
National Association of Child Care Professionals/April 24 - 26, 2013

Orange

Academy of Clinical Research Professionals/Orange County Convention
Center/April 13 - 16, 2013/2000 attendees/over 100 exhibitors
Hearth, Patio and Barbecue Association/Orange County Convention Center/
March 13 - 16, 2013/12000 attendees/over 100 exhibitors
International Cast Polymer Association/Orange County Convention Center/Jan.
29 - 31, 2013/3500 attendees/over 100 exhibitors
National Automobile Dealers Association/Orange County Convention Center/
Feb. 8 - 11, 2013
North American Association of Food Equipment Manufacturers/Orange County
Convention Center/Feb. 7 - 9, 2013/over 100 exhibitors
North American Association of Food Equipment Manufacturers/Orange County
Convention Center/Feb. 9 - 11, 2017
North American Association of Food Equipment Manufacturers/Orange County
Convention Center/Feb. 7 - 9, 2019

Orlando

AABB - American Association of Blood Banks/Oct. 22 - 25, 2016
Academy of Criminal Justice Sciences/Caribe Royale All-Suite Hotel and
Convention Center/March 3 - 7, 2015
Academy of Management/Aug. 9 - 13, 2013
Academy of Pharmaceutical Research and Science/March 28 - 31, 2014
Academy of Physicians in Clinical Research/Orange County Convention
Center/April 13 - 16, 2013
Air Conditioning Contractors of America/Orlando World Center/Feb. 27 -
March 2, 2013
Air Force Association/Rosen Shingle Creek Hotel/Feb. 21 - 22, 2013
Airborne Law Enforcement Association/July 17 - 20, 2013
Aircraft Electronics Association/April 27 - 30, 2016
Airlines Electronic Engineering Committee/Hilton Orlando Lake Buena Vista/
April 22 - 24, 2013
Ambulatory Surgery Center Association/Orlando World Center Marriott/May
13 - 16, 2015/2500 attendees
American Academy of Anesthesiologist Assistants/Caribe Royale Orlando/April
13 - 16, 2013
American Academy of Child and Adolescent Psychiatry/Walt Disney World
Resort/Oct. 22 - 27, 2013
American Academy of Cosmetic Dentistry/April 30 - May 3, 2014
American Academy of Forensic Sciences/Hilton Orlando Lake Buena Vista/Feb.
16 - 21, 2015
American Academy of Implant Dentistry/Peabody Orlando/Nov. 5 - 8, 2014/
over 100 exhibitors
American Academy of Orthotists and Prosthetists/Caribe Royal Resort/Feb. 20
- 23, 2013
American Academy of Orthotists and Prosthetists/Caribe Royale Orlando/
March 9 - 12, 2016
American Academy of Orthotists and Prosthetists/Caribe Royale Orlando/
March 6 - 9, 2019
American Academy of Osteopathy/Rosen Shingle Creek Hotel/March 20 - 24,
2013
American Academy of Osteopathy/Rosen Shingle Creek Resort/March 16 - 20,
2016
American Academy of Pain Management/JW Marriott Orlando Grande Lakes/
Sept. 26 - 29, 2013
American Academy of Pediatric Dentistry/Walt Disney World Resort/May 23 -
26, 2013
American Academy of Pediatrics/Orange County Convention Center/Oct. 26 -
29, 2013
American Association of Colleges for Teacher Education/Rosen Shingle Creek/
Feb. 28 - March 2, 2013
American Association of Colleges of Nursing/Buena Vista Palace/Feb. 20 - 23,
2013
American Association of Collegiate Registrars and Admissions Officers/
Orlando World Center Marriott/March 25 - 28, 2018
American Association of Directors of Psychiatric Residency Training/Hilton
Orlando Bonnet Creek/March 4 - 7, 2015
American Association of Managing General Agents/March 1 - 4, 2014
American Association of Nurse Anesthetists/Orlando World Center Marriott/
Sept. 13 - 16, 2014
American Association of Oral and Maxillofacial Surgeons/Orange County
Convention Center/Oct. 7 - 12, 2013
American Association of Orthodontists/April 29 - May 2, 2016
American Association of Pharmaceutical Scientists/Orlando Convention
Center/Oct. 25 - 29, 2015
American Association of Pharmaceutical Scientists/Orlando Convention
Center/Oct. 22 - 26, 2023
American Association of Port Authorities/Oct. 13 - 17, 2013/51-100 exhibitors
American Association of Swine Veterinarians/Feb. 28 - March 3, 2015/900
attendees/51-100 exhibitors
American Association of Teachers of German/Orange County Convention
Center-Rosen Centre Hotel/Nov. 22 - 24, 2013
American Association of Zoo Keepers/Sept. 8 - 12, 2014
American Association of Zoo Veterinarians/Walt Disney World Resort/Oct. 18
- 24, 2014
American Bankers Association/JW Marriott Orlando Grande Lakes/Feb. 17 -
20, 2013
American Baseball Coaches Association/Marriott World Center/Jan. 2 - 5,
2015/5500 attendees/over 100 exhibitors
American Broncho-Esophagological Association/JW Marriott Orlando Grande
Lakes/April 10 - 14, 2013
American Brush Manufacturers Association/Hyatt Grand Cypress/March 22 -
25, 2017
American Chemical Society/March 31 - April 4, 2019
American Cleaning Institute/JW Marriott Orlando Grande Lakes/Jan. 28 - Feb.
2, 2013/725 attendees

American Cleaning Institute/JW Marriott Orlando Grande Lakes/Jan. 27 - Feb.
1, 2014/725 attendees
American Cleaning Institute/JW Marriott Orlando Grande Lakes/Jan. 26 - 31,
2015/725 attendees
American Cleaning Institute/JW Marriott Orlando Grande Lakes/Jan. 25 - 30,
2016/725 attendees
American Cleaning Institute/JW Marriott Orlando Grande Lakes/Jan. 23 - 28,
2017/725 attendees
American College Health Association/Orlando World Center Marriott/May 26
- 30, 2015
American College of Health Care Administrators/Omni Orlando Resort at
ChampionsGate/April 12 - 16, 2013
American College of Occupational and Environmental Medicine/Shingle Creek/
April 28 - May 1, 2013
American College of Physician Executives/Loews Portofino Bay Hotel/Jan. 25 -
27, 2013
American College of Physicians/April 10 - 12, 2014
American College of Physicians/April 10 - 14, 2014
American College of Physicians Services, Inc./April 10 - 12, 2014
American College of Sports Medicine/May 28 - 31, 2014
American College of Tax Counsel/Jan. 24 - 26, 2013
American College of Toxicology/Hyatt Regency Grand Cypress/Nov. 9 - 12,
2014
American Composites Manufacturers Association/Orange County Convention
Center/Jan. 29 - 31, 2013/3500 attendees/over 100 exhibitors
American Concrete Pipe Association/Rosen Shingle Creek Resort/Feb. 5 - 7,
2015
American Correctional Association/Orlando World Center Marriott/Jan. 5 - 10,
2018
American Council of Engineering Companies/Hilton Orlando Bonnet Creek/
Oct. 15 - 18, 2017
American Council of Life Insurers (ACLI)/Hyatt Regency Grand Cypress/July 17
- 19, 2013
American Council on the Teaching of Foreign Languages/Orange County
Convention Center-Rosen Centre Hotel/Nov. 22 - 24, 2013
American Counseling Association/March 11 - 15, 2015/1-10 exhibitors
American Financial Services Association/Convention Center/The Peabody
Orlando/Feb. 6 - 8, 2013
American Fuel & Petrochemical Manufacturers/Orlando World Center
Marriott/May 21 - 24, 2013
American Gas Association/Gaylord Palms Resort and Convention Center-
Orlando/May 21 - 23, 2013
American Geriatrics Society/Walt Disney World Swan And Dolphin/May 14 -
17, 2014
American Hernia Society/JW Marriott Orlando Grande Lakes/March 13 - 16,
2013
American Institute of Ultrasound in Medicine/March 21 - 25, 2015
American Institute of Ultrasound in Medicine/March 25 - 29, 2017
American Laryngological Association/JW Marriott Orlando Grande Lakes/April
10 - 14, 2013
American Laryngological, Rhinological and Otological Society/JW Marriott
Orlando Grande Lakes/April 10 - 14, 2013
American Library Association/June 23 - 28, 2016
American Medical Group Association/Hilton Orlando Bonnet Creek/March 14
- 16, 2013
American Medical Society for Sports Medicine/Walt Disney World Swan And
Dolphin/April 25 - 29, 2018
American Montessori Society/Hilton Orlando Destination Parkway/March 14 -
17, 2013
American Oil Chemists' Society/Rosen Shingle Creek Hotel/May 3 - 6, 2015
American Organization of Nurse Executives/March 12 - 15, 2014
American Orthopaedic Society for Sports Medicine/Hilton Orlando Bonnet
Creek/July 9 - 12, 2015/51-100 exhibitors
American Osteopathic Association/Oct. 17 - 21, 2015
American Osteopathic Colleges of Ophthalmology and Otolaryngology - Head
and Neck Surgery/Hyatt Regency Grand Cypress/May 8 - 12, 2013
American Osteopathic Colleges of Ophthalmology and Otolaryngology - Head
and Neck Surgery/Ritz Carlton/May 6 - 10, 2015
American Otological Society/JW Marroitt Grande Lakes Resort/April 12 - 14,
2013
American Pet Products Association/Orange County Convention Center/Feb. 20
- 22, 2013/1-10 exhibitors
American Pharmacists Association/March 28 - 31, 2014
American Podiatric Medical Association/Orlando World Center Marriott/July
23 - 26, 2015
American Public Power Association/Sept. 22 - 25, 2013
American Railway Engineering and Maintenance-of-Way Association/Aug. 28
- 31, 2016
American Resort Development Association/Orlando World Center Marriott/
March 24 - 28, 2013
American Rhinologic Society/JW Marriott Orlando Grande Lakes/April 10 - 14,
2013
American School Counselor Association/Walt Disney World Swan And
Dolphin/June 29 - July 2, 2014
American Society for Blood and Marrow Transplantation/Feb. 19 - 23, 2014
American Society for Horticultural Science/Rosen Plaza Hotel/July 28 - 31,
2014
American Society for Training and Development/May 17 - 20, 2015
American Society of Addiction Medicine/April 10 - 13, 2014
American Society of Addiction Medicine/April 10 - 13, 2014
American Society of Anesthesiologists/Oct. 14 - 18, 2017
American Society of Anesthesiologists/Oct. 19 - 23, 2019
American Society of Consultant Pharmacists/Walt Disney World Resort/May
15 - 17, 2013
American Society of Consultant Pharmacists/Gaylord Palms Resort and
Convention Center-Orlando/Nov. 4 - 7, 2014
American Society of Cytopathology/Hilton Orlando Bonnet Creek/Nov. 8 - 12,
2013
American Society of Health-System Pharmacists/Dec. 8 - 12, 2013
American Society of Human Genetics/Oct. 17 - 21, 2017

American Society of Plumbing Engineers/Sept. 19 - 22, 2013
American Society of Safety Engineers/June 8 - 11, 2014
American Soybean Association/Feb. 28 - March 2, 2013
American Speech-Language-Hearing Association/Nov. 20 - 22, 2014
American Thyroid Association/Walt Disney World Swan And Dolphin/Sept. 17 - 23, 2015
American Thyroid Association/Walt Disney World Swan and Dolphin Resort/ Oct. 18 - 23, 2015
American Truck Dealers/Orange County Convention Center/Feb. 8 - 11, 2013
American Trucking Associations/Orlando World Center Marriott/Oct. 19 - 22, 2013
American Urological Association/May 17 - 21, 2014
American Wholesale Marketers Association/Peabody Orlando Hotel/March 6 - 8, 2013
American Wire Producers Association/Hilton Orlando Bonnet Creek/Feb. 18 - 20, 2013
Assistive Technology Industry Association/Caribe Royale Orlando All-Suite Hotel and Convention Center/Jan. 30 - Feb. 2, 2013/51-100 exhibitors
Association for Biblical Higher Education/Hilton Orlando/Feb. 13 - 16, 2013
Association for Biblical Higher Education/Wyndham Orlando Resort/Feb. 19 - 22, 2014
Association for Biblical Higher Education/Wyndham Orlando Resort/Feb. 19 - 22, 2015
Association for Corporate Growth/Rosen Shingle Creek/April 22 - 25, 2013
Association for Research in Vision and Ophthalmology/May 4 - 8, 2014
Association for Specialists in Group Work/Feb. 6 - 9, 2014
Association for Surgical Education/Gaylord Palms Resort and Convention Center-Orlando/April 23 - 27, 2013/700 attendees
Association for Theatre in Higher Education/Hyatt Regency Grand Cypress/ Aug. 1 - 3, 2013/800 attendees/11-25 exhibitors
Association for Unmanned Vehicle Systems International/Orange County Convention Center/May 13 - 16, 2014/8000 attendees/over 100 exhibitors
Association of Clinical Research Professionals/April 12 - 16, 2013
Association of Clinical Research Professionals/Orange County Convention Center/April 13 - 16, 2013/2000 attendees
Association of College and University Housing Officers-International/June 27 - 30, 2015
Association of College Unions International/April 5 - 10, 2014
Association of Energy Services Professionals, International/Hyatt Regency Grand Cypress/Jan. 28 - 31, 2013
Association of Equipment Manufacturers/Hilton Bonnet Creek Resort/Nov. 3 - 5, 2013
Association of Fraternity Advisors/Hilton Orlando Bonnet Creek/Dec. 4 - 8, 2013
Association of Gay and Lesbian Psychiatrists/Walt Disney World Resort/Oct. 22 - 27, 2013
Association of Governing Boards of Universities and Colleges/Convention Center/The Peabody Orlando/April 13 - 15, 2014
Association of Government Accountants/Orlando World Center Marriott/July 13 - 16, 2014
Association of Independent Corrugated Converters/Hilton Bonnet Creek Resort/April 24 - 26, 2013
Association of Industrial Metallizers, Coaters and Laminators/Orange County Convention Center/April 9 - 11, 2013
Association of Insurance Compliance Professionals/Convention Center/The Peabody Orlando/Oct. 2 - 5, 2016
Association of Occupational Health Professionals in Healthcare/Walt Disney World Resorts/Sept. 11 - 14, 2013
Association of Physician Assistants in Cardiovascular Surgery/Jan. 22 - 26, 2014
Association of Private Sector Colleges and Universities (Career College Association)/Rosen Shingle Creek/June 5 - 7, 2013/11-25 exhibitors
Association of Professional Chaplains/Walt Disney World Resort/June 27 - 30, 2013
Association of Program Directors in Surgery/Gaylord Palms Resort and Convention Center-Orlando/April 23 - 27, 2013
Association of Public and Land-Grant Universities (APLU)/Hilton Orlando Bonnet Creek/Nov. 2 - 4, 2014
Association of Rotational Molders International/Hyatt Regency Grand Cypress/ March 17 - 19, 2013
Association of Small Business Development Centers/Hilton Orlando Lake Buena Vista/Sept. 9 - 12, 2013
Association of Teacher Educators/Caribe Royale Orlando/Feb. 10 - 14, 2017
Association of Zoos and Aquariums/Sept. 12 - 17, 2014
Automated Imaging Association/Orlando World Marriott Center/Feb. 20 - 22, 2013
Aviation Insurance Association/Hilton Bonnet Creek Resort/May 4 - 7, 2013
Aviation Technician Education Council/April 13 - 16, 2013
BICSI/Rosen Shingle Creek/Feb. 2 - 6, 2014
BICSI/Orlando World Center Marriott/Feb. 22 - 26, 2015
BICSI/Rosen Shingle Creek/Feb. 7 - 11, 2016
Building Owners and Managers Association International/June 22 - 24, 2014
Business Professionals of America/May 8 - 12, 2013
Campus Safety, Health and Environmental Management Association/The Renaissance Orlando at Sea World/July 12 - 17, 2013
CBA/Orange County Convention Center/June 28 - July 1, 2015
Ceilings and Interior Systems Construction Association/Walt Disney World Resort/March 26 - 29, 2018
Ceilings and Interior Systems Construction Association/March 28 - 29, 2018
Ceilings and Interior Systems Construction Association/March 25 - 28, 2024
Christian Schools International/Buena Vista Palace/Sept. 25 - 27, 2013
Civil Aviation Medical Association/Renaissance Orlando Resort/Oct. 3 - 5, 2013
Clinical Laboratory Management Association/Caribe Royale All-Suite Hotel and Convention Center/April 7 - 10, 2013
College Athletic Business Management Association/Orlando World Center Marriott/June 10 - 13, 2013
College Athletic Business Management Association/Orlando World Center Marriott/June 6 - 9, 2014

College of American Pathologists/Gaylord Palms Resort and Convention Center-Orlando/Oct. 13 - 16, 2013/1400 attendees/over 100 exhibitors
College of Optometrists in Vision Development/Rosen Shingle Creek/Oct. 8 - 12, 2013
College Sports Information Directors of America/June 12 - 15, 2013/26-50 exhibitors
Community College Business Officers/Disney's Contemporary Resort/Sept. 24 - 27, 2016
Competitive Telecommunications Association/Gaylord Palms Resort and Convention Center-Orlando/Sept. 23 - 26, 2013
Computer Measurement Group/Dec. 8 - 13, 2013
Construction Management Association of America/Hilton Bonnet Creek Resort/Oct. 11 - 13, 2015/1000 attendees
Controlled Environment Testing Association/April 12 - 16, 2013
Cooperative Education and Internship Association/DoubleTree by Hilton at the Entrance to Universal Orlando/April 14 - 16, 2013
Council of State Speech-Language-Hearing Association Presidents/Nov. 19, 2014
Dermatology Nurses' Association/Walt Disney World Dolphin/May 1 - 4, 2014
Design-Build Institute of America/Walt Disney World Resort/March 18 - 20, 2013
Design-Build Institute of America/Walt Disney World Resort/March 20 - 22, 2013
Destination Marketing Association International/July 15 - 17, 2013
Direct Selling Association/Peabody Orlando/June 1 - 3, 2014/900 attendees
Direct Selling Association/Peabody Orlando/June 4 - 6, 2017/900 attendees
Distributive Education Clubs of America (DECA)/Disney All-Star Sports Resort/ Feb. 6 - 10, 2013
Distributive Education Clubs of America (DECA)/April 25 - 28, 2015
Diving Equipment and Marketing Association/Orange County Convention Center/Nov. 6 - 9, 2013
Drug & Alcohol Testing Industry Association/Loews Royal Pacific Resort /May 9 - 11, 2013
Edison Electric Institute/Orlando World Center Marriott/Nov. 10 - 13, 2013
Educational Book and Media Association/Ritz-Carlton Orlando, Grande Lakes/ Jan. 14 - 17, 2013
Educause/Sept. 29 - Oct. 2, 2014
Electrical and Computer Engineering Department Heads Association/Buena Vista Hotel/March 22 - 26, 2013
The Electrochemical Society/Hilton Bonnet Creek Resort/May 11 - 16, 2014
Envelope Manufacturers Association/Ritz-Carlton Orlando, Grande Lakes/April 17 - 20, 2013
Environmental Bankers Association/Jan. 19 - 21, 2013
Environmental Mutagen Society/Hilton Orlando Lake Buena Vista/Sept. 13 - 17, 2014
Event Service Professionals Association/Walt Disney Swan and Dolphin Resor/ Jan. 11 - 13, 2013
The Fertilizer Institute/Hyatt Regency Grand Cypress/Feb. 11 - 13, 2013
Financial Management Association International/Hilton Orlando Bonnet Creek/Oct. 14 - 17, 2015
Financial Planning Association/Oct. 19 - 22, 2013
Fire Department Safety Officers Association/Wyndham Lake Buena Vista Resort/Jan. 20 - 23, 2013
Food Marketing Institute/Peabody Orlando/April 30 - May 2, 2013
Food Shippers of America/JW Marriott Orlando Grande Lakes/Feb. 23 - 25, 2014
GAMA International/Orlando World Center Marriott/March 15 - 18, 2015
Gases and Welding Distributors Association/Sept. 15 - 18, 2013
Gases and Welding Distributors Association/Oct. 3 - 9, 2013
Gasket Fabricators Association/Hilton Orlando/March 25 - 27, 2014
Generic Pharmaceutical Association/JW Marriott Orlando Grande Lakes/Feb. 20 - 22, 2013
Gerontological Society of America/Nov. 18 - 22, 2015
Golf Course Superintendents Association of America/Orange County Convention Center/Feb. 5 - 6, 2014
Greeting Card Association/The Villas of Grand Cypress/Oct. 3 - 6, 2013
Health Occupations Students of America/Disney's Coronado Springs Resort/ June 25 - 28, 2014
Healthcare Billing and Management Association/Walt Disney Swan and Dolphin/April 17 - 19, 2013
Healthcare Financial Management Association/Orange County Convention Center/June 16 - 19, 2013
Heart Failure Society of America/Peabody Orlando Hotel/Sept. 22 - 25, 2013
Heating, Airconditioning and Refrigeration Distributors International/JW Marriott Orlando Grande Lakes/Nov. 14 - 17, 2015
Hosa/Disney's Coronado Springs Resort/June 25 - 28, 2014
Ideas America/Sept. 11 - 13, 2013
IEEE Engineering in Medicine and Biology Society/Aug. 30 - Sept. 4, 2016
IEEE - Industry Applications Society/Walt Disney World Dolphin Resort/April 14 - 18, 2013/650 attendees
IEEE Microwave Theory and Techniques Society/April 14 - 16, 2013
Independent Medical Distributors Association/Loews Royal Pacific Resort/June 9 - 11, 2013
InfoComm International/Orange County Convention Center/June 8 - 14, 2013
InSight/Orange County Convention Center/Sept. 24 - 27, 2013
Institute for Professionals in Taxation/Renaissance Orlando at SeaWorld/June 23 - 26, 2013
Institute of Environmental Sciences and Technology/Rosen Shingle Creek Resort/Jan. 28 - 31, 2013
The Institute of Financial Operations/Disney's Coronado Springs Resort/May 19 - 23, 2013
Institute of Mathematical Statistics/Orlando World Center/March 10 - 13, 2013
Institute of Navigation/Renaissance Orlando at SeaWorld/June 10 - 13, 2013/11-25 exhibitors
Institute of Navigation/Renaissance Orlando at SeaWorld/June 16 - 19, 2014
Institute of Real Estate Management/Hilton Orlando Bonnet Creek/Oct. 14 - 18, 2014
Institute of Scrap Recycling Industries, Inc./Orange County Convention Center/ April 9 - 13, 2013

Insurance Accounting and Systems Association/Marriott Orlando World Center/June 4 - 7, 2017

International Association for Human Resource Information Management/Disney's Contemporary Resort/June 2 - 5, 2013

International Association of Airport Duty Free Stores/Orlando Convention Center/April 7 - 11, 2013

International Association of Arson Investigators/Rosen Centre Hotel/May 5 - 10, 2013

International Association of Chiefs of Police/Oct. 25 - 29, 2014/over 100 exhibitors

International Cast Polymer Alliance/Orange County Convention Center/Jan. 29 - 31, 2013

International Dairy Foods Association/JW Marriott Orlando Grande Lakes/Jan. 27 - 30, 2013

International Dairy-Deli-Bakery Association/Orange County Convention Center/June 2 - 4, 2013

International Energy Credit Association/JW Marriott Orlando Grande Lakes/Sept. 29 - Oct. 2, 2013

International Foodservice Distributors Association/Marriott World Center/Oct. 14 - 16, 2013

International Paralegal Management Association/Hyatt Regency Grand Cypress/Oct. 16 - 19, 2013

International Precious Metals Institute/JW Marriott Orlando Grande Lakes/June 7 - 10, 2014

International Sanitary Supply Association/Nov. 4 - 7, 2014

International Sleep Products Association/Disney's Grand Floridian Resort and Spa /March 6 - 7, 2013

International Sleep Products Association/March 16 - 19, 2016

International Society of Arboriculture/Aug. 8 - 12, 2015

International Society of Transport Aircraft Trading/JW Marriott Orlando Grande Lakes/March 10 - 12, 2013

International Ticketing Association/Walt Disney World Resort/Jan. 29 - 31, 2013

International Trademark Association/May 21 - 25, 2016

International Warehouse Logistics Association/Loews Portofino Bay Hotel at Universal Orlando/March 10 - 12, 2013

Jewish Community Centers Association of North America/Rosen Plaza Hotel/March 3 - 6, 2013

Journalism Education Association/Nov. 12 - 16, 2015

Lift Manufacturers Product Section - Material Handling Institute/Florida Hotel and Conference Center/Sept. 30 - Oct. 3, 2013

LOMA/Hyatt Regency Grand Cypress/Sept. 8 - 10, 2013

Marketing Research Association/Walt Disney World Swan/June 10 - 12, 2013/600 attendees

Material Handling Equipment Distributors Association/Loews Portofino Bay Resort/May 3 - 7, 2014

Material Handling Industry of America/Florida Hotel and Conference Center/Sept. 30 - Oct. 3, 2013

Messenger Courier Association of the Americas/The Swan and Dolphin/May 6 - 9, 2015

Metal Injection Molding Association/Hilton Orlando Lake Buena Vista/March 4 - 6, 2013

Metal Powder Industries Federation/Lake Buena Vista Resort Village and Spa / May 18 - 22, 2014

Metal Treating Institute/Disney's Yacht Club Resort/April 9 - 11, 2015

Minor League Baseball/Walt Disney World Swan And Dolphin/Dec. 9 - 12, 2013/3000 attendees/over 100 exhibitors

Mobile Air Conditioning Society Worldwide/Caribe Royale All Suite Hotel and Convention Center/Feb. 7 - 9, 2013

NACE International/Orange County Convention Center/March 17 - 21, 2013/11-25 exhibitors

National Association of Student Personnel Administrators/Orlando World Center Marriott/March 16 - 20, 2013/11-25 exhibitors

National Alliance of State Pharmacy Associations/Oct. 12 - 13, 2013

National Association for Bilingual Education/Walt Disney World Swan And Dolphin/Feb. 5 - 9, 2013

National Association of Black Journalists/Gaylord Palms Resort and Convention Center-Orlando/July 31 - Aug. 4, 2013

National Association of Church Business Administration/Gaylord Palms Resort and Convention Center-Orlando/July 7 - 11, 2015

National Association of College Auxiliary Services/Rosen Shingle Creek/Oct. 14 - 17, 2018

National Association of Colleges and Employers/Marriott World Center/June 4 - 7, 2013

National Association of Collegiate Directors of Athletics/Orlando World Center Marriott/June 13 - 16, 2013

National Association of Collegiate Directors of Athletics/Orlando World Center Marriott/June 9 - 12, 2014

National Association of Collegiate Directors of Athletics/Orlando World Center Marriott/June 15 - 18, 2015

National Association of Collegiate Directors of Athletics/Orlando World Center Marriott/June 12 - 15, 2017

National Association of Collegiate Directors of Athletics/Orlando World Center Marriott/June 10 - 13, 2019

National Association of Collegiate Directors of Athletics/Orlando World Center Marriott/June 14 - 17, 2021

National Association of Collegiate Marketing Administrators/Orlando World Center Marriott/June 10 - 13, 2013

National Association of Collegiate Marketing Administrators/Orlando World Center Marriott/June 6 - 9, 2014

National Association of Collegiate Marketing Administrators/Orlando World Center Marriott/June 15 - 18, 2015

National Association of Collegiate Marketing Administrators/Orlando World Center Marriott/June 12 - 15, 2017

National Association of Collegiate Marketing Administrators/Orlando World Center Marriott/June 10 - 13, 2019

National Association of Collegiate Marketing Administrators/Orlando World Center Marriott/June 14 - 17, 2021

National Association of Congregational Christian Churches/Hilton Lake Buena Vista/June 22 - 25, 2013

National Association of Educational Procurement, Inc./Disney's Contemporary Resort/April 7 - 10, 2013

National Association of Educational Procurement, Inc./Walt Disney World Resorts/April 8 - 11, 2018

National Association of Graduate Admissions Professionals/Gaylord Palms Resort and Convention Center-Orlando/April 24 - 27, 2013

National Association of Health Unit Coordinators/Rosen Plaza Hotel/Aug. 7 - 10, 2013

National Association of Home Builders/Jan. 11 - 14, 2017

National Association of Home Builders/Feb. 22 - 25, 2018

National Association of Independent Life Brokerage Agencies/JW Marriott Orlando Grande Lakes/Nov. 19 - 21, 2015

National Association of Independent Life Brokerage Agencies/JW Marriott Orlando Grande Lakes/Nov. 15 - 17, 2018

National Association of Insurance Women (International)/Caribe Royale All Suites Resort/June 5 - 8, 2013

National Association of Pediatric Nurse Practitioners/Hilton Orlando/April 17 - 20, 2013/1500 attendees/11-25 exhibitors

National Association of Physician Recruiters/Disney's Contemporary Resort/April 10 - 12, 2013

National Association of Principals of Schools for Girls/Feb. 23 - 25, 2014

National Association of Realtors/Nov. 4 - 7, 2016

National Association of Regulatory Utility Commissioners/Hilton Orlando Bonnet Creek/Nov. 17 - 20, 2013

National Association of School Psychologists/Walt Disney World Swan & Dolphin Resort/Feb. 17 - 21, 2015

National Association of State Directors of Migrant Education/April 28 - May 1, 2013/1500 attendees

National Association of State Utility Consumer Advocates (NASUCA)/Nov. 17 - 20, 2013

National Association of Subrogation Professionals/Rosen Shingle Creek/Nov. 8 - 11, 2014

National Association of Uniform Manufacturers and Distributors/The Renaissance Orlando at Sea World/April 4 - 7, 2013/51-100 exhibitors

National Association of Women Lawyers/Walt Disney World Grand Floridian Resort/Feb. 14 - 16, 2013

National Automobile Dealers Association/Feb. 9 - 11, 2013

National Board of Boiler and Pressure Vessel Inspectors/Gaylord Palms Resort and Convention Center-Orlando/May 9 - 13, 2016

National Business Aviation Association/Oct. 21 - 23, 2014

National Catholic Educational Exhibitors/April 7 - 9, 2015

National Cheese Institute/JW Marriott Orlando Grande Lakes/Jan. 27 - 30, 2013/over 100 exhibitors

National Coil Coating Association/Loews Portofino Bay Hotel/April 22 - 24, 2013

National Coil Coating Association/Loews Portofino Bay Hotel/April 18 - 20, 2016

National Community Pharmacists Association/Walt Disney World Swan And Dolphin/Oct. 12 - 16, 2013

National Concrete Burial Vault Association/Gaylord Palms Resort and Convention Center-Orlando/Feb. 23 - 25, 2013

National Defense Transportation Association/Sept. 13 - 17, 2014

National Emergency Number Association/Caribe Royale/Feb. 10 - 13, 2013

National Federation Coaches Association/Jan. 1, 2013

National Federation Coaches Association/Rosen Shingle Creek/Jan. 3 - 6, 2013

National Federation Coaches Association/Jan. 6, 2013

National Federation Coaches Association/Orlando World Center Marriott/Dec. 11 - 15, 2015

National Federation of Municipal Analysts/Disney's Grand Floridian Resort and Spa/May 6 - 9, 2014

National Federation of State High School Associations/Rosen Shingle Creek/Jan. 3 - 6, 2013

National Fire Sprinkler Association/Hilton Bonnet Creek Resort/April 30 - May 2, 2015

National Freight Transportation Association/Omni Orlando Resort at ChampionsGate/March 20 - 24, 2013

National Institute of Governmental Purchasing/Orlando World Center Marriott/Aug. 24 - 28, 2013

National Institute of Governmental Purchasing/Gaylord Palms Resort and Convention Center-Orlando/Aug. 24 - 28, 2018

National Interscholastic Athletic Administrators Association/Orlando World Center Marriott/Dec. 11 - 15, 2015

National League for Nursing/Orlando World Center Marriott/Sept. 21 - 24, 2016

National Minority Supplier Development Council/Orange County Convention Center/Nov. 2 - 5, 2014

National Multi-Housing Council/Hilton Orlando Bonnet Creek/Nov. 17 - 19, 2014

National Orientation Directors Association/Nov. 2 - 5, 2014

National Pest Management Association/Florida Hotel and Conference Center/Jan. 8 - 9, 2013

National Precast Concrete Association/Rosen Shingle Creek Hotel/Feb. 5 - 7, 2015

National Retail Tenants Association/The Renaissance Orlando at Sea World/Sept. 22 - 25, 2013

National Scholastic Press Association/Walt Disney World Swan And Dolphin/Nov. 12 - 16, 2015

National Science Teachers Association/Nov. 6 - 8, 2014

National Society for Histotechnology/Sept. 15 - 20, 2017

National Telecommunications Cooperative Association/Walt Disney World Swan & Dolphin Resort/June 15 - 17, 2014

National Tour Association/Jan. 19 - 23, 2013

National Tour Association/Orange County Convention Center/Jan. 20 - 24, 2013

National Wooden Pallet and Container Association/Loews Portofino Bay Hotel/Feb. 16 - 19, 2013

Newspaper Association of America/Hilton Bonnet Creek Resort/April 14 - 17, 2013

North American Academy of Liturgy/Jan. 2 - 5, 2014

North American Menopause Society/Oct. 5 - 8, 2016

North American Thermal Analysis Society/Aug. 8 - 11, 2016
Opticians Association of America/Buena Vista Palace/Jan. 17 - 19, 2013
Organization for the Promotion and Advancement of Small
Telecommunications Companies/Disney Yacht and Beach Resort/July 13 -
17, 2013
Orthopaedic Section - American Physical Therapy Association/Marriott World
Center/May 2 - 4, 2013
Orthopaedic Trauma Association/Oct. 3 - 6, 2018
Parenteral Drug Association/Peabody Orlando/April 15 - 17, 2013
Pet Industry Distributors Association/Orange County Convention Center/Feb.
20 - 22, 2013/11-25 exhibitors
Pharmaceutical Marketing Research Group/Gaylord Palms Resort and
Convention Center-Orlando/March 9 - 11, 2014
Phi Delta Kappa International/April 26 - 28, 2013
Phycological Society of America/Aug. 4 - 10, 2013
Physician Office Managers Association of America/Walt Disney World Swan/
Sept. 18 - 21, 2013
Powder Metallurgy Parts Association/Hilton Orlando Lake Buena Vista/March
4 - 6, 2013
Powder Metallurgy Parts Association/May 18 - 22, 2014
Professional Convention Management Association/Orange County Convention
Center/Jan. 13 - 16, 2013/3000 attendees
Professional Golfers Association of America/Hilton Orlando/Jan. 22 - 24, 2013
Professional Liability Underwriting Society/Nov. 4 - 6, 2013
Professional Retail Store Maintenance Association/Rosen Shingle Creek/April 6
- 8, 2014
Public Housing Authorities Directors Association/Hyatt Regency Grand
Cypress/Jan. 12 - 15, 2014
Public Investors Arbitration Bar Association/JW Marriott Orlando Grande
Lakes/Oct. 16 - 19, 2013
RCI, Inc./Rosen Shingle Creek Hotel/March 14 - 19, 2013
Research Society on Alcoholism/Grand Cypress/June 22 - 26, 2013
Resource Center for Religious Institutes/Oct. 26 - 30, 2015
Retail Industry Leaders Association/Gaylord Palms Resort and Convention
Center-Orlando/Feb. 17 - 20, 2013/1-10 exhibitors
Robotic Industries Association/Orlando World Center Marriott/Feb. 20 - 22,
2013
SMMA - The Motor and Motion Association/Villas of Grand Cypress Orlando
Hotel/May 7 - 9, 2013
Society for American Archaeology/April 6 - 10, 2016
Society for Applied Learning Technology/Caribe Royale Hotel/March 6 - 8,
2013
Society for Cardiovascular Angiography and Interventions/Convention Center/
The Peabody Orlando/May 8 - 11, 2013
Society for Cardiovascular Angiography and Interventions/Convention Center/
The Peabody Orlando/May 4 - 7, 2013
Society for Experimental Mechanics, Inc./Rosen Plaza Hotel/Feb. 3 - 6, 2013
Society for Gynecologic Investigation/Hilton Orlando Bonnet Creek/March 20
- 23, 2013
Society for Laboratory Automation and Screening/Gaylord Palms Resort and
Convention Center/Jan. 12 - 16, 2013
Society for Marketing Professional Services/July 31 - Aug. 3, 2013/1-10
exhibitors
Society for Pediatric Dermatology/March 2, 2017
Society for Public Health Education/April 17 - 19, 2013
Society for Range Management/Caribe Royal Resort/Feb. 7 - 15, 2014
Society for Simulation in Healthcare/Peabody Orlando/Jan. 26 - 30, 2013
Society for Surgery of the Alimentary Tract/Orange County Convention Center/
May 17 - 21, 2013
Society of Actuaries/Oct. 26 - 29, 2014
Society of American Military Engineers/Jacksonville Post/May 20 - 23, 2014
Society of Competitive Intelligence Professionals/Caribe Royal Resort/May 6 -
9, 2013/500 attendees/51-100 exhibitors
Society for Critical Care Medicine/Orange County Convention Center/Feb. 20 -
24, 2016
Society for Critical Care Medicine/Orange County Convention Center/Feb. 15 -
19, 2020
Society of Forensic Toxicologists/Oct. 26 - Nov. 3, 2013
Society of Forensic Toxicologists/Oct. 27 - Nov. 1, 2013
Society of Government Meeting Professionals/May 22 - 24, 2013
Society of Incentive & Travel Executives/Loews Portofino Bay Hotel at Universal
Orlando/Dec. 7 - 10, 2014
Society of Pharmaceutical and Biotech Trainers/Peabody Orlando/June 10 - 13,
2013/over 100 exhibitors
Specialty Graphic Imaging Association/Orange County Convention Center/Oct.
23 - 25, 2013
Synthetic Turf Council/Renaissance Orlando at SeaWorld/March 20 - 22, 2013
System Safety Society/Renaissance Orlando at SeaWorld/Aug. 6 - 14, 2016
Technology Student Association/Rosen Shingle Creek Hotel/June 28 - July 2,
2013
Transportation Intermediaries Association/April 15 - 18, 2015
Triological Society/JW Marriott Grande Lakes/April 10 - 14, 2013
Undersea and Hyperbaric Medical Society/DoubleTree by Hilton at the
Entrance to Universal Orlando/June 13 - 15, 2013
United Methodist Association of Health and Welfare Ministries/Hilton in the
Walt Disney World(R) Resort/March 4 - 6, 2013
United Motorcoach Association/Orange County Convention Center/Jan. 20 -
24, 2014
United Producers Formulators and Distributors Association/April 23 - 25, 2013
Utilimetrics/Alliance for Advanced Metering & Data Management Solutions/
Sept. 28 - Oct. 1, 2014
Wine and Spirits Wholesalers of America/Grande Lakes/April 28 - 30, 2013
Worldwide ERC/May 7 - 9, 2014

Palm Beach
American Society for Automation in Pharmacy/Breakers Palm Beach/June 26 -
28, 2014
Flavor and Extract Manufacturers Association/Ritz-Carlton/May 5 - 8, 2013
National Association of Chain Drug Stores/The Breakers/April 20 - 23, 2013
National Electrical Manufacturers Association/Breakers Palm Beach/Nov. 8 -
9, 2013

Stable Value Investment Association/Four Seasons Resort Palm Beach/April 14
- 16, 2013
Tag and Label Manufacturers Institute/Four Seasons Resort Palm Beach/March
3 - 6, 2013

Palm Beach Gardens
American Boiler Manufacturers Association/PGA National Hotel, Resort and
Spa/Jan. 18 - 21, 2013
American Concrete Pipe Association/PGA National Resort and Spa/March 10 -
12, 2013
Manufacturers' Agents Association for the Foodservice Industry/PGA National
Resort and Spa/Jan. 15 - 18, 2014
National Sporting Goods Association/PGA National Resort and Spa/May 5 - 8,
2013
Outdoor Power Equipment Aftermarket Association/PGA National Resort and
Spa/Feb. 16 - 19, 2013
Shelf-Stable Food Processors Association/PGA National Resort and Spa/March
10 - 12, 2013

Palm Coast
Apple Processors Association/Hammock Beach Resort/June 16 - 18, 2013

Palm Harbor
Fabricators & Manufacturers Association, International/Innisbrook Golf and
Spa Resort/Feb. 27 - March 1, 2013

Pensacola
National Association of Health and Educational Facilities Finance Authorities/
Hilton Pensacola Beach Gulf Front/April 15 - 17, 2013

Ponte Vedra Beach
American Association of Insurance Services/Ponte Vedra Inn and Club/April 7
- 9, 2013
American Sports Builders Association/Sawgrass Marriott Golf Resort and Spa/
Dec. 6 - 10, 2014
Cookie and Snack Bakers Association/Ponte Vedra Inn and Club/Feb. 17 - 20,
2013
Dental Trade Alliance/Ponte Vedra Beach Resort/Oct. 15 - 18, 2013
National Association of Principals of Schools for Girls/Ponte Vedra Inn and
Club/Feb. 24 - 26, 2013
National Health Council/Ponte Vedra Inn and Club/Feb. 13 - 15, 2013
Secondary Materials and Recycled Textiles Association/Ponte Vedra Inn and
Club/March 17 - 20, 2013

Reunion
Automotive Safety Council/Reunion Resort and Golf Club/March 20 - 24, 2013

Sarasota
Electrical Generating Systems Association/Hyatt Regency Sarasota/March 17 -
19, 2013

St. Augustine
Petroleum Packaging Council/Renaissance Resort at World Golf Village/March
17 - 19, 2013

St. Pete Beach
AMC Institute/Loews Don CeSar Hotel/Feb. 13 - 15, 2013
Association of American Feed Control Officials/Aug. 10 - 12, 2013
The Association of Suppliers to the Paper Industry/Don CeSar Beach Hotel/
Feb. 28 - March 1, 2013
Flexible Intermediate Bulk Container Association/Lowes Don CeSar Beach
Hotel/April 18 - 19, 2013
Flexible Packaging Association/TradeWinds Resort/Feb. 13 - 15, 2013
International Concrete Repair Institute/TradeWinds Island Resort/March 20 -
22, 2013
International Window Cleaning Association/TradeWinds Island Resort/Feb. 13
- 16, 2013/400 attendees
Kappa Psi Pharmaceutical Fraternity, Inc./Trade Winds Resort/July 30 - Aug. 4,
2013
National Animal Supplement Council/TradeWinds Island Grand/May 14 - 16,
2013
National Association of Schools of Dance/Don CeSar Beach Hotel/Sept. 11 -
13, 2013
Optometric Extension Program Foundation/May 2 - 4, 2013
Outdoor Power Equipment and Engine Service Association/Loews Don CeSar
Hotel/March 3 - 6, 2013
Plastics Pipe Institute/May 5 - 8, 2013
Women in Government/Jan. 3 - 5, 2013

St. Petersburg
Airports Council International - North America/Vinoy Renaissance St.
Petersburg Resort and Golf Club/March 5 - 7, 2013
American Accounting Association/Hilton St. Petersburg Bayfront/March 8 - 9,
2013
American Brush Manufacturers Association/Renaissance Vinoy Resort and
Golf Club/March 18 - 21, 2015
Association of American Plant Food Control Officials/Aug. 1 - 4, 2013
Association of Metropolitan Water Agencies/Vinoy Renaissance St. Petersburg
Resort and Golf Club/Oct. 27 - 30, 2013
Hydraulic Institute/Renaissance Vinoy Resort and Golf Club/Feb. 12 - 17, 2015
Information Technology Alliance/Vinoy Renaissance/April 28 - 30, 2013
Inter-Company Marketing Group/Marriott Vinoy Renaissance Resort and Golf
Club/Jan. 29 - 31, 2013
National Hearing Conservation Association/Hilton St. Petersburg Bayfront/Feb.
21 - 23, 2013
Polyurethane Foam Association/Renaissance Vinoy Resort and Golf Club/May
22 - 23, 2013
Process Equipment Manufacturers' Association/April 10 - 14, 2013
Transportation Lawyers Association/Marriott Vinoy Renaissance Resort and
Golf Club/April 29 - May 3, 2014
Xplor International/The TradeWinds Island Grand Hotel/April 17 - 19, 2013

Sunny Isles Beach
Management Association for Private Photogrammetric Surveyors/Trump Hotel/
Jan. 27 - 31, 2013

Tampa
Academy of Managed Care Pharmacy/Tampa Convention Center/April 2 - 4,
2014
Academy of Osseointegration/March 7 - 9, 2013

Academy of Veterinary Homeopathy/Clearwater Beach Hotel/April 26 - 28, 2013

American Animal Hospital Association/March 12 - 15, 2015

American Association for Respiratory Care/Nov. 7 - 10, 2015/5000 attendees/over 100 exhibitors

American Association of Woodturners/Tampa Convention Center/June 28 - 30, 2013

American Bandmasters Association/University of South Florida/March 6 - 9, 2013

American Intellectual Property Law Association/Tampa Marriott Waterside Hotel and Marina/Jan. 30 - Feb. 2, 2013

American Pain Society/Tampa Convention Center/April 30 - May 3, 2014

American Society for Engineering Education/June 16 - 19, 2019

American Society of Abdominal Surgeons/DoubleTree by Hilton Hotel Tampa Airport-Westshore/Nov. 1 - 3, 2013

American Society of Agronomy (ASA, CSSA, SSSA)/Nov. 3 - 6, 2013

American Society of Agronomy (ASA, CSSA, SSSA)/Oct. 22 - 25, 2017

American Sugarbeet Growers Association/Tampa Marriott Waterside Hotel and Marina/Feb. 9 - 11, 2013

American Traffic Safety Service Association/Tampa Convention Center/Feb. 6 - 10, 2015

ASPRS-The Imaging and Geospatial Information Society/Grand Hyatt Tampa Bay/May 4 - 8, 2015

Association Montessori International - United States of America/Grand Hyatt Tampa Bay/Feb. 15 - 18, 2013

Association of American Geographers/April 8 - 12, 2014

BICSI/Tampa Convention Center/Jan. 20 - 24, 2013

Biomedical Engineering Society/Oct. 7 - 10, 2015/3000 attendees/51-100 exhibitors

Conference on College Composition and Communication/March 18 - 21, 2015

Council on Social Work Education/Tampa Convention Center/Oct. 23 - 26, 2014

Crop Science Society of America/Nov. 3 - 6, 2013

Crop Science Society of America/Oct. 22 - 25, 2017

Decision Sciences Institute/Tampa Marriott Waterside Hotel and Marina/Nov. 22 - 25, 2014

The Fertilizer Institute/Tampa Marriott Waterside Hotel/Nov. 19 - 21, 2013

Healthcare Distribution Management Association/Tampa Marriott Waterside Hotel/March 3 - 6, 2013

Institute of Navigation/Tampa Convention Center/Sept. 8 - 14, 2014

Institute of Navigation/Tampa Convention Center/Sept. 14 - 18, 2015

International Association of Assessing Officers/Aug. 28 - 31, 2016

International Cemetery, Cremation and Funeral Association/Tampa Convention Center/April 10 - 13, 2013/over 100 exhibitors

International Federation of Pharmaceutical Wholesalers/Tampa Marriott Waterside Hotel/March 3 - 6, 2013

International Police Mountain Bike Association/May 16 - 23, 2014

NALP - The Association for Legal Career Professionals/Grand Hyatt Tampa Bay/April 24 - 27, 2013

National Association of Elevator Contractors/Tampa Bay Convention Center/Sept. 23 - 26, 2013

National Association of Episcopal Schools/Berkeley Preparatory School/Feb. 7 - 9, 2013

National Cattlemen's Beef Association/Tampa Bay Convention Center/Feb. 6 - 9, 2013/6000 attendees

National Guardianship Association/Grand Hyatt Tampa Bay/Oct. 12 - 15, 2013

National Independent Concessionaires Association/USF Embassy Suites/Feb. 4 - 6, 2013

National School Supply and Equipment Association/March 13 - 15, 2013

National School Supply and Equipment Association/Jan. 15 - 17, 2014

National School Supply and Equipment Association/Oct. 29 - 31, 2014

Orthopaedic Trauma Association/Oct. 15 - 18, 2014

Outdoor Amusement Business Association/Embassy Suites Hotel/Feb. 7 - 8, 2013

Public Risk Management Association/Tampa Bay Convention Center/June 2 - 5, 2013

Recreation Vehicle Industry Association/Tampa Marriott Waterside Hotel and Marina/Jan. 17 - 20, 2013

SMMA - The Motor and Motion Association/Marriott Tampa Airport Hotel/Nov. 5 - 7, 2013

Snack Food Association/Tampa Marriott Waterside Hotel and Marina/March 16 - 19, 2013

The Society for Modeling and Simulation International/Renaissance Tampa International Plaza Hotel/Jan. 28 - Feb. 1, 2013

Society for the History of Discoveries/Tampa Marriott Waterside Hotel and Marina/Oct. 31 - Nov. 2, 2013

Society of Gynecologic Oncologists/Tampa Bay Convention Center/March 23 - 26, 2014

Soil Science Society of America/Nov. 3 - 7, 2013/3200 attendees/over 100 exhibitors

Soil Science Society of America/Oct. 22 - 25, 2017

Venus

Association of Field Ornithologists/March 27 - 30, 2013

West Palm Beach

American Society of Concrete Contractors/Breakers/July 25 - 28, 2013

International Association of Fairs and Expositions/West Palm Beach Marriott/April 25 - 28, 2013

Salt Institute/Ritz Carlton/March 6 - 8, 2013

Weston

International Beverage Dispensing Equipment Association/Hyatt Regency Bonaventure Conference Center and Spa/March 7 - 12, 2013

GEORGIA

Albany

Quail Unlimited/Albany Civic Center/Jan. 24 - 26, 2013

Athens

The Association of Literary Scholars, Critics, and Writers/University Of Georgia/April 5 - 7, 2013

Atlanta

Academy of Clinical Laboratory Physicians and Scientists/Emory University/June 6 - 8, 2013

Academy of Management/Aug. 4 - 8, 2017

ACUTA - The Association for Information Communications Technology Professionals in Higher Education/Hyatt Regency Atlanta/April 19 - 22, 2015

Adhesive and Sealant Council/Hyatt Regency Atlanta/April 21 - 23, 2013

Airports Council International - North America/June 4 - 5, 2013

American Academy of Advertising/March 27 - 30, 2014

American Academy of Clinical Toxicology/Hyatt Regency Atlanta/Sept. 27 - Oct. 2, 2013

American Academy of Religion/Nov. 21 - 24, 2015/10000 attendees/over 100 exhibitors

American Association for Clinical Chemistry, Inc./July 26 - 30, 2015/18000 attendees

American Association for the History of Medicine/May 16 - 19, 2013

American Association of Colleges for Teacher Education/Hilton Atlanta/Feb. 27 - March 1, 2015

American Association of Medical Assistants/Sheraton Atlanta Hotel/Sept. 27 - 30, 2013

American Association of Museums/April 26 - 29, 2015/over 100 exhibitors

American Association of Physical Anthropologists/April 12 - 16, 2016

American Association of Retired Persons/Georgia World Congress Center/Oct. 4 - 5, 2013

American Association of Veterinary Clinicians/Westin Atlanta Airport/March 21 - 22, 2013

American Coatings Association/Georgia World Congress Center/April 7 - 10, 2014/7500 attendees/over 100 exhibitors

American College of Allergy, Asthma and Immunology/Nov. 6 - 11, 2014/51-100 exhibitors

American College of Clinical Pharmacology/Westin Peachtree Plaza, Atlanta/Sept. 14 - 16, 2014

American College of Sports Medicine/April 2 - 5, 2014

American College of Veterinary Pathologists/Atlanta Marriott Marquis/Nov. 8 - 12, 2014

American Conference of Academic Deans/Jan. 23 - 26, 2013

American Council of Life Insurers (ACLI)/The Ritz-Carlton Buckhead/Feb. 23 - 26, 2013

American Craft Council/Cobb Galleria Centre/May 14 - 17, 2013

American Dental Association/Georgia World Congress Center/Oct. 19 - 24, 2017

American Economic Association/Atlanta Marriott Century Center/Jan. 5 - 7, 2018

American Educational Research Association/April 11 - 15, 2013

American Feed Industry Association/Georgia World Congress Center/Jan. 29 - 31, 2013

The American Finance Association/Jan. 5 - 7, 2018

American Health Information Management Association/Sept. 15 - 20, 2013

American Health Information Management Association/Oct. 26 - 30, 2013

American Historical Association/Atlanta Marriott Marquis/Jan. 7 - 10, 2016

American Institute of Certified Planners/April 26 - 29, 2014

American Library Association/Jan. 20 - 24, 2017

American Mathematical Society/Hyatt Regency Atlanta/Jan. 4 - 7, 2017

American Meat Institute/Georgia World Congress Center/Jan. 29 - 31, 2013/25000 attendees/over 100 exhibitors

American Meteorological Society/Feb. 2 - 6, 2014

American Moving and Storage Association/Atlanta Marriott Marquis/March 3 - 6, 2013

American Nuclear Society/Atlanta Marriott Marquis/June 16 - 20, 2013

American Nurses Association/Feb. 6 - 8, 2013

American Planning Association/April 26 - 29, 2014

American Planning Association/April 26 - 30, 2014

American Prepaid Legal Services Institute/Hyatt Regency Atlanta/May 2 - 4, 2013

American Psychiatric Association/May 14 - 18, 2016

American Short Line and Regional Railroad Association/Atlanta Marriott Century Center/April 27 - 30, 2013/1500 attendees/51-100 exhibitors

American Society for Clinical Laboratory Science/July 26 - 30, 2015/19000 attendees/over 100 exhibitors

American Society for Clinical Laboratory Science/July 28 - Aug. 1, 2015

American Society for Clinical Pharmacology and Therapeutics/Atlanta Marriott Marquis/March 19 - 22, 2014

American Society for Engineering Education/June 23 - 26, 2013

American Society for Engineering Education/Georgia World Congress Center/June 23 - 26, 2013/4000 attendees/over 100 exhibitors

American Society for Healthcare Engineering/July 21 - 24, 2013/1-10 exhibitors

American Society for Metabolic and Bariatric Surgery/Georgia World Congress Center/Nov. 11 - 16, 2013

American Society for Neurochemistry/March 13 - 18, 2015

American Society for Therapeutic Radiology and Oncology/Georgia World Congress Center/Sept. 22 - 25, 2013

American Society of Association Executives-The Center for Association Leadership/Aug. 3 - 6, 2013

American Society of Criminology/Atlanta Marriott Century Center/Nov. 20 - 23, 2013

American Society of Criminology/Atlanta Marriott Marquis/Nov. 14 - 17, 2018

American Society of Criminology/Atlanta Marriott Marquis/Nov. 16 - 19, 2022

American Society of Nephrology/Georgia World Congress Center/Nov. 5 - 10, 2013

American Student Dental Association/March 6 - 10, 2013

American Student Dental Association/Westin Peachtree Plaza, Atlanta/March 6 - 9, 2013/400 attendees/51-100 exhibitors

Archivists and Librarians in the History of the Health Sciences/May 15 - 16, 2013

Association for Play Therapy/Renaissance Waverly Atlanta Luxury Hotel/Oct. 6 - 11, 2015

Association for the Study of African American Life and History/Sheraton Atlanta Hotel/Sept. 21 - 27, 2015

Association for Unmanned Vehicle Systems International/Georgia World Congress Center/May 5 - 8, 2015/8000 attendees/over 100 exhibitors

Association of American Colleges and Universities/Hyatt Regency Atlanta/Jan. 23 - 26, 2013/1800 attendees/11-25 exhibitors

Association of Analytical Communities International/Marriott Atlanta Marquis/Sept. 24 - 27, 2017

Association of Asphalt Paving Technologists/Sheraton Atlanta Hotel/March 16 - 19, 2014

Association of Children's Prosthetic-Orthotic Clinics/Grand Hyatt Atlanta In Buckhead/April 10 - 13, 2013

Association of College Unions International/March 15 - 19, 2020

Association of Medical School Pediatric Department Chairs/Hyatt Regency Atlanta/Feb. 28 - March 3, 2013

Association of Procurement Technical Assistance Centers/Sheraton Atlanta Hotel/April 21 - 25, 2013

Association of Professors of Gynecology and Obstetrics/Hyatt Regency Atlanta/Feb. 26 - March 1, 2014

Association of Proposal Management Professionals/The Westin Peachtree Plaza/May 28 - 31, 2013

Association of State Floodplain Managers/Hyatt Regency Atlanta/May 31 - June 1, 2015

Association of Teacher Educators/Hyatt Regency Atlanta/Feb. 15 - 19, 2013

Bearing Specialist Association/Loews Atlanta Hotel/Jan. 27 - 29, 2013

Beta Alpha Psi/Aug. 7 - 9, 2014

CBA/Georgia World Congress Center/June 22 - 25, 2014

Chain Drug Marketing Association/Feb. 23 - 25, 2013

Chain Drug Marketing Association/Hilton Atlanta/Sept. 19 - 22, 2013

Conference of Radiation Control Program Directors/Crowne Plaza Atlanta Perimeter at Ravinia/May 19 - 22, 2014

Conference on Latin American History/Jan. 7 - 10, 2016

Construction Owners Association of America/Grand Hyatt Atlanta In Buckhead/May 8 - 10, 2013

Council for Advancement and Support of Education/Hyatt Regency Atlanta/April 17 - 19, 2013

Council for Advancement and Support of Education/Westin Buckhead Atlanta/May 8 - 10, 2013

Council for Advancement and Support of Education/Georgia Tech Hotel and Conference Center/June 6 - 7, 2013

Council on Social Work Education/Atlanta Marriott Marquis/Nov. 3 - 6, 2016

Distributive Education Clubs of America (DECA)/May 3 - 6, 2014

Division 1-A Athletic Directors Association/Jan. 16 - 19, 2019

Evidence Photographers International Council/Georgia World Congress Center/Jan. 19 - 22, 2013

Express Carriers Association/April 15, 2014

Express Carriers Association/Atlanta Marriott Marquis/April 15 - 17, 2014

Fresh Produce Association of the Americas/Oct. 23 - 26, 2015

Fresh Produce Association of the Americas/Oct. 23 - 25, 2015/18000 attendees

Historians of American Communism/Atlanta Marriott Marquis/Jan. 7 - 10, 2016

Human Capital Institute/Grand Hyatt Atlanta/Feb. 5 - 7, 2013

IEEE Communications Society/Dec. 9 - 13, 2013

Independent Educational Consultants Association/April 10 - 13, 2013

Institute of Nuclear Materials Management/Market Center Inforum/July 19 - 24, 2014/11-25 exhibitors

International Association of Music Libraries, United States Branch/Feb. 24 - March 2, 2014

International Association of Special Investigation Units/Atlanta Marriott Marquis/Sept. 8 - 11, 2013

International Dairy-Deli-Bakery Association/June 7 - 9, 2015

International District Energy Association/Atlanta Marriott Marquis/Feb. 17 - 21, 2014

International Society for Research on Aggression/July 15 - 19, 2014

International Society for Technology in Education/June 29 - July 2, 2014/20000 attendees/over 100 exhibitors

International Studies Association/Atlanta Marriott Marquis/March 16 - 19, 2016

League for Innovation in the Community College/Sheraton Atlanta Hotel/Oct. 27 - 30, 2013

Lift Manufacturers Product Section - Material Handling Institute/Georgia World Congress Center/March 17 - 20, 2014

Marble Institute of America/Georgia World Congress Center/April 29 - May 2, 2013

Materials Handling and Management Society/Georgia World Congress Center/March 17 - 20, 2014/over 100 exhibitors

Mathematical Association of America/Jan. 4 - 7, 2017

Metal Construction Association/Oct. 1 - 3, 2013

Music Library Association/Feb. 24 - March 2, 2014

NALS/Atlanta Marriott Perimeter Center/Oct. 17 - 20, 2013

National Animal Control Association/Atlanta Marriott Marquis/Sept. 5 - 6, 2013

National Association for Business Teacher Education/April 13, 2013

National Association for Alcoholism and Drug Abuse Counselors/InterContinental Buckhead Atlanta/Oct. 11 - 14, 2013

National Association of Biology Teachers/Hyatt Regency Atlanta/Nov. 20 - 23, 2013

National Association of Diaconate Directors/Archdiocese of Atlanta/April 21 - 25, 2014

National Association of Educational Procurement, Inc./Atlanta Hyatt/April 12 - May 15, 2015

National Association of Healthcare Access Management/Hyatt Regency Atlanta/May 15 - 18, 2013

National Association of Professional Organizers/Sheraton Atlanta Hotel/May 18 - 21, 2016

National Business Education Association/Atlanta Marriott Century Center/April 16 - 20, 2013

National Collegiate Athletic Association/Jan. 16 - 19, 2019

National Conference of Bankruptcy Judges/Oct. 30 - Nov. 2, 2013

National Conference of State Legislatures/Aug. 12 - 15, 2013/over 100 exhibitors

National Council of Structural Engineers Associations/Sept. 18 - 21, 2013

National Council on Measurement in Education/April 10 - 14, 2013

National Education Association/July 1 - 6, 2013

National Electrical Manufacturers Representatives Association/Atlanta Marriott Century Center/Feb. 5 - 8, 2014

National Forum for Black Public Administrators/April 20 - 24, 2013/1000 attendees

National Forum for Black Public Administrators/April 20 - 23, 2013

National Glass Association/Georgia World Congress Center/Sept. 10 - 12, 2013/over 100 exhibitors

National Poultry and Food Distributors Association/Hyatt Regency Atlanta/Jan. 29 - Feb. 1, 2013

National Propane Gas Association/Georgia World Congress Center/April 13 - 15, 2013

National Propane Gas Association/Georgia World Congress Center/April 12 - 14, 2014

National Propane Gas Association/Georgia World Congress Center/April 11 - 13, 2015

National Propane Gas Association/Georgia World Congress Center/April 9 - 11, 2016

National School Supply and Equipment Association/Jan. 16 - 18, 2013

National Telecommunications Cooperative Association/InterContinental Buckhead Atlanta/May 19 - 21, 2013

North American Association of Christians in Social Work/Sheraton Atlanta Hotel/Oct. 17 - 20, 2013

North American Society for Cardiovascular Imaging/Atlanta Marriott Marquis/Sept. 28 - Oct. 1, 2013

Obesity Society/Nov. 12 - 16, 2013

Organization of American Historians/April 10 - 13, 2014

Pediatric Orthopedic Society of North America/Atlanta Marriott Century Center/April 29 - May 2, 2015

Produce Marketing Association/Oct. 23 - 26, 2015

Produce Marketing Association/Oct. 23 - 25, 2015/18500 attendees/over 100 exhibitors

Professional Liability Underwriting Society/Nov. 1 - 3, 2017

Professional Photographers of America/Georgia World Congress Center/Jan. 20 - 22, 2013

Refrigerating Engineers and Technicians Association/Nov. 4, 2014

Refrigerating Engineers and Technicians Association/Nov. 4 - 7, 2014

Romance Writers of America/Atlanta Marriott Marquis/July 17 - 21, 2013/2100 attendees

School Nutrition Association/July 9 - 12, 2017

Sewn Products Equipment and Suppliers of the Americas/Georgia World Congress Center/May 13 - 15, 2014/8000 attendees

Society for Academic Emergency Medicine/May 15 - 18, 2013

The Society for Adolescent Medicine/Omni Hotel at CNN Center/March 13 - 16, 2013

The Society for Investigative Dermatology/Hilton Atlanta/May 6 - 9, 2015

Society for Italian Historical Studies/Hilton Atlanta/Marietta Hotel and Conference Center/Jan. 7 - 10, 2016

Society for Physician Assistants in Pediatrics/Sheraton Atlanta Hotel/March 8 - 10, 2013

Society for Radiation Oncology Administration/Sept. 21 - 25, 2013

Society for Technical Communication/Hyatt Regency Atlanta/May 5 - 8, 2013/11-25 exhibitors

Society of Biblical Literature/Nov. 21 - 24, 2015

Society of Biological Psychiatry/May 12 - 14, 2016

Society of Biological Psychiatry/May 14 - 18, 2016

Society of Cardiovascular Anesthesiologists/JW Marriott Atlanta Buckhead/May 6 - 11, 2013

Society of Forensic Toxicologists/Oct. 17 - 25, 2015

Specialty Graphic Imaging Association/Georgia World Congress Center/Nov. 4 - 6, 2015

Specialty Tools and Fasteners Distributors Association/Georgia World Congress Center/Nov. 6 - 8, 2016

Tile Council of North America, Inc./Georgia World Congress Center/April 29 - May 2, 2013/over 100 exhibitors

U.S Poultry and Egg Association/Georgia World Congress Center/Jan. 29 - 31, 2013

United States Psychiatric Rehabilitation Association/Hyatt Regency Atlanta/June 9 - 12, 2013

The Wire Association International, Inc./Georgia World Congress Center/April 23 - 25, 2013

Augusta

American Holistic Veterinary Medical Association/Augusta Marriott at the Convention Center/Oct. 17 - 20, 2015

Braselton

Sports Lawyers Association/Chateau Elan Winery and Resort/May 16 - 18, 2013

Lumpkin

Artist-Blacksmiths' Association of North America/Columbus Ga Convention Center & Westville Village/March 15 - 17, 2013

Savannah

American Accounting Association/Hyatt Regency Savannah/Feb. 21 - 23, 2013

American Association of Neuromuscular and Electrodiagnostic Medicine/Savannah International Trade and Convention Center/Oct. 29 - Nov. 1, 2014

American College of Veterinary Radiology/Savannah Marriott Riverfront/Oct. 8 - 11, 2013

American Physical Society/April 5 - 8, 2014

American Physical Society/Nov. 16 - 20, 2015

American Society for Parenteral and Enteral Nutrition/Savannah International Trade and Convention Center/Jan. 18 - 21, 2014

Association for Information Systems/Aug. 7 - 10, 2014/3000 attendees

Association of Nutrition & Foodservice Professionals/Westin Savannah Harbor Golf Resort and Spa/July 28 - 31, 2013

Certification Board for Urologic Nurses and Associates/Hyatt Regency/March 7 - 9, 2013

Coordinating Research Council/Hyatt Regency/April 29 - May 2, 2013

The Fertilizer Institute/Hyatt Regency/Nov. 18 - 20, 2014

International Association of Clerks, Recorders, Election Officials and Treasurers/The Mulberry Inn/Jan. 10 - 15, 2013

International Association of Workforce Professionals (IAWP)/Hyatt Regency Savannah/June 14 - 17, 2015
Land Improvement Contractors of America/Savannah Marriott Riverfront/Feb. 5 - 10, 2013
National Agricultural Aviation Association/Dec. 7 - 10, 2015
National Air Filtration Association/The Westin Savannah Harbor Golf Resort & Spa/Sept. 25 - 27, 2013
National Association for Court Management/Hyatt Regency Savannah/Feb. 9 - 11, 2014
National Association of Credit Union Supervisory and Auditing Committees/ Hilton Savannah DeSoto Hotel/June 12 - 15, 2013
National Association of Fraternal Insurance Counsellors/Hilton Savannah DeSoto/May 6 - 8, 2013
National Association of Health Unit Coordinators/Hilton Savannah DeSoto/ Aug. 5 - 8, 2015
National Association of State Controlled Substances Authorities/Oct. 21 - 24, 2014
National Association of Truck Stop Operators(NATSO)/Westin Savannah Harbor Golf Resort and Spa/Feb. 2 - 6, 2013
National Conference of Insurance Legislators/Hyatt Regency/March 6 - 9, 2014
National Council of Writing Program Administrators/July 14 - 21, 2013
National Ski and Snowboard Retailers Association/April 30 - May 3, 2014
National Watermelon Association/Savannah Marriott Riverfront/Feb. 19 - 23, 2014
Society of Urologic Nurses and Associates/Hyatt Regency Savannah/March 7 - 9, 2013

Sea Island
Neurosurgical Society of America/Cloisters/April 7 - 10, 2013

HAWAII
Honolulu
American Academy of Advertising/University of Hawaii/May 31 - June 2, 2013
American Association of Endodontists/Hawaii Convention Center/April 17 - 20, 2013/4000 attendees/over 100 exhibitors
American Association of Immunologists/Hawaii Convention Center/May 3 - 7, 2013/700 attendees/over 100 exhibitors
American Association of Neuromuscular and Electrodiagnostic Medicine/ Hawaii Convention Center/Oct. 28 - 31, 2015
American Association of Oral and Maxillofacial Surgeons/Hilton Hawaiian Village Waikiki Beach Resort/Sept. 8 - 13, 2014
American Association of Veterinary Immunologists/May 3 - 7, 2013
American College of Allergy, Asthma and Immunology/Nov. 6 - 11, 2014
American Counseling Association/March 26 - 30, 2014/1-10 exhibitors
American Crystallographic Association/July 20 - 24, 2013
American Institute of Physics/Nov. 3 - 7, 2014
American Podiatric Medical Association/Hilton Hawaiian Village Waikiki Beach Resort/July 24 - 27, 2014
American Society for Blood and Marrow Transplantation./Feb. 18 - 21, 2016
American Society for Reproductive Medicine/Hawaii Convention Center/Oct. 18 - 22, 2014
American Society of Human Genetics/Oct. 18 - 22, 2022
American Society of Limnology and Oceanography/Feb. 23 - 28, 2014
American Wood-Protection Association/Sheraton Waikiki/April 28 - May 1, 2013
Association for Research in Vision and Ophthalmology/April 29 - May 2, 2018
Association of the United States Army/Hilton Hawaiian Village Waikiki Beach Resort/April 7 - 9, 2013
Building Owners and Managers Association International/Sheraton Waikiki/ Jan. 18 - 21, 2013
Controlled Release Society/Hawaii Convention Center/July 21 - 24, 2013
CPCU Society/Sept. 17 - 20, 2016
Information Storage Industry Consortium/Nov. 3 - 7, 2014
International Anesthesia Research Society/Hilton Hawaiian Village Waikiki Beach Resort/March 21 - 24, 2015
International Federation of Fertility Societies/Hawaii Convention Center/Oct. 18 - 24, 2014
International Food, Wine and Travel Writers Association/Hilton Hawaiian Village Waikiki Beach Resort/May 23 - 27, 2013
International Foundation of Employee Benefit Plans/Nov. 8 - 11, 2015
International Foundation of Employee Benefit Plans/Nov. 15 - 18, 2020
International Studies Association/Hilton Hawaiian Village Waikiki Beach Resort/March 25 - 28, 2020
National Association of Elevator Contractors/Sheraton Waikiki/April 18 - 21, 2015
National Conference of State Liquor Administrators/Sheraton Waikiki/June 24 - 26, 2013
National Conference on Public Employee Retirement Systems/Hilton Hawaiian Village Waikiki Beach Resort/May 19 - 23, 2013
National Football League/Jan. 27, 2013
National Guard Association of the U.S./Sept. 20 - 23, 2013
National Guard Executive Directors Association/Jan. 21 - 25, 2013
National Guard Executive Directors Association/Sheraton Waikiki/Jan. 22 - 25, 2013
The Oceanography Society/Feb. 23 - 28, 2014
Pacific Telecommunications Council/Jan. 20 - 23, 2013/1500 attendees
Society for American Archaeology/April 3 - 7, 2013
Society for Industrial and Organizational Psychology Inc./Hilton Hawaiian Village Waikiki Beach Resort/May 15 - 17, 2014
Society for Critical Care Medicine/Hawaii Convention Center/Jan. 21 - 25, 2017
Society of Government Service Urologists/Waikiki Beach Marriott Resort and Spa/Jan. 20 - 25, 2013
Society of Neurointerventional Surgery/Sheraton Waikiki/Feb. 4 - 5, 2013

Kauai
American Association for Hand Surgery/Grand Hyatt Kauai Resort and Spa/ Jan. 8 - 11, 2014/26-50 exhibitors
American College of Real Estate Lawyers/Grand Hyatt Kauai Resort and Spa/ March 27 - 30, 2014
American Society for Reconstructive Microsurgery/Grand Hyatt Kauai/Jan. 11 - 14, 2014

Organization for the Promotion and Advancement of Small Telecommunications Companies/Grand Hyatt Kauai/Jan. 5 - 9, 2013

Kohala Coast
American College of Psychiatrists/Hapuna Beach Prince Hotel/Feb. 20 - 24, 2013
American Judges Association/The Fairmont Orchid/Sept. 22 - 27, 2013
American Real Estate Society/Mauna Lani Bay Hotel and Bungalows Resort/ April 10 - 13, 2013
American Society of Ocularists/Mauna Lani Bay Hotel and Bungalows Resort/ May 9 - 17, 2013

Maui
Academy of Prosthodontics/Sheraton Maui Resort and Spa/April 16 - 20, 2013
American Association for Cancer Research/Hyatt Regency Maui/Feb. 21 - 25, 2013
American College of Trial Lawyers/Grand Wailea/March 3 - 6, 2016
Associated Builders and Contractors/Grand Wailea/Feb. 11 - 12, 2014
Association of Private Enterprise Education/April 14 - 16, 2013
Institute of Electrical and Electronics Engineers (IEEE)/Jan. 11 - 14, 2013
International Association of Defense Counsel/Grand Waila Resort/July 7 - 12, 2013
National Association of State Boards of Accountancy/Oct. 27 - 30, 2013
North American Society for Dialysis and Transplantation/Ritz Carlton Kapalua/July 14 - 18, 2013
Sheet Metal and Air Conditioning Contractors' National Association/Wailea Beach Marriott Resort and Spa/Oct. 20 - 24, 2013
Society of Abdominal Radiology/Grand Waila Resort/Feb. 24 - March 1, 2013

Waikaloa
AMT - The Association For Manufacturing Technology/Hilton Waikaloa Village/March 5 - 8, 2013

Waikoloa
American Association for the Surgery of Trauma/Hilton Waikoloa Village/Sept. 14 - 17, 2016/1000 attendees
American Association of Managing General Agents/Hilton Waikoloa Village/ May 18 - 21, 2014/720 attendees/51-100 exhibitors
American Council of Engineering Companies/Hilton Waikoloa Village/Oct. 22 - 25, 2014
American Peptide Society/Hilton Waikoloa Village/June 22 - 27, 2013
Financial & Insurance Conference Planners/Hilton Waikoloa Village/Nov. 16 - 19, 2014
IEEE Power Electronics Society/June 15 - 19, 2014
International Neuropsychological Society/Hilton Waikoloa Village/Feb. 6 - 9, 2013
International Society for Prosthetics and Orthotics - United States/Waikoloa Beach Marriott Resort and Spa/Jan. 26 - 29, 2014/1-10 exhibitors
National Tooling and Machining Association/Hilton Waikoloa Village/March 5 - 8, 2013

Wailea
National Association of Chapter Thirteen Trustees (NACTT)/Wailea Beach Resort and Spa Marriott/Jan. 24 - 26, 2013

Weimea
Society for Physical Regulation in Biology and Medicine/Hapuna Beach Prince Hotel/Jan. 2 - 5, 2013

IDAHO
Boise
American Society of Plant Taxonomists/July 25 - 31, 2014
Council of Multiple Listing Services/Oct. 2 - 5, 2013
National Association of State Boating Law Administrators/Sept. 15 - 18, 2013
National Association of State Directors of Teacher Education and Certification/ Grove Hotel/Oct. 23 - 25, 2014
National Council of Writing Program Administrators/July 12 - 19, 2015
North American Membrane Society/Grove Hotel/June 8 - 12, 2013

Coeur d#Alene
Cotton Warehouse Association of America/Coeur d'Alene Resort/June 5, 2013
Council of Colleges of Acupuncture and Oriental Medicine/Coeur d' Alene Resort/May 14 - 18, 2013
Council of Producers & Distributors of Agrotechnology/Coeur d'Alene Inn and Conference Center/July 23 - 25, 2015
Forest Landowners Association/Coeur d' Alene Resort/June 5 - 7, 2013
National Association of State Technology Directors/Coeur d'Alene Hotel/Aug. 24 - 28, 2014
Society for Pediatric Dermatology/Coeur d' Alene Resort/July 9 - 12, 2014

Sun Valley
Society of Petroleum Evaluation Engineers/Sun Valley Resort/June 8 - 11, 2013

ILLINOIS
Alton
Xi Psi Phi Dental Fraternity/April 6, 2013
Champaign
IEEE Power Electronics Society/Feb. 22 - 23, 2013
Chicago
AABC Commissioning Group/InterContinental Hotels/April 17 - 19, 2013
Academy of Organizational and Occupational Psychiatry/University Club/April 20 - 21, 2013
Academy of Political Science/Sheraton Chicago Hotel and Towers/Aug. 29 - Sept. 1, 2013
Accordionists and Teachers Guild International/Hyatt Lisle/July 17 - 21, 2013
Air and Waste Management Association/June 25 - 28, 2013
American Academy of Clinical Neuropsychology/Renaissance Chicago Downtown Hotel/June 20 - 22, 2013
American Academy of Matrimonial Lawyers/J.W. Marriott Hotel/Nov. 6 - 9, 2013
American Academy of Ophthalmic Executives/McCormick Place/Oct. 18 - 21, 2014
American Academy of Ophthalmic Executives/McCormick Place/Oct. 15 - 18, 2016

American Academy of Ophthalmic Executives/McCormick Place/Oct. 27 - 30, 2018

American Academy of Ophthalmology/McCormick Place/Oct. 18 - 21, 2014

American Academy of Orthopaedic Surgeons/McCormick Place/March 19 - 23, 2013

American Academy of Orthotists and Prosthetists/Hyatt Regency Chicago/Feb. 26 - March 1, 2014

American Academy of Orthotists and Prosthetists/Hyatt Regency Chicago/March 1 - 4, 2017

American Academy of Pediatrics/Oct. 17 - 20, 2015

American Academy of Periodontology/Fairmont Hotel/April 13 - 14, 2013

American Academy of Psychiatry and the Law/Chicago Marriott Downtown Magnificent Mile/Oct. 23 - 26, 2014

American Academy of Restorative Dentistry/Ritz Carlton Hotel/Feb. 23 - 24, 2013

American Anthropological Association/Hilton Chicago/Nov. 20 - 24, 2013

American Art Therapy Association, Inc./July 6 - 10, 2016

American Association for Clinical Chemistry, Inc./July 27 - 31, 2014/18000 attendees

American Association for the Advancement of Science/Feb. 13 - 17, 2014

American Association for the History of Medicine/May 8 - 11, 2014

American Association of Certified Orthoptists/Oct. 18 - 21, 2014

American Association of Colleges of Pharmacy/Hyatt Regency/July 13 - 17, 2013

American Association of Collegiate Registrars and Admissions Officers/Hilton Chicago/Nov. 10 - 13, 2013

American Association of Corporate and Public Practice Veterinarians/July 22, 2013

The American Association of Dental Boards/ADA Headquarters/April 21 - 22, 2013

The American Association of Dental Boards/ADA Headquarters/April 6 - 7, 2014

The American Association of Eye and Ear Centers of Excellence/Nov. 16 - 18, 2014

The American Association of Eye and Ear Centers of Excellence/Nov. 16 - 18, 2014

American Association of Legal Nurse Consultants/Palmer House a Hilton Hotel/April 4 - 6, 2013

American Association of Oral and Maxillofacial Surgeons/Sheraton Chicago Hotel and Towers/Dec. 5 - 8, 2013

American Association of Oral and Maxillofacial Surgeons/Sheraton Chicago Hotel and Towers/Dec. 4 - 7, 2014

American Association of Oral and Maxillofacial Surgeons/Sheraton Chicago Hotel and Towers/Dec. 3 - 6, 2015

American Association of Physicians of Indian Origin/Sheraton Hotel/May 23 - 27, 2013

American Association of Teachers of Slavic and East European Languages/Jan. 9 - 12, 2014

American Association of Veterinary Parasitologists/July 20 - 23, 2013

American Bar Association/Feb. 5 - 11, 2014

American Bar Association/July 30 - Aug. 4, 2015

American Bar Association/Aug. 2 - 7, 2018

American Baseball Coaches Association/Hyatt Regency/Jan. 3 - 6, 2013/6000 attendees/over 100 exhibitors

American Board of Professional Psychology/Stouffer Renaissance Chicago Hotel/June 20 - 22, 2013

American Burn Association/April 21 - 24, 2015

American Burn Association/April 10 - 13, 2018

American Burn Association/April 6 - 9, 2021

American Butter Institute/Chicago Marriott Downtown Magnificent Mile/April 28 - 30, 2013

American College of Chest Physicians/Oct. 26 - 31, 2013

American College of Emergency Physicians/Oct. 27 - 30, 2014

American College of Nurse-Midwives/May 19 - 24, 2017

American College of Nurse-Midwives/May 20 - 25, 2022

American College of Occupational and Environmental Medicine/Chicago Sheraton Hotel and Towers/April 10 - 13, 2016

American College of Trial Lawyers/Fairmont Chicago Millenium Park/Oct. 1 - 4, 2015

American Council of Life Insurers (ACLI)/April 7 - 9, 2014

American Dairy Products Institute/Chicago Marriott Downtown Magnificent Mile/April 28 - 30, 2013

American Dairy Products Institute/Hyatt Regency Chicago/April 27 - 30, 2014

American Diabetes Association/Hyatt Regency McCormick Place/April 13, 2013

American Economic Association/Hyatt Regency Chicago/Jan. 6 - 8, 2017

American Educational Research Association/April 16 - 20, 2015

American Equilibration Society/Chicago Downtown Marriott/Feb. 20 - 21, 2013

American Equilibration Society/Chicago Downtown Marriott/Feb. 19 - 20, 2014

American Family Therapy Academy/Palmer House Hilton Hotel/June 5 - 8, 2013

The American Finance Association/Jan. 6 - 8, 2017

American Gynecological and Obstetrical Society/InterContinental Hotel/Sept. 18 - 21, 2013

American Institute of Certified Planners/Hyatt Regency Chicago/April 13 - 16, 2013

American Institute of Floral Designers/Hilton Chicago/July 3 - 8, 2014

American Institute of Homeopathy/Hyatt Regency Chicago/Feb. 8 - 10, 2013

American Institute of Physics/Jan. 14 - 18, 2013

American Library Association/June 27 - July 2, 2013

American Library Association/Jan. 23 - 27, 2015

American Library Association/June 22 - 27, 2017

American Medical Association/Hyatt Regency Chicago/June 15 - 19, 2013

American Medical Informatics Association/Hilton Chicago/Nov. 12 - 16, 2016

American Ornithologists' Union/Aug. 14 - 19, 2013

American Orthopaedic Foot and Ankle Society/Hyatt Regency/Sept. 21 - 23, 2014

American Orthopaedic Society for Sports Medicine/Sheraton Chicago Hotel and Towers/July 11 - 14, 2013/51-100 exhibitors

American Osteopathic College of Anesthesiologists/Wyndham Chicago/March 15 - 17, 2013

American Philological Association/Jan. 2 - 5, 2014

American Philosophical Association/Palmer House a Hilton Hotel/Feb. 26 - March 1, 2014

American Planning Association/Hyatt Regency Chicago/April 13 - 17, 2013

American Political Science Association/Sheraton Chicago Hotel and Towers/Aug. 29 - Sept. 1, 2013

American Prosthodontic Society/Swissotel Chicago/Feb. 21 - 23, 2013

American Public Health Association/Nov. 7 - 11, 2015/13000 attendees

American Public Transportation Association/Sept. 29 - Oct. 2, 2013

American Public Works Association/McCormick Place/Aug. 25 - 28, 2013

American Railway Engineering and Maintenance-of-Way Association/Hilton Chicago/Sept. 28 - Oct. 1, 2014

American Railway Engineering and Maintenance-of-Way Association/Sept. 16 - 19, 2018

American Society for Artificial Internal Organs/June 12 - 15, 2013

American Society for Clinical Investigation/Fairmont Chicago Millenium Park/April 26 - 28, 2013

American Society for Clinical Investigation/Fairmont Chicago Millenium Park/April 25 - 27, 2014

American Society for Clinical Laboratory Science/July 27 - 31, 2014/19000 attendees/over 100 exhibitors

American Society for Clinical Laboratory Science/July 29 - Aug. 2, 2014

American Society for Clinical Laboratory Science/July 28 - Aug. 1, 2020

American Society for Clinical Laboratory Science/July 23 - 27, 2024

American Society for Dermatologic Surgery/Hyatt Regency/Oct. 3 - 6, 2013

American Society for Dermatologic Surgery/Hyatt Regency Chicago/Oct. 15 - 18, 2015

American Society for Dermatologic Surgery/Hyatt Regency Chicago/Oct. 5 - 7, 2017

American Society for Healthcare Engineering/Aug. 3 - 6, 2014/1-10 exhibitors

American Society for Histocompatibility and Immunogenetics/Sheraton Chicago Hotel and Towers/Nov. 18 - 22, 2013

American Society of Addiction Medicine/April 25 - 28, 2013

American Society of Addiction Medicine/April 25 - 28, 2013

American Society of Anesthesiologists/Oct. 22 - 26, 2016

American Society of Anesthesiologists/Oct. 26 - 30, 2019

American Society of Baking/Chicago Marriott Downtown Magnificent Mile/March 3 - 6, 2013

American Society of Clinical Oncology/McCormick Place/May 31 - June 4, 2013

American Society of Clinical Oncology/May 30 - June 3, 2014

American Society of Clinical Oncology/May 29 - June 2, 2015

American Society of Clinical Oncology/June 3 - 7, 2016

American Society of Clinical Oncology/June 2 - 6, 2017

American Society of Clinical Oncology/June 1 - 5, 2018

American Society of Clinical Oncology/May 31 - June 4, 2019

American Society of Clinical Oncology/May 29 - June 2, 2020

American Society of Criminology/Palmer House Hilton Hotel/Nov. 17 - 20, 2021

American Society of Dermatopathology/Hilton Chicago/Nov. 6 - 9, 2014

American Society of Hand Therapists/Oct. 24 - 27, 2013

American Society of Landscape Architects/McCormick Place/Nov. 6 - 9, 2015/over 100 exhibitors

American Society of Nuclear Cardiology/Sept. 27 - 30, 2013

American Society of Ocularists/Oct. 17 - 21, 2014

The American Society of Pediatric Hematology/Oncology/Palmer House a Hilton Hotel/May 14 - 17, 2014

American Society of PeriAnesthesia Nurses/Hilton Chicago/April 14 - 18, 2013/2000 attendees/over 100 exhibitors

American Society of Plumbing Engineers/Sept. 19 - 24, 2014

American Society of Transplantation/April 29 - May 3, 2017

American Society on Aging/Hyatt Regency/March 12 - 16, 2013

American Society on Aging/Hyatt Regency/March 23 - 27, 2015

American Society on Aging/Hyatt Regency/March 20 - 24, 2017

American Speech-Language-Hearing Association/Nov. 14 - 16, 2013

American Spinal Injury Association/Swissotel Chicago/May 6 - 8, 2013

American Student Dental Association/Holiday Inn Chicago Mart Plaza/Nov. 15 - 17, 2013/51-100 exhibitors

American Supply Association/Chicago Marriott Downtown Magnificent Mile/Oct. 27 - 29, 2015

American Translators Association/Sheraton Chicago Hotel and Towers/Nov. 5 - 8, 2014

American Urogynecologic Society/Hilton Chicago/July 22 - 27, 2014

American Urogynecologic Society/Hilton Chicago/Oct. 6 - 9, 2015

American Veterinary Medical Association/July 20 - 23, 2013

American Welding Society/Nov. 18 - 21, 2013

Anxiety Disorders Association of America/Chicago Marriott Downtown Magnificent Mile/March 27 - 30, 2014

ASPSN - American Society of Plastic Surgical Nurses/Oct. 10 - 13, 2014

Association for Consumer Research/Oct. 3 - 6, 2013

Association for Governmental Leasing and Finance/DoubleTree Chicago Magnificent Mile/May 7 - 11, 2013

Association for Information Systems/Aug. 15 - 18, 2013/3000 attendees

Association for Library and Information Science Education/Jan. 27 - 30, 2015

The Association for Library Service to Children/June 27 - July 2, 2013

Association for Supervision and Curriculum Development (ASCD)/McCormick Place/March 16 - 18, 2013

Association for Surgical Education/Fairmont Chicago Millenium Park/April 8 - 12, 2014

Association for the Treatment of Sexual Abusers/Sheraton Chicago Hotel and Towers/Oct. 30 - Nov. 2, 2013

Association of American Geographers/April 21 - 25, 2015

Association of American Medical Colleges/Hyatt Regency Chicago/Nov. 7 - 12, 2014

Association of American Physicians/Fairmont Chicago Millenium Park/April 26 - 28, 2013

Association of American Physicians/Fairmont Chicago Millenium Park/April 25 - 27, 2014

Association of Analytical Communities International/Palmer House a Hilton Hotel/Aug. 25 - 28, 2013
Association of Collegiate Business Schools and Programs/Chicago Marriott Downtown Magnificent Mile/June 27 - 30, 2014
Association of Community College Trustees/Oct. 22 - 25, 2014
Association of Healthcare Internal Auditors/Aug. 25 - 28, 2013
Association of Insolvency and Restructuring Advisors/Westin Chicago Northwest/June 5 - 8, 2013
Association of periOperative Registered Nurses/March 29 - April 3, 2014
Association of Program Directors in Surgery/Fairmont Chicago Millenium Park/ April 8 - 12, 2014
Association of Proposal Management Professionals/May 26 - 29, 2014
Association of Specialized and Professional Accreditors/Millennium Knickerbocker Hotel Chicago/April 7 - 9, 2013
Association of Specialized and Professional Accreditors/March 29 - 31, 2015
Association of Specialized and Professional Accreditors/April 2 - 4, 2017
Association of Teacher Educators/Hilton Chicago/Feb. 11 - 17, 2016
Association of University Programs in Health Administration/Palmer House a Hilton Hotel/March 12, 2013
The Association to Advance Collegiate Schools of Business/April 7 - 9, 2013
Business and Institutional Furniture Manufacturers Association International/ June 10 - 12, 2013
Catholic Health Association of the United States/Chicago Marriott Downtown Magnificent Mile/June 22 - 24, 2014
Center for Spiritual and Ethical Education/Cenacle Retreat and Conference Center/June 23 - 28, 2013
Center for Spiritual and Ethical Education/Cenacle Retreat and Conference Center/June 25 - 30, 2013
Central Conference of American Rabbis/Fairmont Chicago Millenium Park/ March 30 - April 2, 2014
College of American Pathologists/Hyatt Regency Chicago/Sept. 7 - 10, 2014/1400 attendees/over 100 exhibitors
Commercial Law League of America/Westin Michigan Avenue Chicago/April 11 - 14, 2013
NAIOP, The Commercial Real Estate Development Association/Hilton Chicago/ April 15 - 17, 2013
Concrete Reinforcing Steel Institute/Swissotel Chicago/Nov. 3 - 6, 2013
Concrete Reinforcing Steel Institute/Swissotel Chicago/Nov. 2 - 5, 2014
Conference of Research Workers in Animal Diseases/Chicago Marriott Downtown Magnificent Mile/Dec. 8 - 10, 2013
Construction Financial Management Association/Sheraton Chicago Hotel and Towers/June 27 - July 1, 2015
Construction Industry CPAs/Consultants Association/CICPAC Annual Conference/July 24 - 26, 2013
Construction Industry Round Table, Inc./Park Hyatt Chicago/Oct. 28 - 30, 2013
Construction Writers Association/Oct. 21 - 23, 2013
Controlled Release Society/The Hilton Chicago/July 13 - 16, 2014
Conveyor Equipment Manufacturers Association/Hilton Chicago O'Hare Airport/Sept. 17 - 18, 2013
Conveyor Equipment Manufacturers Association/Hilton Chicago O'Hare Airport/Sept. 16 - 17, 2014
Council for Advancement and Support of Education/Renaissance Blackstone Hotel/May 1 - 3, 2013
Council for Advancement and Support of Education/Renaissance Blackstone Hotel/June 19 - 21, 2013
Council of State Speech-Language-Hearing Association Presidents/Nov. 13, 2013
Council on Anthropology and Education/Chicago Hilton Indian Lakes Resort/ Nov. 20 - 24, 2013
Council on Foundations/April 28 - 30, 2013
Employee Assistance Society of North America/Hotel Sax Chicago/May 1 - 3, 2013
The Endocrine Society/June 21 - 24, 2014
Eye Bank Association of America/Sheraton Chicago Hotel and Towers/June 5 - 8, 2013
Financial Management Association International/Hyatt Regency Chicago/Oct. 16 - 19, 2013
Food Marketing Institute/McCormick Place/June 10 - 13, 2014/over 100 exhibitors
Food Processing Suppliers Association/McCormick Place/Nov. 3 - 6, 2013/10000 attendees
Gas Technology Institute/Sheraton Chicago Hotel and Towers/Sept. 3 - 6, 2013
Genetics Society of America/Hilton Chicago/March 4 - 8, 2015
Gynecologic Oncology Group/Hyatt Regency/July 18 - 20, 2014
Health Industry Distributors Association/Navy Pier Park/Sept. 17 - 19, 2014
Hispanic Association of Colleges and Universities/Hilton Chicago/Oct. 26 - 28, 2013
History of Science Society/Nov. 6 - 9, 2014
Hoist Manufacturers Institute/McCormick Place/Jan. 21 - 24, 2013/30000 attendees/over 100 exhibitors
Human Factors and Ergonomics Society/Hyatt Regency Chicago/Oct. 27 - 31, 2014/1500 attendees
Human Factors Society/Hyatt Regency Chicago/Oct. 27 - 31, 2014
Hydraulic Institute/Lincolnshire Marriott Resort/June 26 - 28, 2013
IEEE - Nuclear and Plasma Sciences Society/Oct. 9 - 14, 2016
IEEE Engineering in Medicine and Biology Society/Aug. 26 - 30, 2014
IEEE Power Electronics Society/Westin O'Hare/May 12 - 15, 2013
INDA, Association of the Nonwoven Fabrics Industry/Navy Pier Park/Nov. 19 - 21, 2013
Institute of Food Technologists/July 13 - 16, 2013
Institute of Food Technologists/July 11 - 14, 2015
Institute of Mathematical Statistics/McCormick Place/July 30 - Aug. 4, 2016
Insured Retirement Institute/Fairmont Chicago, Millennium Park/Sept. 22 - 24, 2013
Intellectual Property Owners Association/Hyatt Regency/Sept. 27 - 29, 2015/11-25 exhibitors
International Academy of Trial Lawyers/Trump International Hotel/July 17 - 21, 2013
International Association of Conference Centers/March 19 - 22, 2013

International Association of Law Enforcement Intelligence Analysts/Swissotel Chicago/April 8 - 12, 2013
International Association of Personnel in Employment Security/July 7 - 10, 2013
International Association of Workforce Professionals (IAWP)/Fairmont Chicago Millenium Park/July 7 - 10, 2013
International Casual Furnishings Association/Merchandise Mart/July 16 - 18, 2013
International Casual Furnishings Association/Merchandise Mart/Sept. 17 - 20, 2013
International Casual Furnishings Association/Merchandise Mart/July 15 - 17, 2014
International Casual Furnishings Association/Merchandise Mart/Sept. 16 - 19, 2014
International Casual Furnishings Association/The Merchandise Mart/July 14 - 16, 2015
International Casual Furnishings Association/The Merchandise Mart/Sept. 16 - 19, 2015
International Casual Furnishings Association/The Merchandise Mart/July 12 - 14, 2016
International Casual Furnishings Association/The Merchandise Mart/Sept. 20 - 23, 2016
International Casual Furnishings Association/The Merchandise Mart/July 11 - 13, 2017
International Casual Furnishings Association/The Merchandise Mart/Sept. 12 - 15, 2017
International Claim Association/Chicago Marriott Downtown Magnificent Mile/Oct. 13 - 16, 2013
International Concrete Repair Institute/Fairmont Chicago Millenium Park/Nov. 13 - 15, 2013
International Dairy Foods Association/McCormick Place/Nov. 3 - 6, 2013
The International Fluid Power Society/Chicago Marriott O'Hare/Nov. 27 - 29, 2013
International Franchise Association/Chicago Marriott Downtown Magnificent Mile/May 4 - 6, 2014
International Franchise Association/Chicago Marriott Downtown Magnificent Mile/May 6 - 7, 2014
International Franchise Association/Chicago Marriott Downtown Magnificent Mile/May 3 - 5, 2015
International Gay and Lesbian Travel Association/May 2 - 4, 2013
International Housewares Association/McCormick Place/March 2 - 5, 2013/60000 attendees/over 100 exhibitors
International Housewares Association/McCormick Place/March 15 - 18, 2014/60000 attendees/over 100 exhibitors
International Housewares Association/McCormick Place/March 7 - 10, 2015/60000 attendees/over 100 exhibitors
International Housewares Association/McCormick Place/March 5 - 8, 2016/60000 attendees/over 100 exhibitors
International Housewares Representatives Association/March 2 - 5, 2013
International Lactation Consultant Association/Sheraton Chicago Hotel and Towers/July 20 - 23, 2016
International Sanitary Supply Association/Oct. 25 - 28, 2016
International Society of Appraisers/J.W. Marriott Hotel/April 12 - 15, 2013
International Ticketing Association/Sheraton Chicago Hotel and Towers/Jan. 28 - 30, 2014
Investment Management Consultants Association/Marriott Michigan Avenue/ Oct. 7 - 8, 2013
Latin American Studies Association/Palmer House a Hilton Hotel/May 21 - 24, 2014
The Learning Disabilities Association/Feb. 25 - 28, 2015
Legal Netlink Alliance/May 9 - 10, 2013
Lift Manufacturers Product Section - Material Handling Institute/McCormick Place/Jan. 21 - 24, 2013/over 100 exhibitors
Materials Handling and Management Society/McCormick Place/Jan. 21 - 24, 2013/over 100 exhibitors
Medical Library Association/May 16 - 21, 2014
Metal Powder Industries Federation/June 23 - 26, 2013
Metal Powder Industries Federation/Chicago Sheraton Hotel and Towers/June 24 - 27, 2013
Modern Language Association/Jan. 9 - 12, 2014
Music Teachers National Association/Marriott Chicago Downtown/March 22 - 26, 2014
NALP - The Association for Legal Career Professionals/Sheraton Chicago Hotel and Towers/April 22 - 25, 2015
National Academy of Arbitrators/Fairmont Chicago, Millennium Park/May 21 - 24, 2014
National Alliance for Musical Theatre/Chicago Shakespeare Theater/April 4 - 6, 2013
National Association for Poetry Therapy/Cenacle Retreat and Conference Center/April 11 - 14, 2013
National Association of Bar Executives/Feb. 4 - 6, 2014
National Association of Chapter Thirteen Trustees (NACTT)/Chicago Marriott Downtown Magnificent Mile/July 16 - 19, 2014
National Association of Consumer Shows/Hilton Chicago Hotel/May 8 - 10, 2013
National Association of Convenience Stores/InterContinental Chicago O'Hare / April 9 - 11, 2013
National Association of Fire Equipment Distributors/Swissotel Chicago/May 23 - 24, 2013
National Association of Osteopathic Foundations/July 16 - 21, 2013
National Association of Personal Financial Advisors/Hilton Chicago/May 12 - 17, 2014/800 attendees
National Association of Realtors/Nov. 3 - 6, 2017
National Association of School Psychologists/Hyatt Regency/Feb. 13 - 16, 2018
National Association of Schools of Theatre/Swissôtel Chicago/March 20 - 22, 2014
National Association of Spine Specialists/Oct. 14 - 17, 2015
National Association of State Departments of Agriculture/McCormick Place/ May 18 - 21, 2013

National Association of State Departments of Agriculture/McCormick Place/June 10 - 13, 2014

National Business Education Association/Chicago Marriott Downtown Magnificent Mile/March 31 - April 4, 2015

National Business Education Association/Chicago Marriott Downtown Magnificent Mile/April 16 - 20, 2019

National Classification Management Society/Palmer House Hilton Hotel/June 25 - 27, 2014

National Confectioners Association/McCormick Place/May 21 - 23, 2013/over 100 exhibitors

National Conference of Bankruptcy Judges/Oct. 8 - 11, 2014

National Conference of Bar Foundations/Feb. 6 - 8, 2014

National Conference of Bar Foundations/July 30 - Aug. 1, 2015

National Council for Marketing and Public Relations/Fairmont Chicago Millennium Park/March 10 - 13, 2013

National Council for the Social Studies/Hyatt Regency/Nov. 30 - Dec. 2, 2018

National Council of State Housing Agencies/Hyatt Regency Chicago/June 24 - 27, 2014

National Council on Aging/Hyatt Regency Chicago/March 19 - 23, 2013

National Court Reporters Association/Hilton Chicago/July 28 - 31, 2016

National Electrical Contractors Association/Oct. 11 - 14, 2014

National Electrical Contractors Association/Oct. 11 - 14, 2014

National Electrical Manufacturers Representatives Association/Sheraton Chicago Hotel and Towers/Jan. 30 - Feb. 2, 2014

National Fire Protection Association/McCormick Place/June 10 - 13, 2013/over 100 exhibitors

The National Flute Association, Inc./Hilton Chicago/Aug. 7 - 10, 2014

National Guard Association of the U.S./Aug. 22 - 25, 2014

National Guard Executive Directors Association/Jan. 13 - 15, 2014

National Guard Executive Directors Association/Jan. 14 - 16, 2014

National Guardianship Association/Chicago Marriott O'Hare/May 16 - 17, 2013

National Luggage Dealers Association/Navy Pier Park/June 20 - 21, 2013

National Parking Association/Hyatt Regency Chicago/Oct. 7 - 11, 2013

National Restaurant Association/McCormick Place/May 18 - 21, 2013/over 100 exhibitors

National Science Teachers Association/March 26 - 29, 2015

National Telecommunications Cooperative Association/Sheraton Chicago Hotel and Towers/Sept. 15 - 18, 2013

North American Society for Pediatric Gastroenterology, Hepatology and Nutrition/Hilton Chicago/Oct. 10 - 13, 2013

North American Spine Society/Oct. 14 - 17, 2015

NPES, The Association for Suppliers of Printing, Publishing, and Converting Technologies/McCormick Place/Sept. 8 - 12, 2013

NPES, The Association for Suppliers of Printing, Publishing, and Converting Technologies/McCormick Place/Sept. 28 - Oct. 1, 2014

NPTA Alliance/March 17 - 19, 2013

Pension Real Estate Association/Oct. 28 - 30, 2013

Piano Technicians Guild/Hyatt Regency O'Hare/July 10 - 14, 2013

Powder Metallurgy Parts Association/Sheraton Chicago Hotel and Towers/June 24 - 27, 2013

Precast/Prestressed Concrete Institute/Hyatt Magnificant Mile/April 25 - 28, 2013

Precision Metalforming Association/Nov. 18 - 21, 2013

Print Services & Distribution Association/Navy Pier Park/May 7 - 9, 2013/1-10 exhibitors

Professional Liability Underwriting Society/Hyatt Regency Chicago/April 10 - 11, 2013

Professional Liability Underwriting Society/Nov. 9 - 11, 2016

Professional Skaters Association/Hyatt Regency O'Hare/May 23 - 25, 2013

Promotion Marketing Association/Westin Chicago River North/April 3 - 4, 2013

The Psychonomic Society/Nov. 19 - 22, 2015

Radiological Society of North America/McCormick Place/Dec. 1 - 6, 2013

Radiological Society of North America/McCormick Place/Nov. 30 - Dec. 5, 2014

Real Estate Investment Securities Association/Hilton Chicago/May 12 - 17, 2014

Religious Education Association/Nov. 7 - 9, 2014

The Renaissance Society of America/March 30 - April 1, 2017/1500 attendees/over 100 exhibitors

Screen Manufacturers Association/May 2 - 3, 2013

Screen Manufacturers Association/May 6 - 7, 2013

Screen Manufacturers Association/May 2 - 3, 2013

Screen Manufacturers Association/May 5 - 6, 2014

Social Science History Association/Palmer House a Hilton Hotel/Nov. 21 - 24, 2013

Social Science History Association/Palmer House a Hilton Hotel/Nov. 17 - 20, 2016

Social Science History Association/Palmer House a Hilton Hotel/Nov. 21 - 24, 2019

Society for Cinema and Media Studies/The Drake Hotel/March 6 - 10, 2013

Society for College and University Planning/July 11 - 15, 2015

Society for Human Resource Management/June 16 - 19, 2013

Society for Industrial & Applied Mathematics/Palmer House a Hilton Hotel/July 7 - 11, 2014

Society for Italian Historical Studies/Hilton Chicago/Jan. 3 - 6, 2019

Society for Photographic Education/Palmer House Hilton Hotel/March 7 - 10, 2013

Society for Textual Scholarship/Loyola University/March 6 - 8, 2013

Society for the Study of Social Problems/Radisson Blu Aqua Hotel/Aug. 21 - 23, 2015

Society of Christian Ethics/Hilton Chicago/Jan. 3 - 6, 2013/550 attendees/11-25 exhibitors

Society of Gynecologic Oncologists/Hilton Chicago/March 29 - April 1, 2015

Society of Radiologists in Ultrasound/The Westin Michigan Avenue Hotel/Oct. 18 - 20, 2013

Society of Radiologists in Ultrasound/The Westin Michigan Avenue Hotel/Oct. 23 - 25, 2015

Society of Urologic Nurses and Associates/Hyatt Regency/Oct. 11 - 14, 2013

Society of Vacuum Coaters/Hyatt Regency Chicago/May 3 - 8, 2014

Solar Electric Power Association/Hyatt Regency McCormick Place/Oct. 21 - 24, 2013

Solar Electric Power Association/Hyatt Regency McCormick Place/Oct. 26 - 29, 2015

Special Interest Group for University and College Computing Services/Holiday Inn Mart Plaza/Nov. 3 - 8, 2013

Sports Lawyers Association/Fairmont Chicago Millenium Park/May 15 - 17, 2014

Tag and Label Manufacturers Institute/Hyatt Regency Chicago/Sept. 3 - 5, 2013

Turfgrass Producers International/The Drake/July 22 - 25, 2013

Turnaround Management Association/JW Marriott Chicago/May 14 - 16, 2013

United Inventors Association of the U.S.A./March 2 - 5, 2013/65000 attendees/over 100 exhibitors

Utility Communicators International/June 11 - 13, 2013

Warehousing Education and Research Council/Hyatt Regency Chicago/April 27 - 30, 2014

Water Environment Federation/McCormick Place/Oct. 5 - 9, 2013/18000 attendees/over 100 exhibitors

Web Sling and Tie down Association/Sax Chicago – A Thompson Hotel/Oct. 15 - 17, 2013

World Future Society/Hilton Chicago/July 26 - 28, 2013

World Pet Association/Donald Stephens Convention Center Chicago/Sept. 20 - 22, 2013

World Pet Association/Donald Stephens Convention Center Chicago/Sept. 19 - 21, 2014

World Pet Association/Donald Stephens Convention Center Chicago/Sept. 18 - 20, 2015

East Peoria

The Brown Swiss Association/Embassy Suites East Peoria-Hotel and RiverFront Conference Center/June 24 - 28, 2014

Lombard

Society for Experimental Mechanics, Inc./The Westin Lombard Yorktown Center/June 3 - 6, 2013

Normal

National Council of Writing Program Administrators/July 13 - 20, 2014

Northbrook

Optometric Extension Program Foundation/March 3 - 4, 2013

Oak Brook

National Conference of Black Political Scientists/Doubletree Hotel Chicago/March 14 - 16, 2013

Ottawa

United States Parachute Association/Skydive Chicago/Sept. 12 - 24, 2013

Rosemont

American Architectural Manufacturers Association/Hyatt Regency O'Hare/June 9 - 12, 2013

American Coatings Association/Hyatt Regency O'Hare/March 11 - 13, 2013

American College of Clinical Pharmacy/Hyatt Regency O'Hare Hotel/April 11 - 15, 2014

American College of Clinical Pharmacy/Hyatt Regency O'Hare Hotel/April 10 - 14, 2015

Association of Rotational Molders International/Donald E. Stephens Convention Center/Oct. 7 - 9, 2014

Automotive Aftermarket Industry Association/Hyatt Regency O'Hare/May 21 - 22, 2013

Casting Industry Suppliers Association/Westin O'Hare/Nov. 6 - 7, 2013

Council of Medical Specialty Societies/Hyatt Regency O'Hare/May 10 - 11, 2013

Healthcare Compliance Packaging Council/Sofitel Hotel /April 1 - 2, 2013

Institute of Food Technologists/InterContinental Chicago O'Hare/March 27 - 28, 2013

Professional Currency Dealers Association/Crowne Plaza Chicago O'Hare, Rosemont/Nov. 20 - 23, 2013

Schaumburg

American Foundry Society/Renaissance Schaumburg Convention Center Hotel/April 8 - 11, 2014/1800 attendees/over 100 exhibitors

American Mold Builders Association/April 24 - 26, 2013

Billiard Congress of America/Schaumburg Renaissance Hotel and Convention Center/July 10 - 13, 2013

IEEE Aerospace and Electronic Systems Society (AESS)/Sept. 16 - 19, 2013

Metals Service Center Institute/Marriott Renaissance Schaumburg Hotel and Convention Center/Sept. 9 - 10, 2013

Metals Service Center Institute/Renaissance Schaumburg Convention Center Hotel/Sept. 10 - 11, 2013

North American Die Casting Association/Renaissance Schaumburg Convention Center Hotel/April 8 - 11, 2013

Springfield

American Association of Meat Processors/Priarie Capital Convention Center/June 18 - 20, 2015

St. Charles

Holstein Association USA/June 27 - 30, 2015

Urbana

Clay Minerals Society/University of Illinois/Oct. 6 - 10, 2013

INDIANA

Indianapolis

The Acoustical Society of America/Oct. 27 - 31, 2014

ACPA College Student Educators International/March 30 - April 2, 2014

African Studies Association/JW Marriott Indianapolis/Nov. 20 - 23, 2014

American Agricultural Editors Association/Indianapolis Marriott Downtown/July 26 - 30, 2014

American Association of Colleges for Teacher Education/JW Marriott Indianapolis/March 1 - 3, 2014

American Association of Physicists in Medicine/Aug. 4 - 8, 2013

American Astronomical Society/Indiana Convention Center/June 2 - 6, 2013

American Catholic Philosophical Association/Oct. 25 - 27, 2013

American Chemical Society/Sept. 8 - 12, 2013

American Cleft Palate-Craniofacial Association/Indianapolis Marriott Downtown/March 25 - 29, 2014
American College of Sports Medicine/May 29 - June 1, 2013
American College of Veterinary Internal Medicine/June 3 - 6, 2015
American College Personnel Association/March 30 - April 2, 2014
American Concrete Pipe Association/Indianapolis Convention Center/Jan. 11 - 13, 2013
American Correctional Association/Aug. 14 - 19, 2015
American Dairy Science Association/July 8 - 12, 2013
American Fraternal Alliance/JW Marriott Indianapolis/Sept. 10 - 12, 2015
American Institute for Conservation of Historic and Artistic Works/JW Marriott Indianapolis/May 29 - June 1, 2013
American Railway Engineering and Maintenance-of-Way Association/Indianapolis Convention Center/Sept. 29 - Oct. 2, 2013
American Railway Engineering and Maintenance-of-Way Association/Indianapolis Convention Center/Sept. 17 - 20, 2017
American Society for Clinical Pharmacology and Therapeutics/JW Marriott Indianapolis/March 6 - 9, 2013
American Society for Engineering Education/June 15 - 18, 2014
American Society for Mass Spectrometry/June 4 - 8, 2017
American Society for Pain Management Nursing/Oct. 9 - 12, 2013
American Society for Quality/Indiana Convention Center/May 6 - 8, 2013
American Society of Animal Science/Indiana Convention Center/July 8 - 12, 2013/2700 attendees
American Society of Questioned Document Examiners/Embassy Suites Indianapolis-Downtown/Aug. 24 - 29, 2013
American Surgical Association/JW Marriott Indianapolis/April 4 - 6, 2013
American Theatre Critics Association/March 21 - 24, 2013
APSE: The Network on Employment/JW Marriott/June 25 - 27, 2013
ASM International/Indiana Convention Center/Sept. 16 - 18, 2013
Associated Church Press/Sheraton Indianapolis City Centre Hotel/April 3 - 5, 2013
Association for Clinical Pastoral Education/Indianapolis Marriott Downtown/May 11 - 15, 2013
Association for Clinical Pastoral Education/Indianapolis Marriott Downtown/May 15 - 18, 2013
Association for Iron and Steel Technology/Indiana Convention Center/May 5 - 8, 2014
Association of College and Research Libraries/J.W.Marriott/April 10 - 13, 2013/3000 attendees/11-25 exhibitors
Association of College Unions International/March 24 - 29, 2019
Association of Lutheran Development Executives/Indianapolis Marriott Downtown/Feb. 8 - 11, 2013
Association of Old Crows/Indianapolis Convention Center/Oct. 12 - 16, 2014
Association of Organ Procurement Organizations/JW Marriott Indianapolis/June 18 - 21, 2013
Business Professionals of America/April 30 - May 4, 2014
Conference on College Composition and Communication/March 19 - 22, 2014
Council for Advancement and Support of Education/Omni Severin Hotel/June 12 - 14, 2013
CPCU Society/Oct. 3 - 6, 2015
Division 1-A Athletic Directors Association/Jan. 17 - 20, 2018
Educause/Oct. 27 - 30, 2015
Equipment Marketing and Distribution Association/JW Marriott Indianapolis/Oct. 22 - 25, 2013
Holstein Association USA/July 8 - 11, 2013
Institute for Supply Management/May 16 - 18, 2016
Insurance Accounting and Systems Association/Indianapolis Convention Center/June 8 - 11, 2014
Interim Ministry Network/Sheraton Hotel/June 3 - 6, 2013
Interior Design Educators Council/JW Mariott/Feb. 17 - 19, 2013
Interlocking Concrete Pavement Institute/Jan. 11 - 15, 2013
International Association for Food Protection/Indiana Convention Center/Aug. 3 - 6, 2014
International Association of Assessing Officers/Sept. 13 - 16, 2015
International Decorative Artisans League/Sheraton Indianapolis Hotel at Keystone Crossing/Oct. 8 - 12, 2013
LeadingAge (American Association of Homes and Services for the Aging)/Oct. 30 - Nov. 2, 2016
Liability Insurance Research Bureau/March 16 - 19, 2014
Microanalysis Society/Aug. 4 - 8, 2013
Microscopy Society of America/Aug. 4 - 8, 2013
National Association of Student Personnel Administrators/March 12 - 16, 2016
National After School Association/Indianapolis Convention Center/April 7 - 10, 2013
National Association for College Admission Counseling/Sept. 18 - 20, 2014
National Association for College Admission Counseling/Sept. 19 - 21, 2014
National Association for Gifted Children/Nov. 6 - 10, 2013
National Association of Blind Merchants/Indianapolis Marriott Downtown/May 20 - 23, 2013
National Association of College and University Business Officers/July 13 - 16, 2013
National Association of College and University Food Services/July 22 - 25, 2015
National Association of College Auxiliary Services/JW Marriott Indianapolis/Oct. 9 - 12, 2016
National Association of Government Defined Contribution Administrators/JW Marriot Indianapolis/Sept. 25 - Oct. 1, 2015
National Association of Insurance Commissioners/JW Marriott Indianapolis/Aug. 24 - 27, 2013
National Association of Scientific Materials Managers/July 25 - 29, 2014
National Association of State Boards of Geology/Nov. 15, 2014
National Association of Supervisors of Agricultural Education/Oct. 17 - 19, 2016
National Association of Supervisors of Agricultural Education/Oct. 23 - 25, 2017
National Association of Supervisors of Agricultural Education/Oct. 22 - 24, 2018
National Association of Women in Construction/Sept. 3 - 6, 2014
National Athletic Trainers Association/June 25 - July 28, 2014

National Auctioneers Association/JW Marriott Indianapolis/July 16 - 20, 2013
National Auto Auction Association/JW Marriott Indianapolis/Sept. 3 - 6, 2013
National Collegiate Athletic Association/Jan. 17 - 20, 2018
National Concrete Masonry Association/Indiana Convention Center/Jan. 11 - 13, 2013
National Council of Examiners for Engineering and Surveying/Aug. 24 - 27, 2016
National Council on Teacher Retirement/JW Marriott Indianapolis/Oct. 11 - 15, 2014
National Interscholastic Swimming Coaches Association/March 28 - 30, 2013
National Network of Estate Planning Attorneys/Crowne Plaza/April 29 - May 3, 2013
National Organization for the Professional Advancement of Black Chemists and Chemical Engineers/JW Marriott Indianapolis/Oct. 1 - 4, 2013
National Precast Concrete Association/Indiana Convention Center/Jan. 11 - 13, 2013/over 100 exhibitors
National Recreation and Parks Association/Sept. 25 - 27, 2018/7000 attendees/over 100 exhibitors
National Soccer Coaches Association of America/Jan. 16 - 20, 2013/9000 attendees
National Society of Accountants/Hyatt Indianapolis/Aug. 21 - 24, 2013
National Truck Equipment Association/Indiana Convention Center/March 6 - 8, 2013/10000 attendees/over 100 exhibitors
North American Catalysis Society/Sept. 8 - 12, 2013
North American Die Casting Association/Indianapolis Convention Center/Oct. 5 - 7, 2015/5000 attendees/over 100 exhibitors
Pediatric Orthopedic Society of North America/JW Marriott Indianapolis/April 27 - 30, 2016
Percussive Arts Society/Nov. 13 - 16, 2013
Property Loss Research Bureau/March 16 - 19, 2014
Public Library Association/March 11 - 15, 2014
Railway Engineering-Maintenance Suppliers Association/Sept. 29 - Oct. 2, 2013
Railway Supply Institute/Indiana Convention Center/Sept. 29 - Oct. 2, 2013
Railway Systems Suppliers, Inc/Indiana Wesleyan University/Sept. 29 - Oct. 1, 2013/2000 attendees/over 100 exhibitors
Registry of Interpreters for the Deaf/JW Marriott Indianapolis/Aug. 9 - 14, 2013
Religion Communicators Council/Sheraton Indianapolis City Centre Hotel/April 3 - 6, 2013
Sigma Theta Tau International/JW Marriott Indianapolis/Nov. 16 - 20, 2013
Society for Ethnomusicology/Indiana University Bloomington/Nov. 14 - 17, 2013
Society for the Scientific Study of Religion/JW Marriott Indianapolis/Oct. 31 - Nov. 2, 2014
Society of Hispanic Professional Engineers/Oct. 30 - Nov. 3, 2013/5000 attendees
Society of Quality Assurance/JW Marriott Indianapolis/April 28 - May 3, 2013
Sports and Entertainment Alliance in Technology/June 9 - 11, 2013
University Council for Educational Administration/Hyatt Regency Indianapolis/Nov. 7 - 10, 2013/1-10 exhibitors
Water Environment Federation/Hyatt Regency Indianapolis/Feb. 23 - 26, 2013
Water Quality Association/Indianapolis Convention Center/April 2 - 5, 2013
The Wire Association International, Inc./Indianapolis Convention Center/May 6 - 7, 2014

La Porte
Pyrotechnics Guild International/Aug. 6 - 12, 2016

IOWA
Ames
Tau Beta Pi Association/Oct. 31 - Nov. 2, 2013
Des Moines
National Association of County Engineers/Des Moines Marriott Downtown/April 21 - 25, 2013
Dubuque
Holstein Association USA/June 25 - 28, 2014
Mason
Pyrotechnics Guild International/Aug. 9 - 15, 2014

KANSAS
Kansas City
American Holistic Veterinary Medical Association/Kansas City Marriott Downtown/Aug. 24 - 27, 2013
McPherson
American Milking Shorthorn Society/May 29 - June 1, 2013
Overland Park
Council of Educational Facility Planners International/Blue Valley Center for Advanced Professional Studies (CAPS)/Feb. 1 - 2, 2013
Wichita
Society for the Advancement of Material and Process Engineering/Century II Convention Center/Oct. 21 - 24, 2013/over 100 exhibitors

KENTUCKY
Bowling Green
North American Thermal Analysis Society/Holiday Inn University Plaza-Bowling Green/Aug. 4 - 7, 2013
Covington
American Forage and Grassland Council/Marriott RiverCenter/Jan. 6 - 9, 2013
Lexington
Association of American State Geologists/June 8 - 12, 2014
College Language Association/April 10 - 13, 2013
National Extension Association of Family and Consumer Sciences/Hyatt Regency Lexington/Sept. 15 - 19, 2013
Safe and Vault Technicians Association/Hilton Lexington/May 6 - 11, 2013
Louisville
American Academy of Osteopathy/Galt House Hotel and Suites/March 18 - 22, 2015

American Association of Medical Society Executives/July 30 - Aug. 2, 2014
American College of Epidemiology/Galt House Hotel and Suites/Sept. 21 - 24, 2013
American Concrete Institute/Hyatt and Kentucky International Convention Center/March 25 - 29, 2013
American Council of Learned Societies/Nov. 14 - 17, 2013
American Design Drafting Association International and American Digital Design Association/Hampton Inn Downtown/April 8 - 12, 2013
American Jail Association/May 21 - 24, 2017
American Musicological Society/Galt House Hotel/Nov. 12 - 15, 2015
American Philatelic Society/Kentucky International Convention Center/Jan. 18 - 20, 2013
American Philatelic Society/Jan. 24 - 26, 2013
American Society for Automation in Pharmacy/The Brown Hotel/June 13 - 15, 2013
American String Teachers Association/March 5 - 8, 2014
Archery Range and Retailers Organization/Jan. 5 - 6, 2013
Archery Trade Association/Kentucky Exposition Center/Jan. 7 - 9, 2013
ASPRS-The Imaging and Geospatial Information Society/Galt House Hotel and Suites/March 23 - 27, 2014
Association for Business Communication/March 6 - 9, 2013
Association of Food and Drug Officials/Louisville Marriott Downtown/June 8 - 12, 2013
Association of Pediatric Hematology/Oncology Nurses/Kentucky International Convention Center/Sept. 19 - 21, 2013
Grain Elevator and Processing Society/Kentucky International Convention Center/Feb. 23 - 26, 2013
International Association of Administrative Professionals/Kentucky Internat'l Convention Center/July 25 - 29, 2015
International Association of Campus Law Enforcement Administrators/Kentucky International Convention Center/June 28 - July 2, 2013
International Association of Clerks, Recorders, Election Officials and Treasurers/June 27 - July 1, 2013
International Nanny Association/April 12 - 15, 2013
Investigative Reporters and Editors/Hyatt Regency Louisville/Feb. 28 - March 3, 2013
NAFSA: Association of International Educators/Kentucky Exposition Center/May 26 - 31, 2013
National Adult Day Service Association/Sept. 15 - 21, 2013
National Association for Court Management/Louisville Marriott Downtown/July 12 - 16, 2015
National Association for Healthcare Quality/Kentucky International Convention Center/Oct. 6 - 9, 2013
National Association of Educational Procurement, Inc./Louisville Marriott Downtown/May 18 - 21, 2014
National Association of Government Defined Contribution Administrators/Kentucky Exposition Center/Sept. 7 - 11, 2013
National Association of Sports Commissions/Louisville Marriott Downtown/April 22 - 25, 2013
National Association of Supervisors of Agricultural Education/Oct. 28 - 30, 2013
National Association of Supervisors of Agricultural Education/Oct. 27 - 29, 2014
National Association of Supervisors of Agricultural Education/Oct. 26 - 28, 2015
National Conference on Weights and Measures/July 14 - 18, 2013
National Federation of Republican Women/Galt House Hotel/Sept. 20 - 23, 2013
National FFA Organization/Oct. 30 - Nov. 2, 2013
National FFA Organization/Oct. 29 - Nov. 1, 2014
National Postsecondary Agriculture Student Organization/Galt House Hotel/March 18 - 21, 2013
National Rural Health Association/May 7 - 10, 2013
National Sheriffs' Association/June 14 - 19, 2019
North American Die Casting Association/Kentucky International Convention Center/Sept. 16 - 18, 2013/5000 attendees/over 100 exhibitors
North American Equipment Dealers Association/Kentucky Exposition Center/Oct. 23 - 25, 2013
North American Equipment Dealers Association/Kentucky Exposition Center/Oct. 22 - 24, 2014
North American Equipment Dealers Association/Kentucky Exposition Center/Oct. 21 - 23, 2015
Propane Engine Fuel Committee/Propane Education and Research Council/Oct. 22 - 24, 2014
Propane Engine Fuel Committee/Propane Education and Research Council/Oct. 21 - 23, 2015
The Propeller Club of the United States/Oct. 15 - 17, 2014
Society of Diagnostic Medical Sonographers/Kentucky Exposition Center/Sept. 26 - 29, 2014/1100 attendees/over 100 exhibitors
Southeastern Theatre Conference/Galt House Hotel/March 6 - 10, 2013
Student National Medical Association/Galt House Hotel/March 27 - 31, 2013/1000 attendees
United States Equestrian Federation/Louisville Marriott Downtown/Jan. 16 - 19, 2013
University Risk Management and Insurance Association/Louisville Marriott Downtown/Sept. 20 - 24, 2014

LOUISIANA

Baton Rouge
American Council for Construction Education/Hilton Baton Rouge Capitol Center/Feb. 20 - 23, 2013
American Farrier's Association/The Belle of Baton Rouge Hotel/Feb. 25 - March 2, 2013
International Clarinet Association/Campus of Louisiana State University/July 30 - Aug. 3, 2014
International Police Mountain Bike Association/April 27 - May 4, 2013
National Association of African American Studies and Affiliates/Crowne Plaza Executive Center Baton Rouge/Feb. 11 - 16, 2013
National Association of County Engineers/Hilton Baton Rouge Capitol Center/April 13 - 17, 2014

National Association of Hispanic and Latino Studies/Crowne Plaza Executive Center Baton Rouge/Feb. 11 - 16, 2013
National Association of Native American Studies/Crowne Plaza Executive Center Baton Rouge/Feb. 11 - 16, 2013
National Taxidermists Association/Crowne Plaza Baton Rouge/July 15 - 23, 2013

Lafayette
Solution Mining Research Institute/April 21 - 24, 2013

New Orleans
AACE International/Sheraton New Orleans Hotel/June 15 - 18, 2014
Airport Consultants Council/Feb. 6 - 8, 2013
Alpha Kappa Psi/Sheraton New Orleans Hotel/Aug. 7 - 10, 2013
American Academy of Ambulatory Care Nursing/Marriott New Orleans/May 20 - 22, 2014
American Academy of Dental Group Practice/Hilton New Orleans Riverside/Feb. 6 - 9, 2013
American Academy of Fertility Care Professionals/Hotel Monteleone/Aug. 7 - 10, 2013
American Academy of Forensic Sciences/Hyatt Regency/Feb. 13 - 18, 2017
American Academy of Hospice and Palliative Medicine/March 13 - 16, 2013
American Academy of Ophthalmic Executives/Ernest N. Morial Convention Center/Nov. 16 - 19, 2013
American Academy of Ophthalmic Executives/Ernest N. Morial Convention Center/Nov. 11 - 14, 2017
American Academy of Ophthalmology/Ernest N. Morial Convention Center/Nov. 16 - 19, 2013
American Academy of Optometry/Oct. 14 - 17, 2015
American Academy of Orthopaedic Surgeons/March 11 - 15, 2014
American Academy of Orthotists and Prosthetists/Hyatt Regency New Orleans/Feb. 18 - 21, 2015
American Academy of Orthotists and Prosthetists/Hyatt Regency New Orleans/Feb. 14 - 17, 2018
American Academy of Veterinary Acupuncture/Hotel Monteleone/May 16 - 19, 2013
American Accounting Association/New Orleans Marriott/Jan. 10 - 12, 2013
American Accounting Association/New Orleans Marriott/Jan. 17 - 19, 2013
American Accounting Association/Hyatt French Quarter/March 22 - 23, 2013
American Association for Cancer Research/April 16 - 20, 2016
American Association for Justice/Sheraton New Orleans Hotel/Feb. 8 - 12, 2014
American Association for Pediatric Ophthalmology and Strabismus/Hyatt Regency/March 25 - 29, 2015
American Association for Public Opinion Research/Sheraton New Orleans Hotel/May 18 - 21, 2017
American Association of Advertising Agencies/March 11 - 13, 2013
American Association of Bovine Practitioners/Sept. 17 - 19, 2015
American Association of Certified Orthoptists/Nov. 16 - 19, 2013
American Association of Colleges of Nursing/JW Marriott New Orleans/Jan. 17, 2013
American Association of Colleges of Nursing/JW Marriott New Orleans/Jan. 17 - 19, 2013
American Association of Critical-Care Nurses/May 14 - 19, 2016
The American Association of Dental Boards/Oct. 30 - 31, 2013
American Association of Directors of Psychiatric Residency Training/Hilton New Orleans Riverside/Feb. 28 - March 2, 2018
American Association of Endodontists/Morial Convention Center/April 26 - 29, 2017
The American Association of Eye and Ear Centers of Excellence/Nov. 10 - 12, 2013
American Association of Genitourinary Surgeons/Ritz-Carlton/April 3 - 6, 2013
American Association of Healthcare Administrative Management/Sheraton New Orleans Hotel/Oct. 16 - 18, 2013
American Association of Immunologists/May 8 - 12, 2015
American Association of Managing General Agents/New Orleans Downtown Marriott at the Convention Center/May 19 - 22, 2013/720 attendees/51-100 exhibitors
American Association of Neurological Surgeons/Ernest N. Morial Convention Center/April 27 - May 1, 2013
American Association of Neuromuscular and Electrodiagnostic Medicine/Hilton New Orleans Riverside/Sept. 14 - 17, 2016
American Association of Orthodontists/April 25 - 29, 2014
American Association of Pharmaceutical Scientists/Ernest N. Morial Convention Center/Oct. 25 - 29, 2020
American Association of Philosophy Teachers/Riverside Hilton/Feb. 20 - 23, 2013
American Association of Physics Teachers/Jan. 5 - 9, 2013
American Association of Plastic Surgeons/The Roosevelt Hotel/April 20 - 23, 2013
American Association of Teachers of French/July 19 - 22, 2014
American Association of University Women/Sheratan New Orleans Hotel/June 9 - 12, 2013
American Brachytherapy Society/Hyatt Regency New Orleans/April 18 - 20, 2013
American Bryological and Lichenological Society/July 26 - 31, 2013
American Catholic Historical Association/Jan. 3 - 6, 2013
American Chemical Society/April 7 - 11, 2013
American Chemical Society/March 18 - 22, 2018
American College Counseling Association/Sept. 25 - 28, 2013
American College of Nuclear Medicine/Sheraton New Orleans Hotel/Jan. 24 - 27, 2013
American College of Prosthodontists/Hyatt Regency New Orleans/Nov. 5 - 8, 2014
American Congress of Obstetricians and Gynecologists/May 4 - 8, 2013
American Correctional Association/Jan. 22 - 27, 2016
American Correctional Association/Jan. 11 - 16, 2019
American Cotton Shippers Association/Windsor Court Hotel/May 8 - 10, 2013
American Council of Life Insurers (ACLI)/April 15 - 17, 2013
American Dental Association/Ernest N. Morial Convention Center/Oct. 31 - Nov. 3, 2013

American Education Finance Association/InterContinental New Orleans/March 14 - 16, 2013

American Group Psychotherapy Association/New Orleans Marriott Hotel/Feb. 25 - March 2, 2013

American Harp Society/Astor Crowne Plaza New Orleans/June 22 - 25, 2014

American Historical Association/New Orleans Marriott/Jan. 3 - 6, 2013

American Immigration Lawyers Association/June 21 - 24, 2017

American Inns of Court/Hilton New Orleans Riverside/May 16 - 18, 2013

American Institute for International Steel/Hilton Riverside/April 9 - 11, 2013

American Logistics Association/Hyatt Regency New Orleans/Sept. 30 - Oct. 2, 2013

American Marketing Association/Sheraton New Orleans Hotel/March 21 - 23, 2013/1-10 exhibitors

American Mathematical Association of Two Year Colleges/Nov. 19 - 22, 2015

American Medical Society for Sports Medicine/Hyatt Regency New Orleans/ April 5 - 9, 2014

American Meteorological Society/Jan. 10 - 14, 2016

American Meteorological Society/Jan. 10 - 14, 2021

American Meteorological Society/Jan. 12 - 16, 2025

American Meteorological Society/Jan. 7 - 11, 2029

American Mosquito Control Association/March 29 - April 2, 2015

American Nuclear Society/Hyatt Regency New Orleans/June 12 - 16, 2016

American Pain Society/May 8 - 11, 2013

American Petroleum Institute/Jan. 21 - 25, 2013

American Petroleum Institute/Nov. 11 - 15, 2013

American Philological Association/Jan. 8 - 11, 2015

American Philosophical Association/Omni Royal Orleans Hotel/Feb. 20 - 23, 2013

American Physical Society/Oct. 27 - 31, 2014

American Physical Society/March 13 - 17, 2017

American Physical Therapy Association - Private Practice Section/Hyatt Regency New Orleans/Nov. 6 - 9, 2013

American Public Health Association/Nov. 15 - 19, 2014/13000 attendees

American Quarter Horse Association/Hyatt Regency/March 7 - 10, 2014

American Reusable Textile Association/New Orleans Morial Convention Center/June 20 - 22, 2013

American Society for Cell Biology/Dec. 14 - 18, 2013

American Society for Clinical Pharmacology and Therapeutics/Hyatt Regency Austin/March 4 - 7, 2015

American Society for Dermatologic Surgery/Hyatt Regency New Orleans/Nov. 10 - 13, 2016

American Society for Engineering Education/June 26 - 29, 2016

American Society for Ethnohistory/Sept. 11 - 14, 2013

American Society for Political and Legal Philosophy/Jan. 4 - 8, 2013

The American Society for Public Administration/Hilton New Orleans Riverside/ March 15 - 19, 2013

American Society of Anesthesiologists/Oct. 11 - 15, 2014

American Society of Criminology/New Orleans Hilton/Nov. 16 - 19, 2016

American Society of Gene & Cell Therapy/May 13 - 16, 2015

American Society of Limnology and Oceanography/Ernest N. Morial Convention Center/Feb. 17 - 22, 2013

American Society of Ocularists/Nov. 15 - 19, 2013

American Society of Ophthalmic Plastic and Reconstructive Surgery/Hyatt Regency/Nov. 14 - 15, 2013

American Society of Orthopedic Physician Assistants/Hyatt Regency/July 31 - Aug. 3, 2013

American Society of Parasitologists/JW Marriott New Orleans/July 24 - 27, 2014

American Society of Plant Taxonomists/July 21 - Aug. 1, 2013

American Society of Tropical Medicine and Hygiene/Sheraton New Orleans Hotel/Nov. 2 - 6, 2014

American Theological Library Association/June 18 - 21, 2014

American Traffic Safety Service Association/Ernest N. Morial Convention Center/Jan. 29 - Feb. 2, 2016

American Veterinary Dental Society/New Orleans Mariott/Oct. 3 - 6, 2013

Associated Collegiate Press/New Orleans Marriott Hotel/Oct. 23 - 27, 2013

Association for Consumer Research/Oct. 1 - 4, 2015

Association for Healthcare Foodservice/June 5 - 8, 2013

Association for Information and Image Management International/Hyatt Regency New Orleans/March 20 - 22, 2013/1-10 exhibitors

Association for Linen Management/June 20 - 22, 2013

Association for Radiological and Imaging Nursing/April 14 - 17, 2013

Association for Symbolic Logic/Feb. 20 - 23, 2013

Association for Unmanned Vehicle Systems International/New Orleans Convention Center/May 3 - 6, 2016/8000 attendees/over 100 exhibitors

Association of Academic Physiatrists/Hilton New Orleans Riverside Hotel/ March 6 - 10, 2013

Association of American Law Schools/Jan. 4 - 8, 2013

Association of American Law Schools/Hilton New Orleans Riverside/Jan. 4 - 7, 2013

Association of American University Presses/New Orleans Marriott/June 22 - 24, 2014

Association of Arts Administration Educators/Bourbon Orleans Hotel/March 7 - 9, 2013

The Association of Black Psychologists/Astor Crowne Plaza New Orleans/July 23 - 27, 2013

Association of College Unions International/March 20 - 24, 2016

The Association of Collegiate Conference and Events Directors International/ Sheraton Hotel New Orleans/March 23 - 26, 2014

Association of Corporate Contributions Professionals/The Hotel Monteleone/ March 10 - 13, 2013

Association of Family and Conciliation Courts/Hilton New Orleans Riverside/ May 27, 2015

Association of Insurance Compliance Professionals/Hilton New Orleans Riverside/Oct. 10 - 14, 2015

Association of International Education Administrators/The New Orleans Marriott/Feb. 17 - 20, 2013

Association of Kentucky Fried Chicken Franchisees, Inc./Hyatt Regency/Feb. 13 - 16, 2013

Association of Leadership Educators/Astor Crowne Plaza/July 7 - 10, 2013

Association of periOperative Registered Nurses/March 24 - 29, 2018

Association of Progressive Rental Organizations/Astor Crowne Plaza and Morial Convention Center/July 15 - 18, 2013

APCO (Association of Public-Safety Communications Officials) International/ Ernest N. Morial Convention Center/Aug. 3 - 7, 2014

Association of School Business Officials International/The Ritz-Carlton, New Orleans/Feb. 14 - 16, 2013

Association of State Dam Safety Officials/Hyatt Regency/Sept. 13 - 17, 2015

Association of Surgical Technologists/Hilton New Orleans Riverside/May 21 - 25, 2013

Association of University Technology Managers/Hyatt Regency New Orleans/ Feb. 22 - 25, 2015

Association of Vascular and Interventional Radiographers/April 13 - 18, 2013

The Botanical Society of America/July 24 - Aug. 1, 2013

Broadcast Cable Credit Association/The Roosevelt Hotel/May 20 - 23, 2013

Cable & Telecommunications Association for Marketing/Oct. 6 - 8, 2013

Casket and Funeral Supply Association of America/Roosevelt New Orleans, A Waldorf Astoria Hotel/March 14 - 16, 2013

Ceilings and Interior Systems Construction Association/Hyatt Regency New Orleans/April 18 - 21, 2016

Ceilings and Interior Systems Construction Association/April 20 - 21, 2016

Child Life Council/Hilton New Orleans Riverside/May 22 - 25, 2014

College Media Association/Oct. 23 - 27, 2013

College of Healthcare Information Management Executives/Ernest N. Morial Convention Center/March 3 - 7, 2013

Communications Fraud Control Association/Loews New Orleans Hotel/Feb. 19 - 21, 2013

Competitive Carriers Association/New Orleans Marriott/April 17 - 19, 2013

Conference on Latin American History/Jan. 3 - 6, 2013

Conference on Latin American History/Hotel Monteleone/Jan. 3 - 5, 2013

Consortium for Graduate Study in Management/June 7 - 12, 2013

Construction Management Association of America/Sheraton Hotel New Orleans/May 5 - 7, 2013

Council for Advancement and Support of Education/Omni Royal Orleans/Feb. 27 - March 1, 2013

CPCU Society/Oct. 26 - 29, 2013

Dance Masters of America, Inc./New Orleans Marriott/July 14 - 20, 2013

Dermatology Nurses' Association/Sheraton New Orleans Hotel/April 4 - 7, 2013/26-50 exhibitors

Education Credit Union Council/New Orleans Marriott Hotel/Feb. 14 - 18, 2014

Electronic Traders Association/New Orleans Convention Center/April 30 - May 2, 2013

Electronic Transactions Association/New Orleans Convention Center/April 30 - May 2, 2013

Environmental Bankers Association/Astor Crowne Plaza/Jan. 19 - 23, 2013

Environmental Mutagen Society/Sheraton Hotel New Orleans/Sept. 26 - 30, 2015

Federal Bar Association/Westin New Orleans Canal Place/May 1 - 5, 2013

Floor Covering Installation Contractors Association/Bourbon Orleans Hotel/ Feb. 24 - 27, 2013/11-25 exhibitors

Fresh Produce Association of the Americas/Oct. 18 - 21, 2013

Fresh Produce Association of the Americas/Oct. 18 - 20, 2013/18000 attendees

Gasket Fabricators Association/Harrah's Hotel/March 19 - 21, 2013

Gerontological Society of America/Nov. 20 - 24, 2013

Gerontological Society of America/Nov. 16 - 20, 2016

Hearth, Patio and Barbecue Association/March 16 - 19, 2016/12000 attendees/over 100 exhibitors

Historians of American Communism/New Orleans Marriott/Jan. 3 - 6, 2013

Hospice and Palliative Nurses Association/March 13 - 16, 2013

Independent Insurance Agents & Brokers of America, Inc./Roosevelt New Orleans Hotel/Sept. 30 - Oct. 4, 2013

Institute for Supply Management/Feb. 5 - 7, 2013

International Association of Business Communicators/Hilton New Orleans Riverside/June 5 - 8, 2016

International Association of Venue Managers/July 26 - 30, 2013

International Claim Association/New Orleans Marriott/Sept. 21 - 24, 2014

International Council of Fine Arts Deans/Hotel Monteleone/Oct. 23 - 26, 2013/200 attendees

International Dyslexia Association/Ernest N. Morial Convention Center/Nov. 6 - 9, 2013

InterNational Electrical Testing Association/Sheraton New Orleans Hotel/Feb. 18 - 21, 2013

International Facility Management Association/Sept. 16 - 18, 2014

International Foundation of Employee Benefit Plans/Oct. 14 - 17, 2018

International Franchise Association/New Orleans Morial Convention Center/ Feb. 22 - 25, 2014/over 100 exhibitors

International Sleep Products Association/New Orleans Morial Convention Center/March 26 - 29, 2014

International Society for Pharmacoeconomics and Outcomes Research/ Sheraton Hotel New Orleans/May 18 - 22, 2013

International Society of Automation/Astor Crowne Plaza Hotel/Aug. 11 - 13, 2013

International Studies Association/Hilton New Orleans Riverside/Feb. 18 - 21, 2015

International Textile and Apparel Association/Sheraton New Orleans Hotel/ Oct. 15 - 18, 2013

Lamaze International/Astor Crowne Plaza Hotel/Oct. 11 - 13, 2013

Land Trust Alliance/Sept. 17 - 19, 2013

LeadingAge (American Association of Homes and Services for the Aging)/Oct. 29 - Nov. 1, 2017

Life Insurers Council/Omni Royal Orleans Hotel/April 23 - 25, 2013

Local Media Association/Roosevelt New Orleans/Feb. 18 - 20, 2013

Marine Technology Society/Morial Convention Center/Jan. 15 - 17, 2013

Media Financial Management Association/The Roosevelt Hotel/May 20 - 22, 2013

Messenger Courier Association of the Americas/Sheraton Hotel New Orleans/ May 8 - 11, 2013

Middle East Studies Association of North America/Sheraton Hotel New Orleans/Oct. 10 - 13, 2013

Mobile Air Conditioning Society Worldwide/Sheraton New Orleans Hotel/Jan. 16 - 18, 2014

NADCA: The HVAC Inspection, Maintenance and Restoration Association/March 15 - 18, 2013

National Association of Student Personnel Administrators/March 21 - 25, 2015

National Association of Medical Staff Services/Hilton New Orleans Riverside/Sept. 27 - Oct. 1, 2014/11-25 exhibitors

National Association of Agricultural Fair Agencies/The Roosevelt Hotel/June 9 - 13, 2013

National Association of Children's Hospitals and Related Institutions/Marriott New Orleans/Oct. 13 - 16, 2013

National Association of College and University Attorneys/Hotel Monteleone/Jan. 11 - 12, 2013

National Association of Concessionaires/Hilton Riverside Hotel/Aug. 6 - 9, 2013

National Association of Counties/New Orleans Morial Convention Center/July 11 - 14, 2014

National Association of Federal Credit Unions/Hyatt French Quarter/March 12 - 14, 2013

National Association of Hispanic Nurses/Astor Crowne Plaza Hotel/Aug. 6 - 9, 2013

National Association of Insurance and Financial Advisors/Oct. 3 - 6, 2015

National Association of Legal Investigators/June 13 - 15, 2013

National Association of Local Housing Finance Agencies/InterContinental New Orleans/April 4 - 6, 2013

National Association of Orthopaedic Technologists/Hyatt Regency/July 31 - Aug. 3, 2013

National Association of Professional Organizers/Sheraton Hotel New Orleans/April 17 - 20, 2013

National Association of Realtors/Nov. 7 - 10, 2014

National Association of School Psychologists/New Orleans Marriot & Sheraton/Feb. 10 - 13, 2016

National Association of Spine Specialists/Oct. 9 - 12, 2013

National Association of Student Financial Aid Administrators/July 19 - 22, 2015

National Association of Temple Administrators/Nov. 8 - 12, 2014

National Automobile Dealers Association/Jan. 24 - 27, 2014

National Beer Wholesalers Association/Hyatt Regency New Orleans/Sept. 28 - Oct. 1, 2014

National Black Nurses Association/Hyatt Regency New Orleans/July 31 - Aug. 4, 2013

National Conference of State Social Security Administrators/Bourbon Orleans Hotel/July 27 - 30, 2014

National Council for the Social Studies/Ernest N. Morial Convention Center/Nov. 13 - 15, 2015

National Council of Farmer Cooperatives/Roosevelt New Orleans/Feb. 12 - 14, 2014

National Council of Higher Education Loan Programs/St. James Parish/July 23 - 28, 2013

National Council of State Housing Agencies/New Orleans Marriott/Oct. 19 - 22, 2013

National Council of Structural Engineers Associations/Sept. 17 - 20, 2014

National Council of Supervisors of Mathematics/April 7 - 9, 2014

National Council of Teachers of Mathematics/April 9 - 12, 2014

National Council of University Research Administrators/March 10 - 12, 2013

National Dental Association/Hilton New Orleans Riverside Hotel/July 25 - 28, 2014

National Educational Broadband Services Organization/Astor Crowne Plaza/April 2 - 5, 2014

National Exchange Club/Sheraton Hotel New Orleans/July 9 - 12, 2014

National Federation Coaches Association/New Orleans Marriott/June 28 - July 2, 2015

National Federation of State High School Associations/New Orleans Marriott/June 28 - July 2, 2015

The National Flute Association, Inc./New Orleans Marriott/Aug. 8 - 11, 2013

National Hearing Conservation Association/Astor Crowne Plaza Hotel/Feb. 19 - 21, 2015

National Home Furnishings Association/June 2 - 4, 2013

National Peanut Buying Point Association/Feb. 14 - 18, 2013

National Recreation and Parks Association/Sept. 26 - 28, 2017/7000 attendees/over 100 exhibitors

National School Boards Association/April 5 - 7, 2014

National Sheriffs' Association/June 15 - 20, 2018

National Student Employment Association/LePavillon Hotel/Oct. 16 - 18, 2013

National Tour Association/Jan. 17 - 21, 2015

National Watermelon Association/Hyatt Regency/Feb. 24 - 28, 2016

North American Catalysis Society/March 7 - 11, 2013

North American Society for the Psychology of Sport and Physical Activity/Hilton Riverside Hotel/June 13 - 15, 2013

North American Spine Society/Oct. 9 - 12, 2013

Orthopaedic Research Society/Hyatt Regency/March 15 - 18, 2014

Paso Fino Horse Association, Inc./Jan. 11 - 12, 2013

Pierre Fauchard Academy/Oct. 31 - Nov. 5, 2013

Polyurethane Foam Association/New Orleans Downtown Marriott at the Convention Center/Nov. 6 - 7, 2013

Population Association of America/Sheraton New Orleans Hotel/April 11 - 13, 2013

Pressure Sensitive Tape Council/Sheraton New Orleans Hotel/May 13 - 17, 2013

Produce Marketing Association/Oct. 18 - 21, 2013

Produce Marketing Association/Oct. 18 - 20, 2013/18500 attendees/over 100 exhibitors

Production and Operations Management Society/April 26 - 29, 2013

Recognition Professionals International/Hilton New Orleans Riverside/April 27 - May 1, 2013

Registry of Interpreters for the Deaf/Hyatt Regency New Orleans/Aug. 11 - 18, 2015

Renal Physicians Association/March 14 - 17, 2013

The Rural Sociological Society/Roosevelt New Orleans, A Waldorf Astoria Hotel/July 30 - Aug. 3, 2013

Scaffold Industry Association/Loews New Orleans Hotel/Feb. 24 - 26, 2013

Society for Italian Historical Studies/New Orleans Marriott/Jan. 3 - 6, 2013

Society for Maternal-Fetal Medicine/Hilton New Orleans Riverside/Feb. 3 - 8, 2014

Society for Military History/Sheraton Hotel New Orleans/March 14 - 17, 2013

Society for Personality and Social Psychology/Ernest N. Morial Convention Center/Jan. 17 - 19, 2013

Society of Interventional Radiology/April 13 - 18, 2013/11-25 exhibitors

Society of Nuclear Medicine/Sheraton New Orleans Hotel/Jan. 24 - 27, 2013

Society of Pediatric Psychology/April 11 - 13, 2013

Society of Petroleum Engineers/Ernest N. Morial Convention Center/Sept. 30 - Oct. 2, 2013

Society of Petrophysicists and Well Log Analysts/Hyatt Regency Hotel/June 22 - 26, 2013

Society of Research Administrators International/Sheraton Hotel New Orleans/Oct. 26 - 30, 2013

Society of Toxicology/Ernest N. Morial Convention Center/March 13 - 17, 2016

Society of University Surgeons/Roosevelt New Orleans Hotel/Feb. 5 - 7, 2013

Special Care Dentistry/Astor Crowne Plaza New Orleans/April 18 - 21, 2013

Special Care Dentistry Association/Astor Crowne Plaza Hotel/April 18 - 21, 2013

Specialty Graphic Imaging Association/Ernest N. Morial Convention Center/Oct. 10 - 12, 2017

Utilimetrics/Alliance for Advanced Metering & Data Management Solutions/Sept. 8 - 11, 2013

Waste Equipment Technology Association/Ernest N. Morial Convention Center/May 20 - 23, 2013/11000 attendees/over 100 exhibitors

Women Band Directors International/June 19 - 23, 2013

Women's Basketball Coaches Association/April 5 - 9, 2013/51-100 exhibitors

MAINE

Portland

Society for the History of Technology/Oct. 10 - 13, 2013

South Portland

Association for Applied and Clinical Sociology/DoubleTree by Hilton Hotel Portland/Oct. 3 - 5, 2013

MARYLAND

Annapolis

Council of Manufacturing Associations/Loews Annapolis Hotel/Jan. 17 - 18, 2013

National Marine Educators Association/Loews Annapolis Hotel/July 19 - 24, 2014

North American Association of Christians in Social Work/Anne Arundel Medical Center/Nov. 6 - 9, 2014

Transportation Research Forum/Doubletree Hotel Annapolis/March 21 - 23, 2013

Baltimore

Academy Health/June 23 - 25, 2013/2400 attendees/26-50 exhibitors

Academy of Pharmaceutical Research and Science/March 4 - 7, 2016

African Studies Association/Baltimore Marriott Waterfront/Nov. 21 - 24, 2013

American Academy of Dental Sleep Medicine/Hilton Baltimore/May 30 - June 1, 2013

American Academy of Medical Acupuncture/Renaissance Baltimore Harborplace/May 3 - 4, 2013

American Academy of Religion/Nov. 23 - 26, 2013/10000 attendees/over 100 exhibitors

American Architectural Manufacturers Association/Baltimore Marriott Waterfront/Oct. 27 - 30, 2013

American Association for Clinical Chemistry, Inc./April 18 - 19, 2013

American Association for Justice/Baltimore Convention Center/July 26 - 30, 2014

American Association for Laboratory Animal Science/Oct. 27 - 31, 2013

American Association of Colleges of Osteopathic Medicine/Baltimore Marriott Waterfront/April 24 - 27, 2013

American Association of Collegiate Registrars and Admissions Officers/Baltimore Convention Center/March 22 - 25, 2015

American Association of Museums/May 19 - 22, 2013/over 100 exhibitors

American Association of State Colleges and Universities/July 25 - 27, 2013

American College of Allergy, Asthma and Immunology/Nov. 7 - 12, 2013/51-100 exhibitors

American College of Allergy, Asthma and Immunology/Nov. 7 - 12, 2013

American College of Occupational and Environmental Medicine/Hilton Baltimore/May 3 - 6, 2015

American College of Osteopathic Internists/Baltimore Marriott Inner Harbor at Camden Yards/Oct. 15 - 19, 2014

American Council of Learned Societies/Renaissance Baltimore Harborplace Hotel/May 9 - 11, 2013

American Craft Council/Baltimore Convention Center/Feb. 19 - 24, 2013

American Educational Studies Association/Engineers Club/Oct. 31 - Nov. 3, 2013

American Mathematical Society/Hilton Baltimore/Jan. 15 - 18, 2014

American Occupational Therapy Association, Inc./Baltimore Convention Center/April 3 - 6, 2014

American Pediatric Society/April 30 - May 3, 2016

American Pediatric Society/April 27 - 30, 2019

American Pharmacists Association/March 4 - 7, 2016

American Philosophical Association/Baltimore Marriott Waterfront/Dec. 27 - 30, 2013

American Physical Society/Baltimore Convention Center/March 18 - 22, 2013

American Physical Society/April 11 - 14, 2015

American Physical Society/May 2 - 5, 2015

American Physical Society/March 14 - 18, 2016

American Society for Bone and Mineral Research/Oct. 4 - 8, 2013

American Society for Bone and Mineral Research/Oct. 4 - 7, 2013/5000 attendees/over 100 exhibitors

American Society for Investigative Pathology/March 3, 2013
American Society for Mass Spectrometry/June 15 - 19, 2014
American Society for Reproductive Medicine/Hilton Baltimore/Oct. 17 - 21, 2015
American Society of Human Genetics/Oct. 6 - 10, 2015
American Society of Pediatric Nephrology/April 30 - May 3, 2016
American Society of Pediatric Nephrology/April 27 - 30, 2019
American Solar Energy Society/April 15 - 20, 2013
American Solar Energy Society/April 16 - 20, 2013
American Telemedicine Association/May 18 - 20, 2014
Applied Research Ethics National Association/March 18 - 19, 2013
ASPRS-The Imaging and Geospatial Information Society/Baltimore Marriott Waterfront/March 24 - 28, 2013
Associated Professional Sleep Societies/Hilton Baltimore/June 1 - 5, 2013/5000 attendees/over 100 exhibitors
Associated Wire Rope Fabricators/Marriott Waterfront/April 27 - 30, 2014
Association for Commuter Transportation/AAA- Four Diamond Hotel/July 25 - 29, 2015
Association for Consumer Research/Oct. 23 - 26, 2014
Association for Continuing Legal Education/Baltimore Marriott Waterfront/ Aug. 3 - 6, 2013
Association for Death Education and Counseling/Renaissance Baltimore Harborplace Hotel/April 23 - 26, 2014
Association for Research in Otolaryngology/Baltimore Marriott Waterfront/ Feb. 16 - 20, 2013
Association for Research in Otolaryngology/Baltimore Marriott Waterfront/ Feb. 21 - 25, 2015
Association for Research in Vision and Ophthalmology/May 7 - 11, 2017
Association for Research in Vision and Ophthalmology/May 3 - 7, 2020
Association of Academic Museums & Galleries/Gilman Hall/May 18, 2013
Association of Organ Procurement Organizations/Baltimore Marriott Inner Harbor at Camden Yards/June 17 - 20, 2014
Association of Professional Researchers for Advancement/Baltimore Marriott Waterfront/Aug. 7 - 10, 2013/11-25 exhibitors
Association on Higher Education and Disability/Hilton Baltimore/July 8 - 13, 2013
AVS: Science and Technology of Materials, Interfaces, and Processing/ Baltimore Convention Center/Nov. 9 - 14, 2014
Beta Alpha Psi/Marriott Baltimore Waterfront/April 1, 2013
Black Psychiatrists of America/Baltimore Hilton Hotel/March 22 - 23, 2013
Clinical Immunology Society/Hilton Baltimore/April 10 - 13, 2014
Composite Panel Association/Hyatt Regency/Sept. 29 - Oct. 1, 2013
Construction Management Association of America/Harbor Court Baltimore/ May 4 - 6, 2014
Decision Sciences Institute/Baltimore Marriott Waterfront/Nov. 16 - 19, 2013
Ecological Society of America/Hilton Baltimore/Aug. 9 - 15, 2015
Forming and Fabricating Community of SME/June 2 - 4, 2013
Geological Society of America/Nov. 1 - 4, 2015
The Grant Professionals Association/Hyatt Regency Baltimore/Nov. 13 - 16, 2013
Hydraulic Institute/Baltimore's Tremont Plaza Hotel/Oct. 23 - 26, 2013
Industrial Diamond Association of America/Hyatt Regency/May 6 - 8, 2013
Institute of Mathematical Statistics/Baltimore Convention Center/March 16 - 19, 2014
Institute of Mathematical Statistics/Baltimore Convention Center/July 29 - Aug. 3, 2017
International Municipal Lawyers Association/Sept. 8 - 14, 2014
International Society for the Study of Dissociation/Hilton Baltimore Hotel/Nov. 16 - 18, 2013
International Society for the Study of Trauma and Dissociation/Hilton Baltimore Hotel/Nov. 16 - 18, 2013
International Studies Association/Hilton Baltimore/Feb. 22 - 25, 2017
Mathematical Association of America/Jan. 15 - 18, 2014
National Association of Student Personnel Administrators/March 15 - 19, 2014
National Alliance of Medicare Set-Aside Professionals, Inc./Hyatt Regency Baltimore/April 25 - 26, 2013
National Association for Gifted Children/Nov. 13 - 16, 2014
The National Association for the Dually Diagnosed/Oct. 23 - 25, 2013
National Association of College and University Food Services/July 9 - 12, 2014
National Association of College and University Food Services/July 9 - 14, 2014
National Association of Elementary School Principals/Baltimore Convention Center/July 11 - 13, 2013
National Association of Negro Business and Professional Women's Clubs/ Hyatt Regency Baltimore/Aug. 12 - 18, 2013
National Association of Secretaries of State/Hilton Baltimore/July 13 - 16, 2014
National Athletic Trainers Association/June 22 - 25, 2016
National Child Support Enforcement Association/Baltimore Omni Inner Harbor/Aug. 5 - 7, 2013
National Coil Coating Association/Baltimore Marriott Waterfront/Sept. 23 - 25, 2013
National Council on Family Relations/Hilton Baltimore/Nov. 18 - 22, 2014
National Guard Association of the U.S./Sept. 9 - 12, 2016
National Recreation and Parks Association/Sept. 24 - 26, 2019/7000 attendees/over 100 exhibitors
National Sheriffs' Association/June 26 - July 1, 2015
National Soccer Coaches Association of America/Jan. 13 - 17, 2016/9000 attendees
National Soccer Coaches Association of America/Jan. 15 - 19, 2020/9000 attendees
National Stone, Sand, and Gravel Association/March 16 - 18, 2015
National Stone, Sand, and Gravel Association/March 16 - 18, 2016
The North American Rail Shippers Association/Hilton Inner Harbor Hotel/May 29 - 31, 2013
Pediatric Endocrine Society/April 30 - May 3, 2016
Pediatric Endocrine Society/April 27 - 30, 2019
Regulatory Affairs Professionals Society/Oct. 24 - 28, 2015
Social Science History Association/Hyatt Regency Baltimore/Nov. 12 - 15, 2015
Society for Conservation Biology/July 21 - 25, 2013/1600 attendees

Society for Developmental and Behavioral Pediatrics/Renaissance Baltimore Harborplace Hotel/Sept. 27 - 30, 2013
Society for Medical Decision Making/Hilton Baltimore/Oct. 20 - 23, 2013/600 attendees
Society for Pediatric Research/April 30 - May 3, 2016
Society for Pediatric Research/April 27 - 30, 2019
Society for Risk Analysis/Dec. 8 - 11, 2013
Society for Sex Therapy and Research/April 4 - 7, 2013
Society of American Gastrointestinal and Endoscopic Surgeons/Hilton Baltimore/April 17 - 20, 2013
Society of Biblical Literature/Nov. 23 - 26, 2013/3000 attendees
Society of Nuclear Medicine/June 6 - 10, 2015
Society of Rheology/CBD/Oct. 11 - 15, 2015
Society of Teachers of Family Medicine/Baltimore Marriott Waterfront/May 1 - 5, 2013/1500 attendees
Society of Toxicology/Baltimore Convention Center/March 12 - 16, 2017
Society of Women Engineers/Oct. 24 - 26, 2013
SPIE - The International Society for Optical Engineering/Baltimore Convention Center/April 29 - May 3, 2013
Sports Lawyers Association/Marriott Waterfront/May 14 - 16, 2015
Surgical Infection Society/April 29 - May 3, 2014
TESOL International Association/April 5 - 8, 2016
United States and Canadian Academy of Pathology/Baltimore Convention Center/March 2 - 8, 2013/4880 attendees/51-100 exhibitors
Weed Science Society of America/Feb. 4 - 7, 2013
Women's Business Enterprise National Council/Hilton Baltimore/March 13 - 15, 2013

Bethesda

American College of Clinical Pharmacology/Bethesda North Marriott Hotel and Conference Center/Sept. 22 - 24, 2013
American Society for Experimental NeuroTherapeutics/Hyatt Regency Bethesda/Feb. 28 - March 2, 2013
National Council on Radiation Protection and Measurement/March 11 - 12, 2013
Sigma Phi Delta/Bethesda North Marriott Hotel and Conference Center/Aug. 8 - 11, 2013
Society for Cryobiology/Marriott Bethesda North Hotel and Conference Center/July 28 - 31, 2013

Buckeystown

Zero Balancing Health Association/The Claggett Center in Buckeystown/May 3 - 5, 2013

Chesapeake City

KWPN of North America/Hassler Dressage/March 14 - 16, 2013

Ft. Washington

AAGL - Advancing Minimally Invasive Gynecology Worldwide/Gaylord National Resort and Convention Center-National Harbor/Nov. 10 - 14, 2013
Air Traffic Control Association/Gaylord National Resort and Convention Center-National Harbor/Oct. 20 - 23, 2013/3000 attendees
Air Traffic Control Association/Gaylord National Resort and Convention Center-National Harbor/Sept. 28 - Oct. 1, 2014
American Association of Colleges of Pharmacy/Gaylord National Hotel and Convention Center/July 11 - 15, 2015
American Association of Tissue Banks/Gaylord National Hotel and Convention Center/Oct. 2 - 6, 2013
American Immigration Lawyers Association/Gaylord National Hotel and Convention Center/June 17 - 20, 2015
American Medical Association/Gaylord National Hotel and Convention Center/ Nov. 16 - 19, 2013
American Medical Directors Association/March 21 - 24, 2013
American Society of Pension Professionals & Actuaries/Gaylord National Resort and Convention Center-National Harbor/Oct. 27 - 30, 2013
Applied Research Ethics National Association/Dec. 5 - 7, 2014
Applied Research Ethics National Association/Dec. 1 - 3, 2017
Association for Molecular Pathology/Gaylord National Resort and Convention Center-National Harbor/Nov. 13 - 15, 2014/over 100 exhibitors
Association of Clean Water Administrators/Westin Washington National Harbor/March 3 - 5, 2013
Association of Legal Administrators/Gaylord National Resort and Convention Center-National Harbor/April 15 - 18, 2013
Association of the United States Army/Gaylord National Resort and Convention Center-National Harbor/Jan. 9 - 11, 2013
Health Care Compliance Association/Gaylord National Hotel and Convention Center/April 21 - 24, 2013
National Association of Drug Court Professionals/Gaylord National Resort and Convention Center-National Harbor/July 14 - 17, 2013
National Association of Drug Court Professionals/Gaylord National Resort and Convention Center-National Harbor/July 19 - 22, 2015
National Association of Mutual Insurance Companies/Sept. 21 - 24, 2014/1700 attendees/over 100 exhibitors
National Association of Secondary School Principals/Gaylord National Resort and Convention Center-National Harbor/Feb. 28 - March 2, 2013
National Dental Association/Gaylord National Hotel and Convention Center/ July 26 - 30, 2013
National Dental Hygienists' Association/Gaylord National Harbor Resort/July 26 - 30, 2013
National Federation Coaches Association/Gaylord National Resort and Convention Center-National Harbor/Dec. 12 - 16, 2014
National Hospice & Palliative Care Organization/Gaylord National Resort and Convention Center-National Harbor/April 25 - 27, 2013
National Hospice & Palliative Care Organization/Gaylord National Resort and Convention Center-National Harbor/March 27 - 29, 2014
National Hospice & Palliative Care Organization/Gaylord National Resort and Convention Center-National Harbor/April 30 - May 2, 2015
National Hospice & Palliative Care Organization/Gaylord National Resort and Convention Center-National Harbor/April 21 - 23, 2016
National Hospice & Palliative Care Organization/Gaylord National Resort and Convention Center-National Harbor/April 27 - 30, 2017
National Institute of Governmental Purchasing/Gaylord National Hotel and Convention Center/Aug. 19 - 23, 2016

National Interscholastic Athletic Administrators Association/Gaylord National Resort and Convention Center-National Harbor/Dec. 12 - 16, 2013

Navy League of the United States/Gaylord National Resort and Convention Center-National Harbor/April 8 - 10, 2013

Navy League of the United States/Gaylord National Resort and Convention Center-National Harbor/April 7 - 9, 2014

Navy League of the United States/Gaylord National Resort and Convention Center-National Harbor/April 13 - 15, 2015

Navy League of the United States/Gaylord National Resort and Convention Center-National Harbor/April 4 - 6, 2016

Navy League of the United States/Gaylord National Resort and Convention Center-National Harbor/April 3 - 5, 2017

Navy League of the United States/Gaylord National Resort and Convention Center-National Harbor/April 9 - 11, 2018

Network Branded Prepaid Card Association/Gaylord National Hotel and Convention Center/June 26 - 28, 2013

Orthopaedic Trauma Association/Oct. 5 - 8, 2016

Pharmaceutical Marketing Research Group/Gaylord National Hotel and Convention Center/March 15 - 17, 2015

Society for Vascular Surgery/Gaylord National Resort and Convention Center-National Harbor/June 4 - 6, 2015

Society for Critical Care Medicine/Gaylord National Hotel and Convention Center/May 16 - 19, 2013/11-25 exhibitors

Society of Hospital Medicine/Gaylord National Resort & Convention Center/May 16 - 19, 2013

Society of Surgical Oncology/Gaylord National Hotel and Convention Center/March 6 - 9, 2013

Voluntary Protection Programs Participants' Association, Inc./Gaylord National Resort and Convention Center-National Harbor/Aug. 25 - 28, 2014

Greenbelt

American Astronautical Society/March 19 - 21, 2013

Maryland City

National Organization of Nurse Practitioner Faculties/Hilton in Baltimore/April 23 - 26, 2015

McHenry

American Association of Managing General Agents/Wisp Resort/May 17 - 20, 2015/720 attendees/51-100 exhibitors

Potomac

American Academy of Veterinary Pharmacology and Therapeutics/Bolger Center/May 19 - 22, 2013

Rockville

Council of State Speech-Language-Hearing Association Presidents/May 17 - 18, 2013

MASSACHUSETTS

Beverly

Christian College Consortium/Wylie Inn and Conference Center/June 12 - 14, 2013

Boston

AABB - American Association of Blood Banks/Oct. 13 - 16, 2018

Academy for Eating Disorders/Boston Marriott Copley Place/April 23 - 25, 2015

Academy Health/June 26 - 28, 2016

Academy of Legal Studies in Business/Fairmont Copley Plaza Hotel Boston/Aug. 6 - 11, 2013

Academy of Managed Care Pharmacy/Hynes Convention Center/Oct. 8 - 10, 2014

Ambulatory Surgery Center Association/Hynes Convention Center/April 17 - 20, 2013/2500 attendees

American Academy of Optometry/Boston Convention and Exhibition Center/Oct. 4 - 7, 2017

American Academy of Pediatric Dentistry/Sheraton Boston Hotel/May 22 - 25, 2014

American Academy of Periodontology/Boston Marriott Copley Place/June 6 - 9, 2013

American Academy of Physical Medicine and Rehabilitation/Marriott/Sheraton/Oct. 1 - 4, 2015

American Academy of Physician Assistants/May 24 - 29, 2014

American Academy of Religion/Nov. 18 - 21, 2017/10000 attendees/over 100 exhibitors

American Academy of Religion/Nov. 21 - 24, 2020/10000 attendees/over 100 exhibitors

American Association for Cancer Research/Oct. 19 - 23, 2013

American Association for Dental Research/March 11 - 14, 2015

American Association for Pediatric Ophthalmology and Strabismus/Westin Copley Place Boston/April 3 - 7, 2016

American Association for Public Opinion Research/Seaport Boston Hotel/May 16 - 19, 2013

American Association for the Advancement of Science/Feb. 14 - 18, 2013

American Association for the Advancement of Slavic Studies/Boston Marriot Copley Place/Nov. 21 - 24, 2013

American Association for the Study of Liver Diseases/Nov. 7 - 11, 2014

American Association of Anatomists/April 20 - 24, 2013

American Association of Anatomists/March 28 - April 1, 2015

American Association of Critical-Care Nurses/May 18 - 23, 2013

American Association of Pharmaceutical Scientists/Boston Convention and Exposition Center/Oct. 16 - 20, 2022

American Association of Teachers of Slavic and East European Languages/Hyatt Regency Boston/Jan. 3 - 6, 2013

American Bar Association/Aug. 7 - 14, 2014

American Bar Association/Aug. 7 - 12, 2014

American Board of Professional Psychology/July 10 - 13, 2014

American Broncho-Esophagological Association/Sheraton Boston Hotel/April 22 - 26, 2015

American Burn Association/March 25 - 28, 2014

American Burn Association/March 21 - 24, 2017

American Chemical Society/Aug. 16 - 20, 2015

American Chemical Society/Aug. 19 - 23, 2018

American College Health Association/Boston Marriott Copley Place/May 28 - June 1, 2013

American College of Emergency Physicians/Oct. 26 - 29, 2015

American College of Osteopathic Surgeons/Westin Boston Waterfront/Sept. 11 - 14, 2014

American College of Phlebology/John B. Hynes Veterans Memorial Convention Center/Sept. 8 - 13, 2013

American College of Physicians/April 30 - May 2, 2015

American College of Physicians Services, Inc./April 30 - May 2, 2015

American College of Real Estate Lawyers/InterContinental Boston/Oct. 16 - 19, 2014

American College of Sports Medicine/June 1 - 4, 2016

American Correctional Association/Aug. 5 - 10, 2016

American Correctional Association/Aug. 2 - 7, 2019

American Council of Engineering Companies/The Westin Copley Place/Oct. 14 - 17, 2015

American Dental Education Association/Hynes Convention Center/March 7 - 10, 2015

American Dental Hygienists' Association/Sheraton Boston Hotel/June 17 - 27, 2013/over 100 exhibitors

American Dialect Society/Boston Marriott Copley Place/Jan. 3 - 6, 2013

American Economic Association/Jan. 3 - 5, 2015/over 100 exhibitors

American Federation for Medical Research/April 20 - 24, 2014/14000 attendees

The American Finance Association/Jan. 3 - 5, 2015

American Guild of Organists/Boston Marriott Copley Place/June 23 - 27, 2014

American Guild of Organists/June 24 - 27, 2014

American Headache Society/Hynes Convention Center Hotel/June 27 - 30, 2013

American Immigration Lawyers Association/Greater Boston Convention and Visitors Bureau/June 18 - 21, 2014

American Institute of Aeronautics and Astronautics/Boston Park Plaza Hotel and Towers/April 8 - 11, 2013

American Institute of Aeronautics and Astronautics/Boston Marriott Copley Place/Aug. 19 - 22, 2013

American Library Association/Jan. 22 - 26, 2016

American Meteorological Society/Jan. 12 - 16, 2020

American Neuropsychiatric Association/The Boston Park Plaza Hotel/April 3 - 6, 2013

American Physiological Society/April 20 - 24, 2013

American Physiological Society/March 28 - April 1, 2015

American Psychological Association - Division of Psychoanalysis/April 24 - 28, 2013

American Public Gas Association/InterContinental Boston/July 28 - 31, 2013

American Public Health Association/Nov. 2 - 6, 2013/13000 attendees

American Society for Biochemistry and Molecular Biology/Boston Convention and Exhibition Cente/April 20 - 24, 2013/over 100 exhibitors

American Society for Healthcare Engineering/July 12 - 15, 2015/1-10 exhibitors

American Society for Investigative Pathology/Boston Convention and Exhibition Center/April 20 - 24, 2013

American Society for Investigative Pathology/March 28 - April 1, 2015

American Society for Laser Medicine and Surgery/Hynes Convention Center and Sheraton Boston Hotel/April 3 - 7, 2013

American Society for Metabolic and Bariatric Surgery/Nov. 2 - 7, 2014

American Society for Microbiology/Oct. 5 - 9, 2013

American Society for Nutrition/Boston Convention and Exhibition Center/April 20 - 24, 2013

American Society for Nutrition/March 28 - April 1, 2015

American Society for Pharmacology and Experimental Therapeutics/Boston Convention and Exhibition Center/April 20 - 24, 2013

American Society for Pharmacology and Experimental Therapeutics/March 28 - April 1, 2015

American Society for Reproductive Medicine/Boston Convention and Exhibition Cente/Oct. 12 - 17, 2013

American Society for Surgery of the Hand/John B. Hynes Veterans Memorial Convention Center/Sept. 18 - 20, 2014

American Society for Surgery of the Hand/Sept. 13 - 15, 2018

American Society of Anesthesiologists/Oct. 15 - 19, 2016

American Society of Anesthesiologists/Oct. 21 - 25, 2017

American Society of Cataract and Refractive Surgery/April 25 - 29, 2014

American Society of Cataract and Refractive Surgery/April 26 - 30, 2014

American Society of Colon and Rectal Surgeons/Hynes Convention Center and Sheraton Boston Hotel/May 30 - June 3, 2015

American Society of Hand Therapists/Sept. 18 - 20, 2014

American Society of Human Genetics/Oct. 22 - 26, 2013

American Society of Landscape Architects/Boston Convention and Exhibition Cente/Nov. 15 - 18, 2013/over 100 exhibitors

American Society of Ophthalmic Administrators/April 9 - 13, 2014

American Society of Ophthalmic Administrators/April 25 - 28, 2014

American Society of Transplantation/June 11 - 15, 2016

American Society of Transplantation/June 1 - 5, 2019

American Statistical Association/Boston Convention and Exhibition Center/Aug. 2 - 7, 2014/5000 attendees

American Surgical Association/Boston Marriott Copley Place/April 10 - 12, 2014

American Veterinary Medical Association/July 11 - 14, 2015

Analytical and Life Science Systems Association/April 28 - 30, 2013

Applied Research Ethics National Association/Nov. 7 - 9, 2013

Applied Research Ethics National Association/Nov. 13 - 15, 2015

Arthroscopy Association of North America/April 14 - 16, 2016

ASFE/The Geoprofessional Business Association/Boston Marriott Copley Place/Oct. 10 - 12, 2013

ASPSN - American Society of Plastic Surgical Nurses/Oct. 16 - 19, 2015

Association for Continuing Legal Education/Westin Copley Place Boston/Aug. 2 - 5, 2014

Association for Slavic, East European, and Eurasian Studies/Boston Marriott Long Wharf/Nov. 21 - 24, 2013

Association of American University Presses/Seaport Boston Hotel/June 20 - 23, 2013

Association of Clinical Scientists/Omni Parker House Hotel/May 22 - 25, 2013
Association of Community Cancer Centers/Westin Boston Waterfront/Oct. 2 - 5, 2013
The Association of Language Companies/Boston Park Plaza Hotel and Towers/May 15 - 18, 2013
Association of Military Surgeons of the United States/Oct. 26 - 31, 2014
Association of Pathology Chairs/Seaport Boston Hotel/July 10 - 12, 2013/11-25 exhibitors
Association of Pathology Chairs/Seaport Boston Hotel/July 9 - 11, 2014
Association of periOperative Registered Nurses/April 1 - 6, 2017
Association of Proposal Management Professionals/May 25 - 28, 2016
Association of School Business Officials International/Hynes Convention Center/Oct. 25 - 28, 2013
Association of Writers and Writing Programs/Sheraton Boston Hotel/March 6 - 9, 2013/9000 attendees
Automotive Aftermarket Industry Association/Westin Boston Waterfront/Sept. 3 - 5, 2014
Business Professionals of America/May 5 - 9, 2016
Business Professionals of America/May 6 - 9, 2016
Cable & Telecommunications Association for Marketing/Oct. 26 - 28, 2014
College Reading and Learning Association/Nov. 6 - 9, 2013
Conference on English Education/Nov. 21 - 24, 2013
Congress of Neurological Surgeons/Oct. 18 - 23, 2014
Council for Advancement and Support of Education/Hilton Boston Back Bay/Jan. 15 - 17, 2013
Council for Advancement and Support of Education/Hyatt Regency Cambridge, Overlooking Boston/April 30 - May 2, 2013
Drug Information Association/Boston Convention and Exhibition Center/June 23 - 27, 2013/over 100 exhibitors
Federation of State Medical Boards of the United States/Sheraton Boston Hotel/April 18 - 20, 2013
Financial & Insurance Conference Planners/Sheraton Boston Hotel/Nov. 17 - 20, 2013
Financial Management Association International/Boston Marriott Copley Place/Oct. 11 - 14, 2017
Financial Managers Society/Seaport Boston Hotel/June 16 - 18, 2013
Financial Planning Association/Sept. 26 - 29, 2015
Glass Art Society/June 13 - 15, 2013
Heart Rhythm Society/Boston Convention and Exhibition Center/May 13 - 16, 2015
Hispanic Dental Association/Boston Mariott Copley Place/Sept. 27 - 29, 2013
The Histochemical Society/Boston Convention and Exposition Center/April 20, 2013
History of Science Society/Nov. 21 - 24, 2013
Human Capital Institute/Boston Park Plaza/June 10 - 12, 2013
Infusion Nurses Society/Nov. 8 - 10, 2013/600 attendees
Institute of Mathematical Statistics/Boston Convention and Exhibition Center/Aug. 2 - 7, 2014
Institute of Transportation Engineers/Sheraton Boston and Hynes Convention Center/Aug. 4 - 7, 2013
Intellectual Property Owners Association/Sheraton Boston Hotel/Sept. 15 - 17, 2013/11-25 exhibitors
International Association for Dental Research/March 11 - 14, 2015
International City/County Management Association/Massachusetts State House/Sept. 22 - 25, 2013
International Federation of Fertility Societies/Boston Marriot/Oct. 12 - 17, 2013
International Foodservice Distributors Association/Boston Marriott Long Wharf/July 21 - 23, 2013
International Foundation of Employee Benefit Plans/Oct. 12 - 15, 2014
International Fruit Tree Association/Feb. 23 - 28, 2013
International Society of Certified Employee Benefit Specialists/Westin Copley Place Boston/Sept. 22 - 25, 2013
International Trademark Association/Boston Convention and Exhibition Center/May 18 - 22, 2019
Investment Management Consultants Association/John B. Hynes Veterans Memorial Convention Center/May 5 - 7, 2014
Journalism Education Association/Nov. 14 - 18, 2013
Journalism Education Association/Nov. 14 - 17, 2013
Korean American Spine Society/Hyatt Regency Boston/June 27 - 29, 2013
Law and Society Association/Sheraton Boston Hotel/May 30 - June 2, 2013
LeadingAge (American Association of Homes and Services for the Aging)/Nov. 1 - 4, 2015
Liability Insurance Research Bureau/March 17 - 20, 2013
Linguistic Society of America/Boston Marriott Copley Place/Jan. 3 - 6, 2013/1000 attendees
Marketing Science Institute/Taj Hotel/April 11 - 12, 2013
Materials Research Society/Hynes Convention Center/Dec. 1 - 6, 2013
Materials Research Society/Nov. 30 - Dec. 5, 2014
Medical Library Association/Sheraton Boston Hotel/May 3 - 8, 2013
Medieval Academy of America/March 31 - April 2, 2016
Middle East Studies Association of North America/Boston Marriott Copley Place/Nov. 17 - 20, 2016
Modern Language Association/Jan. 3 - 6, 2013/11-25 exhibitors
NAFSA: Association of International Educators/Four Seasons Hotels and Resorts/May 24 - 29, 2015
NALP - The Association for Legal Career Professionals/Hynes Convention Center/April 13 - 16, 2016
National Association of Academies of Science/Feb. 13 - 17, 2013
National Association of Bar Executives/Aug. 5 - 7, 2014
National Association of Electrical Distributors/Boston Marriott Copley Place/May 4 - 7, 2013
National Association of Elevator Contractors/Boston College/Sept. 28 - Oct. 1, 2015
National Association of Federal Credit Unions/Sheraton Boston Hotel/July 9 - 13, 2013
National Association of Pediatric Nurse Practitioners/John B. Hynes Veterans Memorial Convention Center/March 11 - 14, 2014/1500 attendees/11-25 exhibitors
Meetings Association of Realtors/Nov. 2 - 5, 2018

National Association of Spine Specialists/Oct. 26 - 29, 2016
National Association of Teachers of Singing/Boston Marriott Copley Place/July 5 - 9, 2014/11-25 exhibitors
National Association of the Remodeling Industry/Boston Marriott Copley Place/May 28 - June 1, 2013
National Auto Auction Association/Sheraton Boston Hotel/Sept. 23 - 26, 2014
National Business Incubation Association/Sheraton/April 7 - 10, 2013
National Career Development Association/Westin Boston Waterfront/July 8 - 10, 2013
National Conference of Bar Foundations/Aug. 7 - 9, 2014
National Conference of Insurance Legislators/Boston Park Plaza/July 10 - 13, 2014
National Council for the Social Studies/John P. Hynes Veterans Memorial Convention Center/Nov. 21 - 23, 2014
National Council of Real Estate Investment Fiduciaries/Fairmont Copley Plaza/July 9 - 11, 2013
National Council of State Housing Agencies/Sheraton Boston Hotel/Oct. 18 - 21, 2014
National Council of Supervisors of Mathematics/April 13 - 15, 2015
National Council of Teachers of English/Nov. 21 - 24, 2013/1-10 exhibitors
National Council of Teachers of Mathematics/April 15, 2015
National Council of Teachers of Mathematics/April 15 - 18, 2015
National Education Association/June 30 - July 5, 2017
National Federation Coaches Association/Boston Marriott Copley Place/June 28 - July 2, 2014
National Federation of State High School Associations/Boston Marriott Copley Place/June 28 - July 2, 2014
National Lesbian and Gay Journalists Association/The Boston Park Plaza Hotel and Towers/Aug. 22 - 25, 2013
National Scholastic Press Association/Sheraton Boston and Hynes Convention Center/Nov. 14 - 17, 2013
National Science Teachers Association/April 3 - 6, 2014
National Telecommunications Cooperative Association/Sheraton Boston Hotel/Sept. 19 - 23, 2015
North American Spine Society/Oct. 26 - 29, 2016
Population Association of America/Boston Marriott Copley Place/May 1 - 3, 2014
Property Loss Research Bureau/Boston Marriott Copley Place/March 17 - 20, 2013
The Protein Society/July 20 - 24, 2013
The Protein Society/July 25 - 29, 2015
The Psychonomic Society/Nov. 17 - 20, 2016
Radiology Business Management Association/Seaport Boston Hotel/Sept. 8 - 11, 2013
The Recreational Vehicle Aftermarket Association/Omni Parker House/Aug. 13 - 16, 2013
Regulatory Affairs Professionals Society/Sept. 28 - Oct. 2, 2013
Religious Education Association/Nov. 1 - 3, 2013
The Renaissance Society of America/March 31 - April 2, 2016/1500 attendees/over 100 exhibitors
School Nutrition Association/July 12 - 16, 2014
Society for Biomaterials/John B. Hynes Veterans Memorial Convention Center/April 10 - 13, 2013
Society for Clinical Trials/Sheraton Boston Hotel/May 19 - 22, 2013
Society for Epidemiologic Research/The Boston Park Plaza Hotel/June 18 - 21, 2013
Society for Free Radical Biology and Medicine/Westin Waterfront Hotel/Nov. 19 - 22, 2015
Society for Pediatric Dermatology/InterContinental Hotel/July 9 - 12, 2015
Society for Research on Nicotine and Tobacco/Westin Boston Waterfront Hotel/March 13 - 16, 2013
Society for the Scientific Study of Religion/Boston Waterfront Hotel/Nov. 8 - 10, 2013
Society for the Study of Indigenous Languages of the Americas/Boston Marriott Copley Place/Jan. 3 - 6, 2013
Society for Vascular Nursing/Sheraton Boston Hotel/May 8 - 11, 2013
Society for Vascular Surgery/Hynes Convention Center/June 5 - 7, 2014
Society of Biblical Literature/Nov. 18 - 21, 2017
Society of Biblical Literature/Nov. 21 - 24, 2020
Society of Corporate Secretaries and Governance Professionals/Sheraton Boston Hotel/June 25 - 28, 2014
Society of Neurological Surgeons/Brandeis University/June 7 - 11, 2013
Special Libraries Association/June 14 - 17, 2015
Special Libraries Association/June 14 - 16, 2015
Specialty Coffee Association of America/Renaissance Boston Waterfront Hotel/April 10 - 14, 2013
Specialty Coffee Association of America/April 10 - 11, 2013
Specialty Coffee Association of America/Boston Convention and Exhibition Center/April 11 - 14, 2013
System Safety Society/Boston Marriott Copley Place/Aug. 11 - 16, 2013
United States and Canadian Academy of Pathology/John B. Hynes Veterans Memorial Convention Center/March 21 - 27, 2015/4880 attendees/51-100 exhibitors
University Professional & Continuing Education Association/April 3 - 6, 2013
University Professional & Continuing Education Association/Copley Place Marriott/April 3 - 5, 2013
University Professional & Continuing Education Association/Boston Marriott Copley/April 4 - 6, 2013
USENIX: The Advanced Computing Systems Association/Dec. 4 - 9, 2016

Cambridge
Association for Technology in Music Instruction/Oct. 31 - Nov. 3, 2013
College Music Society/Hyatt Regency Cambridge/Oct. 31 - Nov. 3, 2013
International Map Trade Association/Hyatt Regency Cambridge/Sept. 8 - 10, 2013
National Association of Schools of Theatre/Royal Sonesta Hotel/March 21 - 23, 2013
The Risk Management Association/April 17 - 18, 2013
Society for French Historical Studies/Cambridge Marriott Hotel/April 4 - 6, 2013

Easton

American Catholic Historical Association/Stonehill College/April 5 - 6, 2013

Norton

Veterinary Botanical Medical Association/Wheaton College/June 28 - 30, 2013

Springfield

National Farmers Union (Farmers Educational & Co-operative Union of America)/Mass Mutual Center/March 2 - 5, 2013

West Springfield

Percheron Horse Association of America/Eastern States Exposition Fairgrounds/Oct. 6 - 11, 2014

Woods Hole

Society of General Physiologists/Marine Biological Laboratory/Sept. 4 - 8, 2013

Society of General Physiologists/Marine Biological Laboratory/Sept. 3 - 7, 2014

Worcester

Metaphysical Society of America/The College of the Holy Cross/April 11 - 13, 2013

MICHIGAN

Alpena

North American Society for Oceanic History/Holiday Inn Alpena/May 15 - 19, 2013

Ann Arbor

American Men's Studies Association/University of Michigan, Ann Arbor/April 4 - 7, 2013

Association for Documentary Editing/Sheraton Ann Arbor Hotel/July 11 - 13, 2013

Dearborn

Association of Official Seed Certifying Agencies/June 23 - 26, 2013

Society for the History of Technology/Nov. 6 - 9, 2014

Detroit

ADED - The Association for Driver Rehabilitation Specialists/Sept. 16 - 18, 2013

American Concrete Institute/Detroit Marriott at the Renaissance Center/March 26 - 30, 2017

American Society of Association Executives-The Center for Association Leadership/Aug. 8 - 11, 2015

Association for Accounting Administration/June 18 - 21, 2013

Association for Iron and Steel Technology/MGM Grand Detroit/March 26 - 28, 2013

National Conference on Weights and Measures/July 12 - 17, 2014

Society of Automotive Analysts/Cobo Hall/Jan. 13, 2013

Society of Tribologists and Lubrication Engineers/Marroitt Renaissance/May 5 - 9, 2013

Grand Rapids

American Jail Association/Amway Grand Plaza Hotel/May 5 - 9, 2013/1000 attendees

American Philatelic Society/Aug. 20 - 23, 2015

Governors' Highway Safety Association/Amway Grand Plaza Hotel/Sept. 7 - 10, 2014

Independent Insurance Agents & Brokers of America, Inc./Amway Grand Plaza Hotel/Sept. 10 - 14, 2014

International Association of Assessing Officers/Aug. 25 - 28, 2013

International Trumpet Guild/June 11 - 15, 2013

Marine Corps League/Amway Grand Plaza Hotel/Aug. 4 - 9, 2013

National Association of Sports Officials/July 28 - 30, 2013

National Organization of Black Law Enforcement Executives/DeVos Performance Hall/July 12 - 14, 2014

Society for the Study of Reproduction/July 19 - 23, 2014

Society of Forensic Toxicologists/Oct. 18 - 25, 2014

Traverse City

Society of Outdoor Recreation Professionals/Park Place Hotel/May 19 - 23, 2013

MINNESOTA

Bloomington

ADARA/Embassy Suites Bloomington/May 29 - June 1, 2013

American Filtration and Separations Society/May 6 - 9, 2013

Distillers Grains Technology Council/DoubleTree by Hilton Hotel Bloomington/May 15 - 16, 2013

National Association of Health Unit Coordinators/Hilton MSP Airport/Mall of America/Aug. 6 - 9, 2014

Brooklyn Park

World History Association/North Hennepin Community College/June 26 - 29, 2013

Duluth

Society for Wetland Scientists/Duluth Entertainment Convention Center/June 2 - 6, 2013

Minneapolis

Academy Health/June 14 - 16, 2015/2400 attendees/51-100 exhibitors

Adhesive and Sealant Council/Hilton Minneapolis/Oct. 21 - 23, 2013

Agricultural & Applied Economics Association/July 27 - 29, 2014

American Alliance for Health, Physical Education, Recreation and Dance/Minneapolis Convention Center/April 5 - 9, 2016/5000 attendees/1-10 exhibitors

American Association of Thoracic Surgery/Minneapolis Convention Center/May 4 - 8, 2013

American Association of Cereal Chemists International/Oct. 18 - 21, 2015/1000 attendees/11-25 exhibitors

American Association of Collegiate Registrars and Admissions Officers/Minneapolis Convention Center/April 2 - 5, 2017

American Association of Physics Teachers/July 26 - 30, 2014

American College of Veterinary Pathologists/Hyatt Regency Minneapolis/Oct. 17 - 21, 2015

American Concrete Institute/Hilton Minneapolis/April 14 - 17, 2013

American Conference of Cantors/Marriott City Center Hotel/June 30 - July 4, 2013

American Correctional Association/Aug. 3 - 8, 2018

American Diabetes Association/Minneapolis Convention Center/Oct. 12, 2013

American Dialect Society/Hilton Minneapolis/Jan. 2 - 5, 2014

American Phytopathological Society/Aug. 9 - 13, 2014

American Railway Engineering and Maintenance-of-Way Association/Minneapolis Convention Center/Oct. 4 - 7, 2015

American Railway Engineering and Maintenance-of-Way Association/Minneapolis Convention Center/Sept. 22 - 25, 2019

American Society for Mass Spectrometry/June 9 - 13, 2013

American Society of Agronomy (ASA, CSSA, SSSA)/Nov. 15 - 18, 2015

American Society of Echocardiography/Minneapolis Convention Center/June 29 - July 2, 2013

American Telemedicine Association/May 15 - 18, 2016

American Telemedicine Association/May 15 - 17, 2016

Associated Collegiate Press/Radisson Plaza Hotel Minneapolis/Feb. 8 - 10, 2013

Association for Behavior Analysis International/Minneapolis Convention Center/May 24 - 28, 2013

Association for Conflict Resolution/Oct. 9 - 12, 2013

Association for Death Education and Counseling/Hilton Minneapolis/April 13 - 16, 2016

Association for Medical Imaging Management/Minneapolis Convention Center/July 28 - 31, 2013

Association for Middle Level Education/Nov. 7 - 9, 2013

Association of American Medical Colleges/Hennepin/Aug. 9 - 11, 2013

Association of College and University Housing Officers-International/June 15 - 18, 2013

Association of College and University Printers/Radisson Plaza Hotel Minneapolis/May 19 - 23, 2013/100 attendees

Association of Military Surgeons of the United States/Nov. 1 - 5, 2015

Association of Pediatric Oncology Social Workers/Hilton Minneapolis/May 15 - 17, 2013

Association of SIDS and Infant Mortality Programs/Depot Renaissance Minneapolis Hotel/April 18 - 21, 2013

Association of Writers and Writing Programs/Hilton Minneapolis/April 8 - 11, 2015/9000 attendees

Biomedical Engineering Society/Oct. 5 - 8, 2016/3000 attendees/51-100 exhibitors

Casualty Actuarial Society/Hilton Minneapolis/Nov. 2 - 6, 2013

Conference on English Education/Nov. 19 - 22, 2015

Council for Advancement and Support of Education/Hotel Wyndham Grand/June 19 - 21, 2013

Credit Research Foundation/Minneapolis Marriott City Center/Aug. 12 - 14, 2013

Crop Science Society of America/Nov. 15 - 18, 2015

Ecological Society of America/Minneapolis Convention Center/Aug. 4 - 9, 2013

Educational Theatre Association/Depot Renaissance Minneapolis Hotel/Sept. 26 - 30, 2013

Entomological Society of America/Nov. 14 - 18, 2015

Government Finance Officers Association of the United States and Canada/May 18 - 21, 2014/over 100 exhibitors

Government Finance Officers Association, Federal Liaison Center/May 18 - 21, 2014

Hospitality Financial and Technology Professionals/Minneapolis Convention Center/June 24 - 27, 2013

Institute for Operations Research and the Management Sciences/Hilton Minneapolis/Oct. 6 - 9, 2013

International Association for Identification/Aug. 10 - 16, 2014

Law and Society Association/Hilton Minneapolis/May 29 - June 1, 2014

Legal Netlink Alliance/Sept. 26 - 28, 2013

Linguistic Society of America/Hilton Minneapolis/Jan. 2 - 5, 2014/1000 attendees

NAFA Fleet Management Association/Minneapolis Convention Center/April 8 - 11, 2014

National Academic Advising Association/Minneapolis Convention Center/Oct. 8 - 11, 2014

NAMTA - National Art Materials Trade Association/Minneapolis Convention Center/May 1 - 3, 2013/over 100 exhibitors

National Association for Health Care Recruitment/Hyatt Regency Minneapolis/July 16 - 19, 2013/250 attendees/26-50 exhibitors

National Association of College and University Food Services/July 10 - 13, 2013

National Association of Diaconate Directors/Archdiocese of St. Paul/April 13 - 17, 2015

National Association of Residential Property Managers/Hyatt Regency/Oct. 22 - 24, 2014

National Association of Schools of Art and Design/Hyatt Regency Minneapolis/Oct. 16 - 18, 2014

National Association of Workforce Development Professionals/May 19 - 22, 2013

National Conference of State Legislatures/July 20 - 24, 2014/over 100 exhibitors

National Council of Teachers of English/Nov. 19 - 22, 2015/1-10 exhibitors

National Education Association/June 30 - July 5, 2018

National Sheriffs' Association/June 25 - 29, 2016

National Society of Professional Engineers/July 17 - 21, 2013

National Telecommunications Cooperative Association/Hyatt Regency Minneapolis/April 16 - 18, 2013

Neurosurgical Society of America/Sept. 20 - 22, 2013

Nonprofit Technology Network/April 11 - 13, 2013/11-25 exhibitors

North American Academy of Liturgy/Jan. 2 - 5, 2014

Religious Conference Management Association/Jan. 29 - Feb. 1, 2013

Scoliosis Research Society/Sept. 30 - Oct. 4, 2015

Snow & Ice Management Association/Hyatt Regency Minneapolis/June 19 - 22, 2013

Society for Industrial Archeology/The Twin Cities/May 30 - June 2, 2013

Society of North American Goldsmiths/Hilton Minneapolis/April 23 - 26, 2014

Soil Science Society of America/Nov. 15 - 18, 2015/3200 attendees/over 100 exhibitors

Veterinary Cancer Society/Hilton Minneapolis/Oct. 17 - 20, 2013

Women in Agribusiness/Oct. 23 - 24, 2013
Rochester
Society of Neurological Surgeons/Mayo Civic Center/May 18 - 20, 2014
St. Paul
American Craft Council/St. Paul RiverCentre/April 18 - 21, 2013
American Society for Precision Engineering/Crowne Plaza St. Paul Riverfront/
Oct. 20 - 25, 2013
National Christian College Athletic Association/Northwestern College/May 30
- June 1, 2013

MISSISSIPPI

Biloxi
Airports Council International - North America/Beau Rivage Resort and
Casino/April 14 - 16, 2013
Billiard and Bowling Institute of America/Beau Rivage Resort and Casino/April
21 - 23, 2013
Children's Literature Association/IP Casino Resort and Spa/June 13 - 15, 2013
Jackson
National Association of Student Affairs Professionals/Jackson State University/
Jan. 31 - Feb. 2, 2013
Tunica
International Society of Certified Electronics Technicians/Harrah's Veranda
Hotel/July 29 - Aug. 2, 2013
National Electronic Service Dealers Association/Harrah's Veranda Hotel/July
29 - Aug. 2, 2013

MISSOURI

Branson
National Chimney Sweep Guild/Chateau on the Lake Resort Spa and
Convention Center/April 4 - 7, 2013
Columbia
Association for Healthcare Documentation Integrity/Boone Hospital Center/
April 12 - 13, 2013
International Society of Weekly Newspaper Editors/June 24 - 28, 2015
Kansas City
Academy of Criminal Justice Sciences/Kansas City Marriott Downtown/March
28 - April 1, 2017
American Biological Safety Association/Hyatt Regency Crown Center/Oct. 17 -
23, 2013
American Booksellers Association/Feb. 23 - 25, 2013
American Concrete Institute/Kansas City Marriott Downtown/April 12 - 15,
2015
American Dairy Science Association/July 20 - 24, 2014
American Guild of Organists/July 1 - 5, 2018
American Society of Agricultural and Biological Engineers/Kansas City
Convention Center/Jan. 28 - 30, 2013
American Society of Agricultural and Biological Engineers/July 21 - 24, 2013
American Society of Animal Science/July 20 - 24, 2014
American Traffic Safety Service Association/Kansas City Hotel-
InterContinental/Aug. 20 - 22, 2014
Association for Recorded Sound Collections/May 15 - 18, 2013
Association of Family Medicine Residency Directors/Sheraton Kansas City
Hotel at Crown Center/April 5 - 9, 2013
Association of Zoos and Aquariums/Sept. 7 - 12, 2013
Association of Zoos and Aquariums/Sept. 7 - 12, 2013
Biscuit and Cracker Manufacturers' Association/InterContinental Kansas City
At The Plaza/May 5 - 8, 2013
Campus Computer Resellers Alliance/CAMEX/Feb. 22 - 26, 2013
Flexographic Technical Association/Oct. 14 - 16, 2013
The Folk Alliance International/Westin Kansas City at Crown Center/Feb. 19 -
23, 2014
The Folk Alliance International/Westin Kansas City at Crown Center/Feb. 18 -
22, 2015
The Folk Alliance International/Westin Kansas City at Crown Center/Feb. 17 -
21, 2016
The Folk Alliance International/Westin Kansas City at Crown Center/Feb. 15 -
19, 2017
The Folk Alliance International/Westin Kansas City at Crown Center/Feb. 14 -
18, 2018
International City/County Management Association/InterContinental Kansas
City At The Plaza/Sept. 25 - 28, 2016
International Council of Fine Arts Deans/Oct. 22 - 25, 2014
Messenger Courier Association of the Americas/The Westin Crown Center/Oct.
10 - 12, 2013
National Agri-Marketing Association/Sheraton Crown Center/April 17 - 19,
2013
National Association of Foster Grandparent Program Directors/THE EMBASSY
SUITES HOTEL/April 7 - 10, 2013
National Association of Intercollegiate Athletics/Sheraton Kansas City Hotel at
Crown Center/April 19 - 23, 2013
National Association of State Controlled Substances Authorities/Oct. 22 - 25,
2013
National Auctioneers Association/Embassy Suites Kansas City/March 4 - 5,
2013
National Coal Transportation Association/InterContinental at the Plaza/June 11
- 13, 2013
National Farmers Organization/KC Convention Center & Aladdin Holiday Inn
Hotel/Jan. 28 - 31, 2013
National Hospice & Palliative Care Organization/Sheraton Kansas City Hotel at
Crown Center/Sept. 26 - 28, 2013
National Institute of Governmental Purchasing/Kansas City Convention
Center/July 31 - Aug. 5, 2015
North American Gamebird Association/InterContinental Hotel/Feb. 4 - 6, 2013
School Nutrition Association/July 13 - 17, 2013
School Nutrition Association/Kansas City Convention Center/July 14 - 17,
2013
Society for Military History/Sheraton Kansas City Hotel at Crown Center/April
3 - 7, 2014

Sports and Entertainment Alliance in Technology/Aug. 4 - 7, 2013
United States Animal Health Association/Sheraton Kansas City at Crown
Center/Oct. 16 - 22, 2014
United States Custom Harvesters, Inc./Kansas City Convention Center/Jan. 29
- 31, 2013
Springfield
American Dexter Cattle Association/Ozark Empire Fairgrounds/June 13 - 16,
2013
St. Charles
Alliance for Massage Therapy Education/St. Charles Convention Center/July
18 - 20, 2013
St. Louis
American Alliance for Health, Physical Education, Recreation and Dance/
America's Center Convention Complex/March 18 - 22, 2014/5000
attendees/1-10 exhibitors
American Association of Colleges of Nursing/Sheraton Westport Chalet Hotel
St. Louis/April 11 - 13, 2013
American Association of Medical Society Executives/July 17 - 20, 2013
American Chemical Society/Sept. 10 - 14, 2017
American Correctional Association/Aug. 18 - 23, 2017
American Council of Life Insurers (ACLI)/Oct. 27 - 29, 2013
American Feed Industry Association/Hyatt Regency St. Louis at The Arch/Sept.
10 - 12, 2013
American Foundry Society/The Doubletree Hotel and Conference Center/April
6 - 9, 2013/8000 attendees/over 100 exhibitors
American Holistic Medical Association/April 18 - 21, 2013
American Society for Mass Spectrometry/May 31 - June 4, 2015
American Society of Pharmacognosy/July 12 - 18, 2013
Associated Wire Rope Fabricators/Hyatt Regency St. Louis at The Arch/Oct. 26
- 29, 2014
Association for Middle Level Education/Nov. 5 - 7, 2015
Association for Technology in Music Instruction/Oct. 29 - Nov. 2, 2014
Association for the Study of Higher Education/Hyatt at the Arch/Nov. 13 - 16,
2013
Association of College Unions International/St. Louis Renaissance Grand Hotel
& Convention Center/March 10 - 14, 2013
Association of Information Technology Professionals/The Millennium Hotel/
April 4 - 7, 2013
Association of Teacher Educators/Hyatt Regency/Feb. 14 - 18, 2014
CBA/The Doubletree Hotel and Conference Center/June 23 - 26, 2013
College Music Society/Oct. 29 - Nov. 2, 2014
Conductors Guild/St. Louis Union Station Marriott/June 15 - 18, 2013
Council for Exceptional Children/April 13 - 16, 2016
Council on Licensure, Enforcement and Regulation/Hyatt Regency/Oct. 3 - 5,
2013
Electrostatic Discharge Association/Hilton St. Louis Frontenac/June 11 - 16,
2013
Government Finance Officers Association of the United States and Canada/
May 6 - 9, 2018/over 100 exhibitors
Government Finance Officers Association, Federal Liaison Center/May 6 - June
9, 2018
Grain Elevator and Processing Society/America's Center Convention Complex/
March 7 - 10, 2015
International Balloon Association/St. Louis Airport Marriott Hotel/Jan. 27 - 30,
2013
International Council on Hotel, Restaurant and Institutional Education/July 24
- 27, 2013
Labor and Employment Relations Association/Crowne Plaza Hotel/June 6 - 9,
2013
League of American Orchestras/June 17 - 20, 2013
Military Impacted Schools Association/June 23 - 25, 2013
Music Industry Conference/Hilton St. Louis Frontenac/April 10 - 12, 2014
National Academy of Arbitrators/Hilton St. Louis Frontenac/Oct. 18 - 20, 2013
The National Association for Music Education (Formerly MENC)/St. Louis
Union Station Marriott/April 10 - 12, 2014
National Association of Boards of Pharmacy/Hyatt Regency St. Louis at The
Arch/May 18 - 21, 2013
National Association of Judiciary Interpreters and Translators/Clayton
Sheraton/May 17 - 19, 2013
National Association of Schools of Art and Design/Hyatt Regency St. Louis at
The Arch/Oct. 10 - 12, 2013
National Association of Schools of Music/Hyatt Regency at the Arch Hotel/
Nov. 20 - 24, 2015
National Athletic Trainers Association/June 23 - 26, 2015
National Council for the Social Studies/Cervantes Convention Center at
America's Center/Nov. 22 - 24, 2013
National Ice Cream Retailers Association/Hilton St. Louis Frontenac/Nov. 5 - 7,
2013
National Recreation and Parks Association/Oct. 4 - 6, 2016/7000 attendees/
over 100 exhibitors
North - American Interfraternity Conference/Ritz Carlton/April 14 - 15, 2013
Organization of American Historians/April 16 - 19, 2015
Painting and Decorating Contractors of America/Hyatt Regency/March 3 - 6,
2013
Resource Center for Religious Institutes/Nov. 3 - 7, 2014
School Nutrition Association/July 14 - 17, 2019
Society for Economic Anthropology/Campus of Washington University/April 11
- 13, 2013
Society for Healthcare Consumer Advocacy/April 3 - 5, 2013
Society for Historians of the Early American Republic/July 18 - 21, 2013
Society for Medical Decision Making/Hyatt Regency St Louis at the Arch/Oct.
17 - 21, 2013
Society of Allied Weight Engineers/Marriot St. Louis Union Station/May 18 -
20, 2013
Society of Cosmetic Chemists/St. Louis Union Station Marriott/June 6 - 7, 2013
Society of Nuclear Medicine/June 7 - 11, 2014
Structural Stability Research Council/April 16 - 20, 2013
System Safety Society/St. Louis Union Station Marriott/Aug. 1 - 10, 2014
Undersea and Hyperbaric Medical Society/Hyatt Regency St. Louis at The
Arch/June 18 - 21, 2014

United States Junior Chamber (Jaycees)/Jan. 10 - 13, 2013
United States Lactation Consultant Association/St. Louis Science Center/May 3 - 5, 2013
Urban Financial Services Coalition/June 13 - 15, 2013
Veterinary Cancer Society/Hyatt Regency St. Louis at The Arch/Oct. 9 - 12, 2014

MONTANA
Choteau
United Suffolk Sheep Association/Weatherbeater Barn/Sept. 7, 2013

NEBRASKA
Grand Island
American Chianina Association/Holiday Inn Midtown - Grand Island/June 15 - 21, 2013
Lincoln
American Meat Science Association/University of Nebraska, Lincoln/June 14, 2015
Association for Computers and the Humanities/University of Nebraska, Lincoln/July 16 - 19, 2013
National Grange/The Cornhusker/Nov. 3 - 5, 2015
Omaha
American Association of Bovine Practitioners/Sept. 14 - 16, 2017
American Society of Parasitologists/Hilton Omaha/June 25 - 28, 2015
College Theology Society/Creighton University/May 30 - June 2, 2013
Grain Elevator and Processing Society/Quest Center/Feb. 22 - 25, 2014
International Association of Operative Millers/Hilton Omaha/May 19 - 23, 2014/800 attendees
International Institute of Municipal Clerks/May 22 - 25, 2016
Kappa Kappa Iota-National/DoubleTree by Hilton Hotel Omaha Downtown/June 25 - 30, 2013
National Association of Document Examiners/April 25 - 27, 2013
United States Wheat Associates, Inc./DoubleTree Omaha/June 8 - 11, 2014
Wildlife Management Institute/Hilton Omaha/March 8 - 13, 2015

NEVADA
Henderson
International Association of Eating Disorders Professionals/Westin Lake Las Vegas Resort and Spa/March 21 - 24, 2013
International Conference of Funeral Service Examining Boards/Westin Lake Las Vegas Resort and Spa/Feb. 27 - 28, 2013
National Association of Therapeutic Schools and Programs (NATSAP)/Green Valley Ranch/Feb. 6 - 8, 2014
Lake Tahoe
American Glovebox Society/Harrah's Lake Tahoe/July 29 - 31, 2013
American Medical Group Association/Caesar's Palace Hotel and Casino/March 23 - 26, 2015
Las Vegas
AACE International/MGM Grand Hotel and Casino/June 28 - July 1, 2015
Academy of Doctors of Audiology/Red Rock Casino Resort and Spa/Nov. 6 - 8, 2014
ACPA College Student Educators International/March 4 - 8, 2013
ACPA College Student Educators International/Paris Hotel/March 4 - 7, 2013
Air and Expedited Motor Carriers Association/Red Rock Casino/March 10 - 12, 2013/over 100 exhibitors
Aircraft Electronics Association/March 25 - 28, 2013
Airforwarders Association/March 10 - 12, 2013
Airports Council International - North America/Harrah's Las Vegas Casino Hotel/Jan. 9 - 11, 2013
Airports Council International - North America/March 10 - 11, 2013
ALMA - The International Loudspeaker Association/Tuscany Suites and Casino/Jan. 6 - 7, 2013
America's Health Insurance Plans/June 12 - 14, 2013
American Academy of Ambulatory Care Nursing/LVH-Las Vegas Hotel and Casino/April 23 - 25, 2013
American Academy of Cosmetic Surgery/Caesars Palace/Jan. 16 - 19, 2013/700 attendees
American Academy of Dental Practice Administration/The Cosmopolitan Hotel/March 6 - 10, 2013
American Academy of Emergency Medicine/The Cosmopolitan of Las Vegas/Feb. 9 - 13, 2013
American Academy of Emergency Medicine/Sugar Loaf Ct/Feb. 11 - 13, 2013
American Academy of Forensic Sciences/Rio All-Suite Hotel and Casino/Feb. 15 - 20, 2016/over 100 exhibitors
American Academy of Implant Dentistry/Caesars Palace/Oct. 21 - 24, 2015/over 100 exhibitors
American Academy of Medical Administrators/Bally's Las Vegas Hotel and Casino/April 10 - 12, 2013
American Academy of Nurse Practitioners/Venetian and Palazzo Resort, Hotel and Casinos/June 19 - 23, 2013
American Academy of Ophthalmic Executives/Sands Expo and Venetian Hotel/Nov. 14 - 17, 2015
American Academy of Orthopaedic Surgeons/March 24 - 28, 2015
American Academy of Podiatric Sports Medicine/July 21 - 25, 2013
American Association for Respiratory Care/Dec. 9 - 12, 2014/5000 attendees/over 100 exhibitors
American Association of Attorney-Certified Public Accountants/Mandalay Bay Resort and Casino/Nov. 6 - 10, 2013
American Association of Bioanalysts/Golden Nugget Hotel and Casino/May 16 - 18, 2013
American Association of Clinical Endocrinologists/May 14 - 18, 2014
American Association of Colleges for Teacher Education/The Mirage/Feb. 23 - 25, 2016
American Association of Equine Practitioners/Dec. 5 - 9, 2015
American Association of Managing General Agents/Nov. 5 - 7, 2014
American Association of Nurse Anesthetists/The Mirage/Aug. 10 - 13, 2013
American Association of Occupational Health Nurses/Cosmopolitan of Las Vegas/April 15 - 18, 2013/1000 attendees

American Association of Retired Persons/Las Vegas Convention Center/May 31 - June 1, 2013
American Bakers Association/Las Vegas Convention Center/Oct. 6 - 9, 2013
American Broncho-Esophagological Association/Caesars Palace Las Vegas Hotel and Casino/May 14 - 18, 2014
American Burn Association/May 3 - 6, 2016
American Burn Association/April 9 - 12, 2019
American College of Cardiovascular Administrators/Bally's Las Vegas/April 10 - 12, 2013
American College of Chiropractic Orthopedists/Tropicana Casino/April 25 - 27, 2013
American College of Foot and Ankle Surgeons/Mandalay Bay Hotel/Feb. 11 - 14, 2013
American College of Health Plan Management/Bally's Las Vegas/April 10 - 12, 2013
American College of Legal Medicine/Planet Hollywood Resort and Casino/Feb. 21 - 24, 2013
American College of Nurse Practitioners/Oct. 2 - 6, 2013
American College of Osteopathic Family Physicians/The Cosmopolitan Hotel/March 21 - 24, 2013
American College of Osteopathic Family Physicians/Mandalay Bay Hotel/Sept. 30 - Oct. 4, 2013
American College of Osteopathic Surgeons/Caesars Palace/Nov. 14 - 17, 2013
American College of Prosthodontists/Caesars Palace Las Vegas Hotel and Casino/Oct. 9 - 12, 2013
American College of Sports Medicine/March 12 - 15, 2013
American College Personnel Association/Planet Hollywood/March 4 - 7, 2013
American Composites Manufacturers Association/Feb. 2 - 5, 2015
American Concrete Pavement Association/Las Vegas Convention Center/Feb. 5 - 8, 2013
American Concrete Pavement Association/Las Vegas Convention Center/Jan. 21 - 24, 2014
American Concrete Pumping Association/World of Concrete/Feb. 5, 2013
American Conference of Governmental Industrial Hygienists/Las Vegas Convention Center/June 24 - 26, 2013
American Escrow Association/Tuscany Suites Hotel and Casino/June 13 - 15, 2013
American Feed Industry Association/Caesars Palace Las Vegas Hotel and Casino/March 12 - 14, 2014
American Fire Sprinkler Association/Caesars Palace Las Vegas Hotel and Casino/Sept. 18 - 22, 2013
American Gaming Association/SandsExpo and Convention Center/Sept. 24 - 26, 2013
American Gas Association/Red Rock/Sept. 18 - 19, 2014
American Immigration Lawyers Association/June 22 - 25, 2016
American Institute of Floral Designers/Paris Las Vegas Hotel and Casino/June 28 - July 2, 2013
American Institute of Ultrasound in Medicine/March 29 - April 2, 2014
American Institute of Ultrasound in Medicine/March 19 - 23, 2016
American Institute of Ultrasound in Medicine/March 20 - 24, 2016
American Institute of Ultrasound in Medicine/March 17 - 21, 2018
American Library Association/June 26 - July 1, 2014
American Nephrology Nurses Association/Rio All-Suite Hotel and Casino/April 21 - 24, 2013
American Osteopathic Association/Sept. 30 - Oct. 4, 2013
American Petroleum Institute/April 22 - 26, 2013
American Podiatric Medical Association/Venetian Resort Hotel Casino/July 21 - 24, 2013
American Professional Society on the Abuse of Children/Caesar's Palace Hotel/June 25 - 28, 2013
American Rental Association/Sands Expo and Convention Center/Feb. 10 - 13, 2013/11-25 exhibitors
American Securitization Forum/ARIA Hotel and Convention Center/Jan. 27 - 30, 2013
American Shoulder and Elbow Surgeons/Bellagio Hotel/Oct. 12, 2013
American Shoulder and Elbow Surgeons/Bellagio Hotel/Oct. 13 - 15, 2013
American Society for Aesthetic Plastic Surgery/Mandalay Bay Resort & Casino/April 2 - 7, 2016
American Society for Nondestructive Testing/Rio All-Suite Hotel and Casino/Nov. 4 - 8, 2013/over 100 exhibitors
American Society for Training and Development/Jan. 15 - 17, 2014
American Society for Training and Development/Jan. 14 - 16, 2015
American Society of Extra-Corporeal Technology/Red Rock Casino Resort and Spa/March 6 - 9, 2013
American Society of Home Inspectors/Bally's Las Vegas/Jan. 13 - 16, 2013
American Society of Neuroimaging/Caesars Palace Las Vegas Hotel and Casino/Jan. 17 - 20, 2013
American Society of Pension Professionals & Actuaries/Caesars Palace Las Vegas Hotel and Casino/March 3 - 5, 2013
American Society of PeriAnesthesia Nurses/April 27 - May 1, 2014
American Society of Podiatric Medicine/July 21 - 25, 2013
American Society of Safety Engineers/June 10 - 13, 2013
American Society of Safety Engineers/Las Vegas Convention Center/June 24 - 27, 2013
American Society of Trial Consultants/The M Resort Spa Casino/May 29 - June 1, 2013
American Subcontractors Association/Planet Hollywood Resort and Casino/March 21 - 23, 2013
American Supply Association/Bellagio Hotel and Casino/Sept. 9 - 12, 2014
American Urogynecologic Society/Convention Center/Oct. 16 - 19, 2013/900 attendees/51-100 exhibitors
American Wholesale Marketers Association/Paris Las Vegas/Feb. 25 - 27, 2014
American Wholesale Marketers Association/Paris Las Vegas/Feb. 24 - 26, 2015
American Wholesale Marketers Association/Paris Las Vegas/Feb. 16 - 18, 2016
Amusement & Music Operators Association/Las Vegas Convention Center/March 20 - 22, 2013
Antique and Amusement Photographers International/Gold Coast Hotel and Casino/Feb. 5 - 7, 2013
Associated Builders and Contractors/Red Rock Casino Resort and Spa/Nov. 5 - 7, 2013

Associated Equipment Distributors/LVH-Las Vegas Hotel and Casino/Jan. 15 - 17, 2013/26-50 exhibitors

Association for Accounting Marketing/Bellagio Las Vegas/June 9 - 12, 2013

Association for Corporate Growth/ARIA Resort and Casino Hotel/April 28 - 30, 2014

Association for the Advancement of Computing in Education/Oct. 21 - 25, 2013

Association of Alternate Postal Systems/Mandalay Bay Resort and Casino/ April 27 - 30, 2013

Association of Career and Technical Education/Dec. 5 - 7, 2013

Association of Certified Fraud Examiners/ARIA Resort and Casino Hotel/June 23 - 28, 2013

Association of Equipment Management Professionals/March 2 - 4, 2014

Association of Food Industries/April 18 - 21, 2013

Association of Genetic Technologists/The Cosmopolitan of Las Vegas/June 6 - 8, 2013

Association of Independent Corrugated Converters/Encore/Sept. 23 - 25, 2013

Association of State and Provincial Psychology Boards/Paris Las Vegas Hotel and Casino/Oct. 16 - 20, 2013

Association of Teachers of Technical Writing/March 13, 2013

Association of the Wall and Ceiling Industry/March 23 - 27, 2014/over 100 exhibitors

Association of Woodworking and Furnishings Suppliers/Las Vegas Convention Center/July 24 - 27, 2013

Automotive Aftermarket Industry Association/Sands Expo and Convention Center/Nov. 5 - 7, 2013

Automotive Aftermarket Industry Association/The Venetian/Nov. 2 - 4, 2014

Automotive Aftermarket Industry Association/Sands Expo Center/Nov. 4 - 6, 2014

Aviation Suppliers Association/Four Seasons Hotel Las Vegas/July 9 - 11, 2013/11-25 exhibitors

Awards and Recognition Association/Rio All-Suite Hotel and Casino/Jan. 29 - Feb. 1, 2013

BICSI/MGM Grand Hotel and Conference Center/Sept. 15 - 19, 2013

BICSI/Mandalay Bay Hotel and Casino/Sept. 20 - 24, 2015

Broadcast Education Association/Las Vegas Hotel and Casino/April 7 - 10, 2013

Building Stone Institute/Mandalay Bay Convention Center/Jan. 27, 2013

Ceilings and Interior Systems Construction Association/Mandalay Bay Resort and Casino/March 24 - 27, 2014/over 100 exhibitors

Ceilings and Interior Systems Construction Association/March 26 - 27, 2014

Ceilings and Interior Systems Construction Association/Mandalay Bay Resort and Casino/March 20 - 23, 2013

Ceilings and Interior Systems Construction Association/March 22 - 23, 2017

College and University Professional Association for Human Resources/Caesars Palace Las Vegas Hotel and Casino/Oct. 27 - 29, 2013

Color Marketing Group/Mandalay Bay Convention Center/Dec. 31, 2013/1-10 exhibitors

Community College Business Officers/Treasure Island Resort and Casino/Sept. 19 - 22, 2015

Competitive Carriers Association/Sept. 10 - 13, 2013

Competitive Telecommunications Association/Aladdin Las Vegas/March 10 - 13, 2013

Competitive Telecommunications Association/Aria/March 23 - 26, 2014

Concrete Foundations Association/Las Vegas Convention Center/Feb. 4 - 8, 2013

Conference on College Composition and Communication/Hoover Dam Bypass/ March 13 - 16, 2013

Construction Financial Management Association/Caesars Palace/Oct. 23 - 25, 2013

Construction Financial Management Association/Caesars Palace/June 7 - 11, 2014

Construction Financial Management Association/The Cosmopolitan Hotel/June 1 - 5, 2019

Construction Management Association of America/ARIA Resort and Casino at CityCenter/Oct. 6 - 8, 2013/1000 attendees

CoreNet Global/MGM Grand Hotel and Casino/Oct. 20 - 22, 2013

Corporate Facility Advisors, Inc./April 3 - 6, 2013

Corrections, U.S.A./Harrah's Las Vegas Casino Hotel/Feb. 4 - 6, 2013

Cottage Industry Miniaturists Trade Association/Orleans Hotel and Casino/Jan. 28 - 30, 2013

Council of Communication Management/Four Seasons Hotel Las Vegas/April 23 - 26, 2013

Council of Residential Specialists/Caesars Palace/Jan. 30 - Feb. 2, 2013

Council on Chiropractic Orthopedics/Tropicana Hotel and Casino/April 25 - 27, 2013

CPA Associates International/Oct. 27 - 30, 2013

Cremation Association of North America/Signature at MGM Grand/Feb. 6 - 7, 2013

DBA International/ARIA Resort and Casino Hotel/Feb. 5 - 7, 2013

DBA International/ARIA Resort and Casino Hotel/Feb. 5 - 7, 2013/1600 attendees/over 100 exhibitors

DBA International/ARIA Resort and Casino Hotel/Feb. 4 - 6, 2014/1600 attendees/over 100 exhibitors

DBA International/ARIA Resort and Casino Hotel/Feb. 3 - 5, 2015/1600 attendees/over 100 exhibitors

DBA International/ARIA Resort and Casino Hotel/Feb. 9 - 11, 2016/1600 attendees/over 100 exhibitors

Destination Marketing Association International/July 21 - 23, 2014

Digital Imaging Marketing Association/Bally's Las Vegas/Jan. 6 - 7, 2013

Distribution Contractors Association/Bellagio Las Vegas/April 2 - 4, 2013

Diving Equipment and Marketing Association/Las Vegas Convention Center/ Nov. 19 - 22, 2014

Edison Electric Institute/ARIA Resort and Casino Hotel/June 8 - 11, 2014

Education Credit Union Council/Paris Las Vegas/Feb. 16 - 19, 2013

Electric Drive Transportation Association/Las Vegas convention/Jan. 8 - 13, 2013

Electrical Apparatus Service Association/Mandalay Bay Resort and convention/June 30 - July 2, 2013

Electronic Components Industry Association/The Cosmopolitan Hotel/May 6 - 9, 2013

Electronic Distribution Show Corporation/The Cosmopolitan Hotel/May 6 - 9, 2013

Electronic Retailing Association/Wynn Las Vegas/Sept. 24 - 26, 2013

Electronic Traders Association/Mandalay Bay/April 8 - 10, 2014

Electronic Transactions Association/Mandalay Bay/April 8 - 10, 2014

Electrostatic Discharge Association/Rio All-Suite Hotel and Casino/Feb. 5 - 10, 2013

Electrostatic Discharge Association/Rio All-Suite Hotel and Casino/Sept. 4 - 13, 2013

Express Delivery & Logistics Association/Red Rock Casion/March 10 - 13, 2013

Financial Executives International/Caesars Palace/May 4 - 5, 2013

Financial Management Association International/Rio All-Suite Casino Resort/ Oct. 19 - 22, 2016

GAMA International/Rio Las Vegas Hotel and Casino/March 20 - 23, 2016

Game Manufacturers Association/Bally's Las Vegas/March 18 - 22, 2013

Game Manufacturers Association/April 8 - 11, 2013/830 attendees

Geothermal Resources Council/Sept. 29 - Oct. 2, 2013

Health Care Administrators Association/Caesars Palace/Feb. 5 - 7, 2013

Healthcare Compliance Packaging Council/Texas Station/May 1 - 2, 2014

Heart Failure Society of America/Caesars Palace/Sept. 14 - 17, 2014

Helicopter Association International/Las Vegas convention/March 4 - 7, 2013/ over 100 exhibitors

Help Desk Institute/Mandalay Bay Las Vegas/April 16 - 19, 2013/11-25 exhibitors

Human Anatomy and Physiology Society/Mirage Hotel and Casino/May 25 - 30, 2013

IEEE Communications Society/Jan. 11 - 14, 2013

IEEE Consumer Electronics Society/Las Vegas Convention Center/Jan. 11 - 14, 2013

Institute for Supply Management/May 5 - 7, 2014

Institute of Food Technologists/June 21 - 24, 2014

Institute of Nuclear Materials Management/JW Marriott Las Vegas Resort and Spa/July 12 - 16, 2015/11-25 exhibitors

Institute of Scrap Recycling Industries, Inc./Mandalay Bay Resort and Casino/ April 6 - 10, 2014

Institute of Scrap Recycling Industries, Inc./Mandalay Bay Resort and Casino/ April 3 - 7, 2016

Insurance Accounting and Systems Association/Mandalay Bay Resort and Casino/June 7 - 10, 2015

International Academy of Oral Medicine and Toxicology/JW Marriott Resort and Spa/Sept. 5 - 7, 2014

International Association of Broadcast Monitors/Las Vegas Convention Center/ April 6 - 11, 2013/11-25 exhibitors

International Association of Fairs and Expositions/Paris Hotel/Dec. 8 - 12, 2013

International Carwash Association/Sands Expo and Convention Center/April 22 - 24, 2013

International Cast Polymer Alliance/Feb. 2 - 5, 2015

International Cast Polymer Association/Feb. 2 - 5, 2015

International Claim Association/Mirage Hotel and Casino/Sept. 27 - 30, 2015

International Congress of Oral Implantologists/May 16 - 18, 2013

International Council of Shopping Centers/Las Vegas Convention Center/May 19 - 22, 2013

International Foundation of Employee Benefit Plans/Oct. 20 - 23, 2013

International Foundation of Employee Benefit Plans/Oct. 22 - 25, 2013

International Franchise Association/MGM Grand Garden Arena/Feb. 17 - 20, 2013/over 100 exhibitors

International Franchise Association/MGM Grand Garden Arena/Feb. 15 - 18, 2015/over 100 exhibitors

International Health, Racquet and Sportsclub Association/Mandalay Bay/ March 19 - 22, 2013

International Iridology Practitioners Association/Hilton Garden Inn/Feb. 22 - 24, 2013

International Licensing Industry Merchandisers' Association/Mandalay Bay Convention Center/June 18 - 20, 2013/18000 attendees/over 100 exhibitors

International Military Community Executives Association/Mirage Resort and Casino/March 10 - 13, 2013

International Parking Institute/June 29 - July 2, 2015

International Pet and Animal Transportation Association/Paris Las Vegas Hotel and Casino/Nov. 2 - 5, 2013

International Public Management Association for Human Resources/Tropicana Las Vegas/Sept. 21 - 25, 2013

International Sanitary Supply Association/Las Vegas Convention Center/Nov. 18 - 21, 2013

International Sanitary Supply Association/Oct. 20 - 23, 2015

International Sanitary Supply Association/Oct. 17 - 20, 2017

International Sign Association/Mandalay Bay Convention Center/April 3 - 6, 2013/over 100 exhibitors

International Spa Association/Mandalay Bay/Oct. 21 - 23, 2013

International Truck Parts Association/Mirage/Jan. 21 - 24, 2013

Investment Management Consultants Association/ARIA Resort and Casino Hotel/April 27 - 29, 2015

The Kite Trade Association International/Texas Station/Jan. 28 - 31, 2013

Legal Marketing Association/ARIA Resort and Casino Hotel/April 8 - 10, 2013

Local Search Association (fka Yellow Pages Association)/Planet Hollywood Resort and Casino/April 13 - 16, 2013

Manufactured Housing Institute/Paris Hotel/April 16 - 18, 2013

Manufactured Housing Institute/Paris Hotel/April 15 - 17, 2014

Manufactured Housing Institute/Paris Hotel/April 14 - 16, 2015

Manufactured Housing Institute/Caesars Palace/May 3 - 5, 2016

Manufactured Housing Institute/Caesars Palace/May 2 - 4, 2017

Marketing Association of Credit Unions/May 29 - 31, 2013

Mason Contractors Association of America/Feb. 3 - 8, 2013

Mason Contractors Association of America/Jan. 19 - 24, 2014

Masonry Veneer Manufacturers Association/Las Vegas Convention Center/Jan. 22 - 25, 2013

Masonry Veneer Manufacturers Association/Las Vegas Convention Center/Feb. 5 - 8, 2013

United Professional Horsemen's Association/Caesars Palace/Jan. 3 - 5, 2013
United States Conference of Mayors/June 21 - 24, 2013
United States Potato Board/Caesar's Palace/Jan. 9 - 12, 2013
Vacuum Dealers Trade Association/Sewing Dealers Trade Association/Las Vegas Convention Center/Feb. 10 - 12, 2013
Video Electronics Standards Association/South Hall Lower Level/Jan. 8 - 11, 2013
The Vision Council/Oct. 2 - 5, 2013
The Vision Council/Sept. 17 - 20, 2014
The Vision Council/Oct. 1 - 3, 2015
The Vision Council/Sept. 21 - 24, 2016
Wedding and Portrait Photographers International/MGM Grand Hotel and Conference Center/March 7 - 14, 2013/1600 attendees
Western Writers of America/Riviera Hotel and Casino/June 24 - 28, 2013
Wiring Harness Manufacturers Association/Renaissance Las Vegas Hotel/Feb. 20 - 22, 2013
World Pet Association/Mandalay Bay/July 23 - 25, 2013
World Pet Association/Mandalay Bay/July 22 - 24, 2014
World Pet Association/Mandalay Bay/July 21 - 23, 2015
Worldwide ERC/May 6 - 8, 2015

Reno
American Association of Airport Executives/May 5 - 7, 2013
American Association of Airport Executives/Reno-Sparks Convention Center/May 19 - 22, 2013
American College of Clinical Pharmacy/Peppermill Resort Spa Casino/April 19 - 23, 2013
American Concrete Institute/Grand Sierra Resort and Casino/March 23 - 27, 2014
American Embryo Transfer Association/Grand Sierra Resort and Casino/Oct. 10 - 12, 2013
American Miniature Horse Association/Peppermill Resort Spa Casino/Feb. 14 - 17, 2013
American Nuclear Society/Grand Sierra Resort and Casino/June 15 - 19, 2014
American Society of Electroneurodiagnostic Technologists/Peppermill Resort Spa Casino/Aug. 1 - 3, 2013
ASPRS-The Imaging and Geospatial Information Society/Grand Sierra Resort and Casino/April 18 - 22, 2016
Association of College Unions International/March 19 - 23, 2018
Association of Shareware Professionals/Atlantis Casino Resort Spa/Sept. 27 - 29, 2013
CALLERLAB - International Association of Square Dance Callers/April 14 - 16, 2014
International Association of Emergency Managers/Silver Legacy Resort Casino/Oct. 25 - 30, 2013
International Embryo Transfer Society/John Ascuaga's Nugget Hotel Resort Casino/Jan. 11 - 14, 2014
International Society for Performance Improvement/Silver Legacy Resort Casino/April 12 - 17, 2013
Marine Corps Aviation Association/Grand Sierra Hotel & Casino/May 15 - 18, 2013
National Agricultural Aviation Association/Dec. 9 - 12, 2013
National Association for Bilingual Education/March 4 - 6, 2015
National Association for Interpretation/Nov. 8 - 11, 2017
National Association of Educational Procurement, Inc./Peppermill Resort Spa Casino/March 26 - 29, 2017
National Association of Subrogation Professionals/Peppermill Resort and Casino/Nov. 8 - 11, 2015
National Associations of State Directors of Pupil Transportation Services/July 22, 2013
National Federation Coaches Association/Peppermill Resort and Casino/June 28 - July 2, 2016
National Federation of Priests' Councils/April 22 - 25, 2013
National Federation of State High School Associations/Peppermill Resort Spa Casino/June 28 - July 2, 2016
National Network of Estate Planning Attorneys/Oct. 6 - 10, 2014
National Retail Tenants Association/Peppermill Resort Spa Casino/Sept. 7 - 10, 2014
National Sheriffs' Association/June 23 - 28, 2017
Roller Skating Association International/Silver Legacy Resort Casino/May 5 - 8, 2013
Soil and Water Conservation Society/Peppermill Reno/July 21 - 24, 2013
Substance Abuse Librarians and Information Specialists/University of Nevada Reno/April 30 - May 3, 2013
Text and Academic Authors Association/Silver Legacy Hotel/June 21 - 22, 2013
United States Bowling Congress/Silver Legacy Resort Casino/April 30 - May 4, 2013

Stateline
International Energy Credit Association/Harveys Lake Tahoe/March 17 - 19, 2013

Summerlin
American Association for Paralegal Education/Oct. 15 - 18, 2014

Zephyr Cove
Health Ministries Association/Zephyr Point Presbyterian Conference Center/June 10 - 12, 2013

NEW HAMPSHIRE
Bretton Woods
American College of Mortgage Attorneys/Omni-Mount Washington Resort/Sept. 18 - 20, 2014
Manchester
National Grange/Radisson Hotel Manchester/Nov. 12 - 16, 2013
Nashua
Midwives Alliance of North America/Holiday Inn/March 1 - 3, 2013

NEW JERSEY
Atlantic City
American Mosquito Control Association/Trump Taj Mahal/Feb. 24 - 28, 2013
International Institute of Municipal Clerks/May 19 - 23, 2013

International Society of Weighing and Measurement/Trump Plaza Hotel and Casino/March 13 - 15, 2013
Mail Systems Management Association/Tropicana Grand Exhibition Center/April 28 - May 1, 2013
NAFA Fleet Management Association/April 20 - 23, 2013
NAFA Fleet Management Association/Atlantic City Convention Center/April 23 - 26, 2013/11-25 exhibitors
National Association of Independent Fee Appraisers/Golden Nugget Hotels and Casinos/April 10 - 11, 2013
North American Association of State and Provincial Lotteries/Sept. 30 - Oct. 3, 2014
Receptive Services Association of America/Feb. 20 - 21, 2013
World Pet Association/April 10 - 12, 2013
Galloway
Society for the Advancement of American Philosophy/The Richard Stockton College/March 7 - 9, 2013
Jersey City
NAIOP, The Commercial Real Estate Development Association/Hyatt Regency Jersey City on the Hudson/June 12 - 13, 2014
Pharmaceutical Marketing Research Group/Hyatt Regency Jersey City on the Hudson/Oct. 20 - 22, 2013
New Brunswick
American Hungarian Educators Association/Rutgers/May 2 - 5, 2013
Pharmaceutical Marketing Research Group/Hyatt Regency New Brunswick/Oct. 19 - 21, 2014
Newark
The National Network for Social Work Managers/Paul Robeson Campus Center/May 16 - 17, 2013
Teaneck
International Fragrance Association North America/Teaneck Marriott at Glenpointe/Jan. 11, 2013
Weehawken
Organization for the Study of Sex Differences/Sheraton Lincoln Harbor Hotel/April 25 - 29, 2013

NEW MEXICO
Albuquerque
American Crystallographic Association/Albuquerque Convention Center/May 24 - 28, 2014
Society for Imaging Science and Technology/Nov. 4 - 8, 2013
Albuquerue
American Academy of Advertising/Hyatt Regency Albuquerque/April 3 - 7, 2013/200 attendees/11-25 exhibitors
American Association of Bovine Practitioners/Sept. 18 - 20, 2014
American Association of Cereal Chemists International/Sept. 29 - Oct. 2, 2013/1000 attendees/11-25 exhibitors
American College of Clinical Pharmacy/Albuquerque Convention Center/Oct. 13 - 16, 2013
American Society of Ichthyologists and Herpetologists/July 10 - 15, 2013
APPAM - The Association for Public Policy Analysis and Management/Albuquerque Convention Center/Nov. 6 - 8, 2014
Association of American Feed Control Officials/Hyatt Regency Albuquerque/Jan. 22 - 24, 2013
Association of Science-Technology Centers/Embassy Suites Albuquerque-Hotel and Spa/Oct. 19 - 22, 2013
Association of State Drinking Water Administrators/Hyatt Regency Albuquerque/Oct. 19 - 23, 2014
Concrete Foundations Association/Santa Ana Pueblo/July 10 - 13, 2013
Contact Lens Society of America/Hotel Albuquerue/April 12 - 13, 2013
Council of Engineering and Scientific Society Executives/Hyatt Regency Tamaya Resort and Spa/Feb. 24 - 27, 2013
Council of the Great City Schools/Hyatt Regency Albuquerque/Oct. 30 - Nov. 3, 2013
The Herpetologists' League/Albuquerque Convention Center/July 10 - 15, 2013
National Association of Diaconate Directors/Albuquerque Marriott Pyramid North/April 10, 2013
National Conference on Weights and Measures/Jan. 19 - 22, 2014
National Ornamental and Miscellaneous Metals Association/Hyatt Regency Albuquerque/March 20 - 23, 2013
North American Academy of Liturgy/Hyatt Regency Albuquerque/Jan. 3 - 6, 2013
North American Small Business International Trade Educators/Embassy Suites/April 8 - 12, 2013
The Society for Investigative Dermatology/Albuquerque Convention Center/May 7 - 10, 2014
Urban and Regional Information Systems Association/March 4 - 7, 2013
Loretto
National Association of Decorative Fabric Distributors/The Inn and Spa/Aug. 7 - 9, 2013
Santa Ana Pueblo
American Academy of Maxillofacial Prosthetics/Hyatt Regency Tamaya Resort & Spa/Oct. 23 - 27, 2013
American Association of Dental Consultants/Hyatt Regency Tamaya Resort and Spa/May 7 - 10, 2014
American Association of Dental Consultants/Hyatt Regency Tamaya Resort and Spa/May 13 - 16, 2015
American Sugar Alliance/Hyatt Regency Tamaya Resort and Spa/July 31 - Aug. 5, 2015
Gasket Fabricators Association/Hyatt Regency Tamaya Resort and Spa/Oct. 1 - 3, 2013
National Association of State Budget Officers/Hyatt Regency Tamaya Resort and Spa/April 25 - 27, 2013
Santa Fe
American Folklore Society/Santa Fe Convention Center/Nov. 5 - 8, 2014
Federal Bar Association/Hilton Buffalo Thunder/April 11 - 12, 2013
Federal Bar Association/Hilton Buffalo Thunder/April 10 - 11, 2014
IEEE Photonics Society/May 5 - 8, 2013

Institute for Operations Research and the Management Sciences/Eldorado Hotel and Spa/Jan. 6 - 8, 2013
North American Thermal Analysis Society/Sept. 15 - 17, 2014
Society of Independent Professional Earth Scientists/El Dorado Hotel and Spa/June 17 - 20, 2013

NEW YORK

Bolton Landing
Copyright Society of the U.S.A./Sagamore Resort/June 9 - 11, 2013

Buffalo
American Agricultural Editors Association/Hyatt Regency Buffalo Hotel And Conference Center/Aug. 3 - 7, 2013
North American Serials Interest Group/June 6 - 9, 2013
Society of Architectural Historians/April 10 - 16, 2013
Society of Architectural Historians/Hyatt Regency Buffalo Hotel And Conference Center/April 10 - 14, 2013

Ithaca
Institute of Mathematical Statistics/July 15 - 26, 2013

Lake Placid
American Society of Highway Engineers/Crowne Plaza Resort and Golf Club, Lake Placid/June 5 - 8, 2013
Outdoor Writers Association of America/Lake Lure Inn and Spa/Sept. 14 - 16, 2013

Manhattan
College Art Association/Hilton New York in midtown Manhattan/Feb. 13 - 16, 2013

New York City
Academy for Eating Disorders/Sheraton New York Hotel and Towers/March 27 - 29, 2014
The Advertising Research Foundation/New York Marriott Marquis/March 17 - 20, 2013
The Advertising Research Foundation/New York Marriott Marquis/March 24 - 26, 2014
American Academy of Child and Adolescent Psychiatry/Hilton New York and Towers/Oct. 25 - 30, 2016
American Academy of Dermatology/July 30 - Aug. 3, 2013
American Academy of Emergency Medicine/Hilton New York/Feb. 11 - 15, 2014
American Association of Pathologists' Assistants/Waldorf = Astoria/Sept. 6 - 12, 2014
American Bar Association/Aug. 10 - 15, 2017
American Booksellers Association/Jacobs Javits Center/May 30 - June 1, 2013/over 100 exhibitors
American College of Physician Executives/Hilton New York/April 26 - 30, 2013
American Head and Neck Society/New York Marriott Marquis/July 26 - 30, 2014
American Historical Association/Hilton and Sheraton/Jan. 2 - 5, 2015
American Historical Association/Hilton New York/Jan. 3 - 6, 2019
American Historical Association/Hilton New York/Jan. 3 - 6, 2020
American Institute of Ultrasound in Medicine/New York Marriott Downtown/April 6 - 10, 2013/2000 attendees
American Medical Women's Association/New York Palace/March 15 - 17, 2013
American Psychiatric Association/May 3 - 7, 2014
American Psychoanalytic Association/Waldorf Towers/Jan. 15 - 20, 2013
American Psychopathological Association/Grand Hyatt New York/March 7 - 9, 2013
American Society for Aesthetic Plastic Surgery/Jacob K. Javits Convention Center/April 11 - 16, 2013/2600 attendees/over 100 exhibitors
American Society of Heating, Refrigerating and Air Conditioning Engineers (ASHRAE)/Jan. 18 - 22, 2013
American Society of Hypertension, Inc./Hilton New York/May 17 - 20, 2014
American Society of Hypertension, Inc./Hilton New York/May 16 - 19, 2015
American Society of Hypertension, Inc./Hilton New York/May 14 - 17, 2016
American Society of Journalists and Authors/April 25 - 27, 2013/51-100 exhibitors
American Sociological Association/Hilton New York/Aug. 10 - 13, 2013
American Stamp Dealers Association/New Yorker Hotel/April 11 - 14, 2013
American Stamp Dealers Association/National Arts Club/Oct. 10 - 13, 2013
Antiquarian Booksellers Association of America/Park Avenue Armory/April 11 - 14, 2013
ARMA International/Hilton New York/Jan. 29 - 31, 2013
Art Dealers Association of America/Park Avenue Armory/March 6 - 10, 2013
ASPSN - American Society of Plastic Surgical Nurses/April 13 - 14, 2013
Association for Behavioral and Cognitive Therapies/Oct. 27 - 30, 2016
Association for Preservation Technology International/New York Marriott Marquis/Oct. 12 - 15, 2013
Association of American Law Schools/Jan. 3 - 6, 2014
Association of Corporate Travel Executives (ACTE)/April 21 - 23, 2013
Association of Foreign Investors in U.S. Real Estate/Mandarin Oriental, New York/Feb. 13 - 14, 2013
Association of Insolvency and Restructuring Advisors/Arno Ristorante/Jan. 31, 2013
The Association of International Photography Art Dealers/Park Avenue Armory/April 4 - 7, 2013
Association of Performing Arts Presenters/Hilton New York/Jan. 11 - 15, 2013
Association of Theatrical Press Agents and Managers/Sardi's Restaurant/Jan. 25, 2013
Association of Women Surgeons/New York Palace Hotel/March 15 - 17, 2013
Audio Publishers Association/The Jacob K. Javits Convention Center/May 29, 2013
Bibliographical Society of America/Jan. 25, 2013
Biotechnology Industry Organization (BIO)/Waldorf = Astoria/Nov. 11 - 12, 2013
Business for Social Responsibility/Nov. 4 - 7, 2014
Chamber Music America/Westin New York at Times Square/Jan. 17 - 20, 2013
College Art Association/Feb. 13 - 16, 2013
College Media Association/March 14 - 16, 2013

Columbia Scholastic Press Association/Columbia University/March 20 - 22, 2013
Columbia Scholastic Press Association/Columbia University/March 19 - 21, 2014
Conference on Latin American History/Jan. 2 - 5, 2015
Council of American Jewish Museums/March 3 - 5, 2013
The Counselors of Real Estate/Waldorf Astoria Hotels and Resorts/April 28 - May 1, 2013
CRE Finance Council/New York Marriott Marquis/June 10 - 12, 2013
Direct Marketing Association Nonprofit Federation/Grand Hyatt New York/July 17 - 18, 2013
Direct Marketing Association Nonprofit Federation/Grand Hyatt New York/July 16 - 17, 2014
Drug, Chemical and Associated Technologies Association/Waldorf = Astoria/March 11 - 14, 2013
Electrical Equipment Representatives Association/Grand Hyatt New York/June 23 - 26, 2013
Financial Management Association International/St. John's University/May 17, 2013
Foodservice & Packaging Institute, Inc./The Conrad/March 22 - 24, 2013
Global Association of Risk Professionals/March 12 - 13, 2013
Historians of American Communism/Hilton New York/Jan. 2 - 5, 2015
Historians of American Communism/Jan. 3 - 6, 2020
Home Fashion Products Association/March 18 - 21, 2013
Home Fashion Products Association/Sept. 23 - 26, 2013
Home Fashion Products Association/March 24 - 27, 2014
Home Fashion Products Association/Sept. 15 - 18, 2014
Independent Sector/Hilton New York/Sept. 29 - Oct. 1, 2013
Insured Retirement Institute/Hilton New York/Feb. 7 - 13, 2014
Intercollegiate Broadcasting System/New York's Hotel Pennsylvania/March 8 - 10, 2013
International Association of Business Communicators/Hilton New York/June 23 - 26, 2013
International Society for the Performing Arts/Jan. 15 - 17, 2013
International Society for the Performing Arts/June 15 - 17, 2013
International Society for the Performing Arts/Jan. 14 - 16, 2014
International Technology Law Association/May 1, 2014
Investment Management Consultants Association/New York Marriott Marquis/Feb. 4 - 5, 2013
Investment Management Consultants Association/New York Marriott Marquis/Feb. 10 - 11, 2013
Manufacturing Jewelers and Suppliers of America/Hilton New York/March 10 - 12, 2013/over 100 exhibitors
Maritime Law Association of the U.S./April 30 - May 2, 2013
Market Technicians Association/Sentry Centers/April 4 - 5, 2013
Mortgage Bankers Association of America/New York Marriott Marquis/May 5 - 8, 2013
National Association for the Specialty Food Trade/June 30 - July 2, 2013/1-10 exhibitors
National Association for the Specialty Food Trade/June 29 - July 1, 2014/1-10 exhibitors
National Association of Chapter Thirteen Trustees (NACTT)/New York Marriott Marquis/Aug. 3 - 6, 2013
National Association of Consumer Bankruptcy Attorneys/April 9 - 13, 2014
National Association of Corporate Treasurers/Westin Times Square Hotel/May 29 - 31, 2013
National Association of Professors of Hebrew/June 24 - 26, 2013
National Court Reporters Association/Hilton New York/July 30 - Aug. 2, 2015
National Retail Federation/Jacob K. Javits Convention Center/Jan. 13 - 16, 2013/1-10 exhibitors
Professional Liability Underwriting Society/Marriott Marquis Hotel/Feb. 6 - 7, 2013
Propane Engine Fuel Committee/Propane Education and Research Council/July 10 - 11, 2013
The Renaissance Society of America/March 27 - 29, 2014/1500 attendees/over 100 exhibitors
Retail Advertising and Marketing Association International/Jacob K. Javits Convention Center/Jan. 13 - 16, 2013/51-100 exhibitors
Romance Writers of America/New York Marriott Downtown/July 22 - 25, 2015/2100 attendees
The Rural Sociological Society/Sheraton New York Hotel/Aug. 6 - 9, 2013
Society for Italian Historical Studies/Hilton New York/Jan. 2 - 5, 2015
Society for Italian Historical Studies/Hilton New York/Jan. 3 - 5, 2020
Society for Menstrual Cycle Research/Marymount Manhattan College/June 6 - 8, 2013
Society for the Study of Social Problems/Westin New York at Times Square/Aug. 9 - 11, 2013
Society of Biological Psychiatry/May 3 - 7, 2014
Society of Biological Psychiatry/The New York Helmsley Hotel/May 8 - 10, 2014
Society of Biological Psychiatry/May 3 - 5, 2018
Society of Children's Book Writers and Illustrators/Hyatt Regency Grand Central/Feb. 1 - 3, 2013
Society of Laparoendoscopic Surgeons/Sheraton New York Hotel and Towers/Sept. 2 - 5, 2015
Toy Industry Association/Jacob K. Javits Convention Center/Feb. 10 - 13, 2013/over 100 exhibitors
The Vision Council/Javits Center/March 14 - 17, 2013/15000 attendees/11-25 exhibitors
The Vision Council/April 3 - 6, 2014
The Vision Council/March 19 - 22, 2015
The Vision Council/April 14 - 17, 2016

Niagara Falls
National Association of Scientific Materials Managers/July 29 - Aug. 2, 2013

Rochester
International Society of Bassists/June 2 - 8, 2013
SPIE - The International Society for Optical Engineering/Rochester Riverside Convention Center/Oct. 14 - 17, 2013

West Point

Military Operations Research Society/United States Military Academy/June 17 - 20, 2013

NORTH CAROLINA

Asheboro

American Association of Zoo Keepers/Sept. 22 - 26, 2013

Asheville

American Dairy Goat Association/Oct. 12 - 19, 2013

American Society of Electroneurodiagnostic Technologists/Grove Park Inn/Aug. 20 - 23, 2014

National Association of Agricultural Fair Agencies/Inn On Biltmore Estate/Sept. 8 - 13, 2013

National Association of Federal Credit Unions/Renaissance Asheville Hotel/May 15 - 17, 2013

National Association of State Retirement Administrators/Grove Park Inn/Aug. 1 - 6, 2014

National Association of State Treasurers/Grove Park Inn/Oct. 6 - 9, 2013

Veterinary Cancer Society/Grove Park Inn/March 16 - 19, 2014

Boone

American Association of Variable Star Observers/Appalachian State University/May 15 - 18, 2013

Cary

Association of Public Health Nurses/Embassy Suites Raleigh-Durham/Research Triangle/June 6 - 8, 2013

CALLERLAB - International Association of Square Dance Callers/Embassy Suites Raleigh-Durham/Research Triangle hotel/March 25 - 27, 2013

Chapel Hill

Association of Research Libraries/Chapel Hill Hotel/April 30 - May 3, 2013

Charleston

The Association for Science Teacher Education/Francis Marion Hotel/Jan. 9 - 12, 2013

Charlotte

AASHTO: Transportation Center of Excellence/Westin Charlotte/Oct. 23 - 27, 2014

American Alliance for Health, Physical Education, Recreation and Dance/Charlotte Convention Center/April 23 - 27, 2013/5000 attendees/1-10 exhibitors

American Association for Dental Research/March 19 - 22, 2014

American Association for Laboratory Animal Science/Oct. 30 - Nov. 3, 2016

American Association for Physical Activity and Recreation/Westin Charlotte/April 23 - 27, 2013

American Association of Bovine Practitioners/Sept. 15 - 17, 2016

American Association of Colleges of Nursing/April 2 - 3, 2013

American Association of Neuroscience Nurses/Charlotte Convention Center/March 9 - 12, 2013/800 attendees/1-10 exhibitors

American Bus Association/Charlotte Convention Center/Jan. 5 - 9, 2013

American Jail Association/Sheraton Charlotte Airport Hotel/April 19 - 22, 2015/1000 attendees

American Public Works Association/Charlotte Convention Center/April 7 - 10, 2013

American Theological Library Association/June 19 - 22, 2013

Assisted Living Federation of America/Charlotte Convention Center/May 7 - 9, 2013

Association of African American Museums/Aug. 7 - 10, 2013

Construction Specifications Institute/Charlotte Omni Hotel/Feb. 7 - 9, 2013

IEEE Power Electronics Society/March 15 - 19, 2015

Infusion Nurses Society/May 18 - 23, 2013/1200 attendees

International Association for Food Protection/Charlotte Convention Center/July 28 - 31, 2013

International City/County Management Association/Charlotte Marriott SouthPark/Sept. 14 - 17, 2014

International Council for Health, Physical, Education, Recreation, Sport and Dance/April 23 - 27, 2013

International Textile and Apparel Association/Hilton Charlotte Center City/Nov. 11 - 17, 2014

Lift Manufacturers Product Section - Material Handling Institute/Charlotte Marriott City Center/April 7 - 10, 2013

Material Handling Industry of America/Charlotte Marriott City Center/April 7 - 10, 2013

National Association for Environmental Management/Charlotte Convention Center/Oct. 23 - 25, 2013

National Association of Church Business Administration/Holiday Inn Charlotte-Center City/July 11 - 15, 2013

National Association of Counties/Charlotte Convention Center/July 10 - 13, 2015

National Chemical Credit Association/Omni Charlotte Hotel/May 16 - 17, 2013

National Correctional Industries Association/Westin Charlotte/March 24 - 27, 2013

National Emergency Number Association/Charlotte Convention Center/June 15 - 20, 2013

National Recreation and Parks Association/Oct. 14 - 16, 2014/7000 attendees/over 100 exhibitors

National Science Teachers Association/Nov. 7 - 9, 2013

National Sheriffs' Association/June 22 - 26, 2013

National Student Nurses Association/April 3 - 7, 2013/11-25 exhibitors

North American Association of Central Cancer Registries/June 13 - 19, 2015

Plastics Pipe Institute/Sept. 29 - Oct. 2, 2013

Research Chefs Association/March 6 - 9, 2013

Shock Society/Westin Charlotte/June 7 - 10, 2014

Specialty Tools and Fasteners Distributors Association/Charlotte Convention Center/Nov. 9 - 11, 2014

Synthetic Yarn and Fiber Association/Sheraton Airport Hotel/April 18 - 19, 2013

Greensboro

Brick Industry Association/Sheraton Greensboro Hotel at Four Seasons/Jan. 29 - 30, 2013

College Band Directors National Association/Sheraton Greensboro at Four Seasons/March 20 - 23, 2013

National Exchange Club/Sheraton Greensboro at Four Seasons/July 10 - 13, 2013

Greenville

Special Interest Group for Design of Communication/East Carolina University Heart Institute/Feb. 25 - 26, 2013

Lake Junaluska

Church and Synagogue Library Association/Lake Junaluska Conference and Retreat Center/July 28 - 30, 2013

Fellowship of United Methodists in Music and Worship Arts/June 23 - 28, 2013

Fellowship of United Methodists in Music and Worship Arts/June 22 - 27, 2014

Pinehurst

American Leather Chemists Association/June 20 - 23, 2013

American Shoulder and Elbow Surgeons/Pinehurst Resort/Oct. 9 - 12, 2014

Raleigh

Association of Community Health Nursing Educators/June 6 - 8, 2013

Association of Science-Technology Centers/North Carolina State University/Oct. 18 - 21, 2014

The Handcrafted Soapmakers Guild/Hilton North Raleigh/May 17 - 19, 2013

International Association of Wildland Fire/Feb. 18 - 22, 2013

Metal Construction Association/The Umstead/June 24 - 26, 2013

National Council of Writing Program Administrators/July 10 - 17, 2016

United States Association for Computational Mechanics/Raleigh Convention Center/July 22 - 25, 2013

Ridgecrest

Christian Medical & Dental Associations/LifeWay Ridgecrest Conference Center/May 2 - 5, 2013

Winston-Salem

Black Theatre Network/Brookstown Inn/July 26 - 29, 2013

Black Theatre Network/Winston-Salem Marriott/July 29 - Aug. 3, 2013

Commission on Accreditation for Law Enforcement Agencies Incorporation/Nov. 13 - 16, 2013

NORTH DAKOTA

Fargo

National Association for Family and Community Education/Holiday Inn of Fargo/July 18 - 21, 2013

Pyrotechnics Guild International/Aug. 8 - 14, 2015

Medora

National Association of Agricultural Fair Agencies/June 20 - 24, 2013

OHIO

Akron

American Chemical Society - Rubber Division/Hilton Akron/Fairlawn/April 21 - 24, 2013

Bath

Association for Living History, Farm and Agricultural Museums/Hale Farm Village/June 14 - 18, 2013

Cincinnati

American Association of Professional Farriers/Hyatt Regency Hotel/Jan. 30, 2013

American Correctional Association/Aug. 7 - 12, 2020

American Counseling Association/Duke Energy Convention Center/March 20 - 24, 2013/1-10 exhibitors

Association for Conflict Resolution/Oct. 8 - 11, 2014

The Association for Manufacturing Excellence/Oct. 19 - 23, 2015

Educational Theatre Association/Hilton Cincinnati Netherland Plaza/July 24 - 27, 2014

Environmental and Water Resources Institute of the American Society of Civil Engineers/Duke Energy Convention Center/May 20 - 22, 2013

EPS Industry Alliance/Hilton Cincinnati Netherland Plaza Hotel/March 18 - 20, 2013

Monument Builders of North America/Feb. 8 - 10, 2013

National Association of Clean Water Agencies/Hilton Cincinnati Netherland Plaza/July 14 - 17, 2013

National Parent Teachers Association/June 20 - 23, 2013

National Women's Studies Association/Hilton Cincinnati Netherland Plaza/Nov. 7 - 10, 2013

North American Deer Farmers Association/March 14 - 16, 2013

Retail Confectioners International/June 24 - 28, 2013

Special Interest Group on Management Information Systems/May 30 - June 1, 2013

United States Institute for Theatre Technology/Duke Energy Convention Center/March 18 - 21, 2015

Cleaveland

American Association for the History of Nursing/Cleveland Clinic/Sept. 26 - 29, 2013

American Chemical Society - Rubber Division/International Exposition Center/Oct. 8 - 10, 2013/6000 attendees/over 100 exhibitors

American Society for Eighteenth-Century Studies/Renaissance Cleveland Hotel/April 4 - 7, 2013

Association of Rotational Molders International/Renaissance Hotel/Sept. 28 - Oct. 1, 2013

National Rural Economic Developers Association/Wyndham Cleveland Playhouse Square Hotel/July 23 - 25, 2014

Public Radio News Directors Incorporated/Cleveland Playhouse Square Hotel/June 18 - 22, 2013

Society for Vascular Medicine/InterContinental Hotel Suites Cleveland/June 12 - 15, 2013

Columbus

American Association for Agricultural Education/May 21 - 24, 2013

American Association of School Librarians/Oct. 15 - 18, 2015

American College of Osteopathic Pediatricians/Renaissance Columbus Downtown Hotel/April 25 - 28, 2013

American Medical Writers Association/Nov. 6 - 9, 2013

American Society for Engineering Education/June 25 - 28, 2017

Association of Ancient Historians/Ohio State University/May 16 - 19, 2013

Association of Research Libraries/April 29 - May 2, 2014

Business History Conference/Hyatt Regency Columbus/March 21 - 23, 2013
Commission on Accreditation for Law Enforcement Agencies Incorporation/July 31 - Aug. 3, 2013
Forging Industry Association/Greater Columbus Convention Center/March 26 - 28, 2013
Game Manufacturers Association/Greater Columbus Convention Center/June 12 - 16, 2013
Game Manufacturers Association/Greater Columbus Convention Center/June 11 - 15, 2014
Game Manufacturers Association/Greater Columbus Convention Center/June 3 - 7, 2015
International Association of Healthcare Central Service Materiel Management/Columbus Convention Center/May 4 - 7, 2014/11-25 exhibitors
International Technology and Engineering Educators Association/March 7 - 9, 2013
Microanalysis Society/July 24 - 28, 2016
Microscopy Society of America/July 25 - 28, 2016
National Exchange Club/Sheraton Columbus at Capitol Square/July 29 - Aug. 1, 2015
The National NeedleArts Association/Greater Columbus Convention Center/June 22 - 24, 2013
North American Association of Wardens and Superintendents/Hilton Columbus Downtown/May 29 - June 1, 2013
Pressure Vessel Manufacturers Association/Crowne Plaza Columbus North/Sept. 9 - 10, 2013
Retail Print Music Dealers Association/May 1 - 4, 2013/230 attendees/26-50 exhibitors
Society of Composers, Inc./Ohio State University/Feb. 13 - 16, 2013
Mason
Air Conditioning Contractors of America/Cincinnati/March 6 - 8, 2013
Oxford
Association for Integrative Studies/Miami University/Nov. 7 - 10, 2013
Sandusky
National Grange/Kalahari Waterpark Resort and Convention Center/Nov. 11 - 15, 2014

OKLAHOMA

Oklahoma City
American Chamber of Commerce Executives/July 24 - 27, 2013
American Society of Mammalogists/Renaissance Oklahoma City Convention Center Hotel/June 6 - 10, 2014
American Volleyball Coaches Association/Dec. 17 - 21, 2014
Association for Business Simulation and Experiential Learning/The Skirvin hotel/March 6 - 8, 2013
Beef Improvement Federation/June 12 - 15, 2013
International Association of Round Dance Teachers/Meridian Convention Center/June 23 - 26, 2013
International Professional Rodeo Association/Jan. 18 - 20, 2013
NALS/DoubleTree Warren Place/Feb. 27 - March 2, 2013
National Association of Sports Commissions/Oklahoma City Convention and Visitors Bureau/March 31 - April 3, 2014
National Christian School Association/March 6 - 9, 2013
National Lieutenant Governors Association/The Skirvin hotel/July 17 - 19, 2013
Oral History Association/Skirvin Hilton Oklahoma City/Oct. 29 - Nov. 3, 2013
Society for Range Management/Renaissance Oklahoma City Convention Center Hotel/Feb. 3 - 7, 2013
Tulsa
Magnet Schools of America/May 5 - 8, 2013
National School Transportation Association/July 19 - 24, 2013
Palomino Horse Breeders of America/Hyatt Regency Tulsa/March 13 - 16, 2013

OREGON

Eugene
Society for Phenomenology and Existential Philosophy/Oct. 24 - 26, 2013
Mt. Hood
Chemical Coaters Association International/The Resort at the Mountain/June 19 - 21, 2013
Portland
Airports Council International - North America/Hilton Portland and Executive Tower/April 22 - 24, 2013
Alliance of Information and Referral Systems/Portland Hilton and Executive Tower/June 2 - 5, 2013
American Academy of Oral and Maxillofacial Pathology/Hilton Portland and Executive Tower/June 14 - 19, 2013
American Association for Aerosol Research/Oregon Convention Center/Sept. 30 - Oct. 4, 2013
American Association for Applied Linguistics/March 22 - 25, 2014
American Association of Medical Society Executives/July 22 - 25, 2015
American Association of Pathologists' Assistants/Hilton Portland and Executive Tower/Sept. 21 - 27, 2013
American Association of Physics Teachers/July 13 - 17, 2013
American Association of School Personnel Administrators/Oct. 13 - 17, 2014
American Ceramics Society/Hilton Portland and Executive Tower/Aug. 4 - 7, 2013
American Council on Consumer Interests/Benson Hotel/April 10 - 12, 2013
American Dental Education Association/Hilton Portland and Executive Tower/June 8 - 11, 2013
American Diabetes Association/Oregon Convention Center/May 4, 2013
American Holistic Veterinary Medical Association/Red Lion Hotel on the River/Sept. 13 - 16, 2014
American Morgan Horse Association/Benson Hotel/Feb. 20 - 23, 2013
American Oriental Society/Hilton Portland and Executive Tower/March 15 - 18, 2013
American Psychology-Law Society/Hilton Portland & Executive Tower/March 7 - 9, 2013
American Public Power Association/Sept. 14 - 17, 2014
American Society of Limnology and Oceanography/May 18 - 23, 2014

American Society of Plant Biologists/July 12 - 16, 2014
American Water Resources Association/Red Lion Hotel on the River-Jantzen Beach/Nov. 4 - 7, 2013
Association for Applied Psychophysiology and Biofeedback/Hilton Portland Executive Towers/March 14 - 16, 2013
Association for Behavior Analysis International/Portland Marriott Downtown Waterfront Hotel/Jan. 25 - 27, 2013
Association Montessori International - United States of America/Hilton Portland and Executive Tower/July 31 - Aug. 3, 2013
Association of Asphalt Paving Technologists/March 15 - 18, 2015
Association of College and Research Libraries/March 25 - 28, 2015
Association of Community Cancer Centers/Portland Marriott Downtown Waterfront/Oct. 21 - 24, 2013
Association of Metropolitan Planning Organizations/Embassy Suites Portland/Oct. 22 - 25, 2013
Association of Partners for Public Lands/March 10 - 14, 2013
Christian Association for Psychological Studies/Portland Marriott Downtown Waterfront Hotel/April 4 - 6, 2013
Conference of Radiation Control Program Directors/Red Lion Hotel Jantzen/May 20 - 23, 2013/400 attendees
Continua Health Alliance/Embassy Suites Portland-Downtown/March 11 - 15, 2013
Entomological Society of America/Nov. 16 - 19, 2014/3000 attendees/26-50 exhibitors
Eye Bank Association of America/Hilton Portland and Executive Tower/June 25 - 28, 2014
Hearing Loss Association of America/DoubleTree by Hilton/June 27 - 30, 2013
International Association for Business and Society/Marriott Downtown Waterfront Hotel/June 6 - 9, 2013
International Association for Food Protection/Oregon Convention Center/July 26 - 29, 2015
International Association of Workforce Professionals (IAWP)/Red Lion Hotel/June 22 - 25, 2014
Marketing Education Association/Nines Hotel/April 18 - 20, 2013
Mathematical Association of America/Aug. 7 - 9, 2014
Microanalysis Society/Aug. 2 - 6, 2015
Microscopy Society of America/Aug. 3 - 7, 2015
National Association of Legal Assistants/Hilton Portland and Executive Tower/July 10 - 13, 2013
National Association of Parliamentarians/Hilton Portland and Executive Tower/Sept. 6 - 9, 2013
National Association of Professional Band Instrument Repair Technicians/DoubleTree by Hilton/April 4 - 7, 2014
National Association of State Retirement Administrators/Portland Marriott Downtown Waterfront/Aug. 2 - 7, 2013
National Child Support Enforcement Association/Hilton Portland and Executive Tower/Aug. 11 - 13, 2014
National Opera Association/Hilton Portland Executive Towers/Jan. 3 - 6, 2013
National Science Teachers Association/Oct. 24 - 26, 2013
National Truck and Heavy Equipment Claims Council/Oct. 10 - 12, 2013
National Wildlife Rehabilitators Association/DoubleTree by Hilton/March 5 - 9, 2013/400 attendees
North American Conference on British Studies/Nov. 8 - 10, 2013
North American Raspberry & Blackberry Association/Jan. 27 - 30, 2013
Philosophy of Education Society/Benson Hotel/March 14 - 18, 2013
Phycological Society of America/May 18 - 23, 2014
Propane Engine Fuel Committee/Propane Education and Research Council/Oct. 9 - 10, 2013
Society for Nutrition Education and Behavior/Hilton Portland and Executive Tower/Aug. 9 - 12, 2013
Society of Insurance Trainers and Educators/Hilton Portland and Executive Tower/June 22 - 26, 2013
Society of Toxicologic Pathologists/Oregon Convention Center/June 16 - 20, 2013
Society of Toxicologic Pathology/Oregon Convention Center/June 16 - 20, 2013
Solar Electric Power Association/April 16 - 17, 2013
States Organization for Boating Access/Hilton DoubleTree Hotel and Conference Center/Sept. 30 - Oct. 3, 2013
Technical Association of the Graphic Arts/Portland Marriott Downtown Waterfront/Feb. 3 - 6, 2013
TESOL International Association/Oregon Convention Center/March 26 - 29, 2014
Turf and Ornamental Communicators Association/Embassy Suites Portland Hotel/May 7 - 10, 2013
United States Wheat Associates, Inc./Nines Hotel/Nov. 3 - 6, 2013

PENNSYLVANIA

Butler
Pyrotechnics Guild International/Aug. 10 - 16, 2013
Coraopolis
American Academy of Podiatric Practice Management/Pittsburgh Airport Marriott/Feb. 27 - March 3, 2013
Erie
Federation of Diocesan Liturgical Commissions/Sheraton Bayfront/Oct. 8 - 12, 2013
Tall Ships America/Sheraton Erie Bayfront Hotel/Feb. 4 - 6, 2013
Gainey Ranch
Casting Industry Suppliers Association/Hyatt Regency Scottsdale Resort and Spa at Gainey Ranch/May 20 - 22, 2013
Grantham
North American Coalition for Christian Admissions Professionals/Messiah College/May 28 - June 1, 2013
Harrisburg
American Rabbit Breeders Association/Pennsylvania Historical and Museum Commission/Oct. 19 - 23, 2013
Hershey
American Beekeeping Federation/Hershey Lodge/Jan. 8 - 12, 2013
OESP - National Association of Oil and Energy Service Professionals/May 19 - 23, 2013

Lancaster

PMCA: An International Association of Confectioners/Lancaster Convention Center/April 15 - 17, 2013

Latrobe

College Theology Society/Saint Vincent's College/May 29 - June 1, 2014

Philadelphia

AABB - American Association of Blood Banks/Oct. 25 - 28, 2014

Academy of Criminal Justice Sciences/Philadelphia Marriott Downtown/Feb. 18 - 22, 2014

Academy of Management/Aug. 1 - 5, 2014

Academy of Political Science/Philadelphia Marriott Downtown/Sept. 1 - 4, 2016

American Academy of Hospice and Palliative Medicine/Feb. 25 - 28, 2015

American Academy of Neurology/April 26 - May 3, 2014

American Academy of Periodontology/Sept. 28 - Oct. 1, 2013

American Association for Cancer Research/April 18 - 22, 2015

American Association for Clinical Chemistry, Inc./July 24 - 28, 2016/18000 attendees/over 100 exhibitors

American Association for the Advancement of Slavic Studies/Philadelphia Marriott Downtown/Nov. 19 - 22, 2015

American Association for the Surgery of Trauma/Philadelphia Marriott Downtown/Sept. 10 - 13, 2014/1000 attendees

American Association of Orthodontists/Philadelphia Convention Center/May 3 - 7, 2013

American Association of Pharmaceutical Scientists/Pennsylvania Convention Center/Oct. 17 - 21, 2021

American Chemical Society/Aug. 21 - 25, 2016

American Concrete Institute/Philadelphia Marriott Downtown/Oct. 23 - 27, 2016

American Correctional Health Services Association/March 14 - 17, 2013

American Economic Association/Jan. 3 - 5, 2014/over 100 exhibitors

American Educational Research Association/April 3 - 7, 2014

American Epilepsy Society/Pennsylvania Convention Center/Dec. 4 - 8, 2015

American Federation of Labor & Congress of Industrial Organizations/Sheraton Philadelphia Downtown Hotel/Jan. 17 - 21, 2013

The American Finance Association/Jan. 3 - 5, 2014

American Homebrewers Association/June 27 - 29, 2013

American Library Association/Jan. 24 - 28, 2014

American Montessori Society/Philadelphia Marriott Downtown/March 12 - 15, 2015

American Optometric Association/June 25, 2014

American Optometric Student Association/June 25, 2014

American Pediatric Society/May 2 - 5, 2020

American Podiatric Medical Association/Philadelphia Marriott Downtown/July 14 - 17, 2016

American Political Science Association/Philadelphia Marriott Downtown/Sept. 1 - 4, 2016

American School Counselor Association/Pennsylvania Convention Center/June 30 - July 3, 2013

American Society for Cell Biology/Dec. 6 - 10, 2014

American Society for Clinical Laboratory Science/July 24 - 28, 2016/19000 attendees/over 100 exhibitors

American Society for Clinical Laboratory Science/July 26 - 30, 2016

American Society for Clinical Laboratory Science/July 23 - 27, 2019

American Society for Clinical Laboratory Science/July 25 - 29, 2023

American Society of Criminology/Philadelphia Marriott Downtown/Nov. 15 - 18, 2017

American Society of Criminology/Philadelphia Marriott Downtown/Nov. 15 - 18, 2023

American Society of Mammalogists/Philadelphia Marriott Downtown/June 14 - 18, 2013

American Society of Nephrology/Pennsylvania Convention Center/Nov. 11 - 16, 2014

American Society of Pediatric Nephrology/May 2 - 5, 2020

American Society of Professional Estimators/Hyatt Regency/July 17 - 20, 2013

American Society of Transplantation/May 2 - 6, 2015

American Thoracic Society/May 17 - 22, 2013

Anxiety Disorders Association of America/Philadelphia Marriott Downtown/March 31 - April 3, 2016

Associated Collegiate Press/Marriott, Philadelphia/Oct. 29 - Nov. 2, 2014

Association for Asian Studies/March 24 - 30, 2014

Association for Behavioral and Cognitive Therapies/Nov. 20 - 23, 2014

Association for Comparative Economic Studies/Jan. 3 - 5, 2014

Association for Library and Information Science Education/Jan. 21 - 24, 2014

Association for Slavic, East European, and Eurasian Studies/Philadelphia Marriott Downtown/Nov. 19 - 22, 2015

Association for the Advancement of Medical Instrumentation/May 31 - June 2, 2014

Association of Academic Health Sciences Library/Nov. 1 - 6, 2013

Association of American Medical Colleges/Pennsylvania Convention Center/Nov. 1 - 6, 2013

Association of College Unions International/March 19 - 23, 2017

Association of Collegiate Business Schools and Programs/Philadelphia Marriott Downtown/June 12 - 15, 2015

Association of Collegiate Schools of Planning/Loews Philadelphia Hotel/Oct. 30 - Nov. 2, 2014

Association of Regulatory Boards of Optometry/June 22 - 24, 2014

Association of University Research Parks/Sept. 24 - 27, 2013

College Media Association/Oct. 29 - Nov. 1, 2014

Council for Exceptional Children/April 9 - 12, 2014

Council of State Speech-Language-Hearing Association Presidents/Nov. 16, 2016

Dance/USA/June 12 - 15, 2013

Developmental Disabilities Nurses Association/Double Tree by Hilton Hotel/April 26 - 29, 2013

Flavor and Extract Manufacturers Association/Hyatt at The Bellevue/Feb. 12 - 13, 2013

Genetics Society of America/Philadelphia Marriott Downtown/March 2 - 6, 2016

Government Finance Officers Association of the United States and Canada/May 31 - June 3, 2015/over 100 exhibitors

Government Finance Officers Association, Federal Liaison Center/May 31 - June 3, 2015

Hospice and Palliative Nurses Association/Feb. 25 - 28, 2015

Insurance Marketing Communications Association/June 23 - 26, 2013

International Association of Chiefs of Police/Oct. 19 - 23, 2013/51-100 exhibitors

International Economic Development Council/Philadelphia Marriott Downtown/Oct. 6 - 9, 2013

International Facility Management Association/Oct. 2 - 4, 2013

International Society for Pharmacoeconomics and Outcomes Research/Philadelphia Marriott Downtown/May 16 - 20, 2015

International Society for Technology in Education/June 28 - July 1, 2015/over 100 exhibitors

International Society for Traumatic Stress Studies/Philadelphia Marriott Downtown/Nov. 7 - 9, 2013/1300 attendees/1-10 exhibitors

LeadingAge (American Association of Homes and Services for the Aging)/Oct. 28 - 31, 2018

Liability Insurance Research Bureau/April 7 - 10, 2013

Million Dollar Round Table/June 9 - 13, 2013

Million Dollar Round Table/June 9 - 12, 2013

NAFSA: Association of International Educators/May 27 - June 1, 2018

National Association of College and University Attorneys/Philadelphia Marriott Downtown/June 19 - 22, 2013

National Association of Independent Schools/Pennsylvania Convention Center/Feb. 27 - March 1, 2013

National Association of Letter Carriers/Pennsylvania Convention Center/July 21 - 25, 2014

National Association of Professional Geriatric Care Managers/DoubleTree by Hilton Philadelphia Center City/April 17 - 20, 2013

National Association of State Chief Information Officers/Philadelphia Marriott Downtown/Oct. 13 - 16, 2013

National Conference of Insurance Legislators/Philadelphia Marriott Downtown/July 11 - 14, 2013

National Conference of State Social Security Administrators/Sheraton Society Hill Hotel/July 28 - 31, 2013

National Council on Measurement in Education/April 2 - 6, 2014

National Federation of Advanced Information Services/Hyatt at The Bellevue/Feb. 24 - 26, 2013

National Finishing Contractors Association/May 29 - June 1, 2013

National Institute of Governmental Purchasing/Philadelphia Convention Centre/Aug. 22 - 27, 2014

National Soccer Coaches Association of America/Jan. 15 - 19, 2014/9000 attendees

National Soccer Coaches Association of America/Jan. 14 - 18, 2015/9000 attendees

National Soccer Coaches Association of America/Jan. 10 - 14, 2018/9000 attendees

National Speakers Association/Philadelphia Marriott Downtown/July 27 - 30, 2013

Osteoarthritis Research Society International/Marriott Philadelphia DownTown/April 18 - 21, 2013

Osteoarthritis Research Society International/Philadelphia Marriott Downtown/April 25, 2013

Parachute Industry Association/DoubleTree by Hilton Hotel Philadelphia Center City/Aug. 23 - 24, 2013

Pediatric Endocrine Society/May 2 - 5, 2020

Physician Assistant Education Association/Marriott Philadelphia DownTown/Oct. 15 - 19, 2014

Professional Women Controllers/Sheraton Society Hill Hotel/April 8 - 11, 2013

Public Library Association/March 20 - 24, 2018

The Public Relations Society of America/Oct. 26 - 29, 2013

Radiation Therapy Oncology Group/Loews Philadelphia Hotel/June 13 - 16, 2013

Self Storage Association/Mariott Downtown/April 23 - 25, 2013

Society for Industrial and Organizational Psychology Inc./Philadelphia Marriott Downtown/April 23 - 25, 2015

Society for Pediatric Research/April 25 - 28, 2020

Society for Pediatric Research/May 2 - 5, 2020

Society for Research in Child Development/March 19 - 21, 2015

Society for Research in Child Development/March 26 - 28, 2015

Society for Research on Nicotine and Tobacco/Philadelphia Marriott Hotel/Feb. 23 - 28, 2015

Society for the History of Authorship, Reading and Publishing/University of Pennsylvania/July 18 - 21, 2013

Society of Behavioral Medicine/Philadelphia Marriott Downtown/April 23 - 26, 2014

Society of Nuclear Medicine/June 23 - 27, 2018

Society of Rheology/CBD/Oct. 5 - 9, 2014

United States Lacrosse/Philadelphia Courtyard Marriott/Jan. 11 - 13, 2013

United States Lacrosse/Philadelphia Courtyard Marriott/Jan. 10 - 12, 2014

Women's Transportation Seminar (WTS International)/May 15 - 17, 2013

WorldatWork/Pennsylvania Convention Center/April 29 - May 1, 2013

Pittsburgh

The Acoustical Society of America/May 18 - 22, 2015

American Association of Immunologists/May 2 - 6, 2014

American Association of Petroleum Geologists/David L. Lawrence Convention Center/May 19 - 22, 2013

American Ceramics Society/David L. Lawrence Convention Center/Oct. 12 - 16, 2014

American Gas Association/Omni William Penn Hotel/May 20 - 23, 2014

American Musicological Society/Wyndham Grand Pittsburgh Downtown/Nov. 7 - 10, 2013

American Society for Eighteenth-Century Studies/March 29 - April 3, 2016

American Therapeutic Recreation Association/Sheraton Station Square Hotel/Sept. 29 - Oct. 2, 2013

Association for Applied and Clinical Sociology/DoubleTree by Hilton Hotel and Suites Pittsburgh Downtown/Oct. 9 - 11, 2014

Association for Iron and Steel Technology/David L. Lawrence Convention Center/May 6 - 9, 2013/over 100 exhibitors

Association for Iron and Steel Technology/Sheraton Station Square Hotel/June 9 - 11, 2013

Association of Children's Museums/April 30 - May 2, 2013

Association of Departments of Foreign Languages/Carnegie Mellon University and University of Pittsburgh/June 6 - 9, 2013

Catholic Theological Society of America/DoubleTree by Hilton Hotel and Suites Pittsburgh Downtown/June 5 - 8, 2014

Communications Workers of America/April 22 - 23, 2013

Council for Advancement and Support of Education/Renaissance Pittsburgh Hotel/June 10 - 12, 2013

Epsilon Sigma Phi/Sept. 15 - 20, 2013

Fellowship of United Methodists in Music and Worship Arts/July 15 - 18, 2013

IEEE Power Electronics Society/Sept. 15 - 18, 2014

NAMTA - National Art Materials Trade Association/April 30 - May 2, 2014

National Association for Research in Science Teaching/March 30 - April 2, 2015

National Association of Catholic Chaplains/Sheraton Station Square Hotel/April 13 - 16, 2013

National Association of County Agricultural Agents/Sept. 15 - 20, 2013

National Association of Jewelry Appraisers/Aug. 10 - 14, 2013

National Catholic Educational Exhibitors/April 22 - 24, 2014

National Organization of Black Law Enforcement Executives/David L. Lawrence Convention Center/Aug. 3 - 7, 2013

National Organization of Nurse Practitioner Faculties/Wyndham Grand Pittsburgh Downtown/April 11 - 14, 2013

National Real Estate Investors Association/Sheraton Station Square Hotel/June 20, 2013

Pipe Fabrication Institute/Fairmont Pittsburgh/May 29 - June 4, 2013

Society for College and University Planning/July 12 - 16, 2014

Society for Ethnomusicology/University of Pittsburgh/Nov. 13 - 16, 2014

Society for Invertebrate Pathology/Sheraton Hotel at Station Square/Aug. 11 - 15, 2013

Society for Nutrition Education and Behavior/July 25 - 28, 2015

Technology and Maintenance Council of American Trucking Associations/David L. Lawrence Convention Center/Sept. 10 - 13, 2013

The Wildlife Society/Oct. 25 - 30, 2014

Shippensburg

National Speleological Society/Aug. 5 - 9, 2013

State College

Architectural Engineering Institute/Pennsylvania State University/April 3 - 5, 2013

University Park

American Society for Virology/Pennsylvania State University/July 20 - 24, 2013

Valley Forge

American Criminal Justice Association Lambda Alpha Epsilon/Radisson Hotel Valley Forge/April 21 - 26, 2013

West Chester

Eastern Apicultural Society of North America/West Chester University of Pennsylvania/Aug. 5 - 9, 2013

Williamsburg

American College of Laboratory Animal Medicine/Williamsburg Lodge/April 14 - 17, 2013

PUERTO RICO

Fajardo

National Academy of Neuropsychology/El Conquistador Resort, The Waldorf Astoria Collection/Nov. 12 - 16, 2014

Ponce

International Council for Small Business/June 20 - 23, 2013

Rio Grande

American College of Psychiatrists/Rio Mar Beach Resort and Spa/Feb. 17 - 21, 2016

American College of Veterinary Ophthalmologists/Rio Mar Beach Resort and Spa/Nov. 4 - 9, 2013/51-100 exhibitors

American Sports Builders Association/Rio Mar Beach Resort and Spa/Feb. 22 - 25, 2013

North American Neuro-Ophthalmology Society/Rio Mar Beach Resort and Spa/March 1 - 6, 2014

Power-Motion Technology Representatives Association/Rio Mar Beach Resort and Spa/April 17 - 20, 2013

Tire Industry Association/Gran Melia Golf Resort/Feb. 20 - 23, 2013

San Juan

American Association of Physician Specialists/Conrad San Juan Condado Plaza/June 24 - 28, 2013

American College of Medical Toxicology/March 17, 2013

American Society of Primatologists/June 18 - 22, 2013

American Thyroid Association/Sheraton Puerto Rico Hotel and Casino/Oct. 16 - 20, 2013

Caribbean Hotel and Tourism Association/Sheraton Puerto Rico Hotel and Casino/May 7 - 9, 2013

Council of State Governments/Dec. 6 - 9, 2013

Federal Bar Association/Caribe Hilton San Juan/Sept. 26 - 28, 2013

Federation of Defense and Corporate Counsel/Waldorf Astoria El Conquistador/Feb. 14 - March 7, 2015

Institute of Industrial Engineers/Caribe Hilton San Juan/May 18 - 22, 2013

International Association for Computer Information Systems/San Juan Marriott Resort and Stellaris Casino/Oct. 2 - 5, 2013

International Communication Association/May 21 - 25, 2015

National Association for Surface Finishing/InterContinental Hotel/March 11 - 15, 2013

Society for Excellence in Eyecare/The Ritz-Carlton San Juan/Feb. 8 - 12, 2013

Society for Obstetric Anesthesia and Perinatology/Caribe Hilton San Juan/April 24 - 28, 2013/11-25 exhibitors

Society for Critical Care Medicine/Puerto Rico Convention Center/Jan. 19 - 23, 2013

RHODE ISLAND

Newport

Democratic Attorneys General Association/May 9 - 10, 2013

Wilson Ornithological Society/Salve Regina University/May 29 - June 1, 2014

Providence

The Acoustical Society of America/May 5 - 9, 2014

American Association of Cereal Chemists International/Oct. 5 - 8, 2014/1000 attendees/11-25 exhibitors

American Association of Teachers of French/July 11 - 14, 2013

American Folklore Society/Westin Providence/Oct. 16 - 19, 2013

American Hockey League/Dunkin Donuts Center Providence/Jan. 27 - 28, 2013

American Society of Plant Biologists/July 20 - 24, 2013

American String Teachers Association/Feb. 27 - March 2, 2013/11-25 exhibitors

Association of Paroling Authorities International/Renaissance Providence Downtown Hotel/May 19 - 22, 2013

Association of State Dam Safety Officials/Rhode Island Convention Center/Sept. 8 - 12, 2013

Council of Engineering and Scientific Society Executives/July 16 - 19, 2013

Council of Engineering and Scientific Society Executives/Westin Providence/July 16 - 18, 2013

Environmental Design Research Association/The Westin Providence Hotel/May 29 - June 1, 2014

International Association for Identification/Aug. 4 - 10, 2013

National Society for Histotechnology/Sept. 20 - 26, 2013

North American Association of State and Provincial Lotteries/The Westin Providence Hotel/Oct. 1 - 4, 2013

Society for In Vitro Biology/June 15 - 19, 2013

Society of Vacuum Coaters/Rhode Island College/April 20 - 25, 2013

Visual Resources Association/Providence Biltmore/April 3 - 6, 2013

SOUTH CAROLINA

Charleston

American Association of Meat Processors/Embassy Suites Hotel and Convention Center/July 18 - 20, 2013/800 attendees

American Association of Neuropathologists/Charleston Place Hotel/June 20 - 23, 2013

American Osteopathic College of Anesthesiologists/Charleston Place Hotel/Jan. 18 - 20, 2013

American Sheep Industry Association/Charleston Marriott/Jan. 22 - 25, 2014

American Society for Adolescent Psychiatry/Medical University Of South Carolina/March 23 - 24, 2013

American Society for Cytotechnology/Charleston Marriott/April 25 - 27, 2014

Association of Professors of Medicine/Charleston Place Hotel/Feb. 27 - March 2, 2013

Association of Zoos and Aquariums/April 7 - 12, 2013/11-25 exhibitors

Commission on Accreditation for Law Enforcement Agencies Incorporation/March 20 - 23, 2013

Commission on Accreditation of Allied Health Education Programs/Francis Marion Hotel/April 14 - 15, 2013

Community Development Society/Francis Marion Hotel/July 20 - 24, 2013

Hardwood Manufacturers Association/Charleston Place Hotel/March 11 - 13, 2013

Independent Hardee's Franchisee Association/Embassy Suites Hotel Airport and Convention Center/Oct. 8 - 10, 2013

International Academy of Oral Medicine and Toxicology/Wild Dunes Resort/March 14 - 16, 2013

National Association of Foreign Trade Zones/DoubleTree by Hilton/May 12 - 13, 2013

National Association of State Technology Directors/Charleston Marriott/Aug. 26 - 30, 2013

National Conference on Weights and Measures/Jan. 27 - 30, 2013

Web Sling and Tie down Association/DoubleTree by Hilton Hotel and Suites Charleston-Historic District/May 5 - 8, 2013

Columbia

National Council for History Education/Westwood High School/Jan. 25 - 26, 2013

Greenville

American Association of Textile Chemists and Colorists/Hyatt Regency Greenville/April 9 - 11, 2013

Association for Financial Counseling and Planning Education/Nov. 20 - 22, 2013

National Association of Development Organizations/Hyatt Regency Greenville/April 23 - 25, 2013

National Association of Development Organizations/Hyatt Regency Greenville/April 24 - 26, 2013

North American Council of Automotive Teachers/July 21 - 25, 2014

Society for Experimental Mechanics, Inc./Hyatt Regency Greenville/June 2 - 4, 2014

Hilton Head Island

Bearing Specialist Association/Westin Hilton Head Island Resort and Spa/May 3 - 7, 2013

Book Manufacturers' Institute/The Westin Hilton Head Island Resort and Spa/April 28 - 30, 2013

Executive Women's Golf Association/Westin Hilton Head Island Resort and Spa/May 8 - 11, 2013

International Health, Racquet and Sportsclub Association/Westin Hilton Head Island Resort and Spa/March 18 - 22, 2013/6000 attendees/over 100 exhibitors

The New Media Consortium/Hilton Head/June 4 - 7, 2013

Isle of Palms

ASFE/The Geoprofessional Business Association/Wild Dunes Resort/April 25 - 27, 2013

Concrete Reinforcing Steel Institute/Wild Dunes Resort/April 26 - 29, 2014

Kiawah Island

American Society for Automation in Pharmacy/Sanctuary Hotel/Jan. 24 - 26, 2013

Society of Independent Show Organizers/Sacntuary Kiawah Island Golf Resort/
April 8 - 11, 2013

Myrtle Beach

American School Health Association/Hilton Myrtle Beach Resort/Oct. 9 - 12,
2013

Association of Baccalaureate Social Work Program Directors/Hilton and
Embassy Suites Resort/March 6 - 10, 2013

Composite Can and Tube Institute/Myrtle Beach Marriott at Grande Dunes/
March 20 - 21, 2013

International Association for Healthcare Security and Safety/Hilton/May 5 - 9,
2013

Portable Sanitation Association International/Sheraton Myrtle Beach
Convention Center Hotel/Oct. 29 - Nov. 2, 2013/over 100 exhibitors

North Charleston

American Society for Indexing/Charleston Convention Center/April 30 - May 3,
2014

American Society for Nondestructive Testing/Charleston Convention Center/
Oct. 27 - 30, 2014

National Association of Trailer Manufacturers/Charleston Area Convention
Center/Feb. 20 - 23, 2013/26-50 exhibitors

National Weather Association/Charleston Convention Center/Oct. 12 - 17,
2013

Pi Gamma Mu/Crowne Plaza Charleston Airport - Convention Center/Oct. 16
- 18, 2014

SOUTH DAKOTA

Deadwood

Association of American State Geologists/June 9 - 13, 2013

Pierre

R-Calf/Best Western Ramkota Pierre Hotel/Aug. 2 - 3, 2013

Rapid City

National Indian Education Association/Oct. 29 - Nov. 3, 2013

United States Wheat Associates, Inc./Holiday Inn Rapid City-Rushmore Plaza/
June 29 - July 1, 2013

Sioux Falls

Enlisted Association of the National Guard of the United States/Sioux Falls
Convention Center/Aug. 18 - 21, 2013

National Association of County Agricultural Agents/July 12 - 16, 2015

North American Elk Breeders Association/Best Western Plus Ramkota Hotel/
Aug. 1 - 3, 2013

TENNESSEE

Chattanooga

American Society of Ichthyologists and Herpetologists/July 30 - Aug. 3, 2014

American Technical Education Association/Chattanooga Convention Center/
March 20 - 21, 2013/51-100 exhibitors

American Therapeutic Recreation Association/Chattanooga Marriott at the
Convention Center/March 10 - 13, 2013

The Herpetologists' League/July 30 - Aug. 3, 2014

Knoxville

American Association of Physical Anthropologists/April 9 - 13, 2013

Human Biology Association/April 8 - 9, 2013

Human Biology Association/Hilton Knoxville/April 10 - 11, 2013

Medieval Academy of America/University of Tennessee/April 4 - 6, 2013

National Association of RV Parks and Campgrounds/Knoxville Convention
Center/Nov. 6 - 8, 2013

National Council of Writing Program Administrators/July 16 - 23, 2017

Memphis

American Classical League/University of Memphis/June 27 - 29, 2013

American Physical Therapy Association - Private Practice Section/Feb. 21 - 23,
2013

American Society for Nondestructive Testing/Peabody Memphis/March 18 -
21, 2013

American Society of Preventive Oncology/Memphis Peabody Hotel/March 9 -
13, 2013

Commercial Real Estate Women Network/Memphis Peabody Hotel/Jan. 31 -
Feb. 1, 2013

International Horn Society/July 29 - Aug. 3, 2013

International Order of the Golden Rule/The Peabody Memphis/April 25 - 28,
2013

Investment Recovery Association/March 24 - 27, 2013

National Association of Legal Investigators/The Peabody Memphis/Feb. 14 -
16, 2013

National Cotton Council of America/Peabody Memphis/Feb. 7 - 11, 2013

National Council for Geographic Education/Peabody Memphis/July 31 - Aug.
3, 2014

National Frame Building Association/Memphis Cook Convention Center/Feb.
20 - 22, 2013

National Telecommunications Cooperative Association/Peabody Memphis/
Aug. 26 - 29, 2013

Physician Assistant Education Association/Peabody Memphis/Oct. 14 - 19,
2013

Murfreesboro

Audio Engineering Society/Middle Tennessee State University/July 25 - 27,
2013

Nashville

Academy of General Dentistry/June 23 - 30, 2013

Academy of Medical-Surgical Nurses/Gaylord Opryland Resort and Convention
Center/Sept. 25 - 29, 2013/1000 attendees/11-25 exhibitors

Aircraft Electronics Association/March 12 - 15, 2014

Alliance of Area Business Publications/Hilton Nashville Downtown/June 20 -
22, 2013

Ambulatory Surgery Center Association/Gaylord Opryland Resort and
Convention Center/May 14 - 17, 2014/2500 attendees

American Animal Hospital Association/March 20 - 23, 2014

American Association of Cardiovascular and Pulmonary Rehabilitation/Oct. 3
- 5, 2013

American Association of Clinical Endocrinologists/May 13 - 17, 2015

American Association of Colleges of Nursing/Fairmont Washington/March 15
- 16, 2013

American Association of Equine Practitioners/Dec. 7 - 11, 2013

American Baseball Coaches Association/Gaylord Opryland Hotel and
Convention Center Nashville, Tennessee/Jan. 7 - 10, 2016

American Board of Vocational Experts/The Doubletree Hotel Nashville
Downtown/March 28 - 30, 2014

American Bus Association/Nashville Convention Center/Jan. 11 - 15, 2014

American Bus Association/Jan. 17 - 21, 2014

American College of Medical Genetics/March 25 - 29, 2014

American College of Nurse-Midwives/May 30 - June 4, 2013

American College of Veterinary Internal Medicine/June 4 - 7, 2014

American College of Veterinary Surgeons/Gaylord Opryland Resort and
Convention Center/Nov. 5 - 7, 2015

American Collegiate Retailing Association/The Gaylord Opryland/March 20 -
23, 2013

American Farm Bureau Federation/Opryland Hotel/Jan. 13 - 16, 2013

American Fire Sprinkler Association/Gaylord Hotels Resorts and Convention
Centers-Nashville/Sept. 17 - 21, 2014

American Football Coaches Association/Gaylord Opryland Resort and
Convention Center/Jan. 6 - 9, 2013

American Gas Association/Omni Hotel/Sept. 15 - 16, 2016

American Gas Association/The Gaylord Opryland/April 30 - May 3, 2019

American Health Care Association/Oct. 16 - 19, 2016

American Mathematical Association of Two Year Colleges/Nov. 13 - 16, 2014

American Mathematical Association of Two Year Colleges/Nov. 20 - 23, 2014

American Medical Directors Association/Feb. 27 - March 2, 2014

American Public Power Association/Gaylord Hotels Resorts and Convention
Centers-Nashville/June 15 - 19, 2013

American Society of Association Executives-The Center for Association
Leadership/Aug. 9 - 12, 2014

American Specialty Toy Retailing Association/June 16 - 19, 2013

American Traffic Safety Service Association/Loews Vanderbilt Hotel, Nashville/
Aug. 14 - 16, 2013

AscdiNatd/March 6 - 8, 2013

Associated Builders and Contractors/Loews Vanderbilt Hotel Nashville/Aug. 6
- 8, 2014

Association for Behavioral and Cognitive Therapies/Nov. 21 - 24, 2013

Association for Middle Level Education/Nov. 6 - 8, 2014

Association for Vascular Access/Gaylord OprylandResort and Convention
Center/Sept. 20, 2013

Association of Academic Physiatrists/Renaissance Nashville Hotel and
Convention Center/Feb. 25 - March 1, 2014

Association of Career and Technical Education/Nov. 20 - 22, 2014

Association of College and Research Libraries/March 29 - April 1, 2017

Association of Fraternity Advisors/Omni Nashville Hotel/Dec. 3 - 7, 2014

Association of Legal Administrators/Music City Center/May 17 - 20, 2015

Association of Pediatric Program Directors/Renaissance Nashville Hotel and
Nashville Convention Center/April 9 - 13, 2013

Association of Schools of Allied Health Professions/Hilton Nashville
Downtown/Oct. 21 - 22, 2013

Association of Schools of Allied Health Professions/Hilton Nashville
Downtown/Oct. 23 - 24, 2013

Association of Schools of Allied Health Professions/Hilton Nashville
Downtown/Oct. 23 - 25, 2013

Association of Service and Computer Dealers International/Renaissance
Nashville Hotel/March 6 - 8, 2013

Association of Water Technologies/Omni Nashville Hotel and Music Center/
Sept. 9 - 12, 2015

Association of Women's Health, Obstetric and Neonatal Nurses/June 15 - 19,
2013/11-25 exhibitors

Building Owners and Managers Association International/Omni Nashville
Hotel/April 30 - May 2, 2014

College of American Pathologists/The Gaylord Opryland/Oct. 4 - 7, 2015/1400
attendees/over 100 exhibitors

Country Radio Broadcasters, Inc./Nashville Convention Center/Feb. 27 - March
1, 2013

CPCU Society/Oct. 7 - 10, 2017

Emergency Nurses Association/Gaylord Hotels Resorts and Convention
Centers-Nashville/Sept. 17 - 21, 2013

EUCG, Inc./Hilton Nashville Downtown/April 14 - 17, 2013

Evangelical Press Association/May 1 - 3, 2013

Family, Career and Community Leaders of America/July 7 - 11, 2013

Family, Career and Community Leaders of America/July 2 - 6, 2017

Financial Management Association International/Opryland Hotel/Oct. 15 - 18,
2014

Foster Family-Based Treatment Association/Gaylord Opryland Resort and
Convention Center/July 28 - 31, 2013

Future Business Leaders of America - Phi Beta Lambda/June 24 - 27, 2014

Future Business Leaders of America - Phi Beta Lambda/June 29 - July 2, 2014

GAMA International/Gaylord OprylandResort and Convention Center/March
16 - 19, 2014

Governors' Highway Safety Association/Omni Nashville Hotel/Aug. 30 - Sept.
2, 2015

Health Occupations Students of America/Gaylord Opryland Hotel/June 26 -
30, 2013

Health Occupations Students of America/Gaylord Opryland Hotel/June 22 -
25, 2016

Hosa/Gaylord Opryland Hotel and Convention Center Nashville, Tennessee/
June 26 - 30, 2013

Hosa/Gaylord Opryland Hotel and Convention Center Nashville, Tennessee/
June 22 - 25, 2016

Institute of Navigation/Nashville Convention Center/Sept. 16 - 20, 2013

International Association of Campus Law Enforcement Administrators/June 29
- July 3, 2015

International Parking Institute/May 22 - 25, 2016

LeadingAge (American Association of Homes and Services for the Aging)/Oct.
19 - 22, 2014

Metal Treating Institute/Renaissance Nashville Hotel/Oct. 7 - 8, 2014

Metal Treating Institute/Renaissance Nashville Hotel/Oct. 4 - 5, 2016

National Association for Campus Activities/Nashville Convention Center/Feb. 16 - 20, 2013/2000 attendees

National Association for Healthcare Quality/Music City Convention Center, Omni Hotel and Resort/Sept. 7 - 10, 2013

National Association for Information Destruction, Inc./The Gaylord Opryland/March 22 - 24, 2013

National Association of Agricultural Educators/Nov. 18 - 22, 2014

National Association of Black Accountants, Inc./Gaylord Opryland Resort and Convention Center/June 5 - 8, 2013

National Association of Church Business Administration/Gaylord Opryland Hotel and Convention Center Nashville, Tennessee/July 14 - 18, 2014

National Association of College and University Business Officers/July 18 - 21, 2015

National Association of Neonatal Nurses/Nashville Convention Center/Oct. 2 - 5, 2013

National Association of Police Organizations/Millennium Maxwell House Hotel/July 20 - 24, 2013

National Association of State Chief Information Officers/Omni Nashville Hotel/Sept. 28 - Oct. 1, 2014

National Association of Steel Pipe Distributors/Hilton Nashville Downtown/Sept. 19 - 21, 2013

National Association of Student Financial Aid Administrators/June 29 - July 2, 2014

National Association of Women in Construction/Sept. 2 - 5, 2015

National Cancer Registrars Association/May 14 - 17, 2014/26-50 exhibitors

National Cattlemen's Beef Association/Gaylord Hotels Resorts and Convention Centers-Nashville/Feb. 4 - 7, 2014/6000 attendees

National Cattlemen's Beef Association/Feb. 1 - 4, 2017

National Conference of Insurance Legislators/Hilton Nashville Downtown/Nov. 21 - 24, 2013

National Council of Postal Credit Unions/Sheraton Nashville Downtown Hotel/April 14 - 16, 2013

National Council of State Housing Agencies/Omni Nashville Hotel/Sept. 26 - 29, 2015

National Council on Public History/Sheraton Nashville Downtown Hotel/April 15 - 18, 2015

National Court Reporters Association/Gaylord Opryland Resort and Convention Center/Aug. 8 - 11, 2013

National Federation Coaches Association/Gaylord Opryland Hotel and Convention Center Nashville, Tennessee/Dec. 9 - 13, 2016

National Guard Association of the U.S./Sept. 10 - 13, 2015

National Hospice & Palliative Care Organization/Gaylord Opryland Resort and Convention Center/Oct. 27 - 29, 2014

National Interscholastic Athletic Administrators Association/Gaylord Hotels Resorts and Convention Centers-Nashville/Dec. 9 - 15, 2016

National Recreation and Parks Association/Sept. 14 - 16, 2021/7000 attendees/over 100 exhibitors

National Religious Broadcasters/Gaylord Hotels Resorts and Convention Centers-Nashville/March 2, 2013

National Religious Broadcasters/Omni Nashville Hotel/March 2 - 5, 2013

National Religious Broadcasters/Gaylord Hotels Resorts and Convention Centers-Nashville/Feb. 22, 2014

National Religious Broadcasters/Gaylord Hotels Resorts and Convention Centers-Nashville/Feb. 22 - 25, 2014

National Religious Broadcasters/Gaylord Hotels Resorts and Convention Centers-Nashville/Feb. 21, 2015

National Religious Broadcasters/Gaylord Hotels Resorts and Convention Centers-Nashville/Feb. 21 - 25, 2015

National Shellfisheries Association/Renaissance Nashville Hotel/Feb. 21 - 25, 2013

National Strength and Conditioning Association/Renaissance Nashville Hotel/Jan. 4 - 5, 2013/600 attendees

NCSL International/Gaylord Hotels Resorts and Convention Centers-Nashville/July 14 - 18, 2013/51-100 exhibitors

NORA: Association of Responsible Recyclers/June 19 - 21, 2013

Paperboard Packaging Council/April 3 - 5, 2013

Petroleum Packaging Council/Nashville Marriott, Vanderbilt University/Aug. 18 - 20, 2013

Precast/Prestressed Concrete Institute/Gaylord Hotels Resorts and Convention Centers-Nashville/Sept. 19 - 23, 2015

Professional Photographers of America/Gaylord OprylandResort and Convention Center/Feb. 1 - 3, 2015

Professional Photographers of America/Gaylord OprylandResort and Convention Center/Jan. 31 - Feb. 2, 2016

Rheumatology Nurses Society/Gaylord Opryland Resort and Convention Center/Aug. 1 - 3, 2013

Scaffold Industry Association/July 21 - 24, 2013

Society of American Gastrointestinal and Endoscopic Surgeons/Gaylord Hotels Resorts and Convention Centers-Nashville/April 15 - 18, 2015

Society of Environmental Toxicology and Chemistry/Gaylord Opryland Hotel and Convention Center Nashville, Tennessee/Nov. 17 - 21, 2013

Society of Pediatric Nurses/Gaylord Opryland Resort and Convention Center/April 11 - 14, 2013

Society of Teachers of Family Medicine/Opryland Resort/Jan. 30 - Feb. 2, 2014

Society of Urologic Nurses and Associates/Omni Hotel/Feb. 26 - 28, 2015

Technology and Maintenance Council of American Trucking Associations/Opryland Hotel/March 11 - 14, 2013

Vacation Rental Managers Association/Gaylord Opryland Resort and Convention Center/Oct. 19 - 23, 2013

Voluntary Protection Programs Participants' Association, Inc./Gaylord Hotels Resorts and Convention Centers-Nashville/Aug. 26 - 29, 2013

Water Environment Federation/Renaissance Hotel/May 6 - 9, 2013

Women in Aviation International/Gaylord Opryland Resort and Convention Center/March 14 - 16, 2013

World Aquaculture Society/Feb. 21 - 25, 2013/11-25 exhibitors

The Wound, Ostomy and Continence Nurses Society/June 21 - 25, 2014

TEXAS

Addison

International Society for Neuronal Regulation/Intercontinental Dallas Hotel/Sept. 18 - 22, 2013

Amarillo

American Jersey Cattle Association/National All-Jersey Inc./Ambassador Hotel/June 24 - 29, 2013

Antonio

American College of Psychiatrists/Grand Hyatt San Antonio/Feb. 19 - 23, 2014

American Fuel & Petrochemical Manufacturers/Grand Hyatt San Antonio/May 14 - 15, 2014

Gases and Welding Distributors Association/Grand Hyatt San Antonio/April 13 - 16, 2013

Independent Insurance Agents & Brokers of America, Inc./Grand Hyatt San Antonio/Sept. 25 - 29, 2013

Middle East Studies Association of North America/Grand Hyatt San Antonio/Nov. 15 - 18, 2018

National Association of College Auxiliary Services/Grand Hyatt San Antonio/Nov. 1 - 4, 2015/51-100 exhibitors

Society of Thoracic Radiology/Grand Hyatt San Antonio/March 16 - 19, 2014

Austin

American Academy of Medical Hypnoanalysts/Hotel Allandale/April 24 - 28, 2013

American Academy of Orthopaedic Surgeons/Oct. 17 - 20, 2013

American Animal Hospital Association/March 31 - April 3, 2016

American Association for Laboratory Animal Science/Oct. 15 - 19, 2017

American Association for Public Opinion Research/Hilton Austin/May 12 - 15, 2016

American Association of Colleges of Nursing/Omni Austin Hotel Downtown/April 17 - 19, 2013

American Association of Directors of Psychiatric Residency Training/Hilton Austin/March 2 - 5, 2016

American Association of Physicists in Medicine/July 20 - 24, 2014

American Association of Suicidology/Hilton Austin/April 24 - 27, 2013

American Astronomical Society/Jan. 10 - 14, 2016

American Astronomical Society/Jan. 6 - 10, 2020

American College of Chest Physicians/Oct. 25 - 30, 2014

American College of Clinical Pharmacy/Austin Convention Center/Oct. 12 - 15, 2014

American Correctional Association/Jan. 9 - 14, 2015

American Fraternal Alliance/Hilton Austin/Sept. 4 - 6, 2014

American Jail Association/Hilton Austin/May 22 - 25, 2016

American Lighting Association/Hyatt Regency Lost Pines Resort and Spa/Sept. 22 - 24, 2013

American Meteorological Society/Jan. 6 - 10, 2013

American Meteorological Society/Jan. 7 - 11, 2018

American Microscopical Society/Jan. 3 - 7, 2014

American Phytopathological Society/Aug. 10 - 14, 2013

American Society for Enology and Viticulture/Hyatt Regency Austin/June 23 - 27, 2014

American Telemedicine Association/May 5 - 7, 2013

Associated Collegiate Press/Hilton, Hotel/Oct. 28 - Nov. 1, 2015

Association of Healthcare Internal Auditors/Sept. 21 - 24, 2014

Association of Waldorf Schools of North America/June 24 - 27, 2013

Board of Specialty Society/Oct. 16 - 20, 2013

Child Neurology Society/Oct. 30 - Nov. 2, 2013

College Media Association/Oct. 28 - 31, 2015

Common - A Users Group/Hilton Austin/April 7 - 10, 2013

Copyright Society of the U.S.A./Omni Hotel & Resorts Downtown Austin/Feb. 14 - 16, 2013

Emdr International Association/Renaissance Austin Hotel/Sept. 26 - 29, 2013

Entomological Society of America/Austin Convention Center/Nov. 17 - 20, 2013/2500 attendees/51-100 exhibitors

Forest Products Society/June 9 - 11, 2013

Healthcare Convention and Exhibitors Association/Austin Convention Center/June 22 - 25, 2013

Healthcare Convention and Exhibitors Association/Hilton Hotel and Austin Convention Center/June 22 - 25, 2013

Human Factors and Ergonomics Society/JW Marriott/Oct. 9 - 13, 2017

Human Factors Society/JW Marriott/Oct. 9 - 13, 2017

International Bridge, Tunnel and Turnpike Association/Hilton Austin/Sept. 14 - 17, 2014

Juice Products Association/Four Seasons Hotel Austin/Oct. 15 - 16, 2013

Master Brewers Association of the Americas/Hilton Austin/Oct. 23 - 26, 2013

Medical Library Association/May 15 - 20, 2015

Messenger Courier Association of the Americas/Hyatt Regency Lost Pines Resort and Spa/Sept. 18 - 20, 2013

Mycological Society of America/Aug. 10 - 14, 2013

National Alliance for Advanced Transportation Batteries/Renaissance Austin Hotel/Jan. 16 - 18, 2013

National Association for Environmental Management/Hilton Austin/Oct. 22 - 24, 2014

National Association of Container Distributors/Barton Creek Resort & Spa/April 16 - 20, 2013

National Association of Federal Credit Unions/Sheraton Austin Hotel at the Capitol/Feb. 26 - 28, 2013

National Association of State Directors of Teacher Education and Certification/Omni Austin Hotel Downtown/June 6 - 9, 2013

National Business Aviation Association/Feb. 12 - 13, 2013

National Community Pharmacists Association/Austin Convention Center/Oct. 18 - 22, 2014

National Funeral Directors Association/Oct. 20 - 23, 2013

National Notary Association/Renaissance Austin Hotel/June 2 - 5, 2013

National Rural Economic Developers Association/Driskill Hotel/July 17 - 19, 2013

National Society for Histotechnology/Aug. 21 - 27, 2014

National Tank Truck Carriers/Hilton Austin/April 28 - 30, 2013

National Telecommunications Cooperative Association/Hyatt Regency Lost Pines Resort and Spa/March 24 - 26, 2013

North American Association of Central Cancer Registries/June 8 - 14, 2013

North American Society for Sport Management/Hilton Austin/May 28 - June 1, 2013

Plumbing Manufacturers Institute/April 7 - 10, 2013
Regulatory Affairs Professionals Society/Sept. 27 - Oct. 1, 2014
Religion Newswriters Association/Sept. 26 - 28, 2013
Selected Independent Funeral Homes/Omni Austin Hotel Downtown/Oct. 16 - 19, 2013
The Society for Adolescent Medicine/March 23 - 26, 2014
Society for American Archaeology/April 23 - 27, 2014
Society for Anthropology in Community Colleges/April 10 - 13, 2013
Society for Integrative and Comparative Biology/Jan. 3 - 7, 2014
Society for Research on Adolescence/March 20 - 22, 2014
Society of Fire Protection Engineers/Omni Hotel & Resorts Downtown Austin/Oct. 27 - Nov. 1, 2013
United States Cutting Tool Institute/The Driskill/Oct. 12 - 14, 2013

Colonnade

National Association for Chicana and Chicano Studies/Omni San Antonio Hotel/March 20 - 23, 2013

Corpus Christi

Cooling Technology Institute/Omni Corpus Christi Hotel-Bayfront Tower/Feb. 3 - 7, 2013
Poultry Science Association/Omni Corpus Christi Hotel Bayfront Tower/July 14 - 17, 2014
Society for Range Management/Jan. 29 - Feb. 6, 2016

Dallas

Academy of Criminal Justice Sciences/Sheraton Dallas/March 19 - 23, 2013
ACUTA - The Association for Information Communications Technology Professionals in Higher Education/Hyatt Regency Dallas at Reunion/March 30 - April 2, 2014
Aircraft Electronics Association/April 8 - 11, 2015
Ambulatory Surgery Center Association/Gaylord Texan Hotel and Convention Center-Dallas/May 3 - 7, 2017/2500 attendees
American Association for Applied Linguistics/Sheraton Dallas Hotel/March 16 - 19, 2013
American Association of Feline Practitioners/The Sheraton Dallas/Sept. 26 - 29, 2013
American Association of Hip and Knee Surgeons/Sheraton Dallas/Nov. 8 - 10, 2013
American Association of Hip and Knee Surgeons/Nov. 7 - 9, 2014
American Association of Hip and Knee Surgeons/Nov. 6 - 8, 2015
American Association of Hip and Knee Surgeons/Nov. 4 - 6, 2016
American Association of Managing General Agents/Nov. 11 - 13, 2015
American Association of Swine Veterinarians/March 1 - 4, 2014/900 attendees/51-100 exhibitors
American Bar Association/Feb. 6 - 12, 2013
American Baseball Coaches Association/Hilton Anatole Dallas/Jan. 2 - 5, 2014/6000 attendees/over 100 exhibitors
American Camp Association/Hyatt Regency Dallas at Reunion/Feb. 12 - 15, 2013/1-10 exhibitors
American Chemical Society/March 16 - 20, 2014
American Choral Directors Association/March 13 - 16, 2013
American College of Veterinary Radiology/April 13, 2013
American Jail Association/Hilton Anatole Dallas/April 27 - 30, 2014/1000 attendees
American Jail Association/April 22 - 25, 2018
American Medical Society for Sports Medicine/Sheraton Dallas/April 16 - 20, 2016
American Montessori Society/Hilton Anatole Dallas/March 27 - 30, 2014
American Society for Blood and Marrow Transplantation/Feb. 26 - March 2, 2014
American Society for Training and Development/May 19 - 22, 2013/9000 attendees
American Society of Heating, Refrigerating and Air Conditioning Engineers (ASHRAE)/Headquarter Hotel/Jan. 26 - 30, 2013
The Association for Manufacturing Excellence/Oct. 24 - 28, 2016
The Association for Nursing Professional Development/Dallas Convention Center/July 16 - 20, 2013
Association for Vascular Access/Gaylord Texan Hotel and Convention Center-Dallas/Sept. 26 - 29, 2015
Association of Analytical Communities International/Sheraton Dallas Hotel/Sept. 18 - 21, 2016
Association of Camp Nurses/Hyatt Regency Dallas/Feb. 11 - 13, 2013
Association of Energy Services Professionals, International/Westin Galleria Dallas/April 29 - May 1, 2013
Association of Government Accountants/Gaylord Texan Hotel and Convention Center-Dallas/July 14 - 17, 2013
Automotive Aftermarket Industry Association/Omni Hotel/Sept. 9 - 11, 2013
Competitive Telecommunications Association/Gaylord Texan Hotel and Convention Center-Dallas/Oct. 5 - 8, 2014
Council on Social Work Education/Hilton Anatole Dallas/Oct. 23 - Nov. 3, 2013
Division 1-A Athletic Directors Association/Jan. 11 - 14, 2017
Express Carriers Association/April 9, 2013
Express Carriers Association/Intercontinental Dallas/April 9 - 11, 2013
Gas Processors Association/Omni Dallas Hotel/April 13 - 16, 2014/1500 attendees
Gas Processors Suppliers Association/Omni Dallas Hotel/April 13 - 16, 2014
Heating, Airconditioning and Refrigeration Distributors International/Hyatt Regency Dallas/Jan. 27, 2013
Hospitality Financial and Technology Professionals/Hilton Anatole/Oct. 16 - 19, 2013
International Anti-Counterfeiting Coalition/May 1 - 3, 2013
International Food Service Executives' Association/Hyatt Regency Dallas at Reunion/April 11 - 14, 2013
International Trademark Association/Dallas Convention Center/May 4 - 8, 2013
Investment Program Association/The Fairmont/Nov. 5 - 7, 2013
LeadingAge (American Association of Homes and Services for the Aging)/Oct. 27 - 30, 2013
League for Innovation in the Community College/Hilton Anatole Dallas/March 10 - 13, 2013
Literacy Research Association/Dec. 4 - 7, 2013

Mortgage Bankers Association of America/Gaylord Texan Hotel and Convention Center-Dallas/Feb. 19 - 22, 2013
NACE International/Dallas Convention Center/March 15 - 19, 2015
National Association for Developmental Education/Hilton Anatole Dallas/March 5 - 8, 2014
National Association of Bar Executives/Hilton Anatole/Feb. 5 - 7, 2013
National Association of Church Business Administration/Gaylord Texan Hotel and Convention Center-Dallas/July 6 - 10, 2016
National Association of Collegiate Directors of Athletics/Hilton Anatole Dallas/June 13 - 16, 2016
National Association of Collegiate Marketing Administrators/Hilton Anatole Dallas/June 13 - 16, 2016
National Association of Independent Life Brokerage Agencies/Gaylord Texan Hotel and Convention Center-Dallas/Nov. 21 - 23, 2013
National Association of Independent Life Brokerage Agencies/Gaylord Texan Hotel and Convention Center-Dallas/Nov. 17 - 19, 2016
National Association of Independent Life Brokerage Agencies/Gaylord Texan Hotel and Convention Center-Dallas/Nov. 14 - 16, 2019
National Association of Schools of Music/Omni Dallas Hotel/Nov. 18 - 22, 2016
National Association of Temple Administrators/Oct. 19 - 23, 2013
National Collegiate Athletic Association/Jan. 11 - 14, 2017
National Conference of Bar Foundations/Hilton Anatole/Feb. 7 - 9, 2013
National Conference of Bar Presidents/Hilton Anatole Hotel/Feb. 7 - 9, 2013
National Conference of Diocesan Vocation Directors/Sept. 23 - 27, 2013
National Electrical Manufacturers Representatives Association/Hilton Anatole/Feb. 3 - 6, 2016
National Home Infusion Association/Hilton Anatole/April 8 - 11, 2013
National Multi-Housing Council/Four Seasons Hotel/April 23 - 24, 2013
National Multi-Housing Council/Dallas Parkway Hilton/Nov. 11 - 13, 2013
National Truck and Heavy Equipment Claims Council/May 3 - 4, 2013
National Wood Flooring Association/Gaylord Texan Hotel and Convention Center-Dallas/April 2 - 5, 2013
National Wooden Pallet and Container Association/Dallas Marriott City Center/Oct. 11 - 13, 2013
North American Menopause Society/Gaylord Texan Hotel and Convention Center-Dallas/Oct. 9 - 12, 2013
North American Society for Trenchless Technology/Gaylord Texan Hotel and Convention Center-Dallas/March 20 - 24, 2016
Pan American Allergy Society/Dallas Marriott City Center/March 21 - 24, 2013
Pan American Allergy Society/Dallas Marriott City Center/March 20 - 23, 2014
Professional Liability Underwriting Society/Nov. 11 - 13, 2015
Professional Retail Store Maintenance Association/Dallas Convention Center/April 3 - 5, 2013
Snack Food Association/Dallas Convention Center/March 1 - 4, 2014
Society for Academic Emergency Medicine/May 14 - 17, 2014
Society of Clinical and Medical Hair Removal/May 4 - 6, 2013
Society of Forensic Toxicologists/Oct. 15 - 23, 2016
Society of Tribologists and Lubrication Engineers/Omni Hotel/May 17 - 21, 2015
SWANA - Solid Waste Association of North America/Aug. 26, 2014
TESOL International Association/Dallas Convention Center/March 20 - 23, 2013
Theatre Communications Group/June 6 - 8, 2013
Warehousing Education and Research Council/April 28 - May 1, 2013

Denton

Society of Ethnobiology/Univ of North Texas/May 15 - 18, 2013

Frisco

Hemophilia Federation of America/Embassy Suites Dallas-Frisco/ Hotel, Convention Center and Spa/April 25 - 27, 2013
Smocking Arts Guild of America/Embassy Suites Hotel and Conference Center/Oct. 23 - 27, 2013

Ft. Worth

American College of Veterinary Ophthalmologists/Omni Ft. Worth Hotel-Ft. Worth Convention Center/Oct. 8 - 11, 2014
American Feed Industry Association/Omni Ft. Worth Hotel/March 13 - 15, 2013
American Massage Therapy Association/Fort Worth Convention Center/Sept. 25 - 28, 2013
American Quarter Horse Association/Omni Hotels and Resorts/March 6 - 9, 2015
Associated Wire Rope Fabricators/Omni Ft. Worth Hotel/April 28 - May 1, 2013
Association for International Agricultural and Extension Education/Stockyard Station/May 19 - 22, 2013
Association of Fraternity Advisors/Omni Fort Worth Hotel/Dec. 2 - 5, 2015
Association of Science Museum Directors/Botanical Research Institute of Texas/Feb. 21 - 23, 2013
Association of Water Technologies/Fort Worth Convention Center/Oct. 29 - Nov. 1, 2014
Beefmaster Breeders United/Oct. 31, 2013
IEEE Power Electronics Society/March 16 - 20, 2014/2000 attendees
International Economic Development Council/Ft. Worth Convention Center/Oct. 19 - 22, 2014
International Society of Arboriculture/Aug. 13 - 17, 2016
International Society of Explosives Engineers/Omni Fort Worth Hotel/Feb. 10 - 13, 2013
National AMBUCS/July 24 - 27, 2013
National AMBUCS, Inc/July 24 - 27, 2013
National Art Education Association/Fort Worth Convention Center/March 7 - 10, 2013/over 100 exhibitors
National Association of Counties/Fort Worth Convention Center/July 19 - 22, 2013
National Association of County Civil Attorneys/Fort Worth Convention Center/July 19 - 22, 2013
National Association of Tower Erectors/Feb. 18 - 21, 2013
National Sheriffs' Association/June 20 - 25, 2014
North American Serials Interest Group/Hilton Fort Worth/May 1 - 4, 2014
United States Institute for Theatre Technology/Fort Worth Convention Center/March 26 - 29, 2014

Galveston

International Association of Drilling Contractors/Galveston Moody Gardens/ Aug. 20 - 21, 2013

Grapevine

American Academy of Home Care Physicians/Gaylord Texan Resort/May 2 - 3, 2013

American Association of Colleges of Pharmacy/Gaylord Texan Hotel and Convention Center, Dallas Texas/July 26 - 30, 2014

American Gas Association/Gaylord Hotels and Convention Centers/May 19 - 21, 2015

American Gas Association/Gaylord Hotels and Convention Centers/April 25 - 28, 2017

American Geriatrics Society/Gaylord Texan Hotel and Convention Center-Grapevine/May 3 - 5, 2013

American Medical Group Association/Gaylord Texan Hotel and Convention Center, Dallas Texas/April 9 - 12, 2014

American Payroll Association/Gaylord Texan Hotel and Convention Center, Dallas Texas/May 7 - 11, 2013

Dairy Management, Inc./Gaylord Texan Hotel and Convention Center, Dallas Texas/Oct. 27 - 29, 2014

Division 1-A Athletic Directors Association/Jan. 16 - 19, 2013

Health Industry Distributors Association/Gaylord Texan Hotel and Convention Center, Dallas Texas/Sept. 9 - 11, 2015

Health Information Trust Alliance (HITRUST)/Gaylord Texan Resort/May 20 - 22, 2013

Independent Time and Labor Management Association/Gaylord Texan Resort and Convention Center/May 7 - 9, 2013

Institute for Supply Management/April 28 - May 1, 2013

International Dyslexia Association/Gaylord Texan Hotel and Convention Center-Grapevine/Oct. 28 - 31, 2015

International Parking Institute/June 1 - 4, 2014

JAWS Society/Gaylord Texan Hotel and Convention Center, Dallas Texas/April 14 - 17, 2013

National Academy of Elder Law Attorneys, Inc./Embassy Suites Dallas/Jan. 18 - 20, 2013

National Association of Sporting Goods Wholesalers/Gaylord Texan Resort/ Oct. 29 - Nov. 1, 2013

National Collegiate Athletic Association/Jan. 16 - 19, 2013

National Milk Producers Federation/Gaylord Texan Hotel and Convention Center, Dallas Texas/Oct. 27 - 29, 2014

NCSL International/Gaylord Texan Hotel and Convention Center-Grapevine/ July 19 - 23, 2015/51-100 exhibitors

Precast/Prestressed Concrete Institute/Gaylord Texan Hotel and Convention Center-Grapevine/Sept. 21 - 25, 2013

Society for Imaging Informatics in Medicine/Gaylord Texan Hotel and Convention Center, Dallas Texas/June 6 - 9, 2013

Society for Imaging Informatics in Medicine/Gaylord Texan Hotel and Convention Center-Grapevine/June 1 - 4, 2017

Truckload Carriers Association/Gaylord Texan Hotel and Convention Center-Grapevine/March 23 - 26, 2014

Voluntary Protection Programs Participants' Association, Inc./Gaylord Texan Hotel and Convention Center-Grapevine/Aug. 24 - 27, 2015

Houston

American Academy of Allergy, Asthma, and Immunology/Feb. 20 - 24, 2015

American Association for Clinical Chemistry, Inc./July 28 - Aug. 1, 2013

American Association for Clinical Chemistry, Inc./July 23 - 27, 2018/18000 attendees

American Association of Family and Consumer Sciences/June 26 - 29, 2013

American Association of Petroleum Geologists/April 6 - 9, 2014

American Association of Petroleum Geologists/April 2 - 5, 2017

American Association of Port Authorities/Nov. 9 - 13, 2014/51-100 exhibitors

American Bar Association/Feb. 4 - 10, 2015

American Concrete Pipe Association/Hilton Americas-Houston/March 7 - 9, 2014

American Correctional Association/Jan. 25 - 30, 2013

American Epilepsy Society/George R. Brown Convention Center/Dec. 2 - 6, 2016

American Guild of Organists/Hilton Americas-Houston/June 23 - 26, 2016

American Guild of Organists/July 4 - 7, 2016

American Jewish Correctional Chaplains Association/Jan. 26 - 30, 2013

American Meteorological Society/Jan. 23 - 27, 2022

American Meteorological Society/Jan. 25 - 29, 2026

American Meteorological Society/Jan. 27 - 31, 2030

American Petroleum Institute/July 16 - 17, 2013

American Public Transportation Association/Oct. 12 - 15, 2014

American Quarter Horse Association/Hyatt Regency Houston/March 8 - 11, 2013

American Society for Bone and Mineral Research/Sept. 12 - 15, 2014/5000 attendees/over 100 exhibitors

American Society for Clinical Laboratory Science/July 28 - Aug. 1, 2013/19000 attendees/over 100 exhibitors

American Society for Clinical Laboratory Science/July 30 - Aug. 3, 2013

American Society for Clinical Laboratory Science/July 23 - 27, 2018/19000 attendees/over 100 exhibitors

American Society for Clinical Laboratory Science/July 24 - 27, 2018

Asian American Hotel Owners Association/George R. Brown Convention Center/March 26 - 29, 2013

Association for Play Therapy/Westin Galleria Houston/Oct. 7 - 12, 2014

Association of Departments of Foreign Languages/Rice University/June 18 - 21, 2013

Association of Jewish Libraries/June 16 - 19, 2013

Catholic Library Association/George R. Brown Convention Center/April 2 - 4, 2013

Chief Petty Officers Association/Aug. 12 - 15, 2013

Conference on College Composition and Communication/April 6 - 9, 2016

Cooling Technology Institute/Hilton Greenspoint Hotel/Feb. 2 - 6, 2014

Energy Telecommunications and Electrical Association/George R. Brown Center/April 9 - 11, 2013

Exhibition Services and Contractors Association/George R. Brown Convention Center/Dec. 9, 2013

Gas Technology Institute/April 16 - 19, 2013/5000 attendees/over 100 exhibitors

Hispanic Association on Corporate Responsibility/Four Seasons Hotel/April 19 - 23, 2013

Humanities Education and Research Association/Westin Galleria Houston/ March 20 - 23, 2013

Independent Petroleum Association of America/The Westin Houston/Jan. 21, 2013/300 attendees

International Association of Drilling Contractors/Omni Houston Hotel Westside/May 16, 2013

International Association of Exhibitions and Events/George R. Brown Convention Center/Dec. 10 - 13, 2013

International Association of Geophysical Contractors/Norris Conference Center/Feb. 21, 2013

International Dairy-Deli-Bakery Association/June 5 - 8, 2016

International Dairy-Deli-Bakery Association/June 5 - 9, 2016

International Executive Housekeepers Association/Omni Houston Hotel/Feb. 11 - 13, 2013

International Liquid Terminals Association/Hilton Americas-Houston/June 3 - 5, 2013

International Liquid Terminals Association/Hilton Americas-Houston/June 3 - 4, 2014

Laser Institute of America/Hilton Houston North/Feb. 12 - 13, 2013

National Association of Catastrophe Adjusters/Omni Houston Galleria Hotel/ Jan. 20 - 24, 2013

National Association of County Park and Recreation Officials/Oct. 8 - 10, 2013

National Association of Diaconate Directors/Archdiocese of Galveston/April 4 - 8, 2016

National Association of Insurance Commissioners/Hilton Americas-Houston/ April 6 - 9, 2013

National Catholic Educational Association/George R. Brown Convention Center/April 2 - 4, 2013/1-10 exhibitors

National Catholic Educational Exhibitors/George R. Brown Convention Center/ April 2 - 4, 2013

National Chemical Credit Association/Magnolia Hotel/Nov. 21 - 22, 2013

National Conference of Bar Foundations/Feb. 5 - 7, 2015

National Council on Education for the Ceramic Arts/George R. Brown Convention Center/March 20 - 23, 2013

National Education Association/July 2 - 7, 2019

National Exchange Club/Hyatt Regency Houston/July 13 - 16, 2016

The National Industrial Transportation League/Nov. 16 - 20, 2013

The National Industrial Transportation League/Nov. 12 - 16, 2016

National Precast Concrete Association/George R. Brown Convention Center/ March 6 - 8, 2014

National Recreation and Parks Association/Oct. 8 - 10, 2013/7000 attendees/ over 100 exhibitors

National Rifle Association of America/George R. Brown Convention Center/ May 3 - 5, 2013/51-100 exhibitors

North American Academy of Liturgy/Jan. 7 - 10, 2016

North American Association of Wardens and Superintendents/George R. Brown Convention Center/Jan. 25 - 30, 2013

Portfolio Management Institute/Omni Houston Hotel/April 17 - 19, 2013

Public Risk Management Association/George R. Brown Convention Center/ June 6 - 10, 2015

Society for Industrial and Organizational Psychology Inc./Sugar Land Marriott Town Square/April 11 - 13, 2013

Society for the Psychological Study of Ethnic Minority Issues/Royal Sonesta Houston/Jan. 17 - 18, 2013

Society for the Psychological Study of Men and Masculinity/Royal Sonest Hotel/Jan. 18 - 20, 2013

Society of American Military Engineers/Houston-Galveston Post/May 19 - 22, 2015/over 100 exhibitors

Society of Exploration Geophysicists/George R. Brown Convention Center/ Sept. 22 - 27, 2013

Society of Petroleum Engineers/George R. Brown Convention Center/Oct. 12 - 14, 2015

Society of Plastics Engineers/Hilton Houston North/Feb. 24 - 27, 2013/51-100 exhibitors

Society of Surgical Oncology/March 25 - 28, 2015/over 100 exhibitors

Souvenirs, Gifts and Novelties Trade Association/George R. Brown Convention Center/Jan. 19 - 22, 2013

United States Coast Guard Chief Petty Officers Association/Aug. 12 - 15, 2013

Irving

American College of Emergency Physicians/Meetings Registrar/May 18 - 21, 2013

American College of Emergency Physicians/Meetings Registrar/May 19 - 22, 2013

National Association of Real Estate Investment Managers/Four Seasons Resort and Club/Jan. 24 - 25, 2013

Kaufman

American Bashkir Curly Registry/Golden Curls/Aug. 8 - 10, 2013

Omni Hotel

Electronic Components Industry Association/Omni Hotel/March 25 - 28, 2013

San Antonio

Academy of Managed Care Pharmacy/Henry B. Gonzalez Convention Center and the Lila Cockrell Theatre/April 3 - 6, 2013

American Academy of Actuaries/JW Marriott San Antonio Hill Country Resort and Spa/Oct. 20 - 23, 2013

American Academy of Allergy, Asthma, and Immunology/Feb. 22 - 26, 2013/11-25 exhibitors

American Academy of Child and Adolescent Psychiatry/The Henry B. Gonzalez Convention Center/Oct. 27 - Nov. 1, 2015

American Academy of Oral Medicine/Hyatt Regency San Antonio/April 23 - 27, 2013

American Academy of Religion/Nov. 19 - 22, 2016/10000 attendees/over 100 exhibitors

American Academy of Religion/Nov. 20 - 23, 2021/10000 attendees/over 100 exhibitors

American Art Therapy Association, Inc./July 9 - 13, 2014

American Association for Laboratory Animal Science/Oct. 19 - 23, 2014

American Association for the Advancement of Slavic Studies/San Antonio
Marriott Rivercenter/Nov. 20 - 23, 2014
American Association of Airport Executives/May 18 - 21, 2014
American Association of Collegiate Registrars and Admissions Officers/JW
Marriott San Antonio Hill Country Resort and Spa/Nov. 6 - 9, 2016
American Association of Community Colleges/The Henry B. Gonzalez
Convention Center/April 18 - 21, 2015
American Association of Medical Dosimetrists/June 16 - 20, 2013
American Association of Neuromuscular and Electrodiagnostic Medicine/JW
Marriott San Antonio Hill Country Resort and Spa/Oct. 16 - 19, 2013
American Association of Pharmaceutical Scientists/The Henry B. Gonzalez
Convention Center/Nov. 10 - 14, 2013
American Association of Pharmaceutical Scientists/The Henry B. Gonzalez
Convention Center/Nov. 3 - 7, 2019
American Association of Physicians of Indian Origin/June 25 - 29, 2014
American Association of School Personnel Administrators/Oct. 1 - 4, 2013
American Association of Teachers of German/The Henry B. Gonzalez
Convention Center/Nov. 21 - 23, 2014
American Association of Teachers of Spanish and Portuguese/San Antonio
Marriott Rivercenter/July 8 - 11, 2013
American Bladesmith Society/Sheraton Gunter San Antonio/Jan. 25 - 26, 2013
American College Health Association/San Antonio Marriott Rivercenter/May
27 - 31, 2014
American College of Allergy, Asthma and Immunology/Nov. 5 - 10,
2015/51-100 exhibitors
American College of Allergy, Asthma and Immunology/Nov. 5 - 10, 2015
American College of Occupational and Environmental Medicine/San Antonio
Marriott Rivercenter/April 27 - 30, 2014
American College of Toxicology/JW Marriott San Antonio Hill Country Resort
and Spa/Nov. 3 - 6, 2013
American College of Veterinary Surgeons/San Antonio Convention Center/Oct.
23 - 26, 2013/over 100 exhibitors
American Composites Manufacturers Association/Feb. 18 - 20, 2014
American Conference of Governmental Industrial Hygienists/Henry Gonzalez
Convention Center/March 11 - 13, 2013
American Correctional Association/Jan. 20 - 25, 2017
American Council on the Teaching of Foreign Languages/Hyatt Regency Hill
Country Resort and Spa/Nov. 21 - 23, 2014
American Dental Association/The Henry B. Gonzalez Convention Center/Oct.
9 - 14, 2014
American Dental Education Association/The Henry B. Gonzalez Convention
Center/March 15 - 18, 2014
American Diabetes Association/The Henry B. Gonzalez Convention Center/
May 18, 2013
American Education Finance Association/Marriott Rivercenter Hotel/March 6
- 8, 2014
American Farm Bureau Federation/Jan. 12 - 15, 2014
American Fuel & Petrochemical Manufacturers/San Antonio Marriott
Rivercenter/March 17 - 19, 2013
American Fuel & Petrochemical Manufacturers/Grand Hyatt San Antonio/
March 24 - 26, 2013
American Fuel & Petrochemical Manufacturers/Grand Hyatt San Antonio/
March 30 - April 1, 2014
American Fuel & Petrochemical Manufacturers/San Antonio Convention
Center/May 20 - 23, 2014
American Fuel & Petrochemical Manufacturers/Grand Hyatt San Antonio/
March 29 - 31, 2015
American Health Care Association/Oct. 4 - 7, 2015
American Institute of Chemical Engineers/The Grand Hyatt/April 28 - May 2,
2013
American Mathematical Society/San Antonio Convention Center/Jan. 10 - 13,
2015
American Membrane Technology Association/The Henry B. Gonzalez
Convention Center/Feb. 25 - 28, 2013
American Military Retirees Association/El Tropicano Riverwalk Hotel/June 7 -
8, 2013
American Nuclear Society/Grand Hyatt San Antonio/June 7 - 11, 2015
American Oil Chemists' Society/The Henry B. Gonzalez Convention Center/
May 4 - 7, 2014
American Physical Society/March 2 - 6, 2015
American Psychiatric Nurses Association/The Henry B. Gonzalez Convention
Center/Oct. 9 - 12, 2013
American Quarter Horse Association/The Grand Hyatt/March 17 - 20, 2017
American Sheep Industry Association/Hyatt Regency San Antonio Riverwalk/
Jan. 23 - 26, 2013
American Society for Indexing/Hotel Contessa/April 17 - 19, 2013
American Society for Mass Spectrometry/June 5 - 9, 2016
American Society of Andrology/Hyatt Regency San Antonio/April 13 - 16, 2013
American Society of Anesthesiologists/Oct. 17 - 21, 2020
American Soybean Association/Feb. 27 - March 1, 2014
American Sports Builders Association/Grand Hyatt San Antonio/Dec. 6 - 10,
2013
American Traffic Safety Service Association/Henry B. Gonzalez Convention
Center and the Lila Cockrell Theatre/Feb. 21 - 25, 2014
American Translators Association/San Antonio Marriott Rivercenter/Nov. 6 - 9,
2013
American Veterinary Medical Association/Aug. 5 - 8, 2016
American Water Works Association/The Henry B. Gonzalez Convention
Center/Feb. 25 - 28, 2013
Arthroscopy Association of North America/April 25 - 27, 2013
ASM International/Sheraton Gunter/April 3 - 5, 2013
ASPRS-The Imaging and Geospatial Information Society/Crowne Plaza San
Antonio Riverwalk/Oct. 29 - 31, 2013
Association for Commuter Transportation/San Antonio Luxury Hotel /July 27 -
31, 2013
Association for Death Education and Counseling/Grand Hyatt San Antonio/
April 8 - 11, 2015
Association for Financial Technology/Hyatt Regency Hill Country Resort and
Spa/March 16 - 18, 2014

Association for Practical and Professional Ethics/St. Anthony Riverwalk
Wyndham Hotel/Feb. 28 - March 3, 2013
The Association for Science Teacher Education/Jan. 15 - 18, 2014
Association for Slavic, East European, and Eurasian Studies/San Antonio
Marriott Rivercenter/Nov. 20 - 23, 2014
The Association for Social Anthropology in Oceania/St. Anthony RiverWalk
Hotel/Feb. 5 - 9, 2013
Association of College Unions International/April 8 - 12, 2015
Association of Lutheran Secondary Schools/Sheraton Gunter Hotel San
Antonio/March 7 - 10, 2013
Association of the Wall and Ceiling Industry/March 18 - 22, 2013/over 100
exhibitors
Association of University Technology Managers/The Henry B. Gonzalez
Convention Center/Feb. 27 - March 2, 2013
BICSI/The Henry B. Gonzalez Convention Center/Sept. 11 - 16, 2016
Biomedical Engineering Society/Oct. 22 - 25, 2014/3000 attendees/51-100
exhibitors
Bowling Proprietors' Association of America/Hyatt Regency Hill Country Resort
and Spa/Jan. 27 - 31, 2013
Ceilings and Interior Systems Construction Association/Grand Hyatt San
Antonio/March 19 - 22, 2013/over 100 exhibitors
College and University Professional Association for Human Resources/Grand
Hyatt San Antonio/Sept. 28 - 30, 2014
Community College Business Officers/Crowne Plaza San Antonio Riverwalk/
Sept. 20 - 23, 2014
Conference of Consulting Actuaries/JW Marriott San Antonio Hill Country
Resort and Spa/Oct. 20 - 23, 2013
Construction Financial Management Association/JW Marriott San Antonio Hill
Country Resort and Spa/June 25 - 29, 2016
Council for Children with Behavioral Disorders/The Henry B. Gonzalez
Convention Center/April 3 - 6, 2013
Council for Exceptional Children/The Henry B. Gonzalez Convention Center/
April 3 - 6, 2013
Council of Colleges of Arts and Sciences/San Antonio Marriott Rivercenter/
Nov. 5 - 8, 2014
Council of Science Editors/May 2 - 5, 2014
Credit Professionals International/Menger Hotel/June 13 - 16, 2013
Direct Selling Association/JW Marriott San Antonio Hill Country Resort and
Spa/May 31 - June 2, 2015/900 attendees
Division 1-A Athletic Directors Association/Jan. 13 - 16, 2016
Exterior Insulation and Finish Systems Industry Members Association (EIMA)/
ASHRAE Convention/June 23 - 28, 2013
Family, Career and Community Leaders of America/July 6 - 10, 2014
Federation of Defense and Corporate Counsel/Westin La Cantera Hill Country
Resort/March 2 - 9, 2013
Federation of State Boards of Physical Therapy/Westin Riverwalk/Oct. 10 - 12,
2013
Flight Safety Foundation/Grand Hyatt San Antonio/April 17 - 19, 2014
Foodservice Equipment Distributors Association/JW Marriott San Antonio Hill
Country Resort and Spa/April 3 - 7, 2013
Fraternity Executives Association/Grand Hyatt San Antonio/July 6 - 10, 2013
Gas Processors Association/San Antonio Riverwalk/April 7 - 10, 2013/1500
attendees
Gas Processors Association/San Antonio Riverwalk/April 12 - 15, 2015
Gas Processors Association/San Antonio Riverwalk/April 9 - 12, 2017
Gas Processors Suppliers Association/San Antonio Riverwalk/April 7 - 10,
2013
Gas Processors Suppliers Association/San Antonio Riverwalk/April 12 - 15,
2015
Gas Processors Suppliers Association/San Antonio Riverwalk/April 9 - 12,
2017
Global Market Development Center/JW Marriott Hill Country Resort & Spa/
Sept. 5 - 9, 2014
Golf Course Superintendents Association of America/The Henry B. Gonzalez
Convention Center/Feb. 25 - 26, 2015
Gynecologic Oncology Group/San Antonio Marriott Rivercenter/July 19 - 21,
2013
Heating, Airconditioning and Refrigeration Distributors International/JW
Marriott San Antonio Hill Country Resort and Spa/Dec. 6 - 9, 2014
Hispanic Association of Colleges and Universities/Grand Hyatt San Antonio/
Feb. 27 - March 1, 2013
Hispanic Association of Colleges and Universities/Grand Hyatt San Antonio/
Oct. 8 - 10, 2016
Independent Lubricant Manufacturers Association/Hyatt Regency Hill Country
Resort and Spa/Oct. 5 - 8, 2013
Independent Petroleum Association of America/Hyatt Regency Hill Country
Resort and Spa/Nov. 7 - 9, 2013
Institute for Operations Research and the Management Sciences/The Grand
Hyatt San Antonio/April 7 - 9, 2013
Instructional Technology Council/Grand Hyatt San Antonio/Feb. 17 - 20, 2013
Insurance Accounting and Systems Association/San Antonio Convention
Center/June 12 - 15, 2016
International Association of Drilling Contractors/The Westin La Cantera
Resort/Oct. 23 - 24, 2013
International Association of Emergency Managers/Grand Hyatt San Antonio/
Nov. 14 - 19, 2014
International Cast Polymer Alliance/Feb. 18 - 20, 2014
International Cast Polymer Association/Feb. 18 - 20, 2014
International City/County Management Association/Bexar County/Sept. 10 -
13, 2017
International Energy Credit Association/Westin La Cantera Hill Country
Resort/April 6 - 8, 2014
The International Fluid Power Society/Feb. 27 - March 2, 2013
International Hunter Education Association/Hyatt Regency Hill Country Resort
and Spa/April 2 - 6, 2013
International Reading Association/April 19 - 22, 2013
International SalonSpa Business Network (ISBN)/Hyatt Hill Country Resort/
May 19 - 21, 2013
International Society for Technology in Education/June 23 - 26, 2013/20000
attendees/over 100 exhibitors

The Woodlands

Wichita Falls

UTAH

Park City

Salt Lake City

International Society for Magnetic Resonance in Medicine/Salt Palace Convention Center/April 20 - 26, 2013

Minerals, Metals and Materials Society/Salt Lake Marriott Downtown at City Creek/July 7 - 11, 2013

National Academic Advising Association/Salt Palace Convention Center/Oct. 6 - 9, 2013

National Association of Bankruptcy Trustees/Grand America Hotel/Sept. 10 - 14, 2014

National Association of Local Boards of Health/Aug. 14 - 16, 2013

National Organization of Life and Health Insurance Guaranty Association/April 9 - 10, 2013

The Philanthropy Roundtable/Grand America Hotel/Oct. 9 - 11, 2014

School Nutrition Association/July 11 - 15, 2015

Seismological Society of America/Salt Palace Convention Center/April 17 - 19, 2013

Society for Education in Anesthesia/Hilton Salt Lake City Center/May 31 - June 2, 2013

Society for Mining, Metallurgy and Exploration, Inc./Salt Palace Convention Center/Feb. 23 - 26, 2014

Society of American Gastrointestinal and Endoscopic Surgeons/Salt Palace Convention Center/April 2 - 5, 2014

Snowbird

The American Society of Naturalists/July 21 - 25, 2013

North American Neuro-Ophthalmology Society/Snowbird Ski and Summer Resort/Feb. 9 - 14, 2013

PSIA-AASI/April 14 - 18, 2013

Society for the Study of Evolution/June 21 - 25, 2013

VERMONT

Lyndonville

American Society of Dowsers/Lyndon State College/June 7 - 9, 2013

Stowe

American Sugar Alliance/Stowe Mountain Lodge/Aug. 1 - 6, 2014

Shareholder Services Association/Stowe Mountain Lodge/July 16 - 19, 2013

Tunbridge

American Milking Devon Cattle Association/Town Hall/May 11, 2013

VIRGIN ISLANDS

St. Thomas

Power and Communications Contractors Association/Frenchman's Reef Marriott Beach Resort/March 14 - 19, 2014

VIRGINIA

Alexandria

Association of American Veterinary Medical Colleges/Westin Alexandria/March 8 - 10, 2013

Association of Military Colleges and Schools of the United States/Westin Hotel/Feb. 24 - 26, 2013

Association of State Drinking Water Administrators/Hilton Alexandria Old Town/March 10 - 13, 2013

Christian Chiropractors Association/Crowne Plaza Old Town Alexandria Hotel/June 26 - 30, 2013

IEEE Microwave Theory and Techniques Society/Oct. 27 - 31, 2013

National Agricultural Alumni and Development Association/Crowne Plaza Old Town Alexandria Hotel/June 16 - 19, 2013

National Association of Educational Office Professionals/July 21 - 26, 2013

National Association of Planning Councils/Embassy Suites Alexandria-Old Town/April 5 - 7, 2013

National Association of Railroad Passengers/Hilton Alexandria Old Town Hotel/April 22 - 24, 2013

National Association of State Veterans Homes/Embassy Suites Alexandria-Old Town/Feb. 24 - March 1, 2013

National Beauty Culturists' League/Hilton Alexandria Mark Center/July 27 - Aug. 3, 2013

National Family Planning and Reproductive Health Association/Westin Alexandria/April 28 - May 1, 2013/1-10 exhibitors

National Motor Freight Traffic Association, Inc./Hilton Alexandria Old Town/June 2 - 3, 2013

National Motor Freight Traffic Association, Inc./Hilton Alexandria Old Town/Sept. 22 - 23, 2013

Process Equipment Manufacturers' Association/Westin Alexandria/Sept. 9 - 10, 2013

Arlington

Aeronautical Repair Station Association/Ritz-Carlton Hotel/March 20 - 22, 2013

American Society of Group Psychotherapy and Psychodrama/Crystal Gateway Marriott/April 11 - 15, 2013

American Society of Interventional Pain Physicians/Crystal Gateway Marriott/June 8 - 12, 2013

American Society of Naval Engineers/Hyatt Regency Crystal City at Reagan National Airport/Feb. 21 - 22, 2013

Association of American Pesticide Control Officials/Hyatt Regency, Crystal City/March 18 - 20, 2013

Association of College Honor Societies/Hyatt Regency Crystal City at Reagan National Airport/Feb. 14 - 17, 2013

Association of Community Cancer Centers/Hyatt Regency Crystal City at Reagan National Airport/March 31 - April 2, 2014

Association of Community Cancer Centers/Hyatt Regency Crystal City at Reagan National Airport/March 15 - 18, 2015

Association of Pediatric Program Directors/Oct. 2 - 4, 2013

Association of Public Television Stations/The Hyatt Regency Crystal City Hotel/Feb. 24 - 26, 2013

Coalition of Higher Education Assistance Organizations/Ritz Carlton/Jan. 27 - 30, 2013

Council for Affordable and Rural Housing/Ritz-Carlton, Pentagon City/June 9 - 11, 2013

Council for Chemical Research, Inc./May 19 - 21, 2013

The Environmental Information Association/Hyatt Regency Hotel Crystal City/March 24 - 27, 2013/26-50 exhibitors

Federal Bar Association/Westin Arlington Gateway/April 4 - 6, 2013

International Academy of Compounding Pharmacists/Crystal City Marriott at Reagan National Airport/June 1 - 4, 2013

International Consumer Product Health and Safety Organization/Hyatt Regency Crystal City at Reagan National Airport/Feb. 26 - March 1, 2013/500 attendees

Investment Adviser Association/Crystal Gateway Marriott/March 7 - 8, 2013

National Association of Development Organizations/Crystal Gateway Marriott/March 11 - 13, 2013

National Association of Development Organizations/Crystal Gateway Marriott/March 24 - 26, 2014

National Association of Government Communicators/Sheraton Pentagon City Hotel/April 16 - 19, 2013

National Association of Postmasters of the United States/Crystal Gateway Marriott/March 16 - 21, 2013

National Association of Professional Background Screeners/Renaissance Arlington Capital View Hotel/April 13 - 17, 2013/26-50 exhibitors

National Association of Professional Background Screeners/Renaissance Arlington Capital View Hotel/April 6 - 8, 2014/26-50 exhibitors

National Association of Professional Insurance Agents/Crystal City Marriott at Reagan National Airport/April 12 - 13, 2013

National Grants Management Association/Crystal Gateway Marriott/May 5 - 9, 2013

National League of Postmasters of the United States/Crystal City Gateway Marriott/Feb. 3 - 5, 2013

National Newspaper Association/Crystal City Marriott at Reagan National Airport/March 13 - 15, 2013

Plumbing-Heating-Cooling Contractors - National Association/Key Bridge Marriott/May 1 - 2, 2013

SAVE International/Crystal Gateway Marriott/June 24 - 27, 2013

Society for Advancement of Management/Key Bridge Marriott/March 21 - 24, 2013

Society for Historians of American Foreign Relations/Renaissance Arlington Capital View Hotel/June 20 - 22, 2013

Society for Personality Assessment/Westin Arlington Gateway/March 19 - 23, 2014/500 attendees

Society of American Magicians/Mariott Hotel Crystal Gateway/July 3 - 6, 2013

Towing and Recovery Association of America/Crystal City Marriott at Reagan National Airport/March 22 - 23, 2013

Wildlife Management Institute/Crystal Gateway Marriott/March 25 - 30, 2013

Window and Door Manufacturers Association/March 18 - 20, 2013

Women in Aerospace/Key Bridge Marriott/June 14, 2013

Blacksburg

American Society for Virology/Virginia Polytechnic Institute and State University/June 18 - 22, 2016

North American Colleges and Teachers of Agriculture/Virginia Tech/June 25 - 29, 2013

Falls Church

Marine Corps League/Fairview Park Marriott/Feb. 7 - 9, 2013

Herndon

Holistic Dental Association/Hilton Washington Dulles Airport/April 18 - 20, 2013/1-10 exhibitors

Hot Springs

National Precast Concrete Association/Homestead/Oct. 9 - 12, 2013

Leesburg

Giving Institute/Lansdowne Resort/July 25 - 28, 2013

Norfolk

American Holistic Nurses Association/June 6 - 8, 2013

Association of College and University Auditors/Norfolk Waterside Marriott/Sept. 22 - 26, 2013

National Strength and Conditioning Association/Marriott Norfolk Waterside/April 16 - 18, 2013

National Surgical Assistant Association/Marriott Norfolk Waterside/May 3 - 5, 2013

Portsmouth

National Association of Professional Band Instrument Repair Technicians/Renaissance Portsmouth Hotel and Waterfront Conference Center/April 5 - 8, 2013

Reston

National Association of State Departments of Agriculture/Hyatt Regency Reston/Feb. 2 - 7, 2013

Object Management Group/Hyatt Regency Reston/March 18 - 22, 2013

Society of Laparoendoscopic Surgeons/Hyatt Regency Reston/Aug. 28 - 31, 2013

Richmond

Association for the Study of African American Life and History/Marriott/Oct. 4 - 9, 2016

Association of the United States Army/Greater Richmond Convention Center/May 7 - 9, 2013

Clowns of America International/Holiday Inn Midlothian-Richmond Koger Center/April 16 - 21, 2013

Council of Chief State School Officers/Jefferson Hotel/Nov. 14 - 17, 2013

IEEE - Nuclear and Plasma Sciences Society/May 4 - 8, 2015

National Council for History Education/Richmond Marriott/March 21 - 23, 2013/700 attendees/over 100 exhibitors

National Science Teachers Association/Oct. 16 - 18, 2014

Roanoke

Women in Mining National/April 25 - 27, 2013

Vienna

Veterinary Cancer Society/Oct. 15 - 18, 2015

Virginia Beach

Air and Surface Transport Nurses Association/Oct. 21 - 23, 2013

International Association for the Study of Dreams/Virginia Beach Resort Hotel/June 21 - 25, 2013

North American Gaming Regulators Association/Hilton Virginia Beach Oceanfront/June 3 - 7, 2013

Training Officers Consortium/Founders Inn and Spa/April 28 - May 1, 2013

Williamsburg

American Dermatological Association/Colonial Williamsburg/Oct. 8 - 12, 2014

American Society for Eighteenth-Century Studies/Colonial William Lodge/
March 18 - 23, 2014

Electric Utility Fleet Managers Conference/Williamsburg Lodge and
Conference Center/June 2 - 5, 2013

International Association of Bedding and Furniture Law Officials/Williamsburg
Lodge/April 10 - 11, 2013

National Association of Power Engineers/The Woodlands Inn and Suites/June
19 - 23, 2013

National Council of Examiners for Engineering and Surveying/Aug. 19 - 22,
2015

National Governors Association/July 12 - 15, 2013

National Railway Historical Society/Jan. 12 - 13, 2013

Outdoor Power Equipment Institute/Williamsburg Lodge/June 19 - 21, 2013

Pulp and Paper Safety Association/Williamsburg Lodge/June 9 - 12, 2013

Wilson Ornithological Society/College of William and Mary/March 7 - 9, 2013

WASHINGTON

Bellevue

ASM International/Meydenbauer CenterBellevue/April 2 - 5, 2013

Association for Financial Counseling and Planning Education/Nov. 19 - 21,
2014

Electrical Generating Systems Association/Hyatt Regency Bellevue/Sept. 15 -
17, 2013

National Association of Postmasters of the United States/Hyatt Regency
Bellevue/Aug. 17 - 22, 2013

National Association of Women in Construction/Aug. 28 - 31, 2013

National Board of Boiler and Pressure Vessel Inspectors/Hyatt Regency
Bellevue/May 12 - 16, 2014

National Conference of Executives of The ARC/Hyatt Regency Bellevue/Aug. 2
- 5, 2013

Refrigerating Engineers and Technicians Association/Oct. 30 - Nov. 2, 2013

Rehabilitation Engineering and Assistive Technology Society of North America/
Hyatt Regency Beleluve/June 20 - 24, 2013

Teratology Society/Hyatt Regency Bellevue/June 28 - July 2, 2014

Maryland

Pharmaceutical Marketing Research Group/Gaylord National Resort/March 10
- 12, 2013

Seattle

Academy of Osseointegration/March 6 - 8, 2014

Airports Council International - North America/Hyatt at Olive 8/May 15 - 18,
2013

America's Health Insurance Plans/Jan. 11 - 13, 2014

American Academy of Cosmetic Dentistry/April 24 - 27, 2013

American Academy of Forensic Sciences/Washington State Convention Center/
Feb. 17 - 22, 2014/over 100 exhibitors

American Academy of Forensic Sciences/Washington State Convention Center/
Feb. 19 - 24, 2018

American Academy of Optometry/Seattle Conference Center/Oct. 23 - 26, 2013

American Alliance for Health, Physical Education, Recreation and Dance/
Washington State Convention Center/March 17 - 21, 2015/5000
attendees/1-10 exhibitors

American Art Therapy Association, Inc./June 26 - 30, 2013

American Association for Dental Research/March 20 - 23, 2013

American Association of Thoracic Surgery/Washington State Convention
Center/April 25 - 29, 2015

American Association of Endodontists/Washington State Convention and Trade
Center/May 6 - 9, 2015/4000 attendees/over 100 exhibitors

American Association of Medical Dosimetrists/June 1 - 5, 2014

American College of Emergency Physicians/Oct. 14 - 17, 2013

American College of Veterinary Internal Medicine/June 12 - 15, 2013

American College of Veterinary Nutrition/June 12 - 15, 2013

American College of Veterinary Surgeons/Washington State Convention
Center/Oct. 6 - 8, 2014

American Dental Education Association/Washington State Convention Center/
March 16 - 19, 2013

American Diabetes Association/Seattle Conference Center/April 13, 2013

American Epilepsy Society/Washington State Convention Center/Dec. 5 - 9,
2014

American Historical Association/Jan. 5 - 8, 2017

American Intellectual Property Law Association/Westin Seattle/May 15 - 17,
2013

American Library Association/Jan. 25 - 29, 2013

American Mathematical Society/Washington State Convention Center/Jan. 6 -
9, 2016

American Meteorological Society/Jan. 22 - 26, 2017

American Mosquito Control Association/Feb. 2 - 6, 2014

American Orthopaedic Society for Sports Medicine/Washington State
Convention Center/July 10 - 13, 2014/51-100 exhibitors

American Osteopathic Academy of Addiction Medicine/R and T Auditorium,
Harborview Medical Center/March 18, 2013

American Osteopathic Association/Oct. 25 - 29, 2014

American Philological Association/Sheraton Seattle Hotel/Jan. 3 - 6,
2013/2800 attendees/51-100 exhibitors

American Planning Association/April 18 - 22, 2015

American Society for Engineering Education/June 14 - 17, 2015

American Society for Surgery of the Hand/Sept. 10 - 12, 2015

American Society of Colon and Rectal Surgeons/Washington State Convention
Center and Sheraton Seattle Hotel/June 4 - 7, 2016

American Society of Consultant Pharmacists/Washington State Convention
Center/Nov. 19 - 22, 2013

American Society of Head and Neck Radiology/Sheraton Seattle Hotel/Sept. 10
- 14, 2014

American Society of Transplant Surgeons/Washington State Convention and
Trade Center/May 18 - 21, 2013

American Society of Transplantation/Washington State Convention Center/
May 18 - 21, 2013

American Society of Transplantation/June 2 - 6, 2018

American Statistical Association/Washington State Convention Center/Aug. 8
- 13, 2015

American Volleyball Coaches Association/Dec. 18 - 22, 2013

Association for Asian American Studies/The Afterlives of Empire/April 17 - 20,
2013

Association for Library and Information Science Education/Grand Hyatt
Seattle/Jan. 22 - 25, 2013

Association for Research in Vision and Ophthalmology/Washington State
Convention Center/May 5 - 9, 2013/12000 attendees

Association for Research in Vision and Ophthalmology/May 1 - 5, 2016

Association for Surgical Education/Westin Seattle/April 14 - 18, 2015

Association of College and University Housing Officers-International/July 9 -
12, 2016

Association of Community College Trustees/Oct. 2 - 5, 2013

Association of Program Directors in Surgery/Westin Seattle/April 14 - 18, 2015

Association of Real Estate License Law Officials/Westin Seattle/Sept. 18 - 22,
2013

Association of Regulatory Boards of Optometry/June 21 - 23, 2015

Association of Specialized and Cooperative Library Agencies/Jan. 25 - 29, 2013

Association of State Floodplain Managers/Washington State Convention
Center/June 1 - 6, 2014

Association of Writers and Writing Programs/Sheraton Seattle Hotel/Feb. 26 -
March 1, 2014/9000 attendees

Biomedical Engineering Society/Sept. 25 - 28, 2013/3000 attendees/51-100
exhibitors

CFA Institute/May 4 - 7, 2014

Chorus America/June 12 - 15, 2013

NAIOP, The Commercial Real Estate Development Association/Sheraton Seattle
Hotel/May 5 - 7, 2014

Communications Fraud Control Association/Monaco Seattle, a Kimpton Hotel/
Oct. 8 - 10, 2013

Decision Sciences Institute/Sheraton Seattle Hotel/Nov. 21 - 24, 2015

Earthquake Engineering Research Institute/Grand Hyatt Seattle/Feb. 12 - 15,
2013

Financial Planning Association/Sept. 27 - 30, 2014

Independent Sector/Sheraton Seattle Hotel/Nov. 16 - 18, 2014

Institute for Operations Research and the Management Sciences/University of
Washington/June 19 - 21, 2014

Institute of Mathematical Statistics/Washington State Convention and Trade
Center/Aug. 8 - 13, 2015

Institute of Transportation Engineers/Washington State Convention Center/
Aug. 10 - 13, 2014

International Association for Dental Research/March 20 - 23, 2013

International City/County Management Association/King County /Sept. 27 -
30, 2015

International Communication Association/May 22 - 26, 2014

International District Energy Association/Washington State Convention
Center/June 8 - 11, 2014

International Neuropsychological Society/Feb. 12 - 15, 2014

International Trademark Association/Washington State Convention Center/
May 16 - 20, 2020

Investment Management Consultants Association/Washington State
Convention Center/April 29 - May 1, 2013

Law and Society Association/Weston Seattle/May 28 - 31, 2015

NALP - The Association for Legal Career Professionals/Washington State
Convention Center/April 9 - 12, 2014

National Association of College and University Business Officers/July 19 - 22,
2014

National Association of Disability Representatives/Grand Hyatt Seattle/May 1
- 4, 2013

National Association of Mutual Insurance Companies/Sheraton Seattle Hotel/
Sept. 22 - 25, 2013/1700 attendees/over 100 exhibitors

National Association of School Psychologists/Sheraton Seattle Hotel/Feb. 12 -
16, 2013

National Association of State Utility Consumer Advocates (NASUCA)/June 9 -
11, 2013

National Center for Employee Ownership/Westin Seattle/April 24 - 26, 2013

National Council of Examiners for Engineering and Surveying/Aug. 20 - 23,
2014

National Council of State Housing Agencies/Sheraton Seattle Hotel/June 13 -
16, 2016

National Council on Problem Gambling/DoubleTree by Hilton Hotel Seattle
Airport/July 19 - 20, 2013

National Defender Investigator Association/Sheraton Seattle Hotel/April 4 - 5,
2013

National Electrical Contractors Association/Oct. 7 - 10, 2017

National Garden Clubs/Sheraton Seattle Hotel/May 24 - 26, 2013

National Operating Committee for Standards of Athletic Equipment/June 28 -
29, 2013

National Renal Administrators Association/Grand Hyatt Seattle/Sept. 25 - 27,
2013

NIBA - The Belting Association/Seattle Sheraton/Sept. 24 - 27, 2014

Research Society on Alcoholism/Bellevue/June 21 - 25, 2014

Resort Hotel Association/The Edgewater Hotel/July 14 - 17, 2013

The Rural Sociological Society/Hyatt Regency Bellevue on Seattle's Eastside/
Aug. 16 - 21, 2016

Society for Epidemiologic Research/June 24 - 27, 2014

Society for Free Radical Biology and Medicine/Sheraton Seattle Hotel/Nov. 19
- 23, 2014

Society for Pediatric Radiology/Hyatt Regency Bellevue on Seattle's Eastside/
April 27 - May 1, 2015

Society for Research in Child Development/April 18 - 20, 2013

Society for Research on Nicotine and Tobacco/Sheraton Seattle Hotel/Feb. 5 -
8, 2014

Society for the Advancement of Material and Process Engineering/June 2 - 5,
2014

Society of Christian Ethics/Westin Seattle/Jan. 9 - 12, 2014

Society of Corporate Secretaries and Governance Professionals/Seattle
Sheraton Hotel/July 10 - 13, 2013

TESOL International Association/March 21 - 24, 2017
United States Junior Chamber (Jaycees)/June 5 - 8, 2013
Western Economic Association International/Grand Hyatt Seattle/June 28 - July 2, 2013
Women's Classical Caucus/Jan. 3 - 6, 2013
The Wound, Ostomy and Continence Nurses Society/June 22 - 26, 2013

Seattle

American Association of Museums/May 18 - 21, 2014/over 100 exhibitors
American Astronomical Society/Jan. 4 - 8, 2015
American Astronomical Society/Jan. 6 - 10, 2019
American Society of Heating, Refrigerating and Air Conditioning Engineers (ASHRAE)/June 28 - July 2, 2014
American Society of Transplantation/May 18 - 21, 2013
Archaeological Institute of America/Washington State Convention Center/Jan. 3 - 6, 2013
Association of Military Surgeons of the United States/Oct. 31 - Nov. 8, 2013
Association of Proposal Management Professionals/May 26 - 29, 2015
International Transplant-Skin Cancer Collaborative/May 18 - 21, 2013
Mathematical Association of America/Jan. 6 - 9, 2016
National Association of State Boards of Geology/Nov. 2, 2013
National Electrical Contractors Association/Oct. 7 - 10, 2017
National League of Cities/Nov. 12 - 16, 2014
USENIX: The Advanced Computing Systems Association/Nov. 9 - 14, 2014

Walla Walla

National Potato Council/Marcus Whitman Hotel and Conference Center/June 24 - 28, 2013

WEST VIRGINIA

Morgantown

Walnut Council/July 28 - 31, 2013

White Sulphur Springs

Association for Financial Technology/The Greenbrier/Sept. 12 - 14, 2014
Association of Defense Trial Attorneys/Greenbrier/April 17 - 21, 2013
Industrial Truck Association/Greenbrier/Sept. 23 - 25, 2013
National Association of Bankruptcy Trustees/Greenbrier/Aug. 8 - 11, 2013

WISCONSIN

De Pere

International Society of Weekly Newspaper Editors/St. Norbert College/June 10 - 14, 2013

Green Bay

Technical Association of the Pulp and Paper Industry/Hyatt on Main, Green Bay/Sept. 15 - 18, 2013

Keshena

Intertribal Timber Council/June 10 - 13, 2013

Kohler

Council of Chief State School Officers/The American Club/July 20 - 23, 2013

Madison

American Meat Science Association/University of Wisconsin and Oscar Mayer/Kraft Foods/June 15 - 18, 2014
American Society for Virology/Monona Terrace Convention Center/June 24 - 28, 2017
Government Finance Officers Association of the United States and Canada/ University of Wisconsin/July 28 - Aug. 2, 2013
Health Physics Society/June 7 - 11, 2013
Health Physics Society/July 7 - 11, 2013
National Institute for Animal Agriculture/Oct. 1 - 5, 2013
National Institute for Animal Agriculture/Sept. 30 - Oct. 4, 2014
National Institute for Animal Agriculture/Sept. 29 - Oct. 3, 2015
National Institute for Animal Agriculture/Oct. 4 - 8, 2016
Purebred Dairy Cattle Association/Alliant Energy Center/Oct. 1 - 5, 2013
Society for Ecological Restoration International/Monona Terrace Community and Convention Center/Oct. 6 - 11, 2013/1500 attendees

Menomonie

International Graphic Arts Education Association/University of Wisconsin-Stout/July 21 - 25, 2013

Milwaukee

American Academy for Cerebral Palsy and Developmental Medicine/Frontier Airlines Center/Oct. 16 - 19, 2013
American Association for Paralegal Education/Oct. 21 - 24, 2015
American Association of Bovine Practitioners/Sept. 19 - 21, 2013
American Association of Meat Processors/Hilton Milwaukee City Center/June 19 - 21, 2014
American Concrete Institute/Hyatt Regency Milwaukee/April 17 - 21, 2016
American Musicological Society/Hilton Milwaukee City Center/Nov. 6 - 9, 2014
American Philatelic Society/Aug. 8 - 11, 2013
American Society of Head and Neck Radiology/Pfister Hotel/Sept. 25 - 29, 2013
Catholic Theological Society of America/Hyatt Regency Milwaukee/June 11 - 14, 2015
Council of the Great City Schools/Hilton Milwaukee City Center/Oct. 20 - 26, 2014
Electrical Manufacturing and Coil Winding Association/Frontier Airlines Center/May 8 - 9, 2013/over 100 exhibitors
Flying Physicians Association/Hyatt Regency Milwaukee/June 23 - 27, 2013
International Association of Administrative Professionals/Milwaukee Convention Center/July 26 - 30, 2014
International Buckskin Horse Association/Wyndham Milwaukee Airport Hotel and Convention Center/March 14 - 16, 2013
International Institute of Municipal Clerks/May 18 - 22, 2014
International Society of Arboriculture/Aug. 2 - 6, 2014
International Society on Thrombosis and Hemostasis/June 23 - 26, 2014
National Association of Sports Commissions/Visit Milwaukee/April 27 - 30, 2015
National Child Support Enforcement Association/Hilton Milwaukee City Center/Aug. 10 - 12, 2015

National Council on Education for the Ceramic Arts/Frontier Airlines Center/ March 19 - 22, 2014
National Women's Studies Association/Hilton Milwaukee Downtown/Nov. 12 - 15, 2015
Society for Applied Spectroscopy/Sept. 29 - Oct. 4, 2013
Society for Nutrition Education and Behavior/June 28 - July 1, 2014
Society for Pediatric Dermatology/Pfister Hotel/July 11 - 14, 2013
United States Institute for Theatre Technology/Frontier Airlines Center/March 20 - 23, 2013/over 100 exhibitors
The Wildlife Society/Oct. 5 - 9, 2013

Oshkosh

Academy of Accounting Historians/University of Wisconsin Oshkosh/Oct. 14 - 19, 2013

Stevens Point

National Wellness Institute, Inc./University of Wisconsin, Stevens Point/July 15 - 18, 2013

Waukesha

The Brown Swiss Association/Milwaukee Mariott West/July 3 - 6, 2013

WYOMING

Laramie

American Society of Mining and Reclamation/Hilton Garden Inn/June 1 - 6, 2013

Teton Village

American College of Mortgage Attorneys/Four Seasons Resort Jackson Hole/ Sept. 26 - 28, 2013

CANADA

ALBERTA

Banff

Agricultural History Society/June 12 - 15, 2013
Association of Environmental and Resource Economists/Banff Centre/June 6 - 9, 2013
Attorneys' Liability Assurance Society Inc./Fairmont Banff Springs Resort/June 17 - 19, 2015
Federation of Defense and Corporate Counsel/Fairmont Banff Springs Resort/ July 25 - Aug. 1, 2015

Calgary

American Association of Petroleum Geologists/June 19 - 22, 2016
American Association of Physical Anthropologists/April 8 - 12, 2014
Human Biology Association/April 11 - 12, 2014
International Association for Impact Assessment/May 13 - 16, 2013

Edmonton

American Society of Plant Taxonomists/July 24 - 30, 2015
Consortium for North American Higher Education Collaboration/MacEwan University Campus/May 1 - 3, 2013
North American Fuzzy Information Processing Society/University of Alberta/ June 24 - 28, 2013

Montreal

National Environmental Balancing Bureau/Hyatt Regency/May 2 - 4, 2013

BRITISH COLUMBIA

Vancouver

Academy of Management/Aug. 7 - 11, 2015
American Academy of Otolaryngology-Head and Neck Surgery/Vancouver Convention Centre/Sept. 29 - Oct. 2, 2013
American Bar Association/Jan. 31 - Feb. 6, 2018
American Broncho-Esophagological Association/Vancouver Convention Centre/Sept. 29 - Oct. 2, 2013
American College of Real Estate Lawyers/Four Seasons Hotel And Resorts/Oct. 17 - 20, 2013
American Society of Heating, Refrigerating and Air Conditioning Engineers (ASHRAE)/Renaissance Vancouver Hotel/Oct. 15 - 18, 2013
American Society of Human Genetics/Oct. 18 - 22, 2016
American Society of Pediatric Nephrology/May 3 - 6, 2014
Association for Research in Vision and Ophthalmology/April 28 - May 2, 2019
Association of Otolaryngology Administrators/Sept. 25 - 28, 2013
Canola Council of Canada/March 14 - 15, 2013
Casualty Actuarial Society/Westin Bayshore/May 19 - 22, 2013
Fresh Produce Association of the Americas/April 2 - 4, 2014
Geological Society of America/Oct. 19 - 22, 2014
History of Economics Society/University of British Columbia/June 20 - 22, 2013
IEEE Power Electronics Society/Sept. 28 - Oct. 2, 2014
IEEE Signal Processing Society/Vancouver Convention and Exhibition Center / May 26 - 31, 2013
Institute of Mathematical Statistics/July 28 - Aug. 2, 2018
Institute of Scrap Recycling Industries, Inc./Vancouver Convention Center/April 14 - 18, 2015
Intellectual Property Owners Association/Vancouver Convention Centre/Sept. 7 - 9, 2014/11-25 exhibitors
International Association of Movers/Vancouver Convention Center/Oct. 7 - 10, 2013
International Bridge, Tunnel and Turnpike Association/Fairmont Hotel Vancouver/Sept. 22 - 25, 2013
International Society of Protistologists/The Westin Bayshore - Vancouver/July 29 - Aug. 2, 2013
The International Wood Products Association/Westin Bayshore/April 17 - 19, 2013/300 attendees
Islamic Medical Association of North America/Aug. 17 - 21, 2013
The Masonry Society/May 31 - June 3, 2013
The Masonry Society/May 31 - June 2, 2013
The Masonry Society/June 2 - 5, 2013
Mineralogical Society of America/Oct. 19 - 22, 2014

National Academy of Arbitrators/The Fairmont Hotel Vancouver/June 5 - 8, 2013
National Association of County Park and Recreation Officials/June 10 - 15, 2013
North American Academy of Liturgy/Jan. 4 - 7, 2018
OPERA America/May 7 - 11, 2013
Pediatric Endocrine Society/May 3 - 6, 2014
Perennial Plant Association/June 21 - 27, 2013
Professional Communications Society/Walter Gage conference hotel/July 15 - 17, 2013
Society for College and University Planning/July 9 - 13, 2016
Society for Information Display/Vancouver Convention Center/May 19 - 24, 2013
Society for Pediatric Research/May 3 - 6, 2014
Society of Environmental Toxicology and Chemistry/Nov. 9 - 13, 2014
Society of Nuclear Medicine/June 8 - 12, 2013
Society of Otorhinolaryngology and Head-Neck Nurses/Sept. 27 - Oct. 1, 2013
Special Libraries Association/June 8 - 11, 2014
Special Libraries Association/June 8 - 10, 2014

Victoria
American Thyroid Association/The Fairmont Empress and Victoria Conference Center/Oct. 18 - 22, 2017
Association for the Advancement of Computing in Education/June 24 - 28, 2013
North American Case Research Association/The Fairmont Empress Hotel/Oct. 17 - 19, 2013
Western Literature Association/Fairmont Empress/Nov. 4 - 8, 2014

Whistler
College of Diplomates of the American Board of Orthodontics/Fairmont Chateau Whistler Resort/July 11 - 15, 2013
International Council of Shopping Centers/Jan. 27 - 29, 2013

MANITOBA
Winnipeg
International Association of Women Police/Sept. 28 - Oct. 2, 2014
The Wildlife Society/Oct. 17 - 21, 2015

NEWFOUNDLAND
St. John's
Marine Technology Society/Sept. 14 - 19, 2014

NOVA SCOTIA
Halifax
Airports Council International - North America/The Lord Nelson Hotel and Suites/May 12 - 15, 2013
International Association of Fire Fighters/July 28 - 31, 2013
North American Society for Sport History/Saint Mary's University/May 24 - 27, 2013

ONTARIO
London
American Society for Virology/The University of Western Ontario/July 11 - 15, 2015
Niagara Falls
International Association of Operative Millers/Hilton Hotel and Suites Niagara Falls/Fallsview/April 29 - May 3, 2013/800 attendees
Ottawa
American Academy of Appellate Lawyers/Fairmont Chateau Laurier Hotel/April 25 - 27, 2013
IEEE Aerospace and Electronic Systems Society (AESS)/April 29 - May 3, 2013
National Council on Public History/Delta Ottawa City Center/April 17 - 20, 2013
North American Association of Central Cancer Registries/June 21 - 27, 2014
North American Thermal Analysis Society/Aug. 10 - 12, 2015
Professional Convention Management Association/July 28 - 30, 2013
Society for Military History/Ottawa Marriott Hotel/April 14 - 17, 2016
Toronto
AACE International/Sheraton Centre Toronto Hotel/June 26 - 29, 2016
American Academy of Cosmetic Dentistry/April 27 - 30, 2016
American Association for Applied Linguistics/March 21 - 24, 2015
American Association of Thoracic Surgery/Metro Toronto Convention Centre/April 26 - 30, 2014
American Comparative Literature Association/University of Toronto/April 4 - 7, 2013
American Educational Studies Association/Oct. 28 - Nov. 2, 2014
American Philological Association/Jan. 5 - 8, 2017
American Psychiatric Association/May 16 - 20, 2015
American Roentgen Ray Society/Metro Toronto Convention Centre/April 19 - 24, 2015
American Society for Environmental History/Fairmont Royal York Hotel/April 3 - 6, 2013
American Society of Association Executives-The Center for Association Leadership/Aug. 12 - 15, 2017
American Society of Human Genetics/Oct. 22 - 26, 2019
American Society of Pediatric Nephrology/May 5 - 8, 2018
American Studies Association/Sheraton Centre Toronto Hotel/Oct. 8 - 11, 2015
The Association for Manufacturing Excellence/Oct. 21 - 25, 2013
The Association of Collegiate Conference and Events Directors International/Fairmont Royal York/March 16 - 20, 2013/600 attendees
Association of Family and Conciliation Courts/Westin Harbour Castle/May 28 - 31, 2014
Association of Insurance Compliance Professionals/Westin Harbour Castle/Oct. 6 - 9, 2013
Association of Investment Management Sales Executives/Sheraton Centre Toronto Hotel/Jan. 29 - 30, 2013
Association of Legal Administrators/Metro Toronto Convention Centre/May 19 - 22, 2014

Auxiliary to the National Medical Association/July 27 - 31, 2013
Ceilings and Interior Systems Construction Association/Fairmont Royal York/Sept. 25, 2013
NAIOP, The Commercial Real Estate Development Association/Fairmont Royal York/Oct. 13 - 16, 2015
Communications Fraud Control Association/Royal York Hotel/June 4 - 6, 2013
The Electrochemical Society/Sheraton Centre Toronto Hotel/May 12 - 17, 2013
The Folk Alliance International/Delta Chelsea/Feb. 20 - 24, 2013
Fresh Produce Association of the Americas/April 17 - 19, 2013
Government Finance Officers Association of the United States and Canada/May 22 - 25, 2016/over 100 exhibitors
Government Finance Officers Association, Federal Liaison Center/May 22 - 25, 2016
Independent Petroleum Association of America/The Ritz-Carlton/June 11, 2013
Institute of Transportation Engineers/Sheraton Centre Toronto Hotel/July 30 - Aug. 2, 2017
International Association of Business Communicators/Sheraton Centre Toronto Hotel/June 8 - 11, 2014
International Society for Magnetic Resonance in Medicine/May 30 - June 5, 2015
International Society of Arboriculture/Aug. 3 - 7, 2013
International Society of Arthroscopy, Knee Surgery and Orthopaedic Sports Medicine/Metro Toronto Convention Centre/May 12 - 16, 2013
International Society on Thrombosis and Hemostasis/June 20 - 25, 2015
International Studies Association/Sheraton Centre Toronto Hotel/March 26 - 29, 2014/5000 attendees
International Studies Association/Sheraton Centre Toronto Hotel/March 27 - 30, 2019
International Trademark Association/May 21 - 25, 2022
Million Dollar Round Table/June 8 - 12, 2014
National Association for College Admission Counseling/Sept. 19 - 21, 2013
National Association of Steel Pipe Distributors/Hyatt Regency Toronto/June 6 - 8, 2013
Pediatric Endocrine Society/May 5 - 8, 2018
Pediatric Orthopedic Society of North America/Sheraton Centre Toronto Hotel/May 1 - 4, 2013
Physician Insurers Association of America/Fairmont Royal York/May 14 - 16, 2014
The Psychonomic Society/Nov. 14 - 17, 2013
Social Science History Association/Fairmont Royal York/Nov. 6 - 9, 2014
Society for Obstetric Anesthesia and Perinatology/Sheraton Centre Toronto Hotel/May 14 - 18, 2014/11-25 exhibitors
Society for Pediatric Research/May 5 - 8, 2018
Society of Biological Psychiatry/May 14 - 16, 2015
Society of Biological Psychiatry/May 16 - 20, 2015
Society of General Internal Medicine/Sheraton Centre Toronto Hotel/April 22 - 25, 2015
Society of International Business Fellows/Four Seasons/Oct. 3 - 6, 2013
Society of North American Goldsmiths/May 15 - 18, 2013
Special Interest Group for Computer-Human Interaction/April 26 - May 1, 2014
Student Youth and Travel Association/Aug. 21 - 26, 2014
Sugar Industry Technologists/May 18 - 21, 2014
TESOL International Association/Metro Toronto Convention Centre/March 25 - 28, 2015
Turnaround Management Association/Westin Harbour Castle/Sept. 29 - Oct. 1, 2014
United Association for Labor Education/Metropolitan Hotel/April 17 - 20, 2013
Waterloo
Association for Symbolic Logic/May 8 - 11, 2013

QUEBEC
Montreal
Academy for Eating Disorders/Hilton Montreal Bonaventure/May 2 - 4, 2013
The Acoustical Society of America/Palais Des Congres de Montreal/June 2 - 7, 2013
The Acoustical Society of America/July 2 - 7, 2013
Alliance for Aging Research/Oct. 1 - 4, 2013
American Association for Justice/Montreal Convention Centre/July 11 - 15, 2015
American Association of Heart Failure Nurses/Le Centre Sheraton Montreal Hotel/June 27 - 29, 2013
American Ceramics Society/Palais Des Congres de Montreal/Oct. 27 - 31, 2013
American College of Chest Physicians/Oct. 24 - 29, 2015
American College of Veterinary Pathologists/Montreal Convention Center and the LeWestin Montreal Hotel/Nov. 16 - 20, 2013
American Conference of Governmental Industrial Hygienists/May 20 - 22, 2013
American Crystallographic Association/Aug. 5 - 12, 2014
American Oil Chemists' Society/Palais Des Congres de Montreal/April 28 - May 1, 2013
American Orthopaedic Association/June 18 - 21, 2014
American Society for Aesthetic Plastic Surgery/Palais Des Congres de Montreal/May 14 - 19, 2015/2500 attendees
American Society for Engineering Education/June 21 - 24, 2020
American Society for Information Science and Technology/Le Centre Sheraton Montreal Hotel/Nov. 1 - 6, 2013
American Society of Agricultural and Biological Engineers/July 13 - 16, 2014
American Society of Human Genetics/Oct. 19 - 23, 2021
American Society of Neuroradiology/Palais Des Congres de Montreal/May 17 - 22, 2014
American Society of Neurorehabilitation/Palais des congrès/Oct. 1 - 4, 2013
American Statistical Association/Palais Des Congres de Montreal/Aug. 3 - 8, 2013/5000 attendees
Association for Education in Journalism and Mass Communication/Aug. 6 - 9, 2014
Association for the Treatment of Sexual Abusers/Le Centre Sheraton Montreal Hotel/Oct. 13 - 17, 2015
Association of Destination Management Executives/Sheraton Center/Feb. 7 - 9, 2014

Association of Schools of Journalism and Mass Communication/Aug. 6 - 9, 2014
Association of Science-Technology Centers/Montréal Science Centre/Oct. 17 - 20, 2015
Attorneys' Liability Assurance Society Inc./Le Centre Sheraton Montreal Hotel/ June 18 - 20, 2014
Biotechnology Industry Organization (BIO)/June 16 - 19, 2013
Council of Science Editors/May 3 - June 7, 2013
Council of Science Editors/Fairmont The Queen Elizabeth/May 3 - 6, 2013
The Fertilizer Institute/Le Centre Sheraton Montreal Hotel/Sept. 22 - 24, 2013
Flight Safety Foundation/Fairmont, the Queen Elizabeth Hotel/April 10 - 11, 2013
Institute of Mathematical Statistics/Palais Des Congres de Montreal/Aug. 3 - 8, 2013
International Anesthesia Research Society/Fairmont The Queen Elizabeth/ March 17 - 24, 2014
International Association of Campus Law Enforcement Administrators/June 20 - 24, 2014
International Downtown Association/Sept. 19 - 25, 2013
International Listening Association/June 20 - 23, 2013
International Society for Heart and Lung Transplantation/Palais Des Congres de Montreal/April 24 - 27, 2013
International Society for Pharmacoeconomics and Outcomes Research/Palais Des Congres de Montreal/May 31 - June 4, 2014
International Society for Pharmacoepidemiology/Montreal Convention Centre/ Aug. 25 - 28, 2013
National Association of College and University Business Officers/July 16 - 19, 2016
National Association of College Auxiliary Services/Palais Des Congres de Montreal/Oct. 5 - 8, 2014/51-100 exhibitors
Regional Airline Association/May 6 - 9, 2013
Society for Gynecologic Investigation/March 16 - 19, 2016
Society for the Study of Reproduction/July 22 - 26, 2013
Society of Rheology/CBD/Oct. 13 - 17, 2013
SPIE - The International Society for Optical Engineering/Palais des congrès/ June 22 - 27, 2014
Teratology Society/Hilton Montreal Bonaventure/June 27 - July 2, 2015

Québec

American Fisheries Society/Aug. 17 - 21, 2014
American Society of Parasitologists/Loews Hotel Le Concorde/June 27 - 30, 2013
IEEE Signal Processing Society/Sept. 28 - Oct. 1, 2015
North American Council of Automotive Teachers/July 22 - 26, 2013
Potato Association of America/July 28 - Aug. 2, 2013
RNA Society/Centre des Congrès de Québec/June 3 - 8, 2014

MEXICO

DISTRITO
Mexico City

International Sanitary Supply Association/March 6 - 8, 2013
International Sanitary Supply Association/World Trade Center/March 13 - 15, 2013

JALISCO
Guadalajara

Packaging Machinery Manufacturers Institute/Expo Guadalajara/Feb. 27 - March 1, 2013/4000 attendees/51-100 exhibitors

MEXICO STATE
Los Cabos

National Wrestling Coaches Association/Westin Resort and Spa/Aug. 2 - 4, 2013

NAYARIT
Punta Mita

International Society of Barristers/Four Seasons/March 10 - 16, 2013

NUEVO LEON
Monterrey

American Welding Society/Cintermex/May 7 - 9, 2013/9000 attendees/over 100 exhibitors
Precision Metalforming Association/Cintermex/May 7 - 9, 2013/7000 attendees/over 100 exhibitors

QUINTANA ROO
Cancun

American Society for Neurochemistry/Cancun Convention Center/April 20 - 24, 2013
Distribution Contractors Association/Ritz Carlton/Feb. 4 - 9, 2014
The Electrochemical Society/Moon Palace Golf and Spa Resort/Oct. 5 - 10, 2014
Society for Developmental Biology/Cancun Center Conventions and Exhibitions/June 16 - 20, 2013

YUCATAN
Mérida

Association for Behavior Analysis International/Hotel Fiesta Americana/Oct. 6 - 8, 2013

AUSTRALIA

Melbourne

Geoscience and Remote Sensing Society/Melbourne Convention and Exhibition Centre /July 21 - 26, 2013
IEEE Signal Processing Society /Sept. 15 - 19, 2013
Institute of Noise Control Engineering/Melbourne Convention and Exhibition Centre /Nov. 16 - 19, 2014
International Lactation Consultant Association/Melbourne Convention Centre / July 25 - 28, 2013
International Society of Chemical Ecology/Melbourne Convention and Exhibition Centre /Aug. 19 - 22, 2013

Notre Dame

Medieval Academy of America/University of Notre Dame /March 12 - 14, 2015

Sydney

Institute of Mathematical Statistics /July 7 - 11, 2014
International Health, Racquet and Sportsclub Association/Sydney Convention and Exhibition Centre- Darling Harbour /April 19 - 21, 2013
International Liver Transplantation Society/Sydney Convention and Exhibition Centre- Darling Harbour /June 12 - 15, 2013/1200 attendees/over 100 exhibitors
Movement Disorder Society /June 16 - 20, 2013
National Association for Information Destruction, Inc./Sheraton on the Park / Feb. 19, 2013
The Open Group /April 15 - 18, 2013

BERMUDA

Southampton

Attorneys' Liability Assurance Society Inc./Fairmont Southampton /June 19 - 21, 2013
Caribbean Cable Communications/The Fairmont Southampton Hotel /Jan. 22 - 24, 2013
College of Diplomates of the American Board of Orthodontics/Fairmont Southampton /July 21 - 25, 2013
Intermediaries and Reinsurance Underwriters Association/Fairmont Southampton /April 21 - 23, 2013
Professional Insurance Marketing Association/The Fairmont Southampton / July 25 - 28, 2013

CHINA

Beijing

IEEE Circuits and Systems Society/China National Convention Center /May 19 - 23, 2013
IEEE Signal Processing Society /May 5 - 9, 2014
InfoComm International/China National Convention Center /April 10 - 12, 2013
International Planetarium Society/Beijing Planetarium /June 23 - 27, 2014
International Turfgrass Society/Beijing Friendship Hotel /July 14 - 19, 2013
The Sulphur Institute/The Kerry Hotel /April 24, 2013

FRANCE

Paris

American Comparative Literature Association/Université Paris-Sorbonne /July 18 - 24, 2013
IEEE Signal Processing Society /Oct. 27 - 30, 2014
Institute of International Finance /June 25 - 27, 2013
Osteoarthritis Research Society International /April 24 - 27, 2014
PROMAX/BDA /March 11 - 12, 2013
Society for the Advancement of Economic Theory/Mines ParisTech /July 22 - 27, 2013
Special Interest Group for Computer-Human Interaction /April 27 - May 2, 2013

GERMANY

Duesseldorf and Leiden

Society of Pelvic Surgeons /July 7 - 13, 2013

Frankfurt

American Institute of Chemical Engineers/Marriott Frankfurt Hotel /Aug. 26 - 29, 2013
Business History Conference/Frankfurt /March 13 - 15, 2014
Sewn Products Equipment and Suppliers of the Americas /June 10 - 13, 2013

Hanover

International Embryo Transfer Society/Hanover Congress Centrum /Jan. 19 - 22, 2013

Munich

Association of Industrial Metallizers, Coaters and Laminators/Munich Trade Fair Center /March 19 - 21, 2013
International College of Cranio-Mandibular Orthopedics/Four Seasons Munich /Oct. 10 - 12, 2013
International Society for Pharmacoepidemiology/Hilton Munich City /April 11 - 13, 2013
Optoelectronics Industry Development Association /June 17 - 20, 2013

INDIA

Hyderabad

American Crystallographic Association /Aug. 21 - 29, 2017
IEEE Control Systems Society /Aug. 26 - 28, 2013

International Society for Prosthetics and Orthotics - United States/HICC /April 4 - 7, 2013

ITALY

Florence

Geochemical Society/Firenze Fiera congress centre /Aug. 25 - 30, 2013/3000 attendees
IEEE Control Systems Society /Dec. 10 - 13, 2013
IEEE Signal Processing Society/Firenze Fiera Congress and Exhibition Center / May 4 - 9, 2014
The International Association of Forensic Toxicologists /Aug. 30 - Sept. 4, 2015
Society for Gynecologic Investigation /March 26 - 29, 2014
Society for Psychophysiological Research/Firenze Fiera Congress and Exhibition Center /Oct. 2 - 6, 2013

Milan

Healthcare Compliance Packaging Council/New Exhibition Center Fiera Milano /May 19 - 21, 2015
IEEE Engineering in Medicine and Biology Society /Aug. 26 - 31, 2015
IEEE Instrumentation and Measurement Society /July 15 - 17, 2013
International Society for Magnetic Resonance in Medicine /May 10 - 16, 2014
National Glass Association/Fieramilano /Oct. 23 - 26, 2013
World Allergy Organization /June 22 - 26, 2013

JAPAN

Osaka

Biotechnology Industry Organization (BIO)/The Ritz - Carlton, Osaka /Jan. 29 - 30, 2013
IEEE Engineering in Medicine and Biology Society /July 2 - 7, 2013
IEEE Engineering in Medicine and Biology Society/Osaka International Convention Center /July 3 - 7, 2013

Tokyo

Western Economic Association International /March 14 - 17, 2013

NETHERLANDS

Amsterdam

Council for European Studies /June 25 - 27, 2013
Drug Information Association/Amsterdam RAI Exhibition and Convention Centre /March 4 - 6, 2013/3000 attendees
Institute of Mathematical Statistics/VU University /June 10 - 14, 2013
Interactive Multimedia and Collaborative Communications Alliance /Jan. 29 - 31, 2013/over 100 exhibitors
International Association of Drilling Contractors/Movenpick Hotel /Sept. 25 - 26, 2013
International Neuropsychological Society /July 10 - 13, 2013
International Sanitary Supply Association /May 6 - 9, 2014
International Society on Thrombosis and Hemostasis/Amsterdam RAI /June 29 - July 4, 2013
Private Label Manufacturers Association/Amsterdam RAI Exhibition and Convention Centre /May 28 - 29, 2013/over 100 exhibitors
Remanufacturing Institute/Amsterdam RAI Exhibition and Convention Centre / June 16 - 18, 2013
Reusable Industrial Packaging Association/NH Grand Hotel Krasnapolsky / June 5 - 7, 2013
Society of Petroleum Engineers/Amsterdam RAI Exhibition and Convention Centre /Oct. 27 - 29, 2014

NEW ZEALAND

Rotorua

American Association of Small Ruminant Practitioners/Rotorua Convention Centre /Feb. 18 - 22, 2013

POLAND

Wroclaw

International Society for the Performing Arts /June 17 - 22, 2013
International Society for the Performing Arts /June 19 - 22, 2013

REPUBLIC OF KOREA (SOUTH KOREA)

Gwangju

International Association for Hydrogen Energy/Kimdaejung Convention Center /June 15 - 20, 2014/over 100 exhibitors

SOUTH AFRICA

Cape Town

AAGL - Advancing Minimally Invasive Gynecology Worldwide /April 9 - 13, 2013
International Air Transport Association/Cape Town's International Convention Centre /June 2 - 4, 2013
International Association for Dental Research /June 25 - 28, 2014
International Society for Infectious Diseases /April 2 - 5, 2014

SPAIN

Madrid

Air Traffic Control Association /Feb. 12 - 14, 2013
International Association for Mathematical Geosciences /Sept. 2 - 6, 2013
Legal Netlink Alliance /Jan. 25 - 26, 2013
Society for Pediatric Dermatology/Palacio de Congresos de Madrid /Sept. 25 - 27, 2013

SWEDEN

Stockholm

Association of State and Provincial Psychology Boards /July 7 - 9, 2013
Movement Disorder Society /June 8 - 12, 2014

SWITZERLAND

Geneva

National Business Aviation Association /May 14 - 16, 2013
National Business Aviation Association /May 13 - 15, 2014
National Business Aviation Association /May 19 - 21, 2015

UNITED KINGDOM

Edinburgh

Hotel Electronic Distribution Network Association /June 18 - 20, 2013
The Society for Investigative Dermatology/Edinburgh International Conference Centre /May 8 - 11, 2013

London

Audio Engineering Society /Feb. 6 - 8, 2013
International Communication Association /June 15 - 19, 2013
International Communication Association /June 17 - 21, 2013
International Council of Shopping Centers /May 15 - 17, 2013
International Society for Medical Publication Professionals/Etc Venues /April 22 - 23, 2013
Marble Institute of America /April 30 - May 2, 2013
The Open Group /Oct. 21 - 24, 2013
Professional Lighting and Sound Association/Hotel Earls Court /Sept. 8 - 11, 2013/12000 attendees/over 100 exhibitors
Professional Lighting and Sound Association/Hotel Earls Court /Sept. 14 - 17, 2014/12000 attendees/over 100 exhibitors

Manchester

Man and Cybernetics Systems Society/Ramada Manchester Piccadilly Hotel / Oct. 13 - 16, 2013

Meeting Location Trends

Associations are listed here under the cities where they held at least one annual meeting or conference during 2010, 2011, or 2012, followed by the year/s in which they hosted the meeting.

USA

ALABAMA

Andalusia

American Blonde D'Aquitaine Association (2010)

Auburn

Council On Forest Engineering (2010)

Birmingham

American Holistic Veterinary Medical Association (2012)
Catholic Radio Association (2012)
National Federation of Licensed Practical Nurses (2010)
School Science and Mathematics Association (2012)

Decatur

Racking Horse Breeders Association of America (2010, 2012)

Enterprise

Combat Helicopter Pilots Association (2011)

Florence

Floor Covering Installation Contractors Association (2012)

Hoover

International Society for Computerized Electrocardiology (2012)

Huntsville

American Astronautical Society (2012)
Army Aviation Association of America (2012)
International Test and Evaluation Association (2010)
The Society for Modeling and Simulation International (2010)
United States Army Warrant Officers Association (2010)

Mobile

American Association of Port Authorities (2012)
American Farrier's Association (2012)
Association of Clinical Scientists (2012)
Commission on Accreditation for Law Enforcement Agencies Incorporation (2012)
Epsilon Sigma Phi (2012)
International Society of Automation (2011)
Marine Corps League (2012)
National Association of State Boating Law Administrators (2012)

Montgomery

Rubber Manufacturers Association (2012)
Scrap Tire Management Council (2012)

Point Clear

Association for University and College Counseling Center Directors (2012)
Casting Industry Suppliers Association (2011)
National Association of Independent Insurance Adjusters (2011)
National Conference of Insurance Legislators (2012)

ALASKA

Anchorage

Airlines Electronic Engineering Committee (2012)
Alliance of Hazardous Materials Professionals (2012)
American Association of Railroad Superintendents (2012)
American Astronomical Society (2012)
American Indian Science and Engineering Society (2012)
American Telemedicine Association (2011)
Association of Environmental and Engineering Geologists (2011)
Association of Real Estate License Law Officials (2010)

Council of State Speech-Language-Hearing Association Presidents (2012)
International Association of Aquatic and Marine Science Libraries and Information Centers (2012)
International Society of Hair Restoration Surgery (2011)
National Association for Rural Mental Health (2010, 2012)
National Association of State Treasurers (2012)
National Defense Transportation Association (2012)
National Environmental, Safety and Health Training Association (2012)
The National Federation of Paralegal Associations, Inc. (2012)
National Marine Educators Association (2012)
National Tutoring Association (2011)
Native American Contractors Association (2011)
North American Snowsports Journalists Association (2011)
The Oceanography Society (2010)

Fairbanks

Outdoor Writers Association of America (2012)

ARIZONA

Carefree

Billiard and Bowling Institute of America (2010)
Federation of American Societies for Experimental Biology (2012)

Chandler

American College of Radiology (2012)
American Society for Therapeutic Radiology and Oncology (2010)
American Wind Energy Association (AWEA) (2012)
Ceramic Tile Distributors Association (2011)
Education Finance Council (2012)
Materials and Methods Standards Association (2011)
National Association of Long Term Care Administrator Boards (2010)
National Exchange Club (2012)
Radiology Business Management Association (2012)
Shelf-Stable Food Processors Association (2010)

Eloy

United States Parachute Association (2012)

Glendale

American Membrane Technology Association (2012)
EUCG, Inc. (2010)
Fire and Emergency Manufacturers and Services Association (2012)
Fire Apparatus Manufacturers' Association (2012)
International Hearing Society (2012)
International Society of Beverage Technologists (2010)
International Test and Evaluation Association (2010)

Litchfield Park

Association of Home Appliance Manufacturers (2010)
International Builders Exchange Executives/Builders Exchange Network (2012)
Mechanical Power Transmission Association (2010, 2012)
National Freight Transportation Association (2010, 2012)

Marana

Eye Bank Association of America (2011)
Multi-Housing Laundry Association (2012)
National Insulation Association (2011)

Mesa

American Academy of Advertising (2011)
Ideas America (2012)
Indian Arts and Crafts Association (2012)
National Hearing Conservation Association (2011)
National Tactical Officers Association of America (2012)

Nogales

Fresh Produce Association of the Americas (2012)

Paradise Valley

National Institute of Pension Administrators (2012)

Phoenix

Academy of Doctors of Audiology (2012)
Academy of Osseointegration (2012)
Academy of Psychosomatic Medicine (2011)
Airlines Electronic Engineering Committee (2010)
Alpha Kappa Psi (2011)
American Academy of Appellate Lawyers (2010)
American Academy of Optometry (2012)
American Academy of Pain Management (2012)
American Association for Public Opinion Research (2011)
American Association of Airport Executives (2012)
American Association of Cosmetology Schools (2011)
American Association of Dental Consultants (2011)
American Association of Family and Consumer Sciences (2011)
American Association of Naturopathic Physicians (2011)
American Association of Pastoral Counselors (2011)
American Association of Swine Veterinarians (2011)
American Bankers Insurance Association (2012)
American College Health Association (2011)
American College of Allergy, Asthma and Immunology (2010)
American College of Toxicology (2011)
American Copper Council (2012)
American Correctional Association (2012)
American Council for Construction Education (2012)
American Council on Education (2010)
American Dairy Science Association (2012)
American Dental Hygienists' Association (2012)
American Fuel & Petrochemical Manufacturers (2010)
American Honey Producers Association (2012)
American Institute of Ultrasound in Medicine (2012)
American Seniors Housing Association (2011)
American Society for Healthcare Environmental Services (2012)
American Society for Healthcare Human Resources Administration (2011)
American Society for Laser Medicine and Surgery (2010)
American Society for Therapeutic Radiology and Oncology (2012)
American Society of Animal Science (2012)
American Society of Appraisers (2012)
American Society of Clinical Psychopharmacology (2012)
American Society of Consultant Pharmacists (2010)
American Society of Farm Managers and Rural Appraisers (2011)
American Society of Landscape Architects (2012)
American Society of Professional Estimators (2012)
American Therapeutic Recreation Association (2012)
American Trucking Associations (2010)
Architectural Woodwork Institute (2012)
ASFE/The Geoprofessional Business Association (2011)
ASM International (2012)
Association for Childhood Education International (2010)
Association for Healthcare Documentation Integrity (2011)
Association for Healthcare Foodservice (2011)
Association for Management Information in Financial Services (2012)
Association for Retail Environments (2012)
Association for the Treatment of Sexual Abusers (2010)
Association of Academic Physiatrists (2011)
Association of Bridal Consultants (2010)
Association of Fraternity Advisors (2010)
Association of Genetic Technologists (2010)
Association of Governing Boards of Universities and Colleges (2010, 2011)
Association of Independent Corrugated Converters (2012)
Association of Investment Management Sales Executives (2011)
Association of Marketing Service Providers (2012)
Association of Military Surgeons of the United States (2010, 2012)
Association of National Advertisers (2011)
Association of Old Crows (2012)
Association of Oncology Social Work (2010)
Association of Program Directors in Internal Medicine (2012)
Association of School Business Officials International (2012)
Association of State Correctional Administrators (2012)
Association of Test Publishers (2011)
Association of Vision Science Librarians (2012)
Association of Zoos and Aquariums (2012)
Automatic Fire Alarm Association (2012)
Book Manufacturers' Institute (2010)
Casualty Actuarial Society (2012)
Child Life Council (2010)
Commercial Finance Association (2012)
Construction Specifications Institute (2012)
Corporate Facility Advisors, Inc. (2010)
Correctional Education Association (2012)
Council on Occupational Education (2010)
Design-Build Institute of America (2012)
Drug & Alcohol Testing Industry Association (2010)
Edison Electric Institute (2012)
Electrostatic Discharge Association (2012)
Employee Stock Ownership Plan Association (2012)
Fabricators & Manufacturers Association, International (2012)
Financial Executives International (2011)
Financial Managers Society (2011)
Fluid Sealing Association (2012)
Food Industry Association Executives (2012)
Food Marketing Institute (2011)
Foodservice Equipment Distributors Association (2011)
Gas Machinery Research Council (2010)
Global Market Development Center (2010, 2011, 2012)
Independent Electrical Contractors (2010)
Information Systems Security Association (2012)

Institute for Operations Research and the Management Sciences (2012)
Institute for Professionals in Taxation (2010)
Institute for Supply Management (2010)
International Academy of Trial Lawyers (2010)
International Association for Identification (2012)
International Association of Assessing Officers (2011)
International Association of Venue Managers (2011)
International Business Brokers Association (2011)
International City/County Management Association (2012)
International Communication Association (2012)
International Council of Shopping Centers (2011)
International Digital Enterprise Alliance (2012)
International Embryo Transfer Society (2012)
International Facility Management Association (2011)
International Function Point Users Group (2012)
International Life Sciences Institute (2012)
International Microelectronics and Packaging Society - IMAPS (2012)
Investment Program Association (2011)
Irrigation Association (2010)
Jesuit Association of Student Personnel Administrators (2012)
League for Innovation in the Community College (2011, 2012)
Management Association for Private Photogrammetric Surveyors (2012)
Manufactured Housing Institute (2011)
Material Handling Equipment Distributors Association (2011)
Microanalysis Society (2012)
Microscopy Society of America (2012)
Mortgage Bankers Association of America (2011)
National Association of Student Personnel Administrators (2012)
National Association of Addiction Treatment Providers (2011, 2012)
National Association of Commissions for Women (2011)
National Association of County Administrators (2012)
National Association of Dental Plans (2012)
National Association of Development Companies (2011)
National Association of EMS Physicians (2010)
National Association of Energy Service Companies (2010)
National Association of Extension 4-H Agents (2010)
National Association of Independent Life Brokerage Agencies (2011)
National Association of Private Special Education Centers (2012)
National Association of Public Insurance Adjusters (2011)
National Association of Secondary School Principals (2010)
National Association of Subrogation Professionals (2012)
National Association of Temple Educators (2012)
National Conference of State Legislatures (2010)
National Council for Prescription Drug Programs (2011, 2012)
National Council on Family Relations (2012)
National Customs Brokers and Forwarders Association of America (2011)
National Home Infusion Association (2012)
National League of Cities (2011)
National Mobility Equipment Dealers Association (2012)
National Motor Freight Traffic Association, Inc. (2011)
National Multi-Housing Council (2012)
The National NeedleArts Association (2012)
National Operating Committee for Standards of Athletic Equipment (2012)
National Science Teachers Association (2012)
North American Equipment Dealers Association (2011)
Organization Development Network (2012)
Organization of American Kodaly Educators (2012)
Outdoor Advertising Association of America (2010)
Outdoor Power Equipment Aftermarket Association (2012)
Outdoor Power Equipment and Engine Service Association (2010, 2012)
Parenteral Drug Association (2012)
Performance Warehouse Association (2010, 2011, 2012)
Power Transmission Distributors Association (2010)
Product Development and Management Association (2011)
RCI, Inc. (2012)
Religious Research Association (2012)
Research Chefs Association (2010)
Retail Industry Leaders Association (2012)
SAE International (2010)
Safety Pharmacology Society (2012)
Self-Insurance Institute of America, Inc. (2011)
Sheet Metal and Air Conditioning Contractors' National Association (2010)
Snack Food Association (2012)
Society for Academic Emergency Medicine (2010)
Society for Cardiovascular Magnetic Resonance (2010)
Society for Developmental and Behavioral Pediatrics (2012)
Society for Healthcare Strategy and Market Development (2011)
Society for Medical Decision Making (2012)
Society for the Scientific Study of Religion (2012)
Society of American Business Editors and Writers (2010)
Society of Gastroenterology Nurses and Associates (2012)
Society of General Internal Medicine (2011)
Society of Medical Consultants to the Armed Forces (2010, 2012)
Society of North American Goldsmiths (2012)
Society of Professional Benefit Administrators (2010)
Specialty Tools and Fasteners Distributors Association (2010)
Sports Lawyers Association (2010)
SSPC: the Society for Protective Coatings (2010)
State Government Affairs Council (2010)
Strategic Marketplace Initiative (2012)
Tag and Label Manufacturers Institute (2012)
TAUC - The Association of Union Constructors (2010)
TechServe Alliance (2011)
Trade Promotion Management Associates (2010)
Traffic Audit Bureau for Media Measurement, Inc. (2010)
Undersea and Hyperbaric Medical Society (2012)
Vacation Rental Managers Association (2012)
Visiting Nurse Associations of America (2012)
The Wound, Ostomy and Continence Nurses Society (2010)

Prescott

Western Literature Association (2010)

Scottsdale

ACA International, The Association of Credit and Collection Professionals (2010)
Academy of Laser Dentistry (2012)
Academy of Physicians in Clinical Research (2012)
AHS International - The Vertical Flight Society (2010)
Air Conditioning, Heating and Refrigeration Institute (AHRI) (2010)
Alpha Omega International Dental Fraternity (2012)
American Academy of Addiction Psychiatry (2011)
American Academy of Dental Practice Administration (2012)
American Academy of Maxillofacial Prosthetics (2011)
American Academy of Medical Administrators (2011)
American Academy of Nurse Practitioners (2010)
American Association of Endodontists (2012)
American Association of Medical Assistants (2012)
American Association of Presidents of Independent Colleges and Universities (2012)
American Association of Tissue Banks (2012)
American Auditory Society (2011, 2012)
American Bakers Association (2012)
American Boiler Manufacturers Association (2010)
American Business Media (2010)
American College of Health Plan Management (2011)
American College of Healthcare Information Administrators (2011)
American College of Osteopathic Emergency Physicians (2012)
American College of Physician Executives (2011)
American College of Prosthodontists (2011)
American College of Trial Lawyers (2012)
American Copper Council (2010)
American Dental Society of Anesthesiology (2011)
American Headache Society (2011, 2012)
American Home Furnishings Alliance (2010)
American Hotel & Lodging Association (AH&LA) (2010)
American Immigration Lawyers Association (2010)
American Institute of Graphic Arts (2010, 2011)
American Institute of Physics (2011)
American Jewish Press Association (2010)
American Laryngological, Rhinological and Otological Society (2011)
American Lighting Association (2012)
American Moving and Storage Association (2010)
American Sheep Industry Association (2012)
American Shoulder and Elbow Surgeons (2010)
American Society for Apheresis (2011)
American Society for Healthcare Risk Management (2011)
American Society of Consultant Pharmacists (2011)
American Society of Dentist Anesthesiologists (2011)
American Theological Library Association (2012)
American Traffic Safety Service Association (2011)
American Truck Dealers (2011)
Analytical Laboratory Managers Association (2010)
Assisted Living Federation of America (2010)
Association for Dressings and Sauces (2012)
Association for Financial Technology (2012)
Association for University and College Counseling Center Directors (2011)
Association of Equipment Management Professionals (2012)
Association of Forensic Document Examiners (2010, 2012)
Association of Schools of Allied Health Professions (2011)
Association of Steel Distributors (2012)
Association of University Professors of Ophthalmology (2011)
Battery Council International (2012)
Captive Insurance Companies Association (2012)
Cleaning Equipment Trade Association (2011)
NAIOP, The Commercial Real Estate Development Association (2011)
Commission on Accreditation for Law Enforcement Agencies Incorporation (2012)
Communications Fraud Control Association (2012)
Congress of Chiropractic State Associations (2010)
Conveyor Equipment Manufacturers Association (2010)
Copyright Society of the U.S.A. (2010)
The Cordage Institute (2010)
Council of Administrators of Special Education (2012)
Council of American Survey Research Organizations (2012)
Council of Graduate Schools (2011)
Council on Chiropractic Education (2012)
Council on the Safe Transportation of Hazardous Articles (2011)
CPAmerica International (2011)
Crop Insurance Research Bureau (2012)
Distribution Business Management Association (2010)
Energy and Environmental Building Association (2012)
Envelope Manufacturers Association (2012)
The Fertilizer Institute (2010, 2011)
Flexible Intermediate Bulk Container Association (2011)
Flexible Packaging Association (2012)
Fluid Fertilizer Foundation (2010, 2012)
The Foodservice Group, Inc. (2012)
Forging Industry Association (2011)
Geospatial Information Technology Association (2010)
Hardwood Plywood and Veneer Association (2010)
Health Care Compliance Association (2012)
Healthcare Distribution Management Association (2011)
Hydraulic Institute (2011)
Independent Lubricant Manufacturers Association (2012)
Independent Professional Representatives Organization (2010)
Industrial Diamond Association of America (2012)
Information Technology Alliance (2012)
The Institute of Internal Auditors (2012)
International Association of Drilling Contractors (2012)
International Bottled Water Association (2012)

International Card Manufacturers Association (2010)
International Dyslexia Association (2010)
International Foodservice Manufacturers Association (2012)
International Packaged Ice Association (2012)
International Parking Institute (2012)
International Regional Magazine Association (2012)
International Society of Hospitality Consultants (2010)
International Society of Transport Aircraft Trading (2012)
International Zinc Association-America (2010)
Investment Management Consultants Association (2012)
Investment Recovery Association (2011)
ISA -The Association of Learning Providers (2010, 2012)
IT Financial Management Association (2012)
Laboratory Animal Management Association (2011)
Laboratory Products Association (2012)
Mechanical Service Contractors of America (2010)
National Aerosol Association (2012)
National Aircraft Finance Association (2010)
National Aircraft Resale Association (2012)
NAMTA - National Art Materials Trade Association (2011)
National Association for Kinesiology in Higher Education (2010)
National Association of Child Care Professionals (2011)
National Association of Independent Fee Appraisers (2010)
National Association of Multicultural Engineering Program Advocates (2012)
National Association of Neonatal Nurses (2012)
National Association of Parliamentarians (2012)
National Association of Physician Recruiters (2012)
National Association of Professional Employer Organizations (2012)
National Association of Retail Collection Attorneys (2011)
National Association of Schools of Music (2011)
National Association of State Controlled Substances Authorities (2012)
National Association of Wheat Growers (2011)
National Black Caucus of Local Elected Officials (2011)
National Council of Legislators from Gaming States (2010)
National Crop Insurance Services (2012)
National Fastener Distributors Association (2012)
National Federation of Press Women (2012)
National Forest Recreation Association (2010, 2011)
National Institute of Oilseed Products (2011)
National Institute of Pension Administrators (2011)
National Insulation Association (2012)
National Lamb Feeders Association (2012)
National Lipid Association (2012)
National Livestock Producers Association (2012)
National Minority Supplier Development Council (2010)
National Ocean Industries Association (2010, 2012)
National School Supply and Equipment Association (2010)
National Speakers Association (2010)
National Tutoring Association (2012)
North American Association of Educational Negotiators (2010)
North American Meat Association (2010)
North American Skull Base Society (2011)
North American Society for Pediatric Gastroenterology, Hepatology and Nutrition (2010)
Optical Imaging Association (2012)
Petroleum Equipment Suppliers Association (2012)
The Philanthropy Roundtable (2011)
Physician Insurers Association of America (2011)
Securities Industry and Financial Markets Association (SIFMA) (2012)
Semiconductor Environmental Safety and Health Association (2010, 2011)
Society for Clinical Vascular Surgery (2010)
Society for Mining, Metallurgy and Exploration, Inc. (2010)
Society for Simulation in Healthcare (2010)
Society of Abdominal Radiology (2012)
Society of University Otolaryngologists-Head and Neck Surgeons (2010)
Softwood Export Council (2012)
Special Care Dentistry (2012)
Special Care Dentistry Association (2012)
Tag and Label Manufacturers Institute (2011)
Textile Rental Services Association of America (2011)
Toy Industry Association (2011)
Transportation Elevator and Grain Merchants Association (2012)
Turfgrass Producers International (2012)
VITA (2012)

Sedona

American Osteopathic College of Dermatology (2010)

Tempe

American Society for Environmental History (2011)
American Society of International Law (2012)
Association of Psychology Postdoctoral and Internship Centers (2012)
Association of University Research Parks (2011)
Aviation Technician Education Council (2012)
Contact Lens Manufacturers Association (2010)
Federation of Defense and Corporate Counsel (2012)
International College of Cranio-Mandibular Orthopedics (2012)
International Double Reed Society (2011)
International Society of Appraisers (2012)
Medieval Academy of America (2011)
National Association of Local Government Auditors (2012)
National Dance Education Organization (2010)
National Frozen and Refrigerated Foods Association (2012)
National Ready Mixed Concrete Association (2010)
North American Saxophone Alliance (2012)

Tucson

Accredited Gemologists Association (2010, 2011, 2012)
Accrediting Council for Continuing Education & Training (2011)
Airborne Law Enforcement Association (2010)

Aluminum Extruders Council (2010)
American Academy of Psychiatry and the Law (2010)
American College of Osteopathic Obstetricians and Gynecologists (2012)
American College of Physician Executives (2010)
American Gear Manufacturers Association (2010)
American Gem Trade Association (2011)
American Journalism Historians Association (2010)
American Osteopathic Colleges of Ophthalmology and Otolaryngology - Head and Neck Surgery (2011)
American Society for Dental Aesthetics (2012)
American Society for Pain Management Nursing (2011)
American Society of Andrology (2012)
American Sugarbeet Growers Association (2011)
Armed Forces Communications and Electronics Association (2012)
Asphalt Recycling and Reclaiming Association (2011)
Association for High Technology Distribution (2012)
Association of Energy Services Professionals, International (2010)
Association of Free Community Papers (2010)
Association of Life Insurance Counsel (2011)
Association of Nurses in AIDS Care (2012)
Captive Insurance Companies Association (2011)
Civil Aviation Medical Association (2011)
Consumer Credit Industry Association (2011)
Electrostatic Discharge Association (2012)
Environmental and Engineering Geophysical Society (2012)
Equipment Leasing and Finance Association (2010)
Fibre Channel Industry Association (2012)
Financial and Security Products Association (2010)
Flexographic Prepress Platemakers Association (2011)
Flight Safety Foundation (2010)
Foodservice Equipment Distributors Association (2012)
The Foodservice Group, Inc. (2012)
Foodservice Sales & Marketing Association (2012)
Funeral Consumers Alliance (2012)
Garden Writers Association (2012)
Glass Art Society (2011)
Global Cold Chain Alliance (2012)
Harness Tracks of America (2010)
Human Capital Institute (2010)
Human Resource People and Strategy (2011)
Independent Office Products and Furniture Dealers Association (2011)
Independent Petroleum Association of America (2010)
Indian Diamond and Colorstone Association (2012)
International Energy Credit Association (2010)
International Nurses Society on Addititions (2011)
International Precious Metals Institute (2010)
International Society of Psychiatric-Mental Health Nurses (2011)
International Tuba-Euphonium Association (2010)
Interstate Oil and Gas Compact Commission (2010)
Jeweler's Vigilance Committee (2012)
NADCA: The HVAC Inspection, Maintenance and Restoration Association (2010)
National Association of EMS Physicians (2012)
National Association of Jewelry Appraisers (2010, 2011, 2012)
National Association of Pipe Coating Applicators (2012)
National Association of Schools of Dance (2010, 2012)
National Association of Therapeutic Schools and Programs (NATSAP) (2011)
National Coil Coating Association (2012)
National Council on Teacher Retirement (2012)
National Network of Estate Planning Attorneys (2012)
National Oilseed Processors Association (2010)
National Renderers Association (2011)
National Sporting Goods Association (2011)
National Water Resources Association (2011)
National Weather Association (2010)
North American Meat Association (2012)
North American Neuro-Ophthalmology Society (2010)
North American Society for the Psychology of Sport and Physical Activity (2010)
Petroleum Convenience Alliance for Technology Standards (2012)
Pipe Fabrication Institute (2010)
Plastic Pipe and Fittings Association (2011)
Society for Features Journalism (2011)
Society for Mathematical Biology (2012)
Society for Physical Regulation in Biology and Medicine (2010)
Society for Vascular Nursing (2012)
Society of Emergency Medicine Physician Assistants (2010, 2012)
Society of Independent Gasoline Marketers of America (SIGMA) (2010)
Solar Electric Power Association (2012)
Steel Plate Fabricators Association Division of STI/SPFA (2012)
Transportation Intermediaries Association (2010)
Turf and Ornamental Communicators Association (2010)
Water and Wastewater Equipment Manufacturers Association (2011, 2012)

ARKANSAS

Alma

Credit Professionals International (2010)

Fayetteville

Council of Supply Chain Management Professionals (2012)

Hot Springs

National Association of Farm Service Agency County Office Employees (2010)

Little Rock

American Association of Kidney Patients (2011)
Association for Business Simulation and Experiential Learning (2010)
Association for Education and Rehabilitation of the Blind & Visually Impaired (2010)
Association of State Drinking Water Administrators (2012)
Communications Supply Service Association (2012)

Correctional Education Association (2010)
Future Business Leaders of America - Phi Beta Lambda (2011)
International Association of Baptist Colleges and Universities (2012)
International Conference of Funeral Service Examining Boards (2012)
National Association of State Directors of Teacher Education and Certification (2011)
National Council on Student Development (2010)
National Emergency Management Association (2010)
National Organization of Black Law Enforcement Executives (2012)
Pedorthic Footwear Association (2011, 2012)
Religion Communicators Council (2011)
Reusable Industrial Packaging Association (2010)
Soaring Society of America (2010)

Pinetop

American Society for Engineering Management (2010)

CALIFORNIA

Anaheim

AACE International (2011)
AIM Global (2012)
Ambulatory Surgery Center Association (2010)
American Association for Cancer Research (2012)
American Association for Clinical Chemistry, Inc. (2010)
American Association of Anatomists (2010)
American Association of Equine Practitioners (2012)
American Association of Occupational Health Nurses (2010)
American Baseball Coaches Association (2012)
American Biological Safety Association (2011)
American Chemical Society (2011)
American College of Allergy, Asthma and Immunology (2012)
American College of Veterinary Internal Medicine (2010)
American Culinary Federation (2010)
American Evaluation Association (2011)
American Library Association (2012)
American Medical Student Association (2010)
American Osteopathic Academy of Sports Medicine (2010)
American Philological Association (2010)
American Physical Society (2011)
American Psychiatric Nurses Association (2011)
American Public Power Association (2010)
American Public Works Association (2012)
American Society for Clinical Laboratory Science (2010)
American Society for Investigative Pathology (2010)
American Society for Pharmacology and Experimental Therapeutics (2010)
American Society of Consultant Pharmacists (2012)
American Society of Home Inspectors (2011)
American Soybean Association (2010)
American Specialty Toy Retailing Association (2011)
Archaeological Institute of America (2010)
Association for Applied and Therapeutic Humor (2010)
Association for Educational Communications and Technology (2010)
The Association for Library Service to Children (2012)
Association for Research in Otolaryngology (2010, 2012)
Association for the Advancement of Wound Care (2010)
Association of Arts Administration Educators (2012)
Association of College and University Housing Officers-International (2012)
Association of Latino Professionals in Finance and Accounting (2011)
Association of Pediatric Hematology/Oncology Nurses (2011)
Association of Pediatric Oncology Social Workers (2010)
Association of Professional Researchers for Advancement (2010)
Association of Specialized and Cooperative Library Agencies (2012)
Association of Strategic Alliance Professionals, Inc. (2010)
Association of Threat Assessment Professionals (2010, 2011)
Association of University Technology Managers (2012)
The Association to Advance Collegiate Schools of Business (2010)
BICSI (2012)
Business Professionals of America (2010)
Clerkship Directors in Internal Medicine (2011)
Clowns of America International (2011)
College Athletic Business Management Association (2010)
Commercial Vehicle Safety Alliance (2010)
Common - A Users Group (2012)
Council of Real Estate Brokerage Managers (2011)
Council of Residential Specialists (2011)
Dance Masters of America, Inc. (2012)
Educause (2010)
Electrostatic Discharge Association (2011)
Family, Career and Community Leaders of America (2011)
Fresh Produce Association of the Americas (2012)
IEEE - Nuclear and Plasma Sciences Society (2012)
IEEE Communications Society (2012)
IEEE Computer Society (2012)
Information Systems Security Association (2012)
The Institute of Internal Auditors (2010)
Intermodal Association of North America (2012)
International Dairy-Deli-Bakery Association (2011)
The International Fluid Power Society (2012)
International Test and Evaluation Association (2011)
Journalism Education Association (2011)
Laser Institute of America (2010, 2012)
Learning Forward (2011)
Million Dollar Round Table (2012)
Music Distributors Association (2012)
National Association for Information Destruction, Inc. (2012)
The National Association for Music Education (Formerly MENC) (2010)
National Association for the Education of Young Children (2010)
National Association of Biology Teachers (2011)
National Association of Boards of Pharmacy (2010)

National Association of Catering and Events (2012)
National Association of Chapter Thirteen Trustees (NACTT) (2011)
National Association of Collegiate Directors of Athletics (2010)
National Association of Concessionaires (2011)
National Association of County Park and Recreation Officials (2012)
National Association of Educational Procurement, Inc. (2012)
National Association of Realtors (2011)
National Association of State Directors of Migrant Education (2010)
National Catholic Educational Association (2010)
National Corn Growers Association (2010)
The National Flute Association, Inc. (2010)
National Health Care Anti-Fraud Association (2012)
The National Industrial Transportation League (2012)
National Information Standards Organization (2012)
National Recreation and Parks Association (2012)
National Speakers Association (2011)
North American Association of Commencement Officers (2010)
North American Catalysis Society (2011)
Piano Manufacturers Association International (2010)
Produce Marketing Association (2012)
Romance Writers of America (2012)
Society of Experimental Test Pilots (2010, 2012)
Society of Hispanic Professional Engineers (2011)
Society of Mexican American Engineers and Scientists (2010)
Specialty Coffee Association of America (2010)
Voluntary Protection Programs Participants' Association, Inc. (2012)
Women's Council of REALTORS (2011)
Young Adult Library Services Association (2012)

Asilomar

Association for Transpersonal Psychology (2012)

Atherton

Energy Telecommunications and Electrical Association (2011)

Bakersfield

United Farm Workers of America (2012)

Berkeley

Association for Symbolic Logic (2011)
International Association for the Study of Dreams (2012)
The National Campus Ministry Association (2011)
National Hispanic Corporate Council (2012)
National Property Management Association (2012)
North American Fuzzy Information Processing Society (2012)
North American Society for Sport History (2012)

Beverly Hills

Association of Talent Agents (2011)
Democratic Governors Association (2012)

Big Bear Lake

Academy of Behavioral Medicine Research (2010)
American Association of Variable Star Observers (2012)

Buena Park

Association for Ambulatory Behavioral Healthcare (2010)

Burlingame

Consumer Electronics Association (2011, 2012)
IEEE Photonics Society (2012)
National Association of Seventh-Day Adventist Dentists (2012)
National Council on Rehabilitation Education (2012)
National Venture Capital Association (2010)
United Methodist Association of Health and Welfare Ministries (2010)

Carlsbad

American Hotel & Lodging Association (AH&LA) (2012)
American Wind Energy Association (AWEA) (2011)
Building Stone Institute (2012)
Corporate Event Marketing Association (2011, 2012)
Marine Corps Association (2011)
Mechanical Service Contractors of America (2012)
Metal Treating Institute (2010)
National Ski Area Association (2011)
Pipe Line Contractors Association (2012)
Shelf-Stable Food Processors Association (2012)
Society of Abdominal Radiology (2011)
Society of Neurointerventional Surgery (2010)
Specialized Carriers and Rigging Association (2011)
USA Rice Federation (2010)

Carmel

Western Association of Industrial Distributors (2010, 2011)

Charleston

International Test and Evaluation Association (2010)

Claremont

The Association of Literary Scholars, Critics, and Writers (2012)

Coalinga

Supima (2010, 2012)

Concord

Association of Independent Corrugated Converters (2010)
International Warehouse Logistics Association (2010)

Coronado

American Academy of Emergency Medicine (2012)
American College of Radiation Oncology (2011)
American Feed Industry Association (2012)
American Orthopaedic Association (2010)
American Society of Head and Neck Radiology (2011)
Association for Comprehensive Energy Psychology (2012)
Concrete Sawing and Drilling Association (2010)
Corporate Housing Providers Association (2010)
Educational Theatre Association (2012)
Fibre Box Association (2010)
Label Printing Industries of America (2012)
Mortgage Bankers Association of America (2010)
National Association of Steel Pipe Distributors (2012)
National Water Resources Association (2010, 2012)
North American Securities Administrators Association (NASAA) (2012)
Organization for the Promotion and Advancement of Small Telecommunications
    Companies (2010)
Paperboard Packaging Council (2011)
Pet Industry Distributors Association (2011)
Power-Motion Technology Representatives Association (2012)
SOCAP International (2012)
Society of Thoracic Radiology (2010)
Teratology Society (2011)
USA Rice Federation (2012)
Wood Moulding and Millwork Producers Association (2012)

Costa Mesa

National Association of Educational Office Professionals (2012)
Real Estate Investment Securities Association (2012)
Society for Experimental Mechanics, Inc. (2012)
United States Pan Asian American Chamber of Commerce (2012)

Culver City

Campus Safety, Health and Environmental Management Association (2011)

Dana Point

Air Movement and Control Association International (2012)
American Ophthalmological Society (2011)
American Seniors Housing Association (2012)
American Sportfishing Association (2010)
CropLife America (2011)
International Academy of Compounding Pharmacists (2012)
National Association of Educational Procurement, Inc. (2012)
National Coffee Association of the U.S.A. (2010)
National Oilseed Processors Association (2011)
National Renderers Association (2012)
Plastic Pipe and Fittings Association (2012)
Property Casualty Insurers Association of America (2012)
Society of Independent Gasoline Marketers of America (SIGMA) (2011)
Truck Renting and Leasing Association (2012)

Del Mar

Distance Education and Training Council (2010)
North American Millers' Association (2010)

Escondido

Association of Waldorf Schools of North America (2012)

Fallbrook

American Association for Crystal Growth (2010, 2012)

Fish Camp

Natural Colored Wool Growers Association (2010)

Garden Grove

American Psychosocial Oncology Society (2011)
Certified Contractors Network (2012)
Commission on Accreditation for Law Enforcement Agencies Incorporation (2010)
Society for Neuro-Oncology (2011)

Half Moon Bay

Construction Industry Round Table, Inc. (2012)
Semiconductor Equipment and Materials International (2012)
Snack Food Association (2010)
Valve Manufacturers Association of America (2012)

Hollywood

Deep Foundations Institute (2010)
Society of Motion Picture and Television Engineers (2010, 2011, 2012)

Huntington Beach

American Seed Trade Association (2011)
The Association for Academic Surgery (2011)
Association for Chemoreception Sciences (2012)
Child Neurology Society (2012)
Footwear Distributors and Retailers of America (2012)
International Test and Evaluation Association (2012)
National Renal Administrators Association (2010)
Society of Thoracic Radiology (2012)
Society of University Surgeons (2011)
United States Cutting Tool Institute (2010)
United States Lifesaving Association (2010)
Women Networking in Electronic Transactions (2012)

Incline Village

Utility Arborist Association (2011)

Indian Wells

American Board of Trial Advocates (2010)
American College of Nurse Practitioners (2012)

American Concrete Pavement Association (2011)
American Concrete Pipe Association (2010)
American Osteopathic Colleges of Ophthalmology and Otolaryngology - Head and Neck Surgery (2012)
American Thyroid Association (2011)
APMI International (2012)
Association for Commuter Transportation (2010)
Christian College Consortium (2012)
College of Healthcare Information Management Executives (2012)
Dental Trade Alliance (2010)
Foodservice Equipment Distributors Association (2010)
Fraternity Executives Association (2012)
Institute for Professionals in Taxation (2012)
Institute for Responsible Housing Preservation (2012)
International Truck Parts Association (2010)
The International Wood Products Association (2012)
Material Handling Industry of America (2010)
Metal Powder Industries Federation (2012)
National Association of Chapter Thirteen Trustees (NACTT) (2012)
National Association of Graphic and Product Identification Manufacturers (2011)
National Association of Pipe Coating Applicators (2010)
National Association of School Music Dealers (2011)
National Coil Coating Association (2010)
National Crop Insurance Services (2011)
National Leased Housing Association (2010, 2012)
North American Meat Association (2010)
NPES, The Association for Suppliers of Printing, Publishing, and Converting Technologies (2012)
Pet Industry Distributors Association (2010)
Powder Metallurgy Parts Association (2012)
Resistance Welding Manufacturing Alliance (2012)

Industry

AIR Commercial Real Estate Association (2012)
National Academy of Engineering of the United States of America (2012)

Irvine

American Society of Mechanical Engineers (ASME) (2011)
National Finance Adjusters (2012)
Student Youth and Travel Association (2011)
Tilt-up Concrete Association (2010)

La Jolla

American Association of Genitourinary Surgeons (2012)
American Home Furnishings Alliance (2011)
American Institute of Certified Public Accountants (2010)
Association for Governmental Leasing and Finance (2012)
Billiard and Bowling Institute of America (2012)
Civil Aviation Medical Association (2012)
College of Diplomates of the American Board of Orthodontics (2011)
Home Baking Association (2012)
International Society of Hotel Association Executives (2012)
National Association of Professional Background Screeners (2010)
National Association of Therapeutic Schools and Programs (NATSAP) (2010)
National Trailer Dealers Association (2012)
Pet Industry Joint Advisory Council (2012)

La Quinta

Air Conditioning, Heating and Refrigeration Institute (AHRI) (2012)
American Bankruptcy Institute (2011)
Association for Iron and Steel Technology (2012)
Community Financial Services Association of America CFSA (2010)
Conveyor Equipment Manufacturers Association (2011)
Council of State Governments (2012)
International Dairy Foods Association (2012)
National Association of Chemical Distributors (2010)
National Cheese Institute (2012)
United States Professional Tennis Association (2010)

Laguna Beach

American Connemara Pony Society (2012)
Analytical and Life Science Systems Association (2012)
Council for Responsible Nutrition (2012)
International Truck Parts Association (2012)
National Association of Broadcasters (2012)

Lake Arrowhead

Financial Planning Association (2012)

Lake Tahoe

Cross Country Ski Areas Association (2011)
Exhibition Services and Contractors Association (2010)

Long Beach

American Animal Hospital Association (2010)
American Association of Petroleum Geologists (2012)
American Cable Association (2010)
American College of Nurse-Midwives (2012)
American Institute of Aeronautics and Astronautics (2011)
American Medical Directors Association (2010)
American Oil Chemists' Society (2012)
American Society for Metabolic and Bariatric Surgery (2010)
American Society of Agronomy (ASA, CSSA, SSSA) (2010)
American Sportfishing Association (2010)
American Urogynecologic Society (2010)
Association for Molecular Pathology (2012)
Association of Energy Services Professionals, International (2012)
Association of Pedestrian and Bicycle Professionals (2012)
Building Owners and Managers Association International (2010)
Chief Petty Officers Association (2012)

Community Transportation Association of America (2010)
Construction Management Association of America (2012)
Council on Technology Teacher Education (2012)
Crop Science Society of America (2010)
Enlisted Association of the National Guard of the United States (2012)
Geothermal Energy Association (2012)
Handweavers Guild of America, Inc. (2012)
Hispanic American Police Command Officers Association (HAPCOA) (2012)
Instructional Technology Council (2012)
International Flight Services Association (2010, 2012)
International Microelectronics and Packaging Society - IMAPS (2011)
International Society for the Study of Trauma and Dissociation (2012)
International Society of Travel and Tourism Educators (2010)
International Technology and Engineering Educators Association (2012)
Metal Injection Molding Association (2010)
National Association for the Support of Long Term Care (2010)
National Council for Workforce Education (2012)
National Emergency Number Association (2012)
The National NeedleArts Association (2011)
National Onion Association (2010)
Orthopaedic Research Society (2011)
Power Sources Manufacturers Association (2012)
Professional Beauty Association | National Cosmetology Association (2011, 2012)
SEPM - Society for Sedimentary Geology (2012)
Society for the Advancement of Material and Process Engineering (2011)
Society of Environmental Toxicology and Chemistry (2012)
Society of Teachers of Family Medicine (2012)
Soil Science Society of America (2010)
Sports Turf Managers Association (2012)
TASH (2012)
Transportation Research Forum (2011)
United States Coast Guard Chief Petty Officers Association (2012)
United States Institute for Theatre Technology (2012)
Utilimetrics/Alliance for Advanced Metering & Data Management Solutions (2012)
Utilities Telecom Council (2011)
World Airline Entertainment Association (2010, 2012)

Los Alamitos

Producers Guild of America (2010)

Los Angeles

Academy for Eating Disorders (2011)
Alliance for Women in Media (2010)
American Academy of Gold Foil Operators (2010)
American Academy of Orofacial Pain (2012)
American Academy of Periodontology (2012)
American Association for Clinical Chemistry, Inc. (2012)
American Association of Medical Society Executives (2012)
American Association of Physician Specialists (2012)
American Association of Teachers of Slavic and East European Languages (2011)
American Catholic Philosophical Association (2012)
American College of Occupational and Environmental Medicine (2012)
American Council on Education (2012)
American Headache Society (2010, 2012)
American Heart Association (2012)
American Institute of Certified Planners (2012)
American Planning Association (2012)
American Postal Workers Union (2012)
American Society for Clinical Laboratory Science (2012)
American Society of Composers, Authors and Publishers (ASCAP) (2012)
American Society of Radiologic Technologists (2011)
American Society of Travel Agents (2012)
Architectural Woodwork Institute (2010)
Asian American Journalists Association (2010)
Associated Collegiate Press (2011)
Association for Computational Linguistics (2010)
Association for Slavic, East European, and Eurasian Studies (2010)
Association of Academic Museums & Galleries (2010)
Association of Bridal Consultants (2011)
Association of College and University Religious Affairs (2011)
Association of Collegiate Business Schools and Programs (2010)
Association of Graduate Liberal Studies Programs (2012)
Association of Jesuit Colleges and Universities (2012)
Association of Jewish Family & Children's Agencies (2010)
Association of State and Territorial Solid Waste Management Officials (2010)
Caucus for Producers, Writers & Directors (2012)
College Art Association (2012)
Committee of 200 (2010)
Copyright Society of the U.S.A. (2012)
Council of American Jewish Museums (2010)
Council on Foundations (2012)
Craft & Hobby Association (2011)
Credit Research Foundation (2012)
Entertainment Merchants Association (2012)
Entrepreneurs' Organization (2011)
Financial & Insurance Conference Planners (2012)
IEEE Photonics Society (2012)
Infusion Nurses Society (2011)
Institute of Scrap Recycling Industries, Inc. (2011)
Intellectual Property Owners Association (2011)
International Association of Industrial Accident Boards and Commissions (2010)
International Brotherhood of Teamsters (2012)
International Clarinet Association (2011)
International College of Applied Kinesiology (2010)
International Council of Shopping Centers (2012)
International Health, Racquet and Sportsclub Association (2012)
International Society for Astrological Research (2012)
International Society for Clinical Densitometry (2012)
The International Society for Minimally Invasive Cardiothoracic Surgery (2012)

International Society for Traumatic Stress Studies (2012)
Investment Management Consultants Association (2012)
IPC - Association Connecting Electronics Industries (2012)
IPC Washington Office (2012)
Mobile Marketing Association (2011)
Modern Language Association (2011)
National Association of City and County Health Officials (2012)
National Association of County and City Health Officials (2012)
National Association of Directors of Nursing Administration in Long Term Care
   (2012)
National Association of Disability Examiners (2011)
National Association of Recording Merchandisers (NARM) (2012)
National Association of Television Program Executives (2010)
National Association of Video Distributors (2012)
National Association of Women Lawyers (2012)
National Black MBA Association (2010)
National Cable & Telecommunications Association (2010)
National Council of Higher Education Loan Programs (2012)
National Dance Education Organization (2012)
National Pace Association (2011, 2012)
National WIC Association (2012)
North American Society for Cardiovascular Imaging (2012)
Open Mobile Alliance (2012)
OPERA America (2010)
Pension Real Estate Association (2012)
PROMAX/BDA (2010)
Retail Print Music Dealers Association (2012)
Society for Cinema and Media Studies (2010)
Society for Clinical Data Management (2012)
Society for Ethnomusicology (2010)
Society for French Historical Studies (2012)
Society for Information Display (2012)
Society of Cable Telecommunications Engineers (2010)
Society of Children's Book Writers and Illustrators (2010, 2012)
Society of Industrial and Office Realtors (2012)
Society of Laparoendoscopic Surgeons (2011)
Solar Energy Industries Association (SEIA) (2010)
Taxicab, Limousine & Paratransit Association (2010)
Transportation Intermediaries Association (2012)
United States Pan Asian American Chamber of Commerce (2011)
Women's Caucus for Art (2012)

Manhattan Beach

Institute for Supply Management (2012)
National Council on Rehabilitation Education (2011)

Millbrae

1394 Trade Association (2012)

Milpitas

National Plasterers Council (2012)

Mission Bay

Credit Research Foundation (2010)

Modesto

Plastic Shipping Container Institute (2011)

Monterey

American Immigration Lawyers Association (2010)
American Society for Enology and Viticulture (2011)
American Society of Irrigation Consultants (2010)
Association of Alternative Newsweeklies (2011)
Association of Applied IPM Ecologists (2011)
Association of Defense Communities (2012)
Association of Pathology Chairs (2011, 2012)
Council of Graduate Schools (2011)
Filter Manufacturers Council (2012)
Food Industry Suppliers Association (2012)
Institute for Professionals in Taxation (2011)
The International Ecotourism Society (2012)
Midwives Alliance of North America (2012)
The National Association of Dog Obedience Instructors (2010)
Public Agency Risk Managers Association (2012)
Society for Obstetric Anesthesia and Perinatology (2012)
Society for Pediatric Dermatology (2012)
SPIE - The International Society for Optical Engineering (2010, 2011, 2012)
Timber Frame Business Council (2012)
United States Professional Tennis Association (2012)
Western Association of Industrial Distributors (2012)
Wood Machinery Manufacturers of America (2010)
Woodworking Machinery Industry Association (2010)

Morro Bay

Asia America MultiTechnology Association (2010)

Mountain View

Asia America MultiTechnology Association (2012)

Napa

American Veterinary Distributors Association (2010)
Association for Financial Technology (2010)
Association of University Technology Managers (2012)
Contact Lens Manufacturers Association (2012)
Dental Trade Alliance (2012)
Equipment and Tool Institute (2010)
International Energy Credit Association (2012)
National Association of Principals of Schools for Girls (2010)
National College of Probate Judges (2012)
National District Attorneys Association (2010)

Plastic Pipe and Fittings Association (2010)
Sanitary Supply Wholesaling Association (2011)

Napa Valley

Fluid Sealing Association (2011)

Newport Beach

American Association of Birth Centers (2010)
American Association of Critical-Care Nurses (2012)
Asphalt Institute (2011)
Commercial Vehicle Safety Alliance (2012)
Contact Lens Society of America (2012)
Hop Growers of America (2012)
IEEE Ultrasonics, Ferroelectrics and Frequency Control Society (2010)
Institute of Navigation (2012)
Multi-Level Marketing International Association (2010)
National Association of Intercollegiate Athletics (2012)
Society of Teachers of Family Medicine (2011)
Tile Roofing Institute (2010)

Oakland

American Association of Zoo Veterinarians (2012)
Architectural Engineering Institute (2011)
Chief Warrant and Warrant Officers Association, United States Coast Guard
   (2010)
National Women's Studies Association (2012)
North American Association for Environmental Education (2012)
Western History Association (2011)

Ojai

National Association of Public Insurance Adjusters (2010)

Olympic Valley

National Association of State Retirement Administrators (2012)
Society of Gynecologic Oncologists (2012)

Ontario

American Association of Physics Teachers (2012)
American Ground Water Trust (2012)
American Institute of Parliamentarians (2010)
North American Society for Trenchless Technology (2012)
Society for Chaos Theory in Psychology and Life Sciences (2011)

Orange

National Association of Women Judges (2012)

Oxnard

Association of Applied IPM Ecologists (2012)

Pacific Grove

Timber Framers Guild (2012)

Pala

National Lubricating Grease Institute (2012)

Palm Desert

American Academy of Dental Practice Administration (2010)
American Agents Alliance (2012)
American Association of Managing General Agents (2010)
American Bankers Association (2012)
American College of Trial Lawyers (2010)
American Pediatric Surgical Association (2011)
American Sports Builders Association (2011)
Arthroscopy Association of North America (2011)
Credit Union Executives Society (2012)
Edison Electric Institute (2010)
Equipment Leasing and Finance Association (2012)
Federal Managers Association (2011)
Institute of Nuclear Materials Management (2011)
International Association of Special Investigation Units (2012)
Investment Company Institute (2011)
Marketing Association of Credit Unions (2010)
National Aerosol Association (2011)
National Asphalt Pavement Association (2012)
National Association of Nurse Practitioners in Women's Health (2010)
National Lubricating Grease Institute (2011)
National Railroad Construction and Maintenance Association, Inc. (2010)
National Retail Tenants Association (2012)
United Shoe Retailers Association (2010)

Palm Spring

Aircraft Owners and Pilots Association (2012)
American Academy of Pain Medicine (2012)
American Advertising Federation (2011)
American Architectural Manufacturers Association (2010, 2011)
American Bonanza Society (2012)
American Institute of Oral Biology (2010, 2011, 2012)
American Ladder Institute (2011)
American Society for Nondestructive Testing (2011)
American Welara Pony Registry (2010)
Associated Cooperage Industries of America (2011)
Association of American Medical Colleges (2012)
Association of Schools of Allied Health Professions (2012)
Association of Test Publishers (2012)
Association of Water Technologies (2012)
BAFT-IFSA (2011)
Ceramic Tile Distributors Association (2012)
Collision Industry Electronic Commerce Association (2012)
Commercial Finance Association (2010)
Community Associations Institute (CAI) (2012)

Copper and Brass Servicenter Association (2012)
Environmental and Water Resources Institute of the American Society of Civil
    Engineers (2011)
Equipment and Tool Institute (2012)
Exhibit Designers and Producers Association (2012)
Foodservice Sales & Marketing Association (2011)
IDEA, The Health and Fitness Association (2012)
Independent Lubricant Manufacturers Association (2010)
Independent Petroleum Association of America (2011)
Institute for Credentialing Excellence (2012)
International Association of Lighting Management Companies (2012)
International Reprographic Association (2010)
Manufacturers' Agents Association for the Foodservice Industry (2012)
NALP - The Association for Legal Career Professionals (2011)
National Association of Neonatal Nurses (2012)
National Cancer Registrars Association (2010)
National Exchange Club (2010)
National Gerontological Nursing Association (2010)
National Institute of Oilseed Products (2010, 2012)
National Onion Association (2012)
National Trailer Dealers Association (2010)
North American Serials Interest Group (2010)
Osteopathic Cranial Academy (2010)
Refrigerated Foods Association (2012)
Society for Human Resource Management (2012)
Stadium Managers Association (2012)
Western Association for Art Conservation (2012)

Palo Alto

American Association for the Advancement of Artificial Intelligence (2012)
American College of Real Estate Lawyers (2010)
American Volleyball Coaches Association (2010)
National Venture Capital Association (2011, 2012)
TechAmerica (fka Technology Association of America) (2012)

Pasadena

American Association for Physical Activity and Recreation (2012)
American Astronautical Society (2012)
American Institute of Aeronautics and Astronautics (2012)
Institute of Transportation Engineers (2012)
International Professional Groomers (2010)
National Association for Chicana and Chicano Studies (2011)
Society for the History of Discoveries (2012)

Pebble Beach

Neurosurgical Society of America (2010)

Pleasanton

Fresh Produce and Floral Council (2010)

Pomona

Recreation Vehicle Industry Association (2011)

Pt. Mugu

Association of Old Crows (2012)

Rancho Mirage

Agricultural Retailers Association (2010)
American Dental Education Association (2012)
American Wire Producers Association (2012)
Association for Retail Environments (2010)
City and Regional Magazine Association (2012)
Coin Laundry Association (2012)
Concrete Sawing and Drilling Association (2010)
Conference of Consulting Actuaries (2010)
Council for Responsible Nutrition (2011)
Fire Suppression Systems Association (2012)
International Association of Defense Counsel (2012)
International Concrete Repair Institute (2012)
International Map Trade Association (2012)
International SalonSpa Business Network (ISBN) (2012)
International Zinc Association-America (2012)
Maple Flooring Manufacturers Association (2012)
Materials and Methods Standards Association (2012)
National Tile Contractors Association (2012)
Pharmaceutical Care Management Association (2010, 2011)
Precision Machined Products Association (2010)
Tire Industry Association (2012)

Rancho Palos Verdes

Association of Equipment Manufacturers (2012)

Redondo Beach

American Pathology Foundation (2012)
Association of American Feed Control Officials (2010)

Riverside

University and College Designers Association (2012)

Sacramento

American Art Therapy Association, Inc. (2010)
American Medical Writers Association (2012)
American Philatelic Society (2012)
American Society of Primatologists (2012)
ASPRS-The Imaging and Geospatial Information Society (2012)
Association for Play Therapy (2011)
The Association for Science Teacher Education (2010)
Association of Asphalt Paving Technologists (2010)
Association of Biomolecular Resource Facilities (2010)
Association of Commercial Real Estate (2012)

Atlantic Seaboard Wine Association (2012)
Geothermal Energy Association (2010, 2012)
Giant Screen Cinema Association (2012)
Health Physics Society (2012)
Information Systems Audit and Control Association (2012)
International Association of Bedding and Furniture Law Officials (2012)
National Alfalfa Alliance (2012)
National Association for Healthcare Quality (2011)
National Association of State Directors of Developmental Disabilities Services,
    Inc. (2012)
National Association of State Directors of Special Education (2012)
National Association of State Directors of Teacher Education and Certification
    (2011)
National Black Police Association (2010)
National Christmas Tree Association (2012)
NCSL International (2012)
Property Loss Research Bureau (2011)
Public Agency Risk Managers Association (2010)
Society for American Archaeology (2011)
Society for Technical Communication (2011)
Society of Municipal Arborists (2012)
United States Committee on Irrigation and Drainage (2010)
United States Society on Dams (2010)

San Bernardino

Urban Libraries Council (2011)
Vocational Evaluation and Career Assessment Professionals (2012)

San Diego

AABB - American Association of Blood Banks (2011)
Academy of Criminal Justice Sciences (2010)
Academy of General Dentistry (2011)
Academy of Managed Care Pharmacy (2010)
Academy of Nutrition and Dietetics (2011)
The Acoustical Society of America (2011)
ADARA (2011)
Agricultural Retailers Association (2012)
Airports Council International - North America (2011)
Allied Finance Adjusters (2010)
America's Small Business Development Center Network (2011)
American Academy of Audiology (2010)
American Academy of Dermatology (2012)
American Academy of Environmental Medicine (2010)
American Academy of Facial Plastic and Reconstructive Surgery (2012)
American Academy of Oral and Maxillofacial Radiology (2010)
American Academy of Orthopaedic Surgeons (2011)
American Academy of Pediatric Dentistry (2012)
American Alliance for Health, Physical Education, Recreation and Dance (2011)
American Architectural Manufacturers Association (2011)
American Association for Aerosol Research (2010)
American Association for Dental Research (2011)
American Association for Health Education (2011)
American Association for Laboratory Animal Science (2011)
American Association for Pediatric Ophthalmology and Strabismus (2011)
American Association for the Advancement of Science (2010)
American Association for the Study of Hungarian History (2010)
American Association of Anatomists (2012)
American Association of Avian Pathologists (2012)
American Association of Clinical Endocrinologists (2011)
American Association of Colleges for Teacher Education (2011)
American Association of Dental Consultants (2010)
American Association of Directors of Psychiatric Residency Training (2012)
American Association of Endodontists (2010)
American Association of Feline Practitioners (2010)
American Association of Insurance Services (2012)
American Association of Oral and Maxillofacial Surgeons (2012)
American Association of Orthodontists (2011)
American Association of Pathologists' Assistants (2012)
American Association of Pharmaceutical Scientists (2012)
American Association of Teachers of Turkic Languages (2010)
American Association of Tissue Banks (2011)
American Association of Veterinary Parasitologists (2012)
American Association of Zoo Keepers (2011)
American Bankers Association (2012)
American Board of Trial Advocates (2012)
American Board of Vocational Experts (2010)
American Brachytherapy Society (2011)
American Broncho-Esophagological Association (2012)
American Catholic Historical Association (2010)
American Chemical Society (2012)
American College for Advancement in Medicine (2010)
American College of Chiropractic Orthopedists (2012)
American College of Clinical Pharmacology (2012)
American College of Construction Lawyers (2010)
American College of Medical Toxicology (2012)
American College of Neuropsychiatrists (2012)
American College of Osteopathic Family Physicians (2012)
American College of Osteopathic Pediatricians (2012)
American College of Physicians (2011)
American College of Trial Lawyers (2011)
American College of Veterinary Ophthalmologists (2010)
American Dental Education Association (2011)
American Epilepsy Society (2012)
American Frozen Food Institute (2010, 2012)
American Fuel & Petrochemical Manufacturers (2012)
American Group Psychotherapy Association (2010)
American Historical Association (2010)
American Holistic Medical Association (2012)
American Homebrewers Association (2011)
American Horse Publications (2011)

American Humor Studies Association (2010)
American Immigration Lawyers Association (2011)
American Institute of Hydrology (2012)
American Institute of Ultrasound in Medicine (2010, 2012)
American Ladder Institute (2010)
American Land Title Association (2010)
American Laryngological Association (2012)
American Laryngological, Rhinological and Otological Society (2012)
American Library Association (2011)
American Medical Group Association (2012)
American Medical Rehabilitation Providers Association (2012)
American Membrane Technology Association (2010)
American Neurological Association (2011)
American Neurotology Society (2012)
American Nuclear Society (2010, 2012)
American Organization of Nurse Executives (2011)
American Ornithologists' Union (2010)
American Orthopaedic Society for Sports Medicine (2011)
American Osteopathic Academy of Addiction Medicine (2012)
American Osteopathic Academy of Sports Medicine (2012)
American Osteopathic Association (2012)
American Osteopathic College of Dermatology (2012)
American Otological Society (2012)
American Pathology Foundation (2012)
American Petroleum Institute (2011, 2012)
American Philosophical Association (2011)
American Physical Therapy Association (2010)
American Psychological Association (2010)
American Public Gas Association (2010)
American Rhinologic Society (2012)
American Risk and Insurance Association (2011)
American Society for Biochemistry and Molecular Biology (2010, 2012)
American Society for Blood and Marrow Transplantation (2012)
American Society for Bone and Mineral Research (2011)
American Society for Indexing (2012)
American Society for Investigative Pathology (2012)
American Society for Metabolic and Bariatric Surgery (2012)
American Society for Microbiology (2010)
American Society for Nutrition (2012)
American Society for Pharmacology and Experimental Therapeutics (2012)
American Society for Precision Engineering (2012)
American Society for Reproductive Medicine (2012)
American Society of Anesthesia Technologists and Technicians (2010)
American Society of Anesthesiologists (2010)
American Society of Cataract and Refractive Surgery (2011)
American Society of Consulting Arborists (2012)
American Society of Golf Course Architects (2010)
American Society of Hand Therapists (2012)
American Society of Health-System Pharmacists (2010)
American Society of Hematology (2011)
American Society of Landscape Architects (2011)
American Society of Nephrology (2012)
American Society of News Editors (2011)
American Society of Ophthalmic Administrators (2011)
American Society of Orthopedic Physician Assistants (2012)
American Society of Radiologic Technologists (2010)
American Society of Regional Anesthesia and Pain Medicine (2012)
American Society of Transplant Surgeons (2010)
American Society of Women Accountants (ACC) (2012)
American Speech-Language-Hearing Association (2011)
American Statistical Association (2012)
American Subcontractors Association (2010)
American Translators Association (2012)
American Veterinary Medical Association (2012)
Applied Research Ethics National Association (2012)
Armed Forces Communications and Electronics Association (2012)
AscdiNatd (2012)
Asian American Psychological Association (2010)
ASPRS-The Imaging and Geospatial Information Society (2010)
Associated Builders and Contractors (2010)
Association for Applied Psychophysiology and Biofeedback (2010)
Association for Business Simulation and Experiential Learning (2012)
Association for Conflict Resolution (2011)
Association for Corporate Growth (2011)
The Association for Environmental Health and Sciences (2010, 2012)
Association for Hose and Accessories Distribution (2011)
Association for Integrative Studies (2010)
Association for Library and Information Science Education (2011)
Association for Library Collections and Technical Services (2011)
Association for Research in Otolaryngology (2012)
Association for Surgical Education (2012)
Association for Technology in Music Instruction (2012)
Association for the Advancement of Computing in Education (2010)
Association of American Physicians and Surgeons (2012)
Association of American Veterinary Medical Colleges (2012)
Association of Avian Veterinarians (2010)
Association of Camp Nurses (2011)
Association of College Administration Professionals (2010)
Association of College Honor Societies (2012)
Association of Correctional Food Service Affiliates (2010)
Association of Dermatology Administrators & Managers (2012)
Association of Earth Science Editors (2012)
Association of Energy Services Professionals, International (2012)
Association of Girl Scout Executive Staff (2011)
Association of Government Accountants (2012)
Association of Healthcare Internal Auditors (2011)
Association of Insolvency and Restructuring Advisors (2010)
Association of Military Banks of America (2010)
Association of Nutrition & Foodservice Professionals (2012)
Association of Pedestrian and Bicycle Professionals (2012)

Association of Pet Dog Trainers (2011)
Association of Physician Assistants in Cardiovascular Surgery (2011)
Association of Professors of Medicine (2010)
Association of Program Directors in Surgery (2012)
Association of Service and Computer Dealers International (2012)
Association of TeleServices International, Inc. (2010)
Association of University Radiologists (2010)
The Association to Advance Collegiate Schools of Business (2012)
Automatic Fire Alarm Association (2010)
Biophysical Society (2012)
The Brewers Association (2012)
Ceilings and Interior Systems Construction Association (2012)
Chief Administrators of Catholic Education (2012)
Choristers Guild (2010)
Christian Leadership Alliance (2010)
College Music Society (2012)
College of American Pathologists (2012)
College Reading and Learning Association (2011)
College Swimming Coaches Association of America (2011)
Commission on Accreditation of Allied Health Education Programs (2012)
The Conference Board (2012)
Construction Management Association of America (2010)
Controlled Environment Testing Association (2012)
Coordinating Research Council (2010)
Council for Adult and Experiential Learning (2010)
Council for Advancement and Support of Education (2012)
Council for Opportunity in Education (2010)
Council of Administrators of Special Education (2010)
Council of American Survey Research Organizations (2010)
Council of Industrial Boiler Owners (CIBO) (2012)
Council of State Administrators of Vocational Rehabilitators (2012)
Council of State Speech-Language-Hearing Association Presidents (2011)
Council of Supply Chain Management Professionals (2010)
Craft & Hobby Association (2012)
Credit Union National Association, Inc. (2012)
CTIA - The Wireless Association (2011, 2012)
Dairy Management, Inc. (2011)
Decision Sciences Institute (2010)
Defense Research Institute (2010)
Dermatology Nurses' Association (2011)
Distribution Business Management Association (2010)
Driver Employer Council of America (2012)
Earthquake Engineering Research Institute (2011)
EDA Consortium (2010, 2011)
Emergency Nurses Association (2012)
Endocrine Fellows Foundation (2010)
The Endocrine Society (2012)
Entomological Society of America (2010)
Environmental Bankers Association (2010)
The Environmental Information Association (2012)
Event Service Professionals Association (2012)
Federal Bar Association (2012)
The Fertilizer Institute (2010)
Flight Safety Foundation (2011)
The Foodservice Group, Inc. (2012)
Foodservice Sales & Marketing Association (2012)
Gay and Lesbian Medical Association (2010)
Genetics Society of America (2011)
Geothermal Resources Council (2011)
Gerontological Society of America (2012)
Gynecologic Oncology Group (2010, 2011, 2012)
Health Forum (2010)
Hispanic Association of Colleges and Universities (2010)
History of Dermatology Society (2012)
History of Science Society (2012)
IDEA, The Health and Fitness Association (2012)
IEEE Engineering in Medicine and Biology Society (2012)
IEEE Photonics Society (2012)
IEEE Power and Energy Society (2012)
Incentive Marketing Association (2011)
Independent Lubricant Manufacturers Association (2010)
Industrial Fabrics Association International (2011)
Industrial Minerals Association -- North America (2012)
Infectious Diseases Society of America (2012)
Inland Marine Underwriters Association (2012)
InSight (2012)
Institute for Supply Management (2010)
Institute of Behavioral and Applied Management (2010)
Institute of Business Appraisers (2011)
Institute of Scrap Recycling Industries, Inc. (2010)
Insurance Accounting and Systems Association (2012)
Insured Retirement Institute (2012)
International Anti-Counterfeiting Coalition (2012)
International Association for Dental Research (2011)
International Association for Food Protection (2010)
International Association of Administrative Professionals (2011)
International Association of Business Communicators (2011)
International Association of Chiefs of Police (2012)
International Association of Drilling Contractors (2012)
International Association of Fire Fighters (2010)
International Association of Healthcare Central Service Materiel Management (2010)
International Association of Law Enforcement Intelligence Analysts (2012)
International Association of Speakers Bureaus (2011)
International Bridge, Tunnel and Turnpike Association (2010)
International Claim Association (2012)
International Cost Estimating and Analysis Association effective (2010)
International Council of Shopping Centers (2011)
International Federation of Fertility Societies (2012)
International Food Service Executives' Association (2012)

International Foundation for Telemetering (2012)
International Foundation of Employee Benefit Plans (2010, 2012)
International Health, Racquet and Sportsclub Association (2010)
International Institute of Ammonia Refrigeration (2010)
International Lactation Consultant Association (2011)
International Microelectronics and Packaging Society - IMAPS (2012)
International Molded Fibre Association (2012)
International Society for Developmental Psychobiology (2010)
International Society for Heart and Lung Transplantation (2011)
International Society for Technology in Education (2012)
International Society of Beverage Technologists (2012)
International Society of Explosives Engineers (2011)
International Sports Heritage Association (2010)
International Studies Association (2012)
International Titanium Association (2011)
International Writing Centers Association (2012)
Interstate Natural Gas Association of America (2011)
IPC - Association Connecting Electronics Industries (2012)
IPC Washington Office (2012)
Irrigation Association (2011)
Lambda Kappa Sigma (2012)
Land Improvement Contractors of America (2012)
League of Historic American Theatres (2012)
Licensing Executives Society (2011)
Literacy Research Association (2012)
Lutheran Educational Conference of North America (2011)
Major Cities Chiefs Association (2012)
Marine Fabricators Association (2011)
Medical Fitness Association (2010)
Metal Construction Association (2011)
Metal Injection Molding Association (2012)
Middle East Librarians' Association (2010)
Middle East Studies Association of North America (2010)
Monument Builders of North America (2012)
Mortgage Bankers Association of America (2012)
Multi-Housing Laundry Association (2011)
Music Library Association (2010)
Mystery Shopping Providers Association (2012)
NAMM - The International Music Products Association (2010, 2011, 2012)
National Academy of Arbitrators (2011)
National Academy of Elder Law Attorneys, Inc. (2010)
National Air Filtration Association (2012)
National Alliance of State Pharmacy Associations (2012)
National Association for Girls and Women in Sport (2011)
National Association for Kinesiology in Higher Education (2012)
National Association of Black Journalists (2010)
National Association of Boards of Examiners of Long Term Care Administrators (2012)
National Association of Chemical Distributors (2011, 2012)
National Association of College Wind and Percussion Instructors (2012)
National Association of Development Organizations (2010)
National Association of Electrical Distributors (2010)
National Association of Foreign Trade Zones (2012)
National Association of Government Defined Contribution Administrators (2012)
National Association of Healthcare Access Management (2012)
National Association of Hispanic Publications (2012)
National Association of Letter Carriers (2010)
National Association of Long Term Care Administrator Boards (2012)
National Association of Mutual Insurance Companies (2010)
National Association of Professional Organizers (2011)
National Association of Professional Surplus Lines Offices, Ltd. (2011)
National Association of Public Insurance Adjusters (2012)
National Association of Real Estate Editors (2010)
National Association of Real Estate Investment Trusts (NAREIT) (2012)
National Association of Regional Councils (2011)
National Association of Retail Collection Attorneys (2012)
National Association of Schools of Music (2012)
National Association of State Budget Officers (2012)
National Association of State Chief Information Officers (2012)
National Association of State Credit Union Supervisors (2011)
National Association of State Workforce Agencies (2012)
National Beer Wholesalers Association (2012)
National Black Nurses Association (2010)
National Business Aviation Association (2010)
National Business Education Association (2010)
National Community Pharmacists Association (2012)
National Conference of Bankruptcy Judges (2012)
National Council for Community Behavioral Healthcare (2011)
National Council of Exchangors (2011)
National Council of Juvenile and Family Court Judges (2010)
National Council of State Agencies for the Blind (2012)
National Council of State Housing Agencies (2011)
National Council of Supervisors of Mathematics (2010)
National Council of Teachers of Mathematics (2010)
National Council of University Research Administrators (2011)
National Council on Aging (2012)
National Dance Association (2011)
National Electrical Contractors Association (2011)
National Electrical Manufacturers Representatives Association (2012)
National Federation of State High School Associations (2010)
National Health Council (2012)
National Hospice & Palliative Care Organization (2011)
National Indian Education Association (2010)
National Indian Gaming Association (2010)
National Indian Head Start Directors Association (2010)
National Intramural-Recreational Sports Association (2010)
National Investor Relations Institute (2010)
National League of Postmasters of the United States (2010)
National Milk Producers Federation (2011)
The National Network for Social Work Managers (2012)

National Notary Association (2012)
National Optometric Association (2011)
National Public Employer Labor Relations Association (2011)
National Railroad Construction and Maintenance Association, Inc. (2012)
National Retail Federation (2012)
National Shellfisheries Association (2010)
National Sheriffs' Association (2010)
National Society of Genetic Counselors (2011)
National Society of Hispanic MBAs (2011)
National Society of Professional Engineers (2012)
National Student Nurses Association (2012)
National Student Osteopathic Medical Association (2012)
National Telecommunications Cooperative Association (2012)
National Tour Association (2012)
National Training and Simulation Association (2012)
NGVAmerica (2012)
North American Association of Educational Negotiators (2011)
North American Catalysis Society (2012)
North American Electric Reliability Corporation (2012)
North American Gaming Regulators Association (2011)
North American Society for the Sociology of Sport (2010)
Osteoarthritis Research Society International (2011)
Pet Sitters International (2010)
Phi Alpha Theta (2010)
Philosophy of Science Association (2012)
Physician Office Managers Association of America (2011)
Police Executive Research Forum (2012)
Portable Sanitation Association International (2012)
Professional Convention Management Association (2012)
Professional Liability Underwriting Society (2011)
Professional Retail Store Maintenance Association (2012)
The Protein Society (2010, 2012)
Radiation Therapy Oncology Group (2011)
Renal Physicians Association (2012)
Ruth Jackson Orthopaedic Society (2011)
Ryan White Medical Providers Coalition (2012)
Safe and Vault Technicians Association (2010)
SAFE Association (2010)
Schools Interoperability Framework Association (2012)
Search - The National Consortium for Justice Information and Statistics (2012)
Secondary Materials and Recycled Textiles Association (2012)
Seismological Society of America (2012)
Shareholder Services Association (2012)
SMMA - The Motor and Motion Association (2011)
Society for Anthropology in Community Colleges (2012)
Society for Cardiovascular Angiography and Interventions (2010)
Society for Education in Anesthesia (2010)
Society for Free Radical Biology and Medicine (2012)
Society for Gynecologic Investigation (2012)
Society for Human Resource Management (2010)
Society for Industrial and Organizational Psychology Inc. (2012)
Society for Italian Historical Studies (2010)
The Society for Modeling and Simulation International (2010, 2012)
Society for Neuroscience (2010)
Society for Neuroscience in Anesthesiology and Critical Care (2010)
Society for Pediatric Anesthesia (2010, 2011)
Society for Pediatric Dermatology (2012)
Society for Personality and Social Psychology (2012)
Society for Radiation Oncology Administration (2010)
Society for Simulation in Healthcare (2012)
Society for Surgery of the Alimentary Tract (2012)
Society of American Gastrointestinal and Endoscopic Surgeons (2012)
Society of Cardiovascular Anesthesiologists (2010, 2011, 2012)
Society of Computed Body Tomography and Magnetic Resonance (2010)
Society for Critical Care Medicine (2011)
Society of Financial Service Professionals (2011)
Society of Former Special Agents of the Federal Bureau of Investigation (2012)
Society of Hospital Medicine (2012)
Society of Military Orthopaedic Surgeons (2011)
Society of Neurointerventional Surgery (2012)
Society of Professors of Child and Adolescent Psychiatry (2012)
Society of State Leaders of Health and Physical Education (2011)
Society of Thoracic Surgeons (2011)
SPIE - The International Society for Optical Engineering (2010, 2011)
Sports Lawyers Association (2012)
Strategic Account Management Association (2012)
Substance Abuse Program Administrators Association (2012)
SWANA - Solid Waste Association of North America (2010)
Technical Association of the Graphic Arts (2010)
Textile Rental Services Association of America (2010)
Transportation and Logistics Council (2010)
Turnaround Management Association (2011)
United Association for Labor Education (2010)
United States Committee on Irrigation and Drainage (2011)
United States Society on Dams (2011)
USENIX: The Advanced Computing Systems Association (2012)
Veterinary Cancer Society (2010)
Western Economic Association International (2011)
Wireless Innovation Forum (2012)
Women in Mining National (2012)
Workgroup for Electronic Data Interchange (2010)
World Aquaculture Society (2010)
World History Association (2010)
WorldatWork (2011)

San Francisco

Academy of Aphasia (2012)
Academy of Managed Care Pharmacy (2012)
Academy of Rehabilitative Audiology (2010)
Advertising and Marketing International Network (2012)

African Studies Association (2010)
AHS International - The Vertical Flight Society (2012)
Aluminum Extruders Council (2012)
American Academy of Adoption Attorneys (2011)
American Academy of Allergy, Asthma, and Immunology (2011)
American Academy of Child and Adolescent Psychiatry (2012)
American Academy of Optometry (2010)
American Academy of Orthopaedic Surgeons (2012)
American Academy of Otolaryngology-Head and Neck Surgery (2011)
American Academy of Pediatrics (2010)
American Academy of Religion (2011)
American Accounting Association (2010)
American Anthropological Association (2012)
American Assembly for Men in Nursing (2012)
American Association for the Advancement of Artificial Intelligence (2011)
American Association for the Study of Liver Diseases (2011)
American Association of Thoracic Surgery (2012)
American Association of Advertising Agencies (2010)
American Association of Bank Directors (2012)
The American Association of Dental Boards (2012)
American Association of Dental Editors (2012)
American Association of Hip and Knee Surgeons (2012)
American Association of Immunologists (2011)
American Association of Independent Music (2012)
American Association of Neuromuscular and Electrodiagnostic Medicine (2011)
American Association of Nurse Anesthetists (2012)
American Association of Pathologists' Assistants (2011)
American Association of Plastic Surgeons (2012)
American Association of Public Health Physicians (2012)
American Association of State Colleges and Universities (2012)
American Bar Association (2010)
American Business Media (2012)
American Chemical Society (2010)
American College of Dentists (2012)
American College of Forensic Psychiatry (2010)
American College of Osteopathic Internists (2010)
American College of Osteopathic Surgeons (2010)
American College of Physician Executives (2012)
American College of Psychiatrists (2011)
American College of Sports Medicine (2012)
American College of Surgeons (2011)
American College of Theriogenologists (2012)
American Conference of Academic Deans (2011)
American Congress of Obstetricians and Gynecologists (2010)
American Counseling Association (2012)
American Craft Council (2012)
American Dental Association (2012)
American Endodontic Society, Inc. (2012)
American Family Therapy Academy (2012)
American Federation of Teachers (AFL-CIO) (2010)
American Frozen Food Institute (2011)
American Geophysical Union (2010, 2011, 2012)
American Glovebox Society (2011)
American Hernia Society (2011)
American Hospital Association (2012)
American Institute of Chemical Engineers (2010)
American Institute of Graphic Arts (2012)
American Intellectual Property Law Association (2011)
American Judicature Society (2010)
American Law Institute (2011)
American Mathematical Society (2010)
American Montessori Society (2012)
American Musicological Society (2011)
American National Standards Institute (2010)
American Neurological Association (2010)
American Neurotology Society (2011)
American Orthopaedic Foot and Ankle Society (2012)
American Osteopathic Academy of Orthopedics (2010)
American Osteopathic College of Dermatology (2010)
American Osteopathic College of Pathologists (2010)
American Osteopathic College of Radiology (2010)
American Philosophical Association (2010)
American Political Science Association (2011)
American Prepaid Legal Services Institute (2011)
American Psychoanalytic Association (2011)
American Public Health Association (2012)
American Rhinologic Society (2011)
American Rock Mechanics Association (2011)
American Society for Artificial Internal Organs (2012)
American Society for Cell Biology (2012)
American Society for Clinical Pathology (2010)
American Society for Colposcopy and Cervical Pathology (2010, 2012)
American Society for Microbiology (2012)
American Society for Stereotactic and Functional Neurosurgery (2012)
American Society for Therapeutic Radiology and Oncology (2012)
American Society of Addiction Medicine (2010)
American Society of Appraisers (2012)
American Society of Criminology (2010)
American Society of Human Genetics (2012)
American Society of Neuroimaging (2010)
American Society of Retina Specialists (2012)
American Society on Aging (2011)
American Student Dental Association (2012)
American Surgical Association (2012)
American Thoracic Society (2012)
American Urological Association (2010)
American Waterways Operators (2010)
Analytical and Life Science Systems Association (2010)
ARMA International (2010)
Arthroscopy Association of North America (2011)

Association for Continuing Legal Education (2011)
Association for Information and Image Management International (2012)
Association for Radiological and Imaging Nursing (2012)
Association for the Advancement of International Education (2011)
Association of Academic Health Centers (2012)
Association of Academic Health Sciences Library (2012)
Association of American Colleges and Universities (2011)
Association of American Law Schools (2011)
Association of American Medical Colleges (2012)
The Association of Asian American Investment Managers (2010)
Association of Defense Communities (2010)
Association of Gay and Lesbian Psychiatrists (2012)
Association of Insolvency and Restructuring Advisors (2012)
Association of International Education Administrators (2011)
Association of Mental Health Librarians (2010)
Association of Neurosurgical Physician Assistants (2010)
Association of Organ Procurement Organizations (2011)
Association of Osteopathic State Executive Directors (2010)
Association of Otolaryngology Administrators (2011)
Association of Professional Landscape Designers (2012)
Association of Public and Land-Grant Universities (APLU) (2011)
Association of Schools of Public Health (2012)
Association of Small Foundations (2012)
Association of State and Provincial Psychology Boards (2012)
Association of Surgical Technologists (2011)
Association of Teachers of Maternal and Child Health (2012)
Association of Vascular and Interventional Radiographers (2012)
Audio Engineering Society (2012)
Audit Bureau of Circulations (2011)
Automotive Aftermarket Industry Association (2012)
Biophysical Society (2010)
Biotechnology Industry Organization (BIO) (2012)
The Brewers Association (2011)
Business for Social Responsibility (2011)
Care Continuum Alliance (2011)
Case Management Society of America (2012)
Central Conference of American Rabbis (2010)
Certification Board for Urologic Nurses and Associates (2012)
CFA Institute (2012)
Coalition of Essential Schools (2010)
Commercial Real Estate Women Network (2010)
Commercial Vehicle Training Association (2012)
Competitive Telecommunications Association (2012)
Conductors Guild (2011)
The Conference Board (2012)
Congress of Neurological Surgeons (2010)
Council for Advancement and Support of Education (2011, 2012)
Council for Affordable and Rural Housing (2010)
Council on Anthropology and Education (2012)
Council on Foundations (2011)
Council on Licensure, Enforcement and Regulation (2012)
CTIA - The Wireless Association (2010)
Dance/USA (2012)
Decision Sciences Institute (2012)
Design Management Institute (2010)
Direct Marketing Association (2010)
Direct Selling Association (2010)
EDA Consortium (2012)
Education Industry Association (2011)
Education Writers Association (2010)
Energy Bar Association (2012)
Farm Credit Council (2011)
Geothermal Energy Association (2012)
Health Forum (2012)
Heart Rhythm Society (2011)
Holistic Dental Association (2012)
Human Factors and Ergonomics Society (2010)
IEEE Electron Devices Society (2012)
Independent Sector (2012)
Institute of Electrical and Electronics Engineers (IEEE) (2012)
International Association for the Study of Organized Crime (2010)
International Association of Addictions and Offender Counselors (2012)
International Brotherhood of Teamsters (2012)
International College of Dentists, U.S.A. Section (2012)
International Health, Racquet and Sportsclub Association (2011)
International Kitchen Exhaust Cleaning Association (2012)
International Liver Transplantation Society (2012)
International Magnesium Association (2012)
International Municipal Lawyers Association (2010)
International Society for Antiviral Research (2010)
International Society for Performance Improvement (2010)
International Society for Pharmaceutical Engineering (2012)
International Society of Political Psychology (2010)
International Technology Law Association (2011)
International Ticketing Association (2011)
International Trademark Association (2011)
International Union of Toxicology (2012)
Investment Management Consultants Association (2010)
IT Financial Management Association (2012)
Latin American Studies Association (2012)
Law and Society Association (2011)
LeadingAge (American Association of Homes and Services for the Aging) (2011)
Materials Research Society (2010, 2011, 2012)
Meat Importers Council of America (2010)
Messenger Courier Association of the Americas (2012)
Metal Powder Industries Federation (2011)
Metal Treating Institute (2012)
MPA - The Association of Magazine Media (2012)
Natco-The Organization for Transplant Professionals (2011)
National Alliance for Musical Theatre (2011)

National Association for the Specialty Food Trade (2011)
National Association of Medical Staff Services (2012)
National Association of Bankruptcy Trustees (2010)
National Association of Bar Executives (2010)
National Association of Clean Water Agencies (2010)
National Association of College and University Attorneys (2011)
National Association of College and University Business Officers (2010)
National Association of Criminal Defense Lawyers (2012)
National Association of Farmers Market Nutrition Programs (2012)
National Association of Graduate Admissions Professionals (2010)
The National Association of Marine Surveyors, Inc. (2010)
National Association of Professors of Hebrew (2011)
National Association of Public Hospitals and Health Systems (2012)
National Association of Public Insurance Adjusters (2012)
National Association of Real Estate Investment Trusts (NAREIT) (2011)
National Association of School Nurses (2012)
National Association of School Psychologists (2011)
National Association of Secondary School Principals (2011)
National Association of State & Local Equity Funds (2012)
National Association of State Procurement Officials (2010)
National Association of State Utility Consumer Advocates (NASUCA) (2010)
National Association of Women Judges (2010)
National Automobile Dealers Association (2011)
National Center for Asia-Pacific Economic Cooperation (2012)
National Communication Association (2010)
National Conference of Federal Trial Judges (2010)
National Conference of Specialized Court Judges (2010)
National Conference of Women's Bar Associations (2012)
National Council on Aging (2011)
National Federation of Community Broadcasters (2011)
National Foundation for Credit Counseling (2011)
National Frozen and Refrigerated Foods Association (2010)
National Guild for Community Arts Education (2010)
National Institute of Governmental Purchasing (2010)
National Lesbian and Gay Journalists Association (2010)
National Lesbian and Gay Law Association (2010)
National Lipid Association (2010)
National Pace Association (2010)
National School Boards Association (2011)
National Science Education Leadership Association (2011)
National Student Osteopathic Medical Association (2010)
National Tank Truck Carriers (2012)
National Truck and Heavy Equipment Claims Council (2010)
National Tuberculosis Controllers Association (2012)
North American Academy of Liturgy (2011)
North American Catalysis Society (2010)
North American Olive Oil Association (2012)
Nuclear Energy Institute (2010)
Object Management Group (2012)
The Open Group (2012)
Opportunity Finance Network (2010)
Orthopaedic Research Society (2012)
Pension Real Estate Association (2010)
Philosophy of Education Society (2010)
Pierre Fauchard Academy (2012)
PKF North American Network (2012)
Plastic Surgery Research Council (2010)
Population Association of America (2012)
Print Services & Distribution Association (2010)
PROMAX/BDA (2010)
The Public Relations Society of America (2012)
Public Relations Student Society of America (2012)
Refrigerated Foods Association (2010)
Religious Communication Association (2010)
Research Society on Alcoholism (2012)
Retail Advertising and Marketing Association International (2011)
Retail Confectioners International (2012)
Retail Industry Leaders Association (2010)
Ruth Jackson Orthopaedic Society (2012)
Sigma Epsilon Delta Dental Fraternity (2012)
SOCAP International (2010)
Society for Anthropology in Community Colleges (2010)
Society for Imaging Science and Technology (2012)
Society for Industrial Microbiology (2010)
Society for Marketing Professional Services (2012)
Society for Maternal-Fetal Medicine (2011)
Society for Obstetric Anesthesia and Perinatology (2011)
Society for Pediatric Radiology (2012)
Society for Photographic Education (2012)
Society for Public Health Education (2012)
Society for Risk Analysis (2012)
Society for Scholarly Publishing (2010)
Society for Vascular Surgery (2010)
Society of Biblical Literature (2011)
Society of Biological Psychiatry (2011)
Society of Forensic Toxicologists (2011)
Society of Gynecologic Oncologists (2010)
Society of Interventional Radiology (2012)
Society of Invasive Cardiovascular Professionals (2011)
Society of Otorhinolaryngology and Head-Neck Nurses (2011)
Society of Toxicology (2012)
Society of Urologic Nurses and Associates (2012)
Software & Information Industry Association (SIIA) (2010, 2011)
Solar Energy Industries Association (SEIA) (2011, 2012)
Solid-State Circuits Society (2010, 2011, 2012)
SPIE - The International Society for Optical Engineering (2011)
Surface Design Association (2010)
Tax Executives Institute, Inc. (2011)
Taxicab, Limousine & Paratransit Association (2011)
Ultrasonic Industry Association (2012)

Union of American Physicians and Dentists (2012)
United States Fencing Coaches Association (2012)
U.S.-Russia Business Council (2010)
University Professional & Continuing Education Association (2010)
University/Resident Theatre Association (2011)
Western Economic Association International (2012)
Women's Transportation Seminar (WTS International) (2011)
World Federation of Public Health Associations (2012)

San Jose

American Association of Woodturners (2012)
American Cleft Palate-Craniofacial Association (2012)
The American Society for Public Administration (2010)
American Telemedicine Association (2012)
ASM International (2011)
Association for Molecular Pathology (2010)
Beta Alpha Psi (2010)
Business Forms Management Association (2010)
Catholic Theological Society of America (2010)
Council of Educational Facility Planners International (2010)
Federation of Diocesan Liturgical Commissions (2012)
International Association of Privacy Professionals (2012)
International City/County Management Association (2010)
International Neural Network Society (2011)
Laser Institute of America (2011)
National Association of College and University Food Services (2010)
National Parent Teachers Association (2010)
NPES, The Association for Suppliers of Printing, Publishing, and Converting Technologies (2011)
Optical Society of America (2011)
Regulatory Affairs Professionals Society (2010)
Sales and Marketing Executives International, Inc. (2011)
Society for Imaging Science and Technology (2011)
Society for Personality Assessment (2010)
Society of Christian Ethics (2010)
SPIE - The International Society for Optical Engineering (2011)
United States of America Gymnastics (2012)
USENIX: The Advanced Computing Systems Association (2010)

San Mateo

American Osteopathic College of Anesthesiologists (2010)
Feldenkrais Guild of North America (2012)
National Watercolor Society (2010, 2011)
The Society of Wine Educators (2012)

Santa Ana

Advertising and Marketing International Network (2012)

Santa Barbara

American Botanical Council (2012)
American Federation for Aging Research (2010, 2012)
BEMA - The Baking Industry Suppliers Association (2011)
Christian College Consortium (2012)
Council of Petroleum Accountants Societies (2010)
Electronic Commerce Code Management Association (2012)
National Council of Farmer Cooperatives (2010)

Santa Clara

Alliance for Gray Market and Counterfeit Abatement (2012)
American Radio Relay League (2012)
American String Teachers Association (2010)
Clean Technology & Sustainable Industries Organization (CTSI) (2012)
Global Semiconductor Alliance (2010)
IEEE Microwave Theory and Techniques Society (2012)
International Disk Drive Equipment and Materials Association (2010)
International Women's Writing Guild (2010)
Joint Electron Device Engineering Council (2011)
Object Management Group (2011)
Society of Vacuum Coaters (2012)
Solar Energy Industries Association (SEIA) (2012)

Santa Cruz

IEEE Circuits and Systems Society (2012)

Santa Monica

Association of Film Commissioners International (2010)
Environmental Markets Association (2012)
Photo Chemical Machining Institute (2012)

Sausalito

Environmental Council of the States (2010)

Scotts Valley

North American Mycological Association (2012)

Silicon Valley

EDA Consortium (2010, 2012)
Technology Services Industry Association (2010)
Women in Technology International (2010)

Solvang

United States Cutting Tool Institute (2012)

Sonoma

National Association for Medical Direction of Respiratory Care (2012)
North American Association of Food Equipment Manufacturers (2010)

South Lake Tahoe

International Association of Law Enforcement Intelligence Analysts (2010)
North American Snowsports Journalists Association (2012)

Squaw Valley

American Academy of Otolaryngic Allergy (2012)

Truckee

Association of Private Sector Colleges and Universities (Career College Association) (2012)

Walnut Creek

Society for Pediatric Radiology (2012)

COLORADO

Alamosa

National Potato Council (2010)
Tourist Railway Association Inc. (2010)

Arvada

American Industrial Hygiene Association (2012)

Aspen

ACA International, The Association of Credit and Collection Professionals (2012)
American Society of Home Inspectors (2011)
Society of Incentive & Travel Executives (2012)
Toxicology Forum (2012)

Beaver Creek

National Association of Police Organizations (2010)

Boulder

MPA - The Association of Magazine Media (2012)
Society of Woman Geographers (2011)
Special Interest Group on Accessible Computing (2012)
SPIE - The International Society for Optical Engineering (2010)
State Higher Education Executive Officers (2011)

Breckenridge

American Astronautical Society (2011)
Society of Outdoor Recreation Professionals (2011)
Veterinary Orthopedic Society (2010)

Broomfield

The National Association for the Dually Diagnosed (2012)
National Council of Higher Education Loan Programs (2012)

Brownfield

National Sunflower Association (2012)

Colorado Springs

ADSC: The International Association of Foundation Drilling (2010)
American Academy of Appellate Lawyers (2012)
American Chemistry Council (2012)
American Coke and Coal Chemicals Institute (2012)
American Holistic Nurses Association (2010)
The American Institute of Mining, Metallurgical, and Petroleum Engineers (2010)
American Land Title Association (2012)
American Osteopathic Academy of Orthopedics (2012)
American Society of Parasitologists (2010)
Association for Financial Technology (2011)
Association of Educational Service Agencies (2011)
Association of Oil Pipe Lines (2010)
Association of Real Estate License Law Officials (2010)
Association of State and Territorial Health Officials (2010)
Christian Legal Society (2012)
Commercial Food Equipment Service Association (2012)
Commission on Accreditation for Law Enforcement Agencies Incorporation (2011)
Edison Electric Institute (2011)
Evangelical Press Association (2012)
Fellowship of United Methodists in Music and Worship Arts (2012)
Gases and Welding Distributors Association (2012)
Grocery Manufacturers Association (GMA) (2012)
Hardwood Plywood and Veneer Association (2010)
Heating, Airconditioning and Refrigeration Distributors International (2012)
Independent Petroleum Association of America (2010, 2012)
Industrial Asset Management Council (2010)
Institute of Navigation (2012)
International Academy of Behavioral Medicine, Counseling and Psychotherapy (2012)
International Franchise Association (2012)
International Order of the Golden Rule (2010)
National Association for Court Management (2010)
National Association of Bankruptcy Trustees (2012)
National Association of College Auxiliary Services (2010)
National Association of Surety Bond Producers (2011)
National Fisheries Institute (2011)
National Ocean Industries Association (2011)
National Tooling and Machining Association (2011)
North American Building Material Distribution Association (2010)
North American Millers' Association (2011)
Property Casualty Insurers Association of America (2010)
Radiology Business Management Association (2010)
School Science and Mathematics Association (2011)
Self Storage Association (2010)
Sheet Metal and Air Conditioning Contractors' National Association (2011)
Society of Corporate Secretaries and Governance Professionals (2011)
Society of Independent Professional Earth Scientists (2010)
Society of Petroleum Evaluation Engineers (2012)
Society of Urologic Nurses and Associates (2010)
United States Potato Board (2011)

Copper Mountain

National Ski Patrol System (2012)
PSIA-AASI (2012)

Crested Butte

Veterinary Orthopedic Society (2012)
Water Sports Industry Association (2012)

Delta

Hydraulic Institute (2012)

Denver

Academic Pediatric Association (2011)
AGN International North America, Inc (2010)
Agricultural & Applied Economics Association (2010)
Airports Council International - North America (2012)
Algal Biomass Organization (2012)
American Academy of Hospice and Palliative Medicine (2012)
American Accounting Association (2011)
American Association of Birth Centers (2011)
American Association of Law Libraries (2010)
American Association of Swine Veterinarians (2012)
American Association of Teachers of Arabic (2012)
American Association of Teachers of German (2011)
American Astronautical Society (2012)
American Camp Association (2010)
American Case Management Association (2012)
American Chemical Society (2011)
American College of Emergency Physicians (2012)
American College of Veterinary Internal Medicine (2011)
American Conference of Governmental Industrial Hygienists (2010)
American Correctional Association (2012)
American Council on the Teaching of Foreign Languages (2011)
American Dairy Science Association (2010)
American Dental Association (2012)
American Dental Education Association (2012)
American Economic Association (2011)
American Educational Research Association (2010)
American Feed Industry Association (2012)
The American Finance Association (2011)
American Fraternal Alliance (2011)
American Fuel & Petrochemical Manufacturers (2012)
American Highland Cattle Association (2012)
American Judges Association (2010)
American National CattleWomen (2010, 2012)
American Neuropsychiatric Association (2011)
American Pediatric Society (2011)
American Public Health Association (2010)
American Public Power Association (2011)
American Public Works Association (2011)
American Society for Cell Biology (2011)
American Society for Healthcare Human Resources Administration (2012)
American Society for Mass Spectrometry (2011)
American Society for Precision Engineering (2011)
American Society for Reproductive Medicine (2010)
American Society for Training and Development (2012)
American Society of Animal Science (2010)
American Society of Crime Laboratory Directors (2011)
American Society of General Surgeons (2011)
American Society of Health-System Pharmacists (2011)
American Society of Maxillofacial Surgeons (2011)
American Society of Mechanical Engineers (ASME) (2011)
American Society of Nephrology (2010)
American Society of Nuclear Cardiology (2011)
American Society of Pediatric Nephrology (2011)
American Society of Safety Engineers (2012)
American Sociological Association (2012)
American Solar Energy Society (2012)
American Spinal Injury Association (2012)
American Tarentaise Association (2012)
American Thoracic Society (2011)
American Translators Association (2010)
APICS The Association for Operations Management (2012)
Arabian Horse Association (2012)
Architectural Woodwork Institute (2010)
ASFE/The Geoprofessional Business Association (2012)
ASPSN - American Society of Plastic Surgical Nurses (2011)
Association for Comparative Economic Studies (2011)
Association for Continuing Legal Education (2012)
Association for Education in Journalism and Mass Communication (2010)
Association for Evolutionary Economics (2011)
Association for Financial Counseling and Planning Education (2010)
Association for Healthcare Resource and Materials Management (2010)
Association for Preservation Technology International (2010)
Association for the Accreditation of Human Research Protection Programs (2012)
Association for the Advancement of Computing in Education (2012)
Association for the Sociology of Religion (2012)
Association for the Treatment of Sexual Abusers (2012)
Association for Unmanned Vehicle Systems International (2010)
Association of Academic Health Sciences Library (2011)
Association of American Medical Colleges (2011)
Association of Bridal Consultants (2012)
The Association of Collegiate Conference and Events Directors International (2012)
Association of Corporate Counsel (2011)
Association of Credit Union Internal Auditors (2012)
Association of Family and Conciliation Courts (2010)
Association of Organ Procurement Organizations (2011)
Association of Public and Land-Grant Universities (APLU) (2012)

Association of Public Health Laboratories (2012)
Association of Schools of Public Health (2010)
Association of State Dam Safety Officials (2012)
Association of the Wall and Ceiling Industry (2010)
Association of University Anesthesiologists (2010)
Association of Women in the Metal Industries (2012)
Association of Writers and Writing Programs (2010)
Association on Higher Education and Disability (2010)
Automotive Training Managers Council (2010)
Beta Alpha Psi (2011)
Board of Registered Polysomnographic Technologists (2010)
The Brewers Association (2010)
Catholic Health Association of the United States (2010)
Ceilings and Interior Systems Construction Association (2010)
Christian Schools International (2012)
Clinical Orthopaedic Society (2010)
Communications Fraud Control Association (2010)
Correctional Education Association (2012)
Council for Advancement and Support of Education (2012)
Council for Children with Behavioral Disorders (2012)
Council for Exceptional Children (2012)
Council of Colleges of Acupuncture and Oriental Medicine (2012)
Council on Foundations (2010)
Defense Credit Union Council (2012)
Dermatology Nurses' Association (2012)
Econometric Society (2011)
Educause (2012)
Electrical Apparatus Service Association (2011)
Emergency Medicine Residents' Association (2012)
Employee Assistance Professionals Association (2011)
EUCG, Inc. (2012)
Federation of Tax Administrators (2011)
Financial Management Association International (2011)
Financial Planning Association (2010)
Flying Physicians Association (2012)
Foodservice & Packaging Institute, Inc. (2011)
Gasket Fabricators Association (2012)
Geochemical Society (2010)
Geological Society of America (2010)
Geoscience Information Society (2010)
Ground Water Protection Council (2010)
Heart Rhythm Society (2010)
Hospice and Palliative Nurses Association (2012)
Independent Laboratory Distributors Association (2010)
Institute for Business & Home Safety (2011)
Insurance Marketing Communications Association (2012)
Interior Design Educators Council (2011)
International Association of Insurance Receivers (2010)
International Association of Lighting Designers (2010)
International Council on Systems Engineering (2011)
International Festivals and Events Association (2012)
International Ground Source Heat Pump Association (2010)
International Society for Technology in Education (2010)
Jewish Education Service of North America (2011)
LeadingAge (American Association of Homes and Services for the Aging) (2012)
Legal Marketing Association (2010)
Middle East Librarians' Association (2012)
Middle East Studies Association of North America (2012)
National Academic Advising Association (2011)
National Alfalfa and Forage Alliance (2010)
National Association for Bilingual Education (2010)
National Association for Business Economics (2010)
National Association for College Admission Counseling (2012)
National Association for Gifted Children (2012)
National Association for Multicultural Education (2010)
National Association for Rural Mental Health (2010)
National Association of Area Agencies on Aging (2012)
The National Association of Colored Women's Club, Inc. (2010)
National Association of Community Health Centers (2012)
National Association of Consumer Credit Administrators (2011)
National Association of Consumer Shows (2011)
National Association of Criminal Defense Lawyers (2011)
National Association of Educational Procurement, Inc. (2010)
National Association of Equipment Leasing Brokers (2012)
National Association of Health Unit Coordinators (2010)
National Association of Hispanic Journalists (2010)
National Association of Independent Public Finance Advisors (2011)
National Association of Insurance Commissioners (2010)
National Association of Latino Elected and Appointed Officials (2010)
National Association of Professional Background Screeners (2011)
National Association of Public Hospitals and Health Systems (2010)
National Association of Real Estate Editors (2012)
National Association of State Budget Officers (2010)
National Association of State Chief Information Officers (2011)
National Association of State Credit Union Supervisors (2012)
National Association of Student Financial Aid Administrators (2010)
National Association of Women in Construction (2012)
National Bison Association (2012)
National Child Support Enforcement Association (2012)
National Coal Transportation Association (2012)
National Conference of Executives of The ARC (2011)
National Council for the Social Studies (2010)
National Council of State Housing Agencies (2012)
National Council on Measurement in Education (2010)
National Dog Groomers Association of America, Inc. (2010)
National Ecological Observatory Network, Inc (2011)
National Economic Association (2011)
National Hay Association (2012)
National Indian Health Board (2012)
National Institute for Animal Agriculture (2012)

National League of Cities (2010)
National Minority Supplier Development Council (2012)
The National Procurement Institute, Inc (2011)
National Retail Federation (2012)
National Rural Health Association (2012)
National Ski and Snowboard Retailers Association (2011)
National WIC Association (2012)
National Women's Studies Association (2010)
North American Limousin Foundation (2010)
North American South Devon Association (2011)
Pediatric Endocrine Society (2011)
Pediatric Orthopedic Society of North America (2012)
Plant Growth Regulation Society of America (2012)
Plastic Surgery Administrative Association (2011)
Potato Association of America (2012)
Poultry Science Association (2010)
PRBA - The Rechargeable Battery Association (2012)
Public Radio Program Directors Association (2010)
REALTORS Land Institute (2012)
Religion Newswriters Association (2010)
Religious Education Association (2010)
Retail Advertising and Marketing Association International (2012)
School Nutrition Association (2012)
SnowSports Industries America (2010, 2011, 2012)
Society for Disability Studies (2012)
Society for Mining, Metallurgy and Exploration, Inc. (2011)
Society for News Design (2010)
Society for Organic Petrology (2010)
Society for Pediatric Research (2011)
Society for Public Health Education (2010)
Society for Social Work Leadership in Health Care (2012)
Society for the Study of Social Problems (2012)
Society of Broadcast Engineers (2012)
Society of Diagnostic Medical Sonographers (2010)
Society of Ethnobiology (2012)
Society of Exploration Geophysicists (2010)
Society of Petroleum Engineers (2011)
Society of Reproductive Surgeons (2010)
Society of Risk Management Consultants (2012)
Society of Toxicologic Pathologists (2011)
Society of Toxicologic Pathology (2011)
Society of Tribologists and Lubrication Engineers (2012)
State Government Affairs Council (2010)
TASH (2010)
United States Potato Board (2010)
United States Ski and Snowboard Association (2012)
University Council for Educational Administration (2012)
UWC - Strategic Services on Unemployment and Workers' Compensation (2012)
Weed Science Society of America (2010)
Western History Association (2012)
Women's Basketball Coaches Association (2012)
Women's Transportation Seminar (WTS International) (2012)
World's Poultry Science Association, U.S.A. Branch (2010)

Dillon

Beta Beta Beta (2010)

Durango

The American Rambouillet Sheep Breeders Association (2010)

Englewood

ASFE/The Geoprofessional Business Association (2011, 2012)

Estes Park

Organization of Wildlife Planners (2010)
Wilderness Education Association (2010, 2011, 2012)

Ft. Collins

United States Committee on Irrigation and Drainage (2010)

Glenwood Springs

National Speleological Society (2011)
Society of Professional Rope Access Technicians (2012)

Grand Junction

Solution Mining Research Institute (2010)

Keystone

Environmental and Engineering Geophysical Society (2010)
Society of Economic Geologists (2010)

Littleton

Society of Economic Geologists (2012)

Snowmass Village

American College of Cardiology (2012)
Management Association for Private Photogrammetric Surveyors (2012)

Vail

American Association of Professional Landmen (2010)
American College of Radiology (2012)
American Orthopaedic Society for Sports Medicine (2010)
American Society of General Surgeons (2011, 2012)
American Sugar Alliance (2010)
Conference of State Court Administrators (2010)
Council of Producers & Distributors of Agrotechnology (2010)
International Oil Scouts Association (2010)
Investment Management Consultants Association (2010, 2011)
National Conference of Commissioners on Uniform State Laws (2011)
Society of Independent Gasoline Marketers of America (SIGMA) (2012)

Society of Military Orthopaedic Surgeons (2010)

Westminster

American Network of Community Options and Resources (ANCOR) (2011)
American Petroleum Institute (2010)
American Physiological Society (2010, 2012)
Association for Hospital Medical Education (2011)
International Society for the Study of Subtle Energies and Energy Medicine (2010)
National Star Route Mail Contractors Association (2010)
North American Society for Trenchless Technology (2012)

CONNECTICUT

Burlington

International Maintenance Institute (2010)

Cromwell

American Association for Physical Activity and Recreation (2011)

Greenwich

Business Forms Management Association (2012)
International Nurses Society on Addicttions (2010)

Groton

Council of American Maritime Museums (2010)
International Maple Syrup Institute (2010)
North American Maple Syrup Council (2012)
North American Society for Oceanic History (2010)

Hartford

Association for Women Geoscientists (2012)
Biomedical Engineering Society (2011)
National Association of County and City Health Officials (2011)
National Chimney Sweep Guild (2011)
Society for Historians of American Foreign Relations (2012)
Tree Care Industry Association (2011)
United States Rowing Association (2011)

Mystic

National Association of Women Judges (2012)
Scale Manufacturers Association (2010)

New Haven

Building Stone Institute (2010)
Medieval Academy of America (2010)
Mycological Society of America (2012)
National Association for Drama Therapy (2012)
Society of Neurological Surgeons (2010)

Southington

American Society of Home Inspectors (2011)

Stamford

National Institute of American Doll Artists (2012)
Professional Lighting and Sound Association (2012)
Promotion Marketing Association (2012)

Storrs

International Society for Research on Aggression (2010)

Trumbull

AMC Institute (2011)

Uncasville

Conference of Educational Administrators of Schools and Programs for the Deaf (2012)
National Indian Gaming Association (2011)

DELAWARE

Claymont

National Railway Historical Society (2012)

Dover

National Association of State Departments of Agriculture (2010)

Newark

American Philosophical Society (2011)
Phi Mu Alpha Sinfonia (2010)

Smyrna

National Association of State Outdoor Recreation Liaison Officers (2011)

Wilmington

American Public Health Association (2011)
Attention Deficit Disorder Association (2012)
Transworld Advertising Agency Network (2010)

DISTRICT OF COLUMBIA

Washington

AASHTO: Transportation Center of Excellence (2012)
ACA International, The Association of Credit and Collection Professionals (2010, 2012)
Academy Health (2012)
Academy of International Business (2012)
Academy of Osseointegration (2011)
Academy of Pharmaceutical Research and Science (2010)

Academy of Political Science (2012)
Academy of Rail Labor Attorneys (2012)
Advanced Medical Technology Association (AdvaMed) (2011)
Africa Travel Association (2012)
African Studies Association (2011)
Agriculture Council of America (2012)
Air Conditioning, Heating and Refrigeration Institute (AHRI) (2012)
Air Force Association (2010, 2011, 2012)
Aircraft Electronics Association (2012)
Airport Consultants Council (2012)
Airports Council International - North America (2012)
Alliance for Aging Research (2012)
Alliance for Children and Families (2011)
America's Health Insurance Plans (2011, 2012)
American Academy for Cerebral Palsy and Developmental Medicine (2010)
American Academy of Actuaries (2012)
American Academy of Clinical Toxicology (2011)
American Academy of Cosmetic Dentistry (2012)
American Academy of Environmental Engineers (2011)
American Academy of Facial Plastic and Reconstructive Surgery (2012)
American Academy of Implant Dentistry (2012)
American Academy of Nursing (2010, 2011, 2012)
American Academy of Ophthalmology (2011, 2012)
American Academy of Otolaryngic Allergy (2012)
American Academy of Otolaryngology-Head and Neck Surgery (2012)
American Academy of Pain Medicine (2011)
American Accounting Association (2012)
American Ambulance Association (2011)
American Antiquarian Society (2010)
American Apparel & Footwear Association (2010, 2012)
American Association for Cancer Research (2010)
American Association for Dental Research (2010)
American Association for Geriatric Psychiatry (2012)
American Association for Homecare (2010, 2012)
American Association for Respiratory Care (2012)
American Association for the Advancement of Science (2011)
American Association for the Study of Liver Diseases (2011)
American Association of Advertising Agencies (2011)
American Association of Airport Executives (2011, 2012)
American Association of Anatomists (2011)
American Association of Clinical Urologists (2010, 2011, 2012)
American Association of Colleges for Teacher Education (2011)
American Association of Colleges of Nursing (2010, 2011, 2012)
American Association of Colleges of Osteopathic Medicine (2012)
American Association of Community Colleges (2012)
American Association of Crop Insurers (2012)
American Association of Engineering Societies (2012)
American Association of Healthcare Administrative Management (2012)
American Association of Oral and Maxillofacial Surgeons (2011, 2012)
American Association of Orthodontists (2010)
American Association of Pharmaceutical Scientists (2011)
American Association of Physics Teachers (2010)
American Association of Political Consultants (2011)
American Association of Port Authorities (2012)
American Association of Teachers of Arabic (2011)
American Association of Teachers of Spanish and Portuguese (2011)
American Association of University Administrators (2010)
American Association of University Professors (2010, 2011, 2012)
American Association of University Women (2011)
American Automotive Leasing Association (2012)
American Bakers Association (2012)
American Bankers Association (2012)
American Bar Association (2012)
The American Board of Opticianry and the National Contact Lens Examiners (2012)
American Booksellers Association (2010)
American Broncho-Esophagological Association (2012)
American Chiropractic Association (2012)
American Cleaning Institute (2012)
American Clinical Laboratory Association (2010, 2012)
American Coal Council (2011)
American College of Cardiology (2011, 2012)
American College of Gastroenterology (2011)
American College of Nurse-Midwives (2010)
American College of Occupational and Environmental Medicine (2011)
American College of Physicians (2012)
American College of Radiology (2010, 2011, 2012)
American College of Rheumatology (2012)
American College of Sports Medicine (2011)
American College of Surgeons (2012)
American College of Surgeons Professional Association (2012)
American College of Trial Lawyers (2010)
American College of Veterinary Surgeons (2012)
American Composites Manufacturers Association (2012)
American Conference of Academic Deans (2010, 2012)
American Congress of Obstetricians and Gynecologists (2011)
American Corn Growers Association (2012)
American Council of Engineering Companies (2010, 2011, 2012)
American Council of Life Insurers (ACLI) (2012)
American Dental Association (2011)
American Dental Education Association (2010)
American Dermatological Association (2012)
American Diabetes Association (2011)
American Federation of Teachers (AFL-CIO) (2011)
American Foundry Society (2012)
American Frozen Food Institute (2011, 2012)
American Geophysical Union (2012)
American Guild of Organists (2010)
American Highway Users Alliance (2012)
American Hospital Association (2010, 2011, 2012)

American Hotel & Lodging Association (AH&LA) (2011)
American Immigration Lawyers Association (2010, 2011)
American Indian Higher Education Consortium (2012)
American Institute for Medical and Biological Engineering (2012)
American Institute of Aeronautics and Astronautics (2010)
The American Institute of Architects (2012)
American Institute of Certified Public Accountants (2012)
American Institute of Homeopathy (2011)
American Insurance Association (2012)
American Intellectual Property Law Association (2010, 2011, 2012)
American Land Title Association (2012)
American Law Institute (2010, 2012)
American League of Lobbyists (2011)
American Library Association (2010, 2012)
American Logistics Association (2012)
American Lung Association (2012)
American Meat Institute (2012)
American Medical Association (2011, 2012)
American Medical Informatics Association (2010, 2011)
American Medical Student Association (2011)
American Motorcyclist Association (2011)
American Network of Community Options and Resources (ANCOR) (2010, 2011, 2012)
American Neurotology Society (2012)
American Nuclear Society (2011)
American Occupational Therapy Association, Inc. (2011, 2012)
American Orthopaedic Association (2012)
American Orthopsychiatric Association (2012)
American Osteopathic Association (2012)
American Peanut Council (2010, 2011, 2012)
American Pharmacists Association (2010)
American Philosophical Association (2011)
American Physical Society (2010, 2012)
American Physical Therapy Association (2011)
American Physical Therapy Association - Private Practice Section (2010)
American Pilots' Association (2012)
American Podiatric Medical Association (2012)
American Political Science Association (2010, 2012)
American Psychological Association (2011)
American Public Gas Association (2011, 2012)
American Public Power Association (2011, 2012)
American Public Transportation Association (2011, 2012)
American Real Estate and Urban Economics Association (2012)
American Resort Development Association (2010, 2011, 2012)
American Securitization Forum (2010)
American Seed Trade Association (2010)
American Short Line and Regional Railroad Association (2012)
American Small Manufacturers' Coalition (2012)
American Society for Aesthetic Plastic Surgery (2010)
American Society for Artificial Internal Organs (2011)
American Society for Biochemistry and Molecular Biology (2011)
American Society for Bioethics and Humanities (2012)
American Society for Clinical Laboratory Science (2012)
American Society for Clinical Pharmacology and Therapeutics (2012)
American Society for Healthcare Risk Management (2012)
American Society for Investigative Pathology (2011)
American Society for Microbiology (2011)
American Society for Therapeutic Radiology and Oncology (2012)
American Society of Access Professionals (2010)
American Society of Addiction Medicine (2011)
American Society of Anesthesia Technologists and Technicians (2012)
American Society of Anesthesiologists (2012)
American Society of Appraisers (2011)
American Society of Association Executives-The Center for Association Leadership (2010, 2012)
American Society of Criminology (2012)
American Society of Gene & Cell Therapy (2010)
American Society of Human Genetics (2010)
American Society of International Law (2010, 2012)
American Society of Interventional Pain Physicians (2010, 2012)
American Society of Landscape Architects (2010)
American Society of News Editors (2010, 2012)
American Society of Preventive Oncology (2012)
American Society on Aging (2012)
American Spinal Injury Association (2011)
American Staffing Association (2010, 2012)
American Student Dental Association (2012)
American Supply Association (2012)
American Teleservices Association (2011)
American Traffic Safety Service Association (2011, 2012)
American Water Works Association (2011)
American Waterways Operators (2011, 2012)
American Wind Energy Association (AWEA) (2011, 2012)
American Wire Producers Association (2012)
Animal Health Institute (2010)
APHSA - Information Systems Management (2012)
APPAM - The Association for Public Policy Analysis and Management (2011)
Appraisal Institute (2012)
ARMA International (2011)
Armed Forces Communications and Electronics Association (2012)
Asian American Psychological Association (2011)
Assisted Living Federation of America (2012)
Associated Builders and Contractors (2011, 2012)
Associated Wire Rope Fabricators (2012)
Association for Advanced Life Underwriting (2010)
Association for Asian American Studies (2012)
Association for Childhood Education International (2011, 2012)
Association for Clinical Research Training (2010, 2012)
Association for Convention Marketing Executives (2010, 2011, 2012)
Association for Corporate Growth (2012)

Association for Demand Response & Smart Grid (2011, 2012)
Association for Jewish Studies (2011)
Association for Medical Imaging Management (2010)
Association for Prevention Teaching and Research (APTR) (2010, 2012)
Association for Psychological Science (2011)
Association for Slavic, East European, and Eurasian Studies (2011)
Association for Supervision and Curriculum Development (ASCD) (2012)
Association for Symbolic Logic (2011)
Association for Theatre in Higher Education (2012)
Association for Unmanned Vehicle Systems International (2011, 2012)
Association Foundation Group (2011, 2012)
Association Media and Publishing (2010)
Association of Academic Health Centers (2010, 2011, 2012)
Association of Academic Health Sciences Library (2010)
Association of Air Medical Services (2010)
Association of American Chambers of Commerce in Latin America (2011, 2012)
Association of American Colleges and Universities (2012)
Association of American Editorial Cartoonists (2012)
Association of American Geographers (2010)
Association of American Law Schools (2012)
Association of American Medical Colleges (2010, 2012)
Association of American Publishers (2011, 2012)
Association of American Railroads (2012)
Association of Arts Administration Educators (2010)
Association of Asian-Pacific Community Health Organizations (2012)
Association of Bone and Joint Surgeons (2010)
Association of Catholic Colleges and Universities (2011, 2012)
Association of Community Cancer Centers (2011)
Association of Community College Trustees (2010, 2011, 2012)
Association of Ecosystem Research Centers (2012)
Association of Educational Therapists (2012)
Association of Energy Engineers (2010)
Association of Federal Communications Consulting Engineers (2010)
Association of Foreign Investors in U.S. Real Estate (2012)
Association of Governing Boards of Universities and Colleges (2012)
Association of Government Accountants (2010, 2011, 2012)
Association of International Education Administrators (2010, 2012)
Association of Jesuit Colleges and Universities (2012)
Association of Maternal and Child Health Programs (AMCHP) (2012)
Association of Medical Diagnostic Manufacturers (2010)
Association of Medical Education and Research in Substance Abuse (2011)
Association of Meeting Professionals (2010)
Association of Metropolitan Water Agencies (2010, 2011, 2012)
Association of National Advertisers (2012)
Association of Neurosurgical Physician Assistants (2011)
Association of Otolaryngology Administrators (2012)
Association of Physician Assistants in Cardiovascular Surgery (2011)
Association of Private Sector Colleges and Universities (Career College Association) (2011, 2012)
Association of Procurement Technical Assistance Centers (2012)
Association of Professional Investment Consultants (2010)
Association of Public Television Stations (2011, 2012)
Association of Research Libraries (2010, 2011, 2012)
Association of Rheumatology Health Professionals (2012)
Association of Specialized and Professional Accreditors (2011)
Association of State and Territorial Solid Waste Management Officials (2012)
Association of State Dam Safety Officials (2011)
Association of State Energy Research and Technology Transfer Institution (2012)
Association of Surgical Technologists (2012)
Association of the United States Army (2010, 2011, 2012)
Association of Transportation Professionals (2012)
Association of University Centers on Disabilities (AUCD) (2012)
Association of University Research Parks (2011, 2012)
Association of Women in the Metal Industries (2011)
Association of Women's Health, Obstetric and Neonatal Nurses (2012)
Association of Writers and Writing Programs (2011)
Association of Zoos and Aquariums (2012)
Automotive Aftermarket Industry Association (2012)
Automotive Service Association (2010)
Automotive Trade Association Executives (2012)
Auxiliary to the National Medical Association (2012)
Bank Administration Institute (2012)
Bank Insurance and Securities Association (2011, 2012)
Brazilian American Chamber of Commerce (2010)
Building Owners and Managers Association International (2011, 2012)
Business Higher Education Forum (2010)
Business Professionals of America (2010)
Cargo Airline Association (2012)
Catholic Cemetery Conference (2012)
Catholic Charities USA (2010)
CCIM Institute (2012)
Certification Board for Urologic Nurses and Associates (2012)
Chief Officers of State Libraries Agencies (2010)
Child Care Aware of America (2012)
Child Life Council (2012)
Child Welfare League of America (2010, 2011, 2012)
Church and Synagogue Library Association (2011)
CIES - The Food Business Forum (2010)
Coalition for Juvenile Justice (2010)
NAIOP, The Commercial Real Estate Development Association (2011, 2012)
Commission on Professionals in Science and Technology (2010)
Communications Workers of America (2012)
Computer Measurement Group (2011)
Computer Security Institute (2011)
Computing Technology Industry Association (CompTIA) (2011)
Conference of Minority Transportation Officials (2012)
Congress of Neurological Surgeons (2011)
Congressional Internet Caucus Advisory Committee (2012)
Consortium of School Networking (2010, 2012)
Consortium of Social Science Associations (2012)

Construction Industry Round Table, Inc. (2012)
Construction Management Association of America (2011)
Construction Writers Association (2012)
Consumer Electronics Association (2012)
Consumer Healthcare Products Association (2012)
Contact Lens Society of America (2012)
Copper Development Association (2011)
Corporate Council on Africa (2012)
The Corps Network (formerly the National Association of Service and Conservation Corps) (2010, 2011, 2012)
Council for Adult and Experiential Learning (2012)
Council for Advancement and Support of Education (2012)
Council for Christian Colleges and Universities (2011)
Council for Exceptional Children (2011)
Council for Higher Education Accreditation (2012)
Council for Professional Recognition (2012)
Council for Resource Development (2010, 2012)
Council of Chief State School Officers (2012)
Council of Graduate Schools (2010, 2012)
Council of Institutional Investors (2010, 2012)
Council of Large Public Housing Authorities (2012)
Council of Manufacturing Associations (2012)
Council of Medical Specialty Societies (2010, 2012)
Council of Residential Specialists (2012)
Council of State Community Development Agencies (2012)
Council of the Americas (2010, 2012)
Council on Foundations (2011)
Council on Governmental Relations (2010, 2012)
Council on Social Work Education (2012)
The Counselors of Real Estate (2011)
CPCU Society (2012)
CRE Finance Council (2012)
Credit Union National Association, Inc. (2011, 2012)
CropLife America (2011)
Dance/USA (2010)
Defense Research Institute (2011)
Dental Trade Alliance (2011)
Destination Marketing Association International (2010, 2012)
Direct Marketing Association (2011)
Direct Marketing Association Nonprofit Federation (2012)
Document Security Alliance (2010, 2012)
Drug Information Association (2012)
ECRI (2012)
Edison Electric Institute (2011)
Education Finance Council (2011)
Education Industry Association (2011, 2012)
Educational Association of University Centers (2010)
Electricity Consumers Resource Council (ELCON) (2012)
Electronic Retailing Association (2012)
Electronic Security Association (2012)
Emergency Medicine Residents' Association (2012)
Employee Benefit Research Institute (2010, 2011)
Employee Stock Ownership Plan Association (2010, 2011, 2012)
Employers Council on Flexible Compensation (2012)
Energy Bar Association (2010, 2011, 2012)
Entrepreneurs' Organization (2012)
Envelope Manufacturers Association (2011)
Equipment Leasing and Finance Association (2012)
Family, Career and Community Leaders of America (2012)
Farm Credit Council (2012)
Federal Managers Association (2011, 2012)
Federation of American Hospitals (2010, 2011, 2012)
Federation of Tax Administrators (2012)
Financial Executives International (2011, 2012)
Financial Industry Regulatory Authority (FINRA) (2011, 2012)
Financial Markets Association (2010, 2012)
Flavor and Extract Manufacturers Association (2012)
Food and Drug Law Institute (2010, 2012)
Food Industry Association Executives (2012)
The Foodservice Group, Inc. (2012)
Forest Products Society (2012)
Forum of Regional Associations of Grantmakers (2011, 2012)
Foundation for International Meetings (2012)
Fresh Produce Association of the Americas (2012)
Friends of the National Institute of Dental and Craniofacial Research (FNIDCR) (2011, 2012)
Fuel Cell and Hydrogen Energy Association (2011)
Fusion Power Associates (2011, 2012)
GAMA International (2011)
Gasification Technologies Council (2012)
Generic Pharmaceutical Association (2010)
Genetics Society of America (2010)
Geothermal Energy Association (2012)
German American Chamber of Commerce (2011)
Global Cold Chain Alliance (2012)
Global Health Council (2010)
Gridwise Alliance (2011)
Grocery Manufacturers Association (GMA) (2010)
Health Care Education Association (2012)
Healthcare Billing and Management Association (2012)
Healthcare Information and Management Systems Society (2012)
Healthcare Supply Chain Association (2011)
Heating, Airconditioning and Refrigeration Distributors International (2012)
Heavy Duty Manufacturers Association (2012)
Help Desk Institute (2011)
Hispanic Association of Colleges and Universities (2010, 2011, 2012)
Hispanic Elected Local Officials (2012)
Hospitality Sales and Marketing Association International (2010, 2011, 2012)
Housing Education and Research Association (2012)
HUBZone Contractors National Council (2012)

Human Resource People and Strategy (2011)
IEEE Magnetics Society (2010)
Independent Bakers Association (2010)
Independent Electrical Contractors (2010, 2011)
Independent Insurance Agents & Brokers of America, Inc. (2012)
Industrial Minerals Association -- North America (2010)
Industrial Truck Association (2010, 2012)
InfoComm International (2012)
Institute of International Finance (2010, 2011)
Institute of Medicine (2012)
Institute of Real Estate Management (2010, 2011, 2012)
Institute of Scrap Recycling Industries, Inc. (2011)
Insured Retirement Institute (2011, 2012)
Interactive Advertising Bureau (2010, 2011, 2012)
Interactive Multimedia and Collaborative Communications Alliance (2012)
International Academy of Compounding Pharmacists (2010, 2011)
International Anti-Counterfeiting Coalition (2012)
International Association of Financial Crimes Investigators (2010)
International Association of Insurance Receivers (2012)
International Association of Medical Equipment Remarketers and Servicers (IAMERS) (2010, 2012)
International Association of Privacy Professionals (2010, 2012)
International Bottled Water Association (2012)
International Brain Injury Association (2012)
International Consumer Product Health and Safety Organization (2010)
International Council for Small Business (2012)
International Council of Employers of Bricklayers and Allied Craftworkers (2011)
International Dairy Foods Association (2012)
InterNational Electrical Testing Association (2011)
International Emissions Trading Association (2012)
International Facility Management Association (2012)
International Foodservice Editorial Council (2011)
International Franchise Association (2010, 2011, 2012)
International Health, Racquet and Sportsclub Association (2012)
International Liver Transplantation Society (2012)
International Nurses Society on Additictions (2012)
International Order of the Golden Rule (2012)
The International Society for Minimally Invasive Cardiothoracic Surgery (2011)
International Society for Pharmacoeconomics and Outcomes Research (2012)
International Society of Managing and Technical Editors (2010)
The International Stability Operations Association (2011, 2012)
International Technology Law Association (2012)
International Trademark Association (2012)
International Union of Toxicology (2011)
Interstate Council on Water Policy (2012)
Investment Adviser Association (2012)
Investment Company Institute (2010)
Investment Program Association (2011, 2012)
Jewish Educators Assembly (2010)
LeadingAge (American Association of Homes and Services for the Aging) (2012)
Learning Resources Network (2012)
Leather Industries of America (2011)
Liability Insurance Research Bureau (2012)
LOMA (2010)
Major County Sheriffs' Association (2012)
Management Association for Private Photogrammetric Surveyors (2011, 2012)
Manufactured Housing Institute (2010, 2012)
Marketing Science Institute (2011)
Meals on Wheels Association of America (2012)
Medicaid Health Plans of America (2012)
Medical Device Manufacturers Association (2010, 2012)
Medical Library Association (2010)
MEMA Information Services Council (2012)
Mental Health America (2012)
Messenger Courier Association of the Americas (2012)
Middle East Librarians' Association (2011)
Middle East Studies Association of North America (2011)
Military Impacted Schools Association (2010)
Military Officers Association of America (MOAA) (2012)
Mortgage Bankers Association of America (2010, 2011, 2012)
Motor and Equipment Manufacturers Association (2010, 2012)
MPA - The Association of Magazine Media (2010)
NALP - The Association for Legal Career Professionals (2011, 2012)
NAMM - The International Music Products Association (2011, 2012)
Natco-The Organization for Transplant Professionals (2012)
National Academy of Education (2011, 2012)
National Academy of Elder Law Attorneys, Inc. (2012)
National Academy of Engineering of the United States of America (2010, 2012)
National Academy of Public Administration (2011)
National Aeronautic Association (2012)
National Affordable Housing Management Association (2010, 2011, 2012)
National After School Association (2010)
National Alliance for Hispanic Health (2011)
National Alliance for Musical Theatre (2010)
National Alliance of State Pharmacy Associations (2010)
National Apartment Association (2010, 2012)
National Art Education Association (2010)
National Asian Pacific American Bar Association (2012)
National Asphalt Pavement Association (2012)
National Assembly of State Arts Agencies (2012)
National Association for Business Economics (2011)
National Association for Developmental Education (2011)
National Association for Equal Opportunity in Higher Education (2010)
National Association for Ethnic Studies (2010)
National Association for Girls and Women in Sport (2012)
National Association for Poetry Therapy (2010)
National Association for Sport and Physical Education (2010)
National Association for State Community Services Programs (2012)
National Association for the Education of Young Children (2012)
National Association for the Specialty Food Trade (2012)

National Association of Area Agencies on Aging (2011, 2012)
National Association of Attorneys General (2011)
National Association of Black-Owned Broadcasters (2012)
National Association of Chain Drug Stores (2012)
National Association of Chapter Thirteen Trustees (NACTT) (2011)
National Association of Chemical Distributors (2012)
National Association of Children's Hospitals and Related Institutions (2011, 2012)
National Association of Church Business Administration (2011)
National Association of Clean Water Agencies (2012)
National Association of College and University Attorneys (2010)
National Association of College and University Business Officers (2012)
National Association of Conservation Districts (2012)
National Association of Convenience Stores (2012)
National Association of Counties (2012)
National Association of County Administrators (2012)
National Association of County Civil Attorneys (2012)
National Association of County Information Officers (2010, 2011)
National Association of County Recorders, Election Officials and Clerks (2011, 2012)
National Association of Criminal Defense Lawyers (2010)
National Association of Development Companies (2012)
National Association of Drug Court Professionals (2011)
National Association of Electrical Distributors (2012)
National Association of Emergency Medical Technicians (2011)
National Association of Federal Credit Unions (2011, 2012)
National Association of Federal Education Program Administrators (2010, 2011, 2012)
National Association of Federally Impacted Schools (2010, 2011, 2012)
National Association of Government Archives and Records Administrators (2010)
National Association of Government Communicators (2010)
National Association of Graduate Admissions Professionals (2011)
National Association of Home Builders (2012)
National Association of Housing and Redevelopment Officials (2011)
National Association of Independent Colleges and Universities (2010, 2011, 2012)
National Association of Insurance and Financial Advisors (2011)
National Association of Insurance Commissioners (2010, 2012)
National Association of Latino Elected and Appointed Officials (2012)
National Association of Local Housing Finance Agencies (2010)
National Association of Minority Contractors (2011)
National Association of Mortgage Brokers (2011)
National Association of Mutual Insurance Companies (2012)
National Association of Nurse Practitioners in Women's Health (2012)
National Association of Police Organizations (2010, 2011, 2012)
National Association of Psychiatric Health Systems (2010)
National Association of Public Hospitals and Health Systems (2010, 2011)
National Association of Real Estate Editors (2010)
National Association of Real Estate Investment Managers (2010)
National Association of Realtors (2011, 2012)
National Association of Regulatory Utility Commissioners (2011)
National Association of Retail Collection Attorneys (2010, 2012)
National Association of Secretaries of State (2010, 2011, 2012)
National Association of Securities Professionals (2012)
National Association of Shareholder and Consumer Attorneys (2011, 2012)
National Association of State Boards of Education (2012)
National Association of State Directors of Career Technical Education Consortium (2010)
National Association of State Election Directors (2010, 2012)
National Association of State Energy Officials (2012)
National Association of State Personnel Executives (2012)
National Association of State Procurement Officials (2010)
National Association of State Treasurers (2012)
National Association of Surety Bond Producers (2012)
National Association of Temple Administrators (2011)
National Association of Towns and Townships (NATAT) (2010)
National Association of Truck Stop Operators(NATSO) (2012)
National Association of University Women (2010)
National Association of Veterans Research and Education Foundations (2010, 2012)
National Association of Water Companies (NAWC) (2012)
National Association of Wheat Growers (2011, 2012)
National Association of Women Business Owners (2010)
National Association of Workforce Boards (NAWB) (2011, 2012)
National Athletic Trainers Association (2011)
National Beer Wholesalers Association (2010, 2012)
National Black Caucus of State Legislators (2012)
National Black Farmers Association (2010)
National Black Public Relations Society (2012)
National Business Group on Health (2012)
National Chicken Council (2011, 2012)
National Chief Petty Officers' Association (2010)
National Child Support Enforcement Association (2012)
National Committee for Quality Assurance (2012)
National Community Pharmacists Association (2010)
National Confectioners Association (2012)
National Conference of CPA Practitioners (2010)
National Conference of Executives of The ARC (2012)
National Conference of Insurance Legislators (2011)
National Conference of State Historic Preservation Officers (2012)
National Conference of State Liquor Administrators (2012)
National Conference on Public Employee Retirement Systems (2012)
National Contract Management Association (2012)
National Cooperative Business Association (2010)
National Council for Community Behavioral Healthcare (2011)
National Council for International Visitors (2012)
National Council for Research on Women (2011)
National Council for Science and the Environment (2010, 2012)
National Council for the Social Studies (2011)
National Council for Workforce Education (2010)
National Council of Farmer Cooperatives (2012)
National Council of State Housing Agencies (2011, 2012)

National Council of Textile Organizations (2010)
National Council of University Research Administrators (2010, 2011, 2012)
National Council on Aging (2011, 2012)
National Council on International Trade Development (2010, 2012)
National Customs Brokers and Forwarders Association of America (2012)
National Dance Association (2012)
National Defense Transportation Association (2010)
National District Attorneys Association (2010)
National Education Association (2012)
National Electrical Contractors Association (2012)
National Electrical Manufacturers Association (2011)
National Employment Lawyers Association (NELA) (2010)
National Exchange Carrier Association (2012)
National Family Planning and Reproductive Health Association (2012)
National Fisheries Institute (2011)
National Foreign Trade Council, Inc. (2010)
National Foundation for Credit Counseling (2010)
National Funeral Directors Association (2012)
National Grocers Association (2010)
National Ground Water Association (2012)
National Head Start Association (2011, 2012)
National Hispanic Medical Association (2010, 2012)
National Hospice & Palliative Care Organization (2011)
National Housing and Rehabilitation Association (2011)
National Housing Conference (2010)
National Humanities Alliance (2011, 2012)
National Hydropower Association (2010, 2012)
National Independent Laboratory Association (2011, 2012)
National Indian Education Association (2012)
National Indian Gaming Association (2012)
National Institute of Building Sciences (2010, 2011)
National Institute of Packaging, Handling and Logistics Engineers (2012)
National League of Cities (2010, 2011, 2012)
National Leased Housing Association (2012)
National Legal Aid and Defender Association (2011)
National Lieutenant Governors Association (2010, 2011, 2012)
National Lipid Association (2010)
National Lumber and Building Material Dealers Association (2010)
National Mining Association (2010)
National Multi-Housing Council (2010, 2012)
National Ocean Industries Association (2010, 2011)
National Organization for the Professional Advancement of Black Chemists and Chemical Engineers (2012)
National Organization of Nurse Practitioner Faculties (2010)
National Parent Teachers Association (2010, 2012)
National Park Hospitality Association (2011)
National Pawnbrokers Association (2012)
National Perinatal Association (2010)
National Pest Management Association (2011, 2012)
National Pharmaceutical Council (2012)
National Potato Council (2010)
National Propane Gas Association (2010, 2012)
National Railroad Construction and Maintenance Association, Inc. (2012)
National Renal Administrators Association (2011)
National Restaurant Association (2011, 2012)
National Retail Federation (2011, 2012)
National Rural Electric Cooperative Association (2011)
National Rural Health Association (2012)
National Science Education Leadership Association (2010)
National Science Teachers Association (2010)
National Sheriffs' Association (2012)
National Shoe Retailers Association (2012)
National Small Business Association (2012)
National Society of Black Physicists (2010)
National Society of Compliance Professionals (2012)
National Student Osteopathic Medical Association (2012)
National Tax Association (2010)
National Telecommunications Cooperative Association (2012)
National Tour Association (2010)
National Training and Simulation Association (2012)
National Waterways Conference (2012)
National WIC Association (2012)
Natural Products Association (2012)
Naval Enlisted Reserve Association (2010)
Network of Executive Women in Hospitality (2011)
Newspaper Association of America (2012)
North American Membrane Society (2010)
North American Menopause Society (2011)
The North American Rail Shippers Association (2010)
North American Securities Administrators Association (NASAA) (2010)
The Open Group (2012)
Optical Society of America (2011)
Organization for the Promotion and Advancement of Small Telecommunications Companies (2011, 2012)
Organization of American Historians (2010)
Outdoor Industry Association (2012)
Petroleum Marketers Association of America (2010, 2012)
Physician Insurers Association of America (2012)
Pi Gamma Mu (2011)
Plastics Pipe Institute (2012)
Plumbing Manufacturers Institute (2010, 2012)
Police Executive Research Forum (2012)
Population Association of America (2011)
Power Transmission Distributors Association (2011)
Precision Machined Products Association (2012)
Preventive Cardiovascular Nurses Association (2012)
Private Label Manufacturers Association (2010, 2011, 2012)
Professional and Organizational Development Network in Higher Education (2012)
Promotional Products Association International (2011, 2012)

Property Casualty Insurers Association of America (2012)
Property Loss Research Bureau (2012)
Property Records Industry Association (2012)
Public Housing Authorities Directors Association (2012)
The Public Relations Society of America (2010)
Railway Engineering-Maintenance Suppliers Association (2012)
Railway Supply Institute (2012)
The Railway Tie Association (2012)
Real Estate Roundtable (2010, 2012)
Reinsurance Association of America (2012)
The Renaissance Society of America (2012)
Renal Physicians Association (2012)
Republican National Lawyers Association (2012)
Research!America (2012)
Reserve Officers Association of the U.S. (2011, 2012)
Retirement Industry Trust Association (2010)
Risk and Insurance Management Society, Inc. (RIMS) (2011)
The Risk Management Association (2011)
SAE International (2012)
Satellite Industry Association (2012)
School Nutrition Association (2011, 2012)
School Social Work Association of America (2012)
Scribes-The American Society of Legal Writers (2012)
Security Industry Association (2012)
Security Traders Association (2010, 2011, 2012)
Seismological Society of America (2011)
Self-Insurance Institute of America, Inc. (2012)
Senior Army Reserve Commanders Association (2010, 2011, 2012)
Senior Executives Association (2010)
Sheet Metal and Air Conditioning Contractors' National Association (2012)
Silver Users Association (2012)
Smart Card Alliance (2010, 2012)
Society for Education in Anesthesia (2012)
Society for Environmental Graphic Design (2010)
Society for Human Resource Management (2012)
Society for Industrial Microbiology (2012)
Society for Medieval and Renaissance Philosophy (2011, 2012)
Society for Neuro-Oncology (2012)
Society for Neuroscience (2011)
Society for Neuroscience in Anesthesiology and Critical Care (2012)
Society for Nutrition Education and Behavior (2012)
Society for Pediatric Anesthesia (2012)
Society for Pediatric Pathology (2010)
Society for the Exploration of Psychotherapy Integration (2011)
Society for the History of Authorship, Reading and Publishing (2011)
Society of American Florists (2012)
Society of American Gastrointestinal and Endoscopic Surgeons (2010)
Society of Behavioral Medicine (2011)
Society of Chemical Manufacturers and Affiliates Inc. (2012)
Society of Christian Ethics (2012)
Society of Competitive Intelligence Professionals (2010)
Society of Computed Body Tomography and Magnetic Resonance (2011)
Society of Corporate Secretaries and Governance Professionals (2012)
Society of Government Meeting Professionals (2012)
Society of Government Travel Professionals (2010)
Society of Gynecologic Oncologists (2012)
Society of Hospital Medicine (2010)
Society of Independent Gasoline Marketers of America (SIGMA) (2011, 2012)
Society of Insurance Trainers and Educators (2012)
Society of Nuclear Medicine (2012)
Society of Professional Asset-Managers and Record Keepers (2012)
Society of Professional Benefit Administrators (2010, 2011)
Society of Teachers of Family Medicine (2012)
Society of the Plastics Industry (2011)
Society of Thoracic Surgeons (2012)
Society of Toxicology (2011)
Society of University Otolaryngologists-Head and Neck Surgeons (2011)
Society of Urologic Nurses and Associates (2012)
The Society of Wine Educators (2010)
Software & Information Industry Association (SIIA) (2012)
Soil and Water Conservation Society (2011)
Specialized Information Publishers Association (2010, 2012)
Sports and Fitness Industry Association (2010, 2012)
Sports Lawyers Association (2011)
Stable Value Investment Association (2011)
State Capital Group (2011)
Steel Manufacturers Association (2010, 2011, 2012)
Structural Building Components Association (2010)
SWANA - Solid Waste Association of North America (2012)
Tax Executives Institute, Inc. (2010)
TechServe Alliance (2012)
Textile Rental Services Association of America (2012)
Toxicology Forum (2010, 2012)
Transportation Development Association (2012)
United Auto Workers (UAW) (2012)
United Fresh Produce Association (2012)
United Spinal Association (2012)
United States Advanced Ceramics Association (2012)
United States and Canadian Academy of Pathology (2010)
United States Cattlemen's Association (2012)
United States Chamber of Commerce (2012)
United States Conference of Mayors (2012)
United States Energy Association (2011, 2012)
United States Hispanic Chamber of Commerce (2010, 2012)
United States Pan Asian American Chamber of Commerce (2012)
United States Pharmacopeia (2010)
United States-China Business Council (2011, 2012)
University Aviation Association (2012)
Urban Libraries Council (2010)
Vinyl Institute (2012)

Vinyl Siding Institute, Inc. (2012)
Visiting Nurse Associations of America (2012)
Water Systems Council (2012)
White House Correspondents Association (2012)
Window and Door Manufacturers Association (2012)
Wireless Innovation Forum (2011)
Women Construction Owners and Executives, USA (2012)
Women in Government (2011, 2012)
Women in Government Relations, Inc. (2010, 2012)
Women's Council of REALTORS (2010, 2012)
Wood Machinery Manufacturers of America (2011)
Work Colleges Consortium (2012)
World Affairs Councils of America (2010, 2011, 2012)

FLORIDA

Amelia Island

American Association of Orthopaedic Medicine (2010)
American Association of Preferred Provider Organizations (2011, 2012)
American Boiler Manufacturers Association (2011)
American Coke and Coal Chemicals Institute (2012)
American Society for Automation in Pharmacy (2011)
American Society of Consulting Arborists (2010)
American Spice Trade Association (2012)
American Venous Forum (2010)
Book Manufacturers' Institute (2012)
Campus Safety, Health and Environmental Management Association (2010)
Council on Employee Benefits (2012)
CropLife America (2012)
Electrical Equipment Representatives Association (2012)
Executive Women's Golf Association (2011)
Forging Industry Association (2010)
Million Dollar Round Table (2012)
National Association of Bankruptcy Trustees (2011)
National Association of Charter School Authorizers (2011)
National Cottonseed Products Association (2010)
National Tooling and Machining Association (2010)
National Watermelon Association (2012)
Non-Ferrous Founders' Society (2011)
The Philanthropy Roundtable (2010)
Plan Sponsor Council of America (2010)
Polyurethane Manufacturers Association (2011)
Precision Metalforming Association (2010)
The Securities Transfer Association (2012)
Society for Historical Archaeology (2010)
Tilt-up Concrete Association (2012)

Atlantic Beach

American Boiler Manufacturers Association (2011)
Association of Investment Management Sales Executives (2010)

Aventura

American Academy of Addiction Psychiatry (2012)
American Society for Gastrointestinal Endoscopy (2010)
Association of Equipment Manufacturers (2011)
Investment Management Consultants Association (2011)
National Association of Corporate Treasurers (2010)
Professional Landcare Network (2011)

Biscayne

Biscuit and Cracker Manufacturers' Association (2011)
National Council of Self-Insurers (2012)

Boca Raton

Agricultural Retailers Association (2011)
American Academy of Actuaries (2012)
American Association for Hand Surgery (2010)
American Association of Plastic Surgeons (2011)
American Bakers Association (2010)
American Council of Engineering Companies (2012)
American Filtration and Separations Society (2012)
American Iron and Steel Institute (2010)
American Shoulder and Elbow Surgeons (2012)
American Society for Reconstructive Microsurgery (2010)
American Surgical Association (2011)
Association of National Advertisers (2010, 2012)
Conference of Consulting Actuaries (2012)
Equipment Leasing and Finance Association (2010)
Financial Managers Society (2011)
Futures Industry Association (2010, 2012)
Independent Bakers Association (2010)
Local Search Association (fka Yellow Pages Association) (2012)
Marketing Research Association (2010)
National Dental Association (2012)
National Dental Hygienists' Association (2012)
National Multi-Housing Council (2010, 2012)
Personal Care Products Council (2010)
Reusable Industrial Packaging Association (2012)
Steel Shipping Container Institute (2012)

Bonita Springs

Academy of Doctors of Audiology (2011)
Air Conditioning, Heating and Refrigeration Institute (AHRI) (2011)
Airport Consultants Council (2012)
American Association of Healthcare Administrative Management (2012)
American Bearing Manufacturers Association (2012)
American Concrete Pavement Association (2010)
American Gear Manufacturers Association (2012)
Aquatic Plant Management Society, Inc. (2010)
Asphalt Emulsion Manufacturers Association (2012)

Association of Academic Physiatrists (2010)
Bearing Specialist Association (2012)
Casting Industry Suppliers Association (2012)
Composite Panel Association (2010)
Concrete Sawing and Drilling Association (2011)
Consumer Healthcare Products Association (2012)
Copper and Brass Servicenter Association (2010)
International Slurry Surfacing Association (2012)
International Union of Police Associations, AFL-CIO (2012)
National Association of Chemical Distributors (2011)
National Association of EMS Physicians (2011)
National Environmental Balancing Bureau (2010)
National Fluid Power Association (2011)
NORA: Association of Responsible Recyclers (2012)
Pet Industry Distributors Association (2012)
Society of Thoracic Radiology (2011)

Cape Canaveral

American Astronautical Society (2010)
United States Advanced Ceramics Association (2012)

Champions Gate

BMC - A Foodservice Sales and Marketing Council (2012)
National Association of School Music Dealers (2012)
National Freight Transportation Association (2011)
National Ski Area Association (2010)

Clearwater

Academy of Surgical Research (2010)
Aerospace Industries Association of America (2010)
American Association for Adult and Continuing Education (2010)
American College of Healthcare Information Administrators (2010)
American Peanut Research and Education Society, Inc. (2010)
American Society of Group Psychotherapy and Psychodrama (2011)
AscdiNatd (2012)
The Association for Science Teacher Education (2012)
Association of Children's Prosthetic-Orthotic Clinics (2010)
Association of Service and Computer Dealers International (2012)
Coal Technology Association (2010, 2011, 2012)
Communications Media Management Association (2010, 2012)
Electrical and Computer Engineering Department Heads Association (2010)
Electronic Funds Transfer Association (2011)
IEEE Computer Society (2012)
International Association for Orthodontics (2010)
International Digital Enterprise Alliance (2010)
Metal Construction Association (2012)
National Academic Advising Association (2010)
National Fisheries Institute (2012)
National Migrant and Seasonal Head Start Association (2010)
North American Association of Educational Negotiators (2012)
Professional Association of Health Care Office Management (2012)
Society for Industrial Microbiology (2010)
Society for Thermal Medicine (2010)
Thoroughbred Racing Associations of North America (2010, 2012)

Cocoa Beach

IEEE Photonics Society (2012)

Coconut Grove

American Home Furnishings Alliance (2012)
Life Insurers Council (2012)

Coral Gables

Academy of Marketing Science (2011)
American Arbitration Association (2012)
American Institute of Certified Public Accountants (2010)
Compressed Gas Association (2010)
Food Processing Suppliers Association (2012)
Music and Entertainment Industry Educators Association (2010)
Steel Tube Institute of North America (2012)

Daytona Beach

Adhesion Society (2010)
America Outdoors Association (2012)
American Ceramics Society (2012)
American Ostrich Association (2010)
Christian Meetings & Conventions Association (2012)
The Coastal and Estuarine Research Federation (2011)
International Association of Counselors and Therapists (2010, 2011, 2012)
Medical Transcription Industry Association (MTIA) (2010)
National Association of Catastrophe Adjusters (2011)
National Mobility Equipment Dealers Association (2011)
The Paddlesports Industry Association (2012)
Parachute Industry Association (2012)
Portable Sanitation Association International (2010)

Deerfield Beach

National Association of Boards of Examiners of Long Term Care Administrators (2011)
National Association of Long Term Care Administrator Boards (2011)
National Council on Compensation Insurance, Inc. (2012)
Woodworking Machinery Industry Association (2012)

Delray Beach

Association for Retail Technology Standards (2012)
Association of Woodworking and Furnishings Suppliers (2012)
Wallcovering Association (2012)

Destin

American Academy of Anesthesiologist Assistants (2011)

Consumer Credit Industry Association (2010)
Consumer Credit Industry Association (2010)
Food Distribution Research Society (2010)
International Association of Structural Movers (2010)
Maple Flooring Manufacturers Association (2010)
Power-Motion Technology Representatives Association (2011)

Duck Key

American Dental Association (2011)

Florida City

American Association of Directors of Psychiatric Residency Training (2010)
American International Automobile Dealers Association (2010)
Association of Investment Management Sales Executives (2012)
Association of School Business Officials International (2010)
Council of Manufacturing Associations (2012)
Dairy Management, Inc. (2012)
The Institute of Financial Operations (2012)
International Safety Equipment Association (ISEA) (2010)
National Milk Producers Federation (2012)
Water and Sewer Distributors of America (2011)

Ft. Lauderdale

AAGL - Advancing Minimally Invasive Gynecology Worldwide (2012)
ACORD - Association for Cooperative Operations Research and Development (2011)
Air and Surface Transport Nurses Association (2010)
Airport Minority Advisory Council (AMAC) (2011)
American Academy of Disability Evaluating Physicians (2012)
American Association of Healthcare Administrative Management (2010)
American College of Foot and Ankle Surgeons (2011)
American College of Osteopathic Emergency Physicians (2011)
American College of Psychiatrists (2010)
American Composites Manufacturers Association (2011)
American Copper Council (2012)
The American Hair Loss Council (2012)
American Public Transportation Association (2010)
American Society of Retina Specialists (2012)
American Society of Transportation and Logistics (2010)
American Welding Society (2011)
American Wood-Protection Association (2011)
APMI International (2010)
Association for Research in Vision and Ophthalmology (2010, 2011, 2012)
Association of Alternate Postal Systems (2012)
Association of Marina Industries (2011)
Association of Physician Assistants in Cardiovascular Surgery (2012)
Association of Volleyball Professionals (2010)
Consumer Specialty Products Association (2010, 2011, 2012)
Credit Research Foundation (2012)
Global Business Travel Association (2011)
Infusion Nurses Society (2010)
International Association of Airport Duty Free Stores (2010)
International Association of Flight And Critical Care Paramedics (2010)
International Association of Venue Managers (2012)
International Society of Hotel Association Executives (2012)
JAWS Society (2010)
Learning Resources Network (2012)
Manufacturers Standardization Society of the Valve and Fittings Industry (2010)
Messenger Courier Association of the Americas (2012)
Metal Powder Industries Federation (2010)
Natco-The Organization for Transplant Professionals (2010)
National Aircraft Finance Association (2011)
National Association of Consumer Credit Administrators (2012)
National Association of Forensic Economics (2012)
National Association of Ordnance and Explosive Waste Contractors (2012)
National Association of Physician Recruiters (2010)
National Concrete Burial Vault Association (2011)
National Contract Management Association (2010)
National Funeral Directors and Morticians Association (2010)
The National Industrial Transportation League (2010)
National Railroad Construction and Maintenance Association, Inc. (2011)
National Real Estate Investors Association (2012)
National Wooden Pallet and Container Association (2012)
National Wrestling Coaches Association (2012)
Native American Journalists Association (2011)
North American Society for Pediatric Gastroenterology, Hepatology and Nutrition (2010)
Nuclear Suppliers Association (2012)
Professional Service Association (2012)
Public Housing Authorities Directors Association (2012)
Society of Accredited Marine Surveyors (2010)
Society of Clinical and Medical Hair Removal (2012)
Society of Professional Journalists (2012)
Society of Thoracic Surgeons (2010, 2011)
Textile Bag and Packaging Association (2012)

Ft. Myers

American College of Radiation Oncology (2012)
American Society of Brewing Chemists (2011)
American Society of Neuroimaging (2011)
Association for Financial Technology (2011)
Door and Access Systems Manufacturers Association, International (2010)
Flexographic Prepress Platemakers Association (2010)
National Association of Pipe Fabricators (2012)
National Coil Coating Association (2011)
National Criminal Justice Association (2010)
National Funeral Directors Association (2012)
Scale Manufacturers Association (2012)
School Science and Mathematics Association (2010)
Single Ply Roofing Institute (2012)
SMMA - The Motor and Motion Association (2012)

Society of Computed Body Tomography and Magnetic Resonance (2012)
Touchstone Energy Cooperatives (2012)
Web Sling and Tie down Association (2011)

Ft. Walton Beach

American Institute of Aeronautics and Astronautics (2012)
Society of Flight Test Engineers (2012)

Haines City

National Health Association (2011)

Hallandale

Laborers-Employers Cooperation & Education Trust (2012)

Hollywood

ACA International, The Association of Credit and Collection Professionals (2012)
American Academy of Facial Plastic and Reconstructive Surgery (2010)
American Association of Cereal Chemists International (2012)
American College of Clinical Pharmacy (2012)
American College of Neuropsychopharmacology (2012)
American College of Phlebology (2012)
American College of Radiology (2012)
American Nuclear Society (2011)
American Society for Histocompatibility and Immunogenetics (2010)
American Society of Clinical Oncology (2012)
Arthroscopy Association of North America (2010)
Bank Insurance and Securities Association (2010, 2012)
Consumer Bankers Association (2010)
Decorative Plumbing and Hardware Association (2010)
Destination Marketing Association International (2010)
Direct Marketing Association (2012)
Edison Electric Institute (2010)
Eye Bank Association of America (2012)
Flavor and Extract Manufacturers Association (2012)
International Association of Plumbing and Mechanical Officials (2012)
International Cinema Technology Association (2012)
Natco-The Organization for Transplant Professionals (2010)
National Association of Real Estate Investment Trusts (NAREIT) (2012)
National Comprehensive Cancer Network (2010, 2012)
National Coordinating Committee for Multiemployer Plans (2012)
National Customs Brokers and Forwarders Association of America (2012)
National Horsemen's Benevolent and Protective Association (2012)
National Indian Gaming Association (2012)
National Parking Association (2012)
PCIA - The Wireless Infrastructure Association (2010)
Pipe Fabrication Institute (2011)
Portfolio Management Institute (2012)
Tax Executives Institute, Inc. (2012)

Jacksonville

ADED - The Association for Driver Rehabilitation Specialists (2011)
American Association of Physics Teachers (2011)
American Mathematical Association of Two Year Colleges (2012)
American Medical Writers Association (2011)
American Military Retirees Association (2012)
American Moving and Storage Association (2011)
American Society of Transportation and Logistics (2012)
American Trakehner Association (2010)
Association for Consumer Research (2010)
Association for Educational Communications and Technology (2011)
Association for Experiential Education (2011)
Association for Financial Counseling and Planning Education (2011)
Association for Healthcare Documentation Integrity (2011)
Association of Boards of Certification (2010)
Association of College Honor Societies (2011)
Association of Eminent Domain Professionals (2012)
Association of Research Directors (2012)
Association of the United States Navy, Inc. (2010)
Canon Law Society of America (2011)
Commission on Accreditation for Law Enforcement Agencies Incorporation (2012)
Contact Lens Society of America (2010)
Equipment Marketing and Distribution Association (2012)
Financial and Security Products Association (2011)
Forest Resources Association (2012)
International Society of Certified Electronics Technicians (2012)
Literacy Research Association (2011)
National Association of Legal Assistants (2010)
National Council of Structural Engineers Associations (2011)
National Electronic Service Dealers Association (2012)
National Ice Cream Retailers Association (2011)
National Legal Aid and Defender Association (2012)
North American Nature Photography Association (2012)
Object Management Group (2012)
Retail Confectioners International (2012)
The Retired Enlisted Association (2012)
Society for Experimental Mechanics, Inc. (2012)
Society for Healthcare Epidemiology of America (2012)
Society of Infectious Diseases Pharmacists (2012)
Society of Insurance Research (2010)
Society of Petroleum Evaluation Engineers (2011)
Society of Teachers of Family Medicine (2010)
SOLE - The International Society of Logistics (2012)
Technical Association of the Graphic Arts (2012)
Used Truck Association (2010)

Key Biscayne

American Dental Society of Anesthesiology (2010)
American Institute of Steel Construction (2012)
American Society of Emergency Radiology (2011)
Emergency Department Practice Management Association (EDPMA) (2010)

PeerSpan (2012)
The Risk Management Association (2012)
The Vinegar Institute (2011)

Key Largo

Community Managers International Association (2012)
National Association of Decorative Fabric Distributors (2012)
National Tank Truck Carriers (2012)

Key West

Association of Leadership Educators (2012)
Consumer Credit Industry Association (2012)
Council of State Restaurant Associations (2012)
Fire Apparatus Manufacturers' Association (2010)
Public Affairs Council (2011)
Uni-Bell PVC Pipe Association (2012)
United States Cutting Tool Institute (2012)

Kissimmee

American College of Osteopathic Family Physicians (2012)
American Institute of Steel Construction (2010)
American Society for Laser Medicine and Surgery (2012)
American Truck Dealers (2010)
Association of Regulatory Boards of Optometry (2010)
Chain Drug Marketing Association (2012)
Institute for Supply Management (2011)
Institute of Electrical and Electronics Engineers (IEEE) (2012)
International Spa Association (2012)
International Titanium Association (2010)
National Association for Home Care and Hospice (2012)
National Association of Directors of Nursing Administration in Long Term Care
   (2011)
National Bulk Vendors Association (2010)
National Dog Groomers Association of America, Inc. (2012)
Society of Pharmaceutical and Biotech Trainers (2010)
WorldatWork (2012)

Lake Buena Vista

Academy of Hospitality Industry Attorneys (2012)
American Academy of Ambulatory Care Nursing (2012)
American Association of Dental Consultants (2012)
American Association of Medical Assistants (2010)
American Board of Quality Assurance and Utilization Review Physicians, Inc.
   (2010)
American College of Foot & Ankle Orthopedics & Medicine (2010, 2011)
American College of Nuclear Medicine (2012)
American College of Radiation Oncology (2010)
American Federation of Teachers (AFL-CIO) (2010)
American Sugarbeet Growers Association (2012)
Association for Financial Technology (2010)
Association of Diesel Specialists (2012)
Association of Latino Professionals in Finance and Accounting (2010)
Brotherhood of Railroad Signalmen (2010)
Casualty Actuarial Society (2012)
Conference of Radiation Control Program Directors (2011)
Council of Hotel and Restaurant Trainers (2011)
Delta Sigma Delta (2010)
Edison Electric Institute (2011)
Education Credit Union Council (2010)
Employee Services Management Association (2010, 2011)
FAA Managers Association, Inc. (2012)
Fabricators & Manufacturers Association, International (2011)
Food Marketing Institute (2011)
Foster Family-Based Treatment Association (2011)
Ice Skating Institute (2012)
Institute of Transportation Engineers (2011)
International Association of Outsourcing Professionals (2010, 2012)
Mobile Air Conditioning Society Worldwide (2011)
National Association of Professional Process Servers (2010)
National Communication Association (2012)
National Hospice & Palliative Care Organization (2012)
National League of Postmasters of the United States (2012)
National Utility Contractors Association (NUCA) (2010)
North American Society for Sport History (2010)
Organization for the Promotion and Advancement of Small Telecommunications
   Companies (2012)
Orthopaedic Trauma Association (2012)
Pediatric Orthopedic Society of North America (2011)
Power and Communications Contractors Association (2010)
Selected Independent Funeral Homes (2010)
Society for Foodservice Management (2010)
Society for Technological Advancement of Reporting (2010)
Society of Pediatric Nurses (2010)
SPIE - The International Society for Optical Engineering (2011)
Tile Contractors' Association of America (2010)
Tube and Pipe Association, International (2011)
Uniform Retailers Association (2010)
Warehousing Education and Research Council (2011)
Wiring Harness Manufacturers Association (2012)

Lake City

CHA - Certified Horsemanship Association (2010)

Longboat Key

National Association of Architectural Metal Manufacturers (2012)
National Association of Flavors and Food-Ingredient Systems (2010)
Transworld Advertising Agency Network (2012)

Manalapan

National Oilseed Processors Association (2012)

Marathon

Professional Insurance Marketing Association (2010)

Marco Island

Academy of Psychosomatic Medicine (2010)
American Concrete Pavement Association (2012)
Association for Dressings and Sauces (2010)
Association of Internal Management Consultants (2010, 2012)
Aviation Distributors and Manufacturers Association International (2010, 2011, 2012)
Brick Industry Association (2010, 2011)
Casting Industry Suppliers Association (2010)
The Commercial Vehicle Solutions Network (2012)
Hydraulic Institute (2010)
International Claim Association (2010)
International Energy Credit Association (2012)
Label Printing Industries of America (2012)
Material Handling Equipment Distributors Association (2010)
National Academy of Neuropsychology (2011)
National Aerosol Association (2010)
National Alcohol Beverage Control Association (2010, 2012)
National Association for Printing Leadership (2012)
National Association of Collegiate Directors of Athletics (2010, 2011, 2012)
National Association of Collegiate Marketing Administrators (2012)
National Association of Graphic and Product Identification Manufacturers (2012)
National Church Goods Association (2010)
NPES, The Association for Suppliers of Printing, Publishing, and Converting Technologies (2012)
Textile Bag and Packaging Association (2011)
The Transformer Association (2011)
Uni-Bell PVC Pipe Association (2010)
United States Tour Operators Association (2011)
Wood Machinery Manufacturers of America (2011)
Woodworking Machinery Industry Association (2011)

Miami

Academy for Eating Disorders (2011)
Academy of Laser Dentistry (2010)
Air and Expedited Motor Carriers Association (2012)
American Academy of Dermatology (2010)
American Academy of Periodontology (2011)
American Apparel Producer's Network (2011)
American Association for Justice (2011)
American Association of Neurological Surgeons (2012)
American Astronomical Society (2010)
American College of Construction Lawyers (2011)
American College of Sports Medicine (2010)
American Copper Council (2011)
American Fence Association (2012)
American Gastroenterological Association (2012)
The American Institute of Architects (2010)
American Institute of Floral Designers (2012)
American Medical Technologists (2011)
American Medical Women's Association (2012)
American Membrane Technology Association (2011)
American Pancreatic Association (2012)
American Psychology-Law Society (2011)
American Psychosocial Oncology Society (2012)
American Society for Horticultural Science (2012)
American Society for Legal History (2011)
American Society for Metabolic and Bariatric Surgery (2010)
American Society for Microbiology (2010, 2011, 2012)
American Society of Neuroimaging (2012)
American Society of Radiologic Technologists (2011)
American Society of Regional Anesthesia and Pain Medicine (2012)
American Statistical Association (2010)
AMT - The Association For Manufacturing Technology (2010)
Asphalt Emulsion Manufacturers Association (2010)
Association for Death Education and Counseling (2011)
Association for Financial Professionals, Inc. (2012)
Association for Healthcare Foodservice (2012)
Association for Research in Vision and Ophthalmology (2012)
Association of Defense Communities (2012)
Association of Dermatology Administrators & Managers (2010)
Association of Equipment Manufacturers (2011)
Association of Hispanic Advertising Agencies (2010, 2011)
The Association of Language Companies (2010)
Association of Marketing Service Providers (2011)
Association of Ship Brokers and Agents (U.S.A.) (2012)
Association of University Professors of Ophthalmology (2012)
Battery Council International (2011)
Color Marketing Group (2012)
Community Action Partnership (2012)
Copier Dealers Association (2010)
Corporate Housing Providers Association (2012)
Council on Occupational Education (2011)
The Counselors of Real Estate (2012)
CRE Finance Council (2012)
Delta Phi Epsilon (2012)
Direct Selling Association (2011)
Drug & Alcohol Testing Industry Association (2011)
The Endocrine Society (2012)
Express Delivery & Logistics Association (2012)
FCIB-NACM Corporation (2012)
Financial & Insurance Conference Planners (2010)
Fluid Sealing Association (2012)
Human Resource People and Strategy (2010)
IGAF Polaris (2011)
Illuminating Engineering Society of North America (2012)

INDA, Association of the Nonwoven Fabrics Industry (2010)
Independent Distributors Association (2012)
Industrial Heating Equipment Association (2012)
Institute of Certified Professional Managers (2010)
Institute of Mathematical Statistics (2011)
Intercoiffure America/Canada (2011)
Intermediaries and Reinsurance Underwriters Association (2012)
International Association of Ice Cream Vendors (2012)
International Association of Physicians in AIDS Care (2010)
International Association of Professional Security Consultants (2012)
International Card Manufacturers Association (2012)
International Dairy Foods Association (2011)
International District Energy Association (2011)
International Franchise Association (2011)
International Laser Display Association (2010)
International Real Estate Federation - American Chapter (2012)
International Society for Clinical Densitometry (2011)
International Society for Infectious Diseases (2010)
International Society for Prenatal Diagnosis (2012)
Material Handling Equipment Distributors Association (2012)
Natco-The Organization for Transplant Professionals (2012)
National Academy of Arbitrators (2011)
National Association of Development Organizations (2011)
National Association of Foreign Trade Zones (2010)
National Association of Health Services Executives (2012)
National Association of Printing Ink Manufacturers (2011)
National Association of Public Insurance Adjusters (2012)
National Association of Security Companies (NASCO) (2012)
National Association of State Chief Information Officers (2010)
National Association of Television Program Executives (2011, 2012)
National Association of Water Companies (NAWC) (2012)
National Association of Women Judges (2012)
National Conference on Public Employee Retirement Systems (2011)
National Electrical Manufacturers Association (2012)
National Investment Company Service Association (2010, 2012)
National Management Association (2010)
National Real Estate Investors Association (2010)
Office Business Center Association International (2010)
Organization for the Promotion and Advancement of Small Telecommunications Companies (2011)
Outpatient Ophthalmic Surgery Society (2012)
Paper Shipping Sack Manufacturers' Association, Inc. (2012)
Process Equipment Manufacturers' Association (2010)
Professional Records and Information Services Management International (2011)
Public Affairs Council (2011)
Sealant, Waterproofing and Restoration Institute (2010)
Secondary Materials and Recycled Textiles Association (2010)
Society for Clinical Trials (2012)
Society for Gynecologic Investigation (2011)
Society of Clinical and Medical Hair Removal (2010, 2011)
Society for Critical Care Medicine (2010)
Society of Environmental Journalists (2011)
Society of Industrial and Office Realtors (2012)
Society of Insurance Financial Management (2010)
Society of Invasive Cardiovascular Professionals (2012)
Society of Nuclear Medicine (2012)
Society of Quality Assurance (2012)
Specialized Information Publishers Association (2010)
Supply Chain Council (2012)
Truck Renting and Leasing Association (2010)
Uniform Retailers Association (2012)
United States Lifesaving Association (2012)
United States Soccer Federation (2012)
Waste Equipment Technology Association (2012)
Water Environment Federation (2012)
Weather Risk Management Association (2012)
Wholesale Florist and Florist Supplier Association (2010, 2012)

Miami Beach

Aluminum Extruders Council (2012)
American Apparel Producer's Network (2012)
American Association of Pathologists' Assistants (2012)
American College of Neuropsychopharmacology (2010)
American Society of Head and Neck Radiology (2012)
Association for Corporate Growth (2010)
Association of National Advertisers (2012)
Association of Ship Brokers and Agents (U.S.A.) (2010, 2011)
NAIOP, The Commercial Real Estate Development Association (2012)
Communications Fraud Control Association (2012)
Conveyor Equipment Manufacturers Association (2012)
Education Industry Association (2012)
Institute of Business Appraisers (2010)
International Society for Pharmacoepidemiology (2012)
International Superyacht Society (2012)
The International Wood Products Association (2010)
Life Insurance Settlement Association (2010)
National Association of Air Medical Communication Specialists (2010)
National Association of Sign Supply Distributors (2012)
National Weather Service Employees Organization (2010)
Public Affairs Council (2012)
Shock Society (2012)
Specialized Information Publishers Association (2012)
TechServe Alliance (2012)

Miami Lakes

National Association of Sewer Service Companies (2010)

Naples

Aircraft Builders Council (2012)
American Academy of Esthetic Dentistry (2012)

American Architectural Manufacturers Association (2012)
American College of Physician Executives (2012)
American College of Psychiatrists (2012)
The American Hockey Coaches Association (2010, 2012)
American Real Estate Society (2010)
American Spice Trade Association (2010)
Appraisal Institute (2010)
The Association of Suppliers to the Paper Industry (2012)
Biscuit and Cracker Manufacturers' Association (2010)
Book Manufacturers' Institute (2011)
Ceramic Tile Distributors Association (2010)
Concrete Reinforcing Steel Institute (2010)
Construction Industry Round Table, Inc. (2011)
Conveyor Equipment Manufacturers Association (2011)
Flexible Packaging Association (2011)
The Foodservice Group, Inc. (2012)
Foodservice Sales & Marketing Association (2012)
Gravure Association of America (2012)
Independent Office Products and Furniture Dealers Association (2010)
Intercollegiate Tennis Association (2010, 2011, 2012)
International Digital Enterprise Alliance (2010)
International Kitchen Exhaust Cleaning Association (2011)
Interstate Natural Gas Association of America (2012)
Laboratory Products Association (2011)
Manufacturers Standardization Society of the Valve and Fittings Industry (2012)
Metal Construction Association (2010)
National AMBUCS (2010)
National Association for Environmental Management (2012)
National Association of Flavors and Food-Ingredient Systems (2012)
National Council of Farmer Cooperatives (2012)
National Hay Association (2012)
National Renderers Association (2010)
National Tile Contractors Association (2010)
North American Die Casting Association (2012)
Personal Care Products Council (2012)
Petroleum Equipment Suppliers Association (2010)
Pressure Sensitive Tape Council (2011)
Propane Engine Fuel Committee/Propane Education and Research Council (2012)
Refrigerated Foods Association (2011)
Research and Development Associates for Military Food and Packaging Systems (2011)
Retail Industry Leaders Association (2012)
The Risk Management Association (2011)
Safety Glazing Certification Council (2011)
Sealant, Waterproofing and Restoration Institute (2012)
The Securities Transfer Association (2010)
Society of Independent Gasoline Marketers of America (SIGMA) (2012)
Society of Military Orthopaedic Surgeons (2012)
Tag and Label Manufacturers Institute (2012)
Transportation Lawyers Association (2012)
Wild Bird Feeding Industry (2011)

Ocala

Paso Fino Horse Association, Inc. (2010)

Orange

Electrical Generating Systems Association (2012)

Orlando

Academy Health (2012)
Academy of Dental Materials (2012)
Academy of Osseointegration (2010)
ACORD - Association for Cooperative Operations Research and Development (2012)
ACUTA - The Association for Information Communications Technology Professionals in Higher Education (2011)
AFCOM (2011)
Air Diffusion Council (2012)
Air Distribution Institute (2012)
Air Force Association (2010)
Aircraft Electronics Association (2010)
Alliance for Children and Families (2012)
Alliance for Continuing Medical Education (2012)
Alliance for Telecommunications Industry Solutions (2010)
Aluminum Extruders Council (2012)
Ambulatory Surgery Center Association (2011)
American Academy of Allergy, Asthma, and Immunology (2012)
American Academy of Anti-Aging Medicine (2012)
American Academy of Cosmetic Surgery (2010)
American Academy of Dental Group Practice (2011)
American Academy of Emergency Medicine (2011)
American Academy of Family Physicians (2011)
American Academy of Maxillofacial Prosthetics (2010)
American Academy of Medical Acupuncture (2010)
American Academy of Nurse Practitioners (2012)
American Academy of Ophthalmic Executives (2011)
American Academy of Ophthalmology (2011)
American Academy of Orofacial Pain (2010)
American Academy of Orthotists and Prosthetists (2011)
American Academy of Physical Medicine and Rehabilitation (2011)
American Advertising Federation (2010)
American Association for Cancer Research (2011)
American Association for Pediatric Ophthalmology and Strabismus (2010)
American Association for Public Opinion Research (2012)
American Association of Cardiovascular and Pulmonary Rehabilitation (2012)
American Association of Cereal Chemists International (2012)
American Association of Certified Orthoptists (2011)
American Association of Colleges of Pharmacy (2012)
American Association of Collegiate Registrars and Admissions Officers (2012)
American Association of Community Colleges (2012)

American Association of Cosmetology Schools (2010, 2012)
American Association of Critical-Care Nurses (2012)
The American Association of Eye and Ear Centers of Excellence (2011)
American Association of Feline Practitioners (2012)
American Association of Heart Failure Nurses (2010)
American Association of Integrated Healthcare Delivery Systems (2010)
American Association of Managed Care Nurses (2011)
American Association of Neuromuscular and Electrodiagnostic Medicine (2012)
American Association of Retired Persons (2010)
American Association of Suicidology (2010)
American Bar Association (2010)
American Beekeeping Federation (2010)
American Biological Safety Association (2012)
American Board of Veterinary Practitioners (2012)
American Board of Vocational Experts (2011)
American Brush Manufacturers Association (2010)
American Cleaning Institute (2011)
American College Counseling Association (2012)
American College of Counselors (2010)
American College of Dentists (2010)
American College of Foot & Ankle Orthopedics & Medicine (2012)
American College of Forensic Examiners Institute (2010)
American College of Legal Medicine (2010)
American College of Occupational and Environmental Medicine (2010)
American College of Osteopathic Family Physicians (2011)
American College of Osteopathic Internists (2012)
American College of Osteopathic Obstetricians and Gynecologists (2011)
American College of Phlebology (2010)
American College of Preventive Medicine (2012)
American College of Prosthodontists (2010)
American College of Toxicology (2012)
American Concrete Pipe Association (2012)
American Culinary Federation (2010)
American Dental Education Association (2012)
American Feed Industry Association (2012)
American Fence Association (2010)
American Flock Association (2010)
American Foundry Society (2010)
American Geriatrics Society (2010)
American Ground Water Trust (2012)
American Health Information Management Association (2010)
American Institute for CPCU - Insurance Institute of America (2010)
American Institute of Aeronautics and Astronautics (2010)
American Institute of Professional Geologists (2010)
American Intellectual Property Law Association (2011)
American Judicature Society (2010)
American Kinesiotherapy Association (2011)
American Laryngological, Rhinological and Otological Society (2010)
American Logistics Association (2011)
American Meat Institute (2010)
American Medical Directors Association (2011)
American Mental Health Counselors Association (2012)
American Metalcasting Consortium (2012)
American Mold Builders Association (2010)
American Morgan Horse Association (2012)
American Nephrology Nurses Association (2012)
American Nurses Association (2012)
American Occupational Therapy Association, Inc. (2010)
American Optometric Association (2010)
American Optometric Student Association (2010)
American Orthotic and Prosthetic Association (2010)
American Osteopathic Association (2011)
American Osteopathic College of Anesthesiologists (2012)
American Osteopathic Colleges of Ophthalmology and Otolaryngology - Head and Neck Surgery (2010)
American Payroll Association (2012)
American Pediatric Surgical Association (2010)
American Pet Products Association (2011)
American Psychological Association (2012)
American Psychological Association - Division of Psychoanalysis (2012)
American Psychological Association - Society of Clinical Psychology (2012)
American Psychotherapy Association (2010)
American Public Power Association (2010)
American Railway Development Association (2012)
American Railway Engineering and Maintenance-of-Way Association (2010)
American Rental Association (2010)
American Resort Development Association (2011)
American Short Line and Regional Railroad Association (2010)
American Society for Blood and Marrow Transplantation (2010)
American Society for Metabolic and Bariatric Surgery (2011)
American Society for Nondestructive Testing (2012)
American Society for Quality (2010)
American Society for Reproductive Medicine (2011)
American Society for Training and Development (2011)
American Society of Agricultural and Biological Engineers (2010)
American Society of Bariatric Physicians (2012)
American Society of Consultant Pharmacists (2010)
American Society of Extra-Corporeal Technology (2012)
American Society of Farm Managers and Rural Appraisers (2010)
American Society of Hand Therapists (2010)
American Society of Heating, Refrigerating and Air Conditioning Engineers (ASHRAE) (2010)
American Society of Hematology (2010)
American Society of Highway Engineers (2011)
American Society of Ocularists (2010)
American Society of Ophthalmic Registered Nurses (2011)
American Society of Pension Professionals & Actuaries (2010)
American Society of PeriAnesthesia Nurses (2012)
American Society of Plumbing Engineers (2011)
American Sports Builders Association (2012)

American Supply Association (2012)
American Teleservices Association (2010)
American Trauma Society (2012)
American Venous Forum (2012)
American Water Resources Association (2010)
American Wire Producers Association (2011)
AMT - The Association For Manufacturing Technology (2012)
Arabian Horse Association (2010)
Arthroscopy Association of North America (2012)
ASFE/The Geoprofessional Business Association (2012)
ASPRS-The Imaging and Geospatial Information Society (2010)
Assistive Technology Industry Association (2010, 2012)
Associated Air Balance Council (2010)
Associated Collegiate Press (2011)
Associated Equipment Distributors (2011)
Associated General Contractors of America (AGC) (2010)
Associated Locksmiths of America (2010)
Association for Hose and Accessories Distribution (2010)
Association for Information Systems (2012)
Association for Medical Imaging Management (2012)
Association for Skilled and Technical Sciences (2012)
Association for the Advancement of Computing in Education (2010)
Association of Analytical Communities International (2010)
Association of Biomolecular Resource Facilities (2012)
Association of Black Cardiologists (2011)
Association of Certified Fraud Examiners (2012)
Association of College and University Auditors (2011)
Association of College and University Housing Officers-International (2011)
The Association of Collegiate Conference and Events Directors International (2011)
Association of Corporate Contributions Professionals (2012)
Association of Corporate Counsel (2012)
Association of Energy Services Professionals, International (2011)
Association of Equipment Manufacturers (2010)
Association of Family and Conciliation Courts (2011)
Association of Fund-Raising Distributors and Suppliers (2010, 2012)
Association of Governing Boards of Universities and Colleges (2010)
Association of Government Accountants (2010)
Association of Insurance Compliance Professionals (2011)
Association of Legal Administrators (2011)
Association of National Advertisers (2010, 2012)
Association of Opinion Journalists (2012)
Association of Paroling Authorities International (2012)
Association of periOperative Registered Nurses (2012)
Association of Professors of Gynecology and Obstetrics (2010, 2012)
Association of Proposal Management Professionals (2010)
Association of Public Health Laboratories (2012)
APCO (Association of Public-Safety Communications Officials) International (2012)
Association of Rehabilitation Nurses (2010)
Association of Rotational Molders International (2010)
Association of Schools of Allied Health Professions (2012)
Association of State and Provincial Psychology Boards (2011)
Association of Teacher Educators (2011)
Association of TeleServices International, Inc. (2012)
Automated Imaging Association (2010, 2012)
Automotive Recyclers Association (2012)
Automotive Trade Association Executives (2010)
Auxiliary to the National Medical Association (2010)
Bearing Specialist Association (2011)
BICSI (2010, 2012)
Black Coaches & Administrators (2012)
Board Retailers Association (2012)
Bowling Writers Association of America (2011)
BP and AMOCO Marketers Association (2012)
Bridge Grid Flooring Manufacturers Association (2012)
Building Service Contractors Association International (2010)
Cable & Telecommunications Association for Marketing (2012)
Campus Computer Resellers Alliance (2010)
Captive Insurance Companies Association (2010)
CBA (2012)
CCIM Institute (2010)
Chain Drug Marketing Association (2011)
Chlorine Institute (2011)
Christian Leadership Alliance (2012)
Christian Legal Society (2010)
Christian Management Association (2012)
Cleaning Equipment Trade Association (2012)
College and University Professional Association for Human Resources (2011)
College Athletic Business Management Association (2011)
Community College Business Officers (2012)
Competitive Carriers Association (2012)
Computer Measurement Group (2010)
Conference of Radiation Control Program Directors (2012)
Congress of Neurological Surgeons (2012)
Construction Financial Management Association (2011, 2012)
Construction Owners Association of America (2012)
Construction Users Roundtable (2012)
Cookie and Snack Bakers Association (2012)
CoreNet Global (2012)
Council for Affordable and Rural Housing (2011)
Council of Real Estate Brokerage Managers (2012)
Council of Residential Specialists (2012)
Council On State Taxation (2012)
CPCU Society (2010)
Credit Union National Association, Inc. (2010)
CTIA - The Wireless Association (2011)
Dermatology Nurses' Association (2010)
Design-Build Institute of America (2011)
Developmental Disabilities Nurses Association (2012)

Distributive Education Clubs of America (DECA) (2011, 2012)
Diving Equipment and Marketing Association (2011)
Edison Electric Institute (2012)
Electrical Apparatus Service Association (2010)
Electrical Manufacturing and Coil Winding Association (2012)
Electrocoat Association (2012)
Exhibition Services and Contractors Association (2012)
Eye Bank Association of America (2011)
Family, Career and Community Leaders of America (2012)
Federation of Defense and Corporate Counsel (2010)
Financial Executives International (2012)
Fire Department Safety Officers Association (2012)
Flexible Packaging Association (2010)
Flexographic Prepress Platemakers Association (2012)
Food Marketing Institute (2012)
Food Shippers of America (2010, 2012)
The Foodservice Group, Inc. (2012)
Foodservice Sales & Marketing Association (2012)
Future Business Leaders of America - Phi Beta Lambda (2011)
GAMA International (2012)
Gasket Fabricators Association (2010, 2012)
Generic Pharmaceutical Association (2012)
Global Market Development Center (2010, 2011)
Grocery Manufacturers Association (GMA) (2012)
Hardwood Plywood and Veneer Association (2011)
Health Industry Business Communications Council (2012)
Healthcare Convention and Exhibitors Association (2012)
Healthcare Distribution Management Association (2010, 2012)
Healthcare Financial Management Association (2011)
Healthcare Information and Management Systems Society (2011)
Healthcare Supply Chain Association (2010, 2012)
Hearth, Patio and Barbecue Association (2010)
Heating, Airconditioning and Refrigeration Distributors International (2012)
Helicopter Association International (2011)
Help Desk Institute (2010, 2012)
Hospitality Financial and Technology Professionals (2012)
IEEE Control Systems Society (2011)
IEEE - Industry Applications Society (2011)
IEEE Instrumentation and Measurement Society (2010)
IEEE Power Electronics Society (2012)
IGAF Polaris (2012)
Independent Armored Car Operators Association (2012)
Independent Community Bankers of America (2010)
Independent Lubricant Manufacturers Association (2011)
InfoComm International (2011)
Institute Management Accountants (2011)
Institute of Environmental Sciences and Technology (2012)
Institute of Industrial Engineers (2011, 2012)
The Institute of Internal Auditors (2010)
Institute of Management Consultants USA (2012)
Institute of Nuclear Materials Management (2012)
Institute of Real Estate Management (2010)
Intelligent Transportation Society of America (2011)
International Alliance of Theatrical Stage Employees, Moving Picture Technicians, Artists and Allied Crafts of the U.S., Its Territories and Canada (2011)
International Anti-Counterfeiting Coalition (2011)
International Association for Cold Storage Construction (2012)
International Association of Airport Duty Free Stores (2010, 2011, 2012)
International Association of Amusement Parks and Attractions(IAAPA) (2010, 2011, 2012)
International Association of Chiefs of Police (2010)
International Association of Emergency Managers (2012)
International Association of Equine Dentists (2012)
International Association of Exhibitions and Events (2012)
International Association of Insurance Receivers (2010)
International Association of Special Investigation Units (2010)
International Bottled Water Association (2010)
International Bridge, Tunnel and Turnpike Association (2012)
International Business Brokers Association (2010)
International Cinema Technology Association (2010)
International Claim Association (2012)
International College of Dentists, U.S.A. Section (2010)
International Community Corrections Association (2012)
International Congress of Oral Implantologists (2012)
International Consumer Product Health and Safety Organization (2012)
International Cost Estimating and Analysis Association effective (2012)
International Council on Systems Engineering (2012)
International Downtown Association (2012)
International Embryo Transfer Society (2011)
International Executive Housekeepers Association (2010)
The International Fluid Power Society (2011)
International Franchise Association (2012)
International Hearing Society (2010)
International Institute of Ammonia Refrigeration (2011)
International Lactation Consultant Association (2012)
International Microelectronics and Packaging Society - IMAPS (2012)
International Municipal Signal Association (2012)
International Premium Cigar and Pipe Retailers (2012)
International Reading Association (2011)
International Sanitary Supply Association (2010)
International Sign Association (2010)
International Society for Performance Improvement (2011)
International Society for Pharmaceutical Engineering (2010)
International Society of Automation (2012)
International Society of Explosives Engineers (2010)
International Society of Transport Aircraft Trading (2010)
International Test and Evaluation Association (2011)
Interstate Renewable Energy Council (2012)
Investment Company Institute (2012)
Irrigation Association (2012)

Laser Institute of America (2011)
League for Innovation in the Community College (2010)
Legal Marketing Association (2011)
Liability Insurance Research Bureau (2012)
Life Insurance Settlement Association (2012)
Local Media Association (2010)
Lutheran Education Association (2012)
Marble Institute of America (2012)
Marine Fabricators Association (2010)
Marine Retailers Association of America (2012)
Marketing Research Association (2010)
The Masonry Society (2010)
Masonry Veneer Manufacturers Association (2012)
Medical Fitness Association (2011)
Meeting Professionals International (2011)
Metal Injection Molding Association (2012)
Minerals, Metals and Materials Society (2012)
Minor League Baseball (2010)
Modular Building Institute (2010, 2012)
Modular Building Systems Council (2012)
Mortgage Bankers Association of America (2012)
National Academic Advising Association (2010)
National Academy of Elder Law Attorneys, Inc. (2010)
National Alliance for Youth Sports (2011)
National Alliance of Medicare Set-Aside Professionals, Inc. (2012)
NAMTA - National Art Materials Trade Association (2012)
National Association for Court Management (2012)
National Association for Developmental Education (2012)
National Association for Research in Science Teaching (2011)
National Association for the Education of Young Children (2011)
National Association of Medical Staff Services (2010)
National Association of Addiction Treatment Providers (2012)
National Association of Bar Executives (2010)
National Association of Chapter Thirteen Trustees (NACTT) (2012)
National Association of Chronic Disease Directors (2010)
National Association of Church Business Administration (2010)
National Association of College Auxiliary Services (2011)
National Association of College Stores (2010)
National Association of Colleges and Employers (2010)
National Association of Collegiate Directors of Athletics (2011)
National Association of Conservation Districts (2010)
National Association of Convenience Stores (2010)
National Association of Councils on Developmental Disabilities (2010)
National Association of Development Companies (2012)
National Association of Estate Planners and Councils (2012)
National Association of Extension 4-H Agents (2012)
National Association of Field Training Officers (2012)
National Association of Government Guaranteed Lenders (NAGGL) (2012)
National Association of Healthcare Access Management (2010)
National Association of Home Builders (2011, 2012)
National Association of Home Builders Research Center (2012)
National Association of Independent Life Brokerage Agencies (2011, 2012)
National Association of Judiciary Interpreters and Translators (2010)
National Association of Latino Elected and Appointed Officials (2012)
National Association of Legal Investigators (2012)
National Association of Nurse Practitioners in Women's Health (2012)
National Association of Police Athletics/Activities Leagues, Inc. (2012)
National Association of Postal Supervisors (2010)
National Association of Professional Background Screeners (2011)
National Association of Professional Pet Sitters (2010)
National Association of Real Estate Editors (2012)
National Association of Real Estate Investment Trusts (NAREIT) (2010)
National Association of Realtors (2012)
National Association of Sporting Goods Wholesalers (2012)
National Association of State Boards of Accountancy (2012)
National Association of State Foresters (2011)
National Association of State Head Injury Administrators (2011)
National Association of Subrogation Professionals (2011)
National Association of Surety Bond Producers (2012)
National Association of Teachers of Singing (2012)
National Association of Therapeutic Schools and Programs (NATSAP) (2012)
National Association of Tower Erectors (2010)
National Auctioneers Association (2011)
National Auto Auction Association (2012)
National Automobile Dealers Association (2010)
National Black Nurses Association (2012)
National Business Aviation Association (2012)
National Business Incubation Association (2010)
National Cancer Registrars Association (2011)
National Cattlemen's Beef Association (2011)
National Chimney Sweep Guild (2012)
National Classification Management Society (2012)
National Concrete Masonry Association (2012)
National Conference of Bar Presidents (2010)
National Conference of Federal Trial Judges (2010)
National Conference of Specialized Court Judges (2010)
National Cotton Council of America (2012)
National Council for Community Behavioral Healthcare (2010)
National Council of Higher Education Loan Programs (2010)
National Council of Real Estate Investment Fiduciaries (2012)
National Council of State Housing Agencies (2012)
National Council of Teachers of English (2010)
National Council of University Research Administrators (2012)
National Council on Family Relations (2011)
National Frozen and Refrigerated Foods Association (2011)
National Golf Course Owners Association (2011)
National Hemophilia Foundation (2012)
National Insulation Association (2010)
National Interscholastic Athletic Administrators Association (2010)
National League for Nursing (2011)

National Marine Electronics Association (2012)
National Medical Association (2010)
National Ornamental and Miscellaneous Metals Association (2012)
National Potato Council (2012)
National Precast Concrete Association (2012)
National Public Employer Labor Relations Association (2012)
National Roofing Contractors Association (2012)
National Safety Council (2012)
National School Supply and Equipment Association (2010)
National Shippers Strategic Transportation Council (2012)
National Society of Accountants for Cooperatives (2010)
National Society of Black Physicists (2012)
National Society of Hispanic MBAs (2012)
National Society of Professional Engineers (2010)
National Sorghum Producers (2011)
National Speakers Association (2010)
National Strength and Conditioning Association (2010)
National Student Nurses Association (2010)
National Student Osteopathic Medical Association (2011)
National Tractor Parts Dealer Association (2011)
National Training and Simulation Association (2011)
National Wood Flooring Association (2012)
Newspaper Association of America (2010)
NIBA - The Belting Association (2012)
North American Association of Floor Covering Distributors (2012)
North American Association of Food Equipment Manufacturers (2011)
North American Building Material Distribution Association (2012)
North American Die Casting Association (2010)
North American Menopause Society (2012)
North American Spine Society (2010)
Obesity Society (2011)
The Optical Lab Division (2010)
Opticians Association of America (2012)
Organization for the Advancement of Structured Information Standards (2012)
Painting and Decorating Contractors of America (2011)
Paper Shipping Sack Manufacturers' Association, Inc. (2010)
Paperboard Packaging Council (2011)
PCIA - The Wireless Infrastructure Association (2012)
Peanut and Tree Nut Processors Association (2012)
Pediatric Orthopedic Society of North America (2012)
Pedorthic Footwear Association (2010)
Phi Alpha Theta (2012)
Phi Chi Theta (2010)
Phi Mu Alpha Sinfonia (2012)
Pierre Fauchard Academy (2010)
Pine Chemicals Association (2010)
Plumbing Contractors of America (2012)
Power Washers of North America (2012)
Preventive Cardiovascular Nurses Association (2011)
Printing Industry Credit Executives (2011)
Produce Marketing Association (2010)
Product Development and Management Association (2010, 2012)
Professional Retail Store Maintenance Association (2010)
Professional Service Association (2010)
Professional Tennis Registry (2012)
Property Loss Research Bureau (2012)
Public Affairs Council (2010, 2012)
Public Relations Student Society of America (2011)
Public Risk Management Association (2010)
Pulp and Paper Safety Association (2012)
Radio Advertising Bureau (2010)
Radio Technical Commission for Maritime Services (2012)
Radiology Business Management Association (2012)
RCI, Inc. (2010)
REALTORS Land Institute (2012)
Religious Communication Association (2012)
Renewable Fuels Association (2012)
Resource Center for Religious Institutes (2012)
RESPRO (Real Estate Services Providers Council) (2012)
Robotic Industries Association (2010, 2011, 2012)
SAVE International (2012)
Self Storage Association (2012)
Snack Food Association (2011)
SOCAP International (2011)
Society for Applied Learning Technology (2012)
Society for Biomaterials (2011)
Society for Cardiovascular Magnetic Resonance (2012)
Society for Clinical Vascular Surgery (2011)
Society for Free Radical Biology and Medicine (2010)
Society for Gynecologic Investigation (2010)
Society for Imaging Informatics in Medicine (2012)
Society for Maintenance & Reliability Professionals (2012)
The Society for Modeling and Simulation International (2010, 2012)
Society for Pediatric Radiology (2012)
Society for the Teaching of Psychology (2012)
Society for Uroradiology (2010)
Society for Wetland Scientists (2012)
Society of Abdominal Radiology (2010)
Society of American Florists (2010)
Society of Cable Telecommunications Engineers (2012)
Society of Financial Service Professionals (2010)
Society of Gastroenterology Nurses and Associates (2010)
Society of General Internal Medicine (2012)
Society of Industrial and Office Realtors (2010)
Society of Nuclear Medicine (2012)
Society of Reproductive Surgeons (2011)
Society of Research Administrators International (2012)
Society of Surgical Oncology (2012)
Society of Trauma Nurses (2010)
Society of Vacuum Coaters (2010)

Society of Women Engineers (2010)
Solar Electric Power Association (2012)
Solar Energy Industries Association (SEIA) (2012)
Souvenirs, Gifts and Novelties Trade Association (2012)
Special Interest Group on Accessible Computing (2010)
Specialized Carriers and Rigging Association (2010)
Specialty Tools and Fasteners Distributors Association (2012)
SPIE - The International Society for Optical Engineering (2010, 2011)
Sports Turf Managers Association (2010)
Steel Plate Fabricators Association Division of STI/SPFA (2011)
Steel Shipping Container Institute (2010)
Strategic Account Management Association (2011)
Surface Mount Technology Association (2012)
SWANA - Solid Waste Association of North America (2010, 2011)
Tile Council of North America, Inc. (2012)
Transportation Intermediaries Association (2011)
The Travel Institute (2010)
Truckload Carriers Association (2012)
Turnaround Management Association (2010)
United Motorcoach Association (2010)
United Potato Growers of America (2012)
United States Composting Council (2010)
The United States Harness Writers' Association (2012)
United States Swim School Association (2011)
Urban and Regional Information Systems Association (2010)
Utilities Telecom Council (2012)
Valve Manufacturers Association of America (2011)
Valve Repair Council (2011)
Vibration Isolation and Seismic Control Manufacturers Association (2010)
Visiting Nurse Associations of America (2010)
Voluntary Protection Programs Participants' Association, Inc. (2010)
Water Quality Association (2010)
Water Sports Industry Association (2010)
Water Systems Council (2010, 2012)
Wire Fabricators Association (2012)
Wiring Harness Manufacturers Association (2010)
Women in Aviation International (2010)
Women's Business Enterprise National Council (2012)
Women's Council of REALTORS (2012)
Worldwide ERC (2010)

Palm Beach

American Association of Attorney-Certified Public Accountants (2012)
American College of Oral and Maxillofacial Surgeons (2012)
American Radium Society (2011)
American Salvage Pool Association (2010, 2012)
American Society for Automation in Pharmacy (2011)
Association for Retail Environments (2011)
Casualty Actuarial Society (2011)
Commodity Markets Council (2012)
Council of American Survey Research Organizations (2011)
Electronic Traders Association (2012)
Electronic Transactions Association (2012)
Fluid Sealing Association (2010)
Gasket Fabricators Association (2011)
Health Physics Society (2011)
The Institute of Internal Auditors (2010, 2012)
Managed Funds Association (2012)
National Association of Business Political Action Committees (2010, 2012)
National Association of Chain Drug Stores (2010, 2012)
National Association of Investment Companies (2012)
National Association of Police Organizations (2012)
National Association of Resale & Thrift Shops (2010)
National Electrical Manufacturers Association (2010)
National Housing and Rehabilitation Association (2012)
National Parking Association (2010)
National Trailer Dealers Association (2011)
NPES, The Association for Suppliers of Printing, Publishing, and Converting Technologies (2011)
Outdoor Power Equipment and Engine Service Association (2011)
The Philanthropy Roundtable (2012)
Precision Machined Products Association (2012)
Security Traders Association (2011)
Society for Sex Therapy and Research (2011)
Society of American Florists (2012)
Society of Professional Asset-Managers and Record Keepers (2011, 2012)
Surgical Infection Society (2011)
Tag and Label Manufacturers Institute (2010)

Palm Beach Gardens

American Brush Manufacturers Association (2012)
Association of Jewish Aging Services (2012)
Compressed Gas Association (2011)
The Cordage Institute (2012)
KWPN of North America (2010)
National Association of Independent Lighting Distributors (2012)
National Society of Certified Healthcare Business Consultants (2010)
Pressure Sensitive Tape Council (2012)
Resistance Welding Manufacturing Alliance (2011)
Yacht Brokers Association of America (2011)

Palm Coast

Pine Chemicals Association (2012)
Professional Insurance Marketing Association (2011, 2012)
Sanitary Supply Wholesaling Association (2010)
Shareholder Services Association (2010)

Palm Harbor

Black Coaches & Administrators (2010)

Panama City

National Association of Independent Lighting Distributors (2010)
The National Association of Marine Surveyors, Inc. (2012)

Panama City Beach

Civil Aviation Medical Association (2010)
National Defense Industrial Association (2011)

Ponte Vedra

Airport Consultants Council (2010)

Ponte Vedra Beach

American Petroleum Institute (2012)
American Sports Builders Association (2010)
American Veterinary Distributors Association (2011)
Association of Life Insurance Counsel (2012)
Exhibit Designers and Producers Association (2010)
Foodservice Sales & Marketing Association (2011)
Forest Landowners Association (2012)
Forestry Conservation Communications Association (2012)
Intermediaries and Reinsurance Underwriters Association (2010)
International Society of Barristers (2010)
National Association of Elevator Contractors (2010)
National Association of Sign Supply Distributors (2010)
Pellet Fuels Institute (2011)
Plastic Pipe and Fittings Association (2010)

Ruskin

Council of Colleges of Acupuncture and Oriental Medicine (2011)

Safety Harbor

American Society of Pharmacognosy (2010)

Sandestin

Association of Real Estate License Law Officials (2011)

Sandston

North American Council of Automotive Teachers (2010)

Sanibel

Greeting Card Association (2010)
National Fellowship of Child Care Executives (2012)

Santa Rosa Beach

International Furniture Transportation and Logistics Council (2011)

Sarasota

American Edged Products Manufacturers Association (2012)
American Society of Marine Artists (2010)
Association of University Professors of Ophthalmology (2010)
Chemical Coaters Association International (2010)
Federation of Associations of Regulatory Boards (2012)
Glass Association of North America (2012)
International Council of Fine Arts Deans (2010)

Sebring

Light Aircraft Manufacturers Association (2010)

Singer Island

Lightning Protection Institute (2012)
United Lightning Protection Association (2012)

St. Augustine

Society for Vector Ecology (2012)

St. Pete Beach

American Association of Birth Centers (2012)
American College of Laboratory Animal Medicine (2012)
American Society for Automation in Pharmacy (2012)
Association for High Technology Distribution (2010)
Association of American Feed Control Officials (2011)
Association of Free Community Papers (2011)
The Association to Advance Collegiate Schools of Business (2011)
Food Industry Association Executives (2010)
Industrial Fabrics Association International (2011)
National Association for Children's Behavioral Health (NACBH) (2012)
National Association of Schools of Dance (2011)
National Council of Real Estate Investment Fiduciaries (2011)
National Council of Self-Insurers (2010)
National Mastitis Council (2012)
North American Transportation Employee Relations Association (2012)
Resort and Commercial Recreation Association (2012)
Society for Consumer Psychology (2010)
Undersea and Hyperbaric Medical Society (2010)

St. Petersburg

AGN International North America, Inc (2010)
Aircraft Builders Council (2010)
American Academy of Environmental Medicine (2012)
American Association of Community Colleges (2010)
American Board of Nursing Specialties (2012)
American Osteopathic College of Occupational and Preventive Medicine (2012)
American Real Estate Society (2012)
Associated Press Managing Editors (2010)
Association for Chemoreception Sciences (2010, 2011)
Association of University Research Parks (2012)
Black Coaches & Administrators (2011)
Council on the Safe Transportation of Hazardous Articles (2010)

Electrical Generating Systems Association (2010)
Federation of State Humanities Councils (2011)
Fibre Channel Industry Association (2011)
Flexible Packaging Association (2012)
Hydraulic Institute (2012)
Independent Laboratory Distributors Association (2011)
Insured Retirement Institute (2011)
International Dairy Foods Association (2011)
JAWS Society (2012)
Manufacturers Standardization Society of the Valve and Fittings Industry (2011)
National Association of Parliamentarians (2011)
National Eating Disorders Association (2012)
National Wooden Pallet and Container Association (2011)
North American Cartographic Information Society (2010)
North American Transportation Employee Relations Association (2011)
Public Affairs Council (2010)
Society for the Teaching of Psychology (2012)
United Ostomy Associations of America (2012)
Vinyl Siding Institute, Inc. (2012)

Stuart

National Association of Flour Distributors (2010)

Sunny Isles Beach

Asphalt Recycling and Reclaiming Association (2010)
National Association of Graphic and Product Identification Manufacturers (2010)

Tallahassee

The Association to Advance Collegiate Schools of Business (2011)

Tampa

Adhesive and Sealant Council (2011)
American Association for Clinical Chemistry, Inc. (2012)
American Association for Dental Research (2012)
American Association for Respiratory Care (2011)
American Board of Quality Assurance and Utilization Review Physicians, Inc. (2012)
American Coal Ash Association (2012)
American Coal Council (2012)
American College of Mental Health Administration (2012)
American College of Nurse Practitioners (2010)
American Concrete Institute (2011)
American Correctional Association (2010)
American Health Care Association (2012)
American Institute of Hydrology (2012)
American Medical Directors Association (2011)
American Neuropsychiatric Association (2010)
American Physical Therapy Association (2012)
American Seed Trade Association (2012)
American Society for Healthcare Engineering (2010)
American Society for Healthcare Human Resources Administration (2010)
American Society for Healthcare Risk Management (2010)
American Society of Abdominal Surgeons (2010, 2011, 2012)
American Society of Health-System Pharmacists (2010)
American Society of Home Inspectors (2011)
American Soybean Association (2011)
American Telemedicine Association (2011)
American Traffic Safety Service Association (2012)
American Truck Dealers (2012)
American Trucking Associations (2010)
Antique and Amusement Photographers International (2012)
Armed Forces Communications and Electronics Association (2012)
Asian American Convenience Stores Association (2012)
ASPRS-The Imaging and Geospatial Information Society (2012)
Association for the Advancement of Medical Instrumentation (2010)
Association for Wedding Professionals International (2012)
Association of Boards of Certification (2012)
Association of Bone and Joint Surgeons (2011)
Association of Clinical Research Professionals (2010)
Association of Educational Service Agencies (2012)
Association of Vascular and Interventional Radiographers (2010)
The Association to Advance Collegiate Schools of Business (2012)
AVS: Science and Technology of Materials, Interfaces, and Processing (2012)
The Coastal and Estuarine Research Federation (2012)
Construction Owners Association of America (2010)
Convention Industry Council (2012)
Council of the Great City Schools (2010)
Dangerous Goods Advisory Council (2011)
Emergency Nurses Association (2011)
Employee Assistance Professionals Association (2010)
Equipment Marketing and Distribution Association (2011)
Federation of Associations of Regulatory Boards (2011)
Gases and Welding Distributors Association (2011)
Healthcare Distribution Management Association (2011)
Incentive Manufacturers & Representatives Alliance (2012)
Institute for Professionals in Taxation (2012)
International Association of Women in Fire and Emergency Services (2012)
International Biometric Industry Association (2012)
The International Fluid Power Society (2012)
Interstate Council on Water Policy (2010)
Management Association for Private Photogrammetric Surveyors (2012)
Musculoskeletal Tumor Society (2012)
National Accounting and Finance Council (2012)
National Association for Healthcare Quality (2012)
National Association for Retail Marketing Services (2010)
National Association for the Support of Long Term Care (2012)
National Association of College and University Business Officers (2011)
National Association of Elementary School Principals (2011)
National Association of Media and Technology Centers (2012)
National Association of Professional Band Instrument Repair Technicians (2010)

National Association of Secondary School Principals (2012)
National Center for Assisted Living (2012)
National Chemical Credit Association (2012)
National Confectionery Sales Association (2012)
National Conference of Bankruptcy Judges (2011)
National Conference of State Legislatures (2011)
National Council on Education for the Ceramic Arts (2011)
National Credit Reporting Association (2012)
National Intramural-Recreational Sports Association (2012)
National Junior College Athletic Association (2011)
National Motor Freight Traffic Association, Inc. (2010)
National Perinatal Association (2012)
National Rural Electric Cooperative Association (2010)
National School Supply and Equipment Association (2012)
National Sorghum Producers (2011)
National Telecommunications Cooperative Association (2010)
Organization for Safety and Asepsis Procedures (2010)
Phi Alpha Delta (2010)
Radiation Therapy Oncology Group (2010)
The Railway Tie Association (2012)
Retail Industry Leaders Association (2010)
Retail Print Music Dealers Association (2011)
Rheumatology Nurses Society (2012)
Sewn Products Equipment and Suppliers of the Americas (2012)
Society for Pediatric Anesthesia (2012)
Society for Research in Child Development (2012)
Society for Social Work Leadership in Health Care (2010)
Society for the Scientific Study of Sexuality (2012)
Society of Interventional Radiology (2010)
Spill Control Association of America (2010)
SSPC: the Society for Protective Coatings (2012)
Technology and Maintenance Council of American Trucking Associations (2012)
Transportation Research Forum (2012)
United Motorcoach Association (2011)
Workgroup for Electronic Data Interchange (2012)

Venice

American Association of Community Theatre (2010)

Wesley Chapel

National Association for Retail Marketing Services (2012)
Peanut and Tree Nut Processors Association (2010)

West Palm Beach

Alliance for Regenerative Medicine (2012)
American Hanoverian Society (2012)
Association of Christian Librarians (2012)
Council for Christian Colleges and Universities (2010)
Society of Insurance Financial Management (2012)

GEORGIA

Albany

American Connemara Pony Society (2010)

Athens

American Society of International Law (2012)
Business History Conference (2010)
Metaphysical Society of America (2012)
Poultry Science Association (2012)
Psychometric Society (2010, 2011)

Atlanta

AACE International (2010)
Academy of Psychosomatic Medicine (2012)
AIM Global (2012)
Air Force Sergeants Association (2010)
American Academy of Forensic Sciences (2012)
American Academy of Hospice and Palliative Medicine (2010)
American Academy of Neurological and Orthopaedic Surgeons (2012)
American Academy of Orthotists and Prosthetists (2012)
American Academy of Physical Medicine and Rehabilitation (2012)
American Academy of Physician Assistants (2010)
American Academy of Psychotherapists (2012)
American Academy of Religion (2010)
American Accounting Association (2012)
American Association for Applied Linguistics (2010)
American Association for Clinical Chemistry, Inc. (2011)
American Association for Homecare (2010, 2011, 2012)
American Association for Laboratory Animal Science (2010)
American Association for Marriage and Family Therapy (2010)
American Association for the Advancement of Artificial Intelligence (2010)
American Association of Airport Executives (2011)
American Association of Avian Pathologists (2010)
American Association of Colleges for Teacher Education (2010)
American Association of Managing General Agents (2012)
American Association of Medical Dosimetrists (2012)
American Association of Veterinary Clinicians (2011, 2012)
American Association of Veterinary Parasitologists (2010)
American Brachytherapy Society (2010)
American Camp Association (2012)
American Cleaning Institute (2011)
American College of Cardiovascular Administrators (2010)
American College of Chest Physicians (2012)
American College of Osteopathic Surgeons (2011)
American College of Rheumatology (2010)
American Congress of Rehabilitation Medicine (2011)
American Council on Consumer Interests (2010)
American Craft Council (2010)
American Economic Association (2010)

American Farm Bureau Federation (2011)
American Feed Industry Association (2010, 2012)
The American Finance Association (2010)
American Gas Association (2012)
American Industrial Hygiene Association (2010)
American Institute of Aeronautics and Astronautics (2010, 2012)
American Logistics Association (2010)
American Medical Society for Sports Medicine (2012)
American Men's Studies Association (2010)
American Meteorological Society (2010)
American Music Therapy Association (2011)
American Peanut Council (2010)
American Philosophical Association (2012)
American Public Gardens Association (2010)
American Railway Development Association (2011)
American Real Estate and Urban Economics Association (2010)
American Society for Apheresis (2012)
American Society for Clinical Pharmacology and Therapeutics (2010)
American Society for Dermatologic Surgery (2012)
American Society for Legal History (2011)
American Society for Precision Engineering (2010)
American Society of Addiction Medicine (2012)
American Society of Dermatopathology (2010)
The American Society of Forensic Odontology (2012)
American Society of Heating, Refrigerating and Air Conditioning Engineers
    (ASHRAE) (2012)
American Society of Hematology (2012)
American Society of Home Inspectors (2011)
American Society of Law, Medicine and Ethics (2010, 2012)
American Society of Mechanical Engineers (ASME) (2011)
American Society of Tropical Medicine and Hygiene (2010, 2012)
American Sociological Association (2010)
American Speech-Language-Hearing Association (2012)
American String Teachers Association (2012)
American Urological Association (2012)
American Wind Energy Association (AWEA) (2012)
Asian American Hotel Owners Association (2012)
Associated Wire Rope Fabricators (2012)
Association for Applied Sport Psychology (2012)
Association for Clinical Pastoral Education (2012)
Association for Comparative Economic Studies (2010)
Association for Death Education and Counseling (2012)
Association for Evolutionary Economics (2010)
Association for Healthcare Philanthropy (2012)
Association for Iron and Steel Technology (2012)
The Association for Library Service to Children (2010)
Association for Supervision and Curriculum Development (ASCD) (2012)
Association for the Accreditation of Human Research Protection Programs (2010)
Association for the Sociology of Religion (2010)
Association of Baccalaureate Social Work Program Directors (2010)
Association of Camp Nurses (2012)
Association of Career and Technical Education (2012)
Association of College and University Religious Affairs (2010)
Association of Coupon Professionals (2011)
Association of Destination Management Executives (2010)
Association of Environmental and Resource Economists (2010)
Association of Equipment Manufacturers (2011)
Association of Executive and Administrative Professionals (2012)
Association of Free Community Papers (2012)
Association of Genetic Technologists (2012)
Association of Government Accountants (2011)
Association of Independent Corrugated Converters (2012)
Association of Jewish Aging Services (2010)
Association of Life Insurance Counsel (2010)
Association of Old Crows (2010)
Association of Pediatric Oncology Social Workers (2011)
Association of Pet Dog Trainers (2010)
Association of Program Directors in Internal Medicine (2012)
Association of Reproductive Health Professionals (2010)
Association of Rheumatology Health Professionals (2010)
Association of Strategic Alliance Professionals, Inc. (2011)
Association of University Interior Designers (2010)
Association of Water Technologies (2011)
Association of Zoos and Aquariums (2011)
ASTM International (2012)
Biomedical Engineering Society (2012)
Biscuit and Cracker Manufacturers' Association (2012)
Care Continuum Alliance (2012)
Catholic Health Association of the United States (2011)
CBA (2011)
Center for the Polyurethanes Industry (2012)
Certified Claims Professional Accreditation Council (2010)
CFA Institute (2012)
Chlorine Chemistry Council (2012)
Chlorine Institute (2012)
Chorus America (2010)
Clinical and Laboratory Standards Institute (2011)
Clinical Laboratory Management Association (2012)
Conference of State Court Administrators (2011)
Conference on College Composition and Communication (2011)
Construction Management Association of America (2010)
Costume Society of America (2012)
Council for Advancement and Support of Education (2011)
Council for Chemical Research, Inc. (2010)
Council for Christian Colleges and Universities (2010)
Council of Communication Management (2012)
Council of Science Editors (2010)
Council of State Speech-Language-Hearing Association Presidents (2012)
Council of Supply Chain Management Professionals (2012)
Council on Occupational Education (2012)

Council on Social Work Education (2011)
Crane Certification Association of America (2012)
Creative Education Foundation (2012)
Custom Electronic Design and Installation Association (2010)
Directed Energy Professional Society (2011)
Environmental Industry Associations (2010)
Express Carriers Association (2011)
Federation of Tax Administrators (2010)
Financial Management Association International (2012)
Forging Industry Association (2010)
Foster Family-Based Treatment Association (2012)
Government Finance Officers Association of the United States and Canada (2010)
Government Management Information Sciences (2010)
Hearth, Patio and Barbecue Association (2012)
High Technology Crime Investigation Association (2010)
Hospitality Financial and Technology Professionals (2011)
Human Capital Institute (2012)
Independent Educational Consultants Association (2012)
Independent Insurance Agents & Brokers of America, Inc. (2012)
Independent Sector (2010)
Information Systems Security Association (2010)
Institute for Credentialing Excellence (2010)
Institute for Professionals in Taxation (2011, 2012)
Institute of Packaging Professionals (2012)
Institute of Transportation Engineers (2012)
Insurance Accounting and Systems Association (2012)
Insurance Marketing Communications Association (2010)
Intellectual Property Owners Association (2010)
Intercollegiate Men's Choruses, an International Association of Male Choruses
    (2012)
Interior Design Educators Council (2010)
Intermodal Association of North America (2011)
The International Air Cargo Association (2012)
International Association of Chiefs of Police (2010)
International Association of Fire Chiefs (2011)
International Customer Service Association (2010)
International Facility Management Association (2010)
International Fire Photographers Association (2011)
International Society for Pharmacoeconomics and Outcomes Research (2010)
International Society for the Study of Trauma and Dissociation (2010)
International Society of Hospitality Consultants (2012)
International Society of Psychiatric Consultation Liaison Nurses (2012)
International Society of Psychiatric-Mental Health Nurses (2012)
International Titanium Association (2012)
Interstate Council on Water Policy (2012)
Jewish Community Centers Association of North America (2010)
Labor and Employment Relations Association (2010)
Learning Forward (2010)
Meals on Wheels Association of America (2010)
Mechanical Power Transmission Association (2010, 2012)
Media Financial Management Association (2011)
Million Dollar Round Table (2011)
Mortgage Bankers Association of America (2012)
Mulch and Soil Council (2012)
Mystery Shopping Providers Association (2011)
National Association for Family Child Care (2012)
National Association for Gifted Children (2010)
National Association for State Community Services Programs (2012)
National Association for the Education of Young Children (2012)
National Association of Advisors for the Health Professions (2010)
National Association of Agricultural Educators (2012)
National Association of Bar Executives (2011)
National Association of Black Social Workers (2012)
National Association of Blacks in Criminal Justice (2010)
National Association of College Auxiliary Services (2012)
National Association of Convenience Stores (2010, 2012)
National Association of County and City Health Officials (2010)
The National Association of Crime Victim Compensation Boards (2012)
National Association of Dental Plans (2011)
National Association of Environmental Professionals (2010)
National Association of Equipment Leasing Brokers (2010)
National Association of Insurance Commissioners (2012)
National Association of Local Boards of Health (2012)
National Association of Minority and Women Owned Law Firms (2012)
National Association of Professional Mortgage Women (2012)
National Association of Professional Surplus Lines Offices, Ltd. (2010, 2012)
National Association of Professors of Hebrew (2010)
National Association of Real Estate Investment Managers (2010)
National Association of Regulatory Utility Commissioners (2010)
National Association of Shell Marketers (2010)
National Association of State Boards of Education (2011)
National Association of State Utility Consumer Advocates (NASUCA) (2010)
National Association of States United For Aging and Disabilities (2010)
National Association of University Women (2012)
National Black Caucus of State Legislators (2010)
National Black MBA Association (2011)
National Business Aviation Association (2010)
National Business Incubation Association (2012)
National Cheese Institute (2011)
National Coalition of Black Meeting Planners (2012)
National Collegiate Athletic Association (2010)
National Conference of Black Political Scientists (2010)
National Council of State Housing Agencies (2011)
National Defender Investigator Association (2012)
National Environmental, Safety and Health Training Association (2010)
National Fenestration Rating Council (2011)
National Foundation for Women Legislators (2012)
National Garden Clubs (2010)
National Health Care Anti-Fraud Association (2011)
National Independent Living Association (2012)

The National Industrial Transportation League (2011)
National Legal Aid and Defender Association (2010)
National Marine Distributors Association (2012)
National Minority Supplier Development Council (2011)
National Opera Association (2010)
National Organization for the Professional Advancement of Black Chemists and Chemical Engineers (2010)
National Poultry and Food Distributors Association (2010, 2012)
National Recreation and Parks Association (2011)
National Retail Federation (2010, 2012)
National Science Teachers Association (2012)
National Solid Wastes Management Association (2010)
National Sorghum Producers (2011)
National Speakers Association (2010)
National Surgical Assistant Association (2011)
National Tuberculosis Controllers Association (2010, 2012)
North American Equipment Dealers Association (2011)
Organization for Safety and Asepsis Procedures (2012)
Oriental Rug Importers Association of America (2012)
Oriental Rug Retailers of America, Inc. (2012)
Perennial Plant Association (2011)
Petroleum Equipment Institute (2010, 2012)
Phi Delta Kappa International (2011)
PKF North American Network (2010)
Polyurethane Foam Association (2010)
Poultry Breeders of America (2012)
Power and Communications Contractors Association (2012)
Produce Marketing Association (2011)
Professional Housing Management Association (2010)
Rabbinical Assembly (2012)
Radiation Therapy Oncology Group (2012)
Registry of Interpreters for the Deaf (2011)
Religious Education Association (2012)
Research Chefs Association (2011)
Research Society on Alcoholism (2011)
Restoration Industry Association (2010)
The Rural Sociological Society (2010)
Scale Manufacturers Association (2010)
SEAMS Association (2012)
Selected Independent Funeral Homes (2012)
Sewn Products Equipment and Suppliers of the Americas (2010, 2012)
National Association of Small Business Investment Companies (2010)
Smocking Arts Guild of America (2012)
Society for Healthcare Epidemiology of America (2010)
Society for Human Resource Management (2012)
Society for Industrial and Organizational Psychology Inc. (2010)
Society for Information Management (2010)
The Society for Investigative Dermatology (2010)
Society for Pediatric Urology (2012)
Society for Photographic Education (2011)
Society for Public Health Education (2010)
Society for the Study of Social Problems (2010)
Society for the Study of Symbolic Interaction (2010)
Society of American Magicians (2010)
Society of American Military Engineers (2010)
Society of Atherosclerosis Imaging and Prevention (2012)
Society of Biblical Literature (2010)
Society of Diagnostic Medical Sonographers (2011)
Society of Engineering Science (2012)
Society of Infectious Diseases Pharmacists (2012)
Society of Neurological Surgeons (2012)
Society of Tribologists and Lubrication Engineers (2011)
TASH (2011)
Technical Association of the Pulp and Paper Industry (2012)
Truck Renting and Leasing Association (2012)
United States Pan Asian American Chamber of Commerce (2012)
U.S Poultry and Egg Association (2011, 2012)
U.S.-Russia Business Council (2012)
User Experience Professionals Association (2011)
Visual Resources Association (2010)
Warehousing Education and Research Council (2012)
Waste Equipment Technology Association (2010)
WIFS - Women in Insurance and Financial Services (2012)
Wildlife Management Institute (2012)
Wood Component Manufacturers Association (2010)
Woodworking Machinery Industry Association (2010)

Augusta

Environmental Industry Associations (2010)

Buckhead

Congress of Chiropractic State Associations (2012)
Juice Products Association (2012)

Columbus

International Trumpet Guild (2012)

Cordele

American Peanut Shellers Association (2012)

Dalton

American Floorcovering Alliance (2012)

Greensboro

United States Industrial Fabrics Institute (2012)

Jekyll Island

National College of Probate Judges (2011)

Macon

National Society of Newspaper Columnists (2012)
Online Audiovisual Catalogers (2010)

Peachtree

American Medical Directors Association (2011)

Perry

National Swine Registry (2012)

Rome

Association of Third World Studies (2012)

Saint Simons Island

American Coke and Coal Chemicals Institute (2011)
International Association of Personnel in Employment Security (2012)
International Association of Workforce Professionals (IAWP) (2012)

Savannah

Accrediting Council for Continuing Education & Training (2010)
Adhesive and Sealant Council (2010)
Aerospace Industries Association of America (2012)
American Academy of Anesthesiologist Assistants (2010)
American Academy of Oral and Maxillofacial Radiology (2012)
American Anthropological Association (2012)
American Art Therapy Association, Inc. (2012)
American Association for Geriatric Psychiatry (2010)
American Association for Paralegal Education (2012)
American Association for the History of Nursing (2012)
American Association of Cereal Chemists International (2010)
American Petroleum Institute (2011)
American Public Power Association (2011)
American Pyrotechnics Association (2010)
American Railway Development Association (2010)
American Society of Extra-Corporeal Technology (2012)
American Wood-Protection Association (2010)
Association for Commuter Transportation (2012)
Association for the Behavioral Sciences and Medical Education (2010)
Association of Educational Service Agencies (2010)
Association of Oil Pipe Lines (2012)
Association of State and Provincial Psychology Boards (2010)
Catfish Farmers of America (2012)
Commercial Food Equipment Service Association (2010)
Communications Supply Service Association (2010)
Council of Chief State School Officers (2012)
Council on the Safe Transportation of Hazardous Articles (2012)
Driving School Association of America (2012)
Education Credit Union Council (2012)
The Fertilizer Institute (2010)
Floor Covering Installation Contractors Association (2012)
Government Management Information Sciences (2012)
Institute of Nuclear Materials Management (2012)
Institute of Transportation Engineers (2010)
International College of Dentists, U.S.A. Section (2012)
International Safety Equipment Association (ISEA) (2011)
Manufactured Housing Institute (2010)
National Agricultural Aviation Association (2012)
National Aircraft Finance Association (2012)
National Association of Development Companies (2010)
National Association of RV Parks and Campgrounds (2011)
National Council for Geographic Education (2010)
National Dental EDI Council (2012)
National Environmental Balancing Bureau (2011)
National Lumber and Building Material Dealers Association (2012)
National Renal Administrators Association (2012)
National Rural Health Association (2010)
North American Retail Hardware Association (2010)
North American Transportation Employee Relations Association (2010)
Power and Communications Contractors Association (2012)
Society of Cardiovascular Anesthesiologists (2011)
Society of Fire Protection Engineers (2012)
Society of Nematologists (2012)
Society of Trauma Nurses (2012)
Sugar Industry Technologists (2010)
Technical Association of the Pulp and Paper Industry (2012)
Veterinary Hospital Managers Association (2010)

Stone Mountain

American Society of Mechanical Engineers (ASME) (2012)

HAWAII

Big Island

American Dental Society of Anesthesiology (2012)
Central Station Alarm Association (2012)
United States Tour Operators Association (2012)
Weed Science Society of America (2012)

Hilo

International Marine Minerals Society (2011)

Honolulu

American Academy of Neurology (2011)
American Academy of Periodontology (2010)
American Academy of Psychoanalysis and Dynamic Psychiatry (2011)
American Association of Orthodontists (2012)
American College of Chest Physicians (2011)
American Farm Bureau Federation (2012)
American Medical Association (2012)
American Pain Society (2012)

American Phytopathological Society (2011)
American Society for Blood and Marrow Transplantation (2011)
American Society of Nephrology (2012)
Associated General Contractors of America (AGC) (2012)
Association for Applied Sport Psychology (2011)
Association for Asian Studies (2011)
Association for Business Communication (2012)
Association for the Advancement of Computing in Education (2011)
Association for University Business and Economic Research (2012)
Association of Image Consultants International (2012)
Association of Legal Administrators (2012)
Association of Science-Technology Centers (2010)
Cremation Association of North America (2010)
Defense Orientation Conference Association (2012)
The Electrochemical Society (2012)
Geoscience and Remote Sensing Society (2010)
IEEE Communications Society (2010)
International Anesthesia Research Society (2010)
International Boxing Federation (2012)
International Foundation of Employee Benefit Plans (2010)
International Society for Prosthetics and Orthotics - United States (2012)
International Textile and Apparel Association (2012)
Law and Society Association (2012)
National Association of State Boating Law Administrators (2010)
National Dental Association (2010)
National Pest Management Association (2010)
National Rehabilitation Association (2012)
Navy League of the United States (2012)
North American Society for the Psychology of Sport and Physical Activity (2012)
Pacific Telecommunications Council (2012)
Society of American Foresters (2011)
Society of American Law Teachers (2010)
United Producers Formulators and Distributors Association (2010)
Urban Affairs Association (2010)
World Teleport Association (2012)

Ka'anapali

IEEE Engineering in Medicine and Biology Society (2012)

Kahuku

The National Greenhouse Manufacturers Association (2010)

Kailua-Kona

National Association for Interpretation (2012)
Turfgrass Producers International (2010)

Kauai

American Association for the Surgery of Trauma (2012)
American Association of Equine Practitioners (2012)
Surface Mount Technology Association (2010)
United States Swim School Association (2012)

Ko Olina

Distribution Contractors Association (2011, 2012)

Kohala Coast

American Board of Trial Advocates (2012)
Neurosurgical Society of America (2011)

Koloa

Air Movement and Control Association International (2011)
Credit Union Executives Society (2011)

Kona

American Fire Sprinkler Association (2012)
American Geophysical Union (2012)
Construction Financial Management Association (2010)
Oceanic Engineering Society (2011)

Maui

American Academy of Esthetic Dentistry (2010)
American Academy of Matrimonial Lawyers (2011)
American Association for Justice (2010)
American Automatic Control Council (2012)
American Society of Medical Association Counsel (2012)
Association of Defense Trial Attorneys (2011)
Concrete Sawing and Drilling Association (2012)
CPA Associates International (2012)
Distance Education and Training Council (2012)
Gases and Welding Distributors Association (2010)
Heating, Airconditioning and Refrigeration Distributors International (2011)
IEEE Control Systems Society (2012)
International Society for Prosthetics and Orthotics - United States (2010)
Management Association for Private Photogrammetric Surveyors (2010)
National Air Filtration Association (2010)
National Asphalt Pavement Association (2010)
National Association of Marine Services (2010)
National School Transportation Association (2012)
National Society of Accountants (2012)
North American Society for Dialysis and Transplantation (2012)
Radiation Research Society (2010)
Society for Leukocyte Biology (2012)
Web Sling and Tie down Association (2010)
Wilderness Medical Society (2010)

Oahu

Maritime Law Association of the U.S. (2011)

Waikiki

Associated Wire Rope Fabricators (2011)

Waikoloa

American College of Neuropsychopharmacology (2011)
Construction Financial Management Association (2010)
National Tuberculosis Controllers Association (2012)
Pediatric Orthopedic Society of North America (2010)
Tree Care Industry Association (2010)
The Wildlife Society (2011)

IDAHO

Boise

American Council for Construction Education (2010)
American Dairy Goat Association (2012)
Bank Administration Institute (2011)
Community Development Society (2011)
Fibre Channel Industry Association (2012)
National Association of Regional Councils (2012)
National Association of State Emergency Medical Services Officials (2012)
National Grange (2012)

Coeur d#Alene

American Public Gas Association (2011)
American Sugar Alliance (2012)
Association for High Technology Distribution (2010)
Association of State Chamber Professionals (2012)
Independent Sealing Distributors (2010)
National Association of Steel Pipe Distributors (2010)
National Precast Concrete Association (2011)
PeerSpan (2011)
Timber Frame Business Council (2010)
Valve Manufacturers Association of America (2010)

Idaho Falls

Cryogenic Society of America (2011)

Sun Valley

Association of Official Seed Certifying Agencies (2012)
International Bone and Mineral Society (2012)
National District Attorneys Association (2011)

Twin Falls

United States Trout Farmers Association (2011)

ILLINOIS

Alsip

Christian Schools International (2010)

Bloomingdale

Gift Associates Interchange Network (2010)
International Metal Decorators Association (2010)

Carbondale

Society for Asian and Comparative Philosophy (2012)

Champaign

American Dairy Science Association (2010)
American Railway Engineering and Maintenance-of-Way Association (2012)
IEEE Power Electronics Society (2012)
North American Society for Trenchless Technology (2010)

Chicago

ACA International, The Association of Credit and Collection Professionals (2011, 2012)
Academy of Breastfeeding Medicine (2012)
Academy of General Dentistry (2012)
Academy of Homiletics (2012)
Academy of Organizational and Occupational Psychiatry (2010, 2012)
Accordionists and Teachers Guild International (2012)
Accreditation Council for Pharmacy Education (2012)
Advertising and Marketing International Network (2012)
AIM North America (2012)
Air Conditioning, Heating and Refrigeration Institute (AHRI) (2012)
Alliance of Area Business Publications (2012)
Alliance of Artists Communities (2011)
Aluminum Anodizers Council (2012)
The Aluminum Association, Inc. (2012)
America's Health Insurance Plans (2010)
American Academy of Clinical Neuropsychology (2010)
American Academy of Clinical Psychiatrists (2012)
American Academy of Dermatology (2010)
American Academy of Forensic Sciences (2011)
American Academy of Matrimonial Lawyers (2011, 2012)
American Academy of Medical Hypnoanalysts (2010)
American Academy of Ophthalmic Executives (2010, 2012)
American Academy of Ophthalmology (2010, 2012)
American Academy of Oral and Maxillofacial Radiology (2011)
American Academy of Orthotists and Prosthetists (2010, 2011)
American Academy of Pediatric Dentistry (2010)
American Academy of Periodontology (2012)
American Academy of Religion (2012)
American Academy of Restorative Dentistry (2012)
American Alliance for Theatre and Education (2011)
American Architectural Manufacturers Association (2010)
American Association for Applied Linguistics (2011)
American Association for Cancer Research (2012)
American Association for Clinical Chemistry, Inc. (2012)

American Association for Public Opinion Research (2010)
American Association for the Study of Hungarian History (2012)
American Association for the Surgery of Trauma (2011)
American Association of Advertising Agencies (2011)
American Association of Certified Orthoptists (2010, 2012)
American Association of Colleges for Teacher Education (2012)
American Association of Credit Union Leagues (2012)
The American Association of Dental Boards (2012)
The American Association of Eye and Ear Centers of Excellence (2010, 2012)
American Association of Heart Failure Nurses (2012)
American Association of Managing General Agents (2012)
American Association of Neuropathologists (2012)
American Association of Nurse Anesthetists (2010)
American Association of Oral and Maxillofacial Surgeons (2010, 2012)
American Association of Orthodontists (2011)
American Association of Pharmaceutical Scientists (2012)
American Association of School Personnel Administrators (2012)
American Association of Surgical Physician Assistants (2012)
American Association of Teachers of French (2012)
American Association of Veterinary Immunologists (2010)
American Association of Women Dentists (2012)
American Bakers Association (2012)
American Bankruptcy Institute (2012)
American Bar Association (2012)
American Bearing Manufacturers Association (2012)
American Beverage Licensees (2012)
American Board of Nursing Specialties (2012)
American Broncho-Esophagological Association (2011)
American Burn Association (2011)
American Butter Institute (2012)
American Catholic Historical Association (2012)
American Choral Directors Association (2011)
American College Health Association (2012)
American College of Cardiovascular Administrators (2012)
American College of Clinical Pharmacology (2011)
American College of Epidemiology (2012)
American College of Mohs Surgeons (2012)
American College of Osteopathic Family Physicians (2012)
American College of Osteopathic Surgeons (2012)
American College of Physician Executives (2011)
American College of Real Estate Lawyers (2012)
American College of Rheumatology (2011)
American College of Surgeons (2012)
American College of Veterinary Surgeons (2011)
American Concrete Institute (2010)
American Congress of Obstetricians and Gynecologists (2011)
American Crystallographic Association (2010)
American Dairy Products Institute (2010, 2011, 2012)
American Dental Association (2012)
American Economic Association (2012)
American Equilibration Society (2012)
American Federation of Musicians (2012)
The American Finance Association (2012)
American Financial Services Association (2012)
American Forest & Paper Association (2011)
American Fraternal Alliance (2010)
American Galvanizers Association (2011)
American Gear Manufacturers Association (2012)
American Gem Trade Association (2010)
American Handwriting Analysis Foundation (2012)
American Head and Neck Society (2011)
American Health Information Management Association (2011, 2012)
American Horticultural Therapy Association (2010)
American Institute of Chemical Engineers (2012)
American Institute of Constructors (2010)
American Judicature Society (2012)
American Laryngological Association (2011)
American Laryngological, Rhinological and Otological Society (2011)
American Medical Association Alliance, Inc. (2010, 2012)
American Medical Informatics Association (2012)
American Montessori Society (2011)
American Nephrology Nurses Association (2012)
American Neurotology Society (2011)
American Optometric Association (2012)
American Optometric Student Association (2012)
American Osteopathic College of Anesthesiologists (2012)
American Otological Society (2011)
American Pancreatic Association (2010, 2011)
American Philosophical Association (2010, 2012)
American Printing History Association (2012)
American Professional Society on the Abuse of Children (2010, 2012)
American Prosthodontic Society (2010, 2011, 2012)
American Psychoanalytic Association (2012)
American Psychological Association - Division of Psychoanalysis (2010)
American Railway Engineering and Maintenance-of-Way Association (2012)
American Real Estate and Urban Economics Association (2012)
American Rock Mechanics Association (2012)
American Roentgen Ray Society (2011)
American Schools of Oriental Research (2012)
American Seed Trade Association (2011, 2012)
American Seniors Housing Association (2010, 2012)
American Society for Clinical Investigation (2010, 2011, 2012)
American Society for Dermatologic Surgery (2010)
American Society for Microbiology (2011)
American Society for Mohs Histotechnology (2012)
American Society for Quality (2010)
American Society for Surgery of the Hand (2012)
American Society for Therapeutic Radiology and Oncology (2012)
American Society for Training and Development (2010)
American Society of Anesthesiologists (2011)

American Society of Appraisers (2011)
American Society of Association Executives-The Center for Association
    Leadership (2012)
American Society of Cataract and Refractive Surgery (2012)
American Society of Clinical Oncology (2010, 2011, 2012)
American Society of Criminology (2012)
American Society of Dermatopathology (2012)
American Society of Health-System Pharmacists (2012)
American Society of Heating, Refrigerating and Air Conditioning Engineers
    (ASHRAE) (2012)
American Society of Interior Designers (2010)
American Society of Mechanical Engineers (ASME) (2010)
American Society of Ocularists (2010, 2012)
American Society of Ophthalmic Administrators (2012)
American Society of Ophthalmic Plastic and Reconstructive Surgery (2012)
American Society of Ophthalmic Registered Nurses (2010, 2012)
American Society of Radiologic Technologists (2011)
American Society on Aging (2010)
American Student Dental Association (2012)
American Supply Association (2010)
American Theological Library Association (2011)
American Urogynecologic Society (2012)
American Water Works Association (2010)
American Wholesale Marketers Association (2012)
AMT - The Association For Manufacturing Technology (2010, 2012)
APMI International (2011)
Architectural Precast Association (2010)
ARMA International (2012)
Asian American Hotel Owners Association (2010)
Asphalt Recycling and Reclaiming Association (2010)
Associated Collegiate Press (2012)
Associated General Contractors of America (AGC) (2012)
Association for Ambulatory Behavioral Healthcare (2011)
Association for Applied and Therapeutic Humor (2012)
Association for Asian Performance (2011)
Association for Business Communication (2010)
Association for Comparative Economic Studies (2012)
Association for Conflict Resolution (2010)
Association for Education in Journalism and Mass Communication (2012)
Association for Evolutionary Economics (2012)
Association for Governmental Leasing and Finance (2010)
Association for Humanist Sociology (2011)
Association for Institutional Research (2010)
Association for Jewish Studies (2012)
The Association for Manufacturing Excellence (2012)
The Association for Nursing Professional Development (2011)
Association for Psychological Science (2012)
Association for Radiological and Imaging Nursing (2011)
Association for the Advancement of Baltic Studies (2012)
Association for the Sociology of Religion (2011)
Association for Theatre in Higher Education (2011)
Association of Academic Health Centers (2011)
Association of American Physicians (2010, 2011, 2012)
Association of American University Presses (2012)
Association of Attorney-Mediators (2012)
The Association of Black Psychologists (2010, 2012)
Association of Business Owners of America (2012)
Association of Christian Therapists (2012)
Association of College and University Printers (2012)
Association of College Unions International (2011)
Association of Community Health Nursing Educators (2011)
Association of Corporate Travel Executives (ACTE) (2010)
Association of Energy Engineers (2011)
Association of Energy Service Companies (2010)
Association of Family and Conciliation Courts (2012)
Association of Fundraising Professionals (2011)
Association of Jesuit Colleges and Universities (2012)
Association of Latino Professionals in Finance and Accounting (2012)
Association of Muslim Social Scientists of North America (2010)
Association of Organ Procurement Organizations (2012)
Association of Pediatric Program Directors (2010)
Association of Regulatory Boards of Optometry (2012)
Association of Research Libraries (2012)
Association of Schools of Journalism and Mass Communication (2012)
Association of Specialized and Professional Accreditors (2010, 2012)
Association of State and Provincial Psychology Boards (2011)
Association of State Correctional Administrators (2010)
Association of Statisticians of American Religious Bodies (2012)
Association of Teacher Educators (2010)
Association of Technical Personnel in Ophthalmology (2010)
Association of Transportation Professionals (2012)
Association of University Programs in Health Administration (2012)
Association of University Research Parks (2010)
Association of Vascular and Interventional Radiographers (2011)
Association of Women Surgeons (2012)
Association of Writers and Writing Programs (2012)
Automotive Trade Association Executives (2012)
BAFT-IFSA (2012)
Bank Administration Institute (2011)
Bearing Specialist Association (2012)
BEMA - The Baking Industry Suppliers Association (2011, 2012)
BKR International (2012)
The Brewers Association (2010)
Building Service Contractors Association International (2012)
Business Marketing Association (2010, 2012)
Business Professionals of America (2012)
Casualty Actuarial Society (2011, 2012)
Cervical Spine Research Society (2012)
CFA Institute (2012)
Chemical Sources Association (2012)

Child Life Council (2011)
Clinical Immunology Society (2011, 2012)
Clinical Orthopaedic Society (2012)
Club Managers Association of America (2012)
College Art Association (2010)
College Media Association (2012)
College of American Pathologists (2010)
College of Healthcare Information Management Executives (2012)
Commercial Finance Association (2010)
Commercial Food Equipment Service Association (2010)
Commercial Law League of America (2010, 2011, 2012)
Commercial Real Estate Women Network (2012)
Commercial Vehicle Safety Alliance (2011)
Committee of 200 (2012)
Comparative and International Education Society (2010)
Composite Can and Tube Institute (2010, 2012)
Computing Technology Industry Association (CompTIA) (2012)
Concrete Reinforcing Steel Institute (2010, 2012)
Concrete Sawing and Drilling Association (2012)
Conductors Guild (2012)
The Conference Board (2011)
Conference of Research Workers in Animal Diseases (2010, 2011, 2012)
Conference on Latin American History (2012)
Congress of Neurological Surgeons (2012)
Construction Industry CPAs/Consultants Association (2010, 2012)
Construction Management Association of America (2012)
Construction Specifications Institute (2011)
Contract Packaging Association (2012)
Conveyor Equipment Manufacturers Association (2010, 2011, 2012)
Cooperative Education and Internship Association (2012)
Coordinating Council for Women in History (2012)
Council for Adult and Experiential Learning (2011)
Council for Advancement and Support of Education (2012)
Council of American Survey Research Organizations (2010, 2012)
Council of State Restaurant Associations (2010, 2012)
The Counselors of Real Estate (2012)
Credit Research Foundation (2012)
Cremation Association of North America (2011)
Dance/USA (2011)
Distributive Education Clubs of America (DECA) (2011, 2012)
The Door and Hardware Institute (2010)
Drug Information Association (2011)
Econometric Society (2012)
Education Law Association (2011)
Electricity Consumers Resource Council (ELCON) (2011)
Electronic Transactions Association (2011)
Electrostatic Discharge Association (2010)
Employers Council on Flexible Compensation (2012)
Equipment Leasing and Finance Association (2010)
Exhibitor Appointed Contractors Association (2012)
Express Carriers Association (2012)
Eye Bank Association of America (2012)
Family Firm Institute, Inc. (2010)
Family, Career and Community Leaders of America (2010)
FCIB-NACM Corporation (2010)
Federation of State Humanities Councils (2012)
Federation of State Medical Boards of the United States (2010)
The Fertilizer Institute (2011)
Flexible Packaging Association (2012)
Fluid Controls Institute (2011)
Food Processing Suppliers Association (2010, 2011)
Foodservice & Packaging Institute, Inc. (2010)
The Foodservice Group, Inc. (2012)
Futures Industry Association (2010, 2011, 2012)
Gamma Iota Sigma (2012)
Gases and Welding Distributors Association (2010)
Genetics Society of America (2012)
Gerontological Society of America (2011)
Glass Packaging Institute (2012)
Global Offset and Countertrade Association (GOCA) (2010)
Government Finance Officers Association of the United States and Canada (2012)
Government Finance Officers Association, Federal Liaison Center (2012)
Health Care Administrators Association (2012)
Health Industry Distributors Association (2010, 2012)
Health Industry Representatives Association (2012)
Heating, Airconditioning and Refrigeration Distributors International (2012)
Hispanic Association on Corporate Responsibility (2012)
Hispanic Dental Association (2010)
Historians of American Communism (2012)
Home Improvement Research Institute (2010, 2012)
Human Resource People and Strategy (2012)
IGAF Polaris (2012)
In-Plant Printing and Mailing Association (2012)
Incentive Manufacturers & Representatives Alliance (2012)
Incentive Marketing Association (2012)
INDA, Association of the Nonwoven Fabrics Industry (2011, 2012)
Independent Laboratory Distributors Association (2012)
Independent Sector (2011)
Industrial Diamond Association of America (2011)
Industrial Research Institute (2010)
Institute of Environmental Sciences and Technology (2012)
Institute of Food Technologists (2010)
International Association for Human Resource Information Management (2012)
International Association for the Study of Organized Crime (2012)
International Association of Attorneys and Executives in Corporate Real Estate (2010, 2012)
International Association of Business Communicators (2012)
International Association of Chiefs of Police (2011)
International Association of Clerks, Recorders, Election Officials and Treasurers (2010)

International Association of Color Manufacturers (2012)
International Association of Diecutting and Diemaking (2010)
International Association of Fire Chiefs (2010)
International Association of Plastics Distributors (2012)
International Association of Railway Operating Officers (2010)
International Bone and Mineral Society (2011)
International Casual Furnishings Association (2010, 2011, 2012)
International Cinema Technology Association (2010)
International District Energy Association (2012)
International Dyslexia Association (2010)
International Executive Housekeepers Association (2012)
International Facility Management Association (2012)
The International Fluid Power Society (2011)
International Housewares Association (2010, 2011, 2012)
International Housewares Representatives Association (2010)
International Public Management Association for Human Resources (2011)
International Reading Association (2010, 2012)
International Sanitary Supply Association (2012)
International Sign Association (2012)
International Society for Heart and Lung Transplantation (2010)
International Society for Pharmacoepidemiology (2011)
International Society of Arboriculture (2010)
International Society of Political Psychology (2012)
International Society of Refractive Surgery of the American Academy of Ophthalmology (2012)
Investment Company Institute (2012)
Investment Management Consultants Association (2011)
Investment Program Association (2010, 2012)
IPC - Association Connecting Electronics Industries (2012)
IPC Washington Office (2012)
Jesuit Association of Student Personnel Administrators (2010)
Justice Research and Statistics Association (2011)
Labor and Employment Relations Association (2012)
Large Urology Group Practice Association (LUGPA) (2012)
Law and Society Association (2010)
The Learning Disabilities Association (2012)
Licensing Executives Society (2010)
Lift Manufacturers Product Section - Material Handling Institute (2011)
Machinery Dealers National Association (2011, 2012)
Manufacturers' Agents National Association (2012)
Marketing Agencies Association Worldwide (2012)
The Masonry Society (2012)
Meals on Wheels Association of America (2011)
Mortgage Bankers Association of America (2010, 2011, 2012)
Musculoskeletal Tumor Society (2011)
Mystery Shopping Providers Association (2010)
National Association of Student Personnel Administrators (2010)
National Arab-American Medical Association (2012)
National Association for Chicana and Chicano Studies (2012)
National Association for Drama Therapy (2010)
National Association for Poetry Therapy (2012)
National Association for Printing Leadership (2012)
National Association of Architectural Metal Manufacturers (2012)
National Association of Bar Executives (2012)
National Association of Child Care Professionals (2010)
National Association of Clinical Nurse Specialists (2012)
National Association of College and University Attorneys (2012)
National Association of Convenience Stores (2010, 2011)
National Association of Counsel for Children (2012)
The National Association of Crime Victim Compensation Boards (2010)
National Association of Dental Laboratories (2010)
National Association of Electrical Distributors (2010)
National Association of Elevator Safety Authorities International (2010)
National Association of Federal Credit Unions (2010)
National Association of Foster Grandparent Program Directors (2010)
National Association of Graphic and Product Identification Manufacturers (2010)
National Association of Long Term Care Administrator Boards (2011)
National Association of Pediatric Nurse Practitioners (2010)
National Association of Personal Financial Advisors (2010)
National Association of Public Hospitals and Health Systems (2011)
National Association of Real Estate Investment Trusts (NAREIT) (2010)
National Association of Recording Merchandisers (NARM) (2010)
National Association of Retail Collection Attorneys (2011)
National Association of School Nurses (2010)
National Association of School Psychologists (2010)
National Association of Securities Professionals (2010)
National Association of State Boards of Education (2010)
National Association of State Directors of Special Education (2011)
National Association of State Fire Marshals (2010)
National Association of Student Financial Aid Administrators (2012)
National Auto Auction Association (2011)
National Black Caucus of State Legislators (2011)
National Cable & Telecommunications Association (2011)
National Catholic Development Conference (2010)
National Child Support Enforcement Association (2010)
National Club Association (2010)
National Commodity Supplemental Food Program Association (2012)
National Confectioners Association (2010, 2011, 2012)
National Conference of Bar Foundations (2012)
National Conference of Commissioners on Uniform State Laws (2010)
National Conference of State Legislatures (2012)
National Council for Community Behavioral Healthcare (2012)
National Council of Investigative and Security Services Inc. (2010)
National Council of Real Estate Investment Fiduciaries (2010, 2012)
National Council of Teachers of English (2011)
National Council on Aging (2010)
National Court Reporters Association (2010)
National Economic Association (2012)
National Education Association (2011)
National Exchange Carrier Association (2011)

National Fastener Distributors Association (2010)
National Fire Sprinkler Association (2010)
National Fluid Power Association (2012)
National Funeral Directors Association (2011)
National Hardwood Lumber Association (2012)
National Hemophilia Foundation (2011)
National Housing and Rehabilitation Association (2012)
National Housing Conference (2012)
National Human Services Assembly (2011)
National Independent Flag Dealers Association (2012)
National Institute of American Doll Artists (2010)
National Kitchen and Bath Association (2010, 2012)
National Legal Aid and Defender Association (2012)
National Lieutenant Governors Association (2012)
National Lime Association (2010)
National Lipid Association (2010)
National Luggage Dealers Association (2012)
National Notary Association (2010)
National Organization for Associate Degree Nursing (2011)
National Organization of Social Security Claimants' Representatives (2010)
National Parking Association (2012)
National Rehabilitation Association (2012)
National Restaurant Association (2010, 2012)
National Roofing Contractors Association (2010)
National Society of Hispanic MBAs (2010)
National Tank Truck Carriers (2010)
National Tax Association (2010)
North American Association for the Study of Religion (2012)
North American Association of Summer Sessions (2011)
North American Catalysis Society (2011)
North American Meat Association (2011, 2012)
North American Menopause Society (2010)
North American Performing Arts Managers and Agents (2012)
The North American Rail Shippers Association (2012)
North American Spine Society (2011)
North American Wholesale Lumber Association (2010, 2012)
NPES, The Association for Suppliers of Printing, Publishing, and Converting Technologies (2010, 2011, 2012)
NPTA Alliance (2010, 2012)
Ophthalmic Photographers' Society (2010, 2012)
Optometric Extension Program Foundation (2012)
Outpatient Ophthalmic Surgery Society (2012)
Packaging Machinery Manufacturers Institute (2010, 2012)
Patient Centered Primary Care Collaborative (2012)
Pension Real Estate Association (2011)
Petroleum Equipment Institute (2011)
Petroleum Packaging Council (2010)
Photoluminescent Safety Association (2010)
Physician Insurers Association of America (2010)
Picture Archive Council of America (2012)
PKF North American Network (2012)
Plastic Shipping Container Institute (2012)
Police Executive Research Forum (2011)
POPAI The Global Association for Marketing at Retail (2012)
Precision Metalforming Association (2011)
Preventive Cardiovascular Nurses Association (2010)
Printing Industry Credit Executives (2010)
Private Label Manufacturers Association (2010, 2012)
Production and Operations Management Society (2012)
Professional Liability Underwriting Society (2012)
Promotion Marketing Association (2011, 2012)
Property Loss Research Bureau (2011)
Public Affairs Council (2010)
R & E Council of the NAPL (2010, 2012)
Radiological Society of North America (2010, 2011, 2012)
RadTech (2012)
Railway Supply Institute (2010, 2012)
Real Estate Investment Securities Association (2012)
Religion Communicators Council (2010)
Rheumatology Nurses Society (2010)
Robotic Industries Association (2011)
The Rural Sociological Society (2012)
Scoliosis Research Society (2012)
Screen Manufacturers Association (2010, 2012)
Security Hardware Distributors Association (2012)
Self-Insurance Institute of America, Inc. (2010)
Smart Card Alliance (2011)
Social Science History Association (2010)
Society for Academic Emergency Medicine (2012)
Society for College and University Planning (2012)
Society for Education in Anesthesia (2011)
Society for Excellence in Eyecare (2011)
Society for Healthcare Strategy and Market Development (2010)
Society for Human Resource Management (2012)
Society for Industrial and Organizational Psychology Inc. (2011)
Society for Italian Historical Studies (2012)
Society for Marketing Professional Services (2011)
Society for Maternal-Fetal Medicine (2010)
Society for Medical Decision Making (2011)
Society for Neuroscience in Anesthesiology and Critical Care (2011)
Society for Pediatric Anesthesia (2011)
Society for Personality Assessment (2012)
Society for Sex Therapy and Research (2012)
Society for Technical Communication (2012)
Society for the Exploration of Psychotherapy Integration (2012)
Society for the Study of Social Problems (2011)
Society for the Teaching of Psychology (2012)
Society for Vascular Medicine (2012)
Society for Vascular Surgery (2011)
Society for Vascular Ultrasound (2011)

Society of Actuaries (2011)
Society of Architectural Historians (2010)
Society of Biblical Literature (2012)
Society of Corporate Secretaries and Governance Professionals (2010)
Society of Industrial and Office Realtors (2011)
Society of Interventional Radiology (2012)
Society of Radiologists in Ultrasound (2011)
Society of Research Administrators International (2010)
Society of Toxicologic Pathologists (2010)
Society of University Otolaryngologists-Head and Neck Surgeons (2012)
Society of Vacuum Coaters (2011)
Society of Women Engineers (2011)
Special Care Dentistry Association (2010, 2011)
Special Libraries Association (2012)
State Higher Education Executive Officers (2012)
Steel Founders' Society of America (2011)
Steel Tube Institute of North America (2010)
Strategic Account Management Association (2010)
Structural Insulated Panel Association (2010)
Swedish-American Chambers of Commerce of the USA, Inc. (2011)
Tag and Label Manufacturers Institute (2010, 2011)
Tax Executives Institute, Inc. (2010)
Taxicab, Limousine & Paratransit Association (2011)
Textile Bag and Packaging Association (2010, 2012)
Textile Rental Services Association of America (2012)
Tobacco Merchants Association of the United States (2011)
Trade Promotion Management Associates (2010)
The Travel and Tourism Research Association (2012)
Travel Goods Association (2011)
United Cerebral Palsy (2010)
United Inventors Association of the U.S.A. (2012)
United States Dairy Export Council (2011)
United States Hide, Skin and Leather Association (2012)
University Film and Video Association (2012)
University/Resident Theatre Association (2011)
Utility Management & Conservation Association (2012)
Vibration Isolation and Seismic Control Manufacturers Association (2012)
Visitor Studies Association (2011)
Wire Fabricators Association (2012)
Wireless Communications Association International (2010)
World Pet Association (2011, 2012)
WorldatWork (2012)
Zero Balancing Health Association (2012)

DeKalb
American Society of Home Inspectors (2011)

East Peoria
Ductile Iron Society (2012)

Elk Grove Village
Society for Values in Higher Education (2011)

Elmhurst
Economic History Association (2010)

Evanston
American Society of Transplant Surgeons (2012)
Committee of Interns and Residents/ SEIU (2012)
Econometric Society (2011)
National Association for Printing Leadership (2012)

Itasca
Air Movement and Control Association International (2011)
National Association of Printing Ink Manufacturers (2011, 2012)

Lincolnshire
American Association of Candy Technologists (2012)
Closure and Container Manufacturers Association (2012)
Society for Military History (2011)

Lisle
American Society of Concrete Contractors (2012)

Lombard
American Board of Quality Assurance and Utilization Review Physicians, Inc. (2012)
American Society of Safety Engineers (2012)

Naperville
American Dairy Science Association (2012)
Bowling Proprietors' Association of America (2011)

Northbrook
American Bearing Manufacturers Association (2010)
Collision Industry Electronic Commerce Association (2012)

Oak Brook
American Architectural Manufacturers Association (2012)
Christian Legal Society (2011)
National Association of Church Personnel Administrators (2010)
Plastic Shipping Container Institute (2010)

Peoria
Employers Association (2012)

Rolling Meadows
Private Label Manufacturers Association (2011)

Rosemont

American Association of Clinical Urologists (2012)
American Pet Products Association (2011)
Canon Law Society of America (2012)
Casting Industry Suppliers Association (2010, 2011, 2012)
Council of Medical Specialty Societies (2010)
Craft & Hobby Association (2010)
Decorative Plumbing and Hardware Association (2012)
Door and Access Systems Manufacturers Association, International (2010)
Electrocoat Association (2012)
Electronic Components Industry Association (2012)
Fluid Power Distributors Association (2012)
Hobby Manufacturers Association (2010)
Holistic Dental Association (2010)
Institute of Food Technologists (2012)
MEMA Information Services Council (2012)
Metal Construction Association (2012)
National Association of Corporate Treasurers (2012)
National Guild of Professional Paperhangers (2010)
Professional Beauty Association | National Cosmetology Association (2012)
Professional Currency Dealers Association (2011, 2012)
SAE International (2012)
United Union of Roofers, Waterproofers and Allied Workers (2011)

Schaumburg

American Foundry Society (2011, 2012)
American Society of Safety Engineers (2012)
Assembly of Episcopal Healthcare Chaplains (2010)
Association of Professional Chaplains (2010, 2012)
International Food Service Executives' Association (2011)
IPC - Association Connecting Electronics Industries (2011, 2012)
Laser Institute of America (2012)
Liability Insurance Research Bureau (2012)
Metals Service Center Institute (2010)
NGVAmerica (2012)
North American Die Casting Association (2011)
North American Technician Excellence (2012)
Property Loss Research Bureau (2012)
Radiant Panel Association (2012)
Retail Bakers of America (2011)

Schiller Park

International Association for Colon Hydrotherapy (2012)

Springfield

American Berkshire Association (2012)
Church and Synagogue Library Association (2012)
National Taxidermists Association (2010)

St. Charles

American Music Therapy Association (2012)

Streamwood

Association of Professors of Mission (2010, 2011)

Urbana

Brazilian Studies Association (2012)
Walnut Council (2012)

Wheaton

Evangelical Church Library Association (2010, 2012)
National Fluid Power Association (2010)

Wheeling

Consumer Healthcare Products Association (2012)
International Professional Groomers (2010)

Winfield

American Association of Clinical Endocrinologists (2012)

INDIANA

Atlanta

American Society for Clinical Laboratory Science (2011)

Bloomingdale

International Metal Decorators Association (2012)

Bloomington

American Association of Teachers of Italian (2012)
American Folklore Society (2012)
Association for Politics and the Life Sciences (2010)
National Association of Professional Band Instrument Repair Technicians (2012)
National Society of Newspaper Columnists (2010)

Chesterton

Association of Conservation Engineers (2012)

Crawfordsville

National Hereford Hog Record Association (2010)

Danville

National Roadside Vegetation Management Association (2010)

Ft. Wayne

American Dexter Cattle Association (2012)

Greencastle

Electronics Technicians Association International (2012)

Howe

Clydesdale Breeders of the United States (2012)

Indian Wells

National Association of Pipe Coating Applicators (2012)

Indianapolis

AASHTO: Transportation Center of Excellence (2012)
ACUTA - The Association for Information Communications Technology Professionals in Higher Education (2012)
Adhesive and Sealant Council (2011)
American Academy of Gold Foil Operators (2011)
American Academy of Medical Hypnoanalysts (2012)
American Academy of the History of Dentistry (2010)
American Alliance for Health, Physical Education, Recreation and Dance (2010)
American Association for Employment in Education (2011)
American Association for Health Education (2010)
American Association for Paralegal Education (2010)
American Association for State and Local History (2011)
American Association of Diabetes Educators (2012)
American Association of Family and Consumer Sciences (2010, 2012)
American Association of Medical Assistants (2011)
American Association of Pastoral Counselors (2010)
American Association of Pathologists' Assistants (2010)
American Bandmasters Association (2012)
American Coatings Association (2012)
American Foundry Society (2012)
American Health Care Association (2010)
American Institute of Aeronautics and Astronautics (2012)
American Metalcasting Consortium (2012)
American Musicological Society (2010)
American Occupational Therapy Association, Inc. (2012)
American Organization of Nurse Executives (2010)
American Public Power Association (2010, 2012)
American Short Line and Regional Railroad Association (2012)
American Society of Consulting Arborists (2011)
American Society of Farm Managers and Rural Appraisers (2012)
American Technical Education Association (2010)
Archery Trade Association (2011)
Association for Healthcare Documentation Integrity (2012)
The Association for Research in Business Education - Delta Pi Epsilon (2011)
Association for Research on Nonprofit Organizations and Voluntary Action (2012)
Association for the Study of Higher Education (2010)
Association of American Feed Control Officials (2012)
Association of American Medical Colleges (2012)
Association of Clean Water Administrators (2010)
Association of Collegiate Business Schools and Programs (2011)
Association of Fraternity Advisors (2012)
Association of Independent Information Professionals (2012)
Association of Independent Trust Companies (2010)
Association of State Drinking Water Administrators (2010)
Automotive Training Managers Council (2012)
Casket and Funeral Supply Association of America (2011, 2012)
Catholic Academy for Communication Arts Professionals (2012)
Catholic Press Association (2012)
Community Transportation Association of America (2011)
Corporate Event Marketing Association (2012)
Council of the Great City Schools (2012)
Custom Electronic Design and Installation Association (2011, 2012)
Division 1-A Athletic Directors Association (2012)
Electronics Technicians Association International (2011)
EPS Industry Alliance (2012)
Federation of State Boards of Physical Therapy (2012)
The Grant Professionals Association (2012)
Independent Time and Labor Management Association (2012)
Industrial Research Institute (2012)
International District Energy Association (2010)
International Ground Source Heat Pump Association (2012)
International Marking and Identification Association (2010)
International Sleep Products Association (2012)
Kappa Delta Pi (2011)
Metal Construction Association (2012)
NAMTA - National Art Materials Trade Association (2010)
National Association for Environmental Management (2010)
National Association for Health Care Recruitment (2012)
National Association for Research in Science Teaching (2012)
National Association of Basketball Coaches (2010)
National Association of Collegiate Women Athletic Administrators (2012)
National Association of Consumer Credit Administrators (2010)
National Association of Educational Procurement, Inc. (2012)
National Association of Mutual Insurance Companies (2011)
National Association of State Directors of Teacher Education and Certification (2010)
National Association of Supervisors of Agricultural Education (2012)
National Black Association for Speech, Language and Hearing (2011)
National Black MBA Association (2012)
National Chimney Sweep Guild (2010)
National Coil Coating Association (2010)
National Collegiate Athletic Association (2012)
National Cooperative Business Association (2010)
National Corn Growers Association (2012)
National Council of Supervisors of Mathematics (2011)
National Council of Teachers of Mathematics (2011)
National Federation of State High School Associations (2010, 2011)
National FFA Organization (2010, 2011, 2012)
National Interscholastic Athletic Administrators Association (2011)
National League for Nursing (2012)
National Rural Economic Developers Association (2012)

National Science Teachers Association (2012)
National Speakers Association (2012)
National Truck Equipment Association (2011, 2012)
NFHS Music Association (2010)
NFHS Speech Debate and Theatre Association (2011)
North American Association of State and Provincial Lotteries (2011)
North American Die Casting Association (2012)
North American Technician Excellence (2011)
Nursery and Landscape Association Executives of North America (2010)
Percussive Arts Society (2011)
Pi Sigma Epsilon (2012)
Quality Service Contractors (2012)
Robotic Industries Association (2010, 2012)
Scrap Tire Management Council (2012)
Self-Insurance Institute of America, Inc. (2012)
Society for Experimental Mechanics, Inc. (2010)
Society for Mining, Metallurgy and Exploration, Inc. (2012)
Society of American Business Editors and Writers (2012)
Society of Gastroenterology Nurses and Associates (2011)
Society of Insurance Trainers and Educators (2010)
Society of Municipal Arborists (2012)
Society of State Leaders of Health and Physical Education (2010)
Structural Building Components Association (2010)
Tau Beta Pi Association (2011)
United States Meat Export Federation (2012)
Utilities Telecom Council (2010)
Water and Sewer Distributors of America (2012)

La Porte

Pyrotechnics Guild International (2012)

New Harmony

Society for German-American Studies (2010)

Notre Dame

Computer Assisted Language Instruction Consortium (2012)

South Bend

History of Economics Society (2011)

W. Lafayette

National Tank Truck Carriers (2012)

IOWA

Altoona

National Horsemen's Benevolent and Protective Association (2012)

Ames

Association of Veterinary Biologics Companies (2011)
Society of Engineering Science (2010)

Cedar Falls

American Physical Society (2011)

Coralville

National Farmers Organization (2010)

Council Bluffs

National Federation of Press Women (2011)

Davenport

American Animal Hospital Association (2012)

Des Moines

American Emu Association (2010)
American Southdown Breeders Association (2012)
Association of Official Seed Analysts, Inc. (2012)
Energy Bar Association (2012)
The National Association of Colored Women's Club, Inc. (2012)
National Association of State Departments of Agriculture (2012)
National Pork Producers Council (2010)
National Postsecondary Agriculture Student Organization (2012)
National Swine Registry (2010)
Percheron Horse Association of America (2010)
Pony of the Americas Club (2012)
Society of Commercial Seed Technologists (2012)

Dubuque

Association of American State Geologists (2011)
National Association for Rural Mental Health (2011)

Grinnell

National Ballroom and Entertainment Association (2012)

Iowa City

Alpha Chi Sigma Fraternity, Inc. (2012)
American Society of Comparative Law (2012)

Okoboji

International Oil Mill Superintendents Association (2012)

Spencer

American Maine-Anjou Association (2010)

KANSAS

Kansas City

Catholic Academy for Communication Arts Professionals (2011)

Lawrence

The American Geographical Society (2011)

Manhattan

Agricultural History Society (2012)

Overland Park

National Association of County Agricultural Agents (2011)
National Crop Insurance Services (2010, 2012)
National Scholastic Press Association (2010)
Optometric Extension Program Foundation (2012)

Wichita

American Angus Association (2012)
American Rabbit Breeders Association (2012)
Council of Petroleum Accountants Societies (2011)
National Association of State Aviation Officials (2010)
SAE International (2010)

KENTUCKY

Cadiz

American Camp Association (2011)

Covington

Academic Pediatric Association (2012)
Adhesive and Sealant Council (2010)
American Society of Pension Professionals & Actuaries (2012)
American Watchmakers-Clockmakers Institute (2010)
Council on Diagnostic Imaging to the A.C.A. (2010)
Investment Casting Institute (2011)
National Association of Pupil Services Administrators (2011)

Lexington

American Academy of Veterinary Acupuncture (2012)
American Alliance for Theatre and Education (2012)
American Assembly for Men in Nursing (2011)
The American Association of Nurse Attorneys (2010)
American Morgan Horse Association (2010)
American Mosquito Control Association (2010)
Association of Racing Commissioners International (2010)
Chief Officers of State Libraries Agencies (2012)
Delta Omicron (2012)
International Association of Women Police (2011)
Mathematical Association of America (2011)
Mycological Society of America (2010)
National Agricultural Alumni and Development Association (2012)
National Association of County Engineers (2012)
National Association of State Park Directors (2012)
National Hay Association (2010)
National Horsemen's Benevolent and Protective Association (2012)
Northern Nut Growers Association (2012)
Professional Fraternity Association (2010)
Purebred Morab Horse Association (2010, 2012)
Retail Confectioners International (2010)
Tau Beta Pi Association (2012)
Tobacco Merchants Association of the United States (2011)
Water Quality Association (2012)

Louisville

ACPA College Student Educators International (2012)
Adhesive and Sealant Council (2012)
American Academy of Osteopathy (2012)
American Angus Association (2011, 2012)
American Association of Clinical Endocrinologists (2012)
American Beefalo Association (2012)
American Beverage Licensees (2010)
American Boat and Yacht Council (2012)
American Chamber of Commerce Executives (2012)
American College Personnel Association (2012)
American Design Drafting Association International and American Digital Design Association (2010)
American Forage and Grassland Council (2012)
American Holistic Nurses Association (2011)
American Independent Business Alliance (2012)
American Nursery and Landscape Association (2010)
American Osteopathic Academy of Sports Medicine (2012)
American Physical Therapy Association - Private Practice Section (2012)
American Psychiatric Nurses Association (2010)
American Pyrotechnics Association (2012)
American Red Poll Association (2012)
American School Health Association (2011)
American Shropshire Registry Association (2012)
American Society for Automation in Pharmacy (2010)
American Society for Engineering Education (2010)
American Society for Quality (2012)
American Society of Agricultural and Biological Engineers (2011, 2012)
American Society of Electroneurodiagnostic Technologists (2010)
American Theological Library Association (2010)
American Volleyball Coaches Association (2012)
Association for Accounting Administration (2011)
Association for Education in Journalism and Mass Communication (2011)
Association for Educational Communications and Technology (2012)
Association for Linen Management (2010, 2012)
Association for Middle Level Education (2011)
Association for Play Therapy (2010)
Association of Avian Veterinarians (2012)
Association of Clinical Scientists (2011)

The Association of Collegiate Conference and Events Directors International (2010)
Association of Consulting Foresters of America (2010)
Association of Equipment Manufacturers (2011)
Association of Millwork Distributors (2012)
Association of State Dam Safety Officials (2012)
Association of State Floodplain Managers (2011)
Belted Galloway Society (2012)
College Media Association (2010)
Commission on Accreditation of Allied Health Education Programs (2010)
Conference on College Composition and Communication (2010)
Conference on English Education (2010)
Council of Chief State School Officers (2010)
Council of Engineering and Scientific Society Executives (2012)
Delta Sigma Pi (2011)
Democratic Governors Association (2012)
Distributive Education Clubs of America (DECA) (2010)
Electrocoat Association (2010)
Flexographic Technical Association (2010)
Glass Art Society (2010)
Hydraulic Institute (2011)
Independent Electrical Contractors (2011)
Independent Turf and Ornamental Distributors Association (2012)
Infusion Nurses Society (2011)
International Association of Administrative Professionals (2010)
International Association of Healthcare Central Service Materiel Management (2011)
International Association of Round Dance Teachers (2010)
International Community Corrections Association (2010)
International Window Film Association (2012)
Justice Research and Statistics Association (2012)
Lawn and Garden Dealers' Association (2012)
Motorist Information and Services Association (2010)
National Animal Control Association (2012)
National Association of Fraternal Insurance Counsellors (2011)
National Association of Neonatal Nurses (2011)
National Association of School Resource Officers (2010)
National Association of Sporting Goods Wholesalers (2010)
National Association of State Procurement Officials (2012)
National Association of Wastewater Transporters (2010, 2011)
National Council on Student Development (2012)
National Frame Building Association (2010)
National Rural Water Association (2011)
National Science Teachers Association (2012)
National Swine Registry (2012)
National Tank Truck Carriers (2012)
National Taxidermists Association (2012)
National Tutoring Association (2010)
North American Association of Professors of Christian Education (2010)
North American Equipment Dealers Association (2012)
Outdoor Power Equipment Institute (2010, 2012)
Plastic Surgery Research Council (2011)
Professional Association of Volleyball Officials (2012)
Professional Grounds Management Society (2012)
Professional Landcare Network (2010, 2011, 2012)
Propane Engine Fuel Committee/Propane Education and Research Council (2012)
Real Estate Educators Association (2012)
Recreation Vehicle Industry Association (2011, 2012)
Scoliosis Research Society (2011)
Shipbuilders Council of America (2012)
The Society for Freshwater Science (2012)
Society of Accredited Marine Surveyors (2012)
Society of Pelvic Surgeons (2012)
Sports and Fitness Industry Association (2012)
The Technology Institute for Music Educators (2012)
Teratology Society (2010)
Turf and Ornamental Communicators Association (2012)
United States Fencing Coaches Association (2010)
Water Environment Federation (2012)
Wood Component Manufacturers Association (2011)

Richmond

International Society of Weekly Newspaper Editors (2010)

LOUISIANA

Baton Rouge

International Planetarium Society (2012)
National Association of African American Studies and Affiliates (2010, 2011, 2012)
National Association of Hispanic and Latino Studies (2012)
National Ground Water Association (2012)
Society of Outdoor Recreation Professionals (2012)

Breaux Bridge

American Counseling Association (2011)

Indian Wells

Offshore Marine Service Association (2010)

Lafayette

Association of Junior Leagues International (2011)
International Association of Drilling Contractors (2012)
Offshore Marine Service Association (2011, 2012)

Lake Charles

American Red Brangus Association (2010)

New Iberia

American Comparative Literature Association (2010)

New Orleans

Academy of General Dentistry (2010)
Academy of Marketing Science (2012)
Academy of Pharmaceutical Research and Science (2012)
Adhesion Society (2012)
AGN International North America, Inc (2012)
Airborne Law Enforcement Association (2011)
Alliance for Continuing Medical Education (2010)
Alliance of Information and Referral Systems (2012)
America's Small Business Development Center Network (2012)
American Academy of Allergy, Asthma, and Immunology (2010)
American Academy of Dermatology (2011)
American Academy of Neurology (2012)
American Academy of Orthopaedic Surgeons (2010)
American Academy of Pediatrics (2012)
American Academy of Psychiatry and the Law (2010)
American Academy of Psychoanalysis and Dynamic Psychiatry (2010)
American Agricultural Editors Association (2011)
American Anthropological Association (2010)
American Association for Respiratory Care (2012)
American Association for the Advancement of Slavic Studies (2012)
American Association of Children's Residential Centers (2012)
American Association of Collegiate Registrars and Admissions Officers (2010)
American Association of Community Colleges (2011)
American Association of Endodontists (2011)
American Association of Feline Practitioners (2010)
American Association of Hip and Knee Surgeons (2010)
The American Association of Nurse Attorneys (2012)
American Association of Petroleum Geologists (2010)
American Association of Pharmaceutical Scientists (2010)
American Association of State Colleges and Universities (2012)
American Backflow Prevention Association (2010)
American Catholic Historical Association (2012)
American Clinical Neurophysiology Society (2011)
American College of Apothecaries (2012)
American College of Health Care Administrators (2011)
American College of Osteopathic Obstetricians and Gynecologists (2010)
American College of Physicians (2012)
American College of Physicians Services, Inc. (2012)
American College of Veterinary Internal Medicine (2012)
American College of Veterinary Nutrition (2012)
American Concrete Pipe Association (2012)
American Council of Independent Laboratories (2011)
American Crystallographic Association (2011)
American Dairy Science Association (2011)
American Dental Education Association (2012)
American Educational Research Association (2011)
American Folklore Society (2012)
American Fraternal Alliance (2012)
American Institute for International Steel (2012)
The American Institute of Architects (2011)
American Insurance Marketing and Sales Society (2010)
American Judges Association (2012)
American Kinesiotherapy Association (2012)
American Library Association (2011)
American Mathematical Society (2011)
American Medical Group Association (2010)
American Medical Rehabilitation Providers Association (2010)
American Meteorological Society (2012)
American Musicological Society (2012)
American Network of Community Options and Resources (ANCOR) (2010)
American Neuropsychiatric Association (2012)
American Nuclear Society (2010)
American Orthopaedic Foot and Ankle Society (2010)
American Payroll Association (2010)
American Pharmacists Association (2012)
American Planning Association (2010)
American Political Science Association (2012)
American Professional Society on the Abuse of Children (2010)
American Psychiatric Association (2010)
American Psychosocial Oncology Society (2010)
American Public Transportation Association (2011)
American Rental Association (2012)
American Society for Apheresis (2010)
American Society for Gastrointestinal Endoscopy (2010)
American Society for Histocompatibility and Immunogenetics (2011)
American Society for Information Science and Technology (2011, 2012)
American Society of Access Professionals (2012)
American Society of Animal Science (2011)
American Society of Bariatric Physicians (2012)
American Society of Emergency Radiology (2012)
American Society of Extra-Corporeal Technology (2011)
American Society of Health-System Pharmacists (2011)
American Society of Maxillofacial Surgeons (2012)
The American Society of Pediatric Hematology/Oncology (2012)
American Society of Pension Professionals & Actuaries (2012)
American Society of PeriAnesthesia Nurses (2010)
American Society of Regional Anesthesia and Pain Medicine (2011)
American Society of Sanitary Engineering (2011)
American Society of Trial Consultants (2012)
American Staffing Association (2011)
American Telemedicine Association (2012)
American Thoracic Society (2010)
American Urogynecologic Society (2012)
American Water Resources Association (2012)
Analytical Laboratory Managers Association (2011)
APA The Engineered Wood Association (2011)
ASPSN - American Society of Plastic Surgical Nurses (2012)
Associated Owners and Developers (2010)

Association for Accounting Administration (2010)
Association for Applied Psychophysiology and Biofeedback (2011)
Association for Conflict Resolution (2012)
Association for Continuing Legal Education (2012)
Association for Institutional Research (2012)
The Association for Library Service to Children (2011)
Association for Medical Imaging Management (2012)
Association for Professionals in Infection Control and Epidemiology (2010)
Association for Slavic, East European, and Eurasian Studies (2012)
Association of American Law Schools (2010)
The Association of American Seed Control Officials (2012)
Association of Analytical Communities International (2011)
Association of College and University Housing Officers-International (2011)
Association of Collegiate Schools of Architecture (2010)
Association of Consulting Foresters of America (2011)
Association of Correctional Food Service Affiliates (2012)
Association of Defense Trial Attorneys (2012)
Association of Dermatology Administrators & Managers (2011)
Association of Diving Contractors International (2010, 2012)
Association of Educators in Imaging and Radiologic Sciences, Inc (2012)
Association of Executive and Administrative Professionals (2010)
Association of Farmworker Opportunity Programs (2010)
Association of Girl Scout Executive Staff (2010)
Association of Information Technology Professionals (2012)
Association of Jesuit Colleges and Universities (2012)
The Association of Language Companies (2012)
Association of Medical School Pediatric Department Chairs (2012)
Association of periOperative Registered Nurses (2012)
Association of Reproductive Health Professionals (2012)
Association of Small Business Development Centers (2012)
Association of TeleServices International, Inc. (2012)
Association of University Research Parks (2011)
Association of University Technology Managers (2010)
Association on Higher Education and Disability (2012)
The Association to Advance Collegiate Schools of Business (2012)
Automotive Service Association (2012)
Cable & Telecommunications Association for Marketing (2010)
Catholic Academy for Communication Arts Professionals (2010)
Catholic Library Association (2011)
Central Conference of American Rabbis (2011)
Chief Petty Officers Association (2010)
Club Managers Association of America (2012)
College and University Professional Association for Human Resources (2010)
Community Action Partnership (2010)
Community Development Society (2010)
Congress of Neurological Surgeons (2012)
Consortium of School Networking (2011)
Construction Users Roundtable (2012)
Council for Advancement and Support of Education (2012)
Council for Affordable and Rural Housing (2012)
Council of Colleges of Arts and Sciences (2010)
Council of Residential Specialists (2010)
Council on Foundations (2012)
Council on Licensure, Enforcement and Regulation (2010)
Credit Union National Association, Inc. (2010)
Deep Foundations Institute (2012)
Defense Research Institute (2012)
Design-Build Institute of America (2012)
Destination Marketing Association International (2011)
DRI International (2012)
Electrical Generating Systems Association (2012)
Emergency Nurses Association (2012)
Employee Stock Ownership Plan Association (2012)
Entrepreneurs' Organization (2010)
Environmental Markets Association (2010)
Evidence Photographers International Council (2012)
Exhibition Services and Contractors Association (2010)
Federally Employed Women (FEW) (2010)
Federation of Internet Solution Providers of the Americas (2010)
Foil and Specialty Effects Association (2010)
Foodservice Sales & Marketing Association (2012)
Gas Processors Association (2012)
Gas Processors Suppliers Association (2012)
Gerontological Society of America (2010)
Groundwater Management Districts Association (2012)
Hardwood Manufacturers Association (2012)
Healthcare Billing and Management Association (2012)
Healthcare Convention and Exhibitors Association (2010)
IEEE Computer Society (2010)
INDA, Association of the Nonwoven Fabrics Industry (2012)
Independent Free Papers of America (2012)
Independent Hardee's Franchisee Association (2012)
Independent Petroleum Association of America (2012)
Industrial Research Institute (2011)
Institute for Professionals in Taxation (2012)
Institute of Food Technologists (2011)
Institute of Real Estate Management (2012)
Intellectual Property Owners Association (2010)
International Association for Truancy and Dropout Prevention (2012)
International Association of Addictions and Offender Counselors (2011)
International Association of Assessing Officers (2011)
International Association of Attorneys and Executives in Corporate Real Estate (2012)
International Association of Diecutting and Diemaking (2010)
International Association of Exhibitions and Events (2010)
International Bottled Water Association (2012)
International Cemetery, Cremation and Funeral Association (2010)
International Dairy-Deli-Bakery Association (2012)
International Foodservice Editorial Council (2010)
International Foundation of Employee Benefit Plans (2011)

International Health, Racquet and Sportsclub Association (2012)
International Ombudsman Association (2010)
International Packaged Ice Association (2011)
International Reading Association (2010)
International Society for Developmental Psychobiology (2012)
International Society for Quality of Life Research (2012)
International Studies Association (2010)
The International Wood Products Association (2011)
Jewish Community Centers Association of North America (2012)
Learning Resources Network (2011)
Lutheran Educational Conference of North America (2012)
Marine Fabricators Association (2012)
Medical Fitness Association (2011, 2012)
MGMA-ACMPE (2010)
Museum Store Association (2012)
NACE International (2012)
National Affordable Housing Management Association (2010)
National Alliance for Youth Sports (2012)
National Alliance of Black School Educators (2011)
National Alliance of State Pharmacy Associations (2012)
National Apartment Association (2010)
National Association for Bilingual Education (2011)
National Association for College Admission Counseling (2011)
National Association for Court Management (2010)
National Association for Ethnic Studies (2012)
National Association for Gifted Children (2011)
National Association of Public Health Statistics and Information Systems (2011)
National Association of Bar Executives (2012)
National Association of Basketball Coaches (2012)
National Association of Black Journalists (2012)
National Association of Blacks in Criminal Justice (2012)
National Association of Catering and Events (2012)
National Association of Chapter Thirteen Trustees (NACTT) (2012)
National Association of Chronic Disease Directors (2011)
National Association of Convenience Stores (2010)
National Association of Disability Representatives (2012)
National Association of Emergency Medical Technicians (2012)
National Association of Energy Service Companies (2012)
National Association of Fire Equipment Distributors (2012)
National Association of Foreign Trade Zones (2011)
National Association of Health Data Organizations (2012)
National Association of Hispanic Publications (2011)
National Association of Housing Cooperatives (2010)
National Association of Insurance Commissioners (2010, 2012)
National Association of Legal Search Consultants (2012)
National Association of Nutrition and Aging Services Programs (2012)
National Association of Orthopedic Nurses (2012)
National Association of Professional Geriatric Care Managers (2011)
National Association of Professional Pet Sitters (2011)
National Association of Realtors (2010)
National Association of Sewer Service Companies (2012)
National Association of State Personnel Executives (2011)
National Association of Stock Plan Professionals (2012)
National Association of Telecommunications Officers and Advisors (2012)
National Association of Veterans Program Administrators (2012)
National Athletic Trainers Association (2011)
National Automatic Merchandising Association (2012)
National Bankers Association (2012)
National Catholic Educational Association (2011)
National Center for Assisted Living (2012)
National Classification Management Society (2011)
National Communication Association (2011)
National Conference of Bankruptcy Judges (2010)
National Conference of Bar Foundations (2012)
National Conference of Bar Presidents (2012)
National Conference of State Liquor Administrators (2010)
National Conference on Public Employee Retirement Systems (2012)
National Conference on Weights and Measures (2012)
National Council of Higher Education Loan Programs (2012)
National Council of Juvenile and Family Court Judges (2012)
National Council on Measurement in Education (2011)
National Education Association (2010)
National Emergency Management Association (2012)
National Fenestration Rating Council (2010)
National Grocers Association (2012)
National Head Start Association (2011)
National Hearing Conservation Association (2012)
National Hemophilia Foundation (2010)
National Industries for the Blind (2011)
National Lawyers Guild (2010)
National Maritime Safety Association (2010)
National Medical Association (2012)
National Naval Officers Association (2012)
National Organization for Associate Degree Nursing (2012)
National Organization of Social Security Claimants' Representatives (2010)
National Orientation Directors Association (2011)
National Ornamental and Miscellaneous Metals Association (2011)
National Pest Management Association (2011)
National Plasterers Council (2011)
National Poultry and Food Distributors Association (2012)
National Precast Concrete Association (2012)
National Public Employer Labor Relations Association (2010)
National Real Estate Investors Association (2010)
National Rehabilitation Association (2010)
National Retail Federation (2012)
National Reverse Mortgage Lenders Association (2010)
National Roof Deck Contractors Association (2012)
National Roofing Contractors Association (2010)
National Rural Electric Cooperative Association (2012)
National Rural Water Association (2012)

North American Export Grain Association, Inc. (2011)
North American Society for the Sociology of Sport (2012)
Oncology Nursing Society (2012)
Organization Development Network (2010)
Orthopaedic Research Society (2010)
Partnership for Philanthropic Planning (2012)
Perlite Institute (2012)
Pet Sitters International (2011)
Petroleum Equipment Suppliers Association (2011)
Phi Delta Chi (2011)
Pickle Packers International (2012)
Pipe Fabrication Institute (2012)
Plan Sponsor Council of America (2012)
Plastic Surgery Administrative Association (2012)
Plastics Pipe Institute (2011)
Polyurethane Manufacturers Association (2012)
Preventive Cardiovascular Nurses Association (2012)
Professional Photographers of America (2012)
Professional Retail Store Maintenance Association (2012)
Professional Women Controllers (2012)
The Propeller Club of the United States (2012)
Property Casualty Insurers Association of America (2011)
REALTORS Land Institute (2010)
Receptive Services Association of America (2012)
Religious Communication Association (2011)
Research and Development Associates for Military Food and Packaging Systems
     (2011)
Roof Coatings Manufacturers Association (2010)
Rural Telecommunications Group (2012)
Safety Glazing Certification Council (2012)
SEPM - Society for Sedimentary Geology (2010)
The Society for Adolescent Medicine (2012)
Society for Biomaterials (2012)
Society for Cinema and Media Studies (2011)
Society for Ethnomusicology (2012)
Society for Human Resource Management (2010)
Society for Industrial Microbiology (2011)
Society for Neuroscience (2012)
Society for Physician Assistants in Pediatrics (2012)
Society for Psychophysiological Research (2012)
Society for Surgery of the Alimentary Tract (2010)
Society for Technological Advancement of Reporting (2012)
Society for the Psychological Study of Social Issues (2010)
Society for Vascular Nursing (2010)
Society of Accredited Marine Surveyors (2011, 2012)
Society of Architectural Historians (2011)
Society of Behavioral Medicine (2012)
Society of Biological Psychiatry (2010)
Society of Cable Telecommunications Engineers (2010)
Society of Cardiovascular Anesthesiologists (2010)
Society of Christian Ethics (2011)
Society of Fire Protection Engineers (2010)
Society of Government Meeting Professionals (2012)
Society of Independent Gasoline Marketers of America (SIGMA) (2012)
Society of Neurointerventional Surgery (2012)
Society of Professors of Child and Adolescent Psychiatry (2010)
Society of Research Administrators International (2012)
Society of Risk Management Consultants (2010)
Society of Teachers of Family Medicine (2011)
Society of Urologic Nurses and Associates (2011)
Special Libraries Association (2010)
Specialty Graphic Imaging Association (2011)
Standards Engineering Society (2012)
State Capital Group (2012)
Structural Building Components Association (2012)
Teaching-Family Association (2010)
TESOL International Association (2011)
Text and Academic Authors Association (2012)
The Transformer Association (2012)
United Cerebral Palsy (2011)
United Professional Horsemen's Association (2010)
United States Junior Chamber (Jaycees) (2010)
United States Society on Dams (2012)
United States Tour Operators Association (2010)
University Council for Educational Administration (2010)
University Professional & Continuing Education Association (2012)
Urban Affairs Association (2011)
Urban Libraries Council (2011)
Used Truck Association (2012)
Vacuum Dealers Trade Association/Sewing Dealers Trade Association (2012)
Veterinary Hospital Managers Association (2012)
Visual Communications Industry Group (2011)
Voluntary Protection Programs Participants' Association, Inc. (2011)
Water Environment Federation (2010, 2012)
Women's Council of REALTORS (2010)
World Aquaculture Society (2011)
The Wound, Ostomy and Continence Nurses Society (2011)

West Monroe

Industrial Truck Association (2012)

MAINE

Bar Harbor

Association of Biomedical Communications Directors (2012)
Health and Sciences Communications Association (2012)
Society of Independent Professional Earth Scientists (2012)
Steel Founders' Society of America (2010)

Bath

Shipbuilders Council of America (2012)

Gorham

Seaplane Pilots Association (2010)

Portland

Alliance for Children and Families (2010)
International Visual Literacy Association (2012)
Justice Research and Statistics Association (2010)
National Extension Association of Family and Consumer Sciences (2010)
National Student Employment Association (2012)
North American Association of Summer Sessions (2010)
Society for the History of Discoveries (2011)

Rockport

College of Diplomates of the American Board of Orthodontics (2010)

MARYLAND

Annapolis

American Society of Consultant Pharmacists (2011)
Association for Communication Excellence (2012)
Edison Electric Institute (2012)
International Test and Evaluation Association (2011)
Organic Reactions Catalysis Society (2012)
Pipe Fabrication Institute (2010)
Refractory Metals Association (2012)

Arnold

National Association of Power Engineers (2010)

Baltimore

AABB - American Association of Blood Banks (2010)
The Acoustical Society of America (2010)
ACPA College Student Educators International (2011)
American Academy of Audiology (2012)
American Academy of Maxillofacial Prosthetics (2012)
American Accordionists Association (2012)
American Association for Paralegal Education (2011)
American Association of Attorney-Certified Public Accountants (2011)
American Association of Colleges of Osteopathic Medicine (2011)
American Association of Critical-Care Nurses (2012)
American Association of Immunologists (2010)
American Association of Neuroscience Nurses (2010)
American Association of Suicidology (2012)
American Association of Veterinary State Boards (2010)
American Automatic Control Council (2010)
American Catholic Philosophical Association (2010)
American Cleaning Institute (2012)
American Coatings Association (2012)
American College of Clinical Pharmacology (2010)
American College of Prosthodontists (2012)
American College of Sports Medicine (2010)
American College of Toxicology (2010)
American College of Veterinary Pathologists (2010)
American College Personnel Association (2011)
American Council of Life Insurers (ACLI) (2010)
American Dialect Society (2010)
American Epilepsy Society (2011)
American Family Therapy Academy (2011)
American Name Society (2010)
American Occupational Therapy Association, Inc. (2012)
American Orthopaedic Society for Sports Medicine (2012)
American Pain Society (2010)
American Sleep Apnea Association (2012)
American Society for Artificial Internal Organs (2010)
American Society for Information Science and Technology (2012)
American Society for Investigative Pathology (2012)
American Society for Neurochemistry (2012)
American Society for Pain Management Nursing (2012)
American Society of Crime Laboratory Directors (2010)
American Society of Cytopathology (2011)
American Society of Health-System Pharmacists (2012)
American Society of Interior Designers (2011)
American Society of Nuclear Cardiology (2012)
The American Society of Pediatric Hematology/Oncology (2011)
American Studies Association (2011)
American Therapeutic Recreation Association (2012)
Anxiety Disorders Association of America (2010)
APPAM - The Association for Public Policy Analysis and Management (2012)
Aquatic Plant Management Society, Inc. (2011)
Asian American Hotel Owners Association (2012)
Association for Applied Psychophysiology and Biofeedback (2012)
Association for Child Psychoanalysis (2010)
The Association for Manufacturing Excellence (2010)
Association for Professionals in Infection Control and Epidemiology (2011)
Association for Research in Otolaryngology (2011)
Association for the Advancement of Wound Care (2012)
Association of American University Presses (2011)
Association of Bridal Consultants (2011)
Association of Collegiate Business Schools and Programs (2012)
Association of Community Cancer Centers (2010, 2012)
Association of Free Standing Radiation Oncology Centers (2010)
Association of Fundraising Professionals (2010)
Association of Healthcare Internal Auditors (2010)
Association of Independent Corrugated Converters (2010)
The Association of Medical Illustrators (2011)
Association of Nurses in AIDS Care (2011)
Association of Organ Procurement Organizations (2010)
Association of Program Directors in Internal Medicine (2010)

Association of Real Estate License Law Officials (2011)
Association of Science-Technology Centers (2011)
Association of State and Territorial Public Health Nutrition Directors (2010)
Association of Universities for Research in Astronomy, Inc. (2011, 2012)
Beta Alpha Psi (2012)
Binding Industries Association (2010)
Biophysical Society (2011)
Black Data Processing Associates (2012)
Board of Registered Polysomnographic Technologists (2011)
Business Forms Management Association (2012)
Carpet Cushion Council (2010)
Clinical and Laboratory Standards Institute (2010)
Clinical Laboratory Management Association (2011)
Coin Laundry Association (2010)
COLA (2010)
College Swimming Coaches Association of America (2010)
Committee of Interns and Residents/ SEIU (2012)
Communications Fraud Control Association (2010)
Council of Engineering and Scientific Society Executives (2012)
Employee Assistance Professionals Association (2012)
Governors' Highway Safety Association (2012)
Health Care Compliance Association (2011)
Healthcare Billing and Management Association (2010)
Healthcare Distribution Management Association (2010)
Human Factors Society (2012)
IEEE Instrumentation and Measurement Society (2011)
INDA, Association of the Nonwoven Fabrics Industry (2012)
Industrial Fabrics Association International (2011)
Institute for Supply Management (2012)
Institute Management Accountants (2010)
Institute of Nuclear Materials Management (2010)
Interior Design Educators Council (2012)
International Dyslexia Association (2012)
International Pharmaceutical Excipients Council of the Americas (2010)
International Society for Medical Publication Professionals (2012)
International Society for Traumatic Stress Studies (2011)
International Society of Air Safety Investigators (2012)
International Special Events Society (2010)
Kappa Delta Pi (2012)
League for Innovation in the Community College (2010)
Linguistic Society of America (2010)
Masonry Veneer Manufacturers Association (2012)
Medical Transcription Industry Association (MTIA) (2012)
NACHA - The Electronic Payments Association (2012)
NADCA: The HVAC Inspection, Maintenance and Restoration Association (2011)
NASTD - Technology Professionals Serving State Government (2012)
National Art Education Association (2010)
National Association for Court Management (2011)
The National Association for Music Education (Formerly MENC) (2012)
National Association for Relationship and Marriage Education (2012)
National Association of Advisors for the Health Professions (2012)
National Association of Clinical Nurse Specialists (2011)
National Association of Credit Union Chairmen (2010)
National Association of Credit Union Supervisory and Auditing Committees (2010)
National Association of Disability Examiners (2010, 2012)
National Association of Ecumenical and Interreligious Staff (2010)
National Association of Episcopal Schools (2012)
National Association of Medical Examiners (2012)
National Association of Multicultural Engineering Program Advocates (2010)
National Association of Orthopedic Nurses (2011)
National Association of Pediatric Nurse Practitioners (2011)
National Association of Professional Insurance Agents (2012)
National Association of Professional Organizers (2012)
National Association of Pupil Services Administrators (2010)
National Association of Regulatory Utility Commissioners (2012)
National Association of Retail Collection Attorneys (2012)
National Association of State Chief Information Officers (2010, 2012)
National Association of State Directors of Teacher Education and Certification (2012)
National Association of State Technology Directors (2012)
National Association of State Utility Consumer Advocates (NASUCA) (2012)
National Association of Tax Professionals (2012)
National Coil Coating Association (2011)
National Correctional Industries Association (2011)
National Council of Postal Credit Unions (2010)
National Council on Teacher Retirement (2011)
National Court Reporters Association (2012)
National Food Service Security Council (2012)
National Gerontological Nursing Association (2012)
National Industries for the Blind (2012)
National Organization of Black Law Enforcement Executives (2010)
National School Supply and Equipment Association (2012)
National School Transportation Association (2011)
National Shellfisheries Association (2011)
National Soccer Coaches Association of America (2011)
National Technical Association (2012)
National Telecommunications Cooperative Association (2012)
National Truck Leasing System (2012)
North American Securities Administrators Association (NASAA) (2010)
Office Business Center Association International (2012)
Organization for the Study of Sex Differences (2012)
Orthopaedic Trauma Association (2010)
Parenteral Drug Association (2010)
Periodical and Book Association of America (2012)
Phi Delta Kappa International (2012)
Physician Assistant Education Association (2010)
Pi Lambda Theta (2012)
Polyurethane Foam Association (2010, 2012)
Print Services & Distribution Association (2010)

Process Equipment Manufacturers' Association (2012)
Rehabilitation Engineering and Assistive Technology Society of North America (2012)
Renal Physicians Association (2010)
The Risk Management Association (2010)
Society for Applied Anthropology (2012)
Society for Cardiovascular Angiography and Interventions (2011)
Society for Chaos Theory in Psychology and Life Sciences (2012)
Society for Clinical Data Management (2011)
Society for Historians of the Early American Republic (2012)
Society for Historical Archaeology (2012)
Society for Pediatric Dermatology (2011)
Society for Physician Assistants in Pediatrics (2010)
Society for the Scientific Study of Religion (2010)
Society for the Study of Indigenous Languages of the Americas (2010)
Society of Accredited Marine Surveyors (2012)
Society of American Law Teachers (2012)
Society of Chemical Manufacturers and Affiliates Inc. (2012)
Society of Nuclear Medicine (2012)
Society of Radiologists in Ultrasound (2012)
Society of Telecommunications Consultants (2012)
Technology Student Association (2010)
Teratology Society (2012)
Towing and Recovery Association of America (2010)
Tree Care Industry Association (2012)
VITA (2011)
Wallcovering Association (2012)
Water Environment Federation (2012)
Women's Business Enterprise National Council (2010)
Wood Products Manufacturers Association (2012)

Bethesda

American Association of Colleges of Osteopathic Medicine (2010)
American Conference of Governmental Industrial Hygienists (2012)
American Society for Experimental NeuroTherapeutics (2010, 2011)
American Society of Preventive Oncology (2010)
Association of Black Cardiologists (2011)
Association of Medical Diagnostic Manufacturers (2011)
Association of Medical Education and Research in Substance Abuse (2010, 2012)
CCIM Institute (2011)
Commission on Accreditation for Law Enforcement Agencies Incorporation (2011)
Consumer Healthcare Products Association (2010, 2011)
Council of State Administrators of Vocational Rehabilitators (2010)
National Association for State Community Services Programs (2010)
National Contract Management Association (2011)
National Council on Radiation Protection and Measurement (2010)
Parenteral Drug Association (2011)
Religion Newswriters Association (2012)
Society of American Military Engineers (2012)
United States Pan Asian American Chamber of Commerce (2012)

Bowie

International Union of Bricklayers and Allied Craftworkers (2011)

Elkridge

Water Quality Association (2010)

Ellicott City

American Filtration and Separations Society (2010)
United States Psychiatric Rehabilitation Association (2012)

Flintstone

International Society of Arboriculture (2012)

Ft. Washington

Air Traffic Control Association (2011, 2012)
American Bankruptcy Institute (2011)
American Bus Association (2010)
American College of Physician Executives (2010)
American Financial Services Association (2011)
American Geriatrics Society (2011)
American Medical Group Association (2011)
American Payroll Association (2010)
American Physical Therapy Association (2011)
American Seed Trade Association (2012)
American Society for Healthcare Environmental Services (2010)
American Society of Consultant Pharmacists (2012)
American Society of Pension Professionals & Actuaries (2010, 2011, 2012)
Associated Equipment Distributors (2012)
Association for Behavioral and Cognitive Therapies (2012)
Association of Maternal and Child Health Programs (AMCHP) (2010)
Building Service Contractors Association International (2010)
The College Board (2012)
Foster Family-Based Treatment Association (2010)
Healthcare Billing and Management Association (2012)
Intelligent Transportation Society of America (2012)
International Association for Human Resource Information Management (2011)
International Association of Movers (2012)
International Council of Shopping Centers (2012)
Investment Management Consultants Association (2012)
National Association of Councils on Developmental Disabilities (2011)
National Association of Independent Schools (2011)
National Association of Insurance Commissioners (2011)
National Association of State Directors of Developmental Disabilities Services, Inc. (2011)
National Cancer Registrars Association (2012)
National Council of Investigative and Security Services Inc. (2011, 2012)
National Council on Aging (2012)
National Hospice & Palliative Care Organization (2012)
Network Branded Prepaid Card Association (2012)

Precast/Prestressed Concrete Institute (2010)
Project Management Institute (2010)
Society for College and University Planning (2011)
Society for Vascular Surgery (2012)
Society for Vascular Ultrasound (2012)
Society of Actuaries (2012)
Society of American Military Engineers (2011, 2012)
Society of Flight Test Engineers (2010)
State Education Technology Directors Association (2011)

Gaithersburg

American Society of Heating, Refrigerating and Air Conditioning Engineers
   (ASHRAE) (2012)
National Society of Professional Surveyors (2011)

Greenbelt

American Astronautical Society (2010)
Military Officers Association of America (MOAA) (2010)
National Association of Fire Investigators (2012)

Laurel

American Society of Safety Engineers (2012)

Lincolnshire

Society for Clinical Trials (2010)

Linthicum

Certified Contractors Network (2012)
National Association of State Directors of Career Technical Education Consortium
   (2011)

McHenry

American Cable Association (2010)
American Electrology Association (2010)

N. Bethesda

Generic Pharmaceutical Association (2010, 2012)

Ocean City

The Foodservice Group, Inc. (2012)
Service Station Dealers of America and Allied Trades (2010, 2012)

Rockville

Association of Railway Museums (2010)
National Grants Management Association (2010)
Parenteral Drug Association (2011)

St. Michaels

ECRI (2011)

Timonium

Violin Society of America (2011)

MASSACHUSETTS

Acushnet

Computer Assisted Language Instruction Consortium (2010)

Amherst

The Association for Environmental Health and Sciences (2010)
IEEE Computer Society (2012)

Andover

IPC Washington Office (2012)

Boston

AABB - American Association of Blood Banks (2012)
Academy Health (2010)
Academy of Management (2012)
Academy of Medical-Surgical Nurses (2011)
Academy of Nutrition and Dietetics (2010)
ACPA College Student Educators International (2010)
Advanced Medical Technology Association (AdvaMed) (2012)
Alliance for Children and Families (2010)
Alliance of Work/Life Progress (2012)
American Academy of Audiology (2012)
American Academy of Cosmetic Dentistry (2011)
American Academy of Dental Sleep Medicine (2012)
American Academy of Facial Plastic and Reconstructive Surgery (2010)
American Academy of Implant Dentistry (2010)
American Academy of Optometry (2011)
American Academy of Otolaryngic Allergy (2010)
American Academy of Otolaryngology-Head and Neck Surgery (2010)
American Academy of Pediatrics (2011)
American Academy of Psychiatry and the Law (2011)
American Academy of Sleep Medicine (2012)
American Alliance for Health, Physical Education, Recreation and Dance (2012)
American Association for Applied Linguistics (2012)
American Association for the Study of Liver Diseases (2010, 2012)
American Association for the Surgery of Trauma (2010)
American Association of Clinical Endocrinologists (2010)
American Association of Endodontists (2012)
American Association of Immunologists (2012)
American Association of Law Libraries (2012)
American Association of Medical Society Executives (2011)
American Association of Nurse Anesthetists (2011)
American Association of Residential Mortgage Regulators (2012)
American Association of Sleep Technologists (2012)
American Association of Teachers of German (2010)

American Association of Variable Star Observers (2011)
American Astronomical Society (2011)
American Bankers Association (2010)
American Burn Association (2010)
American Catholic Historical Association (2011)
American Chemical Society (2010)
American College of Allergy, Asthma and Immunology (2011)
American College of Osteopathic Surgeons (2012)
American College Personnel Association (2010)
American Collegiate Retailing Association (2011)
American Conference of Cantors (2010)
American Council on the Teaching of Foreign Languages (2010)
American Crystallographic Association (2012)
American Education Finance Association (2012)
American Fiber Manufacturers Association (2012)
American Gas Association (2012)
American Historical Association (2011)
American Institute of Floral Designers (2010)
American Institute of Ultrasound in Medicine (2011)
American Library Association (2010)
American Mathematical Association of Two Year Colleges (2010)
American Mathematical Society (2012)
American Mental Health Counselors Association (2010)
American Montessori Society (2010)
American Morgan Horse Association (2011)
American Neurogastroenterology and Motility Society (2010)
American Neurological Association (2012)
American Organization of Nurse Executives (2012)
American Oriental Society (2012)
American Orthopaedic Association (2011)
American Orthotic and Prosthetic Association (2012)
American Pediatric Society (2012)
American Philosophical Association (2010)
American Physical Society (2012)
American Physical Therapy Association (2010)
American Planning Association (2011)
American Podiatric Medical Association (2011)
American Podiatric Medical Students Association (2011)
American Podiatric Medical Writers Association (2011)
American Prepaid Legal Services Institute (2010)
American Rhinologic Society (2010)
American School Counselor Association (2010)
American Society for Aesthetic Plastic Surgery (2011)
American Society for Artificial Internal Organs (2012)
American Society for Clinical Pathologists (2012)
American Society for Clinical Pathology (2012)
American Society for Surgery of the Hand (2010)
American Society for Therapeutic Radiology and Oncology (2012)
American Society of Cataract and Refractive Surgery (2010)
American Society of Cytopathology (2010)
American Society of Neuroradiology (2010)
American Society of Ophthalmic Administrators (2010)
American Society of Pediatric Nephrology (2012)
American Society of Radiologic Technologists (2012)
American Society of Transplant Surgeons (2012)
American Society of Transplantation (2012)
American Translators Association (2011)
American Veterinary Dental Society (2011)
Analytical and Life Science Systems Association (2012)
Antiquarian Booksellers Association of America (2012)
APPAM - The Association for Public Policy Analysis and Management (2010)
Applied Research Ethics National Association (2012)
Art Libraries Society of North America (2010)
Associated Schools of Construction (2010)
Association for Continuing Legal Education (2011)
Association for Education and Rehabilitation of the Blind & Visually Impaired
   (2011)
Association for Financial Professionals, Inc. (2011)
Association for Healthcare Philanthropy (2011)
Association for Healthcare Resource and Materials Management (2011)
Association for Library and Information Science Education (2010)
The Association for Nursing Professional Development (2012)
Association for Psychological Science (2010)
Association for Surgical Education (2011)
Association for Symbolic Logic (2012)
Association for the Advancement of International Education (2010, 2012)
Association of Boarding Schools (2011)
Association of College and Research Libraries (2010)
Association of College Honor Societies (2010)
Association of College Unions International (2012)
Association of Collegiate Schools of Architecture (2012)
Association of Community College Trustees (2012)
Association of Defense Trial Attorneys (2010)
Association of Farmworker Opportunity Programs (2012)
Association of Gay and Lesbian Psychiatrists (2010)
Association of Independent Commercial Producers (2012)
Association of Independent Manufacturers'/Representatives, Inc. (2012)
Association of Insolvency and Restructuring Advisors (2011)
Association of Institutional Investors (2012)
Association of Jesuit Colleges and Universities (2012)
Association of Legal Administrators (2010)
Association of Occupational Health Professionals in Healthcare (2010)
Association of Oncology Social Work (2011)
Association of Program Directors in Surgery (2011)
Association of Reporters of Judicial Decisions (2011)
Association of University Radiologists (2011)
Automated Imaging Association (2010)
BioCommunications Association (2010)
Biotechnology Industry Organization (BIO) (2012)
BMC - A Foodservice Sales and Marketing Council (2012)

Cable & Telecommunications Association for Marketing (2011)
Catholic Library Association (2012)
Central Conference of American Rabbis (2012)
CFA Institute (2010, 2012)
Chief Officers of State Libraries Agencies (2010)
Children's Literature Association (2012)
Chinese Language Teachers Association (2010)
College and University Professional Association for Human Resources (2012)
Committee of 200 (2011)
Copier Dealers Association (2010)
Council for Advancement and Support of Education (2012)
Council for European Studies (2012)
Council of Development Finance Agencies (2011)
Council of Multiple Listing Services (2012)
Council of the Great City Schools (2011)
Decision Sciences Institute (2011)
Deep Foundations Institute (2011)
Democratic Governors Association (2010)
Design Management Institute (2012)
Direct Marketing Association (2011)
The Electrochemical Society (2011)
The Endocrine Society (2011)
Family Firm Institute, Inc. (2011)
The Fertilizer Institute (2012)
Fiber Society (2012)
The Foodservice Group, Inc. (2012)
Gerontological Society of America (2011)
Global Business Travel Association (2012)
Gynecologic Oncology Group (2010, 2012)
Heart Rhythm Society (2012)
Hospice and Palliative Nurses Association (2010)
Human Factors and Ergonomics Society (2012)
Human Factors Society (2012)
IEEE Engineering in Medicine and Biology Society (2011)
Independent Educational Consultants Association (2012)
Industrial Fabrics Association International (2012)
Infectious Diseases Society of America (2011)
The Institute of Internal Auditors (2012)
Insured Retirement Institute (2011)
International Anesthesia Research Society (2012)
International Association of Administrative Professionals (2010)
International Association of Correctional Training Personnel (2010)
International Aviation Women's Association (2010)
International Communication Association (2011)
International Concatenated Order of Hoo-Hoo (2012)
International Conference of Symphony and Opera Musicians (2010)
International Council for Health, Physical, Education, Recreation, Sport and Dance (2012)
International Federation of Fertility Societies (2012)
International Hearing Society (2011)
International Institute of Forecasters (2012)
International Neuropsychological Society (2011)
International Paralegal Management Association (2011)
International Pediatric Nephrology Association (2012)
International Society for Respiratory Protection (2012)
International Society of Hair Restoration Surgery (2010)
International Trademark Association (2010)
International Transplant-Skin Cancer Collaborative (2012)
Investigative Reporters and Editors (2012)
Learning Forward (2012)
Marketing Research Association (2010)
Marketing Science Institute (2012)
Materials Research Society (2010, 2011, 2012)
Mathematical Association of America (2012)
Metaphysical Society of America (2010)
National Academy of Elder Law Attorneys, Inc. (2011)
National Affordable Housing Management Association (2012)
National Apartment Association (2012)
National Association for Business Teacher Education (2012)
National Association for Campus Activities (2012)
National Association for Proton Therapy (2012)
National Association for Sport and Physical Education (2012)
National Association of College and University Food Services (2012)
National Association of Consumer Advocates (2010)
National Association of Drug Court Professionals (2010)
National Association of Judiciary Interpreters and Translators (2012)
National Association of Professional Process Servers (2012)
National Association of Schools of Music (2010)
National Association of State Election Directors (2012)
National Association of State Energy Officials (2010)
National Association of Student Financial Aid Administrators (2011)
National Business Education Association (2012)
National Cable & Telecommunications Association (2012)
National Catholic Educational Association (2012)
National Collegiate Honors Council (2012)
National Conference of Insurance Legislators (2010)
National Council of Investigative and Security Services Inc. (2012)
National Electrical Contractors Association (2010)
National Electrical Manufacturers Representatives Association (2011)
National Fire Protection Association (2011)
National Guild for Community Arts Education (2011)
National Housing and Rehabilitation Association (2011, 2012)
National Investment Company Service Association (2012)
National League of Cities (2012)
National Marine Educators Association (2011)
National Pest Management Association (2012)
National School Boards Association (2012)
National Society of Genetic Counselors (2012)
National Venture Capital Association (2011)
National Waterways Conference (2010)

The New Media Consortium (2012)
North American Case Research Association (2012)
North American Catalysis Society (2010)
Oncology Nursing Society (2011)
The Open Group (2010)
Organic Trade Association (2010)
Outdoor Industry Association (2012)
Pediatric Endocrine Society (2012)
PeerSpan (2010)
Pension Real Estate Association (2010, 2012)
Perennial Plant Association (2012)
Pine Chemicals Association (2012)
Professional Skaters Association (2012)
The Protein Society (2011)
Risk and Insurance Management Society, Inc. (RIMS) (2010)
The Risk Management Association (2010, 2012)
School Social Work Association of America (2012)
Selected Independent Funeral Homes (2012)
Sleep Research Society (2012)
Social Science History Association (2011)
Society for Academic Emergency Medicine (2011)
Society for Clinical and Experimental Hypnosis (2010)
Society for Developmental and Behavioral Pediatrics (2010)
Society for Information Display (2012)
Society for Italian Historical Studies (2011)
Society for Marketing Professional Services (2010)
The Society for Modeling and Simulation International (2011)
Society for Pediatric Radiology (2010)
Society for Pediatric Research (2012)
Society for Personality Assessment (2012)
Society for Psychophysiological Research (2011)
Society for Radiation Oncology Administration (2012)
Society for Scholarly Publishing (2011)
Society for Sex Therapy and Research (2010)
Society for Vascular Surgery (2010)
Society for Vascular Ultrasound (2010)
Society of Cardiovascular Anesthesiologists (2012)
Society of Computed Body Tomography and Magnetic Resonance (2012)
Society of Environmental Toxicology and Chemistry (2011)
Society of Forensic Toxicologists (2012)
Society of Independent Gasoline Marketers of America (SIGMA) (2010)
Society of International Business Fellows (2010)
Society of Laparoendoscopic Surgeons (2012)
Society of Neurointerventional Surgery (2010)
Society of Otorhinolaryngology and Head-Neck Nurses (2010)
Society of Plastics Engineers (2011)
Society of Toxicologic Pathologists (2012)
Society of Toxicologic Pathology (2012)
Society of Urologic Nurses and Associates (2010)
Special Interest Group on Ada Programming Language (2012)
Specialty Coffee Association of America (2012)
Standards Engineering Society (2010)
State Government Affairs Council (2012)
SWANA - Solid Waste Association of North America (2010)
TESOL International Association (2010)
Theatre Communications Group (2012)
Theta Tau (2012)
Turnaround Management Association (2012)
United Producers Formulators and Distributors Association (2012)
United Professional Horsemen's Association (2011)
United States Grains Council (2010)
United States Psychiatric Rehabilitation Association (2011)
Urban Libraries Council (2010)
USENIX: The Advanced Computing Systems Association (2011, 2012)
WIFS - Women in Insurance and Financial Services (2010)
Women Chefs and Restaurateurs (2011)
World Future Society (2010)

Brewster

Global Offset and Countertrade Association (GOCA) (2012)

Cambridge

Advertising and Marketing International Network (2010)
American Academy of Arts & Sciences (2012)
American Society of Safety Engineers (2011)
Association of Professional Model Makers (2010)
Association of Strategic Alliance Professionals, Inc. (2012)
Chlorobenzene Producers Association (2012)
Edison Electric Institute (2011)
Health Industry Business Communications Council (2011)
Human Milk Banking Association of North America (2010)
Lift Manufacturers Product Section - Material Handling Institute (2011)
Material Handling Industry of America (2011)
Metals Service Center Institute (2012)
National Association for Armenian Studies and Research (2012)
National Association of Schools of Theatre (2010)
National Association of Women Judges (2012)
National Council of State Boards for Nursing (2010)
Object Management Group (2012)
Plasma Protein Therapeutics Association (2012)
Society for Radiation Oncology Administration (2012)
Society of Chemical Manufacturers and Affiliates Inc. (2012)
Telecommunications Industry Association (2010)
Ultrasonic Industry Association (2010)
Window and Door Manufacturers Association (2012)

Cape Cod

The Histochemical Society (2010)

Chatham

New England Club Managers Association (2012)

Dedham

American Association of Clinical Endocrinologists (2012)

Duxbury

Association for the Calligraphic Arts (2010)

Essex

International Transplant-Skin Cancer Collaborative (2012)

Marlborough

Ice Skating Institute (2010)

Medford

Association for Spanish and Portuguese Studies (2012)

Newton

Club Managers Association of America (2012)

Northampton

Children's Book Council (2011)

Peabody

Independent Laboratory Distributors Association (2012)

Sturbridge

American Council of Snowmobile Associations (2012)
Association for Living History, Farm and Agricultural Museums (2010)

Waltham

Medical Device Manufacturers Association (2012)

Wellesley Hills

Conference on Faith and History (2010, 2012)

West Springfield

American Dairy Goat Association (2011)
National Association of Agricultural Fair Agencies (2011)

Winchester

New England Club Managers Association (2012)

Woburn

American Association of Variable Star Observers (2012)
Society of General Physiologists (2010)

Woods Hole

American Antiquarian Society (2011)
The Histochemical Society (2012)
Society of General Physiologists (2012)

Worcester

American Antiquarian Society (2010)
American Sportfishing Association (2011)
ASM International (2012)

MICHIGAN

Acme

American College of Neuropsychiatrists (2011)
Concrete Foundations Association (2011)
National Association of Professional Insurance Agents (2010)

Alpena

Cancer Patient Education Network (2012)

Ann Arbor

Children's Literature Association (2010)
Congress on Research in Dance (2012)
Guild of Artists and Artisans (2011)
International Association of Bridge, Structural, Ornamental and Reinforcing Iron Workers (2012)
Library Binding Institute (2012)
NARSA-The International Heal Transfer Association (2012)
Organization for the Study of Sex Differences (2010)
Plastic Surgery Research Council (2012)
RNA Society (2012)

Bay Harbor

College of Diplomates of the American Board of Orthodontics (2012)

Birmingham

Guild of Artists and Artisans (2010, 2011)

Dearborn

American Gear Manufacturers Association (2012)
Council for Chemical Research, Inc. (2011, 2012)
Equipment and Tool Institute (2012)
IEEE Power Electronics Society (2012)
IFCA International (2012)
Investment Casting Institute (2010)

Detroit

AASHTO: Transportation Center of Excellence (2011)
American Academy of Podiatric Practice Management (2010)
American Federation of Teachers (AFL-CIO) (2012)
Asian American Journalists Association (2011)
Association for Accounting Administration (2012)

Choristers Guild (2010)
Energy Solutions Center (2010)
NAFA Fleet Management Association (2010)
National Association of Independent Public Finance Advisors (2010)
National Association of Pastoral Musicians (2010)
National Association of Temple Administrators (2012)
National Exchange Club (2011)
Original Equipment Suppliers Association (2010, 2011, 2012)
SAE International (2012)
Society of Architectural Historians (2012)
Society of Automotive Analysts (2012)

E. Lansing

American Physical Society (2011)
Institute of Public Utilities (2012)
Phycological Society of America (2010)

Frankenmuth

International Maple Syrup Institute (2011)

Gaylord

Government Management Information Sciences (2012)

Grand Rapids

American Association of Clinical Endocrinologists (2012)
American Dairy Goat Association (2011)
American Mold Builders Association (2012)
American Society of Concrete Contractors (2011)
Association for Integrative Studies (2011)
Association of Fish and Wildlife Agencies (2010)
International Fruit Tree Association (2010)
National Association for Family and Community Education (2010)
National Association for Surface Finishing (2010)
National Association of Postmasters of the United States (2010)
National High School Athletic Coaches Association (2011)
National Onion Association (2012)
North American Association of State and Provincial Lotteries (2010)
Office Furniture Distribution Association (2011)
SAE International (2011)
Society of Christian Philosophers (2010)
Society of Plastics Engineers (2012)
Walnut Council (2010)

Lansing

American Institute of Organbuilders (2012)

Livonia

Automotive Industry Action Group (2012)
Transportation Safety Equipment Institute (2012)

Mount Prospect

The Association of Concert Bands (2011)

Novi

Association of Sewing and Design Professionals (2012)
Automotive Industry Action Group (2012)
PRBA - The Rechargeable Battery Association (2012)

Plymouth

Robotic Industries Association (2011)

Rochester

Association for Integrative Studies (2012)

Southfield

Automotive Industry Action Group (2012)
Society of Automotive Analysts (2012)

Sterling Heights

Automation Alley (2012)
Automotive Industry Action Group (2012)

Traverse City

AASHTO: Transportation Center of Excellence (2012)
Association of State and Territorial Public Health Nutrition Directors (2012)
Concrete Foundations Association (2012)
Interlocking Concrete Pavement Institute (2012)
National Concrete Masonry Association (2012)

Troy

Society of Plastics Engineers (2011)

MINNESOTA

Alexandria

American Oil Chemists' Society (2010)

Anoka

Fabricators & Manufacturers Association, International (2012)

Billings

Public Lands Council (2012)

Bloomington

Holstein Association USA (2010)
National Association of Service Managers (2012)

Duluth

The American Quaternary Association (2012)

Minneapolis

ACA International, The Association of Credit and Collection Professionals (2012)
Academy of Managed Care Pharmacy (2011)
Alliance of Work/Life Progress (2012)
American Academy of Advertising (2010)
American Academy of Dental Sleep Medicine (2011)
American Academy of Environmental Medicine (2011)
American Academy of Oral and Maxillofacial Pathology (2012)
American Academy of Sleep Medicine (2011)
American Academy on Communication in Healthcare (2012)
American Association for Aerosol Research (2012)
American Association for Laboratory Animal Science (2012)
American Association of Food Hygiene Veterinarians (2010)
American Association of Medical Dosimetrists (2010)
American Association of Museums (2012)
American Association of Philosophy Teachers (2011)
American Association of School Librarians (2011)
American Association of Veterinary Laboratory Diagnosticians (2010)
American Dance Therapy Association (2011)
American Diabetes Association (2012)
American Evaluation Association (2012)
The American Geographical Society (2011)
American Homebrewers Association (2010)
American Indian Science and Engineering Society (2011)
American Institute of Aeronautics and Astronautics (2012)
American Institute of Chemical Engineers (2011)
American Massage Therapy Association (2010)
American Men's Studies Association (2012)
American Philosophical Association (2011)
American Rabbit Breeders Association (2010)
American Railway Engineering and Maintenance-of-Way Association (2011)
American Risk and Insurance Association (2012)
American School Counselor Association (2012)
American Sexually Transmitted Diseases Association (2012)
American Society for Bone and Mineral Research (2012)
American Society for Indexing (2010)
American Society for Pain Management Nursing (2010)
American Society for Virology (2011)
American Society of Agricultural Consultants (2010)
American Society of Colon and Rectal Surgeons (2010)
American Society of Ichthyologists and Herpetologists (2011)
American Society of Plant Biologists (2011)
American Society of Trial Consultants (2010)
American Student Dental Association (2012)
American Thyroid Association (2010)
Art Libraries Society of North America (2011)
Associated Collegiate Press (2011, 2012)
Associated Professional Sleep Societies (2010)
The Association for Science Teacher Education (2011)
Association of Academic Museums & Galleries (2012)
Association of Collegiate Schools of Planning (2010)
Association of Credit Union Internal Auditors (2010)
Association of Genetic Technologists (2011)
Association of Occupational Health Professionals in Healthcare (2011)
Association of Pediatric Hematology/Oncology Nurses (2010)
Association of Professional Researchers for Advancement (2012)
APCO (Association of Public-Safety Communications Officials) International (2012)
Association of Rotational Molders International (2012)
Association of Specialized and Professional Accreditors (2012)
Association of State Drinking Water Administrators (2011)
Association of University Programs in Health Administration (2012)
Association of University Research Parks (2010)
Campus Safety, Health and Environmental Management Association (2011)
Catholic Library Association (2010)
Chorus America (2012)
College Music Society (2010)
Council for Advancement and Support of Education (2011)
Council on Technology Teacher Education (2011)
Defense Credit Union Council (2010)
Edison Electric Institute (2011)
Geological Society of America (2011)
Geoscience Information Society (2011)
Illuminating Engineering Society of North America (2012)
Independent Insurance Agents & Brokers of America, Inc. (2011)
Institute for Professionals in Taxation (2012)
International Academy of Oral Medicine and Toxicology (2012)
International Association of Railway Operating Officers (2011)
International Association of Women Police (2010)
International Council of Fine Arts Deans (2012)
International Downtown Association (2012)
International Paralegal Management Association (2010)
International Technology and Engineering Educators Association (2011)
International Transplant Nurses Society (2010)
International Trumpet Guild (2011)
Journalism Education Association (2011)
The Knitting Guild Association (2011)
The Masonry Society (2011)
Master Brewers Association of the Americas (2011)
Medical Library Association (2011)
Mineralogical Society of America (2011)
National Academy of Arbitrators (2012)
National Agri-Marketing Association (2012)
National American Indian Housing Council (2010)
National Association for Court Management (2012)
National Association of Biology Teachers (2010)
National Association of Children's Hospitals and Related Institutions (2010)
National Association of Letter Carriers (2012)
National Association of Manufacturers (2011)

National Association of Scientific Materials Managers (2011)
National Association of State Energy Officials (2012)
National Association of Wheat Growers (2010)
National Catholic Educational Association (2010)
National Center for Employee Ownership (2012)
National Cooperative Business Association (2011)
National Council on Family Relations (2010)
National Emergency Number Association (2011)
National Foundation for Credit Counseling (2010)
National Grocers Association (2012)
National Guardianship Association (2011)
National Horsemen's Benevolent and Protective Association (2010)
National Recreation and Parks Association (2010)
North American Export Grain Association, Inc. (2011)
North American Society for the Sociology of Sport (2011)
Organization for the Promotion and Advancement of Small Telecommunications Companies (2010, 2011, 2012)
Organization of American Kodaly Educators (2011)
Orthopaedic Trauma Association (2012)
Plumbing-Heating-Cooling Contractors - National Association (2011)
Printing Industry Credit Executives (2012)
The Psychonomic Society (2012)
Railway Engineering-Maintenance Suppliers Association (2011)
Railway Supply Institute (2011)
Railway Systems Suppliers, Inc (2011)
Regional Airline Association (2012)
Rhetoric Society of America (2010)
Sleep Research Society (2011)
Society for College and University Planning (2010)
Society for Computers in Psychology (2012)
Society for Epidemiologic Research (2012)
Society for Imaging Informatics in Medicine (2010)
Society for Imaging Science and Technology (2011)
Society for Industrial & Applied Mathematics (2012)
Society for the Study of Amphibians and Reptiles (2011)
Society for Vascular Medicine (2012)
Society of General Internal Medicine (2010)
State Higher Education Executive Officers (2010)
System Safety Society (2012)
Text and Academic Authors Association (2010)
United States Animal Health Association (2010)
United States Grains Council (2012)
United States Lifesaving Association (2012)
United States Psychiatric Rehabilitation Association (2012)
Visual Resources Association (2011)
Web Sling and Tie down Association (2012)

Rochester

American Association for the History of Medicine (2010)
National Network of Depression Centers (2012)
Outdoor Writers Association of America (2010)

Roseville

Christian College Consortium (2012)

Saint Louis Park

Ice Skating Institute (2011)

St. Paul

American Agricultural Editors Association (2010)
American Association of Meat Processors (2012)
American Fisheries Society (2012)
American Society of Electroneurodiagnostic Technologists (2012)
American Technical Education Association (2011)
Association of Children's Museums (2010)
Association of Christian Librarians (2010)
Catholic Medical Association (2012)
Correctional Education Association (2012)
International Police Mountain Bike Association (2012)
National Association for Interpretation (2011)
National Association of Barber Boards of America (2010)
National Association of Catholic Chaplains (2010)
National Association of Parliamentarians (2010)
National Association of State Administrators and Supervisors of Private Schools (2010)
National Conference on Weights and Measures (2010)
National Federation of Community Broadcasters (2010)
Surface Design Association (2011)
University Aviation Association (2010)

MISSISSIPPI

Bay Saint Louis

Land Trust Alliance (2012)

Biloxi

AASHTO: Transportation Center of Excellence (2010)
American Technical Education Association (2012)
National Conference of Insurance Legislators (2012)
National Lieutenant Governors Association (2010)
Newspaper Association Managers (2012)
Society of Air Force Clinical Surgeons (2011)

Gulfport

Council of State Community Development Agencies (2012)

Jackson

Hardwood Manufacturers Association (2010)
National Conference of Black Lawyers (2010)

Natchez

AASHTO: Transportation Center of Excellence (2010)

Robinsonville

National Association for Search and Rescue (2010)

Tunica

Cotton Incorporated (2012)
National Waterways Conference (2012)

Tupelo

American Society of Mining and Reclamation (2012)

MISSOURI

Branson

American Psychotherapy Association (2011)
American Resort Development Association (2012)
Beefmaster Breeders United (2012)
Coin Laundry Association (2012)
Concrete Foundations Association (2010)
International Regional Magazine Association (2010)
NALS (2010)
National Roadside Vegetation Management Association (2012)
National Rural Education Association (2010)
United States Trout Farmers Association (2010)

Brighton

National Fellowship of Child Care Executives (2010)

Chesterfield

National Drilling Association (2010)

Columbia

National Trappers Association (2011)

Kansas City

Academy of Legal Studies in Business (2012)
The Acoustical Society of America (2012)
ADED - The Association for Driver Rehabilitation Specialists (2010, 2012)
Alliance of Artists Communities (2012)
Alliance of Professional Tattooists (2010)
American Academy of Environmental Medicine (2010)
American Academy of Family Physicians (2012)
American Association of Advertising Agencies (2011)
American Association of Meat Processors (2010)
American Association of Neuroscience Nurses (2011)
American Association of Private Railroad Car Owners (2011)
American Council for Construction Education (2012)
American Design Drafting Association International and American Digital Design Association (2011)
American Hereford Association (2012)
American Literary Translators Association (2011)
American Meat Institute (2011)
American School Health Association (2010)
American Seed Trade Association (2011)
American String Teachers Association (2011)
American Volleyball Coaches Association (2010)
Asian/Pacific American Librarians Association (2012)
Association for Clinical Pastoral Education (2010)
Association for Death Education and Counseling (2010)
Association of Family Medicine Administration (2010)
Association of Professional Model Makers (2012)
Chief Officers of State Libraries Agencies (2010)
Clowns of America International (2012)
Costume Society of America (2010)
Council for Advancement and Support of Education (2010)
Crane Certification Association of America (2012)
Distillers Grains Technology Council (2011)
Equipment Marketing and Distribution Association (2010)
Federation of Analytical Chemistry and Spectroscopy Societies (2012)
Food Processing Suppliers Association (2012)
Generic Animal Drug Alliance (2012)
Governors' Highway Safety Association (2010)
In-Plant Printing and Mailing Association (2012)
International Association of Assessing Officers (2012)
International Hunter Education Association (2012)
International League of Electrical Associations (2010)
International Society for Educational Planning (2012)
International Veterinary Academy of Pain Management (2010)
Journalism Education Association (2010)
League for Innovation in the Community College (2012)
Major League Soccer (2012)
Missouri Fox Trotting Horse Breed Association (2010)
NAFSA: Association of International Educators (2010)
National Agri-Marketing Association (2010, 2012)
National Association of Collegiate Women Athletic Administrators (2012)
National Association of Educational Office Professionals (2010)
National Association of Farm Broadcasting (2010, 2012)
National Association of Women Highway Safety Leaders, Inc. (2010)
National Cooperative Business Association (2012)
National Council for History Education (2012)
National Defense Industrial Association (2010)
National Head Start Association (2011)
National Institute for Animal Agriculture (2010)
National Operating Committee for Standards of Athletic Equipment (2012)
National Portable Storage Association (2012)
National Rural Electric Cooperative Association (2010)

National Soccer Coaches Association of America (2012)
Reserve Officers Association of the U.S. (2012)
Society for Applied Spectroscopy (2012)
Society for Nutrition Education and Behavior (2011)
Society of Government Meeting Professionals (2010)
Specialized Carriers and Rigging Association (2012)
Stained Glass Association of America (2010, 2012)
Tilt-up Concrete Association (2011)
Touchstone Energy Cooperatives (2010)
Truckload Carriers Association (2010)
United States Institute for Theatre Technology (2010)
United States Wheat Associates, Inc. (2011)
Wheat Quality Council (2010, 2012)

Lake Ozark

American Institute of Chemical Engineers (2010)

Montreal

The Renaissance Society of America (2011)

Ridgedale

American International Charolais Association (2011)

Riverside

American Federation of School Administrators (2012)
Coalition of Labor Union Women (2012)

Sedalia

The National Association of Dog Obedience Instructors (2012)

Springfield

American Forage and Grassland Council (2010)
American Public Gas Association (2010)
American Society for Ethnohistory (2012)
North American Association of Wardens and Superintendents (2012)
Red Angus Association of America (2010)

St. Charles

The American Association of Code Enforcement (2012)
American Cultural Resources Association (ACRA) (2011)
National Association of Credit Management (2012)
The National NeedleArts Association (2010)
Professional Currency Dealers Association (2010)

St. Louis

Accreditation Board for Engineering and Technology Inc. (2012)
Airport Minority Advisory Council (AMAC) (2012)
Alpha Gamma Rho (2010)
American Association of Bovine Practitioners (2011)
American Association of Medical Dosimetrists (2011)
American Association of Veterinary Parasitologists (2011)
American Board of Veterinary Practitioners (2011)
American Catholic Philosophical Association (2011)
American College Counseling Association (2010)
American Driver and Traffic Safety Education Association (2010)
American Hackney Horse Society (2011)
American Orff-Schulwerk Association (2012)
American Oriental Society (2010)
American Society for Aesthetics (2012)
American Society for Legal History (2011, 2012)
American Society for Neurochemistry (2011)
American Society for Quality (2010)
American Society of Association Executives-The Center for Association Leadership (2011)
American Society of Home Inspectors (2011)
American Society of International Law (2012)
American Society of Plant Taxonomists (2011)
American Veterinary Medical Association (2011)
American Water Works Association (2012)
American Wholesale Marketers Association (2010)
AMT - The Association For Manufacturing Technology (2012)
Architectural Woodwork Institute (2010)
ASFE/The Geoprofessional Business Association (2011)
Asphalt Emulsion Manufacturers Association (2011)
Asphalt Recycling and Reclaiming Association (2012)
Association for Applied and Clinical Sociology (2010)
Association for Consumer Research (2011)
Association for Education in Journalism and Mass Communication (2011)
Association for Financial Counseling and Planning Education (2012)
Association for Healthcare Volunteer Resource Professionals (2010)
Association for Supervision and Curriculum Development (ASCD) (2012)
Association for the Advancement of Wound Care (2012)
Association of Career and Technical Education (2011)
Association of Community Cancer Centers (2010)
Association of Fraternity Advisors (2011)
Association of Information Technology Professionals (2010)
Association of Oncology Social Work (2011)
Association of Personal Historians (2012)
Association of State and Territorial Dental Directors (2010)
Binding Industries Association (2012)
Business History Conference (2011)
Catholic Charities USA (2012)
Catholic Theological Society of America (2012)
CBA (2010)
Classification Society (2010)
College Sports Information Directors of America (2012)
Conference on College Composition and Communication (2012)
Consortium for Advanced Management, International (2012)
Credit Professionals International (2012)
Distillers Grains Technology Council (2012)

Econometric Society (2011)
Enlisted Association of the National Guard of the United States (2010)
Entrepreneurs' Organization (2011)
Equipment Marketing and Distribution Association (2011)
Ethics and Compliance Officer Association (2012)
EUCG, Inc. (2010)
Flexographic Technical Association (2011)
Healthcare Billing and Management Association (2010)
Institute of Certified Professional Managers (2011)
Institute of Packaging Professionals (2010)
Institute of Transportation Engineers (2011)
International Academy of Oral Medicine and Toxicology (2011)
International Association of Audio Information Services (2011)
International Association of Campus Law Enforcement Administrators (2010)
International Association of Jewish Vocational Services (2010)
International Business Music Association (2011)
International Economic Development Council (2012)
International Festivals and Events Association (2010)
International Police Mountain Bike Association (2010)
International Special Events Society (2011)
Investigative Reporters and Editors (2012)
IT Financial Management Association (2011)
Medieval Academy of America (2012)
Meeting Professionals International (2012)
Multi-Level Marketing International Association (2012)
Music Industry Conference (2012)
NAFA Fleet Management Association (2012)
National Asphalt Pavement Association (2011)
National Association for Campus Activities (2011)
National Association for College Admission Counseling (2010)
The National Association for Music Education (Formerly MENC) (2012)
National Association of Agricultural Educators (2011)
National Association of Area Agencies on Aging (2010)
National Association of Credit Union Supervisory and Auditing Committees (2012)
National Association of Fire Equipment Distributors (2010)
National Association of Housing and Redevelopment Officials (2011)
National Association of Personnel Services (2010)
National Association of Regulatory Utility Commissioners (2011)
National Association of Resale & Thrift Shops (2012)
National Association of State Boards of Geology (2010)
National Association of Tax Professionals (2011)
National Association of Vision Professionals (2012)
National Association of Women in Construction (2011)
National Athletic Trainers Association (2012)
National Christian College Athletic Association (2011)
National Coil Coating Association (2012)
National Council for Workforce Education (2011)
National Council of Examiners for Engineering and Surveying (2012)
National Council of Structural Engineers Associations (2012)
National Educational Telecommunications Association (2012)
National Frame Building Association (2012)
National Grain and Feed Association (2012)
National Onsite Wastewater Recycling Association (2010)
National Orientation Directors Association (2010)
National Rifle Association of America (2012)
National Society of Black Engineers (2011)
National Telecommunications Cooperative Association (2010)
National Truck Equipment Association (2010)
North American Association of Christians in Social Work (2012)
North American Blueberry Council (2012)
North American Horticultural Supply Association (2011)
North American Serials Interest Group (2011)
Passenger Vessel Association (2011)
Pet Food Institute (2012)
Philosophy of Education Society (2011)
Porcelain Enamel Institute (2012)
Portland Cement Association (2011)
Poultry Science Association (2011)
Powder Coating Institute (2012)
Professional and Organizational Development Network in Higher Education (2010)
The Psychonomic Society (2010)
Recognition Professionals International (2012)
School Social Work Association of America (2010)
SMMA - The Motor and Motion Association (2010, 2012)
Society for American Archaeology (2010)
Society for In Vitro Biology (2012)
Society for News Design (2011)
Society of American Military Engineers (2012)
Society of American Registered Architects (2012)
Society of Cable Telecommunications Engineers (2010)
Society of Depreciation Professionals (2010)
Society of Pelvic Reconstructive Surgeons (2010)
Society of Professional Benefit Administrators (2011)
Society of Surgical Oncology (2010)
Society of Tribologists and Lubrication Engineers (2012)
Soil and Water Conservation Society (2010)
Steel Plate Fabricators Association Division of STI/SPFA (2012)
Transportation Clubs International (2012)
United Soybean Board (2012)
United States Meat Export Federation (2010)
Water Environment Federation (2012)
Young Adult Library Services Association (2012)

MONTANA

Big Sky

IEEE Aerospace and Electronic Systems Society (AESS) (2012)

Billings

Brotherhood of Locomotive Engineers and Trainmen (2012)
Dude Ranchers' Association (2010)
Society for Range Management (2011)

Bozeman

American Society for Virology (2010)

Choteau

Columbia Sheep Breeders Association of America (2010)

Kalispell

American Journalism Historians Association (2011)

Missoula

Society of Environmental Journalists (2010)

Osage Beach

Electronic Security Association (2012)

Whitefish

National Conference of Appellate Court Clerks (2010)

NEBRASKA

Grand Island

United States Custom Harvesters, Inc. (2011, 2012)

Kearney

Association of Field Ornithologists (2011)

Lincoln

Adjutants General Association of the United States (2012)
Educational Theatre Association (2010)
International Clarinet Association (2012)
National Guard Association of the U.S. (2012)
Psychometric Society (2012)

Omaha

American Agricultural Law Association (2010)
American Association of Railroad Superintendents (2012)
American Association of Swine Veterinarians (2010)
American Society of Mechanical Engineers (ASME) (2012)
Architectural Engineering Institute (2012)
Associated Schools of Construction (2011)
Catholic Cemetery Conference (2010)
Council of State and Territorial Epidemiologists (2012)
Fraternal Field Managers Association (2010)
General Federation of Women's Clubs (2010)
Industrial Asset Management Council (2012)
Military Impacted Schools Association (2011)
National Association of Extension 4-H Agents (2011)
National Association of Fraternal Insurance Counsellors (2010)
National Association of Legal Assistants (2012)
National Association of Local Boards of Health (2010)
National Association of State Boards of Geology (2012)
National Association of State Directors of Career Technical Education Consortium (2012)
National Farmers Union (Farmers Educational & Co-operative Union of America) (2012)
National Grain and Feed Association (2012)
National Hispanic Corporate Council (2011)
National Newspaper Association (2010)
Transportation Elevator and Grain Merchants Association (2010)

NEVADA

Elko

Society of Mineral Analysts (2010, 2012)

Henderson

Appliance Parts Distributors Association (2010)
Association of Metropolitan Water Agencies (2010)
Biscuit and Cracker Manufacturers' Association (2012)
Industrial Diamond Association of America (2010)
National Association for Family Child Care (2011)
National Association of Health Unit Coordinators (2011)
National Association of Seventh-Day Adventist Dentists (2011)
Non-Ferrous Founders' Society (2012)
Pressure Vessel Manufacturers Association (2011)
Railway Industrial Clearance Association (2010)
Society for Human Ecology (2011)
Society for Obstetric Anesthesia and Perinatology (2011)

Incline Village

American Society of Consulting Arborists (2011)
The Railway Tie Association (2011)
Western History Association (2010)

Lake Tahoe

Accrediting Council for Continuing Education & Training (2012)
American College of Chiropractic Orthopedists (2010)
Forest Landowners Association (2010)
Mountain Rescue Association (2012)
Society for Technological Advancement of Reporting (2011)

Las Vegas

AABC Commissioning Group (2010, 2012)

AAGL - Advancing Minimally Invasive Gynecology Worldwide (2012)
ACA International, The Association of Credit and Collection Professionals (2012)
Academy of Medical-Surgical Nurses (2010)
Accrediting Bureau of Health Education Schools (2010, 2012)
Accrediting Council for Independent Colleges and Schools (2010, 2012)
AFCOM (2011)
AGN International North America, Inc (2010)
Air Conditioning Contractors of America (2012)
Air Diffusion Council (2011)
Airport Ground Transportation Association (2012)
Allied Finance Adjusters (2012)
ALMA - The International Loudspeaker Association (2010, 2012)
American Academy for Cerebral Palsy and Developmental Medicine (2011)
American Academy of Actuaries (2011)
American Academy of Ambulatory Care Nursing (2010)
American Academy of Anti-Aging Medicine (2012)
American Academy of Audiology (2012)
American Academy of Clinical Toxicology (2012)
American Academy of Cosmetic Surgery (2012)
American Academy of Dental Group Practice (2012)
American Academy of Emergency Medicine (2010)
American Academy of Implant Dentistry (2011)
American Academy of Matrimonial Lawyers (2012)
American Academy of Neurology (2011, 2012)
American Academy of Pain Management (2010, 2011)
American Academy of Physician Assistants (2011)
American Academy of Professional Coders (2012)
American Ambulance Association (2010, 2011, 2012)
American Amusement Machine Association (2010)
American Association for Adult and Continuing Education (2012)
American Association for Hand Surgery (2012)
American Association for Homecare (2010, 2012)
American Association of Bioanalysts (2010, 2012)
American Association of Cosmetology Schools (2011)
American Association of Dental Editors (2011)
American Association of Feline Practitioners (2012)
American Association of Grain Inspection and Weighing Agencies (2010, 2012)
American Association of Individual Investors (2011)
American Association of Integrated Healthcare Delivery Systems (2012)
American Association of Managed Care Nurses (2010, 2011, 2012)
American Association of Private Lenders (2012)
The American Association of Radon Scientists and Technologists (2012)
American Bakers Association (2010)
American Beekeeping Federation (2012)
American Beverage Association (2012)
American Beverage Licensees (2012)
American Board of Quality Assurance and Utilization Review Physicians, Inc. (2012)
American Board of Veterinary Practitioners (2012)
American Board of Vocational Experts (2012)
American Broncho-Esophagological Association (2010)
American Classical League (2012)
American Coatings Association (2010, 2012)
American College for Advancement in Medicine (2010, 2012)
American College of Chiropractic Orthopedists (2011)
American College of Emergency Physicians (2010)
American College of Foot and Ankle Surgeons (2010)
American College of Forensic Examiners Institute (2012)
American College of Gastroenterology (2012)
American College of Health Care Administrators (2010, 2012)
American College of Mohs Surgeons (2011)
American College of Osteopathic Emergency Physicians (2011)
American College of Osteopathic Family Physicians (2010)
American College of Real Estate Lawyers (2012)
American College of Sports Medicine (2012)
American College of Veterinary Radiology (2012)
American Composites Manufacturers Association (2010, 2012)
American Construction Inspectors Association (2011)
American Council of Engineering Companies (2011)
American Dental Assistants Association (2011)
American Dental Association (2011)
American Dental Hygienists' Association (2010)
American Disc Jockey Association (2012)
The American Fair Credit Council (2011)
American Federation of Government Employees (2012)
American Financial Services Association (2012)
American Gaming Association (2012)
American Gem Trade Association (2010)
American Greyhound Track Operators Association (2010, 2012)
American Head and Neck Society (2010)
American Hellenic Educational Progressive Association (AHEPA) (2012)
American Home Furnishings Alliance (2012)
American Institute for CPCU - Insurance Institute of America (2011)
American Institute of Certified Public Accountants (2010)
American Intellectual Property Law Association (2012)
American International Automobile Dealers Association (2012)
American Laryngological Association (2010)
American Laryngological, Rhinological and Otological Society (2010)
American Lighting Association (2010)
American Medical Technologists (2010)
American Mountain Guides Association (2012)
American Moving and Storage Association (2012)
American Nurses Association (2012)
American Orthotic and Prosthetic Association (2011)
American Osteopathic College of Anesthesiologists (2012)
American Osteopathic College of Radiology (2012)
American Otological Society (2010)
American Pathology Foundation (2011)
American Payroll Association (2010)
American Petroleum Institute (2011)

American Physical Therapy Association - Private Practice Section (2012)
American Pilots' Association (2010)
American Postal Workers Union (2011, 2012)
American Psychotherapy Association (2012)
American Purchasing Society (2011)
American Radium Society (2012)
American Recovery Association (2010, 2011)
American Rental Association (2011)
American Resort Development Association (2010, 2012)
American Reusable Textile Association (2011)
American Securitization Forum (2012)
American Society for Clinical Pathology (2011)
American Society for Colposcopy and Cervical Pathology (2010)
American Society for Metabolic and Bariatric Surgery (2010, 2012)
The American Society for Public Administration (2012)
American Society for Reconstructive Microsurgery (2012)
American Society for Surgery of the Hand (2011)
American Society of Civil Engineers (2010)
American Society of Clinical Hypnosis (2011)
American Society of Cytopathology (2012)
American Society of Health-System Pharmacists (2012)
American Society of Heating, Refrigerating and Air Conditioning Engineers (ASHRAE) (2011)
American Society of Home Inspectors (2010)
American Society of Pension Professionals & Actuaries (2011)
American Society of Preventive Oncology (2011)
American Society of Radiologic Technologists (2012)
American Society of Retina Specialists (2012)
American Society of Travel Agents (2011)
American Sociological Association (2011)
American Sportfishing Association (2010)
American Staffing Association (2012)
American Swimming Coaches Association (2012)
American Truck Dealers (2012)
American Trucking Associations (2012)
American Water Works Association (2011)
American Welding Society (2012)
American Wholesale Marketers Association (2010, 2012)
Amusement & Music Operators Association (2011, 2012)
Antique and Amusement Photographers International (2011)
Asian American Journalists Association (2012)
ASM International (2012)
Associated General Contractors of America (AGC) (2011, 2012)
Associated Locksmiths of America (2012)
The Association for Academic Surgery (2012)
Association for Accounting Administration (2012)
Association for Accounting Marketing (2012)
Association for Hose and Accessories Distribution (2012)
Association for Skilled and Technical Sciences (2010)
Association for Supervision and Curriculum Development (ASCD) (2011)
Association for the Advancement of Automotive Medicine (2010)
Association for the Study of Higher Education (2012)
Association for Unmanned Vehicle Systems International (2012)
Association of Academic Physiatrists (2012)
Association of Analytical Communities International (2012)
Association of Career and Technical Education (2010)
Association of Chiropractic Colleges (2012)
Association of Equipment Manufacturers (2010)
Association of Fund-Raising Distributors and Suppliers (2011)
Association of Independent Manufacturers'/Representatives, Inc. (2010)
Association of Lutheran Secondary Schools (2012)
Association of Management/International Association of Management (2010)
Association of Occupational Health Professionals in Healthcare (2012)
Association of Partners for Public Lands (2012)
Association of Physician Assistants in Obstetrics and Gynecology (2010)
Association of Pilots and Spa Professionals (2011)
Association of Private Enterprise Education (2010, 2012)
Association of Private Sector Colleges and Universities (Career College Association) (2010, 2012)
Association of Rehabilitation Nurses (2011)
Association of Reproductive Health Professionals (2011)
Association of Steel Distributors (2010, 2012)
Association of Strategic Alliance Professionals, Inc. (2012)
Association of TeleServices International, Inc. (2012)
Association of University Technology Managers (2011)
Association of Woodworking and Furnishings Suppliers (2011)
Automatic Transmission Rebuilders Association (2011, 2012)
Automotive Aftermarket Industry Association (2010, 2011, 2012)
Automotive Distribution Network (2012)
Automotive Maintenance and Repair Association (2012)
Automotive Oil Change Association (2010, 2012)
Automotive Parts Remanufacturers Association (2010, 2011, 2012)
Aviation Insurance Association (2012)
Beefmaster Breeders United (2010)
BICSI (2010)
Billiard Congress of America (2010)
The Bluetooth Special Interest Group (2012)
Bowling Proprietors' Association of America (2010)
Bowling Writers Association of America (2010)
Brain Injury Association of America (2010)
Broadcast Cable Credit Association (2012)
Broadcast Education Association (2010, 2011, 2012)
Building Service Contractors Association International (2011)
CALLERLAB - International Association of Square Dance Callers (2011)
Casket and Funeral Supply Association of America (2011)
CCIM Institute (2012)
Cedar Shake and Shingle Bureau (2012)
Chemical Coaters Association International (2012)
City and Regional Magazine Association (2012)
Clinical Laboratory Management Association (2010)

Commission on Accreditation for Law Enforcement Agencies Incorporation (2010)
Communications Fraud Control Association (2012)
Community Associations Institute (CAI) (2010, 2012)
Competitive Carriers Association (2012)
Competitive Telecommunications Association (2011)
Computer Measurement Group (2012)
Concrete Foundations Association (2012)
Concrete Sawing and Drilling Association (2012)
Conference of Consulting Actuaries (2011)
Conference on English Education (2012)
Conference on English Leadership (2012)
Consortium of College and University Media Centers (2012)
Construction Financial Management Association (2011, 2012)
Contact Lens Association of Ophthalmologists (2010)
Cottage Industry Miniaturists Trade Association (2010, 2011, 2012)
Council of American Survey Research Organizations (2012)
Council of Chiropractic Physiological Therapeutics and Rehabilitation (2012)
Council of Communication Management (2011)
Court Information Technology Officer Consortium (2012)
CPA Manufacturing Services Association (2012)
CPCU Society (2011)
Credit Union National Association, Inc. (2010)
Dance Educators of America (2012)
DBA International (2011, 2012)
Design-Build Institute of America (2010)
Direct Marketing Association (2012)
Direct Marketing Association Nonprofit Federation (2012)
Diving Equipment and Marketing Association (2010, 2012)
The Door and Hardware Institute (2012)
Drycleaning & Laundry Institute (2011)
Electric Drive Transportation Association (2012)
The Electrochemical Society (2010)
Electronic Distribution Show Corporation (2010, 2011, 2012)
Electronic Retailing Association (2010, 2012)
Electronic Traders Association (2012)
Electronic Transactions Association (2010, 2012)
Employee Assistance Society of North America (2011)
Employee Stock Ownership Plan Association (2010, 2011)
Exhibit Designers and Producers Association (2011)
Exterior Insulation and Finish Systems Industry Members Association (EIMA) (2011)
FAA Managers Association, Inc. (2011)
Fabricators & Manufacturers Association, International (2012)
Financial Executives International (2010)
Financial Managers Society (2012)
Flexible Intermediate Bulk Container Association (2010, 2012)
Flexographic Technical Association (2010)
Floor Covering Installation Contractors Association (2012)
Fluid Controls Institute (2012)
Foil and Specialty Effects Association (2012)
Food Marketing Institute (2010)
The Foodservice Group, Inc. (2012)
Foodservice Sales & Marketing Association (2012)
GAMA International (2010)
Game Manufacturers Association (2010, 2011, 2012)
Gasket Fabricators Association (2010)
Glass Association of North America (2010, 2011)
Golf Coaches Association of America (2011, 2012)
Golf Course Superintendents Association of America (2012)
The Grant Professionals Association (2011)
Health Care Administrators Association (2012)
Health Care Compliance Association (2012)
Healthcare Convention and Exhibitors Association (2011)
Healthcare Financial Management Association (2012)
Healthcare Information and Management Systems Society (2012)
Heavy Duty Manufacturers Association (2010)
Hotel Brokers International (2010, 2011, 2012)
Hotel Electronic Distribution Network Association (2012)
Human Factors and Ergonomics Society (2011)
Human Milk Banking Association of North America (2012)
Ice Skating Institute (2010)
IEEE Communications Society (2010)
IEEE Consumer Electronics Society (2010)
IEEE Signal Processing Society (2012)
Illuminating Engineering Society of North America (2010)
Imaging Supplies Coalition (2012)
Incentive Manufacturers & Representatives Alliance (2012)
Independent Bakers Association (2012)
Independent Laboratory Distributors Association (2010)
Independent Office Products and Furniture Dealers Association (2012)
Independent Photo Imagers (2011, 2012)
InfoComm International (2012)
Infusion Nurses Society (2012)
Institute for Responsible Housing Preservation (2012)
Institute Management Accountants (2012)
Institute of Food Technologists (2012)
The Institute of Internal Auditors (2010, 2011)
Institute of Scrap Recycling Industries, Inc. (2012)
Insulation Contractors Association of America (2010)
Interactive Multimedia and Collaborative Communications Alliance (2012)
Interior Design Society (2011)
Interlocking Concrete Pavement Institute (2011)
International Academy of Oral Medicine and Toxicology (2011)
International Aloe Science Council (2012)
International and American Associations of Clinical Nutritionists (2010)
International Association for Computer Information Systems (2010)
International Association for Healthcare Security and Safety (2012)
International Association for Human Resource Information Management (2010)
International Association of Administrative Professionals (2012)
International Association of Arson Investigators (2011)

International Association of Broadcast Monitors (2012)
International Association of Emergency Managers (2011)
International Association of Exhibitions and Events (2011)
International Association of Fairs and Expositions (2010, 2011, 2012)
International Association of Operative Millers (2010)
International Association of Used Equipment Dealers (2012)
International Aviation Ground Support Association (2010)
International Beverage Dispensing Equipment Association (2012)
International Business Brokers Association (2010, 2012)
International Carwash Association (2010, 2012)
International Cast Polymer Alliance (2012)
International Cemetery, Cremation and Funeral Association (2011, 2012)
International Claim Association (2010, 2011)
International Coach Federation (2011)
International Council of Air Shows (2010, 2011, 2012)
International Council of Shopping Centers (2012)
International Door Association (2010, 2012)
International Erosion Control Association (2012)
International Executive Housekeepers Association (2011, 2012)
The International Food & Beverage Forum (2012)
International Food, Wine and Travel Writers Association (2012)
International Foodservice Distributors Association (2012)
International Franchise Association (2011)
International Health, Racquet and Sportsclub Association (2012)
International Iridology Practitioners Association (2012)
International Licensing Industry Merchandisers' Association (2010, 2012)
International Nanny Association (2012)
International Packaged Ice Association (2010)
International Parking Institute (2010)
International Precious Metals Institute (2012)
International Sanitary Supply Association (2011)
International Sign Association (2011)
International Society of Automation (2010)
International Society of Beverage Technologists (2012)
International Society of Crime Prevention Practitioners (2012)
International Society of Hotel Association Executives (2010)
International Society of Weighing and Measurement (2012)
International Spa Association (2011)
International Surface Fabricators Association (2011)
International Test and Evaluation Association (2011)
International Truck Parts Association (2010)
Internet Marketing Association (2012)
Investment Management Consultants Association (2011)
IPC - Association Connecting Electronics Industries (2010, 2011)
Juvenile Products Manufacturers Association (2010)
The Kite Trade Association International (2011, 2012)
LeadingAge (American Association of Homes and Services for the Aging) (2010)
Machinery Dealers National Association (2010)
Major Cities Chiefs Association (2012)
Manufactured Housing Institute (2012)
Marble Institute of America (2011, 2012)
Mason Contractors Association of America (2010, 2011, 2012)
Masonry Veneer Manufacturers Association (2012)
Media Financial Management Association (2012)
Medical-Dental-Hospital Business Associates (2012)
Messenger Courier Association of the Americas (2010)
MGMA-ACMPE (2011)
MIDI Manufacturers Association (2012)
Mobile Air Conditioning Society Worldwide (2010, 2012)
NADCA: The HVAC Inspection, Maintenance and Restoration Association (2011)
NARSA-The International Heal Transfer Association (2011, 2012)
National Academy of Elder Law Attorneys, Inc. (2011)
National Agricultural Aviation Association (2011)
National Air Transportation Association (2010)
National American Indian Housing Council (2011, 2012)
National Association for Court Management (2011)
National Association for Health Care Recruitment (2010)
National Association for Home Care and Hospice (2011)
National Association for Information Destruction, Inc. (2010)
National Association for Interpretation (2010)
National Association for Medical Direction of Respiratory Care (2011)
National Association for Sport and Physical Education (2012)
National Association of Agricultural Educators (2010)
National Association of Broadcasters (2010, 2012)
National Association of Casino Party Operators (2010, 2011)
National Association of Catastrophe Adjusters (2012)
National Association of Colleges and Employers (2012)
National Association of Community Health Centers (2011)
National Association of Conservation Districts (2012)
National Association of Consumer Shows (2012)
National Association of Convenience Stores (2011, 2012)
National Association of Credit Management (2010, 2012)
National Association of Credit Union Service Organizations (2012)
National Association of Dental Laboratories (2010, 2012)
National Association of Development Organizations (2012)
National Association of Electrical Distributors (2011)
National Association of Enrolled Agents (2012)
National Association of Fire Equipment Distributors (2010, 2012)
National Association of Fraternal Insurance Counsellors (2012)
National Association of Government Guaranteed Lenders (NAGGL) (2012)
National Association of Home Builders (2010)
National Association of Independent Life Brokerage Agencies (2012)
National Association of Insurance and Financial Advisors (2012)
National Association of Letter Carriers (2011)
National Association of Managed Care Physicians (2011, 2012)
National Association of Mortgage Brokers (2011, 2012)
National Association of Nephrology Technologists and Technicians (2010, 2012)
National Association of Nutrition and Aging Services Programs (2010)
National Association of Personal Financial Advisors (2011)
National Association of Pizzeria Operators (2012)

National Association of Police Organizations (2010, 2012)
National Association of Professional Pet Sitters (2012)
National Association of Real Estate Editors (2010)
National Association of Rehabilitation Providers and Agencies (2012)
National Association of Retail Collection Attorneys (2010)
National Association of RV Parks and Campgrounds (2010, 2012)
National Association of Schools of Public Affairs and Administration (2010)
National Association of Steel Pipe Distributors (2010)
National Association of Subrogation Professionals (2012)
National Association of Tax Professionals (2011)
National Association of Television Program Executives (2010)
National Association of Theatre Owners (2011, 2012)
National Association of Ticket Brokers (2012)
National Association of Truck Stop Operators(NATSO) (2010, 2012)
National Association of Uniform Manufacturers and Distributors (2012)
National Association of Veterans Program Administrators (2010)
National Association of Workforce Development Professionals (2012)
National Auto Auction Association (2010, 2011, 2012)
National Automatic Merchandising Association (2012)
National Automobile Dealers Association (2012)
National Bar Association (2012)
National Beer Wholesalers Association (2011)
National Bicycle Dealers Association (2012)
National Board of Boiler and Pressure Vessel Inspectors (2011)
National Business Aviation Association (2011)
National Candle Association (2011, 2012)
National Center for State Courts (2012)
National Child Care Association (2012)
National Coalition of Black Meeting Planners (2011)
National Concrete Burial Vault Association (2010)
National Conference of Black Political Scientists (2012)
National Conference on Public Employee Retirement Systems (2010)
National Council of Exchangors (2010, 2012)
National Council of Juvenile and Family Court Judges (2010)
National Council of Legislators from Gaming States (2012)
National Council of Postal Credit Unions (2011)
National Council of Teachers of English (2012)
National Court Reporters Association (2011)
National CPA Health Care Advisors Association (2010)
National Credit Reporting Association (2010)
National Defender Investigator Association (2010)
National Demolition Association (2010, 2011)
National Electrical Contractors Association (2012)
National Environmental Health Association (2012)
National Exchange Carrier Association (2010)
National Federation of Licensed Practical Nurses (2012)
National Federation of Municipal Analysts (2012)
National Fire Protection Association (2010, 2012)
The National Flute Association, Inc. (2012)
National Franchisee Association (2010)
National Funeral Directors and Morticians Association (2012)
National Glass Association (2010, 2012)
National Golf Course Owners Association (2012)
National Golf Foundation (2012)
National Grocers Association (2011, 2012)
National Ground Water Association (2010, 2011, 2012)
National Health Care Anti-Fraud Association (2010)
National Independent Automobile Dealers Association (2010, 2011, 2012)
National Independent Fire Alarm Distributors (2012)
National Independent Laboratory Association (2012)
National Institute of Pension Administrators (2010, 2012)
National Investment Banking Association (2011, 2012)
National Kitchen and Bath Association (2011)
National League for Nursing (2010)
National Limousine Association (2010, 2012)
National Mining Association (2012)
National Motor Freight Traffic Association, Inc. (2012)
National Organization of Legal Services Workers (2010, 2012)
National Orientation Directors Association (2012)
National Parking Association (2011)
National Pawnbrokers Association (2010, 2012)
National Potato Council (2011)
The National Procurement Institute, Inc (2010)
National Registry of Environmental Professionals (2010, 2011)
National Retail Hobby Stores Association (2011, 2012)
National Roofing Contractors Association (2011)
National Shoe Retailers Association (2010, 2012)
National Shooting Sports Foundation (2012)
National Society for Histotechnology (2011)
National Society of Accountants for Cooperatives (2012)
National Society of Certified Healthcare Business Consultants (2012)
National Society of Insurance Premium Auditors (2012)
National Society of Professional Surveyors (2012)
National Stone, Sand, and Gravel Association (2011)
National Strength and Conditioning Association (2011)
National Structured Settlements Trade Association (2010)
National Systems Contractors Association (2010)
National Telecommunications Cooperative Association (2012)
National Tour Association (2011)
National United Merchants Beverage Association (2012)
National Weather Service Employees Organization (2012)
Natural Products Association (2010, 2011, 2012)
NIBA - The Belting Association (2011)
Non Commissioned Officers Association (NCOA) (2010, 2012)
North American Association of Floor Covering Distributors (2010)
North American Membrane Society (2011)
North American Neuromodulation Society (2011, 2012)
North American Retail Hardware Association (2011)
North American Skull Base Society (2012)
Not-For-Profit Services Association (2012)

Nuclear Information and Records Management Association (2010)
Office Business Center Association International (2011)
Office Furniture Dealers Alliance (2012)
The Optical Lab Division (2011, 2012)
Packaging Machinery Manufacturers Institute (2011)
Paint and Decorating Retailers Association (2010)
Paperboard Packaging Council (2012)
Petroleum Equipment Institute (2012)
Petroleum Marketers Association of America (2012)
Photo Chemical Machining Institute (2010)
Piano Technicians Guild (2010)
Plumbing-Heating-Cooling Contractors - National Association (2010)
PMA - The Worldwide Community of Imaging Associations (2011)
Polyurethane Manufacturers Association (2010)
Precision Metalforming Association (2012)
Professional Bail Agents of the United States (2010, 2012)
Professional Beauty Association | National Cosmetology Association (2010, 2012)
Professional Convention Management Association (2012)
Professional Golfers Association of America (2010)
Professional Records and Information Services Management International (2012)
Professional Rodeo Cowboys Association (2012)
Promotional Products Association International (2010, 2012)
Public Housing Authorities Directors Association (2010)
Public Radio Program Directors Association (2012)
Qualitative Research Consultants Association (2011)
Radiology Business Management Association (2011)
Real Estate Investment Securities Association (2010, 2012)
Recognition Professionals International (2010)
Recreation Vehicle Dealers Association of North America (2010, 2011, 2012)
Recreation Vehicle Rental Association (2012)
Remanufacturing Institute (2010, 2011)
Restaurant Facility Management Association (2012)
Retail Bakers of America (2012)
Retail Solutions Providers Association (2012)
Roller Skating Association International (2010, 2012)
Rubber Pavements Association (2012)
Satellite Industry Association (2010)
Scaffold Industry Association (2011, 2012)
SCORE Association (2011)
Security Industry Association (2010)
Self Storage Association (2010, 2012)
Service Industry Association (2011)
Sheet Metal and Air Conditioning Contractors' National Association (2012)
Showmen's League of America (2011, 2012)
Society for Advancement of Management (2012)
Society for Cardiovascular Angiography and Interventions (2012)
Society for Clinical Vascular Surgery (2012)
Society for Cross-Cultural Research (2012)
Society for Foodservice Management (2012)
Society for Personality and Social Psychology (2010)
Society for Technological Advancement of Reporting (2010, 2012)
Society for the Scientific Study of Sexuality (2010)
Society for Vascular Medicine (2012)
Society of American Magicians (2012)
Society of Collision Repair Specialists (2012)
Society of Exploration Geophysicists (2012)
Society of Financial Service Professionals (2012)
Society of Glass and Ceramic Decorated Products (2012)
Society of Incentive & Travel Executives (2011, 2012)
Society of Mexican American Engineers and Scientists (2012)
Society of Military Widows (2011)
Society of Professional Journalists (2010)
Society of Radiologists in Ultrasound (2010)
Society of Risk Management Consultants (2012)
Society of Tribologists and Lubrication Engineers (2010)
Society of University Surgeons (2012)
Society of Vertebrate Paleontology (2011)
Souvenir Wholesale Distributors Association (2010)
Specialty Equipment Market Association (2010, 2012)
Specialty Graphic Imaging Association (2010, 2012)
Specialty Sleep Association (2010, 2011, 2012)
SSPC: the Society for Protective Coatings (2011)
Standards Engineering Society (2011)
Steel Deck Institute (2011)
Surgical Infection Society (2010)
System Safety Society (2011)
Taxicab, Limousine & Paratransit Association (2012)
Technology Services Industry Association (2011, 2012)
Tire Industry Association (2011, 2012)
Tobacco Merchants Association of the United States (2012)
Tortilla Industry Association (2010, 2012)
Travel Goods Association (2010, 2012)
Truckload Carriers Association (2010)
Uniform Retailers Association (2011)
Uniformed Services Academy of Family Physicians (2012)
United Producers Formulators and Distributors Association (2012)
United Shoe Retailers Association (2012)
United States Association of Independent Gymnastic Clubs (2011)
United States Clean Heat & Power Association (2011)
United States Soccer Federation (2011)
United States Telecom Association (2012)
United States Trout Farmers Association (2012)
Urban History Association (2010)
User Experience Professionals Association (2012)
Vacuum Dealers Trade Association/Sewing Dealers Trade Association (2010, 2011)
Veterinary Cancer Society (2012)
The Vision Council (2012)
Waste Equipment Technology Association (2012)
Water and Sewer Distributors of America (2012)

Water and Wastewater Equipment Manufacturers Association (2012)
Weather Modification Association (2012)
Wedding and Portrait Photographers International (2012)
Wine and Spirits Wholesalers of America (2010, 2012)
Women's Foodservice Forum (2012)
World Aquaculture Society (2012)
World Floor Covering Association (2012)
World Pet Association (2010, 2012)
World Waterpark Association (2012)
Worldwide ERC (2011)

Laughlin

International Association of Dive Rescue Specialists (2012)

Primm

The Kite Trade Association International (2010)

Reno

Airborne Law Enforcement Association (2012)
Aircraft Electronics Association (2011)
America Outdoors Association (2011)
American Association of Meat Processors (2011)
American Association of School Personnel Administrators (2011)
American Association of Textile Chemists and Colorists (2011)
American Backflow Prevention Association (2012)
American Custom Gunmakers Guild (2012)
American Jail Association (2012)
American Sheep Industry Association (2011)
American Society of Extra-Corporeal Technology (2010)
American Society of Mammalogists (2012)
American Society of Professional Estimators (2012)
Association for Arid Lands Studies (2010)
Association of American Feed Control Officials (2012)
Association of College and University Auditors (2010)
Association of Nurses in AIDS Care (2010)
Association of the Wall and Ceiling Industry (2011)
Association of Water Technologies (2010)
Dairy Management, Inc. (2010)
Developmental Disabilities Nurses Association (2010)
Electrostatic Discharge Association (2010)
Entomological Society of America (2011)
Federation of Analytical Chemistry and Spectroscopy Societies (2011)
Geothermal Energy Association (2012)
Geothermal Resources Council (2012)
Institute of Environmental Sciences and Technology (2010)
Institute of Management Consultants USA (2010)
International Association of Campus Law Enforcement Administrators (2012)
International Community Corrections Association (2011)
International Decorative Artisans League (2012)
International District Energy Association (2010)
International Food Service Executives' Association (2010)
International Institute of Municipal Clerks (2010)
International Window Cleaning Association (2010)
The Knitting Guild Association (2012)
National Alliance of Independent Crop Consultants (2012)
National Animal Control Association (2011)
National Association of Counties (2010)
National Association of County Recorders, Election Officials and Clerks (2010)
National Association of Housing and Redevelopment Officials (2010)
National Association of Housing Cooperatives (2012)
National Association of Postal Supervisors (2010)
National Association of Professional Band Instrument Repair Technicians (2011)
National Association of Rural Health Clinics (2012)
National Association of School Resource Officers (2012)
National Association of Sporting Goods Wholesalers (2011)
National Association of State Workforce Agencies (2012)
National Association of Trailer Manufacturers (2010)
National Council of Juvenile and Family Court Judges (2011)
National Guard Association of the U.S. (2012)
National Guard Executive Directors Association (2012)
National Mobility Equipment Dealers Association (2010)
National Onion Association (2011)
National Translator Association (2010)
North American Gamebird Association (2012)
North American Nature Photography Association (2010)
Paint and Decorating Retailers Association (2012)
Production and Operations Management Society (2011)
Professional Records and Information Services Management International (2010)
Radiant Panel Association (2010)
SAFE Association (2011, 2012)
Soaring Society of America (2012)
Society for Nutrition Education and Behavior (2010)
Spray Polyurethane Foam Alliance (2011)
Substance Abuse Librarians and Information Specialists (2012)
SWANA - Solid Waste Association of North America (2010)
United States Committee on Irrigation and Drainage (2012)
Women in Aviation International (2011)

Stateline

International Energy Credit Association (2011)

Summerlin

Nuclear Information and Records Management Association (2012)

Tahoe

Association of College and University Auditors (2011)

NEW HAMPSHIRE

Manchester

Inter-Society Color Council (2012)
The Knitting Guild Association (2010, 2012)
National Alcohol Beverage Control Association (2012)

Meredith

National Association of State Fire Marshals (2012)

Whitefield

Environmental Council of the States (2010)

NEW JERSEY

Atlantic City

Allied Finance Adjusters (2012)
American Hockey League (2012)
Association of Energy Engineers (2012)
Bowling Proprietors' Association of America (2011)
Brotherhood of Locomotive Engineers and Trainmen (2012)
Concrete Sawing and Drilling Association (2010)
International Association of Auto Theft Investigators (2011)
International Kitchen Exhaust Cleaning Association (2010)
International Society of Weighing and Measurement (2010)
National Association of Elevator Contractors (2012)
National Association of Fire Equipment Distributors (2010, 2012)
National Association of Vertical Transportation Professionals (2012)
Real Estate Buyers Agent Council (2011)
SMMA - The Motor and Motion Association (2011)
World Pet Association (2012)

Bayonne

American Academy of Cosmetic Surgery (2011)

Cape May

Dance Films Association (2011)
Flying Physicians Association (2012)
United States Lifesaving Association (2011)

Cherry Hill

The National Federation of Paralegal Associations, Inc. (2010)

East Brunswick

The Technology Institute for Music Educators (2010)

East Rutherford

International Council of Shopping Centers (2011)

Elizabeth

Council on Undergraduate Research (2012)

Hackensack

Copyright Society of the U.S.A. (2010)

Hamburg

Copyright Society of the U.S.A. (2012)

Hasbrouck Heights

International Fragrance Association North America (2012)

Jersey City

American Society of Group Psychotherapy and Psychodrama (2012)
Flavor and Extract Manufacturers Association (2011)

Livingston

Malignant Hyperthermia Association of the United States (2012)

MacAfee

Society for Values in Higher Education (2012)

Madison

Environmental Industry Associations (2010)

Monroe Twp

American College of Nutrition (2011)

Morristown

American Association of Clinical Endocrinologists (2012)
American College of Nutrition (2012)

New Brunswick

Association of Strategic Alliance Professionals, Inc. (2010)
Consumer Healthcare Products Association (2011)
Healthcare Compliance Packaging Council (2011)

Newark

American Society of Law, Medicine and Ethics (2010)
Chemical Sources Association (2011)
National Association of Women Judges (2011)
Personal Care Products Council (2012)
Society of Flavor Chemists (2012)

Princeton

The Association of Literary Scholars, Critics, and Writers (2010)

Rochester

Cheese Importers Association of America, Inc. (2011)

Saddle Brook

Cheese Importers Association of America, Inc. (2012)

Seaside

American Littoral Society (2012)

Secaucus

Association of Sewing and Design Professionals (2010)
National Association of Independent Fee Appraisers (2012)

Somerset

American Sportfishing Association (2011)
Coblentz Society (2011)

Teaneck

International Fragrance Association North America (2012)

W. Orange

Property Owners Association (2012)
Research Institute for Fragrance Materials (2011, 2012)

NEW MEXICO

Albuquerque

American Association of Bovine Practitioners (2010)
American Association of Physical Anthropologists (2010)
American College of Veterinary Radiology (2011)
American Institute for Conservation of Historic and Artistic Works (2011)
American Society for Eighteenth-Century Studies (2010)
American Society of Heating, Refrigerating and Air Conditioning Engineers (ASHRAE) (2010)
Association of Lutheran Secondary Schools (2010)
Association of TeleServices International, Inc. (2012)
Connected International Meeting Professionals Association (2011)
Environmental and Water Resources Institute of the American Society of Civil Engineers (2012)
Human Biology Association (2010)
International Association of Clerks, Recorders, Election Officials and Treasurers (2012)
International Cost Estimating and Analysis Association effective (2011)
International Microelectronics and Packaging Society - IMAPS (2012)
International Test and Evaluation Association (2010)
Music Teachers National Association (2010)
National Association of Scientific Materials Managers (2012)
National Association of Trailer Manufacturers (2011)
National Environmental Health Association (2010)
Professional Women Controllers (2010)
Society for Cross-Cultural Research (2010)
Society for Developmental Biology (2010)
Vibration Isolation and Seismic Control Manufacturers Association (2010)
Western Music Association (2010)
Young Adult Library Services Association (2010)

Albuquerue

American Agricultural Editors Association (2012)
American Architectural Manufacturers Association (2010)
American Association of Attorney-Certified Public Accountants (2010)
American Board for Certification in Orthotics and Prosthetics, Inc. (ABC) (2011)
American College of Medical Genetics (2010)
American Council for Construction Education (2010)
American Dance Therapy Association (2012)
American Indian Science and Engineering Society (2010)
American Society of Sugar Beet Technologists (2011)
American Water Resources Association (2011)
Animal Behavior Society (2012)
APPA - Leadership in Educational Facilities (2012)
Association for Continuing Higher Education (2010)
The Association for the Study of Play (2012)
Association of Christian Therapists (2010)
Congress on Research in Dance (2012)
Directed Energy Professional Society (2012)
Federation of State Humanities Councils (2010)
Floor Covering Installation Contractors Association (2011)
The Foodservice Group, Inc. (2012)
Handweavers Guild of America, Inc. (2010)
Human Behavior and Evolution Society (2012)
Indian Arts and Crafts Association (2010)
Industrial Asset Management Council (2011)
International Association of Healthcare Central Service Materiel Management (2012)
International Listening Association (2010)
International Society for Computerized Electrocardiology (2010)
International Test and Evaluation Association (2011)
Intertribal Monitoring Association on Indian Trust Funds (2012)
National Association of Government Defined Contribution Administrators (2011)
National Association of Hispanic Publications (2010)
National Association of Professional Geriatric Care Managers (2010)
National Association of Workforce Development Professionals (2010)
National Council for Marketing and Public Relations (2010)
National Extension Association of Family and Consumer Sciences (2011)
National Indian Education Association (2011)
National Mastitis Council (2010)
National Newspaper Association (2011)
National Translator Association (2012)
North American Horticultural Supply Association (2010)
Online Audiovisual Catalogers (2012)
Pedorthic Footwear Association (2011)
Pile Driving Contractors Association (2012)
Restoration Industry Association (2010)
Society for Public Health Education (2011)
Society of American Foresters (2010)
Society of Municipal Arborists (2010)

State Guard Association of the United States (2010)
Text and Academic Authors Association (2011)
United States Hispanic Chamber of Commerce (2011)
Veterinary Cancer Society (2011)
Visual Resources Association (2012)
Western Literature Association (2012)
Western Music Association (2012)
World History Association (2012)

Burro Mountain

Spanish Barb Horse Association (2010)

Carlsbad

North American Corriente Association (2012)

Las Cruces

National Dance Association (2010)

Santa Ana Pueblo

Academy of Prosthodontics (2010)
American Academy of Oral Medicine (2010)
American Architectural Manufacturers Association (2012)
American Association of Acupuncture and Oriental Medicine (2010)
American Association of Genitourinary Surgeons (2010)
American Veterinary Distributors Association (2012)
National Federation of Municipal Analysts (2010)

Santa Fe

American Association for Marriage and Family Therapy (2011)
American Geophysical Union (2011)
American Psychological Association - Division of Psychoanalysis (2012)
American Society for Microbiology (2011)
American Society for Neurochemistry (2010)
American Society of Limnology and Oceanography (2010)
Association for Behavior Analysis International (2012)
Association for Child Psychoanalysis (2012)
Association for Humanist Sociology (2010)
Association for Spiritual, Ethical and Religious Values in Counseling (2012)
Copyright Society of the U.S.A. (2011)
Environmental Bankers Association (2012)
Federal Bar Association (2010)
Independent Turf and Ornamental Distributors Association (2010)
Metal Powder Industries Federation (2010)
National Association of Government Archives and Records Administrators (2012)
National Association of State Park Directors (2010)
National Conference of Insurance Legislators (2011)
Powder Metallurgy Parts Association (2010)
Professional Insurance Marketing Association (2012)
Society for Cultural Anthropology (2010)
The Society for Freshwater Science (2010)
Society for the History of Discoveries (2010)
Society of Rheology (2010)
Society of Risk Management Consultants (2010)
Universities Council on Water Resources (2012)

NEW YORK

Albany

American College of Occupational and Environmental Medicine (2011)
Association of YMCA Professionals (2011)
International Association of Milk Control Agencies (2011)
Iroquois Healthcare Alliance (2012)
National Association of Disability Examiners (2010)

Binghamton

American Folklore Society (2011)
International Association of Personnel in Employment Security (2012)
International Association of Workforce Professionals (IAWP) (2012)

Bolton Landing

Copyright Society of the U.S.A. (2011)
Management Association for Private Photogrammetric Surveyors (2011)

Bronxville

National Association of Personal Financial Advisors (2011)

Brooklyn

American Dance Therapy Association (2010)
American Hungarian Educators Association (2012)
Color Marketing Group (2010)
Freelancers Union (2012)
Romanian-American Chamber of Commerce (2010)

Buffalo

Canon Law Society of America (2010)
Consortium of College and University Media Centers (2010)
Interstate Oil and Gas Compact Commission (2011)
National Association of Academic Advisors for Athletes (2012)
National Garden Clubs (2012)
North American Association for Environmental Education (2010)
Radical Philosophy Association (2012)
United States Animal Health Association (2011)

Chelsea

Association of Real Estate Women (2012)

Coila

Agricultural Stewardship Association (2012)

Corning

American Scientific Glassblowers Society (2012)

E. Elmhurst

Indian Dental Association (USA) (2010)

Flushing

Indian Dental Association (USA) (2012)

Garden City

Subcontractors Trade Association (2012)

Hempstead

Italian American Studies Association (2012)

Hilton

Women in Cable Telecommunications, Inc. (2011)

Ithaca

American Dairy Products Institute (2010)
National Association of Convenience Stores (2012)
North American Flowerbulb Wholesalers Association (2010)
United Fresh Produce Association (2012)

Lake George

Institute on Religion in an Age of Science (2012)
National Volunteer Fire Council (2011)

Lake Placid

American Council of Snowmobile Associations (2012)

New Paltz

Center for Exhibition Industry Research (2011)

New York City

The Academy of American Poets (2010)
Academy of Criminal Justice Sciences (2012)
Academy of Security Educators and Trainers (2010)
The Advertising Research Foundation (2011, 2012)
Africa Travel Association (2010)
Alliance for Children and Families (2010)
American Academy of Appellate Lawyers (2012)
American Academy of Child and Adolescent Psychiatry (2010)
American Academy of Dermatology (2011)
American Academy of Oral Medicine (2012)
American Academy of Pediatric Dentistry (2011)
American Advertising Federation (2011, 2012)
American Artists Professional League (2012)
American Association for Justice (2011)
American Association of Advertising Agencies (2012)
American Association of Attorney-Certified Public Accountants (2011)
American Association of Community Theatre (2012)
American Association of Exporters & Importers (2010)
American Association of Political Consultants (2011)
American Board of Quality Assurance and Utilization Review Physicians, Inc. (2012)
American Booksellers Association (2010)
American Chemical Society (2012)
American Cinema Editors (2010)
American Coal Council (2011, 2012)
American College of Cardiology (2011)
American College of Mohs Surgeons (2010)
American College of Nutrition (2010)
American College of Trial Lawyers (2012)
American Collegiate Retailing Association (2011)
American Council of Independent Laboratories (2012)
American Diabetes Association (2012)
American Group Psychotherapy Association (2011, 2012)
American Harp Society (2012)
American Hernia Society (2012)
American Hotel & Lodging Association (AH&LA) (2010, 2012)
American Import Shippers Association (2011, 2012)
American Institute of Chemical Engineers (2012)
American Institute of Graphic Arts (2010)
American Institute of Marine Underwriters (2012)
American Institute of Ultrasound in Medicine (2011)
American Intellectual Property Law Association (2010)
American Numismatic Society (2010)
American Psychoanalytic Association (2010, 2011, 2012)
American Psychological Association (2010)
American Psychopathological Association (2011)
American Road and Transportation Builders Association (2010)
American Skin Association (2011, 2012)
American Society for Mohs Histotechnology (2010)
American Society for Stereotactic and Functional Neurosurgery (2010)
American Society for the Alexander Technique (2012)
American Society of Clinical Psychopharmacology (2012)
American Society of Geolinguistics (2010)
American Society of Hypertension, Inc. (2010, 2011, 2012)
American Society of Journalists and Authors (2010, 2011, 2012)
American Society of Media Photographers (2012)
American Society of Neuroradiology (2012)
American Society of Pharmacognosy (2012)
American Society of Picture Professionals (2012)
American Stamp Dealers Association (2010, 2011, 2012)
American Waterways Operators (2011)
Analytical and Life Science Systems Association (2010)
Antiquarian Booksellers Association of America (2012)
Appraisers Association of America (2010, 2011, 2012)

Art and Antique Dealers League of America (2012)
Art Dealers Association of America (2010, 2012)
Association for Library Collections and Technical Services (2010)
Association for Retail Environments (2010, 2011)
Association for the Study of Food and Society (2012)
Association for the Study of Nationalities (2010, 2012)
Association of American Geographers (2012)
The Association of Average Adjusters of the United States and Canada (2012)
Association of Cable Communicators (2010)
Association of Educational Publishers (2011)
Association of Executive Search Consultants (2010, 2011, 2012)
Association of Foreign Investors in U.S. Real Estate (2012)
Association of Insolvency and Restructuring Advisors (2011, 2012)
The Association of International Photography Art Dealers (2010, 2012)
Association of Investment Management Sales Executives (2012)
Association of National Advertisers (2012)
Association of Performing Arts Presenters (2010, 2011, 2012)
Association of Professional Design Firms (2010)
Association of Research Libraries (2012)
Association of Theatrical Press Agents and Managers (2011, 2012)
Audio Engineering Society (2011)
Audio Publishers Association (2010, 2012)
Audit Bureau of Circulations (2012)
Bibliographical Society of America (2010, 2011)
Black Retail Action Group (2010)
Book Industry Study Group, Inc. (2010, 2012)
Business for Social Responsibility (2012)
Center for Exhibition Industry Research (2012)
Chamber Music America (2011)
Child Care Aware of America (2011)
Chinese American Medical Society (2010, 2012)
The Clearing House Association (2012)
Coal Trading Association (2012)
College Media Association (2010, 2012)
Columbia Scholastic Press Association (2012)
Commercial Finance Association (2011)
Commercial Law League of America (2010, 2011, 2012)
NAIOP, The Commercial Real Estate Development Association (2012)
Community Action Partnership (2012)
The Concrete Industry Board (2012)
The Conference Board (2011, 2012)
Council for Opportunity in Education (2012)
Council of American Survey Research Organizations (2010, 2012)
Council of Literary Magazines and Presses (2011)
Council of Protocol Executives (2010, 2012)
Council of State Governments (2010)
CRE Finance Council (2010, 2011)
Cremation Association of North America (2011)
Custom Tailors and Designers Association of America (2012)
Dance Critics Association (2012)
Design Management Institute (2011, 2012)
Direct Marketing Association (2012)
Distributive Education Clubs of America (DECA) (2012)
The Door and Hardware Institute (2011)
Educational Theatre Association (2010)
EMTA - Trade Association for the Emerging Markets (2011, 2012)
Evangelical Christian Publishers Association (2012)
Fashion Group International (2011, 2012)
Financial Executives International (2010, 2011, 2012)
Financial Industry Regulatory Authority (FINRA) (2012)
Financial Management Association International (2010)
The Foodservice Group, Inc. (2012)
The Fragrance Foundation (2010, 2011)
Fulfillment Management Association (2012)
Futures Industry Association (2010, 2012)
Gases and Welding Distributors Association (2011)
Global Association of Risk Professionals (2011, 2012)
Greeting Card Association (2010, 2012)
Hedge Fund Association (2011)
Historians of Islamic Art Association (2012)
Home Fashion Products Association (2012)
Human Capital Institute (2012)
Human Resource People and Strategy (2012)
Independent Filmmaker Project (2012)
Institute of General Semantics (2011, 2012)
Institute of Noise Control Engineering (2012)
Institute of Store Planners (2012)
Insured Retirement Institute (2012)
Intercoiffure America/Canada (2010, 2012)
Intercollegiate Broadcasting System (2010)
International Academy of Television Arts and Sciences (2011)
International Association for Corporate and Professional Recruitment (2012)
International Association of Business Communicators (2012)
International Association of Credit Portfolio Managers (2012)
International Association of Culinary Professionals (2012)
International Association of Milk Control Agencies (2011)
International Corrugated Packaging Foundation (2010)
International Council of Shopping Centers (2011, 2012)
International Federation of Pharmaceutical Wholesalers (2012)
International Fine Print Dealers Association (2012)
International Licensing Industry Merchandisers' Association (2011, 2012)
International Newspaper Marketing Association (2010)
International Pediatric Nephrology Association (2010)
International Society for the Performing Arts (2012)
International Swaps and Derivatives Association (2012)
International Women's Writing Guild (2010, 2011, 2012)
Investment Casting Institute (2010)
Investment Company Institute (2011, 2012)
Investment Management Consultants Association (2011)
Ireland Chamber of Commerce in the United States (2010, 2012)

Italian American Studies Association (2010)
Italy-America Chamber of Commerce (2010)
Jewish Book Council (2011)
Jewish Community Centers Association of North America (2011)
Loan Syndication & Trading Association (2012)
Managed Funds Association (2011)
Manufacturing Jewelers and Suppliers of America (2010, 2011, 2012)
Maritime Law Association of the U.S. (2012)
Money Management Institute (2010, 2012)
Mortgage Bankers Association of America (2010)
Music Publishers Association of the United States (2012)
Mutual Fund Education Alliance (2012)
NALP - The Association for Legal Career Professionals (2011, 2012)
National Alliance for Musical Theatre (2010)
National Art Education Association (2012)
National Association for Business Economics (2012)
National Association for Multi-Ethnicity in Communications (2012)
National Association for the Advancement of Psychoanalysis (2012)
National Association for the Specialty Food Trade (2010)
National Association of Corporate Treasurers (2012)
National Association of Legal Search Consultants (2010)
National Association of Professors of Hebrew (2010)
National Association of Publishers' Representatives (2011)
National Association of Real Estate Investment Trusts (NAREIT) (2010, 2011)
National Association of Recording Merchandisers (NARM) (2011)
National Association of State Treasurers (2011)
National Association of Steel Pipe Distributors (2012)
National Association of Women Lawyers (2012)
National Auto Auction Association (2010)
National Club Association (2012)
National Conference on Public Employee Retirement Systems (2012)
National Council of Juvenile and Family Court Judges (2011)
National Electrical Manufacturers Representatives Association (2010)
National Finishing Contractors Association (2010)
National Lipid Association (2011)
National Music Publishers Association (2010)
The National Network for Social Work Managers (2010)
National Retail Federation (2011, 2012)
National Shoe Retailers Association (2011)
New America Alliance (2012)
The New York Academy of Sciences (2011, 2012)
North American Catalysis Society (2012)
NPTA Alliance (2010, 2012)
Phi Delta Epsilon International Medical Fraternity (2012)
Picture Archive Council of America (2010)
Portugal-US Chamber of Commerce (2012)
Professional Liability Underwriting Society (2012)
Professional Women Photographers (2011)
The Public Relations Society of America (2012)
Romance Writers of America (2011)
Romanian-American Chamber of Commerce (2012)
Securities Industry and Financial Markets Association (SIFMA) (2010, 2011, 2012)
Security Industry Association (2010)
Smart Card Alliance (2010)
Social Venture Network (2012)
Society for Ancient Greek Philosophy (2010, 2012)
Society for Sex Therapy and Research (2011, 2012)
Society for the Advancement of American Philosophy (2012)
Society for the Psychological Study of Men and Masculinity (2012)
Society of Actuaries (2010)
Society of American Business Editors and Writers (2010, 2012)
Society of Chemical Manufacturers and Affiliates Inc. (2011)
Society of Children's Book Writers and Illustrators (2012)
Society of Cosmetic Chemists (2010, 2011)
Society of Insurance Financial Management (2010, 2011)
Society of Laparoendoscopic Surgeons (2010)
Society of Motion Picture and Television Engineers (2011)
Society of Neurointerventional Surgery (2012)
Society of Scribes (2011)
Student Youth and Travel Association (2011)
Substance Abuse Librarians and Information Specialists (2010)
Television Bureau of Advertising (2012)
Tennis Industry Association (2012)
Theatre Communications Group (2011)
Toy Industry Association (2011)
United Spinal Association (2012)
United States Association of Importers of Textiles and Apparel (2011, 2012)
United States Tennis Association (2010)
University/Resident Theatre Association (2011)
Urban History Association (2012)
Women in Cable Telecommunications, Inc. (2012)
World Trade Centers Association (2011)

Niagara Falls

Association of Official Seed Certifying Agencies (2010)
CALLERLAB - International Association of Square Dance Callers (2010)
North American Association of Wardens and Superintendents (2010)

Port Jefferson

The Association of Concert Bands (2012)

Poughkeepsie

Environmental Industry Associations (2010)

Queens

Subcontractors Trade Association (2010)

Rochester

Alliance of Information and Referral Systems (2010)
American Edged Products Manufacturers Association (2012)

American Literary Translators Association (2012)
The Association for the Study of Play (2011)
Atlantic Seaboard Wine Association (2011)
National Association of States United For Aging and Disabilities (2010)
Optical Society of America (2010)
Phi Chi Theta (2012)
Society for Historians of the Early American Republic (2010)
Society for Phenomenology and Existential Philosophy (2012)
SPIE - The International Society for Optical Engineering (2011)

Rye Brook

Social Venture Network (2012)

Saratoga Springs

Association of Metropolitan Planning Organizations (2012)
Semiconductor Equipment and Materials International (2012)

Schenectady

League of Historic American Theatres (2011)

Silver Bay

International Association of Conference Center Administrators (2012)

Stony Brook

National Association of Puerto Rican-Hispanic Social Workers (2012)

Suffern

American Sportfishing Association (2011)

Syracuse

American Association of Zoo Keepers (2012)
Epsilon Sigma Phi (2011)
History of Economics Society (2010)

Troy

AVS: Science and Technology of Materials, Interfaces, and Processing (2010)

Uniondale

North American Catalysis Society (2012)
Scientific Equipment and Furniture Association (2012)

Verona

American Association for Physical Activity and Recreation (2011)

White Plains

Club Managers Association of America (2010)

Woodbury

National Association of Diaconate Directors (2012)

NORTH CAROLINA

Aberdeen

International Association of Conference Center Administrators (2010)

Asheville

AGN International North America, Inc (2010)
American Association for Agricultural Education (2012)
American Association for Marriage and Family Therapy (2012)
American Coke and Coal Chemicals Institute (2010)
American College of Veterinary Radiology (2010)
American School Band Directors' Association (2012)
Associated Wire Rope Fabricators (2010)
Association for Financial Technology (2012)
Association of Environmental and Resource Economists (2012)
Association of Marketing Service Providers (2012)
Casting Industry Suppliers Association (2011)
Choristers Guild (2010)
International Association for Business and Society (2012)
International Association for the Study of Dreams (2010)
International Association of Defense Counsel (2012)
National Poultry and Food Distributors Association (2010)
North American Millers' Association (2012)
Pellet Fuels Institute (2010)
Product Liability Advisory Council (2012)
Research and Development Associates for Military Food and Packaging Systems (2012)
Society of International Business Fellows (2012)
Turfgrass Producers International (2012)

Boone

Eastern Apicultural Society of North America (2010)

Cary

Cleveland Bay Horse Society of North America (2012)

Chapel Hill

National Association of Clean Water Agencies (2012)
Ophthalmic Photographers' Society (2012)

Charlotte

Academy of Surgical Research (2012)
American Association for Marriage and Family Therapy (2012)
American Association of Motor Vehicle Administrators (2012)
American Association of Physicists in Medicine (2012)
American Association of Textile Chemists and Colorists (2012)
American College of Medical Genetics (2012)
American Concrete Pipe Association (2011)
American Society of Plumbing Engineers (2012)

American Society of Women Accountants (ACC) (2011)
American Subcontractors Association (2012)
Appliance Parts Distributors Association (2011)
Architectural Woodwork Institute (2011)
ASM International (2012)
Asphalt Recycling and Reclaiming Association (2012)
Association for the Advancement of Medical Instrumentation (2012)
Association for the Study of Higher Education (2011)
Association of Equipment Manufacturers (2012)
Association of Schools of Allied Health Professions (2010)
Association of the Wall and Ceiling Industry (2012)
Automotive Recyclers Association (2011)
Ceilings and Interior Systems Construction Association (2012)
Cervical Spine Research Society (2010)
Communications Media Management Association (2011)
Credit Professionals International (2011)
Electronic Security Association (2011)
EUCG, Inc. (2011)
Federation of State Boards of Physical Therapy (2011)
General Federation of Women's Clubs (2012)
Geochemical Society (2012)
Geological Society of America (2012)
Geoscience Information Society (2012)
Health Industry Distributors Association (2011)
Institute for Operations Research and the Management Sciences (2011)
Institute of Certified Business Counselors (2011)
International Association of Campus Law Enforcement Administrators (2011)
International Association of Dive Rescue Specialists (2010)
International Brotherhood of Teamsters (2012)
International Downtown Association (2011)
International Economic Development Council (2011)
International Society of Certified Employee Benefit Specialists (2010)
International Technology and Engineering Educators Association (2010)
Lift Manufacturers Product Section - Material Handling Institute (2011)
Material Handling Industry of America (2010, 2012)
Mineralogical Society of America (2012)
NAFA Fleet Management Association (2011)
National Association for Campus Activities (2012)
National Conference of State Fleet Administrators (2011)
The National Flute Association, Inc. (2011)
National Foundation for Credit Counseling (2012)
National Funeral Directors Association (2012)
National Grange (2010)
National Lipid Association (2012)
National Rifle Association of America (2010)
National School Public Relations Association (2010)
National Society for Experiential Education (2010)
National Stone, Sand, and Gravel Association (2012)
Nuclear Energy Institute (2010)
Parenting Media Association (2010)
Public Relations Student Society of America (2012)
Quality Service Contractors (2012)
Rubber Pavements Association (2012)
Self Storage Association (2011)
SEPM - Society for Sedimentary Geology (2012)
Single Ply Roofing Institute (2012)
Society for the Advancement of American Philosophy (2010)
SWANA - Solid Waste Association of North America (2010)
Synthetic Yarn and Fiber Association (2012)
Urban Financial Services Coalition (2012)
The Wound, Ostomy and Continence Nurses Society (2012)

Clemmons

American Association for Chinese Studies (2010)
American Classical League (2010)

Concord

American Embryo Transfer Association (2010)
Herb Growing and Marketing Network (2012)
Society of Vertebrate Paleontology (2012)

Durham

Air and Waste Management Association (2012)
American Genetic Association (2012)
Association of Academic Chairmen of Plastic Surgery (2010)
Association of Ancient Historians (2012)
INDA, Association of the Nonwoven Fabrics Industry (2012)
International Society of Automation (2010)
International Society of Protistologists (2012)
National Association of Graduate-Professional Students (2012)
National Association of Science Writers (2012)
Society of Pelvic Surgeons (2010)

Fayetteville

United States Army Warrant Officers Association (2011)

Greensboro

American Association of Veterinary Laboratory Diagnosticians (2012)
Brick Industry Association (2012)
The Knitting Guild Association (2011)
National Auctioneers Association (2010)
National Forum for Black Public Administrators (2010)
Refrigerating Engineers and Technicians Association (2011)
Society for Maintenance & Reliability Professionals (2011)
United States Animal Health Association (2012)
United States Synchronized Swimming (2012)

High Point

National Home Furnishings Association (2012)

Lake Junaluska

Fellowship of United Methodists in Music and Worship Arts (2012)

Myrtle Beach

Association of Industrial Metallizers, Coaters and Laminators (2012)

New Bern

Council On Forest Engineering (2012)

Pinehurst

American Society of Concrete Contractors (2011)
Employee Stock Ownership Plan Association (2012)
Executive Women's Golf Association (2010)
Independent Lubricant Manufacturers Association (2012)
United States Industrial Fabrics Institute (2010)
Waterproofing Contractors Association (2012)

Raleigh

American Aging Association (2011)
American Association for Physical Activity and Recreation (2012)
American Association of Textile Chemists and Colorists (2012)
American Cheese Society (2012)
American Journalism Historians Association (2012)
American Massage Therapy Association (2012)
American Peanut Research and Education Society, Inc. (2012)
American Solar Energy Society (2011)
Association for the Study of African American Life and History (2010)
Cotton Incorporated (2012)
Delta Theta Phi (2011)
Federation of Analytical Chemistry and Spectroscopy Societies (2010)
IEEE Power Electronics Society (2012)
INDA, Association of the Nonwoven Fabrics Industry (2011)
Inter-Society Color Council (2010)
International Microelectronics and Packaging Society - IMAPS (2010)
International Society for Pharmacoepidemiology (2010)
National Black Association for Speech, Language and Hearing (2012)
National Conference of Black Political Scientists (2011)
National Weather Service Employees Organization (2011)
North American Association for Environmental Education (2011)
North American Association of Christians in Social Work (2010)
Parapsychological Association (2012)
Sigma Xi, The Scientific Research Society (2010)
Society for In Vitro Biology (2011)
The Society for Investigative Dermatology (2012)
Society for Vector Ecology (2010)
Special Interest Group on Security, Audit, and Control (2012)
Visitor Studies Association (2012)
Water Environment Federation (2012)

Research Triangle Park

Christian Medical & Dental Associations (2010)

Wilmington

Attention Deficit Disorder Association (2011)
Institute for Business & Home Safety (2011)
League of Historic American Theatres (2010)
National Institute for Farm Safety, Incorporation (2010)
Waterproofing Contractors Association (2010)

Winston-Salem

Black Theatre Network (2011)

NORTH DAKOTA

Bismarck

Lignite Energy Council (2010, 2011)
National Association of State Treasurers (2011)

Fargo

American Meat Science Association (2012)

Minot

Columbia Sheep Breeders Association of America (2010)
United States Durum Growers Association (2011)

W. Fargo

Pyrotechnics Guild International (2011)

OHIO

Athens

Alpha Chi Sigma Fraternity, Inc. (2010)

Blue Ash

Equipment Service Association (2012)

Bowling Green

National Association of Local Boards of Health (2010)

Cincinnati

Academy of Managed Care Pharmacy (2012)
American Chemical Society - Rubber Division (2012)
American Concrete Institute (2011)
American Criminal Justice Association Lambda Alpha Epsilon (2012)
American Gear Manufacturers Association (2011)
American Jail Association (2011)
American Oil Chemists' Society (2011)
American Society of Agronomy (ASA, CSSA, SSSA) (2012)

American Society of Highway Engineers (2010)
American Trakehner Association (2012)
American Wine Society (2010)
ASM International (2011)
Association for Practical and Professional Ethics (2010, 2011, 2012)
The Association for Research in Business Education - Delta Pi Epsilon (2012)
Association of Collegiate Schools of Planning (2012)
Association of Equipment Manufacturers (2010)
Association of Pet Dog Trainers (2012)
Association of Public Health Laboratories (2010)
Association of Women Soil Scientists (2012)
Commission on Accreditation for Law Enforcement Agencies Incorporation (2011)
Community Development Society (2012)
Construction Users Roundtable (2012)
Council for Advancement and Support of Education (2012)
Crop Science Society of America (2012)
Forging Industry Association (2010)
Glass Manufacturing Industry Council (2012)
Governors' Highway Safety Association (2011)
Healthcare Billing and Management Association (2012)
Institute Management Accountants (2011)
International Concrete Repair Institute (2011)
International Council for Small Business (2010)
Lutheran Education Association (2011)
National Association for Pupil Transportation (2011)
National Association of Intercollegiate Athletics (2010)
National Association of Schools of Art and Design (2010)
National Association of Schools of Theatre (2012)
National Association of State Directors of Teacher Education and Certification (2012)
National Conference of Black Mayors (2010)
National Correctional Industries Association (2010)
National Genealogical Society (2012)
National Industries for the Blind (2010)
National Private Truck Council (2010, 2011, 2012)
National Renderers Association (2010)
National Rural Education Association (2012)
National Society for Histotechnology (2011)
National Stone, Sand, and Gravel Association (2010)
National Student Employment Association (2010)
National Student Nurses Association (2010)
Organization of Black Designers (2012)
Railway Systems Suppliers, Inc (2012)
Society for Ear, Nose and Throat Advances in Children (2010)
Society for Industrial Archeology (2012)
Society of Hispanic Professional Engineers (2010)
Society of Quality Assurance (2010)
Soil Science Society of America (2012)
Unfinished Furniture Association (2010)

Cleaveland

American Association of Critical-Care Nurses (2012)
American Association of Family and Consumer Sciences (2010)
American Chemical Society - Rubber Division (2011)
American College of Occupational and Environmental Medicine (2011)
American Hungarian Educators Association (2011)
American Music Therapy Association (2010)
American Prepaid Legal Services Institute (2012)
Association for Education and Rehabilitation of the Blind & Visually Impaired (2011)
Association for Play Therapy (2012)
Association of Independent Information Professionals (2010)
Association of Professional Landscape Designers (2011)
Association of University Anesthesiologists (2012)
Catholic Theological Society of America (2010)
Conference of Minority Transportation Officials (2010)
Council of State Governments (2012)
Ductile Iron Society (2010)
Environmental Design Research Association (2012)
Fluid Controls Institute (2012)
Forging Industry Association (2012)
Healthcare Compliance Packaging Council (2012)
History of Science Society (2011)
Hobby Manufacturers Association (2012)
Hydraulic Institute (2010)
Industrial Heating Equipment Association (2012)
National Academies of Practice (2012)
National Academy of Arbitrators (2010)
National Association of Graphic and Product Identification Manufacturers (2012)
National Association of Health Unit Coordinators (2012)
National Association of Medical Examiners (2010)
National Association of Neighborhoods (2012)
National Association of Regional Councils (2010)
Oral History Association (2012)
Society for News Design (2012)
Society for the History of Technology (2011)
Society for Vascular Medicine (2010)
Society of Rheology (2011)
Violin Society of America (2010)

Columbus

Academy of Accounting Historians (2010)
American Association of Blacks in Energy (2010)
American Association of Credit Union Leagues (2012)
The American Association of Radon Scientists and Technologists (2010)
American Bryological and Lichenological Society (2012)
American Business Media (2012)
American Ceramics Society (2011)
American Cleaning Institute (2012)
American Foundry Society (2012)

American Public Gardens Association (2012)
American Public Power Association (2010)
American Society of Plant Taxonomists (2012)
Archery Range and Retailers Organization (2010, 2012)
Archery Trade Association (2010, 2012)
ASM International (2011)
Association for Behavior Analysis International (2012)
Association of Science-Technology Centers (2012)
Association of Women's Health, Obstetric and Neonatal Nurses (2011)
The Botanical Society of America (2012)
Conference of Radiation Control Program Directors (2010)
Council on Governmental Ethics Laws (2012)
Game Manufacturers Association (2010, 2011, 2012)
Insurance Loss Control Association (2010, 2012)
International Economic Development Council (2010)
International Society for Ecological Modelling-North American Chapter (2012)
National Animal Control Association (2010)
National Association for Developmental Education (2010)
National Association of Disability Examiners (2012)
National Association of Jewelry Appraisers (2010)
National Association of Personal Financial Advisors (2011)
National Association of Professional Organizers (2010)
National Association of State & Local Equity Funds (2011)
National Council of Art Administrators (2012)
National Environmental Health Association (2011)
National Extension Association of Family and Consumer Sciences (2012)
National Ground Water Association (2012)
National Guild of Professional Paperhangers (2012)
National Intramural-Recreational Sports Association (2012)
The National NeedleArts Association (2011)
National School Boards Association (2012)
North American Die Casting Association (2012)
Phi Beta Fraternity (2012)
Power Washers of North America (2010)
Precision Machined Products Association (2011)
Pressure Vessel Manufacturers Association (2011)
Society of Broadcast Engineers (2011)
Society of Composers, Inc. (2012)
Society of Ethnobiology (2011)
Teaching-Family Association (2010)
Violin Society of America (2012)
Women's International Network of Utility Professionals (2012)

Dayton

Association for Hose and Accessories Distribution (2010)
Professional Aviation Maintenance Association (2011)

Dublin

American College of Nurse Practitioners (2011)

Huron

National Christmas Tree Association (2011)

Lima

American Poultry Association (2010)

Loudonville

Society of Chemical Manufacturers and Affiliates Inc. (2012)

Marysville

American Shropshire Registry Association (2011)

Middleburg Heights

U.S.A. Toy Library Association (2012)

Oregon

International Double Reed Society (2012)

Perrysburg

Guild of Artists and Artisans (2011)

Sandusky

North American Raspberry & Blackberry Association (2012)
The Paddlesports Industry Association (2011)

Toledo

Glass Art Society (2012)
North American Deer Farmers Association (2010)

Westerville

Association of Christian Schools International (2012)

Westlake

Guild of Artists and Artisans (2011)

Wooster

Columbia Sheep Breeders Association of America (2012)

Worthington

American Society of Home Inspectors (2011)

OKLAHOMA

Duncan

National Swine Registry (2011, 2012)

Lone Wolf

National Solid Wastes Management Association (2012)

Norman

International Double Reed Society (2010)
National Association of Blacks in Criminal Justice (2012)

Oklahoma City

American Association for State and Local History (2010)
American Association of Advertising Agencies (2011)
American Association of Women Dentists (2011)
American Shire Horse Association (2010)
Association of Public Treasurers of the United States and Canada (2011)
Association of Racing Commissioners International (2012)
Association of Social Work Boards (2011)
Association of State Floodplain Managers (2010)
Communications Supply Service Association (2011)
Council for Community and Economic Research (2012)
Kappa Kappa Iota-National (2010)
Livestock Marketing Association (2010)
National Association of EMS Educators (2012)
National Association of Postmasters of the United States (2012)
National Association of Royalty Owners (2012)
National Association of State Auditors, Comptrollers and Treasurers (2012)
National Council of Structural Engineers Associations (2011)
National Indian Education Association (2012)
National Society of Accountants (2010)
National Truck and Heavy Equipment Claims Council (2012)
Organization for the Study of Sex Differences (2011)
Pinto Horse Association of America (2011, 2012)
Truck-frame and Axle Repair Association (2012)
United States Conference of Mayors (2010)
United States Rowing Association (2012)

Ridgedale

American Poultry Association (2010)

Stillwater

American Dexter Cattle Association (2011)

Tulsa

American Academy of Cosmetic Surgery (2011)
American Buckskin Registry Association (2010)
American Design Drafting Association International and American Digital Design Association (2012)
American Shetland Pony Club/American Miniature Horse Registry (2010)
Association for Women in Communications (2011)
Association of Specialty Cut Flower Growers (2010)
International Academy of Oral Medicine and Toxicology (2012)
Mental Health America (2012)
National Association of County Agricultural Agents (2010)
National Grange (2011)
Palomino Horse Breeders of America (2012)
Welsh Pony and Cob Society of America (2012)

OREGON

Corvallis

Potato Association of America (2010)
Society of Nematologists (2011)

Eugene

Association for Direct Instruction (2010)
Radical Philosophy Association (2010)

Forest Grove

Optometric Extension Program Foundation (2012)

Klamath Falls

United States Potato Board (2012)

Medford

The Foodservice Group, Inc. (2012)

Mississauga

Conference on Faith and History (2010)

Portland

Academy of Marketing Science (2010)
American Academy of Environmental Medicine (2011)
American Association for Aerosol Research (2010)
American Association of Naturopathic Physicians (2010)
American Association of Physics Teachers (2010)
American Association of Suicidology (2011)
American Association of Wildlife Veterinarians (2012)
American Board of Professional Psychology (2010)
American Botanical Council (2012)
American Chiropractic Association (2011)
American College for Advancement in Medicine (2011)
American College of Veterinary Ophthalmologists (2012)
American Criminal Justice Association Lambda Alpha Epsilon (2010)
American Dialect Society (2012)
American Farrier's Association (2012)
American Geophysical Union (2010)
American Hanoverian Society (2011)
American Institute of Building Design (2010)
American Institute of Inspectors (2010, 2011, 2012)
American Jail Association (2010)
American Malting Barley Association (2012)
American Massage Therapy Association (2011)
American Name Society (2012)

American Physical Society (2010)
American Psychosomatic Society (2010)
American Society for Colposcopy and Cervical Pathology (2010)
American Society for Enology and Viticulture (2012)
American Society for Environmental History (2010)
American Society of Brewing Chemists (2012)
American Society of Echocardiography (2011)
American Society of Limnology and Oceanography (2010)
The American Society of Naturalists (2010)
American Wine Society (2012)
APA The Engineered Wood Association (2012)
ASFE/The Geoprofessional Business Association (2010)
Association for Computational Linguistics (2011)
Association for Dressings and Sauces (2010)
Association for Middle Level Education (2012)
The Association for Social Anthropology in Oceania (2011)
Association for University and College Counseling Center Directors (2010)
Association for Women in Psychology (2010)
Association of American Editorial Cartoonists (2010)
Association of Baccalaureate Social Work Program Directors (2012)
Association of Children's Museums (2012)
Association of Community Health Nursing Educators (2012)
Association of Energy Services Professionals, International (2010)
Association of Graduate Liberal Studies Programs (2012)
The Association of Medical Illustrators (2010)
Association of Metropolitan Water Agencies (2012)
Association of Pediatric Oncology Social Workers (2012)
Association of State and Territorial Health Officials (2011)
Association of University Programs in Health Administration (2010)
College Theology Society (2010)
Commercial Vehicle Safety Alliance (2012)
Controlled Release Society (2010)
Council of Development Finance Agencies (2010)
Council of State and Territorial Epidemiologists (2010)
Council on Social Work Education (2010)
Ecological Society of America (2012)
Emergency Nurses Association (2011)
Energy and Environmental Building Association (2010)
Fermenters International Trade Association (2010)
The Foodservice Group, Inc. (2012)
Forest Products Society (2011)
The Handcrafted Soapmakers Guild (2012)
Human Biology Association (2012)
Industrial Designers Society of America (2010)
Institute of Navigation (2010, 2011)
Institute of Noise Control Engineering (2011)
International Association of Approved Basketball Officials, Inc. (2010)
International Association of Culinary Professionals (2010)
The International Ecotourism Society (2010)
International Firestop Council (2012)
International Institute of Municipal Clerks (2012)
International Ombudsman Association (2011)
International Society of Arboriculture (2012)
Journalism Education Association (2010)
Linguistic Society of America (2012)
Marketing and Advertising Global Network (2012)
Microanalysis Society (2010)
Microscopy Society of America (2010)
NALS (2012)
NASTD - Technology Professionals Serving State Government (2010)
National Association for Pupil Transportation (2010)
National Association of Black County Officials (2011)
National Association of Clinical Nurse Specialists (2010)
National Association of Counties (2011)
National Association of County Recorders, Election Officials and Clerks (2011)
National Association of Document Examiners (2010)
National Association of Environmental Professionals (2012)
National Association of Long Term Care Administrator Boards (2010)
National Association of State Budget Officers (2010)
National Association of State Directors of Migrant Education (2012)
National Association of Temple Administrators (2010)
National College of Probate Judges (2010)
National Conference on Weights and Measures (2012)
National Council for Geographic Education (2011)
National Council on Public History (2010)
National Federation of Federal Employees (2012)
National Federation of Federal Employees, Federal Dist. 1, IAMAW, AFL-CIO (2012)
National Guardianship Association (2012)
National Onion Association (2010)
National Rural Economic Developers Association (2010)
National Scholastic Press Association (2010)
National Staff Development and Training Association (2012)
Native American Contractors Association (2011)
North American Association of Central Cancer Registries (2012)
North American Cartographic Information Society (2012)
North American Small Business International Trade Educators (2012)
The Oceanography Society (2010)
Passenger Vessel Association (2012)
Perennial Plant Association (2010)
Public Library Association (2010)
Public Risk Management Association (2011)
Refrigerating Engineers and Technicians Association (2010)
SAVE International (2011)
Seismological Society of America (2010)
Shock Society (2010)
Society for Pediatric Dermatology (2010)
Society for Psychophysiological Research (2010)
Society for the Study of Evolution (2010)
Society for the Study of Indigenous Languages of the Americas (2012)

Society for the Study of Reproduction (2011)
Society for Thermal Medicine (2012)
Society for Values in Higher Education (2010)
Society of Environmental Toxicology and Chemistry (2010)
Society of Fire Protection Engineers (2011)
Society of Neurological Surgeons (2011)
Society of Outdoor Recreation Professionals (2010)
Society of Systematic Biologists (2010)
Society of Wood Science and Technology (2011)
Specialty Coffee Association of America (2012)
TechAmerica (fka Technology Association of America) (2011)
Timber Products Manufacturers Association (2012)
University Professional & Continuing Education Association (2012)
University Risk Management and Insurance Association (2011)
Urban and Regional Information Systems Association (2012)
Victorian Society in America (2011)
Weed Science Society of America (2011)
Western Economic Association International (2010)
The Wildlife Society (2012)

Seaside

CHA - Certified Horsemanship Association (2012)

Sunriver

Resort and Commercial Recreation Association (2010)

Warm Springs

Intertribal Timber Council (2012)

PENNSYLVANIA

Bellefonte

American Philatelic Society (2012)

Chambersburg

Council for Near-Infrared Spectroscopy (2012)

Champion

American Orff-Schulwerk Association (2011)

Devon

American Warmblood Registry (2010)

Erie

Association of Ancient Historians (2011)

Farmington

Professional Services Council (2010)
Resort and Commercial Recreation Association (2011)

Gettysburg

International Association of Approved Basketball Officials, Inc. (2010)

Harrisburg

American British White Park Association (2010)
American Concrete Pavement Association (2012)
Association of Nutrition & Foodservice Professionals (2010)
Holstein Association USA (2011)
IT Financial Management Association (2010)
Paso Fino Horse Association, Inc. (2011)

Hershey

Association of YMCA Professionals (2010)
CPA USA Network (2010)
High Technology Crime Investigation Association (2012)
International Professional Groomers (2010)
National Coal Transportation Association (2012)
National Grants Management Association (2011)
National Guardianship Association (2010)
OESP - National Association of Oil and Energy Service Professionals (2011)
Search - The National Consortium for Justice Information and Statistics (2012)
United States-Taiwan Business Council (2012)
United States Army Warrant Officers Association (2012)

Lake Harmony

American Council of Christian Churches (2011)

Lancaster

PMCA: An International Association of Confectioners (2012)
The Society of Naval Architects and Marine Engineers (2011)

Milford

National Association of State Foresters (2011)

New Wilmington

North American Association for the Study of Religion (2012)

Oaks

American Sportfishing Association (2011)

Philadelphia

Academy of General Dentistry (2012)
Academy of Nutrition and Dietetics (2012)
Aestheticians International Association (2012)
African Studies Association (2012)
Alliance of Associations of Teachers of Japanese (2012)
American Academy of Family Physicians (2012)
American Academy of Gold Foil Operators (2012)
American Academy of Orthopaedic Surgeons (2012)

American Academy of Psychoanalysis and Dynamic Psychiatry (2012)
American Association for the History of Medicine (2011)
American Association of Thoracic Surgery (2011)
American Association of Clinical Endocrinologists (2012)
American Association of Collegiate Registrars and Admissions Officers (2012)
American Association of Law Libraries (2011)
American Association of Neurological Surgeons (2010)
American Association of Neuropathologists (2010)
American Association of Oral and Maxillofacial Surgeons (2011)
American Association of Physicists in Medicine (2010)
American Association of Physics Teachers (2012)
American Association of Teachers of French (2010)
American Association of Teachers of German (2012)
American Association of Teachers of Italian (2012)
American Association of Zoo Keepers (2010)
American Bus Association (2011)
American Chemical Society (2012)
American College Health Association (2010)
American Council of Learned Societies (2010, 2012)
American Council on the Teaching of Foreign Languages (2012)
American Filtration and Separations Society (2012)
American Folklore Society (2011)
American Literary Translators Association (2010)
American Occupational Therapy Association, Inc. (2011)
American Philological Association (2012)
American Psychiatric Association (2012)
American Registry for Internet Numbers (2011)
American Society for Aesthetics (2012)
American Society for Automation in Pharmacy (2012)
American Society for Cell Biology (2010)
American Society for Colposcopy and Cervical Pathology (2010)
American Society for Legal History (2010)
American Society of Consulting Arborists (2012)
American Society of Echocardiography (2011)
American Society of Gene & Cell Therapy (2012)
American Society of Group Psychotherapy and Psychodrama (2010)
American Society of Mechanical Engineers (ASME) (2010)
American Society of Nephrology (2011)
American Society of Nuclear Cardiology (2010)
American Society of Plumbing Engineers (2010)
American Society of Sanitary Engineering (2012)
American Society of Transplant Surgeons (2011)
American Society of Transplantation (2011)
American Society of Tropical Medicine and Hygiene (2011)
American Society on Aging (2010, 2011)
American Speech-Language-Hearing Association (2010)
American Water Resources Association (2010)
Archaeological Institute of America (2012)
Association for Behavior Analysis International (2012)
The Association for Consortium Leadership (2012)
Association for Documentary Editing (2010)
Association for Information and Image Management International (2010)
The Association for Research in Business Education - Delta Pi Epsilon (2010)
Association for Supervision and Curriculum Development (ASCD) (2012)
Association of College and Research Libraries (2011)
Association of Collegiate Schools of Architecture (2012)
Association of Healthcare Internal Auditors (2012)
Association of Independent Research Institutes (2012)
Association of Moving Image Archivists (2010)
Association of periOperative Registered Nurses (2011)
APCO (Association of Public-Safety Communications Officials) International (2011)
Association of University Anesthesiologists (2011)
Black Data Processing Associates (2010)
Business History Conference (2012)
Catholic Health Association of the United States (2012)
Chain Drug Marketing Association (2011)
Chinese Language Teachers Association (2012)
Collaborative Family Healthcare Association (2011)
The Cordage Institute (2012)
Council of American Jewish Museums (2011)
Council of Communication Management (2010)
Council of State Speech-Language-Hearing Association Presidents (2010)
Council of Supply Chain Management Professionals (2011)
Diagnostic Marketing Association (2010)
Drug Information Association (2012)
Educause (2011)
FCIB-NACM Corporation (2012)
Federation of Defense and Corporate Counsel (2010)
Future Business Leaders of America - Phi Beta Lambda (2011)
Gynecologic Oncology Group (2011)
Health Care Compliance Association (2011)
Healthcare Convention and Exhibitors Association (2010)
History of Science Society (2012)
IEEE Computer Society (2012)
INDA, Association of the Nonwoven Fabrics Industry (2012)
The Independent Book Publishers Association (2012)
Independent Educational Consultants Association (2011)
Industrial Asset Management Council (2011)
Industrial Research Institute (2011)
International Alliance of Theatrical Stage Employees, Moving Picture Technicians, Artists and Allied Crafts of the U.S., Its Territories and Canada (2012)
International Association for Corporate and Professional Recruitment (2010)
International Association of Fire Fighters (2012)
International Center for Study of Psychiatry and Psychology (2012)
The International Fluid Power Society (2010)
International Liquid Terminals Association (2011)
International Marking and Identification Association (2012)
International Society of Nurses in Genetics (2012)
International Textile and Apparel Association (2011)

Internet Society (2011)
Laboratory Products Association (2010)
League for Innovation in the Community College (2012)
Marketing and Advertising Global Network (2010)
Marketing Science Institute (2012)
Musculoskeletal Tumor Society (2010)
National Association of Student Personnel Administrators (2011)
National Academy of Arbitrators (2010)
National Association for Multicultural Education (2012)
National Association of Black Social Workers (2010)
National Association of Boards of Pharmacy (2012)
National Association of Government Defined Contribution Administrators (2010)
National Association of Health Services Executives (2012)
National Association of Pupil Services Administrators (2012)
National Association of School Psychologists (2012)
National Athletic Trainers Association (2010)
National Business Incubation Association (2010)
National Chemical Credit Association (2010)
National Coffee Association of the U.S.A. (2012)
National Community Pharmacists Association (2010)
National Comprehensive Cancer Network (2011)
National Council of State Supervisors for Languages (2012)
National Council of Supervisors of Mathematics (2012)
National Council of Teachers of Mathematics (2012)
National Council on Education for the Ceramic Arts (2010)
National Court Reporters Association (2012)
National Federation of Advanced Information Services (2010, 2011, 2012)
National Organization of Social Security Claimants' Representatives (2012)
National Pharmaceutical Council (2012)
National Portable Storage Association (2012)
National Safety Council (2010, 2011)
National Soccer Coaches Association of America (2010)
North American Association of Summer Sessions (2012)
Pharmaceutical Marketing Research Group (2012)
Plumbing-Heating-Cooling Contractors - National Association (2012)
Police Executive Research Forum (2010)
Public Library Association (2012)
Qualitative Research Consultants Association (2010)
Radiation Therapy Oncology Group (2010)
Refrigerated Foods Association (2010)
Religion Communicators Council (2012)
Rhetoric Society of America (2012)
Risk and Insurance Management Society, Inc. (RIMS) (2012)
Scaffold Industry Association (2010)
Smart Card Alliance (2012)
Social Venture Network (2011)
Society for Ethnomusicology (2011)
Society for Healthcare Strategy and Market Development (2012)
Society for Historians of the Early American Republic (2011)
Society for Photographic Education (2010)
Society for Research on Adolescence (2010)
Society for Scholarly Publishing (2010)
Society of American Registered Architects (2010)
Society of Biological Psychiatry (2012)
Society of Chemical Manufacturers and Affiliates Inc. (2012)
Society of Dance History Scholars (2012)
Society of Independent Show Organizers (2011)
Special Interest Group for University and College Computing Services (2011)
Special Libraries Association (2011)
TESOL International Association (2012)
United States Lacrosse (2012)
Utility Arborist Association (2010)
Women's Classical Caucus (2012)

Pittsburgh

AASHTO: Transportation Center of Excellence (2012)
Agricultural & Applied Economics Association (2011)
Airports Council International - North America (2010)
American Association of Immunologists (2012)
American Association of Legal Nurse Consultants (2010)
American Association of Sexuality Educators, Counselors and Therapists (2010)
American Ceramics Society (2012)
American College of Clinical Pharmacy (2011)
American College of Osteopathic Pediatricians (2011)
American Concrete Institute (2010)
American Counseling Association (2010)
American Diabetes Association (2012)
American Dialect Society (2011)
The American Electrophoresis Society (2012)
American Fisheries Society (2010)
American Institute for Conservation of Historic and Artistic Works (2011)
American Institute of Chemical Engineers (2012)
American Psychiatric Nurses Association (2012)
American Society for Information Science and Technology (2010)
American Society of Agricultural and Biological Engineers (2010)
American Society of Mechanical Engineers (ASME) (2010)
American Society of Mining and Reclamation (2010)
American Student Dental Association (2010)
ASM International (2012)
Association for Iron and Steel Technology (2010)
Association for Radiological and Imaging Nursing (2012)
Association for the Study of African American Life and History (2012)
Association of African American Museums (2010)
Association of Pediatric Hematology/Oncology Nurses (2012)
Association of State and Territorial Dental Directors (2011)
Association of State Drinking Water Administrators (2010)
Catholic Academy for Communication Arts Professionals (2011)
Catholic Press Association (2010, 2011)
Classification Society (2011, 2012)
Construction Owners Association of America (2010)

Council of Engineering and Scientific Society Executives (2010)
Council of State and Territorial Epidemiologists (2011)
Ecological Society of America (2010)
Ground Water Protection Council (2010)
Housing Education and Research Association (2012)
InSight (2011)
International Association of Addictions and Offender Counselors (2010)
International Association of Forensic Nurses (2010)
International Association of Marriage and Family Counselors (2010)
International Concrete Repair Institute (2010)
International Reciprocal Trade Association (2010)
Linguistic Society of America (2011)
Mathematical Association of America (2010)
Metal Construction Association (2010)
National Association of Counties (2012)
National Association of County Park and Recreation Officials (2012)
National Association of County Recorders, Election Officials and Clerks (2012)
National Association of Hospital Hospitality Houses (2010)
National Association of Pastoral Musicians (2012)
National Association of Royalty Owners (2010)
National Association of State Alcohol and Drug Abuse Directors (NASADAD) (2012)
National Association of State Directors of Teacher Education and Certification (2010)
National Association of Steel Pipe Distributors (2010)
National Corrugated Steel Pipe Association (2012)
National Mining Association (2012)
National WIC Association (2011)
North American Association of Christians in Social Work (2011)
Philosophy of Education Society (2012)
Retail Confectioners International (2011)
Society for Education in Anesthesia (2010)
Society for Healthcare Consumer Advocacy (2010)
Society for Industrial & Applied Mathematics (2010)
Society for Menstrual Cycle Research (2011)
Society for the Study of Indigenous Languages of the Americas (2011)
Society of Glass and Ceramic Decorated Products (2011)
Society of Insurance Research (2012)
Society of Vertebrate Paleontology (2010)
Tree Care Industry Association (2010)
United Association for Labor Education (2012)
University Council for Educational Administration (2011)
University Risk Management and Insurance Association (2010)
Urban Affairs Association (2012)
The Wildlife Society (2011)

Scranton

National Railway Historical Society (2010)

Seven Springs

American Herbalists Guild (2012)
American Society of Highway Engineers (2012)

Sewickley

Label Printing Industries of America (2012)

State College

Society for Textual Scholarship (2011)
Society for the Study of Reproduction (2012)

Trevose

Naval Enlisted Reserve Association (2012)

Valley Forge

American Criminal Justice Association Lambda Alpha Epsilon (2011)
National Conference of CPA Practitioners (2012)

West Conshohocken

Surface Design Association (2012)

Williamsport

Wood Component Manufacturers Association (2010)

York

National Sunroom Association (2012)

PUERTO RICO

Carolina

Marketing and Advertising Global Network (2012)
National Association of Elevator Contractors (2012)

Fajardo

Pressure Sensitive Tape Council (2010)
Process Equipment Manufacturers' Association (2012)

Las Croabas

American Council of Engineering Companies (2010)
Distribution Contractors Association (2011)
National Utility Contractors Association (NUCA) (2011)

Rio Grande

College of Optometrists in Vision Development (2010)
Contract Packaging Association (2012)
Educational Book and Media Association (2012)
Fire Suppression Systems Association (2011)
International Life Sciences Institute (2010)
NADCA: The HVAC Inspection, Maintenance and Restoration Association (2012)
National Association of Shareholder and Consumer Attorneys (2012)

Textile Bag and Packaging Association (2010)

San Juan

American Academy of Esthetic Dentistry (2011)
American Academy of Oral and Maxillofacial Pathology (2011)
American Academy of Oral Medicine (2011)
American Association of Teachers of Spanish and Portuguese (2012)
American Association of Tissue Banks (2012)
American Cleft Palate-Craniofacial Association (2011)
American College of Eye Surgeons (2010)
American Federation of School Administrators (2012)
American Psychology-Law Society (2012)
American Registry for Internet Numbers (2011)
American Society for Histocompatibility and Immunogenetics (2012)
American Society of Limnology and Oceanography (2011)
American Studies Association (2012)
Association of Professors of Medicine (2011)
Coalition for Juvenile Justice (2012)
Comparative and International Education Society (2012)
Fire Apparatus Manufacturers' Association (2011)
Food Distribution Research Society (2012)
Hispanic Association of Colleges and Universities (2011)
International Association for Orthodontics (2012)
International Association of Rehabilitation Professionals (2012)
International Council of Shopping Centers (2012)
International Council on Hotel, Restaurant and Institutional Education (2010)
International Pharmaceutical Excipients Council of the Americas (2012)
Islamic Medical Association of North America (2011)
NALP - The Association for Legal Career Professionals (2010)
National Association of Hispanic Nurses (2012)
National Association of Housing Cooperatives (2011)
National Association of Reinforcing Steel Contractors (2010)
National Association of Secretaries of State (2012)
National Association of State Workforce Agencies (2011)
National Bankers Association (2010)
National Independent Laboratory Association (2012)
Radiation Research Society (2012)
Society for Physical Regulation in Biology and Medicine (2012)

RHODE ISLAND

Bristol

Association for Living History, Farm and Agricultural Museums (2012)

Newport

American College of Laboratory Animal Medicine (2010)
American Osteopathic Association (2012)
Association of Metropolitan Water Agencies (2011)
International Association of Industrial Accident Boards and Commissions (2012)
International Engraved Graphics Association (2010)
International Sports Heritage Association (2012)
National Conference of Insurance Legislators (2011)
Tall Ships America (2012)
Unified Abrasives Manufacturers Association (2012)
United Abrasives Manufacturers Association, Coated Division (2012)

Providence

Academy of Rehabilitative Audiology (2012)
Alliance of Area Business Publications (2011)
Alliance of Artists Communities (2010)
American Academy on Communication in Healthcare (2010, 2012)
American Comparative Literature Association (2012)
American Fire Sprinkler Association (2010)
American Orthopaedic Society for Sports Medicine (2010)
American Osteopathic Academy of Sports Medicine (2011)
American Physical Society (2012)
American Phytopathological Society (2012)
American Society for Indexing (2011)
American Society of Brewing Chemists (2010)
American Society of Ichthyologists and Herpetologists (2010)
American Society of Plant Taxonomists (2010)
American Specialty Toy Retailing Association (2010)
Association for Applied Sport Psychology (2010)
Association of Food and Drug Officials (2012)
The Botanical Society of America (2010)
Child Neurology Society (2010)
City and Regional Magazine Association (2010)
Coalition of Essential Schools (2011)
Design Management Institute (2010)
Federation of Tax Administrators (2012)
Hearing Loss Association of America (2012)
International Association for Food Protection (2012)
International Council on Hotel, Restaurant and Institutional Education (2012)
Liability Insurance Research Bureau (2012)
Master Brewers Association of the Americas (2010)
National Association of Secretaries of State (2010)
National Association of State Budget Officers (2012)
National Onsite Wastewater Recycling Association (2012)
National Strength and Conditioning Association (2012)
National Tax Association (2012)
NCSL International (2010)
OESP - National Association of Oil and Energy Service Professionals (2010, 2012)
Snow & Ice Management Association (2010)
Society for Experimental Mechanics, Inc. (2010)
The Society of Naval Architects and Marine Engineers (2012)
University Risk Management and Insurance Association (2012)

SOUTH CAROLINA

Charleston

Airports Council International - North America (2012)
Alliance for Massage Therapy Education (2011)
American Academy of Oral Medicine (2012)
American Academy of Veterinary Acupuncture (2012)
American Association of Genitourinary Surgeons (2011)
American Association of State Colleges and Universities (2010)
American Association of Textile Chemists and Colorists (2011)
American Bandmasters Association (2010)
American Coatings Association (2012)
American College of Neuropsychiatrists (2011)
American Cotton Shippers Association (2010)
American Land Title Association (2011)
American Microscopical Society (2012)
American Ophthalmological Society (2012)
American Peanut Shellers Association (2012)
American Society of Questioned Document Examiners (2012)
Associated Cooperage Industries of America (2012)
Associated General Contractors of America (AGC) (2012)
Association for Ambulatory Behavioral Healthcare (2011)
Association for Preservation Technology International (2012)
Association of American Medical Colleges (2012)
Association of Bone and Joint Surgeons (2012)
Association of Bridal Consultants (2012)
Association of Clean Water Administrators (2011)
Association of Environmental and Engineering Geologists (2010)
Association of Marketing Service Providers (2010)
Association of Old Crows (2011)
Association of Organ Procurement Organizations (2011)
Association of Public Treasurers of the United States and Canada (2010)
Biotechnology Industry Organization (BIO) (2012)
Building Stone Institute (2011)
Cleaning Equipment Trade Association (2010)
Council of State Governments (2010)
Council of State Speech-Language-Hearing Association Presidents (2011)
Council on Licensure, Enforcement and Regulation (2012)
Foodservice Sales & Marketing Association (2010)
Groundwater Management Districts Association (2010)
Hardwood Manufacturers Association (2011)
The Hosiery Association (2010)
In-Plant Printing and Mailing Association (2011)
International Association of Clerks, Recorders, Election Officials and Treasurers (2010)
International Association of Eating Disorders Professionals (2012)
International College of Dentists, U.S.A. Section (2010)
International Engraved Graphics Association (2012)
National Academy of Arbitrators (2012)
National Association of Clean Water Agencies (2011)
National Association of County Agricultural Agents (2012)
National Association of Disability Examiners (2010)
The National Association of Marine Surveyors, Inc. (2010)
National Association of Principals of Schools for Girls (2011)
National Association of Regulatory Utility Commissioners (2010)
National Association of State Controlled Substances Authorities (2010)
National Association of State Utility Consumer Advocates (NASUCA) (2012)
National Coffee Association of the U.S.A. (2012)
National College of Probate Judges (2010)
National Conference of Appellate Court Clerks (2012)
National Conference of Insurance Legislators (2010)
National Council of Postal Credit Unions (2012)
National Federation of Municipal Analysts (2011)
National Genealogical Society (2011)
National Grain and Feed Association (2012)
The National Greenhouse Manufacturers Association (2012)
National Newspaper Association (2012)
National Organization of Nurse Practitioner Faculties (2012)
NCSL International (2012)
North American Gamebird Association (2011)
Personal Care Products Council (2012)
Petroleum Packaging Council (2012)
Phycological Society of America (2012)
Pile Driving Contractors Association (2010)
Power Washers of North America (2010)
Power-Motion Technology Representatives Association (2010)
Pulp and Paper Safety Association (2010)
Society for Ear, Nose and Throat Advances in Children (2012)
Society for French Historical Studies (2011)
Society for Integrative and Comparative Biology (2012)
Society for Risk Analysis (2011)
Society of Cosmetic Chemists (2012)
Society of Government Service Urologists (2012)
Taxicab, Limousine & Paratransit Association (2010)
Textile Care Allied Trades Association (2010)
Tile Contractors' Association of America (2012)
United States Court Reporters Association (2012)

Clemson

Gravure Association of America (2010)
International Graphic Arts Education Association (2012)

Columbia

Correctional Education Association (2012)
National District Attorneys Association (2010)
National Recycling Coalition (2011)

Folly Beach

American Canoe Association (2012)

Greenville

American Academy of Fertility Care Professionals (2010)
American Academy of Thermology (2012)
American Association of School Librarians (2012)
American Orthopsychiatric Association (2010, 2011)
IEEE Power Electronics Society (2012)
INDA, Association of the Nonwoven Fabrics Industry (2012)
International Association of Workforce Professionals (IAWP) (2010)
The Masonry Society (2012)
National Christian College Athletic Association (2010, 2012)
National Ice Cream Retailers Association (2012)
Packaging Machinery Manufacturers Institute (2010)

Hilton Head Island

Academy of Prosthodontics (2011)
American Coke and Coal Chemicals Institute (2010)
American College of Veterinary Ophthalmologists (2011)
American Judges Association (2011)
American Society of Echocardiography (2010)
American Society of Transplant Surgeons (2012)
American Sportfishing Association (2012)
Association of Fish and Wildlife Agencies (2012)
Community College Business Officers (2010)
Composite Can and Tube Institute (2010)
Council of Administrators of Special Education (2011)
Education Law Association (2012)
Eye Bank Association of America (2010)
Forest Resources Association (2010)
Institute of Clean Air Companies (2012)
Manufacturers' Agents Association for the Foodservice Industry (2011)
National Association of School Music Dealers (2010)
Non-Ferrous Founders' Society (2010)
Plastic Pipe and Fittings Association (2011)
Polyurethane Foam Association (2012)
Tire Retread and Repair Information Bureau (2012)
Transportation Lawyers Association (2010)

Isle of Palms

Kitchen Cabinet Manufacturers Association (2010)
Refrigeration Service Engineers Society (2012)

Kiawah Island

American Society for Automation in Pharmacy (2010)
Association of Edison Illuminating Companies (2010, 2012)
Snack Food Association (2012)

Mt. Pleasant

Electronic Security Association (2011)

Myrtle Beach

American Academy of Advertising (2012)
American Association of Philosophy Teachers (2010)
American Association of School Personnel Administrators (2010)
Association for Spiritual, Ethical and Religious Values in Counseling (2010)
Association of Applied IPM Ecologists (2010)
Association of Industrial Metallizers, Coaters and Laminators (2010)
Atlantic intra Coastal Waterway Association (2011)
Council for Learning Disabilities (2010)
The Foodservice Group, Inc. (2012)
Institute of Navigation (2012)
International Association for Computer Information Systems (2012)
International Association for Healthcare Security and Safety (2010)
International Concrete Repair Institute (2010)
International Conference of Funeral Service Examining Boards (2011)
National Association for Surface Finishing (2011)
National Association of Activity Professionals (2011)
National Association of Home Inspectors (2012)
Restoration Industry Association (2011, 2012)
Safe and Vault Technicians Association (2012)
School Social Work Association of America (2011)
SEAMS Association (2011, 2012)
Waterproofing Contractors Association (2010)

North Charleston

Society for the Advancement of Material and Process Engineering (2012)
Society of Manufacturing Engineers (2012)

Spartanburg

National Council of Chain Restaurants (2012)

SOUTH DAKOTA

Deadwood

National Sunflower Association (2011)

Rapid City

American Indian Higher Education Consortium (2012)
American Institute of Professional Geologists (2012)
Artist-Blacksmiths' Association of North America (2012)

Sioux Falls

National High School Athletic Coaches Association (2010)
National Taxidermists Association (2011)

TENNESSEE

Alcoa

National Remotivation Therapy Organization (2010)

Athens

American Dexter Cattle Association (2010)

Bristol

EEG and Clinical Neuroscience Society (2012)

Chattanooga

American Association of Private Railroad Car Owners (2012)
American Business Women's Association (2010)
American College of Medical Physics (2011)
American Institute of Graphic Arts (2010)
Association of Railway Museums (2011)
Kappa Kappa Iota-National (2012)
National Hydropower Association (2012)
Southeastern Theatre Conference (2012)

Franklin

Walking Horse Trainers Association (2011, 2012)

Gatlinburg

National Association of Seventh-Day Adventist Dentists (2010)
North American Case Research Association (2010)

Kingsport

American Association of Retirement Communities (2012)
American Council of Christian Churches (2012)

Knoxville

Entomological Society of America (2012)
Society for Mathematical Biology (2012)
Western Writers of America (2010)

Lewisburg

Walking Horse Owners Association of America (2012)

Manchester

National Spotted Saddle Horse Association (2012)

Memphis

Airlines Electronic Engineering Committee (2011)
American Bridge Teachers' Association (2012)
American Business Women's Association (2012)
American College of Osteopathic Pediatricians (2012)
American Conference of Cantors (2010)
American Council on Consumer Interests (2012)
American Criminal Justice Association Lambda Alpha Epsilon (2011)
American Heartworm Society (2010)
American Orthodontic Society (2012)
American Public Power Association (2012)
American Road and Transportation Builders Association (2012)
American Society of Civil Engineers (2011)
Artist-Blacksmiths' Association of North America (2010)
Association of Destination Management Executives (2012)
Association of Family Medicine Residency Directors (2012)
Association of Progressive Rental Organizations (2012)
The Association of Suppliers to the Paper Industry (2010)
Council of State Governments (2011)
Earthquake Engineering Research Institute (2012)
Executive Women International (2010)
Filter Manufacturers Council (2010)
The Folk Alliance International (2011, 2012)
Hydraulic Institute (2012)
International Association of Diecutting and Diemaking (2012)
International Cemetery, Cremation and Funeral Association (2012)
Label Printing Industries of America (2012)
National Association for Pupil Transportation (2012)
National Association of Charter School Authorizers (2012)
National Association of County and City Health Officials (2010)
National Association of Criminal Defense Lawyers (2010)
National Association of Health Services Executives (2010)
National Association of Junior Auxiliaries (2011)
National Association of Teachers of Singing (2012)
National Associations of State Directors of Pupil Transportation Services (2012)
National Conference of Black Lawyers (2010)
National Cotton Ginners' Association (2010)
National Education Association (2012)
National Ground Water Association (2011)
National Hardwood Lumber Association (2011)
National Opera Association (2012)
National Student Nurses Association (2011)
National Young Farmers Education Association (2012)
Paso Fino Horse Association, Inc. (2011)
Regional Airline Association (2011)
Seismological Society of America (2011, 2012)
Society for American Archaeology (2012)
Special Interest Group for University and College Computing Services (2012)
Urban and Regional Information Systems Association (2012)
Utility Communicators International (2012)

Murfreesboro

American Quarter Horse Association (2012)
National Association of Activity Professionals (2012)
National Spotted Saddle Horse Association (2010, 2012)
University Aviation Association (2012)

Nashville

Academy of Clinical Laboratory Physicians and Scientists (2010)
Academy of Hospitality Industry Attorneys (2012)
AFCOM (2012)
American Academy of Professional Coders (2010)
American Agricultural Law Association (2012)

The American Association of Code Enforcement (2011)
American Association of Occupational Health Nurses (2012)
American Baseball Coaches Association (2011)
American Coal Ash Association (2010)
American College of Health Care Administrators (2012)
American College of Veterinary Pathologists (2011)
American Dairy Science Association (2010)
American Fence Association (2012)
American Folklore Society (2010)
American Foundry Society (2012)
American Gas Association (2011)
American Guild of Organists (2012)
American Hackney Horse Society (2012)
American Holistic Medical Association (2010)
American Immigration Lawyers Association (2012)
American Judges Association (2012)
American Paint Horse Association (2010)
American Phytopathological Society (2010)
American Public Power Association (2011)
American Recovery Association (2012)
American Sheep Industry Association (2010)
American Society for Theatre Research (2012)
American Society of Clinical Hypnosis (2010)
American Society of Hand Therapists (2011)
American Society of Military Comptrollers (2010)
American Society of Professional Estimators (2011)
American Soybean Association (2012)
American Spinal Injury Association (2010)
American Woman's Society of Certified Public Accountants (2010)
American Wood-Protection Association (2012)
APICS The Association for Operations Management (2010)
Army Aviation Association of America (2011, 2012)
Assisted Living Federation of America (2011)
Associated Locksmiths of America (2011)
Associated Press Managing Editors (2012)
Association for Humanist Sociology (2010)
Association for the Advancement of Computing in Education (2011)
Association of Administrative Law Judges (2012)
Association of Millwork Distributors (2010, 2011)
Association of Rehabilitation Nurses (2012)
Association of Women's Health, Obstetric and Neonatal Nurses (2010)
AVS: Science and Technology of Materials, Interfaces, and Processing (2011)
Broadcast Cable Credit Association (2010)
CALLERLAB - International Association of Square Dance Callers (2012)
Catholic Cemetery Conference (2011)
Center for the Polyurethanes Industry (2011)
Child Care Aware of America (2011)
Chlorine Institute (2010)
Competitive Telecommunications Association (2010)
Council for Advancement and Support of Education (2011)
Council for Exceptional Children (2010)
Council of Educational Facility Planners International (2011)
Council on Governmental Ethics Laws (2011)
Council on Licensure, Enforcement and Regulation (2010)
Country Music Association (2012)
Country Radio Broadcasters, Inc. (2010, 2012)
Dangerous Goods Advisory Council (2012)
Delta Nu Alpha (2012)
Electrical Apparatus Service Association (2012)
Electronic Security Association (2012)
Enterprise Wireless Alliance (2012)
Ethics and Compliance Officer Association (2010)
Financial and Security Products Association (2012)
Foil and Specialty Effects Association (2011)
Future Business Leaders of America - Phi Beta Lambda (2010)
Gas Machinery Research Council (2011)
Gospel Music Association (2010)
Ground Water Protection Council (2012)
Health Ministries Association (2012)
Healthcare Financial Management Association (2010)
Independent Community Bankers of America (2012)
Independent Free Papers of America (2010)
Indoor Tanning Association (2010, 2011)
Institute of Behavioral and Applied Management (2012)
The Institute of Financial Operations (2012)
Institute of Navigation (2012)
Insurance Accounting and Systems Association (2011)
International Association of Baptist Colleges and Universities (2010)
International Association of Correctional Training Personnel (2011)
International Association of Diecutting and Diemaking (2011)
International Association of Flight And Critical Care Paramedics (2012)
International Association of Law Enforcement Intelligence Analysts (2011)
International Association of Machinists and Aerospace Workers (2011)
International Bluegrass Music Association (2010, 2012)
International Entertainment Buyers Association (2010, 2012)
International Federation of Leather Guilds (2012)
International Foodservice Editorial Council (2012)
International Institute of Municipal Clerks (2011)
International Parking Institute (2012)
International Public Management Association for Human Resources (2012)
International Society of Certified Electronics Technicians (2010)
International Society of Explosives Engineers (2012)
Investment Casting Institute (2012)
Lamaze International (2012)
Lightning Protection Institute (2010)
Metal Powder Industries Federation (2012)
Metal Treating Institute (2012)
Microscopy Society of America (2011)
Midwives Alliance of North America (2010)
Minor League Baseball (2012)

NAMM - The International Music Products Association (2011, 2012)
National Academic Advising Association (2012)
National Academy of Neuropsychology (2012)
National Alliance of Black School Educators (2012)
National Association for Family Child Care (2012)
National Association for Healthcare Quality (2010)
The National Association for the Dually Diagnosed (2010, 2011)
National Association of Credit Management (2012)
National Association of Diaconate Directors (2011)
National Association of Directors of Nursing Administration in Long Term Care (2012)
National Association of Drug Court Professionals (2012)
National Association of Federal Credit Unions (2012)
National Association of Government Archives and Records Administrators (2011)
National Association of Home Inspectors (2010)
National Association of Housing and Redevelopment Officials (2012)
National Association of Local Government Auditors (2012)
National Association of Professional Background Screeners (2012)
National Association of Small Trucking Companies (2012)
National Association of State Aviation Officials (2011)
National Association of State Boards of Accountancy (2011, 2012)
National Association of State Directors of Special Education (2010)
National Association of Wheat Growers (2012)
National Block and Bridle Club (2012)
National Board of Boiler and Pressure Vessel Inspectors (2012)
National Catholic Development Conference (2012)
National Cattlemen's Beef Association (2012)
National Coalition of Girls' Schools (2010)
National Community Pharmacists Association (2011)
National Council of Chain Restaurants (2010)
National Electronic Service Dealers Association (2010)
National Federation of Priests' Councils (2012)
National Federation of State High School Associations (2012)
National Ice Cream Retailers Association (2010)
National Livestock Producers Association (2010)
National Religious Broadcasters (2010, 2012)
National Rural Water Association (2010, 2012)
National Sheriffs' Association (2012)
National Tooling and Machining Association (2012)
National Tractor Parts Dealer Association (2010)
North American Association of Floor Covering Distributors (2011)
North American Deer Farmers Association (2011)
North American Manufacturing Research Institution of SME (2010)
North American Serials Interest Group (2012)
North American Society for Trenchless Technology (2012)
Partnership for Philanthropic Planning (2010)
Physician Office Managers Association of America (2012)
Pipe Fabrication Institute (2012)
Porcelain Enamel Institute (2012)
Post-Tensioning Institute (2012)
Power Washers of North America (2011)
Precast/Prestressed Concrete Institute (2012)
Professional Photographers of America (2010)
Professional Retail Store Maintenance Association (2011)
Protestant Church-Owned Publishers Association (2010, 2011, 2012)
Public Media Business Association (2011)
Public Risk Management Association (2012)
Romance Writers of America (2010)
School Nutrition Association (2011)
Society for Public Health Education (2012)
Society of Glass and Ceramic Decorated Products (2010)
Society of Manufacturing Engineers (2010)
Society of the Plastics Industry (2012)
SWANA - Solid Waste Association of North America (2011)
Technology Student Association (2012)
Theatre Library Association (2012)
Turf and Ornamental Communicators Association (2012)
United Professional Horsemen's Association (2012)
United States Canola Association (2012)
Viola da Gamba Society of America (2012)
Workers' Injury Law and Advocacy Group (2011)

Pigeon Forge

Zoological Association of America (2012)

Wartrace

National Spotted Saddle Horse Association (2012)

White Pine

Walking Horse Trainers Association (2012)

TEXAS

Antonio

Air Force Sergeants Association (2011)
American Academy of Ambulatory Care Nursing (2011)
American Academy of Pain Medicine (2010)
American Association for Pediatric Ophthalmology and Strabismus (2012)
American College of Oral and Maxillofacial Surgeons (2010)
American Fuel & Petrochemical Manufacturers (2012)
American Society of Heating, Refrigerating and Air Conditioning Engineers (ASHRAE) (2012)
American Studies Association (2010)
Association of Home Office Underwriters (2010)
Association of Kentucky Fried Chicken Franchisees, Inc. (2012)
Association of Teacher Educators (2012)
Financial & Insurance Conference Planners (2011)
Hispanic Association of Colleges and Universities (2011)
International Society for Clinical Densitometry (2010)
International Ticketing Association (2012)

National Association of Attorneys General (2011)
National Ski and Snowboard Retailers Association (2012)
National Ski Area Association (2012)
Research and Development Associates for Military Food and Packaging Systems (2012)
Society for Obstetric Anesthesia and Perinatology (2010)
Society for Pediatric Anesthesia (2010)
Society of Industrial and Office Realtors (2010)
Society of Trauma Nurses (2011)
The Travel and Tourism Research Association (2010)

Austin

Academy for Eating Disorders (2012)
Academy of Homiletics (2011)
Academy of Surgical Research (2011)
Air Conditioning Contractors of America (2012)
American Association of Bioanalysts (2011)
American Association of Managing General Agents (2010)
American Association of Philosophy Teachers (2012)
American Association of Political Consultants (2012)
American Association of Sexuality Educators, Counselors and Therapists (2012)
American Astronomical Society (2012)
American Bar Association (2012)
American Brush Manufacturers Association (2011)
American Case Management Association (2012)
American College of Clinical Pharmacy (2010)
American Concrete Pipe Association (2011)
American Herbalists Guild (2010)
American Intellectual Property Law Association (2012)
American Mathematical Association of Two Year Colleges (2011)
American Mosquito Control Association (2012)
American Organization for Bodywork Therapies of Asia (2011)
American Society for Cytotechnology (2010)
American Society of Law, Medicine and Ethics (2010)
American Society of Primatologists (2011)
Associated Air Balance Council (2012)
Associated Builders and Contractors (2012)
Association for Asian American Studies (2010)
Association for Continuing Higher Education (2012)
Association for Healthcare Documentation Integrity (2010)
Association for Healthcare Foodservice (2010)
Association of American State Geologists (2012)
Association of Asphalt Paving Technologists (2012)
Association of College and University Housing Officers-International (2010)
Association of Collegiate Schools of Architecture (2012)
Association of Credit Union Internal Auditors (2011)
Association of Organ Procurement Organizations (2012)
Association of Professional Researchers for Advancement (2011)
Association of Public Health Nurses (2012)
Association of Real Estate License Law Officials (2012)
Association of Small Foundations (2010)
Association of State and Territorial Health Officials (2012)
Automotive Recyclers Association (2010)
Battery Council International (2010)
Biomedical Engineering Society (2010)
Building Stone Institute (2010)
City and Regional Magazine Association (2010)
Collaborative Family Healthcare Association (2012)
Commercial Vehicle Safety Alliance (2011)
Conference of Radiation Control Program Directors (2011)
Consumer Bankers Association (2012)
Council for Learning Disabilities (2011, 2012)
Council for Responsible Nutrition (2010)
Council of Hotel and Restaurant Trainers (2012)
Council of State Governments (2012)
Council On State Taxation (2010)
Crane Certification Association of America (2012)
Ecological Society of America (2011)
Electrical and Computer Engineering Department Heads Association (2012)
Environmental Council of the States (2012)
The Environmental Information Association (2010)
EUCG, Inc. (2012)
Fluid Sealing Association (2010)
Foodservice & Packaging Institute, Inc. (2012)
Gas Machinery Research Council (2012)
Gas Processors Association (2010)
Gas Processors Suppliers Association (2010)
Gasket Fabricators Association (2011)
Ground Water Protection Council (2010)
Health Care Compliance Association (2012)
Herb Society of America (2012)
IEEE Instrumentation and Measurement Society (2010)
Illuminating Engineering Society of North America (2011)
Independent Professional Representatives Organization (2012)
Industrial Asset Management Council (2012)
Institute for Operations Research and the Management Sciences (2010)
International Association for Energy Economics (2012)
International Association of Bedding and Furniture Law Officials (2011)
International Association of Drilling Contractors (2010, 2011)
International Claim Association (2010)
International Municipal Lawyers Association (2012)
Laboratory Animal Management Association (2012)
Local Search Association (fka Yellow Pages Association) (2012)
Museum Store Association (2010)
NACHA - The Electronic Payments Association (2011)
NALP - The Association for Legal Career Professionals (2012)
National Association for Health and Fitness (2010)
National Association of Catastrophe Adjusters (2010)
National Association of Catering and Events (2010)
National Association of Clean Water Agencies (2010)

National Association of Counsel for Children (2010)
National Association of Criminal Defense Lawyers (2010)
National Association of Equipment Leasing Brokers (2011)
National Association of Graduate Admissions Professionals (2012)
National Association of Professional Mortgage Women (2010)
National Association of Schools of Public Affairs and Administration (2012)
National Association of Shell Marketers (2011)
National Association of State Outdoor Recreation Liaison Officers (2012)
National Association of State Procurement Officials (2011)
National Association of Tax Professionals (2010)
National Conference of Insurance Legislators (2010)
National Guard Executive Directors Association (2010)
National Panhellenic Conference (2011)
National Steel Bridge Alliance (2012)
North American Association of Commencement Officers (2012)
North American Gaming Regulators Association (2012)
North American Small Business International Trade Educators (2010)
Percussive Arts Society (2012)
Pet Sitters International (2012)
Powder Coating Institute (2010)
Precision Machined Products Association (2011)
Public Investors Arbitration Bar Association (2012)
Radiology Business Management Association (2010)
Rubber Manufacturers Association (2011)
Semiconductor Equipment and Materials International (2011)
Society for Healthcare Consumer Advocacy (2012)
Society for Historical Archaeology (2012)
Society for Imaging Science and Technology (2010)
Society for Textual Scholarship (2012)
Society for the Psychological Study of Men and Masculinity (2010)
Society of Gynecologic Oncologists (2012)
Society of Insurance Trainers and Educators (2011)
Society of Petrophysicists and Well Log Analysts (2010)
Specialized Carriers and Rigging Association (2012)
Sports Turf Managers Association (2011)
State Government Affairs Council (2011)
State Guard Association of the United States (2011)
State Risk and Insurance Management Association (2012)
The Transformer Association (2010)
United States Association for Energy Economics (2012)
United States Committee on Irrigation and Drainage (2012)
United States Composting Council (2012)
USA Rice Federation (2011)
XBRL US, Inc. (2012)

Bastrop

National Energy Services Association (2011)

Bloomington

Santa Gertrudis Breeders International (2011)

College Station

American Academy of Veterinary Pharmacology and Therapeutics (2012)
American Gelbvieh Association (2010)
American Red Brangus Association (2012)

Corpus Christi

Army Aviation Association of America (2012)

Cypress

National Energy Services Association (2010)

Dallas

ACA International, The Association of Credit and Collection Professionals (2011)
Acute Long Term Hospital Association (2012)
Ambulatory Surgery Center Association (2012)
American Association of Airport Executives (2010)
American Association of Hip and Knee Surgeons (2010, 2012)
American Baseball Coaches Association (2010)
American Chiropractic Association (2012)
American Concrete Institute (2012)
American Gem Trade Association (2012)
American Institute of Biological Sciences (2012)
American Library Association (2012)
American Osteopathic College of Radiology (2010)
American Physical Society (2011)
American Registry for Internet Numbers (2012)
American Society for Clinical Pharmacology and Therapeutics (2011)
American Society of Agricultural and Biological Engineers (2012)
American Society of Association Executives-The Center for Association Leadership (2012)
American Society of Breast Disease (2012)
American Society of Heating, Refrigerating and Air Conditioning Engineers (ASHRAE) (2012)
American Water Works Association (2012)
American Wind Energy Association (AWEA) (2010)
Appliance Parts Distributors Association (2010)
Asian American Hotel Owners Association (2011)
ASIS International (2010)
Assisted Living Federation of America (2012)
Associated Builders and Contractors (2012)
Association for Corporate Growth (2012)
Association for Education in Journalism and Mass Communication (2012)
Association for Healthcare Documentation Integrity (2011)
Association for Healthcare Volunteer Resource Professionals (2012)
Association for Library and Information Science Education (2012)
Association for Library Collections and Technical Services (2012)
The Association for Library Service to Children (2012)
The Association for Manufacturing Excellence (2011)

Association for Population/Family Planning Libraries and Information Centers, International (2010)
Association of Academic Health Centers (2010)
Association of Community College Trustees (2011)
Association of Insurance Compliance Professionals (2010)
Association of Jewish Aging Services (2011)
Association of Library Trustees, Advocates, Friends and Foundations (2012)
Association of Opinion Journalists (2010)
Association of Professional Chaplains (2011)
Association of Professional Landscape Designers (2010)
Association of Proposal Management Professionals (2012)
Association of Public and Land-Grant Universities (APLU) (2010)
Association of YMCA Professionals (2011)
Automotive Oil Change Association (2010)
Automotive Service Association (2010)
BMC - A Foodservice Sales and Marketing Council (2012)
College Athletic Business Management Association (2012)
Commercial Finance Association (2010)
Commercial Vehicle Training Association (2012)
Commission on Accreditation for Law Enforcement Agencies Incorporation (2010)
Competitive Telecommunications Association (2010, 2012)
Congress of Chiropractic State Associations (2011)
Construction Owners Association of America (2012)
Consumer Electronics Association (2012)
Council on Employee Benefits (2010)
Crane Certification Association of America (2012)
Design-Build Institute of America (2010)
Division 1-A Athletic Directors Association (2012)
Edison Welding Institute (2010)
Electronic Security Association (2012)
Energy Solutions Center (2010)
Equipment Marketing and Distribution Association (2010)
Event Service Professionals Association (2010)
Executive Women International (2012)
Food Marketing Institute (2011, 2012)
The Foodservice Group, Inc. (2012)
Foodservice Sales & Marketing Association (2012)
Garden Writers Association (2010)
Gas Technology Institute (2010)
Grocery Manufacturers Association (GMA) (2012)
Health Care Compliance Association (2010)
Helicopter Association International (2012)
Holiday and Decorative Association (2012)
Hydraulic Institute (2011)
IEEE Signal Processing Society (2010)
Independent Distributors Association (2010)
Independent Educational Consultants Association (2011)
Independent Staffing Alliance (2010)
Industrial Fabrics Association International (2011)
Infusion Nurses Society (2012)
Insulation Contractors Association of America (2012)
International Association of Black Professional Fire Fighters (2011)
International Association of Music Libraries, United States Branch (2012)
International Aviation Women's Association (2012)
International Brotherhood of Magicians (2011)
International College of Applied Kinesiology (2012)
International Erosion Control Association (2010)
International Municipal Signal Association (2010)
International Society of Nurses in Genetics (2010)
Liability Insurance Research Bureau (2012)
Marketing Research Association (2012)
Minor League Baseball (2011)
Mortgage Bankers Association of America (2012)
Mulch and Soil Council (2010)
Music Library Association (2012)
National After School Association (2012)
National Association for Bilingual Education (2012)
National Association for Business Economics (2011)
National Association of Medical Staff Services (2011)
National Association of Academic Advisors for Athletes (2011)
National Association of Biology Teachers (2012)
National Association of Broadcasters (2012)
National Association of Certified Valuation Analysts (2012)
National Association of College and University Food Services (2011)
National Association of Collegiate Directors of Athletics (2011)
National Association of Collegiate Marketing Administrators (2012)
National Association of Independent Life Brokerage Agencies (2010)
National Association of Police Organizations (2011)
National Association of Professional Baseball Leagues (2011)
National Association of Real Estate Investment Trusts (NAREIT) (2011)
National Association of Royalty Owners (2012)
National Association of Security Companies (NASCO) (2010)
National Association of Spine Specialists (2012)
National Coalition of Girls' Schools (2012)
National Council of Acoustical Consultants (2012)
National Council of Real Estate Investment Fiduciaries (2010)
National Council of State Boards for Nursing (2012)
National Guild for Community Arts Education (2012)
National Head Start Association (2010, 2012)
National Home Infusion Association (2010)
National Information Standards Organization (2012)
National Multi-Housing Council (2010, 2012)
National Registry of Environmental Professionals (2010)
National Society of Black Engineers (2012)
National Society of Genetic Counselors (2010)
National Speakers Association (2012)
National Systems Contractors Association (2012)
National Telecommunications Cooperative Association (2011)
National Truck and Heavy Equipment Claims Council (2012)
National Watermelon Association (2010)

North American Association of Professors of Christian Education (2012)
North American Deer Farmers Association (2012)
North American Spine Society (2012)
Organization of American Kodaly Educators (2010)
Owner-Operator Independent Drivers Association, Inc. (2010)
Pan American Allergy Society (2012)
PCIA - The Wireless Infrastructure Association (2011)
PeerSpan (2010)
Population Association of America (2010)
Power Transmission Distributors Association (2012)
Professional Association of Christian Educators (2012)
Professional Convention Management Association (2010)
Property Loss Research Bureau (2012)
RCI, Inc. (2012)
Restaurant Facility Management Association (2010)
Retail Industry Leaders Association (2012)
The Risk Management Association (2012)
School Nutrition Association (2010)
Search - The National Consortium for Justice Information and Statistics (2012)
Society for Healthcare Consumer Advocacy (2012)
Society for Healthcare Epidemiology of America (2011)
Society for Maternal-Fetal Medicine (2012)
Society for Technical Communication (2010)
Society for the Psychological Study of Men and Masculinity (2010)
Society of American Business Editors and Writers (2011)
Society of Hospital Medicine (2011)
Society of Interventional Radiology (2012)
Spray Polyurethane Foam Alliance (2012)
Submersible Wastewater Pump Association (2012)
Surgical Infection Society (2012)
Technology Student Association (2011)
Telecommunications Industry Association (2012)
Toy Industry Association (2010)
United Fresh Produce Association (2012)
United States Hispanic Chamber of Commerce (2010)
Water and Sewer Distributors of America (2011)
The Wire Association International, Inc. (2012)
Women in Aviation International (2012)
Women's Foodservice Forum (2012)
WorldatWork (2010)
Young Adult Library Services Association (2012)

Denton

American Harp Society (2011)
International Horn Society (2012)

El Paso

Humanities Education and Research Association (2010)
International Test and Evaluation Association (2011, 2012)

Farmers Branch

Kappa Delta Pi (2012)
Marble Institute of America (2012)

Fredericksburg

Organization of Flying Adjusters (2012)

Frisco

Association of Directory Publishers (2012)

Ft. Worth

AHS International - The Vertical Flight Society (2011, 2012)
American Academy of Craniofacial Pain (2012)
American Aging Association (2012)
American Association for Marriage and Family Therapy (2011)
American Cleft Palate-Craniofacial Association (2010)
American Institute of Parliamentarians (2012)
American Miniature Horse Association (2010, 2012)
American Paint Horse Association (2012)
American Wholesale Marketers Association (2011)
Appaloosa Horse Club (2010, 2012)
Army Aviation Association of America (2010)
Association of Energy Service Companies (2010, 2012)
Baptist Communicators Association (2012)
Catholic Charities USA (2011)
College of Optometrists in Vision Development (2012)
Communications Marketing Association (2012)
Computing Technology Industry Association (CompTIA) (2012)
Environmental Mutagen Society (2010)
Federation of State Medical Boards of the United States (2012)
Independent Electrical Contractors (2012)
International Andalusian and Lusitano Horse Association (2012)
International Downtown Association (2010)
International Festivals and Events Association (2011)
International Foodservice Distributors Association (2011)
Lamaze International (2011)
Literacy Research Association (2010)
National Alliance of Independent Crop Consultants (2011)
National Association of Collegiate Women Athletic Administrators (2010)
National Association of Real Estate Brokers (2010)
National Association of Trailer Manufacturers (2012)
National Automotive Finance Association (2010, 2012)
National Cotton Council of America (2012)
National Dairy Herd Information Association (2012)
National Utility Contractors Association (NUCA) (2012)
National Vehicle Leasing Association (2012)
North American Peruvian Horse Association (2010, 2012)
Palomino Horse Breeders of America (2010)
Post-Tensioning Institute (2010)
Religious Conference Management Association (2010)

SAE International (2012)
Snack Food Association (2010)
Society for the Advancement of Material and Process Engineering (2011)
Society of American Military Engineers (2011)
Society of Hispanic Professional Engineers (2012)
Soil and Water Conservation Society (2012)
Surface Mount Technology Association (2011)
Texas Longhorn Breeders Association of America (2010)
Undersea and Hyperbaric Medical Society (2011)
Web Sling and Tie down Association (2010)

Galveston

American Brahman Breeders Association (2012)
Brotherhood of Locomotive Engineers and Trainmen (2012)
Council of American Maritime Museums (2012)
International Transplant Nurses Society (2012)
League of Historic American Theatres (2010)
North American Society for Oceanic History (2012)

Grapevine

American Academy of Cosmetic Dentistry (2010)
American Bus Association (2012)
American College of Osteopathic Obstetricians and Gynecologists (2012)
American Correctional Association (2011)
American Society for Laser Medicine and Surgery (2011)
American Society of Professional Estimators (2010)
American Society of Transplantation (2012)
American Trucking Associations (2011)
Archery Trade Association (2012)
Association for Medical Imaging Management (2011)
Association for Molecular Pathology (2011)
Association of Diesel Specialists (2010)
Association of Private Sector Colleges and Universities (Career College Association) (2011)
Association of Surgical Technologists (2010)
College of American Pathologists (2011)
Construction Financial Management Association (2011)
Direct Selling Association (2012)
Distribution Contractors Association (2010, 2012)
Electrical Manufacturing and Coil Winding Association (2010)
Insurance Accounting and Systems Association (2010)
International Association of Administrative Professionals (2012)
International Society for Pharmaceutical Engineering (2011)
Investment Program Association (2010)
Legal Marketing Association (2012)
National Academy of Elder Law Attorneys, Inc. (2011, 2012)
National Association for Home Care and Hospice (2012)
National Association of Colleges and Employers (2011)
National Association of Mutual Insurance Companies (2012)
Sigma Theta Tau International (2011)
Structural Stability Research Council (2012)

Houston

Academy of Clinical Research Professionals (2012)
American Association of Petroleum Geologists (2011, 2012)
American Astronautical Society (2011)
American Ceramics Society (2010)
American Fuel & Petrochemical Manufacturers (2012)
American Institute of Chemical Engineers (2012)
American Medical Student Association (2012)
American Petroleum Institute (2012)
American Society for Nondestructive Testing (2010)
American Society of Andrology (2010)
American Society of Head and Neck Radiology (2010)
American Society of Mechanical Engineers (ASME) (2012)
American Society of Orthopedic Physician Assistants (2010)
ASM International (2012)
Association of Clinical Research Professionals (2012)
Association of Jewish Family & Children's Agencies (2012)
APCO (Association of Public-Safety Communications Officials) International (2010)
Association of Zoos and Aquariums (2010)
The Association to Advance Collegiate Schools of Business (2010, 2012)
Beef Improvement Federation (2012)
Business and Institutional Furniture Manufacturers Association International (2012)
Chlorine Institute (2011)
College Reading and Learning Association (2012)
Cooling Technology Institute (2010, 2012)
Council of Petroleum Accountants Societies (2012)
Deep Foundations Institute (2012)
Democratic Governors Association (2010)
The Endocrine Society (2012)
Energy Frontiers International (2012)
Energy Security Council (2012)
Energy Telecommunications and Electrical Association (2010, 2011)
Forging Industry Association (2012)
Fresh Produce Association of the Americas (2012)
Geospatial Information Technology Association (2010, 2011, 2012)
Global Business Travel Association (2010)
Ground Water Protection Council (2012)
Heating, Airconditioning and Refrigeration Distributors International (2010)
IEEE Communications Society (2011)
Independent Bakers Association (2012)
Independent Petroleum Association of America (2012)
The Integrated Ocean Drilling Program (2012)
Intelligent Transportation Society of America (2010)
International Association of Audio Information Services (2012)
International Association of Drilling Contractors (2012)
International Association of Jewish Vocational Services (2012)

International Association of Venue Managers (2010)
International Brangus Breeders Association (2012)
International Concrete Repair Institute (2011)
International Dairy-Deli-Bakery Association (2010)
International Economic Development Council (2012)
International Liquid Terminals Association (2010, 2012)
International Ombudsman Association (2012)
Laser Institute of America (2010, 2011)
Maritime Law Association of the U.S. (2010)
NACE International (2011)
NAFSA: Association of International Educators (2012)
NANDA International (2012)
National Association of Basketball Coaches (2011)
National Association of Black Accountants, Inc. (2010)
National Association of Church Business Administration (2012)
National Association of College Stores (2011)
National Association of Educational Procurement, Inc. (2012)
National Association of Elementary School Principals (2010)
National Association of Health Services Executives (2012)
National Association of Independent Schools (2012)
National Association of Investors Corporation (2012)
National Association of Orthopaedic Technologists (2010)
National Association of Wheat Growers (2012)
National Association of Women Judges (2012)
National BioDiesel Board (2012)
National Black Chamber of Commerce (2010, 2012)
National Energy Services Association (2010)
National Federation of Priests' Councils (2010)
National Organization for the Professional Advancement of Black Chemists and Chemical Engineers (2011)
The National Procurement Institute, Inc (2012)
National Real Estate Investors Association (2011)
Norwegian-American Chamber of Commerce (2012)
Organization of American Historians (2011)
Petroleum Technology Transfer Council (2011)
Pipeline Research Council International, Inc. (2012)
Produce Marketing Association (2012)
Research Association of Minority Professors (2012)
Retail Bakers of America (2012)
Retail Confectioners International (2011)
Society for Pediatric Pathology (2012)
Society for Research on Nicotine and Tobacco (2012)
Society for Critical Care Medicine (2012)
Society of Mexican American Engineers and Scientists (2012)
The Society of Naval Architects and Marine Engineers (2011)
Society of North American Goldsmiths (2010)
Society of Pediatric Nurses (2012)
Society of Petroleum Engineers (2010)
Society of Piping Engineers and Designers (2012)
Society of Plastics Engineers (2012)
Society of Women Engineers (2012)
Specialty Coffee Association of America (2011)
Specialty Steel Industry of North America (2012)
Steel Tank Institute Division of STI/SPFA (2012)
Texas Alliance of Energy Producers (2012)
United Braford Breeders (2011)
United States Wheat Associates, Inc. (2012)
Valve Repair Council (2012)
WaterJet Technology Association - Industrial and Municipal Cleaning Association (2010, 2011, 2012)
Waterways Council, Inc. (2012)
Women in Endocrinology (2012)

Hurst

American Society of Safety Engineers (2012)

Irving

Electronic Transactions Association (2012)
Transportation Elevator and Grain Merchants Association (2012)
USA Rice Federation (2010)

Kerrville

Exotic Wildlife Association (2012)
Mohair Council of America (2012)

Las Colinas

American Association of Credit Union Leagues (2010)

Lost Pines

Bearing Specialist Association (2011)
Water Systems Council (2011)

Lubbock

The American Rambouillet Sheep Breeders Association (2012)
National Sorghum Producers (2011)
Society of Environmental Journalists (2012)
Western Literature Association (2012)

McAllen

Conference of Minority Public Administrators (2012)
North American Nature Photography Association (2011)

Midland

Society of Petroleum Engineers (2012)

Plano

Acute Long Term Hospital Association (2010)
The Association of Concert Bands (2010)
Association of Food and Drug Officials (2011)

Prairie View

The Association of Black Psychologists (2012)

S. Padre Island

American Association of Wildlife Veterinarians (2010)
Consortium of College and University Media Centers (2011)

San Antonio

AACE International (2012)
Academy of Ambulatory Foot and Ankle Surgery (2010)
Academy of Doctors of Audiology (2010)
Academy of Management (2011)
ACUTA - The Association for Information Communications Technology
   Professionals in Higher Education (2010)
ADSC: The International Association of Foundation Drilling (2012)
Air Conditioning Contractors of America (2011)
Airport Ground Transportation Association (2010)
AMC Institute (2010)
America's Small Business Development Center Network (2010)
American Academy of Anesthesiologist Assistants (2012)
American Academy of Dental Practice Administration (2011)
American Academy of Dental Sleep Medicine (2010)
American Academy of Disability Evaluating Physicians (2011)
American Academy of Medical Administrators (2012)
American Academy of Medical Hypnoanalysts (2011)
American Academy of Sleep Medicine (2010)
American Association for Geriatric Psychiatry (2011)
American Association of Colleges of Nursing (2012)
American Association of Colleges of Pharmacy (2011)
American Association of Diabetes Educators (2010)
American Association of Endodontists (2011)
American Association of Equine Practitioners (2011)
American Association of Feline Practitioners (2012)
American Association of Legal Nurse Consultants (2012)
American Association of Managing General Agents (2012)
American Association of Plastic Surgeons (2010)
American Association of Sleep Technologists (2010)
American Association of State Colleges and Universities (2012)
American Backflow Prevention Association (2011)
American Bakers Association (2011)
American Bearing Manufacturers Association (2011)
American Board of Veterinary Practitioners (2012)
American Case Management Association (2010)
American Chemical Society - Rubber Division (2012)
American Clinical and Climatological Association (2010)
American Clinical Neurophysiology Society (2012)
American College of Foot and Ankle Surgeons (2012)
American College of Gastroenterology (2010)
American College of Health Plan Management (2012)
American College of Laboratory Animal Medicine (2011)
American College of Osteopathic Internists (2011)
American College of Trial Lawyers (2011)
American Conference of Governmental Industrial Hygienists (2012)
American Correctional Health Services Association (2012)
American Electrology Association (2012)
American Embryo Transfer Association (2011)
American Epilepsy Society (2010)
American Evaluation Association (2010)
American Filtration and Separations Society (2010)
American Fire Sprinkler Association (2011)
American Football Coaches Association (2012)
American Fuel & Petrochemical Manufacturers (2011, 2012)
American Heart Association (2010)
American Institute of Chemical Engineers (2010)
American Medical Directors Association (2012)
American Medical Technologists (2012)
American Miniature Horse Association (2011)
American Moving and Storage Association (2012)
American National CattleWomen (2012)
American Occupational Therapy Association, Inc. (2012)
American Peanut Research and Education Society, Inc. (2011)
American Pediatric Surgical Association (2012)
American Philological Association (2011)
American Public Transportation Association (2010)
American School Health Association (2012)
American Scientific Glassblowers Society (2010)
American Seed Trade Association (2010)
American Short Line and Regional Railroad Association (2011)
American Society for Dental Aesthetics (2010)
American Society for Eighteenth-Century Studies (2012)
American Society for Engineering Education (2012)
American Society for Healthcare Engineering (2012)
American Society for Microbiology (2012)
American Society of Agronomy (ASA, CSSA, SSSA) (2011)
American Society of Colon and Rectal Surgeons (2012)
American Society of Transplantation (2011)
American Subcontractors Association (2012)
American Telemedicine Association (2010)
American Traffic Safety Service Association (2010)
American Veterinary Dental Society (2010)
American Volleyball Coaches Association (2011)
Analytical Laboratory Managers Association (2012)
Aquarium and Zoo Facilities Association (2011)
Archaeological Institute of America (2011)
Architectural Precast Association (2012)
Associated Equipment Distributors (2010)
Associated Professional Sleep Societies (2010)
The Association for Academic Surgery (2010)

Association for Assessment and Accreditation of Laboratory Animal Care
   International (2011, 2012)
Association for Behavior Analysis International (2010)
Association for Financial Professionals, Inc. (2010)
Association for Healthcare Philanthropy (2010)
Association for Healthcare Resource and Materials Management (2012)
Association for Hospital Medical Education (2010)
Association for Management Information in Financial Services (2010)
Association for Surgical Education (2010)
Association for the Behavioral Sciences and Medical Education (2012)
Association for Vascular Access (2012)
Association of Academic Chairmen of Plastic Surgery (2010)
Association of Biomolecular Resource Facilities (2011)
Association of Bridal Consultants (2011)
Association of College and University Auditors (2012)
Association of Community Cancer Centers (2012)
Association of Corporate Counsel (2010)
Association of Energy Service Companies (2011)
Association of Insurance Compliance Professionals (2012)
Association of Military Surgeons of the United States (2011)
Association of Paroling Authorities International (2011)
Association of Pediatric Program Directors (2012)
Association of Professors of Gynecology and Obstetrics (2011)
Association of Program Directors in Surgery (2010)
Association of State Floodplain Managers (2012)
Association of University Radiologists (2012)
ATM Industry Association (2012)
Automotive Fleet and Leasing Association (2012)
Book Manufacturers' Institute (2011)
Bridge Grid Flooring Manufacturers Association (2010)
Casket and Funeral Supply Association of America (2012)
College Swimming Coaches Association of America (2012)
College Theology Society (2012)
Cooling Technology Institute (2011)
Corporate Facility Advisors, Inc. (2012)
Council of Educational Facility Planners International (2012)
Council of State Speech-Language-Hearing Association Presidents (2010)
Crop Science Society of America (2011)
Dance Masters of America, Inc. (2010)
Drug & Alcohol Testing Industry Association (2012)
Equipment Leasing and Finance Association (2011)
Equipment Service Association (2012)
Financial Planning Association (2012)
Fire Apparatus Manufacturers' Association (2010)
Flexographic Technical Association (2012)
Future Business Leaders of America - Phi Beta Lambda (2012)
Gas Processors Association (2011)
Gas Processors Suppliers Association (2011)
Government Finance Officers Association of the United States and Canada (2011)
Healthcare Distribution Management Association (2012)
Healthcare Financial Management Association (2010)
High Technology Crime Investigation Association (2011)
IEEE Aerospace and Electronic Systems Society (AESS) (2011)
Industrial Heating Equipment Association (2010)
Institute for Professionals in Taxation (2011)
Institute Management Accountants (2012)
Institute of Certified Business Counselors (2010)
The Institute of Financial Operations (2012)
Institute of Industrial Engineers (2010)
Insurance Consumer Affairs Exchange (2012)
Intellectual Property Owners Association (2012)
International Association of Diecutting and Diemaking (2011)
International Association of Emergency Managers (2010)
International Association of Flight And Critical Care Paramedics (2010)
International Association of Law Enforcement Firearms Instructors, Inc. (2010)
International Association of Operative Millers (2011)
International Association of Plumbing and Mechanical Officials (2011)
International Cemetery, Cremation and Funeral Association (2010)
International Claim Association (2012)
International Customer Service Association (2011)
International Facility Management Association (2012)
International Firestop Council (2012)
International Franchise Association (2010)
International Lactation Consultant Association (2010)
International Laser Display Association (2012)
International Liquid Terminals Association (2012)
International Order of the Golden Rule (2010)
International Precious Metals Institute (2011)
International Society of Automation (2010)
Interstate Oil and Gas Compact Commission (2012)
IT Financial Management Association (2011)
Journalism Education Association (2012)
League of Historic American Theatres (2010)
Lift Manufacturers Product Section - Material Handling Institute (2012)
Local Media Association (2012)
Manufactured Housing Institute (2012)
Manufacturers' Agents Association for the Foodservice Industry (2010)
The Masonry Society (2011)
Material Handling Industry of America (2012)
Meat Importers Council of America (2012)
MGMA-ACMPE (2012)
Military Officers Association of America (MOAA) (2011)
NACE International (2010)
NALP - The Association for Legal Career Professionals (2012)
National Association of Addiction Treatment Providers (2010)
National Association of Boards of Pharmacy (2011)
National Association of Child Care Professionals (2012)
National Association of Division Order Analysts (2010)
National Association of Episcopal Schools (2010)
National Association of Exclusive Buyer Agents (2012)

National Association of Free Clinics (2012)
National Association of Healthcare Access Management (2011)
National Association of Healthcare Education Centers (2012)
National Association of Pediatric Nurse Practitioners (2012)
National Association of Personnel Services (2012)
National Association of Professional Background Screeners (2010)
National Association of State Boards of Geology (2011)
National Association of State Utility Consumer Advocates (NASUCA) (2011)
National Association of Surety Bond Producers (2010)
National Association of Temple Educators (2012)
National Association of Tower Erectors (2012)
National Board of Boiler and Pressure Vessel Inspectors (2010)
National Braille Association (2012)
National Chemical Credit Association (2010)
National Collegiate Athletic Association (2011)
National Concrete Masonry Association (2010)
National Conference of State Legislatures (2011)
National Council of Farmer Cooperatives (2011)
National Council on Teacher Retirement (2012)
National Customs Brokers and Forwarders Association of America (2010)
National Demolition Association (2012)
National Energy Services Association (2012)
National Fastener Distributors Association (2010)
National Federation Coaches Association (2012)
National Federation of State High School Associations (2012)
National Ground Water Association (2012)
National Interscholastic Athletic Administrators Association (2012)
National Judges Association (2012)
National Organization of Life and Health Insurance Guaranty Association (2012)
National Reverse Mortgage Lenders Association (2012)
National School Public Relations Association (2011)
National School Supply and Equipment Association (2011)
National Sporting Goods Association (2012)
National Tractor Parts Dealer Association (2012)
National Tuberculosis Controllers Association (2012)
North American Association of Food Equipment Manufacturers (2012)
North American Gamebird Association (2010)
North American Meat Association (2012)
North American Neuro-Ophthalmology Society (2012)
North American Society for Trenchless Technology (2012)
Nursery and Landscape Association Executives of North America (2012)
Obesity Society (2012)
Opportunity Finance Network (2012)
The Optical Lab Division (2011)
Orthopaedic Trauma Association (2011)
Parenting Media Association (2012)
Partnership for Philanthropic Planning (2011)
Plastic Pipe and Fittings Association (2012)
Plastics Pipe Institute (2010)
Portable Sanitation Association International (2011)
Power and Communications Contractors Association (2012)
Precast/Prestressed Concrete Institute (2011)
Printing Industry Credit Executives (2012)
Professional Liability Underwriting Society (2010)
Professional Photographers of America (2011)
Property Loss Research Bureau (2010)
Pulp and Paper Safety Association (2011)
Quality Service Contractors (2012)
Radiant Panel Association (2011)
Refrigerating Engineers and Technicians Association (2012)
Research Chefs Association (2012)
Research Society on Alcoholism (2010)
Risk and Insurance Management Society, Inc. (RIMS) (2012)
Service Specialists Association (2012)
Sleep Research Society (2010)
Society for Ancient Greek Philosophy (2011)
Society for Developmental and Behavioral Pediatrics (2011)
Society for Economic Anthropology (2012)
Society for Education in Anesthesia (2011)
Society for Human Resource Management (2010)
Society for Pediatric Pathology (2011)
Society for Physician Assistants in Pediatrics (2011)
Society for the Psychological Study of Men and Masculinity (2012)
Society of Air Force Physician Assistants (2011)
Society of American Gastrointestinal and Endoscopic Surgeons (2011)
Society of Exploration Geophysicists (2011)
Society of Former Special Agents of the Federal Bureau of Investigation (2010)
Society of Government Service Urologists (2010)
Society of Petroleum Engineers (2012)
Society of Quality Assurance (2011)
Society of Surgical Oncology (2011)
Society of University Surgeons (2010)
Society of Urologic Nurses and Associates (2011)
Soil Science Society of America (2011)
Specialty Tools and Fasteners Distributors Association (2011)
Structural Insulated Panel Association (2012)
Transportation Intermediaries Association (2012)
United Methodist Association of Health and Welfare Ministries (2011)
United States and Canadian Academy of Pathology (2011)
United States Lactation Consultant Association (2010)
Vacation Rental Managers Association (2010)
Veterinary Hospital Managers Association (2011)
Vibration Institute (2011)
Vibration Isolation and Seismic Control Manufacturers Association (2012)
Waste Equipment Technology Association (2010)
Water Quality Association (2011)
Women's Basketball Coaches Association (2010)
World Waterpark Association (2010)
Worldwide ERC (2012)
Zonta International (2010)

San Marcos
    Beefmaster Breeders United (2011)
    National Council for Geographic Education (2012)
    Society for Chaos Theory in Psychology and Life Sciences (2010)

Southlake
    Plastics Pipe Institute (2010, 2012)

Sugar Land
    National Constables Association (2012)

The Woodlands
    American Exploration & Production Council (2012)
    Association of Directory Publishers (2010)
    Council of Petroleum Accountants Societies (2011)
    Energy Security Council (2010)
    Petroleum Packaging Council (2010, 2012)
    Steel Plate Fabricators Association Division of STI/SPFA (2010)

Tyler
    North American Council of Automotive Teachers (2012)

Wichita Falls
    United States Custom Harvesters, Inc. (2010)

Wimberley
    American Red Brangus Association (2012)

UTAH

Deer Valley
    American Association of Managing General Agents (2012)

Ogden
    Association of Field Ornithologists (2010)

Park City
    American Academy of Dental Practice Administration (2010)
    American Society of Ophthalmic Plastic and Reconstructive Surgery (2010)
    Association of Children's Prosthetic-Orthotic Clinics (2011)
    Association of Vascular and Interventional Radiographers (2010)
    Concrete Sawing and Drilling Association (2011)
    Giving Institute (2012)
    Mason Contractors Association of America (2012)
    National Association of Spine Specialists (2012)
    Neurosurgical Society of America (2012)
    States Organization for Boating Access (2010)
    Steel Founders' Society of America (2012)
    United States Ski and Snowboard Association (2010)
    Water Sports Industry Association (2010)
    Wilderness Medical Society (2010, 2011, 2012)

Salt Lake City
    Academy of General Dentistry (2012)
    Academy of Medical-Surgical Nurses (2012)
    America Outdoors Association (2010)
    American Academy of Adoption Attorneys (2012)
    American Academy of Fertility Care Professionals (2012)
    American Apparel & Footwear Association (2010)
    American Association for Employment in Education (2012)
    American Association for State and Local History (2012)
    American Fuel & Petrochemical Manufacturers (2012)
    American Health Information Management Association (2011)
    American Industrial Hygiene Association (2010)
    American Institute of Chemical Engineers (2010)
    American Medical Society for Sports Medicine (2011)
    American Optometric Association (2011)
    American Optometric Student Association (2011)
    American Payroll Association (2011)
    American Society for Mass Spectrometry (2010)
    American Society of Limnology and Oceanography (2012)
    American Wind Energy Association (AWEA) (2010)
    Aquatic Plant Management Society, Inc. (2012)
    Association for Documentary Editing (2011)
    Association of American University Presses (2010)
    Association of Ancient Historians (2010)
    Association of Environmental and Engineering Geologists (2012)
    Association of Independent Corrugated Converters (2011)
    Association of Regulatory Boards of Optometry (2011)
    Campus Computer Resellers Alliance (2012)
    Chain Drug Marketing Association (2012)
    College Reading and Learning Association (2010)
    Council of Petroleum Accountants Societies (2010)
    Distributive Education Clubs of America (DECA) (2012)
    Health Physics Society (2010)
    Hearth, Patio and Barbecue Association (2011)
    Humanities Education and Research Association (2012)
    International Society of Air Safety Investigators (2011)
    Land Trust Alliance (2012)
    Marble Institute of America (2012)
    NACE International (2012)
    National Association of Academic Advisors for Athletes (2010)
    National Association of College Stores (2012)
    National Association of Health Data Organizations (2010)
    National Association of State Aviation Officials (2010)
    National Association of State Departments of Agriculture (2011)
    National Association of Teachers of Singing (2010)
    National Council of State Housing Agencies (2012)

National Genealogical Society (2010)
National Interstate Council of State Boards of Cosmetology (2012)
National Student Nurses Association (2011)
North American Society for Pediatric Gastroenterology, Hepatology and Nutrition (2012)
The Oceanography Society (2012)
Society for Integrative and Comparative Biology (2011)
Society for Risk Analysis (2010)
Society for the Advancement of Material and Process Engineering (2010)
Society for the Advancement of Scandinavian Study (2012)
Society of Gynecologic Oncologists (2010)
Society of Nuclear Medicine (2010)
Society of Toxicology (2010)

Snowbird

American Holistic Nurses Association (2012)
Computing Research Association (2010)
Environmental and Water Resources Institute of the American Society of Civil Engineers (2012)
National Ski Patrol System (2010)
The Wildlife Society (2010)

West Valley City

American Association of Community Theatre (2012)

VERMONT

Arlington

National Association for Printing Leadership (2012)

Burlington

Alpha Gamma Rho (2012)
Association of Alternative Newsweeklies (2012)
Eastern Apicultural Society of North America (2012)
National Association of State Facilities Administrators (2010)
National Conference of Insurance Legislators (2012)

Essex Junction

National Speleological Society (2010)

Montpelier

Building Stone Institute (2011)
Society for Industrial Archeology (2010)

Shelburne

The Brown Swiss Association (2012)

Stowe

American College of Radiology (2012)
American Sugar Alliance (2011)

Tunbridge

American Milking Devon Cattle Association (2012)

Woodstock

Distribution Contractors Association (2011)

VIRGIN ISLANDS

St. Thomas

American College of Eye Surgeons (2011)
Black Psychiatrists of America (2010)
National Tooling and Machining Association (2010)
Spring Manufacturers Institute (2010)

VIRGINIA

Alexandria

Academy for Eating Disorders (2011)
The Aluminum Association, Inc. (2010)
American Academy of Physician Assistants (2012)
American Association of Surgical Physician Assistants (2010)
American Association of Veterinary Clinicians (2010)
American Horticultural Society (2010)
American Institute of Constructors (2012)
American National Standards Institute (2010)
The Association for Consortium Leadership (2010)
The Association for Social Anthropology in Oceania (2010)
Association of American Pesticide Control Officials (2012)
Association of American Veterinary Medical Colleges (2011, 2012)
Association of Clean Water Administrators (2012)
Association of Coupon Professionals (2012)
Association of Military Colleges and Schools of the United States (2010, 2012)
Association of Progressive Rental Organizations (2010)
Association of State Drinking Water Administrators (2012)
Broadcast Technology Society (2012)
Combat Helicopter Pilots Association (2012)
COMISS Network - The Network on Ministry in Specialized Settings (2011, 2012)
Construction Users Roundtable (2012)
Coordinating Research Council (2012)
CPA Manufacturing Services Association (2012)
Ethylene Oxide Sterilization Association, Inc. (2010, 2012)
International Association of Clerks, Recorders, Election Officials and Treasurers (2012)
International Society for Educational Planning (2010)
National Association of Extension 4-H Agents (2012)
National Association of Health Data Organizations (2011)
National Association of Independent Public Finance Advisors (2012)
National Association of Nonprofit Accountants & Consultants (2012)

National Association of Planning Councils (2010, 2011, 2012)
National Association of State Budget Officers (2010, 2012)
National Association of State Directors of Developmental Disabilities Services, Inc. (2010, 2012)
National Association of State Veterans Homes (2011)
National Association of Temple Administrators (2011)
National Association of Temple Educators (2010)
National Board for Certification in Occupational Therapy, Inc. (2012)
National Council of State Boards for Nursing (2011)
National CPA Health Care Advisors Association (2012)
National Emergency Management Association (2010, 2011, 2012)
National Grants Management Association (2012)
National Motor Freight Traffic Association, Inc. (2010, 2011, 2012)
National Property Management Association (2011)
National Rehabilitation Association (2011)
Phi Alpha Delta (2012)
Roof Coatings Manufacturers Association (2010)
Society for Historians of American Foreign Relations (2011)
Society for Industrial Microbiology (2012)
Society of Government Travel Professionals (2011)
United States Court Reporters Association (2010)

Arlington

Academy of Nutrition and Dietetics (2012)
Air Conditioning, Heating and Refrigeration Institute (AHRI) (2010)
American Association for the Advancement of Artificial Intelligence (2012)
American Association of Christian Schools (2012)
American Association of Family and Consumer Sciences (2012)
American Booksellers Association (2012)
American Cleaning Institute (2010)
American College of Preventive Medicine (2010)
American Council on International Personnel (2011)
American Glovebox Society (2012)
American Institute for Medical and Biological Engineering (2011)
American Society of Association Executives-The Center for Association Leadership (2012)
American Society of Interventional Pain Physicians (2011, 2012)
American Society of Naval Engineers (2010, 2012)
American Spice Trade Association (2012)
American Trucking Associations (2010)
American Waterways Operators (2010)
Anxiety Disorders Association of America (2012)
APSE: The Network on Employment (2012)
Army Aviation Association of America (2012)
Asphalt Emulsion Manufacturers Association (2012)
Associated General Contractors of America (AGC) (2012)
Association for Clinical Pastoral Education (2012)
Association for Enterprise Opportunity (2010)
Association of American Pesticide Control Officials (2010, 2011)
Association of Christian Schools International (2012)
Association of Community Health Nursing Educators (2010)
Association of Pediatric Program Directors (2012)
Association of United States Night Vision Manufacturers (2010, 2011, 2012)
Association of University Centers on Disabilities (AUCD) (2010)
Club Managers Association of America (2012)
The Coalition for Government Procurement (2012)
Coalition of Higher Education Assistance Organizations (2012)
Construction Writers Association (2012)
Council for Affordable and Rural Housing (2010, 2012)
Council for Electronic Revenue Communication Advancement (2010, 2012)
Council of Producers & Distributors of Agrotechnology (2012)
Design-Build Institute of America (2012)
The Environmental Information Association (2012)
Equal Justice Works (2012)
Equipment Leasing and Finance Association (2010)
Federal Bar Association (2010)
Federal Managers Association (2010, 2012)
Hearing Loss Association of America (2011)
Institute for Professionals in Taxation (2012)
International District Energy Association (2012)
International Safety Equipment Association (ISEA) (2011, 2012)
International Society for Medical Publication Professionals (2010)
Investment Adviser Association (2010, 2012)
Judge Advocates Association (2012)
Marine Corps Association (2010)
Military Officers Association of America (MOAA) (2010, 2012)
National Academies of Practice (2011, 2012)
National Association for Business Economics (2012)
National Association for the Support of Long Term Care (2012)
National Association of Alcoholism and Drug Abuse Counselors (2010)
National Association of Development Organizations (2010, 2012)
National Association of Healthcare Education Centers (2012)
National Association of Insurance Women (International) (2010)
National Association of Medicaid Directors (2012)
National Association of Postmasters of the United States (2012)
National Association of Professional Employer Organizations (2012)
National Association of Professional Insurance Agents (2012)
National Association of Residential Property Managers (2012)
National Association of Self-Instructional Language Programs (2012)
National Association of State Administrators and Supervisors of Private Schools (2012)
National Association of States United For Aging and Disabilities (2012)
National Council for Accreditation of Teacher Education (2012)
National Council of Higher Education Loan Programs (2012)
National Council of State Agencies for the Blind (2012)
National Council of State Boards for Nursing (2012)
National Council on Rehabilitation Education (2010, 2011, 2012)
National Family Planning and Reproductive Health Association (2010)
National League of Postmasters of the United States (2012)
National Mastitis Council (2011)

National Newspaper Association (2012)
National Risk Retention Association (2012)
National Society of Accountants (2010)
Newspaper Association Managers (2012)
North - American Interfraternity Conference (2012)
Nurses Organization of Veterans Affairs (2010)
Plumbing-Heating-Cooling Contractors - National Association (2012)
Professional Landcare Network (2012)
R & E Council of the NAPL (2012)
Science Fiction and Fantasy Writers of America (2012)
Society for Applied Learning Technology (2010)
Society for Military History (2012)
Society for Public Health Education (2011)
Society for Scholarly Publishing (2012)
Society of Federal Labor and Employee Relations Professionals (2011)
Society of Government Travel Professionals (2011, 2012)
State Education Technology Directors Association (2012)
Transportation Research Forum (2010)
United States Dairy Export Council (2012)
United States Pan Asian American Chamber of Commerce (2011)

Blacksburg

Architectural Woodwork Institute (2011)
National Association of University Fisheries and Wildlife Programs (2010)

Chantilly

Armed Forces Communications and Electronics Association (2012)
National Military Intelligence Association (2012)

Charlottesville

Employee Stock Ownership Plan Association (2012)
Respiratory Nursing Society (2012)

Culpeper

American Devon Cattle Association (2012)

Dulles

National Private Truck Council (2012)

Fairfax

American Society of Home Inspectors (2011)
American Wholesale Marketers Association (2012)
National Association of Area Agencies on Aging (2011)
National Military Intelligence Association (2010)

Falls Church

Marine Corps League (2011)

Ferrum

American Suffolk Horse Association (2010)

Fredericksburg

United Fresh Produce Association (2012)

Ft. Belvoir

National Association for Uniformed Services (2011)
Society of American Military Engineers (2012)
Society of Military Widows (2011)

Hampton

International Decorative Artisans League (2011)
National Association for Interpretation (2012)

Harrisonburg

American Devon Cattle Association (2010)

Herndon

Chief Warrant and Warrant Officers Association, United States Coast Guard (2011)
Management Association for Private Photogrammetric Surveyors (2011)

Hot Springs

Federal Communications Bar Association (2010)
Independent Insurance Agents & Brokers of America, Inc. (2011)
Industrial Asset Management Council (2010)
National Verbatim Reporters Association (2010)

La Jolla

United Synagogue of Conservative Judaism (2011)

Lansdowne

Advertising and Marketing International Network (2010)
American Association of Colleges of Pharmacy (2010)

Leesburg

American Association of Pastoral Counselors (2012)
Professional Insurance Marketing Association (2010)
Timber Frame Business Council (2012)

Lexington

Society for Military History (2010)

McLean

American Association of Physician Specialists (2011)

Norfolk

Association of Food and Drug Officials (2010)
Association of the United States Navy, Inc. (2012)
International Association of Women in Fire and Emergency Services (2012)

International Brotherhood of Magicians (2012)
National Association of State Alcohol and Drug Abuse Directors (NASADAD) (2010)
National Association of State Emergency Medical Services Officials (2010)
National Association of Student Affairs Professionals (2012)
National Counter Intelligence Corps Association (2012)
Oceanic Engineering Society (2012)
Shock Society (2011)
Smocking Arts Guild of America (2010)
Society of Government Meeting Professionals (2011)
Special Interest Group for University and College Computing Services (2010)

Quantico

Military Operations Research Society (2010)

Reston

The American Institute of Mining, Metallurgical, and Petroleum Engineers (2012)
American Press Institute (2011)
American Psychiatric Nurses Association (2012)
Association for Comprehensive Energy Psychology (2011)
Express Delivery & Logistics Association (2012)
InfoComm International (2012)
National Association of Broadcasters (2012)
Object Management Group (2012)
Plasma Protein Therapeutics Association (2010, 2011)
Society for Applied Learning Technology (2012)
Workgroup for Electronic Data Interchange (2010, 2012)

Richmond

American Association for State and Local History (2011)
American Logistics Association (2010)
American Philatelic Society (2010)
American Society of Parasitologists (2012)
Association for Technology in Music Instruction (2011)
Association for the Study of African American Life and History (2011)
Atlantic Seaboard Wine Association (2012)
Choristers Guild (2011)
College Music Society (2011)
Executive Women International (2012)
Holstein Association USA (2011)
International Association of Fairs and Expositions (2010)
International Council of Shopping Centers (2012)
International Customer Service Association (2012)
International Police Mountain Bike Association (2011)
IT Financial Management Association (2010)
National Association of Medical Minority Educators, Inc. (2010)
National Wooden Pallet and Container Association (2010)
Society of Forensic Toxicologists (2010)
Teaching-Family Association (2012)
United States-Taiwan Business Council (2011)

Roanoke

Aquacultural Engineering Society (2010, 2012)
Children's Literature Association (2011)
Housing Education and Research Association (2012)

Springfield

Armed Forces Communications and Electronics Association (2012)
TechAmerica (fka Technology Association of America) (2010)

Sterling

Urban Financial Services Coalition (2012)

Vienna

Case Management Society of America (2011)
National Council on Aging (2011)

Virginia Beach

American Society for Engineering Management (2012)
American Wind Energy Association (AWEA) (2012)
Armed Forces Communications and Electronics Association (2012)
Electronic Security Association (2012)
Independent Insurance Agents & Brokers of America, Inc. (2010)
Marine Technology Society (2012)
National Forum for Black Public Administrators (2012)
National Head Start Association (2010)
Society of Allied Weight Engineers (2010)
The Travel and Tourism Research Association (2012)

Williamsburg

American College of Osteopathic Pediatricians (2010)
American Society for Nondestructive Testing (2010)
Animal Behavior Society (2010)
Association of Bridal Consultants (2011)
Association of Public Treasurers of the United States and Canada (2012)
Book Manufacturers' Institute (2010)
Council of Industrial Boiler Owners (CIBO) (2010)
Distance Education and Training Council (2011)
Federation of Defense and Corporate Counsel (2011)
Inland Marine Underwriters Association (2010)
International Oil Mill Superintendents Association (2010)
Kitchen Cabinet Manufacturers Association (2012)
Master Pools Guild, Inc. (2010)
National Maritime Safety Association (2012)
Textile Care Allied Trades Association (2012)
Vibration Institute (2012)

WASHINGTON

Bellevue

American Logistics Association (2010)
American Medallic Sculpture Association (2012)
Antenna Measurement Techniques Association (2012)
ASM International (2010)
Associated Wire Rope Fabricators (2010)
Association for Education and Rehabilitation of the Blind & Visually Impaired (2012)
Association of Real Estate License Law Officials (2011)
Council of State Governments (2011)
Dangerous Goods Advisory Council (2010)
Environmental Mutagen Society (2012)
Fraternity Executives Association (2010)
IEEE Communications Society (2012)
International Association of Black Professional Fire Fighters (2012)
International League of Electrical Associations (2011)
International Municipal Signal Association (2011)
International Ozone Association-Pan American Group Branch (2010)
National Association of Jewelry Appraisers (2012)
Society for In Vitro Biology (2012)
USENIX: The Advanced Computing Systems Association (2012)

Bellingham

International Society of Weekly Newspaper Editors (2012)

Bremerton

International Listening Association (2012)

Langley

International Association of Home Staging Professionals (2012)

Maryland

National Association of Corporate Directors (2012)

Marysville

Council of Educational Facility Planners International (2012)

Olympia

American Horticultural Therapy Association (2012)

Redmond

Communications Media Management Association (2012)
International Association of Attorneys and Executives in Corporate Real Estate (2011)

Seattle

Academy Health (2011)
Agricultural & Applied Economics Association (2012)
Air and Surface Transport Nurses Association (2012)
American Academy of Clinical Neuropsychology (2012)
American Academy of Forensic Sciences (2010)
American Academy of Home Care Physicians (2012)
American Academy of Physical Medicine and Rehabilitation (2010)
American Association of Attorney-Certified Public Accountants (2012)
American Association of Collegiate Registrars and Admissions Officers (2011)
American Association of Community Colleges (2012)
American Association of Feline Practitioners (2012)
American Association of Medical Society Executives (2010)
American Association of Neuroscience Nurses (2012)
American Association of Nurse Anesthetists (2010)
The American Association of Nurse Attorneys (2011)
American Association of Teachers of Slavic and East European Languages (2012)
American Association of Veterinary State Boards (2012)
American College of Veterinary Pathologists (2012)
American College of Veterinary Surgeons (2010)
American Collegiate Retailing Association (2012)
American Concrete Pavement Association (2012)
American Cultural Resources Association (ACRA) (2012)
American Education Finance Association (2011)
American Educational Studies Association (2012)
American Federation of Teachers (AFL-CIO) (2010)
American Fisheries Society (2011)
American Geriatrics Society (2012)
American Physical Therapy Association - Private Practice Section (2011)
American Public Power Association (2012)
American Public Transportation Association (2012)
American Railway Development Association (2011)
American Real Estate Society (2011)
American Society for Enology and Viticulture (2010)
American Society for Theatre Research (2010)
American Society of Dentist Anesthesiologists (2010)
American Society of Dermatopathology (2011)
American Society of Extra-Corporeal Technology (2012)
American Society of Gene & Cell Therapy (2011)
American Society of Neuroradiology (2011)
American Veterinary Dental Society (2012)
American Waterways Operators (2012)
Associated Collegiate Press (2012)
Association for Behavior Analysis International (2012)
Association for Information Systems (2012)
Association for Medical Imaging Management (2012)
Association for the Advancement of Automotive Medicine (2012)
Association of Air Medical Services (2012)
Association of American Geographers (2011)
Association of Community Cancer Centers (2011)
Association of Government Accountants (2011)
Association of Moving Image Archivists (2012)
Association of Pathology Chairs (2010)
Association of Procurement Technical Assistance Centers (2012)

Association of Progressive Rental Organizations (2012)
Association of Public Health Laboratories (2012)
Association of School Business Officials International (2011)
Association of State and Provincial Psychology Boards (2010)
Association of State Dam Safety Officials (2010)
Association on Higher Education and Disability (2011)
Aviation Suppliers Association (2012)
Catholic Medical Association (2010)
Congress on Research in Dance (2010)
Council of Colleges of Arts and Sciences (2012)
Council of Institutional Investors (2012)
Council of Professional Associations on Federal Statistics (2012)
Council of Science Editors (2012)
Deep Sea Fishermen's Union (2011)
Destination Marketing Association International (2012)
Education Finance Council (2011)
The Electrochemical Society (2012)
Electrostatic Discharge Association (2012)
Environmental Design Research Association (2012)
The Foodservice Group, Inc. (2012)
Heart Failure Society of America (2012)
The History of Education Society (2012)
IEEE Education Society (2012)
Industrial Research Institute (2010)
International Academy of Compounding Pharmacists (2012)
International Association of Chiefs of Police (2012)
International Association of Flight And Critical Care Paramedics (2012)
International Association of Insurance Receivers (2010)
International Association of Plumbing and Mechanical Officials (2010)
International Association of Wildland Fire (2012)
International Cinema Technology Association (2011)
International Flight Services Association (2011)
International Public Management Association for Human Resources (2010)
International Real Estate Federation - American Chapter (2010)
International Society for Advancement Cytometry (2010)
International Society of Exposure Science (2012)
International Society of Protistologists (2011)
International Transplant Nurses Society (2012)
LOMA (2012)
Marine Technology Society (2010)
The Masonry Society (2010)
Minerals, Metals and Materials Society (2010)
Modern Language Association (2012)
NACHA - The Electronic Payments Association (2010)
Natco-The Organization for Transplant Professionals (2012)
National Academy of Elder Law Attorneys, Inc. (2012)
National Association for Chicana and Chicano Studies (2010)
National Association of Credit Union Supervisory and Auditing Committees (2011)
National Association of Dental Plans (2010)
National Association of Government Archives and Records Administrators (2012)
National Association of Independent Schools (2012)
National Association of Insurance and Financial Advisors (2010)
National Association of Insurance Commissioners (2010)
National Association of Orthopedic Nurses (2010)
National Association of Principals of Schools for Girls (2012)
National Association of Professional Geriatric Care Managers (2012)
National Association of Residential Property Managers (2010)
National Association of State Auditors, Comptrollers and Treasurers (2012)
National Association of State Retirement Administrators (2010)
National Association of Temple Educators (2011)
National Bison Association (2012)
National Cooperative Business Association (2012)
National Council for the Social Studies (2012)
National Council of Urban Education Associations (2012)
National Council on Education for the Ceramic Arts (2012)
National Institute of Governmental Purchasing (2012)
National Interstate Council of State Boards of Cosmetology (2010)
National Management Association (2012)
National Marine Electronics Association (2010)
National Organization of Social Security Claimants' Representatives (2012)
National Shellfisheries Association (2012)
National Society of Accountants (2011)
National Telecommunications Cooperative Association (2011)
North American Society for Cardiovascular Imaging (2010)
Oceanic Engineering Society (2010)
Organization for the Promotion and Advancement of Small Telecommunications Companies (2010)
Physician Assistant Education Association (2012)
Piano Technicians Guild (2012)
Pile Driving Contractors Association (2012)
Production Engine Remanufacturers Association (2012)
Professional and Organizational Development Network in Higher Education (2012)
Public Housing Authorities Directors Association (2012)
Regulatory Affairs Professionals Society (2012)
SACNAS (Society for Advancement of Chicanos and Native Americans in Science) (2012)
Sealant, Waterproofing and Restoration Institute (2012)
Society for Applied Anthropology (2011)
Society for Epidemiologic Research (2010)
Society for Industrial Archeology (2011)
Society for Industrial Microbiology (2011)
Society for Information Management (2012)
Society for Integrative and Comparative Biology (2010)
Society for Mining, Metallurgy and Exploration, Inc. (2012)
Society of Accredited Marine Surveyors (2012)
Society of Behavioral Medicine (2010)
Society of Competitive Intelligence Professionals (2011)
Society of Diagnostic Medical Sonographers (2012)

Society of Government Service Urologists (2011)
Society of Infectious Diseases Pharmacists (2012)
Society of North American Goldsmiths (2011)
Society of Plastics Engineers (2012)
Special Interest Group for Design of Communication (2012)
Swedish-American Chambers of Commerce of the USA, Inc. (2010)
Technical Association of the Pulp and Paper Industry (2012)
Theatre Library Association (2010)
Worldwide ERC (2010)

Seattle

American Academy of Orthopaedic Surgeons (2011)
American Association of Colleges of Pharmacy (2010)
American Astronomical Society (2011)
American Burn Association (2012)
American Choral Directors Association (2012)
American Farm Bureau Federation (2010)
American Homebrewers Association (2012)
American Meteorological Society (2011)
American Pharmacists Association (2011)
American Podiatric Medical Students Association (2010)
American Society for Cytotechnology (2012)
American Society of Bariatric Physicians (2010)
American Society of PeriAnesthesia Nurses (2011)
Association for the Advancement of Baltic Studies (2010)
Association of Clinical Research Professionals (2011)
Association of Energy Engineers (2012)
Association of Research Libraries (2010)
Board of Specialty Society (2011)
Building Owners and Managers Association International (2012)
Healthcare Financial Management Association (2010)
Hispanic National Bar Association (2012)
Journalism Education Association (2010)
Marketing Association of Credit Unions (2012)
Medical Library Association (2012)
The National Association for the Dually Diagnosed (2010)
National Association of Elementary School Principals (2012)
National Association of Police Athletics/Activities Leagues, Inc. (2011)
National Association of State Auditors, Comptrollers and Treasurers (2012)
National Institute of Governmental Purchasing (2012)
National Investor Relations Institute (2012)
National Tactical Officers Association of America (2012)
North American Society for Sport Management (2012)
The Psychonomic Society (2011)
RNA Society (2010)
The Society for Adolescent Medicine (2011)
Society for Biomaterials (2010)
Society for Information Display (2010)
The Society of Naval Architects and Marine Engineers (2010)
Society of Teachers of Family Medicine (2012)
World Airline Entertainment Association (2011)

Spokane

American Association of Cereal Chemists International (2012)
American Murray Grey Association (2010)
American Therapeutic Recreation Association (2010)
Council for Professional Recognition (2012)
International Association for Identification (2010)
International Association of Operative Millers (2012)
International Association of Personnel in Employment Security (2012)
International Association of Round Dance Teachers (2012)
International Association of Wildland Fire (2010)
International Association of Workforce Professionals (IAWP) (2012)
National Association of Diaconate Directors (2010)
National Association of University Forest Resources Programs (2012)
National Association of Wheat Growers (2012)
National Auctioneers Association (2012)
Packaging Machinery Manufacturers Institute (2012)
Printing Industries of America (2012)
Society for Range Management (2012)
Society of American Foresters (2012)

Stevenson

American Forest Resource Council (2010)
Forest Landowners Association (2010)
Native American Contractors Association (2012)
Social Venture Network (2012)

Tacoma

Association of Specialty Cut Flower Growers (2012)
Guild of American Luthiers (2011)
International Professional Groomers (2010)
National Interscholastic Swimming Coaches Association (2012)
Society for the History of Technology (2010)

Vancouver

American Association of Critical-Care Nurses (2012)
Association of Independent Information Professionals (2011)
Holistic Dental Association (2011)
International Paralegal Management Association (2012)

WEST VIRGINIA

Charleston

Association for University Business and Economic Research (2010)
Association of State Dam Safety Officials (2010)
Council of State Governments (2012)
Enlisted Association of the National Guard of the United States (2011)
National Association of State Auditors, Comptrollers and Treasurers (2010)

Daniels

National Association of Secretaries of State (2011)

Lewisburg

National Speleological Society (2012)

Shepherdstown

Association of State Wetland Managers (2011)

South Charleston

International Association of Correctional Training Personnel (2012)

Weirton

International Brotherhood of Magicians (2012)

White Sulphur Springs

American Ophthalmological Society (2010)
Apple Processors Association (2012)
Association of Edison Illuminating Companies (2011)
Direct Selling Association (2010)
Envelope Manufacturers Association (2012)
Industrial Fabrics Association International (2011)
Juice Products Association (2012)
National Coal Transportation Association (2012)
Professional Services Council (2012)
Resort Hotel Association (2012)
United States Industrial Fabrics Institute (2011)

WISCONSIN

Appleton

American Driver and Traffic Safety Education Association (2012)
Pyrotechnics Guild International (2010)
United States of Ayrshire Breeders' Association (2012)

Brookfield

American Pinzgauer Association (2012)

Centuria

American Blonde D'Aquitaine Association (2012)

Green Bay

Association of Information Technology Professionals (2012)

Kohler

American Association of Healthcare Consultants (2010)
American College of Mortgage Attorneys (2012)

Lake Geneva

American Leather Chemists Association (2010)
Automotive Market Research Council (2010)
Casting Industry Suppliers Association (2010)
Commercial Vehicle Solutions Network (2010)
The Commercial Vehicle Solutions Network (2010)
National Association of State Retirement Administrators (2011)

Madison

American Academy of Veterinary Pharmacology and Therapeutics (2011)
American Cultural Resources Association (ACRA) (2010)
American Physical Therapy Association - Private Practice Section (2012)
American Society for Environmental History (2012)
American Society for Virology (2012)
Association for Experiential Education (2012)
Association for Symbolic Logic (2012)
Association of University Research Parks (2012)
Dairy Management, Inc. (2010)
Forest Products Society (2010, 2011)
Genetics Society of America (2012)
Holstein Association USA (2011)
Mathematical Association of America (2012)
National Association of Resource Conservation and Development Councils (2012)
National Association of State Emergency Medical Services Officials (2011)
National Institute for Animal Agriculture (2012)
National Weather Association (2012)
North American Cartographic Information Society (2011)
North American Colleges and Teachers of Agriculture (2012)
North American Lake Management Society (2012)
Society for Historians of American Foreign Relations (2010)
United States of Ayrshire Breeders' Association (2012)
Walnut Council (2011)

Merrimac

American Institute of the History of Pharmacy (2012)

Middleton

Transportation Development Association (2012)

Milwaukee

AGN International North America, Inc (2012)
Alliance for Children and Families (2010)
Alliance of Area Business Publications (2012)
American Association of Cardiovascular and Pulmonary Rehabilitation (2010)
American Association of Public Health Dentistry (2012)
American Association of Teachers of German (2012)
American Bankers Association (2012)
American British White Park Association (2010)
American Chemical Society - Rubber Division (2010)
American Federation of State, County and Municipal Employees (2011)

American Institute for Conservation of Historic and Artistic Works (2010)
American Medical Writers Association (2010)
American Pinzgauer Association (2012)
American Society of Composers, Authors and Publishers (ASCAP) (2012)
ASPRS-The Imaging and Geospatial Information Society (2011)
Association for Applied and Clinical Sociology (2012)
Association of Fish and Wildlife Agencies (2010)
Association of State and Territorial Dental Directors (2012)
Electrical Generating Systems Association (2012)
Electrical Manufacturing and Coil Winding Association (2012)
Flexographic Technical Association (2012)
Future Business Leaders of America - Phi Beta Lambda (2011)
Hearing Loss Association of America (2010)
Historians Film Committee/Film & History (2012)
IEEE Power Electronics Society (2012)
International Association for Food Protection (2011)
International Association for Identification (2011)
International City/County Management Association (2011)
International Institute of Ammonia Refrigeration (2012)
International Ozone Association-Pan American Group Branch (2012)
Lamaze International (2010)
National American Legion Press Association (2010)
National Association of Activity Professionals (2010)
National Association of Animal Breeders (2012)
National Association of Catholic Chaplains (2011, 2012)
National Association of Railroad Passengers (2012)
National Association of Schools of Art and Design (2012)
National Association of State Boating Law Administrators (2011)
National Business Incubation Association (2012)
National Council on Public History (2012)
National Guard Association of the U.S. (2011)
National Organization for Human Service (2012)
National School Transportation Association (2012)
National Society for Experiential Education (2012)
National WIC Association (2010)
North American Academy of Liturgy (2010)
Organization of American Historians (2012)
Pi Sigma Epsilon (2010)
Precision Metalforming Association (2012)
Regional Airline Association (2010)
Religious Research Association (2011)
Society for Education in Anesthesia (2012)
Society for Maintenance & Reliability Professionals (2010)
Society for the Scientific Study of Religion (2011)
Society for the Study of Reproduction (2010)
Society of Plastics Engineers (2010)
Special Interest Group on Management Information Systems (2012)
The Wire Association International, Inc. (2010)

Pewaukee

Federation of Environmental Technologists, Inc. (2010, 2012)

Stevens Point

National Wellness Institute, Inc. (2011, 2012)

Willard

American Herbalists Guild (2012)

Wisconsin Dells

National Livestock Producers Association (2011)
Pony of the Americas Club (2011)

WYOMING

Cheyenne

National Association of State Foresters (2012)

Cody

Dude Ranchers' Association (2012)

Gillette

North American Corriente Association (2012)

Jackson Hole

Epsilon Sigma Phi (2010)

Laramie

The American Quaternary Association (2010)
American Society of Mammalogists (2010)

Moran

Society of Computed Body Tomography and Magnetic Resonance (2010)

Teton Village

AASHTO: Transportation Center of Excellence (2012)
Academy of Prosthodontics (2012)

CANADA

ALBERTA

Banff

American Concrete Pavement Association (2012)
Association of Children's Prosthetic-Orthotic Clinics (2012)
Council of Engineering and Scientific Society Executives (2012)
Foodservice & Packaging Institute, Inc. (2010)
Society for Pediatric Pathology (2010)

Calgary

Air and Waste Management Association (2010)
Airports Council International - North America (2012)
American Society of Heating, Refrigerating and Air Conditioning Engineers (ASHRAE) (2012)
Employee Assistance Society of North America (2012)
Fresh Produce Association of the Americas (2012)
International Association of Business Communicators (2012)
International Right of Way Association (2010)
Master Pools Guild, Inc. (2010)
Pipeline Research Council International, Inc. (2012)

Edmonton

National Guild of Professional Paperhangers (2010)
Society for Conservation Biology (2010)

Lake Louise

Web Sling and Tie down Association (2012)

Montreal

Qualitative Research Consultants Association (2012)

BRITISH COLUMBIA

Vancouver

Airports Council International - North America (2012)
American Academy of Gnathologic Orthopedics (2012)
American Academy of Gold Foil Operators (2010)
American Academy of Hospice and Palliative Medicine (2011)
American Association for Geriatric Psychiatry (2012)
American Association for Justice (2010)
American Association for the Advancement of Science (2012)
American Association of Physicists in Medicine (2011)
American College of Chest Physicians (2010)
American College of Medical Genetics (2011)
American Congress of Rehabilitation Medicine (2012)
American Educational Research Association (2012)
American Ground Water Trust (2012)
American Institute of Physics (2012)
American Ornithologists' Union (2012)
American Orthopsychiatric Association (2012)
American Pediatric Society (2010)
American Psychology-Law Society (2010)
American Roentgen Ray Society (2012)
American Society for Aesthetic Plastic Surgery (2012)
American Society for Eighteenth-Century Studies (2011)
American Society for Engineering Education (2011)
American Society for Mass Spectrometry (2012)
American Society of Colon and Rectal Surgeons (2011)
American Society of Ichthyologists and Herpetologists (2012)
American Society of Neurorehabilitation (2012)
American Society of Pediatric Nephrology (2010)
American Society of Retina Specialists (2010)
American Statistical Association (2010)
Animal Transportation Association (2012)
APPA - Leadership in Educational Facilities (2012)
Arabian Horse Association (2011)
ASME International Gas Turbine Institute (2011)
ASPSN - American Society of Plastic Surgical Nurses (2012)
Association for Consumer Research (2012)
Association of Fundraising Professionals (2012)
Association of Image Consultants International (2010)
Automotive Body Parts Association (2012)
Aviation Insurance Association (2010)
The Bluetooth Special Interest Group (2012)
Council of Engineering and Scientific Society Executives (2011)
Economic History Association (2012)
The Electrochemical Society (2010)
The Herpetologists' League (2012)
Hospice and Palliative Nurses Association (2011)
IEEE Magnetics Society (2012)
Infectious Diseases Society of America (2010)
Information Storage Industry Consortium (2012)
International Anesthesia Research Society (2011)
International Association for Healthcare Security and Safety (2012)
International Foundation of Employee Benefit Plans (2011)
Meeting Professionals International (2010)
Metal Powder Industries Federation (2012)
Million Dollar Round Table (2010)
NAFSA: Association of International Educators (2011)
National Academy of Neuropsychology (2010)
National Association of Steel Pipe Distributors (2012)
National Concrete Masonry Association (2011)
National Council for Air and Stream Improvement, Inc. (2011)
National Council of University Research Administrators (2012)
National Council on Measurement in Education (2012)
National Maritime Safety Association (2011)
National Precast Concrete Association (2010)
National Society for Histotechnology (2012)
North American Neuro-Ophthalmology Society (2011)
Production and Operations Management Society (2010)
Project Management Institute (2012)
Risk and Insurance Management Society, Inc. (RIMS) (2011)
Social Science History Association (2012)
Society for Clinical Trials (2011)
Society for Pediatric Pathology (2012)
Society for Pediatric Research (2010)
Society for Research on Adolescence (2012)
Society of Multivariate Experimental Psychology (2012)

Society of Teachers of Family Medicine (2010)
Special Interest Group on Management Information Systems (2010)
United States and Canadian Academy of Pathology (2012)
Veterinary Hospital Managers Association (2012)
World Future Society (2011)

Victoria

American Society for Aesthetics (2010)
American Society of Questioned Document Examiners (2010)
Association for Preservation Technology International (2011)
Computer Assisted Language Instruction Consortium (2011)
International Business Brokers Association (2012)
North American Society of Adlerian Psychology (2011)
Power Transmission Distributors Association (2012)
Society of Cardiovascular Anesthesiologists (2010, 2011)
Society of Ethnobiology (2010)
Society of Petroleum Evaluation Engineers (2010)

Whistler

Attorneys' Liability Assurance Society Inc. (2012)
Federation of Defense and Corporate Counsel (2012)
International Council of Shopping Centers (2012)
Society of Economic Geologists (2012)
Wilderness Medical Society (2012)

MANITOBA

Winnipeg

American Embryo Transfer Association (2012)
North American Council of Automotive Teachers (2011)
The Travel and Tourism Research Association (2012)

NEWFOUNDLAND

Labrador

International Association of Women Police (2012)

St. John's

American Geophysical Union (2011)

NOVA SCOTIA

Halifax

American Association of Port Authorities (2010)
Angel Capital Association (2012)
Association of Real Estate License Law Officials (2012)
Society for Invertebrate Pathology (2011)
Society for Organic Petrology (2011)

ONTARIO

Hamilton

Linguistic Association of Canada and the United States (2010)

Listowel

Red and White Dairy Cattle Association (2012)

Mississauga

Associated Equipment Distributors (2011)
Association of Traumatic Stress Specialists (2010)
Geosynthetic Materials Association (2012)

Niagara Falls

Commercial Vehicle Solutions Network (2012)
National Chemical Credit Association (2012)
Tea Association of the United States of America (2012)
Tea Council of the U.S.A. (2012)

Niagara-on-the-Lake

Society of Risk Management Consultants (2011)

Ottawa

American Society for Ethnohistory (2010)
The American Society of Naturalists (2012)
Association for Canadian Studies in the United States (2011)
Association of Certified Fraud Examiners (2012)
Building Owners and Managers Association International (2012)
Canadian-American Business Council (2012)
Drug Information Association (2012)
Forest Products Society (2011)
Interlocking Concrete Pavement Institute (2010)
International Association of Business Communicators (2012)
National Association of Marine Services (2012)
Society of Systematic Biologists (2012)

Stratford

North American Maple Syrup Council (2010)

Toronto

Academy of Criminal Justice Sciences (2011)
Alliance of Associations of Teachers of Japanese (2012)
American Academy for Cerebral Palsy and Developmental Medicine (2012)
American Academy of Child and Adolescent Psychiatry (2011)
American Academy of Neurology (2010)
American Academy of Physician Assistants (2012)
American Animal Hospital Association (2011)
American Association of Thoracic Surgery (2010)
American Bar Association (2011)

American College of Nurse Practitioners (2012)
American College of Physicians (2010)
American College of Real Estate Lawyers (2011)
American Concrete Institute (2012)
American Head and Neck Society (2012)
American Society for Bone and Mineral Research (2010)
American Society of Nephrology (2011)
American Society of Plastic Surgeons (2010)
American Society of Regional Anesthesia and Pain Medicine (2010)
American Water Works Association (2012)
Art Libraries Society of North America (2012)
ASPSN - American Society of Plastic Surgical Nurses (2010)
Association for Asian Studies (2012)
Association for Behavioral and Cognitive Therapies (2011)
Association for Institutional Research (2011)
Association for Research on Nonprofit Organizations and Voluntary Action (2011)
Association for the Advancement of Computing in Education (2010)
Association for the Treatment of Sexual Abusers (2011)
Association of Alternative Newsweeklies (2010)
Association of Certified Fraud Examiners (2011)
Association of Investment Management Sales Executives (2012)
The Association of Medical Illustrators (2012)
Association of Plastic Surgery Assistants (2010)
Canadian-American Business Council (2011)
Composite Panel Association (2010)
Concrete Foundations Association (2012)
Council for International Tax Education (2011)
Council of State Governments (2010)
FCIB-NACM Corporation (2012)
Fuel Cell and Hydrogen Energy Association (2012)
ICOM, International Communications Agency Network (2011)
The International Alliance for Women (2010)
International Association for Healthcare Security and Safety (2011)
International Association for Hydrogen Energy (2012)
International Association of Business Communicators (2010)
International Association of Clothing Designers and Executives (2010)
International Association of Privacy Professionals (2012)
International Council of Shopping Centers (2011)
International District Energy Association (2011)
International Society for Performance Improvement (2012)
International Society of Appraisers (2010)
International Ticketing Association (2010)
Jean Piaget Society (2012)
Latin American Studies Association (2010)
Licensing Executives Society (2012)
Linguistic Association of Canada and the United States (2012)
Movement Disorder Society (2011)
NALP - The Association for Legal Career Professionals (2012)
The National Association for the Dually Diagnosed (2010)
National Association of Bar Executives (2011)
National Association of Credit Management (2011, 2012)
National Association of Criminal Defense Lawyers (2010)
National Coalition of Black Meeting Planners (2010)
National Conference of Black Lawyers (2012)
National Lesbian and Gay Law Association (2011)
National Optometric Association (2012)
National Society of Black Engineers (2010)
Plastic Surgery Administrative Association (2010)
Religious Education Association (2011)
Retail Confectioners International (2012)
Semiotic Society of America (2012)
The Society for Adolescent Medicine (2010)
Society for Clinical and Experimental Hypnosis (2012)
Society for Humanistic Judaism (2010)
Society for Medical Decision Making (2010)
Society for Research on Nicotine and Tobacco (2011)
Specialty Coffee Association of America (2012)
Truck Writers of North America (2010)
University Professional & Continuing Education Association (2011)
University Professional & Continuing Education Association (2011)
Wi-Fi Alliance (2012)
World Future Society (2012)
WorldatWork (2010, 2012)

QUEBEC

Gatineau

Composite Panel Association (2012)

La Malbaie

National Tank Truck Carriers (2012)

Montebello

Timber Frame Business Council (2010)

Montreal

Academy of Management (2010)
Aluminum Anodizers Council (2010)
American Academy of Psychiatry and the Law (2012)
American Anthropological Association (2011)
American Association of Airport Executives (2012)
American Association of Bovine Practitioners (2012)
American Automatic Control Council (2012)
American Congress of Rehabilitation Medicine (2010)
American Hellenic Educational Progressive Association (AHEPA) (2010)
American Ladder Institute (2012)
American Society for Microbiology (2010, 2012)
American Society of Andrology (2011)
American Society of Civil Engineers (2012)
American Society of Clinical Oncology (2012)

American Society of Heating, Refrigerating and Air Conditioning Engineers (ASHRAE) (2011)
American Society of Human Genetics (2011)
American Society of Mechanical Engineers (ASME) (2012)
American Society of Neurorehabilitation (2010)
The American Society of Pediatric Hematology/Oncology (2010)
American Society of Plant Biologists (2010)
Association for the Advancement of Computing in Education (2012)
Association of Collegiate Schools of Architecture (2011)
Association of Railway Museums (2012)
Association of Research Libraries (2011)
Association of Rotational Molders International (2010)
BICSI (2010)
Cheiron: The International Society for the History of Behavioral and Social Sciences (2012)
Compressed Gas Association (2012)
Council for European Studies (2010)
Council on Botanical and Horticultural Libraries (2012)
The Electrochemical Society (2011)
Employee Assistance Society of North America (2010)
Environmental Mutagen Society (2011)
Geochemical Society (2012)
Gerontological Society of America (2011)
History of Science Society (2010)
International Association for the Study of Pain (2010)
International Association of Forensic Nurses (2011)
International Association of Music Libraries, United States Branch (2012)
International College of Applied Kinesiology (2012)
International Neuropsychological Society (2012)
International Pediatric Transplant Association (2011)
International Pet and Animal Transportation Association (2010)
International Society for Ecological Modelling-North American Chapter (2011)
International Society for Magnetic Resonance in Medicine (2011)
International Society for the Study of Trauma and Dissociation (2011)
International Society for Traumatic Stress Studies (2010)
International Studies Association (2011)
International Textile and Apparel Association (2010)
National Association of Document Examiners (2011)
National Council for Air and Stream Improvement, Inc. (2012)
National Tour Association (2010)
North American Academy of Ecumenists (2010)
North American Academy of Liturgy (2012)
North American Association of State and Provincial Lotteries (2012)
North American Conference on British Studies (2012)
Perlite Institute (2010)
Philosophy of Science Association (2010)
Society for Cultural Anthropology (2011)
Society for Developmental Biology (2012)
Society for Epidemiologic Research (2011)
Society for Phenomenology and Existential Philosophy (2010)
Society of Research Administrators International (2011)
Sugar Industry Technologists (2011)
Theatre Library Association (2011)
Tourist Railway Association Inc. (2012)
University and College Designers Association (2012)
USENIX: The Advanced Computing Systems Association (2012)

Québec

American Association of Neuromuscular and Electrodiagnostic Medicine (2010)
American Association of Wildlife Veterinarians (2011)
American College of Mortgage Attorneys (2010)
American Thyroid Association (2012)
Association for High Technology Distribution (2012)
Controlled Release Society (2012)
Industrial Fabrics Association International (2011)
International Concrete Repair Institute (2012)
National Bison Association (2012)
Sanitary Supply Wholesaling Association (2012)
Society for Imaging Science and Technology (2012)
Wildlife Disease Association (2011)
World Council of Credit Unions, Inc. (2012)

SASKATCHEWAN

Saskatoon

Pierre Fauchard Academy (2012)
Risk and Insurance Management Society, Inc. (RIMS) (2012)

MEXICO

BAJA SOUTH

Los Cabos

National Fire Sprinkler Association (2012)

DISTRITO

Mexico City

Color Marketing Group (2012)
Consortium for North American Higher Education Collaboration (2011)
Entrepreneurs' Organization (2011)
NGVAmerica (2012)
Packaging Machinery Manufacturers Institute (2010, 2012)

GUERRERO

Ixtapa

Transportation Safety Equipment Institute (2010)

JALISCO

Guadalajara

American Association of Teachers of Spanish and Portuguese (2010)
American Medical Women's Association (2012)
Association of Natural Bio-Control Producers (2012)

Puerto Vallarta

Alliance of Area Business Publications (2011, 2012)
North American Export Grain Association, Inc. (2011)

MEXICO STATE

Cabo San Lucas

International Association of Lighting Management Companies (2010)

NUEVO LEON

Monterrey

American Society of Heating, Refrigerating and Air Conditioning Engineers (ASHRAE) (2012)
Institute of Industrial Engineers (2010)
International Association of Used Equipment Dealers (2012)
The Wire Association International, Inc. (2010)

QUERETARO DE ARTEAGA

Queretaro

Fabricators & Manufacturers Association, International (2012)

QUINTANA ROO

Cancun

American Galvanizers Association (2010)
American Medical Society for Sports Medicine (2010)
Association of Alternate Postal Systems (2010)
Copier Dealers Association (2010)
Credit Union Executives Society (2011)
International Federation of Pharmaceutical Wholesalers (2012)
National Onion Association (2011)
Petroleum Equipment Institute (2012)
World Allergy Organization (2011)

Cozumel

Distinguished Restaurants of North America (2012)

Riviera Maya

Wood Moulding and Millwork Producers Association (2010)

VERACRUZ-LLAVE

Veracruz

Inter-American Bar Association (2011)

YUCATAN

Mérida

Society for Applied Anthropology (2010)
Society for Ecological Restoration International (2011)

ARGENTINA

Buenos Aires

AAGL - Advancing Minimally Invasive Gynecology Worldwide (2012)
Americas Association of Cooperative/Mutual Insurance Societies (2012)
PROMAX/BDA (2012)
Society for Invertebrate Pathology (2012)

Mar del Plata

The Coastal and Estuarine Research Federation (2012)

Rosario

Society for Cryobiology (2012)

San Miguel de Tucuman

International Association for Dental Research (2011)

ARMENIA

Yerevan

American Telemedicine Association (2011)

ARUBA

Palm Beach

American Sports Builders Association (2012)

AUSTRALIA

Adelaide

International Association for the Study of Pain (2012)

Brisbane

Bioelectromagnetics Society (2012)
Gemological Institute of America (2012)
International Association for Mathematical Geosciences (2012)
International Road Federation (2011)
Sigma Theta Tau International (2012)

Bunbury

International Concatenated Order of Hoo-Hoo (2012)

Cairns

American Association for Geriatric Psychiatry (2012)
International Psychogeriatric Association (2012)

Canberra

American Society of International Law (2012)

Glenelg

International Life Sciences Institute (2012)

Gold Coast

Entrepreneurs' Organization (2011)
Guild of Natural Science Illustrators (2011)

Kalgoorlie

Society of Economic Geologists (2012)

Melbourne

American Society for Reproductive Medicine (2011)
IEEE Microwave Theory and Techniques Society (2011)
Imaging and Perimetry Society (2012)
International Brain Injury Association (2012)
International Federation of Fertility Societies (2011)
International Society for Magnetic Resonance in Medicine (2012)
National Guardianship Association (2012)
World Aquaculture Society (2012)

Perth

International Desalination Association (2011)

Queensland

International College of Surgeons (2012)

Surfers Paradise

American Association of Cereal Chemists International (2012)

Sydney

IEEE Communications Society (2012)
IEEE Control Systems Society (2012)
IEEE Photonics Society (2012)
InfoComm International (2012)
Institute of Electrical and Electronics Engineers (IEEE) (2012)
International Association for the Study of Dreams (2012)
International Association of Wildland Fire (2012)
International Atherosclerosis Society (2012)
International Swaps and Derivatives Association (2011, 2012)
Turnaround Management Association (2012)

AUSTRIA

Linz

International Tuba-Euphonium Association (2012)

Vienna

American Academy of the History of Dentistry (2012)
ATM Industry Association (2012)
International Health, Racquet and Sportsclub Association (2012)
International Trademark Association (2011)
Wi-Fi Alliance (2012)

BAHAMAS

Paradise Island

Black Entertainment and Sports Lawyers Association (2012)
International Society of Hair Restoration Surgery (2012)

BELGIUM

Brussels

Armed Forces Communications and Electronics Association (2012)
Association for Competitive Technology (ACT) (2011)
Family Firm Institute, Inc. (2012)
FCIB-NACM Corporation (2012)
International Consumer Product Health and Safety Organization (2012)
International Real Estate Federation - American Chapter (2012)
International Society for Pharmaceutical Engineering (2011)
National Association for Information Destruction, Inc. (2012)
Toxicology Forum (2011)

BERMUDA

Southampton

American College of Health Care Administrators (2012)

BOLIVIA

Saint Maarten

United States Superyacht Association (2012)

BRAZIL

Bahia

World's Poultry Science Association, U.S.A. Branch (2012)

Bonito

Association for Tropical Biology and Conservation (2012)

Buzios RJ

North American Calorimetry Conference (2012)

Florianopolis

International Gay and Lesbian Travel Association (2012)

Fortaleza

IEEE - Industry Applications Society (2012)

Porto Alegre

IEEE Computer Society (2012)

Rio de Janeiro

International Academy of Trial Lawyers (2012)
International Association for Dental Research (2012)
International Association of Drilling Contractors (2012)
International Society for Ecological Economics (2012)

Salvador

International Health, Racquet and Sportsclub Association (2012)

Salvador da Bahia

Association of Third World Studies (2011)

São Paulo

Brazilian American Chamber of Commerce (2012)
Food and Drug Law Institute (2012)
International Health, Racquet and Sportsclub Association (2012)
International Licensing Industry Merchandisers' Association (2012)
International Society of Automation (2011)
Mobile Marketing Association (2011)

CAMBODIA

Siem Reap

World History Association (2012)

CAYMAN ISLANDS

Grand Cayman

Society for Excellence in Eyecare (2012)

CHILE

Santiago

Flight Safety Foundation (2012)
International Association of Oral and Maxillofacial Surgeons (2011)
World Airline Entertainment Association (2012)

CHINA

Beijing

American Association of Cereal Chemists International (2012)
American Mushroom Institute (2012)
Association of Foreign Investors in U.S. Real Estate (2012)
ATM Industry Association (2012)
Automotive Industry Action Group (2012)
Automotive Parts Remanufacturers Association (2012)
Biotechnology Industry Organization (BIO) (2012)
Gas Technology Institute (2012)
IEEE Communications Society (2012)
IEEE Computer Society (2012)
International Air Transport Association (2012)
Plastics Pipe Institute (2011)
Society for Organic Petrology (2012)
Society for the Advancement of Material and Process Engineering (2012)
Society of Incentive & Travel Executives (2012)
Society of Wood Science and Technology (2012)

Chengdu

IEEE Computer Society (2012)
Society for Biomaterials (2012)

Guangzhou

American Pet Products Association (2011)

Hong Kong

ASM International (2011)
Association of Certified Fraud Examiners (2012)
EMTA - Trade Association for the Emerging Markets (2012)
International Cinema Technology Association (2012)
International Swaps and Derivatives Association (2011)

Huangshan

IEEE Communications Society (2012)

ShangHai

American Academy of Anti-Aging Medicine (2012)
American Association of State Colleges and Universities (2012)
IEEE Photonics Society (2011, 2012)
International Council of Shopping Centers (2011, 2012)
International Health, Racquet and Sportsclub Association (2012)
International Licensing Industry Merchandisers' Association (2012)
Optoelectronics Industry Development Association (2012)
Private Label Manufacturers Association (2011, 2012)

Shenzhen

AMT - The Association For Manufacturing Technology (2012)
IPC - Association Connecting Electronics Industries (2011)

Suzhou City

International Safe Transit Association (2012)

Tianjin

Special Interest Group for Information Retrieval (2012)

Wuhan-Gongcheng

International Plant Propagators Society (2012)

COLOMBIA

Cartagena

American Oil Chemists' Society (2011)
Professional Records and Information Services Management International (2012)

Medellin

InfoComm International (2011)

COSTA RICA

Herradura

American Academy of Matrimonial Lawyers (2012)
Retail Solutions Providers Association (2012)

CROATIA (HRVATSKA)

Dubrovnik

American Society for Aesthetics (2012)

CZECH REPUBLIC

Brno

International Society of Bassists (2012)

Prague

American Association for Clinical Chemistry, Inc. (2012)
Aviation Industry CBT Committee (2011)
CFA Institute (2012)
International Society for Heart and Lung Transplantation (2012)
World Aquaculture Society (2012)

DENMARK

Copenhagen

ASME International Gas Turbine Institute (2012)

Frederiksberg

Society for Social Studies of Science (2012)

ECUADOR

Cuenca

IEEE Communications Society (2012)

Puerto Ayora

American Geophysical Union (2011)

EGYPT

Cairo

American Hardwood Export Council (2011)

ESTONIA

Tallinn

International Association for Philosophy and Literature (2012)

FINLAND

Helsinki

International Association for Dental Research (2012)

FRANCE

Besançon

IEEE Computer Society (2012)

Cannes

The Open Group (2012)

Lyon

American Association of Wildlife Veterinarians (2012)
Association of Rotational Molders International (2012)
International Bone and Mineral Society (2012)
Wildlife Disease Association (2012)

Nice

American Society of Transplantation (2012)

Paris

Ethics and Compliance Officer Association (2012)
IEEE Communications Society (2012)

Poitiers

Giant Screen Cinema Association (2012)

Villepinte

International Interior Design Association (2012)

GERMANY

Aachen

Association for Assessment and Accreditation of Laboratory Animal Care International (2012)

Bavaria

American Society for Artificial Internal Organs (2012)

Bayreuth

Automotive Parts Remanufacturers Association (2012)

Berlin

American Society for Clinical Laboratory Science (2012)
Association of Test Publishers (2012)
Closure and Container Manufacturers Association (2011)
Electronic Retailing Association (2012)
Institute for Operations Research and the Management Sciences (2012)
International Association of Amusement Parks and Attractions(IAAPA) (2012)
International College of Cranio-Mandibular Orthopedics (2012)
International Council of Shopping Centers (2012)
International Life Sciences Institute (2012)
International Society for Pharmacoeconomics and Outcomes Research (2012)
Railway Engineering-Maintenance Suppliers Association (2012)

Bremen

Solution Mining Research Institute (2012)

Dortmund

International Safe Transit Association (2012)

Dresden

EDA Consortium (2012)
Institute of Electrical and Electronics Engineers (IEEE) (2012)
Semiconductor Equipment and Materials International (2012)

Düsseldorf

FCIB-NACM Corporation (2012)
National Glass Association (2012)

Erfurt

International Microelectronics and Packaging Society - IMAPS (2012)

Essen

IEEE Computer Society (2012)

Frankfurt

American Society of Interior Designers (2012)

Freiburg

International Society of Travel and Tourism Educators (2012)

Hamburg

ASM International (2011)
Association of Service and Computer Dealers International (2011)
Specialty Coffee Association of America (2012)

Leipzig

International Society for Ecological Modelling-North American Chapter (2012)

Manching

Society of Allied Weight Engineers (2012)

Munich

Association of Industrial Metallizers, Coaters and Laminators (2011)
Audio Engineering Society (2012)
Drug Information Association (2012)
Electronics Representatives Association (2012)
International Association of Emergency Managers (2011)
North American Catalysis Society (2012)

Neue Aula

International Isotope Society (2012)

Nuremberg

IEEE Power Electronics Society (2012)
International College of Cranio-Mandibular Orthopedics (2012)

Stuttgart

1394 Trade Association (2012)
Automated Imaging Association (2012)

GREECE

Athens

Academy of Molecular Imaging (2012)
American Psychosomatic Society (2012)
International Society of Refractive Surgery of the American Academy of
	Ophthalmology (2011)

Corfu

American Society for Aesthetics (2012)

Rhodes

International Society of Offshore and Polar Engineers (2012)

Thessaloniki

Music Industry Conference (2012)

HUNGARY

Budapest

American Association of Airport Executives (2012)
IEEE Instrumentation and Measurement Society (2012)
International Contrast Ultrasound Society (2011)
International Council of Shopping Centers (2012)
International Society for Quality of Life Research (2012)

INDIA

Bangalore

International Technology Law Association (2012)
Internet Society (2011)
Semiconductor Equipment and Materials International (2012)
Softwood Export Council (2012)

Bengaluru

IEEE Communications Society (2012)
IEEE Power and Energy Society (2012)
IEEE Power Electronics Society (2012)

Delhi

IEEE Power Electronics Society (2012)

Ghaziabad

Pierre Fauchard Academy (2012)

Hyderabad

World Allergy Organization (2012)

Kanyakumari

American Society of Radiologic Technologists (2011)

Mumbai

Biotechnology Industry Organization (BIO) (2012)

Murthal

IEEE Power Electronics Society (2012)

New Delhi

International Road Federation (2011, 2012)

Pune

Pediatric Orthopedic Society of North America (2012)
Society for Mathematical Biology (2012)

IRAN

Tehran

International Association for Dental Research (2011)

ISRAEL

Haifa

International Desalination Association (2011)

Tel Aviv

The International Society for Minimally Invasive Cardiothoracic Surgery (2011)
International Writing Centers Association (2012)

ITALY

Bologna

American Neurogastroenterology and Motility Society (2012)

Cortina d'Ampezzo

American Society for Reproductive Medicine (2012)

Florence

American Academy of Psychoanalysis and Dynamic Psychiatry (2012)
IEEE Magnetics Society (2012)
IEEE Power Electronics Society (2012)

Milan

American Association of Petroleum Geologists (2011)
International Association for the Study of Pain (2012)
International Council of Shopping Centers (2011)

Palermo

IEEE Computer Society (2012)

Rome

American Bankruptcy Institute (2012)
Association of Catholic Colleges and Universities (2012)
Association of Corporate Travel Executives (ACTE) (2012)
International Council on Systems Engineering (2012)
International Technology Law Association (2012)

Siena

International Society for Third-Sector Research (2012)

Udine

Society for Natural Philosophy (2012)

Venice

Central Station Alarm Association (2011)

JAMAICA

Montego Bay

Black Psychiatrists of America (2012)
Urban and Regional Information Systems Association (2012)

JAPAN

Chiba

The Integrated Ocean Drilling Program (2012)

Fukuoka

IEEE Computer Society (2012)

Kyoto

Generic Pharmaceutical Association (2012)
International Society for Molecular Plant Microbe Interactions (2012)

Nagasaki

IEEE Power Electronics Society (2012)

OITA

IEEE Magnetics Society (2012)

Osaka

AAGL - Advancing Minimally Invasive Gynecology Worldwide (2011)
Robotics and Automation Society (2012)

Sapporo

Pierre Fauchard Academy (2012)

Sendai

IEEE Photonics Society (2011)

Tokyo

Drug Information Association (2012)
Fuel Cell and Hydrogen Energy Association (2012)
Institute of International Finance (2012)
International Swaps and Derivatives Association (2011, 2012)
Wi-Fi Alliance (2012)

LITHUANIA

Launas

International Association of Oral and Maxillofacial Surgeons (2012)

Vilnius

International Council of Shopping Centers (2011)

LUXEMBOURG

Luxembourg City

National Investment Company Service Association (2012)

Walferdange

International Society for Research on Aggression (2012)

MALAYSIA

Kuala Lumpur

AscdiNatd (2012)

Association of Service and Computer Dealers International (2012)
Islamic Medical Association of North America (2012)
The Travel and Tourism Research Association (2012)

MONACO

Monte Carlo
Foil and Specialty Effects Association (2012)

MONGOLIA

Ulaanbaatar
International Association for Dental Research (2011)

MOROCCO

Marrakech
Environmental and Water Resources Institute of the American Society of Civil
Engineers (2012)

Tangier
American Institute for Maghrib Studies (2012)

NETHERLANDS

Amsterdam
FCIB-NACM Corporation (2012)
IEEE Computer Society (2012)
International Sanitary Supply Association (2012)
ISEH Society for Hematology and Stem Cells (2012)
National Fire Protection Association (2012)
National Marine Manufacturers Association (2012)
Private Label Manufacturers Association (2012)

Dam Square
American Peanut Council (2012)

Den Bosch
KWPN of North America (2012)

Hague
Drug Information Association (2012)
International Newspaper Marketing Association (2012)

Tilburg
Society for the Psychological Study of Science Issues (2011)

Utrecht
State Capital Group (2012)

NEW ZEALAND

Auckland
IEEE Power and Energy Society (2012)
Licensing Executives Society (2012)
Sugar Industry Technologists (2012)

Christchurch
International Brotherhood of Magicians (2012)

New Zealand
Society of American Travel Writers (2011)

Wellington
International Council for Small Business (2012)

NIGERIA

Ile-Ife
National Board for Certified Counselors (2012)

NORWAY

Oslo
International Association for Mathematical Geosciences (2012)
International Neuropsychological Society (2012)
International Society of Protistologists (2012)

PANAMA

Panama City
American Association of Heart Failure Nurses (2012)
United States Grains Council (2012)

PERU

Lima
American Society of Travel Agents (2012)
International Council of Shopping Centers (2012)
Society of Economic Geologists (2012)

POLAND

Gdansk
World Council of Credit Unions, Inc. (2012)

Warsaw
American Hardwood Export Council (2011)
The Combustion Institute (2012)
IEEE Aerospace and Electronic Systems Society (AESS) (2012)
International Road Federation (2011)
Materials Research Society (2012)

PORTUGAL

Algarve
Society for Mathematical Biology (2012)

Braga
American Society for Aesthetics (2012)

Cascais
International Society on Thrombosis and Hemostasis (2011)

Lisboa
Society for Hematopathology (2012)

Lisbon
International Newspaper Marketing Association (2011)
International Society for Performance Improvement (2012)
Power Transmission Distributors Association (2012)
Seismological Society of America (2012)
USENIX: The Advanced Computing Systems Association (2012)

Porto
American Astronautical Society (2011)
International Association for Impact Assessment (2012)

QATAR

Doha
International Association of School Librarianship (2012)

REPUBLIC OF KOREA (SOUTH KOREA)

Busan
International Society of Refractive Surgery of the American Academy of
Ophthalmology (2012)

Jeju
Association for Computational Linguistics (2012)

Seoul
IEEE Circuits and Systems Society (2012)
IEEE Computer Society (2012)
IEEE Power Electronics Society (2012)
Institute of Electrical and Electronics Engineers (IEEE) (2012)
International Association for Dental Research (2011)
International Society for the Performing Arts (2012)
Man and Cybernetics Systems Society (2012)

ROMANIA

Bucharest
AAGL - Advancing Minimally Invasive Gynecology Worldwide (2012)
International Health, Racquet and Sportsclub Association (2012)
Internet Society (2011)

Sibiu
Society for Romanian Studies (2012)

RUSSIA

Moscow
Cryogenic Society of America (2012)
General Aviation Manufacturers Association (2012)
International Pediatric Nephrology Association (2012)
NAMM - The International Music Products Association (2012)

St. Petersburg
International Real Estate Federation - American Chapter (2012)
National Center for Asia-Pacific Economic Cooperation (2011)

Ulyanovsk
General Aviation Manufacturers Association (2012)

SINGAPORE

Singapore
Alliance for Gray Market and Counterfeit Abatement (2012)
American Association of Petroleum Geologists (2012)
American Cleaning Institute (2012)
American Coatings Association (2012)
American Geophysical Union (2012)

American Industrial Hygiene Association (2012)
Board Retailers Association (2012)
Electrostatic Discharge Association (2012)
EMTA - Trade Association for the Emerging Markets (2012)
Futures Industry Association (2011, 2012)
Healthcare Information and Management Systems Society (2012)
IEEE Society on Social Implications of Technology (2012)
International Swaps and Derivatives Association (2012)
National Association for Surface Finishing (2012)

Suntec City

Geosynthetic Materials Association (2012)

SLOVENIA

Ljubljana

International Federation of Nurse Anesthetists (2012)

SOUTH AFRICA

Cape Town

American College of Veterinary Anesthesiologists (2012)
Generic Pharmaceutical Association (2011)
United States National Committee of the International Dairy Federation (2012)
World Trade Centers Association (2012)

Johannesburg

Corporate Council on Africa (2012)
Internet Society (2012)
PROMAX/BDA (2012)

Midrand

Computing Technology Industry Association (CompTIA) (2012)

Pretoria

American Swimming Coaches Association (2012)

Rustenburg

Council of International Investigators (2012)

Stellenbosch

ATM Industry Association (2012)

Tanzania

International Institute of Fisheries Economics and Trade (2012)

SPAIN

Barcelona

American Association of Tissue Banks (2011)
GSM Association (2012)
IEEE Aerospace and Electronic Systems Society (AESS) (2011)
IEEE Computer Society (2011)
International Association of Drilling Contractors (2012)
International Desalination Association (2012)
International Society for Pharmacoepidemiology (2012)
National BioDiesel Board (2011)
The Open Group (2012)
Osteoarthritis Research Society International (2012)
Society for Chaos Theory in Psychology and Life Sciences (2012)
Society of Incentive & Travel Executives (2012)
SPIE - The International Society for Optical Engineering (2012)
Weather Risk Management Association (2012)

Bilbao

The Travel and Tourism Research Association (2012)

Granada

Association for Behavior Analysis International (2011)

Madrid

American Crystallographic Association (2011)
AscdiNatd (2012)
Association of Service and Computer Dealers International (2012)
International Association of Credit Portfolio Managers (2012)
International Pet and Animal Transportation Association (2012)
Methanol Institute (2012)
Society of Chemical Manufacturers and Affiliates Inc. (2012)

Seville

International Council of Psychologists (2012)

Tarragona

IEEE Communications Society (2012)

SWEDEN

Gothenburg

Society of Allied Weight Engineers (2012)

Malmo

SAE International (2012)

Stockholm

The Open Group (2011)

SWITZERLAND

Basel

Biotechnology Industry Organization (BIO) (2012)

Geneva

Internet Society (2012)
National Business Aviation Association (2012)

Grindelwald

American Geophysical Union (2011)

Lausanne

International Council on Hotel, Restaurant and Institutional Education (2012)

Lucerne

Adventure Travel Trade Association (2012)
Society for the Advancement of Material and Process Engineering (2012)

Saint Gallen

Fiber Society (2012)

Zurich

FCIB-NACM Corporation (2012)
North American Clinical Dermatologic Society (2012)

TAIWAN

Tainan.

IEEE Communications Society (2012)

Taipei

Consumer Data Industry Association (2012)
Council of Supply Chain Management Professionals (2011)
IEEE Computer Society (2012)
IPC - Association Connecting Electronics Industries (2011)
North American Retail Hardware Association (2012)
The Open Group (2011)
Semiconductor Equipment and Materials International (2012)
Society for Experimental Mechanics, Inc. (2012)
United States Junior Chamber (Jaycees) (2012)

THAILAND

Bangkok

CFA Institute (2012)
Color Marketing Group (2012)
International Association of Drilling Contractors (2011)
International Map Trade Association (2011)
International Neural Network Society (2012)
International Society for Infectious Diseases (2012)

Nakorn Pathom Province

Association for International Agricultural and Extension Education (2012)

TUNISIA

Tunis

IEEE Photonics Society (2012)

TURKEY

Ankara

Metal Powder Industries Federation (2011)

Antalya

International Psycho-Oncology Society (2011)
Psychometric Society (2012)

Istanbul

American Association of Political Consultants (2011)
American Coatings Association (2012)
Institute of Mathematical Statistics (2012)
International Federation of Fertility Societies (2012)
Transworld Advertising Agency Network (2012)

Izmir

Global Offset and Countertrade Association (GOCA) (2012)

UNITED ARAB EMIRATES

Abu Dhabi

Association for Research in Vision and Ophthalmology (2012)
Digital Screenmedia Association (2011)
International Society of Refractive Surgery of the American Academy of Ophthalmology (2012)

Dubai

AACE International (2012)
Community Financial Services Association of America CFSA (2012)
Interactive Multimedia and Collaborative Communications Alliance (2012)
International Association of Drilling Contractors (2012)
International Licensing Industry Merchandisers' Association (2012)
International Society of Beverage Technologists (2011)

UNITED KINGDOM

Birmingham
Associated Schools of Construction (2012)

Brighton
North American Skull Base Society (2012)

Colnbrook
Flight Safety Foundation (2012)

Coventry
American Hardwood Export Council (2011)

Edinburgh
American Society of Appraisers (2011)
Behavior Genetics Association (2012)
Federation of Straight Chiropractors and Organizations (2012)
International Brain Injury Association (2012)
Pipeline Research Council International, Inc. (2012)
SPIE - The International Society for Optical Engineering (2012)

Glasgow
IEEE Aerospace and Electronic Systems Society (AESS) (2012)
The Oceanography Society (2012)

Leeds
American Society for Aesthetics (2012)

London
American Hardwood Export Council (2011)
American Orthopsychiatric Association (2012)
ATM Industry Association (2012)
Aviation Insurance Association (2011)
Computing Technology Industry Association (CompTIA) (2012)
Copper Development Association (2011)
CoreNet Global (2012)
CRE Finance Council (2011)
Digital Screenmedia Association (2012)
Evangelical Christian Publishers Association (2012)
FCIB-NACM Corporation (2012)
Gas Technology Institute (2012)
International Coach Federation (2012)
International Licensing Industry Merchandisers' Association (2012)
International Society of Transport Aircraft Trading (2012)
International Swaps and Derivatives Association (2011, 2012)
National Association of Convenience Stores (2012)
The Open Group (2012)
Professional Lighting and Sound Association (2012)
Software & Information Industry Association (SIIA) (2011)

Manchester
Academy of Accounting Historians (2012)
Association for Symbolic Logic (2012)

Oxford
International Society of Managing and Technical Editors (2012)

Petersfield
Movement Disorder Society (2012)

Shrivenham
Directed Energy Professional Society (2012)

URUGUAY

Colonia del Sacramento
IEEE Photonics Society (2011)

VIETNAM

Hanoi
IEEE Communications Society (2012)